CW00519150

NOTES

NOTES

The Form Book ®

FLAT ANNUAL FOR 2020

THE OFFICIAL FORM BOOK

ALL THE 2019 RETURNS

Complete record of Flat Racing
from 1 January to 31 December 2019

Associated Raceform products

The Form Book is updated weekly. Subscribers receive a binder, together with all the early racing. Weekly sections and a new index are threaded into the binder to keep it up to date.

The data contained in *The Form Book Flat Annual for 2020* is available in paper form or a download. The Raceform Interactive dowload, contains same data as The Flat Form Book, and operates on any PC within a 'Windows' environment. The database is designed to allow access to the information in a number of different ways, and is extremely quick and easy to use.

Published in 2020 by Raceform Ltd
27 Kingfisher Court, Hambridge Road, Newbury, Berkshire RG14 5SJ

A catalogue record for this book is available from the British Library

ISBN 978-1-83950-060-2
Printed in the UK by CPI Group (UK) Ltd, Croydon, CR0 4YY
Full details of all Raceform services and publications are available from:

Raceform Ltd, Sanders Road, Wellingborough, Northants NN8 4BX
Tel: 01933 304858
Email: shop@racingpost.com
www.racingpost.com

Cover picture: Enable wins a thrilling
King George VI and Queen Elizabeth Stakes at Ascot.

CONTENTS

Racereaders

Mark Brown
Cathal Gahan
Steffan Edwards
Walter Glynn
Keith McHugh
Richard Lowther
Tim Mitchell
Jonathan Neesom
David Orton
Darren Owen
Steve Payne
Colin Roberts
Joe Rowntree
Andrew Sheret
David Toft
Ron Wood
Richard Young

The Official Scale of Weight, Age & Distance (Flat)

The following scale should only be used in conjunction with the Official ratings published in this book. Use of any other scale will introduce errors into calculations. The allowances are expressed as the number of pounds that is deemed the average horse in each group falls short of maturity at different dates and distances.

Dist		Jan		Feb		Mar		Apr		May		Jun		Jul		Aug		Sep		Oct		Nov		Dec	
(fur)	Age	1-15	16-31	1-14	15-28	1-15	16-31	1-15	16-30	1-15	16-31	1-15	16-30	1-15	16-31	1-15	16-31	1-15	16-30	1-15	16-31	1-15	16-30	1-15	16-31
5	2	-	-	-	-	-	47	44	41	38	36	34	32	30	28	26	24	22	20	19	18	17	17	16	16
	3	15	15	14	14	13	12	11	10	9	8	7	6	5	4	3	2	1	1	-	-	-	-	-	-
6	2	-	-	-	-	-	-	-	-	44	41	38	36	33	31	28	26	24	22	21	20	19	18	17	17
	3	16	16	15	15	14	13	12	11	10	9	8	7	6	5	4	3	2	2	1	1	-	-	-	-
7	2	-	-	-	-	-	-	-	-	-	-	-	-	38	35	32	30	27	25	23	22	21	20	19	19
	3	18	18	17	17	16	15	14	13	12	11	10	9	8	7	6	5	4	3	2	2	1	1	-	-
8	2	-	-	-	-	-	-	-	-	-	-	-	-	-	-	37	34	31	28	26	24	23	22	21	20
	3	20	20	19	19	18	17	15	14	13	12	11	10	9	8	7	6	5	4	3	3	2	2	1	1
9	3	22	22	21	21	20	19	17	15	14	13	12	11	10	9	8	7	6	5	4	4	3	3	2	2
	4	1	1	-	-	-	-	-	-	-	-	-	-	-	-	-	-	-	-	-	-	-	-	-	-
10	3	23	23	22	22	21	20	19	17	15	14	13	12	10	9	8	7	6	5	4	4	3	3	2	2
	4	1	1	-	-	-	-	-	-	-	-	-	-	-	-	-	-	-	-	-	-	-	-	-	-
11	3	24	24	23	23	22	21	20	19	17	15	14	13	11	10	9	8	7	6	5	5	4	4	3	3
	4	2	2	1	1	-	-	-	-	-	-	-	-	-	-	-	-	-	-	-	-	-	-	-	-
12	3	25	25	24	24	23	22	21	20	19	17	15	14	12	11	10	9	8	7	6	6	5	5	4	4
	4	3	3	2	2	1	1	-	-	-	-	-	-	-	-	-	-	-	-	-	-	-	-	-	-
13	3	26	26	25	25	24	23	22	21	20	19	17	15	13	11	10	9	8	7	6	6	5	5	4	4
	4	3	3	2	2	3	3	2	1	-	-	-	-	-	-	-	-	-	-	-	-	-	-	-	-
14	3	27	27	26	26	25	24	23	22	21	20	18	16	14	12	11	10	9	8	7	7	6	6	5	5
	4	4	4	3	3	2	2	1	1	-	-	-	-	-	-	-	-	-	-	-	-	-	-	-	-
15	3	28	28	27	27	26	25	24	23	22	21	19	17	15	13	12	11	10	8	8	7	6	6	5	5
	4	4	4	3	3	2	2	1	1	-	-	-	-	-	-	-	-	-	-	-	-	-	-	-	-
16	3	29	29	28	28	27	26	25	24	23	22	21	19	17	15	13	12	11	10	9	8	7	7	6	6
	4	5	5	4	4	3	3	2	2	1	1	-	-	-	-	-	-	-	-	-	-	-	-	-	-
18	3	31	31	30	30	29	28	27	26	25	24	23	21	19	17	15	13	12	11	10	9	8	7	6	6
	4	5	5	4	4	3	3	2	2	1	1	0	0	-	-	-	-	-	-	-	-	-	-	-	-
20	3	33	33	32	32	31	30	29	28	27	26	25	23	21	19	17	15	13	12	11	10	9	8	7	7
	4	6	6	5	5	4	4	3	3	2	2	1	1	-	-	-	-	-	-	-	-	-	-	-	-

The Form Book

Welcome to the *The Form Book Flat Annual for 2020*, comprising the complete year's Flat results for 2019.

Race details contain Racing Post Ratings assessing the merit of each individual performance, speed figures for every horse that clocks a worthwhile time, weight-for-age allowances, stall positions for every race and the starting price percentage, in addition to the traditional features.

Race Focus comments are printed below most races, along with the results of stewards' enquiries.

The official record

THE FORM BOOK records comprehensive race details of every domestic race, every major European Group race and every foreign event in which a British-trained runner participated.

MEETING BACK REFERENCE NUMBER is the Raceform number of the last meeting run at the track and is shown to the left of the course name. Abandoned meetings are signified by a dagger.

THE GOING, The Official going, shown at the head of each meeting, is recorded as follows: Turf: Hard; Firm; Good to firm; Good; Good to soft; Soft; Heavy. All-Weather: Fast; Standard to fast; Standard; Standard to slow; Slow. There may be variations for non-British meetings

Where appropriate, a note is included indicating track bias and any differences to the official going indicated by race times.

THE WEATHER is shown below the date for selected meetings.

THE WIND is given as a strength and direction at the Winning Post, classified as follows:
Strength: gale; v.str; str; fresh; mod; slt; almost nil; nil.
Direction: (half) against; (half) bhd; (half) across from or towards stands.

VISIBILITY is good unless otherwise stated.

RACE NUMBERS for foreign races carry the suffix 'a' in the race header and in the index.

RACE TITLE is the name of the race as shown in the Racing Calendar.

COMPETITIVE RACING CLASSIFICATIONS are shown on a scale from Class 1 to Class 7. All Pattern races are Class 1.

THE RACE DISTANCE is given for all races, and is accompanied by (s) for races run on straight courses and (r) for courses where there is a round track of comparable distance. On All-Weather courses (F) for Fibresand or (P) for Polytrack indicates the nature of the artificial surface on which the race is run.

OFFICIAL RACE TIME as published in the Racing Calendar is followed in parentheses by the time when the race actually started. This is followed by the race class, age restrictions, handicap restrictions and the official rating of the top weight.

PRIZE MONEY shows penalty values down to sixth place (where applicable).

THE POSITION OF THE STARTING STALLS is shown against each race, in the form of: High (H), Centre (C) or Low (L). In keeping with all other major racing nations, stalls are now numbered from the inside rail. If the stalls are placed adjacent to the inside rail they are described as low, if against the outside rail they are described as high. Otherwise they are central.

IN THE RACE RESULT, the figures to the far left of each horse (under FORM) show the most recent form figures. The figure in bold is the finishing position in this race as detailed below.

1...40 - finishing positions first to fortieth; **b** - brought down; **c** - carried out; **f** - fell; **p** - pulled up; **r** - refused; **ro** - ran out; **s** - slipped up; **u** - unseated rider; **v** - void race.

THE OFFICIAL DISTANCES between the horses are shown on the left-hand side immediately after their position at the finish.

NUMBER OF DAYS SINCE PREVIOUS RUN is the superscript figure immediately following the horse name and suffix.

PREVIOUS RACEFORM RACE NUMBER is the boxed figure to the right of the horse's name.

THE HORSE'S AGE is shown immediately before the weight carried.

WEIGHTS shown are actual weights carried.

OFFICIAL RATING is the figure in bold type directly after the horse's name in the race result. This figure indicates the Official BHA rating, at entry, after the following adjustments had been made:
(i) Overweight carried by the rider.
(ii) The number of pounds out of the handicap (if applicable).
(iii) Penalties incurred after the publication of the weights.
However, no adjustments have been made for:
(i) Weight-for-age.
(ii) Riders' claims.

HEADGEAR is shown immediately before the jockey's name and in parentheses and expressed as: **b** (blinkers); **v** (visor); **h** (hood); **e** (eyeshield); **c** (eyecover); **p** (sheepskin cheekpieces); **t** (tongue-tie).

THE JOCKEY is shown for every runner followed, in superscript, by apprentice allowances in parentheses.

APPRENTICE ALLOWANCES The holders of apprentice jockeys' licences under the provisions of Rule 60(iii) are permitted to claim the following allowances in Flat races:
7lb until they have won 20 Flat races run under the Rules of any recognised Turf Authority; thereafter 5lb until they have won 50 such Flat races; thereafter 3lb until they have won 95 such Flat races. These allowances can be claimed in the Flat races set out below, with the exception of races confined to apprentice jockeys:
(a) All handicaps other than those Rated stakes which are classified as listed races.
(b) All selling and claiming races.
(b) All weight-for-age races classified 3, 4, 5, 6 and 7.

THE DRAW for places at the start is shown after each jockey's name.

RACING POST RATINGS, which record the level of performance attained in this race for each horse, appear in the end column after each horse. These are the work of handicappers Simon Turner, Sam Walker and Paul Curtis, who head a dedicated team dealing with Flat races for Raceform and sister publication, the *Racing Post*.

THE TRAINER is shown for every runner.

COMMENT-IN-RUNNING is shown for each horse in an abbreviated form. Details of abbreviations appear later in this section.

STARTING PRICES appear below the jockey in the race result. The favourite indicator appears to the right of the Starting Price; 1 for the favourite, 2 for the second-favourite and 3 for third-favourite. Joint favourites share the same number.

RACE TIMES in Great Britain are official times which are electronically recorded and shown to 100th of a second. Figures in parentheses following the time show the number of seconds faster or slower than the Raceform Median Time for the course and distance.

RACEFORM MEDIAN TIMES are compiled from all races run over the course and distance in the preceding five years. Times equal to the median are shown as (0.00). Times under the median are preceded by minus, for instance, 1.8 seconds under the median would be shown (-1.8). Record times are displayed either referring to the juvenile record (2y crse rec) or to the overall record (course record).

TRACK VARIANT appears against each race to allow for changing conditions of the track and ground. It is shown to a hundredth of a second and indicates the adjustment per furlong against the median time. The going based on the going correction is shown in parentheses and is recorded in the following stages:
Turf: HD (Hard); F (Firm); GF (Good to firm); G (Good); GS (Good to soft); S (Soft); HVY (Heavy). All-Weather: FST (Fast); SF (Standard to fast); STD (Standard); SS (Standard to slow); SLW (Slow)

WEIGHT-FOR-AGE allowances are given where applicable for mixed-age races.

STARTING PRICE PERCENTAGE follows the going correction and weight-for-age details, and gives the total SP percentage of all runners that competed. It precedes the number of runners taking part in the race.

SELLING DETAILS (where applicable) and details of any claim are given. Friendly claims are not detailed.

SPEED RATINGS appear below the race time and going correction. They are the work of time expert Dave Bellingham and differ from conventional ratings systems in that they are an expression of a horse's ability in terms of lengths-per-mile, as opposed to pounds in weight. They are not directly comparable with BHA and Racing Post Ratings.

The ratings take no account of the effect of weight, either historically or on the day, and this component is left completely to the user's discretion. What is shown is a speed rating represented in its purest form, rather than one that has been altered for weight using a mathematical formula that treats all types of horses as if they were the same.

A comparison of the rating achieved with the 'par' figure for the grade of race - the rating that should be achievable by an average winner in that class of race - will both provide an at-a-glance indication of whether or not a race was truly run and also highlight the value of the form from a time perspective.

In theory, if a horse has a best speed figure five points superior to another and both run to their best form in a race over a mile, the first horse should beat the second by five lengths. In a race run over two miles, the margin should be ten lengths and so on.

Before the speed figures can be calculated, it is necessary to establish a set of standard or median times for every distance at every track, and this is done by averaging the times of all winners over a particular trip going back several years. No speed ratings are produced when insufficient races have been run over a distance for a reliable median time to be calculated.

Once a meeting has taken place, a raw unadjusted speed rating is calculated for each winner by calculating how many lengths per mile the winning time was faster or slower than the median for the trip. A difference of 0.2 of a second equals one length. The raw speed ratings of all winners on the card are then compared with the 'par' figure for the class of race. The difference between the 'raw' speed rating and the 'par' figure for each race is then noted, and both the fastest and slowest races are discarded before the rest are averaged to produce the going allowance or track variant. This figure gives an idea as to how much the elements, of which the going is one, have affected the final times of each race.

The figure representing the going allowance is then used to adjust the raw speed figures and produce the final ratings, which represent how fast the winners would have run on a perfectly good surface with no external influences, including the weather.

The ratings for beaten horses are worked out by taking the number of lengths they were behind the winner, adjusting that to take into account the distance of the race, and deducting that figure from the winner's rating. The reader is left with a rating which provides an instant impression of the value of a time performance.

The speed 'pars' below act as benchmark with which to compare the speed figures earned by each horse in each race. A horse that has already exceeded the 'par' for the class he is about to run in is of special interest, especially if he has done it more than once, as are horses that have consistently earned higher figures than their rivals.

Class 1 Group One	117
Class 1 Group Two	115
Class 1 Group Three	113
Class 1 Listed	111
Class 2	109
Class 3	107
Class 4	105
Class 5	103
Class 6	101
Class 7	99

Allowances need to be made for younger horses and for fillies. These allowances are as follows.

MONTH	2yo	3yo
Jan / Feb	n/a	-6
Mar / Apr	-11	-5
May / Jun	-10	-4
Jul / Aug	-9	-3
Sep / Oct	-8	-2
Nov / Dec	-7	-1
Races contested by fillies only		-3

Allowances are cumulative. For example, using a combination of the above pars and allowances, the par figure for the Epsom Oaks would be 110. The Group One par is 117, then deduct 4 because the race is confined to three year olds and run in June, then subtract another 3 because the race is confined to fillies.

TOTE prices include £1 stake. Exacta dividends are shown in parentheses. The Computer Straight Forecast dividend is preceded by the letters CSF, Computer Tricast is preceded by CT and Trifecta dividend is preceded by the word Trifecta. Jackpot, Placepot and Quadpot details appear at the end of the meeting to which they refer.

OWNER is followed by the breeder's name and the trainer's location.

STEWARDS' ENQUIRIES are included with the result, and any suspensions and/or fines incurred. Objections by jockeys and officials are included, where relevant.

HISTORICAL FOCUS details occasional points of historical significance.

FOCUS The Focus section helps readers distinguish good races from bad races and reliable form from unreliable form, by drawing together the opinions of handicapper, time expert and paddock watcher and interpreting their views in a punter-friendly manner.

Abbreviations and their meanings

Paddock comments

gd sort - well made, above average on looks
attr - attractive, but not as impressive as good sort
gd bodied - good bodied, well put together
h.d.w - has done well, improved in looks
wl grwn - well grown, has filled to its frame
lengthy - longer than average for its height
tall - tall
rangy - lengthy and tall but in proportion.
cl cpld - close coupled
scope - scope for physical development
str - strong, powerful looking
w'like - workmanlike, ordinary in looks
lt-f - light-framed, not much substance
cmpt - compact
neat - smallish, well put together
leggy - long legs compared with body
angular - unfurnished behind the saddle, not filled to frame
unf - unfurnished in the midriff, not filled to frame
narrow - not as wide as side appearance would suggest
small - lacks any physical scope
nt grwn - not grown
lw - looked fit and well
bkwd - backward in condition
t - tubed
swtg - sweating
b (off fore or nr fore) - bandaged in front
b.hind (off or nr) - bandaged behind

At the start

stdd s - jockey purposely reins back the horse
dwlt - missed the break and left for a short time
s.s - slow to start, left longer than a horse that dwelt
s.v.s - started very slowly
s.i.s - started on terms but took time to get going
ref to r - does not jump off, or travels a few yards then stops
rel to r - tries to pull itself up in mid-race
w.r.s - whipped round start

Position in the race

led - in lead on its own
disp ld - upsides the leader
w ldr - almost upsides the leader

w ldrs - in a line of three or more disputing the lead
prom - on the heels of the leaders, in front third of the field
trckd ldr(s) - just in behind the leaders giving impression that it could lead if asked
chsd ldr - horse in second place
chsd clr ldrs - horse heads main body of field behind two clear leaders
chsd ldrs - horse is in the first four or five but making more of an effort to stay close to the pace than if it were tracking the leaders.
clsd - closed
in tch - close enough to have a chance
hdwy - making ground on the leader
gd hdwy - making ground quickly on the leader, could be a deliberate move
sme hdwy - making some ground but no real impact on the race
w.w - waited with
stdy hdwy - gradually making ground
ev ch - upsides the leaders when the race starts in earnest
rr - at the back of main group but not detached
bhd - detached from the main body of runners
hld up - restrained as a deliberate tactical move
nt rcvr - lost all chance after interference, mistake etc.
wknd - stride shortened as it began to tire
lost tch - had been in the main body but a gap appeared as it tired
lost pl - remains in main body of runners but lost several positions quickly

Riding

effrt - short-lived effort
pushed along - received urgings with hands only, jockey not using legs
rdn - received urgings from saddle, including use of whip
hrd rdn - received maximum assistance from the saddle including use of whip
drvn - received forceful urgings, jockey putting in a lot of effort and using whip
hrd drvn - jockey very animated, plenty of kicking, pushing and reminders

Finishing comments

jst failed - closing rapidly on the winner and probably would have led a stride after the line
r.o - jockey's efforts usually involved to produce an increase in pace without finding an appreciable turn of speed
r.o wl - jockey's efforts usually involved to produce an obvious increase in pace without finding an appreciable turn of speed
unable qckn - not visibly tiring but does not possess a sufficient change of pace
one pce - not tiring but does not find a turn of speed, from a position further out than unable qckn
nt r.o. - did not consent to respond to pressure
styd on - going on well towards the end, utilising stamina
nvr able to chal - unable to produce sufficient to reach a challenging position
nvr nr to chal - in the opinion of the racereader, the horse was never in a suitable position to challenge.
nrst fin - nearer to the winner in distance beaten than at any time since the race had begun in earnest
nvr nrr - nearer to the winner position-wise than at any time since the race had begun in earnest
rallied - responded to pressure to come back with a chance having lost its place
no ex - unable to sustain its run
bttr for r - likely to improve for the run and experience
rn green - inclined to wander and falter through inexperience
too much to do - left with too much leeway to make up

Winning comments

v.easily - a great deal in hand
easily - plenty in hand
comf - something in hand, always holding the others
pushed out - kept up to its work with hands and heels without jockey resorting to whip or kicking along and wins fairly comfortably
rdn out - pushed and kicked out to the line, with the whip employed
drvn out - pushed and kicked out to the line, with considerable effort and the whip employed
all out - nothing to spare, could not have found any more
jst hld on - holding on to a rapidly diminishing lead, could not have found any more if passed
unchal - must either make all or a majority of the running and not be challenged from an early stage

• Complete list of abbreviations

a - always
abt - about
a.p - always prominent
appr - approaching
awrdd - awarded
b.b.v - broke blood-vessel
b.d - brought down
bdly - badly
bef - before
bhd - behind
bk - back
blkd - baulked
blnd - blundered
bmpd - bumped
bnd - bend
btn- beaten
bttr - better
c - came
ch - chance
chal - challenged
chse - chase
chsd - chased
chsng - chasing
circ - circuit
cl - close
clr - clear
clsd - closed
comf - comfortably
cpld - coupled
crse - course
ct - caught
def - definite
dismntd - dismounted
disp - disputed
dist - distance
div - division
drvn - driven
dwlt - dwelt
edgd - edged
effrt - effort

ent - entering
ev ch - every chance
ex - extra
f - furlong
fin - finished
fnd - found
fnl - final
fr - from
gd - good
gng - going
gp - group
grad - gradually
grnd - ground
hd - head
hdd - headed
hdwy - headway
hld - held
hmpd - hampered
imp - impression
ins - inside
j.b - jumped badly
j.w - jumped well
jnd - joined
jst - just
kpt - kept
l - length
ld - lead
ldr - leader
lft - left
mod - moderate
m - mile
m.n.s - made no show
mde - made
mid div - mid division
mstke - mistake
n.d - never dangerous
n.g.t - not go through
n.m.r - not much room
nk - neck
no ex - no extra
nr - near
nrr - nearer
nrst fin - nearest finish
nt - not
nvr - never
one pce - one pace
out - from finish
outpcd - outpaced
p.u - pulled up
pce - pace
pckd - pecked
pl - place
plcd - placed
plld - pulled
press - pressure
prog - progress
prom - prominent
qckly - quickly
qckn - quicken
r - race
racd - raced
rch - reach
rcvr - recover
rdn - ridden
rdr - rider
reard - reared
ref - refused
rn - ran
rnd - round
r.o - ran on
rr - rear
rspnse - response
rt - right
s - start
sddle - saddle
shkn - shaken
slt - slight
sme - some
sn - soon
spd- speed
st - straight
stmbld - stumbled
stdd - steadied
stdy - steady
strly - strongly
styd - stayed
styng - staying
s. u - slipped up
swtchd - switched
swvd - swerved
tk - took
t.k.h - took keen hold
t.o - tailed off
tch - touch
thrght - throughout
trbld - troubled
trckd - tracked
u.p - under pressure
u.str.p- under strong pressure
w - with
w.r.s - whipped round start
wd - wide
whn - when
wknd - weakened
wl - well
wnr - winner
wnt - went
1/2-wy - halfway

Racing Post Ratings

Racing Post Ratings for each horse are shown in the right hand column, headed RPR, and indicate the actual level of performance attained in that race. The figure in the back index represents the BEST public form that Raceform's Handicappers still believe the horse capable of reproducing.

To use the ratings constructively in determining those horses best-in in future events, the following procedure should be followed:

(i) In races where all runners are the same age and are set to carry the same weight, no calculations are necessary. The horse with the highest rating is best-in.

(ii) In races where all runners are the same age but are set to carry different weights, add one point to the Racing Post Rating for every pound less than 10 stone to be carried; deduct one point for every pound more than 10 stone.

For example,

Horse	Age & wt	Adjustment from 10st	Base rating	Adjusted rating
Treclare	3-10-1	-1	78	77
Buchan	3-9-13	+1	80	81
Paper Money	3-9-7	+7	71	78
Archaic	3-8-11	+17	60	77

Therefore Buchan is top-rated (best-in)

(iii) In races concerning horses of different ages the procedure in (ii) should again be followed, but reference must also be made to the Official Scale of Weight-For-Age.

For example,

12 furlongs, July 20th

Horse	Age & wt	Adjustment from 10st	Base rating	Adjusted rating	W-F-A deduct	Final rating
Archaic	5-10-0	0	90	90	Nil	90
Orpheus	4-9-9	+5	88	93	Nil	93
Lemonora	3-9-4	+10	85	95	-12	83
Tamar	4-8-7	+21	73	94	Nil	94

Therefore Tamar is top-rated (best-in)

(A 3-y-o is deemed 12lb less mature than a 4-y-o or older horse on 20th July over 12f. Therefore, the deduction of 12 points is necessary.)

The following symbols are used in conjunction with the ratings:

++: almost certain to prove better

+: likely to prove better

d: disappointing (has run well below best recently)

?: form hard to evaluate

t: tentative rating based on race-time rating may prove unreliable

Weight adjusted ratings for every race are published daily in Raceform Private Handicap.

For subscription terms please contact the Subscription Department on 01933 304858.

Course descriptions

(R.H.) denotes right-hand and (L.H.) left-hand courses.

ASCOT (R.H)

Right-handed triangular track just under 1m 6f in length. The Round course descends from the 1m 4f start into Swinley Bottom, the lowest part of the track. It then turns right-handed and joins the Old Mile Course, which starts on a separate chute. The course then rises to the right-handed home turn over a new underpass to join the straight mile course. The run-in is about 3f, rising slightly to the winning post. The whole course is of a galloping nature with easy turns.

AYR (L.H)

A left-handed, galloping, flat oval track of 1m 4f with a 4f run-in. The straight 6f is essentially flat.

BATH (L.H)

Galloping, left-handed, level oval of 1m 4f 25y, with long, stiff run-in of about 4f which bends to the left. An extended chute provides for races over 5f 11y and 5f 161y.

BEVERLEY (R.H)

A right-handed oval of 1m 3f, generally galloping, with an uphill run-in of two and a half furlongs. The 5f course is very stiff.

BRIGHTON (L.H)

Left-handed, 1m 4f horseshoe with easy turns and a run-in of three and a half furlongs. Undulating and sharp, the track suits handy types.

CARLISLE (R.H)

Right-handed, 1m 4f pear-shaped track. Galloping and undulating with easy turns and a stiff uphill run-in of three and a half furlongs. 6f course begins on an extended chute.

CATTERICK (L.H)

A sharp, left-handed, undulating oval of 1m 180y with a downhill run-in of 3f.

CHEPSTOW (L.H)

A left-handed, undulating oval of about 2m, with easy turns, and a straight run-in of 5f. There is a straight track of 1m 14y.

CHESTER (L.H)

A level, sharp, left-handed, circular course of 1m 73y, with a short run-in of 230y. Chester is a specialists' track which generally suits the sharp-actioned horse.

DONCASTER (L.H)

A left-handed, flat, galloping course of 1m 7f 110y, with a long run-in which extends to a straight mile.

EPSOM (L.H)

Left-handed and undulating with easy turns, and a run-in of just under 4f. The straight 5f course is also undulating and downhill all the way, making it the fastest 5f in the world.

FFOS LAS (L.H)

The track is a 60m wide, basically flat, 1m4f oval with sweeping bends.

GOODWOOD (R.H)

A sharp, undulating, essentially right-handed track with a long run-in. There is also a straight 6f course.

HAMILTON PARK (R.H)

Sharp, undulating, right-handed course of 1m 5f with a five and a half furlong, uphill run-in. There is a straight track of 6f.

HAYDOCK PARK (L.H)

A galloping, almost flat, oval track, 1m 5f round, with a run-in of four and a half furlongs and a straight 6f course.

KEMPTON PARK (R.H)

A floodlit Polytrack circuit opened in March 2006. A 1m 2f outer track accommodates races over 6f, 7f, 1m, 1m 3f, 1m 4f and 2m. The 1m inner track caters for races over 5f and 1m 2f.

LEICESTER (R.H)

Stiff, galloping, right-handed oval of 1m 5f, with a 5f run-in. There is a straight course of 7f.

LINGFIELD PARK (L.H)

Turf Course: A sharp, undulating left-handed circuit, with a 7f 140y straight course.

Polytrack course: left-handed all-weather is 1m 2f round. It is a sharp, level track with a short run-in.

MUSSELBURGH (R.H)

A sharp, level, right-handed oval of 1m 2f, with a run-in of 4f. There is an additional 5f straight course.

NEWBURY (L.H)

Left-handed, oval track of about 1m 7f, with a slightly undulating straight mile. The round course is level and galloping with a four and a half furlong run-in. Races over the round mile and 7f 60y start on the adjoining chute.

NEWCASTLE (L.H)

Galloping, easy, left-handed oval of 1m 6f, with an uphill 4f run-in. There is a straight course of 1m 8y.

NEWMARKET (R.H)

Rowley Mile Course: There is a straight 1m2f course, which is wide and galloping. Races over 1m4f or more are right-handed. The Rowley course has a long run-in and a stiff finish.

July Course: Races up to a mile are run on the Bunbury course, which is straight. Races over 1m2f or more are right-handed, with a 7f run-in. Like the Rowley course, the July track is stiff.

NOTTINGHAM (L.H)

Left-handed, galloping, oval of about 1m 4f, and a run-in of four and a half furlongs. Flat with easy turns.

PONTEFRACT (L.H)

Left-handed oval, undulating course of 2m 133y, with a short run-in of 2f. It is a particularly stiff track with the last 3f uphill.

REDCAR (L.H)

Left-handed, level, galloping, oval course of 1m 6f with a straight run-in of 5f. There is also a straight 1m.

RIPON (R.H)

A sharp, undulating, right-handed oval of 1m 5f, with a 5f run-in. There is also a 6f straight course.

SALISBURY (R.H)

Right-handed and level, with a run-in of 4f. There is a straight 1m track. The last half mile is uphill, providing a stiff test of stamina.

SANDOWN PARK (R.H)

An easy right-handed oval course of 1m 5f with a stiff straight uphill run-in of 4f. Separate straight 5f track is also uphill. Galloping.

SOUTHWELL (L.H)

Left-handed oval, Fibresand course of 1m 2f with a 3f run-in. There is a straight 5f. Sharp and level, Southwell suits front-runners.

THIRSK (L.H)

Left-handed, oval of 1m 2f with sharp turns and an undulating run-in of 4f. There is a straight 6f track.

WARWICK (L.H)

Left-handed, sharp, level track of 1m 6f 32y in circumference, with a run-in of two and a half furlongs. There is also a 6f chute.

WETHERBY (L.H)

Left-handed, galloping track. Circuit 1m4f. 4f straight, slightly uphill.

WINDSOR (Fig. 8)

Figure eight track of 1m 4f 110y. The course is level and sharp with a long run-in. The 6f course is essentially straight.

WOLVERHAMPTON (L.H)

Left-handed oval, Tapeta course of 1m, with a run-in of 380y. A level track with sharp bends.

YARMOUTH (L.H)

Left-handed, level circuit of 1m 4f, with a run-in of 5f. The straight course is 1m long.

YORK (L.H)

Left-handed, level, galloping track, with a straight 6f. There is also an adjoining chute of 7f.

SOUTHWELL (L-H)

Tuesday, January 1

OFFICIAL GOING: Fibresand: standard

Wind: Moderate across Weather: Cloudy

1 BETWAY NOVICE MEDIAN AUCTION STKS 4f 214y(F)

12:35 (12:35) (Class 5) 3-4-Y-0 £4,140 (£1,232; £615; £307) Stalls Centre

Form RPR

605- 1 **Swiss Chime**[28] 9392 3-8-6 56 KieranO'Neill 2 60
(Dean Ivory) *mde all: rdn wl over 1f out: drvn and edgd rt ins fnl f: kpt on wl towards fin (jockey said filly hung right throughout)* **10/1**

2 ¾ **Hanati (IRE)** 3-8-6 0 LukeMorris 4 57
(Simon Crisford) *dwlt: green and wnt lft s: sn chsng ldng pair: rdn along 2f out: drvn and ch ent fnl f: kpt on u.p* **9/4**[2]

2- 3 ¾ **Jungle Secret (IRE)**[17] 9566 3-8-6 0 BarryMcHugh 5 55
(Richard Fahey) *green: sn pushed along and outpcd towards rr: hdwy 1/2-way: rdn along wl over 1f out: kpt on fnl f* **9/2**[3]

222- 4 ¾ **Point Zero (IRE)**[12] 9645 4-9-12 67 (b) AlistairRawlinson 3 63
(Michael Appleby) *cl up: pushed along over 2f out: rdn and ev ch over 1f out: sn drvn and wknd ins fnl f* **6/4**[1]

6- 5 17 **Amliba**[13] 9612 3-8-6 0 JoeFanning 1
(David O'Meara) *dwlt: green and a towards rr: outpcd and bhd fr 1/2-way* **7/1**

58.69s (-1.01) **Going Correction** -0.20s/f (Stan)
WFA 3 from 4yo 15lb 5 Ran SP% 110.5
Speed ratings (Par 103): **100,98,97,96,69**
CSF £32.63 TOTE £11.90: £4.50, £1.80; EX 40.00 Trifecta £139.70.
Owner K T Ivory & Mrs Valerie Hubbard **Bred** Mrs J E Laws **Trained** Radlett, Herts

FOCUS
A moderate novice. The winner has been rated to her AW form, with the third close to her debut figure.

2 BETWAY CASINO H'CAP 6f 16y(F)

1:10 (1:10) (Class 5) (0-75,76) 4-Y-0+
£5,433 (£1,617; £808; £404; £300; £300) Stalls Low

Form RPR

236- 1 **Bellevarde (IRE)**[14] 9597 5-9-4 72 HollieDoyle 7 79
(Richard Price) *cl up: chal over 2f out: led wl over 1f out: sn rdn: drvn ins fnl f: kpt on wl towards fin* **14/1**

150- 2 ¾ **Dollar Value (USA)**[27] 9402 4-8-11 65 (p) JoeFanning 5 70
(Robert Cowell) *led: rdn along 2f out: sn hdd: drvn and ev ch jst over 1f out: kpt on u.p fnl f* **11/2**[3]

206- 3 hd **Jack The Truth (IRE)**[108] 7271 5-9-1 76 JessicaCooley(7) 3 80
(George Scott) *trckd ldrs: effrt and n.m.r 2f out: sn swtchd rt and rdn over 1f out: drvn ent fnl f: kpt on* **5/1**[2]

041- 4 ½ **Global Melody**[12] 9645 4-9-0 68 NicolaCurrie 2 70
(Phil McEntee) *trckd ldrs on inner: hdwy over 2f out: rdn to chal jst over 1f out: ev ch ins fnl f: drvn and no ex last 75yds* **7/2**[1]

002- 5 2 **Amazing Grazing (IRE)**[14] 9597 5-9-7 75 LewisEdmunds 1 71
(Rebecca Bastiman) *dwlt: in tch: rdn along over 2f out: kpt on u.p fnl f (jockey dropped whip approx 1 1/2f out)* **6/1**

614- 6 1 ¾ **Kommander Kirkup**[21] 9491 8-9-1 69 (p) AndrewMullen 9 59
(Michael Herrington) *in tch on outer: pushed along 1/2-way: wd st: rdn to chse ldrs wl over 1f out: sn drvn: edgd lft and no imp* **9/1**

556- 7 ½ **Zapper Cass (FR)**[14] 9596 6-9-4 72 (p) LukeMorris 4 61
(Michael Appleby) *dwlt and towards rr: rdn along 1/2-way: wd st: sn drvn and no hdwy* **5/1**[2]

660- 8 1 ¼ **Tathmeen (IRE)**[27] 9414 4-9-7 75 CamHardie 6 60
(Antony Brittain) *prom: cl up 1/2-way: rdn along wl over 2f out: sn wknd* **25/1**

000- 9 9 **Monks Stand (USA)**[21] 9494 5-9-2 70 (v) BarryMcHugh 8 26
(John Mackie) *sn rdn along in rr: outpcd and bhd fr wl over 2f out* **14/1**

1m 14.71s (-1.79) **Going Correction** -0.20s/f (Stan) 9 Ran SP% 112.4
Speed ratings (Par 103): **103,102,101,101,98 96,95,93,81**
CSF £86.11 CT £444.23 TOTE £13.10: £3.30, £2.40, £2.20; EX 92.00 Trifecta £747.30.
Owner Barry Veasey **Bred** Tally-Ho Stud **Trained** Ullingswick, H'fords

FOCUS
A competitive handicap, but the early gallop wasn't strong and the pace held up pretty well. A small pb from the winner, with the third and fourth rated close to form.

3 BETWAY SPRINT H'CAP 4f 214y(F)

1:45 (1:45) (Class 3) (0-90,90) 4-Y-0+
£10,582 (£3,168; £1,584; £792; £396; £198) Stalls Centre

Form RPR

450- 1 **Moonraker**[11] 9662 7-9-3 86 LukeMorris 6 95
(Michael Appleby) *racd towards stands' side: cl up: led 3f out: rdn and hdd 1 1/2f out: drvn ent fnl f: led and edgd rt last 100yds: kpt on (regarding the apparent improvement in form, trainer's rep said gelding was uited by being able to race more prominently, therefore avoiding any kickback on this occasion)* **15/2**

226- 2 ½ **Watchable**[25] 9446 9-9-7 90 (p) JoeFanning 8 97
(David O'Meara) *racd nr stands' rail: trckd ldrs: hdwy 1/2-way: led 1 1/2f out: sn rdn: drvn and hdd whn sltly hmpd and carried rt ins fnl 100yds: no ex towards fin* **9/1**

442- 3 nk **Ornate**[11] 9662 6-9-3 86 DougieCostello 1 92
(David C Griffiths) *racd towards far side: dwlt: sn chsng ldrs: rdn wl over 1f out: drvn and ev ch ins fnl f: kpt on* **3/1**[2]

105- 4 1 **Jashma (IRE)**[11] 9662 5-8-10 82 (b) FinleyMarsh(3) 2 84
(Richard Hughes) *racd towards far side: towards rr: rdn along and hdwy over 2f out: drvn over 1f out: kpt on fnl f* **11/4**[1]

030- 5 nk **Something Lucky (IRE)**[11] 9662 7-9-0 83 (v) AlistairRawlinson 4 84
(Michael Appleby) *towards rr centre: hdwy 2f out: sn rdn: styd on fnl f* **7/1**[3]

506- 6 hd **Landing Night (IRE)**[3] 9748 7-8-4 78 (tp) RhiainIngram(5) 7 79
(Rebecca Menzies) *racd towards stands' side: chsd ldrs: pushed along 2f out: sn rdn and edgd lft: one pce (jockey said gelding hung left throughout)* **8/1**

131- 7 1 ¼ **You're Cool**[22] 9486 7-8-12 81 (t) LewisEdmunds 3 77
(John Balding) *slt ld centre: hdd 3f out: cl up and rdn 2f out: sn drvn and grad wknd* **9/1**

500- 8 1 **Equimou**[3] 9748 5-8-13 82 HollieDoyle 5 74
(Robert Eddery) *chsd ldrs centre: rdn along over 2f out: sn wknd* **16/1**

58.2s (-1.50) **Going Correction** -0.20s/f (Stan) 8 Ran SP% 112.9
Speed ratings (Par 107): **104,103,102,101,100 100,98,96**
CSF £69.90 CT £247.11 TOTE £8.20: £2.40, £2.00, £1.20; EX 55.60 Trifecta £365.50.
Owner The Kettlelites **Bred** Stratford Place Stud **Trained** Oakham, Rutland

FOCUS
The early speed was more towards the stands' side and the first two were up there from the start. The third has been rated close to his C&D latest.

4 SUNRACING.CO.UK H'CAP 7f 14y(F)

2:20 (2:20) (Class 3) (0-95,88) 4-Y-0+
£10,582 (£3,168; £1,584; £792; £396; £198) Stalls Low

Form RPR

316- 1 **Saint Equiano**[91] 7869 5-9-7 88 CallumRodriguez 6 97
(Keith Dalgleish) *qckly away: mde all: rdn clr wl over 1f out: kpt on strly* **5/1**[3]

005- 2 1 ¼ **Custard The Dragon**[11] 9661 6-9-1 82 (p) JoeFanning 1 87
(John Mackie) *hld up towards rr: hdwy over 2f out: rdn wl over 1f out: drvn to chse wnr ins fnl f: no imp towards fin* **5/1**[3]

204- 3 ½ **Gentlemen**[21] 9494 8-8-11 78 (h) NicolaCurrie 8 82
(Phil McEntee) *chsd wnr: rdn along 2f out: drvn over 1f out: kpt on same pce* **12/1**

/00- 4 2 ¼ **Esprit De Corps**[21] 9494 5-8-10 77 LewisEdmunds 2 75
(David Barron) *in rr: rdn along 3f out: hdwy 2f out: kpt on fnl f* **28/1**

045- 5 5 **Call Out Loud**[26] 9430 7-9-1 82 (vt) AlistairRawlinson 4 66
(Michael Appleby) *trckd ldrs: hdwy and cl up 3f out: wd st: and rdn over 2f out: drvn wl over 1f out: sn wknd* **13/2**

32/- 6 nk **Me Too Nagasaki (IRE)**[449] 7892 5-8-12 86 (t[1]) TobyEley(7) 7 69
(Stuart Williams) *chsd ldrs on wd outside: cl up 1/2-way: rdn along and wd st: wknd 2f out* **8/1**

112- 7 2 ½ **Angel Palanas**[14] 9596 5-8-7 81 (p) JonathanFisher(7) 3 58
(K R Burke) *trckd ldng pair on inner: pushed along 3f out: rdn over 2f out: sn drvn and btn (trainer said regarding the performance, gelding was possibly unsuited by not being able to dominate on this occasion)* **3/1**[1]

215- 8 11 **The Great Wall (USA)**[165] 5158 5-9-3 84 LukeMorris 5 31
(Michael Appleby) *trckd ldng pair: effrt wl over 2f out: sn rdn and wknd (vet said gelding bled from the nose)* **7/2**[2]

1m 27.3s (-3.00) **Going Correction** -0.20s/f (Stan) 8 Ran SP% 116.1
Speed ratings (Par 107): **109,107,107,104,98 98,95,82**
CSF £30.63 CT £287.91 TOTE £5.80: £1.90, £1.70, £3.90; EX 34.70 Trifecta £274.40.
Owner Paul & Clare Rooney **Bred** Usk Valley Stud **Trained** Carluke, S Lanarks

FOCUS
A good performance from the winner, who handled the surface well on his first visit to Southwell. The second has been rated similar to when winning this last year.

5 FOLLOW SUN RACING ON TWITTER H'CAP 1m 13y(F)

2:55 (2:57) (Class 5) (0-75,77) 4-Y-0+
£5,433 (£1,617; £808; £404; £300; £300) Stalls Low

Form RPR

021- 1 **Showboating (IRE)**[21] 9496 11-9-6 72 (p) LewisEdmunds 2 83
(John Balding) *hld up in rr: n.m.r on inner bnd at 1/2-way: hdwy on inner wl over 2f out: rdn to chal over 1f out: led jst ins fnl f: sn clr: kpt on strly* **5/1**[3]

011- 2 2 ¼ **Tagur (IRE)**[32] 9337 5-9-1 72 (p) ThomasGreatrex(5) 5 78
(Kevin Ryan) *cl up: led jst over 2f out: sn rdn: jnd and drvn over 1f out: hdd jst ins fnl f: kpt on same pce* **9/2**[2]

000- 3 2 ¼ **Pearl Spectre (USA)**[6] 9702 8-9-7 73 (v) NicolaCurrie 7 74
(Phil McEntee) *sn ;led: rdn along and hdd over 2f out: drvn wl over 1f out: kpt on one pce* **12/1**

400- 4 6 **Red Touch (USA)**[15] 9585 7-9-5 71 (b) AlistairRawlinson 6 58
(Michael Appleby) *cl up on outer: rdn along wl over 2f out: drvn and outpcd fr wl over 1f out* **12/1**

632- 5 1 ¼ **Thechildren'strust (IRE)**[11] 9656 4-9-11 77 HectorCrouch 4 61
(Gary Moore) *t.k.h: hld up in tch: effrt 3f out: rdn along over 2f out: sn drvn along and n.d (regarding the gelding's performance, trainer could offer no explanation, other than the gelding is an inconsistent type)* **5/4**[1]

034- 6 1 ¾ **Duke Of Alba (IRE)**[14] 9600 4-8-9 61 AndrewMullen 8 41
(John Mackie) *chsd ldrs on outer: rdn along 3f out: sn wknd* **12/1**

620- 7 nk **Sooqaan**[21] 9496 8-8-9 61 (p) CamHardie 3 40
(Antony Brittain) *hld up: a towards rr (jockey said gelding stumbled leaving stalls)* **16/1**

145- 8 4 ½ **Muqarred (USA)**[246] 2206 7-9-5 76 BenSanderson(5) 1 45
(Roger Fell) *cl up: rdn along over 3f out: sn wknd* **22/1**

1m 40.55s (-3.15) **Going Correction** -0.20s/f (Stan) 8 Ran SP% 112.6
Speed ratings (Par 103): **107,104,102,96,95 93,93,88**
CSF £26.81 CT £255.96 TOTE £5.90: £1.50, £1.30, £2.40; EX 24.80 Trifecta £236.50.
Owner M & Mrs L Cooke & A McCabe **Bred** Crone Stud Farms Ltd **Trained** Scrooby, S Yorks

FOCUS
They finished well strung out here. The winner backed up his latest effort here, and the second posted a small pb.

6 LIKE SUN RACING ON FACEBOOK H'CAP 1m 13y(F)

3:30 (3:32) (Class 6) (0-60,59) 4-Y-0+
£3,105 (£924; £461; £300; £300; £300) Stalls Low

Form RPR

001- 1 **Bond Angel**[11] 9659 4-9-0 59 KatherineBegley(7) 11 66
(David Evans) *trckd ldrs: hdwy 3f out: led 1 1/2f out: sn rdn and kpt on wl* **7/1**[2]

005- 2 1 ¼ **Angel's Acclaim (IRE)**[14] 9593 5-9-6 58 (p) BarryMcHugh 6 62
(Kevin Ryan) *dwlt and towards rr: hdwy over 3f out: chsd ldrs 2f out: sn rdn: drvn and styd on wl fnl f* **13/2**[1]

002- 3 shd **Catapult**[12] 9644 4-8-11 49 HollieDoyle 8 53
(Clifford Lines) *led 2f: cl up: led again wl over 2f out: sn rdn and hdd 1 1/2f out: sn drvn and kpt on same pce (one-day ban: failed to ride to draw (15th Jan))* **7/1**[2]

050- 4 2 **Broken Wings (IRE)**[15] 9587 4-9-4 56 (v[1]) CallumRodriguez 2 55
(Keith Dalgleish) *t.k.h: trckd ldrs on inner: hdwy 3f out: rdn along 2f out: drvn over 1f out: kpt on one pce* **14/1**

006- 5 1 **Amity Island**[29] 9381 4-9-1 56 BenRobinson(3) 12 53
(Ollie Pears) *chsd ldrs on wd outside: pushed along over 3f out: rdn along and wd st: drvn 2f out: kpt on* **15/2**[3]

043- 6 2 **Golden Guide**[12] 9643 4-8-2 47 (v) RhonaPindar(7) 3 40
(K R Burke) *in rr tl styd on fnl 2f: n.d* **12/1**

603- 7 *nse* **Luath**[12] 9644 6-9-0 **52** .... NickyMackay 4 44
(Suzzanne France) *towards rr tl styd on fnl 2f* **7/1**[2]

230- 8 *shd* **Alpha Tauri (USA)**[14] 9600 13-9-1 **56** .... NoelGarbutt(3) 7 48
(Charles Smith) *towards rr: hdwy 3f out: rdn along 2f out: sn no imp* **20/1**

040- 9 *1 ¾* **Queen Tomyris**[20] 9501 4-9-2 **54** .... (h[1]) JoeFanning 5 42
(William Jarvis) *a towards rr: wd st and bhd* **10/1**

400- 10 *¾* **Gembari**[24] 9465 4-9-5 **57** .... (v) LewisEdmunds 13 43
(John Balding) *cl up: led after 2f: rdn along 3f out: sn hdd & wknd over 2f out* **28/1**

001- 11 *1 ½* **Candesta (USA)**[12] 9644 9-9-5 **57** .... (t) HectorCrouch 14 40
(Julia Feilden) *chsd ldrs: wd st: rdn along over 2f out: sn wknd* **8/1**

453- 12 *1 ½* **Captain Kissinger**[76] 7159 4-8-9 **54** .... (b) EllieMacKenzie(7) 1 34
(Jo Hughes, France) *in tch on inner: rdn along over 3f out: sn wknd* **18/1**

030- 13 *2 ¼* **Limerick Lord (IRE)**[12] 9643 7-8-12 **50** .... (p) CharlieBennett 10 24
(Julia Feilden) *in tch: effrt 3f out: rdn along over 2f out: sn wknd* **10/1**

1m 41.37s (-2.33) **Going Correction** -0.20s/f (Stan) **13** Ran SP% **119.7**
Speed ratings (Par 101): **101,99,99,97,96 94,94,94,92,92 90,89,86**
CSF £52.14 CT £336.66 TOTE £5.30: £2.30, £2.10, £2.70; EX 23.10 Trifecta £152.30.
Owner M W Lawrence **Bred** R C Bond **Trained** Pandy, Monmouths
■ Stewards' Enquiry : Lewis Edmunds one-day ban: failed to ride to draw (15th Jan)

FOCUS
An ordinary contest.
T/Plt: £335.10 to a £1 stake. Pool: £52,823.39 - 115.07 winning units T/Qpdt: £30.20 to a £1 stake. Pool: £7,410.28 - 181.20 winning units **Joe Rowntree**

7 - 17a (Foreign Racing) - See Raceform Interactive

NEWCASTLE (A.W) (L-H)
Wednesday, January 2

OFFICIAL GOING: Tapeta: standard
Wind: virtually nil Weather: overcast

18 BETWAY CASINO MAIDEN STKS — 1m 2f 42y (Tp)
3:35 (3:37) (Class 5) 4-Y-O+ **£3,752** (£1,116; £557; £278) **Stalls** High

Form RPR

233- 1 **Cloudlam**[25] 9464 4-9-0 69 .... (b[1]) MartinHarley 7 75
(William Haggas) *mde all: rdn over 1f out: sn in command: pushed out ins fnl f* **11/4**[2]

543- 2 *4 ½* **Sajanjl**[63] 8733 4-9-0 69 .... JackMitchell 4 66
(Simon Crisford) *in tch: racd quite keenly: hdwy and trckd ldr 5f out: rdn over 2f out: one pce and hld in 2nd fr appr fnl furlong* **7/4**[1]

2- 3 *1 ¼* **Ice Pyramid (IRE)**[194] 4080 4-9-5 0 .... AndrewMullen 1 69
(Philip Kirby) *dwlt and veered lft s: hld up in tch: pushed along over 3f out: rdn 2f out: edgd lft: styd on same pce ins fnl f* **11/4**[2]

30- 4 *½* **Be Thankful**[46] 9134 4-9-0 0 .... JoeFanning 3 63
(Roger Charlton) *trckd ldr: rdn over 2f out: sn one pce: no ins fnl f and lost 3rd fnl 50yds* **11/2**[3]

5 *14* **Bempton Cliffs (IRE)**[11] 4-9-5 0 .... BarryMcHugh 6 40
(Tony Coyle) *hld up: racd keenly: pushed along over 2f out: wknd over 1f out* **20/1**

05- 6 *10* **Fields Of Fire**[18] 9553 5-9-6 0 .... JamesSullivan 2 19
(Alistair Whillans) *hld up: rdn over 3f out: wknd* **150/1**

000- 7 *nk* **Last Glance (IRE)**[12] 9660 4-9-5 43 .... CamHardie 5 19
(Tracy Waggott) *trckd ldrs: rdn and wknd 3f out* **250/1**

2m 9.32s (-1.08) **Going Correction** +0.15s/f (Slow)
WFA 4 from 5yo 1lb **7** Ran SP% **110.9**
Speed ratings (Par 103): **110,106,105,105,93 85,85**
CSF £7.46 TOTE £3.30: £1.50, £2.20; EX 7.20 Trifecta £23.40.
Owner St Albans Bloodstock Limited **Bred** St Albans Bloodstock Llp **Trained** Newmarket, Suffolk

FOCUS
An ordinary maiden for older horses, which appeared to be run at a routine pace, although the time the winner recorded was decent. The second and fourth have been rated a bit below form for now.

19 SUNRACING.CO.UK H'CAP — 1m 5y (Tp)
4:10 (4:10) (Class 4) (0-85,87) 4-Y-O+
£5,530 (£1,645; £822; £411; £400; £400) **Stalls** Centre

Form RPR

020- 1 **Trevithick**[41] 9204 4-9-7 **85** .... JoeFanning 6 91
(Bryan Smart) *pressed ldr: pushed along to ld over 2f out: rdn appr fnl f: pressed ins fnl f: kpt on: a doing enough* **11/4**[1]

005- 2 *½* **My Target (IRE)**[32] 9358 8-9-9 **87** .... CamHardie 3 92
(Michael Wigham) *hld up in tch: pushed along and hdwy over 1f out: rdn to chal ins fnl f: kpt on but a hld* **8/1**

206- 3 *¾* **Come On Tier (FR)**[28] 9397 4-9-2 **80** .... MartinHarley 5 83
(David Simcock) *hld up in tch: hdwy to chse ldrs over 1f out: rdn and kpt on same pce* **7/2**[3]

541- 4 *1* **Space Bandit**[36] 9277 4-8-12 **76** .... AndrewMullen 2 77
(Michael Appleby) *trckd ldrs: pushed along 3f out: rdn over 1f out: one pce* **14/1**

651- 5 *7* **Dubai Acclaim (IRE)**[35] 9285 4-8-10 **74** .... BarryMcHugh 4 59
(Richard Fahey) *led narrowly: rdn and hdd over 2f out: sn wknd (jockey said gelding stopped quickly, trainers rep could offer no explanation for gelding's poor run)* **3/1**[2]

133- 6 *7* **Breaking Records (IRE)**[21] 9508 4-9-9 **87** .... (h) JackMitchell 1 56
(Hugo Palmer) *trckd ldrs: racd keenly: rdn over 2f out: sn wknd (jockey said gelding ran too free)* **5/1**

1m 39.67s (1.07) **Going Correction** +0.15s/f (Slow) **6** Ran SP% **109.4**
Speed ratings (Par 105): **100,99,98,97,90 83**
CSF £22.89 TOTE £3.10: £2.50, £5.50; EX 24.30 Trifecta £98.90.
Owner Mrs P A Clark **Bred** Mrs P A Clark **Trained** Hambleton, N Yorks

FOCUS
This fair little handicap proved tactical. Muddling form. A length pb from the winner.

20 LADBROKES HOME OF THE ODDS BOOST NOVICE STKS — 7f 14y (Tp)
4:45 (4:45) (Class 5) 3-Y-O **£3,752** (£1,116; £557; £278) **Stalls** Centre

Form RPR

61- 1 **Dutch Pursuit (IRE)**[14] 9612 3-9-7 0 .... CallumRodriguez 3 76
(Michael Dods) *trckd ldrs: pushed along to ld over 1f out: drvn ins fnl f: strly pressed towards fin: all out* **5/1**[3]

244- 2 *nse* **Shanghai Grace**[62] 8783 3-9-2 78 .... CallumShepherd 4 71
(Charles Hills) *trckd ldrs: racd keenly: pushed along over 2f out: rdn ins fnl f: kpt on to chal strly towards fin* **6/1**

03- 3 *shd* **Kentucky Kingdom (IRE)**[42] 9183 3-9-2 0 .... MartinHarley 2 71
(William Haggas) *hld up in midfield: pushed along and hdwy over 1f out: sn chsd ldr: rdn ins fnl f: kpt on* **5/4**[1]

4 *¾* **Solar Park (IRE)** 3-9-2 0 .... AndrewMullen 10 69
(James Tate) *dwlt: in tch: sme hdwy over 1f out: rdn to chal ent fnl f: kpt on same pce* **16/1**

40- 5 *3* **Just Once**[81] 8177 3-8-11 0 .... HectorCrouch 8 56
(Mrs Ilka Gansera-Leveque) *prom: rdn over 2f out: no ex ins fnl f* **50/1**

0- 6 *½* **Amourie**[28] 9411 3-8-11 0 .... JamesSullivan 1 55
(Ray Craggs) *hld up: rdn along over 2f out: styd on ins fnl f* **100/1**

00- 7 *nk* **Benji**[32] 9354 3-9-2 0 .... BarryMcHugh 7 59
(Richard Fahey) *hld up: pushed along over 2f out: kpt on ins fnl f: nvr involved* **50/1**

2- 8 *½* **Fiction Writer (USA)**[47] 9103 3-9-2 0 .... JoeFanning 5 57
(Mark Johnston) *led: rdn over 2f out: hdd over 1f out: wknd ins fnl f* **2/1**[2]

00- 9 *2 ¾* **Half Full**[35] 9283 3-8-9 0 .... JoshQuinn(7) 6 50
(Michael Easterby) *midfield: lost pl 3f out: sn struggling towards rr* **66/1**

0- 10 *2* **Somewhat Sisyphean**[33] 9323 3-9-2 0 .... NathanEvans 9 45
(Wilf Storey) *dwlt: a towards rr* **150/1**

1m 28.11s (1.91) **Going Correction** +0.15s/f (Slow) **10** Ran SP% **121.7**
Speed ratings (Par 97): **95,94,94,93,90 89,89,89,85,83**
CSF £36.10 TOTE £6.00: £1.80, £2.00, £1.10; EX 32.40 Trifecta £80.50.
Owner Geoff & Sandra Turnbull **Bred** Elwick Stud **Trained** Denton, Co Durham

FOCUS
This interesting novice event was another race run at an uneven tempo. The fifth and sixth likely limit the overall form.

21 LADBROKES BET £5 GET £20 H'CAP — 6f (Tp)
5:15 (5:16) (Class 5) (0-70,70) 3-Y-O
£3,752 (£1,116; £557; £400; £400; £400) **Stalls** Centre

Form RPR

022- 1 **Coolagh Magic**[12] 9669 3-9-6 **69** .... (p) BarryMcHugh 5 78
(Richard Fahey) *prom: pushed along to ld wl over 1f out: kpt on wl pushed out: comf* **5/4**[1]

552- 2 *2 ¾* **Caustic Love (IRE)**[14] 9612 3-9-3 **66** .... CallumRodriguez 3 66
(Keith Dalgleish) *trckd ldrs: rdn over 1f out: kpt on but no ch w wnr* **5/2**[2]

0- 3 *shd* **Vrai (IRE)**[32] 3-9-6 **69** .... (b) AndrewMullen 4 69
(Kevin Ryan) *trckd ldrs: racd quite keenly: rdn 2f out: kpt on same pcae* **9/1**

141- 4 *2 ¾* **Lads Order (IRE)**[13] 9646 3-9-7 **70** .... DougieCostello 1 61
(Michael Appleby) *led: rdn and hdd wl over 1f out: no ex ins fnl f* **8/1**[3]

050- 5 *1 ½* **Gunnabedun (IRE)**[14] 9613 3-8-7 **56** .... JoeFanning 2 42
(Iain Jardine) *hld up: rdn over 1f out: nvr threatened* **18/1**

510- 6 *nk* **Popping Corks (IRE)**[35] 9284 3-8-10 **59** .... JamesSullivan 7 44
(Linda Perratt) *s.i.s: sn in tch: rdn 2f out: wknd ins fnl f* **22/1**

515- 7 *shd* **Geography Teacher (IRE)**[14] 9613 3-8-6 **55** .... CamHardie 6 40
(Roger Fell) *hld up: rdn 2f out: nvr threatened* **18/1**

1m 13.26s (0.76) **Going Correction** +0.15s/f (Slow) **7** Ran SP% **109.0**
Speed ratings (Par 97): **100,96,96,92,90 90,90**
CSF £3.94 TOTE £2.00: £1.20, £1.40; EX 5.50 Trifecta £20.10.
Owner Alan Harte **Bred** C J Mills **Trained** Musley Bank, N Yorks

FOCUS
Not the worst 3yo class 6 sprint handicap. This time the stands' side was favoured. It's been rated at face value for now, with the second rated to her recent C&D form and the third to her French figures.

22 FOLLOW TOP TIPSTER TEMPLEGATE AT SUNRACING H'CAP — 1m 5y (Tp)
5:45 (5:46) (Class 5) (0-70,70) 4-Y-O+
£3,752 (£1,116; £557; £400; £400; £400) **Stalls** Centre

Form RPR

300- 1 **Paparazzi**[14] 9614 4-9-0 **63** .... CamHardie 7 76
(Tracy Waggott) *dwlt: hld up: gd hdwy 2f out: pushed along to ld over 1f out: qcknd clr: easily* **12/1**

122- 2 *4 ½* **Zodiakos (IRE)**[22] 9496 6-8-10 **66** .... (p) TristanPrice(7) 4 69
(Roger Fell) *led after 1f: rdn and hdd over 1f out: one pce and no ch w wnr* **11/2**[3]

552- 3 *nk* **Newmarket Warrior (IRE)**[14] 9614 8-9-7 **70** .... (p) JoeFanning 5 72+
(Iain Jardine) *hld up: rdn over 2f out: kpt on to go 3rd ins fnl f* **10/3**[1]

613- 4 *1* **Man Of Verve (IRE)**[25] 9465 5-8-11 **60** .... JackMitchell 9 60
(Philip Kirby) *trckd ldrs: pushed along to chal over 2f out: rdn over 1f out: no ex ins fnl f* **7/2**[2]

200- 5 *4 ½* **Bobby Joe Leg**[14] 9615 5-9-5 **68** .... JamesSullivan 8 57
(Ruth Carr) *led for 1f: trckd ldr: rdn over 2f out: sn outpcd and btn* **10/1**

030- 6 *2* **Decoration Of War (IRE)**[22] 9496 4-9-6 **69** .... AndrewMullen 6 54
(Michael Appleby) *trckd ldrs: rdn along 3f out: wknd over 1f out (a post-race endoscopic examination revealed significant mucus in the gelding's trachea)* **7/2**[2]

104- 7 *hd* **Lucky Violet (IRE)**[54] 8980 7-8-6 **58** .... (h) BenRobinson(3) 10 42
(Linda Perratt) *hld up in tch: rdn over 2f out: wknd fnl f* **9/1**

200- 8 *12* **Escape Clause (IRE)**[14] 9614 5-9-5 **68** .... (h) DougieCostello 3 25
(Grant Tuer) *half-rrd s and s.i.s: racd keenly and sn in tch: rdn over 2f out: sn wknd (jockey said gelding reared as stalls opened)* **50/1**

1m 39.66s (1.06) **Going Correction** +0.15s/f (Slow) **8** Ran SP% **111.7**
Speed ratings (Par 103): **100,95,95,94,89 87,87,75**
CSF £72.50 CT £267.71 TOTE £14.40: £2.20, £2.20, £1.10; EX 85.00 Trifecta £250.00.
Owner Gordon Allan Elsa Crankshaw **Bred** The Columella Partnership **Trained** Spennymoor, Co Durham

FOCUS
A modest handicap. The winner has been rated back to his best.

23 FOLLOW SUNRACING ON TWITTER H'CAP — 7f 14y (Tp)
6:15 (6:16) (Class 5) (0-75,75) 4-Y-O+
£3,752 (£1,116; £557; £400; £400; £400) **Stalls** Centre

Form RPR

052- 1 **Rey Loopy (IRE)**[14] 9615 5-9-6 **74** .... AndrewMullen 7 84
(Ben Haslam) *hld up: pushed along and hdwy over 1f out: rdn to ld 1f out: kpt on wl* **7/2**[3]

200- 2 *2 ¼* **Harvest Day**[14] 9615 4-9-0 **68** .... (t) NathanEvans 6 72
(Michael Easterby) *trckd ldrs: pushed along to chse ldr wl over 1f out: rdn appr fnl f: kpt on same pce* **3/1**[2]

003- 3 *hd* **Dirchill (IRE)**[14] 9615 5-9-7 **75** .... (b) JasonHart 4 78
(David Thompson) *in tch: pushed along 2f out: rdn and kpt on fnl f* **10/1**

001- 4 *3* **Smugglers Creek (IRE)**[54] 8980 5-8-13 **67** .... (v[1]) JoeFanning 1 62
(Iain Jardine) *led: rdn over 1f out: hdd 1f out: wknd ins fnl f* **10/1**

311- 5 *2 ¾* **Chosen World**[14] 9615 5-8-8 **65** .... (p) ConorMcGovern(3) 2 52
(Julie Camacho) *trckd ldrs: rdn over 2f out: wknd over 1f out* **11/4**[1]

000- 6 *3* **Admiral Rooke (IRE)**[22] 9495 4-8-7 **61** .... CamHardie 5 40
(Michael Appleby) *prom: rdn over 2f out: wknd over 1f out* **40/1**

223- 7 1 ½ **Fingal's Cave (IRE)**[15] 9593 7-9-1 **69**............................(p[1]) JackMitchell 3 44
(Philip Kirby) *hld up: rdn over 2f out: sn btn* **9/2**
1m 26.69s (0.49) **Going Correction** +0.15s/f (Slow) 7 Ran SP% **112.7**
Speed ratings (Par 103): **103,100,100,96,93 90,88**
CSF £13.99 TOTE £3.50: £1.90, £2.20; EX 15.50 Trifecta £102.50.
Owner Daniel Shapiro & Mrs C Barclay **Bred** Worldwide Partners **Trained** Middleham Moor, N Yorks

FOCUS
This modest handicap was run at an ordinary pace and again they raced more near side. The second and third have been rated close to form.

24 BETWAY H'CAP 6f (Tp)
6:45 (6:47) (Class 4) (0-85,82) 4-Y-O+
£5,530 (£1,645; £822; £411; £400; £400) **Stalls** Centre

Form RPR
122- 1 **Nick Vedder**[28] 9414 5-9-5 **80**............................(b) CamHardie 1 89
(Michael Wigham) *hld up in rr: gng wl but stl fair bit to do over 1f out: shkn up and r.o wl fnl 110yds: led ld nr fin* **11/2**[3]
661- 2 nk **Equiano Springs**[28] 9414 5-9-3 **78**............................ AndrewMullen 7 86
(Tom Tate) *led narrowly: rdn 2f out: kpt on but hdd nr fin* **9/2**[2]
060- 3 nk **Atholblair Boy (IRE)**[14] 9615 6-8-7 **75**............... FayeMcManoman(7) 5 82
(Nigel Tinkler) *midfield: pushed along and hdwy over 1f out: chal ins fnl f: kpt on* **9/1**
1/1- 4 1 **Royal Prospect (IRE)**[33] 9324 4-9-7 **82**.............. CallumRodriguez 8 86
(Julie Camacho) *dwlt: sn trckd ldrs: pushed along over 1f out: rdn ins fnl f: one pce* **6/4**[1]
21/- 5 ¾ **Global Tango (IRE)**[424] 8587 4-9-5 **80**.............. CallumShepherd 3 81
(Charles Hills) *hld up: rdn over 2f out: hung lft over 1f out: kpt on ins fnl f (jockey said gelding hung left-handed throughout)* **20/1**
020- 6 1 **Katheefa (USA)**[13] 9640 5-9-0 **75**............................ JamesSullivan 4 73
(Ruth Carr) *trckd ldrs: pushed along over 1f out: rdn ins fnl f: no ex* **10/1**
304- 7 ½ **Tommy G**[33] 9324 6-8-12 **80**............................ CoreyMadden(7) 6 77
(Jim Goldie) *pressed ldr: rdn 2f out: no ex fnl f* **11/1**
0/0- 8 5 **Valley Of Fire**[33] 9324 7-9-2 **77**............................ JackMitchell 9 58
(Les Eyre) *midfield: rdn over 2f out: wknd over 1f out* **25/1**
340- 9 22 **Highly Sprung (IRE)**[144] 6013 6-9-4 **79**............... JoeFanning 10
(Les Eyre) *dwlt: hld up: pushed along over 2f out: wknd over 1f out and eased* **40/1**
1m 12.23s (-0.27) **Going Correction** +0.15s/f (Slow) 9 Ran SP% **112.0**
Speed ratings (Par 105): **107,106,106,104,103 102,101,95,65**
CSF £28.70 CT £217.15 TOTE £6.60: £1.60, £1.70, £2.60; EX 29.80 Trifecta £186.30.
Owner David Spratt & Michael Wigham **Bred** Petches Farm Ltd **Trained** Newmarket, Suffolk

FOCUS
This fair sprint handicap was run at a sound pace and it saw a tight three-way finish. A small pb from the second.

25 BETWAY SPRINT H'CAP 5f (Tp)
7:15 (7:16) (Class 6) (0-60,57) 4-Y-O+
£3,105 (£924; £461; £400; £400; £400) **Stalls** Centre

Form RPR
400- 1 **Encoded (IRE)**[30] 9378 6-8-9 **45**............................ JoeFanning 7 51
(Lynn Siddall) *hld up in rr: pushed along and hdwy over 1f out: rdn and r.o fnl f: led nr fin* **9/1**
550- 2 nk **Novabridge**[28] 9416 11-8-8 **47**............................(b) PhilDennis(3) 1 52
(Karen Tutty) *led: rdn and 2 l up ent fnl f: edgd lft ins fnl f: no ex and hdd nr fin* **20/1**
050- 3 1 ½ **Poppy In The Wind**[14] 9617 7-9-7 **57**............................(v) CamHardie 8 57
(Alan Brown) *dwlt: hld up: pushed along over 2f out: stl lot to do over 1f out: rdn and kpt on ins fnl f* **5/1**[3]
005- 4 ¾ **Queen Of Kalahari**[14] 9617 4-9-4 **54**............................(t) JackMitchell 9 51
(Les Eyre) *prom: rdn over 2f out: no ex ins fnl f* **7/2**[1]
000- 5 nse **Bahango (IRE)**[33] 9328 7-9-7 **57**............................(p) CallumRodriguez 2 54
(Patrick Morris) *s.i.s: hld up: hdwy and trckd ldrs 3f out: rdn over 1f out: no ex ins fnl f (jockey said gelding fly leapt leaving the stalls)* **9/1**
404- 6 ¾ **Windforpower (IRE)**[18] 9558 9-9-3 **53**............................(v) BarryMcHugh 10 47
(Tracy Waggott) *midfield on outer: rdn over 2f out: kpt on same pce and nvr threatened ldrs* **9/2**[2]
630- 7 ½ **Star Cracker (IRE)**[18] 9558 7-8-12 **51**............................(p) EoinWalsh(3) 4 43
(Jim Goldie) *midfield: rdn over 2f out: one pce and nvr threatened ldrs* **6/1**
000- 8 2 ¼ **Camanche Grey (IRE)**[18] 9558 8-8-9 **45**............................ NathanEvans 6 29
(Lucinda Egerton) *chsd ldrs: rdn over 2f out: lost pl and btn over 1f out* **33/1**
040- 9 3 ¼ **Fuel Injection**[18] 9558 8-9-0 **50**............................(p) JamesSullivan 3 22
(Ruth Carr) *chsd ldrs: rdn over 2f out: wknd over 1f out* **14/1**
330- 10 3 ¼ **Funkadelic**[28] 9416 4-9-4 **54**............................(p) AndrewMullen 5 15
(Ben Haslam) *chsd ldrs: rdn over 2f out: wknd over 1f out* **12/1**
59.8s (0.30) **Going Correction** +0.15s/f (Slow) 10 Ran SP% **113.4**
Speed ratings (Par 101): **103,102,100,98,98 97,96,93,88,82**
CSF £166.96 CT £1014.51 TOTE £8.10: £3.00, £5.20, £2.50; EX 174.70 Trifecta £1384.80.
Owner Jimmy Kay **Bred** John Cullinan **Trained** Colton, N Yorks

FOCUS
A moderate sprint handicap. The winner has been rated in line with her August C&D run, and the second to his C&D wins early last year.
T/Plt: £39.30 to a £1 stake. Pool: £77,563.64 - 1,440.36 winning units T/Qpdt: £9.30 to a £1 stake. Pool: £13,161.59 - 1,044.66 winning units **Andrew Sheret**

WOLVERHAMPTON (A.W) (L-H)
Wednesday, January 2

OFFICIAL GOING: Tapeta: standard
Wind: Nil Weather: Overcast

26 BETWAY SPRINT CLASSIFIED STKS 5f 21y (Tp)
12:40 (12:40) (Class 6) 3-Y-O+
£3,105 (£924; £461; £300; £300; £300) **Stalls** Low

Form RPR
300- 1 **Captain Ryan**[14] 9606 8-9-8 **48**............................(p[1]) KieranO'Neill 9 55
(Geoffrey Deacon) *hld up: hdwy over 1f out: rdn to ld wl ins fnl f: r.o* **10/1**
226- 2 ½ **Storm Trooper (IRE)**[12] 9668 8-9-8 **46**..............(t) RichardKingscote 10 53
(Charlie Wallis) *w ldr: rdn and ev ch whn edgd rt over 1f out: styd on* **8/1**
546- 3 nk **Brother In Arms (IRE)**[27] 9433 5-9-3 **48**............... PoppyBridgwater(5) 2 52
(Tony Carroll) *s.i.s: hld up: r.o ins fnl f: nt rch ldrs* **3/1**[1]
446- 4 hd **Compton River**[64] 8720 7-9-1 **50**............................ HarryRussell(7) 5 51
(Bryan Smart) *half-rrd s: sn prom: rdn to ld ins fnl f: sn hdd: styd on* **7/1**[3]
404- 5 shd **Storm Lightning**[12] 9668 10-9-5 **48**............................ EoinWalsh(3) 8 51
(Mark Brisbourne) *prom: pushed along over 3f out: rdn over 1f out: r.o* **10/1**
440- 6 ½ **Le Manege Enchante (IRE)**[6] 9722 6-9-8 **48**..........(v) PaddyMathers 4 49
(Derek Shaw) *s.i.s: hld up: r.o u.p ins fnl f: nt rch ldrs* **8/1**
444- 7 ½ **Kemmeridge Bay**[14] 9613 3-8-7 **50**............................(b) HollieDoyle 3 41
(Grant Tuer) *led: rdn and hdd ins fnl f: no ex* **5/1**[2]
005- 8 nk **Velvet Vixen (IRE)**[18] 9566 3-8-7 **46**............................ DavidProbert 6 40
(Jo Hughes, France) *chsd ldrs: rdn over 1f out: no ex wl ins fnl f* **8/1**
300- 9 1 ½ **Shesthedream (IRE)**[12] 9668 6-9-3 **47**............................(h) KevinLundie(5) 7 41
(Lisa Williamson) *s.i.s: hld up: rdn over 1f out: nvr on terms* **20/1**
000- 10 ¾ **Roy's Legacy**[27] 9433 10-9-8 **47**............................ CharlieBennett 1 38
(Shaun Harris) *chsd ldrs: rdn over 1f out: no ex ins fnl f* **16/1**
640- 11 7 **Emjayem**[191] 4185 9-9-8 **50**............................ JoeyHaynes 11 13
(Patrick Chamings) *s.i.s: hld up: hdwy on outer 1/2-way: rdn over 1f out: wknd fnl f* **14/1**
1m 1.82s (-0.08) **Going Correction** -0.025s/f (Stan)
WFA 3 from 5yo+ 15lb 11 Ran SP% **123.0**
Speed ratings (Par 101): **99,98,97,97,97 96,95,95,92,91 80**
CSF £91.73 TOTE £10.90: £3.00, £2.30, £2.60; EX 115.40 Trifecta £817.10.
Owner R J Douglas **Bred** Mrs C Lloyd **Trained** Compton, Berks

FOCUS
A low-grade race but a competitive one. They finished in a heap.

27 BETWAY NOVICE STKS 6f 20y (Tp)
1:10 (1:12) (Class 5) 3-Y-O+
£3,752 (£1,116; £557; £278) **Stalls** Low

Form RPR
3- 1 **Benny And The Jets (IRE)**[21] 9497 3-8-12 **0**..............(t) RobHornby 13 76
(Sylvester Kirk) *a.p: chsd ldr over 4f out: led and hung rt over 1f out: rdn and hdd ins fnl f: rallied to ld towards fin* **7/2**[2]
0- 2 ½ **Probability (IRE)**[216] 3255 3-8-7 **0**............................ EdwardGreatrex 12 69
(Archie Watson) *chsd ldrs: rdn to ld ins fnl f: edgd rt: hdd towards fin* **10/1**
0- 3 3 ¼ **Eufemia**[84] 8106 3-8-7 **0**............................ HollieDoyle 8 59
(Amy Murphy) *led: swtchd lft over 5f out: rdn and hdd over 1f out: no ex ins fnl f* **25/1**
2- 4 1 ¼ **Minuty**[40] 9223 4-9-9 **0**............................ DavidProbert 4 59
(Rae Guest) *chsd ldrs: shkn up over 2f out: styd on same pce fnl f* **9/2**[3]
0- 5 hd **Fort Benton (IRE)**[22] 9490 3-8-12 **0**............................ CliffordLee 5 59
(David Barron) *hld up: pushed along over 3f out: hdwy over 1f out: sn rdn: styd on same pce fnl f* **20/1**
6 hd **Dawn Delight** 4-9-9 **0**............................ JasonWatson 9 58
(Hugo Palmer) *pushed along early in rr: shkn up 1/2-way: r.o ins fnl f: nvr nrr* **10/1**
034- 7 1 ¼ **Superseded (IRE)**[28] 9396 3-8-12 **68**............................(h[1]) RichardKingscote 6 55
(Charles Hills) *hld up: shkn up over 1f out: nt trble ldrs* **13/8**[1]
00- 8 ½ **Hooflepuff (IRE)**[12] 9671 3-8-12 **0**............................ ShaneKelly 2 53
(Robert Cowell) *s.i.s: pushed along over 3f out: nvr nrr* **25/1**
63- 9 2 ½ **Atyaaf**[13] 9645 4-10-0 **0**............................ PaddyMathers 11 49
(Derek Shaw) *hld up: plld hrd: shkn up over 1f out: n.d* **50/1**
050- 10 hd **Tunky**[18] 9566 3-8-7 **61**............................ JoeyHaynes 7 39
(James Given) *chsd ldrs: shkn up over 2f out: wknd fnl f* **50/1**
55- 11 1 **Maid Millie**[34] 9306 3-8-4 **0**............................ EoinWalsh(3) 3 36
(Robert Cowell) *s.i.s: pushed along over 3f out: a in rr* **25/1**
00- 12 1 ¼ **Push Back**[5] 9730 3-8-12 **0**............................(b[1]) KieranO'Neill 10 37
(George Peckham) *s.i.s: rn green and a in rr* **50/1**
0- 13 8 **Mrs Todd**[212] 3431 5-9-9 **0**............................ RobertHavlin 1 11
(Tony Carroll) *plld hrd and prom: hmpd over 5f out: rdn: hung lft and wknd over 1f out: b.b.v (vet said mare bled from the nose)* **100/1**
1m 13.86s (-0.64) **Going Correction** -0.025s/f (Stan)
WFA 3 from 4yo+ 16lb 13 Ran SP% **119.9**
Speed ratings (Par 103): **103,102,98,96,96 95,94,93,90,89 88,86,76**
CSF £34.70 TOTE £4.80: £2.30, £2.50, £4.70; EX 46.80 Trifecta £650.00.
Owner Deauville Daze Partnership **Bred** Pier House Stud **Trained** Upper Lambourn, Berks
■ Stewards' Enquiry : Hollie Doyle two-day ban: careless riding (Jan 16-17)

FOCUS
An ordinary novice. The early pace wasn't that strong and those towards the front dominated throughout. The fourth has been rated close to her debut effort.

28 BETWAY CASINO H'CAP 6f 20y (Tp)
1:45 (1:47) (Class 6) (0-60,62) 4-Y-O+
£3,105 (£924; £461; £300; £300; £300) **Stalls** Low

Form RPR
260- 1 **Santafiora**[14] 9617 5-8-13 **52**............................ KieranO'Neill 7 59
(Julie Camacho) *s.i.s: sn prom: rdn to ld 1f out: hung rt ins fnl f: styd on* **5/1**[2]
600- 2 ¾ **Carpet Time (IRE)**[18] 9558 4-9-7 **60**............................ ShaneKelly 10 65
(David Barron) *hld up in tch: swtchd rt over 1f out: sn rdn: carried rt wl ins fnl f: r.o* **10/1**
011- 3 hd **Peachey Carnehan**[6] 9720 5-9-9 **62** 6ex............................(v) RobertHavlin 8 66+
(Michael Mullineaux) *s.i.s and hmpd s: hld up: swtchd rt over 1f out: rdn and r.o wl ins fnl f: nt quite rch ldrs* **9/4**[1]
042- 4 nk **Fantasy Justifier (IRE)**[39] 9250 8-9-4 **57**............................(p) DavidProbert 11 60
(Ronald Harris) *led: hdd over 3f out: shkn up whn rdr dropped whip 1f out: carried rt wl ins fnl f: styd on* **10/1**
000- 5 ¾ **Spirit Power**[18] 9558 4-9-6 **59**............................(p[1]) RachelRichardson 2 60
(Eric Alston) *plld hrd and prom: shkn up over 1f out: carried rt wl ins fnl f: kpt on (jockey said gelding ran too freely)* **16/1**
400- 6 ½ **Indian Affair**[14] 9606 9-8-12 **58**............................(bt) KerrieRaybould(7) 4 57
(Milton Bradley) *prom: lost pl over 4f out: rdn and r.o ins fnl f* **7/1**[3]
021- 7 2 **Astrophysics**[18] 9560 7-9-6 **59**............................ AdamKirby 13 52
(Lynn Siddall) *chsd ldrs: pushed along over 2f out: styng on same pce whn hmpd wl ins fnl f* **7/1**[3]
000- 8 shd **Whispering Soul (IRE)**[12] 9668 6-8-7 **46** oh1............................(b) LiamJones 9 38
(Brian Baugh) *edgd lft s: hld up: rdn over 1f out: nt trble ldrs* **16/1**
211- 9 ¾ **Toni's A Star**[30] 9379 7-9-0 **58**............................ PoppyBridgwater(5) 1 48
(Tony Carroll) *sn chsng ldr: led over 3f out: rdn and hdd 1f out: edgd rt and wknd ins fnl f (trainers rep said mare was unsuited by the step up in trip to 6f20yds)* **7/1**[3]
300- 10 hd **Dream Ally (IRE)**[22] 9491 9-9-0 **56**............................ PhilDennis(3) 6 45
(John Weymes) *hld up in tch: rdn over 1f out: wknd ins fnl f* **50/1**

/00- **11** *43* **Whigwham**[130] 6539 5-8-7 **46** oh1 EdwardGreatrex 5
(Gary Sanderson) *hld up: pushed along and wknd 1/2-way* **50/1**

1m 14.25s (-0.25) **Going Correction** -0.025s/f (Stan) 11 Ran SP% **114.9**
Speed ratings (Par 101): **100,99,98,98,97 96,94,93,92,92 35**
CSF £52.36 CT £140.54 TOTE £5.80: £2.00, £2.30, £1.10; EX 60.00 Trifecta £202.70.
Owner Judy & Richard Peck & Partner **Bred** Highbury Stud & John Troy **Trained** Norton, N Yorks
■ Stewards' Enquiry : Kieran O'Neill caution: careless riding

FOCUS
Moderate sprinting form. The winner has been rated pretty much to form, and the second to his maiden form.

29 BETWAY HEED YOUR HUNCH H'CAP 1m 1f 104y (Tp)
2:20 (2:20) (Class 4) (0-85,87) 4-Y-O+

£5,530 (£1,645; £822; £411; £300; £300) **Stalls** Low

Form RPR
1/2- **1** **Military Law**[21] 9509 4-10-0 **87** RobertHavlin 6 93+
(John Gosden) *mde all: set stdy pce tl qcknd and hung rt fr over 2f out: sn rdn: styd on (jockey said gelding hung right-handed throughout)* **6/4**[1]

123- **2** *1* **Illustrissime (USA)**[14] 9610 6-9-4 **76** (p) JoeyHaynes 5 80
(Ivan Furtado) *prom: chsd wnr over 6f out: rdn over 1f out: styd on* **7/1**[3]

334- **3** *hd* **This Girl**[30] 9384 4-9-6 **79** RichardKingscote 3 83
(Tom Dascombe) *prom: rdn over 2f out: styd on* **7/1**[3]

500- **4** *3/4* **High Acclaim (USA)**[17] 8487 5-9-6 **78** DavidProbert 4 80
(Roger Teal) *hld up: hdwy 6f out: rdn over 1f out: styd on* **16/1**

300- **5** *1* **Central City (IRE)**[21] 9506 4-9-0 **73** KieranO'Neill 1 73
(Ian Williams) *chsd wnr tl over 6f out: remained handy: rdn over 1f out: no ex ins fnl f* **10/1**

211- **6** *nse* **Michele Strogoff**[18] 9563 6-10-1 **87** AlistairRawlinson 7 87+
(Michael Appleby) *tried to anticipate the s: s.s: hld up: shkn up over 2f out: effrt over 1f out: hung lft ins fnl f: nt trble ldrs (jockey said gelding anticipated the start and subsequently missed the break)* **2/1**[2]

000- **7** *5* **Argus (IRE)**[44] 9155 7-9-1 **73** EdwardGreatrex 2 62
(Alexandra Dunn) *hld up: rdn over 2f out: n.d* **33/1**

2m 0.32s (-0.48) **Going Correction** -0.025s/f (Stan)
WFA 4 from 5yo+ 1lb 7 Ran SP% **116.2**
Speed ratings (Par 105): **101,100,99,99,98 98,93**
CSF £13.36 TOTE £2.20: £1.40, £2.30; EX 11.10 Trifecta £34.70.
Owner Qatar Racing Limited **Bred** Qatar Bloodstock Ltd **Trained** Newmarket, Suffolk

FOCUS
This was steadily run and turned into a dash from the turn in. The form has been rated at face value around the second and third for now.

30 LADBROKES FILLIES' CONDITIONS STKS (ALL-WEATHER CHAMPIONSHIPS FAST-TRACK QUALIFIER) 7f 36y (Tp)
2:50 (2:50) (Class 2) 4-Y-O+ **£12,938** (£3,850; £1,924; £962) **Stalls** High

Form RPR
511- **1** **Island Of Life (USA)**[28] 9398 5-9-0 94 (tp) RichardKingscote 1 105+
(William Haggas) *hld up: hdwy over 1f out: rdn to ld ins fnl f: edgd rt: r.o* **11/4**[1]

061- **2** *3/4* **Castle Hill Cassie (IRE)**[47] 9102 5-9-3 100 JasonWatson 3 105
(Ben Haslam) *hld up: hdwy and nt clr run over 1f out: chsd wnr ins fnl f: r.o* **9/2**[2]

330- **3** *1/2* **Pattie**[10] 9689 5-9-0 97 CharlesBishop 2 101
(Mick Channon) *hld up: hdwy over 1f out: r.o* **6/1**[3]

032- **4** *nk* **Lucymai**[27] 9430 6-9-0 101 JackDuern 4 100
(Dean Ivory) *prom: rdn to ld over 1f out: hdd ins fnl f: styd on* **9/2**[2]

400- **5** *3 1/2* **Peak Princess (IRE)**[42] 9173 5-9-0 92 EdwardGreatrex 6 90
(Archie Watson) *led: hdd over 6f out: chsd ldrs: pushed along 1/2-way: no ex ins fnl f* **10/1**

300- **6** *2 1/2* **Miss Bar Beach (IRE)**[88] 7978 4-9-0 95 ShaneKelly 5 84
(Keith Dalgleish) *s.i.s: hdwy to chse ldr 6f out: rdn and ev ch over 1f out: wknd ins fnl f* **33/1**

211- **7** *1 1/2* **Crossing The Line**[27] 9430 4-9-0 101 DavidProbert 7 80
(Andrew Balding) *led over 6f out: rdn and hdd over 1f out: wknd ins fnl f (jockey said filly stopped quickly)* **11/4**[1]

1m 27.24s (-1.56) **Going Correction** -0.025s/f (Stan) 7 Ran SP% **116.0**
Speed ratings (Par 96): **107,106,105,105,101 98,96**
CSF £15.96 TOTE £3.20: £1.80, £2.80; EX 16.60 Trifecta £112.40.
Owner Hamer, Hawkes & Hellin **Bred** Darley **Trained** Newmarket, Suffolk
■ Stewards' Enquiry : Jason Watson caution: careless riding

FOCUS
A good contest, and it was run to suit the closers. The second has been rated to her previous C&D win.

31 SUNRACING.CO.UK H'CAP 7f 36y (Tp)
3:20 (3:21) (Class 5) (0-70,72) 4-Y-O+

£3,752 (£1,116; £557; £300; £300; £300) **Stalls** High

Form RPR
064- **1** **Inaam (IRE)**[28] 9402 6-9-4 **67** (h) AdamKirby 9 80
(Paul D'Arcy) *stdd s: hld up: racd keenly: hdwy over 1f out: sn swtchd rt: qcknd to ld wl ins fnl f: edgd lft: rdn out* **3/1**[2]

602- **2** *1 1/4* **Dark Alliance (IRE)**[7] 9702 8-9-0 **68** MeganNicholls(5) 1 78
(Mark Loughnane) *hld up in tch: rdn and ev ch wl ins fnl f: r.o (jockey said gelding hung right-handed in the home straight)* **9/4**[1]

002- **3** *2 1/2* **Secondo (FR)**[23] 9483 9-9-9 **72** (v) LiamKeniry 5 75
(Robert Stephens) *hmpd s: hld up: rdn and r.o ins fnl f: wnt 3rd nr fin* **16/1**

003- **4** *nk* **Sir Ottoman (FR)**[14] 9616 6-9-4 **67** JoeyHaynes 8 69
(Ivan Furtado) *prom: chsd ldr over 5f out: rdn over 1f out: styd on same pce ins fnl f* **10/1**

003- **5** *1/2* **Gabrial The Tiger (IRE)**[12] 9656 7-9-3 **71** SebastianWoods(5) 2 72
(Richard Fahey) *led early: chsd ldrs: rdn over 1f out: no ex ins fnl f* **16/1**

004- **6** *nk* **Fast Track**[16] 9587 8-9-7 **70** JasonWatson 10 70
(David Barron) *sn led: rdn over 1f out: hung rt and hdd wl ins fnl f: no ex (jockey said gelding hung right-handed in the home straight)* **10/1**

200- **7** *1/2* **Air Of York (IRE)**[12] 9656 7-9-2 **65** (p) DavidProbert 3 64
(John Flint) *prom: rdn over 2f out: no ex fnl f (jockey said gelding jumped right-handed leaving stalls)* **25/1**

001- **8** *1 1/4* **Creek Harbour (IRE)**[18] 9565 4-9-8 **71** ShaneKelly 7 67
(Richard Hughes) *hmpd s: plld hrd: hdwy over 5f out: rdn over 1f out: no ex fnl f* **7/2**[3]

6/0- **9** *1 3/4* **Dubai Elegance**[15] 9596 5-9-9 **72** PaddyMathers 4 63
(Derek Shaw) *hmpd s: hld up: rdn over 2f out: n.d* **100/1**

500- **10** *7* **Tavener**[12] 9656 7-9-7 **70** (p) AlistairRawlinson 6 42
(David C Griffiths) *hmpd s: a in rr: hung rt and wknd over 2f out* **50/1**

1m 27.7s (-1.10) **Going Correction** -0.025s/f (Stan) 10 Ran SP% **114.7**
Speed ratings (Par 103): **105,103,100,100,99 99,98,97,95,87**
CSF £9.85 CT £90.40 TOTE £3.60: £1.60, £1.30, £3.50; EX 12.20 Trifecta £83.10.
Owner Tramore Tree **Bred** John Doyle **Trained** Newmarket, Suffolk

FOCUS
A fair handicap which set up for those ridden with patience. The second has been rated similar to his latest effort.
T/Jkpt: Not Won. T/Plt: £69.10 to a £1 stake. Pool: £65,057.33 - 686.99 winning units T/Qpdt: £11.40 to a £1 stake. Pool: £7,800.67 - 502.49 winning units **Colin Roberts**

CHELMSFORD (A.W) (L-H)
Thursday, January 3

OFFICIAL GOING: Polytrack: standard
Wind: Light, against Weather: Dry, chilly

32 BET TOTEPLACEPOT AT TOTESPORT.COM NOVICE STKS (PLUS 10 RACE) 1m (P)
4:10 (4:11) (Class 4) 3-Y-O **£5,175** (£1,540; £769; £384) **Stalls** Low

Form RPR
333- **1** **Originaire (IRE)**[44] 9165 3-8-9 79 (p) LiamJones 2 78
(William Haggas) *hld up in tch: clsd to trck ldrs 4f out: wnt 2nd and effrt 2f out: rdn to ld ent fnl f: edgd lft but styd on and in command ins fnl f* **11/10**[1]

- **2** *1 3/4* **Majestic Dawn (IRE)** 3-8-9 0 RaulDaSilva 1 74
(Paul Cole) *led: rdn and hrd pressed over 1f out: hdd ent fnl f: keeping on same pce and hld whn sltly impeded and swtchd rt wl ins fnl f* **2/1**[2]

06- **3** *6* **Biz Markee (IRE)**[15] 9607 3-8-9 0 JosephineGordon 8 60
(Hugo Palmer) *taken down early: broke wl: sn stdd and hld up in tch: pushed along over 2f out: outpcd and hung lft over 1f out: modest 3rd and kpt on same pce ins fnl f (jockey said gelding hung badly left-handed on bend)* **20/1**

0- **4** *3/4* **Mokuba (IRE)**[71] 8548 3-8-9 0 JasonWatson 3 58
(Brian Meehan) *in tch in midfield: rdn wl over 2f out: outpcd and wl hld over 1f out: 4th and plugged on same pce ins fnl f* **12/1**

00- **5** *3 1/4* **Dance To Freedom**[54] 8993 3-8-9 0 (t) MartinDwyer 6 51
(Stuart Williams) *stdd s: pushed along and clsd but v wd bnd 3f out: outpcd and wl btn over 1f out: edgd lft and wknd fnl f* **40/1**

01- **6** *3/4* **The Meter**[70] 8577 3-8-6 0 DarraghKeenan(5) 4 51
(Mohamed Moubarak) *s.i.s and hmpd sn after s: sn rcvrd to chse ldr: rdn over 2f out: 3rd and outpcd u.p over 1f out: wknd ins fnl f* **20/1**

0- **7** *39* **Red Desert (IRE)**[40] 9255 3-8-9 0 JackMitchell 7
(Roger Varian) *hld up in tch: dropped to last and struggling u.p over 2f out: lost tch and virtually p.u ins fnl f (jockey said gelding lost action on bend; vet said gelding had irregular heartbeat)* **6/1**[3]

1m 41.18s (1.28) **Going Correction** +0.05s/f (Slow) 7 Ran SP% **114.9**
Speed ratings (Par 99): **95,93,87,86,83 82,43**
CSF £3.43 TOTE £2.10: £1.30, £1.80; EX 4.60 Trifecta £26.30.
Owner China Horse Club International Limited **Bred** Vimal And Gillian Khosla **Trained** Newmarket, Suffolk

FOCUS
A modest 3yo novice. It was run at a routine pace

33 BET TOTEEXACTA AT TOTESPORT.COM H'CAP 1m (P)
4:45 (4:46) (Class 6) (0-65,67) 4-Y-O+

£3,493 (£1,039; £519; £400; £400; £400) **Stalls** Low

Form RPR
/36- **1** **Philamundo (IRE)**[22] 9507 4-9-7 **65** (b[1]) AdamKirby 11 79+
(Richard Spencer) *nudged leaving stalls: dropped in and hld up in last pair: stl 11th and stl plenty to do whn swtchd rt and effrt 2f out: str run u.p to ld ins fnl f: sn clr: v readily* **9/1**

253- **2** *5* **Classic Charm**[28] 9428 4-9-3 **61** RobertWinston 4 64
(Dean Ivory) *t.k.h: trckd ldrs: nt clr run over 1f out: sn swtchd rt and effrt to chal: drvn to ld ins fnl f: sn hdd and nt match pce of wnr fnl 100yds* **9/4**[1]

400- **3** *1* **Rippling Waters (FR)**[28] 9428 5-9-6 **64** (t[1]) DougieCostello 3 64
(Jamie Osborne) *chsd ldr tl led ent fnl 2f: sn hrd pressed and u.p: hdd ins fnl f and nt match pce of wnr fnl 100yds* **16/1**

155- **4** *1* **Beepeecee**[28] 9428 5-9-9 **67** (p) ShaneKelly 5 64
(Thomas Gallagher) *hld up in tch in midfield: swtchd lft and hdwy u.p to press ldrs ent fnl f: no ex and outpcd by wnr fnl 100yds* **10/1**

502- **5** *1 1/2* **Bubbly**[26] 9458 4-9-7 **65** RichardKingscote 10 59
(Charlie Fellowes) *bmpd leaving stalls: hld up in tch in last quartet: effrt and swtchd rt over 1f out: kpt on ins fnl f: no threat to wnr* **5/1**[3]

360- **6** *nk* **Steal The Scene (IRE)**[43] 9182 7-9-9 **67** JackMitchell 7 60
(Kevin Frost) *wl in tch in midfield: effrt and chsd ldrs ent fnl 2f: unable qck u.p over 1f out: wknd ins fnl f* **6/1**

342- **7** *1 1/4* **Mochalov**[20] 9531 4-8-13 **57** FergusSweeney 8 47
(Jane Chapple-Hyam) *wnt rt leaving stalls: t.k.h: effrt ent fnl 2f: unable qck: lost pl and btn over 1f out: wknd ins fnl f* **12/1**

060- **8** *1 1/4* **King Of Rooks**[19] 9567 6-9-7 **65** (t[1]) RobertHavlin 9 53
(Henry Spiller) *hld up in tch in last trio: effrt towards inner whn nt clrest of runs briefly over 1f out: nvr trbld ldrs* **25/1**

034- **9** *1/2* **Pacific Salt (IRE)**[22] 9510 6-9-4 **62** CallumShepherd 2 48
(Pam Sly) *led: hdd and pushed along 2f out: stl pressing ldrs but unable qck u.p over 1f out: wknd ins fnl f* **4/1**[2]

000- **10** *nk* **Enzo (IRE)**[16] 9593 4-9-5 **63** JoeyHaynes 6 49
(Paul Howling) *in tch in midfield: shkn up 3f out: edgd lft and no hdwy u.p over 1f out: wl btn fnl f* **50/1**

000- **11** *1 1/4* **Echo Brava**[23] 9431 9-9-2 **60** RobHornby 12 43
(Suzi Best) *in rr: effrt 2f out: sn rdn and no imp: nvr involved* **66/1**

000- **12** *3* **Elusif (IRE)**[22] 9504 4-8-8 **52** LiamJones 1 28
(Shaun Keightley) *in tch in midfield: rdn 3f out: sn struggling and lost pl over 1f out: bhd ins fnl f* **25/1**

1m 39.08s (-0.82) **Going Correction** +0.05s/f (Slow) 12 Ran SP% **125.5**
Speed ratings (Par 101): **106,101,100,99,97 97,95,94,94,93 92,89**
CSF £30.59 CT £346.77 TOTE £10.70: £2.90, £1.40, £5.70; EX 43.80 Trifecta £430.30.
Owner Rebel Racing **Bred** Gerard Mullins **Trained** Newmarket, Suffolk

FOCUS
A run-of-the-mill handicap, run at a fair pace.

34 BET TOTEQUADPOT AT TOTESPORT.COM H'CAP 1m (P)
5:20 (5:22) (Class 4) (0-80,80) 4-Y-0+
£6,986 (£2,079; £1,038; £519; £400; £400) Stalls Low

Form RPR
102- **1** **Scofflaw**[20] 9532 5-9-2 76 (v[1]) AdamKirby 1 84
(David Evans) *in tch in midfield: nt clr run and swtchd rt over 1f out: hdwy u.p to ld wl ins fnl f: r.o wl* 8/1
/31- **2** ½ **Holy Heart (IRE)**[22] 9501 4-9-6 80 (t) RobertHavlin 7 87
(John Gosden) *chsd ldr: rdn to ld over 1f out: hdd and one pce wl ins fnl f* 3/1[2]
001- **3** 1 **Glenn Coco**[49] 9070 5-9-5 79 (t) RichardKingscote 2 84
(Stuart Williams) *trckd ldrs: effrt on inner to press ldrs over 1f out: kpt on same pce u.p ins fnl f* 5/1[3]
321- **4** 1 **Glory Of Paris (IRE)**[28] 9428 5-9-6 80 RobertWinston 5 82
(Michael Appleby) *t.k.h: hld up in tch in midfield: effrt over 1f out: chsd ldrs and kpt on u.p ins fnl f: nvr enough pce to threaten ldrs* 15/8[1]
024- **5** 1 **Ambient (IRE)**[22] 9506 4-9-2 76 (p) JFEgan 3 76
(Jane Chapple-Hyam) *hld up in tch in midfield: effrt u.p over 1f out: unable qck and kpt on same pce ins fnl f* 16/1
340- **6** shd **Samphire Coast**[20] 9532 6-9-5 79 (v) PaddyMathers 9 79
(Derek Shaw) *taken down early: stdd s: hld up in last pair: swtchd rt and effrt over 1f out: styd on ins fnl f: nvr threatened ldrs* 16/1
450- **7** ¾ **Lefortovo (FR)**[49] 9090 6-9-6 80 DougieCostello 10 78
(Jo Hughes, France) *stdd and swtchd lft after s: t.k.h: hld up in last pair: kpt on ins fnl f: n.d* 66/1
564- **8** ½ **Glory Awaits (IRE)**[28] 9429 9-9-5 79 (b) CallumShepherd 8 76
(David Simcock) *led: rdn ent fnl 2f: hdd and no ex over 1f out: wknd ins fnl f* 16/1
555- **9** hd **Lacan (IRE)**[29] 9397 8-9-4 78 RossaRyan 4 75
(Brett Johnson) *trckd ldrs: unable qck u.p and outpcd over 1f out: wknd ins fnl f* 9/1
/00- **10** 3¾ **Badenscoth**[252] 2107 5-9-0 77 (h) JackDuern(3) 6 65
(Dean Ivory) *taken down early: stdd s: t.k.h: hld up in last pair: effrt on inner over 1f out: no imp and wknd ins fnl f* 33/1

1m 39.51s (-0.39) **Going Correction** +0.05s/f (Slow) 10 Ran SP% 119.6
Speed ratings (Par 105): **103,102,101,100,99 99,98,98,97,94**
CSF £33.13 CT £140.34 TOTE £6.50: £1.50, £2.20, £1.80; EX 37.00 Trifecta £154.30.
Owner John Abbey & Emma Evans **Bred** Mrs M E Slade **Trained** Pandy, Monmouths

FOCUS
Not a bad handicap and it's straightforward form.

35 BET TOTETRIFECTA AT TOTESPORT.COM H'CAP 5f (P)
5:55 (5:55) (Class 2) (0-105,103) 4-Y-0+ £12,938 (£3,850; £1,924; £962) Stalls Low

Form RPR
005- **1** **Tropics (USA)**[13] 9667 11-9-4 100 (h) RobertWinston 8 107
(Dean Ivory) *dwlt: hdwy to chse ldr after 1f: rdn to ld jst over 1f out: r.o wl and in command fnl 100yds* 10/1
054- **2** ¾ **Royal Birth**[306] 1007 8-9-0 96 (t) RichardKingscote 5 100
(Stuart Williams) *in tch in midfield: effrt over 1f out: drvn to chse wnr 100yds out: styd on but a hld* 4/1[2]
100- **3** 1¼ **Captain Lars (SAF)**[13] 9662 9-8-7 89 (b) HollieDoyle 4 89
(Archie Watson) *chsd ldrs: effrt ent fnl 2f: drvn over 1f out: kpt on same pce ins fnl f* 7/1
000- **4** ¾ **Jumira Bridge**[13] 9667 5-8-12 94 EdwardGreatrex 3 91
(Robert Cowell) *s.i.s: in tch towards rr: effrt u.p over 1f out: styd on ins fnl f: nvr trbld ldrs* 12/1
134- **5** shd **Verne Castle**[30] 9391 6-8-7 94 (h) DarraghKeenan(5) 6 91
(Michael Wigham) *led: rdn over 1f out: sn hdd and drvn: no ex and wknd wl ins fnl f* 4/1[2]
023- **6** 1¼ **Gracious John (IRE)**[13] 9667 6-9-7 103 AdamKirby 2 95
(David Evans) *in tch in midfield: effrt over 2f out: unable qck u.p over 1f out: wl hld and kpt on same pce ins fnl f (trainer's rep could offer no explanation for the gelding's performance)* 9/4[1]
023- **7** 2 **Teruntum Star (FR)**[30] 9391 7-9-1 97 (v) JosephineGordon 7 82
(Kevin Ryan) *dwlt: sn outpcd and pushed along in rr: swtchd rt and no hdwy u.p over 1f out: nvr involved* 6/1[3]

59.46s (-0.74) **Going Correction** +0.05s/f (Slow) 7 Ran SP% 114.3
Speed ratings (Par 109): **107,105,103,102,102 100,97**
CSF £49.34 CT £301.64 TOTE £13.30: £6.20, £3.30; EX 60.10 Trifecta £328.50.
Owner Dean Ivory **Bred** D Konecny, S Branch & A Branch **Trained** Radlett, Herts
■ Stewards' Enquiry : Darragh Keenan two-day ban: failing to ride out to best finish (Jan 17-18)

FOCUS
It paid to be handy in this decent sprint handicap.

36 BET TOTESWINGER AT TOTESPORT.COM H'CAP 5f (P)
6:25 (6:25) (Class 4) (0-80,82) 4-Y-0+
£6,986 (£2,079; £1,038; £519; £400; £400) Stalls Low

Form RPR
216- **1** **Shamshon (IRE)**[24] 9486 8-9-12 82 RichardKingscote 5 91
(Stuart Williams) *trckd ldrs: nt clr run and swtchd rt over 1f out: rdn and clsd to chal ins fnl f: r.o wl to ld wl ins fnl f* 5/2[1]
030- **2** 1 **Red Pike (IRE)**[34] 9324 8-9-0 77 HarryRussell(7) 2 82
(Bryan Smart) *dwlt: wnt rt and cannoned into rival leaving stalls: in tch in rr of main gp: effrt and swtchd rt over 2f out: drvn and bmpd over 1f out: styd on strly and edgd lft ins fnl f: snatched 2nd on post* 8/1
640- **3** nse **Joegogo (IRE)**[21] 9525 4-9-6 76 JFEgan 4 81
(David Evans) *led: drvn over 1f out: hdd wl ins fnl f: no ex and one pce towards fin: lost 2nd on post* 10/1
642- **4** ¾ **Becker**[12] 9682 4-8-11 67 (h) EdwardGreatrex 9 69
(Robert Cowell) *trckd ldrs: effrt and drvn to chal over 1f out: no ex 100yds out and outpcd towards fin* 8/1
004- **5** 1¼ **Golden Salute (IRE)**[12] 9682 4-9-0 70 JasonWatson 1 69
(Andrew Balding) *s.i.s: in tch in rr of main gp: nt clr run and swtchd rt over 1f out: hdwy to chse ldrs ins fnl f: keeping on but hld whn squeezed for room and hmpd wl ins fnl f* 5/1[3]
065- **6** 2 **Moon Song**[14] 9640 4-9-3 73 HectorCrouch 3 63
(Clive Cox) *in tch in midfield: shuffled bk on inner over 2f out: nt clr run and hmpd wl over 1f out: sn rdn and nvr threatened to get on terms: wknd ins fnl f* 4/1[2]

002- **7** nk **The Establishment**[17] 9588 4-8-12 71 (h[1]) EoinWalsh(3) 8 60
(David Evans) *stdd after s and swtchd lft: sn detached in last and pushed along: c wd and racd in centre st: styd on ins fnl f: nvr trbld ldrs (jockey said gelding was outpaced in the early stages)* 10/1
201- **8** nse **It's All A Joke (IRE)**[12] 9682 4-8-13 76 (b) Pierre-LouisJamin(7) 7 65
(Archie Watson) *chsd ldrs: struggling to qckn u.p whn bmpd over 1f out: hung lft and wknd ins fnl f: fin lame (vet reported the gelding to be lame on its left-fore leg)* 10/1
460- **9** 4½ **Midnightly**[21] 9525 5-9-0 70 (t) DavidProbert 6 43
(Rae Guest) *chsd ldr: n.m.r and swtchd rt jst over 1f out: wknd ins fnl f* 25/1

1m 0.04s (-0.16) **Going Correction** +0.05s/f (Slow) 9 Ran SP% 118.6
Speed ratings (Par 105): **103,101,101,100,98 94,94,94,87**
CSF £24.10 CT £174.89 TOTE £3.60: £1.30, £2.80, £3.30; EX 22.40 Trifecta £137.50.
Owner T W Morley & Regents Racing **Bred** Stonethorn Stud Farms Ltd **Trained** Newmarket, Suffolk
■ Stewards' Enquiry : Harry Russell two-day ban: interference & careless riding (Jan 17-18)

FOCUS
This fair sprint handicap saw a tight finish.

37 BET TOTESCOOP6 AT TOTESPORT.COM H'CAP 7f (P)
6:55 (6:57) (Class 6) (0-55,57) 4-Y-0+
£3,493 (£1,039; £519; £400; £400; £400) Stalls Low

Form RPR
000- **1** **African Blessing**[105] 7459 6-9-6 53 KierenFox 3 63+
(John Best) *hld up in tch in midfield: swtchd rt and hdwy 2f out: clsd u.p to chse ldrs 1f out: led ins fnl f: r.o wl* 6/1
044- **2** 2 **Foreign Legion (IRE)**[4] 9765 4-8-12 45 (p) NickyMackay 7 50
(Luke McJannet) *led tl 5f out: chsd ldr tl led again ent fnl 2f: wandered rt u.p over 1f out: hdd and no ex ins fnl f* 3/1[1]
000- **3** ¾ **Rivas Rob Roy**[13] 9664 4-9-7 54 JoeyHaynes 5 57
(John Gallagher) *hld up in tch in midfield: effrt to chse ldrs over 1f out: kpt on same pce u.p ins fnl f* 12/1
264- **4** ¾ **Black Hambleton**[15] 9616 6-8-13 53 HarryRussell(7) 8 54
(Bryan Smart) *chsd ldrs: effrt 2f out: unable qck and kpt on same pce ins fnl f* 12/1
050- **5** ¾ **Zorawar (FR)**[15] 9602 5-9-5 52 (p) AdamKirby 4 52
(David O'Meara) *s.i.s: hld up in last pair: nt clr run and swtchd rt over 1f out: styd on ins fnl f: nvr trbld ldrs (jockey said gelding was denied a clear run for a few strides turning into the home straight)* 5/1[3]
000- **6** nk **Brockey Rise (IRE)**[17] 9587 4-9-4 54 (b) EoinWalsh(3) 6 52
(David Evans) *chsd ldr early: styd prom: effrt and chsd ldr again over 1f out tl 1f out: no ex and wknd ins fnl f* 6/1
335- **7** 2 **Herringswell (FR)**[27] 9441 4-9-7 57 GabrieleMalune(3) 1 49
(Henry Spiller) *hld up in tch in midfield: effrt to chse ldrs and edgd lft over 1f out: no ex and wknd ins fnl f* 9/2[2]
000- **8** 5 **Shamrock Emma (IRE)**[14] 9641 4-8-12 45 HollieDoyle 2 24
(Gary Moore) *in tch in last trio: effrt ent fnl 2f: nvr involved* 33/1
050- **9** 3 **Willsy**[112] 7219 6-8-9 45 FinleyMarsh(3) 10 16
(Frank Bishop) *in tch in midfield: rdn over 2f out: sn struggling and bhd over 1f out* 50/1
533- **10** 1 **Mr Potter**[22] 9504 6-9-4 51 (v) PhilipPrince 9 19
(Richard Guest) *taken down early: stdd s: hld up in last pair: effrt over 1f out: no hdwy and nvr involved (jockey said gelding took a false step approximately a furlong out)* 10/1
600- **11** 3¼ **Summer Angel (IRE)**[14] 9647 4-8-12 45 (p[1]) MartinDwyer 11
(Michael Appleby) *mounted on crse: sn prom: led 5f out tl hdd and rdn ent fnl 2f: sn lost pl and fdd ins fnl f* 25/1

1m 27.1s (-0.10) **Going Correction** +0.05s/f (Slow) 11 Ran SP% 121.6
Speed ratings (Par 101): **102,99,98,98,97 96,94,88,85,84 80**
CSF £24.87 CT £217.32 TOTE £7.10: £2.70, £1.70, £4.70; EX 27.90 Trifecta £278.90.
Owner J Tomkins **Bred** Michael Turner **Trained** Oad Street, Kent

FOCUS
A weak handicap.

38 BUY TICKETS AT CHELMSFORDCITYRACECOURSE.COM H'CAP 1m 6f (P)
7:25 (7:26) (Class 6) (0-65,65) 4-Y-0+
£3,493 (£1,039; £519; £400; £400; £400) Stalls Low

Form RPR
000/ **1** **Geordielad**[206] 7324 5-8-7 46 oh1 EdwardGreatrex 3 55
(Oliver Sherwood) *mde all: rdn and clr w rival over 2f out: styd on and forged clr over 1f out: kpt on and a doing enough ins fnl f* 25/1
222- **2** 1¼ **Your Band**[13] 9665 4-9-3 60 NicolaCurrie 9 67
(Jamie Osborne) *t.k.h: hld up in last trio: effrt over 3f out: hdwy on outer to chse clr ldng pair 2f out: kpt on and chsd clr wnr 150yds out: styd on but nvr getting to wnr* 5/2[1]
525- **3** 3½ **Konigin**[12] 9687 4-9-7 64 (tp) JFEgan 10 66
(John Berry) *chsd ldrs: wnt 2nd 4f out: pressing wnr: rdn and kicked clr over 2f out: no ex and outpcd over 1f out: plugged on same pce ins fnl f* 9/2[3]
004- **4** 1¼ **Goldslinger (FR)**[44] 9159 7-9-4 57 (t[1]) HectorCrouch 4 57
(Gary Moore) *hld up in midfield: outpcd and nt clr run over 2f out: swtchd lft over 1f out: hdwy and swtchd rt ins fnl f: kpt on but no threat to ldrs* 10/1
160- **5** 7 **Carvelas (IRE)**[28] 9431 10-9-10 63 DavidProbert 5 54
(J R Jenkins) *stdd after s: hld up in last pair: effrt on outer over 2f out: nvr threatened to get on terms w ldrs: wknd ins fnl f* 16/1
110/ **6** ¾ **Regal Gait (IRE)**[469] 7319 6-9-12 65 (w) AdamKirby 2 55
(Simon Dow) *midfield: pushed along 7f out: effrt but ldrs kicking clr over 2f out: wknd ins fnl f* 4/1[2]
631- **7** 1 **Affair**[49] 9067 5-9-3 56 CharlieBennett 7 44
(Hughie Morrison) *t.k.h: chsd wnr for 2f: chsd ldrs tl outpcd u.p over 1f out: wknd fnl f* 9/1
052- **8** 5 **Sellingallthetime (IRE)**[7] 9721 8-9-7 63 (p) EoinWalsh(3) 8 44
(Michael Appleby) *s.i.s and nt clr run sn after s: swtchd rt and hdwy to chse wnr after 2f: lost 2nd 4f out and sn rdn: lost pl and bhd whn nt clr run over 1f out: sn wknd* 7/1
500- **9** 52 **Lazarus (IRE)**[22] 9407 5-9-6 59 (t) CharlesBishop 1
(Amy Murphy) *midfield: rdn and reminders over 6f out: dropped to rr and hmpd over 3f out: bhd and virtually p.u over 1f out: t.o (jockey said gelding was never travelling)* 10/1

3m 3.03s (-0.17) **Going Correction** +0.05s/f (Slow)
WFA 4 from 5yo+ 4lb 9 Ran SP% 117.2
Speed ratings (Par 101): **102,101,99,98,94 94,93,90,61**
CSF £88.60 CT £349.73 TOTE £23.70: £5.40, £1.40, £1.70; EX 108.20 Trifecta £1015.70.
Owner A Taylor **Bred** Allan Munnis & Laurance Walwin **Trained** Upper Lambourn, Berks

FOCUS
An ordinary staying handicap in which the winner dictated.

39 2019 MEMBERSHIP AVAILABLE H'CAP 1m 2f (P)
7:55 (7:58) (Class 6) (0-60,61) 4-Y-O+
£3,493 (£1,039; £519; £400; £400; £400) Stalls Low

Form RPR
300- 1 **Baasha**[22] 9512 4-9-7 **61**.....(b) RobertHavlin 8 68
(Ed Dunlop) *stdd after s: hld up in last quartet: clsd and n.m.r wl over 1f out: squeezed through jst over 1f out: ev ch u.p ins fnl f: r.o to ld cl home* **7/1**

161- 2 *nk* **Hard Toffee (IRE)**[21] 9527 8-9-5 **58**..... AdamKirby 7 64
(Louise Allan) *hld up in tch in midfield: clsd and nt clr run ent fnl 2f: gap opened and hdwy wl over 1f out: drvn to ld ins fnl f: kpt on tl hdd and no ex cl home* **9/4**[1]

404- 3 *2 1/4* **Sharp Operator**[21] 9528 6-9-2 **55**.....(h) RichardKingscote 3 57
(Charlie Wallis) *in tch in midfield: clsd to trck ldrs over 2f out: nt clr run and swtchd rt over 1f out: sn drvn and led jst over 1f out: hdd ins fnl f: sn outpcd* **9/2**[2]

536- 4 *3/4* **Mullarkey**[40] 9249 5-9-0 **53**..... KierenFox 10 53
(John Best) *hld up in tch in last pair: hdwy over 2f out: chsd ldrs but unable qck 1f out: outpcd ins fnl f* **6/1**[3]

/05- 5 *2 1/2* **Red Cossack (CAN)**[22] 9510 8-8-9 **51**.....(h) JackDuern(3) 13 46
(Dean Ivory) *stdd and awkward leaving stalls: t.k.h: hld up in last pair: hdwy on outer to chse ldrs and rdn 3f out: no ex ent fnl f: wknd ins fnl f* **10/1**

142- 6 *nk* **Mans Not Trot (IRE)**[13] 9658 4-9-3 **57**.....(p) NicolaCurrie 6 52
(Jamie Osborne) *led: drvn and hdd over 1f out: no ex and wknd ins fnl f (jockey said gelding hung right-handed)* **6/1**[3]

360- 7 *1 1/4* **Stosur (IRE)**[8] 9704 8-8-12 **58**.....(b) TobyEley(7) 2 50
(Gay Kelleway) *t.k.h: chsd ldrs: pressing ldrs but struggling to qckn whn nudged lft over 1f out: wknd ins fnl f (jockey said mare hung right-handed turning in)* **25/1**

605- 8 *1 3/4* **Steel Helmet (IRE)**[21] 9527 5-8-7 **46** oh1..... JosephineGordon 9 35
(Harriet Bethell) *chsd ldrs: rdn over 2f out: unable qck and lost pl jst over 1f out: wknd ins fnl f* **20/1**

624- 9 *1* **Herm (IRE)**[26] 9465 5-9-2 **55**..... JFEgan 11 42
(David Evans) *hld up in tch in last quartet: hdwy and rdn over 2f out: sn struggling and lost pl over 1f out: wknd fnl f* **10/1**

200- 10 *1/2* **New Street (IRE)**[58] 8887 8-9-7 **60**.....(b) RobHornby 4 46
(Suzi Best) *chsd ldr tl unable qck over 1f out: sn lost pl and wknd ins fnl f* **20/1**

00- 11 *2* **Compulsive (IRE)**[43] 9168 4-9-6 **60**.....(v[1]) HectorCrouch 5 42
(Gary Moore) *midfield: rdn over 6f out: drvn over 2f out: nt clr ent fnl f: sn btn and lost pl: bhd ins fnl f* **20/1**

635- 12 *10* **Golconda Prince (IRE)**[79] 8309 5-9-4 **60**..... PaddyBradley(3) 12 22
(Mark Pattinson) *midfield tl dropped to rr and rdn 3f out: sn struggling and bhd ins fnl f* **33/1**

2m 8.34s (-0.26) **Going Correction** +0.05s/f (Slow)
WFA 4 from 5yo+ 1lb **12 Ran SP% 129.3**
Speed ratings (Par 101): **103,102,100,100,98 98,97,95,94,94 92,84**
CSF £23.50 CT £85.91 TOTE £8.40: £2.80, £1.50, £2.30; EX 38.80 Trifecta £229.20.
Owner Mhs Partners & E Dunlop **Bred** Mrs D O'Brien **Trained** Newmarket, Suffolk

FOCUS
This weak handicap was run at a strong pace.
T/Jkpt: Not Won. T/Plt: £304.40 to a £1 stake. Pool: £95,426.52 - 228.80 winning units T/Qpdt: £119.20 to a £1 stake. Pool: £14,071.65 - 87.32 winning units **Steve Payne**

[1]SOUTHWELL (L-H)
Thursday, January 3

OFFICIAL GOING: Fibresand: standard
Wind: Virtually nil Weather: Overcast

40 BETWAY HEED YOUR HUNCH AMATEUR RIDERS' H'CAP 2m 102y(F)
12:55 (12:55) (Class 6) (0-60,60) 4-Y-O+
£2,994 (£928; £464; £300; £300; £300) Stalls Low

Form RPR
403- 1 **Katie Gale**[13] 9663 9-10-13 **59**.....(v) MissGinaAndrews 5 69+
(Robyn Brisland) *hld up in tch: trckd ldrs over 6f out: hdwy on bit on outer over 3f out: sn cl up: led 2f out: rdn clr over 1f out: kpt on strly* **8/1**[3]

041- 2 *6* **Tynecastle Park**[91] 6639 6-10-6 **57**..... MrGeorgeEddery(5) 6 60
(Robert Eddery) *trckd ldrs: hdwy 4f out: cl up over 3f out: rdn along 2f out and ev ch tl drvn over 1f out and kpt on same pce* **11/4**[2]

001- 3 *2 1/2* **Constituent**[13] 9657 4-9-11 **48**.....(v) MissSerenaBrotherton 10 50
(Michael Appleby) *prom: led after 2f: pushed along over 3f out: rdn and hdd 2f out: sn edgd lft: kpt on one pce* **7/4**[1]

400- 4 *9* **Rock N'Stones (IRE)**[16] 8479 8-10-9 **60**..... JoeWilliamson(5) 4 49
(Gillian Boanas) *chsd ldrs: pushed along and sltly outpcd over 5f out: hdwy 4f out: rdn along to chse ldrs over 2f out: sn drvn and outpcd* **50/1**

400- 5 *3* **Bertie Moon**[18] 7959 9-9-13 **50**..... MrMatthewEnnis(5) 12 35
(Tony Forbes) *cl up: rdn along over 3f out: drvn wl over 2f out: sn wknd* **50/1**

000- 6 *3/4* **Boru's Brook (IRE)**[44] 9159 11-9-7 **46** oh1.....(be[1]) MrCiaranJones(7) 9 31
(Emma Owen) *dwlt: a in rr* **80/1**

652- 7 *4* **Ruler Of The Nile**[5] 9751 7-10-8 **54**.....(b) MissBeckySmith 7 34
(Marjorie Fife) *hld up in rr: hdwy on outer over 6f out: trckd ldrs 4f out: rdn along over 3f out: sn btn (vet said gelding finished lame)* **11/4**[2]

0/0- 8 *2 1/4* **Edgar (GER)**[13] 9657 9-10-7 **58**..... MissSarahBowen(5) 8 35
(David Bridgwater) *a towards rr* **40/1**

606- 9 *9* **Animated Hero**[19] 9553 6-9-11 **46** oh1.....(vt) MrAaronAnderson(3) 11 12
(Rebecca Menzies) *chsd ldrs: rdn along over 4f out: wknd over 3f out* **33/1**

000- 10 *35* **Allnite (IRE)**[41] 7841 4-9-4 **46** oh1.....(h w) MissEmilyBullock(5) 3
(Marjorie Fife) *led 2f: prom: rdn along over 6f out: sn lost pl and bhd* **20/1**

3m 42.49s (-3.01) **Going Correction** -0.15s/f (Stan)
WFA 4 from 6yo+ 5lb **10 Ran SP% 116.1**
Speed ratings (Par 101): **101,98,96,92,90 90,88,87,82,65**
CSF £28.82 CT £56.62 TOTE £6.80: £1.80, £1.20, £1.30; EX 33.20 Trifecta £102.00.
Owner Ferrybank Properties Limited **Bred** Netherfield House Stud **Trained** Danethorpe, Notts

FOCUS
A moderate handicap. The winner has been rated back to her spring form, and the second to his August win.

41 PLAY 4 TO SCORE AT BETWAY MAIDEN STKS 1m 4f 14y(F)
1:30 (1:30) (Class 5) 4-Y-O+
£3,752 (£1,116; £557; £278) Stalls Low

Form RPR
502- 1 **Temur Khan**[26] 9464 4-9-5 76..... DavidProbert 2 82
(Tony Carroll) *trckd ldrs: hdwy over 3f out: chal over 2f out: led wl over 1f out: sn rdn clr: kpt on strly* **9/4**[2]

4- 2 *5* **Miss Crick**[26] 9464 8-9-3 0..... MartinHarley 7 68
(Alan King) *trckd ldrs: pushed along and outpcd 4f out: sn rdn: swtchd wd and hdwy over 2f out: styd on to chse wnr ins fnl f: no imp* **5/2**[3]

230- 3 *3/4* **Francophilia**[8] 9706 4-9-0 73..... JoeFanning 4 68
(Mark Johnston) *trckd ldng pair: cl up after 4f: rdn to take slt ld wl over 2f out: hdd wl over 1f out: sn drvn and one pce* **2/1**[1]

6- 4 *7* **Taraayef (IRE)**[103] 7526 4-9-0 0..... AndrewMullen 1 57
(Adrian Nicholls) *trckd ldr: led after 2f: pushed along 4f out: rdn over 3f out: hdd wl over 2f out: sn drvn and wknd* **12/1**

5- 5 *3 1/4* **Utility (GER)**[15] 9464 8-9-3 0..... PoppyBridgwater(5) 5 55
(David Bridgwater) *a in rr* **12/1**

060- 6 *21* **Ejabah (IRE)**[14] 9643 5-9-0 38..... NoelGarbutt(3) 3 17
(Charles Smith) *led 2f: prom: pushed along over 7 out: rdn and lost pl 1/2-way: sn bhd* **200/1**

7 *3 1/4* **Willy Sewell**[195] 6-9-8 0..... AlistairRawlinson 6 17
(Michael Appleby) *trckd ldrs: hdwy 7f out and cl up: rdn along over 3f out: sn wknd and eased (jockey said gelding ran too free and hung right throughout)* **33/1**

2m 38.02s (-2.98) **Going Correction** -0.15s/f (Stan)
WFA 4 from 5yo+ 3lb **7 Ran SP% 111.5**
Speed ratings (Par 103): **103,99,99,94,92 78,76**
CSF £7.87 TOTE £2.70: £1.20, £1.40; EX 8.50 Trifecta £17.10.
Owner Mrs Helen Hogben **Bred** London Thoroughbred Services Ltd **Trained** Cropthorne, Worcs

FOCUS
Not much strength in depth here and an easy win for the top-rated on official ratings. The winner has been rated back to his best, the second to form and third to her AW latest.

42 BETWAY CASINO H'CAP 6f 16y(F)
2:00 (2:00) (Class 6) (0-65,67) 4-Y-O+
£3,105 (£924; £461; £300; £300; £300) Stalls Low

Form RPR
056- 1 **The Golden Cue**[17] 9587 4-8-10 **61**..... TobyEley(7) 3 69
(Steph Hollinshead) *trckd ldrs: hdwy 2f out: rdn over 1f out: drvn to chal ins fnl f: kpt on wl to ld on line (jockey said gelding hung right)* **14/1**

322- 2 *shd* **First Excel**[14] 9649 7-9-5 **66**.....(b) EoinWalsh(3) 5 73
(Roy Bowring) *cl up: rdn 2f out: led wl over 1f out: drvn ins fnl f: hdd on line* **9/2**[2]

212- 3 *1 3/4* **Liamba**[78] 8334 4-9-2 **63**..... ConorMcGovern(3) 8 64
(David O'Meara) *in tch: hdwy over 2f out: rdn wl over 1f out: kpt on fnl f* **9/1**

541- 4 *1/2* **Mr Strutter (IRE)**[14] 9649 5-9-2 **67**..... OliverStammers(7) 6 67+
(Ronald Thompson) *blindfold removed late and lost 5 l s: bhd: rdn and hdwy over 2f out: styng on to chse ldrs ins fnl f: hmpd and swtchd rt towards fin (jockey said gelding reared as stalls opened and blindfold was caught on gelding's ears)* **7/4**[1]

000- 5 *1 1/4* **Always Amazing**[5] 9748 5-9-7 **65**..... PaddyMathers 4 61
(Derek Shaw) *towards rr: rdn along and hdwy on inner over 2f out: chsd ldrs over 1f out: sn drvn and no imp* **10/1**

554- 6 *shd* **Archimedes (IRE)**[14] 9648 6-8-11 **58**.....(tp) PhilDennis(3) 2 53
(David C Griffiths) *led: rdn along over 2f out: hdd wl over 1f out: sn drvn: kpt on same pce: edgd rt towards fin* **20/1**

22-4 7 *7* **Point Zero (IRE)**[2] 1 4-9-9 **67**.....(b) AlistairRawlinson 9 40
(Michael Appleby) *chsd ldng pair on outer: wd st: sn rdn and wknd wl over 1f out* **5/1**[3]

305- 8 *12* **Blistering Dancer (IRE)**[28] 9433 9-8-7 **51** oh6..... DavidProbert 7
(Tony Carroll) *chsd ldrs: rdn along over 3f out: sn wknd* **50/1**

450- 9 *4 1/2* **Grise Lightning (FR)**[15] 9617 4-9-2 **60**..... BarryMcHugh 1
(Richard Fahey) *chsd ldrs on inner: rdn along over 3f out: sn wknd* **9/1**

1m 15.86s (-0.64) **Going Correction** -0.15s/f (Stan) **9 Ran SP% 113.7**
Speed ratings (Par 101): **98,97,95,94,93 93,83,67,61**
CSF £74.72 CT £611.17 TOTE £16.10: £3.50, £1.80, £2.30; EX 83.40 Trifecta £411.20.
Owner The Golden Cue Partnership **Bred** D R Botterill **Trained** Upper Longdon, Staffs

FOCUS
A modest handicap but it produced a thrilling finish and an unlucky loser. The winner has been rated close to last year's turf form, and the second to form.

43 BETWAY SPRINT H'CAP 4f 214y(F)
2:35 (2:35) (Class 5) (0-70,68) 4-Y-O+
£3,752 (£1,116; £557; £300; £300; £300) Stalls Centre

Form RPR
261- 1 **Miningggold**[14] 9648 6-8-13 **65**.....(p) PaulaMuir(5) 2 75
(Michael Dods) *racd towards far side: trckd ldrs: hdwy over 2f out: rdn to ld over 1f out: drvn and kpt on wl fnl f* **11/4**[1]

013- 2 *1* **Piazon**[14] 9649 8-9-1 **62**.....(be) NathanEvans 10 68
(Julia Brooke) *racd centre: chsd ldrs: hdwy wl over 1f out: rdn to chse wnr ins fnl f: drvn and no ex towards fin* **10/1**

035- 3 *3/4* **Crosse Fire**[5] 9748 7-9-2 **68**.....(p) TheodoreLadd(5) 6 71+
(Scott Dixon) *dwlt and bhd: swtchd lft to far rail over 2f out: rdn wl over 1f out: kpt on wl fnl f (jockey said gelding was slowly away)* **7/2**[2]

350- 4 *2 1/4* **Warrior's Valley**[16] 9597 4-9-2 **63**.....(t) AlistairRawlinson 11 58
(David C Griffiths) *racd towards stands' side: chsd ldrs: cl up 1/2-way: led 2f out: sn rdn: edgd lft and hdd over 1f out: grad wknd* **16/1**

600- 5 *nse* **Pearl Acclaim (IRE)**[5] 9748 9-9-1 **65**.....(p) PhilDennis(3) 3 60
(David C Griffiths) *prom centre: rdn along over 2f out: sn drvn and one pce* **20/1**

555- 6 *1 1/2* **Fethiye Boy**[21] 9525 5-9-7 **68**..... DavidProbert 5 58
(Ronald Harris) *racd centre: slt ld: hdd 3f out: cl up: led again briefly over 2f out: sn hdd and grad wknd* **16/1**

005- 7 *1 1/4* **My Name Is Rio (IRE)**[16] 9597 9-9-4 **65**..... BarryMcHugh 8 50
(John Davies) *outpcd and bhd tl styd on fnl f* **14/1**

043- 8 *shd* **Decision Maker (IRE)**[14] 9648 5-8-6 **56**.....(v[1]) EoinWalsh(3) 1 41
(Roy Bowring) *dwlt: racd towards far rail: sn chsng ldrs: cl up 1/2-way: rdn along 2f out: grad wknd over 1f out* **7/1**[3]

160- 9 *3/4* **Fink Hill (USA)**[14] 9649 4-9-2 **63**.....(b) CharlesBishop 9 45
(Richard Spencer) *racd centre: a towards rr* **20/1**

000- **10** 3/4 **Come On Dave (IRE)**[30] 9393 10-9-3 **67**.....................(e[1]) TimClark(3) 4 46
(Paul D'Arcy) *dwlt: a towards rr* **22/1**

000- **F** **Razin' Hell**[40] 9251 8-9-4 **65**.....................(v) LewisEdmunds 7
(John Balding) *cl up centre: slt ld 3f out: rdn along hdd over 2f out: lost pl and fell wl over 1f out: fatally injured* **7/1**[3]

58.89s (-0.81) **Going Correction** -0.15s/f (Stan) **11** Ran SP% **115.3**
Speed ratings (Par 103): **100,98,97,93,93 91,89,88,87,86**
CSF £29.29 CT £100.35 TOTE £3.50: £1.70, £3.60, £1.50; EX 27.90 Trifecta £68.70.

Owner Mrs C E Dods **Bred** Mrs G S Rees **Trained** Denton, Co Durham

FOCUS
A modest contest won by an in-form mare. The second has been rated in line with his recent form.

44 SUNRACING.CO.UK H'CAP — 7f 14y(F)

3:10 (3:12) (Class 4) (0-80,84) 4-Y-O+
£6,080 (£1,809; £904; £452; £300; £300) **Stalls** Low

Form — RPR

512- **1** **Weld Al Emarat**[23] 9494 7-9-7 **80**..................... NathanEvans 3 88+
(Michael Easterby) *trckd ldrs: hdwy over 2f out: rdn to chse ldng pair over 1f out: drvn ins fnl f: styd on wl to ld towards fin* **11/8**[1]

12-0 **2** 1/2 **Angel Palanas**[2] 4 5-9-1 **81**.....................(p) JonathanFisher(7) 4 88
(K R Burke) *cl up: led 2f out: rdn over 1f out: drvn ins fnl f: hdd and no ex towards fin* **5/1**[3]

401- **3** 1 **The Right Choice (IRE)**[23] 9491 4-8-11 **70**.....................(b) BarryMcHugh 1 74
(Richard Fahey) *trckd ldrs on inner: hdwy and cl up over 2f out: rdn and ev ch over 1f out: drvn and kpt on same pce fnl f* **16/1**

033- **4** 1 3/4 **Hammer Gun (USA)**[13] 9661 6-9-6 **79**.....................(v) JasonHart 8 79
(Derek Shaw) *dwlt and bhd: rdn along and hdwy over 2f out: styd on u.p fnl f* **11/2**

311- **5** 5 **Robero**[8] 9702 7-9-4 **84** 6ex.....................(e) TobyEley(7) 7 71
(Gay Kelleway) *in tch: pushed along over 3f out: rdn and sme hdwy over 2f out: sn drvn and n.d (jockey said gelding was never travelling)* **7/2**[2]

231- **6** 6 **Kyllachy Dragon (IRE)**[20] 9535 4-9-5 **78**.....................(h) DavidProbert 6 49
(Ronald Harris) *prom on outer: effrt 3f out: rdn along over 2f out: sn drvn and wknd* **18/1**

000- **7** 2 1/2 **Zaeem**[17] 9585 10-8-11 **70**..................... KieranO'Neill 5 35
(Ivan Furtado) *led: rdn along 3f out: hdd 2f out: sn wknd* **25/1**

000/ **8** 20 **Whirl Me Round**[371] 9437 5-8-1 **67**..................... RPWalsh(7) 2
(Robyn Brisland) *s.i.s and bhd: hdwy to take clsr order 4f out: rdn along over 3f out: sn wknd (jockey said gelding was slowly away)* **66/1**

1m 27.4s (-2.90) **Going Correction** -0.15s/f (Stan) **8** Ran SP% **112.9**
Speed ratings (Par 105): **110,109,108,106,100 93,90,68**
CSF £8.35 CT £72.78 TOTE £2.10: £1.10, £1.40, £3.40; EX 9.00 Trifecta £60.30.

Owner Imperial Racing Partnership No 8 **Bred** Rabbah Bloodstock Limited **Trained** Sheriff Hutton, N Yorks

FOCUS
A fair handicap and a progressive winner. The second and fourth have been rated similar to when meeting the winner here last month.

45 FOLLOW TOP TIPSTER TEMPLEGATE AT SUN RACING H'CAP — 7f 14y(F)

3:45 (3:46) (Class 6) (0-65,65) 4-Y-O+
£3,105 (£924; £461; £300; £300; £300) **Stalls** Low

Form — RPR

503- **1** **Thunder Buddy**[13] 9659 4-8-6 **55**..................... PaulaMuir(5) 10 66
(K R Burke) *prom: cl up 3f out: led wl over 1f out: sn rdn: drvn ins fnl f: kpt on wl towards fin* **9/2**[1]

20-0 **2** 1 1/2 **Sooqaan**[2] 5 8-9-3 **61**.....................(p) CamHardie 9 68
(Antony Brittain) *trckd ldrs: effrt and n.m.r wl over 1f out: sn swtchd rt and rdn: chsd wnr and ch ins fnl f: drvn and kpt on same pce towards fin* **7/1**

040- **3** 2 1/2 **Queens Royale**[54] 8997 5-9-6 **64**.....................(v) AlistairRawlinson 8 65
(Michael Appleby) *cl up: led 4f out: rdn along 3f out: hdd and drvn wl over 1f out: sn edgd lft and kpt on same pce* **15/2**

260- **4** 1 **Break The Silence**[16] 9593 5-8-13 **57**.....................(p) KieranO'Neill 7 55
(Scott Dixon) *led 3f: cl up: rdn along wl over 2f out: drvn wl over 1f out: kpt on same pce* **8/1**

026- **5** 4 **Ticks The Boxes (IRE)**[14] 9649 7-8-2 **46**.....................(v) NathanEvans 11 34
(John Wainwright) *chsd ldrs: rdn along over 2f out: sn drvn and kpt on one pce* **33/1**

300- **6** 3 1/2 **Showmethedough**[29] 9402 4-9-2 **65**.....................(p[1]) SebastianWoods(5) 3 43
(Richard Fahey) *chsd ldrs on inner: rdn along wl over 2f out: sn btn* **13/2**[3]

000/ **7** 1/2 **Adiator**[617] 2082 11-7-10 **47** oh1 ow1.....................(p) FayeMcManoman(7) 1 24
(Seb Spencer) *a towards rr* **100/1**

300- **8** nk **Poyle George Two**[62] 8797 4-9-4 **62**.....................(b) CharlesBishop 6 38
(Ralph Beckett) *a towards rr* **14/1**

003- **9** 1 **Grinty (IRE)**[16] 9600 5-9-2 **60**.....................(p) AndrewMullen 5 34
(Michael Dods) *chsd ldrs on outer: wd st: sn rdn and wknd (jockey said gelding ran flat)* **5/1**[2]

/50- **10** 1 3/4 **Cold Fire (IRE)**[310] 941 6-8-1 **52**..................... RPWalsh(7) 12 21
(Robyn Brisland) *in tch: rdn along 3f out: sn wknd* **50/1**

000- **11** 2 1/2 **Brigand**[16] 9600 4-9-1 **62**..................... TimClark(3) 2 25
(Paul D'Arcy) *rrd and dwlt s: a in rr (jockey said gelding fly-leapt the stalls and was slowly away)* **66/1**

002- **12** 10 **Boots And Spurs**[14] 9643 10-8-5 **54**.....................(v) TheodoreLadd(5) 4
(Scott Dixon) *towards rr: pushed along and outpcd bef 1/2-way: sn bhd (jockey said gelding was never travelling)* **5/1**[2]

1m 28.38s (-1.92) **Going Correction** -0.15s/f (Stan) **12** Ran SP% **114.3**
Speed ratings (Par 101): **104,102,99,98,93 89,89,88,87,85 82,71**
CSF £34.08 CT £229.87 TOTE £4.00: £1.60, £2.40, £2.70; EX 37.00 Trifecta £241.40.

Owner Mrs Elaine M Burke **Bred** J C S Wilson Bloodstock **Trained** Middleham Moor, N Yorks

FOCUS
A moderate handicap but an authoritative winner. The second has been rated in line with his November run here.

T/Plt: £30.40 to a £1 stake. Pool: £92,985.32 - 2,231.71 winning units T/Qpdt: £12.10 to a £1 stake. Pool: £9,482.03 - 576.05 winning units **Joe Rowntree**

DEAUVILLE (R-H)

Thursday, January 3

OFFICIAL GOING: Polytrack: standard

46a PRIX SWAIN (CONDITIONS) (4YO+) (POLYTRACK) — 1m 4f 110y(P)

1:02 4-Y-O+
£9,459 (£3,594; £2,648; £1,513; £756; £567)

RPR

1 **Pascasha D'Or (FR)**[16] 5-9-7 0..................... MorganDelalande 5 86
(S Wattel, France) **14/5**[2]

2 3/4 **Pao Enki (FR)**[8] 5-9-1 0..................... PierreBazire 4 79
(Mme A Rosa, France) **11/1**

3 1 **Rossita (GER)** 5-9-2 0..................... ThomasTrullier 3 78
(Andreas Suborics, Germany) **21/1**

4 3/4 **Sura (IRE)**[50] 4-8-13 0..................... BertrandFlandrin 9 79
(Waldemar Hickst, Germany) **26/1**

5 hd **Edington (GER)**[102] 7594 7-9-5 0..................... ThierryThulliez 7 80
(Frau S Steinberg, Germany) **41/10**[3]

6 snk **Innenminister (GER)** 4-8-11 0..................... JeffersonSmith 10 77
(Dr A Bolte, Germany) **23/1**

7 2 **Echauffour (FR)**[37] 9279 6-9-10 0..................... ThomasHuet 2 81
(J-C Rouget, France) **5/2**[1]

8 3 **Trawangane (FR)**[37] 9279 5-9-1 0..................... MlleLauraGrosso(3) 14 71
(N Clement, France) **15/1**

9 nse **Mr Gallivanter (IRE)**[295] 8-9-1 0..................... StephaneLaurent 12 68
(Mlle B Renk, France) **65/1**

10 hd **Pantomime (IRE)**[35] 7-9-0 0..................... FrankPanicucci 11 66
(Mme G Rarick, France) **58/1**

11 2 **Trancoso (FR)**[765] 8147 6-9-1 0..................... DamienBoche 13 64
(E Leenders, France) **11/1**

12 1 1/4 **Monde Chat Luna (JPN)**[68] 8661 8-9-1 0..................... GlenBraem 15 62
(Hiroo Shimizu, France) **70/1**

13 2 **Blushing Bere (FR)**[584] 8-9-2 0 ow1..................... GeoffreyBoughaita 6 60
(E Leenders, France) **36/1**

14 1 1/4 **Helioblu Bareliere (FR)**[18] 6-9-3 0..................... CEFlannelly 8 59
(Mme G Rarick, France) **108/1**

15 3 1/2 **Pure Country**[73] 8471 4-8-11 0..................... JulesMobian 1 52
(Noel Williams) *wl into stride: disp ld early: settled to trck ldrs: shuffled bk to midfield 7f out: pushed along 3f out: rdn w limited rspnse 2f out: wknd and eased ins fnl f* **33/1**

2m 36.28s
WFA 4 from 5yo+ 3lb **15** Ran SP% **121.0**
PARI-MUTUEL (all including 1 euro stake): WIN 3.80; PLACE 1.80, 4.10, 5.70; DF 22.60; SF 36.20.
Owner J-M Aubry-Dumand **Bred** Aubry-Dumand Elevage **Trained** France

MEYDAN (L-H)

Thursday, January 3

OFFICIAL GOING: Turf: good; dirt: fast

47a LONGINES GENTS RECORD COLLECTION (H'CAP) (TURF) — 1m 4f 11y

2:30 (2:30) (95-107,107) 3-Y-O+
£82,677 (£27,559; £13,779; £6,889; £4,133; £2,755)

RPR

1 **Bin Battuta**[495] 6445 5-9-1 **102**.....................(p) ChristopheSoumillon 1 106+
(Saeed bin Suroor) *trckd ldr: led 1 1/2f out: r.o wl: comf* **11/4**[2]

2 1 1/2 **Ispolini**[221] 3134 4-9-1 **105**.....................(t) JamesDoyle 2 108
(Charlie Appleby) *s.i.s: mid-div: chsd ldrs and ev ch 2f out: r.o fnl 1 1/2f* **5/4**[1]

3 nk **Sharpalo (FR)**[25] 7-9-0 **101**.....................(t) ConnorBeasley 5 102
(A bin Harmash, UAE) *mid-div: r.o wl fnl 1 1/2f: nrst fin* **50/1**

4 1 1/4 **Appeared**[132] 6501 7-8-11 **99**..................... RichardMullen 6 97
(David Simcock) *mid-div: r.o fnl 2f: nrst fin* **25/1**

5 3/4 **Basateen (IRE)**[18] 7-8-13 **100**..................... DaneO'Neill 7 98
(Doug Watson, UAE) *s.i.s: nvr nr to chal but r.o fnl 2f* **11/1**

6 1 1/2 **Maifalki (FR)**[47] 9137 6-8-11 **99**..................... FabriceVeron 9 94
(N Caullery, France) *nvr bttr than mid-div* **25/1**

7 3/4 **Earnshaw (USA)**[292] 1256 8-9-6 **107**.....................(t) MickaelBarzalona 11 101
(S Jadhav, UAE) *nvr nr to chal* **14/1**

8 shd **Big Challenge (IRE)**[84] 8140 5-8-7 **95**..................... HayleyTurner 3 88
(Saeed bin Suroor) *sn led: hdd 2f out: sn btn* **10/3**[3]

9 hd **Jaaref (IRE)**[25] 6-9-3 **104**..................... JimCrowley 8 98
(A R Al Rayhi, UAE) *trckd ldr: led briefly 2f out: hdd & wknd 1 1/2f out* **20/1**

2m 32.41s
WFA 4 from 5yo+ 3lb **9** Ran SP% **123.6**
CSF: 6.83; TRICAST: 143.27.
Owner Godolphin **Bred** Darley **Trained** Newmarket, Suffolk

FOCUS
TRAKUS (metres travelled compared to winner): 2nd +12, 3rd 0, 4th +10, 5th +1, 6th +10, 7th +5, 8th +2, 9th +9. The rail was at its innermost point for the opening fixture of the 2019 Dubai World Cup Carnival, now in its 16th year and with an earlier place in the calendar than usual. The pace was slow early which turned this into the sprint and the winner picked up smartly: 28.09 (400m from standing start), 26.14 (800m), 25.34 (1200m), 25.31 (1600m), 24.43 (2000m), with the winner getting the final 410m in 22.89. The first three have been rated close to their marks.

48a UAE 1000 GUINEAS TRIAL PRESENTED BY LONGINES LA GRANDE CLASSIQUE (CONDITIONS) (FILLIES) (DIRT) — 7f (D)

3:05 (3:05) 3-Y-O
£47,244 (£15,748; £7,874; £3,937; £2,362; £1,574)

RPR

1 **Al Hayette (USA)**[14] 9652 3-9-0 87.....................(h) FabriceVeron 6 91+
(Ismail Mohammed) *settled in rr: rdn 3f out: r.o wl: led fnl 110yds* **14/1**

2 2 **Nashirah**[72] 8512 3-9-0 83..................... JamesDoyle 1 83
(Charlie Appleby) *s.i.s: trckd ldr: rdn to ld 1f out: hdd fnl 110yds* **5/2**[1]

3 1 1/2 **Muthhila (IRE)**[79] 8296 3-9-0 75..................... XavierZiani 5 79
(S Jadhav, UAE) *sn led: hdd 1f out but r.o* **66/1**

4 *1* **Mulhima (IRE)**[86] 8091 3-9-0 70........................ AntonioFresu 9 76
(A bin Harmash, UAE) *trckd ldr: ev ch 2 1/2f out: r.o same pce fnl 2f* **50/1**

5 *1* **Swift Rose (IRE)**[47] 9133 3-9-0 85........................ KevinStott 8 73
(Saeed bin Suroor) *s.i.s: nvr nr to chal but r.o fnl 2f* **11/2**

6 *1 3/4* **Al Shamkhah (USA)**[42] 9217 3-9-0 85........................ MickaelBarzalona 2 68
(S Jadhav, UAE) *nvr nr to chal but r.o fnl 2 1/2f* **9/1**

7 *1/2* **Queen Monaco (IRE)**[14] 9652 3-9-0 0........................(v) ConnorBeasley 7 67
(H Al Alawi, UAE) *a mid-div* **80/1**

8 *2 1/4* **Turn 'n Twirl (USA)**[15] 9603 3-9-0 86........................ JimCrowley 4 61
(Simon Crisford) *trckd ldr tl wknd fnl 2 1/2f* **11/4**[2]

9 *6 3/4* **Lady Wedad (USA)**[42] 9217 3-9-0 0........................ PatDobbs 13 43
(Doug Watson, UAE) *nvr nr to chal* **20/1**

10 *nk* **Oya (IRE)**[14] 9652 3-9-0 0........................ RichardMullen 3 42
(S Seemar, UAE) *s.i.s: a in rr* **80/1**

11 *2 3/4* **Foggy Flight (USA)**[14] 9652 3-9-0 84........................(h) RoystonFfrench 14 35
(S Jadhav, UAE) *nvr nr to chal* **33/1**

12 *6 3/4* **Aqqadeer (USA)**[14] 9652 3-9-0 0........................ ShermanBrown 11 16
(R Bouresly, Kuwait) *s.i.s: a in rr* **100/1**

13 *shd* **Ghost Queen**[86] 8075 3-9-0 78........................(v) DaneO'Neill 10 16
(Simon Crisford) *a in rr* **40/1**

14 *10 1/2* **Dubai Beauty (IRE)**[88] 8024 3-9-0 104........................ ChristopheSoumillon 12
(Saeed bin Suroor) *chsd ldrs tl wknd 3f out* **3/1**[3]

1m 27.22s (2.12) **Going Correction** +0.475s/f (Slow) **14 Ran SP% 129.3**
Speed ratings: **106,103,102,100,99 97,97,94,86,86 83,75,75,63**
CSF: 51.33.
Owner Ismail Mohammed **Bred** Patrick Davis & W S Farish **Trained** Newmarket, Suffolk

FOCUS
TRAKUS: 2nd -5, 3rd -4, 4th +3, 5th +4, 6th +10, 7th -4, 8th 0, 9th +6, 10th -2, 11th +10, 12th +4, 13th +4, 14th +10. The dirt course was consistently fast towards the end of the last carnival, but had been slow in more recent weeks during the latest domestic season and that was again the case this time, so it proved hard work for these young fillies with the pace gradually slowing: 25.07 (400m from standing start), 23.29 (800m), 25.45 (1200m), with the winner getting the final section in 12.98. The seventh and tenth cast doubt on the value of the form.

49a LONGINES LADIES RECORD COLLECTION (H'CAP) (TURF) 5f
3:40 (3:40) (95-110,110) 3-Y-0+

£68,503 (£22,834; £11,417; £5,708; £3,425; £2,283)

RPR

1 **Faatinah (AUS)**[47] 6-9-6 **110**........................(p) JimCrowley 6 113
(David A Hayes, Australia) *chsd ldr: rdn 2 1/2f out: led 1f out: r.o wl* **4/1**[3]

2 *2 1/2* **Hit The Bid**[76] 8397 5-9-6 **110**........................(t) ChrisHayes 2 104
(D J Bunyan, Ire) *trckd ldr: led 2 1/2f out: hdd 1f out: r.o* **7/4**[1]

3 *2* **Ibn Malik (IRE)**[28] 9438 6-8-9 **100**........................ DaneO'Neill 12 86
(M Al Mheiri, UAE) *nvr nr to chal but r.o wl fnl 1 1/2f: nrst fin* **7/2**[2]

4 *nk* **Orvar (IRE)**[100] 7639 6-8-10 **101**........................ LukeMorris 10 86
(Paul Midgley) *settled in rr: r.o fnl 2f: nrst fin* **12/1**

5 *hd* **Dutch Masterpiece**[28] 9438 9-8-13 **103**........................(t) ConnorBeasley 3 88
(Jaber Ramadhan, Bahrain) *trckd ldr: ev ch 1 1/2f out: one pce fnl f* **12/1**

6 *3/4* **Marnie James**[103] 7527 4-9-1 **105**........................(t) JamesDoyle 7 87
(Iain Jardine) *mid-div: r.o same pce fnl 2f* **9/1**

7 *nk* **Yard Line (USA)**[63] 8790 8-8-5 **95**........................ TadhgO'Shea 9 76
(R Bouresly, Kuwait) *s.i.s: nvr nr to chal but r.o fnl 2f* **33/1**

8 *nk* **Waady (IRE)**[14] 9654 7-8-11 **102**........................(b) PatDobbs 8 81
(Doug Watson, UAE) *nvr bttr than mid-div* **12/1**

9 *2* **Alfolk (AUS)**[341] 4-9-4 **108**........................(p) OlivierDoleuze 5 81
(M F De Kock, South Africa) *nvr bttr than mid-div* **22/1**

10 *shd* **Race Day (IRE)**[114] 7155 6-8-5 **98** ow3........................(p) RowanScott(3) 11 71
(Saeed bin Suroor) *a in rr* **14/1**

11 *2 1/4* **Freescape**[62] 8816 4-8-5 **96**........................ SamHitchcott 4 59
(David Marnane, Ire) *s.i.s: a in rr* **14/1**

12 *1/2* **Circle Dream (IRE)**[28] 9438 4-8-5 **95**........................ RichardMullen 1 58
(S Seemar, UAE) *sn led: hdd & wknd 2 1/2f out* **66/1**

57.47s **12 Ran SP% 133.8**
CSF: 12.85; TRICAST: 30.80.
Owner Hamdan Al Maktoum **Bred** Shadwell Stud Australasia Ltd **Trained** Australia

FOCUS
A smart sprint handicap: 23.92, 21.53, with the winner to the line in a slowing 12.03.

50a DUBAWI STKS PRESENTED BY LONGINES LADIES MASTER COLLECTION (GROUP 3) (DIRT) 6f (D)
4:15 (4:15) 3-Y-0+

£94,488 (£31,496; £15,748; £7,874; £4,724; £3,149)

RPR

1 **Raven's Corner (IRE)**[28] 9438 6-9-1 105........................(bt) RichardMullen 6 111
(S Seemar, UAE) *trckd ldr: smooth prog 3f out: led 1 1/2f out: r.o wl* **7/2**[3]

2 *1 3/4* **Drafted (USA)**[28] 9438 5-9-1 110........................ SamHitchcott 5 106+
(Doug Watson, UAE) *settled in rr: rdn 3f out: r.o v wl 1 1/2f out: nrst fin* **7/4**[1]

3 *6 1/2* **My Catch (IRE)**[278] 1524 8-9-1 109........................ PatDobbs 4 85
(Doug Watson, UAE) *sn led: hdd 1 1/2f out: wknd fnl 110yds* **5/2**[2]

4 *2 1/2* **Above The Rest (IRE)**[47] 9127 8-9-1 108........................(h) BenCurtis 3 77+
(David Barron) *s.i.s: a mid-div* **13/2**

5 *3 1/2* **High On Life**[28] 9438 8-9-1 104........................(t) MickaelBarzalona 2 66
(S Jadhav, UAE) *trckd ldr tl wknd fnl 1 1/2f* **12/1**

6 *3/4* **Trickbag (USA)**[71] 5-9-1 95........................(t) CarlosLopez 7 63
(Susanne Berneklint, Sweden) *nvr bttr than mid-div* **66/1**

7 *8 1/2* **Ace Korea (USA)**[46] 4-9-1 104........................(t) DarryllHolland 1 36
(Peter Wolsley, Korea) *slowly away: a in rr* **14/1**

1m 11.68s (0.08) **Going Correction** +0.475s/f (Slow) **7 Ran SP% 116.3**
Speed ratings: **118,115,107,103,99 98,86**
CSF: 10.41.
Owner Touch Gold Racing & Sean Ewing **Bred** Rabbah Bloodstock Ltd **Trained** United Arab Emirates

FOCUS
TRAKUS: 2nd -4, 3rd -5, 4th -7, 5th -6, 6th -2, 7th +2. A good pace over a tiring track: 23.84, 23.28, 24.56. The second has been rated to his latest.

51a SINGSPIEL STKS PRESENTED BY LONGINES V H P COLLECTION (GROUP 3) (TURF) 1m 1f
4:50 (4:50) 3-Y-0+

£94,488 (£31,496; £15,748; £7,874; £4,724; £3,149)

RPR

1 **Dream Castle**[299] 1136 5-9-0 111........................ ChristopheSoumillon 11 114+
(Saeed bin Suroor) *mid-div: smooth prog 2 1/2f out: led 1f out: r.o wl* **12/1**

2 *1 1/2* **Racing History (IRE)**[63] 8794 7-9-0 108........................(v) KevinStott 14 111
(Saeed bin Suroor) *trckd ldr: ev ch 2 1/2f out: hdd 1f out: r.o* **25/1**

3 *hd* **Salsabeel (IRE)**[130] 6606 5-9-0 111........................ BrettDoyle 13 110
(Charlie Appleby) *slowly away: settled in rr: r.o wl fnl 1 1/2f: nrst fin* **12/1**

4 *3* **Team Talk**[299] 1138 6-9-0 108........................(h) PatCosgrave 1 104
(Saeed bin Suroor) *mid-div: r.o same pce fnl 2f* **25/1**

5 *nk* **Bay Of Poets (IRE)**[315] 852 5-9-0 110........................ ColmO'Donoghue 6 104
(Charlie Appleby) *trckd ldrs: ev ch 2f out: one pce fnl 1 1/2f* **15/2**[3]

6 *1 1/4* **Light The Lights (SAF)**[292] 1256 7-9-0 111........................ OlivierDoleuze 16 101
(M F De Kock, South Africa) *nvr nr to chal but r.o fnl 2f* **33/1**

7 *hd* **Escalator**[66] 8695 4-8-13 105........................ StevieDonohoe 10 100
(Charlie Fellowes) *mid-div: r.o same pce fnl 2f* **16/1**

8 *hd* **Furia Cruzada (CHI)**[14] 9653 7-8-9 105........................(t) AntonioFresu 4 95
(E Charpy, UAE) *trckd ldr: ev ch 2 1/2f out: one pce fnl 2f* **33/1**

9 *2 1/4* **Gm Hopkins**[25] 8-9-0 101........................ RobertTart 8 95
(Jaber Ramadhan, Bahrain) *slowly away: nvr nr to chal* **66/1**

10 *nse* **Degas (GER)**[74] 8464 6-9-0 113........................ FabriceVeron 5 95
(Markus Klug, Germany) *nvr bttr than mid-div* **33/1**

11 *3/4* **Deauville (IRE)**[110] 7318 6-9-0 115........................(v) LukeMorris 3 94
(Fawzi Abdulla Nass, Bahrain) *sn led: hdd 2f out: sn btn* **10/1**

12 *1/2* **Key Victory (IRE)**[196] 4025 4-8-13 108........................ JamesDoyle 7 93
(Charlie Appleby) *mid-div: chsd ldrs 2 1/2f out: wknd fnl f* **11/10**[1]

13 *1 3/4* **Hornsby**[25] 6-9-0 104........................ MickaelBarzalona 15 89
(S Jadhav, UAE) *nvr bttr than mid-div* **50/1**

14 *6 1/2* **Settle For Bay (FR)**[197] 3999 5-9-0 107........................ PatDobbs 12 75
(David Marnane, Ire) *nvr bttr than mid-div* **10/3**[2]

15 *6 1/4* **Musaddas**[1036] 812 9-9-0 100........................ ShermanBrown 2 62
(R Bouresly, Kuwait) *trckd ldr: t.k.h: wknd fnl 2f* **100/1**

16 *3/4* **Arod (IRE)**[131] 6520 8-9-0 108........................ JimCrowley 9 61
(David Simcock) *nvr bttr than mid-div* **28/1**

1m 49.4s
WFA 4 from 5yo+ 1lb **16 Ran SP% 137.2**
CSF: 302.46.
Owner Godolphin **Bred** Darley **Trained** Newmarket, Suffolk

FOCUS
TRAKUS: 2nd -5, 3rd -5, 4th -12, 5th -8, 6th -11, 7th -6, 8th -10, 9th -12, 10th -9, 11th -10, 12th -5, 13th -1, 14th -1, 15th -13, 16th -9. They went steady early and sprinted late: 25.99 (400m), 24.7 (800m), 24.67 (1200m), 22.71 (1600m), with the winner home in 11.33. The first three have been rated to their marks.

52a LONGINES MASTER COLLECTION MOON PHASE (H'CAP) (TURF) 7f
5:25 (5:25) (95-114,114) 3-Y-0+

£82,677 (£27,559; £13,779; £6,889; £4,133; £2,755)

RPR

1 **Another Batt (IRE)**[75] 8409 4-8-9 **104**........................ ConnorBeasley 13 109
(George Scott) *mid-div: smooth prog 2 1/2f out: rdn to ld 1f out: r.o wl* **12/1**

2 *1* **Top Score**[131] 6530 5-9-1 **109**........................(p) ChristopheSoumillon 1 112
(Saeed bin Suroor) *trckd ldr: led 1 1/2f out: hdd 1f out: r.o* **9/4**[1]

3 *2* **Ekhtiyaar**[163] 5299 5-8-5 **100**........................ SamHitchcott 3 97
(Doug Watson, UAE) *mid-div: r.o fnl 2f: nrst fin* **12/1**

4 *2 1/4* **Seniority**[96] 7773 5-8-8 **103**........................ ChrisHayes 8 94
(William Haggas) *nvr nr to chal but r.o wl fnl 1 1/2f* **7/1**

5 *shd* **Suyoof (AUS)**[322] 738 6-8-13 **107**........................ DaneO'Neill 9 99
(M F De Kock, South Africa) *nvr nr to chal but r.o wl fnl 2f* **25/1**

6 *nk* **Victory Wave (USA)**[110] 7279 5-8-6 **101**........................(h) HayleyTurner 10 91
(Saeed bin Suroor) *trckd ldr: led 2f out: hdd 1 1/2f out: wknd fnl 110yds* **6/1**[3]

7 *nk* **Amazour (IRE)**[69] 8594 7-8-5 **99**........................ FabriceVeron 4 89
(Ismail Mohammed) *nvr nr to chal but r.o fnl 2f* **20/1**

8 *1 1/2* **Above N Beyond**[25] 6-8-5 **98**........................(t) RichardMullen 11 85
(A bin Harmash, UAE) *a mid-div* **50/1**

9 *1 3/4* **Portamento (IRE)**[14] 9655 7-8-7 **102**........................ FernandoJara 6 82
(A R Al Rayhi, UAE) *nvr bttr than mid-div* **33/1**

10 *1 3/4* **Never Back Down (IRE)**[63] 8768 4-8-7 **102**........................(v) BenCurtis 12 77
(Hugo Palmer) *nvr bttr than mid-div* **16/1**

11 *1 3/4* **Manahir (FR)**[69] 8624 5-8-5 **100**........................ MickaelBarzalona 7 71
(S Jadhav, UAE) *nvr bttr than mid-div* **33/1**

12 *1 1/2* **Aurum (IRE)**[216] 3329 4-8-5 **100**........................(t) BrettDoyle 5 67
(Charlie Appleby) *trckd ldrs tl wknd fnl 2f* **11/4**[2]

13 *2 1/4* **Janoobi (SAF)**[278] 1525 5-9-6 **114**........................ JimCrowley 14 76
(M F De Kock, South Africa) *nvr bttr than mid-div* **9/1**

14 *6 1/2* **Ghaamer (USA)**[419] 8731 9-8-7 **102**........................ AntonioFresu 2 45
(R Bouresly, Kuwait) *sn led: hdd & wknd 2f out* **50/1**

1m 23.48s **14 Ran SP% 133.9**
CSF: 41.39; TRICAST: 373.17; Placepot: 204.10 to a £1 stake. Quadpot: 44.70 to a £1 stake.
Owner Excel Racing **Bred** J W Nicholson **Trained** Newmarket, Suffolk

FOCUS
TRAKUS: 2nd -5, 3rd -8, 4th -3, 5th -2, 6th -6, 7th -8, 8th 0, 9th -4, 10th +1, 11th -5, 12th -10, 13th 0, 14th -10. The pace was a bit too fast: 24.75, 22.63, 23.81, with the winner to the line in a slowing 12.26.

KEMPTON (A.W) (R-H)
Friday, January 4

OFFICIAL GOING: Polytrack: standard to slow
Wind: Light, half against Weather: Fine and crisp

53 WISE BETTING AT RACINGTV.COM H'CAP 6f (P)
2:10 (2:10) (Class 6) (0-55,61) 4-Y-0+

£3,105 (£924; £461; £300; £300; £300) **Stalls** Low

Form RPR

065- 1 **Holdenhurst**[16] 9606 4-9-7 **55**........................ JFEgan 4 61
(Bill Turner) *trckd ldng pair: rdn to take 2nd 2f out: clsd on ldr fnl f: led last 75yds: hld on wl* **10/1**

061- 2 *shd* **Distant Applause (IRE)**[15] 9641 4-9-5 **53**........................ FergusSweeney 1 59
(Dominic Ffrench Davis) *t.k.h: hld up in midfield: swtchd off rail and prog 2f out: rdn to chal ins fnl f: kpt on wl but jst hld* **7/2**[1]

001- 3 *1 1/4* **Mercers**[4] 9776 5-9-13 **61** 6ex........................(b) JasonWatson 11 63
(Paddy Butler) *led: stl gng strly 2f out: rdn over 1f out: hdd and fdd last 75yds* **12/1**

500- 4 *1/2* **Toolatetodelegate**[44] 9176 5-9-1 **52**........................(t) FinleyMarsh(3) 2 53
(Brian Barr) *in tch in midfield: shkn up over 2f out: styd on over 1f out: nrly snatched 3rd* **10/1**

002- **5** *1 ½* **Athassel**[7] 9735 10-8-11 **52**.......................... GinaMangan(7) 3 48
(David Evans) *racd wd in midfield: pushed along over 2f out: hanging and lost grnd sn after: kpt on fnl f* **5/1**[2]

440- **6** *hd* **Swiss Cross**[7] 9735 12-9-7 **55**.......................... JosephineGordon 10 51
(Phil McEntee) *chsd ldrs: rdn and nt qckn over 2f out: one pce after* **14/1**

042- **7** *2 ¼* **Legal Mind**[15] 9641 6-9-4 **52**.......................... AdamKirby 7 41+
(Emma Owen) *bdly hmpd s: mostly in last pair and nvr able to rcvr* **5/1**[2]

0/3- **8** *nk* **Wotamadam**[16] 9606 4-9-7 **55**.......................... MartinDwyer 6 43
(Dean Ivory) *wnt sharply lft s: chsd ldr to 2f out: sn wknd* **9/1**[3]

0/0- **9** *1* **Atalanta Queen**[30] 9401 4-9-2 **50**.......................... ShaneKelly 12 35
(Robyn Brisland) *awkward s and also sltly impeded: hld up in last: snatched up bhd loose horse over 3f out: nvr any prog (jockey said filly was hampered by the loose horse on the final bend)* **66/1**

613- **U** **Magicinthemaking (USA)**[50] 9079 5-9-3 **51**.......................... HollieDoyle 8
(John E Long) *bdly hmpd and uns rdr s* **7/2**[1]

1m 14.06s (0.96) **Going Correction** +0.10s/f (Slow) **10** Ran SP% **121.8**
Speed ratings (Par 101): **97,96,95,94,92 92,89,88,87,**
CSF £47.10 CT £451.26 TOTE £13.90: £3.40, £1.80, £2.30; EX 50.40 Trifecta £477.90.
Owner Ansells Of Watford **Bred** Southill Stud **Trained** Sigwells, Somerset

FOCUS
Modest sprint handicap form.

54 100% PROFIT BOOST AT 32REDSPORT.COM H'CAP 1m (P)
2:45 (2:45) (Class 5) (0-75,75) 4-Y-O+

£3,752 (£1,116; £557; £300; £300; £300) **Stalls** Low

Form RPR

102- **1** **Katie Lee (IRE)**[73] 8508 4-9-7 **75**.......................... FranBerry 8 83+
(Henry Candy) *hld up towards rr: prog and nt clr run briefly wl over 1f out: clsd fnl f: drvn ahd last 100yds: styd on wl* **14/1**

662- **2** *1 ½* **Al Reeh (IRE)**[36] 9316 5-9-5 **73**..........................(p) MarcMonaghan 7 78+
(Marco Botti) *trckd ldr at str pce: led over 2f out and sent for home: hdd and no ex last 100yds* **3/1**[1]

060- **3** *¾* **The Warrior (IRE)**[23] 9506 7-9-4 **75**.......................... PaddyBradley(3) 5 78
(Lee Carter) *hld up in last trio: gd prog on inner 2f out: rdn to chal fnl f: one pce last 100yds* **16/1**

450- **4** *nk* **Brockagh Cailin**[27] 9458 4-8-7 **61** oh2.......................... HollieDoyle 10 63
(J S Moore) *sn urged along in last: prog on outer 2f out: styd on after and nrly snatched 3rd (jockey said filly was never travelling in the early stages; vet reported the filly lost its right hind shoe)* **100/1**

516- **5** *1 ¾* **Blaze Of Hearts (IRE)**[21] 9536 6-9-7 **75**..........................(v) RobertWinston 6 73
(Dean Ivory) *hld up wl in tch: rdn and prog to take 2nd briefly wl over 1f out: fdd fnl f* **5/1**[3]

400- **6** *2 ¾* **Bobby Biscuit (USA)**[30] 9397 4-9-6 **74**.......................... JFEgan 4 66
(Simon Dow) *wl in tch: effrt over 2f out: rdn to dispute 2nd briefly over 1f out: wknd fnl f* **6/1**

504- **7** *2* **Makambe (IRE)**[14] 9661 4-9-5 **73**..........................(p) JoeyHaynes 3 60
(Paul Howling) *chsd ldng pair to 2f out: wknd* **20/1**

414- **8** *nk* **Choral Music**[42] 9228 4-9-7 **75**.......................... RobHornby 2 62
(John E Long) *chsd ldng pair: rdn over 2f out: sn lost pl and btn* **7/1**

050- **9** *2 ¼* **Six Strings**[23] 9506 5-9-4 **75**.......................... JackDuern(3) 1 56
(Dean Ivory) *led at str pce: hdd over 2f out: wknd qckly wl over 1f out* **7/1**

400- **10** *hd* **Martineo**[46] 9157 4-9-7 **75**.......................... AdamKirby 9 56
(Paul D'Arcy) *broke on terms but stdd into rr: hld up and racd wd: pushed along and no prog over 2f out (jockey said colt ran in snatches)* **4/1**[2]

002- **11** *8* **Singing Sheriff**[30] 9406 4-9-0 **68**.......................... LiamKeniry 11 31
(Ed Walker) *taken down early: hld up but sn pushed along: mostly in last trio and lost tch over 2f out: t.o (jockey said gelding was never travelling)* **16/1**

1m 38.58s (-1.22) **Going Correction** +0.10s/f (Slow) **11** Ran SP% **125.1**
Speed ratings (Par 103): **110,108,107,107,105 102,100,100,98,98 90**
CSF £59.49 CT £792.02 TOTE £17.90: £3.20, £1.70, £6.70; EX 31.00 Trifecta £634.60.
Owner M D Poland & H Candy **Bred** Thomas J Murphy **Trained** Kingston Warren, Oxon

FOCUS
A competitive affair with nine of the 11 runners rated within 2lb of the ceiling for the grade. A clear pb from the unexposed winner, with the third and fourth setting the standard.

55 32RED CASINO H'CAP 1m (P)
3:15 (3:15) (Class 4) (0-85,80) 3-Y-O **£6,629** (£2,085; £1,122) **Stalls** Low

Form RPR

641- **1** **Reeth (IRE)**[21] 9530 3-9-5 **78**..........................(b) RobertHavlin 2 83
(John Gosden) *mde all: stretched on 2f out: shkn up and drew further clr fnl f* **10/11**[1]

353- **2** *3 ¼* **Redemptive**[21] 9530 3-8-7 **66**.......................... HollieDoyle 3 65
(David Elsworth) *pressed wnr tl rdn and nt qckn 2f out: steadily outpcd fnl f* **4/1**[3]

201- **3** *3* **Anycity (IRE)**[18] 9591 3-9-7 **80**..........................(b) FrannyNorton 1 71
(Michael Wigham) *a in 3rd: pushed along by 1/2-way: shkn up and lft bhd 2f out: one pce after* **6/1**

533- **F** **Teresita Alvarez (USA)**[14] 9669 3-8-8 **67**.......................... JasonWatson 4
(Jeremy Noseda) *cl up whn stmbld and fell heavily after 100yds* **7/2**[2]

1m 40.35s (0.55) **Going Correction** +0.10s/f (Slow) **4** Ran SP% **108.9**
Speed ratings (Par 99): **101,97,94,**
CSF £4.84 TOTE £1.70; EX 4.60 Trifecta £13.30.
Owner Prince A A Faisal **Bred** Nawara Stud Limited **Trained** Newmarket, Suffolk

FOCUS
A disappointing turn out for this 0-85 and it proved easy pickings for for the odds-on Reeth, whose task was made much simpler by the early fall of his chief market rival. The winner improved again.

56 32RED.COM H'CAP 1m (P)
3:50 (3:50) (Class 3) (0-90,90) 4-Y-O+

£9,337 (£2,796; £1,398; £699; £349; £175) **Stalls** Low

Form RPR

140- **1** **Chiefofchiefs**[181] 4685 6-9-7 **90**..........................(p) RichardKingscote 6 98+
(Charlie Fellowes) *hld up in last trio: prog 2f out: swtchd lft over 1f out and sn chsd ldng pair: rdn and styd on wl fnl f to ld last strides* **3/1**[2]

122- **2** *nk* **Family Fortunes**[23] 9506 5-8-13 **82**.......................... LiamKeniry 5 89
(Michael Madgwick) *t.k.h: trckd ldrs: prog 2f out: pushed into the ld over 1f out: drvn fnl f: hdd last strides* **7/2**[3]

206- **3** *shd* **Al Jellaby**[130] 6623 4-9-4 **87**.......................... AdamKirby 2 94+
(Clive Cox) *sn led and set mod pce tl after 1/2-way: rdn and hdd over 1f out: hrd drvn and rallied fnl f: outpcd nr fin* **6/4**[1]

631- **4** *4* **Unforgiving Minute**[25] 9483 8-9-4 **87**.......................... ShaneKelly 8 85
(Paul D'Arcy) *hld up in last trio: pushed along over 2f out: prog over 1f out: tk 4th fnl f but no imp after* **10/1**

024- **5** *1 ½* **Jellmood**[20] 9564 4-9-0 **86**..........................(t) AaronJones(3) 3 80
(Marco Botti) *t.k.h: trckd ldrs: shkn up on inner 2f out: wknd over 1f out* **10/1**

100- **6** *2 ½* **Able Jack**[181] 4659 6-9-5 **88**.......................... RossaRyan 7 76
(Stuart Williams) *t.k.h: hld up in last: pushed along and no real prog 2f out: nvr in it* **33/1**

060- **7** *½* **Merlin**[28] 9446 5-9-4 **87**.......................... FrannyNorton 1 74
(Michael Bell) *trckd ldng pair: shkn up and cl enough 2f out: wknd over 1f out* **33/1**

010- **8** *2 ½* **Juanito Chico (IRE)**[20] 9564 5-8-10 **79**..........................(t) JosephineGordon 4 60
(Stuart Williams) *t.k.h: trckd ldr: edgd lft and lost 2nd 2f out: wknd* **14/1**

1m 39.01s (-0.79) **Going Correction** +0.10s/f (Slow) **8** Ran SP% **118.0**
Speed ratings (Par 107): **107,106,106,102,101 98,98,95**
CSF £14.53 CT £20.90 TOTE £4.50: £2.40, £1.10, £1.10; EX 16.10 Trifecta £37.30.
Owner Mervyn Ayers **Bred** Executive Bloodlines **Trained** Newmarket, Suffolk

FOCUS
The first three pulled clear and fought out a close finish in this good quality handicap. The winner is rated in line with his turf form, with the runner-up setting the standard.

57 32RED CONDITIONS STKS (PLUS 10 RACE) (ALL-WEATHER CHAMPIONSHIPS FAST-TRACK QUALIFIER) 6f (P)
4:20 (4:21) (Class 2) 3-Y-O

£15,562 (£4,660; £2,330; £1,165; £582; £292) **Stalls** Low

Form RPR

41- **1** **No Nonsense**[23] 9497 3-9-2 0.......................... LiamKeniry 8 98
(David Elsworth) *dwlt: hld up in last: shkn up and prog on outer 2f out: drvn to cl on ldrs fnl f: sustained effrt to ld last strides* **12/1**

101- **2** *shd* **James Street (IRE)**[30] 9394 3-9-2 **88**.......................... JosephineGordon 5 97
(Hugo Palmer) *t.k.h early: chsd clr ldng pair: clsd 2f out: rdn to take narrow ld fnl f: kpt on but hdd last strides* **5/1**[3]

306- **3** *1* **Charming Kid**[27] 9461 3-9-2 **103**.......................... BarryMcHugh 3 94
(Richard Fahey) *led at str pce but sn jnd: hld together 2f out: shkn up and narrowly hdd fnl f: one pce nr fin* **7/1**

455- **4** *1* **Don Armado (IRE)**[14] 9680 3-9-2 **93**..........................(t) RichardKingscote 2 91
(Stuart Williams) *chsd clr ldng pair: clsd 2f out: shkn up and nt qckn jst over 1f out: one pce after* **13/2**

551- **5** *hd* **K Club (IRE)**[5] 9762 3-8-11 **86**.......................... RossaRyan 6 85
(Richard Hannon) *hld up disputing 4th: clsd on ldrs 2f out: cl up and rdn 1f out: nt qckn and fdd last 100yds* **8/1**

211- **6** *hd* **Deep Intrigue**[29] 9427 3-9-2 **90**.......................... FrannyNorton 7 89+
(Mark Johnston) *w ldr at str pce to 2f out: lost pl and btn over 1f out: kpt on again nr fin* **7/2**[2]

013- **7** *1 ¼* **You Never Can Tell (IRE)**[27] 9461 3-9-2 **93**.......................... AdamKirby 1 85
(Richard Spencer) *a in last trio: pushed along 2f out: reminders 1f out and no prog* **9/4**[1]

1m 12.45s (-0.65) **Going Correction** +0.10s/f (Slow) **7** Ran SP% **114.3**
Speed ratings (Par 103): **108,107,106,105,104 104,103**
CSF £69.70 TOTE £12.20: £5.70, £2.40; EX 67.80 Trifecta £526.60.
Owner J C Smith **Bred** Littleton Stud **Trained** Newmarket, Suffolk

FOCUS
The inaugural running of this Fast-Track Qualifier and the outsider of the entire field got the verdict in a photo finish. The first two home had beaten Jamie Osborne's Ricochet in their respective last-time-out C&D wins. Improvement from both the first two.

58 32RED ON THE APP STORE H'CAP (DIV I) 1m 3f 219y(P)
4:50 (4:53) (Class 6) (0-55,55) 4-Y-O+

£3,105 (£924; £461; £300; £300; £300) **Stalls** Low

Form RPR

001- **1** **Apex Predator (IRE)**[14] 9666 4-9-3 **54**..........................(bt) AdamKirby 5 62
(Seamus Durack) *hld up towards rr: prog over 2f out: drvn to chse ldr jst over 1f out: styd on to ld last 50yds* **11/4**[1]

443- **2** *¾* **Arlecchino's Arc (IRE)**[36] 9310 4-9-2 **53**..........................(b[1]) LiamKeniry 9 59
(Mark Usher) *t.k.h: trckd ldrs: led over 2f out and sent for home: 2 l up over 1f out: wilted and hdd last 50yds* **6/1**[2]

036- **3** *1 ¼* **Mistress Nellie**[22] 9527 4-8-9 **46** oh1..........................(p) HollieDoyle 3 50
(William Stone) *t.k.h: hld up and sn in last: sme prog 1/2-way: hdwy and wdst of all bnd 3f out: cajoled along and racd awkwardly over 2f out: styd on to take 3rd ins fnl f (jockey said filly hung both ways)* **11/1**

504- **4** *nk* **Demophon**[14] 9665 5-8-11 **48**.......................... FinleyMarsh(3) 11 50
(Steve Flook) *hld up in midfield: rdn and no prog over 2f out: kpt on over 1f out to take 4th nr fin* **8/1**

026- **5** *½* **Sheila's Empire (IRE)**[8] 9159 4-8-9 **53**.......................... AaronMackay(7) 2 56
(J S Moore) *trckd ldrs: prog on inner over 2f out: one pce over 1f out* **10/1**

/00- **6** *1 ¼* **Sark (IRE)**[20] 9562 6-9-7 **55**.......................... JFEgan 6 55
(David Evans) *hld up in rr: prog arnd rivals bnd 4f out to 3f out: nt qckn over 2f out: shkn up and kpt on again fnl f* **9/1**

210- **7** *nse* **Lady Of York**[146] 6007 5-9-7 **55**.......................... JoeyHaynes 8 54
(Paul Howling) *t.k.h: trckd ldrs: prog to take 2nd briefly over 1f out: sn wknd* **12/1**

603- **8** *1 ¼* **Murhib (IRE)**[50] 9072 7-8-12 **46** oh1..........................(h) RichardKingscote 13 43
(Lydia Richards) *trckd ldr: led briefly wl over 2f out: wknd over 1f out* **7/1**[3]

300- **9** *6* **Altaira**[51] 9047 8-8-12 **46**.......................... FrannyNorton 1 34
(Tony Carroll) *cl up: rdn to take 2nd briefly wl over 1f out: wknd rapidly fnl f* **14/1**

400- **10** *nse* **Gift From God**[85] 8142 6-8-5 **46** oh1..........................(t) AledBeech(7) 7 34
(Hugo Froud) *nvr beyond midfield: rdn and no real prog over 2f out* **25/1**

004- **11** *3 ½* **River Rule**[72] 8530 4-8-4 **46** oh1.......................... RhiainIngram(5) 10 29
(Adrian Wintle) *a in rr: shkn up and brief effrt over 2f out: sn btn* **50/1**

0/0- **12** *19* **Meetings Man (IRE)**[353] 250 12-9-1 **49**.......................... RobHornby 14 1
(Ali Stronge) *nvr bttr than midfield: dropped to rr 4f out: t.o* **100/1**

200- **13** *1* **Loving Your Work**[69] 8650 8-8-13 **54**.......................... TristanPrice(7) 12 4
(Ken Cunningham-Brown) *pressed ldrs: rdn over 4f out: wknd qckly 3f out: t.o* **25/1**

506- **14** *24* **Estibdaad (IRE)**[318] 806 9-9-4 **52**..........................(tp) RobertWinston 4
(Paddy Butler) *led to wl over 2f out: wknd rapidly: t.o (jockey said gelding hung left-handed)* **33/1**

2m 36.08s (1.58) **Going Correction** +0.10s/f (Slow)
WFA 4 from 5yo+ 3lb **14** Ran SP% **119.9**
Speed ratings (Par 101): **98,97,96,96,96 95,95,94,90,90 88,75,74,58**
CSF £17.11 CT £161.22 TOTE £3.30: £1.40, £2.20, £3.00; EX 17.20 Trifecta £171.20.
Owner Mrs Anne Cowley **Bred** Forenaghts Stud **Trained** Upper Lambourn, Berkshire

FOCUS
This looked marginally the stronger of the two divisions. The market got it right.

59 32RED ON THE APP STORE H'CAP (DIV II) 1m 3f 219y(P)
5:20 (5:26) (Class 6) (0-55,55) 4-Y-0+

£3,105 (£924; £461; £300; £300; £300) **Stalls** Low

Form RPR
051- 1 **Tigerfish (IRE)**[30] 9408 5-9-2 **50**.....(p) HollieDoyle 5 56
(William Stone) *trckd ldrs: bmpd 1/2-way: rdn and styd on over 1f out: clsd to ld last 75yds* **7/1**[3]

006- 2 1 1/4 **Gorham's Cave**[51] 9054 5-9-2 **50**.....(h) RichardKingscote 10 54
(Ali Stronge) *t.k.h: hld up in last: stl there over 2f out: rapid prog on outer over 1f out: r.o wl to snatch 2nd last stride: too late* **14/1**

003- 3 nse **Banta Bay**[30] 9408 5-8-12 **46** oh1..... JosephineGordon 12 50
(John Best) *trckd ldr to over 2f out: styd pressing: rdn to ld 1f out: hdd and no ex last 75yds* **10/1**

050- 4 nk **Top Rock Talula (IRE)**[29] 5575 4-8-9 **46** oh1..... FrannyNorton 11 50
(Warren Greatrex) *led: rdn and hdd 2f out: rallied over 1f out: nrly upsides ins fnl f: one pce last 100yds* **8/1**

40- 5 1 **Wally's Wisdom**[30] 9407 7-9-7 **55**..... LiamJones 7 57
(Mark Loughnane) *hld up in midfield: effrt over 2f out: rdn and kpt on fr over 1f out: nt pce to threaten* **13/2**[2]

004- 6 nse **Far Cry**[22] 9527 6-9-3 **51**..... CharlieBennett 9 53
(Hughie Morrison) *hld up in last trio: prog and weaved through fr 2f out: nvr quite pce to rch ldrs fnl f* **14/1**

000- 7 shd **Harry Callahan (IRE)**[13] 9687 4-9-1 **52**..... JFEgan 14 55
(Mick Channon) *racd wd: wl in tch: rdn and nt qckn 2f out: one pce after* **7/1**[3]

640- 8 hd **Sea's Aria (IRE)**[30] 9409 8-8-12 **46** oh1..... RobHornby 4 47
(Mark Hoad) *hld up in last trio: effrt on inner over 2f out: rdn and kpt on fr over 1f out but nvr gng pce to chal* **10/1**

600- 9 hd **Harbour Force (FR)**[45] 9160 5-9-4 **52**..... ShaneKelly 2 53
(Neil Mulholland) *trckd ldng pair: swvd lft 1/2-way: led 2f out: hdd 1f out: wknd and eased last 100yds* **25/1**

40- 10 1/2 **Alcanar (USA)**[28] 8893 6-9-7 **55**..... GeorgeDowning 1 55
(Tony Carroll) *trckd ldrs: rdn over 2f out: wknd fnl f* **4/1**[1]

053- 11 1 **Mulsanne Chase**[14] 9665 5-9-1 **49**.....(p) RobertWinston 8 48
(Conor Dore) *hld up wl in rr: effrt over 2f out: no prog over 1f out* **11/1**

203- 12 8 **Rocket Ronnie (IRE)**[22] 9528 9-8-9 **46**.....(p) FinleyMarsh(3) 13 32
(Adrian Wintle) *a towards rr: rdn and struggling wl over 3f out: sn btn* **16/1**

000- 13 1/2 **Drifting Star (IRE)**[28] 9445 4-8-9 **46** oh1.....(b[1]) JoeyHaynes 3 32
(Gary Moore) *in tch: rdn 4f out: sn lost pl and btn* **25/1**

2m 38.07s (3.57) **Going Correction** +0.10s/f (Slow)
WFA 4 from 5yo+ 3lb **13 Ran SP% 122.9**
Speed ratings (Par 101): **92,91,91,90,90 90,90,90,89,89 88,83,83**
CSF £104.27 CT £986.69 TOTE £5.90: £2.40, £3.90, £3.20; EX 125.00 Trifecta £974.00.
Owner Miss Caroline Scott **Bred** Swordlestown Little **Trained** West Wickham, Cambs

FOCUS
A moderate handicap, in which only two of these had won previously over the distance. They went steadily and the winning time was significantly slower than the first division.
T/Jkpt: Not won. T/Plt: £79.40 to a £1 stake. Pool: £69,773.51 - 640.86 winning units T/Qpdt: £11.60 to a £1 stake. Pool: £6,358.92 - 403.76 winning units **Jonathan Neesom**

[26]WOLVERHAMPTON (A.W) (L-H)
Friday, January 4

OFFICIAL GOING: Tapeta: standard
Wind: Nil Weather: Overcast

60 PLAY 4 TO SCORE AT BETWAY CLASSIFIED STKS 6f 20y (Tp)
4:05 (4:07) (Class 6) 3-Y-0+

£3,105 (£924; £461; £400; £400; £400) **Stalls** Low

Form RPR
064- 1 **New Rich**[7] 9735 9-9-1 50.....(b) GeorgiaDobie(7) 1 58
(Eve Johnson Houghton) *hld up: hdwy over 1f out: shkn up to ld ins fnl f: rdn out* **7/1**

044- 2 3/4 **Ever Rock (IRE)**[17] 9598 3-8-6 49..... KieranO'Neill 5 52
(J S Moore) *led early: chsd ldrs: rdn and ev ch ins fnl f: styd on* **9/2**[3]

000- 3 1 1/4 **Dodgy Bob**[16] 9617 6-9-8 48.....(v) JamesSullivan 11 52
(Michael Mullineaux) *chsd ldr 5f out: rdn and ev ch whn edgd rt over 1f out: edgd lft ins fnl f: styd on same pce* **20/1**

4 nse **Piper Bomb (IRE)**[28] 9451 4-9-8 50.....(t) StevieDonohoe 4 52+
(Adrian McGuinness, Ire) *prom: pushed along over 2f out: r.o u.p ins fnl f* **15/8**[1]

3B0- 5 hd **Dalness Express**[14] 9668 6-9-5 50.....(t) BenRobinson(3) 9 51
(John O'Shea) *chsd ldrs: nt clr run over 1f out: sn rdn: edgd lft and styd on same pce ins fnl f* **16/1**

002- 6 3/4 **Tarseekh**[8] 9720 6-9-8 50.....(b) AndrewMullen 6 49
(Charlie Wallis) *sn led: rdn and edgd rt over 1f out: hdd and no ex ins fnl f* **4/1**[2]

106- 7 1 1/2 **Sugar Plum Fairy**[16] 9606 4-9-8 50..... DavidProbert 10 44
(Tony Carroll) *hld up: running on whn nt clr run wl ins fnl f: nt trble ldrs* **10/1**

050- 8 3 1/2 **Sophisticated Heir (IRE)**[8] 9720 9-9-1 50..... TobyEley(7) 12 33
(Kevin Frost) *hld up in tch: rdn over 1f out: wknd fnl f* **16/1**

550- 9 1 **Foxy Boy**[20] 9558 5-9-8 48..... JasonHart 7 30
(Rebecca Bastiman) *hld up: nt clr run over 2f out: hdwy u.p over 1f out: styng on same pce whn hmpd and eased wl ins fnl f* **12/1**

000- 10 8 **Jacksonfire**[59] 8902 7-9-1 49.....(p) LauraCoughlan(7) 3 4
(Michael Mullineaux) *s.i.s: sn outpcd* **50/1**

1m 14.05s (-0.45) **Going Correction** -0.125s/f (Stan)
WFA 3 from 4yo+ 16lb **10 Ran SP% 120.7**
Speed ratings (Par 101): **98,97,95,95,95 94,92,87,86,75**
CSF £40.02 TOTE £6.60: £2.30, £1.60, £4.10; EX 35.10 Trifecta £398.30.
Owner Eden Racing Club **Bred** Whitsbury Manor Stud And Mrs M E Slade **Trained** Blewbury, Oxon

FOCUS
A weak sprint.

61 BETWAY CASINO H'CAP 1m 4f 51y (Tp)
4:35 (4:35) (Class 5) (0-70,71) 4-Y-0+

£3,752 (£1,116; £557; £400; £400; £400) **Stalls** Low

Form RPR
042- 1 **Ice Canyon**[20] 9562 5-8-12 **64**.....(h) EoinWalsh(3) 7 73
(Mark Brisbourne) *hld up: nt clr run and hdwy over 2f out: shkn up to ld ins fnl f: styd on wl* **8/1**

521- 2 3 1/4 **Para Mio (IRE)**[20] 9555 4-9-2 **68**.....(t) MartinHarley 10 72
(Seamus Durack) *hld up: nt clr run and swtchd rt over 2f out: hdwy over 1f out: sn rdn: styd on same pce ins fnl f* **13/8**[1]

405- 3 shd **Star Ascending (IRE)**[17] 9595 7-9-7 **70**.....(p) JamesSullivan 11 75+
(Jennie Candlish) *hld up: hmpd over 2f out: rdn and r.o wl ins fnl f: wnt 3rd post (jockey said gelding was denied a clear run on the bend turning into the home straight)* **25/1**

346- 4 shd **Tor**[32] 8658 5-9-7 **70**..... JoeFanning 3 73
(Iain Jardine) *led over 3f: chsd ldr: led again over 1f out: sn rdn: hdd ins fnl f: styd on same pce* **4/1**[2]

020- 5 hd **Agent Gibbs**[18] 9585 7-9-1 **71**..... KateLeahy(7) 8 74
(John O'Shea) *s.i.s: hld up: hdwy over 1f out: swtchd lft ent fnl f: styd on* **25/1**

602- 6 2 1/4 **Iftiraaq (IRE)**[34] 9359 8-9-4 **67**.....(p w) EdwardGreatrex 9 67
(David Loughnane) *chsd ldrs: led 8f out: rdn and hdd over 1f out: wknd wl ins fnl f (jockey said gelding hung right)* **7/1**[3]

556- 7 1 3/4 **Epitaph (IRE)**[9] 9706 5-9-0 **63**.....(v) AlistairRawlinson 1 60
(Michael Appleby) *sn drvn along to join ldr: led over 8f out: sn hdd: remained handy: rdn over 3f out: wknd fnl f* **7/1**[3]

000- 8 3/4 **Let's Be Happy (IRE)**[15] 9647 5-8-13 **62**.....(b) KieranO'Neill 5 58
(Mandy Rowland) *s.i.s: hdwy over 10f out: rdn over 1f out: nt clr run and wknd ins fnl f* **33/1**

400- 9 9 **Natch**[16] 9609 4-8-13 **65**..... PaddyMathers 2 46
(Michael Attwater) *prom: rdn over 2f out: sn wknd* **25/1**

600- 10 33 **Qayed (CAN)**[14] 9664 4-8-11 **63**..... DavidProbert 4
(Mark Brisbourne) *chsd ldrs: rdn over 3f out: wknd over 2f out (jockey said gelding stopped quickly)* **14/1**

2m 37.2s (-3.60) **Going Correction** -0.125s/f (Stan)
WFA 4 from 5yo+ 3lb **10 Ran SP% 115.4**
Speed ratings (Par 103): **107,104,104,104,104 103,101,101,95,73**
CSF £20.30 CT £317.98 TOTE £7.40: £2.20, £1.10, £5.10; EX 30.30 Trifecta £277.10.
Owner Derek & Mrs Marie Dean **Bred** Darley **Trained** Great Ness, Shropshire

FOCUS
This was run at a good pace and those held up were favoured. The winner is rated to his summer form.

62 BETWAY HEED YOUR HUNCH CLASSIFIED STKS 1m 1f 104y (Tp)
5:10 (5:11) (Class 6) 4-Y-0+

£3,105 (£924; £461; £400; £400; £400) **Stalls** Low

Form RPR
003- 1 **Diamond Reflection (IRE)**[9] 9704 7-9-1 50.....(t[1]) EdwardGreatrex 2 57
(Alexandra Dunn) *chsd ldrs: wnt 2nd over 2f out: led over 1f out: sn rdn: styd on: eased nr fin* **7/1**[3]

246- 2 1/2 **Don't Do It (IRE)**[14] 9659 4-9-0 50.....(b) AndrewMullen 1 56
(Michael Appleby) *s.i.s: hdwy over 6f out: rdn and hung lft over 1f out: chsd wnr ins fnl f: r.o* **12/1**

550- 3 2 1/2 **Cottingham**[15] 9644 4-9-0 50..... JasonHart 4 51
(Kevin Frost) *hld up: hdwy over 1f out: r.o to go 3rd towards fin: nt rch ldrs* **9/2**[2]

4 3/4 **Taceec (IRE)**[28] 9455 4-9-0 48..... KieranO'Neill 11 50+
(Adrian McGuinness, Ire) *hld up: hdwy over 1f out: sn rdn: styd on same pce ins fnl f* **16/1**

4/0- 5 1/2 **Clive Clifton (IRE)**[25] 9481 6-9-1 50..... MartinHarley 9 49
(Mark Brisbourne) *hld up: r.o ins fnl f: nvr nrr* **16/1**

200- 6 1/2 **Mr Frankie**[80] 8297 8-8-12 49..... EoinWalsh(3) 10 48
(Roy Brotherton) *chsd ldr after 1f: led 3f out: rdn and hdd over 1f out: wknd wl ins fnl f: b.b.v (vet said gelding bled from the nose)* **16/1**

004- 7 1 **Going Native**[32] 9381 4-8-9 50..... DarraghKeenan(5) 6 46
(Olly Williams) *s.i.s: hld up: r.o ins fnl f: nvr on terms (jockey said filly reared as the stalls opened and missed the break as a result)* **10/1**

003- 8 3/4 **Boatrace (IRE)**[59] 8897 4-9-0 49..... StevieDonohoe 7 45
(David Evans) *s.i.s: hdwy over 7f out: pushed along over 3f out: wknd over 1f out* **9/2**[2]

005- 9 nk **Puchita (IRE)**[44] 9181 4-9-0 49..... CamHardie 13 44
(Antony Brittain) *s.i.s: hld up: nvr nrr* **33/1**

000- 10 3 1/4 **Wide Acclaim (IRE)**[93] 7893 4-9-0 50.....(t) AlistairRawlinson 12 38
(Rebecca Menzies) *prom: rdn over 2f out: wknd over 1f out* **33/1**

000- 11 3 **Idol Deputy (FR)**[25] 9481 13-8-10 49.....(p) RachealKneller(5) 3 32
(James Bennett) *prom: pushed along and lost pl over 6f out: effrt and nt clr run over 2f out: rdn and wknd over 1f out (jockey said gelding was never travelling)* **33/1**

342- 12 3 1/2 **Jeremy's Jet (IRE)**[44] 9180 8-8-10 49..... PoppyBridgwater(5) 5 26
(Tony Carroll) *hld up in tch: pld hrd: ct wd fr over 6f out: rdn over 2f out: wknd over 1f out (jockey said gelding was never travelling. Trainers' rep said gelding may have been unsuited by being declared without it's customary tongue strap on this occasion)* **9/4**[1]

600/ 13 11 **Poor Duke (IRE)**[466] 7465 9-8-12 48.....(p) PhilDennis(3) 8 5
(Michael Mullineaux) *led: rdn and hdd 3f out: wknd wl over 1f out* **100/1**

1m 58.9s (-1.90) **Going Correction** -0.125s/f (Stan)
WFA 4 from 6yo+ 1lb **13 Ran SP% 123.9**
Speed ratings (Par 101): **103,102,100,99,99 98,97,97,96,94 91,88,78**
CSF £89.40 TOTE £7.00: £2.80, £3.40, £1.60; EX 46.90 Trifecta £390.10.
Owner Team Dunn **Bred** Barronstown Stud **Trained** West Buckland, Somerset

FOCUS
Low-grade fare.

63 FOLLOW SUN RACING ON TWITTER (S) STKS 1m 142y (Tp)
5:45 (5:45) (Class 6) 4-Y-0+

£3,105 (£924; £461; £400; £400; £400) **Stalls** Low

Form RPR
400- 1 **Mister Music**[69] 8634 10-10-0 86..... PoppyBridgwater(5) 2 73+
(Tony Carroll) *s.i.s: hld up: hdwy and hung lft over 1f out: rdn and r.o to ld nr fin* **3/1**[2]

253- **2** ½ **Skydiving**[7] 9732 4-9-0 73 CharlesBishop 3 54+
(Eve Johnson Houghton) *led: hdd 7f out: chsd ldr tl led again over 1f out: rdn and edgd lft ins fnl f: hdd nr fin* **4/5**[1]

6/4- **3** 2 **Beau Satchel**[16] 9620 9-9-7 59 (tp) KieranO'Neill 5 56+
(Adrian McGuinness, Ire) *chsd ldr 1f: remained handy: rdn over 2f out: styd on (vet said gelding was lame on it's right fore)* **7/1**[3]

000- **4** nk **Stamp Duty (IRE)**[64] 8776 11-8-12 43 (p) BenRobinson(3) 4 49
(Suzzanne France) *prom: rdn over 1f out: styd on* **100/1**

004- **5** 1 ½ **Count Montecristo (FR)**[14] 9658 7-8-10 57 (p) BenSanderson(5) 6 46
(Roger Fell) *s.i.s: hdwy to ld 7f out: rdn and hdd over 1f out: no ex wl ins fnl f* **12/1**

040- **6** 1 ½ **King Of Naples**[17] 9595 6-9-1 65 (p1) JamesSullivan 7 43
(Ruth Carr) *hld up: racd keenly: shkn up and hung lft fr over 1f out: nvr on terms (jockey said gelding ran too free)* **16/1**

500- **7** 14 **Spoken Words**[30] 9415 10-8-10 40 PaddyMathers 1 8
(John David Riches) *prom: racd keenly: stdd and lost pl after 1f: rdn over 2f out: sn wknd* **100/1**

1m 49.55s (-0.55) **Going Correction** -0.125s/f (Stan)
WFA 4 from 6yo+ 1lb **7 Ran SP% 108.6**
Speed ratings (Par 101): **97,96,94,94,93 91,79**
.There was no bid for the winner. Skydiving was claimed by Mr P. S. McEntee for £600\n\x\x
Owner A Sergent & Partner **Bred** Longview Stud & Bloodstock Ltd **Trained** Cropthorne, Worcs

FOCUS
A muddling affair and, with the fourth finishing close up, dubious form.

64 SUNRACING.CO.UK H'CAP 7f 36y (Tp)
6:15 (6:16) (Class 6) (0-60,62) 4-Y-O+
£3,105 (£924; £461; £400; £400; £400) **Stalls High**

Form RPR
505- **1** **Grey Destiny**[24] 9495 9-9-5 **58** (p) CamHardie 11 65
(Antony Brittain) *hld up: plld hrd: rdn over 1f out: str run ins fnl f to ld nr fin (trainers' rep could offer no explanation for the improved performance)* **12/1**

421- **2** ½ **Viola Park**[23] 9504 5-9-2 **55** (p) DavidProbert 1 61
(Ronald Harris) *led: rdn over 1f out: edgd rt ins fnl f: hdd nr fin* **3/1**[1]

200- **3** ½ **Aljunood (IRE)**[35] 9337 5-9-3 **56** (h) DougieCostello 6 61
(John Norton) *hld up: plld hrd: hdwy over 1f out: nt clr run sn after: rdn and r.o ins fnl f (jockey said gelding ran too free)* **5/1**

345- **4** 1 **Shamlan (IRE)**[31] 9387 7-9-6 **59** (b) JackMitchell 7 61
(Kevin Frost) *chsd ldr: rdn and ev ch whn hung rt fr over 1f out: styd on same pce towards fin* **4/1**[3]

500- **5** nse **Ad Vitam (IRE)**[59] 8902 11-8-5 **47** (bt) PhilDennis(3) 3 49
(Suzzanne France) *chsd ldrs: shkn up over 2f out: styd on same pce towards fin* **33/1**

406- **6** ¾ **Bidding War**[87] 8086 4-9-2 **60** KevinLundie(5) 5 60
(Michael Appleby) *chsd ldrs: rdn over 1f out: styd on same pce ins fnl f* **10/1**

300- **7** 2 **Daze Out (IRE)**[254] 2064 4-9-4 **57** PaddyMathers 12 52
(Richard Fahey) *s.i.s: hld up: nvr nrr* **50/1**

11-3 **8** 1 ¼ **Peachey Carnehan**[2] 28 5-9-9 **62** 6ex (v) JamesSullivan 8 55
(Michael Mullineaux) *hdwy over 5f out: rdn over 1f out: edgd lft and wknd fnl f (jockey said gelding was unsuited by being trapped wide without cover throughout)* **7/2**[2]

000- **9** ½ **Tasaaboq**[8] 9720 8-8-8 **47** (tp) EdwardGreatrex 2 38
(Phil McEntee) *s.i.s: nvr on terms (jockey said gelding was slowly away)* **20/1**

000- **10** 2 ½ **Frozen Lake (USA)**[30] 9402 7-9-3 **59** (h) BenRobinson(3) 4 44
(John O'Shea) *hld up: pushed along 1/2-way: wknd over 1f out (jockey said gelding hung right throughout)* **25/1**

1m 28.81s (0.01) **Going Correction** -0.125s/f (Stan) **10 Ran SP% 114.2**
Speed ratings (Par 101): **94,93,92,91,91 90,88,87,86,83**
CSF £45.34 CT £212.54 TOTE £12.30: £2.10, £1.40, £2.20; EX 71.50 Trifecta £440.60.
Owner Antony Brittain **Bred** Northgate Lodge Stud Ltd **Trained** Warthill, N Yorks

FOCUS
This was steadily run but the winner overcame the lack of pace to score.

65 LADBROKES, HOME OF THE ODDS BOOST H'CAP 7f 36y (Tp)
6:45 (6:45) (Class 5) (0-70,71) 3-Y-O
£3,752 (£1,116; £557; £400; £400; £400) **Stalls High**

Form RPR
635- **1** **War and Glory (IRE)**[14] 9671 3-9-3 **65** CallumRodriguez 4 68
(James Tate) *hld up: hdwy over 1f out: sn rdn: r.o to ld nr fin* **7/1**

424- **2** shd **Beryl The Petal (IRE)**[9] 9708 3-9-4 **69** ConorMcGovern(3) 1 71
(David O'Meara) *chsd ldrs: rdn over 1f out: led ins fnl f: hdd nr fin* **5/1**[3]

060- **3** nk **Cadeau D'Amour (IRE)**[49] 9105 3-9-2 **64** PaddyMathers 6 65
(Richard Fahey) *s.i.s: hld up: hdwy and hung rt over 1f out: rdn and edgd lft ins fnl f: r.o* **16/1**

150- **4** 2 **Axel Jacklin**[18] 9591 3-9-6 **68** JoeFanning 2 64
(Mark Johnston) *led: hdd over 5f out: chsd ldr who sn wnt clr: shkn up to cl over 1f out: styd on same pce wl ins fnl f* **12/1**

501- **5** 3 ¼ **Freedom And Wheat (IRE)**[7] 9729 3-9-3 **65** 6ex (v) FergusSweeney 7 52
(Brendan Powell) *racd freely: led over 5f out: sn clr: rdn and c bk to the field over 1f out: wknd and hdd ins fnl f (jockey said colt hung left throughout)* **11/8**[1]

663- **6** 3 ½ **Lahessar**[155] 5656 3-9-9 **71** (w) MartinHarley 5 49
(George Scott) *hld up: shkn up over 2f out: wknd over 1f out* **7/2**[2]

000- **7** 39 **Treasure Quest**[21] 9530 3-9-6 **68** CharlesBishop 3
(Brian Meehan) *chsd ldrs: pushed along 1/2-way: wknd 2f out (jockey said colt stopped quickly)* **14/1**

1m 27.57s (-1.23) **Going Correction** -0.125s/f (Stan) **7 Ran SP% 113.7**
Speed ratings (Par 97): **102,101,101,99,95 91,46**
CSF £40.85 TOTE £6.40: £2.80, £2.10; EX 31.70 Trifecta £276.90.
Owner Saeed Manana **Bred** Kilmoon Syndicate **Trained** Newmarket, Suffolk

FOCUS
The favourite set a scorching pace and this was set up for the closers. There was little between the first three at the line. The winner is rated up a length and the runner-up helps with the standard.

66 LADBROKES NOVICE MEDIAN AUCTION STKS 1m 1f 104y (Tp)
7:15 (7:18) (Class 5) 3-Y-O **£3,752** (£1,116; £557; £278) **Stalls Low**

Form RPR
232- **1** **Robert L'Echelle (IRE)**[13] 9683 3-9-2 76 RobertHavlin 4 78+
(Hughie Morrison) *a.p: chsd ldr over 3f out: led 2f out: rdn clr fnl f* **4/5**[1]

2 3 **Colony Queen** 3-8-11 0 AndrewMullen 8 66
(James Tate) *hld up: hdwy over 2f out: chsd wnr and edgd lft fnl f: no imp* **20/1**

04- **3** 1 **Bolt N Brown**[43] 9205 3-8-4 0 TobyEley(7) 5 64
(Gay Kelleway) *hld up in tch: rdn over 1f out: styd on same pce fnl f* **33/1**

4 1 ¾ **Eclittica (IRE)** 3-8-11 0 MartinHarley 2 60+
(Marco Botti) *s.i.s: hld up: hdwy and swtchd rt 1f out: nt trble ldrs* **14/1**

5- **5** 1 ¼ **Gino Wotimean (USA)**[18] 9590 3-9-2 0 RossaRyan 6 63
(Noel Williams) *free to post: prom: racd keenly: rdn over 2f out: edgd lft over 1f out: styd on same pce* **11/4**[2]

423- **6** ¾ **Stay Forever (FR)**[72] 8547 3-8-11 74 DavidProbert 1 56
(Andrew Balding) *w ldr tl led at stdy pce 7f out: hdd 2f out: wknd fnl f* **9/2**[3]

00- **7** 11 **Ostrich**[18] 9590 3-9-2 0 (p1) EdwardGreatrex 7 38
(Roger Charlton) *s.i.s: pushed along early in rr: shkn up 1/2-way: wknd over 2f out* **25/1**

0- **8** ¾ **Hilbre Lake (USA)**[8] 9726 3-8-9 0 ElishaWhittington(7) 3 36
(Lisa Williamson) *led: hdd 7f out: chsd ldr tl pushed along over 3f out: wknd over 2f out* **100/1**

2m 0.28s (-0.52) **Going Correction** -0.125s/f (Stan) **8 Ran SP% 119.6**
Speed ratings (Par 97): **97,94,93,91,90 90,80,79**
CSF £24.68 TOTE £1.60: £1.02, £4.70, £7.10; EX 21.50 Trifecta £217.90.
Owner A N Solomons **Bred** Macha Bloodstock **Trained** East Ilsley, Berks

FOCUS
This proved straightforward for the well supported favourite, who improved again. The third looks the key to the form.

67 LADBROKES, HOME OF THE ODDS BOOST FILLIES' H'CAP 1m 1f 104y (Tp)
7:45 (7:45) (Class 5) (0-70,71) 4-Y-O+
£3,752 (£1,116; £557; £400; £400; £400) **Stalls Low**

Form RPR
330- **1** **Perfect Refuge**[16] 9609 4-9-9 **69** HectorCrouch 2 78
(Clive Cox) *sn pushed along to chse ldrs: rdn over 1f out: nt clr run ins fnl f: r.o to ld nr fin* **8/1**

021- **2** hd **Proceed (IRE)**[14] 9664 4-9-5 **65** EdwardGreatrex 4 73
(Archie Watson) *w ldr tl settled into 2nd pl over 7f out: led wl over 1f out: rdn and edgd lft ins fnl f: hdd nr fin* **11/4**[2]

003- **3** 1 ¼ **Sunshineandbubbles**[6] 9747 6-9-6 **65** (v) JoeFanning 3 70
(Jennie Candlish) *chsd ldrs: rdn over 1f out: styd on same pce wl ins fnl f* **8/1**

013- **4** nse **Destinys Rock**[14] 9664 4-8-12 **63** MeganNicholls(5) 6 69+
(Mark Loughnane) *hld up: hdwy and nt clr run over 1f out: swtchd rt: nt clr run ins fnl f: r.o (jockey said filly was denied a clear run in the home straight)* **4/1**[3]

550- **5** ½ **Sosian**[15] 9647 4-8-5 **51** (b1) PaddyMathers 10 55+
(Richard Fahey) *s.i.s: hld up: hdwy over 1f out: r.o: nt rch ldrs* **25/1**

153- **6** 2 ½ **Gilded Heaven**[16] 9614 4-9-11 **71** JackMitchell 5 70
(Roger Varian) *hld up in tch: swtchd rt over 1f out: sn rdn and hung lft: styd on same pce* **5/2**[1]

005- **7** nk **Cooperess**[22] 8781 6-7-12 **50** SophieRalston(7) 7 48
(Dai Burchell) *plld hrd and prom: rdn over 1f out: no ex fnl f* **50/1**

323- **8** 2 **Bell Heather (IRE)**[97] 7754 6-9-7 **66** StevieDonohoe 9 60
(Patrick Morris) *hld up: rdn over 1f out: nvr on terms* **14/1**

000- **9** ½ **Cash N Carrie (IRE)**[18] 9592 5-8-12 **57** AlistairRawlinson 1 50
(Michael Appleby) *led: rdn and hdd wl over 1f out: wknd ins fnl f* **50/1**

000- **10** 1 **Perceived**[41] 9253 7-8-10 **55** (p) CamHardie 12 46
(Antony Brittain) *hld up: rdn over 1f out: n.d* **50/1**

11 3 ¼ **Nice To Sea (IRE)**[492] 6604 5-8-6 **53** DavidProbert 11 37
(Olly Murphy) *s.i.s: a in rr* **50/1**

1m 59.76s (-1.04) **Going Correction** -0.125s/f (Stan)
WFA 4 from 5yo+ 1lb **11 Ran SP% 115.8**
Speed ratings (Par 100): **99,98,97,97,97 95,94,92,92,91 88**
CSF £28.98 CT £181.22 TOTE £8.30: £2.60, £1.70, £2.30; EX 32.60 Trifecta £172.30.
Owner Hants and Herts **Bred** Mildmay Bloodstock Ltd **Trained** Lambourn, Berks
■ Stewards' Enquiry : Paddy Mathers two-day ban; misuse of whip (Jan 18-19)

FOCUS
It paid to race close to the pace in this one. The third seems the best guide.
T/Plt: £196.50 to a £1 stake. Pool: £86,892.92 - 322.78 winning units T/Qpdt: £27.70 to a £1 stake. Pool: £11,489.53 - 306.27 winning units **Colin Roberts**

68 - 75a (Foreign Racing) - See Raceform Interactive

46 DEAUVILLE (R-H)
Friday, January 4

OFFICIAL GOING: Polytrack: standard

76a PRIX DE FOLLEVILLE (CLAIMER) (4YO) (ALL-WEATHER TRACK) (POLYTRACK) 1m 4f 110y(P)
12:10 4-Y-O **£8,108** (£3,243; £2,432; £1,621; £810)

RPR
1 **Northern Daggers (ITY)**[431] 4-8-11 0 QuentinPerrette 13 64
(Andrea Marcialis, France) **32/1**

2 ½ **Dubai Empire (FR)**[74] 8476 4-9-1 0 FrankPanicucci 7 67
(Mme G Rarick, France) **9/1**

3 1 ¾ **Akinathor Game (FR)**[19] 4-9-4 0 (p) PierreBazire 4 67
(G Botti, France) **3/1**[1]

4 1 **Rumbo Norte (IRE)**[19] 4-8-8 0 (b) MlleAudeDuporte(3) 9 59
(Gianluca Bietolini, France) **22/1**

5 nk **Madulain (FR)**[56] 4-8-11 0 JulienGuillochon 3 58
(H-A Pantall, France) **19/5**[2]

6 snk **Win Vic (FR)**[19] 4-8-11 0 (b) MarcNobili 10 58
(S Kobayashi, France) **18/1**

7 ½ **Golega (FR)**[37] 4-9-1 0 (p) MorganDelalande 5 61
(P Van De Poele, France) **17/1**

8 snk **Wiseiten (FR)**[42] 4-8-11 0 ThomasTrullier 14 57
(Frank Sheridan, Italy) **58/1**

9 ½ **Shabrice (GER)** 4-8-8 BertrandFlandrin 12 53
(H Blume, Germany) **26/5**

10 12 **Feheriq (FR)**[39] 4-9-4 0 ArnaudBourgeais 2 44
(E Rocton, France) **45/1**

11 hd **Wallflower (IRE)**[36] 9318 4-8-8 0 RaulDaSilva 1 34
(Rae Guest) *wl into stride: led: pushed along and hdd over 2f out: rdn w little rspnse over 1f out: eased ins fnl f* **9/2**[3]

12 6 **Tropezienne (FR)**[58] 4-8-6 0 MlleLauraPoggionovo(2) 11 24
(R Le Dren Doleuze, France) **25/1**

13 15 **Arretez La Musique (FR)** 4-8-11 0 (p) QuentinGervais 8 3
(J-L Bara, France) **94/1**

14 7 **Fergus D'Ana (FR)**[45] 4-8-11 0....(p) JeffersonSmith 6
(F-X Belvisi, France) 109/1
2m 35.71s 14 Ran SP% 118.0
PARI-MUTUEL (all including 1 euro stake): WIN 33.00; PLACE 7.50, 3.50, 2.10; DF 162.20; SF 304.90.
Owner Mme Luciana Gallino **Bred** Antonio Romeo Torsiello **Trained** France

77 - (Foreign Racing) - See Raceform Interactive

53 KEMPTON (A.W) (R-H)

Saturday, January 5

OFFICIAL GOING: Polytrack: standard to slow
Wind: Virtually nil Weather: (Partly cloudy)

78 32RED CASINO FILLIES' NOVICE STKS 7f (P)
4:15 (4:17) (Class 5) 3-Y-O+ **£3,881** (£1,155; £577; £288) **Stalls** Low

Form RPR
0- 1 **Invitational**[17] 9603 3-8-10 0.... JackMitchell 13 77
(Roger Varian) *broke wl and led fr a wd draw: effrt to qckn clr 2f out: sn in command and rdn 1f out: styd on wl* 20/1
2 ½ **Vandella (IRE)** 3-8-10 0.... RobertHavlin 9 75+
(John Gosden) *racd in midfield: smooth prog to chse wnr 3f out: effrt to go 2nd 2f out: rdn to chse wnr over 1f out: styd on wl fnl f and clsng all the way to line: bttr for run* 3/1[1]
- 3 3 ½ **Pacificadora (USA)** 3-8-10 0.... NickyMackay 6 65
(Simon Dow) *hld up on inner: effrt to cl and rn green over 2f out: sn rdn and styd on strly fr over 1f out: nrst fin* 6/1
4 1 ¼ **Dorchester** 3-8-7 0....(b[1]) AaronJones(3) 2 62
(Marco Botti) *dwlt and sn rcvrd to r in midfield: swtchd lft and pushed along to chse wnr 2f out: rdn over 1f out: kpt on one pce fnl f* 9/2[2]
6- 5 ½ **Lucky Lou (IRE)**[29] 9443 3-8-10 0.... MartinDwyer 1 60
(Ken Cunningham-Brown) *racd in midfield: pushed along and green 3f out: rdn and unable qck 2f out: hung rt u.p 1f out: kpt on* 25/1
6 ½ **Solar Heights (IRE)** 3-8-10 0.... LukeMorris 14 59
(James Tate) *hld up: hdwy u.p 2f out: sn rdn and kpt on wl fnl f: no threat to wnr* 5/1[3]
7 ½ **Canasta** 3-8-10 0....(h[1]) JoeFanning 4 58
(James Fanshawe) *racd in midfield: pushed along 2f out: rdn over 1f out: kpt on* 11/1
04- 8 3 ¼ **War No More (USA)**[19] 9592 4-10-0 0.... LiamKeniry 7 53
(Ed Walker) *chsd ldr: rdn and outpcd by wnr 2f out: wknd ins fnl f* 18/1
02- 9 hd **Regal Ambition**[26] 9484 3-8-10 0.... HectorCrouch 11 48
(Clive Cox) *hld up: rdn along 2f out: nvr able to land a blow* 11/1
0- 10 2 ¼ **Cape Cyclone (IRE)**[196] 4132 4-10-0 0.... LouisSteward 5 46
(Stuart Williams) *hld up in rr: rdn along over 2f out: nvr on terms* 16/1
0- 11 ½ **Amor Kethley**[15] 9670 3-8-5 0.... DarraghKeenan(5) 3 41
(Amy Murphy) *chsd wnr early: rdn and outpcd by wnr 2f out: wknd ins fnl f* 100/1
12 3 ¼ **Storm Girl** 3-8-10 0.... RobHornby 10 32
(Michael Attwater) *racd in midfield: rdn and outpcd 3f out: sn struggling in rr* 100/1
0- 13 ¾ **Platinum Coast (USA)**[25] 9490 3-8-10 0.... DavidProbert 8 30
(James Tate) *hld up in tch: pushed along and green 3f out: sn outpcd and wknd fnl f* 25/1
14 nk **Frea** 3-8-10 0.... JosephineGordon 12 29
(Harry Dunlop) *dwlt: a in rr* 66/1
1m 25.3s (-0.70) **Going Correction** 0.0s/f (Stan)
WFA 3 from 4yo 18lb 14 Ran SP% 117.9
Speed ratings (Par 100): **104,103,99,98,97 96,96,92,92,89 89,85,84,84**
CSF £75.08 TOTE £26.20: £5.20, £2.10, £2.30; EX 123.60 Trifecta £1372.30.
Owner Ziad A Galadari **Bred** Galadari Sons Stud Company Limited **Trained** Newmarket, Suffolk
FOCUS
The first two finished nicely clear in this fillies' novice.

79 INTRODUCING RACING TV H'CAP 1m (P)
4:45 (4:49) (Class 6) (0-60,60) 3-Y-O
£3,105 (£924; £461; £400; £400; £400) **Stalls** Low

Form RPR
000- 1 **Brains (IRE)**[42] 9246 3-8-13 52....(b[1]) NicolaCurrie 1 59
(Jamie Osborne) *hld up in tch in midfield: hdwy to chse ldr ldr 2f out: rdn to ld over 1f out and hung rt handed into rail: drvn and hdd 110yds out: rallied wl u.p and hung lft handed away fr whip to ld again cl home (trainer said, as to the apparent improvement in form, the gelding benefitted from a step up in trip from 6 furlongs to a mile and the first-time application of blinkers)* 4/1[2]
000- 2 ½ **Heatherdown (IRE)**[16] 9636 3-8-12 51.... MartinHarley 3 57
(Michael Bell) *trckd ldr: rdn along and upsides w ev ch over 1f out: led briefly 110yds out: sn drvn: carried lft and hdd by wnr cl home* 20/1
004- 3 ½ **Lee Roy**[29] 9444 3-9-7 60.... KierenFox 13 65
(Michael Attwater) *led: rdn along and strly pressed by rivals 2f out: hdd by wnr over 1f out: kpt on wl and carried lft fnl f* 12/1
600- 4 4 ½ **Miss Green Dream**[51] 9073 3-8-12 51....(p[1]) FranBerry 5 45
(Stuart Williams) *settled in midfield: rdn and outpcd by ldng trio 2f out: kpt on fnl f* 33/1
203- 5 1 **Rajman**[23] 9521 3-9-5 58....(h) JackMitchell 11 50
(Tom Clover) *hld up in last: hdwy on rail 2f out: rdn and kpt on fnl f* 8/1
405- 6 ½ **Elysian Lady**[29] 9444 3-9-7 60.... FrannyNorton 14 51
(Michael Wigham) *trckd ldr: rdn and outpcd over 2f out: wknd fnl f* 15/2[3]
000- 7 ½ **Iris's Spirit**[38] 9290 3-8-7 46 oh1.... LukeMorris 7 36
(Tony Carroll) *racd in rr of midfield: pushed along and little prog over 2f out: sn drvn and kpt on* 66/1
004- 8 nk **Drummer Jack (IRE)**[23] 9521 3-9-6 59....(t) MartinDwyer 9 48
(William Muir) *slowly away and hmpd leaving stalls: sn rcvrd to r in midfield on outer: prog arnd field u.p over 2f out: sn one pce and plugged on* 11/4[1]
016- 9 1 ½ **Grandee Daisy**[38] 9292 3-9-5 58.... RobertWinston 6 44
(Jo Hughes, France) *racd in midfield: rdn and outpcd as tempo qcknd 2f out: one pce fnl f* 9/1
006- 10 ¾ **Royal Dancer**[42] 9243 3-9-4 57.... ShaneKelly 2 41
(Sylvester Kirk) *hld up in rr: rdn 2f out: nvr on terms* 20/1
001- 11 nk **Singe Du Nord**[25] 9489 3-8-6 52....(p) FayeMcManoman(7) 12 35
(Nigel Tinkler) *racd in rr of midfield: pushed along and struggling over 2f out: nvr a factor* 20/1

455- 12 5 **Pot Luck**[143] 6151 3-9-7 60.... DavidProbert 4 32
(Andrew Balding) *racd in midfield: rdn and outpcd 3f out: sn bhd (jockey said filly was never travelling)* 14/1
004- 13 2 **The Grey Dancer (IRE)**[60] 8890 3-8-12 51.... HectorCrouch 8 18
(Joseph Tuite) *racd in tch in midfield: rdn along and outpcd over 2f out: wknd fnl f* 14/1
1m 40.0s (0.20) **Going Correction** 0.0s/f (Stan) 13 Ran SP% 119.3
Speed ratings (Par 95): **99,98,98,93,92 92,91,91,89,88 88,83,81**
CSF £88.69 CT £922.85 TOTE £4.70: £2.00, £7.10, £3.70; EX 111.00 Trifecta £1141.50.
Owner The Judges & Partner **Bred** Kilnamoragh Stud **Trained** Upper Lambourn, Berks
■ Stewards' Enquiry : Nicola Currie two-day ban: interference & careless riding (Jan 19, 21)
FOCUS
The first three pulled clear and had a good battle.

80 JOIN RACING TV NOW H'CAP 1m (P)
5:15 (5:18) (Class 6) (0-55,55) 4-Y-O+
£3,105 (£924; £461; £400; £400; £400) **Stalls** Low

Form RPR
460- 1 **With Approval (IRE)**[6] 9767 7-9-7 55....(p) LiamJones 9 62
(Laura Mongan) *mde all: pushed along to qckn tempo 3f out: sn rdn and strly pressed by rival 1f out: styd on gamely ins fnl f: a jst doing enough* 10/1
351- 2 hd **Molten Lava (IRE)**[16] 9643 7-9-5 53....(p) RobertHavlin 14 60
(Steve Gollings) *chsd wnr: rdn upsides and ev ch 1f out: drvn and styd on wl fnl f: a jst hld by wnr* 5/1[2]
353- 3 1 ¾ **Woggle (IRE)**[22] 9531 4-9-2 50....(p) KieranO'Neill 3 53+
(Geoffrey Deacon) *broke wl but bdly hmpd and snatched up after 1f: sn dropped to rr as a result: hdwy on inner u.p 2f out: styd on wl ins fnl f: nt rch ldng pair* 5/1[2]
564- 4 nk **Voice Of A Leader (IRE)**[26] 9481 8-9-5 53....(p) JoeyHaynes 5 55
(Paul Howling) *racd in rr of midfield: pushed along and briefly short of room 3f out: rdn to go 3rd 2f out: kpt on wl fnl f: lost 3rd 50yds out* 6/1[3]
000- 5 3 ¼ **Runaiocht (IRE)**[8] 9735 9-9-3 51....(b) RobertWinston 13 45
(Brian Forsey) *racd in rr: rdn and outpcd over 2f out: kpt on wl passed btn horses fnl f* 25/1
005- 6 1 ½ **Gracie Stansfield**[110] 7356 5-9-7 55.... GeorgeDowning 8 46
(Tony Carroll) *dwlt and racd in last: effrt to cl u.p 2f out: sn rdn and unable qck over 1f out (jockey said mare was slow into stride)* 33/1
022- 7 2 **Luxford**[23] 9527 5-9-3 51.... HectorCrouch 1 37
(Gary Moore) *broke wl but sn restrained into midfield: pushed along over 2f out: rdn and little imp over 1f out: kpt on* 3/1[1]
000- 8 5 **Ramblow**[10] 9704 6-9-5 53....(t) RossaRyan 2 28
(Alexandra Dunn) *racd in midfield: drvn along 2f out: one pce after* 50/1
224- 9 6 **Sir Jamie**[149] 5900 6-9-4 52.... LukeMorris 7 13
(Tony Carroll) *racd in rr of midfield: pushed along and little imp over 2f out: wknd fnl f* 12/1
200- 10 5 **Haabis (USA)**[32] 9387 6-9-3 51.... DavidProbert 10 1
(Patrick Chamings) *trckd ldrs: rdn and outpcd 3 out: wknd fr over 1f out (jockey said gelding hung left-handed throughout)* 14/1
400- 11 1 ¾ **Blue Harmony**[33] 9381 4-9-0 53.... MeganNicholls(5) 6
(Michael Blake) *racd in midfield: outpcd 1/2-way: sn bhd* 14/1
5/5- 12 19 **Achianna (USA)**[248] 2282 4-9-4 52.... JFEgan 4
(Rod Millman) *settled in midfield: lost pl 1/2-way: sn struggling (jockey said filly ran too free; vet reported that the filly lost a tooth)* 20/1
060- 13 30 **Demons And Wizards (IRE)**[33] 9378 4-9-4 52.... EdwardGreatrex 12
(Lydia Richards) *racd in midfield: pushed along arnd outside of field 3f out: sn bhd (jockey said gelding hung left-handed and stopped quickly)* 50/1
1m 40.08s (0.28) **Going Correction** 0.0s/f (Stan) 13 Ran SP% 118.2
Speed ratings (Par 101): **98,97,96,95,92 91,89,84,78,73 71,52,22**
CSF £55.76 CT £292.12 TOTE £12.70: £3.10, £2.10, £1.90; EX 77.50 Trifecta £528.10.
Owner Mrs P J Sheen **Bred** Yeomanstown Stud **Trained** Epsom, Surrey
FOCUS
Few got into this.

81 32RED/EBF STALLIONS BREEDING FILLIES' H'CAP 1m (P)
5:45 (5:45) (Class 3) (0-90,81) 4-Y-O+
£12,450 (£3,728; £1,864; £932; £466; £234) **Stalls** Low

Form RPR
435- 1 **Happy Escape**[33] 9384 5-9-1 75.... FrannyNorton 1 82
(Tony Carroll) *hld up in last trio: smooth prog to trck ldr over 1f out: rdn to ld 1f out: styd on wl fnl f* 5/1[3]
043- 2 1 ¼ **Pure Shores**[9] 9724 5-9-5 79.... KieranO'Neill 7 83
(Ian Williams) *s.i.s and racd in last: pushed along over 2f out: styd on wl u.str.p ins fnl f to snatch 2nd fnl strides* 10/1
213- 3 nse **Roman Spinner**[22] 9532 4-9-5 79....(t) MartinHarley 9 83
(Rae Guest) *hld up: clsd on ldr gng wl over 1f out: sn rdn and fnd little: lost 2nd fnl strides* 9/2[2]
/32- 4 nse **Red Chois (IRE)**[19] 9592 5-9-2 76....(h) DavidProbert 3 80
(William Jarvis) *chsd ldr and ev ch 2f out: kpt on one pce fnl f* 5/1[3]
321- 5 ¾ **Yusra**[16] 9638 4-9-3 77.... LukeMorris 2 79
(Marco Botti) *led: rdn along and strly pressed 2f out: hung lft wh hdd 1f out: wknd fnl f* 4/1[1]
013- 6 1 **Margie's Choice (GER)**[14] 9684 4-9-2 76....(p[1]) RobertHavlin 6 76
(Michael Madgwick) *racd in midfield: rdn and outpcd 2f out: one pce fnl f* 16/1
604- 7 1 ¾ **Autumn Leaves**[14] 9684 4-8-13 73.... AlistairRawlinson 8 69
(Michael Appleby) *trckd ldr: rdn along and unable qck over 1f out: plugged on* 50/1
6/3- 8 nk **Jamaican Jill**[37] 9312 4-9-3 77.... MartinDwyer 4 72
(William Muir) *racd in midfield: pushed along 3f out: sn rdn and wknd ins fnl f* 7/1
245- 9 4 **Ventura Blues (IRE)**[21] 9564 5-9-7 81....(p) RossaRyan 5 67
(Richard Hannon) *hld up: pushed along over 2f out: rdn and little rspnse over 1f out: wknd fnl f (jockey said mare was never travelling)* 6/1
1m 38.92s (-0.88) **Going Correction** 0.0s/f (Stan) 9 Ran SP% 115.2
Speed ratings (Par 104): **104,102,102,102,101 100,99,98,94**
CSF £53.58 CT £242.11 TOTE £6.30: £1.80, £2.60, £1.50; EX 46.60 Trifecta £179.70.
Owner A A Byrne **Bred** Anthony Byrne **Trained** Cropthorne, Worcs

FOCUS
This set up for the closers, the first three being the last three into the turn.

82 32RED H'CAP 1m 7f 218y(P)
6:15 (6:17) (Class 2) (0-105,104) 4-Y-O+
£15,562 (£4,660; £2,330; £1,165; £582; £292) Stalls Low

Form RPR
1- 1 **Amade (IRE)**39 9279 5-9-0 **92**....(b) RobertHavlin 2 101+
(G Botti, France) *dwlt and racd in rr: quick move on outer to take clsr order 6f out: clsd on ldr gng wl 3f out: rdn and qcknd clr over 2f out: sn in command and rdn out fnl f* **2/1**1

030- 2 2 1/4 **Castlelyons (IRE)**21 9552 7-8-12 **90**....(h) CallumShepherd 3 95
(Robert Stephens) *racd in midfield: effrt to cl on inner 2f out: sn drvn and wnt 2nd over 1f out: styd on wl fnl f: no ch w wnr* **10/1**

2/0- 3 1 1/4 **Zubayr (IRE)**14 9686 7-8-8 **86**.... KieranO'Neill 7 89
(Ian Williams) *hld up in last: hdwy u.p 3f out: swtchd wdst of all and drvn 2f out: styd on wl ins fnl f to snatch 3rd fnl strides* **14/1**

506- 4 hd **Eddystone Rock (IRE)**14 9686 7-8-11 **89**.... KierenFox 11 92
(John Best) *hld up in rr: hdwy u.p wd arnd field over 3f out: sn rdn and wnt 3rd 1f out: all out and lost 3rd fnl strides* **33/1**

102- 5 2 **Count Calabash (IRE)**22 9534 5-9-5 **97**.... CharlesBishop 1 98
(Eve Johnson Houghton) *led: rdn along and strly pressed 3f out: drvn and hdd by wnr over 2f out: kpt on one pce fnl f* **9/2**2

423- 6 1 1/4 **Cayirli (FR)**39 9279 7-8-12 **90**....(t1) MartinHarley 8 89
(Seamus Durack) *hld up in rr of midfield: fast forward move arnd outside of field to go 2nd over 4f out: sn rdn and outpcd by wnr over 2f out: wknd fnl f* **9/1**

606- 7 4 1/2 **Cosmelli (ITY)**21 9552 6-9-8 **100**....(v) LukeMorris 10 94
(Gay Kelleway) *trckd ldr: pushed along 4f out: sn rdn and little rspnse: nvr on terms* **40/1**

1UP- 8 2 1/4 **Addicted To You (IRE)**70 8658 5-9-3 **95**.... JasonHart 9 86
(Mark Johnston) *hld up in midfield: hdwy to go 2nd and chse ldr after 6f: rdn and lost pl over 3f out* **18/1**

110- 9 1/2 **Envoy**47 9155 5-8-11 **89**.... RyanTate 6 79
(James Eustace) *racd in midfield: rdn along and unable qck over 2f out: one pce fnl f* **7/1**3

543- 10 18 **Lord George (IRE)**14 9686 6-9-12 **104**....(v) AdamKirby 5 73
(James Fanshawe) *chsd ldr: rdn and outpcd 3f out: sn bhd (trainer could offer no explanation for the gelding's performance)* **7/1**3

/60- 11 44 **Winterlude (IRE)**22 9534 9-8-13 **91**.... JoeFanning 4 7
(Jennie Candlish) *trckd ldr: pushed along and lost action over 2f out: virtually p.u (jockey said gelding stopped quickly)* **20/1**

3m 25.47s (-4.63) **Going Correction** 0.0s/f (Stan) **11 Ran SP% 117.7**
Speed ratings (Par 109): **111,109,109,109,108 107,105,104,103,94 72**
CSF £22.88 CT £226.71 TOTE £2.50: £1.30, £2.90, £5.60; EX 25.20 Trifecta £206.60.
Owner Laurent Dassault **Bred** Eamonn McEvoy **Trained** France

FOCUS
A good performance from the winner, who proved himself a well-handicapped horse on his British debut.

83 32RED ON THE APP STORE H'CAP 6f (P)
6:45 (6:46) (Class 4) (0-85,83) 3-Y-O £6,469 (£1,925; £962; £481; £400) Stalls Low

Form RPR
505- 1 **Xtara (IRE)**17 9611 3-8-12 **74**....(v1) BarryMcHugh 2 78
(Adrian Nicholls) *disp the ld tl pushed along and sltly outpcd 2f out: drvn along over 1f out: kpt on gamely u.str.p to ld again on the post* **5/1**

243- 2 shd **Uncle Jerry**22 9533 3-9-5 **81**....(b) ShaneKelly 5 85
(Richard Hughes) *trckd ldng pair: clsd gng wl 2f out: sn rdn and led ins fnl f: strly pressed and hdd by wnr fnl strides* **9/2**3

014- 3 1 **Beleaguerment (IRE)**22 9533 3-9-0 **76**....(p1) EdwardGreatrex 1 77
(Archie Watson) *trckd ldng pair and plld quite hrd early: rdn upsides wnr and ev ch over 1f out: couldn't sustain effrt fnl 100yds* **5/4**1

021- 4 2 1/2 **Wedding Date**47 9151 3-9-7 **83**.... RossaRyan 4 76
(Richard Hannon) *disp ld tl qcknd tempo to ld 2f out: sn drvn and hdd by wnr ins fnl f: no ex* **4/1**2

340- 5 22 **Showu**91 7983 3-8-7 **69**.... LukeMorris 3
(Tony Carroll) *s.i.s and rdr sn looking down: detached after 1f: mde gd hdwy to cl on rivals 3f out: sn rdn and wknd (jockey said filly was outpaced early and moved poorly; vet reported that the filly was lame left hind)* **11/1**

1m 14.44s (1.34) **Going Correction** 0.0s/f (Stan) **5 Ran SP% 107.6**
Speed ratings (Par 99): **91,90,89,86,56**
CSF £25.03 TOTE £5.80: £2.80, £1.70; EX 25.20.
Owner Sultan Saeed Harib **Bred** Robert Norton **Trained** Sessay, N Yorks

FOCUS
A messy race from a pace perspective.

84 100% PROFIT BOOST AT 32REDSPORT.COM H'CAP 1m 7f 218y(P)
7:15 (7:15) (Class 5) (0-75,75) 4-Y-O+
£3,752 (£1,116; £557; £400; £400; £400) Stalls Low

Form RPR
005- 1 **Blazon**39 9272 6-8-11 **60**....(p) JoeFanning 9 67
(Kim Bailey) *hld up in last: clsd gng wl 3f out: bmpd along 2f out: sn rdn and styd on strly to ld fnl 50yds (trainer said, as to the apparent improvement in form, the gelding benefitted from the step up in trip from 1 1/2 miles to 2 miles and the re-application of cheekpieces)* **14/1**

163/ 2 1 **Red Royalist**35 8078 5-9-12 **75**.... AdamKirby 1 81
(Stuart Edmunds) *racd in midfield: effrt to cl 3f out: rdn to ld 2f out: over 1 l clr 1f out: drvn and hdd by wnr fnl 50yds* **11/2**2

005- 3 1 **East Indies**17 9608 6-9-7 **70**.... HectorCrouch 7 75
(Gary Moore) *hld up in rr: effrt to cl on outer over 2f out: styd on wl fnl f: nt rch ldng pair* **16/1**

325- 4 1/2 **Moon Of Baroda**143 6149 4-9-7 **75**....(b) CallumShepherd 8 79
(Charles Hills) *racd in midfield: effrt to chse ldr over 2f out: rdn and upsides ldr over 1f out: no ex fnl f* **7/1**

210- 5 3 **Spiritual Man (IRE)**31 9400 7-9-4 **67**.... FranBerry 11 68
(Jonjo O'Neill) *racd in midfield: rdn to take clsr order over 2f out: sn drvn and no imp 1f out: kpt on* **25/1**

206- 6 4 **Bird For Life**15 9665 5-8-1 **57**....(p) EllieMacKenzie(7) 6 53
(Mark Usher) *hld up in rr: rdn along over 2f out: sn drvn and little imp 1f out: one pce after* **16/1**

131- 7 3/4 **Ilhabela Fact**29 9447 5-9-8 **71**.... FrannyNorton 10 66
(Tony Carroll) *hld up in tch: smooth hdwy to go 2nd 3f out: rdn and unable qck 2f out: wknd fnl f* **10/3**1

212- 8 13 **Nafaayes (IRE)**17 9608 5-8-11 **60**....(p) MartinDwyer 2 40
(Jean-Rene Auvray) *trckd ldr tl led after 6f: drvn along to maintain ld 3f out: hdd 2f out: sn wknd* **6/1**3

650- 9 34 **Confederate**28 9464 4-9-3 **71**....(t1) LukeMorris 3 12
(Hugo Palmer) *led tl hdd and trckd new ldr after 6f: rdn and reminders 5f out: outpcd 4f out: sn bhd* **11/1**

602- 10 8 **Ardamir (FR)**17 9608 7-9-3 **66**.... LiamJones 4
(Laura Mongan) *trckd ldr: pushed along 5f out: detached 3f out* **9/1**

3m 28.31s (-1.79) **Going Correction** 0.0s/f (Stan)
WFA 4 from 5yo+ 5lb **10 Ran SP% 105.9**
Speed ratings (Par 103): **104,103,103,102,101 99,98,92,75,71**
CSF £76.54 CT £1026.78 TOTE £12.90: £3.80, £2.30, £3.50; EX 91.40.
Owner The Blazing Optimists **Bred** Juddmonte Farms Ltd **Trained** Andoversford, Gloucs
■ Buckle Street was withdrawn. Price at time of withdrawal 11/1. Rule 4 applies to all bets - deduction 5p in the pound

FOCUS
A fair staying handicap.

85 FOLLOW @RACINGTV ON TWITTER H'CAP 1m 3f 219y(P)
7:45 (7:45) (Class 6) (0-65,64) 4-Y-O+
£3,105 (£924; £461; £400; £400; £400) Stalls Low

Form RPR
000- 1 **Sir Prize**24 9511 4-9-2 **62**.... RobertWinston 14 69+
(Dean Ivory) *hld up in rr: hdwy on wd outside over 3f out: sn rdn and prog to chse ldr over 1f out: styd on strly to ld fnl 100yds (trainer said, as to the apparent improvement in form, the gelding has benefitted from gaining experience and being ridden more patiently)* **20/1**

003- 2 1/2 **Double Legend (IRE)**29 9448 4-8-10 **56**....(b) RobertHavlin 8 62
(Amanda Perrett) *trckd ldr: pushed along to chse ldr 3f out: upsides and ev ch 2f out: drvn and responded wl to press to grab 2nd fnl strides* **3/1**1

123- 3 hd **Turn Of Luck (IRE)**6 9769 4-9-3 **63**....(p) NicolaCurrie 5 69
(Jamie Osborne) *led: rdn along and strly pressed by rival 2f out: drvn and hdd by wnr 100yds out: lost 2nd fnl strides (jockey said colt hung left-handed under pressure)* **3/1**1

300- 4 1 1/2 **Foresee (GER)**40 8765 6-9-3 **60**.... FrannyNorton 4 62
(Tony Carroll) *hld up in tch in midfield: rdn and outpcd over 2f out: kpt on one pce fnl f* **12/1**

225- 5 1 1/2 **Power Home (IRE)**24 9511 5-9-2 **59**.... CharlesBishop 1 60
(Denis Coakley) *racd in midfield in tch: rdn and unable qck 2f out: kpt on once pce fnl f* **12/1**

026- 6 1/2 **Famous Dynasty (IRE)**14 9687 5-9-5 **62**.... DavidProbert 6 61
(Michael Blanshard) *settled in midfield: clsd gng wl over 2f out whn briefly short of room: sn rdn and unable qck: one pce fnl f* **16/1**

240- 7 3/4 **Make Good (IRE)**33 9380 4-9-4 **64**....(v) LukeMorris 9 63
(David Dennis) *hld up in rr: rdn along 3f out: sme late hdwy passed btn horses fnl f* **33/1**

430- 8 3 **Highway One (USA)**75 8489 5-9-6 **63**.... AdamKirby 2 56
(George Baker) *trckd ldr: clsd gng wl over 2f out: rdn and little imp over 1f out: wknd fnl f* **6/1**2

000- 9 nk **Boycie**21 9562 6-9-2 **59**....(b) HollieDoyle 13 52
(Adrian Wintle) *racd in midfield: drvn 2f out: outpcd and plugged don fnl f (jockey said gelding hung left-handed throughout)* **50/1**

/00- 10 nk **Tour De Paris (IRE)**23 3950 4-9-4 **64**....(v1) MartinHarley 10 57
(Alan King) *racd in midfield: rdn along over 2f out: hung to fair rail u.p 1f out: nvr on terms* **10/1**3

000- 11 3/4 **Butterfield (IRE)**17 9609 6-9-7 **64**.... LiamJones 7 55
(Tony Carroll) *hld up: rdn and outpcd over 2f out: nvr a factor (jockey said gelding stumbled leaving the stalls)* **20/1**

036- 12 1 3/4 **Happy Ending (IRE)**112 7303 4-8-11 **57**.... RobHornby 11 46
(Seamus Mullins) *hld up: a in rr* **50/1**

04/- 13 8 **Furiously Fast (IRE)**27 261 7-8-12 **60**.... PoppyBridgwater(5) 12 36
(Dai Burchell) *hld up: rdn and detached 3f out* **14/1**

/00- 14 nk **Matravers**19 9585 8-9-1 **58**....(v) JoeyHaynes 3 33
(Martin Keighley) *dwlt and racd in last: a bhd* **25/1**

2m 35.49s (0.99) **Going Correction** 0.0s/f (Stan)
WFA 4 from 5yo+ 3lb **14 Ran SP% 121.5**
Speed ratings (Par 101): **96,95,95,94,93 93,92,90,90,90 89,88,83,83**
CSF £75.73 CT £242.14 TOTE £29.40: £7.30, £1.80, £1.50; EX 155.00 Trifecta £1544.20.
Owner Michael & Heather Yarrow **Bred** Chippenham Lodge Stud **Trained** Radlett, Herts

FOCUS
A good performance from the winner, who came from behind in a race in which otherwise the pace held up.
T/Plt: £1,748.80 to a £1 stake. Pool: £89,911.30 - 37.53 winning units T/Qpdt: £50.20 to a £1 stake. Pool: £13,947.62 - 205.27 winning units **Mark Grantham**

LINGFIELD (L-H)
Saturday, January 5

OFFICIAL GOING: Polytrack: standard to slow
Wind: light, half against Weather: overcast, chilly

86 BETWAY CASINO H'CAP 1m 2f (P)
12:40 (12:42) (Class 5) (0-75,75) 4-Y-O+
£3,752 (£1,116; £557; £300; £300; £300) Stalls Low

Form RPR
052- 1 **Forbidden Planet**85 8159 4-9-1 **69**.... RichardKingscote 3 83+
(Roger Charlton) *chsd ldrs: effrt to cl 2f out: rdn to ld ent fnl f: r.o strly: readily* **6/5**1

250- 2 4 1/2 **Graceful James (IRE)**37 9316 6-9-8 **75**.... KieranO'Neill 8 79
(Jimmy Fox) *dwlt and rousted along early: sn rcvrd and chsd ldrs: wnt 2nd 6f out tl rdn to ld wl over 1f out: hdd ent fnl f: sn brushed aside but plugged on for clr 2nd* **6/1**3

050- 3 6 **King Of The Sand (IRE)**24 9502 4-9-5 **73**.... AdamKirby 9 66
(Gary Moore) *chsd ldr tl led over 7f out: rdn and hdd wl over 1f out: 3rd and wknd fnl f* **3/1**2

103- 4 1 1/4 **Bayston Hill**37 9311 5-9-3 **70**.... DavidProbert 4 60
(Mark Usher) *in tch in midfield: rdn wl over 2f out: sn struggling and outpcd: wl hld over 1f out* **8/1**

416- 5 4 1/2 **Seaborough (IRE)**30 5658 4-9-2 **70**.... MartinHarley 5 52
(Alan King) *hld up in tch in last pair: effrt wl over 2f out: sn outpcd and wl btn over 1f out* **16/1**

/05- 6 3 **Sunbreak (IRE)**7 9747 4-8-13 **67**.... JoeFanning 6 43
(Mark Johnston) *led tl over 7f out: chsd ldr tl 6f out: rdn and outpcd jst over 2f out: sn btn and fdd fnl f* **7/1**

400- 7 53 **Jupiter**[10] 9702 4-8-8 **62** EdwardGreatrex 1
(Alexandra Dunn) *a in rr: pushed along over 4f out: drvn and lost tch 3f out: virtually p.u over 1f out: t.o* 66/1

2m 5.05s (-1.55) **Going Correction** +0.10s/f (Slow)
WFA 4 from 5yo+ 1lb 7 Ran SP% **115.7**
Speed ratings (Par 103): **110,106,101,100,97 94,52**
CSF £9.44 CT £18.10 TOTE £1.90: £1.10, £2.20; EX 8.50 Trifecta £28.20.
Owner Kingwood Stud Management Co Ltd **Bred** David John Brown **Trained** Beckhampton, Wilts

FOCUS
This ordinary handicap revolved around the lightly raced Forbidden Planet on his debut for Roger Charlton. The runner-up is rated close to his reappearance form here, but there are doubts over the field.

87 BETWAY H'CAP 1m 2f (P)
1:15 (1:15) (Class 3) (0-95,96) 4-Y-0 **£7,246** (£2,168; £1,084; £542; £270) **Stalls** Low

Form RPR

211- 1 **Matterhorn (IRE)**[15] 9661 4-9-5 **93** FrannyNorton 2 104+
(Mark Johnston) *pressed ldr: rdn and qcknd to ld jst over 2f out: sn clr: r.o and a in command ins fnl f* 8/11[1]

656- 2 1 ¾ **Mythical Madness**[10] 9705 8-9-9 **96** (v) AdamKirby 4 101
(David O'Meara) *hld up wl in tch: effrt to chse ldng pair jst over 2f out: drvn to chse clr wnr over 1f out: kpt on ins fnl f but nvr threatening wnr* 16/1

501- 3 5 **Lexington Law (IRE)**[24] 9502 6-9-6 **93** (p) DavidProbert 6 88
(Alan King) *dwlt: hld up wl in tch in rr: effrt 2f out: nvr any ch of getting on terms w wnr: wnt 3rd and kpt on same pce ins fnl f* 7/2[2]

246- 4 4 ½ **Guvenor's Choice (IRE)**[9] 9723 4-8-10 **84** (t) LukeMorris 1 71
(K R Burke) *led and set stdy gallop: rdn and hdd jst over 2f out: sn outpcd by wnr: lost 2nd over 1f out: wknd ins fnl f* 8/1[3]

111/ 5 1 ¾ **Shargiah (IRE)**[568] 3785 6-9-8 **95** DougieCostello 5 78
(Michael Appleby) *awkward leaving stalls: chsd ldrs on outer: rdn over 2f out: outpcd and btn whn hung rt bnd wl over 1f out: wknd* 20/1

000- 6 6 **Battle Of Marathon (USA)**[141] 6251 7-9-5 **92** JosephineGordon 3 63
(John Ryan) *dwlt: sn rcvrd and trckd ldrs on inner: rdn over 2f out: sn outpcd and dropped to rr: bhd and eased wl ins fnl f* 9/1

2m 5.35s (-1.25) **Going Correction** +0.10s/f (Slow)
WFA 4 from 6yo+ 1lb 6 Ran SP% **111.9**
Speed ratings (Par 107): **109,107,103,100,98 93**
CSF £14.27 TOTE £1.80: £1.50, £5.70; EX 9.70 Trifecta £28.20.
Owner Sheikh Hamdan bin Mohammed Al Maktoum **Bred** Barronstown Stud **Trained** Middleham Moor, N Yorks

FOCUS
This featured some prolific AW winners, though only a couple of them arrived here in form and there wasn't much depth. They went very steadily and it proved an unsatisfactory affair. The winner was value for extra.

88 BETWAY LIVE CASINO H'CAP 1m 4f (P)
1:45 (1:45) (Class 4) (0-80,80) 4-Y-0+
£5,530 (£1,645; £822; £411; £300; £300) **Stalls** Low

Form RPR

1- 1 **Nylon Speed (IRE)**[40] 6394 5-9-0 **70** (t[1]) MartinHarley 6 78+
(Alan King) *chsd ldrs tl wnt 2nd over 3f out: rdn to ld over 1f out: sn qcknd clr u.p: r.o wl: eased towards fin* 11/10[1]

601- 2 2 **Dutch Uncle**[8] 9728 7-9-10 **80** (p) LukeMorris 4 83
(Olly Murphy) *hld up in tch in last trio: clsd and nt clrest of runs over 2f out: edgd out rt bnd wl over 1f out: sn rdn: drvn to chse wnr wl ins fnl f: kpt on but no threat to wnr* 5/1[3]

150- 3 hd **Tralee Hills**[29] 9447 5-9-6 **76** CharlesBishop 7 79
(Peter Hedger) *dropped in bhd after s: hld up in tch in last trio: hdwy on outer to chse ldrs 5f out: rdn and nudged rt bnd wl over 1f out: kpt on u.p but nvr enough pce to threaten wnr* 4/1[2]

140- 4 1 **Smiley Bagel (IRE)**[24] 9502 6-9-3 **73** LiamKeniry 3 74
(Ed Walker) *t.k.h: hld up wl in tch in midfield: clsd to trck ldrs jst over 2f out: effrt 2f out: kpt on same pce and no threat to wnr ins fnl f* 14/1

636- 5 hd **Bamako Du Chatelet (FR)**[24] 9505 8-8-12 **68** (p) FranBerry 5 69
(Ian Williams) *rousted along leaving stalls: chsd ldr tl led over 10f out: rdn ent fnl 2f: hdd over 1f out: sn outpcd by wnr: kpt on same pce and lost 3 pls wl ins fnl f* 11/2

020/ 6 2 **Stormy Blues**[23] 5220 5-9-5 **75** (t) DougieCostello 2 73
(Nigel Hawke) *awkward leaving stalls and slowly away: sn rcvrd and hld up in tch: effrt on inner over 1f out: kpt on same pce and no imp ins fnl f* 33/1

600- 7 9 **Esspeegee**[29] 9447 6-8-9 **70** DarraghKeenan(5) 8 53
(Alan Bailey) *stdd s: t.k.h: hld up in tch in last pair: rdn over 2f out: sn struggling: wknd over 1f out* 28/1

0/0- 8 18 **Shinghari (IRE)**[8] 9731 7-9-4 **74** RossaRyan 1 29
(Alexandra Dunn) *led tl over 10f out: chsd ldr tl over 3f out: sn pushed along and struggling: bhd over 1f out: wknd* 25/1

2m 35.92s (2.92) **Going Correction** +0.10s/f (Slow) 8 Ran SP% **116.6**
Speed ratings (Par 105): **94,92,92,91,91 90,84,72**
CSF £7.03 CT £16.71 TOTE £2.00: £1.60, £1.30, £1.30; EX 6.90 Trifecta £18.70.
Owner Axom Lxxiv **Bred** Stiftung Gestut Fahrhof **Trained** Barbury Castle, Wilts

FOCUS
A fair middle-distance handicap and plenty to like about the way in which the unexposed favourite settled matters. He has the potential to do better, though it wasn't the most robust field.

89 FOLLOW SUN RACING ON TWITTER CONDITIONS STKS 1m 1y(P)
2:15 (2:15) (Class 2) 4-Y-0+ **£11,827** (£3,541; £1,770; £885; £442) **Stalls** High

Form RPR

424- 1 **Salateen**[30] 9430 7-9-3 102 (t) MartinHarley 3 108
(David O'Meara) *led tl over 6f out: chsd ldr tl led again over 2f out: nudged along and kicked over 2 l clr 2f out: rdn over 1f out: kpt on and in command ins fnl f: eased towards fin* 3/1[2]

115- 2 2 **Straight Right (FR)**[45] 9173 5-9-3 108 (h) RobHornby 2 102
(Andrew Balding) *stdd s: hld up in rr: stl plenty to do and effrt wl over 1f out: nt clr run: swtchd lft and hdwy u.p 1f out: r.o to chse clr wnr wl ins fnl f: nvr getting on terms* 4/5[1]

412- 3 ¾ **Take The Helm**[240] 2573 6-9-3 96 LiamKeniry 4 100
(Brian Meehan) *t.k.h: chsd ldr tl led over 6f out: hdd over 2f out: unable to match pce of wnr and rdn over 1f out: kpt on same pce and a hld: lost 2nd wl ins fnl f* 9/2[3]

501- 4 nk **Calling Out (FR)**[23] 9524 8-9-3 97 StevieDonohoe 5 99
(David Simcock) *hld up in tch in 4th: effrt to chse ldrs ent fnl 2f: drvn and kpt on same pce ins fnl f* 12/1

001- 5 6 **Book Of Dreams (IRE)**[182] 4659 4-9-3 93 DougieCostello 1 85
(Michael Appleby) *chsd ldrs tl rdn and struggling to qckn jst over 2f out: lost pl and dropped to last 1f out: wknd ins fnl f* 16/1

1m 37.57s (-0.63) **Going Correction** +0.10s/f (Slow) 5 Ran SP% **112.3**
Speed ratings (Par 109): **107,105,104,103,97**
CSF £5.99 TOTE £3.10: £1.50, £1.10; EX 7.00 Trifecta £14.30.
Owner Sheikh Abdullah Almalek Alsabah **Bred** Mrs Janis Macpherson **Trained** Upper Helmsley, N Yorks

FOCUS
They went no pace in this good quality conditions contest and it was stolen off the home turn by the forwardly ridden Salateen. He's rated pretty much to his best.

90 LADBROKES NOVICE MEDIAN AUCTION STKS 1m 1y(P)
2:50 (2:51) (Class 6) 3-Y-O **£3,105** (£924; £461; £230) **Stalls** High

Form RPR

02- 1 **Renegade Master**[29] 9443 3-9-2 0 NicolaCurrie 10 80
(George Baker) *taken down early: t.k.h: chsd ldrs tl wnt 2nd over 5f out: effrt to ld over 1f out: rdn clr ins fnl f: eased towards fin* 25/1

5- 2 ½ **Target Zone**[24] 9500 3-9-2 0 DavidProbert 5 80+
(David Elsworth) *t.k.h: chsd ldrs: effrt in 4th 2f out: rn green over 1f out: hdwy ins fnl f to chse wnr 75yds out: styd on wl but nvr getting to wnr* 7/2[3]

41- 3 1 ¼ **Coolagh Forest (IRE)**[50] 9103 3-9-9 0 BarryMcHugh 9 83
(Richard Fahey) *t.k.h: chsd ldr tl led over 6f out: rdn and hdd over 1f out: kpt on same pce and lost 2nd 75yds out* 8/1

3- 4 2 ¾ **Harvey Dent**[14] 9683 3-9-2 0 EdwardGreatrex 1 71+
(Archie Watson) *hld up in tch in midfield: effrt on inner over 1f out: kpt on same pce and no imp ins fnl f* 7/4[1]

\- 5 1 ¾ **Fast Boy (IRE)** 3-9-2 0 MartinHarley 11 66
(David Simcock) *dwlt: hld up towards rr: hdwy on outer to chse ldrs over 2f out: wd and lost pl bnd 2f out: wl hld and kpt on same pce after* 20/1

1- 6 shd **Rectory Road**[51] 9074 3-9-6 0 JoshuaBryan(3) 6 72
(Andrew Balding) *t.k.h: led tl over 6f out: styd chsng ldrs: effrt over 1f out: no ex u.p 1f out: wknd ins fnl f* 2/1[2]

04- 7 2 ¾ **Altar Boy**[45] 9172 3-9-2 0 LukeMorris 3 59
(Sylvester Kirk) *in tch in midfield: rdn jst over 2f out: sn struggling to qckn and outpcd over 1f out: wknd ins fnl f* 10/1

00- 8 1 ½ **Anglesey Penny**[29] 9442 3-8-4 0 GinaMangan(7) 12 51
(J R Jenkins) *hld up in tch in midfield: effrt over 1f out: sn outpcd and wknd ins fnl f* 150/1

0- 9 10 **Twpsyn (IRE)**[28] 9459 3-8-9 0 KatherineBegley(7) 7 33
(David Evans) *hld up in tch towards rr: shkn up over 2f out: sn outpcd and wl btn over 1f out: eased wl ins fnl f: fin lame (jockey said gelding was slow into stride and then lost it's action in the straight. Vet said gelding was coughing post-race and lame on it's left-fore leg)* 66/1

0- 10 2 **Harry The Norseman**[24] 9499 3-9-2 0 HollieDoyle 2 28
(David Elsworth) *restless in stalls: in tch towards rr: rdn over 2f out: sn outpcd: wl bhd fnl f* 33/1

0- 11 hd **Midnite Rendezvous**[9] 9727 3-8-11 0 RaulDaSilva 4 23
(Derek Shaw) *dwlt: a towards rr: rdn over 2f out: sn outpcd: wl bhd fnl f* 100/1

12 45 **Prince Mamillius** 3-9-2 0 CallumShepherd 8
(Derek Shaw) *s.i.s: a in rr: pushed along 4f out: lost tch over 2f out: virtually p.u fnl f: t.o* 100/1

1m 39.78s (1.58) **Going Correction** +0.10s/f (Slow) 12 Ran SP% **127.8**
Speed ratings (Par 95): **96,95,94,91,89 89,86,85,75,73 73,28**
CSF £116.87 TOTE £18.50: £5.10, £1.50, £1.80; EX 119.10 Trifecta £2254.30.
Owner Gwyn Powell **Bred** Gwyn & Samantha Powell **Trained** Chiddingfold, Surrey

FOCUS
An informative novice event, though very few landed a blow with the first three home racing in the first quartet throughout.

91 SUNRACING.CO.UK H'CAP 7f 1y(P)
3:25 (3:26) (Class 5) (0-75,77) 4-Y-0+
£3,752 (£1,116; £557; £300; £300; £300) **Stalls** Low

Form RPR

40- 1 **Kodiline (IRE)**[21] 9564 5-9-2 **77** KatherineBegley(7) 11 83
(David Evans) *stdd and dropped in towards rr after s: hld up in tch: clsd and nt clr run ent fnl 2f: hdwy u.p ent fnl f: wnt 2nd ins fnl f: r.o strly to ld last stride* 8/1

202- 2 nk **Highland Acclaim (IRE)**[8] 9733 8-9-4 **72** (h) EdwardGreatrex 12 77
(David O'Meara) *w ldr tl led over 3f out: rdn and kicked clr over 1f out: drvn ins fnl f: hdd and no ex last strides* 12/1

500- 3 ½ **Real Estate (IRE)**[22] 9536 4-9-0 **68** (p) CallumShepherd 2 72
(Michael Attwater) *t.k.h: hld up in tch in midfield: nt clr run ent fnl 2f tl gap opened and hdwy jst ins fnl f: r.o strly u.p fnl 100yds: nt quite rch ldrs* 33/1

035- 4 ¾ **Bernie's Boy**[8] 9733 6-9-7 **75** (p) NicolaCurrie 3 77
(Phil McEntee) *t.k.h: chsd ldrs tl wnt 2nd wl over 2f out: sn edgd rt: effrt but unable to match pce of ldr over 1f out: kpt on same pce and lost 2 pls ins fnl f (jockey said gelding hung right-handed from 3f out)* 11/1

334- 5 ½ **Espresso Freddo (IRE)**[10] 9702 5-9-5 **73** (v[1]) ShaneKelly 1 73
(Robert Stephens) *dwlt and pushed along leaving stalls: sn in tch in midfield and t.k.h: effrt 2f out: kpt on same pce u.p ins fnl f* 7/1

426- 6 ¾ **Evening Attire**[37] 9317 8-9-4 **72** HollieDoyle 9 70+
(William Stone) *restless in stalls: s.i.s: t.k.h and hld up in rr: clsd and nt clr run over 1f out: sn swtchd lft: styd on wl ins fnl f: nt rch ldrs (jockey said gelding anticipated the start and ran too free)* 5/1[3]

313- 7 ¾ **Critical Thinking (IRE)**[10] 9702 5-9-8 **76** (tp) StevieDonohoe 4 72
(David Loughnane) *chsd ldrs: effrt 2f out: unable to match pce of ldr over 1f out: no ex and outpcd ins fnl f* 5/2[1]

0- 8 ½ **Militry Decoration (IRE)**[85] 8171 4-9-4 **72** RobertWinston 10 67
(Dr Jon Scargill) *niggled along early: in tch in last trio: effrt over 1f out: kpt on ins fnl f: no threat to ldrs* 20/1

060- 9 ¾ **Helen Sherbet**[15] 9656 4-8-11 **65** (v[1]) RichardKingscote 5 58
(K R Burke) *led tl over 3f out: lost 2nd over 2f out and sn u.p: lost pl wl over 1f out: wknd ins fnl f* 16/1

402- 10 shd **Grey Galleon (USA)**[22] 9535 5-9-7 **75** (p) AdamKirby 7 68
(Clive Cox) *hld up in tch: nt clr run ent fnl 2f tl effrt ent fnl f: kpt on but nvr a threat to ldrs* 9/2[2]

100- 11 4 ½ **De Little Engine (IRE)**[10] 9702 5-8-12 **66** RossaRyan 8 47
(Alexandra Dunn) *in tch in midfield on outer: rdn over 2f out: lost pl over 1f out and wknd ins fnl f* 20/1

1m 24.91s (0.11) **Going Correction** +0.10s/f (Slow) 11 Ran SP% **121.4**
Speed ratings (Par 103): **103,102,102,101,100 99,98,98,97,97 92**
CSF £100.10 CT £3055.45 TOTE £9.50: £2.80, £3.00, £10.40; EX 104.30 Trifecta £1777.00.
Owner Mrs E Evans **Bred** Miss Aoife Boland **Trained** Pandy, Monmouths

FOCUS
Not many of these were in form but it looked a competitive race nonetheless. The winner is rated back to his Wolverhampton win.
T/Plt: £153.70 to a £1 stake. Pool: £57,008.77 - 270.76 winning units T/Qpdt: £44.00 to a £1 stake. Pool: £5,509.19 - 92.48 winning units **Steve Payne**

92a-96a (Foreign Racing) - See Raceform Interactive

[47]MEYDAN (L-H)
Saturday, January 5

OFFICIAL GOING: Turf: good; dirt: fast

97a DISTRICT ONE ELEGANCE STRETCH CUP (H'CAP) (DIRT) 7f (D)
2:55 (2:55) 3-Y-O+ **£24,358** (£8,119; £4,465; £2,435; £1,217)

RPR
1 **Bochart**[30] 9440 6-9-11 **85**........(t) RichardMullen 6 101
(S Seemar, UAE) *sn led: a gng wl: rdn clr 2f out: r.o wl: easily* **13/8[1]**
2 6 ½ **Mazeed (USA)**[30] 9439 5-9-3 **78**........(bt) TadhgO'Shea 3 76
(S Seemar, UAE) *settled rr: r.o wl fnl 2f: nrst fin* **10/1**
3 1 **Old Fashioned (CHI)**[16] 9655 6-9-2 **77**........(h) ConnorBeasley 7 72
(A bin Harmash, UAE) *trckd ldr: ev ch 2f out: one pce fnl 1 1/2f* **7/1[3]**
4 ½ **Robin Weathers (USA)**[72] 8578 5-8-13 **74**........ AdriedeVries 9 67
(Fawzi Abdulla Nass, Bahrain) *chsd ldrs: ev ch 2 1/2f out: one pce fnl 2f* **12/1**
5 6 **Denzille Lane (IRE)**[36] 9348 7-9-6 **81**........(b) PatDobbs 2 58
(Doug Watson, UAE) *trckd ldr: ev ch 2 1/2f out: one pce fnl 2f* **11/1**
6 2 ¾ **Muhtaram**[13] 9690 9-9-0 **75**........(b) BenCurtis 1 45
(M Al Mheiri, UAE) *nvr nr to chal* **18/1**
7 6 ½ **Glenglade**[22] 9547 4-9-11 **85**........(t) FabriceVeron 10 38
(Ismail Mohammed) *nvr nr to chal* **18/1**
8 shd **Manthoor (IRE)**[92] 7948 4-9-11 **85**........ AntonioFresu 8 38
(H Al Alawi, UAE) *slowly away: a in rr* **25/1**
9 3 ¾ **Jazirat (IRE)**[13] 9690 4-9-4 **79**........(p) SzczepanMazur 11 21
(S Al Shamsi, UAE) *nvr bttr than mid-div* **33/1**
10 ½ **Cantiniere (USA)**[31] 9406 4-9-4 **79**........ HayleyTurner 5 20
(Saeed bin Suroor) *nvr bttr than mid-div* **10/3[2]**
11 2 ¼ **Gotti (USA)**[21] 9568 4-9-0 **75**........ RonanWhelan 12 10
(A R Al Rayhi, UAE) *nvr bttr than mid-div* **20/1**
12 6 ¾ **Archer's Arrow (USA)**[8] 9738 5-8-13 **74**........ HarryBentley 4
(A bin Harmash, UAE) *s.i.s: a in rr* **28/1**
13 7 ¼ **Mightily**[44] 9222 5-9-5 **80**........(v) SamHitchcott 14
(Doug Watson, UAE) *nvr bttr than mid-div* **14/1**
14 15 **Samharry**[8] 9742 5-9-0 **75**........ PatCosgrave 13
(H Al Alawi, UAE) *a in rr* **28/1**

1m 25.62s (0.52) **Going Correction** +0.65s/f (Slow) **14 Ran SP% 134.4**
Speed ratings: **123,115,114,113,107 103,96,96,92,91 88,81,72,55**
CSF: 20.94; TRICAST: 107.39.
Owner Al Bait Mutawahed Team **Bred** Darley **Trained** United Arab Emirates

98 - (Foreign Racing) - See Raceform Interactive

[18]NEWCASTLE (A.W) (L-H)
Sunday, January 6

OFFICIAL GOING: Tapeta: standard to slow
Wind: Breezy, half against in races on straight course and in over 3f of races on the round course Weather: Cloudy, bright

99 BETWAY H'CAP 2m 56y (Tp)
1:00 (1:01) (Class 6) (0-65,67) 4-Y-O+
£3,493 (£1,039; £519; £400; £400; £400) **Stalls Low**

Form RPR
0/1- 1 **Grey Mist**[22] 9551 5-9-9 **58**........(h) JasonHart 7 65
(Karen McLintock) *dwlt: sn rcvrd to press ldr: led over 3f out to over 2f out: regained ld 1f out: styd on strly* **5/6[1]**
2/1- 2 1 ¼ **Shine Baby Shine**[15] 26 5-9-12 **61**........ JackMitchell 6 67
(Philip Kirby) *hld up: gd hdwy to chse ldrs over 5f out: led over 2f out to 1f out: kpt on same pce fnl 100yds* **5/1[2]**
423- 3 4 **Galileo's Spear (FR)**[10] 9721 6-10-4 **67**........(t) LukeMorris 8 68
(Sir Mark Prescott Bt) *hld up in tch: drvn and outpcd over 4f out: rallied and prom 2f out: kpt on same pce fnl f* **5/1[2]**
206- 4 2 ¾ **Highway Robber**[22] 9551 6-8-9 **49**........(t) PaulaMuir(5) 9 46
(Wilf Storey) *prom tl rdn and wknd fr over 1f out* **12/1[3]**
604- 5 nse **Dizoard**[60] 8319 9-8-10 **45**........ JoeFanning 5 42
(Iain Jardine) *t.k.h: hld up in tch: stdy hdwy over 2f out: rdn over 1f out: sn no imp* **22/1**
220- 6 3 ½ **Seasearch**[15] 9687 4-9-7 **61**........(p) GrahamLee 1 56
(Andrew Balding) *trckd ldrs: rdn over 2f out: wknd wl over 1f out* **20/1**
/66- 7 6 **Isharah (USA)**[18] 9623 6-9-5 **57**........(tp) OisinOrr(3) 2 43
(Noel C Kelly, Ire) *hld up: drvn and struggling over 4f out: nvr on terms* **18/1**
053/ 8 10 **Sigurd (GER)**[96] 3756 7-8-10 **45**........ BarryMcHugh 3 19
(Joanne Foster) *led to over 3f out: rdn and wknd over 2f out* **80/1**

3m 40.92s (5.92) **Going Correction** +0.15s/f (Slow)
WFA 4 from 5yo+ 5lb **8 Ran SP% 111.2**
Speed ratings (Par 101): **91,90,88,87,86 85,82,77**
CSF £4.79 CT £11.82 TOTE £1.70: £1.10, £1.70, £1.60; EX 6.30 Trifecta £19.40.
Owner Alan Lamont & Brian Chicken **Bred** David Jamison Bloodstock And G Roddick **Trained** Ingoe, Northumberland

FOCUS
The going was standard to slow.\n\x\x Stalls - Straight: centre; 1m2f & 1m4f: outside; 2m: inside\n\x\x Ordinary fare in this staying handicap. They did not go a great gallop, but the winner showed tenacity and is one to keep on side.

100 BETWAY HEED YOUR HUNCH AMATEUR RIDERS' H'CAP 1m 4f 98y (Tp)
1:30 (1:30) (Class 6) (0-60,60) 4-Y-O+
£3,369 (£1,044; £522; £400; £400; £400) **Stalls High**

Form RPR
205- 1 **Belabour**[128] 6765 6-10-11 **60**........ MissBeckyBrisbourne(3) 7 70
(Mark Brisbourne) *hld up in rr: stdy hdwy over 2f out: sustained run fnl f to ld nr fin* **11/2[2]**
210- 2 ½ **Nevada**[17] 9647 6-11-0 **60**........(b[1]) MrSimonWalker 4 69
(Steve Gollings) *hld up in midfield: smooth hdwy to trck ldrs over 3f out: led gng wl over 1f out: sn rdn clr: kpt on fnl f: hdd and no ex nr fin* **3/1[1]**
040- 3 6 **Hugoigo**[22] 9551 5-9-7 **46** oh1........ MissShannonWatts(7) 1 46
(Jim Goldie) *t.k.h: hld up: stdy hdwy over 2f out: effrt and chsd clr ldng pair over 1f out: sn no imp* **18/1**
000- 4 1 ¼ **Onda District (IRE)**[107] 7493 7-9-9 **46** oh1........ SophieSmith(5) 11 44
(Stella Barclay) *chsd ldr: led over 3f out to over 1f out: wknd ins fnl f* **28/1**
000- 5 1 ¾ **Kilcoran**[22] 9554 4-9-11 **46** oh1........ MrWilliamEasterby 9 43
(Philip Kirby) *hld up: stdy hdwy 3f out: effrt and edgd lft over 1f out: wknd ins fnl f* **16/1**
455- 6 2 ¾ **Something Brewing (FR)**[8] 9551 5-10-5 **58**........(p) MrNathanSeery(7) 8 50+
(Iain Jardine) *hld up: outpcd over 4f out: rallied against far rail 2f out: sn no imp* **6/1[3]**
060- 7 5 **Emperor Sakhee**[22] 9554 9-9-11 **46** oh1........(h) MrAaronAnderson(3) 12 30
(Karen McLintock) *hld up in midfield: hdwy and prom over 3f out: wknd over 1f out* **12/1**
604- 8 2 **Elite Icon**[22] 9551 5-10-0 **46** oh1........ MissCatherineWalton 3 27
(Jim Goldie) *trckd ldrs: rdn and outpcd over 2f out: sn btn* **8/1**
600- 9 1 ¾ **Hellavashock**[15] 6384 6-9-7 **46** oh1........(v) MrConnorWood(7) 2 25
(Alistair Whillans) *trckd ldrs tl rdn and wknd over 2f out* **80/1**
112/ 10 nk **Rainbow Lad (IRE)**[602] 2671 6-11-0 **60**........ MissSerenaBrotherton 10 38
(Michael Appleby) *hld up towards rr: hdwy and in tch over 3f out: rdn and wknd over 1f out* **6/1[3]**
100- 11 11 **Romantic (IRE)**[58] 8985 10-10-1 **52**........ CharlieTodd(5) 6 14
(Noel C Kelly, Ire) *hld up: struggling over 3f out: sn btn* **40/1**
060- 12 2 ½ **Cross Swords**[34] 9381 4-9-10 **52**........(p) MissRosieHowarth(7) 5 11
(Roger Fell) *t.k.h: led at decent gallop: clr 1/2-way: hdd over 3f out: wknd over 2f out* **14/1**

2m 43.51s (2.41) **Going Correction** +0.15s/f (Slow)
WFA 4 from 5yo+ 3lb **12 Ran SP% 112.7**
Speed ratings (Par 101): **98,97,93,92,91 89,86,85,84,83 76,74**
CSF £20.80 CT £273.45 TOTE £6.80: £1.90, £1.30, £5.70; EX 25.00 Trifecta £302.90.
Owner Mark Brisbourne **Bred** Darley **Trained** Great Ness, Shropshire

FOCUS
A moderate amateur riders' handicap which produced an exciting finish.

101 BETWAY LIVE CASINO H'CAP 1m 4f 98y (Tp)
2:00 (2:00) (Class 5) (0-70,71) 4-Y-O+
£4,140 (£1,232; £615; £400; £400; £400) **Stalls High**

Form RPR
052- 1 **Glan Y Gors (IRE)**[22] 9554 7-9-5 **65**........(p) CliffordLee 4 70
(David Thompson) *t.k.h: cl up: led over 1f out: rdn and hrd pressed fnl f: hld on wl cl home* **16/1**
414- 2 nk **Champarisi**[27] 9487 4-9-4 **67**........ JackMitchell 9 73
(Grant Tuer) *cl up: ev ch over 2f out: rdn and outpcd over 1f out: rallied to take 2nd cl home: jst hld* **3/1[3]**
012- 3 nk **Trautmann (IRE)**[22] 9551 5-9-9 **69**........(tp) AlistairRawlinson 7 74
(Rebecca Menzies) *t.k.h: hld up on outside: smooth hdwy to ld over 2f out: rdn and hdd over 1f out: rallied: no ex and lost 2nd* **5/2[2]**
125- 4 ¾ **Royal Cosmic**[161] 5518 5-9-0 **60**........ TonyHamilton 1 63
(Richard Fahey) *trckd ldrs: rdn whn n.m.r briefly over 2f out: rallied over 1f out: kpt on ins fnl f* **66/1**
315- 5 7 **Pammi**[22] 9554 4-8-4 **56**........ PhilDennis(3) 11 49
(Jim Goldie) *hld up: rdn and outpcd 3f out: rallied over 1f out: no imp fnl f* **12/1**
020- 6 1 ½ **French Heroine**[22] 9554 4-8-10 **59**........ JoeFanning 3 50
(Declan Carroll) *prom: effrt and rdn over 2f out: wknd over 1f out* **33/1**
0/1- 7 ½ **Isle Of Avalon (IRE)**[11] 9706 4-9-8 **71**........ LukeMorris 10 61
(Sir Mark Prescott Bt) *hld up in tch: effrt and rdn over 2f out: wknd over 1f out (jockey said filly ran flat)* **2/1[1]**
344- 8 9 **Middlescence (IRE)**[22] 9553 5-9-5 **65**........ KieranO'Neill 6 40
(Lucinda Egerton) *led to over 2f out: rdn and wknd over 1f out* **14/1**
9 14 **Fearaun (IRE)**[83] 8287 4-9-3 **66**........ JasonHart 5 19
(Stella Barclay) *hld up: drvn and struggling over 3f out: btn fnl 2f* **100/1**

2m 42.24s (1.14) **Going Correction** +0.15s/f (Slow)
WFA 4 from 5yo+ 3lb **9 Ran SP% 112.6**
Speed ratings (Par 103): **102,101,101,101,96 95,95,89,79**
CSF £61.99 CT £163.61 TOTE £17.40: £3.50, £1.20, £1.20; EX 95.90 Trifecta £502.40.
Owner B Lapham & J Souster **Bred** Colm McEvoy **Trained** Bolam, Co Durham

FOCUS
A fair middle-distance handicap which run saw the winner fend off the rallying runner-up.

102 BETWAY CASINO H'CAP 1m 2f 42y (Tp)
2:30 (2:31) (Class 5) (0-75,77) 4-Y-O+
£4,140 (£1,232; £615; £400; £400; £400) **Stalls High**

Form RPR
411- 1 **Elysees Palace**[247] 2391 5-9-8 **74**........ LukeMorris 1 83
(Sir Mark Prescott Bt) *hld up in tch: stdy hdwy 3f out: effrt and pushed along over 1f out: drvn to ld ins fnl f: styd on wl* **8/11[1]**
606- 2 ¾ **Dommersen (IRE)**[18] 9610 6-9-6 **77**........ BenSanderson(5) 8 84
(Roger Fell) *prom: smooth hdwy to ld over 2f out: rdn and hrd pressed over 1f out: hdd ins fnl f* **14/1**
452- 3 1 **Mr Carbonator**[19] 9595 4-9-1 **68**........ JackMitchell 6 74
(Philip Kirby) *hld up: hdwy over 2f out: rdn and ev ch over 1f out: one pce ins fnl f* **5/1[2]**
305- 4 3 ¾ **Rockwood**[122] 6978 8-9-4 **70**........(v) JasonHart 2 68
(Karen McLintock) *dwlt: hld up: hdwy to chse clr ldng trio over 1f out: no imp fnl f* **25/1**
501- 5 1 ¼ **Remmy D (IRE)**[61] 8900 4-8-11 **71**........ CoreyMadden(7) 7 67
(Jim Goldie) *dwlt: hld up: effrt and pushed along over 2f out: no imp fr over 1f out* **40/1**
016- 6 1 **God Willing**[17] 9642 8-9-6 **72**........(t) JoeFanning 9 65
(Declan Carroll) *t.k.h: hld up on outside: effrt over 2f out: no further imp fr over 1f out* **25/1**
550- 7 3 ¼ **Bahkit (IRE)**[32] 9410 5-8-12 **64**........ AndrewMullen 5 51
(Philip Kirby) *led 3f: cl up tl rdn and wknd over 1f out* **14/1**
612- 8 1 **Berlusca (IRE)**[20] 9585 10-8-4 **63**........ MarkCrehan(7) 3 48
(David Loughnane) *led after 3f: hdd over 2f out: wknd over 1f out* **25/1**
252- 9 1 **Mametz Wood (IRE)**[19] 9593 4-8-13 **73**........(p) JonathanFisher(7) 4 57
(K R Burke) *t.k.h: chsd ldrs: rdn and wknd over 2f out* **12/1[3]**

2m 9.34s (-1.06) **Going Correction** +0.15s/f (Slow)
WFA 4 from 5yo+ 1lb **9 Ran SP% 109.6**
Speed ratings (Par 103): **110,109,108,105,104 103,101,100,99**
CSF £10.47 CT £28.19 TOTE £1.60: £1.02, £2.40, £1.80; EX 11.50 Trifecta £46.90.
Owner J Fishpool - Osborne House **Bred** Meon Valley Stud **Trained** Newmarket, Suffolk

FOCUS
A fair handicap which saw the unexposed winner grind it out. The runner-up had dropped to a lenient mark so the form looks solid.

103 LADBROKES HOME OF THE ODDS BOOST NOVICE STKS 1m 2f 42y (Tp)
3:00 (3:01) (Class 5) 3-Y-O £4,140 (£1,232; £615; £307) Stalls High

Form				RPR
	1		**One Vision (IRE)** 3-9-2 0 ... JackMitchell 1 (Charlie Appleby) *hld up: stdy hdwy to chse ldr over 1f out: rdn and kpt on wl fnl f to ld cl home* 9/4[1]	85
5-	2	hd	**Top Power (FR)**[37] 9323 3-9-2 0 ... GrahamLee 8 (Andrew Balding) *t.k.h early: cl up: led after 1f: rdn over 1f out: kpt on fnl f: hdd cl home* 11/2	84
4-	3	2 3/4	**War Tiger (USA)**[50] 9131 3-9-2 0 ... TonyHamilton 6 (Richard Fahey) *t.k.h early: prom: effrt and pushed along 2f out: kpt on fnl f: nt pce of first two* 11/2	79
	4	1 1/4	**Miss Morocco** 3-8-11 0 ... RobertHavlin 2 (John Gosden) *t.k.h: hld up: stdy hdwy over 2f out: effrt over 1f out: no imp fnl f* 4/1[2]	71
13-	5	1 3/4	**Kheros**[20] 9590 3-9-7 0 ... EdwardGreatrex 4 (Archie Watson) *prom: rdn over 2f out: wknd fnl f* 9/2[3]	78
0-	6	3 1/4	**Trapani**[25] 9500 3-8-11 0 ... KieranO'Neill 5 (John Gosden) *led 1f: cl up tl rdn and wknd over 1f out* 15/2	61
6-	7	4 1/2	**Gate City (USA)**[17] 9635 3-9-2 0 ...(v[1]) AndrewMullen 7 (Adrian Nicholls) *dwlt: sn cl up: rdn over 2f out: wknd over 1f out* 100/1	57
	8	3/4	**Lizzie Loch** 3-8-11 0 ... CamHardie 3 (Alistair Whillans) *hld up: struggling over 3f out: sn btn* 66/1	51
0-	9	18	**Amber**[22] 9556 3-8-8 0 ... BenRobinson(3) 9 (Peter Niven) *hld up: rdn and struggling over 3f out: lost tch fnl 2f* 200/1	15

2m 11.15s (0.75) **Going Correction** +0.15s/f (Slow) 9 Ran SP% 114.5
Speed ratings (Par 97): **103,102,100,99,98 95,92,91,77**
CSF £15.08 TOTE £3.40: £1.10, £2.00, £1.80; EX 15.30 Trifecta £38.70.
Owner Godolphin **Bred** Godolphin **Trained** Newmarket, Suffolk
FOCUS
An interesting novice event containing some nicely-bred sorts so it would be no surprise to see the race throw up a few winners.

104 SUNRACING.CO.UK H'CAP 7f 14y (Tp)
3:30 (3:30) (Class 4) (0-80,82) 4-Y-O+
£6,727 (£2,002; £1,000; £500; £400; £400) Stalls Centre

Form				RPR
506-	1		**Made Of Honour (IRE)**[10] 9724 5-9-5 78 ...(p[1]) CliffordLee 4 (K R Burke) *t.k.h: hld up in tch: stdy hdwy to press ldr over 1f out: kpt on wl fnl f to ld cl home* 7/1	85
45-5	2	shd	**Call Out Loud**[5] 4 7-9-9 82 ...(vt) AlistairRawlinson 3 (Michael Appleby) *led: rdn over 1f out: kpt on fnl f: hdd cl home* 11/4[3]	89
010-	3	3	**Portledge (IRE)**[37] 9324 5-9-5 78 ...(b) JoeFanning 1 (James Bethell) *hld up in tch: stdy hdwy to trck ldrs over 1f out: rdn and one pce ins fnl f* 9/4[1]	77
000-	4	8	**Supreme Power (IRE)**[61] 8897 5-8-3 62 ...(p) LukeMorris 2 (Tracy Waggott) *prom: rdn over 2f out: wknd over 1f out* 14/1	39
2/0-	5	nk	**Fuwairt (IRE)**[74] 8557 7-9-0 80 ... MarkCrehan(7) 6 (David Loughnane) *dwlt: sn prom: rdn over 2f out: wknd over 1f out* 5/2[2]	56
000-	6	16	**Andalusite**[17] 9638 6-8-3 62 ...(v) AndrewMullen 5 (John Gallagher) *cl up: rdn and outpcd over 2f out: lost tch over 1f out* 40/1	

1m 26.44s (0.24) **Going Correction** +0.15s/f (Slow) 6 Ran SP% 107.6
Speed ratings (Par 105): **104,103,100,91,90 72**
CSF £24.25 TOTE £5.30: £2.50, £1.70; EX 19.10 Trifecta £62.40.
Owner Ontoawinner, D Mackay & Mrs E Burke **Bred** Limetree Stud **Trained** Middleham Moor, N Yorks
■ Stewards' Enquiry : Clifford Lee two-day ban: used whip above the permitted level (Jan 21-22)
FOCUS
A decent finale, but only half the field were involved in the finish and the winner showed plenty of resolution to prevail.
T/Plt: £18.30 to a £1 stake. Pool: £92,945.62 - 3,697.15 winning units T/Qpdt: £8.40 to a £1 stake. Pool: £7,467.68 - 654.67 winning units **Richard Young**

105a-114a (Foreign Racing) - See Raceform Interactive

76 DEAUVILLE (R-H)
Saturday, January 5

OFFICIAL GOING: Polytrack: standard

115a PRIX DE BEAUFOSSE (CLAIMER) (5YO+) (ALL-WEATHER TRACK) (POLYTRACK) 7f 110y(P)
10:45 5-Y-O+ £8,108 (£3,243; £2,432; £1,621; £810)

			RPR
1		**Acrux**[56] 8996 6-9-1 0 ... GlenBraem 4 (L Rovisse, France) 217/10	81
2	3/4	**Wow (GER)**[23] 5-9-8 0 ... ThomasTrullier 12 (Andreas Suborics, Germany) 3/1[2]	86
3	1 1/4	**Constantino (IRE)**[112] 7279 6-9-1 0 ... JeffersonSmith 3 (Mark Loughnane) *prom: outpcd and dropped into midfield over 3f out: drvn and styd on fr 1 1/2f out: chsd ldr into fnl f: kpt on at same pce: lost 2nd fnl 50yds* 14/5[1]	76
4	1 1/4	**Desert Heights (IRE)**[21] 9567 5-8-11 0 ... JeremieMonteiro 13 (Mme V Deiss, France) 55/1	69
5	shd	**Inglorious**[82] 8264 5-9-1 0 ...(b) PierreBazire 2 (E Lyon, France) 10/1	73
6	hd	**Saint Pois (FR)**[18] 8-9-4 0 ... FrankPanicucci 6 (J-P Sauvage, France) 26/5	75
7	3/4	**Beama (FR)**[21] 9567 6-9-2 0 ...(p) BenjaminHubert 11 (P Monfort, France) 48/10[3]	71
8	1 1/4	**Colibri Cael (FR)**[35] 7-8-11 0 ...(b) QuentinPerrette 10 (P Leblanc, France) 22/1	63
9	1 1/4	**Samagace Du Vivien (FR)** 5-8-11 0 ... JulienGuillochon 14 (S Gouvaze, France) 112/1	60
10	4 1/2	**Vitor (FR)**[275] 7-8-11 0 ...(p) EnzoCorallo 5 (O De Montzey, France) 23/1	49
11	2	**Magicienmake Myday**[22] 8-8-11 0 ...(b) EmmanuelEtienne 9 (H De Nicolay, France) 39/1	44
12	1	**Tallinski (IRE)**[94] 7903 5-9-1 0 ... GijsSnijders 8 (Stal Vie En Rose, Belgium) 27/1	45
13	4	**Pont Neuilly (FR)**[22] 9-8-11 0 ...(p) MarcNobili 1 (H De Nicolay, France) 15/1	31
14	1 3/4	**Bromley Cross (IRE)**[113] 6-8-11 0 ...(b) DamienGibelloSacco 7 (Emilie Varin, France) 160/1	27

1m 26.39s 14 Ran SP% 119.8
PARI-MUTUEL (all including 1 euro stake): WIN 22.70; PLACE 4.80, 1.70, 1.80; DF 45.50; SF 105.20.
Owner Willy Van Der Auwera **Bred** Niarchos Family **Trained** France

60 WOLVERHAMPTON (A.W) (L-H)
Monday, January 7

OFFICIAL GOING: Tapeta: standard
Wind: Fresh behind Weather: Overcast

116 LIKE SUN RACING ON FACEBOOK APPRENTICE H'CAP 7f 36y (Tp)
4:15 (4:15) (Class 6) (0-55,55) 4-Y-O+
£3,105 (£924; £461; £400; £400; £400) Stalls High

Form				RPR
4	1		**Taceec (IRE)**[3] 62 4-9-0 48 ... ConorMcGovern 2 (Adrian McGuinness, Ire) *a.p: swtchd rt over 1f out: rdn to chse ldr fnl f: styd on to ld towards fin* 7/2[2]	55+
00-3	2	3/4	**Dodgy Bob**[3] 60 6-9-0 48 ...(v) PhilDennis 6 (Michael Mullineaux) *a.p: chsd ldr over 5f out: led over 2f out: rdn over 1f out: edgd rt: hdd towards fin* 7/1	53
060-	3	nk	**Classy Cailin (IRE)**[52] 9098 4-9-4 52 ... EoinWalsh 5 (Mark Loughnane) *s.i.s: hld up: plld hrd: hdwy over 1f out: sn rdn: r.o* 25/1	56
050-	4	1 1/4	**Kellington Kitty (USA)**[26] 9504 4-9-1 52 ... TheodoreLadd(3) 1 (Mike Murphy) *hld up in tch: rdn over 1f out: styd on same pce ins fnl f* 12/1	53
000-	5	nk	**Shovel It On (IRE)**[28] 9483 4-9-2 50 ...(w) FinleyMarsh 10 (Steve Flook) *s.i.s: hld up: rdn and r.o ins fnl f: nt rch ldrs* 50/1	50
026-	6	hd	**Harbour Patrol (IRE)**[67] 8779 7-8-13 47 ...(b) BenRobinson 12 (Rebecca Bastiman) *hld up: hdwy over 1f out: r.o: nt rch ldrs* 20/1	47
000-	7	1/2	**Mr Andros**[18] 9634 6-8-11 50 ...(v) ScottMcCullagh(5) 4 (Brendan Powell) *chsd ldr tl over 5f out: remained handy: rdn over 1f out: edgd lft and styd on same pce ins fnl f* 10/1	49
4	8	3/4	**Piper Bomb (IRE)**[3] 60 4-9-2 50 ...(t[1]) WilliamCox 3 (Adrian McGuinness, Ire) *led: shkn up and hdd over 2f out: no ex ins fnl f* 3/1[1]	47
204-	9	1	**Malaysian Boleh**[10] 9734 9-8-6 47 ...(be) GraceMcEntee(7) 7 (Phil McEntee) *s.i.s: pushed along early in rr: shkn up over 2f out: n.d* 8/1	41
000-	10	1 3/4	**Castlerea Tess**[11] 9720 6-8-13 50 ...(p) GabrieleMalune(3) 8 (Sarah Hollinshead) *hld up: rdn over 2f out: hung lft ins fnl f: n.d* 25/1	40
000-	11	2	**Tidal Surge (IRE)**[25] 9527 4-9-7 55 ... JaneElliott 11 (Les Eyre) *trckd ldrs: pushed along 1/2-way: wknd over 1f out* 100/1	40
503-	12	3 1/4	**Musbaq (USA)**[17] 9660 4-8-11 52 ...(p) TristanPrice(7) 9 (Ben Haslam) *s.i.s: hdwy over 5f out: pushed along 1/2-way: wknd over 1f out (trainer rep could offer no explanation for gelding's poor performance other than it stopped quickly. post-race examination failed to reveal any abnormalities)* 5/1[3]	29

1m 28.43s (-0.37) **Going Correction** -0.15s/f (Stan) 12 Ran SP% 119.7
Speed ratings (Par 101): **96,95,94,93,93 92,92,91,90,88 85,82**
CSF £26.96 CT £539.91 TOTE £3.00: £1.40, £2.90, £6.50; EX 32.10 Trifecta £575.70.
Owner Taceec Syndicate **Bred** Aidan Connolly **Trained** Lusk, Co Dublin
FOCUS
A weak handicap. The form has a straightforward feel.

117 SUN RACING TOP TIPS & PREVIEWS NOVICE STKS 7f 36y (Tp)
4:45 (4:46) (Class 5) 4-Y-O+ £3,752 (£1,116; £557; £278) Stalls High

Form				RPR
346-	1		**Blame Culture (USA)**[105] 7606 4-9-2 77 ... DavidProbert 9 (George Margarson) *hld up: racd keenly: hdwy and edgd lft over 2f out: swtchd rt wl over 1f out: sn shkn up and edgd lft: rdn to ld wl ins fnl f: styd on* 4/5[1]	74
61/	2	1/2	**Followthesteps (IRE)**[560] 4160 4-9-9 0 ... TonyHamilton 7 (Ivan Furtado) *chsd ldr 1f: remained handy: led over 1f out: rdn: edgd lft and hdd wl ins fnl f: styd on* 4/1[2]	79
4-	3	2 1/2	**Orient Express**[20] 9594 4-9-2 0 ... BarryMcHugh 6 (Richard Fahey) *hld up: hdwy over 1f out: styd on same pce wl ins fnl f* 7/1[3]	65
5-	4	1/2	**My Town Chicago (USA)**[23] 9565 4-9-2 0 ... JackMitchell 10 (Kevin Frost) *s.i.s: hld up: hdwy over 1f out: sn rdn: styd on same pce ins fnl f* 25/1	64
	5	shd	**Master Diver** 4-9-2 0 ... LukeMorris 5 (Sir Mark Prescott Bt) *s.i.s and swvd lft s: bhd: pushed along: nt clr run and swtchd rt over 2f out: hdwy and hung lft fr over 1f out: r.o: nt rch ldrs* 8/1	64+
505-	6	9	**Mystical Moon (IRE)**[18] 9645 4-8-8 42 ...(v[1]) PhilDennis(3) 2 (David C Griffiths) *led: hdd over 5f out: led again 3f out: rdn and hdd over 1f out: wknd fnl f* 50/1	34
/5-	7	1/2	**Purbeck Gem**[111] 7402 5-8-4 0 ... RPWalsh(7) 11 (Robyn Brisland) *s.i.s: rcvrd to ld over 5f out: hdd 3f out: rdn over 2f out: wknd fnl f* 33/1	33
53/	8	4	**Strawberryandcream**[410] 8914 4-8-11 0 ... NicolaCurrie 8 (James Bethell) *s.i.s: nvr on terms* 14/1	22
50-	9	nse	**Lambrini Lullaby**[20] 9594 4-8-7 0 ow1 ... KevinLundie(5) 4 (Lisa Williamson) *prom: rdn over 2f out: wknd over 1f out* 100/1	23
00-	10	3/4	**Geneva Trumpet**[65] 8824 8-8-9 0 ... HarryRussell(7) 1 (Seb Spencer) *s.i.s: sn pushed along and a in rr* 100/1	25
00-	11	27	**Suttonwood Sally**[31] 9445 5-8-11 0 ... KieranO'Neill 3 (Geoffrey Deacon) *prom: pushed along 1/2-way: nt clr run and stmbld over 2f out: sn wknd and eased (vet said mare lost left fore shoe)* 100/1	

1m 27.57s (-1.23) **Going Correction** -0.15s/f (Stan) 11 Ran SP% 117.6
Speed ratings (Par 103): **101,100,97,97,96 86,86,81,81,80 49**
CSF £3.93 TOTE £1.60: £1.30, £1.40, £1.70; EX 4.70 Trifecta £18.10.
Owner Mangiacapra, Hill, Hook Partnership **Bred** Summerhill Farm **Trained** Newmarket, Suffolk

FOCUS
This was run at a solid gallop. It's ordinary novice form, with little depth, and the winner did not need to match his best to get off the mark.

118 BETWAY SPRINT H'CAP 5f 21y (Tp)
5:15 (5:15) (Class 6) (0-55,55) 4-Y-O+

£3,105 (£924; £461; £400; £400; £400) Stalls Low

Form RPR

00-1 1 **Captain Ryan**[5] 26 8-9-6 54 6ex..........................(p) KieranO'Neill 1 62
(Geoffrey Deacon) *trckd ldrs: swtchd rt over 1f out: rdn and r.o to ld towards fin* 4/1[3]

441- 2 3/4 **Alaskan Bay (IRE)**[17] 9668 4-9-7 55........................ MartinHarley 2 60
(Rae Guest) *led 1f: led again 2f out: rdn over 1f out: hdd towards fin* 3/1[1]

26-2 3 hd **Storm Trooper (IRE)**[5] 26 8-8-12 46........................(t) DavidProbert 6 51
(Charlie Wallis) *chsd ldrs: led 4f out: hdd 2f out: rdn and ev ch ins fnl f: unable qck nr fin* 3/1[1]

323- 4 2 3/4 **Red Stripes (USA)**[11] 9722 7-8-11 52........................(b) ElishaWhittington(7) 4 47
(Lisa Williamson) *prom: hmpd over 3f out: rdn over 1f out: nt pce to chal (jockey said gelding ran too freely)* 7/2[2]

000- 5 hd **Barnsdale**[18] 9641 6-8-5 46 oh1........................ MeganEllingworth(7) 5 40
(Steph Hollinshead) *hld up: r.o ins fnl f: nvr nrr* 50/1

00-0 6 1/2 **Shesthedream (IRE)**[5] 26 6-8-13 47........................(p[1]) CamHardie 9 39
(Lisa Williamson) *s.i.s and hmpd s: hld up: plld hrd: rdn over 1f out: r.o ins fnl f: nvr on terms (jockey said mare ran too freely)* 33/1

456- 7 nk **Zipedeedodah (IRE)**[35] 9379 7-9-3 51........................ NicolaCurrie 8 42
(Joseph Tuite) *s.i.s and edgd rt s: in r: r.o ins fnl f: nvr nrr* 7/1

003- 8 2 1/4 **Celerity (IRE)**[7] 9777 5-8-7 46 oh1........................(p) KevinLundie(5) 11 29
(Lisa Williamson) *hld up: effrt on outer 1/2-way: nt trble ldrs* 33/1

00-0 9 nk **Whispering Soul (IRE)**[5] 28 6-8-12 46 oh1........................(b) LukeMorris 7 28
(Brian Baugh) *prom: pushed along over 3f out: wknd fnl f* 25/1

605- 10 2 1/2 **Beaming**[107] 7547 5-8-12 46 oh1........................ RobHornby 3 19
(Peter Hiatt) *chsd ldrs: rdn over 1f out: wknd fnl f* 25/1

600- 11 3 **Minty Jones**[61] 8935 10-8-9 46 oh1........................(v) PhilDennis(3) 10 8
(Michael Mullineaux) *s.i.s and edgd lft s: sn chsng ldrs: rdn and wknd over 1f out* 100/1

1m 1.0s (-0.90) **Going Correction** -0.15s/f (Stan) 11 Ran SP% 121.2
Speed ratings (Par 101): **101,99,99,95,94 93,93,89,89,85 80**
CSF £16.06 CT £42.71 TOTE £5.30: £1.70, £1.40, £1.50; EX 19.40 Trifecta £63.50.
Owner R J Douglas **Bred** Mrs C Lloyd **Trained** Compton, Berks

FOCUS
The pace held up pretty well here.

119 BETWAY LIVE CASINO H'CAP 1m 5f 219y (Tp)
5:45 (5:45) (Class 5) (0-75,75) 4-Y-O+

£3,752 (£1,116; £557; £400; £400; £400) Stalls Low

Form RPR

412- 1 **Given Choice (IRE)**[18] 9639 4-9-8 75........................ JackMitchell 5 86
(Simon Crisford) *chsd ldr: led on bit over 3f out: pushed clr over 2f out: eased towards fin* 1/1[1]

056- 2 5 **Falcon Cliffs (IRE)**[19] 9608 5-8-12 66........................ PoppyBridgwater(5) 4 70
(Tony Carroll) *s.i.s: hld up: hdwy and nt clr run over 2f out: rdn to go 2nd 1f out: no ch w wnr* 8/1[3]

624- 3 3 **Tidal Watch (IRE)**[19] 9608 5-9-9 72........................(p[1]) FranBerry 6 72
(Jonjo O'Neill) *prom: rdn over 3f out: chsd wnr over 2f out: sn outpcd: lost 2nd 1f out* 3/1[2]

331- 4 8 **Yasir (USA)**[23] 9562 11-8-7 56........................ DavidProbert 2 45
(Sophie Leech) *s.s: hld up: hdwy over 4f out: wknd over 2f out (jockey said gelding hung right-handed)* 8/1[3]

000- 5 shd **Dream Magic (IRE)**[52] 9100 5-9-3 66........................ AndrewMullen 1 54
(Mark Loughnane) *led: rdn and hdd over 3f out: wknd 2f out* 12/1

000- 6 122 **Jack Bear**[28] 9487 8-9-8 71........................(v[1]) RobertWinston 3
(Roger Teal) *chsd ldrs: pushed along 5f out: wknd over 3f out (jockey said gelding moved poorly and stopped quickly. post-race examination failed to reveal any abnormalities)* 14/1

2m 57.83s (-3.17) **Going Correction** -0.15s/f (Stan)
WFA 4 from 5yo+ 4lb 6 Ran SP% 111.6
Speed ratings (Par 103): **103,100,98,93,93**
CSF £9.76 TOTE £1.50: £1.30, £3.70; EX 7.60 Trifecta £16.60.
Owner Moulton Stud Partnership **Bred** Shadwell Estate Company Limited **Trained** Newmarket, Suffolk

FOCUS
This proved very straightforward for the favourite, who built on her recent form.

120 BETWAY CASINO H'CAP 1m 1f 104y (Tp)
6:15 (6:15) (Class 6) (0-60,60) 4-Y-O+

£3,105 (£924; £461; £400; £400; £400) Stalls Low

Form RPR

/43- 1 **Bollihope**[304] 1097 7-9-7 60........................ RobertHavlin 3 74
(Shaun Keightley) *a.p: chsd ldr 2f out: led over 1f out: rdn clr* 5/1[2]

101- 2 5 **False Id**[12] 9703 6-9-5 58........................(b) DavidProbert 13 62
(David Loughnane) *hld up: hdwy over 1f out: r.o to go 2nd wl ins fnl f: no ch w wnr* 8/1

402- 3 3/4 **Arrowzone**[12] 9703 8-9-6 59........................(b) JasonHart 6 62
(Kevin Frost) *trckd ldrs: racd keenly: rdn and hmpd over 1f out: styd on same pce fnl f* 5/1[2]

261- 4 nk **Champagne Rules**[12] 9704 8-9-4 60........................ PhilDennis(3) 7 62
(Sharon Watt) *s.i.s: hld up: swtchd rt and hdwy over 1f out: rdn and hung rt ins fnl f: nt rch ldrs (jockey said gelding hung right-handed)* 4/1[1]

600- 5 nk **La Sioux (IRE)**[30] 9465 5-9-2 55........................(b[1]) TonyHamilton 4 56
(Richard Fahey) *led: rdn and hdd over 1f out: no ex ins fnl f* 16/1

5- 6 1 1/4 **Kodi Koh (IRE)**[12] 9704 4-9-0 54........................ JFEgan 1 53
(David Evans) *hld up in tch: rdn and edgd rt over 1f out: no ex ins fnl f* 8/1

334- 7 4 1/2 **Final Attack (IRE)**[12] 9703 8-8-11 53........................(p) GabrieleMalune(3) 11 44
(Sarah Hollinshead) *s.i.s: hld up: rdn over 1f out: nvr on terms* 11/2[3]

350- 8 1 3/4 **Lifeboat (IRE)**[20] 8335 4-8-13 53........................ LukeMorris 5 40
(Kevin Frost) *hld up: rdn over 2f out: wknd over 1f out* 33/1

/64- 9 7 **Midnight Vixen**[24] 9531 5-9-6 59........................ StevieDonohoe 10 33
(David Simcock) *hld up in tch: drvn along on outer over 2f out: wknd over 1f out* 16/1

605- 10 1 1/4 **Takiah**[47] 9180 4-8-6 46........................ AndrewMullen 12 18
(Peter Hiatt) *s.i.s: hld up: a in rr* 25/1

600- 11 nse **Beadlam (IRE)**[20] 9600 6-8-8 52........................(p) BenSanderson(5) 8 23
(Roger Fell) *sn chsng ldr: rdn and ev ch over 2f out: wknd over 1f out* 25/1

600- 12 20 **Island Flame (IRE)**[51] 9136 6-9-3 56........................(p) RobertWinston 9
(Les Eyre) *racd keenly: prom: rdn over 2f out: sn wknd (jockey said mare stopped quickly. vet said mare had finished lame on left hind)* 20/1

1m 58.17s (-2.63) **Going Correction** -0.15s/f (Stan)
WFA 4 from 5yo+ 1lb 12 Ran SP% 118.1
Speed ratings (Par 101): **105,100,99,99,99 98,94,92,86,85 85,67**
CSF £42.23 CT £212.66 TOTE £6.30: £2.10, £2.60, £1.80; EX 56.00 Trifecta £249.90.
Owner Simon Lockyer **Bred** Minster Stud And Mrs H Dalgety **Trained** Newmarket, Suffolk

FOCUS
An ordinary handicap, but it was won well. The winner looks to have rediscovered his 2017 level.

121 BETWAY CONDITIONS STKS 1m 1f 104y (Tp)
6:45 (6:45) (Class 2) 4-Y-O+ £11,971 (£3,583; £1,791; £896; £446) Stalls Low

Form RPR

023- 1 **Hathal (USA)**[22] 9571 7-9-1 107........................ NicolaCurrie 1 100
(Jamie Osborne) *trckd ldrs: wnt 2nd over 3f out: rdn to ld over 1f out: hung lft ins fnl f: r.o* 6/4[1]

244- 2 2 3/4 **Goring (GER)**[16] 9685 7-9-1 102........................(v) CharlesBishop 3 94
(Eve Johnson Houghton) *hld up in tch: shkn up over 2f out: rdn over 1f out: styd on to go 2nd wl ins fnl f* 13/8[2]

11-6 3 1/2 **Michele Strogoff**[5] 29 6-9-1 87........................ AlistairRawlinson 6 93
(Michael Appleby) *led: clr over 6f out tl over 2f out: rdn and hdd over 1f out: styd on same pce ins fnl f* 6/1[3]

004- 4 1 **Dragon Mall (USA)**[34] 9390 6-9-1 87........................(t) StevieDonohoe 4 91
(Rebecca Menzies) *s.i.s: hld up: hdwy and edgd lft over 1f out: r.o: nt rch ldrs* 33/1

500- 5 12 **Gold Hunter (IRE)**[111] 7391 9-9-1 76........................ FinleyMarsh 5 66
(Steve Flook) *sn chsng ldr: lost 2nd over 3f out: sn rdn: wknd over 1f out* 66/1

000- 6 1 1/2 **Carry On Deryck**[319] 851 7-9-1 107........................(w) BenRobinson 2 63
(Ollie Pears) *prom: lost pl 7f out: shkn up over 3f out: hung rt and wknd over 2f out (jockey said gelding hung right-handed throughout)* 10/1

1m 57.18s (-3.62) **Going Correction** -0.15s/f (Stan) 6 Ran SP% 105.9
Speed ratings (Par 109): **110,107,107,106,95 94**
CSF £3.65 TOTE £2.10: £1.10, £1.30; EX 3.70 Trifecta £5.40.
Owner Dr A Sedrati and Partner **Bred** Tenth Street Stables Llc **Trained** Upper Lambourn, Berks

FOCUS
A bit of a tactical affair. It's rated around the third and the form isn't rock solid.

122 LADBROKES HOME OF THE ODDS BOOST H'CAP 1m 1f 104y (Tp)
7:15 (7:16) (Class 6) (0-65,67) 3-Y-O

£3,105 (£924; £461; £400; £400; £400) Stalls Low

Form RPR

052- 1 **Hermocrates (FR)**[31] 9444 3-9-7 65........................ RossaRyan 6 70
(Richard Hannon) *chsd ldrs: rdn and edgd lft over 1f out: r.o u.p to ld nr fin* 5/2[1]

603- 2 hd **Navadir (JPN)**[25] 9522 3-9-5 66........................(t) GabrieleMalune(3) 5 70
(Marco Botti) *hld up in tch: lost pl 7f out: hdwy 2f out: chsd ldr over 1f out: rdn to ld ins fnl f: edgd lft: hdd nr fin* 5/1[3]

022- 3 2 1/4 **Fenjal (IRE)**[9] 9744 3-9-9 67........................(p) LukeMorris 3 67
(Hugo Palmer) *led: drvn along fr over 3f out: hdd and no ex ins fnl f* 4/1[2]

506- 4 1/2 **Margaret J**[27] 9489 3-8-2 46 oh1........................(p) NicolaCurrie 9 45
(Phil McEntee) *hld up: hdwy and nt clr run over 1f out: r.o: nt rch ldrs* 33/1

00- 5 nk **Tails I Win (CAN)**[33] 9411 3-8-11 60........................ BenSanderson(5) 7 58
(Roger Fell) *s.i.s: hld up: hdwy over 1f out: r.o: nrst fin* 25/1

004- 6 2 1/4 **Lethal Guest**[19] 9611 3-9-5 66........................ BenRobinson(3) 1 60
(Ollie Pears) *chsd ldrs: rdn over 1f out: no ex ins fnl f* 6/1

403- 7 2 3/4 **Peters Pudding (IRE)**[21] 9591 3-9-4 62........................(b) JFEgan 2 51
(David Evans) *plld hrd: w ldr 1f: remained handy: rdn over 1f out: wknd fnl f* 7/1

060- 8 2 **George Hastings**[27] 9489 3-8-3 47........................ AndrewMullen 4 32
(K R Burke) *s.i.s: hdwy over 4f out: rdn over 3f out: wknd wl over 1f out* 12/1

004- 9 1 1/4 **Vin D'Honneur (IRE)**[38] 9325 3-8-10 54........................(v) FranBerry 10 37
(Stuart Williams) *s.i.s: pushed along to go prom 7f out: chsd ldr over 6f out: rdn over 1f out: hmpd and wknd sn after* 12/1

2m 0.24s (-0.56) **Going Correction** -0.15s/f (Stan) 9 Ran SP% 114.2
Speed ratings (Par 95): **96,95,93,93,93 91,88,86,85**
CSF £14.86 CT £47.54 TOTE £2.40: £1.10, £2.80, £1.50; EX 18.20 Trifecta £97.60.
Owner Michael Pescod **Bred** D R Tucker & Silfield Bloodstock **Trained** East Everleigh, Wilts
■ Stewards' Enquiry : Gabriele Malune caution: careless riding

FOCUS
A modest affair, but the first two were unexposed and look open to further improvement.

123 LADBROKES FILLIES' H'CAP 7f 36y (Tp)
7:45 (7:46) (Class 5) (0-75,75) 4-Y-O+

£3,752 (£1,116; £557; £400; £400; £400) Stalls High

Form RPR

301- 1 **Zafaranah (USA)**[44] 9257 5-9-6 74........................ RobHornby 1 82
(Pam Sly) *hld up in tch: nt clr run over 1f out: rdn to ld ins fnl f: hung rt: drvn out* 7/4[1]

555- 2 shd **Zoraya (FR)**[12] 9702 4-9-7 75........................(t[1]) RaulDaSilva 2 82
(Paul Cole) *hld up: hdwy over 1f out: rdn to chse wnr ins fnl f: sn ev ch: r.o* 7/2[2]

236- 3 2 3/4 **Elenora Delight**[18] 9638 4-9-1 69........................(t) MarcMonaghan 3 69
(Marco Botti) *s.i.s: sn prom: rdn over 1f out: hmpd ins fnl f: styd on same pce* 5/1[3]

023- 4 shd **Wind Storm**[20] 9594 4-8-8 62........................ JasonHart 8 61
(K R Burke) *prom: chsd ldr over 5f out: led over 1f out: rdn and hdd ins fnl f: hmpd sn after: styd on same pce* 14/1

560- 5 1/2 **Thorntoun Lady (USA)**[19] 9617 9-8-2 56 oh1........................ NicolaCurrie 7 54
(Jim Goldie) *hld up: carried wd over 2f out: r.o ins fnl f: nvr nrr* 25/1

000- 6 1 1/2 **Rizzle Dizzle**[192] 4344 4-8-12 66........................ CamHardie 4 60
(Rebecca Menzies) *chsd ldr tl over 5f out: remained handy: rdn over 1f out: no ex ins fnl f* 50/1

235- 7 2 1/2 **Curious Fox**[33] 9404 6-9-4 72........................ DavidProbert 9 59
(Anthony Carson) *s.i.s: hld up: hdwy over 1f out: wknd wl ins fnl f* 16/1

5/0- 8 2 1/2 **Queens Care (IRE)**[35] 9380 4-8-7 61........................ KieranO'Neill 6 41
(Julie Camacho) *plld hrd and prom: stdd and lost pl over 5f out: rdn and hung rt over 2f out: sn wknd* 50/1

612- 9 3 1/2 **Wirral Girl (IRE)**[33] 9404 4-9-7 75........................ LukeMorris 5 46
(Denis Quinn) *sn led: rdn and hdd over 1f out: wknd ins fnl f (jockey said filly ran too freely)* 10/1

042- R **One More Chance (IRE)**[20] 9600 4-8-8 **62**.................. AndrewMullen 10
(Michael Appleby) *ref to r* **8/1**
1m 28.17s (-0.63) **Going Correction** -0.15s/f (Stan) **10** Ran SP% **115.8**
Speed ratings (Par 100): **97,96,93,93,93 91,88,85,81,**
CSF £7.47 CT £24.52 TOTE £2.30: £1.30, £1.70, £3.20; EX 7.70 Trifecta £26.20.
Owner Pam's People **Bred** Shadwell Farm LLC **Trained** Thorney, Cambs
■ Stewards' Enquiry : Rob Hornby two-day ban: careless riding (Jan 21-22)

FOCUS
This was steadily run and developed into a dash for home from the turn in. The winner found a bit extra on her November win.
T/Plt: £14.00 to a £1 stake. Pool: £105,623.22 - 5,472.65 winning units T/Qpdt: £3.70 to a £1 stake. Pool: £15,007.03 - 2,995.00 winning units **Colin Roberts**

[99]NEWCASTLE (A.W) (L-H)

Tuesday, January 8

OFFICIAL GOING: Tapeta: standard
Wind: Light against Weather: Fine

124 BETWAY LIVE CASINO H'CAP — 2m 56y (Tp)
3:40 (3:40) (Class 5) (0-75,77) 4-Y-0+
£4,140 (£1,232; £615; £400; £400; £400) **Stalls** Low

Form RPR
231- **1** **Loud And Clear**[20] 9610 8-9-7 **77**.................. PhilDennis(3) 6 84
(Jim Goldie) *hld up: pushed along and hdwy on outer over 2f out: rdn to chal appr fnl f: led ins fnl f: styd on: pushed out towards fin* **7/4**[1]
304- **2** ½ **Ajman Prince (IRE)**[20] 9610 6-9-10 **77**.................. PJMcDonald 4 83
(Alistair Whillans) *in tch: smooth hdwy 3f out: led 2f out: sn edgd rt and rdn: pressed appr fnl f: drvn and hdd ins fnl f: styd on* **9/4**[2]
342- **3** 5 **River Glades**[189] 4507 4-9-4 **76**.................. JamesSullivan 2 76
(Tom Tate) *led: rdn and hdd 2f out: no ex in 3rd fr appr fnl f* **14/1**
012- **4** 1¼ **Lopes Dancer (IRE)**[20] 9610 7-9-6 **73**.................. AlistairRawlinson 5 72
(Harriet Bethell) *in tch: lost pl sltly over 5f out: rdn over 2f out: plugged on fnl f: nvr a threat* **3/1**[3]
650- **5** shd **River Dart (IRE)**[57] 5898 7-9-2 **69**..................(w) RobertWinston 1 67
(Tony Carroll) *trckd ldrs: rdn along 3f out: outpcd 2f out: plugged on ins fnl f* **28/1**
230- **6** 7 **Archive (FR)**[20] 9610 9-9-1 **71**.................. BenRobinson(3) 3 61
(Brian Ellison) *hld up: rdn over 2f out: wknd over 1f out* **16/1**
3m 32.68s (-2.32) **Going Correction** +0.225s/f (Slow) **6** Ran SP% **108.1**
WFA 4 from 6yo+ 5lb
Speed ratings (Par 103): **114,113,111,110,110 107**
CSF £5.44 TOTE £3.20: £1.70, £1.40; EX 6.70.
Owner Mr & Mrs Philip C Smith **Bred** Philip Newton **Trained** Uplawmoor, E Renfrews

FOCUS
Dry, windy conditions following just a millimetre of rain on Monday. The stalls were in the centre for all races bar this long-distance opener (inner), which was run at just a steady tempo until well past halfway. The winner continues to progress, and the runner-up is rated to form.

125 SUNRACING.CO.UK H'CAP — 1m 5y (Tp)
4:10 (4:12) (Class 6) (0-65,69) 4-Y-0+
£3,493 (£1,039; £519; £400; £400; £400) **Stalls** Centre

Form RPR
36P- **1** **Servo (IRE)**[151] 5976 5-9-6 **63**.................. CallumRodriguez 14 73
(Lynn Siddall) *hld up: racd keenly: gd hdwy towards nr side over 1f out: pushed along to ld 110yds out: edgd lft: kpt on wl* **14/1**
00-1 **2** ¾ **Paparazzi**[6] 22 4-9-12 **69** 6ex.................. PJMcDonald 1 77
(Tracy Waggott) *hld up: gd hdwy towards far side over 1f out: pushed along to ld narrowly 1f out: rdn and hdd 110yds out: kpt on* **6/4**[1]
160- **3** 2 **King Oswald (USA)**[13] 9703 6-9-2 **59**..................(tp) LiamJones 2 63
(James Unett) *trckd ldrs: rdn to ld narrowly appr fnl f: hdd 1f out: one pce* **17/2**[3]
055- **4** ½ **Don't Be Surprised**[54] 9086 4-8-10 **56**..................(p[1]) BenRobinson(3) 5 59
(Seb Spencer) *dwlt: sn in midfield racing keenly: shuffled towards rr over 4f out: pushed along and hdwy appr fnl f: short of room ins fnl f and swtchd lft: rdn and kpt on wl (jockey said gelding was denied a clear run inside the final furlong)* **28/1**
303- **5** ½ **Traveller (FR)**[34] 9410 5-9-3 **60**..................(t) CamHardie 11 62
(Antony Brittain) *midfield: hdwy 2f out: rdn and ev ch 1f out: no ex ins fnl f* **9/1**
204- **6** ½ **Corked (IRE)**[20] 9614 6-9-3 **60**.................. DougieCostello 13 61
(Alistair Whillans) *dwlt: hld up: rdn 2f out: kpt on ins fnl f* **12/1**
144- **7** ½ **Silverturnstogold**[49] 9166 4-9-4 **61**.................. FrannyNorton 12 61
(Tony Carroll) *sn trckd ldrs racing keenly: rdn 2f out: no ex ins fnl f* **13/2**[2]
441- **8** ½ **Squire**[59] 8998 8-9-3 **60**..................(tp) LukeMorris 3 59
(Marjorie Fife) *led narrowly: rdn 2f out: hdd appr fnl f: sn no ex* **9/1**
526- **9** 1¾ **Somewhere Secret**[20] 9614 5-9-5 **62**..................(p) JamesSullivan 7 57
(Michael Mullineaux) *trckd ldrs: keen early: rdn over 2f out: wknd ins fnl f* **11/1**
060- **10** ¾ **Kingofmerrows (IRE)**[19] 9634 5-9-2 **59**..................(p) CliffordLee 4 52
(Karen Tutty) *prom: rdn along over 2f out: wkng and btn whn hmpd 110yds out* **25/1**
020- **11** 1½ **Military Madame (IRE)**[91] 8069 4-9-5 **62**.................. JasonHart 8 52
(John Quinn) *midfield: racd quite keenly: pushed along 3f out: wknd fnl f* **50/1**
460- **12** 11 **Prancing Oscar (IRE)**[88] 8159 5-9-7 **64**..................(p) AndrewMullen 6 30
(Ben Haslam) *trckd ldrs: pushed along over 3f out: wknd over 1f out* **14/1**
000- **13** ½ **Cosmic Ray**[66] 8828 7-9-0 **57**..................(h) JoeFanning 10 21
(Les Eyre) *trckd ldrs: racd keenly: pressed ldr 5f out: lost pl 2f out and wknd qckly* **50/1**
1m 41.58s (2.98) **Going Correction** +0.225s/f (Slow) **13** Ran SP% **124.4**
Speed ratings (Par 101): **94,93,91,90,90 89,89,88,87,86 84,73,73**
CSF £35.84 CT £214.03 TOTE £14.40: £4.70, £1.30, £3.60; EX 51.40 Trifecta £380.40.
Owner Jimmy Kay **Bred** Finbar & Noel O'Reilly **Trained** Colton, N Yorks
■ Valentino Boy was withdrawn, price at time of withdrawal 20/1. Rule 4 does not apply.

FOCUS
A moderate but competitive straight mile handicap, in which the initial pace was ordinary. The first two were produced on opposite sides of the track. The form is taken at face value.

126 LADBROKES HOME OF THE ODDS BOOST H'CAP — 7f 14y (Tp)
4:45 (4:47) (Class 3) (0-90,87) 3-Y-O **£11,026** (£3,300; £1,650; £826; £411) **Stalls** Centre

Form RPR
223- **1** **Zip**[28] 9490 3-8-6 **72**.................. BarryMcHugh 2 77
(Richard Fahey) *trckd ldrs: racd keenly: rdn to ld over 1f out: drvn and kpt on wl* **9/4**[2]
401- **2** 1¾ **Mardle**[39] 9323 3-9-0 **80**.................. CliffordLee 3 80
(K R Burke) *hld up: pushed along and hdwy 2f out: rdn to chal appr fnl f: one pce fnl 110yds* **15/8**[1]
113- **3** ½ **Woodside Wonder**[9] 9762 3-9-7 **87**..................(p) CallumRodriguez 1 86
(Keith Dalgleish) *wnt lft s but sn led: rdn over 2f out: hdd over 1f out: drvn and sn outpcd: plugged on fnl f* **11/2**
230- **4** ½ **Material Girl**[18] 9669 3-8-7 **73**..................(p) LukeMorris 4 71
(Richard Spencer) *prom: pushed along over 2f out: hung lft and sn outpcd: rdn over 1f out: plugged on fnl f* **10/1**
041- **5** 17 **Seductive Moment (GER)**[8] 9770 3-8-13 **79** 6ex.................. JoeFanning 5 31
(Mark Johnston) *dwlt: sn trckd ldrs: rdn over 2f out: wknd over 1f out (trainers' rep could offer no explanation for the poor performance)* **9/2**[3]
1m 27.85s (1.65) **Going Correction** +0.225s/f (Slow) **5** Ran SP% **108.2**
Speed ratings (Par 101): **99,97,96,95,76**
CSF £6.62 TOTE £3.00: £2.20, £1.30; EX 7.00 Trifecta £18.90.
Owner The Knavesmire Partnership **Bred** Worksop Manor Stud **Trained** Musley Bank, N Yorks

FOCUS
Tightly knit on the face of it, with only 1lb separating the quintet on adjusted RPRs, but not a conspicuously strong event for the class with only one competitor rated fewer than 10lb below the ceiling. Once again, the initial pace was nothing special. The third helps set the standard.

127 BETWAY SPRINT H'CAP — 5f (Tp)
5:15 (5:15) (Class 3) (0-95,97) 4-Y-0+ **£11,320** (£3,368; £1,683; £841) **Stalls** Centre

Form RPR
612- **1** **Outrage**[32] 9446 7-9-4 **90**..................(b) KieranO'Neill 1 99
(Daniel Kubler) *midfield: pushed along and hdwy appr fnl f: led ins fnl f: sn rdn: wandered sltly but kpt on wl* **11/2**[2]
016- **2** ¾ **Foolaad**[73] 8632 8-9-10 **96**..................(t) LiamKeniry 9 102
(Roy Bowring) *prom: rdn 2f out: kpt on* **9/2**[1]
200- **3** ½ **Equitation**[88] 8167 5-8-9 **81**..................(t[1]) MartinDwyer 4 85+
(Stuart Williams) *s.i.s: hld up in rr: pushed along 3f out: sme hdwy over 1f out: rdn and kpt on wl fnl f: nrst fin* **9/1**
26-2 **4** hd **Watchable**[7] 3 9-9-4 **90**..................(p) JoeFanning 8 93
(David O'Meara) *led: pushed along over 2f out: rdn over 1f out: hdd ins fnl f: no ex* **13/2**[3]
551- **5** ½ **Primo's Comet**[68] 8784 4-8-4 **79**..................(p) PhilDennis(3) 3 81
(Jim Goldie) *hld up: rdn over 1f out: kpt on ins fnl f: nvr a threat* **11/1**
000- **6** nk **Bengali Boys (IRE)**[39] 9324 4-8-13 **85**.................. TonyHamilton 10 86
(Richard Fahey) *chsd ldrs: rdn 2f out: one pce* **14/1**
303- **7** 1 **Boom The Groom (IRE)**[134] 6620 8-9-3 **89**..................(w) RobertWinston 5 86
(Tony Carroll) *chsd ldrs: rdn 2f out: no ex ins fnl f* **8/1**
313- **8** ¾ **El Hombre**[9] 9763 5-9-7 **93**.................. CallumRodriguez 2 87
(Keith Dalgleish) *prom: rdn 2f out: wknd ins fnl f* **9/2**[1]
130- **9** ½ **Dynamo Walt (IRE)**[18] 9667 8-9-1 **87**..................(v) PaddyMathers 7 80
(Derek Shaw) *midfield: rdn 2f out: wknd fnl f* **33/1**
054- **10** 2 **Atletico (IRE)**[13] 9707 7-9-4 **97**.................. KatherineBegley(7) 6 82
(David Evans) *midfield: rdn 2f out: wknd fnl f* **9/1**
59.18s (-0.32) **Going Correction** +0.225s/f (Slow) **10** Ran SP% **114.1**
Speed ratings (Par 107): **111,109,109,108,107 107,105,104,103,100**
CSF £29.77 CT £223.11 TOTE £4.70: £1.70, £1.90, £3.60; EX 31.40 Trifecta £430.70.
Owner Capture The Moment Vi **Bred** Trickledown Stud Limited **Trained** Lambourn, Berks

FOCUS
A nicely competitive sprint handicap for the grade, and a decent pace on from the outset. The winner is getting back towards his old best.

128 LADBROKES NOVICE STKS (PLUS 10 RACE) — 1m 5y (Tp)
5:45 (5:46) (Class 4) 3-Y-O **£6,727** (£2,002; £1,000; £500) **Stalls** Centre

Form RPR
1- **1** **Set Piece**[27] 9499 3-9-9 0.................. LukeMorris 2 89+
(Hugo Palmer) *dwlt: sn trckd ldrs: led gng wl 2f out: sn jnd: pushed clr ins fnl f: readily* **1/1**[1]
2 3 **Sparkle In His Eye** 3-9-2 0.................. JoeFanning 1 75+
(William Haggas) *dwlt: hld up: rdn along and hdwy over 2f out: jnd ldr over 1f out: kpt on but sn outpcd by wnr ins fnl f* **9/2**[3]
0- **3** 2½ **Social Network (IRE)**[41] 9290 3-8-11 0.................. PJMcDonald 5 64+
(James Tate) *trckd ldrs: pushed along over 2f out: chal 2f out: one pce in 3rd fnl f* **33/1**
3- **4** 4½ **Sils Maria**[66] 8826 3-8-11 0.................. FrannyNorton 3 53
(Ann Duffield) *hld up: pushed along over 2f out: kpt on fnl f: nvr involved* **100/1**
- **5** ¾ **Will Of Iron** 3-9-2 0.................. RobertHavlin 4 56+
(John Gosden) *dwlt: hld up: reminder and green early: hdwy and trckd ldrs over 5f out: pushed along over 2f out: sn outpcd and btn* **3/1**[2]
4- **6** 3 **Lilligram**[26] 9522 3-8-11 0.................. JackMitchell 7 44
(Roger Varian) *led: rdn and hdd 2f out: sn wknd* **6/1**
7 19 **Initial Approach (IRE)** 3-8-8 0.................. BenRobinson(3) 6
(Alan Brown) *prom: pushed along over 2f out: wknd and bhd* **250/1**
1m 42.35s (3.75) **Going Correction** +0.225s/f (Slow) **7** Ran SP% **111.8**
Speed ratings (Par 99): **90,87,84,80,79 76,57**
CSF £5.71 TOTE £1.70: £1.10, £2.70; EX 6.00 Trifecta £44.50.
Owner K Abdullah **Bred** Juddmonte Farms (east) Ltd **Trained** Newmarket, Suffolk

FOCUS
Not that deep a novice event by any means, and a winning time 0.77 seconds slower than the earlier 0-65, but the winner will have learned plenty. The first two are both well related and capable of better.

129 BETWAY CASINO H'CAP — 5f (Tp)
6:15 (6:15) (Class 6) (0-60,60) 4-Y-0+
£3,493 (£1,039; £519; £400; £400; £400) **Stalls** Centre

Form RPR
54-6 **1** **Archimedes (IRE)**[5] 42 6-9-5 **58**..................(tp) RobertWinston 12 66
(David C Griffiths) *prom: pushed along 2f out: rdn to ld 110yds out: kpt on* **8/1**

405- **2** 1 **Steelriver (IRE)**^{124} 7002 9-9-7 **60**........ JasonHart 6 64
(Michael Herrington) *hld up: pushed along and hdwy appr fnl f: kpt on wl fnl f: wnt 2nd towards fin* **8/1**

00-1 **3** 1 **Encoded (IRE)**^{6} 25 6-8-12 **51** 6ex........ JoeFanning 4 52
(Lynn Siddall) *midfield: pushed along and hdwy over 1f out: rdn and kpt on fnl f* **7/1**^{3}

50-2 **4** 1/2 **Novabridge**^{6} 25 11-8-5 **47**........(b) PhilDennis$^{(3)}$ 1 46
(Karen Tutty) *led: pushed along 2f out: rdn and hdd 110yds out: no ex* **8/1**

04-6 **5** nk **Windforpower (IRE)**^{6} 25 9-9-0 **53**........(v) BarryMcHugh 2 51
(Tracy Waggott) *chsd ldrs: rdn 2f out: one pce* **6/1**^{2}

335- **6** nk **Cherry Oak (IRE)**^{62} 8928 4-9-7 **60**........ GrahamLee 7 57
(Ben Haslam) *midfield: rdn along 2f out: kpt on same pce fnl f* **6/1**^{2}

000- **7** 3/4 **Argon**^{19} 9641 4-8-7 **46** oh1........(p) AndrewMullen 3 40
(Noel Wilson) *in tch: rdn and outpcd over 1f out: plugged on fnl f* **80/1**

50-3 **8** 1/2 **Poppy In The Wind**^{6} 25 7-9-4 **57**........(v) CamHardie 9 49
(Alan Brown) *s.i.s: hld up: pushed along 3f out: kpt on ins fnl f: nvr involved* **5/1**^{1}

30-0 **9** 1/2 **Star Cracker (IRE)**^{6} 25 7-8-12 **51**........(p) PJMcDonald 11 42
(Jim Goldie) *chsd ldrs: rdn along 2f out: sn outpcd and no threat after* **6/1**^{2}

40-0 **10** 1 **Fuel Injection**^{6} 25 8-8-11 **50**........(p) JamesSullivan 8 37
(Ruth Carr) *dwlt: hld up: nvr threatened* **40/1**

/00- **11** 1/2 **Sir Walter (IRE)**^{18} 9659 4-8-7 **46** oh1........ RachelRichardson 10 31
(Eric Alston) *midfield: rdn 2f out: wknd fnl f* **25/1**

644- **12** nk **Amazing Amaya**^{130} 6749 4-8-10 **49**........(h) PaddyMathers 5 33
(Derek Shaw) *hld up: rdn over 1f out: edgd lft and sn btn* **33/1**

1m 0.11s (0.61) **Going Correction** +0.225s/f (Slow) **12** Ran SP% **115.8**
Speed ratings (Par 101): **104,102,100,100,99 99,97,97,96,94 93,93**
CSF £66.93 CT £478.47 TOTE £10.30: £3.00, £3.20, £2.30; EX 85.30 Trifecta £1181.50.
Owner Ladies And The Tramps **Bred** Paddy Twomey & Irish National Stud **Trained** Bawtry, S Yorks

FOCUS
A decent pace throughout but a winning time just under a second slower than that of the earlier 0-95 sprint feature, and relatively few got into it. The winner figured on a good mark.

130 LADBROKES HOME OF THE ODDS BOOST NOVICE STKS 5f (Tp)
6:45 (6:45) (Class 5) 3-Y-O £4,140 (£1,232; £615; £307) **Stalls** Centre

Form RPR

12- **1** **Lorna Cole (IRE)**^{38} 9353 3-9-4 0........ MartinDwyer 2 74
(William Muir) *trckd ldrs: led gng wl 2f out: pressed ent fnl f: rdn and kpt on* **4/6**^{1}

04- **2** 1/2 **Kyllachy Warrior (IRE)**^{18} 9671 3-8-13 0........ PhilDennis$^{(3)}$ 3 70
(Lawrence Mullaney) *hld up in tch: pushed along and hdwy over 1f out: rdn to chal ent fnl f: kpt on* **11/1**

3 nk **Olympic Spirit** 3-9-2 0........ PJMcDonald 5 69
(David Barron) *dwlt: sn chsd ldrs: pushed along and bit outpcd 2f out: rdn and kpt on wl fnl f* **7/1**^{3}

000- **4** 7 **White Iverson (IRE)**^{19} 9646 3-9-2 67........(b) LukeMorris 6 44
(Richard Spencer) *led: rdn and hdd 2f out: wknd ins fnl f* **25/1**

6- **5** 3 **Shug**^{34} 9394 3-9-2 0........ LiamKeniry 4 33
(Ed Walker) *prom: pushed along over 2f out: wknd over 1f out* **10/3**^{2}

64- **6** nk **Chillon Castle**^{10} 9745 3-8-8 0........ ConorMcGovern$^{(3)}$ 1 27
(David O'Meara) *s.i.s: hld up: pushed along over 2f out: rdn over 1f out: wknd* **50/1**

1m 1.15s (1.65) **Going Correction** +0.225s/f (Slow) **6** Ran SP% **109.7**
Speed ratings (Par 97): **95,94,93,82,77 77**
CSF £8.85 TOTE £1.60: £1.10, £4.70; EX 7.10 Trifecta £21.90.
Owner John O'Mulloy **Bred** J Waldron & J Barton **Trained** Lambourn, Berks

FOCUS
In all likelihood a moderate novice event, and slower than the preceding low-grade handicap by over a second. The form's rated around the 1-2.

131 BETWAY SPRINT H'CAP 5f (Tp)
7:15 (7:18) (Class 5) (0-75,76) 4-Y-O+
£4,140 (£1,232; £615; £400; £400; £400) **Stalls** Centre

Form RPR

235- **1** **Pea Shooter**^{41} 9288 10-9-3 **71**........ CallumRodriguez 9 79
(Brian Ellison) *trckd ldrs: rdn to ld 1f out: kpt on* **11/1**

22-2 **2** 1/2 **First Excel**^{5} 42 7-8-12 **66**........(b) EoinWalsh 7 72
(Roy Bowring) *prom: rdn over 1f out: kpt on* **6/1**^{3}

205- **3** 1 1/2 **Miracle Works**^{25} 9536 4-9-2 **70**........ LiamKeniry 3 71
(Ed Walker) *midfield: rdn over 1f out: kpt on fnl f* **9/1**

000- **4** nse **Jan Van Hoof (IRE)**^{41} 9288 8-9-4 **72**........(h) BarryMcHugh 5 73
(Michael Herrington) *dwlt: hld up: pushed along and hdwy over 1f out: rdn and kpt on fnl f* **22/1**

302- **5** 1/2 **Wiff Waff**^{41} 9288 4-9-6 **74**........ PJMcDonald 2 73+
(Stuart Williams) *dwlt: hld up: rdn over 1f out: swtchd lft ins fnl f: r.o fnl 110yds: nrst fin* **11/2**^{2}

212- **6** nse **Another Angel (IRE)**^{24} 9558 5-9-1 **69**........ CamHardie 8 68
(Antony Brittain) *led: drvn over 1f out: hdd 1f out: wknd fnl 110yds* **7/2**^{1}

014- **7** 1 1/2 **Laubali**^{11} 9733 4-9-8 **76**........(p) JoeFanning 1 70
(David O'Meara) *hld up in midfield: rdn along 2f out: no imp* **9/1**

035- **8** 1 1/2 **Lord Of The Glen**^{29} 9486 4-9-1 **72**........(b) PhilDennis$^{(3)}$ 6 62
(Jim Goldie) *hld up in midfield: pushed along over 2f out: outpcd and btn over 1f out* **8/1**

60-0 **9** 1 1/2 **Fink Hill (USA)**^{5} 43 4-8-9 **63**........(p^{1}) LukeMorris 4 48
(Richard Spencer) *trckd ldrs: rdn along over 2f out: wknd over 1f out* **25/1**

59.97s (0.47) **Going Correction** +0.225s/f (Slow) **9** Ran SP% **99.5**
Speed ratings (Par 103): **105,104,101,101,100 100,98,96,93**
CSF £55.84 CT £386.94 TOTE £9.90: £2.80, £2.20, £2.60; EX 58.10 Trifecta £973.20.
Owner Mrs Andrea Mallinson **Bred** R F And S D Knipe **Trained** Norton, N Yorks

■ Casterbridge was withdrawn, price at time of withdrawal 11/2. Rule 4 applies to all bets. Deduction of 15p in the pound.
■ Stewards' Enquiry : Eoin Walsh two-day ban; misuse of whip (Jan 22-23)

FOCUS
It paid to sit just off the early leaders in this competitive but modest finale. This was up with the winner's best form since 2016. Casterbridge proved unruly at the start and cannot run again until passing a stalls test.
T/Jkpt: Not Won. T/Plt: £71.30 to a £1 stake. Pool: £82,124.25 - 840.02 winning units T/Qpdt: £25.50 to a £1 stake. Pool: £10,947.73 - 316.91 winning units **Andrew Sheret**

^{78}KEMPTON (A.W) (R-H)
Wednesday, January 9

OFFICIAL GOING: Polytrack: standard to slow
Wind: Clear Weather: Cold

132 TALKSPORT H'CAP 7f (P)
4:15 (4:16) (Class 7) (0-50,50) 4-Y-O+ £2,587 (£770; £384; £192) **Stalls** Low

Form RPR

344- **1** **Cool Echo**^{42} 9286 5-9-4 **48**........(p) DavidProbert 8 58
(J R Jenkins) *racd in rr-div: shkn up and tk clsr order 3f out: effrt bhd ldr 2f out: led over 1f out where briefly pressed: asserted fnl f and rdn out* **8/1**^{3}

603- **2** 2 1/2 **Admirable Art (IRE)**^{39} 9356 9-9-6 **50**........ AdamKirby 6 54
(Tony Carroll) *hld up in rr on inner: shkn up 3f out: rdn to chse wnr over 1f out and briefly chal: no imp sn after and shuffled along last 150yds* **5/2**^{1}

005- **3** 4 1/2 **Star Attraction (FR)**^{164} 5531 4-8-13 **48**........ PoppyBridgwater$^{(5)}$ 1 40
(Tony Carroll) *bhd ldrs: effrt out wd wl over 2f out: plugged on one pce: tk 3rd wl ins fnl f* **8/1**^{3}

034- **4** 1 1/4 **Fairway To Heaven (IRE)**^{25} 9559 10-8-11 **46**........(t^{1}) RhiainIngram$^{(5)}$ 10 35
(Paul George) *racd in mid-div: rdn over 2f out: plugged on in dual for 3rd ent fnl f: no ex last 100yds* **14/1**

366- **5** shd **Be Bold**^{116} 7309 7-9-2 **46**........(b) CharlesBishop 7 34
(Rebecca Bastiman) *sn led: 3 l clr 3f out: effrt over 2f out: no ex over 1f out and hdd: plugged on tl wknd qckly ins fnl f* **10/1**

200- **6** nk **Makofitwhatyouwill**^{19} 9660 4-9-6 **50**........ JamesSullivan 9 38
(Ruth Carr) *outpcd in rr: effrt 3f out: sme prog ent fnl f* **18/1**

000- **7** nse **Whatdoesnotkillyou**^{102} 7753 5-9-6 **50**........ PJMcDonald 12 37
(John Mackie) *pushed along leaving stalls: in rr: effrt wl over 3f out: no imp in st* **8/1**^{3}

000- **8** 9 **Shifting Star (IRE)**^{36} 9387 14-9-5 **49**........(vt) KieranO'Neill 5 13
(John Bridger) *bhd ldr: effrt 3f out: nt qckn and wknd fr 2f out* **25/1**

500- **P** **Father McKenzie**^{21} 9602 5-9-6 **50**........ LukeMorris 2
(James Eustace) *bhd ldrs: wnt wrong 4f out and immediately eased: p.u and dismntd 3f out* **11/4**^{2}

1m 26.47s (0.47) **Going Correction** -0.025s/f (Stan) **9** Ran SP% **113.4**
Speed ratings (Par 97): **96,93,88,86,86 86,86,75,**
CSF £27.80 CT £167.43 TOTE £6.10: £1.80, £1.20, £2.40; EX 19.30 Trifecta £123.20.
Owner M K P Turner **Bred** Michael Turner **Trained** Royston, Herts

FOCUS
A moderate affair, but it was run at a good gallop.

133 32RED ON THE APP STORE NOVICE STKS 1m (P)
4:45 (4:47) (Class 5) 3-Y-O £3,881 (£1,155; £577; £288) **Stalls** Low

Form RPR

3- **1** **Creationist (USA)**^{28} 9499 3-9-2 0........ AdamMcNamara 2 83
(Roger Charlton) *bhd ldrs on inner: effrt in centre 2f out: kpt on wl over 1f out and narrowly led jst ins fnl f in three-way fin: jst hld on* **5/1**^{3}

32- **2** shd **Enchanting Man**^{12} 9730 3-9-2 0........ AdamKirby 3 82+
(Charlie Appleby) *covered up bhd ldrs: rdn on outer and chal over 1f out: sltly intimidated by eventual 3rd and edgd lft to stands' side rail: ev ch in three-way fin thrght fnl f and tk 2nd post: jst failed* **3/1**^{2}

02- **3** shd **White Coat**^{13} 9725 3-9-2 0........ RobertHavlin 6 82
(John Gosden) *narrowly led: shkn up 2f out: rdn over 1f out and hung lft: hdd jst ins fnl fbut stl ev ch in three-way fin: kpt on wl tl lost 2nd post (jockey said colt hung left-handed from entering the home straight)* **13/8**^{1}

4 9 **Kingdom Of Dubai (FR)** 3-9-2 0........ JackMitchell 5 61
(Roger Varian) *cl up chsng ldrs: cl enough whn rdn over 2f out: plugged on one pce over 1f out* **25/1**

32- **5** 1 **Fox Kasper (IRE)**^{29} 9490 3-9-2 0........ RyanMoore 8 59
(Richard Hannon) *w ldr on outer: pushed along over 3f out: no imp and one pce over 1f out* **10/1**

- **6** 1/2 **Lady Mascara** 3-8-11 0........ PJMcDonald 13 52+
(James Fanshawe) *s.s: in rr: effrt over 2f out w a bit to do: pleasing hdwy fr over 1f out: nvr nrr* **125/1**

7 2 **Dobrianka** 3-8-11 0........ DavidProbert 9 48
(Ralph Beckett) *bhd ldrs but w no cover and rn green thrght: effrt over 2f out: again rn green and shuffled along after: can do bttr* **20/1**

8 1 3/4 **Yvette** 3-8-11 0........ LukeMorris 7 44
(Sir Mark Prescott Bt) *hld up in rr-div: green and niggled along 4f out: shuffled along over 2f out* **6/1**

- **9** 1/2 **Breakfast Time** 3-8-11 0........ EdwardGreatrex 12 43
(Archie Watson) *racd in mid-div between horses: rdn over 2f out: no imp 2f out* **66/1**

10 2 3/4 **Capofaro** 3-9-2 0........ NicolaCurrie 11 41
(Jamie Osborne) *s.s and in rr: rdn along over 3f out: plugged on in st (jockey said gelding was slowly away and ran green)* **50/1**

11 1 1/2 **Spotton (IRE)** 3-9-2 0........ FranBerry 4 38
(William Haggas) *s.s: in rr-div: rn green and racd on and off the bit for 2f: effrt over 3f out: sn hld* **16/1**

12 3/4 **Evie May** 3-8-11 0........ FrannyNorton 14 31
(Mick Channon) *a in rr: t.k.h at times: no ex fr 2f out* **100/1**

1m 38.92s (-0.88) **Going Correction** -0.025s/f (Stan) **12** Ran SP% **122.9**
Speed ratings (Par 97): **103,102,102,93,92 92,90,88,88,85 83,83**
CSF £20.43 TOTE £7.40: £1.70, £1.20, £1.10; EX 24.20 Trifecta £49.00.
Owner Nick Bradley Racing 38 & Sohi **Bred** Courtlandt Farm **Trained** Beckhampton, Wilts

FOCUS
The first three finished well clear and had a good battle. There's a doubt over the depth of the race.

134 WISE BETTING AT RACINGTV.COM H'CAP 1m (P)
5:15 (5:15) (Class 5) (0-75,76) 3-Y-O
£3,752 (£1,116; £557; £400; £400; £400) **Stalls** Low

Form RPR

006- **1** **Alkaamel**^{105} 7669 3-8-10 **64**........ FranBerry 3 72+
(William Haggas) *t.k.h in rr-div on inner: shkn up over 2f out and smooth hdwy: rdn to ld wl over 1f out: drvn out fnl f: comf (trainers' rep could offer no explanation for the app imp in form)* **2/1**^{1}

025- **2** 2 1/4 **Spirit Warning**^{157} 5770 3-9-4 **75**........ JoshuaBryan$^{(3)}$ 6 77
(Andrew Balding) *bhd ldrs and t.k.h early: travelling wl on heels waiting for gap jst over 2f out: rdn 2f out to chse wnr: briefly threatened ent fnl f: sn hld* **11/2**^{3}

The Form Book Flat 2019, Raceform Ltd, Newbury, RG14 5SJ

330- **3** ½ **Four Mile Bridge (IRE)**[77] 8553 3-9-2 **70**.................... RobertWinston 2 71
(Charles Hills) *hld up in rr: prog gng wl over 2f out: rdn 2f out: kpt on wl fnl f to press runner-up last 100yds* **10/1**

600- **4** 3¾ **Sir Ox (USA)**[55] 9085 3-8-4 **58**..(p¹) LukeMorris 9 50
(Robert Cowell) *t.k.h bhd ldrs tl briefly led after 2f: settled bhd ldrs after: effrt on outer over 2f out: no imp over 1f out and plugged on one pce* **50/1**

600- **5** hd **Quduraat**[29] 9490 3-8-13 **67**.. AlistairRawlinson 1 59
(Michael Appleby) *hld up in rr-div: rdn over 2f out: one pce over 1f out* **66/1**

462- **6** 1 **Emma Point (USA)**[20] 9637 3-9-2 **70**......................(h) MarcMonaghan 10 59
(Marco Botti) *t.k.h and plld way into narrow ld gng into first bnd: shkn up 2f out: wnr sn wnt by: plugged on one pce after* **13/2**

006- **7** 1¾ **Classic Star**[19] 9669 3-8-8 **65**.. JackDuern(3) 8 50
(Dean Ivory) *hld up in rr-div and racd wd: pushed along on outer over 2f out: ev ch whn rdn 2f out: sn dropped out* **10/1**

366- **8** 7 **Love Kisses (IRE)**[21] 9611 3-9-1 **69**................................ PJMcDonald 7 38
(Mark Johnston) *hld up in rr-div: pushed along over 3f out: no imp fr 2f out* **20/1**

055- **9** 5 **Numero Uno**[26] 9530 3-9-1 **69**..(b¹) RobHornby 4 27
(Martyn Meade) *pushed along leaving stalls: tk fierce hold in rr-div and rapid prog on outer to dispute ld after 2f: rdn over 2f out and wknd sn after (trainers' rep could offer no explanation for the poor performance)* **3/1²**

1m 39.41s (-0.39) **Going Correction** -0.025s/f (Stan) **9** Ran SP% **113.4**
Speed ratings (Par 97): **100,97,97,93,93 92,90,83,78**
CSF £12.92 CT £86.41 TOTE £2.60: £1.10, £2.00, £3.50; EX 13.00 Trifecta £90.50.
Owner Hamdan Al Maktoum **Bred** Coln Valley Stud **Trained** Newmarket, Suffolk

FOCUS
Nothing really wanted to go on and it was a messy early gallop.The first three are all bred to do better.

135 32RED CASINO H'CAP 1m 2f 219y(P)
5:45 (5:46) (Class 5) (0-70,70) 4-Y-0+

£3,752 (£1,116; £557; £400; £400; £400) **Stalls** Low

Form RPR

440- **1** **My Brother Mike (IRE)**[83] 8349 5-8-13 **62**.................... PJMcDonald 12 70
(Kevin Frost) *hld up in last: shkn up wl over 2f out and swtchd to outer: plenty to do whn stylish prog over 1f out: qcknd up wl ent fnl f and edgd rt: upsides last 100yds and drvn to ld cl home: easily* **16/1**

163- **2** ¾ **Unit Of Assessment (IRE)**[33] 9447 5-9-6 **69**..............(vt) AdamKirby 11 76
(William Knight) *bhd ldr: rdn to ld 2f out: kpt on wl and two l up 1f out: chal last 100yds: stuck on tl hdd cl home* **7/2¹**

006- **3** 1¾ **Mary Elise (IRE)**[32] 9464 4-9-1 **66**.................................. CharlesBishop 10 70
(Eve Johnson Houghton) *cl up on outer: rdn 2f out: kpt on to take 3rd fnl f* **16/1**

422- **4** ½ **Beauty Salon**[10] 9766 4-9-2 **67**......................................(t) DavidProbert 6 70
(James Fanshawe) *s.s: hld up in rr: rdn over 2f out: no ch w ldng paid and plugged on fnl f (jockey said filly was slowly away)* **6/1³**

321- **5** hd **Magic Mirror**[35] 9400 6-9-7 **70**..(p) RobHornby 1 73+
(Mark Rimell) *racd in rr-div on inner: rdn 2f out: kpt on wl fnl f* **7/2¹**

030- **6** 1¾ **Mood For Mischief**[28] 9510 4-8-12 **63**.............................. LiamKeniry 2 63
(Ed Walker) *hld up in rr-div and t.k.h: rdn over 2f out w a bit to do: kpt on wl fnl f* **9/1**

050- **7** nk **Gendarme (IRE)**[26] 9535 4-9-4 **69**.................................... RossaRyan 5 68
(Richard Hannon) *racd bhd ldrs: rdn over 2f out: plugged on fr over 1f out* **20/1**

8 1¼ **Distingo (IRE)**[13] 6-9-7 **70**..(p) HectorCrouch 3 67
(Gary Moore) *racd in mid-div on inner: niggled along to hold pl fr 5f out: effrt over 3f out: plugged on* **5/1²**

534- **9** hd **Rainbow Jazz (IRE)**[18] 9687 4-8-12 **63**........................(be) CharlieBennett 9 60
(Adam West) *led: rdn over 2f out: hdd 2f: wknd ent fnl f* **22/1**

/40- **10** 2½ **Royal Goldie (IRE)**[239] 2738 4-9-3 **68**........................(t¹ w) RobertHavlin 8 61
(Lydia Richards) *chsd ldr: rdn over 2f out: no imp over 1f out* **66/1**

650- **11** ¾ **Global Style (IRE)**[116] 7282 4-9-4 **69**............................ GeorgeDowning 7 60
(Tony Carroll) *hld up in rr-div: shkn up over 2f out: travelling okay but n.m.r on heels over 1f out: eased fnl f (jockey said gelding hung badly right-handed throughout)* **16/1**

000- **12** 9 **Sonnetist**[25] 6687 5-9-7 **70**..(v¹) FranBerry 4 46
(David Evans) *pushed along leaving stalls and briefly led: sn bhd ldr: rdn 2f out and gng okay: emptied qckly (jockey said gelding stopped quickly)* **16/1**

2m 20.75s (-0.25) **Going Correction** -0.025s/f (Stan)
WFA 4 from 5yo+ 2lb **12** Ran SP% **119.5**
Speed ratings (Par 103): **103,102,101,100,100 99,99,98,98,96 95,89**
CSF £70.64 CT £941.95 TOTE £27.10: £5.70, £1.80, £5.60; EX 121.00 Trifecta £1236.80.
Owner J T Stimpson **Bred** D & J Dwan **Trained** Newcastle-under-Lyme, Staffs

FOCUS
They went an honest pace and four of the first six were at the back of the field turning in.

136 32RED CONDITIONS STKS 6f (P)
6:15 (6:15) (Class 2) 4-Y-0+ **£15,562** (£4,660; £2,330; £1,165; £582) **Stalls** Low

Form RPR

/00- **1** **Keystroke**[342] 517 7-9-2 103...(t¹) PJMcDonald 4 109
(Stuart Williams) *hld up in last: shkn up and smooth hdwy over 1f out: cl up whn effrt between horses 1f out: sn led: kpt on wl last 100yds: jst hld on* **11/2³**

112- **2** shd **Cenotaph (USA)**[91] 8103 7-9-2 108.................................... RyanMoore 5 108
(Jeremy Noseda) *hld up in 4th: pushed along over 1f out on outer: no immediate imp tl kpt on wl ins fnl f: jst failed* **8/11¹**

022- **3** 1½ **Gulliver**[14] 9707 5-9-2 102..(tp) AdamKirby 6 103
(David O'Meara) *bhd ldr on outer: rdn 2f out: briefly led 1f out: sn dropped to 3rd* **11/1**

233- **4** ¾ **Danzan (IRE)**[14] 9707 4-9-2 99.. DavidProbert 2 100
(Andrew Balding) *led: rdn 2f out: pressed either side over 1f out: hdd 1f out and no imp after* **12/1**

610- **5** 1¼ **Corinthia Knight (IRE)**[19] 9667 4-9-5 109.................. EdwardGreatrex 3 99
(Archie Watson) *bhd ldr on inner: rdn over 2f out: briefly threatened over 1f out: no ex 1f out and plugged on (jockey said gelding hung left-handed under pressure)* **4/1²**

1m 13.06s (-0.04) **Going Correction** -0.025s/f (Stan) **5** Ran SP% **109.3**
Speed ratings (Par 109): **99,98,96,95,94**
CSF £9.98 TOTE £8.50: £3.50, £1.10; EX 10.20 Trifecta £53.20.
Owner Front Runner Racing III **Bred** Cheveley Park Stud Ltd **Trained** Newmarket, Suffolk

FOCUS
A good race and a smart performance from the winner, who at the age of seven was having his first start in a sprint. The form could be rated a bit better through the third and fourth.

137 32RED.COM H'CAP 6f (P)
6:45 (6:47) (Class 6) (0-60,60) 3-Y-0

£3,105 (£924; £461; £400; £400; £400) **Stalls** Low

Form RPR

604- **1** **Halle's Harbour**[25] 9566 3-8-12 **51**..............................(v) EdwardGreatrex 1 58
(Paul George) *racd in mid-div on inner: niggled along to go pce at times: shkn up and gd prog over 2f out: rdn 2f out and led over 1f out: rdn out fnl f* **7/2²**

500- **2** 2 **Delagate The Lady**[12] 9729 3-8-9 **48**.............................. KierenFox 8 49
(Michael Attwater) *hld up in rr-div: shkn up over 2f out: rdn 2f out: kpt on to take 2nd cl home* **16/1**

226- **3** nk **Nananita (IRE)**[42] 9289 3-9-4 **57**................................... LiamJones 5 57
(Mark Loughnane) *t.k.h to post: racd bhd clr ldr: lft in ld over 2f out: rdn 2f out: hdd over 1f out: plugged on but lost 2nd cl home* **9/4¹**

040- **4** nk **Cherry Cola**[172] 5225 3-8-13 **52**.................................. CallumShepherd 2 51
(Mick Channon) *hld up in rr: outpcd wl over 3f out: plenty to do 2f out: stuck on fr over 1f out: nrst fin* **7/1**

664- **5** nk **Quicksilver**[21] 9612 3-9-7 **60**.. LiamKeniry 9 58
(Ed Walker) *bhd ldrs: rdn over 2f out: kpt on one pce fr over 1f out* **7/1**

003- **6** 1¼ **Zeebad (IRE)**[22] 9598 3-8-7 **46**.................................(b) LukeMorris 10 43
(Paul D'Arcy) *racd in mid-div: shkn up over 2f out: prog travelling wl whn checked and veered lft over 1f out: lost ch and shuffled along after* **10/1**

006- **7** ½ **Wye Bother (IRE)**[22] 9599 3-8-7 **46** oh1............................(t) RaulDaSilva 7 39
(Milton Bradley) *racd in rr-div: rdn over 2f out: no immediate imp over 1f out: styd on again ins fnl f* **100/1**

440- **8** 4½ **Quarto Cavallo**[175] 5079 3-9-5 **58**................................ CharlieBennett 3 37
(Adam West) *racd in rr-div: rdn 2f out: plugged on* **16/1**

004- **9** 1½ **Dotty Grand**[118] 7214 3-8-12 **51**................................... NicolaCurrie 6 26
(Jamie Osborne) *bhd ldrs: rdn over 2f out: nt qckn (jockey said filly stopped quickly)* **6/1³**

500- **10** 20 **Clevedon (IRE)**[25] 9566 3-9-1 **54**..............................(b) GeorgeDowning 4
(Ronald Harris) *qckly away and blazed a trail in ld: 5 l clr whn swung v wd into st: hdd over 2f out and no ex over 1f out (jockey said gelding hung left-handed throughout and ran wide on the bend)* **33/1**

1m 13.37s (0.27) **Going Correction** -0.025s/f (Stan) **10** Ran SP% **117.1**
Speed ratings (Par 95): **97,94,93,93,93 91,90,84,82,56**
CSF £58.34 CT £157.55 TOTE £4.10: £1.40, £4.80, £1.30; EX 71.30 Trifecta £194.90.
Owner D Boddy, E Foster And Karen George **Bred** Steve Lock **Trained** Crediton, Devon
■ Stewards' Enquiry : Edward Greatrex two-day ban; misuse of whip (Jan 24-25)

FOCUS
A moderate handicap run at a strong pace that favoured those held up.

138 WATCH RACE REPLAYS AT RACINGTV.COM H'CAP 7f (P)
7:15 (7:18) (Class 6) (0-65,67) 4-Y-0+

£3,105 (£924; £461; £400; £400; £400) **Stalls** Low

Form RPR

014- **1** **Briyouni (FR)**[46] 9244 6-9-7 **63**...................................... RobHornby 1 73+
(Ralph Beckett) *hld up in rr on inner: shkn up over 2f out waiting for gap: rdn and gd prog over 1f out: led jst ins fnl f: styd on wl* **11/4¹**

005- **2** 1¼ **Cashel (IRE)**[28] 9504 4-9-2 **58**.................................... AlistairRawlinson 8 65
(Michael Appleby) *hld up in rr-div on outer: effrt out wd over 2f out w a bit to do: no immediate imp tl qcknd over 1f out: no ch w wnr fnl f and pushed out to take 2nd nr fin* **16/1**

025- **3** ¾ **Hic Bibi**[20] 9638 4-8-13 **62**.. LauraCoughlan(7) 5 67
(David Loughnane) *led: shkn up in clr ld 2f out: nursed along and edgd lft over 1f out: hdd jst ins fnl f and lost 2nd nr fin* **16/1**

21-2 **4** hd **Viola Park**[5] 64 5-8-13 **55**..(p) DavidProbert 3 59
(Ronald Harris) *hld up in rr-div: rdn 2f out: kpt on fnl f* **4/1²**

223- **5** 1½ **Lady Marigold (IRE)**[36] 9386 4-8-11 **60**..................(t¹) GeorgiaDobie(7) 10 60
(Eve Johnson Houghton) *hld up in rr: rdn over 2f out: styd on wl fr over 1f out: nvr nrr* **20/1**

/52- **6** ½ **Ventriloquist**[10] 9764 7-9-6 **62**...................................... LukeMorris 9 61
(Simon Dow) *racd in mid-div: rdn 2f out and no ex sn after* **9/1**

423- **7** nse **Stand N Deliver**[25] 9565 5-9-6 **62**..............................(b¹) AdamKirby 7 61
(Clive Cox) *racd in mid-div: one pce fr over 1f out* **11/1**

045- **8** ¾ **Dark Magic**[10] 9765 5-9-5 **61**.....................................(v) RobertWinston 4 58
(Dean Ivory) *bhd ldr: rdn over 2f out: no imp sn after* **5/1³**

120- **9** ½ **Mezmaar**[34] 9428 10-9-6 **62**..(v¹) LiamKeniry 6 59
(Mark Usher) *tk fierce hold for 2f in rr-div: on heels and effrt 2f out: n.m.r between horses over 1f out: no ex* **20/1**

2/0- **10** 1½ **Perfect Soldier (IRE)**[11] 9747 5-9-11 **67**........................ LiamJones 2 59
(Shaun Keightley) *racd in mid-div: rdn over 2f out: sn hld* **40/1**

221- **11** ¾ **Chetan**[28] 9512 7-9-4 **67**... TobyEley(7) 11 57
(Tony Carroll) *bhd ldr on outer: struggling over 3f out: wknd over 1f out* **8/1**

1m 25.69s (-0.31) **Going Correction** -0.025s/f (Stan) **11** Ran SP% **116.5**
Speed ratings (Par 101): **100,98,97,97,95 95,95,94,93,92 91**
CSF £47.97 CT £609.67 TOTE £3.70: £1.80, £4.60, £4.80; EX 51.90 Trifecta £725.60.
Owner Mrs Ralph Beckett **Bred** S C E A Elevage De La Croix De Place **Trained** Kimpton, Hants

FOCUS
A modest heat.

139 100% PROFIT BOOST AT 32REDSPORT.COM AMATEUR RIDERS' H'CAP 6f (P)
7:45 (7:45) (Class 4) (0-85,86) 4-Y-0+

£6,239 (£1,935; £967; £484; £400; £400) **Stalls** Low

Form RPR

230- **1** **Choice Encounter**[20] 9640 4-10-4 **75**................ MissBrodieHampson 1 78
(Archie Watson) *jinked rt leaving stalls and jockey did wl to hold on: sn rcvrd and racd in rr-div: effrt 2f out w a bit to do: gd hdwy over 1f out: styd on wl last 150yds to ld cl home: shade cosily at fin: gd ride* **5/2²**

000- **2** nk **Peggy's Angel**[32] 9462 4-9-10 **72**.................................(h) TomMidgley(5) 7 74
(Jo Hughes, France) *racd in mid-div: effrt 2f out: kpt on wl fr over 1f out: styd on jst ins fnl f between horses and tk 2nd last strides* **50/1**

0- **3** ½ **National Glory (IRE)**[22] 9596 4-10-6 **77**.................(p¹) MrSimonWalker 4 77+
(Archie Watson) *sn led: shkn up 2f out: three l clr over 1f out: hrd rdn and began to weaken last 150yds: hdd cl home and lost 2nd last strides* **11/2³**

026- **4** hd **Madrinho (IRE)**[36] 9389 6-10-1 **77**....................... MissSarahBowen(5) 6 77
(Tony Carroll) *awkward s: hld up in rr-div: effrt w plenty to do 2f out: kpt on wl fr over 1f out and gaining at fin: nvr nrr* **6/1**

326- **5** *3* **Human Nature (IRE)**[41] 9305 6-11-0 **85**....................(t) MrRossBirkett 5 75
(Stuart Williams) *bhd ldr: effrt 2f out: kpt on wl tl wknd ins fnl f* **15/8**[1]

030- **6** *1 ¼* **Drakefell (IRE)**[33] 9446 4-10-11 **82**.......... MissSerenaBrotherton 2 68
(Richard Hannon) *bhd ldr: rdn 2f out: kpt on wl tl no ex and wknd ins fnl f* **6/1**

032- **7** *6* **Regulator (IRE)**[101] 7807 4-10-10 **86**.......... MissHannahWelch(5) 9 53
(Alexandra Dunn) *a in rr: effrt and sme hdwy over 1f out* **25/1**

000- **8** *4* **Concur (IRE)**[12] 9734 6-10-0 **71** oh26....................(tp) MrPatrickMillman 8 25
(Rod Millman) *in rr: no imp 2f out* **100/1**

000- **9** *3 ½* **All Or Nothin (IRE)**[20] 9634 10-9-9 **71** oh26..(p) MissMichelleBryant(5) 3 14
(Paddy Butler) *mid-div: no ex 2f out* **150/1**

1m 12.88s (-0.22) **Going Correction** -0.025s/f (Stan) **9** Ran SP% **114.8**
Speed ratings (Par 105): **100,99,98,98,94 93,85,79,75**
CSF £117.86 CT £644.20 TOTE £3.60: £1.30, £12.10, £1.60; EX 150.90 Trifecta £1017.10.
Owner Greenfield Racing **Bred** Stratford Place Stud & Willow Bloodstock **Trained** Upper Lambourn, W Berks

FOCUS
The leader set a good gallop and the first two and fourth came from off the pace. The form could be rated a shade better using the winner and fourth.
T/Jkpt: Not won. T/Plt: £27.60 to a £1 stake. Pool: £94,411.31 - 2494.64 winning units T/Qpdt: £14.50 to a £1 stake. Pool: £11,998.82 - 611.22 winning units **Cathal Gahan**

[86]LINGFIELD (L-H)
Wednesday, January 9

OFFICIAL GOING: Polytrack: standard
Wind: medium, against Weather: overcast, chilly

140 LADBROKES HOME OF THE ODDS BOOST H'CAP 7f 1y(P)
12:50 (12:50) (Class 5) (0-75,74) 3-Y-O
£3,752 (£1,116; £557; £300; £300; £300) **Stalls** Low

Form RPR

026- **1** **Black Medick**[28] 9498 3-9-0 **74**.................... SeamusCronin(7) 7 78+
(Richard Hannon) *hld up wl in tch in midfield: nt clr run 2f out tl gap opened 1f out: rdn and str run ins fnl f to ld 75yds out: gng away at fin* **12/1**

400- **2** *¾* **Hypnos (IRE)**[86] 8277 3-8-13 **66**.................... StevieDonohoe 4 68
(David Simcock) *chsd ldr: effrt ent fnl 2f: drvn and stydd on to ld ins fnl f: sn hdd and nt match pce of wnr towards fin* **9/1**

332- **3** *nk* **Ballistic (IRE)**[20] 9646 3-9-7 **74**....................(p) RaulDaSilva 2 75
(Robert Cowell) *trckd ldrs on inner: effrt and edgd lft u.p over 1f out: ev ch ins fnl f: styd on same pce towards fin* **3/1**[2]

50-4 **4** *nk* **Axel Jacklin**[5] 65 3-9-1 **68**.................... JoeFanning 5 68+
(Mark Johnston) *restless in stalls and s.i.s: hld up in tch in rr: clsd and nt clr run wl over 1f out tl effrt u.p ent fnl f: r.o wl fnl 100yds: nt rch ldrs* **9/2**[3]

105- **5** *1* **So Hi Storm (IRE)**[47] 9226 3-9-1 **68**.................... JFEgan 1 65
(K R Burke) *led: rdn over 1f out: drvn and hdd ins fnl f: no ex and wknd towards fin* **9/4**[1]

665- **6** *5* **Grandstand (IRE)**[35] 9396 3-9-4 **71**....................(p1) DavidProbert 3 55
(Andrew Balding) *dwlt: in tch in last pair: shkn up 2f out: drvn over 1f out: no imp: nt clr run and swtchd rt over 1f out: no prog and wl hld fnl f* **7/1**

354- **7** *½* **Temple Of Wonder (IRE)**[20] 9646 3-9-1 **68**.......... RobertWinston 6 51
(Charlie Wallis) *broke wl: sn retrained and t.k.h: in tch on outer: rdn and unable qck over 1f out: wknd ins fnl f (jockey said gelding ran too free)* **8/1**

1m 25.23s (0.43) **Going Correction** 0.0s/f (Stan) **7** Ran SP% **115.3**
Speed ratings (Par 97): **97,96,95,95,94 88,88**
CSF £111.59 TOTE £12.90: £5.20, £5.80; EX 174.40.
Owner Rockcliffe Stud **Bred** Rockcliffe Stud **Trained** East Everleigh, Wilts
■ Stewards' Enquiry : Robert Winston one-day ban; weighing in procedures (Jan 23)

FOCUS
Quite a bunched finish, and modest form. The time was 3sec outsde the standard.

141 BETWAY NOVICE MEDIAN AUCTION STKS 6f 1y(P)
1:25 (1:25) (Class 6) 3-5-Y-O **£3,105** (£924; £461; £230) **Stalls** Low

Form RPR

0- **1** **Minoria**[158] 5715 4-9-9 0.................... MartinHarley 6 75
(Rae Guest) *chsd ldrs: wnt 3rd 3f out: effrt wl over 1f out: chsd ldr ins fnl f: styd on wl u.p to ld cl home* **11/1**

532- **2** *½* **Secret Ace**[13] 9727 3-8-7 70.................... EdwardGreatrex 11 69
(Archie Watson) *chsd ldr: effrt over 1f out: drvn and upsides 1f out: edgd lft and led ins fnl f: hrd drvn and kpt on: hdd and no ex cl home* **5/4**[1]

5- **3** *3 ½* **Spirit Of Lucerne (IRE)**[76] 8577 3-8-7 0.................... NicolaCurrie 9 59
(Phil McEntee) *midfield: effrt in 5th and rn green 2f out: kpt on ins fnl f to go 3rd towards fin: no threat to ldrs* **20/1**

46- **4** *1 ¼* **Dancing Ballerina (IRE)**[13] 9727 3-8-7 0.................... DavidProbert 10 55
(K R Burke) *led: rdn and edgd lft over 1f out: hdd ins fnl f: sn wknd (jockey said filly hung left-handed under pressure)* **3/1**[2]

600- **5** *1 ¼* **Brogans Bay (IRE)**[127] 6905 4-9-9 40.................... NickyMackay 8 55
(Simon Dow) *stdd s: t.k.h: hld up off the pce in midfield: nt clr run over 1f out: kpt on ins fnl f: nvr trbld ldrs* **50/1**

66- **6** *2 ¼* **Miss Pollyanna (IRE)**[74] 8637 3-8-2 0.................... RhiainIngram(5) 4 44
(Roger Ingram) *chsd ldng pair tl 3f out: unable qck and outpcd over 1f out: wknd ins fnl f* **12/1**

00- **7** *½* **Laguna Spirit**[12] 9730 3-8-7 0....................(h1) JFEgan 1 43
(Pat Phelan) *stdd s: hld up off the pce: nvr involved* **50/1**

040- **8** *nk* **Reignite**[26] 9529 4-10-0 62....................(h1) EoinWalsh 2 51
(Emma Owen) *hld up off the pce in midfield: hmpd and lost pl over 4f out: rdn and wd bnd 2f out: kpt on ins fnl f: nvr involved (jockey said colt was outpaced throughout)* **4/1**[3]

00- **9** *½* **Magnetic (IRE)**[35] 9417 3-8-5 0.................... AaronMackay(7) 5 45
(J S Moore) *hld up off the pce in last quartet: effrt over 1f out: edgd lft u.p ins fnl f: nvr involved* **25/1**

00/ **10** *5* **Singer In The Sand (IRE)**[392] 9200 4-9-2 0.......... SophieRalston(7) 7 29
(Pat Phelan) *a off pce: bhd fnl f* **66/1**

0- **P** **Check In Check Out (IRE)**[13] 9727 3-8-0 0. ThoreHammerHansen(7) 3
(Richard Hannon) *sn dropped to rr: rdn and lost tch 3f out: eased 2f out: t.o whn p.u and dismntd ins fnl f* **16/1**

1m 12.0s (0.10) **Going Correction** 0.0s/f (Stan)
WFA 3 from 4yo 16lb **11** Ran SP% **125.4**
Speed ratings (Par 101): **99,98,93,92,90 87,86,86,85,78**
CSF £26.10 TOTE £12.40: £2.70, £1.10, £4.90; EX 34.30 Trifecta £691.40.
Owner C J Mills **Bred** C J Mills **Trained** Newmarket, Suffolk
■ Stewards' Enquiry : Thore Hammer Hansen eight-day ban; continuing on an exhausted/lame horse (Jan 23-26,28-31)
Edward Greatrex one-day ban; failure to ride to draw (Jan 23)
David Probert one-day ban; failure to ride to draw (Jan 23)

FOCUS
All but two of the field in this very modest event were fillies. They went a decent gallop and winning rider Martin Harley said that it rode more like a 5f race.

142 LADBROKES H'CAP 6f 1y(P)
1:55 (1:55) (Class 4) (0-80,81) 3-Y-O **£5,530** (£1,645; £822; £411; £300) **Stalls** Low

Form RPR

030- **1** **Artair (IRE)**[60] 9006 3-9-5 **74**.................... LouisSteward 1 77
(Michael Bell) *chsd ldrs tl wnt 2nd 4f out: effrt ent fnl f: styd on u.p and ev ch ins fnl f: led towards fin* **12/1**

14-3 **2** *nk* **Beleaguerment (IRE)**[4] 83 3-9-7 **76**....................(p) EdwardGreatrex 3 78+
(Archie Watson) *outpcd in 4th early: clsd to chse ldrs 2f out: chsd ldng pair jst ins fnl f: styd on strly fnl 100yds: snatched 2nd last stride: nt quite rch wnr* **5/2**[2]

43-2 **3** *shd* **Uncle Jerry**[4] 83 3-9-12 **81**....................(b) ShaneKelly 4 83
(Richard Hughes) *led: rdn and edgd rt over 1f out: hrd drvn ins fnl f: hdd towards fin: no ex and lost 2nd last stride* **2/1**[1]

154- **4** *3 ½* **London Rock (IRE)**[10] 9762 3-8-9 **71**.......... ThoreHammerHansen(7) 5 61
(Richard Hannon) *anticipated s and rdr unable to remove hood immediately: slowly away: in tch in rr: effrt ent fnl 2f: kpt on same pce and no imp ins fnl f (jockey said blindfold got stuck in the bridle meaning it took two attempts to remove it)* **5/1**

652- **5** *2* **Champion Brogie (IRE)**[10] 9762 3-9-6 **75**.................... RobertWinston 2 59
(J S Moore) *chsd ldr for 1f: chsd ldrs after tl unable qck and outpcd over 1f out: wknd ins fnl f* **11/4**[3]

1m 11.65s (-0.25) **Going Correction** 0.0s/f (Stan) **5** Ran SP% **112.9**
Speed ratings (Par 99): **101,100,100,95,93**
CSF £42.48 TOTE £8.60: £3.10, £1.20; EX 28.20 Trifecta £77.10.
Owner Secular Stagnation And Partner **Bred** Tally-Ho Stud **Trained** Newmarket, Suffolk

FOCUS
A fair handicap, run slightly quicker than the preceding novice event. The third dictates the form.

143 BETWAY CONDITIONS STKS 1m 4f (P)
2:30 (2:30) (Class 2) 4-Y-O+ **£11,971** (£3,583) **Stalls** Low

Form RPR

224- **1** **Court House (IRE)**[14] 9705 4-9-2 105.................... RobertHavlin 1 111+
(John Gosden) *mde all: rdn and qckning 2f out: increased advantage over 1f out: in command and r.o wl fnl f* **8/11**[1]

423- **2** *4 ½* **Scarlet Dragon**[18] 9685 6-9-5 106.................... MartinHarley 2 103
(Alan King) *dropped in bhd rival after s: t.k.h: trckd rival: effrt wl over 1f out: sn rdn and no imp: wl hld ins fnl f* **Evs**[2]

2m 33.73s (0.73) **Going Correction** 0.0s/f (Stan)
WFA 4 from 5yo+ 3lb **2** Ran SP% **107.9**
Speed ratings (Par 109): **97,94**
TOTE £1.20.
Owner HRH Princess Haya Of Jordan **Bred** Nanallac Stud **Trained** Newmarket, Suffolk

FOCUS
A good-quality conditions event, but with just two runners it was always likely to be falsely run. The time was 6.75 slower than the standard, respectable in the circumstances. Not form to take too literally

144 BETWAY H'CAP 6f 1y(P)
3:05 (3:05) (Class 6) (0-65,69) 4-Y-O+
£3,105 (£924; £461; £300; £300; £300) **Stalls** Low

Form RPR

031- **1** **Deeds Not Words (IRE)**[9] 9773 8-9-11 **69** 6ex....................(p) JFEgan 3 75
(Michael Wigham) *bmpd leaving stalls: in tch in midfield: effrt and clsd over 1f out: hdwy u.p to chse ldr 100yds out: r.o wl to ld on post* **15/2**

042- **2** *shd* **Very Honest (IRE)**[36] 9388 6-9-7 **65**....................(v) RossaRyan 10 71
(Brett Johnson) *led and crossed to inner: rdn and edgd rt over 1f out: drvn ins fnl f: kpt on but hdd last stride* **13/2**

535- **3** *½* **Independence Day (IRE)**[23] 9587 6-9-9 **67**.................... JoeyHaynes 8 71
(Paul Howling) *stdd bk after s: hld up in tch in last quartet: hdwy over 1f out: edgd lft but styd on wl ins fnl f: nt quite rch ldrs* **5/1**[2]

620- **4** *1 ¼* **Majorette**[36] 9388 5-9-3 **64**.................... FinleyMarsh(3) 4 64
(Brian Barr) *wnt lft leaving stalls: t.k.h: wl in tch in midfield: impeded after 1f: effrt over 1f out: kpt on same pce ins fnl f* **16/1**

530- **5** *hd* **First Link (USA)**[28] 9504 4-8-6 **57**.................... TobyEley(7) 9 57
(Jean-Rene Auvray) *stdd and awkward leaving stalls: hld up in last pair: shkn up over 1f out: rdn and hdwy ent fnl f: sltly impeded ins fnl f but kpt on wl fnl 100yds: nt rch ldrs (jockey said filly was slowly away)* **11/1**

504- **6** *½* **Aguerooo (IRE)**[10] 9764 6-9-7 **65**....................(tp) JoeFanning 7 63
(Charlie Wallis) *stdd after s: hld up in last quartet: hdwy over 1f out: rdn and kpt on ins fnl f: nt rch ldrs* **11/2**[3]

600- **7** *hd* **Flirtare (IRE)**[219] 3435 4-9-5 **63**.................... RobertHavlin 12 61
(Amanda Perrett) *chsd ldrs: wnt 2nd after 1f: rdn over 1f out: drvn and pressing wnr 1f out: lost 2nd and no ex 100yds out: wknd towards fin* **16/1**

00-6 **8** *½* **Indian Affair**[7] 28 9-9-0 **58**....................(bt) RobertWinston 1 54
(Milton Bradley) *t.k.h: chsd ldrs: effrt on inner over 1f out: drvn and kpt on same pce ins fnl f* **14/1**

644- **9** *3* **Spenny's Lass**[23] 9588 4-9-3 **61**....................(p) StevieDonohoe 6 48
(John Ryan) *midfield: effrt and wd bnd 2f out: no imp: wl hld and kpt on same pce fnl f (jockey said filly lost it's action)* **10/1**

020- **10** *1 ½* **Picket Line**[26] 9529 7-9-6 **64**....................(b) LiamKeniry 2 47
(Geoffrey Deacon) *in tch in midfield: effrt on inner over 1f out: no imp and wknd ins fnl f* **17/2**

000- **11** *hd* **Just An Idea (IRE)**[79] 8484 5-9-6 **64**.................... NickyMackay 11 46
(Roger Ingram) *sn outpcd and dropped to rr: nvr involved* **40/1**

060- **12** *3 ¾* **Fiery Breath**[14] 9702 4-9-6 **64**.................... MartinHarley 5 35
(Robert Eddery) *t.k.h: chsd ldrs: effrt 2f out: sn struggling and outpcd over 1f out: wknd fnl f (jockey said gelding stopped quickly)* **4/1**[1]

1m 11.73s (-0.17) **Going Correction** 0.0s/f (Stan) **12** Ran SP% **126.0**
Speed ratings (Par 101): **101,100,100,98,98 97,97,96,92,90 90,85**
CSF £59.35 CT £281.79 TOTE £5.60: £2.50, £1.60, £2.30; EX 25.90 Trifecta £158.30.
Owner D Hassan, Ali Tait, M Wigham **Bred** B Holland, S Hillen & J Cullinan **Trained** Newmarket, Suffolk
■ Stewards' Enquiry : Rossa Ryan caution; careless riding

FOCUS
Moderate sprint handicap form, with a busy finish. The winner is edging towards his 2017 high.

145 BETWAY CASINO H'CAP — 1m 2f (P)
3:40 (3:40) (Class 6) (0-65,65) 4-Y-0+
£3,105 (£924; £461; £300; £300; £300) Stalls Low

Form — RPR

/00- 1 **Jafetica**[21] 9609 5-9-8 **65** ... JoeFanning 6 — 73
(Mark Johnston) *hld up in tch towards rr: gd hdwy on outer bnd 2f out: rdn and chsd ldr over 1f out: led 1f out: r.o wl and in command ins fnl f (trainers' rep said, reg app imp in form, mare benefitted from a drop in class. Vet said mare lost it's left-fore shoe)* **14/1**

614- 2 1 1/4 **Global Wonder (IRE)**[34] 9428 4-9-7 **65** ... MartinHarley 5 — 72
(Gay Kelleway) *taken down early: hld up in tch in midfield: clsd and nt clr run ent fnl 2f: swtchd lft and rdn to chse ldrs over 1f out: chsd wnr ins fnl f: kpt on but a hld* **6/4[1]**

30-0 3 1 **Highway One (USA)**[4] 85 5-9-6 **63** ... (p[1]) LiamKeniry 8 — 67
(George Baker) *pushed lft and stmbld sltly leaving stalls: rousted along and rcvrd to chse ldr after 1f: led over 6f out: pushed along and kicked clr ent fnl 2f: hdd 1f out: 3rd and one pce ins fnl f* **5/1[3]**

601- 4 3/4 **Tobacco Road (IRE)**[58] 8489 9-9-5 **62** ... (t) HectorCrouch 2 — 64
(Mark Pattinson) *in tch in midfield: nt clr run and hmpd jst over 2f out: swtchd rt and rallied jst over 1f out: styd on wl u.p ins fnl f: nvr quite getting on terms w ldrs* **10/1**

00-0 5 1 3/4 **New Street (IRE)**[6] 39 8-9-3 **60** ... RobHornby 4 — 59
(Suzi Best) *hld up in last trio: effrt over 1f out: swtchd rt and rdn ins fnl f: styd on but no threat to ldrs* **10/1**

0/6- 6 5 **Spring Ability (IRE)**[12] 9732 4-9-4 **62** ... LiamJones 7 — 52
(Laura Mongan) *wnt rt leaving stalls: chsd ldrs: effrt on inner ent fnl 2f: unable qck and btn 1f out: wknd ins fnl f* **18/1**

000- 7 1 3/4 **Spring Dixie (IRE)**[19] 9666 7-8-1 **51** oh6 ... ThoreHammerHansen(7) 1 — 37
(Natalie Lloyd-Beavis) *dwlt: hld up in rr: effrt on inner over 1f out: no imp and nvr involved* **66/1**

000- 8 2 **The Bearfighter (IRE)**[28] 9512 4-9-0 **58** ... StevieDonohoe 3 — 41
(Charlie Fellowes) *led tl over 6f out: chsd ldr: rdn over 2f out: lost pl over 1f out: wknd ins fnl f* **4/1[2]**

560- 9 3/4 **Khazix (IRE)**[20] 9634 4-9-1 **59** ... (v[1]) CallumShepherd 9 — 41
(Harry Dunlop) *pushed rt leaving stalls: hdwy to chse ldrs after 1f out: lost pl qckly over 1f out: wknd and bhd ins fnl f* **12/1**

2m 5.7s (-0.90) **Going Correction** 0.0s/f (Stan)
WFA 4 from 5yo+ 1lb — **9 Ran SP% 116.0**
Speed ratings (Par 101): **103,102,101,100,99 95,93,92,91**
CSF £35.62 CT £126.68 TOTE £11.00: £3.30, £1.20, £1.60; EX 31.90 Trifecta £98.10.
Owner A D Spence & M B Spence **Bred** Rabbah Bloodstock Limited **Trained** Middleham Moor, N Yorks

FOCUS
This was run at what appeared to be a reasonable gallop. The winner got near her old form.
T/Plt: £255.70 to a £1 stake Pool: £53,175.13 - 151.79 winning units T/Qpdt: £15.70 to a £1 stake. Pool: £6,376.94 - 300.54 winning units **Steve Payne**

146 - 153a (Foreign Racing) - See Raceform Interactive

[32]CHELMSFORD (A.W) (L-H)
Thursday, January 10

OFFICIAL GOING: Polytrack: standard
Wind: light, half against Weather: light rain, chilly

154 £20 FREE BETS AT TOTESPORT.COM "HANDS & HEELS" APPRENTICE H'CAP (A RACING EXCELLENCE INITIATIVE) — 1m (P)
4:15 (4:15) (Class 5) (0-75,72) 4-Y-0+
£5,433 (£1,617; £808; £404; £400; £400) Stalls Low

003- 1 **Lunar Deity**[31] 9488 10-9-2 **72** ... GraceMcEntee(5) 5 — 76
(Stuart Williams) *s.i.s and pushed along leaving stalls: hld up in last pair: clsd to chse ldrs over 2f out: effrt to chal 1f out: styd on wl to ld towards fin* **7/1**

01-0 2 1/2 **Creek Harbour (IRE)**[8] 31 4-9-3 **71** ... GeorgeRooke(3) 6 — 74
(Richard Hughes) *t.k.h: w ldr tl pushed into ld over 1f out: kpt on wl ins fnl f: hdd and one pce towards fin* **5/1[3]**

664- 3 nse **Caledonia Duchess**[70] 8781 6-8-9 **60** ... (p) EllieMacKenzie 1 — 63
(Jo Hughes, France) *chsd ldng pair: nt clrest of runs over 1f out: gap opened and effrt to chal 1f out: kpt on wl ins fnl f: no ex towards fin* **6/1**

102- 4 2 **Sweet Nature (IRE)**[21] 9638 4-8-13 **69** ... GianlucaSanna(5) 3 — 67
(William Haggas) *hld up in last pair: effrt over 1f out: chsd ldrs and kpt on same pce ins fnl f* **9/4[2]**

121- 5 2 3/4 **Channel Packet**[64] 8918 5-9-3 **68** ... MarkCrehan 4 — 60
(Michael Appleby) *led: pushed along and hdd over 1f out: wknd ins fnl f* **7/4[1]**

000- 6 6 **Prince Consort (IRE)**[20] 9659 4-8-4 **58** oh13 ... (h) RhonaPindar(3) 2 — 36
(John Wainwright) *in tch in midfield tl dropped to rr over 2f out: pushed along and btn over 1f out: wknd ins fnl f* **66/1**

1m 40.67s (0.77) **Going Correction** +0.075s/f (Slow) — **6 Ran SP% 112.1**
Speed ratings (Par 103): **99,98,98,96,93 87**
CSF £40.39 TOTE £6.40: £3.30, £2.50; EX 38.60 Trifecta £143.70.
Owner W E Enticknap & Partner **Bred** Hermes Services Ltd **Trained** Newmarket, Suffolk

FOCUS
A fair handicap run at a steady pace.

155 TOTEPOOL CASHBACK CLUB AT TOTESPORT.COM H'CAP — 1m (P)
4:45 (4:50) (Class 7) (0-50,50) 3-Y-0+ £2,911 (£866; £432; £216) Stalls Low

Form — RPR

44-2 1 **Foreign Legion (IRE)**[7] 37 4-9-9 **45** ... (p) NickyMackay 6 — 53
(Luke McJannet) *prom in main gp tl clsd to trck ldrs over 2f out: rdn to chal over 1f out: forged ahd u.p ins fnl f: styd on* **3/1[1]**

006- 2 1 1/2 **Satchville Flyer**[13] 9734 8-10-0 **50** ... JackMitchell 4 — 55
(David Evans) *stdd s: t.k.h: hld up off the pce in rr: clsd over 1f out: chsd clr ldng pair 1f out: hung lft and racd awkwardly but kpt on ins fnl f to go 2nd towards fin: nvr getting to wnr* **5/1[2]**

602- 3 1/2 **Foxrush Take Time (FR)**[20] 9660 4-9-9 **45** ... (e) AdamKirby 9 — 49
(Richard Guest) *chsd clr ldr: clsd and rdn to ld over 2f out: clr w wnr over 1f out: hdd ins fnl f: no ex and one pce fnl 100yds: lost 2nd towards fin* **14/1**

000- 4 3 1/2 **Gone With The Wind (GER)**[62] 8978 8-9-9 **45** ... (p) MartinHarley 2 — 41
(Rebecca Bastiman) *midfield: effrt over 2f out: swtchd rt over 1f out and chse clr ldng pair ent fnl f: no imp and sn lost 3rd: wl hld and plugged on same pce ins fnl f* **20/1**

003- 5 nk **Born To Reason (IRE)**[20] 9658 5-9-12 **48** ... (b) LiamJones 7 — 44
(Kevin Frost) *hld up in midfield: swtchd lft and effrt u.p over 1f out: kpt on ins fnl f: nvr any threat to ldrs* **16/1**

600- 6 4 **Nicky Baby (IRE)**[28] 9528 5-9-9 **45** ... (p) RobertHavlin 13 — 32
(Dean Ivory) *prom in chsng gp: rdn and struggling to qckn over 2f out: losing pl whn short of room over 1f out: wknd ins fnl f* **16/1**

606- 7 1 1/2 **African Showgirl**[21] 9644 6-9-2 **45** ... (p[1]) GeorgiaDobie(7) 10 — 29
(Ivan Furtado) *pushed lft leaving stalls: t.k.h and dashed up into midfield after 1f: rdn over 2f out: sn struggling and lost pl over 1f out: wknd ins fnl f* **25/1**

000- 8 3 1/4 **Pass The Cristal (IRE)**[22] 9602 5-9-13 **49** ... MartinDwyer 14 — 25
(William Muir) *stdd s: hld up off the pce in rr: effrt on outer and sme hdwy over 2f out: no imp and btn over 1f out: wknd ins fnl f (jockey said gelding moved poorly throughout)* **16/1**

561- 9 1 **Ertidaad (IRE)**[28] 9523 7-9-13 **49** ... (v) EoinWalsh 12 — 23
(Emma Owen) *midfield: no imp u.p and swtchd lft over 1f out: nvr threatened ldrs and wknd ins fnl f (jockey said gelding was denied clear run in home straight)* **8/1**

636- 10 2 3/4 **Joyful Dream (IRE)**[50] 9181 5-9-9 **45** ... (v) ShaneKelly 11 — 13
(Paul D'Arcy) *wnt sharply lft leaving stalls: prom in chsng gp: rdn 3f out: sn struggling and lost pl over 1f out: wknd fnl f* **16/1**

000- 11 nk **Invisible Shadow**[29] 9501 4-9-2 **45** ... ScottMcCullagh(7) 5 — 12
(Richard Spencer) *sn rdn: a towards rr: nvr involved (jockey said gelding ran flat)* **7/1[3]**

000- 12 3 **Amaranth (IRE)**[15] 9703 6-10-0 **50** ... CallumShepherd 3 — 11
(Michael Scudamore) *led and sn clr: rdn and hdd over 2f out: lost pl and btn over 1f out: wknd fnl f* **5/1[2]**

000- 13 1 1/4 **Jasmine B (IRE)**[129] 6875 3-7-10 **45** ... LauraPearson(7) 8
(John Ryan) *a towards rr: nvr involved* **33/1**

504- 14 nk **Admiral Anson**[107] 7642 5-9-2 **45** ... (p[1]) MarkCrehan(7) 15 — 2
(Michael Appleby) *a towards rr: nvr involved* **50/1**

0/6- 15 11 **Compton Brave**[274] 1728 5-9-9 **45** ... DavidProbert 1
(J R Jenkins) *prom in chsng gp: drvn 3f out and sn lost pl: bhd and eased ins fnl f* **25/1**

1m 41.42s (1.52) **Going Correction** +0.075s/f (Slow)
WFA 3 from 4yo+ 20lb — **15 Ran SP% 129.5**
Speed ratings (Par 97): **95,93,93,89,89 85,83,80,79,76 76,73,72,71,60**
CSF £17.16 CT £196.87 TOTE £3.30: £1.80, £1.90, £4.10; EX 20.20 Trifecta £171.00.
Owner Ivor Collier **Bred** Norelands Bloodstock **Trained** Newmarket, Suffolk

FOCUS
An open if modest handicap run at a strong tempo.

156 EXTRA PLACES AT TOTESPORT.COM NOVICE STKS (PLUS 10 RACE) — 1m 2f (P)
5:15 (5:20) (Class 4) 3-Y-0 £6,210 (£1,848; £923; £461) Stalls Low

Form — RPR

1- 1 **Themaxwecan (IRE)**[101] 7830 3-9-9 0 ... PJMcDonald 4 — 89
(Mark Johnston) *midfield: effrt to chse ldrs over 2f out: clsd u.p and edgd lft ins fnl f: led wl ins fnl f: styd on wl* **4/1[2]**

2 3/4 **American Graffiti (FR)** 3-9-2 0 ... JackMitchell 2 — 80
(Charlie Appleby) *midfield on inner: effrt and stl plenty to do over 2f out: rdn and clsd jst over 1f out: styng on and swtchd rt ins fnl f: gng on wl at fin and snatched 2nd last strides* **10/1**

41- 3 nk **New King**[33] 9459 3-9-9 0 ... RobertHavlin 1 — 86
(John Gosden) *chsd ldrs: effrt to chse ldr over 2f out: styd on and clsd to chal ins fnl f: no ex towards fin* **1/1[1]**

4 nk **Kinver Edge (USA)** 3-9-2 0 ... AdamKirby 9 — 78+
(Charlie Appleby) *chsd ldr: clsd to ld over 3f out: rdn and kicked clr over 2f out: rn green and hung rt over 1f out: hrd pressed ins fnl f: hdd and no ex 50yds out: lost 2 pls cl home* **8/1[3]**

5 5 **Blood Eagle (IRE)** 3-9-2 0 ... DavidProbert 5 — 68+
(Andrew Balding) *stdd and short of room leaving stalls: hld up towards rr: short of room and hmpd wl over 7f out: clsd but stl plenty to do over 2f out: swtchd rt and pushed along over 2f out: rn green and no imp fnl f* **8/1[3]**

5- 6 1 1/2 **Holy Kingdom (IRE)**[21] 9637 3-9-2 0 ... LukeMorris 8 — 65
(Tom Clover) *chsd ldng trio tl clsd to chse ldr wl over 2f out: 3rd and drvn ent fnl 2f: no imp and btn over 1f out: wknd ins fnl f* **14/1**

03- 7 8 **Ring Cycle**[21] 9635 3-9-2 0 ... LiamKeniry 7 — 49
(Sylvester Kirk) *stdd and awkward leaving stalls: hld up in rr: effrt over 2f out: sn struggling: wknd over 1f out* **33/1**

0- 8 5 **Philonikia**[57] 9048 3-8-11 0 ... RobHornby 11 — 34
(Ralph Beckett) *wnt rt leaving stalls: midfield but wd: rdn 3f out: sn struggling and bhd over 1f out* **16/1**

0- 9 12 **Hammy End (IRE)**[24] 9590 3-9-2 0 ... (h) MartinDwyer 6 — 15
(William Muir) *hld up towards rr: hung rt and wd fr over 7f out: bhd 2f out: sn wl bhd (jockey said gelding hung right-handed)* **100/1**

06- 10 21 **Red Skye Delight (IRE)**[21] 9636 3-8-11 0 ... MartinHarley 10
(Luke McJannet) *led and sn clr: hdd over 3f out: lost pl over 2f out: wl bhd fnl f: t.o* **100/1**

0- 11 31 **Path To The Stars (GER)**[14] 9726 3-9-2 0 ... (v[1]) CallumShepherd 3
(James Tate) *uns rdr and loose briefly bef s: awkward leaving stalls: bhd: rdn over 4f out: lost tch and eased wl over 1f out: t.o* **66/1**

2m 8.9s (0.30) **Going Correction** +0.075s/f (Slow) — **11 Ran SP% 120.3**
Speed ratings (Par 99): **101,100,100,99,95 94,88,84,74,57 33**
CSF £44.26 TOTE £5.60: £1.60, £2.90, £1.10; EX 50.10 Trifecta £120.20.
Owner Douglas Livingston **Bred** Niarchos Family **Trained** Middleham Moor, N Yorks

FOCUS
An interesting contest.

157 £2.5 MILLION SCOOP6 THIS SATURDAY H'CAP — 1m 2f (P)
5:50 (5:50) (Class 4) (0-85,84) 4-Y-0+
£6,986 (£2,079; £1,038; £519; £400; £400) Stalls Low

Form — RPR

032- 1 **Star Of Southwold (FR)**[14] 9723 4-9-6 **84** ... LukeMorris 5 — 91
(Michael Appleby) *mde all: wnt clr w runner-up over 2f out: hrd drvn and battled on gamely ins fnl f: all out* **3/1[1]**

303- 2 hd **Global Art**[29] 9505 4-9-0 **78** ... RobertHavlin 3 — 84
(Ed Dunlop) *trckd wnr: pushed along and kicked clr w wnr over 2f out: hrd drvn and kpt on wl ins fnl f: jst hld* **10/3[2]**

121- 3 nk **Claire Underwood (IRE)**[14] 9723 4-9-1 **79** ... TonyHamilton 2 — 84+
(Richard Fahey) *wnt rt leaving stalls: chsd ldrs: rdn and outpcd over 2f out: rallied u.p ins fnl f: styd on strly towards fin: nt quite rch ldrs* **3/1[1]**

020- 4 5 **Brittanic (IRE)**[14] 9723 5-9-7 **84** ... StevieDonohoe 4 — 78
(David Simcock) *stdd s: hld up in rr: effrt but outpcd by ldrs over 2f out: edgd lft and no imp over 1f out* **12/1**

The Form Book Flat 2019, Raceform Ltd, Newbury, RG14 5SJ

40-6 **5** *1* **Samphire Coast**[7] 34 6-9-2 **79**................................(v) PaddyMathers 1 71
(Derek Shaw) *taken down early: t.k.h: hld up in tch: rdn and outpcd over 2f out: no threat to ldrs after* **7/1**

/05- **6** *17* **Perpetrator (IRE)**[170] 5322 4-8-9 **73**................................(p[1]) DavidProbert 6 32
(Roger Charlton) *hld up in tch: rdn over 3f out: sn struggling and hung rt: bhd and lost tch over 1f out (jockey said gelding hung right-handed)* **5/1**[3]

2m 8.02s (-0.58) **Going Correction** +0.075s/f (Slow) **6** Ran SP% **109.9**
WFA 4 from 5yo+ 1lb
Speed ratings (Par 105): **105,104,104,100,99 86**
CSF £12.65 TOTE £3.40: £1.40, £2.20; EX 10.90 Trifecta £28.60.
Owner Middleham Park Racing XXXIII **Bred** S C Snig Elevage **Trained** Oakham, Rutland

FOCUS
A competitive handicap run at an even pace. The first three home finished clear.

158 BET IN PLAY AT TOTESPORT.COM H'CAP 7f (P)

6:25 (6:27) (Class 5) (0-75,74) 4-Y-0+

£5,433 (£1,617; £808; £404; £400; £400) **Stalls** Low

Form RPR

00-3 **1** **Pearl Spectre (USA)**[9] 5 8-9-2 **70**................................(v) NicolaCurrie 8 76
(Phil McEntee) *led: rdn and jnd over 1f out: sn drvn and hdd 1f out: battled bk gamely to ld again towards fin* **6/1**[3]

331- **2** *nk* **Enthaar**[94] 8046 4-9-6 **74**................................(t[1]) PJMcDonald 3 79+
(Stuart Williams) *t.k.h: chsd wnr for over 1f: styd trcking ldrs tl wnt 2nd again and switching rt ent fnl 2f: upsides wnr and hld together over 1f out: pushed into ld 1f out: sn rdn: drvn 100yds: hdd towards fin* **7/2**[2]

000- **3** *½* **Titan Goddess**[42] 9317 7-9-4 **72**................................ RossaRyan 5 76
(Mike Murphy) *hld up in tch in midfield: effrt over 2f out: sltly outpcd over 1f out: rallied u.p ins fnl f: styd on strly towards fin: nt quite rch ldrs* **14/1**

534- **4** *¾* **Kadrizzi (FR)**[42] 9317 6-9-6 **74**................................ RobertHavlin 1 76
(Dean Ivory) *in tch in midfield: effrt on inner over 2f out: rdn to chse ldrs over 1f out: kpt on but nvr quite getting on terms w ldrs ins fnl f: hld and nt clrest of runs cl home* **11/8**[1]

200- **5** *4½* **Archie (IRE)**[98] 7934 7-9-3 **74**................................(t[1]) FinleyMarsh(3) 7 64
(Brian Barr) *hld up in tch towards rr: swtchd rt and effrt over 1f out: no imp and wl hld whn hung lft ins fnl f* **33/1**

56-0 **6** *8* **Zapper Cass (FR)**[9] 2 6-9-4 **72**................................(p) LukeMorris 2 40
(Michael Appleby) *t.k.h: hld up towards rr: swtchd rt and hdwy over 4f out: lost pl 2f out: hung rt and wknd over 1f out (jockey said gelding ran too free)* **11/1**

410- **7** *2¼* **Rockies Spirit**[19] 9682 4-9-5 **73**................................(p) AdamKirby 6 35
(Denis Quinn) *t.k.h: chsd wnr over 5f out tl over 2f out: lost pl u.p over 1f out: wknd fnl f* **14/1**

000- **8** *nk* **Makaarim**[12] 9747 5-9-5 **73**................................(h[1]) MartinHarley 4 34
(Seamus Durack) *wnt rt leaving stalls: nvr travelling wl in rr: rdn and clsd 3f out: sn struggling and outpcd: bhd over 1f out (trainers rep said gelding made a noise)* **8/1**

1m 26.62s (-0.58) **Going Correction** +0.075s/f (Slow) **8** Ran SP% **114.3**
Speed ratings (Par 103): **106,105,105,104,99 89,87,87**
CSF £27.28 CT £283.34 TOTE £4.30: £1.50, £1.30, £4.20; EX 31.00 Trifecta £395.90.
Owner Steve Jakes **Bred** Estate Of Edward P Evans **Trained** Newmarket, Suffolk

FOCUS
A fair race for the grade with all eight runners rated within 5lb of the ceiling.

159 MILLIONAIRE MAKER THIS SATURDAY'S SCOOP6 H'CAP 7f (P)

6:55 (6:58) (Class 6) (0-60,59) 4-Y-0+

£3,493 (£1,039; £519; £400; £400; £400) **Stalls** Low

Form RPR

250- **1** **Amor Fati (IRE)**[28] 9523 4-8-9 **45**................................ NicolaCurrie 6 55
(David Evans) *t.k.h: hld up in tch in midfield: clsd to chse ldrs and swtchd rt over 1f out: chsd ldr 1f out: clsd u.p to ld ins fnl f: sn in command and r.o wl (trainers rep said, regarding improvement in form, that the gelding appreciated the removal of the visor)* **14/1**

00-1 **2** *1¾* **African Blessing**[7] 37 6-9-9 **59** 6ex................................ KierenFox 11 64
(John Best) *dropped in bhd after s: t.k.h: clsd: nt clrest of runs and swtchd rt 2f out: hdwy u.p over 1f out: r.o to chse wnr wl ins fnl f: nvr getting on terms* **3/1**[1]

642- **3** *1¾* **Daring Guest (IRE)**[13] 9734 5-9-7 **57**................................ JackMitchell 10 57
(Tom Clover) *styd wd early: chsd ldrs: effrt ent fnl 2f: rdn to ld over 1f out: hdd and no ex ins fnl f: lost 2nd wl ins fnl f and wknd towards fin* **4/1**[2]

04-0 **4** *nk* **Malaysian Boleh**[3] 116 9-8-4 **47**................................(be) GraceMcEntee(7) 1 47
(Phil McEntee) *in tch in midfield: effrt to chse ldrs over 2f out: rdn over 1f out: kpt on same pce ins fnl f* **12/1**

430- **5** *nk* **Napping**[34] 9441 6-9-3 **56**................................(p) GabrieleMalune(3) 5 55
(Amy Murphy) *t.k.h: hld up in tch in midfield: effrt over 1f out: kpt on u.p ins fnl f: nvr enough pce to rch ldrs* **16/1**

000- **6** *2¼* **Tellovoi (IRE)**[12] 9749 11-9-2 **52**................................(p) PJMcDonald 3 45
(Richard Guest) *taken down early: led: rdn and hdd over 1f out: no ex and wknd ins fnl f* **7/1**

266- **7** *½* **Caledonia Laird**[56] 9078 8-9-4 **54**................................(p) DavidProbert 9 46
(Jo Hughes, France) *hld up in tch in last quartet: wd and lost pl bnd 2f out: effrt u.p over 1f out: nvr threatened to get on terms and kpt on same pce ins fnl f* **10/1**

300- **8** *½* **Misu Pete**[65] 8887 7-8-13 **56**................................(p) EllieMacKenzie(7) 7 46
(Mark Usher) *t.k.h: in tch in midfield: effrt over 2f out: struggling to qckn whn sltly impeded and swtchd lft over 1f out: no imp and wl hld ins fnl f* **8/1**

000- **9** *7* **Lord Del Boy**[29] 9509 4-8-9 **45**................................ LukeMorris 8 17
(Michael Attwater) *sn dropped to rr and nvr travelling wl: wl bhd over 1f out: eased wl ins fnl f* **40/1**

536- **10** *2½* **Shyarch**[56] 9080 5-9-0 **50**................................(p) RobertHavlin 2 16
(Christine Dunnett) *chsd ldr: ev ch and rdn wl over 1f out: sn btn and lost pl: bhd and eased wl ins fnl f (jockey said gelding stopped quickly)* **5/1**[3]

006- **11** *2½* **Henrietta's Dream**[36] 9415 5-8-9 **45**................................(b) PaddyMathers 4 4
(John Wainwright) *rousted along leaving stalls: chsd ldrs: losing pl u.p whn hmpd 2f out: no ch after: bhd and eased wl ins fnl f* **66/1**

1m 27.02s (-0.18) **Going Correction** +0.075s/f (Slow) **11** Ran SP% **118.5**
Speed ratings (Par 101): **104,102,100,99,99 96,96,95,87,84 81**
CSF £56.30 CT £210.48 TOTE £13.60: £3.20, £1.40, £1.50; EX 73.60 Trifecta £265.00.
Owner Mrs Catherine Gannon **Bred** Tony O'Meara **Trained** Pandy, Monmouths
■ Stewards' Enquiry : Nicola Currie two-day ban: careless riding (Jan 24-25)

FOCUS
A moderate handicap but probably quite strong for the grade among the leaders.

160 BOOK TICKETS AT CHELMSFORDCITYRACECOURSE.COM H'CAP 1m 6f (P)

7:25 (7:27) (Class 6) (0-60,60) 4-Y-0+

£3,493 (£1,039; £519; £400; £400; £400) **Stalls** Low

Form RPR

22-2 **1** **Your Band**[7] 38 4-9-3 **60**................................ NicolaCurrie 1 77
(Jamie Osborne) *s.i.s: racd in last pair: swtchd rt: pushed along and hdwy on outer to chse ldr 4f out: led ent fnl 3f: sn rdn clr: in n.d but wandering rt 1f out: v easily* **1/1**[1]

034- **2** *14* **Heron (USA)**[38] 9383 5-9-6 **59**................................(p) JackMitchell 4 56
(Brett Johnson) *hld up in last quartet: nt clr run wl over 2f out: swtchd rt and effrt wl over 1f out: kpt on to go 2nd ins fnl f: no ch w wnr* **5/1**[2]

606- **3** *2¼* **Thahab Ifraj (IRE)**[11] 8785 6-8-7 **46** oh1................................ LukeMorris 5 40
(Alexandra Dunn) *reminder sn after s: hld up towards rr: clsd on outer 4f out: rdn to chse clr wnr over 2f out: no imp: plugged on same pce and lost wl btn 2nd ins fnl f* **10/1**

306- **4** *nk* **Alexis Carrington (IRE)**[20] 9663 4-8-13 **56**................................(v) JasonHart 8 51
(John Quinn) *in tch in midfield: effrt 3f out: no ch w wnr and kpt on same pce u.p fr over 1f out* **14/1**

200- **5** *¾* **Caracas**[165] 5525 5-9-1 **54**................................(p) PJMcDonald 2 47
(Kevin Frost) *hld up in last quartet: effrt and swtchd rt over 2f out: no ch w wnr and kpt on same pce u.p fr over 1f out* **20/1**

023- **6** *4* **Contingency Fee**[13] 9728 4-8-7 **57**................................(p) GraceMcEntee(7) 13 46
(Phil McEntee) *styd wd early: in tch in midfield: chsd ldrs 5f out: 3rd and unable to match pce of wnr over 2f out and sn wl btn: wknd ins fnl f* **20/1**

066- **7** *6* **Chorus of Lies**[12] 9750 7-8-0 **46** oh1......(bt[1]) ThoreHammerHansen(7) 11 26
(Alexandra Dunn) *s.i.s: hdwy to chse ldr after 3f tl lost 2nd jst over 3f out: sn outpcd and wknd over 1f out* **80/1**

010- **8** *26* **Lumen**[38] 9383 4-8-7 **50**................................(bt[1]) RobHornby 12
(Roger Charlton) *t.k.h: pressed ldr tl led after 2f: hdd ent fnl 3f and sn outpcd: wknd and wl bhd over 1f out: eased ins fnl f: t.o* **7/1**[3]

006- **9** *15* **More Harry**[155] 5861 4-8-3 **46** oh1................................ PaddyMathers 3
(Martin Smith) *t.k.h: hld up in midfield: lost tch 3f out: t.o and virtually p.u over 1f out* **40/1**

136- **10** *5* **Duration (IRE)**[85] 8312 4-9-1 **58**................................(v[1]) DavidProbert 9
(J R Jenkins) *led for 2f: chsd ldrs tl 8f out: sn u.p and lost pl: lost tch 4f out: t.o* **14/1**

26-5 **11** *38* **Sheila's Empire (IRE)**[6] 58 4-8-3 **53**................................ AaronMackay(7) 10
(J S Moore) *restless in stalls: chsd ldrs tl 5f out: rdn and dropped to rr over 3f out: t.o and virtually p.u over 1f out* **16/1**

3m 2.93s (-0.27) **Going Correction** +0.075s/f (Slow) **11** Ran SP% **120.7**
WFA 4 from 5yo+ 4lb
Speed ratings (Par 101): **103,95,93,93,93 90,87,72,63,61 39**
CSF £5.88 CT £34.59 TOTE £1.90: £1.10, £2.00, £1.80; EX 7.90 Trifecta £52.60.
Owner Frank McGrath **Bred** Miss A J Rawding & P M Crane **Trained** Upper Lambourn, Berks

FOCUS
Not a strong contest but the winner thrashed his rivals.

161 CELEBRATE VALENTINES DAY HERE H'CAP 6f (P)

7:55 (7:56) (Class 6) (0-52,52) 3-Y-0+

£3,493 (£1,039; £519; £400; £400; £400) **Stalls** Centre

Form RPR

13-U **1** **Magicinthemaking (USA)**[6] 53 5-9-11 **51**................................ RobertHavlin 11 57
(John E Long) *in tch in midfield: clsd to trck ldrs over 2f out: effrt over 1f out: drvn and str chal ins fnl f: kpt on wl to ld last strides* **4/1**[1]

40-6 **2** *hd* **Le Manege Enchante (IRE)**[8] 26 6-9-8 **48**..........(v) PaddyMathers 5 53
(Derek Shaw) *t.k.h: prom: chsd ldr over 3f out: effrt and ev ch over 1f out: drvn and maintained chal ins fnl f: led cl home: hdd last strides* **10/1**

040- **3** *shd* **Charlie Alpha (IRE)**[38] 9385 5-9-1 **46** oh1..............(b) RhiainIngram(5) 8 51
(Roger Ingram) *t.k.h: chsd ldr tl led over 4f out: hrd pressed and rdn over 1f out: kpt on u.p: hdd and lost 2 pls cl home* **10/1**

064- **4** *2¾* **Krazy Paving**[14] 9720 7-9-9 **49**................................(b) LukeMorris 2 46
(Olly Murphy) *chsd ldrs: rdn over 2f out: kpt on same pce u.p ins fnl f* **6/1**

300- **5** *¾* **Sybil Grand**[71] 8730 3-8-10 **52**................................(b[1]) NicolaCurrie 4 43
(Jamie Osborne) *in tch in midfield: effrt ent fnl 2f: unable qck over 1f out: kpt on u.p ins fnl f: nvr enough pce to get on terms* **9/2**[2]

500- **6** *hd* **Sovereign State**[14] 9722 4-9-11 **51**................................ EoinWalsh 10 45
(Tony Newcombe) *short of room sn after s: midfield: effrt over 1f out: hung lft and kpt on ins fnl f: no threat to ldrs (jockey said gelding hung left-handed)* **12/1**

00-0 **7** *1¾* **Tasaaboq**[6] 64 8-8-13 **46**................................(t) GraceMcEntee(7) 7 35
(Phil McEntee) *taken down early and led to s: hld up in tch towards rr: clsd over 1f out: rdn and swtchd lft ins fnl f: kpt on but no threat to ldrs* **25/1**

463- **8** *hd* **Black Truffle (FR)**[36] 9401 9-8-13 **46**..................(v) EllieMacKenzie(7) 9 34
(Mark Usher) *dwlt: in tch in rr: effrt over 1f out: hdwy and swtchd lft 1f out: kpt on ins fnl f: nvr trbld ldrs (jockey said gelding was short of room leaving stalls)* **11/1**

012- **9** *½* **Poppy May (IRE)**[12] 9749 5-9-12 **52**................................ PJMcDonald 14 39
(James Given) *in tch in midfield on outer: lost pl bnd 2f out: bhd and nt clrest of runs ent fnl f: kpt on ins fnl f: nvr trbld ldrs* **5/1**[3]

340- **10** *shd* **Plucky Dip**[21] 9634 8-9-4 **51**................................(p) LauraPearson(7) 12 37
(John Ryan) *bhd: effrt on inner over 1f out: kpt on ins fnl f: nvr trbld ldrs* **12/1**

000- **11** *2¼* **Ballesteros**[21] 9648 10-9-10 **50**................................ LiamKeniry 6 30
(Suzi Best) *led tl 4f out: chsd ldr tl over 4f out: lost pl u.p over 1f out: wknd ins fnl f* **50/1**

003- **12** *1* **Secret Asset (IRE)**[78] 8535 14-9-6 **46** oh1................................(b) RobHornby 3 23
(Lisa Williamson) *t.k.h: chsd ldrs: rdn and struggling to qckn over 2f out: lost pl over 1f out: wknd ins fnl f* **25/1**

006- **13** *hd* **Premium Pink (IRE)**[43] 9293 4-9-5 **52**................................ JessicaCooley(7) 1 28
(Luke McJannet) *pushed along early: towards rr on inner: effrt and sme hdwy over 1f out but nvr getting on terms: wknd ins fnl f* **12/1**

1m 14.5s (0.80) **Going Correction** +0.075s/f (Slow) **13** Ran SP% **128.4**
WFA 3 from 4yo+ 16lb
Speed ratings (Par 101): **97,96,96,92,91 91,89,89,88,88 85,83,83**
CSF £47.53 CT £404.34 TOTE £5.10: £1.70, £3.80, £4.50; EX 46.40 Trifecta £380.80.
Owner Martin J Gibbs & R D John **Bred** Janice Woods **Trained** Brighton, East Sussex

FOCUS
A weak handicap run at a solid pace. The race is rated around the front trio and can't be rated any higher.
T/Jkpt: Not won. T/Plt: £55.10 to a £1 stake. Pool: £86,771.75. 1,149.10 winning units. T/Qpdt: £6.70 to a £1 stake. Pool: £14,896.93. 1,636.18 winning units. **Steve Payne**

[40]SOUTHWELL (L-H)
Thursday, January 10

OFFICIAL GOING: Fibresand: standard
Wind: Virtually nil Weather: Overcast

162 BETWAY CASINO H'CAP — 1m 4f 14y(F)
12:45 (12:45) (Class 5) (0-75,75) 4-Y-0+
£3,752 (£1,116; £557; £300; £300; £300) **Stalls** Low

Form | | | RPR
001- **1** **Azari**[23] 9595 7-9-8 **73**..............(b[1]) RossaRyan 2 85
(Alexandra Dunn) *mde all: rdn clr wl over 2f out: kpt on strly* **4/1**[2]
061- **2** 7 **Love Rat**[12] 9750 4-8-4 **63**..............(v) TheodoreLadd(5) 3 64
(Scott Dixon) *trckd wnr: pushed along 3f out: rdn 2f out: sn edgd lft and drvn: plugged on: no ch w wnr (jockey said gelding hung left home straight)* **5/1**[3]
025- **3** ¾ **Saint Mac**[114] 7380 4-8-7 **61** oh3.............. AndrewMullen 7 61
(Michael Appleby) *pushed along s: sn trcking ldrs on outer: pushed along and wd st: rdn and hung lft 2f out: sn drvn and one pce* **5/2**[1]
213- **4** 4½ **Princess Harley (IRE)**[30] 9492 4-9-1 **69**.............. CharlesBishop 4 61
(Mick Quinn) *trckd ldrs: pushed along 4f out: rdn over 3f out: sn drvn and outpcd fnl 2f* **4/1**[2]
144/ **5** 1½ **Sleepy Haven (IRE)**[43] 4499 9-8-10 **61** oh3..............(p) JoeFanning 1 51
(Jennie Candlish) *trckd ldng pair on inner: pushed along wl over 3f out: rdn wl over 2f out: sn wknd (jockey said gelding became unbalanced on final bend)* **10/1**
600/ **6** 1¼ **Toboggan's Fire**[35] 8315 6-9-3 **75**.............. EllaMcCain(7) 5 63
(Donald McCain) *hld up in tch: pushed along over 4f out: rdn over 3f out: sn wknd* **50/1**
561- **7** 5 **Scrafton**[14] 9721 8-8-10 **66**.............. PoppyBridgwater(5) 6 46
(Tony Carroll) *t.k.h early: hld up in rr: hdwy on outer 5f out: trckd ldrs over 3f out: rdn along and wd st: sn btn (vet said gelding was lame right fore)* **6/1**

2m 37.46s (-3.54) **Going Correction** -0.05s/f (Stan)
WFA 4 from 6yo+ 3lb — **7** Ran SP% **110.6**
Speed ratings (Par 103): **109,104,103,100,99 99,95**
CSF £22.42 TOTE £4.80: £2.00, £4.20; EX 29.90 Trifecta £64.90.
Owner B B S & Lot 51 **Bred** Yeguada De Milagro Sa **Trained** West Buckland, Somerset

FOCUS
A fair handicap that looked open beforehand but was processional from the home straight.

163 BETWAY SPRINT H'CAP — 4f 214y(F)
1:20 (1:20) (Class 4) (0-85,86) 4-Y-0+
£6,080 (£1,809; £904; £452; £300; £300) **Stalls** Centre

Form | | | RPR
42-3 **1** **Ornate**[9] 3 6-9-5 **86**.............. PhilDennis(3) 6 99
(David C Griffiths) *mde all centre: rdn over 1f out: drvn ins fnl f: kpt on strly towards fin* **6/1**[2]
021- **2** 2 **Acclaim The Nation (IRE)**[20] 9662 6-9-2 **80**..............(p) JasonHart 1 86
(Eric Alston) *cl up centre: rdn over 1f out: ev ch ent fnl f: sn drvn and kpt on same pce towards fin* **15/8**[1]
101- **3** nk **Eternal Sun**[23] 9597 4-8-9 **76**.............. GabrieleMalune(3) 2 81
(Ivan Furtado) *racd towards far side: chsd ldrs: hdwy over 2f out: rdn wl over 1f out: ev ch ent fnl f: sn drvn and kpt on same pce towards fin* **8/1**
000- **4** 2¼ **Midnight Malibu (IRE)**[49] 9206 6-9-6 **84**.............. JamesSullivan 4 81
(Tim Easterby) *in tch centre: pushed along 1/2-way: hdwy 2f out: chsd ldrs and rdn over 1f out: no imp fnl f* **7/1**
301- **5** 1¼ **Classic Pursuit**[12] 9748 8-9-3 **81**..............(v) LukeMorris 3 73
(Michael Appleby) *chsd ldrs centre: rdn along 2f out: sn drvn and wknd over 1f out* **8/1**
204- **6** ¾ **Erissimus Maximus (FR)**[20] 9662 5-9-7 **85**..............(b) NicolaCurrie 5 75
(Amy Murphy) *chsd ldrs centre: rdn along 2f out: swtchd rt and drvn over 1f out: sn wknd* **13/2**[3]
610- **7** 13 **Jacob's Pillow**[108] 7602 8-8-3 **72**.............. TheodoreLadd(5) 7 15
(Rebecca Bastiman) *sn outpcd and bhd fr 1/2-way* **50/1**
432- **U** **Samovar**[12] 9748 4-8-11 **75**..............(b) KieranO'Neill 8
(Scott Dixon) *uns rdr s* **7/1**

58.31s (-1.39) **Going Correction** -0.05s/f (Stan) — **8** Ran SP% **111.6**
Speed ratings (Par 105): **109,105,105,101,99 98,77,**
CSF £16.79 CT £88.13 TOTE £5.20: £1.70, £1.10, £3.20; EX 19.20 Trifecta £89.00.
Owner Kings Road Racing Partnership **Bred** Cheveley Park Stud Ltd **Trained** Bawtry, S Yorks

FOCUS
A useful sprint won in serene fashion after an eventful start where Samovar stumbled and unseated his jockey as the stalls opened.

164 SUNRACING.CO.UK H'CAP — 1m 13y(F)
1:55 (1:55) (Class 3) (0-90,91) 4-Y-0-£9,451 (£2,829; £1,414; £708; £352) **Stalls** Low

Form | | | RPR
422- **1** **Three Weeks (USA)**[20] 9661 4-9-7 **86**..............(p) JoeFanning 6 94+
(David O'Meara) *sn slt ld: hdd 5f out and cl up: effrt and slt ld wl over 2f out: rdn over 1f out: edgd lft ent fnl f: kpt on* **5/4**[1]
21-1 **2** ½ **Showboating (IRE)**[9] 5 11-8-13 **78** 6ex..............(p) CamHardie 5 85
(John Balding) *dwlt and towards rr: pushed along over 3f out: rdn and hdwy 2f out: chsd wnr whn n.m.r on inner ent fnl f: sn swtchd rt: drvn and styd on wl towards fin* **4/1**[3]
605- **3** 3¼ **Mama Africa (IRE)**[14] 9724 5-8-8 **76**.............. JaneElliott(3) 1 76
(David Barron) *trckd ldrs on inner: pushed along 3f out: hdwy over 2f out: rdn and ev ch over 1f out: kpt on same pce fnl f* **16/1**
242- **4** 1¾ **Mr Top Hat**[15] 9705 4-9-5 **91**.............. KatherineBegley(7) 4 87
(David Evans) *cl up: slt ld after 3f: rdn along 3f out: sn hdd: drvn and wknd wl over 1f out* **9/4**[2]
0V4- **5** 6 **Barrington (IRE)**[49] 9213 5-9-4 **83**..............(v) LukeMorris 2 65
(Michael Appleby) *dwlt: t.k.h: sn chsng ldng pair: rdn along wl over 2f out: sn wknd* **12/1**

1m 42.16s (-1.54) **Going Correction** -0.05s/f (Stan) — **5** Ran SP% **108.8**
Speed ratings (Par 107): **105,104,101,99,93**
CSF £6.44 TOTE £2.00: £1.10, £2.80; EX 6.40 Trifecta £20.20.
Owner Apple Tree Stud **Bred** Apple Tree Stud **Trained** Upper Helmsley, N Yorks

FOCUS
The complexion of this race changed with the morning withdrawal of likely hot favourite Weld Al Emarat but it was a useful handicap nonetheless.

165 BETWAY H'CAP — 6f 16y(F)
2:25 (2:25) (Class 4) (0-80,80) 4-Y-0+
£5,922 (£1,772; £886; £443; £300; £300) **Stalls** Low

Form | | | RPR
01-3 **1** **The Right Choice (IRE)**[7] 44 4-8-11 **70**..............(b) PaddyMathers 1 79
(Richard Fahey) *in tch: rdn along and sltly outpcd 1/2-way: hdwy over 2f out: chsd ldrs over 1f out: drvn to ld ins fnl f: kpt on strly* **9/2**[2]
35-3 **2** 1¾ **Crosse Fire**[7] 43 7-8-3 **67**..............(p) TheodoreLadd(5) 6 70
(Scott Dixon) *cl up: rdn to ld wl over 1f out: drvn and hdd ins fnl f: kpt on same pce towards fin* **12/1**
131- **3** 3 **Black Salt**[23] 9596 5-9-5 **78**.............. RobertWinston 3 71
(David Barron) *trckd ldrs: hdwy and wd st: rdn and edgd lft over 1f out: sn drvn: no imp fnl f* **1/1**[1]
36-1 **4** 1 **Bellevarde (IRE)**[9] 2 5-8-12 **78** 6ex.............. JonathanFisher(7) 2 68
(Richard Price) *trckd ldrs: hdwy wl over 2f out: sn cl up: rdn wl over 1f out: grad wknd appr fnl f* **16/1**
231- **5** 2¼ **Tan**[13] 9733 5-9-7 **80**.............. AlistairRawlinson 5 63
(Michael Appleby) *led: rdn along over 2f out: drvn and hdd wl over 1f out: sn wknd* **11/2**[3]
06-3 **6** 2¾ **Jack The Truth (IRE)**[9] 2 5-8-10 **76**.............. JessicaCooley(7) 7 50
(George Scott) *prom: cl up on outer 1/2-way: wd st: rdn over 2f out: sn wknd* **8/1**
000- **7** 6 **Guardia Svizzera (IRE)**[30] 9494 5-9-0 **73**..............(h) CamHardie 4 28
(Roger Fell) *in tch: pushed along over 4f out: rdn over 3f out: wd st: sn outpcd and bhd* **33/1**

1m 15.03s (-1.47) **Going Correction** -0.05s/f (Stan) — **7** Ran SP% **111.2**
Speed ratings (Par 105): **107,104,100,99,96 92,84**
CSF £51.15 TOTE £5.60: £2.00, £3.10; EX 24.30 Trifecta £122.00.
Owner The Fairweather Foursome **Bred** Mrs E Fitzsimons **Trained** Musley Bank, N Yorks

FOCUS
A modest heat and something of a turn-up with the hot favourite only third.

166 PLAY 4 TO SCORE AT BETWAY H'CAP — 6f 16y(F)
3:00 (3:00) (Class 6) (0-60,62) 4-Y-0+
£3,105 (£924; £461; £300; £300; £300) **Stalls** Low

Form | | | RPR
00-5 **1** **Pearl Acclaim (IRE)**[7] 43 9-9-10 **62**..............(p) PhilDennis(3) 10 69
(David C Griffiths) *trckd ldng pair: hdwy and cl up 1/2-way: rdn to ld 2f out: drvn ins fnl f: hld on wl towards fin* **11/2**[3]
516- **2** ½ **Jazz Legend (USA)**[12] 9749 6-8-13 **51**.............. WilliamCox(3) 2 57
(Mandy Rowland) *slt ld: pushed along over 2f out and sn hdd: rdn wl over 1f out: drvn and rallied gamely ins fnl f: kpt on wl* **9/2**[1]
020- **3** 1½ **Diamond Pursuit**[12] 9749 4-9-0 **52**.............. GabrieleMalune(3) 3 53
(Ivan Furtado) *trckd ldrs: rdn along over 2f out: drvn wl over 1f out: kpt on same pce fnl f* **9/2**[1]
063- **4** 1½ **Alligator**[13] 9735 5-8-5 **45**.............. PoppyBridgwater(5) 5 42
(Tony Carroll) *in tch: hdwy and wd st: rdn to chse ldrs whn carried sltly lft wl over 1f out: sn no imp* **5/1**[2]
060- **5** nk **Mountain Of Stars**[21] 9648 4-8-10 **45**..............(p) JamesSullivan 9 41
(Suzzanne France) *dwlt and swtchd rt to outer: in tch: hdwy and wd st: rdn to chse ldrs and edgd lft over 1f out: sn drvn and one pce* **14/1**
05-0 **6** 2¼ **Blistering Dancer (IRE)**[7] 42 9-8-10 **45**.............. JohnFahy 1 34
(Tony Carroll) *dwlt and towards rr: rdn along 1/2-way: kpt on u.p fnl 2f: n.d (vet said gelding lost left hind shoe)* **10/1**
054- **7** ½ **Westfield Wonder**[12] 9749 4-8-10 **45**..............(b) KieranO'Neill 7 32
(Ronald Thompson) *cl up: rdn along over 2f out: drvn wl over 1f out: sn wknd* **7/1**
00-0 **8** 3¼ **Dream Ally (IRE)**[8] 28 9-9-7 **56**.............. CliffordLee 4 34
(John Weymes) *chsd ldrs: rdn along over 2f out: sn wknd* **9/1**
200- **9** 2 **Juan Horsepower**[19] 9681 5-9-4 **56**..............(b) TimClark(3) 6 28
(Richard Phillips) *dwlt: a outpcd and bhd (jockey said gelding was slowly away)* **16/1**
000- **10** 20 **Luduamf (IRE)**[149] 6128 5-8-10 **45**.............. DannyBrock 8
(Michael Chapman) *dwlt: a outpcd and bhd* **100/1**

1m 16.62s (0.12) **Going Correction** -0.05s/f (Stan) — **10** Ran SP% **113.5**
Speed ratings (Par 101): **97,96,94,92,91 88,88,83,81,54**
CSF £29.60 CT £122.48 TOTE £4.70: £2.30, £1.90, £2.00; EX 32.60 Trifecta £126.80.
Owner Ontoawinner 2 & Partner **Bred** Awbeg Stud **Trained** Bawtry, S Yorks

FOCUS
Moderate stuff but an exciting finish and a double on the day for trainer and jockey. The straightforward level is set around the second and third.

167 BETWAY "HANDS AND HEELS" SERIES APPRENTICE H'CAP (PART OF THE RACING EXCELLENCE INITIATIVE) — 4f 214y(F)
3:35 (3:35) (Class 6) (0-60,62) 4-Y-0+
£3,105 (£924; £461; £300; £300; £300) **Stalls** Centre

335- **1** **Gorgeous General**[26] 9558 4-9-2 **48**.............. WilliamCarver(3) 4 53
(Lawrence Mullaney) *prom centre: effrt 2f out: rdn over 1f out: styd on wl to ld towards fin* **10/3**[2]
016- **2** nk **Divine Call**[21] 9648 12-9-12 **55**.............. TristanPrice 3 59
(Charlie Wallis) *trckd ldrs: n.m.r and swtchd lft towards far side over 3f out: hdwy 2f out: rdn to ld over 1f out: hdd and no ex towards fin* **14/1**
00-0 **3** ½ **Sir Walter (IRE)**[2] 129 4-9-2 **45**.............. EllaMcCain 6 47
(Eric Alston) *prom: cl up over 2f out: rdn over 1f out: ev ch tl no ex towards fin* **16/1**
13-2 **4** 1 **Piazon**[7] 43 8-10-2 **62**..............(be) HarryRussell(3) 1 61
(Julia Brooke) *cl up: slt ld 2f out: sn rdn: hdd over 1f out: kpt on same pce (vet said gelding lost right fore shoe)* **5/4**[1]
064- **5** ½ **Coiste Bodhar (IRE)**[21] 9649 8-9-3 **46**..............(p) JessicaCooley 5 43
(Scott Dixon) *led: rdn along: hdd and outpcd over 2f out: kpt on fnl f* **14/1**
042- **6** ¾ **Furni Factors**[21] 9648 4-9-5 **51**..............(b) AmeliaGlass(3) 7 45
(Ronald Thompson) *racd towards stands' side: dwlt: in tch: hdwy and cl up 2f out: rdn over 1f out: one pce fnl f* **7/2**[3]

59.96s (0.26) **Going Correction** -0.05s/f (Stan) — **6** Ran SP% **109.0**
Speed ratings (Par 101): **95,94,93,92,91 90**
CSF £41.08 TOTE £3.90: £1.70, £5.20; EX 37.80 Trifecta £272.20.
Owner Shaun Humphries **Bred** Shaun & Leanne Humphries **Trained** Great Habton, N Yorks

FOCUS
A moderate finish to proceedings but credit should go to the winner who shed his maiden tag at the 14th attempt. Weak form.

T/Plt: £147.70 to a £1 stake. Pool: £46,294.80. 313.31 winning units. T/Qpdt: £28.00 to a £1 stake. Pool: £4,435.01. 158.39 winning units. **Joe Rowntree**

92 MEYDAN (L-H)

Thursday, January 10

OFFICIAL GOING: Turf: good; dirt: fast

168a DUBAI TROPHY SPONSORED BY MASDAR (CONDITIONS) (TURF) 7f

3:05 (3:05) 3-Y-O

£47,244 (£15,748; £7,874; £3,937; £2,362; £1,574)

RPR

1 **Good Fortune**113 7423 3-9-3 94.....(t) JamesDoyle 12 97
(Charlie Appleby) *mid-div: smooth prog 2 1/2f out: led 1 1/2f out: r.o wl* **7/2**3

2 3/4 **Woven**123 7099 3-9-3 83..... JimCrowley 8 95
(David Simcock) *hmpd sn after s: mid-div: smooth prog 3f out: r.o wl fnl 1 1/2f: nrst fin* **15/2**

3 1 1/4 **Trolius (IRE)**55 9106 3-9-5 89.....(p) ChrisHayes 14 94
(Simon Crisford) *mid-div: r.o wl fnl 2f: nrst fin* **20/1**

4 1 3/4 **Irish Trilogy (IRE)**84 3-9-5 85..... CarlosLopez 5 89
(Andrew Kidney, Sweden) *trckd ldr: ev ch 2f out: r.o same pce fnl 1 1/2f* **40/1**

5 1 1/4 **Shining Armor**27 9533 3-9-0 95..... DarraghKeenan(5) 15 86
(John Ryan) *sn led: hdd 1 1/2f out: wknd fnl f* **25/1**

6 nse **Prince Elzaam (IRE)**121 7143 3-9-5 86..... DaneO'Neill 16 85+
(Jaber Ramadhan, Bahrain) *mid-div: r.o same pce fnl 2f* **40/1**

7 2 1/2 **Al Fajir Mukbile (IRE)**78 8553 3-9-3 83..... FabriceVeron 3 77
(Ismail Mohammed) *s.i.s: a mid-div* **28/1**

8 1 1/4 **Estihdaaf (USA)**86 8305 3-9-3 89..... ChristopheSoumillon 6 73
(Saeed bin Suroor) *a mid-div* **7/4**1

9 nse **Dream With You (FR)**83 3-8-9 87.....(t) AntonioFresu 4 65
(N Caullery, France) *sed awkwardly: nvr bttr than mid-div* **33/1**

10 shd **Iskandarani (USA)**35 9436 3-9-0 0.....(b) ShermanBrown 11 70
(R Bouresly, Kuwait) *a in rr* **80/1**

11 hd **Bosconero (IRE)**41 9352 3-8-8 0.....(t) SaeedAlMazrooei(6) 7 69
(A R Al Rayhi, UAE) *nvr nr to chal* **80/1**

12 1 **Sporting Chance**89 8214 3-9-5 105.....(p) PatCosgrave 1 72
(Simon Crisford) *s.i.s: trckd ldrs tl wknd fnl 1 1/2f* **5/2**2

13 2 3/4 **Magic Image**22 9603 3-8-9 84..... DarryllHolland 9 54
(Saeed bin Suroor) *nvr bttr than mid-div* **14/1**

14 8 3/4 **King Lothbrok (FR)**108 7623 3-9-0 79..... ConnorBeasley 13 36
(A bin Harmash, UAE) *nvr bttr than mid-div* **80/1**

15 13 **Al Mortajaz (FR)**35 9436 3-9-0 73.....(b) BenCurtis 2
(Ismail Mohammed) *trckd ldr tl wknd fnl 2 1/2f* **33/1**

16 19 1/2 **Mneef (USA)**13 9741 3-9-0 0..... MickaelBarzalona 10
(S Jadhav, UAE) *a in rr* **66/1**

1m 24.12s (0.02) **Going Correction** +0.30s/f (Good) **16 Ran SP% 133.6**
Speed ratings: **111,110,108,106,105 105,102,100,100,100 100,99,96,86,71 49**
CSF: 30.44.
Owner Godolphin **Bred** Rabbah Bloodstock Ltd **Trained** Newmarket, Suffolk

FOCUS
TRAKUS (metres travelled compared to winner): 2nd -6, 3rd -3, 4th -3, 5th -7, 6th +1, 7th -15, 8th +1, 9th -7, 10th -6, 11th +3, 12th -6, 13th -6, 14th +3, 15th -9, 16th -1. The rail was out four metres on the turf course. One of two new races to bolster the 3yo turf programme at the carnival and the form looks quite useful. This was a fast early/slow late pace scenario: 24.47 (400m from standing start), 22.98 (800m), 24.08 (1200m), 12.59 (line).

169a UAE 2000 GUINEAS TRIAL SPONSORED BY STRATA (CONDITIONS) (DIRT) 1m (D)

3:40 (3:40) 3-Y-O

£47,244 (£15,748; £7,874; £3,937; £2,362; £1,574)

RPR

1 **Walking Thunder (USA)**35 9436 3-8-9 95.....(h) ConnorBeasley 13 106+
(A bin Harmash, UAE) *trckd ldr: led gng wl 3f out: r.o wl: easily* **10/3**2

2 9 **Manguzi (FR)**13 9741 3-8-9 75..... FernandoJara 11 85
(A R Al Rayhi, UAE) *chsd ldrs: r.o wl fnl 2f but no ch w wnr* **33/1**

3 6 **Al Seel Legacy's (USA)**21 9650 3-8-9 85..... PatDobbs 7 71+
(Doug Watson, UAE) *settled in rr: r.o wl fnl 2f: nrst fin* **12/1**3

4 1 **Royal Marine (IRE)**95 8025 3-9-1 113..... ChristopheSoumillon 6 75+
(Saeed bin Suroor) *s.i.s: mid-div: r.o same pce fnl 2 1/2f* **5/6**1

5 2 **Power Link (USA)**111 7497 3-8-9 85.....(p) MickaelBarzalona 4 64
(S Jadhav, UAE) *sn led: hdd 3f out: wknd fnl 1 1/2f* **25/1**

6 3/4 **Red Cactus (USA)**84 3-8-11 80 ow2..... CarlosLopez 5 64+
(Bent Olsen, Denmark) *nvr nr to chal but r.o fnl 2f* **66/1**

7 3/4 **Burj**75 8644 3-8-9 87..... KevinStott 3 61
(Saeed bin Suroor) *s.i.s: a mid-div* **16/1**

8 4 **Giant Hero (USA)**173 3-8-9 85.....(t) ChrisHayes 12 51
(N Bachalard, UAE) *nvr nr to chal* **14/1**

9 1 1/4 **Rayig**97 7957 3-8-9 72..... RonanWhelan 1 49
(A R Al Rayhi, UAE) *s.i.s: nvr nr to chal* **66/1**

10 1 1/2 **Faith And Fortune (ARG)**154 3-9-5 97..... OlivierDoleuze 8 39
(M F De Kock, South Africa) *nvr bttr than mid-div* **14/1**

11 1 **Dark Thunder (IRE)**94 8056 3-8-9 77.....(p) SamHitchcott 10 43
(Doug Watson, UAE) *chsd ldrs tl wknd fnl 2 1/2f* **33/1**

12 1 **Galaxy Road (USA)** 3-8-9 0..... BenCurtis 2 41
(M Al Mheiri, UAE) *nvr bttr than mid-div* **25/1**

13 5 1/4 **Nitro (USA)** 3-8-9 0.....(b) DaneO'Neill 9 28
(Doug Watson, UAE) *slowly away: a in rr* **40/1**

1m 38.43s (0.93) **Going Correction** +0.35s/f (Slow) **13 Ran SP% 123.5**
Speed ratings: **109,100,94,93,91 90,89,85,84,82 81,80,75**
CSF: 119.75.
Owner Phoenix Ladies Syndicate **Bred** Golden Legacy Stable **Trained** United Arab Emirates

FOCUS
TRAKUS: 2nd +6, 3rd -5, 4th +6, 5th -6, 6th +5, 7th -4, 8th +9, 9th +5, 10th -5, 11th +2, 12th -1, 13th +4. The distance of this race was up from 7f. A fast early/slow late pace: 24.19 (quicker than later older-horse Group 2), 23.17, 24.79, 26.28.

170a CLEVELAND CLINIC ABU DHABI WORLD EALTHCARE CUP (H'CAP) (TURF) 6f

4:15 (4:15) (95-108,108) 3-Y-O+

£82,677 (£27,559; £13,779; £6,889; £4,133; £2,755)

RPR

1 **Dream Today (IRE)**94 8050 4-8-7 **96**..... ChrisHayes 7 100
(Jamie Osborne) *trckd ldr: rdn 2f out: r.o wl to ld cl home* **16/1**

2 shd **Abrantes (SPA)**81 6-8-11 **100**..... VaclavJanacek 11 104
(G Arizkorreta Elosegui, Spain) *settled in rr: smooth prog 2f out: led 1f out: hdd cl home* **20/1**

3 shd **Intisaab**54 9127 8-9-6 **108**.....(p) JamesDoyle 1 113
(David O'Meara) *mid-div: r.o wl fnl 2f: nrst fin* **7/1**

4 hd **Alfredo Arcano (IRE)**27 9541 5-8-6 **95**.....(t) ConnorBeasley 4 98
(David Marnane, Ire) *trckd ldr: ev ch 1 1/2f out: r.o wl: jst failed* **10/1**

5 nk **Roussel (IRE)**133 6717 4-8-10 **99**.....(p) ColmO'Donoghue 5 101
(Charlie Appleby) *sn led: hdd 1f out but r.o wl* **9/1**

6 3/4 **Glenamoy Lad**26 9561 5-8-8 **97**.....(t) RichardMullen 3 97
(Michael Wigham) *slowly away: mid-div: r.o fnl 2f: nrst fin* **10/3**2

7 3 1/2 **Above The Rest (IRE)**7 50 8-9-6 **108**.....(h) BenCurtis 6 97
(David Barron) *nvr bttr than mid-div* **6/1**3

8 nk **Major Partnership (IRE)**96 7998 4-9-0 **102**...(t) ChristopheSoumillon 2 91
(Saeed bin Suroor) *s.i.s: trckd ldr tl outpcd fnl 2f* **2/1**1

9 2 3/4 **Ghaamer (USA)**7 52 9-8-6 **95**.....(t) BrettDoyle 8 74
(R Bouresly, Kuwait) *trckd ldr tl wknd 4f out* **80/1**

10 1 3/4 **Waady (IRE)**7 49 7-8-9 **98**.....(h) DaneO'Neill 10 71
(Doug Watson, UAE) *a in rr* **16/1**

11 nk **Raafid**5 95 6-8-8 **97**..... FernandoJara 12 69
(A R Al Rayhi, UAE) *a in rr* **28/1**

12 8 3/4 **Emirates Skycargo (IRE)**55 9117 7-8-8 **97**... PierantonioConvertino 13 41
(R Bouresly, Kuwait) *a in rr* **80/1**

1m 11.0s (2.00) **Going Correction** +0.30s/f (Good) **12 Ran SP% 124.7**
Speed ratings: **98,97,97,97,97 96,91,91,87,85 84,72**
CSF: 308.10; TRICAST: 2,484.36.
Owner Melbourne 10 Racing **Bred** Ballylinch Stud **Trained** Upper Lambourn, Berks

FOCUS
A competitive sprint handicap, if short of unexposed types, and the pace was strong, in particular the middle section: 24.87 (from standing start), 22.03, 24.1. The first six have all been rated close to their marks.

171a AL MAKTOUM CHALLENGE R1 SPONSORED BY MUBADALA (GROUP 2) (DIRT) 1m (D)

4:50 (4:50) 3-Y-O+

£165,354 (£55,118; £27,559; £13,779; £8,267; £5,511)

RPR

1 **North America**285 1527 7-9-0 118.....(t) RichardMullen 2 118
(S Seemar, UAE) *wl away: sn led: skipped clr 3 1/2f out: r.o wl: easily* **6/1**

2 9 **Kimbear (USA)**35 9438 5-9-0 109..... PatDobbs 1 98
(Doug Watson, UAE) *trckd ldr: rdn 4f out: r.o wl fnl 3f but no ch w wnr* **5/2**1

3 1 3/4 **Muntazah**32 6-9-0 110..... JimCrowley 4 94
(Doug Watson, UAE) *mid-div: r.o fnl 3f but no ch w wnr* **7/1**

4 1 3/4 **Gold Town**285 1522 4-9-0 113.....(p) JamesDoyle 8 90
(Charlie Appleby) *mid-div: r.o same pce fnl 3f* **9/2**3

5 2 3/4 **African Ride**103 7759 5-9-0 105.....(t) ChristopheSoumillon 6 83
(Simon Crisford) *a mid-div* **8/1**

6 2 1/4 **Dolkong (USA)**32 5-9-0 100..... PatCosgrave 5 78
(Simon Foster, Korea) *s.i.s: a in rr* **66/1**

7 10 1/4 **Etijaah (USA)**21 9653 9-9-0 106.....(h) DaneO'Neill 9 54
(Doug Watson, UAE) *a in rr* **25/1**

8 6 **Masaarr (USA)**147 6218 4-9-0 109.....(b) ChrisHayes 3 41
(N Bachalard, UAE) *nvr nr to chal* **25/1**

9 6 1/2 **Heavy Metal**285 1520 9-9-0 114..... MickaelBarzalona 7 26
(S Jadhav, UAE) *trckd ldr: rdn 4f out: wknd fnl 3f* **3/1**2

1m 35.88s (-1.62) **Going Correction** +0.35s/f (Slow) **9 Ran SP% 118.8**
Speed ratings: **122,113,111,109,106 104,94,88,81**
CSF: 21.76.
Owner Ramzan Kadyrov **Bred** Qatar Bloodstock Ltd **Trained** United Arab Emirates

FOCUS
TRAKUS: 2nd 0, 3rd +3, 4th +10, 5th +9, 6th +8, 7th +5, 8th +3, 9th +6. The track seemed quicker than in recent weeks but even so this was an extremely good time from the winner, backing up a stunning visual impression. The splits were 24.45, 22.6, 23.83, 25.00, which made for a 2.55sec quicker final time than Walking Thunder earlier on the card. The runner-up looks the best guide to the form.

172a SPECIAL OLYMPICS CUP (H'CAP) (DIRT) 1m 1f 110y(D)

5:25 (5:25) (90-111,111) 3-Y-O+

£82,677 (£27,559; £13,779; £6,889; £4,133; £2,755)

RPR

1 **New Trails (USA)**21 9653 5-8-7 **99**.....(t) ConnorBeasley 7 112+
(A bin Harmash, UAE) *mid-div: smooth prog 4 1/2f out: led 3 1/2f out: r.o wl: easily* **7/2**1

2 10 1/2 **Tried And True (USA)**13 9737 7-8-5 **97**.....(v) SamHitchcott 5 89
(Doug Watson, UAE) *settled in rr: r.o wl fnl 3f but no ch w wnr* **13/2**3

3 2 1/4 **Key Bid**5 98 5-8-5 **92**.....(t) FernandoJara 6 84
(A R Al Rayhi, UAE) *mid-div: r.o fnl 2f but no ch w first two* **16/1**

4 1 1/2 **Saltarin Dubai (ARG)**21 9653 6-9-0 **105**.....(bt) RichardMullen 4 90
(S Seemar, UAE) *trckd ldr: led 4f out: hdd 3 1/2f out: r.o same pce fnl 2 1/2f* **11/2**2

5 2 **Welsh Lord**71 8736 4-8-5 **95** ow3..... RowanScott(3) 2 82+
(Saeed bin Suroor) *s.i.s: mid-div: r.o same pce fnl 2f* **9/1**

6 3/4 **Light The Lights (SAF)**7 51 7-9-6 **111**..... AdriedeVries 3 90
(M F De Kock, South Africa) *a mid-div* **8/1**

7 1/2 **Montsarrat (IRE)**21 9653 6-8-5 **97**.....(b) MickaelBarzalona 11 74
(S Jadhav, UAE) *rdn to ld: hdd & wknd 4f out* **12/1**

8 9 3/4 **Street Of Dreams**35 9437 6-8-5 **90**..... ChrisHayes 1 54
(Doug Watson, UAE) *nvr bttr than mid-div* **8/1**

9 25 **Syphax (USA)**21 9653 5-8-5 **94**..... RoystonFfrench 10 3
(S Jadhav, UAE) *slowly away: a in rr* **33/1**

10 dist **Active Spirit (IRE)**[49] 9220 8-8-5 **91**..................(vt) TadhgO'Shea 9
(Doug Watson, UAE) *nvr bttr than mid-div: virtually p.u 2 1/2f out* **40/1**
11 dist **Glassy Waters (USA)**[37] 9390 5-8-5 **96**.................. HayleyTurner 8
(Saeed bin Suroor) *a in rr* **7/2**[1]
1m 59.26s (0.46) **Going Correction** +0.35s/f (Slow)
WFA 4 from 5yo+ 1lb 11 Ran SP% **124.3**
Speed ratings: **112,103,101,100,99 98,98,90,70,**
CSF: 28.15; TRICAST: 335.99.
Owner Hamdan Sultan Ali Alsabousi **Bred** Darley **Trained** United Arab Emirates
FOCUS
TRAKUS: 2nd +8, 3rd +1, 4th -5, 5th -8, 6th -9, 7th -8, 8th -6, 9th 0, 10th +20, 11th +4. This was run at a true pace: 25.31, 23.87, 25.71, 25.16, 19.21 (final 300m). Another wide-margin winner, as in all the dirt races on the day.

173a CEPSA ENERGY CUP (H'CAP) (TURF) 1m
6:00 (6:00) (95-105,105) 3-Y-O+
£63,779 (£21,259; £10,629; £5,314; £3,188; £2,125)

RPR
1 **Baroot**[301] 1223 7-9-0 **99**.................. AdriedeVries 8 106+
(M F De Kock, South Africa) *mid-div: smooth prog 2 1/2f out: rdn to ld fnl 110yds* **33/1**
2 2 **On The Warpath**[159] 5731 4-8-10 **96**.................. ColmO'Donoghue 9 97
(Charlie Appleby) *trckd ldr: led 4f out: r.o wl but hdd fnl 110yds* **5/2**[1]
3 nse **Silent Attack**[243] 2632 6-9-4 **103**.................. ChristopheSoumillon 7 105
(Saeed bin Suroor) *mid-div: chsd ldrs 2 1/2f out: r.o fnl 1 1/2f: nrst fin* **10/3**[2]
4 ¾ **Cliffs Of Capri**[97] 7953 5-8-11 **97**.................. ChrisHayes 10 96
(Jamie Osborne) *settled in rr: r.o wl fnl 2f: nrst fin* **20/1**
5 ½ **Kronprinz (GER)**[42] 9321 4-9-5 **104**.................. AntonioFresu 16 103
(E Charpy, UAE) *mid-div: r.o same pce fnl 2f* **50/1**
6 hd **Eshtiraak (AUS)**[55] 4-9-0 **99**.................. JimCrowley 4 98
(David A Hayes, Australia) *nvr bttr than mid-div* **10/1**
7 shd **Taamol (IRE)**[21] 9655 5-9-1 **100**..................(t) FernandoJara 11 98
(A R Al Rayhi, UAE) *nvr nr to chal but r.o fnl 2 1/2f* **33/1**
8 shd **Zainhom (USA)**[13] 9739 5-9-0 **99**..................(p) DaneO'Neill 14 97
(M Al Mheiri, UAE) *mid-div: r.o same pce fnl 2f* **20/1**
9 nk **King's Field (IRE)**[34] 9453 4-9-6 **105**.................. RonanWhelan 3 102
(Joseph Patrick O'Brien, Ire) *trckd ldrs tl wknd 2f out* **8/1**[3]
10 1 **Bold Rex (SAF)**[327] 782 5-8-13 **98**.................. OlivierDoleuze 5 93
(M F De Kock, South Africa) *a mid-div* **28/1**
11 nk **Hors De Combat**[113] 7424 8-9-4 **103**.................. TadhgO'Shea 6 97
(Denis Coakley) *nvr nr to chal* **10/1**
12 3¾ **Mailshot (USA)**[32] 5-8-11 **97**.................. MickaelBarzalona 13 82
(S Jadhav, UAE) *nvr nr to chal* **20/1**
13 2 **Gm Hopkins**[7] 51 8-9-1 **100**.................. RobertTart 15 81
(Jaber Ramadhan, Bahrain) *nvr bttr than mid-div* **33/1**
14 5½ **Equitant**[34] 9453 4-8-11 **97**.................. PatCosgrave 12 65
(Joseph Patrick O'Brien, Ire) *nvr bttr than mid-div* **16/1**
15 1¼ **Original Choice (IRE)**[40] 9358 5-9-3 **102**..................(p) BenCurtis 1 68
(William Haggas) *sn led: hdd & wknd 4f out* **9/1**
16 2 **Good Effort (IRE)**[86] 8304 4-9-1 **100**.................. FabriceVeron 2 61
(Ismail Mohammed) *nvr bttr than mid-div* **14/1**
1m 36.41s (-1.09) **Going Correction** +0.30s/f (Good) **16** Ran SP% **132.0**
Speed ratings: **117,115,114,114,113 113,113,113,113,112 111,107,105,100,99 97**
CSF: 114.72; TRICAST: 383.25; Placepot: 2,897.20 to a £1 stake. Quadpot: 59.40 to a £1 stake.
Owner Sh Ahmed bin Mohd bin Khalifa Al Maktoum **Bred** W & R Barnett Ltd **Trained** South Africa
FOCUS
TRAKUS: 2nd 0, 3rd +3, 4th -4, 5th +3, 6th +3, 7th +2, 8th +7, 9th -1, 10th -1, 11th -3, 12th +6, 13th +7, 14th +6, 15th -5, 16th -5. The splits were 25.25, 23.18, 24.09, before the winner quickened up in 23.28. The third helps with the form, rated to his turf pick.

140 LINGFIELD (L-H)
Friday, January 11
OFFICIAL GOING: Polytrack: standard
Wind: light, across Weather: bright spells

174 LADBROKES HOME OF THE ODDS BOOST H'CAP 1m 1y(P)
1:10 (1:10) (Class 6) (0-65,67) 3-Y-O
£3,105 (£924; £461; £300; £300; £300) **Stalls** High

Form RPR
123- 1 **Dancing Jo**[51] 9169 3-9-7 **65**.................. CharlesBishop 7 69
(Mick Channon) *in tch in midfield: effrt on inner ent fnl 2f: swtchd rt and chsd ldrs over 1f out: clsd u.p to chse ldr ins fnl f: r.o wl to ld cl home* **9/4**[1]
065- 2 nk **Wall Of Sapphire (IRE)**[15] 9726 3-9-9 **67**.................. JackMitchell 1 70
(Hugo Palmer) *led: sn hdd and trckd ldrs: effrt to chse ldr and swtchd rt ent fnl 2f: rdn to ld over 1f out: drvn 1f out: kpt on u.p: hdd and no ex cl home* **9/2**[2]
460- 3 ½ **Bug Boy (IRE)**[73] 8728 3-9-5 **63**..................(p[1]) JFEgan 3 65
(Paul George) *dwlt: t.k.h: hld up in last trio: clsd and nt clr run 2f out tl swtchd rt ent fnl f: hdwy u.p to chse ldng pair 100yds out: styd on strly towards fin: nt quite rch ldrs* **10/1**
005- 4 3 **Patronus**[25] 9591 3-8-6 **50**..................(b) KieranO'Neill 5 45
(Brian Meehan) *dwlt and pushed along leaving stalls: hdwy to ld over 6f out: rdn and hdd over 1f out: no ex u.p and wknd ins fnl f* **20/1**
132- 5 ½ **Um Shama (IRE)**[11] 9770 3-9-2 **60**.................. JosephineGordon 9 54
(David Loughnane) *stdd s: hld up in tch in last trio: clsd and nt clr run bnd wl over 1f out: swtchd rt over 1f out: edgd lft and styd on wl ins fnl f: no threat to ldrs (jockey said filly ran too free and hung left-handed in the straight)* **5/1**[3]
04-0 6 2¼ **Drummer Jack (IRE)**[6] 79 3-9-1 **59**..................(t) MartinDwyer 2 48
(William Muir) *dwlt: in tch in rr: pushed along 4f out: hdwy u.p on inner over 1f out: no imp and wl hld fnl f* **9/2**[2]
006- 7 4½ **Red Archangel (IRE)**[35] 9444 3-9-3 **61**..................(p[1]) AdamKirby 4 39
(Richard Spencer) *rousted along leaving stalls: sn led: hdd over 6f out: chsd ldr: rdn over 3f out: lost 2nd ent fnl 2f and sn struggling: wknd fnl f* **7/1**
004- 8 4½ **Uponastar (IRE)**[32] 9484 3-9-5 **63**.................. MartinHarley 8 31
(Amy Murphy) *dwlt: in tch in midfield: rdn 2f out: sn outpcd and btn over 1f out: wknd fnl f* **14/1**
045- 9 16 **The Galla Girl (IRE)**[43] 9307 3-9-0 **61**..................(h) AaronJones(3) 6
(Denis Quinn) *chsd ldrs on outer: rdn and lost pl bnd 2f out: sn bhd* **33/1**
1m 37.32s (-0.88) **Going Correction** -0.075s/f (Stan) **9** Ran SP% **119.8**
Speed ratings (Par 95): **101,100,100,97,96 94,89,85,69**
CSF £12.93 CT £86.60 TOTE £2.40: £1.10, £1.70, £5.00; EX 12.30 Trifecta £147.10.
Owner R E F Ten **Bred** A S Palmer **Trained** West Ilsley, Berks
FOCUS
A modest but competitive looking 3yo handicap, although the first three came clear and the form looks reasonable for the grade, rated around the second.

175 LIKE SUN RACING ON FACEBOOK H'CAP 1m 1y(P)
1:40 (1:40) (Class 6) (0-65,71) 4-Y-O+
£3,105 (£924; £461; £300; £300; £300) **Stalls** High

Form RPR
161- 1 **Mr Mac**[38] 9387 5-9-4 **62**.................. CharlesBishop 6 72+
(Peter Hedger) *stdd after s: hld up in rr: shkn up and clsd ent fnl 2f: rdn and hdwy to chse ldrs 1f out: sn chalng: r.o wl to ld 50yds out: gng away at fin* **11/2**[3]
012- 2 1¼ **Delicate Kiss**[12] 9767 5-9-2 **60**..................(b) LiamJones 5 67
(John Bridger) *in tch in midfield on outer: rdn and clsd to chse ldrs 2f out: drvn to ld 1f out: hung lft but kpt on ins fnl f: hdd and nt match pce of wnr fnl 50yds* **6/1**
003- 3 1¾ **Screaming Gemini (IRE)**[34] 9458 5-9-3 **66**.......... PoppyBridgwater(5) 7 70
(Tony Carroll) *chsd ldng trio: nt clrest of run briefly over 1f out: clsd u.p to chse ldrs 1f out: no ex and sltly impeded ins fnl f: kpt on same pce after* **9/1**
416- 4 1 **Cuttin' Edge (IRE)**[36] 9428 5-9-7 **65**.................. MartinDwyer 9 66
(William Muir) *t.k.h: chsd ldrs tl wnt 2nd over 6f out: rdn and ev ch wl over 1f out tl no ex jst ins fnl f: outpcd fnl 100yds* **3/1**[2]
460- 5 1½ **Accomplice**[108] 7651 5-9-8 **66**.................. DavidProbert 8 63
(Michael Blanshard) *dwlt: hld up in tch in last trio: effrt over 1f out: rdn and kpt on ins fnl f: nvr trbld ldrs* **66/1**
42-0 6 shd **Mochalov**[8] 33 4-8-13 **57**.................. DannyBrock 3 54
(Jane Chapple-Hyam) *chsd ldr for over 1f: styd trcking ldrs on inner: effrt over 1f out: pressed ldrs briefly 1f out: no ex and outpcd ins fnl f* **20/1**
000- 7 shd **Purple Paddy**[70] 8797 4-8-7 **51** oh6.................. JohnFahy 2 48
(Jimmy Fox) *dwlt: t.k.h: sn rcvrd and in tch in midfield: effrt on inner over 1f out: nt clr run and swtchd rt 1f out: kpt on but no threat to ldrs ins fnl f* **33/1**
310- 8 4½ **Aqua Libre**[109] 7618 6-9-4 **62**..................(p) EdwardGreatrex 1 49
(Jennie Candlish) *led: rdn over 1f out: hdd 1f out: sn btn and wknd ins fnl f* **20/1**
36-1 9 8 **Philamundo (IRE)**[8] 33 4-9-13 **71** 6ex..................(b) AdamKirby 4 39
(Richard Spencer) *stdd after s: plld hrd: hld up in last trio: effrt over 2f out: no prog and bhd whn hung lft over 1f out: wknd fnl f (jockey said gelding ran too free)* **6/4**[1]
1m 37.06s (-1.14) **Going Correction** -0.075s/f (Stan) **9** Ran SP% **118.6**
Speed ratings (Par 101): **102,100,99,98,96 96,96,91,83**
CSF £37.39 CT £296.60 TOTE £6.90: £2.60, £1.80, £2.40; EX 34.00 Trifecta £169.50.
Owner P C F Racing Ltd **Bred** J J Whelan **Trained** Hook, Hampshire
FOCUS
This modest handicap for older horses was run 0.26 secs faster than the opening 3yo contest. The winner came from last 3f out and it's quite straightforward form for the grade.

176 SUN RACING H'CAP 7f 1y(P)
2:10 (2:10) (Class 2) (0-105,96) 4-Y-O+ £11,971 (£3,583; £1,791; £896; £446) **Stalls** Low

Form RPR
031- 1 **Keyser Soze (IRE)**[30] 9508 5-9-7 **96**.................. AdamKirby 8 106+
(Richard Spencer) *s.i.s: hld up in tch in rr: clsd and swtchd rt over 1f out: shifting lft and qcknd u.p to ld ins fnl f: sn in command (vet reported the gelding had sustained a small wound to its left-fore fetlock)* **4/5**[1]
225- 2 1 **Areen Heart (FR)**[11] 9774 5-8-13 **88**..................(h) MartinHarley 7 95
(David O'Meara) *mounted in the chute and taken down early: led: urged along over 1f out: hdd and rdn ins fnl f: kpt on same pce towards fin* **8/1**[3]
V43- 3 1¼ **Swift Approval (IRE)**[11] 9772 7-8-10 **85**..................(p) DavidProbert 9 89
(Stuart Williams) *chsd ldrs on outer: wnt 2nd over 3f out: rdn over 1f out: unable qck and lost 2nd ins fnl f: kpt on same pce fnl 100yds* **9/1**
412- 4 1 **Intransigent**[104] 7750 10-8-8 **86**..................(b) WilliamCox(3) 6 87
(Andrew Balding) *hld up wl in tch in midfield: shkn up over 1f out: sn rdn: kpt on same pce ins fnl f* **25/1**
000- 5 nse **Reckless Endeavour (IRE)**[41] 9357 6-8-12 **87**.................. FranBerry 2 88
(David Barron) *in tch in midfield: effrt ent fnl 2f: nt clr run and swtchd lft ent fnl f: sn rdn and kpt on same pce after* **10/1**
004- 6 ½ **Mickey (IRE)**[27] 9561 6-8-13 **88**..................(v) RichardKingscote 5 88
(Tom Dascombe) *dwlt: hld up in tch in last trio: effrt and wd bnd 2f out: kpt on ins fnl f: no threat to wnr* **8/1**[3]
000- 7 nk **Mr Scaramanga**[93] 8105 5-8-8 **90**.................. LeviWilliams(7) 1 89
(Simon Dow) *stdd after s: hld up in tch in last trio: effrt and hdwy on inner over 1f out: no imp ins fnl f* **33/1**
12-3 8 1 **Take The Helm**[6] 89 6-9-7 **96**.................. LiamKeniry 4 92
(Brian Meehan) *trckd ldr tl 3f out: rdn ent fnl 2f: no ex 1f out: wknd ins fnl f* **11/2**[2]
1m 22.53s (-2.27) **Going Correction** -0.075s/f (Stan) **8** Ran SP% **119.0**
Speed ratings (Par 109): **109,107,106,105,105 104,104,103**
CSF £8.70 CT £38.01 TOTE £1.60: £1.10, £2.50, £2.50; EX 8.00 Trifecta £40.70.
Owner Rebel Racing (2) **Bred** J Hanly **Trained** Newmarket, Suffolk
FOCUS
The feature race and a good handicap but not that competitive according to the betting and the well-backed favourite came from last to first. It's been rated around the second.

177 PLAY 4 TO SCORE AT BETWAY CLAIMING STKS 6f 1y(P)
2:40 (2:40) (Class 6) 4-Y-O+
£3,105 (£924; £461; £300; £300; £300) **Stalls** Low

Form RPR
31-1 1 **Deeds Not Words (IRE)**[2] 144 8-9-0 63..................(p) JFEgan 4 61+
(Michael Wigham) *hld up in tch: swtchd rt and clsd over 2f out: chsd ldrs: swtchd lft and rdn over 1f out: hdwy to ld ins fnl f: r.o wl* **4/1**[2]
35-4 2 ¾ **Bernie's Boy**[6] 91 6-8-11 75..................(p) GraceMcEntee(7) 5 63+
(Phil McEntee) *led: rdn over 1f out: hdd and kpt on same pce ins fnl f* **9/2**[3]
060- 3 hd **Knockout Blow**[12] 9765 4-9-2 65.................. CharlieBennett 6 60+
(Jim Boyle) *dwlt: rcvrd and hdwy to press ldr after 1f: rdn over 1f out: kpt on same pce ins fnl f* **20/1**

45-0 **4** *1* **Ventura Blues (IRE)**[6] 81 5-8-5 81.........(p) ThoreHammerHansen(7) 1 53+
(Richard Hannon) *chsd ldr for 1f: styd trcking ldrs on inner: effrt over 1f out: ev ch ins fnl f: no ex and outpcd towards fin* **1/1**[1]

320- **5** *½* **Sweet And Dandy (IRE)**[95] 8047 4-9-2 71...................... KieranO'Neill 3 56+
(Jimmy Fox) *s.i.s: in tch in last pair: effrt on inner over 1f out: nt clr run and swtchd rt 1f out: edgd rt and kpt on same pce u.p ins fnl f* **5/1**

322- **6** *nk* **Stopdworldnletmeof**[11] 9777 5-8-6 46.................... EllieMacKenzie(7) 2 52
(David Flood) *broke wl and prom: restrained and grad lost pl: wl in tch in last pair and effrt over 1f out: kpt on ins fnl f: no threat to wnr* **50/1**

1m 11.31s (-0.59) **Going Correction** -0.075s/f (Stan) **6** Ran SP% **111.6**
Speed ratings (Par 101): **100,99,98,97,96 96**
CSF £21.60 TOTE £4.00: £1.90, £2.10; EX 13.90 Trifecta £129.30.Deeds Not Words was claimed by Mr David Tate for £8,000. Ventura Blues was claimed by Mrs Alex Dunn for £11,000.
Owner D Hassan, Ali Tait, M Wigham **Bred** B Holland, S Hillen & J Cullinan **Trained** Newmarket, Suffolk

FOCUS
The usual mixed levels of ability amongst those contesting this claimer and they finished in a heap, suggesting that the form needs taking with a pinch of salt. The prominence of the sixth governs the bare form's worth.

178 BETWAY NOVICE STKS 6f 1y(P)
3:10 (3:10) (Class 5) 4-Y-O+ £3,752 (£1,116; £557; £278) **Stalls** Low

Form RPR
434- **1** **Ballyquin (IRE)**[44] 9287 4-9-0 75 ow1.................. JoshuaBryan(3) 3 78+
(Andrew Balding) *trckd ldr for 1f: styd trcking ldrs tl wnt 2nd again jst over 2f out: swtchd rt and shkn up to chal over 1f out: sn rdn to ld: r.o wl and asserted ins fnl f* **2/1**[1]

0- **2** *2* **Barritus**[350] 418 4-9-2 0.. FranBerry 7 69
(George Baker) *t.k.h: midfield on outer: hdwy to chse ldrs 4f out: led 3f out: rdn and hrd pressed over 1f out: sn hdd and kpt on same pce ins fnl f* **5/1**

01- **3** *½* **Always A Drama (IRE)**[77] 8601 4-9-2 0.................. RobertWinston 2 67
(Charles Hills) *t.k.h: wl in tch in midfield: nt clrest of runs jst over 2f out: sn clsd to chse ldrs: hung lft and kpt on same pce ins fnl f (jockey said filly hung left-handed in the straight)* **11/4**[2]

2-4 **4** *2* **Minuty**[9] 27 4-8-11 0.. MartinHarley 6 56
(Rae Guest) *wl in tch in midfield: lost pl on outer bnd 2f out: pushed along and reminder over 1f out: kpt on steadily under hands and heels riding ins fnl f: no threat to wnr* **9/2**[3]

4- **5** *shd* **Favori Royal (FR)**[22] 9645 4-9-2 0............................ EdwardGreatrex 1 60+
(Archie Watson) *led for 1f: grad shuffled bk and 6th whn rdn ent fnl 2f: nt clr run and swtchd rt 2f out: kpt on same pce and no threat to ldrs ins fnl f* **6/1**

06- **6** *¾* **Farl (IRE)**[27] 9565 4-8-11 0.......................... RichardKingscote 8 53+
(Ed Walker) *s.i.s: outpcd in rr: clsd and in tch but stl in rr over 2f out: pushed along over 1f out: kpt on same pce under hands and heels riding and no threat to ldrs ins fnl f* **20/1**

6- **7** *3* **Paminah**[13] 9746 4-8-11 0.. CharlieBennett 4 43
(Hughie Morrison) *sn outpcd in last pair: clsd and in tch over 2f out: outpcd again and btn over 1f out: wknd ins fnl f* **33/1**

0- **8** *10* **Dunstall Dreamer**[27] 9565 4-9-2 0........................ KieranO'Neill 5 16
(Denis Quinn) *hdwy to ld after 1f: hdd 3f out: lost pl ent fnl 2f: sn wknd and wl bhd ins fnl f* **100/1**

1m 11.13s (-0.77) **Going Correction** -0.075s/f (Stan) **8** Ran SP% **117.8**
Speed ratings (Par 103): **102,99,98,96,95 94,90,77**
CSF £12.85 TOTE £2.80: £1.10, £1.60, £1.40; EX 12.20 Trifecta £48.60.
Owner J Palmer-Brown **Bred** Brucetown Farms Ltd **Trained** Kingsclere, Hants

FOCUS
Mostly inexperienced types contesting this 4yo+ novice stakes. The time was 0.18 secs faster than the preceding claimer. The third has been rated close to her modest Kempton win.

179 BETWAY HEED YOUR HUNCH APPRENTICE H'CAP 5f 6y(P)
3:40 (3:40) (Class 6) (0-65,66) 4-Y-O+
£3,105 (£924; £461; £300; £300; £300) **Stalls** High

Form RPR
303- **1** **Pharoh Jake**[11] 9776 11-8-10 46.......................... EllieMacKenzie 4 55
(John Bridger) *in tch in rr of main gp: effrt and clsd over 1f out: hdwy and rdn to ld ins fnl f: r.o strly* **12/1**

000- **2** *2* **Entertaining Ben**[24] 9597 6-9-7 64..........................(p) GraceMcEntee(7) 6 66
(Amy Murphy) *led: rdn over 1f out: hdd and one pce ins fnl f* **8/1**

000- **3** *¾* **Pranceabootthetoon (IRE)**[22] 9641 4-8-6 45..........(t) AmeliaGlass(3) 3 44
(Milton Bradley) *in rr of main gp: outpcd and detached 3f out: pushed along and clsd over 1f out: swtchd rt and r.o wl ins fnl f to snatch 3rd cl home* **33/1**

061- **4** *nk* **Impart**[11] 9777 5-9-13 66 6ex..................................(v) GavinAshton(3) 1 64
(Laura Mongan) *in tch in midfield on inner: nt clr run and swtchd rt 2f out: kpt on same pce ins fnl f (two-day ban: interference & careless riding (Jan 25-26, 28-30))* **3/1**[1]

56-0 **5** *¾* **Zipedeedodah (IRE)**[4] 118 7-8-12 51..................(p¹) WilliamCarver(3) 5 46
(Joseph Tuite) *pressed ldr on inner: rdn and ev ch over 1f out tl no ex jst ins fnl f: wknd wl ins fnl f (seven-day ban: interference & careless riding (Jan 25-26, 28-31, Feb 1))* **6/1**[3]

100- **6** *nk* **Jorvik Prince**[15] 9722 5-10-0 64.............................. JessicaCooley 10 58
(Karen Tutty) *pressed ldrs on outer: struggling to qckn u.p whn rdr dropped whip 1f out: wknd wl ins fnl f* **6/1**[3]

244- **7** *2* **Avon Green**[51] 9176 4-9-13 63.................................. MarkCrehan 7 50
(Joseph Tuite) *wd: in tch in midfield: wd and rdn bnd 2f out: lost pl and n.d after* **10/1**

0/5- **8** *13* **Little Miss Daisy**[223] 3365 5-9-12 62.................... Pierre-LouisJamin 9 +
(William Muir) *rdr struggling to remove hood and v.s.a: nvr on terms (jockey said the mare had reared as the stalls opened meaning he was unable to remove the blind)* **14/1**

050- **U** **Temple Road (IRE)**[11] 9776 11-9-7 62..................(bt) KerrieRaybould(5) 8 +
(Milton Bradley) *stdd and swtchd lft after s: bdly hmpd and uns rdr after 150yds* **14/1**

01-3 **F** **Mercers**[7] 53 5-9-11 61 6ex..(b) TristanPrice 2 +
(Paddy Butler) *chsd ldrs tl clipped heels and fell after 150yds* **7/2**[2]

58.87s (0.07) **Going Correction** -0.075s/f (Stan) **10** Ran SP% **120.0**
Speed ratings (Par 101): **96,92,91,91,89 89,86,65,,**
CSF £107.30 CT £3091.71 TOTE £12.70: £3.60, £2.40, £13.60; EX 167.30 Trifecta £2911.00.
Owner J J Bridger Mrs J Stamp **Bred** J J Bridger **Trained** Liphook, Hants

FOCUS
A moderate but competitive apprentice handicap with a number of multiple course winners taking part. It was a messy race though, with a couple coming down early on and the market leaders being well held. The winner is rated to his 2018 high.
T/Jkpt: Not won. T/Plt: £352.80 to a £1 stake. Pool: £72,366.28 - 149.70 winning units. T/Qpdt: £80.90 to a £1 stake. Pool: £8,080.34 - 73.86 winning units. **Steve Payne**

[116] WOLVERHAMPTON (A.W) (L-H)
Friday, January 11

OFFICIAL GOING: Tapeta: standard
Wind: light breeze Weather: cloudy and cool

180 SUN RACING NO1 RACING SITE APPRENTICE H'CAP 1m 142y (Tp)
4:10 (4:10) (Class 6) (0-60,59) 4-Y-O+
£3,105 (£924; £461; £400; £400; £400) **Stalls** Low

Form RPR
231- **1** **Cape Greco (USA)**[14] 9734 4-9-4 59........................ GeorgiaDobie(5) 5 66
(Jo Hughes, France) *trckd ldrs: pushed along in 4th 2f out: rdn to chal 1f out: led 1/2f out: rdn clr* **11/4**[1]

233- **2** *1* **Big Bad Lol (IRE)**[30] 9512 5-9-5 59....................(p) OliverStammers(5) 7 64
(Ed Walker) *led: 1 l ld 2f out: rdn 1 1/2f out: 1 l ld 1f out: hdd 1/2f out: no ex* **7/2**[2]

50-1 **3** *1 ½* **Amor Fati (IRE)**[1] 159 4-8-12 51 6ex..................... KieranSchofield(3) 1 53
(David Evans) *hld up: pushed along and hdwy over 1f out: drvn fnl f: rdn into 3rd last two strides* **5/1**[3]

536- **4** *shd* **Sir Lancelott**[22] 9634 7-8-10 45.. PaulaMuir 2 47
(Adrian Nicholls) *trckd ldrs: pushed along in 5th 2f out: drvn over 1f out: swtchd to outer and rdn fnl f: kpt on* **6/1**

063- **5** *hd* **Cockney Boy**[22] 9634 6-9-1 50................................(v) TheodoreLadd 4 51
(Michael Appleby) *t.k.h: prom: trckd ldrs 1/2-way: pushed along in 3rd 2f out: drvn over 1f out: rdn and no ex fnl f: lost two pls last few strides* **10/1**

065- **6** *1* **Snooker Jim**[12] 9767 4-9-6 59.....................................(t) TobyEley(3) 6 58
(Steph Hollinshead) *mid-div: drvn 2f out: rdn over 1f out: one pce fnl f (jockey said gelding hung right-handed)* **10/1**

030- **7** *1 ¼* **Madame Jo Jo**[41] 9356 4-8-6 47............................(p) EllaMcCain(5) 11 43
(Sarah Hollinshead) *chsd ldrs: wnt prom after 3f: 1 l 2nd 2f out: reminders over 1f out: sn wknd* **33/1**

50- **8** *2 ¼* **Polly's Gold (IRE)**[12] 9767 4-9-2 52..........................(p) RhiainIngram 8 44
(Paul George) *mid-div on outer: drvn 2f out: no imp* **33/1**

50-0 **9** *½* **Willsy**[8] 37 6-8-7 45.. SeamusCronin(3) 13 36
(Frank Bishop) *slowly away: bhd: last 2f out: drvn over 1f out: rdn fnl f: one pce* **100/1**

005- **10** *½* **Moonbi Creek (IRE)**[15] 9720 12-8-7 45..................... JonathanFisher(3) 12 35
(Stella Barclay) *t.k.h: hld up: drvn over 1f out: rdn fnl f: no imp* **50/1**

456- **11** *hd* **Lord Murphy (IRE)**[12] 9767 6-9-4 56....................(t) ScottMcCullagh(3) 9 45
(Mark Loughnane) *hld up: pushed along over 2f out: sn drvn: rdn over 1f out: no imp* **10/1**

00-0 **12** *1* **Jacksonfire**[7] 60 7-8-9 49..................................(p) LauraCoughlan(5) 10 36
(Michael Mullineaux) *hld up: pushed along 1 1/2f out: sn rdn: wknd fnl f* **100/1**

600- **13** *shd* **Cookie Ring (IRE)**[37] 9413 8-8-5 45............................(t) RhonaPindar(5) 3 32
(Andrew Crook) *a bhd* **50/1**

1m 49.44s (-0.66) **Going Correction** -0.075s/f (Stan)
WFA 4 from 5yo+ 1lb **13** Ran SP% **118.9**
Speed ratings (Par 101): **99,98,96,96,96 95,94,92,92,91 91,90,90**
CSF £11.68 CT £47.41 TOTE £3.40: £1.60, £1.50, £2.00; EX 14.10 Trifecta £70.50.
Owner Joe Smith, Jimmy Smith, Jo Hughes **Bred** Petaluma Bloodstock **Trained** France

FOCUS
A modest apprentice riders' handicap on standard Tapeta. The winning time was over four seconds outside of standard and it paid to be handy enough. The likes of the second and fourth help set a straightforward level.

181 FOLLOW TOP TIPSTERS AT SUN RACING CLASSIFIED (S) STKS 1m 142y (Tp)
4:45 (4:45) (Class 5) 4-Y-O+
£3,752 (£1,116; £557; £400; £400; £400) **Stalls** Low

Form RPR
545- **1** **Arabic Culture (USA)**[36] 9431 5-8-12 66..................... NicolaCurrie 6 70
(Jamie Osborne) *mde all: pushed along and qcknd pce in 3 l ld 2f out: rdn 1 1/2f out: 4 l ld 1f out: c further clr fnl f: easily* **11/8**[1]

330- **2** *6* **Roman De Brut (IRE)**[13] 9747 7-8-5 66.......................... TobyEley(7) 5 57
(Ivan Furtado) *t.k.h: chsd ldr: sn settled in mid-div: lost pl and drvn over 3f out: hdwy on outer 2f out: rdn into 2nd over 1f out: 4 l 2nd 1f out: kpt on fnl f: no ch w wnr* **5/1**[3]

536- **3** *1* **Red Gunner**[34] 9458 5-8-12 58.. LukeMorris 2 55
(Mark Loughnane) *hld up: pushed along in last 2f out: sn drvn: hdwy on inner 1 1/2f out: rdn into 3rd 1f out: kpt on fnl f* **7/1**

06/ **4** *3* **Blue Skimmer (IRE)**[11] 2624 7-8-12 57........................ MarcMonaghan 3 49
(Alastair Ralph) *hld up: wnt prom 1/2-way: rdn and lost pl over 2f out: no ex fr over 1f out* **20/1**

416- **5** *8* **Mr Red Clubs (IRE)**[16] 9703 10-8-7 66.....................(p) RhiainIngram(5) 4 32
(Henry Tett) *mid-div: drvn and lost pl over 2f out: reminder in last 1f out: no ex* **7/1**

425- **6** *6* **The Groove**[42] 9335 6-8-12 68.. RossaRyan 1 20
(David Evans) *t.k.h: trckd ldrs: drvn in 3 l 2nd 2f out: rdn and wknd over 1f out: sn eased: bled fr nose (vet said gelding had bled from the nose)* **3/1**[2]

1m 49.36s (-0.74) **Going Correction** -0.075s/f (Stan) **6** Ran SP% **113.5**
Speed ratings (Par 103): **100,94,93,91,84 78**
CSF £8.94 TOTE £2.00: £1.60, £1.70; EX 7.80 Trifecta £40.20.The winner was sold to Grant Tuer for 8,200gns.
Owner David N Reynolds & Chris Watkins **Bred** Darley **Trained** Upper Lambourn, Berks

FOCUS
An ordinary seller. The modest pace increased approaching 4f out and the favourite kicked clear from over 2f out. The winner and fourth offer some perspective on the level of the form.

182 LADBROKES H'CAP 5f 21y (Tp)
5:15 (5:15) (Class 4) (0-85,87) 3-Y-O £5,530 (£1,645; £822; £411) **Stalls** Low

Form RPR
312- **1** **Rock Bottom**[13] 9745 3-8-2 67.......................... GeorgeRooke(7) 1 73
(Richard Hughes) *mde all: 1 l ld 2f out: pushed into 3 l ld 1f out: r.o wl fnl f: ld diminishing nr fin but nvr in danger: comf* **9/4**[2]

241- **2** *1* **Dragon Beat (IRE)**[25] 9589 3-8-12 70.......................... DougieCostello 2 72
(Michael Appleby) *trckd ldrs: drvn into 2nd 1 1/2f out: 3 l 2nd 1f out: rdn fnl f: kpt on wl to cl on wnr but nvr a threat* **3/1**[3]

421- **3** *1* **Klass Action (IRE)**[16] 9709 3-9-7 79.......................... LukeMorris 3 77+
(Sir Mark Prescott Bt) *in rr: pushed along 2f out: drvn and racd wd 1 1/2f out: wnt 3rd over 1f out: rdn fnl f: one pce* **11/10**[1]

060- 4 3 1/4 **Yolo Again (IRE)**[53] 9151 3-9-10 **87** BenSanderson(5) 4 74
(Roger Fell) *chsd ldr: drvn in 1 l 2nd 2f out: rdn and dropped to last over 1f out: wknd fnl f* **16/1**

1m 0.97s (-0.93) **Going Correction** -0.075s/f (Stan) 4 Ran SP% **109.3**
Speed ratings (Par 99): **104,102,100,95**
CSF £9.04 TOTE £3.10; EX 6.70 Trifecta £11.10.
Owner R P Gallagher & Partner **Bred** Whitsbury Manor Stud **Trained** Upper Lambourn, Berks

FOCUS
A decent little 3yo sprint handicap. The second-favourite made all in a fairly good time. It's been rated around the second to her C&D latest.

183 LADBROKES HOME OF THE ODDS BOOST H'CAP 1m 1f 104y (Tp)
5:45 (5:45) (Class 6) (0-60,60) 3-Y-O
£3,105 (£924; £461; £400; £400; £400) **Stalls** Low

Form RPR

044- 1 **Warrior Display (IRE)**[11] 9770 3-8-12 **58** (p) AaronMackay(7) 7 62
(J S Moore) *trckd ldrs: drvn in 3rd 1 1/2f out: sn rdn: hdwy to dispute ld fnl f: r.o wl u.p: led last stride* **33/1**

006- 2 shd **Tabou Beach Boy**[15] 9725 3-9-1 **54** NathanEvans 8 58
(Michael Easterby) *led: drvn in 1/2 l ld 2f out: rdn over 1f out: narrow ld 1f out: jnd and kpt on wl fnl f: hdd last stride* **4/1**[2]

066- 3 1 1/2 **Willkommen**[25] 9591 3-8-10 **56** (b[1]) StefanoCherchi(7) 5 57
(Marco Botti) *hld up: drvn 2f out: rdn and hdwy over 1f out: r.o wl fnl f: tk 3rd last 100yds* **25/1**

000- 4 1/2 **Comeonfeeltheforce (IRE)**[14] 9729 3-9-2 **55** (t) RaulDaSilva 9 55+
(Adam West) *hld up: hdwy on outer 4f out: drvn in cl 2nd 3f out: rdn 2f out: ev ch 1f out: no ex fnl f* **50/1**

000- 5 nk **Greyzee (IRE)**[213] 3706 3-8-12 **51** JoeyHaynes 13 50
(Rod Millman) *slowly away: bhd: drvn and hdwy on outer over 1f out: r.o fnl f: nvr nrr* **33/1**

04-0 6 1/2 **Vin D'Honneur (IRE)**[4] 122 3-9-1 **54** CallumRodriguez 3 52
(Stuart Williams) *mid-div on inner: rdn 1 1/2f out: one pce* **7/2**[1]

550- 7 1 1/4 **Whimsical Dream**[125] 7081 3-8-12 **51** JoeFanning 1 47
(Michael Bell) *hld up: hdwy on outer 3f out: drvn into 4th 2f out: rdn 1 1/2f out: wknd fnl f* **8/1**

000- 8 nse **Miss Havana**[14] 9730 3-9-4 **57** CharlesBishop 10 53
(Eve Johnson Houghton) *trckd ldrs: drvn in 5th 2f out: rdn over 1f out: no ex* **20/1**

000- 9 1 1/4 **Usanecolt (IRE)**[99] 7943 3-9-3 **56** NicolaCurrie 2 50
(Jamie Osborne) *hld up: pushed along over 2f out: one pce under hand riding fr over 1f out* **5/1**[3]

660- 9 dht **Melissa (FR)**[15] 9725 3-8-9 **51** JaneElliott(3) 6 45
(Ivan Furtado) *hld up: pushed along over 2f out: reminder over 1f out: no imp* **16/1**

324- 11 3 **Global Goddess (IRE)**[14] 9729 3-9-7 **60** LukeMorris 11 48
(Gay Kelleway) *mid-div: drvn and lost pl over 2f out: rn wd 1 1/2f out: wknd* **10/1**

000- 12 3/4 **Liberata Bella**[31] 9489 3-9-2 **55** DavidProbert 4 42
(George Scott) *hld up: drvn 3f out: rdn in rr 1 1/2f out: no rspnse* **12/1**

000- 13 1 3/4 **Gamba (IRE)**[28] 9530 3-9-7 **60** (b) RossaRyan 12 43
(Richard Hannon) *prom: drvn and lost pl 3f out: sn rdn and wknd: eased and dropped to last fnl f (jockey said filly was never travelling)* **7/1**

2m 1.94s (1.14) **Going Correction** -0.075s/f (Stan) 13 Ran SP% **121.6**
Speed ratings (Par 95): **91,90,89,89,88 88,87,87,86,86 83,82,81**
WIN: 52.90 Warrior Display; PL: 10.90 Warrior Display 6.60 Willkommen 1.40 Tabou Beach Boy; EX: 303.30; CSF: 157.70; TC: 3442.39; TF: 1885.70 CSF £157.70 CT £3442.39 TOTE £52.90: £10.90, £1.40, £6.60; EX 303.30 Trifecta £1885.70.
Owner Mrs Wendy O'Leary & J S Moore **Bred** David And Leslie Laverty **Trained** Upper Lambourn, Berks

FOCUS
A modest 3yo handicap. The winning time was slow and it paid to race prominently. The bare form looks very modest.

184 PLAY 4 TO SCORE AT BETWAY H'CAP 1m 4f 51y (Tp)
6:15 (6:15) (Class 4) (0-85,87) 4-Y-O+
£5,530 (£1,645; £822; £411; £400; £400) **Stalls** Low

Form RPR

/52- 1 **Flaming Marvel (IRE)**[35] 9447 5-9-3 **81** DavidProbert 1 90+
(James Fanshawe) *mid-div: pushed along and hdwy 1 1/2f out: drvn to chal 1f out: rdn fnl f: r.o wl: led last 25yds* **10/11**[1]

101- 2 nk **Amitie Waltz (FR)**[42] 9332 7-9-0 **78** ShaneKelly 3 86
(Richard Hughes) *mid-div: hdwy 3f out: pushed into 1 l 2nd 2f out: drvn into ld 1f out: rdn fnl f: kpt on wl: hdd last 25yds* **8/1**

363- 3 2 1/4 **Wimpole Hall**[30] 9502 6-9-3 **81** (p) JoeFanning 6 85
(William Jarvis) *hld up: pushed along and hdwy 1 1/2f out: sn rdn: r.o into 3rd fnl f but no threat to first two home* **7/1**[3]

120/ 4 4 **White Shaheen**[888] 5147 6-9-7 **85** NicolaCurrie 2 83
(William Muir) *trckd ldrs: pushed along and lost pl over 2f out: rdn fnl f: one pce* **25/1**

23-2 5 1/2 **Illustrissime (USA)**[9] 29 6-8-12 **76** (p) JoeyHaynes 5 73
(Ivan Furtado) *t.k.h: trckd ldr: led over 2f out: pushed along in 1 l ld 2f out: sn drvn: rdn and hdd 1f out: wknd fnl f* **12/1**

625- 6 3 1/4 **Derek Duval (USA)**[15] 9723 5-9-3 **81** (t) RossaRyan 8 73
(Stuart Williams) *hld up: drvn 3f out: rdn on outer 1 1/2f out: no imp (jockey said gelding hung right-handed throughout)* **8/1**

121/ 7 1 1/2 **Alabaster**[568] 4004 5-9-9 **87** (p) LukeMorris 4 77
(Sir Mark Prescott Bt) *led: drvn and hdd over 2f out: wknd* **5/1**[2]

200/ 8 13 **Sporty Yankee (USA)**[28] 6323 6-8-0 **71** oh1 (p) SophieRalston(7) 7 40
(Aytach Sadik) *in rr: rdn and lost tch 4f out* **100/1**

2m 37.08s (-3.72) **Going Correction** -0.075s/f (Stan) 8 Ran SP% **116.3**
Speed ratings (Par 105): **109,108,107,104,104 102,101,92**
CSF £9.41 CT £34.30 TOTE £1.90: £1.10, £2.40, £2.20; EX 8.90 Trifecta £38.30.
Owner Merry Fox Stud Limited **Bred** Merry Fox Stud Limited **Trained** Newmarket, Suffolk

FOCUS
A decent middle-distance handicap. The favourite swooped late to win narrowly in the quickest comparative time on the card. The first two have been rated to their recent form.

185 BETWAY STAYERS' H'CAP 2m 120y (Tp)
6:45 (6:45) (Class 6) (0-55,55) 4-Y-O+
£3,105 (£924; £461; £400; £400; £400) **Stalls** Low

Form RPR

060- 1 **Lady Makfi (IRE)**[27] 9562 7-9-7 **55** (p) DavidProbert 10 60
(Johnny Farrelly) *hld up: drvn and hdwy over 2f out: rdn to ld over 1f out: hung lft fnl f: r.o: hld on wl nr fin* **10/1**

051- 2 hd **Betancourt (IRE)**[39] 9383 9-9-7 **55** (p) LiamKeniry 13 60
(Stef Keniry) *mid-div: smooth hdwy into 3rd 3f out: rdn in 2 1/2 l 2nd 2f out: ev ch 1f out: cl 2nd ent fnl f: r.o wl: jst hld* **5/1**[3]

005- 3 2 1/4 **Helf (IRE)**[40] 6180 5-9-7 **55** (tp) NathanEvans 3 57
(Oliver Greenall) *hld up: drvn and hdwy 3f out: 4th 2f out: sn rdn: ev ch over 1f out: one pce fnl f* **20/1**

200- 4 nk **Normandy Blue**[43] 9310 4-8-12 **51** CallumShepherd 2 55
(Louise Allan) *hld up: drvn and hdwy 3f out: 3rd 2f out: rdn over 1f out: one pce fnl f* **16/1**

6/0- 5 2 1/4 **Templier (IRE)**[37] 9407 6-9-6 **54** ShaneKelly 5 53
(Gary Moore) *led: rdn in 2 1/2 l ld 2f out: hdd over 1f out: no ex fnl f* **8/1**

000- 6 5 **Silvington**[21] 9666 4-8-7 **46** oh1 NicolaCurrie 6 41
(Mark Loughnane) *in rr: drvn and effrt 3f out: rdn 1 1/2f out: no ex fr over 1f out* **25/1**

/00- 7 12 **Anton Dolin (IRE)**[36] 4848 11-8-9 **46** oh1 (b) PhilDennis(3) 1 25
(Michael Mullineaux) *trckd ldrs: drvn and lost pl 4f out: wknd* **100/1**

8 1 **Awesome Gal (IRE)**[510] 6218 5-8-12 **46** oh1 LukeMorris 12 24
(Sir Mark Prescott Bt) *t.k.h: chsd ldr: drvn 4f out: rdn 3f out: sn lost pl: eased over 1f out* **3/1**[1]

650- 9 8 **Mistress Viz (IRE)**[21] 9665 5-8-9 **46** oh1 (p) NoelGarbutt(3) 4 14
(Sarah Hollinshead) *hld up: pushed along 3f out: sn drvn: no imp* **50/1**

000- 10 7 **Iconic Boy**[21] 9657 4-8-7 **46** oh1 CamHardie 8 8
(Alexandra Dunn) *mid-div: rdn 4f out: wknd* **33/1**

500- 11 4 **Essgee Nics (IRE)**[34] 9464 6-8-7 **46** oh1 (p) RhiainIngram(5) 9
(Paul George) *hld up: rdn 3f out: sn wl bhd* **33/1**

01-3 12 85 **Constituent**[8] 40 4-8-9 **48** (v) LiamJones 7
(Michael Appleby) *hld up: drvn on outer 1/2-way: sn rdn and dropped away* **6/1**

043- 13 dist **Thresholdofadream (IRE)**[52] 9159 4-9-2 **55** JoeFanning 11
(Amanda Perrett) *chsd ldrs: lost pl over 5f out: sn dropped to rr and eased* **7/2**[2]

3m 36.64s (-2.66) **Going Correction** -0.075s/f (Stan)
WFA 4 from 5yo+ 5lb 13 Ran SP% **121.7**
Speed ratings (Par 101): **113,112,111,111,110 108,102,102,98,95 93,53,6**
CSF £56.99 CT £1006.40 TOTE £12.10: £2.80, £2.00, £6.30; EX 49.20 Trifecta £1319.10.
Owner John McMahon **Bred** Coleman Bloodstock Limited **Trained** Midford, Avon

FOCUS
A moderate staying handicap. The winning time compared favourably with most of the races on the card. The first two have been rated to their recent best.

186 BETWAY NOVICE STKS 5f 21y (Tp)
7:15 (7:15) (Class 5) 3-Y-O+
£3,752 (£1,116; £557; £278) **Stalls** Low

Form RPR

2 1 **Hanati (IRE)**[10] 1 3-8-8 0 LukeMorris 7 67+
(Simon Crisford) *mde all: pushed along in 1 l ld 2f out: drvn in 2 l ld 1f out: r.o wl under hand riding fnl f: comf* **13/8**[2]

053- 2 1 1/4 **Kadiz (IRE)**[25] 9589 3-8-8 70 (b) NicolaCurrie 1 62
(Richard Hughes) *prom: drvn 2f out: rdn in 2 l 2nd 1f out: kpt on but no imp on wnr fnl f* **1/1**[1]

04- 3 1 **Lieutenant Conde**[22] 9636 3-8-13 0 CharlieBennett 6 63+
(Hughie Morrison) *bhd: pushed along 2f out: drvn and hdwy over 1f out: kpt on wl into 3rd fnl f: gng on at fin* **7/1**[3]

6-5 4 1 **Amliba**[10] 1 3-8-8 0 CamHardie 2 54
(David O'Meara) *mid-div: pushed along in 4th 2f out: drvn into 3rd on inner 1 1/2f out: one pce and lost 3rd ins fnl f* **50/1**

00- 5 1 1/2 **Speed Skater**[23] 9604 3-8-8 0 JoeFanning 4 49
(Amanda Perrett) *hld up: pushed along 3f out: effrt on outer over 2f out: sn pushed along: no ex fr over 1f out* **20/1**

00- 6 1/2 **Storm Blitz (IRE)**[38] 9392 3-8-13 0 EdwardGreatrex 8 52
(Robert Cowell) *chsd ldrs: drvn 2f out: wknd over 1f out* **14/1**

7 nk **Inverarity** 3-8-10 0 FinleyMarsh(3) 5 51
(Frank Bishop) *slowly away: in rr: drvn on outer 1 1/2f out: no imp* **50/1**

00- 8 1 3/4 **Graceful (IRE)**[49] 9224 3-8-5 0 PhilDennis(3) 3 40
(Richard Hannon) *racd in 5th: lost pl over 2f out: sn drvn: dropped to last 1f out* **33/1**

1m 2.45s (0.55) **Going Correction** -0.075s/f (Stan) 8 Ran SP% **118.9**
Speed ratings (Par 103): **92,90,88,86,84 83,83,80**
CSF £3.64 TOTE £2.10: £1.10, £1.02, £2.10; EX 3.80 Trifecta £8.80.
Owner Sultan Ali **Bred** Michael Downey & Roalso Ltd **Trained** Newmarket, Suffolk

FOCUS
Effectively a fair 3yo novice sprint contest. The second-favourite quickened up about 2f out to dominate off her own tempo on the lead. The runner-up has been rated below form.

187 BETWAY LIVE CASINO H'CAP 6f 20y (Tp)
7:45 (7:45) (Class 5) (0-70,72) 4-Y-O+
£3,752 (£1,116; £557; £400; £400; £400) **Stalls** Low

Form RPR

252- 1 **A Sure Welcome**[25] 9587 5-9-7 **70** (b[1]) LiamKeniry 10 76
(John Spearing) *t.k.h: prom: 1/2 l 2nd 2f out: pushed along to chal over 1f out: rdn to ld jst ins fnl f: sn strly pressed and r.o wl: jst hld on* **7/1**[3]

365- 2 nse **Kupa River (IRE)**[24] 9596 5-9-4 **67** (h) CamHardie 4 73+
(Roger Fell) *hld up: drvn 1 1/2f out: hdwy over 1f out: rdn to chal wnr ins fnl f: r.o wl: jst hld* **4/1**[1]

600- 3 1/2 **Dotted Swiss (IRE)**[24] 9597 4-9-6 **69** EdwardGreatrex 8 73
(Archie Watson) *hld up: pushed along 2f out: drvn on outer 1 1/2f out: rdn and hdwy over 1f out: r.o strly into 3rd wl ins fnl f* **14/1**

3/0- 4 1 **Miracle Garden**[14] 9733 7-9-9 **72** (p) StevieDonohoe 7 73
(Ian Williams) *trckd ldrs: drvn in 4th 2f out: rdn fnl f: kpt on* **9/2**[2]

303- 5 shd **Hollander**[14] 9733 5-9-6 **69** (t) NicolaCurrie 5 70
(William Muir) *mid-div: pushed along 2f out: sn drvn: rdn fnl f: one pce* **7/1**[3]

03-4 6 nk **Sir Ottoman (FR)**[9] 31 6-9-4 **67** LiamJones 9 67
(Ivan Furtado) *prom: led after 1f: pushed along in 1/2 l ld 2f out: sn drvn: rdn over 1f out: narrow ld 1f out: hdd jst ins fnl f: sn wknd* **7/1**[3]

000- 7 1 3/4 **Letmestopyouthere (IRE)**[14] 9733 5-9-0 **68** ThomasGreatrex(5) 2 62
(Archie Watson) *hld up: drvn 2f out: reminder over 1f out: no imp* **8/1**

360- 8 1/2 **Indian Pursuit (IRE)**[24] 9597 6-9-5 **68** (v) JasonHart 1 61
(John Quinn) *led 1f: trckd ldrs whn hdd: pushed along in 3rd 2f out: sn drvn: rdn 1f out: wknd fnl f* **14/1**

056- 9 1 **Stoneyford Lane (IRE)**[16] 9702 5-8-9 **65** (v) TobyEley(7) 3 54
(Steph Hollinshead) *in rr: rdn 1 1/2f out: no rspnse* **8/1**

100- 10 1 1/2 **Our Man In Havana**[16] 9702 4-8-13 **65** (v[1]) WilliamCox(3) 6 50
(Richard Price) *hld up: drvn 2f out: rdn 1 1/2f out: no rspnse* **12/1**

1m 13.31s (-1.19) **Going Correction** -0.075s/f (Stan) 10 Ran SP% **118.9**
Speed ratings (Par 103): **104,103,103,101,101 101,99,98,97,95**
CSF £35.91 CT £397.66 TOTE £5.30: £2.70, £2.20, £4.40; EX 45.10 Trifecta £414.60.
Owner Kinnersley Partnership 3 **Bred** Richard Evans Bloodstock **Trained** Kinnersley, Worcs

■ Stewards' Enquiry : Liam Keniry two-day ban: misuse of whip (Jan 25-26)

FOCUS

An ordinary sprint handicap. The favourite couldn't quite get up in a truly-run contest. The second has been rated close to his November C&D form.

T/Plt: £148.70 to a £1 stake. Pool: £81,275.67 - 398.75 winning units. T/Qpdt: £91.40 to a £1 stake. Pool: £8,599.29 - 69.59 winning units. **Keith McHugh**

188 - 195a (Foreign Racing) - See Raceform Interactive

JEBEL ALI (L-H)

Friday, January 11

OFFICIAL GOING: Dirt: fast

196a AL SHAFAR INVESTMENT LLC (H'CAP) (DIRT) 6f (D)

10:15 (10:15) (65-85,84) 3-Y-O+ **£12,179** (£4,059; £2,232; £1,217; £608)

RPR

1 **Pinter**[14] 9740 7-8-11 **72**....(p) AntonioFresu 1 81
(E Charpy, UAE) *mid-div: rdn 2 1/2f out: led 1f out: r.o wl* **5/1**[2]

2 ½ **Kidd Malibu (USA)**[14] 9742 6-8-11 **72**.... DaneO'Neill 5 79
(M Al Mheiri, UAE) *chsd ldrs: led far side 2 1/2f out: hdd 1f out but r.o wl* **8/1**

3 3½ **Guernsey (USA)**[35] 9457 5-8-13 **73**.... PatDobbs 6 70
(Doug Watson, UAE) *mid-div: r.o fnl 2f but no ch w first two* **13/2**[3]

4 2 **Beachcomber (USA)**[14] 9738 5-9-3 **77**....(tp) TadhgO'Shea 14 67
(S Seemar, UAE) *chsd ldrs: led nrside 2 1/2f out: r.o wl fnl 2f* **12/1**

5 shd **Gervais (USA)**[36] 9439 5-8-11 **72**....(bt) FernandoJara 13 61
(A R Al Rayhi, UAE) *mid-div: r.o fnl 2f but nvr nr to chal* **16/1**

6 2¼ **Ejbaar**[14] 9742 7-9-7 **81**....(v) RichardMullen 4 64
(S Seemar, UAE) *slowly away: nvr nr to chal but r.o fnl 2 1/2f* **8/1**

7 nk **Mutawakked (IRE)**[35] 9457 5-8-9 **70**.... BenCurtis 10 51
(M Al Mheiri, UAE) *a mid-div* **14/1**

8 hd **Sahaafy (USA)**[42] 9348 7-9-11 **84**....(v) JimCrowley 8 66
(M Al Mheiri, UAE) *chsd ldrs tl outpcd fnl 2f* **10/3**[1]

9 2½ **Salvadori (IRE)**[6] 95 8-9-7 **81**.... GeraldAvranche 9 54
(R Bouresly, Kuwait) *nvr nr to chal* **10/1**

10 1¾ **Rich And Famous (USA)**[14] 9742 5-8-9 **70**....(tp) RoystonFfrench 2 37
(S Jadhav, UAE) *chsd ldrs tl wknd 3f out* **28/1**

11 1¼ **Ajwad**[6] 96 6-8-5 **65**.... ElioneChaves 3 29
(R Bouresly, Kuwait) *led far side tl wknd 2 1/2f out* **9/1**

12 18 **Mutahaddith**[22] 9654 9-9-3 **77**....(t) RonanWhelan 7
(A R Al Rayhi, UAE) *trckd ldr tl wknd 3f out* **14/1**

13 7¼ **Yabrave**[77] 8623 5-9-11 **84**....(t) ChrisHayes 15
(N Bachalard, UAE) *a in rr* **20/1**

14 4¼ **Wazin**[57] 9070 4-8-13 **73**....(v) PatCosgrave 12
(Simon Crisford) *s.i.s: nvr nr to chal* **14/1**

15 22 **Kion (IRE)**[14] 9742 4-8-9 **70**....(b) SamHitchcott 16
(Jaber Ramadhan, Bahrain) *nvr able to chal* **28/1**

16 34 **Silent Bullet (IRE)**[64] 8972 8-8-9 **70**.... BernardoPinheiro 11
(R Bouresly, Kuwait) *trckd ldr tl wknd 3f out* **50/1**

1m 12.45s (-0.96) **16** Ran SP% **141.6**
CSF: 51.01; TRICAST: 231.55.
Owner Sheikh Ahmed bin Mohammed Al Maktoum **Bred** New England, Mount Coote & P Barrett **Trained** United Arab Emirates

197a COMMERCIAL BANK OF DUBAI (H'CAP) (DIRT) 1m (D)

10:45 (10:45) (75-88,88) 4-Y-O+ **£12,820** (£4,273; £2,350; £1,282; £641)

RPR

1 **Craving (IRE)**[57] 9069 4-8-7 **77**.... ConnorBeasley 10 86
(Simon Crisford) *trckd ldr: led 1 1/2f out: r.o wl: comf* **9/1**

2 1¾ **Untold Secret**[14] 9738 7-8-10 **80**.... RoystonFfrench 3 85
(S Jadhav, UAE) *mid-div: chsd ldrs and ev ch 2 1/2f out: r.o wl fnl 1 1/2f* **9/4**[1]

3 2½ **Aleko**[14] 9738 6-8-5 **75**....(bt) AntonioFresu 12 74
(E Charpy, UAE) *nvr nr to chal but r.o wl fnl 2f: nrst fin* **14/1**

4 ¾ **Berkshire Boy (IRE)**[14] 9737 5-9-0 **83**....(v) WJLee 1 82
(H Al Alawi, UAE) *settled in rr: chsd ldrs 2 1/2f out: one pce fnl 1 1/2f* **11/1**

5 2¼ **Invincible Strike (IRE)**[13] 8-8-7 **77**.... RichardMullen 8 69
(S Seemar, UAE) *sn led: hdd & wknd 1 1/2f out* **12/1**

6 3½ **Timeless Flight**[6] 96 5-8-9 **84**....(t) SaeedAlMazrooei[(6)] 2 69
(A R Al Rayhi, UAE) *nvr bttr than mid-div* **28/1**

7 2 **Jazirat (IRE)**[6] 97 4-8-6 **76**.... SzczepanMazur 5 56
(S Al Shamsi, UAE) *broke awkwardly: nvr nr to chal* **18/1**

8 10 **Jahaafel (FR)**[128] 6952 4-8-13 **82**.... JimCrowley 11 40
(M Al Mheiri, UAE) *trckd ldr tl wknd 2 1/2f out* **13/2**[3]

9 ½ **Sharamm (IRE)**[161] 5686 4-9-5 **88**....(t) ChrisHayes 4 45
(N Bachalard, UAE) *nvr bttr than mid-div* **7/2**[2]

10 5¼ **Trenchard (USA)**[27] 9568 5-8-10 **80**....(v) PatDobbs 6 23
(Doug Watson, UAE) *a in rr* **8/1**

11 27 **Maghaweer (IRE)**[202] 4135 4-9-0 **83**....(v) TadhgO'Shea 7
(H Al Alawi, UAE) *nvr bttr than mid-div* **16/1**

12 16½ **Important Mission (USA)**[485] 7053 5-9-5 **88**.... XavierZiani 9
(S Jadhav, UAE) *chsd ldr: wd 6f out: wknd 3 1/2f out* **14/1**

1m 37.35s **12** Ran SP% **131.4**
CSF: 32.77; TRICAST: 313.31.
Owner Sultan Ali **Bred** Lynn Lodge Stud **Trained** Newmarket, Suffolk

198 - 201a (Foreign Racing) - See Raceform Interactive

174

LINGFIELD (L-H)

Saturday, January 12

OFFICIAL GOING: Polytrack: standard

Wind: Fresh, across (towards stands) Weather: Overcast

202 LADBROKES HOME OF THE ODDS BOOST FILLIES' H'CAP 1m 1y(P)

12:50 (12:50) (Class 5) (0-70,69) 4-Y-O+

£3,752 (£1,116; £557; £300; £300; £300) **Stalls** High

Form RPR

223- 1 **Lady Alavesa**[23] 9638 4-9-5 **67**....(p) JosephineGordon 8 75
(Gay Kelleway) *hld up in last: prog and swtchd towards inner over 1f out: shkn up to ld jst ins fnl f: pushed out: comf* **11/4**[2]

601- 2 1¾ **Dashing Poet**[25] 9593 5-9-3 **65**.... CharlesBishop 2 69
(Heather Main) *t.k.h: hld up in tch: rdn and clsd 2f out: led briefly 1f out: one pce fnl f* **13/8**[1]

003- 3 hd **Mrs Benson (IRE)**[31] 9501 4-9-5 **67**.... DavidProbert 3 71
(Michael Blanshard) *trckd ldrs: prog on outer over 3f out: led over 2f out but hung rt bnd sn after and jnd: hdd 1f out: kpt on (jockey said filly hung right-handed in the straight)* **7/1**

02-5 4 ½ **Bubbly**[9] 33 4-9-2 **64**.... StevieDonohoe 6 67
(Charlie Fellowes) *hld up: prog on outer over 2f out: drvn to chal jst over 1f out: nt qckn and one pce fnl f* **3/1**[3]

000- 5 1½ **Peace Prevails**[13] 9769 4-8-12 **60**.... CharlieBennett 5 59
(Jim Boyle) *hanging rt thrght: led after 1f to over 2f out: stl upsides jst over 1f out: wknd fnl f* **25/1**

234- 6 5 **Spiced**[100] 7936 4-9-0 **62**....(p) PhilipPrince 1 50
(Ron Hodges) *stmbld sltly s: hld up in tch: shkn up over 2f out: no prog and btn over 1f out* **20/1**

065- 7 4½ **Black Lace**[31] 9509 4-8-2 **50** oh5....(p) NicolaCurrie 4 28
(Steve Woodman) *led 1f: chsd ldr to 3f out: wknd 2f out* **33/1**

1m 37.3s (-0.90) **Going Correction** -0.075s/f (Stan) **7** Ran SP% **113.8**
Speed ratings (Par 100): **101,99,99,98,97 92,87**
CSF £7.51 CT £25.99 TOTE £3.30: £1.80, £1.70; EX 7.20 Trifecta £24.80.
Owner N Scandrett & Strictly Fun Racing Club **Bred** A C M Spalding **Trained** Exning, Suffolk

FOCUS

A modest fillies' handicap. The pace picked up after the first two furlongs and the second-favourite swooped late to win quite readily. It's been rated around the third and fourth.

203 BETWAY H'CAP 6f 1y(P)

1:25 (1:25) (Class 3) (0-95,94) 4-Y-O- **£7,246** (£2,168; £1,084; £542; £270) **Stalls** Low

Form RPR

502- 1 **Alsvinder**[13] 9763 6-9-7 **94**....(t) AdamKirby 4 101
(David O'Meara) *trckd ldr: drvn to ld jst ins fnl f: edgd lft after: kpt on wl nr fin* **7/1**

051- 2 nk **Merhoob (IRE)**[13] 9763 7-9-5 **92**.... LukeMorris 5 98
(John Ryan) *t.k.h: trckd ldng pair: rdn over 1f out: grad clsd u.p fnl f: tk 2nd last 75yds: a jst hld* **9/4**[1]

245- 3 1 **Gorgeous Noora (IRE)**[91] 8190 5-9-4 **91**.... HollieDoyle 1 95+
(Archie Watson) *hld up in last pair: pushed along over 1f out: trying to cl whn nt clr run ins fnl f: kpt on to take 3rd last stride (jockey said mare was denied a clear run)* **3/1**[3]

540- 4 nse **Reflektor (IRE)**[28] 9561 6-9-5 **92**.... RichardKingscote 6 95
(Tom Dascombe) *led fr wdst draw: urged along 2f out: hdd jst ins fnl f: one pce (jockey said gelding moved poorly)* **8/1**

002- 5 ¾ **Desert Doctor (IRE)**[28] 9561 4-9-3 **90**.... LiamKeniry 2 90
(Ed Walker) *stdd s: t.k.h and hld up in last: stl there and shkn up over 1f out: styd on fnl 100yds: too late* **5/2**[2]

034- 6 1¼ **Zac Brown (IRE)**[13] 9763 8-8-7 **87**....(t) SeamusCronin[(7)] 3 83
(Charlie Wallis) *t.k.h: trckd ldng pair: effrt on inner wl over 1f out: wknd ins fnl f* **14/1**

1m 10.72s (-1.18) **Going Correction** -0.075s/f (Stan) **6** Ran SP% **114.6**
Speed ratings (Par 107): **104,103,102,102,101 99**
CSF £23.82 TOTE £7.00: £2.60, £2.80; EX 15.90 Trifecta £67.00.
Owner F Gillespie **Bred** Northern Bloodstock Inc **Trained** Upper Helmsley, N Yorks
■ Stewards' Enquiry : Adam Kirby two-day ban: careless riding (Jan 26,28)

FOCUS

A fairly good sprint handicap. A stacking pace picked up notably from the 3f marker and it produced a busy finish. The first two have been rated to their best.

204 BETWAY LIVE CASINO (S) STKS 1m 4f (P)

2:00 (2:00) (Class 6) 4-Y-O+ **£3,105** (£924; £461; £300; £300) **Stalls** Low

Form RPR

01-2 1 **Dutch Uncle**[7] 88 7-9-2 **80**....(p) LukeMorris 5 57+
(Olly Murphy) *hld up and last to 5f out: trckd ldr 3f out: cajoled along to cl over 1f out: led last 100yds: pushed out* **1/3**[1]

23-6 2 ½ **Contingency Fee**[2] 160 4-8-6 **57**....(p) GraceMcEntee[(7)] 4 57
(Phil McEntee) *led after 2f: urged along over 2f out: kpt on steadily but hdd and hld last 100yds* **12/1**[3]

350- 3 2¾ **Noble Expression**[44] 9313 4-8-13 **80**....(v[1]) CharlieBennett 2 52
(Jim Boyle) *led 2f: trckd ldr to over 3f out: sn outpcd u.p and dropped to 4th: styd on to take 3rd again fnl f* **3/1**[2]

645- 4 2¾ **London Grammar (IRE)**[15] 9728 5-8-4 **45**.... ThoreHammerHansen[(7)] 3 42
(Ralph J Smith) *trckd ldr 2f: styd wl in tch: rdn on outer over 3f out and sn outpcd: no hdwy fnl 2f* **100/1**

003- 5 4 **Sea Tea Dea**[26] 9586 5-8-11 **45**....(t) JosephineGordon 1 36
(Katy Price) *hld up in tch: dropped to last 5f out: pushed along and no prog 3f out* **50/1**

2m 32.86s (-0.14) **Going Correction** -0.075s/f (Stan)
WFA 4 from 5yo+ 3lb **5** Ran SP% **110.7**
Speed ratings (Par 101): **97,96,94,93,90**
CSF £5.87 TOTE £1.20: £1.10, £3.10; EX 5.30.The winner was bought in for £5,000
Owner Mrs F Shaw **Bred** Cheveley Park Stud Ltd **Trained** Wilmcote, Warks

FOCUS

A fair little middle-distance seller. The odds-on favourite could do no more than win from off another highly tactical gallop. The form could possibly be rated 5lb better around the second and fourth.

205 SUN RACING TOP TIPS AND PREVIEWS H'CAP 1m 1y(P)

2:35 (2:35) (Class 2) (0-105,96) 4-Y-O- **£11,971** (£3,583; £1,791; £896; £446) **Stalls** High

Form RPR

005- 1 **Apex King (IRE)**[12] 9772 5-7-9 **77** oh1.... LauraCoughlan[(7)] 6 84
(David Loughnane) *t.k.h: trckd ldr: led jst over 2f out: shkn up and 2 l ahd over 1f out: pushed along and styd on steadily after* **13/2**

011- 2 1 **Breden (IRE)**[37] 9429 9-9-7 **96**.... RobertWinston 5 101+
(Linda Jewell) *hld up in last: prog wl over 1f out: urged along to chse wnr jst ins fnl f: styd on but nvr able to chal (jockey said gelding was hampered leaving the stalls)* **2/1**[1]

032- 3 1¾ **Chevallier**[12] 9774 7-9-4 **93**.... LukeMorris 7 94
(Archie Watson) *trckd ldng pair: rdn 2f out: chsd wnr over 1f out to jst ins fnl f: one pce* **4/1**[3]

024- 4 ¾ **Isomer (USA)**[54] 9154 5-8-6 **88**....(h[1]) WilliamCarver[(7)] 3 87
(Andrew Balding) *trckd ldng pair: styd on inner in st and no imp on ldrs over 1f out: one pce* **7/1**

05-2 5 2½ **My Target (IRE)**[10] 19 8-8-12 **87**.... JFEgan 4 81
(Michael Wigham) *s.i.s and pushed along early in last pair: effrt on outer 3f out: rdn and no prog over 2f out: one pce after (jockey said gelding moved poorly)* **9/4**[2]

660- **6** ½ **Contrast (IRE)**[17] 9705 5-8-6 **88** .... JoshQuinn(7) 2 80
(Michael Easterby) *led to jst over 2f out: wknd jst over 1f out* **20/1**

1m 35.69s (-2.51) **Going Correction** -0.075s/f (Stan) **6** Ran SP% **114.7**
Speed ratings (Par 109): **109,108,106,105,103 102**
CSF £20.57 TOTE £7.90: £3.30, £1.10; EX 25.30 Trifecta £91.80.
Owner G B & G H Firmager **Bred** Dr W O'Brien **Trained** Tern Hill, Shropshire

FOCUS
The feature contest was a good handicap. The winning time was just outside standard and the favourite reached a relatively close second from a modest position turning in. The form could be rated a bit higher based on the third's recent form.

206 SUNRACING.CO.UK NOVICE STKS 1m 1y(P)
3:10 (3:10) (Class 5) 4-Y-O+ **£3,752** (£1,116; £557; £278) **Stalls** High

Form RPR

34- **1** **Shamlahar**[201] 4202 4-8-11 0 .... JackMitchell 6 73+
(Simon Crisford) *plld hrd early and wnt prom 6f out: trckd ldr 5f out: chal over 2f out but hung rt bnd sn after: narrow ld wl over 1f out: hrd rdn and swished tail: hld on* **5/4**[1]

032- **2** nk **Oneovdem**[15] 9732 5-9-2 74 .... JoeyHaynes 2 77
(Tim Pinfield) *led 2f: styd cl up: rdn 2f out: chal fnl f: chsd wnr last 100yds: nt qckn nr fin* **10/3**[2]

300- **3** ½ **Pheidippides**[28] 9563 4-9-2 77 .... (b[1]) LukeMorris 4 76
(Tom Clover) *trckd ldrs: rdn over 2f out: drvn to try to chal fnl f: kpt on but jst hld* **5/1**

24- **4** ¾ **Yimou (IRE)**[36] 9445 4-9-2 0 .... MartinDwyer 7 74
(Dean Ivory) *dwlt: t.k.h: prog to ld after 2f: drvn and hdd wl over 1f out: pressed wnr tl no ex last 100yds* **4/1**[3]

00- **5** 12 **The Celtic Machine**[15] 9732 4-9-0 0 ow1 .... PaddyBradley(3) 5 47
(Pat Phelan) *hld up in last pair: pushed along and lft bhd 3f out: tk remote 5th last strides: nvr in it* **50/1**

/ **6** ½ **Beyond The Fringe (IRE)** 4-8-11 0 .... RossaRyan 3 40
(Phil McEntee) *cl up: lost pl over 5f out: rdn over 2f out: sn wknd* **14/1**

0- **7** 9 **Dubai Eye**[14] 9746 4-8-8 0 .... (b[1]) NoelGarbutt(3) 1 20
(Hugo Palmer) *in tch in rr to 3f out: sn bhd* **33/1**

1m 36.77s (-1.43) **Going Correction** -0.075s/f (Stan) **7** Ran SP% **115.8**
Speed ratings (Par 103): **104,103,103,102,90 89,80**
CSF £5.84 TOTE £2.10: £1.40, £1.60; EX 5.30 Trifecta £20.70.
Owner Hussain Alabbas Lootah **Bred** Barry Walters **Trained** Newmarket, Suffolk

FOCUS
A fair novice contest. The winning time was no better than average and the market principals finished in a bit of heap after a near four-way go in the final furlong. The second and fourth help set the standard.

207 BETWAY CASINO H'CAP 1m 2f (P)
3:40 (3:40) (Class 6) (0-55,56) 4-Y-O+
£3,105 (£924; £461; £300; £300; £300) **Stalls** Low

Form RPR

500- **1** **Cold Harbour**[148] 6236 4-9-3 **51** .... (t[1]) KieranO'Neill 8 57
(Robyn Brisland) *wl in tch in midfield: rdn and prog over 2f out: gap appeared and drvn to ld 1f out: jst hld on (trainer said, regarding the apparent improvement in form, that gelding had benefitted from the application of a first-time tongue tie, a weak race, and the yard being in better form)* **12/1**

04-3 **2** hd **Sharp Operator**[9] 39 6-9-8 **55** .... (h) RichardKingscote 9 60
(Charlie Wallis) *reluctant to enter stalls: hld up in rr: gng strly over 3f out: pushed along and prog over 2f out: trckd ldrs over 1f out but nt clr run: r.o fnl f and jnd wnr nr fin: nt qckn last strides* **9/2**[2]

004- **3** 1¾ **Prerogative (IRE)**[44] 9319 5-8-10 **48** .... (b) PoppyBridgwater(5) 5 49
(Tony Carroll) *prom: trckd ldng pair over 4f out: led over 2f out and wd bnd sn after: hdd and nt qckn 1f out* **11/2**

003- **4** 1¾ **Affluence (IRE)**[30] 9527 4-9-3 **51** .... ShaneKelly 7 50
(Martin Smith) *trckd ldrs: rdn over 2f out and wdst of all bnd sn after: tried to mount a chal over 1f out: one pce* **5/1**[3]

/03- **5** ¾ **Dove Mountain (IRE)**[53] 4820 8-9-9 **56** .... (bt) LukeMorris 10 53
(Olly Murphy) *slowly away: hld up wl in rr: rdn over 2f out: only modest prog and hanging over 1f out: r.o fnl f: nrst fin* **33/1**

03-1 **6** 1½ **Diamond Reflection (IRE)**[8] 62 7-9-5 **52** .... (tp) RossaRyan 6 46
(Alexandra Dunn) *led at set str pce early: hdd over 4f out: styd w ldr: rdn 3f out: drvn and stl upsides jst over 1f out: fdd fnl f* **6/1**

020- **7** ½ **Ahfad**[30] 9523 4-9-1 **49** .... (b) HectorCrouch 14 43
(Gary Moore) *pushed up fr wdst draw to press ldr: led over 4f out to over 2f out: wknd fnl f* **25/1**

066- **8** ½ **Stay In The Light**[44] 9319 4-8-13 **47** .... JackMitchell 4 40
(Roger Ingram) *hld up towards rr: tried to make prog on inner and shkn up over 2f out: nvr clrest of runs after: no ch whn no room and snatched up last 75yds (jockey said filly was denied a clear run on several occasions in the home straight)* **16/1**

605- **9** nk **Tesorina (IRE)**[13] 9769 4-9-5 **53** .... AdamKirby 2 45
(William Knight) *cl up bhd ldrs: rdn over 2f out: stl in tch on inner over 1f out: wknd fnl f* **10/3**[1]

040- **10** 3 **Voice Of Dubai**[254] 2352 4-8-9 **46** oh1 .... (p) NoelGarbutt(3) 12 33
(Hugo Palmer) *dwlt: mostly in last pair: rdn over 2f out: racing v awkwardly over 1f out and no prog* **50/1**

000- **11** nk **Gracious George (IRE)**[81] 8494 9-8-7 **47** oh1 ow1... MarkCrehan(7) 13 32
(Jimmy Fox) *hld up wl in rr: pushed along on outer over 3f out: no prog u.p 2f out* **33/1**

610- **12** nk **Lady Of Authority**[21] 9687 4-9-5 **53** .... DannyBrock 3 38
(Richard Phillips) *trckd ldng pair to over 4f out: rdn wl over 2f out: wknd over 1f out* **10/1**

006- **13** shd **Feel The Vibes**[136] 6686 5-8-13 **46** oh1 .... DavidProbert 1 30
(Michael Blanshard) *dwlt: a in rr: struggling over 2f out (jockey said gelding hung right-handed)* **25/1**

300- **14** 23 **Tabla**[283] 1594 7-9-5 **52** .... RobertWinston 11
(Lee Carter) *towards rr: no prog over 3f out: wknd qckly over 2f out: t.o (jockey said mare had stopped quickly)* **22/1**

2m 4.85s (-1.75) **Going Correction** -0.075s/f (Stan)
WFA 4 from 5yo+ 1lb **14** Ran SP% **130.1**
Speed ratings (Par 101): **104,103,102,101,100 99,98,98,98,95 95,95,95,76**
CSF £66.13 CT £349.80 TOTE £14.20: £4.50, £2.10, £2.20; EX 86.00 Trifecta £733.60.
Owner Mrs Jackie Cornwell And Mrs Jo Brisland **Bred** Exors Of The Late Mrs Liz Nelson **Trained** Danethorpe, Notts

FOCUS
A moderate handicap. The even pace picked up over 3f out and two horses came from further back through to fight it out.
T/Plt: £28.30 to a £1 stake. Pool: £55,161.25 - 1,419.53 winning units T/Qpdt: £12.60 to a £1 stake. Pool: £4,645.94 - 270.72 winning units **Jonathan Neesom**

124 NEWCASTLE (A.W) (L-H)
Saturday, January 12

OFFICIAL GOING: Tapeta: standard to slow
Wind: Breezy, half against in races on the straight course and in over 3f of home straight in races on the

208 BETWAY CASINO H'CAP 1m 4f 98y (Tp)
3:30 (3:30) (Class 7) (0-50,50) 3-Y-O+ **£2,264** (£673; £336; £168) **Stalls** High

Form RPR

502- **1** **Splash Of Verve (IRE)**[17] 9704 7-9-4 **48** .... TobyEley(7) 6 54
(David Thompson) *t.k.h: hld up: smooth hdwy on wd outside to ld over 2f out: rdn and clr over 1f out: kpt on wl fnl f* **25/1**

40-3 **2** 2¼ **Hugoigo**[6] 100 5-9-1 **45** .... CoreyMadden(7) 9 48
(Jim Goldie) *hld up: effrt on outside over 2f out: chsd wnr last 50yds: styd on: nt pce to chal* **7/1**[2]

/00- **3** nk **Manomine**[24] 9625 10-9-12 **49** .... GrahamLee 1 52
(R K Watson, Ire) *trckd ldrs: effrt and chsd wnr over 1f out to last 50yds: one pce* **11/1**

623- **4** 1½ **Traditional Dancer (IRE)**[33] 7584 7-9-10 **47** .... (p) JoeFanning 10 47
(Iain Jardine) *hld up in midfield on outside: stdy hdwy and ev ch briefly over 2f out: sn rdn: kpt on same pce ins fnl f* **15/2**[3]

005- **5** hd **Sweetest Smile (IRE)**[22] 9665 4-9-3 **46** .... BenRobinson(3) 14 47
(Ed de Giles) *in tch: rdn over 2f out: rallied over 1f out: one pce ins fnl f* **8/1**

06-4 **6** ¾ **Highway Robber**[6] 99 6-9-7 **49** .... (t) PaulaMuir(5) 11 48
(Wilf Storey) *hld up: rdn along 3f out: effrt over 1f out: kpt on fnl f: nt pce to chal (jockey said gelding missed the break and was therefore unable to make the running)* **8/1**

/0-5 **7** shd **Clive Clifton (IRE)**[8] 62 6-9-12 **49** .... PJMcDonald 3 48
(Mark Brisbourne) *hld up: effrt and rdn over 2f out: kpt on fnl f: no imp* **10/1**

05-6 **8** 2¾ **Fields Of Fire**[10] 18 5-9-10 **47** .... AndrewMullen 5 42
(Alistair Whillans) *midfield: drvn and outpcd over 2f out: no imp fr over 1f out* **100/1**

6/0- **9** hd **Bigbadboy (IRE)**[64] 8978 6-9-6 **50** .... (w) HarryRussell(7) 12 44
(Clive Mulhall) *led: rdn and hdd over 2f out: wknd over 1f out* **40/1**

05-0 **10** 1½ **Puchita (IRE)**[8] 62 4-9-7 **47** .... (b[1]) CamHardie 13 40
(Antony Brittain) *hld up: pushed along over 3f out: no imp fr 2f out* **33/1**

225- **11** 4 **Good Man (IRE)**[51] 9202 6-9-13 **50** .... (v[1]) JasonHart 8 36
(Karen McLintock) *t.k.h: cl up tl rdn and wknd wl over 1f out* **3/1**[1]

04-0 **12** ½ **Going Native**[8] 62 4-9-9 **49** .... DougieCostello 2 35
(Olly Williams) *t.k.h in midfield: drvn and outpcd over 2f out: sn wknd* **25/1**

500- **13** 21 **Rajapur**[36] 2345 6-9-10 **47** .... (p) CallumRodriguez 7 1
(David Thompson) *hld up: rdn along 3f out: sn wknd: t.o* **33/1**

424- **14** 139 **Glasgon**[28] 9554 9-9-12 **49** .... (p) JamesSullivan 4
(Ray Craggs) *in tch: rdn 1/2-way: lost pl over 4f out: lost tch and eased fnl 3f (jockey said gelding weakened quickly turning into the home straight)* **10/1**

2m 45.95s (4.85) **Going Correction** +0.55s/f (Slow)
WFA 4 from 5yo+ 3lb **14** Ran SP% **115.0**
Speed ratings (Par 97): **105,103,103,102,102 101,101,99,99,98 95,95,81,**
CSF £176.01 CT £2050.46 TOTE £14.60: £5.20, £3.20, £3.60; EX 209.40 Trifecta £1525.70.
Owner Horsingaround **Bred** J Donnelly **Trained** Bolam, Co Durham

FOCUS
A basement-level handicap.

209 SUNRACING.CO.UK H'CAP 1m 5y (Tp)
4:00 (4:00) (Class 4) (0-80,79) 4-Y-O+
£5,530 (£1,645; £822; £411; £400; £400) **Stalls** Centre

Form RPR

0-12 **1** **Paparazzi**[4] 125 4-8-13 **71** .... CamHardie 3 83
(Tracy Waggott) *hld up: hdwy to ld over 1f out: pushed out fnl f* **11/4**[3]

52-1 **2** 1¾ **Rey Loopy (IRE)**[10] 23 5-9-6 **78** .... AndrewMullen 7 86+
(Ben Haslam) *t.k.h: hld up: hdwy over 2f out: effrt and ev ch briefly appr fnl f: one pce last 100yds* **5/2**[2]

21-4 **3** 1½ **Glory Of Paris (IRE)**[9] 34 5-9-7 **79** .... AlistairRawlinson 5 84+
(Michael Appleby) *rrd and lost several l s: plld hrd and rcvrd to ld after 2f: rdn and hdd over 1f out: sn one pce* **9/4**[1]

52-3 **4** 1¼ **Newmarket Warrior (IRE)**[10] 22 8-8-12 **70** .... (p) JoeFanning 4 72
(Iain Jardine) *t.k.h early: prom: effrt and pushed along over 1f out: outpcd ins fnl f* **5/1**

666- **5** 1¼ **Mont Kinabalu (IRE)**[120] 7234 4-9-6 **78** .... GrahamLee 1 77
(Kevin Ryan) *hld up in tch: rdn and outpcd over 1f out: n.d after* **16/1**

/0-0 **6** 13 **Dubai Elegance**[10] 31 5-8-9 **67** .... PaddyMathers 2 36
(Derek Shaw) *cl up: rdn over 2f out: wknd over 1f out* **80/1**

45-0 **7** 2¼ **Muqarred (USA)**[11] 5 7-8-11 **74** .... BenSanderson(5) 6 38
(Roger Fell) *led at slow pce for 2f: chsd wnr: drvn and struggling over 2f out: sn wknd* **50/1**

1m 45.31s (6.71) **Going Correction** +0.55s/f (Slow) **7** Ran SP% **111.8**
Speed ratings (Par 105): **88,86,84,83,82 69,67**
CSF £9.58 TOTE £4.50: £2.60, £1.70; EX 11.20 Trifecta £25.20.
Owner Gordon Allan Elsa Crankshaw **Bred** The Columella Partnership **Trained** Spennymoor, Co Durham

FOCUS
There was no pace on early. The winner has been rated in line with the better view of his previous C&D win.

210 FOLLOW TOP TIPSTER TEMPLEGATE AT SUNRACING H'CAP 1m 5y (Tp)
4:30 (4:30) (Class 6) (0-55,55) 4-Y-O+
£3,105 (£924; £461; £400; £400; £400) **Stalls** Centre

Form RPR

364- **1** **Betty Grable (IRE)**[24] 9617 5-8-12 **46** .... NathanEvans 10 52
(Wilf Storey) *hld up on nr side of gp: smooth hdwy to ld over 1f out: rdn and drifted lft ins fnl f: kpt on wl* **10/1**

455- **2** ½ **Thecornishbarron (IRE)**[28] 9555 7-8-12 **46** oh1 .... CamHardie 5 51
(Brian Ellison) *dwlt: hld up: angled to nr side of gp and effrt over 1f out: chsd wnr ins fnl f: r.o: hld nr fin* **11/2**[3]

005- **3** nse **Top Offer**[33] 9481 10-9-6 **54** .... (p) GrahamLee 9 59
(Patrick Morris) *hld up in centre of gp: smooth hdwy over 1f out: effrt and disp 2nd pl ins fnl f: kpt on: hld nr fin* **16/1**

The Form Book Flat 2019, Raceform Ltd, Newbury, RG14 5SJ

231- **4** 3/4 **I Am Dandy (IRE)**[38] 9412 4-9-1 **52**..........................(t) BenRobinson(3) 1 55
(James Ewart) *prom in centre of gp: effrt and chsd wnr over 1f out to ins fnl f: sn one pce* **17/2**

300- **5** 2 1/2 **Highwayman**[28] 9555 6-9-3 **51**..............................(h) CallumRodriguez 13 49
(David Thompson) *hld up: effrt on far side of gp wl over 1f out: rdn and no imp fnl f* **5/1**[2]

51-2 **6** 3 3/4 **Molten Lava (IRE)**[7] 80 7-9-7 **55**..............................(p) JoeFanning 3 44
(Steve Gollings) *t.k.h early: in tch on nr side of gp: effrt and rdn over 1f out: wknd ins fnl f* **7/2**[1]

500- **7** 1/2 **Cardaw Lily (IRE)**[32] 9493 4-8-12 **46**.............................. JamesSullivan 14 34
(Ruth Carr) *hld up: pushed along over 2f out: effrt on far side of gp over 1f out: no imp fnl f* **40/1**

400- **8** 3 **Totally Magic (IRE)**[25] 9600 7-9-1 **49**..........................(b[1]) BarryMcHugh 6 31
(Richard Whitaker) *t.k.h: cl up in centre of gp: rdn and led briefly over 1f out: wknd ins fnl f* **11/2**[3]

250- **9** 1 1/4 **Kavora**[23] 9643 4-8-11 **48**.............................. AaronJones(3) 11 27
(Micky Hammond) *led in centre of gp: rdn and hdd over 1f out: sn wknd* **20/1**

43-6 **10** nk **Golden Guide**[11] 6 4-8-12 **46**.............................. CliffordLee 7 24
(K R Burke) *hld up on nr side of gp: drvn and outpcd over 2f out: sn btn* **10/1**

006- **11** 2 3/4 **Benaras (USA)**[22] 9660 4-8-13 **52**.............................. BenSanderson(5) 12 24
(Roger Fell) *hld up: drvn along on far side of gp over 2f out: sn wknd* **100/1**

300- **12** 12 **Deolali**[277] 1707 5-9-4 **52**.............................. PaddyMathers 4
(Stella Barclay) *trckd ldrs on far side of gp tl rdn and wknd over 2f out: eased* **125/1**

000- **13** 1 1/2 **Glorious Rocket**[72] 8778 5-9-6 **54**..............................(h) DougieCostello 8
(John Hodge) *missed break: plld hrd in midfield on far side of gp: struggling over 2f out: sn wknd (jockey said gelding ran too free)* **80/1**

1m 42.65s (4.05) **Going Correction** +0.55s/f (Slow) **13 Ran SP% 114.5**
Speed ratings (Par 101): **101,100,100,99,97 93,92,89,88,88 85,73,72**
CSF £59.95 CT £876.47 TOTE £12.10: £3.20, £2.70, £5.80; EX 90.50 Trifecta £864.70.
Owner W Storey **Bred** Tally-Ho Stud **Trained** Muggleswick, Co Durham

FOCUS
Another low-level handicap.

211 LADBROKES HOME OF THE ODDS BOOST NOVICE STKS (PLUS 10 RACE) 6f (Tp)
5:00 (5:00) (Class 4) 3-Y-O **£5,530** (£1,645; £822; £411) **Stalls** Centre

Form RPR

23- **1** **Kareena Kapoor (USA)**[197] 4332 3-8-11 0.............................. JoeFanning 2 75+
(Simon Crisford) *trckd ldrs: led gng wl over 1f out: shkn up ins fnl f: comf* **4/7**[1]

2 1/2 **Plumette** 3-8-11 0.............................. PJMcDonald 1 71+
(Richard Fahey) *in tch: effrt and edgd lft over 1f out: chsd wnr ins fnl f: kpt on fin* **25/1**

3 3 1/4 **Compton's Finale**[8] 70 3-9-2 72..............................(t[1]) GrahamLee 5 66
(Adrian Paul Keatley, Ire) *trckd ldrs: effrt and rdn over 1f out: kpt on same pce fnl f* **7/2**[2]

0-3 **4** 1/2 **Eufemia**[10] 27 3-8-11 0..............................(t[1]) AlistairRawlinson 3 59
(Amy Murphy) *t.k.h: led: rdn and hdd over 1f out: kpt on same pce* **18/1**

5 hd **Call Me Ginger** 3-8-9 0.............................. CoreyMadden(7) 11 63+
(Jim Goldie) *s.i.s: hld up: green and outpcd over 2f out: gd hdwy fnl f: kpt on fin* **33/1**

00- **6** 2 1/2 **Firsteen**[24] 9612 3-8-11 0.............................. CamHardie 8 50
(Alistair Whillans) *hld up: pushed along over 2f out: wknd over 1f out* **150/1**

65- **7** nk **Zaula**[110] 7608 3-8-6 0.............................. ThomasGreatrex(5) 10 49
(Archie Watson) *trckd ldr to over 2f out: wknd over 1f out (jockey said filly stopped quickly)* **11/2**[3]

06- **8** 3 3/4 **Petite Magician (IRE)**[42] 9353 3-8-11 0.............................. JasonHart 9 37
(David Barron) *hld up: pushed along over 2f out: sn wknd* **80/1**

0-6 **9** 1 3/4 **Amourie**[10] 20 3-8-11 0.............................. JamesSullivan 4 32
(Ray Craggs) *hld up: rdn and struggling over 2f out: sn btn* **50/1**

10 13 **Gatesy (IRE)** 3-8-13 0.............................. BenRobinson(3) 7
(John Davies) *missed break: hld up: rdn and struggling over 2f out: sn lost tch (jockey said gelding was slowly away and then ran too free)* **80/1**

1m 15.27s (2.77) **Going Correction** +0.55s/f (Slow) **10 Ran SP% 118.4**
Speed ratings (Par 99): **103,102,98,97,97 93,93,88,86,68**
CSF £25.94 TOTE £1.40: £1.10, £4.10, £1.40; EX 18.60 Trifecta £45.20.
Owner Hussain Alabbas Lootah **Bred** China Horse Club International Limited **Trained** Newmarket, Suffolk

■ Sharrabang was withdrawn. Price at time of withdrawal 66/1. Rule 4 does not apply

FOCUS
The bare form looks ordinary, but a few of these should improve. The winner has been rated in line with his turf runs, and the fourth to her latest.

212 FOLLOW SUNRACING ON TWITTER H'CAP 1m 5y (Tp)
5:30 (5:30) (Class 3) (0-95,94) 4-Y-O+ **£7,439** (£2,213; £1,106; £553) **Stalls** Centre

Form RPR

134- **1** **Tough Remedy (IRE)**[12] 9774 4-9-0 **87**.............................. PJMcDonald 4 93
(Keith Dalgleish) *dwlt: sn prom: drvn and outpcd over 2f out: rallied to ld ins fnl f: styd on wl* **10/11**[1]

042- **2** 1 **Azzeccagarbugli (IRE)**[30] 9524 6-9-7 **94**..............................(p) GrahamLee 1 98
(Marco Botti) *led at ordinary gallop: rdn and hdd over 2f out: rallied and ev ch ins fnl f: kpt on same pce towards fin* **3/1**[2]

000- **3** 1/2 **Ballard Down (IRE)**[198] 4299 6-9-7 **94**.............................. CallumRodriguez 3 97
(David O'Meara) *cl up: led over 2f out: rdn and hdd ins fnl f: kpt on same pce* **5/1**[3]

506- **4** nk **Qaffaal (USA)**[189] 4681 8-9-7 **94**.............................. NathanEvans 5 96
(Michael Easterby) *hld up in tch: effrt and rdn over 1f out: kpt on fnl f: no further imp towards fin* **9/1**

000- **5** 21 **Steel Train (FR)**[33] 9483 8-9-0 **90**.............................. ConorMcGovern(3) 2 44
(David O'Meara) *plld hrd: cl up: rdn and outpcd over 2f out: lost tch over 1f out* **20/1**

1m 42.57s (3.97) **Going Correction** +0.55s/f (Slow) **5 Ran SP% 108.8**
Speed ratings (Par 107): **102,101,100,100,79**
CSF £3.74 TOTE £1.70: £1.40, £1.10; EX 4.00 Trifecta £11.30.
Owner Titanium Racing Club **Bred** Mrs Noreen Maher **Trained** Carluke, S Lanarks

FOCUS
Just five runners; an ordinary race of its type. The second has been rated to his latest.

213 LIKE SUNRACING ON FACEBOOK H'CAP 7f 14y (Tp)
6:00 (6:00) (Class 4) (0-85,83) 4-Y-O+ **£5,530** (£1,645; £822; £411; £400) **Stalls** Centre

Form RPR

10-3 **1** **Portledge (IRE)**[6] 104 5-9-2 **78**..............................(b) PJMcDonald 2 86
(James Bethell) *dwlt: sn trcking ldrs: led gng wl over 1f out: drvn out fnl f* **7/2**[3]

430- **2** 1 **Luis Vaz De Torres (IRE)**[44] 9305 7-8-13 **75**.............................. TonyHamilton 3 80
(Richard Fahey) *t.k.h: hld up in last pl: effrt and hdwy over 1f out: pressed wnr ins fnl f: kpt on: hld nr fin* **18/1**

403- **3** 3/4 **Helovaplan (IRE)**[95] 8095 5-9-7 **83**.............................. GrahamLee 1 86
(Bryan Smart) *led: rdn: edgd lft and hdd over 1f out: rallied: one pce ins fnl f* **5/1**

5-52 **4** 10 **Call Out Loud**[6] 104 7-9-4 **80**..............................(vt) AlistairRawlinson 5 56
(Michael Appleby) *pressed ldr tl rdn and wknd over 1f out* **6/4**[1]

05-2 **5** 4 1/2 **Custard The Dragon**[11] 4 6-9-6 **82**..............................(p) JoeFanning 4 46
(John Mackie) *prom: rdn along over 2f out: wknd wl over 1f out* **11/4**[2]

1m 29.65s (3.45) **Going Correction** +0.55s/f (Slow) **5 Ran SP% 110.8**
Speed ratings (Par 105): **102,100,100,88,83**
CSF £47.67 TOTE £5.90: £2.40, £5.20; EX 41.40 Trifecta £130.10.
Owner Tony Buckingham **Bred** S P Hussain **Trained** Middleham Moor, N Yorks

FOCUS
The winner blew the start, the second was keen, the third has shown his best form over further and the fourth and fifth did not give their true running, so this doesn't look robust form. The winner has been rated to his best.

214 BETWAY H'CAP 6f (Tp)
6:30 (6:30) (Class 5) (0-75,76) 4-Y-O+
£3,752 (£1,116; £557; £400; £400; £400) **Stalls** Centre

Form RPR

60-3 **1** **Athollblair Boy (IRE)**[10] 24 6-9-1 **76**.............................. FayeMcManoman(7) 9 85
(Nigel Tinkler) *hld up: hdwy to ld appr fnl f: pushed along and edgd lft last 100yds: hld on wl* **2/1**[1]

210- **2** shd **Duke Cosimo**[24] 9616 9-8-5 **62**.............................. PhilDennis(3) 4 69
(Michael Herrington) *hld up: hdwy over 1f out: shkn up and squeezed through to chse wnr ins fnl f: kpt on fin: jst hld* **14/1**

402- **3** 3 **Avenue Of Stars**[24] 9616 6-8-8 **62**..............................(v) JasonHart 5 59
(Karen McLintock) *led: rdn and hdd appr fnl f: sn one pce* **11/2**[3]

000- **4** 1/2 **Kentuckyconnection (USA)**[101] 7890 6-8-7 **68**....(p) HarryRussell(7) 8 64
(Bryan Smart) *hld up: rdn and hdwy 2f out: kpt on same pce ins fnl f* **16/1**

506- **5** 1 1/2 **Johnny Cavagin**[26] 9588 10-8-11 **65**.............................. JoeFanning 2 56+
(Paul Midgley) *t.k.h: hld up: pushed along and outpcd 2f out: rallied ins fnl f: no imp* **14/1**

102- **6** 1 3/4 **Lucky Lodge**[24] 9617 9-9-2 **70**..............................(b) CamHardie 3 55
(Antony Brittain) *prom: rdn along over 2f out: rallied: outpcd appr fnl f: sn btn* **17/2**

203- **7** 1/2 **Capla Demon**[32] 9491 4-9-0 **68**..............................(p) CallumRodriguez 7 52
(Antony Brittain) *trckd ldrs: rdn over 2f out: wknd fnl f* **9/1**

20-6 **8** 6 **Katheefa (USA)**[10] 24 5-9-5 **73**..............................(p[1]) JamesSullivan 6 38
(Ruth Carr) *t.k.h: in tch: lost nr-side cheekpiece over 2f out: effrt over 1f out: wknd fnl f* **4/1**[2]

14-6 **9** 3 1/4 **Kommander Kirkup**[11] 2 8-9-0 **68**..............................(p) AndrewMullen 1 22
(Michael Herrington) *in tch: rdn and outpcd over 2f out: btn over 1f out* **33/1**

1m 14.16s (1.66) **Going Correction** +0.55s/f (Slow) **9 Ran SP% 111.4**
Speed ratings (Par 103): **110,109,105,105,103 100,100,92,87**
CSF £30.83 CT £130.12 TOTE £3.60: £1.80, £3.40, £1.20; EX 30.80 Trifecta £142.80.
Owner The Geezaaah Partnership **Bred** Ms Ashley O'Leary **Trained** Langton, N Yorks

FOCUS
Fair form. The winner has been rated close to his best, and the second in line with his recent form.

215 LADBROKES H'CAP 5f (Tp)
7:00 (7:00) (Class 6) (0-65,67) 3-Y-O
£3,105 (£924; £461; £400; £400; £400) **Stalls** Centre

Form RPR

604- **1** **Giacomo Casanova (IRE)**[87] 8323 3-8-13 **55**.............................. AndrewMullen 11 64
(Kevin Ryan) *trckd ldrs: hdwy to ld over 1f out: pushed clr ins fnl f: comf* **13/2**

144- **2** 2 1/4 **Hanakotoba (USA)**[44] 9307 3-9-6 **62**..............................(t) CallumRodriguez 6 63
(Stuart Williams) *veered bdly lft s: t.k.h: sn pressing ldr: rdn and ev ch briefly over 1f out: kpt on ins fnl f: nt rch wnr (jockey said filly hung badly left leaving the stalls)* **5/1**[3]

546- **3** nk **Madame Vitesse (FR)**[39] 9392 3-9-7 **63**.............................. TonyHamilton 9 63
(Richard Fahey) *t.k.h: hld up in midfield: effrt and angled lft over 1f out: kpt on fnl f (jockey said filly suffered interference leaving the stalls)* **11/1**

50-5 **4** nse **Gunnabedun (IRE)**[10] 21 3-8-10 **52**.............................. JoeFanning 10 52
(Iain Jardine) *hld up: hdwy over 1f out: rdn and kpt on same pce wl ins fnl f* **14/1**

550- **5** 1 **Pink Flamingo**[63] 9006 3-9-11 **67**.............................. PJMcDonald 3 64
(Mark Johnston) *hmpd s: hld up: rdn and hdwy over 1f out: kpt on fnl f: no imp* **16/1**

262- **6** 1/2 **Willow Brook**[45] 9284 3-9-0 **56**..............................(h) GrahamLee 1 50
(Julie Camacho) *hmpd s: hld up in midfield: effrt and pushed along over 1f out: keeping on whn n.m.r briefly ins fnl f: r.o (jockey said filly suffered interference leaving the stalls)* **7/2**[1]

651- **6** dht **Klopp**[45] 9284 3-9-7 **63**.............................. CamHardie 4 57
(Antony Brittain) *hmpd s: t.k.h in tch: rdn over 2f out: one pce ins fnl f* **4/1**[2]

600- **8** 1 **Sing Bertie (IRE)**[45] 9284 3-8-5 **47**.............................. PaddyMathers 8 38
(Derek Shaw) *t.k.h: hld up: effrt and rdn over 1f out: no imp fnl f (jockey said gelding ran too free)* **40/1**

006- **9** 1 1/2 **Global Myth (USA)**[82] 8470 3-8-10 **52**..............................(p[1]) JasonHart 7 37
(Robert Cowell) *led: rdn and hdd over 1f out: wknd ins fnl f* **6/1**

000- **10** 5 **Cool Walk**[25] 9598 3-8-3 **45**.............................. JamesSullivan 5 12
(Derek Shaw) *t.k.h: hld up: rdn and outpcd 2f out: sn btn* **100/1**

546- **11** 2 1/2 **Oxygenic**[26] 9589 3-8-12 **57**.............................. ConorMcGovern(3) 2 15
(David O'Meara) *hmpd s: hld up on outside: struggling over 2f out: sn btn* **33/1**

1m 2.77s (3.27) **Going Correction** +0.55s/f (Slow) **11 Ran SP% 113.8**
Speed ratings (Par 95): **95,91,90,90,89 88,88,86,84,76 72**
WIN: 7.90 Giacomo Casanova; PL: 3.50 Madame Vitesse 1.40 Hanakotoba 2.60 Giacomo Casanova; EX: 40.70; CSF: 37.30; TC: 356.89 CSF £37.30 CT £356.89 TOTE £7.90: £2.60, £1.40, £3.50; EX 40.70.
Owner Giacomo Casanova Partners **Bred** P Kelly **Trained** Hambleton, N Yorks

FOCUS
A modest sprint handicap, and four of the unplaced horses - the runners from the bottom four stalls - were hampered by the runner-up soon after the start, but the winner did this well.
T/Plt: £308.00 to a £1 stake. Pool: £64,020.17 - 151.73 winning units T/Qpdt: £28.80 to a £1 stake. Pool: £11,333.43 - 290.48 winning units **Richard Young**

CHANTILLY (R-H)
Saturday, January 12
OFFICIAL GOING: Polytrack: standard

216a PRIX DE LA PORTE DES MARCHANDS (CLAIMER) (3YO) (ALL-WEATHER TRACK) (POLYTRACK) 1m (P)
1:57 (1:57) 3-Y-O £9,009 (£3,603; £2,702; £1,801; £900)

RPR
1 **Cleostorm (FR)**[20] 3-8-11 0............................(b) MaxímeGuyon 7 71
(P Monfort, France) **21/10**[1]
2 2 **Ana Gold (FR)**[17] 3-8-7 0............................(b[1]) ThomasTrullier(6) 5 68
(Laurent Loisel, France) **16/1**
3 hd **Chacha Boy (FR)**[25] 3-8-11 0............................(p) MlleAlisonMassin(4) 1 70
(Y Barberot, France) **15/1**
4 snk **Ale Tango (FR)**[20] 3-9-1 0............................ CristianDemuro 15 70
(G Botti, France) **47/10**[3]
5 1 **Ursus Arctos (IRE)**[17] 3-8-11 0............................ SebastienMaillot 9 63
(N Clement, France) **13/1**
6 3 **She's A Stunner (IRE)** 3-8-8 0............................(p) EddyHardouin 16 53
(Matthieu Palussiere, France) **69/1**
7 hd **What Secret (IRE)** 3-9-4 0............................(b[1]) TonyPiccone 11 63
(Matthieu Palussiere, France) **42/1**
8 3 ½ **Still In Deauville (IRE)** 3-8-11 0............................ PierreBazire 14 48
(Miss V Haigh, France) *in rr: outpcd and pushed along over 3f out: swtchd outside rivals 2f out: plugged on past btn rivals fr 1 1/2f out: nvr a factor* **54/1**
9 1 ¼ **Exclusive Oro (FR)**[29] 3-8-8 0............................ AurelienLemaitre 10 42
(Mme Pia Brandt, France) **16/1**
10 2 **Run Ashore (FR)**[93] 8250 3-9-4 0............................ IoritzMendizabal 6 47
(J S Moore) *cl up early but sn outpcd and dropped into midfield: 6th and drvn 3f out: rdn 1 1/2f out: sing to stay on whn squeezed out by two rivals ent fnl f: qckly eased* **22/5**[2]
11 2 **Division (FR)**[199] 3-9-1 0............................ ThierryThulliez 3 40
(R Le Gal, France) **17/1**
12 4 **Fifty Days Fire (FR)**[25] 3-9-1 0............................(b) MickaelForest 8 31
(D Allard, France) **84/1**
13 2 ½ **Palmina (FR)**[25] 3-8-8 0............................ AnthonyCrastus 12 18
(D Zarroli, Italy) **67/1**
14 8 **Cold Light Of Day (FR)**[17] 3-7-13 0............................ MlleLeaBails(9) 13
(Robert Collet, France) **101/1**
15 dist **Hurricane Gold (FR)**[223] 3412 3-9-4 0............................ AntoineHamelin 2
(Matthieu Palussiere, France) **77/10**

1m 39.8s **15 Ran SP% 119.7**
PARI-MUTUEL (all including 1 euro stake): WIN 3.10; PLACE 1.60, 3.70, 3.70; DF 20.50.
Owner Jean-Paul Boin **Bred** J-P Boin **Trained** France

217a PRIX DE CHASSELOUP (MAIDEN) (3YO) (ALL-WEATHER TRACK) (POLYTRACK) 6f 110y(P)
3:10 3-Y-O £11,261 (£4,504; £3,378; £2,252; £1,126)

RPR
1 **Becquagold (FR)**[25] 9601 3-9-2 0............................ IoritzMendizabal 5 79
(O Trigodet, France) **57/10**[3]
2 snk **Glorious Emaraty (FR)**[22] 9671 3-9-2 0............ Pierre-CharlesBoudot 10 78
(Clive Cox) *hld up in midfield: nt clr run over 2f out: stdd and angled out w 1 1/2f to run: drvn to cl over 1f out: virtually upsides ldng pair last 150yds: styd on u.p: no ex cl home* **2/1**[1]
3 1 ½ **Adelante (FR)**[16] 9727 3-8-13 0............................ MaximeGuyon 4 71
(George Baker) *settled in midfield: 5th whn a little outpcd and drvn w under 2f to run: sn rdn: styd on fnl f: nt rch front two* **11/1**
4 snk **Gardol Man (IRE)**[17] 3-9-2 0............................ CristianDemuro 7 74
(G Botti, France) **27/10**[2]
5 snk **Hinemoa (FR)** 3-7-13 0............................ MlleLauraGrosso(9) 9 65
(N Clement, France) **26/1**
6 hd **Realityhacking (FR)**[17] 3-8-7 0............................(b) MlleMarieVelon(9) 8 73
(F Chappet, France) **68/10**
7 1 ½ **A Delight (FR)**[244] 3-8-13 0............................ AntoineHamelin 1 65
(Matthieu Palussiere, France) **21/1**
8 ¾ **Mortirolo (FR)** 3-8-6 0............................ QuentinPerrette(5) 6 61
(Andrea Marcialis, France) **33/1**
9 ¾ **Little Jo (FR)**[30] 3-9-2 0............................ EddyHardouin 3 64
(P Monfort, France) **55/1**
10 2 **Porthos (FR)**[17] 3-8-13 0............................ DelphineSantiago(3) 12 58
(Mme G Rarick, France) **58/1**
11 1 ¼ **Pleasant Gesture (IRE)**[38] 9417 3-8-7 0............ ThomasTrullier(6) 11 51
(J S Moore) *w.w towards rr: moved into midfield bef 1/2-way: rdn and no further imp over 1 1/2f out: sn wknd* **16/1**
12 3 **La Miura (FR)** 3-8-8 0............................ VincentCheminaud 2 38
(T Castanheira, France) **35/1**

1m 19.43s **12 Ran SP% 119.8**
PARI-MUTUEL (all including 1 euro stake): WIN 6.70; PLACE 2.00, 1.80, 2.70; DF 10.20.
Owner Mme V Becquart, P Schlienger & R Schlienger **Bred** B Becquart, R Schlienger & P Schlienger **Trained** France

218 - 227a (Foreign Racing) - See Raceform Interactive

[162]SOUTHWELL (L-H)
Sunday, January 13
OFFICIAL GOING: Fibresand: standard
Wind: Strong behind Weather: Overcast

228 LADBROKES HOME OF THE ODDS BOOST H'CAP 7f 14y(F)
12:20 (12:20) (Class 6) (0-65,67) 3-Y-O
£3,105 (£924; £461; £400; £400; £400) **Stalls Low**

Form RPR
040- 1 **Sylviacliffs (FR)**[15] 9744 3-8-9 **53**............................ AndrewMullen 1 56
(K R Burke) *midfield: n.m.r and pushed along 1/2-way: rdn and hdwy 2f out: sn swtchd lft and chsd ldrs over 1f out: drvn to chal ins fnl f: kpt on u.p to ld last 50yds (trainer said, as to the apparent improvement in form, the filly benefitted from a trouble-free run on this occasion)* **22/1**
005- 2 hd **Arriba De Toda (IRE)**[15] 9744 3-8-2 **46** oh1............(b[1]) CamHardie 8 48
(Brian Ellison) *towards rr: pushed along 3f out: wd st: hdwy and swtchd lft over 2f out: sn rdn: chsd ldrs over 1f out: drvn to chal ins fnl f: ev ch: jst hld* **33/1**
001- 3 ½ **Rusper Dreams (IRE)**[31] 9521 3-9-2 **60**............................ DougieCostello 10 61
(Jamie Osborne) *prom: led 2f out: rdn over 1f out: jnd and drvn ins fnl f: hdd and no ex last 50yds* **7/2**[1]
35-1 4 nk **War and Glory (IRE)**[9] 65 3-9-9 **67**............................ LukeMorris 7 67
(James Tate) *trckd ldrs: hdwy and wd st: rdn 2f out: drvn and edgd rt to stands' rail over 1f out: ch ins fnl f: kpt on same pce* **5/1**[2]
000- 5 1 ¼ **Robeam (IRE)**[16] 9729 3-8-11 **55**............................ TonyHamilton 6 52
(Richard Fahey) *sn pushed along in rr: rdn along at 1/2-way: hdwy on inner 2f out: kpt on wl fnl f* **13/2**[3]
043- 6 shd **Bawtry Lady**[15] 9749 3-8-2 **49**............................(b) PhilDennis(3) 14 46
(David C Griffiths) *prom: led after 1f: rdn along and wd st: hdd 2f out: sn drvn and grad wknd* **25/1**
503- 7 ¾ **Dolly Dupree**[26] 9599 3-8-7 **51**............................ HollieDoyle 11 46
(Paul D'Arcy) *chsd ldrs on inner: rdn along wl over 2f out: sn drvn and grad wknd* **20/1**
03-0 8 6 **Peters Pudding (IRE)**[6] 122 3-8-11 **62**............(v) KatherineBegley(7) 3 41
(David Evans) *reminders s and sn rdn along: in tch and n.m.r bnd after 3f: chsd ldrs on inner 3f out: sn rdn and wknd over 2f out (jockey said gelding didn't face the kickback)* **7/1**
631- 9 1 **Champagne Mondays**[15] 9749 3-8-9 **53**............................(p) NicolaCurrie 2 30
(Scott Dixon) *led 1f: prom: rdn along 3f out: wknd over 2f out* **10/1**
505- 10 2 ¾ **Uh Oh Chongo**[18] 9709 3-9-6 **64**............................ NathanEvans 9 34
(Michael Easterby) *dwlt: a towards rr* **8/1**
006- 11 ½ **Agent Smith (IRE)**[159] 5815 3-8-10 **54**............................ CliffordLee 12 22
(K R Burke) *clsd up: rdn along 3f out: drvn 2f out: sn wknd* **20/1**
000- 12 1 ¾ **Symphony (IRE)**[46] 9289 3-8-12 **56**............................ JosephineGordon 13 20
(James Unett) *towards rr: wd st: rdn and hung lft 2f out: nvr a factor* **33/1**
000- 13 3 **Eagre**[96] 8092 3-8-2 **46** oh1............................(v) PaddyMathers 4 2
(Derek Shaw) *a in rr* **66/1**
003- 14 3 **Dothraki (IRE)**[15] 9744 3-8-12 **56**............................(e) GrahamLee 5 4
(Ronald Thompson) *a in rr* **14/1**

1m 30.71s (0.41) **Going Correction** -0.05s/f (Stan) **14 Ran SP% 116.7**
Speed ratings (Par 95): **95,94,94,93,92 92,91,84,83,80 79,77,74,70**
CSF £564.15 CT £3221.75 TOTE £28.50: £7.00, £8.30, £3.80; EX 835.70 Trifecta £1492.90.
Owner The Mount Racing Club & Mrs E Burke **Bred** P Lemarie & S A R L Ecurie Silgezam **Trained** Middleham Moor, N Yorks

■ Stewards' Enquiry : Phil Dennis caution: careless riding

FOCUS
A moderate handicap run at a strong-looking pace.

229 LADBROKES NOVICE STKS 7f 14y(F)
12:50 (12:50) (Class 5) 3-Y-O £3,752 (£1,116; £557; £278) **Stalls Low**

Form RPR
4- 1 **Eve Harrington (USA)**[33] 9490 3-8-11 0............................ LukeMorris 5 66
(Sir Mark Prescott Bt) *dwlt and pushed along s: sn trcking ldrs: hdwy on inner 3f out: rdn along 2f out: chal over 1f out: drvn ins fnl f: led last 120yds: jst hld on* **5/4**[1]
320- 2 nse **Barossa Red (IRE)**[143] 6455 3-8-13 82............................ JoshuaBryan(3) 6 71
(Andrew Balding) *trckd ldrs: pushed along and hdwy over 3f out: sn cl up: led 2f out and sn rdn: drvn ent fnl f: hdd last 120yds: rallied gamely towards fin: jst hld* **2/1**[2]
3 hd **Sense Of Direction** 3-8-11 0............................ CliffordLee 8 65+
(K R Burke) *cl up on outer: rn green: pushed along and outpcd after 3f: hdwy and wd st: chsd ldrs over 2f out: rdn wl over 1f out: styd on to chal ent fnl f: ev ch tl no ex towards fin* **11/1**
45- 4 ½ **Ivory Charm**[16] 9730 3-8-11 0............................ PJMcDonald 2 64+
(Richard Fahey) *in rr and sn swtchd rt to wd outside: outpcd and detached 1/2-way: rdn along and wd st: gd hdwy over 1f out: styd on strly fnl f: nrst fin* **9/1**[3]
0-0 5 1 **Twpsyn (IRE)**[8] 90 3-8-9 0............................ GinaMangan(7) 7 66
(David Evans) *cl up: rdn along 3f out: drvn wl over 1f out: grad wknd appr fnl f* **100/1**
023- 6 5 **Cheap Jack**[39] 9411 3-9-2 67............................(e[1]) GrahamLee 4 53
(Ronald Thompson) *led: rdn along 3f out: hdd 2f out: sn drvn: wknd appr fnl f* **12/1**
56- 7 1 ¼ **Sarasota Star (IRE)**[27] 9590 3-9-2 0............................ JoeyHaynes 9 50
(Martin Keighley) *trckd ldrs: rapid hdwy on outer and cl up 3f out: disp ld over 2f out: sn rdn: wknd wl over 1f out* **18/1**
8 9 **Georgearthurhenry** 3-9-2 0............................ MartinHarley 3 26
(Amy Murphy) *cl up on inner: rdn along 3f out: sn wknd* **25/1**
00- 9 ½ **So I'm Told (IRE)**[43] 9354 3-9-2 0............................ JackMitchell 1 25
(George Scott) *in rr and sn swtchd rt to wd outside: outpcd and detached fr 1/2-way* **50/1**

1m 29.65s (-0.65) **Going Correction** -0.05s/f (Stan) **9 Ran SP% 115.9**
Speed ratings (Par 97): **101,100,100,100,99 93,91,81,81**
CSF £3.79 TOTE £2.10: £1.20, £1.60, £1.90; EX 4.30 Trifecta £23.40.
Owner Sir Mark Prescott **Bred** John R Penn & Frank Penn **Trained** Newmarket, Suffolk

FOCUS
Little more than 1.5l covered the first five at the line, so probably just ordinary bare form, but some nice types. The second has been rated a bit below his 2yo form for now.

230 BETWAY SPRINT H'CAP 4f 214y(F)
1:25 (1:25) (Class 4) (0-85,92) 4-Y-O+

£6,080 (£1,809; £904; £452; £400; £400) **Stalls** Centre

Form RPR
2-31 **1** **Ornate**[3] [163] 6-10-0 **92** 6ex.................................. PhilDennis(3) 7 101
(David C Griffiths) *mde all towards centre: rdn over 1f out: drvn ins fnl f: edgd lft: kpt on wl towards fin* **5/2**[1]

5-32 **2** 1/2 **Crosse Fire**[3] [165] 7-8-7 **68** oh1............................(p) KieranO'Neill 5 76
(Scott Dixon) *cl up centre: rdn to chal over 1f out: drvn and ev ch ins fnl f: edgd rt and no ex towards fin* **7/1**

61-1 **3** 1 **Miningold**[10] [43] 6-8-3 **69**.......................................(p) PaulaMuir(5) 1 73
(Michael Dods) *racd towards far side: cl up: effrt to chal over 1f out: sn rdn: drvn and ev ch ins fnl f: no ex towards fin* **13/2**[3]

104- **4** 3 3/4 **Chookie Dunedin**[15] [9748] 4-9-7 **82**............... CallumRodriguez 3 73
(Keith Dalgleish) *cl up in centre: rdn along wl over 1f out: grad wknd* **7/2**[2]

30-5 **5** 1 **Something Lucky (IRE)**[12] [3] 7-9-7 **82**...........(v) AlistairRawlinson 6 69
(Michael Appleby) *sn swtchd rt to r towards stands' side: sn outpcd and bhd: rdn along over 2f out: kpt on fnl f* **12/1**

210- **6** 3 1/2 **Cool Spirit**[59] [9084] 4-9-4 **79**.. PJMcDonald 2 53
(James Given) *cl up in centre: rdn along 1/2-way: sn outpcd* **25/1**

32-U **7** 2 1/4 **Samovar**[3] [163] 4-8-9 **75**...................................(b) TheodoreLadd(5) 4 41
(Scott Dixon) *s.i.s and lost several l s: a bhd (jockey said the gelding put its head in the adjacent stall as the start was effected, causing the gelding to be slowly away and lose many lengths as a result)* **7/2**[2]

57.99s (-1.71) **Going Correction** -0.05s/f (Stan) 7 Ran SP% **110.4**
Speed ratings (Par 105): **111,110,108,102,101 95,91**
CSF £18.99 TOTE £3.90: £2.60, £3.00; EX 16.80 Trifecta £59.00.
Owner Kings Road Racing Partnership **Bred** Cheveley Park Stud Ltd **Trained** Bawtry, S Yorks

FOCUS
A useful sprint handicap. The second and third have been rated close to their recent form.

231 BETWAY CASINO H'CAP 1m 4f 14y(F)
1:55 (1:55) (Class 3) (0-90,91) 4-Y-O+ **£9,451** (£2,829; £1,414; £708; £352) **Stalls** Low

Form RPR
01-1 **1** **Azari**[3] [162] 7-9-0 **79** 6ex.......................................(b) RossaRyan 4 86
(Alexandra Dunn) *cl up: led after 2 1/2f: pushed along over 3f out: rdn wl over 2f out: drvn over 1f out: edgd rt ins fnl f: hld on wl towards fin (caution: careless riding)* **5/4**[1]

631- **2** 1 **Vivernus (USA)**[24] [9642] 6-9-5 **84**................................... AndrewMullen 1 89
(Adrian Nicholls) *led 2f: cl up: pushed along 4f out: rdn to chal wl over 2f out: sn edgd lft: drvn and ev ch over 1f out: hrd drvn ins fnl f: no ex towards fin* **15/8**[2]

045- **3** 2 **Ezanak (IRE)**[16] [9731] 6-8-10 **75**..............................(b) LukeMorris 5 77
(Michael Appleby) *pushed along s: sn trcking ldng pair: pushed along over 4f out: rdn over 3f out: drvn over 2f out: kpt on same pce* **12/1**

001- **4** nk **Mixboy (FR)**[12] [8716] 9-9-12 **91**.. JoeFanning 3 92
(Keith Dalgleish) *hld up: pushed along 4f out: rdn and hdwy over 2f out: drvn over 1f out: kpt on fnl f* **5/1**[3]

366- **5** 15 **Great Hall**[17] [9053] 9-9-10 **89**..................................... DougieCostello 2 66
(Mick Quinn) *in tch: pushed along over 4f out: rdn over 3f out: sn outpcd* **16/1**

2m 38.7s (-2.30) **Going Correction** -0.05s/f (Stan) 5 Ran SP% **109.5**
Speed ratings (Par 107): **105,104,103,102,92**
CSF £3.79 TOTE £1.60: £1.10, £2.10; EX 4.00 Trifecta £14.30.
Owner B B S & Lot 51 **Bred** Yeguada De Milagro Sa **Trained** West Buckland, Somerset

FOCUS
A fair handicap. The winner has been rated similar to his win three days earlier.

232 FOLLOW SUNRACING ON TWITTER H'CAP 1m 13y(F)
2:30 (2:30) (Class 6) (0-65,76) 4-Y-O+

£3,105 (£924; £461; £400; £400; £400) **Stalls** Low

Form RPR
062- **1** **Long Socks**[24] [9647] 5-9-3 **61**... MartinHarley 1 68
(Alan King) *trckd ldrs: hdwy over 3f out: led 1 1/2f out: sn rdn: drvn ins fnl f: kpt on strly* **6/1**[3]

04/- **2** 1 1/2 **Havelock (IRE)**[106] [7792] 5-8-11 **55**.................................. LukeMorris 5 59
(Peter Fahey, Ire) *n.m.r after s and towards rr: hdwy at 1/2-way: trckd ldrs 3f out: effrt on inner and rdn 2f out: drvn to chse wnr ins fnl f: no imp towards fin* **11/1**

01-1 **3** 1 1/2 **Bond Angel**[12] [6] 4-8-12 **63**.............................. KatherineBegley(7) 6 63+
(David Evans) *n.m.r after s and towards rr: hdwy on outer and v wd st: rdn and hdwy 2f out: styd on wl fnl f* **8/1**

03-1 **4** 4 1/2 **Thunder Buddy**[10] [45] 4-8-9 **60**................................ RhonaPindar(7) 7 50
(K R Burke) *cl up: led 3f out: rdn over 2f out: hdd wl over 1f out: sn drvn and grad wknd* **7/2**[1]

0-02 **5** 1/2 **Sooqaan**[10] [45] 8-9-4 **62**..(p) CamHardie 9 51
(Antony Brittain) *trckd ldrs: hdwy 3f out: rdn along 2f out: sn drvn and one pce* **13/2**

036- **6** 1/2 **Eponina (IRE)**[23] [9656] 5-9-3 **61**................................. AlistairRawlinson 4 48
(Michael Appleby) *cl up: led over 6f out: pushed along 4f out: rdn and hdd 3f out: drvn over 2f out: grad wknd* **16/1**

064- **7** 3 **Alonso Cano (IRE)**[36] [9458] 4-9-4 **62**........................(b) PJMcDonald 10 43
(Jo Hughes, France) *prom: rdn along wl over 3f out: sn outpcd* **5/1**[2]

02-0 **8** 6 **Boots And Spurs**[10] [45] 10-8-4 **53**...................(v) TheodoreLadd(5) 3 20
(Scott Dixon) *slt ld early: hdd and pushed along over 6f out: sn lost pl and bhd (jockey said gelding was never travelling)* **20/1**

100- **9** 9 **Major Crispies**[151] [6146] 8-9-7 **65**...................(w) CallumRodriguez 14 11
(Ronald Thompson) *cl up on outer: rdn along and wd st: sn wknd* **33/1**

1/5- **10** 10 **King Christophe (IRE)**[47] [9271] 7-9-0 **58**.......................... JFEgan 11
(Peter Fahey, Ire) *dwlt: sn chsng ldrs: rdn along wl over 3f out: sn wknd (jockey said gelding was never travelling; vet reported the gelding was lame on its right hind)* **6/1**[3]

1m 43.88s (0.18) **Going Correction** -0.05s/f (Stan) 10 Ran SP% **113.8**
Speed ratings (Par 101): **97,95,94,89,89 88,85,79,70,60**
CSF £68.19 CT £528.62 TOTE £5.40: £1.80, £4.30, £2.00; EX 66.20 Trifecta £974.70.
Owner Ray Bailey **Bred** Ray Bailey **Trained** Barbury Castle, Wilts
■ Stewards' Enquiry : Rhona Pindar three-day ban: interference & careless riding (Jan 28-30)

FOCUS
This looked a reasonable race for the grade.

233 SUNRACING.CO.UK H'CAP 7f 14y(F)
3:00 (3:00) (Class 6) (0-65,65) 4-Y-O+

£3,105 (£924; £461; £400; £400; £400) **Stalls** Low

Form RPR
05-1 **1** **Grey Destiny**[9] [64] 9-9-2 **60**..(p) CamHardie 14 68
(Antony Brittain) *stdd s and sn swtchd lft: hld up towards rr: gd hdwy wl over 2f out: rdn to chse ldr over 1f out: led ent fnl f: kpt on strly* **16/1**

650- **2** 1 1/4 **Bee Machine (IRE)**[23] [9659] 4-8-3 **54**..................(t) ZakWheatley(7) 9 59
(Declan Carroll) *in tch: wd st: rdn to chse ldrs and edgd lft over 2f out: led wl over 1f: hdd and drvn ent fnl f: kpt on same pce* **25/1**

/26- **3** 1/2 **Baron Run**[255] [2357] 9-8-3 **54** ow1...................................... RhonaPindar(7) 4 57
(K R Burke) *t.k.h: trckd ldrs on inner: hdwy over 2f out: rdn over 1f out: kpt on fnl f* **18/1**

50-2 **4** 1 3/4 **Dollar Value (USA)**[12] [2] 4-9-7 **65**.............................(p) JoeFanning 5 64
(Robert Cowell) *trckd ldrs: effrt 3f out: rdn along over 2f out: drvn over 1f out: kpt on same pce* **3/1**[1]

60-4 **5** 1/2 **Break The Silence**[10] [45] 5-8-6 **55**......................(b) TheodoreLadd(5) 11 53
(Scott Dixon) *chsd ldrs on outer: wd st: rdn over 2f out: kpt on same pce* **6/1**[2]

060- **6** nse **Bold Spirit**[23] [9656] 8-8-9 **60**...........................(bt) CianMacRedmond(7) 6 58
(Declan Carroll) *towards rr: rdn along over 2f out: kpt on fnl f* **14/1**

600- **7** 1 1/2 **Alba Del Sole (IRE)**[23] [9656] 4-9-5 **63**.................................... JoeyHaynes 10 57
(Ivan Furtado) *dwlt: a towards rr* **40/1**

040- **8** 3 **Essential**[62] [9034] 5-8-7 **58**... TobyEley(7) 2 44
(Olly Williams) *cl up: led 4f out: rdn along 3f out: sn hdd: wknd fnl 2f (jockey said gelding hung left in the final furlong)* **16/1**

40-3 **9** 3/4 **Queens Royale**[10] [45] 5-9-4 **62**...........................(v) RobertWinston 13 46
(Michael Appleby) *trckd ldrs: hdwy on outer over 3f out: led wl over 2f out: rdn along and hdd wl over 1f out: sn wknd (vet reported the mare finished lame on its right hind)* **6/1**[2]

60-0 **10** 7 **Helen Sherbet**[8] [91] 4-8-11 **62**................................ JonathanFisher(7) 3 28
(K R Burke) *a towards rr (jockey said filly was slowly away)* **8/1**[3]

03-0 **11** 12 **Grinty (IRE)**[10] [45] 5-9-1 **59**..........................(v[1]) CallumRodriguez 1
(Michael Dods) *cl up on inner: rdn along wl over 2f out: sn wknd* **8/1**[3]

0/ **12** 1/2 **Eadbhard (IRE)**[153] [6110] 4-9-6 **64**..(h) JFEgan 7
(Peter Fahey, Ire) *dwlt: a bhd* **10/1**

50-4 **13** 1/2 **Broken Wings (IRE)**[12] [6] 4-8-10 **54**..............................(v) LukeMorris 8
(Keith Dalgleish) *slt ld 2f: cl up: rdn along 3f out: sn wknd: bhd and eased fnl 2f* **16/1**

1m 29.93s (-0.37) **Going Correction** -0.05s/f (Stan) 13 Ran SP% **120.7**
Speed ratings (Par 101): **100,98,98,96,95 95,93,90,89,81 67,67,66**
CSF £367.50 CT £7280.24 TOTE £14.00: £3.10, £7.40, £4.70; EX 584.70 Trifecta £2068.20.
Owner Antony Brittain **Bred** Northgate Lodge Stud Ltd **Trained** Warthill, N Yorks
■ Stewards' Enquiry : Zak Wheatley two-day ban: used whip above the permitted level (Jan 28-29)

FOCUS
A modest handicap, but competitive.
T/Jkpt: Not won. T/Plt: £259.00 to a £1 stake. Pool: £90,469.07 - 254.96 winning units T/Qpdt: £66.90 to a £1 stake. Pool: £12,021.92 - 132.80 winning units **Joe Rowntree**

234 - (Foreign Racing) - See Raceform Interactive

180 WOLVERHAMPTON (A.W) (L-H)
Monday, January 14

OFFICIAL GOING: Tapeta: standard
Wind: Light across Weather: Overcast

235 LADBROKES HOME OF THE ODDS BOOST H'CAP 6f 20y (Tp)
4:40 (4:40) (Class 6) (0-65,65) 3-Y-O

£3,105 (£924; £461; £400; £400; £400) **Stalls** Low

Form RPR
000- **1** **Deconso**[54] [9183] 3-8-2 **46** oh1.. HollieDoyle 5 51
(Christopher Kellett) *chsd ldrs: rdn to ld and edgd lft wl ins fnl f: r.o (trainer said, as to the apparent improvement in form, the gelding had benefitted from dropping back in trip to 6 furlongs 20 yards, having run too keenly over 7 furlongs 36 yards on its previous start)* **50/1**

040- **2** 1/2 **Second Collection**[38] [9444] 3-9-4 **62**.......................(h) DavidProbert 6 66
(Tony Carroll) *hld up: hdwy over 1f out: rdn and ev ch wl ins fnl f: r.o* **7/2**[1]

062- **3** 1 1/2 **Alban's Dream**[47] [9289] 3-8-13 **62**......................(b) DarraghKeenan(5) 10 61
(Robert Eddery) *edgd lft s: sn led: rdn over 1f out: hdd and unable qck wl ins fnl f* **4/1**[2]

06-0 **4** nk **Wye Bother (IRE)**[5] [137] 3-8-2 **46** oh1............................(t) KieranO'Neill 7 44
(Milton Bradley) *led early: chsd ldrs: rdn and swtchd rt over 1f out: styd on same pce wl ins fnl f* **50/1**

006- **5** 1 3/4 **Valley Belle (IRE)**[25] [9646] 3-9-0 **58**...............................(v) NicolaCurrie 1 53
(Phil McEntee) *hld up in tch: shkn up over 1f out: nt clr run ins fnl f: nvr able to chal* **5/1**[3]

065- **6** hd **Sister Of The Sign (IRE)**[47] [9289] 3-9-1 **59**........... RichardKingscote 11 51
(James Given) *sn chsng ldr: rdn over 1f out: no ex ins fnl f* **7/1**

400- **7** 1 1/2 **Nguni**[33] [9498] 3-9-4 **62**...(t[1]) RaulDaSilva 3 50
(Paul Cole) *hld up: hdwy and hung lft fr over 1f out: nt rch ldrs* **8/1**

8 1 **Kodi Dream**[103] [7913] 3-8-9 **58**................................. BenSanderson(5) 8 43
(Roger Fell) *hld up: pushed along on outer over 2f out: nvr nrr* **4/1**[2]

64P- **9** 3/4 **Piccothepack**[229] [3225] 3-8-12 **56**.. TonyHamilton 13 39
(Richard Fahey) *s.i.s: styd on fr over 1f out: nvr on terms* **33/1**

500- **10** 2 3/4 **Macho Lady (IRE)**[28] [9589] 3-8-12 **56**................................. MartinHarley 2 30
(David O'Meara) *hld up in tch: lost pl over 3f out: n.d after* **12/1**

004- **11** nse **Awake In Asia**[19] [9709] 3-9-7 **65**.. LukeMorris 9 39
(Charlie Wallis) *hmpd s: hld up in tch: rdn over 2f out: wknd fnl f* **10/1**

1m 14.07s (-0.43) **Going Correction** -0.20s/f (Stan) 11 Ran SP% **126.1**
Speed ratings (Par 95): **94,93,91,90,88 88,86,85,84,80 80**
CSF £233.30 CT £922.56 TOTE £117.90: £30.40, £1.90, £1.60; EX 816.90.
Owner Andy Bell & Fergus Lyons **Bred** Llety Farms **Trained** Lathom, Lancs
■ Good Tyne Girl was withdrawn. Price at time of withdrawal 16-1. Rule 4 does not apply.
■ Stewards' Enquiry : Darragh Keenan two-day ban: used whip with arm above shoulder height (Jan 28-29)

FOCUS
Not much to dwell on in a very ordinary handicap. The early gallop wasn't overly strong and the majority of those held up were at a disadvantage. The balance of the second, third and fourth suggests this will prove very modest low-grade form.

236 BETWAY SPRINT H'CAP 6f 20y (Tp)
5:15 (5:15) (Class 6) (0-65,65) 4-Y-0+
£3,105 (£924; £461; £400; £400; £400) **Stalls** Low

Form RPR
60-1 **1** **Santafiora**[12] 28 5-8-11 **55**.......... KieranO'Neill 1 62
(Julie Camacho) *chsd ldrs: edgd lft over 1f out: rdn to ld sn after: hung rt ins fnl f: jst hld on* **6/1**[2]
00-5 **2** *nk* **Always Amazing**[11] 42 5-9-2 **60**.......... RaulDaSilva 3 66
(Derek Shaw) *s.i.s: hdwy over 4f out: nt clr run over 1f out: sn rdn: r.o* **10/1**
42-2 **3** *½* **Very Honest (IRE)**[5] 144 6-9-7 **65**..........(p[1]) AdamKirby 4 70
(Brett Johnson) *chsd ldrs: rdn over 1f out: ev ch ins fnl f: styd on* **13/8**[1]
403- **4** *1* **Mother Of Dragons (IRE)**[14] 9773 4-9-5 **63**..........(v) RossaRyan 5 65
(Phil McEntee) *mid-div: pushed along and hdwy over 2f out: swtchd rt over 1f out: styd on u.p* **25/1**
60-5 **5** *shd* **Thorntoun Lady (USA)**[7] 123 9-8-11 **55**..........(p) NicolaCurrie 8 56
(Jim Goldie) *s.i.s: sn pushed along in rr: r.o ins fnl f: nt rch ldrs (jockey said mare was outpaced in the early stages)* **12/1**
032- **6** *nk* **Time To Reason (IRE)**[18] 9722 6-9-7 **65**..........(p) RichardKingscote 13 66
(Charlie Wallis) *hld up: r.o ins fnl f: nrst fin* **8/1**[3]
060- **7** *1 ¼* **Red Invader (IRE)**[14] 9773 9-9-0 **61**.......... TimClark[(3)] 10 58
(Paul D'Arcy) *s.i.s: hld up: hdwy over 1f out: nt clr run ins fnl f: styd on same pce (jockey said gelding was denied a clear run approximately 1f out)* **100/1**
00-5 **8** *½* **Spirit Power**[12] 28 4-9-0 **58**..........(p) JasonHart 7 53
(Eric Alston) *hld up in tch: rdn over 1f out: styd on same pce ins fnl f* **16/1**
000- **9** *nk* **Oriental Relation (IRE)**[28] 9587 8-9-4 **62**..........(v) LukeMorris 9 56
(John Balding) *led: hdd over 4f out: chsd ldr tl rdn over 1f out: no ex ins fnl f* **50/1**
00-0 **10** *1 ½* **Our Man In Havana**[3] 187 4-9-7 **65**.......... HollieDoyle 6 55
(Richard Price) *hld up: hdwy and nt clr fr over 1f out tl swtchd rt ins fnl f: no ex (jockey said gelding was denied a clear run approximately 1f out)* **8/1**[3]
6/5- **11** *2 ¼* **Filbert Street**[361] 284 4-9-2 **60**..........(p[1]) JFEgan 2 43
(Roy Brotherton) *chsd ldr tl led over 4f out: rdn and hdd over 1f out: wknd ins fnl f* **25/1**
00-2 **12** *shd* **Carpet Time (IRE)**[12] 28 4-9-2 **60**.......... ShaneKelly 11 43
(David Barron) *hld up: pushed along over 2f out: nvr on terms* **20/1**
1m 13.5s (-1.00) **Going Correction** -0.20s/f (Stan) 12 Ran SP% 112.7
Speed ratings (Par 101): **98,97,96,95,95 95,93,92,92,90 87,87**
CSF £57.22 CT £139.83 TOTE £7.40: £2.50, £3.30, £1.10; EX 67.10 Trifecta £186.00.
Owner Judy & Richard Peck & Partner **Bred** Highbury Stud & John Troy **Trained** Norton, N Yorks

FOCUS
Mainly exposed performers in a modest handicap. The gallop was reasonable but the first six finished in a bit of a heap. The likes of the second, third and fourth confirm the straightforward level.

237 FOLLOW SUN RACING ON TWITTER CLASSIFIED CLAIMING STKS 7f 36y (Tp)
5:45 (5:45) (Class 6) 4-Y-0+
£3,105 (£924; £461; £400; £400; £400) **Stalls** High

Form RPR
02-2 **1** **Dark Alliance (IRE)**[12] 31 8-8-10 71.......... MeganNicholls[(5)] 4 77
(Mark Loughnane) *hld up: hdwy over 2f out: shkn up to ld and edgd rt ins fnl f: r.o wl* **13/8**[1]
6-06 **2** *1 ¾* **Zapper Cass (FR)**[4] 158 6-9-1 70.......... LukeMorris 1 73
(Michael Appleby) *sn chsng ldrs: n.m.r over 5f out: rdn to chse ldr over 1f out: ev ch ins fnl f: styd on same pce* **14/1**
04-6 **3** *2 ¾* **Fast Track**[12] 31 8-8-10 69.......... ShaneKelly 5 61
(David Barron) *s.i.s: hld up: nt clr run over 2f out: hdwy over 1f out: sn rdn: styd on same pce ins fnl f (jockey said gelding was slowly away)* **7/1**
02-3 **4** *shd* **Secondo (FR)**[12] 31 9-9-1 71..........(v) CallumShepherd 8 66
(Robert Stephens) *prom: racd keenly: wnt 2nd over 5f out: led over 2f out: rdn over 1f out: hdd and no ex ins fnl f* **7/1**
554- **5** *4* **Majestic Moon (IRE)**[16] 9747 9-8-8 73.......... TobyEley[(7)] 3 56
(Julia Feilden) *prom: rdn over 2f out: wknd fnl f* **5/1**[2]
553- **6** *¾* **Misty Birnam (SAF)**[35] 9483 5-9-1 71..........(p) StevieDonohoe 7 54
(Ian Williams) *prom: lost pl over 5f out: pushed along and hdwy 2f out: sn swtchd rt and rdn: wknd fnl f* **11/2**[3]
00-0 **7** *14* **Guardia Svizzera (IRE)**[4] 165 5-9-2 73..........(h) BenSanderson[(5)] 2 26
(Roger Fell) *led over 4f: wknd over 1f out (jockey said gelding hung right-handed)* **25/1**
500- **8** *6* **Mr Wing (IRE)**[24] 9660 4-8-9 23..........(p[1]) NathanEvans 6
(John Wainwright) *hld up: pushed along over 4f out: wknd 1/2-way* **100/1**
1m 27.17s (-1.63) **Going Correction** -0.20s/f (Stan) 8 Ran SP% 106.6
Speed ratings (Par 101): **101,99,95,95,91 90,74,67**
CSF £23.01 TOTE £2.40: £1.10, £3.00, £2.20; EX 18.90 Trifecta £101.60.
Owner Andy Holding Speed Figures Co Uk **Bred** Yeomanstown Stud **Trained** Rock, Worcs

FOCUS
A fair claimer in which the gallop was a reasonable one and the first two pulled clear in the closing stages. The winner has been rated to form.

238 BETWAY CONDITIONS STKS (ALL-WEATHER CHAMPIONSHIPS FAST-TRACK QUALIFIER) 2m 120y (Tp)
6:15 (6:15) (Class 2) 4-Y-0+
£11,827 (£3,541; £1,770; £885; £442; £222) **Stalls** Low

Form RPR
411- **1** **Aircraft Carrier (IRE)**[25] 9639 4-9-0 90..........(p) MartinHarley 4 109
(John Ryan) *hld up: hdwy on outer over 2f out: rdn to ld and edgd rt ins fnl f: styd on u.p* **7/4**[1]
/12- **2** *¾* **Festival Of Ages (USA)**[30] 9552 5-9-5 98.......... AdamKirby 1 108
(Charlie Appleby) *chsd ldrs: rdn on outer to go 2nd over 2f out: carried wd and led over 1f out: hdd ins fnl f: edgd lft: styd on u.p* **7/4**[1]
414- **3** *5* **Watersmeet**[30] 9552 8-9-5 104.......... JoeFanning 5 102
(Mark Johnston) *led early: chsd ldr: hmpd 7f out: led again over 6f out: rn wd and hdd over 1f out: no ex ins fnl f* **3/1**[2]
015- **4** *12* **Alfredo (IRE)**[30] 9552 7-9-5 94..........(bt[1]) LukeMorris 3 88
(Seamus Durack) *s.i.s: hdwy to join ldrs 1/2-way: edgd lft 7f out: rdn over 3f out: wknd wl over 1f out* **16/1**[3]
12- **5** *5* **Arch My Boy**[56] 9152 5-9-5 0.......... HectorCrouch 6 82
(Martin Smith) *s.i.s: sn rcvrd to ld: hmpd 7f out: hdd over 6f out: chsd ldr: rdn over 3f out: lost 2nd over 2f out: wknd wl over 1f out* **25/1**
040- **6** *77* **Golden Wolf (IRE)**[30] 9552 5-9-5 91..........(t[1]) DougieCostello 2
(Iain Jardine) *hld up: plld hrd: wknd over 4f out (jockey said gelding stopped quickly)* **40/1**
3m 31.18s (-8.12) **Going Correction** -0.20s/f (Stan) course record
WFA 4 from 5yo+ 5lb 6 Ran SP% 109.9
Speed ratings (Par 109): **111,110,108,102,100 64**
CSF £4.75 TOTE £2.30: £1.20, £1.20; EX 5.40 Trifecta £8.40.
Owner John Stocker **Bred** Lynch Bages Ltd **Trained** Newmarket, Suffolk
■ Stewards' Enquiry : Luke Morris caution: careless riding

FOCUS
A good-quality event run in a course record time in which the gallop soon steadied before picking up again around halfway. The first two, who are ones to keep on the right side, pulled clear in the closing stages.

239 BETWAY NOVICE STKS 1m 1f 104y (Tp)
6:45 (6:45) (Class 5) 4-Y-0+ £3,752 (£1,116; £557; £278) **Stalls** Low

Form RPR
06- **1** **Cosmic Landscape**[15] 9766 4-9-2 0.......... CallumShepherd 2 79
(Dominic Ffrench Davis) *a.p: rdn to chse ldr over 1f out: n.m.r wl ins fnl f: r.o to ld nr fin* **25/1**
422- **2** *hd* **Simple Thought (IRE)**[38] 9445 4-8-11 79.......... JoeFanning 3 74
(Simon Crisford) *led: rdn over 1f out: edgd lft ins fnl f: hdd nr fin* **13/8**[2]
6- **3** *1* **Tappity Tap**[38] 9445 4-8-11 0..........(h) KieranO'Neill 9 72
(Daniel Kubler) *s.i.s: hld up: pushed along and hdwy over 2f out: edgd lft ins fnl f: r.o* **50/1**
334- **4** *6* **Mount Ararat (IRE)**[188] 4795 4-9-2 0.......... CliffordLee 6 64
(K R Burke) *sn w ldr tl settled into 2nd over 6f out: rdn over 2f out: lost 2nd over 1f out: wknd wl ins fnl f* **10/11**[1]
3- **5** *1 ¾* **Tofan**[38] 9445 4-9-2 0..........(t) LukeMorris 10 61
(Marco Botti) *chsd ldrs: rdn over 2f out: wknd fnl f* **7/1**[3]
5-4 **6** *2* **My Town Chicago (USA)**[7] 117 4-9-2 0.......... JasonHart 4 56
(Kevin Frost) *trckd ldrs: racd keenly: wknd ins fnl f* **20/1**
00- **7** *10* **Ice Cool Cullis (IRE)**[30] 9565 4-9-2 0.......... LiamJones 8 35
(Mark Loughnane) *hmpd sn after s: outpcd* **100/1**
0- **8** *5* **Interrogation (FR)**[31] 9531 4-8-13 0.......... TimClark[(3)] 1 25
(Alan Bailey) *sn pushed along towards rr: rdn over 3f out: sn wknd (jockey said gelding was never travelling)* **100/1**
9 *2* **Flight To Nowhere**[240] 7-8-12 0.......... StevieDonohoe 5 16
(Richard Price) *s.s outpcd* **66/1**
00- **10** *4* **Hellofagame**[30] 9565 4-9-2 0.......... HollieDoyle 7 12
(Richard Price) *wnt rt s: sn pushed along and prom: wknd over 3f out* **100/1**
1m 58.27s (-2.53) **Going Correction** -0.20s/f (Stan)
WFA 4 from 7yo 1lb 10 Ran SP% 118.0
Speed ratings (Par 103): **103,102,101,96,95 93,84,79,78,74**
CSF £66.28 TOTE £39.90: £5.10, £1.10, £17.70; EX 147.80 Trifecta £2260.40.
Owner Kingwood Stud Management Co Ltd **Bred** Mehmet Kurt **Trained** Lambourn, Berks

FOCUS
The market leader disappointed but still fair form from the first three, who pulled clear of the remainder in the last furlong. The early gallop was just an ordinary one. The second has been rated similar to her two previous C&D runs.

240 BETWAY CASINO H'CAP 1m 1f 104y (Tp)
7:15 (7:15) (Class 3) (0-95,96) 4-Y-0 £7,246 (£2,168; £1,084; £542; £270) **Stalls** Low

Form RPR
1-63 **1** **Michele Strogoff**[7] 121 6-9-0 **87**.......... AlistairRawlinson 1 96
(Michael Appleby) *mde all: racd freely and sn clr: rdn over 1f out: unchal* **15/8**[1]
04-4 **2** *2 ½* **Dragon Mall (USA)**[7] 121 6-9-0 **87**..........(t) StevieDonohoe 2 90
(Rebecca Menzies) *s.i.s: hld up: hdwy to go 2nd over 1f out: edgd lft: r.o: no ch w wnr* **7/2**[3]
425- **3** *5* **Nonios (IRE)**[19] 9705 7-9-7 **94**..........(h) MartinHarley 5 87
(David Simcock) *hld up: swtchd rt over 1f out: r.o to go 3rd ins fnl f: nvr on terms* **3/1**[2]
56-2 **4** *2 ½* **Mythical Madness**[9] 87 8-9-9 **96**..........(p) AdamKirby 3 83
(David O'Meara) *chsd wnr who sn wnt clr: rdn over 2f out: lost 2nd over 1f out: wknd fnl f* **5/1**
00-6 **5** *2 ¾* **Battle Of Marathon (USA)**[9] 87 7-8-9 **89**.......... LauraPearson[(7)] 4 70
(John Ryan) *hld up: hdwy 6f out: wknd over 1f out* **14/1**
1m 57.14s (-3.66) **Going Correction** -0.20s/f (Stan) 5 Ran SP% 105.3
Speed ratings (Par 107): **108,105,101,99,96**
CSF £7.81 TOTE £2.40: £1.30, £1.90; EX 8.00 Trifecta £19.70.
Owner Stephen Louch **Bred** Razza Del Sole Societa Agricola Srl **Trained** Oakham, Rutland

FOCUS
A valuable contest but a very one-sided one given the winner was allowed a huge amount of rope in front and the bare form doesn't look entirely reliable. The winner has been rated back to his old best.

241 BETWAY LIVE CASINO H'CAP 1m 1f 104y (Tp)
7:45 (7:45) (Class 6) (0-60,66) 4-Y-0+
£3,105 (£924; £461; £400; £400; £400) **Stalls** Low

Form RPR
61-4 **1** **Champagne Rules**[7] 120 8-9-4 **60**.......... PhilDennis[(3)] 9 69+
(Sharon Watt) *s.i.s: hld up: swtchd rt and hdwy over 1f out: r.o to ld wl ins fnl f: sn clr* **8/1**[3]
43-1 **2** *3* **Bollihope**[7] 120 7-9-13 **66** 6ex.......... RobertHavlin 1 69
(Shaun Keightley) *a.p: nt clr run over 2f out: swtchd rt over 1f out: rdn to ld ins fnl f: sn hdd: styd on same pce* **1/1**[1]
34-6 **3** *1 ¼* **Duke Of Alba (IRE)**[13] 5 4-9-5 **59**.......... LukeMorris 4 60
(John Mackie) *chsd ldrs: rdn and hung lft over 1f out: styd on same pce ins fnl f* **9/1**
000- **4** *nk* **Sea Shack**[15] 9767 5-8-10 **56**..........(t[1]) ThoreHammerHansen[(7)] 13 56
(Julia Feilden) *led: rdn over 1f out: hdd and no ex ins fnl f* **50/1**
01-2 **5** *1 ½* **False Id**[7] 120 6-9-5 **58**..........(b) DavidProbert 11 56
(David Loughnane) *s.i.s: hld up: hdwy and nt clr run over 1f out: sn rdn: styd on same pce ins fnl f* **6/1**[2]
653- **6** *2* **Pike Corner Cross (IRE)**[19] 9703 7-9-7 **60**.......... CallumShepherd 8 54
(Ed de Giles) *hld up in tch: rdn over 1f out: wknd ins fnl f* **8/1**[3]
060- **7** *1 ½* **Muraaqeb**[108] 7717 5-8-7 **46** oh1..........(p) KieranO'Neill 5 37
(Milton Bradley) *prom: chsd ldr over 6f out: rdn over 2f out: nt clr run over 1f out: wknd ins fnl f* **66/1**
456- **8** *nk* **Mac O'Polo (IRE)**[130] 6992 5-8-12 **58**..........(p w) EllaMcCain[(7)] 2 48
(Donald McCain) *hld up in tch: rdn over 1f out: wknd fnl f* **16/1**

The Form Book Flat 2019, Raceform Ltd, Newbury, RG14 5SJ

500- **9** 1½ **Marble Bar**[13] 8309 4-9-6 **60** .... JoeFanning 3 48
(Iain Jardine) *racd keenly in 2nd pl tl over 6f out: remained handy: rdn over 1f out: wknd ins fnl f* **33/1**

000- **10** 4½ **Bridge Of Sighs**[116] 7461 7-8-4 **50** .... TobyEley(7) 10 29
(Steph Hollinshead) *hld up: rdn over 2f out: wknd fnl f (jockey said gelding was never travelling)* **50/1**

000- **11** 4½ **Tha'ir (IRE)**[45] 9326 9-9-7 **60** .... DougieCostello 12 30
(Olly Williams) *hld up: shkn up over 2f out: sn wknd* **40/1**

445- **12** ¾ **Wicklow Warrior**[40] 9412 4-8-6 **46** oh1 .... (p) NathanEvans 7 15
(Peter Niven) *unruly in stalls: hld up: rdn over 2f out: sn wknd (jockey said gelding was restless in the stalls)* **25/1**

000- **13** 2 **Just Heather (IRE)**[40] 9413 5-8-7 **46** oh1 .... (v) CamHardie 6 11
(John Wainwright) *s.i.s: hld up: rdn over 3f out: wknd over 2f out* **100/1**

1m 59.01s (-1.79) **Going Correction** -0.20s/f (Stan) **13 Ran SP% 118.0**
WFA 4 from 5yo+ 1lb
Speed ratings (Par 101): **99,96,95,94,93 91,90,90,88,84 80,80,78**
CSF £15.55 CT £78.61 TOTE £7.80: £2.30, £1.10, £2.60; EX 21.20 Trifecta £174.00.
Owner Rosey Hill Partnership **Bred** Heather Raw **Trained** Brompton-on-Swale, N Yorks
■ Stewards' Enquiry : Thore Hammer Hansen one-day ban: failure to ride to their draw (Feb 1)

FOCUS
Exposed performers in a modest finale. The gallop was just an ordinary one to the home turn and the winner deserves credit for coming from an unpromising position. The winner last rated this highly in 2014.
T/Plt: £28.10 to a £1 stake. Pool: £97,553.24 - 2,527.97 winning units T/Qpdt: £6.70 to a £1 stake. Pool: £12,820.08 - 1,396.88 winning units **Colin Roberts**

132 KEMPTON (A.W) (R-H)
Tuesday, January 15

OFFICIAL GOING: Polytrack: standard to slow
Wind: Virtually nil Weather: Overcast

242 32RED CASINO NOVICE STKS 1m 3f 219y(P)
4:10 (4:13) (Class 5) 4-Y-0+
£3,881 (£1,155; £577; £288) **Stalls Low**

Form RPR

4/ **1** **Ulster (IRE)**[432] 8704 4-9-2 0 .... EdwardGreatrex 1 90
(Archie Watson) *broke wl and mde all: 2 l clr and gng wl 3f out: rdn and in command over 1f out: pushed out: comf* **2/1[2]**

1- **2** 5 **Ramsbury**[38] 9464 4-9-9 0 .... StevieDonohoe 13 90
(Charlie Fellowes) *racd keenly in midfield: stdy prog to go 2nd 3f out: rdn along to chse wnr 2f out: kpt on but no imp fnl f* **4/5[1]**

3 2½ **Knight Crusader**[45] 7-9-5 0 .... LukeMorris 11 77
(John O'Shea) *racd in midfield: pushed along to go clsr 4f out: rdn and styd on wl fr 2f out: no ch w front pair* **50/1**

33- **4** 8 **Arctic Chief**[103] 800 9-9-5 0 .... (t) RobertHavlin 12 64
(Richard Phillips) *restrained and racd in last trio: hdwy to go 6th over 2f out: rdn and kpt on for remote 4th fnl f* **16/1**

5 2 **Dimmesdale**[40] 4-9-2 0 .... LiamJones 6 62
(John O'Shea) *hld up in last: pushed along and outpcd 4f out: rdn and sme late hdwy passed btn horses fnl f* **40/1**

6 3 **Grange Walk (IRE)**[11] 4-8-13 0 .... PaddyBradley(3) 9 57
(Pat Phelan) *hld up: hdwy u.p 3f out: sn rdn and kpt on one pce fr 2f out* **66/1**

0/- **7** 5 **Harbour Quay**[678] 1083 5-8-12 0 .... RPWalsh(7) 10 48
(Robyn Brisland) *hld up in rr: pushed along and forced wd arnd home bnd: sn rdn and plugged on fnl f* **33/1**

8 5 **Oborne Lady (IRE)**[203] 6-9-0 0 .... RobHornby 4 35
(Seamus Mullins) *racd in tch in midfield: rdn and unable qck over 2f out: no ex fnl f* **100/1**

330- **9** 3¼ **Mobham (IRE)**[119] 7378 4-9-2 75 .... DavidProbert 8 36
(J R Jenkins) *trckd wnr: rdn and outpcd over 2f out: wknd fnl f* **20/1**

1/ **10** 27 **Power Surge (IRE)**[502] 6633 5-9-12 0 .... AdamKirby 7
(Robert Stephens) *racd in tch in 4th: rdn along 3f out: wknd fr over 1f out (trainer could offer no explanation for the poor performance)* **10/1[3]**

0- **11** nk **Signsealdelivered**[17] 9746 5-9-0 0 .... DarraghKeenan(5) 2
(Clifford Lines) *trckd wnr early: rdn along and outpcd 3f out: sn struggling and bhd* **100/1**

0- **12** 19 **Evadala (FR)**[34] 9509 4-8-11 0 .... FergusSweeney 3
(Michael Blanshard) *racd in midfield: rdn and unable qck 3f out: sn struggling and wknd fnl f* **100/1**

0- **13** 6 **Golden Etoile (FR)**[16] 9766 5-9-0 0 .... (t) JosephineGordon 14
(Colin Tizzard) *racd in midfield on outer: pushed along and reminders 1/2-way: wd home bnd: nvr on terms* **100/1**

00- **U** **Irving's Girl**[16] 9766 4-8-11 0 .... RossaRyan 5
(Brett Johnson) *hld up: lost action and uns rdr over 3f out (filly sustained an injury in running and unseated rider)* **66/1**

2m 34.3s (-0.20) **Going Correction** +0.15s/f (Slow) **14 Ran SP% 122.9**
WFA 4 from 5yo+ 3lb
Speed ratings (Par 103): **106,102,101,95,94 92,89,85,83,65 65,52,48,**
CSF £3.78 TOTE £2.70: £1.10, £1.10, £9.70; EX 4.50 Trifecta £76.70.
Owner J Allison, S Barrow & Partner **Bred** Stowell Hill Ltd & D Ludlow **Trained** Upper Lambourn, W Berks

FOCUS
The early pace wasn't the strongest but they finished well strung out in this novice.

243 100% PROFIT BOOST AT 32REDSPORT.COM H'CAP 7f (P)
4:45 (4:47) (Class 6) (0-60,60) 4-Y-0+
£3,105 (£924; £461; £400; £400; £400) **Stalls Low**

Form RPR

23- **1** **Astrospeed (IRE)**[16] 9765 4-9-6 **59** .... (h) AdamKirby 2 68+
(James Fanshawe) *racd in midfield on inner: clsd gng wl over 2f out: swtchd lft and rdn to chse ldr 2f out: led 1f out and sn in command: rdn out* **10/11[1]**

560- **2** 3¼ **Rapid Rise (IRE)**[160] 5858 5-8-7 **46** oh1 .... (p[1]) FrannyNorton 4 47
(Milton Bradley) *hld up: hdwy u.p 3f out: rdn along and styd on wl ins fnl f: no ch w wnr* **50/1**

45-4 **3** ¾ **Shamlan (IRE)**[11] 64 7-9-5 **58** .... (p) JasonHart 1 57
(Kevin Frost) *trckd ldr: effrt to cl whn briefly short of room 2f out: sn rdn and kpt on wl fnl f* **7/1[3]**

300- **4** hd **Billie Beane**[91] 8297 4-8-13 **52** .... RobertWinston 6 51
(Dr Jon Scargill) *hld up in rr: pushed along 3f out: sn rdn and mde gd late hdwy passed btn horses fnl f* **16/1**

660- **5** nk **Little Miss Kodi (IRE)**[18] 9734 6-8-13 **52** .... (t) LiamJones 7 50
(Mark Loughnane) *trckd ldr: rdn along to chse ldr 3f out: drvn and led 2f out: hdd by wnr 1f out and no ex fnl f* **12/1**

1-24 **6** 1¼ **Viola Park**[6] 138 5-9-2 **55** .... (p) DavidProbert 5 50
(Ronald Harris) *hld up in rr of midfield: rdn along and outpcd 2f out: plugged on fnl f (jockey said gelding ran flat)* **7/2[2]**

600- **7** nk **Clement (IRE)**[41] 9402 9-9-0 **60** .... (b) KateLeahy(7) 3 54
(John O'Shea) *hld up: rdn 3f out: minor prog fnl f: n.d* **16/1**

050- **8** shd **More Salutes (IRE)**[16] 9764 4-9-2 **55** .... LukeMorris 10 48
(Michael Attwater) *hld up in last: hdwy u.p 2f out: swtchd rt to far rail over 1f out: kpt on fnl f* **33/1**

00U- **9** 1¾ **Lisnamoyle Lady (IRE)**[61] 9078 4-8-7 **46** oh1 .... (bt) DannyBrock 11 35
(Martin Smith) *dwlt but sn rcvrd to chse ldr: pushed along 3f out: rdn and led briefly over 2f out: sn hdd & wknd fnl f* **150/1**

040- **10** 2 **Rising Sunshine (IRE)**[61] 9077 6-8-7 **46** oh1 .... (bt) RaulDaSilva 8 30
(Milton Bradley) *hld up: rdn over 2f out: nvr on terms* **40/1**

00-6 **11** 5 **Admiral Rooke (IRE)**[13] 23 4-9-5 **58** .... (v[1]) AlistairRawlinson 9 29
(Michael Appleby) *led: stl on bit 3f out: rdn and hdd over 2f out: wknd over 1f out* **20/1**

0/0- **12** 13 **Mahna Mahna (IRE)**[18] 9735 5-8-0 **46** oh1 .... (h[1]) EllieMacKenzie(7) 13
(David W Drinkwater) *racd in midfield: rdn and lost pl 3f out: sn bhd (jockey said gelding stopped quickly)* **66/1**

1m 26.59s (0.59) **Going Correction** +0.15s/f (Slow) **12 Ran SP% 120.8**
Speed ratings (Par 101): **102,98,97,97,96 95,95,94,92,90 84,70**
CSF £85.72 CT £242.60 TOTE £1.80: £1.10, £12.30, £2.20; EX 65.30 Trifecta £406.50.
Owner Dragon Gate **Bred** Noel Cogan **Trained** Newmarket, Suffolk

FOCUS
A moderate handicap, but it was won by an improving lightly raced sort.

244 32RED ON THE APP STORE H'CAP 6f (P)
5:15 (5:17) (Class 6) (0-55,52) 4-Y-0+
£3,105 (£924; £461; £400; £400; £400) **Stalls Low**

Form RPR

000- **1** **Deer Song**[15] 9773 6-9-0 **45** .... (b) LiamJones 2 52
(John Bridger) *racd in midfield on inner: effrt to cl and wnt 3rd over 1f out: sn drvn and led 100yds out: styd on wl* **9/1**

64-1 **2** 1½ **New Rich**[11] 60 9-9-0 **52** .... (b) GeorgiaDobie(7) 4 55
(Eve Johnson Houghton) *hld up in rr: hdwy u.p to go 6th 2f out: sn rdn and short of room 1f out: swtchd lft fnl 100yds and styd on strly to grab 2nd cl home: nt rch wnr* **7/2[1]**

330- **3** nk **Monarch Maid**[40] 9433 8-9-0 **45** .... KieranO'Neill 10 47
(Peter Hiatt) *broke wl fr wd draw to ld: rdn along to maintain short advantage 2f out: sn drvn and hdd by wnr 100yds out: lost 2nd fnl strides* **14/1**

246- **4** ¾ **Compton Prince**[26] 9641 10-9-0 **45** .... (b) LukeMorris 1 44
(Milton Bradley) *trckd ldr: rdn along and almost upsides ldr 2f out: drvn and ev ch over 1f out: no ex fnl f* **10/1**

42-0 **5** nk **Legal Mind**[11] 53 6-9-7 **52** .... AdamKirby 6 50
(Emma Owen) *trckd ldr: rdn along to chse ldr 2f out: sn drvn and no imp 1f out: one pce fnl f* **6/1[3]**

060- **6** ¾ **Burauq**[89] 8342 7-9-0 **45** .... (v) FrannyNorton 5 43
(Milton Bradley) *racd in midfield: rdn and outpcd over 2f out: kpt on one pce fnl f* **16/1**

26-5 **7** ½ **Ticks The Boxes (IRE)**[12] 45 7-9-0 **45** .... (v) RobertWinston 9 40
(John Wainwright) *trckd ldr: briefly snatched up whn short of room exiting bk st: rdn and little imp 2f out: one pce fnl f* **10/1**

000- **8** shd **Caledonian Gold**[55] 9177 6-8-9 **45** .... (b) KevinLundie(5) 3 39
(Lisa Williamson) *sltly hmpd leaving stalls and racd in rr: outpcd 3f out: nvr on terms* **20/1**

46-3 **9** 2¼ **Brother In Arms (IRE)**[13] 26 5-8-11 **47** .... PoppyBridgwater(5) 11 35
(Tony Carroll) *racd in midfield: drvn along and lost pl over 2f out: wknd fnl f* **11/2[2]**

00-4 **10** 1¼ **Toolatetodelegate**[11] 53 5-9-3 **51** .... (tp) FinleyMarsh(3) 7 35
(Brian Barr) *hld up in rr: a bhd* **7/1**

00-5 **11** 4½ **Barnsdale**[8] 118 6-8-7 **45** .... MeganEllingworth(7) 8 15
(Steph Hollinshead) *hld up: outpcd 1/2-way: sn in rr and struggling* **40/1**

1m 13.84s (0.74) **Going Correction** +0.15s/f (Slow) **11 Ran SP% 112.3**
Speed ratings (Par 101): **101,99,98,97,97 96,95,95,92,90 84**
CSF £38.60 CT £445.96 TOTE £11.00: £3.20, £3.00, £4.20; EX 49.20 Trifecta £404.30.
Owner The Deer's Hut **Bred** J Khan & P Wilson **Trained** Liphook, Hants

FOCUS
Low grade fare. The winner has been rated near his autumn 2017 level.

245 INTRODUCING RACING TV CLASSIFIED STKS 1m 3f 219y(P)
5:45 (5:49) (Class 6) 3-Y-0+
£3,105 (£924; £461; £400; £400; £400) **Stalls Low**

Form RPR

50-4 **1** **Top Rock Talula (IRE)**[11] 59 4-9-8 46 .... EdwardGreatrex 5 59
(Warren Greatrex) *settled wl in 4th: hdwy into 3rd 3f out: clsd on ldr qckly 2f out: pushed into ld over 1f out: sn in command and rdn out fnl f* **5/1[2]**

00-0 **2** 2¼ **Harry Callahan (IRE)**[11] 59 4-9-8 50 .... (v[1]) CallumShepherd 14 56+
(Mick Channon) *hld up in rr: stl gng wl whn short of room 3f out: rdn along once in clr 2f out: sn drvn and styd on strly ins fnl f: no ch w wnr* **11/2[3]**

064- **3** 2¼ **Croeso Cymraeg**[17] 9750 5-9-11 41 .... RaulDaSilva 3 51
(James Evans) *hld up in last: short of room whn stl on bit and last 3f out: swtchd lft to far rail at cutaway 2f out: rdn and styd on strly fr over 1f out: no ch w wnr (jockey said gelding ran too free)* **25/1**

000- **4** nse **Alate (IRE)**[17] 9744 3-8-0 49 .... LukeMorris 7 50
(Sir Mark Prescott Bt) *racd in midfield: pushed along 5f out: rdn and reminders over 3f out: kpt on one pce fr over 1f out* **10/1**

500- **5** 1 **Falls Creek (USA)**[39] 9445 4-9-8 35 .... (b[1]) DavidProbert 4 50+
(Andrew Balding) *hld up in rr: pushed along over 2f out: sn drvn and sme late prog passed btn horses ins fnl f* **25/1**

05-5 **6** 3 **Red Cossack (CAN)**[12] 39 8-9-8 49 .... JackDuern(3) 13 45
(Dean Ivory) *s.i.s: pushed up arnd field to ld after 2f out: pushed along and 5 l clr 3f out: sn drvn and strly pressed by wnr 2f out: hdd over 1f out: wknd fnl f* **13/2**

04-6 **7** 2¾ **Far Cry**[11] 59 6-9-11 50 .... CharlieBennett 10 40
(Hughie Morrison) *hld up: rdn along 1/2-way: minor prog fnl f but n.d* **16/1**

06-2 **8** shd **Gorham's Cave**[11] 59 5-9-11 50 .... (h) RichardKingscote 2 40
(Ali Stronge) *racd in midfield: hdwy u.p into 5th 3f out: sn drvn and no imp: wknd fnl f* **11/2[3]**

46-2 **9** ½ **Don't Do It (IRE)**[11] 62 4-9-8 50 .... (b) AndrewMullen 8 40
(Michael Appleby) *dwlt sltly but sn rcvrd to trck ldr: wnt 2nd 6f out: 5 l down on clr ldr 3f out: sn rdn to cl and ev ch 2f out: wknd fnl f (jockey said gelding ran too free)* **9/2[1]**

The Form Book Flat 2019, Raceform Ltd, Newbury, RG14 5SJ

550- **10** *4* **Passing Clouds**[16] 9767 4-9-8 **44**........................ KierenFox 12 34
(Michael Attwater) *racd in midfield: rdn and outpcd 3f out: nvr able to get on terms* **40/1**
6/6- **11** *16* **Solitary Sister (IRE)**[33] 9528 5-9-11 **45**........................ NicolaCurrie 6
(John Berry) *hld up: a in rr (jockey said mare hung left-handed. Trainer said mare didn't handle going right handed)* **14/1**
00-0 **12** *3 3/4* **Drifting Star (IRE)**[11] 59 4-9-8 **43**........................(vt) HectorCrouch 9
(Gary Moore) *racd in rr of midfield: rdn along 5f out: nvr a factor* **66/1**
000- **13** *1* **Seventii**[26] 9647 5-9-6 **50**........................(p[1]) DarraghKeenan(5) 1
(Robert Eddery) *hld up: a in rr* **14/1**
060- **14** *28* **Tilsworth Rose**[159] 5926 5-9-8 **35**........................ WilliamCox(3) 11
(J R Jenkins) *led for 2f bef trcking new ldr: rdn and lost pl qckly 4f out: sn detached (jockey said mare was never travelling)* **100/1**

2m 36.75s (2.25) **Going Correction** +0.15s/f (Slow)
WFA 3 from 4yo 25lb 4 from 5yo+ 3lb **14** Ran SP% **119.9**
Speed ratings (Par 101): **98,96,95,94,94 92,90,90,90,87 76,74,73,54**
CSF £31.25 TOTE £6.00: £2.30, £2.20, £6.90; EX 42.00 Trifecta £794.20.
Owner Fitorfat Racing **Bred** Maurice Regan **Trained** Upper Lambourn, Berks

FOCUS
A weak race but it was run at a good gallop. The third, fourth and fifth anchor the form.

246 32RED.COM H'CAP — 1m 3f 219y(P)
6:15 (6:18) (Class 5) (0-70,72) 4-Y-0+
£3,752 (£1,116; £557; £400; £400; £400) **Stalls** Low

Form RPR
63-2 **1** **Unit Of Assessment (IRE)**[6] 135 5-9-6 **69**........................(vt) AdamKirby 1 79
(William Knight) *settled wl in 4th: hdwy under hands and heels into 3rd 3f out: rdn to ld over 1f out: sn in command and rdn out* **5/4**[1]
300- **2** *3* **Continuum**[27] 8735 10-9-5 **68**........................(b) NicolaCurrie 5 73
(Peter Hedger) *v.s.a and detached by 10 l early: latched onto main gp in last after 4f: stl last 3f out: sn rdn and mde stdy hdwy through field 2f out: styd on wl to take 2nd ins fnl f: no ch w wnr (jockey said gelding was slowly away)* **8/1**[3]
05- **3** *1 3/4* **Subliminal**[18] 9732 4-8-11 **63**........................ NickyMackay 3 65
(Simon Dow) *settled in 5th: rdn and outpcd over 2f out: kpt on wl u.p ins fnl f* **16/1**
400- **4** *1/2* **Incredible Dream (IRE)**[202] 4255 6-8-11 **63**........................ JackDuern(3) 2 64
(Dean Ivory) *dwlt and racd in rr: rdn along over 2f out: styd on wl fnl f (jockey said gelding was slowly away)* **16/1**
000- **5** *2 3/4* **Zenith One (IRE)**[41] 9400 4-9-1 **67**........................(t) FergusSweeney 7 64
(Seamus Durack) *racd in midfield: pushed along over 2f out: rdn and unable qck over 1f out: kpt on one pce* **12/1**
00- **6** *1* **Roar (IRE)**[20] 9706 5-9-9 **72**........................ CallumShepherd 8 67
(Ed de Giles) *led: rdn along and strly pressed by rivals either side 2f out: sn hdd by wnr and wknd fnl f* **9/1**
021- **7** *1/2* **Taurean Dancer (IRE)**[24] 9687 4-8-12 **64**........................(p[1]) RossaRyan 6 58
(Roger Teal) *trckd ldr: clsd gng wl 3f out: rdn and upsides w ev ch 2f out: outpcd by wnr over 1f out: wknd fnl f* **6/1**[2]
006- **8** *1/2* **Gravity Wave (IRE)**[27] 9609 5-9-2 **70**........................ PoppyBridgwater(5) 4 63
(Sylvester Kirk) *racd in midfield: hdwy to go 2nd 4f out: rdn and little imp over 2f out: wknd fnl f* **14/1**
000- **9** *5* **Chief Sittingbull**[60] 9097 6-8-8 **57**........................ DavidProbert 9 42
(Tony Carroll) *racd in rr of midfield: rdn and lost pl over 2f out: n.d* **66/1**
20-5 **10** *4* **Agent Gibbs**[11] 61 7-9-7 **70**........................(b[1]) LukeMorris 10 49
(John O'Shea) *racd in midfield: rdn and outpcd over 2f out: sn struggling* **12/1**

2m 35.6s (1.10) **Going Correction** +0.15s/f (Slow)
WFA 4 from 5yo+ 3lb **10** Ran SP% **115.1**
Speed ratings (Par 103): **102,100,98,98,96 96,95,95,92,89**
CSF £11.50 CT £109.36 TOTE £1.80: £1.10, £1.60, £4.50; EX 12.40 Trifecta £94.80.
Owner A Hetherton **Bred** Barouche Stud (IRE) Ltd **Trained** Angmering, W Sussex

FOCUS
Compensation for the winner, who was denied in the closing stages here last time. A small pb from the winner.

247 32RED H'CAP — 6f (P)
6:45 (6:47) (Class 4) (0-85,84) 4-Y-0+
£6,469 (£1,925; £962; £481; £400; £400) **Stalls** Low

Form RPR
333- **1** **Busby (IRE)**[26] 9640 4-8-13 **76**........................(p) MartinDwyer 3 84
(Conrad Allen) *trckd ldr: upsides gng wl 2f out: sn rdn and led over 1f out: in command and rdn out fnl f* **11/8**[1]
340- **2** *1* **Upavon**[235] 3043 9-9-7 **84**........................ AdamKirby 2 89
(Tony Carroll) *hld up in last: effrt to chse wnr 2f out: drvn in 4th over 1f out: styd on wl fnl f* **16/1**
206- **3** *1 3/4* **Excellent George**[40] 9432 7-9-7 **84**........................(t[1]) PJMcDonald 4 83
(Stuart Williams) *led: pushed along and strly pressed by rivals either side 2f out: drvn and hdd by wnr over 1f out: kpt on fnl f* **10/1**
103- **4** *2* **Fivetwoeight**[80] 8636 5-9-1 **78**........................ LukeMorris 5 71
(Peter Chapple-Hyam) *racd in midfield: stl gng wl 2f out: rdn and fnd little over 1f out: kpt on* **8/1**
5-42 **5** *nk* **Bernie's Boy**[4] 177 6-8-4 **74**........................(p) GraceMcEntee(7) 1 66
(Phil McEntee) *trckd ldr: rdn along and ev ch on inner over 1f out: wknd fnl f* **7/1**[3]
121- **6** *1/2* **Compas Scoobie**[89] 8350 6-9-0 **77**........................ RichardKingscote 6 67+
(Stuart Williams) *racd in 4th on the outer: rdn and unable qck 2f out: one pce fnl f* **5/2**[2]

1m 13.14s (0.04) **Going Correction** +0.15s/f (Slow) **6** Ran SP% **109.3**
Speed ratings (Par 105): **105,103,101,98,98 97**
CSF £22.49 TOTE £2.40: £1.30, £7.10; EX 28.80 Trifecta £158.20.
Owner John C Davies **Bred** J C Davies **Trained** Newmarket, Suffolk

FOCUS
Not much pace on early and it was an advantage to be handy. The second has been rated close to last winter's form.

248 32RED CASINO H'CAP — 1m (P)
7:15 (7:16) (Class 5) (0-70,71) 4-Y-0+
£3,752 (£1,116; £557; £400; £400; £400) **Stalls** Low

Form RPR
201- **1** **Divine Messenger**[34] 9510 5-9-5 **68**........................(p[1]) PJMcDonald 2 80
(Emma Owen) *trckd ldr on inner: clsd gng strly 2f out: pushed into ld over 1f out: sn clr: readily* **9/4**[2]
411- **2** *6* **Tamerlane (IRE)**[32] 9536 4-9-7 **70**........................(b) AdamKirby 4 68
(Clive Cox) *led: rdn and hdd by wnr over 1f out: kpt on one pce fnl f* **4/5**[1]
30-4 **3** *1 1/4* **Be Thankful**[13] 18 4-9-2 **65**........................ AdamMcNamara 8 60
(Roger Charlton) *trckd ldr: rdn along and outpcd by front pair 2f out: kpt on one pce fnl f* **10/1**[3]
212/ **4** *3/4* **Choral Clan (IRE)**[390] 9338 8-9-7 **70**........................ RobertHavlin 5 64
(Brendan Powell) *settled in 5th: effrt to chse wnr 2f out: sn drvn and unable qck: one pce fnl f* **14/1**
200- **5** *2 3/4* **Cherbourg (FR)**[76] 8733 7-9-4 **67**........................(p) RobertWinston 9 54
(Dr Jon Scargill) *racd in 4th: rdn and outpcd 2f out: kpt on one pce fnl f* **20/1**
060- **6** *10* **Face Like Thunder**[32] 9535 4-9-5 **68**........................ LiamKeniry 6 32
(Paul D'Arcy) *racd keenly in last: drvn and no imp 2f out: sn struggling* **50/1**
500- **P** **Kafeel (USA)**[16] 9765 8-9-2 **65**........................ HectorCrouch 7
(Gary Moore) *hld up: rdn and outpcd 3f out: lost action and p.u 1f out (jockey said gelding lost it's action)* **40/1**

1m 39.8s **Going Correction** +0.15s/f (Slow) **7** Ran SP% **111.2**
Speed ratings (Par 103): **106,100,98,98,95 85,**
CSF £4.09 CT £10.22 TOTE £3.20: £1.30, £1.10; EX 4.60 Trifecta £15.80.
Owner Miss Emma L Owen **Bred** P J J Eddery **Trained** Nether Winchendon, Bucks

FOCUS
The market made this a two-horse race and the second-favourite proved much the best. A clear pb from the winner, but the form can't be taken too seriously given the lack of depth.

249 RACINGTV.COM H'CAP — 7f (P)
7:45 (7:45) (Class 5) (0-70,77) 4-Y-0+
£3,752 (£1,116; £557; £400; £400; £400) **Stalls** Low

Form RPR
020- **1** **In The Red (IRE)**[15] 9772 6-9-9 **72**........................(p) AdamKirby 2 80
(Martin Smith) *trckd ldr: rdn along to ld over 1f out: hung rt u.str.p ins fnl f: a holding on* **11/2**
50-0 **2** *1/2* **Six Strings**[11] 54 5-9-9 **72**........................(p[1]) RobertWinston 1 78
(Dean Ivory) *trckd ldr on inner: clsd gng wl 2f out: rdn to chse wnr 1f out: styd on wl fnl f: a hld by wnr* **5/2**[1]
031- **3** *1 1/2* **Storm Melody**[16] 9764 6-9-0 **63**........................(p) CharlesBishop 4 65
(Ali Stronge) *racd in midfield: rdn to chse wnr 2f out: sn outpcd over 1f out: kpt on fnl f* **7/2**[2]
400- **4** *1* **Mount Wellington (IRE)**[30] 9569 4-9-7 **70**........................ RobertHavlin 8 69
(Henry Spiller) *dwlt and racd in rr: rdn along 2f out: styd on wl fnl f: nt rch ldrs* **16/1**
401- **5** *1 1/4* **Wilson (IRE)**[41] 9402 4-9-5 **68**........................(p) ShelleyBirkett 5 64
(Julia Feilden) *racd in midfield: rdn and unable qck 2f out: one pce fnl f (trainer said gelding was unsuited by the standard to slow going and would prefer a quicker surface)* **8/1**
0-31 **6** *1* **Pearl Spectre (USA)**[5] 158 8-10-0 **77** 6ex........................(v) NicolaCurrie 3 70
(Phil McEntee) *led: rdn along and hdd by wnr over 1f out: wknd fnl f* **4/1**[3]
625- **7** *6* **Mr Gent (IRE)**[109] 7727 4-9-5 **68**........................(b) FrannyNorton 6 45
(Ed Dunlop) *hld up: drvn along over 2f out: sn struggling: eased fnl 100yds* **12/1**
0/0- **8** *2 3/4* **Blue Candy**[232] 3177 4-9-7 **70**........................(w) KieranO'Neill 7 40
(Ivan Furtado) *racd keenly in last: rdn and little rspnse over 2f out: nvr on terms* **33/1**

1m 27.04s (1.04) **Going Correction** +0.15s/f (Slow) **8** Ran SP% **113.8**
Speed ratings (Par 103): **100,99,97,96,95 94,87,84**
CSF £19.47 CT £54.33 TOTE £6.10: £1.90, £1.40, £1.40; EX 19.00 Trifecta £73.40.
Owner Sunville Rail Limited **Bred** Airlie Stud **Trained** Newmarket, Suffolk

FOCUS
This was quite steadily run early on and it was an advantage to race prominently. It's been rated around the second to his best for his current yard.
T/Jkpt: £16,768.20 to a £1 stake. Pool: £167,682.13 - 10.00 winning units T/Plt: £118.10 to a £1 stake. Pool: £81,336.50 - 502.42 winning units T/Qpdt: £51.30 to a £1 stake. Pool: £11,417.66 - 164.59 winning units **Mark Grantham**

242 KEMPTON (A.W) (R-H)
Wednesday, January 16

OFFICIAL GOING: Polytrack: standard to slow
Wind: LIGHT, ACROSS Weather: SHOWERS

250 INTRODUCING RACING TV H'CAP — 1m (P)
4:30 (4:30) (Class 6) (0-60,60) 4-Y-0+
£3,105 (£924; £461; £400; £400; £400) **Stalls** Low

Form RPR
05-2 **1** **Cashel (IRE)**[7] 138 4-9-5 **58**........................ AlistairRawlinson 2 69
(Michael Appleby) *trckd ldrs: effrt to press ldr 2f out: rdn to ld over 1f out: hrd pressed but styd on wl ins fnl f* **4/1**[2]
242- **2** *1/2* **Gas Monkey**[93] 8282 4-9-6 **59**........................ ShelleyBirkett 10 69+
(Julia Feilden) *broke wl and prom early: sn stdd and hld up in rr after 2f: impeded over 2f out: effrt jst over 2f out: gd hdwy and swtchd rt jst over 1f out: str chal u.p ins fnl f: hld towards fin* **7/1**[3]
31-1 **3** *1/2* **Cape Greco (USA)**[5] 180 4-9-6 **59**........................ RobertWinston 1 68
(Jo Hughes, France) *chsd ldrs: effrt to press ldrs 2f out: pressing wnr and ev ch ent fnl f: kpt on same pce ins fnl f* **11/8**[1]
00-3 **4** *5* **Rivas Rob Roy**[13] 37 4-9-1 **54**........................ JoeyHaynes 14 51
(John Gallagher) *t.k.h: chsd ldrs: effrt ent fnl 2f: unable qck u.p and outpcd over 1f out: wl hld and kpt on same pce ins fnl f* **33/1**
50-4 **5** *1* **Brockagh Cailin**[12] 54 4-9-0 **60**........................ AaronMackay(7) 5 55
(J S Moore) *dwlt: sn rcvrd and in tch in midfield: unable qck over 1f out: wl hld and kpt on same pce ins fnl f* **12/1**
030- **6** *3 3/4* **Sebastiano Ricci (IRE)**[40] 9448 4-9-6 **59**........................ EoinWalsh 9 45
(Mark Loughnane) *hld up towards rr: impeded over 2f out: sme hdwy over 1f out: swtchd rt and kpt on ins fnl f: no threat to ldrs (jockey said gelding suffered interference 2 1/2f out)* **16/1**
60-1 **7** *1 1/4* **With Approval (IRE)**[11] 80 7-9-5 **58**........................(p) LiamJones 6 41
(Laura Mongan) *led: rdn ent fnl 2: hdd over 1f out: sn outpcd and wknd ins fnl f* **16/1**
000- **8** *1/2* **Naralsaif (IRE)**[56] 9177 5-8-13 **52**........................(v) PaddyMathers 8 34
(Derek Shaw) *chsd ldr tl 2f out: sn u.p and outpcd: wknd ins fnl f* **66/1**
010- **9** *1 3/4* **Solveig's Song**[43] 9387 7-9-3 **56**........................(p) NicolaCurrie 7 34
(Steve Woodman) *midfield: dropped bk to rr of main gp and swtchd rt 1/2-way: effrt on inner and swtchd rt 2f: nvr threatened to get on terms* **33/1**
646- **10** *5* **Phobos**[120] 7384 4-9-4 **57**........................ FergusSweeney 12 24
(Michael Blanshard) *t.k.h: hld up towards rr on outer: nvr involved* **100/1**

00-0 **11** *2 1/4* **Tidal Surge (IRE)**[9] 116 4-8-13 **55**..............................(b[1]) JaneElliott(3) 4 17
(Les Eyre) *midfield: rdn 1/2-way: wandering rt and outpcd over 2f out: sn btn and wknd over 1f out* **40/1**

36-3 **12** *3 3/4* **Red Gunner**[5] 181 5-9-5 **58**.............................. LukeMorris 13 11+
(Mark Loughnane) *v.s.a: in rr: carried v wd bnd 4f out: no ch after (jockey said gelding was badly hampered and carried wide on the final bend by the loose horse)* **10/1**

556- **U** **Cristal Pallas Cat (IRE)**[79] 8688 4-8-11 **50**..................(h) KieranO'Neill 3
(Roger Ingram) *restless in stalls: anticipated s: lurchd forward: stmbld and uns rdr leaving stalls* **14/1**

1m 39.15s (-0.65) **Going Correction** +0.025s/f (Slow) **13** Ran SP% **120.6**
Speed ratings (Par 101): **104,103,103,98,97 93,92,91,89,84 82,78,**
CSF £31.65 CT £59.48 TOTE £4.90: £1.90, £2.60, £1.10; EX 32.00 Trifecta £83.30.
Owner Laurence Bellman **Bred** Kildaragh Stud & M Downey **Trained** Oakham, Rutland
■ Stewards' Enquiry : Jane Elliott caution: careless riding

FOCUS
A modest handicap. The winning time was just over three seconds above par on standard to slow Polytrack. The winner has been rated back to his best.

251 32RED ON THE APP STORE MAIDEN STKS 1m (P)
5:00 (5:01) (Class 5) 3-Y-O **£3,881** (£1,155; £577; £288) **Stalls** Low

Form RPR

5-2 **1** **Target Zone**[11] 90 3-9-5 0.............................. DavidProbert 8 82
(David Elsworth) *chsd ldr tl rdn to ld 2f out: clr and sustained duel w runner-up fr wl over 1f out: forged ahd ins fnl f: styd on wl and drew clr fnl 75yds* **2/1[2]**

2 *2 1/4* **Battle of Paradise (USA)** 3-9-5 0.............................. LukeMorris 14 77
(Sir Mark Prescott Bt) *chsd ldrs and wd early: effrt to chal wl over 1f out: sustained duel w wnr tl no ex ins fnl f: outpcd fnl 75yds* **11/2[3]**

3 *4 1/2* **Ifreet (QA)** 3-9-5 0.............................. RossaRyan 5 66+
(Richard Hannon) *midfield: pushed along over 3f out: styd on to chse clr ldng ldng pair 1f out: kpt on for clr 3rd but no imp ins fnl f* **40/1**

3- **4** *2 3/4* **Woods (IRE)**[19] 9730 3-9-5 0.............................. RyanMoore 6 60
(William Haggas) *chsd ldrs: effrt ent fnl 2f: no imp and sn outpcd by ldrs: wl hld 4th and kpt on same pce ins fnl f* **7/4[1]**

5 *1 3/4* **Ardimento (IRE)** 3-9-5 0.............................. JoeyHaynes 13 56+
(Rod Millman) *stdd s: hld up in rr: pushed along out: hdwy over 1f out: swtchd rt and kpt on wl ins fnl f: nvr trbld ldrs* **150/1**

0- **6** *1/2* **Fly Lightly**[35] 9500 3-9-5 0.............................. EoinWalsh 1 55
(Robert Cowell) *dwlt: midfield: effrt jst over 2f out: no real imp but kpt on ins fnl f: nvr threatened ldrs* **40/1**

- **7** *2 1/2* **Farzeen** 3-9-0 0.............................. FranBerry 11 44
(Roger Varian) *stdd s: t.k.h: hld up in rr: hdwy into midfield 1/2-way: outpcd u.p and btn over 1f out: sn wknd (jockey said filly ran too free; vet said filly had been struck into on its left fore)* **14/1**

64- **8** *2 1/4* **Great Shout (IRE)**[28] 9604 3-9-0 0..............................(t) MartinHarley 4 39
(Amy Murphy) *mounted in the chute: t.k.h: led tl rdn and hdd 2f out: sn outpcd and lost wl btn 3rd 1f out: fdd ins fnl f (jockey said filly ran too free; trainer said filly had breathing problem)* **14/1**

9 *3 1/2* **Percy Alexander** 3-9-5 0.............................. PJMcDonald 9 36
(James Tate) *rn green in midfield: rdn and outpcd jst over 2f out: sn wl btn and wknd over 1f out* **16/1**

0- **10** *nk* **Wan Chai (USA)**[35] 9499 3-9-0 0.............................. RichardKingscote 3 30
(Ralph Beckett) *a towards rr: pushed along over 2f out: no prog and sn outpcd: nvr involved and wl btn over 1f out* **40/1**

11 *3/4* **Winter Snowdrop (IRE)** 3-9-0 0.............................. ShelleyBirkett 10 29
(Julia Feilden) *stdd after s: hld up towards rr: effrt and short of room 2f out: no real imp over 1f out: wknd fnl f* **100/1**

12 *4 1/2* **Dubai Metro** 3-9-5 0..............................(h[1]) GeorgeWood 12 23
(George Scott) *a towards rr: effrt over 2f out: sn outpcd and wl bhd over 1f out* **100/1**

13 *6* **Aquarius Miracle** 3-9-5 0.............................. RobertHavlin 2 9
(George Scott) *chsd ldrs: rdn and struggling over 2f out: sn lost pl: dropped towards rr over 1f out: fdd* **33/1**

0- **14** *16* **Poet Pete (IRE)**[19] 9730 3-9-5 0.............................. FergusSweeney 7
(Brendan Powell) *rn green in midfield: dropped to rr and wd bnd 3f out: sn lost tch and t.o* **100/1**

1m 38.78s (-1.02) **Going Correction** +0.025s/f (Slow) **14** Ran SP% **118.2**
Speed ratings (Par 97): **106,103,99,96,94 94,91,89,86,85 84,80,74,58**
CSF £12.82 TOTE £2.60: £1.10, £1.90, £11.10; EX 13.90 Trifecta £269.70.
Owner G B Partnership **Bred** G B Partnership **Trained** Newmarket, Suffolk

FOCUS
A fair 3yo maiden. The second-favourite came through to readily account for the most fancied of the many newcomers in the second half of the straight. The winning time was the quickest of three opening 1m contests. The level is a bit fluid.

252 100% PROFIT BOOST AT 32REDSPORT.COM H'CAP 1m (P)
5:30 (5:31) (Class 4) (0-85,82) 4-Y-O+

£6,469 (£1,925; £962; £481; £400; £400) **Stalls** Low

Form RPR

31-2 **1** **Holy Heart (IRE)**[13] 34 4-9-7 **82**..............................(t) RobertHavlin 2 91+
(John Gosden) *led for 1f: trckd ldrs tl wnt 2nd again over 3f out: led 2f out: sn rdn: kpt on wl and a doing enough ins fnl f: rdn out* **6/4[1]**

10-0 **2** *3/4* **Juanito Chico (IRE)**[12] 56 5-9-3 **78**..............................(t) PJMcDonald 5 84
(Stuart Williams) *stdd s: t.k.h: hld up in tch in midfield: clsd and swtchd rt 2f out: rdn to press wnr jst over 1f out: kpt on u.p but a hld ins fnl f* **9/1**

110- **3** *2 1/4* **Sun Hat (IRE)**[42] 9397 4-9-6 **81**..............................(p) RyanMoore 1 82
(Simon Crisford) *hld up wl in tch in midfield: effrt ent fnl 2f: chsd clr pair u.p 1f out: kpt on same pce and no imp ins fnl f* **4/1[2]**

06-3 **4** *shd* **Come On Tier (FR)**[14] 19 4-9-4 **79**.............................. StevieDonohoe 7 80
(David Simcock) *stdd s: hld up in tch in rr: effrt ent fnl 2f: swtchd rt and hdwy u.p jst over 1f out: kpt on same pce and no imp ins fnl f* **6/1[3]**

306- **5** *1/2* **Enzemble (IRE)**[72] 8882 4-9-5 **80**.............................. AdamKirby 6 79
(James Fanshawe) *stdd s: hld up in tch in last trio: effrt and reminder 2f out: swtchd lft over 1f out: kpt on ins fnl f but nvr enough pce to get on terms* **4/1[2]**

530- **6** *2* **Noble Peace**[74] 8835 6-8-13 **74**.............................. DavidProbert 3 69
(Lydia Pearce) *led after 1f: hdd and rdn 2f out: outpcd and lost 3rd 1f out: wknd ins fnl f* **20/1**

144- **7** *48* **Carouse (IRE)**[13] 1159 4-9-5 **80**.............................. LukeMorris 4
(Evan Williams) *chsd ldr: rdn and lost pl over 3f out: dropped to rr over 2f out: sn lost tch and virtually p.u over 1f out: t.o (jockey said gelding stopped quickly)* **50/1**

1m 39.53s (-0.27) **Going Correction** +0.025s/f (Slow) **7** Ran SP% **111.0**
Speed ratings (Par 105): **102,101,99,98,98 96,48**
CSF £15.31 TOTE £1.90: £1.50, £4.30; EX 17.70 Trifecta £66.50.

Owner Gestut Ammerland **Bred** Ammerland Verwaltung Gmbh & Co Kg **Trained** Newmarket, Suffolk

FOCUS
A fair handicap but the favourite recorded the slowest winning time from the three opening 1m contests on the card. The third has been rated back to form.

253 32RED CASINO H'CAP 6f (P)
6:00 (6:00) (Class 5) (0-75,77) 4-Y-O+

£2,434 (£2,434; £557; £400; £400; £400) **Stalls** Low

Form RPR

365- **1** **Little Palaver**[25] 9682 7-8-13 **74**..............................(p) AmeliaGlass(7) 3 80
(Clive Cox) *chsd ldrs: swtchd rt and effrt on inner 2f out: clsd and ev ch u.p 1f out: led wl ins fnl f: edgd lft towards fin and jnd to dead-heat on post* **11/1**

030- **1** *dht* **Mont Kiara (FR)**[100] 8047 6-9-4 **72**.............................. AdamKirby 2 78
(Simon Dow) *t.k.h: hld up in midfield: swtchd lft and effrt 2f out: hdwy u.p jst over 1f out: clsd and ev ch wl ins fnl f: r.o to join rival and dead-heat on post* **10/1**

423- **3** *shd* **Treacherous**[33] 9536 5-9-7 **75**.............................. CallumShepherd 12 81+
(Ed de Giles) *stdd and dropped in bhd after s: effrt and hdwy over 1f out: ev ch ins fnl f: r.o wl towards fin: jst hld* **7/1**

111- **4** *hd* **Soar Above**[33] 9529 4-8-10 **67**..............................(p) TimClark(3) 9 72
(Paul D'Arcy) *bustled along leaving stalls: chsd ldrs: effrt and rdn to ld but hrd pressed over 1f out: hld on u.p tl hdd wl ins fnl f: edgd rt and no ex last strides* **10/3[1]**

000- **5** *3/4* **Rock Of Estonia (IRE)**[49] 9288 4-9-3 **71**.............................. RichardKingscote 5 74+
(Charles Hills) *stdd s: hld up in tch towards rr: nt clrest of runs 2f out: hdwy over 1f out: clsd whn nt clr run ent fnl f: swtchd rt ins fnl f: styd on wl towards fin: nt quite rch ldrs* **9/1**

006- **6** *nk* **Princely**[27] 9640 4-9-7 **75**.............................. LukeMorris 6 77
(Michael Appleby) *chsd ldr: effrt and ev ch over 1f out: sn drvn and maintained chal tl no ex wl ins fnl f: jst getting outpcd whn squeezed for room and hmpd towards fin* **20/1**

26-4 **7** *1/2* **Madrinho (IRE)**[7] 139 6-9-4 **77**.............................. PoppyBridgwater(5) 8 79+
(Tony Carroll) *hld up in last trio: swtchd rt and hdwy over 1f out: clsng ins fnl f: pressing ldrs and styng on but running out of time whn nt clr run and snatched up cl home (jockey said gelding suffered interference on run to line)* **9/2[2]**

05-3 **8** *nk* **Miracle Works**[8] 131 4-9-2 **70**.............................. LiamKeniry 7 72+
(Ed Walker) *hld up towards rr: effrt nt clrest of runs 2f out: hdwy over 1f out: chsng ldrs u.p ins fnl f: keeping on same pce and hld whn squeezed for room and eased wl ins fnl f* **11/2[3]**

510- **9** *2 3/4* **Full Intention**[48] 9305 5-9-5 **73**.............................. PJMcDonald 10 64
(Lydia Pearce) *in tch in midfield: unable qck over 1f out: wknd ins fnl f* **20/1**

143- **10** *2 3/4* **Anonymous John (IRE)**[39] 9462 7-9-6 **74**.............................. JFEgan 4 56
(Dominic Ffrench Davis) *midfield: rdn over 2f out: sn struggling and outpcd over 1f out: wknd ins fnl f* **10/1**

/30- **11** *1 1/2* **Hello Girl**[39] 9462 4-9-4 **72**.............................. RobertHavlin 11 49
(Dean Ivory) *led tl rdn and hdd over 1f out: sn outpcd: wknd ins fnl f* **20/1**

1m 12.48s (-0.62) **Going Correction** +0.025s/f (Slow) **11** Ran SP% **119.9**
Speed ratings (Par 103): **105,105,104,104,103 103,102,102,98,94 92**
WIN: Mont Kiara 6.60, Little Palaver 5.80; PL: Treacherous 2.40, MK 4.20, LP 3.40; EX: LP/MK 57.10, MK/LP 55.60; CSF: LP/MK 57.23, MK/LP 56.58; TC: LP/MK/T 418.77, MK/LP/T 415.72; TF: LP/MK/T 404.10, MK/LP/T 512.80;.
Owner J C G Chua **Bred** Guy Pariente Holding Sprl **Trained** Epsom, Surrey
Owner Trevor Fox **Bred** Mrs Sandra Fox **Trained** Lambourn, Berks

FOCUS
A fair sprint handicap. The decent gallop produced a particularly competitive finish and the first eight home were covered by about two lengths at the line. Little Palaver has been rated in line with his recent form, and the fourth close to form.

254 32RED.COM H'CAP 6f (P)
6:30 (6:33) (Class 4) (0-85,85) 4-Y-O+

£6,469 (£1,925; £962; £481; £400; £400) **Stalls** Low

Form RPR

336- **1** **Doc Sportello (IRE)**[17] 9763 7-9-7 **85**.............................. RobertWinston 6 90
(Tony Carroll) *t.k.h: stdd and dropped in bhd after s: clsd 2f out: wnt between rivals to ld jst ins fnl f: r.o wl and a doing enough ins fnl f* **10/1**

-425 **2** *1/2* **Bernie's Boy**[1] 247 6-8-3 **74**..............................(p) GraceMcEntee(7) 2 77
(Phil McEntee) *led: sn hdd: chsd ldrs: effrt to chal over 1f out: rdn to ld briefly 1f out: sn hdd: kpt on u.p but a hld ins fnl f* **11/1**

00-5 **3** *3/4* **Gold Hunter (IRE)**[9] 121 9-8-9 **76**.............................. FinleyMarsh(3) 4 77
(Steve Flook) *sn led: drvn and hrd pressed over 1f out: hdd 1f out: cl up in 3rd and kpt on same pce u.p ins fnl f* **25/1**

040- **4** *2* **Al Asef**[16] 9772 4-9-2 **80**.............................. LukeMorris 3 74
(Marco Botti) *wl in tch in last pair: effrt ent fnl 2f: drvn and unable qck over 1f out: kpt on same pce ins fnl f* **2/1[2]**

00-2 **5** *2* **Peggy's Angel**[7] 139 4-8-8 **72**..............................(h) JFEgan 1 60
(Jo Hughes, France) *t.k.h: hld up in tch: hdwy to chse ldr over 3f out tl lost pl over 1f out: wknd ins fnl f* **4/1[3]**

641- **6** *10* **King Robert**[27] 9640 6-9-5 **83**.............................. RyanMoore 5 39
(Charlie Wallis) *chsd ldrs on outer tl lost pl over 3f out: bhd and edgd rt over 1f out: sn wknd (jockey said gelding ran flat)* **15/8[1]**

1m 12.96s (-0.14) **Going Correction** +0.025s/f (Slow) **6** Ran SP% **109.4**
Speed ratings (Par 105): **101,100,99,96,94 80**
CSF £97.49 TOTE £6.70: £3.40, £4.20; EX 61.80 Trifecta £337.50.
Owner George Nixon **Bred** J Hutchinson **Trained** Cropthorne, Worcs

FOCUS
A decent sprint handicap but the previous 6f contest was about half-a-second quicker. It's been rated around the first two to their recent bests.

255 32RED H'CAP 7f (P)
7:00 (7:00) (Class 3) (0-95,95) 4-Y-O+

£9,337 (£2,796; £1,398; £699; £349; £175) **Stalls** Low

Form RPR

35-1 **1** **Happy Escape**[11] 81 5-8-4 **78**.............................. HollieDoyle 6 87
(Tony Carroll) *hld up in tch: clsd over 1f out: rdn and qcknd to ld 1f out: in command and r.o strly ins fnl f* **7/2[2]**

33-4 **2** *1 1/4* **Hammer Gun (USA)**[13] 44 6-8-3 **77**..............................(v) PaddyMathers 7 82
(Derek Shaw) *hld up in last pair: hdwy and swtchd lft ent fnl f: r.o wl u.p to go 2nd towards fin: no threat to wnr* **20/1**

011- **3** *nk* **Exchequer (IRE)**[40] 9446 8-9-3 **91**..............................(p) FrannyNorton 3 **95**
(Richard Guest) *t.k.h: chsd ldr and styd wd early: clsd and rdn to ld over 1f out: sn hdd and unable to match pce of wnr: kpt on same pce and lost 2nd towards fin* **7/2**[2]

04-3 **4** *3/4* **Gentlemen**[15] 4 8-8-3 **77**..............................(h) NicolaCurrie 5 **79**
(Phil McEntee) *chsd ldrs: clsd and effrt on inner 2f out: unable qck and kpt on same pce ins fnl f* **7/1**[3]

01-5 **5** *1* **Book Of Dreams (IRE)**[11] 89 4-9-5 **93**.................... DougieCostello 1 **92**
(Michael Appleby) *led: rdn ent fnl 2f: hdd over 1f out: no ex and outpcd ins fnl f* **25/1**

163- **6** *1/2* **Eljaddaaf (IRE)**[16] 9774 8-9-4 **95**..............................(h) JackDuern(3) 8 **93**
(Dean Ivory) *t.k.h: hld up in tch in midfield: hung rt and nt clrest of runs whn effrt over 1f out: kpt on same pce and no imp ins fnl f (jockey said gelding hung right-handed; vet said gelding had bled from nose)* **7/1**[3]

/50- **7** *2* **Burguillos**[202] 4307 6-9-2 **90**..............................(t) PJMcDonald 2 **83**
(Stuart Williams) *stdd s: hld up in tch in last pair: effrt over 1f out: nvr trbld ldrs* **11/4**[1]

50-0 **8** *2* **Lefortovo (FR)**[13] 34 6-8-5 **79** ow1.............................. JFEgan 4 **66**
(Jo Hughes, France) *stdd s: hld up in tch: hdwy on outer into midfield over 3f out: rdn over 2f out: lost pl over 1f out: bhd ins fnl f* **7/1**[3]

1m 24.98s (-1.02) **Going Correction** +0.025s/f (Slow) **8** Ran SP% **117.2**
Speed ratings (Par 107): **106,104,104,103,102 101,99,97**
CSF £69.15 CT £266.64 TOTE £4.90: £1.10, £5.00, £1.40; EX 75.20 Trifecta £342.10.
Owner A A Byrne **Bred** Anthony Byrne **Trained** Cropthorne, Worcs

FOCUS
The feature contest was a good handicap. They went quite hard up front and more restrained runners prospered in the best comparative time on the night. A pb from the winner, with the second rated in line with his recent Southwell form and the third to his recent win.

256 JOIN RACING TV NOW FILLIES' H'CAP 7f (P)
7:30 (7:32) (Class 5) (0-70,69) 4-Y-O+

£3,752 (£1,116; £557; £400; £400; £400) **Stalls** Low

Form RPR

151- **1** **Chloellie**[75] 8797 4-9-6 **68**.............................. DavidProbert 6 **76**
(J R Jenkins) *t.k.h: hld up in tch in midfield: effrt over 1f out: str run u.p to ld wl ins fnl f: r.o wl* **3/1**[2]

022- **2** *nk* **Violet's Lads (IRE)**[17] 9765 5-8-13 **61**.............................. RossaRyan 5 **68**
(Brett Johnson) *t.k.h: hld up in tch in midfield: clsd over 2f out: rdn to ld 1f out: hdd wl ins fnl f: kpt on but hld towards fin* **9/2**[3]

221- **3** *1 1/2* **Chica De La Noche**[17] 9765 5-9-2 **64**..............................(p) NickyMackay 1 **67**
(Simon Dow) *hld up in tch in midfield: effrt and str chal u.p over 1f out: no ex ins fnl f: rdn and outpcd wl ins fnl f* **5/2**[1]

400- **4** *1* **The Special One (IRE)**[28] 9606 6-8-4 **59**..............................(h) GraceMcEntee(7) 4 **59**
(Phil McEntee) *hld up in tch in rr of main gp: clsd over 2f out: nt clrest of runs over 1f out tl ins fnl f: kpt on towards fin but unable to chal* **25/1**

04-0 **5** *1/2* **Autumn Leaves**[11] 81 4-9-7 **69**.............................. LukeMorris 3 **68**
(Michael Appleby) *chsd ldr tl 4f out: styd prom: ev ch u.p over 1f out: drvn and unable qck 1f out: wknd ins fnl f* **7/1**

000- **6** *1* **Hit The Beat**[43] 9393 4-9-5 **67**.............................. AdamKirby 7 **63**
(Clive Cox) *led: rdn ent fnl 2f: drvn over 1f out: hdd 1f out: sn outpcd and wknd ins fnl f* **14/1**

64-3 **7** *2 1/2* **Caledonia Duchess**[6] 154 6-8-12 **60**..............................(p) PJMcDonald 9 **49**
(Jo Hughes, France) *chsd ldrs: wnt 2nd 4f out: drvn jst over 2f out: lost pl over 1f out: wknd ins fnl f* **5/1**

443- **8** *5* **Natalie Express (FR)**[188] 4854 5-9-4 **66**..............................(h) DougieCostello 8 **42**
(Henry Spiller) *v.s.a: t.k.h: hld up in last pair: clsd and effrt on inner 2f out: no imp over 1f out: wknd ins fnl f (jockey said mare was slowly away)* **25/1**

/5-0 **9** *26* **Achianna (USA)**[11] 80 4-8-2 **50** oh1..............................(t[1]) NicolaCurrie 2
(Rod Millman) *racd awkwardly dropped to last pair whn veered lft over 5f out: effrt over 2f out: sn btn and lost tch (jockey said filly ducked left a furlong after start)* **66/1**

1m 26.16s (0.16) **Going Correction** +0.025s/f (Slow) **9** Ran SP% **116.8**
Speed ratings (Par 100): **100,99,97,96,96 95,92,86,56**
CSF £16.88 CT £38.39 TOTE £3.80: £1.40, £1.80, £1.30; EX 19.00 Trifecta £44.40.
Owner Mrs Veronica Bullard & Mrs Wendy Jenkins **Bred** Mrs Wendy Jenkins **Trained** Royston, Herts

FOCUS
A modest fillies' handicap. The second-favourite continued her love affair with this Sunbury track. The second and third have been rated close to their Lingfield latest.

257 EVERY RACE LIVE ON RACING TV H'CAP 1m 3f 219y(P)
8:00 (8:00) (Class 6) (0-55,55) 4-Y-O+

£3,105 (£924; £461; £400; £400; £400) **Stalls** Low

Form RPR

225- **1** **Cosmogyral (IRE)**[18] 9750 4-9-2 **53**..............................(b) CallumShepherd 3 **59**
(Dominic Ffrench Davis) *midfield: swtchd lft and clsd 3f out: sn pressing ldrs: led wl over 1f out: drvn over 1f out: hdd ins fnl f: battled bk and sn led again: hld on towards fin* **7/1**[3]

031- **2** *1/2* **Ember's Glow**[26] 9665 5-9-4 **52**.............................. EoinWalsh 5 **56**
(Mark Loughnane) *in tch in midfield: clsd u.p to chse ldrs 1f out: nt clr run and swtchd lft ins fnl f: styd on strly towards fin (jockey said gelding was denied clear run)* **6/1**[2]

055- **3** *shd* **Singing The Blues (IRE)**[26] 9664 4-9-2 **53**.............................. JoeyHaynes 4 **58**
(Rod Millman) *led early: sn hdd and stdd bk and t.k.h in midfield: clsd 2f out: ev ch u.p ins fnl f: kpt on wl towards fin* **11/4**[1]

03-0 **4** *shd* **Murhib (IRE)**[12] 58 7-8-12 **46** oh1..............................(h) RobertHavlin 7 **50**
(Lydia Richards) *wl in tch in midfield: trying to switch out lft over 2f out: effrt and ev ch wl over 1f out: drvn and led ins fnl f: sn hdd: kpt on but lost 2 pls last strides* **9/1**

024- **5** *1* **Creative Talent (IRE)**[21] 9704 7-9-2 **55**.............................. PoppyBridgwater(5) 11 **57**
(Tony Carroll) *squeezed for room sn after s: sn dropped in bhd: swtchd lft and effrt over 2f out: hdwy ent fnl 2f: styd on wl but nvr quite getting to ldrs* **8/1**

040- **6** *1 1/4* **Clovelly Bay (IRE)**[25] 9687 8-9-0 **55**.............................. TylerSaunders(7) 8 **55**
(Marcus Tregoning) *t.k.h: sn chsng ldrs: wnt 2nd 6f out tl led ent fnl 2f: sn rdn and hdd over 1f out: no ex ins fnl f: wknd towards fin* **8/1**

53-0 **7** *1* **Captain Kissinger**[15] 6 4-8-13 **50**..............................(b) JFEgan 12 **50**
(Jo Hughes, France) *in tch in midfield: clsd on outer over 3f out: clsd u.p to chse ldrs 1f out: kpt on same pce ins fnl f* **33/1**

04-4 **8** *hd* **Demophon**[12] 58 5-8-10 **47**.............................. FinleyMarsh(3) 14 **45**
(Steve Flook) *dropped in bhd after s: hld up in rr: swtchd rt and clsd 2f out: hdwy u.p over 1f out: no real imp ins fnl f* **8/1**

503- **9** *3* **Telekinetic**[34] 9526 4-9-0 **51**.............................. ShelleyBirkett 1 **46**
(Julia Feilden) *t.k.h: hld up in last quartet: shkn up and effrt ent fnl 2f: kpt on steadily ins fnl f but nvr threatened to get on terms* **28/1**

36-3 **10** *2 3/4* **Mistress Nellie**[12] 58 4-8-9 **46** oh1..............................(p) HollieDoyle 2 **36**
(William Stone) *dropped in bhd after s: t.k.h: hld up in last quartet: effrt over 2f out: no hdwy u.p over 1f out: nvr involved (jockey said filly ran too free)* **8/1**

001- **11** *8* **Millie May**[42] 9407 5-8-13 **47**.............................. JohnFahy 10 **23**
(Jimmy Fox) *sn led: hdd over 9f out: chsd ldr tl 6f out: styd chsng ldrs tl lost pl u.p over 1f out: sn wknd* **25/1**

600- **12** *3 1/4* **Iona Island**[42] 9408 6-9-4 **52**..............................(p) RossaRyan 13 **23**
(Jean-Rene Auvray) *bustled along leaving stalls: sn prom: led over 9f out tl hdd ent fnl 2f: lost pl over 1f out: bhd ins fnl f* **66/1**

200- **13** *3 1/2* **River Cafe (IRE)**[34] 9527 4-8-8 **52**..............................(p) GraceMcEntee(7) 6 **19**
(Phil McEntee) *chsd ldrs: lost pl qckly 2f out and sn bhd: wknd fnl f* **50/1**

2m 34.86s (0.36) **Going Correction** +0.025s/f (Slow)
WFA 4 from 5yo+ 3lb **13** Ran SP% **121.6**
Speed ratings (Par 101): **99,98,98,98,97 97,96,96,94,92 87,84,82**
CSF £47.53 CT £146.83 TOTE £7.10: £1.70, £3.30, £1.60; EX 47.20 Trifecta £229.80.
Owner Kingwood Stud Management Co Ltd **Bred** Rathasker Stud **Trained** Lambourn, Berks

FOCUS
A moderate middle-distance handicap. The top three in the market came to the fore. The balance of the first four suggests the form can't be rated much higher.
T/Plt: £233.20 to a £1 stake. Pool: £86,560.69 - 270.89 winning units T/Qpdt: £93.00 to a £1 stake. Pool: £13,300.30 - 105.80 winning units **Steve Payne**

202 LINGFIELD (L-H)
Wednesday, January 16

OFFICIAL GOING: Polytrack: standard
Wind: Strong, half behind Weather: Overcast, drizzly

258 LADBROKES HOME OF THE ODDS BOOST H'CAP 1m 2f (P)
1:20 (1:20) (Class 5) (0-75,77) 3-Y-O

£3,752 (£1,116; £557; £300; £300; £300) **Stalls** Low

Form RPR

02-1 **1** **Renegade Master**[11] 90 3-9-9 **77**.............................. NicolaCurrie 5 **83**
(George Baker) *t.k.h: pressed ldr: led over 2f out and sent for home: 4 l up over 1f out: edgd rt fnl f: jst clung on* **9/2**[3]

535- **2** *nse* **Water's Edge (IRE)**[25] 9683 3-9-7 **75**.............................. PJMcDonald 2 **81+**
(James Tate) *hld up disputing 5th: prog towards inner 2f out to chse clr ldr (and wnr) over 1f out: hanging but clsd fnl f: edgd rt nr fin: jst pipped* **10/3**[2]

501- **3** *3 1/4* **Debbonair (IRE)**[40] 9444 3-9-1 **69**.............................. RyanMoore 1 **68**
(Hugo Palmer) *trckd ldng pair: rdn over 2f out: hanging and quite wd bnd sn after: nt qckn over 1f out and no imp after* **2/1**[1]

033- **4** *1/2* **Il Capitano (FR)**[20] 9726 3-9-6 **74**.............................. AdamMcNamara 6 **72**
(Roger Charlton) *hld up disputing 5th: effrt and nt clr run briefly 2f out: hdwy to dispute 3rd fnl f: one pce after* **5/1**

600- **5** *3 1/4* **Bonneville (IRE)**[132] 6995 3-8-5 **59**.............................. KieranO'Neill 3 **51**
(Rod Millman) *won early battle for ld: tried to kick on 3f out: hdd over 2f out: lost 2nd and wknd over 1f out* **20/1**

006- **6** *2* **Repulse Bay (IRE)**[46] 9355 3-8-7 **61**.............................. RobHornby 7 **49**
(Ralph Beckett) *dwlt: hld up in last pair: pushed along and bdly outpcd over 2f out: no ch after: kpt on ins fnl f* **25/1**

005- **7** *1/2* **Royal Guild (IRE)**[198] 4482 3-8-9 **63**..............................(p[1]) LukeMorris 8 **50**
(Sir Mark Prescott Bt) *dwlt: rousted fr wd draw but forced to trck ldng pair: rdn over 2f out: wd bnd sn after: wknd over 1f out* **6/1**

000- **8** *23* **Romany Rose (IRE)**[36] 9489 3-7-13 **56** oh11..........(p[1]) NoelGarbutt(3) 4
(Conor Dore) *hld up in last pair: rdn and wknd 3f out: t.o* **100/1**

2m 6.97s (0.37) **Going Correction** -0.075s/f (Stan) **8** Ran SP% **115.1**
Speed ratings (Par 97): **95,94,92,91,89 87,87,68**
CSF £19.67 CT £38.63 TOTE £5.40: £1.40, £1.10, £2.10; EX 20.30 Trifecta £49.40.
Owner Gwyn Powell **Bred** Gwyn & Samantha Powell **Trained** Chiddingfold, Surrey

FOCUS
The early gallop was an ordinary one and it developed into a sprint from the turn in. Muddling form. The third and fourth have been rated close to form.

259 LADBROKES MAIDEN AUCTION STKS 1m 4f (P)
1:50 (1:50) (Class 6) 3-Y-O **£3,105** (£924; £461; £230) **Stalls** Low

Form RPR

3- **1** **Paradise Boy (FR)**[27] 9637 3-9-0 0.............................. RobHornby 7 **70+**
(Andrew Balding) *t.k.h early: trckd ldr after 2f: led over 2f out and sn 2 l ahd: pushed out fnl f: comf* **4/9**[1]

2 *2 1/4* **Ydra** 3-8-13 0.............................. EdwardGreatrex 6 **64+**
(Archie Watson) *hld up towards rr: prog 2f out: shkn up and styd on to take 2nd ins fnl f: no imp on wnr after* **7/2**[2]

04-3 **3** *hd* **Bolt N Brown**[12] 66 3-8-8 64.............................. JosephineGordon 2 **58**
(Gay Kelleway) *t.k.h early: trckd ldr 2f: styd cl up: rdn over 2f out: chsd wnr over 1f out: no imp and lost 2nd ins fnl f: kpt on* **10/1**[3]

0- **4** *3 1/4* **Maiden Navigator**[26] 9670 3-8-8 0..............................(h[1]) HollieDoyle 1 **53**
(David Simcock) *hld up towards rr: outpcd whn taken wd bnd 2f out: shkn up and prog to take 4th ins fnl f: styd on steadily* **20/1**

60- **5** *4* **Snow In Spring**[25] 9683 3-9-2 0.............................. RichardKingscote 8 **55**
(Ralph Beckett) *chsd ldrs: rdn over 2f out: sn lost pl and wknd* **10/1**

06-4 **6** *1/2* **Margaret J**[9] 122 3-8-8 42..............................(p) NicolaCurrie 3 **46**
(Phil McEntee) *led: shkn up and hdd over 2f out: lost 2nd and wknd over 1f out* **20/1**

7 *2* **Perique** 3-9-5 0.............................. LukeMorris 4 **54**
(Ed Dunlop) *s.s: v green early: a in last pair: shkn up 3f out: no ch whn racd v awkwardly over 1f out (jockey said gelding was slowly away)* **8/1**[3]

8 *hd* **Enyama (GER)** 3-8-8 0.............................. DavidProbert 5 **42**
(Michael Attwater) *rn green early in last pair: pushed along and prog on outer to chse ldrs over 3f out: wknd over 2f out (jockey said filly ran green)* **33/1**

2m 33.89s (0.89) **Going Correction** -0.075s/f (Stan) **8** Ran SP% **133.2**
Speed ratings (Par 95): **94,92,92,90,87 87,85,85**
CSF £3.11 TOTE £1.40: £1.02, £2.00, £3.10; EX 3.40 Trifecta £14.20.
Owner Gerry Rafferty **Bred** H Honore & S A R L Crispin De Moubray **Trained** Kingsclere, Hants

FOCUS
This didn't take a lot of winning. The pace steadied in the middle part of the race.

260 SUN RACING NO1 RACING SITE H'CAP 7f 1y(P)
2:25 (2:25) (Class 4) (0-85,85) 4-Y-O+
£3,588 (£3,588; £822; £411; £300; £300) Stalls Low

Form RPR
0V3- 1 **Florencio**[48] 9305 6-9-6 **84**..............................(p) DougieCostello 9 90
(Jamie Osborne) *hld up in midfield: prog over 2f out: clsd on ldr w one other fnl f: drvn to dead-heat last stride* **5/1**[2]
02-2 1 *dht* **Highland Acclaim (IRE)**[11] 91 8-8-9 **73**..............(h) DavidProbert 2 79
(David O'Meara) *mde all: sent for home over 2f out and 2 l ahd: drvn fnl f: jnd last stride* **11/2**[3]
13-0 3 *shd* **Critical Thinking (IRE)**[11] 91 5-8-11 **75**..............(tp) PJMcDonald 3 81
(David Loughnane) *trckd ldrs: shkn up to chse ldr 2f out: drvn and clsd fnl f: jst hld and also lost 2nd last strides* **7/2**[1]
11-5 4 3 ¼ **Robero**[13] 44 7-9-0 **85**..............................(e) TobyEley(7) 6 82
(Gay Kelleway) *t.k.h early: trckd ldrs: nt qckn over 2f out: wl hld in 4th and no imp over 1f out* **6/1**
40-1 5 1 **Kodiline (IRE)**[11] 91 5-8-8 **79**.............................. KatherineBegley(7) 5 74
(David Evans) *dwlt: hld up in last: shkn up over 2f out and lot to do: kpt on but nvr a factor (jockey said gelding hung right-handed throughout)* **7/2**[1]
110- 6 *shd* **Murdanova (IRE)**[273] 1892 6-9-1 **79**.............................. ShaneKelly 8 73
(Ivan Furtado) *hld up in last pair: prog on wd outside 1/2-way: no hdwy 2f out: fdd* **9/1**
045- 7 5 **Smokey Lane (IRE)**[69] 8958 5-9-5 **83**.............................. LukeMorris 4 64
(Sam Thomas) *towards rr: urged along 1/2-way: struggling after* **9/1**
550- 8 2 ¾ **Red Cymbal**[29] 9596 4-8-8 **72**..............................(p) JosephineGordon 1 45
(David C Griffiths) *hld up in rr: plenty to do whn nt clr run briefly on inner 2f out: no prog and nvr in it* **20/1**
000- P **Spare Parts (IRE)**[16] 9772 5-9-7 **85**..............................(t[1]) NicolaCurrie 7
(Phil McEntee) *chsd ldr to 2f out: lost action bdly and p.u after* **16/1**

1m 23.69s (-1.11) **Going Correction** -0.075s/f (Stan) **9** Ran SP% **121.4**
Speed ratings (Par 105): **103,103,102,99,98 97,92,89,**
WIN: 2.90 Florencio, 3.10 Highland Acclaim; PL: F 1.80, HA 2.20, Critical Thinking 1.10; EX: F/HA 13.30, HA/F 13.80; CSF: F/HA 17.24, HA/F 17.50; TC: F/HA/CT 56.04, HA/F/CT 56.73; TF: F/HA/CT 47.50, HA/F/CT 53.60.
Owner Evan M Sutherland **Bred** Rathbarry Stud **Trained** Upper Helmsley, N Yorks
Owner Melbourne 10 Racing **Bred** Newsells Park Stud **Trained** Upper Lambourn, Berks

FOCUS
This was run at a fairly steady early gallop and few were able to get involved, but there was a tight finish and the judge couldn't split the first two. The dead-heating pair and the third have been rated close to their recent bests.

261 LADBROKES H'CAP 6f 1y(P)
3:00 (3:00) (Class 3) (0-90,90) 3-Y-O £7,246 (£2,168; £1,084; £542; £270) Stalls Low

Form RPR
11-6 1 **Deep Intrigue**[12] 57 3-9-7 **90**.............................. PJMcDonald 4 96
(Mark Johnston) *mde all: sent for home over 2f out: drvn over 1f out: kpt on wl and a holding on* **3/1**[3]
01-2 2 1 **James Street (IRE)**[12] 57 3-9-5 **88**.............................. JosephineGordon 2 91+
(Hugo Palmer) *sn pushed along in 4th: unable to make inroads tl prog over 1f out: styd on to take 2nd last 75yds* **5/4**[1]
225- 3 *nk* **Isaan Queen (IRE)**[17] 9762 3-9-3 **86**.............................. EdwardGreatrex 3 88
(Archie Watson) *trckd ldng pair: rdn over 2f out: effrt on inner and drvn to chse wnr ins fnl f: kpt on but lost 2nd last 75yds* **15/2**
4-32 4 1 ½ **Beleaguerment (IRE)**[7] 142 3-8-7 **76**..............................(p) HollieDoyle 1 73
(Archie Watson) *hld up in detached last: pushed along to cl over 2f out: rdn and nt qckn over 1f out: kpt on same pce fnl f (jockey said gelding was outpaced in the early stages)* **9/4**[2]
51-5 5 ½ **K Club (IRE)**[12] 57 3-9-5 **88**.............................. RyanMoore 5 84
(Richard Hannon) *chsd wnr: rdn over 2f out: no imp over 1f out: lost 2nd and wknd ins fnl f* **7/1**

1m 11.01s (-0.89) **Going Correction** -0.075s/f (Stan) **5** Ran SP% **124.5**
Speed ratings (Par 101): **102,100,100,98,97**
CSF £8.34 TOTE £4.70: £2.60, £1.10; EX 10.90 Trifecta £41.90.
Owner Clipper Logistics **Bred** Mr & Mrs J Davis & P Mitchell B'Stock **Trained** Middleham Moor, N Yorks

FOCUS
Quite a tight little handicap, but the winner dominated from the start. The third has been rated to form.

262 BETWAY H'CAP 1m 5f (P)
3:30 (3:30) (Class 6) (0-65,66) 4-Y-O+
£3,105 (£924; £461; £300; £300; £300) Stalls Low

Form RPR
230- 1 **Pivotal Flame (IRE)**[17] 9769 6-9-3 **61**..............................(v) PaddyBradley(3) 3 68
(Pat Phelan) *hld up in midfield: prog over 2f out gng wl: chsd ldr over 1f out: rdn to ld last 150yds: sn in command* **4/1**[2]
340- 2 1 ½ **Rare (IRE)**[36] 9492 4-9-3 **66**.............................. ThomasGreatrex(5) 8 71
(Archie Watson) *chsd ldr 2f: styd prom: shkn up and lost pl over 2f out: rallied over 1f out: drvn and styd on fnl f to take 2nd last stride* **14/1**
054- 3 *shd* **Attain**[17] 9769 10-9-3 **65**.............................. Pierre-LouisJamin(7) 4 70+
(Archie Watson) *slowly away and urged along early: mostly in last tl prog on outer over 3f out: rdn to chse ldr 2f out: led over 1f out: hdd and no ex last 150yds: lost 2nd fnl stride* **8/1**
535- 4 *nk* **Queen Of Paris**[17] 9766 4-9-7 **65**.............................. CallumShepherd 1 69
(William Knight) *hld up towards rr: shkn up over 2f out: prog and rdn over 1f out: styd on fnl f to press for a pl nr fin* **5/1**[3]
430- 5 2 ½ **Dolphin Village (IRE)**[25] 9687 9-8-10 **51** oh6..............(h) CharlieBennett 5 51
(Shaun Harris) *hld up: last over 2f out but gng wl enough: pushed along and prog over 1f out: kpt on fnl f but no ch to be involved* **25/1**
030- 6 1 **Vanity Vanity (USA)**[42] 9407 4-9-3 **61**.............................. CharlesBishop 6 60
(Denis Coakley) *prom in chsng gp: rdn to chse ldr 3f out to 2f out: wknd over 1f out* **5/1**[3]
60-5 7 2 ¼ **Carvelas (IRE)**[13] 38 10-9-7 **62**.............................. DavidProbert 10 58
(J R Jenkins) *hld up towards rr: shkn up over 2f out: no real prog on outer over 1f out: wknd fnl f* **16/1**
353- 8 4 **Galitello**[86] 8479 4-9-6 **64**.............................. PJMcDonald 7 54
(Mark Johnston) *chsd clr ldr after 2f to 3f out: lost pl u.p 2f out: wknd fnl f* **2/1**[1]
44-0 9 5 **Middlescence (IRE)**[10] 101 5-9-5 **65**..............(t) PoppyBridgwater(5) 2 47
(Lucinda Egerton) *racd freely: led and clr: stl 12 l ahd 4f out: c bk to rivals over 2f out: hdd & wknd rapidly over 1f out* **20/1**

2m 43.6s (-2.40) **Going Correction** -0.075s/f (Stan)
WFA 4 from 5yo+ 3lb **9** Ran SP% **118.9**
Speed ratings (Par 101): **104,103,103,102,101 100,99,96,93**
CSF £59.80 CT £434.83 TOTE £6.40: £1.50, £2.60, £2.30; EX 97.00 Trifecta £906.70.
Owner Hugh J F Lang **Bred** Rabbah Bloodstock Limited **Trained** Epsom, Surrey

FOCUS
The runaway leader set a good gallop and this set up for a closer. Straightforward form, with the winner rated to her mark.

263 FOLLOW TOP TIPSTERS AT SUN RACING APPRENTICE H'CAP 7f 1y(P)
4:00 (4:00) (Class 6) (0-55,55) 4-Y-O+
£3,105 (£924; £461; £300; £300; £300) Stalls Low

Form RPR
00-6 1 **Brockey Rise (IRE)**[13] 37 4-9-9 **52**..............................(b) KatherineBegley 2 58
(David Evans) *chsd ldng pair: rdn 2f out: clsd on inner over 1f out: wnt 2nd ins fnl f: styd on to ld last 50yds* **15/2**
40-6 2 *nk* **Swiss Cross**[12] 53 12-9-5 **53**..............................(p) GraceMcEntee(5) 1 58
(Phil McEntee) *w ldr: led jst over 2f out: kpt on wl whn hrd pressed over 1f out: hdd last 50yds* **8/1**
000- 3 1 ¼ **Secret Glance**[76] 8779 7-9-0 **46**..............................(p[1]) MarkCrehan(3) 8 48
(Adrian Wintle) *narrow ldr to jst over 2f out: kpt pressing ldr tl no ex ins fnl f* **14/1**
63-0 4 *nk* **Black Truffle (FR)**[6] 161 9-9-0 **46**..............................(p) EllieMacKenzie(3) 5 47
(Mark Usher) *chsd ldrs: plenty to do in 5th over 2f out: rdn to take 4th over 1f out: kpt on and nrst fin but nvr able to chal* **4/1**[1]
000- 5 1 **Haraz (IRE)**[19] 9735 6-9-3 **46** oh1..............................(bt[1]) SeamusCronin 7 44+
(Paddy Butler) *hld up in last trio: prog wl over 1f out: styd on to take 5th nr fin: too late to threaten* **25/1**
00-0 6 1 ½ **Concur (IRE)**[7] 139 6-8-10 **46** oh1..............................(bt) OliverSearle(7) 6 40
(Rod Millman) *dwlt but sn chsd ldng trio: rdn over 2f out: fdd over 1f out* **33/1**
003- 7 *hd* **Baby Gal**[19] 9734 5-8-12 **46**..............................(v) IsobelFrancis(5) 13 40
(Jim Boyle) *stdd s: swtchd to inner fr wd draw and hld up in last: stl there wl over 1f out and no ch: r.o fnl f: all too late (enq held into running and riding, jockey stated her instructions were to ride the race as she found it, but as she was slowly away from a wide draw, she decided to drop in and go the shortest way home. Trainer's rep stated that he was satisfied that the* **4/1**[1]
40-0 8 1 ¾ **Plucky Dip**[6] 161 8-9-3 **51**..............................(p) LauraPearson(5) 3 40
(John Ryan) *hld up towards rr: pushed along and sme prog into midfield over 2f out: no hdwy over 1f out* **5/1**[2]
40-0 9 1 ¼ **Rising Sunshine (IRE)**[1] 243 6-8-12 **46** oh1..............(bt) AmeliaGlass(5) 11 32
(Milton Bradley) *taken down early: reluctant to enter stalls: nvr beyond midfield on outer: no prog and btn 2f out* **12/1**
00-0 10 *hd* **Camanche Grey (IRE)**[14] 25 8-9-0 **46** oh1..............(t[1]) WilliamCarver(3) 9 32
(Lucinda Egerton) *taken down early: hld up in rr: no prog over 2f out: no ch after* **25/1**
35-0 11 1 ¾ **Herringswell (FR)**[13] 37 4-9-12 **55**.............................. ScottMcCullagh 4 36
(Henry Spiller) *a in rr: no prog and btn 2f out* **7/1**[3]
04/- 12 2 ½ **Twistsandturns (IRE)**[456] 8134 8-8-12 **46** oh1.............. GeorgiaDobie(5) 14 21
(Adrian Wintle) *awkward s: a in rr: no prog 2f out* **25/1**

1m 24.0s (-0.80) **Going Correction** -0.075s/f (Stan) **12** Ran SP% **120.9**
Speed ratings (Par 101): **101,100,99,98,97 96,95,93,92,92 90,87**
CSF £64.63 CT £846.78 TOTE £9.00: £2.70, £2.50, £4.80; EX 67.30 Trifecta £1069.00.
Owner John Abbey & Emma Evans **Bred** P O'Rourke **Trained** Pandy, Monmouths
■ Stewards' Enquiry : Isobel Francis ten-day ban; failure to achieve best possible placing (Jan 30-31,Feb 1-8)

FOCUS
Few got into this, with the pace holding up pretty well. Modest form.
T/Plt: £26.70 to a £1 stake. Pool: £64,901.13 - 1,768.01 winning units T/Qpdt: £17.90 to a £1 stake. Pool: £5,886.74 - 242.41 winning units **Jonathan Neesom**

264a-271a (Foreign Racing) - See Raceform Interactive

208 NEWCASTLE (A.W) (L-H)
Thursday, January 17

OFFICIAL GOING: Tapeta: standard
Wind: Almost nil Weather: Dry

272 PLAY 4 TO SCORE AT BETWAY H'CAP 1m 4f 98y (Tp)
3:55 (3:55) (Class 5) (0-75,80) 4-Y-O+
£3,752 (£1,116; £557; £400; £400; £400) Stalls High

Form RPR
52-1 1 **Glan Y Gors (IRE)**[11] 101 7-9-7 **71** 6ex..............................(p) CliffordLee 9 78
(David Thompson) *t.k.h: trckd ldr: led over 2f out: hrd pressed fr over 1f out: rdn and hld on wl fnl f* **13/2**[2]
06-2 2 *nk* **Dommersen (IRE)**[11] 102 6-9-8 **77**.............................. BenSanderson(5) 5 83
(Roger Fell) *t.k.h: hld up: hdwy far side over 2f out: rdn to chal over 1f out: kpt on fnl f: hld nr fin* **7/1**[3]
11-1 3 1 ¼ **Elysees Palace**[11] 102 5-10-2 **80** 6ex..............................(p[1]) LukeMorris 8 84+
(Sir Mark Prescott Bt) *in tch: stdy hdwy and angled rt 3f out: effrt and rdn wl over 1f out: kpt on same pce ins fnl f* **8/13**[1]
620- 4 ½ **Thawry**[86] 8508 4-9-4 **71**.............................. CamHardie 7 74
(Antony Brittain) *dwlt: hld up: effrt on outside wl over 1f out: kpt on same pce last 100yds* **22/1**
50-0 5 *nk* **Confederate**[12] 84 4-9-2 **69**..............................(bt[1]) PJMcDonald 2 72
(Hugo Palmer) *t.k.h: chsd ldrs: rdn over 2f out: hung lft and no ex fr over 1f out* **25/1**
610- 6 1 **Kyoto Star (FR)**[29] 9608 5-9-8 **72**.............................. RobertHavlin 12 73
(Henry Spiller) *hld up in midfield: effrt whn nt clr run wl over 1f out: rdn and no imp fnl f* **8/1**
6/0- 7 1 ¼ **Brokopondo (IRE)**[48] 9345 7-8-5 **60** oh7.............................. PaulaMuir(5) 6 59
(Miss Clare Louise Cannon, Ire) *hld up in midfield: effrt on outside and prom over 2f out: sn rdn: wknd ins fnl f* **18/1**
440- 8 ½ **Apache Blaze**[43] 9400 4-8-12 **65**.............................. AndrewMullen 4 63
(Robyn Brisland) *t.k.h in midfield: drvn over 2f out: wknd over 1f out* **28/1**
/00- 9 8 **Paris Protocol**[29] 9610 6-9-10 **74**..............................(p) JasonHart 3 60
(Mark Walford) *hld up: rdn and outpcd wl over 2f out: sn btn* **20/1**
260/ 10 2 ½ **Stanarley Pic**[454] 8214 8-8-7 **60** oh2.............................. PhilDennis(3) 1 42
(Susan Corbett) *led to over 2f out: sn rdn and wknd* **150/1**

450- **11** *5* **Starplex**[16] 9610 9-9-13 **77**......(t[1]) GrahamLee 10 51
(Kenny Johnson) *midfield on outside: stdy hdwy and prom 1/2-way: rdn and outpcd over 2f out: sn btn* **250/1**

450- **12** *11* **Abel Tasman**[21] 9723 5-9-12 **76**...... EoinWalsh 11 32
(Stef Keniry) *missed break: hld up: struggling over 5f out: sn btn* **80/1**

2m 45.13s (4.03) **Going Correction** +0.25s/f (Slow)
WFA 4 from 5yo+ 3lb **12** Ran SP% **122.8**
Speed ratings (Par 103): **96,95,94,94,94 93,92,92,87,85 82,74**
CSF £50.25 CT £68.22 TOTE £5.50: £2.10, £2.10, £1.10; EX 52.80 Trifecta £91.40.

Owner B Lapham & J Souster **Bred** Colm McEvoy **Trained** Bolam, Co Durham

FOCUS

This modest handicap proved tactical and it saw a tight finish, although that was dominated by the first pair. Muddling form.

273 SUNRACING.CO.UK H'CAP 1m 5y (Tp)

4:25 (4:25) (Class 7) (0-50,50) 3-Y-O+ **£2,264** (£673; £336; £168) **Stalls** Centre

Form RPR

204- **1** **Miss Bates**[35] 9523 5-9-12 **50**...... JoeFanning 10 58
(Ann Duffield) *hld up on far side of gp: cruised through to ld appr fnl f: shkn up and sn qcknd clr: kpt on wl* **9/2[2]**

440- **2** *1 3/4* **Irish Times**[203] 4295 4-9-12 **50**...... RobertHavlin 11 54
(Henry Spiller) *hld up on nr side of gp: rdn over 2f out: hdwy over 1f out: chsd (clr) wnr ins fnl f: r.o* **12/1**

26-6 **3** *1 1/2* **Harbour Patrol (IRE)**[10] 116 7-9-6 **47**......(b) PhilDennis(3) 3 48
(Rebecca Bastiman) *t.k.h: hld up on far side of gp: smooth hdwy and prom over 2f out: rdn over 1f out: one pce ins fnl f* **20/1**

50-0 **4** *1/2* **Cold Fire (IRE)**[14] 45 6-9-4 **49**...... RPWalsh(7) 9 49
(Robyn Brisland) *hld up: rdn along over 2f out: hdwy and hung lft over 1f out: kpt on fnl f: nt pce to chal* **18/1**

05-0 **5** *3/4* **Moonbi Creek (IRE)**[6] 180 12-9-7 **45**...... CallumRodriguez 2 43
(Stella Barclay) *missed break: hld up on far side of gp: hdwy over 2f out: rdn and one pce ins fnl f (jockey said gelding was slowly away)* **20/1**

530- **6** *1/2* **Song Of Summer**[28] 9643 4-9-3 **46**...... PaulaMuir(5) 7 43
(Iain Jardine) *cl up in centre of gp: led over 2f out to over 1f out: no ex ins fnl f* **16/1**

4/4- **7** *3/4* **Our Manekineko**[28] 9643 9-9-0 **45**......(bt) GearoidBrouder(7) 13 40
(Stephen Michael Hanlon, Ire) *hld up in tch in centre of gp: rdn to ld briefly over 1f out: no ex ins fnl f* **5/1[3]**

02-3 **8** *3 3/4* **Foxrush Take Time (FR)**[7] 155 4-9-7 **45**......(e[1]) FrannyNorton 1 32
(Richard Guest) *prom on far side of gp: rdn over 2f out: wknd over 1f out* **8/1**

00-0 **9** *3/4* **Wide Acclaim (IRE)**[13] 62 4-9-10 **48**......(t[1]) AlistairRawlinson 14 33
(Rebecca Menzies) *hld up on nr side of gp: rdn over 2f out: wknd over 1f out* **22/1**

41 **10** *7* **Taceec (IRE)**[10] 116 4-9-5 **46**...... ConorMcGovern(3) 5 16
(Adrian McGuinness, Ire) *hld up in midfield in centre of gp: rdn over 2f out: wknd wl over 1f out (jockey said gelding stopped quickly; vet reported the gelding had scoped dirty during a post-race endoscopic examination)* **5/2[1]**

4- **11** *1/2* **Effernock Fizz (IRE)**[21] 9676 4-9-12 **50**...... LukeMorris 8 19
(Miss Katy Brown, Ire) *prom on nr side of gp: rdn and outpcd over 2f out: sn wknd* **40/1**

100- **12** *22* **Little Choosey**[28] 9644 9-9-12 **50**......(bt) RobertWinston 6
(Roy Bowring) *led on far side of gp to over 2f out: wknd over 1f out: eased (jockey said mare hung left and stopped quickly)* **10/1**

13 *7* **Shandon (IRE)**[7] 7745 4-9-7 **45**......(t[1]) LiamJones 4
(Lucinda Egerton) *chsd ldrs in centre of gp: struggling over 3f out: sn btn* **100/1**

1m 42.2s (3.60) **Going Correction** +0.25s/f (Slow) **13** Ran SP% **119.8**
Speed ratings (Par 97): **92,90,88,88,87 87,86,82,81,74 74,52,45**
CSF £53.66 CT £1022.50 TOTE £5.60: £2.70, £3.80, £3.10; EX 61.70 Trifecta £1107.80.

Owner Evelyn Duchess Of Sutherland **Bred** Tirnaskea Stud **Trained** Constable Burton, N Yorks

■ Stewards' Enquiry : Gearoid Brouder two-day ban: used whip above the permitted level (Jan 31, Feb 1)

FOCUS

This bottom-drawer handicap was run at an average pace. The second has been rated roughly to his mark.

274 LADBROKES H'CAP 7f 14y (Tp)

4:55 (4:55) (Class 5) (0-70,70) 3-Y-O **£3,752** (£1,116; £557; £400; £400; £400) **Stalls** Centre

Form RPR

013- **1** **Rich Approach (IRE)**[29] 9613 3-8-12 **61**...... PJMcDonald 1 70+
(James Bethell) *hld up: hdwy to ld over 1f out: rdn and edgd rt ins fnl f: r.o wl* **13/8[1]**

0-44 **2** *1 3/4* **Axel Jacklin**[8] 140 3-9-3 **66**......(b[1]) JoeFanning 8 69
(Mark Johnston) *t.k.h early: chsd ldr: rdn and ev ch briefly over 1f out: sn chsng wnr: one pce ins fnl f* **15/2**

24-2 **3** *2 1/4* **Beryl The Petal (IRE)**[13] 65 3-9-4 **70**...... ConorMcGovern(3) 7 67
(David O'Meara) *in tch: effrt over 2f out: rdn over 1f out: sn one pce* **7/2[2]**

055- **4** *3* **Picture Poet (IRE)**[75] 8825 3-9-0 **63**......(v) RobertHavlin 5 52
(Henry Spiller) *hld up: stdy hdwy over 2f out: rdn and outpcd over 1f out: no imp ins fnl f* **6/1[3]**

0-3 **5** *1 1/4* **Vrai (IRE)**[15] 21 3-9-5 **68**......(b) AndrewMullen 2 53
(Kevin Ryan) *t.k.h: led: rdn and hdd over 1f out: wknd ins fnl f* **7/1**

00-0 **6** *4 1/2* **Benji**[15] 20 3-8-13 **62**...... TonyHamilton 4 35
(Richard Fahey) *hld up in tch: lost pl over 2f out: sn struggling: n.d after* **16/1**

020- **7** *2 1/2* **Teodula (IRE)**[49] 9306 3-9-4 **67**...... LukeMorris 6 34
(Henry Spiller) *hld up: effrt over 2f out: wknd over 1f out* **40/1**

200- **8** *2* **Cool Kitty**[30] 9598 3-8-0 **54**...... PaulaMuir(5) 3 15
(Rebecca Menzies) *s.i.s: t.k.h and sn cl up: rdn and struggling 2f out: sn btn* **33/1**

1m 28.28s (2.08) **Going Correction** +0.25s/f (Slow) **8** Ran SP% **110.1**
Speed ratings (Par 97): **98,96,93,90,88 83,80,78**
CSF £13.42 CT £34.39 TOTE £2.60: £1.10, £1.60, £1.60; EX 13.90 Trifecta £34.90.

Owner The Vickers & Clark Racing Partnership **Bred** The Kiss Me Goodbye Syndicate **Trained** Middleham Moor, N Yorks

FOCUS

This tight 3yo handicap was run at a fair enough pace. The second has been rated close to form.

275 BETWAY NOVICE STKS 6f (Tp)

5:25 (5:25) (Class 5) 4-Y-O+ **£3,752** (£1,116; £557; £278) **Stalls** Centre

Form RPR

6 **1** **Dawn Delight**[15] 27 4-8-11 0...... JoeFanning 7 68+
(Hugo Palmer) *prom chsng gp: wnt 2nd over 2f out: effrt and rdn over 1f out: led ins fnl f: kpt on strly* **11/4[2]**

5 **2** *3 1/4* **Master Diver**[10] 117 4-9-2 0...... LukeMorris 1 63+
(Sir Mark Prescott Bt) *racd against far rail jst away fr main gp: led and sn clr: rdn 2f out: hdd ins fnl f: kpt on same pce* **10/3[3]**

05- **3** *1 1/4* **Proceeding**[50] 9287 4-9-2 0...... CamHardie 4 59
(Tracy Waggott) *prom: effrt and rdn over 2f out: kpt on same pce over 1f out* **25/1**

/5-0 **4** *2 3/4* **Purbeck Gem**[10] 117 5-8-4 0...... RPWalsh(7) 8 45
(Robyn Brisland) *chsd clr ldr to over 2f out: rdn and outpcd over 1f out* **50/1**

5- **5** *2* **Polished Article**[30] 9594 4-8-8 0...... PhilDennis(3) 2 39
(Lawrence Mullaney) *t.k.h: hld up: effrt and rdn over 2f out: sn no imp* **50/1**

02/ **6** *7* **Sporting Bill (IRE)**[444] 8466 4-9-2 0...... PJMcDonald 3 21
(James Fanshawe) *hld up: stdy hdwy over 2f out: rdn and wknd over 1f out* **1/1[1]**

- **7** *6* **Savlad** 4-9-2 0...... CliffordLee 5 2
(Shaun Harris) *s.i.s: hld up in tch: rdn and outpcd over 2f out: sn btn* **100/1**

1m 13.48s (0.98) **Going Correction** +0.25s/f (Slow) **7** Ran SP% **108.5**
Speed ratings (Par 103): **103,98,97,93,90 81,73**
CSF £10.75 TOTE £3.40: £1.50, £2.70; EX 11.90 Trifecta £65.60.

Owner Hamad Rashed Bin Ghedayer **Bred** Rabbah Bloodstock Limited **Trained** Newmarket, Suffolk

FOCUS

Visually this was a messy novice sprint, with the first pair dominating on the far side. It's been rated cautiously.

276 FOLLOW TOP TIPSTER TEMPLEGATE AT SUNRACING H'CAP 1m 5y (Tp)

5:55 (5:55) (Class 4) (0-85,87) 4-Y-O+ **£5,387** (£1,612; £806; £403; £400) **Stalls** Centre

Form RPR

1-43 **1** **Glory Of Paris (IRE)**[5] 209 5-9-5 **79**...... LukeMorris 1 86
(Michael Appleby) *t.k.h: trckd ldr: led and hrd pressed fr over 1f out: rdn and r.o wl fnl f* **11/10[1]**

654- **2** *1/2* **Fayez (IRE)**[21] 9723 5-9-13 **87**......(p) CamHardie 3 93
(David O'Meara) *hld up in tch: hdwy to dispute ld over 1f out: kpt on same pce wl ins fnl f* **5/2[2]**

106- **3** *1 1/2* **Sheila's Treat (IRE)**[27] 9661 6-9-4 **78**...... JasonHart 2 81
(Ivan Furtado) *t.k.h: stdd bhd ldng pair: effrt and rdn over 1f out: kpt on same pce ins fnl f* **7/2[3]**

504- **4** *4 1/2* **Malaspina (ITY)**[36] 7306 7-9-7 **81**...... DayversonDeBarros 4 73
(Ivan Furtado) *led at slow gallop: rdn and hdd 2f out: sn wknd* **33/1**

600- **5** *3 3/4* **Gabrial's Kaka (IRE)**[101] 8052 9-8-11 **71**...... PaddyMathers 5 55
(Patrick Morris) *t.k.h: hld up in last pl: effrt over 2f out: rdn and wknd over 1f out* **22/1**

1m 40.85s (2.25) **Going Correction** +0.25s/f (Slow) **5** Ran SP% **105.7**
Speed ratings (Par 105): **98,97,96,91,87**
CSF £3.69 TOTE £1.60: £1.10, £1.30; EX 4.00 Trifecta £6.50.

Owner C L Bacon **Bred** Peter Grimes & The Late Jackie Grimes **Trained** Oakham, Rutland

FOCUS

The two market leaders fought out this feature handicap, which proved tactical. A small pb from the winner, with the second rated to his recent form.

277 BETWAY CASINO H'CAP 6f (Tp)

6:25 (6:25) (Class 6) (0-60,62) 4-Y-O+

£3,105 (£924; £461; £400; £400; £400) **Stalls** Centre

Form RPR

416- **1** **Dandy Highwayman (IRE)**[29] 9617 5-9-2 **62**......(tp) HarryRussell(7) 9 69
(Ollie Pears) *in tch on nr side of gp: hdwy to ld over 1f out: hrd pressed ins fnl f: hld on wl cl home* **11/1**

0/ **2** *nse* **Ken's Sam's (IRE)**[6] 188 6-9-4 **60** 6ex......(p) ConorMcGovern(3) 13 67
(Adrian McGuinness, Ire) *hld up: hdwy on nr side of gp over 1f out: pressed wnr ins fnl f: kpt on wl: jst hld* **9/4[1]**

21-0 **3** *1 3/4* **Astrophysics**[15] 28 7-9-6 **59**...... CallumRodriguez 1 61
(Lynn Siddall) *hld up: hdwy on far side of gp over 1f out: chsng ldrs whn rdn and edgd rt ins fnl f: no ex (jockey said gelding hung right)* **9/1**

346- **4** *3/4* **Skyva**[29] 9616 4-9-2 **58**......(v[1]) BenRobinson(3) 7 58
(Brian Ellison) *prom in centre of gp: effrt and rdn 2f out: kpt on same pce ins fnl f (jockey said gelding ran too free)* **7/1**

400- **5** *nk* **Leeshaan (IRE)**[159] 5996 4-9-5 **58**...... JoeFanning 4 57
(Rebecca Bastiman) *hld up in centre of gp: effrt whn nt clr run briefly over 1f out and ins fnl f: kpt on: nvr able to chal* **33/1**

240- **6** *nse* **Nutopia**[33] 9559 4-8-9 **48**...... CamHardie 5 46
(Antony Brittain) *hld up: hdwy far side of gp over 1f out: sn rdn: no imp fnl f (jockey said filly was slowly away)* **16/1**

541- **7** *1/2* **Roaring Rory**[48] 9329 6-9-2 **60**...... SebastianWoods(5) 2 57
(Ollie Pears) *in tch towards far side of gp: drvn over 2f out: kpt on fnl f: no imp* **13/2[3]**

006- **8** *3/4* **Trulove**[45] 9378 6-8-7 **46** oh1......(b) PaddyMathers 8 41
(John David Riches) *in tch on nr side of gp: rdn over 2f out: one pce fnl f* **80/1**

003- **9** *1 1/2* **Scenery**[29] 9617 4-9-6 **59**...... BarryMcHugh 12 49
(Marjorie Fife) *hld up in centre of gp: effrt and rdn whn n.m.r briefly over 1f out: sn no imp* **11/1**

003- **10** *3/4* **High Anxiety**[291] 1536 5-8-7 **46** oh1...... LukeMorris 6 34
(Andrew Crook) *cl up: rdn over 1f out: outpcd whn checked ins fnl f: sn btn* **66/1**

012- **11** *nk* **Breathoffreshair**[43] 9415 5-9-5 **58**......(tp) FrannyNorton 10 45
(Richard Guest) *hld up on nr side of gp: drvn along 2f out: sn btn* **11/2[2]**

0-00 **12** *1/2* **Camanche Grey (IRE)**[1] 263 8-8-7 **46** oh1......(t) LiamJones 11 32
(Lucinda Egerton) *led on nr side of gp: rdn and hdd over 1f out: sn wknd* **66/1**

006/ **13** *24* **Miss Rebero**[1598] 6015 9-8-0 **46** oh1...... FayeMcManoman(7) 3
(Gary Sanderson) *bhd on far side of gp: struggling over 2f out: sn lost tch: t.o* **200/1**

1m 13.23s (0.73) **Going Correction** +0.25s/f (Slow) **13** Ran SP% **112.2**
Speed ratings (Par 101): **105,104,102,101,101 101,100,99,97,96 96,95,63**
CSF £33.40 CT £242.15 TOTE £13.90: £4.90, £1.30, £3.80; EX 38.90 Trifecta £295.70.

Owner Ontoawinner & Ollie Pears **Bred** Michael M Byrne **Trained** Norton, N Yorks

FOCUS
Not a bad sprint handicap for the grade and there was a sound pace on. The third has been rated near his recent form.

278 BETWAY SPRINT H'CAP 5f (Tp)
6:55 (6:55) (Class 5) (0-75,77) 4-Y-O+

£3,752 (£1,116; £557; £400; £400; £400) **Stalls Centre**

Form				RPR
12-6	1		**Another Angel (IRE)**[9] 131 5-9-1 **69** CamHardie 7 (Antony Brittain) *trckd ldrs on nr side of gp: effrt and rdn over 1f out: led ins fnl f: r.o wl* **5/1**[2]	78
02-5	2	3/4	**Amazing Grazing (IRE)**[16] 2 5-9-4 **75** BenRobinson(3) 5 (Rebecca Bastiman) *prom in centre of gp: effrt and pushed along over 1f out: kpt on fnl f to take 2nd towards fin: nt rch wnr* **16/1**	81
2-22	3	1	**First Excel**[9] 131 7-8-13 **67** (b) EoinWalsh 6 (Roy Bowring) *trckd ldr on nr side of gp: effrt over 1f out: led briefly ins fnl f: no ex and lost 2nd towards fin* **6/1**[3]	69
02-5	4	1/2	**Wiff Waff**[9] 131 4-9-6 **74** CallumRodriguez 8 (Stuart Williams) *hld up in centre: effrt and pushed along over 1f out: kpt on fnl f: nvr able to chal* **4/1**[1]	75+
50-4	5	1/2	**Warrior's Valley**[14] 43 4-8-5 **62** (t) PhilDennis(3) 10 (David C Griffiths) *led on nr side of gp: rdn over 1f out: hdd ins fnl f: sn btn* **25/1**	61
06-6	6	nk	**Landing Night (IRE)**[16] 3 7-9-8 **76** (tp) PJMcDonald 11 (Rebecca Menzies) *hld up: stdy hdwy on nr side of gp over 1f out: rdn and no imp fnl f* **6/1**[3]	74
35-0	7	1/2	**Lord Of The Glen**[9] 131 4-9-4 **72** (b) JoeFanning 4 (Jim Goldie) *hld up in centre of gp: effrt over 1f out: sn n.d* **10/1**	68
344-	8	1	**Gamesome (FR)**[90] 8383 8-9-1 **69** DougieCostello 9 (Paul Midgley) *hld up in centre of gp: shortlived effrt over 2f out: wknd ins fnl f* **14/1**	61
30-2	9	1	**Red Pike (IRE)**[14] 36 8-9-2 **77** HarryRussell(7) 3 (Bryan Smart) *prom on far side of gp: rdn and edgd lft wl over 1f out: sn btn* **13/2**	66
366-	10	1/2	**Gnaad (IRE)**[27] 9662 5-9-8 **76** JoeyHaynes 2 (Alan Bailey) *hld up on far side of gp: struggling 2f out: sn btn* **8/1**	63

59.21s (-0.29) **Going Correction** +0.25s/f (Slow) **10 Ran SP% 115.2**
Speed ratings (Par 103): **104,102,101,100,99 99,98,96,95,94**
CSF £80.22 CT £490.17 TOTE £5.40: £2.00, £4.70, £1.60; EX 77.70 Trifecta £497.00.
Owner Antony Brittain **Bred** Yeomanstown Stud **Trained** Warthill, N Yorks

FOCUS
The early pace stood up in this open-looking sprint handicap. The runner-up helps set the level, with the third rated close to his recent form.

279 BETWAY H'CAP 5f (Tp)
7:25 (7:25) (Class 6) (0-65,66) 4-Y-O+

£3,105 (£924; £461; £400; £400; £400) **Stalls Centre**

Form				RPR
4-61	1		**Archimedes (IRE)**[9] 129 6-9-6 **62** 6ex (tp) RobertWinston 11 (David C Griffiths) *cl up on nr side of gp: led over 1f out: rdn and kpt on wl fnl f* **5/1**[2]	68
030-	2	nk	**Cuppacoco**[29] 9617 4-9-6 **62** JoeFanning 6 (Ann Duffield) *led in centre of gp: rdn: edgd lft and hdd over 1f out: rallied and ev ch fnl f: kpt on: hld nr fin* **10/1**	67
05-2	3	nk	**Steelriver (IRE)**[9] 129 9-9-4 **60** JasonHart 12 (Michael Herrington) *hld up on nr side of gp: hdwy over 1f out: chsng ldrs and drifted lft ins fnl f: kpt on: hld cl home* **6/1**[3]	64
525-	4	3/4	**Royal Mezyan (IRE)**[21] 9722 8-9-5 **61** RobertHavlin 9 (Henry Spiller) *hld up in centre of gp: rdn and hdwy over 1f out: kpt on fnl f: nt pce to chal* **10/1**	62
12-3	5	3/4	**Liamba**[14] 42 4-9-7 **63** CamHardie 4 (David O'Meara) *prom in centre of gp: rdn 2f out: kpt on ins fnl f* **12/1**	61
001-	6	1/2	**Astraea**[33] 9558 4-9-5 **61** NathanEvans 3 (Michael Easterby) *hld up in midfield on far side of gp: effrt and drvn along 2f out: edgd lft: no imp fnl f* **3/1**[1]	58
6/3-	7	1 1/4	**Blue Suede (IRE)**[33] 9558 5-8-1 **48** PaulaMuir(5) 10 (R K Watson, Ire) *prom towards nr side of gp: rdn along 2f out: edgd lft and wknd ins fnl f* **10/1**	40
4-65	8	1	**Windforpower (IRE)**[9] 129 9-8-8 **50** (v) BarryMcHugh 7 (Tracy Waggott) *hld up in centre of gp: effrt and rdn over 2f out: no imp fr over 1f out* **9/1**	39
50-0	9	3	**Grise Lightning (FR)**[14] 42 4-9-1 **57** TonyHamilton 8 (Richard Fahey) *prom in centre of gp tl rdn and wknd over 1f out* **25/1**	35
111-	10	1/2	**Social Butterfly (IRE)**[26] 9681 4-9-10 **66** (h) FrannyNorton 2 (Mick Channon) *hld up on far side of gp: drvn along over 2f out: nvr on terms (trainer could offer no explanation for the filly's performance)* **7/1**	42
00-0	11	1	**Spoken Words**[13] 63 10-7-10 **45** (p) RPWalsh(7) 5 (John David Riches) *hld up towards far side of gp: struggling over 2f out: sn btn* **200/1**	17

59.69s (0.19) **Going Correction** +0.25s/f (Slow) **11 Ran SP% 117.8**
Speed ratings (Par 101): **100,99,99,97,96 95,93,92,87,86 85**
CSF £54.42 CT £314.17 TOTE £4.50: £1.50, £4.10, £2.30; EX 63.70 Trifecta £401.40.
Owner Ladies And The Tramps **Bred** Paddy Twomey & Irish National Stud **Trained** Bawtry, S Yorks

FOCUS
This moderate sprint handicap was run at a solid pace and it developed far side.
T/Plt: £32.60 to a £1 stake. Pool: £55,692.04 - 1706.94 winning units T/Qpdt: £5.40 to a £1 stake. Pool: £10,005.19 - 1848.58 winning units **Richard Young**

[168]MEYDAN (L-H)
Thursday, January 17

OFFICIAL GOING: Dirt: fast; turf: good

280a AZIZI FARISHTA (H'CAP) (DIRT) 6f (D)
2:30 (2:30) (90-105,105) 3-Y-O+

£63,779 (£21,259; £10,629; £5,314; £3,188; £2,125)

			RPR
1		**I Kirk (SWE)**[186] 4986 5-9-6 **105** CarlosLopez 4 (Susanne Berneklint, Sweden) *sn led: kicked clr 2f out: r.o wl: easily* **13/2**	110+
2	3 1/4	**Honorable Treasure (USA)**[55] 4-9-4 **103** (b) PatCosgrave 7 (Kenneth McPeek, U.S.A) *mid-div: r.o wl fnl 1 1/2f: nrst fin* **6/1**[3]	98
3	2	**Laieth**[56] 9213 4-8-5 **90** SamHitchcott 2 (Saeed bin Suroor) *mid-div: r.o same pce fnl 2 1/2f* **13/2**	78
4	1	**Pop The Hood (USA)**[160] 7-8-9 **95** PatDobbs 3 (Doug Watson, UAE) *s.i.s: a mid-div* **15/8**[1]	79
5	1 3/4	**Wasim (IRE)**[42] 9438 4-8-13 **98** FabriceVeron 6 (Ismail Mohammed) *s.i.s: nvr nr to chal* **10/1**	77
6	3 3/4	**Almanaara (IRE)**[42] 9438 6-8-11 **97** (v) JimCrowley 1 (Doug Watson, UAE) *trckd ldr: ev ch 2 1/2f out: wknd fnl 1 1/2f* **5/2**[2]	63
7	5	**Ennobled Friend (USA)**[20] 9739 9-8-6 **92** (bt) ConnorBeasley 5 (A bin Harmash, UAE) *a in rr* **28/1**	42

1m 12.96s (1.36) **Going Correction** +0.40s/f (Slow) **7 Ran SP% 116.8**
Speed ratings: **106,101,99,97,95 90,83**
CSF: 45.89; TRICAST: 266.10.
Owner Hastgruppen I Lund AB **Bred** Loberods Hastklinik AB **Trained** Sweden

FOCUS
TRAKUS (metres travelled compared to winner): 2nd +10, 3rd 0, 4th +4, 5th +5, 6th +6, 7th +10. This looked a decent, interesting handicap but nothing could live with the winner, who took them through strong early fractions: 24.20 (400m from standing start), 22.97 (800m), 25.79 (line).

281a AZIZI RIVIERA (H'CAP) (TURF) 1m 6f 11y
3:05 (3:05) (95-105,105) 3-Y-O+

£82,677 (£27,559; £13,779; £6,889; £4,133; £2,755)

			RPR
1		**Ispolini**[14] 47 4-9-1 **105** (t) JamesDoyle 4 (Charlie Appleby) *settled in rr: smooth prog 2 1/2f out: led 2f out: r.o wl: comf* **1/1**[1]	110+
2	1 1/4	**Suspicious Mind (DEN)**[73] 6-8-9 **95** (t) ElioneChaves 3 (Andrew Kidney, Sweden) *mid-div: chsd ldrs and ev ch 3f out: r.o wl fnl 2f* **33/1**	96
3	2 1/2	**Red Galileo**[292] 1521 8-9-6 **105** ChristopheSoumillon 5 (Saeed bin Suroor) *sn led: hdd 2f out: r.o same pce* **11/4**[2]	104
4	1 1/4	**Appeared**[14] 47 7-9-0 **99** RichardMullen 2 (David Simcock) *s.i.s: nvr nr to chal but r.o fnl 2 1/2f* **12/1**	96
5	nk	**Rio Tigre (IRE)**[12] 98 8-8-9 **95** MickaelBarzalona 6 (S Jadhav, UAE) *nvr nr to chal but r.o fnl 3f* **12/1**	91
6	6 1/4	**Speedo Boy (FR)**[47] 8188 5-8-13 **98** JimCrowley 1 (Ian Williams) *nvr bttr than mid-div* **5/1**[3]	86
7	3	**Jukebox Jive (FR)**[125] 7242 5-8-10 **96** ChrisHayes 7 (Jamie Osborne) *trckd ldr tl wknd 2 1/2f out* **16/1**	79

2m 57.14s
WFA 4 from 5yo+ 4lb **7 Ran SP% 117.5**
CSF: 41.28.
Owner Godolphin **Bred** Newsells Park Stud **Trained** Newmarket, Suffolk

FOCUS
TRAKUS: 2nd -1, 3rd -6, 4th -11, 5th - 7, 6th -10, 7th 0. The rail on the turf course was out 12 metres. A steadily run race, with the winner getting the last section in 24.09 and nothing else making up significant ground.

282a AZIZI ALIYAH (H'CAP) (DIRT) 1m (D)
3:40 (3:40) (90-105,105) 3-Y-O+

£63,779 (£21,259; £10,629; £5,314; £3,188; £2,125)

			RPR
1		**Capezzano (USA)**[28] 9651 5-8-10 **96** (h) RoystonFfrench 9 (S Jadhav, UAE) *mid-div: smooth prog 3f out: rdn to ld fnl 110yds: comf* **20/1**	105
2	2 1/4	**Thegreatcollection (USA)**[28] 9651 5-8-11 **97** (b) SamHitchcott 1 (Doug Watson, UAE) *mid-div: r.o wl fnl 2f: nrst fin* **6/1**[3]	101
3	3/4	**Galvanize (USA)**[28] 9655 6-9-1 **100** PatDobbs 2 (Doug Watson, UAE) *sn led: kicked clr 2 1/2f out: hdd fnl 110yds but kpt on wl* **7/2**[2]	103
4	5	**Secret Ambition**[28] 9651 6-9-6 **105** (t) RichardMullen 4 (S Seemar, UAE) *s.i.s: nvr nr to chal but r.o fnl 2 1/2f* **11/4**[1]	97
5	3/4	**Plata O Plomo (USA)**[95] 5-8-13 **98** (vt) CarlosLopez 8 (Susanne Berneklint, Sweden) *nvr nr to chal but r.o fnl 2 1/2f* **14/1**	88
6	3 1/4	**Rodaini (USA)**[28] 9651 5-9-1 **100** (t) ConnorBeasley 7 (A bin Harmash, UAE) *trckd ldr tl wknd 3f out* **8/1**	82
7	hd	**Draco (USA)**[34] 9547 4-8-11 **97** ChrisHayes 10 (N Bachalard, UAE) *wl away: trckd ldr tl wknd 2 1/2f out* **13/2**	78
8	14	**Hornsby**[14] 51 6-8-5 **91** (p) MickaelBarzalona 3 (S Jadhav, UAE) *a in rr* **16/1**	40
9	1/2	**Irish Freedom (USA)**[194] 5-9-3 **102** (bt) TadhgO'Shea 11 (S Seemar, UAE) *a in rr* **16/1**	50
10	nk	**Desert Frost (IRE)**[87] 8472 5-8-5 **90** (p) AntonioFresu 5 (Saeed bin Suroor) *nvr bttr than mid-div* **14/1**	38
11	nse	**Fitzgerald (USA)**[371] 171 7-9-3 **102** (t) XavierZiani 6 (S Jadhav, UAE) *a in rr* **33/1**	50

1m 38.06s (0.56) **Going Correction** +0.40s/f (Slow) **11 Ran SP% 120.4**
Speed ratings: **113,110,110,105,104 101,100,86,86,86 85**
CSF: 138.90; TRICAST: 541.31.
Owner Sultan Ali **Bred** Darley **Trained** United Arab Emirates

FOCUS
TRAKUS: 2nd -12, 3rd -15, 4th -8, 5th +3, 6th -9, 7th -3, 8th -5, 9th +2, 10th -6, 11th -1. The pace was rapid early - quicker to halfway than North America in the previous week's Group 2 - before slowing but still quite a decent-looking final time for the grade: 24.33, 22.6, 24.76, with the winner to the line in 26.2.

283a CAPE VERDI SPONSORED BY AZIZI DEVELOPMENTS (GROUP 2) (F&M) (TURF) 1m
4:15 (4:15) 3-Y-O+

£118,110 (£39,370; £19,685; £9,842; £5,905; £3,937)

			RPR
1		**Poetic Charm**[90] 8403 4-9-0 103 JamesDoyle 2 (Charlie Appleby) *settled in rr: smooth prog 3f out: led 1f out: r.o wl: easily* **11/10**[1]	109+
2	4	**Asoof**[103] 7985 4-9-0 96 ChristopheSoumillon 3 (Saeed bin Suroor) *trckd ldr: led 2f out: hdd 1f out but kpt on wl* **10/3**[2]	100
3	1 3/4	**Furia Cruzada (CHI)**[14] 51 7-9-0 105 (t) AntonioFresu 1 (E Charpy, UAE) *mid-div: chsd ldrs and ev ch 2 1/2f out: r.o same pce fnl 2f* **6/1**	96
4	2 1/2	**Victory Wave (USA)**[14] 52 5-9-0 101 (h) KevinStott 5 (Saeed bin Suroor) *s.i.s: nvr nr to chal but r.o fnl 2f* **9/2**[3]	90
5	3 3/4	**Peri Lina (TUR)**[82] 4-9-0 101 (h) SelimKaya 7 (Hasan Boyraz, Turkey) *nvr bttr than mid-div* **16/1**	82

6 ½ **Monza (IRE)**[91] 4-9-0 95 ....(p) CarlosLopez 4 80
(Bent Olsen, Denmark) *sn led: hdd & wknd 2f out* **50/1**
7 hd **Mia Tesoro (IRE)**[111] 7733 6-9-0 97 ....(h) StevieDonohoe 6 80
(Charlie Fellowes) *a in rr* **16/1**

1m 36.46s (-1.04) **Going Correction** +0.40s/f (Good) **7** Ran SP% **116.9**
Speed ratings: **121,117,115,112,109 108,108**
CSF: 5.22.
Owner Godolphin **Bred** Godolphin **Trained** Newmarket, Suffolk

FOCUS
TRAKUS: 2nd -1, 3rd -1, 4th +4, 5th +3, 6th -2, 7th +3. They went a modest pace - 25.8, 23.93, 23.9 - before the winner quickened up in 22.59. The final time was good all considered, being 0.38sec quicker than a more evenly run handicap later on the card. The winner has been rated in line with the best view of her French 3yo form.

284a AZIZI STAR (H'CAP) (TURF) 1m 2f
4:50 (4:50) (95-105,104) 3-Y-O+

£63,779 (£21,259; £10,629; £5,314; £3,188; £2,125)

RPR

1 **First Nation**[117] 7532 5-9-3 101 .... BrettDoyle 8 110
(Charlie Appleby) *slowly away: settled in rr: smooth prog 2 1/2f out: rdn to ld 1f out: r.o wl: easily* **8/1**
2 4 ½ **Nordic Lights**[210] 4025 4-9-5 104 .... ColmO'Donoghue 1 105
(Charlie Appleby) *sn led: rdn 2 1/2f out: hdd 1f out but kpt on wl* **4/1**[3]
3 1 ¾ **Earnshaw (USA)**[14] 47 8-9-6 104 ....(t) MickaelBarzalona 3 101
(S Jadhav, UAE) *trckd ldr: ev ch 2f out: r.o same pce fnl 1 1/2f* **12/1**
4 1 ¼ **Jaaref (IRE)**[14] 47 6-9-5 103 .... JimCrowley 2 97
(A R Al Rayhi, UAE) *mid-div: chsd ldrs 2 1/2f out: r.o same pce fnl 2f* **16/1**
5 ½ **Mountain Hunter (USA)**[110] 7773 5-9-5 103 ...... ChristopheSoumillon 7 96
(Saeed bin Suroor) *mid-div: r.o same pce fnl 2 1/2f* **5/2**[1]
6 2 **Harlan Strong (ARG)**[91] 4-9-3 101 .... DaneO'Neill 4 90
(Kenneth McPeek, U.S.A) *trckd ldrs tl wknd fnl 3f* **25/1**
7 shd **Dark Red (IRE)**[170] 5582 7-9-3 101 .... ChrisHayes 9 90
(Ed Dunlop) *a mid-div* **16/1**
8 nk **Big Challenge (IRE)**[14] 47 5-8-10 95 .... KevinStott 6 82
(Saeed bin Suroor) *nvr bttr than mid-div* **8/1**
9 2 **Buhwarui Banseok (USA)**[39] 6-9-0 98 ....(b) BernardFayd'Herbe 10 82
(Bart Rice, Korea) *a in rr* **66/1**
10 nk **Celestial Spheres (IRE)**[256] 2450 5-8-13 97 ....(p) JamesDoyle 5 81
(Charlie Appleby) *nvr nr to chal* **3/1**[2]

2m 1.95s (-0.75) **Going Correction** +0.40s/f (Good)
WFA 4 from 5yo+ 1lb **10** Ran SP% **120.6**
Speed ratings: **119,115,114,113,112 111,110,110,109,108**
CSF: 41.50; TRICAST: 393.44.
Owner Godolphin **Bred** Darley **Trained** Newmarket, Suffolk

FOCUS
TRAKUS: 2nd +2, 3rd 0, 4th 0, 5th +4, 6th +4, 7th +8, 8th +4, 9th +5, 10th +4. The runner-up set a modest overall tempo - 26.77, 23.41, 24.15, 23.81 - before the winner picked up in 23.13.

285a AZIZI MINA (H'CAP) (TURF) 1m
5:25 (5:25) (95-107,107) 3-Y-O+

£82,677 (£27,559; £13,779; £6,889; £4,133; £2,755)

RPR

1 **Desert Fire (IRE)**[182] 5140 4-8-7 95 .... ChrisHayes 11 100
(Saeed bin Suroor) *trckd ldr: rdn 2 1/2f out: r.o wl to ld fnl 55yds* **5/1**[3]
2 nk **Race Day (IRE)**[14] 49 6-8-5 96 ow1 ....(p) RowanScott(3) 5 100
(Saeed bin Suroor) *trckd ldr: led 2f out: r.o wl but hdd fnl 55yds* **25/1**
3 1 **Bedouin's Story**[83] 8611 4-8-7 95 ....(h) TadhgO'Shea 7 98+
(Saeed bin Suroor) *slowly away: settled in rr: smooth prog 2f out: n.m.r 1f out: r.o wl* **7/1**
4 shd **Key Victory (IRE)**[14] 51 4-9-6 107 .... JamesDoyle 4 109
(Charlie Appleby) *settled in rr: rdn to chal ldrs 3f out: r.o fnl 2f* **9/4**[1]
5 2 ½ **Fly At Dawn (USA)**[371] 172 5-9-4 105 ....(t) ColmO'Donoghue 8 102
(Charlie Appleby) *mid-div: r.o same pce fnl 2 1/2f* **14/1**
6 ½ **Stratton Street (USA)**[392] 9359 5-8-7 95 .... RichardMullen 2 90
(S Seemar, UAE) *mid-div: chsd ldrs and ev ch 2f out: one pce fnl f* **66/1**
7 shd **Poet's Society**[117] 7525 5-8-10 98 .... ConnorBeasley 6 92
(A bin Harmash, UAE) *sn led: hdd 2f out: sn btn* **25/1**
8 2 **Settle For Bay (FR)**[14] 51 5-9-6 107 ....(t) WJLee 3 98
(David Marnane, Ire) *nvr bttr than mid-div* **4/1**[2]
9 2 ½ **Suyoof (AUS)**[14] 52 6-9-6 107 .... DaneO'Neill 1 92
(M F De Kock, South Africa) *nvr bttr than mid-div* **6/1**
10 2 ¾ **Muraaqeb (AUS)**[61] 4-9-4 105 ....(b) JimCrowley 10 84
(David A Hayes, Australia) *a in rr* **12/1**
11 7 ¼ **Fire Away (USA)**[214] 7-9-4 105 ....(b) OlivierDoleuze 9 67
(M F De Kock, South Africa) *s.i.s: a in rr* **14/1**

1m 36.84s (-0.66) **Going Correction** +0.40s/f (Good) **11** Ran SP% **124.4**
Speed ratings: **119,118,117,117,115 114,114,112,110,107 100**
CSF: 130.35; TRICAST: 910.93; PLACEPOT: 175.70 to a £1 stake. QUADPOT: 32.30 to a £1 stake.
Owner Godolphin **Bred** Godolphin **Trained** Newmarket, Suffolk

FOCUS
TRAKUS: 2nd -7, 3rd -5, 4th -4, 5th -3, 6th -7, 7th -4, 8th -2, 9th -4, 10th 0, 11th +1. This looked a strong handicap and a few of these shaped better than the result - this should produce some winners. The pace soon picked up to be fair: 26.03, 23.58, 23.52, with the winner home in 23.67.

250 KEMPTON (A.W) (R-H)
Friday, January 18

OFFICIAL GOING: Polytrack: standard to slow
Wind: Moderate tail wind Weather: Overcast

286 RACINGTV.COM H'CAP 5f (P)
4:10 (4:12) (Class 6) (0-60,62) 4-Y-O+

£3,105 (£924; £461; £400; £400; £400) **Stalls** Low

Form RPR

0-50 1 **Spirit Power**[4] 236 4-9-7 58 .... JasonHart 5 68+
(Eric Alston) *mde most: effrt to qckn tempo and wnt a l clr 2f out: kpt up to work under hands and heels ins fnl f: a doing enough* **5/2**[1]
366- 2 1 ¼ **Dandilion (IRE)**[124] 7327 6-9-4 58 ....(t w) JoshuaBryan(3) 6 63
(Alex Hales) *hld up: hdwy u.p to go 5th 2f out: rdn between rivals over 1f out: styd on wl to go 2nd wl ins fnl f: no ch w wnr* **15/2**
11-0 3 nk **Toni's A Star**[16] 28 7-9-2 58 .... PoppyBridgwater(5) 1 62
(Tony Carroll) *trckd ldng pair on inner: swtchd lft off rail and rdn to chse wnr in 2nd over 1f out: drvn and kpt on one pce fnl f: lost 2nd cl home* **7/2**[3]
60-3 4 3 ¼ **Knockout Blow**[7] 177 4-9-11 62 .... CharlieBennett 8 54
(Jim Boyle) *trckd wnr: rdn and outpcd over 1f out: kpt on one pce fnl f* **3/1**[2]
03-0 5 2 ½ **Celerity (IRE)**[11] 118 5-8-1 45 ....(v) ElishaWhittington(7) 9 28
(Lisa Williamson) *hld up in rr of midfield: rdn and outpcd over 2f out: nvr cl enough to get involved* **50/1**
006- 6 hd **Ask The Guru**[18] 9777 9-9-0 51 ....(v) KierenFox 4 34
(Michael Attwater) *chsd wnr and upsides at times: rdn and lost pl over 1f out: wknd fnl f* **16/1**
050- 7 ¾ **Precious Plum**[58] 9177 5-9-3 61 ....(p) ScottMcCullagh(7) 7 41
(Charlie Wallis) *hld up: a in rr* **16/1**
0-03 8 2 ¾ **Sir Walter (IRE)**[8] 167 4-8-1 45 ....(p) RobertDodsworth(7) 3 15+
(Eric Alston) *rrd as stalls opened and racd in last: nvr on terms (jockey said gelding jumped awkwardly from the stalls)* **8/1**

59.51s (-0.99) **Going Correction** -0.125s/f (Stan) **8** Ran SP% **112.4**
Speed ratings (Par 101): **102,100,99,94,90 90,88,84**
CSF £21.13 CT £64.66 TOTE £3.10: £1.20, £1.90, £1.30; EX 21.70 Trifecta £79.10.
Owner The Selebians **Bred** Lordship Stud **Trained** Longton, Lancs

FOCUS
Not a bad race for the grade. It's been rated around the third near her recent best.

287 100% PROFIT BOOST AT 32REDSPORT.COM H'CAP 5f (P)
4:45 (4:45) (Class 5) (0-75,73) 3-Y-O

£3,752 (£1,116; £557; £400; £400; £400) **Stalls** Low

Form RPR

206- 1 **Kingi Compton**[32] 9589 3-8-8 60 ....(b) EdwardGreatrex 1 65
(Archie Watson) *broke wl and mde all: gng strly and 3 l clr over 1f out: drvn to maintain advantage ins fnl f and a in command* **9/2**[2]
12-1 2 2 **Rock Bottom**[7] 182 3-9-0 73 6ex .... GeorgeRooke(7) 2 71
(Richard Hughes) *dwlt sltly and trckd wnr on rail: rdn to chse wnr and hung lft handed over 1f out: kpt on fnl f but no match for wnr* **10/11**[1]
44-2 3 nk **Hanakotoba (USA)**[6] 215 3-8-10 62 ....(t) RichardKingscote 6 59
(Stuart Williams) *settled wl in 4th: pushed along to chse wnr 2f out: sn rdn and styd on one pce fnl f* **11/2**[3]
05-0 4 1 ½ **Velvet Vixen (IRE)**[16] 26 3-7-9 54 oh9 .... RPWalsh(7) 3 45
(Jo Hughes, France) *dwlt and racd in rr: pushed along arnd outer of field 2f out: sn rdn and unable qck over 1f out: kpt on* **40/1**
340- 5 4 ½ **Arcadian Rocks (IRE)**[244] 2842 3-9-0 73 .... ScottMcCullagh(7) 5 48
(Mick Channon) *hld up: pushed along and outpcd 1/2-way: rdn and detached appr fnl f: plugged on* **16/1**
05-1 6 ½ **Swiss Chime**[17] 1 3-8-8 60 .... KieranO'Neill 4 33
(Dean Ivory) *chsd wnr: rdn and lost pl over 1f out: wknd fnl f (jockey said filly hung both ways)* **6/1**

59.44s (-1.06) **Going Correction** -0.125s/f (Stan) **6** Ran SP% **108.6**
Speed ratings (Par 97): **103,99,99,96,89 88**
CSF £8.43 TOTE £5.10: £2.10, £1.20; EX 9.70 Trifecta £26.00.
Owner Wood Family & Partner **Bred** Mrs J A Prescott **Trained** Upper Lambourn, W Berks

FOCUS
A fair handicap. The winner has been rated back to his early form.

288 JOIN RACING TV NOW H'CAP 1m 1f 219y(P)
5:15 (5:20) (Class 6) (0-55,55) 4-Y-O+

£3,105 (£924; £461; £400; £400; £400) **Stalls** Low

Form RPR

36-4 1 **Mullarkey**[15] 39 5-9-4 52 ....(t[1]) KierenFox 14 58
(John Best) *mde all: pushed along to qckn tempo over 2f out: rdn and 3 l clr 1f out: rdn out fnl f and a doing enough* **8/1**[3]
05-0 2 1 ¼ **Tesorina (IRE)**[6] 207 4-9-4 53 ....(v[1]) AdamKirby 8 58
(William Knight) *trckd wnr: pushed along to cl in 4th 3f out: rdn and wnt 2nd 2f out: stl 3 l down on wnr appr fnl f: kpt on and clsd gap but nvr getting to wnr ins fnl f* **8/1**[3]
550- 3 nse **Monsieur Fox**[92] 8338 4-9-6 55 .... RobertHavlin 10 60
(Lydia Richards) *hld up in rr: hdwy u.p and wd arnd home bnd 2f out: sn rdn and styd on wl ins fnl f to snatch 3rd cl home* **28/1**
604- 4 nse **Don't Cry About It (IRE)**[21] 9728 4-9-6 55 ....(bt) CharlesBishop 12 59
(Ali Stronge) *hld up in last: pushed along and clsd on outer 2f out: rdn and styd on wl ins fnl f: nrst fin* **20/1**
03-5 5 3 **Born To Reason (IRE)**[8] 155 5-9-0 48 ....(b) LiamJones 9 46
(Kevin Frost) *racd in midfield on outer: rdn along 2f out: sn drvn and kpt on one pce fnl f* **16/1**
4-32 6 1 ¼ **Sharp Operator**[6] 207 6-9-7 55 ....(h) RichardKingscote 1 54+
(Charlie Wallis) *racd keenly on the inner in midfield: gng wl in 8th 2f out: briefly short of room over 1f out: fnlly in clr ins fnl f but all ch gone: styd on (jockey said gelding was denied a clear run)* **11/10**[1]
560- 7 2 **Amy Kane**[74] 8881 5-9-1 49 .... HollieDoyle 6 41
(Jimmy Fox) *hld up: rdn and hung lft handed u.p 2f out: drvn and plugged on fnl f* **33/1**
00-5 8 ¾ **Runaiocht (IRE)**[13] 80 9-9-1 49 ....(b) RobertWinston 3 39
(Brian Forsey) *wnt to post early: racd in midfield: pushed along to cl and briefly short of room off home bnd 2f out: rdn to cl and wnt 3rd over 1f out: wknd fnl f* **12/1**
00-0 9 1 ¼ **Loving Your Work**[14] 58 8-9-1 52 .... FinleyMarsh(3) 4 40
(Ken Cunningham-Brown) *racd in midfield on inner: rdn and outpcd 2f out: briefly short of room and hmpd by rival wl over 1f out: swtchd rt to rail and plugged on fnl f* **33/1**
00-0 10 2 **Harbour Force (FR)**[14] 59 5-9-3 51 ....(b) ShaneKelly 13 35
(Neil Mulholland) *s.i.s and rdn to chse wnr early: drvn and little rspnse 2f out: wknd fr over 1f out* **14/1**
060- 11 1 ¾ **Dawn Commando**[221] 3688 4-9-4 53 ....(b[1]) KieranO'Neill 7 35
(Daniel Kubler) *s.i.s and qckly circled field to trck wnr: rdn and outpcd over 2f out: lost pl and wknd fnl f* **7/1**[2]
50-0 12 1 **Lifeboat (IRE)**[11] 120 4-9-1 53 ....(h[1]) JoshuaBryan(3) 2 33
(Kevin Frost) *dwlt and racd in rr: a bhd (jockey said gelding found little when asked for an effort)* **28/1**

2m 7.29s (-0.71) **Going Correction** -0.125s/f (Stan)
WFA 4 from 5yo+ 1lb **12** Ran SP% **120.1**
Speed ratings (Par 101): **97,96,95,95,93 92,90,90,89,87 86,85**
CSF £66.73 CT £1709.57 TOTE £8.50: £2.50, £2.40, £8.30; EX 38.60 Trifecta £552.70.
Owner Thomson & Partners **Bred** Best Breeding **Trained** Oad Street, Kent

■ Estibdaad and True Calling were withdrawn Prices at time of withdrawal 66-1 and 50-1 respectively. Rule 4 does not apply.

FOCUS
A modest handicap. The third and fourth help pin the level.

289 32RED CASINO NOVICE STKS 7f (P)
5:45 (5:51) (Class 5) 3-Y-O £3,881 (£1,155; £577; £288) Stalls Low

Form RPR

1-6 **1** **Rectory Road**[13] 90 3-9-7 0 DavidProbert 11 87+
(Andrew Balding) *racd in midfield: swtchd lft arnd rivals and clsd gng wl over 2f out: pushed along to ld over 1f out: rdn out ins fnl f: readily* **6/1**

44-2 **2** 2 **Shanghai Grace**[16] 20 3-9-2 75 CallumShepherd 4 76
(Charles Hills) *racd in midfield: hdwy u.p to chse ldr over 2f out: sn rdn and unable to match the pce of wnr over 1f out: kpt on wl for clr 2nd* **7/1**

225- **3** 2 ½ **Fume (IRE)**[37] 9498 3-9-2 74 RichardKingscote 5 69
(Ralph Beckett) *led: rdn along and hung lft over 2f out: sn strly pressed and hdd by wnr over 1f out: one pce fnl f* **4/1[3]**

4 **4** ¾ **Kingdom Of Dubai (FR)**[9] 133 3-9-2 0 LukeMorris 1 67
(Roger Varian) *settled wl in tch in 4th: rdn along over 2f out: drvn and unable qck over 1f out: one pce fnl f (trainer could offer no explanation for the colt's performance)* **7/2[2]**

2-0 **5** shd **Fiction Writer (USA)**[16] 20 3-9-2 0 PJMcDonald 6 67
(Mark Johnston) *chsd ldr: rdn and outpcd 2f out: drvn and kpt on one pce fnl f* **20/1**

0- **6** 3 ¾ **Nefyn Beach (IRE)**[30] 9603 3-8-11 0 FrannyNorton 2 52
(Jo Hughes, France) *dwlt and racd in rr: pushed along to cl over 2f out: sn rdn and kpt on one pce fr over 1f out: n.d* **50/1**

01- **7** 5 **Engrossed (IRE)**[39] 9485 3-9-4 0 RobHornby 8 45
(Martyn Meade) *hld up in rr: pushed along over 2f out: rdn and mde sme late hdwy ins fnl f* **14/1**

8 ½ **Cockney Hill** 3-9-2 0 FranBerry 7 42
(Joseph Tuite) *dwlt and racd in rr: minor hdwy u.p over 2f out: rdn and little imp over 1f out: n.d* **100/1**

00- **9** 1 **Dark Poet**[48] 9355 3-9-2 0 AdamKirby 10 39
(Clive Cox) *hld up in rr: drvn along over 2f out: nvr on terms* **33/1**

0 **10** 1 ¼ **Frea**[13] 78 3-8-11 0 NicolaCurrie 12 31
(Harry Dunlop) *trckd ldr: rdn along and unable qck 2f out: lost pl and wknd ins fnl f* **150/1**

256- **11** 2 ½ **Alatia (IRE)**[159] 6075 3-9-2 89 RobertWinston 13 29
(Jo Hughes, France) *racd in rr of midfield: drvn over 2f out: nvr able to get on terms* **20/1**

12 8 **Passive (IRE)** 3-9-2 0 LiamKeniry 9 7
(David Elsworth) *dwlt and racd in rr: a bhd* **50/1**

0- **13** 8 **With Pride**[58] 9183 3-9-2 0 ShaneKelly 14
(Neil Mulholland) *hld up: a in rr: eased fnl f* **150/1**

6- **14** 2 ¾ **Crown Of Flowers**[22] 9726 3-8-11 0 RyanMoore 3
(Richard Hannon) *racd in tch in midfield: bmpd by rival and sltly short of room 3f out: c wd off home bnd: rdr sn looking down and heavily eased fr over 1f out (jockey said filly hung left-handed)* **11/4[1]**

1m 25.14s (-0.86) **Going Correction** -0.125s/f (Stan) **14 Ran SP% 121.0**
Speed ratings (Par 97): **99,96,93,93,92 88,82,82,81,79 76,67,58,55**
CSF £45.22 TOTE £7.40: £2.00, £2.10, £1.70; EX 55.30 Trifecta £181.80.
Owner Park House Partnership **Bred** Addington Bloodstock Ltd **Trained** Kingsclere, Hants

FOCUS
An open event run at a sound pace. The third has been rated to his C&D handicap latest, and the second back to his debut run.

290 32RED ON THE APP STORE H'CAP 1m (P)
6:15 (6:19) (Class 5) (0-75,75) 3-Y-O £3,752 (£1,116; £557; £400) Stalls Low

Form RPR

25-2 **1** **Spirit Warning**[9] 134 3-9-4 75 JoshuaBryan(3) 4 82
(Andrew Balding) *trckd ldr in 3rd: smooth prog to press ldr 2f out: rdn and led wl over 1f out: rdn out ins fnl f and a doing enough* **11/4[2]**

430- **2** 1 **My Dear Friend**[221] 3685 3-9-5 73 RichardKingscote 1 77
(Ralph Beckett) *led and racd a little keenly: pushed along to qckn tempo over 2f out: rdn and hdd by wnr wl over 1f out: rallied wl u.p to chal wnr again ins fnl f but a hld* **10/3[3]**

040- **3** 3 ¾ **Spirit Kingdom (USA)**[56] 9227 3-8-12 66 FrannyNorton 3 61
(Mark Johnston) *racd in last: rdn along to go 3rd over 1f out: kpt on one pce ins fnl f: no match for front pair* **25/1**

03-3 **4** 2 ¾ **Kentucky Kingdom (IRE)**[16] 20 3-9-6 74 RyanMoore 2 63
(William Haggas) *trckd ldr: rdn and fnd little 2f out: dropped to last over 1f out: wknd fnl f* **10/11[1]**

1m 39.39s (-0.41) **Going Correction** -0.125s/f (Stan) **4 Ran SP% 106.0**
Speed ratings (Par 97): **97,96,92,89**
CSF £11.08 TOTE £3.50; EX 11.20 Trifecta £33.60.
Owner Kingsclere Racing Club **Bred** Kingsclere Stud **Trained** Kingsclere, Hants

FOCUS
A fair handicap despite the small field.

291 32RED H'CAP 1m 7f 218y(P)
6:45 (6:49) (Class 4) (0-85,82) 4-Y-O+
£6,469 (£1,925; £962; £481; £400; £400) Stalls Low

Form RPR

001- **1** **Dalileo (IRE)**[32] 9586 4-9-5 80 FrannyNorton 1 88
(Mark Johnston) *racd in midfield: stdy hdwy to chse ldr 2f out: rdn to ld 1f out: kpt on wl u.str.p ins fnl f: a doing enough* **12/1**

260- **2** 1 ¼ **Navajo Star (IRE)**[107] 7902 5-9-0 70 KieranO'Neill 4 76
(Robyn Brisland) *settled wl in 4th: clsd gng wl on outer over 2f out: pushed into ld 2f out: sn drvn and hdd by wnr 1f out: kpt on wl fnl f but no match for wnr* **25/1**

040- **3** nk **Champagne Champ**[37] 9503 7-9-9 79 RichardKingscote 2 84
(Rod Millman) *trckd ldr in 3rd: rdn and outpcd as tempo increased 2f out: kpt on wl ins fnl f but no match for wnr* **10/1**

106- **4** ½ **Diocletian (IRE)**[29] 9639 4-9-7 82 RobHornby 3 86
(Andrew Balding) *dwlt and racd in rr: effrt to cl on ldrs over 2f out: rdn and ev ch over 1f out: kpt on fnl f* **15/8[2]**

12-1 **5** 12 **Given Choice (IRE)**[11] 119 4-9-1 81 6ex CameronNoble(5) 5 71
(Simon Crisford) *led: rdn along and hdd 2f out: wknd ins fnl f (trainer's rep said filly did not stay the trip of 2m)* **7/4[1]**

202- **6** 21 **Final Choice**[14] 9215 6-9-3 73 (vt) LukeMorris 6 38
(Adam West) *hld up: pushed along over 3f out: rdn along and racd wd off home bnd: sn detached and eased fnl f (jockey said gelding was slowly away)* **33/1**

034- **7** 25 **Sunblazer (IRE)**[37] 9503 9-9-9 79 (t) AdamKirby 7 14
(Kim Bailey) *trckd ldr: rdn along and little rspnse 3f out: sn drvn and wknd 2f out: eased fnl f (trainer's rep said gelding had a breathing problem)* **13/2[3]**

3m 27.49s (-2.61) **Going Correction** -0.125s/f (Stan)
WFA 4 from 5yo+ 5lb **7 Ran SP% 108.1**
Speed ratings (Par 105): **101,100,100,99,93 83,70**
CSF £212.91 TOTE £8.90: £4.20, £7.10; EX 189.60 Trifecta £2361.00.
Owner Kingsley Park Owners Club **Bred** Barronstown Stud **Trained** Middleham Moor, N Yorks

FOCUS
They went a steady pace for this fair handicap. The second has been rated to form.

292 32RED.COM H'CAP 1m 2f 219y(P)
7:15 (7:17) (Class 5) (0-75,77) 4-Y-O+
£3,752 (£1,116; £557; £400; £400; £400) Stalls Low

Form RPR

00-5 **1** **Central City (IRE)**[16] 29 4-9-1 71 (p) KieranO'Neill 8 78
(Ian Williams) *hld up in rr and t.k.h at times: effrt to cl on ldrs over 2f out: swtchd wdst of all and rdn over 1f out: styd on strly ins fnl f to ld fnl strides (jockey said gelding hung right-handed in the closing stages)* **14/1**

010- **2** nk **Dono Di Dio**[37] 9505 4-8-10 73 ScottMcCullagh(7) 4 79
(Michael Madgwick) *racd in midfield: pushed along to cl on ldrs 2f out: waited for gap and c w str run between rivals to ld 100yds out: hdd by wnr fnl strides* **12/1**

204- **3** ¾ **Berrahri (IRE)**[146] 6515 8-9-4 72 KierenFox 10 77
(John Best) *led: drvn along and hdd jst over 1f out: kpt on wl for press ins fnl f but no match for wnr* **25/1**

1-1 **4** ¾ **Nylon Speed (IRE)**[13] 88 5-9-7 75 (t) MartinHarley 12 79
(Alan King) *trckd ldr: rdn along and ev ch over 1f out: kpt on one pce fnl f: no ex* **2/1[1]**

00-6 **5** shd **Bobby Biscuit (USA)**[14] 54 4-9-1 71 JFEgan 11 75
(Simon Dow) *restrained in last: hdwy u.p into midfield over 2f out: swtchd rt to far rail 1f out: styd on wl fnl f: nt rch ldrs* **12/1**

146- **6** ½ **Surrey Blaze (IRE)**[149] 6407 4-9-6 76 FranBerry 1 79
(Joseph Tuite) *racd in midfield: gd prog to chse ldr 2f out: sn rdn and led briefly 1f out: hdd & wknd 100yds out* **12/1**

613- **6** dht **Long Call**[60] 7400 6-8-9 68 PoppyBridgwater(5) 2 74+
(Tony Carroll) *hld up: rdn along and making gd hdwy whn briefly short of room over 1f out: ct on heels and nowhere to go ins fnl f: fin on bridle (jockey said regarding running and riding that the gelding was hanging badly right-handed, which she reported to scales on her return, and had to continually correct her mount in order to ensure continued in a straight line and did not interfere with the* **9/1[3]**

403- **8** 1 **New Agenda**[85] 8102 7-9-9 77 AdamKirby 3 78
(Paul Webber) *racd in midfield: rdn to chse ldr 2f out: sn drvn and ev ch 1f out: no ex fnl f* **3/1[2]**

653- **9** 5 **Presence Process**[30] 9609 5-8-12 66 CharlieBennett 7 59
(Pat Phelan) *trckd ldr: rdn along and outpcd 2f out: wknd fnl f* **25/1**

644/ **10** 2 ½ **Sir George Somers (USA)**[443] 2557 6-9-4 72 LiamKeniry 5 60
(Nigel Twiston-Davies) *hld up: rdn and outpcd 3f out: nvr on terms* **40/1**

642- **11** 6 **Tangramm**[139] 6819 7-9-7 75 RobertWinston 9 53
(Dean Ivory) *settled wl in 4th early: rdn and unable qck 2f out: wknd whn btn ins fnl f* **16/1**

320- **12** 2 ½ **Vampish**[173] 5529 4-9-3 73 DavidProbert 6 47
(Philip McBride) *hld up: a in rr* **25/1**

2m 21.19s (0.19) **Going Correction** -0.125s/f (Stan)
WFA 4 from 5yo+ 2lb **12 Ran SP% 117.9**
Speed ratings (Par 103): **97,96,96,95,95 95,95,94,90,89 84,82**
CSF £162.86 CT £4114.82 TOTE £18.90: £4.60, £5.00, £4.40; EX 181.30 Trifecta £2879.50.
Owner Spencer Coomes **Bred** Mattock Stud **Trained** Portway, Worcs

FOCUS
A fair handicap which saw a bunch finish. The winner has been rated to his Doncaster win, the second similar to her course win in November, and the third to last summer's form.

293 INTRODUCING RACING TV H'CAP 6f (P)
7:45 (7:49) (Class 7) (0-50,53) 4-Y-O+ £2,587 (£770; £384; £192) Stalls Low

Form RPR

4-21 **1** **Foreign Legion (IRE)**[8] 155 4-9-10 53 6ex (p) NickyMackay 2 59
(Luke McJannet) *racd in midfield: hdwy u.p over 2f out: rdn and styd on wl to ld ins fnl f: drvn out* **7/4[1]**

30-3 **2** nk **Monarch Maid**[3] 244 8-9-2 45 KieranO'Neill 9 50
(Peter Hiatt) *led: rdn and strly pressed by wnr over 1f out: hdd ins fnl f but kpt on wl for press* **11/1**

006- **3** 2 ¾ **Elliot The Dragon (IRE)**[22] 9720 4-9-2 45 CallumShepherd 1 42
(Derek Shaw) *hld up: short of room and racd keenly as a result leaving bk st: pushed along over 2f out: rdn and kpt on one pce ins fnl f (jockey said gelding ran too free)* **10/1**

06-0 **4** ½ **Sugar Plum Fairy**[14] 60 4-9-7 50 NicolaCurrie 3 45+
(Tony Carroll) *hld up in rr: pushed along 1/2-way: swtchd rt to far rail and rdn over 2f out: briefly short of room and plld off rail over 1f out: rdn and styd on wl fnl f (jockey said filly was denied a clear run)* **7/1[3]**

0-62 **5** ½ **Le Manege Enchante (IRE)**[8] 161 6-9-4 47 (v) RaulDaSilva 4 41
(Derek Shaw) *dwlt and racd in rr: pushed along over 2f out: rdn and kpt on fnl f: nvr able to chal* **3/1[2]**

603- **6** ½ **Nuzha**[29] 9641 5-9-2 45 (p) ShaneKelly 6 37
(Tony Newcombe) *racd in midfield: rdn and ev ch wl over 1f out: one pce fnl f* **16/1**

423- **7** ½ **Isabella Ruby**[22] 9720 4-8-13 47 (h) KevinLundie(5) 12 38
(Lisa Williamson) *trckd ldr: rdn and outpcd over 2f out: sn drvn and no imp: wknd fnl f* **20/1**

000- **8** ½ **Dolydaydream**[88] 8482 4-8-13 45 (p) PaddyBradley(3) 5 34
(Pat Phelan) *trckd ldr early: rdn and ev ch in 2nd over 1f out: wknd ins fnl f* **25/1**

46-4 **9** 3 **Compton Prince**[3] 244 10-9-2 45 (b) FrannyNorton 11 25
(Milton Bradley) *hld up in rr of midfield: c wdst of all off home bnd: stl gng wl 2f out: sn rdn and fnd little: no ex fnl f* **11/1**

500- **10** 10 **Cape Hill Cotter (FR)**[72] 8926 4-9-6 49 (p[1]) AdamKirby 10
(Ann Duffield) *settled in 4th: rdn along and no imp 2f out: sn eased whn btn fnl f* **50/1**

000- **R** **Free Talkin**[18] 9776 4-9-2 45 (p) KierenFox 7
(Michael Attwater) *ref to r* **100/1**

1m 12.33s (-0.77) **Going Correction** -0.125s/f (Stan) **11 Ran SP% 117.1**
Speed ratings (Par 97): **100,99,95,95,94 93,93,92,88,75**
CSF £21.86 CT £156.83 TOTE £2.60: £1.30, £2.90, £2.90; EX 18.50 Trifecta £148.90.
Owner Ivor Collier **Bred** Norelands Bloodstock **Trained** Newmarket, Suffolk

FOCUS
A modest handicap.
T/Plt: £714.70 to a £1 stake. Pool: £77,099.59 - 78.75 winning units T/Qpdt: £133.70 to a £1 stake. Pool: £9,964.73 - 55.12 winning units **Mark Grantham**

[258] LINGFIELD (L-H)
Friday, January 18

OFFICIAL GOING: Polytrack: standard
Wind: Fresh, behind Weather: Fine

294 SUN RACING H'CAP — 1m 1y(P)
12:55 (12:55) (Class 5) (0-75,77) 4-Y-O+
£3,752 (£1,116; £557; £300; £300; £300) **Stalls High**

Form — RPR

060- **1** **Shyron**[18] [9772] 8-9-6 **74**.......... RobertWinston 7 — 81
(Lee Carter) *awkward s: t.k.h: hld up in last pair: prog jst over 2f out: urged along and clsd qckly fnl f to ld last 100yds: sn clr* **12/1**

50-2 **2** 1 ¼ **Graceful James (IRE)**[13] [86] 6-9-7 **75**.......... KieranO'Neill 6 — 79
(Jimmy Fox) *led: rdn and hrd pressed fr 2f out: kpt on but hdd and outpcd last 100yds* **2/1**[1]

24-5 **3** ¾ **Ambient (IRE)**[15] [34] 4-9-7 **75**..........(b[1]) AdamKirby 5 — 77
(Jane Chapple-Hyam) *sn chsd ldr: rdn to chal and upsides jst over 2f out to over 1f out: nt qckn and lost 2nd ins fnl f* **7/2**[2]

00-4 **4** ¾ **High Acclaim (USA)**[16] [29] 5-9-2 **77**.......... SeamusCronin[(7)] 3 — 78
(Roger Teal) *in tch: pushed along 3f out: chsd ldng pair on inner over 1f out to fnl f: one pce* **4/1**[3]

60-3 **5** 2 ½ **The Warrior (IRE)**[14] [54] 7-9-4 **75**.......... PaddyBradley[(3)] 2 — 70
(Lee Carter) *hld up and sn in last: pushed along over 1f out: passed two rivals fnl f but nvr remotely involved* **10/1**

546- **6** 1 **Chikoko Trail**[20] [6884] 4-8-12 **66**.......... ShaneKelly 4 — 59
(Gary Moore) *chsd ldng pair: rdn over 2f out: lost 3rd and wknd over 1f out* **25/1**

32-5 **7** 2 ¾ **Thechildren'strust (IRE)**[17] [5] 4-9-9 **77**.......... HectorCrouch 1 — 63
(Gary Moore) *plld hrd: hld up: hmpd after 1f: drvn 3f out: fnd nil and btn whn wd bnd 2f out* **7/2**[2]

1m 36.08s (-2.12) **Going Correction** -0.125s/f (Stan) **7 Ran SP% 118.4**
Speed ratings (Par 103): **105,103,103,102,99 98,96**
CSF £38.28 TOTE £18.80: £5.40, £1.50; EX 32.70 Trifecta £371.70.
Owner John Joseph Smith **Bred** F Butler **Trained** Epsom, Surrey
■ Stewards' Enquiry : Kieran O'Neill two-day ban: interference & careless riding (Feb 1-2)

FOCUS
A good performance from the winner, who bounced back to form on his first start for Lee Carter. It's been rated around the second.

295 SUNRACING.CO.UK H'CAP — 1m 1y(P)
1:25 (1:25) (Class 6) (0-62,68) 4-Y-O+
£3,105 (£924; £461; £300; £300; £300) **Stalls High**

Form — RPR

002- **1** **Weloof (FR)**[45] [9386] 5-9-7 **62**.......... AdamKirby 11 — 70
(Paul D'Arcy) *hld up towards rr: prog over 2f out: rdn and clsd to ld 1f out: drvn out* **13/8**[1]

61-1 **2** ½ **Mr Mac**[7] [175] 5-9-13 **68** 6ex.......... CharlesBishop 10 — 75
(Peter Hedger) *hld up in last trio: rdn and prog wl over 1f out: fin strly fnl f to take 2nd last stride: too late* **7/4**[2]

256- **3** shd **Barrsbrook**[37] [9512] 5-9-7 **62**..........(v) HectorCrouch 5 — 69
(Gary Moore) *trckd ldrs: shkn up over 2f out: prog to ld wl over 1f out: hdd 1f out: styd on but lost 2nd last stride* **12/1**

00P- **4** 4 **Spiritual Star (IRE)**[239] [3011] 10-9-9 **64**..........(t) JFEgan 4 — 61
(Paul George) *s.i.s: hld up in rr: nt clr run jst over 2f out: sme prog over 1f out: kpt on but no ch w ldrs* **20/1**

5-6 **5** 2 **Kodi Koh (IRE)**[11] [120] 4-8-13 **54**..........(v[1]) NicolaCurrie 7 — 47
(David Evans) *pressed ldr: led over 2f out: wd bnd sn after and hdd wl over 1f out: fdd (jockey said filly hung right-handed rounding the bend)* **20/1**

60-0 **6** nk **King Of Rooks**[15] [33] 6-9-7 **62**.......... RobertHavlin 1 — 54
(Henry Spiller) *hld up in midfield: gng wl enough over 2f out: prog to chse ldrs over 1f out: wknd tamely fnl f (vet reported the gelding had lost its left hind shoe)* **25/1**

500- **7** 2 **Scrutiny**[72] [8936] 8-9-6 **61**..........(p) JosephineGordon 9 — 49
(Kevin Ryan) *sn in last and pushed along early: effrt over 2f out: trying to make prog but no ch whn nt clr run 1f out* **25/1**

0-03 **8** 1 **Highway One (USA)**[9] [145] 5-9-5 **60**..........(p) LiamKeniry 2 — 45
(George Baker) *led to over 2f out: wknd over 1f out* **17/2**[3]

560- **9** 10 **Ubla (IRE)**[49] [9322] 6-8-13 **61**..........(p) TobyEley[(7)] 6 — 23+
(Gay Kelleway) *pressed ldng pair on outer to over 2f out: sddle slipped and sn wknd (jockey said his saddle slipped)* **12/1**

52-6 **10** 32 **Ventriloquist**[9] [138] 7-9-7 **62**.......... LukeMorris 3
(Simon Dow) *awkward s: sn chsd ldrs: drvn 3f out: wknd rapidly 2f out: t.o (vet reported the gelding had bled from the nose)* **10/1**

4/4- **11** 1 ½ **King Torus (IRE)**[149] [6435] 11-9-4 **59**..........(vt) RobertWinston 8
(Lee Carter) *hld up in midfield and racd wd: lost pl 3f out: eased 2f out and t.o* **33/1**

1m 36.77s (-1.43) **Going Correction** -0.125s/f (Stan) **11 Ran SP% 129.6**
Speed ratings (Par 101): **102,101,101,97,95 95,93,92,82,50 48**
CSF £4.87 CT £28.60 TOTE £2.70: £1.20, £2.10, £3.00; EX 5.80 Trifecta £46.90.
Owner Tramore Tree **Bred** Dream With Me Stable Inc **Trained** Newmarket, Suffolk

FOCUS
The first three finished clear in this modest heat.

296 LADBROKES HOME OF THE ODDS BOOST H'CAP — 6f 1y(P)
2:00 (2:00) (Class 6) (0-55,56) 3-Y-O
£3,105 (£924; £461; £300; £300; £300) **Stalls Low**

Form — RPR

000- **1** **Lincoln Spirit**[51] [9284] 3-9-7 **53**.......... AdamKirby 9 — 56
(David O'Meara) *pressed ldr over 4f out: sltly wd bnd 2f out and lost 2nd over 1f out: styd on terms w ldrs: drvn and r.o fnl f to ld last strides* **8/1**

000- **2** hd **Not So Shy**[52] [9276] 3-9-10 **56**.......... NicolaCurrie 1 — 59
(David Evans) *cl up on inner: chal over 1f out: w ldr fnl f: jst outpcd last strides* **12/1**

030- **3** shd **Yfenni (IRE)**[154] [6261] 3-8-13 **45**.......... RobertWinston 4 — 48
(Milton Bradley) *led: rdn and jnd over 1f out: kpt on wl but jst outpcd nr fin* **33/1**

00-2 **4** ½ **Delagate The Lady**[9] [137] 3-9-2 **48**.......... KierenFox 5 — 50
(Michael Attwater) *hld up in last trio: shkn up over 2f out: prog on outer jst over 1f out: r.o to take 4th last strides: too late* **8/1**

44-2 **5** shd **Ever Rock (IRE)**[14] [60] 3-8-11 **50**.......... AaronMackay[(7)] 6 — 51
(J S Moore) *chsd ldrs: rdn over 2f out: styd on fnl f but nvr able to chal* **9/2**[3]

000- **6** nk **Tintern Spirit (IRE)**[31] [9598] 3-8-13 **45**.......... KieranO'Neill 7 — 45
(Milton Bradley) *pressed ldr to over 4f out: styd chsng ldrs: rdn 2f out: kpt on but lost pls nr fin* **33/1**

600- **7** hd **Gregarious Girl**[86] [8532] 3-9-7 **53**.......... RichardKingscote 3 — 52
(Stuart Williams) *hld up in midfield: gng wl enough over 2f out: rdn over 1f out: hanging lft and nt qckn: kpt on ins fnl f* **11/4**[1]

040- **8** 1 ¼ **Bridlemere Court (IRE)**[36] [9521] 3-9-2 **48**.......... HollieDoyle 2 — 43
(David Elsworth) *nt that wl away: sn in midfield: shkn up over 2f out: nt qckn and no prog over 1f out: kpt on* **6/1**

053- **9** ½ **Milldean Panther**[34] [9566] 3-9-10 **56**.......... LiamKeniry 10 — 50
(Suzi Best) *hld up in last trio: shkn up over 2f out: one pce and nvr able to threaten* **7/2**[2]

40-4 **10** 3 ½ **Cherry Cola**[9] [137] 3-9-6 **52**.......... CallumShepherd 8 — 35
(Mick Channon) *in tch: rdn over 2f out: sn btn (trainer's rep said the filly may have been unsuited by the sharp 6 furlongs at Lingfield)* **9/1**

004- **11** 5 **Scenic Lady**[174] [5472] 3-9-0 **46**..........(h[1]) LukeMorris 11 — 14
(Michael Attwater) *nvr gng wl and a bhd* **33/1**

1m 13.31s (1.41) **Going Correction** -0.125s/f (Stan) **11 Ran SP% 130.1**
Speed ratings (Par 95): **85,84,84,83,83 83,83,81,80,76 69**
CSF £108.63 CT £3069.79 TOTE £12.80: £3.10, £3.60, £9.60; EX 96.10 Trifecta £1881.00.
Owner G P S Heart of Racing (Bloodstock) Ltd **Bred** Pc Coaches Of Lincoln Ltd **Trained** Upper Helmsley, N Yorks

FOCUS
This was steadily run in the early stages and it was an advantage to race prominently.

297 PLAY 4 TO SCORE AT BETWAY H'CAP — 6f 1y(P)
2:30 (2:30) (Class 2) (0-105,103) 4-Y-O+
£11,827 (£3,541; £1,770; £885; £442; £222) **Stalls Low**

Form — RPR

45-3 **1** **Gorgeous Noora (IRE)**[6] [203] 5-8-9 **91**.......... HollieDoyle 6 — 103
(Archie Watson) *chsd ldr: shkn up over 2f out: clsd to ld over 1f out: drvn clr fnl f: readily* **7/4**[1]

16-1 **2** 3 **Shamshon (IRE)**[15] [36] 8-8-3 **85**.......... NicolaCurrie 2 — 87
(Stuart Williams) *hld up in 5th: urged along and plenty to do over 2f out: r.o fr over 1f out: tk 2nd last strides* **5/1**[3]

6-24 **3** ½ **Watchable**[10] [127] 9-8-8 **90**..........(p) JoeFanning 3 — 90
(David O'Meara) *chsd ldng pair: shkn up over 2f out: chsd wnr on inner 1f out: sn outpcd: lost 2nd last strides* **9/2**[2]

31-5 **4** ½ **Tan**[8] [165] 5-8-2 **84** oh4.......... LukeMorris 1 — 83
(Michael Appleby) *led: kicked on over 2f out: hdd over 1f out: outpcd after* **5/1**[3]

401/ **5** 6 **Giogiobbo**[80] 6-9-7 **103**..........(bt) AdamKirby 5 — 83
(Nick Littmoden) *hld up in 4th: shkn up over 2f out: sn wknd* **13/2**

23-0 **6** 13 **Teruntum Star (FR)**[15] [35] 7-8-13 **95**..........(p) JosephineGordon 4 — 33
(Kevin Ryan) *a in last and nvr gng wl: t.o (jockey said gelding was never travelling)* **7/1**

1m 9.69s (-2.21) **Going Correction** -0.125s/f (Stan) **6 Ran SP% 113.7**
Speed ratings (Par 109): **109,105,104,103,95 78**
CSF £11.09 TOTE £2.00: £1.10, £2.90; EX 10.50 Trifecta £37.00.
Owner David Howden & David Redvers **Bred** Kabansk Ltd & Rathbarry Stud **Trained** Upper Lambourn, W Berks

FOCUS
An interesting sprint handicap, and it was won in impressive fashion. The fourth has been rated close to form.

298 BETWAY H'CAP — 5f 6y(P)
3:05 (3:05) (Class 6) (0-58,58) 3-Y-O+
£3,105 (£924; £461; £300; £300; £300) **Stalls High**

Form — RPR

023- **1** **Sandfrankskipsgo**[27] [9681] 10-10-0 **58**.......... ShaneKelly 2 — 64
(Peter Crate) *mde all: rdn 2f out: edgd rt fnl f: drvn out and kpt on wl* **15/2**

03-1 **2** 1 **Pharoh Jake**[7] [179] 11-8-9 **46** oh1.......... EllieMacKenzie[(7)] 1 — 48
(John Bridger) *chsd ldng pair on inner: hit rail over 2f out: rdn over 1f out: kpt on fnl f to win battle for 2nd: a jst hld* **9/2**[3]

004- **3** shd **Hula Girl**[18] [9773] 4-9-12 **56**..........(b) LukeMorris 10 — 58
(Charles Hills) *chsd ldng trio: urged along over 2f out: clsd u.p fnl f: nrly snatched 2nd* **15/2**

000- **4** hd **Thegreyvtrain**[34] [9566] 3-8-8 **53**.......... DavidProbert 3 — 48
(Ronald Harris) *chsd wnr: rdn 2f out: kpt on but a hld: lost 2 pls nr fin* **16/1**

/04- **5** shd **Shackled N Drawn (USA)**[18] [9777] 7-9-12 **56**..........(bt) AdamKirby 4 — 57
(Peter Hedger) *hld up: n.m.r on inner after 1f: prog over 1f out: urged along and pressed for a pl fnl f: no ex nr fin* **4/1**[2]

41-2 **6** 1 **Alaskan Bay (IRE)**[11] [118] 4-9-4 **55**.......... SeamusCronin[(7)] 6 — 52+
(Rae Guest) *racd on outer in midfield: rdn 2f out: nvr on terms w ldrs but kpt on fnl f* **11/2**

602- **7** nk **Fareeq**[18] [9776] 5-10-0 **58**..........(bt) RichardKingscote 7 — 54+
(Charlie Wallis) *hld up in rr: pushed along 2f out: styd on fnl f on inner but nvr really in it* **11/4**[1]

004- **8** 2 **Chicago School (IRE)**[18] [9776] 6-8-13 **46** oh1..........(vt) JaneElliott[(3)] 8 — 35+
(Nikki Evans) *s.s: detached in last: pushed along 2f out: nvr able to rch ldrs* **33/1**

005- **9** 7 **Waneen (IRE)**[18] [9777] 6-9-13 **57**..........(p[1]) LiamKeniry 5 — 21
(Paul D'Arcy) *racd wd v wd in midfield: pushed along bef 1/2-way: wknd 2f out: t.o* **10/1**

58.33s (-0.47) **Going Correction** -0.125s/f (Stan)
WFA 3 from 4yo+ 15lb **9 Ran SP% 121.7**
Speed ratings (Par 101): **98,96,96,95,95 94,93,90,79**
CSF £43.54 CT £271.88 TOTE £8.40: £2.60, £2.30, £2.90; EX 42.40 Trifecta £254.70.
Owner Peter Crate **Bred** Peter Crate **Trained** Newdigate, Surrey
■ Stewards' Enquiry : Seamus Cronin two-day ban: interference & careless riding (Feb 1-2)

FOCUS
The pace held up in this ordinary sprint, and it was a one-two for the veterans in the line-up.

299 LADBROKES HOME OF THE ODDS BOOST NOVICE STKS 1m 2f (P)
3:40 (3:40) (Class 5) 3-Y-O **£3,752** (£1,116; £557; £278) **Stalls** Low

Form RPR

5- **1** **Marhaban (IRE)**[41] 9459 3-9-2 0....(b) AdamKirby 2 81
(Charlie Appleby) *mde all: jinked rt bnd over 8f out: pushed 3 l clr over 2f out: rdn and ld dwindled fnl f but a holding on* **3/1**[3]

02- **2** *3/4* **Gantier**[63] 9104 3-9-2 0....(p) RobertHavlin 4 79
(John Gosden) *dwlt and rousted early: carried rt bnd over 8f out: chsd ldng trio after: shkn up over 3f out: grad clsd on wnr fr over 1f out: tk 2nd ins fnl f: nvr able to chal* **2/1**[2]

3 *nk* **Allocator (FR)** 3-9-2 0....RyanMoore 6 78
(Richard Hannon) *s.s: hld up in 5th: pushed along over 3f out: prog to chse wnr over 2f out: grad clsd fr over 1f out but lost 2nd ins fnl f* **5/4**[1]

60- **4** *5* **Thunderoad**[22] 9725 3-8-13 0....AaronJones(3) 5 68
(Marco Botti) *chsd wnr: carried rt bnd over 8f out: lost 2nd over 2f out: fdd* **33/1**

5 *10* **Resounding Silence (USA)** 3-8-11 0....PJMcDonald 1 43
(James Tate) *chsd ldng pair to over 3f out: sn btn* **18/1**

0- **6** *1 1/2* **Munstead Moonshine**[32] 9590 3-8-11 0....RobHornby 3 40
(Andrew Balding) *mostly in last: lft bhd over 3f out* **33/1**

2m 4.09s (-2.51) **Going Correction** -0.125s/f (Stan) **6 Ran SP% 113.9**
Speed ratings (Par 97): **105,104,104,100,92 90**
CSF £9.68 TOTE £3.90: £1.50, £1.30; EX 9.40 Trifecta £16.50.
Owner Godolphin **Bred** Rabbah Bloodstock Limited **Trained** Newmarket, Suffolk

FOCUS
This was dominated by the leader, who had an easy time of it. The form makes sense, with the second and fourth rated close to their marks.
T/Plt: £214.20 to a £1 stake. Pool: £72,820.74 - 248.06 winning units T/Qpdt: £64.50 to a £1 stake. Pool: £8,173.96 - 93.77 winning units **Jonathan Neesom**

300 - 305a (Foreign Racing) - See Raceform Interactive

188 DUNDALK (A.W) (L-H)
Friday, January 18

OFFICIAL GOING: Polytrack: standard

306a J DUFFY SERVICES RACE 6f (P)
8:00 (8:00) 3-Y-O **£8,601** (£2,667; £1,270; £572; £223)

RPR

1 **Charming Kid**[14] 57 3-9-2 99....BarryMcHugh 6 102+
(Richard Fahey) *edgd sltly rt s: sn swtchd lft to trck ldr in 2nd: impr travelling wl to ld over 1f out: pushed out and extended advantage ins fnl f where in command: eased cl home: easily* **6/4**[1]

2 *2 3/4* **Empire Line (IRE)**[14] 70 3-8-12 84....(p[1]) WayneLordan 5 82
(J A Stack, Ire) *chsd ldrs: 5th 1/2-way: hdwy gng wl bhd ldrs 2f out: sn rdn and clsd u.p into 2nd ins fnl f where no imp on easy wnr: kpt on wl* **9/4**[2]

3 *2 1/2* **Cityman**[112] 7740 3-8-7 76....BenCoen(5) 4 74
(Andrew Slattery, Ire) *chsd ldrs: 4th 1/2-way: rdn disputing 3rd under 2f out and no imp on easy wnr u.p in 3rd ins fnl f: kpt on same pce* **5/1**[3]

4 *1 1/2* **That's Not Me (IRE)**[28] 9672 3-8-6 76....DannySheehy(5) 3 68
(Anthony McCann, Ire) *led: over 1 l clr at 1/2-way: rdn and strly pressed under 2f out: hdd over 1f out and sn wknd into 4th* **8/1**

5 *1 3/4* **Snow Hope**[28] 9674 3-8-4 0....(h[1]) KillianLeonard(3) 2 59
(A Oliver, Ire) *hld up: pushed along in 6th fr bef 1/2-way: struggling in 6th into st: sme hdwy far side under 2f out: no imp on ldrs in 5th 1f out: kpt on under hands and heels ins fnl f* **33/1**

6 *1 1/4* **Lavengro Lad (IRE)**[28] 9672 3-8-2 0....PaddyHarnett(10) 7 60
(Andrew Slattery, Ire) *sltly impeded s and sn swtchd lft in rr: gng wl in 7th at 1/2-way: pushed along over 2f out and no imp on ldrs u.p in 6th ins fnl f: kpt on one pce (jockey said gelding hung right in hme str)* **66/1**

7 *4 1/2* **Pass The Vino (IRE)**[14] 70 3-8-12 0....MarkGallagher 8 45
(D J Bunyan, Ire) *chsd ldrs: 3rd 1/2-way: rdn and wknd 2f out: lame (jockey said that his mount travelled well into the straight, changed legs and lost action; vet reported the animal to be lame right front post race)* **5/1**[3]

8 *13* **James' Will**[28] 9674 3-8-12 0....GaryHalpin 1 4
(David Marnane, Ire) *pushed along briefly early: sn settled towards rr: pushed along and dropped to rr bef 1/2-way: sn detached and wknd: nvr a factor* **66/1**

1m 11.97s (-0.43) **Going Correction** +0.30s/f (Slow) **8 Ran SP% 121.1**
Speed ratings: **108,104,101,99,96 95,89,71**
CSF £5.48 TOTE £2.20: £1.02, £3.60, £1.80; DF 5.00 Trifecta £22.60.
Owner The Cool Silk Partnership **Bred** Biddestone Stud Ltd **Trained** Musley Bank, N Yorks

FOCUS
The winner was entitled to do this and seems to be back on song. It's been rated around the balance of the first five.

307a FAST SHIPPING H'CAP 6f (P)
8:30 (8:31) 3-Y-O+ **£6,936** (£2,150; £1,024; £461; £39; £39)

RPR

1 **Dandys Gold (IRE)**[14] 71 5-8-13 74....DMSimmonson(7) 9 83
(William J Fitzpatrick, Ire) *hld up in tch: 6th at 1/2-way: hdwy nr side over 1f out: rdn to ld ins fnl f where edgd lft and kpt on wl clsng stages* **9/1**

2 *1 1/4* **View The Bay (IRE)**[14] 68 4-8-10 69....BenCoen(5) 1 74
(Andrew Slattery, Ire) *chsd ldrs: disp 4th at 1/2-way: hdwy to chal far side 1 1/2f out: sn disp and led narrowly briefly ins fnl f tl sn hdd: no imp on wnr clsng stages: jst hld 2nd* **11/2**[1]

3 *nse* **Billyfairplay (IRE)**[35] 9542 5-9-7 75....(p) MarkGallagher 11 80+
(John James Feane, Ire) *chsd ldrs: 3rd 1/2-way: impr to chal nr side u.p over 1f out: no imp on wnr in 3rd wl ins fnl f: kpt on: jst hld for 2nd* **7/1**[3]

4 *1/2* **Kasbah (IRE)**[14] 71 7-9-7 75....RoryCleary 7 78
(Adrian McGuinness, Ire) *got upset in stalls briefly: hld up: 9th 1/2-way: prog 2f out: n.m.r briefly 1 1/2f out and impr between horses to chal over 1f out where u.p: no imp on wnr u.p in 4th wl ins fnl f: kpt on* **8/1**

5 *shd* **Hee Haw (IRE)**[14] 71 5-8-12 69....TomMadden(3) 2 72
(Adrian McGuinness, Ire) *s.i.s: in rr: last at 1/2-way: r.o u.p far side fr over 1f out to chse ldrs ins fnl f: kpt on same pce in 5th clsng stages: jnd for 5th on line (jockey said that his mount was slowly away)* **8/1**

5 *dht* **Lily's Prince (IRE)**[7] 194 9-8-10 64....ShaneFoley 4 67
(Garvan Donnelly, Ire) *hooded to load: hld up: 8th 1/2-way: gng wl over 2f out: n.m.r fr under 2f out and tk clsr order: rdn in 6th wl ins fnl f and r.o clsng stages to dead-heat for 5th on line: nrst fin* **10/1**

7 *1 1/2* **The Right Choice (IRE)**[8] 165 4-9-7 75....(b) BarryMcHugh 12 73
(Richard Fahey) *mid-div: 7th 1/2-way: rdn nr side under 2f out and no imp on ldrs ent fnl f: kpt on ins fnl f: eased cl home* **6/1**[2]

8 *1 1/4* **My Good Brother (IRE)**[108] 7881 10-8-7 61....(v) WayneLordan 13 55
(T G McCourt, Ire) *s.i.s: towards rr: 12th 1/2-way: drvn in rr over 2f out and no imp: sn swtchd rt and kpt on u.p ins fnl f: nvr nrr* **40/1**

9 *hd* **Captain Power (IRE)**[72] 8937 7-9-5 73....RobbieColgan 5 66
(D Broad, Ire) *w.w in rr of mid-div early: 11th 1/2-way: pushed along over 2f out: rdn over 1f out and kpt on one pce* **28/1**

10 *shd* **Togoville (IRE)**[14] 68 9-9-7 80....(b) DonaghO'Connor(5) 6 73
(Anthony McCann, Ire) *cl up bhd ldr and sn disp ld: cl 2nd at 1/2-way: rdn to dispute ld fr 2f out tl hdd over 1f out: wknd ins fnl f* **28/1**

11 *1 1/4* **Smart Stinger (USA)**[7] 188 5-8-3 64....(b) AndrewSlattery(7) 3 53
(Andrew Slattery, Ire) *chsd ldrs: disp 4th at 1/2-way: gng wl bhd ldrs over 2f out: pushed along under 2f out and hmpd 1 1/2f out: no imp after: sn rdn and one pce ins fnl f where short of room briefly* **8/1**

12 *1/2* **Clare Island (IRE)**[49] 9343 5-8-8 67....DannySheehy(5) 8 55
(Edward Lynam, Ire) *s.i.s: towards rr early: 10th 1/2-way: drvn over 2f out and no imp ins fnl f where short of room briefly: kpt on one pce: nvr a factor* **14/1**

13 *5* **Snow Patch (IRE)**[7] 188 4-8-5 62....KillianLeonard(3) 10 34
(D J Bunyan, Ire) *broke wl to ld briefly tl sn jnd: narrow advantage at 1/2-way: jnd fr 2f out: sn rdn and hdd over 1f out: wknd and eased ins fnl f* **6/1**[2]

1m 12.36s (-0.04) **Going Correction** +0.30s/f (Slow) **13 Ran SP% 124.9**
Speed ratings: **106,104,104,103,103 103,101,99,99,99 97,97,90**
Tote Aggregate: 2019: 138,031.00 - 2018: 150,245.00. Pick Six: Not won. Pool of 2,786.75 carried forward CSF £59.66 CT £391.27 TOTE £9.20: £2.50, £2.00, £2.70; DF 74.10 Trifecta £382.70.
Owner George Halford **Bred** George Halford **Trained** Rathangan, Co Kildare

FOCUS
Any amount of these held chances inside the last but the winner got the clearest passage down the outside. The standard is set by the first five.
T/Jkpt: @3,500.00. Pool: @5,000.00 T/Plt: Part won. @25,374.30 to @1 stake. Pool: @36,249.07 **Brian Fleming**

308 - (Foreign Racing) - See Raceform Interactive

294 LINGFIELD (L-H)
Saturday, January 19

OFFICIAL GOING: Polytrack: standard
Wind: MEDIUM, BEHIND Weather: OVERCAST

309 BETWAY LIVE CASINO H'CAP 1m 2f (P)
12:50 (12:50) (Class 6) (0-65,67) 4-Y-O+
£3,105 (£924; £461; £300; £300; £300) **Stalls** Low

Form RPR

14-2 **1** **Global Wonder (IRE)**[10] 145 4-9-8 66....MartinHarley 4 74
(Gay Kelleway) *taken down early: t.k.h early: in tch in midfield: swtchd rt and hdwy 3f out: ev ch and rdn over 1f out: unable to match pce of ldr and sltly impeded jst ins fnl f: rallied u.p to ld cl home* **3/1**[1]

441- **2** *nk* **Narjes**[20] 9769 5-9-9 66....(h) LukeMorris 6 72
(Laura Mongan) *hld up in tch in last trio: hdwy on outer over 2f out: chalng u.p over 1f out: sn led: drvn almost 2 l clr and hanging lft ins fnl f: hdd and no ex last strides* **5/1**[2]

00-0 **3** *2 3/4* **Natch**[15] 61 4-9-4 62....(p) CallumShepherd 8 64
(Michael Attwater) *restless in stalls: wl in tch in midfield: nt clrest of runs and swtchd rt 2f out: kpt on wl u.p ins fnl f: snatched 3rd last strides: no threat to ldrs* **33/1**

200- **4** *hd* **Freebe Rocks (IRE)**[20] 9764 4-9-5 63....(p) StevieDonohoe 1 65
(Ian Williams) *t.k.h: clsd on inner to chse ldrs ent fnl 2f: outpcd and drvn over 1f out: swtchd rt 1f out: chsd clr ldng pair jst ins fnl f kpt on but no threat to ldrs: lost 3rd last strides* **12/1**[3]

30-1 **5** *shd* **Pivotal Flame (IRE)**[3] 262 6-9-7 67 6ex....(v) PaddyBradley(3) 2 69
(Pat Phelan) *hld up in last pair: clsd and nt clr run 2f out: swtchd rt and effrt over 1f out: kpt on ins fnl f: no threat to ldrs* **3/1**[1]

23-3 **6** *4 1/2* **Turn Of Luck (IRE)**[14] 85 4-9-6 64....(p) NicolaCurrie 9 57
(Jamie Osborne) *s.i.s: rcvrd and hdwy on outer first bnd to chse ldr over 7f out: led over 3f out: rdn and hdd over 1f out: sn outpcd and wknd ins fnl f (jockey said colt had no more to give)* **3/1**[1]

4-00 **7** *6* **Middlescence (IRE)**[3] 262 5-9-4 61....(t) LiamJones 10 42
(Lucinda Egerton) *wl in tch in midfield: hdwy to chse ldrs 6f out: upsides ldr over 3f out tl unable qck u.p 2f out: outpcd over 1f out: wknd fnl f* **20/1**

030- **8** *9* **Viento De Condor (IRE)**[22] 9732 4-9-6 64....(v) AdamKirby 7 29
(Tom Clover) *midfield: swtchd rt and hdwy after 1f: led 8f out tl over 3f out: short of room and losing pl sn after: rdn and outpcd 2f out: wl btn over 1f out (vet reported the gelding had lost its right-fore shoe)* **20/1**

0-05 **9** *2* **New Street (IRE)**[10] 145 8-9-0 57....RobHornby 3 17
(Suzi Best) *sn in rr: struggling 3f out: sn lost tch and no ch over 1f out* **25/1**

/00- **10** *50* **Shanakill Star (IRE)**[197] 4607 5-8-3 46 oh1....KieranO'Neill 5
(Dean Ivory) *plld hrd: led for 2f: chsd ldrs tl lost pl and towards rr whn impeded over 2f out: lost tch and eased over 1f out: t.o* **25/1**

2m 3.71s (-2.89) **Going Correction** -0.10s/f (Stan)
WFA 4 from 5yo+ 1lb **10 Ran SP% 119.5**
Speed ratings (Par 101): **107,106,104,104,104 100,95,88,87,47**
CSF £17.43 CT £419.68 TOTE £3.30: £1.30, £2.30, £9.50; EX 18.90 Trifecta £321.00.
Owner Dr Johnny Hon **Bred** Gervin Creaner **Trained** Exning, Suffolk

FOCUS
There was a good pace on early and that set things up for the closers.

310 BETWAY HEED YOUR HUNCH H'CAP 1m 2f (P)
1:25 (1:25) (Class 4) (0-85,86) 4-Y-O+
£5,530 (£1,645; £822; £411; £300; £300) **Stalls** Low

Form RPR

52-1 **1** **Forbidden Planet**[14] 86 4-9-1 78....RyanMoore 5 86+
(Roger Charlton) *trckd ldrs: pushed along and clsd to press ldrs and carried rt bnd 2f out: rdn to ld 1f out: reminders and r.o wl whn pressed ins fnl f* **4/5**[1]

22-2 **2** 3/4 **Family Fortunes**[15] 56 5-9-8 **84**........................ LiamKeniry 6 89
(Michael Madgwick) *stdd s: hld up in tch in last pair: clsd to trck ldrs 2f out: swtchd rt and effrt over 1f out: chsd wnr ins fnl f: kpt on u.p but a hld* **9/2**[2]

2- **3** 3/4 **Sheberghan (IRE)**[210] 4147 4-9-6 **83**........................ EdwardGreatrex 3 87
(Archie Watson) *s.i.s and bustled along leaving stalls: in tch in rr: clsd whn nt clr run and swtchd rt wl over 1f out: swtchd lft and hdwy 1f out: chsd ldng pair and kpt on same pce ins fnl f* **8/1**

440- **4** 2 3/4 **Emenem**[110] 7848 5-9-8 **84**........................ LukeMorris 1 82
(Simon Dow) *led for 1f: chsd ldr: rdn and ev ch whn drifted rt bnd 2f out: unable qck jst over 1f out: no ex and wknd ins fnl f* **12/1**

454- **5** 1 **Voi**[23] 9724 5-8-10 **72**........................(t) MartinDwyer 4 68
(Conrad Allen) *trckd ldrs on inner: effrt ent fnl 2f: unable qck jst over 1f out: no ex and wknd ins fnl f* **33/1**

222- **6** 1/2 **Maybe Today**[47] 9382 4-9-9 **86**........................(p[1]) RobertHavlin 2 82
(Simon Crisford) *rousted along to ld after 1f: rdn and hrd pressed ent fnl 2f: hdd 1f out: no ex and wknd ins fnl f* **5/1**[3]

2m 4.34s (-2.26) **Going Correction** -0.10s/f (Stan)
WFA 4 from 5yo 1lb **6** Ran SP% **112.1**
Speed ratings (Par 105): **105,104,103,101,100 100**
CSF £4.76 TOTE £1.70: £1.10, £2.70; EX 5.00 Trifecta £27.50.
Owner Kingwood Stud Management Co Ltd **Bred** David John Brown **Trained** Beckhampton, Wilts

FOCUS
This was won by a progressive sort. The second has been rated to form.

311 BETWAY CASINO H'CAP 1m 4f (P)
2:00 (2:00) (Class 2) (0-105,103) 4-Y-O+
£11,827 (£3,541; £1,770; £885; £442; £222) **Stalls** Low

Form RPR

125- **1** **Soghan (IRE)**[238] 3091 5-8-10 **89**........................(t) ShaneKelly 5 95
(Richard Hughes) *stdd s: hld up in tch in last pair: effrt on inner and rdn to chal jst over 1f out: drvn to ld ins fnl f: edgd rt but r.o wl u.p* **10/1**

004- **2** nk **Primero (FR)**[28] 9686 6-9-7 **100**........................ AdamKirby 6 105
(David O'Meara) *stdd s: in rr: pushed along and clsd ent fnl 2f: nt clr run ent fnl f: swtchd lft and hdwy ins fnl f: str run to press wnr towards fin: clsng at fin but nvr quite getting to wnr* **5/1**[2]

43-0 **3** nk **Lord George (IRE)**[14] 82 6-9-10 **103**........................(p[1]) RyanMoore 4 108
(James Fanshawe) *chsd ldr: upsides and rdn ent fnl 2f: led over 1f out: hdd ins fnl f: kpt on u.p but hld and lost 2nd towards fin* **8/1**

011- **4** nk **Redicean**[28] 9686 5-9-4 **97**........................ MartinHarley 2 101
(Alan King) *trckd ldrs: hemmed in bnd 2f out: switching out rt and nudging rival over 1f out: in the clr and drvn 1f out: kpt on wl u.p ins fnl f* **8/11**[1]

523- **5** 1/2 **Seafarer (IRE)**[19] 9775 5-9-0 **93**........................(v) MartinDwyer 3 96
(Marcus Tregoning) *wl in tch in midfield: effrt ent fnl 2f: nudged rt over 1f out: hrd drvn and kpt on u.p ins fnl f* **6/1**[3]

116- **6** 5 **India**[106] 7951 4-8-6 **88**........................(h) LukeMorris 1 83
(Michael Bell) *led: rdn and hrd pressed over 2f out: hdd over 1f out: no ex and dropped to rr 100yds out: wknd and eased towards fin* **20/1**

2m 29.04s (-3.96) **Going Correction** -0.10s/f (Stan)
WFA 4 from 5yo+ 3lb **6** Ran SP% **113.8**
Speed ratings (Par 109): **109,108,108,108,108 104**
CSF £58.41 TOTE £10.90: £4.40, £2.60; EX 61.30 Trifecta £1133.00.
Owner The Queens **Bred** Ballyreddin Stud **Trained** Upper Lambourn, Berks

FOCUS
This was run at a good gallop and, while it was a bunched finish, it was the two held up at the back who came through to finish first and second. The second and third have been rated to their recent bests.

312 LADBROKES HOME OF THE ODDS BOOST H'CAP 1m 1y(P)
2:35 (2:35) (Class 3) (0-90,87) 3-Y-O **£7,246** (£2,168; £1,084) **Stalls** High

Form RPR

604- **1** **Forseti**[148] 6484 3-8-10 **79**........................(h) JoshuaBryan(3) 3 81+
(Andrew Balding) *stdd s: t.k.h in detached last: clsd to trck ldrs 6f out: effrt 2f out: ev ch whn edgd lft ins fnl f: edgd bk rt u.p wl ins fnl f but r.o wl to ld on post* **3/1**[2]

33-1 **2** nse **Originaire (IRE)**[16] 32 3-9-0 **80**........................(p) RyanMoore 1 80
(William Haggas) *t.k.h: trckd ldr: effrt as ldr qcknd ent fnl 2f: rdn and ev ch ent fnl f: edgd lft u.p but kpt on to ld wl ins fnl f: hdd on post* **4/9**[1]

200- **3** 2 **Amplify (IRE)**[85] 8606 3-9-7 **87**........................ AdamKirby 2 84
(Brian Meehan) *led: stdd gallop after 3f: rdn and qcknd ent fnl 2f: drvn and hrd pressed ent fnl f: hdd and squeezed for room wl ins fnl f: no ex and outpcd towards fin* **11/2**[3]

1m 37.26s (-0.94) **Going Correction** -0.10s/f (Stan) **3** Ran SP% **109.6**
Speed ratings (Par 101): **100,99,97**
CSF £5.06 TOTE £3.40; EX 5.50 Trifecta £4.30.
Owner Mick and Janice Mariscotti **Bred** Deerfield Farm **Trained** Kingsclere, Hants

FOCUS
Just the three runners but there was a tight finish. The second has been rated in line with his recent C&D form, with the third close to his debut run.

313 BETWAY MEDIAN AUCTION MAIDEN STKS 6f 1y(P)
3:10 (3:10) (Class 6) 3-5-Y-O **£3,105** (£924; £461; £230) **Stalls** Low

Form RPR

0-2 **1** **Probability (IRE)**[17] 27 3-8-7 0........................ EdwardGreatrex 2 74+
(Archie Watson) *mde all: pushed along and qcknd clr over 1f out: r.o strly ins fnl f: comf* **4/5**[1]

0- **2** 2 **Sea Of Reality (IRE)**[43] 9442 3-8-7 0........................ LiamJones 7 65
(William Haggas) *wnt rt leaving stalls and slowly away: switching to inner and hdwy into midfield over 4f out: wnt 2nd and rdn 2f out: drvn and no imp over 1f out: kpt on but no threat to wnr* **4/1**[2]

0-0 **3** 1 1/4 **Amor Kethley**[14] 78 3-8-7 0........................ GeorgeWood 3 61
(Amy Murphy) *t.k.h: chsd ldrs: effrt and hdwy over 1f out: 3rd and kpt on same pce u.p ins fnl f* **50/1**

4 1 **Reggae Runner (FR)** 3-8-12 0........................ FrannyNorton 8 63+
(Mark Johnston) *pushed rt leaving stalls and s.i.s: rn green in rr: 6th and effrt 2f out: swtchd rt over 1f out: hdwy and styd on wl ins fnl f: no threat to wnr* **8/1**

405- **5** 1 1/2 **Maximum Power (FR)**[36] 9529 4-9-7 63........................ WilliamCarver(7) 6 63
(Tim Pinfield) *chsd ldrs on outer: outpcd u.p over 1f out: wknd ins fnl f* **7/1**[3]

- **6** 1/2 **Major Blue** 3-8-12 0........................ HollieDoyle 1 57+
(James Eustace) *s.i.s: rn green early: in rr and t.k.h after 2f: effrt on inner over 1f out: no threat to ldrs but kpt on ins fnl f* **12/1**

5- **7** 3 1/4 **Remembering You (IRE)**[29] 9670 3-8-7 0........................ RobHornby 4 42
(Clive Cox) *midfield tl dropped to last trio 4f out: 7th and rdn 2f out: no prog and nvr involved* **8/1**

0- **8** hd **What A Dazzler**[64] 9093 3-8-0 0........................ ThoreHammerHansen(7) 5 42
(Bill Turner) *chsd wnr tl 2f out: sn outpcd and wknd ins fnl f* **100/1**

1m 12.07s (0.17) **Going Correction** -0.10s/f (Stan)
WFA 3 from 4yo 16lb **8** Ran SP% **120.9**
Speed ratings (Par 101): **94,91,89,88,86 85,81,81**
CSF £4.71 TOTE £1.70: £1.10, £1.10, £11.10; EX 5.60 Trifecta £96.80.
Owner Mrs C Cashman **Bred** Marie & Mossy Fahy **Trained** Upper Lambourn, W Berks

FOCUS
A modest maiden won comfortably by the odds-on favourite.

314 BETWAY H'CAP 6f 1y(P)
3:40 (3:40) (Class 5) (0-70,70) 4-Y-O+ **£3,752** (£1,116; £557; £300; £300) **Stalls** Low

Form RPR

04-6 **1** **Aguerooo (IRE)**[10] 144 6-9-0 **63**........................(tp) FrannyNorton 6 71
(Charlie Wallis) *stdd s: hld up in tch in rr: clsd and nt clr run over 1f out: gap opened and readily qcknd through to ld ins fnl f: sn in command* **11/4**[2]

00-3 **2** 1 **Real Estate (IRE)**[14] 91 4-9-5 **68**........................(p) CallumShepherd 2 73
(Michael Attwater) *chsd ldrs: nt clr run on inner 2f out: effrt on inner 2f out: hdwy over 1f out: ev ch u.p ins fnl f: unable to match pce of wnr fnl 75yds: kpt on* **3/1**[3]

440- **3** 1/2 **Lalania**[37] 9525 4-9-7 **70**........................(h) EdwardGreatrex 5 73
(Stuart Williams) *mounted in chute and taken down early: chsd ldr: pushed along over 2f out: edgd lft over 1f out: ev ch ins fnl f: one pce fnl 75yds* **7/1**

300- **4** nk **Big Time Maybe (IRE)**[82] 8689 4-9-6 **69**........................(p w) AdamKirby 1 71
(Michael Attwater) *led: rdn over 1f out: hdd and no ex ins fnl f: outpcd towards fin* **10/1**

00-3 **5** 2 1/2 **Dotted Swiss (IRE)**[8] 187 4-9-6 **69**........................(b) HollieDoyle 3 63+
(Archie Watson) *dwlt: in tch in last pair: rdn: hdwy on outer and pressed ldrs 2f out: unable qck over 1f out: wknd ins fnl f (jockey said filly stopped quickly)* **13/8**[1]

1m 10.9s (-1.00) **Going Correction** -0.10s/f (Stan) **5** Ran SP% **111.4**
Speed ratings (Par 103): **102,100,100,99,96**
CSF £11.41 TOTE £3.40: £1.60, £1.70; EX 12.60 Trifecta £53.20.
Owner P E Axon **Bred** Cooneen Stud **Trained** Ardleigh, Essex

FOCUS
They went a decent enough gallop and it set up nicely for the well-backed winner. The second has been rated to his recent form.
T/Plt: £440.40 to a £1 stake. Pool: £53,801.79 - 89.18 winning units T/Qpdt: £72.70 to a £1 stake. Pool: £3,891.04 - 39.58 winning units **Steve Payne**

235 WOLVERHAMPTON (A.W) (L-H)
Saturday, January 19

OFFICIAL GOING: Tapeta: standard
Wind: breezy Weather: showers, cold

315 LIKE SUN RACING ON FACEBOOK APPRENTICE H'CAP 7f 36y (Tp)
4:40 (4:40) (Class 6) (0-65,65) 4-Y-O+
£3,105 (£924; £461; £400; £400; £400) **Stalls** High

Form RPR

406- **1** **Mooroverthebridge**[158] 6121 5-9-1 **59**........................ FinleyMarsh 1 65
(Grace Harris) *led: hdd after 3f: remained prom: disp ld 3f out: drvn into 1/2 l ld 2f out: sn rdn: 1 l ld 1f out: ld reduced fnl f but r.o wl to hold on* **50/1**

032- **2** nk **Blessed To Empress (IRE)**[70] 8997 4-9-3 **61**........................ NicolaCurrie 5 66
(Amy Murphy) *chsd ldr: led after 3f: disp ld 3f out: 1/2 l 2nd 2f out: sn drvn: rdn over 1f out: 1 l 2nd 1f out: r.o wl to cl on wnr fnl f but nvr getting there* **13/2**

366- **3** 1/2 **Energia Flavio (BRZ)**[33] 9585 8-9-1 **62**........................ CameronNoble(3) 6 66
(Patrick Morris) *chsd ldrs: pushed along in 3rd 2f out: drvn over 1f out: sn rdn: r.o fnl f* **11/1**

066- **4** 1/2 **Muatadel**[52] 9281 6-9-4 **65**........................(p) BenSanderson(3) 10 68
(Roger Fell) *hld up: pushed along 2f out: rdn and hdwy fnl f: r.o to secure 4th nr fin* **20/1**

60-6 **5** hd **Steal The Scene (IRE)**[16] 33 7-9-7 **65**........................(p) CliffordLee 2 69
(Kevin Frost) *mid-div: drvn 1 1/2f out: rdn fnl f: kpt on (jockey said gelding was denied a clear run approaching the final furlong)* **4/1**[2]

661- **6** hd **Anif (IRE)**[20] 9767 5-9-0 **63**........................ KieranSchofield(5) 4 65
(David Evans) *mid-div: pushed along in 4th 2f out: rdn over 1f out: one pce (jockey said gelding was slowly away)* **11/4**[1]

330- **7** 1 1/4 **Newstead Abbey**[50] 9335 9-9-5 **63**........................ PhilDennis 7 62
(Rebecca Bastiman) *mid-div: pushed along 2f out: rdn over 1f out: no imp* **16/1**

42-R **8** shd **One More Chance (IRE)**[12] 123 4-8-11 **62**........................ MarkCrehan(7) 9 61
(Michael Appleby) *dwlt losing several l: bhd: drvn 1 1/2f out: sn rdn: sme late hdwy but nvr a threat (jockey said filly was very slowly away)* **18/1**

650- **9** 2 **Takeonefortheteam**[20] 9765 4-9-6 **64**........................ EoinWalsh 12 58
(Mark Loughnane) *t.k.h: rdn on outer 1 1/2f out: no imp (jockey said gelding hung right throughout)* **20/1**

000- **10** 2 3/4 **Tuscany (IRE)**[82] 8694 5-9-1 **62**........................(p) MeganNicholls(3) 11 49
(Grace Harris) *bhd: drvn 3f out: rdn over 1f out: no rspnse (jockey said gelding was never travelling)* **28/1**

00-0 **11** 4 1/2 **Air Of York (IRE)**[17] 31 7-9-2 **63**........................(p) DarraghKeenan(3) 8 39
(John Flint) *prom on outer: drvn and lost pl 2f out: dropped away over 1f out* **11/1**

00-3 **12** 1/2 **Aljunood (IRE)**[15] 64 5-8-7 **56**........................(h) JoshQuinn(5) 3 31
(John Norton) *t.k.h: hld up on outer: hdwy 3f out: drvn and lost pl 2f out: rn wd 1 1/2f out: wknd (jockey said gelding ran too free and was unsuited by racing wide without cover throughout)* **6/1**[3]

1m 28.76s (-0.04) **Going Correction** -0.075s/f (Stan) **12** Ran SP% **117.0**
Speed ratings (Par 101): **97,96,96,95,95 95,93,93,91,88 82,82**
CSF £336.06 CT £3903.91 TOTE £64.30: £12.80, £2.10, £3.60; EX 627.40 Trifecta £3725.70.
Owner Grace Harris Racing **Bred** D J And Mrs Deer **Trained** Shirenewton, Monmouthshire

FOCUS
Exposed performers in an ordinary handicap. The steady pace meant those held up were at a disadvantage and the first six finished in a heap. Limited form in behind the winner.

316 SUN RACING TOP TIPS & PREVIEWS MAIDEN STKS 7f 36y (Tp)
5:15 (5:15) (Class 5) 3-Y-O+ £3,752 (£1,116; £557; £278) Stalls High

Form RPR
24- 1 **Liberation Day**[210] 4136 3-8-10 0 AlistairRawlinson 10 69
(Tom Dascombe) *prom: drvn in 1 l 2nd 2f out: rdn to ld 1f out: kpt on wl fnl f: jst hld on* **11/4**[2]

2 *hd* **Kodiac Harbour (IRE)** 4-10-0 0 (p[1]) JFEgan 6 73
(Paul George) *hld up: pushed along and hdwy 2f out: swtchd to outer over 1f out: rdn fnl f: r.o strly to gain on wnr: jst failed* **40/1**

6- 3 *hd* **Wanaasah**[100] 8139 3-8-5 0 JoeFanning 5 63
(Mark Johnston) *t.k.h: prom: pushed along in 4th 2f out: rdn over 1f out: r.o wl fnl f* **7/2**[3]

4- 4 *1* **Paddy's Pursuit (IRE)**[19] 9771 3-8-10 0 KieranO'Neill 8 65
(Mark Loughnane) *led: drvn in 1 l ld 2f out: rdn over 1f out: hdd 1f out: no ex fnl f* **20/1**

5- 5 *1 1/2* **Designated**[66] 9050 3-8-5 0 LukeMorris 4 56
(Clive Cox) *trckd ldrs: drvn in 3rd 2f out: rdn 1f out: no ex and lost two pls fnl f* **2/1**[1]

5/0- 6 *1/2* **Haader (FR)**[259] 2412 4-10-0 0 RaulDaSilva 12 65
(Derek Shaw) *t.k.h: mid-div: pushed along in 5th 2f out: rdn over 1f out: one pce fnl f: lost shoe (vet reported the gelding lost its right hind shoe)* **100/1**

45- 7 *2 1/4* **Smoki Smoka (IRE)**[221] 3714 3-8-10 0 DavidProbert 2 54
(Tom Dascombe) *hld up: pushed along 2f out: rdn over 1f out: no imp (jockey said gelding was slowly away)* **4/1**

00- 8 *1/2* **Peruvian Summer (IRE)**[49] 9355 3-8-10 0 CliffordLee 11 52
(Kevin Frost) *hld up: drvn 1 1/2f out: sn rdn: no imp* **100/1**

00- 9 *1/2* **Jungle Warfare (IRE)**[31] 9607 3-8-10 0 RossaRyan 3 51
(Richard Hannon) *hld up: drvn 2f out: no imp* **40/1**

45- 10 *hd* **Doris Bleasedale (IRE)**[197] 4620 3-8-5 0 PaddyMathers 7 45
(Richard Fahey) *hld up: pushed along over 2f out: nvr involved* **28/1**

0- 11 *12* **Dream Model (IRE)**[23] 9727 3-8-6 ow1 EoinWalsh 9 14
(Mark Loughnane) *in rr: rdn 1 1/2f out: no rspnse (vet reported the filly was lame on its left hind)* **100/1**

0 12 *6* **Prince Mamillius**[14] 90 3-8-10 0 JamesSullivan 1 2
(Derek Shaw) *mid-div: pushed along 3f out: reminder and lost pl over 2f out: sn rdn and wknd* **200/1**

1m 30.33s (1.53) **Going Correction** -0.075s/f (Stan)
WFA 3 from 4yo 18lb 12 Ran SP% **118.8**
Speed ratings (Par 103): **88,87,87,86,84 84,81,80,80,80 66,59**
CSF £112.74 TOTE £4.10: £1.50, £10.60, £1.60; EX 134.10 Trifecta £661.40.
Owner Fdcholdings Nolan Rcg Rutherford **Bred** Horizon Bloodstock Limited **Trained** Malpas, Cheshire

FOCUS
No more than a fair maiden and one in which the first six finished in a bit of a heap, The gallop was an ordinary one and the performance of the runner-up needs upgrading.

317 BETWAY H'CAP 5f 21y (Tp)
5:45 (5:45) (Class 5) (0-75,75) 4-Y-O+ £3,752 (£1,116; £557; £400; £400; £400) Stalls Low

Form RPR
104- 1 **Union Rose**[56] 9251 7-9-2 70 (p) DavidProbert 7 79
(Ronald Harris) *prom: 1 l 2nd 2f out: pushed into ld over 1f out: rdn fnl f: r.o wl* **16/1**

52-1 2 *1 1/4* **A Sure Welcome**[8] 187 5-9-4 72 (b) LiamKeniry 2 76+
(John Spearing) *t.k.h: slowly away: bhd: hdwy 2f out: sn drvn: rdn fnl f: r.o wl: tk 2nd last stride* **13/8**[1]

01-0 3 *nse* **It's All A Joke (IRE)**[16] 36 4-9-0 75 (b) Pierre-LouisJamin(7) 1 79
(Archie Watson) *chsd ldr: drvn 1 1/2f out: sn rdn: wnt 2nd 1f out: kpt on fnl f: lost 2nd last stride* **7/1**

04-5 4 *nk* **Golden Salute (IRE)**[16] 36 4-8-11 68 WilliamCox(3) 5 71
(Andrew Balding) *mid-div: 4th 2f out: drvn over 1f out: rdn fnl f: kpt on* **10/1**

60-0 5 *1 3/4* **Midnightly**[16] 36 5-8-13 67 (bt[1]) FranBerry 8 64
(Rae Guest) *bhd: hmpd over 2f out: drvn 1 1/2f out: rdn fnl f: r.o* **20/1**

42-4 6 *nk* **Becker**[16] 36 4-8-12 66 (h) LukeMorris 9 62
(Robert Cowell) *bhd: hmpd rival over 2f out: sn drvn: rdn and one pce fnl f* **13/2**[3]

035- 7 *3/4* **Look Surprised**[82] 8689 6-8-7 68 EllieMacKenzie(7) 10 61
(Roger Teal) *in rr: drvn on outer 1 1/2f out: rdn over 1f out: one pce fnl f* **33/1**

0-60 8 *1* **Katheefa (USA)**[7] 214 5-9-2 70 (p) JamesSullivan 3 59
(Ruth Carr) *hld up: pushed along and nt clr run 1 1/2f out: no imp fnl f (jockey said gelding was denied a clear run in the home straight)* **4/1**[2]

00-2 9 *1 1/4* **Entertaining Ben**[8] 179 6-8-10 64 (p) NicolaCurrie 4 49
(Amy Murphy) *led: drvn in 1 l ld 2f out: rdn and hdd over 1f out: wknd fnl f* **16/1**

041- 10 *3 3/4* **Brandy Station (IRE)**[23] 9722 4-8-7 66 (h) KevinLundie(5) 11 37
(Lisa Williamson) *mid-div on outer: drvn 2f out: rdn and wknd over 1f out (jockey said gelding hung right)* **16/1**

10-0 11 *3 3/4* **Rockies Spirit**[9] 158 4-9-4 72 (p) DannyBrock 6 30
(Denis Quinn) *chsd ldrs: pushed along 2f out: sn drvn and wknd* **25/1**

1m 0.6s (-1.30) **Going Correction** -0.075s/f (Stan) 11 Ran SP% **122.2**
Speed ratings (Par 103): **107,105,104,104,101 101,99,98,96,90 84**
CSF £43.13 CT £220.48 TOTE £18.60: £3.80, £1.10, £2.30; EX 56.90 Trifecta £328.90.
Owner Adrian Evans **Bred** Home Farm **Trained** Earlswood, Monmouths
■ Stewards' Enquiry : Luke Morris two-day ban: interference & careless riding (Feb 2-3)

FOCUS
A decent gallop but another race on the card that favoured those up with the pace.

318 BETWAY LIVE CASINO H'CAP 2m 120y (Tp)
6:15 (6:15) (Class 5) (0-70,71) 4-Y-O+ £3,752 (£1,116; £557; £400; £400; £400) Stalls Low

Form RPR
05-1 1 **Blazon**[14] 84 6-9-5 63 (p) JoeFanning 7 72+
(Kim Bailey) *hld up: hdwy gng wl over 2f out: pushed along in 2 l 2nd 2f out: drvn to chal over 1f out: led ent fnl f: sn clr: comf* **7/4**[2]

56-2 2 *4 1/2* **Falcon Cliffs (IRE)**[12] 119 5-9-7 65 RobertWinston 1 69
(Tony Carroll) *trckd ldrs: wnt 2nd 3f out: pushed into ld over 2f out: 2 l ld 2f out: drvn over 1f out: rdn and hdd ent fnl f: no ex* **9/2**[3]

2-21 3 *2 3/4* **Your Band**[9] 160 4-9-6 69 NicolaCurrie 4 72
(Jamie Osborne) *hld up: pushed along in 5th 3f out: drvn in 4th 2f out: rdn into 3rd 1 1/2f out: one pce fnl f* **13/8**[1]

300- 4 *7* **Angel Gabrial (IRE)**[92] 8375 10-9-12 70 FranBerry 9 62
(Patrick Morris) *in rr: pushed along over 2f out: drvn into 4th over 1f out: no ex fnl f* **33/1**

131- 5 *14* **The Way You Dance (IRE)**[192] 4816 7-9-13 71 (v) ShaneKelly 8 47
(Neil Mulholland) *prom: led over 6f out: qcknd pce 4f out: drvn and hdd over 2f out: wknd* **14/1**

220- 6 *15* **Marshall Aid (IRE)**[29] 9666 6-9-1 59 JosephineGordon 3 17
(Mark Usher) *mid-div: hdwy to chse ldr 6f out: pushed along in 3rd 3f out: sn drvn and dropped to rr* **40/1**

02-6 P **Iftiraaq (IRE)**[15] 61 8-9-8 66 (p) DavidProbert 6
(David Loughnane) *led at mod gallop: sn racing wd: c to stands' rail 1/2-way: dropped to rr over 6f out: wl bhd whn p.u: lame (jockey said gelding hung very badly; vet reported the gelding was found to be lame on its left fore)* **12/1**

3m 40.36s (1.06) **Going Correction** -0.075s/f (Stan)
WFA 4 from 5yo+ 5lb 7 Ran SP% **112.4**
Speed ratings (Par 103): **94,91,90,87,80 73,**
CSF £9.77 CT £13.82 TOTE £2.60: £1.50, £2.20; EX 10.60 Trifecta £20.60.
Owner The Blazing Optimists **Bred** Juddmonte Farms Ltd **Trained** Andoversford, Gloucs

FOCUS
Not much in the way of pace and the market leader proved a bit of a disappointment but an improved effort from Blazon, who won with a fair bit in hand.

319 LADBROKES HOME OF THE ODDS BOOST H'CAP 1m 142y (Tp)
6:45 (6:45) (Class 6) (0-60,59) 3-Y-O £3,105 (£924; £461; £400; £400; £400) Stalls Low

Form RPR
32-5 1 **Um Shama (IRE)**[8] 174 3-9-0 59 LauraCoughlan(7) 5 64
(David Loughnane) *hld up: hdwy over 2f out: pushed into ld 1 1/2f out: 3 l ld 1f out: pushed out fnl f: comf* **5/1**[3]

062- 2 *1* **Precision Prince (IRE)**[22] 9729 3-9-6 58 LiamJones 13 61
(Mark Loughnane) *hld up: drvn 2f out: effrt on outer 1 1/2f out: rdn to chse wnr ins fnl f: r.o (jockey said colt hung left)* **8/1**

00-5 3 *1/2* **Tails I Win (CAN)**[12] 122 3-9-2 59 (h[1]) BenSanderson(5) 2 61
(Roger Fell) *hld up: drvn 1 1/2f out: rdn on outer 1f out: r.o wl fnl f: tk 3rd last 25yds* **9/1**

00-4 4 *1/2* **Comeonfeeltheforce (IRE)**[8] 183 3-9-2 54 (t) RaulDaSilva 3 56+
(Adam West) *mid-div: pushed along 2f out: sn drvn: nt clr run over 1f out: rdn and r.o fnl f: tk 4th nr fin (jockey said filly was denied a clear run in the home straight)* **11/1**

5 *hd* **Act Of Magic (IRE)**[71] 8986 3-8-9 52 DarraghKeenan(5) 10 52
(Mohamed Moubarak) *mid-div on outer: tk clsr order 1/2-way: pushed along in cl 2nd 2f out: rdn and lost pl 1f out: no ex fnl f* **4/1**[1]

430- 6 *2 1/4* **Fflur**[39] 9489 3-9-1 53 CliffordLee 4 50
(K R Burke) *trckd ldrs: drvn 2f out: nt clr run over 1f out: no ex fnl f* **11/1**

300- 7 *1 1/2* **Riviera Claire**[43] 9444 3-9-7 59 (t[1]) DougieCostello 7 52
(Jamie Osborne) *bhd: drvn 1 1/2f out: rdn over 1f out: no imp* **8/1**

50-0 8 *1/2* **Tunky**[17] 27 3-9-5 57 FranBerry 11 48
(James Given) *bhd: pushed along over 2f out: rdn 1 1/2f out: no imp* **33/1**

445- 9 *2 3/4* **Freesia Gold (IRE)**[22] 9729 3-9-4 56 RobertWinston 8 42
(Daniel Kubler) *led: pushed along in narrow ld 2f out: drvn and hdd 1 1/2f out: wknd fnl f* **9/1**

06-0 10 *3 3/4* **Agent Smith (IRE)**[6] 228 3-9-2 54 (h[1]) DavidProbert 9 32
(K R Burke) *prom: drvn in cl 3rd 2f out: sn lost pl: rdn and wknd over 1f out* **33/1**

606- 11 *3* **Power Of Life (USA)**[49] 9354 3-9-6 58 LouisSteward 1 30
(Michael Bell) *trckd ldrs: pushed along 2f out: wknd 1 1/2f out (jockey said gelding was denied a clear run approaching the 1 furlong marker)* **9/2**[2]

003- 12 *39* **Casting (IRE)**[56] 9243 3-8-11 56 MarkCrehan(7) 6
(Richard Hannon) *mid-div: rdn on outer 3f out: sn dropped to rr: no ch whn rn wd 1 1/2f out (jockey said colt moved poorly)* **18/1**

1m 50.22s (0.12) **Going Correction** -0.075s/f (Stan) 12 Ran SP% **124.9**
Speed ratings (Par 95): **96,95,94,94,94 92,90,90,87,84 81,47**
CSF £47.53 CT £364.17 TOTE £7.20: £1.90, £2.80, £3.10; EX 56.00 Trifecta £259.00.
Owner G B & G H Firmager **Bred** C & M Murphy **Trained** Tern Hill, Shropshire

FOCUS
A couple of unexposed sorts in a moderate handicap. The gallop was reasonable and the first five finished in a bit of a heap. It's been rated as straightforward modest form.

320 LADBROKES H'CAP 7f 36y (Tp)
7:15 (7:15) (Class 4) (0-85,86) 3-Y-O £5,530 (£1,645; £822; £411; £400) Stalls High

Form RPR
034- 1 **Nefarious (IRE)**[38] 9497 3-9-5 80 FranBerry 3 85
(Henry Candy) *disp ld 1f: trckd ldr whn hdd: dropped to 3rd over 3f out: drvn into 3 l 2nd 2f out: rdn to cl on ldr 1f out: r.o wl to ld 75yds out: sn clr* **2/1**[1]

123- 2 *1 1/4* **Times Past (IRE)**[31] 9605 3-8-12 78 ThomasGreatrex(5) 7 79
(Archie Watson) *disp ld tl led on own after 1f: pushed along in 3 l ld 2f out: rdn in reduced ld 1f out: hdd 75yds out: no ex* **7/2**[3]

624- 3 *nse* **Lady Cosette (FR)**[22] 9730 3-9-2 77 (b) ShaneKelly 2 78
(Jeremy Noseda) *hld up in rr: pushed along 2f out: drvn and hdwy over 1f out: 3rd ent fnl f: sn rdn: kpt on* **5/2**[2]

26-1 4 *1 1/4* **Black Medick**[10] 140 3-8-9 77 SeamusCronin(7) 4 75
(Richard Hannon) *t.k.h: prom: sn positioned bhd ldrs: pushed along on outer 2f out: rdn in 4th over 1f out: no imp fnl f* **9/2**

46- 5 *6* **Facethepuckout (IRE)**[51] 9314 3-9-3 78 (p) StevieDonohoe 5 59
(John Ryan) *prom: 2nd 3f out: drvn and lost pl 2f out: sn dropped to rr* **7/1**

1m 28.28s (-0.52) **Going Correction** -0.075s/f (Stan) 5 Ran SP% **114.8**
Speed ratings (Par 99): **99,97,97,96,89**
CSF £9.77 TOTE £3.20: £1.60, £1.70; EX 10.50 Trifecta £22.30.
Owner A Davis **Bred** Ms Ashley O'Leary **Trained** Kingston Warren, Oxon

FOCUS
An ordinary turn out for a fairly valuable event and a muddling gallop means this bare form isn't entirely reliable.

321 BETWAY CASINO H'CAP — 1m 4f 51y (Tp)
7:45 (7:45) (Class 6) (0-60,60) 4-Y-O+
£3,105 (£924; £461; £400; £400; £400) **Stalls** Low

Form / RPR

060- **1** **Tetradrachm**[65] 9067 6-9-2 **55**..............(t[1]) StevieDonohoe 9 68+
(Rebecca Menzies) *bhd: swift move on outer over 2f out: sn led: 2 l ld 2f out: drvn 6 l clr 1f out: rdn further clr fnl f* **6/1**[1]

01-1 **2** *7* **Apex Predator (IRE)**[15] 58 4-9-1 **57**..............(bt) LukeMorris 11 60
(Seamus Durack) *hld up: drvn and hdwy 1 1/2f out: rdn into 6 l 2nd 1f out: kpt on fnl f: no ch w wnr* **6/1**[1]

000- **3** *nk* **Rail Dancer**[23] 9721 7-9-7 **60**..............(p) LiamJones 10 62
(Shaun Keightley) *hld up: drvn on outer 1 1/2f out: rdn and hdwy ent fnl f: r.o: tk 3rd 100yds out* **16/1**

052- **4** *4* **Music Major**[28] 9687 6-9-4 **57**..............(p[1]) LiamKeniry 8 53
(Michael Attwater) *hld up: pushed along and hdwy 2f out: rdn 1 1/2f out: 3rd 1f out: no ex fnl f: lost 3rd 100yds out* **11/1**

00-0 **5** *3/4* **Qayed (CAN)**[15] 61 4-9-4 **60**..............(p[1]) ShaneKelly 4 55
(Mark Brisbourne) *hld up: drvn 1 1/2f out: styd on fnl f* **25/1**

104- **6** *1* **Iley Boy**[29] 9666 5-9-3 **56**..............(p) JoeyHaynes 2 49
(John Gallagher) *chsd ldrs: drvn into 2 l 2nd 2f out: sn rdn: wknd fnl f* **9/1**

50-5 **7** *1 1/4* **Sosian**[15] 67 4-8-9 **51**..............(b) PaddyMathers 1 43
(Richard Fahey) *chsd ldrs: pushed along 2f out: drvn 1 1/2f out: no imp* **7/1**[3]

06/4 **8** *10* **Blue Skimmer (IRE)**[8] 181 7-9-1 **54**.............. MarcMonaghan 6 30
(Alastair Ralph) *prom: disp ld 1/2-way: hdd over 2f out: sn rdn and wknd (jockey said gelding hung right)* **14/1**

053- **9** *2 1/4* **Warofindependence (USA)**[29] 9666 7-9-0 **53**..............(p) RossaRyan 3 26
(John O'Shea) *bhd: lost footing after 1f: drvn over 2f out: reminder over 1f out: no rspnse (jockey said gelding hung left throughout)* **11/1**

31-0 **10** *nk* **Wallflower (IRE)**[15] 76 4-9-3 **59**.............. FranBerry 5 32
(Rae Guest) *led: jnd 1/2-way: led over 2f out: sn hdd: wknd qckly (jockey said filly had no more to give in the final furlong)* **7/1**[3]

4-40 **11** *19* **Demophon**[3] 257 5-8-8 **47**.............. JosephineGordon 7
(Steve Flook) *chsd ldrs: lost pl 1/2-way: rdn and rallied 4f out: wknd over 2f out* **13/2**[2]

00-4 **12** *13* **Onda District (IRE)**[13] 100 7-8-7 **46** oh1.............. KieranO'Neill 12
(Stella Barclay) *mid-div on outer: drvn and lost pl over 3f out: sn dropped to rr* **16/1**

2m 37.7s (-3.10) **Going Correction** -0.075s/f (Stan)
WFA 4 from 5yo+ 3lb — **12** Ran SP% **115.8**
Speed ratings (Par 101): **107,102,102,99,98 98,97,90,89,89 76,67**
CSF £39.98 CT £548.94 TOTE £6.70: £2.50, £1.90, £5.20; EX 45.70 Trifecta £574.10.
Owner Stoneleigh Racing **Bred** Paramount Bloodstock **Trained** Mordon, Durham
■ Stewards' Enquiry : Stevie Donohoe caution: careless riding

FOCUS
An ordinary handicap was taken apart by Tetradrachm, who made a decisive move around the home turn. The gallop was an ordinary one up to that point. It's been rated conservatively around the second and third.

322 BETWAY HEED YOUR HUNCH H'CAP — 5f 21y (Tp)
8:15 (8:15) (Class 7) (0-50,58) 4-Y-O+ — **£2,264** (£673; £336; £168) **Stalls** Low

Form / RPR

50-0 **1** **Foxy Boy**[15] 60 5-9-4 **47**..............(b[1]) DavidProbert 10 55
(Rebecca Bastiman) *chsd ldr: pushed into ld 1 1/2f out: 2 l ld 1f out: rdn and in command fnl f: comf* **13/2**[3]

0-00 **2** *1 3/4* **Fuel Injection**[11] 129 8-9-4 **47**..............(b) JamesSullivan 3 49
(Ruth Carr) *bhd: pushed along and hdwy 2f out: sn drvn: wnt 3rd 150yds out: r.o wl to go 2nd last few strides* **9/1**

44-0 **3** *nk* **Amazing Amaya**[11] 129 4-9-4 **47**..............(h) PaddyMathers 4 48
(Derek Shaw) *mid-div: hdwy into 3rd 2f out: rdn to chse wnr ent fnl f: kpt on: lost 2nd last few strides* **12/1**

00-3 **4** *2 1/2* **Pranceabootthetoon (IRE)**[8] 179 4-8-9 **45**..............(t) AmeliaGlass[(7)] 1 37
(Milton Bradley) *hld up: hdwy on inner 1 1/2f out: 4th ent fnl f: one pce* **10/1**

04-5 **5** *nse* **Storm Lightning**[17] 26 10-9-4 **47**.............. EoinWalsh 5 38
(Mark Brisbourne) *bhd: drvn 2f out: rdn in rr 1 1/2f out: kpt on past btn horses fnl f* **7/2**[2]

556- **6** *2 1/4* **Teepee Time**[23] 9722 6-8-13 **45**..............(b) PhilDennis[(3)] 11 28
(Michael Mullineaux) *chsd ldrs: drvn and dropped to 4th 2f out: sn rdn and no ex* **10/1**

060- **7** *nk* **Men United (FR)**[149] 6446 6-9-2 **45**..............(b) LiamKeniry 2 27
(Roy Bowring) *led: pushed along in 1/2 l ld 2f out: drvn and hdd 1 1/2f out: wknd 1f out* **20/1**

0-06 **8** *2 3/4* **Shesthedream (IRE)**[12] 118 6-9-2 **45**..............(p) LukeMorris 9 17
(Lisa Williamson) *slowly away: sn rcvrd to r in mid-div: drvn 2f out: rdn over 1f out: wknd* **14/1**

0-11 **9** *1 3/4* **Captain Ryan**[12] 118 8-10-1 **58**..............(p) KieranO'Neill 8 24
(Geoffrey Deacon) *in rr: effrt on outer over 2f out: reminder over 1f out: no rspnse (jockey said gelding hung right; trainer said gelding ran flat)* **15/8**[1]

1m 1.27s (-0.63) **Going Correction** -0.075s/f (Stan) — **9** Ran SP% **117.6**
Speed ratings (Par 97): **102,99,98,94,94 91,90,86,83**
CSF £64.44 CT £697.23 TOTE £7.30: £2.10, £2.80, £3.40; EX 50.60 Trifecta £624.20.
Owner Grange Park Racing Club And Partner **Bred** Giles W Pritchard-Gordon (farming) Ltd **Trained** Cowthorpe, N Yorks
■ Stewards' Enquiry : David Probert one-day ban: failure to ride to the draw (Feb 2)

FOCUS
A low-grade handicap which didn't take as much winning as seemed likely with the market leader underperforming. The gallop was reasonable but very few figured. Very modest form in behind the winner.
T/Plt: £113.20 to a £1 stake. Pool: £85,938.27 - 553.75 winning units T/Qpdt: £13.70 to a £1 stake. Pool: £13,982.38 - 753.03 winning units **Keith McHugh**

323a-340a (Foreign Racing) - See Raceform Interactive

315 WOLVERHAMPTON (A.W) (L-H)
Monday, January 21
OFFICIAL GOING: Tapeta: standard
Wind: Medium behind

341 LADBROKES HOME OF THE ODDS BOOST H'CAP — 7f 36y (Tp)
4:15 (4:15) (Class 6) (0-55,55) 3-Y-O
£3,105 (£692; £692; £400; £400; £400) **Stalls** High

Form / RPR

00-2 **1** **Heatherdown (IRE)**[16] 79 3-9-2 **55**.............. CameronNoble[(5)] 3 59+
(Michael Bell) *hld up in midfield: rdn over 2f out: r.o wl fnl f: led last strides* **15/8**[1]

530- **2** *1/2* **Micronize (IRE)**[54] 9289 3-9-7 **55**.............. TonyHamilton 1 58
(Richard Fahey) *led: hung lft over 1f out: kpt on u.p fnl f: hdd and jnd for 2nd last strides* **7/1**[3]

005- **2** *dht* **Macs Blessings (IRE)**[89] 8540 3-9-4 **52**..............(p) LiamKeniry 7 55+
(Stef Keniry) *s.i.s: towards rr: rdn over 2f out: r.o wl up inner fnl f: jst hld* **18/1**

020- **4** *nk* **Farump**[23] 9749 3-8-9 **48**.............. DarraghKeenan[(5)] 5 50
(Robert Eddery) *trckd ldr: rdn 2f out: kpt on same pce: lost 2 pls nr fin* **20/1**

15-0 **5** *3/4* **Geography Teacher (IRE)**[19] 21 3-9-0 **53**.............. BenSanderson[(5)] 2 53
(Roger Fell) *trckd ldrs: rdn over 2f out: unable qck and lost 2 pls ins fnl f* **12/1**

00-0 **6** *nk* **Cool Kitty**[4] 274 3-8-13 **54**.............. ThoreHammerHansen[(7)] 4 53
(Rebecca Menzies) *s.i.s: sn in midfield: nt clr run and swtchd rt over 1f out: unable qck fnl f* **14/1**

7 *hd* **Bellepower (IRE)**[52] 9338 3-8-12 **46** oh1..............(p) LukeMorris 9 45
(John James Feane, Ire) *towards rr: chsd along at times: rdn and hdwy 2f out: nt clr run over 1f out: swtchd rt early ins fnl f: edgd lft and r.o: nrst fin* **7/2**[2]

000- **8** *1 1/4* **Isabella Red (IRE)**[54] 9289 3-9-4 **52**.............. PJMcDonald 11 48
(David Evans) *hld up: rdn 2f out: styd on fnl f: nvr able to chal* **33/1**

9 *2 3/4* **Lady Greta (IRE)**[10] 195 3-9-7 **55**.............. AdamKirby 12 44
(Adrian McGuinness, Ire) *trckd ldrs on outer: rdn over 2f out: wknd fnl f* **17/2**

44-0 **10** *10* **Kemmeridge Bay**[19] 26 3-9-0 **48**..............(b) SamJames 8 13
(Grant Tuer) *prom 2f: midfield after: lost pl over 2f out: sn rdn and wknd* **40/1**

00-0 **11** *10* **Anglesey Penny**[16] 90 3-9-1 **49**.............. DavidProbert 6
(J R Jenkins) *hld up: rdn 2f out: sn btn (jockey said filly suffered interference approx 3f and stopped quickly. post-race examination failed to reveal any abnormalities)* **25/1**

1m 30.36s (1.56) **Going Correction** -0.10s/f (Stan) — **11** Ran SP% **113.6**
Speed ratings (Par 95): **87,86,86,86,85 84,84,83,80,68 57**
EX: HD/MB 19.20, HD/MIC 6.40; CSF: HD/MB 18.01, HD/MIC 6.93; TC: HD/MIC/MB 89.73, HD/MB/MIC 99.51; TF: HD/MB/MIC 108.80, HD/MIC/MB 83.00 TOTE £2.50: £1.10, £2.10, £4.30.
Owner The Heatherdonians **Bred** Tally-Ho Stud **Trained** Newmarket, Suffolk

FOCUS
A moderate 3yo handicap with only one previous winner in the field. It proved hard to come from off the pace and the principals finished in a heap.

342 LADBROKES H'CAP — 5f 21y (Tp)
4:50 (4:50) (Class 4) (0-85,84) 3-Y-O
£5,530 (£1,645; £822; £411; £400; £400) **Stalls** Low

Form / RPR

60-4 **1** **Yolo Again (IRE)**[10] 182 3-9-2 **84**.............. BenSanderson[(5)] 2 87
(Roger Fell) *led narrowly: drvn over 1f out: hdd ins fnl f: rallied to ld again cl home (trainer rep said, regarding improved form shown, filly had stripped fitter for its reappearance)* **40/1**

21-4 **2** *shd* **Wedding Date**[16] 83 3-9-4 **81**.............. RossaRyan 5 84
(Richard Hannon) *cl up in 2nd: rdn 2f out: led narrowly ins fnl f: kpt on: hdd cl home* **10/1**

3-23 **3** *hd* **Uncle Jerry**[12] 142 3-9-3 **83**..............(b) FinleyMarsh[(3)] 7 85+
(Richard Hughes) *hld up: rdn and hdwy 2f out: r.o wl towards fin: jst hld* **7/2**[1]

122- **4** *1/2* **Sandridge Lad (IRE)**[35] 9589 3-8-13 **76**.............. StevieDonohoe 1 76
(John Ryan) *half-rrd s and s.i.s: hld up: hit rail over 3f out: rdn and clsd 2f out: r.o fnl f: nvr quite able to chal (jockey said gelding reared as stalls opened and subsequently missed the break)* **4/1**[2]

5 *1 1/4* **Annabelle Rock (IRE)**[31] 9672 3-8-4 **67**.............. KieranO'Neill 4 63
(Adrian McGuinness, Ire) *chsd ldrs: rdn 2f out: kpt on same pce fnl f* **17/2**

12-1 **6** *1* **Lorna Cole (IRE)**[13] 130 3-8-12 **75**.............. MartinDwyer 3 67
(William Muir) *trckd ldrs: rdn 2f out: nt clr run over 1f out: outpcd fnl f* **7/2**[1]

41-2 **7** *5* **Dragon Beat (IRE)**[10] 182 3-8-8 **71**.............. JoeFanning 8 45
(Michael Appleby) *wnt to post early: hld up: rdn 2f out: outpcd and no ch fnl f (trainer said, regarding poor performance, filly was trapped wide throughout from stall eight)* **5/1**[3]

310- **8** *2 1/2* **Kapono**[212] 4105 3-9-2 **79**.............. AdamKirby 6 44
(Amy Murphy) *chsd ldrs: rdn over 2f out: wknd appr fnl f* **10/1**

1m 1.31s (-0.59) **Going Correction** -0.10s/f (Stan) — **8** Ran SP% **112.3**
Speed ratings (Par 99): **100,99,99,98,96 95,87,83**
CSF £373.10 CT £1779.52 TOTE £36.80: £8.50, £2.50, £1.40; EX 305.10 Trifecta £1264.80.
Owner Nick Bradley Racing 28 **Bred** The Suite Partnership **Trained** Nawton, N Yorks

FOCUS
A fair 3yo sprint handicap and another tight finish. The front pair dominated throughout. The fourth helps set the standard

343 LADBROKES HOME OF THE ODDS BOOST NOVICE STKS — 1m 1f 104y (Tp)
5:25 (5:25) (Class 5) 3-Y-O — **£3,752** (£1,116; £557; £278) **Stalls** Low

Form / RPR

4-3 **1** **War Tiger (USA)**[15] 103 3-9-2 0.............. TonyHamilton 4 87
(Richard Fahey) *mde all: shkn up wl over 1f out: rdn fnl f: comf* **3/1**[2]

4 **2** *3 1/2* **Kinver Edge (USA)**[11] 156 3-9-2 0.............. AdamKirby 6 81
(Charlie Appleby) *trckd ldrs: wnt 2nd after 2f: rdn 2f out: nt qckn and hld fnl f* **4/11**[1]

5-5 **3** *8* **Gino Wotimean (USA)**[17] 66 3-9-2 0.............. RossaRyan 2 63
(Noel Williams) *t.k.h early: trckd wnr 2f: rdn in 3rd over 2f out: one pce and no ch w ldng over 1f out* **25/1**

0-0 **4** *14* **Midnite Rendezvous**[16] 90 3-8-11 0.............. RaulDaSilva 5 29
(Derek Shaw) *a in 4th: rdn over 3f out: wknd 2f out* **200/1**

5 17 **Withoutdestination** 3-9-2 0...............(p[1]) MarcMonaghan 1
(Marco Botti) *s.s: in rr: early reminders: drvn along 5f out: wknd 3f out: eased over 1f out: t.o* **12/1**[3]

1m 58.51s (-2.29) **Going Correction** -0.10s/f (Stan) **5** Ran SP% **110.3**
Speed ratings (Par 97): **106,102,95,83,68**
CSF £4.50 TOTE £4.30: £1.70, £1.10; EX 5.20 Trifecta £10.80.
Owner Mrs Richard Henry **Bred** Premier Bloodstock **Trained** Musley Bank, N Yorks

FOCUS
November's Melbourne Cup winner Cross Counter took this 3yo novice event last year. A small field, but a big range of odds and this time the long-odds-on Godolphin representative was floored. The winner looks a nice prospect. They raced in more or less the same order throughout.

344 BETWAY HEED YOUR HUNCH H'CAP 1m 1f 104y (Tp)
5:55 (5:55) (Class 5) (0-70,68) 4-Y-O+
£3,752 (£1,116; £557; £400; £400; £400) **Stalls** Low

Form RPR

1 **Manfadh (IRE)**[237] 3217 4-9-3 **65**............ ShaneKelly 5 74+
(Mark Brisbourne) *upset in stalls: s.i.s: t.k.h early: sn in midfield: drvn and hdwy on outer 2f out: led ins fnl f: readily* **40/1**

1- 2 2 **Captain Dan (IRE)**[49] 9385 5-9-6 **67**............ LukeMorris 3 72+
(John James Feane, Ire) *trckd ldrs: drvn 2f out: ev ch ins fnl f: sn hung lft and outpcd by wnr* **5/2**[2]

40-6 3 ¾ **King Of Naples**[17] 63 6-9-1 **62**............ JamesSullivan 2 66
(Ruth Carr) *t.k.h: hld up: hdwy 2f out: rdn over 1f out: unable qck ins fnl f: wnt 3rd cl home* **40/1**

43-2 4 nk **Sajanji**[19] 18 4-9-6 **68**............ AdamKirby 10 71
(Simon Crisford) *sltly hmpd leaving stalls: chsd ldrs tl led 7f out: drvn 2f out: hdd and no ex ins fnl f: lost 3rd cl home* **15/8**[1]

244- 5 1 ½ **Zephyros (GER)**[236] 3237 8-9-0 **66**............ PoppyBridgwater(5) 4 66
(David Bridgwater) *hld up: rdn on outer over 2f out: styd on fnl f: nvr able to chal* **22/1**

663- 6 shd **Ghazan (IRE)**[23] 9746 4-9-5 **67**............ JasonHart 7 67
(Kevin Frost) *t.k.h: prom: led 8f out to 7f out: chsd ldrs: drvn and disp 2nd 2f out: fdd fnl f* **14/1**

23-0 7 nk **Bell Heather (IRE)**[17] 67 6-9-4 **65**............ DougieCostello 6 64
(Patrick Morris) *led tl restrained and hdd 8f out: chsd ldrs: rdn 3f out: styd on u.p tl no ex ins fnl f* **16/1**

001- 8 nk **Tagle (IRE)**[44] 9458 4-9-0 **62**............(b) PJMcDonald 1 60
(Ivan Furtado) *midfield: rdn 4f out: outpcd over 2f out: edgd lft and styd on fnl f* **8/1**[3]

12-0 9 2 ¾ **Berlusca (IRE)**[15] 102 10-9-1 **62**............ DavidProbert 9 55
(David Loughnane) *wnt to post early: s.s: t.k.h in last: rdn over 2f out: no imp: wknd ent fnl f (jockey said gelding ran too freely and hung badly left-handed)* **12/1**

03-3 10 1 **Sunshineandbubbles**[17] 67 6-9-4 **65**............(v) JoeFanning 11 56
(Jennie Candlish) *wnt lft leaving stalls: prom on outer: trckd ldr 5f out: rdn 2f out: sn lost 2nd: wknd fnl f* **10/1**

1m 59.73s (-1.07) **Going Correction** -0.10s/f (Stan) **10** Ran SP% **113.0**
WFA 4 from 5yo+ 1lb
Speed ratings (Par 103): **100,98,97,97,95 95,95,95,92,92**
CSF £133.26 CT £4108.82 TOTE £73.80: £15.10, £1.20, £8.40; EX 332.60 Trifecta £4756.50.
Owner Derek & Mrs Marie Dean **Bred** Shadwell Estate Company Limited **Trained** Great Ness, Shropshire

FOCUS
An ordinary handicap which had little depth to it and it a two-horse race according to the market. However, a muddling race resulted in another big-priced winner.

345 BETWAY LIVE CASINO H'CAP 1m 4f 51y (Tp)
6:25 (6:25) (Class 4) (0-85,87) 4-Y-O+
£5,530 (£1,645; £822; £411; £400; £400) **Stalls** Low

Form RPR

311- 1 **Fearsome**[22] 9768 5-9-2 **80**............ AdamKirby 7 93+
(Nick Littmoden) *hld up: shkn up and hdwy 2f out: qcknd to ld 1f out: r.o strly and sn clr: eased nr fin* **5/2**[2]

504- 2 5 **Technological**[21] 9775 4-9-3 **84**............ LukeMorris 2 89
(George Margarson) *trckd ldr: drvn to ld 2f out: hdd 1f out: sn hung rt and outpcd by wnr (vet said colt spread its left fore plate)* **10/3**[3]

632- 3 2 **Thaqaffa (IRE)**[22] 9768 6-9-3 **81**............(h) MartinHarley 1 82
(Amy Murphy) *racd keenly: trckd ldrs: rdn over 1f out: sn outpcd by ldng pair: hld on for 3rd towards fin* **8/1**

133- 4 ½ **Kaser (IRE)**[25] 9723 4-8-11 **78**............ PJMcDonald 8 79
(David Loughnane) *hld up in tch: rdn over 2f out: styd on fnl f: no ch w ldrs* **2/1**[1]

5/0- 5 2 **Gawdawpalin (IRE)**[44] 9463 6-9-4 **85**............(t[1]) GaryMahon(3) 6 82?
(Sylvester Kirk) *led: rdn over 2f out: sn hdd: wknd fnl f* **25/1**

045- 6 3 ¼ **Tenedos**[126] 7370 4-8-12 **79**............ CallumShepherd 4 72
(Ed de Giles) *hld up: rdn over 2f out: no imp on ldrs* **14/1**

60-0 7 2 ½ **Winterlude (IRE)**[16] 82 9-9-9 **87**............(t[1]) JoeFanning 5 75
(Jennie Candlish) *trckd ldrs: rdn on outer over 2f out: hung rt over 1f out: wknd (jockey said gelding stopped quickly. post-race examination failed to reveal any abnormalities)* **12/1**

00/0 8 7 **Sporty Yankee (USA)**[10] 184 6-8-7 **71** oh7............(p) JamesSullivan 3 47
(Aytach Sadik) *s.i.s: in tch towards rr: rdn 4f out: wknd over 2f out* **250/1**

2m 38.71s (-2.09) **Going Correction** -0.10s/f (Stan) **8** Ran SP% **114.7**
WFA 4 from 5yo+ 3lb
Speed ratings (Par 105): **102,98,97,97,95 93,91,87**
CSF £11.38 CT £56.33 TOTE £2.80: £1.10, £1.40, £2.20; EX 10.40 Trifecta £52.40.
Owner G F Chesneaux & Nick Littmoden **Bred** Newhall Estate Farm **Trained** Newmarket, Suffolk

FOCUS
A fair middle-distance handicap, though a few of these had something to prove. The pace wasn't that strong, but the winner was most impressive. The runner-up ran his race and sets the standard.

346 BETWAY H'CAP 1m 4f 51y (Tp)
6:55 (6:55) (Class 5) (0-70,72) 4-Y-O+
£3,752 (£1,116; £557; £400; £400; £400) **Stalls** Low

Form RPR

05-3 1 **Star Ascending (IRE)**[17] 61 7-9-7 **70**............(p) JoeFanning 6 77
(Jennie Candlish) *t.k.h: trckd ldrs: wnt 2nd 2f out: rdn to ld 1f out: r.o* **5/1**[3]

42-1 2 nk **Ice Canyon**[17] 61 5-9-5 **68**............(h) EoinWalsh 1 75
(Mark Brisbourne) *t.k.h in midfield: hdwy 2f out: rdn over 1f out: ev ch ins fnl f: unable qck towards fin* **11/2**

543- 3 1 ½ **Flood Defence (IRE)**[26] 9706 5-8-10 **62**............ PhilDennis(3) 2 67
(Iain Jardine) *hld up: nt clr run over 2f out: rdn over 1f out: r.o fnl f: wnt 3rd cl home* **7/2**[2]

14-2 4 nk **Champarisi**[15] 101 4-9-1 **67**............ SamJames 4 73+
(Grant Tuer) *led and set stdy pce: rdn 2f out: hdd 1f out: disputing 2nd whn hmpd ins fnl f: ct for 3rd cl home* **9/4**[1]

20/6 5 ¾ **Stormy Blues**[16] 88 5-9-9 **72**............(t) DougieCostello 5 75
(Nigel Hawke) *hld up: rdn over 2f out: styd on fnl f: nvr able to chal* **28/1**

40-4 6 7 **Smiley Bagel (IRE)**[16] 88 6-9-2 **72**............ OliverStammers(7) 9 64
(Ed Walker) *hld up in tch: rdn over 2f out: wknd over 1f out* **20/1**

104- 7 3 ½ **Carp Kid (IRE)**[26] 9706 4-9-4 **70**............(p) LukeMorris 7 57
(John Flint) *t.k.h: prom: trckd ldr after 3f: rdn: hung rt and lost 2nd over 2f out: wknd over 1f out* **8/1**

606- 8 2 ¼ **Brexitmeansbrexit**[24] 9731 4-9-6 **72**............ RossaRyan 3 56
(Richard Hannon) *trckd ldr 3f: remained cl up: rdn over 2f out: wknd 1f out* **12/1**

52-0 9 ¾ **Sellingallthetime (IRE)**[18] 38 8-9-2 **65**............(p) AlistairRawlinson 8 46
(Michael Appleby) *s.i.s: towards rr: gd hdwy on outer to chse ldrs 5f out: rdn 3f out: wknd 2f out* **18/1**

0 10 31 **Fearaun (IRE)**[15] 101 4-8-8 **60**............ JamesSullivan 10
(Stella Barclay) *chsd ldrs on outer: rdn over 4f out and qckly lost pl: bhd fnl 3f: t.o* **100/1**

2m 37.3s (-3.50) **Going Correction** -0.10s/f (Stan)
WFA 4 from 5yo+ 3lb **10** Ran SP% **118.3**
Speed ratings (Par 103): **107,106,105,105,105 100,98,96,96,75**
CSF £32.61 CT £109.89 TOTE £5.20: £1.60, £1.60, £1.70; EX 24.20 Trifecta £130.20.
Owner Paul Wright-Bevans **Bred** Philip Gilligan & Anne Gilligan **Trained** Basford Green, Staffs
■ Stewards' Enquiry : Joe Fanning caution: careless riding

FOCUS
A lesser handicap than the previous race over the same trip, but run at a stronger gallop resulting in a time 1.41sec quicker.

347 BETWAY SPRINT H'CAP 6f 20y (Tp)
7:25 (7:25) (Class 5) (0-75,74) 4-Y-O+
£3,752 (£1,116; £557; £400; £400; £400) **Stalls** Low

Form RPR

00-0 1 **Martineo**[17] 54 4-9-4 **71**............ AdamKirby 2 78+
(Paul D'Arcy) *s.i.s: hld up: rdn over 1f out: sn swtchd rt: r.o down outer to ld cl home* **7/1**[3]

65-2 2 nk **Kupa River (IRE)**[10] 187 5-9-1 **68**............(h) LukeMorris 1 74
(Roger Fell) *racd keenly: trckd ldrs: rdn 2f out: led 1f out: r.o: hdd cl home* **15/8**[1]

240- 3 nk **Monumental Man**[34] 9596 10-9-4 **71**............(p) DougieCostello 7 76
(Jamie Osborne) *led: rdn 2f out: hdd 1f out: kpt on: unable qck towards fin* **15/2**

610- 4 2 ¾ **Burtonwood**[35] 9588 7-8-10 **66**............(v) ConorMcGovern(3) 9 62
(Julie Camacho) *hld up: rdn 2f out: r.o fnl f: tk 4th last strides* **20/1**

14-0 5 nk **Laubali**[13] 131 4-9-7 **74**............(v[1]) MartinHarley 3 69
(David O'Meara) *hld up in tch: rdn to go 3rd 1f out: wknd fnl 100yds (jockey said gelding moved poorly)* **9/2**[2]

43-0 6 2 **Anonymous John (IRE)**[5] 253 7-9-7 **74**............ JFEgan 4 63
(Dominic Ffrench Davis) *chsd ldr: rdn wl over 2f out: lost 2nd 2f out: wknd fnl f* **8/1**

1/1- 7 5 **Ahundrednotout**[17] 71 5-9-3 **70**............(p) StevieDonohoe 8 43
(John James Feane, Ire) *chsd ldrs: rdn over 2f out: sn outpcd: wknd fnl f* **9/2**[2]

1m 13.38s (-1.12) **Going Correction** -0.10s/f (Stan) **7** Ran SP% **111.3**
Speed ratings (Par 103): **103,102,102,98,98 95,88**
CSF £19.47 CT £97.88 TOTE £7.90: £3.20, £1.60; EX 21.10 Trifecta £107.00.
Owner Power Geneva Ltd **Bred** Saleh Al Homaizi & Imad Al Sagar **Trained** Newmarket, Suffolk

FOCUS
An ordinary sprint handicap weakened further by the absence of Inaam, who would probably have gone off favourite, but his stable still took the prize with Adam Kirby switching to the winner.

348 SUN RACING NO1 RACING SITE H'CAP 1m 142y (Tp)
7:55 (7:55) (Class 6) (0-60,60) 4-Y-O+
£3,105 (£924; £461; £400; £400; £400) **Stalls** Low

Form RPR

02-3 1 **Arrowzone**[14] 120 8-9-6 **59**............(b) JasonHart 3 65
(Kevin Frost) *led 2f: chsd ldrs: drvn to ld again on inner 1f out: r.o* **8/1**

10-0 2 ½ **Aqua Libre**[10] 175 6-9-7 **60**............(p) JoeFanning 7 65
(Jennie Candlish) *s.i.s: towards rr: hdwy whn nt clr run 2f out: rdn over 1f out: r.o ins fnl f: wnt 2nd last strides* **22/1**

33-2 3 ½ **Big Bad Lol (IRE)**[10] 180 5-9-7 **60**............ DavidProbert 10 64
(Ed Walker) *chsd ldrs: wnt 2nd after 3f: rdn over 2f out: lost 2nd over 2f out: kpt on: unable qck ins fnl f* **4/1**[2]

23-0 4 nk **Stand N Deliver**[12] 138 5-9-7 **60**............(b) AdamKirby 5 63
(Clive Cox) *chsd ldrs tl led after 2f: rdn over 2f out: hdd 1f out: kpt on u.p tl no ex and lost 2 pls nr fin* **9/1**

210- 5 nk **Mossy's Lodge**[26] 9704 6-9-6 **59**............(tp) StevieDonohoe 8 62
(Rebecca Menzies) *chsd ldrs: rdn over 2f out: styd on down outer fnl f: unable to chal* **20/1**

13-4 6 hd **Man Of Verve (IRE)**[19] 22 5-9-7 **60**............ PJMcDonald 2 62
(Philip Kirby) *chsd ldrs: nt clr run and swtchd lft appr fnl f: swtchd rt sn after: unable qck ins fnl f (jockey said gelding denied clear run in str)* **11/2**[3]

00-5 7 1 ¾ **La Sioux (IRE)**[14] 120 5-9-1 **54**............(b) TonyHamilton 4 53
(Richard Fahey) *wnt to post early: towards rr: rdn over 2f out: styd on fnl f: nvr a threat* **18/1**

100- 8 ½ **Ainne**[48] 9386 4-8-13 **56**............(bt) GaryMahon(3) 1 53
(Sylvester Kirk) *midfield: rdn 2f out: sme hdwy on inner over 1f out: fdd fnl f* **33/1**

0-30 9 3 ¼ **Aljunood (IRE)**[2] 315 5-9-3 **56**............(h) DougieCostello 6 47
(John Norton) *s.i.s: t.k.h in rr: rdn over 2f out: hung rt over 1f out: no imp (jockey said gelding ran too freely and hung right-handed)* **14/1**

300- 10 2 ¼ **Pecheurs De Perles (IRE)**[23] 9751 5-9-0 **53**............ ShaneKelly 9 39
(Paul D'Arcy) *t.k.h: prom: rdn over 2f out: wknd over 1f out* **33/1**

06-6 11 nk **Bidding War**[17] 64 4-9-4 **58**............ RobertWinston 12 43
(Michael Appleby) *s.i.s: towards rr: hdwy on outer 4f out: rdn over 2f out: wknd over 1f out* **16/1**

21/ 12 25 **Turn On The Tears (USA)**[17] 69 6-9-2 **55**............ LukeMorris 11
(John James Feane, Ire) *hld up: rdn over 3f out: wknd 2f out: eased fnl f: t.o (jockey said mare was never travelling. post-race examination failed to reveal any abnormalities)* **3/1**[1]

1m 49.32s (-0.78) **Going Correction** -0.10s/f (Stan)
WFA 4 from 5yo+ 1lb **12** Ran SP% **114.3**
Speed ratings (Par 101): **99,98,98,97,97 97,95,95,92,90 90,68**
CSF £172.47 CT £810.78 TOTE £8.70: £2.50, £6.60, £1.30; EX 191.20 Trifecta £1357.00.
Owner Robert Greenwood Racing **Bred** J K Beckitt & Son **Trained** Newcastle-under-Lyme, Staffs

FOCUS
A moderate handicap to end and, as with many races of its type around here, not a lot to separate the principals. The favourite ran a shocker but that mare aside, the form looks fairly reliable.
T/Jkpt: Not won. T/Plt: £26.40 to a £1 stake. Pool: £111,652.23 - 3,078.06 winning units T/Qpdt: £5.20 to a £1 stake. Pool: £17,776.43 - 2,528.00 winning units **Richard Lowther**

[272]NEWCASTLE (A.W) (L-H)
Tuesday, January 22

OFFICIAL GOING: Tapeta: standard
Wind: Virtually nil Weather: Cloudy & dry

349 BETWAY LIVE CASINO H'CAP — 2m 56y (Tp)
4:10 (4:10) (Class 2) (0-100,100) 4£15,752 (£4,715; £2,357; £1,180; £587) **Stalls** Low

Form — RPR
234- **1** **Busy Street**[53] 9333 7-9-0 **88** .... AlistairRawlinson 6 — 96
(Michael Appleby) *trckd ldrs: hdwy on outer 3f out: led wl over 1f out: sn jnd and rdn: drvn and kpt on wl fnl f* **6/1**[3]
021- **2** *3/4* **Stargazer (IRE)**[38] 9552 6-9-12 **100** .... RobertWinston 3 — 107
(Philip Kirby) *hld up towards rr: t.k.h 1/2-way: hdwy on inner 3f out: effrt wl over 1f out: sn chal and rdn: drvn and ev ch ins fnl f: kpt on same pce towards fin* **6/5**[1]
31-1 **3** *3* **Loud And Clear**[14] 124 8-8-4 **81** oh2 .... PhilDennis(3) 5 — 84
(Jim Goldie) *hld up and bhd: hdwy 3f out: sn swtchd rt to outer: rdn along 2f out: styd on fnl f* **6/1**[3]
/0-3 **4** *nk* **Zubayr (IRE)**[17] 82 7-8-12 **86** .... (p) KieranO'Neill 7 — 89
(Ian Williams) *t.k.h early: trckd ldr: hdwy and cl up over 4f out: led 3f out: sn rdn: hdd wl over 1f out: sn drvn and kpt on one pce* **11/2**[2]
06-0 **5** *1/2* **Cosmelli (ITY)**[17] 82 6-9-10 **98** .... (b) LukeMorris 4 — 100
(Gay Kelleway) *trckd ldng pair: pushed along 4f out: rdn 3f out: drvn over 1f out and sn one pce* **11/1**
06-4 **6** *1/2* **Eddystone Rock (IRE)**[17] 82 7-9-1 **89** .... KierenFox 1 — 91
(John Best) *trckd ldng pair: pushed along over 4f out: rdn 3f out: drvn and one pce fnl 2f* **14/1**
350/ **7** *1 1/4* **Red Tornado (FR)**[154] 1068 7-8-11 **85** .... JoeFanning 8 — 85
(Chris Fairhurst) *hld up towards rr: pushed along and outpcd over 3f out: hdwy and in tch 2f out: sn rdn and n.m.r over 1f out: no imp* **50/1**
UP-0 **8** *10* **Addicted To You (IRE)**[17] 82 5-9-5 **93** .... (v[1]) JasonHart 2 — 81
(Mark Johnston) *sn led: racd freely and sn clr: pushed along 4f out: rdn and hdd 3f out: sn wknd* **14/1**

3m 31.89s (-3.11) **Going Correction** +0.15s/f (Slow) 8 Ran SP% **113.0**
Speed ratings (Par 109): **113,112,111,110,110 110,109,104**
CSF £13.29 CT £44.40 TOTE £6.40: £2.10, £1.10, £2.00; EX 15.70 Trifecta £61.60.
Owner Khdrp & Martyn Elvin **Bred** Juddmonte Farms Ltd **Trained** Oakham, Rutland

FOCUS
A good staying handicap with the winner appreciating a step up in trip. A decent initial gallop visibly slowed in the middle part of the race, before the tempo increased again entering the home straight. The overall winning time was nearly six seconds above standard.

350 FOLLOW TOP TIPSTER TEMPLEGATE AT SUNRACING H'CAP — 1m 5y (Tp)
4:45 (4:45) (Class 4) (0-85,87) 4-Y-O+
£6,727 (£2,002; £1,000; £500; £400; £400) **Stalls** Centre

Form — RPR
2-12 **1** **Rey Loopy (IRE)**[10] 209 5-9-4 **79** .... AndrewMullen 1 — 85
(Ben Haslam) *wnt lft s: hld up in rr: hdwy 2f out: chsd ldrs over 1f out: sn chal and rdn led ins fnl f: kpt on wl towards fin* **9/2**[3]
20-1 **2** *nk* **Trevithick**[20] 19 4-9-12 **87** .... GrahamLee 6 — 92
(Bryan Smart) *led: pushed along 2f out: rdn over 1f out: hdd ins fnl f: sn drvn and rallied towards fin* **5/2**[2]
46-1 **3** *shd* **Blame Culture (USA)**[15] 117 4-9-2 **77** .... PJMcDonald 7 — 81
(George Margarson) *trckd ldrs: hdwy to chse ldr 2f out: rdn to chal over 1f out: drvn and ev ch ins fnl f: no ex towards fin* **9/4**[1]
66-5 **4** *1 1/4* **Mont Kinabalu (IRE)**[10] 209 4-9-1 **76** .... DougieCostello 3 — 77
(Kevin Ryan) *hld up in rr: hdwy 2f out: effrt to chse ldrs over 1f out: rdn and kpt on fnl f* **16/1**
20-4 **5** *1 1/2* **Brittanic (IRE)**[12] 157 5-9-7 **82** .... (p[1]) StevieDonohoe 2 — 80
(David Simcock) *trckd ldrs: pushed along over 2f out: rdn wl over 1f out: grad wknd* **8/1**
420- **6** *2 1/2* **Testa Rossa (IRE)**[34] 9614 9-8-11 **75** .... (b) PhilDennis(3) 4 — 67
(Jim Goldie) *trckd ldrs: pushed along wl over 2f out: rdn wl over 1f out: sn wknd* **13/2**
600- **7** *2 1/4* **Rioja Day (IRE)**[50] 8776 9-8-0 **68** oh23 .... (p) CoreyMadden(7) 5 — 55
(Jim Goldie) *cl up: pushed along 3f out: rdn over 2f out: sn wknd* **150/1**

1m 40.65s (2.05) **Going Correction** +0.15s/f (Slow) 7 Ran SP% **108.5**
Speed ratings (Par 105): **95,94,94,93,91 89,87**
CSF £14.46 TOTE £3.70: £2.00, £1.60; EX 13.20 Trifecta £33.10.
Owner Daniel Shapiro & Mrs C Barclay **Bred** Worldwide Partners **Trained** Middleham Moor, N Yorks

FOCUS
A decent handicap. The second-favourite set an honest tempo after a modest first furlong, but set the race up for another course-specialist in the narrow winner.

351 SUNRACING.CO.UK H'CAP — 7f 14y (Tp)
5:15 (5:15) (Class 2) (0-105,107) 4£15,752 (£4,715; £2,357; £1,180; £587) **Stalls** Centre

Form — RPR
211- **1** **Pinnata (IRE)**[39] 9532 5-8-6 **90** .... (t) JoeFanning 9 — 100
(Stuart Williams) *prom: effrt to ld jst over 2f out: rdn over 1f out: kpt on strly* **2/1**[1]
15-2 **2** *1 1/2* **Straight Right (FR)**[17] 89 5-9-9 **107** .... (h) PJMcDonald 6 — 113
(Andrew Balding) *t.k.h early: hld up: hdwy 3f out: n.m.r and swtchd rt towards stands' rail and rdn to chse ldng pair over 1f out: drvn ent fnl f: kpt on same pce* **9/4**[2]
25-2 **3** *hd* **Areen Heart (FR)**[11] 176 5-8-5 **89** .... (h) LukeMorris 5 — 94
(David O'Meara) *t.k.h early: trckd ldng pair: hdwy over 2f out: rdn to chse wnr wl over 1f out: sn drvn and edgd rt: kpt on same pce fnl f* **10/1**
122/ **4** *shd* **Battered**[493] 7149 5-9-1 **99** .... CallumRodriguez 4 — 104
(Ralph Beckett) *hld up towards rr: hdwy and pushed along 3f out: swtchd lft and rdn to chse ldrs over 1f out: kpt on u.p fnl f* **9/1**
020- **5** *1* **Starlight Romance (IRE)**[99] 8265 5-8-7 **91** .... BarryMcHugh 8 — 93
(Richard Fahey) *hld up in rr: hdwy and pushed along 3f out: rdn to chse ldrs and swtchd lft over 1f out: kpt on u.p fnl f* **28/1**
32-4 **6** *hd* **Lucymai**[20] 30 6-9-2 **100** .... RobertWinston 2 — 102
(Dean Ivory) *trckd ldrs: pushed along 3f out: rdn 2f out: drvn over 1f out: grad wknd* **10/1**
361- **7** *1/2* **Gallipoli (IRE)**[96] 8346 6-8-6 **90** .... PaddyMathers 3 — 91
(Richard Fahey) *chsd ldrs: pushed along 3f out: rdn over 2f out: sn drvn and btn* **13/2**[3]
60-6 **8** *5* **Contrast (IRE)**[10] 205 5-8-2 **86** oh2 .... NathanEvans 1 — 73
(Michael Easterby) *led: pushed along 3f out: rdn and hdd jst over 2f out: sn drvn and wknd* **25/1**

1m 25.07s (-1.13) **Going Correction** +0.15s/f (Slow) 8 Ran SP% **112.9**
Speed ratings (Par 109): **112,110,110,109,108 108,108,102**
CSF £6.49 CT £32.67 TOTE £2.70: £1.20, £1.10, £2.20; EX 7.20 Trifecta £35.90.
Owner David N Reynolds & C D Watkins **Bred** Ammerland Verwaltung Gmbh & Co Kg **Trained** Newmarket, Suffolk

FOCUS
Another good quality handicap. The favourite won readily in a good comparative time after pouring on the pressure approaching the final two furlongs. The third helps to set the standard.

352 BETWAY CONDITIONS STKS (ALL-WEATHER CHAMPIONSHIPS FAST-TRACK QUALIFIER) — 5f (Tp)
5:45 (5:45) (Class 2) 4-Y-O+ **£18,903** (£5,658; £2,829; £1,416; £705) **Stalls** Centre

Form — RPR
112- **1** **Encore D'Or**[95] 8397 7-9-0 109 .... LukeMorris 6 — 101
(Robert Cowell) *trckd ldrs: hdwy to chse ldr 2f out: rdn over 1f out: sn chal: drvn to ld fnl 100yds: kpt on* **9/4**[1]
-311 **2** *nk* **Ornate**[9] 230 6-9-0 92 .... PhilDennis 7 — 100
(David C Griffiths) *led: rdn over 1f out and edgd lft: sn jnd and drvn: hdd fnl 100yds: kpt on gamely u.p towards fin* **11/1**
006- **3** *1/2* **Stone Of Destiny**[150] 6530 4-9-0 105 .... PJMcDonald 3 — 98
(Andrew Balding) *dwlt: t.k.h: hld up towards rr: hdwy over 2f out: rdn over 1f out: drvn and ch ent fnl f: kpt on* **7/2**[2]
12-1 **4** *nk* **Outrage**[14] 127 7-9-0 94 .... (b) KieranO'Neill 1 — 97
(Daniel Kubler) *hld up in rr: hdwy 2f out: rdn to chse ldrs whn n.m.r and swtchd lft 1f out: drvn and kpt on wl towards fin* **7/2**[2]
415- **5** *1 1/4* **Suzi's Connoisseur**[27] 9707 8-9-0 86 .... (b) PaulMulrennan 2 — 93
(Jane Chapple-Hyam) *trckd ldng pair: rdn along 2f out: drvn over 1f out: wknd fnl f* **33/1**
51-2 **6** *1/2* **Merhoob (IRE)**[10] 203 7-9-0 93 .... StevieDonohoe 5 — 91
(John Ryan) *trckd ldrs: pushed along over 2f out: rdn wl over 1f out: sn one pce* **8/1**
05-1 **7** *6* **Tropics (USA)**[19] 35 11-9-0 104 .... (h) RobertWinston 4 — 69
(Dean Ivory) *cl up: rdn along over 2f out: wknd wl over 1f out: hld whn n.m.r and hmpd ent fnl f (jockey said gelding ran flat)* **11/2**[3]

58.27s (-1.23) **Going Correction** +0.15s/f (Slow) 7 Ran SP% **113.0**
Speed ratings (Par 109): **115,114,113,113,111 110,100**
CSF £27.32 TOTE £2.60: £1.60, £4.80; EX 17.70 Trifecta £79.40.
Owner Mrs Morley,G Johnson,Newsells Park Stud **Bred** Newsells Park Stud **Trained** Six Mile Bottom, Cambs

■ Stewards' Enquiry : Phil Dennis two-day ban; careless riding (Feb 5-6)

FOCUS
The feature race was a good quality conditions sprint although the proximity of the fifth limits the form somewhat. The favourite came through to deny the wayward front-runner in the final furlong. It took just over 58 seconds to win it.

353 BETWAY SPRINT H'CAP — 5f (Tp)
6:15 (6:15) (Class 4) (0-85,87) 4-Y-O+
£6,727 (£2,002; £1,000; £500; £400; £400) **Stalls** Centre

Form — RPR
030- **1** **Fendale**[102] 8167 7-9-5 **83** .... GrahamLee 3 — 92
(Bryan Smart) *trckd ldr: effrt and cl up over 1f out: chal ent fnl f: led fnl 120yds: pushed out: cleverly* **5/1**[3]
650- **2** *1/2* **Bowson Fred**[32] 9662 7-8-9 **80** .... JoshQuinn(7) 4 — 87
(Michael Easterby) *led: rdn along wl over 1f out: jnd and drvn ent fnl f: hdd fnl 120yds: kpt on* **9/1**
51-5 **3** *3/4* **Primo's Comet**[14] 127 4-9-1 **79** .... JoeFanning 8 — 83+
(Jim Goldie) *hld up in rr: hdwy 2f out: swtchd lft to far rail and rdn over 1f out: drvn and styd on fnl f* **10/3**[2]
30-0 **4** *3/4* **Dynamo Walt (IRE)**[14] 127 8-9-7 **85** .... (v) PaddyMathers 7 — 87
(Derek Shaw) *chsd ldrs: rdn along wl over 1f out: drvn and kpt on same pce fnl f* **33/1**
350- **5** *nk* **Saaheq**[47] 9432 5-9-3 **81** .... LukeMorris 1 — 82
(Michael Appleby) *chsd ldng pair: rdn along 2f out: sn drvn and kpt on same pce* **12/1**
/1-4 **6** *1 1/4* **Royal Prospect (IRE)**[20] 24 4-9-4 **82** .... PaulMulrennan 5 — 78
(Julie Camacho) *dwlt and towards rr: t.k.h and sn chsng ldrs: swtchd lft towards far rail 1/2-way: rdn along wl over 1f out: sn drvn and btn (jockey said gelding hung left after the first furlong)* **9/4**[1]
22- **7** *1 1/4* **Foxy Forever (IRE)**[32] 9667 9-9-9 **87** .... (t) FrannyNorton 6 — 79
(Michael Wigham) *chsd ldrs: rdn along 2f out: sn wknd (jockey said gelding hung left)* **5/1**[3]
00-4 **8** *nse* **Jan Van Hoof (IRE)**[14] 131 8-8-7 **71** .... (h) BarryMcHugh 2 — 62
(Michael Herrington) *dwlt: a in rr* **22/1**

59.27s (-0.23) **Going Correction** +0.15s/f (Slow) 8 Ran SP% **112.2**
Speed ratings (Par 105): **107,106,105,103,103 101,99,99**
CSF £46.66 CT £170.41 TOTE £6.10: £1.50, £2.80, £1.40; EX 49.00 Trifecta £189.70.
Owner S Chappell & Partner **Bred** Cheveley Park Stud Ltd **Trained** Hambleton, N Yorks

FOCUS
Another decent sprint handicap. The pace increased notably after the first furlong and it paid to race prominently. The favourite was disappointing after racing keenly and hanging.

354 LADBROKES NOVICE STKS — 7f 14y (Tp)
6:45 (6:45) (Class 5) 3-Y-O **£4,140** (£1,232; £615; £307) **Stalls** Centre

Form — RPR
043- **1** **Havana Rocket (IRE)**[128] 7333 3-9-2 83 .... (w) PJMcDonald 1 — 79
(Andrew Balding) *mde all: shkn up wl over 1f out: rdn and kpt on strly fnl f* **4/6**[1]
4 **2** *2 1/2* **Solar Park (IRE)**[20] 20 3-9-2 0 .... LukeMorris 4 — 72
(James Tate) *t.k.h: trckd ldng pair: effrt to chse wnr wl over 1f out: drvn and kpt on same pce fnl f* **3/1**[2]
3- **3** *1 1/4* **Dream Chick (IRE)**[91] 8502 3-8-11 0 .... AndrewMullen 2 — 64
(Kevin Ryan) *hld up in rr: hdwy over 2f out: rdn to chse ldng pair over 1f out: sn drvn and no imp* **12/1**
4 *10* **Mustadun** 3-9-2 0 .... FrannyNorton 3 — 42
(Mark Johnston) *cl up: pushed along 3f out: rdn over 2f out: sn wknd* **7/1**[3]

5 3 1/4 **Parker's Pride** 3-9-2 0 .... NathanEvans 5 33
(Brian Rothwell) *chsd ldng pair: rdn along wl over 2f out: sn outpcd* **66/1**

1m 28.4s (2.20) **Going Correction** +0.15s/f (Slow) **5** Ran SP% **106.7**
Speed ratings (Par 97): **93,90,88,77,73**
CSF £2.65 TOTE £1.50: £1.02, £1.60; EX 3.00 Trifecta £7.00.
Owner Rocket Racing **Bred** Ballyhane Stud **Trained** Kingsclere, Hants

FOCUS
A fair little 3yo novice contest. The odds-on favourite got off the mark in fine style from off his own increasing tempo after a slow first two furlongs. The runner-up ran to his mark so the form looks sound.

355 FOLLOW SUNRACING ON TWITTER H'CAP 7f 14y (Tp)
7:15 (7:15) (Class 5) (0-75,74) 4-Y-0+
£4,140 (£1,232; £615; £400; £400; £400) **Stalls** Centre

Form RPR
00-2 **1** **Harvest Day**[20] [23] 4-9-1 **68** ....(t) NathanEvans 8 78+
(Michael Easterby) *trckd ldrs: hdwy over 2f out: led wl over 1f out: sn rdn and kpt on strly* **7/2[1]**

2-34 **2** 2 **Newmarket Warrior (IRE)**[10] [209] 8-9-2 **69** ....(p) TonyHamilton 4 73+
(Iain Jardine) *dwlt and hld up towards rr: hdwy 3f out: swtchd rt and rdn 2f out: styd on to chse wnr ins fnl f: no imp towards fin* **14/1**

010- **3** 1 1/4 **Mudawwan (IRE)**[55] [9285] 5-9-5 **72** ....(tp) PJMcDonald 7 72
(James Bethell) *led: pushed along over 2f out: sn rdn and hdd wl over 1f out: drvn and kpt on same pce fnl f* **11/2[2]**

255- **4** 2 **Elixsoft (IRE)**[237] [3241] 4-8-12 **65** .... LukeMorris 6 60
(Roger Fell) *chsd ldrs: rdn along 2f out: sn drvn and kpt on same pce* **33/1**

560- **5** nk **The British Lion (IRE)**[34] [9615] 4-9-1 **68** .... JoeFanning 5 62
(Mark Johnston) *prom: trckd wnr 1/2-way: rdn along over 2f out: drvn over 1f out: grad wknd* **15/2[3]**

03-3 **6** 3/4 **Dirchill (IRE)**[20] [23] 5-9-7 **74** .... JasonHart 3 66
(David Thompson) *dwlt: plld hrd and sn chsng ldrs: rdn along over 2f out: sn wknd* **11/2[2]**

034- **7** 1/2 **Gun Case**[34] [9615] 7-8-10 **63** ....(v) BarryMcHugh 9 54
(Alistair Whillans) *a towards rr* **8/1**

14-1 **8** nse **Briyouni (FR)**[13] [138] 6-9-1 **68** .... CallumRodriguez 1 59
(Ralph Beckett) *dwlt: hld up: a towards rr (jockey said gelding was unsuited by the slow early pace)* **7/2[1]**

004- **9** 1/2 **Dream Mount (IRE)**[32] [9656] 4-8-12 **65** ....(be) GrahamLee 2 54
(Julie Camacho) *trckd ldrs: pushed along 3f out: rdn wl over 1f out: sn wknd* **14/1**

1m 27.77s (1.57) **Going Correction** +0.15s/f (Slow) **9** Ran SP% **114.4**
Speed ratings (Par 97): **97,94,93,91,90 89,89,89,88**
CSF £54.61 CT £264.92 TOTE £4.70: £1.30, £3.50, £2.50; EX 46.60 Trifecta £270.20.
Owner Mrs C E Mason & Partner **Bred** Howard Barton Stud **Trained** Sheriff Hutton, N Yorks
■ Stewards' Enquiry : P J McDonald two-day ban; misuse of whip (Jan 26,Feb 6)

FOCUS
A fair handicap. One of the joint-favourites won easily from off another increasing tempo after a slow first two furlongs.

356 BETWAY CASINO H'CAP 6f (Tp)
7:45 (7:45) (Class 6) (0-65,66) 4-Y-0+
£3,493 (£1,039; £519; £400; £400; £400) **Stalls** Centre

Form RPR
02-3 **1** **Avenue Of Stars**[10] [214] 6-9-3 **61** ....(v) JasonHart 13 70
(Karen McLintock) *racd towards stands' side: prom: cl up over 2f out: led wl over 1f out: rdn and kpt on strly fnl f* **9/2[1]**

00-5 **2** 1 3/4 **Bobby Joe Leg**[20] [22] 5-9-8 **66** ....(b[1]) JamesSullivan 6 70
(Ruth Carr) *t.k.h early in midfield: hdwy 2f out: rdn over 1f out: swtchd lft and drvn fnl f: fin wl* **15/2**

620- **3** nse **Epeius (IRE)**[42] [9491] 6-9-7 **65** .... AndrewMullen 8 69
(Ben Haslam) *hld up towards rr: hdwy 3f out: swtchd rt and rdn to chse ldrs wl over 1f out: kpt on fnl f* **9/2[1]**

002- **4** nk **Soldier Blue (FR)**[177] [5524] 5-8-5 **52** ....(v) BenRobinson(3) 3 55
(Brian Ellison) *dwlt and towards rr: hdwy 1/2-way: chsd ldrs 2f out: rdn wl over 1f out: drvn and kpt on same pce fnl f* **16/1**

01-4 **5** 3/4 **Smugglers Creek (IRE)**[20] [23] 5-9-8 **66** ....(p) JoeFanning 11 66
(Iain Jardine) *racd centre: led: rdn along over 2f out: hdd wl over 1f out: sn drvn and kpt on same pce* **7/1[3]**

10-2 **6** nk **Duke Cosimo**[10] [214] 9-9-4 **65** .... PhilDennis(3) 9 65
(Michael Herrington) *towards rr: pushed along 3f out: rdn and hdwy 2f out: kpt on fnl f* **13/2[2]**

00-4 **7** 1 **Kentuckyconnection (USA)**[10] [214] 6-9-1 **66** ....(p) HarryRussell(7) 5 63
(Bryan Smart) *chsd ldrs: rdn along 2f out: sn drvn and kpt on same pce* **12/1**

546- **8** 2 1/2 **Rock Warbler (IRE)**[116] [7728] 6-9-6 **64** .... CallumRodriguez 10 53
(Michael Mullineaux) *in tch: pushed along wl over 2f out: sn rdn and grad wknd* **10/1**

06-5 **9** 2 **Johnny Cavagin**[10] [214] 10-9-5 **63** .... GrahamLee 2 46
(Paul Midgley) *dwlt: sn in tch: rdn along wl over 2f out: sn wknd* **14/1**

00-6 **10** 1 1/4 **Rizzle Dizzle**[15] [123] 4-9-4 **62** .... StevieDonohoe 7 41
(Rebecca Menzies) *cl up: rdn along wl over 2f out: sn wknd* **12/1**

0-40 **11** 2 1/4 **Broken Wings (IRE)**[9] [233] 4-8-10 **54** ....(v) LukeMorris 4 27
(Keith Dalgleish) *towards rr: pushed along 1/2-way: rdn and hung lft 2f out: nvr a factor* **50/1**

05-0 **12** 1 **My Name Is Rio (IRE)**[19] [43] 9-9-5 **63** .... BarryMcHugh 12 33
(John Davies) *prom: rdn along 1/2-way: sn wknd* **25/1**

0-06 **13** 4 **Dubai Elegance**[10] [209] 5-9-2 **60** .... PaddyMathers 1 18
(Derek Shaw) *dwlt: sn in tch: rdn along over 2f out: sn wknd* **50/1**

1m 12.62s (0.12) **Going Correction** +0.15s/f (Slow) **13** Ran SP% **118.8**
Speed ratings (Par 101): **105,102,102,102,101 100,99,96,93,91 88,87,82**
CSF £36.88 CT £166.98 TOTE £4.50: £1.90, £3.30, £1.90; EX 42.70 Trifecta £259.90.
Owner Don Eddy **Bred** Steve Lock & Redmyre Bloodstock **Trained** Ingoe, Northumberland

FOCUS
A modest sprint handicap. One of the joint-favourites gamely dominated the second part of the race in a fair time for the grade.
T/Jkpt: £6,666.60 to a £1 stake. Pool: £10,000.00 - 1.5 winning units T/Plt: £24.40 to a £1 stake. Pool: £105,193.29 - 3,145.47 winning units T/Qpdt: £11.20 to a £1 stake. Pool: £14,908.49 - 979.46 winning units **Joe Rowntree**

286 KEMPTON (A.W) (R-H)
Wednesday, January 23

OFFICIAL GOING: Polytrack: standard to slow
Weather: Cold

357 RACINGTV.COM H'CAP 6f (P)
4:40 (4:40) (Class 7) (0-50,51) 4-Y-0+
£2,587 (£770; £384; £192) **Stalls** Low

Form RPR
06-3 **1** **Elliot The Dragon (IRE)**[5] [293] 4-9-2 **45** .... CallumShepherd 5 51
(Derek Shaw) *plld hrd thrght in rr-div: shkn up 2f out: rdn on outer over 1f out: kpt on wl ins fnl f: pushed out to ld cl home (jockey said gelding ran too free and hung both ways)* **7/1[3]**

B0-5 **2** nk **Dalness Express**[19] [60] 6-9-6 **49** ....(tp) FergusSweeney 3 54
(John O'Shea) *hld up in rr: swtchd to outer 2f out and rdn: outpcd w a bit to do over 1f out: picked up wl ins fnl f and tk 2nd last strides* **7/1[3]**

4-55 **3** 1/2 **Storm Lightning**[4] [322] 10-9-4 **47** .... EoinWalsh 2 51
(Mark Brisbourne) *trckd ldr: shkn up 2f out: rdn to ld over 1f out: stuck on wl w narrow advantage tl hdd cl home and lost 2nd last strides* **6/1[2]**

6-30 **4** 3/4 **Brother In Arms (IRE)**[8] [244] 5-9-4 **47** ....(p) RossaRyan 10 48
(Tony Carroll) *hld up in rr: rdn 2f out: outpcd and wdst over 1f out w a bit to do: kpt on wl ins fnl f* **14/1**

604- **5** 3/4 **Kyllukey**[113] [7873] 6-9-3 **46** ....(t) AdamKirby 4 45
(Charlie Wallis) *cl up in mid-div: effrt 2f out: ev ch ent fnl f: no ex last 110yds and eased cl home (jockey said gelding suffered slight interference on the run to the line)* **7/2[1]**

234- **6** nk **Slipalongtrevaskis**[34] [9641] 6-9-4 **47** ....(e) JoeyHaynes 7 45
(Paul Howling) *half-rrd s and in rr: tk clsr order over 2f out on inner: rdn at cutaway: on heels of ldr ent fnl f: no ex sn after and wknd* **6/1[2]**

63-4 **7** 1 1/4 **Alligator**[13] [166] 5-8-11 **45** .... PoppyBridgwater(5) 1 46+
(Tony Carroll) *mid-div on inner: gng okay but unable to be rdn on heels fr over 1f out: briefly shkn up ins fnl f: again n.m.r and eased fnl 110yds (jockey said gelding was denied a clear run)* **15/2**

22-6 **8** 1 **Stopdworldnletmeof**[12] [177] 5-9-3 **46** .... JFEgan 9 37
(David Flood) *led: rdn 2f out: hdd over 1f out: one pce after* **18/1**

33-0 **9** 1/2 **Mr Potter**[20] [37] 6-9-7 **50** ....(v) PhilipPrince 12 40
(Richard Guest) *loaded wout jockey: trckd ldr: rdn 2f out: no imp ent fnl f and wknd* **20/1**

00-1 **10** 2 1/4 **Deer Song**[8] [244] 6-9-8 **51** 6ex ....(b) LiamJones 6 34
(John Bridger) *mid-div but a bit wd w little cover: shkn up 2f out: one pce whn a sltly squeezed up over 1f out: fdd sn after* **10/1**

1m 13.8s (0.70) **Going Correction** +0.10s/f (Slow) **10** Ran SP% **113.3**
Speed ratings (Par 97): **99,98,97,96,95 95,93,92,91,88**
CSF £53.65 CT £310.32 TOTE £8.80: £2.90, £2.60, £2.20; EX 61.80 Trifecta £347.80.
Owner Derek Shaw **Bred** Rathbarry Stud **Trained** Sproxton, Leics

FOCUS
They finished in a bit of a heap, the hold-up horses coming through at the finish. The first two, fourth and sixth trailed the field going into the turn.

358 32RED ON THE APP STORE NOVICE STKS (PLUS 10 RACE) 1m 3f 219y(P)
5:15 (5:17) (Class 5) 3-Y-0
£3,881 (£1,155; £577; £288) **Stalls** Low

Form RPR
1 **Almost Midnight** 3-9-2 0 .... StevieDonohoe 1 79+
(David Simcock) *hld up in 5th: green and niggled along wl over 3f out: shkn up over 2f out: picked up smartly 2f out and sn led: in complete command fnl f and pushed out: eased cl home: v easily: promising type* **8/1**

05- **2** 2 3/4 **Natsovia**[41] [9522] 3-8-11 0 .... NicolaCurrie 5 66
(Jamie Osborne) *hld up in last trio: shkn up over 2f out: rdn 2f out w a bit to do: tk 2nd ins fnl f: kpt on wl but no ch w v easy wnr (jockey said filly was slow into stride)* **16/1**

3 1 3/4 **Alpasu (IRE)** 3-9-2 0 ....(t[1] w) EdwardGreatrex 8 68
(Archie Watson) *led after 1f: narrow ldr and set mod pce: jinked sltly lft at 1/2-way: shkn up over 3f out: rdn over 2f out: hdd over 1f out: lost 2nd ins fnl f: plugged on one pce* **13/2[3]**

0- **4** 1 **Seeusoon (IRE)**[55] [9308] 3-9-2 0 .... DavidProbert 2 67
(Andrew Balding) *bhd ldng pair: shkn up over 2f out: rdn to chal 2f out: sltly green and outpcd over 1f out: kpt on again ins fnl f* **7/2[2]**

5 2 1/4 **Hen (IRE)** 3-8-11 0 .... AdamMcNamara 7 58
(Jamie Osborne) *in last and 5 l adrift of nrest rival: clsr at 1/2-way: shuffled along over 2f out: plugged on* **33/1**

0-6 **6** shd **Trapani**[17] [103] 3-8-11 0 ....(p[1]) RobertHavlin 3 58
(John Gosden) *bhd ldr tl disp on outer after 2f: carried sltly lft at 1/2-way: effrt over 2f out: no ex over 1f out and fdd* **7/4[1]**

0- **7** 2 **Moonlit Sea**[27] [9726] 3-9-2 0 .... LukeMorris 4 60
(James Tate) *racd in 4th and keen at times: shkn up over 2f out: sn sltly hmpd: green and one pce after* **7/2[2]**

05- **8** 18 **Astromerry**[165] [6001] 3-8-4 0 .... TobyEley(7) 6 26
(Mark H Tompkins) *hld up in last trio: effrt wl over 2f out: hld 2f out: sn eased* **150/1**

2m 36.0s (1.50) **Going Correction** +0.10s/f (Slow) **8** Ran SP% **114.7**
Speed ratings (Par 97): **99,97,96,95,93 93,92,80**
CSF £122.34 TOTE £9.00: £2.50, £4.20, £1.80; EX 86.80 Trifecta £617.70.
Owner The Almost Midnight Partnership **Bred** Card Bloodstock **Trained** Newmarket, Suffolk

FOCUS
An ordinary novice and the form is open to question but the winner showed impressive pace to skip clear.

359 BET AT RACINGTV.COM MAIDEN STKS 7f (P)
5:45 (5:47) (Class 5) 3-Y-0+
£3,881 (£1,155; £577; £288) **Stalls** Low

Form RPR
1 **Songkran (IRE)** 3-8-10 0 .... DavidProbert 10 70+
(David Elsworth) *mid-div: bdly hmpd on two occasions in cl succession after 2f: dropped to rr-div: shkn up and smooth prog over 2f out: rdn over 1f out on wl on outer ins fnl f: led post: gd ride* **4/1[2]**

0- **2** shd **Assimilation (IRE)**[63] [9183] 3-8-10 0 .... LiamKeniry 5 69+
(Ed Walker) *racd in mid-div: cl and rdn 2f out: styd on ent fnl f to chse ldr: fin wl last 100yds between horses and jst denied* **10/1**

3 shd **Tulloona** 3-8-10 0 .... LukeMorris 2 68
(Tom Clover) *t.k.h early: bhd ldr: rdn 2f out: led over 1f out and sn 2 l clr: kpt on wl ins fnl f: ld reduced fnl 110yds and hdd last strides: jst lost 2nd* **25/1**

The Form Book Flat 2019, Raceform Ltd, Newbury, RG14 5SJ

4 1¾ **I'm Available (IRE)** 3-8-5 0 ... MartinDwyer 11 58+
(Andrew Balding) *hld up in rr-div: shkn up over 2f out: gd hdwy fr over 1f out being pushed along: shaped wl fnl f* **10/1**

0- 5 nk **Fox Happy (IRE)**[42] 9497 3-8-10 0 ... RossaRyan 13 63+
(Richard Hannon) *racd in mid-div: effrt 2f out: kpt on wl over 1f out: no ex last 150yds* **6/1**

6 2½ **Charlie Arthur (IRE)** 3-8-10 0 ... (h[1]) ShaneKelly 6 56+
(Richard Hughes) *v awkward s and in rr: bhd and plenty to do over 3f out: shkn up over 2f out: kpt on w promise fr over 1f out* **9/4[1]**

7 2½ **Circle Of Stars (IRE)** 3-8-10 0 ... StevieDonohoe 12 49
(Charlie Fellowes) *racd in rr-div: effrt over 2f out: kpt on one pce fr over 1f out* **11/1**

00- 8 4½ **Spirit Of Angel (IRE)**[55] 9315 3-8-10 0 ... NicolaCurrie 4 37
(Marcus Tregoning) *a towards rr: shuffled along fr 2f out (jockey said gelding was slow into stride and ran green)* **5/1[3]**

000- 9 ¾ **Valentine Mist (IRE)**[130] 7269 7-9-4 39 ... PoppyBridgwater(5) 9 35
(James Grassick) *sn led: rdn over 2f out: hdd over 1f out: fdd fnl f* **200/1**

00- 10 5 **Spirit Of Epsom**[306] 1326 5-9-7 0 ... LeviWilliams(7) 7 27
(Brett Johnson) *t.k.h nt wanting to ld: sn bhd ldr: effrt 3f out: fdd 2f out* **125/1**

00- 11 11 **Storm Boy**[61] 9223 4-10-0 0 ... RobHornby 8
(Michael Attwater) *bhd ldr: effrt 3f out and struggling: no ex in st* **66/1**

12 2½ **Doti** 3-8-5 0 ... KieranO'Neill 3
(Rod Millman) *cl up and plld hrd: no ex over 2f out: fdd sn after (vet reported the filly had been struck into on its left hind)* **20/1**

13 70 **Sionnach Rua** 4-9-2 0 ... MarkCrehan(7) 1
(Jimmy Fox) *missed break: wl detached in rr after 2f: allowed to come home in own time: t.o (jockey said filly was slowly away and ran green)* **200/1**

1m 26.66s (0.66) **Going Correction** +0.10s/f (Slow)
WFA 3 from 4yo+ 18lb **13** Ran SP% **120.1**
Speed ratings (Par 103): **100,99,99,97,97 94,91,86,85,80 67,64,**
CSF £42.37 TOTE £4.70: £1.10, £3.60, £7.00; EX 50.90 Trifecta £867.30.
Owner King Power Racing Co Ltd **Bred** J F Tuthill **Trained** Newmarket, Suffolk

FOCUS
There was a three-way photo to this maiden. The bare form looks modest although the winner did well to overcome a troubled passage.

360 32RED CASINO H'CAP 7f (P)
6:15 (6:16) (Class 5) (0-75,77) 3-Y-O
£3,752 (£1,116; £557; £400; £400; £400) **Stalls** Low

Form RPR

32-3 1 **Ballistic (IRE)**[14] 140 3-9-7 **74** ... (p) RaulDaSilva 5 82
(Robert Cowell) *disp ld: rdn 2f out and edgd into ld: clr ldr over 1f out: asserted ins fnl f: easily* **3/1[2]**

062- 2 3¾ **Brandon (FR)**[160] 6200 3-9-7 **77** ... AaronJones(3) 3 75
(Marco Botti) *hld up in rr-div: rdn 2f out: chal up inner over 1f out: no ch w wnr ins fnl f* **7/1[3]**

536- 3 1 **Urban Highway (IRE)**[96] 8385 3-8-12 **65** ... DavidProbert 4 60
(Tony Carroll) *in rr: rdn over 2f out: a bit to do over 1f out: styd on fnl f to take 3rd cl home* **10/1**

033- 4 nk **French Twist**[69] 9085 3-8-13 **66** ... PJMcDonald 7 60
(Mark Johnston) *bhd ldrs: rdn 2f out: kpt on one pce fnl f* **12/1**

566- 5 1 **Hua Hin (IRE)**[49] 9396 3-8-13 **66** ... (t) RossaRyan 6 58
(Richard Hannon) *in rr-div on outer: rdn over 2f out: outpcd over 1f out: kpt on again fnl f* **20/1**

23-6 6 2 **Stay Forever (FR)**[19] 66 3-9-3 **73** ... WilliamCox(3) 2 59
(Andrew Balding) *bhd ldrs: rdn 2f out: one pce* **10/1**

324- 7 1¼ **Toffee Galore**[145] 6758 3-9-7 **74** ... EdwardGreatrex 1 57
(Archie Watson) *narrow ldr: rdn 2f out and narrowly hdd: began to weaken over 1f out: fdd tamely ins fnl f (jockey said filly stopped quickly)* **11/8[1]**

1m 26.28s (0.28) **Going Correction** +0.10s/f (Slow) **7** Ran SP% **110.2**
Speed ratings (Par 97): **102,97,96,96,95 92,91**
CSF £22.11 TOTE £3.90: £1.20, £3.70; EX 17.30 Trifecta £172.90.
Owner Mrs Fitri Hay **Bred** Tally-Ho Stud **Trained** Six Mile Bottom, Cambs

FOCUS
A fair handicap and a good performance from the winner. The runner-up appeared to a similar level to his Wolverhampton second and is the benchmark.

361 32RED H'CAP 6f (P)
6:45 (6:47) (Class 4) (0-85,82) 4-Y-O+
£6,469 (£1,925; £962; £481; £400; £400) **Stalls** Low

Form RPR

30-1 1 **Choice Encounter**[14] 139 4-9-2 **77** ... HollieDoyle 6 83
(Archie Watson) *mounted in chute: hld up in rr-div: shkn up 2f out: effrt over 1f out: stuck on wl and led 100yds out: jst hld on* **11/4[1]**

405- 2 nse **Last Page**[228] 3599 4-8-11 **79** ... LauraCoughlan(7) 4 84
(David Loughnane) *t.k.h and led after 1f: rdn and edgd lft 2f out: hdd over 1f out: fought bk ins fnl f and jst denied (jockey said gelding hung left-handed in the straight)* **13/2**

153- 3 ½ **Kamra (USA)**[50] 9389 5-9-5 **80** ... (bt) AdamKirby 1 83
(Henry Spiller) *trckd ldrs: rdn 2f out: led over 1f out: hdd 110yds out and dropped to 3rd cl home* **3/1[2]**

311- 4 hd **Red Alert**[129] 7327 5-9-2 **82** ... (p) PoppyBridgwater(5) 3 85
(Tony Carroll) *sn bhd ldr: effrt on outer 2f out: kpt on wl fnl f* **14/1**

1/-5 5 ¾ **Global Tango (IRE)**[21] 24 4-9-4 **79** ... CallumShepherd 2 79
(Charles Hills) *hld up in rr-div on inner: effrt wl over 1f out: kpt on tl no ex last 100yds (jockey said gelding hung left-handed in the straight)* **7/2[3]**

0-3 6 1¼ **National Glory (IRE)**[14] 139 4-9-2 **77** ... (p) EdwardGreatrex 5 73
(Archie Watson) *hld up in last: rdn at cutaway: kpt on over 1f out: no ex ins fnl f* **11/2**

003- 7 2 **Nezar (IRE)**[82] 8800 8-8-12 **76** ... JackDuern(3) 7 66
(Dean Ivory) *bhd ldr on outer: shkn up over 2f out: rdn 2f out: outpcd over 1f out: plugged on* **20/1**

1m 13.17s (0.07) **Going Correction** +0.10s/f (Slow) **7** Ran SP% **114.0**
Speed ratings (Par 105): **103,102,102,102,101 99,96**
CSF £20.84 TOTE £3.50: £2.80, £4.40; EX 25.20 Trifecta £89.70.
Owner Greenfield Racing **Bred** Stratford Place Stud & Willow Bloodstock **Trained** Upper Lambourn, W Berks

FOCUS
The early pace wasn't that strong and they finished in a heap. The winner may be even better in a strongly-run event.

362 32RED.COM H'CAP 1m 2f 219y(P)
7:15 (7:16) (Class 5) (0-70,77) 4-Y-O+
£3,752 (£1,116; £557; £400; £400; £400) **Stalls** Low

Form RPR

00-1 1 **Sir Prize**[18] 85 4-9-2 **64** ... RobertWinston 10 76
(Dean Ivory) *racd in mid-div and t.k.h at times: rdn on outer 2f out: sustained effrt and led 100yds out: kpt on in narrow ld* **5/1[3]**

31-0 2 nk **Ilhabela Fact**[18] 84 5-9-11 **71** ... LukeMorris 6 82
(Tony Carroll) *bhd ldr on outer: effrt 2f out: led over 1f out: hdd 100yds out: fought on but no ex* **15/8[1]**

02-0 3 2¼ **Singing Sheriff**[19] 54 4-9-3 **65** ... LiamKeniry 5 73
(Ed Walker) *t.k.h in mid-div: gng wl 2f out: shkn up wl over 1f out between horses: rdn 1f out and kpt on wl between horses tl n.m.r fnl 100yds: pushed out* **25/1**

00-1 4 1¼ **Baasha**[20] 39 4-9-2 **64** ... (b) RobertHavlin 3 69
(Ed Dunlop) *hld up in rr-div: prog and gng okay whn shuffled along ent fnl f: nvr involved* **7/1**

50-0 5 shd **Gendarme (IRE)**[14] 135 4-9-4 **66** ... RossaRyan 7 71
(Richard Hannon) *early ldr: sn bhd ldr: rdn wl over 1f out on heels of ldr: one pce ent fnl f* **16/1**

40-1 6 nk **My Brother Mike (IRE)**[14] 135 5-9-6 **66** ... PJMcDonald 8 70
(Kevin Frost) *dropped out leaving stalls and hld up in last pair: shkn up on outer and prog on outer wl over 1f out: unable qck and plugged on* **11/2**

3-21 7 3½ **Unit Of Assessment (IRE)**[8] 246 5-10-3 **77** 6ex ... (vt) AdamKirby 11 75
(William Knight) *bhd ldrs on outer: effrt and outpcd 2f out: no imp over 1f out* **7/2[2]**

00-0 8 7 **Espeegee**[18] 88 6-9-2 **67** ... DarraghKeenan(5) 2 54
(Alan Bailey) *in last: struggling and 10 l off pack over 3f out: plugged on fnl f* **66/1**

0/0- 9 6 **Petra's Pony (IRE)**[105] 8100 4-9-0 **62** ... MartinDwyer 9 38
(Brian Meehan) *sn led: rdn over 2f out: hdd wl over 1f out: wknd qckly* **33/1**

2m 23.6s (2.60) **Going Correction** +0.10s/f (Slow)
WFA 4 from 5yo+ 2lb **9** Ran SP% **115.7**
Speed ratings (Par 103): **97,96,95,94,94 93,91,86,81**
CSF £14.63 CT £213.08 TOTE £5.50: £1.70, £1.10, £7.10; EX 17.70 Trifecta £192.40.
Owner Michael & Heather Yarrow **Bred** Chippenham Lodge Stud **Trained** Radlett, Herts

FOCUS
An ordinary handicap which was run at a muddling pace. The winner may progress again.

363 INTRODUCING RACING TV H'CAP 1m 3f 219y(P)
7:45 (7:51) (Class 6) (0-55,55) 4-Y-O+
£3,105 (£924; £461; £400; £400; £400) **Stalls** Low

Form RPR

31-2 1 **Ember's Glow**[7] 257 5-9-4 **52** ... EoinWalsh 2 60
(Mark Loughnane) *racd in mid-div on inner: gd prog and clsr wl over 2f out: rdn 2f out: led over 1f out: clr and drvn out fnl f* **3/1[2]**

06-6 2 2½ **Bird For Life**[18] 84 5-9-0 **55** ... (p) EllieMacKenzie(7) 6 59
(Mark Usher) *hld up in last pair: rdn and wnt wd over 3f out: outpcd and plenty to do whn picked up wl fr over 1f out: gaining ins fnl f: nvr nrr* **8/1**

0-02 3 ½ **Harry Callahan (IRE)**[8] 245 4-8-13 **50** ... (v) CallumShepherd 9 54
(Mick Channon) *racd in mid-div: drvn along wl over 3f out: outpcd over 2f out: styd on wl over 1f out: nvr nrr* **6/1[3]**

00-5 4 1½ **Caracas**[13] 160 5-9-1 **52** ... (p) JoshuaBryan(3) 4 53
(Kevin Frost) *bhd ldrs: effrt wl over 2f out: plugged on fr over 1f: nt pce of ldrs* **16/1**

03-3 5 ½ **Banta Bay**[19] 59 5-8-12 **46** ... JosephineGordon 12 46
(John Best) *bhd ldrs: move to ld at 1/2-way: rdn over 2f out: hdd over 1f out: plugged on one pce after* **20/1**

55-3 6 2¾ **Singing The Blues (IRE)**[7] 257 4-9-2 **53** ... (p[1]) LukeMorris 7 50
(Rod Millman) *cl up: disp ld 4f out and niggled along: rdn wl over 2f out plugged on one pce* **5/2[1]**

43-2 7 1 **Arlecchino's Arc (IRE)**[19] 58 4-9-3 **54** ... (b) LiamKeniry 14 49
(Mark Usher) *hld up in rr: rdn wl over 2f out and outpcd: styd on wl fr over 1f out: nrst fin* **10/1**

060- 8 1¾ **Slowfoot (GER)**[49] 9409 11-9-2 **50** ... RobHornby 8 41
(Suzi Best) *racd in rr-div: effrt wl over 2f out: kpt on one pce* **66/1**

010/ 9 nk **Tractive Effort**[588] 3724 6-9-1 **49** ... KierenFox 1 40
(Michael Attwater) *bhd ldrs: rdn over 3f out: no imp and one pce over 1f out (jockey said gelding hung badly left-handed in the straight)* **50/1**

400- 10 ¾ **Tyrsal (IRE)**[55] 9318 8-9-2 **50** ... HollieDoyle 11 40
(Clifford Lines) *hld up in rr-div: cl 3f out: rdn over 2f out: fdd qckly over 1f out* **33/1**

31-0 11 3¾ **Affair**[20] 38 5-9-7 **55** ... CharlieBennett 13 39
(Hughie Morrison) *racd in mid-div: rdn along wl over 3f out: no imp over 2f out* **33/1**

05-6 12 15 **Gracie Stansfield**[18] 80 5-9-4 **52** ... GeorgeDowning 10 12
(Tony Carroll) *mid-div: effrt out wd 4f out: no imp in st* **40/1**

000- 13 2½ **Sargento**[105] 8100 4-8-8 **52** ... LeviWilliams(7) 3 9
(Simon Dow) *racd in mid-div: niggled along 5f out: rdn over 3f out: sn hld* **66/1**

10-0 14 2 **Lady Of York**[19] 58 5-9-6 **54** ... JoeyHaynes 5 6+
(Paul Howling) *led: hdd at 1/2-way: rdn over 4f out: no ex 3f out and eased* **12/1**

2m 34.34s (-0.16) **Going Correction** +0.10s/f (Slow)
WFA 4 from 5yo+ 3lb **14** Ran SP% **119.7**
Speed ratings (Par 101): **104,102,102,101,100 98,98,97,96,96 93,83,82,80**
CSF £25.58 CT £137.91 TOTE £4.00: £1.50, £2.20, £2.20; EX 31.50 Trifecta £183.90.
Owner Trevor Johnson **Bred** Darley **Trained** Rock, Worcs

FOCUS
Low-grade fare in which the winner got the run of things.

364 100% PROFIT BOOST AT 32REDSPORT.COM H'CAP 1m (P)
8:15 (8:18) (Class 5) (0-70,72) 4-Y-O+
£3,752 (£1,116; £557; £400; £400; £400) **Stalls** Low

Form RPR

36-3 1 **Elenora Delight**[16] 123 4-9-4 **67** ... (t[1]) MarcMonaghan 5 76
(Marco Botti) *sn led: mde rest: rdn 2f out: asserted ins fnl f* **6/1[3]**

21-5 **2** 2 1/4 **Magic Mirror**[14] 135 6-9-6 **69**..................(p) RobHornby 3 73
(Mark Rimell) *racd in mid-div: effrt 2f out: kpt on to take 2nd ins fnl f but no ch w wnr* **5/2**[1]

50-0 **3** 1/2 **Global Style (IRE)**[14] 135 4-9-4 **67**.................. GeorgeDowning 6 70
(Tony Carroll) *hld up in rr-div: rdn over 2f out: kpt on fr over 1f out* **20/1**

34-5 **4** 1/2 **Espresso Freddo (IRE)**[18] 91 5-9-8 **71**..................(p) AdamKirby 8 73
(Robert Stephens) *hld up in rr: shkn up 2f out gng wl: angled to outer and rdn over 1f out: styd on wl but too much to do last 150yds and shuffled along* **7/2**[2]

6-30 **5** 3/4 **Red Gunner**[7] 250 5-8-8 **57**.................. LukeMorris 1 57
(Mark Loughnane) *racd in mid-div: effrt over 2f out: plugged on* **8/1**

003- **6** hd **Claudine (IRE)**[106] 8070 4-8-7 **63**.................. AmeliaGlass(7) 2 63
(Henry Candy) *early ldr: sn trckd ldr: rdn 2f out: fdd fnl f* **14/1**

03-3 **7** 3 **Mrs Benson (IRE)**[11] 202 4-9-4 **67**.................. DavidProbert 4 60
(Michael Blanshard) *bhd ldr: effrt over 2f out: no ex ent fnl f and fdd* **8/1**

53-2 **8** 3 3/4 **Skydiving**[19] 63 4-9-7 **70**.................. DougieCostello 7 54
(Jamie Osborne) *hld up in rr: shkn up in last over 2f out: no imp and shuffled along over 1f out* **13/2**

00-5 **9** 7 **Archie (IRE)**[13] 158 7-9-4 **72**..................(tp) PoppyBridgwater(5) 9 40
(Brian Barr) *t.k.h on outer in mid-div w no cover: scrubbed along over 3f out: no imp and wknd over 1f out* **33/1**

1m 39.86s (0.06) **Going Correction** +0.10s/f (Slow) **9 Ran SP% 115.0**
Speed ratings (Par 103): **103,100,100,99,99 98,95,92,85**
CSF £21.28 CT £282.41 TOTE £7.00: £2.40, £1.70, £5.70; EX 19.60 Trifecta £266.40.
Owner Les Boyer Partnership **Bred** Saleh Al Homaizi & Imad Al Sagar **Trained** Newmarket, Suffolk

FOCUS
This was steadily run and dominated by the leader.
T/Plt: £556.50 to a £1 stake. Pool: £113,425.42. 148.77 winning units. T/Qpdt: £43.30 to a £1 stake. Pool: £17,423.62. 297.34 winning units. **Cathal Gahan**

309 **LINGFIELD** (L-H)
Wednesday, January 23

OFFICIAL GOING: Polytrack: standard
Wind: light, against Weather: overcast, cold

365 LIKE SUN RACING ON FACEBOOK H'CAP 7f 1y(P)
1:00 (1:00) (Class 6) (0-55,55) 3-Y-O+
£3,105 (£924; £461; £300; £300; £300) **Stalls Low**

Form RPR

00-0 **1** **Mr Andros**[16] 116 6-9-7 **48**..................(bt) ShaneKelly 12 56
(Brendan Powell) *hld up in rr: stl last wl over 1f out: swtchd rt: pushed along and effrt ent fnl f: qcknd and str run ins fnl f to ld wl ins fnl f: sn in command* **10/1**

03-0 **2** 1 3/4 **Baby Gal**[7] 263 5-9-5 **46**..................(b[1]) CharlieBennett 4 49
(Jim Boyle) *in tch in midfield: effrt ent fnl 2f: drvn and clsd to press ldrs and edgd lft ins fnl f: unable to match pce of wnr and one pce wl ins fnl f: snatched 2nd on post (jockey said mare hung left-handed under pressure)* **10/1**

02-3 **3** nse **Catapult**[22] 6 4-9-8 **49**.................. HollieDoyle 1 52
(Clifford Lines) *led: drvn over 1f out: hdd and unable to match pce of wnr wl ins fnl f: kpt on same pce and lost 2nd on post* **7/1**[2]

325- **4** nse **Locommotion**[35] 9602 7-10-0 **55**.................. LukeMorris 6 58
(Matthew Salaman) *hld up in tch in midfield: nt clr run ent fnl 2f: hdwy on inner over 1f out: styd on to press ldrs ins fnl f: unable to match pce of wnr and one pce wl ins fnl f* **4/1**[1]

00-5 **5** 1/2 **Haraz (IRE)**[7] 263 6-8-12 **46** oh1..................(bt) SeamusCronin(7) 9 48
(Paddy Butler) *wl in tch in midfield: effrt to chse ldr jst over 2f out: drvn over 1f out: kpt on to press wnr 100yds out: unable to match pce of wnr and one pce wl ins fnl f* **20/1**

405- **6** nk **Seaquinn**[26] 9735 4-9-5 **46** oh1.................. KierenFox 10 47
(John Best) *hld up in tch in last trio: swtchd rt and effrt u.p over 1f out: hdwy u.p ins fnl f: styd on wl towards fin* **16/1**

0-62 **7** hd **Swiss Cross**[7] 263 12-9-5 **53**..................(p) GraceMcEntee(7) 3 54
(Phil McEntee) *rousted along leaving stalls: hld up in tch in midfield: nt clr run and shuffled bk ent fnl 2f: swtchd rt and rdn over 1f out: styd on wl ins fnl f* **8/1**[3]

004- **8** 1/2 **Gold Club**[23] 9773 8-10-0 **55**..................(p) RobertWinston 13 54
(Lee Carter) *broke wl: sn restrained and hld wl in tch on outer: effrt to chse ldrs and wd bnd 2f out: rallied u.p 1f out: styd on ins fnl f* **12/1**

265- **9** nse **Maazel (IRE)**[24] 9764 5-9-6 **54**.................. TobyEley(7) 5 53
(Julia Feilden) *hld up in tch towards rr: nt clrest of runs and edgd out rt 2f out: hdwy jst over 1f out: chsng ldrs ins fnl f: unable to match pce of wnr and one pce whn bmpd and hmpd wl ins fnl f* **4/1**[1]

02-5 **10** nk **Athassel**[19] 53 10-9-4 **52**.................. KatherineBegley(7) 14 50
(David Evans) *hld up in tch in midfield: nt clr run ent fnl 2f: swtchd rt: effrt and hdwy jst over 1f out: keeping on and chsng ldrs whn swtchd rt: nt clr run: bdly hmpd and eased wl ins fnl f (jockey said gelding was denied a clear run)* **14/1**

44-1 **11** hd **Cool Echo**[14] 132 5-9-13 **54**..................(p) DavidProbert 2 52
(J R Jenkins) *trckd ldrs: effrt 2f out: 3rd and drvn over 1f out: no ex ins fnl f and outpcd fnl 75yds* **7/1**[2]

12 3 **Coffeemeanscoffee (IRE)**[12] 189 4-9-2 **46** oh1.(p[1]) KillianLeonard(3) 7 36
(W J Martin, Ire) *hld up in midfield: effrt whn nt clr run ent fnl 2f: kpt on same pce and no imp ins fnl f* **33/1**

00-5 **13** 2 1/4 **Brogans Bay (IRE)**[14] 141 4-9-13 **54**.................. NickyMackay 11 38
(Simon Dow) *t.k.h: rdn over 2f out: lost pl qckly over 1f out: bhd and eased wl ins fnl f* **16/1**

000- **14** 4 1/2 **Flourishable**[23] 9771 3-8-1 **46** oh1.................. KieranO'Neill 8 14
(Tony Carroll) *chsd ldr tl jst over 2f out: lost pl u.p and bhd 1f out: wknd and eased wl ins fnl f* **50/1**

1m 25.09s (0.29) **Going Correction** -0.025s/f (Stan)
WFA 3 from 4yo+ 18lb **14 Ran SP% 130.1**
Speed ratings (Par 101): **97,95,94,94,94 93,93,93,93,92 92,89,86,81**
CSF £113.26 CT £788.65 TOTE £12.20: £4.40, £3.30, £2.60; EX 120.40 Trifecta £921.20.
Owner BP Racing Club (The Dublin Flyers) **Bred** A Christou **Trained** Upper Lambourn, Berks

FOCUS
This looked wide open. It was run at a sound pace and saw a blanket finish, with the winner swooping late.

366 LADBROKES HOME OF THE ODDS BOOST FILLIES' H'CAP 7f 1y(P)
1:30 (1:30) (Class 5) (0-70,69) 4-Y-O+
£3,752 (£1,116; £557; £300; £300; £300) **Stalls Low**

Form RPR

30-5 **1** **First Link (USA)**[14] 144 4-8-8 **56**.................. HollieDoyle 4 65+
(Jean-Rene Auvray) *stdd s: t.k.h: hld up in tch in rr: v wd and clsd bnd 2f out: hdwy u.p 1f out: hung lft but str run to ld wl ins fnl f: sn in command: readily (vet said filly lost it's right-fore shoe)* **13/2**

21-3 **2** 1 1/2 **Chica De La Noche**[7] 256 5-9-2 **64**..................(p) AdamKirby 3 69
(Simon Dow) *hld up in tch in midfield: nt clrest of runs: swtchd lft and hdwy over 1f out: str chal u.p ins fnl f tl unable to match pce of wnr wl ins fnl f* **3/1**[1]

363- **3** nk **Playful Spirit**[56] 9287 4-9-7 **69**.................. RobertHavlin 8 73
(John Gosden) *led: rdn over 1f out: drvn 1f out: hdd and unable to match pce of wnr wl ins fnl f* **4/1**[2]

25-3 **4** 1 1/4 **Hic Bibi**[14] 138 4-8-7 **62**.................. LauraCoughlan(7) 7 64
(David Loughnane) *taken down early: hld up in tch in last trio: effrt u.p and impeded over 1f out: kpt on ins fnl f: nvr enough pce to threaten ldrs* **7/1**

02-4 **5** 1/2 **Sweet Nature (IRE)**[13] 154 4-9-7 **69**..................(p[1]) MartinHarley 5 68
(William Haggas) *chsd ldrs: effrt 2f out: chsd wnr over 1f out tl ins fnl f: no ex and wknd wl ins fnl f* **5/1**[3]

00-4 **6** 1 **The Special One (IRE)**[7] 256 6-8-4 **59**..................(h) GraceMcEntee(7) 9 56
(Phil McEntee) *pushed along briefly sn after s: in tch in midfield: effrt over 1f out: keeping on whn sltly short of room ins fnl f: wl hld and kpt on same pce after* **20/1**

010- **7** 1/2 **Time Stands Still**[40] 9538 5-8-12 **63**.................. KillianLeonard(3) 10 58
(W J Martin, Ire) *chsd ldr: rdn and ev ch over 2f out tl outpcd and lost pl over 1f out: wknd ins fnl f* **14/1**

320- **8** 3 3/4 **Sonnet Rose (IRE)**[90] 8578 5-9-7 **69**..................(bt) MartinDwyer 6 60
(Conrad Allen) *chsd ldrs: effrt jst over 2f out: unable qck over 1f out: hld whn squeezed for room and hmpd ins fnl f* **8/1**

23-5 **9** 3 **Lady Marigold (IRE)**[14] 138 4-8-4 **59**..................(p) GeorgiaDobie(7) 1 36
(Eve Johnson Houghton) *pushed along leaving stalls: a towards rr: nvr involved* **8/1**

1m 23.85s (-0.95) **Going Correction** -0.025s/f (Stan) **9 Ran SP% 121.2**
Speed ratings (Par 100): **104,102,101,100,99 98,98,93,90**
CSF £27.74 CT £91.71 TOTE £6.50: £2.10, £1.90, £1.70; EX 27.10 Trifecta £161.00.
Owner Stuart McPhee **Bred** Juddmonte Farms Inc **Trained** Calne, Wilts
■ Stewards' Enquiry : Adam Kirby caution; careless riding
Hollie Doyle two-day ban; careless riding (Feb 6-7)

FOCUS
They were soon strung out in modest fillies' handicap. The winner got a good ride and was the second consecutive winner to come from last place.

367 LADBROKES NOVICE STKS 6f 1y(P)
2:05 (2:05) (Class 5) 3-Y-O
£3,752 (£1,116; £557; £278) **Stalls Low**

Form RPR

305- **1** **St Peters Basilica (IRE)**[43] 9490 3-9-2 **75**..................(b[1]) RobertHavlin 1 74
(John Gosden) *mde all: shkn up and readily wnt clr over 1f out: sn in command and in n.d ins fnl f* **1/1**[1]

0- **2** 2 1/2 **Derry Boy**[174] 5642 3-9-2 **0**.................. EoinWalsh 6 66
(David Evans) *taken down early and led to post: sn chsng wnr: rdn and edgd rt bnd 2f out: outpcd over 1f out: hld but kpt on for clr 2nd ins fnl f* **12/1**

3 2 **Bequest** 3-8-11 **0**.................. DavidProbert 3 55
(Ron Hodges) *sn outpcd in last trio and rn green: effrt wl over 1f out: kpt on wl ins fnl f to go 3rd last strides: no threat to wnr* **20/1**

4 nk **Fury And Fire** 3-9-2 **0**.................. LukeMorris 5 59
(William Jarvis) *chsd ldng pair: rdn ent fnl 2f: unable to match pce of wnr and kpt on same pce fr over 1f out: lost 3rd last strides* **9/1**[3]

6-5 **5** 1 3/4 **Shug**[15] 130 3-9-2 **0**.................. LiamKeniry 7 53
(Ed Walker) *stdd s: sn in tch in midfield: shkn up: rn green and edgd lft over 1f out: wl hld and kpt on same pce ins fnl f* **16/1**

6 5 **Turn To Rock (IRE)** 3-9-2 **0**.................. NicolaCurrie 2 37
(Ed Walker) *midfield tl outpcd in last trio over 4f out: bhd and rn green bnd 2f out: no ch after but kpt on wl ins fnl f (jockey said gelding ran green)* **7/4**[2]

00- **7** 1 1/2 **The Man Of Mode (IRE)**[137] 7051 3-9-2 **0**.................. CallumShepherd 4 32
(Michael Attwater) *outpcd in last trio: rdn ent fnl 2f: no prog and wl hld over 1f out: wknd ins fnl f* **40/1**

1m 12.49s (0.59) **Going Correction** -0.025s/f (Stan) **7 Ran SP% 117.1**
Speed ratings (Par 97): **95,91,89,88,86 79,77**
CSF £15.75 TOTE £1.90: £1.10, £5.00; EX 13.30 Trifecta £92.70.
Owner Lady Bamford, Magnier, Smith & Tabor **Bred** Orpendale,Wynatt,Chelston & Daylesford **Trained** Newmarket, Suffolk

FOCUS
A moderate novice sprint and a routine victory for the Gosden hotpot.

368 BETWAY H'CAP 1m 2f (P)
2:40 (2:40) (Class 2) (0-105,102) 4-Y-O+
£11,827 (£3,541; £1,770; £885; £442; £222) **Stalls Low**

Form RPR

101- **1** **Pactolus (IRE)**[28] 9705 8-9-10 **102**..................(t) AdamKirby 1 107
(Stuart Williams) *trckd ldrs: effrt to press ldr wl over 1f out: rdn to ld 1f out: drvn: edging rt but kpt on wl ins fnl f* **5/1**

431- **2** 1/2 **Cosmeapolitan**[23] 9775 6-9-2 **94**.................. DavidProbert 6 98+
(Alan King) *hld up wl in tch in rr: clsd and wd bnd 2f out: hdwy 1f out: r.o strly ins fnl f to go 2nd last strides: nvr quite getting to wnr* **9/2**[3]

112- **3** nk **Caspar The Cub (IRE)**[23] 9775 4-9-1 **94**..................(p) MartinHarley 2 98+
(Alan King) *wl in tch in midfield: stl travelling wl whn nt clr run: swtchd rt and wd bnd 2f out: hdwy 1f out: r.o wl ins fnl f: wnt 2nd towards fin: nt quite getting to wnr and lost 2nd last strides* **11/4**[1]

145- **4** 1/2 **C Note (IRE)**[40] 9534 6-8-10 **88**..................(t) LukeMorris 3 90
(Heather Main) *led and set stdy gallop: rdn and qcknd wl over 2f out: drvn and hdd 1f out: edging rt and kpt on same pce ins fnl f: lost 2 pls towards fin* **11/1**

01-4 **5** 3/4 **Calling Out (FR)**[18] 89 8-9-5 **97**.................. StevieDonohoe 5 98
(David Simcock) *hld up wl in tch: effrt jst over 2f out: chsd ldrs ent fnl f: kpt on same pce ins fnl f* **22/1**

330- **6** 1 1/4 **Abe Lincoln (USA)**[116] 7773 6-9-8 **100**........................(tp) RobertHavlin 8 98
(Jeremy Noseda) *hld up wl in tch: clsd on outer to chse ldrs 4f out: rdn and outpcd over 1f out: kpt on same pce and no imp ins fnl f* **7/2**[2]

642- **7** 1 1/2 **Kyllachy Gala**[14] 8198 6-9-6 **98**.............................. EdwardGreatrex 7 93
(Warren Greatrex) *pressed ldr: rdn wl over 2f out: lost 2nd and unable qck wl over 1f out: wknd ins fnl f* **12/1**

552- **8** 3 3/4 **Speed Company (IRE)**[11] 8899 6-8-6 **84**......................... KieranO'Neill 4 72
(Ian Williams) *t.k.h: hld up wl in tch: last and rdn ent fnl 2f: no imp and wknd ins fnl f* **7/1**

2m 6.68s (0.08) **Going Correction** -0.025s/f (Stan)
WFA 4 from 6yo+ 1lb **8 Ran SP% 116.6**
Speed ratings (Par 109): **98,97,97,96,96 95,94,91**
CSF £28.32 CT £74.35 TOTE £5.90: £2.60, £2.60, £1.10; EX 26.80 Trifecta £62.60.
Owner T W Morley & Mrs J Morley **Bred** Tom McDonald **Trained** Newmarket, Suffolk

FOCUS
This feature handicap was run at an ordinary pace until 3f out. Pactolus was winning from a three-figure mark for the first time, despite his advancing years.

369 BETWAY CASINO H'CAP 1m 7f 169y(P)
3:10 (3:10) (Class 6) (0-60,60) 4-Y-O+

£3,105 (£924; £461; £300; £300; £300) **Stalls** Low

Form RPR

004- **1** **Casa Comigo (IRE)**[47] 9448 4-8-11 **52**.............................. KierenFox 8 61+
(John Best) *wnt rt leaving stalls: t.k.h: in tch in midfield: clsd to chse ldrs 9f out: nt clr run 2f out: gap opened: rdn and qcknd to ld 1f out: r.o wl* **9/2**[3]

12-0 **2** 1 3/4 **Nafaayes (IRE)**[18] 84 5-9-3 **60**.............................(p) TobyEley(7) 9 64
(Jean-Rene Auvray) *hmpd leaving stalls: t.k.h: hld up in last pair: hdwy on outer 5f out: effrt to chse ldrs 2f: rdn and chsd wnr ins fnl f: kpt on (jockey said mare was hampered leaving the stalls)* **7/1**

002- **3** 2 1/4 **Argyle (IRE)**[17] 9409 6-9-9 **59**.......................................(v) AdamKirby 10 60
(Gary Moore) *hmpd leaving stalls and pushed along early: midfield: hdwy on outer 5f out: rdn over 3f out: drvn and ev ch 2f out tl unable qck 1f out: outpcd ins fnl f* **4/1**[2]

3-62 **4** nk **Contingency Fee**[11] 204 4-8-7 **55**.........................(p) GraceMcEntee(7) 12 58
(Phil McEntee) *hld up in midfield on outer: clsd to press ldrs 4f out: rdn and ev ch jst over 2f out tl unable qck 1f out: outpcd ins fnl f* **20/1**

364- **5** hd **Tilsworth Sammy**[41] 9526 4-8-11 **52**............................... DavidProbert 4 55
(J R Jenkins) *sn towards rr: last and rdn over 4f out: hdwy into midfield 2f out: styd on strly ins fnl f: nt rch ldrs* **33/1**

0-41 **6** 1/2 **Top Rock Talula (IRE)**[8] 245 4-8-11 **52** 6ex.......... EdwardGreatrex 14 54
(Warren Greatrex) *chsd ldrs tl wnt 2nd 9f out: led over 3f out: hrd pressed and drvn over 2f out: hdd 1f out and wknd ins fnl f* **11/4**[1]

41-2 **7** shd **Tynecastle Park**[20] 40 6-9-2 **57**.............................. DarraghKeenan(5) 3 57
(Robert Eddery) *trckd ldrs on inner: shuffled bk bhd wkng rival 3f out: tried to rally u.p over 1f out: swtchd rt and kpt on wl ins fnl f: nvr getting bk on terms w ldrs* **7/1**

40-0 **8** 1/2 **Sea's Aria (IRE)**[19] 59 8-8-10 **46** oh1.............................. KieranO'Neill 6 45
(Mark Hoad) *hld up towards rr: hdwy on outer 5f out: rdn and chsd ldrs ent fnl 2f: unable qck over 1f out: wknd ins fnl f* **16/1**

0/4- **9** hd **Schindlers Ark (USA)**[166] 5964 5-8-11 **47**........................ NicolaCurrie 5 46
(Jane Chapple-Hyam) *w ldr tl over 9f out: steadily lost pl and midfield whn rdn over 2f out: rallied and keeping on ins fnl f: nt clr run and eased towards fin (jockey said gelding was denied a clear run on the run to the line)* **11/1**

444- **10** 1 1/4 **Planetoid (IRE)**[33] 9657 11-9-4 **54**..................................(p) RobHornby 7 52
(Suzi Best) *hld up in rr: nt clr run over 2f out: hdwy on inner over 1f out: swtchd rt 1f out: no threat to ldrs but kpt on ins fnl f* **20/1**

0/0- **11** 5 **Netley Abbey**[55] 9318 5-8-5 **46** oh1..........................(t[1]) RhiainIngram(5) 2 38
(Paul George) *hld up towards rr: hmpd 3f out: continually hmpd after and lost any ch: rdn over 1f out: no imp (jockey said gelding was denied a clear run three furlongs out)* **33/1**

405- **12** 7 **Magojiro (USA)**[60] 9252 4-8-5 **49**............................(v[1]) KillianLeonard(3) 13 34
(W J Martin, Ire) *s.i.s: hld up towards rr: nt clr run: edgd lft and hmpd over 2f out: lost any ch and wl btn fnl 2f* **25/1**

45-4 **13** 8 **London Grammar (IRE)**[11] 204 5-8-5 **48** oh1 ow2 SeamusCronin(7) 1 22
(Ralph J Smith) *t.k.h: led tl over 9f out: steadily lost pl: midfield and rdn over 2f out: sn btn and wknd over 1f out* **50/1**

00-0 **14** 6 **Gift From God**[19] 58 6-8-10 **46** oh1...................................(t) JohnFahy 11 12
(Hugo Froud) *chsd ldrs tl led over 9f out: hdd over 3f out: sn lost pl: bhd over 1f out: wknd* **50/1**

3m 22.88s (-2.82) **Going Correction** -0.025s/f (Stan)
WFA 4 from 5yo+ 5lb **14 Ran SP% 127.2**
Speed ratings (Par 101): **106,105,104,103,103 103,103,103,103,102 99,96,92,89**
CSF £35.44 CT £141.93 TOTE £5.80: £2.10, £2.80, £1.40; EX 43.80 Trifecta £164.80.
Owner Simon Malcolm **Bred** Simon Malcom **Trained** Oad Street, Kent

FOCUS
A moderate staying handicap, run at a brisk early pace. Straightforward enough form which should work out.

370 LADBROKES HOME OF THE ODDS BOOST FILLIES' NOVICE STKS 1m 1y(P)
3:45 (3:45) (Class 5) 3-Y-O+ **£3,752** (£1,116; £557; £278) **Stalls** High

Form RPR

4/2- **1** **Capriolette (IRE)**[212] 4196 4-10-0 0.............................. LiamKeniry 8 82
(Ed Walker) *sn w ldr: rdn and kicked clr w ldr 2f out: led jst over 1f out: sn asserted but hung lft: in command and r.o wl ins fnl f* **8/1**[2]

2 **2** 3 1/4 **Vandella (IRE)**[18] 78 3-8-8 0.............................. RobertHavlin 7 72
(John Gosden) *sn led: rdn and kicked clr w wnr 2f out: hdd jst over 1f out and hmpd: swtchd rt and kpt on same pce ins fnl f* **4/11**[1]

3 5 **Red Fedora** 3-8-8 0.............................. DavidProbert 9 58
(Clive Cox) *chsd ldrs: 5th and outpcd ent fnl 2f: no ch w ldng pair but kpt on ins fnl f to snatch 3rd last strides* **8/1**[2]

0- **4** hd **Mrs Meader**[35] 9604 3-8-8 0.............................. KieranO'Neill 12 58
(Seamus Mullins) *midfield: hdwy on outer to chse ldrs over 2f out: 3rd and outpcd 2f out: no ch w ldng pair after and kpt on same pce: lost 3rd last strides* **66/1**

6- **5** 1/2 **Gold Fleece**[27] 9725 3-8-8 0.............................. JosephineGordon 10 56+
(Hugo Palmer) *sn dropped to last trio and pushed along over 4f out: 10th and wl off the pce 2f out: swtchd rt over 1f out: no ch w ldng pair but r.o strly ins fnl f* **25/1**

6- **6** 1 1/4 **Perfect Grace**[44] 9485 3-8-8 0.............................. EdwardGreatrex 1 54
(Archie Watson) *in tch in midfield 6th and outpcd jst over 2f out: wl hld and plugged on same pce after* **14/1**[3]

05- **7** nk **Loch Lady**[35] 9607 3-8-8 0.............................. RobHornby 5 53
(Ralph Beckett) *midfield: outpcd jst over 2f out: 7th and wl btn whn rn green over 1f out: plugged on* **20/1**

0 **8** 1 1/4 **Yvette**[14] 133 3-8-8 0.............................. LukeMorris 2 50
(Sir Mark Prescott Bt) *chsd ldrs: 4th and outpcd 2f out: sn btn and wknd ins fnl f* **20/1**

-0 **9** nk **Breakfast Time**[14] 133 3-8-8 0.............................. HollieDoyle 6 49
(Archie Watson) *broke wl: sn stdd bk and in last quartet after 2f: rdn over 2f out: nvr involved* **25/1**

0 **10** 8 **Evie May**[14] 133 3-8-8 0.............................. JohnFahy 4 31
(Mick Channon) *t.k.h: hld up in tch in midfield: rdn: lost pl and rn green over 2f out: wknd wl over 1f out* **66/1**

11 2 3/4 **Tanzerin (IRE)** 3-8-8 0.............................. NicolaCurrie 3 25
(Charlie Fellowes) *sn outpcd in last pair: nvr involved* **16/1**

12 11 **Puzzle Cache**[252] 5-10-0 0.............................. CharlieBennett 11 4
(Rod Millman) *s.i.s: a outpcd in rr* **150/1**

1m 37.54s (-0.66) **Going Correction** -0.025s/f (Stan)
WFA 3 from 4yo+ 20lb **12 Ran SP% 128.9**
Speed ratings (Par 100): **102,98,93,93,93 91,91,90,89,81 79,68**
CSF £11.68 TOTE £9.50: £2.00, £1.02, £2.30; EX 22.60 Trifecta £93.90.
Owner Mr & Mrs Andrew Blaxland **Bred** Tom Wallace **Trained** Upper Lambourn, Berks

FOCUS
The market leaders dominated this fillies' novice contest although the odds-on favourite had to give best despite receiving over a stone from the winner.
T/Jkpt: Not won. T/Plt: £27.80 to a £1 stake. Pool: £119,778.10. 3,145.11 winning units. T/Qpdt: £3.60 to a £1 stake. Pool: £17,637.73. 3,553.39 winning units. **Steve Payne**

371 - 378a (Foreign Racing) - See Raceform Interactive

154 CHELMSFORD (A.W) (L-H)
Thursday, January 24

OFFICIAL GOING: Polytrack: standard
Wind: light, across Weather: overcast, chilly

379 BET TOTEPLACEPOT AT TOTESPORT.COM ALL-WEATHER "HANDS AND HEELS" APPRENTICE H'CAP 7f (P)
4:25 (4:26) (Class 7) (0-50,51) 4-Y-O+ **£2,911** (£866; £432; £216) **Stalls** Low

Form RPR

1 **Lion Hearted (IRE)**[143] 6889 5-9-2 **45**.............................. MarkCrehan 6 63+
(Michael Appleby) *pressed ldr for over 1f: chsd ldrs after: rdn over 2f out: clsd to ld 1f out: styd on strly and drew clr ins fnl f: readily* **11/10**[1]

0-13 **2** 6 **Amor Fati (IRE)**[13] 180 4-9-8 **51**.............................. WilliamCarver 7 53+
(David Evans) *v.s.a: hld up in rr: nt clr run and hmpd 3f out: hdwy to chse ldng quartet over 1f out: kpt on wl and wnt 2nd wl ins fnl f: no ch w wnr (jockey said gelding was slowly away)* **7/2**[2]

00-6 **3** 2 **Tellovoi (IRE)**[14] 159 11-9-7 **50**..............................(p) OliverStammers 3 45
(Richard Guest) *chsd ldr over 5f out: swtchd out rt and effrt to chal wl over 1f out: chsd wnr but outpcd jst ins fnl f: wl hld after and lost 2nd wl ins fnl f* **12/1**

36-4 **4** nk **Sir Lancelott**[13] 180 7-9-2 **45**.............................. LauraCoughlan 13 39
(Adrian Nicholls) *dwlt: styd wd and in tch: swtchd rt and effrt wl over 1f out: styd on steadily ins fnl f to go 2nd towards fin: no ch w wnr* **8/1**[3]

005- **5** 3/4 **Canimar**[42] 9523 4-9-0 **46**..............................(p) GavinAshton(3) 8 38
(Shaun Keightley) *led: rdn and hrd pressed over 1f out: hdd 1f out and sn outpcd by wnr: wknd fnl 100yds* **12/1**

4-04 **6** 3/4 **Malaysian Boleh**[14] 159 9-9-0 **46**..............................(be) GraceMcEntee(3) 1 36
(Phil McEntee) *hld up in tch: nt clr run and shuffled bk over 2f out: effrt and hdwy over 1f out: swtchd lft and kpt on ins fnl f: no ch w wnr* **9/1**

05-6 **7** 3/4 **Mystical Moon (IRE)**[17] 117 4-9-2 **45**..............................(v) EllaMcCain 12 33
(David C Griffiths) *midfield: hdwy to chse ldrs 4f out: pressing ldr jst over 2f out tl no ex 1f out: wknd ins fnl f* **33/1**

12-0 **8** 2 1/4 **Poppy May (IRE)**[14] 161 5-9-8 **51**.............................. TobyEley 10 33
(James Given) *hld up in rr: wd and effrt bnd 2f out: plugged on ins fnl f: nvr trbld ldrs (jockey said mare was never travelling)* **16/1**

/6-0 **9** 5 **Compton Brave**[14] 155 5-9-2 **45**.............................. AmeliaGlass 11 14
(J R Jenkins) *t.k.h: hld up in tch in midfield: effrt wl over 1f out: sn outpcd and wkng whn hung lft ins fnl f* **33/1**

000- **10** nk **Tally's Song**[64] 9177 6-8-13 **45**..............................(t[1]) ElishaWhittington(3) 2 14
(Grace Harris) *pushed along leaving stalls: a towards rr: n.m.r and impeded over 2f out: bhd 2f out (jockey said mare suffered interference rounding the bend)* **50/1**

06-0 **11** 3 1/2 **Premium Pink (IRE)**[14] 161 4-9-7 **50**..............................(p[1]) JessicaCooley 5 9
(Luke McJannet) *in tch in midfield: rdn and lost pl over 1f out: wknd fnl f* **50/1**

506- **12** 12 **Jampower**[262] 2518 4-9-2 **45**.............................. EllieMacKenzie 4
(Natalie Lloyd-Beavis) *chsd ldrs for 3f: rdn and losing pl over 2f out: bhd and hung rt ins fnl f* **50/1**

1m 26.2s (-1.00) **Going Correction** -0.05s/f (Stan) **12 Ran SP% 124.0**
Speed ratings (Par 97): **103,96,93,93,92 91,90,88,82,82 78,64**
CSF £4.85 CT £31.00 TOTE £2.00: £1.10, £1.20, £3.90; EX 7.00 Trifecta £32.70.
Owner Slipstream Racing **Bred** Dowager Countess Harrington **Trained** Oakham, Rutland

FOCUS
One-way traffic in this lowly 'hands and heels' race.

380 BET TOTEEXACTA AT TOTESPORT.COM FILLIES' NOVICE STKS 7f (P)
4:55 (4:56) (Class 4) 3-Y-O+ **£5,530** (£1,645; £822; £411) **Stalls** Low

Form RPR

-3 **1** **Pacificadora (USA)**[19] 78 3-8-10 0.............................. NickyMackay 4 67+
(Simon Dow) *hld up wl in tch: effrt and shifted lft jst over 1f out: sn chalng and led ins fnl f: r.o wl* **11/4**[2]

0- **2** 1 1/2 **Miaella**[77] 8959 4-10-0 0.............................. JoeyHaynes 3 68
(Paul Howling) *broke wl: sn restrained: t.k.h and trckd ldrs: swtchd rt: nt clr run and hmpd over 1f out: gap opened and effrt 1f out: hdwy to chse wnr wl ins fnl f: kpt on wl but nvr getting on terms w wnr* **66/1**

06- **3** 3/4 **Hanbury Dreams**[24] 9771 3-8-10 0.............................. MartinDwyer 8 62
(Tom Clover) *stdd s: t.k.h: dropped in after 1f out and hld up in tch: clsd: nt clr run and hmpd over 1f out: hdwy ins fnl f: kpt on wl to go 3rd last strides: nvr getting on terms w wnr* **33/1**

5- **4** nk **Sundiata**[36] 9604 3-8-10 0.............................. CallumShepherd 6 60
(Charles Hills) *dwlt and flashed tail leaving stalls: sn rcvrd to chse ldrs on outer: effrt and ev ch over 1f out: led and edgd rt 1f out: hdd ins fnl f: no ex and lost 2 pls wl ins fnl f* **2/1**[1]

5 2 1/4 **J'Ouvert (IRE)** 3-8-10 0.............................. StevieDonohoe 7 54
(David Simcock) *t.k.h: hld up in tch in midfield: effrt and rn green over 1f out: sltly impeded 1f out: kpt on ins fnl f: no threat to wnr* **7/1**

50- **6** hd **Beehaar**[36] 9604 3-8-10 0.............................. RobertHavlin 9 53
(John Gosden) *pressed ldr: ev ch and rdn over 1f out: hdd 1f out: no ex and wknd ins fnl f* **10/1**

7 shd **April Wine** 3-8-10 0 HectorCrouch 2 53
(Clive Cox) *rn v green: sn pushed along outpcd and detached in last: clsd jst over 1f out: swtchd rt and kpt on wl ins fnl f: nvr trbld ldrs* **16/1**

4 8 3/4 **Dorchester**[19] 78 3-8-10 0 (b) LukeMorris 5 51
(Marco Botti) *led: hrd pressed and rdn ent fnl 2f: hdd over 1f out: no ex and wknd ins fnl f* **4/1[3]**

0- 9 1 1/4 **Duplicitous (IRE)**[28] 9725 3-8-10 0 ShaneKelly 1 48
(James Tate) *dwlt: in tch in midfield: rdn 3f out: effrt u.p over 1f out: no imp 1f out and wknd ins fnl f* **16/1**

1m 27.01s (-0.19) **Going Correction** -0.05s/f (Stan) 9 Ran SP% **117.8**
WFA 3 from 4yo 18lb
Speed ratings (Par 102): **99,97,96,96,93 93,93,92,90**
CSF £148.55 TOTE £3.80: £1.10, £17.70, £14.90; EX 154.10 Trifecta £5524.00.
Owner Robert Moss **Bred** Martha Jane Mulholland Et Al **Trained** Epsom, Surrey

FOCUS
Not sure how strong a novice this was, with the the two rank outsiders filling the places.

381 BET TOTEQUADPOT AT TOTESPORT.COM H'CAP 7f (P)
5:25 (5:25) (Class 4) (0-85,85) 4-Y-0+
£6,986 (£2,079; £1,038; £519; £400; £400) **Stalls** Low

Form RPR

01-3 1 **Glenn Coco**[21] 34 5-9-1 79 (t) CallumRodriguez 3 87
(Stuart Williams) *wl in tch in midfield: effrt to press ldrs 1f out: rdn to ld 1f out: kpt on wl ins fnl f: rdn out* **3/1[1]**

34-4 2 3/4 **Kadrizzi (FR)**[14] 158 6-8-9 73 (v) RobertHavlin 8 79
(Dean Ivory) *hld up in tch: effrt in centre over 1f out: hdwy u.p to chse wnr 100yds out: kpt on wl but a hld* **5/1[2]**

02-1 3 1 1/4 **Scofflaw**[21] 34 5-9-2 80 (v) AdamKirby 5 83
(David Evans) *sn dropped to last pair and outpcd early: effrd and hdwy into midfield over 2f out: hdwy u.p 1f out: chsd ldrs and kpt on fnl 100yds* **3/1[1]**

4-34 4 1 1/2 **Gentlemen**[8] 255 8-8-6 77 (h) GraceMcEntee(7) 9 76
(Phil McEntee) *led: sn hdd and chsd ldrs: effrt to press ldr 2f out tl unable qck and edgd rt 1f out: nt match pce of wnr and lost 2nd 100yds out: wknd towards fin* **10/1**

26-6 5 3 1/4 **Evening Attire**[19] 91 8-8-7 71 HollieDoyle 11 61
(William Stone) *sn led: rdn over 1f out: hdd 1f out: no ex and wknd ins fnl f* **10/1**

00-5 6 1/2 **Steel Train (FR)**[12] 212 8-9-7 85 LukeMorris 1 73
(David O'Meara) *dwlt: pushed along and outpcd in rr early: clsd: in tch and t.k.h 1/2-way: nt clr run 3f out: forced way between horses over 1f out: kpt on same pce u.p ins fnl f* **25/1**

204- 7 3 1/2 **Los Camachos (IRE)**[45] 9483 4-8-8 79 GinaMangan(7) 6 58
(David Evans) *prom: chsd ldr over 4f out tl unable qck u.p over 1f out: wknd ins fnl f* **9/1[3]**

3-42 8 hd **Hammer Gun (USA)**[8] 255 6-8-13 77 (v) PaddyMathers 7 55
(Derek Shaw) *in tch in midfield: rdn over 2f out: unable qck and pushed lft over 1f out: no imp and wknd ins fnl f* **5/1[2]**

314- 9 3 3/4 **It Must Be Faith**[255] 2702 9-8-11 75 (p) LiamJones 10 43
(Michael Appleby) *wl in tch in midfield: unable qck u.p and btn over 1f out: wknd fnl f* **33/1**

40-0 10 3/4 **Highly Sprung (IRE)**[22] 24 6-8-13 77 DougieCostello 4 43
(Les Eyre) *a towards rr: rdn over 3f out: bhd over 1f out* **50/1**

50-0 11 6 **Red Cymbal**[8] 260 4-8-8 72 (p) MartinDwyer 2 22
(David C Griffiths) *pushed along towards rr: unable qck u.p and btn over 1f out: wknd fnl f* **25/1**

1m 24.98s (-2.22) **Going Correction** -0.05s/f (Stan) 11 Ran SP% **124.1**
Speed ratings (Par 105): **110,109,107,106,102 101,97,97,93,92 85**
CSF £18.60 CT £51.95 TOTE £3.20: £1.40, £2.00, £1.40; EX 21.70 Trifecta £74.70.
Owner Miss Emily Stevens Partnership **Bred** Old Mill Stud And S C Williams **Trained** Newmarket, Suffolk

FOCUS
Ordinary form where the winner confirmed the form with the runner up on worse terms.

382 BET TOTETRIFECTA AT TOTESPORT.COM H'CAP 6f (P)
5:55 (5:55) (Class 3) (0-95,96) 4-Y-0+ £9,703 (£2,887; £1,443; £721) **Stalls** Centre

Form RPR

02-5 1 **Desert Doctor (IRE)**[12] 203 4-9-1 89 LukeMorris 1 98
(Ed Walker) *in tch in midfield: swtchd lft and effrt over 1f out: rdn to chal 1f out: sustained effrt u.p ins fnl f to ld cl home* **7/2[1]**

26-5 2 hd **Human Nature (IRE)**[15] 139 6-8-2 83 (t) GraceMcEntee(7) 6 91
(Stuart Williams) *led: hrd pressed and reminders over 1f out: edgd rt ins fnl f: kpt on tl hdd and no ex cl home* **6/1**

41-6 3 1 1/2 **King Robert**[8] 254 6-8-2 83 WilliamCarver(7) 7 87
(Charlie Wallis) *trckd ldrs: effrt and ev ch over 1f out tl no ex ins fnl f: outpcd fnl 100yds* **12/1**

406- 4 hd **Ultimate Avenue (IRE)**[49] 9430 5-9-5 93 StevieDonohoe 4 96
(David Simcock) *stdd after s: hld up in rr: effrt over 1f out: hdwy 1f out: kpt on wl u.p ins fnl f: nvr getting on terms w ldrs* **25/1**

101- 5 nk **How Far (IRE)**[178] 5548 4-9-5 93 RobertHavlin 5 95
(Simon Crisford) *trckd ldrs: effrt u.p and ev ch over 1f out tl no ex and outpcd fnl 100yds* **4/1[2]**

43-3 6 hd **Swift Approval (IRE)**[13] 176 7-8-10 84 (p) DavidProbert 9 85
(Stuart Williams) *chsd ldr: rdn and ev ch over 1f out: jst getting outpcd whn sltly impeded ins fnl f: outpcd fnl 100yds* **9/2[3]**

0-55 7 nk **Something Lucky (IRE)**[11] 230 7-8-8 82 LiamJones 3 82
(Michael Appleby) *hld up in tch in midfield: swtchd rt and effrt over 1f out: swtchd bk lft 1f out: kpt on same pce ins fnl f* **20/1**

54-0 8 4 1/2 **Atletico (IRE)**[16] 127 7-9-7 95 EoinWalsh 8 81
(David Evans) *stdd s: hld up in last pair: effrt and reminder over 1f out: no imp: nvr involved* **33/1**

02-1 9 3/4 **Alsvinder**[12] 203 6-9-8 96 (t) AdamKirby 2 80
(David O'Meara) *anticipated s and s.i.s: a towards rr: effrt and reminder over 1f out: no prog and sn btn: nvr involved* **7/2[1]**

1m 11.5s (-2.20) **Going Correction** -0.05s/f (Stan) 9 Ran SP% **116.2**
Speed ratings (Par 107): **112,111,109,109,109 108,108,102,101**
CSF £24.38 CT £228.17 TOTE £4.00: £1.30, £1.90, £4.30; EX 24.90 Trifecta £169.30.
Owner Mrs Fitri Hay **Bred** Skeaghmore Hill **Trained** Upper Lambourn, Berks
■ Stewards' Enquiry : Grace McEntee caution: careless riding
Adam Kirby jockey said horse anticipated the start and was slowly away as a result

FOCUS
Plenty had their chance in this decent sprint.

383 BET TOTESWINGER AT TOTESPORT.COM H'CAP 6f (P)
6:25 (6:25) (Class 6) (0-60,60) 4-Y-0+
£3,493 (£1,039; £519; £400; £400; £400) **Stalls** Centre

Form RPR

052- 1 **At Your Service**[24] 9773 5-9-5 58 JoeyHaynes 10 65
(Paul Howling) *hld up in tch: hdwy u.p and hung lft ins fnl f: led wl ins fnl f: r.o wl* **4/1[2]**

65-1 2 1 1/4 **Holdenhurst**[20] 53 4-8-12 58 SeamusCronin(7) 4 61
(Bill Turner) *chsd ldrs on inner: nt clr run 2f out: sn swtchd rt and effrt: kpt on u.p ins fnl f to chse wnr towards fin: no imp cl home* **9/1**

002- 3 1 **Invisible Storm**[40] 9560 4-9-1 54 (b) HollieDoyle 3 54
(William Stone) *t.k.h: led: rdn over 1f out: hdd wl ins fnl f: sn lost 2nd and outpcd towards fin* **7/1[3]**

016- 4 1/2 **Billyoakes (IRE)**[24] 9773 7-9-7 60 (p) LukeMorris 5 59
(Charlie Wallis) *in tch in midfield: effrt over 1f out: hrd drvn and kpt on ins fnl f: nvr quite getting on terms w ldrs* **10/1**

61-2 5 hd **Distant Applause (IRE)**[20] 53 4-9-2 55 FergusSweeney 6 53
(Dominic Ffrench Davis) *chsd ldrs: effrt to chse ldr over 1f out tl no ex and lost 2nd ins fnl f: wknd towards fin* **4/1[2]**

44-0 6 nk **Spenny's Lass**[15] 144 4-9-7 60 (p) StevieDonohoe 11 57
(John Ryan) *in rr of main gp: effrt and hdwy over 1f out: kpt on ins fnl f: nvr getting on terms w ldrs* **16/1**

006- 7 1 **Theydon Spirit**[55] 9337 4-8-13 52 MarcMonaghan 9 46
(Henry Spiller) *dwlt: in rr of main gp: clsd into midfield over 2f out: nt clr run over 1f out: kpt on same pce ins fnl f* **22/1**

00-0 8 1 3/4 **Caledonian Gold**[9] 244 6-8-0 46 oh1 (b) LauraCoughlan(7) 7 35
(Lisa Williamson) *taken down early: restrained and awkward leaving stalls: hld up in detached last: effrt towards inner over 1f out: hdwy and swtchd rt ins fnl f: nvr trbld ldrs* **66/1**

0-52 9 3 **Always Amazing**[10] 236 5-9-7 60 RaulDaSilva 2 40
(Derek Shaw) *chsd ldrs tl rdn to chse ldr 2f out tl lost pl u.p over 1f out: wknd ins fnl f (trainer could offer no explanation for the gelding's performance other than that the gelding may be better ridden with more restrain)* **2/1[1]**

0-00 10 4 1/2 **Fink Hill (USA)**[16] 131 4-9-7 60 (b[1]) AdamKirby 8 27
(Richard Spencer) *chsd ldr tl 2f out: losing pl and wnt lft over 1f out: bhd and eased ins fnl f* **14/1**

00-0 11 2 1/4 **Just An Idea (IRE)**[15] 144 5-9-2 60 RhiainIngram(5) 12 20
(Roger Ingram) *a towards rr: hung lft and bhd over 1f out* **66/1**

1m 12.73s (-0.97) **Going Correction** -0.05s/f (Stan) 11 Ran SP% **124.8**
Speed ratings (Par 101): **104,102,101,100,100 99,98,96,92,86 83**
CSF £42.27 CT £257.06 TOTE £5.30: £1.60, £3.10, £2.00; EX 40.00 Trifecta £229.80.
Owner Chelsea Banham Pre Training Ltd **Bred** Qatar Bloodstock Ltd **Trained** Cowlinge, Suffolk
■ Stewards' Enquiry : Joey Haynes four-day ban: used whip above the permitted level (Feb 7-10)

FOCUS
Run at a good gallop, this sprint set up for the closers and the winner challenged widest.

384 BET TOTESCOOP6 AT TOTESPORT.COM NOVICE STKS 6f (P)
6:55 (6:56) (Class 4) 3-Y-0+ £5,530 (£1,645; £822; £411) **Stalls** Centre

Form RPR

1 **Dahawi** 3-8-12 0 LukeMorris 5 71+
(Hugo Palmer) *wl in tch in midfield: effrt over 2f out: swtchd rt and hdwy to chse ldr over 1f out: styd on strly wl ins fnl f: led last stride* **6/4[1]**

0-2 2 shd **Sea Of Reality (IRE)**[5] 313 3-8-7 0 LiamJones 7 65
(William Haggas) *restless in stalls: led: rdn over 1f out: kpt on u.p ins fnl f: hdd last stride* **4/1[2]**

6- 3 2 1/4 **Spiritually**[63] 9207 3-8-7 0 GeorgeWood 3 58
(Chris Wall) *in tch in rr of main gp: effrt and clsd to chse ldrs whn swtchd lft ent fnl f: kpt on same pce fnl 150yds* **16/1**

4-5 4 2 **Favori Royal (FR)**[13] 178 4-10-0 0 HollieDoyle 2 60
(Archie Watson) *t.k.h: chsd ldrs: effrt u.p over 1f out: unable qck 1f out and kpt on same pce ins fnl f* **5/1**

5-3 5 1 3/4 **Spirit Of Lucerne (IRE)**[15] 141 3-8-8 0 ow1 RossaRyan 8 47
(Phil McEntee) *t.k.h: chsd ldr tl 3f out: unable qck u.p over 1f out: wknd ins fnl f* **25/1**

6 1 1/2 **Easy Money (IRE)** 4-10-0 0 DavidProbert 6 50
(Ed Walker) *t.k.h: chsd ldrs tl hdwy to chse ldr 3f out tl over 1f out: sn unable qck and wknd ins fnl f (jockey said gelding ran too free)* **9/2[3]**

7 4 1/2 **Guiding Spirit (IRE)** 3-8-12 0 HectorCrouch 4 32
(Clive Cox) *s.i.s and rn green in detached last: kpt on ins fnl f: nvr involved* **10/1**

0-0 8 2 **Dunstall Dreamer**[13] 178 4-10-0 0 KieranO'Neill 1 29
(Denis Quinn) *sn dropped to last pair: effrt ent fnl 2f: no imp and wknd fnl f* **66/1**

1m 13.61s (-0.09) **Going Correction** -0.05s/f (Stan) 8 Ran SP% **115.2**
WFA 3 from 4yo 16lb
Speed ratings (Par 105): **98,97,94,92,89 87,81,79**
CSF £7.69 TOTE £2.10: £1.10, £1.40, £3.80; EX 8.80 Trifecta £49.80.
Owner M M Stables **Bred** Richard Kent & Robert Percival **Trained** Newmarket, Suffolk
■ Stewards' Enquiry : Liam Jones caution: careless riding

FOCUS
An average novice but the right horses came to the fore.

385 DANNY AND FRANK PRESTON'S NORTHERN H'CAP 2m (P)
7:25 (7:28) (Class 5) (0-70,70) 4-Y-0+
£5,433 (£1,617; £808; £404; £400; £400) **Stalls** Low

Form RPR

60-2 1 **Navajo Star (IRE)**[6] 291 5-9-12 70 (v) KieranO'Neill 7 76
(Robyn Brisland) *hld up wl in tch: travelling strly whn nt clr run 3f out: swtchd rt and bumping rival to get out over 1f out: shkn up and hdwy to ld 1f out: kpt on wl u.p ins fnl f: drvn out (jockey said mare hung right-handed in the home straight)* **15/8[1]**

30-6 2 1/2 **Mood For Mischief**[15] 135 4-8-12 61 LiamKeniry 5 66
(Ed Walker) *t.k.h: chsd ldr tl led after 2f: hdd after 3f and trckd ldrs after: swtchd rt and effrt ent fnl 2f: bmpd by wnr over 1f out: kpt on u.p ins fnl f: wnt 2nd towards fin* **5/1[3]**

41- 3 1/2 **Colwood**[34] 9663 5-9-4 67 DarraghKeenan(5) 2 71
(Robert Eddery) *hld up in tch in last pair: hdwy u.p on inner to chse ldrs 1f out: wnt 2nd ins fnl f: kpt on but lost 2nd towards fin* **4/1[2]**

655- 4 1/2 **Masters Apprentice (IRE)**[45] 9487 4-9-1 64 LukeMorris 6 67
(Sylvester Kirk) *chsd ldr after 4f out: rdn and ev ch ent fnl 2f: led over 1f out: hdd 1f out and kpt on same pce ins fnl f* **5/1[3]**

046- **5** *nse* **Mundersfield**[29] 9704 5-8-9 **60**....(h) GeorgeBass(7) 4 63
(David Simcock) *stdd s: t.k.h: hld up wl in tch in midfield: clsd to chse ldrs whn squeezed for room and swtchd lft over 1f out: swtchd rt and kpt on same pce u.p ins fnl f* **14/1**

522- **6** *1 1/2* **Whinging Willie (IRE)**[27] 9728 10-9-3 **68**....(v) RhysClutterbuck(7) 9 70
(Gary Moore) *t.k.h: led: sn hdd and trckd ldrs after 3f: effrt over 2f out: unable qck over 1f out: kpt on same pce ins fnl f* **9/1**

521/ **7** *4* **Oxford Blu**[24] 6343 5-9-10 **68**....(p) DavidProbert 8 65
(Olly Murphy) *chsd ldrs tl led after 3f: rdn and hrd pressed ent fnl 2f: hdd over 1f out: no ex and wknd ins fnl f* **10/1**

00-0 **8** *47* **Spring Dixie (IRE)**[15] 145 7-8-2 **51** oh6.... RhiainIngram(5) 3
(Natalie Lloyd-Beavis) *dwlt: t.k.h: hld up wl in tch in last pair: hdwy on outer 7f out: rdn and struggling over 3f out: bhd fnl 2f: t.o and eased fnl f* **66/1**

3m 34.54s (4.54) **Going Correction** -0.05s/f (Stan)
WFA 4 from 5yo+ 5lb **8** Ran SP% **115.4**
Speed ratings (Par 103): **86,85,85,85,85 84,82,58**
CSF £11.68 CT £33.38 TOTE £2.70: £1.20, £1.70, £1.40; EX 12.40 Trifecta £51.10.
Owner Ferrybank Properties Limited **Bred** Robert Dunne **Trained** Danethorpe, Notts
■ Stewards' Enquiry : Kieran O'Neill four-day ban: interference & careless riding (Feb 7-10)

FOCUS
Any one of five or six had a chance approaching the last furlong, with the favourite just picking up best. There was a stewards inquiry called, but the result was never going to be altered.

386 ENJOY VALENTINES DAY HERE H'CAP 1m (P)
7:55 (7:56) (Class 6) (0-65,73) 4-Y-O+
£3,493 (£1,039; £519; £400; £400; £400) **Stalls** Low

Form RPR

00-3 **1** **Rippling Waters (FR)**[21] 33 5-9-5 **63**.... DougieCostello 3 70
(Jamie Osborne) *trckd ldrs on inner: swtchd lft and rdn to ld narrowly over 1f out: sustained battle w rivals after: hld on gamely wl ins fnl f: all out* **7/2**[2]

60-5 **2** *hd* **Accomplice**[13] 175 5-9-5 **63**.... DavidProbert 4 70
(Michael Blanshard) *hld up in tch: clsd nt clr run and swtchd rt over 1f out: hdwy to chse ldrs 1f out: ev ch ins fnl f: kpt on wl to go 2nd last strides* **9/1**

41-0 **3** *hd* **Squire**[16] 125 8-9-1 **59**....(tp) LukeMorris 9 65
(Marjorie Fife) *t.k.h: hld up wl in tch in midfield: nt clr run over 2f out: pushed along and clsd to chse ldrs 2f out: drvn and ev ch over 1f out: sustained chal u.p: no ex towards fin and lost 2nd cl home* **3/1**[1]

020- **4** *1 1/2* **Sir Gnet (IRE)**[178] 5568 5-9-6 **64**....(h) RobertHavlin 6 67
(Ed Dunlop) *t.k.h: hld up in tch in midfield: swtchd rt over 1f out: swtchd bk lft and hdwy 1f out: chsd ldrs ins fnl f: kpt on same pce towards fin* **6/1**[3]

254- **5** *1 1/2* **Duchess Of Avon**[27] 9732 4-9-7 **65**.... HectorCrouch 7 64
(Gary Moore) *in tch in midfield: effrt u.p over 1f out: kpt on ins fnl f: nvr enough pce to threaten ldrs* **12/1**

004- **6** *2 3/4* **Dukes Meadow**[64] 9181 8-8-2 **51** oh6.... RhiainIngram(5) 2 45
(Roger Ingram) *sn dropped to rr: swtchd to outer 6f out: dashed up on outer to chse ldrs 3f out: rdn and ev ch 2f out tl over 1f out: no ex 1f out: wknd ins fnl f* **16/1**

63-5 **7** *6* **Cockney Boy**[13] 180 6-8-7 **51** oh2....(v) HollieDoyle 1 30
(Michael Appleby) *led: rdn and hdd over 1f out: sn lost pl and btn 1f out: wknd ins fnl f (vet reported the gelding had bled from the nose)* **7/2**[2]

00-0 **8** *8* **Zaeem**[21] 44 10-9-9 **67**.... JoeyHaynes 10 28
(Ivan Furtado) *chsd ldrs tl wnt over 5f out: rdn and outpcd jst over 2f out: wknd over 1f out and bhd fnl f* **16/1**

/0-0 **9** *2* **Perfect Soldier (IRE)**[15] 138 5-9-5 **63**.... LiamJones 8 19
(Shaun Keightley) *pressed ldr tl over 2f out: rdn 3f out: lost pl and bhd 2f out: sn wknd* **16/1**

1m 40.12s (0.22) **Going Correction** -0.05s/f (Stan) **9** Ran SP% **119.1**
Speed ratings (Par 101): **96,95,95,94,92 89,83,75,73**
CSF £36.21 CT £107.23 TOTE £3.90: £1.50, £2.00, £1.40; EX 37.30 Trifecta £125.50.
Owner Melbourne 10 Racing **Bred** E A R L Elevage Des Loges **Trained** Upper Lambourn, Berks

FOCUS
A cracking finish to this modest event, three of them duelling to the line.
T/Jkpt: £5,000 to a £1 stake. Pool: £14,084.51 - 2.0 winning units T/Plt: £54.30 to a £1 stake. Pool: £103,267.77 - 1,387.50 winning units T/Qpdt: £16.40 to a £1 stake. Pool: £17,327.29 - 777.15 winning units **Steve Payne**

228 SOUTHWELL (L-H)
Thursday, January 24
OFFICIAL GOING: Fibresand: standard
Wind: Virtually nil Weather: Cloudy

387 PLAY 4 TO SCORE AT BETWAY H'CAP 1m 4f 14y(F)
1:15 (1:15) (Class 6) (0-65,66) 4-Y-O+
£3,105 (£924; £461; £300; £300; £300) **Stalls** Low

Form RPR

25-4 **1** **Royal Cosmic**[18] 101 5-9-5 **59**.... SebastianWoods(5) 7 65
(Richard Fahey) *trckd ldrs on inner: hdwy over 3f out: chal over 2f out: rdn to ld and edgd rt 1 1/2f out: drvn and wandered ins fnl f: kpt on towards fin* **10/1**

141- **2** *1/2* **Anna Jammeela**[26] 9751 4-9-6 **58**....(t) DavidProbert 3 64
(Lucy Wadham) *hld up towards rr: hdwy over 4f out: chsd ldrs over 2f out: rdn wl over 1f out: drvn and kpt on wl fnl f* **7/2**[1]

20-6 **3** *nk* **Seasearch**[18] 99 4-9-3 **58**....(p) JoshuaBryan(3) 6 64
(Andrew Balding) *trckd ldrs: hdwy to chse ldr 4f out: led wl over 2f out: rdn along wl over 1f out: sn hdd: drvn and kpt on wl fnl f* **6/1**[3]

05-2 **4** *4* **Angel's Acclaim (IRE)**[23] 6 5-9-9 **58**.... BarryMcHugh 2 57
(Kevin Ryan) *towards rr: hdwy 4f out: chsd ldrs 3f out: rdn over 2f out: drvn over 1f out: nt rch ldrs* **13/2**

004- **5** *7* **Lean On Pete (IRE)**[35] 9647 10-9-7 **59**.... BenRobinson(3) 4 47
(Ollie Pears) *prom: rdn along and outpcd 5f out: hdwy u.p to chse ldrs 3f out: drvn and one pce fnl 2f* **14/1**

633- **6** *1 1/2* **Di's Gift**[26] 9750 10-9-3 **57**....(v) KevinLundie(5) 9 43
(Michael Appleby) *dwlt: sn chsng ldrs: cl up after 3f: led over 5f out: rdn along over 3f out: hdd wl over 2f out: sn drvn and outpcd* **7/1**

3-60 **7** *7* **Golden Guide**[12] 210 4-8-7 **45**....(p) AndrewMullen 8 22
(K R Burke) *towards rr: hdwy over 3f out: rdn along over 2f out: sn no imp* **25/1**

304- **8** *4 1/2* **Tingo In The Tale (IRE)**[26] 9751 10-8-10 **45**....(p) EoinWalsh 13 14
(Tony Forbes) *a towards rr* **50/1**

500- **9** *19* **Tilly Devine**[58] 9271 5-8-10 **45**....(b) PaddyMathers 11
(Scott Dixon) *cl up: rdn along over 4f out: sn lost pl and bhd* **40/1**

300- **10** *5* **Oceanus (IRE)**[35] 9647 5-9-8 **57**.... ShelleyBirkett 1
(Julia Feilden) *a towards rr: bhd fnl 3f (jockey said gelding was never travelling)* **22/1**

655- **11** *1/2* **Chica Da Silva**[26] 9751 4-8-11 **49**....(p) KieranO'Neill 5
(Scott Dixon) *prom: rdn along 5f out: sn lost pl and bhd fnl 3f* **33/1**

001- **12** *3/4* **Handsome Bob (IRE)**[35] 9647 4-10-0 **66**....(b) CallumRodriguez 10
(Keith Dalgleish) *sn led: hdd over 5f out: rdn along 4f out: sn wknd (trainer's rep said gelding was unsuited by being taken on for the lead)* **4/1**[2]

2m 40.77s (-0.23) **Going Correction** +0.10s/f (Slow)
WFA 4 from 5yo+ 3lb **12** Ran SP% **113.6**
Speed ratings (Par 101): **104,103,103,100,96 95,90,87,74,71 71,70**
CSF £40.77 CT £230.75 TOTE £10.20: £3.20, £1.60, £1.90; EX 52.00 Trifecta £233.60.
Owner The Cosmic Cases **Bred** The Cosmic Cases **Trained** Musley Bank, N Yorks

FOCUS
The track was expected to ride slower and deeper than normal due to the work needed to ward off overnight frost, and the opening time seemed to bear that out. The initial gallop was quite quick but the form looks quite reliable with the right horses to the fore.

388 BETWAY NOVICE STKS 4f 214y(F)
1:45 (1:45) (Class 5) 3-Y-O+
£3,752 (£1,116; £557; £278) **Stalls** Centre

Form RPR

2-40 **1** **Point Zero (IRE)**[21] 42 4-9-13 64....(be) AlistairRawlinson 7 71
(Michael Appleby) *racd centre: slt ld: hdd over 3f out: rdn wl over 1f out: sn edgd lft: drvn to ld ins fnl f: kpt on* **6/1**[3]

21 **2** *3/4* **Hanati (IRE)**[13] 186 3-9-0 0.... LukeMorris 8 64
(Simon Crisford) *racd towards stands' side: chsd ldng pair: pushed along and sltly outpcd over 2f out: rdn wl over 1f out and sn hung lft: drvn ins fnl f: rdn on wl towards fin* **2/1**[1]

53-2 **3** *1* **Kadiz (IRE)**[13] 186 3-8-0 69....(b) GeorgeRooke(7) 2 54
(Richard Hughes) *racd towards far side: wnt lft s: cl up: led over 3f out: clr over 2f out: rdn over 1f out: edgd lft and hdd ins fnl f: kpt on same pce* **11/4**[2]

000- **4** *3 3/4* **Atwaar**[79] 9001 3-8-4 54.... NoelGarbutt(3) 3 40
(Charles Smith) *racd centre: in rr: sme hdwy over 2f out: sn rdn along and nvr nr ldrs* **66/1**

43-6 **5** *3* **Bawtry Lady**[11] 228 3-8-4 49....(bt) PhilDennis(3) 5 29
(David C Griffiths) *chsd ldrs centre: rdn along 1/2-way: sn outpcd* **25/1**

0 **6** *1* **Inverarity**[13] 186 3-8-9 0.... FinleyMarsh(3) 1 31
(Frank Bishop) *wnt lft s: a in rr far side* **50/1**

/30- **7** *4* **Mayfair Rock (IRE)**[350] 624 4-9-8 0.... CliffordLee 6 17
(K R Burke) *dwlt and wnt rt s: racd towards stands' side: a in rr* **14/1**

1m 1.05s (1.35) **Going Correction** +0.10s/f (Slow)
WFA 3 from 4yo 15lb **7** Ran SP% **88.3**
Speed ratings (Par 103): **93,91,90,84,79 77,71**
CSF £10.59 TOTE £5.80: £1.90, £1.20; EX 11.20 Trifecta £20.80.
Owner The Horse Watchers **Bred** Tom Foley **Trained** Oakham, Rutland
■ So Hi Speed was withdrawn. Price at time of withdrawal 7/2. Rule 4 applies to all bets - deduction 20p in the pound.

FOCUS
This took less winning than it would have had So Hi Speed gone into the stalls. Modest form.

389 BETWAY SPRINT H'CAP 4f 214y(F)
2:20 (2:20) (Class 3) (0-95,97) 4-Y-O+ **£9,703** (£2,887; £1,443; £721) **Stalls** Centre

Form RPR

00-4 **1** **Midnight Malibu (IRE)**[14] 163 6-8-11 **82**.... RachelRichardson 4 92
(Tim Easterby) *cl up centre: rdn to take slt ld over 1f out: drvn and edgd lft ins fnl f: kpt on wl* **15/2**

16-2 **2** *1/2* **Foolaad**[16] 127 8-9-12 **97**....(t) RobertWinston 1 105
(Roy Bowring) *racd towards far side: cl up: effrt 2f out: sn rdn to chal: ev ch ins fnl f: no ex towards fin (vet said gelding lost right fore shoe)* **6/4**[1]

50-1 **3** *1* **Moonraker**[23] 3 7-9-3 **88**.... LukeMorris 6 93
(Michael Appleby) *racd towards stands' side: sn slt ld: rdn along over 2f out: hdd and drvn over 1f out: edgd lft ins fnl f: kpt on same pce* **11/2**[2]

2-U0 **4** *1/2* **Samovar**[11] 230 4-8-4 **75**....(b) KieranO'Neill 7 78
(Scott Dixon) *cl up centre: rdn and ev ch over 1f out: drvn ent fnl f: kpt on same pce* **10/1**

00-4 **5** *4* **Jumira Bridge**[21] 35 5-9-7 **92**.... PJMcDonald 5 80
(Robert Cowell) *chsd ldrs centre: rdn along over 2f out: sn one pce* **11/1**

33-4 **6** *nk* **Danzan (IRE)**[15] 136 4-9-9 **97**.... JoshuaBryan(3) 3 84
(Andrew Balding) *racd towards far side: prom: rdn along over 2f out: sn wknd (trainer's rep said gelding was unsuited by surface and lost left fore shoe)* **6/1**[3]

01-5 **7** *5* **Classic Pursuit**[14] 163 8-8-10 **81**....(b) AndrewMullen 2 50
(Michael Appleby) *dwlt and n.m.r s: sn swtchd markedly rt to stands' side: a in rr* **17/2**

59.63s (-0.07) **Going Correction** +0.10s/f (Slow) **7** Ran SP% **109.4**
Speed ratings (Par 107): **104,103,101,100,94 93,85**
CSF £17.57 TOTE £8.00: £4.50, £1.30; EX 19.80 Trifecta £107.10.
Owner D A West & Partner **Bred** Kabansk Ltd & Rathbarry Stud **Trained** Great Habton, N Yorks

FOCUS
Decent sprint handicap form with two course specialists fighting it out.

390 BETWAY LIVE CASINO H'CAP 1m 4f 14y(F)
2:55 (2:55) (Class 4) (0-80,79) 4-Y-O+
£6,080 (£1,809; £904; £452; £300; £300) **Stalls** Low

Form RPR

02-1 **1** **Temur Khan**[21] 41 4-9-5 77.... DavidProbert 7 84
(Tony Carroll) *prom: hdwy 3f out: led over 2f out: rdn and hdd 1 1/2f out: cl up and drvn ent fnl f: rallied gamely to ld nr fin* **9/4**[1]

6-22 **2** *nse* **Dommersen (IRE)**[7] 272 6-9-5 **79**.... BenSanderson(5) 8 85
(Roger Fell) *dwlt and hld up in rr: hdwy over 3f out: chal on outer wl over 2f out: rdn to take slt ld 1 1/2f out: sn edgd lft: drvn ins fnl f: hdd and no ex nr fin* **11/2**[3]

25-3 **3** *1* **Saint Mac**[14] 162 4-8-7 **65** oh6.... AndrewMullen 3 69
(Michael Appleby) *hld up in rr: hdwy over 3f out: rdn along over 2f out: chsd ldrs whn nt clr run and swtchd rt to outer jst over 1f out: sn drvn and styd on wl towards fin* **7/1**

402- **4** *shd* **Second Page**[145] 6822 5-8-11 **73**....(b) SeamusCronin(7) 5 77
(Richard Hannon) *trckd ldrs: hdwy over 3f out: rdn along 2f out: n.m.r and swtchd lft over 1f out: sn drvn and kpt on same pce* **12/1**

240- **5** *1* **Purple Rock (IRE)**[29] 9706 7-8-10 **72**....(e[1]) FayeMcManoman(7) 9 74
(Gay Kelleway) *led: pushed along over 3f out: rdn and hdd wl over 2f out: sn drvn and grad wknd* **8/1**

 The Form Book Flat 2019, Raceform Ltd, Newbury, RG14 5SJ

52-3 **6** 2 1/4 **Mr Carbonator**[18] 102 4-8-7 **68**................................ PhilDennis(3) 6 68
(Philip Kirby) *trckd ldrs: hdwy over 3f out: rdn along over 2f out: drvn over 1f out: kpt on one pce* **10/3**[2]

024- **7** 1 1/4 **High Command (IRE)**[38] 9586 6-9-4 **73**................ AlistairRawlinson 1 70
(Michael Appleby) *hld up in rr: hdwy 4f out: wd st: rdn along over 2f out: sn wknd* **14/1**

105- **8** 11 **Sociologist (FR)**[35] 9642 4-8-12 **70**....................(b[1]) KieranO'Neill 2 50
(Scott Dixon) *chsd ldr: pushed along 4f out: rdn over 3f out: sn drvn and wknd (jockey said gelding ran too free in first-time blinkers)* **25/1**

/0-0 **9** 24 **Shinghari (IRE)**[19] 88 7-9-0 **69**................................ RossaRyan 4 10
(Alexandra Dunn) *chsd ldrs: rdn along 5f out: sn wknd* **66/1**

2m 40.76s (-0.24) **Going Correction** +0.10s/f (Slow) 9 Ran SP% **112.5**
WFA 4 from 5yo+ 3lb
Speed ratings (Par 105): **104,103,103,103,102 101,100,92,76**
CSF £14.39 CT £72.42 TOTE £2.70: £1.20, £2.10, £2.00; EX 12.30 Trifecta £56.10.
Owner Mrs Helen Hogben **Bred** London Thoroughbred Services Ltd **Trained** Cropthorne, Worcs
■ Stewards' Enquiry : Faye McManoman three-day ban: interference (7-9 Feb)

FOCUS
The time was virtually identical to that of the opening Class 6 handicap.

391 LADBROKES HOME OF THE ODDS BOOST H'CAP 1m 13y(F)
3:30 (3:30) (Class 3) (0-95,91) 3-Y-O £7,470 (£2,236; £1,118) **Stalls Low**

Form RPR

211- **1** **Jahbath**[79] 8888 3-9-7 **91**................................ PJMcDonald 3 106
(William Haggas) *trckd ldr: cl up over 3f out: led on bit over 2f out: qcknd clr over 1f out: impressive* **8/15**[1]

321- **2** 7 **Whenapoet**[26] 9744 3-8-2 **72** oh3..............................(p) AndrewMullen 1 69
(Michael Appleby) *led: jnd and rdn along over 3f out: hdd over 2f out: sn drvn and kpt on: no ch w wnr* **5/1**[3]

41-3 **3** 1 3/4 **Coolagh Forest (IRE)**[19] 90 3-8-10 **80**................ TonyHamilton 2 72
(Richard Fahey) *trckd ldng pair: pushed along over 4f out: rdn and outpcd 3f out: kpt on fnl f* **3/1**[2]

1m 42.31s (-1.39) **Going Correction** +0.10s/f (Slow) 3 Ran SP% **106.9**
Speed ratings (Par 101): **110,103,101**
CSF £3.34 TOTE £1.20; EX 2.90 Trifecta £2.50.
Owner Hamdan Al Maktoum **Bred** Exors Of The Late Sir Eric Parker, Crimbourne Stud **Trained** Newmarket, Suffolk

FOCUS
Not the most competitive of handicaps, but a very useful winner who will prove better than this grade in time.

392 FOLLOW TOP TIPSTER TEMPLEGATE AT SUNRACING H'CAP 1m 13y(F)
4:05 (4:05) (Class 5) (0-75,75) 4-Y-O+ £3,752 (£1,116; £557; £300; £300; £300) **Stalls Low**

Form RPR

251- **1** **Side Effect**[34] 9658 4-9-1 **69**..............................(p) AndrewMullen 1 77
(Michael Appleby) *trckd ldrs: effrt and cl up over 2f out: rdn to ld 1 1/2f out: sn edgd lft: drvn and hung lft to inner ail ins fnl f: kpt on wl towards fin* **4/1**[2]

05-3 **2** 3/4 **Mama Africa (IRE)**[14] 164 5-9-4 **75**................ JaneElliott(3) 3 81
(David Barron) *led 2f: prom: effrt over 2f out: chsd ldrs whn swtchd lft over 1f out: sn rdn: styd on wl fnl f* **8/1**

01-2 **3** hd **Dashing Poet**[12] 202 5-8-11 **65**................................ PJMcDonald 4 72
(Heather Main) *dwlt: trckd ldrs on inner: hdwy 3f out: cl up wl over 1f out: rdn to chal ent fnl f: ev ch whn n.m.r and hmpd ins fnl f: sn swtchd rt and kpt on: lost 2nd nr line* **3/1**[1]

54-5 **4** 1 1/2 **Majestic Moon (IRE)**[10] 237 9-9-5 **73**..............(p) ShelleyBirkett 5 75
(Julia Feilden) *cl up: wd st: rdn to ld briefly 2f out: sn drvn and edgd rt over 1f out: kpt on same pce* **7/1**[3]

52-0 **5** 3 1/4 **Mametz Wood (IRE)**[18] 102 4-8-10 **71**..............(v) JonathanFisher(7) 2 66
(K R Burke) *trckd ldrs: pushed along 3f out: rdn over 2f out: sn drvn and btn (jockey said gelding wouldn't face the kickback having been slowly away)* **3/1**[1]

-316 **6** 4 **Pearl Spectre (USA)**[9] 249 8-9-4 **72**..............(v) JosephineGordon 7 57
(Phil McEntee) *chsd ldrs on outer: led after 2f: rdn along 3f out: hdd over 2f out: sn drvn and wknd* **7/1**[3]

5-00 **7** 8 **Muqarred (USA)**[12] 209 7-8-11 **70**..............(p) BenSanderson(5) 6 37
(Roger Fell) *trckd ldrs: pushed along over 3f out: rdn wl over 2f out: sn outpcd and bhd* **16/1**

1m 43.47s (-0.23) **Going Correction** +0.10s/f (Slow) 7 Ran SP% **112.0**
Speed ratings (Par 103): **105,104,104,102,99 95,87**
CSF £33.49 CT £106.73 TOTE £4.90: £2.20, £3.10; EX 21.90 Trifecta £61.20.
Owner Robin Oliver **Bred** The Fame Is The Spur Partnership **Trained** Oakham, Rutland
■ Stewards' Enquiry : Andrew Mullen three-day ban: interference (7-9 Feb)

FOCUS
An ordinary handicap.
T/Plt: £ to a £1 stake. Pool: £ - winning units T/Qpdt: £ to a £1 stake. Pool: £ - winning units
Joe Rowntree

323 MEYDAN (L-H)
Thursday, January 24
OFFICIAL GOING: Turf: good; dirt: standard

393a EGA BILLETS TROPHY (H'CAP) (TURF) 5f (T)
2:30 (2:30) (95-113,113) 3-Y-O+ £82,677 (£27,559; £13,779; £6,889; £4,133; £2,755)

RPR

1 **Mazzini**[106] 8103 6-8-5 **95**................................ TadhgO'Shea 8 101
(Fawzi Abdulla Nass, Bahrain) *sn led: rdn 2 1/2f out: r.o wl* **16/1**

2 nk **Hit The Bid**[21] 49 5-9-3 **110**..............................(t) ChrisHayes 5 112
(D J Bunyan, Ire) *trckd ldrs: ev ch 1 1/2f out: r.o wl* **13/8**[2]

3 1 1/2 **Faatinah (AUS)**[21] 49 6-9-6 **113**..............................(p) JimCrowley 7 110
(David A Hayes, Australia) *chsd ldrs: ev ch 2 1/2f out: r.o fnl 2f: nrst fin* **11/8**[1]

4 2 3/4 **Orvar (IRE)**[21] 49 6-8-7 **101**................................ ConnorBeasley 3 87
(Paul Midgley) *mid-div: r.o same pce fnl 2f* **12/1**[3]

5 1 **Rebel Streak**[124] 7535 4-8-9 **103**..............................(v) MickaelBarzalona 4 85
(Ali Jan, Qatar) *trckd ldr tl wknd 2f out* **16/1**

6 1/2 **Dutch Masterpiece**[21] 49 9-8-8 **102** ow1..............................(t) RobertTart 2 82
(Jaber Ramadhan, Bahrain) *s.i.s: nvr nr to chal* **20/1**

7 3/4 **Alfolk (AUS)**[21] 49 4-8-13 **106**..............................(tp) DaneO'Neill 6 85
(M F De Kock, South Africa) *nvr nr to chal* **33/1**

8 3 1/4 **Marnie James**[21] 49 4-8-11 **105**..............................(t) GeraldMosse 1 71
(Iain Jardine) *nvr bttr than mid-div* **16/1**

57.23s (0.13) **Going Correction** +0.375s/f (Good) 8 Ran SP% **113.2**
Speed ratings: **114,113,111,106,105 104,103,97**
CSF: 41.76; TRICAST: 61.45.
Owner Ahmed Al-Qattan & Fawzi Nass **Bred** Jan & Peter Hopper **Trained** Bahrain

FOCUS
The winner made all, helped by a sensible opening split: 24.17, 21.3, 11.76. The first two and fourth help set the level.

394a AL BASTAKIYA TRIAL SPONSORED BY EMIRATES GLOBAL ALUMINIUM (CONDITIONS) (DIRT) 1m 1f 110y(D)
3:05 (3:05) 3-Y-O £47,244 (£15,748; £7,874; £3,937; £2,362; £1,574)

RPR

1 **Manguzi (FR)**[14] 169 3-8-13 **90**................................ FernandoJara 3 104
(A R Al Rayhi, UAE) *sn led: kicked clr 2 1/2f out: kpt on wl: jst hld on* **5/1**[3]

2 1/2 **Estihdaaf (USA)**[14] 168 3-8-13 **86**................ ChristopheSoumillon 1 103+
(Saeed bin Suroor) *mid-div: rdn 3f out: kpt on wl fnl 1 1/2f: jst failed* **4/1**[1]

3 12 1/2 **Victory Command (IRE)**[117] 7770 3-9-1 **102**................ RoystonFfrench 13 82+
(Mark Johnston) *mid-div: kpt on fnl 2f but no ch w first two* **14/1**

4 4 1/2 **Grecko (ARG)**[208] 3-9-11 **107**................................ PatCosgrave 6 73
(Kenneth McPeek, U.S.A) *mid-div: r.o same pce fnl 2 1/2f* **9/2**[2]

5 2 **Superior (USA)**[77] 8967 3-8-13 **85**................................ ConnorBeasley 4 64
(A bin Harmash, UAE) *trckd ldr: ev ch 2 1/2f out: wknd fnl 1 1/2f* **5/1**[3]

6 1 1/4 **Tone Broke (CAN)**[38] 3-9-1 **95**..............................(t) JimCrowley 8 63
(Steven Asmussen, U.S.A) *mid-div: r.o same pce fnl 2 1/2f* **14/1**

7 nk **Obeyaan (USA)**[19] 92 3-8-9 **0**..............................(v) RichardMullen 2 57
(Fawzi Abdulla Nass, Bahrain) *s.i.s: nvr nr to chal* **33/1**

8 1 1/4 **Raayan (USA)**[19] 92 3-8-9 **0**................................ AntonioFresu 7 54
(A R Al Rayhi, UAE) *s.i.s: nvr nr to chal* **16/1**

9 1/2 **Al Seel Legacy's (USA)**[14] 169 3-8-13 **85**................ PatDobbs 10 57
(Doug Watson, UAE) *mid-div: chsd ldrs 3f out: wknd fnl 2 1/2f* **8/1**

10 6 1/4 **Shanty Star (USA)**[19] 92 3-8-9 **0**................................ IKoyuncu 9 40
(R Bouresly, Kuwait) *s.i.s: nvr nr to chal* **50/1**

11 3 1/4 **Alla Mahlak (USA)**[19] 92 3-8-9 **75**................ PierantonioConvertino 11 34
(R Bouresly, Kuwait) *nvr nr to chal* **66/1**

12 3 **Bila Shak (USA)**[49] 9436 3-8-9 **80**................................ AdriedeVries 12 28
(Fawzi Abdulla Nass, Bahrain) *slowly away: a in rr* **7/1**

13 1 1/2 **Alda'iya (USA)**[19] 92 3-8-9 **0**................................ SamHitchcott 5 25
(Doug Watson, UAE) *nvr bttr than mid-div* **66/1**

14 12 1/2 **Iskandarani (USA)**[14] 168 3-8-9 **0**..............................(b) BrettDoyle 14
(R Bouresly, Kuwait) *a in rr* **66/1**

1m 59.59s (0.79) **Going Correction** +0.375s/f (Slow) 14 Ran SP% **123.7**
Speed ratings: **111,110,100,97,95 94,94,93,92,87 85,82,81,71**
CSF: 25.61.
Owner Ahmad Al Shaikh **Bred** Ecurie Haras De Beauvoir **Trained** UAE

FOCUS
TRAKUS (metres travelled compared to winner): 2nd -1, 3rd +24, 4th +9, 5th +9, 6th +18, 7th +4, 8th +16, 9th +20, 10th +30, 11th +27, 12th +17, 13th 0, 14th +30. The winner set a sensible pace: 26.17 (400m from standing start), 24.39 (800m), 24.67 (1200m), 25.08 (1600m).

395a AL RASHIDIYA SPONSORED BY EMIRATES GLOBAL ALUMINIUM (GROUP 2) (TURF) 1m 1f (T)
3:40 (3:40) 3-Y-O+ £118,110 (£39,370; £19,685; £9,842; £5,905; £3,937)

RPR

1 **Dream Castle**[21] 51 5-9-0 **114**................ ChristopheSoumillon 3 116
(Saeed bin Suroor) *mid-div: smooth prog 3 1/2f out: rdn to ld 2f out: r.o wl: easily* **7/4**[1]

2 3 **Leshlaa (USA)**[219] 3966 5-9-0 **111**................................ PatCosgrave 7 110+
(Saeed bin Suroor) *mid-div: r.o fnl 2f but no ch w wnr* **10/1**

3 nse **Racing History (IRE)**[21] 51 7-9-0 **111**..............................(v) KevinStott 6 110+
(Saeed bin Suroor) *trckd ldr: ev ch 2f out: r.o wl but no ch w wnr* **8/1**

4 1 1/2 **Blair House (IRE)**[75] 9012 6-9-0 **116**..............................(b) JamesDoyle 1 107+
(Charlie Appleby) *settled in rr: r.o fnl 2 1/2f: nrst fin* **9/4**[2]

5 1 **Euginio (IRE)**[103] 8191 5-9-0 **109**................................ FabriceVeron 5 105
(Fawzi Abdulla Nass, Bahrain) *s.i.s: nvr nr to chal but r.o fnl 2f* **25/1**

6 3/4 **Deauville (IRE)**[21] 51 6-9-0 **113**................................ AdriedeVries 9 103
(Fawzi Abdulla Nass, Bahrain) *nvr bttr than mid-div* **25/1**

7 5 3/4 **First Contact (IRE)**[138] 7095 4-8-13 **109**................ ColmO'Donoghue 8 91
(Charlie Appleby) *a in rr* **7/1**[3]

8 hd **Bay Of Poets (IRE)**[21] 51 5-9-0 **110**................................ BrettDoyle 4 91
(Charlie Appleby) *sn led: hdd & wknd 2f out* **16/1**

9 11 **Arod (IRE)**[21] 51 8-9-0 **105**................................ JimCrowley 2 68
(David Simcock) *trckd ldr tl wknd 3f out* **40/1**

1m 48.24s (-0.86) **Going Correction** +0.375s/f (Good) 9 Ran SP% **115.8**
WFA 4 from 5yo+ 1lb
Speed ratings: **118,115,115,113,113 112,107,107,97**
CSF: 20.12.
Owner Godolphin **Bred** Darley **Trained** Newmarket, Suffolk

FOCUS
TRAKUS: 2nd +1, 3rd +2, 4th +1, 5th +3, 6th +3, 7th +5, 8th +1, 9th +2. A faster pace than in the C&D Singspiel three weeks earlier but still not a strong gallop and the winner quickened smartly again: 25.53, 23.69, 24.33, 22.92, 11.77. The second and third help set the level.

396a EGA JEBEL ALI TROPHY (H'CAP) (DIRT) 1m 2f (D)
4:15 (4:15) (92-108,108) 3-Y-O+ £63,779 (£21,259; £10,629; £5,314; £3,188; £2,125)

RPR

1 **Saltarin Dubai (ARG)**[14] 172 6-9-0 **102**..............................(bt) RichardMullen 1 109
(S Seemar, UAE) *sn led: kicked clr 2 1/2f out: r.o wl* **5/1**[3]

2 1 1/4 **Montsarrat (IRE)**[14] 172 6-8-6 **95**..............................(b) MickaelBarzalona 7 98+
(S Jadhav, UAE) *mid-div: r.o wl fnl 2f: nrst fin* **12/1**

3 1/2 **Dolkong (USA)**[14] 171 5-8-11 **100**................................ OlivierDoleuze 2 102+
(Simon Foster, Korea) *mid-div: r.o wl fnl 1 1/2f: nrst fin* **8/1**

4 5 3/4 **Key Bid**[14] 172 5-8-6 **93** ow1..............................(t) FernandoJara 6 86
(A R Al Rayhi, UAE) *trckd ldrs: ev ch 2 1/2f out: one pce fnl 2f* **15/2**

5 hd **Mystique Moon**[26] 5-8-6 **95**................................ SamHitchcott 5 85
(Doug Watson, UAE) *mid-div: n.m.r 3f out: r.o same pce fnl 2 1/2f* **9/2**[2]

6 shd **Senior Investment (USA)**[83] 8823 5-9-6 **108**................ PatCosgrave 9 99
(Kenneth McPeek, U.S.A) *nvr nr to chal* **20/1**

7 1 3/4 **Welsh Lord**[14] 172 4-8-5 **92**................................ ChrisHayes 3 82
(Saeed bin Suroor) *trckd ldr tl wknd fnl 2 1/2f* **8/1**

8 4 3/4 **Tried And True (USA)**[14] 172 7-8-9 **98** ow1....................(v) PatDobbs 8 75
(Doug Watson, UAE) *nvr nr to chal* **11/4**[1]

9 12 1/2 **Aquarium**[89] 8649 4-9-1 **104**.. JamesDoyle 4 58
(Mark Johnston) *slowly away: a in rr* **9/1**

2m 5.79s (1.09) **Going Correction** +0.375s/f (Slow)
WFA 4 from 5yo+ 1lb **9** Ran SP% **118.0**
Speed ratings: **110,109,108,104,103 103,102,98,88**
CSF: 64.14; TRICAST: 477.38.

Owner Sheikh Mohammed Bin Khalifa Al Maktoum **Bred** Haras Firmamento **Trained** United Arab Emirates

FOCUS
TRAKUS: 2nd +19, 3rd -2, 4th +17, 5th +7, 6th +9, 7th +7, 8th +19, 9th +23. The winner made all through even splits: 26.65, 24.81, 24.48, 24.96, 24.89. The winner has been rated to his best.

397a AL FAHIDI FORT SPONSORED BY EMIRATES GLOBAL ALUMINIUM (GROUP 2) (TURF) 7f
4:50 (4:50) 3-Y-O+

£118,110 (£39,370; £14,763; £14,763; £5,905; £3,937)

RPR

1 **D'bai (IRE)**[104] 8147 5-9-0 111.......................................(bt) JamesDoyle 7 115+
(Charlie Appleby) *mid-div: smooth prog 2 1/2f out: led 1 1/2f out: r.o wl* **2/1**[1]

2 1 3/4 **Mythical Magic (IRE)**[111] 7970 4-9-0 106................ ColmO'Donoghue 4 109+
(Charlie Appleby) *mid-div: chsd ldrs 3f out: r.o wl 2f out: nrst fin* **13/2**[3]

3 1/2 **Lansky (IRE)**[106] 8103 4-9-0 100............................ MickaelBarzalona 12 108
(S Jadhav, UAE) *trckd ldrs: ev ch 2f out: wknd fnl f* **50/1**

3 dht **Bravo Zolo (IRE)**[341] 779 7-9-0 111........................... BrettDoyle 8 108
(Charlie Appleby) *bmpd at s: mid-div: r.o fnl 1 1/2f: nrst fin* **12/1**

5 1 3/4 **Top Score**[21] 52 5-9-0 110...............................(p) ChristopheSoumillon 1 103
(Saeed bin Suroor) *nvr nr to chal but r.o fnl 2f* **11/4**[2]

6 nk **Championship (IRE)**[299] 1525 8-9-0 112..................(t) ConnorBeasley 13 102
(A bin Harmash, UAE) *trckd ldr: led 2 1/2f out: hdd 1 1/2f out: r.o same pce* **20/1**

7 nk **Comin' Through (AUS)**[46] 9476 5-9-3 117...............(bt) PatCosgrave 9 105
(Chris Waller, Australia) *trckd ldr: ev ch 3f out: one pce fnl 2 1/2f* **33/1**

8 1 **Another Batt (IRE)**[21] 52 4-9-0 108............................ SamHitchcott 11 99
(George Scott) *nvr bttr than mid-div* **15/2**

9 hd **Marinaresco (SAF)**[362] 6-9-0 118.......................(b) BernardFayd'Herbe 6 98
(M F De Kock, South Africa) *a in rr* **33/1**

10 1/2 **Portamento (IRE)**[21] 52 7-9-0 101............................ FernandoJara 3 97
(A R Al Rayhi, UAE) *trckd ldr tl wknd fnl 3f* **66/1**

11 3 3/4 **Janoobi (SAF)**[21] 52 5-9-0 112................................ JimCrowley 10 87
(M F De Kock, South Africa) *sn led: hdd & wknd 2 1/2f out* **10/1**

12 4 **Degas (GER)**[21] 51 6-9-0 113.................................... AdriedeVries 2 76
(Markus Klug, Germany) *nvr bttr than mid-div* **66/1**

13 5 1/4 **Intisaab**[14] 170 8-9-0 109.......................................(p) MartinHarley 5 62
(David O'Meara) *nvr nr to chal* **20/1**

1m 23.4s (-0.70) **Going Correction** +0.375s/f (Good) **13** Ran SP% **122.2**
Speed ratings: **119,117,116,116,114 114,113,112,112,111 107,102,96**
CSF: 14.86.

Owner Godolphin **Bred** Lodge Park Stud **Trained** Newmarket, Suffolk

FOCUS
TRAKUS: 2nd -3, 3rd +2, 4th +2, 5th -4, 6th -2, 7th -3, 8th +1, 9th +1, 10th -7, 11th -6, 12th -8, 13th -3. The pace was steady early and gradually picked up: 25.68, 23.06, 22.71, 11.96.

398a EGA AL TAWEELAH TROPHY (H'CAP) (TURF) 1m 4f 11y(T)
5:25 (5:25) (95-106,106) 3-Y-O+

£63,779 (£21,259; £10,629; £5,314; £3,188; £2,125)

RPR

1 **Spotify (FR)**[129] 7373 5-9-5 **105**..................................(p) JamesDoyle 2 110
(Charlie Appleby) *sn led: kicked clr 2 1/2f out: r.o wl: jst hld on* **9/4**[2]

2 nk **Sharpalo (FR)**[21] 47 7-9-1 **101**.................................(t) ConnorBeasley 5 106+
(A bin Harmash, UAE) *settled in rr: smooth prog 3 1/2f out: r.o wl fnl 2f: nrst fin* **16/1**

3 5 3/4 **Bin Battuta**[21] 47 5-9-6 **106**.......................(p) ChristopheSoumillon 7 103
(Saeed bin Suroor) *mid-div: chsd ldrs 2 1/2f out: r.o same pce fnl 2f* **11/8**[1]

4 3 **Zamaam**[313] 1256 9-8-11 **98**......................................(t) JimCrowley 10 88
(E Charpy, UAE) *settled in rr: smooth prog to chse ldr 4f out: ev ch 2 1/2f out: one pce fnl 2f* **40/1**

5 1 1/4 **Parsifal (SPA)**[95] 6-8-8 **95**.. BenCurtis 3 83
(G Arizkorreta Elosegui, Spain) *broke awkwardly: chsd ldrs: r.o same pce fnl 2 1/2f* **66/1**

6 4 **Dubhe**[272] 2122 4-8-9 **99**...(tp) BrettDoyle 4 82
(Charlie Appleby) *a in mid-div* **5/1**[3]

7 5 **North Face (IRE)**[50] 9405 4-8-10 **100**.....................(t) MickaelBarzalona 1 75
(Marco Botti) *trckd ldr tl wknd fnl 2 1/2f* **12/1**

8 6 1/2 **Harlan Strong (ARG)**[7] 284 4-9-0 **100**........................ PatCosgrave 8 64
(Kenneth McPeek, U.S.A) *nvr bttr than mid-div* **66/1**

9 29 **Maifalki (FR)**[21] 47 6-8-11 **98**.................................. FabriceVeron 6 15
(N Caullery, France) *trckd ldr tl wknd fnl 2 1/2f* **25/1**

10 12 **Wadigor**[580] 4033 6-9-4 **104**.. ChrisHayes 9
(N Bachalard, UAE) *s.i.s: a in rr* **20/1**

2m 30.78s (-1.02) **Going Correction** +0.375s/f (Good)
WFA 4 from 5yo+ 3lb **10** Ran SP% **117.1**
Speed ratings: **118,117,114,112,111 108,105,100,81,73**
CSF: 34.54; TRICAST: 65.78; PLACEPOT: £34.00 to a £1 stake. Pool of £6,074.60 - 130.25 winning units; QUADPOT: £22.30 to a £1 stake. Pool of £495.90 - 16.40 winning units.

Owner Godolphin **Bred** Wertheimer & Frere **Trained** Newmarket, Suffolk

FOCUS
TRAKUS: 2nd +10, 3rd +15, 4th +16, 5th +7, 6th +3, 7th +1, 8th +14, 9th +9, 10th +9. The winner was soon setting a fair pace: 27.39, 24.87, 24.85, 24.73, 23.69, 25.25.

[365]LINGFIELD (L-H)
Friday, January 25

OFFICIAL GOING: Polytrack: standard
Wind: Moderate, half behind Weather: Cloudy, mild

399 SUN RACING H'CAP 1m 1y(P)
1:15 (1:15) (Class 6) (0-55,55) 4-Y-O+

£3,105 (£924; £461; £300; £300; £300) **Stalls** High

Form RPR

046- 1 **Collate**[26] 9765 4-9-4 **53**...(v) DavidProbert 2 60
(Amy Murphy) *t.k.h: hld up in midfield: prog 2f out to trck ldr over 1f out: sn clsd: rdn to ld last 100yds: fnd enough to assert nr fin* **5/1**[1]

3-16 2 1 **Diamond Reflection (IRE)**[13] 207 7-9-3 **52**..............(tp) RossaRyan 8 57
(Alexandra Dunn) *trckd ldr after 2f: led 2f out and kicked for home: drvn and hdd last 100yds: styd on but hld nr fin* **7/1**

24-0 3 2 **Herm (IRE)**[22] 39 5-9-5 **54**...(v[1]) NicolaCurrie 3 54
(David Evans) *t.k.h: hld up in midfield: rdn over 2f out: styd on fr over 1f out to take 3rd ins fnl f: no threat to ldng pair* **7/1**

125- 4 nk **Three C's (IRE)**[28] 9734 5-9-4 **53**.................................(p) HollieDoyle 1 52
(Adrian Wintle) *w ldr 2f: styd cl up: rdn and nt qckn over 2f out: kpt on same pce fr over 1f out* **13/2**[3]

621- 5 1/2 **Hidden Dream (IRE)**[71] 9071 4-8-12 **52**...................(p) KevinLundie[(5)] 4 50
(Christine Dunnett) *led to 2f out: lost 2nd over 1f out: fdd fnl f* **12/1**

400- 6 1 1/2 **Multitask**[170] 5856 9-9-6 **55**...(p) AdamKirby 12 50+
(Gary Moore) *t.k.h: dropped in fr wdst draw and hld up in last: pushed along over 1f out: late prog but nvr remotely involved* **10/1**

24-0 7 2 1/4 **Sir Jamie**[20] 80 6-9-2 **51**.. LukeMorris 10 41
(Tony Carroll) *s.i.s: hld up in rr: pushed along 2f out: no great prog whn reminders fnl f* **14/1**

000- 8 nk **No Approval (IRE)**[55] 9356 6-8-12 **52**............... PoppyBridgwater[(5)] 5 41
(David Bridgwater) *dwlt: t.k.h: hld up in last trio: brief effrt on inner over 1f out: no real prog* **12/1**

60-0 9 1 **Stosur (IRE)**[22] 39 8-8-13 **55**..................................(b) TobyEley[(7)] 9 42
(Gay Kelleway) *t.k.h: chsd ldrs on outer: rdn over 2f out: lost pl sn after: fdd (jockey said mare stopped quickly)* **11/1**

64-4 10 1/2 **Voice Of A Leader (IRE)**[20] 80 8-9-4 **53**...................... JoeyHaynes 7 38
(Paul Howling) *hld up in last trio: rdn on outer over 2f out: wd bnd sn after: no prog (jockey said gelding ran too free)* **8/1**

06-6 11 3 1/4 **Farl (IRE)**[14] 178 4-9-4 **53**.. RichardKingscote 6 31
(Ed Walker) *chsd ldrs: rdn wl over 2f out: wknd qckly wl over 1f out* **11/2**[2]

1m 36.99s (-1.21) **Going Correction** -0.15s/f (Stan) **11** Ran SP% **121.0**
Speed ratings (Par 101): **100,99,97,96,96 94,92,92,91,90 87**
CSF £40.93 CT £255.28 TOTE £4.80: £2.10, £2.00, £2.00; EX 41.10 Trifecta £189.60.

Owner Bill Tillett **Bred** Juddmonte Farms Ltd **Trained** Newmarket, Suffolk

FOCUS
An open, moderate handicap opened a low-key card. The second has been rated to his recent level.

400 LADBROKES HOME OF THE ODDS BOOST H'CAP 1m 1y(P)
1:45 (1:45) (Class 6) (0-60,58) 3-Y-O

£3,105 (£924; £461; £300; £300; £300) **Stalls** High

Form RPR

00-4 1 **Sir Ox (USA)**[16] 134 3-9-4 **55**.......................................(p) LukeMorris 8 63+
(Robert Cowell) *mostly trckd ldr: rdn over 2f out: clsd to ld jst over 1f out: drvn clr fnl f* **10/1**

05-6 2 2 3/4 **Elysian Lady**[20] 79 3-9-7 **58**.. AdamKirby 4 60
(Michael Wigham) *chsd ldrs: urged along bef 1/2-way: rdn and prog 2f out: kpt on to take 2nd ins fnl f: no ch w wnr* **9/2**[3]

00-4 3 nse **Miss Green Dream**[20] 79 3-8-12 **49**..........................(p) DavidProbert 6 51
(Stuart Williams) *s.i.s: towards rr: prog 2f out: rdn and styd on fr over 1f out: tk 3rd nr fin and nrly snatched 2nd* **12/1**

4-06 4 1 3/4 **Drummer Jack (IRE)**[14] 174 3-9-5 **56**......................(b[1]) RobertHavlin 7 54
(William Muir) *led at decent pce: rdn 2f out: hdd jst over 1f out: wknd fnl f* **6/1**

003- 5 nk **Ignatius (IRE)**[49] 9444 3-9-3 **54**...................................... KierenFox 12 51
(John Best) *cl up: trckd ldng pair over 2f out: swtchd to outer and rdn over 1f out: limited rspnse and wl hld fnl f* **9/4**[1]

613- 6 2 3/4 **Keep It Country Tv**[28] 9729 3-9-0 **54**.................... PaddyBradley[(3)] 1 45
(Pat Phelan) *hld up in midfield: pushed along and sltly outpcd over 2f out: effrt on outer wl over 1f out: no real prog (jockey said gelding ran flat)* **10/3**[2]

55-0 7 3/4 **Pot Luck**[20] 79 3-9-7 **58**...(b[1]) RobHornby 3 47
(Andrew Balding) *chsd ldrs: urged along bef 1/2-way: no prog 2f out: wknd on inner jst over 1f out* **20/1**

000- 8 1/2 **Ring Out The Bells (IRE)**[51] 9394 3-9-3 **57**............... WilliamCox[(3)] 10 45
(Charles Hills) *t.k.h: disp 2nd pl to over 2f out: wknd over 1f out* **50/1**

00-0 9 nse **Isabella Red (IRE)**[4] 341 3-9-1 **52**............................... NicolaCurrie 5 40
(David Evans) *s.i.s: hld up in last pair: rdn on inner and no prog over 1f out* **16/1**

000- 10 1/2 **Crazy Spin**[105] 8163 3-8-8 **45**.. JoeyHaynes 9 31
(Ivan Furtado) *racd on outer: in tch: rdn over 3f out: sn struggling* **33/1**

000- 11 5 **Supreme Chance**[37] 9607 3-8-8 **45**................................... EoinWalsh 11 20
(Michael Blanshard) *dropped in fr wd draw and hld up in rr: rdn and no prog over 2f out* **66/1**

04-0 12 15 **Scenic Lady**[7] 296 3-8-9 **46**...(h) HollieDoyle 2
(Michael Attwater) *a in rr: bhd after 1/2-way: t.o (jockey said filly was never travelling)* **66/1**

1m 36.96s (-1.24) **Going Correction** -0.15s/f (Stan) **12** Ran SP% **121.6**
Speed ratings (Par 95): **100,97,97,95,95 92,91,91,91,90 85,70**
CSF £54.28 CT £560.61 TOTE £10.10: £3.00, £1.50, £2.70; EX 53.30 Trifecta £1063.80.

Owner Khalifa Dasmal **Bred** Machmer Hall **Trained** Six Mile Bottom, Cambs

FOCUS
Extremely moderate fare with only one previous winner taking their chance. Lots were off the bridle at halfway.

401 LADBROKES CLAIMING STKS 7f 1y(P)
2:20 (2:20) (Class 6) 3-Y-O

£3,105 (£924; £461; £300; £300; £300) **Stalls** Low

Form RPR

-442 1 **Axel Jacklin**[8] 274 3-9-10 67...(b) AdamKirby 9 71
(Mark Johnston) *sn pressed ldr: rdn to ld jst over 2f out: drvn clr 1f out: styd on* **11/8**[1]

250- **2** 1 3/4 **Elieden (IRE)**79 8929 3-8-8 58......................(h1) TobyEley(7) 1 57
(Gay Kelleway) *slowly away: in tch: prog 2f out: rdn and styd on to take 2nd last 150yds: unable to chal (jockey said filly was very slowly away)* **8/13**

65-6 **3** 2 1/2 **Grandstand (IRE)**16 140 3-8-11 67.................. JoshuaBryan(3) 8 49
(Andrew Balding) *chsd ldng pair: rdn over 2f out: nt qckn wl over 1f out: one pce after* **11/42**

3-00 **4** 1 **Peters Pudding (IRE)**12 228 3-9-0 61..................(v) EoinWalsh 10 47
(David Evans) *won battle for ld fr wdst draw: grad edgd across to inner: rdn and hdd jst over 2f out: wknd jst ins fnl f* **8/13**

40-0 **5** 2 1/4 **Bridlemere Court (IRE)**7 296 3-9-0 48....................(v1) HollieDoyle 3 40
(David Elsworth) *rousted early but unable to hold prom pl: shkn up over 2f out: no prog and wl btn over 1f out* **25/1**

40-5 **6** 2 3/4 **Arcadian Rocks (IRE)**7 287 3-8-13 73................. ScottMcCullagh(7) 2 39
(Mick Channon) *chsd ldng pair to over 2f out: pushed along and wknd on inner over 1f out* **20/1**

7 2 1/4 **Morro Castle** 3-9-10 0.................................... NicolaCurrie 6 37
(Jamie Osborne) *a in last pair: pushed along 1/2-way: no prog (jockey said gelding ran green; vet reported the gelding was lame on it right fore)* **10/1**

0- **8** 1 1/2 **Red's Comet**63 9225 3-9-1 0.............................. RichardKingscote 5 24
(Laura Mongan) *in rr whn impeded over 5f out: no prog over 2f out* **50/1**

53-0 **U** **Pleasant Gesture (IRE)**13 217 3-8-6 65.................. AaronMackay(7) 4
(J S Moore) *in tch whn stmbld and uns rdr over 5f out* **10/1**

1m 24.56s (-0.24) **Going Correction** -0.15s/f (Stan) **9 Ran SP% 119.7**
Speed ratings (Par 95): **95,93,90,89,86 83,80,79,**
CSF £13.87 TOTE £2.00: £1.10, £2.40, £1.10; EX 14.20 Trifecta £43.60.Axel Jacklin was claimed by Paul Howling for £10,000. Grandstand was claimed by R. J. Price for £5,000
Owner Middleham Park Racing III **Bred** Godolphin **Trained** Middleham Moor, N Yorks
■ Stewards' Enquiry : Eoin Walsh caution: careless riding

FOCUS
A typically weak claimer.

402 PLAY 4 TO SCORE AT BETWAY H'CAP — 6f 1y(P)
2:55 (2:55) (Class 6) (0-55,54) 3-Y-O+
£3,105 (£924; £461; £300; £300; £300) **Stalls Low**

Form RPR

0-61 **1** **Brockey Rise (IRE)**9 263 4-9-3 52....................(b) KatherineBegley(7) 8 62
(David Evans) *hld up in rr: prog on wd outside over 1f out: str run to ld last 75yds: sn clr* **9/21**

4-25 **2** 1 1/2 **Ever Rock (IRE)**7 296 3-8-6 50.......................... JoeyHaynes 2 51
(J S Moore) *chsd ldrs: clsd over 2f out: rdn to ld jst over 1f out: styd on but hdd and outpcd last 75yds* **7/1**

-620 **3** 1 1/2 **Swiss Cross**2 365 12-9-4 53..........................(p) GraceMcEntee(7) 12 54
(Phil McEntee) *chsd ldrs on outer: shkn up and cl up 2f out: nt qckn over 1f out: kpt on fnl f* **14/1**

0-32 **4** 1/2 **Monarch Maid**7 293 8-9-3 45.............................. AdamKirby 10 44
(Peter Hiatt) *w ldr at str pce: led briefly over 1f out: outpcd fnl f: did best of those forcing the pce* **13/23**

0-24 **5** nk **Delagate The Lady**7 296 3-8-4 48.......................... LukeMorris 9 42
(Michael Attwater) *chsd ldrs: pushed along bef 1/2-way: lost pl 2f out: kpt on u.p fnl f* **6/12**

/3-0 **6** 1/2 **Wotamadam**21 53 4-9-11 53.................................. RobertHavlin 5 50
(Dean Ivory) *hld up in midfield: effrt over 1f out: nt qckn and no imp on ldrs fnl f* **10/1**

000- **7** 3/4 **Red Snapper**29 9720 4-9-5 47................................(p) HollieDoyle 7 42
(William Stone) *t.k.h: hld up towards rr: urged along wl over 1f out: styd on last 100yds: n.d* **25/1**

021- **8** 1/2 **Prominna**113 7946 9-9-12 54.............................. DavidProbert 4 47
(Tony Carroll) *hld up in rr: trying to make prog towards inner whn nt clr run thrght fnl f: no ch* **8/1**

40-3 **9** 3/4 **Charlie Alpha (IRE)**15 161 5-9-0 47......................(b) RhiainIngram(5) 3 38
(Roger Ingram) *t.k.h: mde most at str pce: hdd & wknd over 1f out* **7/1**

02-6 **10** hd **Tarseekh**21 60 6-9-7 49..........................(b) RichardKingscote 11 39
(Charlie Wallis) *stdd s fr wd draw: hld up and last of main gp: nudged along on inner and nt clr run fnl f: nvr involved (jockey said gelding was denied a clear run)* **13/23**

00-0 **11** 2 3/4 **Dolydaydream**7 293 4-9-0 45..........................(v1) PaddyBradley(3) 1 27
(Pat Phelan) *w ldng pair to over 3f out: lost pl over 2f out: wknd u.p fnl f* **20/1**

04-0 **12** 25 **Dotty Grand**16 137 3-8-5 49..............................(p) NicolaCurrie 6
(Jamie Osborne) *sn bhd: t.o bef 1/2-way (jockey said filly was never travelling)* **16/1**

1m 11.4s (-0.50) **Going Correction** -0.15s/f (Stan) **12 Ran SP% 125.5**
WFA 3 from 4yo+ 16lb
Speed ratings (Par 101): **97,95,93,92,91 91,90,89,88,88 84,51**
CSF £37.84 CT £430.70 TOTE £5.70: £1.50, £2.90, £4.60; EX 43.80 Trifecta £309.30.
Owner John Abbey & Emma Evans **Bred** P O'Rourke **Trained** Pandy, Monmouths

FOCUS
An open moderate sprint handicap. The winner was building on his recent win, and beat the third by a wider margin this time.

403 LADBROKES HOME OF THE ODDS BOOST NOVICE MEDIAN AUCTION STKS — 1m 2f (P)
3:25 (3:25) (Class 6) 3-Y-O
£3,105 (£924; £461; £230) **Stalls Low**

Form RPR

3-4 **1** **Harvey Dent**20 90 3-9-2 0.................................. HollieDoyle 5 71+
(Archie Watson) *t.k.h: mde all: shkn up and drew clr 2f out: in n.d after: eased nr fin (jockey said gelding hung left-handed throughout)* **8/151**

2 **2** 3 1/2 **Colony Queen**21 66 3-8-11 0.............................. LukeMorris 8 56
(James Tate) *t.k.h early: trckd ldng pair: pushed along 4f out: rdn over 2f out: tk 2nd jst over 1f out: kpt on but no ch w wnr* **9/22**

0- **3** 3/4 **Boutonniere (USA)**29 9726 3-9-2 0........................ RobHornby 9 60
(Andrew Balding) *pressed wnr to over 2f out: outpcd after: lost 2nd jst over 1f out: kpt on* **7/1**

000- **4** 4 **Mr Fox**28 9729 3-9-2 45.................................... DavidProbert 4 52
(Michael Attwater) *hld up in midfield: outpcd over 2f out: shkn up and nvr on terms after: kpt on* **100/1**

0-0 **5** 1/2 **Hammy End (IRE)**15 156 3-9-2 0..........................(h) RobertHavlin 3 51
(William Muir) *hld up in last trio: pushed along over 2f out: nvr on terms w ldrs but kpt on steadily fnl f* **50/1**

4 **6** 1 1/2 **Eclittica (IRE)**21 66 3-8-8 0........................ AaronJones(3) 10 43
(Marco Botti) *dwlt: hld up in rr: pushed along and wd bnd 2f out: no real prog (jockey said filly was slowly away)* **16/1**

4- **7** 6 **Astrosparkle**167 6001 3-8-11 0............................ MarcMonaghan 6 32
(Mark H Tompkins) *dwlt: in tch in midfield: rdn and wknd over 2f out* **100/1**

8 33 **Phoenix Queen** 3-8-11 0.................................. JosephineGordon 2
(Gay Kelleway) *s.i.s: a bhd: t.o* **40/1**

04- **9** 1 1/4 **Little Rock (IRE)**49 9442 3-9-2 0........................ ShaneKelly 7
(Richard Hughes) *chsd ldrs: shkn up over 2f out: wknd rapidly wl over 1f out: t.o (jockey said gelding stopped quickly)* **6/13**

2m 5.33s (-1.27) **Going Correction** -0.15s/f (Stan) **9 Ran SP% 122.5**
Speed ratings (Par 95): **99,96,95,92,92 90,86,59,58**
CSF £3.76 TOTE £1.70: £1.10, £1.40, £2.10; EX 4.00 Trifecta £16.30.
Owner Saxon Thoroughbreds **Bred** Mrs D O Joly **Trained** Upper Lambourn, W Berks

FOCUS
A one-sided novice. The likes of the fourth, fifth and seventh limit the form.

404 BETWAY AMATEUR RIDERS' H'CAP — 1m 4f (P)
3:55 (3:55) (Class 5) (0-75,75) 4-Y-O+
£3,743 (£1,161; £580; £300; £300; £300) **Stalls Low**

Form RPR

035- **1** **French Mix (USA)**39 9585 5-10-0 66.................. MissHannahWelch(5) 2 75
(Alexandra Dunn) *trckd ldrs: trapped bhd wkng rival over 2f out and dropped to 6th: prog on inner over 1f out: clsd to ld 150yds out: sn clr* **12/1**

54-3 **2** 3 **Attain**9 262 10-10-4 65...................................... MrSimonWalker 8 69
(Archie Watson) *in tch in midfield: pushed along over 3f out: effrt over 2f out: rdn and kpt on over 1f out to take 2nd last stride: no ch w wnr* **5/21**

0-15 **3** nse **Pivotal Flame (IRE)**6 309 6-10-6 67 6ex.....(v) MissSerenaBrotherton 3 71
(Pat Phelan) *trckd ldrs thrght: wnt 3rd 3f out: rdn over 1f out: chsd wnr 100yds out but no imp: lost 2nd last stride* **7/23**

055- **4** 1 3/4 **Take Two**26 9768 10-10-8 74.............................. MrJamieBrace(5) 6 75
(Alex Hales) *wl in rr: rdn over 3f out: styd on over 2f out: tk 4th last stride: nrst fin* **14/1**

612- **5** 1/2 **Country'N'Western (FR)**36 9642 7-10-9 75.............. MrGeorgeEddery(5) 7 76
(Robert Eddery) *dwlt: sn trckd ldrs: wnt 2nd over 3f out: led over 2f out and sent for home: floundered fnl f: sn hdd & wknd* **13/2**

222- **6** 2 3/4 **Strictly Art (IRE)**161 6237 6-10-0 68........................ MissEmmaJack(7) 4 64
(Alan Bailey) *sn in last: virtually t.o 1/2-way and urged along: sed to run on 2f out: fin wl but no ch* **20/1**

400- **7** 3 3/4 **Blame Me Forever (USA)**84 8798 4-10-9 73...........(b1) MrRossBirkett 5 64
(Don Cantillon) *rapid prog to join ldr after 2f: led 1/2-way: hdd and lost pl qckly over 3f out* **14/1**

21-2 **8** 1 **Proceed (IRE)**21 67 4-10-3 67..........................(p1) MissBrodieHampson 9 57
(Archie Watson) *t.k.h: trckd ldr 2f and again over 5f out: led over 3f out to over 2f out: wknd rapidly (jockey said filly hung badly left-handed)* **10/32**

001- **9** 7 **Mouchee (IRE)**37 9609 4-10-6 70........................(v) MrPatrickMillman 10 48
(Michael Blake) *a in last trio: lost tch over 3f out (jockey said gelding hung right-handed throughout)* **10/1**

00- **10** 25 **Aegeus (IRE)**43 9528 6-9-10 62 oh16 ow1....(bt) MissMichelleBryant(5) 1
(Paddy Butler) *led to 1/2-way: wknd qckly: t.o* **100/1**

2m 30.63s (-2.37) **Going Correction** -0.15s/f (Stan) **10 Ran SP% 123.1**
WFA 4 from 5yo+ 3lb
Speed ratings (Par 103): **101,99,98,97,97 95,93,92,87,71**
CSF £44.60 CT £135.33 TOTE £14.40: £5.10, £1.10, £2.20; EX 51.70 Trifecta £273.10.
Owner Mrs G Welch **Bred** Calumet Farm **Trained** West Buckland, Somerset
■ Stewards' Enquiry : Mr George Eddery five-day ban: failing to ride out (Feb 8-9 & 19, Mar 15 & 25)

FOCUS
A modest event for amateur riders. The winner has been rated back to her old Irish form, and the second to his recent effort.
T/Jkpt: Not Won. T/Plt: £56.80 to a £1 stake. Pool: £70,959.03 - 911.82 winning units T/Qpdt: £4.80 to a £1 stake. Pool: £7,625.34 - 1,175.49 winning units **Jonathan Neesom**

349 NEWCASTLE (A.W) (L-H)
Friday, January 25

OFFICIAL GOING: Tapeta: standard to slow
Wind: Breezy, half against Weather: Dry

405 LADBROKES MAIDEN STKS — 1m 5y (Tp)
4:15 (4:15) (Class 5) 3-Y-O
£3,752 (£1,116; £557; £278) **Stalls Centre**

Form RPR

2 **1** **Sparkle In His Eye**17 128 3-9-5 0........................ DanielTudhope 8 78+
(William Haggas) *hld up towards far side of gp: effrt and swtchd rt over 1f out: led wl ins fnl f: pushed out: comf* **8/151**

6- **2** 1/2 **You Little Ripper (IRE)**93 8548 3-9-5 0.................. PaulMulrennan 2 76+
(Peter Chapple-Hyam) *prom on far side of gp: stdy hdwy and led over 1f out: rdn: edgd rt and hdd wl ins fnl f: one pce nr fin* **10/32**

0- **3** 3 1/2 **Elikapeka (FR)**147 6758 3-9-0 0.......................... GrahamLee 11 63
(Kevin Ryan) *led in centre of gp to over 1f out: rallied: outpcd ins fnl f* **100/1**

0- **4** 2 1/4 **Dreams And Visions (IRE)**41 9556 3-8-12 0.............. JoshQuinn(7) 9 63
(Michael Easterby) *dwlt: hld up in midfield in centre of gp: shkn up and effrt over 1f out: kpt on fnl f: nt rch first three* **50/1**

0- **5** hd **Art Of Diplomacy**41 9556 3-9-5 0........................ NathanEvans 10 62
(Michael Easterby) *dwlt: hld up towards rr on nr side of gp: effrt and shkn up whn nt clr run briefly over 1f out: kpt on fnl f: nt pce to chal (jockey said gelding was denied a clear run approaching the final 1 1/2f)* **33/1**

63- **6** 3/4 **Mushaageb (IRE)**29 9725 3-9-5 0.......................... JoeFanning 7 60
(Roger Varian) *cl up on far side of gp: effrt and ev ch over 1f out: wknd ins fnl f* **9/23**

7 2 1/4 **Beresford (IRE)** 3-9-5 0.................................... TonyHamilton 6 55
(Richard Fahey) *dwlt: t.k.h in rr: shkn up and effrt on far side of gp over 1f out: nvr able to chal* **28/1**

8 nk **Three Castles** 3-9-5 0.................................... CallumRodriguez 5 54
(Keith Dalgleish) *missed break: hld up in centre of gp: pushed along over 2f out: effrt over 1f out: kpt on fnl f: no imp* **20/1**

9 1 1/4 **Half Bolly** 3-9-5 0.. DougieCostello 3 51
(Mark Walford) *hld up on far side of gp: rdn over 2f out: sn no imp* **150/1**

10 3/4 **Zoom Out** 3-8-12 0.................................... FayeMcManoman(7) 4 49
(Nigel Tinkler) *hld up on nr side of gp: pushed along and outpcd 2f out: sn btn* **150/1**

11 2 **Simul Amicis** 3-9-0 0.. JamesSullivan 1 40
(Dianne Sayer) *hld up in centre of gp: struggling over 2f out: sn btn* **200/1**

0- **12** 2¾ **Showshutai**[65] 9183 3-9-5 0 KieranO'Neill 12 38
(Christopher Kellett) *t.k.h: cl up in centre of gp tl rdn and wknd over 1f out* **250/1**

6-0 **13** ½ **Gate City (USA)**[19] 103 3-9-5 0 (v) AndrewMullen 13 37
(Adrian Nicholls) *cl up on nr side of gp tl rdn and wknd fr 2f out* **150/1**

1m 45.38s (6.78) **Going Correction** +0.45s/f (Slow) **13** Ran SP% **123.5**
Speed ratings (Par 97): **84,83,80,77,77 76,74,74,73,72 70,67,67**
CSF £2.64 TOTE £1.60: £1.10, £1.10, £15.70; EX 3.40 Trifecta £100.10.
Owner A E Oppenheimer **Bred** Hascombe And Valiant Studs **Trained** Newmarket, Suffolk

FOCUS
A fair 3yo maiden on standard to slow Tapeta. There was a stiff head wind blowing down the track into the runners faces. The odds-on favourite picked up strongly in the final 100 yards to prevail. The winning time was modest off a steady gallop. Muddling form. The level is fluid in behind the first two.

406 LADBROKES HOME OF THE ODDS BOOST H'CAP 6f (Tp)
4:45 (4:45) (Class 6) (0-60,58) 3-Y-O
£3,105 (£924; £461; £400; £400; £400) **Stalls** Centre

Form RPR

000- **1** **Scandinavian Lady (IRE)**[62] 9254 3-9-2 **53** JasonHart 5 60
(Ivan Furtado) *hld up in tch in centre of gp: drvn over 2f out: rallied over 1f out: led last 30yds: kpt on* **11/1**

004- **2** 1 **Arishka (IRE)**[161] 6261 3-9-7 **58** RobertWinston 2 62
(Daniel Kubler) *led in centre of gp: rdn and qcknd over 1f out: hdd and no ex last 30yds* **22/1**

00-6 **3** ¾ **Firsteen**[13] 211 3-9-2 **53** GrahamLee 4 55
(Alistair Whillans) *hld up in centre of gp: rdn over 2f out: hdwy over 1f out: kpt on fnl f: nrst fin* **25/1**

64-5 **4** ¾ **Quicksilver**[16] 137 3-9-7 **58** PJMcDonald 6 58
(Ed Walker) *t.k.h: trckd ldr: rdn 2f out: lost 2nd and one pce ins fnl f* **4/1**[2]

0-54 **5** 3½ **Gunnabedun (IRE)**[13] 215 3-9-1 **52** JoeFanning 11 41
(Iain Jardine) *hld up: effrt on nr side of gp 2f out: no imp fnl f* **5/2**[1]

560- **6** 2 **Where's Perle**[28] 9729 3-9-2 **53** FrannyNorton 3 36
(Michael Wigham) *chsd ldrs on far side of gp: effrt and rdn 2f out: wknd ins fnl f* **10/1**

00-1 **7** nk **Deconso**[11] 235 3-9-0 **51** 6ex KieranO'Neill 8 33
(Christopher Kellett) *reluctant to enter stalls: prom on nr side of gp: rdn over 2f out: wknd over 1f out* **5/1**[3]

000- **8** 2¼ **Sittin Handy (IRE)**[48] 9460 3-9-5 **56** LiamJones 7 31
(Mark Loughnane) *hld up: rdn along in centre of gp over 2f out: sn no imp: btn over 1f out* **10/1**

6-54 **9** 1¼ **Amliba**[14] 186 3-9-5 **56** DanielTudhope 10 28
(David O'Meara) *hld up on far side of gp: rdn and hung lft over 2f out: sn wknd (jockey said filly was slowly away)* **20/1**

005- **10** ½ **Lethal Laura**[38] 9598 3-9-0 **51** BarryMcHugh 1 21
(James Given) *t.k.h: hld up in tch on far side of gp: struggling over 2f out: sn btn* **12/1**

1m 15.59s (3.09) **Going Correction** +0.45s/f (Slow) **10** Ran SP% **112.4**
Speed ratings (Par 95): **97,95,94,93,89 86,85,82,81,80**
CSF £222.10 CT £5732.43 TOTE £13.70: £3.50, £5.70, £7.90; EX 249.60 Trifecta £5620.60.
Owner The Giggle Factor Partnership **Bred** Kildaragh Stud **Trained** Wiseton, Nottinghamshire

FOCUS
A modest 3yo sprint handicap. One of the many fillies in the race finished her race off more powerfully than the rest in a one-two-three-four for her sex.

407 PLAY 4 TOSCORE AT BETWAY H'CAP 6f (Tp)
5:15 (5:15) (Class 4) (0-80,83) 4-Y-O+
£5,530 (£1,645; £822; £411; £400; £400) **Stalls** Centre

Form RPR

23-3 **1** **Treacherous**[9] 253 5-9-2 **75** CallumShepherd 8 88
(Ed de Giles) *t.k.h: in tch: smooth hdwy 2f out: led and rdn 1f out: edgd lft and flashed tail ins fnl f: r.o* **7/2**[2]

61-2 **2** 1¼ **Equiano Springs**[23] 24 5-9-7 **80** AndrewMullen 4 89
(Tom Tate) *s.i.s: sn rcvrd and led: rdn and hdd 1f out: kpt on same pce* **10/3**[1]

0-31 **3** 1 **Athollblair Boy (IRE)**[13] 214 6-9-0 **80** FayeMcManoman(7) 7 86
(Nigel Tinkler) *trckd ldrs: effrt and rdn over 1f out: kpt on same pce ins fnl f* **4/1**[3]

024- **4** 1½ **Russian Realm**[87] 8719 9-9-6 **79** GrahamLee 9 80
(Paul Midgley) *hld up: effrt and pushed along over 1f out: no imp fnl f* **9/1**

31-3 **5** hd **Black Salt**[15] 165 5-9-5 **78** RobertWinston 2 78
(David Barron) *hld up: rdn and effrt over 1f out: no imp ins fnl f* **9/1**

000- **6** 1 **Tricky Dicky**[35] 9662 6-9-2 **78** PhilDennis(3) 6 75
(Olly Williams) *cl up tl rdn and outpcd wl over 1f out: n.d after* **25/1**

1-11 **7** 2 **Deeds Not Words (IRE)**[14] 177 8-8-12 **71** BarryMcHugh 5 62
(Tracy Waggott) *hld up in tch: rdn over 2f out: wknd over 1f out* **25/1**

04-0 **8** 2¼ **Tommy G**[23] 24 6-9-6 **79** JoeFanning 3 63
(Jim Goldie) *hld up: rdn along 2f out: sn no imp: btn fnl f (trainer was informed that the gelding could not run until the day after passing a stalls test)* **5/1**

1m 13.97s (1.47) **Going Correction** +0.45s/f (Slow) **8** Ran SP% **109.7**
Speed ratings (Par 105): **108,106,105,103,102 101,98,95**
CSF £14.24 CT £42.99 TOTE £3.50: £1.30, £1.50, £1.50; EX 15.70 Trifecta £54.50.
Owner Woodham Walter Partnership **Bred** P M Hicks **Trained** Ledbury, H'fords

FOCUS
The feature race was a fairly decent sprint handicap and the second-favourite won well in a favourable time on the night. A small pb from the winner, with the third rated close to his latest effort.

408 LADBROKES NOVICE STKS 5f (Tp)
5:45 (5:45) (Class 5) 3-Y-O £3,752 (£1,116; £557; £278) **Stalls** Centre

Form RPR

1 **Metal Exchange** 3-8-11 0 AndrewMullen 2 67+
(Kevin Ryan) *s.i.s: hld up: effrt and rdn over 1f out: edgd lft and kpt on wl fnl f to ld nr fin* **25/1**

3 **2** hd **Olympic Spirit**[17] 130 3-9-2 0 PJMcDonald 8 71
(David Barron) *prom: rdn to ld ins fnl f: kpt on: hdd nr fin* **11/4**[2]

3 **3** 1¼ **Compton's Finale**[13] 211 3-9-2 70 (tp) GrahamLee 6 66
(Adrian Paul Keatley, Ire) *led: rdn over 1f out: hdd ins fnl f: kpt on same pce* **7/2**[3]

6- **4** 1¼ **Ghost Buy (FR)**[30] 9709 3-9-2 0 DayversonDeBarros 5 62
(Ivan Furtado) *cl up: rdn and edgd lft over 1f out: sn one pce* **25/1**

04-2 **5** 2 **Kyllachy Warrior (IRE)**[17] 130 3-8-13 70 PhilDennis(3) 1 54
(Lawrence Mullaney) *prom: drvn along 2f out: outpcd fnl f* **13/2**

232- **6** ½ **Antonia Clara**[30] 9709 3-8-11 70 JoeFanning 4 48
(Stuart Williams) *t.k.h: hld up in tch: effrt and rdn 2f out: sn no imp: btn fnl f* **11/8**[1]

7 nk **Fortunate Move** 3-8-11 0 CliffordLee 7 46
(Richard Fahey) *bhd: rn green and outpcd 1/2-way: nvr on terms* **33/1**

50- **8** 7 **Football Friend**[51] 9411 3-8-9 0 KieranSchofield(7) 3 26
(Antony Brittain) *bhd: struggling wl over 2f out: sn btn* **150/1**

1m 1.96s (2.46) **Going Correction** +0.45s/f (Slow) **8** Ran SP% **115.6**
Speed ratings (Par 97): **98,97,95,93,90 89,89,78**
CSF £92.28 TOTE £24.40: £5.70, £1.30, £1.10; EX 155.70 Trifecta £567.70.
Owner T A Rahman **Bred** N E F Luck **Trained** Hambleton, N Yorks

FOCUS
A fair 3yo novice sprint. The shock winner grabbed the second-favourite late on in a reasonable comparative time for these relatively young horses. It's been rated through the consistent third to his latest.

409 LADBROKES HOME OF THE ODDS BOOST H'CAP 1m 5y (Tp)
6:15 (6:15) (Class 5) (0-75,73) 3-Y-O
£3,752 (£1,116; £557; £400; £400; £400) **Stalls** Centre

Form RPR

06-1 **1** **Alkaamel**[16] 134 3-9-4 **70** DanielTudhope 1 86+
(William Haggas) *stdd in last pl: smooth hdwy to ld over 1f out: qcknd clr on bit ins fnl f: v easily* **4/11**[1]

05-5 **2** 3¼ **So Hi Storm (IRE)**[16] 140 3-9-1 **67** CliffordLee 6 68
(K R Burke) *t.k.h: trckd ldrs: effrt and ev ch briefly over 1f out: chsd (clr) wnr ins fnl f: no imp* **10/1**[2]

40-3 **3** 1¾ **Spirit Kingdom (USA)**[7] 290 3-9-0 **66** FrannyNorton 4 63
(Mark Johnston) *led at modest gallop: rdn 2f out: hdd over 1f out: no ex ins fnl f* **25/1**

432- **4** nse **Fayetta**[29] 9726 3-9-5 **71** PJMcDonald 5 68
(David Loughnane) *prom: rdn and outpcd 2f out: rallied fnl f: nt pce to chal* **11/1**[3]

0- **5** 3 **Joza (IRE)**[42] 9539 3-9-4 **70** (be) GrahamLee 7 59
(Adrian Paul Keatley, Ire) *dwlt and wnt rt s: t.k.h: hld up in tch: rdn over 2f out: no imp over 1f out* **18/1**

302- **6** 3¾ **Curfewed (IRE)**[37] 9611 3-9-7 **73** PaulMulrennan 3 53
(Tracy Waggott) *t.k.h: hld up: rdn and outpcd over 2f out: btn over 1f out (jockey said gelding ran too free)* **12/1**

00-5 **7** 4½ **Quduraat**[16] 134 3-8-12 **64** AlistairRawlinson 2 34
(Michael Appleby) *t.k.h: pressed ldr tl rdn and wknd qckly over 1f out* **40/1**

1m 44.36s (5.76) **Going Correction** +0.45s/f (Slow) **7** Ran SP% **110.0**
Speed ratings (Par 97): **89,85,84,83,80 77,72**
CSF £4.35 TOTE £1.30: £1.10, £3.30; EX 4.70 Trifecta £35.30.
Owner Hamdan Al Maktoum **Bred** Coln Valley Stud **Trained** Newmarket, Suffolk

FOCUS
An ordinary 3yo handicap. They went a steady gallop and the overall winning time was modest, but there was plenty to like about how the odds-on favourite outclassed his opponents. The second has been rated in line with his better form.

410 SUNRACING.CO.UK H'CAP 7f 14y (Tp)
6:45 (6:45) (Class 6) (0-60,60) 4-Y-O+
£3,105 (£924; £461; £400; £400; £400) **Stalls** Centre

Form RPR

060- **1** **Porrima (IRE)**[140] 7035 4-9-4 **57** AndrewMullen 10 65
(Ben Haslam) *hld up: hdwy nr side of gp wl over 1f out: led last 50yds: r.o* **14/1**

03-0 **2** ¾ **Scenery**[8] 277 4-9-5 **58** BarryMcHugh 5 64
(Marjorie Fife) *hld up: hdwy nr side of gp over 2f out: led over 1f out to last 50yds: kpt on same pce* **14/1**

010- **3** nk **Magical Molly Joe**[46] 9481 5-8-11 **53** (h) JaneElliott(3) 13 58
(David Barron) *hld up in centre of gp: effrt whn nt clr run briefly over 1f out: gd hdwy fnl f: kpt on: hld nr fin (jockey said mare was denied a clear run 1½f out)* **12/1**

320- **4** 1½ **Kroy**[37] 9616 5-9-0 **56** (p) BenRobinson(3) 7 58
(Ollie Pears) *t.k.h: hld up in tch in centre of gp: smooth hdwy to ld briefly over 1f out: sn rdn: one pce ins fnl f* **6/1**[2]

000- **5** 2 **Pretty Passe**[156] 6415 5-9-7 **60** CallumRodriguez 1 57
(Martin Todhunter) *hld up: effrt in centre of gp 2f out: kpt on same pce ins fnl f* **33/1**

1-25 **6** ½ **False Id**[11] 241 6-8-12 **58** (b) LauraCoughlan(7) 9 53
(David Loughnane) *hld up on far side of gp: drvn along over 2f out: rallied over 1f out: kpt on fin* **6/1**[2]

12-0 **7** ½ **Breathoffreshair**[8] 277 5-9-5 **58** (t) PhilipPrince 4 52
(Richard Guest) *in tch on far side of gp: drvn and outpcd 3f out: rallied over 1f out: no ex ins fnl f* **16/1**

600- **8** 2¼ **Iberica Road (USA)**[148] 6706 6-9-0 **53** SamJames 2 42
(Grant Tuer) *midfield on far side of gp: rdn and outpcd over 2f out: n.d after* **9/1**

00-0 **9** 1 **Daze Out (IRE)**[21] 64 4-9-2 **55** TonyHamilton 12 41
(Richard Fahey) *midfield on nr side of gp: drvn and outpcd over 2f out: sn n.d* **40/1**

40-0 **10** nk **Essential**[12] 233 5-9-2 **58** PhilDennis(3) 8 43
(Olly Williams) *prom on nr side of gp: hdwy and ev ch briefly over 1f out: wknd ins fnl f* **20/1**

/05- **11** 1½ **The Mcgregornator (IRE)**[15] 4460 5-9-3 **56** (p) GrahamLee 14 38
(Adrian Paul Keatley, Ire) *midfield on nr side of gp: drvn and outpcd over 2f out: sn btn* **25/1**

233- **12** ¾ **Great Colaci**[98] 8381 6-9-0 **53** KieranO'Neill 11 33
(Gillian Boanas) *led 1f: cl up on nr side of gp: regained ld over 2f out: edgd lft and hdd over 1f out: sn wknd (jockey said gelding hung left)* **5/1**[1]

26-3 **13** 6 **Baron Run**[12] 233 9-8-7 **53** RhonaPindar(7) 3 18
(K R Burke) *t.k.h: led on far side of gp after 1f to over 2f out: wknd over 1f out* **16/1**

00-4 **14** 5 **Supreme Power (IRE)**[19] 104 5-9-7 **60** (p) PaulMulrennan 6 12
(Tracy Waggott) *cl up in centre of gp: rdn over 2f out: wknd wl over 1f out* **15/2**[3]

1m 28.99s (2.79) **Going Correction** +0.45s/f (Slow) **14** Ran SP% **113.8**
Speed ratings (Par 101): **102,101,100,99,96 96,95,93,91,91 89,89,82,76**
CSF £178.05 CT £2474.15 TOTE £16.00: £5.50, £5.40, £4.40; EX 199.90 Trifecta £844.00.
Owner Daniel Shapiro & Partners **Bred** Tally-Ho Stud **Trained** Middleham Moor, N Yorks

■ Stewards' Enquiry : Philip Prince two-day ban: failing to obtain the best possible placing (tba)

FOCUS
A modest handicap. A strong gallop suited those ridden from well of the pace and the winning time compared favourably on the night. The second has been rated in line with his summer turf form.

411 BETWAY SPRINT H'CAP — 5f (Tp)
7:15 (7:15) (Class 6) (0-60,67) 4-Y-O+

£3,105 (£924; £461; £400; £400; £400) **Stalls** Centre

Form				RPR
35-1	**1**		**Gorgeous General**[15] [167] 4-8-9 **49** .... PhilDennis(3) 11	58
(Lawrence Mullaney) *trckd ldr on nr side of gp: led over 1f out: pushed out fnl f: comf* **9/1**
-501 | **2** | 1 1/2 | **Spirit Power**[7] [286] 4-9-13 **64** 6ex........................ JasonHart 9 | 68
(Eric Alston) *led on nr side of gp: rdn and hdd over 1f out: kpt on same pce ins fnl f* **9/2[2]**
0-13 | **3** | 1 1/4 | **Encoded (IRE)**[17] [129] 6-8-11 **48**........................ JoeFanning 2 | 47
(Lynn Siddall) *hld up in centre of gp: rdn and hdwy over 1f out: r.o ins fnl f* **9/1**
0-30 | **4** | 2 1/4 | **Poppy In The Wind**[17] [129] 7-9-3 **54**..................(b) AndrewMullen 5 | 45
(Alan Brown) *dwlt and swtchd rt s: hld up on nr side of gp: effrt over 2f out: kpt on same pce fnl f* **10/1**
0-24 | **5** | shd | **Novabridge**[17] [129] 11-8-10 **47**..................(b) ShaneGray 6 | 38
(Karen Tutty) *prom in centre of gp: drvn and effrt over 1f out: one pce ins fnl f* **14/1**
-030 | **6** | 1 | **Sir Walter (IRE)**[7] [286] 4-8-8 **45**........................ RachelRichardson 4 | 32
(Eric Alston) *prom on far side of gp: rdn and edgd lft over 1f out: sn outpcd* **20/1**
04-3 | **7** | 3 | **Hula Girl**[7] [298] 4-9-5 **56**..................(b) CallumShepherd 1 | 32
(Charles Hills) *hld up on far side of gp: rdn and outpcd 2f out: sn btn* **11/1**
06-0 | **8** | 2 | **Trulove**[8] [277] 6-8-8 **45**........................ PaddyMathers 7 | 14
(John David Riches) *prom tl rdn and wknd wl over 1f out* **33/1**
-002 | **9** | 1 | **Fuel Injection**[6] [322] 8-8-10 **47**..................(b) JamesSullivan 3 | 12
(Ruth Carr) *hld up in centre: drvn along 1/2-way: nvr on terms* **25/1**
35-6 | **10** | 2 1/2 | **Cherry Oak (IRE)**[17] [129] 4-9-7 **58**........................ PaulMulrennan 10 | 14
(Ben Haslam) *in tch: drvn and struggling 1/2-way: sn btn* **6/1[3]**
-611 | **U** | | **Archimedes (IRE)**[8] [279] 6-10-2 **67** 6ex..................(tp) RobertWinston 8 |
(David C Griffiths) *rdr unbalanced and uns as stall opened* **11/4[1]**

1m 1.36s (1.86) **Going Correction** +0.45s/f (Slow) 11 Ran SP% **114.8**
Speed ratings (Par 101): **103,100,98,95,94 93,88,85,83,79**
CSF £46.87 CT £383.86 TOTE £9.80: £2.20, £2.00, £3.00; EX 70.30 Trifecta £718.30.
Owner Shaun Humphries **Bred** Shaun & Leanne Humphries **Trained** Great Habton, N Yorks

FOCUS
A modest sprint handicap. The winner won well in a relatively good comparative time for the grade, proceeded by the loose-running favourite who had unseated his jockey leaving the gates. The second has been rated to his Kempton win.

412 LADBROKES H'CAP — 5f (Tp)
7:45 (7:45) (Class 6) (0-65,67) 3-Y-O

£3,105 (£924; £461; £400; £400; £400) **Stalls** Centre

Form				RPR
51-6	**1**		**Klopp**[13] [215] 3-8-12 **63**..................(h[1]) KieranSchofield(7) 9	68
(Antony Brittain) *t.k.h: hld up: hdwy nr side over 1f out: led ins fnl f: edgd lft: pushed out* **3/1[1]**
00-0 | **2** | 1/2 | **Gregarious Girl**[7] [296] 3-8-9 **53**..................(t[1]) JoeFanning 8 | 56
(Stuart Williams) *trckd ldr: led over 1f out: drifted lft and hdd ins fnl f: hld towards fin* **10/1**
50-5 | **3** | 2 3/4 | **Pink Flamingo**[13] [215] 3-9-7 **65**........................ PJMcDonald 3 | 58
(Mark Johnston) *led: rdn along and hdd over 1f out: kpt on same pce ins fnl f* **11/2**
653- | **4** | nse | **Ginvincible**[30] [9709] 3-9-9 **67**........................ BarryMcHugh 7 | 60
(James Given) *cl up: effrt and ev ch briefly over 1f out: no ex ins fnl f* **4/1[3]**
34-0 | **5** | 4 1/2 | **Superseded (IRE)**[23] [27] 3-9-8 **66**........................ CallumShepherd 1 | 43
(Charles Hills) *hld up bhd ldng gp: drvn and outpcd 1/2-way: sme late hdwy: nvr on terms* **10/3[2]**
040- | **6** | 3 3/4 | **Kyroc (IRE)**[108] [8074] 3-9-3 **61**........................ PaulMulrennan 4 | 24
(Susan Corbett) *bhd: drvn and outpcd 1/2-way: nvr on terms* **80/1**
00-0 | **7** | 3 1/4 | **Sing Bertie (IRE)**[13] [215] 3-8-2 **46** oh1........................ PaddyMathers 2 |
(Derek Shaw) *hld up: rdn and struggling over 2f out: sn btn* **20/1**
46-4 | **8** | 1/2 | **Dancing Ballerina (IRE)**[16] [141] 3-9-2 **60**........................ CliffordLee 6 | 10
(K R Burke) *prom: rdn over 2f out: edgd lft and wknd over 1f out* **7/1**

1m 1.61s (2.11) **Going Correction** +0.45s/f (Slow) 8 Ran SP% **111.1**
Speed ratings (Par 95): **101,100,95,95,88 82,77,76**
CSF £31.37 CT £150.36 TOTE £3.60: £1.30, £3.00, £1.60; EX 31.80 Trifecta £178.60.
Owner Antony Brittain **Bred** Northgate Lodge Stud Ltd **Trained** Warthill, N Yorks

FOCUS
An ordinary sprint handicap. The comparative winning time was fair for the grade. The second has been rated near last year's best.
T/Plt: £220.40 to a £1 stake. Pool: £78,077.71 - 258.53 winning units T/Qpdt: £14.90 to a £1 stake. Pool: £14,517.65 - 720.23 winning units **Richard Young**

413 - 418a (Foreign Racing) - See Raceform Interactive

300 DUNDALK (A.W) (L-H)
Friday, January 25

OFFICIAL GOING: Polytrack: standard

419a KENNEDY'S BAR & RESTAURANT APPRENTICE MAIDEN — 7f (P)
8:00 (8:02) 4-Y-O+ £6,936 (£2,150; £1,024; £461; £180)

| | | | RPR
---|---|---|---|---
| **1** | | **Master Diver**[8] [275] 4-9-7 0........................ TomMadden 3 | 78+
(Sir Mark Prescott Bt) *hooded to load: chsd ldrs: 3rd 1/2-way: gng wl almost on terms 2f out: led narrowly over 1f out: rdn briefly and extended advantage ins fnl f: comf* **5/4[1]**
| **2** | 3 | **Twenty Minutes**[14] [191] 4-9-7 74........................ DonaghO'Connor 12 | 69
(Damian Joseph English, Ire) *sn led briefly tl jnd after 2f: narrow advantage at 1/2-way: rdn 2f out and strly pressed: hdd narrowly over 1f out: no imp on easy wnr ins fnl f: kpt on same pce* **3/1[2]**
| **3** | 2 | **Lewandowski (IRE)** 5-9-7 0........................ OisinOrr 2 | 64
(Edward Lynam, Ire) *hld up towards rr early: tk clsr order after 2f: 7th 1/2-way: prog far side 2f out to chse ldrs: rdn in 3rd over 1f out and no imp on easy wnr ins fnl f: kpt on same pce: jst hld 4th* **16/1**
| **4** | nk | **Al Batal**[42] [9540] 6-9-0 66..................(t[1]) MikeO'Connor(7) 10 | 63
(John C McConnell, Ire) *prom early tl sn hdd briefly: disp ld again after 2f: cl 2nd at 1/2-way: drvn bhd ldrs 2f out and no imp on easy wnr u.p in 4th 1f out: kpt on same pce: jst hld for 3rd* **10/1**
| **5** | 2 | **Eagle Reel (IRE)**[82] [8861] 4-9-7 0..................(t) BenCoen 6 | 57
(Luke Comer, Ire) *reluctant to load: chsd ldrs: disp 4th at 1/2-way: drvn 2f out and no imp on ldrs in 5th ins fnl f: kpt on one pce* **40/1**
| **6** | 2 1/2 | **Fairy Tango (IRE)** 4-9-2 0..................(t[1]) DannySheehy 5 | 46
(Sarah Lynam, Ire) *s.i.s and pushed along in rr early: 10th 1/2-way: pushed along and swtchd lft 2f out: sme hdwy far side 1f out: rdn briefly ins fnl f and kpt on one pce in 6th: nvr trbld ldrs* **33/1**
| **7** | hd | **Iseebreeze (IRE)**[42] [9540] 4-8-12 0........................ NathanCrosse(4) 7 | 45
(Anthony Mulholland, Ire) *hld up in tch: disp 4th between horses over 3f out: lost pl into st: drvn and no imp 2f out: one pce fnl f* **50/1**
| **8** | 2 | **Proud And Elated (FR)**[63] [9237] 4-8-12 63..................(bt) AlanPersse(4) 8 | 40
(Joseph Patrick O'Brien, Ire) *chsd ldrs: racd keenly: disp 4th briefly over 3f out: rdn nr side over 2f out and sn no ex* **6/1[3]**
| **9** | 2 1/2 | **Ingelara (IRE)**[35] [9676] 4-8-9 0..................(t) HughHorgan(7) 11 | 33
(Joseph Patrick O'Brien, Ire) *mid-div and t.k.h early: disp 9th at 1/2-way: rdn and swtchd lft 2f out: no ex over 1f out: one pce after* **66/1**
| **10** | 1/2 | **UAE Soldier (USA)**[450] [8508] 4-9-3 0..................(t[1]) AndrewSlattery(4) 9 | 37
(R P Cody, Ire) *hld up: disp 9th at 1/2-way: rdn far side 2f out and no imp ent fnl f* **40/1**
| **11** | 1 3/4 | **Kris Black (IRE)**[35] [9676] 6-9-3 0........................ AdamFarragher(4) 1 | 32
(Kieran P Cotter, Ire) *in rr: last at 1/2-way: rdn and no imp fr over 2f out: nvr a factor (jockey said that his mount made a noise in running)* **100/1**

1m 26.4s (1.30) **Going Correction** +0.325s/f (Slow) 11 Ran SP% **111.0**
Speed ratings: **105,101,99,98,96 93,93,91,88,87 85**
CSF £4.15 TOTE £1.70: £1.02, £1.40, £3.40; DF 4.50 Trifecta £39.10.
Owner Lee,Mrs Baxter,Bouverie,Chisholm,Howard **Bred** Wardley Bloodstock **Trained** Newmarket, Suffolk
■ Stewards' Enquiry : Donagh O'Connor caution: careless riding

FOCUS
Straightforward in the end for the British raider. The fifth, sixth and 11th limit the level.

420 - (Foreign Racing) - See Raceform Interactive

216 CHANTILLY (R-H)
Friday, January 25

OFFICIAL GOING: Polytrack: standard

421a PRIX ARTUS (MAIDEN) (3YO COLTS & GELDINGS) (ALL-WEATHER TRACK) (POLYTRACK) — 1m 1f 110y(P)
1:37 3-Y-O £11,261 (£4,504; £3,378; £2,252; £1,126)

| | | RPR
---|---|---|---
1 | | **Fairmont (FR)** 3-9-2 0........................ ChristopheSoumillon 6 | 83
(C Ferland, France) **17/10[1]**
2 | 3 1/2 | **Albiceleste (FR)**[21] 3-8-8 0........................ MohammedLyesTabti(8) 10 | 76
(C Lerner, France) **50/1**
3 | shd | **Beeswax (FR)**[57] [9315] 3-9-2 0........................ StephanePasquier 8 | 76
(Ed Walker) *settled towards rr of midfield: urged along over 2f out: rdn and hdwy over 1f out: styd on u.p ins fnl f: no ch w wnr* **56/10[3]**
4 | 3/4 | **Iskanderhon (USA)**[12] 3-9-2 0..................(p) TonyPiccone 7 | 74
(I Endaltsev, Czech Republic) **78/10**
5 | 1 1/4 | **Camprond (FR)**[41] 3-8-10 0........................ JeremieMonteiro(6) 4 | 72
(Mme Pia Brandt, France) **51/10[2]**
6 | 2 1/2 | **Paraponera Jem (FR)** 3-8-11 0........................ EddyHardouin 11 | 62
(S Jesus, France) **74/1**
7 | 3 | **Qaabil (IRE)**[93] [8564] 3-9-2 0........................ HugoJourniac 16 | 61
(J-C Rouget, France) *hld up towards rr: pushed along over 2f out: rdn w limited rspnse over 1f out: no ex ins fnl f* **9/1**
8 | 1 1/2 | **Into The Sound (IRE)**[21] 3-9-2 0........................ CristianDemuro 12 | 58
(G Botti, France) **74/10**
9 | 1 1/4 | **Long Game (FR)** 3-9-2 0..................(p) GregoryBenoist 2 | 55
(P Decouz, France) **36/1**
10 | 1/2 | **Hello Is You (FR)**[38] [9601] 3-9-2 0........................ AurelienLemaitre 5 | 54
(F Head, France) **25/1**
11 | 2 | **Koroneki (IRE)**[38] 3-8-7 0..................(b) MlleOphelieThiebaut(9) 3 | 50
(M Delcher Sanchez, France) **168/1**
12 | shd | **Penn Kalet (FR)**[38] [9601] 3-8-8 0........................ JackyNicoleau(8) 1 | 50
(B Legros, France) **166/1**
13 | 1 3/4 | **Fersen (FR)**[21] 3-9-2 0........................ ClementLecoeuvre 9 | 46
(F Chappet, France) **59/1**
14 | 1 1/2 | **Know It's Possible (FR)**[41] 3-9-2 0........................ VincentCheminaud 15 | 43
(H-A Pantall, France) **41/1**
15 | dist | **Nicco (FR)**[38] 3-9-2 0........................ BertrandFlandrin 13 |
(S Smrczek, Germany) **42/1**

1m 55.38s 15 Ran SP% **119.3**
PARI-MUTUEL (all including 1 euro stake): WIN 2.70; PLACE 1.70, 8.10, 2.30; DF 57.20;.
Owner Michael Motschmann **Bred** M Motschmann **Trained** France

422a-424a (Foreign Racing) - See Raceform Interactive

196 JEBEL ALI (L-H)
Friday, January 25

OFFICIAL GOING: Dirt: fast

425a JEBEL ALI MILE SPONSORED BY SHADWELL (GROUP 3) (DIRT) — 1m (D)
11:30 (11:30) 3-Y-O+

£73,717 (£24,572; £12,286; £6,143; £3,685; £2,457)

| | | RPR
---|---|---|---
1 | | **Secret Ambition**[8] [282] 6-9-0 103..................(t) RichardMullen 7 | 107
(S Seemar, UAE) *s.i.s: mid-div: smooth prog to ld 2 1/2f out: r.o wl* **2/1[1]**
2 | 1 3/4 | **Shamaal Nibras (USA)**[47] 10-9-0 103........................ PatDobbs 2 | 103
(Doug Watson, UAE) *slowly away: settled in rr: smooth prog 3f out: n.m.r 2f out: r.o wl once clr: nrst fin* **5/1**
3 | nk | **Behavioral Bias (USA)**[159] 5-9-0 100..................(bt) TadhgO'Shea 4 | 102
(S Seemar, UAE) *mid-div: chsd ldrs and ev ch 2 1/2f out: r.o fnl 1 1/2f* **13/2**
4 | 1 3/4 | **Forjatt (IRE)**[47] 11-9-0 105........................ ChrisHayes 5 | 98
(N Bachalard, UAE) *settled in rr: smooth prog 2 1/2f out: ev ch 1 1/2f out: one pce fnl f* **4/1[2]**
5 | 5 1/4 | **Rocket Power**[6] [327] 6-9-0 95........................ ConnorBeasley 6 | 86
(A bin Harmash, UAE) *mid-div: chsd ldrs and ev ch 1 1/2f out: wknd 1f out* **9/2[3]**

6 3 1/4 **Fitzgerald (USA)**[8] 282 7-9-0 95 .... XavierZiani 1 79
(S Jadhav, UAE) *trckd ldr: t.k.h: wd 6f out: wknd fnl 3 1/2f* 25/1

7 9 1/4 **Just A Penny (IRE)**[28] 9739 7-9-0 105 .... SamHitchcott 9 57
(Doug Watson, UAE) *sn led: hdd 2 1/2f out: wknd fnl f* 8/1

8 2 1/2 **Mailshot (USA)**[15] 173 5-9-0 95 .... RoystonFfrench 8 52
(S Jadhav, UAE) *s.i.s: a in rr* 20/1

9 14 **Musaddas**[22] 51 9-9-0 96 .... GeraldAvranche 3 19
(R Bouresly, Kuwait) *nvr bttr than mid-div* 40/1

1m 36.88s **9 Ran SP% 123.7**
CSF: 13.19.
Owner Nasir Askar **Bred** Darley **Trained** United Arab Emirates

426 - 428a (Foreign Racing) - See Raceform Interactive

[379] CHELMSFORD (A.W) (L-H)
Saturday, January 26

OFFICIAL GOING: Polytrack: standard
Wind: Virtually nil Weather: Overcast with showers

429 £20 FREE BETS AT TOTESPORT.COM APPRENTICE H'CAP 1m (P)
4:40 (4:40) (Class 5) (0-75,77) 4-Y-O+
£5,433 (£1,617; £808; £404; £400; £400) Stalls Low

Form RPR

6-10 1 **Philamundo (IRE)**[15] 175 4-9-4 **76** ....(b) ScottMcCullagh(5) 10 87+
(Richard Spencer) *hld up in last: gd hdwy arnd field to go 5th 2f out: rdn and clsd qckly on ldrs over 1f out: led wl ins fnl f: rdn out* 10/1

22-2 2 2 3/4 **Zodiakos (IRE)**[24] 22 6-8-10 **66** ....(p) BenSanderson(3) 4 71
(Roger Fell) *led: pushed along whn strly pressed by rival 2f out: sn drvn and hdd by wnr ins fnl f: kpt on* 5/1[3]

64-0 3 hd **Glory Awaits (IRE)**[23] 34 9-9-3 **77** ....(b) GeorgeBass(7) 1 82
(David Simcock) *broke wl and trckd ldrs racing keenly: gng wl in 3rd and swtchd lft over 1f out: sn rdn and hung lft u.p 1f out: one pce fnl f* 6/1

500- 4 hd **Regular Income (IRE)**[46] 9495 4-8-9 **67** ....(p) TobyEley(5) 8 71
(Adam West) *hld up: hdwy u.p over 2f out: rdn along to go 4th 2f out: briefly short of room over 1f out: swtchd rt off rail and styd on ins fnl f (jockey said gelding was slowly away and denied a clear run)* 16/1

4-53 5 5 **Ambient (IRE)**[8] 294 4-9-2 **74** ....(b) SeamusCronin(5) 3 67
(Jane Chapple-Hyam) *chsd ldr: rdn along 2f out: sn drvn and wknd ins fnl f* 9/2[2]

21-5 6 nk **Channel Packet**[16] 154 5-8-8 **68** .... MarkCrehan(7) 9 60
(Michael Appleby) *racd promly on the outer: pushed along and outpcd 3f out: rdn and little imp 2f out: kpt on fnl f (vet reported the horse lost its left fore shoe)* 10/1

03-1 7 5 **Lunar Deity**[16] 154 10-8-13 **73** .... GraceMcEntee(7) 6 53
(Stuart Williams) *trckd ldrs: pushed along over 2f out: drvn over 1f out: wknd fnl f* 6/1

00-0 8 3/4 **Badenscoth**[23] 34 5-9-6 **73** ....(h) JackDuern 7 52
(Dean Ivory) *dwlt and racd in rr: rdn 1/2-way: nvr on terms* 14/1

/0-0 9 27 **Blue Candy**[11] 249 4-8-12 **65** ....(p1) PhilDennis 5
(Ivan Furtado) *dwlt: pushed along to chse ldrs: rdn over 2f out: wknd and t.o over 1f out* 50/1

00-3 10 25 **Titan Goddess**[16] 158 7-9-5 **72** .... NicolaCurrie 2
(Mike Murphy) *slowly away and hld up: in rr whn heavily eased 2f out (jockey said mare lost its action in the home straight where she eased the mare to the line)* 11/4[1]

1m 38.98s (-0.92) **Going Correction** -0.075s/f (Stan) **10 Ran SP% 122.8**
Speed ratings (Par 103): **101,98,98,97,92 92,87,86,59,34**
CSF £62.66 CT £343.72 TOTE £13.50: £3.70, £1.80, £2.60; EX 94.10 Trifecta £827.00.
Owner Rebel Racing **Bred** Gerard Mullins **Trained** Newmarket, Suffolk

FOCUS
A fair apprentice handicap and they went a decent clip. The second and third have been rated in line with their recent form.

430 TOTEPOOL CASHBACK CLUB AT TOTESPORT.COM H'CAP 7f (P)
5:15 (5:15) (Class 6) (0-65,67) 4-Y-O+
£3,493 (£1,039; £519; £400; £400; £400) Stalls Low

Form RPR

065- 1 **Harbour Vision**[109] 8096 4-9-8 **66** .... PaddyMathers 5 73
(Derek Shaw) *hld up in rr: rdn and hdwy u.p on outer wl over 1f out: styd on wl to ld wl ins fnl f* 12/1

503- 2 1 **Pindaric**[42] 9560 5-7-11 **46** oh1 .... RhiainIngram(5) 10 50
(Declan Carroll) *trckd ldr and racd keenly: rdn along to chal 2f out: drvn along to ld jst ins fnl f: kpt on but hdd by wnr fnl 75yds* 16/1

021- 3 3/4 **Garth Rockett**[86] 8772 5-9-7 **65** ....(tp) ShaneKelly 3 67
(Brendan Powell) *racd in tch in midfield: rdn along and ev ch over 1f out: drvn and no ex ins fnl f* 4/1[2]

633- 4 1/2 **Kraka (IRE)**[53] 9388 4-9-7 **65** ....(p) KieranO'Neill 2 66
(Christine Dunnett) *trckd ldr in 4th: hdwy u.p to take a narrow ld over 1f out: rdn and hdd jst ins fnl f: no ex* 6/1[3]

0-46 5 1 **The Special One (IRE)**[3] 366 6-8-6 **57** ....(h) GraceMcEntee(7) 1 56
(Phil McEntee) *racd in midfield on inner: rdn along to cl wl over 1f out: drvn and ev ch ins fnl f* 14/1

520- 6 1 1/4 **Dreamboat Annie**[37] 9649 4-9-4 **62** ....(p) RobertHavlin 9 57
(Mark Usher) *led: rdn along and hdd over 1f out: wknd ins fnl f* 25/1

53-2 7 1/2 **Classic Charm**[23] 33 4-9-3 **61** .... RobertWinston 7 55
(Dean Ivory) *settled in midfield: effrt to chse ldrs wl over 1f out: rdn whn briefly short of room ins fnl f: no ex (jockey said filly had no more to give)* 3/1[1]

0-12 8 1/2 **African Blessing**[16] 159 6-9-2 **60** .... KierenFox 8 53
(John Best) *racd in rr of midfield: rdn along and c wdst of all into home st: sn drvn and wknd ins fnl f (jockey said gelding ran too free)* 4/1[2]

03-5 9 nk **Hollander**[15] 187 5-9-9 **67** ....(t) NicolaCurrie 4 59
(William Muir) *hld up: niggled along 1/2-way: rdn wl over 2f out: drvn and little imp over 1f out: nvr on terms (jockey said gelding was never travelling)* 9/1

60-0 10 8 **Ubla (IRE)**[8] 295 6-8-10 **61** ....(p) TobyEley(7) 6 32
(Gay Kelleway) *chsd ldr: rdn along 2f out: wknd and lost pl ins fnl f* 16/1

1m 26.47s (-0.73) **Going Correction** -0.075s/f (Stan) **10 Ran SP% 119.3**
Speed ratings (Par 101): **101,99,99,98,97 95,95,94,94,85**
CSF £190.63 CT £929.20 TOTE £10.40: £3.80, £4.50, £1.90; EX 173.20 Trifecta £2957.70.
Owner New Vision Bloodstock **Bred** Newsells Park Stud **Trained** Sproxton, Leics

FOCUS
A modest handicap and the early pace was not strong. They fanned across the centre of the track and plenty had a chance with 1f to run. The winner has been rated near his best.

431 EXTRA PLACES AT TOTESPORT.COM NOVICE STKS 6f (P)
5:45 (5:45) (Class 4) 3-Y-O+ £5,530 (£1,645; £822; £411) Stalls Centre

Form RPR

513- 1 **Nubough (IRE)**[92] 8592 3-8-12 84 ....(h) RichardKingscote 4 83
(Charles Hills) *racd in midfield: stdy prog 2f out: pushed along to go 2nd over 1f out: rdn fnl f to ld 110yds out and readily asserted* 2/7[1]

0-35 2 3 1/2 **Vrai (IRE)**[9] 274 3-8-7 66 ....(p1) JosephineGordon 1 67
(Kevin Ryan) *led: rdn along and strly pressed by wnr 1f out: hdd fnl 110yds and no ex* 6/1[2]

0-05 3 8 **Twpsyn (IRE)**[13] 229 3-8-12 68 .... EoinWalsh 5 46
(David Evans) *hld up in rr: rdn and outpcd over 2f out: styd on wl ins fnl f to snatch 3rd cl home: no ch w front pair (jockey said gelding was short for room shortly after the start)* 22/1

4 nk **Snooze Button (IRE)** 4-10-0 0 .... NicolaCurrie 3 49
(Jamie Osborne) *hld up and squeezed for room after 1f: rdn and outpcd 2f out: styd on ins fnl f to chal for remote 3rd: no ch w front pair* 10/1[3]

0-0 5 2 1/2 **Platinum Coast (USA)**[21] 78 3-8-7 0 .... HollieDoyle 2 32
(James Tate) *trckd ldr: rdn along and outpcd 2f out: wknd ins fnl f* 33/1

/0-6 6 1 1/4 **Haader (FR)**[7] 316 4-10-0 72 .... PaddyMathers 6 37
(Derek Shaw) *racd cl up in 4th: rdn along to chse ldr 2f out: lost pl and wknd fnl f* 20/1

/6 7 2 **Beyond The Fringe (IRE)**[14] 206 4-9-9 0 .... RossaRyan 7 26
(Phil McEntee) *chsd ldr racing keenly: rdn and outpcd 2f out: drvn and lost pl over 1f out: wknd fnl f (jockey said filly ran too free in the early stages)* 66/1

1m 12.68s (-1.02) **Going Correction** -0.075s/f (Stan)
WFA 3 from 4yo 16lb **7 Ran SP% 114.7**
Speed ratings (Par 105): **103,98,87,87,83 82,79**
CSF £2.33 TOTE £1.20: £1.10, £1.80; EX 2.90 Trifecta £10.40.
Owner Hamdan Al Maktoum **Bred** Shadwell Estate Company Limited **Trained** Lambourn, Berks

FOCUS
Little strength in depth and the well-supported winner did this with little fuss. The early gallop was modest. The second has been rated to her recent form.

432 IRISH LOTTO AT TOTESPORT.COM H'CAP 1m 6f (P)
6:15 (6:15) (Class 4) (0-85,86) 4-Y-O+ £6,986 (£2,079; £1,038; £519) Stalls Low

Form RPR

666- 1 **West Coast Flyer**[43] 9534 6-10-0 **86** .... StevieDonohoe 3 92
(David Simcock) *hld up in last: quick hdwy on outer to go 2nd 2f out: sn rdn to ld over 1f out and hung lft handed u.p: rdn out fnl f and a doing enough* 6/4[1]

000- 2 nk **Stamford Raffles**[176] 5684 6-9-11 **83** .... AdamKirby 4 88
(Jane Chapple-Hyam) *trckd ldr: rdn along and dropped to last 2f out: sn drvn and styd on wl ins fnl f: nt rch wnr* 6/1

414- 3 1 1/2 **Cry Wolf**[29] 9731 6-9-6 **78** ....(p) RossaRyan 2 82
(Alexandra Dunn) *trckd ldr: pushed along to ld 2f out: str pressed and hdd by wnr over 1f out: carried lft by wnr 1f out: no ex fnl f* 13/8[2]

45-3 4 3 1/4 **Ezanak (IRE)**[13] 231 6-9-2 **74** ....(b) LukeMorris 1 72
(Michael Appleby) *led at a stdy pce: effrt to qckn tempo 3f out: sn drvn and hdd 2f out: wknd fnl f* 9/2[3]

3m 4.3s (1.10) **Going Correction** -0.075s/f (Stan) **4 Ran SP% 110.6**
Speed ratings (Par 105): **93,92,91,90**
CSF £10.03 TOTE £2.10; EX 9.10 Trifecta £13.00.
Owner Ali Saeed **Bred** Miss K Rausing **Trained** Newmarket, Suffolk

■ Stewards' Enquiry : Stevie Donohoe three-day ban: interference & careless riding (Feb 11-13)

FOCUS
A fair handicap and the pace was not strong. It turned into something of a sprint. Muddling form, with the second the key.

433 BET IN PLAY AT TOTESPORT.COM H'CAP 5f (P)
6:45 (6:45) (Class 5) (0-75,77) 4-Y-O+
£5,433 (£1,617; £808; £404; £400; £400) Stalls Low

Form RPR

40-3 1 **Joegogo (IRE)**[23] 36 4-9-0 **75** .... SeamusCronin(7) 5 85
(David Evans) *mde all: rdn to maintain advantage over 1f out: styd on wl fnl f* 3/1[1]

400- 2 1 1/2 **Cappananty Con**[145] 6879 5-9-7 **75** .... RichardKingscote 2 80
(Charlie Wallis) *trckd wnr: drvn along to chse wnr over 1f out: kpt on wl fnl f* 6/1[3]

2-54 3 1/2 **Wiff Waff**[9] 278 4-9-5 **73** .... DanielMuscutt 8 76
(Stuart Williams) *hld up in last pair: swtchd to outer and rdn to chse wnr over 1f out: styd on wl fnl f: nt rch ldng pair* 6/1[3]

1-03 4 1 **It's All A Joke (IRE)**[7] 317 4-9-0 **75** ....(b) Pierre-LouisJamin(7) 4 75
(Archie Watson) *racd promly: rdn along over 2f out: drvn over 1f out: kpt on one pce fnl f* 3/1[1]

140- 5 1 1/4 **Top Boy**[81] 8892 9-9-9 **77** ....(v) PaddyMathers 7 72
(Derek Shaw) *hld up in last pair: rdn wl over 1f out: one pce fnl f: nvr on terms* 9/1

06-6 6 nk **Princely**[10] 253 4-9-6 **74** .... LukeMorris 3 68
(Michael Appleby) *trckd wnr: rdn along over 1f out: lost pl and wknd fr 1f out* 4/1[2]

/5-0 7 3 **Little Miss Daisy**[15] 179 5-8-8 **62** .... MartinDwyer 1 45
(William Muir) *chsd wnr on inner: rdn along and outpcd 2f out: wknd fnl f* 33/1

0-51 8 3/4 **Pearl Acclaim (IRE)**[16] 166 9-8-8 **65** ....(p) PhilDennis(3) 6 46
(David C Griffiths) *racd in midfield: c wdst of all into home st: rdn over 1f out: wknd fnl f (jockey said gelding hung right-handed throughout)* 20/1

59.33s (-0.87) **Going Correction** -0.075s/f (Stan) **8 Ran SP% 116.3**
Speed ratings (Par 103): **103,100,99,98,96 95,90,89**
CSF £21.97 CT £103.02 TOTE £3.50: £1.20, £2.30, £1.80; EX 18.00 Trifecta £138.90.
Owner Wayne Clifford **Bred** Barry Noonan And Denis Noonan **Trained** Pandy, Monmouths

FOCUS
Competitive for the grade and a fair sprint. The winner made all. The winner has been rated to his winter best.

434 DOUBLE DELIGHT HAT-TRICK HEAVEN AT TOTESPORT.COM H'CAP — 1m 2f (P)
7:15 (7:15) (Class 4) (0-80,79) 4-Y-0+ — **£5,175** (£1,540; £769; £384) **Stalls Low**

Form — RPR

-222 **1** **Dommersen (IRE)**[2] 390 6-9-2 **79**........................ BenSanderson(5) 5 — 86
(Roger Fell) *hld up: hdwy u.p on outer over 1f out: drvn and stdy on strly to ld clsng stages: jst got up* **4/1**[3]

25-6 **2** *nk* **Derek Duval (USA)**[15] 184 5-9-7 **79**....................(vt[1]) DanielMuscutt 4 — 85
(Stuart Williams) *trckd ldr: pushed along to cl on ldr 2f out: rdn to ld 1f out: kpt on but hdd by wnr fnl strides* **8/1**

421- **3** *1 1/4* **Involved**[47] 9482 4-9-1 **74**........................ RichardKingscote 3 — 79
(Daniel Kubler) *racd in midfield: rdn along and ev ch over 1f out: kpt on one pce ins fnl f* **6/1**

032- **4** *2* **Cuillin (USA)**[51] 9431 4-8-12 **71**........................ GeorgeWood 6 — 72
(James Fanshawe) *racd in midfield: effrt to cl on inner over 1f out: rdn and kpt on one pce ins fnl f* **6/1**

03-2 **5** *1 3/4* **Global Art**[16] 157 4-9-5 **78**........................(p) RobertHavlin 2 — 75
(Ed Dunlop) *chsd ldr: pushed along and upsides ldr 2f out: sn rdn over 1f out: one pce fnl f* **3/1**[2]

41-4 **6** *4* **Space Bandit**[24] 19 4-9-2 **75**........................ AlistairRawlinson 1 — 64
(Michael Appleby) *led: rdn and strly pressed over 1f out: hdd 1f out: wknd ins fnl f* **5/2**[1]

2m 5.92s (-2.68) **Going Correction** -0.075s/f (Stan)
WFA 4 from 5yo+ 1lb — **6 Ran SP% 113.3**
Speed ratings (Par 105): **107,106,105,104,102 99**
CSF £34.38 TOTE £4.80: £2.30, £3.50; EX 42.00 Trifecta £104.90.
Owner Middleham Park Racing X & Partner **Bred** The Lavington Stud **Trained** Nawton, N Yorks
■ Stewards' Enquiry : Robert Havlin caution: careless riding

FOCUS
Quite competitive for the grade and they came down the centre of the track. Fair form. The second has been rated to his recent best.

435 CELEBRATE JANUARY'S HERO TYLER HART NOVICE MEDIAN AUCTION STKS — 1m 2f (P)
7:45 (7:45) (Class 5) 4-5-Y-0 — **£4,948** (£1,472; £735; £367) **Stalls Low**

Form — RPR

1- **1** **Plait**[155] 6480 4-8-11 0........................ SaraDelFabbro(7) 3 — 90+
(Michael Bell) *led for 2f tl trckd new ldr: cruised bk into the ld 2f out: drew effrtlessly clr: wl in command fnl f: easily* **15/8**[1]

362- **2** *12* **White Turf (IRE)**[157] 6420 4-9-2 75........................ DavidProbert 9 — 64
(Andrew Balding) *trckd wnr bef ldng after 2f out: rdn and hdd by wnr 2f out: kpt on fnl f but no match for easy wnr* **11/4**[3]

0/-0 **3** *1* **Harbour Quay**[11] 242 5-9-3 0........................ KieranO'Neill 8 — 61
(Robyn Brisland) *chsd ldr: rdn and outpcd by wnr 2f out: kpt on one pce fnl f for remote 3rd* **12/1**

4 *1/2* **Ripplet**[25] 4-8-11 0........................ CharlieBennett 2 — 56
(Hughie Morrison) *racd in tch: rdn along and outpcd over 2f out: kpt on one pce: nvr on terms* **8/1**

644- **5** *2* **Echo Cove (IRE)**[36] 9664 4-9-2 66........................(b[1]) JFEgan 7 — 57
(Jane Chapple-Hyam) *racd in tch in midfield: rdn and outpcd 2f out: one pce fnl f* **2/1**[2]

0- **6** *3 1/2* **Zahraani**[27] 9766 4-9-2 0........................ DannyBrock 1 — 50
(J R Jenkins) *hld up: nvr able to get on terms* **50/1**

0-0 **7** *18* **Interrogation (FR)**[12] 239 4-8-13 0........................ TimClark(3) 6 — 14
(Alan Bailey) *a in rr: t.o 2f out* **66/1**

60- **8** *4* **Brecqhou Island**[68] 9152 4-9-2 0........................ DanielMuscutt 4
(Mark Pattinson) *racd in midfield: rdn and lost pl over 2f out: sn bhd* **28/1**

0- **9** *34* **Lord Digby**[71] 9097 4-9-2 0........................ PaddyMathers 5
(Adam West) *racd in midfield: rdn and lost pl 4f out: sn t.o* **50/1**

2m 6.26s (-2.34) **Going Correction** -0.075s/f (Stan)
WFA 4 from 5yo 1lb — **9 Ran SP% 122.4**
Speed ratings: **106,96,95,95,93 90,76,73,46**
CSF £7.91 TOTE £2.60: £1.20, £1.10, £4.10; EX 8.30 Trifecta £66.50.
Owner Mrs Michael Bell **Bred** Juddmonte Farms Ltd **Trained** Newmarket, Suffolk

FOCUS
A modest novice median auction event which the winner turned into a rout. The worth of the form is open to question.

436 BLACK NOTLEY H'CAP — 1m 2f (P)
8:15 (8:17) (Class 7) (0-50,50) 4-Y-0+ — **£2,911** (£866; £432; £216) **Stalls Low**

Form — RPR

04-3 **1** **Prerogative (IRE)**[14] 207 5-9-0 **48**........................(p) PoppyBridgwater(5) 3 — 54
(Tony Carroll) *trckd ldr: clsd gng wl 2f out: sn rdn and led over 1f out: rdn out and stdy on wl fnl f* **7/2**[2]

6-20 **2** *3/4* **Don't Do It (IRE)**[11] 245 4-9-6 **50**........................ LukeMorris 16 — 55
(Michael Appleby) *racd in tch in midfield: hdwy to go 3rd 2f out: sn rdn to chse wnr and ev ch over 1f out: kpt on wl and clsng all the way to the line: nt rch wnr* **12/1**

03-4 **3** *1 1/4* **Affluence (IRE)**[14] 207 4-9-6 **50**........................ AdamKirby 9 — 52
(Martin Smith) *racd in midfield: hdwy u.p 2f out: sn drvn and kpt on wl fnl f: nt rch ldng pair* **5/2**[1]

00-5 **4** *3* **Highwayman**[14] 210 6-9-6 **49**........................(h) JFEgan 7 — 45
(David Thompson) *hld up: effrt to cl 2f out: sn rdn and stdy on wl fnl f: no ch w front pair* **7/1**[3]

03-0 **5** *nse* **Rocket Ronnie (IRE)**[22] 59 9-9-2 **45**........................(p) HollieDoyle 1 — 40
(Adrian Wintle) *racd in midfield: rdn and outpcd 2f out: kpt on one pce fr 1f out: nvr on terms* **16/1**

61-0 **6** *2 1/2* **Ertidaad (IRE)**[16] 155 7-9-5 **48**........................(v) EoinWalsh 12 — 39
(Emma Owen) *trckd ldr early: rdn along over 2f out: one pce 1f out: plugged on* **33/1**

53-0 **7** *nk* **Mulsanne Chase**[22] 59 5-9-5 **48**........................(p) RossaRyan 14 — 38
(Conor Dore) *racd in midfield: rdn along over 1f out: plugged on one pce ins fnl f: nvr on terms* **20/1**

00-6 **8** *2 1/4* **Nicky Baby (IRE)**[16] 155 5-9-2 **45**........................(p) RobertHavlin 2 — 31
(Dean Ivory) *trckd ldrs early: rdn and no imp over 1f out: wknd ins fnl f* **20/1**

0-50 **9** *1/2* **Clive Clifton (IRE)**[14] 208 6-9-4 **47**........................ CharlieBennett 4 — 32
(Mark Brisbourne) *hld up: rdn and outpcd over 2f out: nvr on terms* **7/1**[3]

/6-0 **10** *1* **Solitary Sister (IRE)**[11] 245 5-9-2 **45**........................ NicolaCurrie 5 — 28
(John Berry) *racd in midfield: pushed along over 2f out: rdn over 1f out: nvr on terms* **25/1**

000- **11** *1 3/4* **Outlaw Torn (IRE)**[31] 9704 10-9-2 **45**........................ PhilipPrince 10 — 25
(Richard Guest) *chsd ldr early: pushed along to ld 3f out: drvn and hdd over 1f out: wknd ins fnl f* **33/1**

0-04 **12** *4 1/2* **Cold Fire (IRE)**[9] 273 6-9-4 **47**........................ KieranO'Neill 13 — 18
(Robyn Brisland) *hld up: niggled along over 4f out: rdn 2f out: nvr a factor* **14/1**

500- **13** *5* **Imperial Act**[112] 8001 4-9-3 **47**........................(h) DavidProbert 15 — 10
(Andrew Balding) *dwlt but sn rcvrd to r in midfield: rdn along 2f out: wknd over 1f out* **8/1**

000- **14** *2 1/2* **Velvet Voice**[60] 8537 5-9-2 **45**........................ MarcMonaghan 6 — 2
(Mark H Tompkins) *dwlt and a in rr* **22/1**

400- **15** *5* **Gannicus**[20] 9634 8-9-3 **46**........................(tp) ShaneKelly 11
(Brendan Powell) *hld up in rr of midfield: rdn and lost pl 3f out: sn bhd* **12/1**

000- **16** *25* **Understory (USA)**[94] 8537 12-9-2 **45**........................ MartinDwyer 8
(Tim McCarthy) *led: rdn and hdd 3f out: lost pl over 2f out: t.o* **66/1**

2m 7.37s (-1.23) **Going Correction** -0.075s/f (Stan)
WFA 4 from 5yo+ 1lb — **16 Ran SP% 139.9**
Speed ratings (Par 97): **101,100,99,97,96 94,94,92,92,91 90,86,82,80,76 56**
CSF £49.02 CT £135.34 TOTE £3.80: £1.40, £2.70, £1.30, £2.10; EX 60.90 Trifecta £270.90.
Owner Six Pack **Bred** Robin Moyles **Trained** Cropthorne, Worcs

FOCUS
A very low-grade handicap. The pace was fair and the winner was always to the fore. The third has been rated near the balance of his recent form since upped to 1m2f.
T/Plt: £206.90 to a £1 stake. Pool: £85,044.27 - 299.95 winning units T/Qpdt: £14.70 to a £1 stake. Pool: £12,791.18 - 641.96 winning units **Mark Grantham**

399 LINGFIELD (L-H)
Saturday, January 26

OFFICIAL GOING: Polytrack: standard
Wind: medium, half behind, increasing and light showers after race 3 Weather: overcast, light showers from race 3

437 LADBROKES HOME OF THE ODDS BOOST H'CAP — 7f 1y(P)
1:20 (1:20) (Class 6) (0-60,61) 3-Y-0 — **£3,105** (£924; £461; £300; £300; £300) **Stalls Low**

Form — RPR

03-5 **1** **Rajman**[21] 79 3-9-5 **58**........................(h) LukeMorris 9 — 64
(Tom Clover) *t.k.h: chsd ldrs: effrt and wd bnd 2f out: styd on to chal ins fnl f: sn drvn to ld: r.o wl* **5/1**[2]

00-1 **2** *1 1/2* **Lincoln Spirit**[8] 296 3-9-1 **54**........................ AdamKirby 4 — 56
(David O'Meara) *trckd ldrs on inner: effrt and nt clrest of runs 2f out: swtchd rt and effrt over 1f out: chsd ldr ent fnl f: sn chalng: chsd wnr and kpt on same pce wl ins fnl f* **6/1**[3]

00-0 **3** *1 1/4* **Nguni**[12] 235 3-9-6 **59**........................(t) RaulDaSilva 5 — 58
(Paul Cole) *w ldr tl led over 5f out: rdn over 1f out: sn drvn: hdd and outpcd ins fnl f* **16/1**

01-3 **4** *hd* **Rusper Dreams (IRE)**[13] 228 3-9-8 **61**........................ DougieCostello 13 — 59
(Jamie Osborne) *in tch in midfield on outer: effrt jst over 2f out: hdwy u.p ins fnl f: styd on but no threat to ldrs* **3/1**[1]

600- **5** *1/2* **Ample Plenty**[59] 9290 3-9-7 **60**........................ StevieDonohoe 8 — 57+
(David Simcock) *in tch in midfield: swtchd rt and bmpd rival over 2f out: effrt 2f out: styd on wl u.p ins fnl f: nt rch ldrs* **10/1**

26-3 **6** *nk* **Nananita (IRE)**[17] 137 3-8-13 **57**........................ MeganNicholls(5) 1 — 53+
(Mark Loughnane) *stdd and t.k.h early: grad reined bk and hld up in last quartet: swtchd rt and effrt over 1f out: styd on wl ins fnl f: nvr trbld ldrs* **5/1**[2]

000- **7** *nk* **Global Acclamation**[50] 9444 3-9-3 **56**........................(b[1]) RobertHavlin 14 — 51
(Ed Dunlop) *stdd leaving stalls and sn swtchd sharply lft: hld up in rr: effrt over 1f out: hdwy and drifting lft ent fnl f: stl shifting lft but kpt on wl ins fnl f: nvr trbld ldrs* **7/1**

040- **8** *nk* **Lysander Belle (IRE)**[59] 9289 3-9-6 **59**........................ DavidProbert 10 — 54
(Sophie Leech) *led tl over 5f out: pressed ldr tl unable qck w ldr over 1f out: 4th and btn jst ins fnl f: wknd fnl 100yds* **12/1**

40-0 **9** *1 1/4* **Quarto Cavallo**[17] 137 3-9-2 **55**........................ CharlieBennett 3 — 46
(Adam West) *s.i.s: sn rcvrd and in tch in midfield: effrt over 1f out: unable qck: wl hld and kpt on same pce ins fnl f* **25/1**

00-0 **10** *3* **Jasmine B (IRE)**[16] 155 3-8-2 **46** oh1........................ DarraghKeenan(5) 6 — 30
(John Ryan) *in tch in midfield: rdn and unable qck over 1f out: sn outpcd and wknd ins fnl f* **40/1**

000- **11** *3/4* **Hurricane Speed (IRE)**[219] 4044 3-8-7 **46** oh1........................(p[1]) FrannyNorton 2 — 28
(Kevin Ryan) *s.i.s: rousted along and sn rcvrd to r in tch in midfield: lost pl u.p over 1f out: wknd fnl f* **8/1**

000- **12** *1/2* **Dancing Jaquetta (IRE)**[36] 9671 3-8-11 **50**........................ LiamJones 12 — 30
(Mark Loughnane) *hld up in rr: swtchd lft after 1f out: effrt on inner over 1f out: no prog and nvr involved* **33/1**

00-0 **13** *3/4* **Magnetic (IRE)**[17] 141 3-9-4 **57**........................ LiamKeniry 11 — 35
(J S Moore) *midfield on outer: bmpd over 2f out: wd and dropped to rr bnd 2f out: n.d* **66/1**

1m 25.04s (0.24) **Going Correction** -0.10s/f (Stan) — **13 Ran SP% 129.6**
Speed ratings (Par 95): **94,92,90,90,90 89,89,89,87,84 83,82,81**
CSF £37.52 CT £472.57 TOTE £6.00: £2.10, £2.40, £5.80; EX 29.00 Trifecta £591.20.
Owner R S Matharu **Bred** Highclere Stud & Jake Warren Ltd **Trained** Newmarket, Suffolk
■ Stewards' Enquiry : Stevie Donohoe two-day ban: used whip above the permitted level (Feb 9-10)

FOCUS
A very ordinary handicap, and messy form.

438 FOLLOW TOP TIPSTERS AT SUN RACING MAIDEN STKS — 7f 1y(P)
1:55 (1:55) (Class 5) 3-Y-0+ — **£3,752** (£1,116; £557; £278) **Stalls Low**

Form — RPR

1 **Moongazer** 3-8-5 0........................ JoeFanning 5 — 65
(Charles Hills) *trckd ldng pair: switching out rt ent fnl 2f: qcknd between rivals to chal ent fnl f: sustained duel w rival fnl f: r.o wl to ld cl home* **5/4**[1]

0- **2** *1/2* **Shake Me Handy**[29] 9732 4-9-7 0........................ SeamusCronin(7) 7 — 74
(Roger Teal) *s.i.s: hld up in tch in last pair: clsd over 2f out: qcknd through on inner to ld ent fnl f: sn clr w wnr and sustained duel ins fnl f: hdd and no ex cl home* **11/1**

40- **3** *5* **Haze**[73] 9050 3-8-5 0........................ RaulDaSilva 6 — 51
(Paul Cole) *in tch in midfield: shkn up over 2f out: outpcd and btn over 1f out: no ch w ldng pair but plugged on to go 3rd ins fnl f* **10/3**[3]

4 1 1/4 **Thedevilinneville** 3-8-10 0.. CharlieBennett 4 52
(Adam West) *s.i.s: detached in last: pushed along and rn green early: clsd on to rr of field: t.k.h over 4f out: rdn and outpcd 2f out: no ch w ldrs but plugged on ins fnl f to snatch 4th last strides* **12/1**

05- 5 *hd* **Haitian Spirit**[38] 9603 3-8-5 0.. HollieDoyle 1 47
(Gary Moore) *taken down early: led: rdn and hdd ent fnl f: sn btn and wknd ins fnl f* **3/1[2]**

00- 6 1 1/2 **Beg For Mercy**[26] 9771 3-8-10 0.. RobertHavlin 3 48
(Michael Attwater) *t.k.h: chsd ldr: rdn and ev ch ent fnl 2f: hung rt bnd 2f out: outpcd over 1f out: sn btn and wknd ins fnl f* **33/1**

1m 23.81s (-0.99) **Going Correction** -0.10s/f (Stan)
WFA 3 from 4yo 18lb 6 Ran SP% **111.5**
Speed ratings (Par 103): **101,100,94,93,93 91**
CSF £16.08 TOTE £2.00: £1.30, £4.50; EX 11.00 Trifecta £51.30.
Owner Mrs Mary-Anne Parker **Bred** Charley Knoll Partnership **Trained** Lambourn, Berks

FOCUS
This looked weak on paper - the second favourite, Haitian Spirit, having run to an RPR of just 60 in defeat here prior to Christmas. The first two pulled well clear.

439 BETWAY CASINO H'CAP 6f 1y(P)
2:30 (2:30) (Class 6) (0-65,66) 4-Y-O+
£3,105 (£924; £461; £300; £300; £300) **Stalls** Low

Form RPR

4-61 1 **Aguerooo (IRE)**[7] 314 6-9-8 **66**..(tp) FrannyNorton 3 74
(Charlie Wallis) *hld up off the pce in last quartet: clsd and swtchd lft over 1f out: r.o u.p to ld wl ins fnl f: r.o and a jst doing enough after* **7/2[1]**

001- 2 *nk* **Pushkin Museum (IRE)**[63] 9250 8-9-4 **62**.. AdamKirby 6 69
(Paul D'Arcy) *hld up in midfield: effrt and clsd over 1f out: hdwy u.p 1f out: led 100yds out: sn hdd: kpt on wl but a hld after* **7/2[1]**

45-0 3 3/4 **Dark Magic**[17] 138 5-8-8 **59**..(v) SophieRalston(7) 2 64
(Dean Ivory) *off the pce in rr: nt clr run briefly bnd wl over 1f out: clsd on inner over 1f out: swtchd rt and kpt on wl ins fnl f (jockey said gelding was denied a clear run rounding the home bend)* **11/2[3]**

20-4 4 *nk* **Majorette**[17] 144 5-9-2 **63**.. FinleyMarsh(3) 1 67
(Brian Barr) *broke wl: sn restrained and off the pce in midfield: clsd over 1f out: styd on and ev ch u.p briefly 100yds out: no ex and one pce towards fin* **17/2**

00-0 5 1 3/4 **Flirtare (IRE)**[17] 144 4-9-3 **61**..(v[1]) RobertHavlin 4 60
(Amanda Perrett) *chsd clr ldng pair: clsd to chse ldr wl over 1f out: sn upsides tl led 1f out: drvn ins fnl f: hdd 100yds out: no ex and wknd towards fin* **11/2[3]**

060- 6 3/4 **Lord Cooper**[75] 9034 5-8-13 **57**.. BarryMcHugh 7 53
(Marjorie Fife) *hld up off the pce in last trio: effrt over 1f out: hdwy u.p ins fnl f: nvr getting to ldrs* **4/1[2]**

00-0 7 1 1/4 **Tavener**[24] 31 7-9-4 **65**..(p) PhilDennis(3) 9 58+
(David C Griffiths) *led and sn clr w rival: rdn over 1f out: hdd 1f out: no ex and wknd ins fnl f* **16/1**

162- 8 7 **Midnight Guest (IRE)**[66] 9178 4-9-0 **65**.. GinaMangan(7) 10 37
(David Evans) *off the pce in midfield: rdn and no hdwy over 1f out: nvr involved and wknd fnl f* **16/1**

0/4- 9 3/4 **Nelson's Hill**[379] 184 9-8-2 **49** ow3.. AaronJones(3) 8 18
(William de Best-Turner) *chsd ldng trio but nt on terms w ldrs: rdn: no imp and edgd lft over 1f out: wknd fnl f* **100/1**

350- 10 1 **Aaliya**[114] 7946 4-9-5 **63**.. GeorgeWood 5 29
(Amy Murphy) *s.i.s and flashed tail leaving stalls: a in rr: nvr involved* **28/1**

61-4 11 1 **Impart**[15] 179 5-9-6 **64**..(v) LiamJones 11 27+
(Laura Mongan) *sn w ldr and dashed clr w ldr: lost 2nd and hung rt bnd wl over 1f out: sn dropped out and wknd fnl f* **16/1**

1m 10.61s (-1.29) **Going Correction** -0.10s/f (Stan) 11 Ran SP% **127.8**
Speed ratings (Par 101): **104,103,102,102,99 98,97,87,86,85 84**
CSF £17.25 CT £70.92 TOTE £3.90: £1.50, £1.50, £1.90; EX 18.90 Trifecta £111.50.
Owner P E Axon **Bred** Cooneen Stud **Trained** Ardleigh, Essex

FOCUS
A typically competitive race of its' nature. It was run at a scorching early pace and was set up perfectly for the closers. Solid form for the grade.

440 BETWAY LIVE CASINO H'CAP 1m 4f (P)
3:05 (3:05) (Class 3) (0-95,92) 4-Y-O+ **£7,246** (£2,168; £1,084; £542) **Stalls** Low

Form RPR

11-1 1 **Fearsome**[5] 345 5-9-1 **86** 6ex.. JoshuaBryan(3) 3 93+
(Nick Littmoden) *stdd s: hld up off the pce in 3rd: clsd 1/2-way: effrt and shifting out rt 2f out: pushed into ld ins fnl f: r.o wl: eased towards fin: comf* **1/1[1]**

22-1 2 1 **Three Weeks (USA)**[16] 164 4-9-7 **92**.. DanielTudhope 2 96
(David O'Meara) *chsd ldr: pushed along and clsd to press ldr 2f out: rdn to ld over 1f out: hdd and kpt on same pce ins fnl f* **5/2[2]**

0-65 3 3/4 **Battle Of Marathon (USA)**[12] 240 7-8-12 **85**.. DarraghKeenan(5) 1 87
(John Ryan) *stdd s: hld up off the pce in rr: clsd and in tch 1/2-way: effrt whn nt clr run and swtchd rt over 1f out: kpt on ins fnl f* **25/1[3]**

346- 4 2 1/2 **Come On Come On (IRE)**[119] 7769 5-9-2 **84**..(b[1]) AdamKirby 4 82
(Clive Cox) *sn led: stdd gallop 1/2-way: rdn and qcknd 3f out: sn drvn: hdd over 1f out: sn btn and wknd ins fnl f* **5/2[2]**

2m 30.48s (-2.52) **Going Correction** -0.10s/f (Stan)
WFA 4 from 5yo+ 3lb 4 Ran SP% **111.0**
Speed ratings (Par 107): **104,103,102,101**
CSF £3.96 TOTE £1.60; EX 3.30 Trifecta £10.90.
Owner G F Chesneaux & Nick Littmoden **Bred** Newhall Estate Farm **Trained** Newmarket, Suffolk

FOCUS
A good quality handicap, despite the small field. The second has been rated to form for now.

441 SUN RACING NO1 RACING SITE H'CAP 1m 1y(P)
3:40 (3:40) (Class 3) (0-95,94) 4-Y-O+ **£7,246** (£2,168; £1,084; £542; £270) **Stalls** High

Form RPR

00-0 1 **Mr Scaramanga**[15] 176 5-8-7 **87**.. LeviWilliams(7) 7 95
(Simon Dow) *chsd ldrs: pressing ldrs whn carried rt bnd 2f out: hdwy to ld and edgd lft 1f out: stl edging sltly lft: pushed along and hld on wl ins fnl f* **20/1**

366- 2 *hd* **Insurgence**[96] 8472 4-9-0 **87**.. DanielMuscutt 1 94
(James Fanshawe) *hld up wl in tch in last quartet: gap opened and hdwy on inner over 1f out: ev ch 1f out: edgd rt and kpt on wl ins fnl f: jst hld towards fin* **13/2[2]**

00-3 3 1/2 **Ballard Down (IRE)**[14] 212 6-9-7 **94**.. DanielTudhope 10 100
(David O'Meara) *stdd s: t.k.h: hld up in tch in rr: hdwy to chse ldrs whn nt clr run and switching rt ent fnl f: swtchd bk lft and chsd ldrs jst ins fnl f: kpt on same pce towards fin* **8/1[3]**

32-3 4 1 **Chevallier**[14] 205 7-9-6 **93**..(p) LukeMorris 4 97
(Archie Watson) *broke wl: grad restrained and wl in tch in midfield: nt clr run over 2f out: chsng ldrs whn sltly impeded 1f out: sn swtchd rt: kpt on u.p fnl 100yds: nt rch ldrs* **8/1[3]**

06-3 5 *nk* **Al Jellaby**[22] 56 4-9-2 **89**.. AdamKirby 8 95+
(Clive Cox) *dwlt and pushed along leaving stalls: rcvrd to chse ldr after 2f: drvn to ld ent fnl 2f: sn hdd but stl ev ch whn edgd lft u.p 1f out: keeping on same pce whn squeezed for room towards fin* **7/4[1]**

V50- 6 3/4 **Sea Fox (IRE)**[45] 9508 5-8-9 **89**.. GinaMangan(7) 11 91
(David Evans) *sn led: hdd ent fnl 2f: sn led again and rdn over 1f out: hdd 1f out: no ex and wknd wl ins fnl f* **25/1**

24-4 7 2 **Isomer (USA)**[14] 205 5-8-11 **87**..(h) JoshuaBryan(3) 3 84
(Andrew Balding) *hld up in tch in last pair: effrt over 1f out: kpt on same pce u.p ins fnl f: nvr trbld ldrs* **10/1**

120- 8 2 1/4 **Key Player**[245] 3095 4-8-13 **86**.. EdwardGreatrex 5 78
(Eve Johnson Houghton) *sn chsng ldrs and t.k.h: effrt over 1f out: struggling to qckn whn nt clr run and hmpd 1f out: no threat to ldrs after and eased wl ins fnl f (jockey said gelding hung right-handed throughout)* **10/1**

5-25 9 *hd* **My Target (IRE)**[14] 205 8-8-13 **86**..(p[1]) FrannyNorton 2 77
(Michael Wigham) *in tch in midfield: rdn and struggling to qckn 2f out: lost pl and bhd ins fnl f* **17/2**

V3-1 10 1 1/2 **Florencio**[10] 260 6-8-13 **86**..(p) DougieCostello 6 74
(Jamie Osborne) *hld up in tch in last trio: effrt over 2f out: no prog and bhd ins fnl f* **8/1[3]**

1m 35.29s (-2.91) **Going Correction** -0.10s/f (Stan) 10 Ran SP% **120.3**
Speed ratings (Par 107): **110,109,109,108,108 107,105,103,102,101**
CSF £148.99 CT £1173.89 TOTE £35.80: £7.20, £2.20, £3.40; EX 123.20 Trifecta £2487.30.
Owner Robert Moss **Bred** Lordship Stud **Trained** Epsom, Surrey
■ Stewards' Enquiry : Levi Williams three-day ban: interference & careless riding (tba)

FOCUS
There weren't too many of these at the peak of their powers coming into this and it's probably wise to treat the form with some suspicion. The winner has been rated to his best since early last year.

442 LADBROKES NOVICE AUCTION STKS 1m 1y(P)
4:15 (4:15) (Class 6) 3-Y-O **£3,105** (£924; £461; £230) **Stalls** High

Form RPR

46- 1 **Gold Bere (FR)**[153] 6579 3-8-13.. LiamKeniry 3 73+
(George Baker) *impeded leaving stalls: sn rcvrd and trckd ldrs: effrt to press ldrs wl over 1f out: rdn to ld 1f out: hrd pressed and edgd lft u.p ins fnl f: bumping w runner-up towards fin: hld on* **9/4[1]**

5-6 2 *shd* **Holy Kingdom (IRE)**[16] 156 3-9-2 0.. LukeMorris 2 75
(Tom Clover) *chsd ldrs: effrt on inner over 1f out: drvn and ev ch ins fnl f: edging sltly rt and bmpd wl ins fnl f: jst hld towards fin* **5/2[2]**

04-0 3 2 3/4 **Altar Boy**[21] 90 3-8-12 69.. GaryMahon(3) 7 68
(Sylvester Kirk) *sn led: hdd over 4f out but styd pressing ldr: rdn to ld again over 1f out: hdd 1f out: no ex and wknd ins fnl f* **7/1**

223- 4 *nk* **Aleeka (USA)**[26] 9770 3-8-6 67.. DavidProbert 9 58
(David O'Meara) *in tch in midfield: effrt 2f out: kpt on u.p ins fnl f* **11/1**

3- 5 3/4 **Lethal Lover**[50] 9443 3-8-11 0.. HectorCrouch 10 62
(Clive Cox) *t.k.h: chsd ldrs on outer: wd bnd 2f out: sn u.p and no imp: kpt on same pce ins fnl f* **6/1[3]**

6 6 **Newton Kyme (IRE)** 3-8-12 0.. StevieDonohoe 1 49
(David Simcock) *s.i.s: sn rcvrd and in tch in midfield: rdn and outpcd 2f out: sn btn and wknd ins fnl f* **20/1**

7 1/2 **Chutzpah (IRE)**[106] 8168 3-8-8 61.. AaronJones(3) 6 47
(Mark Hoad) *hld up in rr: pushed along over 2f out: sn outpcd and no threat to ldrs after* **66/1**

8 2 3/4 **Copper Rose (IRE)** 3-8-10 0.. JoeFanning 4 39
(Mark Johnston) *hdwy to press ldr after 1f: led on inner over 4f out: hdd and hung lft over 1f out: sn btn and wknd fnl f* **7/1**

9 1/2 **Watch And Learn** 3-8-5 0.. MartinDwyer 5 33
(Andrew Balding) *v.s.a: rn green in rr: nvr on terms* **16/1**

10 *nse* **Newsflash** 3-8-2 0.. DarraghKeenan(5) 8 35
(Amy Murphy) *dropped to last trio and pushed along over 4f out: rdn over 2f out: sn outpcd and btn* **33/1**

1m 38.13s (-0.07) **Going Correction** -0.10s/f (Stan) 10 Ran SP% **122.0**
Speed ratings (Par 95): **96,95,93,92,92 86,85,82,82,82**
CSF £8.34 TOTE £2.80: £1.10, £1.40, £2.70; EX 9.60 Trifecta £46.70.
Owner P Bowden **Bred** S N C Regnier **Trained** Chiddingfold, Surrey
■ Stewards' Enquiry : Liam Keniry two-day ban: interference & careless riding (Feb 9-10)

FOCUS
This lacked depth and didn't take much winning. The winner has been rated in keeping with his debut, while the third and fourth offer some perspective.
T/Plt: £283.60 to a £1 stake. Pool: £61,301.30 - 157.75 winning units T/Qpdt: £37.50 to a £1 stake. Pool: £5,426.74 - 107.06 winning units **Steve Payne**

443 - (Foreign Racing) - See Raceform Interactive

GULFSTREAM PARK (L-H)
Saturday, January 26

OFFICIAL GOING: Dirt: sloppy (sealed); turf: yielding

444a PEGASUS WORLD CUP TURF INVITATIONAL STKS (GRADE 1) (3YO+) (TURF) 1m 1f 110y(T)
9:51 3-Y-O+
£2,091,535 (£627,460; £453,166; £383,444; £348,588; £275,590)

RPR

1 **Bricks And Mortar (USA)**[35] 5-8-12 0.. IradOrtizJr 7 119+
(Chad C Brown, U.S.A) *midfield: stdy hdwy fr 2 1/2f out: rdn 2f out: chsd ldrs whn drvn over 1f out: led 150yds: kpt on strly and drew clr* **14/5[2]**

2 2 1/2 **Magic Wand (IRE)**[84] 8844 4-8-0 0.. WayneLordan 1 104+
(A P O'Brien, Ire) *in tch: dropped to midfield 3f out: rdn and styd on fr over 2f out: drvn to take 2nd 50yds out: no ch w wnr* **94/10**

3 *nk* **Delta Prince (USA)**[85] 6-8-12 0.. FrankieDettori 8 113
(James Jerkens, U.S.A) *hld up towards rr: hdwy into midfield 1/2-way: trckd ldrs 2 1/2f out: wnt 2nd 2f out: rdn under 2f out: led 1 1/2f out: drvn fnl f: hdd 150yds out: no ex last 75yds: lost 2nd 50yds out* **93/10**

4 1 3/4 **Catapult (USA)**[84] 8846 6-8-12 0.. JoelRosario 9 109
(John W Sadler, U.S.A) *towards rr of midfield: forward move to ld 1/2-way: rdn 2f out: hdd 1 1/2f out: wknd steadily fnl f* **67/10[3]**

5 2 **Channel Maker (CAN)**[84] 8848 5-8-5 0..(b) JavierCastellano 3 98
(William Mott, U.S.A) *hld up towards rr: stdy hdwy on outer fr 3 1/2f out: rdn and kpt on same pce fr 2f out* **15/2**

6 *hd* **Yoshida (JPN)**[84] 8849 5-8-12 0........................ JoseLOrtiz 2 105
(William Mott, U.S.A) *hld up in rr: rdn and kpt on wl fr over 2f out: nvr in contention* **2/1**[1]

7 *5 1/4* **Next Shares (USA)**[21] 6-8-12 0........................(b) TylerGaffalione 5 94
(Amy Dollase, U.S.A) *racd keenly in midfield: dropped towards rr 3f out: rdn and effrt under 2f out: no ex fnl f* **173/10**

8 *nse* **Dubby Dubbie (USA)**[64] 4-8-12 0........................(b) LucaPanici 10 96
(Robert B Hess Jr, U.S.A) *trckd ldrs: rdn to chse ldr over 3f out: lost pl 2f out: sn btn* **119/1**

9 *10* **Aerolithe (JPN)**[69] 9139 5-8-0 0........................ FlorentGeroux 4 62
(Takanori Kikuzawa, Japan) *chsd ldr: dropped to 4th 4f out: lost pl 3f out: sn wl btn* **9/1**

10 *11 1/2* **Fahan Mura (USA)**[28] 5-8-7 0........................(b) EdwinAMaldonado 6 45
(Vladimir Cerin, U.S.A) *led: hdd 1/2-way: lost pl under 3f out: sn wl btn* **43/1**

1m 54.59s
WFA 4 from 5yo+ 1lb **10** Ran SP% **122.3**
PARI-MUTUEL (all including 2 unit stake): WIN 7.60; PLACE (1-2) 4.20, 9.00; SHOW (1-2-3) 3.20, 6.40, 6.60; SF 60.40.
Owner Klaravich Stables Inc & William H Lawrence **Bred** George Strawbridge Jr **Trained** USA

FOCUS
A new race, replacing the Gulfstream Park Turf Handicap. It rained for much of the day, so yielding going on the outer turf track. This wasn't a bad field for an inaugural running.

445a PEGASUS WORLD CUP INVITATIONAL STKS (GRADE 1) (3YO+) (MAIN TRACK) (DIRT) 1m 1f (D)
10:36 3-Y-O+
£3,149,606 (£984,251; £708,661; £551,181; £433,070; £196,850)

RPR

1 **City Of Light (USA)**[84] 8843 5-8-12 0........................ JavierCastellano 3 125+
(Michael McCarthy, U.S.A) *chsd ldr: led under 4f out: rdn 2f out: drew wl clr fr 1 1/2f out: pushed out* **19/10**[2]

2 *5 3/4* **Seeking The Soul (USA)**[64] 9240 6-8-12 0........................ JohnRVelazquez 4 113
(Dallas Stewart, U.S.A) *hld up towards rr: rdn and styd on fr 2f out: wnt 2nd 150yds out: no ch w clr wnr* **34/1**

3 *1 1/2* **Accelerate (USA)**[84] 8849 6-8-12 0........................(b) JoelRosario 5 110
(John W Sadler, U.S.A) *trckd ldrs: pushed along to chse ldr 3f out: rdn under 2f out: lft bhd by clr wnr fr 1 1/2f out: no ex fnl f: lost 2nd 150yds out* **6/4**[1]

4 *4 3/4* **Bravazo (USA)**[64] 9240 4-8-12 0........................ LuisSaez 1 101
(D Wayne Lukas, U.S.A) *in tch: rdn 3 1/2f out: outpcd over 2f out: drvn and kpt on fr 1 1/2f out: no ex fnl f* **101/10**

5 *nk* **Audible (USA)**[42] 4-8-12 0........................ FlavienPrat 10 100
(Todd Pletcher, U.S.A) *towards rr: rdn and hdwy fr 2f out: wknd fnl f* **91/10**[3]

6 *3/4* **Gunnevera (USA)**[84] 8849 5-8-12 0........................(b) IradOrtizJr 8 98
(Antonio Sano, U.S.A) *dwlt: towards rr of midfield: rdn and plugged on fr 2 1/2f out* **19/2**

7 *12 1/4* **True Timber (USA)**[56] 9362 5-8-12 0........................ JoeBravo 7 72
(Kiaran McLaughlin, U.S.A) *midfield on outer: rdn 3f out: wknd under 2f out* **74/1**

8 *3/4* **Imperative (USA)**[50] 9-8-12 0........................(b) TylerGaffalione 11 70
(Anthony T Quartarolo, U.S.A) *a towards rr* **196/1**

9 *1 1/4* **Tom's D'Etat (USA)**[35] 6-8-12 0........................(b) ShaunBridgmohan 6 68
(Albert M Stall Jr, U.S.A) *trckd ldrs: rdn over 3f out: wknd and wl btn over 2f out* **195/10**

10 *1* **Something Awesome (CAN)**[71] 8-8-12 0........................(b) EdgarSPrado 2 66
(Jose Corrales, U.S.A) *in tch in midfield: rdn and briefly wnt 3rd 2f out: wknd qckly 1 1/2f out* **89/1**

11 *3 3/4* **Kukulkan (MEX)**[49] 4-8-12 0........................ FrankieDettori 9 59
(Fausto Gutierrez, Mexico) *a towards rr: struggling fr over 2f out* **269/10**

12 *15 1/4* **Patternrecognition (USA)**[56] 9362 6-8-12 0........................ JoseLOrtiz 12 26
(Chad C Brown, U.S.A) *led: hdd under 4f out: lost pl qckly over 3f out: t.o* **202/10**

1m 47.71s (-1.46)
WFA 4 from 5yo+ 1lb **12** Ran SP% **121.9**
PARI-MUTUEL (all including 2 unit stake): WIN 5.80; PLACE (1-2) 4.20, 19.20; SHOW (1-2-3) 3.00, 8.20, 2.80; SF 82.20.
Owner Mr & Mrs William K Warren Jr **Bred** Ann Marie Farm **Trained** USA

FOCUS
A reduced purse this time, with the owners putting up $500,000 instead of $1M in the first two years, but still a hugely valuable race, and another good field with two last-time-out Breeders' Cup winners heading the betting. It was run in near darkness and in driving rain over a sloppy track, and the winner was awesome. The second has been rated to his best.

446a-456a (Foreign Racing) - See Raceform Interactive

341 WOLVERHAMPTON (A.W) (L-H)
Monday, January 28

OFFICIAL GOING: Tapeta: standard
Wind: negligible Weather: mainly clear skies, cold

457 BETWAY CASINO AMATEUR RIDERS' H'CAP 1m 5f 219y (Tp)
4:50 (4:50) (Class 5) (0-70,72) 4-Y-O+
£3,618 (£1,122; £560; £400; £400; £400) **Stalls** Low

Form RPR

35-1 1 **French Mix (USA)**[3] 404 5-10-11 **72** 6ex........... MissHannahWelch(5) 9 81
(Alexandra Dunn) *led: hdd after 1f: trckd ldrs: pushed along in 1/2 l 2nd 2f out: reminders and led 1f out: rdr dropped whip: pushed clr fnl f: comf (vet reported the mare had been struck into on its left hind)* **5/2**[1]

340- 2 *3 1/4* **Party Royal**[54] 9409 9-10-3 **59**........................(p) MrDavidDunsdon 7 63
(Nick Gifford) *trckd ldr: led after 1f: set modest gallop: disp ld as pce qcknd over 4f out: pushed along in 1/2 l 2f out: hdd 1f out: sn rdn: no ex* **12/1**

020- 3 *3* **Punkawallah**[82] 8936 5-10-7 **70**........................(p) MrTambyWelch(7) 3 70
(Alexandra Dunn) *hld up: plenty to do 3f out: reminders over 2f out: sn rdn: hdwy over 1f out: styd on into 3rd fnl f* **12/1**

40-2 4 *nk* **Rare (IRE)**[12] 262 4-10-6 **66**........................ MrSimonWalker 1 67
(Archie Watson) *trckd ldrs: pushed along in 4th 2f out: sn drvn: rdn in 3rd 1f out: wknd fnl f* **4/1**[3]

606/ 5 *4 1/2* **Uncle Bernie (IRE)**[582] 4120 9-10-7 **70**..............(p) MrSeanHawkins(7) 8 63
(Sarah Hollinshead) *in rr: hdwy to chse ldrs 4f out: drvn and effrt on outer 2f out: racd wd 1 1/2f out: no ex fr over 1f out* **66/1**

12/0 6 *3/4* **Rainbow Lad (IRE)**[22] 100 6-10-2 **58**........... MissSerenaBrotherton 10 50
(Michael Appleby) *mid-div: pushed along and lost pl 2f out: rdn ent fnl f: one pce* **20/1**

0-50 7 *1 3/4* **Agent Gibbs**[13] 246 7-10-12 **68**........................ MissBrodieHampson 11 58
(John O'Shea) *hld up: hdwy over 5f out: disp ld over 4f out: rdn and lost pl over 2f out: grad wknd* **12/1**

05-1 8 *1 1/2* **Belabour**[22] 100 6-10-8 **64**........................ MissBeckyBrisbourne 4 51
(Mark Brisbourne) *hld up: pushed along 2f out: no imp (jockey said gelding ran too freely and was unsuited by the slow early pace)* **3/1**[2]

31-4 9 *2 1/4* **Yasir (USA)**[21] 119 11-9-13 **55**........................ MissBeckySmith 2 39
(Sophie Leech) *hld up: drvn 2f out: reminder over 1f out: no imp* **15/2**

200- P **Diamonds A Dancing**[164] 6225 9-10-6 **69**.......(h) MissMeganJordan(7) 5
(Laura Morgan) *hld up: in rr and lost tch over 3f out: wl bhd whn p.u over 1f out: lame (vet reported the gelding finished lame on its right fore)* **25/1**

3m 12.21s (11.21) **Going Correction** -0.10s/f (Stan)
WFA 4 from 5yo+ 4lb **10** Ran SP% **118.5**
Speed ratings (Par 103): **64,62,60,60,57 57,56,55,54,**
CSF £33.92 CT £311.18 TOTE £3.30: £1.20, £3.30, £3.80; EX 28.60 Trifecta £349.10.
Owner Mrs G Welch **Bred** Calumet Farm **Trained** West Buckland, Somerset

FOCUS
A steadily run handicap which suited those ridden prominently. Muddling form. The second has been rated to last year's C&D run.

458 LADBROKES HOME OF THE ODDS BOOST CLAIMING STKS 6f 20y (Tp)
5:25 (5:25) (Class 6) 3-Y-O
£3,105 (£924; £461; £400; £400; £400) **Stalls** Low

Form RPR

643- 1 **Slowmo (IRE)**[62] 9276 3-9-3 70........................ RichardKingscote 2 70+
(Tom Dascombe) *mde all: pushed along in 1 1/2 l ld 2f out: reminder in 3 l ld 1f out: pushed out fnl f: readily* **1/1**[1]

00-5 2 *2 1/4* **Sybil Grand**[18] 161 3-8-3 50 ow3........................(b) NicolaCurrie 1 49
(Jamie Osborne) *chsd ldrs: drvn in 3rd 2f out: rdn over 1f out: r.o into 2nd fnl f: nvr nr wnr* **14/1**

32-2 3 *3* **Secret Ace**[19] 141 3-9-2 70........................ EdwardGreatrex 4 53
(Archie Watson) *prom: drvn in 1 1/2 l 2nd 2f out: rdn over 1f out: no ex and lost 2nd fnl f (jockey said filly hung left-handed in the home straight)* **11/4**[2]

4-00 4 *nk* **Dotty Grand**[3] 402 3-8-0 49........................(b[1]) HollieDoyle 3 36
(Jamie Osborne) *hld up: pushed along in 5th 2f out: sn drvn: rdn over 1f out: kpt on into 4th fnl f* **66/1**

106- 5 *1 1/2* **Islay Mist**[96] 8532 3-8-3 61........................(t) GraceMcEntee(7) 6 42
(Amy Murphy) *hld up: pushed along 2f out: rdn and racd wd over 1f out: no imp* **28/1**

54-4 5 *dht* **London Rock (IRE)**[19] 142 3-9-0 70........................ SeamusCronin(7) 7 53
(Richard Hannon) *chsd ldrs on outer: drvn in 4th 2f out: rdn 1 1/2f out: wknd fnl f* **4/1**[3]

005- 7 *1 1/2* **Haggswood Boy**[30] 9745 3-8-2 28........................(b[1]) WilliamCox(3) 8 32
(Ronald Thompson) *slowly away: bhd: drvn in rr and hit rail over 2f out: nvr a factor (jockey said gelding was never travelling)* **150/1**

1m 13.7s (-0.80) **Going Correction** -0.10s/f (Stan) **7** Ran SP% **108.9**
Speed ratings (Par 95): **101,98,94,93,91 91,89**
CSF £15.21 TOTE £1.60: £1.02, £8.40; EX 12.30 Trifecta £29.20.Slowmo was claimed by Mr Antony Brittain for £10,000. Sybil Grand was claimed by Miss Katy Jane Price for £4,000
Owner Chasemore Farm LLP & Owen Promotions Ltd **Bred** Tally-Ho Stud **Trained** Malpas, Cheshire

FOCUS
A strongly run claimer. The second and seventh highlight the potential limitations of the form.

459 LADBROKES FILLIES' H'CAP 1m 1f 104y (Tp)
5:55 (5:55) (Class 5) (0-75,74) 4-Y-O+
£3,752 (£1,116; £557; £400; £400; £400) **Stalls** Low

Form RPR

33-1 1 **Cloudlam**[26] 18 4-9-5 **70**........................(b) RichardKingscote 4 79
(William Haggas) *hld up: hdwy on outer over 2f out: 1 l 2nd 2f out: shkn up and reminder to ld over 1f out: kpt up to work to assert fnl f* **5/6**[1]

30-1 2 *1 1/4* **Perfect Refuge**[24] 67 4-9-7 **72**........................ HectorCrouch 3 78
(Clive Cox) *hld up: pushed along in 5th 2f out: drvn on outer 1 1/2f out: rdn into 2nd ins fnl f: r.o but a hld* **9/2**[3]

00-0 3 *2 3/4* **Cash N Carrie (IRE)**[24] 67 5-8-5 **55** oh1...................(p[1]) LiamJones 6 55
(Michael Appleby) *in rr: drvn 3f out: rdn over 2f out: hdwy over 1f out: kpt on fnl f: tk 3rd last 50yds* **66/1**

310- 4 *nk* **Lulu Star (IRE)**[116] 7936 4-8-5 **56**........................ ShelleyBirkett 7 56
(Julia Feilden) *prom: drvn over 2f out: lost pl 1 1/2f out: sn rdn: one pce* **33/1**

406- 5 *1/2* **Barbara Villiers**[121] 3266 4-8-12 **63**........................ EoinWalsh 1 62
(David Evans) *led: drvn in 1 l ld 2f out: sn rdn: hdd over 1f out: wknd fnl f* **16/1**

202- 6 *4* **Ruby Gates (IRE)**[32] 9724 6-9-7 **74**........................(p) TimClark(3) 2 64
(Paul D'Arcy) *trckd ldr: drvn and lost pl 2f out: sn rdn: wknd fnl f (trainer could offer no explanation for the poor form shown)* **4/1**[2]

/3-0 7 *10* **Jamaican Jill**[23] 81 4-9-9 **74**........................ MartinDwyer 5 43
(William Muir) *mid-div on outer: drvn and lost pl over 2f out: sn rdn and dropped to last* **8/1**

1m 58.48s (-2.32) **Going Correction** -0.10s/f (Stan)
WFA 4 from 5yo+ 1lb **7** Ran SP% **114.2**
Speed ratings (Par 100): **106,104,102,102,101 98,89**
CSF £4.99 TOTE £1.70: £1.10, £1.70; EX 4.90 Trifecta £131.40.
Owner St Albans Bloodstock Limited **Bred** St Albans Bloodstock Llp **Trained** Newmarket, Suffolk

FOCUS
The pace was sound for this fair handicap. The second has been rated to form.

460 LADBROKES EBF FILLIES' H'CAP 1m 142y (Tp)
6:25 (6:25) (Class 2) (0-105,100) 4-Y-O+
£16,807 (£5,032; £2,516; £1,258; £629; £315) **Stalls** Low

Form RPR

61-2 1 **Castle Hill Cassie (IRE)**[26] 30 5-9-10 **100**........................ GrahamLee 1 105
(Ben Haslam) *chsd ldrs: 3rd 2f out: pushed along to chal 1 1/2f out: led 1f out: rdn and briefly lugged rt fnl f: r.o wl* **2/1**[1]

532- 2 *3/4* **Pride's Gold (USA)**[37] 9684 4-8-11 **88**........................ RobertHavlin 4 91
(Simon Crisford) *led: qcknd pce 3f out: pushed along in 1 1/2 l ld 2f out: drvn and edgd rt over 1f out: sn hdd: rdn fnl f: one pce* **2/1**[1]

23-1 3 *nk* **Lady Alavesa**[16] 202 4-8-4 **81** oh10........................(p) JosephineGordon 3 84
(Gay Kelleway) *hld up: last 2f out: drvn and hdwy 1 1/2f out: rdn into 3rd fnl f: kpt on* **10/1**

5-04 **4** ¾ **Ventura Blues (IRE)**[17] 177 5-8-5 **81** oh4....................(p) JoeFanning 2 82?
(Alexandra Dunn) *hld up: 5th 2f out: drvn to chse ldrs 1 1/2f out: briefly nt clr run over 1f out: one pce fnl f* **25/1**

34-3 **5** 1 **This Girl**[26] 29 4-8-4 **81** oh2.. LukeMorris 5 80
(Tom Dascombe) *prom: drvn 3f out: rdn in 2nd over 2f out: 1 1/2 l 2nd 2f out: lost pl over 1f out: no ex fnl f* **7/2**[2]

00-5 **6** 3½ **Peak Princess (IRE)**[26] 30 5-8-9 **90**..............(b) ThomasGreatrex(5) 6 81
(Archie Watson) *mid-div on outer: pushed along 2f out: drvn 1 1/2f out: dropped to last 1f out* **6/1**[3]

1m 49.03s (-1.07) **Going Correction** -0.10s/f (Stan)
WFA 4 from 5yo 1lb **6** Ran SP% **116.1**
Speed ratings (Par 96): **100,99,99,98,97 94**
CSF £6.47 TOTE £2.40: £1.50, £1.40; EX 8.30 Trifecta £28.90.
Owner D Howden, S Lock & D Redvers **Bred** Yeomanstown Stud **Trained** Middleham Moor, N Yorks

FOCUS
Only one of the field was rated within 15lb of the ceiling, whilst three of the six runners were racing from out of the handicap, but it was still a fair handicap which saw an exciting finish. The winner has been rated to her recent form.

461 LADBROKES HOME OF THE ODDS BOOST H'CAP 1m 142y (Tp)
6:55 (6:55) (Class 5) (0-70,71) 3-Y-O

£3,752 (£1,116; £557; £400; £400; £400) **Stalls Low**

Form RPR

22-3 **1** **Fenjal (IRE)**[21] 122 3-9-5 **67**..............................(b¹) EdwardGreatrex 4 73
(Hugo Palmer) *mde all: drvn 3f out: rdn in 1 l ld 2f out: 2 l ld 1f out: r.o wl fnl f* **5/1**[2]

45-0 **2** 1¼ **Smoki Smoka (IRE)**[9] 316 3-9-7 **69**.................... RichardKingscote 11 73
(Tom Dascombe) *forward move fr wd draw to go prom: drvn over 2f out: 1 l 2nd 2f out: sn rdn: 2 l 2nd 1f out: kpt on fnl f* **9/1**

4-23 **3** nk **Beryl The Petal (IRE)**[11] 274 3-9-4 **69**................ ConorMcGovern(3) 1 72
(David O'Meara) *trckd ldrs: pushed along in 3rd 2f out: rdn over 1f out: one pce fnl f* **8/1**

65-2 **4** ¾ **Wall Of Sapphire (IRE)**[17] 174 3-9-6 **68**....................(p¹) JoeFanning 6 69
(Hugo Palmer) *trckd ldrs: drvn in 4th 2f out: sn rdn: no imp fnl f* **4/1**[1]

5-14 **5** 1 **War and Glory (IRE)**[15] 228 3-9-6 **68**.................... CallumRodriguez 8 67
(James Tate) *hld up: rdn and hdwy over 1f out: one pce fnl f* **11/2**[3]

23-6 **6** nk **Cheap Jack**[15] 229 3-9-4 **66**.. GrahamLee 13 65
(Ronald Thompson) *bhd: pushed along on outer 1 1/2f out: rdn and mod hdwy fnl f* **33/1**

060- **7** nk **Ned Mackay**[102] 8354 3-9-7 **69**..............................(b¹) AdamMcNamara 12 67
(Roger Charlton) *dwlt losing several l: bhd: in rr 3f out: pushed along 2f out: hdwy 1 1/2f out: rdn and kpt on fnl f (jockey said gelding was slowly away)* **16/1**

05-0 **8** 3¼ **Royal Guild (IRE)**[12] 258 3-8-13 **61**..............................(b¹) LukeMorris 2 52
(Sir Mark Prescott Bt) *mid-div: drvn over 2f out: rdn and wknd fnl f* **16/1**

66-0 **9** 1¼ **Love Kisses (IRE)**[19] 134 3-9-3 **65**............................... PJMcDonald 3 54
(Mark Johnston) *mid-div: drvn in 5th 2f out: sn rdn and wknd* **20/1**

33-F **10** 9 **Teresita Alvarez (USA)**[24] 55 3-9-5 **67**........................ ShaneKelly 9 37
(Jeremy Noseda) *hld up: pushed along 2f out: last 1 1/2f out: nvr involved* **5/1**[2]

2-51 **11** 11 **Um Shama (IRE)**[9] 319 3-8-9 **64**........................ LauraCoughlan(7) 10 11+
(David Loughnane) *t.k.h: mid-div: pushed along and lost pl over 2f out: dropped to last over 1f out (jockey said the saddle slipped)* **9/1**

1m 49.41s (-0.69) **Going Correction** -0.10s/f (Stan) **11** Ran SP% **119.3**
Speed ratings (Par 97): **99,97,97,96,96 95,95,92,91,83 73**
CSF £50.39 CT £367.93 TOTE £4.00: £1.60, £3.80, £2.00; EX 53.40 Trifecta £384.30.
Owner Al Shaqab Racing **Bred** Linacre House Ltd **Trained** Newmarket, Suffolk

FOCUS
An open handicap in which the prominent runners dominated. Ordinary form rated around those in behind the first two.

462 FOLLOW SUN RACING ON TWITTER (S) H'CAP 1m 142y (Tp)
7:25 (7:25) (Class 6) (0-65,62) 4-6-Y-O

£3,105 (£924; £461; £400; £400; £400) **Stalls Low**

Form RPR

100- **1** **Foxy Lady**[51] 9465 4-9-4 **58**..(p) ShaneGray 2 64
(Kevin Ryan) *mid-div: drvn and hdwy over 1f out: rdn to ld 1f out: r.o wl u.p fnl f (trainer said, as to the apparent improvement in form, the filly was contesting a weaker race on this occasion)* **14/1**

56-0 **2** nk **Lord Murphy (IRE)**[17] 180 6-9-1 **54**..............................(t¹) LiamJones 10 59
(Mark Loughnane) *hld up: drvn and hdwy over 1f out: rdn to chal wl ins fnl f: r.o wl* **10/1**

42-6 **3** 1 **Mans Not Trot (IRE)**[25] 39 4-9-2 **56**..........................(p) NicolaCurrie 5 59
(Jamie Osborne) *led: drvn in 1/2 l ld 2f out: rdn and hdd 1f out: kpt on fnl f* **3/1**[1]

36-0 **4** nk **Joyful Dream (IRE)**[18] 155 5-8-6 **45**.............................. HollieDoyle 11 48
(Paul D'Arcy) *trckd ldrs: 4th 2f out: drvn on outer 1 1/2f out: rdn fnl f: kpt on (jockey said mare hung left and right-handed in the home straight)* **28/1**

20-0 **5** ½ **Military Madame (IRE)**[20] 125 4-9-5 **59**.....................(p¹) PJMcDonald 7 62
(John Quinn) *mid-div: drvn 2f out: rdn fnl f: one pce (jockey said filly was denied a clear run turning into the home straight)* **14/1**

030- **6** hd **One Liner**[38] 9665 5-8-6 **45**... DavidProbert 8 46
(John O'Shea) *bhd: drvn and plenty to do 1 1/2f out: rdn over 1f out: r.o fnl f: nvr nrr* **16/1**

10-5 **7** ¾ **Mossy's Lodge**[7] 348 6-9-6 **59**..................................(tp) StevieDonohoe 3 59
(Rebecca Menzies) *slowly away: bhd: pushed along 2f out: drvn on outer 1 1/2f out: rdn fnl f: one pce (jockey said mare became unsettled in the stalls and as a result was slowly away)* **3/1**[1]

000- **8** ¾ **Majestic Man (IRE)**[58] 7840 6-8-3 **45**........................ WilliamCox(3) 12 43
(Ronald Thompson) *chsd ldr: rdn in 1/2 l 2nd 2f out: lost pl 1 1/2f out: wknd fnl f* **100/1**

00-0 **9** ½ **Ainne**[7] 348 4-8-13 **56**..(bt) GaryMahon(3) 6 53
(Sylvester Kirk) *trckd ldrs: pushed along in 3rd 2f out: sn drvn: rdn and ev ch over 1f out: wknd fnl f* **9/1**[3]

004- **10** 2½ **Unsuspected Girl (IRE)**[153] 6651 6-8-6 **45**...............(t¹) RaulDaSilva 13 37
(Milton Bradley) *bhd: drvn 1 1/2f out: sn rdn: no imp* **80/1**

4-00 **11** 2 **Going Native**[16] 208 4-8-6 **46**..(p¹) LukeMorris 4 34
(Olly Williams) *hld up: drvn on outer over 2f out: reminder ent fnl f: no rspnse* **9/1**[3]

60-0 **12** 16 **Prancing Oscar (IRE)**[20] 125 5-9-8 **61**........................(p) PaulMulrennan 9 15
(Ben Haslam) *prom: on outer over 2f out: sn lost pl: dropped to last over 1f out (jockey said gelding stopped quickly)* **13/2**[2]

1m 49.64s (-0.46) **Going Correction** -0.10s/f (Stan)
WFA 4 from 5yo+ 1lb **12** Ran SP% **117.3**
Speed ratings: **98,97,96,96,96 95,95,94,94,91 90,75**
CSF £144.40 CT £544.86 TOTE £10.80: £3.30, £2.40, £1.50; EX 113.10 Trifecta £812.10.There was no bid for the winner
Owner K&J Bloodstock Ltd **Bred** Mrs F M Gordon **Trained** Hambleton, N Yorks
■ Stewards' Enquiry : Nicola Currie caution: careless riding

FOCUS
A modest handicap.

463 FOLLOW TOP TIPSTERS AT SUN RACING H'CAP 7f 36y (Tp)
7:55 (7:55) (Class 5) (0-70,70) 4-Y-O+

£3,752 (£1,116; £557; £400; £400; £400) **Stalls High**

Form RPR

60-5 **1** **The British Lion (IRE)**[6] 355 4-9-5 **68**.............................. JoeFanning 5 75
(Mark Johnston) *mid-div: hdwy gng wl over 2f out: drvn to chal on outer 1 1/2f out: led 1f out: rdn fnl f: r.o wl and sn 1 l clr: ld diminishing nr fin: hld on* **11/4**[1]

5-11 **2** nk **Grey Destiny**[15] 233 9-8-8 **64**................................(p) KieranSchofield(7) 1 70
(Antony Brittain) *hld up: pushed along and effrt over 1f out: drvn to chal wl ins fnl f: str late run: clsng on wnr nr fin* **13/2**

156- **3** nk **The King's Steed**[65] 9257 6-8-13 **62**..........................(bt) NicolaCurrie 2 67
(Shaun Lycett) *chsd ldrs: 3rd 2f out: drvn 1 1/2f out: sn rdn: ev ch ent fnl f: kpt on u.p* **15/2**

03-5 **4** ½ **Gabrial The Tiger (IRE)**[26] 31 7-9-2 **70**............ SebastianWoods(5) 3 74
(Richard Fahey) *led: pushed along in 1/2 l ld 2f out: sn rdn: hdd 1f out: no ex* **10/1**

0-24 **5** ½ **Dollar Value (USA)**[15] 233 4-9-1 **64**.................................(p) LukeMorris 4 66
(Robert Cowell) *prom: drvn in 1/2 l 2nd 2f out: lost pl over 1f out: n.m.r ins fnl f: no ex last 100yds (vet reported the gelding lost its left fore shoe)* **13/2**

420- **6** 2½ **Global Humor (USA)**[31] 9733 4-9-3 **66**.......................... RobertHavlin 7 62
(Ed Dunlop) *hld up: pushed along 2f out: chsd ldrs over 1f out: sn rdn and wknd* **11/2**[3]

00-5 **7** 1½ **Gabrial's Kaka (IRE)**[11] 276 9-9-5 **68**........................ PaddyMathers 10 60
(Patrick Morris) *slowly away: bhd: drvn 1 1/2f out: no imp* **100/1**

/0-4 **8** 3½ **Miracle Garden**[17] 187 7-9-7 **70**..............................(p) StevieDonohoe 9 52
(Ian Williams) *hld up: drvn over 2f out: sn rdn: no imp* **5/1**[2]

02/6 **9** 1¼ **Sporting Bill (IRE)**[11] 275 4-9-7 **70**........................(v¹) DanielMuscutt 11 49
(James Fanshawe) *hld up: pushed along in 6th 2f out: rdn and wknd over 1f out (jockey said gelding moved poorly under pressure in the home straight)* **16/1**

400- **10** 10 **Deadly Accurate**[30] 9747 4-9-7 **70**.................................... EoinWalsh 8 22
(Roy Brotherton) *bhd: rdn over 2f out: no ch fr over 1f out* **66/1**

300- **11** 5 **Bouclier (IRE)**[208] 4525 9-9-4 **67**.............................(p) DavidProbert 12 5
(James Unett) *mid-div on outer: drvn and lost pl over 2f out: dropped to last 1 1/2f out* **28/1**

1m 27.06s (-1.74) **Going Correction** -0.10s/f (Stan) **11** Ran SP% **118.1**
Speed ratings (Par 103): **105,104,104,103,103 100,98,94,93,81 76**
CSF £20.77 CT £122.31 TOTE £3.60: £1.60, £1.70, £3.20; EX 24.10 Trifecta £122.60.
Owner John Brown & Megan Dennis **Bred** Barronstown Stud And Mrs T Stack **Trained** Middleham Moor, N Yorks

FOCUS
A fair handicap. The winner has been rated close to his early 3yo form, while the third and fourth help set the level.

464 LIKE SUN RACING ON FACEBOOK NOVICE STKS 7f 36y (Tp)
8:25 (8:25) (Class 5) 4-Y-O+ £3,752 (£1,116; £557; £278) **Stalls High**

Form RPR

2- **1** **Tiger Eye (IRE)**[44] 9565 4-8-11 0...................................... GeorgeWood 5 79+
(James Fanshawe) *chsd ldrs: wnt 2nd over 2f out: pushed into ld 1 1/2f out: drvn into 3 l ld 1f out: kpt up to work and r.o wl fnl f* **11/10**[1]

0-1 **2** 2½ **Minoria**[19] 141 4-9-2 0.. DavidProbert 1 76
(Rae Guest) *hld up: hdwy into 3rd 2f out: wnt 2nd 1 1/2f out: sn rdn: kpt on fnl f but nvr nr wnr* **9/1**

61 **3** 2½ **Dawn Delight**[11] 275 4-9-4 0.. JoeFanning 2 71
(Hugo Palmer) *hld up: pushed along in last 2f out: drvn on outer 1 1/2f out: rdn fnl f: kpt on: tk 3rd last stride* **9/4**[2]

333- **4** nse **Gates Pass**[29] 9766 4-9-2 74....................................(p¹) NicolaCurrie 3 69
(Jamie Osborne) *prom: drvn in 3rd over 2f out: sn dropped to 4th: wnt 3rd ent fnl f: no ex and lost 3rd last stride* **7/2**[3]

400- **5** 4½ **Lope De Loop (IRE)**[90] 8729 4-8-11 49..........................(t¹) EoinWalsh 4 52?
(Aytach Sadik) *led: pushed along 2f out: hdd 1/2f out: sn rdn and wknd* **100/1**

1m 27.98s (-0.82) **Going Correction** -0.10s/f (Stan) **5** Ran SP% **111.6**
Speed ratings (Par 103): **100,97,94,94,89**
CSF £11.86 TOTE £1.80: £1.20, £2.80; EX 9.50 Trifecta £19.80.
Owner Qatar Racing Limited **Bred** Orpendale,Wynatt,Chelston & Daylesford **Trained** Newmarket, Suffolk

FOCUS
An interesting novice. The second has been rated in line with her Lingfield win.
T/Jkpt: £5,000 to a £1 stake. Pool: £10,000.00 - 2 winning units T/Plt: £52.80 to a £1 stake. Pool: £126,749.53 - 1749.13 winning units T/Qpdt: £8.80 to a £1 stake. Pool: £17,135.28 - 1426.95 winning units **Keith McHugh**

457 WOLVERHAMPTON (A.W) (L-H)
Tuesday, January 29

OFFICIAL GOING: Tapeta: standard
Wind: Light behind Weather: Snow showers

465 LIKE SUN RACING ON FACEBOOK H'CAP 1m 142y (Tp)
4:35 (4:35) (Class 6) (0-60,64) 4-Y-O+

£3,105 (£924; £461; £400; £400; £400) **Stalls Low**

Form RPR

-326 **1** **Sharp Operator**[11] 288 6-9-4 **57**..............................(h) RichardKingscote 8 62
(Charlie Wallis) *hld up: hmpd 7f out: hdwy 2f out: rdn to ld ins fnl f: edgd rt: jst hld on* **5/1**[3]

000- **2** shd **Zarkavon**[166] 6184 5-8-0 **46** oh1.............................. FayeMcManoman(7) 10 51
(John Wainwright) *s.i.s: hld up: hdwy over 1f out: n.m.r and swtchd lft ins fnl f: r.o wl* **150/1**

416- **3** *1 1/2* **Blyton Lass**[110] 8142 4-8-13 **53**........................ BarryMcHugh 11 55
(James Given) *hld up: hdwy over 1f out: swtchd lft ins fnl f: r.o* **12/1**

-132 **4** *1 1/4* **Amor Fati (IRE)**[5] 379 4-8-11 **51**........................ NicolaCurrie 1 50
(David Evans) *hld up: plld hrd: hdwy over 3f out: rdn over 1f out: styd on* **9/4**[1]

2-31 **5** *1/2* **Arrowzone**[8] 348 8-9-8 **64** 6ex........................(b) JoshuaBryan(3) 6 62
(Kevin Frost) *led: racd keenly: hdd over 6f out: chsd ldr: shkn up to ld 1f out: rdn and hdd ins fnl f: edgd rt and no ex* **9/2**[2]

4-40 **6** *nk* **Voice Of A Leader (IRE)**[4] 399 8-9-0 **53**........................ JoeyHaynes 12 50
(Paul Howling) *s.i.s: sn prom: led over 6f out: shkn up over 2f out: hdd 1f out: styd on same pce ins fnl f* **11/1**

340- **7** *1* **Zahirah**[30] 9767 5-9-4 **57**........................ DannyBrock 2 52
(J R Jenkins) *w ldr 1f: remained handy: rdn over 1f out: no ex ins fnl f* **9/1**

66-3 **8** *3* **Energia Flavio (BRZ)**[10] 315 8-9-3 **61**........................ CameronNoble(5) 7 50
(Patrick Morris) *prom: chsd ldr over 5f out tl shkn up over 1f out: wknd ins fnl f* **9/2**[2]

500- **9** *3 1/4* **Thundercloud**[48] 9511 4-9-6 **60**........................(p) KieranO'Neill 5 42
(Scott Dixon) *plld hrd and prom: rdn over 2f out: wknd over 1f out* **20/1**

000- **10** *1 3/4* **Les Gar Gan (IRE)**[84] 8905 8-8-7 **46** oh1........................ HollieDoyle 13 24
(Ray Peacock) *hld up: rdn over 2f out: nvr on terms (jockey said mare ran in snatches)* **150/1**

00-0 **11** *3 1/2* **Mr Wing (IRE)**[15] 237 4-8-6 **46** oh1........................(p) JamesSullivan 3 17
(John Wainwright) *plld hrd and prom: hmpd and lost pl 7f out: pushed along over 3f out: wknd over 1f out* **200/1**

00-0 **12** *1 3/4* **Cookie Ring (IRE)**[18] 180 8-8-2 **46** oh1........................(bt) PaulaMuir(5) 9 13
(Andrew Crook) *s.i.s: plld hrd: hdwy over 5f out: rdn over 2f out: sn wknd* **66/1**

1m 49.31s (-0.79) **Going Correction** -0.125s/f (Stan) 12 Ran SP% **117.9**
WFA 4 from 5yo+ 1lb
Speed ratings (Par 101): **98,97,96,95,95 94,93,91,88,86 83,82**
CSF £622.94 CT £8294.37 TOTE £4.50: £1.50, £43.80, £3.80; EX 367.90.
Owner Lee Brooks **Bred** Bumble Bloodstock & Mrs S Nicholls **Trained** Ardleigh, Essex

FOCUS
The early pace was slow but picked up markedly down the back and it was the closers who came through at the finish. Ordinary form, with the runner-up recording a 7lb pb.

466 FOLLOW SUN RACING ON TWITTER CLAIMING STKS 1m 142y (Tp)
5:10 (5:10) (Class 5) 4-Y-O+ £3,752 (£1,116; £557; £400; £400) **Stalls Low**

Form RPR

04-0 **1** **Los Camachos (IRE)**[5] 381 4-9-0 79........................ KatherineBegley(5) 5 75
(David Evans) *mde all: set stdy pce tl qcknd over 2f out: rdn out* **9/2**[3]

00-1 **2** *hd* **Mister Music**[25] 63 10-8-13 85........................ PoppyBridgwater(5) 3 73+
(Tony Carroll) *hld up: hdwy over 1f out: rdn to chse wnr wl ins fnl f: edgd lft: r.o* **7/4**[1]

25-6 **3** *3/4* **The Groove**[18] 181 6-8-6 66........................ GinaMangan(7) 2 66
(David Evans) *plld hrd: trckd wnr over 5f: rdn over 1f out: r.o* **20/1**

2-21 **4** *3/4* **Dark Alliance (IRE)**[15] 237 8-8-13 72........................ MeganNicholls(5) 6 69
(Mark Loughnane) *plld hrd and prom: wnt 2nd 3f out: rdn over 1f out: styd on same pce ins fnl f* **15/8**[2]

0-56 **5** *10* **Steel Train (FR)**[5] 381 8-9-4 85........................(h[1]) DanielTudhope 1 48+
(David O'Meara) *s.s: hld up: shkn up over 2f out: hung lft and wknd over 1f out (jockey said gelding moved poorly; vet said gelding was lame on its right fore)* **6/1**

1m 52.41s (2.31) **Going Correction** -0.125s/f (Stan) 5 Ran SP% **108.4**
WFA 4 from 5yo+ 1lb
Speed ratings (Par 103): **84,83,83,82,73**
CSF £12.42 TOTE £5.80: £2.20, £1.10; EX 15.10 Trifecta £104.30.
Owner Mrs Penny Keble White & Emma Evans **Bred** Hardys Of Kilkeel Ltd **Trained** Pandy, Monmouths

FOCUS
A tactical affair, dominated from the front by the winner.

467 SUNRACING.CO.UK H'CAP 7f 36y (Tp)
5:45 (5:45) (Class 6) (0-60,61) 4-Y-O+ £3,105 (£924; £461; £400; £400; £400) **Stalls High**

Form RPR

-211 **1** **Foreign Legion (IRE)**[11] 293 4-9-3 **56**........................(p) NickyMackay 9 65+
(Luke McJannet) *nt clr run sn after s: hld up: hdwy over 4f out: shkn up and hung rt fr over 1f out: rdn and r.o to ld wl ins fnl f* **7/2**[1]

5-43 **2** *1/2* **Shamlan (IRE)**[14] 243 7-9-1 **57**........................(p) JoshuaBryan(3) 2 63
(Kevin Frost) *prom: lost pl over 5f out: pushed along 1/2-way: hdwy over 1f out: sn rdn: r.o wl* **5/1**[2]

42-3 **3** *3/4* **Daring Guest (IRE)**[19] 159 5-9-4 **57**........................(b[1]) LukeMorris 7 61
(Tom Clover) *sn prom: chsd ldr over 4f out: rdn to ld over 1f out: edgd rt: hdd and unable qck wl ins fnl f* **11/2**[3]

06-1 **4** *1/2* **Mooroverthebridge**[10] 315 5-9-4 **60**........................ FinleyMarsh(3) 5 64+
(Grace Harris) *s.i.s: hld up: nt clr run over 1f out: r.o ins fnl f: nt rch ldrs* **6/1**

-611 **5** *3/4* **Brockey Rise (IRE)**[4] 402 4-9-1 **61** 6ex........................(b) GinaMangan(7) 12 63
(David Evans) *hld up: hdwy over 2f out: nt clr run over 1f out: sn rdn: styd on* **11/1**

34-6 **6** *1/2* **Spiced**[17] 202 4-9-7 **60**........................(p[1]) DavidProbert 4 60
(Ron Hodges) *led 1f: chsd ldrs: rdn over 1f out: styd on same pce ins fnl f* **16/1**

025- **7** *nk* **Holy Tiber (IRE)**[29] 9776 4-9-6 **59**........................ JoeyHaynes 1 59
(Paul Howling) *hld up: shkn up over 1f out: nt clr run and swtchd lft ins fnl f: nvr nr to chal (jockey said filly was denied a clear run 1f out)* **14/1**

450- **8** *nse* **Chez Vegas**[42] 9600 6-9-5 **58**........................ KieranO'Neill 8 57
(Scott Dixon) *led 6f out: sn hdd: remained handy: rdn and ev ch over 1f out: no ex ins fnl f* **25/1**

050- **9** *1/2* **Big Amigo (IRE)**[188] 5350 6-9-4 **57**........................ EoinWalsh 3 55
(Ken Wingrove) *hld up: rdn over 1f out: nt trble ldrs (jockey said gelding was denied a clear run on the bend entering the home straight)* **100/1**

034- **10** *3/4* **First Call (FR)**[115] 8001 4-8-12 **51**........................ StevieDonohoe 6 47
(Ian Williams) *s.i.s: hld up: n.d* **6/1**

00-0 **11** *1 1/2* **Clement (IRE)**[14] 243 9-8-11 **57**........................(v) KateLeahy(7) 10 49
(John O'Shea) *sn prom: rdn over 2f out: wknd fnl f* **25/1**

36-6 **12** *1 1/4* **Eponina (IRE)**[16] 232 5-9-6 **59**........................ AlistairRawlinson 11 48
(Michael Appleby) *sn pushed along and prom: led over 5f out: rdn and hdd over 1f out: wknd ins fnl f* **14/1**

1m 28.13s (-0.67) **Going Correction** -0.125s/f (Stan) 12 Ran SP% **119.1**
Speed ratings (Par 101): **98,97,96,95 94,94,94,93,92 91,89**
CSF £20.12 CT £97.53 TOTE £4.40: £1.80, £1.80, £1.70; EX 26.00 Trifecta £134.80.
Owner Ivor Collier **Bred** Norelands Bloodstock **Trained** Newmarket, Suffolk

FOCUS
A moderate handicap, but a competitive one. The level is straightforward.

468 BETWAY H'CAP 6f 20y (Tp)
6:15 (6:15) (Class 5) (0-70,70) 4-Y-O+ £3,752 (£1,116; £557; £400; £400; £400) **Stalls Low**

Form RPR

501- **1** **Turanga Leela**[43] 9588 5-9-2 **65**........................(b) StevieDonohoe 8 78
(John Mackie) *mde all: rdn and edgd rt over 1f out: r.o wl* **25/1**

00-4 **2** *3 1/2* **Mount Wellington (IRE)**[14] 249 4-9-5 **68**........................(p) RobertHavlin 1 70
(Henry Spiller) *hld up in tch: rdn over 1f out: styd on to go 2nd nr fin* **7/2**[1]

00-4 **3** *nk* **Big Time Maybe (IRE)**[10] 314 4-9-4 **67**........................(p) AdamKirby 3 68
(Michael Attwater) *prom: racd keenly: rdn to chse wnr ins fnl f: styd on same pce: lost 2nd nr fin* **12/1**

4-63 **4** *1/2* **Fast Track**[15] 237 8-9-5 **68**........................ CallumRodriguez 13 67
(David Barron) *chsd wnr: rdn and edgd rt over 1f out: lost 2nd ins fnl f: styd on same pce* **10/1**

020- **5** *1 1/2* **Van Gerwen**[91] 8719 6-9-7 **70**........................(b[1]) DanielTudhope 6 65
(Les Eyre) *prom: rdn over 1f out: no ex ins fnl f* **14/1**

0-11 **6** *1* **Santafiora**[15] 236 5-8-9 **58**........................ KieranO'Neill 7 49
(Julie Camacho) *hld up: pushed along and hdwy 2f out: sn rdn: no imp fnl f* **5/1**[2]

35-3 **7** *3/4* **Independence Day (IRE)**[20] 144 6-9-4 **67**........................ JoeyHaynes 2 56
(Paul Howling) *hld up: shkn up and swtchd rt over 1f out: nvr nrr* **7/2**[1]

46-0 **8** *1 1/2* **Rock Warbler (IRE)**[7] 356 6-9-1 **64**........................(e[1]) JamesSullivan 9 48
(Michael Mullineaux) *hld up: shkn up over 1f out: nvr on terms* **33/1**

0-00 **9** *nk* **Our Man In Havana**[15] 236 4-8-11 **63**........................ JoshuaBryan(3) 4 46
(Richard Price) *hld up: rdn over 1f out: wknd fnl f* **18/1**

-062 **10** *shd* **Zapper Cass (FR)**[15] 237 6-9-5 **68**........................(p) LukeMorris 10 51
(Michael Appleby) *sn prom: shkn up over 2f out: wknd fnl f (jockey said gelding hung right throughout)* **9/1**[3]

00-0 **11** *2 1/4* **Letmestopyouthere (IRE)**[18] 187 5-9-3 **66**........................ HollieDoyle 11 42
(Archie Watson) *sn pushed along and a in rr (jockey said gelding was never travelling)* **20/1**

151- **12** *9* **Ty Rock Brandy (IRE)**[25] 68 4-9-5 **68**........................(h[1]) ShaneKelly 5 15
(Adrian McGuinness, Ire) *hld up: plld hrd: rdn over 2f out: wknd over 1f out: eased fnl f (jockey said filly hung right)* **14/1**

1m 13.07s (-1.43) **Going Correction** -0.125s/f (Stan) 12 Ran SP% **118.0**
Speed ratings (Par 103): **104,99,98,98,96 94,93,91,91,91 88,76**
CSF £108.41 CT £1155.49 TOTE £25.80: £6.70, £1.90, £3.90; EX 249.60 Trifecta £1879.60.
Owner Eventmasters Racing **Bred** Chasemore Farm **Trained** Church Broughton, Derbys
■ Stewards' Enquiry : Stevie Donohoe one-day ban: failure to ride to draw (Feb 14)

FOCUS
Few got into this, the winner dominating from the front and those held up never getting involved.

469 BETWAY LIVE CASINO H'CAP 1m 5f 219y (Tp)
6:45 (6:45) (Class 5) (0-75,76) 4-Y-O+ £3,752 (£1,116; £557; £400; £400; £400) **Stalls Low**

Form RPR

50-3 **1** **Noble Expression**[17] 204 4-9-7 **74**........................(p[1]) CharlieBennett 3 85
(Jim Boyle) *led early: chsd ldrs: led 3f out: rdn clr fnl 2f: eased nr fin* **16/1**

/1-0 **2** *8* **Isle Of Avalon (IRE)**[23] 101 4-9-4 **71**........................(b[1]) LukeMorris 10 71
(Sir Mark Prescott Bt) *hld up in tch: rdn over 2f out: sn outpcd* **4/1**[2]

223- **3** *hd* **Tommy Docc (IRE)**[30] 9768 7-9-10 **73**........................ CallumRodriguez 9 73
(Keith Dalgleish) *sn chsng ldr: led over 3f out: sn hdd: rdn over 2f out: sn outpcd* **3/1**[1]

3-0 **4** *5* **Pure Country**[26] 46 4-9-9 **76**........................(p[1]) RossaRyan 1 69
(Noel Williams) *chsd ldrs: shkn up over 6f out: wknd 2f out* **3/1**[1]

355- **5** *1 1/4* **All My Love (IRE)**[28] 9295 7-9-8 **71**........................ RobHornby 8 62
(Pam Sly) *s.i.s: hld up: hdwy over 4f out: rdn over 2f out: wkng whn hung lft over 1f out (jockey said that the mare anticipated the start, and thought that this could have jammed the gates causing his stall to open fractionally slow)* **15/2**

5-34 **6** *36* **Ezanak (IRE)**[3] 432 6-9-11 **74**........................(b) LiamJones 5 14
(Michael Appleby) *sn pushed along to ld: rdn and hdd over 3f out: wkng whn hmpd over 2f out* **8/1**

0/00 **7** *4* **Sporty Yankee (USA)**[8] 345 6-9-1 **64**........................(p) JamesSullivan 6
(Aytach Sadik) *s.i.s: hld up: rdn over 4f out: wkng whn hmpd over 2f out* **150/1**

00-4 **8** *3* **Angel Gabrial (IRE)**[10] 318 10-9-4 **67**........................ StevieDonohoe 7
(Patrick Morris) *hld up: rdn and wkng whn hmpd over 2f out* **20/1**

36-5 **F** **Bamako Du Chatelet (FR)**[24] 88 8-9-4 **67**........................(p) FranBerry 4
(Ian Williams) *hld up: hdwy u.p to dispute 5th whn fell over 2f out* **6/1**[3]

2m 58.38s (-2.62) **Going Correction** -0.125s/f (Stan) 9 Ran SP% **118.5**
WFA 4 from 6yo+ 4lb
Speed ratings (Par 103): **102,97,97,94,93 73,70,69,**
CSF £81.08 CT £252.31 TOTE £15.60: £4.50, £1.20, £1.90; EX 101.20 Trifecta £615.80.
Owner The Waterboys **Bred** Horizon Bloodstock Limited **Trained** Epsom, Surrey

FOCUS
The winner drew clear in this staying contest. The winner has been rated back to his early form for Roger Varian, with the third close to his recent form.

470 BETWAY HEED YOUR HUNCH H'CAP 6f 20y (Tp)
7:15 (7:15) (Class 2) (0-105,100) 3-Y-O+ £12,450 (£3,728; £1,864; £932; £466; £234) **Stalls Low**

Form RPR

6-12 **1** **Shamshon (IRE)**[11] 297 8-8-13 **85**........................ RichardKingscote 3 93
(Stuart Williams) *a.p: chsd ldr over 1f out: shkn up to ld wl ins fnl f: r.o* **6/1**[3]

11-3 **2** *1* **Exchequer (IRE)**[13] 255 8-9-4 **90**........................(p) JoeFanning 4 95
(Richard Guest) *led: rdn over 1f out: hdd wl ins fnl f: styd on same pce* **15/2**

/01- **3** *1/2* **Sanaadh**[45] 9557 6-9-6 **92**........................(t) FrannyNorton 5 95+
(Michael Wigham) *s.i.s: hld up: hdwy and hung lft over 1f out: swtchd rt ins fnl f: r.o (jockey said gelding hung left in the home straight)* **3/1**[2]

22-3 **4** *1* **Gulliver**[20] 136 5-10-0 **100**........................(tp) DanielTudhope 8 100
(David O'Meara) *chsd ldrs: shkn up over 2f out: styd on* **13/2**

1-22 **5** *1/2* **James Street (IRE)**[13] 261 3-8-1 **89**........................ LukeMorris 6 84
(Hugo Palmer) *chsd ldr: shkn up over 2f out: lost 2nd over 1f out: styd on same pce ins fnl f* **6/5**[1]

045- **6** *5* **Mokaatil**[30] 9763 4-9-4 **90**........................(t) StevieDonohoe 7 73
(Ian Williams) *hld up: rdn and edgd lft over 1f out: rdr dropped reins ins fnl f: nvr on terms* **33/1**

The Form Book Flat 2019, Raceform Ltd, Newbury, RG14 5SJ

106- 7 1 1/2 **Udontdodou**[34] 9707 6-9-12 **98** .... PhilipPrince 1 76
(Richard Guest) *hld up: racd keenly: hung rt over 2f out: sn wknd* **25/1**

1m 11.85s (-2.65) **Going Correction** -0.125s/f (Stan)
WFA 3 from 4yo+ 16lb **7 Ran SP% 116.6**
Speed ratings (Par 109): **112,110,110,108,108 101,99**
CSF £50.56 CT £162.11 TOTE £7.10: £2.80, £2.90; EX 51.10 Trifecta £146.40.
Owner T W Morley & Regents Racing **Bred** Stonethorn Stud Farms Ltd **Trained** Newmarket, Suffolk
FOCUS
It didn't pay to be too far off the pace here. The second has been rated to form.

471 BETWAY SPRINT H'CAP — 5f 21y (Tp)
7:45 (7:45) (Class 4) (0-80,81) 4-Y-O+
£6,080 (£1,809; £904; £452; £400; £400) **Stalls** Low

Form RPR
21-2 1 **Acclaim The Nation (IRE)**[19] 163 6-9-7 **80** .... (p) LukeMorris 5 90
(Eric Alston) *mde all: shkn up over 1f out: drvn out* **13/2**
0-31 2 1 3/4 **Joegogo (IRE)**[3] 433 4-9-1 **81** 6ex .... SeamusCronin(7) 3 85
(David Evans) *sn prom: nt clr run 1/2-way: rdn over 1f out: styd on to go 2nd wl ins fnl f* **3/1**[1]
2-12 3 *nk* **A Sure Welcome**[10] 317 5-8-13 **72** .... (b) LiamKeniry 6 75
(John Spearing) *s.i.s: hld up: hdwy 1/2-way: swtchd rt over 1f out: r.o u.p* **7/2**[2]
-U04 4 1 1/4 **Samovar**[5] 389 4-9-2 **75** .... (b) KieranO'Neill 4 73
(Scott Dixon) *chsd wnr: rdn over 1f out: no ex and lost 2nd wl ins fnl f* **14/1**
-550 5 1 1/2 **Something Lucky (IRE)**[5] 382 7-9-7 **80** .... (b) AlistairRawlinson 1 73
(Michael Appleby) *s.i.s: bhd: r.o towards fin: nt rch ldrs (jockey said gelding was slowly away and never travelling)* **4/1**[3]
1-54 6 1/2 **Tan**[11] 297 5-9-0 **80** .... MarkCrehan(7) 2 71
(Michael Appleby) *chsd ldrs: swtchd rt over 3f out: rdn over 1f out: no ex* **9/2**
04-1 7 *nse* **Union Rose**[10] 317 7-9-1 **74** .... (p) DavidProbert 7 65
(Ronald Harris) *prom: nt clr run and lost pl over 3f out: n.d after* **8/1**
23-4 8 2 **Red Stripes (USA)**[22] 118 7-8-0 **62** oh10 ow1 .... (b) AaronJones(3) 8 46
(Lisa Williamson) *hld up: n.d* **66/1**

(-1.90) **Going Correction** -0.125s/f (Stan) **8 Ran SP% 118.0**
Speed ratings (Par 105): **110,107,106,104,102 101,101,98**
CSF £27.27 CT £80.83 TOTE £5.50: £1.80, £1.60, £1.60; EX 31.20 Trifecta £138.80.
Owner Con Harrington **Bred** Con Harrington **Trained** Longton, Lancs
■ Stewards' Enquiry : Seamus Cronin four-day ban: use of whip (Feb 12-15)
FOCUS
There looked to be plenty of front-runners in the line-up, but the winner bagged the lead and made all. The winner has been rated up a length on his recent form, with the second rated to his Chelmsford win and the third close to form.

472 LADBROKES HOME OF THE ODDS BOOST NOVICE STKS — 1m 142y (Tp)
8:15 (8:15) (Class 5) 3-Y-O
£3,752 (£1,116; £557; £278) **Stalls** Low

Form RPR
56- 1 **Red Bond (IRE)**[38] 9683 3-9-2 0 .... CallumRodriguez 7 78
(Keith Dalgleish) *mde all: hung lft sn after s: qckng 2f out: rdn out* **8/1**[3]
2 2 1/2 **American Graffiti (FR)**[19] 156 3-9-2 0 .... AdamKirby 4 77
(Charlie Appleby) *chsd ldrs: shkn up over 2f out: rdn to chse wnr fnl f: edgd lft: styd on* **4/11**[1]
3 5 **William McKinley** 3-9-2 0 .... (b[1]) LukeMorris 5 66
(Hugo Palmer) *s.i.s: rcvrd to chse wnr over 7f out: shkn up over 3f out: rdn and lost 2nd 1f out: sn edgd lft and no ex* **9/2**[2]
4 3/4 **Cardano (USA)** 3-9-2 0 .... KieranO'Neill 2 64
(Ian Williams) *hld up: shkn up over 2f out: n.d (jockey said gelding ran green)* **20/1**
5 2 **Al Daayen (FR)** 3-8-11 0 .... PJMcDonald 3 54
(Mark Johnston) *chsd ldrs: rdn over 1f out: wknd fnl f* **28/1**
6 1/2 **Shaleela's Dream** 3-9-2 0 .... (b[1]) MarcMonaghan 6 58
(Marco Botti) *s.i.s: hld up: rdn over 1f out: nvr on terms* **25/1**
0- 7 10 **Redemptress (IRE)**[33] 9727 3-8-11 0 .... LiamJones 1 30
(John O'Shea) *prom: lost pl after 1f: pushed along 1/2-way: wknd over 2f out* **200/1**

1m 49.52s (-0.58) **Going Correction** -0.125s/f (Stan) **7 Ran SP% 115.2**
Speed ratings (Par 97): **97,96,92,91,89 89,80**
CSF £11.62 TOTE £9.60: £2.50, £1.10; EX 17.30 Trifecta £44.00.
Owner Middleham Park Racing XXVII **Bred** Mrs Colette Todd **Trained** Carluke, S Lanarks
FOCUS
A fair novice, but a tactical affair. The second has been rated in line with his debut form.
T/Jkpt: Not won. T/Plt: £652.70 to a £1 stake. Pool £107,179.54 - 119.87 winning units T/Qpdt: £57.80 to a £1 stake. Pool: £20,293.30 - 259.71 winning units **Colin Roberts**

437 LINGFIELD (L-H)
Wednesday, January 30
OFFICIAL GOING: Polytrack: standard to slow
Wind: Almost nil Weather: Sunny, cold

473 BETWAY LIVE CASINO H'CAP — 1m 2f (P)
1:50 (1:50) (Class 5) (0-70,72) 4-Y-O+
£3,752 (£1,116; £557; £300; £300; £300) **Stalls** Low

Form RPR
41-2 1 **Narjes**[11] 309 5-9-6 **68** .... (h) LukeMorris 10 74
(Laura Mongan) *hld up in midfield: prog over 1f out: cajoled along to chal fnl f: led fnl 100yds: kpt on* **11/2**[3]
0/65 2 *nk* **Stormy Blues**[9] 346 5-9-10 **72** .... (t[1]) RossaRyan 3 77
(Nigel Hawke) *cl up on inner: rdn 2f out: chal between rivals fnl f: kpt on but hld nr fin* **7/1**
321- 3 1/2 **Rakematiz**[49] 9511 5-9-7 **69** .... CallumShepherd 11 73
(Brett Johnson) *racd wd early: prog to ld after 3f: drvn for home over 2f out: hdd and one pce ins fnl f* **7/2**[2]
04-0 4 1 1/4 **Makambe (IRE)**[26] 54 4-9-7 **70** .... JoeyHaynes 4 72
(Paul Howling) *hld up in last pair: cajoled along wl over 1f out: prog to take 4th ins fnl f: nt pce to rch ldrs* **8/1**
040- 5 3/4 **Ripley (IRE)**[56] 9402 4-9-1 **64** .... (t) RichardKingscote 5 64
(Charles Hills) *stdd s: hld up in last pair: drvn wl over 1f out: no prog tl r.o fnl 150yds: nvr nrr* **20/1**
0-65 6 *nse* **Bobby Biscuit (USA)**[12] 292 4-9-7 **70** .... JFEgan 2 70
(Simon Dow) *t.k.h: hld up in midfield: rdn on inner wl over 1f out: nt qckn and no imp on ldrs (vet said colt bled from the nose)* **5/2**[1]
40-0 7 3/4 **Royal Goldie (IRE)**[21] 135 4-9-1 **64** .... (t) RobertHavlin 9 62
(Lydia Richards) *hld up in last trio: urged along 2f out: one pce and nvr able to threaten* **33/1**
4-21 8 1/2 **Global Wonder (IRE)**[11] 309 4-9-6 **69** .... (p) AdamKirby 1 66
(Gay Kelleway) *led 3f: chsd ldr: rdn over 3f out: lost pl over 1f out: fdd (trainer could offer no explanation for the gelding's performance)* **7/2**[2]
44/0 9 9 **Sir George Somers (USA)**[12] 292 6-9-7 **69** .... LiamKeniry 6 48
(Nigel Twiston-Davies) *pressed ldrs tl wknd qckly over 2f out* **25/1**

2m 7.04s (0.44) **Going Correction** -0.025s/f (Stan)
WFA 4 from 5yo+ 1lb **9 Ran SP% 123.6**
Speed ratings (Par 103): **97,96,96,95,94 94,94,93,86**
CSF £45.54 CT £158.54 TOTE £6.20: £1.70, £2.10, £1.50; EX 45.80 Trifecta £283.00.
Owner Peter Robert Howell **Bred** Rabbah Bloodstock Limited **Trained** Epsom, Surrey
■ Chetan was withdrawn, price at time of withdrawal 16/1. Rule 4 does not apply.
FOCUS
Modest form and the pace was a steady one. The first three have been rated as finding a bit on their recent form.

474 LADBROKES MAIDEN FILLIES' STKS — 1m 2f (P)
2:20 (2:20) (Class 5) 3-Y-O+
£3,752 (£1,116; £557; £278) **Stalls** Low

Form RPR
0- 1 **Anapurna**[34] 9725 3-8-5 0 .... KieranO'Neill 4 86
(John Gosden) *trckd ldrs: led over 2f out and kicked on: clr fnl f: hung bdly rt nr fin (jockey said filly ran green)* **6/1**
2 5 **Dawn Crusade (IRE)** 3-8-2 0 .... WilliamCox(3) 1 76
(Charlie Appleby) *trckd ldng trio: effrt over 2f out: reminder to chse wnr wl over 1f out but then hung bdly lft: no imp after (jockey said filly ran green)* **15/8**[1]
0- 3 1 3/4 **Royal Family (FR)**[62] 9314 3-8-5 0 .... NickyMackay 7 72
(John Gosden) *dwlt: hld up in 5th: pushed along and outpcd over 2f out: rdn and kpt on to take 3rd 1f out: no threat* **7/2**[3]
22-2 4 7 **Simple Thought (IRE)**[16] 239 4-9-13 77 .... AdamKirby 2 64
(Simon Crisford) *trckd ldr: rdn and no rspnse wl over 2f out: sn lost pl and btn* **5/2**[2]
53-2 5 4 1/2 **Redemptive**[26] 55 3-8-0 66 .... DarraghKeenan(5) 6 49
(David Elsworth) *mde most to over 2f out: pushed along and wknd qckly over 1f out* **8/1**
00- 6 9 **Gladden (IRE)**[33] 9732 4-9-10 0 .... PaddyBradley(3) 3 37
(Lee Carter) *dwlt: hld up in last: shkn up 3f out: sn lft bhd* **100/1**

2m 4.34s (-2.26) **Going Correction** -0.025s/f (Stan)
WFA 3 from 4yo 23lb **6 Ran SP% 112.0**
Speed ratings (Par 100): **108,104,102,97,93 86**
CSF £17.64 TOTE £8.10: £3.30, £1.10; EX 23.40 Trifecta £101.30.
Owner Helena Springfield Ltd **Bred** Meon Valley Stud **Trained** Newmarket, Suffolk
FOCUS
Time may show this was a fairly decent maiden and the winner was rather impressive. The level is a bit fluid.

475 LADBROKES HOME OF THE ODDS BOOST/EBF FILLIES' H'CAP — 7f 1y(P)
2:50 (2:50) (Class 3) (0-90,82) 4-Y-O+
£9,766 (£2,923; £1,461; £731) **Stalls** Low

Form RPR
06-1 1 **Made Of Honour (IRE)**[24] 104 5-9-5 **80** .... (p) CliffordLee 4 86
(K R Burke) *trckd ldr after 2f: urged along over 2f out and sn chalng: drvn ahd jst ins fnl f: styd on wl* **10/3**[3]
103- 2 1 1/4 **Treasure Me**[96] 8603 4-9-7 **82** .... (p) StevieDonohoe 3 85
(Charlie Fellowes) *s.i.s: rcvrd to ld after 1f: rdn wl over 1f out: hdd and one pce jst ins fnl f* **3/1**[2]
5-11 3 1/2 **Happy Escape**[14] 255 5-9-7 **82** .... AdamKirby 2 84
(Tony Carroll) *hld up in last: shkn up and nt qckn wl over 1f out: styd on to take 3rd ins fnl f: nvr able to chal* **5/4**[1]
51-1 4 3/4 **Side Effect**[6] 392 4-9-0 **75** 6ex .... (p) AlistairRawlinson 1 75
(Michael Appleby) *t.k.h: led 1f: short of room briefly and dropped to 3rd 5f out: shkn up on inner wl over 1f out: one pce after* **5/1**

1m 25.13s (0.33) **Going Correction** -0.025s/f (Stan) **4 Ran SP% 109.2**
Speed ratings (Par 104): **97,95,95,94**
CSF £12.96 TOTE £3.90; EX 12.50 Trifecta £18.10.
Owner Ontoawinner, D Mackay & Mrs E Burke **Bred** Limetree Stud **Trained** Middleham Moor, N Yorks
FOCUS
No great gallop on here and all four still held a chance with 1f to run. The second has been rated to form.

476 SUNRACING.CO.UK MAIDEN H'CAP — 7f 1y(P)
3:20 (3:20) (Class 6) (0-60,62) 3-Y-O+
£3,105 (£924; £461; £300; £300; £300) **Stalls** Low

Form RPR
2-33 1 **Catapult**[7] 365 4-9-3 **49** .... HollieDoyle 12 57
(Clifford Lines) *v fast away: mde all: 2 l clr wl over 1f out: drvn out fnl f: a holding on* **4/1**[1]
24-0 2 3/4 **Global Goddess (IRE)**[19] 183 3-8-5 **58** .... (p) WilliamCox(3) 6 59
(Gay Kelleway) *hld up in midfield: rdn and prog over 1f out: styd on to take 2nd fnl 75yds: clsd on wnr nr fin but a hld* **16/1**
23-4 3 1 **Wind Storm**[23] 123 4-10-0 **60** .... CliffordLee 8 63
(K R Burke) *chsd wnr: rdn over 2f out: no imp over 1f out: kpt on but lost 2nd fnl 75yds* **7/1**[3]
540- 4 1 1/4 **Your Mothers' Eyes**[70] 9169 3-8-11 **61** .... JoeyHaynes 3 56
(Alan Bailey) *trckd ldrs: rdn over 2f out: one pce and nvr able to cl* **7/1**[3]
40-0 5 *hd* **Reignite**[21] 141 4-10-0 **60** .... AdamKirby 5 60+
(Emma Owen) *taken steadily to post: hld up in last trio: stl there 2f out: rdn over 1f out: fin strly but too late* **9/1**
050- 6 3/4 **Kath's Boy (IRE)**[165] 6282 5-9-0 **46** oh1 .... (p[1]) GeorgeDowning 4 44
(Tony Carroll) *wl plcd: 5th and pushed along 2f out: no imp on ldrs whn rdn ins fnl f* **25/1**
0/0- 7 *nk* **Paco Dawn**[76] 9079 5-9-0 **46** oh1 .... RossaRyan 13 43
(Tony Carroll) *hld up in rr: sme prog on inner 2f out: rdn and kpt on fnl f but nt pce to threaten (jockey said mare was denied a clear run)* **80/1**
22-2 8 *nk* **Violet's Lads (IRE)**[14] 256 5-9-13 **62** .... PaddyBradley(3) 11 66+
(Brett Johnson) *hld up in rr: swtchd to inner over 1f out: nt clr run after: nvr in it but kpt on nr fin (jockey said mare was denied a clear run)* **4/1**[1]
20-4 9 1 1/4 **Farump**[9] 341 3-7-9 **50** oh2 .... DarraghKeenan(5) 2 38
(Robert Eddery) *in tch: rdn wl over 2f out: no prog over 1f out: fdd* **20/1**
2-44 10 *shd* **Minuty**[19] 178 4-9-12 **58** .... RobertHavlin 1 51
(Rae Guest) *prom: rdn over 2f out: disp 3rd on inner over 1f out: wknd fnl f* **6/1**[2]
0-34 11 1/2 **Eufemia**[18] 211 3-8-10 **60** .... (t) GeorgeWood 9 46
(Amy Murphy) *hld up in midfield: rdn over 2f out: no prog* **8/1**

00-5 **12** *1 ¼* **Speed Skater**[19] 186 3-8-8 **58** .... JoeFanning 14 41
(Amanda Perrett) *racd on outer: nvr beyond midfield: rdn and no prog over 2f out: wknd fnl f* **16/1**

5-60 **13** *nk* **Mystical Moon (IRE)**[6] 379 4-9-0 **46** oh1 ....(v) StevieDonohoe 7 33
(David C Griffiths) *hld up in last trio: rdn over 2f out and no prog after* **33/1**

060- **14** *1 ¼* **Breezing**[63] 9291 3-8-7 **57** .... MartinDwyer 10 36
(Sylvester Kirk) *s.i.s: nvr gng wl and a last* **33/1**

1m 24.99s (0.19) **Going Correction** -0.025s/f (Stan) **14 Ran SP% 127.9**
WFA 3 from 4yo+ 18lb
Speed ratings (Par 101): **97,96,95,93,93 92,92,91,90,90 89,88,87,86**
CSF £74.40 CT £467.25 TOTE £4.90: £1.90, £4.60, £3.00; EX 74.00 Trifecta £523.20.
Owner Prima Racing Partnership **Bred** Owen O'Brien **Trained** Exning, Suffolk

FOCUS
Moderate form and little got into it, with Catapult making all and giving Clifford Lines a winner with his final runner as a trainer. The second has been rated near her best.

477 LADBROKES NOVICE AUCTION STKS — 6f 1y(P)
3:50 (3:50) (Class 6) 3-Y-O **£3,105** (£924; £461; £230) **Stalls Low**

Form RPR

1 **With Caution (IRE)** 3-8-11 0 .... PJMcDonald 5 68+
(James Tate) *in tch in 5th: urged along 2f out: sltly green but picked up and prog over 1f out: chsd ldr ins fnl f: r.o to ld fnl 50yds* **11/2**[3]

40-2 **2** *½* **Second Collection**[16] 235 3-8-11 64 ....(h) RichardKingscote 4 66
(Tony Carroll) *cl up on inner: wnt 2nd 2f out: shkn up to ld over 1f out: styd on but hdd and outpcd fnl 50yds* **4/1**[2]

3- **3** *2* **Scorched Breath**[56] 9395 3-9-2 0 .... StevieDonohoe 1 65
(Charlie Fellowes) *chsd ldr: lost 2nd and nt qckn 2f out: sn outpcd: kpt on ins fnl f* **8/15**[1]

0- **4** *¾* **Sussudio**[81] 9000 3-8-11 0 .... MartinDwyer 3 58
(Richard Spencer) *led: rdn and hdd over 1f out: fdd fnl f* **20/1**

0- **5** *5* **Estranged (IRE)**[34] 9727 3-8-11 0 .... JoeFanning 2 43
(Tom Clover) *hld up in last: outpcd and shkn up 2f out: fdd* **33/1**

0-5 **6** *½* **Fort Benton (IRE)**[28] 27 3-9-2 0 .... CliffordLee 6 46
(David Barron) *racd wd: chsd ldng pair: rdn over 2f out: losing pl whn v wd bnd sn after: bhd fnl f* **14/1**

1m 11.7s (-0.20) **Going Correction** -0.025s/f (Stan) **6 Ran SP% 115.0**
Speed ratings (Par 95): **100,99,96,95,89 88**
CSF £28.13 TOTE £6.10: £2.30, £1.90; EX 22.30 Trifecta £40.40.
Owner Saeed Manana **Bred** Ballyphilip Stud **Trained** Newmarket, Suffolk

FOCUS
Modest novice form, with the runner-up rated just 64.

478 BETWAY H'CAP — 5f 6y(P)
4:20 (4:20) (Class 7) (0-50,50) 3-Y-O+ **£2,264** (£673; £336; £168) **Stalls High**

Form RPR

006- **1** **Skip To My Lou**[118] 7946 4-9-5 **45** .... KierenFox 8 56
(Peter Crate) *chsd ldr: shkn up 2f out: rdn to chal over 1f out: styd on to ld fnl 100yds (trainer said regarding apparent improvement in from that filly had been slow in maturing and this race was a drop in class)* **9/2**[3]

3-12 **2** *1 ½* **Pharoh Jake**[12] 298 11-9-2 **49** .... EllieMacKenzie(7) 2 55
(John Bridger) *chsd ldr: rdn to ld over 1f out: hdd and outpcd fnl 100yds: styd on* **4/1**[2]

000- **3** *2 ¼* **Compton Abbey**[34] 9720 5-9-10 **50** ....(v[1]) RossaRyan 9 48
(Alexandra Dunn) *slowly away: wl in rr: wdst of all bnd 2f out: drvn and styd on over 1f out to take 3rd nr fin* **14/1**

5-06 **4** *½* **Blistering Dancer (IRE)**[20] 166 9-9-5 **45** ....(p) PJMcDonald 4 41
(Tony Carroll) *chsd ldrs but nt on terms: rdn on inner over 1f out: kpt on to take 3rd briefly ins fnl f: n.d* **10/1**

046- **5** *½* **Hurricane Alert**[30] 9776 7-9-6 **49** .... WilliamCox(3) 10 43
(Mark Hoad) *chsd ldng trio: rdn 2f out: kpt on same pce and disp 3rd briefly ins fnl f: n.d* **16/1**

4-03 **6** *1* **Amazing Amaya**[11] 322 4-9-7 **47** ....(h) CallumShepherd 5 38
(Derek Shaw) *hld up in rr: shkn up 2f out: no great prog and nvr involved* **9/1**

6-23 **7** *½* **Storm Trooper (IRE)**[23] 118 8-9-6 **46** ....(t) RichardKingscote 1 35
(Charlie Wallis) *led: rdn and hdd over 1f out: hanging and wknd fnl f* **3/1**[1]

-046 **8** *hd* **Malaysian Boleh**[6] 379 9-9-6 **46** ....(v) StevieDonohoe 6 34
(Phil McEntee) *mostly in last pl and struggling tl r.o fnl 150yds* **3/1**[1]

000- **9** *½* **Hornby**[30] 9777 4-9-2 **45** ....(t[1]) JoshuaBryan(3) 7 31
(Michael Attwater) *nvr beyond midfield: rdn and no prog over 1f out* **33/1**

04-0 **10** *1 ¾* **Chicago School (IRE)**[12] 298 6-9-5 **45** ....(vt) AlistairRawlinson 3 25
(Nikki Evans) *restless stalls: slowly away: a towards rr: rdn and no prog over 1f out* **16/1**

58.58s (-0.22) **Going Correction** -0.025s/f (Stan) **10 Ran SP% 128.6**
Speed ratings (Par 97): **100,97,94,93,92 90,90,89,88,86**
CSF £25.59 CT £254.39 TOTE £6.30: £2.00, £1.60, £3.90; EX 31.80 Trifecta £338.40.
Owner Peter Crate **Bred** Peter Crate **Trained** Newdigate, Surrey

FOCUS
Lowly sprinting form, but a winner on the up. The second has been rated to his recent C&D winning figure.
T/Plt: £725.10 to a £1 stake. Pool: £131,665.67 - 132.55 winning units T/Qpdt: £101.90 to a £1 stake. Pool: £13,215.34 - 95.89 winning units **Jonathan Neesom**

465 WOLVERHAMPTON (A.W) (L-H)
Wednesday, January 30

OFFICIAL GOING: Tapeta: standard
Wind: Nil Weather: Fine

479 BETWAY APPRENTICE H'CAP — 1m 1f 104y (Tp)
4:45 (4:45) (Class 6) (0-60,60) 4-Y-O+ **£3,105** (£924; £461; £400; £400; £400) **Stalls Low**

Form RPR

4-30 **1** **Caledonia Duchess**[14] 256 6-9-1 **59** ....(v) GeorgiaDobie(5) 6 65
(Jo Hughes, France) *trckd ldrs: racd keenly: wnt 2nd over 1f out: rdn to ld wl ins fnl f: styd on (trainers' rep said, reg app imp in form, mare may have benefitted from the reapplication of a the visor)* **11/1**

00-4 **2** *½* **Sea Shack**[16] 241 5-8-12 **54** ....(tp) ScottMcCullagh(3) 7 59
(Julia Feilden) *chsd ldr tl led over 2f out: rdn and hdd wl ins fnl f: kpt on* **12/1**

03-5 **3** *nk* **Traveller (FR)**[22] 125 5-9-3 **59** ....(t) KieranSchofield(3) 8 63
(Antony Brittain) *hld up in tch: rdn over 1f out: r.o* **13/2**[2]

4 *nk* **Chaparral Dream (IRE)**[84] 8943 4-8-9 **54** .... MarkCrehan(5) 3 58+
(Adrian McGuinness, Ire) *chsd ldrs: rdn over 1f out: edgd rt ins fnl f: r.o* **9/4**[1]

6-44 **5** *1 ¼* **Sir Lancelott**[6] 379 7-8-2 **46** oh1 .... LauraCoughlan(5) 10 48
(Adrian Nicholls) *hld up: hdwy over 1f out: r.o: nt rch ldrs* **8/1**

60-3 **6** *nk* **King Oswald (USA)**[22] 125 6-9-3 **59** ....(p) TobyEley(3) 9 60+
(James Unett) *s.i.s: hld up: hdwy over 1f out: r.o: nt rch ldrs (jockey said gelding was slowly away)* **15/2**[3]

00-0 **7** *2* **Boycie**[25] 85 6-9-3 **56** ....(p) MeganNicholls 1 53
(Adrian Wintle) *hld up: hdwy over 1f out: sn rdn: styd on same pce ins fnl f* **18/1**

04-6 **8** *3* **Corked (IRE)**[22] 125 6-9-6 **59** .... CameronNoble 11 50
(Alistair Whillans) *hld up: rdn over 1f out: n.d* **11/1**

105- **9** *¾* **Blue Rocks**[314] 1309 5-9-7 **60** .... SebastianWoods 4 50
(Lisa Williamson) *led: hdd over 2f out: wknd ins fnl f* **33/1**

00-0 **10** *2 ¼* **Altaira**[26] 58 8-8-7 **46** oh1 ....(b) PoppyBridgwater 12 35
(Tony Carroll) *hld up in tch: hmpd over 3f out: shkn up over 1f out: wknd fnl f* **40/1**

66-0 **11** *4 ½* **Stay In The Light**[18] 207 4-8-6 **46** .... RhiainIngram 13 23
(Roger Ingram) *s.i.s: hld up: hdwy and hung lft over 3f out: wknd over 2f out* **18/1**

600- **12** *¾* **Box And Cox**[163] 6355 4-8-9 **52** ....(t[1] w) JonathanFisher(3) 2 28
(Stef Keniry) *s.s: hld up: swtchd rt over 4f out: wknd over 2f out (jockey said gelding was slowly away)* **22/1**

2m 0.31s (-0.49) **Going Correction** 0.0s/f (Stan) **12 Ran SP% 111.6**
WFA 4 from 5yo+ 1lb
Speed ratings (Par 101): **102,101,101,101,99 99,97,95,94,92 88,87**
CSF £125.43 CT £913.60 TOTE £11.70: £4.00, £4.20, £2.30; EX 153.30 Trifecta £1262.90.
Owner Isla & Colin Cage **Bred** Mrs I M Cage And Mr C J Cage **Trained** France

FOCUS
A modest race in which the principals raced close to the pace. The second and third help set the level.

480 BETWAY STAYERS' H'CAP — 2m 120y (Tp)
5:15 (5:15) (Class 4) (0-85,84) 4-Y-O+ **£5,530** (£1,645; £822; £411; £400) **Stalls Low**

Form RPR

25-4 **1** **Moon Of Baroda**[25] 84 4-9-0 **75** ....(b) DavidProbert 5 81
(Charles Hills) *hld up: hdwy over 3f out: led over 1f out: rdn and edgd rt ins fnl f: styd on* **9/4**[1]

102- **2** *¾* **Markhan (USA)**[26] 72 6-9-12 **82** ....(t) JamieSpencer 1 87
(Gordon Elliott, Ire) *trckd ldrs: rdn over 1f out: chsd wnr ins fnl f: styd on* **7/2**[3]

054- **3** *1 ¼* **Chocolate Box (IRE)**[21] 6984 5-9-12 **82** .... LiamJones 2 85
(Mark Loughnane) *racd keenly in 2nd pl tl led over 10f out: qcknd over 3f out: rdn and hdd over 2f out: styd on same pce ins fnl f* **9/1**

63/2 **4** *1 ¼* **Red Royalist**[25] 84 5-9-6 **76** .... ShaneKelly 3 78
(Stuart Edmunds) *sn led at stdy pce: hdd over 10f out: chsd ldr tl led again over 2f out: rdn and hdd over 1f out: no ex wl ins fnl f* **3/1**[2]

21/0 **5** *12* **Alabaster**[19] 184 5-10-0 **84** ....(p) LukeMorris 4 71
(Sir Mark Prescott Bt) *prom: shkn up over 3f out: wknd over 2f out (jockey said gelding hung right-handed throughout)* **9/2**

3m 42.88s (3.58) **Going Correction** 0.0s/f (Stan) **5 Ran SP% 106.2**
WFA 4 from 5yo+ 5lb
Speed ratings (Par 105): **91,90,90,89,83**
CSF £9.49 TOTE £2.50: £1.40, £1.80; EX 9.30 Trifecta £37.80.
Owner Tony Wechsler & Ann Plummer **Bred** Fittocks Stud **Trained** Lambourn, Berks

FOCUS
A fair handicap but it wasn't a proper test, with the time 10.38sec slower than standard. Muddling form.

481 BETWAY CLASSIFIED CLAIMING STKS — 1m 4f 51y (Tp)
5:45 (5:45) (Class 5) 4-Y-O+ **£3,752** (£1,116; £557; £400; £400; £400) **Stalls Low**

Form RPR

56-0 **1** **Epitaph (IRE)**[26] 61 5-8-12 60 ....(b) AndrewMullen 7 66
(Michael Appleby) *hld up: hdwy 3f out: nt clr run and swtchd lft over 1f out: rdn and r.o to ld wl ins fnl f* **12/1**

00-5 **2** *nk* **Dream Magic (IRE)**[23] 119 5-8-12 62 .... EoinWalsh 9 66
(Mark Loughnane) *chsd ldr over 2f: remained handy: led 2f out: sn rdn: edgd lft and hdd wl ins fnl f* **9/1**

06-0 **3** *2 ¼* **Gravity Wave (IRE)**[15] 246 5-8-8 69 .... LukeMorris 8 58
(Sylvester Kirk) *hld up in tch: drvn along over 2f out: edgd lft u.p fnl f: styd on same pce* **10/3**[2]

504- **4** *5* **Hussar Ballad (USA)**[46] 9555 10-7-11 56 .... KieranSchofield(7) 3 46
(Antony Brittain) *awkward s: hld up: hdwy over 6f out: nt clr run and lost pl over 3f out: hdwy over 1f out: sn rdn: styd on same pce fnl f* **7/1**

53-6 **5** *½* **Pike Corner Cross (IRE)**[16] 241 7-7-12 59 ow1 ..... LauraCoughlan(7) 4 46
(Ed de Giles) *s.s: hld up and bhd: swtchd lft and hdwy over 1f out: nt trble ldrs (jockey said gelding was slowly away)* **13/2**[3]

065- **6** *8* **Raashdy (IRE)**[34] 9721 6-8-13 61 ....(p) PoppyBridgwater(5) 10 46
(Peter Hiatt) *prom: chsd ldr over 9f out: led 8f out: rdn and hdd 2f out: edgd rt and wknd fnl f* **28/1**

0-00 **7** *1 ¾* **Spring Dixie (IRE)**[6] 385 7-8-5 35 .... RhiainIngram(5) 2 36
(Natalie Lloyd-Beavis) *s.i.s: hld up: wknd over 2f out* **300/1**

061- **8** *nk* **Brigadoon**[203] 4802 12-8-4 67 .... LiamJones 1 29
(Michael Appleby) *chsd ldrs: rdn over 4f out: wknd over 2f out* **14/1**

00-0 **9** *hd* **Tha'ir (IRE)**[16] 241 9-8-5 55 .... PhilDennis(3) 6 33
(Olly Williams) *led 4f: chsd ldr tl rdn over 2f out: wknd over 1f out* **100/1**

-213 **10** *65* **Your Band**[11] 318 4-9-1 69 ....(p[1]) NicolaCurrie 5
(Jamie Osborne) *sn pushed along in rr: hdwy 10f out: lost pl 7f out: wknd over 4f out: eased fnl 2f (jockey said gelding ran flat. Vet said gelding was suffering from cardiac arrhythmia)* **15/8**[1]

2m 36.01s (-4.79) **Going Correction** 0.0s/f (Stan) **10 Ran SP% 112.8**
WFA 4 from 5yo+ 3lb
Speed ratings (Par 103): **112,111,110,106,106 101,100,99,99,56**
CSF £110.45 TOTE £14.40: £2.70, £2.50, £1.30; EX 139.40 Trifecta £728.40.
Owner Looksarnteverything Partnership **Bred** Whisperview Trading Ltd **Trained** Oakham, Rutland
■ Gravity Wave was claimed by Mr J. L. Flint for £6000.

The Form Book Flat 2019, Raceform Ltd, Newbury, RG14 5SJ

FOCUS
Very moderate form, anchored by the seventh.

482 BETWAY LIVE CASINO H'CAP 1m 5f 219y (Tp)
6:15 (6:15) (Class 6) (0-55,55) 4-Y-O+
£3,105 (£924; £461; £400; £400; £400) Stalls Low

Form RPR
354- 1 **Clearance**[14] 9318 5-8-13 **47**........................ HectorCrouch 4 52+
(Gary Moore) *hld up: hdwy over 1f out: rdn and r.o to ld wl ins fnl f* **10/3**[1]
00-5 2 1 **Falls Creek (USA)**[15] 245 4-8-8 **46** oh1..............(b) DavidProbert 11 52
(Andrew Balding) *chsd ldrs: rdn to ld 1f out: sn edgd lft: hdd wl ins fnl f* **13/2**[3]
610- 3 *shd* **Picture Painter (IRE)**[23] 8613 6-9-4 **55**.............. FinleyMarsh(3) 10 58
(David Pipe) *chsd ldrs: edgd lft after 3f: rdn and ev ch fr over 1f out: kpt on* **14/1**
40-5 4 *nk* **Wally's Wisdom**[26] 59 7-9-6 **54**........................ LiamJones 1 57
(Mark Loughnane) *hld up in tch: lost pl over 6f out: pushed along and hdwy over 1f out: styd on* **9/2**[2]
00-0 5 2 **Chief Sittingbull**[15] 246 6-9-2 **50**..............(t[1]) KieranO'Neill 7 50
(Tony Carroll) *sn led: rdn over 2f out: hdd 1f out: no ex ins fnl f* **11/1**
-400 6 *shd* **Demophon**[11] 321 5-8-12 **46** oh1........................ NicolaCurrie 12 46
(Steve Flook) *sn w ldr: rdn over 2f out: ev ch over 1f out: edgd rt and styd on same pce ins fnl f* **14/1**
/56- 7 *shd* **Oromo (IRE)**[69] 8319 6-8-12 **46** oh1..............(t) LukeMorris 6 47
(Karl Thornton, Ire) *prom: nt clr run and swtchd rt over 1f out: sn rdn: edgd lft and styd on same pce fnl f* **9/1**
03-5 8 *nk* **Sea Tea Dea**[18] 204 5-8-12 **46** oh1..............(t) ShaneKelly 5 47
(Katy Price) *chsd ldrs: hmpd after 3f: nt clr run and swtchd lft over 1f out: nt clr run again ins fnl f: no ex* **66/1**
06-4 9 2 ¼ **Alexis Carrington (IRE)**[20] 160 4-9-2 **54**..............(v) JamieSpencer 13 54
(John Quinn) *hld up: shkn up and hdwy over 1f out: nt clr run ins fnl f: eased* **13/2**[3]
00-0 10 ¾ **Iona Island**[14] 257 6-8-7 **48**..............(t[1]) TobyEley(7) 2 43
(Jean-Rene Auvray) *s.i.s: hld up: n.d (jockey said mare hung left-handed)* **50/1**
36-0 11 2 ¾ **Happy Ending (IRE)**[25] 85 4-9-3 **55**........................ RobHornby 8 48
(Seamus Mullins) *hld up: pushed along and hdwy on outer over 2f out: carried wd sn after: wknd over 1f out* **33/1**
56-0 12 4 **Mac O'Polo (IRE)**[16] 241 5-9-0 **55**........................ EllaMcCain(7) 9 41
(Donald McCain) *hld up in tch: hung rt over 7f out: hmpd over 2f out: wknd over 1f out* **11/1**
066- 13 24 **Oenophile (GER)**[27] 4501 4-9-2 **54**........................ AndrewMullen 3 8
(Tom Gretton) *s.i.s: hld up: hdwy over 5f out: rdn 3f out: sn wknd (jockey said filly ran too freely)* **50/1**

3m 6.01s (5.01) **Going Correction** 0.0s/f (Stan)
WFA 4 from 5yo+ 4lb **13 Ran SP% 116.3**
Speed ratings (Par 101): **85,84,84,84,83 83,82,82,81,81 79,77,63**
CSF £23.46 CT £268.13 TOTE £4.00: £1.60, £2.30, £4.40; EX 27.90 Trifecta £354.60.
Owner G L Moore **Bred** Richard W Farleigh **Trained** Lower Beeding, W Sussex
■ Stewards' Enquiry : Finley Marsh caution; careless riding

FOCUS
They didn't go a great gallop in this very modest event. The third and fourth help pin a straightforward level.

483 BETWAY H'CAP 6f 20y (Tp)
6:45 (6:45) (Class 6) (0-60,61) 4-Y-O+
£3,105 (£924; £461; £400; £400; £400) Stalls Low

Form RPR
0-60 1 **Indian Affair**[21] 144 9-9-2 **55**..............(bt) KieranO'Neill 9 61
(Milton Bradley) *led early: w ldr: rdn over 1f out: r.o u.p to ld post* **14/1**
0-32 2 *nse* **Dodgy Bob**[23] 116 6-8-6 **48**..............(v) PhilDennis(3) 5 54
(Michael Mullineaux) *sn led: rdn over 1f out: edgd rt and hdd ins fnl f: rallied to ld nr fin: hdd post* **10/1**
0-34 3 *hd* **Knockout Blow**[12] 286 4-9-7 **60**..............(p[1]) CharlieBennett 1 65+
(Jim Boyle) *hld up: plld hrd: nt clr run: hdwy and swtchd rt over 1f out: sn rdn: r.o wl* **15/2**[3]
065- 4 ½ **Coastal Cyclone**[112] 8104 5-9-2 **55**........................ ShaneKelly 2 59
(Harry Dunlop) *chsd ldrs: rdn to ld ins fnl f: edgd lft: hdd nr fin* **10/1**
16-4 5 ½ **Billyoakes (IRE)**[6] 383 7-9-7 **60**..............(p) LukeMorris 7 62
(Charlie Wallis) *chsd ldrs: rdn over 2f out: styd on u.p* **7/1**[2]
-625 6 1 ¼ **Le Manege Enchante (IRE)**[12] 293 6-8-9 **48**..............(v) PaddyMathers 10 47
(Derek Shaw) *s.i.s: hld up: hdwy u.p over 1f out: nt rch ldrs* **25/1**
001- 7 *shd* **Cuban Spirit**[46] 9559 4-9-6 **59**........................ NicolaCurrie 3 57
(Henry Candy) *s.i.s: hld up: shkn up over 2f out: hdwy u.p over 1f out: nt clr run ins fnl f: nt trble ldrs (jockey said gelding was slowly away and hung left-handed)* **11/8**[1]
42-4 8 *nk* **Fantasy Justifier (IRE)**[28] 28 8-9-4 **57**..............(p) DavidProbert 11 54
(Ronald Harris) *hld up: plld hrd: hdwy over 1f out: nt trble ldrs (jockey said gelding ran too freely)* **11/1**
50-0 9 2 ½ **Precious Plum**[12] 286 5-9-5 **58**..............(p) AndrewMullen 8 48
(Charlie Wallis) *hld up on outer: plld hrd: shkn up over 1f out: nvr trbld ldrs* **66/1**
23-0 10 2 **Isabella Ruby**[12] 293 4-8-0 **46**..............(h) KieranSchofield(7) 6 30
(Lisa Williamson) *hld up in tch on outer: plld hrd: pushed along over 2f out: wknd fnl f (jockey said filly stopped quickly)* **16/1**

1m 13.41s (-1.09) **Going Correction** 0.0s/f (Stan) **10 Ran SP% 110.8**
Speed ratings (Par 101): **107,106,106,106,105 103,103,103,99,97**
CSF £137.83 CT £1114.48 TOTE £11.80: £2.50, £2.10, £2.80; EX 113.00 Trifecta £880.20.
Owner J M Bradley **Bred** Mette Campbell-Andenaes **Trained** Sedbury, Gloucs

FOCUS
A frantic finish to this low-grade sprint.

484 SUNRACING.CO.UK H'CAP 7f 36y (Tp)
7:15 (7:15) (Class 6) (0-55,55) 4-Y-O+
£3,105 (£924; £461; £400; £400; £400) Stalls High

Form RPR
245/ 1 **Hungarian Rhapsody**[537] 5892 5-9-5 **55**........................ NicolaCurrie 4 61
(Jamie Osborne) *mde virtually all: rdn over 1f out: styd on* **2/1**[1]
0-34 2 *nse* **Rivas Rob Roy**[14] 250 4-9-4 **54**........................ JoeyHaynes 2 60
(John Gallagher) *trckd ldrs: ev ch fr over 1f out: sn rdn: styd on (vet said gelding lost it's left fore shoe)* **8/1**
-246 3 2 ½ **Viola Park**[15] 243 5-9-4 **54**........................ DavidProbert 8 54
(Ronald Harris) *hld up: rdn and r.o to go 3rd wl ins fnl f: nt rch ldrs* **7/1**[3]
/30- 4 1 **Seanie (IRE)**[70] 9184 10-9-5 **55**..............(t) LukeMorris 3 52
(Karl Thornton, Ire) *chsd wnr tl over 1f out: no ex ins fnl f* **33/1**
100- 5 ½ **Seaforth (IRE)**[149] 6860 7-8-13 **52**........................ FinleyMarsh(3) 10 48
(Adrian Wintle) *hld up in tch: rdn over 1f out: styd on same pce fnl f* **80/1**
135- 6 ½ **Imbucato**[113] 8070 5-9-3 **53**........................ GeorgeDowning 6 48
(Tony Carroll) *hld up in tch: rdn over 1f out: styd on same pce fnl f* **33/1**
20-3 7 *nse* **Diamond Pursuit**[20] 166 4-9-2 **52**........................ KieranO'Neill 12 47
(Ivan Furtado) *prom: shkn up over 2f out: styd on same pce fnl f* **25/1**
60-3 8 1 **Classy Cailin (IRE)**[23] 116 4-9-2 **52**........................ EoinWalsh 7 44
(Mark Loughnane) *hld up: rdn over 1f out: nvr nrr* **14/1**
10-3 9 ½ **Magical Molly Joe**[5] 410 5-9-0 **53**..............(h) JaneElliott(3) 1 44+
(David Barron) *hld up: racd keenly: nt clr run fr over 2f out: nvr trbld ldrs (jockey said mare was denied a clear run)* **7/2**[2]
4-12 10 ½ **New Rich**[15] 244 9-8-9 **52**..............(b) GeorgiaDobie(7) 9 42
(Eve Johnson Houghton) *hld up: plld hrd: hdwy on outer 1/2-way: rdn over 1f out: wknd fnl f (jockey said gelding ran too freely)* **25/1**
00-0 11 1 **Marble Bar**[16] 241 4-9-5 **55**........................ CallumRodriguez 11 42
(Iain Jardine) *hld up: nvr on terms* **25/1**
2-50 12 *hd* **Athassel**[7] 365 10-9-2 **52**........................ ShaneKelly 5 39
(David Evans) *s.i.s: hld up: nvr on terms* **15/2**

1m 28.53s (-0.27) **Going Correction** 0.0s/f (Stan) **12 Ran SP% 116.3**
Speed ratings (Par 101): **101,100,98,96,96 95,95,94,94,93 92,92**
CSF £16.67 CT £96.41 TOTE £2.50: £1.60, £2.90, £2.30; EX 20.50 Trifecta £152.40.
Owner J A Osborne **Bred** W And R Barnett Ltd **Trained** Upper Lambourn, Berks
■ Stewards' Enquiry : Eoin Walsh two-day ban; misuse of whip (Feb 13-14)

FOCUS
Pace held up in this routine handicap. The second has been rated near this winter's best.

485 FOLLOW TOP TIPSTER TEMPLEGATE AT SUN RACING H'CAP 1m 142y (Tp)
7:45 (7:45) (Class 7) (0-50,50) 4-Y-O+ £2,264 (£673; £336; £168) Stalls Low

Form RPR
30-0 1 **Limerick Lord (IRE)**[29] 6 7-9-2 **47**..............(p) ShelleyBirkett 8 54
(Julia Feilden) *mde all: rdn and edgd rt ins fnl f: styd on (trainer said, reg app imp in form, gelding benefitted from being switched to the Tapeta surface having raced exclusively on Fibresand in recent runs, and also appreciated an uncontested lead on this occasion)* **16/1**
00-0 2 2 **Blue Harmony**[25] 80 4-8-11 **48**..............(p) MeganNicholls(5) 13 51
(Michael Blake) *plld hrd and prom: wnt 2nd over 6f out tl over 4f out: chsd wnr again over 3f out: rdn and edgd lft fr over 1f out: styd on* **28/1**
00-6 3 ¾ **Mr Frankie**[26] 62 8-9-4 **49**..............(p) EoinWalsh 10 50
(Roy Brotherton) *s.i.s: hld up: hung lft over 2f out: hdwy over 1f out: rdn and r.o to go 3rd ins fnl f: nt rch ldrs* **8/1**
20-0 4 *nk* **Ahfad**[18] 207 4-9-2 **48**..............(b) HectorCrouch 4 49
(Gary Moore) *hld up: hdwy over 2f out: nt clr run over 1f out: r.o* **13/2**
42-0 5 *hd* **Jeremy's Jet (IRE)**[26] 62 8-9-4 **49**..............(t) DavidProbert 6 49+
(Tony Carroll) *s.i.s: hld up: nt clr run over 2f out: hdwy over 1f out: r.o: nt rch ldrs* **7/2**[1]
0-00 6 *hd* **Plucky Dip**[14] 263 8-8-9 **47**........................ LauraPearson(7) 3 47
(John Ryan) *prom: hmpd over 2f out: rdn over 1f out: styd on same pce ins fnl f* **14/1**
50-4 7 ½ **Kellington Kitty (USA)**[23] 116 4-9-4 **50**........................ RossaRyan 7 49
(Mike Murphy) *chsd wnr 2f: remained handy: rdn and edgd rt over 1f out: styd on same pce fnl f* **11/2**[3]
00-0 8 2 **Little Choosey**[13] 273 9-9-5 **50**..............(bt) RobHornby 1 45
(Roy Bowring) *hld up: rdn and r.o ins fnl f: nvr nrr* **20/1**
53-3 9 2 **Woggle (IRE)**[25] 80 4-9-4 **50**..............(b) KieranO'Neill 5 40
(Geoffrey Deacon) *s.i.s: hld up: hmpd over 2f out: n.d (jockey said filly was denied a clear run approaching the home turn)* **5/1**[2]
00-5 10 2 **Shovel It On (IRE)**[23] 116 4-9-3 **49**........................ NicolaCurrie 11 35
(Steve Flook) *hld up: nvr on terms (jockey said gelding didn't face the kickback)* **18/1**
00-0 11 3 **Idol Deputy (FR)**[26] 62 13-8-11 **47**..............(p) RachealKneller(5) 2 27
(James Bennett) *prom: sn pushed along: lost pl over 5f out: rdn over 4f out: hmpd over 2f out: n.d after* **28/1**
00-0 12 11 **Whatdoesnotkillyou**[21] 132 5-9-2 **47**..............(v[1]) LukeMorris 12 4
(John Mackie) *hld up: hdwy over 5f out: rdn and wknd over 2f out (vet said gelding finished lame on it's right hind)* **40/1**
13 22 **Lady Scathach (IRE)**[40] 9678 4-9-2 **48**..............(p) ShaneKelly 9
(T G McCourt, Ire) *s.i.s: pushed along and hdwy over 7f out: chsd ldr over 4f out tl rdn over 3f out: hung lft and wknd over 2f out (jockey said filly stopped quickly and hung left-handed in the home straight)* **16/1**

1m 49.3s (-0.80) **Going Correction** 0.0s/f (Stan)
WFA 4 from 5yo+ 1lb **13 Ran SP% 116.5**
Speed ratings (Par 97): **103,101,100,100,100 99,99,97,95,94 91,81,62**
CSF £405.73 CT £3804.76 TOTE £21.70: £6.60, £8.70, £2.60; EX 652.70 Trifecta £2640.60.
Owner Steve Clarke & Partner **Bred** R N Auld **Trained** Exning, Suffolk

FOCUS
A bottom-grade handicap. The race has been rated with feet on the ground.

486 LADBROKES HOME OF THE ODDS BOOST NOVICE STKS 1m 142y (Tp)
8:15 (8:15) (Class 5) 3-Y-O £3,752 (£1,116; £557; £278) Stalls Low

Form RPR
044- 1 **Albert Finney**[40] 9669 3-9-2 72..............(h) RobertHavlin 3 71+
(John Gosden) *mde all: qcknd over 2f out: shkn up over 1f out: edgd lft ins fnl f: r.o wl* **5/4**[1]
000- 2 2 ¾ **Time Immemorial (IRE)**[74] 9122 3-9-2 27..............(b[1]) DavidProbert 1 64
(Roger Varian) *chsd ldrs: rdn to chse wnr over 1f out: styd on same pce fnl f* **25/1**
3 1 ¼ **Counting Sheep (IRE)**[97] 8584 3-9-2 0........................ JamieSpencer 7 61
(Gordon Elliott, Ire) *hld up: hdwy over 2f out: rdn and edgd lft over 1f out: styd on same pce fnl f* **13/8**[2]
5- 4 4 ½ **Htilominlo**[67] 9254 3-9-2 0........................ ShaneKelly 5 50
(Sylvester Kirk) *chsd wnr: rdn over 2f out: lost 2nd over 1f out: wknd fnl f* **10/3**[3]
0-0 5 10 **Path To The Stars (GER)**[20] 156 3-9-2 0........................ LukeMorris 6 27
(James Tate) *s.i.s: hld up: shkn up over 3f out: wknd over 2f out* **50/1**

1m 50.42s (0.32) **Going Correction** 0.0s/f (Stan) **5 Ran SP% 111.4**
Speed ratings (Par 97): **98,95,94,90,81**
CSF £27.03 TOTE £1.70: £1.10, £6.20; EX 17.90 Trifecta £56.90.
Owner Ms Rachel D S Hood **Bred** Ms Rachel Hood **Trained** Newmarket, Suffolk
■ Stewards' Enquiry : David Probert two-day ban; misuse of whip (Feb 3,14)

FOCUS
This wasn't strongly run, the time 1.12sec slower than the preceding Class 7 handicap. It's been rated around the winner, with the third a bit below form.
T/Jkpt: Not Won. T/Plt: £234.60 to a £1 stake. Pool: £132,229.76 - 411.43 winning units T/Qpdt: £40.20 to a £1 stake. Pool: £18,508.84 - 340.46 winning units **Colin Roberts**

487 - 494a (Foreign Racing) - See Raceform Interactive

[405]NEWCASTLE (A.W) (L-H)

Thursday, January 31

OFFICIAL GOING: Tapeta: standard
Wind: Almost nil Weather: Dry, cold

495 BETWAY CASINO H'CAP — 1m 4f 98y (Tp)
4:05 (4:05) (Class 5) (0-75,72) 4-Y-O+

£3,752 (£1,116; £557; £400; £400; £400) **Stalls** High

Form / RPR

12-4 **1** **Lopes Dancer (IRE)**[23] 124 7-9-7 **72** .... JoeFanning 4 — 78
(Harriet Bethell) *mde all at ordinary gallop: hrd pressed and pushed along fr 2f out: asserted ins fnl f: styd on wl towards fin* **9/4**[1]

1-41 **2** ½ **Champagne Rules**[17] 241 8-8-13 **67** .... BenRobinson[(3)] 5 — 72
(Sharon Watt) *dwlt: plld hrd in tch: smooth hdwy to chal 2 out: sn rdn: kpt on fnl f: hld towards fin (jockey said gelding ran too free)* **11/2**[3]

12-3 **3** ¾ **Trautmann (IRE)**[25] 101 5-9-4 **69** ....(tp) AlistairRawlinson 2 — 73
(Rebecca Menzies) *dwlt: hld up in last pl: effrt and hdwy over 1f out: kpt on fnl f: nt pce to chal (jockey said gelding hung left-handed in the final three furlongs)* **9/4**[1]

243- **4** 1 **Home Before Dusk**[71] 9179 4-9-0 **68** .... CallumRodriguez 1 — 70
(Keith Dalgleish) *hld up in tch: rdn over 2f out: rallied: kpt on fnl f: no imp* **5/1**[2]

20-4 **5** 2 ¼ **Thawry**[14] 272 4-8-10 **71** .... KieranSchofield[(7)] 3 — 70
(Antony Brittain) *t.k.h: chsd wnr to over 2f out: sn rdn along: outpcd fnl f* **5/1**[2]

00-6 **6** 4 ½ **Prince Consort (IRE)**[21] 154 4-8-0 **59** oh13 ow1.......(h) PaulaMuir[(5)] 7 — 50
(John Wainwright) *trckd ldrs: rdn along over 2f out: wknd over 1f out* **200/1**

2m 43.95s (2.85) **Going Correction** +0.10s/f (Slow)
WFA 4 from 5yo+ 3lb — 6 Ran SP% **110.8**
Speed ratings (Par 103): **94,93,93,92,91 88**
CSF £14.86 TOTE £2.70: £1.70, £2.30; EX 14.70 Trifecta £36.60.
Owner W A Bethell **Bred** Carol Burke & Lope De Vega Syndicate **Trained** Arnold, E Yorks

FOCUS
A steadily run affair, dominated by the winner.

496 BETWAY APPRENTICE H'CAP — 6f (Tp)
4:40 (4:40) (Class 5) (0-75,77) 4-Y-O+

£3,752 (£1,116; £418; £418; £400; £400) **Stalls** Centre

Form / RPR

20-3 **1** **Epeius (IRE)**[9] 356 6-9-2 **65** ....(v[1]) SebastianWoods 5 — 71
(Ben Haslam) *hld up: effrt in centre of trck whn nt clr run over 2f out: effrt over 1f out: edgd lft ins fnl f: led nr fin* **9/2**[2]

0-52 **2** nk **Bobby Joe Leg**[9] 356 5-9-3 **66** ....(b) PaulaMuir 4 — 71
(Ruth Carr) *s.i.s: hld up: effrt on far side of trck over 1f out: kpt on fnl f to take 2nd nr fin: jst hld* **4/1**[1]

02-6 **3** hd **Lucky Lodge**[19] 214 9-9-3 **69** ....(b) KieranSchofield[(3)] 3 — 73
(Antony Brittain) *chsd wnr in centre of trck: rdn along 2f out: carried lft ins fnl f: kpt on: hld nr fin* **7/1**

020- **3** dht **Gowanbuster**[44] 9596 4-9-0 **66** ....(t) JoshQuinn[(3)] 2 — 70
(Susan Corbett) *led and sn clr: pushed along and drifted to far rail over 1f out: wknd and hdd nr fin* **12/1**

2-52 **5** 2 **Amazing Grazing (IRE)**[14] 278 5-9-12 **75** .... RhiainIngram 1 — 73
(Rebecca Bastiman) *in tch: effrt on far side of trck over 1f out: kpt on same pce ins fnl f* **9/1**

10-6 **6** 4 ½ **Murdanova (IRE)**[15] 260 6-10-0 **77** .... CameronNoble 8 — 60
(Ivan Furtado) *hld up: rdn on nr side of trck over 2f out: wknd over 1f out* **13/2**[3]

3-36 **7** 1 **Dirchill (IRE)**[9] 355 5-9-8 **74** .... JonathanFisher[(3)] 7 — 54
(David Thompson) *hld up in tch: rdn on nr side of trck over 2f out: wknd over 1f out* **4/1**[1]

634- **8** 6 **Mansfield**[35] 9722 6-8-13 **62** .... PoppyBridgwater 6 — 23
(Stella Barclay) *prom in centre of trck: rdn over 2f out: wknd over 1f out* **9/1**

1m 11.7s (-0.80) **Going Correction** +0.10s/f (Slow) — 8 Ran SP% **111.7**
Speed ratings (Par 103): **109,108,108,108,105 99,98,90**
WIN: 4.60 Epeius; PL: 1.60 Epeius; 1.70 Bobby Joe Leg; 1.20 Lucky Lodge 2.00 Gowanbuster EX: 22.00; CSF: 21.72; TC: 97.67 60.12; TF: 101.10 62.40 CSF £21.72 TOTE £4.60: £1.60, £1.70; EX 22.00.
Owner Ben Haslam Racing Syndicate **Bred** Mrs Dolores Gleeson **Trained** Middleham Moor, N Yorks

■ Stewards' Enquiry : Sebastian Woods two-day ban; careless riding (Feb 14-15)

FOCUS
A good finish to this sprint handicap, which was run at a decent gallop.

497 LADBROKES H'CAP — 5f (Tp)
5:15 (5:15) (Class 6) (0-60,59) 3-Y-O **£3,105** (£924; £461; £400; £400) **Stalls** Centre

Form / RPR

65-6 **1** **Sister Of The Sign (IRE)**[17] 235 3-9-5 **57** .... BarryMcHugh 2 — 62
(James Given) *t.k.h: mde all at modest tempo: rdn over 1f out: edgd rt ins fnl f: kpt on wl: unchal* **10/1**

62-6 **2** 1 **Willow Brook**[19] 215 3-9-4 **56** ....(h) GrahamLee 3 — 56
(Julie Camacho) *in tch: stdy hdwy over 2f out: rdn and sltly outpcd over 1f out: rallied ins fnl f: tk 2nd nr fin: nt rch wnr (jockey said filly hung right-handed in the final furlong)* **4/1**[3]

10-6 **3** nse **Popping Corks (IRE)**[29] 21 3-9-3 **58** .... BenRobinson[(3)] 4 — 58
(Linda Perratt) *stdd in last pl (in tch): effrt and hdwy over 1f out: disp 2nd pl ins fnl f: one pce towards fin* **11/1**

0-02 **4** hd **Gregarious Girl**[6] 412 3-9-0 **52** ....(t) JoeFanning 5 — 52
(Stuart Williams) *t.k.h: chsd ldrs: effrt and pushed along over 1f out: chsd wnr ins fnl f tl no ex nr fin* **13/8**[1]

501- **5** ¾ **One One Seven (IRE)**[99] 8542 3-9-0 **59** .... KieranSchofield[(7)] 1 — 56
(Antony Brittain) *t.k.h: chsd wnr: rdn over 1f out: no ex last 100yds* **15/8**[2]

1m 1.61s (2.11) **Going Correction** +0.10s/f (Slow) — 5 Ran SP% **110.3**
Speed ratings (Par 95): **87,85,85,85,83**
CSF £47.22 TOTE £11.80: £5.50, £1.60; EX 45.80 Trifecta £196.20.
Owner The Cool Silk Partnership **Bred** Mrs Claire Doyle **Trained** Willoughton, Lincs

FOCUS
They went slow and then dashed home, finishing in a heap. The winner rates back to her best.

498 BETWAY SPRINT H'CAP — 5f (Tp)
5:50 (5:50) (Class 5) (0-70,72) 4-Y-O+

£3,752 (£1,116; £557; £400; £400; £400) **Stalls** Centre

Form / RPR

60-0 **1** **Tathmeen (IRE)**[30] 2 4-9-7 **70** .... CallumRodriguez 3 — 77
(Antony Brittain) *hld up: hdwy on far side of gp to ld over 1f out: rdn and hld on wl fnl f (trainers' rep said, reg app imp in form, gelding appreciated being dropped back in trip from 6f to 5f)* **12/1**

611U **2** nk **Archimedes (IRE)**[6] 411 6-8-12 **64** ....(tp) PhilDennis[(3)] 7 — 70
(David C Griffiths) *prom: effrt on nr side of gp over 1f out: chsd wnr ins fnl f: kpt on: hld nr fin* **13/2**[3]

-600 **3** hd **Katheefa (USA)**[12] 317 5-9-6 **69** ....(p) JamesSullivan 6 — 74
(Ruth Carr) *hld up: nt clr run 1/2-way: effrt towards nr side of gp over 1f out: kpt on fnl f: no ex cl home* **9/1**

2-61 **4** 1 ¼ **Another Angel (IRE)**[14] 278 5-9-2 **72** .... KieranSchofield[(7)] 8 — 73
(Antony Brittain) *cl up in centre of gp: led 1/2-way to over 1f out: kpt on same pce ins fnl f* **2/1**[1]

5-00 **5** 2 **Lord Of The Glen**[14] 278 4-9-3 **69** ....(v) JamieGormley[(3)] 4 — 62
(Jim Goldie) *in tch in centre of gp: drvn along 1/2-way: kpt on same pce appr fnl f* **7/1**

10-0 **6** 1 ½ **Jacob's Pillow**[21] 163 8-9-6 **69** ....(p) DanielTudhope 2 — 57
(Rebecca Bastiman) *led in centre of gp to 1/2-way: drvn and no ex fr over 1f out* **66/1**

30-2 **7** ½ **Cuppacoco**[14] 279 4-9-0 **63** .... JoeFanning 5 — 49
(Ann Duffield) *dwlt: sn prom on far side of gp: rdn and outpcd over 1f out: sn btn* **11/2**[2]

59.08s (-0.42) **Going Correction** +0.10s/f (Slow) — 7 Ran SP% **93.7**
Speed ratings (Par 103): **107,106,106,104,101 98,97**
CSF £55.94 CT £385.40 TOTE £12.40: £5.10, £1.80; EX 63.80 Trifecta £363.50.
Owner Antony Brittain **Bred** Shadwell Estate Company Limited **Trained** Warthill, N Yorks

■ Nigg Bay was withdrawn. Price at time of withdrawal 5/1. Rule 4 applies to all bets - deduction 15p in the pound.

FOCUS
A competitive heat and it was the bigger priced of the two Antony Brittain-trained runners who came through to win.

499 SUNRACING.CO.UK H'CAP — 7f 14y (Tp)
6:25 (6:25) (Class 4) (0-85,85) 4-Y-O+

£5,387 (£1,612; £806; £403; £400; £400) **Stalls** Centre

Form / RPR

5-25 **1** **Custard The Dragon**[19] 213 6-9-3 **81** ....(v[1]) JoeFanning 5 — 89
(John Mackie) *prom: smooth hdwy to ld over 1f out: rdn and r.o wl fnl f (trainer said, reg app imp in form, gelding benefited from the application of a first time visor)* **12/1**

0-31 **2** ½ **Portledge (IRE)**[19] 213 5-9-2 **80** ....(b) PJMcDonald 7 — 87
(James Bethell) *hld up: smooth hdwy to chal over 1f out: rdn fnl f: no ex last 50yds* **3/1**[2]

00-5 **3** 3 **Reckless Endeavour (IRE)**[20] 176 6-9-7 **85** ....(p) AndrewMullen 4 — 84
(David Barron) *hld up: effrt and hdwy over 1f out: chsd clr ldng pair ins fnl f: kpt on: no imp* **5/1**

213- **4** hd **Deansgate (IRE)**[57] 9414 6-9-1 **79** .... PaulMulrennan 6 — 77
(Julie Camacho) *plld hrd: hld up: stdy hdwy whn nt clr run briefly over 1f out: rdn and no ex ins fnl f (jockey said gelding ran too free)* **2/1**[1]

61/2 **5** 1 ½ **Followthesteps (IRE)**[24] 117 4-9-0 **78** .... TonyHamilton 3 — 72
(Ivan Furtado) *chsd ldr: rdn and ev ch briefly over 1f out: wknd ins fnl f* **4/1**[3]

15-0 **6** 1 ¼ **The Great Wall (USA)**[30] 4 5-9-6 **84** .... LukeMorris 1 — 75
(Michael Appleby) *in tch: rdn over 2f out: edgd lft and wknd over 1f out* **18/1**

04-4 **7** ½ **Malaspina (ITY)**[14] 276 7-8-13 **77** .... DayversonDeBarros 2 — 67
(Ivan Furtado) *led: rdn and over 2 l clr over 2f out: hdd over 1f out: sn wknd* **33/1**

1m 25.29s (-0.91) **Going Correction** +0.10s/f (Slow) — 7 Ran SP% **110.9**
Speed ratings (Par 105): **109,108,105,104,103 101,101**
CSF £45.03 TOTE £14.50: £4.30, £2.10; EX 51.90 Trifecta £184.10.
Owner Derbyshire Racing **Bred** Mr & Mrs Kevan Watts **Trained** Church Broughton, Derbys

FOCUS
The first two finished nicely clear here.

500 FOLLOW TOP TIPSTER TEMPLEGATE AT SUNRACING NOVICE STKS — 7f 14y (Tp)
7:00 (7:00) (Class 5) 3-Y-O+ **£3,752** (£1,116; £557; £278) **Stalls** Centre

Form / RPR

56- **1** **Devil's Angel**[195] 5156 3-8-10 0 .... PJMcDonald 6 — 69
(Jedd O'Keeffe) *hld up: shkn up and hdwy over 1f out: rdn to ld ins fnl f: r.o wl* **13/2**[3]

4-1 **2** 1 ¼ **Eve Harrington (USA)**[18] 229 3-8-12 0 .... LukeMorris 4 — 68
(Sir Mark Prescott Bt) *t.k.h: led: rdn over 1f out: hdd ins fnl f: kpt on same pce* **6/4**[1]

0- **3** 2 **Divied (USA)**[64] 9282 3-8-10 0 .... BarryMcHugh 3 — 61
(John Quinn) *hld up: effrt on outside over 1f out: chsd clr ldng pair ins fnl f: kpt on: no imp* **16/1**

4 1 **Bay Of Naples (IRE)** 3-8-10 0 .... JoeFanning 2 — 58
(Mark Johnston) *chsd ldr: rdn over 2f out: one pce fr over 1f out* **7/4**[2]

4-3 **5** 3 ¼ **Orient Express**[24] 117 4-10-0 0 .... TonyHamilton 5 — 54
(Richard Fahey) *in tch: effrt and rdn 2f out: wknd ins fnl f* **15/2**

-0 **6** 2 **Savlad**[14] 275 4-10-0 0 .... ShaneGray 7 — 49
(Shaun Harris) *chsd ldrs: rdn over 2f out: wknd over 1f out* **250/1**

R **Desai**[55] 5-10-0 ....(t) JackGarritty 1
(Noel Wilson) *ref to r* **40/1**

1m 27.79s (1.59) **Going Correction** +0.10s/f (Slow)
WFA 3 from 4yo+ 18lb — 7 Ran SP% **110.2**
Speed ratings (Par 103): **94,92,90,89,85 83,**
CSF £15.49 TOTE £8.20: £4.20, £1.10; EX 16.00 Trifecta £94.70.
Owner John Dance **Bred** Ed's Stud Ltd **Trained** Middleham Moor, N Yorks

FOCUS
A modest affair.

501 FOLLOW SUNRACING ON TWITTER H'CAP 7f 14y (Tp)
7:30 (7:30) (Class 7) (0-50,50) 3-Y-O+ **£2,264** (£673; £336; £168) **Stalls Centre**

Form RPR

1 **1** **Lion Hearted (IRE)**[7] 379 5-9-7 **45**........................ AlistairRawlinson 12 64+
(Michael Appleby) *in tch nr side of gp: shkn up and hdwy over 1f out: led ins fnl f: pushed clr: readily* **1/3**[1]

00-0 **2** *3 1/4* **Totally Magic (IRE)**[19] 210 7-9-5 **46**..........................(b) PhilDennis(3) 3 54
(Richard Whitaker) *led in centre of gp: rdn over 1f out: hdd ins fnl f: no ch w ready wnr* **12/1**[3]

055- **3** *1 1/2* **Twiggy**[89] 8830 5-9-7 **45**.. PJMcDonald 13 49
(Karen McLintock) *hld up on far side of gp: hdwy to chse ldng pair over 1f out: kpt on same pce ins fnl f* **14/1**

00-0 **4** *2 1/2* **Deolali**[19] 210 5-9-8 **46**.. JackGarritty 1 44
(Stella Barclay) *hld up: hdwy on far side of gp over 1f out: kpt on same pce fnl f* **100/1**

00-6 **5** *1 3/4* **Makofitwhatyouwill**[22] 132 4-9-10 **48**........................ JamesSullivan 4 42
(Ruth Carr) *in tch on far side of gp: rdn and effrt 2f out: wknd ins fnl f* **40/1**

302- **6** *nk* **You Little Beauty**[91] 8777 3-8-5 **47**..............................(p) LukeMorris 10 35
(Ann Duffield) *t.k.h: cl up on nr side of gp: rdn over 2f out: wknd over 1f out* **22/1**

30-6 **7** *1 3/4* **Song Of Summer**[14] 273 4-9-7 **45**.............................. JoeFanning 6 34
(Iain Jardine) *hmpd s: hld up: effrt on far side of gp 2f out: no imp fnl f* **22/1**

466- **8** *2 1/4* **Let Right Be Done**[64] 9286 7-9-7 **45**..............................(b) GrahamLee 7 28
(Linda Perratt) *t.k.h: hld up in centre of gp: effrt and pushed along over 1f out: sn n.d* **50/1**

6-63 **9** *6* **Harbour Patrol (IRE)**[14] 273 7-9-8 **46**.....................(b) DanielTudhope 9 14
(Rebecca Bastiman) *t.k.h in midfield in centre of gp: rdn over 2f out: wknd over 1f out (starter reported that gelding was unruly in the stalls. Jockey said gelding weakened quickly inside the final two furlongs)* **11/1**[2]

004- **10** *3 1/4* **Royal Rattle**[57] 9412 4-9-8 **46**.............................. PaulMulrennan 5 6
(John Norton) *prom in centre of gp: drvn and outpcd over 2f out: btn over 1f out* **20/1**

050- **11** *1/2* **Wontgetfooledagen (IRE)**[143] 7126 3-8-6 **48**.......(v[1]) PaddyMathers 11
(Ivan Furtado) *hld up towards nr side of gp: struggling over 2f out: sn btn* **33/1**

020- **12** *1 1/4* **Jennies Gem**[42] 9644 6-9-4 **45**.............................. BenRobinson(3) 8
(Ollie Pears) *racd on nr side of gp: w ldr to 1/2-way: cl up tl rdn and wknd over 1f out* **22/1**

03-0 **13** *2* **Musbaq (USA)**[24] 116 4-9-12 **50**..........................(v[1]) AndrewMullen 14
(Ben Haslam) *hld up on nr side of gp: struggling over 2f out: sn btn* **16/1**

1m 26.12s (-0.08) **Going Correction** +0.10s/f (Slow)
WFA 3 from 4yo+ 18lb **13 Ran SP% 129.7**
Speed ratings (Par 97): **104,100,98,95,93 93,91,88,81,78 77,76,73**
CSF £5.45 CT £41.03 TOTE £1.30: £1.10, £2.90, £3.70; EX 7.30 Trifecta £50.30.
Owner Slipstream Racing **Bred** Dowager Countess Harrington **Trained** Oakham, Rutland

FOCUS
A weak race, and the hot favourite confirmed himself way ahead of his mark.

502 PLAY 4 TO SCORE AT BETWAY H'CAP 6f (Tp)
8:00 (8:00) (Class 6) (0-60,60) 4-Y-O+
£3,105 (£924; £461; £400; £400; £400) **Stalls Centre**

Form RPR

650- **1** **Ginger Jam**[94] 8703 4-8-8 **54**.............................. FayeMcManoman(7) 3 61
(Nigel Tinkler) *hld up in centre of gp: hdwy 2f out: led ins fnl f: pushed out: comf* **7/1**

120- **2** *1* **Your Pal Tal**[173] 5996 9-8-12 **54**..........................(v) DonaghO'Connor(3) 5 58
(J F Levins, Ire) *led on nr side of gp: rdn over 2f out: hrd pressed over 1f out: hdd ins fnl f: kpt on same pce towards fin* **12/1**

0-55 **3** *nse* **Thorntoun Lady (USA)**[17] 236 9-8-8 **54**.................. CoreyMadden(7) 4 58
(Jim Goldie) *s.i.s: hld up on far side of gp: rdn and gd hdwy fnl f: nrst fin* **12/1**

41-0 **4** *1 3/4* **Roaring Rory**[14] 277 6-9-4 **60**.............................. BenRobinson(3) 8 59
(Ollie Pears) *hld up on nr side of gp: rdn over 2f out: hdwy over 1f out: kpt on fnl f: no imp (jockey said gelding was never travelling)* **4/1**[1]

560- **5** *1* **Picks Pinta**[177] 5825 8-8-0 **46** oh1..............................(b) RPWalsh(7) 1 42
(John David Riches) *t.k.h: cl up on nr side of gp: effrt and ev ch over 1f out to ins fnl f: wknd last 75yds* **33/1**

40-6 **6** *hd* **Nutopia**[14] 277 4-8-0 **46**.............................. KieranSchofield(7) 9 41
(Antony Brittain) *in tch in centre of gp: rdn and effrt 2f out: wknd ins fnl f* **4/1**[1]

2-00 **7** *2* **Breathoffreshair**[6] 410 5-9-5 **58**..............................(t) PhilipPrince 6 47
(Richard Guest) *prom on far side of gp: effrt over 2f out: wknd fnl f* **9/2**[2]

00-5 **8** *2 1/4* **Leeshaan (IRE)**[14] 277 4-9-3 **56**.............................. JoeFanning 7 38
(Rebecca Bastiman) *t.k.h: prom on nr side of gp: outpcd over 2f out: btn over 1f out* **11/2**[3]

350- **9** *nse* **Maureb (IRE)**[140] 7219 7-9-3 **56**..............................(p) BarryMcHugh 2 38
(Tony Coyle) *in tch on far side of gp tl rdn and wknd fr 2f out* **9/1**

1m 12.44s (-0.06) **Going Correction** +0.10s/f (Slow) **9 Ran SP% 114.4**
Speed ratings (Par 101): **104,102,102,100,98 98,96,93,92**
CSF £85.65 CT £987.45 TOTE £6.70: £2.30, £3.50, £3.60; EX 106.40 Trifecta £768.90.
Owner Walter Veti **Bred** Bearstone Stud Ltd **Trained** Langton, N Yorks
■ Stewards' Enquiry : Donagh O'Connor two-day ban; misuse of whip (Feb 14-15)

FOCUS
A moderate handicap won by the least exposed runner in the line-up. The form could be rated slightly higher through the third and fourth.
T/Plt: £435.90 to a £1 stake. Pool: £85,843.48 - 143.75 winning units T/Qpdt: £115.40 to a £1 stake. Pool: £16,973.09 - 108.82 winning units **Richard Young**

387 SOUTHWELL (L-H)
Thursday, January 31

OFFICIAL GOING: Fibresand: standard to slow
Wind: Nil Weather: Freezing fog

503 BETWAY SPRINT H'CAP 4f 214y(F)
1:35 (1:35) (Class 6) (0-60,62) 4-Y-O+
£3,105 (£924; £461; £300; £300; £300) **Stalls Centre**

Form RPR

0-45 **1** **Warrior's Valley**[14] 278 4-9-7 **60**..............................(t[1]) StevieDonohoe 2 70
(David C Griffiths) *mde all centre: rdn over 1f out: kpt on strly* **5/2**[2]

5-11 **2** *2* **Gorgeous General**[6] 411 4-8-13 **55** 6ex.............................. PhilDennis(3) 10 58
(Lawrence Mullaney) *racd towards stands' rail: in tch: hdwy over 2f out: rdn to chse ldrs and edgd lft to centre wl over 1f out: kpt on u.p fnl f* **2/1**[1]

3-24 **3** *shd* **Piazon**[21] 167 8-9-2 **62**..............................(be) HarryRussell(7) 7 65
(Julia Brooke) *prom centre: effrt to chse wnr wl over 1f out: sn rdn: drvn and kpt on same pce fnl f: lost 2nd nr line* **6/1**[3]

/5-0 **4** *2 3/4* **Filbert Street**[17] 236 4-9-4 **57**..............................(p) JFEgan 5 50
(Roy Brotherton) *chsd wnr centre: rdn along 2f out: sn drvn and kpt on one pce* **20/1**

0306 **5** *1 3/4* **Sir Walter (IRE)**[6] 411 4-8-7 **46** oh1.............................. RachelRichardson 9 32
(Eric Alston) *racd towards stands' side: in tch: hdwy over 2f out: sn rdn and edgd lft towards centre: drvn over 1f out: no imp* **11/1**

03-0 **6** *1 3/4* **High Anxiety**[14] 277 5-8-2 **46** oh1.............................. AndrewBreslin(5) 1 26
(Andrew Crook) *racd nr far rail: dwlt and towards rr tl rdn and styd on fr over 1f out: n.d* **25/1**

16-2 **7** *2 1/2* **Divine Call**[21] 167 12-9-2 **55**.............................. HollieDoyle 4 26
(Charlie Wallis) *in tch centre: effrt over 2f out: sn rdn along and btn (jockey said gelding was never travelling)* **8/1**

560- **8** *3/4* **Pearl Noir**[62] 9330 9-8-9 **48**..............................(b) NicolaCurrie 8 16
(Scott Dixon) *in tch: rdn along bef 1/2-way: sn wknd* **16/1**

3-05 **9** *3 1/2* **Celerity (IRE)**[13] 286 5-8-0 **46** oh1..................(p) FayeMcManoman(7) 6 2
(Lisa Williamson) *chsd ldrs: rdn along 1/2-way: sn wknd* **100/1**

-060 **10** *5* **Shesthedream (IRE)**[12] 322 6-8-7 **46** oh1.............................. JoeyHaynes 3
(Lisa Williamson) *dwlt: sn chsng ldrs towards centre: rdn along bef 1/2-way: sn wknd* **50/1**

1m 1.59s (1.89) **Going Correction** +0.275s/f (Slow) **10 Ran SP% 113.1**
Speed ratings (Par 101): **95,91,91,87,84 81,77,76,70,62**
CSF £7.30 CT £25.30 TOTE £3.20: £1.10, £1.10, £1.90; EX 8.00 Trifecta £31.20.
Owner N Davies, D Clarke & Eros **Bred** P Balding **Trained** Bawtry, S Yorks

FOCUS
The Fibresand was officially standard to slow following overnight work on it, when temperatures got down to -6C, but Phil Dennis thought it was riding close to standard. Visibility wasn't great on a foggy day. The winner dominated the opening sprint and is rated to last year's form.

504 PLAY 4 TO SCORE AT BETWAY H'CAP 1m 4f 14y(F)
2:05 (2:05) (Class 6) (0-55,56) 4-Y-O+
£3,105 (£924; £461; £300; £300; £300) **Stalls Low**

Form RPR

64-3 **1** **Croeso Cymraeg**[16] 245 5-8-12 **46**.............................. RaulDaSilva 4 52
(James Evans) *t.k.h early: hld up towards rr: stdy hdwy 7f out: trckd ldrs over 3f out: cl up over 2f out: led wl over 1f out: rdn and kpt on wl fnl f* **4/1**[1]

-624 **2** *1 1/4* **Contingency Fee**[8] 369 4-8-11 **55**..............................(p) GraceMcEntee(7) 8 60
(Phil McEntee) *trckd ldrs: cl up 1/2-way: led over 4f out: pushed along over 2f out: sn rdn and hdd wl over 1f out: kpt on wl u.p fnl f* **7/1**

042- **3** *2* **Siyahamba (IRE)**[41] 9657 5-8-6 **47** oh1 ow1.............. HarryRussell(7) 5 48
(Bryan Smart) *in tch: hdwy 5f out: chsd ldr 3f out: chal over 2f out: sn rdn and ev ch: drvn over 1f out: kpt on same pce* **8/1**

033- **4** *8* **Filament Of Gold (USA)**[42] 9647 8-9-4 **52**..............................(b) EoinWalsh 6 41
(Roy Brotherton) *dwlt and towards rr: hdwy over 5f out: chsd ldrs 3f out: rdn along 2f out: sn drvn and no imp* **5/1**[3]

00-0 **5** *5* **Tilly Devine**[7] 387 5-8-9 **47** oh1..............................(b) JaneElliott(3) 10 28
(Scott Dixon) *cl up: led over 6f out: hdd over 4f out: sn pushed along: rdn 3f out and grad wknd* **33/1**

40-0 **6** *2 3/4* **Alcanar (USA)**[27] 59 6-9-5 **53**..............................(t[1]) RossaRyan 2 31
(Tony Carroll) *hld up towards rr: smooth hdwy 1/2-way: chsd ldng pair 4f out: rdn along 3f out: sn drvn and btn (jockey said gelding had no more to give from 3f out)* **9/2**[2]

063- **7** *1 1/2* **The Lock Master (IRE)**[33] 9751 12-8-12 **46** oh1.....(p) AndrewMullen 12 21
(Michael Appleby) *dwlt: racd wd and towards rr: hdwy over 5f out: rdn along to chse ldrs 3f out: sn drvn and btn* **12/1**

55-0 **8** *27* **Chica Da Silva**[7] 387 4-8-12 **49**..............................(b[1]) NicolaCurrie 9
(Scott Dixon) *led: pushed along and hdd over 6f out: sn lost pl and bhd* **40/1**

000- **9** *3 3/4* **Harlequin Dancer (IRE)**[42] 9644 4-8-2 **46** oh1(p[1]) FayeMcManoman(7) 3
(Lawrence Mullaney) *dwlt: a in rr (jockey said filly was never travelling)* **100/1**

210- **10** *15* **Urban Spirit (IRE)**[114] 8076 5-9-3 **54**..............................(w) PhilDennis(3) 13
(Lawrence Mullaney) *chsd ldng pair: pushed along over 5f out: rdn over 4f out: sn lost pl and bhd* **12/1**

0/ **11** *14* **Rockafilly (FR)**[71] 9185 4-8-9 **46** oh1.............................. ShaneKelly 1
(J A Nash, Ire) *chsd ldrs: rdn along 1/2-way: sn outpcd and bhd (jockey said filly was never travelling)* **50/1**

44/5 **12** *2 1/2* **Sleepy Haven (IRE)**[21] 162 9-9-8 **56**..............................(tp) CallumShepherd 14
(Jennie Candlish) *dwlt: a in rr: rdn along and outpcd over 5f out: sn detached* **9/1**

06-0 **13** *3* **More Harry**[21] 160 4-8-9 **46** oh1..............................(t[1]) DannyBrock 11
(Martin Smith) *a in rr: outpcd and bhd fnl 4f* **66/1**

2m 45.36s (4.36) **Going Correction** +0.275s/f (Slow)
WFA 4 from 5yo+ 3lb **13 Ran SP% 113.7**
Speed ratings (Par 101): **96,95,93,88,85 83,82,64,61,51 42,40,38**
CSF £29.46 CT £211.68 TOTE £4.50: £1.40, £2.30, £2.30; EX 29.50 Trifecta £95.70.
Owner R R Evans **Bred** Richard Evans **Trained** Broadwas, Worcs

FOCUS
They finished strung out in this very modest handicap, in which the winner's time was 11.36sec outside standard.

505 LADBROKES H'CAP 6f 16y(F)
2:40 (2:40) (Class 6) (0-65,66) 3-Y-O
£3,105 (£924; £461; £300; £300; £300) **Stalls Low**

Form RPR

5-05 **1** **Geography Teacher (IRE)**[10] 341 3-8-9 **53**.............................. HollieDoyle 7 59
(Roger Fell) *dwlt and bhd: pushed along and gd hdwy wl over 2f out: swtchd lft and rdn to chse ldrs over 1f out: styd on strly fnl f to ld last 75yds* **13/2**[3]

31-0 **2** *2* **Champagne Mondays**[18] 228 3-8-8 **52**..............................(p) NicolaCurrie 9 52
(Scott Dixon) *chsd ldrs: rdn along and hdwy 2f out: chsd ldng pair and drvn ent fnl f: kpt on same pce* **12/1**

451- **3** *3/4* **Melgate Magic**[44] 9598 3-9-7 **65**..............................(bt) NathanEvans 5 63+
(Michael Easterby) *sn cl up: disp ld over 3f out: slt ld wl over 2f out: sn rdn: drvn over 1f out: edgd rt ent fnl f: hdd last 75yds* **6/4**[1]

331- **4** *nk* **Tobeeornottobee**[43] 9613 3-9-8 **66**.............................. CallumShepherd 4 63+
(Declan Carroll) *slt ld and set str pce: pushed along 3f out: sn hdd and rdn: drvn and edgd rt over 1f out: wknd ins fnl f* **2/1**[2]

06-5 **5** 2 1/2 **Valley Belle (IRE)**[17] [235] 3-8-12 **56**......................(v) JosephineGordon 8 45
(Phil McEntee) *in tch: hdwy and wd st: rdn along and chsd ldrs 2f out: sn drvn: edgd lft and no imp* **16/1**

00-2 **6** 1/2 **Not So Shy**[13] [296] 3-8-12 **56**.. EoinWalsh 1 44
(David Evans) *in tch on inner: rdn along wl over 2f out: sn drvn and n.d* **18/1**

3-65 **7** 2 1/2 **Bawtry Lady**[7] [388] 3-8-1 **48**..............................(be) WilliamCox(3) 2 28
(David C Griffiths) *chsd ldrs: rdn along wl over 2f out: sn drvn and one pce* **25/1**

4P-0 **8** 1 1/4 **Piccothepack**[17] [235] 3-8-9 **53**................................ PaddyMathers 6 30
(Richard Fahey) *a in rr* **25/1**

1m 19.27s (2.77) **Going Correction** +0.275s/f (Slow) 8 Ran SP% **113.2**
Speed ratings (Par 95): **92,89,88,87,84 83,80,78**
CSF £77.57 CT £176.24 TOTE £7.70: £2.00, £2.90, £1.10; EX 73.80 Trifecta £196.10.
Owner Northern Marking Ltd & Partners **Bred** E Higgins **Trained** Nawton, N Yorks

FOCUS
The two form horses went hammer and tongs up front, with the winner coming from well off the pace. There are doubts over the form, but it's been rated at something like face value around the runner-up.

506 LADBROKES HOME OF THE ODDS BOOST H'CAP 4f 214y(F)
3:10 (3:10) (Class 5) (0-75,76) 3-Y-O **£3,752** (£1,116; £557; £300) **Stalls** Centre

Form RPR

22-1 **1** **Coolagh Magic**[29] [21] 3-9-7 **75**..................................(p) TonyHamilton 4 83
(Richard Fahey) *cl up: led over 2f out: rdn over 1f out: kpt on strly* **4/1**[3]

601- **2** 2 1/4 **Scale Force**[33] [9745] 3-8-7 **68**.. TobyEley(7) 1 68
(Gay Kelleway) *t.k.h early: cl up: effrt 2f out: sn rdn and ev ch: kpt on same pce fnl f* **10/11**[1]

54-0 **3** 5 **Temple Of Wonder (IRE)**[22] [140] 3-8-8 **67** ow2(h[1]) SeamusCronin(7) 2 51
(Charlie Wallis) *chsd ldrs: rdn along and outpcd over 2f out: styd on fnl f* **10/1**

22-4 **4** 3 **Sandridge Lad (IRE)**[10] [342] 3-9-8 **76**......................... StevieDonohoe 3 47
(John Ryan) *led: pushed along and hdd over 2f out: rdn wl over 1f out: drvn over 1f out: sn wknd (trainer's rep could offer no explanation for the gelding's performance)* **11/4**[2]

1m 0.63s (0.93) **Going Correction** +0.275s/f (Slow) 4 Ran SP% **108.1**
Speed ratings (Par 97): **103,99,91,86**
CSF £8.20 TOTE £3.10; EX 6.70 Trifecta £22.20.
Owner Alan Harte **Bred** C J Mills **Trained** Musley Bank, N Yorks
■ Stewards' Enquiry : Seamus Cronin three-day ban: weighed in 2lb over (16 & 18-19 Feb)

FOCUS
This was around a second quicker than the opening Class 6 handicap.

507 FOLLOW SUN RACING ON TWITTER H'CAP 1m 13y(F)
3:40 (3:40) (Class 5) (0-70,71) 4-Y-O+
£3,752 (£1,116; £557; £300; £300; £300) **Stalls** Low

Form RPR

330- **1** **Mr Coco Bean (USA)**[51] [9495] 5-8-11 **63**........................ JoshuaBryan(3) 3 71
(David Barron) *midfield: hdwy 3f out: rdn to chse ldrs 1 1/2f out: drvn to chal and edgd lft ins fnl f: kpt on wl to ld nr fin* **8/1**

1-13 **2** hd **Bond Angel**[18] [232] 4-8-9 **63**................................ KatherineBegley(5) 10 70
(David Evans) *sn led: jnd and rdn 2f out: cl up: drvn ent fnl f: edgd rt last 75yds: hdd nr fin* **8/1**

1-23 **3** 1 1/4 **Dashing Poet**[7] [392] 5-8-13 **65**...................................... JaneElliott(3) 13 69
(Heather Main) *trckd ldrs: hdwy to chse ldr 3f out: chal 2f out and sn rdn: ev ch ent fnl f: sn drvn and kpt on same pce* **11/2**[3]

0-45 **4** 1 1/2 **Break The Silence**[18] [233] 5-8-7 **56** oh2..............(b) JosephineGordon 1 56
(Scott Dixon) *chsd ldrs on inner: rdn along over 3f out: swtchd markedly rt to outer over 2f out: sn rdn on u.p fnl f* **25/1**

2-22 **5** 1 1/4 **Zodiakos (IRE)**[5] [429] 6-8-12 **66**..........................(p) BenSanderson(5) 7 63
(Roger Fell) *trckd ldrs: pushed along over 3f out: rdn wl over 2f out: sn drvn and one pce* **3/1**[1]

45-1 **6** nk **Arabic Culture (USA)**[20] [181] 5-9-5 **68**.......................... SamJames 8 65
(Grant Tuer) *cl up: pushed along 4f out: rdn over 3f out: sn drvn and grad wknd* **9/2**[2]

4/-2 **7** 11 **Havelock (IRE)**[18] [232] 5-8-8 **57**..................................... ShaneKelly 2 28
(Peter Fahey, Ire) *dwlt: a towards rr (jockey said gelding was never travelling)* **11/2**[3]

400- **8** hd **Shearian**[33] [9747] 9-8-10 **66**.............................. CianMacRedmond(7) 11 37
(Declan Carroll) *dwlt: a towards rr* **28/1**

00-0 **9** 4 1/2 **Makaarim**[21] [158] 5-9-8 **71**...(h) JamieSpencer 6 32
(Seamus Durack) *dwlt: a in rr* **12/1**

200- **10** 25 **Kyllachys Tale (IRE)**[15] [8598] 5-9-7 **70**....................(p) CallumShepherd 5
(Roger Teal) *a towards rr* **50/1**

60-6 **11** 7 **Face Like Thunder**[16] [248] 4-8-13 **65**...........................(e[1]) TimClark(3) 9
(Paul D'Arcy) *chsd ldrs: rdn along wl over 3f out: sn wknd* **66/1**

1m 44.98s (1.28) **Going Correction** +0.275s/f (Slow) 11 Ran SP% **114.6**
Speed ratings (Par 103): **104,103,102,101,99 99,88,88,83,58 51**
CSF £66.39 CT £391.25 TOTE £9.10: £2.50, £2.40, £1.70; EX 78.00 Trifecta £300.60.
Owner S Raines **Bred** Stewart Larkin Armstrong **Trained** Maunby, N Yorks
■ Stewards' Enquiry : Joshua Bryan two-day ban: used whip above permitted level (14-15 Feb)

FOCUS
Very ordinary form.

508 SUNRACING.CO.UK APPRENTICE H'CAP 7f 14y(F)
4:10 (4:10) (Class 5) (0-75,76) 4-Y-O+
£3,752 (£1,116; £557; £300; £300; £300) **Stalls** Low

Form RPR

1-46 **1** **Space Bandit**[5] [434] 4-9-3 **75**.. MarkCrehan(7) 4 91
(Michael Appleby) *trckd ldng pair: cl up 1/2-way: led 3f out: pushed along over 2f out: rdn wl over 1f out: clr whn edgd rt fnl f: kpt on strly* **5/2**[1]

00-4 **2** 5 **Esprit De Corps**[30] [4] 5-9-10 **75**.................................. JoshuaBryan 1 77
(David Barron) *hld up: hdwy over 3f out: sn chsng ldrs: effrt and ev ch 2f out: sn rdn: edgd lft ent fnl f: kpt on same pce* **9/2**[3]

-322 **3** 2 1/2 **Crosse Fire**[18] [230] 7-9-4 **69**.......................................(p) NicolaCurrie 8 64
(Scott Dixon) *cl up on outer: rdn and edgd lft 2f out: sn drvn and kpt on same pce fnl f* **12/1**

-025 **4** 1/2 **Sooqaan**[18] [232] 8-8-10 **61**..(p) WilliamCox 3 55
(Antony Brittain) *trckd ldrs: hdwy 3f out: effrt whn n.m.r and sltly hmpd 2f out: sn swtchd rt and rdn: kpt on same pce fnl f* **7/1**

1-02 **5** 2 3/4 **Creek Harbour (IRE)**[21] [154] 4-8-13 **71**.......................... GeorgeRooke(7) 2 57
(Richard Hughes) *led 1f: prom: pushed along over 3f out: rdn wl over 2f out: sn drvn and grad wknd* **5/1**

-344 **6** 5 **Gentlemen**[7] [381] 8-9-4 **76**.......................................(h) GraceMcEntee(7) 6 49
(Phil McEntee) *cl up: led after 1f: pushed along and hdd 3f out: rdn over 2f out: sn wknd* **4/1**[2]

30-2 **7** 3 3/4 **Luis Vaz De Torres (IRE)**[19] [213] 7-9-3 **75**.............. RussellHarris(7) 5 38
(Richard Fahey) *hld up in tch: hdwy 3f out: effrt whn n.m.r and swtchd rt towards stands' rail 2f out: sn rdn and n.d (jockey said gelding was never travelling)* **8/1**

005- **8** 38 **Port Lairge**[248] [2354] 9-8-10 **61** oh16.................................... EoinWalsh 7
(Michael Chapman) *rel to r and lost 20 l s: a t.o* **250/1**

1m 30.59s (0.29) **Going Correction** +0.275s/f (Slow) 8 Ran SP% **115.1**
Speed ratings (Par 103): **109,103,100,99,96 91,86,43**
CSF £14.10 CT £112.77 TOTE £2.80: £1.10, £1.70, £2.50; EX 13.10 Trifecta £116.40.
Owner Rod In Pickle Partnership **Bred** Newsells Park Stud **Trained** Oakham, Rutland

FOCUS
A dominant winner of this fair handicap.
T/Jkpt: Not won. T/Plt: £54.70 to a £1 stake. Pool: £146,936.83 - 1,960.76 winning units T/Qpdt: £24.20 to a £1 stake. Pool: £12,442.61 - 380.31 winning units **Joe Rowntree**

421 CHANTILLY (R-H)
Thursday, January 31

OFFICIAL GOING: Polytrack: slow

509a PRIX DU ROND FILLE DE L'AIR (MAIDEN) (3YO FILLIES) (ALL-WEATHER TRACK) (POLYTRACK) 1m (P)
12:25 3-Y-O **£11,261** (£4,504; £3,378; £2,252; £1,126)

RPR

1 **Schhili (IRE)**[26] 3-9-2 0...................................... Pierre-CharlesBoudot 8 74
(H-A Pantall, France) **22/5**[2]

2 shd **Grace Bere (FR)** 3-8-11 0.. CristianDemuro 1 69
(S Cerulis, France) **21/1**

3 2 **Krunch** 3-8-11 0.. IoritzMendizabal 5 64
(X Thomas-Demeaulte, France) **31/5**

4 nk **Adelante (FR)**[19] [217] 3-9-2 0.. MaximeGuyon 2 68
(George Baker) *wl away: led tl jnd 1/2-way: pushed along into 2f out: rdn w narrow ld appr 1f out: no ex whn hdd fnl 100yds: lost 3rd cl home* **8/5**[1]

5 2 **Dukessa (FR)**[48] 3-9-2 0.. GregoryBenoist 10 64
(D Smaga, France) **14/1**

6 nse **Flaming Heart (FR)**[63] [9320] 3-9-2 0......................... VincentCheminaud 12 64
(H-A Pantall, France) **15/1**

7 3/4 **La Miura (FR)**[19] [217] 3-8-8 0.................................... TeddyHautbois(8) 11 62
(T Castanheira, France) **114/1**

8 1 3/4 **Poetic Diva (FR)**[18] 3-9-2 0...................................... SebastienMaillot 6 58
(N Clement, France) **23/1**

9 2 **Vento Di Fronda (IRE)** 3-8-4 0........................... AlexandreChesneau(7) 9 48
(G Botti, France) **35/1**

10 nk **Icebee (IRE)**[26] 3-8-13 0...................................... MlleCoraliePacaut(3) 4 53
(Vaclav Luka Jr, Czech Republic) **14/1**

11 1/2 **Dragonfly (FR)** 3-8-11 0.. MickaelBerto 3 47
(D Windrif, France) **80/1**

12 hd **Terrestre (FR)** 3-8-11 0.. AurelienLemaitre 7 46
(F Head, France) **11/2**[3]

1m 40.95s 12 Ran SP% **119.4**
PARI-MUTUEL (all including 1 euro stake): WIN 5.40; PLACE 2.10, 4.60, 2.40; DF 46.30;.
Owner Paul Nataf **Bred** Haras D'Etreham **Trained** France

393 MEYDAN (L-H)
Thursday, January 31

OFFICIAL GOING: Dirt: fast; turf: good

510a UAE 1000 GUINEAS SPONSORED BY DP WORLD UAE REGION (LISTED RACE) (FILLIES) (DIRT) 1m (D)
3:05 (3:05) 3-Y-O
£118,110 (£39,370; £19,685; £9,842; £5,905; £3,937)

RPR

1 **Silva (IRE)**[48] 3-9-0 **82**.. OisinMurphy 4 100+
(Mme Pia Brandt, France) *trckd ldr: rdn to ld 1 1/2f out: r.o wl: easily* **33/1**

2 9 3/4 **Divine Image (USA)**[49] [9522] 3-9-0 **97**............................. WilliamBuick 7 78+
(Charlie Appleby) *slowly away: nvr nr to chal but r.o wl fnl 2f: nrst fin* **6/4**[1]

3 hd **Lady Parma (USA)**[42] [9652] 3-9-0 **75**............................ RichardMullen 8 77
(S Seemar, UAE) *sn led: hdd 1 1/2f out but kpt on* **12/1**

4 1 **Dubai Beauty (IRE)**[28] [48] 3-9-0 **100**..............(h) ChristopheSoumillon 2 75+
(Saeed bin Suroor) *mid-div: r.o fnl 2f but nvr nr to chal* **12/1**

5 2 **Starry Eyes (USA)**[128] [7645] 3-9-0 **90**............................ PatCosgrave 3 70
(Simon Crisford) *mid-div: r.o same pce fnl 2 1/2f* **16/1**

6 3/4 **Habah (USA)**[42] [9652] 3-9-0 **75**................................... SamHitchcott 10 68
(Doug Watson, UAE) *mid-div: r.o same pce fnl 2f* **66/1**

7 1 **Al Shamkhah (USA)**[28] [48] 3-9-0 **85**......................... MickaelBarzalona 1 66
(S Jadhav, UAE) *mid-div: r.o same pce fnl 2 1/2f* **14/1**

8 3 3/4 **Mulhima (IRE)**[28] [48] 3-9-0 **87**...................................... ConnorBeasley 14 58
(A bin Harmash, UAE) *nvr bttr than mid-div* **40/1**

9 nk **Muthhila (IRE)**[28] [48] 3-9-0 **89**................................... RoystonFfrench 11 57
(S Jadhav, UAE) *trckd ldr tl wknd fnl 2 1/2f* **33/1**

10 6 1/4 **Al Hayette (USA)**[28] [48] 3-9-0 **97**................................(h) FabriceVeron 15 43
(Ismail Mohammed) *nvr nr to chal* **9/2**[3]

11 1/2 **Razeena (CAN)**[42] [9652] 3-9-0 **79**...................................... PatDobbs 9 41
(Doug Watson, UAE) *nvr nr to chal* **14/1**

12 3 **Foggy Flight (USA)**[28] [48] 3-9-0 **80**............................(h) XavierZiani 12 34
(S Jadhav, UAE) *chsd ldrs tl wknd fnl 2 1/2f* **80/1**

13 4 3/4 **Lover's Knot**[203] [4872] 3-9-0 **86**..................................(p) JamesDoyle 5 24
(Charlie Appleby) *nvr bttr than mid-div* **7/2**[2]

14 13 **Swift Rose (IRE)**[28] [48] 3-9-0 **85**...................................... KevinStott 13
(Saeed bin Suroor) *nvr bttr than mid-div* **25/1**

15 5 3/4 **Emma Point (USA)**[22] [134] 3-9-0 **75**........................(b) AntonioFresu 6
(Marco Botti) *nvr bttr than mid-div* **100/1**

1m 39.62s (2.12) **Going Correction** +0.475s/f (Slow) 15 Ran SP% **130.9**
Speed ratings: **108,98,98,97,95 94,93,89,89,83 82,79,74,61,56**
CSF: 87.31.
Owner Zalim Bifov **Bred** Zalim Bifov **Trained** France

FOCUS
TRAKUS (metres travelled compared to winner): 2nd +2, 3rd 0, 4th -2, 5th +5, 6th +15, 7th +6, 8th +15, 9th +5, 10th +13, 11th +3, 12th +11, 13th +4, 14th +9, 15th +8. They went a strong pace that gradually slowed: 24.55 (400m from standing start), 23.38 (800m), 25.28 (1200m), with the winner to the line in 26.33. The third probably limits the standard.

511a MEYDAN CLASSIC TRIAL SPONSORED BY MINA RASHID MARINA (CONDITIONS) (TURF) 7f
3:40 (3:40) 3-Y-O

£47,244 (£15,748; £7,874; £3,937; £2,362; £1,574)

RPR

1 **Golden Jaguar (USA)**[20] [198] 3-8-9 83 ....(h) ConnorBeasley 15 92+
(A bin Harmash, UAE) *slowly away: settled in rr: smooth prog 2 1/2f out: led 1 1/2f out: r.o wl* **12/1**

2 *2* **Irish Trilogy (IRE)**[21] [168] 3-8-11 89 ow2 .... CarlosLopez 3 89
(Andrew Kidney, Sweden) *mid-div: r.o wl fnl 2f: nrst fin but no ch w wnr* **25/1**

3 *nk* **Sporting Chance**[21] [168] 3-8-10 103 .... PatCosgrave 2 87
(Simon Crisford) *trckd ldr: ev ch 2f out: r.o but no ch w wnr* **9/1**[3]

4 *1/2* **Prince Elzaam (IRE)**[21] [168] 3-8-9 86 .... OisinMurphy 13 85
(Jaber Ramadhan, Bahrain) *mid-div: r.o fnl 2f: nrst fin* **14/1**

5 *nk* **Nashirah**[28] [48] 3-8-5 92 .... BrettDoyle 7 80
(Charlie Appleby) *trckd ldrs: led 2f out: hdd 1 1/2f out: kpt on same pce* **5/1**[2]

6 *3/4* **Trolius (IRE)**[21] [168] 3-8-9 93 ....(p) ChrisHayes 10 82
(Simon Crisford) *mid-div: r.o same pce fnl 2f* **5/1**[2]

7 *1* **Nayslayer (IRE)**[96] [8644] 3-8-10 73 ow1 .... AdriedeVries 5 80
(Ali Jan, Qatar) *nvr nr to chal but r.o fnl 2 1/2f* **50/1**

8 *hd* **Tabarak (USA)** 3-8-9 0 .... BenCurtis 8 79
(R Bouresly, Kuwait) *nvr nr to chal but r.o fnl 2 1/2f* **66/1**

9 *1* **Al Fajir Mukbile (IRE)**[21] [168] 3-8-9 83 .... FabriceVeron 12 76
(Ismail Mohammed) *nvr bttr than mid-div* **25/1**

10 *2* **Woven**[21] [168] 3-8-9 94 .... JimCrowley 9 71
(David Simcock) *nvr nr to chal* **7/4**[1]

11 *2 1/4* **Burj**[21] [169] 3-8-9 87 .... KevinStott 6 65
(Saeed bin Suroor) *nvr nr to chal* **12/1**

12 *5 1/2* **Shining Armor**[21] [168] 3-8-4 95 .... DarraghKeenan(5) 14 51
(John Ryan) *nvr bttr than mid-div* **20/1**

13 *5* **Shanaghai City (USA)**[20] [198] 3-8-9 72 ....(t) JRosales 4 36
(R Bouresly, Kuwait) *trckd ldr tl wknd fnl 2 1/2f* **66/1**

14 *hd* **Magic Image**[21] [168] 3-8-5 80 .... HayleyTurner 11 32
(Saeed bin Suroor) *nvr bttr than mid-div* **25/1**

15 *7 1/2* **Faith And Fortune (ARG)**[21] [169] 3-9-5 90 .... OlivierDoleuze 1 12
(M F De Kock, South Africa) *sn led: hdd & wknd fnl 2f* **25/1**

1m 24.29s **15 Ran SP% 126.8**
CSF: 292.59.
Owner Phoenix Ladies Syndicate **Bred** William J Betz & Peter V Lamantia **Trained** United Arab Emirates

FOCUS
TRAKUS: 2nd -5, 3rd -8, 4th -3, 5th -5, 6th -6, 7th -8, 8th -7, 9th -3, 10th -3, 11th -7, 12th 0, 13th -4, 14th -7, 15th -7. The rail was out four metres on the turf track. A solidly run race: 24.43, 23.35, 24.25, 12.26.

512a AL SHINDAGHA SPRINT SPONSORED BY JEBEL ALI PORT (GROUP 3) (DIRT) 6f (D)
4:15 (4:15) 3-Y-O+

£94,488 (£31,496; £15,748; £7,874; £4,724; £3,149)

RPR

1 **Drafted (USA)**[28] [50] 5-9-0 108 .... PatDobbs 4 112
(Doug Watson, UAE) *settled in rr: smooth prog 3f out: rdn to ld fnl 165yds: r.o wl* **13/8**[1]

2 *3/4* **Tato Key (ARG)**[224] 4-9-0 109 ....(t) ShaneFoley 3 110
(David Marnane, Ire) *mid-div: rdn to ld 1 1/2f out: hdd fnl 165yds: kpt on wl* **13/2**

3 *1 1/4* **Ibn Malik (IRE)**[28] [49] 6-9-0 107 .... JimCrowley 1 106
(M Al Mheiri, UAE) *trckd ldr: ev ch 2f out: r.o same pce fnl 1 1/2f* **4/1**[3]

4 *4 3/4* **Nine Below Zero**[12] [325] 4-9-0 99 .... AdriedeVries 2 91
(Fawzi Abdulla Nass, Bahrain) *nvr nr to chal* **14/1**

5 *1 3/4* **My Catch (IRE)**[28] [50] 8-9-0 107 .... SamHitchcott 5 85
(Doug Watson, UAE) *wl away: sn led: hdd & wknd fnl 1 1/2f* **10/1**

6 *1 1/4* **Switzerland (USA)**[70] 5-9-2 109 ....(t) RyanMoore 6 83
(Steven Asmussen, U.S.A) *trckd ldr tl wknd 1 1/2f out* **11/4**[2]

1m 12.34s (0.74) **Going Correction** +0.475s/f (Slow) **6 Ran SP% 113.9**
Speed ratings: **114,113,111,105,102 101**
CSF: 13.12.
Owner Misty Hollow Farm **Bred** John Foster, Barbara Hooker & Field Commission Par **Trained** United Arab Emirates

FOCUS
TRAKUS: 2nd -3, 3rd -7, 4th -6, 5th -9, 6th -6. A good, strongly run race: 23.84, 23.09, with the winner home in 24.98.

513a MINA RASHID (H'CAP) (DIRT) 1m (D)
4:50 (4:50) (90-107,107) 3-Y-O+

£82,677 (£27,559; £13,779; £6,889; £4,133; £2,755)

RPR

1 **Capezzano (USA)**[14] [282] 5-9-0 101 ....(h) MickaelBarzalona 4 118+
(S Jadhav, UAE) *sn led: skipped clr 2 1/2f out: r.o wl: easily* **7/1**[3]

2 *14* **Thegreatcollection (USA)**[14] [282] 5-8-9 97 ....(b) SamHitchcott 10 81
(Doug Watson, UAE) *mid-div: r.o wl fnl 2 1/2f but no ch w wnr* **22/1**

3 *3* **African Ride**[21] [171] 5-9-4 105 ....(t) ChristopheSoumillon 14 83
(Simon Crisford) *mid-div: chsd wnr 3f out: r.o same pce fnl 2 1/2f* **16/1**

4 *2 1/2* **Gold Town**[21] [171] 4-9-6 107 ....(b) WilliamBuick 7 79
(Charlie Appleby) *trckd ldr: ev ch 3f out: one pce fnl 2 1/2f* **3/1**[1]

5 *nse* **Plata O Plomo (USA)**[14] [282] 5-8-11 99 ow2 ....(vt) CarlosLopez 8 70
(Susanne Berneklint, Sweden) *mid-div: r.o same pce fnl 2 1/2f* **33/1**

6 *1 1/2* **Galvanize (USA)**[14] [282] 6-8-13 100 .... PatDobbs 2 69
(Doug Watson, UAE) *a mid-div* **7/1**[3]

7 *nk* **Moqarrar (USA)**[12] [324] 4-8-8 96 ow1 .... JimCrowley 11 63
(E Charpy, UAE) *a mid-div* **8/1**

8 *5 3/4* **Honorable Treasure (USA)**[14] [280] 4-9-2 103 ....(b) PatCosgrave 1 58
(Kenneth McPeek, U.S.A) *nvr bttr than mid-div* **12/1**

9 *1 3/4* **Pillar Of Society (IRE)**[12] [327] 5-8-6 91 ow1 .... RoystonFfrench 9 44
(Doug Watson, UAE) *nvr nr to chal* **40/1**

10 *11 1/2* **Bochart**[26] [97] 6-8-7 95 ....(t) RichardMullen 3 18
(S Seemar, UAE) *stmbld at s: trckd ldr tl wknd fnl 4f* **5/1**[2]

11 *3 1/4* **Big Challenge (IRE)**[14] [284] 5-8-5 91 ....(v) HarryBentley 6 9
(Saeed bin Suroor) *slowly away: a in rr* **33/1**

12 *1 3/4* **Fly At Dawn (USA)**[14] [285] 5-9-3 104 ....(t) JamesDoyle 5 17
(Charlie Appleby) *nvr nr to chal* **15/2**

13 *1 1/2* **Equitant**[21] [173] 4-8-8 96 ....(b) TadhgO'Shea 13
(Joseph Patrick O'Brien, Ire) *nvr bttr than mid-div* **22/1**

14 *1 3/4* **Laieth**[14] [280] 4-8-5 90 .... ChrisHayes 12
(Saeed bin Suroor) *nvr bttr than mid-div* **14/1**

1m 36.95s (-0.55) **Going Correction** +0.475s/f (Slow) **14 Ran SP% 126.8**
Speed ratings: **121,107,104,101,101 99,99,93,92,80 77,75,74,72**
CSF: 164.32; TRICAST: 2,471.56.
Owner Sultan Ali **Bred** Darley **Trained** United Arab Emirates

FOCUS
TRAKUS: 2nd +5, 3rd +5, 4th +5, 5th +10, 6th +8, 7th +9, 8th +3, 9th +6, 10th 0, 11th +1, 12th +3, 13th +14, 14th +18. The winner covered the first 6f in 1:11.68, which was quicker than the preceding Group 3 over that trip, albeit on different parts of the track - and he'd done the same last time as well, going quicker than a 6f handicap.

514a JAFZA (H'CAP) (TURF) 1m 2f
5:25 (5:25) (95-111,111) 3-Y-O+

£82,677 (£27,559; £13,779; £6,889; £4,133; £2,755)

RPR

1 **Oasis Charm**[271] [2415] 5-8-13 104 ....(p) WilliamBuick 6 109+
(Charlie Appleby) *mid-div: smooth prog 3f out: led fnl 1 1/2f: r.o wl* **2/1**[1]

2 *3/4* **Team Talk**[28] [51] 6-9-3 108 ....(h) ChristopheSoumillon 11 111
(Saeed bin Suroor) *s.i.s: settled in rr: r.o wl fnl 2f: nrst fin* **11/2**[3]

3 *hd* **Zaman**[139] [7267] 4-9-1 107 ....(b) BrettDoyle 5 111
(Charlie Appleby) *mid-div: chsd ldrs 2 1/2f out: r.o same pce fnl 1 1/2f* **14/1**

4 *3 1/2* **Earnshaw (USA)**[14] [284] 8-8-10 102 ....(t) MickaelBarzalona 7 97
(S Jadhav, UAE) *mid-div: r.o same pce fnl 2f* **16/1**

5 *shd* **Stage Magic (IRE)**[131] [7567] 4-8-9 102 .... ColmO'Donoghue 9 97
(Charlie Appleby) *sn led: hdd 1 1/2f out: r.o same pce* **40/1**

6 *1/2* **Dark Red (IRE)**[14] [284] 7-8-8 100 ....(b) ChrisHayes 1 93
(Ed Dunlop) *mid-div: chsd ldrs 3f out: r.o same pce fnl 2f* **25/1**

7 *shd* **Euginio (IRE)**[7] [395] 5-9-4 109 .... OisinMurphy 3 103
(Fawzi Abdulla Nass, Bahrain) *nvr bttr than mid-div* **15/2**

8 *6* **Key Victory (IRE)**[14] [285] 4-9-1 107 ....(p) JamesDoyle 13 90
(Charlie Appleby) *nvr nr to chal* **11/4**[2]

9 *1 1/2* **Ventura Knight (IRE)**[36] [9705] 4-8-5 98 .... RoystonFfrench 10 77
(Mark Johnston) *nvr bttr than mid-div* **40/1**

10 *6 3/4* **Silent Attack**[21] [173] 6-8-13 104 .... KevinStott 2 70
(Saeed bin Suroor) *nvr bttr than mid-div* **20/1**

11 *2* **Astronomer (IRE)**[111] [8149] 4-9-3 109 .... OlivierDoleuze 8 72
(M F De Kock, South Africa) *nvr nr to chal* **12/1**

12 *10* **Light The Lights (SAF)**[21] [172] 7-9-6 111 ....(t) PatCosgrave 4 53
(M F De Kock, South Africa) *nvr bttr than mid-div* **14/1**

13 *1 3/4* **North Face (IRE)**[7] [398] 4-8-5 97 ....(b) AntonioFresu 12 36
(Marco Botti) *nvr nr to chal* **66/1**

14 *9 3/4* **Deauville (IRE)**[7] [395] 6-9-5 110 ....(v) AdriedeVries 14 29
(Fawzi Abdulla Nass, Bahrain) *trckd ldr tl wknd fnl 2 1/2f* **25/1**

2m 2.27s
WFA 4 from 5yo+ 1lb **14 Ran SP% 132.9**
CSF: 14.02; TRICAST: 138.71.
Owner Godolphin **Bred** Miss K Rausing & Juddmonte Farms Ltd **Trained** Newmarket, Suffolk

FOCUS
TRAKUS: 2nd -1, 3rd +3, 4th +1, 5th -7, 6th -8, 7th -3, 8th -2, 9th -2, 10th -6, 11th -6, 12th -2, 13th +2, 14th 0. This was run at a solid pace: 25.49, 23.06, 24.39, 24.58, with the winner to the line in 24.58.

515a HAMDAN BIN MOHAMMED CRUISE TERMINAL (H'CAP) (TURF) 1m
6:00 (6:00) (95-105,105) 3-Y-O+

£63,779 (£21,259; £10,629; £5,314; £3,188; £2,125)

RPR

1 **Escalator**[28] [51] 4-9-6 105 .... ChrisHayes 15 111+
(Charlie Fellowes) *settled in rr: smooth prog 2f out: rdn to ld fnl 110yds: r.o wl* **12/1**

2 *1 1/2* **Above N Beyond**[28] [52] 6-8-11 97 ....(vt) ConnorBeasley 13 99
(A bin Harmash, UAE) *mid-div: rdn to ld 3f out: r.o wl but hdd fnl 110yds* **33/1**

3 *3/4* **On The Warpath**[21] [173] 4-8-11 97 .... WilliamBuick 16 97
(Charlie Appleby) *trckd ldr: ev ch 3f out: r.o wl fnl 1 1/2f* **4/1**[2]

4 *nk* **Bedouin's Story**[14] [285] 4-8-10 96 ....(h) OisinMurphy 12 95
(Saeed bin Suroor) *s.i.s: nvr nr to chal but r.o wl fnl 1 1/2f: nrst fin* **4/1**[2]

5 *1/2* **Eshtiraak (AUS)**[21] [173] 4-9-0 99 ....(p) JimCrowley 6 98
(David A Hayes, Australia) *mid-div: chsd ldrs 1 1/2f out: r.o same pce fnl f* **25/1**

6 *nse* **Hornsby**[14] [282] 6-9-3 102 ....(p) MickaelBarzalona 4 101
(S Jadhav, UAE) *s.i.s: nvr nr to chal but r.o fnl 2f* **33/1**

7 *2 1/2* **Barot**[21] [173] 7-9-5 104 .... AdriedeVries 7 97
(M F De Kock, South Africa) *nvr nr to chal but r.o fnl 2 1/2f* **6/1**[3]

8 *1 1/4* **Seniority**[28] [52] 5-9-4 103 .... RyanMoore 1 93
(William Haggas) *a mid-div* **7/2**[1]

9 *1* **Hors De Combat**[21] [173] 8-9-4 103 .... TadhgO'Shea 10 91
(Denis Coakley) *a mid-div* **16/1**

10 *3/4* **Major Partnership (IRE)**[21] [170] 4-9-2 101 .....(t) ChristopheSoumillon 2 87
(Saeed bin Suroor) *trckd ldr tl wknd fnl 3f* **12/1**

11 *nk* **Mutawathea**[264] [2645] 8-8-10 96 ....(p) HarryBentley 9 81
(Simon Crisford) *nvr nr to chal* **50/1**

12 *4* **Bold Rex (SAF)**[21] [173] 5-8-11 97 .... OlivierDoleuze 5 72
(M F De Kock, South Africa) *nvr bttr than mid-div* **20/1**

13 *1/2* **Kronprinz (GER)**[21] [173] 4-9-5 104 .... AntonioFresu 14 79
(E Charpy, UAE) *nvr bttr than mid-div* **40/1**

14 *1 1/4* **Aqabah (USA)**[484] [7754] 4-9-2 101 .... JamesDoyle 11 73
(Charlie Appleby) *nvr bttr than mid-div* **8/1**

15 *5 3/4* **Jaaref (IRE)**[14] [284] 6-9-3 102 .... DaneO'Neill 8 61
(A R Al Rayhi, UAE) *nvr bttr than mid-div* **33/1**

16 *5* **Love Dreams (IRE)**[108] [8265] 5-8-13 98 ....(b) RoystonFfrench 3 46
(Mark Johnston) *sn led: hdd & wknd 2 1/2f out* **66/1**

1m 36.67s **16 Ran SP% 132.2**
CSF: 382.97; TRICAST: 1,327.78. PLACEPOT: £1,032.10 to a £1 stake. QUADPOT: £134.80 to a £1 stake..
Owner Saeed bel Obaida **Bred** Rabbah Bloodstock Limited **Trained** Newmarket, Suffolk

The Form Book Flat 2019, Raceform Ltd, Newbury, RG14 5SJ

FOCUS
TRAKUS: 2nd +3, 3rd 0, 4th +5, 5th 0, 6th -3, 7th +2, 8th -1, 9th +7, 10th -3, 11th +2, 12th +2, 13th +5, 14th +2, 15th +6, 16th -3. The winner picked up well off a good gallop: 24.59, 23.15, 24.62, 23.47.

473 LINGFIELD (L-H)
Friday, February 1

OFFICIAL GOING: Polytrack: standard
Wind: Fresh, half against Weather: Overcast, drizzly, cold

516 LADBROKES HOME OF THE ODDS BOOST FILLIES' H'CAP — 1m 1y(P)
1:45 (1:45) (Class 5) (0-75,77) 4-Y-O+ **£3,752** (£1,116; £557; £300; £300) **Stalls** High

Form — RPR
12-2 **1** **Delicate Kiss**[21] 175 5-8-9 **63** ....(b) LiamJones 3 75
(John Bridger) *t.k.h: trckd ldng pair: pushed along 2f out: clsd to ld 1f out: sn rdn clr* **2/1**[2]
21-5 **2** 4 ½ **Yusra**[27] 81 4-9-9 **77** .... DanielMuscutt 7 79
(Marco Botti) *trckd ldr: shkn up to ld over 1f out: hdd 1f out and immediately outpcd* **11/10**[1]
422- **3** ¾ **Indiscretion (IRE)**[215] 4433 4-9-7 **75** .... RobHornby 1 75
(Jonathan Portman) *trckd ldng pair: shkn up and nt qckn over 1f out: kpt on same pce fnl f* **5/1**[3]
13-6 **4** 1 ¼ **Margie's Choice (GER)**[27] 81 4-9-2 **75** .... CameronNoble(5) 2 72
(Michael Madgwick) *led: styd on inner and hdd over 1f out: hrd rdn and wknd* **5/1**[3]
00-0 **5** 18 **Suttonwood Sally**[25] 117 5-7-13 **56** oh11 .... NoelGarbutt(3) 6 12
(Geoffrey Deacon) *outpcd and a bhd: t.o* **50/1**
1m 36.83s (-1.37) **Going Correction** +0.025s/f (Slow) 5 Ran SP% **116.2**
Speed ratings (Par 100): **107,102,101,100,82**
CSF £4.93 TOTE £2.70: £1.40, £1.30; EX 5.00 Trifecta £13.70.
Owner Dbd Partnership **Bred** T Ellison, B Olkowicz And C Speller **Trained** Liphook, Hants
FOCUS
This looked fairly competitive but the winner ran away from them inside the last.

517 FOLLOW SUN RACING ON TWITTER CLAIMING STKS — 7f 1y(P)
2:20 (2:20) (Class 6) 4-Y-O+ **£3,105** (£924; £461; £300) **Stalls** Low

Form — RPR
4-01 **1** **Los Camachos (IRE)**[3] 466 4-9-9 79 .... KatherineBegley(5) 3 84
(David Evans) *mde all: rdn 2f out: edgd rt fnl f but kpt on wl* **5/4**[1]
551- **2** 1 ½ **Loyalty**[295] 1760 12-9-4 85 ....(v) CallumShepherd 2 70
(Derek Shaw) *trckd wnr: poised to chal over 1f out and apparently gng easily: rdn and no rspnse fnl f: readily hld after* **2/1**[2]
30-6 **3** ½ **Drakefell (IRE)**[23] 139 4-9-7 80 .... MarkCrehan(7) 1 79
(Richard Hannon) *chsd ldng pair: pushed along 2f out and nt on terms: rdn on inner fnl f: kpt on but nvr nr to chal* **7/2**[3]
2-60 **4** 8 **Ventriloquist**[14] 295 7-8-7 62 .... LeviWilliams(7) 4 43
(Simon Dow) *s.i.s: a last and nvr on terms: bhd fnl 2f* **7/1**
1m 24.2s (-0.60) **Going Correction** +0.025s/f (Slow) 4 Ran SP% **112.5**
Speed ratings (Par 101): **104,102,101,92**
CSF £4.26 TOTE £2.30; EX 6.30.
Owner Mrs Penny Keble White & Emma Evans **Bred** Hardys Of Kilkeel Ltd **Trained** Pandy, Monmouths
■ Stewards' Enquiry : Mark Crehan caution: careless riding
FOCUS
A fair claimer.

518 LADBROKES NOVICE STKS — 1m 2f (P)
2:55 (2:55) (Class 5) 3-Y-O **£3,752** (£1,116; £557; £278) **Stalls** Low

Form — RPR
35-2 **1** **Water's Edge (IRE)**[16] 258 3-9-2 80 .... RyanMoore 7 75+
(James Tate) *trckd ldr after 2f: led over 2f out and sn lft clr: pushed out firmly fnl f* **4/9**[1]
2 2 ¾ **Heavenly Tale (IRE)** 3-8-11 0 .... OisinMurphy 2 64+
(Ralph Beckett) *trckd ldr 2f: styd cl up: chsd wnr over 2f out: rn green and no imp over 1f out: kpt on* **4/1**[2]
3 3 ¼ **Hendrix (IRE)** 3-9-2 0 .... RobHornby 1 62
(Hughie Morrison) *s.s: in tch in last pair: outpcd 3f out: pushed along to take 3rd wl over 1f out: kpt on steadily* **16/1**
0 **4** 1 ½ **Perique**[16] 259 3-9-2 0 .... DanielMuscutt 5 59
(Ed Dunlop) *dwlt: in tch: chsd ldng pair over 2f out but green and wd bnd sn after: dropped to 4th wl over 1f out* **33/1**
5 46 **Mallet Head** 3-9-2 0 .... DannyBrock 6
(Philip McBride) *s.s: in tch in rr to over 3f out: wknd rapidly: t.o* **33/1**
-5 **P** **Fast Boy (IRE)**[27] 90 3-9-2 0 .... JamieSpencer 4
(David Simcock) *led: set mod pce to 4f out: hdd over 2f out: lost action sn after and p.u* **9/2**[3]
2m 12.75s (6.15) **Going Correction** +0.025s/f (Slow) 6 Ran SP% **119.2**
Speed ratings (Par 97): **76,73,71,70,33**
CSF £3.07 TOTE £1.30: £1.10, £1.70; EX 3.10 Trifecta £12.90.
Owner Saeed Manana **Bred** John Fielding **Trained** Newmarket, Suffolk
FOCUS
This was slowly run and developed into a dash from the turn in.

519 BETWAY CONDITIONS STKS — 1m 7f 169y(P)
3:25 (3:25) (Class 2) 4-Y-O+ **£11,827** (£3,541; £1,770; £885) **Stalls** Low

Form — RPR
031- **1** **Grey Britain**[55] 9463 5-9-5 106 .... AdamKirby 5 110
(John Ryan) *hld up in last: clsd up fr 4f out: trckd ldr over 1f out: rdn to ld last 150yds: asserted nr fin* **7/4**[1]
14-3 **2** 1 ¼ **Watersmeet**[18] 238 8-9-5 103 .... JoeFanning 3 108
(Mark Johnston) *trckd ldr: led 3f out: rdn 2f out: hdd last 150yds: tried to respond but no ex nr fin* **9/4**[2]
21-2 **3** 5 **Stargazer (IRE)**[10] 349 6-9-5 100 .... RossaRyan 4 102
(Philip Kirby) *hld up in 3rd: moved up to press ldng pair on outer over 3f out: rdn to chse ldr wl over 2f out to over 1f out: fdd* **11/4**[3]
3-03 **4** 19 **Lord George (IRE)**[13] 311 6-9-5 103 ....(v) RyanMoore 1 79
(James Fanshawe) *led at gd pce: urged along and hdd 3f out: wknd qckly sn after (trainer's rep could offer no explanation for the gelding's performance)* **9/2**
3m 18.95s (-6.75) **Going Correction** +0.025s/f (Slow) 4 Ran SP% **112.0**
Speed ratings (Par 109): **117,116,113,104**
CSF £6.19 TOTE £2.30; EX 6.20 Trifecta £14.60.
Owner G Smith-Bernal **Bred** D R Tucker **Trained** Newmarket, Suffolk
FOCUS
This was a proper test at the trip.

520 PLAY 4 TO SCORE AT BETWAY NOVICE STKS — 5f 6y(P)
3:55 (3:55) (Class 5) 3-Y-O+ **£3,752** (£1,116; £557; £278) **Stalls** High

Form — RPR
2- **1** **Key To Power**[258] 2862 3-8-7 0 .... JoeFanning 2 72+
(Mark Johnston) *mde all: pushed clr over 1f out: comf* **4/9**[1]
40- **2** 4 ½ **Turquoise Friendly**[58] 9394 3-8-12 0 .... RossaRyan 1 60
(Robert Cowell) *chsd wnr: easily outpcd over 1f out: kpt on (jockey said colt hung right-handed rounding the bend)* **5/2**[2]
0-50 **3** 1 ¾ **Brogans Bay (IRE)**[9] 365 4-9-7 54 .... NickyMackay 4 55
(Simon Dow) *t.k.h early: hld up in last: effrt on inner 2f out: tk 3rd jst over 1f out: no hdwy after* **33/1**
346- **4** nk **Starchant**[122] 7874 3-8-7 70 .... LiamJones 7 48
(John Bridger) *chsd ldng pair 2f: dropped to last and rdn 1/2-way: one pce over 1f out* **10/1**[3]
000- **5** 4 **Chocco Star (IRE)**[43] 9636 3-8-7 0 .... JoeyHaynes 6 34
(Paul Howling) *s.i.s: racd v wd thrght: effrt to dispute 2nd over 2f out: wd bnd sn after and wknd over 1f out* **40/1**
59.72s (0.92) **Going Correction** +0.025s/f (Slow) 5 Ran SP% **112.3**
WFA 3 from 4yo 14lb
Speed ratings (Par 103): **93,85,83,82,76**
CSF £1.90 TOTE £1.30: £1.10, £1.30; EX 2.00 Trifecta £7.90.
Owner Sheikh Hamdan bin Mohammed Al Maktoum **Bred** Godolphin **Trained** Middleham Moor, N Yorks
FOCUS
The winner was found a good opportunity, enjoyed the run of the race and won with the minimum of fuss.

521 BETWAY APPRENTICE H'CAP — 1m 2f (P)
4:30 (4:30) (Class 3) (0-90,91) 4-Y-O **£7,246** (£2,168; £1,084; £542; £270) **Stalls** Low

Form — RPR
25-3 **1** **Nonios (IRE)**[18] 240 7-9-12 **91** ....(h) DylanHogan(3) 3 98
(David Simcock) *dwlt: hld up in last pair: prog over 2f out: pushed into ld over 1f out: idled and urged along fnl f: jst hld on* **15/2**
4-40 **2** hd **Isomer (USA)**[6] 441 5-9-11 **87** .... JoshuaBryan 5 93
(Andrew Balding) *cl up: trckd ldr 1/2-way: led over 2f out: drvn and hdd over 1f out: rallied fnl f: jst hld* **3/1**[2]
0-51 **3** ¾ **Central City (IRE)**[14] 292 4-8-12 **74** ....(p) WilliamCox 1 78
(Ian Williams) *t.k.h: trckd ldr to 1/2-way: lost pl on inner 2f out and outpcd over 1f out: drvn and clsd on ldng pair fnl f: too late* **6/1**
45-4 **4** 2 ½ **C Note (IRE)**[9] 368 6-9-5 **88** ....(t) EllieMacKenzie(7) 4 87
(Heather Main) *mde most to over 2f out: sn lost pl and btn (trainer's rep said gelding ran flat)* **11/10**[1]
54-2 **5** ½ **Fayez (IRE)**[15] 276 5-9-11 **87** ....(p) ConorMcGovern 2 85
(David O'Meara) *hld up in last pair: effrt on outer 2f out: rdn and no rspnse over 1f out* **9/2**[3]
2m 5.35s (-1.25) **Going Correction** +0.025s/f (Slow) 5 Ran SP% **116.9**
Speed ratings (Par 107): **106,105,105,103,102**
CSF £31.21 TOTE £5.40: £2.20, £2.00; EX 24.70 Trifecta £105.90.
Owner Millingbrook Racing **Bred** Sheikh Sultan Bin Khalifa Al Nayhan **Trained** Newmarket, Suffolk
FOCUS
A bit of a tactical affair, and there was a tight finish.
T/Plt: £29.30 to a £1 stake. Pool: £85,434.06 - 2,123.72 winning units T/Qpdt: £9.40 to a £1 stake. Pool: £7,883.86 - 617.15 winning units **Jonathan Neesom**

495 NEWCASTLE (A.W) (L-H)
Friday, February 1

OFFICIAL GOING: Tapeta: standard to slow (racing abandoned after race 5 (6.15) due to heavy snow)
Wind: Almost nil Weather: Dry, cold

522 PLAY 4 TO SCORE AT BETWAY H'CAP — 1m 4f 98y (Tp)
4:15 (4:15) (Class 4) (0-85,87) 4-Y-O+ **£5,530** (£1,645; £822; £411; £400; £400) **Stalls** High

Form — RPR
21-3 **1** **Claire Underwood (IRE)**[22] 157 4-9-4 **79** .... TonyHamilton 4 86+
(Richard Fahey) *prom chsng gp: hdwy and cl up over 2f out: rdn and sltly outpcd over 1f out: rallied to ld ins fnl f: kpt on wl* **5/2**[1]
1-13 **2** hd **Loud And Clear**[10] 349 8-9-3 **79** .... PhilDennis(3) 2 85
(Jim Goldie) *hld up: hdwy and ev ch over 2f out: rdn over 1f out: kpt on fnl f to press wnr cl home: jst hld* **11/2**[2]
400- **3** nse **Desert Ruler**[130] 7620 6-9-7 **80** .... JackGarritty 6 86
(Jedd O'Keeffe) *hld up: smooth hdwy on outside to ld over 2f out: rdn over 1f out: hdd ins fnl f: rallied: hld cl home* **8/1**[3]
243- **4** 9 **Native Fighter (IRE)**[177] 5871 5-9-9 **82** .... PJMcDonald 5 74
(Jedd O'Keeffe) *hld up: hdwy over 2f out: effrt and chsd clr ldng trio over 1f out: edgd lft: no imp fnl f* **5/2**[1]
2-11 **5** ½ **Glan Y Gors (IRE)**[15] 272 7-8-8 **74** ....(p) TobyEley(7) 1 65
(David Thompson) *t.k.h: prom chsng gp: effrt and pushed along over 2f out: wknd over 1f out* **11/1**
054- **6** 8 **Petitioner (IRE)**[104] 8419 5-9-6 **79** .... SamJames 3 57
(John Davies) *chsd clr ldr to over 2f out: rdn and wknd wl over 1f out* **8/1**[3]
40-6 **7** 16 **Golden Wolf (IRE)**[18] 238 5-10-0 **87** ....(t[1]) RachaelBlackmore 7 39
(Iain Jardine) *plld hrd: led and sn wl clr: hdd over 2f out: sn wknd: t.o (trainer said that the gelding ran too free and then weakened quickly turning into the home straight)* **11/1**
2m 40.45s (-0.65) **Going Correction** +0.375s/f (Slow) 7 Ran SP% **111.4**
WFA 4 from 5yo+ 2lb
Speed ratings (Par 105): **110,109,109,103,103 98,87**
CSF £15.73 TOTE £3.60: £1.90, £2.30; EX 16.90 Trifecta £104.10.
Owner Parker Partnership **Bred** Sindjara Partnership **Trained** Musley Bank, N Yorks
FOCUS
A modest event in which the leader was 15 lengths clear at halfway. Three came away from the others in the last couple of furlongs.

523 LADBROKES NOVICE STKS — 1m 5y (Tp)
4:45 (4:45) (Class 5) 3-Y-O **£3,752** (£1,116; £557) **Stalls** Centre

Form — RPR
3-1 **1** **Creationist (USA)**[23] 133 3-9-9 0 .... AdamMcNamara 2 88+
(Roger Charlton) *t.k.h: pressed ldr: led over 2f out: pushed out fnl f: comf* **1/3**[1]

2 1 1/4 **Formal Order**[21] [190] 3-9-2 0..(t) FrannyNorton 3 75
(J P Murtagh, Ire) *led at modest gallop: hdd and rdn over 2f out: kpt on same pce fnl f* **3/1**[2]

0 3 11 **Three Castles**[7] [405] 3-9-2 0.. CallumRodriguez 1 49
(Keith Dalgleish) *dwlt: trckd ldrs: rdn over 2f out: wknd fnl f* **16/1**[3]

1m 44.95s (6.35) **Going Correction** +0.375s/f (Slow) **3** Ran SP% **105.9**
Speed ratings (Par 97): **83,81,70**
CSF £1.57 TOTE £1.20; EX 1.40 Trifecta £1.50.

Owner Nick Bradley Racing 38 & Sohi **Bred** Courtlandt Farm **Trained** Beckhampton, Wilts

FOCUS
Not much of a contest, this was steadily run in a time 8.45 slower than standard. A deer ran across the track in front of the runners after a couple of furlongs, but no harm was done.

524 LADBROKES HOME OF THE ODDS BOOST H'CAP 7f 14y (Tp)
5:15 (5:15) (Class 6) (0-65,67) 3-Y-O

£3,105 (£924; £461; £400; £400; £400) **Stalls** Centre

Form RPR

0 1 **Kodi Dream**[18] [235] 3-8-7 **56**.. BenSanderson(5) 6 60
(Roger Fell) *dwlt and checked s: t.k.h in rr: rdn and hdwy over 1f out: led ins fnl f: hld on wl* **9/1**

020- 2 nk **Klipperty Klopp**[63] [9325] 3-8-8 **59**.. KieranSchofield(7) 4 62
(Antony Brittain) *chsd ldr: effrt over 2f out: sltly outpcd over 1f out: rallied and chsd wnr wl ins fnl f: kpt on fin* **9/1**

05-0 3 nk **Uh Oh Chongo**[19] [228] 3-9-3 **61**.. NathanEvans 1 63
(Michael Easterby) *t.k.h: hld up: pushed along over 2f out: hdwy on far side of gp over 1f out: edgd lft ins fnl f: r.o* **16/1**

0-33 4 nk **Spirit Kingdom (USA)**[7] [409] 3-9-6 **64**.. FrannyNorton 3 66
(Mark Johnston) *led at ordinary gallop: rdn over 1f out: hdd ins fnl f: one pce towards fin* **13/2**

5 1/2 **Duhallow Noelie (IRE)**[63] [9338] 3-8-10 **61**.. CierenFallon(7) 8 61
(Adrian Paul Keatley, Ire) *hld up: rdn over 2f out: effrt on nr side of gp over 1f out: one pce ins fnl f* **7/2**[1]

060- 6 1 **Fanfaronade (USA)**[44] [9603] 3-9-9 **67**.. RobertHavlin 7 65
(John Gosden) *chsd ldrs: rdn and outpcd over 1f out: no imp fnl f* **6/1**[3]

60-3 7 nk **Cadeau D'Amour (IRE)**[28] [65] 3-9-7 **65**................(p1) TonyHamilton 2 62
(Richard Fahey) *in tch: effrt and rdn over 1f out: edgd lft: outpcd fnl f* **7/2**[1]

000- 8 1 1/4 **Joey Boy (IRE)**[87] [8904] 3-9-3 **61**.. DougieCostello 5 55
(Kevin Ryan) *dwlt and checked s: hld up in tch: rdn over 2f out: wknd over 1f out* **11/2**[2]

1m 29.12s (2.92) **Going Correction** +0.375s/f (Slow) **8** Ran SP% **113.3**
Speed ratings (Par 95): **98,97,97,96,96 95,94,93**
CSF £83.94 CT £1278.12 TOTE £12.70: £3.40, £2.80, £5.50; EX 94.80 Trifecta £736.10.

Owner Nick Bradley Racing 29 & Partner **Bred** Whatcote Farm Stud **Trained** Nawton, N Yorks

FOCUS
A modest gallop led to something of a blanket finish. It has to rate as ordinary form for the grade.

525 LADBROKES FILLIES' H'CAP 7f 14y (Tp)
5:45 (5:45) (Class 5) (0-70,70) 4-Y-O+

£3,752 (£1,116; £557; £400; £400; £400) **Stalls** Centre

Form RPR

60-1 1 **Porrima (IRE)**[7] [410] 4-9-0 **63** 6ex.. AndrewMullen 5 70
(Ben Haslam) *dwlt and fly-jmpd s: hld up in last pl: rdn over 2f out: hdwy over 1f out: led ins fnl f: r.o* **11/4**[2]

63-3 2 1 1/2 **Playfull Spirit**[9] [366] 4-9-6 **69**..(p1) RobertHavlin 6 72
(John Gosden) *chsd ldr: rdn over 2f out: effrt and ev ch briefly ins fnl f: one pce towards fin* **11/8**[1]

55-4 3 1 **Elixsoft (IRE)**[10] [355] 4-9-2 **65**.. CallumRodriguez 3 65
(Roger Fell) *hld up in tch: rdn over 2f out: effrt over 1f out: kpt on same pce ins fnl f* **6/1**[3]

6-60 4 hd **Eponina (IRE)**[3] [467] 5-8-5 **59**.. KevinLundie(5) 4 59
(Michael Appleby) *led: qcknd 1/2-way: rdn 2f out: hdd and no ex ins fnl f* **9/1**

/35- 5 1 3/4 **Hippeia (IRE)**[284] [2026] 4-9-7 **70**.. SamJames 2 65
(Grant Tuer) *t.k.h: hld up: rdn and outpcd over 2f out: rallied fnl f: no imp* **28/1**

04-0 6 3 **Lucky Violet (IRE)**[30] [22] 7-8-5 **57**.. JamieGormley(3) 1 44
(Linda Perratt) *chsd ldrs: rdn over 2f out: effrt over 1f out: wknd fnl f* **9/1**

1m 27.83s (1.63) **Going Correction** +0.375s/f (Slow) **6** Ran SP% **106.5**
Speed ratings (Par 100): **105,103,102,101,99 96**
CSF £6.16 TOTE £3.70: £1.60, £1.20; EX 8.70 Trifecta £24.60.

Owner Daniel Shapiro & Partners **Bred** Tally-Ho Stud **Trained** Middleham Moor, N Yorks

FOCUS
This was 1.29sec quicker than the preceding Class 6 event.

526 SUNRACING.CO.UK H'CAP 1m 5y (Tp)
6:15 (6:15) (Class 4) (0-80,81) 4-Y-O+ **£5,530** (£1,645; £822; £411; £400) **Stalls** Centre

Form RPR

33- 1 **Executive Force**[86] [8918] 5-9-0 **71**..(p) FrannyNorton 2 82
(Michael Wigham) *cl up: shkn up to ld appr fnl f: kpt on wl* **11/4**[2]

6-13 2 2 **Blame Culture (USA)**[10] [350] 4-9-6 **77**.. PJMcDonald 4 83
(George Margarson) *led at modest gallop 3f: pressed ldr: effrt and ev ch appr fnl f: sn pressing wnr: one pce ins fnl f* **13/8**[1]

-431 3 1 1/2 **Glory Of Paris (IRE)**[15] [276] 5-9-10 **81**.. AndrewMullen 3 84
(Michael Appleby) *dwlt: plld hrd and sn cl up: taken wd and led after 3f: rdn and hdd appr fnl f: sn one pce* **11/4**[2]

/36- 4 3 3/4 **Prosecution**[19] [8018] 5-9-7 **78**..(b) RobertHavlin 1 72
(J P Murtagh, Ire) *hld up in tch: rdn along and outpcd wl over 1f out: no imp fnl f* **11/2**[3]

000- 5 3 3/4 **Tiercel**[134] [7447] 6-9-0 **74**.. PhilDennis(3) 5 59
(Rebecca Bastiman) *hld up: effrt over 2f out: wknd over 1f out* **33/1**

1m 42.22s (3.62) **Going Correction** +0.375s/f (Slow) **5** Ran SP% **109.8**
Speed ratings (Par 105): **96,94,92,88,85**
CSF £7.61 TOTE £4.40: £2.10, £1.30; EX 8.40 Trifecta £14.80.

Owner Tugay Akman **Bred** Rabbah Bloodstock Limited **Trained** Newmarket, Suffolk

FOCUS
It was snowing at this stage. This was steadily run and became tactical. All the runners raced down the centre of the track from halfway.

527 FOLLOW SUNRACING ON TWITTER APPRENTICE H'CAP 1m 5y (Tp)
(6:45) (Class 6) (0-65,) 4-Y-O+

£

528 LADBROKES FILLIES' NOVICE STKS 6f (Tp)
(7:15) (Class 5) 3-Y-O+ £

529 BETWAY H'CAP 6f (Tp)
(7:45) (Class 7) (0-50,) 3-Y-O+ £

T/Plt: £58.50 to a £1 stake. Pool: £74,341.74 - 926.61 winning units T/Qpdt: £19.30 to a £1 stake. Pool: £12,345.20 - 472.51 winning units **Richard Young**

479 WOLVERHAMPTON (A.W) (L-H)
Friday, February 1

OFFICIAL GOING: Tapeta: standard
Wind: Fresh against Weather: Overcast

530 FOLLOW TOP TIPSTER TEMPLEGATE AT SUN RACING H'CAP (DIV I) 7f 36y (Tp)
1:00 (1:00) (Class 6) (0-52,54) 4-Y-O+

£3,752 (£1,116; £557; £300; £300; £300) **Stalls** High

Form RPR

60-2 1 **Rapid Rise (IRE)**[17] [243] 5-9-1 **46**..(p) RaulDaSilva 6 51
(Milton Bradley) *prom: racd keenly: lost pl over 5f out: pushed along and hdwy over 2f out: nt clr run over 1f out: sn swtchd rt: rdn and r.o to ld wl ins fnl f* **8/1**

66-5 2 1 **Be Bold**[23] [132] 7-9-1 **46** oh1..(b) DavidProbert 4 49
(Rebecca Bastiman) *chsd ldr: rdn to ld ins fnl f: sn hdd: styd on same pce* **5/1**[3]

0-30 3 1/2 **Classy Cailin (IRE)**[2] [484] 4-9-7 **52**.. EoinWalsh 8 53
(Mark Loughnane) *s.i.s: plld hrd and hdwy over 5f out: rdn over 1f out: r.o* **6/1**

0-00 4 hd **Tasaaboq**[22] [161] 8-8-8 **46** oh1..(tp) GraceMcEntee(7) 5 47
(Phil McEntee) *s.i.s: hld up: racd keenly: hdwy over 1f out: sn rdn: r.o* **12/1**

00-3 5 3/4 **Secret Glance**[16] [263] 7-9-1 **46**..(p) StevieDonohoe 1 45
(Adrian Wintle) *led: rdn over 1f out: hdd and no ex ins fnl f* **9/4**[1]

5-05 6 1 3/4 **Moonbi Creek (IRE)**[15] [273] 12-9-1 **46** oh1.. JamesSullivan 2 41
(Stella Barclay) *s.i.s: hld up: shkn up over 2f out: no trble ldrs* **14/1**

03-2 7 4 1/2 **Admirable Art (IRE)**[23] [132] 9-9-5 **50**.. LiamKeniry 3 34
(Tony Carroll) *sn chsng ldrs: pushed along 1/2-way: rdn over 1f out: wknd fnl f (jockey said gelding was never travelling; trainer could offer no further explanation for the gelding's performance)* **7/2**[2]

1m 30.67s (1.87) **Going Correction** +0.25s/f (Slow) **7** Ran SP% **109.4**
Speed ratings (Par 101): **99,97,97,97,96 94,89**
CSF £43.01 CT £236.06 TOTE £8.70: £4.50, £2.50; EX 34.70 Trifecta £220.60.
Owner M G Ridley **Bred** Eleanor Brazill **Trained** Sedbury, Gloucs

FOCUS
A meeting arranged at short notice. The first leg of a lowly handicap and the form's viewed a shade negatively.

531 FOLLOW TOP TIPSTER TEMPLEGATE AT SUN RACING H'CAP (DIV II) 7f 36y (Tp)
1:30 (1:30) (Class 6) (0-52,53) 4-Y-O+

£3,752 (£1,116; £557; £300; £300; £300) **Stalls** High

Form RPR

3-04 1 **Black Truffle (FR)**[16] [263] 9-9-1 **46** oh1..(v) ShaneGray 8 51
(Mark Usher) *hld up: hdwy over 1f out: sn swtchd lft: shkn up to ld wl ins fnl f: rdn out* **9/2**[3]

3-02 2 nk **Baby Gal**[9] [365] 5-9-1 **46**..(b) CharlieBennett 4 50
(Jim Boyle) *chsd ldrs: rdn and hung rt over 1f out: r.o* **7/2**[2]

2-05 3 hd **Legal Mind**[17] [244] 6-9-6 **51**..(p1) EoinWalsh 5 55
(Emma Owen) *chsd ldr: rdn over 1f out: ev ch ins fnl f: styd on* **15/2**

0-00 4 3/4 **Rising Sunshine (IRE)**[16] [263] 6-9-1 **46** oh1..(bt) DavidProbert 1 48
(Milton Bradley) *hld up in tch: rdn over 2f out: r.o*

6203 5 1 **Swiss Cross**[7] [402] 12-9-1 **53**..(p) GraceMcEntee(7) 2 52
(Phil McEntee) *sn pushed along to ld: rdn over 1f out: edgd rt: hdd and no ex wl ins fnl f* **3/1**[1]

0-00 6 nse **Caledonian Gold**[8] [383] 6-9-1 **46** oh1..(b) HectorCrouch 7 45
(Lisa Williamson) *s.s: hld up: rdn over 1f out: r.o ins fnl f: nt rch ldrs* **33/1**

30-0 7 1/2 **Madame Jo Jo**[21] [180] 4-9-1 **46**..(p) ShaneKelly 3 44
(Sarah Hollinshead) *chsd ldrs: rdn over 1f out: no ex wl ins fnl f* **6/1**

4/-0 8 27 **Twistsandturns (IRE)**[16] [263] 8-9-1 **46** oh1.. StevieDonohoe 9
(Adrian Wintle) *sn outpcd* **50/1**

1m 30.36s (1.56) **Going Correction** +0.25s/f (Slow) **8** Ran SP% **110.6**
Speed ratings (Par 101): **101,100,100,99,98 98,97,66**
CSF £19.22 CT £107.56 TOTE £5.20: £1.40, £1.70, £2.30; EX 17.90 Trifecta £78.30.
Owner The Mark Usher Racing Club **Bred** Peter Harris **Trained** Upper Lambourn, Berks

FOCUS
Any one of five still held a chance inside the last furlong. The second and third set a straightforward level.

532 SUN RACING CLASSIFIED STKS (DIV I) 1m 142y (Tp)
2:05 (2:05) (Class 6) 3-Y-O+

£3,752 (£1,116; £557; £300; £300; £300) **Stalls** Low

Form RPR

50-5 1 **Zorawar (FR)**[29] [37] 5-9-10 50.. ShaneGray 5 58+
(David O'Meara) *trckd ldrs: edgd lft sn after s: lost pl over 6f out: hdwy over 2f out: led on bit over 1f out: shkn up: edgd lft and sn clr: easily* **4/1**[2]

30-6 2 6 **One Liner**[4] [462] 5-9-10 42.. ShaneKelly 2 45
(John O'Shea) *prom: hmpd and lost pl 8f out: hdwy over 6f out: rdn over 1f out: styd on same pce: wnt 2nd nr fin* **6/1**

5-56 3 1/2 **Red Cossack (CAN)**[17] [245] 8-9-7 49.. JackDuern(3) 11 44
(Dean Ivory) *s.i.s: hld up: hdwy on outer over 3f out: led over 1f out: sn rdn: edgd lft and hdd: no ex* **3/1**[1]

50-0 **4** *1 ¼* **Whimsical Dream**[21] [183] 3-8-3 49............................ PaddyMathers 1 36
(Michael Bell) *awkward leaving stalls: pushed along early then hld up and racd keenly: swtchd rt over 2f out: hdwy over 1f out: sn rdn: styd on same pce fnl f* **5/1**[3]

00-0 **5** *hd* **Imperial Act**[6] [436] 4-9-10 45.......................(h) DavidProbert 3 41
(Andrew Balding) *s.i.s: hld up: hdwy: nt clr run and swtchd rt over 1f out: nt trble ldrs* **11/2**

00-4 **6** *3* **Gone With The Wind (GER)**[22] [155] 8-9-10 42......(p) WilliamCarson 8 35
(Rebecca Bastiman) *edgd rt s: chsd ldr 1f: remained handy: rdn over 2f out: wknd ins fnl f* **14/1**

000- **7** *2* **Cala Sveva (IRE)**[42] [9670] 3-8-3 45............................ RaulDaSilva 9 25
(Mark Usher) *hmpd s: chsd ldr over 7f out tl shkn up over 2f out: wknd ins fnl f* **28/1**

00-0 **8** *1* **Outlaw Torn (IRE)**[6] [436] 10-9-10 38............................ PhilipPrince 7 28
(Richard Guest) *led: clr over 5f out tl rdn over 2f out: hdd over 1f out: wknd fnl f* **16/1**

000- **9** *16* **Late For The Sky**[239] [3497] 5-9-10 43............................ JamesSullivan 10
(Stella Barclay) *s.i.s: hld up: bhd and pushed along over 6f out: rdn over 3f out: sn wknd* **100/1**

000- **10** *8* **Kheleyf's Girl**[34] [9088] 4-9-10 41.......................(p[1]) StevieDonohoe 4
(Clare Ellam) *pushed along to chse ldrs: nt clr run sn after s: rdn and wknd over 2f out* **100/1**

000- **11** *3 ¾* **Coral Caye**[35] [9734] 5-9-10 38.......................(v[1]) ShelleyBirkett 6
(Steph Hollinshead) *s.i.s: hdwy 7f out: rdn and wknd over 3f out* **100/1**

1m 51.18s (1.08) **Going Correction** +0.25s/f (Slow) **11** Ran SP% **110.3**
WFA 3 from 4yo+ 21lb
Speed ratings (Par 101): **105,99,99,98,97 95,93,92,78,71 67**
CSF £25.99 TOTE £5.50: £1.90, £2.20, £1.50; EX 29.20 Trifecta £88.90.
Owner Evan M Sutherland **Bred** S C H H The Aga Khan's Studs **Trained** Upper Helmsley, N Yorks
■ Stewards' Enquiry : Shane Gray caution: careless riding

FOCUS
One-way traffic in this weak contest, and the winner could have been rated a few lengths higher.

533 SUN RACING CLASSIFIED STKS (DIV II) 1m 142y (Tp)
2:40 (2:40) (Class 6) 3-Y-O+
£3,752 (£1,116; £557; £300; £300; £300) **Stalls** Low

Form RPR

60-0 **1** **Muraaqeb**[18] [241] 5-9-10 37............................(p) DavidProbert 10 50
(Milton Bradley) *chsd ldr after 1f tl over 4f out: led over 2f out: rdn and hdd over 1f out: rallied to ld nr fin* **16/1**

2-30 **2** *hd* **Foxrush Take Time (FR)**[15] [273] 4-9-10 44.................(e) PhilipPrince 8 50
(Richard Guest) *chsd ldrs: nt clr run over 2f out: rdn over 1f out: r.o* **12/1**

-445 **3** *nk* **Sir Lancelott**[2] [479] 7-9-3 44............................ LauraCoughlan(7) 3 49
(Adrian Nicholls) *chsd ldrs: led over 1f out: rdn ins fnl f: hdd nr fin* **5/2**[1]

6-46 **4** *1 ½* **Margaret J**[16] [259] 3-8-3 46.......................(p) PaddyMathers 1 41
(Phil McEntee) *hld up in tch: pushed along and lost pl over 4f out: hdwy over 1f out: r.o u.p* **5/1**[3]

0-50 **5** *1 ¼* **Sosian**[13] [321] 4-9-3 49.......................(b) RussellHarris(7) 5 43
(Richard Fahey) *s.i.s: hld up: hdwy over 3f out: rdn over 1f out: styd on same pce ins fnl f (jockey said filly was slowly away)* **11/4**[2]

00-0 **6** *4* **Cardaw Lily (IRE)**[20] [210] 4-9-10 44............................ JamesSullivan 7 35
(Ruth Carr) *s.i.s: hld up: nt clr run: swtchd rt and hdwy over 1f out: hung lft and wknd ins fnl f* **14/1**

0-00 **7** *4 ½* **Willsy**[21] [180] 6-9-10 42............................ ShaneKelly 2 25
(Frank Bishop) *hld up: effrt over 1f out: wknd fnl f* **28/1**

00-0 **8** *hd* **No Approval (IRE)**[7] [399] 6-9-5 50.......................(p[1]) PoppyBridgwater(5) 9 25
(David Bridgwater) *plld hrd and sn prom: wnt 2nd over 4f out: led 3f out: sn hdd: wknd fnl f (jockey said gelding had no more to give)* **7/1**

0-06 **9** *9* **Concur (IRE)**[16] [263] 6-9-3 40.......................(tp) OliverSearle(7) 4 6
(Rod Millman) *sn led: hdd 3f out: wknd over 1f out* **40/1**

1m 52.43s (2.33) **Going Correction** +0.25s/f (Slow) **9** Ran SP% **110.5**
WFA 3 from 4yo+ 21lb
Speed ratings (Par 101): **99,98,98,97,96 92,88,88,80**
CSF £179.34 TOTE £16.10: £3.40, £3.00, £1.30; EX 112.10 Trifecta £581.30.
Owner E A Hayward **Bred** Peter Winkworth **Trained** Sedbury, Gloucs
■ Stewards' Enquiry : Philip Prince two-day ban: used whip above the permitted level (Feb 15-16)

FOCUS
A bit of a turn-up here in division two, with the winner carrying an official rating of just 37. The form is rated around the second and third.

534 LIKE SUN RACING ON FACEBOOK MAIDEN STKS 1m 142y (Tp)
3:10 (3:10) (Class 5) 3-Y-O+ **£4,625** (£1,376; £687; £343) **Stalls** Low

Form RPR

0- **1** **Wings Of Time**[126] [7736] 3-8-7 0............................ DavidProbert 1 74+
(Charlie Appleby) *hld up: hdwy and nt clr run over 2f out: shkn up to ld ins fnl f: pushed out* **4/9**[1]

4 **2** *½* **Reggae Runner (FR)**[13] [313] 3-8-2 0............................ AndrewBreslin(5) 6 73+
(Mark Johnston) *led: hung rt fr over 2f out: rdn: wnt rt and hdd ins fnl f: r.o* **14/1**

6 **3** *3* **Solar Heights (IRE)**[27] [78] 3-8-2 0............................ JamesSullivan 2 62
(James Tate) *hld up: hdwy over 2f out: hmpd ins fnl f: styd on same pce* **9/2**[2]

5 **4** *1* **Ardimento (IRE)**[16] [251] 3-8-7 0............................ EoinWalsh 4 64
(Rod Millman) *s.i.s: sn plld hrd and prom: wnt 2nd 5f out: rdn and nt clr run 1f out: swtchd lft: styd on same pce (jockey said gelding ran greenly)* **7/1**[3]

4 **5** *8* **Thedevilinneville**[6] [438] 3-8-7 0............................ CharlieBennett 3 45
(Adam West) *racd keenly in 2nd pl tl 5f out: remained handy: rdn over 1f out: wkng whn hung rt fnl f (jockey said gelding ran too freely)* **80/1**

6 *nk* **Golden Grenade (FR)** 3-8-7 0............................ JohnFahy 8 45
(Ian Williams) *s.s: rn green and a in rr* **50/1**

1m 51.96s (1.86) **Going Correction** +0.25s/f (Slow) **6** Ran SP% **109.8**
Speed ratings (Par 103): **101,100,97,97,89 89**
CSF £7.91 TOTE £1.40: £1.10, £3.90; EX 6.70 Trifecta £11.70.
Owner Godolphin **Bred** Godolphin **Trained** Newmarket, Suffolk

FOCUS
Little more than an average maiden.

535 BETWAY STAYERS' H'CAP 2m 120y (Tp)
3:40 (3:40) (Class 6) (0-65,65) 4-Y-O+ **£3,752** (£1,116; £557; £300; £300) **Stalls** Low

Form RPR

05-5 **1** **Sweetest Smile (IRE)**[20] [208] 4-8-0 46 oh1............................ JaneElliott(3) 2 52
(Ed de Giles) *chsd ldrs: led 3f out: rdn clr over 1f out* **2/1**[2]

000- **2** *4 ½* **Hediddodinthe (IRE)**[102] [8480] 5-9-5 65............................ RPWalsh(7) 5 64
(Peter Winks) *s.i.s: hld up: hdwy over 3f out: rdn over 2f out: edgd lft and chsd wnr fnl f: styd on same pce* **10/1**

6-22 **3** *5* **Falcon Cliffs (IRE)**[13] [318] 5-9-12 65............................ LiamKeniry 7 58
(Tony Carroll) *chsd ldr tl led over 13f out: hdd 3f out: sn rdn: wknd fnl f* **4/5**[1]

00 **4** *8* **Fearaun (IRE)**[11] [346] 4-8-12 55............................ StevieDonohoe 3 40
(Stella Barclay) *led at stdy pce: hdd over 13f out: chsd ldr tl rdn over 3f out: wknd over 2f out* **66/1**

00-6 **5** *7* **Silvington**[21] [185] 4-8-3 46 oh1............................ JamesSullivan 6 23
(Mark Loughnane) *hld up: pushed along over 5f out: wknd 3f out* **9/1**[3]

3m 47.85s (8.55) **Going Correction** +0.25s/f (Slow) **5** Ran SP% **109.5**
WFA 4 from 5yo+ 4lb
Speed ratings (Par 101): **89,86,84,80,77**
CSF £19.52 TOTE £2.90: £1.10, £3.00; EX 16.70 Trifecta £26.20.
Owner The LAM Partnership **Bred** J Wigan & London Thoroughbred Services **Trained** Ledbury, H'fords
■ Stewards' Enquiry : Stevie Donohoe caution: careless riding

FOCUS
Lowly staying form with the favourite failing to run her race, but the form could be rated up to 6lb better. The pace was a steady one.

536 BETWAY HEED YOUR HUNCH H'CAP 1m 1f 104y (Tp)
4:10 (4:10) (Class 5) (0-75,76) 4-Y-O+
£4,625 (£1,376; £687; £343; £300; £300) **Stalls** Low

Form RPR

00-4 **1** **Regular Income (IRE)**[6] [429] 4-8-13 67.................(p) CharlieBennett 10 74
(Adam West) *hld up: hdwy and rn wd over 1f out: rdn and hung lft ins fnl f: r.o to ld nr fin (jockey said gelding hung right-handed from halfway)* **11/2**[3]

40-0 **2** *¾* **Apache Blaze**[15] [272] 4-8-9 63............................ ShaneKelly 7 68
(Robyn Brisland) *hld up: hdwy on outer over 2f out: led over 1f out: rdn and hdd nr fin* **11/1**

0-63 **3** *¾* **King Of Naples**[11] [344] 6-8-7 61.......................(h[1]) JamesSullivan 2 65+
(Ruth Carr) *s.i.s: hld up: hdwy and nt clr run fr over 1f out tl wl ins fnl f: r.o (jockey said gelding was denied a clear run until approaching the half furlong marker)* **9/1**

30-3 **4** *¾* **Francophilia**[29] [41] 4-8-11 70............................ AndrewBreslin(5) 5 72
(Mark Johnston) *sn led: hdd over 4f out: remained w ldr: rdn and ev ch over 1f out: no ex towards fin* **6/1**

4/0- **5** *½* **Harlow**[112] [8172] 5-9-8 76............................ StevieDonohoe 8 77
(Ian Williams) *chsd ldrs: rdn over 2f out: no ex wl ins fnl f* **7/2**[2]

050- **6** *1 ½* **Doctor Wonderful**[172] [6101] 4-8-11 65............................ WilliamCarson 6 63
(Kevin Frost) *hld up: shkn up and nt clr run over 2f out: styd on fr over 1f out: nt trble ldrs* **33/1**

42-0 **7** *1 ¾* **Tangramm**[14] [292] 7-9-1 72............................ JackDuern(3) 1 66
(Dean Ivory) *stdd s: hld up: shkn up over 1f out: nvr nr to chal (jockey said gelding was never travelling)* **10/1**

560- **8** *½* **Captain Pugwash (IRE)**[34] [9311] 5-9-4 72.................(p[1]) LiamKeniry 3 65
(Stef Keniry) *trckd ldrs: rdn whn nt clr run over 1f out: no ex fnl f* **16/1**

13-4 **9** *2* **Destinys Rock**[28] [67] 4-8-4 63............................ MeganNicholls(5) 9 52
(Mark Loughnane) *plld hrd and prom: led over 4f out: hdd over 1f out: wknd ins fnl f (jockey said filly ran too freely)* **10/3**[1]

2m 1.64s (0.84) **Going Correction** +0.25s/f (Slow) **9** Ran SP% **111.2**
Speed ratings (Par 103): **106,105,104,104,103 102,100,100,98**
CSF £60.33 CT £516.73 TOTE £5.00: £2.20, £2.40, £2.20; EX 49.20 Trifecta £429.00.
Owner Ian & Amanda Maybrey And Partners **Bred** Garrett O'Neill **Trained** Epsom, Surrey

FOCUS
An ordinary handicap that set up for the closers.

537 LADBROKES HOME OF THE ODDS BOOST H'CAP 1m 1f 104y (Tp)
4:40 (4:40) (Class 6) (0-60,59) 3-Y-O
£3,752 (£1,116; £557; £300; £300; £300) **Stalls** Low

Form RPR

62-2 **1** **Precision Prince (IRE)**[13] [319] 3-9-7 59............................ EoinWalsh 9 65
(Mark Loughnane) *hld up: hdwy over 1f out: sn rdn and hung lft: nt clr run ins fnl f: r.o to ld towards fin* **9/4**[1]

00-5 **2** *nk* **Greyzee (IRE)**[21] [183] 3-8-13 51............................ AlistairRawlinson 1 56
(Rod Millman) *chsd ldrs: led over 1f out: sn rdn: hdd towards fin* **9/4**[1]

05-2 **3** *hd* **Macs Blessings (IRE)**[11] [341] 3-9-0 52.......................(p) LiamKeniry 2 57
(Stef Keniry) *hld up in tch: racd keenly: rdn and ev ch whn hung rt ins fnl f: styd on* **6/1**[2]

5-00 **4** *2 ¼* **Pot Luck**[7] [400] 3-9-3 55.......................(b) DavidProbert 4 55
(Andrew Balding) *chsd ldr: led 2f out: rdn and hdd over 1f out: edgd lft ins fnl f: no ex towards fin* **10/1**

0-44 **5** *4* **Comeonfeeltheforce (IRE)**[13] [319] 3-9-2 54..........(t) CharlieBennett 11 47
(Adam West) *hld up: rdn over 2f out: rn wd over 1f out: nt trble ldrs* **10/1**

00-0 **6** *½* **Symphony (IRE)**[19] [228] 3-9-2 54............................ ShaneKelly 10 46
(James Unett) *hld up in tch: plld hrd: rdn and hung lft over 1f out: no ex fnl f* **33/1**

00-5 **7** *2* **Bonneville (IRE)**[16] [258] 3-9-0 57............................ PoppyBridgwater(5) 3 45
(Rod Millman) *sn led: hdd 2f out: wknd ins fnl f* **9/1**[3]

000- **8** *3 ¼* **Made In Lewisham (IRE)**[118] [7995] 3-9-4 56............................ HectorCrouch 6 38
(David Evans) *hld up: rdn and wknd over 2f out* **33/1**

0-04 **9** *13* **Midnite Rendezvous**[11] [343] 3-8-7 45............................ RaulDaSilva 8
(Derek Shaw) *s.i.s: hdwy over 7f out: rdn over 3f out: wkng whn hung rt over 2f out* **66/1**

6-00 **10** *6* **Gate City (USA)**[7] [405] 3-8-8 53.......................(v) LauraCoughlan(7) 7
(Adrian Nicholls) *s.i.s: hld up: wknd over 2f out* **20/1**

2m 3.55s (2.75) **Going Correction** +0.25s/f (Slow) **10** Ran SP% **116.1**
Speed ratings (Par 95): **97,96,96,94,91 90,88,85,74,69**
CSF £6.45 CT £25.55 TOTE £3.30: £1.20, £1.40, £1.60; EX 8.40 Trifecta £38.10.
Owner Precision Facades Ltd **Bred** J O'Haire **Trained** Rock, Worcs

FOCUS
The right horses came to the fore of this moderate 3yo handicap, which had a bit more depth than most races on the card.
T/Jkpt: Not Won. T/Plt: £115.70 to a £1 stake. Pool: £83,558.75 - 527 winning units T/Qpdt: £12.00 to a £1 stake. Pool: £11,878.28 - 726.72 winning units **Colin Roberts**

538 - 546a (Foreign Racing) - See Raceform Interactive

[429]CHELMSFORD (A.W) (L-H)

Saturday, February 2

OFFICIAL GOING: Polytrack: standard

Weather: Fine

547 £20 FREE BETS AT TOTESPORT.COM MAIDEN FILLIES' STKS 7f (P)

1:00 (1:09) (Class 5) 3-Y-O+ £4,140 (£1,232; £615; £307) Stalls Low

Form RPR

2- **1** **Orchid Star**[144] 7151 3-8-11 0 WilliamBuick 4 80+
(Charlie Appleby) *mde all: shkn up and qcknd over 2f out: clr fr over 1f out: comf* **1/8**[1]

5 **2** *5* **J'Ouvert (IRE)**[9] 380 3-8-11 0 StevieDonohoe 5 65
(David Simcock) *racd keenly in 2nd pl: rdn over 1f out: styd on same pce* **5/1**[2]

40 **3** *3* **Dorchester**[9] 380 3-8-11 0 MarcMonaghan 3 56
(Marco Botti) *prom: racd keenly: rdn over 1f out: no ex* **9/1**[3]

4 *5* **Jazzy Card (IRE)** 3-8-11 0 CallumShepherd 1 43
(Linda Jewell) *hld up: shkn up over 2f out: sn outpcd* **66/1**

5 *18* **Crazy Daisy** 3-8-11 0 DannyBrock 2
(Jane Chapple-Hyam) *s.s: hld up: rdn and wknd over 2f out* **25/1**

1m 27.01s (-0.19) **Going Correction** 0.0s/f (Stan) **5 Ran SP% 120.9**
Speed ratings (Par 100): **101,95,91,86,65**
CSF £1.86 TOTE £1.10: £1.10, £1.60; EX 1.80 Trifecta £5.20.
Owner Godolphin **Bred** Godolphin **Trained** Newmarket, Suffolk

FOCUS
This 3yo fillies' maiden was all about the winner.

548 TOTEPOOL CASHBACK CLUB AT TOTESPORT.COM H'CAP 7f (P)

1:35 (1:40) (Class 4) (0-80,82) 4-Y-O+
£6,727 (£2,002; £1,000; £500; £300; £300) Stalls Low

Form RPR

224- **1** **Field Gun (USA)**[107] 8346 4-9-4 76 (t[1]) RossaRyan 4 81
(Stuart Williams) *plld hrd and prom: rdn over 1f out: led wl ins fnl f: jst hld on* **5/2**[1]

14-0 **2** *hd* **It Must Be Faith**[9] 381 9-8-12 73 (p) JaneElliott[(3)] 7 77
(Michael Appleby) *led: rdn and hung rt over 1f out: hdd wl ins fnl f: styd on* **66/1**

-101 **3** *shd* **Philamundo (IRE)**[7] 429 4-9-3 82 (b) ScottMcCullagh[(7)] 1 86
(Richard Spencer) *stdd s: hld up: shkn up over 2f out: hdwy on outer over 1f out: sn rdn: r.o* **7/2**[2]

65-1 **4** *shd* **Harbour Vision**[7] 430 4-8-11 69 PaddyMathers 5 72
(Derek Shaw) *hld up: shkn up over 2f out: rdn: hung lft and r.o ins fnl f: nt quite rch ldrs* **7/2**[2]

1-13 **5** *1 1/4* **Cape Greco (USA)**[17] 250 4-7-13 64 ow1 GeorgiaDobie[(7)] 3 64
(Jo Hughes, France) *chsd ldrs: rdn and nt clr run over 1f out: hmpd ins fnl f: styd on same pce* **9/2**[3]

4-03 **6** *nk* **Glory Awaits (IRE)**[7] 429 9-9-0 77 (b) DylanHogan[(5)] 6 76
(David Simcock) *plld hrd in 2nd: rdn and nt clr run over 1f out: styd on same pce ins fnl f* **6/1**

000- **7** *6* **Sword Exceed (GER)**[33] 9772 5-9-7 79 DayversonDeBarros 2 62
(Ivan Furtado) *broke wl: sn stdd and lost pl: hld up: effrt over 1f out: hung lft and wknd fnl f* **11/1**

1m 25.51s (-1.69) **Going Correction** 0.0s/f (Stan) **7 Ran SP% 115.3**
Speed ratings (Par 105): **109,108,108,108,107 106,99**
CSF £124.68 TOTE £2.90: £1.90, £3.80; EX 55.30 Trifecta £443.50.
Owner T W Morley **Bred** Forging Oaks Farm Llc **Trained** Newmarket, Suffolk

FOCUS
They didn't hang around in this modest handicap and it saw a tight finish.

549 EXTRA PLACES AT TOTESPORT.COM CLASSIFIED STKS 1m 5f 66y(P)

2:10 (2:15) (Class 6) 4-Y-O+
£3,105 (£924; £461; £300; £300; £300) Stalls Low

Form RPR

-023 **1** **Harry Callahan (IRE)**[10] 363 4-9-0 49 (v) CallumShepherd 3 56
(Mick Channon) *trckd ldrs: lost pl 5f out: hdwy on outer over 2f out: rdn to chse ldr over 1f out: edgd lft ins fnl f: styd on u.p to ld post* **7/4**[1]

3-35 **2** *hd* **Banta Bay**[10] 363 5-9-2 46 JosephineGordon 9 54
(John Best) *led at stdy pce after 1f: hdd 5f out: led again 4f out: rdn and hung rt over 1f out: hdd post* **5/1**[3]

00-4 **3** *5* **Normandy Blue**[22] 185 4-9-0 50 KieranO'Neill 4 49
(Louise Allan) *led 1f: chsd ldrs: rdn over 2f out: hung rt over 1f out: styd on same pce fnl f (jockey said gelding hung right-handed in the home straight)* **4/1**[2]

3-04 **4** *2 1/4* **Murhib (IRE)**[17] 257 7-9-2 46 (h) HectorCrouch 6 44
(Lydia Richards) *hld up: hdwy to ld 5f out: hdd 4f out: rdn over 1f out: wknd ins fnl f* **4/1**[2]

60-0 **5** *1 1/2* **Slowfoot (GER)**[10] 363 11-8-11 44 (b) ThomasGreatrex[(5)] 2 41
(Suzi Best) *hld up: hdwy over 4f out: rdn over 1f out: wknd fnl f* **16/1**

00-0 **6** *9* **Seventii**[18] 245 5-8-11 46 DarraghKeenan[(5)] 5 29
(Robert Eddery) *hld up in tch: lost pl over 6f out: rdn over 2f out: wknd over 1f out* **25/1**

04-0 **7** *3* **Unsuspected Girl (IRE)**[5] 462 6-9-2 42 (tp) FrannyNorton 1 25
(Milton Bradley) *hld up: hdwy over 6f out: lost pl over 4f out: rdn and wknd over 1f out* **25/1**

3-00 **8** *7* **Mulsanne Chase**[7] 436 5-9-2 45 (p) RossaRyan 8 15
(Conor Dore) *chsd ldrs: rdn over 2f out: wknd over 1f out* **9/1**

2m 58.8s (5.20) **Going Correction** 0.0s/f (Stan)
WFA 4 from 5yo+ 2lb **8 Ran SP% 116.6**
Speed ratings (Par 101): **84,83,80,79,78 72,71,66**
CSF £11.15 TOTE £2.20: £1.10, £1.70, £1.50; EX 11.30 Trifecta £34.20.
Owner Chelsea Thoroughbreds- Dirty Harry **Bred** Corduff Stud **Trained** West Ilsley, Berks

FOCUS
This weak staying event was run at an uneven pace.

550 IRISH LOTTO AT TOTESPORT.COM H'CAP 6f (P)

2:45 (2:53) (Class 6) (0-58,60) 3-Y-O
£3,105 (£924; £461; £300; £300; £300) Stalls Centre

Form RPR

00-0 **1** **Global Acclamation**[7] 437 3-9-5 54 (b) LiamKeniry 8 60
(Ed Dunlop) *pushed along early in rr: hdwy 2f out: rdn to ld and edgd lft wl ins fnl f: r.o* **6/1**[3]

0-03 **2** *1/2* **Amor Kethley**[14] 313 3-9-11 60 GeorgeWood 7 65
(Amy Murphy) *chsd ldrs: rdn to ld over 1f out: hdd wl ins fnl f* **12/1**

6-55 **3** *nk* **Valley Belle (IRE)**[2] 505 3-9-7 56 (v) CallumShepherd 6 60
(Phil McEntee) *hld up: hdwy over 1f out: r.o* **4/1**[2]

550- **4** *3/4* **Farol**[114] 8138 3-9-4 53 BarryMcHugh 4 54
(James Given) *hld up: hdwy over 1f out: sn rdn: nt rch ldrs* **10/1**

5-35 **5** *3/4* **Spirit Of Lucerne (IRE)**[9] 384 3-9-11 60 (p[1]) RossaRyan 2 59
(Phil McEntee) *trckd ldrs: rdn over 1f out: kpt on* **16/1**

30-3 **6** *nse* **Yfenni (IRE)**[15] 296 3-8-10 45 FrannyNorton 3 45
(Milton Bradley) *w ldrs tl over 4f out: remained handy: nt clr run over 1f out: styd on same pce ins fnl f* **10/1**

16-0 **7** *1* **Grandee Daisy**[28] 79 3-9-0 56 GeorgiaDobie[(7)] 5 52
(Jo Hughes, France) *s.i.s: nt clr run and swtchd rt ins fnl f: nt trble ldrs* **6/1**[3]

00-6 **8** *2 3/4* **Tintern Spirit (IRE)**[15] 296 3-8-10 45 RaulDaSilva 9 33
(Milton Bradley) *led: rdn and hdd over 1f out: wknd ins fnl f* **33/1**

04-2 **9** *2* **Arishka (IRE)**[8] 406 3-9-11 60 KieranO'Neill 1 42
(Daniel Kubler) *w ldr: rdn and ev ch over 1f out: wknd ins fnl f* **15/8**[1]

1m 13.61s (-0.09) **Going Correction** 0.0s/f (Stan) **9 Ran SP% 118.1**
Speed ratings (Par 95): **100,99,98,97,96 96,95,91,89**
CSF £76.35 CT £325.08 TOTE £6.20: £2.10, £3.20, £1.30; EX 57.20 Trifecta £453.90.
Owner Global Group Lifestyle And Sports Club **Bred** Highclere Stud **Trained** Newmarket, Suffolk

FOCUS
A moderate sprint handicap.

551 BET IN PLAY AT TOTESPORT.COM H'CAP 5f (P)

3:20 (3:25) (Class 3) (0-90,88) 4-Y-O+ £9,703 (£2,887; £1,443; £721) Stalls Low

Form RPR

50-5 **1** **Saaheq**[11] 353 5-8-12 79 AlistairRawlinson 4 90
(Michael Appleby) *edgd rt s: chsd ldrs: nt clr run over 1f out: rdn to ld ins fnl f: r.o wl* **11/4**[1]

0-04 **2** *2* **Dynamo Walt (IRE)**[11] 353 8-9-2 83 (v) PaddyMathers 6 87
(Derek Shaw) *hld up in tch: rdn and ev ch ins fnl f: styd on same pce* **7/1**

03-0 **3** *hd* **Boom The Groom (IRE)**[25] 127 8-9-6 87 RossaRyan 7 90
(Tony Carroll) *led: hdd over 3f out: remained w ldr: led over 1f out: rdn and hdd ins fnl f: styd on same pce* **4/1**[2]

22-0 **4** *nse* **Foxy Forever (IRE)**[11] 353 9-9-5 86 (bt) FrannyNorton 3 89
(Michael Wigham) *broke wl enough: nt clr run and lost pl over 4f out: hdwy over 1f out: sn rdn: styd on* **7/1**

06-3 **5** *1 1/4* **Excellent George**[18] 247 7-9-2 83 (t) IrineuGoncalves 2 81
(Stuart Williams) *chsd ldrs: nt clr run and swtchd rt over 1f out: styd on same pce ins fnl f* **5/1**

/40- **6** *nk* **Green Door (IRE)**[273] 2410 8-9-0 88 (p) JonathanFisher[(7)] 1 85
(Robert Cowell) *hld up: effrt and nt clr run over 1f out: no imp ins fnl f* **9/1**

00-3 **7** *2 1/2* **Captain Lars (SAF)**[30] 35 9-9-2 88 (b) ThomasGreatrex[(5)] 5 76
(Archie Watson) *sn w ldr: led over 3f out: rdn and hdd over 1f out: wknd ins fnl f* **9/2**[3]

59.51s (-0.69) **Going Correction** 0.0s/f (Stan) **7 Ran SP% 116.5**
Speed ratings (Par 107): **105,101,101,101,99 98,94**
CSF £23.27 TOTE £3.00: £1.70, £3.40; EX 25.10 Trifecta £120.20.
Owner The Horse Watchers **Bred** Cliveden Stud Ltd **Trained** Oakham, Rutland

FOCUS
This feature sprint handicap saw another tight finish.

552 DOUBLE DELIGHT HAT-TRICK HEAVEN AT TOTESPORT.COM H'CAP 1m 2f (P)

3:55 (4:00) (Class 4) (0-80,80) 4-Y-O+
£6,727 (£2,002; £1,000; £500; £300; £300) Stalls Low

Form RPR

-513 **1** **Central City (IRE)**[1] 521 4-9-1 74 (p) KieranO'Neill 2 81
(Ian Williams) *chsd ldr: pushed along over 2f out: rdn to ld over 1f out: edgd rt ins fnl f: styd on u.p* **13/8**[1]

1-03 **2** *1 1/2* **Squire**[9] 386 8-7-13 61 oh2 (tp) JaneElliott[(3)] 3 65
(Marjorie Fife) *edgd rt s: led: rdn and hdd over 1f out: styd on same pce wl ins fnl f* **5/1**[3]

/05- **3** *2 1/4* **Astrologist (IRE)**[141] 7261 4-9-1 74 JosephineGordon 6 74
(Olly Murphy) *hld up: pushed along over 3f out: styd on to go 3rd ins fnl f: nt trble ldrs* **16/1**

1-21 **4** *5* **Dutch Uncle**[21] 204 7-9-2 80 (p) MeganNicholls[(5)] 1 70
(Olly Murphy) *trckd ldrs: racd keenly: wknd fnl f* **7/1**

3-25 **5** *1* **Global Art**[7] 434 4-9-5 78 (b) LiamKeniry 5 66
(Ed Dunlop) *prom: rdn over 1f out: wknd fnl f* **5/1**[3]

6-34 **6** *1 3/4* **Come On Tier (FR)**[17] 252 4-9-0 78 (t[1]) DylanHogan[(5)] 4 62
(David Simcock) *s.i.s: hld up: racd keenly: shkn up over 2f out: n.d* **3/1**[2]

2m 7.66s (-0.94) **Going Correction** 0.0s/f (Stan) **6 Ran SP% 114.8**
Speed ratings (Par 105): **103,101,100,96,95 93**
CSF £10.60 TOTE £2.60: £1.50, £2.60; EX 9.20 Trifecta £74.30.
Owner Spencer Coomes **Bred** Mattock Stud **Trained** Portway, Worcs

FOCUS
Only two of these mattered for pretty much all the race.
T/Plt: £79.20 to a £1 stake. Pool: £52,553.47 - 483.85 winning units T/Qpdt: £25.00 to a £1 stake. Pool: £5,381.00 - 159.20 winning units **Colin Roberts**

[357]KEMPTON (A.W) (R-H)

Saturday, February 2

OFFICIAL GOING: Polytrack: standard to slow

Wind: breezy Weather: cloudy and cold

553 RASHER FRITH MEMORIAL H'CAP 7f (P)

4:45 (4:46) (Class 7) (0-50,64) 4-Y-O+ £2,587 (£770; £384; £192) Stalls Low

Form RPR

00-0 **1** **Naralsaif (IRE)**[17] 250 5-9-3 48 (v) RaulDaSilva 2 54
(Derek Shaw) *trckd ldrs: pushed along 2f out: rdn over 1f out: chal ent fnl f: led 1/2f out: r.o wl* **6/1**

60-5 **2** *nk* **Little Miss Kodi (IRE)**[18] 243 6-9-5 50 (t) ShaneKelly 9 55
(Mark Loughnane) *mid-div: pushed along 2f out: rdn to chal fnl f: wnt 2nd 1/2f out: kpt on wl: hld nr fin* **5/1**[3]

-322 **3** *1/2* **Dodgy Bob**[3] 483 6-9-0 48 (v) PhilDennis[(3)] 4 52
(Michael Mullineaux) *led: pushed along 2f out: drvn and jnd 1f out: hdd 1/2f out: no ex* **3/1**[1]

36-0 **4** *nk* **Shyarch**[23] [159] 5-9-3 **48**......(p) RobertHavlin 10 52
(Christine Dunnett) *hld up: pushed along and plenty to do 2f out: hdwy whn nt clr run over 1f out: in clr fnl f: drvn and r.o wl: tk 4th last two strides (jockey said gelding was denied a clear run)* **10/1**

00-0 **5** ½ **Elusif (IRE)**[30] [33] 4-9-2 **47**......(v[1]) LiamJones 8 49
(Shaun Keightley) *cl 2nd: drvn 2f out: rdn over 1f out: disp ld 1f out: hdd 1/2f out: wknd last 100yds* **16/1**

06-2 **6** *hd* **Satchville Flyer**[23] [155] 8-9-5 **50**...... EoinWalsh 3 51
(David Evans) *hld up: pushed along 2f out: hdwy over 1f out: kpt on fnl f (jockey said gelding was denied a clear run)* **9/2**[2]

60-0 **7** *nk* **Dawn Commando**[15] [288] 4-9-4 **49**......(b) CallumShepherd 6 50
(Daniel Kubler) *hld up: effrt on outer over 3f out: drvn over 2f out: sn rdn: hdwy over 1f out: one pce fnl f (jockey said gelding was denied a clear run)* **16/1**

0-52 **8** 3¾ **Dalness Express**[10] [357] 6-9-5 **50**......(tp) FergusSweeney 1 41
(John O'Shea) *mid-div: pushed along on inner over 2f out: sn drvn: rdn and wknd fnl f* **11/2**

0-10 **9** 4½ **Deer Song**[10] [357] 6-9-1 **49**......(b) PaddyBradley[(3)] 11 28
(John Bridger) *in rr: pushed along in last 2f out: nvr involved* **40/1**

000- **10** *1* **My Girl Maisie (IRE)**[67] [9273] 5-9-5 **50**...... GeraldMosse 14 27
(Richard Guest) *trckd across fr wd draw to chse ldrs: drvn and lost pl 2f out: sn wknd and eased* **50/1**

05-3 **11** *5* **Star Attraction (FR)**[24] [132] 4-9-2 **47**...... DavidProbert 7 11
(Tony Carroll) *hld up: drvn over 2f out: sn dropped to last* **16/1**

1m 27.34s (1.34) **Going Correction** +0.20s/f (Slow) **11 Ran SP% 120.7**
Speed ratings (Par 97): **100,99,99,98,98 97,97,93,88,87 81**
CSF £37.12 CT £111.53 TOTE £7.60: £2.60, £1.80, £2.10; EX 45.70 Trifecta £196.10.
Owner Shawthing Racing Partnership (d Shaw) **Bred** Shadwell Estate Company Limited **Trained** Sproxton, Leics

FOCUS
A bottom-grade handicap.

554 32RED ON THE APP STORE NOVICE STKS 7f (P)
5:15 (5:19) (Class 5) 3-Y-O+ £3,881 (£1,155; £577; £288) Stalls Low

Form RPR

1- **1** **Golden Spectrum**[73] [9171] 3-9-4 0...... GeraldMosse 11 87+
(Gay Kelleway) *qckly trckd across fr wd draw: mde all: qcknd clr over 1f out: 3 l ld 1f out: pushed out fnl f: readily* **4/6**[1]

0-2 **2** 1½ **Derry Boy**[10] [367] 3-8-11 0...... EoinWalsh 12 73
(David Evans) *prom: drvn 2f out: wnt 2nd 1f out: r.o fnl f: nvr nr wnr* **33/1**

0- **3** *3* **Chop Chop (IRE)**[101] [8546] 3-8-6 0...... HollieDoyle 7 60+
(Roger Charlton) *hld up: pushed along 2f out: hdwy over 1f out: wnt 3rd 1f out: no ex fnl f* **10/1**

0-5 **4** *4* **Fox Happy (IRE)**[10] [359] 3-8-11 0...... RossaRyan 10 54
(Richard Hannon) *t.k.h: trckd ldrs: sn racing in 2nd: drvn over 2f out: rdn and wknd over 1f out* **10/1**

62-2 **5** 1½ **Brandon (FR)**[10] [360] 3-8-8 77...... AaronJones[(3)] 9 50
(Marco Botti) *trckd ldr: sn racing in 3rd: drvn over 2f out: sn rdn and wknd* **11/2**[2]

0 **6** ¾ **Capofaro**[24] [133] 3-8-11 0...... NicolaCurrie 4 48+
(Jamie Osborne) *mid-div: pushed along and effrt on inner 2f out: reminders over 1f out: wknd fnl f* **20/1**

7 *2* **Angel Black (IRE)** 3-8-11 0...... LiamJones 2 43
(Shaun Keightley) *hld up: drvn 2f out: no imp* **50/1**

8 ½ **Plum Duff** 3-8-6 0...... JoeyHaynes 1 36
(Rod Millman) *hld up: pushed along over 3f out: lost tch fr 2f out* **50/1**

9 *6* **Sacred Warner (IRE)** 3-8-11 0......(w) HectorCrouch 6 25
(Clive Cox) *bhd: drvn over 3f out: reminder over 1f out: no rspnse* **9/1**[3]

6 **10** 4½ **Newton Kyme (IRE)**[7] [442] 3-8-11 0...... CallumShepherd 5 13
(David Simcock) *t.k.h: hld up: pushed along in rr 3f out: sn drvn and lost tch (jockey said gelding suffered interference in the back straight and moved poorly in the home straight)* **25/1**

1m 27.04s (1.04) **Going Correction** +0.20s/f (Slow)
WFA 3 from 4yo 17lb **10 Ran SP% 119.0**
Speed ratings (Par 103): **102,100,96,92,90 89,87,86,80,74**
CSF £40.39 TOTE £1.50: £1.10, £5.40, £2.60; EX 23.00 Trifecta £154.80.
Owner Dr Johnny Hon **Bred** Newsells Park Stud **Trained** Exning, Suffolk
■ Catheadans Gift was withdrawn. Price at time of withdrawal 150/1. Rule 4 does not apply

FOCUS
The odds-on favourite dominated throughout.

555 32RED CASINO H'CAP 6f (P)
5:45 (5:49) (Class 5) (0-75,77) 3-Y-O
£3,752 (£1,116; £557; £400; £400; £400) Stalls Low

Form RPR

003- **1** **Distant Mirage**[43] [9671] 3-9-0 **66**...... LukeMorris 2 71
(James Tate) *t.k.h: chsd ldrs on inner: pushed along in 3rd 1 1/2f out: drvn to chal 1f out: rdn fnl f: r.o wl to ld last 50yds: gng away at fin* **5/2**[2]

05-1 **2** ¾ **Xtara (IRE)**[28] [83] 3-9-11 **77**......(v) BarryMcHugh 3 80
(Adrian Nicholls) *led: pushed along 2f out: rdn in narrow ld 1f out: r.o fnl f: hdd last 50yds: no ex* **9/4**[1]

0-21 **3** 1¾ **Probability (IRE)**[14] [313] 3-9-7 **73**...... EdwardGreatrex 1 70
(Archie Watson) *chsd ldr: cl 2nd 2f out: rdn and ev ch 1f out: no ex fnl f* **5/2**[2]

65-0 **4** *1* **Zaula**[21] [211] 3-9-4 **70**......(p[1]) HollieDoyle 4 64
(Archie Watson) *mid-div: chsd ldrs 2f out: drvn in 4th over 1f out: no ex fnl f (jockey said filly lugged right-handed in the straight)* **16/1**

230- **5** 1¾ **Under Curfew**[134] [7497] 3-9-2 **68**...... FrannyNorton 8 57
(Tony Carroll) *hld up in rr: last 2f out: pushed along over 1f out: kpt on past btn horses fnl f* **40/1**

36-3 **6** 1½ **Urban Highway (IRE)**[10] [360] 3-8-11 **63**...... DavidProbert 5 47
(Tony Carroll) *hld up: drvn in 5th 1 1/2f out: sn rdn: no imp* **8/1**[3]

256- **7** *2* **Haats Off**[34] [9762] 3-9-1 **67**...... NicolaCurrie 7 44
(Brian Barr) *t.k.h: slowly away: bhd: pushed along 2f out: rdn and wknd over 1f out (jockey said filly was slowly away and ran too freely)* **25/1**

40-0 **8** *2* **Lysander Belle (IRE)**[7] [437] 3-8-5 **57**...... NickyMackay 6 28
(Sophie Leech) *hld up: drvn over 2f out: rdn and wknd over 1f out* **50/1**

1m 14.37s (1.27) **Going Correction** +0.20s/f (Slow) **8 Ran SP% 113.2**
Speed ratings (Par 97): **99,98,95,94,92 90,87,84**
CSF £8.32 CT £14.15 TOTE £3.30: £1.20, £1.10, £1.30; EX 9.80 Trifecta £23.40.
Owner Saeed Manana **Bred** D J And Mrs Deer **Trained** Newmarket, Suffolk

FOCUS
A modest handicap fought out by the market leaders.

556 WISE BETTING AT RACINGTV.COM FILLIES' NOVICE STKS 1m (P)
6:15 (6:21) (Class 5) 3-Y-O+ £3,881 (£1,155; £577; £288) Stalls Low

Form RPR

5- **1** **Yimkin (IRE)**[115] [8098] 3-8-9 0...... OisinMurphy 4 74+
(Roger Charlton) *led 1f: trckd ldrs whn hdd: pushed into ld over 1f out: rdn clr fnl f* **13/8**[2]

0- **2** 1¼ **Vegatina**[45] [9607] 3-8-9 0......(t) NickyMackay 10 71
(John Gosden) *prom: led 3f out: shkn up 2f out: rdn and hdd over 1f out: kpt on fnl f* **16/1**

04- **3** ½ **Cabarita**[49] [9556] 3-8-9 0...... PJMcDonald 3 70
(Ralph Beckett) *trckd ldrs: pushed along 2f out: drvn on inner 1 1/2f out: hdwy into 3rd 1f out: one pce fnl f (jockey said filly hung left-handed)* **6/4**[1]

4 *2* **Any Smile (IRE)** 3-8-9 0...... JamieSpencer 8 65
(Michael Bell) *chsd ldrs: drvn 2f out: 4th 1f out: one pce fnl f* **33/1**

5 1¼ **Elisheba (IRE)** 3-8-9 0...... RobertHavlin 6 62+
(John Gosden) *v.s.a losing several l: bhd: last 3f out: pushed along and hdwy over 1f out: r.o steadily fnl f: nvr nrr (jockey said filly was slowly away)* **5/1**[3]

0 **6** *2* **Tanzerin (IRE)**[10] [370] 3-8-9 0...... NicolaCurrie 7 57
(Charlie Fellowes) *prom: led after 1f: hdd 3f out: drvn and wknd 2f out* **100/1**

7 *shd* **Dusty Damsel** 3-8-9 0...... RossaRyan 1 57+
(Mike Murphy) *dwlt: bhd: drvn in last 2f out: pushed along and r.o wl fnl f: nvr nrr (jockey said filly hung left-handed)* **25/1**

0- **8** *nse* **Something Blond (IRE)**[54] [9485] 3-8-6 0...... AaronJones[(3)] 2 57
(Marco Botti) *hld up: pushed along 2f out: one pce fnl f* **50/1**

05- **9** 1¼ **Crimson Kiss (IRE)**[44] [9636] 3-8-2 0...... JoeBradnam[(7)] 5 54
(Michael Bell) *mid-div: pushed along 2f out: no imp* **50/1**

0- **10** *nk* **Maisie Moo**[121] [7943] 3-8-9 0...... LiamJones 13 53
(Shaun Keightley) *reluctant to load: t.k.h: hld up: tk clsr order 1/2-way: 3rd 3f out: pushed along and lost pl 1 1/2f out: reminder over 1f out: reminders and wknd fnl f* **200/1**

0- **11** ¾ **Sweet Poem**[144] [7151] 3-8-9 0......(w) LukeMorris 9 52
(Clive Cox) *hld up: drvn 3f out: reminder and wknd over 1f out* **66/1**

12 ¾ **Gabriela Laura** 3-8-9 0...... DavidProbert 14 50
(Clive Cox) *slowly away: bhd: drvn 2f out: wknd over 1f out* **33/1**

-00 **13** 1¾ **Breakfast Time**[10] [370] 3-8-9 0...... HollieDoyle 11 46
(Archie Watson) *hld up: drvn 3f out: rdn and dropped to last over 1f out* **66/1**

1m 42.92s (3.12) **Going Correction** +0.20s/f (Slow) **13 Ran SP% 118.8**
Speed ratings (Par 100): **92,90,90,88,87 85,84,84,83,83 82,81,80**
CSF £25.18 TOTE £2.50: £1.10, £3.30, £1.10; EX 31.70 Trifecta £60.70.
Owner Prince A A Faisal **Bred** Nawara Stud Limited **Trained** Beckhampton, Wilts

FOCUS
An ordinary novice.

557 32RED.COM H'CAP (LONDON MILE SERIES QUALIFIER) 1m (P)
6:45 (6:48) (Class 4) (0-85,86) 4-Y-O+
£6,469 (£1,925; £962; £481; £400; £400) Stalls Low

Form RPR

2-22 **1** **Family Fortunes**[14] [310] 5-9-0 **85**...... ScottMcCullagh[(7)] 11 95
(Michael Madgwick) *hld up: plenty to do 3f out: hdwy 2f out: rdn in 4th 1f out: r.o strly fnl f: led last stride* **6/1**[2]

004- **2** *shd* **Intrepidly (USA)**[65] [9313] 5-9-6 **84**......(p[1]) AdamKirby 5 93
(Charlie Fellowes) *trckd ldrs: 3rd 3f out: pushed along on inner 2f out: drvn to ld over 1f out: rdn fnl f: r.o: hdd last stride* **5/2**[1]

06-5 **3** *2* **Enzemble (IRE)**[17] [252] 4-9-1 **79**...... GeraldMosse 4 83
(James Fanshawe) *mid-div: pushed along and hdwy 2f out: drvn in 5th 1f out: r.o fnl f: tk 3rd last few strides* **8/1**

2-13 **4** *nk* **Scofflaw**[9] [381] 5-8-11 **80**......(v) KatherineBegley[(5)] 6 83
(David Evans) *t.k.h: prom: 2nd 2f out: drvn over 1f out: rdn fnl f: one pce: lost 3rd last few strides* **9/1**

60-1 **5** 2¼ **Shyron**[15] [294] 8-8-11 **78**...... PaddyBradley[(3)] 9 76
(Lee Carter) *slowly away: bhd: last 3f out: pushed along and nt clr run 1f out: r.o wl fnl f: nvr nrr (jockey said gelding was denied a clear run)* **10/1**

01-1 **6** *nk* **Divine Messenger**[18] [248] 5-9-0 **78**......(p) PJMcDonald 10 75
(Emma Owen) *mid-div on outer: drvn over 2f out: sn rdn: one pce fnl f* **6/1**[2]

00-6 **7** *nk* **Able Jack**[29] [56] 6-9-8 **86**...... RossaRyan 7 83
(Stuart Williams) *led: pushed along in 1 l ld 2f out: rdn and hdd over 1f out: wknd fnl f* **16/1**

0-02 **8** 1¼ **Juanito Chico (IRE)**[17] [252] 5-9-2 **80**......(t) OisinMurphy 2 74
(Stuart Williams) *t.k.h: mid-div: pushed along and effrt 2f out: rdn over 1f out: wknd fnl f* **13/2**[3]

-420 **9** 3½ **Hammer Gun (USA)**[9] [381] 6-8-12 **76**......(v) PaddyMathers 3 62
(Derek Shaw) *chsd ldrs: drvn and lost pl 2f out: sn rdn and wknd* **25/1**

200- **10** *1* **Poetic Force (IRE)**[99] [8611] 5-9-3 **86**......(t) PoppyBridgwater[(5)] 12 70
(Tony Carroll) *hld up on outer: pushed along 2f out: sn drvn: no rspnse* **80/1**

000- **11** ½ **Gossiping**[65] [9309] 7-8-10 **74**...... ShaneKelly 1 56
(Gary Moore) *hld up on inner: pushed along and lost pl 2f out: dropped away fnl f* **20/1**

1m 39.26s (-0.54) **Going Correction** +0.20s/f (Slow) **11 Ran SP% 116.4**
Speed ratings (Par 105): **110,109,107,107,105 105,104,103,100,99 98**
CSF £20.68 CT £124.67 TOTE £6.40: £2.40, £1.70, £3.00; EX 24.40 Trifecta £152.40.
Owner Los Leader **Bred** A Parrish & Mrs L Sadler **Trained** Denmead, Hants

FOCUS
Solid handicap form.

558 32RED H'CAP 1m 7f 218y(P)
7:15 (7:15) (Class 3) (0-90,91) 4-Y-O+
£9,337 (£2,796; £1,398; £699; £349; £175) Stalls Low

Form RPR

23-6 **1** **Cayirli (FR)**[28] [82] 7-9-10 **88**...... FergusSweeney 1 95
(Seamus Durack) *trckd ldrs: pushed into ld ent fnl 2f: drvn in 1 l ld 1f out: pushed out to assert fnl f: readily* **7/1**

114- **2** *2* **Lucky Deal**[44] [9639] 4-9-9 **91**...... FrannyNorton 4 96
(Mark Johnston) *chsd ldr: pushed along in 2nd over 2f out: rdn and lost pl 2f out: rallied into 1 l 2nd 1f out: no ex fnl f* **2/1**[1]

66-1 **3** ¾ **West Coast Flyer**[7] [432] 6-9-10 **88**...... JamieSpencer 5 92
(David Simcock) *hld up in last: pushed along 2f out: drvn and lugged lft briefly over 1f out: rdn fnl f: r.o: tk 3rd last stride* **4/1**[3]

30-2 **4** *hd* **Castlelyons (IRE)**[28] 82 7-9-13 **91**........................(h) CallumShepherd 2 95
(Robert Stephens) *racd in 4th: pushed along over 2f out: hdwy and ev ch over 1 1/2f out: sn rdn: 3rd 1f out: no ex fnl f: lost 3rd last stride* **6/1**

322- **5** *2 1/4* **Jabbaar**[98] 8631 6-9-12 **90**.. AdamKirby 6 91
(Iain Jardine) *hld up: pushed along in 5th 2f out: sn drvn: no imp* **25/1**

06-4 **6** *1 3/4* **Diocletian (IRE)**[15] 291 4-8-13 **81**.................................. OisinMurphy 3 80
(Andrew Balding) *led: pushed along 2f out: sn hdd: wknd and dropped to last fnl f* **5/2**[2]

3m 34.35s (4.25) **Going Correction** +0.20s/f (Slow)
WFA 4 from 6yo+ 4lb **6** Ran SP% **112.5**
Speed ratings (Par 107): **97,96,95,95,94 93**
CSF £21.58 TOTE £9.10: £2.90, £1.60; EX 24.20 Trifecta £86.50.
Owner Stephen Tucker **Bred** Haras De Son Altesse L'Aga Khan S C E A **Trained** Upper Lambourn, Berkshire

FOCUS
Not a bad staying contest.

559 100% PROFIT BOOST AT 32REDSPORT.COM H'CAP 1m 3f 219y(P)
7:45 (7:46) (Class 5) (0-70,74) 4-Y-0+
£3,752 (£1,116; £557; £400; £400; £400) **Stalls** Low

Form RPR

1-02 **1** **Ilhabela Fact**[10] 362 5-9-11 **74**.. AdamKirby 7 81
(Tony Carroll) *trckd ldrs: sn racing in 2nd: drvn to ld ent fnl 2f: rdn in 1 l ld 1f out: rdn and r.o fnl f: a doing enough* **11/8**[1]

331- **2** *3/4* **Houlton**[65] 9310 4-8-12 **70**.......................(tp) StefanoCherchi(7) 6 75
(Marco Botti) *led: narrow ld 2f out: pushed along and hdd 1 1/2f out: kpt on wl fnl f* **6/1**[3]

40-0 **3** *1/2* **Make Good (IRE)**[28] 85 4-8-11 **62**......................(vt) CallumShepherd 5 66
(David Dennis) *hld up: drvn over 2f out: sn rdn: wandered over 1f out: kpt on fnl f: gaining on front two nr fin (jockey said gelding hung right-handed in the straight)* **20/1**

402- **4** *2 1/2* **Rubensian**[54] 9488 6-9-7 **70**..............................(p) JamieSpencer 1 70
(David Simcock) *hld up: 6th 3f out: drvn on outer 2f out: hdwy into 3rd 1f out: rdn and wknd fnl f: eased nr fin* **12/1**

05-3 **5** *3 1/4* **Subliminal**[18] 246 4-8-10 **61**.. NickyMackay 3 56
(Simon Dow) *t.k.h: chsd ldr: sn racing in 3rd: drvn 2f out: sn rdn and lost pl: wknd fnl f* **9/2**[2]

204- **6** *7* **Emerald Rocket (IRE)**[114] 8130 4-9-4 **69**....................(p) LukeMorris 2 53
(Olly Murphy) *hld up: drvn in 5th 3f out: rdn and dropped away 1f out* **20/1**

00-2 **P** **Continuum**[18] 246 10-9-5 **68**..(p) NicolaCurrie 4
(Peter Hedger) *dwlt: racd in last: bhd whn appeared to go wrong and p.u 1/2-way: lame (jockey said the gelding felt wrong behind; vet reported the gelding was found to be lame left fore)* **9/2**[2]

2m 35.07s (0.57) **Going Correction** +0.20s/f (Slow)
WFA 4 from 5yo+ 2lb **7** Ran SP% **110.0**
Speed ratings (Par 103): **106,105,105,103,101 96,**
CSF £9.22 TOTE £2.10: £1.30, £2.80; EX 9.60 Trifecta £95.60.
Owner Cooke & Millen **Bred** Robert Nahas **Trained** Cropthorne, Worcs

FOCUS
The winner got the job done cosily enough.

560 BET AT RACINGTV.COM H'CAP 1m 3f 219y(P)
8:15 (8:19) (Class 6) (0-60,60) 4-Y-0+
£3,105 (£924; £461; £400; £400; £400) **Stalls** Low

Form RPR

03-2 **1** **Double Legend (IRE)**[28] 85 4-9-2 **57**..........................(b) RobertHavlin 8 64
(Amanda Perrett) *chsd ldr: pushed along in 2nd over 2f out: drvn to ld 2f out: rdn in 1 1/2 l ld 1f out: r.o wl fnl f* **7/2**[1]

030- **2** *1 3/4* **Zamperini (IRE)**[28] 8316 7-9-6 **59**.................................. HectorCrouch 5 62
(Gary Moore) *mid-div: drvn 3f out: hdwy 2f out: rdn over 1f out: r.o into 2nd fnl f* **9/1**

04-6 **3** *1/2* **Iley Boy**[14] 321 5-9-2 **55**...(p) PJMcDonald 12 57
(John Gallagher) *hld up: pushed along on outer and plenty to do 2f out: drvn and hdwy over 1f out: rdn fnl f: r.o wl: tk 3rd last 25yds* **16/1**

6-62 **4** *1/2* **Bird For Life**[10] 363 5-8-9 **55**..........................(p) EllieMacKenzie(7) 4 57
(Mark Usher) *slowly away: bhd: pushed along 2f out: rdn on outer over 1f out: r.o strly fnl f: nvr nrr* **8/1**

00-3 **5** *nk* **Rail Dancer**[14] 321 7-9-6 **59**...(v) LiamJones 9 60
(Shaun Keightley) *chsd ldrs: pushed into 4th 3f out: rdn over 2f out: tk 3rd 1f out: no ex and lost two pls fnl f* **11/1**

00-4 **6** *1/2* **Foresee (GER)**[28] 85 6-9-6 **59**.. AdamKirby 6 59
(Tony Carroll) *trckd ldrs: hdwy to ld 3f out: sn drvn: hdd 2f out: sn rdn: wknd fnl f* **10/1**

1-21 **7** *1 3/4* **Ember's Glow**[10] 363 5-9-2 **55**.. EoinWalsh 1 53
(Mark Loughnane) *hld up: pushed along 2f out: rdn over 1f out: no imp (jockey said gelding ran flat)* **4/1**[2]

34-2 **8** *hd* **Heron (USA)**[23] 160 5-9-6 **59**..(p) RossaRyan 3 56
(Brett Johnson) *hld up: drvn 2f out: rdn over 1f out: no imp* **12/1**

00-0 **9** *3/4* **Lazarus (IRE)**[30] 38 5-9-3 **56**.. DavidProbert 14 52
(Amy Murphy) *hld up: pushed along and effrt on inner 2f out: sn rdn and wknd* **40/1**

000- **10** *6* **Multigifted**[61] 8893 6-8-13 **59**..........................(p) ScottMcCullagh(7) 11 45
(Michael Madgwick) *slowly away: bhd: pushed along in last 3f out: rdn 2f out: no rspnse* **66/1**

614/ **11** *7* **Hallings Comet**[445] 806 10-9-4 **57**.................................... JamieSpencer 7 32
(Shaun Lycett) *led: rdn 3f out: sn hdd: wknd and eased 2f out* **25/1**

600- **12** *32* **Ross Raith Rover**[34] 9769 6-9-4 **60**............................(b) PaddyBradley(3) 2
(Lee Carter) *mid-div: 5th 3f out: drvn and lost pl over 2f out: rdn over 1f out: wknd and heavily eased fnl f (jockey said gelding lost its action)* **6/1**[3]

2m 36.15s (1.65) **Going Correction** +0.20s/f (Slow)
WFA 4 from 5yo+ 2lb **12** Ran SP% **116.4**
Speed ratings (Par 101): **102,100,100,100,99 99,98,98,97,93 89,67**
CSF £34.19 CT £446.82 TOTE £4.50: £1.50, £3.20, £4.90; EX 30.20 Trifecta £271.00.
Owner Dean Angell And Partner **Bred** Myles Sunderland **Trained** Pulborough, W Sussex
■ Spring Ability was withdrawn. Price at time of withdrawal 50/1. Rule 4 does not apply

FOCUS
An ordinary handicap.
T/Plt: £11.40 to a £1 stake. Pool: £103,627.17 - 6,619.21 winning units T/Qpdt: £4.60 to a £1 stake. Pool: £14,201.31 - 2,242.13 winning units **Keith McHugh**

516 LINGFIELD (L-H)
Saturday, February 2

OFFICIAL GOING: Polytrack: standard
Wind: medium, against Weather: overcast, chilly

561 LADBROKES HOME OF THE ODDS BOOST H'CAP 7f 1y(P)
12:35 (12:35) (Class 5) (0-75,77) 3-Y-0 **£3,752** (£1,116; £557; £300) **Stalls** Low

Form RPR

5-21 **1** **Spirit Warning**[15] 290 3-9-9 **77**.. JoshuaBryan(3) 1 82
(Andrew Balding) *t.k.h: mde all: rdn over 1f out: styd on and a doing enough ins fnl f* **7/4**[1]

00-2 **2** *1* **Hypnos (IRE)**[24] 140 3-9-1 **66**.. JamieSpencer 5 68
(David Simcock) *t.k.h: trckd ldrs tl wnt 2nd 4f out: effrt ent fnl 2f: drvn over 1f out: kpt on but a readily hld ins fnl f* **3/1**[3]

010- **3** *nk* **Port Of Leith (IRE)**[52] 9498 3-9-7 **72**................................ JoeFanning 2 73
(Mark Johnston) *s.i.s and wnt rt leaving stalls: t.k.h: sn rcvrd and trckd wnr tl 4f out: effrt on inner 2f out: kpt on and swtchd rt ins fnl f: nvr quite enough pce to chal* **6/1**

04-3 **4** *2 3/4* **Lieutenant Conde**[22] 186 3-8-13 **64**............................ CharlieBennett 4 58
(Hughie Morrison) *t.k.h: hld up in tch in rr: rdn over 2f out: no imp over 1f out: kpt on same pce after* **2/1**[2]

1m 25.82s (1.02) **Going Correction** -0.05s/f (Stan) **4** Ran SP% **109.0**
Speed ratings (Par 97): **92,90,90,87**
CSF £7.18 TOTE £2.00; EX 6.60 Trifecta £13.30.
Owner Kingsclere Racing Club **Bred** Kingsclere Stud **Trained** Kingsclere, Hants

FOCUS
A fair little 3yo handicap on standard Polytrack. The favourite successfully controlled a stop-start gallop into a reported head wind in the home straight. He's rated to his Lingfield win.

562 BETWAY LIVE CASINO MAIDEN STKS 1m 4f (P)
1:10 (1:10) (Class 5) 4-Y-0+ **£3,752** (£1,116; £557; £278) **Stalls** Low

Form RPR

554- **1** **Endlessly (IRE)**[128] 7706 4-9-5 72................................(w) JamieSpencer 2 75
(Olly Murphy) *prom in chsng gp: effrt in 3rd ent fnl 2f: chsd clr ldr and hung lft over 1f out: swtchd rt and styd on ins fnl f to ld towards fin: eased whn hitting the front* **2/1**[1]

500- **2** *3/4* **Hidden Depths (IRE)**[103] 8485 4-9-5 70............................ NicolaCurrie 7 74
(Jamie Osborne) *t.k.h: led and sn wnt clr: rdn 2f out: stl clr and drvn ent fnl f: hdd towards fin and sn btn* **5/2**[2]

30-0 **3** *3 1/4* **Mobham (IRE)**[18] 242 4-9-5 70.................................... RobertHavlin 9 69
(J R Jenkins) *stdd s: dropped in bhd and t.k.h early: wl off the pce in last pair: hdwy on inner into midfield over 2f out: modest 4th over 1f out: rdn and kpt on wl ins fnl f to go 3rd 100yds out: nvr getting to ldrs* **20/1**

3 **4** *1 1/2* **Knight Crusader**[18] 242 7-9-7 0...................................... LukeMorris 3 65
(John O'Shea) *chsd clr ldr: rdn over 3f out: drvn and lost btn 2nd over 1f out: kpt on same pce after and lost 3rd 100yds out* **2/1**[1]

0 **5** *8* **Oborne Lady (IRE)**[18] 242 6-9-2 0.................................... ShaneKelly 8 48
(Seamus Mullins) *prom in chsng gp: rdn and no imp in 4th 2f out: wl btn over 1f out* **66/1**

6 **6** *1 1/2* **Grange Walk (IRE)**[18] 242 4-9-2 0.......................... PaddyBradley(3) 4 51
(Pat Phelan) *hld up wl off the pce in midfield of main gp: no imp over 2f out: nvr involved* **12/1**[3]

6/0- **7** *2 1/2* **Faraway Fields (USA)**[187] 5553 4-9-5 0............................ EoinWalsh 1 47
(Peter Hiatt) *hld up wl off the pce: effrt over 2f out: no prog and nvr involved* **12/1**[3]

0-6 **8** *2 3/4* **Zahraani**[7] 435 4-8-12 0.. GinaMangan(7) 6 43
(J R Jenkins) *hld up wl off the pce in rr: nvr involved* **66/1**

2m 32.88s (-0.12) **Going Correction** -0.05s/f (Stan)
WFA 4 from 6yo+ 2lb **8** Ran SP% **118.4**
Speed ratings (Par 103): **98,97,95,94,89 88,86,84**
CSF £7.56 TOTE £2.40: £1.10, £1.30, £4.10; EX 7.90 Trifecta £54.50.
Owner Raymond Treacy **Bred** Ladyswood Stud **Trained** Wilmcote, Warks

FOCUS
An ordinary middle-distance maiden. One of the joint-favourites picked up the long-time leader in the final 50 yards from off a searching gallop. The first two are rated close to their form for previous yards.

563 BETWAY CLEVES STKS (LISTED RACE) (ALL-WEATHER CHAMPIONSHIPS FAST-TRACK QUALIFIER) 6f 1y(P)
1:45 (1:45) (Class 1) 4-Y-0+
£25,519 (£9,675; £4,842; £2,412; £1,210; £607) **Stalls** Low

Form RPR

051- **1** **Kachy**[38] 9707 6-9-0 112.................................. RichardKingscote 8 117
(Tom Dascombe) *broke fast: crossed to inner and mde all: rdn and kicked clr over 1f out: in command and styd on ins fnl f: rdn out* **10/11**[1]

5-31 **2** *3 1/2* **Gorgeous Noora (IRE)**[15] 297 5-8-9 98........................ HollieDoyle 5 101
(Archie Watson) *chsd ldrs: effrt in 3rd over 2f out: drvn to chse clr wnr 1f out: kpt on u.p to hold 2nd but no real imp on wnr* **8/1**[3]

06-3 **3** *3/4* **Stone Of Destiny**[11] 352 4-9-0 102............................ OisinMurphy 6 103
(Andrew Balding) *dwlt: hld up in tch: effrt on outer bnd 2f out: hdwy 1f out: styd on ins fnl f: no threat to wnr* **14/1**

60/- **4** *1* **Mokarris (USA)**[640] 2289 5-9-0 100..........................(w) RobertHavlin 9 100
(Simon Crisford) *stdd and swtchd lft after s: hld up in last pair: nt clr run wl over 1f out: hdwy and switching lft ent fnl f: kpt on wl ins fnl f: no threat to wnr* **17/2**

113- **5** *shd* **Sir Thomas Gresham (IRE)**[70] 9245 4-9-0 100.............. MartinDwyer 4 100
(Tim Pinfield) *rousted along leaving stalls: sn chsng wnr: rdn over 2f out: unable to match pce of wnr over 1f out: lost 2nd and wl hld 1f out: lost 2 pls ins fnl f* **16/1**

12-2 **6** *1/2* **Cenotaph (USA)**[24] 136 7-9-0 107.................................. RyanMoore 3 98
(Jeremy Noseda) *hld up in tch in midfield: effrt 2f out: sn switching rt and unable qck over 1f out: keeping on same pce and wl hld whn nt clrest of runs ins fnl f: eased towards fin* **4/1**[2]

414- **7** *4* **Roman River**[227] 4019 4-9-0 90...................................... GeraldMosse 1 85
(Martin Smith) *hld up in tch in midfield: effrt 2f out: hmpd and shuffled bk over 1f out: swtchd rt and no prog 1f out* **40/1**

10-5 **8** *1 3/4* **Corinthia Knight (IRE)**[24] 136 4-9-0 108.................. EdwardGreatrex 7 80
(Archie Watson) *s.i.s and hmpd sn after s: in rr: nt clr run on inner 2f out: stl in rr whn bdly hmpd 1f out: nvr involved (jockey said gelding was slowly away)* **20/1**

000- **9** *nk* **Lancelot Du Lac (ITY)**[140] 7290 9-9-0 109.....................(h) AdamKirby 2 79
(Dean Ivory) *taken down early: rousted along leaving stalls: chsd ldrs: rdn over 2f out: sn struggling and lost pl over 1f out: carried lft ent fnl f: wknd* **14/1**

1m 8.32s (-3.58) **Going Correction** -0.05s/f (Stan) course record 9 Ran SP% **120.4**
Speed ratings (Par 111): **121,116,115,114,113 113,107,105,105**
CSF £9.78 TOTE £1.60: £1.10, £1.90, £3.50; EX 10.30 Trifecta £50.60.

Owner David Lowe **Bred** Denniff Farms Ltd **Trained** Malpas, Cheshire

■ Stewards' Enquiry : Robert Havlin two-day ban: interference & careless riding (Feb 16 & 18)

FOCUS
A good quality Listed sprint. Last year's winner, and the odds-on favourite, dominated impressively from the front in a course-record time. At face value this could be rated another pb from Kachy.

564 BETWAY H'CAP 6f 1y(P)
2:20 (2:20) (Class 4) (0-80,77) 4-Y-0+
£5,530 (£1,645; £822; £411; £300; £300) **Stalls** Low

Form RPR

2-21 **1** **Highland Acclaim (IRE)**[17] 260 8-9-5 **75**.....................(h) DavidProbert 6 83
(David O'Meara) *chsd ldrs tl wnt 2nd over 2f out: shkn up and clsd jst over 1f out: rdn to ld 100yds out: in command after and pushed out towards fin* **7/1**

64-1 **2** *1* **Inaam (IRE)**[31] 31 6-9-4 **74**.....................(h) AdamKirby 2 79
(Paul D'Arcy) *chsd ldrs: effrt over 2f out: kpt on u.p to chse wnr wl ins fnl f: no imp towards fin* **7/2**[2]

34-1 **3** *nk* **Ballyquin (IRE)**[22] 178 4-9-2 **75**..................... JoshuaBryan(3) 1 79
(Andrew Balding) *led: sn hdd and chsd ldr tl over 2f out: styd chsng ldrs: effrt on inner over 1f out: chsd wnr wl ins fnl f: kpt on same pce and lost 2nd wl ins fnl f* **3/1**[1]

65-1 **4** *½* **Little Palaver**[17] 253 7-8-12 **75**.....................(p) AmeliaGlass(7) 7 77
(Clive Cox) *midfield: effrt wl over 1f out: hdwy and swtchd lft ins fnl f: kpt on wl towards fin: nvr getting to wnr* **12/1**

02-0 **5** *¾* **The Establishment**[30] 36 4-9-1 **71**.....................(h) EoinWalsh 9 71
(David Evans) *bustled long to ld sn after s and crossed to inner: rdn over 1f out: hdd and no ex 100yds out: wknd towards fin* **14/1**

01-1 **6** *nk* **Zafaranah (USA)**[26] 123 5-9-7 **77**..................... ShaneKelly 4 76
(Pam Sly) *midfield: short of room and impeded after 1f: pushed along over 3f out: drvn and unable qck over 1f out: kpt on u.p ins fnl f: nvr enough pce to threaten ldrs (jockey said mare suffered interference on the first bend)* **7/1**

0-53 **7** *½* **Gold Hunter (IRE)**[17] 254 9-9-1 **74**..................... FinleyMarsh(3) 5 71
(Steve Flook) *midfield tl squeezed for room: hmpd and dropped to last pair after 1f: effrt over 1f out: styd on ins fnl f: nvr trbld ldrs* **25/1**

401- **7** *dht* **Gold Stone**[60] 9393 4-9-2 **72**..................... JamieSpencer 10 69
(Kevin Ryan) *stdd s: hld up in last pair: effrt over 1f out: styd on ins fnl f: nvr trbld ldrs* **10/1**

30-1 **9** *1¼* **Mont Kiara (FR)**[17] 253 6-9-3 **73**..................... LukeMorris 8 66
(Simon Dow) *swtchd lft after s: hld up: hdwy into midfield over 4f out: unable qck over 1f out: wknd ins fnl f* **14/1**

0-36 **10** *nk* **National Glory (IRE)**[10] 361 4-9-7 **77**.....................(p) OisinMurphy 3 69
(Archie Watson) *t.k.h: hld up in midfield: effrt on inner over 1f out: no imp and bhd ins fnl f* **11/2**[3]

1m 10.71s (-1.19) **Going Correction** -0.05s/f (Stan) 10 Ran SP% **121.6**
Speed ratings (Par 105): **105,103,103,102,101 101,100,100,98,98**
WIN: 8.10 Highland Acclaim; PL: 1.40 Ballyquin 2.50 Highland Acclaim 2.60 Inaam; EX: 37.60; CSF: 33.19; TC: 94.00; TF: 158.10 CSF £33.19 CT £94.00 TOTE £8.10: £2.50, £2.60, £1.40; EX 37.60 Trifecta £158.10.

Owner Evan M Sutherland **Bred** Rathbarry Stud **Trained** Upper Helmsley, N Yorks

FOCUS
A fair sprint handicap. The winning time was respectable for the grade and the winner built on his latest form.

565 BETWAY WINTER DERBY TRIAL STKS (LISTED RACE) (ALL-WEATHER CHAMPIONSHIPS FAST-TRACK QUALIFIER) 1m 2f (P)
2:55 (2:55) (Class 1) 4-Y-0+
£25,519 (£9,675; £4,842; £2,412; £1,210; £607) **Stalls** Low

Form RPR

111- **1** **Wissahickon (USA)**[42] 9685 4-9-3 117..................... FrankieDettori 2 119+
(John Gosden) *chsd ldrs: clsd to trck ldrs 4f out: nt clr run: hemmed in and hmpd wl over 1f out: swtchd out rt ent fnl f: pushed along: qckned smartly to ld wl ins fnl f and coasted home: easily* **8/15**[1]

522- **2** *¾* **Big Country (IRE)**[42] 9685 6-9-0 109.....................(p) LukeMorris 7 110
(Michael Appleby) *chsd ldr: clsd to press ldr 4f out: shkn up 2f out but styd pressing ldr: drvn to ld jst ins fnl f: hdd and readily brushed aside by wnr wl ins fnl f* **5/1**[2]

24-1 **3** *2¼* **Court House (IRE)**[24] 143 4-9-0 105..................... RobertHavlin 3 105
(John Gosden) *led: pressed 4f out: rdn ent fnl 2f: hdd jst ins fnl f: no ex and outpcd fnl 100yds out* **5/1**[2]

40-1 **4** *2* **Chiefofchiefs**[29] 56 6-9-0 93.....................(p) RichardKingscote 1 101
(Charlie Fellowes) *chsd ldng trio: effrt over 2f out: clsd and swtchd rt over 1f out: kpt on but no imp ins fnl f* **14/1**[3]

30-6 **5** *2¾* **Abe Lincoln (USA)**[10] 368 6-9-0 98.....................(tp) RyanMoore 8 96
(Jeremy Noseda) *hld up in midfield: effrt over 2f out: no imp over 1f out: nvr threatened ldrs* **18/1**

/34- **6** *1* **In The Lope (IRE)**[46] 5-9-0 100..................... AdamKirby 9 94
(Mme Pia Brandt, France) *stdd and dropped in after s: hld up in last pair: swtchd rt and shkn up over 2f out: nvr involved* **16/1**

120- **7** *1½* **Main Street**[226] 4025 4-9-0 99..................... DavidProbert 6 92
(David Elsworth) *hld up in last trio: effrt over 2f out: reminder and no prog over 1f out: wknd ins fnl f* **20/1**

000- **8** *31* **Time To Study (FR)**[141] 7241 5-9-0 101.....................(p¹) JamieSpencer 4 29
(Ian Williams) *stdd s: a in rr: lost tch 4f out: t.o and eased fnl 2f* **33/1**

2m 1.53s (-5.07) **Going Correction** -0.05s/f (Stan) 8 Ran SP% **124.1**
Speed ratings (Par 111): **118,117,115,114,111 111,109,85**
CSF £4.34 TOTE £1.50: £1.02, £1.50, £1.50; EX 4.00 Trifecta £10.80.

Owner George Strawbridge **Bred** Augustin Stable **Trained** Newmarket, Suffolk

FOCUS
The feature contest was a good quality Listed race. The odds-on favourite clocked a winning time about half-a-second outside of standard despite being stopped in his run at the top of the straight. The fourth lends just a slight doubt to the form.

566 BETWAY STAYERS H'CAP 1m 7f 169y(P)
3:30 (3:30) (Class 5) (0-75,71) 4-Y-0+ **£3,752** (£1,116; £557; £300; £300) **Stalls** Low

Form RPR

53-0 **1** **Galitello**[17] 262 4-8-12 **62**..................... PJMcDonald 4 67
(Mark Johnston) *led for over 1f: chsd ldr: ev ch and drvn wl over 2f out: led ent fnl f: hld on wl u.p ins fnl f* **5/1**

46-5 **2** *nse* **Mundersfield**[9] 385 5-9-0 **60**.....................(h) JamieSpencer 1 65
(David Simcock) *stdd s: hld up in tch in rr: clsd and nt clrest of runs 2f out: sn switching rt: rdn and hdwy over 1f out: ev ch and edgd lft ins fnl f: kpt on wl: jst hld* **5/2**[2]

43-0 **3** *½* **Thresholdofadream (IRE)**[22] 185 4-8-4 **54**..................... NicolaCurrie 3 58
(Amanda Perrett) *chsd ldrs: effrt ent fnl 2f: sltly outpcd wl over 1f out: rallied and clsd to chse ldrs whn nt clr run and swtchd lft wl ins fnl f: kpt on u.p towards fin* **9/2**[3]

/00- **4** *hd* **Knight Commander**[45] 7455 6-8-11 **57**..................... HollieDoyle 2 60
(Steve Flook) *hld up in tch: clsd to trck ldrs 4f out: effrt on inner over 2f out: ev ch u.p ent fnl f: unable qck wl ins fnl f (jockey said gelding was denied a clear run)* **16/1**

1-02 **5** *2¼* **Isle Of Avalon (IRE)**[4] 469 4-9-7 **71**.....................(b) LukeMorris 5 71
(Sir Mark Prescott Bt) *t.k.h: led over 14f out: hrd pressed and rdn jst over 2f out: hdd ent fnl f: sn btn and wknd ins fnl f* **11/8**[1]

3m 24.59s (-1.11) **Going Correction** -0.05s/f (Stan)
WFA 4 from 5yo+ 4lb 5 Ran SP% **111.4**
Speed ratings (Par 97): **100,99,99,99,98**
CSF £17.91 TOTE £4.30: £2.70, £1.50; EX 17.20 Trifecta £48.30.
Owner Kingsley Park 12 - Ready To Run **Bred** The Lavington Stud **Trained** Middleham Moor, N Yorks

FOCUS
A modest staying handicap. They went a muddling gallop and, while the favourite dropped away, the rest of the field still had chances in the final furlong in a tight photo-finish. It can't be rated as solid form.

567 LADBROKES H'CAP 1m 2f (P)
4:05 (4:05) (Class 5) (0-75,77) 3-Y-O **£3,752** (£1,116; £557; £300) **Stalls** Low

Form RPR

253- **1** **Murray River (USA)**[87] 8932 3-10-0 **76**.....................(b) FrankieDettori 4 86
(John Gosden) *wl in tch in rr: pushed along and clsd on outer to join ldrs 3f out: rdn to ld over 1f out: r.o strly and drew clr fnl f* **10/11**[1]

01-3 **2** *4* **Debbonair (IRE)**[17] 258 3-9-7 **69**..................... OisinMurphy 1 70
(Hugo Palmer) *led: hrd pressed and rdn over 2f out: hdd over 1f out: no match for wnr and kpt on same pce ins fnl f* **9/4**[2]

03-2 **3** *1½* **Navadir (JPN)**[26] 122 3-9-7 **69**.....................(h) DanielMuscutt 3 67
(Marco Botti) *trckd ldrs: effrt on inner 2f out: 3rd and unable qck u.p over 1f out: wl hld and kpt on same pce ins fnl f (trainer's rep said filly had a breathing problem)* **4/1**[3]

44-1 **4** *7* **Warrior Display (IRE)**[22] 183 3-8-6 **61**.....................(p) AaronMackay(7) 5 45
(J S Moore) *chsd ldr: rdn and ev ch over 2f out: outpcd and squeezed for room over 1f out: sn bhd and wknd fnl f* **20/1**

2m 6.13s (-0.47) **Going Correction** -0.05s/f (Stan) 4 Ran SP% **107.9**
Speed ratings (Par 97): **99,95,94,89**
CSF £3.20 TOTE £1.60; EX 3.00 Trifecta £4.30.
Owner HH Sheikha Al Jalila Racing **Bred** Mt Brilliant Farm **Trained** Newmarket, Suffolk

FOCUS
A fair little 3yo handicap. The favourite came readily clear once given his head from off a muddling gallop over 2f out. The form is rated around the second and third.
T/Plt: £13.20 to a £1 stake. Pool: £76,048.81 - 4,197.67 winning units T/Qpdt: £3.00 to a £1 stake. Pool: £7,737.28 - 1,869.10 winning units **Steve Payne**

568 - 569a (Foreign Racing) - See Raceform Interactive

510 MEYDAN (L-H)
Saturday, February 2

OFFICIAL GOING: Dirt: fast; turf: good

570a SPECIAL OLYMPICS WORLD GAMES CUP (MAIDEN) (TURF) 1m 1f
1:10 (1:10) 3-Y-O **£21,153** (£7,051; £3,878; £2,115; £1,057)

RPR

1 **Bila Shak (USA)**[9] 394 3-9-0 75.....................(v) AdriedeVries 3 73
(Fawzi Abdulla Nass, Bahrain) *s.i.s: settled in rr: smooth prog 4f out: r.o wl fnl 1 1/2f: led cl home* **3/1**[2]

2 *nk* **Shanty Star (USA)**[9] 394 3-9-0 0..................... PierantonioConvertino 6 72
(R Bouresly, Kuwait) *trckd ldr: n.m.r 3f out: rdn to ld 1f out: hdd cl home* **20/1**

3 *1½* **Dark Thunder (IRE)**[23] 169 3-9-0 77..................... PatDobbs 1 69
(Doug Watson, UAE) *mid-div: chsd ldrs 2 1/2f out: r.o wl fnl 1 1/2f* **4/1**[3]

4 *nk* **Bosconero (IRE)**[6] 446 3-8-8 70.....................(t) SaeedAlMazrooei(6) 10 69
(A R Al Rayhi, UAE) *mid-div: chsd ldrs 3f out: led 2f out: hdd 1f out but kpt on* **20/1**

5 *3* **Phalasteen (USA)** 3-9-0 0..................... SzczepanMazur 2 62
(R Bouresly, Kuwait) *mid-div: r.o same pce fnl 2f* **25/1**

6 *1½* **Raayan (USA)**[9] 394 3-9-0 73..................... FernandoJara 9 59
(A R Al Rayhi, UAE) *s.i.s: nvr nr to chal* **6/1**

7 *nk* **Luxor Temple (USA)**[6] 446 3-9-0 68..................... BenCurtis 4 59
(A R Al Rayhi, UAE) *s.i.s: nvr nr to chal but r.o fnl 2f* **18/1**

8 *1* **Refulgence Star (IRE)**[22] 198 3-9-0 69.....................(b) RichardMullen 14 56
(S Seemar, UAE) *mid-div: chsd ldrs and ev ch 2f out: wknd fnl f* **11/4**[1]

9 *8* **Tammam Boss (IRE)**[22] 198 3-9-0 0.....................(b) TadhgO'Shea 13 40
(S Seemar, UAE) *trckd ldr: led 2 1/2f out: hdd & wknd 2f out* **28/1**

10 *4* **Private Ryan (USA)**[22] 198 3-9-0 64.....................(vt) WJLee 8 31
(H Al Alawi, UAE) *nvr bttr than mid-div* **20/1**

11 *nk* **King Lothbrok (FR)**[23] 168 3-9-0 79.....................(h) ConnorBeasley 11 31
(A bin Harmash, UAE) *nvr bttr than mid-div* **15/2**

12 *9¾* **Mneef (USA)**[23] 168 3-9-0 55.....................(b) RoystonFfrench 12 10
(S Jadhav, UAE) *nvr bttr than mid-div* **25/1**

13 *26* **Al Mortajaz (FR)**[23] 168 3-9-0 73.....................(bt) FabriceVeron 7
(Ismail Mohammed) *sn led: hdd & wknd 2 1/2f out* **12/1**

14 *7½* **La Petite Sauvage (USA)**[44] 9652 3-8-9 0..................... ChrisHayes 5
(A bin Harmash, UAE) *in rr: hmpd after 1 1/2f: nvr able to chal* **33/1**

1m 52.74s 14 Ran SP% **139.0**
CSF: 74.18.

Owner Fawzi Abdulla Nass **Bred** Dancing Trieste Syndicate **Trained** Bahrain

571a-572a (Foreign Racing) - See Raceform Interactive

573a YAHSAT TROPHY (H'CAP) (DIRT) 1m
2:55 (2:55) (76-89,89) 3-Y-O+ **£23,717** (£7,905; £4,348; £2,371; £1,185)

RPR

1 **Mazeed (USA)**[14] [328] 5-8-7 **77**..........(bt) TadhgO'Shea 14 83
(S Seemar, UAE) *mid-div: rdn 3f out: r.o wl to ld fnl 110yds* **12/1**

2 *1* **Quartier Francais (USA)**[14] [326] 5-8-11 **81**..........(b) FernandoJara 1 85
(A R Al Rayhi, UAE) *settled in rr: rdn 4f out: r.o v wl fnl 2f: nrst fin* **7/2**[1]

3 *¾* **Welford**[14] [324] 6-9-1 **84**..........(bt) RichardMullen 10 87
(S Seemar, UAE) *mid-div: chsd ldrs 2 1/2f out: ev ch 1 1/2f out: r.o wl* **11/2**

4 *shd* **Craving (IRE)**[22] [197] 4-9-0 **83**.......... ConnorBeasley 12 86
(Simon Crisford) *trckd ldr: led 1f out: r.o wl but hdd fnl 110yds* **7/1**

5 *2* **Pirate's Cove (IRE)**[14] [325] 6-9-2 **85**..........(p) RoystonFfrench 11 83
(S Jadhav, UAE) *sn led: hdd 1f out: wknd fnl 110yds* **8/1**

6 *nk* **Old Fashioned (CHI)**[28] [97] 6-8-6 **76**..........(h) FabriceVeron 13 73
(A bin Harmash, UAE) *mid-div: chsd ldrs and ev ch 2f out: wknd fnl f* **16/1**

7 *3* **Native Appeal (IRE)**[41] [9690] 4-8-11 **81** ow1..........(t) DaneO'Neill 9 71
(Doug Watson, UAE) *s.i.s: nvr nr to chal* **20/1**

8 *½* **Grand Argentier (FR)**[28] [96] 7-9-4 **87**..........(v) PatDobbs 4 77
(Doug Watson, UAE) *trckd ldrs tl wknd 3f out* **9/2**[2]

9 *8* **Hold Sway (IRE)**[36] [9737] 5-8-8 **78**.......... SamHitchcott 5 48
(Doug Watson, UAE) *a in rr* **25/1**

10 *6¼* **Timeless Flight**[22] [197] 5-8-6 **82**..........(t) SaeedAlMazrooei(5) 8 38
(A R Al Rayhi, UAE) *s.i.s: a in rr* **25/1**

11 *2½* **Litigation**[28] [98] 4-9-3 **86**..........(b) ChrisHayes 7 37
(Jaber Ramadhan, Bahrain) *trckd ldr tl wknd 3f out* **20/1**

12 *6¼* **Manthoor (IRE)**[13] [330] 4-8-13 **82**.......... WJLee 2 19
(H Al Alawi, UAE) *nvr bttr than mid-div* **20/1**

13 *8½* **Fawaareq (IRE)**[14] [325] 6-9-0 **83**.......... JimCrowley 3
(Doug Watson, UAE) *s.i.s: nvr nr to chal* **14/1**

14 *4* **Welsh Lord**[9] [396] 4-9-6 **89**..........(h) PatCosgrave 6
(Saeed bin Suroor) *s.i.s: a in rr* **5/1**[3]

1m 40.11s **14 Ran SP% 138.3**
CSF: 57.65; TRICAST: 284.07.
Owner Sheikh Mohammed Bin Khalifa Al Maktoum **Bred** Whisper Hill Farm Llc **Trained** United Arab Emirates

574 - 584a (Foreign Racing) - See Raceform Interactive

503 SOUTHWELL (L-H)
Sunday, February 3

OFFICIAL GOING: Fibresand: standard to slow
Wind: Light across Weather: Fine & dry

585 LADBROKES HOME OF THE ODDS BOOST H'CAP 7f 14y(F)
1:00 (1:00) (Class 6) (0-60,62) 3-Y-O
£3,493 (£1,039; £519; £400; £400; £400) **Stalls Low**

Form RPR

03-0 1 **Dolly Dupree**[21] [228] 3-8-9 **49**.......... TheodoreLadd(5) 7 56
(Paul D'Arcy) *trckd ldrs on outer: pushed along and wd st: hdwy 2f out: rdn and edgd lft over 1f out: chsd ldrs and hung lft ins fnl f: kpt on strly to ld fnl 50yds* **8/1**

004- 2 *¾* **Pandora Star**[36] [9744] 3-9-3 **52**..........(v) JasonHart 3 57
(John Quinn) *t.k.h: cl up: slt ld after 1f: rdn along 2f out: drvn jst over 1f out: hdd and no ex fnl 50yds* **20/1**

40-1 3 *1½* **Sylviacliffs (FR)**[21] [228] 3-9-7 **56**.......... AndrewMullen 1 57
(K R Burke) *trckd ldrs on inner: pushed along 2f out: rdn over 1f out: drvn to chal ent fnl f: ev ch tl kpt on same pce fnl 100yds* **6/1**[3]

01 4 *½* **Kodi Dream**[2] [524] 3-9-8 **62** 6ex.......... BenSanderson(5) 9 62
(Roger Fell) *dwlt and towards rr: hdwy on outer to chse ldrs over 3f out: rdn along 2f out: drvn appr fnl f: kpt on same pce* **3/1**[2]

000- 5 *¾* **Trouble Shooter (IRE)**[51] [9530] 3-9-5 **54**..........(v[1]) LiamJones 6 52
(Shaun Keightley) *trckd ldrs: pushed along wl over 2f out: rdn and hung lft over 1f out: drvn and hung lft to inner rail ent fnl f: kpt on same pce* **28/1**

1-02 6 *3* **Champagne Mondays**[3] [505] 3-9-3 **52**..........(p) NicolaCurrie 8 42
(Scott Dixon) *slt ld 1f: cl up: rdn over 2f out: drvn wl over 1f out: grad wknd appr fnl f* **7/1**

7 *11* **Miss Wow (IRE)**[111] [8286] 3-8-11 **46**.......... LiamKeniry 5 8
(Stef Keniry) *a in rr* **20/1**

05-2 8 *¾* **Arriba De Toda (IRE)**[21] [228] 3-8-13 **48**..........(b) CallumRodriguez 2 8
(Brian Ellison) *chsd ldrs: rdn along over 2f out: sn drvn and wknd (trainer said the gelding didn't face the kickback)* **11/4**[1]

050- 9 *1¾* **Maddfourmaggy (IRE)**[143] [7214] 3-8-3 **45**.......... TobyEley(7) 4
(Steph Hollinshead) *a in rr (jockey said the filly didn't face the kickback)* **100/1**

600- 10 *1¼* **Russian Rum**[130] [7669] 3-9-3 **52**.......... BarryMcHugh 10 4
(James Given) *a in rr* **11/1**

1m 33.72s (3.42) **Going Correction** +0.40s/f (Slow) **10 Ran SP% 111.9**
Speed ratings (Par 95): **96,95,93,92,92 88,76,75,73,71**
CSF £151.39 CT £1033.71 TOTE £7.20: £2.00, £4.10, £1.80; EX 187.50 Trifecta £1045.70.
Owner K Snell **Bred** K Snell **Trained** Newmarket, Suffolk

FOCUS
Probably a fair race at a moderate level.

586 BETWAY HEED YOUR HUNCH H'CAP 6f 16y(F)
1:35 (1:35) (Class 6) (0-65,67) 4-Y-O+
£3,105 (£924; £461; £400; £400; £400) **Stalls Low**

Form RPR

30-0 1 **Newstead Abbey**[15] [315] 9-8-12 **61**..........(p) TheodoreLadd(5) 13 69
(Rebecca Bastiman) *hld up towards rr: hdwy 1/2-way: chsd ldrs wl over 1f out: swtchd lft to inner and drvn ent fnl f: led fnl 75yds* **10/1**

66-4 2 *½* **Muatadel**[15] [315] 6-9-1 **64**..........(p) BenSanderson(5) 5 71
(Roger Fell) *trckd ldrs: n.m.r after 1f: hdwy over 2f out: rdn to chal wl over af out: led appr fnl f: sn drvn: hdd and no ex fnl 75yds* **6/1**[2]

56-1 3 *¾* **The Golden Cue**[31] [42] 4-8-12 **63**.......... TobyEley(7) 2 67
(Steph Hollinshead) *trckd ldng pair: hdwy to chse ldr wl over 2f out: rdn wl over 1f out: drvn and kpt on same pce fnl f (jockey said gelding hung right)* **6/1**[2]

044- 4 *1¼* **Poet's Pride**[165] [6416] 4-9-3 **64**.......... JoshuaBryan(3) 10 65
(David Barron) *prom whn hmpd after 1f: chsd ldrs whn n.m.r and hmpd over 4f out: swtchd to outer and wd st: sn rdn: styd on fnl 2f: nrst fin* **6/1**[2]

-223 5 *¾* **First Excel**[17] [278] 7-9-9 **67**..........(v) EoinWalsh 3 65+
(Roy Bowring) *sn led: rdn along 2f out: sn jnd: hdd and drvn over 1f out: grad wknd* **4/1**[1]

00-0 6 *¾* **Major Crispies**[21] [232] 8-9-4 **62**.......... CallumRodriguez 9 58
(Ronald Thompson) *hld up towards rr: hdwy over 2f out: rdn over 1f out: kpt on fnl f: nrst fin* **40/1**

514- 7 *1¼* **Fly True**[59] [9433] 6-8-6 **50**.......... NickyMackay 1 42
(Ivan Furtado) *dwlt and towards rr: hdwy on inner to chse ldrs over 3f out: rdn along 2f out: drvn over 1f out: sn no imp (jockey said mare had no more to give)* **13/2**[3]

-510 8 *3½* **Pearl Acclaim (IRE)**[8] [433] 9-9-4 **65**..........(p) PhilDennis(3) 8 47
(David C Griffiths) *prom whn hmpd after 1f: sn pushed along and in tch: rdn over 2f out and sn wknd* **14/1**

64-5 9 *¾* **Coiste Bodhar (IRE)**[24] [167] 8-8-2 **46** oh1..........(p) NicolaCurrie 11 28
(Scott Dixon) *prom on outer whn edgd lft after 1f: chsd ldrs whn n.m.r bnd over 4f out: rdn and wd st: sn wknd (jockey said gelding hung right off the home bend)* **40/1**

03-0 10 *1* **Capla Demon**[22] [214] 4-9-8 **66**..........(p) CamHardie 7 43
(Antony Brittain) *a in rr* **11/1**

400- 11 *13* **Sir Geoffrey (IRE)**[45] [9649] 13-7-11 **46** oh1..........(b) DarraghKeenan(5) 4
(Scott Dixon) *clsd up: sltly hmpd after 1f: rdn along 3f out: wknd over 2f out* **66/1**

/00- 12 *3¾* **Interchoice Star**[297] [1772] 14-8-2 **46** oh1..........(p) NathanEvans 14
(Ray Peacock) *chsd ldrs on outer: rdn along over 3f out: sn wknd* **250/1**

4-60 13 *39* **Kommander Kirkup**[22] [214] 8-9-8 **66**..........(p) AndrewMullen 6
(Michael Herrington) *trckd ldrs whn hmpd and lost pl after 1f: bhd whn eased and detached bef 1/2-way* **12/1**

1m 19.03s (2.53) **Going Correction** +0.40s/f (Slow) **13 Ran SP% 114.7**
Speed ratings (Par 101): **99,98,97,95,94 93,92,87,86,85 67,62,10**
CSF £65.53 CT £407.10 TOTE £9.60: £3.00, £2.00, £2.60; EX 61.00 Trifecta £349.30.
Owner Lets Be Lucky Racing 20 And Partner **Bred** Grasshopper 2000 Ltd **Trained** Cowthorpe, N Yorks

■ Stewards' Enquiry : Nicola Currie six-day ban: interference & careless riding (Feb 18-23)

FOCUS
A well run sprint handicap, where the winner came fast and late to nudge to the front.

587 BETWAY (S) STKS 4f 214y(F)
2:10 (2:10) (Class 5) 4-Y-O+
£3,752 (£1,116; £557; £400; £400; £400) **Stalls Centre**

Form RPR

-401 1 **Point Zero (IRE)**[10] [388] 4-9-6 66..........(be) AlistairRawlinson 2 57
(Michael Appleby) *racd towards far side: mde all: rdn over 1f out: hld on wl towards fin* **4/6**[1]

6-50 2 *½* **Ticks The Boxes (IRE)**[19] [244] 7-9-0 44..........(b) NathanEvans 1 49
(John Wainwright) *racd nr far rail: chsd wnr: rdn to chal over 1f out: drvn and ev ch ins fnl f: kpt on same pce towards fin* **14/1**

-004 3 *4½* **Tasaaboq**[2] [530] 8-8-13 43..........(tp) GraceMcEntee(7) 7 39
(Phil McEntee) *racd centre: in tch: hdwy over 2f out: rdn wl over 1f out: kpt on same pce* **33/1**

6-20 4 *1¼* **Divine Call**[3] [503] 12-9-3 55.......... SeamusCronin(7) 3 38
(Charlie Wallis) *racd towards far side: chsd ldng pair: rdn along 2f out: sn drvn and btn* **9/1**

54-0 5 *2¼* **Westfield Wonder**[24] [166] 4-9-0 44..........(t[1]) NicolaCurrie 4 20
(Ronald Thompson) *racd centre: in tch: rdn along bef 1/2-way: sn outpcd* **20/1**

040- 6 *shd* **French**[50] [9560] 6-8-9 50..........(p) CamHardie 6 15
(Antony Brittain) *chsd ldrs centre: rdn along 1/2-way: sn outpcd* **7/1**[3]

0-30 7 *7* **Diamond Pursuit**[4] [484] 4-8-9 52..........(t[1]) JasonHart 5
(Ivan Furtado) *dwlt: a bhd (jockey said filly was restless in the stalls)* **3/1**[2]

0-00 8 *5* **Mr Wing (IRE)**[5] [465] 4-9-0 23..........(p) PaulMulrennan 8
(John Wainwright) *sn outpcd and bhd* **125/1**

1m 1.6s (1.90) **Going Correction** +0.40s/f (Slow) **8 Ran SP% 122.7**
Speed ratings (Par 103): **100,99,92,90,86 86,75,67**
CSF £14.10 TOTE £1.60: £1.10, £3.60, £9.10; EX 10.20 Trifecta £158.50.The winner was bought in for £3800. Ticks The Boxes was claimed by Mr Brian Ellison for £5000.
Owner The Horse Watchers **Bred** Tom Foley **Trained** Oakham, Rutland

FOCUS
This looked at the mercy of the market leader on these terms and he just about got the job done. The action unfolded towards the inside of the track. The runner-up is the key, with his back form worth more.

588 BETWAY SPRINT H'CAP 4f 214y(F)
2:45 (2:45) (Class 2) (0-100,98) 3-Y-O+
£12,450 (£3,728; £1,864; £932; £466; £234) **Stalls Centre**

Form RPR

0-13 1 **Moonraker**[10] [389] 7-9-4 **88**.......... AlistairRawlinson 4 101
(Michael Appleby) *racd towards far side: cl up: led 1/2-way: rdn over 1f out: kpt on strly fnl f* **5/1**[3]

3112 2 *3½* **Ornate**[12] [352] 6-9-8 **95**.......... PhilDennis(3) 6 95
(David C Griffiths) *racd towards stands' side: prom: chsd wnr and rdn over 1f out: drvn ent fnl f: kpt on same pce (vet reported the gelding lost its left fore shoe)* **9/4**[1]

15-5 3 *¾* **Suzi's Connoisseur**[12] [352] 8-9-2 **86**..........(b) PaulMulrennan 2 84
(Jane Chapple-Hyam) *chsd ldrs centre: rdn along wl over 1f out: kpt on fnl f* **16/1**

6-22 4 *2¾* **Foolaad**[10] [389] 8-10-0 **98**..........(t) LiamKeniry 1 86
(Roy Bowring) *racd towards far side: slt ld: hdd 1/2-way: rdn along 2f out: drvn wl over 1f out: kpt on one pce* **4/1**[2]

-233 5 *1* **Uncle Jerry**[13] [342] 3-8-0 **84** oh1..........(b) PaddyMathers 7 62
(Richard Hughes) *chsd ldrs centre: rdn along 2f out: sn one pce* **15/2**

04-6 6 *¾* **Erissimus Maximus (FR)**[24] [163] 5-9-0 **84**..........(b) NicolaCurrie 8 66
(Amy Murphy) *racd nr stands' side: a in rr* **16/1**

U044 7 *1* **Samovar**[5] [471] 4-8-4 **79** oh6..........(b) TheodoreLadd(5) 3 57+
(Scott Dixon) *s.i.s: hdwy and in tch on far side after 1f: rdn along 2f out: sn drvn and wknd (jockey said gelding anticipated the start and missed the break as a result)* **8/1**

0-41 8 *3* **Midnight Malibu (IRE)**[10] [389] 6-9-1 **85**.......... RachelRichardson 9 52+
(Tim Easterby) *s.i.s: racd nr stands' rail: a bhd (jockey said mare anticipated the start and missed the break as a result)* **10/1**

4-00 **9** 4 **Atletico (IRE)**[10] 382 7-9-3 **92** KatherineBegley(5) 5 45
(David Evans) *in tch centre: rdn along bef 1/2-way: sn outpcd (jockey said gelding was outpaced throughout; vet reported the gelding bled from the nose)* **33/1**

1m 0.11s (0.41) **Going Correction** +0.40s/f (Slow) 9 Ran SP% **114.1**
WFA 3 from 4yo+ 14lb
Speed ratings (Par 109): **112,106,105,100,99 98,96,91,85**
CSF £16.42 CT £166.58 TOTE £5.40: £1.90, £1.20, £3.00; EX 18.70 Trifecta £239.60.
Owner The Kettlelites **Bred** Stratford Place Stud **Trained** Oakham, Rutland

FOCUS
This was the strongest event on the card, with plenty of these fully proven at the course.

589 BETWAY CASINO H'CAP 1m 6f 21y(F)
3:20 (3:20) (Class 6) (0-60,61) 4-Y-0+
£3,105 (£924; £461; £400; £400; £400) **Stalls** Low

Form RPR

0-63 **1** **Seasearch**[10] 387 4-9-4 **59** (p) JoshuaBryan(3) 14 70
(Andrew Balding) *hld up: stdy hdwy 5f out: trckd ldrs 3f out: cl up 2f out: shkn up to ld jst ins fnl f: eased towards fin: comf* **2/1**[1]

1-20 **2** nk **Tynecastle Park**[11] 369 6-9-3 **57** DarraghKeenan(5) 13 64
(Robert Eddery) *trckd ldrs: hdwy on outer 1/2-way: cl up 4f out: chal wl over 2f out: rdn wl over 1f out: drvn and slt ld appr fnl f: sn hdd: rallied u.p towards fin* **7/2**[2]

6242 **3** 3 **Contingency Fee**[3] 504 4-8-10 **55** (p) GraceMcEntee(7) 4 60
(Phil McEntee) *prom: led after 6f: pushed along 3f out: jnd and rdn over 2f out: drvn wl over 1f out: hdd appr fnl f: grad wknd* **7/2**[2]

/4-0 **4** 16 **Schindlers Ark (USA)**[11] 369 5-8-12 **47** DannyBrock 11 29
(Jane Chapple-Hyam) *prom: cl up over 4f out: rdn along over 3f out: drvn over 2f out: kpt on one pce* **12/1**

66-0 **5** nk **Isharah (USA)**[28] 99 6-9-1 **53** (bt) OisinOrr(3) 6 35
(Noel C Kelly, Ire) *midfield: pushed along and hdwy over 4f out: rdn along and in tch 3f out: drvn over 2f out: n.d* **15/2**[3]

0/6- **6** 3 1/4 **Unonothinjonsnow**[36] 9751 5-8-3 **45** (p) FayeMcManoman(7) 12 22
(Frank Bishop) *prom: chsd ldr over 6f out: rdn along 4f out: wknd 3f out* **80/1**

/00- **7** 8 **Esme Kate (IRE)**[66] 9310 4-8-7 **45** (tp[1]) PaddyMathers 1 14
(Ivan Furtado) *trckd ldrs on inner: pushed along over 6f out: rdn over 4f out: sn outpcd* **33/1**

52-0 **8** 16 **Ruler Of The Nile**[31] 40 7-9-6 **55** (b) BarryMcHugh 8
(Marjorie Fife) *trckd ldrs: hdwy and cl up over 4f out: rdn along over 3f out: drvn over 2f out: sn wknd* **20/1**

00-6 **9** 14 **Boru's Brook (IRE)**[31] 40 11-8-3 **45** (be) RPWalsh(7) 2
(Emma Owen) *a bhd* **150/1**

00-4 **10** hd **Incredible Dream (IRE)**[19] 246 6-9-9 **61** (p) JackDuern(3) 5
(Dean Ivory) *dwlt and towards rr: hdwy on outer 1/2-way: chsd ldrs over 4f out: rdn along over 3f out: sn btn (jockey said gelding moved poorly in the home straight)* **11/1**

00-4 **11** 2 **Rock N'Stones (IRE)**[31] 40 8-9-1 **57** OliverStammers(7) 3
(Gillian Boanas) *led 6f: cl up: rdn along over 5f out: sn wknd* **50/1**

5-60 **12** 2 **Fields Of Fire**[22] 208 5-8-10 **45** AndrewMullen 7
(Alistair Whillans) *a in rr* **40/1**

3m 13.36s (5.06) **Going Correction** +0.40s/f (Slow) 12 Ran SP% **119.6**
WFA 4 from 5yo+ 3lb
Speed ratings (Par 101): **101,100,99,89,89 87,83,74,66,66 64,63**
CSF £8.55 CT £23.46 TOTE £3.10: £1.50, £1.50, £1.50; EX 10.20 Trifecta £28.80.
Owner Kingsclere Racing Club **Bred** Kingsclere Stud **Trained** Kingsclere, Hants

FOCUS
A moderate staying event, in which the early gallop seemed decent enough. Straightforward form.

590 SUNRACING.CO.UK H'CAP 1m 13y(F)
3:50 (3:50) (Class 6) (0-60,57) 4-Y-0+
£3,105 (£924; £461; £400; £400; £400) **Stalls** Low

Form RPR

30-0 **1** **Alpha Tauri (USA)**[33] 6 13-8-12 **53** BenSanderson(5) 12 63
(Charles Smith) *prom: cl up 1/2-way: led 3f out: rdn clr wl over 1f out: styd on strly* **10/1**

-000 **2** 3 3/4 **Going Native**[6] 462 4-8-10 **46** RachelRichardson 5 48
(Olly Williams) *trckd ldrs on inner: hdwy 3f out: rdn to chse ldng pair wl over 1f out: drvn and kpt on fnl f* **20/1**

50-2 **3** 3 **Bee Machine (IRE)**[21] 233 4-8-12 **55** (t) ZakWheatley(7) 7 50
(Declan Carroll) *cl up: led 4f out: rdn along and hdd 3f out: drvn 2f out: kpt on one pce* **13/2**[3]

00-0 **4** 4 **Pecheurs De Perles (IRE)**[13] 348 5-8-10 **46** PaddyMathers 8 33
(Paul D'Arcy) *t.k.h early: trckd ldrs: pushed along and sltly outpcd over 3f out: rdn wl over 2f out: plugged on u.p appr fnl f: n.d* **12/1**

06-5 **5** 1 3/4 **Amity Island**[33] 6 4-8-10 **53** (p) HarryRussell(7) 9 36
(Ollie Pears) *chsd ldrs: effrt on outer to chse ldng pair 3f out: rdn over 2f out: sn drvn and one pce* **5/1**[2]

03-0 **6** 1 1/2 **Luath**[33] 6 6-9-1 **51** NickyMackay 2 30
(Suzzanne France) *towards rr: pushed along and hdwy on inner 3f out: rdn over 2f out: drvn wl over 1f out: nvr nr ldrs* **17/2**

-454 **7** 3/4 **Break The Silence**[3] 507 5-9-4 **54** (b) JosephineGordon 3 32
(Scott Dixon) *trckd ldrs: pushed along and lost pl 5f out: towards rr and swtchd wd home turn: sn rdn: sme late hdwy (trainer could offer no explanation other than the gelding may have ran flat on this occasion following its run three days earlier)* **2/1**[1]

01-0 **8** 10 **Candesta (USA)**[33] 6 9-9-7 **57** (tp) DanielMuscutt 10 13
(Julia Feilden) *dwlt: hdwy and chsd ldrs over 4f out: rdn wl over 3f out: wd st and sn wknd (jockey said gelding anticipated the start and was slowly away as a result)* **16/1**

5-65 **9** 9 **Kodi Koh (IRE)**[16] 295 4-8-10 **51** (v) KatherineBegley(5) 4
(David Evans) *led: pushed along and hdd 4f out: chsd ldrs: rdn 3f out: sn wknd (jockey said filly hung right on the home bend)* **8/1**

00-0 **10** 15 **Les Gar Gan (IRE)**[5] 465 8-8-9 **45** NicolaCurrie 11
(Ray Peacock) *in tch rdn along 1/2-way: sn outpcd and bhd (jockey said mare stopped quickly)* **125/1**

1m 45.86s (2.16) **Going Correction** +0.40s/f (Slow) 10 Ran SP% **113.2**
Speed ratings (Par 101): **105,101,98,94,92 91,90,80,71,56**
CSF £184.08 CT £1421.82 TOTE £12.70: £3.80, £5.30, £2.30; EX 210.00 Trifecta £2454.50.
Owner J R Theaker **Bred** Flaxman Holdings Ltd **Trained** Temple Bruer, Lincs

FOCUS
Nothing more than a moderate handicap.
T/Jkpt: Not Won. T/Plt: £90.60 to a £1 stake. Pool: £131,983.70 - 1,063.37 winning units T/Qpdt: £8.80 to a £1 stake. Pool: £20,653.78 - 1,720.45 winning units **Joe Rowntree**

591 - (Foreign Racing) - See Raceform Interactive

ST MORITZ (R-H)
Sunday, February 3

OFFICIAL GOING: Snow: frozen

592a GROSSER PREIS LONGINES (CONDITIONS) (4YO+) (SNOW) 1m 1f
12:30 4-Y-0+
£6,720 (£3,360; £2,400; £1,600; £800; £480)

RPR

1 **New Agenda**[16] 292 7-9-0 0 (h) DennisSchiergen 3 64
(Paul Webber) *mde all: kicked 3 l clr w 2f to run: styd on gamely u.p fnl f: jst hld on* **56/10**

2 nk **Fiesta (SWI)**[350] 796 5-8-10 0 TimBurgin(4) 1 63
(P Schaerer, Switzerland) **69/10**

3 dist **Berrahri (IRE)**[16] 292 8-9-8 0 RaphaelLingg 2
(John Best) *chsd ldr in share of 2nd: outpcd and niggled along fr 3f out: plugged on but lost tch w front pair* **5/2**[2]

4 dist **Nimrod (IRE)**[350] 796 6-9-11 0 KieranO'Neill 6
(M Weiss, Switzerland) **11/10**[1]

5 10 **Daisy Bere (FR)**[214] 6-8-10 0 (b) NicolasGuilbert 4
(Flurina Wullschleger, Germany) **141/10**

6 dist **Zyrjann (IRE)**[72] 714 7-9-0 0 AntoineCoutier 5
(Meret Kaderli, Switzerland) **134/10**

7 dist **Cornwall Cottage** 5-9-2 0 ClementLheureux 7
(A Schaerer, Switzerland) **13/5**[3]

2m 7.32s 7 Ran SP% **145.3**
Owner The New Agenda Syndicate **Bred** Juddmonte Farms Ltd **Trained** Mollington, Oxon

547 **CHELMSFORD (A.W)** (L-H)
Monday, February 4

OFFICIAL GOING: Polytrack: standard
Wind: light, half behind Weather: rain

593 DOUBLE DELIGHT HAT-TRICK HEAVEN AT TOTESPORT.COM H'CAP 1m 2f (P)
2:00 (2:02) (Class 7) (0-50,51) 3-Y-0+
£2,587 (£770; £384; £192) **Stalls** Low

Form RPR

005- **1** **Chakrii (IRE)**[163] 6513 3-8-6 **49** (p) HollieDoyle 6 50+
(Henry Spiller) *awkward leaving stalls and dwlt: hld up in last pair: effrt over 2f out: swtchd rt and str run on outer to ld over 1f out: edging lft but r.o wl ins fnl f* **10/1**

3-43 **2** 3/4 **Affluence (IRE)**[9] 436 4-9-9 **49** (p[1]) RhiainIngram(5) 3 55
(Martin Smith) *short of room sn after s and dropped to rr: hld up in last pair: clsd and nt clr run over 2f out: swtchd rt: nt clr run over 1f out: sn swtchd lft: hmpd ins fnl f: swtchd lft: r.o to go 2nd towards fin (jockey said gelding was denied a clear run in the home straight)* **9/4**[1]

0-00 **3** 1 1/2 **Outlaw Torn (IRE)**[3] 532 10-9-10 **45** (e) PhilipPrince 1 46
(Richard Guest) *taken down early: plld hrd: chsd ldr tl over 8f out: styd handy: ev ch and drvn over 1f out: nt match pce of wnr ins fnl f: kpt on same pce and lost 2nd wl ins fnl f* **25/1**

-202 **4** 3/4 **Don't Do It (IRE)**[9] 436 4-10-2 **51** LukeMorris 9 52
(Michael Appleby) *in tch in midfield: nt clr run 3f out: switching rt and effrt over 1f out: keeping on same pce u.p and hld whn sltly impeded ins fnl f* **11/4**[2]

05-0 **5** 2 **Steel Helmet (IRE)**[32] 39 5-9-10 **45** JosephineGordon 2 41
(Harriet Bethell) *bustled along leaving stalls: sn prom: short of room and hmpd over 8f out: swtchd rt and hdwy on outer to press ldrs 7f out: rdn ent fnl 2f: unable qck over 1f out: wknd ins fnl f* **8/1**

21-5 **6** 1 1/4 **Hidden Dream (IRE)**[10] 399 4-9-11 **51** (p) KevinLundie(5) 4 46
(Christine Dunnett) *wl in tch in midfield: unable qck u.p over 1f out: wknd ins fnl f* **6/1**[3]

0-60 **7** 3 1/2 **Nicky Baby (IRE)**[9] 436 5-9-10 **45** (b) RobertHavlin 5 32
(Dean Ivory) *sn led: rdn ent fnl 2f: hdd over 1f out: no ex and wknd ins fnl f* **16/1**

00-0 **8** 1 3/4 **Iberica Road (USA)**[10] 410 6-10-2 **51** SamJames 7 35
(Grant Tuer) *sn prom: chsd ldr over 8f out tl unable qck and lost pl over 1f out: wknd ins fnl f* **8/1**

644- **9** 3 1/4 **Cloud Nine (FR)**[334] 1064 6-9-10 **45** KieranO'Neill 8 22
(Tony Carroll) *t.k.h early: chsd ldrs tl restrained and hld up in last trio over 7f out: effrt over 2f out: sn struggling and bhd over 1f out* **33/1**

2m 7.16s (-1.44) **Going Correction** -0.10s/f (Stan) 9 Ran SP% **115.7**
WFA 3 from 4yo+ 22lb
Speed ratings (Par 97): **101,100,99,98,97 96,93,91,89**
CSF £32.91 CT £560.28 TOTE £10.90: £2.50, £1.30, £6.40; EX 38.30 Trifecta £693.90.
Owner Brendan Boyle **Bred** Austin Curran **Trained** Newmarket, Suffolk
■ Stewards' Enquiry : Robert Havlin caution: careless riding

FOCUS
A weak handicap which was won in good style by the only 3yo.

594 BET IN-PLAY AT TOTESPORT.COM H'CAP 7f (P)
2:30 (2:32) (Class 7) (0-50,52) 3-Y-0+
£2,587 (£770; £384; £192) **Stalls** Low

Form RPR

2-60 **1** **Tarseekh**[10] 402 6-9-4 **49** (b) SeamusCronin(7) 8 55
(Charlie Wallis) *mde all: wnt lft sn after s: rdn over 1f out: sustained duel w rival fnl f: battled on u.p and forged ahd towards fin* **6/1**[2]

000- **2** 1/2 **Percy Toplis**[89] 8917 5-9-2 **45** (p) KevinLundie(5) 11 50
(Christine Dunnett) *chsd ldrs: clsd to trck ldrs over 2f out: effrt to go 2nd over 1f out: ev ch and sustained duel w wnr fnl f: kpt on u.p: jst outpcd towards fin* **40/1**

-006 **3** shd **Caledonian Gold**[3] 531 6-9-7 **45** HectorCrouch 6 49
(Lisa Williamson) *taken down early: hmpd sn after s: hld up in tch in midfield: switching rt and barging match w rival over 1f out: hdwy to chse ldrs 1f out: kpt on wl u.p fnl 100yds* **33/1**

0-52 **4** 3/4 **Little Miss Kodi (IRE)**[2] 553 6-9-12 **50** (t) LiamJones 1 52
(Mark Loughnane) *chsd ldrs: nt clrest of runs ent fnl f: kpt on same pce u.p and lost 3rd towards fin (jockey said mare was denied a clear run)* **10/3**[1]

34-6 **5** ½ **Slipalongtrevaskis**[12] 357 6-9-8 **46**..........(p) JoeyHaynes 15 47
(Paul Howling) *hld up in tch in midfield: effrt and barging match w rival over 1f out: kpt on ins fnl f: nvr getting on terms w ldrs* **7/1**[3]

000- **6** ½ **Melo Pearl**[130] 7691 3-8-4 **45**..........(b[1]) PaddyMathers 16 42
(Mrs Ilka Gansera-Leveque) *stdd and dropped in bhd after s: hld up in rr: clsd: nt clr run over 1f out: gap opened and hdwy ins fnl f: styd on wl fnl 100yds: nt rch ldrs (jockey said filly was denied a clear run approaching the final furlong)* **33/1**

000- **7** 1 **Jack Louie**[203] 5017 3-8-2 **46** ow1.......... JackDuern(3) 12 38
(Dean Ivory) *hld up in tch in rr: effrt on inner and hdwy over 1f out: kpt on same pce and no imp ins fnl f* **20/1**

05-6 **8** ¾ **Seaquinn**[12] 365 4-9-7 **45**.......... KierenFox 3 42
(John Best) *hld up in tch in midfield: nt clr run over 1f out: gap opened 1f out: styd on ins fnl f: no threat to ldrs (jockey said filly was denied a clear run)* **6/1**[2]

0043 **9** nse **Tasaaboq**[1] 587 8-9-7 **45**..........(tp) RossaRyan 14 40
(Phil McEntee) *hld up in tch in last quartet: effrt over 2f out: rdn edging lft over 1f out: keeping on same pce and wl hld whn sltly impeded wl ins fnl f* **20/1**

-022 **10** 1 **Baby Gal**[3] 531 5-9-8 **46**..........(b) CharlieBennett 13 39
(Jim Boyle) *stdd s: t.k.h: hld up in tch towards rr: effrt ent fnl 2f: kpt on u.p ins fnl f: nvr trbld ldrs* **7/1**[3]

6-52 **11** 3½ **Be Bold**[3] 530 7-9-7 **45**..........(b) WilliamCarson 10 29
(Rebecca Bastiman) *t.k.h: w wnr tl lost pl u.p over 1f out: wknd ins fnl f* **10/1**

-004 **12** 3½ **Dotty Grand**[7] 458 3-8-6 **47**..........(b) HollieDoyle 4 16
(Jamie Osborne) *t.k.h: chsd ldrs tl hung rt: wd and lost pl over 2f out: bhd fnl f (jockey said filly hung right off the final bend)* **25/1**

3-20 **13** 1¾ **Admirable Art (IRE)**[3] 530 9-9-12 **50**.......... JFEgan 9 20
(Tony Carroll) *rn in snatches: midfield on outer: rdn over 3f out: edgd out rt and no prog wl over 1f out: wl btn and eased ins fnl f (jockey said gelding moved poorly)* **12/1**

1m 26.42s (-0.78) **Going Correction** -0.10s/f (Stan)
WFA 3 from 4yo+ 17lb **13** Ran SP% **115.1**
Speed ratings (Par 97): **100,99,99,98,97 97,96,95,95,94 90,86,84**
CSF £219.34 CT £6135.25 TOTE £5.90: £2.00, £17.90, £15.40; EX 241.60 Trifecta £922.70.
Owner P E Axon **Bred** Cheveley Park Stud Ltd **Trained** Ardleigh, Essex

■ Mr Potter (14-1) and Quarto Cavallo (25-1) were withdrawn. Rule 4 applies to all bets - deduction 5p in the pound.

■ Stewards' Enquiry : Seamus Cronin four-day ban: interference & careless riding (Feb 20-23); four-day ban: used whip above the permitted level (Feb 25-28); one-day ban: failure to ride to their draw (Mar 1)

FOCUS
Another basement level handicap in which it paid to race prominently, and the level is straightforward.

595 TOTEPOOL CASHBACK CLUB AT TOTESPORT.COM H'CAP 1m (P)
3:00 (3:02) (Class 6) (0-55,63) 3-Y-0+

£3,493 (£1,039; £519; £300; £300; £300) **Stalls** Low

Form RPR

00-0 **1** **Misu Pete**[25] 159 7-9-6 **54**..........(p) EllieMacKenzie(7) 3 60
(Mark Usher) *mde all: rdn over 1f out: edgd rt u.p but hld on gamely ins fnl f* **4/1**[2]

2-06 **2** nk **Mochalov**[24] 175 4-9-13 **54**.......... DannyBrock 9 59
(Jane Chapple-Hyam) *pressed wnr thrght: rdn and edgd sltly lft over 1f out: kpt on u.p ins fnl f: a jst hld (vet reported the gelding had been struck into on his right hind)* **6/1**

-465 **3** ½ **The Special One (IRE)**[9] 430 6-10-0 **55**..........(h) RossaRyan 4 60
(Phil McEntee) *in tch in midfield: effrt jst over 2f out: nt clr run and swtchd rt over 1f out: chsd ldng pair ins fnl f: swtchd rt and styd on wl u.p towards fin* **5/1**[3]

0-46 **4** 1½ **Gone With The Wind (GER)**[3] 532 8-9-5 **46** oh1...(p) WilliamCarson 2 47
(Rebecca Bastiman) *t.k.h: chsd ldrs: effrt in 4th ent fnl 2f: kpt on ins fnl f: nvr enough pce to rch ldrs* **9/1**

000- **5** ½ **Lesanti**[256] 3016 5-9-5 **46** oh1.......... CallumShepherd 1 46
(Ed de Giles) *trckd ldrs on inner: effrt over 1f out: sn drvn and unable qck: kpt on same pce ins fnl f* **25/1**

3261 **6** 1¾ **Sharp Operator**[6] 465 6-10-1 **63** 6ex..........(h) SeamusCronin(7) 11 59
(Charlie Wallis) *in tch in midfield on outer: effrt over 1f out: kpt on ins fnl f: nvr getting on terms w ldrs (jockey said gelding ran flat; vet reported the gelding had lost a left fore shoe)* **10/3**[1]

5-00 **7** hd **Herringswell (FR)**[19] 263 4-9-7 **53**..........(p[1]) CameronNoble(5) 7 48
(Henry Spiller) *impeded s: hld up in tch in midfield: effrt on inner over 1f out: kpt on ins fnl f: no threat to ldrs* **20/1**

04-0 **8** shd **Gold Club**[12] 365 8-9-13 **54**..........(p) LiamKeniry 8 49
(Lee Carter) *wnt lft s: hld up in tch in midfield: effrt over 2f out: struggling to qckn and no imp whn nt clrest of runs over 1f out: kpt on same pce ins fnl f (starter reported that colt was the subject of a third criteria failure; trainer was informed that the colt could not run until the day after passing a stalls test)* **20/1**

04-6 **9** ¾ **Dukes Meadow**[11] 386 8-9-0 **46** oh1.......... RhiainIngram(5) 5 40
(Roger Ingram) *dwlt: hld up in tch in rr: effrt: nt clr run and swtchd rt over 1f out: kpt on ins fnl f: nvr trbld ldrs* **12/1**

-305 **10** nk **Red Gunner**[12] 364 5-10-0 **55**.......... LiamJones 13 47
(Mark Loughnane) *dwlt: hld up in tch in rr: clsd and nt clr run over 1f out: nvr any enough room and no prog tl swtchd lft ins fnl f: nvr trbld ldrs (jockey said gelding was denied a clear run)* **9/1**

4-00 **11** 6 **Sir Jamie**[10] 399 6-9-9 **50**..........(b) KieranO'Neill 12 29
(Tony Carroll) *stdd s: t.k.h: hld up in rr: no hdwy u.p over 1f out: wknd fnl f* **14/1**

04-0 **12** 1½ **Admiral Anson**[25] 155 5-9-0 **46** oh1..........(v[1]) KevinLundie(5) 10 21
(Michael Appleby) *t.k.h: midfield on outer: clsd to chse ldrs over 4f out: rdn and lost pl over 2f out: bhd ins fnl f* **66/1**

00-0 **13** 3½ **Eagre**[22] 228 3-8-0 **46** oh1..........(v) PaddyMathers 6 8
(Derek Shaw) *impeded s: a in rr: no hdwy u.p over 1f out: wknd fnl f* **40/1**

1m 40.85s (0.95) **Going Correction** -0.10s/f (Stan)
WFA 3 from 4yo+ 19lb **13** Ran SP% **125.7**
Speed ratings (Par 101): **91,90,90,88,88 86,86,86,85,85 79,77,74**
CSF £28.12 CT £131.61 TOTE £4.90: £1.60, £2.40, £2.20; EX 34.20 Trifecta £216.40.
Owner The Mark Usher Racing Club **Bred** A C M Spalding **Trained** Upper Lambourn, Berks

FOCUS
This moderate handicap was dominated by the front-runners; straightforward form rated around the principals.

596 EXTRA PLACES AT TOTESPORT.COM H'CAP 6f (P)
3:30 (3:32) (Class 6) (0-60,62) 4-Y-0+

£3,493 (£1,039; £519; £300; £300; £300) **Stalls** Centre

Form RPR

2111 **1** **Foreign Legion (IRE)**[6] 467 4-9-9 **62** 6ex..........(p) NickyMackay 9 69
(Luke McJannet) *swtchd lft sn after s: in tch in midfield: effrt and hdwy on inner over 1f out: chsd ldr and swtchd rt ent fnl f: r.o u.p to ld 100yds out: rdn out* **7/2**[1]

25-0 **2** 1¾ **Holy Tiber (IRE)**[6] 467 4-9-6 **59**..........(t) JoeyHaynes 2 61
(Paul Howling) *stdd s: hld up in tch in midfield: rdn over 2f out: nt clr run over 1f out: swtchd lft and hdwy ins fnl f: r.o to chse wnr wl ins fnl f: nvr getting on terms* **7/1**[3]

00-0 **3** ½ **Red Snapper**[10] 402 4-8-7 **46** oh1..........(p) HollieDoyle 6 46
(William Stone) *short of room leaving stalls: off the pce in last pair: swtchd rt and hdwy over 1f out: edging lft but styd on wl ins fnl f: no threat to wnr (jockey said filly hung left in the home straight)* **50/1**

02-0 **4** 1¼ **Fareeq**[17] 298 5-8-12 **58**..........(bt) SeamusCronin(7) 3 54
(Charlie Wallis) *led: rdn over 1f out: drvn and hdd 100yds out: sn outpcd: lost 2 pls and wknd towards fin* **7/1**[3]

6-45 **5** ½ **Billyoakes (IRE)**[5] 483 7-9-6 **59**..........(p) AndrewMullen 8 54
(Charlie Wallis) *chsd ldrs: unable qck over 1f out: kpt on same pce ins fnl f* **7/1**[3]

5-03 **6** hd **Dark Magic**[9] 439 5-9-3 **59**..........(v) JackDuern(3) 4 53
(Dean Ivory) *off the pce in last trio: effrt and stl plenty to do wl over 1f out: hdwy and styd on ins fnl f: nvr trbld ldrs* **4/1**[2]

-343 **7** 3½ **Knockout Blow**[5] 483 4-9-7 **60**..........(p) CharlieBennett 5 44
(Jim Boyle) *pressed ldr tl unable qck and outpcd u.p over 1f out: wknd ins fnl f* **7/2**[1]

6-04 **8** 1½ **Sugar Plum Fairy**[17] 293 4-8-10 **49**.......... KieranO'Neill 1 28
(Tony Carroll) *chsd ldrs: effrt in 3rd ent fnl 2f: unable qck u.p over 1f out: wknd ins fnl f* **11/1**

03-4 **9** 4½ **Mother Of Dragons (IRE)**[21] 236 4-9-9 **62**..........(v) RossaRyan 7 28
(Phil McEntee) *hmpd after stert and sn in rr: nvr travelling wl: hung rt: wd and lost tch over 2f out (jockey said filly hung right handed throughout)* **16/1**

1m 12.59s (-1.11) **Going Correction** -0.10s/f (Stan) **9** Ran SP% **118.1**
Speed ratings (Par 101): **103,100,100,98,97 97,92,90,84**
CSF £29.23 CT £1054.47 TOTE £4.30: £1.30, £2.30, £3.70; EX 33.30 Trifecta £629.80.
Owner Ivor Collier **Bred** Norelands Bloodstock **Trained** Newmarket, Suffolk
■ Stewards' Enquiry : Nicky Mackay two-day ban: interference & careless riding (Feb 18-19)

FOCUS
An ordinary sprint handicap but won by an improving sort; straightforward form behind.

597 £20 FREE BETS AT TOTESPORT.COM H'CAP 5f (P)
4:00 (4:02) (Class 6) (0-55,54) 3-Y-0+

£3,493 (£1,039; £519; £300; £300; £300) **Stalls** Low

Form RPR

3-40 **1** **Red Stripes (USA)**[6] 471 7-9-2 **51**..........(b) SeamusCronin(7) 6 60
(Lisa Williamson) *pressed ldr: rdn to ld jst over 1f out: hanging lft but forged ahd ins fnl f: hrd pressed towards fin: a hanging on* **4/1**[2]

06-1 **2** nk **Skip To My Lou**[5] 478 4-9-9 **51** 6ex.......... KierenFox 11 59
(Peter Crate) *chsd ldrs: outpcd over 2f out: effrt over 1f out: hdwy and edging lft ins fnl f: chsd wnr wl ins fnl f: r.o strly towards fin but nvr quite getting to wnr (jockey said filly felt sore upon pulling up)* **5/2**[1]

5-04 **3** 2½ **Velvet Vixen (IRE)**[17] 287 3-8-6 **48**.......... JosephineGordon 4 41
(Jo Hughes, France) *led: rdn and hdd over 1f out: no ex and btn ins fnl f: lost 2nd and wknd wl ins fnl f* **16/1**

0-01 **4** ½ **Foxy Boy**[16] 322 5-9-10 **52**..........(b) WilliamCarson 5 50
(Rebecca Bastiman) *chsd ldrs: effrt jst over 2f out: swtchd rt over 1f out: kpt on same pce ins fnl f* **9/1**

63-0 **5** ½ **Atyaaf**[33] 27 4-9-8 **50**.......... PaddyMathers 9 45
(Derek Shaw) *hld up in rr of main gp: effrt over 1f out: clsng whn swtchd lft ins fnl f: styng on but no threat to ldrs whn nt clr run and forced to ease towards fin (jockey said gelding was denied a clear run on the run to the line)* **14/1**

21-0 **6** ¾ **Prominna**[10] 402 9-9-12 **54**.......... RossaRyan 8 47
(Tony Carroll) *stdd s: t.k.h: hld up in rr of main gp: hdwy u.p and hanging lft 1f out: stl racing awkwardly but kpt on ins fnl f: nvr trbld ldrs (jockey said gelding hung left in the final furlong)* **9/1**

02-3 **7** shd **Invisible Storm**[11] 383 4-9-12 **54**..........(b) HollieDoyle 12 46
(William Stone) *midfield on outer: effrt over 1f out: kpt on ins fnl f: nvr trbld ldrs* **8/1**

2-60 **8** 2 **Stopdworldnletmeof**[12] 357 5-9-3 **45**..........(be) JFEgan 7 30
(David Flood) *in tch in midfield: unable qck over 1f out: wknd ins fnl f* **20/1**

-230 **9** ¾ **Storm Trooper (IRE)**[5] 478 8-9-4 **46**..........(t) AndrewMullen 3 28
(Charlie Wallis) *awkward leaving stalls: towards rr of main gp: effrt u.p over 1f out: no imp whn nt clr run 1f out: wknd ins fnl f* **12/1**

-050 **10** ½ **Celerity (IRE)**[4] 503 5-9-3 **45**..........(p) HectorCrouch 10 26
(Lisa Williamson) *in rr of main gp: rdn and no hdwy over 1f out: wl hld and plugged on same pce ins fnl f* **100/1**

0-30 **11** 1 **Charlie Alpha (IRE)**[10] 402 5-9-0 **47**..........(b) RhiainIngram(5) 2 24
(Roger Ingram) *midfield: effrt on inner over 1f out: no prog and wknd ins fnl f* **6/1**[3]

00-0 **12** 9 **The Man Of Mode (IRE)**[12] 367 3-7-11 **46**..........(p[1]) SophieRalston(7) 1
(Michael Attwater) *sn outpcd and a detached in last (jockey said gelding was slowly away)* **40/1**

59.74s (-0.46) **Going Correction** -0.10s/f (Stan)
WFA 3 from 4yo+ 14lb **12** Ran SP% **122.4**
Speed ratings (Par 101): **99,98,94,93,92 91,91,88,87,86 84,70**
CSF £14.69 CT £152.12 TOTE £5.90: £1.80, £1.60, £3.90; EX 17.60 Trifecta £282.70.
Owner E H Jones (paints) Ltd **Bred** Tim Ahearn **Trained** Taporley, Wrexham

FOCUS
A low-grade sprint handicap where again those racing close to the pace dominated.

598 IRISH LOTTO AT TOTESPORT.COM MAIDEN STKS 1m 2f (P)
4:30 (4:30) (Class 5) 3-Y-0+ **£4,787** (£1,424; £711; £355) **Stalls** Low

Form RPR

02-2 **1** **Gantier**[17] 299 3-8-6 79..........(b[1]) NickyMackay 1 75
(John Gosden) *dwlt and swtchd rt sn after s: jnd ldrs after 2f: rdn and kicked clr w ldr over 2f out: drvn to ld ins fnl f: forged ahd u.str.p towards fin* **4/11**[1]

2 1 **Redemptorist (IRE)**[112] 8291 4-9-7 0........................ SeamusCronin(7) 4 78
(Olly Murphy) *chsd ldrs: swtchd rt and hdwy to join ldr after 2f: led 7f out: rdn and kicked clr w wnr over 2f out: edgd rt and hdd ins fnl f: no ex towards fin* **4/1**[3]

32-4 3 2 ½ **Fayetta**[10] 409 3-7-10 69 ow2........................ LauraCoughlan(7) 2 65
(David Loughnane) *w ldr for 2f: dropped to rr and hld up in tch 7f out: effrt between horses to chse clr ldng pair over 2f out: kpt on but nvr getting bk on terms* **7/2**[2]

00- 4 10 **Velvet Vista**[53] 9522 3-8-1 0........................ HollieDoyle 5 43
(Mark H Tompkins) *t.k.h early: in tch: rdn and outpcd over 2f out: sn btn and wknd over 1f out* **33/1**

00- 5 2 **Freedom's Breath**[104] 8510 3-7-12 0........................ JaneElliott(3) 3 39
(Michael Appleby) *led tl 7f out: chsd ldrs tl rdn and outpcd over 2f out: sn btn and wknd over 1f out* **100/1**

2m 8.07s (-0.53) **Going Correction** -0.10s/f (Stan)
WFA 3 from 4yo 22lb **5 Ran SP% 119.5**
Speed ratings (Par 103): **98,97,95,87,85**
CSF £2.83 TOTE £1.20: £1.10, £1.70; EX 2.40 Trifecta £4.70.
Owner K Abdullah **Bred** Juddmonte Farms Ltd **Trained** Newmarket, Suffolk

FOCUS
This uncompetitive, small-field maiden was run nearly a second slower than the opening Class 7 handicap. The form needs treating with caution.
T/Jkpt: £41,288.90 to a £1 stake. Pool: £61,933.34 - 1.50 winning units T/Plt: £134.60 to a £1 stake. Pool: £81,142.04 - 439.75 winning units T/Qpdt: £11.50 to a £1 stake. Pool: £9,868.10 - 633.02 winning units **Steve Payne**

530 **WOLVERHAMPTON (A.W)** (L-H)
Monday, February 4

OFFICIAL GOING: Tapeta: standard
Wind: Almost nil Weather: Cloudy

599 SUNRACING.CO.UK ALL WEATHER "HANDS AND HEELS" SERIES APPRENTICE H'CAP (RE INITIATIVE) 7f 36y (Tp)
4:55 (4:55) (Class 6) (0-55,55) 4-Y-O+
£3,105 (£924; £461; £400; £400; £400) **Stalls High**

Form RPR

66-0 1 **Caledonia Laird**[25] 159 8-9-1 52........................(v) GeorgiaDobie(3) 8 62
(Jo Hughes, France) *hld up in tch: lost pl 3f out: hdwy over 1f out: shkn up to ld wl ins fnl f: r.o wl* **5/1**[2]

05-5 2 3 **Canimar**[11] 379 4-8-9 46 oh1........................(v[1]) GavinAshton(3) 6 49
(Shaun Keightley) *chsd ldr: led 1/2-way: edgd lft over 2f out: sn wnt clr: shkn up and hdd wl ins fnl f: styd on same pce (jockey said filly hung left-handed round the final bend)* **6/1**

60-6 3 2 **Lord Cooper**[9] 439 5-9-7 55........................(b[1]) MarkCrehan 2 53
(Marjorie Fife) *hld up: hdwy on outer over 2f out: nt clr run over 1f out: styd on to go 3rd nr fin* **9/2**[1]

064- 4 nk **Dark Confidant (IRE)**[95] 8776 6-8-12 46........................(p) EllaMcCain 4 43
(Donald McCain) *chsd ldrs: shkn up over 1f out: styd on same pce ins fnl f* **11/2**[3]

632- 5 ¾ **Secret Lightning (FR)**[255] 3069 7-9-3 54........................(v) CierenFallon(3) 12 49
(Michael Appleby) *sn led: hdd 1/2-way: nt clr run over 2f out: no ex fnl f* **14/1**

-304 6 ¾ **Brother In Arms (IRE)**[12] 357 5-8-7 46........................ GraceMcEntee(5) 5 39
(Tony Carroll) *hld up: pushed along on outer over 2f out: nvr nrr* **9/2**[1]

400- 7 nk **Captain Marmalade (IRE)**[26] 8338 7-8-7 46 oh1........ SeanKirrane(5) 9 39
(Jimmy Fox) *s.i.s: hld up: pushed along over 2f out: edgd lft over 1f out: nvr on terms* **40/1**

5-04 8 ½ **Purbeck Gem**[18] 275 5-9-3 51........................ AmeliaGlass 10 42
(Robyn Brisland) *prom: pushed along over 2f out: wknd ins fnl f: b.b.v (vet reported the mare had bled from the nose)* **20/1**

00-0 9 1 ¼ **Frozen Lake (USA)**[31] 64 7-9-2 55........................(vt[1]) KateLeahy(5) 11 44
(John O'Shea) *s.i.s: plld hrd: hdwy over 5f out: nt clr run and wknd over 1f out* **33/1**

006- 10 2 **Play With Me**[63] 9385 5-8-12 46 oh1........................ JessicaCooley 1 29
(Ken Wingrove) *mid-div: lost pl 4f out: nt clr run over 2f out: n.d after* **100/1**

-300 11 1 ¾ **Aljunood (IRE)**[14] 348 5-9-5 53........................(h) TobyEley 7 32
(John Norton) *s.s: nvr on terms (jockey said gelding was slowly away)* **11/2**[3]

1m 29.16s (0.36) **Going Correction** 0.0s/f (Stan) **11 Ran SP% 115.9**
Speed ratings (Par 101): **97,93,91,90,90 89,88,88,86,84 82**
CSF £33.41 CT £147.92 TOTE £6.20: £1.90, £2.60, £1.80; EX 39.50.
Owner Isla & Colin Cage **Bred** Mrs I M Cage And Mr C J Cage **Trained** France

FOCUS
A low-grade handicap; straightforward form.

600 LIKE SUN RACING ON FACEBOOK CLASSIFIED (S) STKS 7f 36y (Tp)
5:25 (5:25) (Class 6) 4-Y-O+
£3,105 (£924; £461; £400; £400; £400) **Stalls High**

Form RPR

5-63 1 **The Groove**[6] 466 6-8-5 66........................ GinaMangan(7) 8 59+
(David Evans) *hld up: hdwy on outer over 2f out: led over 1f out: rdn out* **9/2**[3]

0-00 2 2 ¼ **Madame Jo Jo**[3] 531 4-8-7 46........................(p) KatherineBegley(5) 1 53
(Sarah Hollinshead) *chsd ldr tl over 5f out: remained handy: rdn and ev ch over 1f out: styd on same pce ins fnl f* **40/1**

2-34 3 nk **Secondo (FR)**[21] 237 9-8-12 69........................(v) DavidProbert 7 52
(Robert Stephens) *hld up: hdwy over 1f out: rdn and edgd lft ins fnl f: styd on: nt rch ldrs* **13/8**[1]

0620 4 1 ½ **Zapper Cass (FR)**[6] 468 6-8-12 68........................(p) LukeMorris 2 49
(Michael Appleby) *s.i.s: hld up: hdwy over 2f out: nt clr run sn after: rdn over 1f out: styd on same pce* **5/2**[2]

0-00 5 4 ½ **Clement (IRE)**[6] 467 9-8-12 57........................(v) FergusSweeney 4 38
(John O'Shea) *prom: rdn over 2f out: wknd over 1f out* **20/1**

3-20 6 1 **Skydiving**[12] 364 4-8-12 67........................(b[1]) DougieCostello 6 35
(Jamie Osborne) *led: plld hrd: rdn and hdd over 1f out: wknd ins fnl f* **11/2**

005- 7 7 **Invinsible (IRE)**[24] 193 4-8-12 38........................ StevieDonohoe 3 18
(Keith Henry Clarke, Ire) *plld hrd and prom: wnt 2nd over 5f out tl 1/2-way: rdn over 2f out: wknd wl over 1f out* **100/1**

1m 28.29s (-0.51) **Going Correction** 0.0s/f (Stan) **7 Ran SP% 108.4**
Speed ratings (Par 101): **102,99,99,97,92 91,83**
CSF £128.31 TOTE £6.40: £1.90, £7.60; EX 61.20.There was no bid for the winner
Owner Dave & Emma Evans **Bred** Cheveley Park Stud Ltd **Trained** Pandy, Monmouths

FOCUS
A bit of a messy race, perhaps not form to trust.

601 SUNRACING.CO.UK CONDITIONS STKS 1m 142y (Tp)
5:55 (5:55) (Class 2) 4-Y-O+ £11,827 (£3,541; £1,770; £885; £442) **Stalls Low**

Form RPR

23-1 1 **Hathal (USA)**[28] 121 7-9-5 107........................ NicolaCurrie 5 111
(Jamie Osborne) *s.i.s: hld up: hdwy and hung lft fr over 1f out: swtchd rt ins fnl f: rdn and r.o to ld towards fin* **2/1**[2]

326- 2 1 ½ **Oh This Is Us (IRE)**[106] 8464 6-9-8 111........................ RyanMoore 1 110
(Richard Hannon) *hld up: hdwy over 2f out: shkn up to ld wl ins fnl f: hdd towards fin* **9/2**

105- 3 nk **Silver Quartz**[50] 9571 4-9-5 100........................ OisinMurphy 4 106
(Archie Watson) *chsd ldrs: led 2f out: rdn and hdd wl ins fnl f* **4/1**[3]

-631 4 7 **Michele Strogoff**[21] 240 6-9-5 90........................ AlistairRawlinson 6 90
(Michael Appleby) *led: rdn and hdd 2f out: wknd ins fnl f* **25/1**

001- 5 30 **Arcanada (IRE)**[35] 9774 6-9-5 109........................(p) RichardKingscote 2 21
(Tom Dascombe) *chsd ldr: shkn up and hung lft over 3f out: lost 2nd over 2f out: wknd wl over 1f out (trainer's rep could offer no explanation for the gelding's performance other than it may have been unsuited by not being able to dominate on this occasion)* **7/4**[1]

1m 47.52s (-2.58) **Going Correction** 0.0s/f (Stan) **5 Ran SP% 111.7**
Speed ratings (Par 109): **111,109,109,103,76**
CSF £11.30 TOTE £3.40: £1.50, £1.70; EX 15.00 Trifecta £29.60.
Owner Dr A Sedrati and Partner **Bred** Tenth Street Stables Llc **Trained** Upper Lambourn, Berks

FOCUS
A good race and it was run at a strong gallop. It's been rated around the third to his best, with the winner matching last year's best.

602 BETWAY CASINO H'CAP 1m 4f 51y (Tp)
6:25 (6:25) (Class 6) (0-52,52) 4-Y-O+
£3,105 (£924; £461; £400; £400; £400) **Stalls Low**

Form RPR

30-5 1 **Dolphin Village (IRE)**[19] 262 9-9-1 46........................(h) PaulMulrennan 12 52
(Shaun Harris) *hld up in tch: racd keenly: chsd ldr over 1f out: nt clr run and swtchd rt ins fnl f: styd on u.p to ld nr fin* **10/1**

/00- 2 nk **Quite Subunctious (IRE)**[31] 74 4-9-1 48........................ StevieDonohoe 4 55
(Keith Henry Clarke, Ire) *trckd ldrs: racd keenly: led over 7f out: rdn over 1f out: edgd rt ins fnl f: hdd nr fin (jockey said filly ran too freely and hung right-handed)* **17/2**

0 3 shd **Nice To Sea (IRE)**[31] 67 5-9-5 50........................(p[1]) DavidProbert 10 56
(Olly Murphy) *s.i.s: hld up: hdwy and nt clr run over 1f out: nt clr run and swtchd rt ins fnl f: sn rdn: r.o wl* **14/1**

02-1 4 nk **Splash Of Verve (IRE)**[23] 208 7-8-13 51........................ TobyEley(7) 2 56
(David Thompson) *trckd ldrs: plld hrd: lost pl over 6f out: nt clr run over 2f out: hdwy over 1f out: sn rdn: ev ch wl ins fnl f: styd on (jockey said gelding ran too freely and was denied a clear run entering the home straight)* **3/1**[1]

020- 5 2 **Pablow**[53] 9528 4-8-8 46........................(b) DarraghKeenan(5) 8 49
(Alan Bailey) *s.i.s: rcvrd to ld at stdy pce tl hdd over 7f out: remained handy: rdn and edgd rt fr over 1f out: styd on same pce ins fnl f* **16/1**

4-31 6 nk **Prerogative (IRE)**[9] 436 5-9-1 51........................(p) PoppyBridgwater(5) 7 52
(Tony Carroll) *led 1f: chsd ldrs: hmpd and lost pl over 2f out: rallied over 1f out: styd on same pce wl ins fnl f* **11/2**[3]

03-0 7 shd **Boatrace (IRE)**[31] 62 4-9-1 48........................(t[1]) EoinWalsh 9 50
(David Evans) *hld up: pushed along over 2f out: hdwy over 1f out: nt rch ldrs* **14/1**

432- 8 4 **Mrs Burbidge**[21] 7959 9-9-6 51........................(tp) AdamKirby 5 46+
(Neil Mulholland) *hld up: hdwy over 2f out: sn rdn: wknd ins fnl f* **5/1**[2]

9 2 ¼ **Vocal Heir (IRE)**[107] 4464 7-9-4 49........................(p) LukeMorris 11 41
(Olly Murphy) *sn pushed along and prom: chsd ldr over 9f out tl over 7f out: wnt 2nd again over 6f out tl rdn over 2f out: wkng whn hmpd ins fnl f* **50/1**

53-0 10 5 **Warofindependence (USA)**[16] 321 7-9-7 52......(p) FergusSweeney 3 35
(John O'Shea) *hld up: racd keenly: nvr on terms (jockey said gelding hung left-handed throughout)* **20/1**

600- 11 3 ¼ **Cuckoo's Calling**[37] 9750 5-9-4 49........................ CallumRodriguez 6 27
(Keith Dalgleish) *s.i.s: hdwy over 7f out: rdn over 2f out: sn wknd* **15/2**

60-0 12 2 ¾ **Amy Kane**[17] 288 5-9-1 46........................ NicolaCurrie 1 19
(Jimmy Fox) *hld up: wknd over 3f out (jockey said mare ran in snatches)* **80/1**

2m 40.7s (-0.10) **Going Correction** 0.0s/f (Stan)
WFA 4 from 5yo+ 2lb **12 Ran SP% 115.6**
Speed ratings (Par 101): **100,99,99,99,98 98,97,95,93,90 88,86**
CSF £88.77 CT £1192.78 TOTE £8.40: £3.20, £2.70, £5.10; EX 98.00 Trifecta £1888.20.
Owner Nottinghamshire Racing **Bred** Gerrardstown House Stud **Trained** Carburton, Notts
■ Stewards' Enquiry : Poppy Bridgwater one-day ban: failure to ride to their draw (Feb 18)

FOCUS
A moderate handicap run at a steady early gallop.

603 BETWAY HEED YOUR HUNCH CLASSIFIED CLAIMING STKS 1m 1f 104y (Tp)
6:55 (6:55) (Class 6) 4-Y-O+
£3,105 (£924; £461; £400; £400; £400) **Stalls Low**

Form RPR

61-6 1 **Anif (IRE)**[16] 315 5-8-9 63........................ EoinWalsh 2 66
(David Evans) *sn chsng ldrs: wnt 2nd over 3f out: led 2f out: rdn out* **13/8**[1]

06-0 2 nk **Brexitmeansbrexit**[14] 346 4-8-10 70........................ ThoreHammerHansen(7) 3 73
(Richard Hannon) *hld up: hdwy over 2f out: rdn and ev ch over 1f out: r.o* **13/2**[3]

3-65 3 4 ½ **Pike Corner Cross (IRE)**[5] 481 7-8-9 59........................ CallumShepherd 4 57
(Alastair Ralph) *led 1f: remained handy: swtchd rt over 2f out: rdn over 1f out: no ex ins fnl f* **4/1**[2]

00-4 4 1 ¼ **Red Touch (USA)**[34] 5 7-8-9 69........................(v) LukeMorris 1 55
(Michael Appleby) *prom: lost pl over 7f out: rdn over 2f out: hung lft ins fnl f: nt trble ldrs* **7/1**

004- 5 5 **Street Poet (IRE)**[66] 9326 6-9-0 67........................(p) PhilDennis(3) 5 53
(Michael Herrington) *led after 1f: hdd over 5f out: chsd ldr tl over 3f out: rdn over 2f out: wknd ins fnl f* **13/2**[3]

2-00 6 5 **Berlusca (IRE)**[14] 344 10-8-9 62........................ NicolaCurrie 6 36
(David Loughnane) *dwlt: hdwy to chse ldr over 7f out: led over 5f out: shkn up and hdd 2f out: wknd fnl f (jockey said gelding moved poorly and had no more to give)* **9/1**

2m 0.55s (-0.25) **Going Correction** 0.0s/f (Stan) **6 Ran SP% 107.3**
Speed ratings (Par 101): **101,100,96,95,91 86**
CSF £11.31 TOTE £2.20: £1.30, £3.30; EX 11.30.

Owner Dave & Emma Evans **Bred** Shadwell Estate Company Limited **Trained** Pandy, Monmouths

FOCUS
The first two pulled clear in this claimer and the winner has been rated to his recent level.

604 BETWAY NOVICE MEDIAN AUCTION STKS 6f 20y (Tp)
7:25 (7:25) (Class 6) 3-5-Y-O £3,105 (£924; £461; £230) Stalls Low

Form RPR

42 1 **Solar Park (IRE)**[13] 354 3-8-11 0 PJMcDonald 8 77+
(James Tate) *chsd ldr: led wl over 2f out: wnt readily clr fr over 1f out: easily* **1/8**[1]

0- 2 13 **Piccolita**[98] 8696 3-8-6 0 CharlieBennett 4 30
(Hughie Morrison) *pushed along early towards rr: hdwy to go 3rd over 3f out: rdn and hung lft fr over 1f out: wkng whn wnt 2nd ins fnl f* **7/1**[2]

0- 3 3 1/2 **Shesadabber**[172] 6199 3-8-6 0 EoinWalsh 6 19
(Brian Baugh) *s.s: in rr and drvn along 1/2-way: wnt 3rd wl ins fnl f: nvr nrr* **80/1**

4 1 1/2 **Purely Prosecco** 3-8-3 0 AaronJones(3) 2 15
(Derek Shaw) *s.s: pushed along 1/2-way: wnt 4th nr fin: nvr on terms (jockey said filly ran greenly)* **11/1**[3]

040- 5 1 3/4 **Bluella**[63] 9378 4-9-7 42 DavidProbert 7 13
(Robyn Brisland) *led: hdd wl over 2f out: wknd over 1f out: lost 2nd ins fnl f* **18/1**

00 6 29 **Prince Mamillius**[16] 316 3-8-11 0 CallumShepherd 1
(Derek Shaw) *pushed along to chse ldrs: lost pl over 3f out: wknd wl over 2f out* **100/1**

1m 14.02s (-0.48) **Going Correction** 0.0s/f (Stan)
WFA 3 from 4yo+ 15lb 6 Ran SP% 117.2
Speed ratings (Par 101): **103,85,81,79,76 38**
CSF £2.13 TOTE £1.10: £1.02, £2.60; EX 2.50 Trifecta £19.20.
Owner Saeed Manana **Bred** Kildaragh Stud **Trained** Newmarket, Suffolk

FOCUS
A simple task for the heavy odds-on favourite, who proved much too good for some ordinary rivals and he has been rated as improving slightly.

605 LADBROKES H'CAP 5f 21y (Tp)
7:55 (7:55) (Class 6) (0-65,63) 3-Y-O £3,105 (£924; £461; £400; £400; £400) Stalls Low

Form RPR

4-23 1 **Hanakotoba (USA)**[17] 287 3-9-6 62 (t) OisinMurphy 5 68
(Stuart Williams) *chsd ldr: led over 1f out: rdn out* **2/1**[1]

0-53 2 3/4 **Pink Flamingo**[10] 412 3-9-7 63 JoeFanning 4 66
(Mark Johnston) *hld up: shkn up to chse wnr fnl f: sn rdn and edgd lft: r.o* **11/4**[2]

46-0 3 1 1/4 **Oxygenic**[23] 215 3-8-9 54 ow1 ConorMcGovern(3) 6 53
(David O'Meara) *sn pushed along in rr: hdwy over 1f out: r.o: nt rch ldrs* **50/1**

04-0 4 1 3/4 **Awake In Asia**[21] 235 3-9-6 62 (v[1]) AdamKirby 2 54
(Charlie Wallis) *prom: pushed along 1/2-way: rdn and hung lft over 1f out: no ex ins fnl f* **8/1**

0-26 5 3/4 **Not So Shy**[4] 505 3-8-9 56 KatherineBegley(5) 7 46
(David Evans) *n.m.r after s: sn pushed along into mid-div: rdn and nt clr run over 1f out: styd on same pce fnl f* **12/1**

545- 6 hd **North Korea (IRE)**[126] 7828 3-9-6 62 LukeMorris 9 51
(Brian Baugh) *s.i.s: sn pushed along in rr: r.o towards fin: nvr nrr* **40/1**

00-4 7 3/4 **Thegreyvtrain**[17] 298 3-8-11 53 PJMcDonald 8 39
(Ronald Harris) *wnt lft s: chsd ldrs: rdn over 1f out: wknd ins fnl f* **12/1**

62-3 8 1 1/2 **Alban's Dream**[21] 235 3-9-1 62 (b) DarraghKeenan(5) 1 43
(Robert Eddery) *led: rdn and hdd over 1f out: wknd ins fnl f (trainer said filly had been unsuited by having to be ridden along early in order to make the running on this drop back in trip to 5 furlongs 21 yards)* **9/2**[3]

560- 9 2 1/4 **Carla Koala**[38] 9730 3-8-12 57 AaronJones(3) 11 30
(Natalie Lloyd-Beavis) *s.i.s: in rr: rdn over 1f out: n.d (jockey said filly hung right-handed)* **125/1**

600- 10 7 **Brother Bentley**[125] 7874 3-9-4 60 DavidProbert 3 7
(Ronald Harris) *dwlt: outpcd: a in rr* **16/1**

1m 1.55s (-0.35) **Going Correction** 0.0s/f (Stan) 10 Ran SP% 115.8
Speed ratings (Par 95): **102,100,98,96,94 94,93,90,87,76**
CSF £7.36 CT £196.67 TOTE £2.70: £1.10, £2.00, £6.40; EX 8.40 Trifecta £270.60.
Owner Mrs J Morley **Bred** Elise Handler & Matthew Schering **Trained** Newmarket, Suffolk

FOCUS
A modest sprint run at a sound pace.

606 LADBROKES HOME OF THE ODDS BOOST NOVICE STKS 1m 1f 104y (Tp)
8:25 (8:25) (Class 5) 3-Y-O £3,752 (£1,116; £557; £278) Stalls Low

Form RPR

5-1 1 **Marhaban (IRE)**[17] 299 3-9-9 0 AdamKirby 4 90+
(Charlie Appleby) *mde all: shkn up over 1f out: styd on* **1/2**[1]

2 3/4 **Cirque Royal** 3-9-2 0 DavidProbert 1 80
(Charlie Appleby) *a.p: chsd wnr over 3f out: shkn up over 2f out: styd on* **15/8**[2]

6- 3 24 **Maria Magdalena (IRE)**[167] 6388 3-8-8 0 AaronJones(3) 6 25
(Marco Botti) *s.i.s: hld up: wknd 3f out: wnt 3rd wl ins fnl f* **25/1**[3]

4 2 1/2 **Kiowa** 3-9-2 0 DannyBrock 5 25
(Philip McBride) *edgd rt s: sn prom: rdn and wknd over 2f out* **80/1**

60- 5 3 3/4 **Simba Samba**[65] 9354 3-9-2 0 NicolaCurrie 2 17
(Philip McBride) *s.i.s: hdwy on outer over 7f out: chsd wnr over 6f out tl over 3f out: wknd over 2f out (jockey said gelding was slowly away)* **50/1**

6 1 1/2 **Shamrad (FR)** 3-9-2 0 StevieDonohoe 7 14
(Ian Williams) *s.i.s: pushed along and a in rr: wknd 3f out* **40/1**

0-0 7 2 **With Pride**[17] 289 3-8-11 0 SeanPalmer(5) 3 10
(Neil Mulholland) *plld hrd in 2nd: lost pl over 6f out: wknd 3f out (jockey said colt ran too freely in the early stages)* **150/1**

2m 1.98s (1.18) **Going Correction** 0.0s/f (Stan) 7 Ran SP% 111.6
Speed ratings (Par 97): **94,93,72,69,66 65,63**
CSF £1.54 TOTE £1.30: £1.10, £1.30; EX 1.70 Trifecta £6.10.
Owner Godolphin **Bred** Rabbah Bloodstock Limited **Trained** Newmarket, Suffolk

FOCUS
Effectively a match between the two Godolphin horses.
T/Plt: £847.80 to a £1 stake. Pool: £98,846.30 - 85.11 winning units T/Qpdt: £71.00 to a £1 stake. Pool: £14,501.99 - 150.95 winning units **Colin Roberts**

522 NEWCASTLE (A.W) (L-H)
Tuesday, February 5

OFFICIAL GOING: Tapeta: standard to slow
Wind: Virtually nil Weather: Heavy rain

607 BETWAY HEED YOUR HUNCH H'CAP 1m 4f 98y (Tp)
4:10 (4:10) (Class 6) (0-65,64) 4-Y-O+ £3,105 (£924; £461; £300; £300; £300) Stalls High

Form RPR

5-41 1 **Royal Cosmic**[12] 387 5-9-2 62 SebastianWoods(5) 8 73+
(Richard Fahey) *trckd ldrs: hdwy 3f out: chsd ldr over 2f out: rdn to ld and hung lft appr fnl f: sn clr* **9/2**[3]

25-0 2 7 **Good Man (IRE)**[24] 208 6-8-7 48 (v) BarryMcHugh 4 48
(Karen McLintock) *s.i.s and lost 10 l s: bhd: tk clsr order 1/2-way: hdwy to chse ldrs 3f out: rdn 2f out: styd on to chse wnr fnl f: no imp (jockey said gelding was awkward leaving the stalls and as a result was slowly away)* **10/1**

0-32 3 1/2 **Hugoigo**[24] 208 5-8-1 45 JamieGormley(3) 1 44
(Jim Goldie) *trckd ldrs: pushed along on inner and sltly outpcd over 3f out: swtchd rt and rdn 2f out: kpt on u.p fnl f* **7/1**

60-1 4 1 1/2 **Tetradrachm**[17] 321 6-9-9 64 (tp) StevieDonohoe 7 61
(Rebecca Menzies) *hld up in rr: stdy hdwy over 5f out: trckd ldrs over 3f out: effrt to ld over 2f out: jnd and rdn over 1f out: hdd: n.m.r and hmpd appr fnl f: sn wknd* **11/8**[1]

04-0 5 1/2 **Elite Icon**[30] 100 5-7-13 45 AndrewBreslin(5) 10 41
(Jim Goldie) *hld up and bhd: hdwy 5f out: rdn along to chse ldrs 2f out: sn drvn and kpt on same pce* **25/1**

43-3 6 3 1/2 **Flood Defence (IRE)**[15] 346 5-9-2 62 TheodoreLadd(5) 5 53
(Iain Jardine) *in tch: pushed along 4f out: rdn 3f out: sn drvn and btn (jockey said mare ran too free then hung left under pressure)* **3/1**[2]

1/0- 7 6 **Judith Gardenier**[168] 6385 7-8-5 46 (p) JamesSullivan 9 28
(R Mike Smith) *trckd ldrs: hdwy and cl up on outer over 4f out: pushed along over 3f out: sn rdn and wknd* **66/1**

00-0 8 3/4 **Just Heather (IRE)**[22] 241 5-8-4 45 (v) CamHardie 6 26
(John Wainwright) *prom: trckd ldr 5f out: rdn along 3f out: sn drvn and wknd* **100/1**

0 9 1 1/4 **Awesome Gal (IRE)**[25] 185 5-8-4 45 (b[1]) LukeMorris 3 24
(Sir Mark Prescott Bt) *led: pushed along over 3f out: sn rdn: hdd over 2f out and sn wknd* **12/1**

000- 10 1 **Lots Ov (IRE)**[173] 6180 5-7-13 45 FayeMcManoman(5) 2 23
(John Wainwright) *trckd ldrs on inner: pushed along over 3f out: sn rdn and wknd* **100/1**

2m 43.65s (2.55) **Going Correction** +0.125s/f (Slow) 10 Ran SP% 121.9
Speed ratings (Par 101): **96,91,91,90,89 87,83,82,82,81**
CSF £49.91 CT £318.04 TOTE £4.60: £1.80, £3.40, £1.70; EX 56.50 Trifecta £302.90.
Owner The Cosmic Cases **Bred** The Cosmic Cases **Trained** Musley Bank, N Yorks
■ Stewards' Enquiry : Sebastian Woods three-day ban; careless riding (Feb 19-21)

FOCUS
The snow that had caused Friday evening's meeting to be called off after the fifth race had cleared leaving Tapeta which was described as 'Standard to Slow'. \n\x\x The market got this moderate handicap all wrong with the winner proving easy to back and the well-backed favourite a disappointing fourth.

608 SUN RACING TOP TIPS AND PREVIEWS NOVICE STKS 1m 5y (Tp)
4:45 (4:45) (Class 5) 4-Y-O+ £3,752 (£1,116; £557; £278) Stalls Centre

Form RPR

01- 1 **Merchant Of Venice**[53] 9531 4-9-7 0 GeorgeWood 7 73+
(James Fanshawe) *trckd ldrs: cl up 3f out: chal wl over 1f out: rdn to ld ins fnl f: kpt on wl* **6/1**[3]

2 1 1/4 **Blindingly (GER)** 4-9-2 0 AndrewMullen 6 66+
(Ben Haslam) *t.k.h early: hld up towards rr: hdwy to trck ldrs 1/2-way: swtchd rt and effrt whn nt clr run over 1f out: sn swtchd lft and rdn: kpt on wl fnl f (jockey said gelding was denied a clear run 1f out)* **14/1**

/62- 3 1/2 **Tum Tum**[38] 9746 4-9-2 76 (h) PaulMulrennan 1 63
(Michael Herrington) *dwlt and towards rr: hdwy over 3f out: chsd ldrs 2f out: sn rdn and kpt on fnl f* **9/4**[2]

3-24 4 3/4 **Sajanji**[15] 344 4-8-11 67 PJMcDonald 8 57
(Simon Crisford) *trckd ldr: cl up 1/2-way: led 2f out: rdn along 1 1/2f out and sn edgd rt: drvn ent fnl f: sn hdd and kpt on same pce* **10/11**[1]

R 5 3/4 **Desai**[5] 500 5-9-2 0 GrahamLee 5 60
(Noel Wilson) *trckd ldng pair: cl up 3f out: rdn along over 2f out: drvn over 1f out: wknd fnl f (vet said gelding lost it's right hind shoe)* **66/1**

/ 6 nk **Scots Sonnet**[326] 5-9-2 0 (h) AlistairRawlinson 3 59+
(Jim Goldie) *towards rr: hdwy over 2f out: rdn over 1f out: styd on fnl f: nrst fin* **40/1**

0- 7 2 3/4 **Harbour Bay**[120] 8055 4-9-2 0 JackGarritty 9 53
(Jedd O'Keeffe) *in tch: pushed along over 3f out: rdn wl over 2f out: sn one pce* **6/1**[3]

606/ 8 11 **Dream On Dreamer (IRE)**[35] 5009 5-8-6 60 (t) FayeMcManoman(5) 4 23
(Lucinda Egerton) *led: rdn along and hdd 3f out: wknd 2f out (jockey said mare ran too free)* **50/1**

5- 9 8 **Nicky Nook**[57] 9482 6-8-11 0 StevieDonohoe 2
(Stella Barclay) *in tch: pushed along 3f out: sn rdn and wknd* **100/1**

1m 39.49s (0.89) **Going Correction** +0.125s/f (Slow) 9 Ran SP% 125.3
Speed ratings (Par 103): **100,98,98,97,96 96,93,82,74**
CSF £86.51 TOTE £6.30: £1.80, £3.30, £1.10; EX 44.00 Trifecta £111.50.
Owner Mr & Mrs P Hopper, Mr & Mrs M Morris **Bred** Mr & Mrs P Hopper & Mr & Mrs M Morris **Trained** Newmarket, Suffolk

FOCUS
A decidedly ordinary novice event, although the winner is going the right way.

609 FOLLOW SUNRACING ON TWITTER H'CAP 7f 14y (Tp)
5:15 (5:15) (Class 5) (0-75,75) 4-Y-O+ £3,752 (£1,116; £557; £300; £300; £300) Stalls Centre

Form RPR

3446 1 **Gentlemen**[5] 508 8-9-7 75 (h) JosephineGordon 2 81
(Phil McEntee) *mde all: rdn over 1f out: kpt on wl towards fin (trainer could offer no explanation for the app imp in form)* **7/1**

11-5 2 hd **Chosen World**[34] 23 5-8-8 65 (p) ConorMcGovern(3) 1 70
(Julie Camacho) *trckd ldng pair: hdwy 2f out: rdn to chal ent fnl f: sn drvn and ev ch tl no ex nr fin* **5/1**

-522 **3** 3/4 **Bobby Joe Leg**[5] 496 5-8-12 **66**..............................(b) JamesSullivan 3 69
(Ruth Carr) *trckd ldrs: hdwy 2f out: rdn to chse wnr over 1f out: drvn and ev ch ins fnl f: kpt on same pce towards fin* **10/3**[1]
10-3 **4** 1 1/4 **Mudawwan (IRE)**[14] 355 5-9-3 **71**..............................(tp) PJMcDonald 6 71
(James Bethell) *trckd wnr: cl up 3f out: rdn along 2f out: sn drvn and wknd appr fnl f* **10/3**[1]
250- **5** *nk* **Insurplus (IRE)**[48] 9616 6-8-4 **61**.............................. JamieGormley(3) 5 60
(Jim Goldie) *trckd ldng pair: pushed along over 2f out: rdn wl over 1f out: sn no imp* **4/1**[2]
-112 **6** 1 3/4 **Grey Destiny**[8] 463 9-8-10 **64**..............................(p) CamHardie 4 58
(Antony Brittain) *s.i.s: a in rr* **9/2**[3]
1m 27.76s (1.56) **Going Correction** +0.125s/f (Slow) **6** Ran SP% **113.5**
Speed ratings (Par 103): **96,95,94,93,93 91**
CSF £41.25 TOTE £8.50: £3.90, £2.70; EX 41.90 Trifecta £183.00.
Owner Trevor Johnson **Bred** Mrs Eleanor Kent **Trained** Newmarket, Suffolk
FOCUS
A modest handicap. There was no pace and the best ride won the race.

610 BETWAY SPRINT H'CAP 5f (Tp)
5:45 (5:45) (Class 5) (0-75,76) 4-Y-O+

£3,752 (£1,116; £557; £300; £300; £300) **Stalls** Centre

Form RPR
-614 **1** **Another Angel (IRE)**[5] 498 5-9-4 **72**.............................. CamHardie 7 81
(Antony Brittain) *trckd ldr: cl up 2f out: rdn to ld over 1f out: drvn and kpt on wl fnl f* **3/1**[1]
35-1 **2** *nk* **Pea Shooter**[28] 131 10-9-6 **74**.............................. CallumRodriguez 9 82
(Brian Ellison) *trckd ldrs: hdwy 2f out: rdn to chal over 1f out: drvn and ev ch ins fnl f: no ex towards fin* **7/1**
6-36 **3** 1 3/4 **Jack The Truth (IRE)**[26] 165 5-9-7 **75**.............................. LukeMorris 5 77
(George Scott) *trckd ldrs: hdwy 2f out: rdn over 1f out: drvn and kpt on same pce fnl f* **8/1**
01-3 **4** *nk* **Eternal Sun**[26] 163 4-9-8 **76**.............................. JasonHart 6 77
(Ivan Furtado) *hld up in tch: swtchd rt and hdwy 2f out: rdn to chse ldrs over 1f out: drvn and kpt on fnl f* **4/1**[2]
6-66 **5** 1 **Landing Night (IRE)**[19] 278 7-9-6 **74**..............................(tp) PJMcDonald 3 71
(Rebecca Menzies) *hld up towards rr: hdwy 2f out: rdn over 1f out: styd on fnl f: nrst fin* **8/1**
44-0 **6** 1/2 **Gamesome (FR)**[19] 278 8-9-0 **68**.............................. DougieCostello 4 63
(Paul Midgley) *dwlt: a towards rr* **20/1**
4252 **7** 1/2 **Bernie's Boy**[20] 254 6-9-6 **74**..............................(p) JosephineGordon 8 67
(Phil McEntee) *led: rdn along over 2f out: hdd and drvn over 1f out: sn wknd* **16/1**
6003 **8** 1 1/2 **Katheefa (USA)**[5] 498 5-9-1 **69**..............................(b[1]) JamesSullivan 1 57
(Ruth Carr) *dwlt: sn chsng ldrs: rdn along 2f out: grad wknd* **9/2**[3]
11U2 **9** 3/4 **Archimedes (IRE)**[5] 498 6-8-10 **64**..............................(tp) StevieDonohoe 2 49
(David C Griffiths) *a towards rr (jockey was slow to remove the blindfold and explained blindfold was stuck on the first attempt to remove it)* **8/1**
000- **10** 3 **Orient Class**[129] 7780 8-9-6 **74**..............................(w) GrahamLee 10 49
(Paul Midgley) *chsd ldrs: rdn along over 2f out: sn wknd* **25/1**
59.04s (-0.46) **Going Correction** +0.125s/f (Slow) **10** Ran SP% **123.5**
Speed ratings (Par 103): **108,107,104,104,102 101,101,98,97,92**
CSF £26.28 CT £159.86 TOTE £4.40: £1.50, £2.40, £2.80; EX 37.50 Trifecta £269.90.
Owner Antony Brittain **Bred** Yeomanstown Stud **Trained** Warthill, N Yorks
FOCUS
Quite a competitive class 5 sprint for the time of year and it seemed to favour those who were prominent early.

611 SUNRACING.CO.UK H'CAP 1m 5y (Tp)
6:15 (6:15) (Class 4) (0-80,82) 4-Y-O+

£6,080 (£1,809; £904; £452; £300; £300) **Stalls** Centre

Form RPR
33-1 **1** **Executive Force**[4] 526 5-9-4 **77** 6ex..............................(p) FrannyNorton 1 93+
(Michael Wigham) *trckd ldrs: smooth hdwy to ld wl over 1f out: pushed out* **1/1**[1]
-121 **2** 1 1/2 **Rey Loopy (IRE)**[14] 350 5-9-7 **80**.............................. AndrewMullen 4 92
(Ben Haslam) *t.k.h: hld up towards rr: swtchd rt and hdwy 2f out: rdn to chse wnr over 1f out: sn drvn and kpt on: no imp towards fin* **13/8**[2]
3166 **3** 6 **Pearl Spectre (USA)**[12] 392 8-8-12 **71**..............................(v) JosephineGordon 3 69
(Phil McEntee) *led: rdn along over 2f out: hdd wl over 1f out: sn drvn and kpt on one pce* **25/1**
20-6 **4** 1 1/2 **Testa Rossa (IRE)**[14] 350 9-8-7 **73**..............................(b) CoreyMadden(7) 7 68
(Jim Goldie) *trckd ldng pair: chsd ldr over 2f out: sn rdn and one pce* **11/1**
00-0 **5** 6 **Rioja Day (IRE)**[14] 350 9-7-13 **61** oh16..............................(p) JamieGormley(3) 2 42
(Jim Goldie) *trckd ldr: pushed along 3f out: rdn over 2f out: sn drvn and wknd* **100/1**
445- **6** 5 **I'm Improving (IRE)**[21] 7870 4-9-9 **82**.............................. CallumRodriguez 5 51
(Keith Dalgleish) *chsd ldrs: rdn along 3f out: sn drvn and wknd* **15/2**[3]
1m 38.34s (-0.26) **Going Correction** +0.125s/f (Slow) **6** Ran SP% **113.0**
Speed ratings (Par 105): **106,104,98,97,91 86**
CSF £2.90 TOTE £2.70: £1.10, £1.50; EX 2.80 Trifecta £17.80.
Owner Tugay Akman **Bred** Rabbah Bloodstock Limited **Trained** Newmarket, Suffolk
FOCUS
Despite the small field this was probably a fair handicap, with the front two coming clear.

612 LADBROKES HOME OF THE ODDS BOOST H'CAP 1m 5y (Tp)
6:45 (6:45) (Class 6) (0-60,61) 3-Y-O

£3,105 (£924; £461; £300; £300; £300) **Stalls** Centre

Form RPR
5-23 **1** **Macs Blessings (IRE)**[4] 537 3-9-3 **52**..............................(p) LiamKeniry 8 58
(Stef Keniry) *trckd ldrs: hdwy 2f out: rdn to chal ent fnl f: led fnl 100yds* **7/2**[1]
325- **2** 1 1/4 **Lexikon**[56] 9489 3-8-8 **46**.............................. JamieGormley(3) 10 49
(Ollie Pears) *led: pushed along 2f out: jnd and rdn over 1f out: drvn ins fnl f: hdd fnl 100yds: kpt on same pce* **13/2**
403- **3** 3/4 **Blazing Dreams (IRE)**[104] 8540 3-9-4 **53**..............................(p) PaulMulrennan 3 55
(Ben Haslam) *hld up towards rr: gd hdwy 2f out: rdn over 1f out: drvn and kpt on wl fnl f* **6/1**
0-00 **4** *hd* **Tunky**[17] 319 3-9-4 **53**.............................. CallumRodriguez 7 54
(James Given) *trckd ldrs: effrt 2f out: sn rdn: drvn and kpt on same pce fnl f* **14/1**
00-5 **5** *nk* **Robeam (IRE)**[23] 228 3-9-5 **54**..............................(p[1]) TonyHamilton 4 55
(Richard Fahey) *in tch: hdwy on outer 2f out: rdn over 1f out: drvn and chsd ldrs ins fnl f: kpt on* **9/2**[2]
30-6 **6** 2 1/4 **Fflur**[17] 319 3-9-3 **52**..............................(p[1]) PJMcDonald 12 48
(K R Burke) *sn trcking ldr: effrt wl over 2f out and sn pushed along: rdn wl over 1f out: drvn and wknd ent fnl f* **5/1**[3]
5-20 **7** 2 1/4 **Arriba De Toda (IRE)**[2] 585 3-8-6 **48**..............................(b) KieranSchofield(7) 6 39
(Brian Ellison) *trckd ldrs: pushed along and sltly outpcd 3f out: drvn along 2f out: n.d* **16/1**
00-0 **8** 3/4 **Half Full**[34] 20 3-9-5 **54**.............................. NathanEvans 11 43
(Michael Easterby) *a towards rr* **14/1**
06-0 **9** *hd* **Power Of Life (USA)**[17] 319 3-9-7 **56**.............................. LouisSteward 9 45
(Michael Bell) *nvr bttr than midfield* **11/1**
00-0 **10** 1/2 **Hurricane Speed (IRE)**[10] 437 3-8-10 **45**..............................(p) ShaneGray 1 32
(Kevin Ryan) *trckd ldng pair: effrt and cl up 3f out: rdn along over 2f out: sn drvn and wknd over 1f out (vet said gelding lost it's right hind shoe)* **33/1**
003- **11** 2 3/4 **Alfred The Grey (IRE)**[119] 8092 3-9-12 **61**.............................. CamHardie 2 42
(Tracy Waggott) *hld up: a in rr* **14/1**
040- **12** 5 **Spring To Freedom (IRE)**[152] 6980 3-9-3 **52**..............................(p[1]) DougieCostello 5 22
(Mark Walford) *towards rr: rdn along and sme hdwy on over 3f out: sn drvn and wknd* **25/1**
1m 39.55s (0.95) **Going Correction** +0.125s/f (Slow) **12** Ran SP% **125.7**
Speed ratings (Par 95): **100,98,98,97,97 95,93,92,92,91 88,83**
CSF £28.03 CT £141.10 TOTE £4.10: £1.60, £3.00, £2.50; EX 34.20 Trifecta £136.10.
Owner From The Front Racing And Stef Keniry **Bred** Miss Jill Finegan **Trained** Middleham, N Yorks
FOCUS
A maiden handicap in all but name and, while it was pretty open, it's surely only moderate form.

613 BETWAY CLASSIFIED STKS 6f (Tp)
7:15 (7:15) (Class 6) 3-Y-O+

£3,105 (£924; £461; £300; £300; £300) **Stalls** Centre

Form RPR
60-5 **1** **Picks Pinta**[5] 502 8-9-3 **43**..............................(b) RPWalsh(7) 9 53
(John David Riches) *t.k.h early: hld up and bhd: swtchd markedly rt 2f out: rdn and str run nr stands' rails ent fnl f: kpt on wl to ld fnl 50yds* **4/1**[1]
0-00 **2** *nk* **Star Cracker (IRE)**[28] 129 7-9-10 **49**..............................(p) PJMcDonald 6 52
(Jim Goldie) *led 1f: trckd ldr: cl up 2f out: rdn to ld over 1f out: drvn ins fnl f: hdd and no ex fnl 50yds* **9/2**[2]
0-63 **3** *hd* **Tellovoi (IRE)**[12] 379 11-9-10 **49**..............................(p) PhilipPrince 1 52
(Richard Guest) *dwlt: sn chsng ldrs: led after 1f: rdn along 2f out: hdd over 1f out: drvn and rallied ins fnl f: kpt on wl towards fin* **6/1**[3]
0460 **4** *nk* **Malaysian Boleh**[6] 478 9-9-3 **45**..............................(be) GraceMcEntee(7) 5 51
(Phil McEntee) *t.k.h early: chsd ldrs: hdwy 2f out: rdn ent fnl f: kpt on same pce towards fin* **8/1**
-056 **5** *hd* **Moonbi Creek (IRE)**[4] 530 12-9-10 **44**.............................. CallumRodriguez 2 50
(Stella Barclay) *dwlt and towards rr: hdwy over 2f out: rdn to chse ldrs over 1f out: styd on fnl f* **16/1**
00-0 **6** 2 1/4 **My Girl Maisie (IRE)**[3] 553 5-9-5 **50**.............................. SebastianWoods(5) 8 43
(Richard Guest) *hld up towards rr: hdwy 2f out: rdn and ch ent fnl f: sn drvn and wknd and kpt on same pce* **20/1**
630- **7** *nse* **First Breath**[46] 9659 4-9-10 **44**..............................(p[1]) AndrewMullen 4 43
(Ben Haslam) *chsd ldrs: rdn along over 2f out: sn wknd* **6/1**[3]
-650 **8** 1 **Windforpower (IRE)**[19] 279 9-9-10 **48**..............................(p) BarryMcHugh 11 40+
(Tracy Waggott) *chsd ldrs: rdn along 2f out: sn wknd* **4/1**[1]
06-0 **9** 1 **Henrietta's Dream**[26] 159 5-9-10 **40**..............................(b) ShaneGray 7 37
(John Wainwright) *chsd ldrs: rdn along over 2f out: sn wknd* **33/1**
0- **10** 1 1/2 **Sokudo (IRE)**[25] 195 3-8-4 **43**..............................(b) AndrewBreslin(5) 10 29
(Madeleine Tylicki, Ire) *a towards rr* **8/1**
1m 12.5s **Going Correction** +0.125s/f (Slow)
WFA 3 from 4yo+ 15lb **10** Ran SP% **122.6**
Speed ratings (Par 101): **105,104,104,103,103 100,100,99,97,95**
CSF £23.28 TOTE £5.50: £2.10, £1.70, £2.10; EX 27.70 Trifecta £142.60.
Owner J R Racing **Bred** Heatherwold Stud **Trained** Pilling, Lancashire
FOCUS
A poor classified event closed the card. As betting suggested, it was wide open and there was a bunched finish.
T/Jkpt: Not Won. T/Plt: £178.20 to a £1 stake. Pool: £106,828.68 - 437.42 winning units T/Qpdt: £24.30 to a £1 stake. Pool: £18,321.94 - 557.32 winning units **Joe Rowntree**

553 KEMPTON (A.W) (R-H)
Wednesday, February 6

OFFICIAL GOING: Polytrack: standard to slow
Wind: Nil Weather: Mild

614 MOVE OVER TO MATCHBOOK H'CAP 1m (P)
1:50 (1:50) (Class 6) (0-65,66) 3-Y-O

£3,105 (£924; £461; £300; £300; £300) **Stalls** Low

Form RPR
0-41 **1** **Sir Ox (USA)**[12] 400 3-9-4 **61**..............................(p) LukeMorris 5 68+
(Robert Cowell) *bhd ldr: shkn up over 2f out: rdn 2f out: led over 1f out: briefly pressed ent fnl f: asserted sn after: eased cl home: comf* **2/1**[1]
55-4 **2** 2 **Picture Poet (IRE)**[20] 274 3-9-4 **61**.............................. DavidProbert 2 63
(Henry Spiller) *cl up bhd ldrs on inner: rdn 2f out: styd on to take 2nd wl ins fnl f but no ch w wnr* **8/1**
-510 **3** 1 3/4 **Um Shama (IRE)**[9] 461 3-9-0 **64**.............................. LauraCoughlan(7) 6 62
(David Loughnane) *racd in mid-div: rdn wdst over 2f out: stuck on and briefly chal over 1f out: one pce sn after and lost 2nd wl ins fnl f (vet said filly lost it's right hind shoe)* **12/1**
4-34 **4** *shd* **Lieutenant Conde**[4] 561 3-9-7 **64**.............................. CharlieBennett 1 62
(Hughie Morrison) *hld up in rr-div: rdn 2f out: outpcd over 1f out w a bit to do: styd on ins fnl f to take 4th* **11/2**[3]
06-3 **5** 1/2 **Biz Markee (IRE)**[34] 32 3-9-9 **66**..............................(p[1]) OisinMurphy 3 64
(Hugo Palmer) *racd in last pair on inner: shkn up 2f out: effrt wl over 1f w a plenty to do: gd prog ins fnl f being shuffled along: nvr nrr* **5/2**[2]
00-0 **6** *hd* **Iris's Spirit**[32] 79 3-8-2 **45**.............................. FrannyNorton 7 42
(Tony Carroll) *bhd ldr on outer: effrt over 2f out and outpcd: plugged on fr over 1f out* **33/1**
604- **7** 4 **Maared (IRE)**[104] 8575 3-9-6 **63**..............................(p) KieranO'Neill 11 50
(Luke McJannet) *w ldr: rdn over 2f out: no ex over 1f out and wknd* **33/1**
04-0 **8** 5 **Uponastar (IRE)**[26] 174 3-9-1 **58**..............................(p[1]) NicolaCurrie 10 34
(Amy Murphy) *led at stdy pce: rdn over 2f out: hdd over 1f out and wknd qckly ent fnl f* **100/1**

400- 9 139 **Gabrial The Giant (IRE)**[119] 8109 3-9-9 **66**................ StevieDonohoe 9 +
(Ian Williams) *hld up in last: bdly hmpd by faller wl over 3f out and eased: virtually plld: t.o (jockey said gelding suffered interference rounding the bend)* **25/1**

50-6 F **Beehaar**[13] 380 3-9-3 **60**..(p[1]) RobertHavlin 8 +
(John Gosden) *t.k.h in last trio: clipped heels wl over 3f out and fell: fatally injured* **12/1**

1m 41.67s (1.87) **Going Correction** +0.10s/f (Slow) **10** Ran SP% **114.5**
Speed ratings (Par 95): **94,92,90,90,89 89,85,80, ,**
CSF £17.86 CT £152.17 TOTE £2.80: £1.20, £2.30, £3.50; EX 17.10 Trifecta £125.10.
Owner Khalifa Dasmal **Bred** Machmer Hall **Trained** Six Mile Bottom, Cambs
■ Stewards' Enquiry : Charlie Bennett 12-day ban; careless riding (Feb 20-23,25-28,Mar 1-2,4-5)

FOCUS
This handicap was marred by a nasty incident on the bend.

615 MATCHBOOK TIME TO MOVE OVER NOVICE STKS 1m (P)
2:20 (2:37) (Class 5) 3-Y-O **£3,881** (£1,155; £577; £288) **Stalls** Low

Form RPR

1 **Don Jupp (USA)** 3-9-2 0.. DanielMuscutt 1 78+
(Marco Botti) *bhd ldr and a travelling best: shkn up wl over 1f out: smooth prog and rdn to ld 1f out: sn in control: easily* **6/4**[1]

6-5 2 2 **Gold Fleece**[14] 370 3-8-11 0.................................. JosephineGordon 7 67
(Hugo Palmer) *w narrow ldr on outer: rdn over 2f out: led 2f out: hdd 1f out: styd on* **6/1**[2]

0-0 3 3 ½ **Wan Chai (USA)**[21] 251 3-8-11 0.............................. OisinMurphy 5 59
(Ralph Beckett) *bhd ldrs on outer: effrt 2f out: shuffled along fr over 1f out to hold 3rd* **16/1**

0-0 4 ¾ **Moonlit Sea**[14] 358 3-9-2 0.. AdamKirby 8 62
(James Tate) *t.k.h in mid-div on outer: settled bttr in rr-div at 1/2-way: rdn 2f out: gd prog tl 1f out: shuffled along after* **6/1**[2]

0 5 3 ¼ **Percy Alexander**[21] 251 3-9-2 0.................................. LukeMorris 3 54
(James Tate) *sn narrow ldr: rdn 3f out to hold pl: hdd 2f out: plugged on* **13/2**[3]

0- 6 shd **Tavus (IRE)**[77] 9171 3-9-2 0.................................. AdamMcNamara 6 54
(Roger Charlton) *racd in last pair of gp: shkn up over 2f out: pushed out fr over 1f out: styd on wl fnl f (jockey said gelding ran green)* **8/1**

7 ½ **Poor Auld Paddy** 3-9-2 0.. DavidProbert 4 53
(David Elsworth) *in rr of gp and rn green: plenty to do at 1/2-way: styd on fr 2f out* **8/1**

00- 8 ¾ **Pinctada**[259] 2983 3-8-11 0...................................... KieranO'Neill 9 46
(John Bridger) *racd in mid-div: effrt over 2f out: nt qckn and fdd* **150/1**

9 45 **Carriageway** 3-8-11 0.. NicolaCurrie 2
(Jonathan Portman) *missed break and sn detached in rr: nvr raised a gallop: t.o (jockey said filly ran green and was never travelling)* **33/1**

1m 40.85s (1.05) **Going Correction** +0.10s/f (Slow) **9** Ran SP% **113.6**
Speed ratings (Par 97): **98,96,92,91,88 88,87,87,42**
CSF £10.53 TOTE £2.40: £1.40, £1.70, £3.80; EX 10.40 Trifecta £101.20.
Owner Gute Freunde Partnership **Bred** Tenth Street Stables **Trained** Newmarket, Suffolk

FOCUS
A modest novice, but won in smooth fashion.

616 MATCHBOOK VIP FILLIES' H'CAP 1m 2f 219y(P)
2:55 (3:02) (Class 5) (0-70,70) 4-Y-O+
£3,752 (£1,116; £557; £300; £300; £300) **Stalls** Low

Form RPR

54-5 1 **Voi**[18] 310 5-9-6 **69**..(t) MartinDwyer 1 77
(Conrad Allen) *niggled along leaving stalls: hld up towards rr: travelling wl and briefly ct on heels over 2f out: swtchd to inner and rdn 2f out: gd prog and led 1f out: edgd lft whn strly pressed fnl 110yds: on top cl home* **4/1**[2]

1-52 2 ¾ **Magic Mirror**[14] 364 6-9-6 **69**.................................(p) AdamKirby 10 76
(Mark Rimell) *hld up in rr-div on outer: shkn up over 2f out: smooth prog wl over 1f out: rdn over 1f out: chal fnl 110yds: no ex last strides* **11/4**[1]

-030 3 1 **Highway One (USA)**[19] 295 5-8-12 **61**............................ LiamKeniry 2 66
(George Baker) *early ldr: sn hld up bhd ldrs on inner: effrt 2f out: rdn over 1f out and ev ch: one pce fnl 110yds* **6/1**

25-5 4 1 ¾ **Power Home (IRE)**[32] 85 5-8-9 **58**............................ OisinMurphy 8 61
(Denis Coakley) *bhd ldr: sltly hmpd 1/2-way: rdn 2f out: styd on wl and briefly led ent fnl f: kpt on* **5/1**[3]

203- 5 2 ½ **Chantresse (IRE)**[113] 8309 4-9-3 **67**......................(p[1]) DavidProbert 7 65
(Mark Usher) *racd in mid-div: rdn wl over 2f out: kpt on one pce fr over 1f out* **10/1**

452- 6 nse **Alacritas**[55] 9526 4-8-9 **59**...................................... LukeMorris 11 57
(David Simcock) *hld up in rr: effrt on outer over 2f out: nt qckn tl styd on wl ins fnl f* **16/1**

10-4 7 2 **Lulu Star (IRE)**[9] 459 4-8-6 **56**............................. ShelleyBirkett 3 50
(Julia Feilden) *sn led: jinked lft at 1/2-way: rdn over 2f out: stuck on wl tl hdd ent fnl f: wknd qckly after* **16/1**

00-0 8 hd **Blame Me Forever (USA)**[12] 404 4-9-6 **70**.................. RossaRyan 6 64
(Don Cantillon) *awkward s: in last: rdn wl over 3f out: no ex 2f out* **16/1**

0-03 9 nse **Cash N Carrie (IRE)**[9] 459 5-8-7 **56** oh2...................(p) NicolaCurrie 4 50
(Michael Appleby) *racd in mid-div: niggled along on bnd over 4f out: effrt over 2f out: nt qckn (jockey said mare was unsuited by the slow early pace)* **16/1**

13-4 10 ¾ **Princess Harley (IRE)**[27] 162 4-9-3 **67**..................(p[1]) FrannyNorton 9 60
(Mick Quinn) *plld hrd thrght: sn bhd ldrs: pressed ldr wl over 3f out: rdn 2f out: wknd over 1f out* **10/1**

2m 23.02s (2.02) **Going Correction** +0.10s/f (Slow)
WFA 4 from 5yo+ 1lb **10** Ran SP% **119.3**
Speed ratings (Par 100): **99,98,97,96,94 94,93,93,92,92**
CSF £15.83 CT £66.51 TOTE £4.80: £1.40, £1.70, £3.20; EX 21.30 Trifecta £146.70.
Owner B Homewood & Partners **Bred** Al Asayl Bloodstock Ltd **Trained** Newmarket, Suffolk
■ Stewards' Enquiry : Martin Dwyer four-day ban; careless riding (Feb 20-23)

FOCUS
This played into the hands of those ridden off the pace.

617 MATCHBOOK CASINO H'CAP (LONDON MIDDLE DISTANCE QUALIFIER) 1m 2f 219y(P)
3:25 (3:30) (Class 4) (0-85,86) 4-Y-O+
£6,469 (£1,925; £962; £481; £300; £300) **Stalls** Low

Form RPR

04-2 1 **Technological**[16] 345 4-9-6 **84**................................... OisinMurphy 3 94+
(George Margarson) *bhd ldr: drvn to ld over 1f out: rdn 1f out and wandered bdly (rt: then lft): corrected and hrd drvn fnl 100yds: jst hld on* **9/4**[1]

110- 2 nse **Red Force One**[158] 6810 4-9-3 **86**.......................(p w) MeganNicholls(5) 2 95
(Paul Nicholls) *led: rdn 2f out: hdd over 1f out: edgd lft appr fnl f: kpt on wl fnl f edging rt and jst failed (jockey said gelding hung left-handed throughout)* **5/1**[3]

516- 3 4 ½ **Villette (IRE)**[46] 9685 5-9-9 **86**.................................. AdamKirby 8 86
(Dean Ivory) *mid-div on outer: effrt out wd over 2f out: kpt on wl fr over 1f out but no match for ldng pair* **5/1**[3]

146/ 4 1 **Jodies Jem**[568] 2819 9-9-5 **82**...................................... LiamKeniry 1 81
(Stuart Edmunds) *mid-div on inner: rdn 2f out: plugged on over 1f out* **50/1**

/14- 5 ½ **Galactic Spirit**[278] 2390 4-9-0 **78**............................ DanielMuscutt 9 77
(Marco Botti) *bhd ldr: rdn 2f out: outpcd and no ex over 1f out* **10/1**

63-3 6 1 **Wimpole Hall**[26] 184 6-9-4 **81**..............................(p) DavidProbert 4 77
(William Jarvis) *in rr and t.k.h at times: effrt 2f out: no room on heels over 1f out an eased tl wl ins fnl f: nvr involved (jockey said gelding was denied a clear run)* **9/2**[2]

33-4 7 1 ½ **Kaser (IRE)**[16] 345 4-9-0 **78**..............................(t[1]) EdwardGreatrex 7 73
(David Loughnane) *a toward rr: effrt 2f out: no imp over 1f out* **9/1**

32-3 8 3 **Thaqaffa (IRE)**[16] 345 6-9-4 **81**............................(h) TomQueally 6 69
(Amy Murphy) *cl up in mid-div: rdn 2f out: ch over 1f out: fdd sn after* **14/1**

/0-5 9 2 ¾ **Gawdawpalin (IRE)**[16] 345 6-9-2 **82**...................... GaryMahon(3) 5 66
(Sylvester Kirk) *missed break and a in rr: effrt 2f out: no ex over 1f out* **20/1**

2m 21.33s (0.33) **Going Correction** +0.10s/f (Slow)
WFA 4 from 5yo+ 1lb **9** Ran SP% **114.8**
Speed ratings (Par 105): **106,105,102,101,101 100,99,97,95**
CSF £13.40 CT £50.23 TOTE £3.50: £1.40, £1.70, £2.10; EX 12.90 Trifecta £45.70.
Owner Abdulla Al Mansoori **Bred** Stephen K Isaac **Trained** Newmarket, Suffolk

FOCUS
This was steadily run and the first two were prominent throughout.

618 MATCHBOOK BETTING PODCAST H'CAP 7f (P)
4:00 (4:00) (Class 4) (0-85,86) 4-Y-O+
£6,469 (£1,925; £962; £481; £300; £300) **Stalls** Low

Form RPR

/0-5 1 **Fuwairt (IRE)**[31] 104 7-8-13 **78**......................... CameronNoble(5) 1 84+
(David Loughnane) *hld up in last: shkn up 2f out and smooth prog on outer: rdn over 1f out and led wl ins fnl f: hld on last strides (trainers' rep said, reg app imp in form, gelding benefitted from more cover on this occasion)* **5/1**[3]

13-3 2 hd **Roman Spinner**[32] 81 4-9-5 **79**..............................(t) LukeMorris 4 84
(Rae Guest) *racd in 5th: rdn 2f out: n.m.r over 1f out and swtchd to outer ent fnl f: kpt on wl and gaining w each stride fnl 75yds: jst failed* **11/4**[1]

45-0 3 1 ½ **Smokey Lane (IRE)**[21] 260 5-9-7 **81**.....................(b[1]) OisinMurphy 2 82
(Sam Thomas) *sn led: rdn 2f out: outpcd and hdd over 1f out: styd on again fnl f to take 3rd nr fin (jockey said gelding hung left-handed throughout)* **8/1**

31-2 4 hd **Enthaar**[27] 158 4-9-1 **75**......................................(t) RossaRyan 6 75
(Stuart Williams) *bhd ldr on inner: rdn 2f out: led over 1f out: hdd ins fnl f: wknd qckly last 100yds* **11/4**[1]

3-10 5 2 ¼ **Florencio**[11] 441 6-9-12 **86**.............................(p) DougieCostello 5 80
(Jamie Osborne) *racd in 4th: rdn 2f out on inner: outpcd over 1f out: one pce fnl f* **6/1**

31-6 6 1 ¾ **Kyllachy Dragon (IRE)**[34] 44 4-9-4 **78**.................(h) DavidProbert 3 68
(Ronald Harris) *w ldr on outer: rdn 2f out: outpcd over 1f out: plugged on (jockey said gelding stopped quickly)* **4/1**[2]

1m 25.34s (-0.66) **Going Correction** +0.10s/f (Slow) **6** Ran SP% **115.4**
Speed ratings (Par 105): **107,106,105,104,102 100**
CSF £19.78 TOTE £7.10: £4.00, £1.80; EX 21.40 Trifecta £125.20.
Owner Lowe, Lewis And Hoyland **Bred** Tommy Burns **Trained** Tern Hill, Shropshire

FOCUS
This was run at a good pace and suited those held up.

619 MATCHBOOK BEST VALUE EXCHANGE H'CAP 1m 7f 218y(P)
4:30 (4:30) (Class 6) (0-65,66) 4-Y-O+
£3,105 (£924; £461; £300; £300; £300) **Stalls** Low

Form RPR

553- 1 **Atomic Jack**[141] 7388 4-9-4 **61**.................................... NicolaCurrie 5 69+
(George Baker) *bhd ldr on inner: smooth prog over 2f out: rdn to ld 2f out: styd on wl fnl f* **5/2**[1]

035- 2 2 **Tin Fandango**[69] 9310 4-9-4 **61**......................(p) JosephineGordon 9 66
(Mark Usher) *led: rdn over 2f out: hdd 2f out: stuck on wl fr over 1f out but no match w wnr* **12/1**

136- 3 2 ¼ **The Detainee**[167] 5977 6-9-12 **65**..........................(p) AdamKirby 2 65
(Neil Mulholland) *bhd ldr: rdn over 2f out: kpt on* **16/1**

00-0 4 ¾ **Butterfield (IRE)**[32] 85 6-9-7 **60**.............................. FrannyNorton 7 59
(Tony Carroll) *racd in mid-div: rdn over 2f out: styd on fr over 1f out: no imp on plcd horses* **14/1**

04-1 5 ½ **Casa Comigo (IRE)**[14] 369 4-8-12 **55**.......................... KierenFox 13 55+
(John Best) *racd in mid-div: gng okay whn swtchd out and rdn over 2f out: stuck on fr over 1f out* **11/4**[2]

35-4 6 1 **Queen Of Paris**[21] 262 4-9-8 **65**............................ DavidProbert 12 64
(William Knight) *hld up in rr: rdn over 2f out: kpt on* **7/1**[3]

035- 7 shd **Crindle Carr (IRE)**[47] 9657 5-8-12 **51**..................(b) DanielMuscutt 10 48
(John Flint) *w ldrs: effrt over 2f out: plugged on* **25/1**

10/6 8 1 ¼ **Regal Gait (IRE)**[34] 38 6-9-3 **63**........................ LeviWilliams(7) 4 59
(Simon Dow) *in rr: swtchd to outer and rdn wl over 2f out: kpt on w plenty to do fr over 1f out: nvr nrr* **16/1**

020- 9 6 **Betsalottie**[22] 9407 6-9-6 **59**..............................(p) KieranO'Neill 11 47
(John Bridger) *bhd ldr: rdn over 3f out: one pce 2f out* **33/1**

55-4 10 5 **Masters Apprentice (IRE)**[13] 385 4-9-3 **63**.................. GaryMahon(3) 6 47
(Sylvester Kirk) *hld up in rr: rdn 2f out: one pce fr over 1f out* **8/1**

000- 11 4 ½ **Art Of Swing (IRE)**[46] 9687 7-9-7 **60**............................ LiamKeniry 14 37
(Lee Carter) *a towards rr* **100/1**

0-24 12 nk **Rare (IRE)**[9] 457 4-9-9 **66**.. OisinMurphy 8 45
(Archie Watson) *w ldr: rdn 3f out: struggling 2f out: no ex sn after and eased* **10/1**

0/0- 13 5 **Tsundoku (IRE)**[39] 9751 8-8-12 **51**............................ HectorCrouch 3 22
(Alexandra Dunn) *a towards rr* **66/1**

3m 32.94s (2.84) **Going Correction** +0.10s/f (Slow)
WFA 4 from 5yo+ 4lb **13** Ran SP% **123.3**
Speed ratings (Par 101): **96,95,93,93,93 92,92,92,89,86 84,84,81**
CSF £34.50 CT £418.85 TOTE £3.60: £1.20, £3.90, £4.20; EX 38.50 Trifecta £400.50.
Owner George Baker And Partners - Super Six **Bred** Newsells Park Stud **Trained** Chiddingfold, Surrey

FOCUS
No great pace on here and the first four raced on the rail most of the way, switching positions slightly.
T/Jkpt: Not Won. T/Plt: £34.30 to a £1 stake. Pool: £66,976.28 - 1421.45 winning units T/Qpdt: £17.30 to a 31 stake. Pool: £7,027.42 - 299.40 winning units **Cathal Gahan**

599 WOLVERHAMPTON (A.W) (L-H)
Wednesday, February 6

OFFICIAL GOING: Tapeta: standard to slow
Wind: moderate across Weather: dry

620 LADBROKES HOME OF THE ODDS BOOST H'CAP — 6f 20y (Tp)
5:10 (5:10) (Class 6) (0-65,67) 3-Y-O
£3,105 (£924; £461; £400; £400; £400) Stalls Low

Form RPR
0-10 1 **Deconso**12 406 3-8-6 50 HollieDoyle 5 57
(Christopher Kellett) *a.p: led 2f out: sn clr: rdn ins fnl f: kpt on wl (trainer could offer no explanation for the app imp in form)* 8/1
362- 2 1 3/4 **Eye Of The Water (IRE)**55 9521 3-8-8 52 PaddyMathers 9 54
(Ronald Harris) *mid-div: hdwy over 2f out: rdn in 4th over 1f out: kpt on ins fnl f: wnt 2nd towards fin* 7/2[1]
-265 3 3/4 **Not So Shy**2 605 3-8-12 56 EoinWalsh 7 56
(David Evans) *racd keenly: prom: trckd ldrs 3f out: rdn over 1f out: kpt on ins fnl f but nt pce to threaten: lost 2nd towards fin* 11/1
6-04 4 1 **Wye Bother (IRE)**23 235 3-8-2 46 oh1 (t[1]) RaulDaSilva 1 43
(Milton Bradley) *led: rdn and hdd 2f out: no ex ins fnl f* 16/1
-252 5 shd **Ever Rock (IRE)**12 402 3-8-6 50 JoeyHaynes 4 46
(J S Moore) *hld up: hdwy 2f out: sn rdn: kpt on same pce fnl f* 13/2[3]
46-3 6 3/4 **Madame Vitesse (FR)**25 215 3-9-0 63 SebastianWoods(5) 10 59
(Richard Fahey) *hld up in mid-div: snatched up whn tight for room ent st: no ch after but kpt on fnl f* 15/2
0-12 7 1/2 **Lincoln Spirit**11 437 3-8-11 55 ShaneGray 2 49
(David O'Meara) *mid-div: lost pl after 2f: towards rr: hdwy over 1f out: one pce fnl f (jockey said filly was never travelling)* 8/1
3-0U 8 2 3/4 **Pleasant Gesture (IRE)**12 401 3-9-0 65 AaronMackay(7) 3 49
(J S Moore) *mid-div: rdn over 2f out: wknd fnl f (vet said filly lost it's right hind shoe)* 18/1
66-5 9 hd **Hua Hin (IRE)**14 360 3-8-12 63 (t) ThoreHammerHansen(7) 6 47
(Richard Hannon) *sn outpcd in rr: nvr on terms (jockey said colt was never travelling)* 4/1[2]
000- 10 1 **Awa Bomba**103 8592 3-9-1 59 GeorgeDowning 12 40
(Tony Carroll) *s.i.s: bhd: midfield after 2f: sn hung lft: lost pl coming wd ent st: no threat after (jockey said gelding hung left-handed)* 18/1
00-0 11 4 **Dancing Jaquetta (IRE)**11 437 3-8-3 47 LiamJones 11 16
(Mark Loughnane) *trckd ldrs: rdn over 2f out: sn lost pl: wknd over 1f out* 80/1

1m 15.28s (0.78) **Going Correction** +0.025s/f (Slow) 11 Ran SP% **115.5**
Speed ratings (Par 95): **95,92,91,90,90 89,88,84,84,83 77**
CSF £35.42 CT £312.15 TOTE £10.90: £2.90, £1.40, £3.10; EX 47.40 Trifecta £359.90.
Owner Andy Bell & Fergus Lyons **Bred** Llety Farms **Trained** Lathom, Lancs
■ Stewards' Enquiry : Liam Jones two-day ban; careless riding (Feb 20-21)

FOCUS
A moderate 3yo sprint handicap, rated around the runner-up.

621 BETWAY NOVICE MEDIAN AUCTION STKS — 6f 20y (Tp)
5:45 (5:45) (Class 6) 3-4-Y-O £3,105 (£924; £461; £230) Stalls Low

Form RPR
-6 1 **Major Blue**18 313 3-8-13 0 HollieDoyle 7 64+
(James Eustace) *trckd ldrs: led ent fnl f: kpt on wl: pushed out* 3/1[2]
- 2 nk **Empty Promises** 3-8-10 0 FinleyMarsh(3) 8 63+
(Frank Bishop) *broke wl: stdd into last trio after 1f: hdwy 2f out: rdn to chse ldrs over 1f out: edging lft but r.o ins fnl f: hld cl home (jockey said colt hung left-handed round the bend)* 40/1
01- 3 1 **Phoenix Star (IRE)**238 3754 3-9-6 0 GeorgeWood 2 67
(Amy Murphy) *racd keenly: prom: led over 2f out: rdn over 1f out: hdd ent fnl f: no ex fnl 120yds (jockey said colt ran too freely)* 9/2[3]
4 2 1/4 **Rakastava (IRE)** 3-8-13 0 CallumShepherd 4 55+
(Mick Channon) *s.i.s: in last pair: in tch travelling wl 3f out: nt clr run on heels of ldrs turning in: shkn up over 1f out: nt qckn* 8/11[1]
50-0 5 1 3/4 **Lambrini Lullaby**30 117 4-9-9 36 CamHardie 3 47
(Lisa Williamson) *stdd s: in last pair: nt clr run whn making prog 2f out: sn rdn: one pce fnl f* 80/1
6 9 **Killer Queen** 4-9-6 0 PhilDennis(3) 1 20
(David C Griffiths) *narrow advantage tl rdn over 2f out: wknd over 1f out* 16/1
0-0 7 5 **Hilbre Lake (USA)**33 66 3-8-6 0 (b[1]) SeamusCronin(7) 6
(Lisa Williamson) *prom: hung rt and lost pl turning in: sn wknd* 66/1

1m 15.54s (1.04) **Going Correction** +0.025s/f (Slow) 7 Ran SP% **112.1**
WFA 3 from 4yo 15lb
Speed ratings (Par 101): **94,93,92,89,86 74,68**
CSF £82.39 TOTE £4.50: £1.80, £11.70; EX 112.70 Trifecta £642.20.
Owner J C Smith **Bred** Littleton Stud **Trained** Newmarket, Suffolk

FOCUS
This novice has been rated cautiously to begin with, as the time was ordinary and the fifth anchors the form.

622 BETWAY HEED YOUR HUNCH H'CAP — 1m 5f 219y (Tp)
6:15 (6:15) (Class 5) (0-75,80) 4-Y-O+ £3,752 (£1,116; £557; £400; £400) Stalls Low

Form RPR
23-3 1 **Tommy Docc (IRE)**8 469 7-9-11 73 (v[1]) CallumRodriguez 6 81
(Keith Dalgleish) *trckd ldrs: chal ins fnl 3f: led jst over 2f out: styd on wl: rdn out* 10/3[2]
10-5 2 1 1/4 **Spiritual Man (IRE)**32 84 7-9-4 66 HollieDoyle 4 71
(Jonjo O'Neill) *racd keenly: hld up last but in tch: hdwy over 2f out: rdn over 1f out: styd on to chse wnr jst ins fnl f: nt pce to chal* 5/1
316- 3 2 1/4 **True Destiny**69 9310 4-8-13 64 (bt w) AdamMcNamara 5 66
(Roger Charlton) *trckd ldrs: rdn 2f out: sn chsng wnr: lost 2nd jst ins fnl f: kpt on same pce* 4/1[3]
0-31 4 2 1/2 **Noble Expression**8 469 4-10-1 80 6ex (p) CharlieBennett 2 79
(Jim Boyle) *prom: led jst over 3f out: rdn and hdd jst over 2f out: sn hld: wknd fnl f (jockey said gelding ran flat)* 11/10[1]
2-00 5 3 1/4 **Sellingallthetime (IRE)**16 346 8-8-10 63 (p) TheodoreLadd(5) 1 57
(Michael Appleby) *led tl jst over 3f out: sn rdn: wknd over 1f out* 20/1

3m 5.26s (4.26) **Going Correction** +0.025s/f (Slow)
WFA 4 from 7yo+ 3lb 5 Ran SP% **112.1**
Speed ratings (Par 103): **88,87,86,84,82**
CSF £19.58 TOTE £3.70: £2.00, £2.80; EX 17.50 Trifecta £48.80.
Owner Ronnie Docherty **Bred** Gerry O'Brien **Trained** Carluke, S Lanarks
■ Stewards' Enquiry : Callum Rodriguez two-day ban; misuse of whip (Feb 20-21)

FOCUS
A modest little staying handicap. The winner earned his best figure since early last year.

623 SUNRACING.CO.UK H'CAP — 7f 36y (Tp)
6:45 (6:45) (Class 3) (0-95,94) 4-Y-O- £7,246 (£2,168; £1,084; £542; £270) Stalls High

Form RPR
561- 1 **Documenting**37 9772 6-9-3 90 JasonHart 7 107
(Kevin Frost) *hld up bhd ldrs off str pce: c wd turning in and gd hdwy: led on bridle jst over 1f out: sauntered clr: impressive* 5/2[2]
224- 2 7 **Sha La La La Lee**202 5129 4-8-12 85 RichardKingscote 1 83
(Tom Dascombe) *set str pce: rdn and hdd jst over 1f out: sn no ch w v easy wnr* 2/1[1]
42-4 3 3 1/2 **Mr Top Hat**27 164 4-8-12 90 (v[1]) KatherineBegley(5) 5 79
(David Evans) *prom: hanging sltly rt over 2f out: sn rdn: kpt on same pce fr over 1f out (jockey said gelding hung right-handed off the final bend)* 15/2
04-6 4 hd **Mickey (IRE)**26 176 6-8-11 87 (v) JaneElliott(3) 2 75
(Tom Dascombe) *trckd ldrs: rdn 2f out: sn one pce* 11/1
5-23 5 2 3/4 **Areen Heart (FR)**15 351 5-9-2 89 (h) JoeFanning 4 70
(David O'Meara) *racd keenly trcking ldrs: rdn 2f out: nt pce to chal: wknd ins fnl f* 4/1[3]
3-03 6 2 1/4 **Critical Thinking (IRE)**21 260 5-8-0 80 oh4 (tp) LauraCoughlan(7) 6 55
(David Loughnane) *sn outpcd: nvr on terms* 20/1

1m 26.71s (-2.09) **Going Correction** +0.025s/f (Slow) 6 Ran SP% **106.8**
Speed ratings (Par 107): **112,104,100,99,96 94**
CSF £7.07 TOTE £6.00: £2.30, £1.10; EX 8.80 Trifecta £32.40.
Owner Kevin Frost Racing Club & M A Humphreys **Bred** Millsec Limited **Trained** Newcastle-under-Lyme, Staffs

FOCUS
This feature handicap was run at a decent pace, and improved form from the impressive winner.

624 FOLLOW TOP TIPSTER TEMPLEGATE AT SUN RACING H'CAP — 1m 142y (Tp)
7:15 (7:15) (Class 6) (0-55,56) 4-Y-O+
£3,105 (£924; £461; £400; £400; £400) Stalls Low

Form RPR
0-51 1 **Zorawar (FR)**5 532 5-9-8 56 6ex ShaneGray 8 66
(David O'Meara) *travelled wl: trckd ldrs: led gng best ent fnl f: pushed clr: comf* 1/1[1]
0-42 2 2 1/4 **Sea Shack**7 479 5-8-13 54 (tp) ScottMcCullagh(7) 11 57
(Julia Feilden) *led: strly pressed fr over 2f out: sn rdn: hdd ent fnl f: kpt on but nt pce of wnr* 6/1[2]
06-0 3 nk **Benaras (USA)**25 210 4-8-12 46 HollieDoyle 4 48
(Roger Fell) *trckd ldrs: chal over 2f out: rdn and ev ch ent fnl f: kpt on but nt pce of wnr* 50/1
200- 4 nk **Compass Point**135 7619 4-9-8 56 AndrewMullen 5 58
(Robyn Brisland) *trckd ldrs: rdn 2f out: kpt on same pce* 12/1
1324 5 nk **Amor Fati (IRE)**8 465 4-8-12 51 KatherineBegley(5) 1 52
(David Evans) *mid-div: rdn 2f out: kpt on on fnl f but nt pce to get involved* 13/2[3]
2-05 6 1/2 **Jeremy's Jet (IRE)**7 485 8-9-1 49 (t) RichardKingscote 2 49
(Tony Carroll) *hld up in last trio: rdn 2f out: little imp tl r.o ins fnl f* 13/2[3]
04-1 7 shd **Miss Bates**20 273 5-9-7 55 JoeFanning 7 55+
(Ann Duffield) *s.i.s: last: hdwy over 1f out but hanging lft: r.o fnl f nt clrest of runs fnl 100yds (jockey said mare hung left-handed in the home straight)* 9/1
6-02 8 3 **Lord Murphy (IRE)**9 462 6-9-6 54 (tp) LiamJones 9 48+
(Mark Loughnane) *a towards rr* 14/1
400- 9 17 **Emigrated (IRE)**77 9180 6-9-0 48 (vt) PaddyMathers 6 6
(Derek Shaw) *racd keenly in midfield: effrt over 2f out: wknd wl over 1f out* 40/1

1m 50.17s (0.07) **Going Correction** +0.025s/f (Slow) 9 Ran SP% **119.7**
Speed ratings (Par 101): **100,98,97,97,97 96,96,94,78**
CSF £7.86 CT £193.22 TOTE £1.60: £1.10, £2.80, £6.30; EX 9.80 Trifecta £359.90.
Owner Evan M Sutherland **Bred** S C H H The Aga Khan's Studs **Trained** Upper Helmsley, N Yorks

FOCUS
They went a solid pace in this weak handicap. The balance of the second, third and fourth sets the level behind the winner.

625 BETWAY CASINO H'CAP — 1m 1f 104y (Tp)
7:45 (7:45) (Class 4) (0-85,85) 4-Y-O+ £5,530 (£1,645; £822; £411; £400) Stalls Low

Form RPR
4-42 1 **Dragon Mall (USA)**23 240 6-9-7 85 (t) StevieDonohoe 3 96
(Rebecca Menzies) *awkwardly away: last: tk str hold and hdwy to trck ldrs over 5f out: rdn to ld ent fnl f: drifted lft: r.o strly: readily* 11/2[3]
32-1 2 3 1/2 **Star Of Southwold (FR)**27 157 4-9-7 85 LukeMorris 2 89
(Michael Appleby) *prom early: trckd ldrs 1/2-way: pushed along over 3f out: rdn 2f out: ev ch briefly ent fnl f: kpt on but nt pce of wnr* 2/1[1]
46-4 3 1 **Guvenor's Choice (IRE)**32 87 4-9-4 82 (t) CliffordLee 5 84
(K R Burke) *led: rdn over 1f out: hdd ent fnl f: no ex* 8/1
2-3 4 2 1/2 **Sheberghan (IRE)**18 310 4-9-5 83 (p[1]) EdwardGreatrex 4 80
(Archie Watson) *racd keenly: trckd ldrs: pressed ldr after 5f tl rdn over 2f out: hld over 1f out: fdd ins fnl f (jockey said gelding hung right-handed throughout)* 9/4[2]
-134 5 1/2 **Scofflaw**4 557 5-9-2 80 EoinWalsh 1 76
(David Evans) *wnt rt s: in last pair but in tch: effrt over 2f out: kpt on but nt pce to get involved (jockey said gelding anticipated the start and jumped awkwardly from the stalls before then hanging left-handed from three furlongs out)* 11/2[3]

1m 59.15s (-1.65) **Going Correction** +0.025s/f (Slow) 5 Ran SP% **106.0**
Speed ratings (Par 105): **108,104,104,101,101**
CSF £15.61 TOTE £5.70: £1.90, £1.10; EX 14.60 Trifecta £60.30.
Owner Mr & Mrs Ian Hall **Bred** Breffni Farm & Marula Park Stud **Trained** Mordon, Durham

FOCUS
With two confirmed front-runners not surprisingly this fair little handicap proved a solid test. The winner was well in on his best.

626 BETWAY SPRINT H'CAP — 5f 21y (Tp)
8:15 (8:15) (Class 6) (0-65,65) 4-Y-O+

£3,105 (£924; £461; £400; £400; £400) **Stalls** Low

Form — RPR

1-03 **1** **Toni's A Star**[19] 286 7-8-8 **57** PoppyBridgwater(5) 8 — 63
(Tony Carroll) *trckd ldrs: rdn to ld ent fnl f: r.o wl* **10/1**

560- **2** 1 ½ **Secret Potion**[54] 9529 5-9-5 **63** PaddyMathers 2 — 64
(Ronald Harris) *hld up: rdn and hdwy jst over 1f out: r.o ins fnl f: fin strly to snatch 2nd nring fin* **10/1**

32-6 **3** nk **Time To Reason (IRE)**[23] 236 6-9-7 **65** (p) RichardKingscote 3 — 65
(Charlie Wallis) *mid-div: rdn wl over 1f out: little imp tl r.o ins fnl f: wnt 3rd cl home* **5/2**[1]

25-4 **4** ½ **Royal Mezyan (IRE)**[20] 279 8-9-2 **60** EdwardGreatrex 5 — 58
(Henry Spiller) *hld up bhd: rdn and hdwy ent fnl f: r.o but nvr threatening to get on terms: wnt 4th cl home (jockey said gelding was slowly away and never travelling)* **4/1**[2]

00-0 **5** nk **Come On Dave (IRE)**[34] 43 10-9-6 **64** (b) DanielMuscutt 10 — 61+
(Paul D'Arcy) *chsd ldr: rdn and ev ch ent fnl f: sn hld: no ex fnl 120yds* **22/1**

0-05 **6** hd **Midnightly**[18] 317 5-9-7 **65** (t) LukeMorris 4 — 61
(Rae Guest) *chsd ldrs: rdn 2f out: kpt on same pce fnl f* **8/1**

55-6 **7** ¾ **Fethiye Boy**[34] 43 5-9-7 **65** ShaneGray 9 — 58+
(Ronald Harris) *led: rdn and hdd ent fnl f: sn no ex* **10/1**

0-00 **8** 2 ½ **Tavener**[11] 439 7-9-5 **63** (p) StevieDonohoe 7 — 47
(David C Griffiths) *mid-div: struggling whn coming wdst into st: n.d after* **11/2**[3]

300- **9** 4 **Swendab (IRE)**[51] 9588 11-8-6 **55** (b) ThomasGreatrex(5) 6 — 25
(John O'Shea) *slowly away and squeezed up s: a towards rr* **40/1**

62-0 **10** 6 **Midnight Guest (IRE)**[11] 439 4-9-2 **65** (v) KatherineBegley(5) 1 — 13
(David Evans) *mid-div: rdn over 2f out: wknd over 1f out* **14/1**

1m 1.35s (-0.55) **Going Correction** +0.025s/f (Slow) **10 Ran SP% 115.8**
Speed ratings (Par 101): **105,102,102,101,100 100,99,95,88,79**
CSF £104.73 CT £335.99 TOTE £7.90: £1.70, £3.20, £1.30; EX 142.80 Trifecta £477.00.
Owner A Star Recruitment Ltd **Bred** Paul Green **Trained** Cropthorne, Worcs
■ Stewards' Enquiry : Shane Gray caution; careless riding

FOCUS
An ordinary sprint handicap, run at a frantic pace.
T/Plt: £344.00 to a £1 stake. Pool: £95,855.23 - 203.36 winning units T/Qpdt: £16.20 to a £1 stake. Pool: £15,410.33 - 702.23 winning units **Tim Mitchell**

593 CHELMSFORD (A.W) (L-H)
Thursday, February 7

627 Meeting Abandoned - Equine Flu Outbreak

568 MEYDAN (L-H)
Thursday, February 7

OFFICIAL GOING: Dirt: fast; turf: good

634a AL NABOODAH COMMERCIAL GROUP (MAIDEN) (DIRT) — 7f (D)
2:30 (2:30) 3-4-Y-O

£21,259 (£7,086; £3,543; £1,771; £1,062; £708)

RPR

1 **Tabarak (USA)**[7] 511 3-8-6 0 RoystonFfrench 2 — 88+
(R Bouresly, Kuwait) *sn led: rdn 2 1/2f out: kpt on wl: comf* **5/2**[2]

2 2 **Midnight Sands (USA)**[196] 5378 3-8-6 82 SamHitchcott 5 — 83
(Doug Watson, UAE) *trckd ldr: ev ch 2f out: r.o same pce fnl 1 1/2f* **15/8**[1]

3 9 ¾ **Karaginsky**[294] 1927 4-9-6 0 (t) RichardMullen 8 — 59
(S Seemar, UAE) *mid-div: r.o same pce fnl 2 1/2f: no ch w front pair* **7/2**[3]

4 2 ¾ **Al Wafi (IRE)**[145] 7268 3-8-6 68 FernandoJara 6 — 49
(A R Al Rayhi, UAE) *mid-div: r.o same pce fnl 2f* **12/1**

5 2 ¼ **Antiguan Rock**[19] 323 4-9-6 56 TadhgO'Shea 1 — 45
(H Al Alawi, UAE) *slowly away: nvr nr to chal* **33/1**

6 5 ¾ **Nibras Time (USA)**[27] 201 4-9-6 0 (b) FabriceVeron 9 — 29
(Ismail Mohammed) *nvr bttr than mid-div* **16/1**

7 4 ¼ **Multicurrency (USA)**[27] 201 4-9-6 61 (t) AntonioFresu 7 — 18
(H Al Alawi, UAE) *nvr bttr than mid-div* **16/1**

8 shd **Alshahhad (IRE)**[55] 9550 4-9-6 0 WJLee 4 — 18
(H Al Alawi, UAE) *a in rr* **33/1**

9 dist **Town Bee (USA)**[33] 92 3-8-6 0 (t) ChrisHayes 3
(Doug Watson, UAE) *trckd ldr tl wknd 4f out* **13/2**

1m 25.28s (0.18) **Going Correction** +0.45s/f (Slow)
WFA 3 from 4yo 17lb **9 Ran SP% 124.2**
Speed ratings: **117,114,103,100,97 91,86,86,**
CSF: 8.32.
Owner Bouresly Racing Syndicate **Bred** Peter E Blum Thoroughbreds Llc **Trained** Kuwait

FOCUS
TRAKUS: 2nd +3, 3rd +3, 4th +6, 5th +8, 6th +6, 7th +6, 8th +15, 9th +4. A strongly run race - 24.69 (400m from standing start), 23.23 (800m), 24.52 (1200m), 12.84 (line) - and two above-average looking types pulled clear in a good battle.

635a AL NABOODAH HONEYWELL PARTNERSHIP (H'CAP) (TURF) — 2m
3:05 (3:05) (95-104,104) 3-Y-O+

£82,677 (£27,559; £13,779; £6,889; £4,133; £2,755)

RPR

1 **Dubhe**[14] 398 4-8-8 **99** (tp) WilliamBuick 3 — 103+
(Charlie Appleby) *trckd ldr: smooth prog 2 1/2f out: led 1 1/2f out: r.o wl: easily* **9/4**[2]

2 4 **Red Galileo**[21] 281 8-9-6 **104** ChristopheSoumillon 5 — 104+
(Saeed bin Suroor) *mid-div: smooth prog 3 1/2f out: ev ch 2f out: r.o fnl 1 1/2f but no ch w wnr* **5/4**[1]

3 8 ½ **Jukebox Jive (FR)**[21] 281 5-8-10 **95** ChrisHayes 2 — 84
(Jamie Osborne) *sn led: hdd & wknd 1 1/2f out* **20/1**

4 12 **Zamaam**[14] 398 9-9-0 **98** (t) JimCrowley 4 — 74
(E Charpy, UAE) *nvr nr to chal* **13/2**

5 3 ¾ **Earnshaw (USA)**[7] 514 8-9-2 **100** (t) MickaelBarzalona 1 — 71
(S Jadhav, UAE) *trckd ldr tl wknd 2 1/2f out* **10/1**

6 16 ½ **Speedo Boy (FR)**[21] 281 5-8-10 **95** (t) BenCurtis 6 — 45
(Ian Williams) *a in rr* **6/1**[3]

3m 20.88s (-3.62) **Going Correction** +0.45s/f (Yiel)
WFA 4 from 5yo+ 4lb **6 Ran SP% 116.7**
Speed ratings: **118,116,111,105,103 95**
CSF: 5.77.
Owner Godolphin **Bred** Kincorth Investments Inc **Trained** Newmarket, Suffolk

FOCUS
TRAKUS: 2nd -3, 3rd -7, 4th -7, 5th -8, 6th +1. Not a complete stamina test, with the winner quickening to the line in 23.7sec over the final 400 metres.

636a UAE 2000 GUINEAS SPONSORED BY AL NABOODAH ASHOK LEYLAND PARTNERSHIP (GROUP 3) (DIRT) — 1m (D)
3:40 (3:40) 3-Y-O

£118,110 (£39,370; £19,685; £9,842; £5,905; £3,937)

RPR

1 **Estihdaaf (USA)**[14] 394 3-9-0 98 (v) ChristopheSoumillon 1 — 108+
(Saeed bin Suroor) *s.i.s but rdn to ld: kicked clr 2f out: r.o wl: easily* **13/2**[3]

2 5 ½ **Walking Thunder (USA)**[28] 169 3-9-0 106 (h) ConnorBeasley 5 — 95
(A bin Harmash, UAE) *mid-div: smooth prog 4f out: r.o fnl 2 1/2f but no ch w wnr* **4/11**[1]

3 2 ¼ **Red Cactus (USA)**[28] 169 3-9-0 84 CarlosLopez 4 — 90+
(Bent Olsen, Denmark) *nvr nr to chal r.o wl fnl 2f* **80/1**

4 2 ¼ **Sporting Chance**[7] 511 3-9-0 100 PatCosgrave 7 — 85
(Simon Crisford) *trckd ldr: ev ch 2f out: wknd fnl f* **20/1**

5 6 ½ **Fintas**[119] 8139 3-9-0 95 ShaneKelly 2 — 70
(Richard Hughes) *trckd ldr tl wknd 3f out* **14/1**

6 1 ½ **Moshaher (USA)**[33] 92 3-9-0 93 PatDobbs 6 — 66
(Doug Watson, UAE) *nvr bttr than mid-div* **4/1**[2]

7 3 **Eyelool (IRE)**[27] 198 3-9-0 80 ChrisHayes 8 — 60
(N Bachalard, UAE) *nvr nr to chal* **66/1**

8 33 **Mulfit (USA)**[49] 9650 3-9-0 83 MickaelBarzalona 3
(S Jadhav, UAE) *chsd ldrs tl wknd 4f out* **33/1**

1m 39.87s (2.37) **Going Correction** +0.45s/f (Slow) **8 Ran SP% 123.7**
Speed ratings: **106,100,98,96,89 88,85,52**
CSF: 10.06.
Owner Godolphin **Bred** Godolphin **Trained** Newmarket, Suffolk

FOCUS
TRAKUS: 2nd +12, 3rd +8, 4th +10, 5th +8, 6th +6, 7th +14, 8th +11. The opening split was sensible but the second quarter was strong and they finished slowly for a poor overall time for the level: 25.16, 22.84, 25.32, 26.55.

637a AL NABOODAH TRAVEL (H'CAP) (TURF) — 1m 1f (T)
4:15 (4:15) (95-105,105) 3-Y-O+

£63,779 (£21,259; £10,629; £5,314; £3,188; £2,125)

RPR

1 **Nordic Lights**[21] 284 4-9-5 **104** WilliamBuick 3 — 107
(Charlie Appleby) *sn led: kicked clr 3f out: r.o wl* **11/4**[2]

2 2 ¼ **Desert Fire (IRE)**[21] 285 4-9-0 **99** ChristopheSoumillon 9 — 97
(Saeed bin Suroor) *mid-div: chsd ldr 3f out: r.o wl fnl 2f but no ch w wnr* **5/2**[1]

3 1 ½ **Baroot**[7] 515 7-9-5 **104** AdriedeVries 10 — 99+
(M F De Kock, South Africa) *settled in rr: r.o wl fnl 2f: nrst fin* **9/1**

4 1 ¾ **Symbolization (IRE)**[118] 8176 4-9-6 **105** JamesDoyle 4 — 96+
(Charlie Appleby) *nvr nr to chal but r.o fnl 2f* **3/1**[3]

5 nk **Kronprinz (GER)**[7] 515 4-9-3 **102** AntonioFresu 6 — 93+
(E Charpy, UAE) *mid-div: r.o same pce fnl 2 1/2f* **80/1**

6 nse **Connect**[164] 6622 4-9-1 **100** (h) ConnorBeasley 1 — 90+
(A bin Harmash, UAE) *nvr nr to chal* **14/1**

7 ¾ **Zorion**[110] 8429 5-9-4 **103** (p) ColmO'Donoghue 7 — 92+
(Charlie Appleby) *a mid-div* **9/1**

8 2 ¼ **Original Choice (IRE)**[28] 173 5-9-1 **100** (p) DanielTudhope 5 — 84+
(William Haggas) *nvr bttr than mid-div* **20/1**

9 2 **Bold Rex (SAF)**[7] 515 5-8-9 **95** SamHitchcott 2 — 74+
(M F De Kock, South Africa) *nvr bttr than mid-div* **66/1**

10 3 ¾ **Walk In The Sun (USA)**[70] 9321 4-9-2 **101** MickaelBarzalona 11 — 73+
(S Jadhav, UAE) *a in rr* **16/1**

11 2 **Aquarium**[14] 396 4-9-5 **104** RoystonFfrench 12 — 72+
(Mark Johnston) *trckd ldr tl wknd 2 1/2f out* **33/1**

12 23 **Ventura Knight (IRE)**[7] 514 4-8-11 **97** OisinMurphy 8 — 16+
(Mark Johnston) *mid-div tl wknd 3 1/2f out* **33/1**

1m 49.69s (0.59) **Going Correction** +0.45s/f (Yiel) **12 Ran SP% 126.2**
Speed ratings: **115,113,111,110,109 109,109,107,105,102 100,79**
CSF: 10.41; TRICAST: 58.69.
Owner Godolphin **Bred** Shutford Stud **Trained** Newmarket, Suffolk

FOCUS
TRAKUS: 2nd 0, 3rd +5, 4th -1, 5th +2, 6th 0, 7th +7, 8th +3, 9th -1, 10th +4, 11th +4, 12th +9. The winner made all but did so through muddling splits, with the second section quite demanding and he finished slowly: 26.06, 22.91, 24.1, 23.78, 12.84.

638a AL MAKTOUM CHALLENGE R2 SPONSORED BY AL NABOODAH ALLIED PRODUCTS DIVISION (GROUP 2) (DIRT) — 1m 1f 110y(D)
4:50 (4:50) 3-Y-O+ **£212,598** (£70,866; £35,433; £17,716; £10,629)

RPR

1 **North America**[28] 171 7-9-0 118 (t) RichardMullen 5 — 116
(S Seemar, UAE) *wl away: sn led: skipped clr 3 1/2f out: r.o wl: easily* **1/3**[1]

2 2 ¼ **New Trails (USA)**[28] 172 5-9-0 106 (t) ConnorBeasley 4 — 112
(A bin Harmash, UAE) *mid-div: r.o wl fnl 1 1/2f: nrst fin* **6/1**[3]

3 4 ¾ **Cosmo Charlie (USA)**[49] 9653 5-9-0 110 PatDobbs 6 — 102
(Doug Watson, UAE) *trckd ldr: ev ch 3 1/2f out: wknd fnl f* **5/1**[2]

4 1 ¼ **Senior Investment (USA)**[14] 396 5-9-0 105 (t) PatCosgrave 2 — 99
(Kenneth McPeek, U.S.A) *nvr nr to chal* **40/1**

5 ¾ **Etijaah (USA)**[28] 171 9-9-0 104 (h) JimCrowley 3 — 98
(Doug Watson, UAE) *nvr bttr than mid-div* **20/1**

6 7 **Second Summer (USA)**[49] 9653 7-9-0 109 (t) RoystonFfrench 1 — 84
(A R Al Rayhi, UAE) *a in rr* **66/1**

1m 58.65s (-0.15) **Going Correction** +0.45s/f (Slow) **6 Ran SP% 114.7**
Speed ratings: **118,116,112,111,110 105**
CSF: 3.05.
Owner Ramzan Kadyrov **Bred** Qatar Bloodstock Ltd **Trained** United Arab Emirates

FOCUS
TRAKUS: 2nd +9, 3rd +4, 4th +12, 5th -7, 6th +1. The winner made all through ordinary splits: 26.55, 23.99, 24.41, 24.1.

639a AL NABOODAH AUTOMOTIVE DIVISION (H'CAP) (TURF) 6f
5:25 (5:25) (96-109,109) 3-Y-O+
£82,677 (£27,559; £13,779; £6,889; £4,133; £2,755)

RPR

1 **Mazzini**^{14} [393] 6-8-10 100 .... AdriedeVries 12 115+
(Fawzi Abdulla Nass, Bahrain) *slowly away: settled in rr: smooth prog 2 1/2f out: led 1 1/2f out: r.o wl* 9/2^{3}

2 2 1/2 **High On Life**^{13} [424] 8-8-10 100 ....(t) MickaelBarzalona 11 107
(S Jadhav, UAE) *sn led: hdd 1 1/2f out but kpt on wl* 16/1

3 1 1/2 **Dream Today (IRE)**^{28} [170] 4-8-8 98 .... ChrisHayes 5 100
(Jamie Osborne) *chsd ldr: ev ch 2f out: r.o same pce fnl 1 1/2f* 12/1

4 1 1/2 **Another Batt (IRE)**^{14} [397] 4-9-4 107 .... ConnorBeasley 2 105
(George Scott) *mid-div: r.o same pce fnl 2f: nrst fin* 14/1

5 1 1/4 **Ibn Malik (IRE)**^{7} [512] 6-8-10 100 .... JimCrowley 7 93
(M Al Mheiri, UAE) *mid-div: r.o same pce fnl 2f* 4/1^{2}

6 2 **Rebel Streak**^{14} [393] 4-8-13 102 ....(v) OisinMurphy 9 90
(Ali Jan, Qatar) *nvr nr to chal but r.o fnl 2f* 14/1

7 1/2 **Alfredo Arcano (IRE)**^{28} [170] 5-8-6 96 ....(t) BenCurtis 4 81
(David Marnane, Ire) *chsd ldrs tl wknd 1 1/2f out* 11/1

8 2 **Glenamoy Lad**^{28} [170] 5-8-7 97 ....(t) RichardMullen 3 76
(Michael Wigham) *nvr nr to chal* 6/1

9 1 **Manahir (FR)**^{13} [426] 5-8-7 97 ....(t) RoystonFfrench 1 73
(S Jadhav, UAE) *a in rr* 66/1

10 2 **Double Up**^{48} [9667] 8-8-6 96 ....(v) TadhgO'Shea 6 65
(Ian Williams) *chsd ldrs tl wknd 2f out* 33/1

11 2 **Top Score**^{14} [397] 5-9-6 109 ....(p) ChristopheSoumillon 8 73
(Saeed bin Suroor) *trckd ldr tl wknd 2f out* 10/3^{1}

12 19 **Intisaab**^{14} [397] 8-9-5 108 ....(p) DanielTudhope 10 11
(David O'Meara) *s.i.s: a in rr* 16/1

1m 10.37s (1.37) **Going Correction** +0.45s/f (Yiel) 12 Ran SP% 121.1
Speed ratings: **108,104,102,100,99 96,95,93,91,89 86,61**
CSF: 76.39; TRICAST: 837.51.
Owner Ahmed Al-Qattan & Fawzi Nass **Bred** Jan & Peter Hopper **Trained** Bahrain

FOCUS
There were two groups early, five runners stands' side including the first two finishers who were drawn closest to that near rail, and the others a bit off the fence, before they merged in the closing stages. A strongly run race: 24.4, 21.74, with the winner to the line in a slowing 23.99.

640a AL NABOODAH CARGO (H'CAP) (TURF) 7f
6:00 (6:00) (95-105,105) 3-Y-O+
£63,779 (£21,259; £10,629; £5,314; £3,188; £2,125)

RPR

1 **Mubtasim (IRE)**^{122} [8044] 5-8-13 98 ....(h) WilliamBuick 14 110
(Charlie Appleby) *sn led: rdn 2 1/2f out: r.o wl* 4/1^{1}

2 3/4 **Poet's Society**^{21} [285] 5-8-11 97 .... ConnorBeasley 4 106
(A bin Harmash, UAE) *mid-div: r.o wl fnl 2f: nrst fin* 14/1

3 1 3/4 **Freescape**^{35} [49] 4-8-11 97 ow1 ....(b) WJLee 2 101
(David Marnane, Ire) *mid-div: r.o fnl 2f: nrst fin* 20/1

4 1/2 **Cliffs Of Capri**^{28} [173] 5-8-11 97 ....(p) ChrisHayes 3 100
(Jamie Osborne) *nvr nr to chal but r.o fnl 1 1/2f* 4/1^{1}

5 3/4 **Lansky (IRE)**^{14} [397] 4-9-6 105 .... MickaelBarzalona 10 107
(S Jadhav, UAE) *mid-div: r.o same pce fnl 2f: nrst fin* 4/1^{1}

6 shd **Victory Wave (USA)**^{21} [283] 5-9-0 99 ....(h) PatCosgrave 8 101
(Saeed bin Suroor) *mid-div: chsd ldr and ev ch 2 1/2f out: one pce fnl 1 1/2f* 13/2^{3}

7 2 3/4 **Good Effort (IRE)**^{28} [173] 4-8-11 97 .... FabriceVeron 9 90
(Ismail Mohammed) *trckd ldr: ev ch 2 1/2f out: wknd fnl 1 1/2f* 28/1

8 1/2 **Race Day (IRE)**^{21} [285] 6-8-13 98 ....(p) ChristopheSoumillon 6 91
(Saeed bin Suroor) *a mid-div* 9/2^{2}

9 3 **Alfoik (AUS)**^{14} [393] 4-9-2 101 ....(t) JimCrowley 5 86
(M F De Kock, South Africa) *nvr bttr than mid-div* 40/1

10 2 **Trickbag (USA)**^{35} [50] 5-8-11 97 ow2 ....(t) CarlosLopez 7 75
(Susanne Berneklint, Sweden) *nvr bttr than mid-div* 80/1

11 3 1/4 **Fas (IRE)**^{103} [8654] 5-9-1 100 .... OisinMurphy 13 71
(Mme Pia Brandt, France) *a in rr* 12/1

12 3 **Never Back Down (IRE)**^{35} [52] 4-9-1 100 ....(p) JamesDoyle 12 62
(Hugo Palmer) *mid-div: t.k.h: wknd fnl 2 1/2f* 20/1

13 8 3/4 **Amazour (IRE)**^{35} [52] 7-9-0 99 .... BenCurtis 11 38
(Ismail Mohammed) *s.i.s: a in rr* 33/1

1m 24.06s (-0.04) **Going Correction** +0.45s/f (Yiel) 13 Ran SP% 125.5
Speed ratings: **118,117,115,114,113 113,110,109,106,104 100,97,87**
CSF: 59.69; TRICAST: 1,065.66; PLACEPOT: £6.00 to a £1 stake. QUADPOT: £4.40 to a £1 stake..
Owner Godolphin **Bred** Mrs Natasha Drennan **Trained** Newmarket, Suffolk
■ Love Dreams was withdrawn. Price at time of withdrawal 50/1. Rule 4 does not apply

FOCUS
TRAKUS: 2nd -4, 3rd -4, 4th -3, 5th +4, 6th 0, 7th 0, 8th -4, 9th 0, 10th +4, 11th +1, 12th +4, 13th +5. The winner set a fast, gradually slowing pace: 24.69 (from standing start), 23.2, 23.47, 12.7.

641a-651a (Foreign Racing) - See Raceform Interactive

607 NEWCASTLE (A.W) (L-H)
Friday, February 8
652 Meeting Abandoned - Equine Flu Outbreak

585 SOUTHWELL (L-H)
Friday, February 8
659 Meeting Abandoned - Equine Flu Outbreak

665 - 681a (Foreign Racing) - See Raceform Interactive

CAGNES-SUR-MER
Sunday, February 10
OFFICIAL GOING: Polytrack: standard; turf: very soft

682a GRAND PRIX DE LA RIVIERA COTE D'AZUR - JACQUES BOUCHARA (LISTED RACE) (4YO+) (POLYTRACK) 1m 2f (P)
1:17 4-Y-O+
£27,027 (£10,810; £8,108; £5,405; £2,702)

RPR

1 **Pump Pump Palace (FR)**^{20} 6-8-13 0 .... Pierre-CharlesBoudot 15 103
(J-P Gauvin, France) 4/1^{1}

2 3/4 **Pretorio (IRE)**^{37} 7-8-13 0 .... HugoJourniac 5 102
(M Nigge, France) 7/1

3 1 **Roc Angel (FR)**^{20} 5-8-13 0 .... TonyPiccone 8 100
(F Chappet, France) 11/1

4 hd **Nice To See You (FR)**^{79} [9239] 6-9-3 0 .... AurelienLemaitre 1 103
(Robert Collet, France) 32/1

5 1 1/4 **Lady Sidney (FR)**^{73} [9321] 5-8-9 0 ....(b) StephanePasquier 4 93
(R Le Dren Doleuze, France) 16/1

6 snk **Aubevoye (FR)**^{20} 4-9-3 0 .... CristianDemuro 14 101
(J-C Rouget, France) 61/10^{2}

7 1 3/4 **Palace Prince (GER)**^{20} 7-8-13 0 ....(p) EddyHardouin 3 93
(Jean-Pierre Carvalho, Germany) 21/1

8 shd **Tabularasa (FR)**^{122} 4-8-13 .... VincentCheminaud 7 94
(N Caullery, France) 24/1

8 dht **Skalleti (FR)** 4-8-13 .... NicolasPerret 10 94
(J Reynier, France) 10/1

10 1 **Mango Tango (FR)**^{50} [9685] 6-8-9 0 ....(p) EdwardGreatrex 6 87
(Archie Watson) *t.k.h early: hld up in mid-div on inner: pushed along over 2f out: swtchd lft ent fnl f: kpt on but n.d clsng stages* 20/1

11 3/4 **Allez Henri (IRE)**^{54} 8-8-13 0 ....(p) AnthonyCrastus 11 89
(D & P Prod'Homme, France) 16/1

12 snk **Magari (FR)**^{20} 6-8-13 0 .... ThierryThulliez 12 89
(Charley Rossi, France) 23/1

13 nk **Cnicht (FR)**^{120} 5-8-13 0 ....(b) Roberto-CarlosMontenegro 16 88
(D Henderson, France) 105/1

14 3 **Plait**^{15} [435] 4-8-9 0 .... MaximeGuyon 13 79
(Michael Bell) *mid-div on outer: asked for effrt 3f out: drvn over 2f out: unable qck and btn ent fnl f: eased clsng stages* 67/10^{3}

15 nk **Alwaysandforever (IRE)**^{63} [9480] 5-8-9 0 ....(b) RyanMoore 9 78
(Gavin Hernon, France) *slowly away: racd in fnl trio on inner: pushed along over 2f out: limited rspnse and sn rdn: wl btn ent fnl f: nvr a factor* 11/1

16 1/2 **Dioresse (IRE)**^{289} 4-8-9 0 ....(p) MickaelForest 2 78
(M Figge, Germany) 150/1

1m 58.44s 16 Ran SP% 119.2
PARI-MUTUEL (all including 1 euro stake): WIN 5.00 PLACE 1.90, 2.40, 3.00 DF 15.80 SF 41.20.
Owner Benoit Bouret **Bred** J-C Bouret & B Bouret **Trained** France

683a PRIX DE LA CALIFORNIE (LISTED RACE) (3YO) (POLYTRACK) 1m (P)
3:42 3-Y-O
£24,774 (£9,909; £7,432; £4,954; £2,477)

RPR

1 **Barys**^{85} [9122] 3-8-13 ....(b) EdwardGreatrex 7 97
(Archie Watson) *led after 1f: asked to qckn over 2f out: rdn 1 1/2f out: chal ent fnl f: kpt on strly u.p clsng stages: in command fnl 110yds* 10/1

2 1 3/4 **Transcendent (ITY)**^{28} 3-8-13 0 .... Pierre-CharlesBoudot 9 93
(F Chappet, France) 6/1

3 1 **Walhaan (IRE)**^{22} 3-8-13 0 .... Jean-BernardEyquem 3 91
(J-C Rouget, France) *slowly away: prog on inner to r in mid-div: pushed along 2f out: swtchd off rail and rdn to chse ldng pair over 1f out: kpt on: nt quite pce to chal* 58/10^{3}

4 3/4 **Trouville (FR)**^{25} 3-8-13 0 .... CristianDemuro 10 89
(C Ferland, France) 11/5^{1}

5 hd **Isalys (FR)**^{22} 3-8-9 0 .... AlexandreGavilan 1 85
(D Guillemin, France) 4/1^{2}

6 1/2 **Dezba**^{28} 3-8-9 0 .... HugoJourniac 2 83
(M Nigge, France) 14/1

7 3 **Helcia (IRE)**^{22} 3-8-9 0 .... JulienAuge 5 76
(C Ferland, France) 9/1

8 1 **High Cliff (FR)**^{22} 3-8-9 0 .... MaximeGuyon 8 74
(F Vermeulen, France) 12/1

9 1 1/4 **Marie's Picnic (FR)**^{56} [9570] 3-8-9 0 .... NicolasPerret 6 71
(J Reynier, France) 46/1

10 5 1/2 **Eyes That Dazzle**^{26} 3-8-9 0 .... AntoineHamelin 4 59
(Matthieu Palussiere, France) 46/1

11 3 1/2 **Lyronada**^{22} 3-8-9 0 .... AnthonyCrastus 11 51
(M Figge, Germany) 61/1

1m 34.34s 11 Ran SP% 119.6
PARI-MUTUEL (all including 1 euro stake): WIN 11.10 PLACE 3.40, 2.70, 2.40 DF 20.70 SF 41.70.
Owner Nurlan Bizakov **Bred** Hesmonds Stud Ltd **Trained** Upper Lambourn, W Berks

684 - 693a (Foreign Racing) - See Raceform Interactive

592 ST MORITZ (R-H)
Sunday, February 10
OFFICIAL GOING: Snow: frozen

694a GROSSER PREIS LONGINES (CONDITIONS) (4YO+) (SNOW) 1m 1f
12:30 4-Y-O+
£5,040 (£2,520; £1,800; £1,200; £600)

RPR

1 **Berrahri (IRE)**^{7} [592] 8-9-11 0 .... DennisSchiergen 4
(John Best) *led after 1f: hdd bef 1/2-way and nudged along to keep tabs on ldr: regained ld over 3f out: drvn 2f out: kpt on gamely u.p ins fnl f: all out* 8/5^{1}

2 1/2 **Fiesta (SWI)**^{7} [592] 5-9-1 0 .... RaphaelLingg 5
(P Schaerer, Switzerland) 9/5^{2}

3 3 **Sleeping Giant (GER)**^{357} [797] 9-7-12 0 ....(p) JennyLanghard$^{(7)}$ 2
(P Schaerer, Switzerland) 51/10

The Form Book Flat 2019, Raceform Ltd, Newbury, RG14 5SJ

4 20 **Samurai (IRE)**[202] 6-9-11 0 MilanZatloukal 1
(M Weiss, Switzerland) 3/1
5 dist **Cornwall Cottage**[7] 592 5-9-4 0 (p) ClementLheureux 6
(A Schaerer, Switzerland) 12/5[3]
2m 13.53s 5 Ran SP% **145.0**
PARI-MUTUEL (all including 1 euro stake): WIN 2.60 PLACE 1.40, 1.30 SF 8.40.
Owner Mark Curtis & Stephen Purdew **Bred** Kilnamoragh Stud **Trained** Oad Street, Kent

614 KEMPTON (A.W) (R-H)
Wednesday, February 13

OFFICIAL GOING: Polytrack: standard to slow
Wind: Moderate, across Weather: Clear

695 RACING TV APPRENTICE H'CAP 1m 2f 219y(P)
5:15 (5:24) (Class 7) (0-50,55) 3-Y-O+ £2,587 (£770; £384; £192) Stalls Low

Form RPR
54-1 1 **Clearance**[14] 482 5-9-7 **50** RhysClutterbuck(7) 2 58
(Gary Moore) *hld up in rr: in last pair over 3f out but gd prog towards inner over 2f out: led over 1f out: styd on wl* 11/2[3]
-432 2 1 1/2 **Affluence (IRE)**[9] 593 4-9-12 **49** (p) RhiainIngram 10 56+
(Martin Smith) *hld up in last pair: stl there and nt clr run over 2f out: pushed along and hdwy over 1f out: r.o to take 2nd last 100yds: too late to threaten wnr* 9/2[1]
05-1 3 1 1/2 **Chakrii (IRE)**[9] 593 3-8-3 **55** 6ex (p) LauraPearson(7) 11 55
(Henry Spiller) *s.s: hld up in last pair tl wl after 1/2-way: rdn over 2f out: prog on outer: tk 2nd briefly ins fnl f: one pce* 6/1
50-0 4 1/2 **Passing Clouds**[29] 245 4-9-8 **46** oh1 GabrieleMalune 8 48
(Michael Attwater) *restless stalls: led 4f: chsd ldr to over 4f out: sn pushed along and looked like dropping away: kpt on and stl ch 2f out: one pce after (jockey said gelding reared as stalls opened)* 25/1
006- 5 1 1/2 **Lady Wolf**[47] 9729 3-7-13 **49** (p) LauraCoughlan(5) 4 46
(Rod Millman) *trckd ldrs: rdn and prog to ld over 2f out: hdd over 1f out: wknd ins fnl f* 12/1
25- 6 1 1/4 **Sheldon Cooper (IRE)**[54] 9666 6-9-6 **45** (t[1]) SeamusCronin(3) 7 42
(David Dennis) *trapped out wd: hld up in rr: prog 1/2-way: rdn over 2f out and tried to cl: no imp 1f out: wknd* 5/1[2]
00-0 7 3/4 **So I'm Told (IRE)**[31] 229 3-8-2 **47** (v[1]) TheodoreLadd 12 40
(George Scott) *nvr bttr than midfield: rdn and no prog over 2f out: plugged on* 8/1
20-5 8 1/2 **Pablow**[9] 602 4-9-2 **46** (bt) CierenFallon(7) 1 42
(Alan Bailey) *chsd ldrs: rdn to cl over 2f out: no imp over 1f out: wknd* 15/2
3-00 9 6 **Boatrace (IRE)**[9] 602 4-9-8 **48** (t) KatherineBegley(3) 14 34
(David Evans) *t.k.h: prom: led over 3f out to over 2f out: wknd qckly over 1f out* 14/1
00-5 10 2 1/2 **The Celtic Machine**[32] 206 4-9-11 **48** ThomasGreatrex 9 30
(Pat Phelan) *wl in tch tl wknd 2f out* 12/1
004/ 11 5 **Rebel Woods (FR)**[659] 2056 6-9-7 **46** (b[1]) ScottMcCullagh(3) 3 18
(Joseph Tuite) *uns rdr and bolted bef s: in tch tl wknd over 2f out (vet said gelding had bled from the nose)* 40/1
05-0 12 4 **Takiah**[37] 120 4-9-3 **46** oh1 AmeliaGlass(5) 13 12
(Peter Hiatt) *t.k.h: trckd ldr: led after 4f to over 3f out: wknd over 2f out* 66/1
2m 21.97s (0.97) **Going Correction** +0.025s/f (Slow)
WFA 3 from 4yo 23lb 4 from 5yo+ 1lb 12 Ran SP% **117.2**
Speed ratings (Par 97): **100,98,97,97,96 95,94,94,90,88 84,81**
CSF £29.68 CT £155.07 TOTE £5.60: £2.30, £1.40, £2.40; EX 25.60 Trifecta £140.30.
Owner G L Moore **Bred** Richard W Farleigh **Trained** Lower Beeding, W Sussex
FOCUS
A modest handicap which suited the closers. A pb from the winner.

696 32RED ON THE APP STORE NOVICE STKS 1m 3f 219y(P)
5:45 (5:48) (Class 5) 4-Y-O+ £3,881 (£1,155; £577; £288) Stalls Low

Form RPR
4/1 1 **Ulster (IRE)**[29] 242 4-9-9 0 EdwardGreatrex 1 95+
(Archie Watson) *t.k.h: led 1f: trckd ldng pair tl swift move to ld 2f out: pushed out after: readily* 8/11[1]
4-2 2 1 3/4 **Miss Crick**[41] 41 8-8-13 0 DavidProbert 7 78
(Alan King) *hld up in midfield: prog to take cl 2nd wl over 1f out: styd on but readily hld by wnr fnl f* 9/1
34 3 3 **Knight Crusader**[11] 562 7-9-4 0 AdamKirby 3 78
(John O'Shea) *hld up in last trio: shkn up and prog over 2f out: tk 3rd over 1f out: kpt on same pce and no imp on ldng pair* 16/1
34-4 4 10 **Mount Ararat (IRE)**[30] 239 4-9-2 85 CliffordLee 4 63
(K R Burke) *t.k.h: led after 1f to 2f out: wknd qckly over 1f out* 9/2[3]
6- 5 5 **Ace Cheetah (USA)**[63] 9509 5-9-4 0 DannyBrock 9 54
(J R Jenkins) *hld up in last trio: rdn wl over 2f out: sn wknd* 150/1
5 6 1/2 **Dimmesdale**[29] 242 4-9-2 0 LiamJones 6 54
(John O'Shea) *mostly in last: shkn up 3f out: sn bhd* 66/1
7 1 1/4 **Sorbet**[41] 4-8-11 0 LukeMorris 2 47
(Lucy Wadham) *s.i.s: sn chsd ldng trio: rdn and wknd over 2f out* 33/1
4/5- 8 2 **Must Be Magic (IRE)**[292] 2121 4-8-11 0 OisinMurphy 5 44
(Andrew Balding) *chsd ldr after 1f to over 2f out: wknd rapidly (jockey said filly stopped quickly)* 7/2[2]
2m 33.09s (-1.41) **Going Correction** +0.025s/f (Slow)
WFA 4 from 5yo+ 2lb 8 Ran SP% **119.3**
Speed ratings (Par 103): **105,103,101,95,91 91,90,89**
CSF £9.43 TOTE £1.50: £1.02, £1.90, £4.50; EX 9.30 Trifecta £25.40.
Owner J Allison, S Barrow & Partner **Bred** Stowell Hill Ltd & D Ludlow **Trained** Upper Lambourn, W Berks
FOCUS
An uncompetitive novice.

697 100% PROFIT BOOST AT 32REDSPORT.COM FILLIES' H'CAP 7f (P)
6:15 (6:16) (Class 5) (0-70,72) 4-Y-O+ £3,752 (£1,116; £557; £400; £400; £400) Stalls Low

Form RPR
1-32 1 **Chica De La Noche**[21] 366 5-9-4 **64** (p) AdamKirby 4 72
(Simon Dow) *chsd ldng trio: pushed along 3f out: rdn to chse ldng pair over 1f out: styd on wl u.p to cl fnl f: led post* 9/4[2]
51-1 2 hd **Chloellie**[28] 256 4-9-11 **71** DavidProbert 3 78
(J R Jenkins) *trckd ldng pair: chsd ldr 2f out: rdn and grad clsd fnl f: led last strides: hdd post* 2/1[1]
20-0 3 1/2 **Sonnet Rose (IRE)**[21] 366 5-9-7 **67** (bt) MartinDwyer 6 73
(Conrad Allen) *pressed ldr: led 3f out: rdn for home wl over 1f out and 2 l up: kpt on but worn down last strides* 8/1
6-60 4 1 1/2 **Bidding War**[23] 348 4-8-10 **56** (p[1]) LukeMorris 2 58
(Michael Appleby) *hld up in 5th: rdn 2f out: chsd ldng trio: u.p jst over 1f out: kpt on but nvr able to chal* 14/1
0-31 5 2 1/2 **Rippling Waters (FR)**[20] 386 5-9-4 **64** (t) DougieCostello 5 59
(Jamie Osborne) *hld up towards rr: rdn over 2f out: no imp on ldrs and btn over 1f out* 6/1[3]
0-30 6 3/4 **Titan Goddess**[18] 429 7-9-12 **72** TomMarquand 8 65
(Mike Murphy) *dwlt: mostly in last pair and shoved along after 3f: nvr gng wl enough to make prog (jockey said mare accelerated the gate and was subsequently slowly away)* 8/1
43-0 7 5 **Natalie Express (FR)**[28] 256 5-9-4 **64** EdwardGreatrex 7 44
(Henry Spiller) *s.s: tk fierce hold and hld up in last pair: effrt on inner 2f out: wknd qckly over 1f out (jockey said mare was slowly away and ran too freely)* 25/1
00-0 8 7 **Valentine Mist (IRE)**[21] 359 7-7-11 **48** oh3 RhiainIngram(5) 1 9
(James Grassick) *led to 3f out: wknd rapidly 2f out* 150/1
1m 26.65s (0.65) **Going Correction** +0.025s/f (Slow) 8 Ran SP% **111.8**
Speed ratings (Par 100): **97,96,96,94,91 90,85,77**
CSF £6.79 CT £26.97 TOTE £2.70: £1.10, £1.10, £2.70; EX 7.50 Trifecta £32.20.
Owner Robert Moss **Bred** Horizon Bloodstock Limited **Trained** Epsom, Surrey
FOCUS
A fair handicap.

698 32RED.COM H'CAP 1m (P)
6:45 (6:47) (Class 5) (0-75,77) 3-Y-O £3,752 (£1,116; £557; £400; £400; £400) Stalls Low

Form RPR
30-2 1 **My Dear Friend**[26] 290 3-9-5 **73** OisinMurphy 6 78
(Ralph Beckett) *led after nthing else seemingly wanted to: dictated stdy pce: kicked on over 2f out: drvn over 1f out: hrd pressed fnl f: jst hld on* 7/2[2]
04-3 2 shd **Lee Roy**[39] 79 3-8-10 **64** KierenFox 7 68
(Michael Attwater) *hld up in last pair: nt clr run briefly over 2f out: rdn on outer over 1f out and prog after: styd on strly fnl f to take 2nd last strides: jst failed* 9/1
-411 3 1/2 **Sir Ox (USA)**[7] 614 3-8-13 **67** 6ex (p) LukeMorris 2 70
(Robert Cowell) *t.k.h: mostly chsd wnr: rdn over 1f out: tried to chal on inner after: kpt on but lost 2nd last strides* 5/1
13-1 4 nk **Rich Approach (IRE)**[27] 274 3-9-0 **68** PJMcDonald 5 70
(James Bethell) *hld up in last pair: prog over 2f out: chsd ldng pair over 1f out: kpt on but nvr quite able to chal: lost 3rd nr fin* 9/2[3]
46-1 5 nk **Gold Bere (FR)**[18] 442 3-9-8 **76** AdamKirby 4 77
(George Baker) *chsd ldrs on outer: pushed along sn after 1/2-way: rdn 2f out: kpt on after and nrst fin but nvr gng pce to chal* 5/2[1]
32-5 6 2 **Fox Kasper (IRE)**[35] 133 3-9-7 **75** (b[1]) SeanLevey 1 72
(Richard Hannon) *trckd ldrs: rdn 2f out: tried to mount an effrt over 1f out: one pce fnl f* 10/1
02-0 7 3 1/2 **Regal Ambition**[39] 78 3-8-7 **61** HollieDoyle 3 50
(Clive Cox) *disp 2nd pl to over 1f out: wknd* 25/1
102- 8 4 **Annecy** 9442 3-9-4 **77** DylanHogan(5) 8 56
(David Simcock) *racd wd: hld up: lost tch w main gp 2f out (jockey said filly stopped quickly)* 20/1
1m 39.86s (0.06) **Going Correction** +0.025s/f (Slow) 8 Ran SP% **113.3**
Speed ratings (Par 97): **100,99,99,99,98 96,93,89**
CSF £33.93 CT £157.06 TOTE £4.30: £2.10, £1.90, £1.80; EX 31.10 Trifecta £136.70.
Owner King Power Racing Co Ltd **Bred** W & R Barnett Ltd **Trained** Kimpton, Hants
FOCUS
A fair handicap run at a steady pace. They finished in a bit of a heap.

699 32RED H'CAP (LONDON MILE QUALIFIER) 1m (P)
7:15 (7:15) (Class 4) (0-85,85) 4-Y-O+ £6,469 (£1,925; £962; £481; £400; £400) Stalls Low

Form RPR
0-65 1 **Samphire Coast**[34] 157 6-8-13 **77** (v) PaddyMathers 5 85
(Derek Shaw) *t.k.h: hld up in midfield: prog on inner jst over 2f out: drvn to ld over 1f out: styd on strly fnl f* 7/1[3]
3-64 2 1 3/4 **Margie's Choice (GER)**[12] 516 4-8-9 **73** (b) GeorgeWood 4 77
(Michael Madgwick) *plld hrd: led to 2f out: sn shkn up: kpt on fnl f to regain 2nd nr fin* 11/1
1-16 3 nk **Divine Messenger**[11] 557 5-9-0 **78** (p) PJMcDonald 1 81
(Emma Owen) *trckd ldng trio: urged along and lost pl over 2f out: struggling over 1f out: styd on again fnl f: tk 3rd last strides* 9/4[2]
-044 4 nk **Ventura Blues (IRE)**[16] 460 5-8-11 **75** (b[1]) RossaRyan 2 78
(Alexandra Dunn) *trckd ldng pair: clsd to ld 2f out: rdn over 1f out: hdd last 150yds: lost 2 pls nr fin* 9/1
2/-6 5 1 1/4 **Me Too Nagasaki (IRE)**[43] 4 5-9-5 **83** (t) OisinMurphy 3 83
(Stuart Williams) *trckd ldr to jst over 2f out: sn rdn and nt qckn: one pce over 1f out* 2/1[1]
4-54 6 2 1/4 **Espresso Freddo (IRE)**[21] 364 5-8-7 **71** oh1 (p) DavidProbert 7 66
(Robert Stephens) *hld up in last: rdn and no prog over 2f out: nvr a factor (jockey said gelding was unruly in the stalls and subsequently slowly away)* 15/2
32-0 7 1/2 **Regulator (IRE)**[35] 139 4-9-7 **85** EdwardGreatrex 6 78
(Alexandra Dunn) *hld up in last trio: effrt on inner over 2f out: hrd rdn and no prog over 1f out* 50/1
V06- 8 1 1/2 **Albishr (IRE)**[63] 9502 4-8-9 **80** LeviWilliams(7) 8 70
(Simon Dow) *hld up in last trio: rdn and no prog over 2f out: wl btn over 1f out* 14/1
1m 40.55s (0.75) **Going Correction** +0.025s/f (Slow) 8 Ran SP% **115.3**
Speed ratings (Par 105): **97,95,94,94,93 91,90,89**
CSF £79.81 CT £229.71 TOTE £10.30: £2.10, £3.10, £1.40; EX 93.20 Trifecta £278.10.
Owner Paddy Barrett **Bred** P E Barrett **Trained** Sproxton, Leics

FOCUS
A competitive handicap.

700 32RED CASINO H'CAP 1m 7f 218y(P)
7:45 (7:45) (Class 5) (0-75,76) 4-Y-O+
£3,752 (£1,116; £557; £400; £400; £400) Stalls Low

Form RPR
110- 1 **Le Torrent**284 2407 7-9-11 71 TomMarquand 9 78
(Simon Dow) *towards rr: urged along 4f out: looked to be struggling wl over 2f out: prog on outer wl over 1f out: drvn to dispute ld fnl f: gained upper hand last 100yds* 14/1

31-2 2 ½ **Houlton**11 559 4-9-3 70 (tp) GabrieleMalune(3) 4 76
(Marco Botti) *t.k.h: hld up in midfield: shkn up over 2f out and sn prog on outer: clsd to dispute ld 1f out: styd on but hdd and hld last 100yds* 11/4[2]

41-3 3 2¾ **Colwood**20 385 5-9-2 67 DarraghKeenan(5) 1 70
(Robert Eddery) *trckd ldrs: hung lft bnd 4f out: wd bnd 3f out and dropped to rr: styd on again over 1f out against nr side rail to take 3rd nr fin* 5/1[3]

5-41 4 ¾ **Moon Of Baroda**14 480 4-9-12 76 (b) DavidProbert 5 78
(Charles Hills) *hld up in midfield: carried lft 4f out but sn trckd ldrs: smooth prog to ld jst over 2f out: idled in front and drvn over 1f out: hdd and fnd nil 1f out* 6/4[1]

/40- 5 1¼ **Akavit (IRE)**310 1701 7-9-12 72 CallumShepherd 6 72
(Ed de Giles) *hld up in last pair: hrd rdn and prog over 2f out: chsd ldrs over 1f out: fdd fnl f* 40/1

23-3 6 1¼ **Galileo's Spear (FR)**38 99 6-9-6 66 (t) LukeMorris 3 65
(Sir Mark Prescott Bt) *cl up: chsd ldr 4f out to over 2f out: fdd over 1f out* 9/1

661/ 7 nk **Mere Anarchy (IRE)**45 6889 8-9-5 70 (p) PoppyBridgwater(5) 8 68
(Robert Stephens) *sn trckd ldr: led after 7f: hdd over 2f out and sn btn* 14/1

300- 8 1 **Conkering Hero (IRE)**63 9503 5-10-2 76 (b1) RobHornby 2 73
(Joseph Tuite) *led 7f: chsd ldr to 4f out: rdn over 2f out: steadily wknd* 25/1

260/ 9 71 **Beau Knight**452 6716 7-9-0 60 RossaRyan 7
(Alexandra Dunn) *in tch in last to 5f out: sn wknd: t.o* 100/1

3m 29.66s (-0.44) **Going Correction** +0.025s/f (Slow)
WFA 4 from 5yo+ 4lb 9 Ran SP% 113.9
Speed ratings (Par 103): **102,101,100,100,99 98,98,98,62**
CSF £51.46 CT £224.63 TOTE £12.90: £2.10, £1.20, £1.80; EX 56.80 Trifecta £252.90.
Owner Paul G Jacobs **Bred** Moutonshoek Investments (Pty) Ltd **Trained** Epsom, Surrey

FOCUS
The pace was honest for this fair handicap.

701 JOIN RACING TV NOW H'CAP 7f (P)
8:15 (8:19) (Class 6) (0-65,65) 4-Y-O+
£3,105 (£924; £461; £400; £400; £400) Stalls Low

Form RPR
0-05 1 **Elusif (IRE)**11 553 4-8-2 46 oh1 HollieDoyle 7 54
(Shaun Keightley) *mde all: rdn over 1f out: hrd pressed after: styd on wl and in command last 100yds* 8/1[3]

3-46 2 1 **Sir Ottoman (FR)**33 187 6-9-7 65 (t1) JasonHart 1 70
(Ivan Furtado) *trckd ldrs on inner: prog 2f out: rdn and styd on over 1f out to take 2nd nr fin: nvr able to chal* 10/3[1]

5-34 3 ¾ **Hic Bibi**21 366 4-8-10 61 LauraCoughlan(7) 2 64
(David Loughnane) *trckd ldng pair tl wnt 2nd over 2f out: rdn to chal on inner jst over 1f out: nt qckn fnl f: lost 2nd nr fin* 4/1[2]

0-06 4 ½ **King Of Rooks**26 295 6-9-0 58 DavidProbert 4 60
(Henry Spiller) *hld up in rr: prog towards inner 2f out: rdn and kpt on to dispute 3rd fnl f: one pce nr fin* 8/1[3]

50-0 5 shd **More Salutes (IRE)**29 243 4-8-7 51 RobHornby 6 53
(Michael Attwater) *hld up in rr: gd prog 2f out: clsd on ldrs ins fnl f: one pce last 75yds* 16/1

0P-4 6 1 **Spiritual Star (IRE)**26 295 10-9-5 63 (t) JFEgan 12 63
(Paul George) *dismntd and led to post: hld up in last trio: prog towards inner wl over 1f out: styng on but wl hld whn nt clr run last 100yds (jockey said gelding was denied clear run in closing stages)* 16/1

32-2 7 1¼ **Blessed To Empress (IRE)**25 315 4-9-3 61 NicolaCurrie 13 57
(Amy Murphy) *t.k.h: trapped on outer in midfield: nt qckn 2f out: n.d after: plugged on* 12/1

31-3 8 ¾ **Storm Melody**29 249 6-9-5 63 (p) TomMarquand 11 57
(Ali Stronge) *hld up in last trio: drvn on outer and tried to make prog 2f out: no great hdwy* 8/1[3]

6-14 9 nse **Mooroverthebridge**15 467 5-9-2 60 LukeMorris 10 54
(Grace Harris) *chsd wnr to over 2f out: steadily wknd u.p* 12/1

-041 10 ½ **Black Truffle (FR)**12 531 9-7-12 47 (v) DarraghKeenan(5) 8 40
(Mark Usher) *prom: rdn over 2f out: steadily wknd over 1f out* 20/1

600- 11 ½ **Barca (USA)**298 1984 5-8-10 61 TylerSaunders(7) 9 52
(Marcus Tregoning) *s.i.s: detached in last and nt gng: fnlly r.o last 150yds* 20/1

5/0- 12 1½ **Footstepsintherain (IRE)**403 102 9-9-3 61 LiamJones 5 48
(J R Jenkins) *wl in tch in midfield: shkn up and no prog over 2f out: wknd over 1f out* 25/1

00-0 13 nk **De Little Engine (IRE)**39 91 5-9-7 65 (p) RossaRyan 14 52
(Alexandra Dunn) *chsd ldrs on outer 5f: sn wknd* 33/1

1m 26.35s (0.35) **Going Correction** +0.025s/f (Slow) 13 Ran SP% 119.9
Speed ratings (Par 101): **99,97,97,96,96 95,93,92,92,92 91,89,89**
CSF £33.06 CT £126.41 TOTE £10.00: £3.20, £1.60, £1.60; EX 43.10 Trifecta £185.10.
Owner Simon Lockyer & Tim Clarke **Bred** Miss Y Jacques **Trained** Newmarket, Suffolk

FOCUS
An open handicap in which it paid to race handy.
T/Jkpt: Not won. T/Plt: £24.40 to a £1 stake. Pool: £94,567.09. 2,818.1 winning units. T/Qpdt: £12.00 to a £1 stake. Pool: £11,218.01. 686.57 winning units. **Jonathan Neesom**

585 SOUTHWELL (L-H)
Wednesday, February 13

OFFICIAL GOING: Fibresand: standard to slow
Wind: moderate across Weather: Cloudy

702 BETWAY APPRENTICE H'CAP 6f 16y(F)
2:00 (2:00) (Class 6) (0-60,62) 4-Y-O+ £2,264 (£673; £336; £168) Stalls Low

Form RPR
-112 1 **Gorgeous General**13 503 4-9-0 55 WilliamCarver(7) 6 65
(Lawrence Mullaney) *cl up: rdn wl over 1f out: slt ld ins fnl f: kpt on wl towards fin* 2/1[2]

2-35 2 nk **Liamba**27 279 4-9-12 60 ConorMcGovern 4 69
(David O'Meara) *cl up: shkn up and slt ld over 2f out: rdn wl over 1f out: drvn and hdd narrowly ins fnl f: ev ch: kpt on gamely towards fin* 6/4[1]

0-00 3 5 **Dream Ally (IRE)**34 166 9-8-13 52 JonathanFisher(5) 1 46
(John Weymes) *slt ld on inner: pushed along 3f out: sn hdd: cl up and rdn wl over 1f out: edgd rt and kpt on same pce fnl f* 33/1

5-52 4 ½ **Canimar**9 599 4-8-5 46 oh1 (v) GavinAshton(7) 8 39
(Shaun Keightley) *sn chsng ldrs: rdn along over 2f out: drvn and edgd lft over 1f out: kpt on one pce (vet said that the filly lost its right hind shoe)* 15/2

354- 5 1¼ **Qallaab (IRE)**46 9746 4-9-7 62 MarkCrehan(7) 5 51
(Michael Appleby) *awkward s and dwlt: rdn along in rr and wd st: kpt on u.p fnl f: n.d* 6/1[3]

0430 6 1¼ **Tasaaboq**9 594 8-8-5 46 oh1 (tp) GraceMcEntee(7) 2 31
(Phil McEntee) *sn rdn along and a outpcd in rr* 16/1

00-0 7 5 **Sir Geoffrey (IRE)**10 586 13-8-12 46 oh1 (b) NicolaCurrie 3 16
(Scott Dixon) *chsd ldrs on inner: rdn along over 3f out: sn lost pl and bhd* 50/1

1m 15.54s (-0.96) **Going Correction** -0.15s/f (Stan) 7 Ran SP% 110.2
Speed ratings (Par 101): **100,99,92,92,90 88,82**
CSF £4.92 CT £56.59 TOTE £2.90: £1.50, £1.10; EX 4.40 Trifecta £59.50.
Owner Shaun Humphries **Bred** Shaun & Leanne Humphries **Trained** Great Habton, N Yorks

FOCUS
A moderate sprint handicap in which the principals were always up there. The second has been rated to her previous best.

703 BETWAY CASINO H'CAP 1m 4f 14y(F)
2:30 (2:30) (Class 5) (0-75,76) 4-Y-O+ £2,911 (£866; £432; £216) Stalls Low

Form RPR
40-5 1 **Purple Rock (IRE)**20 390 7-9-4 70 (e) DanielMuscutt 6 80
(Gay Kelleway) *led after 1f and set stdy pce: pushed along 3f out: rdn 2f out: clr whn drvn and edgd rt ent fnl f: kpt on strly* 3/1[2]

12-5 2 3¾ **Country'N'Western (FR)**19 404 7-9-1 72 DarraghKeenan(5) 4 76
(Robert Eddery) *trckd ldng pair: hdwy to chse wnr and wd st: rdn along 2f out: drvn and edgd lft over 1f out: kpt on same pce* 2/1[1]

00-2 3 5 **Hidden Depths (IRE)**11 562 4-9-2 70 NicolaCurrie 5 67
(Jamie Osborne) *hld up in rr: hdwy 4f out: chsd ldng pair and wd st: rdn over 2f out: sn drvn and one pce (jockey said gelding was slowly away)* 3/1[2]

4/6- 4 16 **Primogeniture (IRE)**29 9295 8-9-10 76 (tp) JoeFanning 7 46
(Martin Keighley) *trckd ldrs: pushed along wl over 4f out: sn lost pl and bhd* 16/1

304- 5 23 **Luv U Whatever**57 9595 9-9-3 69 BarryMcHugh 3 3
(Marjorie Fife) *led 1f: trckd wnr: pushed along over 3f out: sn rdn and wknd* 4/1[3]

2m 36.61s (-4.39) **Going Correction** -0.15s/f (Stan)
WFA 4 from 5yo+ 2lb 5 Ran SP% 109.2
Speed ratings (Par 103): **108,105,102,91,76**
CSF £9.25 TOTE £3.20: £1.40, £1.30; EX 9.40 Trifecta £23.30.
Owner Strictly Fun Racing Club **Bred** Barronstown Stud **Trained** Exning, Suffolk

FOCUS
This modest handicap was another race where you had to be handy due to an uneven pace. The winner has been rated close to his November C&D mark.

704 BETWAY LIVE CASINO H'CAP 2m 102y(F)
3:00 (3:00) (Class 3) (0-90,91) 4-Y-O+ £9,703 (£2,887; £1,443; £721) Stalls Low

Form RPR
314/ 1 **Rainbow Dreamer**46 3928 6-9-12 91 (p) HollieDoyle 7 99
(Alan King) *trckd ldrs: pushed along 3f out: rdn on outer over 2f out: drvn and hdwy over 1f out: styd on wl fnl f to ld towards fin (jockey said gelding hung left throughout)* 15/2

02-4 2 nk **Second Page**20 390 5-8-1 73 (b) ThoreHammerHansen(7) 6 80
(Richard Hannon) *trckd ldng pair: hdwy 3f out and sn cl up: rdn wl over 1f out: drvn to take slt ld ins fnl f: hdd and no ex towards fin* 9/1

34-1 3 1¼ **Busy Street**22 349 7-9-12 91 AlistairRawlinson 3 96
(Michael Appleby) *trckd ldrs: smooth hdwy 3f out: sn cl up: shkn up to take slt ld over 1f out: sn rdn: hdd and drvn ins fnl f: kpt on same pce towards fin* 9/4[1]

01-2 4 1 **Amitie Waltz (FR)**33 184 7-9-1 80 ShaneKelly 2 84
(Richard Hughes) *hld up in rr: hdwy 3f out: trckd ldrs over 2f out: effrt whn n.m.r appr fnl f: sn rdn and kpt on same pce* 5/2[2]

1-11 5 3¼ **Azari**31 231 7-9-2 81 (b) RossaRyan 1 81
(Alexandra Dunn) *t.k.h: led: pushed along 3f out: rdn 2f out: hdd over 1f out: sn drvn and wknd* 13/2

004- 6 58 **World War (IRE)**94 4776 5-9-3 82 (t1) DanielMuscutt 5 12
(Martin Keighley) *cl up: rdn along over 4f out: sn wknd (jockey said gelding ran in snatches)* 66/1

P-00 7 106 **Addicted To You (IRE)**22 349 5-9-11 90 JoeFanning 4
(Mark Johnston) *dwlt and reminders in rr: hdwy to join field after 3f: cl up after 5f: pushed along over 6f out: sn rdn: lost pl and bhd (jockey said gelding was never travelling)* 6/1[3]

3m 37.89s (-7.61) **Going Correction** -0.15s/f (Stan) 7 Ran SP% 110.2
Speed ratings (Par 107): **113,112,112,111,110 81,**
CSF £65.10 TOTE £6.60: £3.70, £3.60; EX 51.60 Trifecta £302.00.
Owner The Maple Street Partnership **Bred** Rabbah Bloodstock Limited **Trained** Barbury Castle, Wilts

The Form Book Flat 2019, Raceform Ltd, Newbury, RG14 5SJ

FOCUS
This feature staying handicap saw a cracking finish. A pb from the second, with the third rated to his Newcastle latest.

705 SUNRACING.CO.UK H'CAP 7f 14y(F)
3:30 (3:30) (Class 5) (0-70,66) 4-Y-O+ **£2,911** (£866; £432; £216) **Stalls** Low

Form RPR
0254 **1** **Sooqaan**[13] [508] 8-8-11 **59**..........................(p) WilliamCox(3) 3 68
(Antony Brittain) *cl up: led 2f out: rdn clr appr fnl f: kpt on strly* **9/4**[1]
6-30 **2** 2 ¼ **Baron Run**[19] [410] 9-8-4 **56** ow3.......................... RhonaPindar(7) 2 58
(K R Burke) *t.k.h: slt ld: rdn along and hdd 2f out: kpt on u.p f* **6/1**[3]
1126 **3** ½ **Grey Destiny**[8] [609] 9-9-6 **65**..........................(p) CamHardie 5 66
(Antony Brittain) *trckd ldng pair: hdwy and cl up over 2f out: effrt and rdn wl over 1f out: kpt on same pce fnl f* **3/1**[2]
-600 **4** 8 **Kommander Kirkup**[10] [586] 8-9-7 **66**.......................... AndrewMullen 1 45
(Michael Herrington) *trckd ldrs: hdwy 3f out: rdn along 2f out: drvn and wknd over 1f out* **12/1**
03-3 **5** 1 ¾ **Screaming Gemini (IRE)**[33] [175] 5-9-1 **65**......(b) PoppyBridgwater(5) 4 39
(Tony Carroll) *t.k.h: trckd ldrs: n.m.r and swtchd rt whn sltly hmpd after 1f: sn pushed along in rr: hdwy and wd st: rdn to chse ldrs and hung lft wl over 1f out: sn wknd (trainer's rep said gelding was slowly away and subsequently resented the kickback from not gaining an early prominent position)* **9/4**[1]

1m 28.87s (-1.43) **Going Correction** -0.15s/f (Stan) **5** Ran SP% **108.5**
Speed ratings (Par 103): **102,99,98,89,87**
CSF £15.06 TOTE £2.80: £1.50, £3.10; EX 9.20 Trifecta £31.40.
Owner Antony Brittain **Bred** J A And Mrs Duffy **Trained** Warthill, N Yorks

FOCUS
This tight-looking handicap was run at a fair pace. The winner has been rated to his best recent form, and the second in line with his last C&D run.

706 BETWAY NOVICE STKS 6f 16y(F)
4:00 (4:00) (Class 5) 4-Y-O+ **£2,911** (£866; £432; £216) **Stalls** Low

Form RPR
3-32 **1** **Playfull Spirit**[12] [525] 4-8-11 69..........................(p) KieranO'Neill 4 69
(John Gosden) *slt ld on outer: hdd narrowly 3f out: led 2f out: rdn over 1f out: drvn ent fnl f: kpt on strly* **1/1**[1]
44-4 **2** 2 **Poet's Pride**[10] [586] 4-9-2 64.......................... BenCurtis 1 68
(David Barron) *cl up on inner: narrow ld 3f out: rdn along and hdd 2f out: drvn and ev ch over 1f out: kpt on same pce fnl f* **6/5**[2]
0-66 **3** 8 **Haader (FR)**[18] [431] 4-9-2 70.......................... RaulDaSilva 5 42
(Derek Shaw) *chsd ldrs: pushed along and wd st: sn rdn and outpcd: kpt on fr over 1f out: n.d* **20/1**
5-5 **4** 1 ½ **Polished Article**[27] [275] 4-8-8 0.......................... PhilDennis(3) 3 33
(Lawrence Mullaney) *cl up: rdn along 3f out: wknd fnl 2f* **80/1**
4 **5** shd **Snooze Button (IRE)**[18] [431] 4-9-2 0.......................... NicolaCurrie 2 37
(Jamie Osborne) *trckd ldrs: pushed along on inner and sltly outpcd over 3f out: kpt on u.p fnl 2f* **16/1**[3]

1m 15.48s (-1.02) **Going Correction** -0.15s/f (Stan) **5** Ran SP% **107.3**
Speed ratings (Par 103): **100,97,86,84,84**
CSF £2.29 TOTE £1.70: £1.02, £1.40; EX 2.30 Trifecta £5.20.
Owner Merry Fox Stud Limited **Bred** Merry Fox Stud Limited **Trained** Newmarket, Suffolk

FOCUS
A weak novice event dominated by the market leaders. The second has been rated back to his best.

707 BETWAY SPRINT H'CAP 4f 214y(F)
4:30 (4:30) (Class 6) (0-65,72) 4-Y-O+ **£2,264** (£673; £336; £168) **Stalls** Centre

Form RPR
5012 **1** **Spirit Power**[19] [411] 4-9-5 **65**.......................... JasonHart 5 70
(Eric Alston) *racd towards stands' side: chsd ldng pair: rdn along over 2f out: hdwy over 1f out: drvn and edgd lft ent fnl f: styd on wl to ld nr fin* **2/1**[2]
1U20 **2** nk **Archimedes (IRE)**[8] [610] 6-9-2 **65**..........................(tp) PhilDennis(3) 3 69
(David C Griffiths) *dwlt: sn chsng ldr towards far side: rdn wl over 1f out: drvn ent fnl f: ev ch last 100yds: kpt on* **9/4**[3]
4011 **3** hd **Point Zero (IRE)**[10] [587] 4-9-12 **72** 6ex..........(be) AlistairRawlinson 2 75
(Michael Appleby) *racd towards far side: led: rdn and edgd lft over 1f out: drvn ins fnl f: hdd and no ex towards fin* **7/4**[1]
0-06 **4** 9 **Jacob's Pillow**[13] [498] 8-9-6 **66**..........................(p) DanielTudhope 4 37
(Rebecca Bastiman) *racd centre: chsd ldr: sn rdn along: outpcd over 3f out: sn bhd* **10/1**

58.98s (-0.72) **Going Correction** -0.15s/f (Stan) **4** Ran SP% **109.6**
Speed ratings (Par 101): **99,98,98,83**
CSF £6.85 TOTE £2.80; EX 7.40 Trifecta £10.80.
Owner The Selebians **Bred** Lordship Stud **Trained** Longton, Lancs

FOCUS
This little sprint handicap had a tight look about it.
T/Plt: £74.90 to a £1 stake. Pool: £64,178.88. 625.25 winning units. T/Qpdt: £54.90 to a £1 stake. Pool: £Pool: £4,154.37. 55.99 winning units. **Joe Rowntree**

708 - 716a (Foreign Racing) - See Raceform Interactive

593 CHELMSFORD (A.W) (L-H)
Thursday, February 14

OFFICIAL GOING: Polytrack: standard
Wind: Virtually nil Weather: Dry

717 £20 FREE BETS AT TOTESPORT.COM CLASSIFIED STKS 1m (P)
4:45 (4:47) (Class 6) 4-Y-O+
£3,105 (£924; £461; £400; £400; £400) **Stalls** Low

Form RPR
40-2 **1** **Irish Times**[28] [273] 4-8-9 50.......................... DylanHogan(5) 1 56
(Henry Spiller) *trckd ldrs and travelled wl: effrt on inner over 1f out: rdn to ld 150yds out: kpt on and a doing enough towards fin* **5/1**[2]
3-00 **2** nk **Captain Kissinger**[17] [257] 4-8-7 50..........................(v[1]) GeorgiaDobie(7) 6 55
(Jo Hughes, France) *chsd ldrs: effrt over 1f out: hdwy u.p to chse wnr ins fnl f: styd on wl towards fin: nvr quite getting to wnr* **10/1**
56-U **3** 1 ½ **Cristal Pallas Cat (IRE)**[29] [250] 4-8-9 50..........(h) RhiainIngram(5) 2 52
(Roger Ingram) *led: rdn over 1f out: hdd 150yds out: no ex and lost 2nd wl ins fnl f: wknd towards fin* **5/1**[2]
-563 **4** 1 ¼ **Red Cossack (CAN)**[13] [532] 8-9-0 47.......................... ShaneKelly 10 49
(Dean Ivory) *taken down early: stdd and dropped in bhd after s: hld up towards rr: clsd 2f out: edgd lft and hdwy over 1f out: stl edging lft but kpt on u.p ins fnl f: nt rch ldrs* **9/2**[1]
0-40 **5** ½ **Kellington Kitty (USA)**[15] [485] 4-9-0 48.......................... RossaRyan 7 48
(Mike Murphy) *pressed ldr: rdn and ev ch ent fnl 2f: 3rd and no ex 1f out: wknd ins fnl f* **11/1**
0-00 **6** 1 **Dawn Commando**[12] [553] 4-9-0 48..........................(b) KieranO'Neill 12 46
(Daniel Kubler) *hld up in last quartet: effrt 2f out: hdwy u.p ins fnl f: styd on: nvr trbld ldrs* **6/1**[3]
0-05 **7** shd **Imperial Act**[13] [532] 4-9-0 45..........................(h) RobHornby 13 45
(Andrew Balding) *stdd s: hld up in last quartet: effrt whn nt clr run and hmpd over 1f out: sn swtchd sltly lft: hdwy ins fnl f: styd on: nvr trbld ldrs* **14/1**
6-26 **8** nk **Satchville Flyer**[12] [553] 8-9-0 50.......................... PJMcDonald 11 45
(David Evans) *s.i.s: effrt whn nt clr run and swtchd rt over 1f out: styd on ins fnl f: nvr trbld ldrs* **5/1**[2]
60-0 **9** 4 ½ **Demons And Wizards (IRE)**[40] [80] 4-9-0 48.......................... LukeMorris 3 34
(Lydia Richards) *t.k.h: in tch in midfield: effrt jst over 2f out: sn struggling and outpcd over 1f out: wknd ins fnl f (vet reported gelding lost its right hind shoe)* **33/1**
00-0 **10** 5 **Emigrated (IRE)**[8] [624] 6-9-0 48..........................(vt) PaddyMathers 5 23
(Derek Shaw) *in tch in midfield: rdn 3f out: struggling whn short of room and hmpd over 1f out: sn dropped out and btn: wknd fnl f* **25/1**
00-0 **11** 9 **Tabla**[33] [207] 7-9-0 50.......................... LiamJones 9 2
(Lee Carter) *chsd ldrs on outer: rdn and lost pl over 2f out: wl bhd ins fnl f (jockey said mare stopped quickly)* **50/1**
00-0 **12** ½ **Pass The Cristal (IRE)**[35] [155] 5-9-0 44.......................... MartinDwyer 8 1
(William Muir) *taken down early: midfield but hung rt thrght: niggled along and lost pl 4f out: wd and bhd bnd 2f out: sn wl bhd (jockey said gelding moved poorly)* **12/1**

1m 38.76s (-1.14) **Going Correction** -0.10s/f (Stan) **12** Ran SP% **123.0**
Speed ratings (Par 101): **101,100,99,97,97 96,96,96,91,86 77,77**
CSF £55.71 TOTE £4.70: £2.00, £2.90, £2.10; EX 75.60 Trifecta £498.20.
Owner D Forrester **Bred** Shortgrove Manor Stud **Trained** Newmarket, Suffolk

FOCUS
This low-key event was run in a respectable 2.76sec outside standard. The winner has been rated in keeping with his most recent effort.

718 TOTEPOOL CASHBACK CLUB AT TOTESPORT.COM H'CAP (DIV I) 7f (P)
5:20 (5:21) (Class 6) (0-52,54) 4-Y-O+
£3,105 (£924; £461; £400; £400; £400) **Stalls** Low

Form RPR
-062 **1** **Mochalov**[10] [595] 4-9-9 **54**.......................... DannyBrock 3 67+
(Jane Chapple-Hyam) *trckd ldrs and travelled wl: effrt between rivals to ld ent fnl 2f: rdn clr over 1f out: in command and kpt on wl ins fnl f: comf* **9/4**[1]
3-U1 **2** 3 ¼ **Magicinthemaking (USA)**[35] [161] 5-9-8 **53**.......................... HollieDoyle 7 57
(John E Long) *chsd ldr for 2f: styd chsng ldrs: effrt in 4th over 2f out: chsd clr wnr over 1f out: kpt on same pce and no imp ins fnl f* **5/2**[2]
0-02 **3** 1 ¼ **Blue Harmony**[15] [485] 4-8-12 **48**..........................(p) MeganNicholls(5) 8 49
(Michael Blake) *in tch in midfield: effrt over 1f out: hung lft u.p jst over 1f out: styd on to chse clr ldng pair ins fnl f: kpt on but no threat to wnr* **12/1**
0063 **4** ¾ **Caledonian Gold**[10] [594] 6-8-8 **46** oh1.......................... AledBeech(7) 5 45
(Lisa Williamson) *taken down early and led to post: stdd and edgd rt leaving s: hld up in last trio: clsd and nt clr run 2f out: edgd lft and effrt ent fnl f: rdn and kpt on ins fnl f: nvr trbld ldrs* **14/1**
03-2 **5** 2 **Pindaric**[19] [430] 5-8-8 **46**.......................... CianMacRedmond(7) 9 40
(Declan Carroll) *chsd ldrs on outer: wnt 2nd 6f out: effrt and pressing ldrs ent fnl 2f: unable qck and outpcd u.p over 1f out: wknd ins fnl f* **11/4**[3]
60-0 **6** 2 ¼ **Tilsworth Rose**[30] [245] 5-9-1 **46** oh1.......................... RaulDaSilva 4 34
(J R Jenkins) *led: rdn and hrd pressed over 2f out: sn hdd and btn over 1f out: wknd ins fnl f* **66/1**
6-60 **7** 2 **Farl (IRE)**[20] [399] 4-9-5 **50**..........................(b[1]) LukeMorris 2 33
(Ed Walker) *in tch in midfield: rdn and struggling to qckn over 2f out: lost pl and btn whn edgd rt over 1f out: wknd fnl f* **14/1**
3-06 **8** ½ **Wotamadam**[20] [402] 4-9-6 **51**.......................... MartinDwyer 10 33
(Dean Ivory) *stdd and swtchd sltly lft after s: t.k.h: hld up in last trio: rdn over 2f out: sn struggling and wl btn over 1f out* **14/1**
05-0 **9** nk **Beaming**[38] [118] 5-8-8 **46** oh1.......................... SophieRalston(7) 6 27
(Peter Hiatt) *dwlt and sltly impeded leaving stalls: a towards rr: rdn and struggling over 2f out: sn struggling and wl btn over 1f out* **50/1**

1m 25.82s (-1.38) **Going Correction** -0.10s/f (Stan) **9** Ran SP% **117.2**
Speed ratings (Par 101): **103,99,97,97,94 92,89,89,88**
CSF £8.24 CT £54.09 TOTE £2.50: £1.10, £1.30, £3.00; EX 7.50 Trifecta £43.30.
Owner Mrs Jane Chapple-Hyam **Bred** D H Brailsford **Trained** Dalham, Suffolk

FOCUS
The first division of a lowly handicap. The second has been rated to her recent level.

719 TOTEPOOL CASHBACK CLUB AT TOTESPORT.COM H'CAP (DIV II) 7f (P)
5:55 (5:59) (Class 6) (0-52,54) 4-Y-O+
£3,105 (£924; £461; £400; £400; £400) **Stalls** Low

Form RPR
0-01 **1** **Naralsaif (IRE)**[12] [553] 5-9-5 **50**..........................(v) PaddyMathers 5 56
(Derek Shaw) *trckd ldrs: nt clr run 2f out: effrt u.p ent fnl f: styd on wl u.p to ld cl home* **4/1**[2]
-524 **2** nk **Little Miss Kodi (IRE)**[10] [594] 6-9-6 **51**..........................(t) ShaneKelly 2 56
(Mark Loughnane) *hld up in tch: clsd and nt clr run ent fnl 2f: swtchd rt and effrt wl over 1f out: hdwy u.p 1f out: ev ch wl ins fnl f: led towards fin: sn hdd and no ex cl home* **5/1**[3]
25-4 **3** nk **Three C's (IRE)**[20] [399] 5-9-7 **52**..........................(p) HollieDoyle 1 56
(Adrian Wintle) *pressed ldr early: settled bk to trck ldrs: effrt between horses over 1f out: rdn to ld ent fnl f: hdd and no ex towards fin* **3/1**[1]
4604 **4** ¾ **Malaysian Boleh**[9] [613] 9-8-8 **46** oh1..........(be) GraceMcEntee(7) 8 48
(Phil McEntee) *hld up in tch on outer: nudged rt wl over 1f out: effrt u.p 1f out: kpt on ins fnl f: nt rch ldrs* **12/1**
1-06 **5** ¾ **Ertidaad (IRE)**[19] [436] 7-9-3 **48**..........................(v) AdamKirby 9 49
(Emma Owen) *roused along to go prom fr wd draw: w ldr over 5f out: drvn ent fnl 2f and styd pressing ldrs tl no ex 1f out: wknd fnl 100yds* **5/1**[3]
-500 **6** ½ **Athassel**[15] [484] 10-9-0 **50**.......................... KatherineBegley(5) 4 50
(David Evans) *niggled along leaving stalls and dropped to last pair: hdwy u.p on inner over 1f out: nt clr run: hmpd and swtchd rt ins fnl f: kpt on same pce fnl 100yds* **8/1**
32-5 **7** 1 **Secret Lightning (FR)**[10] [599] 7-9-9 **54**..........(v) AlistairRawlinson 7 51
(Michael Appleby) *in tch in midfield on outer: unable qck u.p over 1f out: keeping on same pce whn short of room and impeded ins fnl f: wknd fnl 100yds* **11/1**

The Form Book Flat 2019, Raceform Ltd, Newbury, RG14 5SJ

0-00 **8** 1 1/4 **No Approval (IRE)**[13] [533] 6-8-10 **46**..............(p) PoppyBridgwater(5) 3 39
(David Bridgwater) *led: drvn and hdd ent fnl f: sn edgd lft and outpcd: wknd ins fnl f* **12/1**

600- **9** 3/4 **Only Ten Per Cent (IRE)**[56] [9641] 11-9-1 **46** oh1.............. JasonHart 6 37
(J R Jenkins) *dwlt and hmpd leaving stalls: in tch in last pair: effrt over 2f out: rdn and unable qck over 1f out: kpt on same pce and no imp ins fnl f* **33/1**

1m 26.39s (-0.81) **Going Correction** -0.10s/f (Stan) **9** Ran SP% **116.1**
Speed ratings (Par 101): **100,99,99,98,97 97,95,94,93**
CSF £24.51 CT £68.30 TOTE £4.30: £1.40, £1.90, £1.50; EX 27.80 Trifecta £61.60.
Owner Derek Shaw **Bred** Shadwell Estate Company Limited **Trained** Sproxton, Leics

FOCUS
The slower division by 0.57sec. Straightforward form in behind the winner.

720 EXTRA PLACES AT TOTESPORT.COM H'CAP 6f (P)
6:30 (6:30) (Class 5) (0-75,76) 3-Y-O **£4,851** (£1,443; £721; £400; £400) **Stalls** Centre

Form RPR

-213 **1** **Probability (IRE)**[12] [555] 3-9-7 **73**.............................. EdwardGreatrex 3 78
(Archie Watson) *mde all: rdn and qcknd clr over 1f out: r.o and a in command ins fnl f* **5/1**[3]

32-6 **2** 1 1/2 **Antonia Clara**[20] [408] 3-9-3 **69**.............................. PJMcDonald 2 68
(Stuart Williams) *dwlt: sn rcvrd and wl in tch: effrt jst over 2f out: unable to match pce of wnr over 1f out: rallied u.p to chse wnr wl ins fnl f: styd on but nvr threatened wnr* **9/2**[2]

31-4 **3** 1/2 **Tobeeornottobee**[14] [505] 3-9-0 **66**.............................. CallumShepherd 5 63
(Declan Carroll) *chsd wnr: rdn over 2f out: unable to match pce of wnr u.p over 1f out: kpt on same pce and lost 2nd wl ins fnl f* **5/1**[3]

445- **4** 1 1/4 **On The Line (IRE)**[141] [7667] 3-9-10 **76**..............(t w) LukeMorris 1 69
(Hugo Palmer) *niggled along leaving stalls: chsd ldrs: rdn over 2f out: unable qck over 1f out: wl hld and one pce ins fnl f* **10/11**[1]

505- **5** 1 1/4 **Sepahi**[132] [7960] 3-9-0 **66**.............................. HollieDoyle 4 55
(Henry Spiller) *stdd s: hld up in tch in rr: effrt over 1f out: nt clr run and swtchd lft 1f out: no imp ins fnl f: eased towards fin* **14/1**

1m 12.86s (-0.84) **Going Correction** -0.10s/f (Stan) **5** Ran SP% **110.6**
Speed ratings (Par 97): **101,99,98,96,95**
CSF £26.30 TOTE £6.60: £3.50, £3.10; EX 17.30 Trifecta £33.00.
Owner Mrs C Cashman **Bred** Marie & Mossy Fahy **Trained** Upper Lambourn, W Berks

FOCUS
Just a fair sprint handicap. The second has been rated to her C&D handicap form.

721 IRISH LOTTO AT TOTESPORT.COM CLASSIFIED STKS 1m 5f 66y(P)
7:00 (7:02) (Class 6) 4-Y-O+
£3,105 (£924; £461; £400; £400; £400) **Stalls** Low

Form RPR

4-31 **1** **Croeso Cymraeg**[14] [504] 5-9-2 50.............................. RaulDaSilva 5 59+
(James Evans) *hld up off the pce in rr: clsd and in tch 8f out: hdwy and nt clr run over 1f out: gap opened and rdn to chse ldr over 1f out: led ins fnl f: r.o strly: readily* **7/4**[1]

-352 **2** 2 **Banta Bay**[12] [549] 5-9-2 49.............................. JosephineGordon 2 54
(John Best) *led: drvn over 1f out: hdd and one pce ins fnl f* **4/1**[2]

0-54 **3** 1 1/2 **Caracas**[22] [363] 5-9-0 50 ow1..............(p) JoshuaBryan(3) 3 53
(Kevin Frost) *chsd ldrs: effrt over 1f out: unable qck and kpt on same pce ins fnl f* **9/2**[3]

0-00 **4** nk **Sea's Aria (IRE)**[22] [369] 8-8-9 44.............................. TobyEley(7) 6 51
(Mark Hoad) *dwlt and short of room leaving stalls: in tch in rr of main gp: clsd on inner over 2f out: hdwy u.p over 1f out: kpt on same pce ins fnl f (jockey said gelding was slowly away)* **14/1**

604- **5** 1/2 **Gemologist (IRE)**[35] [1771] 4-9-0 50.............................. PJMcDonald 1 53
(Mark Johnston) *bustled along leaving stalls: sn chsng ldrs: unable qck u.p over 1f out: kpt on same pce ins fnl f* **7/1**

3-05 **6** 3 1/4 **Rocket Ronnie (IRE)**[19] [436] 9-9-2 43..............(p) HollieDoyle 7 46
(Adrian Wintle) *t.k.h: hld up in midfield: clsd on outer over 2f out: unable qck u.p over 1f out: sn outpcd and wknd ins fnl f* **20/1**

0-52 **7** 2 3/4 **Falls Creek (USA)**[15] [482] 4-9-0 46..............(b) RobHornby 4 44
(Andrew Balding) *pressed ldr tl rdn and outpcd over 1f out: wknd ins fnl f* **6/1**

6-00 **8** 1 1/2 **Solitary Sister (IRE)**[19] [436] 5-9-2 40.............................. NicolaCurrie 9 40
(John Berry) *off the pce in last pair: clsd and in tch 8f out: effrt over 1f out: no imp: wknd fnl f (jockey said mare was outpaced early)* **50/1**

63-0 **9** 17 **The Lock Master (IRE)**[14] [504] 12-9-2 44..............(v) LukeMorris 8 15
(Michael Appleby) *wnt lft leaving stalls: in tch in midfield on outer: rdn over 3f out: sn struggling: wl bhd and eased ins fnl f* **33/1**

2m 52.61s (-0.99) **Going Correction** -0.10s/f (Stan)
WFA 4 from 5yo+ 2lb **9** Ran SP% **117.7**
Speed ratings (Par 101): **99,97,96,96,96 94,92,91,81**
CSF £8.79 TOTE £2.70: £1.20, £1.60, £1.60; EX 8.60 Trifecta £24.80.
Owner Richard Evans Bloodstock **Bred** Richard Evans **Trained** Broadwas, Worcs

FOCUS
A decent race of its type, this was steadily run. The second has been rated near his recent form.

722 BET IN PLAY AT TOTESPORT.COM H'CAP 1m 2f (P)
7:30 (7:32) (Class 4) (0-80,82) 4-Y-O+
£5,530 (£1,645; £822; £411; £400; £400) **Stalls** Low

Form RPR

3-11 **1** **Executive Force**[9] [611] 5-9-10 **82** 6ex..............(p) FrannyNorton 1 93+
(Michael Wigham) *hld up wl in tch in midfield: clsd to press ldr and hld together over 1f out: shkn up to ld ins fnl f: sn qcknd clr and r.o strly: v readily* **13/8**[1]

42-2 **2** 2 1/2 **Gas Monkey**[29] [250] 4-8-7 **65** oh2..............(p[1]) ShelleyBirkett 2 69
(Julia Feilden) *wl in tch in midfield: effrt over 1f out: edging lft but kpt on to go 2nd 100yds out: no ch w wnr* **10/3**[2]

-020 **3** 1 1/2 **Juanito Chico (IRE)**[12] [557] 5-9-7 **79**..............(t[1]) PJMcDonald 5 80
(Stuart Williams) *stdd leaving stalls: t.k.h: hld up in last pair: effrt over 2f out: hdwy u.p whn nt clr run and swtchd rt 1f out: swtchd lft ins fnl f: kpt on to snatch 3rd last strides: no ch w wnr* **8/1**

3-12 **4** nk **Bollihope**[31] [241] 7-8-10 **68**.............................. JasonHart 4 68
(Shaun Keightley) *led: rdn over 1f out: hdd and nt match pce of wnr ins fnl f: lost btn 2nd 100yds out: wknd towards fin* **4/1**[3]

16-6 **5** 1 3/4 **God Willing**[39] [102] 8-8-5 **70**..............(t) ZakWheatley(7) 7 67
(Declan Carroll) *chsd ldr over 8f out tl outpcd u.p over 1f out: wknd ins fnl f* **33/1**

0-35 **6** shd **The Warrior (IRE)**[27] [294] 7-9-2 **74**.............................. LiamJones 6 71
(Lee Carter) *stdd s: t.k.h: hld up in tch in last pair: effrt over 2f out: sn outpcd and no threat to ldrs after* **22/1**

0-14 **7** 7 **Baasha**[22] [362] 4-8-7 **65** oh1..............(b) LukeMorris 3 49
(Ed Dunlop) *t.k.h: pressed ldr tl settled in 3rd over 8f out: rdn over 2f out: lost pl and bhd 1f out: wknd and eased wl ins fnl f: fin lame (vet reported gelding was lame right hind)* **8/1**

2m 6.85s (-1.75) **Going Correction** -0.10s/f (Stan) **7** Ran SP% **110.7**
Speed ratings (Par 105): **103,101,99,99,98 98,92**
CSF £6.63 TOTE £2.10: £1.40, £1.80; EX 6.80 Trifecta £36.60.
Owner Tugay Akman **Bred** Rabbah Bloodstock Limited **Trained** Newmarket, Suffolk

FOCUS
Fairly useful handicap form.

723 DOUBLE DELIGHT HAT-TRICK HEAVEN AT TOTESPORT.COM NOVICE STKS (PLUS 10 RACE) 1m 2f (P)
8:00 (8:03) (Class 4) 3-Y-O **£5,757** (£1,713; £856; £428) **Stalls** Low

Form RPR

2 **1** **Cirque Royal**[10] [606] 3-9-2 0.............................. AdamKirby 1 82+
(Charlie Appleby) *restless in stalls: mde virtually all: rdn jst over 2f out: drifted rt over 1f out: asserted ins fnl f: styd on strly and drew clr fnl 100yds* **1/3**[1]

2 2 1/2 **Ragnar** 3-9-2 0.............................. CallumShepherd 2 77
(Dominic Ffrench Davis) *trckd ldrs: wnt 2nd and nt clrest of runs 2f out: swtchd lft and effrt to press wnr over 1f out: no ex and outpcd fnl 100yds* **12/1**[3]

3 1 3/4 **Persuading (IRE)** 3-9-2 0.............................. ShaneKelly 4 74+
(Charlie Appleby) *dwlt: wnt lft and rn green early: in tch in last pair: hdwy on inner into midfield 4f out: effrt to chse ldng trio 2f out: edgd rt 1f out: swtchd lft and kpt on ins fnl f to snatch 3rd last strides* **11/4**[2]

0 **4** hd **Copper Rose (IRE)**[19] [442] 3-8-11 0.............................. PJMcDonald 9 68
(Mark Johnston) *pressed ldrs tl dropped in and settled in 4th over 7f out: effrt to chse wnr over 2f out tl over 1f out: 3rd and outpcd whn swtchd lft 1f out: kpt on same pce and lost 3rd last strides* **25/1**

6 **5** 8 **Shaleela's Dream**[16] [472] 3-9-2 0..............(b) MarcMonaghan 7 57
(Marco Botti) *hld up in tch: effrt over 2f out: outpcd by ldng quartet over 1f out: wl hld 5th and hung rt 1f out* **25/1**

5 **6** 3/4 **Withoutdestination**[24] [343] 3-8-13 0..............(b[1]) AaronJones(3) 6 56
(Marco Botti) *s.i.s: effrt over 2f out: drvn and wl outpcd over 1f out: plugged on to pass btn horses ins fnl f: nvr involved* **50/1**

04 **7** 1 1/4 **Perique**[13] [518] 3-9-2 0.............................. DanielMuscutt 5 53
(Ed Dunlop) *t.k.h: hld up in tch in midfield: rdn over 2f out: sn outpcd and wl hld whn wandered over 1f out: wknd fnl f* **12/1**[3]

0-6 **8** 1 1/4 **Munstead Moonshine**[27] [299] 3-8-11 0.............................. RobHornby 8 46
(Andrew Balding) *wnt lft leaving stalls: in tch in midfield: effrt over 2f out: sn outpcd and wl btn over 1f out: wknd fnl f* **80/1**

0 **9** 5 **Georgearthurhenry**[32] [229] 3-9-2 0.............................. GeorgeWood 10 41
(Amy Murphy) *t.k.h: in tch in midfield on outer: effrt over 2f out: sn outpcd and wl btn over 1f out: wknd fnl f* **66/1**

0 **10** 1 3/4 **Newsflash**[19] [442] 3-8-6 0.............................. DarraghKeenan(5) 3 32
(Amy Murphy) *chsd wnr tl rdn and lost 2nd over 2f out and sn outpcd: wl btn over 1f out: wknd fnl f* **66/1**

2m 8.02s (-0.58) **Going Correction** -0.10s/f (Stan) **10** Ran SP% **130.9**
Speed ratings (Par 99): **98,96,94,94,88 87,86,85,81,80**
CSF £7.93 TOTE £1.20: £1.02, £2.80, £1.10; EX 12.90 Trifecta £20.60.
Owner Godolphin **Bred** Godolphin **Trained** Newmarket, Suffolk

FOCUS
The first four finished a long way clear in this novice event, in which the winner set a modest pace. The time was 1.17sec slower than the preceding Class 4 handicap. The winner has been rated as stepping up a little on his debut run.

724 BOOK TICKETS AT CHELMSFORDCITYRACECOURSE.COM H'CAP 1m 2f (P)
8:30 (8:34) (Class 6) (0-60,63) 4-Y-O+
£3,105 (£924; £461; £400; £400; £400) **Stalls** Low

Form RPR

2024 **1** **Don't Do It (IRE)**[10] [593] 4-8-12 **51**..............(v[1]) AlistairRawlinson 12 60+
(Michael Appleby) *hld up in tch in midfield: effrt u.p over 1f out: drvn to ld and edgd lft ins fnl f: hld on towards fin* **7/1**

-511 **2** nk **Zorawar (FR)**[8] [624] 5-9-10 **63** 6ex.............................. ShaneGray 14 71+
(David O'Meara) *t.k.h: hld up in tch in midfield: nt clrest of runs and swtchd rt over 1f out: clsd to chse ldrs 1f out: effrt to press wnr ins fnl f: styd on but hld towards fin* **5/2**[1]

01-4 **3** 2 **Tobacco Road (IRE)**[36] [145] 9-9-4 **60**..............(t) JoshuaBryan(3) 11 64
(Mark Pattinson) *hld up in last quartet: hdwy u.p over 1f out: ev ch 1f out: no ex and outpcd fnl 100yds* **22/1**

0-03 **4** 2 **Natch**[26] [309] 4-9-8 **61**..............(p) CallumShepherd 7 62
(Michael Attwater) *trckd ldrs tl clsd to press ldr 5f out: rdn to ld over 1f out: hdd ins fnl f: sn outpcd and wknd wl ins fnl f* **16/1**

440- **5** 1/2 **Kilbaha Lady (IRE)**[57] [9614] 5-9-8 **61**.............................. JasonHart 3 62
(Nigel Tinkler) *hld up in tch in midfield: nt clr run and hmpd over 1f out: shkn up 1f out: swtchd rt and styd on ins fnl f: no ch w ldrs (jockey said mare was denied a clear run)* **16/1**

-301 **6** 1/2 **Caledonia Duchess**[15] [479] 6-9-1 **61**..............(v) GeorgiaDobie(7) 4 59
(Jo Hughes, France) *restless in stalls: t.k.h: wl in tch in midfield: clsd to press ldrs 3f out: ev ch u.p over 1f out tl no ex ins fnl f: wknd wl ins fnl f* **12/1**

06-5 **7** 1 **Barbara Villiers**[17] [459] 4-9-8 **61**.............................. PJMcDonald 13 58
(David Evans) *pressed ldr 5f out: styd prom tl unable qck over 1f out: wknd ins fnl f* **33/1**

0-00 **8** nse **Harbour Force (FR)**[27] [288] 5-8-10 **49**.............................. ShaneKelly 8 45
(Neil Mulholland) *in tch in midfield: effrt jst over 2f out: swtchd rt and drvn 1f out: kpt on same pce ins fnl f* **50/1**

6-41 **9** 1 **Mullarkey**[27] [288] 5-9-2 **55**..............(t) KierenFox 1 49
(John Best) *trckd ldrs: effrt u.p over 1f out: unable qck and wknd ins fnl f* **4/1**[2]

20-6 **10** 1 **Marshall Aid (IRE)**[26] [318] 6-9-3 **56**.............................. NicolaCurrie 2 49
(Mark Usher) *sn towards rr: rdn and outpcd over 3f out: sme prog and wnt lft over 1f out: nvr trbld ldrs* **16/1**

4-60 **11** 3 1/2 **Dukes Meadow**[10] [595] 8-8-2 **46** oh1..............RhiainIngram(5) 10 32
(Roger Ingram) *hld up in last quartet: effrt over 1f out: no prog and nvr involved* **50/1**

61-2 **12** 3/4 **Hard Toffee (IRE)**[42] [39] 8-9-7 **60**.............................. AdamKirby 15 44
(Louise Allan) *midfield on outer: effrt u.p over 2f out: btn over 1f out and wknd ins fnl f* **6/1**

-032 **13** 2 1/4 **Squire**[12] [552] 8-9-8 **61**..............(tp) LukeMorris 5 41
(Marjorie Fife) *t.k.h: led tl over 1f out: sn lost pl and wknd ins fnl f* **5/1**[3]

/00- **14** *91* **Davina**[213] 5030 4-8-0 **46** oh1 ThoreHammerHansen(7) 9
(Bill Turner) *sn towards rr: rdn over 7f out: lost tch 4f out: t.o (jockey said filly was never travelling)* **100/1**
2m 5.84s (-2.76) **Going Correction** -0.10s/f (Stan) **14** Ran **SP% 129.6**
Speed ratings (Par 101): **107,106,105,103,103 102,101,101,101,100 97,96,95,22**
CSF £26.00 CT £396.75 TOTE £8.10: £2.20, £2.10, £6.30; EX 50.70 Trifecta £897.60.
Owner ThornleyNaylorGriffithsMulhernJohnson **Bred** L O'Donovan **Trained** Oakham, Rutland
FOCUS
A competitive event for the grade. A minor pb from the winner.
T/Jkpt: £714.20 to a £1 stake. Pool: £10,000.00 - 14.00 winning units T/Plt: £20.80 to a £1 stake. Pool: £84,105.31 - 2,939.24 winning units T/Qpdt: £8.40 to a £1 stake. Pool: £15,637.07 - 1,362.32 winning units **Steve Payne**

634 MEYDAN (L-H)
Thursday, February 14
OFFICIAL GOING: Turf: good; dirt: fast

725a MEYDAN SPRINT SPONSORED BY GULF NEWS (GROUP 2) (TURF) 5f (T)
3:05 (3:05) 3-Y-O+
£118,110 (£39,370; £19,685; £9,842; £5,905; £3,937)

RPR
1 **Blue Point (IRE)**[174] 6504 5-9-0 **120** WilliamBuick 1 121+
(Charlie Appleby) *trckd ldr: rdn to ld 2f out: r.o wl: easily* **1/4**[1]
2 *5* **Faatinah (AUS)**[21] 393 6-9-0 **112** (b) JimCrowley 4 102
(David A Hayes, Australia) *sn led: hdd 2f out: r.o wl but no ch w wnr* **3/1**[2]
3 *2* **Portamento (IRE)**[4] 681 7-9-0 **100** FernandoJara 2 95
(A R Al Rayhi, UAE) *nvr nr to chal but r.o wl fnl 2f* **50/1**
4 *4 1/2* **Mujaafy (AUS)**[397] 4-9-0 **105** PatCosgrave 3 79
(M F De Kock, South Africa) *trckd ldr tl wknd 2 1/2f out* **22/1**
5 *1 1/2* **Rebel Streak**[7] 639 4-9-0 **100** (b) MickaelBarzalona 5 73
(Ali Jan, Qatar) *chsd ldr tl wknd 2 1/2f out* **33/1**
6 *17* **Johann Strauss**[721] 892 8-9-0 **100** RoystonFfrench 6 12
(R Bouresly, Kuwait) *slowly away: a in rr* **80/1**
56.52s (-0.58) **Going Correction** +0.425s/f (Yiel) **6** Ran **SP% 115.5**
Speed ratings: **121,113,109,102,100 73**
CSF: 1.38.
Owner Godolphin **Bred** Oak Lodge Bloodstock **Trained** Newmarket, Suffolk
FOCUS
There was a lightning-quick second section - 24.09 (400m from standing start), 20.95 (800m), 11.48 (line) - and the Group 1-class winner was way too good for the others. The third limits the form.

726a FIREBREAK STKS SPONSORED BY REACH BY GULF NEWS (GROUP 3) (DIRT) 1m (D)
3:40 (3:40) 3-Y-O+
£94,488 (£31,496; £15,748; £7,874; £4,724; £3,149)

RPR
1 **Muntazah**[35] 171 6-9-0 **109** JimCrowley 7 115
(Doug Watson, UAE) *mid-div: smooth prog 3f out: led 1 1/2f out: r.o wl: easily* **7/2**[3]
2 *4 1/4* **Secret Ambition**[20] 425 6-9-2 **106** (t) RichardMullen 2 107+
(S Seemar, UAE) *s.i.s: trckd ldr: ev ch 2 1/2f out: r.o same pce fnl 2f* **15/2**
3 *3 1/4* **Heavy Metal**[35] 171 9-9-0 **114** MickaelBarzalona 1 98
(S Jadhav, UAE) *wl away: sn led: hdd 1 1/2f out: wknd fnl 110yds* **13/8**[1]
4 *1 1/4* **Kimbear (USA)**[35] 171 5-9-0 **109** PatDobbs 5 95+
(Doug Watson, UAE) *mid-div: r.o same pce fnl 2f* **11/4**[2]
5 *19* **Behavioral Bias (USA)**[20] 425 5-9-0 **102** (bt) TadhgO'Shea 3 51
(S Seemar, UAE) *trckd ldr tl wknd 3f out* **22/1**
6 *12* **Janoobi (SAF)**[21] 397 5-9-0 **109** (t) SamHitchcott 6 23
(M F De Kock, South Africa) *a in rr* **25/1**
7 *3 1/2* **Silent Attack**[14] 514 6-9-0 **103** (p) ChristopheSoumillon 4 15
(Saeed bin Suroor) *a in rr* **16/1**
1m 38.21s (0.71) **Going Correction** +0.425s/f (Slow) **7** Ran **SP% 112.8**
Speed ratings: **113,108,105,104,85 73,69**
CSF: 28.45.
Owner Hamdan Al Maktoum **Bred** Shadwell Estate Co Ltd **Trained** United Arab Emirates
FOCUS
TRAKUS: 2nd -3, 3rd -8, 4th +3, 5th +3, 6th +3, 7th -1. A strong early pace over a tiring track, and they finished slowly: 24.23, 22.35, 24.94, 26.69. A pb from the winner, with the second helping to set the level.

727a MEYDAN TROPHY SPONSORED BY FRIDAY (CONDITIONS) (TURF) 1m 1f 110y
4:15 (4:15) 3-Y-O
£47,244 (£15,748; £7,874; £3,937; £2,362; £1,574)

RPR
1 **Art Du Val**[113] 8563 3-9-3 **101** WilliamBuick 10 91+
(Charlie Appleby) *mid-div: smooth prog 3f out: led 1 1/2f out: r.o wl: easily* **1/1**[1]
2 *4* **Bila Shak (USA)**[12] 570 3-9-3 **81** (v) OisinMurphy 1 77
(Fawzi Abdulla Nass, Bahrain) *trckd ldr: ev ch 3f out: r.o fnl 2f: no ch w wnr* **11/1**
3 *nk* **Trolius (IRE)**[14] 511 3-9-5 **93** (tp) ChrisHayes 8 79
(Simon Crisford) *mid-div: chsd ldr 2 1/2f out: r.o fnl 2f: no ch w wnr* **15/2**[3]
4 *3 1/4* **Dobbia (USA)**[40] 92 3-9-0 **0** AntonioFresu 6 67
(A bin Harmash, UAE) *s.i.s: nvr nr to chal but r.o fnl 2 1/2f out: nrst fin* **80/1**
5 *1* **Burj**[14] 511 3-9-5 **83** (h) ChristopheSoumillon 4 70
(Saeed bin Suroor) *sn led: hdd 1 1/2f out: wknd fnl 110yds* **28/1**
6 *2* **Alla Mahlak (USA)**[21] 394 3-9-0 **70** SzczepanMazur 9 61
(R Bouresly, Kuwait) *nvr nr to chal* **100/1**
7 *shd* **Emma Point (USA)**[14] 510 3-8-9 **75** (h) TadhgO'Shea 2 56
(Marco Botti) *nvr nr to chal* **80/1**
8 *1 1/4* **Phalasteen (USA)**[12] 570 3-9-0 **0** ConnorBeasley 5 58
(R Bouresly, Kuwait) *nvr nr to chal* **50/1**
9 *10 3/4* **Victory Command (IRE)**[21] 394 3-9-5 **101** RoystonFfrench 3 41
(Mark Johnston) *trckd ldr tl wknd 3f out* **5/2**[2]
10 *1 1/2* **Bosconero (IRE)**[12] 570 3-8-8 **76** (bt) SaeedAlMazrooei(6) 7 33
(A R Al Rayhi, UAE) *slowly away: a in rr* **66/1**
11 *1 3/4* **Luxor Temple (USA)**[12] 570 3-9-0 **68** (b) FernandoJara 11 29
(A R Al Rayhi, UAE) *nvr bttr than mid-div* **100/1**
12 *22* **Promise Of Success**[78] 9291 3-8-9 **0** PatCosgrave 12
(Saeed bin Suroor) *nvr bttr than mid-div* **8/1**
1m 56.94s **12** Ran **SP% 121.1**
CSF: 14.82.
Owner Godolphin **Bred** D J And Mrs Deer **Trained** Newmarket, Suffolk
FOCUS
TRAKUS: 2nd -6, 3rd +1, 4th -5, 5th -6, 6th 0, 7th -3, 8th -3, 9th -1, 10th +9, 11th +4, 12th +4. A new race, uncompetitive but with a good winner, and it was strongly run: 25.3 (400m from standing start), 23.11 (800m), 24.65 (1200m), 24.8 (1600m). The second, fourth, sixth and eighth limit the form.

728a BALANCHINE SPONSORED BY GULFNEWS.COM (GROUP 2) (F&M) (TURF) 1m 1f (T)
4:50 (4:50) 3-Y-O+
£118,110 (£39,370; £19,685; £9,842; £5,905; £3,937)

RPR
1 **Poetic Charm**[28] 283 4-9-3 **107** WilliamBuick 6 109+
(Charlie Appleby) *s.i.s: settled in rr: smooth prog 2 1/2f out: led 1 1/2f out: r.o wl: easily* **2/7**[1]
2 *2 3/4* **Mia Tesoro (IRE)**[28] 283 6-9-0 **95** ChrisHayes 2 99
(Charlie Fellowes) *settled in rr: r.o fnl 2f but no ch w wnr: nrst fin* **50/1**
3 *3/4* **Peri Lina (TUR)**[28] 283 4-9-0 **97** (h) SelimKaya 3 97
(Hasan Boyraz, Turkey) *broke awkwardly: mid-div: t.k.h: r.o fnl 2f: no ch w wnr* **50/1**
4 *2 1/2* **Asoof**[28] 283 4-9-0 **98** ChristopheSoumillon 1 92
(Saeed bin Suroor) *sn led: hdd 3 1/2f out: led again 2 1/2f out: hdd & wknd 1 1/2f out* **10/3**[2]
5 *3/4* **Furia Cruzada (CHI)**[28] 283 7-9-0 **103** (t) AntonioFresu 5 91
(E Charpy, UAE) *mid-div: chsd ldrs and ev ch 2 1/2f out: wknd fnl f* **11/1**[3]
6 *9 1/4* **Monza (IRE)**[28] 283 4-9-0 **95** (p) CarlosLopez 4 71
(Bent Olsen, Denmark) *trckd ldr: led briefly 3 1/2f out: hdd & wknd 2 1/2f out* **80/1**
1m 49.6s (0.50) **Going Correction** +0.425s/f (Yiel) **6** Ran **SP% 114.3**
Speed ratings: **114,111,110,108,108 99**
CSF: 25.32.
Owner Godolphin **Bred** Godolphin **Trained** Newmarket, Suffolk
FOCUS
TRAKUS: 2nd -4, 3rd -5, 4th -6, 5th 0, 6th -1. Another weak race with a good winner, and there was something of a muddling tempo: 25.71, 23.34, 24.84, 23.63, 12.08.

729a INSIDEOUT (H'CAP) (DIRT) 6f (D)
5:25 (5:25) (90-108,108) 3-Y-O+
£63,779 (£21,259; £10,629; £5,314; £3,188; £2,125)

RPR
1 **Lavaspin**[84] 9218 5-8-5 **92** (b) RichardMullen 2 101
(S Seemar, UAE) *sn led: rdn 3f out: r.o wl* **4/1**[2]
2 *2 1/4* **Switzerland (USA)**[14] 512 5-9-5 **107** (t) MickaelBarzalona 7 108
(Steven Asmussen, U.S.A) *trckd ldr: ev ch 2 1/2f out: r.o same pce fnl 2f* **11/2**
3 *nk* **Nine Below Zero**[14] 512 4-8-10 **99** TadhgO'Shea 8 98
(Fawzi Abdulla Nass, Bahrain) *mid-div: r.o fnl 2f: nrst fin* **10/3**[1]
4 *1/2* **Good Curry (TUR)**[117] 7-9-6 **108** HalisKaratas 3 106+
(Bayram Kocakaya, Turkey) *mid-div: r.o wl fnl 1 1/2f: nrst fin* **8/1**
5 *3/4* **Almanaara (IRE)**[28] 280 6-8-5 **94** (v) SamHitchcott 9 89+
(Doug Watson, UAE) *mid-div: r.o same pce fnl 2 1/2f* **18/1**
6 *1* **Pop The Hood (USA)**[28] 280 7-8-6 **95** (bt) ConnorBeasley 6 87
(Doug Watson, UAE) *mid-div: chsd ldrs and ev ch 2 1/2f out: wknd fnl f* **11/2**
7 *3* **Taamol (IRE)**[4] 681 5-8-6 **92** ow1 FernandoJara 5 77
(A R Al Rayhi, UAE) *squeezed at s: nvr nr to chal* **25/1**
8 *3/4* **Glenamoy Lad**[7] 639 5-8-6 **95** (t) ChrisHayes 1 75
(Michael Wigham) *nvr nr to chal* **18/1**
9 *7 3/4* **Victory Wave (USA)**[7] 640 5-8-9 **98** PatCosgrave 4 53
(Saeed bin Suroor) *a in rr* **9/2**[3]
10 *1 1/4* **Ace Korea (USA)**[42] 50 4-8-11 **100** (t) FabriceVeron 10 51
(Peter Wolsley, Korea) *s.i.s: a in rr* **40/1**
1m 11.98s (0.38) **Going Correction** +0.425s/f (Slow) **10** Ran **SP% 120.0**
Speed ratings: **114,111,110,109,108 107,103,102,92,90**
CSF: 27.25; TRICAST: 84.37.
Owner Mohd Khaleel Ahmed **Bred** Darley **Trained** United Arab Emirates
FOCUS
TRAKUS: 2nd +6, 3rd +9, 4th +2, 5th +7, 6th +8, 7th +14, 8th +3, 9th +11, 10th +11. The winner made all through fast early-slow late splits: 24.01, 22.68, 25.29.

730a WHEELS (H'CAP) (TURF) 1m 4f 11y(T)
6:00 (6:00) (95-109,109) 3-Y-O+
£82,677 (£27,559; £13,779; £6,889; £4,133; £2,755)

RPR
1 **Mountain Hunter (USA)**[28] 284 5-9-1 **102** ChristopheSoumillon 7 107+
(Saeed bin Suroor) *trckd ldr: led 2f out: r.o wl* **11/2**[3]
2 *1 1/2* **Red Galileo**[7] 635 8-8-11 **102** RowanScott(4) 4 104
(Saeed bin Suroor) *mid-div: r.o fnl 2f: nrst fin* **10/1**
3 *nse* **Walton Street**[153] 7241 5-9-5 **106** (p) WilliamBuick 1 108
(Charlie Appleby) *mid-div: smooth prog 2 1/2f out: r.o fnl 2f* **2/1**[1]
4 *3/4* **Sharpalo (FR)**[21] 398 7-9-3 **104** (t) ConnorBeasley 5 105
(A bin Harmash, UAE) *settled in rr: r.o fnl 2 1/2f out: nrst fin* **8/1**
5 *6 1/2* **Zaman**[14] 514 4-9-5 **108** (b) JamesDoyle 2 99
(Charlie Appleby) *mid-div: r.o same pce fnl 2 1/2f* **10/3**[2]
6 *3* **Rio Tigre (IRE)**[12] 572 8-8-7 **95** MickaelBarzalona 11 80
(S Jadhav, UAE) *nvr nr to chal* **25/1**
7 *2 1/4* **Stage Magic (IRE)**[14] 514 4-8-13 **102** ColmO'Donoghue 14 85
(Charlie Appleby) *mid-div: smooth prog to ld 5f out: hdd & wknd 4f out* **33/1**
8 *1 3/4* **Very Talented (IRE)**[138] 7773 6-9-3 **104** PatCosgrave 10 83
(Saeed bin Suroor) *nvr bttr than mid-div* **12/1**
9 *2 1/4* **Celestial Spheres (IRE)**[28] 284 5-8-9 **97** (p) BrettDoyle 13 72+
(Charlie Appleby) *slowly away: nvr nr to chal* **25/1**
10 *6 1/2* **Parsifal (SPA)**[21] 398 6-8-7 **95** FernandoJara 3 59
(G Arizkorreta Elosegui, Spain) *slowly away: a in rr* **50/1**
11 *3 1/2* **Maifalki (FR)**[21] 398 6-8-7 **95** (e) TadhgO'Shea 6 54
(N Caullery, France) *a in rr* **66/1**
12 *2 1/2* **Appeared**[28] 281 7-8-9 **97** ChrisHayes 8 52
(David Simcock) *trckd ldr tl wknd fnl 2 1/2f* **16/1**

13	21	**Buhwarui Banseok (USA)**[28] [284] 6-8-7 **95**..........(b) RichardMullen 12	16
		(Bart Rice, Korea) *s.i.s: nvr bttr than mid-div* 80/1	
14	11 1/2	**Astronomer (IRE)**[14] [514] 4-9-6 **109**..........(bt) OlivierDoleuze 9	14
		(M F De Kock, South Africa) *sn led: hdd 5f out: wknd fnl 3 1/2f out* 22/1	

2m 29.32s (-2.68) **Going Correction** +0.425s/f (Yiel)
WFA 4 from 5yo+ 2lb **14** Ran SP% **125.2**
Speed ratings: **125,124,123,123,119 117,115,114,112,108 106,104,90,82**
CSF: 58.35; TRICAST: 151.30; PLACEPOT: £14.20 to a £1 stake. Pool: £4,531.75 - 229.75 winning units; QUADPOT: £10.10 to a £1 stake. Pool: £758.30 - 55.40 winning units.
Owner Godolphin **Bred** Darley **Trained** Newmarket, Suffolk

FOCUS
TRAKUS: 2nd +2, 3rd +2, 4th +3, 5th +13, 6th +16, 7th +10, 8th +14, 9th +20, 10th +14, 11th +17, 12th +12, 13th +23, 14th +3. This was a solid test of stamina: 26.31, 25.00, 24.29, 23.69, 24.79, with the winner to the line in 24.91.

561 LINGFIELD (L-H)
Friday, February 15

OFFICIAL GOING: Polytrack: standard
Wind: light, behind Weather: fine

731 BETWAY HEED YOUR HUNCH H'CAP — 1m 7f 169y(P)
2:00 (2:00) (Class 6) (0-60,67) 4-Y-O+ **£2,264** (£673; £336; £168) **Stalls** Low

Form				RPR
3-03	1		**Thresholdofadream (IRE)**[13] [566] 4-8-13 **53**.............. JoeFanning 11	59+
			(Amanda Perrett) *midfield early: sn stdd and hld up towards rr: nt clr run over 2f out: clsd ent fnl 2f: chsd ldrs 1f out: r.o u.p to ld wl ins fnl f* 16/1	
53-1	2	hd	**Atomic Jack**[9] [619] 4-9-13 **67** 6ex.............. NicolaCurrie 1	75+
			(George Baker) *s.i.s: t.k.h and hdwy to chse ldrs after 2f: led after 3f tl over 9f out: shuffled bk over 4f out: nt clr run over 2f out: hdwy and swtchd rt 1f out: r.o strly to go 2nd cl home: nt quite rch winne (jockey said gelding ran too free and was denied a clear run)* 13/8[1]	
02-3	3	3/4	**Argyle (IRE)**[23] [369] 6-9-9 **59**..............(v) ShaneKelly 14	62
			(Gary Moore) *t.k.h: wl in tch in midfield: hdwy to ld over 4f out: rdn and drifted rt over 1f out: hdd and no ex wl ins fnl f (vet reported the gelding lost its left fore shoe)* 9/1	
0-62	4	nse	**Mood For Mischief**[22] [385] 4-9-8 **62**.............. LukeMorris 2	67
			(Ed Walker) *wl in tch in midfield: clsd to chse ldrs and pushed along 4f out: 3rd and drvn ent fnl 2f: pressed ldrs ins fnl f: no ex and one pce wl ins fnl f* 5/1[2]	
-624	5	1/2	**Bird For Life**[13] [560] 5-8-12 **55**..............(p) EllieMacKenzie(7) 12	57
			(Mark Usher) *in tch towards rr: pushed along over 6f out: hdwy but v wd 3f out: clsng and swtchd lft jst ins fnl f: styd on wl: nt rch ldrs* 9/1	
2-02	6	1 1/4	**Nafaayes (IRE)**[23] [369] 5-9-4 **61**..............(p) TobyEley(7) 13	62
			(Jean-Rene Auvray) *t.k.h: w ldr early: restrained into midfield but stl keen: hdwy to press ldrs again over 4f out: rdn and ev ch over 2f out: unable qck over 1f out: wknd ins fnl f* 8/1[3]	
4-20	7	hd	**Heron (USA)**[13] [560] 5-9-8 **58**..............(p) DanielMuscutt 10	58
			(Brett Johnson) *t.k.h: wl in tch in midfield: trckd ldrs 5f out: rdn over 2f out: kpt on same pce ins fnl f* 16/1	
64-5	8	1 3/4	**Tilsworth Sammy**[23] [369] 4-8-10 **50**.............. DavidProbert 6	50
			(J R Jenkins) *in tch towards rr: swtchd rt and effrt over 2f out: nt clrest of runs ent fnl 2f: drvn over 1f out: kpt on ins fnl f: nvr trbld ldrs* 12/1	
00-0	9	1	**Multigifted**[13] [560] 6-8-13 **56**..............(h) ScottMcCullagh(7) 7	53
			(Michael Madgwick) *stdd s: hld up in rr: effrt over 1f out: kpt on ins fnl f: nvr trbld ldrs* 25/1	
/0-0	10	nse	**Netley Abbey**[23] [369] 5-8-5 **46** oh1..............(tp) RhiainIngram(5) 3	43
			(Paul George) *led for 3f: styd chsng ldrs: u.p and struggling to qckn over 2f out: lost pl and btn over 1f out: plugged on same pce fnl f* 33/1	
004-	11	3 3/4	**Shaji**[25] [9310] 4-9-1 **60**..............(p[1]) PoppyBridgwater(5) 5	55
			(David Bridgwater) *wl in tch in midfield: hdwy to join ldr over 8f out: led 5f out: sn hdd: rdn over 2f out: losing pl whn short of room over 1f out: wknd fnl f* 33/1	
-631	12	hd	**Seasearch**[12] [589] 4-9-4 **65** 6ex..............(p) WilliamCarver(7) 8	59
			(Andrew Balding) *hld up in tch in midfield on outer: pushed along and effrt 3f out: rdn and no prog ent fnl 2f: sn outpcd and btn over 1f out: wknd fnl f (jockey said gelding was unsuited by the track, which in their opinion was too sharp for the gelding)* 8/1[3]	
	13	2 1/4	**Lamh Ar Lamh (IRE)**[31] [1442] 5-8-10 **46** oh1..............(t) HollieDoyle 4	36
			(Nigel Hawke) *a in rr-div: bhd and u.p: no prog and wl btn over 1f out (jockey said mare was never travelling)* 50/1	
500/	14	1 1/4	**Sixties Idol**[40] [1082] 6-8-11 **47** oh1 ow1..............(bt) StevieDonohoe 9	35
			(Sheena West) *towards rr: swtchd rt and hdwy after 2f: jnd ldr after 3f tl led over 9f out: hdd 5f out: rdn and lost pl 3f out: bhd over 1f out* 50/1	

3m 25.4s (-0.30) **Going Correction** -0.025s/f (Stan)
WFA 4 from 5yo+ 4lb **14** Ran SP% **130.1**
Speed ratings (Par 101): **99,98,98,98,98 97,97,96,96,96 94,94,93,92**
CSF £44.20 CT £279.34 TOTE £12.70: £3.20, £1.10, £3.60; EX 44.30 Trifecta £425.70.
Owner D M James & Woodcote Stud **Bred** Woodcote Stud **Trained** Pulborough, W Sussex

FOCUS
They went steady early on and the pace picked up significantly running down the hill.

732 SUN RACING TOP TIPS AND PREVIEWS NOVICE STKS — 1m 1y(P)
2:35 (2:35) (Class 5) 4-Y-O+ **£2,911** (£866; £432; £216) **Stalls** High

Form				RPR
2	1		**Kodiac Harbour (IRE)**[27] [316] 4-9-2 0.............. JFEgan 2	75
			(Paul George) *plld hrd: chsd ldrs: effrt 2f out: swtchd lft over 1f out: sn chalng u.p: nosed ahd ins fnl f: styd on wl and hld on gamely after* 5/2[2]	
00-3	2	nk	**Pheidippides**[34] [206] 4-9-2 74..............(b) LukeMorris 5	74
			(Tom Clover) *led for over 1f out: chsd ldr tl rdn to chal ent fnl 2f: drvn and led jst over 1f out: hdd ins fnl f: kpt on u.p but a hld* 9/4[1]	
4-	3	nk	**Iconic Girl**[99] [8959] 4-8-11 0.............. DavidProbert 1	68
			(Andrew Balding) *in tch in midfield: clsd to trck ldrs 2f out: effrt and ev ch jst over 1f out: kpt on but unable qck wl ins fnl f* 11/4[3]	
33-4	4	2 3/4	**Gates Pass**[18] [464] 4-9-2 71..............(p) NicolaCurrie 3	67
			(Jamie Osborne) *dwlt: bustled along and rcvrd to ld over 6f out: rdn and hrd pressed ent fnl 2f: drvn and hdd jst over 1f out: wknd ins fnl f* 4/1	
	5	3/4	**Velvet Morn (IRE)** 4-8-11 0.............. CallumShepherd 6	60
			(William Knight) *hld up in last pair: nudged along and outpcd ent fnl f: no threat to ldrs after but kpt on steadily ins fnl f* 28/1	
0-0	6	15	**Lord Digby**[20] [435] 4-9-2 0.............. PaddyMathers 7	31
			(Adam West) *dropped in bhd after s: in tch in rr: rdn over 2f out: sn outpcd and wknd over 1f out* 100/1	

1m 37.02s (-1.18) **Going Correction** -0.025s/f (Stan) **6** Ran SP% **110.4**
Speed ratings (Par 103): **104,103,103,100,99 84**
CSF £8.25 TOTE £2.90: £1.10, £1.60; EX 7.30 Trifecta £16.50.
Owner Mike Hocking And Paul George **Bred** Tally-Ho Stud **Trained** Crediton, Devon

FOCUS
The market principals had a good battle from the turn in.

733 LADBROKES HOME OF THE ODDS BOOST NOVICE STKS — 7f 1y(P)
3:10 (3:10) (Class 5) 3-Y-O **£2,911** (£866; £432; £216) **Stalls** Low

Form				RPR
4	1		**Bay Of Naples (IRE)**[15] [500] 3-9-2 0.............. JoeFanning 2	76
			(Mark Johnston) *mde all: rdn over 1f out: hld on gamely ins fnl f* 14/1	
0-2	2	shd	**Assimilation (IRE)**[23] [359] 3-9-2 0.............. LukeMorris 7	75
			(Ed Walker) *chsd wnr: effrt ent fnl 2f: hrd drvn and ev ch ins fnl f: kpt on: jst hld* 5/1	
4-22	3	1	**Shanghai Grace**[28] [289] 3-9-2 77.............. RichardKingscote 1	73
			(Charles Hills) *trckd ldrs on inner: effrt wl over 1f out: drvn and pressed ldr 1f out: ev ch ins fnl f: unable qck and outpcd towards fin* 7/4[1]	
	4	hd	**Lestrade** 3-9-2 0..............(h[1]) CallumShepherd 9	72+
			(William Jarvis) *stdd and dropped in bhd after s: hld up in rr: clsd and swtchd rt over 1f out: rdn and hdwy 1f out: str run fnl 100yds out: gng on strly at fin: nt rch ldrs* 33/1	
1	5	2 1/4	**Songkran (IRE)**[23] [359] 3-9-9 0.............. DavidProbert 8	73
			(David Elsworth) *chsd ldrs: effrt in cl 4th 2f out: unable qck and outpcd over 1f out: wl hld and kpt on same pce ins fnl f* 7/2[3]	
3-4	6	1/2	**Woods (IRE)**[30] [251] 3-9-2 0.............. TomMarquand 6	65
			(William Haggas) *wl in tch in midfield: effrt 2f out: outpcd over 1f out: wl hld and kpt on same pce ins fnl f* 11/4[2]	
	7	1/2	**Theban Air** 3-8-11 0.............. StevieDonohoe 5	58
			(Lucy Wadham) *rn green: in tch in last trio: effrt whn drifted wd bnd 2f out: kpt on same pce after* 25/1	
06	8	11	**Capofaro**[13] [554] 3-9-2 0.............. NicolaCurrie 3	34
			(Jamie Osborne) *stdd after s: hld up in last pair: effrt jst over 2f out: sn outpcd: wknd over 1f out (jockey said gelding became unbalanced on the side of the track)* 50/1	
00-	9	1 1/2	**Cachaca**[70] [9443] 3-8-11 0.............. KierenFox 4	25
			(John Best) *t.k.h: hld up wl in tch in midfield: effrt over 2f out: sn outpcd and lost pl: wknd over 1f out* 100/1	

1m 25.31s (0.51) **Going Correction** -0.025s/f (Stan) **9** Ran SP% **118.3**
Speed ratings (Par 97): **96,95,94,94,91 91,90,78,76**
CSF £81.98 TOTE £8.00: £3.30, £1.80, £1.10; EX 56.80 Trifecta £209.60.
Owner Sheikh Hamdan bin Mohammed Al Maktoum **Bred** Godolphin **Trained** Middleham Moor, N Yorks

FOCUS
The early pace wasn't strong and those up front dominated throughout.

734 LIKE SUN RACING ON FACEBOOK H'CAP — 7f 1y(P)
3:40 (3:40) (Class 4) (0-85,86) 4-Y-O+ **£4,690** (£1,395; £697; £348) **Stalls** Low

Form				RPR
51-2	1		**Loyalty**[14] [517] 12-9-7 **83**..............(v) PaddyMathers 1	90+
			(Derek Shaw) *taken down early: led: hdd over 4f out but styd upsides ldr on inner: led again wl over 1f out: sn rdn and kicked over 1 l clr: styd on wl and a doing enough ins fnl f: rdn out* 14/1	
-105	2	1	**Florencio**[9] [618] 6-9-10 **86**..............(p) DougieCostello 3	89
			(Jamie Osborne) *chsd wnr for 1f: wl in tch in midfield after: effrt over 1f out: drvn to chse ldng pair 1f out: wnt 2nd and swtchd rt wl ins fnl f: styd on but nvr getting to wnr* 3/1[2]	
05-2	3	1/2	**Last Page**[23] [361] 4-8-10 **79**.............. LauraCoughlan(7) 6	81
			(David Loughnane) *t.k.h to post: t.k.h on outer: jnd wnr 5f out: led over 4f out tl wl over 1f out: sn rdn and unable to match pce of wnr: kpt on same pce and lost 2nd wl ins fnl f: burst blood vessel (vet reported the gelding bled from the nose)* 7/2	
-211	4	2 3/4	**Highland Acclaim (IRE)**[13] [564] 8-9-3 **79**..............(h) DavidProbert 5	74
			(David O'Meara) *stdd s: t.k.h: sn chsng ldrs: rdn: hung lft and unable qck over 1f out: wknd ins fnl f (jockey said gelding ran too free and hung left-handed)* 2/1[1]	
0-15	5	3/4	**Kodiline (IRE)**[30] [260] 5-9-3 **79**.............. HollieDoyle 4	72
			(David Evans) *awkward leaving stalls: rcvrd to chse wnr after 1f tl 5f out: dropped to last pair and rdn wl over 2f out: outpcd and btn over 1f out (jockey said gelding was never travelling)* 10/3[3]	
/00-	6	2 1/4	**Until Midnight (IRE)**[99] [8958] 9-8-12 **74**.............. NicolaCurrie 2	60
			(Eugene Stanford) *hld up in detached last: clsd 3f out: rdn over 1f out: sn btn and wknd fnl f* 33/1	

1m 23.66s (-1.14) **Going Correction** -0.025s/f (Stan) **6** Ran SP% **113.2**
Speed ratings (Par 105): **105,103,103,100,99 96**
CSF £56.15 TOTE £13.20: £5.20, £2.70; EX 55.20 Trifecta £233.00.
Owner Derek Shaw **Bred** Ecoutila Partnership **Trained** Sproxton, Leics

FOCUS
A fair contest.

735 PLAY 4 TO SCORE AT BETWAY H'CAP — 1m 4f (P)
4:15 (4:15) (Class 4) (0-85,85) 4-Y-O+ **£4,690** (£1,395; £697; £348) **Stalls** Low

Form				RPR
50-3	1		**Tralee Hills**[41] [88] 5-8-13 **75**..............(t[1]) TomMarquand 6	81
			(Peter Hedger) *stdd s: hld up in rr: clsd and lft handy over 4f out: effrt 2f out: swtchd rt over 1f out: str run u.p ins fnl f to ld last stride* 5/1[2]	
1-13	2	shd	**Elysees Palace**[29] [272] 5-9-4 **80**.............. LukeMorris 3	85
			(Sir Mark Prescott Bt) *chsd ldr tl led 10f out: wnt clr over 7f out: allowed rivals to cl 5f out: jnd over 2f out: rdn 2f out: forged ahd 1f out: hrd drvn ins fnl f: hdd last stride* 1/2[1]	
14-3	3	1/2	**Cry Wolf**[20] [432] 6-9-2 **78**..............(p) RossaRyan 7	82
			(Alexandra Dunn) *stdd and awkward leaving stalls: hld up in tch: clsd and lft cl 3rd over 4f out: sn chsng ldr: ev ch and rdn ent fnl 2f: kpt on same pce wl ins fnl f* 7/1[3]	
1/4-	4	1/2	**Wapping (USA)**[393] [277] 6-9-2 **85**.............. AaronMackay(7) 5	88
			(Barry Brennan) *t.k.h: chsd ldrs: lft 2nd briefly over 4f out: nt clrest of runs on inner over 2f out: effrt to press ldrs 1f out: edgd rt and kpt on same pce ins fnl f* 40/1	
110-	5	3	**Ravenous**[133] [7952] 8-8-7 **76**.............. SophieRalston(7) 4	75
			(Luke Dace) *midfield: lft cl up over 4f out: outpcd and wd wl over 1f out: wl hld and kpt on same pce ins fnl f* 25/1	
20/4	P		**White Shaheen**[35] [184] 6-9-6 **82**.............. NicolaCurrie 2	
			(William Muir) *led for 2f: chsd ldr after tl eased and p.u over 4f out: lame (vet reported the gelding was lame on its left fore)* 8/1	

2m 36.05s (3.05) **Going Correction** -0.025s/f (Stan) **6** Ran SP% **113.2**
Speed ratings (Par 105): **88,87,87,87,85**
CSF £8.09 TOTE £5.70: £2.20, £1.10; EX 9.30 Trifecta £25.20.
Owner P C F Racing Ltd **Bred** Natton House Thoroughbreds **Trained** Hook, Hampshire

FOCUS
This was steadily run and turned into a sprint. They finished in a heap.

736 BETWAY H'CAP 1m 4f (P)
4:50 (4:50) (Class 6) (0-55,57) 4-Y-O+ £2,264 (£673; £336; £168) Stalls Low

Form RPR
5-02 1 **Tesorina (IRE)**[28] 288 4-9-3 53 (v) RichardKingscote 3 59
(William Knight) *mde all: rdn ent fnl 2f: clr ins fnl f: a holding on towards fin* 7/1
-416 2 nk **Top Rock Talula (IRE)**[23] 369 4-9-4 54 EdwardGreatrex 1 60
(Warren Greatrex) *pushed along leaving stalls: in tch in midfield: effrt in 5th 2f out: swtchd rt and hdwy ins fnl f: chsd wnr wl ins fnl f: styd on wl but nvr quite getting to wnr* 9/2[1]
3-20 3 1 1/4 **Arlecchino's Arc (IRE)**[23] 363 4-9-3 53 (b) TomMarquand 14 57
(Mark Usher) *rousted along leaving stalls and early reminder: styd wd tl hdwy to chse wnr and moved towards inner 10f out: rdn ent fnl 2f: unable to match pce of wnr 1f out: edgd lft and lost 2nd wl ins fnl f* 15/2
52-4 4 hd **Music Major**[27] 321 6-9-8 56 (p) CallumShepherd 9 59+
(Michael Attwater) *hld up in rr: stl bhd and nt clr run over 2f out: rdn and hdwy 1f out: r.o strly ins fnl f: nt rch ldrs* 7/1
004- 5 3/4 **Luna Magic**[72] 9408 5-9-4 57 DarraghKeenan(5) 8 58
(Lydia Pearce) *awkward leaving stalls: hld up in tch in midfield: nt clrest of run jst over 2f out: hdwy and swtchd rt 1f out: styd on u.p ins fnl f: short of room and swtchd rt cl home (jockey said mare jumped awkwardly from the stalls)* 16/1
200- 6 hd **Tommys Geal**[51] 9054 7-8-13 54 ScottMcCullagh(7) 6 55+
(Michael Madgwick) *pushed along leaving stalls: hld up in last pair: nt clr run ent fnl 2f: hdwy over 1f out: styd on u.p ins fnl f: n.m.r towards fin: fin lame (vet reported the mare was lame on its left fore)* 14/1
1-12 7 3/4 **Apex Predator (IRE)**[27] 321 4-9-6 56 (bt) LukeMorris 5 56
(Seamus Durack) *t.k.h: chsd ldrs: effrt 2f out: drvn and fnd little over 1f out: wknd ins fnl f* 6/1[3]
51-1 8 2 **Tigerfish (IRE)**[42] 59 5-9-4 52 (p) HollieDoyle 13 48
(William Stone) *t.k.h: midfield tl grad stdd bk and in tch in last trio 8f out: stl last pair jst over 2f out: forced wd and effrt bnd 2f out: kpt on ins fnl f: no threat to ldrs* 5/1[2]
006- 9 3/4 **Willow Grace**[130] 8059 4-9-3 53 NicolaCurrie 12 49
(George Baker) *chsd ldrs: rdn and struggling to qckn ent fnl 2f: lost pl over 1f out: wknd ins fnl f* 12/1
5-40 10 1/2 **London Grammar (IRE)**[23] 369 5-8-5 46 oh1 ThoreHammerHansen(7) 11 40
(Ralph J Smith) *chsd wnr tl 10f out: wl in tch in midfield after: rdn over 2f out: unable qck and lost pl over 1f out: wknd ins fnl f* 66/1
-044 11 1 **Murhib (IRE)**[13] 549 7-8-12 46 (h) DavidProbert 15 39
(Lydia Richards) *hld up in tch in midfield: effrt jst over 2f out: unable qck and btn over 1f out: wknd ins fnl f* 8/1
00/0 12 2 3/4 **Singer In The Sand (IRE)**[37] 141 4-8-13 52 PaddyBradley(3) 10 41
(Pat Phelan) *hld up in tch in midfield: rdn jst over 2f out: sn outpcd and lost pl over 1f out: wknd fnl f* 66/1
00-6 P **Sark (IRE)**[42] 58 6-9-5 53 EoinWalsh 7
(David Evans) *hld up in tch in last quartet: eased and p.u over 3f out: bandage c loose (jockey said gelding was pulled up due the bandage on the right fore coming loose approaching 4 furlongs out)* 14/1

2m 31.25s (-1.75) **Going Correction** -0.025s/f (Stan)
WFA 4 from 5yo+ 2lb 13 Ran SP% 126.9
Speed ratings (Par 101): **104,103,102,102,102 102,101,100,99,99 98,97,**
CSF £41.01 CT £254.07 TOTE £7.90: £2.30, £2.10, £3.00; EX 38.50 Trifecta £421.50.
Owner Angmering Park Thoroughbreds Vi **Bred** Karis Bloodstock Ltd & Rathbarry Stud **Trained** Angmering, W Sussex

FOCUS
A moderate handicap in which it was an advantage to be up with the pace. Straightforward form, with the first two rated near their recent best.
T/Jkpt: Not Won. T/Plt: £64.00 to a £1 stake. Pool: £66,163.12 - 754.39 winning units T/Qpdt: £21.70 to a £1 stake. Pool: £7,483.62 - 254.09 winning units **Steve Payne**

607 NEWCASTLE (A.W) (L-H)
Friday, February 15

OFFICIAL GOING: Tapeta: standard to slow
Wind: Breezy, half behind on the straight course and in over 3f of home straight in race on the round cour Weather: Dry

737 BETWAY CASINO H'CAP 1m 4f 98y (Tp)
4:45 (4:45) (Class 4) (0-85,85) 4-Y-O+ £4,690 (£1,395; £697; £348) Stalls High

Form RPR
-115 1 **Glan Y Gors (IRE)**[14] 522 7-8-12 74 (p) CliffordLee 5 82
(David Thompson) *t.k.h early: trckd ldr: rdn along over 2f out: led ins fnl f: kpt on wl* 11/2
2-12 2 1 1/4 **Star Of Southwold (FR)**[9] 625 4-9-7 85 AlistairRawlinson 3 91
(Michael Appleby) *led at ordinary gallop: rdn 2f out: edgd lft and hdd ins fnl f: kpt on same pce* 7/4[1]
-411 3 2 **Royal Cosmic**[10] 607 5-8-4 71 6ex SeanDavis(5) 1 74
(Richard Fahey) *trckd ldrs: rdn along over 2f out: kpt on same pce fnl f* 4/1[3]
50/0 4 4 **Red Tornado (FR)**[24] 349 7-9-6 82 JasonHart 2 79
(Chris Fairhurst) *prom: rdn and outpcd 2f out: sn n.d* 12/1
43-4 5 1/2 **Native Fighter (IRE)**[14] 522 5-9-4 80 JackGarritty 6 76
(Jedd O'Keeffe) *stdd and swtchd lft s: hld up: effrt and pushed along over 2f out: no imp fr over 1f out* 7/2[2]
045- 6 3/4 **Restive (IRE)**[58] 9610 6-8-6 71 oh1 JamieGormley(3) 4 66
(Jim Goldie) *hld up in tch: rdn and outpcd over 2f out: btn over 1f out* 12/1

2m 45.48s (4.38) **Going Correction** +0.225s/f (Slow)
WFA 4 from 5yo+ 2lb 6 Ran SP% 109.4
Speed ratings (Par 105): **94,93,91,89,88 88**
CSF £14.79 TOTE £6.90: £3.20, £1.10; EX 17.40 Trifecta £58.10.
Owner B Lapham & J Souster **Bred** Colm McEvoy **Trained** Bolam, Co Durham

FOCUS
The track was decompacted last week and the going was duly given as standard to slow. They went a modest gallop in this opener, the three that mattered in those positions for much of the race.

738 SUNRACING.CO.UK APPRENTICE H'CAP 7f 14y (Tp)
5:15 (5:15) (Class 6) (0-60,62) 4-Y-O+ £2,264 (£673; £336; £168) Stalls Centre

Form RPR
11 1 **Lion Hearted (IRE)**[15] 501 5-9-3 58 MarkCrehan(3) 2 78+
(Michael Appleby) *racd in centre of gp: mde all: pushed clr fr 2f out: readily* 4/7[1]
33-0 2 6 **Great Colaci**[21] 410 6-8-11 52 OliverStammers(3) 11 55
(Gillian Boanas) *cl up on nr side of gp: chsd wnr over 2f out: rdn and kpt on fnl f: nt pce to chal* 20/1
3-14 3 1 1/4 **Thunder Buddy**[33] 232 4-9-7 59 JonathanFisher 7 59
(K R Burke) *prom in centre of gp: drvn along over 2f out: kpt on ins fnl f: no imp* 10/1[2]
1-04 4 1/2 **Roaring Rory**[15] 502 6-9-7 59 BenSanderson 6 58
(Ollie Pears) *hld up towards centre of gp: drvn along over 2f out: kpt on fnl f: no imp* 25/1
-553 5 1/2 **Thorntoun Lady (USA)**[15] 502 9-8-11 54 CoreyMadden(5) 3 51
(Jim Goldie) *hld up: pushed along in centre of gp over 2f out: kpt on fnl f: nvr rchd ldrs* 25/1
31-4 6 1 3/4 **I Am Dandy (IRE)**[34] 210 4-8-11 52 (t) RussellHarris(3) 9 45
(James Ewart) *chsd wnr on nr side of gp to over 2f out: rallied: outpcd fnl f* 14/1
64-4 7 nk **Black Hambleton**[43] 37 6-8-11 52 HarryRussell(3) 8 44
(Bryan Smart) *hld up on nr side of gp: drvn and outpcd over 2f out: rallied ins fnl f: n.d* 22/1
34-0 8 1/2 **Gun Case**[24] 355 7-9-10 62 (v) AndrewBreslin 1 53
(Alistair Whillans) *hld up on far side of gp: drvn and outpcd over 2f out: sme late hdwy: nvr on terms* 16/1
3-02 9 nse **Scenery**[21] 410 4-9-7 59 MeganNicholls 5 50
(Marjorie Fife) *cl up in centre of gp: rdn over 2f out: wknd ins fnl f* 12/1[3]
0-66 10 3/4 **Nutopia**[15] 502 4-8-7 45 KieranSchofield 4 34
(Antony Brittain) *hld up in midfield on far side of gp: drvn over 2f out: wknd over 1f out* 33/1
0-65 11 nk **Makofitwhatyouwill**[15] 501 4-8-7 45 PaulaMuir 10 33
(Ruth Carr) *missed break: bhd on nr side of gp: drvn over 2f out: sn no imp: btn over 1f out (jockey said gelding was slowly away)* 28/1

1m 27.1s (0.90) **Going Correction** +0.225s/f (Slow) 11 Ran SP% 116.2
Speed ratings (Par 101): **103,96,94,94,93 91,91,90,90,89 89**
CSF £19.45 CT £68.68 TOTE £1.50: £1.02, £5.10, £2.80; EX 13.80 Trifecta £88.60.
Owner Slipstream Racing **Bred** Dowager Countess Harrington **Trained** Oakham, Rutland

FOCUS
A deeply one-sided apprentice handicap.

739 LADBROKES FILLIES' NOVICE STKS 1m 5y (Tp)
5:45 (5:45) (Class 5) 3-Y-O+ £2,911 (£866; £432; £216) Stalls Centre

Form RPR
2-1 1 **Orchid Star**[13] 547 3-9-0 0 DanielTudhope 1 69+
(Charlie Appleby) *mde all: shkn up and clr ins fnl f: comf* 1/12[1]
2 3 **Farrdhana** 3-8-7 0 NathanEvans 4 55
(Bryan Smart) *dwlt: hld up: smooth hdwy over 2f out: effrt and chsd wnr over 1f out: one pce ins fnl f* 16/1[3]
5 3 1/2 **Al Daayen (FR)**[17] 472 3-8-7 0 FrannyNorton 5 54
(Mark Johnston) *pressed wnr to over 1f out: edgd lft: one pce ins fnl f* 16/1[3]
0 4 1 1/2 **Lizzie Loch**[40] 103 3-8-7 0 PaulHanagan 2 51
(Alistair Whillans) *hld up in tch: pushed along over 2f out: edgd lft and no imp over 1f out* 66/1
5 7 **Quila Saeda (GER)**[230] 5-10-5 0 AlistairRawlinson 3 47
(Michael Appleby) *reluctant to enter stalls: cl up: drvn and outpcd over 2f out: btn over 1f out* 7/1[2]

1m 41.1s (2.50) **Going Correction** +0.225s/f (Slow)
WFA 3 from 5yo 19lb 5 Ran SP% 118.1
Speed ratings (Par 100): **96,93,92,91,84**
CSF £4.32 TOTE £1.02: £1.02, £4.60; EX 3.40 Trifecta £10.20.
Owner Godolphin **Bred** Godolphin **Trained** Newmarket, Suffolk

FOCUS
A novice that was all about the winner, a smart sort in prospect.

740 FOLLOW SUNRACING ON TWITTER H'CAP 1m 5y (Tp)
6:15 (6:15) (Class 4) (0-80,82) 4-Y-O+ £4,568 (£1,367; £683; £342; £170) Stalls Centre

Form RPR
03-3 1 **Helovaplan (IRE)**[34] 213 5-9-11 82 GrahamLee 4 85
(Bryan Smart) *cl up: led gng wl over 2f out: hrd pressed fr over 1f out: hld on wl towards fin* 11/10[1]
210- 2 nk **Intense Style (IRE)**[139] 7750 7-9-7 78 DanielTudhope 5 80
(Les Eyre) *t.k.h: hld up in tch: shkn up over 2f out: hung lft and chal over 1f out: kpt on fnl f: hld towards fin* 7/1
326- 3 2 3/4 **Saisons D'Or (IRE)**[129] 8096 4-9-2 73 JackGarritty 2 69
(Jedd O'Keeffe) *plld hrd: cl up: taken wd briefly after 2f: effrt and rdn 2f out: outpcd fnl f* 11/4[2]
01-5 4 nk **Remmy D (IRE)**[40] 102 4-8-6 70 CoreyMadden(7) 3 65
(Jim Goldie) *hld up in last pl: effrt and hdwy over 1f out: rdn and no imp fnl f* 10/1
0-60 5 4 1/2 **Contrast (IRE)**[24] 351 5-9-4 82 JoshQuinn(7) 1 67
(Michael Easterby) *led to over 2f out: rdn and wknd over 1f out* 13/2[3]

1m 40.01s (1.41) **Going Correction** +0.225s/f (Slow) 5 Ran SP% 109.2
Speed ratings (Par 105): **101,100,97,97,93**
CSF £9.10 TOTE £1.70: £1.10, £3.10; EX 9.30 Trifecta £18.90.
Owner The Smart Set **Bred** Ross Moorhead **Trained** Hambleton, N Yorks

FOCUS
Few of these arrived in top form and it turned into a bit of a sprint.

741 BETWAY H'CAP 6f (Tp)
6:45 (6:45) (Class 5) (0-75,77) 4-Y-O+ £2,911 (£866; £432; £216) Stalls Centre

Form RPR
0-31 1 **Epeius (IRE)**[15] 496 6-8-13 67 (v) AndrewMullen 6 74
(Ben Haslam) *t.k.h: hld up in tch: rdn and hdwy over 1f out: led ins fnl f: hld on wl towards fin* 10/3[1]
2-63 2 nk **Lucky Lodge**[15] 496 9-9-1 69 (b) CamHardie 4 75
(Antony Brittain) *t.k.h: led to over 1f out: rallied and ev ch briefly ins fnl f: sn pressing wnr: kpt on: hld nr fin* 9/2[3]

4-00 **3** *1* **Tommy G**[21] 407 6-9-6 **77**.................. PhilDennis(3) 7 80
(Jim Goldie) *hld up: smooth hdwy over 1f out: sn rdn: kpt on ins fnl f: nt rch first two* **9/2**[3]

613 **4** *nk* **Dawn Delight**[18] 464 4-9-3 **71**.................. PaulMulrennan 5 73
(Hugo Palmer) *prom: rdn and outpcd over 1f out: rallied ins fnl f: kpt on fin* **9/2**[3]

-363 **5** *½* **Jack The Truth (IRE)**[10] 610 5-9-7 **75**.................. GeorgeWood 2 75
(George Scott) *t.k.h: pressed ldr: led over 1f out to ins fnl f: sn outpcd* **7/2**[2]

6-66 **6** *nk* **Princely**[20] 433 4-9-4 **72**.................. (p[1]) AlistairRawlinson 3 71
(Michael Appleby) *prom: effrt and rdn over 1f out: fdd ins fnl f* **10/1**

-110 **7** *nk* **Deeds Not Words (IRE)**[21] 407 8-9-2 **70**.................. BarryMcHugh 1 68
(Tracy Waggott) *hld up: rdn and outpcd over 1f out: n.d after* **40/1**

1m 12.6s (0.10) **Going Correction** +0.225s/f (Slow) 7 Ran SP% **111.4**
Speed ratings (Par 103): **108,107,106,105,105 104,104**
CSF £17.57 TOTE £3.20: £1.70, £4.00; EX 20.00 Trifecta £79.00.
Owner Ben Haslam Racing Syndicate **Bred** Mrs Dolores Gleeson **Trained** Middleham Moor, N Yorks

FOCUS
A fairly muddling sprint, albeit there is reason to think the result is solid enough.

742 PLAY 4 TO SCORE AT BETWAY H'CAP 6f (Tp)
7:15 (7:15) (Class 6) (0-60,60) 4-Y-O+ **£2,264** (£673; £336; £168) **Stalls** Centre

Form RPR

201- **1** **Rockley Point**[108] 8715 6-9-5 **58**.................. JasonHart 3 64
(Katie Scott) *mde all in centre of gp: rdn over 1f out: hrd pressed last 100yds: hld on wl* **12/1**

5-23 **2** *nk* **Steelriver (IRE)**[29] 279 9-9-4 **60**.................. PhilDennis(3) 4 65
(Michael Herrington) *hld up in centre of gp: hdwy and angled rt over 1f out: effrt and chsd wnr ins fnl f: kpt on: hld nr fin* **11/2**[2]

0-00 **3** *½* **Essential**[21] 410 5-9-0 **53**.................. (b[1]) RachelRichardson 9 57
(Olly Williams) *hld up in tch on nr side of gp: effrt and chsd wnr over 1f out to ins fnl f: sn one pce* **12/1**

50-1 **4** *½* **Ginger Jam**[15] 502 4-9-1 **59**.................. FayeMcManoman(5) 2 61
(Nigel Tinkler) *hld up on far side of gp: stdy hdwy over 2f out: effrt and rdn over 1f out: one pce ins fnl f* **11/10**[1]

-002 **5** *1 ¼* **Star Cracker (IRE)**[10] 613 7-8-7 **49**.................. (p) JamieGormley(3) 6 47
(Jim Goldie) *hld up on nr side of gp: drvn along over 2f out: rallied over 1f out: kpt on same pce last 75yds (jockey said gelding anticipated the start hit its head on the stalls and as a result missed the break)* **7/1**[3]

3-06 **6** *½* **High Anxiety**[15] 503 5-8-2 **46** oh1.................. (h[1]) AndrewBreslin(5) 7 43
(Andrew Crook) *chsd wnr to over 1f out: sn outpcd: n.d after* **50/1**

05-4 **7** *1 ½* **Queen Of Kalahari**[44] 25 4-8-13 **52**.................. JamesSullivan 8 44
(Les Eyre) *t.k.h: in tch in centre of gp: rdn 2f out: fdd ins fnl f* **14/1**

050- **8** *1 ¼* **Milton Road**[219] 4807 4-9-7 **60**.................. (w) DanielTudhope 5 49
(Rebecca Bastiman) *in tch in centre of gp: rdn over 2f out: wknd over 1f out* **8/1**

0-63 **9** *½* **Lord Cooper**[11] 599 5-9-2 **55**.................. (p) BarryMcHugh 1 42
(Marjorie Fife) *s.i.s: bhd on far side of gp: struggling over 2f out: nvr on terms* **14/1**

1m 12.69s (0.19) **Going Correction** +0.225s/f (Slow) 9 Ran SP% **117.3**
Speed ratings (Par 101): **107,106,105,105,103 102,100,99,98**
CSF £77.67 CT £826.44 TOTE £13.80: £3.40, £1.70, £3.30; EX 62.30 Trifecta £503.60.
Owner The Vintage Flyers **Bred** Newsells Park Stud **Trained** Galasheils, Scottish Borders

FOCUS
A modest sprint which was decided by a deft ride on the all-the-way winner.

743 BETWAY SPRINT H'CAP 5f (Tp)
7:45 (7:45) (Class 5) (0-70,72) 4-Y-O+ **£2,911** (£866; £432; £216) **Stalls** Centre

Form RPR

0-40 **1** **Jan Van Hoof (IRE)**[24] 353 8-9-6 **68**.................. BarryMcHugh 5 76+
(Michael Herrington) *awkward s: hld up in last pl: smooth hdwy to chse ldr over 1f out: led last 50yds: hld on wl* **8/1**

U202 **2** *shd* **Archimedes (IRE)**[2] 707 6-9-0 **65**.................. (tp) PhilDennis(3) 1 72
(David C Griffiths) *led at ordinary gallop: rdn over 1f out: hdd last 50yds: kpt on: jst hld* **5/1**

0-01 **3** *¾* **Tathmeen (IRE)**[15] 498 4-9-10 **72**.................. CamHardie 3 76
(Antony Brittain) *hld up: hdwy and rdn over 1f out: kpt on ins fnl f: hld towards fin* **4/1**[2]

20-3 **4** *1 ½* **Gowanbuster**[15] 496 4-9-4 **66**.................. (t) PaulMulrennan 2 65
(Susan Corbett) *t.k.h: pressed ldr to over 1f out: no ex ins fnl f* **9/4**[1]

-005 **5** *¾* **Lord Of The Glen**[15] 498 4-9-2 **67**.................. JamieGormley(3) 6 63
(Jim Goldie) *t.k.h: hld up in tch: effrt and pushed along over 1f out: no imp ins fnl f* **9/2**[3]

1-13 **6** *2 ¼* **Mininggold**[33] 230 6-9-2 **69**.................. (p) PaulaMuir(5) 7 57
(Michael Dods) *prom tl rdn and wknd appr fnl f* **11/2**

1m 0.24s (0.74) **Going Correction** +0.225s/f (Slow) 6 Ran SP% **112.1**
Speed ratings (Par 103): **103,102,101,99,98 94**
CSF £45.99 TOTE £9.10: £2.80, £2.60; EX 58.50 Trifecta £164.20.
Owner Mrs H Lloyd-Herrington **Bred** Old Carhue Stud **Trained** Cold Kirby, N Yorks

FOCUS
A fair sprint in which a well-handicapped sort just got the better of two of the form picks.
T/Plt: £61.00 to a £1 stake. Pool: £68,085.44 - 813.87 winning units T/Qpdt: £18.10 to a £1 stake. Pool: £9,198.54 - 375.12 winning units **Richard Young**

744 - 747a (Foreign Racing) - See Raceform Interactive

665

DUNDALK (A.W) (L-H)
Friday, February 15

OFFICIAL GOING: Polytrack: standard

748a CORAL BEST PRICE GUARANTEED ALL UK & IRISH RACES H'CAP 6f (P)
7:00 (7:02) 4-Y-O+ **£14,405** (£4,450; £2,108; £936; £351)

RPR

1 **Togoville (IRE)**[28] 307 9-8-6 **76**.................. (b) AndrewSlattery(7) 9 89+
(Anthony McCann, Ire) *sltly impeded s: sn trckd ldr: cl 2nd at 1/2-way: pushed along nr side over 2f out: sn rdn and kpt on wl u.p to ld wl ins fnl f (trainer said regarding apparent improvement in form that his charge was a renowned course specialist and was helped tonight by the surface riding slow which kept the gelding in the race)* **33/1**

2 *1 ¼* **View The Bay (IRE)**[14] 538 4-8-7 **75**.................. BenCoen(5) 4 84
(Andrew Slattery, Ire) *prom tl sn settled bhd ldrs: 5th 1/2-way: hdwy to chal 1 1/2f out: rdn to ld ent fnl f: hdd u.p wl ins fnl f and no ex* **4/1**[3]

3 *½* **Billyfairplay (IRE)**[7] 666 5-8-13 **76**.................. (p) MarkGallagher 6 83
(John James Feane, Ire) *chsd ldrs: 3rd 1/2-way: impr to ld fr 2f out: sn rdn and hdd ent fnl f: no imp on wnr u.p in 3rd wl ins fnl f* **7/2**[2]

4 *1* **Amanaat (IRE)**[14] 538 6-9-6 **86**.................. (t) RossCoakley(3) 8 90
(Denis Gerard Hogan, Ire) *hld up: disp 7th at 1/2-way: gng wl over 2f out: sn rdn and r.o u.p nr side ins fnl f into nvr threatening 4th cl home* **11/1**

5 *½* **Geological (IRE)**[35] 191 7-9-7 **84**.................. ShaneFoley 13 87
(Damian Joseph English, Ire) *tacked over early to sn ld: narrow advantage at 1/2-way: rdn and hdd 2f out: no ex u.p bhd ldrs ent fnl f: one pce clsng stages* **16/1**

6 *½* **Nick Vedder**[44] 24 5-9-7 **84**.................. (b) ColinKeane 10 85
(Michael Wigham) *dwlt sltly: towards rr: 10th 1/2-way: last into st where hung sltly: pushed along under 2f out and wnt 10th 1f out: r.o nr side wl ins fnl f: nrst fin (jockey said that his mount hung left in the straight)* **5/2**[1]

7 *shd* **Plough Boy (IRE)**[14] 538 8-9-0 **80**.................. OisinOrr(3) 2 81
(Garvan Donnelly, Ire) *dwlt sltly: hld up towards rr: 9th 1/2-way: pushed along 2f out and sme hdwy over 1f out where rdn: kpt on one pce ins fnl f* **20/1**

8 *nk* **Lily's Prince (IRE)**[14] 545 9-8-7 **70**.................. WayneLordan 5 70
(Garvan Donnelly, Ire) *mid-div: 6th 1/2-way: gng wl into st: pushed along fr 2f out and no ex u.p over 1f out: one pce after* **8/1**

9 *nk* **Master Speaker (IRE)**[140] 7742 9-9-2 **89**.................. DaireDavis(10) 3 88
(Adrian McGuinness, Ire) *dwlt: towards rr: last at 1/2-way: tk clsr order far side over 2f out: sn rdn and no ex in mid-div ins fnl f: wknd clsng stages* **10/1**

10 *½* **Verhoyen**[14] 538 4-8-9 **72**.................. (h) NGMcCullagh 1 69
(M C Grassick, Ire) *hld up: disp 7th at 1/2-way: rdn far side 2f out and no ex ent fnl f: wknd* **33/1**

11 *6* **Eastern Racer (IRE)**[14] 538 7-9-7 **84**.................. KevinManning 7 62
(Denis Gerard Hogan, Ire) *chsd ldrs: 4th 1/2-way: rdn over 2f out and sn wknd* **25/1**

1m 11.87s (-0.53) **Going Correction** +0.25s/f (Slow) 11 Ran SP% **119.7**
Speed ratings: **113,111,110,109,108 108,107,107,107,106 98**
CSF £158.79 CT £608.67 TOTE £47.10: £6.50, £1.50, £1.60; DF 288.20 Trifecta £1180.80.
Owner Patrick Joseph McCann **Bred** Steven Nolan **Trained** Castleblaney, Co. Monaghan
■ Stewards' Enquiry : Shane Foley caution: careless riding
Ben Coen one-day ban: failing to keep a straight course to the marker poles (tba)

FOCUS
A blast from the past as the winner became the first horse to win ten races on this surface here. The placed horses set the level.

749 - 751a (Foreign Racing) - See Raceform Interactive

695

KEMPTON (A.W) (R-H)
Saturday, February 16

OFFICIAL GOING: Polytrack: standard to slow
Wind: Light behind Weather: Overcast

752 32RED ON THE APP STORE NOVICE STKS (DIV I) 6f (P)
4:40 (4:47) (Class 5) 3-Y-O+ **£3,881** (£1,155; £577; £288) **Stalls** Low

Form RPR

1 **1** **Dahawi**[23] 384 3-9-6 **0**.................. LukeMorris 2 81
(Hugo Palmer) *chsd ldrs: rdn to ld over 1f out: styd on* **4/6**[1]

065- **2** *1* **Orange Blossom**[92] 9093 3-8-8 **77**.................. BarryMcHugh 8 66
(James Given) *led 1f: chsd ldr: rdn over 1f out: styd on* **10/1**

3 *1 ½* **Brigadier** 3-8-13 **0**.................. JoeFanning 3 66
(Robert Cowell) *led 5f out: rdn: hung lft and hdd over 1f out: no ex ins fnl f* **9/4**[2]

0 **4** *1 ¼* **Guiding Spirit (IRE)**[23] 384 3-8-13 **0**.................. HollieDoyle 5 62
(Clive Cox) *edgd rt s: sn chsng ldrs: rdn over 1f out: styd on same pce* **33/1**

4 **5** *hd* **Fury And Fire**[24] 367 3-8-13 **0**.................. CallumShepherd 1 61
(William Jarvis) *s.i.s: in rr: hdwy over 1f out: nt trble ldrs* **7/1**[3]

000- **6** *12* **Apron Strings**[107] 8771 3-8-5 **54**.................. GabrieleMalune(3) 9 18
(Michael Attwater) *hld up: effrt over 2f out: sn wknd* **100/1**

6 **7** *¾* **Turn To Rock (IRE)**[24] 367 3-8-13 **0**.................. DavidProbert 6 21
(Ed Walker) *in rr and pushed along over 4f out: shkn up and carried hd high over 2f out: nt run on* **16/1**

0 **8** *1 ¼* **Passive (IRE)**[29] 289 3-8-8 **0**.................. DarraghKeenan(5) 7 17
(David Elsworth) *s.i.s: sn pushed along and a in rr* **50/1**

0/0- **9** *1 ½* **Western Dynamisme (FR)**[192] 5867 4-9-2 **5**.................. LeviWilliams(7) 4 11
(Simon Dow) *s.i.s and hmpd s: sn in tch: pushed along over 2f out: wknd wl over 1f out* **150/1**

1m 12.93s (-0.17) **Going Correction** +0.025s/f (Slow) 9 Ran SP% **124.8**
WFA 3 from 4yo 15lb
Speed ratings (Par 103): **102,100,98,97,96 80,79,78,76**
CSF £10.72 TOTE £1.50: £1.02, £2.30, £1.30; EX 8.40 Trifecta £24.00.
Owner M M Stables **Bred** Richard Kent & Robert Percival **Trained** Newmarket, Suffolk

FOCUS
The Polytrack was riding standard to slow ahead of the first division of the novice sprint, in which they didn't go flat out and the first five came clear.

753 32RED ON THE APP STORE NOVICE STKS (DIV II) 6f (P)
5:15 (5:20) (Class 5) 3-Y-O+ **£3,881** (£1,155; £577; £288) **Stalls** Low

Form RPR

0 **1** **Cockney Hill**[29] 289 3-8-13 **0**.................. OisinMurphy 1 78
(Joseph Tuite) *mde all: shkn up and qcknd clr 2f out: easily (trainer could offer no explanation for the gelding's improved form other than being gelded and coming on from its first run)* **13/8**[1]

0-0 **2** *8* **Cape Cyclone (IRE)**[42] 78 4-9-9 **0**.................. DanielMuscutt 5 51
(Stuart Williams) *prom: chsd wnr over 1f out: styd on same pce* **16/1**

040- **3** *¾* **Alicia Darcy (IRE)**[218] 4911 3-8-8 **81**.................. BarryMcHugh 8 45
(James Given) *prom: shkn up over 2f out: sn outpcd: styd on to go 3rd wl ins fnl f* **5/2**[2]

45 **4** *½* **Snooze Button (IRE)**[3] 706 4-10-0 **0**.................. AdamMcNamara 3 52
(Jamie Osborne) *racd keenly in 2nd: shkn up over 2f out: sn outpcd: lost 2nd over 1f out* **16/1**

00- **5** *¾* **Talk Like This (USA)**[66] 9497 3-8-8 **0**.................. TheodoreLadd(5) 4 46
(Tim Pinfield) *prom: racd keenly: shkn up over 1f out: wknd ins fnl f* **20/1**

6 **6** *3* **Charlie Arthur (IRE)**[24] 359 3-8-13 **0**.................. (h) ShaneKelly 9 36
(Richard Hughes) *s.i.s: hld up: rdn over 2f out: no rspnse: edgd rt over 1f out* **7/2**[3]

4 **7** *1* **Purely Prosecco**[12] 604 3-8-8 **0**.................. PaddyMathers 7 28
(Derek Shaw) *s.i.s: hld up: plld hrd: swtchd rt 5f out: sme hdwy u.p over 2f out: wknd over 1f out (jockey said filly ran too freely)* **66/1**

45 **8** *4* **Thedevilinneville**[15] 534 3-8-13 0 CharlieBennett 6 20
(Adam West) *s.i.s: hld up: plld hrd: wknd over 2f out (jockey said gelding ran too freely)* **50/1**

1m 12.86s (-0.24) **Going Correction** +0.025s/f (Slow)
WFA 3 from 4yo 15lb **8** Ran SP% **108.9**
Speed ratings (Par 103): **102,91,90,89,88 84,83,78**
CSF £26.13 TOTE £2.20: £1.10, £3.80, £1.10; EX 23.50 Trifecta £58.20.
Owner David Klein **Bred** D J And Mrs Deer **Trained** Lambourn, Berks
■ Red Moon Lady was withdrawn. Price at time of withdrawal 12/1. Rule 4 applies to all bets - deduction 5p in the pound

FOCUS
The second division of the novice sprint run fractionally quicker then the first, and won convincingly by the heavily backed favourite.

754 32RED CASINO H'CAP 1m 3f 219y(P)
5:45 (5:48) (Class 5) (0-75,75) 4-Y-0+
£3,752 (£1,116; £557; £400; £400; £400) **Stalls** Low

Form RPR

-210 **1** **Unit Of Assessment (IRE)**[24] 362 5-9-5 **73** (vt) AdamKirby 2 82
(William Knight) *mde al: set stdy pce tl shkn up and qcknd over 2f out: rdn over 1f out: edgd rt ins fnl f: styd on wl* **11/2**[3]

10-2 **2** *2 1/2* **Dono Di Dio**[29] 292 4-8-11 **74** ScottMcCullagh(7) 11 79
(Michael Madgwick) *chsd ldrs: rdn over 1f out: styd on to go 2nd nr fin* **12/1**

1-14 **3** *nse* **Nylon Speed (IRE)**[29] 292 5-9-6 **74** (t) DavidProbert 14 79
(Alan King) *chsd wnr: rdn over 2f out: styd on same pce ins fnl f* **5/1**[2]

0-11 **4** *1 1/4* **Sir Prize**[24] 362 4-8-12 **68** RobHornby 3 71+
(Dean Ivory) *hld up: rdn over 1f out: r.o ins fnl f: nt rch ldrs* **2/1**[1]

/0-5 **5** *1* **Harlow**[15] 536 5-9-6 **74** StevieDonohoe 4 75
(Ian Williams) *prom: rdn over 1f out: styd on same pce fnl f* **12/1**

46-6 **6** *3/4* **Surrey Blaze (IRE)**[29] 292 4-9-5 **75** OisinMurphy 12 75+
(Joseph Tuite) *hld up: rdn over 2f out: styd on ins fnl f: nvr nrr* **8/1**

116- **7** *1* **Outofthequestion**[38] 6301 5-9-2 **70** TomMarquand 10 69
(Alan King) *hld up: pushed along over 3f out: r.o ins fnl f: nvr nrr* **25/1**

0-16 **8** *nk* **My Brother Mike (IRE)**[24] 362 5-8-13 **67** CliffordLee 7 65
(Kevin Frost) *hld up in tch: rdn over 2f out: no ex fnl f* **12/1**

10-6 **9** *1 1/2* **Kyoto Star (FR)**[30] 272 5-9-3 **71** (p[1]) LukeMorris 1 67
(Henry Spiller) *racd keenly: prom: rdn over 2f out: wknd ins fnl f* **16/1**

0-46 **10** *hd* **Smiley Bagel (IRE)**[26] 346 6-9-1 **69** RichardKingscote 5 64
(Ed Walker) *hld up: nt clr run over 2f out: hdwy over 1f out: wknd fnl f* **16/1**

0-41 **11** *2 1/4* **Regular Income (IRE)**[15] 536 4-9-0 **70** (p) CharlieBennett 9 62
(Adam West) *s.i.s: hld up: rdn over 2f out: nvr on terms* **25/1**

0-00 **12** *5* **Esspeegee**[24] 362 6-8-6 **65** DarraghKeenan(5) 6 49
(Alan Bailey) *hld up: pushed along over 4f out: wknd over 2f out* **100/1**

2m 34.99s (0.49) **Going Correction** +0.025s/f (Slow)
WFA 4 from 5yo+ 2lb **12** Ran SP% **120.0**
Speed ratings (Par 103): **99,97,97,96,95 95,94,94,93,93 91,88**
CSF £69.62 CT £356.51 TOTE £5.60: £1.70, £3.20, £2.20; EX 71.30 Trifecta £365.00.
Owner A Hetherton **Bred** Barouche Stud (IRE) Ltd **Trained** Angmering, W Sussex

FOCUS
A fair handicap featuring several improving AW types, but they went a crawl and the winner made all.

755 32RED.COM H'CAP 6f (P)
6:15 (6:16) (Class 4) (0-85,83) 4-Y-0+
£6,469 (£1,925; £962; £481; £400; £400) **Stalls** Low

Form RPR

3-31 **1** **Treacherous**[22] 407 5-9-3 **79** CallumShepherd 5 85+
(Ed de Giles) *s.i.s: hld up: rdn over 1f out: r.o u.p ins fnl f: to ld post* **5/2**[1]

120- **2** *nse* **Rose Berry**[116] 8498 5-9-4 **83** (h) JoshuaBryan(3) 2 89
(Charlie Wallis) *chsd ldrs: rdn to ld over 1f out: edgd lft ins fnl f: hdd post* **16/1**

21-6 **3** *3/4* **Compas Scoobie**[32] 247 6-9-1 **77** OisinMurphy 1 81
(Stuart Williams) *hld up in tch: nt clr run over 1f out: r.o* **9/2**[2]

0-11 **4** *nk* **Choice Encounter**[24] 361 4-9-2 **78** HollieDoyle 3 81
(Archie Watson) *chsd ldrs: shkn up over 2f out: rdn over 1f out: r.o* **5/2**[1]

-360 **5** *1 3/4* **National Glory (IRE)**[14] 564 4-8-13 **75** (p) EdwardGreatrex 4 72
(Archie Watson) *led: shkn up and qcknd 2f out: hdd over 1f out: edgd lft and no ex ins fnl f (vet reported the gelding lost its left fore shoe)* **20/1**

5-14 **6** *3/4* **Little Palaver**[14] 564 7-8-6 **75** (p) AmeliaGlass(7) 6 70
(Clive Cox) *chsd ldr tl rdn over 1f out: no ex whn hmpd ins fnl f* **10/1**

00-5 **7** *nk* **Rock Of Estonia (IRE)**[31] 253 4-8-9 **71** DavidProbert 7 65
(Charles Hills) *s.i.s and edgd lft s: hld up: rdn over 1f out: nt trble ldrs (jockey said gelding jumped awkwardly from the stalls)* **11/2**[3]

1m 12.14s (-0.96) **Going Correction** +0.025s/f (Slow) **7** Ran SP% **110.4**
Speed ratings (Par 105): **107,106,105,105,103 102,101**
CSF £40.79 TOTE £3.30: £2.10, £8.40; EX 30.80 Trifecta £190.70.
Owner Woodham Walter Partnership **Bred** P M Hicks **Trained** Ledbury, H'fords

FOCUS
A tight little sprint featuring a couple of in-form winners, and there was a tight finish. They went a fair pace.

756 32RED/EBFSTALLIONS.COM FILLIES' H'CAP 7f (P)
6:45 (6:48) (Class 3) (0-95,97) 4-Y-0+
£12,450 (£3,728; £1,864; £932; £466; £234) **Stalls** Low

Form RPR

326- **1** **Toy Theatre**[161] 7075 5-8-1 **76** JaneElliott(3) 5 84
(Michael Appleby) *sn led: hdd 6f out: remained handy: chsd ldr over 2f out: led wl over 1f out: rdn out* **20/1**

03-2 **2** *1 1/4* **Treasure Me**[17] 475 4-8-10 **82** (p) StevieDonohoe 6 87
(Charlie Fellowes) *hld up in tch: shkn up over 2f out: nt clr run over 1f out: styd on u.p to go 2nd post* **10/1**

30-3 **3** *shd* **Pattie**[45] 30 5-9-11 **97** CallumShepherd 3 101
(Mick Channon) *prom: lost pl 6f out: hdwy 2f out: chsd wnr over 1f out: sn rdn: styd on same pce wl ins fnl f* **10/1**

3-32 **4** *2* **Roman Spinner**[10] 618 4-8-8 **80** (t) LukeMorris 1 79
(Rae Guest) *hld up: hdwy u.p over 1f out: styd on same pce wl ins fnl f* **9/2**[2]

6-11 **5** *1/2* **Made Of Honour (IRE)**[17] 475 5-8-11 **83** (p) CliffordLee 4 81
(K R Burke) *s.i.s: pushed along early in rr: shkn up over 2f out: styd on wl ins fnl f: nvr nrr (vet reported the mare lost its right fore shoe)* **7/1**[3]

0-56 **6** *1 1/2* **Peak Princess (IRE)**[19] 460 5-9-2 **88** (b) DanielTudhope 8 82
(Archie Watson) *chsd ldrs: rdn over 1f out: no ex ins fnl f* **12/1**

00-6 **7** *nk* **Miss Bar Beach (IRE)**[45] 30 4-9-7 **93** CallumRodriguez 7 86
(Keith Dalgleish) *led 6f out: rdn and hdd wl over 1f out: no ex ins fnl f* **25/1**

55-2 **8** *1* **Zoraya (FR)**[40] 123 4-8-5 **77** (tp) RaulDaSilva 10 67
(Paul Cole) *chsd ldr over 5f out tl rdn over 2f out: wknd fnl f* **20/1**

/2-1 **9** *nk* **Capriolette (IRE)**[24] 370 4-8-11 **83** DavidProbert 2 72
(Ed Walker) *s.i.s: hld up: plld hrd: shkn up over 1f out: n.d (jockey said filly jumped awkwardly leaving the stalls and was slowly away)* **15/8**[1]

-113 **10** *10* **Happy Escape**[17] 475 5-8-10 **82** TomMarquand 9 44
(Tony Carroll) *hld up: rdn over 2f out: sn wknd (jockey said mare stopped quickly)* **10/1**

1m 25.08s (-0.92) **Going Correction** +0.025s/f (Slow) **10** Ran SP% **113.8**
Speed ratings (Par 104): **106,104,104,102,101 99,99,98,98,86**
CSF £196.21 CT £2117.73 TOTE £20.60: £4.90, £3.10, £2.60; EX 175.30 Trifecta £883.00.
Owner L J Vaessen **Bred** Darley **Trained** Oakham, Rutland

FOCUS
A warm fillies' handicap despite a disappointing short-priced favourite. They went an even tempo.

757 32RED CONDITIONS STKS (ALL WEATHER CHAMPIONSHIPS FAST-TRACK QUALIFIER) 1m 7f 218y(P)
7:15 (7:15) (Class 2) 4-Y-0+ **£15,562** (£4,660; £2,330; £1,165; £582) **Stalls** Low

Form RPR

00-2 **1** **Stamford Raffles**[21] 432 6-9-7 84 RichardKingscote 2 96
(Jane Chapple-Hyam) *mde all: set stdy pce tl qcknd over 3f out: rdn over 1f out: jst hld on* **33/1**

51- **2** *shd* **Spark Plug (IRE)**[73] 9399 8-9-10 107 (p) TomMarquand 5 99
(Brian Meehan) *hld up: rdn over 1f out: r.o ins fnl f: jst failed* **9/2**[3]

31-1 **3** *1 3/4* **Grey Britain**[15] 519 5-9-7 106 AdamKirby 6 94
(John Ryan) *hld up: hdwy u.p over 1f out: styd on same pce wl ins fnl f* **1/1**[1]

023- **4** *1/2* **Higher Power**[63] 9552 7-9-7 105 GeorgeWood 1 93
(James Fanshawe) *chsd ldr over 6f: remained handy: rdn over 1f out: no ex wl ins fnl f* **7/2**[2]

11-4 **5** *1/2* **Redicean**[28] 311 5-9-7 97 DavidProbert 4 93
(Alan King) *prom: chsd ldr over 9f out: rdn and ev ch over 1f out: no ex wl ins fnl f* **11/2**

3m 32.93s (2.83) **Going Correction** +0.025s/f (Slow) **5** Ran SP% **108.7**
Speed ratings (Par 109): **93,92,92,91,91**
CSF £158.82 TOTE £19.40: £6.00, £2.80; EX 69.90 Trifecta £452.40.
Owner Jane Chapple-Hyam & Bryan Hirst **Bred** C A Cyzer **Trained** Dalham, Suffolk

FOCUS
A fast-track qualifier for the marathon race on finals day, and it again paid to race prominently.

758 100% PROFIT BOOST AT 32REDSPORT.COM H'CAP 1m 3f 219y(P)
7:45 (7:48) (Class 2) (0-105,97) 4-Y-0+ **£16,172** (£4,812; £2,405; £1,202) **Stalls** Low

Form RPR

02-5 **1** **Count Calabash (IRE)**[42] 82 5-9-12 **97** JoeFanning 5 109
(Eve Johnson Houghton) *mde all: pushed clr fr over 2f out: easily (vet reported the gelding lost its left hind shoe)* **7/2**[3]

12-3 **2** *6* **Caspar The Cub (IRE)**[24] 368 4-9-7 **94** (p) TomMarquand 4 97
(Alan King) *s.i.s: hld up: swtchd lft over 2f out: hdwy to go 2nd over 1f out: sn rdn and hung rt: no ch w wnr* **2/1**[1]

6-13 **3** *2 1/2* **West Coast Flyer**[14] 558 6-9-3 **88** StevieDonohoe 6 86
(David Simcock) *s.i.s: hld up: pushed along and hdwy over 1f out: nvr on terms* **10/1**

143- **4** *2 1/4* **Pipes Of Peace (IRE)**[64] 9534 5-9-11 **96** (t) OisinMurphy 3 90
(Seamus Durack) *chsd wnr: rdn over 2f out: lost 2nd over 1f out: wknd fnl f* **3/1**[2]

40-4 **5** *3/4* **Emenem**[28] 310 5-8-11 **82** LukeMorris 1 75
(Simon Dow) *chsd ldrs: pushed along over 4f out: rdn over 2f out: wknd fnl f* **10/1**

01-3 **6** *nse* **Lexington Law (IRE)**[42] 87 6-9-8 **93** (p) DavidProbert 2 86
(Alan King) *prom: rdn over 2f out: wknd over 1f out* **7/1**

2m 30.26s (-4.24) **Going Correction** +0.025s/f (Slow)
WFA 4 from 5yo+ 2lb **6** Ran SP% **111.2**
Speed ratings (Par 109): **115,111,109,107,107 107**
CSF £10.73 TOTE £4.30: £2.20, £1.30; EX 12.20 Trifecta £61.80.
Owner Trish & Colin Fletcher-Hall **Bred** Miss S Von Schilcher **Trained** Blewbury, Oxon

FOCUS
A fair middle-distance handicap despite the top-weight being 8lb below the ceiling, and another all-the-way winner on the card.

759 RACINGTV.COM H'CAP 6f (P)
8:15 (8:15) (Class 6) (0-65,66) 4-Y-0+
£3,105 (£924; £461; £400; £400; £400) **Stalls** Low

Form RPR

01-3 **1** **Always A Drama (IRE)**[36] 178 4-9-9 **66** RichardKingscote 6 72
(Charles Hills) *chsd ldrs: led over 1f out: rdn out* **6/1**[2]

05-5 **2** *3/4* **Maximum Power (FR)**[28] 313 4-9-0 **62** TheodoreLadd(5) 10 66
(Tim Pinfield) *sn led: rdn and hung lft over 1f out: sn hdd: kpt on* **16/1**

33-4 **3** *nk* **Kraka (IRE)**[21] 430 4-9-2 **64** (v) KevinLundie(5) 4 67
(Christine Dunnett) *hld up: hdwy over 1f out: sn rdn: r.o* **5/1**[1]

330- **4** *1 1/2* **Bond Street Beau**[66] 9507 4-9-2 **59** DanielTudhope 1 59
(Philip McBride) *prom: hmpd over 1f out: styd on same pce ins fnl f (jockey said gelding suffered interference in running)* **6/1**[2]

2-46 **5** *1 1/2* **Becker**[28] 317 4-9-7 **64** (h) LukeMorris 12 58
(Robert Cowell) *sn prom: chsd ldr over 4f out: rdn and edgd lft over 1f out: no ex ins fnl f* **10/1**

65-4 **6** *2* **Coastal Cyclone**[17] 483 5-8-11 **54** ShaneKelly 7 42
(Harry Dunlop) *chsd ldrs: rdn and hung rt fr over 1f out: styd on same pce* **14/1**

0-00 **7** *3/4* **Letmestopyouthere (IRE)**[18] 468 5-9-6 **63** HollieDoyle 5 49
(Archie Watson) *s.i.s: hdwy over 1f out: nt trble ldrs* **7/1**[3]

0-44 **8** *2 3/4* **Majorette**[21] 439 5-9-5 **62** AdamKirby 2 40
(Brian Barr) *edgd lft s: hld up: nvr on terms* **5/1**[1]

-520 **9** *nse* **Always Amazing**[23] 383 5-9-5 **62** PaddyMathers 9 39
(Derek Shaw) *s.i.s: hld up: rdn over 2f out: n.d* **20/1**

00-6 **10** *3* **Hit The Beat**[31] 256 4-8-13 **63** AmeliaGlass(7) 8 31
(Clive Cox) *prom tl wknd over 1f out* **25/1**

034- **11** *6* **Show The Money**[63] 9565 4-9-5 **62** SeanLevey 3 12
(Eugene Stanford) *s.i.s and hmpd s: hld up: wknd over 1f out: hung lft fnl f (jockey said gelding hung left-handed)* **5/1**[1]

1m 12.48s (-0.62) **Going Correction** +0.025s/f (Slow) **11** Ran SP% **121.3**
Speed ratings (Par 101): **105,104,103,101,99 96,95,92,92,88 80**
CSF £100.72 CT £532.81 TOTE £5.10: £2.10, £4.60, £1.70; EX 116.20 Trifecta £451.00.
Owner B W Neill **Bred** Patrick Kelly **Trained** Lambourn, Berks

FOCUS
A moderate sprint and it paid to race prominently. It's been rated around the second to his best AW form to date.
T/Plt: £935.90 to a £1 stake. Pool: £69,478.81 - 54.19 winning units T/Qpdt: £329.40 to a £1 stake. Pool: £11,291.73 - 25.36 winning units **Colin Roberts**

[731]LINGFIELD (L-H)
Saturday, February 16

OFFICIAL GOING: Polytrack: standard
Wind: medium, behind Weather: overcast

760 SUN RACING NO1 RACING SITE H'CAP — 1m 1y(P)
1:30 (1:30) (Class 6) (0-60,62) 4-Y-O+ **£2,264** (£673; £336; £168) **Stalls** High

Form RPR
0-51 **1** **First Link (USA)**[24] 366 4-9-8 **61** .... HollieDoyle 4 73+
(Jean-Rene Auvray) *broke wl: restrained into last trio and t.k.h: gd hdwy on outer bnd 2f out: rdn to ld 1f out: in command and reminder ins fnl f: pushed out towards fin: comf* **6/4**[1]

042- **2** 1 1/4 **Jai Hanuman (IRE)**[73] 9413 5-8-8 **47** ....(t) FrannyNorton 3 53
(Michael Wigham) *taken down early: hld up in tch in midfield: nt clr run and swtchd rt over 1f out: styd on ins fnl f: wnt 2nd towards fin: no threat to wnr* **13/2**[3]

0-01 **3** 3/4 **Limerick Lord (IRE)**[17] 485 7-8-12 **51** ....(p) ShelleyBirkett 9 55
(Julia Feilden) *chsd ldr tl led ent fnl 2f: rdn over 1f out: hdd 1f out: no ex and one pce after: lost 2nd towards fin* **20/1**

0-00 **4** 1 1/4 **Ubla (IRE)**[21] 430 6-9-2 **58** ....(e[1]) WilliamCox(3) 10 59
(Gay Kelleway) *stdd after s and dropped in bhd: hld up in rr: effrt on outer wl over 1f out: styd on u.p ins fnl f: no threat to wnr* **25/1**

3-23 **5** nk **Big Bad Lol (IRE)**[26] 348 5-9-7 **60** ....(p) RichardKingscote 5 61
(Ed Walker) *wnt rt leaving stalls and impeded: hld up in tch in last trio: nt clrest of runs over 1f out: pushed along and hdwy 1f out: styd on ins fnl f: no threat to wnr (jockey said gelding suffered interference leaving the stalls)* **5/2**[2]

4-03 **6** nk **Herm (IRE)**[22] 399 5-9-0 **53** ....(v) EoinWalsh 7 53
(David Evans) *sltly impeded leaving stalls: t.k.h: chsd ldng trio: effrt ent fnl 2f: unable qck over 1f out: kpt on same pce ins fnl f* **9/1**

0-55 **7** 1 **Haraz (IRE)**[24] 365 6-8-0 **46** oh1 ....(bt) ThoreHammerHansen(7) 1 44
(Paddy Butler) *in tch in midfield on inner: effrt over 1f out: swtchd lft and no imp ins fnl f* **33/1**

03-6 **8** 1/2 **Claudine (IRE)**[24] 364 4-9-9 **62** .... RossaRyan 2 59
(Alexandra Dunn) *trckd ldrs on inner: rdn over 1f out: unable qck and wknd ins fnl f* **33/1**

310- **9** 7 **Soaring Spirits (IRE)**[48] 9764 9-9-6 **59** ....(b) AdamKirby 8 39
(Dean Ivory) *wnt lft leaving stalls: led: hdd and rdn ent fnl 2f: no ex u.p over 1f out: fdd ins fnl f* **16/1**

00-P **10** 1 1/4 **Kafeel (USA)**[32] 248 8-9-9 **62** .... ShaneKelly 6 40
(Gary Moore) *hmpd and dropped to rr sn after s: hdwy into midfield after 2f: rdn over 2f out: swtchd rt and no hdwy over 1f out: fdd fnl f (jockey said gelding suffered interference leaving the stalls)* **12/1**

1m 36.45s (-1.75) **Going Correction** -0.20s/f (Stan) **10 Ran SP% 120.0**
Speed ratings (Par 101): **100,98,98,96,96 96,95,94,87,86**
CSF £11.81 CT £144.63 TOTE £2.50: £1.10, £2.80, £3.60; EX 11.80 Trifecta £93.60.
Owner Stuart McPhee **Bred** Juddmonte Farms Inc **Trained** Calne, Wilts

FOCUS
This looks solid form for the lowly level. Straightforward form in behind the winner.

761 LADBROKES HOME OF THE ODDS BOOST NOVICE STKS — 1m 1y(P)
2:05 (2:05) (Class 5) 3-Y-O **£2,911** (£866; £432; £216) **Stalls** High

Form RPR
42 **1** **Reggae Runner (FR)**[15] 534 3-9-2 **0** .... FrannyNorton 9 85+
(Mark Johnston) *sn led and mde rest: asserting and hung rt wl over 1f out: in command and styd on strly ins fnl f* **7/2**[2]

4 **2** 2 1/2 **I'm Available (IRE)**[24] 359 3-8-11 **0** .... WilliamBuick 5 75
(Andrew Balding) *chsd ldrs tl wnt 2nd over 5f out: effrt to press wnr 2f out: struggling to qckn and swtchd lft over 1f out: wl hld and kpt on same pce ins fnl f* **3/1**[1]

0 **3** 3/4 **Dobrianka**[38] 133 3-8-11 **0** .... RichardKingscote 6 73
(Ralph Beckett) *t.k.h: chsd ldrs: effrt and outpcd in 4th ent fnl 2f: wnt 3rd 1f out: kpt on ins fnl f but no threat to wnr* **7/2**[2]

0-22 **4** 3 **Derry Boy**[14] 554 3-9-2 **73** .... EoinWalsh 2 71
(David Evans) *taken down early and led to post: chsd wnr tl over 5f out: chsd ldrs after: rdn and unable qck over 1f out: wknd ins fnl f* **7/2**[2]

3 **5** 4 1/2 **Red Fedora**[24] 370 3-8-11 **0** .... DavidProbert 1 56
(Clive Cox) *in tch in midfield: rdn and outpcd jst over 2f out: wl btn over 1f out* **14/1**

0-3 **6** nk **Chop Chop (IRE)**[14] 554 3-8-11 **0** .... AdamMcNamara 3 55
(Roger Charlton) *rdr briefly unbalanced leaving stalls: hld up in last quartet: shkn up and outpcd over 2f out: nvr involved* **7/1**[3]

6-6 **7** 1 **Perfect Grace**[24] 370 3-8-11 **0** .... EdwardGreatrex 4 53
(Archie Watson) *restless in stalls: hld up in last trio: pushed along and outpcd over 2f out: nvr involved (jockey said filly was restless in the stalls and slowly away)* **20/1**

8 hd **Sir Canford (IRE)** 3-9-2 **0** .... TomMarquand 8 57
(Ali Stronge) *dropped in after s: a in rr: shkn up over 2f out: sn outpcd and wl btn* **50/1**

0 **9** nk **Watch And Learn**[21] 442 3-8-11 **0** .... RobHornby 7 52
(Andrew Balding) *dwlt: hld up in rr: shkn up over 2f out: sn outpcd and wl btn* **100/1**

1m 36.17s (-2.03) **Going Correction** -0.20s/f (Stan) **9 Ran SP% 118.5**
Speed ratings (Par 97): **102,99,98,95,91 90,89,89,89**
CSF £14.73 TOTE £4.50: £1.70, £1.40, £1.60; EX 16.00 Trifecta £98.70.
Owner Hugh Hart **Bred** Hugh Hart **Trained** Middleham Moor, N Yorks

FOCUS
Few got seriously competitive behind the front-running winner and the bare form is probably just fair.

762 BETWAY H'CAP — 6f 1y(P)
2:40 (2:40) (Class 2) (0-105,101) 4-Y-O+ **£11,971** (£3,583; £1,791; £896; £446) **Stalls** Low

Form RPR
2-10 **1** **Alsvinder**[23] 382 6-9-2 **96** ....(t) AdamKirby 5 102
(David O'Meara) *broke fast to ld: rdn jst over 2f out: drvn over 1f out: hdd jst ins fnl f: battled bk gamely u.p towards fin to ld again on post* **7/1**[2]

1-26 **2** nse **Merhoob (IRE)**[25] 352 7-8-8 **93** .... DarraghKeenan(5) 1 99
(John Ryan) *sn trcking ldrs on inner: effrt to chal over 1f out: sn rdn and led jst ins fnl f: kpt on u.p but hdd on post* **7/2**[1]

2-34 **3** nk **Gulliver**[18] 470 5-9-5 **99** ....(tp) DanielTudhope 8 104
(David O'Meara) *hld up in midfield: effrt and wd 2f out: hdwy u.p ins fnl f: styd on strly towards fin: nt quite rch ldrs* **7/2**[1]

322- **4** hd **Raucous**[213] 5096 6-9-5 **99** ....(tp) RichardKingscote 3 103
(Robert Cowell) *hld up in tch in midfield: effrt over 1f out: styd on wl u.p fnl 100yds: nt quite rch ldrs* **7/2**[1]

2-51 **5** shd **Desert Doctor (IRE)**[23] 382 4-8-12 **92** .... LukeMorris 4 96
(Ed Walker) *in tch in midfield: effrt in 5th ent fnl 2f: chsd ldrs and drvn whn swtchd lft ins fnl f: kpt on towards fin* **7/2**[1]

-000 **6** 1 1/4 **Atletico (IRE)**[13] 588 7-8-12 **92** .... EoinWalsh 2 92
(David Evans) *hld up in last pair: effrt over 1f out: kpt on and swtchd sltly lft ins fnl f: nvr getting on terms w ldrs and eased towards fin* **25/1**

06-4 **7** nk **Ultimate Avenue (IRE)**[23] 382 5-8-12 **92** ....(h) StevieDonohoe 6 91
(David Simcock) *sn off the pce in rr: clsd and effrt over 1f out: kpt on ins fnl f: nvr trbld ldrs* **12/1**[3]

01/5 **8** 1/2 **Giogiobbo**[29] 297 6-9-4 **101** ....(b) JoshuaBryan(3) 7 99
(Nick Littmoden) *chsd wnr tl over 1f out: sn rdn and unable qck: wknd ins fnl f* **25/1**

1m 9.25s (-2.65) **Going Correction** -0.20s/f (Stan) **8 Ran SP% 116.8**
Speed ratings (Par 109): **109,108,108,108,108 106,106,105**
CSF £32.45 CT £100.56 TOTE £7.10: £1.90, £1.40, £1.50; EX 37.60 Trifecta £188.00.
Owner F Gillespie **Bred** Northern Bloodstock Inc **Trained** Upper Helmsley, N Yorks

FOCUS
A busy finish to this good, competitive sprint handicap.

763 BETWAY SPRINT H'CAP — 5f 6y(P)
3:15 (3:15) (Class 4) (0-80,80) 4-Y-O+ **£4,690** (£1,395; £697; £348) **Stalls** High

Form RPR
-034 **1** **It's All A Joke (IRE)**[21] 433 4-8-8 **74** ....(b) Pierre-LouisJamin(7) 6 81
(Archie Watson) *chsd ldrs: wnt 2nd jst over 3f out: rdn and ev ch over 1f out: struck by rivals whip 1f out: led and edgd lft ins fnl f: hld on gamely* **4/1**[3]

5505 **2** hd **Something Lucky (IRE)**[18] 471 7-9-5 **78** ....(v) AlistairRawlinson 3 84+
(Michael Appleby) *dwlt: outpcd in rr: effrt over 1f out: hdwy ins fnl f: styd on strly to go 2nd cl home: nt quite rch wnr* **5/1**

-312 **3** nk **Joegogo (IRE)**[18] 471 4-9-7 **80** .... JFEgan 4 85
(David Evans) *sn bustled along to ld: rdn jst over 2f out: hdd ins fnl f: kpt on wl: no ex and lost 2nd cl home* **5/2**[2]

142- **4** 1/2 **Spring Romance (IRE)**[213] 5089 4-9-4 **77** .... AdamKirby 5 80
(Dean Ivory) *chsd ldr tl jst over 3f out: effrt in 3rd on inner over 1f out: kpt on ins fnl f but nvr quite enough pce to get to ldrs* **2/1**[1]

0-10 **5** nse **Mont Kiara (FR)**[14] 564 6-9-0 **73** .... TomMarquand 2 76
(Simon Dow) *chsd ldrs tl lost pl and impeded after 1f: effrt in 4th 2f out: styd on ins fnl f: nt rch ldrs* **15/2**

35-0 **P** **Look Surprised**[28] 317 6-8-7 **66** .... NicolaCurrie 1
(Roger Teal) *chsd ldrs for 1f: effrt in 5th 2f out: sn eased: p.u and dismntd over 1f out: burst blood vessel (vet reported the mare had bled from the nose)* **25/1**

57.6s (-1.20) **Going Correction** -0.20s/f (Stan) **6 Ran SP% 114.2**
Speed ratings (Par 105): **101,100,100,99,99**
CSF £24.29 TOTE £4.60: £1.80, £2.50; EX 20.40 Trifecta £71.50.
Owner Greenfield Racing **Bred** M Phelan **Trained** Upper Lambourn, W Berks

FOCUS
A fair, competitive sprint handicap.

764 BETWAY CASINO H'CAP — 1m 2f (P)
3:50 (3:50) (Class 3) (0-95,95) 4-Y-O+ **£7,246** (£2,168; £1,084; £542; £270) **Stalls** Low

Form RPR
1-55 **1** **Book Of Dreams (IRE)**[31] 255 4-9-3 **91** .... DougieCostello 1 97
(Michael Appleby) *mde all and dictated gallop: pushed along 2f out: rdn and jst over 1 length clr ent fnl f: styd on wl* **14/1**

2-43 **2** 1 **Mr Top Hat**[10] 623 4-9-1 **89** .... EoinWalsh 4 93
(David Evans) *t.k.h early: chsd wnr thrght: effrt over 1f out: drvn ent fnl f: kpt on but a hld* **9/2**

5-31 **3** nk **Nonios (IRE)**[15] 521 7-9-0 **93** ....(h) DylanHogan(5) 3 96
(David Simcock) *stdd s: hld up in last pair: nt clr run on inner 2f out: swtchd rt and in the clr 1f out: rdn ins fnl f: kpt on but nvr enough pce to rch wnr* **11/4**[2]

0-15 **4** 1 3/4 **Shyron**[14] 557 8-8-7 **81** oh3 .... LiamJones 2 81
(Lee Carter) *t.k.h: chsd ldng pair: effrt over 1f out: kpt on same pce ins fnl f* **8/1**

6-24 **5** 1/2 **Mythical Madness**[33] 240 8-9-7 **95** ....(v) DanielTudhope 6 94
(David O'Meara) *stdd s: hld up in last pair: effrt over 1f out: kpt on ins fnl f: nvr getting on term w wnr* **7/2**[3]

-402 **6** nk **Isomer (USA)**[15] 521 5-8-12 **88** ow1 .... JoshuaBryan(3) 5 87
(Andrew Balding) *midfield: effrt 2f out: unable qck u.p over 1f out: kpt on same pce ins fnl f (vet reported the gelding to be mildly lame on its left-fore leg)* **9/4**[1]

2m 5.78s (-0.82) **Going Correction** -0.20s/f (Stan) **6 Ran SP% 115.6**
Speed ratings (Par 107): **95,94,93,92,92 91**
CSF £76.15 TOTE £13.40: £4.00, £2.60; EX 70.60 Trifecta £161.60.
Owner Craig Buckingham **Bred** Mrs Mary Rose Hayes **Trained** Oakham, Rutland

FOCUS
The one-two filled those positions pretty much throughout; muddling form.

765 LADBROKES H'CAP — 1m 4f (P)
4:25 (4:25) (Class 6) (0-65,60) 3-Y-O **£2,264** (£673; £336; £168) **Stalls** Low

Form RPR
000- **1** **Ginge N Tonic**[102] 8890 3-8-7 **45** ow1 .... ThoreHammerHansen 9 50
(Adam West) *rousted along leaving stalls: hdwy to ld over 10f out: mde rest: rdn 2f out: drvn ins fnl f: hld on wl towards fin* **25/1**

4-06 **2** 1/2 **Vin D'Honneur (IRE)**[36] 183 3-8-13 **52** ....(p[1]) SeanLevey 2 55
(Stuart Williams) *t.k.h early: led tl over 10f out: stdd bk and wl in tch in midfield: effrt in 5th 2f out: hdwy u.p to chse wnr ins fnl f: clsng towards fin but nvr quite getting to wnr* **6/1**[3]

0-43 **3** 2 1/4 **Miss Green Dream**[22] 400 3-8-10 **49** .... ShelleyBirkett 6 50
(Julia Feilden) *hld up in midfield: effrt over 2f out: hung lft over 1f out: clsng whn nt clr run and swtchd rt 1f out: kpt on ins fnl f: no threat to ldng pair (jockey said filly hung left-handed in the straight)* **7/1**

0-50 **4** 1/2 **Bonneville (IRE)**[15] 537 3-9-0 **53** ....(b[1]) AlistairRawlinson 4 52
(Rod Millman) *in tch in midfield: clipped heels and stmbld 10f out: effrt in 4th 2f out: wandered 1f out: kpt on same pce u.p ins fnl f (jockey said gelding ran too free and clipped heels shortly after the start)* **9/2**[2]

4-14 **5** *nse* **Warrior Display (IRE)**[14] 567 3-9-0 **60**..................(p) AaronMackay(7) 8 59
(J S Moore) *chsd ldrs: wnt 2nd 5f out: rdn and pressing wnr 2f out tl hung lft: no ex jst ins fnl f: wknd wl ins fnl f (jockey said gelding hung left-handed under pressure)* **16/1**

000- **6** *½* **Moon Artist (FR)**[50] 9729 3-8-7 **46**.......................... JosephineGordon 7 44
(Michael Blanshard) *hld up in last quartet: 9th and effrt wl over 1f out: hdwy ins fnl f: styd on wl fnl 100yds: nvr trbld ldrs* **33/1**

000- **7** *1* **Ede's**[59] 9607 3-9-4 **60**.. PaddyBradley(3) 1 56
(Pat Phelan) *hld up in tch in midfield: effrt in 7th 3f out: sn rdn: no imp and rn green bnd 2f out: drvn over 1f out: hung lft and kpt on ins fnl f: nvr threatened ldrs (jockey said gelding hung left-handed under pressure)* **3/1**[1]

-445 **8** *shd* **Comeonfeeltheforce (IRE)**[15] 537 3-8-13 **52**..........(t) RaulDaSilva 10 48
(Adam West) *chsd ldrs: wnt 2nd 9f out tl 5f out: styd prom: unable qck over 1f out: wknd ins fnl f* **10/1**

040- **9** *1* **Brinkleys Katie**[91] 9132 3-9-4 **57**................................ JFEgan 3 53
(Paul George) *hld up in last quartet: 8th and effrt over 1f out: kpt on ins fnl f: nvr trbld ldrs and eased towards fin (jockey said filly hung badly right-handed)* **9/1**

0-05 **10** *6* **Hammy End (IRE)**[22] 403 3-9-2 **55**............................(h) NicolaCurrie 11 40
(William Muir) *stdd and wnt rt leaving stalls: hld up off the pce in rr: clsd 1/2-way: rdn 2f out: sn btn (jockey said gelding hung right-handed throughout)* **8/1**

60-0 **11** *25* **George Hastings**[40] 122 3-8-6 **45**.............................. AndrewMullen 5
(K R Burke) *s.i.s and swtchd lft leaving stalls: a towards rr: lost tch over 2f out: t.o* **9/1**

2m 30.79s (-2.21) **Going Correction** -0.20s/f (Stan) **11** Ran SP% **122.8**
Speed ratings (Par 95): **99,98,97,96,96 96,95,95,95,91 74**
CSF £175.94 CT £1195.60 TOTE £36.30: £8.20, £2.60, £2.30; EX 420.30 Trifecta £3382.30.
Owner Steve & Jolene De'Lemos **Bred** C A Cyzer **Trained** Epsom, Surrey

FOCUS
A moderate 3yo handicap. Straightforward form.
T/Plt: £384.60 to a £1 stake. Pool: £65,738.51 - 124.77 winning units T/Qpdt: £72.60 to a £1 stake. Pool; £6,426.92 - 65.45 winning units **Steve Payne**

766 - 779a (Foreign Racing) - See Raceform Interactive

[694] ST MORITZ (R-H)
Sunday, February 17

OFFICIAL GOING: Snow: frozen

780a LONGINES 80TH GROSSER PREIS VON ST. MORITZ (LOCAL GROUP 2) (4YO+) (SNOW) 1m 2f
12:00 4-Y-O+
£37,332 (£18,666; £13,332; £8,888; £4,444; £2,666)

RPR

1 **Berrahri (IRE)**[7] 694 8-9-4 0.. KierenFox 6
(John Best) *w.w towards rr: tk clsr order after 1/2-way: drvn to chse clr ldr fr 2f out: led ent fnl f: drvn clr* **73/10**

2 *5* **Jungleboogie (GER)**[23] 7-9-0 0.................................. EddyHardouin 10
(Carina Fey, France) **111/10**

3 *nk* **Nimrod (IRE)**[14] 592 6-9-8 0.. KieranO'Neill 5
(M Weiss, Switzerland) **71/10**

4 *½* **Jacksun (FR)**[8] 5-9-0 0.. AntoineCoutier 4
(M Figge, Germany) **179/10**

5 *1 ¼* **Filou (SWI)**[200] 8-9-0 0.. RaphaelLingg 4
(P Schaerer, Switzerland) **7/2**[2]

6 *10* **Daisy Bere (FR)**[14] 592 6-8-8 0.................................(b) NicolasGuilbert 2
(Flurina Wullschleger, Germany) **184/10**

7 *1 ¾* **Fiesta (SWI)**[7] 694 5-8-8 0...................................... ClementLheureux 8
(P Schaerer, Switzerland) **36/5**

8 *dist* **Take A Guess (FR)**[200] 7-8-11 0..................................(p) TimBurgin 1
(Claudia Erni, Switzerland) **69/10**

9 *nk* **Manipur (GER)**[550] 6084 5-8-11 0................................ MaximPecheur 9
(Markus Klug, Germany) **48/10**[3]

10 *dist* **New Agenda**[14] 592 7-8-11 0.................................... DennisSchiergen 7
(Paul Webber) *chsd ldng gp: nvr gng wl: lost pl bef 1/2-way: sn wl bhd* **17/10**[1]

2m 13.94s **10** Ran SP% **144.5**
PARI-MUTUEL (all including 1 euro stake): WIN 8.30 PLACE 2.80, 2.30, 2.20 DF 40.80 SF 387.10.
Owner Mark Curtis & Stephen Purdew **Bred** Kilnamoragh Stud **Trained** Oad Street, Kent

781 - (Foreign Racing) - See Raceform Interactive

[737] NEWCASTLE (A.W) (L-H)
Monday, February 18

OFFICIAL GOING: Tapeta: standard to slow
Wind: Strong half against easing after race 3 Weather: Cloudy

782 BETWAY CASINO H'CAP 1m 4f 98y (Tp)
5:00 (5:00) (Class 6) (0-65,64) 4-Y-O+ **£2,587** (£770; £384; £192) **Stalls High**

Form RPR

450- **1** **Echo (IRE)**[45] 9201 4-8-13 **56**.................................(b¹) JackGarritty 12 65
(Jedd O'Keeffe) *trckd ldng pair: hdwy to chse clr ldr 3f out: sn pushed along: rdn wl over 1f out: led jst ins fnl f: drvn out* **33/1**

10-2 **2** *2* **Nevada**[43] 100 6-9-8 **63**..(b) AndrewMullen 11 68
(Steve Gollings) *hld up in rr: hdwy over 2f out: chsd ldrs 1 1/2f out: sn rdn: drvn and kpt on wl fnl f* **4/1**[2]

40-5 **3** *2* **Ripley (IRE)**[19] 473 4-9-4 **61**.......................................(t) LukeMorris 4 64
(Charles Hills) *hld up in midfield: hdwy over 3f out: rdn along to chse ldrs wl over 1f out: drvn and kpt on fnl f* **22/1**

0-14 **4** *nk* **Tetradrachm**[13] 607 6-9-9 **64**.................................(tp) StevieDonohoe 9 66
(Rebecca Menzies) *trckd ldrs: hdwy over 4f out: led wl over 2f out: rdn and hdd 1 1/2f out: drvn and edgd lft fnl f: one pce* **6/1**[3]

2-14 **5** *shd* **Splash Of Verve (IRE)**[14] 602 7-8-10 **51**.................. JamesSullivan 13 52
(David Thompson) *trckd ldrs: hdwy over 3f out: rdn to ld 1 1/2f out: drvn and hdd jst ins fnl f: kpt on one pce* **9/1**

5-02 **6** *2 ½* **Good Man (IRE)**[13] 607 6-8-7 **48**............................(p) BarryMcHugh 6 46
(Karen McLintock) *hld up in rr: hdwy wl over 2f out: nt clr run and swtchd lft over 1f out: sn rdn: styng on whn nt clr run and hmpd on inner ins fnl f: one pce after* **9/1**

04-4 **7** *½* **Hussar Ballad (USA)**[19] 481 10-8-13 **54**.......................... CamHardie 7 51
(Antony Brittain) *hld up: hdwy on outer 3f out: rdn along over 2f out: sn drvn and no imp* **18/1**

0/ **8** *2 ¾* **Camile (IRE)**[12] 3483 6-9-4 **59**...................................... JoeFanning 10 52
(Iain Jardine) *hld up: hdwy 3f out: rdn along 2f out: sn drvn and n.d* **10/3**[1]

-323 **9** *nk* **Hugoigo**[13] 607 5-8-1 **45**.. JaneElliott(3) 1 37
(Jim Goldie) *hld up in tch: hdwy over 4f out: pushed along over 3f out: rdn wl over 2f out: sn wknd* **16/1**

00-2 **10** *4* **Quite Subunctious (IRE)**[14] 602 4-8-5 **48**..................... MartinDwyer 2 35
(Keith Henry Clarke, Ire) *t.k.h: sn led: clr 7f out: pushed along over 3f out: hdd wl over 2f out: sn wknd* **14/1**

0-66 **11** *½* **Prince Consort (IRE)**[18] 495 4-8-2 **45**.....................(h) NathanEvans 14 32
(John Wainwright) *a in rr* **100/1**

5-10 **12** *hd* **Belabour**[21] 457 6-9-9 **64**.. EoinWalsh 3 49
(Mark Brisbourne) *a towards rr* **12/1**

4-05 **13** *1* **Elite Icon**[13] 607 5-8-1 **45**.. JamieGormley(3) 8 29
(Jim Goldie) *chsd ldrs: rdn along over 3f out: sn wknd* **33/1**

6-46 **14** *¾* **Highway Robber**[37] 208 6-8-1 **47**...............................(t) PaulaMuir(5) 5 30
(Wilf Storey) *trckd ldr: pushed along over 4f out: rdn over 3f out: sn wknd* **25/1**

2m 43.87s (2.77) **Going Correction** +0.225s/f (Slow)
WFA 4 from 5yo+ 2lb **14** Ran SP% **117.9**
Speed ratings (Par 101): **99,97,96,96,96 94,94,92,92,89 89,88,88,87**
CSF £153.01 CT £3028.71 TOTE £24.00: £7.30, £1.80, £5.60; EX 193.30 Trifecta £2420.40.
Owner Miss S E Hall & C Platts **Bred** Pat McCarthy **Trained** Middleham Moor, N Yorks

FOCUS
More competitive than many a race in this grade with several posting decent efforts last time. \bQuite Subunctious\p set quite stiff fractions on the front end and was understandably swallowed up in the straight. The form could be worth a shade better.

783 LADBROKES H'CAP 5f (Tp)
5:30 (5:30) (Class 6) (0-60,62) 3-Y-O **£2,264** (£673; £336; £168) **Stalls Centre**

Form RPR

04-1 **1** **Giacomo Casanova (IRE)**[37] 215 3-9-9 **62**............... AndrewMullen 1 67
(Kevin Ryan) *trckd ldng pair: smooth hdwy over 2f out: led 1 1/2f out: rdn and edgd rt ins fnl f: kpt on* **2/1**[1]

00-0 **2** *½* **Joey Boy (IRE)**[17] 524 3-9-5 **58**..................................(b¹) ShaneGray 4 61
(Kevin Ryan) *trckd ldrs: hdwy 2f out: rdn over 1f out: styd on wl fnl f* **10/1**

006- **3** *1 ¾* **Secret Picnic (FR)**[117] 8540 3-9-0 **53**.............................. JasonHart 2 50
(John Quinn) *trckd ldrs: hdwy on inner wl over 1f out: rdn and styng on whn n.m.r and sltly hmpd ins fnl f: kpt on same pce after* **11/4**[2]

5-61 **4** *1 ¼* **Sister Of The Sign (IRE)**[18] 497 3-9-7 **60**.............. BarryMcHugh 3 52
(James Given) *t.k.h: sn led: pushed along over 2f out: sn rdn and hdd 1 1/2f out: sn drvn and wknd* **4/1**[3]

01-5 **5** *1* **One One Seven (IRE)**[18] 497 3-9-6 **59**.......................... CamHardie 5 48
(Antony Brittain) *hld up in rr: hdwy over 2f out: rdn along wl over 1f out: no imp* **4/1**[3]

40-6 **6** *8* **Kyroc (IRE)**[24] 412 3-9-5 **58**.................................... PaulMulrennan 6 18
(Susan Corbett) *cl up: rdn along 1/2-way: sn outpcd and bhd* **80/1**

1m 0.64s (1.14) **Going Correction** +0.225s/f (Slow) **6** Ran SP% **110.3**
Speed ratings (Par 95): **99,98,95,93,91 79**
CSF £21.37 TOTE £2.30: £1.20, £3.50; EX 15.60 Trifecta £71.80.
Owner Giacomo Casanova Partners **Bred** P Kelly **Trained** Hambleton, N Yorks

FOCUS
Not a bad little sprint for the grade with one or two in here worth keeping an eye on. The winner more than confirmed previous C&D improvement.

784 SUNRACING.CO.UK H'CAP 1m 5y (Tp)
6:00 (6:00) (Class 5) (0-70,70) 4-Y-O+ **£2,911** (£866; £432; £216) **Stalls Centre**

Form RPR

111 **1** **Lion Hearted (IRE)**[3] 738 5-8-9 **58**.................................... LukeMorris 7 73+
(Michael Appleby) *trckd ldrs: smooth hdwy to ld 2f out: rdn over 1f out and sn edgd rt: kpt on wl towards fin* **2/7**[1]

5-43 **2** *2* **Elixsoft (IRE)**[17] 525 4-9-0 **63**.................................. CallumRodriguez 10 73
(Roger Fell) *trckd ldrs: hdwy 2f out: rdn over 1f out: kpt on wl fnl f* **9/1**[2]

0-36 **3** *1 ¾* **King Oswald (USA)**[19] 479 6-8-10 **59**........................(tp) AndrewMullen 12 65
(James Unett) *dwlt and hld up towards rr: gd hdwy 3f out: chsd wnr and rdn whn n.m.r on inner and sltly hmpd appr fnl f: sn swtchd lft: kpt on same pce* **16/1**[3]

5-16 **4** *1 ½* **Arabic Culture (USA)**[18] 507 5-9-3 **66**............................ SamJames 4 69
(Grant Tuer) *trckd ldng pair: effrt and hdwy over 2f out: rdn wl over 1f out: drvn appr fnl f: kpt on same pce* **9/1**[2]

5 *5* **Delegating**[17] 543 5-8-7 **56** oh1.. MartinDwyer 1 47
(Keith Henry Clarke, Ire) *midfield: hdwy towards far side over 2f out: sn rdn and no imp* **50/1**

520- **6** *½* **Celtic Artisan (IRE)**[104] 8910 8-9-0 **63**..............................(t) CamHardie 9 53
(Rebecca Menzies) *hld up towards rr: hdwy wl over 2f out: sn rdn and n.d* **40/1**

3/6- **7** *2* **Lucy's Law (IRE)**[269] 3069 5-9-4 **67**............................ JamesSullivan 11 52
(Tom Tate) *hld up: a towards rr* **22/1**

05-6 **8** *nk* **Sunbreak (IRE)**[44] 86 4-8-9 **65**.................................. OliverStammers(7) 2 50
(Mark Johnston) *chsd ldrs: rdn along wl over 2f out: sn wknd* **28/1**

000- **9** *1* **Passionate Love (IRE)**[154] 7371 4-8-7 **56**.......................... NathanEvans 13 38
(Mark Walford) *trckd ldrs: pushed along 3f out: rdn over 2f out: sn wknd* **66/1**

04-5 **10** *3 ¾* **Street Poet (IRE)**[14] 603 6-8-13 **65**...........................(p) PhilDennis(3) 14 39
(Michael Herrington) *cl up: chal over 2f out: sn rdn and ev ch: drvn and wknd over 1f out* **33/1**

661/ **11** *4* **Rock Island Line**[468] 8662 5-8-11 **60**..........................(p) PaulHanagan 8 24
(Mark Walford) *chsd ldrs: rdn along over 2f out: sn drvn and wknd* **20/1**

550- **12** *2* **Mighty Mac (IRE)**[282] 2658 4-9-4 **70**........................(p¹) JamieGormley(3) 3 30
(Karen McLintock) *led: pushed along 3f out: rdn over 2f out: sn hdd & wknd* **25/1**

026/ **13** *2 ¾* **Graphite (IRE)**[478] 8434 5-9-4 **67**.................................... ShaneGray 5 21
(Geoffrey Harker) *a towards rr* **66/1**

53/0 **14** *½* **Strawberryandcream**[42] 117 4-8-11 **60**................. RachelRichardson 6 12
(James Bethell) *a towards rr* **66/1**

1m 40.22s (1.62) **Going Correction** +0.225s/f (Slow) **14** Ran SP% **131.9**
Speed ratings (Par 103): **100,98,96,94,89 89,87,86,85,82 78,76,73,72**
CSF £3.77 CT £27.65 TOTE £1.20: £1.02, £2.50, £3.80; EX 6.10 Trifecta £37.70.
Owner Slipstream Racing **Bred** Dowager Countess Harrington **Trained** Oakham, Rutland

FOCUS
One outstanding candidate in an otherwise modest event, even for this grade, and he justified his extremely cramped odds. The front four pulled a fair way clear. The runner-up is rated in line with last spring's form.

785 FOLLOW TOP TIPSTER TEMPLEGATE AT SUN RACING NOVICE STKS 7f 14y (Tp)
6:30 (6:30) (Class 5) 3-Y-O+ £2,911 (£866; £432; £216) Stalls Centre

Form RPR
4 1 **Mustadun**[27] [354] 3-8-6 0 JoeFanning 13 73
(Mark Johnston) *trckd ldng pair: hdwy and cl up 1/2-way: led 3f out: rdn wl over 1f out: drvn ins fnl f: hld on wl towards fin* **12/1**
2 nk **Conaglen** 3-8-6 0 PaulHanagan 10 72
(James Bethell) *green and s.i.s: t.k.h and towards rr: hdwy 1/2-way: chsd ldrs 2f out: rdn over 1f out: styd on to chal ins fnl f: ev ch tl no ex towards fin* **4/1**[2]
44 3 5 **Kingdom Of Dubai (FR)**[31] [289] 3-8-6 0 LukeMorris 12 59
(Roger Varian) *trckd ldrs: pushed along and hdwy 3f out: rdn wl over 1f out: sn drvn and kpt on same pce* **5/4**[1]
4 1 1/2 **Picture Your Dream**[44] 4-9-4 0 NathanEvans 5 55
(Seb Spencer) *hld up: hdwy 3f out: chsd ldrs 2f out: sn rdn and kpt on fnl f* **40/1**
5 3/4 **Muhallab (IRE)** 3-8-6 0 AndrewMullen 2 52
(Adrian Nicholls) *led: jnd and pushed along 1/2-way: hdd 3f out and sn rdn: wknd over 1f out* **5/1**[3]
R5 6 2 1/2 **Desai**[13] [608] 5-9-9 0 GrahamLee 8 52
(Noel Wilson) *chsd ldrs: rdn along over 2f out: grad wknd* **22/1**
7 2 **Vita Vivet** 3-8-1 0 JamesSullivan 3 35
(Dianne Sayer) *dwlt and in rr tl sme late hdwy* **50/1**
5 8 shd **Parker's Pride**[27] [354] 3-8-3 0 JamieGormley(3) 11 40
(Brian Rothwell) *a towards rr* **100/1**
05- 9 1 3/4 **Brahma Kamal**[189] [6107] 3-8-1 0 AndrewBreslin(5) 7 35
(Keith Dalgleish) *chsd ldrs: rdn along wl over 2f out: sn wknd* **40/1**
0 10 nk **Beresford (IRE)**[24] [405] 3-8-6 0 BarryMcHugh 9 34
(Richard Fahey) *chsd ldrs: rdn along over 2f out: sn wknd* **5/1**[3]
0 11 8 **Simul Amicis**[24] [405] 3-8-1 0 CamHardie 6 8
(Dianne Sayer) *a towards rr* **80/1**
-06 12 7 **Savlad**[18] [500] 4-9-9 0 PaulMulrennan 1
(Shaun Harris) *a in rr* **150/1**
1m 28.34s (2.14) **Going Correction** +0.225s/f (Slow)
WFA 3 from 4yo+ 17lb 12 Ran SP% 119.5
Speed ratings (Par 103): **96,95,89,88,87 84,82,82,80,79 70,62**
CSF £58.62 TOTE £8.20: £2.20, £1.90, £1.10; EX 81.60 Trifecta £251.10.
Owner Ewan And Anna Hyslop **Bred** Biddestone Stud Ltd **Trained** Middleham Moor, N Yorks

FOCUS
Not a particularly strong novice event but the front two pulled nicely clear. The runner-up ran a huge race on debut and is one to keep on side next time. The form looks fluid.

786 BETWAY HEED YOUR HUNCH H'CAP 6f (Tp)
7:00 (7:00) (Class 3) (0-95,96) 4-Y-O+
£9,337 (£2,796; £1,398; £699; £349; £175) Stalls Centre

Form RPR
1-22 1 **Equiano Springs**[24] [407] 5-8-7 81 AndrewMullen 1 89
(Tom Tate) *cl up: led over 3f out: rdn wl over 1f out: drvn and kpt on wl fnl f* **4/1**[1]
-313 2 1/2 **Athollblair Boy (IRE)**[24] [407] 6-8-2 81 oh2 FayeMcManoman(5) 8 87
(Nigel Tinkler) *hld up in rr: swtchd lft and hdwy 2f out: rdn over 1f out: chal ins fnl f: kpt on* **11/2**[2]
250- 3 1 1/4 **Visionary (IRE)**[233] [4388] 5-9-8 96 LukeMorris 10 98
(Robert Cowell) *trckd ldrs: hdwy over 2f out: rdn wl over 1f out: drvn and kpt on fnl f* **12/1**
2-14 4 hd **Outrage**[27] [352] 7-9-6 94 (b) KieranO'Neill 7 96
(Daniel Kubler) *trckd ldrs: hdwy over 2f out: rdn over 1f out: drvn and kpt on same pce fnl f* **11/2**[2]
04-4 5 1 1/2 **Chookie Dunedin**[36] [230] 4-8-7 81 oh1 JoeFanning 2 78
(Keith Dalgleish) *trckd ldrs: hdwy to chse ldng pair over 2f out: rdn wl over 1f out: wknd ent fnl f* **10/1**
00-3 6 1 1/4 **Equitation**[41] [127] 5-8-7 81 (t) MartinDwyer 9 74
(Stuart Williams) *hld up towards rr: t.k.h on outer 1/2-way: effrt over 2f out: sn rdn and n.d* **4/1**[1]
3-46 7 1 **Danzan (IRE)**[25] [389] 4-9-8 96 GrahamLee 3 86
(Andrew Balding) *led: hdd over 3f out: rdn along wl over 2f out: sn drvn and wknd* **12/1**
-131 8 3 1/2 **Moonraker**[15] [588] 7-9-7 95 AlistairRawlinson 4 74
(Michael Appleby) *chsd ldrs: rdn along over 2f out: sn wknd* **6/1**[3]
505- 9 1 3/4 **Oriental Lilly**[101] [8977] 5-8-4 81 oh3 JamieGormley(3) 6 54
(Jim Goldie) *in tch: rdn along 3f out: sn wknd* **14/1**
1m 12.16s (-0.34) **Going Correction** +0.225s/f (Slow) 9 Ran SP% 116.2
Speed ratings (Par 107): **111,110,108,108,106 104,103,98,96**
CSF £26.07 CT £244.37 TOTE £4.70: £2.60, £1.90, £3.90; EX 31.10 Trifecta £239.20.
Owner T T Racing **Bred** Paddock Space **Trained** Tadcaster, N Yorks

FOCUS
A warm heat but, although the pace looked even enough, not many got into it. The winner confirmed C&D latest with the runner-up.

787 BETWAY (S) STKS 5f (Tp)
7:30 (7:30) (Class 5) 3-Y-O+ £2,911 (£866; £324; £324) Stalls Centre

Form RPR
0-30 1 **Captain Lars (SAF)**[16] [551] 9-9-9 86 (b) ThomasGreatrex(5) 4 71
(Archie Watson) *cl up: slt ld 3f out: rdn wl over 1f out: drvn and kpt on wl fnl f* **1/1**[1]
6204 2 1/2 **Zapper Cass (FR)**[14] [600] 6-9-2 64 (b) MarkCrehan(7) 1 64
(Michael Appleby) *trckd ldrs: hdwy wl over 1f out: rdn ent fnl f: kpt on wl towards fin* **9/2**[3]
/00- 3 nk **Discreet Hero (IRE)**[70] [9486] 6-9-6 79 (t) GrahamLee 2 60
(Noel Wilson) *hld up: hdwy 2f out: rdn over 1f out: drvn and kpt on fnl f* **20/1**
223- 3 dht **Harperelle**[153] [7389] 3-8-1 73 AndrewMullen 3 49
(K R Burke) *slt ld: hdd over 3f out: cl up: rdn wl over 1f out: ev ch tl drvn ins fnl f and no ex last 75yds* **13/8**[2]
00-0 5 3 **Roy's Legacy**[47] [26] 10-9-4 44 GinaMangan(7) 5 54
(Shaun Harris) *chsd ldng pair: rdn along wl over 2f out: sn wknd* **80/1**
1m 0.62s (1.12) **Going Correction** +0.225s/f (Slow)
WFA 3 from 6yo+ 14lb 5 Ran SP% 112.3
Speed ratings (Par 103): **100,99,98,98,93**
CSF £6.26 TOTE £2.20: £1.30, £1.60; EX 5.00 Trifecta £13.50.There was no bid for the winner. Harperelle was claimed by Mr A. C. Whillans for £7400
Owner Greenfield Racing **Bred** Klawervlei Stud **Trained** Upper Lambourn, W Berks

FOCUS
The market suggested this would be a cakewalk for the favourite and although he got the job done, he was forced to work quite hard for it. The fifth limits the form.

788 BETWAY LIVE CASINO H'CAP 6f (Tp)
8:00 (8:00) (Class 6) (0-65,66) 4-Y-O+ £1,468 (£1,468; £336; £168) Stalls Centre

Form RPR
6-42 1 **Muatadel**[15] [586] 6-9-2 65 (p) BenSanderson(5) 5 71
(Roger Fell) *hld up towards rr: swtchd lft and hdwy over 1f out: sn rdn: styd on strly fnl f to ld last 50yds: jnd on line* **5/1**[2]
0-26 1 dht **Duke Cosimo**[27] [356] 9-9-3 64 PhilDennis(3) 6 70
(Michael Herrington) *hld up towards rr: hdwy wl over 1f out: rdn and styd on wl fnl f: jnd ldr last stride* **5/1**[2]
0-34 3 1 **Gowanbuster**[3] [743] 4-9-8 66 (t) PaulMulrennan 4 69
(Susan Corbett) *qckly away and clr: rdn over 1f out: drvn ins fnl f: hdd and no ex last 50yds* **5/1**[2]
2-31 4 1 1/2 **Avenue Of Stars**[27] [356] 6-9-8 66 (v) JasonHart 1 65
(Karen McLintock) *chsd clr ldr: hdwy 2f out: rdn over 1f out: drvn and kpt on same pce fnl f* **3/1**[1]
16-1 5 3/4 **Dandy Highwayman (IRE)**[32] [277] 5-9-0 65 (tp) HarryRussell(7) 8 61
(Ollie Pears) *chsd ldrs: hdwy 2f out: rdn over 1f out: drvn and no imp fnl f* **8/1**
0-06 6 3/4 **Major Crispies**[15] [586] 8-9-2 60 (t) CallumRodriguez 9 54
(Ronald Thompson) *chsd ldrs: rdn wl over 1f out: sn drvn and grad wknd* **12/1**
-000 7 1 1/2 **Breathoffreshair**[18] [502] 5-8-12 56 (t) PhilipPrince 10 46
(Richard Guest) *a towards rr* **14/1**
5535 8 nk **Thorntoun Lady (USA)**[3] [738] 9-8-7 54 JamieGormley(3) 7 43
(Jim Goldie) *chsd ldrs: rdn along wl over 1f out: grad wknd* **7/1**[3]
3-00 9 3 **Capla Demon**[15] [586] 4-9-5 63 (v[1]) CamHardie 3 43
(Antony Brittain) *dwlt: a in rr* **25/1**
1m 13.32s (0.82) **Going Correction** +0.225s/f (Slow) 9 Ran SP% 116.8
Speed ratings (Par 101): **103,103,101,99,98 97,95,95,91**
WIN: 2.30 Muatadel 2.60 Duke Cosimo; PL: 1.90 Gowanbuster 1.90 Muatadel 1.80 Duke Cosimo; EX: 15.90 15.60; CSF: 15.30 15.30; TC: 66.14 66.14; TF: 74.40 76.70 CSF £15.30 CT £66.14 TOTE £2.30: £1.90, £1.90; EX 15.90 Trifecta £74.40.
Owner R G Fell **Bred** Lofts Hall Stud & B Sangster **Trained** Nawton, N Yorks
Owner Stuart Herrington **Bred** Cheveley Park Stud Ltd **Trained** Cold Kirby, N Yorks

FOCUS
A reasonable heat for the grade, with the top four all coming here in decent form. They couldn't split the front two on the line. The first three are all rated near their recent bests.
T/Plt: £24.40 to a £1 stake. Pool: £84,700.99 - 2,528.01 winning units T/Qpdt: £4.80 to a £1 stake. Pool: £12,585.34 - 1,907.60 winning units **Joe Rowntree**

620 WOLVERHAMPTON (A.W) (L-H)
Tuesday, February 19

OFFICIAL GOING: Tapeta: standard
Wind: Light behind Weather: Cloudy

789 BETWAY HEED YOUR HUNCH AMATEUR RIDERS' H'CAP 1m 4f 51y (Tp)
5:30 (5:30) (Class 6) (0-55,55) 4-Y-O+ £2,183 (£677; £338; £169) Stalls Low

Form RPR
5-36 1 **Singing The Blues (IRE)**[27] [363] 4-10-10 53 MrPatrickMillman 5 65+
(Rod Millman) *racd keenly: led early: led again over 10f out: hdd over 9f out: chsd ldr tl led again over 3f out: rdn clr fr over 1f out: eased towards fin* **5/4**[1]
0-00 2 3 3/4 **Boycie**[20] [479] 6-10-8 54 (p) HarriettLees(5) 4 57
(Adrian Wintle) *hld up: nt clr run over 2f out: rdn over 1f out: nt clr run: swtchd lft and r.o to go 2nd wl ins fnl f: no ch w wnr* **12/1**
2/06 3 1 3/4 **Rainbow Lad (IRE)**[22] [457] 6-11-0 55 MissSerenaBrotherton 11 54
(Michael Appleby) *pushed along early in rr: swtchd rt over 5f out: hdwy over 4f out: chsd wnr over 2f out: rdn over 1f out: styd on same pce: lost 2nd wl ins fnl f* **7/1**
006- 4 nk **Pullman Brown (USA)**[49] [7603] 7-10-4 50 TomMidgley(5) 1 49
(Philip Kirby) *hld up in tch: lost pl over 6f out: nt clr run over 2f out: shkn up over 1f out: edgd lft and styd on ins fnl f: nt trble ldrs (jockey said gelding was denied a clear run approaching the home turn)* **11/2**[2]
300- 5 1 1/2 **Torch**[236] [4293] 6-10-7 48 TabithaWorsley 6 44
(Laura Morgan) *prom: lost pl over 7f out: hdwy on outer over 2f out: edgd lft and no ex fnl f* **20/1**
0-00 6 1 **Lazarus (IRE)**[17] [560] 5-10-5 53 (t) MissMintyBloss(7) 10 48
(Amy Murphy) *sn prom: pushed along over 3f out: edgd lft and no ex fnl f (vet said gelding lost it's left fore shoe)* **14/1**
004 7 3 **Fearaun (IRE)**[18] [535] 4-10-2 50 SophieSmith(5) 12 41
(Stella Barclay) *plld hrd and prom: led at stdy pce over 9f out: hdd over 3f out: wknd fnl f* **50/1**
10-3 8 nk **Picture Painter (IRE)**[20] [482] 6-10-7 55 MrFergusGillard(7) 7 45
(David Pipe) *sn pushed along towards rr: hdwy over 6f out: nt clr run: swtchd lft and rdn over 1f out: wknd fnl f* **6/1**[3]
360- 9 1/2 **Sigrid Nansen**[55] [9703] 4-10-7 53 (p) MissHannahWelch(3) 8 43
(Alexandra Dunn) *sn led: hdd over 10f out: chsd ldrs: rdn over 2f out: wknd over 1f out* **16/1**
6-00 10 8 **Happy Ending (IRE)**[20] [482] 4-10-5 53 MrMatthewFielding(5) 2 30
(Seamus Mullins) *hld up: hdwy on outer wl over 1f out: sn rdn: edgd lft and wknd fnl f* **33/1**
3-00 11 15 **Warofindependence (USA)**[15] [602] 7-10-9 50 (p) MissBrodieHampson 3 2
(John O'Shea) *plld hrd and prom: clipped heels wl over 10f out: led briefly over 3f out: wknd over 1f out (jockey said gelding hung badly left-handed throughout)* **16/1**
2m 41.42s (0.62) **Going Correction** 0.0s/f (Stan)
WFA 4 from 5yo+ 2lb 11 Ran SP% 122.4
Speed ratings (Par 101): **97,94,93,93,92 91,89,89,88,83 73**
CSF £19.10 CT £85.53 TOTE £2.10: £1.40, £4.20, £2.10; EX 18.20 Trifecta £91.90.
Owner Rod Millman & Andy Smith **Bred** Lynn Lodge Stud **Trained** Kentisbeare, Devon

The Form Book Flat 2019, Raceform Ltd, Newbury, RG14 5SJ

FOCUS
A moderate contest, but a gamble was landed on the winner. Straightforward form in behind the winner.

790 BETWAY H'CAP 6f 20y (Tp)
6:00 (6:00) (Class 5) (0-75,77) 4-Y-0+ £2,911 (£866; £432; £216) Stalls Low

Form RPR

2-05 **1** **The Establishment**[17] 564 4-9-4 **70**......(h) EoinWalsh 8 78
(David Evans) *hld up: plld hrd: nt clr run and swtchd rt over 1f out: hdwy sn after: rdn and r.o to ld towards fin* **7/2**[2]

6-40 **2** *½* **Madrinho (IRE)**[34] 253 6-9-6 **77**...... PoppyBridgwater(5) 11 83
(Tony Carroll) *hld up: hdwy: nt clr run and swtchd rt ins fnl f: r.o* **12/1**

40-3 **3** *½* **Monumental Man**[29] 347 10-9-5 **71**......(p) DougieCostello 5 76
(Jamie Osborne) *chsd ldrs: rdn over 1f out: ev ch ins fnl f: styd on* **8/1**[3]

1/25 **4** *hd* **Followthesteps (IRE)**[19] 499 4-9-10 **76**...... AdamKirby 6 80
(Ivan Furtado) *chsd ldrs: shkn up over 2f out: rdn to ld ins fnl f: hdd towards fin* **5/2**[1]

-123 **5** *nk* **A Sure Welcome**[21] 471 5-9-5 **71**......(b) LukeMorris 13 74
(John Spearing) *sn led: rdn over 1f out: hdd and edgd lft ins fnl f: styd on same pce* **16/1**

0-32 **6** *nk* **Real Estate (IRE)**[31] 314 4-9-2 **68**......(p) CallumShepherd 9 70
(Michael Attwater) *hld up in tch: racd keenly: rdn over 1f out: styd on* **12/1**

-611 **7** *1* **Aguerooo (IRE)**[24] 439 6-9-3 **69**......(tp) OisinMurphy 1 69
(Charlie Wallis) *s.i.s: sn prom: shkn up and nt clr run ins fnl f: nvr able to chal (jockey said gelding was denied a clear run in the home straight)* **8/1**[3]

1-30 **8** *½* **Peachey Carnehan**[46] 64 5-8-10 **62**......(v) JamesSullivan 4 59
(Michael Mullineaux) *hld up: rdn and nt clr run over 1f out: nt rch ldrs* **14/1**

623- **9** *shd* **Mutabaahy (IRE)**[123] 8382 4-9-7 **73**......(h) CamHardie 12 70
(Antony Brittain) *broke wl enough: sn stdd and lost pl: hld up: plld hrd: effrt on outer over 1f out: nt trble ldrs* **16/1**

5-30 **10** *2 ¼* **Independence Day (IRE)**[21] 468 6-9-0 **66**...... JoeyHaynes 7 56
(Paul Howling) *hld up: shkn up over 2f out: nvr nr to chal* **11/1**

052- **11** *1 ¼* **Vimy Ridge**[153] 7421 7-9-0 **71**......(tp) DarraghKeenan(5) 2 57
(Alan Bailey) *s.i.s: hld up: effrt over 1f out: n.d* **50/1**

20-5 **12** *2 ¾* **Van Gerwen**[21] 468 6-9-1 **67**......(v[1]) JoeFanning 10 44
(Les Eyre) *broke wl: settled to chse ldrs: shkn up over 1f out: eased whn btn ins fnl f (jockey said gelding moved poorly in the home straight)* **20/1**

1m 13.69s (-0.81) **Going Correction** 0.0s/f (Stan) **12 Ran SP% 121.9**
Speed ratings (Par 103): **105,104,103,103,103 102,101,100,100,97 95,92**
CSF £47.04 CT £330.14 TOTE £4.50: £1.90, £3.60, £2.60; EX 57.90 Trifecta £432.10.
Owner Power Geneva Ltd & Partner **Bred** S A Douch **Trained** Pandy, Monmouths

■ Laubali was withdrawn, price at time of withdrawal 11/1. Rule 4 applies to all bets struck prior to withdrawal, but not to SP bets. Deduction - 5p in the pound. New market formed.

FOCUS
A good gallop set things up for the closers. The winner has been rated close to his early form, and the second close to form.

791 BETWAY SPRINT H'CAP 5f 21y (Tp)
6:30 (6:30) (Class 4) (0-85,84) 4-Y-0+ £4,690 (£1,395; £697; £348) Stalls Low

Form RPR

460- **1** **Just That Lord**[60] 9662 6-9-7 **84**...... LukeMorris 8 92
(Michael Attwater) *mde all: rdn over 1f out: styd on u.p* **8/1**

5052 **2** *½* **Something Lucky (IRE)**[3] 763 7-9-1 **78**......(v) AlistairRawlinson 4 84
(Michael Appleby) *a.p: shkn up over 1f out: chsd wnr wl ins fnl f: r.o* **5/2**[1]

6141 **3** *½* **Another Angel (IRE)**[14] 610 5-8-13 **76**...... CamHardie 7 80
(Antony Brittain) *a.p: chsd wnr 4f out: rdn over 1f out: styd on: lost 2nd wl ins fnl f* **11/2**[3]

1-53 **4** *nse* **Primo's Comet**[28] 353 4-8-13 **79**...... PhilDennis(3) 11 83+
(Jim Goldie) *hld up: rdn and r.o ins fnl f: nt rch ldrs* **5/1**[2]

31-0 **5** *½* **You're Cool**[49] 3 7-9-4 **81**......(t) LewisEdmunds 2 83
(John Balding) *w wnr 1f: remained handy: rdn over 1f out: styd on same pce wl ins fnl f* **10/1**

550- **6** *½* **Poyle Vinnie**[143] 7766 9-9-7 **84**...... JamesSullivan 1 85
(Ruth Carr) *hld up in tch: racd keenly: shkn up and edgd lft over 1f out: kpt on* **7/1**

050- **7** *1 ¾* **George Dryden (IRE)**[127] 8254 7-9-6 **83**......(t w) DanielTudhope 3 77
(Charlie Wallis) *s.i.s: hld up: rdn over 1f out: nvr on terms* **13/2**

-042 **8** *¾* **Dynamo Walt (IRE)**[17] 551 8-9-6 **83**......(v) PaddyMathers 5 75
(Derek Shaw) *hld up: rdn over 1f out: nt trble ldrs* **8/1**

1m 0.63s (-1.27) **Going Correction** 0.0s/f (Stan) **8 Ran SP% 117.8**
Speed ratings (Par 105): **110,109,108,108,107 106,103,102**
CSF £29.29 CT £122.90 TOTE £10.30: £2.60, £1.20, £1.70; EX 30.10 Trifecta £248.00.
Owner Mrs M S Teversham **Bred** Mrs Monica Teversham **Trained** Epsom, Surrey

FOCUS
This was dominated by the winner, who made every yard. The winner has been rated to his best.

792 BETWAY LIVE CASINO H'CAP 1m 1f 104y (Tp)
7:00 (7:00) (Class 6) (0-55,57) 4-Y-0+ £2,264 (£673; £336; £168) Stalls Low

Form RPR

3245 **1** **Amor Fati (IRE)**[13] 624 4-9-2 **50**...... AdamKirby 8 56
(David Evans) *chsd ldrs: pushed along to ld 2f out: hrd rdn fr over 1f out: all out* **6/1**[3]

24-5 **2** *nse* **Creative Talent (IRE)**[34] 257 7-9-6 **54**...... TomMarquand 4 60+
(Tony Carroll) *prom: lost pl over 7f out: hmpd 2f out: hdwy u.p and hung lft fr over 1f out: r.o (jockey said gelding hung left-handed)* **4/1**[2]

10-0 **3** *nk* **Lady Of Authority**[38] 207 4-8-10 **51**...... GeorgiaDobie(7) 5 56
(Richard Phillips) *hld up: hdwy on outer and edgd lft over 2f out: chsd wnr over 1f out: sn rdn: r.o* **14/1**

0241 **4** *1 ¾* **Don't Do It (IRE)**[5] 724 4-9-9 **57** 6ex......(v) AlistairRawlinson 3 59
(Michael Appleby) *prom: nt clr run over 2f out: rdn over 1f out: styd on same pce wl ins fnl f (jockey said gelding was denied a clear run approaching the home turn)* **5/2**[1]

16-3 **5** *shd* **Blyton Lass**[21] 465 4-9-5 **53**...... BarryMcHugh 12 56
(James Given) *s.i.s: in rr: nt clr run over 1f out: edgd lft and r.o ins fnl f: nrst fin* **14/1**

05-3 **6** *2* **Top Offer**[38] 210 10-9-7 **55**......(p) OisinMurphy 6 53
(Patrick Morris) *hld up: nt clr run over 1f out: styd on ins fnl f: nvr nrr* **10/1**

0-63 **7** *1 ¾* **Mr Frankie**[20] 485 8-9-0 **48**......(p) EoinWalsh 13 44
(Roy Brotherton) *swtchd lft sn after s: hld up: nt clr run over 1f out: nt trble ldrs (jockey said gelding was denied a clear run on two occasions in the home straight. Trainer said gelding lost it's left fore shoe)* **28/1**

00-0 **8** *1* **Perceived**[46] 67 7-9-4 **52**......(p) CamHardie 11 46
(Antony Brittain) *chsd ldrs: hmpd 2f out: rdn over 1f out: wknd ins fnl f* **33/1**

-422 **9** *4* **Sea Shack**[13] 624 5-8-13 **54**......(tp) ScottMcCullagh(7) 9 39
(Julia Feilden) *led after 1f: hdd 5f out: led again over 3f out: hdd 2f out: wknd fnl f* **8/1**

00-0 **10** *6* **Cosmic Ray**[42] 125 7-9-6 **54**......(h) JoeFanning 2 28
(Les Eyre) *led 1f: remained w ldr: led again 5f out tl over 3f out: rdn over 2f out: wknd over 1f out* **33/1**

-162 **11** *2 ¼* **Diamond Reflection (IRE)**[25] 399 7-9-6 **54**......(tp) RossaRyan 1 24
(Alexandra Dunn) *chsd ldrs: shkn up over 2f out: nt clr run over 1f out: wknd fnl f (trainer could offer no explanation for the poor form shown)* **8/1**

365- **12** *7* **Allleedsaren'Twe**[196] 5840 4-8-11 **52**......(w) RPWalsh(7) 7 8
(Shaun Harris) *plld hrd and prom: stdd and lost pl after 1f: effrt on outer over 2f out: sn wknd* **66/1**

1m 59.53s (-1.27) **Going Correction** 0.0s/f (Stan) **12 Ran SP% 118.3**
Speed ratings (Par 101): **105,104,104,103,103 101,99,98,95,89 87,81**
CSF £29.32 CT £327.45 TOTE £6.20: £2.50, £1.40, £5.80; EX 31.60 Trifecta £394.40.
Owner Mrs Catherine Gannon **Bred** Tony O'Meara **Trained** Pandy, Monmouths

FOCUS
A bit of a messy race, with the pace picking up down the back, leading to those up front beginning to tire on the turn in and causing some bunching in behind. The second and third help pin the limited level.

793 BETWAY CASINO H'CAP 1m 1f 104y (Tp)
7:30 (7:30) (Class 5) (0-75,75) 4-Y-0+ £2,911 (£866; £432; £216) Stalls Low

Form RPR

3-25 **1** **Illustrissime (USA)**[39] 184 6-9-7 **75**......(p) JasonHart 4 87+
(Ivan Furtado) *prom: lost pl over 3f out: nt clr run over 2f out: shkn up and hdwy over 1f out: rdn to ld ins fnl f: r.o wl* **4/1**[1]

2-03 **2** *3* **Singing Sheriff**[27] 362 4-8-12 **66**...... LukeMorris 11 71
(Ed Walker) *s.i.s: hld up: hdwy over 3f out: shkn up over 2f out: hung lft and r.o ins fnl f* **12/1**

22-4 **3** *nk* **Beauty Salon**[41] 135 4-8-12 **66**...... OisinMurphy 1 70
(James Fanshawe) *chsd ldrs: rdn to ld over 1f out: hdd ins fnl f: styd on same pce* **4/1**[1]

0-45 **4** *¾* **Thawry**[19] 495 4-9-2 **70**...... CamHardie 7 73
(Antony Brittain) *hld up: hdwy over 1f out: styd on* **11/1**

0-02 **5** *1 ½* **Apache Blaze**[18] 536 4-8-10 **64**...... AndrewMullen 10 64
(Robyn Brisland) *chsd ldrs: nt clr run and swtchd lft ins fnl f: styd on same pce (jockey said filly was denied a clear run in the home straight)* **10/1**[3]

02-6 **6** *1* **Ruby Gates (IRE)**[22] 459 6-9-3 **74**......(p) TimClark(3) 2 72
(Paul D'Arcy) *pushed along to ld at stdy pce after 1f: hdd over 3f out: led again 2f out: rdn and hdd over 1f out: wknd wl ins fnl f* **18/1**

1 **7** *1* **Manfadh (IRE)**[29] 344 4-9-1 **69**...... ShaneKelly 9 64
(Mark Brisbourne) *hld up: racd keenly: hdwy over 5f out: rdn over 1f out: wknd ins fnl f* **5/1**[2]

05-0 **8** *½* **Blue Rocks**[20] 479 5-8-4 **61** oh4...... GabrieleMalune(3) 8 55
(Lisa Williamson) *led 1f: chsd ldr tl led again over 3f out: rdn and hdd 2f out: wknd ins fnl f* **66/1**

2-00 **9** *1 ¾* **Tangramm**[18] 536 7-9-1 **69**......(p) MartinDwyer 13 60
(Dean Ivory) *hld up: rdn over 1f out: n.d* **25/1**

0-12 **10** *3 ¼* **Perfect Refuge**[22] 459 4-9-4 **72**...... HectorCrouch 5 56
(Clive Cox) *hld up: racd keenly: rdn and swtchd rt over 2f out: wknd fnl f (jockey said filly ran too freely)* **4/1**[1]

-633 **11** *1 ¾* **King Of Naples**[18] 536 6-8-7 **61**......(h) JamesSullivan 3 41
(Ruth Carr) *hld up: racd keenly: wd and carried rt over 2f out: wknd fnl f* **11/1**

2m 0.2s (-0.60) **Going Correction** 0.0s/f (Stan) **11 Ran SP% 120.7**
Speed ratings (Par 103): **102,99,99,98,97 96,95,94,93,90 88**
CSF £55.44 CT £208.79 TOTE £5.60: £1.60, £3.90, £2.00; EX 63.80 Trifecta £177.00.
Owner Carl Hodgson **Bred** Goldmark Farm Llc **Trained** Wiseton, Nottinghamshire

FOCUS
They went fairly steady early on but the pace picked up leaving the back straight. The second, third and fourth have been rated close to their recent marks.

794 LADBROKES HOME OF THE ODDS BOOST FILLIES' NOVICE STKS 1m 1f 104y (Tp)
8:00 (8:00) (Class 5) 3-Y-0+ £2,911 (£866; £432; £216) Stalls Low

Form RPR

5 **1** **Elisheba (IRE)**[17] 556 3-8-7 0...... KieranO'Neill 8 70+
(John Gosden) *s.i.s: sn chsng ldrs: rdn over 1f out: hung lft and styd on to ld wl ins fnl f* **2/1**[2]

2 **2** *1* **Dawn Crusade (IRE)**[20] 474 3-8-7 0...... DavidProbert 1 68
(Charlie Appleby) *led at stdy pce: qcknd over 2f out: rdn over 1f out: hdd wl ins fnl f* **4/5**[1]

3 *1 ¾* **Caen Na Coille (USA)** 3-8-7 0...... GeorgeWood 5 64
(Ed Dunlop) *hld up: racd keenly: shkn up over 1f out: styd on to go 3rd nr fin: nt rch ldrs* **40/1**

2-43 **4** *nk* **Fayetta**[15] 598 3-8-7 **68**...... EdwardGreatrex 7 64
(David Loughnane) *chsd ldr: pushed along over 3f out: rdn and lost 2nd over 1f out: hmpd ins fnl f: styd on same pce* **16/1**

5 *¾* **Teodora De Vega (IRE)** 3-8-7 0...... RobHornby 3 62
(Ralph Beckett) *s.i.s: hld up: shkn up over 2f out: styd on ins fnl f: nt trble ldrs* **6/1**[3]

6-4 **6** *1 ½* **Taraayef (IRE)**[47] 41 4-10-0 0...... AndrewMullen 2 65
(Adrian Nicholls) *chsd ldrs: pushed along over 3f out: styd on same pce fr over 1f out* **66/1**

5 **7** *½* **Hen (IRE)**[27] 358 3-8-7 0...... JoeFanning 6 58
(Jamie Osborne) *dwlt: hld up: shkn up over 2f out: nvr on terms* **40/1**

2m 1.38s (0.58) **Going Correction** 0.0s/f (Stan)
WFA 3 from 4yo 21lb **7 Ran SP% 115.4**
Speed ratings (Par 100): **97,96,94,94,93 92,91**
CSF £4.00 TOTE £2.90: £1.60, £1.10; EX 4.80 Trifecta £68.20.
Owner Angus Dundee Distillers plc **Bred** Triermore Stud **Trained** Newmarket, Suffolk

FOCUS
The early pace was steady and the winner did well to run down the second. The winner has been rated a bit below her debut effort. The fourth helps set the standard, while the sixth and seventh have been rated in line with their previous form.

795 LADBROKES FILLIES' NOVICE STKS 7f 36y (Tp)
8:30 (8:30) (Class 5) 3-Y-0+ £2,911 (£866; £432; £216) Stalls High

Form RPR

1 **Nabeyla** 3-8-11 0...... OisinMurphy 7 81+
(Roger Varian) *chsd ldr: led wl over 1f out: edgd lft and sn pushed clr* **7/4**[1]

0- **2** 6 **Soul Searching**[269] [3089] 3-8-11 0........................ TomMarquand 4 65
(James Tate) *prom: rdn over 1f out: sn hung lft: styd on same pce: wnt 2nd wl ins fnl f* **3/1**[2]

4 **3** 1 3/4 **Any Smile (IRE)**[17] [556] 3-8-11 0........................ JamieSpencer 6 60
(Michael Bell) *led: rdn and hdd over 1f out: no ex fnl f* **15/2**[3]

4 nk **Di Matteo** 3-8-11 0........................ MarcMonaghan 2 59
(Marco Botti) *pushed along in rr early: hdwy u.p over 1f out: nt trble ldrs* **14/1**

3- **5** 1 **Aigiarne (IRE)**[61] [9636] 3-8-11 0........................ HectorCrouch 11 56
(Clive Cox) *hld up in tch: plld hrd: rdn over 1f out: sn outpcd: hung rt ins fnl f* **15/2**[3]

0 **6** 4 **Fortunate Move**[25] [408] 3-8-11 0........................ BarryMcHugh 3 46
(Richard Fahey) *chsd ldrs: rdn over 2f out: wknd fnl f* **66/1**

7 1/2 **Whims Of Desire** 3-8-11 0........................ LukeMorris 1 44
(Sir Mark Prescott Bt) *sn pushed along in rr: nvr on terms* **22/1**

0-2 **8** 1 **Piccolita**[15] [604] 3-8-11 0........................ CharlieBennett 5 42
(Hughie Morrison) *hld up: shkn up over 2f out: wknd over 1f out* **66/1**

52 **9** 2 1/4 **J'Ouvert (IRE)**[17] [547] 3-8-11 0........................ StevieDonohoe 10 36
(David Simcock) *chsd ldrs: rdn over 2f out: wknd over 1f out* **11/1**

0 **10** 1 3/4 **Initial Approach (IRE)**[42] [128] 3-8-8 0........................ BenRobinson(3) 9 31
(Alan Brown) *a in rr* **150/1**

11 3 1/2 **Honey Bear (IRE)** 3-8-11 0........................ JoeFanning 8 21
(Mark Johnston) *s.s: outpcd* **8/1**

12 nk **Hurricane Heidi** 3-8-11 0........................ PaddyMathers 12 21
(Derek Shaw) *s.s: outpcd* **125/1**

1m 28.81s (0.01) **Going Correction** 0.0s/f (Stan) 12 Ran SP% **119.8**
Speed ratings (Par 100): **99,92,90,89,88 84,83,82,79,77 73,73**
CSF £6.74 TOTE £2.20: £1.20, £1.60, £2.20; EX 8.10 Trifecta £52.90.
Owner Sheikh Ahmed Al Maktoum **Bred** Godolphin **Trained** Newmarket, Suffolk

FOCUS
The two for money filled the first two places but in truth the winner proved in a different league. It's been rated at face value, with the third and fifth close to their debut figures.
T/Plt: £86.70 to a £1 stake. Pool: £109,787.86 - 924.04 winning units T/Qpdt: £14.30 to a £1 stake. Pool: £14,296.88 - 735.78 winning units **Colin Roberts**

[717] CHELMSFORD (A.W) (L-H)
Wednesday, February 20

OFFICIAL GOING: Polytrack: standard
Wind: virtually nil Weather: dry

796 £20 FREE BETS AT TOTESPORT.COM NOVICE STKS 6f (P)
5:15 (5:16) (Class 5) 3-Y-O+ **£3,752** (£1,116; £557; £278) **Stalls** Centre

Form RPR

1 **Fen Breeze** 3-8-8 0........................ NickyMackay 2 75
(Rae Guest) *trckd ldr for 1f: styd handy: effrt on inner to chal over 1f out: rdn to ld 1f out: asserting and edgd rt ins fnl f: r.o strly* **20/1**

2-1 **2** 2 3/4 **Key To Power**[19] [520] 3-9-1 0........................ JoeFanning 1 73
(Mark Johnston) *led: drifted rt wl over 1f out: sn rdn and hrd pressed: hdd 1f out: no ex and outpcd ins fnl f* **4/5**[1]

3 **3** 1 1/4 **Tulloona**[28] [359] 3-8-13 0........................ OisinMurphy 4 67
(Tom Clover) *stmbld and wnt rt leaving stalls: sn rcvrd to chse ldr after 1f and t.k.h: effrt and c towards centre wl over 1f out: 3rd and outpcd ins fnl f (jockey said gelding stumbled leaving the stalls)* **5/1**[3]

55- **4** nk **Revolutionise (IRE)**[84] [9282] 3-8-13 0........................(h) CharlieBennett 3 66
(Roger Varian) *hld up wl in tch in rr: effrt 2f out: no imp over 1f out: wl hld and one pce ins fnl f* **9/4**[2]

1m 14.25s (0.55) **Going Correction** -0.025s/f (Stan) 4 Ran SP% **107.8**
Speed ratings (Par 103): **95,91,89,89**
CSF £37.50 TOTE £35.90; EX 32.30 Trifecta £98.90.
Owner C J Murfitt **Bred** Pantile Stud **Trained** Newmarket, Suffolk

FOCUS
An ordinary novice event, but a taking performance from the only newcomer in the field. The second, third and fourth have been rated close to their marks.

797 TOTEPOOL CASHBACK CLUB AT TOTESPORT.COM H'CAP 6f (P)
5:45 (5:47) (Class 4) (0-85,82) 4-Y-O+
£5,530 (£1,645; £822; £411; £300; £300) **Stalls** Centre

Form RPR

4461 **1** **Gentlemen**[15] [609] 8-9-1 76........................(h) JosephineGordon 3 84
(Phil McEntee) *s.i.s: in rr: rdn over 3f out: clsd: nt clr run and swtchd rt over 1f out: hdwy u.p to chal ins fnl f: r.o wl to ld towards fin* **5/1**

1-63 **2** 3/4 **King Robert**[27] [382] 6-9-7 82........................ JoeFanning 4 88
(Charlie Wallis) *trckd ldrs: clsd and switching out rt 2f out: shkn up to ld jst over 1f out: rdn ins fnl f: hdd and no ex towards fin* **3/1**[2]

11-4 **3** 2 **Red Alert**[28] [361] 5-9-2 82........................ PoppyBridgwater(5) 5 82
(Tony Carroll) *in tch in last pair: rdn over 3f out: clsd over 1f out: wnt 3rd ins fnl f: kpt on same pce and no imp after* **6/1**

5-03 **4** 1 3/4 **Smokey Lane (IRE)**[14] [618] 5-9-5 80........................(b) OisinMurphy 1 74
(Sam Thomas) *led: rdn over 1f out: hdd 1f out: sn outpcd and wknd ins fnl f* **4/1**[3]

1-50 **5** shd **Classic Pursuit**[27] [389] 8-9-0 80........................(v) TheodoreLadd(5) 6 74
(Michael Appleby) *t.k.h: sn prom on outer: rdn and unable qck over 1f out: wknd ins fnl f* **20/1**

40-4 **6** 2 1/4 **Al Asef**[35] [254] 4-9-3 78........................(p[1]) RyanMoore 2 64
(Marco Botti) *t.k.h: w ldr: rdn and ev ch over 1f out tl no ex 1f out: sn btn and wknd ins fnl f (jockey said colt ran too free)* **2/1**[1]

1m 12.2s (-1.50) **Going Correction** -0.025s/f (Stan) 6 Ran SP% **114.0**
Speed ratings (Par 105): **109,108,105,103,102 99**
CSF £20.74 TOTE £6.10: £2.60, £1.60; EX 22.90 Trifecta £88.90.
Owner Trevor Johnson **Bred** Mrs Eleanor Kent **Trained** Newmarket, Suffolk

FOCUS
A fair little sprint handicap, but the two leaders may have done too much early and paid for it, while the winner came from a detached last. The winner has been rated in line with his winter best, with the second to his C&D run.

798 EXTRA PLACES AT TOTESPORT.COM H'CAP 7f (P)
6:15 (6:16) (Class 5) (0-75,75) 3-Y-O
£3,752 (£1,116; £557; £300; £300; £300) **Stalls** Low

Form RPR

350- **1** **Zmhar (IRE)**[188] [6199] 3-9-6 74........................(h[1]) OisinMurphy 6 88+
(James Tate) *dwlt and short of room leaving stalls: towards rr: effrt and qcknd to cl over 1f out: led ins fnl f: r.o strly and drew clr: v readily* **5/1**[2]

050- **2** 6 **Bubbelah (IRE)**[201] [5683] 3-8-10 64........................ JamieSpencer 3 62
(David Simcock) *dwlt: hld up in midfield: swtchd lft and effrt over 1f out: kpt on same pce u.p to go 2nd towards fin: no ch w wnr* **5/4**[1]

-553 **3** nk **Valley Belle (IRE)**[18] [550] 3-8-2 56........................(v) JosephineGordon 5 53
(Phil McEntee) *chsd ldrs tl clsd to join ldr after over 1f out: rdn and ev ch over 1f out tl nt match pce of wnr jst ins fnl f: battling for 2nd and kpt on same pce after* **25/1**

103- **4** 1/2 **Diva D (IRE)**[109] [8825] 3-9-3 71........................ JoeFanning 4 67
(Mark Johnston) *t.k.h: led: rdn over 1f out: hdd and nt match pce of wnr jst ins fnl f: kpt on same pce after and lost 2 pls ins fnl f* **8/1**

-233 **5** 2 1/2 **Beryl The Petal (IRE)**[23] [461] 3-8-12 69........................ ConorMcGovern(3) 1 58
(David O'Meara) *trckd ldr for over 1f out: styd handy tl rdn and unable qck over 1f out: wknd ins fnl f* **8/1**

45-4 **6** 1 1/4 **Ivory Charm**[38] [229] 3-8-11 65........................(p[1]) BarryMcHugh 9 51
(Richard Fahey) *in tch in rr of main gp: effrt and no imp over 1f out: sn outpcd and wknd ins fnl f* **7/1**[3]

2-25 **7** 3/4 **Brandon (FR)**[18] [554] 3-9-7 75........................(p) RyanMoore 2 58
(Marco Botti) *chsd ldrs: effrt ent fnl 2f: drvn and unable qck over 1f out: wknd ins fnl f* **9/1**

243- **8** nk **Molly Mai**[128] [8278] 3-8-12 66........................ DannyBrock 8 49
(Philip McBride) *dwlt and swtchd lft after s: a bhd: nvr involved* **25/1**

06-3 **9** hd **Hanbury Dreams**[27] [380] 3-8-11 65........................ KieranO'Neill 7 47
(Tom Clover) *chsd ldrs: rdn ent fnl 2f: outpcd u.p and btn over 1f out: wknd ins fnl f* **16/1**

1m 25.45s (-1.75) **Going Correction** -0.025s/f (Stan) 9 Ran SP% **119.4**
Speed ratings (Par 97): **109,102,101,101,98 96,96,95,95**
CSF £12.05 CT £141.48 TOTE £5.80: £1.90, £1.10, £7.60; EX 15.90 Trifecta £168.60.
Owner Saeed Manana **Bred** Rabbah Bloodstock Limited **Trained** Newmarket, Suffolk

FOCUS
A modest 3yo handicap taken apart by the winner. The first two, both making their handicap debuts, made their efforts closest to the inside rail. The winner has been rated in line with his July C&D form.

799 IRISH LOTTO AT TOTESPORT.COM H'CAP 2m (P)
6:45 (6:47) (Class 2) (0-100,101) 4-Y-O+ **£12,291** (£3,657; £1,827; £913) **Stalls** Low

Form RPR

14-2 **1** **Lucky Deal**[18] [558] 4-8-13 91........................ JoeFanning 5 101+
(Mark Johnston) *dwlt: sn rcvrd to chse ldr: clsd and trckd ldr 10f out tl led wl over 1f out: clr 1f out: r.o strly: heavily eased towards fin: v easily* **6/4**[1]

4-13 **2** 3 **Busy Street**[7] [704] 7-9-3 91........................ AlistairRawlinson 3 95
(Michael Appleby) *hld up in 4th clsd and wl in tch 10f out: effrt 2f out: chsd clr wnr 1f out: styd on for clr 2nd but no ch w wnr* **5/2**[2]

-115 **3** 3 3/4 **Azari**[7] [704] 7-8-0 81........................(b) ThoreHammerHansen(7) 4 81
(Alexandra Dunn) *led and clr tl 10f out: rdn and hdd over 1f out: sn outpcd and btn: wknd ins fnl f* **12/1**

04-2 **4** 1/2 **Primero (FR)**[32] [311] 6-9-13 101........................ RyanMoore 2 100
(David O'Meara) *broke wl: sn retrained into 3rd and t.k.h: clsd to trck ldrs 10f out: rdn over 2f out: unable qck over 1f out: wknd ins fnl f* **4/1**[3]

1/05 **5** 1 1/4 **Alabaster**[21] [480] 5-8-0 81........................ GavinAshton(7) 1 79
(Sir Mark Prescott Bt) *t.k.h: hld up in rr: clsd and wl in tch 10f out: rdn and outpcd over 2f out: no ch after but kpt on again ins fnl f* **8/1**

3m 32.46s (2.46) **Going Correction** -0.025s/f (Stan)
WFA 4 from 5yo+ 4lb 5 Ran SP% **107.4**
Speed ratings (Par 109): **92,90,88,88,87**
CSF £5.16 TOTE £2.20: £1.30, £1.70; EX 4.10 Trifecta £14.90.
Owner Kai Fai Leung **Bred** Fittocks Stud **Trained** Middleham Moor, N Yorks

FOCUS
A slightly disappointing turnout for a race of its value. A solid early gallop had steadied significantly by halfway.

800 BET IN PLAY TOTESPORT.COM H'CAP 1m (P)
7:15 (7:16) (Class 2) (0-100,99) 4-Y-O+ **£12,291** (£3,657; £1,827; £913) **Stalls** Low

Form RPR

11-1 **1** **Matterhorn (IRE)**[46] [87] 4-9-7 99........................ JoeFanning 3 112+
(Mark Johnston) *sn chsng ldr: rdn to ld over 1f out: sn wnt clr and r.o wl ins fnl f: v readily* **5/4**[1]

34-1 **2** 3 1/4 **Tough Remedy (IRE)**[39] [212] 4-8-6 89........................ AndrewBreslin(5) 1 94
(Keith Dalgleish) *hld up in last trio: effrt and stl plenty to do ent fnl 2f: sme hdwy on inner over 1f out: styd on ins fnl f to go 2nd towards fin: no ch w wnr* **7/1**

6314 **3** 3/4 **Michele Strogoff**[16] [601] 6-8-12 90........................ AlistairRawlinson 5 93
(Michael Appleby) *led: rdn and hrd pressed over 2f out: hdd over 1f out sn outpcd and wl hld ins fnl f: kpt on same pce and lost 2nd towards fin* **7/1**

11-2 **4** nk **Breden (IRE)**[39] [205] 9-9-7 99........................ AdamKirby 6 101
(Linda Jewell) *in tch in midfield: effrt in 3rd over 2f out: no ch w wnr and kpt on same pce ins fnl f* **5/1**[3]

22/4 **5** 7 **Battered**[29] [351] 5-9-7 99........................ OisinMurphy 4 85
(Ralph Beckett) *t.k.h: hld up in last trio: outpcd over 2f out: no imp and wl hld whn carried rt over 1f out: no ch fnl f* **4/1**[2]

1-45 **6** 4 1/2 **Calling Out (FR)**[28] [368] 8-9-4 96........................ JamieSpencer 2 72
(David Simcock) *hld up in tch in midfield: rdn and outpcd over 2f out: no imp and wl hld whn drifted rt over 1f out: wknd fnl f* **16/1**

63-6 **7** 4 1/2 **Eljaddaaf (IRE)**[35] [255] 8-9-0 95........................(h) JackDuern(3) 7 61
(Dean Ivory) *s.i.s and bustled along early: hung rt and wd thrght: clsd and t.k.h after 2f: hdwy into midfield 4f out: sn rdn and struggling: bhd over 1f out (jockey said gelding hung right throughout)* **33/1**

1m 37.21s (-2.69) **Going Correction** -0.025s/f (Stan) 7 Ran SP% **114.9**
Speed ratings (Par 109): **112,108,108,107,100 96,91**
CSF £11.02 TOTE £1.80: £1.40, £2.50; EX 9.60 Trifecta £44.50.
Owner Sheikh Hamdan bin Mohammed Al Maktoum **Bred** Barronstown Stud **Trained** Middleham Moor, N Yorks

FOCUS
A decent 0-100 handicap won easily by an improving colt in a good time. Not many got into it.

801 DOUBLE DELIGHT HAT-TRICK HEAVEN AT TOTESPORT.COM H'CAP 1m (P)
7:45 (7:47) (Class 5) (0-70,70) 4-Y-O+
£3,752 (£1,116; £557; £300; £300; £300) **Stalls** Low

Form RPR

5-14 **1** **Harbour Vision**[18] [548] 4-9-6 69........................ PaddyMathers 9 77+
(Derek Shaw) *stdd and dropped in bhd after s: hld up in rr: clsd whn nt clr run and swtchd lft 1f out: rdn and r.o to ld wl ins fnl f: gng way at fin* **5/1**[2]

4653 **2** *1 ½* **The Special One (IRE)**[16] 595 6-8-7 **56** oh1......(h) JosephineGordon 8 61
(Phil McEntee) *hld up in last quartet: clsd and effrt jst over 2f out: hdwy u.p 1f out: kpt on to go 2nd last strides* **20/1**

1-56 **3** *nk* **Channel Packet**[25] 429 5-8-13 **67**..........................(p) TheodoreLadd(5) 6 71
(Michael Appleby) *t.k.h: chsd ldr tl led over 1f out: hung lft 1f out: hdd and no ex wl ins fnl f: lost 2nd last strides* **7/1**[3]

5112 **4** *½* **Zorawar (FR)**[6] 724 5-9-4 **67**.. AdamKirby 5 70
(David O'Meara) *dwlt: hld up in tch in last quartet: clsd and swtchd rt 2f out: hdwy to chse ldr jst ins fnl f: ev ch ins fnl f: sn no ex and one pce towards fin* **13/8**[1]

04-0 **5** *1 ½* **Dream Mount (IRE)**[29] 355 4-8-10 **62**.............(be) ConorMcGovern(3) 1 62
(Julie Camacho) *t.k.h: effrt over 1f out: sn u.p and edging lft: wknd ins fnl f* **10/1**

0-51 **6** *¾* **The British Lion (IRE)**[23] 463 4-9-7 **70**......................... RossaRyan 10 68
(Alexandra Dunn) *dropped in after s: hld up in last pair: effrt on outer over 2f out: edging lft and no imp ins fnl f* **25/1**

0-40 **7** *1 ¼* **Miracle Garden**[23] 463 7-9-5 **68**.................................(p) JamieSpencer 4 63
(Ian Williams) *hld up in tch in midfield: nt clrest of runs over 1f out: edgd lft over 1f out: nvr enough room: unable to cl and nudged lft ins fnl f: wl hld and eased wl ins fnl f* **7/1**[3]

/04- **8** *5* **Tebay (IRE)**[203] 5621 4-9-4 **67**.. EoinWalsh 3 51
(Luke McJannet) *in tch in midfield: effrt on inner whn bdly hmpd and snatched up over 1f out: nt rcvr and wl btn fnl f* **25/1**

150- **9** *nk* **Tundra**[62] 9640 5-9-0 **70**.. CierenFallon(7) 7 53
(Anthony Carson) *dwlt: sn rcvrd to chse ldrs and t.k.h on outer: rdn and unable qck over 1f out: wknd ins fnl f* **20/1**

6-65 **10** *4 ½* **Evening Attire**[27] 381 8-9-6 **69**... HectorCrouch 2 42
(William Stone) *led: rdn and hdd over 1f out: sn impeded and dropped out: wknd fnl f* **8/1**

1m 39.07s (-0.83) **Going Correction** -0.025s/f (Stan) **10** Ran SP% **117.2**
Speed ratings (Par 103): **103,101,101,100,99 98,97,92,91,87**
CSF £102.89 CT £695.28 TOTE £4.50: £1.60, £3.40, £2.30; EX 117.10 Trifecta £458.30.
Owner New Vision Bloodstock **Bred** Newsells Park Stud **Trained** Sproxton, Leics

FOCUS
An ordinary handicap and several had a chance passing the furlong pole.

802 LITTLE LEIGHS H'CAP — 1m 2f (P)
8:15 (8:17) (Class 6) (0-60,62) 3-Y-O
£3,105 (£924; £461; £300; £300; £300) **Stalls** Low

Form RPR

06-5 **1** **Lady Wolf**[7] 695 3-9-0 **49**..(p) RobHornby 3 53
(Rod Millman) *chsd ldrs early: restrained and hld up in tch in midfield: swtchd lft and hdwy over 1f out: drvn and ev ch ent fnl f: styd on wl to ld last strides* **10/1**

5-13 **2** *hd* **Chakrii (IRE)**[7] 695 3-8-12 **52**...................................... DylanHogan(5) 8 56
(Henry Spiller) *short of room leaving stalls: hld up in last pair: swtchd rt and effrt over 2f out: clsd and swtchd rt again 2f out: hdwy u.p to ld and edging lft ent fnl f: kpt on wl: hdd last strides* **3/1**[2]

2-21 **3** *2* **Precision Prince (IRE)**[19] 537 3-9-13 **62**........................ EoinWalsh 2 62
(Mark Loughnane) *stdd s: t.k.h: restrained and hld up in tch in midfield: clsd over 2f out: hdwy and rdn to chal ent fnl f tl no ex and outpcd wl ins fnl f* **15/8**[1]

060- **4** *1 ¾* **Archdeacon**[211] 5298 3-9-7 **56**... AdamKirby 13 53
(Dean Ivory) *stdd s: t.k.h: hld up in last trio: clsd and nt clrest of runs ent fnl 2f: swtchd rt over 1f out: hdwy u.p ins fnl f: styd on but no threat to ldrs* **5/1**[3]

50-0 **5** *4 ½* **Wontgetfooledagen (IRE)**[20] 501 3-8-10 **45**.........(t[1]) PaddyMathers 1 33
(Ivan Furtado) *t.k.h: hld up in tch in midfield: nt clr run and hmpd 2f out: stl nt clr run and swtchd rt over 1f out: swtchd lft and kpt on between rivals ins fnl f: no ch w ldrs (jockey said gelding was denied a clear run rounding the bend into the home straight)* **33/1**

055- **6** *1* **Mendeleev**[167] 6980 3-8-12 **47**.. BarryMcHugh 10 33
(James Given) *chsd ldr tl led over 8f out: rdn over 1f out: sn hdd & wknd ins fnl f* **33/1**

0-00 **7** *nk* **Jasmine B (IRE)**[25] 437 3-8-5 **45**.............................. DarraghKeenan(5) 7 31
(John Ryan) *bmpd leaving stalls: sn led and crossed to inner: hdd over 8f out but styd chsng ldrs: rdn and pressing ldr over 1f out: sn outpcd and wknd ins fnl f* **50/1**

036- **8** *2* **Silk Island (IRE)**[53] 9744 3-8-13 **48**................................... RossaRyan 12 30
(Michael Wigham) *chsd ldrs: wnt 2nd over 7f out tl over 1f out: sn outpcd and wknd ins fnl f* **33/1**

66-3 **9** *1 ¼* **Willkommen**[40] 183 3-9-0 **56**.................................(b) StefanoCherchi(7) 9 35
(Marco Botti) *a in rr: rdn and struggling over 3f out: sn outpcd and no ch after* **10/1**

04-0 **10** *¾* **Maared (IRE)**[14] 614 3-9-12 **61**.. KieranO'Neill 4 39
(Luke McJannet) *t.k.h: prom: sn restrained and hld up in tch: unable qck u.p and btn over 1f out: wknd ins fnl f* **20/1**

-464 **11** *4* **Margaret J**[19] 533 3-8-10 **45**...............................(p) JosephineGordon 5 15
(Phil McEntee) *wnt rt and bmpd rival leaving stalls: clsd to chse ldrs on outer 4f out: rdn and losing pl over 2f out: bhd ins fnl f* **12/1**

2m 8.8s (0.20) **Going Correction** -0.025s/f (Stan) **11** Ran SP% **117.9**
Speed ratings (Par 95): **98,97,96,94,91 90,90,88,87,87 83**
CSF £38.35 CT £82.96 TOTE £11.50: £2.70, £1.30, £2.00; EX 50.70 Trifecta £274.40.
Owner Howard Barton Stud **Bred** Howard Barton Stud **Trained** Kentisbeare, Devon

FOCUS
A moderate 3yo handicap. The first two took contrasting routes and the result would probably have been different had the roles been reversed. The first four pulled clear. The winner has been rated back near her debut effort.
T/Plt: £1592.50 to a £1 stake. Pool: £55,738.75 - 25.55 winning units T/Qpdt: £12.40 to a £1 stake. Pool: £8,813.06 - 525.10 winning units **Steve Payne**

782 NEWCASTLE (A.W) (L-H)
Wednesday, February 20

OFFICIAL GOING: Tapeta: standard to slow
Wind: Breezy, half against in races on the straight course and in over 3f of home straight in races on the Weather: Overcast, showers

803 BETWAY H'CAP — 1m 4f 98y (Tp)
2:00 (2:00) (Class 4) (0-80,81) 4-Y-O+ **£4,883** (£1,461; £730; £365; £182) **Stalls** High

Form RPR

00-3 **1** **Desert Ruler**[19] 522 6-9-10 **81**... JackGarritty 8 90
(Jedd O'Keeffe) *hld up in last pl: smooth hdwy on outside over 2f out: rdn to ld ins fnl f: kpt on wl* **9/2**[3]

1-31 **2** *½* **Claire Underwood (IRE)**[19] 522 4-9-3 **81**..................... SeanDavis(5) 7 89
(Richard Fahey) *hld up in tch: hdwy on outside over 2f out: led over 1f out to ins fnl f: kpt on: hld nr fin* **3/1**[2]

-132 **3** *2* **Elysees Palace**[5] 735 5-9-9 **80**.......................................(p) LukeMorris 9 85
(Sir Mark Prescott Bt) *s.i.s: hld up: hdwy and edgd lft over 2f out: chsd ldrs over 1f out: effrt and ev ch whn hung lft ins fnl f: one pce* **5/2**[1]

2-41 **4** *2* **Lopes Dancer (IRE)**[20] 495 7-9-2 **73**......................... DanielTudhope 4 75
(Harriet Bethell) *pressed ldr: drvn and ev ch over 2f out to over 1f out: no ex ins fnl f* **8/1**

4-24 **5** *hd* **Champarisi**[30] 346 4-8-8 **67**... SamJames 5 68
(Grant Tuer) *led: rdn and hrd pressed over 2f out: hdd over 1f out: sn outpcd* **8/1**

2-33 **6** *1 ¾* **Trautmann (IRE)**[20] 495 5-8-12 **69**..............................(tp) CamHardie 2 67
(Rebecca Menzies) *dwlt: t.k.h: hld up: stdy hdwy over 2f out: rdn and hung lft over 1f out: sn outpcd* **14/1**

106- **7** *4 ½* **Iconic Belle**[22] 5942 5-9-6 **77**.................................... CallumRodriguez 10 68
(Philip Kirby) *trckd ldrs: rdn over 2f out: wknd over 1f out* **25/1**

5-31 **8** *2* **Star Ascending (IRE)**[30] 346 7-9-2 **73**....................(p) JamesSullivan 6 61
(Jennie Candlish) *t.k.h: prom: rdn over 2f out: wknd over 1f out* **16/1**

60-0 **9** *1* **Captain Pugwash (IRE)**[19] 536 5-8-13 **70**........................ GrahamLee 1 56
(Stef Keniry) *prom: rdn along over 2f out: sn lost pl and struggling* **50/1**

45-6 **10** *4 ½* **Tenedos**[30] 345 4-9-4-4 **77**.. AdamKirby 3 56
(Ed de Giles) *hld up: rdn and struggling 3f out: btn fnl 2f* **25/1**

2m 42.84s (1.74) **Going Correction** +0.325s/f (Slow)
WFA 4 from 5yo+ 2lb **10** Ran SP% **116.2**
Speed ratings (Par 105): **107,106,105,104,103 102,99,98,97,94**
CSF £17.98 CT £40.80 TOTE £4.90: £1.70, £1.10, £1.90; EX 22.10 Trifecta £54.60.
Owner Highbeck Racing 4 **Bred** Mrs J M Quy **Trained** Middleham Moor, N Yorks

FOCUS
A decent race for the level, featuring three last-time-out winners. However, the time was 7.14 seconds slower than standard. Muddling form, but the third has been rated to form.

804 LADBROKES NOVICE STKS — 1m 2f 42y (Tp)
2:35 (2:35) (Class 5) 3-Y-O **£3,234** (£962; £481; £240) **Stalls** High

Form RPR

22 **1** **American Graffiti (FR)**[22] 472 3-9-2 0.............................. AdamKirby 3 86
(Charlie Appleby) *chsd ldrs: pushed along over 3f out: led over 2f out: clr over 1f out: pushed out: unchal* **13/8**[2]

2 **2** *6* **Battle of Paradise (USA)**[35] 251 3-9-2 0......................... LukeMorris 5 74
(Sir Mark Prescott Bt) *hld up in tch: effrt and pushed along 3f out: rdn to chse (clr) wnr over 1f out: hung lft ins fnl f: one pce* **1/2**[1]

555- **3** *2 ¼* **Cormier (IRE)**[124] 8378 3-9-2 71..................................... GrahamLee 1 69
(Stef Keniry) *led at ordinary gallop: rdn and hdd over 2f out: lost 2nd and one pce over 1f out* **40/1**

02-6 **4** *6* **Curfewed (IRE)**[26] 409 3-9-2 72.. CamHardie 4 57
(Tracy Waggott) *hld up: drvn and outpcd over 2f out: n.d after* **33/1**[3]

0-0 **5** *15* **Amber**[45] 103 3-8-11 0.. JamesSullivan 2 22
(Peter Niven) *pressed ldr to over 3f out: rdn and wknd over 2f out* **250/1**

2m 12.26s (1.86) **Going Correction** +0.325s/f (Slow) **5** Ran SP% **110.5**
Speed ratings (Par 97): **105,100,98,93,81**
CSF £2.80 TOTE £2.00: £1.10, £1.02; EX 3.20 Trifecta £5.90.
Owner Godolphin **Bred** Dayton Investments Limited **Trained** Newmarket, Suffolk

FOCUS
A two-horse race considering the betting (around 100.0 bar two on the exchanges at the off), with the second in the market proving best. The third has been rated close to form.

805 SUNRACING.CO.UK H'CAP — 7f 14y (Tp)
3:10 (3:10) (Class 2) 4-Y-O+
£28,012 (£8,388; £4,194; £2,097; £1,048; £526) **Stalls** Centre

Form RPR

31-1 **1** **Keyser Soze (IRE)**[40] 176 5-9-10 **101**................................ AdamKirby 5 109+
(Richard Spencer) *hld up: hdwy on outside over 1f out: rdn to ld ins fnl f: r.o wl* **13/8**[1]

61-0 **2** *¾* **Gallipoli (IRE)**[29] 351 6-8-13 **90**..............................(b) TonyHamilton 6 96
(Richard Fahey) *prom: rdn over 2f out: hdwy to ld over 1f out to ins fnl f: kpt on: hld nr fin* **12/1**

11-1 **3** *¾* **Pinnata (IRE)**[29] 351 5-9-4 **95**..(t) SeanLevey 4 99
(Stuart Williams) *pressed ldr: rdn and led briefly over 1f out: kpt on same pce ins fnl f* **3/1**[2]

01-3 **4** *nk* **Sanaadh**[22] 470 6-9-1 **92**...(t) CamHardie 9 95
(Michael Wigham) *stdd s: hld up: stdy hdwy over 1f out: rdn and r.o fnl f: nrst fin* **10/1**

316- **5** *½* **Breathless Times**[51] 9774 4-9-8 **99**.......................(t) AdamMcNamara 8 101
(Roger Charlton) *hld up in tch: rdn over 2f out: r.o ins fnl f: nvr able to chal (jockey said gelding ran too freely)* **15/2**[3]

-251 **6** *½* **Custard The Dragon**[20] 499 6-8-7 **84**........................(v) AndrewMullen 2 84
(John Mackie) *dwlt: hld up in tch: effrt and rdn over 1f out: no ex ins fnl f* **25/1**

20-5 **7** *4 ½* **Starlight Romance (IRE)**[29] 351 5-8-13 **90**..................... PaulHanagan 1 78
(Richard Fahey) *prom: rdn over 2f out: wknd over 1f out* **33/1**

1-32 **8** *¾* **Exchequer (IRE)**[22] 470 8-8-13 **90**..(p) JFEgan 3 76
(Richard Guest) *led at modest gallop: qcknd over 2f out: rdn and hdd over 1f out: sn wknd* **33/1**

0-33 **9** *3 ¼* **Ballard Down (IRE)**[25] 441 6-9-3 **94**........................(v) DanielTudhope 7 72
(David O'Meara) *hld up: rdn and outpcd over 2f out: edgd lft and btn over 1f out* **11/1**

1m 27.32s (1.12) **Going Correction** +0.325s/f (Slow) **9** Ran SP% **109.7**
Speed ratings (Par 109): **106,105,104,103,103 102,97,96,93**
CSF £20.54 CT £48.78 TOTE £2.20: £1.20, £3.50, £1.20; EX 20.80 Trifecta £63.50.
Owner Rebel Racing (2) **Bred** J Hanly **Trained** Newmarket, Suffolk

FOCUS
A really competitive handicap at a decent level and the early pace appeared decent enough. The third and fourth has been rated close to form.

806 LADBROKES HOME OF THE ODDS BOOST CONDITIONS STKS (PLUS 10 RACE) (AW CHAMPIONSHIPS FAST-TRACK QUAL) — 6f (Tp)
3:45 (3:45) (Class 2) 3-Y-O **£18,675** (£5,592; £2,796; £1,398; £699; £3515) **Stalls** Centre

1-61 **1** **Deep Intrigue**[35] 261 3-9-0 94....................................... DanielTudhope 2 86
(Mark Johnston) *pressed ldr: effrt and rdn over 1f out: led ins fnl f: drvn out* **5/2**[2]

5 **2** *nk* **Call Me Ginger**[39] 211 3-9-0 0... JamieGormley 3 85
(Jim Goldie) *hld up: hdwy over 1f out: chsd wnr ins fnl f: r.o* **100/1**

55-4 **3** *½* **Don Armado (IRE)**[47] 57 3-9-0 92.........................(t) CallumRodriguez 7 83
(Stuart Williams) *hld up in tch: rdn and effrt over 1f out: r.o ins fnl f* **7/1**

321- 4 ¾ Barbill (IRE)[99] 9045 3-9-3 103 JFEgan 1 84
(Mick Channon) prom: effrt and ev ch over 1f out to ins fnl f: r.o same pce 13/8[1]

150- 5 nk Quiet Endeavour (IRE)[74] 9461 3-9-0 99 HollieDoyle 5 80
(Archie Watson) led: rdn and hrd pressed over 1f out: edgd rt and hdd ins fnl f: one pce 11/1

13-0 6 1 You Never Can Tell (IRE)[47] 57 3-9-0 92 (p[1]) GrahamLee 4 79
(Richard Spencer) t.k.h: prom: rdn over 2f out: one pce whn checked ins fnl f 6/1[3]

510- 7 1 ¼ Walkman (IRE)[161] 7168 3-9-0 79 RaulDaSilva 6 77?
(Michael Appleby) t.k.h: chsd ldrs: rdn over 2f out: one pce whn hmpd and snatched up ins fnl f: sn btn 18/1

1m 13.46s (0.96) **Going Correction** +0.325s/f (Slow) 7 Ran SP% 108.0
Speed ratings (Par 103): **106,105,104,103,103 102,100**
CSF £125.03 TOTE £3.30: £1.80, £14.50; EX 122.30 Trifecta £973.80.
Owner Clipper Logistics **Bred** Mr & Mrs J Davis & P Mitchell B'Stock **Trained** Middleham Moor, N Yorks

FOCUS
A hot sprint, but they all finished quite close together. The third has been rated close to his latest form.

807 FOLLOW TOP TIPSTER TEMPLEGATE AT SUNRACING H'CAP 1m 5y (Tp)
4:20 (4:20) (Class 4) (0-85,87) 4-Y-0+ **£4,883** (£1,461; £730; £365; £182) **Stalls** Centre

Form RPR
-524 1 Call Out Loud[39] 213 7-9-5 82 JFEgan 3 90
(Michael Appleby) mde all and sn clr: pushed along over 1f out: hrd pressed ins fnl f: edgd rt and hld on wl cl home 14/1

1212 2 shd Rey Loopy (IRE)[15] 611 5-9-3 80 AndrewMullen 1 87+
(Ben Haslam) stdd s: t.k.h: hld up in tch: hdwy to press wnr fnl f: ev ch last 75yds: keeping on whn n.m.r cl home 2/1[1]

521 3 1 ½ Master Diver[26] 419 4-9-4 81 LukeMorris 5 84
(Sir Mark Prescott Bt) dwlt: sn chsng (clr) wnr: effrt and rdn 2f out: edgd lft and kpt on same pce ins fnl f 9/2[3]

4-25 4 5 Fayez (IRE)[19] 521 5-9-10 87 (p) DanielTudhope 8 79
(David O'Meara) hld up: rdn over 2f out: no imp over 1f out 13/2

0-64 5 2 ¼ Testa Rossa (IRE)[15] 611 9-8-5 71 (b) PhilDennis(3) 6 58
(Jim Goldie) hld up: rdn and outpcd over 2f out: n.d after 12/1

1013 6 1 ¼ Philamundo (IRE)[18] 548 4-9-5 82 (b) AdamKirby 7 66
(Richard Spencer) dwlt: sn chsng clr ldng pair: rdn over 2f out: edgd lft and wknd over 1f out 10/3[2]

-250 7 15 My Target (IRE)[25] 441 8-9-7 84 CamHardie 4 33
(Michael Wigham) hld up: drvn and outpcd over 2f out: sn btn 11/1

1m 42.65s (4.05) **Going Correction** +0.325s/f (Slow) 7 Ran SP% 110.6
Speed ratings (Par 105): **92,91,90,85,83 81,66**
CSF £39.70 CT £143.00 TOTE £15.40: £5.90, £2.40; EX 38.90 Trifecta £282.90.
Owner Kings Head Duffield Racing Partnership **Bred** Rabbah Bloodstock Limited **Trained** Oakham, Rutland

FOCUS
This had looked a decent race for the class but hardly anything got into it. The winner has been rated back to his old best.

808 LIKE SUNRACING ON FACEBOOK H'CAP 7f 14y (Tp)
4:50 (4:50) (Class 5) (0-70,72) 4-Y-0+ **£3,234** (£962; £481; £240) **Stalls** Centre

Form RPR
1-52 1 Chosen World[15] 609 5-9-5 65 (p) CallumRodriguez 7 76
(Julie Camacho) hld up: smooth hdwy to ld over 1f out: pushed clr: readily 15/8[1]

0-11 2 3 ¾ Porrima (IRE)[19] 525 4-9-7 67 AndrewMullen 5 68
(Ben Haslam) fly-jmpd s: hld up in last pl: hdwy to chse wnr fnl f: kpt on: nt pce to chal 10/3[3]

-360 3 2 ½ Dirchill (IRE)[20] 496 5-9-12 72 (b) CliffordLee 2 66
(David Thompson) chsd ldrs: drvn and ev ch briefly over 1f out: edgd lft: one pce ins fnl f 12/1

430/ 4 1 ¼ Annie Fior (IRE)[12] 666 5-9-4 64 DanielTudhope 6 55
(B A Murphy, Ire) cl up: rdn and outpcd whn checked over 1f out: no imp fnl f 3/1[2]

360- 5 shd Equidae[118] 8578 4-9-7 67 (t[1]) LukeMorris 4 57
(Iain Jardine) dwlt: t.k.h: prom: effrt and rdn 2f out: sn one pce 33/1

50-5 6 nk Insurplus (IRE)[15] 609 6-8-10 59 JamieGormley(3) 1 49
(Jim Goldie) led to over 1f out: sn outpcd 9/1

153- 7 3 ¾ Christmas Night[151] 7553 4-9-2 65 BenRobinson(3) 3 45
(Ollie Pears) cl up: drvn and ev ch briefly over 1f out: wknd fnl f 10/1

1m 27.83s (1.63) **Going Correction** +0.325s/f (Slow) 7 Ran SP% 112.6
Speed ratings (Par 103): **103,98,95,94,94 93,89**
CSF £8.05 TOTE £4.90: £2.70, £3.20; EX 8.10 Trifecta £43.80.
Owner The Kirkham Partnership **Bred** North Bradon Stud **Trained** Norton, N Yorks

FOCUS
A modest event won easily by the market leader. The form has been near face value, with the runner-up close to her latest form.
T/Plt: £13.50 to a £1 stake. Pool: £69,347.65 - 3728.86 winning units T/Qpdt: £12.00 to a £1 stake. Pool: £4,502.21 - 276.97 winning units **Richard Young**

789 WOLVERHAMPTON (A.W) (L-H)
Wednesday, February 20

OFFICIAL GOING: Tapeta: standard
Wind: Fresh behind Weather: OVERCAST

809 BETWAY CASINO HANDS AND HEELS APPRENTICE H'CAP (RACING EXCELLENCE INITIATIVE) 6f 20y (Tp)
5:30 (5:30) (Class 7) (0-50,52) 4-Y-0+ **£1,940** (£577; £288; £72; £72) **Stalls** Low

Form RPR
34-4 1 Fairway To Heaven (IRE)[42] 132 10-9-2 45 (tp) Pierre-LouisJamin 2 51
(Paul George) prom: hdwy over 5f out: swtchd rt over 2f out: shkn up on outer over 1f out: led ins fnl f: r.o 10/1

50-0 2 1 Kavora[39] 210 4-9-2 45 OliverStammers 10 48
(Micky Hammond) s.i.s: hld up: hdwy on outer over 2f out: shkn up and ev ch ins fnl f: styd on same pce towards fin 6/1[2]

3-40 3 ¾ Alligator[28] 357 5-8-13 45 ElishaWhittington(3) 9 46
(Tony Carroll) prom: lost pl 5f out: sn hung rt: shkn up over 1f out: r.o ins fnl f: wnt 3rd post: nt rch ldrs 9/1

0-51 4 nk Picks Pinta[15] 613 8-9-2 48 (b) AaronMackay(3) 4 50
(John David Riches) s.i.s: in rr: pushed along and hdwy over 1f out: nt clr run and swtchd lft ins fnl f: r.o 13/2[3]

0-00 4 dht Marble Bar[21] 484 4-9-9 52 EllaMcCain 5 53
(Iain Jardine) prom: racd keenly: hmpd over 5f out: nt clr run over 1f out: sn shkn up: styd on 9/1

-553 6 1 Storm Lightning[28] 357 10-9-0 46 GraceMcEntee(3) 12 43
(Mark Brisbourne) led early: chsd ldrs: ev ch ins fnl f: styd on same pce 22/1

0-40 7 hd Toolatetodelegate[36] 244 5-9-4 50 (vt) SeanKirrane(3) 13 46
(Brian Barr) prom: lost pl over 5f out: r.o ins fnl f 50/1

02-4 8 nk Soldier Blue (FR)[29] 356 5-9-8 51 (v) WilliamCarver 3 47
(Brian Ellison) s.i.s: hld up: nt clr run and swtchd rt ins fnl f: r.o: nt rch ldrs 9/4[1]

3-00 9 ½ Isabella Ruby[21] 483 4-9-2 45 (h) RussellHarris 8 39
(Lisa Williamson) prom: shkn up over 1f out: styd on same pce fnl f 22/1

60-6 10 1 Burauq[36] 244 7-9-2 45 (v) AmeliaGlass 1 37
(Milton Bradley) prom: hmpd and lost pl over 5f out: hdwy over 1f out: styng on same pce whn hmpd ins fnl f 28/1

-014 11 nk Foxy Boy[16] 597 5-9-8 51 (b) HarryRussell 7 41
(Rebecca Bastiman) sn led: shkn up over 1f out: hdd ins fnl f: wknd towards fin 12/1

6-40 12 hd Compton Prince[33] 293 10-9-2 45 (b) EllieMacKenzie 6 34
(Milton Bradley) chsd ldr: swtchd lft over 5f out: shkn up over 1f out: wknd ins fnl f 25/1

/0-0 13 1 Atalanta Queen[47] 53 4-9-4 47 (v) MarkCrehan 11 33
(Robyn Brisland) pushed along early towards rr: shkn up over 2f out: n.d 50/1

1m 15.25s (0.75) **Going Correction** +0.05s/f (Slow) 13 Ran SP% 115.1
Speed ratings (Par 97): **97,95,94,94,94 92,92,92,91,90 89,89,88**
WIN: 11.50 Fairway To Heaven; PL: 3.20 Fairway To Heaven 2.00 Kavora 2.50 Alligator; EX: 79.70; CSF: 60.87; TC: 577.14; TF: 450.70 CSF £60.87 CT £577.14 TOTE £11.50: £3.20, £2.00, £2.50; EX 79.70 Trifecta £450.70.
Owner Miss Karen George **Bred** J Cullinan **Trained** Crediton, Devon
■ Stewards' Enquiry : Ellie MacKenzie four-day ban: interference & careless riding (Mar 5-8)
Aaron Mackay five-day ban: interference & careless riding (Mar 6-9, 11)

FOCUS
A moderate apprentice riders' handicap on standard Tapeta. The winning time was over three seconds above standard off a muddling initial gallop.

810 BETWAY LIVE CASINO H'CAP 1m 5f 219y (Tp)
6:00 (6:00) (Class 6) (0-60,60) 4-Y-0+ **£2,749** (£818; £408; £204) **Stalls** Low

Form RPR
00-0 1 Tour De Paris (IRE)[46] 85 4-9-4 60 (v) TomMarquand 6 69
(Alan King) hld up in tch: rdn and hung rt over 1f out: hung lft and led wl ins fnl f: drvn out 10/1

00/1 2 1 ½ Geordielad[48] 38 5-8-12 51 EdwardGreatrex 8 56
(Oliver Sherwood) led at stdy pce: shkn up and qcknd over 2f out: rdn over 1f out: edgd rt and hdd wl ins fnl f 13/8[1]

00-4 3 1 ½ Knight Commander[18] 566 6-9-1 57 FinleyMarsh(3) 11 60
(Steve Flook) broke wl enough: sn pushed along and lost pl: hdwy on outer over 1f out: edgd lft ins fnl f: r.o 22/1

1-40 4 1 Yasir (USA)[23] 457 11-9-2 55 DougieCostello 1 58
(Sophie Leech) s.i.s: hld up: nt clr run fr over 1f out tl ins fnl f: r.o to go 4th nr fin: nt rch ldrs (jockey said gelding was denied a clear run approaching the final furlong) 40/1

51-2 5 nk Betancourt (IRE)[40] 185 9-9-3 56 (p) JasonHart 7 57
(Stef Keniry) sn prom: chsd ldr over 8f out: rdn and hung rt over 1f out: no ex ins fnl f 3/1[2]

0-04 6 ¾ Butterfield (IRE)[14] 619 6-9-5 58 PaulMulrennan 3 59
(Tony Carroll) chsd ldrs: lost pl over 7f out: pushed along over 3f out: nt clr run over 2f out: hdwy over 1f out: sn rdn: styd on same pce ins fnl f 5/1[3]

0-05 7 2 ¼ Qayed (CAN)[32] 321 4-9-1 57 (p) ShaneKelly 5 56
(Mark Brisbourne) hld up: hdwy over 4f out: shkn up on outer over 2f out: styd on same pce fr over 1f out 16/1

0-60 8 1 Marshall Aid (IRE)[6] 724 6-9-3 56 DanielMuscutt 4 52
(Mark Usher) pushed along early towards rr: sme hdwy u.p over 1f out: hmpd and wknd ins fnl f 16/1

040- 9 4 ½ Last Chance Paddy (USA)[134] 8089 5-8-13 52 StevieDonohoe 9 42
(Sarah-Jayne Davies) plld hrd in 2nd pl: lost 2nd over 8f out: remained handy: rdn over 2f out: wknd fnl f 66/1

640- 10 1 Palermo (IRE)[126] 8319 5-9-1 54 (t w) GeorgeWood 13 43
(Michael Wigham) s.i.s: hdwy over 9f out: rdn on outer over 2f out: wknd over 1f out 16/1

3m 4.22s (3.22) **Going Correction** +0.05s/f (Slow)
WFA 4 from 5yo+ 3lb 10 Ran SP% 114.8
Speed ratings (Par 101): **92,91,90,89,89 89,87,87,84,84**
CSF £25.88 CT £359.71 TOTE £8.90: £2.20, £1.60, £3.20; EX 37.40 Trifecta £321.40.
Owner HP Racing Tour De Paris **Bred** Paul Hancock **Trained** Barbury Castle, Wilts
■ Stewards' Enquiry : Dougie Costello caution: careless riding

FOCUS
A modest staying handicap. The favourite couldn't quite dominate off his own muddling gallop. The winning time was over six seconds outside of standard. The likes of the fourth help pin the level.

811 BETWAY NOVICE STKS 5f 21y (Tp)
6:30 (6:30) (Class 5) 4-Y-0+ **£3,396** (£1,010; £505; £252) **Stalls** Low

Form RPR
4-42 1 Poet's Pride[7] 706 4-9-2 63 TomMarquand 7 65
(David Barron) chsd ldr: rdn to ld ins fnl f: r.o 8/15[1]

25-0 2 2 ¼ Mr Gent (IRE)[36] 249 4-9-2 65 (p[1]) PaulMulrennan 4 57
(Ed Dunlop) chsd ldrs: pushed along 1/2-way: swtchd rt over 1f out: styd on u.p to go 2nd wl ins fnl f 7/2[3]

0-0 3 hd Mrs Todd[49] 27 5-8-11 0 FergusSweeney 8 51
(Tony Carroll) plld hrd and sn prom: hung lft fr 1/2-way: rdn over 1f out: styd on 33/1

40-5 4 3 ¼ Bluella[16] 604 4-8-11 42 LewisEdmunds 6 40
(Robyn Brisland) led: rdn whn rdr dropped whip over 1f out: hdd and no ex ins fnl f 33/1

056- 5 nse Angel Eyes[178] 6578 4-8-4 39 RPWalsh(7) 3 39
(John David Riches) hld up: racd keenly: nt clr run 2f out: styd on ins fnl f: nt trble ldrs 66/1

-440 6 1 ½ Minuty[21] 476 4-8-11 56 (b[1]) DavidProbert 1 34
(Rae Guest) s.i.s: sn pushed along in rr: rdn over 1f out: nvr nrr 5/2[2]

0500 7 nk Celerity (IRE)[16] 597 5-8-4 38 GeorgiaDobie(7) 2 33
(Lisa Williamson) hld up: nt clr run over 3f out: n.d 40/1

250- 8 9 **Go Sandy**[168] 6940 4-8-4 48 (b) ElishaWhittington(7) 5 1
(Lisa Williamson) *s.s: a in rr: wknd over 1f out* 80/1

1m 1.95s (0.05) **Going Correction** +0.05s/f (Slow) 8 Ran SP% **127.1**
Speed ratings (Par 103): **101,97,97,91,91 89,88,74**
CSF £3.48 TOTE £1.10: £1.10, £1.60, £12.60; EX 4.30 Trifecta £48.20.
Owner Laurence O'Kane/Harrowgate BloodstockLtd **Bred** Swettenham Stud Bloodstock Ltd **Trained** Maunby, N Yorks

FOCUS
An ordinary novice sprint contest. The odds-on favourite came home strongly in the home straight after a modest initial gallop.

812 FOLLOW TOP TIPSTERS AT SUN RACING H'CAP 7f 36y (Tp)
7:00 (7:00) (Class 4) (0-80,81) 4-Y-O+ **£5,175** (£1,540; £769; £384) **Stalls** High

Form RPR
-132 1 **Blame Culture (USA)**[19] 526 4-9-5 77 DavidProbert 7 86
(George Margarson) *plld hrd: wnt 2nd 6f out tl over 4f out: remained handy: rdn to ld and hung lft wl ins fnl f* 7/4[1]

4313 2 nk **Glory Of Paris (IRE)**[19] 526 5-9-2 81 MarkCrehan(7) 12 89
(Michael Appleby) *s.s: hdwy on outer to chse ldr over 4f out: led 3f out: rdn: hung lft and hdd wl ins fnl f (jockey said gelding was slowly away)* 15/2[3]

0-66 3 1 1/4 **Murdanova (IRE)**[20] 496 6-9-3 75 JasonHart 6 79
(Ivan Furtado) *chsd ldrs: rdn over 1f out: r.o* 11/1

0-42 4 1/2 **Esprit De Corps**[20] 508 5-9-2 74 TomMarquand 1 77
(David Barron) *chsd ldrs: rdn over 1f out: no ex wl ins fnl f* 11/2[2]

1-16 5 1/2 **Zafaranah (USA)**[18] 564 5-9-5 77 CallumShepherd 11 79
(Pam Sly) *hld up: rdn over 1f out: edgd lft and r.o ins fnl f: nt rch ldrs* 9/1

4200 6 nk **Hammer Gun (USA)**[18] 557 6-8-13 74 (v) AaronJones(3) 2 75
(Derek Shaw) *stdd s: hld up: racd keenly: hdwy over 1f out: nt rch ldrs (jockey said gelding ran too freely)* 12/1

-036 7 3/4 **Critical Thinking (IRE)**[14] 623 5-9-3 75 (tp) TrevorWhelan 5 74
(David Loughnane) *trckd ldrs: lost pl over 4f out: pushed along and hdwy over 1f out: sn rdn: styd on same pce ins fnl f* 10/1

6-54 8 3/4 **Mont Kinabalu (IRE)**[29] 350 4-9-2 74 (p[1]) DougieCostello 8 71
(Kevin Ryan) *hld up: shkn up and swtchd rt over 1f out: nt trble ldrs* 12/1

106- 9 1 1/2 **Logi (IRE)**[159] 7235 5-9-7 79 (b) LewisEdmunds 3 72
(Rebecca Bastiman) *led 4f: chsd ldr: rdn over 1f out: wknd ins fnl f* 20/1

650- 10 1 3/4 **Fire Diamond**[67] 9564 6-9-4 76 (p) PaulMulrennan 10 64
(Tom Dascombe) *s.i.s: hld up: nvr on terms* 80/1

530- 11 5 **Laqab (IRE)**[53] 9747 6-8-5 66 GabrieleMalune(3) 4 41
(Derek Shaw) *s.i.s: hld up: plld hrd: hdwy over 4f out: rdn and wknd over 1f out* 40/1

235- 12 6 **Rosarno (IRE)**[107] 8885 5-9-4 76 JoeyHaynes 9 34
(Paul Howling) *hdwy on outer over 4f out: pushed along 1/2-way: wknd over 2f out* 66/1

1m 28.28s (-0.52) **Going Correction** +0.05s/f (Slow) 12 Ran SP% **116.2**
Speed ratings (Par 105): **104,103,102,101,101 100,99,99,97,95 89,82**
CSF £14.12 CT £114.91 TOTE £2.10: £1.20, £1.90, £2.60; EX 14.20 Trifecta £87.10.
Owner Mangiacapra, Hill, Hook Partnership **Bred** Summerhill Farm **Trained** Newmarket, Suffolk

FOCUS
The feature contest was a fair handicap. The favourite came home well off an initially muddling gallop to narrowly get the better of an old rival in the best comparative time on the night.

813 LADBROKES H'CAP 6f 20y (Tp)
7:30 (7:30) (Class 6) (0-65,65) 3-Y-O **£2,749** (£818; £408; £204) **Stalls** Low

Form RPR
62-2 1 **Eye Of The Water (IRE)**[14] 620 3-8-9 53 DavidProbert 1 58
(Ronald Harris) *chsd ldr 1f: remained handy: rdn to ld and edgd lft wl ins fnl f: styd on* 5/2[1]

-032 2 1/2 **Amor Kethley**[18] 550 3-9-3 61 GeorgeWood 10 65
(Amy Murphy) *prom: chsd ldr 5f out: led over 1f out: rdn and hdd wl ins fnl f: kpt on* 14/1

-120 3 nk **Lincoln Spirit**[14] 620 3-8-11 55 LewisEdmunds 4 58
(David O'Meara) *hld up: hdwy over 1f out: sn rdn: r.o to go 3rd nr fin: nt rch ldrs (jockey said filly hung right-handed throughout)* 12/1

04-1 4 1/2 **Halle's Harbour**[42] 137 3-8-13 57 (v) EdwardGreatrex 2 58
(Paul George) *s.i.s: sn prom: rdn and hung lft ins fnl f: n.m.r sn after: styd on* 9/2[2]

000- 5 1/2 **Good Tyne Girl (IRE)**[68] 9530 3-9-6 64 TomMarquand 5 64
(Heather Main) *hld up: rdn over 1f out: r.o ins fnl f: nt rch ldrs* 20/1

360- 6 nk **Fast Endeavour**[69] 9521 3-8-7 54 (p[1]) GabrieleMalune(3) 3 53
(Ian Williams) *hld up: hdwy over 1f out: r.o ins fnl f: nt trble ldrs* 12/1

-101 7 1 1/2 **Deconso**[14] 620 3-8-12 56 StevieDonohoe 7 53
(Christopher Kellett) *led: rdn and hdd over 1f out: styng on same pce whn hmpd wl ins fnl f* 11/2[3]

6-36 8 1 1/4 **Madame Vitesse (FR)**[14] 620 3-8-11 62 RussellHarris(7) 13 52+
(Richard Fahey) *s.i.s: hld up: plld hrd: racd on outer: rdn over 1f out: edgd lft and styd on ins fnl f: n.d (vet reported the filly lost its right fore shoe)* 20/1

600- 9 1 1/4 **Kickham Street**[113] 8714 3-9-7 65 JasonHart 9 52
(John Quinn) *stdd s: hld up: plld hrd: shkn up over 2f out: nvr on terms (jockey said gelding ran too freely)* 6/1

45-6 10 1 1/2 **North Korea (IRE)**[16] 605 3-9-2 60 WilliamCarson 6 42
(Brian Baugh) *prom: rdn over 1f out: wknd fnl f* 33/1

060- 11 3 **Potenza (IRE)**[146] 7707 3-9-0 58 ShaneKelly 8 31
(Stef Keniry) *sn prom: rdn over 2f out: wknd over 1f out* 20/1

1m 14.97s (0.47) **Going Correction** +0.05s/f (Slow) 11 Ran SP% **115.7**
Speed ratings (Par 95): **98,97,96,96,95 95,93,91,89,87 83**
CSF £36.94 CT £362.55 TOTE £2.50: £1.10, £4.90, £3.90; EX 33.30 Trifecta £308.80.
Owner Malcolm E Wright **Bred** M Fahy **Trained** Earlswood, Monmouths

FOCUS
A modest 3yo sprint handicap. The favourite held a handy position throughout and won a shade cosily. A small pb from the third.

814 LADBROKES HOME OF THE ODDS BOOST FILLIES' H'CAP 1m 142y (Tp)
8:00 (8:00) (Class 5) (0-70,72) 4-Y-O+ **£3,396** (£1,010; £505; £252) **Stalls** Low

Form RPR
154- 1 **American Endeavour (USA)**[68] 9536 4-10-2 72 (h) MarcMonaghan 1 78+
(Marco Botti) *racd keenly: a.p: swtchd rt over 1f out: rdn to ld 1f out: styd on u.p* 5/2[1]

4-60 2 1 **Corked (IRE)**[21] 479 6-9-1 57 DougieCostello 3 60
(Alistair Whillans) *hld up in tch: hld up over 4f out: hdwy and swtchd rt over 1f out: sn rdn: styd on to go 2nd nr fin* 15/2

2-R0 3 hd **One More Chance (IRE)**[32] 315 4-8-13 62 (b[1]) MarkCrehan(7) 6 64
(Michael Appleby) *s.i.s: sn prom: led over 5f out: rdn and hdd 1f out: styd on same pce towards fin* 12/1

0-50 4 hd **La Sioux (IRE)**[30] 348 5-8-5 52 (b) RhiainIngram(5) 5 54
(Richard Fahey) *sn led: hdd over 5f out: chsd ldr: rdn: carried rt and lost 2nd over 1f out: styd on same pce wl ins fnl f (jockey said mare suffered interference in running)* 11/1

20-0 5 3/4 **Vampish**[33] 292 4-10-1 71 JasonHart 2 72
(Philip McBride) *prom: lost pl after 1f: rdn over 1f out: swtchd lft and r.o ins fnl f* 28/1

3-00 6 hd **Bell Heather (IRE)**[30] 344 6-9-7 63 StevieDonohoe 7 63
(Patrick Morris) *hld up: hdwy over 4f out: rdn over 1f out: styd on* 10/1

0-02 7 nk **Aqua Libre**[30] 348 6-9-5 61 (p) EdwardGreatrex 8 61
(Jennie Candlish) *dwlt: hld up: racd keenly: r.o u.p and carried lft ins fnl f: nt clr run towards fin: nt trble ldrs (jockey said mare was slowly away)* 4/1[2]

00-1 8 nk **Foxy Lady**[23] 462 4-9-4 60 (p) ShaneGray 9 58
(Kevin Ryan) *chsd ldrs: rdn over 2f out: styd on* 11/1

6-50 9 3 **Barbara Villiers**[6] 724 4-9-0 61 KatherineBegley(5) 4 52
(David Evans) *s.i.s: hld up: hdwy over 3f out: rdn on outer over 2f out: hung lft and wknd fnl f* 6/1[3]

1m 49.41s (-0.69) **Going Correction** +0.05s/f (Slow) 9 Ran SP% **111.5**
Speed ratings (Par 100): **105,104,103,103,103 102,102,102,99**
CSF £20.54 CT £182.11 TOTE £2.50: £1.10, £2.50, £3.90; EX 23.00 Trifecta £216.60.
Owner A J Suited & Gute Freunde Partnership **Bred** Baumann Stables **Trained** Newmarket, Suffolk

FOCUS
An ordinary fillies' handicap. The favourite was switched off the rail after racing prominently and strongly asserted in the final furlong.
T/Jkpt: Not won T/Plt: £60.20 to a £1 stake. Pool: £69,165.29 - 1,148.37 winning units T/Qpdt: £5.10 to a £1 stake. Pool: £8,927.38 - 1,731.31 winning units **Colin Roberts**

815a-822a (Foreign Racing) - See Raceform Interactive

796 CHELMSFORD (A.W) (L-H)
Thursday, February 21

OFFICIAL GOING: Polytrack: standard
Wind: virtually nil Weather: dry

823 BET TOTEPLACEPOT AT TOTESPORT.COM APPRENTICE H'CAP 5f (P)
5:50 (5:50) (Class 6) (0-65,66) 4-Y-O+
£3,105 (£924; £461; £400; £400; £400) **Stalls** Low

Form RPR
2-63 1 **Time To Reason (IRE)**[15] 626 6-9-4 64 (p) Pierre-LouisJamin(3) 1 71
(Charlie Wallis) *dwlt: sn rcvrd and in midfield: swtchd lft and effrt u.p over 1f out: rdn to ld ent fnl f: hld on wl and a doing enough ins fnl f* 3/1[1]

0-43 2 1/2 **Big Time Maybe (IRE)**[23] 468 4-9-9 66 (p) ScottMcCullagh 3 71
(Michael Attwater) *chsd ldr: effrt u.p to ld jst over 1f out: sn hdd: kpt on u.p but a jst hld ins fnl f* 5/1[3]

46-5 3 1/2 **Hurricane Alert**[22] 478 7-8-4 47 AledBeech 6 50
(Mark Hoad) *taken down early: midfield: effrt and reminders ent fnl 2f: styd on u.p to press ldng pair ins fnl f: kpt on same pce towards fin* 25/1

66-2 4 1 **Dandilion (IRE)**[34] 286 6-8-10 58 (t) CierenFallon(5) 4 58
(Alex Hales) *racd in last pair: rdn jst over 2f out: hdwy over 1f out: chsd ldrs and kpt on same pce fnl 100yds* 7/2[2]

0113 5 1 3/4 **Point Zero (IRE)**[8] 707 4-9-6 66 (v[1]) MarkCrehan(3) 2 60
(Michael Appleby) *taken down early: chsd ldr: rdn and sltly squeezed for room over 1f out: edgd lft and wknd ins fnl f* 3/1[1]

0-20 6 2 1/2 **Entertaining Ben**[33] 317 6-9-0 62 (p) GraceMcEntee(5) 7 47+
(Amy Murphy) *pushed along to ld and set str gallop: rdn and hdd jst over 1f out: wknd ins fnl f* 10/1

-401 7 nse **Red Stripes (USA)**[17] 597 7-8-10 56 (b) EllieMacKenzie(3) 5 40
(Lisa Williamson) *dwlt and rousted along leaving stalls: a in rr: nvr involved and wl hld whn hung lft 1f out* 7/1

59.58s (-0.62) **Going Correction** -0.10s/f (Stan) 7 Ran SP% **114.3**
Speed ratings (Par 101): **100,99,98,96,94 90,89**
CSF £18.34 TOTE £4.70: £2.10, £2.50; EX 21.50 Trifecta £200.30.
Owner J E Titley & J Goddard **Bred** Glenvale Stud **Trained** Ardleigh, Essex

FOCUS
This was run at a good gallop. The winner has been rated towards the balance of his better 2018 form.

824 BET TOTEEXACTA AT TOTESPORT.COM FILLIES' H'CAP 6f (P)
6:25 (6:25) (Class 5) (0-70,72) 4-Y-O+
£4,851 (£1,443; £721; £400; £400; £400) **Stalls** Centre

Form RPR
1-31 1 **Always A Drama (IRE)**[5] 759 4-9-3 72 6ex CierenFallon(7) 1 82+
(Charles Hills) *trckd ldrs: pressing ldr and waiting for gap on inner over 1f out: pushed along and hdwy to ld 150yds out: r.o wl and in command after: comf* 4/6[1]

40-3 2 1 3/4 **Lalania**[33] 314 4-9-7 69 SeanLevey 4 73
(Stuart Williams) *sn led: drvn over 1f out: hdd 150yds out: kpt on same pce and comf hld by wnr ins fnl f* 6/1[2]

20-6 3 1 1/2 **Dreamboat Annie**[26] 430 4-8-12 60 (p) TomMarquand 3 59
(Mark Usher) *swtchd rt sn after s: sn chsng ldr and wd: rdn over 1f out: unable qck and wl hld in 3rd ins fnl f* 8/1[3]

0-35 4 1 1/4 **Dotted Swiss (IRE)**[33] 314 4-9-6 68 (b) HollieDoyle 2 63
(Archie Watson) *in tch in midfield: drvn over 1f out: unable qck and no ex 1f out: wknd ins fnl f* 6/1[2]

44-0 5 1 3/4 **Avon Green**[41] 179 4-9-0 62 ShaneKelly 5 52
(Joseph Tuite) *wnt sltly rt leaving stalls: a in last pair: no imp u.p over 1f out: wknd ins fnl f* 25/1

04-0 6 3/4 **War No More (USA)**[47] 78 4-9-1 63 CharlieBennett 6 50
(Roger Varian) *wnt rt leaving s: a in rr: rdn over 2f out: outpcd and btn over 1f out: wknd ins fnl f* 10/1

1m 12.44s (-1.26) **Going Correction** -0.10s/f (Stan) 6 Ran SP% **112.6**
Speed ratings (Par 100): **104,101,99,98,95 94**
CSF £5.26 TOTE £1.40: £1.10, £3.00; EX 4.70 Trifecta £21.60.
Owner B W Neill **Bred** Patrick Kelly **Trained** Lambourn, Berks

FOCUS
This proved straightforward for the odds-on favourite.

825 BET TOTEQUADPOT AT TOTESPORT.COM H'CAP 1m 2f (P)
6:55 (6:57) (Class 4) (0-85,88) 4-Y-O+ **£5,530** (£1,645; £822; £411) **Stalls** Low

Form RPR
-111 1 **Executive Force**[7] 722 5-9-11 88 6ex (p) JFEgan 2 96
(Michael Wigham) *stdd s: hld up in rr: swtchd rt and effrt over 1f out: clsd to ld ins fnl f but edging lft: stl edging sltly lft but r.o wl* 9/4[2]

2-11 **2** *nk* **Forbidden Planet**[33] 310 4-9-7 **84**.................... RyanMoore 4 91
(Roger Charlton) *chsd ldr: drvn to chal over 1f out: led jst ins fnl f: sn hdd and carried sltly lft: short of room and wandered cl home: kpt on* **10/11**[1]

3-36 **3** *1 ½* **Wimpole Hall**[15] 617 6-8-10 **80**....................(p) CierenFallon(7) 1 84
(William Jarvis) *t.k.h: trckd ldrs: effrt on inner over 1f out: ev ch 1f out: keeping on same pce whn sltly squeezed for room ins fnl f* **5/1**[3]

5131 **4** *nk* **Central City (IRE)**[19] 552 4-9-0 **77**....................(p) StevieDonohoe 3 81
(Ian Williams) *t.k.h: led: drvn over 1f out: hdd jst ins fnl f: keeping on same pce whn squeezed for room ins fnl f* **10/1**

2m 7.5s (-1.10) **Going Correction** -0.10s/f (Stan) 4 Ran SP% **108.9**
Speed ratings (Par 105): **100,99,98,98**
CSF £4.77 TOTE £3.10; EX 5.00 Trifecta £5.00.
Owner Tugay Akman **Bred** Rabbah Bloodstock Limited **Trained** Newmarket, Suffolk
■ Stewards' Enquiry : J F Egan two-day ban: careless riding (Mar 7-8)

FOCUS
This was steadily run and turned into a test of speed.

826 BET TOTETRIFECTA AT TOTESPORT.COM H'CAP 1m 2f (P)
7:25 (7:27) (Class 5) (0-75,77) 3-Y-O
£4,851 (£1,443; £721; £400; £400; £400) **Stalls** Low

Form RPR

56-1 **1** **Red Bond (IRE)**[23] 472 3-9-7 **75**.................... SeanLevey 3 81
(Keith Dalgleish) *mde all and dictated stdy gallop: rdn over 1f out: drvn jst ins fnl f: kpt on wl: jst hld on cl home* **8/1**

3-41 **2** *hd* **Harvey Dent**[27] 403 3-9-9 **77**.................... HollieDoyle 4 82
(Archie Watson) *t.k.h: sn pressing wnr: rdn over 1f out: edgd lft but sustained effrt u.p: kpt on wl cl home: jst hld (jockey said gelding hung left-handed under pressure)* **5/2**[2]

44-1 **3** *nse* **Albert Finney**[22] 486 3-9-5 **73**....................(h) RyanMoore 5 78
(John Gosden) *t.k.h: wl in tch in midfield: effrt over 1f out: chsd ldrs and hrd drvn jst ins fnl f: styd on towards fin* **6/4**[1]

031- **4** *2 ½* **Torolight**[107] 8890 3-9-0 **68**.................... ShaneKelly 2 68
(Richard Hughes) *jostled leaving stalls: hld up in tch in 5th: swtchd rt and effrt ent fnl 2f: hung lft and no imp ins fnl f* **4/1**[3]

5-24 **5** *3* **Wall Of Sapphire (IRE)**[24] 461 3-9-0 **68**....................(b[1]) TomMarquand 1 62
(Hugo Palmer) *trckd ldrs: effrt over 1f out: lost 3rd and no ex u.p 1f out: wknd ins fnl f* **12/1**

21-2 **6** *4* **Whenapoet**[28] 391 3-8-8 **69**....................(p) MarkCrehan(7) 6 55
(Michael Appleby) *stdd and awkward leaving stalls: a in rr: rdn over 3f out: no threat to ldrs after (jockey said colt was slowly away)* **20/1**

2m 7.29s (-1.31) **Going Correction** -0.10s/f (Stan) 6 Ran SP% **112.1**
Speed ratings (Par 97): **101,100,100,98,96 93**
CSF £28.19 TOTE £8.30: £3.30, £1.50; EX 28.30 Trifecta £81.00.
Owner Middleham Park Racing XXVII **Bred** Mrs Colette Todd **Trained** Carluke, S Lanarks

FOCUS
This was steadily run and favoured those up front.

827 BET TOTESWINGER AT TOTESPORT.COM NOVICE STKS 1m (P)
7:55 (7:57) (Class 4) 3-Y-O+ **£5,530** (£1,645; £822; £411) **Stalls** Low

Form RPR

42 **1** **Kinver Edge (USA)**[31] 343 3-8-9 **0**.................... ShaneKelly 7 87+
(Charlie Appleby) *mde all: rdn over 1f out: in command and styd on strly ins fnl f* **3/1**[2]

02-3 **2** *2 ¾* **White Coat**[43] 133 3-8-9 **80**.................... RyanMoore 8 81+
(John Gosden) *chsd wnr: rdn over 1f out: unable qck and styd on same pce ins fnl f* **1/2**[1]

20- **3** *3* **Lovely Approach**[351] 1060 4-10-0 **0**....................(h[1]) TomMarquand 3 80
(Hugo Palmer) *midfield: 5th and drvn over 2f out: no threat to ldng pair but kpt on to go 3rd wl ins fnl f* **20/1**

20-2 **4** *¾* **Barossa Red (IRE)**[39] 229 3-8-6 **80**.................... WilliamCox(3) 4 72
(Andrew Balding) *chsd ldng trio: effrt in 3rd 2f out: no imp and wl hld whn edgd lft ins fnl f: lost 3rd wl ins fnl f* **5/1**[3]

5 *4 ½* **Love Explodes** 3-8-1 **0**.................... JaneElliott(3) 5 57
(Ed Vaughan) *dwlt: hld up in rr: effrt and wd 2f out: nvr involved and wl hld whn edgd lft ins fnl f* **12/1**

6 *2* **Bawaader (IRE)** 4-10-0 **0**.................... DanielMuscutt 2 63
(Ed Dunlop) *s.i.s: hld up in last pair: effrt over 2f out: sn outpcd and wl hld over 1f out* **20/1**

00 **7** *4 ½* **Georgearthurhenry**[7] 723 3-8-9 **0**.................... GeorgeWood 1 47
(Amy Murphy) *chsd ldrs: rdn and lost 3rd 2f out: sn lost pl and wknd fnl f* **100/1**

8 *1* **Noel (IRE)** 4-10-0 **0**.................... FergusSweeney 6 51
(Daniel Kubler) *a last trio: rdn over 2f out: sn struggling: bhd ins fnl f* **50/1**

1m 38.32s (-1.58) **Going Correction** -0.10s/f (Stan)
WFA 3 from 4yo 19lb 8 Ran SP% **128.5**
Speed ratings (Par 105): **103,100,97,96,92 90,85,84**
CSF £5.43 TOTE £3.30: £1.10, £1.02, £6.70; EX 6.50 Trifecta £30.50.
Owner Godolphin **Bred** Bridlewood Farm **Trained** Newmarket, Suffolk

FOCUS
Not a bad novice, the favourite setting a fair standard and appearing to run his race in second.

828 BET TOTESCOOP6 AT TOTESPORT.COM H'CAP 1m (P)
8:25 (8:27) (Class 6) (0-65,65) 4-Y-O+
£3,105 (£924; £461; £400; £400; £400) **Stalls** Low

Form RPR

5-21 **1** **Cashel (IRE)**[36] 250 4-9-5 **63**.................... TomMarquand 4 73+
(Michael Appleby) *chsd ldr over 6f out: rdn to ld over 1f out: styd on strly and drew clr ins fnl f* **1/1**[1]

0-52 **2** *2 ¾* **Accomplice**[28] 386 5-9-5 **63**.................... FergusSweeney 7 67
(Michael Blanshard) *stdd s: t.k.h: hld up in tch in last pair: effrt and clsd ent fnl 2f: drvn over 1f out: kpt on ins fnl f to go 2nd towards fin: no ch w wnr* **14/1**

3-20 **3** *nk* **Classic Charm**[26] 430 4-9-2 **60**.................... ShaneKelly 2 63
(Dean Ivory) *hld up in tch in midfield: effrt and clsd to press ldrs 2f out: drvn and ev ch over 1f out tl unable to match pce of wnr 1f out: kpt on same pce after and lost 2nd towards fin* **6/1**[3]

56-3 **4** *2 ¾* **The King's Steed**[24] 463 6-8-11 **62**....................(bt) CierenFallon(7) 3 59
(Shaun Lycett) *sn led: rdn and hdd over 1f out: sn outpcd and wknd ins fnl f* **3/1**[2]

0634 **5** *nk* **Caledonian Gold**[7] 718 6-8-7 **51** oh6....................(h) JoeyHaynes 5 47
(Lisa Williamson) *stdd s: t.k.h: hld up in tch in last pair: nt clrest of runs 2f out: sn rdn and unable qck: wknd ins fnl f* **66/1**

-315 **6** *4 ½* **Rippling Waters (FR)**[8] 697 5-9-6 **64**....................(t) DougieCostello 1 50
(Jamie Osborne) *chsd ldr for over 1f out: rdn and lost pl over 1f out: bhd 1f out and wknd ins fnl f* **6/1**[3]

1m 38.93s (-0.97) **Going Correction** -0.10s/f (Stan) 6 Ran SP% **111.7**
Speed ratings (Par 101): **100,97,96,94,93 89**
CSF £16.71 TOTE £1.70: £1.10, £4.30; EX 14.50 Trifecta £42.00.
Owner Laurence Bellman **Bred** Kildaragh Stud & M Downey **Trained** Oakham, Rutland

FOCUS
A modest handicap but the winner is on the up. The second has been rated to form.
T/Plt: £34.30 to a £1 stake. Pool: £55,901.17 - 1,189.34 winning units T/Qpdt: £9.00 to a £1 stake. Pool: £5,858.07 - 481.43 winning units **Steve Payne**

702 SOUTHWELL (L-H)
Thursday, February 21

OFFICIAL GOING: Fibresand: standard to slow
Wind: Light across Weather: Fine & dry

829 SUNRACING.CO.UK H'CAP 1m 13y(F)
2:25 (2:25) (Class 6) (0-55,55) 3-Y-O+ **£2,587** (£770; £384; £192) **Stalls** Low

Form RPR

-302 **1** **Baron Run**[8] 705 9-9-5 **53**.................... RhonaPindar(7) 12 63
(K R Burke) *trckd ldrs: cl up 1/2-way: led wl over 2f out: rdn clr appr fnl f: kpt on strly* **12/1**

0-52 **2** *2 ¼* **Greyzee (IRE)**[20] 537 3-8-7 **53**.................... JoeyHaynes 9 52
(Rod Millman) *trckd ldrs: hdwy 3f out: rdn over 1f out: swtchd rt and drvn ent fnl f: styd on* **3/1**[1]

-302 **3** *nk* **Foxrush Take Time (FR)**[20] 533 4-9-5 **46** oh1............(e) PhilipPrince 2 50
(Richard Guest) *sn slt ld: pushed along over 3f out: hdd wl over 2f out and sn rdn: drvn and kpt on fnl f* **18/1**

4540 **4** *½* **Break The Silence**[18] 590 5-9-7 **53**....................(b) TheodoreLadd(5) 14 56
(Scott Dixon) *trckd ldrs on outer: hdwy and wd st: chsd ldng pair and rdn wl over 1f out: drvn and kpt on same pce fnl f* **12/1**

00-4 **5** *¾* **Compass Point**[15] 624 4-10-0 **55**.................... AndrewMullen 3 56
(Robyn Brisland) *midfield: hdwy on inner: 3f out: chsd ldrs wl over 1f out: sn rdn and kpt on same pce* **14/1**

0002 **6** *¾* **Going Native**[18] 590 4-9-5 **46**.................... RachelRichardson 13 46
(Olly Williams) *dwlt and swtchd lft s: towards rr: hdwy on inner over 2f out: rdn wl over 1f out: kpt on fnl f* **12/1**

00-5 **7** *1 ¾* **Trouble Shooter (IRE)**[18] 585 3-8-6 **52**....................(v) HollieDoyle 1 42
(Shaun Keightley) *in tch: pushed along and lost pl 1/2-way: rdn and hdwy over 2f out: kpt on fnl f* **17/2**[3]

5 **8** *¾* **Act Of Magic (IRE)**[33] 319 3-8-6 **52**.................... KieranO'Neill 5 40
(Mohamed Moubarak) *dwlt and swtchd rt s: sn pushed along in rr: bhd and wd st: rdn and hdwy wl over 2f out: kpt on: n.d (jockey said gelding missed the break)* **4/1**[2]

0-23 **9** *1 ¾* **Bee Machine (IRE)**[18] 590 4-9-7 **55**....................(t) ZakWheatley(7) 10 45
(Declan Carroll) *chsd ldrs: hdwy 3f out: rdn over 2f out: grad wknd* **12/1**

1-26 **10** *3 ¾* **Molten Lava (IRE)**[40] 210 7-9-13 **54**....................(p) LukeMorris 7 35
(Steve Gollings) *trckd ldrs towards inner: pushed along over 3f out: rdn wl over 2f out: sn drvn and btn* **14/1**

0-00 **11** *2* **Iberica Road (USA)**[17] 593 6-9-7 **48**....................(b) SamJames 4 25
(Grant Tuer) *cl up: pushed along wl over 3f out: rdn 3f out: sn wknd* **22/1**

-030 **12** *¾* **Cash N Carrie (IRE)**[15] 616 5-9-10 **51**.................... LewisEdmunds 6 26+
(Michael Appleby) *trckd ldrs: pushed along wl over 3f: sn rdn and wknd (jockey said mare suffered interference on the bend turning in to the home straight)* **20/1**

200- **13** *1* **Ronni Layne**[154] 7460 5-9-5 **46**.................... CallumShepherd 11 19
(Louise Allan) *a towards rr* **66/1**

00-0 **14** *4* **Made In Lewisham (IRE)**[20] 537 3-8-5 **51**............(b[1]) PaddyMathers 8 8
(David Evans) *a towards rr* **66/1**

1m 42.8s (-0.90) **Going Correction** -0.125s/f (Stan)
WFA 3 from 4yo+ 19lb 14 Ran SP% **117.0**
Speed ratings (Par 101): **99,96,96,95,95 94,92,91,90,86 84,83,82,78**
CSF £44.91 CT £677.23 TOTE £12.80: £4.20, £2.30, £5.20; EX 64.20 Trifecta £1130.80.
Owner Eric Burke & Partner **Bred** Mrs D Hughes **Trained** Middleham Moor, N Yorks

FOCUS
A modest handicap run at a sound pace. It looked hard work inside the final furlong. The third is among those that help pin the level.

830 FOLLOW SUN RACING ON TWITTER H'CAP 7f 14y(F)
3:00 (3:00) (Class 6) (0-65,65) 4-Y-O+ **£2,587** (£770; £384; £192) **Stalls** Low

Form RPR

-143 **1** **Thunder Buddy**[6] 738 4-9-1 **59**....................(p[1]) CliffordLee 10 67
(K R Burke) *cl up: chal 3f out: led 2f out: rdn over 1f out: drvn ins fnl f: kpt on wl towards fin* **5/2**[1]

-331 **2** *¾* **Catapult**[22] 476 4-8-8 **52**.................... HollieDoyle 9 58
(Shaun Keightley) *cl up: led over 3f out: hdd 2f out: sn rdn: drvn and ev ch ins fnl f: no ex last 75yds* **6/1**[3]

-132 **3** *2 ¼* **Bond Angel**[21] 507 4-9-2 **65**.................... KatherineBegley(5) 6 65
(David Evans) *in tch: hdwy 3f out: rdn 2f out: edgd lft over 1f out: styd on u.p fnl f (vet said filly lost left fore shoe)* **7/2**[2]

0-01 **4** *1* **Newstead Abbey**[18] 586 9-9-3 **64**....................(p) PhilDennis(3) 2 61
(Rebecca Bastiman) *in tch: hdwy on inner 3f out: rdn along 2f out: kpt on fnl f* **16/1**

0-01 **5** *nse* **Alpha Tauri (USA)**[18] 590 13-8-11 **60**.................... BenSanderson(5) 7 57
(Charles Smith) *chsd ldrs: hdwy 3f out: rdn 2f out: drvn over 1f out: kpt on same pce* **11/1**

2541 **6** *4* **Sooqaan**[8] 705 8-9-7 **65** 6ex....................(p) CamHardie 4 51
(Antony Brittain) *prom: rdn along 3f out: drvn 2f out: sn wknd* **8/1**

3-00 **7** *1 ¾* **Grinty (IRE)**[39] 233 5-8-13 **57**....................(p) PaulMulrennan 3 39
(Michael Dods) *sn outpcd and bhd: wd st: rdn over 2f out: kpt on fnl f* **33/1**

1263 **8** *nk* **Grey Destiny**[8] 705 9-8-13 **64**....................(p) KieranSchofield(7) 5 45
(Antony Brittain) *midfield: effrt on inner 3f out: sn rdn along and n.d* **10/1**

00-0 **9** *hd* **Shearian**[21] 507 9-8-12 **63**.................... CianMacRedmond(7) 14 43
(Declan Carroll) *prom: rdn along 3f out: wknd 2f out* **40/1**

0-00 **10** *5* **Daze Out (IRE)**[27] 410 4-8-8 **52**....................(p) PaddyMathers 12 19
(Richard Fahey) *dwlt: a towards rr* **50/1**

4-50 **11** *½* **Coiste Bodhar (IRE)**[18] 586 8-7-13 **46** oh1.........(p) JamieGormley(3) 8 11
(Scott Dixon) *a towards rr* **66/1**

5-60 **12** *nk* **Seaquinn**[17] 594 4-8-2 **46** oh1.................... LukeMorris 13 11
(John Best) *dwlt: a towards rr* **25/1**

100- **13** *3* **War Of Succession**[113] 8733 5-9-0 **58**.................... CallumShepherd 11 14
(Tony Newcombe) *dwlt and in rr: bhd and wd st (vet said gelding lost left fore shoe)* **25/1**

010- **14** *29* **Astrojewel**[55] 9734 4-8-9 **58**.................................... TheodoreLadd(5) 1
(Mark H Tompkins) *led: rdn along hdd over 3f out: sn wknd (jockey said filly stopped quickly)* **33/1**

1m 28.44s (-1.86) **Going Correction** -0.125s/f (Stan) **14** Ran SP% **119.0**
Speed ratings (Par 101): **105,104,101,100,100 95,93,93,93,87 86,86,83,50**
CSF £16.02 CT £53.58 TOTE £3.50: £1.70, £1.70, £1.50; EX 19.30 Trifecta £83.80.
Owner Mrs Elaine M Burke **Bred** J C S Wilson Bloodstock **Trained** Middleham Moor, N Yorks

FOCUS
A modest handicap run at a sound pace. Minor personal bests from the first two.

831 BETWAY MAIDEN STKS — 4f 214y(F)
3:35 (3:35) (Class 5) 3-Y-0+ — £2,911 (£866; £432; £216) **Stalls** Centre

Form RPR

60- **1** **Fair Alibi**[107] 8895 3-9-0 0.................................... JamesSullivan 5 70+
(Tom Tate) *chsd ldrs centre: pushed along 2f out: swtchd rt and hdwy over 1f out: sn rdn: styd on wl fnl f to ld towards fin* **10/1**

654- **2** *1* **So Hi Speed (USA)**[206] 5562 3-9-0 73.................................... LukeMorris 3 66
(Robert Cowell) *prom centre: led 3f out: rdn and hdd 2f out: cl up: drvn over 1f out: led last 100yds: hdd and no ex towards fin* **11/8**[1]

3 *1* **Gupta** 3-9-0 0.................................... PaulMulrennan 6 63
(David Brown) *wnt rt s: racd towards centre and slt ld 2f: cl up: led again 2f out: rdn over 1f out: green and edgd lft ent fnl f: hdd and no ex last 100yds* **7/1**[3]

3-23 **4** *½* **Kadiz (IRE)**[28] 388 3-8-6 66....................................(b) FinleyMarsh(3) 4 56
(Richard Hughes) *wnt lft s: in tch centre: hdwy 1/2-way: chsd ldrs wl over 1f out: rdn and ev ch ins fnl f: sn drvn and kpt on same pce* **13/8**[2]

5 *3* **Termonator** 3-9-0 0.................................... SamJames 1 50
(Grant Tuer) *racd towards far side: chsd ldrs: rdn along over 2f out: sn one pce* **25/1**

00-4 **6** *¾* **Atwaar**[28] 388 3-8-6 51.................................... NoelGarbutt(3) 8 43
(Charles Smith) *racd towards stands' side: chsd ldrs: rdn along 1/2-way: drvn 2f out: sn wknd* **33/1**

6 **7** *4* **Killer Queen**[15] 621 4-9-6 0.................................... PhilDennis(3) 2 34
(David C Griffiths) *wnt lft s: racd towards far side: prom: rdn along over 2f out: sn wknd* **66/1**

8 *28* **Abbi Dab** 3-8-5 0 ow1.................................... KevinLundie(5) 7
(Michael Appleby) *green and dwlt: sn outpcd and bhd* **14/1**

59.33s (-0.37) **Going Correction** -0.125s/f (Stan)
WFA 3 from 4yo 14lb **8** Ran SP% **116.7**
Speed ratings (Par 103): **97,95,93,93,88 87,80,35**
CSF £24.64 TOTE £10.60: £2.10, £1.10, £2.30; EX 29.70 Trifecta £213.70.
Owner T T Racing **Bred** Biddestone Stud Ltd **Trained** Tadcaster, N Yorks

FOCUS
A weak maiden.

832 BETWAY HEED YOUR HUNCH H'CAP — 6f 16y(F)
4:10 (4:10) (Class 4) (0-85,86) 4-Y-0+ — £5,175 (£1,540; £769; £384) **Stalls** Low

Form RPR

000- **1** **Zylan (IRE)**[174] 6761 7-9-6 **86**.................................... BenSanderson(5) 4 98
(Roger Fell) *trckd ldrs: hdwy over 2f out: led wl over 1f out: rdn clr jst ins fnl f: kpt on strly* **9/1**

3223 **2** *3¼* **Crosse Fire**[21] 508 7-8-3 **69**....................................(p) TheodoreLadd(5) 3 71
(Scott Dixon) *hld up in tch: n.m.r wl over 2f out and sn swtchd lft: hdwy on inner wl over 1f out: sn rdn: styd on strly fnl f* **7/1**

5-06 **3** *hd* **The Great Wall (USA)**[21] 499 5-9-6 **81**....................................(p[1]) AndrewMullen 7 82
(Michael Appleby) *reminders s: chsd ldrs: pushed along whn n.m.r and swtchd rt wl over 2f out: rdn and sltly outpcd wl over 1f out: styd on u.p fnl f* **11/2**[3]

0440 **4** *1½* **Samovar**[18] 588 4-8-8 **72**....................................(b) JamieGormley(3) 5 68
(Scott Dixon) *slt ld: rdn along 2f out: sn hdd: drvn over 1f out: kpt on u.p fnl f* **16/1**

53-3 **5** *hd* **Kamra (USA)**[29] 361 5-9-4 **79**....................................(bt) DanielMuscutt 1 75
(Henry Spiller) *in tch on inner: pushed along over 3f out: rdn to chse ldrs 2f out: sn drvn and kpt on same pce* **6/1**

2-02 **6** *1* **Angel Palanas**[49] 44 5-9-0 **82**....................................(p) JonathanFisher(7) 8 74
(K R Burke) *cl up: chal 3f out: rdn over 2f out: drvn over 1f out: grad wknd* **7/2**[2]

40-5 **7** *1* **Top Boy**[26] 433 9-9-0 **75**....................................(v) PaddyMathers 6 64
(Derek Shaw) *chsd ldrs: rdn along wl over 2f out: sn wknd* **33/1**

060- **8** *3¼* **Related**[107] 8892 9-9-1 **76**.................................... PaulMulrennan 2 55
(Paul Midgley) *sn outpcd and a in rr* **33/1**

1-35 **9** *nk* **Black Salt**[27] 407 5-9-1 **76**.................................... LewisEdmunds 10 54
(David Barron) *chsd ldrs on wd outside: hdwy 1/2-way: rdn along over 2f out: sn drvn and btn (trainer's rep said gelding could offer no explanation for the performance)* **11/4**[1]

24-4 **10** *1* **Russian Realm**[27] 407 9-9-3 **78**.................................... GrahamLee 9 53
(Paul Midgley) *chsd ldrs: rdn along 3f out: sn wknd* **16/1**

1m 14.83s (-1.67) **Going Correction** -0.125s/f (Stan) **10** Ran SP% **118.7**
Speed ratings (Par 105): **106,101,101,99,99 97,96,92,91,90**
CSF £71.89 CT £382.18 TOTE £17.30: £4.50, £1.50, £1.60; EX 77.60 Trifecta £507.00.
Owner R G Fell **Bred** Philip And Mrs Jane Myerscough **Trained** Nawton, N Yorks

FOCUS
A competitive handicap run at a sound pace.

833 BETWAY CASINO H'CAP — 1m 4f 14y(F)
4:45 (4:45) (Class 5) (0-75,74) 4-Y-0+ — £3,234 (£962; £481; £240) **Stalls** Low

Form RPR

00-0 **1** **Argus (IRE)**[50] 29 7-8-13 **71**.................................... ThoreHammerHansen(7) 5 79
(Alexandra Dunn) *trckd ldr: hdwy and cl up 3f out: wd st: rdn to chal over 2f out: drvn over 1f out: led ins fnl f: styd on strly towards fin* **10/1**

/-03 **2** *2¾* **Harbour Quay**[26] 435 5-8-13 **64**.................................... PaulMulrennan 1 67
(Robyn Brisland) *set gd pce: pushed along 3f out: rdn wl over 1f out: drvn: edgd lft and hdd 1f out: kpt on same pce* **8/1**

6-01 **3** *7* **Epitaph (IRE)**[22] 481 5-9-0 **65**....................................(v) AndrewMullen 2 57
(Michael Appleby) *in tch: rdn along over 4f out: outpcd over 3f out: sn drvn: styd on u.p fnl f* **7/4**[1]

213- **4** *2* **Mearing**[118] 8597 4-9-4 **74**....................................(p) JamieGormley(3) 7 64
(Iain Jardine) *trckd ldrs: pushed along and hdwy over 4f out: rdn along 3f out: drvn and kpt on one pce fnl 2f* **11/4**[2]

61-2 **5** *¾* **Love Rat**[42] 162 4-8-4 **62**....................................(v) TheodoreLadd(5) 3 50
(Scott Dixon) *chsd ldng pair: pushed along over 3f out: rdn over 2f out: sn drvn and kpt on one pce* **7/2**[3]

660/ **6** *75* **Shades Of Silver**[447] 8505 9-9-4 **72**.................................... BenRobinson(3) 4
(Alexandra Dunn) *a bhd: t.o fnl 3f* **40/1**

2m 37.19s (-3.81) **Going Correction** -0.125s/f (Stan)
WFA 4 from 5yo+ 2lb **6** Ran SP% **107.9**
Speed ratings (Par 103): **107,105,100,99,98 48**
CSF £75.16 TOTE £10.60: £4.80, £4.00; EX 69.10 Trifecta £243.20.
Owner N McCloskey **Bred** Grangecon Stud **Trained** West Buckland, Somerset

FOCUS
The pace was sound for this fair handicap.

834 PLAY 4 TO SCORE AT BETWAY H'CAP — 4f 214y(F)
5:20 (5:20) (Class 6) (0-55,57) 3-Y-0+ — £2,587 (£770; £384; £192) **Stalls** Centre

Form RPR

1121 **1** **Gorgeous General**[8] 702 4-9-3 **55**.................................... WilliamCarver(7) 4 65
(Lawrence Mullaney) *cl up centre: led 2f out: rdn over 1f out: drvn ins fnl f: kpt on wl towards fin* **1/1**[1]

054- **2** *¾* **Twentysvnthlancers**[101] 9031 6-9-11 **56**.................................... PaulMulrennan 1 63
(Paul Midgley) *racd towards centre: chsd ldrs: hdwy over 2f out: rdn to chal over 1f out: ev ch ins fnl f: sn drvn and kpt on same pce last 75yds* **11/1**

060/ **3** *2* **Intense Starlet (IRE)**[142] 7881 8-8-12 **46** oh1.........(p) BenRobinson(3) 2 46
(Brian Ellison) *racd towards far side: in tch: hdwy to chse ldrs over 2f out: rdn whn rdr dropped whip wl over 1f out: chsd ldng pair and edgd rt ins fnl f: kpt on* **12/1**

04-5 **4** *1¾* **Kyllukey**[29] 357 6-8-10 **46** oh1....................................(t) TheodoreLadd(5) 8 40
(Charlie Wallis) *prom centre: rdn along and sltly outpcd wl over 1f out: kpt on u.p fnl f* **11/2**[2]

-245 **5** *½* **Novabridge**[27] 411 11-9-1 **46**....................................(b) CliffordLee 13 38
(Karen Tutty) *racd nr stands' rail: prom: rdn along wl over 1f out: drvn and kpt on same pce fnl f* **25/1**

-051 **6** *½* **Geography Teacher (IRE)**[21] 505 3-8-9 **57**......... JamieGormley(3) 10 41
(Roger Fell) *racd towards stands' rail: sn outpcd and bhd: rdn along 1/2-way: hdwy wl over 1f out: drvn and hung lft ent fnl f: kpt on* **6/1**[3]

7 *3½* **Ascot Dreamer**[69] 9539 3-8-10 **53** ow2............(p[1]) DayversonDeBarros 7 26
(David Brown) *chsd ldrs centre: rdn along over 2f out: grad wknd* **16/1**

-026 **8** *¾* **Champagne Mondays**[18] 585 3-8-6 **51**.................(p) JamesSullivan 11 20
(Scott Dixon) *racd towards stands' side: prom: rdn along over 2f out: grad wknd* **20/1**

060- **9** *1* **Tina Teaspoon**[63] 9648 5-9-1 **46** oh1....................................(h) RaulDaSilva 6 17
(Derek Shaw) *towards rr centre: hdwy 2f out: sn rdn and kpt on fnl f* **50/1**

00-0 **10** *1* **Tally's Song**[28] 379 6-8-8 **46** oh1....................................(p) KeelanBaker(7) 3 13
(Grace Harris) *racd far side: sn outpcd: sme late hdwy* **100/1**

0-50 **11** *2* **Leeshaan (IRE)**[21] 502 4-9-5 **53**.................................... PhilDennis(3) 9 13
(Rebecca Bastiman) *racd towards centre: chsd ldrs: rdn along 1/2-way: sn wknd* **25/1**

500- **12** *3½* **Archie Stevens**[101] 9031 9-9-2 **50**.................................... TimClark(3) 5
(Clare Ellam) *racd centre: led: rdn along and hdd 2f out: sn wknd* **50/1**

/00- **13** *9* **Crikeyitswhykie**[54] 9749 4-9-2 **47**....................................(v[1]) PaddyMathers 12
(Derek Shaw) *dwlt: racd towards stands' side: a outpcd and bhd* **40/1**

59.29s (-0.41) **Going Correction** -0.125s/f (Stan)
WFA 3 from 4yo+ 14lb **13** Ran SP% **121.4**
Speed ratings (Par 101): **98,96,93,90,90 89,83,82,80,79 76,70,56**
CSF £12.67 CT £95.28 TOTE £1.90: £1.40, £2.30, £2.70; EX 14.40 Trifecta £92.40.
Owner Shaun Humphries **Bred** Shaun & Leanne Humphries **Trained** Great Habton, N Yorks

FOCUS
Not a bad race for the grade. The action unfolded middle-to-far side. Routine form in behind the winner.
T/Jkpt: Not won. T/Plt: £153.20 to a £1 stake. Pool: £72,353.41 - 344.61 winning units T/Qpdt: £58.10 to a £1 stake. Pool: £6,798.81 - 86.56 winning units **Joe Rowntree**

[809]WOLVERHAMPTON (A.W) (L-H)
Thursday, February 21

OFFICIAL GOING: Tapeta: standard
Wind: Light behind Weather: Fine

835 BETWAY HEED YOUR HUNCH H'CAP — 1m 1f 104y (Tp)
5:05 (5:05) (Class 6) (0-65,64) 4-Y-0+
£3,105 (£924; £461; £300; £300; £300) **Stalls** Low

Form RPR

400- **1** **Citta D'Oro**[114] 8726 4-9-0 **57**....................................(p[1]) RobHornby 9 63
(James Unett) *chsd ldr 2f: remained handy: led over 2f out: rdn over 1f out: styd on* **28/1**

4-63 **2** *hd* **Duke Of Alba (IRE)**[38] 241 4-9-1 **58**.................................... JoeFanning 3 64
(John Mackie) *a.p: chsd wnr over 2f out: rdn and edgd lft over 1f out: r.o* **7/4**[1]

40-5 **3** *2½* **Kilbaha Lady (IRE)**[7] 724 5-9-4 **61**.................................... JasonHart 10 62
(Nigel Tinkler) *hld up: pushed along and hdwy over 2f out: rdn over 1f out: r.o to go 3rd wl ins fnl f: nt rch ldrs* **15/2**[3]

1-61 **4** *1* **Anif (IRE)**[17] 603 5-9-6 **63**.................................... EoinWalsh 4 62
(David Evans) *led: hdd 6f out: led again over 3f out: hdd over 2f out: sn rdn: styd on same pce fnl f* **11/4**[2]

00-2 **5** *1½* **Zarkavon**[23] 465 5-8-0 **48** ow2.................................... FayeMcManoman(5) 12 45
(John Wainwright) *hld up: pushed along over 2f out: r.o ins fnl f: nvr nrr* **18/1**

3-40 **6** *1¾* **Destinys Rock**[20] 536 4-9-5 **62**.................................... LiamJones 5 55
(Mark Loughnane) *s.i.s: hdwy over 6f out: rdn over 1f out: edgd rt and no ex fnl f* **10/1**

-500 **7** *½* **Clive Clifton (IRE)**[26] 436 6-8-2 **45**....................................(p[1]) KieranO'Neill 8 37
(Mark Brisbourne) *s.i.s: sn mid-div: pushed along 6f out: hdwy over 2f out: rdn over 1f out: styng on same pce whn nt clr run and swtchd lft ins fnl f* **9/1**

50-6 **8** *6* **Doctor Wonderful**[20] 536 4-9-2 **62**.................................... JoshuaBryan(3) 2 43
(Kevin Frost) *s.i.s: hld up: nt clr run over 2f out: nvr on terms* **12/1**

000- **9** *¾* **Vincent's Forever**[55] 8886 6-9-4 **61**.................................... DavidProbert 13 40
(Sophie Leech) *hld up: shkn up over 2f out: n.d* **66/1**

54-5 **10** *1½* **Duchess Of Avon**[28] 386 4-9-5 **62**.................................... HectorCrouch 11 39
(Gary Moore) *hld up in tch: rdn on outer over 2f out: wknd over 1f out* **16/1**

050- **11** *20* **Reshaan (IRE)**[128] 8301 4-9-7 **64**.................................... RossaRyan 1 3
(Alexandra Dunn) *unruly in stalls: chsd ldrs: rdn over 3f out: wknd over 2f out: eased over 1f out* **25/1**

0-00 **12** *5* **Blue Candy**[26] 429 4-8-11 **57**....................(h[1]) GabrieleMalune(3) 7
(Ivan Furtado) *plld hrd and sn prom: led 6f out: hdd over 3f out: wknd 2f out: eased (jockey said gelding ran too freely)* **50/1**

1m 59.62s (-1.18) **Going Correction** +0.025s/f (Slow) 12 Ran SP% **123.5**
Speed ratings (Par 101): **106,105,103,102,101 99,99,94,93,92 74,69**
CSF £78.93 CT £445.76 TOTE £34.40: £5.50, £1.40, £2.70; EX 218.70 Trifecta £1262.30.
Owner P S Burke **Bred** P & Mrs N Burke **Trained** Wolverhampton, West Midlands

FOCUS
Typical form for the grade. The pace lifted mid-race and the time was 3.46sec quicker than the following novice stakes. The second has been rated close to form.

836 BETWAY CASINO NOVICE AUCTION STKS 1m 1f 104y (Tp)
5:40 (5:40) (Class 5) 3-4-Y-O **£3,752** (£1,116; £557; £278) **Stalls** Low

Form RPR
22 **1** **Colony Queen**[27] 403 3-8-2 0.................... KieranO'Neill 1 60
(James Tate) *w ldr tl n.m.r over 7f out: remained handy: shkn up over 3f out: nt clr run and swtchd rt ins fnl f: rdn and r.o to ld post* **4/1**[3]

3-1 **2** *nk* **Paradise Boy (FR)**[36] 259 3-9-0 0.................... RobHornby 3 71
(Andrew Balding) *led at stdy pce: qcknd over 3f out: rdn and hung lft ins fnl f: hdd post* **11/10**[1]

0-03 **3** *hd* **Global Style (IRE)**[29] 364 4-10-0 66.................... GeorgeDowning 7 70
(Tony Carroll) *a.p: chsd ldr 7f out: rdn over 2f out: ev ch ins fnl f: r.o* **14/1**

0- **4** *2 1/2* **Oliver Hardy**[280] 2780 3-8-7 0....................(w) DavidProbert 6 59
(Paul Cole) *prom: rdn over 2f out: styd on: nt pce to chal* **3/1**[2]

5 *1 1/2* **Mi Manchi (IRE)** 3-8-0 0 ow1.................... GabrieleMalune(3) 8 52
(Marco Botti) *s.i.s: hld up: pushed along and hdwy over 2f out: nt trble ldrs* **22/1**

0- **6** *nk* **Truckingby**[120] 8543 3-8-7 0....................(b[1]) JoeFanning 4 55
(Mark Johnston) *s.i.s: sn pushed along and prom: shkn up over 4f out: outpcd over 2f out: kpt on fnl f* **20/1**

7 *1* **Fields Of Dreams** 3-8-7 0.................... EdwardGreatrex 2 53
(Roger Charlton) *s.i.s: hld up: shkn up over 2f out: nt trble ldrs* **12/1**

0-4 **8** *1* **Maiden Navigator**[36] 259 3-7-11 0....................(h) DarraghKeenan(5) 5 46
(David Simcock) *s.i.s: hld up: shkn up and an rn wd turning for home: nvr trbld ldrs* **50/1**

2m 3.08s (2.28) **Going Correction** +0.025s/f (Slow)
WFA 3 from 4yo 21lb 8 Ran SP% **118.0**
Speed ratings (Par 103): **90,89,89,87,86 85,84,83**
CSF £8.94 TOTE £4.00: £1.10, £1.10, £4.40; EX 12.30 Trifecta £56.60.
Owner Saeed Manana **Bred** Mrs J A Cornwell **Trained** Newmarket, Suffolk

FOCUS
This was 3.46sec slower than the preceding Class 6 handicap. The principals were always prominent.

837 BETWAY H'CAP 5f 21y (Tp)
6:10 (6:10) (Class 2) (0-105,107) 4-Y-O+ **£12,291** (£3,657; £1,827; £913) **Stalls** Low

Form RPR
3-03 **1** **Boom The Groom (IRE)**[19] 551 8-8-3 **87**.................... LiamJones 6 93
(Tony Carroll) *a.p: plld hrd early: rdn to ld and edgd lft ins fnl f: r.o* **8/1**

-121 **2** *1/2* **Shamshon (IRE)**[23] 470 8-8-4 **88**.................... KieranO'Neill 8 92
(Stuart Williams) *hld up: swtchd lft sn after s: hdwy 2f out: rdn and swtchd lft ins fnl f: nt rch wnr* **3/1**[1]

5-10 **3** *1* **Tropics (USA)**[30] 352 11-9-3 **104**....................(h) JackDuern(3) 5 105
(Dean Ivory) *sn pushed along to join ldr: rdn to ld over 1f out: hdd ins fnl f: edgd lft: no ex nr fin* **20/1**

00-0 **4** *nk* **Lancelot Du Lac (ITY)**[19] 563 9-9-9 **107**....................(h) AdamKirby 3 108
(Dean Ivory) *prom: nt clr run and lost pl over 4f out: shkn up over 1f out: rdn: edgd lft and r.o ins fnl f* **15/2**[3]

45-6 **5** *1 1/4* **Mokaatil**[23] 470 4-8-3 **87**.................... JoeFanning 4 82
(Ian Williams) *s.i.s: hld up: nt clr run and swtchd rt ins fnl f: r.o: nt trble ldrs* **17/2**

2-04 **6** *nk* **Foxy Forever (IRE)**[19] 551 9-8-2 **86**....................(bt) CamHardie 7 80
(Michael Wigham) *prom: ct out wd: shkn up and lost pl 2f out: n.d after* **14/1**

1-44 **7** *hd* **Orvar (IRE)**[28] 393 6-9-1 **99**.................... LukeMorris 2 94
(Paul Midgley) *led 1f: chsd ldrs: rdn and ev ch 1f out: styng on same pce whn hmpd wl ins fnl f* **7/2**[2]

001- **8** *2* **Doctor Sardonicus**[62] 9667 8-9-9 **107**.................... AlistairRawlinson 1 93
(Tom Dascombe) *slipped s: rcvrd to ld after 1f: rdn and hdd over 1f out: wknd wl ins fnl f (jockey said gelding was slowly into stride)* **3/1**[1]

1m 0.25s (-1.65) **Going Correction** +0.025s/f (Slow) 8 Ran SP% **117.1**
Speed ratings (Par 109): **114,113,111,111,109 108,108,105**
CSF £33.10 CT £472.30 TOTE £7.30: £2.10, £1.30, £6.60; EX 37.80 Trifecta £403.60.
Owner B J Millen **Bred** John Foley **Trained** Cropthorne, Worcs

FOCUS
A classy sprint handicap run at a strong gallop, in a time only 0.65sec outside the standard.

838 LADBROKES, HOME OF THE ODDS BOOST H'CAP 6f 20y (Tp)
6:40 (6:40) (Class 3) (0-90,92) 3-Y-O **£7,439** (£2,213; £1,106; £553) **Stalls** Low

Form RPR
24-1 **1** **Liberation Day**[33] 316 3-8-9 **77**....................(p[1]) DavidProbert 7 80
(Tom Dascombe) *chsd ldr after 1f: rdn to ld wl ins fnl f: r.o* **11/2**[3]

2335 **2** *nk* **Uncle Jerry**[18] 588 3-8-12 **83**....................(b) FinleyMarsh(3) 4 85
(Richard Hughes) *chsd ldrs: rdn over 1f out: r.o* **9/2**[2]

2-11 **3** *3/4* **Coolagh Magic**[21] 506 3-8-13 **81**....................(p) PaulHanagan 2 81+
(Richard Fahey) *awkward leaving stalls: hld up: shkn up and swtchd rt 1f out: r.o wl ins fnl f: wnt 3rd post: nt rch ldrs (jockey said colt anticipated the start and as a result was slowly away)* **5/2**[1]

140- **4** *shd* **Oberyn Martell**[182] 6455 3-9-3 **92**.................... GeorgiaDobie(7) 6 91
(Eve Johnson Houghton) *led: rdn over 1f out: hdd wl ins fnl f* **10/1**

-324 **5** *nk* **Beleaguerment (IRE)**[36] 261 3-8-10 **78**....................(b) EdwardGreatrex 3 76+
(Archie Watson) *hld up: rdn over 1f out: r.o ins fnl f: nt rch ldrs* **10/1**

341- **6** *1/2* **Fares Kodiac (IRE)**[100] 9037 3-9-7 **89**.................... MarcMonaghan 5 86
(Marco Botti) *plld hrd in 2nd pl 1f: remained handy: rdn over 1f out: styd on same pce ins fnl f* **9/2**[2]

21-3 **7** *1* **Klass Action (IRE)**[41] 182 3-8-9 **77**....................(p[1]) LukeMorris 8 71
(Sir Mark Prescott Bt) *hld up: rdn over 1f out: styd on same pce wl ins fnl f* **8/1**

510- **8** *4* **Lovin (USA)**[143] 7851 3-9-2 **84**.................... DanielTudhope 1 65
(David O'Meara) *prom: rdn over 1f out: wknd and eased ins fnl f* **12/1**

1m 15.09s (0.59) **Going Correction** +0.025s/f (Slow) 8 Ran SP% **117.3**
Speed ratings (Par 101): **97,96,95,95,95 94,93,87**
CSF £31.26 CT £78.24 TOTE £5.50: £1.40, £1.90, £2.00; EX 40.10 Trifecta £143.20.
Owner Fdcholdings Nolan Rcg Rutherford **Bred** Horizon Bloodstock Limited **Trained** Malpas, Cheshire

FOCUS
Fair handicap form.

839 LADBROKES H'CAP 1m 1f 104y (Tp)
7:10 (7:10) (Class 4) (0-85,82) 3-Y-O **£5,530** (£1,645; £822; £411) **Stalls** Low

Form RPR
4-31 **1** **War Tiger (USA)**[31] 343 3-9-7 **82**.................... TonyHamilton 3 88+
(Richard Fahey) *chsd ldr 1f: dropped to rr over 6f out: hdwy on outer over 2f out: shkn up to ld 1f out: r.o: comf* **8/11**[1]

2-21 **2** *3/4* **Gantier**[17] 598 3-9-4 **79**....................(b) KieranO'Neill 4 82
(John Gosden) *s.i.s: pushed along to chse ldr after 1f: rdn over 2f out: ev ch over 1f out: styd on* **3/1**[2]

5-21 **3** *3 1/4* **Water's Edge (IRE)**[20] 518 3-9-5 **80**.................... AdamKirby 2 76
(James Tate) *hld up: hdwy to go 3rd over 6f out: shkn up and swtchd lft over 1f out: sn rdn and ev ch: no ex ins fnl f* **4/1**[3]

5-02 **4** *2* **Smoki Smoka (IRE)**[24] 461 3-8-9 **70**.................... LukeMorris 1 62
(Tom Dascombe) *led: qcknd 3f out: rdn: hung lft and hdd over 1f out: wknd ins fnl f* **12/1**

1m 59.19s (-1.61) **Going Correction** +0.025s/f (Slow) 4 Ran SP% **110.6**
Speed ratings (Par 99): **108,107,104,102**
CSF £3.32 TOTE £1.60; EX 3.40 Trifecta £7.80.
Owner Mrs Richard Henry **Bred** Premier Bloodstock **Trained** Musley Bank, N Yorks

FOCUS
An interesting handicap, and the quickest of the three races over the trip.

840 SUNRACING.CO.UK H'CAP 7f 36y (Tp)
7:40 (7:40) (Class 5) (0-75,77) 4-Y-O+
£3,752 (£1,116; £557; £300; £300; £300) **Stalls** High

Form RPR
3-54 **1** **Gabrial The Tiger (IRE)**[24] 463 7-9-1 **69**.................... PaulHanagan 4 74
(Richard Fahey) *led: shkn up and hdd over 1f out: rallied to ld wl ins fnl f: r.o* **9/2**[3]

3/0- **2** *1/2* **Call Me Grumpy (IRE)**[84] 9309 5-9-7 **75**....................(b[1]) LukeMorris 2 79
(Roger Varian) *s.i.s: hld up: hdwy over 2f out: shkn up to ld over 1f out: rdn and hdd wl ins fnl f* **11/8**[1]

026- **3** *hd* **Mr Minerals**[72] 9494 5-9-9 **77**....................(t) RossaRyan 5 80
(Alexandra Dunn) *hld up: hdwy over 1f out: r.o u.p* **12/1**

-214 **4** *1 1/4* **Dark Alliance (IRE)**[23] 466 8-8-12 **71**.................... MeganNicholls(5) 1 71
(Mark Loughnane) *plld hrd: trckd wnr tl over 5f out: remained handy: shkn up over 1f out: styd on (jockey said gelding ran too freely)* **2/1**[2]

0-00 **5** *2 1/2* **Highly Sprung (IRE)**[28] 381 6-9-3 **74**.................... ConorMcGovern(3) 6 67
(Les Eyre) *chsd wnr over 5f out tl rdn over 1f out: styd on same pce* **40/1**

4-40 **6** *2 1/4* **Malaspina (ITY)**[21] 499 7-9-2 **73**.................... GabrieleMalune(3) 8 60
(Ivan Furtado) *hdwy over 5f out: rdn over 1f out: edgd lft and styd on same pce* **20/1**

200- **7** *9* **Showdance Kid**[189] 6204 5-8-10 **64**.................... JasonHart 3 27
(Kevin Frost) *prom: lost pl over 5f out: wknd over 1f out* **14/1**

1m 28.45s (-0.35) **Going Correction** +0.025s/f (Slow) 7 Ran SP% **115.2**
Speed ratings (Par 103): **103,102,102,100,97 95,85**
CSF £11.31 CT £68.14 TOTE £3.20: £1.80, £1.90; EX 12.90 Trifecta £56.60.
Owner Dr Marwan Koukash **Bred** Kenneth Heelan **Trained** Musley Bank, N Yorks

FOCUS
Ordinary handicap form.

841 FOLLOW SUN RACING ON TWITTER NOVICE STKS 7f 36y (Tp)
8:10 (8:10) (Class 5) 3-Y-O+ **£4,237** (£1,260; £630; £315) **Stalls** High

Form RPR
1 **Masked Identity** 4-10-0 0.................... JoeFanning 4 80+
(Kevin Frost) *s.i.s: hld up: hdwy on outer over 2f out: swtchd lft over 1f out: shkn up to ld ins fnl f: r.o wl: comf* **10/1**

2 **2** *1 1/4* **Plumette**[40] 211 3-8-6 0.................... BarryMcHugh 2 66
(Richard Fahey) *led: shkn up over 1f out: rdn and hdd ins fnl f: styd on same pce* **8/13**[1]

-053 **3** *1 3/4* **Twpsyn (IRE)**[26] 431 3-8-11 67.................... EoinWalsh 5 66
(David Evans) *chsd ldrs: rdn over 1f out: styd on same pce* **12/1**

5-0 **4** *nk* **Remembering You (IRE)**[33] 313 3-8-6 0.................... DavidProbert 7 60
(Clive Cox) *prom: chsd ldr over 5f out: rdn and ev ch wl over 1f out: edgd lft and no ex wl ins fnl f* **28/1**

0 **5** *3 1/2* **April Wine**[28] 380 3-8-6 0.................... LukeMorris 6 51
(Clive Cox) *hld up in tch: rdn over 2f out: hung lft and no ex fr over 1f out* **13/2**[3]

6 *2 1/4* **Sharrabang** 3-8-9 0 ow1.................... FinleyMarsh(3) 3 51
(Stella Barclay) *s.i.s: hld up: shkn up over 2f out: n.d* **66/1**

4-4 **7** *1 3/4* **Paddy's Pursuit (IRE)**[33] 316 3-8-11 0.................... LiamJones 1 45
(Mark Loughnane) *plld hrd and prom: rdn over 2f out: wknd over 1f out* **5/1**[2]

1m 29.49s (0.69) **Going Correction** +0.025s/f (Slow)
WFA 3 from 4yo 17lb 7 Ran SP% **113.6**
Speed ratings (Par 103): **97,95,93,93,89 86,84**
CSF £16.52 TOTE £9.00: £4.70, £1.10; EX 24.40 Trifecta £141.90.
Owner D S Lovatt **Bred** Cheveley Park Stud Ltd **Trained** Newcastle-under-Lyme, Staffs

FOCUS
A modest novice event.
T/Plt: £47.60 to a £1 stake. Pool: £72,686.23 - 1,112.91 winning units T/Qpdt: £15.10 to a £1 stake. Pool: £6,972.76 - 340.54 winning units **Colin Roberts**

725 MEYDAN (L-H)
Thursday, February 21

OFFICIAL GOING: Dirt: fast; turf: good

842a JAGUAR F PACE (H'CAP) (DIRT) 7f (D)
2:30 (2:30) (90-105,104) 3-Y-O+
£63,779 (£21,259; £10,629; £5,314; £3,188; £2,125)

RPR
1 **Rodaini (USA)**[11] 681 5-8-13 **97**....................(t) ConnorBeasley 3 108
(A bin Harmash, UAE) *chased leaders, rdn to ld 1f out, ran on well* **6/1**

2 *shd* **Moqarrab (USA)**[164] 7129 4-8-9 **94** ow1.................... DaneO'Neill 10 104+
(M Al Mheiri, UAE) *settled rear, ran on wl fnl 1 1/2f, nrst finish* **12/1**

3 *1 3/4* **Almanaara (IRE)**[7] 729 6-8-9 **94**....................(v) JimCrowley 4 99
(Doug Watson, UAE) *soon led, kicked clr 2 1/2f out, hdd 1f out, wknd fnl 100yds* **7/1**

The Form Book Flat 2019, Raceform Ltd, Newbury, RG14 5SJ

4 2 **Nine Below Zero**[7] 729 4-9-1 **99** AdriedeVries 2 100
(Fawzi Abdulla Nass, Bahrain) *mid-division, chsd leaders and ev ch 2 1/2f out, ran on same pace fnl 2f* **4/1**[3]

5 1 1/4 **Bochart**[21] 513 6-8-10 **95** (t) RichardMullen 5 91
(S Seemar, UAE) *tracked ldr til wknd fnl 1 1/2f* **3/1**[1]

6 1/2 **Aqabah (USA)**[21] 515 4-9-0 **98** JamesDoyle 8 94+
(Charlie Appleby) *mid-division, ran on same pace fnl 3f* **8/1**

7 1 3/4 **Gold Town**[21] 513 4-9-6 **104** (b) WilliamBuick 6 95
(Charlie Appleby) *never nr to challenge* **7/2**[2]

8 1 **Trickbag (USA)**[14] 640 5-8-13 **98** ow3 (vt) CarlosLopez 9 85
(Susanne Berneklint, Sweden) *always in rear* **40/1**

9 5 3/4 **Honorable Treasure (USA)**[21] 513 4-9-2 **100** (bt) FernandoJara 1 73
(Kenneth McPeek, U.S.A) *slowly into strd, al in rear* **25/1**

10 1 1/4 **Good Effort (IRE)**[14] 640 4-8-10 **95** FabriceVeron 7 64
(Ismail Mohammed) *slowly into strd, mid-division, chsd leaders 2 1/2f out, one pace fnl 1 1/2f* **20/1**

1m 25.26s (0.16) **Going Correction** +0.50s/f (Slow) **10** Ran SP% **123.9**
Speed ratings: **119,118,116,114,113 112,110,109,102,101**
CSF: 77.91; TRICAST: 543.37.

Owner Abdullah Saeed Al Naboodah **Bred** Greenwood Lodge Farm **Trained** United Arab Emirates

FOCUS
TRAKUS (metres travelled compared to winner): 2nd +12, 3rd 0, 4th -1, 5th +7, 6th +10, 7th +4, 8th +8, 9th +2, 10th +5. A good, competitive handicap run at a strong pace leading to a slow finish: 24.04 (400m from standing start), 22.6 (800m), 24.98 (1200m), 13.64 (line). It's been rated around the winner, third and fourth.

843a LAND ROVER DISCOVERY (H'CAP) (TURF) 6f
3:05 (3:05) (95-108,107) 3-Y-O+

£63,779 (£21,259; £10,629; £5,314; £3,188; £2,125)

RPR

1 **Ekhtiyaar**[49] 52 5-8-13 **100** JimCrowley 2 116
(Doug Watson, UAE) *chased ldr, led 1 1/2f out, ran on well* **7/2**[1]

2 5 1/4 **Riflescope (IRE)**[19] 574 6-8-7 **95** (tp) RichardMullen 7 93
(S Seemar, UAE) *slowly into strd, settled rear, smooth prog 2 1/2f out, ran on wl fnl 2f but no ch wth winner* **7/2**[1]

3 2 1/4 **Dream Today (IRE)**[14] 639 4-8-10 **98** (tp) ChrisHayes 4 89
(Jamie Osborne) *tracked ldr, ev ch 2 1/2f out, ran on same pace fnl 2f* **11/2**[2]

4 nk **Legendary Lunch (IRE)**[11] 681 5-9-0 **101** AdriedeVries 10 92
(Fawzi Abdulla Nass, Bahrain) *chased ldr, ev ch 2f out, ran on same pace fnl 1f* **7/2**[1]

5 1 1/2 **Another Batt (IRE)**[14] 639 4-9-6 **107** ConnorBeasley 6 93
(George Scott) *mid-division, ran on same pace fnl 3f* **12/1**[3]

6 nk **Alfredo Arcano (IRE)**[14] 639 5-8-7 **95** (t) BenCurtis 8 79
(David Marnane, Ire) *chased ldr, ran on same pace fnl 2 1/2f* **16/1**

7 1 **Glenamoy Lad**[7] 729 5-8-7 **95** (t) FrannyNorton 12 76
(Michael Wigham) *never better than mid-division* **12/1**[3]

8 1/2 **Quayside**[105] 8965 4-8-9 **97** (bt) TadhgO'Shea 14 76
(S Seemar, UAE) *soon led, hdd and wknd fnl 1 1/2f* **33/1**

9 1 3/4 **Love Dreams (IRE)**[21] 515 5-8-7 **95** (b) RoystonFfrench 3 69
(Mark Johnston) *always in rear* **33/1**

10 9 1/4 **Log Out Island (IRE)**[97] 9117 6-9-5 **106** AntonioFresu 13 51
(S Seemar, UAE) *chased ldr til wknd 2 1/2f out* **50/1**

11 nk **Double Up**[14] 639 8-8-7 **95** (v) SamHitchcott 1 38
(Ian Williams) *always in rear* **33/1**

12 1 **Never Back Down (IRE)**[14] 640 4-8-9 **97** (v) PatCosgrave 5 37
(Hugo Palmer) *always in rear* **33/1**

13 12 **Fas (IRE)**[14] 640 5-8-10 **98** OisinMurphy 9
(Mme Pia Brandt, France) *never better than mid-division* **12/1**[3]

14 6 3/4 **Intisaab**[14] 639 8-9-5 **106** (v) JamesDoyle 11
(David O'Meara) *never better than mid-division* **25/1**

1m 10.18s (1.18) **Going Correction** +0.50s/f (Yiel) **14** Ran SP% **128.6**
Speed ratings: **112,105,102,101,99 99,97,97,94,82 82,80,64,55**
CSF: 15.09; TRICAST: 71.23.

Owner Hamdan Al Maktoum **Bred** James Ortega Bloodstock **Trained** United Arab Emirates

FOCUS
A strongly run sprint handicap: 24.21, 21.88, 24.07.

844a DUBAI MILLENNIUM STKS SPONSORED BY JAGUAR (GROUP 3) (TURF) 1m 2f
3:40 (3:40) 3-Y-O+

£94,488 (£31,496; £15,748; £7,874; £4,724; £3,149)

RPR

1 **Spotify (FR)**[28] 398 5-9-0 109 (p) JamesDoyle 3 110
(Charlie Appleby) *soon led, kicked clr 2 1/2f out, ran on wl, jst hld on* **8/1**

2 shd **Racing History (IRE)**[28] 395 7-9-0 111 (v) ChristopheSoumillon 2 110
(Saeed bin Suroor) *tracked ldr, ran on wl fnl 1 1/2f, jst failed* **5/1**[2]

3 1 1/2 **First Nation**[35] 284 5-9-0 109 WilliamBuick 5 107+
(Charlie Appleby) *mid-division, chsd ldr and ev ch 3f out, one pace fnl 1 1/2f* **10/11**[1]

4 nse **Team Talk**[21] 514 6-9-0 109 (h) PatCosgrave 7 107+
(Saeed bin Suroor) *never nr to chal but ran on wl fnl 1 1/2f, nrst finish* **14/1**

5 1 **Oasis Charm**[21] 514 5-9-0 108 (p) BrettDoyle 6 105
(Charlie Appleby) *tracked ldr, keen, ev ch 2f out, wknd fnl 1f* **8/1**

6 2 3/4 **Muzdawaj**[19] 572 6-9-0 96 JimCrowley 1 99
(M Al Mheiri, UAE) *never better than mid-division* **33/1**

7 1/2 **Vintager**[215] 5221 4-8-13 112 ColmO'Donoghue 8 98
(Charlie Appleby) *never nr to challenge* **13/2**[3]

8 8 **Connect**[14] 637 4-8-13 100 (h) ConnorBeasley 4 82
(A bin Harmash, UAE) *never better than mid-division* **50/1**

2m 5.55s (2.85) **Going Correction** +0.50s/f (Yiel) **8** Ran SP% **116.2**
Speed ratings: **108,107,106,106,105 103,103,96**
CSF: 48.30.

Owner Godolphin **Bred** Wertheimer & Frere **Trained** Newmarket, Suffolk

FOCUS
TRAKUS: 2nd 0, 3rd +4, 4th +3, 5th +4, 6th +1, 7th +1, 8th +8. The winner jogged round in an uncontested lead before sprinting home: 27.7, 25.54, 25.83, 23.78, 22.7. The standard is set by the first two and sixth.

845a UAE OAKS SPONSORED BY RANGE ROVER (GROUP 3) (FILLIES) (DIRT) 1m 1f 110y(D)
4:15 (4:15) 3-Y-O

£118,110 (£39,370; £19,685; £9,842; £5,905; £3,937)

RPR

1 **Divine Image (USA)**[21] 510 3-9-0 97 WilliamBuick 4 94+
(Charlie Appleby) *mid-division, smooth prog 3f out, kpt on wl fnl 2f, led cl home* **5/6**[1]

2 nk **Swift Rose (IRE)**[21] 510 3-9-0 79 (p) HayleyTurner 2 89
(Saeed bin Suroor) *soon led, kicked clr 2 1/2f out, kpt on wl but hdd fnl 50m* **40/1**

3 3 1/2 **Razeena (CAN)**[21] 510 3-9-0 79 PatDobbs 11 82
(Doug Watson, UAE) *mid-division, chsd leaders and ev ch 3f out, kpt on same pace fnl 2f* **40/1**

4 2 **Habah (USA)**[21] 510 3-9-0 81 SamHitchcott 8 78
(Doug Watson, UAE) *slowly into strd, nvr nr to chal but kpt on wl fnl 2 1/2f* **40/1**

5 nk **Al Hayette (USA)**[21] 510 3-9-0 95 (h) FabriceVeron 6 77
(Ismail Mohammed) *never nr to chal but kpt on fnl 2 1/2f* **12/1**[3]

6 1 3/4 **Al Shamkhah (USA)**[21] 510 3-9-0 83 (b) MickaelBarzalona 1 74
(S Jadhav, UAE) *mid-division, kpt on same pace fnl 2 1/2f* **25/1**

7 2 1/2 **Starry Eyes (USA)**[21] 510 3-9-0 90 PatCosgrave 7 69
(Simon Crisford) *never better than mid-division* **25/1**

8 2 **Silva (IRE)**[21] 510 3-9-0 104 OisinMurphy 9 64
(Mme Pia Brandt, France) *tracked ldr til wknd fnl 2 1/2f* **13/8**[2]

9 20 **Dream With You (FR)**[42] 168 3-9-0 83 (t) AdriedeVries 5 23
(N Caullery, France) *never better than mid-division* **66/1**

10 1 3/4 **Mulhima (IRE)**[21] 510 3-9-0 85 ConnorBeasley 10 20
(A bin Harmash, UAE) *tracked leaders til wknd fnl 2f* **66/1**

11 dist **Dubai Beauty (IRE)**[21] 510 3-9-0 95 (h) ChristopheSoumillon 3
(Saeed bin Suroor) *slowly into strd, nvr nr to chal, virtually pld up 3 1/2f out* **20/1**

2m 1.76s (2.96) **Going Correction** +0.50s/f (Slow) **11** Ran SP% **123.1**
Speed ratings: **108,107,104,103,103 101,99,98,82,80**
CSF:55.56.

Owner Godolphin **Bred** Peter Magnier **Trained** Newmarket, Suffolk

FOCUS
TRAKUS: 2nd -9, 3rd +16, 4th -4, 5th +6, 6th -7, 7th +17, 8th +1, 9th 0, 10th +14, 11th -1. They went fast early and finished slowly: 25.53 (400m from standing start), 24.22 (800m), 24.61 (1200m), 26.75 (1600m) - the winner's final quarter was 26.93. The final time was the second slowest over C&D from 43 races to date, only better than the 2017 Oaks won by Nomorerichblondes.

846a ZABEEL MILE SPONSORED BY AL TAYER MOTORS (GROUP 2) (TURF) 1m
4:50 (4:50) 3-Y-O+

£118,110 (£39,370; £19,685; £9,842; £5,905; £3,937)

RPR

1 **Mythical Magic (IRE)**[28] 397 4-9-0 106 WilliamBuick 2 115
(Charlie Appleby) *mid-division, smooth prog 3 1/2f out, led 2f out, ran on wl, easily* **5/2**[2]

2 3 **Century Dream (IRE)**[124] 8407 5-9-0 116 (t) OisinMurphy 8 108
(Simon Crisford) *tracked ldr, led 5f out, hdd 2f out but ran on well* **15/8**[1]

3 3/4 **First Contact (IRE)**[28] 395 4-9-0 107 ColmO'Donoghue 5 106+
(Charlie Appleby) *tracked leaders, ev ch 3 1/2f out, ran on same pace fnl 2f* **12/1**

4 hd **Wootton (FR)**[117] 8662 4-9-0 112 JamesDoyle 6 106+
(Charlie Appleby) *never nr to chal but ran on fnl 2 1/2f* **7/2**[3]

5 2 1/4 **Marinaresco (SAF)**[28] 397 6-9-0 115 (b) BernardFayd'Herbe 7 101
(M F De Kock, South Africa) *settled rear, smooth prog 2 1/2f out, ev ch 2f out, wknd fnl 1f* **14/1**

6 3/4 **Janoobi (SAF)**[7] 726 5-9-0 109 JimCrowley 1 99+
(M F De Kock, South Africa) *never better than mid-division* **33/1**

7 6 1/4 **Comin' Through (AUS)**[28] 397 5-9-3 115 (bt) PatCosgrave 4 89
(Chris Waller, Australia) *never better than mid-division* **40/1**

8 8 1/2 **Championship (IRE)**[28] 397 8-9-0 110 (t) ConnorBeasley 3 65
(A bin Harmash, UAE) *never better than mid-division* **12/1**

9 2 **Top Score**[14] 639 5-9-0 107 (tp) ChristopheSoumillon 9 60
(Saeed bin Suroor) *soon led, hdd 5f out, sn beaten* **16/1**

1m 36.39s (-1.11) **Going Correction** +0.50s/f (Yiel) **9** Ran SP% **118.9**
Speed ratings: **119,116,115,115,112 112,105,97,95**
CSF: 7.86.

Owner Godolphin **Bred** Peter Kelly And Ms Wendy Daly **Trained** Newmarket, Suffolk

FOCUS
TRAKUS: 2nd -2, 3rd -5, 4th -3, 5th +2, 6th -2, 7th +4, 8th +1, 9th -3. A fair gallop to this Group 2: 24.96, 23.05, 23.98, with the winner home in 24.27. Another small step up from the winner.

847a RANGE ROVER VELAR (H'CAP) (TURF) 1m
5:25 (5:25) (95-105,105) 3-Y-O+

£63,779 (£21,259; £10,629; £5,314; £3,188; £2,125)

RPR

1 **Major Partnership (IRE)**[21] 515 4-8-13 **98** (tp) KevinStott 6 101
(Saeed bin Suroor) *mid-division, smooth prog 2 1/2f out, led 1f out, ran on well* **33/1**

2 nk **Above N Beyond**[21] 515 6-8-13 **98** (vt) ConnorBeasley 8 101
(A bin Harmash, UAE) *tracked ldr, led 2f out, hdd 1f out but ran on well* **12/1**

3 nk **Cliffs Of Capri**[14] 640 5-8-11 **97** (p) PatDobbs 11 98
(Jamie Osborne) *mid-division, ran on wl fnl 1 1/2f, nrst finish* **12/1**

4 1 1/4 **Freescape**[14] 640 4-8-11 **97** (b) WJLee 16 95
(David Marnane, Ire) *mid-division, ran on same pace fnl 2 1/2f* **16/1**

5 shd **Bedouin's Story**[21] 515 4-8-10 **96** PatCosgrave 14 94
(Saeed bin Suroor) *slowly into strd, nvr nr to chal but ran on fnl 2f* **9/2**[2]

6 hd **Forjatt (IRE)**[27] 425 11-9-4 **103** ChrisHayes 15 101
(N Bachalard, UAE) *never nr to chal but ran on wl fnl 1 1/2f* **33/1**

7 nk **Eshtiraak (AUS)**[21] 515 4-8-13 **98** (b) JimCrowley 2 96
(David A Hayes, Australia) *mid-div, ran on same pace fnl 2f* **20/1**

8 1 1/4 **Jaaref (IRE)**[21] 515 6-9-1 **100** DaneO'Neill 3 95
(A R Al Rayhi, UAE) *mid-division, ran on same pace fnl 2 1/2f* **50/1**

9 ½ **Kronprinz (GER)**[14] 637 4-9-1 **100** .... AntonioFresu 10 94
(E Charpy, UAE) *never better than mid-division* 33/1
10 shd **Hors De Combat**[21] 515 8-9-2 **101** .... OisinMurphy 5 94
(Denis Coakley) *never better than mid-division* 14/1
11 ½ **Dark Red (IRE)**[21] 514 7-8-13 **98** ....(b) BenCurtis 9 90
(Ed Dunlop) *never nr to challenge* 33/1
12 hd **Mutawathea**[21] 515 8-8-9 **95** ....(p) FrannyNorton 1 86
(Simon Crisford) *tracked ldr, ev ch 2 1/2f out, wknd fnl 2f* 50/1
13 ½ **Rocket Power**[27] 425 6-8-9 **95** .... MickaelBarzalona 13 85
(A bin Harmash, UAE) *never better than mid-division* 33/1
14 4¼ **Symbolization (IRE)**[14] 637 4-9-6 **105** ....(p) WilliamBuick 4 86
(Charlie Appleby) *soon led, hdd and wknd 2f out* 11/8[1]
15 2¾ **Aurum (IRE)**[49] 52 4-9-0 **99** ....(t) JamesDoyle 12 74
(Charlie Appleby) *never better than mid-division* 14/1
16 10 **Completion (IRE)**[136] 8050 4-8-9 **95** .... BrettDoyle 7 46
(Charlie Appleby) *never better than mid-division* 8/1[3]

1m 37.19s (-0.31) **Going Correction** +0.50s/f (Yiel) 16 Ran SP% **129.4**
Speed ratings: **115,114,114,113,113 112,112,111,110,110 110,110,109,105,102 92**
CSF: 389.15; TRICAST: 5,004.50; PLACEPOT: £57.60 to a £1 stake. QUADPOT: £10.90 to a £1 stake.
Owner Godolphin **Bred** Eyrefield Stud **Trained** Newmarket, Suffolk

FOCUS
TRAKUS: 2nd -1, 3rd -8, 4th -5, 5th -2, 6th -6, 7th -5, 8th -7, 9th +2, 10th -4, 11th 0, 12th -8, 13th 0, 14th -6, 15th -2, 16th -1. Similarly run to the preceding Group 2 but a 0.80sec slower final time: 25.09, 23.5, 24.08, with the winner to the line in 24.37.

823 CHELMSFORD (A.W) (L-H)
Friday, February 22

OFFICIAL GOING: Polytrack: standard (abandoned after race 2 (6.15) due to safety concerns caused by fog)
Wind: Virtually nil Weather: Foggy

848 BET TOTEPLACEPOT AT TOTESPORT.COM H'CAP 5f (P)
5:45 (5:45) (Class 7) (0-50,52) 3-Y-O+ £2,587 (£770; £384; £192) Stalls Low

Form RPR
3-05 1 **Atyaaf**[18] 597 4-9-10 **50** .... PaddyMathers 3 61+
(Derek Shaw) *travelled strly: wl in tch in midfield: upsides ldr 100yds out: sn led and r.o strly* 15/8[1]
0-05 2 1¼ **Roy's Legacy**[4] 787 10-9-5 **45** .... CharlieBennett 1 51
(Shaun Harris) *mde most: hrd pressed and u.p 100yds out: sn hdd and outpcd towards fin* 8/1[3]
000- 3 1 **Pentland Lad (IRE)**[213] 5298 3-8-8 **48** ....(t[1]) StevieDonohoe 5 44
(Charlie Fellowes) *in last quartet after 1f: r.o ins fnl f to snatch 3rd last stride: nt rch ldng pair* 2/1[2]
2300 4 shd **Storm Trooper (IRE)**[18] 597 8-9-5 **45** ....(t) LukeMorris 4 47
(Charlie Wallis) *taken down early: trckd ldrs: chsng ldrs and kpt on same pce fnl 100yds* 14/1
600- 5 1½ **Camino**[115] 8725 6-9-0 **45** .... DylanHogan[(5)] 7 42
(Andi Brown) *last quartet after 1f: r.o ins fnl f: nt rch ldrs* 80/1
0-06 6 1½ **Tilsworth Rose**[8] 718 5-9-5 **45** ....(b[1]) DannyBrock 9 36
(J R Jenkins) *chsd ldrs: rdn over 2f out: wknd ins fnl f* 50/1
2035 7 ½ **Swiss Cross**[21] 531 12-9-5 **52** ....(p) GraceMcEntee[(7)] 8 41
(Phil McEntee) *a midfield: nvr threatened ldrs* 8/1[3]
5000 8 1 **Celerity (IRE)**[2] 811 5-8-12 **45** ....(b) ElishaWhittington[(7)] 10 31
(Lisa Williamson) *prom after 1f: wknd and wl btn ins fnl f* 66/1
-044 9 1½ **Wye Bother (IRE)**[16] 620 3-8-5 **45** ....(tp) RaulDaSilva 6 19
(Milton Bradley) *w ldr: rdn ent fnl 2f: wknd ins fnl f* 20/1
3046 10 1 **Brother In Arms (IRE)**[18] 599 5-9-5 **45** ....(b[1]) TomMarquand 11 22
(Tony Carroll) *outpcd in rr after 1f: nvr involved* 8/1[3]
003- 11 6 **Spring Holly (IRE)**[121] 8542 3-7-13 **46** .... AledBeech[(7)] 12
(Milton Bradley) *a towards rr: nvr involved* 50/1

1m 0.42s (0.22) **Going Correction** -0.025s/f (Stan) 11 Ran SP% **119.5**
WFA 3 from 4yo+ 14lb
Speed ratings (Par 97): **97,95,93,93,90 88,87,86,83,82 72**
CSF £17.49 CT £33.90 TOTE £2.60: £1.10, £2.70, £1.60; EX 15.90 Trifecta £75.50.
Owner Gb Civil Engineering (leicester) Ltd **Bred** Shadwell Estate Company Limited **Trained** Sproxton, Leics

FOCUS
Thick fog meant the runners were only in view for two brief periods on the turn, and for about the last 50yds or so.

849 BET TOTEEXACTA AT TOTESPORT.COM H'CAP 5f (P)
6:15 (6:16) (Class 5) (0-75,74) 4-Y-O+ £3,752 (£1,116; £557; £400; £400; £400) Stalls Low

Form RPR
5-30 1 **Miracle Works**[37] 253 4-9-1 **68** .... TomMarquand 2 80
(Robert Cowell) *t.k.h: hld up in tch in midfield: in ld wl ins fnl f: r.o strly: readily* 11/4[1]
-451 2 2 **Warrior's Valley**[22] 503 4-8-13 **66** ....(tp) StevieDonohoe 3 71
(David C Griffiths) *taken down early: t.k.h: led: hdd ins fnl f: no ex and outpcd towards fin* 6/1[3]
3635 3 nk **Jack The Truth (IRE)**[7] 741 5-9-7 **74** .... LukeMorris 4 78
(George Scott) *t.k.h: chsd ldrs: ev ch and hrd drvn ins fnl f: no ex and outpcd towards fin* 11/4[1]
4-02 4 ¾ **It Must Be Faith**[20] 548 9-9-3 **73** ....(p) JaneElliott[(3)] 1 74
(Michael Appleby) *t.k.h: chsd ldrs: hld in 4th and one pce ins fnl f* 8/1
00-2 5 ½ **Cappananty Con**[27] 433 5-9-7 **74** .... AdamKirby 5 73
(Charlie Wallis) *racd in last pair: 5th and kpt on same pce ins fnl f* 3/1[2]
30-0 6 7 **Hello Girl**[37] 253 4-9-1 **68** .... JFEgan 6 42
(Dean Ivory) *midfield: wd and struggling bnd 2f out: bhd ins fnl f* 20/1
3-50 7 ½ **Hollander**[27] 430 5-8-12 **65** ....(t) AlistairRawlinson 7 37
(Alexandra Dunn) *a outpcd in rr* 25/1

59.8s (-0.40) **Going Correction** -0.025s/f (Stan) 7 Ran SP% **112.3**
Speed ratings (Par 103): **102,98,98,97,96 85,84**
CSF £18.89 TOTE £2.90: £2.00, £3.20; EX 19.90 Trifecta £71.20.
Owner T W Morley **Bred** Worksop Manor Stud **Trained** Six Mile Bottom, Cambs

FOCUS
Again, limited visibility due to fog, and the remainder of the card was abandoned following this race.

850 BET TOTEQUADPOT AT TOTESPORT.COM H'CAP 5f (P)
(6:45) (Class 3) (0-95,) 4-Y-O+ £

851 BET TOTETRIFECTA AT TOTESPORT.COM MAIDEN STKS 1m (P)
(7:15) (Class 5) 3-Y-O+ £

852 BET TOTESWINGER AT TOTESPORT.COM H'CAP 7f (P)
(7:45) (Class 6) (0-65,) 4-Y-O+ £

853 BET TOTESCOOP6 AT TOTESPORT.COM H'CAP 1m 6f (P)
(8:15) (Class 7) (0-50,) 4-Y-O+ £

T/Plt: £3.00 to a £1 stake. Pool: £75,850.56 - 18,007.31 winning units **Steve Payne**

760 LINGFIELD (L-H)
Friday, February 22

OFFICIAL GOING: Polytrack: standard
Wind: Virtually nil Weather: Overcast with sunny spells

854 LADBROKES H'CAP 5f 6y(P)
1:50 (1:50) (Class 5) (0-70,69) 3-Y-O £2,911 (£866; £432; £216) Stalls High

Form RPR
-532 1 **Pink Flamingo**[18] 605 3-9-3 **65** ....(b[1]) JoeFanning 4 67
(Mark Johnston) *mde all: pushed along to qckn tempo over 1f out: rdn out ins fnl f: a in command* 6/4[1]
4-03 2 ¾ **Temple Of Wonder (IRE)**[22] 506 3-9-3 **65** ....(h) LukeMorris 5 64
(Charlie Wallis) *racd in midfield: pushed along over 2f out: rdn and swtchd rt 1f out: r.o wl ins fnl f: nt rch wnr* 10/1
5-16 3 shd **Swiss Chime**[35] 287 3-8-5 **58** .... MeganNicholls[(5)] 8 57
(Dean Ivory) *trckd ldr: rdn along to chse wnr over 1f out: kpt on one pce ins fnl f* 14/1
06-1 4 nse **Kingi Compton**[35] 287 3-9-4 **66** ....(b) EdwardGreatrex 2 65+
(Archie Watson) *dwlt and racd in rr: hdwy on bridle on inner 2f out: sn rdn and kpt on one pce ins fnl f (jockey said gelding jumped awkwardly)* 2/1[2]
46-4 5 ½ **Starchant**[21] 520 3-9-6 **68** .... KieranO'Neill 3 65
(John Bridger) *t.k.h to post: trckd ldr on inner: rdn and unable qck over 1f out: one pce ins fnl f* 14/1
040- 6 ¾ **Dandy Lad (IRE)**[72] 9498 3-9-1 **66** .... FinleyMarsh[(3)] 6 64+
(Richard Hughes) *hld up in last: hdwy u.p 2f out: making prog whn short of room 1f out: sn bdly hmpd ins fnl f: nt rcvr (jockey said gelding was denied a clear run)* 5/1[3]

59.02s (0.22) **Going Correction** -0.05s/f (Stan) 6 Ran SP% **112.4**
Speed ratings (Par 97): **96,94,94,94,93 92**
CSF £17.12 CT £149.64 TOTE £1.90: £1.30, £4.30; EX 9.40.
Owner Lowther Racing & Partner **Bred** Lowther Racing **Trained** Middleham Moor, N Yorks

FOCUS
A modest sprint, dominated by the winner. The second has been rated close to his Southwell form.

855 LADBROKES HOME OF THE ODDS BOOST H'CAP 1m 1y(P)
2:25 (2:25) (Class 6) (0-60,61) 3-Y-O £2,264 (£673; £336; £168) Stalls High

Form RPR
535- 1 **Red Phoenix (IRE)**[84] 9325 3-9-9 **61** .... JoeFanning 10 68
(Mark Johnston) *mde all: rdn along to qckn 2f out: swung wd off home bnd and sn drvn: drifted lft handed u.str.p ins fnl f but a doing enough* 2/1[1]
6-55 2 1 **Shug**[30] 367 3-9-6 **58** .... LiamKeniry 2 63+
(Ed Walker) *settled wl in midfield on inner: swtchd rt gng wl over 2f out: hdwy u.p over 1f out: drvn and styd on wl ins fnl f: no ch w wnr* 16/1
5 3 nk **Duhallow Noelie (IRE)**[27] 524 3-9-2 **61** ....(t) CierenFallon[(7)] 7 65
(Adrian Paul Keatley, Ire) *trckd wnr: rdn and outpcd by wnr 2f out: kpt on one pce ins fnl f* 4/1[3]
000- 4 nk **What Will Be (IRE)**[122] 8496 3-9-7 **59** .... DavidProbert 6 62+
(Olly Murphy) *racd promly in 5th: hdwy into 3rd 2f out: sn drvn to chse wnr over 1f out: one pce fnl f* 5/2[2]
645- 5 2¾ **Lippy Lady (IRE)**[114] 8730 3-8-9 **52** .... RhiainIngram[(5)] 8 49
(Paul George) *walked to post: hld up and racd wd thrght: minor hdwy wdst of all into home st over 1f out: kpt on fnl f* 16/1
005- 6 4½ **Miss Communicate**[53] 9771 3-9-7 **59** .... AdamKirby 3 46
(Lydia Pearce) *racd wl in tch in 4th: pushed along and unable qck 2f out: sn bhd and pushed out fnl f* 14/1
066- 7 hd **Another Reason (IRE)**[116] 8690 3-9-9 **61** .... LukeMorris 5 47
(Olly Murphy) *racd in midfield: pushed along and racd lazily 1/2-way: rdn 2f out: kpt on one pce fnl f* 20/1
00-0 8 2 **Laguna Spirit**[44] 141 3-8-12 **50** .... CharlieBennett 4 32
(Pat Phelan) *dwlt and racd in last: minor hdwy u.p 2f out: n.d (vet reported the filly had lost its left-fore shoe)* 33/1
400- 9 nse **Cauthen (IRE)**[93] 9169 3-9-7 **59** .... RobHornby 9 40
(Ken Cunningham-Brown) *hld up: racd wd: pushed along over 2f out: sn rdn and no imp fr over 1f out* 25/1
302- 10 3½ **Kenoughty (FR)**[162] 7213 3-9-1 **53** ....(p[1]) ShaneKelly 11 26
(Richard Hughes) *hld up: pushed along and dropped to last 2f out: nvr a factor* 8/1
00-0 11 hd **Pinctada**[16] 615 3-8-12 **50** .... KieranO'Neill 1 23
(John Bridger) *trckd ldr: rdn along and lost pl over 2f out: wknd over 1f out* 50/1

1m 38.23s (0.03) **Going Correction** -0.05s/f (Stan) 11 Ran SP% **125.0**
Speed ratings (Par 95): **97,96,95,95,92 88,87,85,85,82 82**
CSF £37.95 CT £130.87 TOTE £2.80: £1.90, £2.80, £1.50; EX 33.90 Trifecta £98.20.
Owner Sheikh Hamdan bin Mohammed Al Maktoum **Bred** Godolphin **Trained** Middleham Moor, N Yorks

FOCUS
An ordinary handicap. The early pace was steady but was gradually wound up by the winner. A minor step up from the winner.

856 SUNRACING.CO.UK H'CAP 7f 1y(P)
3:00 (3:00) (Class 3) (0-90,89) 4-Y-O- **£7,246** (£2,168; £1,084; £542; £270) **Stalls** Low

Form RPR
656- **1** **Maksab (IRE)**[181] 6528 4-8-10 **85**........................... ScottMcCullagh(7) 2 93
(Mick Channon) *trckd ldng pair: pushed along to ld over 1f out: sn drvn and kpt on wl fnl f: a doing enough* **8/1**
015- **2** *nk* **Motajaasid (IRE)**[63] 9656 4-8-1 **76**...............(t) ThoreHammerHansen(7) 4 83
(Richard Hughes) *rn c wdst of all off home bnd 2f out: hdwy u.p into 4th over 1f out: drvn and styd on wl fnl f: nt rch wnr* **6/1**
-235 **3** *2* **Areen Heart (FR)**[16] 623 5-9-6 **88**........................ AdamKirby 1 90
(David O'Meara) *settled wl in midfield: rdn to chse wnr and ev ch over 1f out: kpt on one pce fnl f* **4/1**[1]
0-01 **4** *½* **Mr Scaramanga**[27] 441 5-9-0 **89**........................ LeviWilliams(7) 6 89+
(Simon Dow) *hld up: smooth hdwy onto heels of ldrs 1f out: briefly short of room: pushed out ins fnl f (jockey said horse was denied a clear run)* **11/2**[3]
50-6 **5** *¾* **Sea Fox (IRE)**[27] 441 5-8-13 **88**........................ GinaMangan(7) 5 86
(David Evans) *racd in midfield: niggled along at times: rdn and outpcd 2f out: one pce fnl f* **16/1**
0-51 **6** *¾* **Fuwairt (IRE)**[16] 618 7-8-8 **81**........................ CameronNoble(5) 3 77
(David Loughnane) *restrained in last pair: hdwy on inner u.p 2f out: briefly short of room 1f out: rdn and one pce fnl f* **6/1**
0/2- **7** *1* **Confrontational (IRE)**[28] 418 5-9-1 **83**........................(p) JoeFanning 7 77
(Jennie Candlish) *led: rdn along and strly pressed by rival 2f out: sn hdd and lost pl over 1f out: wknd fnl f* **4/1**[1]
3-36 **8** *1 ¼* **Swift Approval (IRE)**[29] 382 7-9-1 **83**........................(p) SeanLevey 8 73
(Stuart Williams) *chsd ldr: rdn along and lost pl over 1f out: wknd fnl f* **5/1**[2]

1m 22.69s (-2.11) **Going Correction** -0.05s/f (Stan) **8 Ran SP% 117.6**
Speed ratings (Par 107): **110,109,107,106,105 105,103,102**
CSF £56.53 CT £223.47 TOTE £9.20: £3.70, £1.90, £1.90; EX 55.30 Trifecta £409.70.
Owner Capt A Pratt **Bred** D J And Mrs Deer **Trained** West Ilsley, Berks

FOCUS
The leaders took each other on and set an unsustainable gallop. The third has been rated a bit below his sound recent C&D form.

857 BETWAY H'CAP 6f 1y(P)
3:30 (3:30) (Class 6) (0-60,60) 4-Y-O+ **£2,264** (£673; £336; £168) **Stalls** Low

Form RPR
133- **1** **Spirit Of Zebedee (IRE)**[84] 9328 6-9-2 **55**........................(v) JasonHart 1 61
(John Quinn) *trckd ldr: rdn along between rivals to ld wl ins fnl f: drvn clsng stages and strly pressed: jst hld on* **5/1**[2]
-036 **2** *shd* **Dark Magic**[18] 596 5-9-5 **58**........................(b[1]) AdamKirby 8 64+
(Dean Ivory) *hld up in rr: hdwy whn short of room over 1f out: waited for gap to appear between rivals and rdn to chse wnr 1f out: styd on strly: jst failed* **4/1**[1]
115 **3** *½* **Brockey Rise (IRE)**[24] 467 4-8-13 **57**...............(b) KatherineBegley(5) 5 61
(David Evans) *trckd ldng pair: rdn along to chse ldr 2f out: drvn and kpt on one pce ins fnl f* **6/1**
-120 **4** *nk* **African Blessing**[27] 430 6-9-7 **60**........................ KierenFox 6 63
(John Best) *hld up: effrt to cl 2f out: briefly short of room over 1f out: sn drvn and kpt on wl fnl f: no ch w wnr (jockey said gelding was denied a clear run)* **5/1**[2]
-000 **5** *hd* **Tavener**[16] 626 7-9-6 **59**........................(p) DougieCostello 3 62+
(David C Griffiths) *racd in midfield: pushed along 2f out: rdn and no imp over 1f out: kpt on one pce fnl f* **8/1**
30-4 **6** *nk* **Bond Street Beau**[6] 759 4-9-6 **59**........................ DavidProbert 7 61
(Philip McBride) *hld up: pushed along and racd wdst of all off home bnd over 1f out: sn rdn and kpt on fnl f* **7/1**
-122 **7** *½* **Pharoh Jake**[23] 478 11-8-3 **49**........................ EllieMacKenzie(7) 10 49
(John Bridger) *trckd ldr: pushed along and almost upsides ldr 2f out: rdn and ev ch 1f out: wknd fnl f* **25/1**
5-12 **8** *nk* **Holdenhurst**[29] 383 4-9-5 **58**........................ JFEgan 2 57
(Bill Turner) *led: rdn and strly pressed by rival 2f out: drvn and hdd ins fnl f: wknd once hdd* **11/2**[3]
04-5 **9** *1* **Shackled N Drawn (USA)**[35] 298 7-9-2 **55**...................(t) JoeFanning 4 51
(Peter Hedger) *dwlt sltly and rcvrd to r in midfield: rdn along over 1f out: btn whn eased fnl 100yds* **12/1**

1m 11.76s (-0.14) **Going Correction** -0.05s/f (Stan) **9 Ran SP% 118.2**
Speed ratings (Par 101): **98,97,97,96,96 96,95,95,93**
CSF £25.99 CT £125.03 TOTE £4.30: £1.70, £1.30, £2.40; EX 28.30 Trifecta £111.30.
Owner Malcolm Walker **Bred** N Hartery **Trained** Settrington, N Yorks

FOCUS
An open race on paper and in the race itself they finished in a tight bunch. It's hard to imagine the form being any stronger than rated.

858 LADBROKES NOVICE STKS (PLUS 10 RACE) 1m 4f (P)
4:05 (4:05) (Class 5) 3-Y-O **£2,911** (£866; £432; £216) **Stalls** Low

Form RPR
0- **1** **Baltic Song (IRE)**[64] 9637 3-9-2 0........................ KieranO'Neill 4 77+
(John Gosden) *settled wl in 4th: hdwy u.p to chse ldr over 1f out: sn rdn and led wl ins fnl f: kpt up to work* **2/1**[2]
3 **2** *1 ¾* **Alpasu (IRE)**[30] 358 3-8-9 0........................(t) Pierre-LouisJamin(7) 6 74
(Archie Watson) *dwlt and hld up in last: niggled along 6f out: hdwy to take clsr order over 3f out: effrt to cl in 3rd 2f out: rdn and kpt on wl fnl f* **12/1**
2 **3** *3 ¾* **Ydra**[37] 259 3-9-2 0........................ EdwardGreatrex 7 68+
(Archie Watson) *trckd ldr: rdn along to ld over 2f out: drvn and hdd by wnr wl ins fnl f: no ex* **11/1**[3]
5-2 **4** *7* **Top Power (FR)**[47] 103 3-9-2 0........................ RobHornby 2 57
(Andrew Balding) *led: rdn along and hdd over 2f out: sn lost pl over 1f out: wknd fnl f (jockey said colt stopped quickly; trainer's rep could offer no further explanation for the colt's performance)* **4/6**[1]
0- **5** *3* **Surrey Breeze (IRE)**[106] 8956 3-9-2 0........................ HollieDoyle 5 52
(Archie Watson) *restless in stalls: pushed along early: rdn along over 2f out: sn struggling: no imp fnl f (jockey said colt was never travelling)* **25/1**
0 **6** *19* **Enyama (GER)**[37] 259 3-8-11 0........................ DavidProbert 1 17
(Michael Attwater) *settled in midfield: rdn along and unable qck over 2f out: wknd fr over 1f out* **100/1**
4-0 **7** *57* **Astrosparkle**[28] 403 3-8-11 0........................ MarcMonaghan 3
(Mark H Tompkins) *racd in rr: rdn along and dropped to last 6f out: sn t.o (trainer's rep said filly had a breathing problem)* **100/1**

2m 29.61s (-3.39) **Going Correction** -0.05s/f (Stan) **7 Ran SP% 115.2**
Speed ratings (Par 97): **109,107,105,100,98 86,48**
CSF £24.88 TOTE £3.80: £1.10, £4.30; EX 23.20 Trifecta £81.80.
Owner Gestut Ammerland **Bred** Gestut Ammerland **Trained** Newmarket, Suffolk

FOCUS
With the favourite disappointing, this was no more than a fair heat, but it was run at a good gallop. The third has been rated in line with the better view of his latest form.

859 PLAY 4 TO SCORE AT BETWAY H'CAP 1m 4f (P)
4:40 (4:40) (Class 6) (0-65,67) 4-Y-O+ **£2,264** (£673; £336; £84; £84) **Stalls** Low

Form RPR
2-44 **1** **Music Major**[7] 736 6-9-0 **56**........................ CallumShepherd 11 62
(Michael Attwater) *racd in midfield: hdwy u.p to cl on ldrs over 1f out: rdn to ld wl ins fnl f: jst got up* **7/1**[3]
0-05 **2** *nse* **Gendarme (IRE)**[30] 362 4-9-6 **64**........................ RossaRyan 4 71
(Alexandra Dunn) *trckd ldr on inner: rdn along to chse ldr 2f out: drvn to ld 1f out: hdd by wnr wl ins fnl f: rallied wl: jst failed* **25/1**
30-6 **3** *1 ¼* **Vanity Vanity (USA)**[37] 262 4-9-2 **60**........................ ShaneKelly 8 65
(Denis Coakley) *racd in tch in midfield: pushed along 3f out: rdn along in 4th 2f out: responded wl to press ins fnl f and kpt on all the way to the line* **20/1**
26-6 **4** *nk* **Famous Dynasty (IRE)**[48] 85 5-9-5 **61**........................ RobHornby 14 65+
(Michael Blanshard) *hld up: hdwy on bit on inner over 2f out: swtchd rt over 1f out: rdn and styd on wl ins fnl f: nt rch ldng pair* **25/1**
40-6 **4** *dht* **Clovelly Bay (IRE)**[37] 257 8-8-4 **53**........................ CierenFallon(7) 1 57
(Marcus Tregoning) *hld up in tch in 5th on inner: pushed along whn briefly short of room over 1f out: rdn and kpt on wl fnl f* **7/1**[3]
53-0 **6** *½* **Presence Process**[35] 292 5-9-6 **65**........................ PaddyBradley(3) 13 69
(Pat Phelan) *trckd ldr: rdn along and ev ch over 1f out: kpt on one pce fnl f* **14/1**
03-5 **7** *¾* **Chantresse (IRE)**[16] 616 4-9-8 **66**........................(p) DanielMuscutt 9 69
(Mark Usher) *led: rdn along to maintain ld 2f out: drvn and hdd 1f out: no ex fnl f* **20/1**
325- **8** *½* **Enmeshing**[109] 8886 6-9-9 **65**........................ GeorgeWood 5 66
(Alexandra Dunn) *hld up: hdwy u.p on outer over 1f out: sn rdn and unable qck 1f out: plugged on* **16/1**
4-32 **9** *1 ½* **Attain**[28] 404 10-9-1 **64**........................ Pierre-LouisJamin(7) 2 62
(Archie Watson) *racd in midfield: shuffled bk to rr after 4f: rdn along and no imp 2f out: one pce fnl f* **13/2**[2]
4/0- **10** *2* **Cracker Factory**[69] 2108 4-9-9 **67**........................ DavidProbert 7 63
(Alan King) *hld up: swtchd rt on to outer of field 4f out: rdn and little rspnse over 2f out: n.d (jockey said gelding suffered interference after the start)* **10/11**[1]
20-0 **11** *nk* **Betsalottie**[16] 619 6-9-0 **56**........................(p) LiamJones 10 51
(John Bridger) *dwlt and racd in last trio: big forward move arnd outside of field to go 2nd over 6f out: rdn along and lost pl 2f out: wknd fnl f* **33/1**
000- **12** *12* **Wynfaul The Wizard (USA)**[260] 3496 4-8-0 **51** oh6(h) ThoreHammerHansen(7) 3 27
(Laura Morgan) *racd in midfield: rdn along and lost pl 3f out: sn detached* **20/1**
-000 **13** *shd* **Spring Dixie (IRE)**[23] 481 7-8-4 **51** oh6........................ RhiainIngram(5) 12 26
(Natalie Lloyd-Beavis) *hld up: mde forward move arnd outside of field to go 5th over 6f out: rdn and lost pl over 3f out: t.o* **100/1**

2m 32.91s (-0.09) **Going Correction** -0.05s/f (Stan)
WFA 4 from 5yo+ 2lb **13 Ran SP% 129.2**
Speed ratings (Par 101): **98,97,97,96,96 96,96,95,94,93 93,85,85**
WIN: 6.70 Music Major; PL: 7.70 Gendarme 4.70 Vanity Vanity 2.20 Music Major; EX: 237.20; CSF: 180.00; TC: 3383.06; TF: 4179.70 CSF £180.00 CT £3383.06 TOTE £6.70: £2.20, £7.70, £4.70; EX 237.20 Trifecta £4179.70.
Owner The Attwater Partnership **Bred** Kevin Daniel Crabb **Trained** Epsom, Surrey

FOCUS
Ordinary handicap form. The winner has been rated to his recent best.
T/Plt: £354.40 to a £1 stake. Pool: £63,222.62 - 130.20 winning units T/Qpdt: £149.70 to a £1 stake. Pool: £6,615.47 - 32.68 winning units **Mark Grantham**

860 - 867a (Foreign Racing) - See Raceform Interactive

509 CHANTILLY (R-H)
Friday, February 22

OFFICIAL GOING: Polytrack: standard

868a PRIX PIC HARDI (MAIDEN) (3YO COLTS & GELDINGS) (ALL-WEATHER TRACK) (POLYTRACK) 1m (P)
11:25 3-Y-O **£11,261** (£4,504; £3,378; £2,252; £1,126)

RPR
1 **Flambeur (USA)**[120] 3-9-2 0........................ MaximeGuyon 1 79
(C Laffon-Parias, France) **4/5**[1]
2 *nk* **Septems (FR)**[22] 3-9-2 0........................ AurelienLemaitre 8 78
(H-A Pantall, France) **81/10**
3 *¾* **Tribhuvan (FR)**[66] 9601 3-9-2 0........................ GregoryBenoist 7 77
(H-A Pantall, France) **11/1**
4 *nse* **Inattendu (FR)**[124] 8447 3-9-2 0........................ StephanePasquier 3 76
(F Chappet, France) **245/10**
5 *2* **Highest Mountain (FR)** 3-8-11 0........................ AlexisBadel 5 67
(Joseph Tuite) *wl into stride: sn led: urged along and hdd over 1f out: drvn and kpt on same pce fnl f* **111/10**
6 *1 ¼* **Carolingien (FR)**[22] 3-9-2 0........................ ChristopheSoumillon 4 69
(F Vermeulen, France) **5/1**[2]
7 *3 ½* **Ayeth (FR)**[157] 3-9-2 0........................ VincentCheminaud 6 61
(A Fabre, France) **61/10**[3]
8 *8* **Kavakney (BEL)**[22] 3-9-2 0........................ StefaanFrancois 2 43
(Gerard Aidant, France) **81/1**

1m 37.1s **8 Ran SP% 119.0**
PARI-MUTUEL (all including 1 euro stake): WIN 1.80; PLACE 1.20, 1.60, 1.80; DF 6.80;.
Owner Wertheimer & Frere **Bred** Wertheimer & Frere **Trained** Chantilly, France

DOHA

Friday, February 22

OFFICIAL GOING: Turf: good

869a IRISH THOROUGHBRED MARKETING CUP (LOCAL GROUP 2) (4YO+) (TURF) 1m (T)

4:15 4-Y-0+ **£89,763** (£34,645; £17,322; £9,448; £6,299)

RPR

1 **Marianafoot (FR)**[68] 9571 4-9-2 0 ....(t) Pierre-CharlesBoudot 6 102
(J Reynier, France)

2 *nk* **Black Granite (IRE)**[364] 875 7-9-2 0 ....(b) OisinMurphy 3 101
(Jassim Mohammed Ghazali, Qatar)

3 *1* **Top Face (USA)**[477] 6-9-2 0 .... TomLukasek 1 99
(H Al Ramzani, Qatar)

4 *nk* **Diplomat (GER)**[110] 8866 8-9-2 0 .... EddyHardouin 5 98
(Carina Fey, France)

5 *1 1/2* **Vitally Important (IRE)**[364] 875 9-9-2 0 ....(t) RonanThomas 14 95
(H Al Ramzani, Qatar)

6 *1 1/4* **Roman Legend (IRE)**[687] 8-9-2 0 ....(t) GeraldAvranche 7 92
(Jassim Mohammed Ghazali, Qatar)

7 *shd* **Copleys Walk (IRE)**[477] 7-9-2 0 .... CristianDemuro 10 92
(Mohammed Hussain, Qatar)

8 *2 1/2* **Nordic Dream (IRE)**[517] 7416 6-9-2 0 .... J-PGuillambert 2 86
(Jassim Mohammed Ghazali, Qatar)

9 *nk* **Yu Change (JPN)**[56] 6-9-2 0 ....(b) RyuAbe 15 85
(Hideyuki Mori, Japan)

10 *2* **Al Mohalhal (IRE)**[364] 875 6-9-2 0 ....(p) Jean-BaptisteHamel 11 81
(R Al Jehani, Qatar)

11 *10 1/2* **Warring States (JPN)**[600] 4422 5-9-2 0 .... HarryBentley 12 57
(Mohammed Jassim Ghazali, Qatar)

12 *shd* **Salateen**[48] 89 7-9-2 0 ....(t) JamesDoyle 8 56
(David O'Meara) *prom: trckd front rnk: pushed along appr 3f out: sn rdn and no rspnse: wl bhd whn eased fnl 150yds*

13 *hd* **Topsy Turvy (IRE)**[364] 875 7-9-2 0 ....(b) EduardoPedroza 4 56
(Ibrahim Al Malki, Qatar)

14 *3 3/4* **Hammerindown (USA)**[805] 8299 8-9-2 0 .... AmurAlRasbi 9 47
(Mohamed Al Farsi, Oman)

1m 35.53s **14** Ran

Owner Jean-Claude Seroul **Bred** J C Seroul **Trained** France

870 - 875a (Foreign Racing) - See Raceform Interactive

854 LINGFIELD (L-H)

Saturday, February 23

OFFICIAL GOING: Polytrack: standard

Wind: LIGHT, ACROSS Weather: SUNNY

876 BETWAY LIVE CASINO H'CAP 1m 2f (P)

1:30 (1:30) (Class 5) (0-70,71) 4-Y-0+ **£2,911** (£866; £432; £216) **Stalls** Low

Form RPR

21-3 1 **Rakematiz**[24] 473 5-9-6 **69** .... CallumShepherd 3 77
(Brett Johnson) *trckd ldrs: effrt on inner over 1f out: sn led: hdd ins fnl f: battled bk wl u.p to ld again last strides* **7/2**[2]

114- 2 *hd* **Hackbridge**[73] 9505 4-9-4 **70** .... PaddyBradley(3) 6 77
(Pat Phelan) *hld up in tch in midfield on outer: clsd to trck ldrs: effrt to chal ent fnl f: led ins fnl f: kpt on wl but hdd and no ex last strides* **5/1**[3]

1-21 3 *1 1/4* **Narjes**[24] 473 5-9-8 **71** ....(h) LukeMorris 9 75
(Laura Mongan) *dwlt and rousted along leaving stalls: towards rr: clsng but nt clr run over 2f out: hdwy on inner to chse ldrs over 1f out: kpt on ins fnl f: nvr quite enough pce to get on terms* **13/2**

000- 4 *3/4* **Time Zone**[68] 9588 5-9-4 **67** .... HollieDoyle 11 70
(Louise Allan) *led to s: midfield: hdwy but v wd first bnd: led over 7f out: pushed along and hdd ent fnl f: no ex: hung lft and outpcd ins fnl f (jockey said gelding hung left-handed in the straight)* **25/1**

21-0 5 *1/2* **Chetan**[45] 138 7-9-4 **67** .... TomMarquand 7 69
(Tony Carroll) *mounted in chute and taken down early: chsd ldr tl over 8f out: styd prom tl outpcd u.p 2f out: swtchd rt and rallied ins fnl f: kpt on but no threat to ldrs (vet reported gelding lost its left-hind shoe)* **16/1**

4-04 6 *1 1/4* **Makambe (IRE)**[24] 473 4-9-6 **69** .... JoeyHaynes 4 68
(Paul Howling) *hld up in tch: effrt and edging lft jst over 1f out: kpt on u.p ins fnl f: no threat to ldrs* **8/1**

1-43 7 *2 1/2* **Tobacco Road (IRE)**[9] 724 9-8-11 **60** ....(t) WilliamCarson 10 54
(Mark Pattinson) *hld up in last pair: nt clr run and sltly impeded ent fnl 2f: swtchd rt over 1f out: kpt on but nvr involved* **11/1**

03-4 8 *1 1/4* **Bayston Hill**[49] 86 5-9-6 **69** .... DanielMuscutt 5 61
(Mark Usher) *hld up in tch towards rr: effrt whn nt clr run and impeded bnd 2f: no imp u.p over 1f out: nvr involved (vet reported gelding lost its left-hind shoe)* **11/1**

/0-0 9 *1 1/2* **Petra's Pony (IRE)**[31] 362 4-8-8 **57** .... MartinDwyer 1 46
(Brian Meehan) *broke wl: sn restrained and hld up in tch: effrt whn racd awkwardly and edgd rt bnd 2f out: no imp and wl hld over 1f out* **50/1**

0-23 10 *hd* **Hidden Depths (IRE)**[10] 703 4-9-7 **70** .... AdamKirby 2 58
(Jamie Osborne) *led tl over 7f out: chsd ldr: rdn over 2f out: lost pl and btn over 1f out: wknd ins fnl f* **3/1**[1]

3-30 11 *54* **Sunshineandbubbles**[33] 344 6-9-1 **64** ....(p) JoeFanning 8
(Jennie Candlish) *chsd ldrs early: wl in tch in midfield tl dropped to rr over 2f out: sn lost tch and eased: t.o* **20/1**

2m 4.25s (-2.35) **Going Correction** -0.125s/f (Stan) **11** Ran SP% **121.5**

Speed ratings (Par 103): **104,103,102,102,101 100,98,97,96,96 53**

CSF £21.80 CT £112.43 TOTE £4.20: £1.80, £2.10, £2.00; EX 28.70 Trifecta £84.30.

Owner Colin Westley **Bred** Cheveley Park Stud Ltd **Trained** Epsom, Surrey

FOCUS

A reduced card, with a trainers' boycott over prize money issues forcing one race to become a walkover and another to be scrapped completely. This was a modest but competitive handicap to start. The first three have all been rated up a bit on their recent form.

877 BETWAY HEVER SPRINT STKS (LISTED RACE) 5f 6y(P)

2:05 (2:05) (Class 1) 4-Y-0+

£25,519 (£9,675; £4,842; £2,412; £1,210; £607) **Stalls** High

Form RPR

-312 1 **Gorgeous Noora (IRE)**[21] 563 5-8-9 98 .... HollieDoyle 2 103
(Archie Watson) *awkward leaving stalls: niggled along early: in tch in rr: swtchd rt and effrt over 1f out: hdwy u.p to chal ins fnl f: r.o wl to ld towards fin* **2/1**[2]

54-2 2 *3/4* **Royal Birth**[51] 35 8-9-0 97 ....(t) SeanLevey 5 105
(Stuart Williams) *hld up in tch: edgd rt bnd wl over 1f out: effrt over 1f out: sn pressing wnr: rdn to ld ins fnl f: hdd and no ex towards fin (jockey said gelding hung right-handed off the bend)* **10/1**

0-50 3 *1 1/4* **Corinthia Knight (IRE)**[21] 563 4-9-0 107 .... EdwardGreatrex 1 101
(Archie Watson) *dwlt: in tch in last pair: effrt and hdwy on inner over 1f out: kpt on same pce u.p ins fnl f* **5/1**[3]

23-6 4 *nk* **Gracious John (IRE)**[51] 35 6-9-0 102 .... EoinWalsh 4 99
(David Evans) *w ldr tl led 2f out: rdn over 1f out: hdd ins fnl f no ex and outpcd towards fin* **12/1**

1122 5 *2 3/4* **Ornate**[20] 588 6-9-0 95 .... TomMarquand 6 90
(David C Griffiths) *led on outer: hdd 2f out: outpcd over 1f out and wknd ins fnl f* **9/1**

12-1 6 *14* **Encore D'Or**[32] 352 7-9-0 109 .... LukeMorris 3 39
(Robert Cowell) *w ldrs on inner tl dropped to 3rd and rdn over 2f out: bhd and btn 1f out: sn eased (jockey said gelding stopped quickly. vet reported gelding had an irregular heart beat)* **7/4**[1]

56.92s (-1.88) **Going Correction** -0.125s/f (Stan) **6** Ran SP% **113.1**

Speed ratings (Par 111): **110,108,106,106,101 79**

CSF £21.58 TOTE £2.80: £1.20, £5.90; EX 21.60 Trifecta £103.50.

Owner David Howden & David Redvers **Bred** Kabansk Ltd & Rathbarry Stud **Trained** Upper Lambourn, W Berks

FOCUS

A solid Listed race that set up for the closers. The second sets the standard, rated to last winter's form.

878 BETWAY CASINO H'CAP 1m 4f (P)

2:35 (2:35) (Class 3) (0-95,95) 4-Y-0 **£7,246** (£2,168; £1,084; £542; £270) **Stalls** Low

Form RPR

014- 1 *hd* **Exceeding Power**[71] 9534 8-9-3 **89** .... GeorgeWood 1 96
(Martin Bosley) *pressed ldr: rdn to ld over 1f out: nudged lft and hdd ins fnl f: kpt on u.p: bmpd and jst hld cl home: awrdd r after stewards' inquiry* **16/1**

000- 2 **Petite Jack**[38] 8957 6-9-6 **92** ....(b) SeanLevey 6 99
(Neil King) *midfield: effrt to press ldrs over 1f out: rdn to chal 1f out: awkward hd carriage and hung lft but led ins fnl f: stl wanting to hang and bmpd rival towards fin: jst prevailed: demoted to 2nd after stewards' inquiry (jockey said gelding hung left-handed)* **9/1**

31-2 3 *1/2* **Cosmeapolitan**[31] 368 6-9-9 **95** .... DavidProbert 2 101
(Alan King) *trckd ldrs: effrt over 1f out: sn rdn to chal 1f out: keeping on but hld whn short of room cl home* **11/4**[2]

6-46 4 *3/4* **Eddystone Rock (IRE)**[32] 349 7-9-1 **87** .... KierenFox 4 92
(John Best) *hld up wl in tch in last pair: pushed rt bnd wl over 1f out: sn rdn: styd on wl ins fnl f: nt rch ldrs (jockey said gelding was taken wide on the bend)* **7/1**

1-11 5 *1* **Fearsome**[28] 440 5-9-5 **91** .... AdamKirby 3 94
(Nick Littmoden) *stdd s: hld up in tch in last pair: nt clr run 2f: sn swtchd rt and plenty to do whn drvn in 5th over 1f out: styd on ins fnl f: nvr getting on terms* **2/1**[1]

4-21 6 *2 1/4* **Technological**[17] 617 4-9-0 **88** ....(p[1]) TomQueally 5 88
(George Margarson) *led and set stdy gallop: rdn and hdd over 1f out: wknd ins fnl f* **7/2**[3]

2m 34.58s (1.58) **Going Correction** -0.125s/f (Stan)

WFA 4 from 5yo+ 2lb **6** Ran SP% **110.6**

Speed ratings (Par 107): **88,89,88,88,87 85**

CSF £134.93 TOTE £25.30: £4.30, £5.00; EX 118.70 Trifecta £769.00.

Owner The Chalfonts **Bred** Rabbah Bloodstock Limited **Trained** Chalfont St Giles, Bucks

FOCUS

The pace looked steady for much of the way and there was a tight finish, with the stewards needed. Muddling and far from solid form.

879 BETWAY WINTER DERBY STKS (GROUP 3) (ALL-WEATHER CHAMPIONSHIPS FAST-TRACK QUALIFIER) 1m 2f (P)

3:15 (3:15) (Class 1) 4-Y-0+

£56,710 (£21,500; £10,760; £5,360; £2,690; £1,350) **Stalls** Low

Form RPR

11-1 1 **Wissahickon (USA)**[21] 565 4-9-0 117 .... FrankieDettori 3 118+
(John Gosden) *hld up in midfield: clsd and pushed along to chse ldr 2f out: rdn to ld over 1f out: in command and r.o wl ins fnl f: comf* **1/4**[1]

4-13 2 *3 1/4* **Court House (IRE)**[21] 565 4-9-0 105 .... WilliamBuick 4 111
(John Gosden) *dwlt and short of room leaving stalls: hdwy to chse ldr 8f out: led 7f out: rdn ent fnl 2f: hdd over 1f out: no ch w wnr but kpt on for clr 2nd ins fnl f* **14/1**

01-1 3 *3 1/2* **Pactolus (IRE)**[31] 368 8-9-0 104 ....(t) CallumRodriguez 7 104
(Stuart Williams) *swtchd lft after s: hld up in rr: effrt ent fnl 2f: kpt on u.p to snatch 3rd last strides: no ch w ldng pair* **40/1**

22-2 4 *hd* **Big Country (IRE)**[21] 565 6-9-0 109 ....(p) LukeMorris 5 103
(Michael Appleby) *chsd ldr for 2f: styd prom tl chsd ldr again 6f out tl 2f out: sn outpcd u.p and wl hld ins fnl f: lost 3rd last strides* **10/1**[3]

0-14 5 *nse* **Chiefofchiefs**[21] 565 6-9-0 100 ....(p) DavidProbert 2 103
(Charlie Fellowes) *stdd s and hld up in last pair: effrt ent fnl 2f: kpt on u.p ins fnl f: no ch w ldng pair* **40/1**

601- 6 *hd* **Master The World (IRE)**[98] 9126 8-9-0 107 ....(p) SeanLevey 6 103
(David Elsworth) *hld up in last trio: effrt 2f out: kpt on u.p ins fnl f: no ch w ldng pair* **16/1**

3-11 7 *8* **Hathal (USA)**[19] 601 7-9-0 107 .... AdamKirby 1 87
(Jamie Osborne) *led for 2f: chsd ldr tl 6f out: styd chsng ldrs: rdn 3f out: outpcd in 4th 2f out: bhd and eased ins fnl f* **8/1**[2]

2m 1.28s (-5.32) **Going Correction** -0.125s/f (Stan) **7** Ran SP% **117.6**

Speed ratings (Par 113): **116,113,110,110,110 110,103**

CSF £6.17 TOTE £1.10: £1.10, £4.20; EX 5.60 Trifecta £64.10.

Owner George Strawbridge **Bred** Augustin Stable **Trained** Newmarket, Suffolk

FOCUS
An uncompetitive running of the Winter Derby, with the good winner on a different level to his rivals, and a one-two for John Gosden. The second has been rated to form, and the third close to his recent efforts.

880 FOLLOW SUN RACING ON TWITTER H'CAP 1m 1y(P)
3:50 (3:50) (Class 2) (0-105,110) 4-Y-£11,971 (£3,583; £1,791; £896; £446) Stalls High

Form RPR

26-2 **1** **Oh This Is Us (IRE)**[19] 601 6-9-12 **110** .... TomMarquand 6 117
(Richard Hannon) *stdd and dropped in after s: hld up in rr: swtchd rt and effrt over 1f out: str run to ld ins fnl f: gng away at fin* **2/1**[1]

05-1 **2** 1 1/4 **Apex King (IRE)**[42] 205 5-7-9 **86** oh4 .... LauraCoughlan(7) 2 90
(David Loughnane) *led to s: awkward as stalls opened and slowly away: sn rcvrd to chse ldr and t.k.h: lost 2nd 2f out and sn rdn: kpt on and ev ch again ins fnl f: nt pce of wnr towards fin: wnt 2nd again cl home* **8/1**

20-0 **3** 1/2 **Main Street**[21] 565 4-8-13 **97** .... DavidProbert 4 100
(David Elsworth) *dwlt: hld up in tch: clsd on inner to chse ldr 2f out: swtchd rt and effrt over 1f out: styd on and ev ch ins fnl f: nt match pce of wnr after and lost 2nd cl home* **5/1**

2-34 **4** 3/4 **Chevallier**[28] 441 7-8-8 **92** ....(p) LukeMorris 1 93
(Archie Watson) *led: 2 l clr and rdn 2f out: hrd drvn and hrd pressed 1f out: hdd ins fnl f: sn outpcd* **8/1**

44-2 **5** 1 1/4 **Goring (GER)**[47] 121 7-8-10 **101** ....(v) GeorgiaDobie(7) 3 99
(Eve Johnson Houghton) *chsd ldr early: sn restrained and hld up in tch: swtchd lft and effrt over 1f out: drvn and chsd ldrs ins fnl f: hld whn short of room cl home* **4/1**[3]

-014 **6** 1 1/4 **Mr Scaramanga**[1] 856 5-7-12 **89** .... LeviWilliams(7) 5 84
(Simon Dow) *stdd s: t.k.h: hdwy to chse ldrs on outer 5f out: lost pl 2f out: bhd fnl f (jockey said horse ran too free)* **10/3**[2]

1m 36.24s (-1.96) **Going Correction** -0.125s/f (Stan) **6** Ran SP% **115.3**
Speed ratings (Par 109): **104,102,102,101,100 99**
CSF £19.21 TOTE £2.10: £1.70, £3.30; EX 14.70 Trifecta £81.80.
Owner Team Wallop **Bred** Herbertstown House Stud **Trained** East Everleigh, Wilts

FOCUS
They went steady early in this decent handicap. The winner has been rated in line with the better view of his form.

881 LADBROKES HOME OF THE ODDS BOOST NOVICE STKS 1m 1y(P)
4:10 (4:10) (Class 5) 3-Y-O £2,911 Stalls High

Form RPR

05- **1** **Greybychoice (IRE)**[233] 4579 3-9-2 0 .... EoinWalsh 1
(Nick Littmoden) *walked over*

(-98.20) **Going Correction** 0.0s/f (Stan) **1** Ran

Owner A A Goodman **Bred** Sherborough Developments Co Ltd **Trained** Newmarket, Suffolk

T/Plt: £424.20 to a £1 stake. Pool: £30,162.24 - 51.90 winning units T/Qpdt: £39.50 to a £1 stake. Pool: £1,712.17 - 32.05 winning units **Steve Payne**

835 WOLVERHAMPTON (A.W) (L-H)
Saturday, February 23

OFFICIAL GOING: Tapeta: standard
Wind: Almost nil Weather: Fine

882 BETWAY H'CAP 6f 20y (Tp)
5:30 (5:30) (Class 6) (0-60,61) 4-Y-O+ £2,425 (£721; £360; £180) Stalls Low

Form RPR

-232 **1** **Steelriver (IRE)**[8] 742 9-9-5 **61** .... PhilDennis(3) 2 76+
(Michael Herrington) *hld up: hdwy and nt clr run over 1f out: shkn up to ld ins fnl f: qcknd clr* **3/1**[2]

0-60 **2** 4 **Admiral Rooke (IRE)**[39] 243 4-8-9 **55** ....(p) MarkCrehan(7) 8 54
(Michael Appleby) *a.p: chsd ldr over 2f out: led over 1f out: rdn and hdd ins fnl f: styd on same pce* **16/1**

5200 **3** 1 3/4 **Always Amazing**[7] 759 5-9-7 **60** .... RaulDaSilva 1 54
(Derek Shaw) *prom: lost pl after 1f: nt clr run over 2f out: swtchd lft and hdwy over 1f out: styd on to go 3rd wl ins fnl f* **7/1**

2-40 **4** 1 1/4 **Fantasy Justifier (IRE)**[24] 483 8-9-3 **56** ....(p) PaddyMathers 5 46
(Ronald Harris) *s.i.s: hld up: plld hrd: rdn and r.o ins fnl f: nrst fin* **12/1**

-066 **5** 1 **Major Crispies**[5] 788 8-9-0 **60** .... RPWalsh(7) 3 46
(Ronald Thompson) *s.i.s: hld up: hdwy on outer over 2f out: shkn up and carried hd high fr over 1f out: nt run on* **14/1**

-004 **6** nk **Marble Bar**[3] 809 4-8-10 **52** .... JamieGormley(3) 7 37
(Iain Jardine) *sn prom: plld hrd: nt clr run and lost pl over 2f out: shkn up and swtchd rt over 1f out: n.d after (jockey said gelding ran too freely)* **4/1**[3]

-601 **7** 1 **Indian Affair**[24] 483 9-9-3 **56** ....(bt) KieranO'Neill 12 38
(Milton Bradley) *led early: chsd ldrs: rdn whn hmpd over 1f out: sn wknd* **12/1**

00-5 **8** hd **Bahango (IRE)**[52] 25 7-9-1 **54** ....(p) ShaneGray 4 36
(Patrick Morris) *restless in stalls: plld hrd and w ldr 1f: remained handy: rdn over 1f out: wknd fnl f* **28/1**

454 **9** 2 **Snooze Button (IRE)**[7] 753 4-9-2 **55** .... AdamMcNamara 10 30
(Jamie Osborne) *chsd ldrs: rdn over 1f out: wknd fnl f* **25/1**

600- **10** 3 1/4 **Tiger Lyon (USA)**[87] 9296 4-9-6 **59** ....(t) JFEgan 9 24
(Paul D'Arcy) *sn led: rdn and hdd over 1f out: wknd ins fnl f (trainer's rep said gelding had a breathing problem)* **11/4**[1]

1m 14.07s (-0.43) **Going Correction** -0.05s/f (Stan) **10** Ran SP% **119.4**
Speed ratings (Par 101): **100,94,92,90,89 88,87,87,84,80**
CSF £51.70 CT £325.80 TOTE £3.30: £1.30, £6.40, £2.50; EX 53.60 Trifecta £268.50.
Owner Mrs H Lloyd-Herrington **Bred** Kildaragh Stud **Trained** Cold Kirby, N Yorks
■ Stewards' Enquiry : Phil Dennis two-day ban: interference & careless riding (Mar 9, 11)

FOCUS
A competitive Class 6 sprint with a well-supported ex-John Butler favourite.

883 BETWAY CASINO CLASSIFIED (S) STKS 6f 20y (Tp)
6:00 (6:00) (Class 5) 3-Y-O+ £3,072 (£914; £456; £228) Stalls Low

Form RPR

-631 **1** **The Groove**[19] 600 6-9-3 66 .... GinaMangan(7) 5 74
(David Evans) *hld up in tch on outer: shkn up over 1f out: led and edgd lft ins fnl f: rdn out: b.b.v (vet reported the gelding had bled from the nose)* **6/1**[3]

-343 **2** 1/2 **Secondo (FR)**[19] 600 9-8-13 66 ....(v) PoppyBridgwater(5) 1 66
(Robert Stephens) *chsd ldrs: rdn and ev ch ins fnl f: kpt on* **6/1**[3]

0-33 **3** 1 **Monumental Man**[4] 790 10-9-4 71 ....(p) DougieCostello 3 63
(Jamie Osborne) *led: shkn up over 1f out: rdn and hdd ins fnl f: styd on same pce* **11/10**[1]

-634 **4** 1 **Fast Track**[25] 468 8-8-11 66 .... MarkCrehan(7) 6 60
(David Barron) *chsd ldr tl shkn up over 1f out: styd on same pce ins fnl f* **5/1**[2]

040- **5** nse **Ninjago**[126] 8412 9-9-4 68 .... PaulMulrennan 2 60
(Paul Midgley) *prom: shkn up over 1f out: styd on same pce ins fnl f* **6/1**[3]

1m 14.57s (0.07) **Going Correction** -0.05s/f (Stan) **5** Ran SP% **107.1**
Speed ratings (Par 103): **97,96,95,93,93**
CSF £36.04 TOTE £7.50: £3.70, £2.90; EX 27.70 Trifecta £68.50.There was no bid for the winner
Owner Dave & Emma Evans **Bred** Cheveley Park Stud Ltd **Trained** Pandy, Monmouths

FOCUS
A seller with all five pretty closely matched but not convincing form at all. The winner has been rated as matching his turf form.

884 LADBROKES MAIDEN FILLIES' STKS 1m 4f 51y (Tp)
6:30 (6:30) (Class 5) 3-Y-O+ £3,234 (£962; £481; £240) Stalls Low

Form RPR

4-22 **1** **Miss Crick**[10] 696 8-10-0 71 .... DougieCostello 4 78
(Alan King) *chsd ldrs: rdn to ld over 1f out: sn hung lft: styd on* **1/1**[1]

24-3 **2** 1 **Lady Cosette (FR)**[35] 320 3-8-4 77 .... CamHardie 6 73
(Harry Dunlop) *stdd s: hld up: hdwy over 1f out: sn rdn and ev ch: styd on same pce wl ins fnl f* **6/1**[3]

504- **3** 5 **Dalakina (IRE)**[129] 8328 3-8-4 70 .... ShaneGray 1 65
(Roger Varian) *led 4f: chsd ldr: rdn and ev ch over 1f out: wknd wl ins fnl f* **3/1**[2]

220- **4** 1 1/4 **The Jean Genie**[130] 8309 5-10-0 74 .... HollieDoyle 2 66
(William Stone) *racd keenly in 2nd tl led 8f out: rdn and hdd over 1f out: wknd ins fnl f (jockey said mare ran too freely)* **11/1**

6-3 **5** hd **Maria Magdalena (IRE)**[19] 606 3-8-1 0 .... AaronJones(3) 3 63
(Marco Botti) *prom: rdn over 3f out: wkng whn hung lft fnl f* **40/1**

6 11 **Matilda Bay (IRE)** 3-8-4 0 .... JosephineGordon 5 45
(Jamie Osborne) *s.s: bhd: hdwy to latch on to the bk of the gp over 5f out: outpcd fr over 3f out (jockey said filly felt short in its action on pulling up)* **10/1**

2m 39.73s (-1.07) **Going Correction** -0.05s/f (Stan)
WFA 3 from 4yo 24lb 4 from 5yo+ 2lb **6** Ran SP% **109.1**
Speed ratings (Par 100): **101,100,97,96,96 88**
CSF £7.09 TOTE £1.80: £1.10, £2.70; EX 7.20 Trifecta £14.50.
Owner David Sewell **Bred** Simon Dutfield **Trained** Barbury Castle, Wilts

FOCUS
An interesting fillies' maiden with an almighty late plunge landed. The winner has been rated as backing up her Kempton latest.

885 LADBROKES HOME OF THE ODDS BOOST H'CAP 1m 142y (Tp)
7:00 (7:00) (Class 4) (0-85,81) 3-Y-O £5,013 (£1,491; £745; £372) Stalls Low

Form RPR

6-11 **1** **Alkaamel**[29] 409 3-9-0 **81** .... CierenFallon(7) 2 86+
(William Haggas) *trckd ldrs: racd keenly: wnt 2nd over 6f out: shkn up to ld over 1f out: rdn ins fnl f: jst hld on* **8/11**[1]

123- **2** hd **Balance Of Power**[147] 7779 3-9-5 **79** .... JasonHart 3 82
(John Quinn) *chsd ldr 2f: remained handy: rdn and swtchd rt over 1f out: r.o wl towards fin* **17/2**

0-22 **3** 1 1/2 **Hypnos (IRE)**[21] 561 3-8-6 **66** .... HollieDoyle 5 66
(David Simcock) *s.i.s: hld up: shkn up over 3f out: rdn and edgd lft over 1f out: r.o to go 3rd post: nt rch ldrs (jockey said gelding was never travelling)* **15/2**[3]

-211 **4** nk **Spirit Warning**[21] 561 3-9-3 **80** .... JoshuaBryan(3) 4 79
(Andrew Balding) *led at stdy pce: qcknd over 2f out: rdn and hdd over 1f out: styd on same pce ins fnl f* **11/4**[2]

1m 49.29s (-0.81) **Going Correction** -0.05s/f (Stan) **4** Ran SP% **106.9**
Speed ratings (Par 99): **101,100,99,99**
CSF £6.96 TOTE £1.40; EX 5.30 Trifecta £17.60.
Owner Hamdan Al Maktoum **Bred** Coln Valley Stud **Trained** Newmarket, Suffolk

FOCUS
Not many runners but lots of good recent form on display for this 3yo handicap. The winner has been rated as confirming his Newcastle figure.

886 SUNRACING.CO.UK H'CAP 1m 142y (Tp)
7:30 (7:30) (Class 5) (0-75,77) 4-Y-O+ £3,234 (£962; £481; £240) Stalls Low

Form RPR

32-2 **1** **Oneovdem**[42] 206 5-9-2 **74** .... TheodoreLadd(5) 2 81
(Tim Pinfield) *mde all: rdn over 1f out: edgd rt ins fnl f: styd on* **7/2**[2]

620- **2** 3/4 **Billy Roberts (IRE)**[129] 8325 6-8-10 **63** .... JasonHart 3 68
(Richard Whitaker) *chsd wnr: rdn over 1f out: styd on* **7/2**[2]

-546 **3** 3/4 **Espresso Freddo (IRE)**[10] 699 5-8-10 **68** ....(p) PoppyBridgwater(5) 4 71
(Robert Stephens) *hld up in tch: racd keenly: swtchd rt over 2f out: rdn over 1f out: styd on* **8/1**[3]

30-0 **4** nk **Laqab (IRE)**[3] 812 6-8-13 **66** .... PaddyMathers 9 69
(Derek Shaw) *hld up: hdwy over 2f out: rdn over 1f out: r.o to go 4th post: nt rch ldrs* **80/1**

30-2 **5** hd **Roman De Brut (IRE)**[43] 181 7-8-9 **65** .... JaneElliott(3) 1 67
(Ivan Furtado) *chsd ldrs: shkn up over 1f out: ev ch whn hmpd ins fnl f: styd on same pce* **9/1**

30-6 **6** 1/2 **Decoration Of War (IRE)**[52] 22 4-9-2 **69** .... AlistairRawlinson 6 73+
(Michael Appleby) *s.i.s: hld up: hdwy over 2f out: nt clr run fr over 1f out tl swtchd lft wl ins fnl f: nvr able to chal* **9/4**[1]

62-3 **7** 3 3/4 **Tum Tum**[18] 608 4-9-2 **72** ....(h) PhilDennis(3) 12 64
(Michael Herrington) *hld up in tch: ct out wd: shkn up over 2f out: styd on same pce fr over 1f out* **12/1**

0-50 **8** nk **Archie (IRE)**[31] 364 7-9-2 **69** ....(t) TrevorWhelan 7 61
(Brian Barr) *restless in stalls: s.i.s: hld up: hdwy u.p over 1f out: no ex ins fnl f (jockey said gelding was slowly into stride)* **100/1**

600- **9** hd **Sioux Frontier (IRE)**[143] 7901 4-9-0 **67** ....(p) LewisEdmunds 5 58
(Iain Jardine) *hld up in tch: lost pl over 3f out: n.d after* **16/1**

000- **10** 1 **Blacklooks (IRE)**[58] 9723 4-9-10 **77** .... KieranO'Neill 11 66
(Ivan Furtado) *s.i.s: hld up: shkn up over 1f out: nvr on terms* **25/1**

000- **11** 2 1/4 **Jack Of Diamonds (IRE)**[171] 6930 10-8-12 **65** ....(p) HollieDoyle 10 49
(Roger Teal) *s.i.s: hld up: rdn over 1f out: edgd lft fnl f: n.d* **66/1**

35-5 **12** 19 **Hippeia (IRE)**[22] 525 4-9-0 **67** .... SamJames 8 7
(Grant Tuer) *chsd ldrs tl rdn and wknd over 2f out* **50/1**

1m 48.52s (-1.58) **Going Correction** -0.05s/f (Stan) **12** Ran SP% **119.4**
Speed ratings (Par 103): **105,104,103,103,103 102,99,99,99,98 96,79**
CSF £16.01 CT £89.21 TOTE £5.20: £2.10, £1.80, £2.00; EX 22.20 Trifecta £145.90.
Owner Arion Equine Limited **Bred** P Balding **Trained** Upper Lambourn, Berks
■ Stewards' Enquiry : Theodore Ladd three-day ban: interference & careless riding (Mar 9, 11-12)

FOCUS
A competitive 0-75 with several coming in for support. The winner has been rated in line with his better Lingfield form, with the second close to last year's turf best and third to his recent form.

887 FOLLOW TOP TIPSTER TEMPLEGATE AT SUN RACING CLASSIFIED STKS — 7f 36y (Tp)
8:00 (8:00) (Class 6) 3-Y-O+ £2,425 (£721; £360; £180) Stalls High

Form RPR
-011 **1** **Naralsaif (IRE)**[9] 719 5-9-10 52.....(v) PaddyMathers 1 60
(Derek Shaw) *chsd ldrs: rdn to ld ins fnl f: r.o* 2/1[1]
0-52 **2** 1 1/2 **Sybil Grand**[26] 458 3-8-2 50.....(b) GabrieleMalune(3) 6 48
(Katy Price) *hld up in tch: nt clr run over 1f out: sn rdn: r.o to 2nd post* 9/1
3223 **3** shd **Dodgy Bob**[21] 553 6-9-5 48.....(v) PhilDennis(3) 5 53
(Michael Mullineaux) *disp ld tl wnt on over 2f out: rdn and hung rt over 1f out: hdd ins fnl f: styd on same pce* 13/2[2]
-300 **4** 1/2 **Diamond Pursuit**[20] 587 4-9-8 50..... JasonHart 3 52
(Ivan Furtado) *chsd ldrs: rdn over 2f out: styd on* 20/1
6-04 **5** 1 **Shyarch**[21] 553 5-9-3 48.....(p) KevinLundie(5) 8 49
(Christine Dunnett) *rrd s: in rr: nt clr run over 1f out: r.o ins fnl f: nt trble ldrs* 15/2
0-21 **6** nk **Rapid Rise (IRE)**[22] 530 5-9-8 48.....(p) RaulDaSilva 9 48
(Milton Bradley) *sn pushed along in rr: hdwy over 1f out: styd on same pce ins fnl f* 14/1
5242 **7** nk **Little Miss Kodi (IRE)**[9] 719 6-9-10 52.....(t) ShaneKelly 10 50
(Mark Loughnane) *hld up in tch: racd keenly: rdn over 1f out: styd on same pce ins fnl f* 9/1
-002 **8** 1/2 **Captain Kissinger**[9] 717 4-9-9 51.....(v) JFEgan 11 47
(Jo Hughes, France) *prom: rdn over 2f out: rn wd over 1f out: styd on same pce fnl f* 7/1[3]
0-00 **9** shd **Isabella Red (IRE)**[29] 400 3-8-5 49.....(v[1]) EoinWalsh 7 40
(David Evans) *s.i.s: hld up: rdn over 1f out: nt trble ldrs* 20/1
03-6 **10** 7 **Zeebad (IRE)**[45] 137 3-8-5 45.....(h[1]) HollieDoyle 2 21
(Paul D'Arcy) *disp ld over 4f: wknd fnl f* 13/2[2]
P-00 **11** 44 **Piccothepack**[23] 505 3-8-5 49..... JosephineGordon 4
(Richard Fahey) *s.i.s: outpcd* 33/1

1m 28.59s (-0.21) **Going Correction** -0.05s/f (Stan) 11 Ran SP% 123.4
WFA 3 from 4yo+ 17lb
Speed ratings (Par 101): **99,97,97,96,95 95,94,94,94,86 35**
CSF £21.67 TOTE £3.70: £1.60, £3.40, £2.40; EX 34.80 Trifecta £171.10.
Owner Derek Shaw **Bred** Shadwell Estate Company Limited **Trained** Sproxton, Leics

FOCUS
A competitive classified stakes to close but an in-form mare completed a quick hat-trick. The second and third have been rated close to their recent course form.
T/Plt: £122.20 to a £1 stake. Pool: £90,275.20 - 539.17 winning units T/Qpdt: £5.20 to a £1 stake. Pool: £11,274.63 - 1,587.72 winning units **Colin Roberts**

888 - 891a (Foreign Racing) - See Raceform Interactive

869 DOHA
Saturday, February 23

OFFICIAL GOING: Turf: good

892a DUKHAN SPRINT (LOCAL GROUP 3) (3YO+) (TURF) — 6f (T)
11:00 3-Y-O+ £112,204 (£43,307; £21,653; £11,811; £7,874)

RPR
1 **Anima Rock (FR)**[338] 4-9-2 0..... TheoBachelot 1 106
(Jassim Mohammed Ghazali, Qatar)
2 1 1/4 **Stone Of Destiny**[21] 563 4-9-2 0..... OisinMurphy 3 102
(Andrew Balding) *slowly away: hld up last: prog whn forced to snatch up after 1f: pushed along in fnl trio 2f out: swtchd lft and gd hdwy 1 1/2f out: kpt on wl and clsng rapidly fnl f but too late: unlucky*
3 3/4 **Izzthatright (IRE)**[364] 901 7-9-2 0..... HarryBentley 7 100
(Jassim Mohammed Ghazali, Qatar)
4 2 3/4 **Cristofano Allori (IRE)**[497] 8055 5-9-2 0..... StephaneLadjadj 6 91
(Abdulaziz Al-Kathiri, Qatar)
5 1 1/4 **Harry's Dancer (IRE)**[303] 7-8-11 0..... RyuAbe 2 82
(Osama Omer E Al-Dafea, Qatar)
6 nse **Julio (GER)**[111] 8868 4-9-2 0..... EduardoPedroza 4 87
(Mario Hofer, Germany)
7 2 1/2 **Darkanna (IRE)**[133] 8190 4-8-11 0..... Jean-BaptisteHamel 8 74
(Mohammed Hussain, Qatar)
8 4 1/4 **My Sharona**[364] 901 10-8-11 0.....(b) J-PGuillambert 5 60
(Jassim Mohammed Ghazali, Qatar)

1m 9.48s 8 Ran
Owner Khalifa Bin Sheail Al Kuwari **Bred** M Daguzan-Garros **Trained** Qatar

893a AL BIDDAH MILE (LOCAL GROUP 2) (3YO) (TURF) — 1m (T)
11:35 3-Y-O £112,204 (£43,307; £21,653; £11,811; £7,874)

RPR
1 **Golden Spectrum**[21] 554 3-9-2..... GeraldMosse 3 93+
(Gay Kelleway) *urged along early: midfield tl pushed along and prog ins fnl 1 1/2f: gd hdwy whn rdn fnl f: led ins fnl 100yds*
2 1/2 **Luchador**[64] 9680 3-8-11 0..... J-PGuillambert 12 87
(Jassim Mohammed Ghazali, Qatar)
3 2 **Cococabala (IRE)**[197] 5948 3-9-2 0..... IvanRossi 1 87
(Tareq Abdulla, Qatar)
4 1 **Admiral Rous (IRE)**[29] 3-9-2 0..... CristianDemuro 11 85+
(E J O'Neill, France)
5 1 **Ours Puissant (IRE)**[69] 9570 3-9-2 0..... OisinMurphy 10 83
(Hugo Palmer) *sn pressing ldr on outer: c wd into st 2f out and lost pl: kpt on u.p fnl f: nt pce to get bk on terms*
6 hd **Arabic Channel (USA)**[64] 9680 3-9-2 0.....(b) RonanThomas 4 82
(H Al Ramzani, Qatar)
7 3 3/4 **Jacko (IRE)**[124] 8474 3-9-2 0..... TheoBachelot 5 74
(Jassim Mohammed Ghazali, Qatar)
8 2 1/2 **Concierge (IRE)**[64] 9680 3-9-2 0..... JamesDoyle 8 68
(George Scott) *racd in rr of mid-div: nudged along appr 3f out: pushed along 2f out: rdn and one pce fnl 1 1/2f*
9 1/2 **Julius Limbani (IRE)**[127] 8402 3-9-2 0..... HarryBentley 7 67
(Jassim Mohammed Ghazali, Qatar)
10 1 3/4 **Cloak And Dagger (IRE)**[64] 9680 3-9-2 0..... EduardoPedroza 14 63
(Ibrahim Al Malki, Qatar)
11 2 1/2 **Hadeer (IRE)**[99] 9105 3-9-2 0..... Jean-BaptisteHamel 9 57
(R Al Jehani, Qatar)
12 3 1/2 **Dark Pursuit**[125] 8438 3-9-2 0..... CarloFiocchi 6 49
(S Ibido, Qatar)
13 1 1/2 **Izzer (IRE)**[64] 9680 3-9-2 0..... StephaneLadjadj 2 46
(Osama Omer E Al-Dafea, Qatar)
U **Rex Place (IRE)**[155] 7504 3-9-2 0..... FalehBughanaim 13
(H Al Ramzani, Qatar)

1m 35.29s 14 Ran
Owner Dr Johnny Hon **Bred** Newsells Park Stud **Trained** Exning, Suffolk

894a H.H THE AMIR TROPHY (LOCAL GROUP 1) (4YO+) (TURF) — 1m 4f
1:15 4-Y-O+ £448,818 (£173,228; £86,614; £47,244; £31,496)

RPR
1 **French King**[119] 8661 4-9-0 0..... OlivierPeslier 9 110
(H-A Pantall, France) *racd keenly and mde virtually all: rdn to assert ins fnl 2f: qcknd and sn clr ent fnl f: kpt on wl*
2 1 1/2 **Royal Julius (IRE)**[111] 8865 6-9-2 0..... GeraldMosse 8 107+
(J Reynier, France)
3 1 1/4 **Hunting Horn (IRE)**[28] 443 4-9-0 0..... RyanMoore 6 106
(A P O'Brien, Ire) *a.p: cl 5th between horses whn shkn up 3f fr home: c sltly wd into st: styd on u.p to chse clr ldr 1f out: kpt on but lost 2nd cl home*
4 3/4 **The Blue Eye**[364] 903 7-9-2 0..... HarryBentley 10 104
(Jassim Mohammed Ghazali, Qatar)
5 1/2 **Es'hail (USA)**[63] 9688 4-9-0 0..... GeraldAvranche 2 104
(R Al Jehani, Qatar)
6 shd **Raymond Tusk (IRE)**[125] 8463 4-9-0 0..... JamieSpencer 15 104
(Richard Hannon) *cl up on outer: pressed ldr after 1/2-way: rdn 2f out and c sltly wd into st: kpt on u.p: fdd late on*
7 2 **Duke Of Dundee (FR)**[364] 903 7-9-2 0..... AdriedeVries 7 100
(A De Mieulle, Qatar)
8 3/4 **Noor Al Hawa (FR)**[140] 8011 6-9-2 0..... MaximeGuyon 12 98
(G E Mikhalides, France)
9 3/4 **Pazeer (FR)**[420] 9460 5-9-2 0..... EduardoPedroza 11 97
(Ibrahim Al Malki, Qatar)
10 shd **Alhazm (FR)**[63] 9688 4-9-0 0..... RonanThomas 3 98
(A De Mieulle, Qatar)
11 1 **Giuseppe Garibaldi (IRE)**[30] 4-9-0 0.....(t) RyanCuratolo 13 96
(Ahmed Kobeissi, Qatar) *hld up towards rr: dropped to rr 5f out: short of racing room whn pushed along over 2f out: sn swtchd to outer: passed btn rivals u.p fr over 1f out: nvr a factor*
12 1 1/4 **Veranda (FR)**[420] 9460 5-9-2 0..... CristianDemuro 14 93
(S Ibido, Qatar)
13 3/4 **Heshem (IRE)**[226] 6-9-2 0..... FalehBughanaim 1 92
(A De Mieulle, Qatar)
14 9 1/4 **Liam The Charmer (USA)**[49] 6-9-2 0.....(b) TylerGaffalione 5 77
(Michael McCarthy, U.S.A)

2m 26.12s 14 Ran
WFA 4 from 5yo+ 2lb
Owner H H Sheikh Abdulla Bin Khalifa Al Thani **Bred** Umm Qarn Farms **Trained** France

FOCUS
The winner dominated throughout.

895 - 905a (Foreign Racing) - See Raceform Interactive

882 WOLVERHAMPTON (A.W) (L-H)
Monday, February 25

OFFICIAL GOING: Tapeta: standard
Wind: Nil Weather: Fine

906 LADBROKES H'CAP — 5f 21y (Tp)
5:25 (5:25) (Class 6) (0-65,66) 3-Y-O £2,264 (£673; £336; £168) Stalls Low

Form RPR
004- **1** **The Defiant**[124] 8542 3-8-7 51..... BarryMcHugh 4 57+
(Paul Midgley) *s.i.s: hld up: plld hrd: hdwy 1/2-way: shkn up to ld over 1f out: rdn out (vet said gelding had been struck into on it's left hind)* 5/1[3]
0-00 **2** 1/2 **Sing Bertie (IRE)**[31] 412 3-8-2 46 oh1..... PaddyMathers 2 48
(Derek Shaw) *s.i.s: hld up: racd keenly: hdwy over 1f out: r.o to go 2nd nr fin* 14/1
4-04 **3** hd **Awake In Asia**[21] 605 3-9-2 60.....(p[1]) LukeMorris 8 61
(Charlie Wallis) *hld up: pushed along 1/2-way: hdwy u.p over 1f out: edgd rt: chsd wnr ins fnl f: r.o* 16/1
032- **4** 1/2 **Griggy (IRE)**[68] 9613 3-9-7 65..... AdamKirby 9 64+
(Paul D'Arcy) *s.i.s: hld up: racd keenly: rdn and r.o ins fnl f: edgd lft: nt rch ldrs* 2/1[1]
00-0 **5** 3/4 **Brother Bentley**[21] 605 3-8-11 55.....(p[1]) JohnFahy 11 51
(Ronald Harris) *pushed along early in rr: racd wd: hdwy over 1f out: styd on same pce wl ins fnl f* 66/1
0-36 **6** 1 1/2 **Yfenni (IRE)**[23] 550 3-8-2 46 oh1..... KieranO'Neill 6 37
(Milton Bradley) *sn led: hdd 4f out: chsd ldrs: shkn up over 1f out: rdn and edgd lft ins fnl f: no ex* 20/1
-540 **7** hd **Amliba**[31] 406 3-8-10 54..... BenCurtis 5 45
(David O'Meara) *prom: racd keenly: hmpd over 4f out: rdn whn hmpd 1f out: styd on same pce* 20/1
6-14 **8** 1 1/2 **Kingi Compton**[3] 854 3-9-8 66.....(b) EdwardGreatrex 3 51
(Archie Watson) *chsd ldrs: edgd rt over 4f out: chsd ldr 3f out: shkn up to ld over 1f out: sn hdd: wknd ins fnl f* 5/2[2]
0-40 **9** 1 1/2 **Thegreyvtrain**[21] 605 3-8-8 52..... DavidProbert 1 31
(Ronald Harris) *led early: chsd ldrs: nt clr run 1/2-way: rdn over 1f out: wknd ins fnl f* 12/1
00-5 **10** shd **Talk Like This (USA)**[9] 753 3-8-9 53..... MartinDwyer 10 32
(Tim Pinfield) *hld up: nvr on terms* 20/1
03-0 **11** 1 1/2 **Spring Holly (IRE)**[3] 848 3-8-2 46..... RaulDaSilva 7 20
(Milton Bradley) *led 4f out: rdn and hdd over 1f out: wknd ins fnl f* 66/1

1m 2.37s (0.47) **Going Correction** -0.025s/f (Stan) 11 Ran SP% 116.1
Speed ratings (Par 95): **95,94,93,93,91 89,89,86,84,84 81**
CSF £64.94 CT £1049.84 TOTE £6.70: £1.90, £5.20, £3.30; EX 89.00 Trifecta £695.40.
Owner Frank Brady **Bred** Frank Brady **Trained** Westow, N Yorks

FOCUS
A modest 3yo sprint handicap on standard Tapeta. Plenty were keen enough early on off a muddling gallop. The winning time was nearly three seconds above standard.

907 BETWAY SPRINT H'CAP — 5f 21y (Tp)
5:55 (5:55) (Class 5) (0-75,77) 4-Y-0+ £2,911 (£866; £432; £216) Stalls Low

Form — RPR

-013 **1** **Tathmeen (IRE)**[10] 743 4-9-4 **72** CamHardie 10 — 81
(Antony Brittain) *s.i.s: hld up: pushed along: hdwy and hung lft fr over 1f out: rdn to ld wl ins fnl f: r.o* 12/1

-525 **2** ¾ **Amazing Grazing (IRE)**[25] 496 5-9-7 **75** LewisEdmunds 5 — 81
(Rebecca Bastiman) *hld up in tch: rdn over 1f out: hung lft and led wl ins fnl f: sn hdd and unable qck* 6/1[2]

1235 **3** ¾ **A Sure Welcome**[6] 790 5-9-3 **71** (b) LukeMorris 11 — 76+
(John Spearing) *half-rrd s: hld up: pushed along and hdwy over 1f out: nt clr run sn after: hmpd and swtchd rt ins fnl f: r.o to go 3rd nr fin* 6/1[2]

0-63 **4** 1¼ **Drakefell (IRE)**[24] 517 4-9-9 **77** (b[1]) SeanLevey 9 — 76
(Richard Hannon) *prom: chsd ldr over 3f out: led over 1f out: rdn: edgd lft and hdd wl ins fnl f: styd on same pce* 16/1

60-2 **5** 2 **Secret Potion**[19] 626 5-8-9 **63** DavidProbert 4 — 55
(Ronald Harris) *sn pushed along and prom: outpcd 2f out: hung lft over 1f out: rdn and swtchd rt ins fnl f: styd on* 10/1

0341 **6** ¾ **It's All A Joke (IRE)**[9] 763 4-9-1 **76** (b) Pierre-LouisJamin(7) 2 — 65
(Archie Watson) *chsd ldrs: nt clr run over 1f out: hmpd: swtchd rt and no ex ins fnl f* 6/1[2]

4512 **7** ½ **Warrior's Valley**[3] 849 4-8-12 **66** (tp) OisinMurphy 1 — 53
(David C Griffiths) *led: rdn and hdd over 1f out: styng on same pce whn hmpd wl ins fnl f* 3/1[1]

34-0 **8** ¾ **Mansfield**[25] 496 6-8-7 **61** PaddyMathers 6 — 45
(Stella Barclay) *s.i.s: nvr on terms* 16/1

430- **8** dht **Gift In Time (IRE)**[102] 9084 4-9-3 **74** ConorMcGovern(3) 7 — 58
(Paul Collins) *s.i.s: outpcd* 50/1

4-06 **10** nk **Gamesome (FR)**[20] 610 8-8-12 **66** PaulMulrennan 8 — 49
(Paul Midgley) *sn prom: ct out wd: shkn up 1/2-way: wknd fnl f* 20/1

5-12 **11** 4 **Pea Shooter**[20] 610 10-9-9 **77** CallumRodriguez 3 — 46
(Brian Ellison) *chsd ldrs: pushed along 1/2-way: wknd fnl f (jockey said gelding hung right-handed throughout)* 7/1[3]

1m 0.74s (-1.16) **Going Correction** -0.025s/f (Stan) 11 Ran SP% 115.6
Speed ratings (Par 103): **108,106,105,103,100 99,98,97,97,96 90**
CSF £80.97 CT £488.09 TOTE £14.00: £4.40, £2.40, £1.80; EX 110.40 Trifecta £608.90.
Owner Antony Brittain **Bred** Shadwell Estate Company Limited **Trained** Warthill, N Yorks

FOCUS
A fair sprint handicap. They went a decent gallop and the winning time was only about a second above standard. The winner picked up strongly from off the pace. The second has been rated to form.

908 BETWAY NOVICE STKS — 6f 20y (Tp)
6:25 (6:25) (Class 5) 3-Y-0+ £2,911 (£866; £432; £216) Stalls Low

Form — RPR

1 **1** **With Caution (IRE)**[26] 477 3-8-13 **0** OisinMurphy 8 — 81+
(James Tate) *chsd ldr: shkn up to ld over 1f out: edgd lft and wnt clr ins fnl f* 4/7[1]

4 **2** 5 **Rakastava (IRE)**[19] 621 3-8-13 **0** CallumShepherd 1 — 64
(Mick Channon) *chsd ldrs: rdn over 1f out: wnt 2nd ins fnl f: styd on same pce* 4/1[2]

-2 **3** 1¾ **Empty Promises**[19] 621 3-8-10 **0** FinleyMarsh(3) 7 — 58
(Frank Bishop) *sn led at stdy pce: qcknd over 2f out: hung rt and hdd over 1f out: no ex ins fnl f (jockey said colt hung right handed off the home bend)* 14/1

0-3 **4** 4½ **Shesadabber**[21] 604 3-8-8 **0** RobHornby 4 — 39
(Brian Baugh) *chsd ldrs: pushed along 1/2-way: wknd over 1f out* 66/1

0-3 **5** ¾ **Divied (USA)**[25] 500 3-8-13 **0** JasonHart 3 — 42
(John Quinn) *s.i.s: hld up: effrt over 1f out: nvr on terms* 8/1[3]

0- **6** 2 **The Numismatist (IRE)**[257] 3725 3-8-13 **0** NicolaCurrie 5 — 35
(Jamie Osborne) *s.i.s: outpcd* 10/1

40 **7** 1¼ **Purely Prosecco**[9] 753 3-8-8 **0** PaddyMathers 6 — 26
(Derek Shaw) *s.i.s: hld up: plld hrd: shkn up over 2f out: n.d* 100/1

1m 14.77s (0.27) **Going Correction** -0.025s/f (Stan) 7 Ran SP% 113.0
Speed ratings (Par 103): **97,90,88,82,81 78,76**
CSF £3.08 TOTE £1.40: £1.20, £1.90; EX 3.70 Trifecta £13.30.
Owner Saeed Manana **Bred** Ballyphilip Stud **Trained** Newmarket, Suffolk

FOCUS
Effectively, an ordinary 3yo novice contest but the odds-on favourite stretched powerfully clear in the final furlong in a race that turned into a sprint from over 2f out.

909 BETWAY HEED YOUR HUNCH H'CAP — 6f 20y (Tp)
6:55 (6:55) (Class 2) (0-105,100) 4-Y-0+ £11,827 (£3,541; £1,770; £885; £442; £222) Stalls Low

Form — RPR

-262 **1** **Merhoob (IRE)**[9] 762 7-9-1 **94** LukeMorris 5 — 104
(John Ryan) *sn pushed along and prom: rdn over 1f out: led wl ins fnl f: r.o wl* 10/1

13-0 **2** 2¼ **El Hombre**[48] 127 5-8-13 **92** CallumRodriguez 1 — 95
(Keith Dalgleish) *chsd ldr 2f: remained handy: wnt 2nd again over 1f out: rdn and ev ch ins fnl f: styd on same pce* 5/1

22-4 **3** nk **Raucous**[9] 762 6-9-6 **99** (tp) OisinMurphy 4 — 101
(Robert Cowell) *hld up: rdn over 1f out: r.o ins fnl f: wnt 3rd post* 9/2[3]

0-53 **4** shd **Reckless Endeavour (IRE)**[25] 499 6-8-4 **83** JoeFanning 3 — 85+
(David Barron) *s.i.s: hld up: rdn over 1f out: r.o wl ins fnl f: nt rch ldrs* 4/1[2]

13-5 **5** nk **Sir Thomas Gresham (IRE)**[23] 563 4-9-7 **100** MartinDwyer 7 — 101
(Tim Pinfield) *led: shkn up over 1f out: rdn and hdd wl ins fnl f: no ex* 3/1[1]

0006 **6** 1 **Atletico (IRE)**[9] 762 7-8-11 **90** EoinWalsh 8 — 88
(David Evans) *hld up: styd on ins fnl f: nt trble ldrs* 16/1

-343 **7** nk **Gulliver**[9] 762 5-9-6 **99** (tp) AdamKirby 2 — 96
(David O'Meara) *hld up: pushed along and hdwy 2f out: rdn and hung lft ins fnl f: no ex* 5/1

40-4 **8** 2¼ **Reflektor (IRE)**[44] 203 6-8-12 **91** BenCurtis 9 — 80
(Tom Dascombe) *chsd ldrs: wnt 2nd 4f out tl rdn over 1f out: wknd ins fnl f* 16/1

1/50 **9** 1 **Giogiobbo**[9] 762 6-9-2 **98** (b) JoshuaBryan(3) 6 — 84
(Nick Littmoden) *hld up in tch: rdn over 1f out: wknd fnl f (jockey said horse did not handle the home bend)* 50/1

1m 12.2s (-2.30) **Going Correction** -0.025s/f (Stan) 9 Ran SP% 119.3
Speed ratings (Par 109): **114,111,110,110,110 108,108,105,104**
CSF £61.33 CT £263.77 TOTE £9.40: £2.40, £2.70, £2.20; EX 67.50 Trifecta £455.00.
Owner Gerry McGladery **Bred** Airlie Stud **Trained** Newmarket, Suffolk
■ Stewards' Enquiry : Luke Morris two-day ban; misuse of whip (Mar 11-12)

FOCUS
The feature race was a good sprint handicap and it produced a comprehensive winner in the best comparative time on the night. The second and third have been rated close to form.

910 BETWAY CASINO H'CAP — 1m 4f 51y (Tp)
7:25 (7:25) (Class 6) (0-60,60) 4-Y-0+ £2,425 (£721; £360; £180) Stalls Low

Form — RPR

5-54 **1** **Power Home (IRE)**[19] 616 5-9-5 **58** OisinMurphy 1 — 65
(Denis Coakley) *led 1f: chsd ldrs: wnt 2nd over 1f out: rdn to ld wl ins fnl f: r.o* 5/1[3]

03 **2** 1¼ **Nice To Sea (IRE)**[21] 602 5-8-11 **50** (p) DavidProbert 10 — 55
(Olly Murphy) *a.p: chsd ldr 10f out tl led wl over 1f out: rdn and hdd wl ins fnl f* 9/4[1]

-120 **3** nk **Apex Predator (IRE)**[10] 736 4-9-1 **56** (bt) TomQueally 3 — 60
(Seamus Durack) *chsd ldrs: rdn over 1f out: r.o* 8/1

65-6 **4** 1 **Raashdy (IRE)**[26] 481 6-9-6 **59** (p) LukeMorris 8 — 62
(Peter Hiatt) *hld up in tch: racd keenly: rdn over 1f out: r.o* 20/1

1-10 **5** 1 **Tigerfish (IRE)**[10] 736 5-8-13 **52** (p) HollieDoyle 6 — 53
(William Stone) *chsd ldrs: rdn over 1f out: styd on same pce ins fnl f* 10/1

-210 **6** 1 **Ember's Glow**[23] 560 5-9-2 **55** EoinWalsh 9 — 55+
(Mark Loughnane) *hld up: hdwy on outer over 4f out: rdn over 1f out: styd on same pce* 4/1[2]

03-5 **7** ½ **Dove Mountain (IRE)**[44] 207 8-8-9 **53** (tp) MeganNicholls(5) 4 — 52+
(Olly Murphy) *s.s: hld up: swtchd lft over 1f out: styd on ins fnl f: nvr nrr (jockey said gelding was slowly away)* 20/1

-256 **8** nse **False Id**[31] 410 6-9-4 **57** (b) TrevorWhelan 11 — 56+
(David Loughnane) *s.s: hld up: styd on fnl f: nvr on terms* 25/1

655- **9** 1¾ **Admiral Spice (IRE)**[31] 6264 4-9-5 **60** (p) DougieCostello 7 — 56+
(Sophie Leech) *hld up: rdn over 2f out: hung lft fnl f: n.d* 50/1

04-0 **10** 1½ **Shaji**[10] 731 4-8-12 **58** (p) PoppyBridgwater(5) 12 — 52
(David Bridgwater) *led at stdy pce after 1f: hdd wl over 2f out: wknd ins fnl f* 33/1

3-46 **11** 1 **Man Of Verve (IRE)**[35] 348 5-9-6 **59** AdamKirby 2 — 53+
(Philip Kirby) *dwlt: hld up: effrt over 1f out: hmpd ins fnl f: eased* 6/1

00-0 **12** 3 **Ross Raith Rover**[23] 560 6-9-5 **58** (v[1]) LiamJones 5 — 45+
(Lee Carter) *hld up: pushed along over 3f out: rdn over 1f out: btn whn hmpd ins fnl f* 16/1

2m 43.17s (2.37) **Going Correction** -0.025s/f (Stan)
WFA 4 from 5yo+ 2lb 12 Ran SP% 126.1
Speed ratings (Par 101): **91,90,89,89,88 87,87,87,86,85 84,82**
CSF £16.68 CT £94.97 TOTE £5.80: £1.90, £1.40, £3.00; EX 26.60 Trifecta £229.60.
Owner Poachers' Dozen **Bred** C Farrell **Trained** West Ilsley, Berks

FOCUS
A modest middle-distance handicap and a race which turned into a 3f sprint off a slow gallop. The winning time was over eight seconds outside standard. Muddling form. The second has been rated close to her latest, with the third to his last C&D run.

911 BETWAY LIVE CASINO H'CAP — 1m 1f 104y (Tp)
7:55 (7:55) (Class 6) (0-65,65) 4-Y-0+ £2,264 (£673; £336; £168) Stalls Low

Form — RPR

6330 **1** **King Of Naples**[6] 793 6-9-3 **61** (h) JackGarritty 9 — 67
(Ruth Carr) *hld up: hdwy over 1f out: carried hd high and hung lft ins fnl f: r.o to ld nr fin (trainers' rep could offer no explanation for the app imp in form other than this race was a drop in class for the gelding)* 8/1

0-50 **2** hd **Mossy's Lodge**[28] 462 6-9-0 **58** (tp) StevieDonohoe 4 — 63
(Rebecca Menzies) *hld up in tch: rdn over 1f out: ev ch ins fnl f: r.o* 12/1

3-53 **3** nse **Traveller (FR)**[26] 479 5-9-0 **58** (t) CamHardie 7 — 63
(Antony Brittain) *chsd ldr: rdn to ld ins fnl f: hdd nr fin* 3/1[2]

-020 **4** 2¼ **Aqua Libre**[5] 814 6-9-3 **61** (p) JoeFanning 5 — 61
(Jennie Candlish) *trckd ldrs: racd keenly: shkn up over 1f out: styd on same pce ins fnl f* 5/2[1]

300- **5** 3 **Baashiq (IRE)**[81] 9431 5-9-6 **64** LukeMorris 2 — 58
(Peter Hiatt) *led: rdn and hdd ins fnl f: no ex* 5/1[3]

44-5 **6** hd **Zephyros (GER)**[35] 344 8-9-2 **65** PoppyBridgwater(5) 1 — 59
(David Bridgwater) *s.i.s: hld up: shkn up over 1f out: nt trble ldrs* 10/1

-140 **7** ½ **Baasha**[11] 722 4-9-6 **64** (b) OisinMurphy 6 — 57
(Ed Dunlop) *prom: rdn over 1f out: no ex ins fnl f* 6/1

440- **8** ½ **Noneedtotellme (IRE)**[177] 6816 6-8-7 **51** oh6 KieranO'Neill 3 — 42
(James Unett) *chsd ldrs: rdn over 2f out: nt clr run and no ex ins fnl f* 25/1

4/00 **9** ½ **Sir George Somers (USA)**[26] 473 6-9-5 **63** (p[1]) LiamKeniry 11 — 53
(Nigel Twiston-Davies) *hld up: rdn and hung lft over 1f out: nvr on terms* 40/1

00-0 **10** 20 **Tuscany (IRE)**[37] 315 5-8-8 **59** (p) KeelanBaker(7) 8 — 7
(Grace Harris) *s.i.s: hld up: hdwy on outer over 4f out: rdn over 2f out: sn wknd* 50/1

2m 0.12s (-0.68) **Going Correction** -0.025s/f (Stan) 10 Ran SP% 120.7
Speed ratings (Par 101): **102,101,101,99,97 96,96,96,95,77**
CSF £100.56 CT £358.20 TOTE £10.50: £2.80, £3.10, £1.20; EX 94.10 Trifecta £360.50.
Owner The Beer Stalkers & Ruth Carr **Bred** Meon Valley Stud **Trained** Huby, N Yorks

FOCUS
A modest handicap. The winning time was ordinary but there was an exciting three-way photo-finish. The second and third set the level.
T/Jkpt: Not won. T/Plt: £305.80 to a £1 stake. Pool: £110,235.03 - 263.14 winning units T/Qpdt: £11.00 to a £1 stake. Pool: £18,627.05 - 1,252.88 winning units **Colin Roberts**

906 WOLVERHAMPTON (A.W) (L-H)
Tuesday, February 26

OFFICIAL GOING: Tapeta: standard
Wind: light breeze Weather: clear and warm

912 FOLLOW TOP TIPSTERS AT SUN RACING H'CAP — 1m 142y (Tp)
5:00 (5:00) (Class 6) (0-60,60) 4-Y-0+ £2,264 (£673; £336; £168) Stalls Low

Form — RPR

/4-0 **1** **Our Manekineko**[40] 273 9-8-7 **46** oh1 (bt) DavidProbert 10 — 54
(Stephen Michael Hanlon, Ire) *hld up: hdwy on outer over 1f out: pushed along to chal ins fnl f: led 100yds out: rdn to assert nr fin* 14/1

34-0 **2** ¾ **Final Attack (IRE)**[50] 120 8-8-10 **52** (p) GabrieleMalune(3) 4 — 58
(Sarah Hollinshead) *mid-div: pushed along on inner 2f out: trckd ldrs over 1f out: drvn to chal ins fnl f: wnt 2nd 100yds out: rdn and kpt on* 7/1[3]

-013 **3** 1¼ **Limerick Lord (IRE)**[10] 760 7-8-12 **51** (p) ShelleyBirkett 12 — 54
(Julia Feilden) *prom: led over 2f out: rdn ent fnl f: hdd 100yds out: one pce* 8/1

2616 **4** *nk* **Sharp Operator**[22] 595 6-9-5 58 (h) LukeMorris 8 60
(Charlie Wallis) *chsd ldrs: pushed along 2f out: rdn and ev ch 1f out and ins fnl f: wknd last 150yds* 7/1[3]

-653 **5** *2* **Pike Corner Cross (IRE)**[22] 603 7-9-4 57 CallumShepherd 11 55
(Alastair Ralph) *in rr: pushed along and plenty to do 1 1/2f out: sn drvn: rdn and hdwy ent fnl f: no ex last 1/2 f* 8/1

6-30 **6** *1 1/4* **Energia Flavio (BRZ)**[28] 465 8-9-7 60 (p) OisinMurphy 2 55
(Patrick Morris) *chsd ldrs: pushed into 2nd 1 1/2f out: rdn 1f out: wknd fnl f* 6/1[2]

-630 **7** *1 1/2* **Lord Cooper**[11] 742 5-8-13 52 (p) HollieDoyle 3 44
(Marjorie Fife) *hld up: drvn 1 1/2f out: sn rdn: no imp* 12/1

0-50 **8** *nse* **Shovel It On (IRE)**[27] 485 4-8-1 47 SophieRalston(7) 1 38
(Steve Flook) *hld up: drvn over 2f out: effrt on inner 1 1/2f out: rdn and no ex fnl f* 50/1

-502 **9** *2 3/4* **Mossy's Lodge**[1] 911 6-9-0 58 (tp) PaulaMuir(5) 5 43
(Rebecca Menzies) *slowly away: bhd: drvn in rr over 2f out: sn rdn: no rspnse (jockey said mare sat down in the stalls and as a result was slowly away)* 4/1[1]

360- **10** *1/2* **John Caesar (IRE)**[154] 7643 8-8-2 46 oh1 (tp) TheodoreLadd(5) 9 30
(Rebecca Bastiman) *hld up on outer: drvn 2f out: rdn and dropped away over 1f out* 25/1

410- **11** *1* **Adventureman**[213] 5482 7-9-7 60 (p) JackGarritty 7 42
(Ruth Carr) *led: pushed along and hdd over 2f out: sn wknd* 8/1

1m 48.92s (-1.18) **Going Correction** -0.125s/f (Stan) **11** Ran SP% **112.8**
Speed ratings (Par 101): **100,99,98,97,96 95,93,93,91,90 89**
CSF £104.30 CT £858.26 TOTE £15.90: £4.60, £2.40, £3.10; EX 135.20 Trifecta £1037.00.
Owner Stephen Michael Hanlon **Bred** Cheveley Park Stud Ltd **Trained** Suncroft, Co. Kildare

FOCUS
A moderate handicap run at a solid gallop.

913 SUN RACING NOVICE STKS 7f 36y (Tp)
5:30 (5:30) (Class 5) 3-Y-0+ £2,911 (£866; £432; £216) **Stalls High**

Form RPR

41 **1** **Bay Of Naples (IRE)**[11] 733 3-9-4 0 JoeFanning 6 78+
(Mark Johnston) *mde all: pushed along and qckned pce 2f out: rdn in narrow ld 1f out: jnd ins fnl f: r.o resolutely to ld and assert nr fin* 5/6[1]

0/2- **2** *nk* **Sarasota (IRE)**[143] 7996 4-9-9 0 NicolaCurrie 2 71
(Jamie Osborne) *trckd ldrs: pushed along in 3rd 2f out: wnt 2nd 1 1/2f out: drvn to chal 1f out: rdn and jnd wnr ins fnl f: r.o wl: hdd as wnr asserted nr fin* 11/2[2]

0-0 **3** *3* **Maisie Moo**[24] 556 3-8-6 0 HollieDoyle 3 57
(Shaun Keightley) *t.k.h: prom: pushed along in 2nd 2f out: drvn and dropped to 3rd 1 1/2f out: rdn 1f out: one pce fnl f (jockey said filly hung left-handed in the home straight)* 66/1

4 **4** *4 1/2* **Cardano (USA)**[28] 472 3-8-11 0 KieranO'Neill 9 50
(Ian Williams) *mid-div: drvn in 5th 2f out: wnt 4th over 1f out: no ex fnl f (jockey said gelding hung left-handed)* 6/1[3]

5 *nk* **Laulloir (IRE)** 3-8-6 0 ShaneGray 12 44
(Kevin Ryan) *chsd ldrs on outer: drvn in 4th 2f out: reminder 1 1/2f out: rdn and no ex fnl f* 25/1

05 **6** *1* **Percy Alexander**[20] 615 3-8-11 0 TomMarquand 1 46
(James Tate) *hld up: drvn in mid-div 2f out: reminder 1 1/2f out: no ex fr over 1f out* 8/1

0-0 **7** *3/4* **Showshutai**[32] 405 3-8-11 0 PaddyMathers 10 44
(Christopher Kellett) *t.k.h: hld up: pushed along over 2f out: wknd over 1f out* 100/1

0 **8** *shd* **Angel Black (IRE)**[24] 554 3-8-11 0 LiamJones 7 44
(Shaun Keightley) *hld up: drvn 1 1/2f out: no imp (jockey said colt was denied a clear run in the home straight)* 33/1

0- **9** *1 1/4* **Irish Charm (FR)**[119] 8729 5-9-11 0 GabrieleMalune(3) 5 47
(Ivan Furtado) *hld up: nvr involved (enq held into the running and riding of the horse which after breaking slowly from the stalls and settling slightly worse than midfield had stayed on under apparent tender handling to finish ninth of twelve, beaten by 11 lengths. Jockey stated that he h* 6/1[3]

54- **10** *1 3/4* **Born In Thorne**[259] 3718 6-9-6 0 JaneElliott(3) 4 37
(Ivan Furtado) *hld up: pushed along over 2f out: reminder 1 1/2f out: no rspnse* 40/1

11 *nk* **Risk Mitigation (USA)** 3-8-11 0 EoinWalsh 8 35
(David Evans) *hld up: pushed along 3f out: sn drvn: no imp (jockey said colt ran greenly)* 33/1

0- **12** *15* **Angel Dundee**[61] 9727 3-8-1 0 (h) DarraghKeenan(5) 11
(Phil McEntee) *t.k.h: bhd: rn v wd after 1f: sn bk w rest of field but in rr: rn v wd over 2f out: no ch after (jockey said filly hung badly right-handed throughout)* 100/1

1m 30.75s (1.95) **Going Correction** -0.125s/f (Stan) **12** Ran SP% **125.3**
WFA 3 from 4yo+ 17lb
Speed ratings (Par 103): **83,82,79,74,73 72,71,71,70,68 67,50**
CSF £6.06 TOTE £2.10: £1.10, £1.40, £16.90; EX 8.70 Trifecta £267.60.
Owner Sheikh Hamdan bin Mohammed Al Maktoum **Bred** Godolphin **Trained** Middleham Moor, N Yorks

FOCUS
They went a steady early gallop and few got into this. The second has been rated to her previous form.

914 LIKE SUN RACING ON FACEBOOK H'CAP 7f 36y (Tp)
6:00 (6:00) (Class 5) (0-75,75) 4-Y-0+ £2,911 (£866; £432; £216) **Stalls High**

Form RPR

0-01 **1** **Martineo**[36] 347 4-9-5 73 AdamKirby 3 85+
(Paul D'Arcy) *mid-div: hdwy 1 1/2f out: drvn to ld 1f out: rdn clr fnl f: comf* 10/11[1]

-632 **2** *1 3/4* **Lucky Lodge**[11] 741 9-9-2 70 (v) CamHardie 4 77
(Antony Brittain) *trckd ldrs: rdn in 4th 2f out: drvn on outer 1 1/2f out: r.o wl to take 2nd ins fnl furlon: nvr a threat to wnr* 8/1[3]

00-6 **3** *2 1/4* **Tricky Dicky**[32] 407 6-9-4 75 PhilDennis(3) 12 76
(Olly Williams) *chsd ldr: pushed along in 1 l 2nd 2f out: rdn and ev ch over 1f out: sn lft bhd by first two but kpt on for 3rd fnl f* 25/1

03-0 **4** *1/2* **Nezar (IRE)**[34] 361 8-9-4 75 JackDuern(3) 10 75
(Dean Ivory) *chsd ldrs: drvn to chal 1 1/2f out: sn rdn and led briefly over 1f out: hdd 1f out: wknd fnl f* 20/1

111- **5** *3 1/4* **Arlecchino's Leap**[341] 1321 7-9-7 75 DavidProbert 1 66
(Mark Usher) *hld up: pushed along 2f out: rdn over 1f out: kpt on fnl f* 12/1

6-00 **6** *1/2* **Rock Warbler (IRE)**[28] 468 6-8-7 61 (h[1]) HollieDoyle 8 50
(Michael Mullineaux) *in rr: drvn over 2f out: rdn on outer over 1f out: mod hdwy fnl f (jockey said gelding was never travelling)* 14/1

-530 **7** *hd* **Gold Hunter (IRE)**[24] 564 9-9-4 72 TomMarquand 2 61
(Steve Flook) *led: pushed along in 1 l ld 2f out: rdn and hdd over 1f out: wknd fnl f (jockey said gelding stopped quickly)* 10/1

0360 **8** *1 1/2* **Critical Thinking (IRE)**[6] 812 5-9-7 75 (tp) TrevorWhelan 9 60
(David Loughnane) *mid-div: drvn and reminders over 2f out: rdn and wknd over 1f out (jockey said gelding hung right-handed)* 5/1[2]

5-00 **9** *nse* **Blue Rocks**[7] 793 5-8-4 61 oh4 GabrieleMalune(3) 6 46
(Lisa Williamson) *hld up: drvn over 2f out: rdn over 1f out: no rspnse* 33/1

-663 **10** *1 1/2* **Haader (FR)**[13] 706 4-8-13 67 PaddyMathers 5 48
(Derek Shaw) *hld up: drvn 3f out: rdn 1 1/2f out: dropped to last fnl f* 20/1

1m 27.05s (-1.75) **Going Correction** -0.125s/f (Stan) **10** Ran SP% **119.9**
Speed ratings (Par 103): **105,103,100,99,96 95,95,93,93,91**
CSF £8.56 CT £120.70 TOTE £1.80: £1.10, £1.50, £5.40; EX 9.50 Trifecta £94.90.
Owner Power Geneva Ltd **Bred** Saleh Al Homaizi & Imad Al Sagar **Trained** Newmarket, Suffolk

FOCUS
This was run at a good gallop and the winner once again finished strongly to score. The second has been rated back to his old C&D best.

915 BETWAY H'CAP 1m 1f 104y (Tp)
6:30 (6:30) (Class 3) (0-95,90) 4-Y-0+ £7,439 (£2,213; £1,106; £553) **Stalls Low**

Form RPR

426- **1** **Swiss Storm**[172] 7019 5-9-5 88 DavidProbert 5 94+
(Michael Bell) *hld up: pushed along and hdwy on outer 1 1/2f out: drvn to chal 1f out: reminder and led jst ins fnl f: drvn clr last 1/2 f* 7/2[2]

20-0 **2** *1 1/4* **Key Player**[31] 441 4-9-1 84 JoeFanning 1 87
(Eve Johnson Houghton) *trckd ldrs: 3rd 2f out: drvn in cl 3rd over 1f out: rdn into 2nd fnl f: chsd wnr last 1/2 f: kpt on* 8/1

0203 **3** *nk* **Juanito Chico (IRE)**[12] 722 5-8-9 78 (t) OisinMurphy 3 80
(Stuart Williams) *hld up: 5th 2f out: trcking ldrs and looking for room 1 1/2f out: in clr and rdn fnl f: r.o wl to take 3rd nr fin* 6/1[3]

3143 **4** *1/2* **Michele Strogoff**[6] 800 6-9-7 90 AlistairRawlinson 4 91
(Michael Appleby) *led: drvn over 2f out: rdn in 1 l ld 2f out: narrow ld 1f out: hdd jst ins fnl f: sn wknd* 1/1[1]

-432 **5** *3/4* **Mr Top Hat**[10] 764 4-9-6 89 EoinWalsh 6 89
(David Evans) *chsd ldr: rdn in 1 l 2nd 2f out: wknd and dropped to 5th over 1f out (jockey said gelding ran flat)* 8/1

240/ **6** *36* **Corinthian**[872] 7123 6-8-13 82 (v[1]) PaddyMathers 2 6
(Derek Shaw) *in rr: lost tch 1/2-way: sn wl bhd and position accepted* 33/1

1m 57.62s (-3.18) **Going Correction** -0.125s/f (Stan) **6** Ran SP% **111.7**
Speed ratings (Par 107): **109,107,107,107,106 74**
CSF £29.53 TOTE £4.00: £2.00, £2.80; EX 34.10 Trifecta £125.40.
Owner Lordship Stud **Bred** Lordship Stud **Trained** Newmarket, Suffolk

FOCUS
Not a bad handicap, and a welcome return to form by the winner. The third has been rated to his latest.

916 BETWAY LIVE CASINO H'CAP 1m 5f 219y (Tp)
7:00 (7:00) (Class 4) (0-85,87) 4-Y-0+ £4,690 (£1,395; £697; £348) **Stalls Low**

Form RPR

52-1 **1** **Flaming Marvel (IRE)**[46] 184 5-9-12 85 DavidProbert 4 95+
(James Fanshawe) *hld up in rr: hdwy into 4 l 2nd 2f out: sn drvn and clsd on ldr: rdn to join issue fnl f: r.o wl to ld last two strides* 6/4[2]

4/11 **2** *hd* **Ulster (IRE)**[13] 696 4-9-11 87 EdwardGreatrex 5 98+
(Archie Watson) *led: qcknd pce 3f out: drvn in 4 l ld 2f out: 2 l ld over 1f out: rdn and jnd by wnr fnl f: kpt on wl: hdd last two strides* 11/8[1]

034- **3** *9* **Elysees (IRE)**[73] 7100 4-9-2 78 TomMarquand 2 76
(Alan King) *hld up: drvn 3f out: rdn in 4th 2f out: kpt on into distant 3rd fnl f* 4/1[3]

0-21 **4** *4 1/2* **Navajo Star (IRE)**[33] 385 5-8-13 72 (v) KieranO'Neill 6 63
(Robyn Brisland) *trckd ldr: drvn in 2nd 3f out: rdn and dropped to 3rd 2f out: no ex fr over 1f out* 16/1

342- **5** *2 1/2* **Omotesando**[213] 5468 9-8-8 67 (p) CharlieBennett 1 55
(Oliver Greenall) *trckd ldr: drvn 3f out: dropped to last 2f out: sn rdn and no ex* 40/1

2m 58.88s (-2.12) **Going Correction** -0.125s/f (Stan)
WFA 4 from 5yo+ 3lb **5** Ran SP% **110.4**
Speed ratings (Par 105): **101,100,95,93,91**
CSF £3.94 TOTE £2.50: £1.10, £1.40; EX 3.90 Trifecta £5.80.
Owner Merry Fox Stud Limited **Bred** Merry Fox Stud Limited **Trained** Newmarket, Suffolk

FOCUS
The first two in the market had this between them late on. Both look progressive and should be kept on side. The second's Kempton win has been franked by the runner-up since, and he's been rated in line with the better view of that form.

917 LADBROKES HOME OF THE ODDS BOOST H'CAP 1m 4f 51y (Tp)
7:30 (7:30) (Class 5) (0-75,72) 3-Y-O £2,911 (£866; £432; £216) **Stalls Low**

Form RPR

05-2 **1** **Natsovia**[34] 358 3-9-3 68 NicolaCurrie 5 71+
(Jamie Osborne) *in rr: pushed along 4f out: drvn 3f out: last 2f out: hdwy on inner over 1f out: rdn and str run fnl f: led last few strides* 6/1[3]

60-4 **2** *nk* **Thunderoad**[39] 299 3-9-2 70 AaronJones(3) 3 73+
(Marco Botti) *hld up: pushed along and hdwy on outer 1 1/2f out: drvn to ld 1f out: sn 1 l clr: drvn in reduced ld last 100yds: hdd last few strides* 12/1

-434 **3** *1* **Fayetta**[7] 794 3-9-3 68 (p[1]) TrevorWhelan 1 68
(David Loughnane) *hld up: pushed along in 4th 2f out: hdwy over 1f out: rdn and ev ch 1f out: one pce fnl f* 20/1

036- **4** *1 1/2* **Lord Lamington**[131] 8343 3-9-0 65 JoeFanning 6 63
(Mark Johnston) *led: drvn in 2 l ld 2f out: rdn in narrow ld over 1f out: hdd 1f out: sn wknd* 11/4[2]

1-32 **5** *hd* **Debbonair (IRE)**[24] 567 3-9-4 69 BenCurtis 7 66
(Hugo Palmer) *hld up: rdn in 5th 2f out: rdn fnl f: no imp (vet said gelding lost it's right fore shoe)* 15/8[1]

24-0 **6** *6* **Toffee Galore**[34] 360 3-9-7 72 OisinMurphy 2 60
(Archie Watson) *trckd ldr: pushed along in 2 l 2nd 2f out: drvn over 1f out: sn rdn and wknd* 8/1

-062 **7** *2 1/2* **Vin D'Honneur (IRE)**[10] 765 3-8-4 55 (p) LukeMorris 4 39
(Stuart Williams) *trckd ldr: drvn 3f out: sn rdn: wknd 1 1/2f out: dropped to last 1f out* 6/1[3]

2m 38.29s (-2.51) **Going Correction** -0.125s/f (Stan) **7** Ran SP% **113.6**
Speed ratings (Par 97): **103,102,102,101,101 97,95**
CSF £70.09 TOTE £7.10: £2.70, £4.70; EX 66.70 Trifecta £491.50.
Owner H J Shipton **Bred** Sahara Group Holdings **Trained** Upper Lambourn, Berks

FOCUS
The first two raced in the last two positions most of the way and benefited from a pace collapse. The fourth has been rated to form and the third close to form.

T/Plt: £323.70 to a £1 stake. Pool: £93,523.07 - 210.89 winning units T/Qpdt: £64.80 to a £1 stake. Pool: £13,398.70 - 152.91 winning units **Keith McHugh**

[752]KEMPTON (A.W) (R-H)

Wednesday, February 27

OFFICIAL GOING: Polytrack: standard to slow

Wind: Nil Weather: Fine

918 100% PROFIT BOOST AT 32REDSPORT.COM APPRENTICE H'CAP 6f (P)

4:55 (4:56) (Class 6) (0-60,60) 3-Y-O

£3,105 (£924; £461; £400; £400; £400) **Stalls** Low

Form RPR

-340 **1** **Eufemia**[28] 476 3-9-5 **58**............(p[1]) GabrieleMalune 7 63
(Amy Murphy) *wnt rt s: sn cl up: rdn wl over 2f out to keep tabs on ldr: prog over 1f out: picked up wl ins fnl f and led cl home: jst hld on* **9/1**

6-00 **2** *hd* **Grandee Daisy**[25] 550 3-8-7 **53**............(v[1]) GeorgiaDobie[(7)] 6 57
(Jo Hughes, France) *racd in rr-div: briefly rdn over 4f out: effrt over 2f out: no immediate imp tl picked up wl on inner fr 1f out: hrd rdn cl home: jst failed* **6/1**[2]

5533 **3** *shd* **Valley Belle (IRE)**[7] 798 3-8-7 **56**............(v) GraceMcEntee[(10)] 1 60
(Phil McEntee) *sn led: effrt wl over 1f out and gng best: stuck on tl fdd last 75yds and hdd cl home* **13/8**[1]

60-6 **4** 1 ¾ **Fast Endeavour**[7] 813 3-9-1 **54**............ CameronNoble 4 53
(Ian Williams) *racd on inner in mid-div: rdn in centre jst over 2f out: stuck fr over 1f out and clsng nr fin* **10/1**

0-02 **5** 2 **Joey Boy (IRE)**[9] 783 3-9-5 **58**............(b) ThomasGreatrex 11 51
(Kevin Ryan) *hld up in rr: effrt over 2f out: no immediate imp tl picked up wl whn swtchd to outer over 1f out: kpt on fnl f* **17/2**

065- **6** *nse* **Nervous Nerys (IRE)**[60] 9749 3-8-13 **52**............ DylanHogan 2 45
(Alex Hales) *restless in stalls and awkward s: in rr on inner: effrt over 2f out: styd on one pce on inner fr over 1f out* **12/1**

605- **7** 1 ¼ **Camachess (IRE)**[126] 8533 3-9-4 **60**............ ScottMcCullagh[(3)] 10 49
(Philip McBride) *hld up in rr: shkn up over 2f out: shuffled along fr over 1f out: prog fnl f: nvr involved* **25/1**

06-3 **8** 1 **Secret Picnic (FR)**[9] 783 3-9-0 **53**............(p[1]) MeganNicholls 12 39
(John Quinn) *wl away fr wd draw and cl up: effrt over 2f out: nt qckn over 1f out and fdd (trainer's rep said gelding had a breathing problem)* **15/2**[3]

2653 **9** 1 ¾ **Not So Shy**[21] 620 3-8-11 **55**............(v[1]) CierenFallon[(5)] 3 36
(David Evans) *bhd ldr: rdn on outer wl over 2f out: nt qckn and wknd over 1f out* **10/1**

00-6 **10** ¾ **Apron Strings**[11] 752 3-8-10 **52**............ Pierre-LouisJamin[(3)] 8 31
(Michael Attwater) *in rr-div: pushed along over 4f out: rdn 3f out: no imp* **125/1**

0-50 **11** 1 **Speed Skater**[28] 476 3-8-10 **54**............(p[1]) OliverStammers[(5)] 9 30
(Amanda Perrett) *dropped in leaving stalls: in last: rdn wl over 2f out: no imp* **33/1**

1m 13.56s (0.46) **Going Correction** +0.075s/f (Slow) 11 Ran SP% 118.1
Speed ratings (Par 95): **99,98,98,96,93 93,91,90,88,87 85**
CSF £61.73 CT £135.64 TOTE £12.60: £3.40, £2.10, £1.10; EX 76.10 Trifecta £197.60.
Owner R S Hoskins And Partners **Bred** Saleh Al Homaizi & Imad Al Sagar **Trained** Newmarket, Suffolk

■ Stewards' Enquiry : Georgia Dobie two-day ban: used whip above the permitted level (Mar 13-14)

FOCUS
An unseasonably warm day gave way to a clear evening and the Polytrack was given an official description of 'standard to slow'. \n\x\x A close finish in this modest apprentice handicap. Nearly half the field were trying headgear for the first time.

919 32RED ON THE APP STORE H'CAP (DIV I) 6f (P)

5:30 (5:30) (Class 6) (0-60,61) 4-Y-O+

£3,105 (£924; £461; £400; £400; £400) **Stalls** Low

Form RPR

0-46 **1** **Bond Street Beau**[5] 857 4-9-6 **58**............ OisinMurphy 3 64
(Philip McBride) *bhd ldr: rdn 2f out: led over 1f out: stuck on wl cl home: jst hld on* **9/4**[1]

-U12 **2** *hd* **Magicinthemaking (USA)**[13] 718 5-9-1 **53**............ HollieDoyle 6 58
(John E Long) *hld up in mid-div: shkn up 2f and gng wl: effrt over 1f out between horses: wandered sltly ent fnl f: gathered up and gd run on outer wl ins fnl f: jst failed: gng on at fin* **3/1**[2]

00-0 **3** *shd* **Storm Boy**[35] 359 4-8-12 **50**............(b[1]) LukeMorris 8 55
(Michael Attwater) *hld up in rr-div: rdn 2f out w a bit to do: gd prog between runners over 1f out: chal on inner fnl f: no ex last strides* **50/1**

54-5 **4** 1 **Qallaab (IRE)**[14] 702 4-9-0 **59**............(bt[1]) ScottMcCullagh[(7)] 7 60
(Michael Appleby) *hld up in rr: effrt 2f out: n.m.r over 1f out: keeping on strly fnl f* **16/1**

-204 **5** *nse* **Divine Call**[24] 587 12-9-2 **54**............ FrannyNorton 10 55
(Charlie Wallis) *bhd ldrs: rdn 2f out: kpt on fr over 1f out: no ex fnl f* **66/1**

-324 **6** ½ **Monarch Maid**[33] 402 8-8-7 **45**............ KieranO'Neill 5 45
(Peter Hiatt) *led: rdn 2f out: hdd over 1f out: stuck on tl fdd last 110yds* **5/1**[3]

-064 **7** 1 ¾ **King Of Rooks**[14] 701 6-8-13 **56**............ DylanHogan[(5)] 11 50
(Henry Spiller) *hld up in rr-div: effrt 2f out on outer: nt qckn over 1f out: styd on tl no ex and eased last 100yds* **10/1**

0-34 **8** 5 **Pranceabootthetoon (IRE)**[39] 322 4-8-7 **45**............(t[1]) NicolaCurrie 9 23
(Milton Bradley) *bhd ldr: ev ch 2f out: stl there over 1f out: sn no ex and wknd* **50/1**

-100 **9** ½ **Deer Song**[25] 553 6-8-9 **47**............(b) LiamJones 2 24
(John Bridger) *mid-div: rdn 2f out: hld over 1f out* **16/1**

6-31 **10** 3 ¼ **Elliot The Dragon (IRE)**[35] 357 4-8-9 **47**............ CallumShepherd 1 13+
(Derek Shaw) *missed break and detached: prog but keen in rr at 1/2-way: effrt over 2f out: no ex sn after (jockey said gelding was slowly away)* **5/1**[3]

1m 13.56s (0.46) **Going Correction** +0.075s/f (Slow) 10 Ran SP% 115.4
Speed ratings (Par 101): **99,98,98,97,97 96,94,87,86,82**
CSF £8.80 CT £250.99 TOTE £3.30: £1.10, £1.80, £11.50; EX 10.00 Trifecta £260.70.
Owner Chris Budgett & P J McBride **Bred** Mrs Mary Taylor & Kirtlington Stud **Trained** Newmarket, Suffolk

FOCUS
A desperate finish to this moderate race, with the winner clinging on after taking it up early in the straight. Straightforward form.

920 32RED ON THE APP STORE H'CAP (DIV II) 6f (P)

6:00 (6:00) (Class 6) (0-60,59) 4-Y-O+

£3,105 (£924; £461; £400; £400; £400) **Stalls** Low

Form RPR

64-4 **1** **Krazy Paving**[48] 161 7-8-5 **48**............(b) MeganNicholls[(5)] 6 57
(Olly Murphy) *cl up w ldrs on outer: effrt 2f out: led ent fnl f: sn clr* **10/1**

-404 **2** 2 **Fantasy Justifier (IRE)**[4] 882 8-9-4 **56**............(p) DavidProbert 3 59+
(Ronald Harris) *hld up towards rr and t.k.h early: shkn up 2f out: smooth prog over 1f out between horses and sltly checked bef being rdn ent fnl f: tk 2nd cl home: nvr nrr (jockey said gelding ran too free)* **5/1**[3]

5-00 **3** ½ **Little Miss Daisy**[32] 433 5-9-6 **58**............ TomMarquand 10 59
(William Muir) *hld up in rr: shkn up and clsr over 2f out: effrt 2f out and darted to inner: chal over 1f out: stuck on fnl f: lost 2nd cl home* **40/1**

4-54 **4** *nk* **Kyllukey**[6] 834 6-8-7 **45**............(t) FrannyNorton 1 45
(Charlie Wallis) *bhd ldr: waiting for gap jst over 2f out: sn rdn: kpt on one pce fnl f* **3/1**[1]

0350 **5** 1 ¾ **Swiss Cross**[5] 848 12-9-0 **52**............(p) CallumShepherd 5 46
(Phil McEntee) *bhd ldr on rail: rdn 2f out: kpt on over 1f out: no ex ins fnl f* **9/1**

3430 **6** ½ **Knockout Blow**[23] 596 4-9-7 **59**............(p) CharlieBennett 4 52
(Jim Boyle) *racd in rr-div: rdn on outer 2f: one pce after* **11/2**

00-0 **7** 1 ¼ **Swendab (IRE)**[21] 626 11-9-1 **53**............(b) RossaRyan 11 42
(John O'Shea) *qckly away fr wd draw and sn led: rdn 2f out: hdd ent fnl f: wknd qckly* **66/1**

2-33 **8** *nk* **Daring Guest (IRE)**[29] 467 5-9-4 **56**............(b) LukeMorris 8 44
(Tom Clover) *w ldr: rdn 2f out: fdd over 1f out (jockey said gelding ran too free)* **9/2**[2]

0U-0 **9** *shd* **Lisnamoyle Lady (IRE)**[43] 243 4-8-8 **46** ow1............(bt) DannyBrock 2 34
(Martin Smith) *a towards rr: effrt 2f out: no imp* **12/1**

0-60 **10** 1 ¾ **Burauq**[7] 809 7-8-7 **45**............(v) JosephineGordon 7 27
(Milton Bradley) *in rr-div: rdn wd over 2f out: plugged on* **28/1**

40- **11** 7 **Give Em A Clump (IRE)**[84] 9401 4-8-4 **47**............(v) RhiainIngram[(5)] 9 7
(Paul George) *a in rr* **16/1**

1m 13.18s (0.08) **Going Correction** +0.075s/f (Slow) 11 Ran SP% 115.3
Speed ratings (Par 101): **102,99,98,98,95 95,93,93,93,90 81**
CSF £57.57 CT £1949.43 TOTE £9.40: £2.90, £2.00, £8.70; EX 57.20 Trifecta £2056.00.
Owner All The Kings Horses & Aiden Murphy **Bred** Trebles Holford Farm Thoroughbreds **Trained** Wilmcote, Warks

FOCUS
Quicker than the opening two 6f handicaps, but these were fully exposed sorts in a moderate race.

921 32RED CASINO NOVICE STKS 1m 3f 219y(P)

6:30 (6:31) (Class 5) 4-Y-O+ **£3,881** (£1,155; £577; £288) **Stalls** Low

Form RPR

1 **Gumball (FR)**[88] 5-9-4 0............(h[1]) OisinMurphy 2 86
(Philip Hobbs) *mde most: swtchd to wd outside away fr rivals sn after s: sn clr ldr: ld reduced at 1/2-way: increased pce wl over 3f out: kicked for home 2f out: stuck on wl fnl f* **4/1**[2]

12- **2** 1 ¾ **Verdana Blue (IRE)**[63] 9399 7-9-6 0............ LukeMorris 7 85
(Nicky Henderson) *bhd wnr: rdn 2f out: kpt on wl chsng wnr fr over 1f out but no imp fnl f* **1/3**[1]

3 10 **Et Moi Alors (FR)**[14] 5-9-4 0............ HectorCrouch 5 67
(Gary Moore) *hld up in rr-div: dropped to rr wl over 4f out: rdn wl over 2f out: prog to take remote 3rd ent fnl f* **25/1**

6-5 **4** 3 ¾ **Ace Cheetah (USA)**[14] 696 5-9-4 0............ DannyBrock 8 61
(J R Jenkins) *early ldr: settled bhd wnr: rdn wl over 2f out: sn lft bhd by ldng pair: lost 3rd ent fnl f* **250/1**

41- **5** 2 **Twist (IRE)**[59] 9766 4-9-9 0............ AdamKirby 6 65
(Nicky Henderson) *racd in mid-div: rdn wl over 2f out: no imp over 1f out* **7/1**[3]

05 **6** ¾ **Oborne Lady (IRE)**[25] 562 6-8-13 0............ RobHornby 4 52
(Seamus Mullins) *racd in mid-div: rdn wl over 2f out: plugged on after* **250/1**

6 *dht* **Lawyersgunsn'money**[33] 4-9-2 0............ DavidProbert 9 57
(Roger Teal) *in rr-div: rdn wl over 2f out: one pce after* **200/1**

4- **8** 1 ½ **Sacred Sprite**[77] 9509 4-8-11 0............ JFEgan 1 49
(John Berry) *hld up in last: rdn wl over 2f out: no imp* **50/1**

0 **9** ¾ **Puzzle Cache**[35] 370 5-8-13 0............(b) CharlieBennett 3 48
(Rod Millman) *hld up in rr-div: rdn wl over 2f: one pce* **150/1**

2m 36.59s (2.09) **Going Correction** +0.075s/f (Slow)
WFA 4 from 5yo+ 2lb 9 Ran SP% 115.3
Speed ratings (Par 103): **96,94,88,85,84 83,83,82,82**
CSF £5.85 TOTE £6.40: £1.20, £1.02, £3.00; EX 7.50 Trifecta £41.80.
Owner Terry Warner **Bred** J Gallorini, Mlle M Bilesimo Et Al **Trained** Withycombe, Somerset

FOCUS
A staying novice which was dominated by horses usually seen over hurdles.

922 32RED H'CAP (LONDON MILE SERIES QUALIFIER) 1m (P)

7:00 (7:01) (Class 4) (0-85,87) 4-Y-O+

£6,469 (£1,925; £962; £481; £400; £400) **Stalls** Low

Form RPR

213- **1** **Rampant Lion (IRE)**[85] 9390 4-9-6 **82**............(p) DavidProbert 7 90+
(William Jarvis) *racd in mid-div on inner: shkn up and swtchd to outer wl over 1f out: rdn ent fnl f: led 110yds out: pushed out to maintain narrow advantage: snugly* **11/2**[2]

00-0 **2** ½ **Poetic Force (IRE)**[25] 557 5-9-7 **83**............(t) GeorgeDowning 1 90
(Tony Carroll) *bhd ldrs: shkn up 2f out and sn in firing line between horses: rdn over 1f out to ld: pressed jst ins fnl f: hdd 110yds out: stuck on (jockey said gelding hung left-handed under pressure)* **12/1**

1345 **3** *nk* **Scofflaw**[21] 625 5-9-2 **78**............(v) HectorCrouch 9 84
(David Evans) *hld up in rr: shkn up and swtchd to outer over 2f out: rdn 2f out: no immediate imp w plenty to do: qcknd wl over 1f out: gaining fnl 150yds: nvr nrr* **12/1**

6-53 **4** 2 ½ **Enzemble (IRE)**[25] 557 4-9-3 **79**............ DanielMuscutt 11 80
(James Fanshawe) *w ldr and t.k.h: marginal ld 2f out: rdn wl over 1f out and sn hdd: no ex sn after* **7/1**

-651 **5** *nk* **Samphire Coast**[14] 699 6-9-5 **81**............(v) PaddyMathers 10 81
(Derek Shaw) *hld up in mid-div between horses: tk fierce hold at times: rdn over 1f out: kpt on tl no ex last 110yds* **8/1**

/-65 **6** 4 ½ **Me Too Nagasaki (IRE)**[14] 699 5-9-4 **80**............(t) OisinMurphy 6 70
(Stuart Williams) *t.k.h early in ld: hdd 2f out: no ex ent fnl f* **13/2**[3]

-155 **7** *1* **Kodiline (IRE)**[12] 734 5-9-2 **78**........................ EoinWalsh 3 65
(David Evans) *bhd ldrs: rdn jst over 2f out: plugged on fr over 1f out (jockey said gelding ran too free)* **33/1**

0-45 **8** *2 3/4* **Brittanic (IRE)**[36] 350 5-9-2 **78**........................ JamieSpencer 8 59
(David Simcock) *s.s and in rr: rdn over 2f out and swtchd to inner: kpt on one pce* **9/1**

04-2 **9** *3 3/4* **Intrepidly (USA)**[25] 557 5-9-11 **87**........................(p) AdamKirby 13 59
(Charlie Fellowes) *cl up on outer: rdn over 2f out: no ex over 1f out* **11/4**[1]

325- **10** *1 3/4* **Rock Icon**[180] 6771 6-9-6 **82**........................ JFEgan 4 50
(Jo Hughes, France) *cl up and t.k.h: pushed along wl over 3f out to hold pl: sme prog over 1f out: no ex and eased fr 1f out (jockey said gelding ran too free)* **20/1**

2-00 **11** *2* **Regulator (IRE)**[14] 699 4-9-4 **80**........................ RossaRyan 5 44
(Alexandra Dunn) *hld up in rr-div: wkng fr wl over 2f out: no ex in rr 2f out* **66/1**

10-2 **12** *1/2* **Intense Style (IRE)**[12] 740 7-9-1 **80**........................ JaneElliott[(3)] 12 42
(Les Eyre) *racd far too wd in rr-div and duly fdd qckly over 2f out* **28/1**

1m 39.08s (-0.72) **Going Correction** +0.075s/f (Slow) **12 Ran SP% 117.0**
Speed ratings (Par 105): **106,105,105,102,102 97,96,94,90,88 86,86**
CSF £65.88 CT £774.87 TOTE £4.70: £2.20, £4.20, £2.90; EX 62.20 Trifecta £451.10.
Owner Dr J Walker **Bred** R J Cornelius **Trained** Newmarket, Suffolk

FOCUS
Easily the best race on the evening and it looked a fair, competitive handicap

923 WISE BETTING AT RACINGTV.COM H'CAP — 1m 2f 219y(P)
7:30 (7:32) (Class 6) (0-60,60) 4-Y-O+
£3,105 (£924; £461; £400; £400; £400) Stalls Low

Form RPR

-361 **1** **Singing The Blues (IRE)**[8] 789 4-9-5 **59** 6ex........................ OisinMurphy 7 66+
(Rod Millman) *bhd ldr: shkn up 2f out: rdn to ld over 1f out: pressed either side thrght fnl f but stuck wl on u.str ride* **2/1**[1]

0-35 **2** *1/2* **Rail Dancer**[25] 560 7-9-5 **58**........................(v) AdamKirby 4 63
(Shaun Keightley) *hld up in mid-div: rdn 2f out: chal wnr on inner thrght fnl f but nt get past* **5/1**[2]

4-63 **3** *3/4* **Iley Boy**[25] 560 5-9-2 **55**........................(p) JoeyHaynes 3 59
(John Gallagher) *cl up in mid-div: rdn 2f out: chal wnr on outer thrght fnl f but no ex in 3rd last 55yds* **10/1**

30-2 **4** *1/2* **Zamperini (IRE)**[25] 560 7-9-6 **59**........................ HectorCrouch 5 62
(Gary Moore) *on outer of mid-div: effrt jst over 2f out: nt qckn tl picked up wl ent fnl f: keeping on at fin* **11/2**[3]

5-35 **5** *1 3/4* **Subliminal**[25] 559 4-9-6 **60**........................ TomMarquand 12 61
(Simon Dow) *wl away fr wd drawn and sn led: effrt 2f out: hdd over 1f out: no ex fnl f* **12/1**

00-1 **6** *1 1/2* **Cold Harbour**[46] 207 4-9-0 **54**........................(t) KieranO'Neill 11 53
(Robyn Brisland) *hld up in rr: rdn 2f out: kpt on wl fr over 1f out: nvr nrr* **8/1**

04-4 **7** *3/4* **Don't Cry About It (IRE)**[40] 288 4-9-1 **55**........................(bt) GeorgeWood 10 52
(Ali Stronge) *hld up in rr: rdn 2f out w a bit to do: kpt on wl fr over 1f out: nvr nrr (jockey said gelding was slowly away)* **25/1**

0-50 **8** *2 1/2* **Carvelas (IRE)**[42] 262 10-9-7 **60**........................ DavidProbert 8 52
(J R Jenkins) *on inner in rr-div: effrt 2f out: plugged on* **33/1**

50-3 **9** *1 3/4* **Monsieur Fox**[40] 288 4-9-1 **55**........................ LukeMorris 6 45
(Lydia Richards) *bhd ldr: effrt 3f out: one pce after* **20/1**

-002 **10** *2 1/2* **Boycie**[8] 789 6-9-1 **54**........................(p) HollieDoyle 9 39
(Adrian Wintle) *hld up in rr: rdn over 2f out: no imp (jockey said gelding ran in snatches; vet reported the gelding lost its left hind shoe)* **16/1**

00-0 **11** *3/4* **Art Of Swing (IRE)**[21] 619 7-9-5 **58**........................ LiamJones 13 42
(Lee Carter) *a towards rr* **66/1**

3-60 **12** *1* **Claudine (IRE)**[11] 760 4-9-1 **60**........................ ThomasGreatrex[(5)] 2 43
(Alexandra Dunn) *cl up in mid-div: effrt 2f out: wknd qckly on inner over 1f out (jockey said filly hung left-handed under pressure)* **50/1**

13 *hd* **Sin Sin (IRE)**[127] 8832 5-9-5 **58**........................ RossaRyan 1 40
(Nigel Hawke) *bhd ldr: effrt 2f out: no ex sn after* **25/1**

2m 22.94s (1.94) **Going Correction** +0.075s/f (Slow) **13 Ran SP% 118.0**
WFA 4 from 5yo+ 1lb
Speed ratings (Par 101): **99,98,98,97,96 95,94,93,91,89 89,88,88**
CSF £10.10 CT £81.86 TOTE £4.00: £1.20, £2.00, £2.90; EX 13.50 Trifecta £78.00.
Owner Rod Millman & Andy Smith **Bred** Lynn Lodge Stud **Trained** Kentisbeare, Devon

FOCUS
Punters only wanted to know about one horse in this moderate handicap and the favourite duly got the best of a driving finish.

924 32RED.COM H'CAP (DIV I) — 7f (P)
8:00 (8:03) (Class 6) (0-60,62) 4-Y-O+
£3,105 (£924; £461; £400; £400; £400) Stalls Low

Form RPR

-051 **1** **Elusif (IRE)**[14] 701 4-8-12 **50**........................(v) HollieDoyle 3 61+
(Shaun Keightley) *early ldr: disp after tl led over 4f out: rdn 2f out and sn in command* **9/4**[1]

-004 **2** *2 1/2* **Rising Sunshine (IRE)**[26] 531 6-8-7 **45**........................(vt[1]) LukeMorris 2 49
(Milton Bradley) *squeezed up and pushed along leaving stalls: sn bhd ldrs: rdn to chse wnr fr 2f out: kpt on wl but no ch fnl f* **33/1**

1-30 **3** *2 3/4* **Storm Melody**[14] 701 6-9-10 **62**........................(p) TomMarquand 10 59
(Ali Stronge) *hld up in rr-div: effrt on outer over 2f out: kpt on wl fr over 1f out* **14/1**

46-1 **4** *1/2* **Collate**[33] 399 4-9-6 **58**........................(v) DavidProbert 4 55
(Amy Murphy) *hld up in rr-div: gng wl w plenty to do whn ct on heels over 2f out: rdn over 1f out and shuffled along ins fnl f to take 4th (jockey said filly was denied a clear run)* **11/2**

000- **5** *nk* **Merdon Castle (IRE)**[91] 9286 7-8-4 **47**........................ FayeMcManoman[(5)] 1 41
(Frank Bishop) *cl up in mid-div: effrt 2 out: plugged on fr over 1f out* **33/1**

65-0 **6** *2 1/2* **Maazel (IRE)**[35] 365 5-9-1 **53**........................ LiamJones 7 41
(Lee Carter) *mid-div: clsr over 2f out: rdn to chse ldrs 2f out: kpt on wl tl no ex fnl f* **12/1**

0-05 **7** *2 1/4* **Reignite**[28] 476 4-9-7 **59**........................(h) AdamKirby 8 41
(Emma Owen) *in rr and struggling: sme prog fr over 2f out (trainer could offer no explanation for the gelding's performance)* **9/2**[3]

5-30 **8** *6* **Star Attraction (FR)**[25] 553 4-8-7 **45**........................ KieranO'Neill 11 10
(Tony Carroll) *in rr-div: effrt 2f out: no ex over 1f out* **66/1**

00-2 **9** *2* **Percy Toplis**[23] 594 5-8-4 **47** ow2........................(p) KevinLundie[(5)] 5 7
(Christine Dunnett) *racd in mid-div: effrt over 2f: no imp over 1f out* **16/1**

45/1 **10** *1/2* **Hungarian Rhapsody**[28] 484 5-9-6 **58**........................ NicolaCurrie 9 17
(Jamie Osborne) *disp ld tl 2nd over 4f out: fdd fr 2f out (jockey said gelding had no more to give)* **7/2**[2]

6532 **11** *3 1/4* **The Special One (IRE)**[7] 801 6-8-10 **55**........................(h) GraceMcEntee[(7)] 13 5
(Phil McEntee) *a in rr-div: no imp fr 2f out* **16/1**

1m 25.75s (-0.25) **Going Correction** +0.075s/f (Slow) **11 Ran SP% 120.1**
Speed ratings (Par 101): **104,101,98,97,97 94,91,84,82,81 78**
CSF £91.47 CT £898.14 TOTE £2.50: £1.30, £6.90, £3.40; EX 54.90 Trifecta £758.40.
Owner Simon Lockyer & Tim Clarke **Bred** Miss Y Jacques **Trained** Newmarket, Suffolk

FOCUS
Three of these came into this off the back of a win and it may rate a shade better than the majority of 0-60s.

925 32RED.COM H'CAP (DIV II) — 7f (P)
8:30 (8:31) (Class 6) (0-60,60) 4-Y-O+
£3,105 (£924; £461; £400; £400; £400) Stalls Low

Form RPR

2463 **1** **Viola Park**[28] 484 5-9-1 **54**........................(p) DavidProbert 1 63
(Ronald Harris) *bhd ldr: shkn up 2f out: rdn to ld over 1f out: kpt on wl fnl f* **11/4**[1]

3-04 **2** *1 1/4* **Stand N Deliver**[37] 348 5-9-6 **59**........................(v[1]) AdamKirby 8 65
(Clive Cox) *bhd ldrs: rdn 2f out on outer: stuck on fr over 1f out and tk 2nd cl home* **5/1**[3]

-342 **3** *shd* **Rivas Rob Roy**[28] 484 4-9-3 **56**........................ JoeyHaynes 6 61
(John Gallagher) *t.k.h early bhd ldr: rdn 2f out: ev ch over 1f out: kpt on fnl f tl no ex and lost 2nd cl home* **7/2**[2]

-400 **4** *3 1/4* **Compton Prince**[7] 809 10-8-7 **46** oh1........................(v) LukeMorris 2 43
(Milton Bradley) *bhd ldrs: effrt on inner 2f out: ev ch over 1f out: plugged on one pce fnl f* **33/1**

20-0 **5** *1/2* **Mezmaar**[49] 138 10-9-4 **60**........................ GaryMahon[(3)] 7 55
(Mark Usher) *racd in rr-div on inner: effrt wl over 2f out: stuck on fr over 1f out to take poor 5th post* **9/1**

/0-0 **6** *nk* **Footstepsintherain (IRE)**[14] 701 9-9-4 **57**........................ LiamJones 4 51
(J R Jenkins) *reluctant to load: sn led: rdn 2f out: hdd over 1f out: plugged on tl wknd jst ins fnl f* **16/1**

0-05 **7** *nk* **More Salutes (IRE)**[14] 701 4-8-11 **50**........................ RobHornby 3 44
(Michael Attwater) *restless in stalls: racd in rr-div: rdn over 2f out: sme prog over 1f out: one pce ent fnl f (jockey said colt may have knocked itself in the stalls; vet reported the colt had a graze on its right fore leg)* **6/1**

6-01 **8** *3/4* **Caledonia Laird**[23] 599 8-8-12 **58**........................(v) GeorgiaDobie[(7)] 11 50
(Jo Hughes, France) *hld up in rr: sltly outpcd 1/2-way: effrt over 2f out w plenty to do: kpt on* **16/1**

6044 **9** *shd* **Malaysian Boleh**[13] 719 9-8-7 **46** oh1........................(be) NicolaCurrie 10 37
(Phil McEntee) *racd in rr on outer: effrt over 2f out: plugged on fr over 1f out* **20/1**

4306 **10** *1 1/4* **Tasaaboq**[14] 702 8-8-7 **46** oh1........................(tp) JosephineGordon 12 34
(Phil McEntee) *in rr and sltly outpcd at 1/2-way: rdn 3f out: no imp* **66/1**

-005 **11** *1 1/4* **Clement (IRE)**[23] 600 9-8-6 **52**........................ KateLeahy[(7)] 9 37
(John O'Shea) *mid-div on outer: rdn to hold pl 4f out: no ex 2f out* **25/1**

0-00 **12** *10* **Demons And Wizards (IRE)**[13] 717 4-8-7 **46**........................(b) KieranO'Neill 5 4
(Lydia Richards) *racd in rr-div: pushed along 4f out: taken off heels ent st: no ex over 1f out* **20/1**

1m 25.84s (-0.16) **Going Correction** +0.075s/f (Slow) **12 Ran SP% 119.4**
Speed ratings (Par 101): **103,101,101,97,97 96,96,95,95,94 92,81**
CSF £15.44 CT £50.89 TOTE £3.20: £1.60, £2.10, £1.70; EX 18.60 Trifecta £55.20.
Owner John & Margaret Hatherell & RHS Ltd **Bred** Limestone Stud **Trained** Earlswood, Monmouths

FOCUS
Little to choose between those at the top of the market and the front three pulled clear. It was slightly slower than the first division.
T/Plt: £43.80 to a £1 stake. Pool: £84,269.71. 1,401.44 winning units. T/Qpdt: £20.30 to a £1 stake. Pool: £13,528.83. 491.94 winning units. **Cathal Gahan**

829 SOUTHWELL (L-H)
Wednesday, February 27

OFFICIAL GOING: Fibresand: standard to slow
Wind: Light, across Weather: Fine & dry

926 BETWAY CASINO H'CAP — 4f 214y(F)
2:30 (2:30) (Class 6) (0-60,63) 4-Y-O+
£2,264 (£673; £336; £168) Stalls Centre

Form RPR

50-6 **1** **Kath's Boy (IRE)**[28] 476 5-8-0 **46** oh1........................(b[1]) ElishaWhittington[(7)] 8 54
(Tony Carroll) *towards rr: hdwy in centre over 2f out: chsd ldrs over 1f out: rdn to ld ins fnl f: kpt on strly* **33/1**

-243 **2** *2 3/4* **Piazon**[27] 503 8-9-9 **62**........................(be) PaulHanagan 2 60
(Julia Brooke) *cl up centre: led 3f out: pushed along 2f out: rdn over 1f out: drvn and hdd ins fnl f: edgd lft and kpt on one pce* **11/4**[2]

0-54 **3** *1/2* **Bluella**[7] 811 4-8-7 **46** oh1........................ AndrewMullen 7 42
(Robyn Brisland) *racd towards stands' side: prom: effrt and cl up wl over 1f out: rdn and ev ch ent fnl f: sn drvn and kpt on same pce* **33/1**

1211 **4** *1/2* **Gorgeous General**[6] 834 4-9-3 **63** 6ex........................ WilliamCarver[(7)] 1 57
(Lawrence Mullaney) *racd towards far side: trckd ldrs: pushed along 2f out: rdn wl over 1f out: drvn and edgd lft ent fnl f: kpt on one pce* **11/8**[1]

14-0 **5** *1 1/2* **Fly True**[24] 586 6-8-10 **49**........................ NickyMackay 5 38
(Ivan Furtado) *in rr and sn pushed along: rdn over 2f out: styd on u.p appr fnl f: nrst fin* **10/1**

-031 **6** *3/4* **Toni's A Star**[21] 626 7-9-4 **62**........................ PoppyBridgwater[(5)] 6 48
(Tony Carroll) *slt ld centre: hdd 3f out: cl up rdn 2f out: drvn over 1f out: sn wknd* **12/1**

01-6 **7** *nk* **Astraea**[41] 279 4-9-7 **60**........................ NathanEvans 3 45
(Michael Easterby) *dwlt: in rr and sn swtchd lft to far rail: bhd and rdn along over 2f out: kpt on u.p fnl f (jockey said filly became upset in the stalls)* **8/1**[3]

-000 **8** *1/2* **Letmestopyouthere (IRE)**[11] 759 5-9-7 **60**........................ EdwardGreatrex 9 43
(Archie Watson) *racd towards stands' side: chsd ldrs: rdn along over 2f out: sn drvn and wknd (jockey said gelding hung left throughout)* **11/1**

000- **9** *9* **Ritas Legacy**[78] 9493 5-8-7 **46** oh1........................(p[1]) EoinWalsh 4
(Roy Brotherton) *chsd ldrs centre: rdn along over 2f out: sn wknd* **100/1**

58.21s (-1.49) **Going Correction** -0.25s/f (Stan) **9 Ran SP% 111.9**
Speed ratings (Par 101): **101,96,95,95,92 91,90,90,75**
CSF £117.90 CT £3074.73 TOTE £45.00: £7.00, £1.30, £6.80; EX 179.50 Trifecta £1816.20.
Owner C J Wheeler **Bred** Mrs Eleanor Commins **Trained** Cropthorne, Worcs

FOCUS
A modest sprint handicap on standard to slow Fibresand. An outsider won going away towards the centre from a high draw and the winning time was under a second outside standard.

927 BETWAY LIVE CASINO H'CAP 1m 4f 14y(F)
3:05 (3:05) (Class 5) (0-75,73) 4-Y-0+ £2,911 (£866; £432; £216) Stalls Low

Form RPR
0-51 **1** **Purple Rock (IRE)**[14] 703 7-9-9 **73**..........(e) DanielMuscutt 1 84
(Gay Kelleway) *mde all: rdn along wl over 2f out: drvn clr over 1f out: kpt on strly* **15/8**[1]
-013 **2** *7* **Epitaph (IRE)**[6] 833 5-9-1 **65**..........(b) AndrewMullen 5 65
(Michael Appleby) *chsd ldng pair: pushed along 4f out: rdn and outpcd 3f out: drvn 2f out: kpt on u.p fnl f: tk 2nd nr fin* **6/1**
-032 **3** *1/2* **Harbour Quay**[6] 833 5-9-0 **64**.......... PaulMulrennan 6 63
(Robyn Brisland) *cl up: chal 3f out: rdn and ev ch over 2f out: drvn over 1f out: kpt on same pce: lost 2nd nr fin* **11/4**[2]
6310 **4** *3/4* **Seasearch**[12] 731 4-8-9 **64**..........(p) WilliamCox(3) 2 62
(Andrew Balding) *trckd ldng pair: pushed along on inner over 3f out: rdn wl over 2f out: sn drvn and kpt on same pce* **9/2**[3]
01-0 **5** *17* **Handsome Bob (IRE)**[34] 387 4-9-0 **66**..........(b) CallumRodriguez 3 37
(Keith Dalgleish) *chsd ldrs: pushed along over 5f out: rdn 4f out: sn outpcd* **16/1**
4-0 **6** *3/4* **High Command (IRE)**[34] 390 6-9-2 **71**.......... KevinLundie(5) 4 41
(Michael Appleby) *dwlt: a bhd (jockey said gelding hung both ways throughout)* **10/1**

2m 34.74s (-6.26) **Going Correction** -0.25s/f (Stan)
WFA 4 from 5yo+ 2lb **6** Ran SP% **108.9**
Speed ratings (Par 103): **110,105,105,104,93 92**
CSF £12.62 TOTE £2.20: £2.20, £2.30; EX 10.40 Trifecta £31.60.
Owner Strictly Fun Racing Club **Bred** Barronstown Stud **Trained** Exning, Suffolk

FOCUS
An ordinary middle-distance handicap. The favourite cleared away from the front in the final two furlongs in a fair winning time. The winner was backing up his C&D latest and has been rated close to his old best.

928 BETWAY H'CAP 6f 16y(F)
3:35 (3:35) (Class 5) (0-75,73) 4-Y-0+ £2,911 (£866; £432; £216) Stalls Low

Form RPR
1135 **1** **Point Zero (IRE)**[6] 823 4-9-6 **72**..........(be) AlistairRawlinson 4 78
(Michael Appleby) *mde virtually all: rdn clr over 1f out: drvn out* **7/2**[1]
133- **2** *1 1/4* **Granny Roz**[156] 7602 5-9-7 **73**.......... PaulMulrennan 3 75
(Ray Craggs) *chsd wnr: rdn along over 2f out: drvn over 1f out: kpt on same pce u.p fnl f* **11/2**[3]
203- **3** *1/2* **Global Exceed**[236] 4601 4-9-4 **70**.......... JoeFanning 6 70
(Robert Cowell) *chsd ldrs: hdwy 3f out: rdn wl over 1f out: drvn and kpt on fnl f* **4/1**[2]
510- **4** *1* **Vallarta (IRE)**[121] 8704 9-8-11 **63**.......... AndrewMullen 2 60
(Ruth Carr) *chsd ldng pair: effrt over 2f out and sn rdn: drvn over 1f out: kpt on same pce fnl f* **8/1**
00-0 **5** *1/2* **Alba Del Sole (IRE)**[45] 233 4-8-9 **61**..........(p) JasonHart 5 56
(Ivan Furtado) *dwlt: hdwy on outer to chse ldrs 1/2-way: rdn along over 2f out: drvn over 1f out: kpt on same pce* **4/1**[2]
3605 **6** *nk* **National Glory (IRE)**[11] 755 4-9-7 **73**..........(p) EdwardGreatrex 1 67
(Archie Watson) *towards rr: pushed along and effrt on inner 3f out: rdn over 2f out: sn drvn and no imp* **7/2**[1]

1m 15.62s (-0.88) **Going Correction** -0.25s/f (Stan) **6** Ran SP% **110.9**
Speed ratings (Par 103): **95,93,92,91,90 90**
CSF £22.01 TOTE £3.60: £1.20, £4.10; EX 14.60 Trifecta £56.00.
Owner The Horse Watchers **Bred** Tom Foley **Trained** Oakham, Rutland

FOCUS
An ordinary handicap. One of the joint-favourites made most, with a fast third-furlong grabbing an advantage that he defended gamely in the second part of the race. The second and third have been rated close to form.

929 SUNRACING.CO.UK H'CAP 7f 14y(F)
4:10 (4:10) (Class 2) (0-105,95) 4-Y-0+
£12,450 (£3,728; £1,864; £932; £466; £234) Stalls Low

Form RPR
12-1 **1** **Weld Al Emarat**[55] 44 7-8-9 **83**.......... NathanEvans 3 94
(Michael Easterby) *hld up: hdwy whn n.m.r and swtchd rt to outer 2f out: rdn to chse ldrs over 1f out: chal ins fnl f: drvn and kpt on wl to ld nr line* **5/2**[1]
-461 **2** *hd* **Space Bandit**[27] 508 4-8-4 **83**.......... TheodoreLadd(5) 4 93
(Michael Appleby) *prom on inner: cl up over 2f out: led over 1f out and sn rdn: drvn ins fnl f: hdd and no ex nr fin* **11/4**[2]
0-12 **3** *1 3/4* **Mister Music**[29] 466 10-8-4 **83**.......... PoppyBridgwater(5) 2 89
(Tony Carroll) *dwlt and in rr: hdwy on inner over 2f out: rdn to chse ldrs over 1f out: ch ins fnl f: kpt on same pce last 75yds* **20/1**
2-12 **4** *1 1/2* **Three Weeks (USA)**[32] 440 4-9-5 **93**..........(p) JoeFanning 7 95
(David O'Meara) *prom: chsd ldr 1/2-way: cl up 3f out: rdn to ld 2f out: hdd and drvn over 1f out: edgd lft and kpt on same pce fnl f* **11/1**
1-54 **5** *3* **Robero**[42] 260 7-8-3 **84**..........(e) SeanKirrane(7) 5 78
(Gay Kelleway) *chsd ldrs: rdn along over 2f out: drvn over 1f out: kpt on one pce* **33/1**
2516 **6** *2 1/2* **Custard The Dragon**[7] 805 6-8-10 **84**..........(v) AndrewMullen 1 71
(John Mackie) *towards rr: hdwy whn n.m.r 2f out: swtchd rt and rdn over 1f out: sn drvn and n.d* **10/1**
-026 **7** *4* **Angel Palanas**[6] 832 5-8-2 **83** ow1..........(p) RhonaPindar(7) 6 59
(K R Burke) *dwlt: sn chsng ldrs: cl up on outer over 3f out: rdn along over 2f out: sn wknd* **9/1**
16-1 **8** *2 1/4* **Saint Equiano**[57] 4 5-9-4 **92**.......... CallumRodriguez 9 62
(Keith Dalgleish) *led: rdn along over 2f out: sn hdd & wknd (jockey said gelding stopped quickly. Vet said gelding was lame on it's right hind)* **4/1**[3]
252- **9** *4* **Gurkha Friend**[151] 7764 7-9-7 **95**.......... JasonHart 8 54
(Karen McLintock) *dwlt and reminders s: chsd ldrs after 1f: rdn along over 3f out: wknd over 2f out* **33/1**

1m 26.29s (-4.01) **Going Correction** -0.25s/f (Stan) course record **9** Ran SP% **113.3**
Speed ratings (Par 109): **112,111,109,108,104 101,97,94,90**
CSF £9.08 CT £104.02 TOTE £2.90: £1.30, £2.20, £3.40; EX 10.80 Trifecta £112.90.
Owner Imperial Racing Partnership No 8 **Bred** Rabbah Bloodstock Limited **Trained** Sheriff Hutton, N Yorks

FOCUS
The feature contest was a good handicap. The favourite grabbed the second favourite close home and dipped under the course-record time. Strong form, with the winner rated back to his early level.

930 FOLLOW TOP TIPSTER TEMPLEGATE AT SUN RACING NOVICE MEDIAN AUCTION STKS 1m 13y(F)
4:40 (4:40) (Class 4) 3-4-Y-0 £5,175 (£1,540; £769; £384) Stalls Low

Form RPR
04-0 **1** **Little Rock (IRE)**[33] 403 3-8-9 0.......... ShaneKelly 4 76
(Richard Hughes) *prom: led over 4f out: pushed along and wd st: rdn and hung lft to inner rail 2f out: drvn ent fnl f: kpt on strly* **5/1**[3]
3-66 **2** *2 3/4* **Stay Forever (FR)**[35] 360 3-8-4 70.......... MartinDwyer 2 65
(Andrew Balding) *in tch: gd hdwy on inner to trck ldrs over 3f out: chsd wnr and wd st: rdn 2f out and ev ch: drvn and edgd lft ent fnl f: kpt on same pce* **2/1**[1]
53 **3** *19* **Al Daayen (FR)**[12] 739 3-8-4 0.......... JoeFanning 8 21
(Mark Johnston) *sn slt ld: hdd over 4f out: cl up: rdn along 3f out: kpt on one pce* **11/2**
4 *2 1/4* **Copper And Five** 3-8-9 0.......... NickyMackay 9 21
(John Gosden) *dwlt and in rr: hdwy and cl up on outer whn bmpd bnd 4f out: green and wd st: sn rdn and kpt on one pce* **5/2**[2]
0 **5** *1* **Zoom Out**[33] 405 3-8-4 0.......... FayeMcManoman(5) 3 19
(Nigel Tinkler) *in rr: hdwy on inner 3f out: sn rdn and plugged on: n.d* **20/1**
6 *4 1/2* **Oblate** 3-8-4 0.......... AndrewMullen 7
(Robyn Brisland) *dwlt: hdwy to chse ldrs after 3f: edgd rt and bmpd bnd 4f out: sn rdn along and outpcd* **14/1**
0 **7** *3* **Phoenix Queen**[33] 403 3-8-4 0.......... ShelleyBirkett 6
(Gay Kelleway) *chsd ldrs: rdn along over 3f out: outpcd and wd st* **50/1**
00 **8** *10* **Beresford (IRE)**[9] 785 3-8-9 0.......... PaulHanagan 1
(Richard Fahey) *prom: pushed along after 2f: lost pl over 4f out: sn bhd* **12/1**

1m 40.52s (-3.18) **Going Correction** -0.25s/f (Stan) **8** Ran SP% **115.0**
Speed ratings (Par 105): **105,102,83,81,80 75,72,62**
CSF £15.54 TOTE £4.10: £1.10, £2.10, £1.20; EX 16.10 Trifecta £82.50.
Owner M H Dixon **Bred** M H Dixon **Trained** Upper Lambourn, Berks

FOCUS
Effectively, an ordinary 3yo novice contest. Only two horses mattered for win purposes from over 2f out in a race that fell apart to a large degree. The winning time was the second slowest comparatively on the card, but over two seconds quicker than the following handicap over this trip. The second has been rated up a bit on her recent form.

931 LADBROKES HOME OF THE ODDS BOOST APPRENTICE H'CAP 1m 13y(F)
5:10 (5:10) (Class 6) (0-60,60) 3-Y-0 £2,264 (£673; £336; £168) Stalls Low

Form RPR
3-01 **1** **Dolly Dupree**[24] 585 3-9-3 **53**.......... TheodoreLadd 7 58+
(Paul D'Arcy) *hld up in rr: hdwy 2f out: sn n.m.r and swtchd rt to outer over 1f out: sn rdn: styd on strly fnl f to ld nr fin* **5/1**[1]
04-2 **2** *1/2* **Pandora Star**[24] 585 3-9-1 **54**..........(v) ThoreHammerHansen(3) 8 58
(John Quinn) *cl up: led 2f out: rdn wl over 1f out: drvn and edgd rt ins fnl f: hdd and no ex nr fin* **8/1**
00-0 **3** *shd* **Crazy Spin**[33] 400 3-8-5 **46** oh1..........(p[1]) WilliamCarver(5) 2 50
(Ivan Furtado) *in tch: hdwy over 3f out: chsd ldrs 2f out and sn rdn: drvn and styd on to chal ins fnl f: kpt on same pce towards fin* **25/1**
-504 **4** *1* **Bonneville (IRE)**[11] 765 3-8-9 **52**..........(p[1]) OliverSearle(7) 10 53
(Rod Millman) *prom: rdn along 3f out: chsd ldr and drvn wl over 1f out: swtchd lft ins fnl f: kpt on same pce* **16/1**
0-13 **5** *nk* **Sylviacliffs (FR)**[24] 585 3-9-2 **55**..........(p[1]) JonathanFisher(3) 4 56
(K R Burke) *chsd ldrs: rdn along over 2f out: drvn wl over 1f out: kpt on same pce fnl f* **7/1**[3]
2-00 **6** *1 3/4* **Regal Ambition**[14] 698 3-9-3 **58**.......... AmeliaGlass(5) 5 55
(Clive Cox) *dwlt and towards rr: hdwy 3f out: sn rdn: styd on u.p fnl 2f: nrst fin* **14/1**
01-0 **7** *hd* **Singe Du Nord**[53] 79 3-8-9 **52**..........(p) IzzyClifton(7) 3 48
(Nigel Tinkler) *towards rr: hdwy on inner over 3f out: rdn along 2f out: kpt on u.p fnl f: nrst fin* **9/1**
00-5 **8** *2 1/2* **Freedom's Breath**[23] 598 3-8-7 **48** oh1 ow2.......... MarkCrehan(5) 6 39
(Michael Appleby) *midfield: effrt and sme hdwy whn wd st: sn rdn and n.d* **50/1**
25-2 **9** *3/4* **Lexikon**[22] 612 3-8-10 **46**.......... BenRobinson 9 35
(Ollie Pears) *slt ld: rdn along 3f out: hdd 2f out: grad wknd* **6/1**[2]
20-2 **10** *3/4* **Klipperty Klopp**[26] 524 3-9-7 **60**.......... KieranSchofield(3) 1 47
(Antony Brittain) *a towards rr* **10/1**
1-34 **11** *2* **Rusper Dreams (IRE)**[32] 437 3-9-10 **60**.......... AaronJones 11 42
(Jamie Osborne) *dwlt: a in rr* **6/1**[2]
-004 **12** *15* **Pot Luck**[26] 537 3-9-3 **53**..........(b) JoshuaBryan 13
(Andrew Balding) *chsd ldrs: rdn along over 3f out: sn wknd* **8/1**

1m 43.15s (-0.55) **Going Correction** -0.25s/f (Stan) **12** Ran SP% **117.4**
Speed ratings (Par 95): **92,91,91,90,90 88,88,85,84,84 82,67**
CSF £44.05 CT £928.20 TOTE £9.40: £2.40, £2.60, £9.70; EX 41.90 Trifecta £1829.00.
Owner K Snell **Bred** K Snell **Trained** Newmarket, Suffolk

FOCUS
A modest 3yo apprentice riders' handicap. The winning time was nearly three seconds slower than the previous novice contest for this age-group over this trip. The level is set around the second, fourth and fifth.
T/Plt: £182.30 to a £1 stake. Pool: £81,147.38. 324.78 winning units. T/Qpdt: £26.30 to a £1 stake. Pool: £7,385.58. 207.55 winning units. **Joe Rowntree**

932 - 939a (Foreign Racing) - See Raceform Interactive

918 KEMPTON (A.W) (R-H)
Thursday, February 28

OFFICIAL GOING: Polytrack: standard to slow
Wind: virtually nil Weather: overcast

940 100% PROFIT BOOST AT 32REDSPORT.COM H'CAP (DIV I) 1m (P)
4:50 (4:54) (Class 6) (0-55,57) 3-Y-0+
£3,105 (£924; £461; £300; £300; £300) Stalls Low

Form RPR
-040 **1** **Cold Fire (IRE)**[33] 436 6-9-5 **46** oh1..........(v[1]) KieranO'Neill 2 58+
(Robyn Brisland) *chsd ldrs: effrt u.p 2f out: clsd to ld jst over 1f out: r.o strly and drew clr ins fnl f: readily (trainer said, reg app imp in form, gelding appreciated the first-time visor and the return to Kempton, where gelding has run well previously)* **4/1**[2]

 The Form Book Flat 2019, Raceform Ltd, Newbury, RG14 5SJ

0-04 **2** 3 ¼ **Ahfad**[29] 485 4-9-6 **47**..............................(b) HectorCrouch 7 50
(Gary Moore) *s.i.s and pushed along in rr early: hdwy into midfield 1/2-way: hdwy u.p over 1f out: styd on to go 2nd wl ins fnl f: no ch w wnr* **11/1**

2-63 **3** 1 ¼ **Mans Not Trot (IRE)**[31] 462 4-10-0 **55**..............................(p) NicolaCurrie 1 55
(Jamie Osborne) *sn led: drvn over 1f out: sn hdd and no ex: outpcd by wnr and lost 2nd wl ins fnl f* **11/4**[1]

10-0 **4** 1 **Solveig's Song**[43] 250 7-10-0 **55**..............................(p) AdamKirby 14 53
(Steve Woodman) *broke wl: restrained and hld up in rr: effrt ent fnl 2f: rdn and hdwy over 1f out: styd on ins fnl f: nvr trbld ldrs* **20/1**

-000 **5** 1 **Herringswell (FR)**[24] 595 4-9-5 **51**..............................(p) DylanHogan(5) 8 47
(Henry Spiller) *midfield: effrt and swtchd lft jst over 2f out: styd on u.p ins fnl f: nvr trbld ldrs* **14/1**

1203 **6** ¾ **Lincoln Spirit**[8] 813 3-8-9 **55**.............................. DavidProbert 3 43
(David O'Meara) *taken down early: broke wl: restrained and hld up in midfield: effrt ent fnl 2f: unable qck over 1f out: wknd ins fnl f* **8/1**[3]

5-00 **7** ½ **Takiah**[15] 695 4-9-5 **46** oh1.............................. LiamKeniry 4 39
(Peter Hiatt) *t.k.h: hld up in tch in midfield: effrt on inner 2f out: no imp u.p over 1f out: wknd ins fnl f* **25/1**

0-00 **8** 1 ¾ **Ainne**[31] 462 4-9-9 **53**..............................(bt) GaryMahon(3) 5 42
(Sylvester Kirk) *sn pressing ldr: ev ch and rdn 2f out: edgd lft u.p and btn over 1f out: wknd ins fnl f* **10/1**

000- **9** 3 ¼ **We Are All Dottie**[143] 8040 3-7-12 **51**.............................. SophieRalston(7) 12 26
(Pat Phelan) *s.i.s: a towards rr: rdn over 2f out: sn outpcd and wknd over 1f out* **50/1**

0-00 **10** nk **With Pride**[24] 606 3-8-0 **46** oh1..............................(t[1]) HollieDoyle 9 20
(Neil Mulholland) *t.k.h: hld up in tch in midfield: rdn and lost pl over 2f out: sn hung lft and no ch over 1f out (jockey said colt ran too free and hung left-handed)* **20/1**

000- **11** nk **Dr Julius No**[150] 7834 5-9-13 **54**.............................. ShaneKelly 13 34
(Murty McGrath) *hld up in tch in midfield: effrt u.p 2f out: unable qck and sn outpcd: wknd fnl f* **16/1**

0-00 **12** ¾ **Amy Kane**[24] 602 5-9-5 **46** oh1.............................. JohnFahy 10 24
(Jimmy Fox) *chsd ldrs: rdn jst over 2f out: sn outpcd and wknd over 1f out* **50/1**

003- **13** 2 ½ **Shining Valley (IRE)**[300] 2376 5-9-9 **57**.............................. ScottMcCullagh(7) 6 29
(Brett Johnson) *dwlt: hld up in rr: hung lft and wd bnd 4f out: no ch fnl 2f (jockey said gelding ran too free and hung left-handed)* **12/1**

005- **14** 23 **Lone Voice (IRE)**[64] 9703 4-9-5 **46** oh1.............................. TomMarquand 11
(Tony Carroll) *t.k.h: midfield on outer: pushed along over 3f out: sn hung lft and bhd: lost tch 2f: eased ins fnl f: t.o (jockey said gelding ran too free and hung left-handed)* **10/1**

1m 40.6s (0.80) **Going Correction** +0.125s/f (Slow) **14 Ran SP% 121.8**
WFA 3 from 4yo+ 19lb
Speed ratings (Par 101): **101,97,96,95,94 93,93,91,88,87 87,86,84,61**
CSF £45.11 CT £146.45 TOTE £5.20: £1.60, £3.60, £1.50; EX 51.00 Trifecta £171.10.
Owner Dallas Racing And Partners **Bred** Mrs J A Cornwell **Trained** Danethorpe, Notts

FOCUS
Few landed a real blow in this weak handicap. Straightforward form behind the winner.

941 100% PROFIT BOOST AT 32REDSPORT.COM H'CAP (DIV II) 1m (P)
5:20 (5:23) (Class 6) (0-55,57) 3-Y-O+
£3,105 (£924; £461; £300; £300; £300) Stalls Low

Form RPR
00-0 **1** **Purple Paddy**[48] 175 4-9-5 **46** oh1.............................. JohnFahy 5 55+
(Jimmy Fox) *stdd s: t.k.h: hld up towards rr: swtchd lft over 6f out: effrt and hdwy on outer bnd 3f out: clsd to chal 2f out: sn led: r.o wl and clr ins fnl f: eased towards fin* **9/1**

0-01 **2** 1 ½ **Misu Pete**[24] 595 7-9-7 **55**..............................(p) EllieMacKenzie(7) 2 60
(Mark Usher) *sn led: rdn ent fnl 2f: hdd over 1f out: unable to match pce of wnr and one pce ins fnl f* **7/2**[2]

6-04 **3** nse **Joyful Dream (IRE)**[31] 462 5-9-5 **46** oh1.............................. ShaneKelly 6 50
(Paul D'Arcy) *hld up in tch in midfield: hdwy u.p over 1f out: battling for 2nd and kpt on ins fnl f: nvr threatened wnr* **33/1**

-056 **4** ¾ **Jeremy's Jet (IRE)**[22] 624 8-9-6 **47**..............................(t) RichardKingscote 3 50
(Tony Carroll) *dwlt: pushed along and sn rcvrd to r in midfield: effrt and clsd to chse ldrs 2f out: kpt on but no threat to wnr ins fnl f* **7/1**[3]

3050 **5** 1 ½ **Red Gunner**[24] 595 5-9-12 **53**.............................. LiamJones 10 52
(Mark Loughnane) *hld up in tch in midfield: clsd and swtchd rt 2f out: no ex u.p over 1f out: wknd ins fnl f* **11/1**

45-0 **6** hd **Freesia Gold (IRE)**[40] 319 3-8-7 **53**.............................. KieranO'Neill 7 46
(Daniel Kubler) *midfield: rdn and unable qck over 2f out: rallied u.p 1f out: no threat to wnr but kpt on ins fnl f* **8/1**

00-0 **7** 2 **Jack Louie**[24] 594 3-8-0 **46** oh1.............................. HollieDoyle 8 34
(Dean Ivory) *chsd ldrs: rdn over 2f out: sn struggling to qckn and outpcd 2f out: plugged on same pce after* **8/1**

00-6 **8** ¾ **Multitask**[34] 399 9-9-12 **53**..............................(p) AdamKirby 9 47
(Gary Moore) *t.k.h: hld up towards rr: clsd and nt clr run 2f out: effrt over 1f out: nvr getting on terms* **10/3**[1]

-500 **9** ½ **Shovel It On (IRE)**[2] 912 4-8-13 **47**.............................. SophieRalston(7) 4 38
(Steve Flook) *in rr: effrt over 2f out: plugged on but nvr involved* **20/1**

00-5 **10** 1 **Lesanti**[24] 595 5-9-5 **46** oh1..............................(b) CallumShepherd 12 35
(Ed de Giles) *led: sn hdd but pressed ldr tl jst over 2f out: sn outpcd and wknd fnl f* **40/1**

0-00 **11** 2 ¼ **Altaira**[29] 479 8-9-5 **46** oh1..............................(b) TomMarquand 11 30
(Tony Carroll) *stdd after s: hld up in last pair: effrt over 2f out: no prog: nvr involved* **66/1**

00-6 **12** 1 ¼ **Melo Pearl**[24] 594 3-8-0 **46** oh1..............................(b) PaddyMathers 13 21
(Mrs Ilka Gansera-Leveque) *stdd s: t.k.h: hld up in rr: effrt over 2f out: no prog: nvr involved* **33/1**

4-10 **13** nk **Cool Echo**[36] 365 5-9-13 **54**..............................(p) DavidProbert 14 34
(J R Jenkins) *midfield: rdn and lost pl over 2f out: no ch fnl 2f* **16/1**

35-0 **14** 1 **Golconda Prince (IRE)**[56] 39 5-9-13 **57**.............................. JoshuaBryan(3) 1 35
(Mark Pattinson) *chsd ldrs: lost pl u.p over 1f out: wknd fnl f* **25/1**

1m 41.08s (1.28) **Going Correction** +0.125s/f (Slow) **14 Ran SP% 122.7**
WFA 3 from 4yo+ 19lb
Speed ratings (Par 101): **98,96,96,95,94 94,92,91,90,89 87,86,85,84**
CSF £38.65 CT £1031.43 TOTE £10.20: £3.20, £2.10, £6.30; EX 43.30 Trifecta £687.90.
Owner Mrs Barbara Fuller **Bred** Babs Fuller **Trained** Collingbourne Ducis, Wilts

FOCUS
This second division of the weak 1m handicap was 0.48 secs slower than the opener. Straightforward form in behind the winner, with the second replicating his recent Chelmsford win.

942 32RED CASINO H'CAP 1m (P)
5:55 (5:58) (Class 5) (0-70,71) 4-Y-O+
£3,752 (£1,116; £557; £300; £300; £300) Stalls Low

Form RPR
-522 **1** **Magic Mirror**[22] 616 6-9-8 **71**..............................(p) TomMarquand 4 79
(Mark Rimell) *chsd ldrs: effrt to chal over 1f out: led ins fnl f: battled on gamely: all out* **5/1**[3]

00-5 **2** shd **Baashiq (IRE)**[3] 911 5-9-1 **64**..............................(p[1]) KieranO'Neill 13 71
(Peter Hiatt) *t.k.h: chsd ldr: effrt ent fnl 2f: drvn to chal over 1f out: led 1f out: hdd ins fnl f: rallied gamely towards fin: jst hld* **33/1**

11-2 **3** 2 ¼ **Tamerlane (IRE)**[44] 248 4-9-7 **70**..............................(b) AdamKirby 6 72
(Clive Cox) *chsd ldrs: drvn in 4th over 1f out: kpt on to chse ldng pair 150yds out: no imp* **11/4**[2]

0-00 **4** ½ **Badenscoth**[33] 429 5-9-4 **67**.............................. FrannyNorton 3 68
(Dean Ivory) *stdd s: t.k.h: hld up off the pce towards rr: effrt but stl plenty to do ent fnl 2f: hdwy over 1f out: styd on ins fnl f: nvr getting on terms w ldrs* **10/1**

260- **5** 1 ¼ **Lothario**[76] 9536 5-9-1 **64**.............................. MartinDwyer 10 62
(Dean Ivory) *stdd s: t.k.h: hld up off the pce in last pair: effrt ent fnl 2f: hdwy over 1f out: kpt on ins fnl f: nvr trbld ldrs* **16/1**

-306 **6** 1 ¾ **Titan Goddess**[15] 697 7-9-7 **70**.............................. HollieDoyle 2 64
(Mike Murphy) *reluctant to go to s and eventually led rdrless to s: sn led: rdn and hrd pressed over 1f out: hdd 1f out: wknd ins fnl f* **20/1**

300- **7** ½ **Pendo**[187] 6514 8-9-5 **68**.............................. JosephineGordon 7 61
(John Best) *chsd ldrs: effrt ent fnl 2f: sn outpcd: wl hld and plugged on same pce ins fnl f* **25/1**

-211 **8** 1 **Cashel (IRE)**[7] 828 4-8-13 **69** 6ex.............................. CierenFallon(7) 11 59
(Michael Appleby) *rrd as stalls opened: rdr lost irons briefly and sn bhd: swtchd lft and effrt ent fnl 2f: kpt on ins fnl f but nvr any ch (jockey said gelding reared as the stalls opened causing him to lose his irons for several strides)* **13/8**[1]

536- **9** 4 ½ **The Eagle's Nest (IRE)**[34] 9431 5-9-7 **70**..............................(t) EdwardGreatrex 1 50
(Alexandra Dunn) *midfield: rdn and struggling to qckn over 2f out: sn outpcd and wknd over 1f out* **20/1**

P-46 **10** 2 ¾ **Spiritual Star (IRE)**[15] 701 10-8-12 **61**..............................(t) JFEgan 8 35
(Paul George) *midfield: rdn over 2f out: sn btn* **20/1**

60-0 **11** 6 **Brecqhou Island**[33] 435 4-8-10 **59**.............................. WilliamCarson 9 19
(Mark Pattinson) *midfield tl dropped to rr over 2f out: lost tch wl over 1f out* **50/1**

0-00 **12** shd **Valentine Mist (IRE)**[15] 697 7-8-7 **56** oh11.............................. GeorgeWood 5 16
(James Grassick) *midfield: lost pl u.p over 2f out: wknd over 1f out* **100/1**

1m 38.72s (-1.08) **Going Correction** +0.125s/f (Slow) **12 Ran SP% 120.4**
Speed ratings (Par 103): **110,109,107,107,105 104,103,102,98,95 89,89**
CSF £163.97 CT £557.69 TOTE £10.10: £2.20, £6.90, £1.20; EX 116.00 Trifecta £514.00.
Owner William Wood **Bred** Hesmonds Stud Ltd **Trained** Leafield, Oxon

FOCUS
Due to an uneven pace it paid to be handy in this modest handicap. A pb from the winner, with the third rated a bit below his recent form.

943 32RED ON THE APP STORE MAIDEN STKS 6f (P)
6:30 (6:31) (Class 5) 3-Y-O+
£3,881 (£1,155; £577; £288) Stalls Low

Form RPR
1 **Eardley Road (IRE)** 3-8-13 0.............................. HectorCrouch 6 80+
(Clive Cox) *rn green early and off the pce in rr: gd hdwy over 1f out: led ins fnl f: sn clr and r.o strly: readily* **6/1**[3]

60 **2** 3 **Turn To Rock (IRE)**[12] 752 3-8-13 0.............................. LiamKeniry 4 68
(Ed Walker) *rn green and off the pce in rr: effrt and clsd 2f out: hdwy and rdn over 1f out: chsd clr wnr ins fnl f: kpt on* **33/1**

3 ¾ **Creek Island (IRE)** 3-8-13 0.............................. FrannyNorton 11 65+
(Mark Johnston) *midfield: nt clr run and swtchd lft over 2f out: effrt over 1f out: kpt on to go 3rd ins fnl f: no threat to wnr* **12/1**

055- **4** 1 **Invincible One (IRE)**[171] 7127 3-8-10 **75**.............................. GaryMahon(3) 2 62
(Sylvester Kirk) *sn clr in ldng trio: outpcd u.p over 1f out: wl hld and kpt on same pce ins fnl f* **11/4**[2]

5 ½ **Physics (IRE)** 3-8-13 0..............................(t[1]) RaulDaSilva 1 60
(Paul Cole) *led and clr w two rivals: asserted 2f out and clr whn rdn over 1f out: hdd ins fnl f: sn btn and wknd after* **15/8**[1]

6 shd **Puzzle** 3-8-13 0.............................. ShaneKelly 5 60+
(Richard Hughes) *s.i.s: rn green: bhd and wl off the pce: hdwy and swtchd rt over 1f out: kpt on ins fnl f: no threat to wnr* **8/1**

03- **7** 3 ¼ **Invincible Sea (IRE)**[59] 9771 3-8-5 0.............................. WilliamCox(3) 9 45
(Linda Jewell) *in tch in midfield: effrt over 2f out: unable qck over 1f out: wknd ins fnl f* **50/1**

0- **8** 2 ¾ **Formally**[148] 7906 3-8-13 0.............................. TomMarquand 12 41
(Tony Carroll) *midfield: effrt and struggling whn hmpd over 2f out: sn btn and wknd fnl f* **50/1**

0-6 **9** ½ **The Numismatist (IRE)**[3] 908 3-8-13 0.............................. NicolaCurrie 8 39
(Jamie Osborne) *dwlt: off the pce in rr: effrt 2f out: no imp and sn outpcd: no ch whn nt clr run and swtchd rt ins fnl f* **33/1**

5-04 **10** 2 **Zaula**[26] 555 3-8-8 **68**..............................(b[1]) EdwardGreatrex 10 28
(Archie Watson) *w ldng pair and clr of field tl 2f out: lost pl u.p over 1f out: wknd fnl f* **10/1**

0 **11** 2 ¼ **Doti**[36] 359 3-8-8 0.............................. RobHornby 3 21
(Rod Millman) *chsd clr ldng trio: rdn and clsd ent fnl 2f: lost pl over 1f out: fdd fnl f* **50/1**

0-0 **12** 9 **What A Dazzler**[40] 313 3-8-8 0..............................(h[1]) WilliamCarson 7
(Bill Turner) *chsd ldrs for 2f: steadily lost pl: bhd fnl f* **100/1**

1m 13.3s (0.20) **Going Correction** +0.125s/f (Slow) **12 Ran SP% 116.4**
Speed ratings (Par 103): **103,99,98,96,96 95,91,87,87,84 81,69**
CSF £192.21 TOTE £5.50: £1.80, £11.40, £2.90; EX 185.80 Trifecta £1755.80.
Owner Paul Smith **Bred** Emiliano Colabolleta **Trained** Lambourn, Berks

FOCUS
The leaders went off too hard in this interesting 3yo sprint maiden. The level is a bit fluid.

944 32RED.COM H'CAP 7f (P)
7:00 (7:00) (Class 5) (0-70,71) 4-Y-O+
£3,752 (£1,116; £557; £300; £300; £300) Stalls Low

Form RPR
23-1 **1** **Astrospeed (IRE)**[44] 243 4-9-6 **69**..............................(h) GeorgeWood 3 76+
(James Fanshawe) *taken down early: dwlt: t.k.h: hld up wl in tch in midfield: effrt to chal over 1f out: sn led: hld on wl u.p ins fnl f* **6/4**[1]

The Form Book Flat 2019, Raceform Ltd, Newbury, RG14 5SJ

11-4 **2** *nk* **Soar Above**[43] 253 4-9-1 **67**..........(p) TimClark(3) 4 73+
(Paul D'Arcy) *t.k.h: chsd ldr: effrt over 1f out: ev ch ins fnl f: r.o wl but hld towards fin* **5/2**[2]

023- **3** *3/4* **Golden Nectar**[217] 5397 5-9-6 **69**.......... LiamJones 6 73
(Laura Mongan) *hld up in tch in midfield: effrt ent fnl 2f: kpt on u.p ins fnl f: wnt 3rd towards fin* **25/1**

10-0 **4** *hd* **Full Intention**[43] 253 5-9-8 **71**.......... AdamKirby 5 74
(Lydia Pearce) *hld up in tch in rr: effrt on inner over 1f out: kpt on u.p ins fnl f: wnt 4th towards fin* **16/1**

0-65 **5** *1/2* **Steal The Scene (IRE)**[40] 315 7-8-12 **64**..........(p) JoshuaBryan(3) 2 66
(Kevin Frost) *t.k.h: chsd ldrs: drvn and pressed ldrs over 1f out: kpt on same pce ins fnl f: lost 2 pls towards fin* **11/2**[3]

1663 **6** *nk* **Pearl Spectre (USA)**[23] 611 8-9-7 **70**..........(v) JosephineGordon 7 71
(Phil McEntee) *sn led and set stdy gallop: drvn and hrd pressed over 1f out: sn hdd & wknd wl ins fnl f* **25/1**

0-00 **7** *7* **Makaarim**[28] 507 5-9-4 **67**..........(h) TomQueally 1 49
(Seamus Durack) *t.k.h: hld up in rr: effrt and reminders over 2f out: no hdwy and sn btn* **20/1**

16-4 **8** *1/2* **Cuttin' Edge (IRE)**[48] 175 5-9-1 **64**..........(p[1]) MartinDwyer 8 45
(William Muir) *midfield on outer: rdn ent fnl 2f: sn struggling and outpcd: wknd over 1f out* **7/1**

1m 27.36s (1.36) **Going Correction** +0.125s/f (Slow) **8 Ran SP% 114.8**
Speed ratings (Par 103): **97,96,95,95,95 94,86,86**
CSF £5.18 CT £56.70 TOTE £2.00: £1.10, £1.10, £5.90; EX 5.90 Trifecta £67.60.
Owner Dragon Gate **Bred** Noel Cogan **Trained** Newmarket, Suffolk

FOCUS
This modest handicap saw a tight finish due to a stop-start tempo. The third has been rated close to form.

945 32RED H'CAP (LONDON MIDDLE DISTANCE SERIES QUALIFIER) 1m 2f 219y(P)
7:30 (7:30) (Class 4) (0-85,86) 4-Y-0+
£6,469 (£1,925; £962; £481; £300; £300) **Stalls Low**

Form RPR

-021 **1** **Ilhabela Fact**[26] 559 5-9-4 **76**.......... TomMarquand 5 87+
(Tony Carroll) *trckd ldrs: effrt and led ent fnl f: clr and r.o strly ins fnl f: readily* **11/4**[1]

030- **2** *2 1/2* **Valentino Dancer**[124] 8640 4-9-0 **80**.......... CierenFallon(7) 3 85
(Olly Murphy) *hld up in tch in midfield: effrt u.p over 1f out: hdwy between rivals to chse clr wnr ins fnl f: kpt on but no threat to ldrs* **6/1**[3]

305- **3** *2* **Lawn Ranger**[141] 8102 4-9-6 **79**.......... RichardKingscote 8 81
(Michael Attwater) *sn chsng ldr: rdn ent fnl 2f: drvn over 1f out: kpt on same pce ins fnl f* **7/1**

2- **4** *2 1/4* **Escapability (IRE)**[125] 8596 4-9-7 **80**.......... DavidProbert 9 79
(Alan King) *t.k.h early: hld up in tch in midfield: pushed along 3f out: unable qck u.p over 1f out: wl hld but kpt on ins fnl f* **10/1**

4-51 **5** *shd* **Voi**[22] 616 5-9-0 **72**..........(t) MartinDwyer 10 70
(Conrad Allen) *stdd s and dropped in bhd: hld up in rr: effrt ent fnl 2f: kpt on ins fnl f: nvr trbld ldrs* **20/1**

06-1 **6** *shd* **Cosmic Landscape**[45] 239 4-9-5 **78**.......... CallumShepherd 6 76
(William Jarvis) *t.k.h: led: drvn over 1f out: sn hdd and no ex: wknd ins fnl f* **8/1**

16-3 **7** *3* **Villette (IRE)**[22] 617 5-10-0 **86**..........(p[1]) AdamKirby 4 79
(Dean Ivory) *chsd ldrs: effrt on inner 2f out: no ex u.p over 1f out: wknd ins fnl f* **5/1**[2]

2-12 **8** *nk* **Ice Canyon**[38] 346 5-8-12 **70**..........(h) EoinWalsh 1 62
(Mark Brisbourne) *t.k.h: hld up in tch in midfield: unable qck u.p over 1f out: wknd ins fnl f (jockey said gelding ran too free)* **10/1**

226- **9** *shd* **El Borracho (IRE)**[139] 8149 4-9-5 **78**..........(h) HollieDoyle 2 70
(Simon Dow) *hld up in last pair: effrt over 2f out: no imp and wl btn over 1f out* **8/1**

2-30 **10** *1* **Thaqaffa (IRE)**[22] 617 6-9-8 **80**..........(h) TomQueally 7 70
(Amy Murphy) *mounted in the chute: t.k.h: hld up in last trio: effrt over 2f out: no imp over 1f out and wknd fnl f* **33/1**

2m 19.31s (-1.69) **Going Correction** +0.125s/f (Slow)
WFA 4 from 5yo+ 1lb **10 Ran SP% 118.2**
Speed ratings (Par 105): **114,112,110,109,109 108,106,106,106,105**
CSF £19.47 CT £106.26 TOTE £3.20: £1.50, £2.30, £2.40; EX 23.80 Trifecta £202.00.
Owner Cooke & Millen **Bred** Robert Nahas **Trained** Cropthorne, Worcs
■ Stewards' Enquiry : Cieren Fallon two-day ban; misuse of whip (Mar 14-15)

FOCUS
This fair handicap was run at an okay pace. The second has been rated close to form, and the third similar to his C&D effort when last seen.

946 RACING TV H'CAP (DIV I) 1m 7f 218y(P)
8:00 (8:01) (Class 6) (0-65,67) 4-Y-0+
£3,105 (£924; £461; £300; £300; £300) **Stalls Low**

Form RPR

5-11 **1** **Blazon**[40] 318 6-9-13 **66**..........(p) AdamKirby 9 73+
(Kim Bailey) *hld up in tch in last trio: clsd on inner over 2f out: swtchd rt and clsd to chse ldrs 2f out: drvn to ld ins fnl f: r.o wl* **5/4**[1]

35-2 **2** *1 3/4* **Tin Fandango**[22] 619 4-9-5 **62**..........(p) JosephineGordon 3 67
(Mark Usher) *led: rdn ent fnl 2f: hdd and unable to match pce of wnr and kpt on same pce ins fnl f* **9/1**

613- **3** *nk* **Percy Prosecco**[47] 6449 4-9-3 **60**.......... RobHornby 8 65
(Noel Williams) *hld up in tch in midfield: clsd over 2f out: rdn to chal over 1f out: unable to match pce of wnr and kpt on same pce ins fnl f* **9/2**[2]

5-46 **4** *nk* **Queen Of Paris**[22] 619 4-9-0 **64**..........(t[1]) Pierre-LouisJamin(7) 2 68
(William Knight) *hld up in tch in midfield: swtchd lft and effrt over 2f out: hdwy to chse ldrs ins fnl f: kpt on but no threat to wnr* **7/1**[3]

-026 **5** *1 3/4* **Nafaayes (IRE)**[13] 731 5-9-8 **61**..........(p) HollieDoyle 10 61
(Jean-Rene Auvray) *stdd s: t.k.h: hld up in tch in last pair: effrt jst over 2f out: hdwy 1f out: kpt on ins fnl f: nvr trbld ldrs* **14/1**

440- **6** *3/4* **Paddys Runner**[51] 4816 7-9-12 **65**..........(b) TomMarquand 5 64
(Graeme McPherson) *dropped in after s: hld up in rr: hdwy on outer to chse ldr 10f out: rdn over 2f out: unable qck and outpcd over 1f out: kpt on same pce ins fnl f* **16/1**

22-6 **7** *2* **Strictly Art (IRE)**[34] 404 6-9-11 **67**.......... JoshuaBryan(3) 1 64
(Alan Bailey) *chsd ldrs: effrt ent fnl 2f: unable qck and outpcd ent fnl f: sn wknd* **12/1**

-100 **8** *1/2* **Belabour**[10] 782 6-9-11 **64**.......... EoinWalsh 4 60
(Mark Brisbourne) *stdd s: hld up in tch: effrt wl over 2f out: unable qck: wl hld and kpt on same pce fr over 1f out* **33/1**

0-43 **9** *2 1/4* **Normandy Blue**[26] 549 4-8-6 **49**.......... KieranO'Neill 11 44
(Louise Allan) *chsd ldr tl 10f out: rdn over 2f out: lost pl and btn over 1f out: wknd ins fnl f* **25/1**

5-51 **10** *3 1/2* **Sweetest Smile (IRE)**[27] 535 4-8-4 **50**.......... WilliamCox(3) 6 41
(Ed de Giles) *chsd ldrs rdn wl over 2f out: sn struggling and lost pl 2f out: bhd and hung lft ins fnl f* **14/1**

3m 35.5s (5.40) **Going Correction** +0.125s/f (Slow)
WFA 4 from 5yo+ 4lb **10 Ran SP% 118.8**
Speed ratings (Par 101): **91,90,89,89,88 88,87,87,86,84**
CSF £13.91 CT £41.96 TOTE £1.80: £1.10, £3.10, £1.80; EX 14.20 Trifecta £51.60.
Owner The Blazing Optimists **Bred** Juddmonte Farms Ltd **Trained** Andoversford, Gloucs
■ Thresholdofadream was withdrawn. Price at time of withdrawal 14/1. Rule 4 applies to all bets - deduction 5p in the pound

FOCUS
They went steadily in this moderate staying handicap. Straightforward form in behind the winner.

947 RACING TV H'CAP (DIV II) 1m 7f 218y(P)
8:30 (8:32) (Class 6) (0-65,67) 4-Y-0+
£3,105 (£924; £461; £300; £300; £300) **Stalls Low**

Form RPR

16-3 **1** **True Destiny**[22] 622 4-9-6 **63**.......... AdamMcNamara 1 73+
(Roger Charlton) *taken down early: hld up in tch in midfield: clsd ent fnl 2f: rdn to press ldng pair jst over 1f out: led ins fnl f: r.o wl* **7/2**[2]

4006 **2** *1 1/4* **Demophon**[8] 482 5-8-7 **46** oh1.......... RaulDaSilva 6 50
(Steve Flook) *chsd ldrs: effrt on inner ent fnl 2f: drvn and ev ch over 1f out: led 1f out: hdd and one pce ins fnl f* **50/1**

201- **3** *2* **Unblinking**[38] 8893 6-9-9 **62**..........(t) TomQueally 10 64
(Nigel Twiston-Davies) *hld up in last quartet: effrt jst over 2f out: hdwy u.p over 1f out: styd on wl ins fnl f: nt rch ldrs* **3/1**[1]

3522 **4** *1 3/4* **Banta Bay**[14] 721 5-8-10 **49**.......... JosephineGordon 9 49
(John Best) *led after 2f and clr tl 6f out: rdn and kicked on ent fnl 2f: hdd 1f out: no ex and wknd ins fnl f* **16/1**

6245 **5** *1 1/4* **Bird For Life**[13] 731 5-8-9 **55**..........(p) EllieMacKenzie(7) 5 53
(Mark Usher) *hld up in last pair: effrt over 2f out: hdwy u.p over 1f out: kpt on wl ins fnl f: nvr trbld ldrs* **6/1**

0/60 **6** *1 1/4* **Regal Gait (IRE)**[22] 619 6-9-7 **60**.......... TomMarquand 4 57
(Simon Dow) *hld up in last pair: effrt and swtchd rt ent fnl 2f: no imp u.p over 1f out: wknd ins fnl f* **6/1**

36-3 **7** *1/2* **The Detainee**[22] 619 6-9-12 **65**..........(p) AdamKirby 3 61
(Neil Mulholland) *led for 2f: chsd ldr: clsd and pressing ldr whn str reminders 4f out: sn rdn: no ex and outpcd over 1f out: wknd ins fnl f* **5/1**[3]

03-1 **8** *10* **Katie Gale**[56] 40 9-9-12 **65**..........(v) KieranO'Neill 8 49
(Robyn Brisland) *prom in chsng gp: clsd and chsng ldr 6f out: rdn wl over 2f out: sn struggling and outpcd: bhd fnl f* **20/1**

50-5 **9** *3* **River Dart (IRE)**[51] 124 7-10-0 **67**.......... RichardKingscote 2 47
(Tony Carroll) *t.k.h: hld up in midfield: rdn over 2f out: sn struggling: bhd ins fnl f* **8/1**

413/ **10** *18* **Dltripleseven (IRE)**[780] 141 6-9-6 **59**.......... WilliamCarson 7 18
(David W Drinkwater) *t.k.h: hld up in last trio: effrt u.p over 2f out: sn btn and wl bhd fnl f: t.o* **40/1**

3m 30.85s (0.75) **Going Correction** +0.125s/f (Slow)
WFA 4 from 5yo+ 4lb **10 Ran SP% 118.6**
Speed ratings (Par 101): **103,102,101,100,99 99,99,94,92,83**
CSF £172.85 CT £592.70 TOTE £4.30: £1.70, £12.60, £1.80; EX 190.00 Trifecta £1265.30.
Owner H R H Sultan Ahmad Shah **Bred** M J & L A Taylor Llp **Trained** Beckhampton, Wilts

FOCUS
The second division of the ordinary staying handicap. Straightforward form in behind the winner.
T/Jkpt: Not Won. T/Plt: £83.50 to a £1 stake. Pool: £67,922.20 - 593.63 winning units T/Qpdt: £13.20 to a £1 stake. Pool: £12,628.60 - 706.86 winning units **Steve Payne**

803 NEWCASTLE (A.W) (L-H)
Thursday, February 28

OFFICIAL GOING: Tapeta: standard to slow
Wind: virtually nil Weather: overcast

948 BETWAY LIVE CASINO H'CAP 1m 4f 98y (Tp)
4:05 (4:05) (Class 4) (0-85,80) 4-Y-0+ £4,883 (£1,461; £730; £365; £182) **Stalls High**

Form RPR

4-33 **1** **Cry Wolf**[13] 735 6-9-0 **78**.......... ThoreHammerHansen(5) 3 86
(Alexandra Dunn) *in tch: qcknd to ld wl over 1f out: rdn and kpt on wl* **7/1**

1151 **2** *2 1/4* **Glan Y Gors (IRE)**[13] 737 7-9-5 **78**..........(p) CliffordLee 4 82
(David Thompson) *prom: rdn to ld 2f out: sn hdd: edgd lft and kpt on same pce* **3/1**[3]

-132 **3** *shd* **Loud And Clear**[27] 522 8-9-4 **80**.......... PhilDennis(3) 6 84
(Jim Goldie) *hld up: rdn 2f out: styd on to go 3rd ins fnl f: nrst fin* **15/8**[1]

30-6 **4** *2 3/4* **Archive (FR)**[51] 124 9-8-3 **69**..........(w) KieranSchofield(7) 1 68
(Brian Ellison) *trckd ldrs: rdn 2f out: sn outpcd* **50/1**

002- **5** *2 1/4* **Nietzsche**[68] 8808 6-9-0 **76**..........(t w) BenRobinson(3) 5 72
(Brian Ellison) *dwlt: hld up in rr: unable qck whn pce increased over 2f out: nvr involved* **9/4**[2]

2/ **6** *11* **Tommy Hallinan (IRE)**[234] 2415 5-9-2 **75**.......... BarryMcHugh 2 53
(Marjorie Fife) *led at stdy pce: rdn and hdd 2f out: wknd* **18/1**

2m 45.47s (4.37) **Going Correction** +0.35s/f (Slow) **6 Ran SP% 110.3**
Speed ratings (Par 105): **99,97,97,95,94 86**
CSF £27.07 TOTE £6.80: £3.10, £1.70; EX 22.50 Trifecta £62.50.
Owner W B B & G J Daly **Bred** Darley **Trained** West Buckland, Somerset

FOCUS
A fairly useful handicap with not much pace on, won in clearcut style by a Somerset raider making the long trip north.

949 LADBROKES NOVICE STKS 1m 2f 42y (Tp)
4:40 (4:40) (Class 5) 3-Y-0
£3,234 (£962; £481; £240) **Stalls High**

Form RPR

042- **1** **Forest Of Dean**[113] 8923 3-9-2 83.......... NickyMackay 3 81+
(John Gosden) *prom: led 3f out: pushed along and sn pressed: rdn over 1f out: kpt on wl to draw clr ins fnl f* **11/8**[2]

1 **2** *4* **Almost Midnight**[36] 358 3-9-9 0.......... JamieSpencer 2 82+
(David Simcock) *trckd ldrs: chal over 2f out: rdn along 2f out: drvn appr fnl f: one pce ins fnl f: eased towards fin* **5/6**[1]

3 *3 1/4* **Autumn Pride (IRE)** 3-9-2 0.......... JoeFanning 4 67
(Mark Johnston) *midfield: pushed along over 3f out: kpt on in 3rd fr over 1f out* **7/2**[3]

0- **4** *2 1/2* **Battle Of Pembroke (USA)**[112] 8954 3-9-2 0.......... StevieDonohoe 8 62
(David Simcock) *in tch: pushed along over 3f out: outpcd over 2f out: kpt on ins fnl f* **20/1**

0-6 5 1/2 **Truckingby**[7] 836 3-9-2 0 (b) JasonHart 7 61
(Mark Johnston) *led: rdn along and hdd 3f out: wknd over 1f out* 66/1

03 6 4 **Three Castles**[27] 523 3-9-2 0 CallumRodriguez 5 53
(Keith Dalgleish) *hld up: pushed along over 2f out: hung lft: nvr threatened* 66/1

7 2 **Black Kraken** 3-9-2 0 PaulMulrennan 6 49
(Ben Haslam) *hld up: pushed along over 2f out: hung lft: nvr threatened (vet said colt lost it's right hind shoe)* 40/1

8 13 **Fast'n Furious (GER)** 3-9-2 0 AndrewMullen 1 23
(Adrian Nicholls) *slowly away: hld up: rdn over 2f out: wknd and bhd appr fnl f* 66/1

2m 19.2s (8.80) **Going Correction** +0.35s/f (Slow) 8 Ran SP% **130.6**
Speed ratings (Par 97): **78,74,72,70,69 66,65,54**
CSF £3.38 TOTE £2.90: £1.10, £1.02, £1.60; EX 4.40 Trifecta £8.80.
Owner HRH Princess Haya Of Jordan **Bred** Car Colston Hall Stud **Trained** Newmarket, Suffolk

FOCUS
The betting market struggled to split the big two Newmarket raiders but this was ultimately quite one-sided.

950 BETWAY CASINO H'CAP 1m 2f 42y (Tp)
5:10 (5:10) (Class 4) (0-80,82) 4-Y-O+ £5,013 (£1,491; £745; £372) Stalls High

Form RPR
-454 1 **Thawry**[9] 793 4-9-5 70 CamHardie 4 76
(Antony Brittain) *hld up in tch: hdwy over 2f out: rdn to chal strly over 1f out: drvn to ld 75yds out: all out* 6/1[3]

2221 2 1/2 **Dommersen (IRE)**[33] 434 6-9-12 82 BenSanderson(5) 1 87+
(Roger Fell) *dwlt: hld up in rr: gng wl but stl plenty to do over 2f out: rdn over 1f out: kpt on wl: nrst fin* 7/4[1]

1-54 3 hd **Remmy D (IRE)**[13] 740 4-8-11 69 CoreyMadden(7) 2 73
(Jim Goldie) *hld up in tch: gd hdwy on outer over 2f out: rdn to ld narrowly over 1f out: edgd lft and hdd 75yds out: one pce* 16/1

05-4 4 3 1/2 **Rockwood**[53] 102 8-9-2 67 (v) JasonHart 5 64
(Karen McLintock) *trckd ldrs: rdn over 2f out: outpcd over 1f out: plugged on ins fnl f* 3/1[2]

410- 5 2 1/2 **Winged Spur (IRE)**[129] 8486 4-10-3 82 JoeFanning 3 74
(Mark Johnston) *trckd ldrs: rdn 2f out: wknd over 1f out* 10/1

45-6 6 1 1/2 **Restive (IRE)**[13] 737 6-9-2 67 AlistairRawlinson 7 56
(Jim Goldie) *led: rdn and hdd over 1f out: sn wknd* 10/1

16-5 7 19 **Seaborough (IRE)**[54] 86 4-9-2 67 CliffordLee 6 18
(David Thompson) *prom: racd keenly: rdn over 2f out: wknd and bhd (jockey said gelding race awkwardly in the early stages)* 10/1

2m 11.47s (1.07) **Going Correction** +0.35s/f (Slow) 7 Ran SP% **108.8**
Speed ratings (Par 105): **109,108,108,105,103 102,87**
CSF £15.29 TOTE £5.80: £2.40, £1.50; EX 18.50 Trifecta £103.60.
Owner Antony Brittain **Bred** Rabbah Bloodstock Limited **Trained** Warthill, N Yorks

FOCUS
A fair handicap that produced a thrilling finish.

951 LADBROKES FILLIES' H'CAP 1m 5y (Tp)
5:45 (5:45) (Class 3) (0-95,82) 4-Y-O+ £15,562 (£4,660; £2,330; £1,165; £582; £292) Stalls Centre

Form RPR
26-1 1 **Toy Theatre**[12] 756 5-9-2 80 JaneElliott(3) 3 93
(Michael Appleby) *trckd ldrs: led 2f out: pushed along and sn qcknd clr: rdn out ins fnl f: easily* 2/1[2]

0444 2 4 **Ventura Blues (IRE)**[15] 699 5-8-13 74 (p) RossaRyan 2 78
(Alexandra Dunn) *dwlt: hld up: sme hdwy 2f out: rdn to go 2nd ins fnl f: kpt on but no ch w wnr* 15/2

3-22 3 3/4 **Treasure Me**[12] 756 4-9-7 82 (p) StevieDonohoe 1 84
(Charlie Fellowes) *in tch: rdn 2f out: drvn to chse clr ldr over 1f out: one pce ins fnl f* 15/8[1]

140- 4 2 1/4 **Alexandrakollontai (IRE)**[111] 8974 9-8-12 78 (b) ConnorMurtagh(5) 4 75
(Alistair Whillans) *in tch: rdn over 2f out: outpcd over 1f out: plugged on ins fnl f* 25/1

221- 5 1 1/2 **Beatbybeatbybeat**[202] 5976 6-8-13 74 (v) CamHardie 6 68
(Antony Brittain) *hld up: rdn 2f out: nvr threatened* 12/1

0-00 6 3 1/2 **Just Heather (IRE)**[23] 607 5-8-2 63 oh18 (v) NathanEvans 7 49
(John Wainwright) *prom: rdn wl over 2f out: wknd over 1f out* 200/1

5-32 7 2 1/4 **Mama Africa (IRE)**[35] 392 5-9-0 75 JoeFanning 5 55
(David Barron) *led: rdn and hdd 2f out: wknd appr fnl f (jockey said mare anticipated the start and hit her head on the stalls)* 5/1[3]

1m 40.51s (1.91) **Going Correction** +0.35s/f (Slow) 7 Ran SP% **108.6**
Speed ratings (Par 104): **104,100,99,97,95 92,89**
CSF £15.40 TOTE £2.20: £1.20, £3.50; EX 13.70 Trifecta £33.40.
Owner L J Vaessen **Bred** Darley **Trained** Oakham, Rutland

FOCUS
A useful handicap and an emphatic winner.

952 SUNRACING.CO.UK H'CAP 7f 14y (Tp)
6:15 (6:15) (Class 4) (0-85,85) 4-Y-O+ £5,013 (£1,491; £745; £372) Stalls Centre

Form RPR
-312 1 **Portledge (IRE)**[28] 499 5-9-3 81 (b) JamieSpencer 1 91
(James Bethell) *trckd ldr: racd quite keenly: led 1f out: kpt on pushed out: cosily* 3/1[1]

-424 2 1 3/4 **Esprit De Corps**[8] 812 5-8-10 74 JoeFanning 2 79
(David Barron) *led: rdn 2f out: hdd 1f out: kpt on same pce* 11/2[3]

3132 3 1/2 **Athollblair Boy (IRE)**[10] 786 6-8-10 79 FayeMcManoman(5) 8 83
(Nigel Tinkler) *in tch: rdn over 1f out: kpt on ins fnl f* 4/1[2]

26-3 4 1 1/2 **Mr Minerals**[7] 840 5-8-13 77 RossaRyan 5 77
(Alexandra Dunn) *trckd ldr: rdn 2f out: one pce* 6/1

13-4 5 nk **Deansgate (IRE)**[28] 499 6-9-1 79 PaulMulrennan 3 78
(Julie Camacho) *stdd s: hld up: racd keenly: pushed along 2f out: n.m.r and swtchd rt jst ins fnl f: kpt on: nrst fin (jockey said gelding ran too free)* 6/1

3603 6 2 1/4 **Dirchill (IRE)**[8] 808 5-8-8 72 (b) CamHardie 4 65
(David Thompson) *in tch: rdn over 1f out: wknd ins fnl f* 20/1

0U4/ 7 1/2 **Tarnhelm**[460] 8954 4-8-7 71 oh4 NathanEvans 9 62
(Wilf Storey) *hld up: rdn 2f out: nvr threatened* 200/1

0-20 8 2 1/2 **Luis Vaz De Torres (IRE)**[28] 508 7-8-10 74 TonyHamilton 7 59
(Richard Fahey) *hld up: racd keenly: rdn 2f out: wknd 1f out* 12/1

010- 9 shd **Big Les (IRE)**[152] 7767 4-9-7 85 JasonHart 6 69
(Karen McLintock) *in tch: rdn over 2f out: wknd appr fnl f* 11/1

1m 27.6s (1.40) **Going Correction** +0.35s/f (Slow) 9 Ran SP% **110.2**
Speed ratings (Par 105): **106,104,103,101,101 98,98,95,95**
CSF £18.15 CT £61.04 TOTE £3.80: £1.30, £2.00, £1.20; EX 19.00 Trifecta £83.30.
Owner Tony Buckingham **Bred** S P Hussain **Trained** Middleham Moor, N Yorks

FOCUS
A fair handicap and not too many concerns for favourite backers.

953 BETWAY HEED YOUR HUNCH H'CAP 5f (Tp)
6:45 (6:45) (Class 4) (0-85,86) 4-Y-O+ £5,013 (£1,491; £745; £372) Stalls Centre

Form RPR
-534 1 **Primo's Comet**[9] 791 4-9-6 79 AlistairRawlinson 10 86
(Jim Goldie) *hld up: pushed along and hdwy over 1f out: rdn ins fnl f: r.o wl fnl 110yds: led nr fin* 3/1[1]

30-1 2 nk **Fendale**[37] 353 7-9-6 86 HarryRussell(7) 3 92
(Bryan Smart) *trckd ldrs: pushed along to chal jst ins fnl f: rdn to ld 75yds out: kpt on but hdd nr fin* 7/2[2]

1413 3 1/2 **Another Angel (IRE)**[9] 791 5-9-3 76 CamHardie 9 80
(Antony Brittain) *led narrowly: drvn over 1f out: hdd 75yds out: kpt on* 5/1[3]

01-0 4 nse **Gold Stone**[26] 564 4-8-13 72 JamieSpencer 6 76
(Kevin Ryan) *dwlt: hld up in rr: swtchd rt over 1f out and sn pushed along: rdn and r.o ins fnl f: nrst fin* 9/1

016- 5 hd **Nibras Again**[148] 7903 5-9-1 74 CallumRodriguez 7 77
(Paul Midgley) *chsd ldrs: rdn over 1f out: kpt on* 14/1

552- 6 nk **Justice Lady (IRE)**[142] 8093 6-9-3 76 LukeMorris 4 78
(Robert Cowell) *hld up in tch: racd quite keenly: pushed along and sme hdwy appr fnl f: rdn ins fnl f: kpt on: bit short of room nr fin* 28/1

-003 7 1 3/4 **Tommy G**[13] 741 6-9-1 77 PhilDennis(3) 5 73
(Jim Goldie) *prom: rdn 2f out: wknd ins fnl f* 12/1

-546 8 nse **Tan**[30] 471 5-9-1 79 TheodoreLadd(5) 11 75
(Michael Appleby) *w ldr: rdn over 1f out: wknd ins fnl f (jockey said gelding hung left throughout)* 9/1

00-0 9 4 **Orient Class**[23] 610 8-8-10 72 BenRobinson(3) 2 53
(Paul Midgley) *in tch: rdn over 1f out: sn wknd (jockey said gelding hung left throughout)* 40/1

406- 10 1/2 **Dapper Man (IRE)**[154] 7713 5-9-2 80 BenSanderson(5) 1 60
(Roger Fell) *prom: rdn 2f out: wknd fnl f (jockey said gelding hung right-handed)* 40/1

050- 11 22 **Rumshak (IRE)**[105] 9084 4-9-4 77 (b) PaulMulrennan 8
(Michael Dods) *dwlt: sn chsd ldrs: pushed along and lost pl 1/2-way: wknd over 1f out: eased (jockey said gelding was unsuited by being unable to dominate)* 10/1

58.91s (-0.59) **Going Correction** +0.35s/f (Slow) 11 Ran SP% **115.7**
Speed ratings (Par 105): **111,110,109,109,109 108,106,105,99,98 63**
CSF £12.84 CT £49.83 TOTE £3.70: £1.40, £1.80, £1.50; EX 17.80 Trifecta £82.60.
Owner The Reluctant Suitor's **Bred** Jim Goldie **Trained** Uplawmoor, E Renfrews

FOCUS
A thrilling finish to a useful handicap with hardly anything separating the first six home.

954 BETWAY NOVICE STKS 6f (Tp)
7:15 (7:15) (Class 5) 3-Y-O+ £2,911 (£866; £432; £216) Stalls Centre

Form RPR
1 **Sandret (IRE)** 3-8-13 0 CamHardie 7 67
(Ben Haslam) *hld up: pushed along and hdwy over 1f out: rdn ins fnl f: kpt on wl: led towards fin* 22/1

2 1/2 **Wise Words** 3-8-8 0 LukeMorris 2 60
(James Tate) *midfield: rdn over 2f out: hdwy over 1f out: led jst ins fnl f: edgd rt: kpt on but hdd nr fin* 15/8[2]

5 3 2 1/2 **Muhallab (IRE)**[10] 785 3-8-13 0 AndrewMullen 5 57
(Adrian Nicholls) *trckd ldr: rdn over 1f out: drvn and one pce fnl f* 12/1

5- 4 shd **Global Destination (IRE)**[203] 5924 3-8-13 0 DanielMuscutt 3 57
(Ed Dunlop) *trckd ldr: rdn to chal strly appr fnl f: drvn and one pce ins fnl f* 11/8[1]

6-00 5 1 3/4 **Henrietta's Dream**[23] 613 5-9-2 40 (b) HarryRussell(7) 6 50?
(John Wainwright) *led: rdn 2f out: hdd jst ins fnl f: sn no ex and already btn in 5th whn sltly hmpd 75yds out* 100/1

0/ 6 3/4 **One Last Hug**[698] 1496 4-9-7 0 CoreyMadden(7) 9 53
(Jim Goldie) *hld up: pushed along over 2f out: kpt on fnl f: nvr threatened* 50/1

7 1 1/2 **Mea Culpa (IRE)** 3-8-13 0 CallumRodriguez 4 44
(Julie Camacho) *slowly away: hld up: nvr threatened* 11/2[3]

8 4 **Marvel** 3-8-13 0 PaulMulrennan 8 31
(Julie Camacho) *midfield: pushed along over 2f out: wknd over 1f out* 14/1

9 1/2 **Opera Kiss (IRE)** 3-8-5 0 PhilDennis(3) 1 24
(Lawrence Mullaney) *s.i.s: pushed along over 2f out: wknd over 1f out* 33/1

1m 13.99s (1.49) **Going Correction** +0.35s/f (Slow) 9 Ran SP% **116.9**
WFA 3 from 4yo+ 15lb
Speed ratings (Par 103): **97,96,93,92,90 89,87,82,81**
CSF £63.52 TOTE £22.50: £5.50, £1.20, £2.50; EX 88.70 Trifecta £727.50.
Owner Ben Haslam Racing Syndicate **Bred** Tally-Ho Stud **Trained** Middleham Moor, N Yorks

FOCUS
A surprise to end the card and a victory for trainer form.
T/Plt: £19.10 to a £1 stake. Pool: £61,122.55 - 2,329.48 winning units T/Qpdt: £5.20 to a £1 stake. Pool: £7,947.09 - 1,130.04 winning units **Andrew Sheret**

LYON-LA SOIE (R-H)
Thursday, February 28

OFFICIAL GOING: Viscoride: standard

955a PRIX ROBERT CHRISTOPHE (CLAIMER) (3YO) (VISCORIDE) 1m 2f 165y(P)
5:07 3-Y-O £6,306 (£2,522; £1,891; £1,261; £630)

RPR
1 **Viomenil (FR)** 3-9-1 0 (p) Pierre-CharlesBoudot 7 70
(J-P Gauvin, France) 97/10

2 nk **Anycity (IRE)**[55] 55 3-9-1 0 (b) TonyPiccone 4 69
(Michael Wigham) *wl into stride: trckd ldrs: jnd ldr after 1f and disp ld: pushed along to ld over 2f out: rdn to extend ld over 1f out: drvn and strly chal ins fnl f: hdd fnl 50yds* 21/10[1]

3 1/2 **Foxy Power (FR)** 3-8-11 0 (b) MaximeGuyon 6 64
(C Escuder, France) 21/10[1]

4 2 **Via Pellegrina (FR)**[126] 3-8-11 0 GabrieleCongiu 9 60
(J-P Gauvin, France) 53/1

5 1/2 **Coco Chamelle (IRE)** 3-8-13 0 (b) StephanePasquier 5 61
(Y Durepaire, France) 11/2[3]

The Form Book Flat 2019, Raceform Ltd, Newbury, RG14 5SJ

6 4 **Le Moqueur (FR)** 3-9-4 0 .... GuillaumeMillet 2 58
(K Borgel, France) 49/1
7 3/4 **Ashwagandha (FR)**[138] 3-8-8 0 .... EddyHardouin 1 47
(K Borgel, France) 48/10[2]
8 3 1/2 **Slivio (FR)** 3-8-11 0 .... FranckBlondel 3 43
(F Rossi, France) 176/10
9 dist **Laredo Chop (FR)**[140] 3-8-11 0 .... (p) CyrilleStefan 8
(J-M Capitte, France) 29/1

2m 18.54s (0.54) 9 Ran SP% **119.0**
PARI-MUTUEL (all including 1 euro stake): WIN 8.90; PLACE 2.40, 1.40, 1.20; DF 15.60;.
Owner Bertrand Milliere **Bred** Mme H Devin **Trained** France

[842]MEYDAN (L-H)

Thursday, February 28

OFFICIAL GOING: Dirt: fast; turf: good

956a MEYDAN CLASSIC SPONSORED BY MOHAMMED BIN RASHID AL MAKTOUM CITY DISTRICT ONE (LISTED RACE) (TURF) 1m

3:05 (3:05) 3-Y-0

£82,677 (£27,559; £13,779; £6,889; £4,133; £2,755)

RPR

1 **Sporting Chance**[21] 636 3-9-0 100 .... PatCosgrave 6 92
(Simon Crisford) *trckd ldrs: led 2f out: hdd 1f out but r.o to ld again fnl 55yds* 14/1
2 nk **Golden Jaguar (USA)**[28] 511 3-9-0 99 .... (h) ConnorBeasley 11 92
(A bin Harmash, UAE) *s.i.s: settled in rr: wd 2 1/2f out: smooth prog 2f out: led 1f out: hdd fnl 55yds* 2/1[2]
3 nk **Irish Trilogy (IRE)**[28] 511 3-9-0 95 .... CarlosLopez 1 91
(Andrew Kidney, Sweden) *mid-div: chsd ldrs 2 1/2f out: r.o wl fnl 2f* 16/1
4 nk **Shanty Star (USA)**[26] 570 3-9-0 80 .... AhmetCelik 4 90
(R Bouresly, Kuwait) *s.i.s: nvr nr to chal but r.o fnl 1 1/2f* 80/1
5 1 1/4 **Nayslayer (IRE)**[28] 511 3-9-0 87 .... PatDobbs 3 87
(Ali Jan, Qatar) *settled in rr: chsd ldrs 2 1/2f out: r.o fnl 2f* 33/1
6 3 1/2 **Good Fortune**[49] 168 3-9-0 96 .... (t) WilliamBuick 5 79
(Charlie Appleby) *nvr nr to chal but r.o same pce fnl 2f* 10/11[1]
7 2 1/2 **Prince Elzaam (IRE)**[28] 511 3-9-0 91 .... OisinMurphy 12 74
(Jaber Ramadhan, Bahrain) *nvr bttr than mid-div* 25/1
8 3 3/4 **Burj**[14] 727 3-9-0 83 .... ChristopheSoumillon 13 65
(Saeed bin Suroor) *sn led: hdd & wknd 2f out* 20/1
9 5 1/4 **Trolius (IRE)**[14] 727 3-9-0 93 .... (vt) JamesDoyle 10 53
(Simon Crisford) *chsd ldrs tl wknd fnl 2f* 10/1[3]
10 5 3/4 **Lady Parma (USA)**[28] 510 3-8-9 87 .... RichardMullen 2 35
(S Seemar, UAE) *nvr nr to chal* 33/1
11 2 1/2 **Al Fajir Mukbile (IRE)**[28] 511 3-9-0 83 .... (b) FabriceVeron 8 34
(Ismail Mohammed) *s.i.s: a in rr* 66/1
12 6 **Victory Command (IRE)**[14] 727 3-9-0 98 .... RoystonFfrench 9 20
(Mark Johnston) *trckd ldr tl wknd 2 1/2f out* 16/1
13 21 **Muthhila (IRE)**[28] 510 3-8-9 87 .... MickaelBarzalona 7
(S Jadhav, UAE) *nvr nr to chal* 50/1

1m 38.31s (0.81) **Going Correction** +0.475s/f (Yiel) 13 Ran SP% **132.4**
Speed ratings: **114,113,113,113,111 108,105,102,96,91 88,82,61**
CSF: 45.09.
Owner Abdulla Al Mansoori **Bred** Ropsley Bloodstock & St Albans Bloodstck **Trained** Newmarket, Suffolk
■ Salayel was withdrawn. Price at time of withdrawal 28/1. Rule 4 does not apply

FOCUS
TRAKUS (metres covered compared to winner): 2nd +6, 3rd -5, 4th -3, 5th -5, 6th 0, 7th +6, 8th -5, 9th +2, 10th -2, 11th +6, 12th 0, 13th +3. Probably form to view negatively, as the first two did things wrong, the favourite disappointed and a few horses anchor the level. The splits were 25.22, 23.84, 24.8, 24.45.

957a DISTRICT ONE CRYSTAL LAGOON TROPHY (H'CAP) (DIRT) 1m (D)

3:40 (3:40) (90-108,107) 3-Y-0+

£63,779 (£21,259; £10,629; £5,314; £3,188; £2,125)

RPR

1 **African Ride**[28] 513 5-9-1 102 .... (t) ChristopheSoumillon 7 109
(Simon Crisford) *trckd ldrs: led 2f out: r.o wl: easily* 9/2[2]
2 3 1/2 **Bochart**[7] 842 6-8-5 93 .... (t) RichardMullen 10 91
(S Seemar, UAE) *mid-div: chsd ldrs 2 1/2f out: r.o wl fnl 2f but no ch w wnr* 8/1
3 3/4 **Ibn Malik (IRE)**[21] 639 6-9-6 107 .... JimCrowley 2 104+
(M Al Mheiri, UAE) *mid-div: r.o wl fnl 2 1/2f: nrst fin* 9/2[2]
4 2 3/4 **Thegreatcollection (USA)**[28] 513 5-8-9 97 .... (b) SamHitchcott 3 87
(Doug Watson, UAE) *nvr nr to chal but r.o fnl 2 1/2f* 11/2[3]
5 2 3/4 **Mystique Moon**[20] 676 5-9-0 101 .... PatDobbs 8 86
(Doug Watson, UAE) *mid-div: r.o same pce fnl 3f* 3/1[1]
6 3/4 **Plata O Plomo (USA)**[28] 513 5-8-8 96 .... (vt) ElioneChaves 4 78
(Susanne Berneklint, Sweden) *a mid-div* 33/1
7 2 1/4 **Moqarrar (USA)**[6] 872 4-8-5 90 .... (b) AntonioFresu 1 70
(E Charpy, UAE) *trckd ldr: led 4 1/2f out: hdd & wknd fnl 2f* 15/2
8 20 **Walk In The Sun (USA)**[21] 637 4-8-10 98 .... MickaelBarzalona 9 29
(S Jadhav, UAE) *nvr bttr than mid-div* 12/1
9 2 3/4 **Connect**[7] 844 4-8-13 100 .... (h) ConnorBeasley 5 25
(A bin Harmash, UAE) *s.i.s: a in rr* 25/1
10 14 1/2 **Broadcast (USA)**[18] 681 4-8-5 90 .... (b) TadhgO'Shea 11
(S Seemar, UAE) *nvr nr to chal* 33/1
11 nk **Pop The Hood (USA)**[14] 729 7-8-5 92 .... (bt) RoystonFfrench 6
(Doug Watson, UAE) *sn led: hdd & wknd 4 1/2f out* 12/1

1m 39.44s (1.94) **Going Correction** +0.475s/f (Slow) 11 Ran SP% **124.7**
Speed ratings: **109,105,104,102,99 98,96,76,73,59 58**
CSF: 42.39; TRICAST: 178.44.
Owner Nabil Mourad **Bred** Wertheimer Et Frere **Trained** Newmarket, Suffolk

FOCUS
TRAKUS: 2nd -6, 3rd -1, 4th -5, 5th +1, 6th +3, 7th -7, 8th +6, 9th +1, 10th +10, 11th -1. They went fast early and finished slowly: 24.08 (400m from standing start), 22.95 (800m), 25.71 (1200m), with the winner to the line in 26.61.

958a NAD AL SHEBA TROPHY SPONSORED BY MOHAMMED BIN RASHID AL MAKTOUM CITY DISTRICT ONE (GROUP 3) (TURF) 1m 6f 11y

4:15 (4:15) 3-Y-0+

£141,732 (£47,244; £23,622; £11,811; £7,086; £4,724)

RPR

1 **Ispolini**[42] 281 4-8-9 109 .... (t) MickaelBarzalona 1 116+
(Charlie Appleby) *settled in rr: smooth prog 2 1/2f out: led 1 1/2f out: easily* 5/2[2]
2 10 1/2 **Red Galileo**[14] 730 8-9-0 102 .... PatCosgrave 6 101
(Saeed bin Suroor) *sn led: hdd 1 1/2f out but kpt on* 12/1
3 11 1/2 **Bin Battuta**[35] 398 5-9-0 106 .... (p) ChristopheSoumillon 4 85
(Saeed bin Suroor) *a mid-div* 9/2[3]
4 shd **Suspicious Mind (DEN)**[42] 281 6-9-0 96 .... (t) ElioneChaves 5 85
(Andrew Kidney, Sweden) *a mid-div* 33/1
5 4 **Zamaam**[21] 635 9-9-0 95 .... (t) JimCrowley 2 79
(E Charpy, UAE) *trckd ldrs tl wknd fnl 2 1/2f* 66/1
6 dist **Pinzolo**[663] 2398 8-9-0 102 .... FabriceVeron 3
(Ismail Mohammed) *a in rr* 50/1
P **Brundtland (IRE)**[123] 8667 4-8-9 114 .... (p) WilliamBuick 7
(Charlie Appleby) *trckd ldr: stmbld and p.u 4 1/2f out: fatally injured* 4/5[1]

2m 55.96s
WFA 4 from 5yo+ 3lb 7 Ran SP% **116.4**
CSF: 30.74.
Owner Godolphin **Bred** Newsells Park Stud **Trained** Newmarket, Suffolk

FOCUS
TRAKUS: 2nd -3, 3rd +2, 4th +9, 5th -2, 6th +16. Essentially a trial for the Dubai Gold Cup - Vazirabad was second in the 2017 and 2018 runnings before winning the main event. This season's race was marred with the favourite going amiss, but still quite an impressive performance from the winner, who got the final section in 24.46 off a reasonable gallop.

959a CURLIN H'CAP SPONSORED BY MOHAMMED BIN RASHID AL MAKTOUM CITY DISTRICT ONE (LISTED HCAP) (DIRT) 1m 2f (D)

4:50 (4:50) (95-105,105) 3-Y-0+

£75,590 (£25,196; £12,598; £6,299; £3,779; £2,519)

RPR

1 **Dolkong (USA)**[35] 396 5-9-1 100 .... OlivierDoleuze 3 108
(Simon Foster, Korea) *mid-div: smooth prog 2 1/2f out: led 1 1/2f out: r.o wl: easily* 9/2[3]
2 9 1/2 **Etijaah (USA)**[21] 638 9-9-2 101 .... (h) JimCrowley 7 90
(Doug Watson, UAE) *nvr nr to chal but r.o wl fnl 2f: no ch w wnr* 9/2[3]
3 4 **Galvanize (USA)**[28] 513 6-8-13 98 .... PatDobbs 1 79
(Doug Watson, UAE) *trckd ldr: smooth prog to ld 2 1/2f out: hdd 1 1/2f out: wknd fnl f* 10/3[2]
4 5 **Key Bid**[6] 872 5-8-9 95 .... (t) FernandoJara 6 65
(A R Al Rayhi, UAE) *s.i.s: nvr nr to chal but r.o fnl 1 1/2f* 12/1
5 1 3/4 **Earnshaw (USA)**[21] 635 8-8-13 98 .... (bt) MickaelBarzalona 2 66
(S Jadhav, UAE) *sn led: hdd 2 1/2f out: wknd fnl f* 20/1
6 13 **Saltarin Dubai (ARG)**[35] 396 6-9-6 105 .... (bt) RichardMullen 4 47
(S Seemar, UAE) *trckd ldr: rdn 4f out: sn btn* 11/4[1]
7 1 1/2 **Irish Freedom (USA)**[42] 282 5-9-1 100 .... (bt) TadhgO'Shea 9 39
(S Seemar, UAE) *nvr bttr than mid-div* 25/1
8 dist **Parsifal (SPA)**[14] 730 6-8-9 95 .... BenCurtis 8
(G Arizkorreta Elosegui, Spain) *s.i.s: a in rr* 50/1
9 dist **Very Talented (IRE)**[14] 730 6-9-1 100 .... ChristopheSoumillon 5
(Saeed bin Suroor) *a in rr* 13/2

2m 5.37s (0.67) **Going Correction** +0.475s/f (Slow) 9 Ran SP% **117.7**
Speed ratings: **116,108,105,101,99 89,88, ,**
CSF: 25.03.
Owner Lee Tae In **Bred** Ellen B Kill Kelley **Trained** Korea

FOCUS
TRAKUS: 2nd +13, 3rd +3, 4th +8, 5th -1, 6th +10, 7th +20, 8th +21, 9th +11. A race named for the 2008 winner who followed up in the Dubai World Cup at Nad Al Sheba, and California Chrome won the 2016 edition. But there was nothing of their quality this time and the race lacked depth, even with the winners of the last two runnings in here. The pace gradually slackened before the winner picked up well: 24.19 (from standing start), 24.39, 25.33, 25.65, with the winner to the line in 24.71.

960a DISTRICT ONE ELEGANCE STRETCH CUP (H'CAP) (TURF) 7f

5:25 (5:25) (95-104,104) 3-Y-0+

£82,677 (£27,559; £13,779; £6,889; £4,133; £2,755)

RPR

1 **On The Warpath**[28] 515 4-8-13 97 .... WilliamBuick 8 107
(Charlie Appleby) *chsd ldrs: rdn to ld 1f out: r.o wl* 9/4[1]
2 1 **Mubtasim (IRE)**[21] 640 5-9-5 103 .... (h) JamesDoyle 3 110
(Charlie Appleby) *trckd ldr: led 1 1/2f out: hdd 1f out but kpt on wl* 11/4[2]
3 1 **Wasim (IRE)**[18] 681 4-9-0 98 .... FabriceVeron 4 102
(Ismail Mohammed) *trckd ldr: led 2 1/2f out: hdd 1 1/2f out but r.o wl* 16/1
4 2 1/4 **Above N Beyond**[7] 847 6-9-3 101 .... (vt) ConnorBeasley 7 99
(A bin Harmash, UAE) *mid-div: r.o same pce fnl 2 1/2f* 9/1
5 shd **Lansky (IRE)**[21] 640 4-9-6 104 .... MickaelBarzalona 10 102
(S Jadhav, UAE) *mid-div: chsd ldrs 2 1/2f out: r.o same pce fnl 2f* 8/1
6 1/2 **Bedouin's Story**[7] 847 4-8-11 96 .... (v) KevinStott 12 92
(Saeed bin Suroor) *s.i.s: nvr nr to chal but r.o wl* 13/2[3]
7 hd **Eshtiraak (AUS)**[7] 847 4-8-11 96 .... (b) DaneO'Neill 9 91
(David A Hayes, Australia) *nvr nr to chal but r.o fnl 2 1/2f* 33/1
8 nk **Dream Today (IRE)**[7] 843 4-8-11 96 .... (t) PatDobbs 13 90
(Jamie Osborne) *mid-div: r.o same pce fnl 2 1/2f* 12/1
9 1 3/4 **Freescape**[7] 847 4-8-13 97 .... (b) WJLee 11 88
(David Marnane, Ire) *nvr bttr than mid-div* 12/1
10 1 1/4 **Musaddas**[34] 425 9-8-11 96 .... AhmetCelik 6 82
(R Bouresly, Kuwait) *nvr nr to chal* 66/1
11 3/4 **Muraaqeb (AUS)**[42] 285 4-9-5 103 .... (b) JimCrowley 1 88
(David A Hayes, Australia) *mid-div tl wknd fnl 2f* 25/1
12 3 1/2 **Liquid Mercury (SAF)**[392] 518 7-9-2 100 .... BernardoPinheiro 2 76
(R Bouresly, Kuwait) *a in rr* 66/1
13 1 **Victory Wave (USA)**[14] 729 5-9-0 98 .... (p) ChristopheSoumillon 5 71
(Saeed bin Suroor) *sn led: hdd & wknd 2 1/2f out* 14/1

14 21 **Johann Strauss**[14] 725 8-9-2 **100**.......................... RoystonFfrench 14 16
(R Bouresly, Kuwait) *a in rr* **66/1**

1m 23.52s (-0.58) **Going Correction** +0.475s/f (Yiel) **14** Ran SP% **131.1**
Speed ratings: **122,120,119,117,117 116,116,115,113,112 111,107,106,82**
CSF: 8.90; TRICAST 86.81.
Owner Godolphin **Bred** Sahara Group & Eurowest Bloodstock **Trained** Newmarket, Suffolk
FOCUS
TRAKUS: 2nd -5, 3rd 0, 4th -4, 5th 0, 6th 0, 7th -4, 8th +3, 9th +2, 10th -3, 11th -3, 12th -7, 13th -4, 14th +4. The first five finishers were positioned 4-3-2-7-6 after 400 metres and the splits were: 25.08, 23.2, 23.1, 12.14.

961a DISTRICT ONE WORLD UN (H'CAP) (TURF) 1m 2f
6:00 (6:00) (95-108,107) 3-Y-0+
£63,779 (£21,259; £10,629; £5,314; £3,188; £2,125)

RPR
1 **Mountain Hunter (USA)**[14] 730 5-9-5 **105**...... ChristopheSoumillon 13 110
(Saeed bin Suroor) *chsd ldrs: rdn to ld fnl f: r.o* **5/2**[1]
2 ¾ **Zorion**[21] 637 5-9-1 **101**.......................................(p) JamesDoyle 1 104
(Charlie Appleby) *sn led: rdn 2 1/2f out: r.o wl but hdd fnl f* **12/1**
3 ¾ **Desert Fire (IRE)**[21] 637 4-8-11 **99**........................(v) PatCosgrave 9 100
(Saeed bin Suroor) *trckd ldr: ev ch 2f out: r.o same pce fnl 1 1/2f* **5/2**[1]
4 1¾ **Gm Hopkins**[49] 173 8-8-10 **97**............................(t) ConnorBeasley 6 94+
(Jaber Ramadhan, Bahrain) *nvr nr to chal but r.o wl fnl 1 1/2f* **40/1**
5 nk **Original Choice (IRE)**[21] 637 5-8-11 **98**......................(t) OisinMurphy 5 94
(William Haggas) *chsd ldrs: ev ch 2f out: wknd fnl f* **22/1**
6 5¾ **Baroot**[21] 637 7-9-3 **103**.................................... AdriedeVries 10 89
(M F De Kock, South Africa) *mid-div: r.o same pce fnl 2f* **15/2**[3]
7 1 **Silent Attack**[14] 726 6-9-3 **103**...............................(p) KevinStott 11 87
(Saeed bin Suroor) *nvr nr to chal but r.o fnl 2 1/2f* **25/1**
8 ¾ **Aquarium**[21] 637 4-8-11 **99**.................................. RoystonFfrench 3 80
(Mark Johnston) *slowly away: chsd ldrs 2 1/2f out: wknd fnl 2f* **33/1**
9 2½ **Mia Tesoro (IRE)**[14] 728 6-8-11 **98**.......................... JimCrowley 12 74
(Charlie Fellowes) *nvr nr to chal* **12/1**
10 1¼ **Hermoso Mundo (SAF)**[215] 6-9-4 **104**.................. BernardFayd'Herbe 7 79
(M F De Kock, South Africa) *nvr nr to chal* **40/1**
11 nk **Key Victory (IRE)**[28] 514 4-9-6 **107**.......................(p) WilliamBuick 8 81
(Charlie Appleby) *nvr bttr than mid-div* **7/1**[2]
12 2¼ **Cliffs Of Capri**[7] 847 5-8-13 **99**...............................(p) PatDobbs 14 69
(Jamie Osborne) *a in rr* **10/1**
13 7 **Peri Lina (TUR)**[14] 728 4-8-9 **97**................................(h) AhmetCelik 2 52
(Hasan Boyraz, Turkey) *broke awkwardly: nvr bttr than mid-div* **20/1**
14 dist **Harlan Strong (ARG)**[35] 398 4-8-9 **96**.......................(t) FernandoJara 4
(Kenneth McPeek, U.S.A) *nvr bttr than mid-div* **80/1**

2m 3.75s (1.05) **Going Correction** +0.475s/f (Yiel) **14** Ran SP% **127.9**
Speed ratings: **114,113,112,111,111 106,105,105,103,102 101,100,94,**
CSF: 37.21; TRIFECTA: 88.56. PLACEPOT: £62.70 to a £1 stake. QUADPOT: £15.30 to a £1 stake..
Owner Godolphin **Bred** Darley **Trained** Newmarket, Suffolk
FOCUS
TRAKUS: 2nd -2, 3rd 0, 4th -1, 5th -3, 6th +5, 7th +1, 8th -3, 9th +3, 10th +2, 11th +5, 12th +2, 13th 0, 14th -1. The runner-up set a slow pace so few got into this: 26.18, 24.38, 25.8, 23.78, with the winner home in 23.38.

[876]LINGFIELD (L-H)
Friday, March 1

OFFICIAL GOING: Polytrack: standard
Wind: Light, across Weather: Cloudy

962 LIKE SUN RACING ON FACEBOOK H'CAP 1m 1y(P)
2:00 (2:00) (Class 5) (0-75,77) 4-Y-0+ **£2,911** (£866; £432; £216) **Stalls** High

Form RPR
0-32 1 **Pheidippides**[14] 732 4-9-6 **74**..................................(b) LukeMorris 4 83
(Tom Clover) *chsd ldng pair: cajoled along over 2f out: brought between rivals to ld last 150yds: styd on wl* **6/1**[3]
20-1 2 1¾ **In The Red (IRE)**[45] 249 6-9-7 **75**...........................(p) AdamKirby 7 80
(Martin Smith) *led 2f: chsd ldr: rdn to ld again wl over 1f out: hdd and one pce last 150yds* **12/1**
-535 3 1 **Ambient (IRE)**[34] 429 4-9-5 **73**.............................. RichardKingscote 10 76
(Jane Chapple-Hyam) *hld up towards rr: rdn 2f out: prog over 1f out: styd on to take 3rd last 100yds: no ch to chal* **7/1**
2144 4 ½ **Dark Alliance (IRE)**[8] 840 8-9-3 **71**.............................. OisinMurphy 11 73
(Mark Loughnane) *stdd s: hld up in last pair: shkn up 2f out: styd on fnl f: nvr nrr but no ch* **11/1**
55-0 5 shd **Lacan (IRE)**[57] 34 8-9-8 **76**.................................. CallumShepherd 5 77
(Brett Johnson) *hld up off the pce in midfield: rdn 2f out: kpt on fnl f but no ch* **12/1**
330- 6 nk **Blazed (IRE)**[98] 9228 5-9-8 **76**...........................(t) StevieDonohoe 2 77
(Ed Vaughan) *taken down early: sltly mistimed s: sn in midfield: rdn and no imp 2f out: kpt on fnl f (jockey said gelding accelerated the gate)* **12/1**
0-44 7 ¾ **High Acclaim (USA)**[42] 294 5-9-7 **75**........................(p) DavidProbert 8 74
(Roger Teal) *taken down early: dwlt: pushed up to chse ldng trio: rdn over 2f out: nt able to cl: fdd fnl f* **5/1**[2]
15-2 8 ½ **Motajaasid (IRE)**[7] 856 4-9-5 **76**.......................(t) FinleyMarsh[(3)] 9 74
(Richard Hughes) *led after 2f: rdn and hdd wl over 1f out: styd on inner and wknd rapidly fnl f (jockey said gelding stopped quickly)* **11/4**[1]
1-12 9 2 **Mr Mac**[42] 295 5-9-3 **71**.................................... TomMarquand 12 64
(Peter Hedger) *hld up in last pair: rdn 2f out: no prog (trainer said gelding ran flat)* **5/1**[2]
/0-0 10 5 **Faraway Fields (USA)**[27] 562 4-8-13 **67**........................ EoinWalsh 6 49
(Peter Hiatt) *stdd s: hld up in last pair: no prog over 2f out: bhd over 1f out* **50/1**

1m 36.2s (-2.00) **Going Correction** -0.10s/f (Stan) **10** Ran SP% **120.2**
Speed ratings (Par 103): **106,104,103,102,102 102,101,101,99,94**
CSF £77.82 CT £534.28 TOTE £10.70: £2.00, £3.60, £2.90; EX 64.00 Trifecta £385.40.
Owner Dr O Rangabashyam **Bred** Farmers Hill Stud **Trained** Newmarket, Suffolk

FOCUS
They went a fair gallop here. The second has been rated to his latest form.

963 SUN RACING NOVICE STKS 7f 1y(P)
2:30 (2:30) (Class 5) 4-Y-0+ **£2,911** (£866; £432; £216) **Stalls** Low

Form RPR
2-1 1 **Tiger Eye (IRE)**[32] 464 4-9-4 0........................ OisinMurphy 4 86+
(James Fanshawe) *hld up bhd ldng pair: brought wd bnd 2f out: clsd to ld 1f out: sn drew clr: readily (jockey said filly hung left-handed under pressure)* **4/6**[1]
0-2 2 hd **Shake Me Handy**[34] 438 4-9-2 0........................... AdamKirby 1 75
(Roger Teal) *led: tk fierce hold: stdd and hdd over 5f out: settled bttr after: rdn to chal over 1f out: squeezed out sn after: kpt on to press runner-up nr fin: fin 3rd: promoted to 2nd* **5/1**[3]
253- 3 3¼ **Your Choice**[61] 9764 4-8-11 **63**...............................(p) LiamJones 3 69
(Laura Mongan) *led over 5f out: rdn over 2f out: edgd rt over 1f out and sn hdd: kpt on same pce: fin 2nd: disqualified and plcd 3rd* **12/1**
4-3 4 1½ **Iconic Girl**[14] 732 4-8-11 0.................................... DavidProbert 2 64
(Andrew Balding) *hld up bhd ldng pair: shkn up 2f out: nt qckn over 1f out and no imp after* **3/1**[2]

1m 24.08s (-0.72) **Going Correction** -0.10s/f (Stan) **4** Ran SP% **109.3**
Speed ratings (Par 103): **100,96,96,94**
CSF £4.46 TOTE £1.40; EX 4.90 Trifecta £11.30.
Owner Qatar Racing Limited **Bred** Orpendale,Wynatt,Chelston & Daylesford **Trained** Newmarket, Suffolk
■ Stewards' Enquiry : Liam Jones caution: careless riding
FOCUS
This proved easy enough for the odds-on favourite. You Choice has been rated to her mark, and Shake Me Handy close to his latest.

964 BETWAY H'CAP 6f 1y(P)
3:05 (3:05) (Class 3) (0-95,100) 4-Y-0+ **£7,246** (£2,168; £1,084; £542; £270) **Stalls** Low

Form RPR
-243 1 **Watchable**[42] 297 9-9-2 **89**....................................(p) AdamKirby 5 95
(David O'Meara) *mde all: kicked 3 l clr 2f out: drvn fnl f: clung on wl* **5/1**[3]
0522 2 nk **Something Lucky (IRE)**[10] 791 7-8-6 **79**.....................(b) HollieDoyle 3 84
(Michael Appleby) *hld up in last pair: prog on outer 2f out: chsd wnr jst over 1f out: styd on and clsd nr fin: jst too late* **8/1**
5-53 3 1¾ **Suzi's Connoisseur**[26] 588 8-8-13 **86**................(b) RichardKingscote 7 85
(Jane Chapple-Hyam) *trckd ldng pair: shkn up 2f out: disp 2nd briefly over 1f out but nt qckn after: styd on same pce* **2/1**[1]
2-16 4 hd **Nick Vedder**[14] 748 5-8-11 **84**..................................(b) OisinMurphy 6 83
(Michael Wigham) *s.i.s: hld up in last pair: shkn up 2f out: sme prog on inner fnl f: nvr nr to chal* **9/4**[2]
2114 5 5 **Highland Acclaim (IRE)**[14] 734 8-8-6 **79**....................(h) DavidProbert 1 62
(David O'Meara) *t.k.h: trckd ldng pair: short of room on inner over 2f out and lost pl: wknd over 1f out (starter reported that the gelding was the subject of a third criteria failure; trainer was informed the gelding could not run until the day after passing a stalls test)* **6/1**
34-6 6 nk **Zac Brown (IRE)**[48] 203 8-8-12 **85**............................(t w) JFEgan 2 67
(Charlie Wallis) *dwlt: pushed up to chse wnr and then t.k.h: edgd lft over 2f out: lost 2nd and wknd rapidly jst over 1f out (jockey said gelding had no more to give)* **16/1**

1m 9.82s (-2.08) **Going Correction** -0.10s/f (Stan) **6** Ran SP% **112.0**
Speed ratings (Par 107): **109,108,106,106,99 98**
CSF £41.62 TOTE £5.20: £2.10, £2.00; EX 24.50 Trifecta £65.50.
Owner Hambleton Xxxix P Bamford Roses Partners **Bred** Cheveley Park Stud Ltd **Trained** Upper Helmsley, N Yorks
■ Stewards' Enquiry : J F Egan two-day ban: interference & careless riding (Mar 15-16)
FOCUS
A fairly competitive sprint on paper, but the winner dictated matters from the front. The winner has been rated to his recent best.

965 PLAY 4 TO SCORE AT BETWAY CLASSIFIED CLAIMING STKS 1m 2f (P)
3:35 (3:35) (Class 5) 4-Y-0+ **£2,911** (£866; £432; £216) **Stalls** Low

Form RPR
6-02 1 **Brexitmeansbrexit**[25] 603 4-9-0 **70**.............. ThoreHammerHansen[(5)] 6 71
(Richard Hannon) *hld up in last pair: prog on outer 2f out: shkn up and clsd over 1f out: rdn to ld last 100yds: styd on wl* **11/4**[1]
1124 2 ¾ **Zorawar (FR)**[9] 801 5-9-10 **67**................................. DavidProbert 5 74
(David O'Meara) *trckd ldrs: stl cruising 2f out: brought to ld 1f out but immediately chal: hdd and nt qckn last 100yds* **16/5**[3]
0303 3 ¾ **Highway One (USA)**[23] 616 5-9-3 **62**........................... LiamKeniry 3 66
(George Baker) *led 2f: chsd ldr: rdn to chal 2f out: outpcd by ldng pair fnl f but styd on* **8/1**
-320 4 hd **Attain**[7] 859 10-8-7 **64**.................................... Pierre-LouisJamin[(7)] 1 62
(Archie Watson) *dwlt and pushed along early: in tch: shkn up and prog 2f out: clsd on ldrs 1f out: styd on fnl f but nvr able to chal* **9/2**
-025 5 1¼ **Creek Harbour (IRE)**[29] 508 4-9-3 **69**............................ ShaneKelly 8 63
(Richard Hughes) *led after 2f: rdn over 2f out: hdd & wknd 1f out* **3/1**[2]
0-44 6 2½ **Red Touch (USA)**[25] 603 7-9-0 **67**.............................(p) LukeMorris 4 55
(Michael Appleby) *chsd ldrs: rdn over 3f out: fdd u.p on inner over 1f out* **16/1**
06-0 7 25 **Willow Grace**[14] 736 4-8-12 **50**................................ NicolaCurrie 7
(George Baker) *hld up in last pair: wknd over 3f out: t.o (jockey said filly stopped quickly)* **25/1**
0-05 8 shd **Suttonwood Sally**[28] 516 5-8-9 **24**............................ NoelGarbutt[(3)] 2
(Geoffrey Deacon) *chsd ldrs: urged along 1/2-way: wknd over 3f out: t.o* **100/1**

2m 3.92s (-2.68) **Going Correction** -0.10s/f (Stan) **8** Ran SP% **115.5**
Speed ratings (Par 103): **106,105,104,104,103 101,81,81**
CSF £12.01 TOTE £4.20: £1.10, £1.80, £2.50; EX 11.30 Trifecta £53.50.
Owner M Stewkesbury **Bred** Mervyn Stewkesbury **Trained** East Everleigh, Wilts
FOCUS
They finished in a bit of a heap in this claimer. The level is set by the second and third.

966 LADBROKES HOME OF THE ODDS BOOST H'CAP 7f 1y(P)
4:10 (4:10) (Class 5) (0-75,80) 3-Y-0 **£2,911** (£866; £432; £216) **Stalls** Low

Form RPR
50-1 1 **Zmhar (IRE)**[9] 798 3-9-12 **80** 6ex.............................(h) OisinMurphy 8 89+
(James Tate) *t.k.h: hld up in rr: prog to trck ldng pair over 2f out: pushed along over 1f out: led jst ins fnl f: sn clr: comf* **30/100**[1]
45-4 2 2¾ **On The Line (IRE)**[15] 720 3-9-6 **74**............................(bt[1]) LukeMorris 5 76
(Hugo Palmer) *trckd ldr after 2f: rdn to ld wl over 1f out: hdd u.p jst ins fnl f: no ch w wnr but kpt on (vet reported the colt lost its left hind shoe)* **5/1**[2]

4-03 **3** ½ **Altar Boy**[34] 442 3-8-12 **69**........ GaryMahon(3) 7 69
(Sylvester Kirk) *led after 1f to wl over 1f out: kpt on wl on inner after but no ch w wnr* **14/1**

005- **4** 2¼ **Laxmi (IRE)**[128] 8553 3-9-2 **70**........ CallumShepherd 3 64+
(Brian Meehan) *hld up in rr: detached in last and pushed along over 2f out: styd on fnl f to take modest 4th last strides: nvr in it* **17/2**[3]

40-3 **5** hd **Alicia Darcy (IRE)**[13] 753 3-9-7 **75**........ RichardKingscote 4 69
(James Given) *trckd ldrs: stl gng wl enough 2f out: shkn up and no rspnse over 1f out: fdd* **10/1**

6-14 **6** nk **Black Medick**[41] 320 3-9-9 **77**........ LiamJones 2 70
(Laura Mongan) *in tch: rdn over 2f out: outpcd over 1f out: no ch after* **11/1**

00-0 **7** 1 **Gabrial The Giant (IRE)**[23] 614 3-8-12 **66**........ StevieDonohoe 1 56
(Ian Williams) *led 1f: chsd ldrs: rdn over 2f out: fdd on inner over 1f out* **50/1**

540- **8** 3½ **Mitigator**[69] 9683 3-9-8 **76**........(p[1]) AdamKirby 9 57
(Lydia Pearce) *stmbld bdly s: in tch in last pair: rdn over 2f out: wknd over 1f out (jockey said colt stumbled leaving the stalls)* **25/1**

1m 24.91s (0.11) **Going Correction** -0.10s/f (Stan) **8 Ran SP% 134.0**
Speed ratings (Par 98): **95,91,91,88,88 88,87,83**
CSF £3.51 CT £15.03 TOTE £1.20: £1.02, £1.50, £4.10; EX 3.50 Trifecta £18.60.
Owner Saeed Manana **Bred** Rabbah Bloodstock Limited **Trained** Newmarket, Suffolk

FOCUS
The odds-on favourite confirmed himself well ahead of his mark. It's been rated around the second and third.

967 LADBROKES NOVICE STKS 1m 2f (P)
4:40 (4:40) (Class 5) 3-Y-O **£2,911** (£866; £432; £216) **Stalls** Low

Form RPR

1- **1** **Moonlight Spirit (IRE)**[99] 9203 3-9-9 0........ AdamKirby 1 81
(Charlie Appleby) *trckd ldr: chal 2f out: shkn up to ld 1f out: hrd pressed after: drvn and hld on nr fin* **2/11**[1]

0-6 **2** hd **Fly Lightly**[44] 251 3-9-2 0........ LukeMorris 5 73
(Robert Cowell) *led: rdn 2f out: narrowly hdd 1f out: kpt on wl u.p and pressed wnr hrd: jst hld* **16/1**[3]

3 3½ **Thelonious** 3-9-2 0........ OisinMurphy 3 66
(Michael Bell) *chsd ldng pair: pushed along over 2f out: no imp but kpt on steadily fr over 1f out* **11/4**[2]

6 **4** 16 **Golden Grenade (FR)**[28] 534 3-9-2 0........ StevieDonohoe 4 34
(Ian Williams) *in tch tl wknd 3f out: sn bhd* **66/1**

50 **5** 93 **Hen (IRE)**[10] 794 3-8-11 0........ NicolaCurrie 2
(Jamie Osborne) *ref to r tl rest had covered 300yds: nvr mde any grnd* **40/1**

2m 7.14s (0.54) **Going Correction** -0.10s/f (Stan) **5 Ran SP% 121.1**
Speed ratings (Par 98): **93,92,90,77,2**
CSF £7.06 TOTE £1.10: £1.10, £3.80; EX 4.80 Trifecta £7.30.
Owner Godolphin **Bred** Godolphin **Trained** Newmarket, Suffolk

FOCUS
There was a good battle between the first two in this novice. Muddling form, with the second the key.
T/Plt: £32.70 to a £1 stake. Pool: £68,222.81 - 1,520.99 winning units T/Qpdt: £7.20 to a £1 stake. Pool: £7,300.84 - 741.21 winning units **Jonathan Neesom**

948 NEWCASTLE (A.W) (L-H)
Friday, March 1

OFFICIAL GOING: Tapeta: standard
Wind: Almost nil Weather: Dry

968 BETWAY LIVE CASINO NOVICE STKS 1m 2f 42y (Tp)
5:30 (5:30) (Class 5) 4-Y-O+ **£3,460** (£1,029; £514; £257) **Stalls** High

Form RPR

2-43 **1** **Beauty Salon**[10] 793 4-8-11 66........ GeorgeWood 5 68
(James Fanshawe) *in tch: smooth hdwy over 2f out: led over 1f out: edgd rt briefly ins fnl f: drvn and kpt on wl* **7/2**[2]

5/3- **2** nk **Allieyf**[303] 2295 4-9-2 0........ PaulMulrennan 4 72
(William Haggas) *t.k.h: pressed ldr: led over 2f out to over 1f out: rallied and edgd lft ins fnl f: kpt on: hld nr fin* **1/1**[1]

10- **3** nk **Tamreer**[264] 3646 4-8-13 0........(h) BenSanderson(5) 9 73
(Roger Fell) *hld up on outside: smooth hdwy over 2f out: effrt and ev ch over 1f out: rdn and kpt on fnl f: hld nr fin* **10/1**[3]

4 4½ **Captain Scott (IRE)** 4-8-13 0........ JaneElliott(3) 10 62
(Heather Main) *unruly in paddock and reluctant to enter stall: prom on outside: effrt and ev ch over 1f out: outpcd whn rdr dropped whip ins fnl f* **25/1**

0-0 **5** ½ **Harbour Bay**[24] 608 4-9-2 0........ JackGarritty 2 61
(Jedd O'Keeffe) *t.k.h: led at stdy gallop: rdn and hdd over 2f out: hung lft and outpcd over 1f out* **25/1**

6 2½ **Bravantina**[34] 4-8-11 0........ JasonHart 6 51
(Mark Walford) *dwlt: hld up: shkn up wl over 1f out: nvr nr ldrs* **100/1**

7 4½ **Kaizer**[38] 4-9-2 0........ DougieCostello 7 47
(Alistair Whillans) *plld hrd: prom: rdn over 2f out: wknd over 1f out* **50/1**

8 14 **Put The Law On You (IRE)**[45] 4-9-2 0........ BarryMcHugh 8 19
(Alistair Whillans) *s.i.s: hld up: rdn and outpcd over 2f out: sn btn* **66/1**

2m 16.28s (5.88) **Going Correction** +0.10s/f (Slow) **8 Ran SP% 93.4**
Speed ratings (Par 103): **80,79,79,75,75 73,69,58**
CSF £4.41 TOTE £3.80: £1.10, £1.02, £1.90; EX 5.40 Trifecta £16.30.
Owner Clipper Logistics **Bred** B Flay Thoroughbreds Inc **Trained** Newmarket, Suffolk
■ Charles Kingsley was withdrawn. Price at time of withdrawal 2-1. Rule 4 applies to all bets - deduction 30p in the pound.

FOCUS
A fair novice contest on standard Tapeta which turned into a sprint from over 2f out off a particularly slow gallop and produced a three-way photo-finish.

969 SUNRACING.CO.UK H'CAP 1m 5y (Tp)
6:00 (6:00) (Class 7) (0-50,50) 3-Y-O+ **£2,814** (£837; £418; £209) **Stalls** Centre

Form RPR

42-2 **1** **Jai Hanuman (IRE)**[13] 760 5-9-10 **48**........(t) FrannyNorton 6 59+
(Michael Wigham) *in tch in centre of gp: shkn up and hdwy over 1f out: led ins fnl f: drvn clr* **2/1**[1]

-633 **2** 3¾ **Tellovoi (IRE)**[24] 613 11-9-9 **47**........(p) PhilipPrince 11 50
(Richard Guest) *led on nr side of gp: hdd over 2f out: rallied and ev ch over 1f out to ins fnl f: kpt on same pce last 100yds* **8/1**

650- **3** nk **Lukoutoldmakezebak**[222] 5242 6-9-5 **46**........(p) JamieGormley(3) 9 48
(David Thompson) *cl up in centre of gp: led over 2f out to ins fnl f: kpt on same pce* **5/1**[3]

4-40 **4** 2¾ **Black Hambleton**[14] 738 6-9-5 **50**........ HarryRussell(7) 10 46
(Bryan Smart) *dwlt: hld up in centre of gp: rdn over 2f out: hdwy over 1f out: no imp fnl f* **13/2**

0-00 **5** 1½ **Little Choosey**[30] 485 9-9-8 **49**........(p) TimClark(3) 2 42
(Roy Bowring) *prom on far side of gp: rdn over 2f out: wknd appr fnl f* **28/1**

000- **6** 1½ **Moretti (IRE)**[78] 9528 4-9-12 **50**........ JoeFanning 4 39
(Les Eyre) *dwlt: hld up on far side of gp: hdwy and prom over 3f out: rdn and wknd over 1f out* **20/1**

00-0 **7** nse **Box And Cox**[30] 479 4-9-11 **49**........(t) DavidNolan 13 38
(Stef Keniry) *hld up in centre of gp: rdn and hdwy over 1f out: no imp fnl f* **20/1**

023- **8** 2 **Lord Rob**[302] 2350 8-9-5 **48**........ ConnorMurtagh(5) 14 33
(David Thompson) *hld up on nr side of gp: rdn along over 2f out: no imp fr over 1f out* **20/1**

0-54 **9** ¾ **Highwayman**[34] 436 6-9-10 **48**........(h) CliffordLee 8 31
(David Thompson) *hld up towards centre of gp: drvn and outpcd over 2f out: hung lft: n.d after* **3/1**[2]

000- **10** 21 **Harbour Sunrise**[78] 9527 4-9-7 **45**........ PaulMulrennan 1
(Shaun Harris) *hld up on far side of gp: drvn and struggling over 2f out: sn btn* **66/1**

066- **11** shd **Ruled By The Moon**[185] 6651 5-9-11 **49**........ JasonHart 12
(Ivan Furtado) *prom on nr side of gp tl rdn and wknd qckly over 2f out* **8/1**

1m 39.6s (1.00) **Going Correction** +0.10s/f (Slow) **11 Ran SP% 129.8**
Speed ratings (Par 97): **99,95,94,92,90 89,89,87,86,65 65**
CSF £20.11 CT £79.14 TOTE £2.80: £1.20, £2.60, £2.00; EX 23.10 Trifecta £143.20.
Owner Ms I D Heerowa **Bred** Lynn Lodge Stud **Trained** Newmarket, Suffolk

FOCUS
A moderate handicap. The clear favourite was the only one to keep going purposefully from off a decent gallop and drew clear in the final furlong. It's been rated with feet on the ground.

970 PLAY 4 TO SCORE AT BETWAY H'CAP 5f (Tp)
6:30 (6:30) (Class 5) (0-70,71) 4-Y-O+ **£3,460** (£1,029; £514; £257) **Stalls** Centre

Form RPR

2042 **1** **Zapper Cass (FR)**[11] 787 6-9-1 **64**........(b) AlistairRawlinson 10 73
(Michael Appleby) *cl up: hdwy on nr side of gp to ld over 1f out: sn hrd pressed: hld on wl fnl f* **5/1**[3]

500- **2** 1 **Canford Bay (IRE)**[156] 7671 5-9-8 **71**........ CamHardie 4 76
(Antony Brittain) *hld up in tch: smooth hdwy and ev ch over 1f out: sn rdn: kpt on same pce last 50yds* **6/1**

-401 **3** 1 **Jan Van Hoof (IRE)**[14] 743 8-9-7 **70**........ BarryMcHugh 5 71
(Michael Herrington) *hld up in rr: smooth hdwy over 1f out: sn rdn along: edgd lft ins fnl f: r.o* **11/4**[2]

0-50 **4** 1½ **Van Gerwen**[10] 790 6-9-4 **67**........ JoeFanning 3 63
(Les Eyre) *prom: drvn and outpcd 2f out: rallied ins fnl f: r.o* **16/1**

-311 **5** nk **Epeius (IRE)**[14] 741 6-9-7 **70**........(v) AndrewMullen 1 65
(Ben Haslam) *hld up on far side of gp: drvn over 2f out: rallied over 1f out: no imp ins fnl f* **9/4**[1]

0030 **6** ½ **Katheefa (USA)**[24] 610 5-9-5 **68**........(p) JackGarritty 2 61
(Ruth Carr) *hld up: smooth hdwy over 1f out: sn rdn: no imp fnl f* **13/2**

00-6 **7** nk **Jorvik Prince**[49] 179 5-9-0 **63**........ NathanEvans 9 55
(Julia Brooke) *led 1f: cl up tl rdn and outpcd over 1f out: btn fnl f (vet said gelding had lost its left fore shoe)* **22/1**

2022 **8** ½ **Archimedes (IRE)**[14] 743 6-9-0 **66**........(tp) PhilDennis(3) 8 56
(David C Griffiths) *cl up: led after 1f to over 1f out: wknd ins fnl f* **15/2**

58.78s (-0.72) **Going Correction** +0.10s/f (Slow) **8 Ran SP% 123.7**
Speed ratings (Par 103): **109,107,105,103,102 102,101,100**
CSF £37.96 CT £102.97 TOTE £5.00: £1.80, £1.90, £1.70; EX 37.40 Trifecta £183.80.
Owner Stephen Louch **Bred** Arunas Cicenas **Trained** Oakham, Rutland

FOCUS
An ordinary sprint handicap. The winning time was under a second outside of standard as the race developed towards the near rail. The winner has been rated to his recent best, with the second close to his last AW start.

971 FOLLOW TOP TIPSTER TEMPLEGATE AT SUNRACING MAIDEN STKS 1m 5y (Tp)
7:00 (7:00) (Class 5) 3-Y-O+ **£3,460** (£1,029; £514; £257) **Stalls** Centre

Form RPR

1 **Severnaya (IRE)** 3-8-5 0........ NickyMackay 12 74+
(John Gosden) *dwlt: sn led: shkn up and qcknd clr in centre of gp 2f out: drifted lft ins fnl f: unchal* **4/7**[1]

/6 **2** 6 **Scots Sonnet**[24] 608 5-10-0 0........(h) AlistairRawlinson 3 71
(Jim Goldie) *hld up on far side of gp: effrt over 2f out: chsd (clr) wnr over 1f out: no imp fnl f* **20/1**

2 **3** 1¼ **Blindingly (GER)**[24] 608 4-10-0 0........ AndrewMullen 6 68
(Ben Haslam) *plld hrd: in tch on nr side of gp: rdn over 2f out: hdwy over 1f out: no imp fnl f* **3/1**[2]

4 3¾ **Nine Elms (USA)** 4-9-11 0........ TimClark(3) 2 59
(Roy Bowring) *dwlt: sn chsng wnr: rdn over 2f out: edgd lft and outpcd fr over 1f out* **25/1**

5 nse **Menina Atrevida** 3-8-5 0........ PaddyMathers 7 48
(Ivan Furtado) *hld up: rdn in centre of gp 3f out: kpt on fnl f: nvr able to chal* **50/1**

6 1½ **Hikayah** 3-8-5 0........ CamHardie 9 45
(David O'Meara) *hld up in centre of gp: rdn along 1/2-way: sme late hdwy: n.d* **25/1**

0 **7** nk **Half Bolly**[35] 405 3-8-10 0........ JasonHart 11 49
(Mark Walford) *dwlt: hld up in centre of gp: rdn and outpcd over 2f out: sme late hdwy: nvr on terms* **66/1**

4- **8** nse **Menin Gate (IRE)**[213] 5574 3-8-10 0........ TonyHamilton 1 49
(Richard Fahey) *cl up in centre of gp: rdn over 2f out: wknd over 1f out* **4/1**[3]

9 2¾ **Star Of Valour (IRE)**[254] 4-10-0 0........ DougieCostello 5 49
(David C Griffiths) *hld up in midfield in centre: drvn and outpcd over 2f out: sn btn* **11/1**

04 **10** 2½ **Lizzie Loch**[14] 739 3-8-5 0........ JoeFanning 4 32
(Alistair Whillans) *t.k.h: prom on nr side of gp: rdn over 2f out: wknd wl over 1f out* **33/1**

0-0 **11** 3 **Somewhat Sisyphean**[58] 20 3-8-10 0........ NathanEvans 8 30
(Wilf Storey) *plld hrd: hld up: effrt on far side of gp 1/2-way: wknd fr 2f out (jockey said gelding ran too free)* **150/1**

000/ **12** *hd* **Whisper A Word (IRE)**[601] 4623 5-9-4 42........ FayeMcManoman(5) 10 31
(Lucinda Egerton) *early ldr: sn in tch on nr side of gp: struggling over 2f out: sn btn* **150/1**

1m 40.2s (1.60) **Going Correction** +0.10s/f (Slow) 12 Ran SP% **137.2**
WFA 3 from 4yo+ 18lb
Speed ratings (Par 103): **96,90,88,85,84 83,83,83,80,77 74,74**
CSF £24.51 TOTE £1.50: £1.10, £3.90, £1.40; EX 20.50 Trifecta £66.50.
Owner HH Sheikha Al Jalila Racing **Bred** Godolphin **Trained** Newmarket, Suffolk

FOCUS
An ordinary maiden. The winning debutante was backed as if defeat was out of the question and she certainly showed why, despite having to make most of the running after a moderate initial gallop. The level is a bit fluid.

972 LADBROKES H'CAP — 6f (Tp)
7:30 (7:30) (Class 5) (0-75,77) 3-Y-O — **£3,460** (£1,029; £514; £257) **Stalls** Centre

Form — RPR
421 **1** **Solar Park (IRE)**[25] 604 3-9-7 **75**.............................. CallumRodriguez 4 77
(James Tate) *trckd ldrs: effrt and rdn over 1f out: led ent fnl f: sn hrd pressed: hld on wl cl home* **5/6**[1]

1-61 **2** *hd* **Klopp**[35] 412 3-8-13 **67**..............................(h) CamHardie 2 68
(Antony Brittain) *dwlt and wnt rt s: t.k.h: hld up in last pl: pushed along over 2f out: hdwy over 1f out: kpt on fnl f to take 2nd towards fin: jst hld* **8/1**[3]

521- **3** *hd* **Edgewood**[111] 9001 3-9-9 **77**.............................. PaulMulrennan 1 77
(James Bethell) *t.k.h: hld up in tch: rdn over 2f out: hdwy over 1f out: kpt on fnl f: hld nr fin* **11/8**[2]

000- **4** *½* **Evangeline Samos**[158] 7622 3-8-9 **63**.............................. ShaneGray 5 62
(Kevin Ryan) *pressed ldr: led 2f out: edgd lft and hdd ent fnl f: sn one pce* **20/1**

5 *3¼* **Dancing Mountain (IRE)**[128] 8555 3-8-6 **63**............ JamieGormley(3) 3 51
(Roger Fell) *led to 2f out: rallied: drvn and wknd fnl f* **16/1**

1m 13.26s (0.76) **Going Correction** +0.10s/f (Slow) 5 Ran SP% **118.4**
Speed ratings (Par 98): **98,97,97,96,92**
CSF £9.33 TOTE £1.70: £1.70, £2.60; EX 6.60 Trifecta £13.50.
Owner Saeed Manana **Bred** Kildaragh Stud **Trained** Newmarket, Suffolk

FOCUS
A fair 3yo handicap. The favourite won narrowly in nearly three seconds outside of standard time after a modest gallop over the first two furlongs. It's been rated around the second.

973 BETWAY CASINO H'CAP — 5f (Tp)
8:00 (8:00) (Class 7) (0-50,50) 3-Y-O+ — **£2,814** (£837; £418; £209) **Stalls** Centre

Form — RPR
42-6 **1** **Furni Factors**[50] 167 4-9-10 **50**..............................(b) CallumRodriguez 10 60
(Ronald Thompson) *racd in centre of gp: mde all: drvn over 1f out: clr ins fnl f: r.o wl* **5/1**[3]

0025 **2** *2½* **Star Cracker (IRE)**[14] 742 7-9-7 **47**..............................(p) AlistairRawlinson 11 48
(Jim Goldie) *in tch in centre of gp: drvn along 2f out: hdwy to chse (clr) wnr ins fnl f: kpt on: nt pce to chal* **4/1**[2]

2455 **3** *¾* **Novabridge**[8] 834 11-9-6 **46**..............................(b) CliffordLee 14 44
(Karen Tutty) *chsd ldrs on nr side of gp: effrt over 2f out: chsd wnr over 1f out to ins fnl f: kpt on same pce* **5/1**[3]

410- **4** *½* **Displaying Amber**[149] 7895 4-9-9 **49**..............................(p) AndrewMullen 8 46
(Ben Haslam) *midfield towards far side of gp: drvn and outpcd 2f out: rallied ins fnl f: r.o* **8/1**

-036 **5** *hd* **Amazing Amaya**[30] 478 4-9-5 **45**..............................(h) PaddyMathers 4 41+
(Derek Shaw) *bhd in centre of gp: rdn along 1/2-way: hdwy fnl f: nrst fin* **16/1**

6500 **6** *½* **Windforpower (IRE)**[24] 613 9-9-6 **46**..............................(v) KevinStott 6 40
(Tracy Waggott) *hld up on far side of gp: rdn 2f out: kpt on fnl f: n.d* **5/1**[3]

000- **7** *hd* **Excel Mate**[80] 9493 5-9-2 **45**.............................. TimClark(3) 3 38
(Roy Bowring) *pressed wnr in centre of gp to over 1f out: edgd lft: wknd ins fnl f (jockey said mare ran too free)* **16/1**

-514 **8** *1¼* **Picks Pinta**[9] 809 8-9-1 **48**..............................(b) RPWalsh(7) 5 37
(John David Riches) *dwlt: hld up on nr side of gp: effrt and drvn along wl over 1f out: sn no imp* **13/2**

050/ **9** *nse* **Major Muscari (IRE)**[557] 6271 11-9-5 **45**..............................(p) DavidNolan 12 34
(Shaun Harris) *dwlt: hld up in centre of gp: drvn along over 2f out: no imp fr over 1f out* **66/1**

0-06 **10** *1½* **My Girl Maisie (IRE)**[24] 613 5-9-5 **45**.............................. PhilipPrince 7 28
(Richard Guest) *bhd towards far side of gp: struggling over 2f out: nvr on terms* **28/1**

60/3 **11** *½* **Intense Starlet (IRE)**[8] 834 8-9-2 **45**..............................(p) BenRobinson(3) 13 26
(Brian Ellison) *hld up in midfield on nr side of gp: drvn along over 2f out: wknd over 1f out (jockey said mare ran flat)* **7/2**[1]

00-0 **12** *19* **Crikeyitswhykie**[8] 834 4-9-7 **47**.............................. LewisEdmunds 2
(Derek Shaw) *bhd on far side of gp: hung lft and struggling wl over 2f out: sn lost tch (jockey said gelding hung left throughout)* **66/1**

59.53s (0.03) **Going Correction** +0.10s/f (Slow) 12 Ran SP% **134.9**
Speed ratings (Par 97): **103,99,97,97,96 95,95,93,93,91 90,59**
CSF £29.04 CT £114.15 TOTE £6.10: £2.10, £1.60, £2.40; EX 37.00 Trifecta £217.60.
Owner B Bruce & R Thompson **Bred** Winterbeck Manor Stud **Trained** Stainforth, S Yorks

FOCUS
A moderate sprint handicap. The winning time was fair for the grade and one of the more fancied runners won decisively. The winner has been rated within a length of last year's best.
T/Plt: £9.40 to a £1 stake. Pool: £107,888.86 - 8,307.61 winning units T/Qpdt: £7.20 to a £1 stake. Pool: £12,065.91 - 1,228.21 winning units **Richard Young**

974 - 976a (Foreign Racing) - See Raceform Interactive

115 DEAUVILLE (R-H)
Friday, March 1

OFFICIAL GOING: Polytrack: standard

977a PRIX DU VAL-DE-REUIL (MAIDEN) (3YO FILLIES) (ALL-WEATHER TRACK) (POLYTRACK) — 1m 1f 110y(P)
1:37 3-Y-O — **£11,261** (£4,504; £3,378; £2,252; £1,126)

RPR
1 **Princess Isla**[157] 3-9-2 0.............................. HugoJourniac 5 72
(J-C Rouget, France) **27/10**[2]

2 *¾* **Krunch**[29] 509 3-9-2 0.............................. IoritzMendizabal 7 70
(X Thomas-Demeaulte, France) **12/5**[1]

3 *1¾* **Sky Orchid (FR)**[163] 3-9-2 0.............................. AurelienLemaitre 9 67
(F Head, France) **39/10**

4 *1½* **Jaliska (FR)**[73] 3-9-2 0..............................(b) GlenBraem 2 64
(S Cerulis, France) **179/10**

5 *2½* **Libline (FR)** 3-9-2 0.............................. AlexisBadel 8 59
(H-F Devin, France) **37/10**[3]

6 *1* **Just Once**[58] 20 3-9-2 0.............................. AntoineHamelin 4 57
(Mrs Ilka Gansera-Leveque) *wl into stride: led: rdn along and hdd over 1f out: wknd ins fnl f* **114/10**

7 *½* **Lala Dance (FR)**[94] 3-8-8 0.............................. MohammedLyesTabti(8) 3 56
(C Lerner, France) **59/1**

8 *hd* **Laura Game (FR)**[78] 3-8-10 0.............................. QuentinPerrette(6) 10 55
(M Brasme, France) **59/1**

9 *7* **Sea Countess (IRE)**[14] 3-9-2 0.............................. MorganDelalande 6 41
(J-V Toux, France) **128/1**

10 *10* **Galzoche (FR)**[22] 3-8-13 0..............................(p) MlleMickaelleMichel(3) 1 21
(Mme C Barande-Barbe, France) **31/1**

1m 58.37s 10 Ran SP% **118.7**
PARI-MUTUEL (all including 1 euro stake): WIN 3.70; PLACE 1.40, 1.30, 1.60; DF 5.70;.
Owner George Baker **Bred** Dayton Investments Ltd **Trained** Pau, France

848 CHELMSFORD (A.W) (L-H)
Saturday, March 2

OFFICIAL GOING: Polytrack: standard
Wind: medium, half behind Weather: overcast, dry

978 £20 FREE BETS AT TOTESPORT.COM NOVICE STKS — 7f (P)
5:30 (5:31) (Class 4) 3-Y-O+ — **£5,530** (£1,645; £822; £411) **Stalls** Low

Form — RPR
-223 **1** **Shanghai Grace**[15] 733 3-8-12 **75**.............................. RichardKingscote 5 78
(Charles Hills) *sn led and mde rest: rdn over 1f out: kpt on u.p and a doing enough ins fnl f* **5/6**[1]

41 **2** *1* **Mustadun**[12] 785 3-9-5 0.............................. JoeFanning 2 82
(Mark Johnston) *broke wl: sn hdd and chsd wnr: effrt 2f out: rdn and pressing wnr over 1f out: kpt on but a hld ins fnl f* **9/2**[3]

3 *8* **Moftris** 3-8-12 0.............................. TomMarquand 4 53
(William Haggas) *s.i.s: t.k.h: chsd ldng pair after 1f: rdn over 2f out: sn outpcd and btn over 1f out: wknd fnl f (jockey said colt was colty in the preliminaries)* **15/8**[2]

4 *14* **Jeanette May** 3-8-7 0.............................. JosephineGordon 3 11
(William Stone) *t.k.h: dropped to last after 1f: rdn over 3f out: sn struggling and wl bhd over 1f out* **50/1**

1m 27.26s (0.06) **Going Correction** +0.05s/f (Slow) 4 Ran SP% **109.5**
Speed ratings (Par 105): **101,99,90,74**
CSF £5.06 TOTE £1.70; EX 4.30 Trifecta £5.90.
Owner Kangyu International Racing (HK) Limited **Bred** Wellsummers Stud **Trained** Lambourn, Berks

FOCUS
The first two dominated this novice stakes, which was run just under 4sec outside the standard. The winner has been rated close to form.

979 TOTEPOOL CASHBACK CLUB AT TOTESPORT.COM NOVICE STKS — 1m (P)
6:00 (6:05) (Class 4) 3-Y-O+ — **£5,530** (£1,645; £822; £411) **Stalls** Low

Form — RPR
63 **1** **Solar Heights (IRE)**[29] 534 3-8-5 0.............................. FrannyNorton 3 74
(James Tate) *chsd ldrs on inner: effrt to chse ldr 2f out: switching rt and rdn over 1f out: stl almost 2 l down and looked hld ins fnl f tl styd on strly cl home to ld on post* **4/1**[2]

2-32 **2** *nse* **White Coat**[9] 827 3-8-10 **80**.............................. KieranO'Neill 8 79
(John Gosden) *led: rdn over 2f out: stl almost 2 l clr and drvn ins fnl f: looked to be doing enough tl no ex towards fin and hdd on post* **4/11**[1]

0 **3** *6* **Willy Sewell**[58] 41 6-9-9 0.............................. TheodoreLadd(5) 9 71
(Michael Appleby) *taken down early and led to s: t.k.h: chsd ldr tl 2f out: sn rdn and outpcd over 1f out: wl hld ins fnl f (jockey said gelding hung right-handed and ran too free)* **100/1**

4 *2* **Mohtarrif (IRE)** 3-8-10 0.............................. MartinDwyer 14 61+
(Marcus Tregoning) *stdd and dropped in after s: t.k.h: hld up towards rr: impeded after 1f: effrt but stl plenty to do whn swtchd rt over 1f out: edging lft kpt on wl under hands and heels riding ins fnl f: nvr trbld ldrs* **10/1**[3]

5 *3¼* **I'm British**[36] 6-10-0 0.............................. RossaRyan 1 59
(Don Cantillon) *in tch in midfield: effrt to chse ldrs ent fnl 2f: sn outpcd and wknd fnl f* **66/1**

0- **6** *nk* **Exoptable**[131] 8469 3-8-5 0.............................. LiamJones 10 47
(William Haggas) *t.k.h: hld up in midfield: edgd lft after 1f: rdn over 2f out: sn struggling and outpcd over 1f out: wknd fnl f* **16/1**

7 *¾* **Vipin (FR)** 4-10-0 0.............................. RichardKingscote 2 57
(William Muir) *dwlt: sn rcvrd and in tch in midfield: impeded after 1f: pushed along over 2f out: sn outpcd and wl hld over 1f out* **33/1**

0 **8** *¾* **Dusty Damsel**[28] 556 3-8-5 0.............................. HayleyTurner 7 44
(Mike Murphy) *rn green early: chsd ldrs: rdn and outpcd over 2f out: wl btn over 1f out: wknd fnl f (jockey said filly ran green in the early stages)* **16/1**

50- **9** *2½* **West Newton**[80] 9500 3-8-10 0.............................. AdamMcNamara 11 43
(Roger Charlton) *midfield: rdn and outpcd over 2f out: wl btn over 1f out: wknd fnl f* **33/1**

06 **10** *1¼* **Tanzerin (IRE)**[28] 556 3-7-12 0.............................. AledBeech(7) 13 35
(Charlie Fellowes) *t.k.h: hld up towards rr: effrt on inner over 1f out: no imp and nvr involved* **80/1**

0 **11** *2* **Dubai Metro**[45] 251 3-8-10 0..............................(h) GeorgeWood 4 36
(George Scott) *midfield: effrt over 2f out: outpcd and wl hld whn sltly impeded over 1f out: sn wknd* **33/1**

12 *4½* **San Diaco (IRE)** 3-8-10 0.............................. JosephineGordon 5 25
(Ed Dunlop) *a towards rr: outpcd and wl bhd over 1f out* **33/1**

0 **13** *8* **Whims Of Desire**[11] 795 3-8-5 0.............................. LukeMorris 12
(Sir Mark Prescott Bt) *swtchd lft and impeded after 1f: rn green and bhd over 5f out: lost tch over 1f out* **40/1**

1m 40.72s (0.82) **Going Correction** +0.05s/f (Slow) 13 Ran SP% **132.1**
WFA 3 from 4yo+ 18lb
Speed ratings (Par 105): **97,96,90,88,85 85,84,83,81,80 78,73,65**
CSF £6.17 TOTE £6.20: £1.50, £1.02, £31.50; EX 11.40 Trifecta £498.70.
Owner Saeed Manana **Bred** Norelands Bloodstock & Yarraman Park **Trained** Newmarket, Suffolk
■ Native Silver was withdrawn. Price at time of withdrawal 40/1. Rule 4 does not apply

FOCUS
The first three were always prominent, in a race probably lacking depth. The first two were clear of the big-priced third. The level is a bit fluid.

980 EXTRA PLACES AT TOTESPORT.COM H'CAP 1m 6f (P)
6:30 (6:32) (Class 3) (0-95,92) 4-Y-0+ **£9,703** (£2,887; £1,443; £721) **Stalls** Low

Form RPR

1-24 **1** **Amitie Waltz (FR)**[17] 704 7-8-11 **80**.......... FinleyMarsh[(3)] 4 88+
(Richard Hughes) *chsd ldrs: clsd and nt clrest of runs on inner 2f out: gap opened and hdwy to chal over 1f out: led and edgd rt jst ins fnl f: r.o strly and asserted towards fin* **15/8**[1]

-216 **2** 2 **Technological**[7] 878 4-9-6 **88**.......... OisinMurphy 7 93
(George Margarson) *broke wl: sn hdd and chsd ldr: effrt wl over 1f out: ev ch 1f out tl no ex and outpcd by wnr wl ins fnl f* **5/1**[3]

0-21 **3** 1 **Stamford Raffles**[14] 757 6-9-12 **92**.......... RichardKingscote 5 96
(Jane Chapple-Hyam) *sn led: rdn ent fnl 2f: hdd jst ins fnl f: jst getting outpcd whn sltly short of room ins fnl f: kpt on same pce after* **5/1**[3]

2-11 **4** 3/4 **Temur Khan**[37] 390 4-8-13 **81**.......... DavidProbert 6 84
(Tony Carroll) *in tch in midfield: clsd and rdn to press ldrs 2f out: no ex u.p and hung rt 1f out: kpt on same pce ins fnl f (jockey said gelding hung right up the home straight)* **10/1**

23-5 **5** 1/2 **Seafarer (IRE)**[42] 311 5-9-12 **92**..........(v) MartinDwyer 8 94
(Marcus Tregoning) *stdd s: hld up in tch in rr: clsd on outer 4f out: rdn to chse ldrs 2f out tl no ex ent fnl f: kpt on same pce after* **8/1**

-133 **6** 4 **West Coast Flyer**[14] 758 6-9-8 **88**.......... JamieSpencer 1 84
(David Simcock) *hld up in tch: effrt ent fnl 2f: no imp u.p over 1f out: wl hld and eased towards fin* **7/2**[2]

265- **7** 2 1/4 **Baydar**[101] 9174 6-9-1 **88**.......... LukeCatton[(7)] 3 81
(Ian Williams) *dwlt: hld up in tch in rr: effrt over 2f out: no imp and no threat to ldrs fnl 2f* **22/1**

3m 4.98s (1.78) **Going Correction** +0.05s/f (Slow)
WFA 4 from 5yo+ 2lb 7 Ran SP% **114.9**
Speed ratings (Par 107): **96,94,94,93,93 91,90**
CSF £11.79 CT £39.84 TOTE £2.60: £1.80, £4.20; EX 14.70 Trifecta £69.50.
Owner Third Time Lucky **Bred** Ecurie La Vallee Martigny **Trained** Upper Lambourn, Berks

FOCUS
They didn't go much of a gallop in this decent staying handicap. Straightforward form, with the second rated close to form and the third confirming his surprise Kempton win.

981 IRISH LOTTO AT TOTESPORT.COM H'CAP 6f (P)
7:00 (7:02) (Class 4) (0-85,86) 4-Y-0+ **£5,530** (£1,645; £822; £411; £400; £400) **Stalls** Centre

Form RPR

112- **1** **Walk On Walter (IRE)**[72] 9640 4-9-5 **83**..........(h) RobHornby 1 95
(Jonathan Portman) *mde most: rdn over 1f out: fnd ex: clr and in command 1f out: r.o strly: eased towards fin* **2/1**[1]

116- **2** 3 **Little Boy Blue**[182] 6800 4-9-1 **86**..........(h) SeamusCronin[(7)] 8 87
(Bill Turner) *t.k.h: hld up in tch: effrt and swtchd rt over 1f out: kpt on u.p to chse wnr wl ins fnl f: nvr a threat* **25/1**

4611 **3** 1 **Gentlemen**[10] 797 8-9-1 **79**..........(h) JosephineGordon 5 77
(Phil McEntee) *rrd as stalls opened and slowly away: bhd: rdn 3f out: c wd st and clsd u.p 1f out: styd on to go 3rd towards fin: no threat to wnr* **5/1**

0-51 **4** 3/4 **Saaheq**[28] 551 5-9-7 **85**.......... AlistairRawlinson 2 80
(Michael Appleby) *t.k.h early: trckd ldrs: swtchd rt and chsd wnr wl over 1f out: sn rdn but unable to match pce of wnr: wl hld and kpt on same pce ins fnl f: lost 2 pls wl ins fnl f: burst blood vessel (vet reported the gelding had bled from the nose)* **9/4**[2]

6-52 **5** 1 **Human Nature (IRE)**[37] 382 6-9-7 **85**..........(t) OisinMurphy 7 77
(Stuart Williams) *t.k.h: chsd ldrs: effrt u.p over 1f out: unable qck and wl hld ins fnl f* **10/3**[3]

061- **6** nk **Arzaak (IRE)**[107] 9084 5-9-1 **79**..........(p) JoeFanning 6 70
(Charlie Wallis) *hld up in tch: effrt over 1f out: no imp: wl hld and kpt on same pce ins fnl f* **25/1**

2520 **7** 11 **Bernie's Boy**[25] 610 6-8-2 **73**..........(p) GraceMcEntee[(7)] 4 29
(Phil McEntee) *restless in stalls: w wnr tl wl over 1f out: sn u.p and lost pl: bhd and wknd fnl f* **20/1**

1m 12.36s (-1.34) **Going Correction** +0.05s/f (Slow) 7 Ran SP% **116.3**
Speed ratings (Par 105): **110,106,104,103,102 101,87**
CSF £53.04 CT £220.27 TOTE £3.00: £1.50, £7.70; EX 32.70 Trifecta £154.00.
Owner Philip Simpson **Bred** Sandro Garavelli **Trained** Upper Lambourn, Berks

FOCUS
A fair sprint handicap, run in a decent time.

982 BET IN PLAY AT TOTESPORT.COM H'CAP 6f (P)
7:30 (7:30) (Class 5) (0-70,72) 4-Y-0+ **£5,175** (£1,540; £769; £400; £400; £400) **Stalls** Centre

Form RPR

-326 **1** **Real Estate (IRE)**[11] 790 4-9-4 **67**..........(p) CallumShepherd 1 75
(Michael Attwater) *t.k.h: hld up in tch in midfield: nt clrest of runs and edgd out rt over 1f out: hdwy u.p to chal ent fnl f: sn led and r.o wl ins fnl f* **7/1**

3-43 **2** nk **Kraka (IRE)**[14] 759 4-9-1 **64**..........(v) KieranO'Neill 5 71
(Christine Dunnett) *t.k.h: led: sn hdd and chsd ldrs: rdn to chal over 1f out: sustained duel w wnr and kpt on u.p ins fnl f: a jst hld* **4/1**[1]

0-42 **3** 3 **Mount Wellington (IRE)**[32] 468 4-9-5 **68**..........(p) OisinMurphy 9 65
(Henry Spiller) *t.k.h: sn led: rdn over 1f out: hdd and no ex u.p jst ins fnl f: outpcd fnl 100yds* **8/1**

-543 **4** 1/2 **Wiff Waff**[35] 433 4-9-9 **72**.......... DanielMuscutt 3 68
(Stuart Williams) *restless in stalls: dwlt: hld up in tch: effrt over 1f out: kpt on u.p ins fnl f: no threat to ldrs* **9/1**

0621 **5** shd **Mochalov**[16] 718 4-8-13 **62**.......... DannyBrock 4 57
(Jane Chapple-Hyam) *s.i.s: hld up in tch in rr: swtchd lft and hdwy 1f out: kpt on ins fnl f: nvr trbld ldrs* **6/1**[3]

6110 **6** shd **Aguerooo (IRE)**[11] 790 6-9-6 **69**..........(tp) FrannyNorton 10 64+
(Charlie Wallis) *stdd after s: in tch in midfield on outer: effrt jst over 1f out: kpt on same pce and no threat to ldrs ins fnl f* **10/1**

-261 **7** 3/4 **Duke Cosimo**[12] 788 9-9-0 **66**.......... PhilDennis[(3)] 2 59
(Michael Herrington) *in tch in midfield: nt clr run over 1f out: swtchd lft ins fnl f: kpt on but no threat to ldrs* **7/1**

-666 **8** 1 3/4 **Princely**[15] 741 4-9-7 **70**..........(p) LukeMorris 6 57
(Michael Appleby) *t.k.h: chsd ldrs: rdn ent fnl 2f: unable qck and btn whn hung lft jst ins fnl f: sn wknd (jockey said colt jumped right-handed out of the stalls)* **14/1**

-300 **9** 1 1/4 **Independence Day (IRE)**[11] 790 6-9-1 **64**.......... JoeyHaynes 7 47
(Paul Howling) *stdd and short of room leaving stalls: hld up in tch towards rr: effrt over 1f out: no imp u.p 1f out: nvr trbld ldrs (jockey said horse suffered interference shortly after the start)* **14/1**

1111 **10** 1/2 **Foreign Legion (IRE)**[26] 596 4-9-4 **67**..........(p) NickyMackay 11 49
(Luke McJannet) *a towards rr and stuck wd: effrt over 1f out: no imp and nvr involved (jockey said gelding ran flat)* **5/1**[2]

00/0 **11** 1 3/4 **Whirl Me Round**[58] 44 5-8-11 **63**..........(p[1]) AaronJones[(3)] 8 39
(Robyn Brisland) *chsd ldrs: wnt 2nd 4f out tl wl over 1f out: sn lost pl: bhd ins fnl f* **40/1**

1m 13.24s (-0.46) **Going Correction** +0.05s/f (Slow) 11 Ran SP% **121.9**
Speed ratings (Par 103): **105,104,100,99,99 99,98,96,94,94 91**
CSF £36.51 CT £240.67 TOTE £7.80: £2.70, £1.70, £2.60; EX 39.00 Trifecta £339.50.
Owner Christian Main **Bred** Rabbah Bloodstock Limited **Trained** Epsom, Surrey

FOCUS
A couple of well supported runners fought out the finish of this modest handicap. The first five all raced on the rail in the first half of the race. Pretty ordinary form, with the winner rated as stepping up slightly on his recent efforts.

983 DOUBLE DELIGHT HAT-TRICK HEAVEN AT TOTESPORT.COM H'CAP (DIV I) 1m 2f (P)
8:00 (8:01) (Class 6) (0-55,55) 4-Y-0+
£3,105 (£924; £461; £400; £400; £400) **Stalls** Low

Form RPR

-203 **1** **Arlecchino's Arc (IRE)**[15] 736 4-9-5 **53**..........(v) DavidProbert 2 59
(Mark Usher) *sn pushed into ld and mde rest: rdn and edgd rt over 1f out: kpt on u.p and doing enough ins fnl f* **3/1**[2]

34-0 **2** 3/4 **First Call (FR)**[32] 467 4-9-1 **49**..........(p) KieranO'Neill 8 54
(Ian Williams) *t.k.h: wl in tch in midfield: effrt to chse wnr over 1f out: pressing wnr but awkward hd carriage ins fnl f: kpt on same pce and a hld* **9/2**[3]

-003 **3** 2 1/2 **Outlaw Torn (IRE)**[26] 593 10-8-12 **46** oh1..........(e) PhilipPrince 6 46
(Richard Guest) *taken down early: t.k.h: hld up in tch in midfield: effrt u.p over 2f out: hdwy to chse clr ldng pair 1f out: edgd lft and no imp ins fnl f* **25/1**

5634 **4** 2 1/4 **Red Cossack (CAN)**[16] 717 8-8-9 **46**..........(p[1]) JackDuern[(3)] 5 42
(Dean Ivory) *taken down early: niggled along early: t.k.h after 2f and hld up in tch: clsd on outer 4f out: rdn over 2f out: unable qck over 1f out: wl hld and plugged on same pce fnl f* **6/1**

-145 **5** 1/2 **Splash Of Verve (IRE)**[12] 782 7-9-0 **51**..........(p[1]) PhilDennis[(3)] 3 46
(David Thompson) *t.k.h: hld up in tch towards rr: effrt u.p over 1f out: unable qck: wl hld and kpt on same pce ins fnl f* **5/1**

-660 **6** 3 1/4 **Prince Consort (IRE)**[12] 782 4-8-7 **46** oh1...(p[1]) FayeMcManoman[(5)] 1 34
(John Wainwright) *chsd ldrs: unable qck u.p over 1f out: wknd ins fnl f* **66/1**

0-40 **7** 9 **Lulu Star (IRE)**[24] 616 4-9-4 **55**.......... JoshuaBryan[(3)] 7 26
(Julia Feilden) *rousted along leaving stalls: pressed wnr tl over 1f out: sn lost pl u.p: bhd and eased ins fnl f (jockey said filly was never travelling)* **12/1**

-316 **8** 6 **Prerogative (IRE)**[26] 602 5-8-12 **51**..........(p) PoppyBridgwater[(5)] 4 11
(Tony Carroll) *niggled along early and sn dropped to rr: rn in snatches after: rdn over 3f out: bhd over 1f out (trainer's rep said gelding was slowly away and was never travelling)* **9/4**[1]

2m 7.48s (-1.12) **Going Correction** +0.05s/f (Slow) 8 Ran SP% **117.9**
Speed ratings (Par 101): **106,105,103,101,101 98,91,86**
CSF £17.62 CT £285.42 TOTE £4.00: £1.40, £1.70, £4.50; EX 19.60 Trifecta £382.50.
Owner K Senior **Bred** Mrs Eithne Hamilton **Trained** Upper Lambourn, Berks

FOCUS
Low-grade handicap form, but slightly the quicker of the two divisions. The winner has been rated to his recent best. Straightforward, limited form in behind him.

984 DOUBLE DELIGHT HAT-TRICK HEAVEN AT TOTESPORT.COM H'CAP (DIV II) 1m 2f (P)
8:30 (8:31) (Class 6) (0-55,55) 4-Y-0+
£3,105 (£924; £461; £400; £400; £400) **Stalls** Low

Form RPR

2414 **1** **Don't Do It (IRE)**[11] 792 4-9-2 **55**..........(v) TheodoreLadd[(5)] 1 61
(Michael Appleby) *hld up in tch: clsd and nt clr run 2f out: hdwy on inner and chal over 1f out: led u.p ins fnl f: kpt on whn pressed towards fin* **6/4**[1]

3023 **2** nk **Foxrush Take Time (FR)**[9] 829 4-8-12 **46** oh1..........(e) PhilipPrince 5 51
(Richard Guest) *wl in tch in midfield: swtchd rt and effrt u.p over 1f out: wnt 2nd ins fnl f: kpt on but nvr quite getting to wnr* **10/1**

-505 **3** 3/4 **Sosian**[29] 533 4-8-12 **46**..........(b) TonyHamilton 9 50
(Richard Fahey) *wnt lft and bmpd leaving stalls: sn swtchd lft and hld up in rr: effrt on outer over 1f out: hung lft 1f out: kpt on to go 3rd nr fin* **14/1**

6-35 **4** 1/2 **Blyton Lass**[11] 792 4-9-4 **52**.......... BarryMcHugh 4 55
(James Given) *t.k.h: chsd ldr tl 6f out: styd chsng ldrs: ev ch u.p over 1f out: led ent fnl f: sn hdd: kpt on same pce and lost 2 pls wl ins fnl f* **5/1**[3]

0-51 **5** 1/2 **Dolphin Village (IRE)**[26] 602 9-8-13 **47**..........(h) CharlieBennett 3 49
(Shaun Harris) *trckd ldrs: rdn over 3f out: swtchd lft and drvn to chal over 1f out tl no ex and outpcd ins fnl f* **16/1**

1-56 **6** 8 **Hidden Dream (IRE)**[26] 593 4-9-2 **50**..........(p) KieranO'Neill 2 37
(Christine Dunnett) *t.k.h: led: rdn and edgd rt over 1f out: hdd ent fnl f: wknd ins fnl f* **8/1**

00-0 **7** 4 1/2 **Gembari**[60] 6 4-9-6 **54**..........(p) JosephineGordon 6 32
(David Brown) *chsd ldrs on outer: hdwy to join ldr 6f out: lost pl and short of room over 1f out: wknd fnl f* **11/4**[2]

00-0 **8** 4 **Passionate Love (IRE)**[12] 784 4-9-3 **51**.......... DougieCostello 7 22
(Mark Walford) *hld up in tch in midfield: effrt over 2f out: no imp and btn whn hung lft over 1f out: wknd fnl f* **40/1**

00-0 **9** 3 **Lots Ov (IRE)**[25] 607 5-8-7 **46** oh1.......... FayeMcManoman[(5)] 8 11
(John Wainwright) *a towards rr: bhd and rdn over 2f out: wl bhd over 1f out* **100/1**

2m 7.87s (-0.73) **Going Correction** +0.05s/f (Slow) 9 Ran SP% **119.5**
Speed ratings (Par 101): **104,103,103,102,102 95,92,89,86**
CSF £19.30 CT £161.63 TOTE £2.40: £1.10, £2.20, £3.30; EX 16.20 Trifecta £142.10.
Owner ThornleyNaylorGriffithsMulhernJohnson **Bred** L O'Donovan **Trained** Oakham, Rutland

FOCUS
Marginally the slower division, and pretty weak form. Straightforward form, with the likes of the second and fourth helping to pin the level.

T/Plt: £104.10 to a £1 stake. Pool: £76,516.27 - 536.43 winning units T/Qpdt: £42.60 to a £1 stake. Pool: £10,093.01 - 175.12 winning units **Steve Payne**

962 LINGFIELD (L-H)

Saturday, March 2

OFFICIAL GOING: Polytrack: standard
Wind: Light across Weather: Overcast

985 BETWAY LIVE CASINO H'CAP — 1m 4f (P)
1:35 (1:35) (Class 5) (0-70,71) 4-Y-0+ **£3,428** (£1,020; £509; £254) **Stalls** Low

Form — RPR

1 **King's Advice**[183] 5-9-9 **71** .... JoeFanning 4 — 79+
(Mark Johnston) *led at stdy pce tl hdd over 2f out: rallied to ld over 1f out: r.o strly: eased nr fin* **11/8**[1]

-460 2 3 **Smiley Bagel (IRE)**[14] [754] 6-9-6 **68** .... RichardKingscote 2 — 71
(Ed Walker) *prom: chsd wnr 10f out: led over 2f out: rdn and hdd over 1f out: no ex wl ins fnl f* **11/2**[2]

000- 3 ½ **Sotomayor**[33] [9585] 4-9-1 **64** .... TomMarquand 3 — 66
(Jane Chapple-Hyam) *s.s: hld up: rdn over 1f out: r.o ins fnl f: wnt 3rd post: nt rch ldrs* **10/1**

-046 4 nse **Makambe (IRE)**[7] [876] 4-9-5 **68** .... JoeyHaynes 6 — 70
(Paul Howling) *hld up: hdwy over 1f out: sn rdn: styd on* **8/1**

3-06 5 shd **Presence Process**[8] [859] 5-8-13 **64** .... PaddyBradley(3) 1 — 66
(Pat Phelan) *chsd wnr 2f: remained handy: rdn over 1f out: styd on* **13/2**

00-4 6 2 **Freebe Rocks (IRE)**[42] [309] 4-8-13 **62** ....(p) KieranO'Neill 7 — 61
(Ian Williams) *hld up: rdn over 2f out: nt trble ldrs* **6/1**[3]

01-0 7 nse **Mouchee (IRE)**[36] [404] 4-9-2 **70** ....(v) MeganNicholls(5) 5 — 69
(Michael Blake) *chsd ldrs: rdn over 2f out: no ex fnl f* **14/1**

2m 33.47s (0.47) **Going Correction** -0.025s/f (Stan) — 7 Ran SP% **112.0**
WFA 4 from 5yo+ 1lb
Speed ratings (Par 103): **97,95,94,94,94 93,93**
CSF £8.78 TOTE £1.80: £1.10, £3.30; EX 8.70 Trifecta £73.20.
Owner Saeed Jaber **Bred** Rabbah Bloodstock Limited **Trained** Middleham Moor, N Yorks

■ Stewards' Enquiry : Joey Haynes two-day ban: used whip above the permitted level (Mar 16, 22)

FOCUS
The one-two filled those positions for most of the way but this looked a fair race for the level. It's been rated a bit negatively.

986 BETWAY HEED YOUR HUNCH H'CAP — 5f 6y(P)
2:10 (2:10) (Class 6) (0-55,57) 4-Y-0+ **£2,264** (£673; £336; £168) **Stalls** High

Form — RPR

6-53 1 **Hurricane Alert**[9] [823] 7-9-0 **46** .... DavidProbert 10 — 52
(Mark Hoad) *w ldrs: led over 1f out: rdn ins fnl f: jst hld on* **6/1**

1-06 2 nk **Prominna**[26] [597] 9-9-2 **53** .... PoppyBridgwater(5) 8 — 58
(Tony Carroll) *half-rrd s: hld up: racd keenly: hdwy over 1f out: sn rdn: r.o* **5/2**[1]

1220 3 nk **Pharoh Jake**[8] [857] 11-8-10 **49** .... EllieMacKenzie(7) 6 — 53
(John Bridger) *chsd ldrs: rdn and r.o wl ins fnl f* **7/1**

-110 4 1 **Captain Ryan**[42] [322] 8-9-11 **57** ....(p) KieranO'Neill 5 — 57
(Geoffrey Deacon) *trckd ldrs: rdn over 1f out: styd on same pce wl ins fnl f* **8/1**

-052 5 ½ **Roy's Legacy**[8] [848] 10-8-13 **45** .... CharlieBennett 1 — 43
(Shaun Harris) *led: rdn: hung rt and hdd over 1f out: no ex wl ins fnl f (jockey said horse hung right-handed throughout)* **5/1**[3]

4-50 6 1¼ **Shackled N Drawn (USA)**[8] [857] 7-9-7 **53** ....(tp) OisinMurphy 9 — 47
(Peter Hedger) *s.i.s: hld up: r.o towards fin: nt trble ldrs (jockey said gelding was slowly away)* **7/2**[2]

06-6 7 hd **Ask The Guru**[43] [286] 9-9-2 **48** ....(b) LukeMorris 4 — 41
(Michael Attwater) *sn w ldrs: rdn over 1f out: no ex ins fnl f* **16/1**

60-0 8 hd **Tina Teaspoon**[9] [834] 5-8-13 **45** ....(h) RaulDaSilva 7 — 38
(Derek Shaw) *hld up: styng on whn nt clr run wl ins fnl f: n.d* **33/1**

00-0 9 39 **Hornby**[31] [478] 4-8-13 **45** ....(t) CallumShepherd 3
(Michael Attwater) *s.i.s: sn pushed along in rr: bhd fnl 3f (jockey said gelding was never travelling)* **25/1**

57.98s (-0.82) **Going Correction** -0.025s/f (Stan) — 9 Ran SP% **118.0**
Speed ratings (Par 101): **105,104,104,102,101 99,99,99,36**
CSF £21.90 CT £110.18 TOTE £5.90: £2.10, £1.30, £2.00; EX 26.70 Trifecta £156.50.
Owner Michael Baldry **Bred** Lady S K Marchwood **Trained** Lewes, E Sussex

FOCUS
A moderate but competitive sprint handicap. The second has been rated to his recent best.

987 BETWAY CASINO H'CAP — 5f 6y(P)
2:50 (2:50) (Class 2) (0-105,105) 4-Y-0+ **£11,971** (£3,583; £1,791; £896; £446) **Stalls** High

Form — RPR

4-22 1 **Royal Birth**[7] [877] 8-9-2 **100** ....(t) OisinMurphy 3 — 106+
(Stuart Williams) *s.i.s: hld up: hdwy on inner over 1f out: led 1f out: rdn out* **6/5**[1]

-503 2 nk **Corinthia Knight (IRE)**[7] [877] 4-9-7 **105** .... EdwardGreatrex 4 — 109
(Archie Watson) *trckd ldrs: rdn to chse wnr ins fnl f: r.o* **4/1**[2]

3-64 3 ½ **Gracious John (IRE)**[7] [877] 6-9-2 **100** .... JFEgan 6 — 102
(David Evans) *sn pushed along to ld: hung rt wl over 1f out: sn rdn: hdd 1f out: styd on (jockey said gelding hung right-handed round the bend and into the straight)* **5/1**[3]

420- 4 nk **Harry Hurricane**[88] [9389] 7-8-2 **86** oh6 .... NicolaCurrie 1 — 87
(George Baker) *awkward s: hld up: r.o ins fnl f: nt rch ldrs* **14/1**

-301 5 1 **Captain Lars (SAF)**[12] [787] 9-8-2 **86** oh1 ....(b) LukeMorris 7 — 83
(Archie Watson) *chsd ldr tl shkn up and carried wd wl over 1f out: styd on same pce fnl f* **25/1**

-031 6 hd **Boom The Groom (IRE)**[9] [837] 8-8-7 **91** .... LiamJones 8 — 88
(Tony Carroll) *chsd ldrs: edgd rt: pushed along 1/2-way: wd and lost pl over 1f out* **8/1**

34-5 7 nk **Verne Castle**[58] [35] 6-8-9 **93** ....(h) FrannyNorton 2 — 89
(Michael Wigham) *trckd ldrs: racd keenly: rdn over 1f out: no ex ins fnl f* **8/1**

56.9s (-1.90) **Going Correction** -0.025s/f (Stan) — 7 Ran SP% **114.9**
Speed ratings (Par 109): **114,113,112,112,110 110,109**
CSF £6.27 CT £17.15 TOTE £2.20: £1.20, £2.80; EX 6.30 Trifecta £15.50.
Owner The Morley Family **Bred** Old Mill Stud & S Williams & J Parry **Trained** Newmarket, Suffolk

FOCUS
A decent sprint handicap. The second and third have been rated close to form.

988 SUN RACING NO1 RACING SITE H'CAP — 1m 1y(P)
3:20 (3:20) (Class 3) (0-95,93) 4-Y-O **£7,246** (£2,168; £1,084; £542; £270) **Stalls** High

Form — RPR

24-2 1 **Sha La La La Lee**[24] [623] 4-8-13 **85** .... RichardKingscote 3 — 92
(Tom Dascombe) *mde all: set stdy pce tl shkn up and qcknd over 2f out: rdn and hung rt ins fnl f: styd on* **5/2**[1]

-221 2 nk **Family Fortunes**[28] [557] 5-8-10 **89** .... ScottMcCullagh(7) 4 — 95
(Michael Madgwick) *s.i.s: hld up: hdwy on outer over 2f out: rdn and r.o to go 2nd post: nt quite rch wnr* **11/4**[2]

66-2 3 nk **Insurgence**[35] [441] 4-9-2 **88** .... DanielMuscutt 2 — 93
(James Fanshawe) *trckd ldrs: rdn to chse wnr ins fnl f: styd on: lost 2nd post* **5/2**[1]

-344 4 ½ **Chevallier**[7] [880] 7-9-4 **90** ....(p) LukeMorris 6 — 94
(Archie Watson) *chsd wnr: shkn up to chal 2f out: rdn and lost 2nd ins fnl f: styd on same pce* **13/2**[3]

-245 5 ¾ **Mythical Madness**[14] [764] 8-9-0 **93** ....(v) CierenFallon(7) 1 — 95
(David O'Meara) *rrd s: and slowly away: hld up: hdwy over 1f out: styd on same pce towards fin (jockey said gelding reared as the stalls opened and was slowly away as a result)* **14/1**

0-65 6 1½ **Sea Fox (IRE)**[8] [856] 5-9-0 **86** .... JFEgan 5 — 85
(David Evans) *prom: racd keenly: shkn up over 2f out: styd on same pce fr over 1f out* **11/1**

1m 37.83s (-0.37) **Going Correction** -0.025s/f (Stan) — 6 Ran SP% **112.1**
Speed ratings (Par 107): **100,99,99,98,98 96**
CSF £9.68 TOTE £2.40: £1.20, £2.00; EX 9.10 Trifecta £25.10.
Owner Nigel And Sharon Mather & Charles Ledigo **Bred** Lady Juliet Tadgell **Trained** Malpas, Cheshire

FOCUS
The winner set a steady early pace. A clear pb from the winner, with the second and third rated to form.

989 LADBROKES SPRING CUP STKS (LISTED RACE) — 7f 1y(P)
3:50 (3:50) (Class 1) 3-Y-O
£25,519 (£9,675; £4,842; £2,412; £1,210; £607) **Stalls** Low

Form — RPR

024- 1 **Fanaar (IRE)**[126] [8646] 3-9-2 **96** .... JimCrowley 3 — 99+
(William Haggas) *s.i.s: sn prom: shkn up over 1f out: rdn to ld wl ins fnl f: r.o* **10/11**[1]

-611 2 nk **Deep Intrigue**[10] [806] 3-9-2 **94** .... PJMcDonald 4 — 98
(Mark Johnston) *racd keenly in 2nd: rdn to ld 1f out: hdd wl ins fnl f: r.o* **15/8**[2]

3-06 3 2 **You Never Can Tell (IRE)**[10] [806] 3-9-2 **91** ....(p) TomQueally 1 — 92
(Richard Spencer) *chsd ldrs: rdn over 1f out: styd on: wnt 3rd nr fin* **20/1**

50-5 4 nk **Quiet Endeavour (IRE)**[10] [806] 3-9-2 **95** ....(p[1]) HollieDoyle 2 — 91
(Archie Watson) *led at stdy pce: qcknd over 2f out: rdn and hdd 1f out: styd on same pce ins fnl f* **16/1**

322- 5 1½ **Chynna**[120] [8805] 3-8-11 **95** .... CallumShepherd 5 — 81
(Mick Channon) *hld up: shkn up 2f out: rdn ins fnl f: nt trble ldrs* **16/1**

5-43 6 34 **Don Armado (IRE)**[10] [806] 3-9-2 **92** ....(t) OisinMurphy 6 — 67
(Stuart Williams) *hld up: shkn up over 2f out: sn wknd and eased (jockey said colt lost its action)* **12/1**[3]

1m 23.44s (-1.36) **Going Correction** -0.025s/f (Stan) — 6 Ran SP% **111.4**
Speed ratings (Par 106): **106,105,103,103,101 62**
CSF £2.73 TOTE £1.50: £1.10, £1.40; EX 3.20 Trifecta £15.70.
Owner Hamdan Al Maktoum **Bred** Bakewell Bloodstock & Freynetown **Trained** Newmarket, Suffolk

FOCUS
A substandard-looking edition of this 3yo Listed race, and they didn't look to go that quick early. It's been rated around the third.

990 BETWAY MAIDEN STKS — 6f 1y(P)
4:25 (4:25) (Class 5) 3-Y-O+ **£3,428** (£1,020; £509; £254) **Stalls** Low

Form — RPR

026- 1 **Swiss Pride (IRE)**[131] [8483] 3-9-0 **76** .... ShaneKelly 3 — 79
(Richard Hughes) *led early: sn stdd and lost pl: hdwy and edgd lft wl over 1f out: sn chsng ldrs: shkn up to ld ins fnl f: qcknd clr* **7/4**[2]

2-62 2 5 **Antonia Clara**[16] [720] 3-8-9 **69** .... OisinMurphy 2 — 58
(Stuart Williams) *led at stdy pce: qcknd over 2f out: rdn and hdd ins fnl f: sn outpcd* **4/5**[1]

0- 3 1 **Zorro's Girl**[100] [9205] 3-8-9 **0** .... HollieDoyle 5 — 55
(Archie Watson) *s.i.s: sn rcvrd to chse ldr: rdn over 1f out: styd on same pce* **6/1**[3]

/4-0 4 8 **Nelson's Hill**[35] [439] 9-9-11 **46** .... AaronJones(3) 1 — 38
(William de Best-Turner) *chsd ldrs: shkn up whn n.m.r wl over 1f out: sn wknd* **100/1**

1m 11.46s (-0.44) **Going Correction** -0.025s/f (Stan) — 4 Ran SP% **107.2**
WFA 3 from 9yo 14lb
Speed ratings (Par 103): **101,94,93,82**
CSF £3.48 TOTE £2.50; EX 3.20 Trifecta £4.20.
Owner Don Churston & Ray Greatorex **Bred** Edward Lynam & John Cullinan **Trained** Upper Lambourn, Berks

FOCUS
Only four runners but this looked useful enough from the winner. It's been rated around the winner to the level he ran to on his one previous AW start.

991 BETWAY STAYERS' APPRENTICE H'CAP (HANDS AND HEELS FINAL) (RACING EXCELLENCE INITIATIVE) — 1m 7f 169y(P)
5:00 (5:00) (Class 4) (0-80,78) 4-Y-0+
£6,553 (£1,961; £980; £490; £300; £300) **Stalls** Low

Form — RPR

-214 1 **Navajo Star (IRE)**[4] [916] 5-9-12 **72** ....(v) WilliamCarver 7 — 79
(Robyn Brisland) *racd keenly in 2nd pl 3f: remained handy: led over 6f out: clr and in command fr over 4f out: shkn up and edgd rt fr over 1f out* **16/1**

3-12 2 2 **Atomic Jack**[15] [731] 4-9-5 **68** .... CierenFallon 4 — 73
(George Baker) *led at stdy pce 5f: chsd ldr tl over 6f out: racd in 3rd pl and wl off the wnr over 4f out: shkn up over 2f out: r.o to go 2nd ins fnl f: no ch w wnr (jockey said gelding hung right-handed)* **4/5**[1]

/055 3 ¾ **Alabaster**[10] [799] 5-10-1 **78** ....(p) GavinAshton(3) 8 — 82
(Sir Mark Prescott Bt) *wnt prom after 2f: led 11f out: hdd over 6f out: chsd wnr: lost grnd on wnr over 4f out: pushed along over 2f out: styd on but lost 2nd ins fnl f (jockey said his saddle slipped)* **12/1**

1-33 **4** *1* **Colwood**[17] 700 5-9-7 **67** .... JessicaCooley 3 70
(Robert Eddery) *chsd ldrs: pushed along over 3f out: styd on fr over 1f out* **7/1**[3]

-223 **5** *3 ¼* **Falcon Cliffs (IRE)**[29] 535 5-9-0 **63** .... ElishaWhittington(3) 1 62
(Tony Carroll) *prom: n.m.r and stmbld after 1f: sn lost pl: pushed along over 3f out: r.o ins fnl f: nt rch ldrs* **12/1**

6-52 **6** *2 ¾* **Mundersfield**[28] 566 5-9-0 **60** .... (h) MarkCrehan 6 55
(David Simcock) *s.s: hld up: bhd 12f out: sme hdwy over 1f out: nvr on terms* **11/1**

02-6 **7** *6* **Final Choice**[43] 291 6-9-12 **72** .... (b) AmeliaGlass 2 60
(Adam West) *wnt prom after 1f: pushed along over 3f out: wknd over 2f out* **33/1**

10-1 **8** *10* **Le Torrent**[17] 700 7-9-9 **74** .... LeviWilliams(5) 5 50
(Simon Dow) *plld hrd and prom: stdd and lost pl after 1f: bhd 12f out: no ch after (jockey said gelding was never travelling)* **6/1**[2]

3m 21.47s (-4.23) **Going Correction** -0.025s/f (Stan)
WFA 4 from 5yo+ 3lb **8** Ran SP% **114.9**
Speed ratings (Par 105): **109,108,107,107,105 104,101,96**
CSF £29.66 CT £175.52 TOTE £11.90: £3.20, £1.10, £2.70; EX 28.00 Trifecta £185.80.
Owner Ferrybank Properties Limited **Bred** Robert Dunne **Trained** Danethorpe, Notts

FOCUS
Muddling form; the lead changed a few times, with the pace not strong, and the decisive move came when the winner went to the front over 6f out and gradually opened up a big lead. The form has been rated cautiously, with the winner having been held off similar marks recently.
T/Plt: £23.60 to a £1 stake. Pool: £56,123.29 - 1,734.12 winning units T/Qpdt: £7.10 to a £1 stake. Pool: £4,680.80 - 485.02 winning units **Colin Roberts**

868 CHANTILLY (R-H)
Saturday, March 2

OFFICIAL GOING: Polytrack: standard

992a PRIX DE LESSARD-ET-LE-CHENE (CLAIMER) (4YO) (ALL-WEATHER TRACK) (POLYTRACK) 7f 110y(P)
12:45 4-Y-O £8,558 (£3,423; £2,567; £1,711; £855)

RPR

1 **Royal Gift (FR)**[17] 4-9-1 0 .... (p) AntoineHamelin 4 80
(Matthieu Palussiere, France) **186/10**

2 *1 ¼* **Mon Paris (FR)** 4-8-9 0 .... JimmyTastayre(6) 3 77
(Edouard Thueux, France) **67/1**

3 *nk* **Caliste**[17] 4-8-11 0 .... (b[1]) Pierre-CharlesBoudot 2 72
(H-A Pantall, France) **5/1**[3]

4 *½* **Karsador**[128] 4-8-9 0 .... QuentinPerrette(6) 1 75
(M Nigge, France) **91/10**

5 *2* **Digicode (FR)**[122] 4-8-13 0 .... (p) JeromeMoutard(3) 5 71
(P Monfort, France) **235/10**

6 *1* **Gone Solo (IRE)**[23] 4-9-2 0 .... (b) MlleAlisonMassin(3) 8 71
(Robert Collet, France) **16/1**

7 *hd* **Admiral Thrawn (IRE)**[23] 4-9-5 0 .... StephanePasquier 10 71
(Andrea Marcialis, France) **12/5**[1]

8 *3* **Dixit Confucius (FR)**[76] 9569 4-8-9 0 .... MlleAudeDuporte(9) 11 62
(F Chappet, France) **40/1**

9 *2* **Zoraya (FR)**[14] 756 4-8-8 0 .... (b[1]) IoritzMendizabal 12 47
(Paul Cole) *racd keenly: hld up towards rr: stdy hdwy on outside fr 4f out: in tch 2 1/2f out: rdn and unable qck 2f out: sn btn: eased fnl 100yds* **23/5**[2]

10 *3* **Cool The Jets**[23] 4-9-1 0 .... CristianDemuro 7 47
(F Vermeulen, France) **101/10**

11 *2* **Black Cat (FR)**[23] 4-9-0 0 .... (p) MlleLauraPoggionovo(8) 6 49
(Mlle A Wattel, France) **54/10**

12 *10* **Animalinhereyes (IRE)**[18] 4-8-5 0 .... MlleCoraliePacaut(3) 9 10
(Mme G Rarick, France) **64/1**

1m 33.15s **12** Ran SP% **119.0**
PARI-MUTUEL (all including 1 euro stake): WIN 19.60; PLACE 6.00, 13.70, 2.50; DF 284.20.
Owner Mrs Theresa Marnane **Bred** Haras De Grandcamp Earl **Trained** France

993a PRIX DE SAINT-VALERY (MAIDEN) (3YO FILLIES) (ALL-WEATHER TRACK) (POLYTRACK) 7f 110y(P)
2:32 3-Y-O £11,261 (£4,504; £3,378; £2,252; £1,126)

RPR

1 **Last Edition (FR)** 3-9-2 0 .... Pierre-CharlesBoudot 8 74
(A Fabre, France) **13/2**[3]

2 *2 ½* **Adelante (FR)**[30] 509 3-9-2 0 .... IoritzMendizabal 4 68
(George Baker) *in tch in midfield: smooth hdwy to trck ldrs over 2f out: rdn and ev ch 1 1/2f out: kpt on wl: nt pce of wnr fnl f* **31/5**[2]

3 *shd* **Torrealta (FR)** 3-9-2 0 .... AlexisBadel 6 68
(H-F Devin, France) **136/10**

4 *nk* **Miss Spotsy (FR)**[57] 3-9-2 0 .... VincentCheminaud 9 67
(H-A Pantall, France) **114/10**

5 *nk* **Persona (FR)**[76] 3-9-2 0 .... HugoJourniac 7 66
(J-C Rouget, France) **5/2**[1]

6 *¾* **Meri Senshi (FR)**[94] 3-9-2 0 .... CristianDemuro 10 64
(S Wattel, France) **207/10**

7 *hd* **Hinemoa (FR)**[23] 3-8-7 .... MlleLauraGrosso(9) 1 64
(N Clement, France) *trckd ldrs: prog to sit 2nd appr home turn: pushed along 2f out: fdd u.p ins fnl f* **9/1**

8 *nse* **Kawkabba (USA)**[23] 3-9-2 0 .... EddyHardouin 3 64
(P Monfort, France) **167/10**

9 *nk* **Glad Memory (GER)**[74] 3-9-2 0 .... AurelienLemaitre 11 63
(F Head, France) **31/5**[2]

10 *8* **Happy Bean (USA)**[94] 3-9-2 0 .... MaximeGuyon 5 43
(C Laffon-Parias, France) **78/10**

11 *½* **Queen's Way (FR)** 3-9-2 0 .... LudovicBoisseau 2
(J-L Guillochon, France) **47/1**

1m 34.58s **11** Ran SP% **118.3**
PARI-MUTUEL (all including 1 euro stake): WIN 7.50; PLACE 2.60, 2.10, 4.20; DF 20.70.
Owner Moussa Mbacke **Bred** M Mbacke **Trained** Chantilly, France

994 - 996a (Foreign Racing) - See Raceform Interactive

956 MEYDAN (L-H)
Saturday, March 2

OFFICIAL GOING: Dirt: fast; turf: good

997 MINA HAMRIYA (H'CAP) (DIRT) 7f (D)
12:35 (12:35) (64-90,79) 3-Y-O £21,794 (£7,264; £3,995; £2,179; £1,089)

Form RPR

100/ **1** **Iftitah (IRE)**[8] 875 5-9-6 **79** .... (bt) TadhgO'Shea 4 88
(S Seemar, UAE) *trckd ldr: r.o wl fnl 1 1/2f: led on line* **11/4**[1]

5 **2** *nse* **Gervais (USA)**[50] 196 5-8-13 **72** .... (bt) FernandoJara 5 81
(A R Al Rayhi, UAE) *sn led: r.o wl fnl 3f but hdd on line* **8/1**

351/ **3** *2 ¼* **Naaeebb (USA)**[28] 569 5-8-8 **68** ow1 .... (t) ConnorBeasley 10 70
(A bin Harmash, UAE) *mid-div: r.o wl fnl 2f: nrst fin* **14/1**

3 **4** *nk* **Guernsey (USA)**[28] 571 5-8-13 **72** .... PatDobbs 14 74
(Doug Watson, UAE) *mid-div: r.o same pce fnl 2 1/2f* **7/1**[3]

0- **5** *nk* **Mayaadeen (IRE)**[171] 7184 4-9-6 **79** .... DaneO'Neill 6 80
(Doug Watson, UAE) *mid-div: r.o same pce fnl 2f* **9/2**[2]

2/ **6** *8 ½* **Tobaco (ARG)**[50] 200 6-9-0 **73** .... (v) SamHitchcott 11 51
(Doug Watson, UAE) *trckd ldr tl wknd 1 1/2f out* **14/1**

0/4- **7** *1* **Speedy Move (IRE)**[28] 571 7-9-1 **74** .... RichardMullen 12 50
(S Seemar, UAE) *trckd ldr tl wknd fnl 1 1/2f* **7/1**[3]

100- **8** *1 ¾* **Extra Large**[157] 7681 4-9-3 **76** .... FabriceVeron 8 47
(M Al Mheiri, UAE) *s.i.s: nvr nr to chal* **12/1**

25-0 **9** *1* **Samharry**[36] 427 5-8-8 **68** .... (t) AntonioFresu 1 35
(H Al Alawi, UAE) *nvr bttr than mid-div* **11/1**

5/ **10** *½* **Right Flank (USA)**[464] 8922 5-9-0 **73** .... AdriedeVries 7 40
(Doug Watson, UAE) *a in rr* **20/1**

212- **11** *1 ½* **Dosc (IRE)**[22] 679 4-8-13 **72** .... (t) BenCurtis 9 35
(M Al Mheiri, UAE) *s.i.s: a in rr* **20/1**

13-0 **12** *2* **Ghost Queen**[58] 48 3-8-5 **75** .... (b) RoystonFfrench 13 31
(Simon Crisford) *a in rr* **12/1**

00-0 **13** *8 ½* **Maghaweer (IRE)**[36] 426 4-8-10 **70** .... (v) SzczepanMazur 3 3
(H Al Alawi, UAE) *nvr bttr than mid-div* **28/1**

636/ **14** *11 ½* **Moseeb (IRE)**[64] 9742 4-8-5 **70** ow5 .... AdamMcLean(7) 2
(A bin Harmash, UAE) *a in rr* **28/1**

1m 25.71s (0.61) **Going Correction** +0.45s/f (Slow)
WFA 3 from 4yo+ 16lb **14** Ran SP% **134.4**
Speed ratings: **114,113,111,111,110 100,99,97,96,96 94,92,82,69**
CSF: 27.08; TRICAST: 292.99.
Owner Nasir Askar **Bred** Palmerston Bloodstock Ltd **Trained** United Arab Emirates

998a-1000a (Foreign Racing) - See Raceform Interactive

1001 MINA RASHID (H'CAP) (DIRT) 1m (D)
2:55 (2:55) (75-94,89) 3-Y-O+ £24,358 (£8,119; £4,465; £2,435; £1,217)

Form RPR

512- **1** **George Villiers (IRE)**[42] 327 4-9-1 **84** .... (b) RichardMullen 9 92
(S Seemar, UAE) *mid-div: smooth prog 2 1/2f out: rdn to ld 165yds out: r.o wl* **6/1**[3]

/5-0 **2** *¾* **Pillar Of Society (IRE)**[30] 513 5-9-6 **89** .... PatDobbs 4 95
(Doug Watson, UAE) *wl away: sn led: clr 2 1/2f out: hdd 165yds out but r.o wl* **8/1**

60- **3** *2 ¾* **Daffg (USA)**[48] 234 4-8-9 **79** .... (vt) AntonioFresu 5 78
(A bin Harmash, UAE) *mid-div: r.o wl fnl 2 1/2f* **18/1**

5-21 **4** *hd* **Mazeed (USA)**[28] 573 5-8-11 **81** .... (bt) TadhgO'Shea 11 79
(S Seemar, UAE) *mid-div: r.o wl fnl 2 1/2f* **3/1**[2]

501- **5** *4* **Etisalat**[8] 871 4-8-9 **79** .... DaneO'Neill 3 68
(A R Al Rayhi, UAE) *nvr nr to chal but r.o fnl 2f* **8/1**

255/ **6** *2 ¼* **King Cole (USA)**[723] 1116 6-8-11 **81** .... SamHitchcott 7 65
(Doug Watson, UAE) *a mid-div* **12/1**

500- **7** *nk* **Arroway (USA)**[8] 873 4-8-6 **76** .... (b) XavierZiani 10 59
(S Jadhav, UAE) *nvr nr to chal* **16/1**

440- **8** *¾* **El Chapo**[56] 96 4-9-3 **86** .... (v) AdriedeVries 2 68
(Fawzi Abdulla Nass, Bahrain) *s.i.s: nvr nr to chal* **20/1**

/02- **9** *1 ¼* **To Dibba**[36] 423 5-9-4 **87** .... (bt) FernandoJara 6 67
(N Bachalard, UAE) *trckd ldr tl wknd 2 1/2f out* **14/1**

3-14 **10** *3* **Craving (IRE)**[28] 573 4-9-0 **83** .... ConnorBeasley 1 56
(Simon Crisford) *nvr bttr than mid-div* **9/4**[1]

304/ **11** *3 ¼* **Chess Master (IRE)**[8] 875 6-8-10 **80** .... (t) BenCurtis 8 44
(M Al Mheiri, UAE) *nvr bttr than mid-div* **9/1**

1m 37.69s (0.19) **Going Correction** +0.45s/f (Slow) **11** Ran SP% **132.5**
Speed ratings: **117,116,113,113,109 107,106,106,104,101 98**
CSF: 60.74; TRICAST: 868.95.
Owner Mohd Khalifa Al Basti **Bred** Floors Farming & The Duke Of Devonshire **Trained** United Arab Emirates

1002 - 1014a (Foreign Racing) - See Raceform Interactive

912 WOLVERHAMPTON (A.W) (L-H)
Monday, March 4

OFFICIAL GOING: Tapeta: standard
Wind: medium tailwind in the home straight Weather: Rain race 6

1015 BETWAY LIVE CASINO H'CAP 1m 1f 104y (Tp)
5:45 (5:45) (Class 6) (0-60,60) 4-Y-O+ £2,264 (£673; £336; £168) Stalls Low

Form RPR

4-52 **1** **Creative Talent (IRE)**[13] 792 7-9-2 **55** .... TomMarquand 8 62
(Tony Carroll) *hld up: bmpd 3f out: hdwy on outer over 2f out: r.o to ld jst over 1f out: rdn out* **7/2**[1]

0-53 **2** *1* **Kilbaha Lady (IRE)**[11] 835 5-9-6 **59** .... AndrewMullen 2 64+
(Nigel Tinkler) *s.i.s: hld up: edgd rt and bmpd 3f out: rdn and swtchd rt over 1f out: r.o ins fnl f: wnt 2nd nr fin: nt rch wnr* **5/1**[3]

4-02 **3** *nk* **Final Attack (IRE)**[6] 912 8-8-10 **52** .... (p) GabrieleMalune(3) 6 57
(Sarah Hollinshead) *t.k.h: chsd ldrs: drvn 2f out: kpt on to dispute 2nd ins fnl f: unable qck* **7/1**

-533 **4** *nk* **Traveller (FR)**[7] 911 5-9-5 **58** .... (t) CamHardie 9 62
(Antony Brittain) *led tl hdd 6f out: trckd ldr tl led 2nd 4f out: drvn over 1f out: disp 2nd again ins fnl f: unable qck* **5/1**[3]

6164 **5** *1* **Sharp Operator**[6] 912 6-9-5 **58** .... (h) RichardKingscote 12 61
(Charlie Wallis) *hld up: hdwy over 2f out: nt clr run ins fnl f: shkn up towards fin: nvr able to chal (jockey said gelding was denied a clear run until inside the final 110yds)* **15/2**

00-0 **6** *shd* **Barca (USA)**^{19} 701 5-9-6 **59** .... MartinDwyer 3 61
(Marcus Tregoning) *s.i.s: sn in midfield: drvn over 1f out: styd on same pce fnl f* **9/2**^{2}

0-01 **7** *nk* **Muraaqeb**^{31} 533 5-8-7 **46** .... (p) KieranO'Neill 5 49
(Milton Bradley) *trckd ldrs: rdn and lost pl over 2f out: trying to rally whn nt clr run ins fnl f: eased (jockey said gelding was denied a clear run inside the final 110yds)* **16/1**

5000 **8** *hd* **Clive Clifton (IRE)**^{11} 835 6-8-7 **46** oh1 .... (v) EoinWalsh 11 47
(Mark Brisbourne) *s.s and early reminder: hdwy after 2f: led 6f out: drvn 2f out: hdd jst over 1f out: wknd ins fnl f* **50/1**

05-0 **9** *½* **Cooperess**^{59} 67 6-8-10 **49** .... DavidProbert 13 49
(Dai Burchell) *t.k.h: prom: chsd ldr 4f out: rdn over 2f out: ev ch ent fnl f: sn wknd* **66/1**

4453 **10** *1* **Sir Lancelott**^{31} 533 7-8-0 **46** oh1 .... LauraCoughlan$^{(7)}$ 4 45
(Adrian Nicholls) *chsd ldrs tl lost pl after 3f: hdwy on ins over 1f out tl nt clr run and eased ins fnl f (jockey said gelding was denied a clear run in the early part of the home straight and again inside the final half furlong)* **20/1**

-315 **11** *5* **Arrowzone**^{34} 465 8-9-7 **60** .... (b) JasonHart 7 49
(Kevin Frost) *hld up: hmpd bnd after 2f: hdwy 5f out: rdn over 2f out: sn wknd* **7/1**

2m 0.42s (-0.38) **Going Correction** -0.15s/f (Stan) **11** Ran SP% **124.6**
Speed ratings (Par 101): **95,94,93,93,92 92,92,92,91,90 86**
CSF £22.13 CT £122.03 TOTE £4.60: £1.50, £2.20, £2.90; EX 27.80 Trifecta £181.10.
Owner The Rebelle Boys **Bred** Pitrizzia Partnership **Trained** Cropthorne, Worcs
■ Stewards' Enquiry : Andrew Mullen caution: careless riding

FOCUS
This moderate handicap was set up for the closers. Sound form for the class. Straightforward form in behind the winner.

1016 BETWAY H'CAP 6f 20y (Tp)
6:15 (6:15) (Class 5) (0-70,72) 4-Y-O+ **£2,911** (£866; £432; £216) **Stalls** Low

Form RPR

5-22 **1** **Kupa River (IRE)**^{42} 347 5-9-6 **69** .... (h) LukeMorris 8 76
(Roger Fell) *racd keenly: chsd ldr: rdn to ld over 1f out: drvn fnl f: jst hld on* **3/1**^{1}

1106 **2** *shd* **Aguerooo (IRE)**^{2} 982 6-9-6 **69** .... (tp) FrannyNorton 4 75
(Charlie Wallis) *chsd ldrs: rdn over 1f out: r.o fnl f: jst failed* **6/1**

2321 **3** *1¾* **Steelriver (IRE)**^{9} 882 9-9-2 **68** .... PhilDennis$^{(3)}$ 7 68+
(Michael Herrington) *sltly hmpd leaving stalls: hld up in last: rdn over 1f out: hung lft and r.o fnl f: wnt 3rd post* **7/2**^{2}

-333 **4** *shd* **Monumental Man**^{9} 883 10-9-7 **70** .... (p) DougieCostello 9 70
(Jamie Osborne) *led: rdn and hdd over 1f out: kpt on same pce fnl f: lost 3rd post (vet said gelding lost right hind shoe)* **11/1**

5223 **5** *½* **Bobby Joe Leg**^{27} 609 5-9-3 **66** .... (b) JamesSullivan 1 64
(Ruth Carr) *chsd ldng pair: drvn wl over 2f out: lost 3rd 1f out: kpt on* **8/1**

23-0 **6** *hd* **Mutabaahy (IRE)**^{13} 790 4-9-9 **72** .... (h) CamHardie 5 70
(Antony Brittain) *s.i.s: hld up: rdn and hdwy 2f out: nt qckn fnl f* **4/1**^{3}

-014 **7** *2¼* **Newstead Abbey**^{11} 830 9-8-10 **64** .... (p) TheodoreLadd$^{(5)}$ 2 55
(Rebecca Bastiman) *half-rrd s: hld up: rdn over 1f out: no imp* **15/2**

2003 **8** *1¼* **Always Amazing**^{9} 882 5-8-10 **59** .... RaulDaSilva 3 46
(Derek Shaw) *midfield: drvn over 2f out: wknd ins fnl f* **16/1**

/40- **9** *14* **Sandytown (IRE)**^{310} 2129 4-8-11 **60** ow2 .... (w) LewisEdmunds 6 2
(David C Griffiths) *midfield: rdn over 2f out: wknd over 1f out* **80/1**

1m 13.12s (-1.38) **Going Correction** -0.15s/f (Stan) **9** Ran SP% **119.8**
Speed ratings (Par 103): **103,102,100,100,99 99,96,94,76**
CSF £22.45 CT £67.33 TOTE £3.70: £1.30, £2.20, £1.70; EX 24.50 Trifecta £90.90.
Owner Middleham Park Racing Lxxii & Partner **Bred** Airlie Stud & Mrs S Rogers **Trained** Nawton, N Yorks

FOCUS
This ordinary sprint handicap was another strongly run affair. The runner-up has been rated in line with his best form over the past year.

1017 BETWAY CASINO H'CAP 1m 4f 51y (Tp)
6:45 (6:45) (Class 2) (0-105,105) 4-Y-O+
£11,827 (£3,541; £1,770; £885; £442; £222) **Stalls** Low

Form RPR

511- **1** **Mootasadir**^{157} 7743 4-9-9 **105** .... OisinMurphy 7 114+
(Hugo Palmer) *trckd ldr tl led 1/2-way: shkn up and qcknd 2f out: drvn and r.o fnl f* **1/1**^{1}

213- **2** *1¾* **Kelly's Dino (FR)**^{192} 6501 6-9-1 **96** .... (p) CliffordLee 4 101
(K R Burke) *trckd ldrs: wnt 2nd 3f out: rdn 2f out: kpt on wl but a being hld by wnr* **10/3**^{2}

-115 **3** *1¼* **Fearsome**^{9} 878 5-8-10 **91** .... TomMarquand 2 94+
(Nick Littmoden) *hld up: rdn and hdwy over 2f out: ro to go 3rd 1f out: no imp on ldng pair* **5/1**^{3}

100- **4** *2¾* **Amazing Red (IRE)**^{226} 5212 6-9-7 **102** .... PJMcDonald 6 101
(Ed Dunlop) *s.i.s: sn in midfield: rdn to chse ldng pair over 2f out: sn no imp: kpt on same pce and lost 3rd 1f out* **18/1**

1-36 **5** *2* **Lexington Law (IRE)**^{16} 758 6-8-11 **92** .... (p) DavidProbert 3 87
(Alan King) *s.i.s: hld up: rdn and outpcd over 2f out: styd on fnl f but nvr a threat (jockey said gelding was slowly away)* **12/1**

6-05 **6** *½* **Cosmelli (ITY)**^{41} 349 6-9-1 **96** .... (e^{1}) DanielMuscutt 8 91
(Gay Kelleway) *led to 1/2-way: lost 2nd and rdn 3f out: wknd 1f out* **16/1**

4-24 **7** *12* **Primero (FR)**^{12} 799 6-9-6 **101** .... AdamKirby 1 76
(David O'Meara) *hld up: rdn over 2f out: sn outpcd: wknd over 1f out (trainer's rep could offer no explanation for the gelding's performance)* **10/1**

/50- **8** *21* **High Language (IRE)**^{138} 8313 5-8-9 **90** .... DannyBrock 5 32
(Philip McBride) *racd keenly: chsd ldrs: rdn 3f out: sn wknd: t.o* **80/1**

2m 35.11s (-5.69) **Going Correction** -0.15s/f (Stan)
WFA 4 from 5yo+ 1lb **8** Ran SP% **118.9**
Speed ratings (Par 109): **112,110,110,108,106 106,98,84**
CSF £4.73 CT £11.61 TOTE £1.80: £1.10, £1.20, £2.00; EX 6.10 Trifecta £18.90.
Owner Sheikh Mohammed Bin Khalifa Al Maktoum **Bred** Essafinaat Ltd **Trained** Newmarket, Suffolk

FOCUS
This good-quality handicap was run at a routine pace. Solid form. The third has been rated close to his recent form.

1018 FOLLOW SUN RACING ON TWITTER CLAIMING STKS 1m 142y (Tp)
7:15 (7:15) (Class 6) 4-Y-O+ **£2,264** (£673; £336; £168) **Stalls** Low

Form RPR

3444 **1** **Chevallier**^{2} 988 7-9-10 **90** .... (p) LukeMorris 1 87
(Archie Watson) *trckd ldr: led over 1f out: drvn clr fnl f: eased nr fin* **5/4**^{1}

-011 **2** *3½* **Los Camachos (IRE)**^{31} 517 4-9-1 **78** .... KatherineBegley$^{(5)}$ 7 76
(David Evans) *led: rdn over 2f out: hdd over 1f out: drvn and outpcd by wnr fnl f* **9/4**^{2}

5-00 **3** *2¾* **Puchita (IRE)**^{51} 208 4-8-0 **44** .... CamHardie 3 50
(Antony Brittain) *chsd ldrs: rdn in 3rd over 2f out: one pce and no real imp* **50/1**

0-00 **4** *2½* **Petra's Pony (IRE)**^{9} 876 4-8-5 **52** .... (h^{1}) MartinDwyer 5 50
(Brian Meehan) *hld up: rdn over 3f out: outpcd over 2f out: styd on to go 4th ins fnl f* **25/1**

2500 **5** *1¼* **My Target (IRE)**^{12} 807 8-9-10 **82** .... (b^{1}) FrannyNorton 6 66
(Michael Wigham) *t.k.h towards rr: clsd after 2f: rdn over 2f out: wknd over 1f out (jockey said gelding hung left-handed)* **4/1**^{3}

1-66 **6** *19* **Kyllachy Dragon (IRE)**^{26} 618 4-9-6 **77** .... (h) DavidProbert 4 22
(Ronald Harris) *chsd ldrs: rdn over 3f out: wknd over 2f out: eased fnl f (jockey said gelding hung right-handed; vet said gelding finished lame right fore)* **9/1**

1m 47.95s (-2.15) **Going Correction** -0.15s/f (Stan) **6** Ran SP% **111.0**
Speed ratings (Par 101): **103,99,97,95,94 77**
CSF £4.17 TOTE £2.10: £1.10, £1.50; EX 4.00.Chevallier was claimed by Mr Christian Main for £12,000; Los Camachos was claimed by Mr J. Gallagher for £10,000
Owner The Chevallier Partnership II **Bred** Kincorth Investments Inc **Trained** Upper Lambourn, W Berks

FOCUS
It paid to be handy in this interesting claimer. The third has been rated to her recent best.

1019 LADBROKES NOVICE STKS 1m 1f 104y (Tp)
7:45 (7:45) (Class 5) 3-Y-O **£2,911** (£866; £432; £216) **Stalls** Low

Form RPR

1 **Questionare** 3-9-2 0 .... (t^{1}) NickyMackay 7 76
(John Gosden) *s.s: sn in midfield: shkn up over 3f out: rdn and clsd over 2f out: chsd wnr 1f out: r.o to ld post* **6/4**^{1}

6-3 **2** *shd* **Wanaasah**^{44} 316 3-8-11 0 .... KieranO'Neill 6 70
(David Loughnane) *led: 4 l clr after 4f: reduced ld and rdn over 2f out: r.o u.p: ct post* **3/1**^{2}

65 **3** *3* **Shaleela's Dream**^{18} 723 3-8-13 0 .... GabrieleMalune$^{(3)}$ 3 69
(Marco Botti) *chsd ldrs: rdn over 2f out: wnt 2nd 2f out to 1f out: kpt on same pce* **7/1**^{3}

4 *4½* **Tsarmina (IRE)** 3-8-11 0 .... EoinWalsh 4 55
(David Evans) *chsd ldrs: rn green and niggled along at times: rdn 3f out: nt pce of ldrs fnl 2f* **40/1**

5 *4* **So Hi Cardi (FR)** 3-8-11 0 .... AdamMcNamara 9 46
(Roger Charlton) *s.s: in rr: rdn 3f out: styd on appr fnl f: nvr nrr* **14/1**

6 *1¼* **Necoleta** 3-8-12 0 ow1 .... LiamKeniry 11 45
(Sylvester Kirk) *v.s.a: in rr: rdn over 3f out: styd on fnl f* **100/1**

6 **7** *7* **Shamrad (FR)**^{28} 606 3-9-2 0 .... PJMcDonald 10 34
(Ian Williams) *midfield: rdn over 2f out: wknd over 1f out* **100/1**

4 **8** *1¼* **Kiowa**^{28} 606 3-9-2 0 .... DannyBrock 1 31
(Philip McBride) *chsd ldr: rdn 3f out: lost 2nd 2f out: wknd appr fnl f* **33/1**

9 *3¼* **Bacon's Rebellion** 3-9-2 0 .... CallumShepherd 12 24
(Ed de Giles) *hld up: chsd along briefly after 3f: rdn 3f out: wknd over 2f out* **33/1**

10 *1¼* **Atlantic City (IRE)** 3-8-13 0 .... GaryMahon$^{(3)}$ 8 22
(Sylvester Kirk) *towards rr: drvn and wknd over 2f out* **33/1**

2m 0.38s (-0.42) **Going Correction** -0.15s/f (Stan) **10** Ran SP% **97.4**
Speed ratings (Par 98): **95,94,92,88,84 83,77,76,73,72**
CSF £3.71 TOTE £2.30: £1.10, £1.10, £2.00; EX 4.60 Trifecta £15.10.
Owner Lady Bamford **Bred** Lady Bamford **Trained** Newmarket, Suffolk
■ Nathanielhawthorne was withdrawn. Price at time of withdrawal 7-2. Rule 4 applies to all bets - deduction 20p in the pound.

FOCUS
This uncompetitive novice event was run at a decent pace. The level is fluid.

1020 LADBROKES HOME OF THE ODDS BOOST FILLIES' NOVICE STKS 6f 20y (Tp)
8:15 (8:15) (Class 5) 3-Y-O+ **£2,911** (£866; £432; £216) **Stalls** Low

Form RPR

0-22 **1** **Second Collection**^{33} 477 3-8-11 **64** .... (h) TomMarquand 7 61+
(Tony Carroll) *hld up: rdn over 2f out: hdwy and nt clr run over 1f out: r.o wl fnl f: led last strides* **7/2**^{3}

5-4 **2** *½* **Sundiata**^{39} 380 3-8-11 0 .... OisinMurphy 3 59+
(Charles Hills) *s.i.s: sn in midfield: hdwy over 2f out: rdn to ld jst ins fnl f: sn drvn: ct last strides* **6/4**^{1}

3 **3** *1¼* **Bequest**^{40} 367 3-8-11 0 .... DavidProbert 1 55
(Ron Hodges) *prom: rdn to chse ldr over 2f out: lost 2nd over 1f out: kpt on* **9/1**

0-4 **4** *nk* **Sussudio**^{33} 477 3-8-4 0 .... (p^{1}) SeanKirrane$^{(7)}$ 10 54+
(Richard Spencer) *s.s: in rr: shkn up and hdwy on outer over 1f out: rdn and r.o fnl f: nvr nrr* **20/1**

56-5 **5** *1* **Angel Eyes**^{12} 811 4-9-4 **42** .... RPWalsh$^{(7)}$ 9 55
(John David Riches) *sn led: drvn and 3 l clr 2f out: hdd jst ins fnl f: no ex* **200/1**

-600 **6** *shd* **Mystical Moon (IRE)**^{33} 476 4-9-8 **40** .... PhilDennis$^{(3)}$ 6 54
(David C Griffiths) *midfield: rdn to chse ldrs over 2f out: kpt on same pce fnl f* **100/1**

5-5 **7** *6* **Designated**^{44} 316 3-8-11 0 .... HectorCrouch 2 31
(Clive Cox) *led early: trckd ldrs: rdn and outpcd over 2f out: wknd 1f out* **5/1**

0-05 **8** *½* **Lambrini Lullaby**^{26} 621 4-9-11 **45** .... CamHardie 5 34
(Lisa Williamson) *hld up: rdn over 2f out: no imp* **150/1**

1 **9** *¾* **Metal Exchange**^{38} 408 3-9-4 0 .... AndrewMullen 8 34
(Kevin Ryan) *chsd ldrs: rdn over 2f out: grad wknd* **10/3**^{2}

00-5 **10** *3* **Lope De Loop (IRE)**^{35} 464 4-9-11 **49** .... (t^{1}) EoinWalsh 4 22
(Aytach Sadik) *prom: chsd ldr after 2f: rdn and lost 2nd over 2f out: wknd over 1f out* **200/1**

1m 13.67s (-0.83) **Going Correction** -0.15s/f (Stan)
WFA 3 from 4yo 14lb **10** Ran SP% **119.4**
Speed ratings (Par 100): **99,98,96,96,94 94,86,86,85,81**
CSF £9.41 TOTE £4.30: £1.30, £1.20, £3.10; EX 11.70 Trifecta £54.30.
Owner A A Byrne **Bred** Anthony Byrne **Trained** Cropthorne, Worcs

FOCUS
This modest fillies' novice event saw changing fortunes inside the final furlong. The fifth and sixth highlight the limitations of the form.
T/Jkpt: £630.50 to a £1 stake. Pool: £14,084.51 - 15.86 winning units. T/Plt: £4.10 to a £1 stake Pool: £126,459.63 - 22,468.95 T/Qpdt: £1.70 to a £1 stake. Pool: £12,838.32 - 5379.14 winning units **Richard Lowther**

[1015]WOLVERHAMPTON (A.W) (L-H)

Tuesday, March 5

OFFICIAL GOING: Tapeta: standard

Wind: Fresh behind Weather: Overcast

1021 BETWAY CASINO H'CAP — 6f 20y (Tp)

5:00 (5:00) (Class 6) (0-60,60) 3-Y-O+

£3,105 (£924; £461; £300; £300; £300) Stalls Low

Form RPR

-300 1 **Peachey Carnehan**[14] 790 5-9-9 60 ....(v) JamesSullivan 11 68
(Michael Mullineaux) *hld up: hdwy over 1f out: rdn to ld wl ins fnl f: r.o* 12/1

2-04 2 ¾ **Fareeq**[29] 596 5-9-6 57 ....(bt) RichardKingscote 4 63
(Charlie Wallis) *dwlt: hld up: hdwy over 1f out: rdn and ev ch wl ins fnl f: styd on* 7/2[1]

50-0 3 ¾ **Milton Road**[18] 742 4-9-6 57 .... AdamKirby 9 61
(Rebecca Bastiman) *hld up: rdn over 1f out: r.o u.p ins fnl f: wnt 3rd towards fin* 10/1

3312 4 1 ¼ **Catapult**[12] 830 4-9-3 54 ....(p) NicolaCurrie 12 54
(Shaun Keightley) *led early: remained w ldr: rdn over 1f out: led briefly wl ins fnl f: styd on same pce* 6/1[2]

6010 5 shd **Indian Affair**[10] 882 9-9-5 56 ....(bt) KieranO'Neill 2 55
(Milton Bradley) *pushed along and prom: nt clr run and lost pl after 1f: shkn up and hdwy over 1f out: swtchd lft ins fnl f: styd on* 10/1

0005 6 ½ **Tavener**[11] 857 7-9-4 58 ....(p) PhilDennis(3) 7 56
(David C Griffiths) *sn led: rdn and hdd wl ins fnl f: styd on same pce* 6/1[2]

600- 7 1 ¼ **Formiga (IRE)**[91] 9387 4-9-6 57 ....(vt) RaulDaSilva 10 51+
(Seamus Durack) *prom: hmpd and lost pl sn after s: hld up: r.o ins fnl f: nt trble ldrs* 40/1

153 8 ½ **Brockey Rise (IRE)**[11] 857 4-8-13 57 ....(b) GinaMangan(7) 6 50
(David Evans) *prom: rdn over 1f out: no ex ins fnl f* 8/1

30-4 9 nk **Seanie (IRE)**[34] 484 10-9-2 53 ....(t) LukeMorris 3 45
(Karl Thornton, Ire) *chsd ldrs: rdn over 2f out: hung lft and no ex ins fnl f (jockey said gelding hung left throughout)* 20/1

-602 10 ¾ **Admiral Rooke (IRE)**[10] 882 4-8-11 55 ....(p) MarkCrehan(7) 8 45
(Michael Appleby) *sn pushed along and prom: ct out wd: rdn over 2f out: wknd ins fnl f* 7/1[3]

600- 11 nk **Jessie Allan (IRE)**[141] 8263 8-8-11 55 .... CoreyMadden(7) 5 44
(Jim Goldie) *s.i.s: hld up: racd keenly: nvr on terms* 66/1

1-60 12 2 **Astraea**[6] 926 4-9-9 60 .... NathanEvans 1 43
(Michael Easterby) *chsd ldrs: rdn over 2f out: wknd fnl f* 6/1[2]

13 22 **Dragon Girl (IRE)**[141] 8287 4-9-8 59 .... EoinWalsh 13
(Roy Brotherton) *racd wd: mid-div: rdn over 3f out: sn wknd* 100/1

1m 14.12s (-0.38) **Going Correction** -0.075s/f (Stan) 13 Ran SP% 124.2

Speed ratings (Par 101): **99,98,97,95,95 94,92,92,91,90 90,87,58**

CSF £54.93 CT £472.70 TOTE £14.00: £3.80, £1.40, £4.30; EX 97.90 Trifecta £690.60.

Owner Keith Jones **Bred** J M Duggan & The Late T Duggan **Trained** Alpraham, Cheshire

FOCUS

The first three all came from the latter half of the field in this well-run sprint handicap. The winner has been rated as doing a bit better than his previous best this winter.

1022 BETWAY HEED YOUR HUNCH H'CAP — 1m 5f 219y (Tp)

5:30 (5:30) (Class 5) (0-75,76) 4-Y-O+

£3,752 (£1,116; £557; £300; £300; £300) Stalls Low

Form RPR

54-1 1 **Endlessly (IRE)**[31] 562 4-9-10 73 ....(h[1]) JamieSpencer 4 81+
(Olly Murphy) *s.i.s: hld up: hdwy on outer and hung lft fr over 1f out: styd on to ld wl ins fnl f: comf* 6/4[1]

25-0 2 ¾ **Enmeshing**[11] 859 6-9-3 64 .... RossaRyan 3 70
(Alexandra Dunn) *s.i.s: hld up: hdwy over 2f out: rdn to ld and hung lft fr over 1f out: hdd wl ins fnl f (vet said gelding lost its right hind shoe)* 10/1

0-52 3 1 **Spiritual Man (IRE)**[27] 622 7-9-6 67 .... LukeMorris 6 72
(Jonjo O'Neill) *chsd ldr: rdn over 2f out: ev ch over 1f out: edgd lft ins fnl f: styd on same pce* 8/1

-414 4 nk **Moon Of Baroda**[20] 700 4-9-13 76 ....(b) DavidProbert 5 80
(Charles Hills) *hld up: nt clr run over 2f out: hdwy and nt clr run over 1f out: sn rdn: kpt on (jockey said gelding hung left throughout)* 5/2[2]

2130 5 1 ¼ **Your Band**[34] 481 4-9-6 69 .... NicolaCurrie 10 71
(Jamie Osborne) *s.i.s: hld up: r.o ins fnl f: nvr trbld ldrs* 14/1

43-4 6 4 ½ **Home Before Dusk**[33] 495 4-9-3 66 ....(p[1]) CallumRodriguez 1 62
(Keith Dalgleish) *led at stdy pce: qcknd 3f out: rdn and hdd over 1f out: wknd ins fnl f* 6/1[3]

60-1 7 2 **Lady Makfi (IRE)**[53] 185 7-8-10 57 ....(p) KieranO'Neill 2 50
(Johnny Farrelly) *chsd ldrs who wnt clr 12f out: tk clsr order over 6f out: rdn over 2f out: wknd fnl f* 25/1

0-03 8 1 ¾ **Mobham (IRE)**[31] 562 4-9-4 67 .... AdamKirby 9 58
(J R Jenkins) *broke wl: sn stdd and lost pl: tk clsr order over 6f out: shkn up over 2f out: wknd over 1f out* 25/1

0-40 9 18 **Angel Gabrial (IRE)**[35] 469 10-9-4 65 .... StevieDonohoe 8 31
(Patrick Morris) *hld up: pushed along and bhd fnl 8f* 100/1

3m 5.76s (4.76) **Going Correction** -0.075s/f (Stan)

WFA 4 from 6yo+ 2lb 9 Ran SP% 118.4

Speed ratings (Par 103): **83,82,82,81,81 78,77,76,66**

CSF £18.46 CT £95.92 TOTE £1.80: £1.10, £2.40, £1.60; EX 17.60 Trifecta £90.00.

Owner Raymond Treacy **Bred** Ladyswood Stud **Trained** Wilmcote, Warks

FOCUS

This wasn't strongly run and it became more of a test of finishing speed than it should have been. Muddling form, with an ordinary standard set around the second, third and fourth.

1023 BETWAY SPRINT H'CAP — 5f 21y (Tp)

6:00 (6:00) (Class 5) (0-70,70) 3-Y-O+

£3,752 (£1,116; £557; £300; £300; £300) Stalls Low

Form RPR

2353 1 **A Sure Welcome**[8] 907 5-10-0 70 ....(b) LukeMorris 2 80
(John Spearing) *chsd ldrs: shkn up over 1f out: rdn: edgd lft and r.o to ld wl ins fnl f* 2/1[1]

005- 2 1 **Qaaraat**[167] 7436 4-9-12 68 .... CamHardie 11 74
(Antony Brittain) *hld up: swtchd lft over 4f out: hdwy over 1f out: rdn to ld ins fnl f: sn hdd: styd on same pce towards fin* 14/1

-432 3 3 **Big Time Maybe (IRE)**[12] 823 4-9-10 66 ....(p) AdamKirby 3 62
(Michael Attwater) *prom: rdn over 1f out: styd on u.p to go 3rd towards fin* 3/1[2]

311- 4 ¾ **Poeta Brasileiro (IRE)**[78] 9587 4-9-13 69 .... RaulDaSilva 7 62
(Seamus Durack) *led over 4f out: rdn over 1f out: hdd ins fnl f: wknd towards fin* 5/1[3]

5-60 5 ½ **Fethiye Boy**[27] 626 5-9-6 62 .... DavidProbert 1 53
(Ronald Harris) *led: hdd over 4f out: chsd ldrs: rdn over 1f out: wknd ins fnl f* 8/1

0-06 6 2 ¼ **Hello Girl**[11] 849 4-9-8 64 .... FrannyNorton 9 47
(Dean Ivory) *hld up in tch: shkn up over 1f out: nt trble ldrs* 25/1

5321 7 1 ¼ **Pink Flamingo**[11] 854 3-8-13 68 ....(b) JoeFanning 4 41
(Mark Johnston) *s.i.s and hmpd s: nt clr run 4f out: shkn up over 1f out: nt trble ldrs (jockey said filly was slowly into stride)* 6/1

020- 8 ¾ **Krystallite**[104] 9176 6-9-3 64 ....(b) TheodoreLadd(5) 10 40
(Scott Dixon) *chsd ldr over 3f out: rdn and ev ch over 1f out: wknd ins fnl f* 50/1

52-0 9 1 **Vimy Ridge**[14] 790 7-9-8 69 ....(t) DarraghKeenan(5) 6 41
(Alan Bailey) *in rr: pushed along 1/2-way: nvr on terms* 50/1

23-3 10 ¾ **Harperelle**[15] 787 3-9-0 69 .... AndrewMullen 5 33
(Alistair Whillans) *sn pushed along in rr: bhd fr 1/2-way* 40/1

-064 11 ½ **Jacob's Pillow**[20] 707 8-9-4 63 ....(p) PhilDennis(3) 8 31
(Rebecca Bastiman) *hmpd sn after s: towards rr and ct wd 1/2-way: wknd over 1f out* 66/1

1m 0.52s (-1.38) **Going Correction** -0.075s/f (Stan)

WFA 3 from 4yo+ 13lb 11 Ran SP% 118.8

Speed ratings (Par 103): **108,106,101,100,99 96,94,92,91,90 89**

CSF £31.89 CT £87.24 TOTE £2.40: £1.30, £4.10, £1.40; EX 31.40 Trifecta £136.50.

Owner Kinnersley Partnership 3 **Bred** Richard Evans Bloodstock **Trained** Kinnersley, Worcs

FOCUS

There was plenty of pace on in this routine handicap, which was run less than a second outside the standard. The winner has been rated in line with the better view of his form.

1024 BETWAY LIVE CASINO H'CAP — 1m 4f 51y (Tp)

6:30 (6:30) (Class 6) (0-65,65) 4-Y-O+

£3,105 (£924; £461; £300; £300; £300) Stalls Low

Form RPR

-164 1 **Arabic Culture (USA)**[15] 784 5-9-7 65 .... SamJames 7 74
(Grant Tuer) *hld up: hdwy on outer over 2f out: rdn to ld ins fnl f: r.o: eased nr fin* 6/1[3]

0-03 2 3 **Make Good (IRE)**[31] 559 4-9-2 61 ....(bt[1]) DavidProbert 9 66
(David Dennis) *chsd ldr: rdn and hmpd over 1f out: styd on same pce ins fnl f* 12/1

-624 3 1 ½ **Mood For Mischief**[18] 731 4-9-3 62 ....(p[1]) LiamKeniry 6 65
(Ed Walker) *prom: rdn whn hmpd over 1f out: styd on* 8/1

0-52 4 ½ **Dream Magic (IRE)**[34] 481 5-9-4 62 .... AndrewMullen 5 63
(Mark Loughnane) *led at stdy pce: qcknd over 3f out: rdn and hung rt over 1f out: hdd and no ex ins fnl f* 7/2[1]

3-36 5 2 ¼ **Flood Defence (IRE)**[28] 607 5-9-3 61 .... AdamKirby 2 58
(Iain Jardine) *trckd ldrs: rdn over 2f out: wknd ins fnl f* 7/2[1]

-144 6 nse **Tetradrachm**[15] 782 6-9-5 63 ....(tp) StevieDonohoe 3 60
(Rebecca Menzies) *hld up: pushed along over 2f out: hdwy over 1f out: styd on same pce ins fnl f* 4/1[2]

3-50 7 3 ¼ **Chantresse (IRE)**[11] 859 4-9-5 64 ....(p) JosephineGordon 4 57
(Mark Usher) *s.i.s: hld up: shkn up over 2f out: nt trble ldrs (jockey said filly sat in the stalls and was slowly away as a result)* 33/1

0-53 8 3 ½ **Ripley (IRE)**[15] 782 4-9-1 60 ....(t) RichardKingscote 1 48
(Charles Hills) *hld up: shkn up over 2f out: sn outpcd* 8/1

5-40 9 1 ¼ **Masters Apprentice (IRE)**[27] 619 4-9-0 62 ....(b[1]) GaryMahon(3) 10 48
(Sylvester Kirk) *hld up: hdwy on outer 5f out: rdn over 3f out: wknd over 1f out* 16/1

600- 10 12 **Eurato (FR)**[161] 7650 9-9-4 62 ....(p) PaddyMathers 12 27
(Derek Shaw) *s.i.s: a in rr: bhd fnl 4f* 100/1

620- 11 14 **Folies Bergeres**[43] 9664 4-9-4 63 .... RobHornby 8 7
(Grace Harris) *chsd ldrs tl rdn and wknd over 3f out* 66/1

2m 38.12s (-2.68) **Going Correction** -0.075s/f (Stan)

WFA 4 from 5yo+ 1lb 11 Ran SP% 120.0

Speed ratings (Par 101): **105,103,102,101,100 100,97,95,94,86 77**

CSF £76.63 CT £587.77 TOTE £6.60: £2.60, £3.10, £3.30; EX 68.90 Trifecta £362.50.

Owner Grant Tuer **Bred** Darley **Trained** Birkby, N Yorks

FOCUS

Ordinary handicap form. Straightforward form in behind the winner.

1025 SUNRACING.CO.UK H'CAP — 1m 142y (Tp)

7:00 (7:00) (Class 4) (0-80,82) 4-Y-O+

£5,530 (£1,645; £822; £411; £300; £300) Stalls Low

Form RPR

000- 1 **International Law**[104] 9182 5-8-10 67 .... CamHardie 7 74
(Antony Brittain) *chsd ldrs: shkn up over 2f out: rdn over 1f out: r.o to ld wl ins fnl f* 10/1

-440 2 1 **High Acclaim (USA)**[4] 962 5-9-4 75 ....(p) DavidProbert 10 80
(Roger Teal) *chsd ldr over 7f out: rdn to ld over 1f out: hdd wl ins fnl f* 5/1[2]

/2-0 3 1 ½ **Confrontational (IRE)**[11] 856 5-9-11 82 ....(p) JoeFanning 1 84
(Jennie Candlish) *led at stdy pce: qcknd over 2f out: hdd over 1f out: styd on same pce ins fnl f* 6/1[3]

0-25 4 1 ¼ **Roman De Brut (IRE)**[10] 886 7-8-4 64 .... JaneElliott(3) 3 63
(Ivan Furtado) *chsd ldrs: swtchd lft over 1f out: sn rdn: no ex ins fnl f* 7/1

0-66 5 ½ **Decoration Of War (IRE)**[10] 886 4-8-11 68 .... LukeMorris 8 66
(Michael Appleby) *hld up: rdn over 2f out: nt trble ldrs* 13/8[1]

-346 6 ½ **Come On Tier (FR)**[31] 552 4-9-5 76 .... JamieSpencer 5 73
(David Simcock) *hld up: hdwy over 3f out: rdn over 1f out: styd on same pce* 5/1[2]

-033 7 ¾ **Global Style (IRE)**[12] 836 4-8-11 68 .... GeorgeDowning 9 63
(Tony Carroll) *hld up: bhd and pushed along over 2f out: styd on towards fin* 8/1

0-50 8 hd **Gabrial's Kaka (IRE)**[36] 463 9-8-8 65 .... PaddyMathers 6 59
(Patrick Morris) *hld up: rdn over 1f out: n.d* 100/1

00-0 9 3 ¼ **Blacklooks (IRE)**[10] 886 4-9-1 72 .... KieranO'Neill 2 59
(Ivan Furtado) *s.s: hld up: shkn up over 1f out: wknd ins fnl f (jockey said gelding was slowly away)* 33/1

1m 47.91s (-2.19) **Going Correction** -0.075s/f (Stan) 9 Ran SP% 122.3

Speed ratings (Par 105): **106,105,103,102,102 101,101,100,98**

CSF £62.91 CT £338.55 TOTE £13.40: £3.10, £1.90, £1.70; EX 86.90 Trifecta £503.20.

Owner John And Tony Jarvis And Partner **Bred** Ed's Stud Ltd **Trained** Warthill, N Yorks

FOCUS
Nothing got involved from the rear with the first four always filling the same positions, albeit in a different order. Muddling form. This is the best the winner has been rated since his Newcastle win last February, while the second has been rated to his best since his Spring Mile win. The third has been rated to form.

1026 FOLLOW TOP TIPSTER TEMPLEGATE AT SUN RACING H'CAP 7f 36y (Tp)
7:30 (7:30) (Class 6) (0-52,52) 3-Y-0+
£3,105 (£924; £461; £300; £300; £300) **Stalls High**

Form RPR
00-5 **1** **Seaforth (IRE)**[34] 484 7-9-5 **50**.......................... FinleyMarsh(3) 7 57
(Adrian Wintle) *hld up: shkn up over 1f out: hung lft and r.o ins fnl f to ld towards fin* **8/1**
2233 **2** 1 **Dodgy Bob**[10] 887 6-9-4 **49**..........................(v) PhilDennis(3) 12 54
(Michael Mullineaux) *chsd ldr: rdn to ld wl ins fnl f: hdd towards fin* **7/1**[3]
-601 **3** 1 1/4 **Tarseekh**[29] 594 6-9-2 **51**..........................(b) SeamusCronin(7) 11 52
(Charlie Wallis) *pushed along to ld: rdn over 1f out: hdd wl ins fnl f* **10/1**
5350 **4** nk **Thorntoun Lady (USA)**[15] 788 9-9-10 **52**.......... AlistairRawlinson 1 53
(Jim Goldie) *hld up in tch: swtchd rt over 1f out: sn rdn: hmpd ins fnl f: styd on* **6/1**[2]
-216 **5** 3/4 **Rapid Rise (IRE)**[10] 887 5-9-6 **48**..........................(p) KieranO'Neill 3 47
(Milton Bradley) *chsd ldrs: drvn along over 2f out: nt clr run wl ins fnl f: styd on* **6/1**[2]
-303 **6** shd **Classy Cailin (IRE)**[32] 530 4-9-9 **51**.......................... EoinWalsh 4 51
(Mark Loughnane) *hld up: nt clr run over 2f out: hdwy over 1f out: nt rch ldrs* **6/1**[2]
65-0 **7** 1 1/4 **Allleedsaren'Twe**[14] 792 4-9-3 **48**.......................... JaneElliott(3) 10 44
(Shaun Harris) *chsd ldrs: rdn over 2f out: hmpd ins fnl f: styd on same pce* **66/1**
140- **8** 3/4 **Ancient Astronaut**[104] 9189 6-9-6 **48**..........................(h) LukeMorris 8 42
(Karl Thornton, Ire) *hld up: shkn up over 1f out: nt trble ldrs* **8/1**
3004 **9** hd **Diamond Pursuit**[10] 887 4-9-7 **49**.......................... JasonHart 2 42
(Ivan Furtado) *chsd ldrs: rdn over 1f out: hmpd and no ex wl ins fnl f* **4/1**[1]
550- **10** shd **Sunnyside Lady**[68] 9720 4-9-6 **48**..........................(t) NathanEvans 6 41
(Michael Easterby) *hld up: hdwy on outer over 2f out: rdn over 1f out: wknd ins fnl f* **10/1**
-000 **11** 3/4 **Daze Out (IRE)**[12] 830 4-9-6 **48**..........................(b[1]) TonyHamilton 5 39
(Richard Fahey) *s.s: n.d* **16/1**
-200 **12** 2 3/4 **Admirable Art (IRE)**[29] 594 9-9-7 **49**.......................... AdamKirby 9 33
(Tony Carroll) *hld up: rdn over 1f out: eased whn btn ins fnl f* **20/1**
1m 28.47s (-0.33) **Going Correction** -0.075s/f (Stan) **12 Ran SP% 127.9**
Speed ratings (Par 101): **98,96,95,95,94 94,92,91,91,91 90,87**
CSF £68.30 CT £594.88 TOTE £11.00: £4.30, £3.00, £3.60; EX 84.30 Trifecta £751.90.
Owner Wintle Racing Club **Bred** W Maxwell Ervine **Trained** Westbury-On-Severn, Gloucs

FOCUS
This lowly handicap was run at what looked a good gallop. The second has been rated in line with his low grade Brighton win.
T/Plt: £537.40 to a £1 stake. Pool: £102,262.12 - 138.89 winning units T/Qpdt: £59.70 to a £1 stake. Pool: £16,143.54 - 199.97 winning units **Colin Roberts**

1027 - (Foreign Racing) - See Raceform Interactive

992 CHANTILLY (R-H)
Tuesday, March 5

OFFICIAL GOING: Polytrack: standard

1028a PRIX DU BOIS BONNET (CLAIMER) (3YO) (ALL-WEATHER TRACK) (POLYTRACK) 6f 110y(P)
1:55 3-Y-0 **£12,162** (£4,864; £3,648; £2,432; £1,216)

RPR
1 **Big Boots (IRE)**[31] 3-9-4 0.......................... MaximeGuyon 1 85
(F Rossi, France) **6/5**[1]
2 1/2 **Footstepsanpie (IRE)**[121] 8863 3-8-11 0.......................... CristianDemuro 7 77
(A Botti, Italy) **37/10**[2]
3 3 **Beleaguerment (IRE)**[12] 838 3-8-8..........................(b) HollieDoyle(3) 2 68
(Archie Watson) *pushed along early to trck ldrs: urged along 2f out: rdn to chse ldrs against far rail over 1f out: chsd wnr and kpt on ins fnl f* **74/10**[3]
4 1 1/4 **Realityhacking (FR)**[52] 217 3-8-11 0.......... Pierre-CharlesBoudot 6 64
(F Chappet, France) **181/10**
5 3/4 **Enough Said**[13] 3-9-4 0.......................... AntoineHamelin 8 69
(Matthieu Palussiere, France) **18/1**
6 nse **Tiptop (FR)**[135] 3-9-2 0.......................... VincentCheminaud 5 67
(Hue & Lamotte D'Argy, France) **126/10**
7 1 1/4 **Brandon (FR)**[13] 798 3-8-11 0.......................... MickaelBarzalona 10 58
(Marco Botti) *hld up towards rr: hdwy 2f out: rdn and ev ch over 1f out: drvn but no ex ins fnl f* **25/1**
8 3 **Stade Velodrome (FR)**[24] 3-8-11 0.......................... StephanePasquier 9 50
(K Borgel, France) **102/10**
9 2 **Oh My Oh My (IRE)**[20] 3-8-11 0..........................(p) EddyHardouin 4 44
(Matthieu Palussiere, France) **49/1**
10 1/2 **Synchrone (FR)** 3-9-1 0.......................... AnthonyCrastus 3 46
(Cedric Rossi, France) **103/10**
1m 18.57s **10 Ran SP% 120.1**
PARI-MUTUEL (all including 1 euro stake): WIN 2.20; PLACE 1.20, 1.50, 1.80; DF 3.80;.
Owner L Haegel **Bred** A Malone **Trained** France

1029a-1030a (Foreign Racing) - See Raceform Interactive

940 KEMPTON (A.W) (R-H)
Wednesday, March 6

OFFICIAL GOING: Polytrack: standard to slow
Wind: Fresh, mostly across (away from stands) Weather: Overcast, heavy shower during race 2

1031 MOVE OVER TO MATCHBOOK H'CAP 1m 1f 219y(P)
4:55 (4:58) (Class 2) (0-105,107) 4-Y-0+
£15,562 (£4,660; £2,330; £1,165; £582; £292) **Stalls Low**

Form RPR
1-11 **1** **Matterhorn (IRE)**[14] 800 4-9-9 **107**.......................... JoeFanning 2 118+
(Mark Johnston) *mde virtually all: drew clr 2f out: pushed out fnl f: comf* **8/11**[1]
1111 **2** 5 **Executive Force**[13] 825 5-8-7 **91**..........................(p) FrannyNorton 4 92+
(Michael Wigham) *hld up in last pair: waiting for room on inner fr 3f out to 2f out: prog over 1f out: styd on to take 2nd ins fnl f: no ch w wnr (jockey said gelding was denied a clear run on the first and final bends)* **4/1**[2]
-313 **3** 3 1/4 **Nonios (IRE)**[18] 764 7-8-9 **93**..........................(h) KieranO'Neill 3 88
(David Simcock) *dwlt: hld up in last: rdn and prog on wd outside 2f out: chsd clr wnr over 1f out: no imp and lost 2nd ins fnl f* **14/1**
231- **4** 4 1/2 **Oasis Fantasy (IRE)**[169] 7387 8-8-3 **87**.......................... LukeMorris 5 73
(David Simcock) *chsd wnr 2f: styd in tch: rdn 3f out: wknd over 1f out* **25/1**
-060 **5** 1 **Dark Red (IRE)**[13] 847 7-8-11 **95**..........................(p[1]) TomMarquand 6 79
(Ed Dunlop) *prom: prog to chse wnr over 4f out: rdn over 2f out lost 2nd and wknd over 1f out* **7/1**[3]
421- **6** 7 **Ghayadh**[172] 7274 4-8-4 **88**..........................(t[1]) MartinDwyer 1 58
(Stuart Williams) *plld hrd: cl up tl wknd qckly u.p 2f out (jockey said gelding ran too freely and hung right-handed)* **16/1**
42-0 **7** 3 **Kyllachy Gala**[42] 368 6-8-11 **95**..........................(p[1]) OisinMurphy 7 59
(Warren Greatrex) *dwlt: rousted to chse wnr after 2f to over 4f out: wknd over 3f out: sn bhd* **20/1**
2m 3.98s (-4.02) **Going Correction** -0.025s/f (Stan) **7 Ran SP% 111.6**
Speed ratings (Par 109): **115,111,108,104,104 98,96**
CSF £3.60 TOTE £1.30: £1.10, £1.70; EX 4.10 Trifecta £12.30.
Owner Sheikh Hamdan bin Mohammed Al Maktoum **Bred** Barronstown Stud **Trained** Middleham Moor, N Yorks

FOCUS
Plain sailing for the favourite, who defied a high mark but had the run of the race. The race could be rated higher at face value.

1032 MATCHBOOK TIME TO MOVE OVER H'CAP 1m (P)
5:30 (5:30) (Class 7) (0-50,54) 4-Y-0+ **£2,587** (£770; £384; £192) **Stalls Low**

Form RPR
2-21 **1** **Jai Hanuman (IRE)**[5] 969 5-9-11 **54** 6ex..........................(t) FrannyNorton 3 69
(Michael Wigham) *hld up in midfield: prog over 2f out: rdn to cl over 1f out: led ins fnl f: r.o and sn clr* **13/8**[1]
-006 **2** 4 1/2 **Dawn Commando**[20] 717 4-9-3 **46**..........................(b) AdamKirby 6 51
(Daniel Kubler) *led after 100yds: drvn clr over 2f out: hdd ins fnl f: sn btn and jst clung on for 2nd* **9/1**
0-01 **3** hd **Purple Paddy**[6] 941 4-9-8 **51** 6ex.......................... JohnFahy 11 55
(Jimmy Fox) *hld up wl in rr: prog arnd rivals bnd over 3f out: rdn over 2f out: styd on to take 3rd nr fin and nrly snatched 2nd* **10/3**[2]
-045 **4** 1 1/4 **Shyarch**[11] 887 5-9-5 **48**..........................(p) EoinWalsh 2 49
(Christine Dunnett) *t.k.h: led 100yds: trckd ldrs after: drvn to take 2nd 2f out to 1f out: wknd (jockey said gelding hung left-handed)* **12/1**
-042 **5** 3 1/2 **Ahfad**[6] 940 4-9-4 **47**..........................(b) HectorCrouch 12 40
(Gary Moore) *hld up in rr: rdn over 2f out: kpt on one pce over 1f out: n.d* **16/1**
0564 **6** 1 1/2 **Jeremy's Jet (IRE)**[6] 941 8-9-4 **47**..........................(t) RichardKingscote 5 37
(Tony Carroll) *chsd ldr after 1f to 2f out: wknd u.p* **6/1**[3]
3-30 **7** 3/4 **Woggle (IRE)**[35] 485 4-9-6 **49**..........................(b) KieranO'Neill 4 37
(Geoffrey Deacon) *chsd ldrs: urged along over 3f out: hanging and racd awkwardly whn rdn over 2f out: no prog* **12/1**
5-60 **8** 1 1/4 **Gracie Stansfield**[42] 363 5-9-5 **48**.......................... GeorgeDowning 7 33
(Tony Carroll) *s.i.s: nvr gng wl: a towards rr* **33/1**
0-50 **9** 1/2 **Runaiocht (IRE)**[47] 288 9-9-3 **46**..........................(b) OisinMurphy 8 30
(Brian Forsey) *t.k.h: trapped out wd in midfield: lost pl over 2f out: nudged along and fdd* **25/1**
00 **10** 3/4 **Mr Potter**[42] 357 6-9-5 **48**..........................(v) TomMarquand 9 30
(Richard Guest) *hld up in last: pushed along and no prog 3f out: no ch after* **40/1**
-002 **11** 3 1/2 **Madame Jo Jo**[30] 600 4-8-13 **47**..........................(p) KatherineBegley(5) 10 21
(Sarah Hollinshead) *chsd ldrs: hanging lft bnd 4f out: wknd over 2f out (jockey said filly ran too freely and hung left-handed)* **25/1**
0040 **12** 7 **Fearaun (IRE)**[15] 789 4-9-2 **45**..........................(t[1]) PaddyMathers 1
(Stella Barclay) *nvr bttr than midfield: wknd over 3f out: bhd fnl 2f* **25/1**
1m 39.63s (-0.17) **Going Correction** -0.025s/f (Stan) **12 Ran SP% 123.6**
Speed ratings (Par 97): **99,94,94,93,89 88,87,86,85,84 81,74**
CSF £17.26 CT £48.63 TOTE £2.50: £1.40, £2.20, £1.30; EX 21.30 Trifecta £89.70.
Owner Ms I D Heerowa **Bred** Lynn Lodge Stud **Trained** Newmarket, Suffolk

FOCUS
This was solidly run and they finished fairly strung out.

1033 MATCHBOOK CASINO NOVICE STKS (DIV I) 1m (P)
6:00 (6:04) (Class 5) 3-Y-0 **£3,881** (£1,155; £577; £288) **Stalls Low**

Form RPR
42 **1** **I'm Available (IRE)**[18] 761 3-8-11 0.......................... OisinMurphy 9 73
(Andrew Balding) *mde all: clr w runner-up fr 2f out: rdn and styd on fnl f: readily* **6/1**[3]
1 **2** 2 1/2 **Moongazer**[39] 438 3-9-4 0.......................... RichardKingscote 10 74
(Charles Hills) *chsd wnr: only threat fr 2f out: tried to mount a chal on inner over 1f out: styd on same pce fnl f an readily hld* **25/1**
3 4 1/2 **Ironclad** 3-9-2 0.......................... JimCrowley 1 62+
(Hugo Palmer) *dwlt: wl in rr: urged along and rn green over 2f out: prog over 1f out: styd on fnl f to take 3rd last strides* **10/11**[1]
0- **4** nk **Swiss Cheer (FR)**[187] 6753 3-9-2 0.......................... LukeMorris 11 61+
(Jonathan Portman) *dwlt: wl in rr: rn into trble briefly over 2f out and rn green after: shkn up and styd on fnl f* **66/1**
5 1/2 **Lumination** 3-9-2 0.......................... RobHornby 6 60+
(Martyn Meade) *sn in midfield: pushed along over 2f out: rn green but styd on ins fnl f: no ch* **16/1**
1- **6** hd **Roma Bangkok**[188] 6713 3-9-9 0.......................... AndreaAtzeni 5 67
(Marco Botti) *chsd ldng pair: lft bhd fr 2f out: no imp after: lost 3 pls nr fin* **15/8**[2]
0 **7** 1 1/4 **Poor Auld Paddy**[28] 615 3-9-2 0.......................... DavidProbert 7 57
(David Elsworth) *chsd ldng trio: rdn over 2f out: wknd over 1f out* **50/1**
54 **8** 6 **Ardimento (IRE)**[33] 534 3-9-2 0.......................... AlistairRawlinson 8 43
(Rod Millman) *hld up and sn in last: pushed along over 2f out: no great prog and nvr involved (jockey said gelding ran too freely)* **40/1**
54- **9** 2 3/4 **Achaeus (GER)**[97] 9308 3-9-2 0.......................... JosephineGordon 3 37
(Ed Dunlop) *nvr beyond midfield: wknd over 2f out* **50/1**
0-4 **10** 3/4 **Oliver Hardy**[13] 836 3-9-2 0..........................(t[1]) RaulDaSilva 4 35
(Paul Cole) *broke w ldrs but heavily restrained and sn in last pair: no prog over 2f out* **33/1**
1m 40.55s (0.75) **Going Correction** -0.025s/f (Stan) **10 Ran SP% 122.0**
Speed ratings (Par 98): **95,92,88,87,87 87,85,79,77,76**
CSF £137.11 TOTE £7.00: £1.90, £3.20, £1.10; EX 57.80 Trifecta £176.80.
Owner George Strawbridge **Bred** George Strawbridge **Trained** Kingsclere, Hants

FOCUS
Few got into this, the first two having it between them in the straight. The winner has been rated up a bit on her Lingfield latest.

1034 MATCHBOOK CASINO NOVICE STKS (DIV II) 1m (P)
6:30 (6:35) (Class 5) 3-Y-O **£3,881** (£1,155; £577; £288) **Stalls** Low

Form RPR

1 **Ebury** 3-9-2 0 RobHornby 9 82+
(Martyn Meade) *s.s: racd in last quartet tl gd prog on outer over 2f out: pushed into ld over 1f out: rdn and styd on wl fnl f: promising debut* **6/1**[3]

-2 **2** *2 ¾* **Majestic Dawn (IRE)**[62] 32 3-9-2 0 RaulDaSilva 7 75
(Paul Cole) *led: rdn 2f out: edgd lft fr over 1f out: sn hdd and outpcd* **3/1**[2]

5-4 **3** *1* **Htilominlo**[35] 486 3-9-2 0 (t[1]) OisinMurphy 4 73
(Sylvester Kirk) *chsd ldng quartet: shkn up and prog 2f out: tk 3rd fnl f: kpt on same pce* **25/1**

4 *1 ¼* **Global Falcon** 3-9-2 0 JimCrowley 11 74+
(Charles Hills) *dwlt: sn in midfield: prog over 2f out: shkn up and cl 3rd whn squeezed out jst over 1f out: nt rcvr but styd on* **20/1**

5 *9* **Liliofthelamplight (IRE)** 3-8-11 0 JoeFanning 3 44
(Mark Johnston) *s.s: rn green in last pair: nudged along over 2f out: sn lft bhd: kpt on past wkng rivals to take remote 5th nr fin* **11/1**

1 **6** *1* **Don Jupp (USA)**[28] 615 3-9-9 0 DanielMuscutt 6 54
(Marco Botti) *trckd ldrs: moved up stylishly to chal over 2f out: sn shkn up and fnd nil: lost pl wl over 1f out then hmpd: wknd (jockey said colt suffered interference in the home straight. Vet said colt bled from the nose)* **1/1**[1]

0 **7** *¾* **Sir Canford (IRE)**[18] 761 3-9-2 0 TomMarquand 2 45
(Ali Stronge) *a in last quartet: no prog over 2f out* **66/1**

0- **8** *shd* **Martin King**[77] 9607 3-9-2 0 AdamKirby 5 45
(Clive Cox) *chsd ldng pair: rdn over 2f out: lost pl and wknd over 1f out* **12/1**

04- **9** *2 ¼* **Show The World**[216] 5656 3-9-2 0 (h[1]) StevieDonohoe 1 40
(Charlie Fellowes) *dwlt: t.k.h: hld up in last pair: no prog over 2f out: wknd* **33/1**

00- **10** *13* **Freedreams**[65] 9771 3-8-11 0 LukeMorris 10 5
(Tony Carroll) *chsd ldr to over 2f out: wknd rapidly: t.o* **100/1**

1m 39.79s (-0.01) **Going Correction** -0.025s/f (Stan) **10** Ran SP% **119.3**
Speed ratings (Par 98): **99,96,95,94,85 84,83,83,80,67**
CSF £23.98 TOTE £7.30: £1.50, £1.20, £4.60; EX 28.50 Trifecta £353.30.
Owner Chelsea Thoroughbreds - M E R **Bred** Miss K Rausing **Trained** Manton, Wilts

FOCUS
The quicker of the two divisions by 0.76sec. It's been rated around the second and third, but the level is a bit fluid.

1035 "ROAD TO THE KENTUCKY DERBY" CONDITIONS STKS (PLUS 10 RACE) 1m (P)
7:00 (7:05) (Class 2) 3-Y-O
£43,575 (£13,048; £6,524; £3,262; £1,631; £819) **Stalls** Low

Form RPR

11-1 **1** **Jahbath**[41] 391 3-9-5 102 JimCrowley 5 100+
(William Haggas) *trckd ldr: shkn up over 2f out: led wl over 1f out: rdn clr sn after: styd on stoutly fnl f* **8/13**[1]

400- **2** *2* **Getchagetchagetcha**[171] 7346 3-9-5 100 AdamKirby 6 95
(Clive Cox) *chsd ldrs: urged along over 3f out: prog wl over 1f out: tk 2nd ins fnl f: styd on but no real imp on wnr* **20/1**

5-21 **3** *½* **Target Zone**[49] 251 3-9-5 83 DavidProbert 3 94
(David Elsworth) *t.k.h: cl up: rdn 2f out: tk 2nd briefly fnl f: styd on* **4/1**[2]

16- **4** *nk* **Chairmanoftheboard (IRE)**[130] 8646 3-9-5 0 CallumShepherd 7 93
(Mick Channon) *in tch: shkn up over 2f out: prog over 1f out: pressed for a pl fnl f: kpt on* **8/1**

31- **5** *½* **Spanish Mission (USA)**[116] 8994 3-9-5 0 JamieSpencer 1 92
(David Simcock) *hld up in last pair: pushed along over 2f out: prog over 1f out: pressed for a pl fnl f: no ex nr fin: nt disgracd* **6/1**[3]

00-3 **6** *6* **Amplify (IRE)**[46] 312 3-9-5 86 TomMarquand 2 78
(Brian Meehan) *led at brisk pce: kicked on over 2f out: hdd wl over 1f out: lost 2nd and wknd qckly fnl f* **66/1**

05-1 **7** *4 ½* **Greybychoice (IRE)**[11] 881 3-9-5 0 EoinWalsh 9 68
(Nick Littmoden) *v.s.i.s: mostly in last and nvr able to figure* **100/1**

253- **8** *5* **Daafr (IRE)**[146] 8139 3-9-5 89 (p w) AndreaAtzeni 8 56
(John Gosden) *racd v wd first 3f: w ldrs tl wknd rapidly wl over 1f out* **14/1**

1m 38.78s (-1.02) **Going Correction** -0.025s/f (Stan) **8** Ran SP% **121.2**
Speed ratings (Par 104): **104,102,101,101,100 94,90,85**
CSF £19.71 TOTE £1.30: £1.10, £4.10, £1.50; EX 16.40 Trifecta £52.80.
Owner Hamdan Al Maktoum **Bred** Exors Of The Late Sir Eric Parker, Crimbourne Stud **Trained** Newmarket, Suffolk

FOCUS
A good race, and a pleasing performance from Jahbath, who continues to impress this AW season and may well have booked his ticket for World Cup night at Meydan. The level looks sound rated around the second, fourth and fifth.

1036 MATCHBOOK VIP H'CAP 7f (P)
7:30 (7:33) (Class 4) (0-80,81) 4-Y-O+
£6,469 (£1,925; £962; £481; £400; £400) **Stalls** Low

Form RPR

640- **1** **La Maquina**[147] 8101 4-9-4 77 (t w) NicolaCurrie 9 86+
(George Baker) *stdd s and dropped in fr wd draw: hld up in last: gd prog on inner 2f out: rdn over 1f out: sustained effrt fnl f to ld last 75yds* **7/1**

015- **2** *½* **The Lamplighter (FR)**[82] 9535 4-8-9 75 (t) WilliamCarver[(7)] 1 82
(George Baker) *trckd ldrs: wnt 2nd 2f out: chal over 1f out: upsides ins fnl f: jst outpcd nr fin* **11/2**[3]

0-12 **3** *shd* **In The Red (IRE)**[5] 962 6-9-2 75 (p) AdamKirby 10 81
(Martin Smith) *led: rdn over 2f out: hrd pressed over 1f out: kpt on wl but hdd last 75yds* **13/2**

/-55 **4** *1 ¼* **Global Tango (IRE)**[42] 361 4-9-4 77 JimCrowley 2 80
(Charles Hills) *trckd ldng pair: rdn and nt qckn 2f out: kpt on same pce after* **8/1**

5213 **5** *¾* **Master Diver**[14] 807 4-9-7 80 LukeMorris 4 81
(Sir Mark Prescott Bt) *t.k.h: hld up in midfield: rdn and sme prog over 2f out: chsd ldrs over 1f out: no hdwy after* **9/2**[2]

2006 **6** *1 ¾* **Hammer Gun (USA)**[14] 812 6-9-0 73 (v) PaddyMathers 7 69
(Derek Shaw) *hld up in rr: rdn and prog over 2f out to chse ldrs over 1f out: no hdwy after: fdd ins fnl f* **14/1**

1321 **7** *2 ¼* **Blame Culture (USA)**[14] 812 4-9-8 81 DavidProbert 6 71
(George Margarson) *hld up in midfield: urged along and nt qckn over 2f out: no prog (jockey said gelding hung left-handed under pressure)* **3/1**[1]

0/0- **8** *2 ¾* **Fighting Temeraire (IRE)**[426] 41 6-8-13 72 RobHornby 5 55
(Dean Ivory) *chsd ldr to 2f out: wknd* **20/1**

-516 **9** *½* **The British Lion (IRE)**[14] 801 4-8-11 70 RossaRyan 8 51
(Alexandra Dunn) *hld up wl in rr: rdn and no prog over 2f out* **33/1**

1-63 **10** *2 ¼* **Compas Scoobie**[18] 755 6-9-4 77 OisinMurphy 11 52
(Stuart Williams) *plld hrd: hld up in rr: no prog over 2f out: wknd and eased* **16/1**

00-6 **11** *3 ¼* **Until Midnight (IRE)**[19] 734 9-8-2 68 CierenFallon[(7)] 3 35
(Eugene Stanford) *chsd ldrs to over 2f out: wknd qckly over 1f out* **50/1**

1m 25.57s (-0.43) **Going Correction** -0.025s/f (Stan) **11** Ran SP% **117.7**
Speed ratings (Par 105): **101,100,100,98,98 96,93,90,89,87 83**
CSF £44.53 CT £270.60 TOTE £8.00: £2.80, £2.10, £2.40; EX 47.40 Trifecta £329.70.
Owner George Baker And Partners - Super Six **Bred** Equine Breeding Limited **Trained** Chiddingfold, Surrey

FOCUS
A competitive affair. It's been rated around the second, third and fourth.

1037 MATCHBOOK BETTING PODCAST H'CAP (DIV I) 6f (P)
8:00 (8:01) (Class 6) (0-65,66) 4-Y-O+
£3,105 (£924; £461; £400; £400; £400) **Stalls** Low

Form RPR

-462 **1** **Sir Ottoman (FR)**[21] 701 6-9-7 65 (tp) JasonHart 6 71
(Ivan Furtado) *led or disp ld thrght: drvn over 1f out: narrow ld last 100yds: jst prevailed* **4/1**[3]

-432 **2** *nse* **Kraka (IRE)**[4] 982 4-9-6 64 (v) KieranO'Neill 8 70
(Christine Dunnett) *plld hrd: disp ld thrght: rdn 2f out: narrow deficit 100yds out: rallied nr fin: pipped on the nod* **7/4**[1]

0-25 **3** *½* **Secret Potion**[9] 907 5-9-5 63 DavidProbert 1 67
(Ronald Harris) *chsd ldrs on inner: rdn to take 3rd wl over 1f out: steadily clsd fnl f but nvr quite able to chal* **9/1**

55-4 **4** *½* **Beepeecee**[62] 33 5-9-8 66 (p) LiamKeniry 7 69
(Thomas Gallagher) *hld up in rr: effrt over 2f out: nt clr run and swtchd lft over 1f out: rdn and styd on fnl f: nrst fin* **16/1**

0362 **5** *shd* **Dark Magic**[12] 857 5-9-1 59 (b) AdamKirby 9 62
(Dean Ivory) *towards rr: rdn over 2f out: kpt on fr over 1f out: nrst fin but nvr able to chal* **8/1**

-303 **6** *1* **Storm Melody**[7] 924 6-9-4 62 (p) TomMarquand 2 62
(Ali Stronge) *prom: rdn and nt qckn 2f out: styd chsng ldng pair tl fdd fnl f* **7/2**[2]

3-40 **7** *3 ½* **Mother Of Dragons (IRE)**[30] 596 4-9-3 61 (v) JosephineGordon 4 50
(Phil McEntee) *slowly away: mostly in last: effrt on inner 2f out: nvr on terms* **40/1**

5-02 **8** *13* **Mr Gent (IRE)**[14] 811 4-9-4 62 (p) PaulMulrennan 3 12
(Ed Dunlop) *t.k.h early: chsd ldng pair to over 2f out: wknd qckly: t.o* **20/1**

650- **9** *12* **Following Breeze (IRE)**[173] 7247 4-8-0 51 oh6 (p) IsobelFrancis[(7)] 5
(Jim Boyle) *chsd ldrs but trapped out wd: hung lft and v wd bnd 3f out: sn bhd: t.o* **66/1**

1m 13.11s (0.01) **Going Correction** -0.025s/f (Stan) **9** Ran SP% **114.3**
Speed ratings (Par 101): **98,97,97,96,96 95,90,73,57**
CSF £11.09 CT £57.71 TOTE £4.50: £1.70, £1.10, £2.90; EX 12.90 Trifecta £85.40.
Owner Carl Hodgson **Bred** Madame Marie-Therese Mimouni **Trained** Wiseton, Nottinghamshire

FOCUS
The first two were side by side throughout and there was little in it at the line.

1038 MATCHBOOK BETTING PODCAST H'CAP (DIV II) 6f (P)
8:30 (8:30) (Class 6) (0-65,65) 4-Y-O+
£3,105 (£924; £461; £400; £400; £400) **Stalls** Low

Form RPR

-400 **1** **Miracle Garden**[14] 801 7-9-7 65 (b) RichardKingscote 3 72
(Ian Williams) *hld up in 5th: prog 2f out: rdn to ld jst over 1f out: styd on to draw clr fnl f* **9/4**[2]

-500 **2** *2 ¼* **Hollander**[12] 849 5-9-5 63 (t) RossaRyan 7 63
(Alexandra Dunn) *chsd ldng trio: rdn over 2f out: responded to cl over 1f out: kpt on to take 2nd last 100yds: no ch w wnr (vet said gelding lost it's left hind shoe)* **40/1**

3246 **3** *½* **Monarch Maid**[7] 919 8-8-7 51 oh6 KieranO'Neill 5 50
(Peter Hiatt) *t.k.h: led: rdn 2f out: hdd jst over 1f out: one pce and lost 2nd last 100yds* **20/1**

510/ **4** *1 ¾* **Just For The Craic (IRE)**[475] 8795 4-9-7 65 AdamKirby 1 59
(Neil Mulholland) *dwlt: hld up in last: effrt on inner 2f out: cl enough over 1f out: fdd ins fnl f* **20/1**

1204 **5** *nk* **African Blessing**[12] 857 6-9-2 60 JamieSpencer 2 53
(John Best) *stdd s: hld up in 6th: shkn up and nt qckn jst over 2f out: kpt on fnl f but n.d* **7/2**[3]

5-52 **6** *hd* **Maximum Power (FR)**[18] 759 4-8-13 62 TheodoreLadd[(5)] 4 54
(Tim Pinfield) *trckd ldng pair: wnt 2nd 2f out to over 1f out: nt qckn and wl hld whn checked ins fnl f: fdd (jockey said gelding was denied a clear run in the closing stages)* **11/8**[1]

0-63 **7** *5* **Dreamboat Annie**[13] 824 4-9-0 58 (p) TomMarquand 9 35
(Mark Usher) *rousted to chse ldr: lost 2nd and wknd u.p 2f out* **16/1**

1m 12.7s (-0.40) **Going Correction** -0.025s/f (Stan) **7** Ran SP% **112.9**
Speed ratings (Par 101): **101,98,97,95,94 94,87**
CSF £84.26 CT £1429.59 TOTE £2.50: £2.20, £15.70; EX 51.10 Trifecta £416.70.
Owner M A Geobey **Bred** W And R Barnett Ltd **Trained** Portway, Worcs

FOCUS
A sound early pace and the faster of the two divisions by 0.41sec.
T/Jkpt: £4,000.00 to a £1 stake. Pool: £14,084.51 - 2.50 winning units T/Plt: £19.80 to a £1 stake. Pool: £83,341.61 - 3,071.20 winning units T/Qpdt: £11.60 to a £1 stake. Pool: £10,450.14 - 666.16 winning units **Jonathan Neesom**

[985] LINGFIELD (L-H)
Wednesday, March 6

OFFICIAL GOING: Polytrack: standard
Wind: LIGHT, BEHIND Weather: OVERCAST, LIGHT RAIN

1039 LADBROKES HOME OF THE ODDS BOOST H'CAP 1m 4f (P)
2:30 (2:30) (Class 6) (0-60,61) 3-Y-O **£3,105** (£924) **Stalls** Low

Form RPR

500- **1** **Glutnforpunishment**[123] 8834 3-9-9 61 DannyBrock 2 63
(Nick Littmoden) *t.k.h: mde virtually all and dictated stdy gallop: rdn ent fnl 2f: r.o and a doing enough ins fnl f* **4/7**[1]

The Form Book Flat 2019, Raceform Ltd, Newbury, RG14 5SJ

40-0 **2** *1 ¼* **Brinkleys Katie**[18] 765 3-8-11 **54**........................ RhiainIngram(5) 1 54
(Paul George) *t.k.h and hung rt thrght: swtchd rt over 8f out: upsides ldr 5f out tl hung rt bnd wl over 1f out: kpt on same pce after (jockey said filly hung right-handed)* **5/4**[2]

2m 41.69s (8.69) **Going Correction** +0.45s/f (Slow) **2** Ran SP% **108.1**
Speed ratings (Par 96): **89,88**
TOTE £1.30.
Owner A A Goodman **Bred** Rabbah Bloodstock Limited **Trained** Newmarket, Suffolk

FOCUS
A decimated card in terms of runners owing to the ongoing prize money protest. The first race was a moderate 3yo middle-distance match handicap on standard Polytrack. They went a slow gallop until the tempo increased over 3f out. A token rating has been given.

1040 BETWAY H'CAP 1m 4f (P)
3:00 (3:00) (Class 4) (0-85,78) 4-Y-O+ **£5,530** (£1,645; £822) **Stalls Low**

Form RPR
1-25 **1** **Love Rat**[13] 833 4-8-7 **64** oh2........................(v) PhilipPrince 3 66
(Scott Dixon) *chsd ldr: niggled along over 5f out: dropped to last wl over 3f out: sn rdn: 4 l 3rd 2f out: swtchd rt over 1f out: plugged on to ld ins fnl f: sn clr* **5/2**[2]

143- **2** *4* **Orobas (IRE)**[174] 7222 7-8-8 **64** oh4........................(v) MirkoSanna 2 60
(Lucinda Egerton) *led: clr 8f out tl jnd over 2f out: hdd and rdn 2f out: led again jst ins fnl f: sn hdd and btn: eased towards fin* **7/2**[3]

-154 **3** *7* **Shyron**[8] 764 8-9-8 **78**........................ DannyBrock 1 67
(Lee Carter) *stdd s: hld up in last: clsd to chse ldr wl over 3f out: upsides over 2f out: rdn to ld 2f out: hdd jst ins fnl f: sn btn and eased wl ins fnl f (jockey said gelding was slowly away)* **4/6**[1]

2m 32.3s (-0.70) **Going Correction** +0.45s/f (Slow)
WFA 4 from 6yo+ 1lb **3** Ran SP% **110.8**
Speed ratings (Par 105): **105,102,97**
CSF £9.23 TOTE £3.50; EX 8.60 Trifecta £7.90.
Owner The Love Rat Partnership **Bred** Dr A Gillespie **Trained** Babworth, Notts

FOCUS
A fair little middle-distance handicap. The winning time was considerably quicker than the first race over this C&D. The whole complexion of the race changed in the final 250 yards. It's been rated negatively.

1041 LADBROKES NOVICE STKS 1m 2f (P)
3:30 (3:30) (Class 5) 3-Y-O **£3,752** (£1,116) **Stalls Low**

Form RPR
066- **1** **Sea Of Marengo (IRE)**[88] 9459 3-8-11 **64**........................ RhiainIngram(5) 2 51+
(Paul George) *mde all and set stdy gallop: pressed and nudged along over 2f out: pushed along and asserted over 1f out: r.o wl and in command ins fnl f* **1/5**[1]

000- **2** *1 ½* **Abenaki**[138] 8384 3-9-2 **52**........................ DannyBrock 1 46
(Sheena West) *chsd wnr: shkn up 3f out: sn ev ch tl unable to match pce of wnr over 1f out: hld and one pce fnl f* **10/3**[2]

2m 15.3s (8.70) **Going Correction** +0.45s/f (Slow) **2** Ran SP% **106.4**
Speed ratings (Par 98): **83,81**
TOTE £1.10.
Owner Mrs V James **Bred** Samuel William Ormsby **Trained** Crediton, Devon

FOCUS
A modest 3yo novice match and understandably tactical. The long-odds on favourite increased the slow speed of the gallop well over 2f out and ran out a commanding winner.

1042 FOLLOW TOP TIPSTERS AT SUN RACING H'CAP 1m 1y(P)
4:00 (4:00) (Class 6) (0-65,67) 4-Y-O+ **£3,105** (£924; £461; £300) **Stalls High**

Form RPR
462- **1** **Toriano**[179] 7079 6-9-10 **66**........................ DylanAlberca-Gavilan(5) 6 70+
(Nick Littmoden) *chsd ldr: effrt wl over 1f out: rdn to ld ent fnl f: r.o wl: comf* **6/4**[1]

-000 **2** *2 ¾* **Middlescence (IRE)**[3] 309 5-9-7 **58**........................(t) MirkoSanna 3 56
(Lucinda Egerton) *led: rdn over 1f out: sn hdd and nt match pce of wnr ins fnl f* **7/1**

2-45 **3** *2 ¼* **Sweet Nature (IRE)**[42] 366 4-10-2 **67**........................ PhilipPrince 5 60
(Laura Mongan) *hld up in tch: rdn over 3f out: drvn and outpcd wl over 1f out: plugged on into 3rd ins fnl f: no ch w wnr* **7/4**[2]

0-06 **4** *2 ½* **Footstepsintherain (IRE)**[7] 925 9-9-6 **57**........................ DannyBrock 4 44
(J R Jenkins) *dwlt: sn rcvrd to trck ldrs: shkn up over 2f out: drvn and outpcd over 1f out: wknd fnl f* **4/1**[3]

1m 37.35s (-0.85) **Going Correction** +0.45s/f (Slow) **4** Ran SP% **108.9**
Speed ratings (Par 101): **101,98,96,93**
CSF £10.95 TOTE £2.90; EX 11.80 Trifecta £16.80.
Owner Chesneaux, Hassiakos & Littmoden **Bred** Southill Stud **Trained** Newmarket, Suffolk

FOCUS
A modest little handicap. The favourite ran out a ready winner in a truly-run contest. It's been rated negatively.

1043 LADBROKES H'CAP 6f 1y(P)
4:30 (4:30) (Class 3) (0-95,64) 3-Y-O **£7,246** (£2,168) **Stalls Low**

Form RPR
0260 **1** **Champagne Mondays**[13] 834 3-8-7 **50**........................(p) PhilipPrince 2 52
(Scott Dixon) *chsd ldr: rdn and ev ch over 2f out: drifted rt but led bnd 2f out: pricking ears in front but asserted and reminder 1f out: wnt clr fnl 100yds: eased cl home* **11/10**[2]

56-0 **2** *2 ¼* **Haats Off**[32] 555 3-9-7 **64**........................ DannyBrock 1 59
(Brian Barr) *sn pushed along to ld: jnd and rdn over 2f out: hdd 2f out and sn unable qck 1f out: outpcd fnl 100yds: eased cl home* **8/11**[1]

1m 13.31s (1.41) **Going Correction** +0.45s/f (Slow) **2** Ran SP% **105.5**
Speed ratings (Par 102): **99,96**
TOTE £1.70.
Owner William A Robinson & Partners **Bred** Mrs Yvette Dixon **Trained** Babworth, Notts

FOCUS
The feature race was a modest 3yo match handicap. The winning time was just over four seconds outside standard from off a muddling gallop. The winner has been rated to his Southwell form, but with little confidence.

1044 BETWAY STAYERS' H'CAP 1m 7f 169y(P)
5:00 (5:00) (Class 6) (0-60,47) 4-Y-O+ **£3,105** (£924) **Stalls Low**

Form RPR
-004 **1** **Sea's Aria (IRE)**[20] 721 8-9-6 **47**........................ MirkoSanna 3 50+
(Mark Hoad) *led and set stdy gallop: hdd over 1f out: shkn up and qcknd to ld again ins fnl f: sn in command and eased towards fin* **1/5**[1]

060/ **2** *1 ¼* **Ledbury (IRE)**[671] 2332 7-9-4 **45**........................ DannyBrock 1 45
(J R Jenkins) *stdd s: trckd wnr: rdn to chal ent fnl 2f: led over 1f out: hdd ins fnl f: sn brushed aside and eased cl home* **7/2**[2]

3m 38.87s (13.17) **Going Correction** +0.45s/f (Slow)
WFA 4 from 7yo+ 3lb **2** Ran SP% **105.6**
Speed ratings (Par 101): **85,84**
TOTE £1.10.
Owner Mrs K B Tester **Bred** Sunderland Holdings Inc **Trained** Lewes, E Sussex

FOCUS
A moderate staying match handicap. The long-odds on favourite had the superior speed in a race which turned into a sprint. A token rating has been given.
T/Plt: £53.00 to a £1 stake. Pool: £36,984.30 - 509.18 winning units T/Qpdt: £10.20 to a £1 stake. Pool: £1,601.12 - 115.07 winning units **Steve Payne**

1045 - 1048a (Foreign Racing) - See Raceform Interactive

974 DUNDALK (A.W) (L-H)
Wednesday, March 6

OFFICIAL GOING: Polytrack: standard

1049a BETVICTOR PATTON STKS (LISTED RACE) 1m (P)
7:15 (7:16) 3-Y-O

£39,864 (£12,837; £6,081; £2,702; £1,351; £675)

RPR
1 **Playa Del Puente (IRE)**[77] 9622 3-9-3 98........................ RonanWhelan 2 104+
(M Halford, Ire) *settled bhd ldrs in 3rd: racd keenly early: disp 3rd at 1/2-way: rdn in 3rd 2f out and clsd u.p to chal whn sltly hmpd 1f out: sn disp and led wl ins fnl f: kpt on wl clsng stages* **11/4**[2]

2 *½* **Western Australia (IRE)**[130] 8633 3-9-3 110........................ RyanMoore 7 103
(A P O'Brien, Ire) *trckd ldr: rdn in 2nd 2f out and ev ch ent fnl f where bmpd and hmpd: sn disp ld briefly tl hdd wl ins fnl f: hld cl home* **6/4**[1]

3 *1 ¾* **Numerian (IRE)**[26] 667 3-9-3 89........................ WayneLordan 4 99
(Joseph Patrick O'Brien, Ire) *w.w in rr: last at 1/2-way: tk clsr order and rdn far side 2f out: u.p in 4th ent fnl f: kpt on ins fnl f into 3rd fnl stride: nvr trbld ldrs* **20/1**

4 *nse* **Van Beethoven (CAN)**[172] 7292 3-9-8 107........................ DonnachaO'Brien 1 104
(A P O'Brien, Ire) *hld up in tch: racd keenly early: disp 5th at 1/2-way: gng wl in 5th 3f out: pushed along in 4th over 2f out: sn rdn and no imp on ldrs in 5th wl ins fnl f: kpt on into 4th fnl strides: jst failed for 3rd* **6/1**

5 *hd* **Colfer Me (IRE)**[26] 667 3-9-3 94........................(b) ShaneFoley 5 98
(Joseph Patrick O'Brien, Ire) *led: over 3 l clr bef st: rdn nr side under 2f out and wandered: edgd lft and sltly bmpd rival 1f out: jnd and hdd wl ins fnl f where sn no ex in 3rd: wknd into 5th cl home (jockey said colt ran around in front)* **12/1**

6 *2 ¾* **Manjeer (IRE)**[130] 8652 3-9-3 0........................ RossCoakley 6 92
(John M Oxx, Ire) *hld up: 7th 1/2-way: rdn and no imp on ldrs under 2f out: one pce after* **33/1**

7 *1 ¾* **Barys**[24] 683 3-9-3 100........................(b) EdwardGreatrex 3 88
(Archie Watson) *dwlt and bmpd sltly s: sn chsd ldrs in 4th: disp 3rd at 1/2-way: drvn bhd ldrs into st: sn rdn and no imp 2f out: one pce after (vet said colt was coughing post race)* **4/1**[3]

8 *1 ¼* **Albuquerque (IRE)**[134] 8518 3-9-3 0........................ SeamieHeffernan 8 85
(A P O'Brien, Ire) *hld up: disp 5th at 1/2-way: rdn towards rr 2f out and sn no ex: one pce after* **10/1**

1m 37.37s (-1.43) **Going Correction** +0.30s/f (Slow) **8** Ran SP% **125.4**
Speed ratings: **114,113,111,111,111 108,107,105**
CSF £8.14 TOTE £3.20: £1.30, £1.30, £6.40; DF 9.60 Trifecta £98.80.
Owner Huang Kai Wen **Bred** Dermot Kelly **Trained** Doneany, Co Kildare

FOCUS
The winner showed himself to be a very progressive colt and should have a considerable future. The balance of the third, fourth and fifth govern the level.

1050 - 1059a (Foreign Racing) - See Raceform Interactive

978 CHELMSFORD (A.W) (L-H)
Thursday, March 7

OFFICIAL GOING: Polytrack: standard
Wind: STRONG, ACROSS Weather: rain

1060 BET TOTEPLACEPOT AT TOTESPORT.COM APPRENTICE H'CAP 1m (P)
5:25 (5:31) (Class 6) (0-55,57) 4-Y-O+

£3,105 (£924; £461; £400; £400; £400) **Stalls Low**

Form RPR
0-21 **1** **Irish Times**[21] 717 4-9-4 **52**........................ DylanHogan 11 58
(Henry Spiller) *hld up in rr of main gp: dropped in bhd after 1f: hdwy on inner over 2f out: rdn to ld 1f out: in command ins fnl f: eased towards fin* **9/1**

040- **2** *1* **Captain Peaky**[206] 6096 6-8-12 **46** oh1........................ PaulaMuir 9 50
(Liam Bailey) *hld up in rr of main gp: effrt but v wd bnd 2f out: hdwy over 1f out: edging lft and kpt on ins fnl f to go 2nd cl home: nvr getting to wnr* **25/1**

4220 **3** *½* **Sea Shack**[16] 792 5-9-3 **54**........................(tp) ScottMcCullagh(3) 12 57
(Julia Feilden) *chsd ldrs: wnt 2nd over 2f out: rdn and ev ch over 1f out tl no ex and one pce ins fnl f* **16/1**

0111 **4** *nk* **Naralsaif (IRE)**[12] 887 5-9-5 **56**........................(v) KatherineBegley(3) 10 58+
(Derek Shaw) *t.k.h: chsd ldr tl led over 5f out: clr over 3f out tl pressed 2f out: edgd rt and sn u.p: hdd 1f out: no ex and kpt on same pce ins fnl f (jockey said mare hung right-handed)* **8/1**

-004 **5** *½* **Ubla (IRE)**[19] 760 6-9-3 **56**........................(e) SeanKirrane(5) 1 58
(Gay Kelleway) *hld up in rr of main gp: clsd on inner over 2f out: effrt over 1f out: kpt on ins fnl f: nvr getting on terms w wnr* **5/1**[2]

4530 **6** *1 ½* **Sir Lancelott**[3] 1015 7-8-7 **46** oh1........................ LauraCoughlan(5) 6 43
(Adrian Nicholls) *hld up wl in tch in midfield: effrt over 1f out: kpt on same pce ins fnl f* **9/1**

2451 **7** *4* **Amor Fati (IRE)**[16] 792 4-8-13 **52**........................ TristanPrice(5) 2 40
(David Evans) *t.k.h: hld up in midfield on inner: dropped to rr of main gp over 2f out: pushed along and hdwy ent fnl f: kpt on but nvr any threat to ldrs* **3/1**[1]

6-U3 **8** *¾* **Cristal Pallas Cat (IRE)**[21] 717 4-9-1 **49**........................(h) RhiainIngram 4 35
(Roger Ingram) *led tl over 5f out: chsd ldr tl over 2f out: unable qck and outpcd over 1f out: wknd ins fnl f (jockey said gelding stopped quickly)* **9/1**

5320 **9** ½ **The Special One (IRE)**[8] 924 6-9-3 **56**................(h) GraceMcEntee(5) 8 41
(Phil McEntee) *hld up towards rr of main gp: clsd on outer over 2f out: rdn and no hdwy over 1f out: wl hld fnl f* **14/1**

-006 **10** 6 **Plucky Dip**[36] 485 8-8-7 **46** oh1...................... LauraPearson(5) 13 17
(John Ryan) *midfield on outer: rdn 2f out: sn lost pl: wknd fnl f* **25/1**

455- **11** ¾ **The Third Man**[187] 6817 8-9-4 **57**.................................. MarkCrehan(5) 7 27
(Henry Spiller) *in tch in midfield: rdn 3f out: sn struggling and wl btn over 1f out: wknd fnl f* **16/1**

0-00 **12** nk **Atalanta Queen**[15] 809 4-8-7 **46** oh1..........................(v) CierenFallon(5) 5 15
(Robyn Brisland) *in tch in midfield: rdn over 2f out: sn struggling and lost pl over 1f out: wknd fnl f* **33/1**

6345 **13** 9 **Caledonian Gold**[14] 828 6-8-7 **46** oh1.............. ElishaWhittington(5) 14
(Lisa Williamson) *taken down early and led to post: chsd ldrs: rdn and lost pl qckly over 2f out: bhd fnl f* **66/1**

-633 **14** 24 **Mans Not Trot (IRE)**[7] 940 4-9-0 **55**..........................(p) EmmaTaff(7) 3 +
(Jamie Osborne) *awkward leaving stalls: slowly away and rdr lost irons: a wl detached in last: t.o (jockey said gelding jumped awkwardly from stalls causing her to lose her irons throughout the race)* **6/1**[3]

1m 40.77s (0.87) **Going Correction** +0.025s/f (Slow) **14** Ran SP% **127.6**
Speed ratings (Par 101): **96,95,94,94,93 92,88,87,86,80 80,79,70,46**
CSF £230.91 CT £3561.91 TOTE £6.80: £3.00, £8.10, £5.40; EX 234.60 Trifecta £3771.10.
Owner D Forrester **Bred** Shortgrove Manor Stud **Trained** Newmarket, Suffolk

FOCUS
A moderate affair.

1061 BET TOTEEXACTA AT TOTESPORT.COM H'CAP 6f (P)

5:55 (6:02) (Class 5) (0-75,76) 4-Y-0+

£5,175 (£1,540; £769; £400; £400; £400) **Stalls** Centre

Form RPR

4-13 **1** **Ballyquin (IRE)**[33] 564 4-9-4 **75**................................ JoshuaBryan(3) 10 85
(Andrew Balding) *mde all: rdn over 1f out: styd on wl u.p ins fnl f* **6/1**[3]

1-24 **2** 1 **Enthaar**[29] 618 4-9-6 **74**..(t) SeanLevey 4 81
(Stuart Williams) *chsd wnr: effrt over 1f out: kpt on u.p but a hld ins fnl f* **9/4**[1]

0-25 **3** ¾ **Cappananty Con**[13] 849 5-9-5 **73**......................... RichardKingscote 5 78
(Charlie Wallis) *wl in tch in midfield: effrt over 1f out: kpt on u.p ins fnl f: snatched 3rd last stride: nvr getting to ldng pair* **4/1**[2]

0056 **4** shd **Tavener**[2] 1021 7-8-4 **61** oh3..(p) PhilDennis(3) 1 65
(David C Griffiths) *t.k.h: chsd ldrs: effrt over 1f out: swtchd rt and kpt on u.p ins fnl f* **10/1**

6353 **5** 1 ¼ **Jack The Truth (IRE)**[13] 849 5-8-12 **73**.................. JessicaCooley(7) 2 73
(George Scott) *t.k.h: hld up in midfield: effrt on inner over 1f out: drvn and kpt on same pce ins fnl f* **6/1**[3]

600- **6** ¾ **Charming Guest (IRE)**[155] 7900 4-9-6 **74**................ CallumShepherd 3 72
(Mick Channon) *in tch in midfield: rdn 2f out: hdwy and swtchd rt jst ins fnl f: styd on fnl 100yds: nvr trbld ldrs* **10/1**

-105 **7** ¾ **Mont Kiara (FR)**[19] 763 6-9-4 **72**................................ TomMarquand 8 67
(Simon Dow) *hld up in last trio: effrt u.p over 1f out: edgd lft but styd on ins fnl f: nvr trbld ldrs* **16/1**

4-06 **8** nk **Spenny's Lass**[42] 383 4-8-7 **61** oh2.............................. KieranO'Neill 11 56
(John Ryan) *chsd ldrs: rdn over 1f out: sn drvn and unable qck ent fnl f: wknd ins fnl f* **50/1**

42-4 **9** 1 ¼ **Spring Romance (IRE)**[19] 763 4-9-8 **76**.......................... AdamKirby 12 67
(Dean Ivory) *t.k.h: hld up in tch in midfield on outer: unable qck u.p and btn over 1f out: wknd ins fnl f* **10/1**

0-46 **10** hd **Al Asef**[15] 797 4-9-8 **76**.. LukeMorris 9 66
(Marco Botti) *t.k.h: hld up in last trio: effrt over 1f out: sn drvn and edgd lft 1f out: nvr trbld ldrs* **16/1**

41- **11** ¾ **Rotherhithe**[207] 6052 4-8-11 **70**...................................(h[1]) DylanHogan(5) 7 57
(Henry Spiller) *taken down early: restless in stalls: stdd s: hld up in rr: effrt over 1f out: no prog: nvr involved (jockey said filly hung right-handed up home straight)* **25/1**

440- **12** ½ **Strategic Heights (IRE)**[170] 7401 10-8-5 **66**...........(b) SeanKirrane(7) 14 52
(Richard Spencer) *stdd s: hld up in rr: effrt over 1f out: rdn ent fnl f: no imp: n.d* **66/1**

1m 12.42s (-1.28) **Going Correction** +0.025s/f (Slow) **12** Ran SP% **125.7**
Speed ratings (Par 103): **109,107,106,106,104 103,102,102,100,100 99,98**
CSF £20.89 CT £65.42 TOTE £5.90: £1.80, £1.40, £1.70; EX 26.50 Trifecta £144.50.
Owner J Palmer-Brown **Bred** Brucetown Farms Ltd **Trained** Kingsclere, Hants

FOCUS
The early pace was ordinary and it proved hard to make up ground from behind.

1062 BET TOTEQUADPOT AT TOTESPORT.COM CONDITIONS STKS (AW CHAMPIONSHIPS FAST-TRACK QUALIFIER) 2m (P)

6:25 (6:30) (Class 2) 4-Y-0+ **£12,938** (£3,850; £1,924; £962) **Stalls** Low

Form RPR

1-1 **1** **Amade (IRE)**[61] 82 5-9-6 97......................................(b) AndreaAtzeni 1 112
(G Botti, France) *stdd s: hld up in last pair: rdn and clsd over 2f out: styd on to chse ldr 1f out: sn led: r.o strly and sn clr* **2/1**[1]

122- **2** 3 ½ **Elegiac**[117] 8995 4-9-3 104.. FrannyNorton 5 108
(Mark Johnston) *chsd ldr: effrt to press ldr over 2f out: rdn to ld over 1f out: hdd ins fnl f: nt match pce of wnr* **5/2**[2]

23-4 **3** 2 ¼ **Higher Power**[19] 757 7-9-6 102.. GeorgeWood 6 105
(James Fanshawe) *wl in tch in midfield: effrt ent fnl 2f: pressed ldng pair u.p 1f out: sn outpcd and wknd ins fnl f* **16/1**

11-1 **4** 2 **Aircraft Carrier (IRE)**[52] 238 4-9-3 100.........................(p) TomQueally 4 103
(John Ryan) *nvr travelled wl: in last pair: rdn over 3f out: sme hdwy and edgd lft 1f out: no imp ins fnl f* **4/1**

1-13 **5** 4 ½ **Grey Britain**[19] 757 5-9-6 105...................................... AdamKirby 3 98
(John Ryan) *stmbld leaving stalls: led: rdn and qcknd over 2f out: hdd over 1f out: sn btn and wknd fnl f* **7/2**[3]

/00- **6** 4 **To Be Wild (IRE)**[88] 9480 6-9-6 99...........................(b[1]) TomMarquand 2 93
(Hugo Palmer) *t.k.h: chsd ldrs: rdn 3f out: outpcd and dropped to rr over 1f out: wknd fnl f* **16/1**

3m 27.21s (-2.79) **Going Correction** +0.025s/f (Slow)
WFA 4 from 5yo+ 3lb **6** Ran SP% **115.9**
Speed ratings (Par 109): **107,105,104,103,100 98**
CSF £7.67 TOTE £2.80: £1.50, £1.80; EX 7.50 Trifecta £36.90.
Owner Laurent Dassault **Bred** Eamonn McEvoy **Trained** France

FOCUS
A solidly run affair and they finished fairly well strung out.

1063 BET TOTETRIFECTA AT TOTESPORT.COM FILLIES' CONDITIONS STKS (AW CHAMPIONSHIPS FAST-TRACK QUALIFIER) 1m (P)

6:55 (6:59) (Class 2) 4-Y-0+ **£12,938** (£3,850; £1,924; £962) **Stalls** Low

Form RPR

115- **1** **Clon Coulis (IRE)**[187] 6811 5-9-3 101...........................(h) JamieSpencer 2 96
(David Barron) *stdd s: hld up in rr: wnt 3rd over 6f out: effrt and clsd over 1f out: chal 1f out: rdn to ld ins fnl f: r.o wl and gng away at fin* **4/7**[1]

0-33 **2** 1 ¾ **Pattie**[19] 756 5-9-0 97.. CallumShepherd 4 89
(Mick Channon) *chsd clr ldr: clsd over 2f out: drvn to ld ent fnl f: hdd ins fnl f: outpcd towards fin* **11/4**[2]

110- **3** 2 ½ **Emily Goldfinch**[145] 8190 6-9-0 83..............................(p) RossaRyan 1 83
(Phil McEntee) *t.k.h: led and sn clr: hrd pressed and drvn over 1f out: sn hdd: wknd fnl 100yds* **20/1**

-511 **4** 1 **First Link (USA)**[19] 760 4-9-0 66...................................... HollieDoyle 5 81
(Jean-Rene Auvray) *t.k.h: hld up mainly in last pair: effrt and swtchd lft over 1f out: no imp u.p fnl f* **11/1**[3]

3-13 **5** 1 ¾ **Lady Alavesa**[38] 460 4-9-0 75..............................(p) JosephineGordon 3 76
(Gay Kelleway) *hld up in last pair: rdn over 2f out: no hdwy u.p over 1f out: nvr trbld ldrs* **12/1**

1m 39.86s (-0.04) **Going Correction** +0.025s/f (Slow) **5** Ran SP% **111.1**
Speed ratings (Par 96): **101,99,96,95,94**
CSF £2.42 TOTE £1.50: £1.10, £1.30; EX 2.50 Trifecta £15.50.
Owner Ms Colette Twomey **Bred** Collette Twomey **Trained** Maunby, N Yorks

FOCUS
The first two stood out at the weights and they finished in market order.

1064 BET TOTESWINGER AT TOTESPORT.COM FILLIES' NOVICE STKS 1m 2f (P)

7:25 (7:27) (Class 4) 3-Y-0+ **£5,530** (£1,645; £822; £411) **Stalls** Low

Form RPR

23- **1** **Frisella**[99] 9291 3-8-7 0..(h[1]) NickyMackay 5 76+
(John Gosden) *t.k.h: hld up in tch in rr: swtchd rt and effrt over 1f out: racd awkwardly briefly over 1f out: hdwy to chse clr ldr 1f out: edgd lft u.p but qcknd up to ld wl ins fnl f: sn clr* **1/4**[1]

04 **2** 2 ¾ **Copper Rose (IRE)**[21] 723 3-8-7 0.............................. JoeFanning 3 71
(Mark Johnston) *led: shkn up over 1f out: hung lft ins fnl f: sn hdd and outpcd* **6/1**[3]

6-3 **3** 3 ½ **Tappity Tap**[52] 239 4-10-0 0..(h) KieranO'Neill 4 69
(Daniel Kubler) *hld up in tch: effrt 3f out: unable qck u.p over 1f out: wknd ins fnl f* **5/1**[2]

0-4 **4** ¾ **Mrs Meader**[43] 370 3-8-7 0.. RobHornby 2 62
(Seamus Mullins) *stdd s: t.k.h: chsd ldng pair: effrt jst over 2f out: unable qck over 1f out: wknd ins fnl f* **40/1**

4 **5** 1 ¼ **Ripplet**[40] 435 4-10-0 0.. CharlieBennett 1 65
(Hughie Morrison) *t.k.h: chsd ldr: rdn over 2f out: unable qck over 1f out: btn whn lost 2nd 1f out: wknd ins fnl f* **20/1**

2m 10.87s (2.27) **Going Correction** +0.025s/f (Slow)
WFA 3 from 4yo 21lb **5** Ran SP% **118.2**
Speed ratings (Par 102): **91,88,86,85,84**
CSF £2.95 TOTE £1.20: £1.10, £1.80; EX 2.40 Trifecta £4.70.
Owner K Abdullah **Bred** Juddmonte Farms Ltd **Trained** Newmarket, Suffolk

FOCUS
The early gallop wasn't strong but they raced in single file for a fair way, before sprinting from the turn in. The winner picked up well to come from last to first.

1065 BET TOTESCOOP6 AT TOTESPORT.COM H'CAP 1m 2f (P)

7:55 (7:58) (Class 5) (0-70,71) 4-Y-0+

£5,175 (£1,540; £769; £400; £400; £400) **Stalls** Low

Form RPR

100- **1** **The Night King**[77] 9639 4-9-7 **70**.................................. AdamKirby 10 78
(Mick Quinn) *hld up in last pair: clsd over 2f out: hdwy and swtchd lft over 1f out: str run u.p ins fnl f to ld towards fin* **8/1**

3-00 **2** nk **Jamaican Jill**[38] 459 4-9-7 **70**...................................... TomMarquand 7 77
(William Muir) *in tch in midfield: effrt and rdn to chse ldrs over 2f out: steadily clsd u.p and ev ch wl ins fnl f: kpt on* **16/1**

-563 **3** 1 **Channel Packet**[15] 801 5-8-10 **66**..........................(p) MarkCrehan(7) 4 71
(Michael Appleby) *led: rdn over 1f out and forged clr: hdd and no ex towards fin* **7/2**[2]

-025 **4** ½ **Apache Blaze**[16] 793 4-8-7 **63**............................... WilliamCarver(7) 14 67
(Robyn Brisland) *in tch in midfield: outpcd over 2f out: effrt over 1f out: edging lft but kpt on wl ins fnl f: nvr quite getting to ldrs* **20/1**

20-4 **5** 2 ½ **The Jean Genie**[12] 884 5-9-8 **71**.................................. HollieDoyle 12 71
(William Stone) *chsd ldng pair: nt clr run and shuffled bk over 2f out: rallied u.p 1f out: swtchd lft and kpt on ins fnl f: nvr getting bk on terms w ldrs* **33/1**

3-44 **6** hd **Gates Pass**[20] 732 4-9-5 **68**...................................(t[1]) NicolaCurrie 9 67
(Jamie Osborne) *chsd ldrs: hung rt and unable qck over 1f out: lost btn 2nd jst ins fnl f: sn wknd* **10/1**

-410 **7** ½ **Regular Income (IRE)**[19] 754 4-9-7 **70**..................(p) CharlieBennett 5 68
(Adam West) *t.k.h: hld up in tch in last quintet: clsd but swtchd rt and wd bnd 2f out: kpt on ins fnl f: nvr trbld ldrs (jockey said gelding hung right-handed throughout)* **12/1**

2-22 **8** ½ **Gas Monkey**[21] 722 4-9-0 **63**.................................(p) ShelleyBirkett 11 60
(Julia Feilden) *t.k.h: hld up in tch in midfield: squeezed for room wl over 7f out: effrt and wd ent fnl 2f: kpt on same pce and nvr getting on terms w ldrs (jockey said gelding ran too free)* **5/2**[1]

-210 **9** nk **Global Wonder (IRE)**[36] 473 4-9-6 **69**...................(e[1]) EdwardGreatrex 3 65
(Gay Kelleway) *taken down early: hld up in tch in last quintet: effrt but forced wd bnd 2f out: kpt on ins fnl f: nvr trbld ldrs* **10/1**

606- **10** 1 ½ **Club Tropicana**[29] 9380 4-8-11 **67**......................... SeanKirrane(7) 15 60
(Richard Spencer) *hld up in tch in last trio: nt clrest of runs over 2f out: effrt over 1f out: rdn 1f out: nvr involved* **66/1**

-363 **11** nk **King Oswald (USA)**[17] 784 6-8-10 **59**........................(tp) LiamJones 1 51
(James Unett) *in tch in midfield: effrt over 2f out: hung lft u.p over 1f out: wknd ins fnl f* **12/1**

0-04 **12** 2 **Laqab (IRE)**[12] 886 6-9-2 **65**.. PaddyMathers 13 53
(Derek Shaw) *stdd s: t.k.h: hld up in rr: effrt on inner over 1f out: nvr on terms and wknd ins fnl f* **25/1**

6-46 **13** 15 **Taraayef (IRE)**[16] 794 4-9-3 **66**.................................. AndrewMullen 6 24
(Adrian Nicholls) *chsd ldr: rdn 3f out: sn struggling and losing pl: bhd and eased ins fnl f* **33/1**

0-34 **14** ½ **Francophilia**[34] [536] 4-9-5 **68**..............................(b[1]) FrannyNorton 8 25
(Mark Johnston) *t.k.h: hld up in tch in midfield: swtchd rt over 7f out: hdwy to chse ldrs 6f out tl lost pl qckly over 2f out: bhd and eased ins fnl f (jockey said filly ran too free)* **7/1[3]**

2m 6.69s (-1.91) **Going Correction** +0.025s/f (Slow) 14 Ran SP% **129.8**
Speed ratings (Par 103): **108,107,106,106,104 104,104,103,103,102 101,100,88,87**
CSF £131.93 CT £545.82 TOTE £7.50: £2.80, £15.50, £1.70; EX 179.60 Trifecta £1357.30.
Owner Andy Viner, John Quorn, Mick Quinn **Bred** Vincenzo De Siero **Trained** Newmarket, Suffolk
■ Stewards' Enquiry : Mark Crehan four-day ban: using whip above permitted level (Mar 22-23, 25-26)

FOCUS
A competitive heat run at a fair gallop.

1066 COFCO INTERNATIONAL SUPPORTING PROSTATE CANCER UK H'CAP 1m 2f (P)
8:25 (8:30) (Class 6) (0-65,66) 3-Y-O
£3,105 (£924; £461; £400; £400; £400) **Stalls** Low

Form RPR

00-4 **1** **Mr Fox**[41] [403] 3-8-11 **55**.............................. CallumShepherd 11 60
(Michael Attwater) *stdd and swtchd lft after s: hld up in rr: effrt ent fnl 2f: hdwy u.p whn nt clr run 1f out: gap opened and clsd u.p ins fnl f: led wl ins fnl f: hld on wl* **33/1**

221 **2** *hd* **Colony Queen**[14] [836] 3-9-7 **65**.............................. JamieSpencer 8 70
(James Tate) *wl in tch in midfield: shuffled bk: forced to switch rt and effrt wd bnd 2f out: clsd u.p and edgd lft 1f out: ev ch ins fnl f: r.o wl but hld towards fin* **5/1[2]**

60-6 **3** 1¼ **Fanfaronade (USA)**[34] [524] 3-9-6 **64**.............................. KieranO'Neill 7 66
(John Gosden) *w ldr tl led over 8f out: rdn over 2f out: hung lft u.p and hdd wl ins fnl f: wknd towards fin* **7/1[3]**

0-50 **4** 1½ **Trouble Shooter (IRE)**[14] [829] 3-8-6 **50**..............................(v) LiamJones 14 50
(Shaun Keightley) *chsd ldrs but stuck wd: rdn over 3f out: hrd drvn and chsd ldr ent fnl f: hung lft and wknd ins fnl f* **25/1**

-132 **5** 1¾ **Chakrii (IRE)**[15] [802] 3-8-11 **55**.............................. DavidProbert 2 52
(Henry Spiller) *hld up in tch in last pair: clsd on inner and nt clrest of runs over 2f out: hdwy u.p to chse ldrs 1f out: no ex ins fnl f: wknd towards fin* **11/4[1]**

-223 **6** 2 **Hypnos (IRE)**[12] [885] 3-9-3 **66**.............................. DylanHogan(5) 5 59
(David Simcock) *hld up in tch in last quartet: shkn up 2f out: sme hdwy u.p over 1f out: kpt on same pce ins fnl f* **5/1[2]**

6-51 **7** ½ **Lady Wolf**[15] [802] 3-8-9 **53**..............................(p) RobHornby 1 45
(Rod Millman) *hld up in tch: effrt to cl and nt clrest of runs jst over 1f out: carried lft and squeezed for room ins fnl f: kpt on same pce u.p after* **8/1**

00-2 **8** 1¼ **Time Immemorial (IRE)**[36] [486] 3-9-7 **65**..............................(b) AndreaAtzeni 10 55
(Roger Varian) *hld up wl in tch in midfield: hdwy to chse ldr 6f out: unable qck u.p over 1f out: lost 2nd and wknd ins fnl f* **8/1**

60-4 **9** 1 **Archdeacon**[15] [802] 3-8-10 **54**.............................. TomMarquand 13 42
(Dean Ivory) *mostly chsd ldr tl 6f out: styd handy tl unable qck u.p over 1f out: wknd ins fnl f* **7/1[3]**

-000 **10** 4½ **Jasmine B (IRE)**[15] [802] 3-7-11 **46** oh1.............................. DarraghKeenan(5) 6 26
(John Ryan) *led for over 1f: styd chsng ldrs: rdn and unable qck over 1f out: wknd ins fnl f* **100/1**

6-35 **11** 3¾ **Biz Markee (IRE)**[29] [614] 3-9-8 **66**..............................(p) LukeMorris 4 39
(Hugo Palmer) *rousted along leaving stalls: midfield: lost pl and rdn over 2f out: sn btn and bhd fnl f* **10/1**

0-05 **12** 2 **Wontgetfooledagen (IRE)**[15] [802] 3-8-2 **46** oh1..(tp) PaddyMathers 15 16
(Ivan Furtado) *a towards rr: rdn 4f out: bhd over 1f out* **50/1**

060- **13** *nk* **Exousia**[202] [6246] 3-8-4 **48**..............................(p[1]) JoeFanning 9 17
(Henry Spiller) *dwlt and short of room leaving stalls: t.k.h and hld up in midfield: hung lft and btn over 1f out: wknd fnl f* **33/1**

2m 8.22s (-0.38) **Going Correction** +0.025s/f (Slow) 13 Ran SP% **129.0**
Speed ratings (Par 96): **102,101,100,99,98 96,96,95,94,90 87,86,86**
CSF £201.33 CT £1343.57 TOTE £135.00: £17.70, £2.00, £2.40; EX 323.30 Trifecta £3008.70.
Owner The Attwater Partnership **Bred** Mark Benton **Trained** Epsom, Surrey

FOCUS
A bit of a turn-up here. The third and fourth guide the level of the form.
T/Plt: £70.40 to a £1 stake. Pool: £84,529.56 - 876.31 winning units T/Qpdt: £7.00 to a £1 stake. Pool: £11,511.91 - 1,204.86 winning units **Steve Payne**

926 SOUTHWELL (L-H)
Thursday, March 7

OFFICIAL GOING: Fibresand: standard
Wind: Strong across Weather: Heavy cloud and windy

1067 LADBROKES HOME OF THE ODDS BOOST H'CAP 1m 13y(F)
3:00 (3:00) (Class 5) (0-75,71) 3-Y-O **£3,752** (£1,116; £557) **Stalls** Low

Form RPR

200- **1** **Love Your Work (IRE)**[153] [7957] 3-9-0 **71**..............................(b[1]) RPWalsh(7) 2 74
(Adam West) *rdn along s: t.k.h: led after 1f: clr 1/2-way: rdn along over 2f out: drvn over 1f out: kpt on wl towards fin* **2/1[2]**

-011 **2** 1½ **Dolly Dupree**[8] [931] 3-8-5 **55** ow2.............................. DannyBrock 3 55
(Paul D'Arcy) *hld up in rr: pushed along 1/2-way: hdwy and wd st: rdn to chse wnr wl over 1f out: drvn appr fnl f: sn edgd lft and kpt on same pce towards fin* **5/4[1]**

635- **3** 13 **Cromwell**[154] [7942] 3-9-0 **64**.............................. PhilipPrince 1 34
(Luke Dace) *led 1f: chsd wnr: pushed along over 3f out: wd st: sn rdn and edgd lft 2f: wknd* **9/4[3]**

1m 42.8s (-0.90) **Going Correction** +0.025s/f (Slow) 3 Ran SP% **108.5**
Speed ratings (Par 98): **105,103,90**
CSF £4.83 TOTE £3.00; EX 4.50 Trifecta £6.30.
Owner Mrs J West **Bred** Gerard Mullins **Trained** Epsom, Surrey

FOCUS
Another meeting this week decimated by a lack of runners - just 19 throughout the card - due to an on-going prize money protest. The winner took apart this moderate 3yo handicap.

1068 BETWAY LIVE CASINO (S) STKS 1m 4f 14y(F)
3:35 (3:35) (Class 6) 4-Y-O+ **£3,105** (£924; £461) **Stalls** Low

Form RPR

00-0 **1** **Rajapur**[54] [208] 6-9-0 45..............................(e[1]) DannyBrock 3 47
(David Thompson) *t.k.h early: trckd ldng pair: hdwy on outer 4f out: led 3f out: rdn and edgd lft over 2f out: sn clr: kpt on strly* **5/6[1]**

60-6 **2** 5 **Ejabah (IRE)**[63] [41] 5-8-2 38.............................. RPWalsh(7) 1 30
(Charles Smith) *t.k.h early: led: pushed along 4f out: rdn and hdd 3f out: drvn and kpt on same pce fnl 2f* **6/4[2]**

006- **3** *hd* **Unique Company (IRE)**[291] [2885] 4-8-13 38.............................. PhilipPrince 2 36
(David Thompson) *trckd ldr: cl up 4f out: rdn along 3f out: drvn 2f out: kpt on same pce* **15/2[3]**

2m 42.93s (1.93) **Going Correction** +0.025s/f (Slow)
WFA 4 from 5yo+ 1lb 3 Ran SP% **106.3**
Speed ratings (Par 101): **94,90,90**
CSF £2.34 TOTE £1.50; EX 2.00 Trifecta £2.50.There was no bid for the winner
Owner B Lapham **Bred** J & W Hoyer **Trained** Bolam, Co Durham

FOCUS
They went an average pace in this desperately weak seller. A token rating has been given.

1069 SUNRACING.CO.UK H'CAP 7f 14y(F)
4:05 (4:05) (Class 5) (0-70,59) 4-Y-O+ **£3,752** (£1,116; £557) **Stalls** Low

Form RPR

-015 **1** **Alpha Tauri (USA)**[14] [830] 13-9-0 **59**.............................. RPWalsh(7) 2 65
(Charles Smith) *cl up: wd st: led wl over 2f out: jnd and rdn 2f out: drvn and edgd rt ins fnl f: kpt on wl towards fin* **13/8[2]**

5-06 **2** ½ **Maazel (IRE)**[8] [924] 5-9-1 **53**.............................. DannyBrock 3 58
(Lee Carter) *dwlt: trckd ldng pair: hdwy on outer and cl up over 3f out: wd st: sn chal: rdn wl over 1f out: drvn and ev ch ins fnl f: no ex towards fin* **6/1[3]**

5404 **3** 2½ **Break The Silence**[14] [829] 5-9-0 **52**..............................(b) PhilipPrince 1 50
(Scott Dixon) *slt ld on inner: pushed along over 3f out: sn rdn and hdd wl over 2f out: styd towards far rail: drvn and kpt on one pce fnl f* **5/6[1]**

1m 28.45s (-1.85) **Going Correction** +0.025s/f (Slow) 3 Ran SP% **106.9**
Speed ratings (Par 103): **111,110,107**
CSF £8.02 TOTE £2.20; EX 5.60 Trifecta £7.40.
Owner J R Theaker **Bred** Flaxman Holdings Ltd **Trained** Temple Bruer, Lincs

FOCUS
Despite just three runners this moderate handicap was run at a fair pace. It's been rated conservatively, with the winner in line with this winter's form.

1070 FOLLOW SUNRACING ON TWITTER MEDIAN AUCTION MAIDEN STKS 1m 13y(F)
4:40 (4:40) (Class 5) 3-5-Y-O **£3,752** (£1,116; £557; £278) **Stalls** Low

Form RPR

1 **Lennybe** 3-8-10 0.............................. MirkoSanna 4 64+
(David Brown) *cl up: led over 3f out: pushed clr wl over 1f out: kpt on strly: easily* **5/4[2]**

630- **2** 8 **Ipcress File**[192] [6639] 4-10-0 48..............................(b[1]) PhilipPrince 3 49
(Scott Dixon) *t.k.h early: trckd ldng pair: swtchd rt and pushed along 1/2-way: rdn and outpcd whn wd st: styd on u.p fnl 2f: no ch w wnr* **10/1[3]**

53- **3** 18 **Dories Delight (IRE)**[112] [9086] 4-10-0 63.............................. DannyBrock 2 8
(Scott Dixon) *led: pushed along 4f out: rdn and hdd over 3f out: drvn over 2f out: sn wknd (jockey said gelding hung left throughout)* **1/1[1]**

0-06 **4** 2 **Lord Digby**[20] [732] 4-9-7 32..............................(b[1]) RPWalsh(7) 1 3
(Adam West) *a outpcd in rr: bhd fnl 3f* **33/1**

1m 43.29s (-0.41) **Going Correction** +0.025s/f (Slow)
WFA 3 from 4yo 18lb 4 Ran SP% **106.5**
Speed ratings (Par 103): **103,95,77,75**
CSF £11.26 TOTE £1.70; EX 10.60.
Owner Ron Hull **Bred** M Massarella **Trained** Averham Park, Notts

FOCUS
Another race where it paid to be handy. It's been rated around the second, but with little confidence.

1071 PLAY 4 TO SCORE AT BETWAY H'CAP 6f 16y(F)
5:10 (5:10) (Class 6) (0-52,52) 3-Y-O+ **£3,105** (£924; £461; £300) **Stalls** Low

Form RPR

16-2 **1** **Jazz Legend (USA)**[56] [166] 6-9-9 **51**.............................. MirkoSanna 5 58
(Mandy Rowland) *cl up on outer: wd and chal 3f out: led wl over 2f out: rdn over 1f out: edgd lft ins fnl f: kpt on* **11/8[2]**

450 **2** 1 **Thedevilinneville**[19] [753] 3-8-3 **52**.............................. RPWalsh(7) 4 50
(Adam West) *dwlt and rdn along in rr: outpcd and bhd over 3f out: hdwy on inner over 2f out: styd on u.p ent fnl f: sn swtchd rt and drvn: kpt on* **8/1[3]**

6332 **3** 1 **Tellovoi (IRE)**[6] [969] 11-9-5 **47**..............................(p) PhilipPrince 3 46
(Richard Guest) *cl up: disp ld 4f out: rdn along over 3f out and wd st: drvn over 2f out: kpt on same pce* **11/10[1]**

60-0 **4** 8 **Pearl Noir**[35] [503] 9-9-4 **46** oh1..............................(p) DannyBrock 2 21
(Scott Dixon) *slt ld on inner: rdn along 1/2-way: hdd wl over 2f out: drvn wl over 1f out: sn wknd* **12/1**

1m 16.12s (-0.38) **Going Correction** +0.025s/f (Slow)
WFA 3 from 6yo+ 14lb 4 Ran SP% **108.5**
Speed ratings (Par 101): **103,101,100,89**
CSF £10.86 TOTE £1.90; EX 6.70.
Owner Miss M E Rowland **Bred** Two Hearts Farm LLC & Four Legacy LLC **Trained** Lower Blidworth, Notts

FOCUS
A weak sprint handicap, run at a frantic pace.

1072 BETWAY H'CAP 4f 214y(F)
5:40 (5:40) (Class 4) (0-85,75) 4-Y-O+ **£5,530** (£1,645) **Stalls** Centre

Form RPR

0-63 **1** **Tricky Dicky**[9] [914] 6-9-0 **75**.............................. RPWalsh(7) 2 79
(Olly Williams) *wnt 10 l clr s: mde all* **2/5[1]**

4404 **2** 10 **Samovar**[14] [832] 4-9-2 **70**..............................(b) DannyBrock 1 38
(Scott Dixon) *dwlt: awkward and rel to r: lost 10 l s: a bhd (jockey said gelding had its head to one side and jumped awkwardly from the stalls, and was slowly away as a result)* **2/1[2]**

1m 0.03s (0.33) **Going Correction** +0.025s/f (Slow) 2 Ran SP% **104.8**
Speed ratings (Par 105): **98,82**
TOTE £1.40.
Owner Eight Gents and a Lady **Bred** Onslow, Stratton & Parry **Trained** Market Rasen, Lincs

FOCUS
This feature sprint handicap was just a match, and the second favourite gave it away at the start, so it's form to ignore.
T/Plt: £341.80 to a £1 stake. Pool: £37,633.26 - 80.36 winning units T/Qpdt: £41.40 to a £1 stake. Pool: £2,795.55 - 49.85 winning units **Joe Rowntree**

FONTAINEBLEAU
Thursday, March 7

OFFICIAL GOING: Turf: heavy

1073a PRIX DE FONTAINEBLEAU TOURISME (CLAIMER) (4YO+) (TURF) 1m 3f
1:55 4-Y-O+ £8,558 (£3,423; £2,567; £1,711; £855)

			RPR
1		**Rogue Runner (GER)**[22] 7-8-11 0 EddyHardouin 4 (Carina Fey, France) **10/1**	70
2	1 1/4	**Freiheit (IRE)**[14] 4-8-11 0 TheoBachelot 7 (Y Barberot, France) **53/10[3]**	69
3	1/2	**Marcelle (FR)**[35] 4-9-1 0 Pierre-CharlesBoudot 6 (M Seror, France) **5/1[2]**	72
4	1	**Ever Love (FR)**[24] 4-8-5 0 MlleMarylineEon(3) 9 (J Boisnard, France) **12/1**	63
5	1 1/4	**Lodi (FR)**[98] 5-9-1 0 ChristopheSoumillon 10 (C Lerner, France) **11/1**	67
6	hd	**Aiseolas (IRE)**[185] 6892 4-8-8 0 StephanePasquier 5 (Gavin Hernon, France) **14/5[1]**	61
7	snk	**Man Of Letters (FR)**[98] 5-8-11 0 AnthonyCrastus 1 (R Chotard, France) **24/1**	62
8	6	**Danse A Rio (FR)**[699] 5-8-11 0 CyrilleStefan 3 (J Bossert, France) **55/1**	52
9	3/4	**Purple Rock (IRE)**[8] 927 7-8-11 0 DanielMuscutt 11 (Gay Kelleway) *sn prom: trckd ldr: urged along over 2f out: rdn but no rspnse over 1f out: wknd and eased fnl f* **11/1**	50
10	12	**Matador (FR)**[25] 4-8-11 0 (p) AntoineHamelin 13 (Matthieu Palussiere, France) **36/1**	30
11	1 1/2	**Vienna Woods (FR)**[217] 5-8-8 0 MaximeGuyon 12 (Y Barberot, France) **13/1**	23
12	20	**Baguera De Vaige (FR)**[14] 4-8-11 0 MathieuAndrouin 2 (O Regley, France) **132/1**	
13	dist	**Blue Diamond (FR)**[20] 7-9-5 0 MickaelBarzalona 8 (S Smrczek, Germany) **8/1**	

PARI-MUTUEL (all including 1 euro stake): WIN 11.20; PLACE 2.60, 2.40, 2.30; DF 30.20;.
Owner Eckhard Sauren **Bred** Stiftung Gestut Fahrhof **Trained** France

1039 LINGFIELD (L-H)
Friday, March 8

OFFICIAL GOING: Polytrack: standard
Wind: medium to strong, half behind Weather: overcast, breezy

1074 SUN RACING H'CAP 1m 1y(P)
2:10 (2:10) (Class 5) (0-75,77) 4-Y-O+ £4,690 (£1,395; £697; £348) Stalls High

Form				RPR
-163	1		**Divine Messenger**[23] 699 5-9-9 77 (p) AdamKirby 4 (Emma Owen) *sn chsng ldr: rdn and clsd over 2f out: drvn to ld over 1f out: in command whn hung rt towards fin* **8/15[1]**	84
4-54	2	1 3/4	**Majestic Moon (IRE)**[43] 392 9-9-3 71 (p) ShelleyBirkett 3 (Julia Feilden) *sn led and clr tl pressed and rdn ent fnl 2f: hdd and unable qck over 1f out: kpt on same pce ins fnl f* **5/1[3]**	74
14-0	3	1/2	**Choral Music**[63] 54 4-9-7 75 RobHornby 1 (John E Long) *broke wl: sn restrained and hld up in 3rd: effrt 2f out: rdn 1f out: kpt on but nvr threatening wnr* **10/3[2]**	77
430-	4	6	**Zapateado**[116] 9029 4-8-8 67 (t) RhiainIngram(5) 2 (Paul George) *dwlt: t.k.h: hld up in rr: effrt 2f out: no imp: wknd ins fnl f (jockey said filly was slowly away)* **12/1**	55

1m 37.18s (-1.02) **Going Correction** -0.05s/f (Stan) 4 Ran SP% **112.7**
Speed ratings (Par 103): **103,101,100,94**
CSF £3.94 TOTE £1.30; EX 2.60 Trifecta £5.40.
Owner Miss Emma L Owen **Bred** P J J Eddery **Trained** Nether Winchendon, Bucks

FOCUS
A straightforward enough success for the odds-on favourite.

1075 FOLLOW SUN RACING ON TWITTER H'CAP 7f 1y(P)
2:40 (2:40) (Class 6) (0-60,62) 4-Y-O+ £3,105 (£924; £461; £300; £300; £300) Stalls Low

Form				RPR
-062	1		**Maazel (IRE)**[1] 1069 5-9-1 53 DannyBrock 3 (Lee Carter) *stdd s: hld up in tch in last pair: clsd on inner over 1f out: rdn and hdwy to chal ins fnl f: hung rt but r.o u.p to ld cl home* **16/1**	60
0564	2	nk	**Tavener**[1] 1061 7-9-6 58 (p) LewisEdmunds 1 (David C Griffiths) *trckd ldr: effrt over 1f out: ev ch 1f out: drvn to ld 100yds out: kpt on: hdd cl home* **9/2[3]**	64
0133	3	3/4	**Limerick Lord (IRE)**[10] 912 7-8-13 51 (p) ShelleyBirkett 7 (Julia Feilden) *sn led: rdn wl over 1f out: drvn 1f out: hdd 100yds out: no ex and one pce towards fin* **8/1**	55
3423	4	1/2	**Rivas Rob Roy**[9] 925 4-9-1 56 FinleyMarsh(3) 4 (John Gallagher) *t.k.h: chsd ldrs: shkn up 2f out: ev ch over 1f out tl unable qck and outpcd fnl 100yds* **13/8[1]**	59
2-20	5	1/2	**Violet's Lads (IRE)**[37] 476 5-9-10 62 RossaRyan 8 (Brett Johnson) *stdd s: hld up in tch in last pair: swtchd rt and effrt over 1f out: hung lft 1f out: kpt on u.p ins fnl f: nvr getting to ldrs* **3/1[2]**	63
043-	6	1/2	**Helfire**[68] 9767 6-9-4 56 (t w) CharlieBennett 6 (Martin Bosley) *taken down early and led to post: hld up in tch in midfield: effrt over 1f out: drvn and one pce fnl f* **7/1**	56
5-02	7	3/4	**Holy Tiber (IRE)**[32] 596 4-9-7 59 (t) JoeyHaynes 2 (Paul Howling) *hld up in tch in midfield: pushed along 2f out: unable qck u.p 1f out: wknd ins fnl f* **10/1**	57

1m 24.23s (-0.57) **Going Correction** -0.05s/f (Stan) 7 Ran SP% **119.9**
Speed ratings (Par 101): **101,100,99,99,98 98,97**
CSF £90.43 CT £637.82 TOTE £26.60: £11.10, £2.80; EX 136.10 Trifecta £720.50.
Owner John Joseph Smith **Bred** Myles Haughney **Trained** Epsom, Surrey
■ Stewards' Enquiry : Danny Brock two-day ban: used whip down the shoulder in the forehand (Mar 22-23)
Finley Marsh £650 fine: changing his boots after weighing out

FOCUS
The early pace wasn't that strong, it turned into a bit of a dash from the turn in and they finished in a heap. The second, third and fourth were prominent throughout so the winner did well to run them down.

1076 BETWAY HEED YOUR HUNCH H'CAP 5f 6y(P)
3:15 (3:15) (Class 5) (0-75,66) 4-Y-O+ £3,752 (£1,116; £557; £300; £300) Stalls High

Form				RPR
5120	1		**Warrior's Valley**[11] 907 4-9-7 66 (tp) LewisEdmunds 5 (David C Griffiths) *mde all: wnt clr 3f out: rdn over 1f out: reminders and rdr looking arnd ins fnl f: reduced advantage but nvr gng to be ct: eased cl home* **8/15[1]**	75
-440	2	1 3/4	**Majorette**[20] 759 5-9-2 61 DannyBrock 2 (Brian Barr) *chsd ldng pair: effrt 2f out: chsd clr wnr ins fnl f: styd on and clsng wl ins fnl f: nvr getting on terms w wnr* **4/1[2]**	63
4010	3	1 1/4	**Red Stripes (USA)**[15] 823 7-8-7 55 (b) GabrieleMalune(3) 6 (Lisa Williamson) *chsd wnr: rdn over 1f out: no imp: lost 2nd and edgd lft ins fnl f* **4/1[2]**	52
050-	4	2 3/4	**Terri Rules (IRE)**[154] 7955 4-9-3 62 ShelleyBirkett 4 (Julia Feilden) *awkward as stalls opened and slowly away: a in last pair: effrt and plenty to do wl over 1f out: no imp: n.d (jockey said filly fly-leapt leaving the stalls and was slowly away)* **14/1[3]**	49
50-0	5	21	**Go Sandy**[16] 811 4-8-0 52 oh6 (h[1]) ElishaWhittington(7) 3 (Lisa Williamson) *a in rr: rdn wl over 2f out: sn struggling: wl bhd and eased ins fnl f (starter reported that filly was the subject of a third criteria failure; trainer was informed that the filly could not run until the day after passing a stalls test)* **66/1**	

57.99s (-0.81) **Going Correction** -0.05s/f (Stan) 5 Ran SP% **113.4**
Speed ratings (Par 103): **104,101,99,94,61**
CSF £3.29 TOTE £1.30: £1.10, £2.20; EX 3.20 Trifecta £6.30.
Owner N Davies, D Clarke & Eros **Bred** P Balding **Trained** Bawtry, S Yorks

FOCUS
This proved straightforward for the short-priced favourite.

1077 LADBROKES FILLIES' NOVICE MEDIAN AUCTION STKS 1m 4f (P)
3:50 (3:50) (Class 6) 3-Y-O £3,105 (£924; £461; £230) Stalls Low

Form				RPR
0-	1		**Break The Rules**[135] 8549 3-8-12 0 DannyBrock 4 (Martin Smith) *s.i.s: hld up wl in tch in rr: clsd on outer 4f out: rdn to chse ldr over 2f out: drvn 1f out: styd on u.p to ld towards fin* **33/1**	68
323-	2	hd	**Air Force Amy**[160] 7763 3-8-12 76 CallumShepherd 3 (Mick Channon) *t.k.h: chsd ldr tl led 3f out: rdn and awkward hd carriage over 1f out: drvn 1f out: kpt on same pce and hdd towards fin* **1/7[1]**	68
5	3	7	**Mi Manchi (IRE)**[15] 836 3-8-5 0 StefanoCherchi(7) 1 (Marco Botti) *t.k.h early: trckd ldrs: trying to switch rt but hemmed in 4f out: last: rdn and outpcd over 2f out: chsd clr ldng pair and hung lft 1f out: no hdwy and wl btn fnl f* **7/1[2]**	57
0	4	11	**Winter Snowdrop (IRE)**[51] 251 3-8-12 0 ShelleyBirkett 2 (Julia Feilden) *led and set stdy gallop: hdd 3f out: 3rd and outpcd over 2f out: wknd over 1f out* **12/1[3]**	39

2m 34.92s (1.92) **Going Correction** -0.05s/f (Stan) 4 Ran SP% **110.6**
Speed ratings (Par 93): **91,90,86,78**
CSF £42.26 TOTE £24.60; EX 33.90 Trifecta £63.60.
Owner Robert P Clarke And Partners **Bred** Wood Farm Stud (Waresley) **Trained** Newmarket, Suffolk

FOCUS
Quite a turn-up here, with the long odds-on favourite narrowly beaten by the outsider of the field. The early pace was steady. The winner, third and fourth will confirm whether the level is right in time.

1078 PLAY 4 TO SCORE AT BETWAY H'CAP 1m 2f (P)
4:20 (4:20) (Class 6) (0-55,57) 4-Y-O+ £3,105 (£924; £461; £300; £300; £300) Stalls Low

Form				RPR
4322	1		**Affluence (IRE)**[23] 695 4-9-5 50 (p) DannyBrock 3 (Martin Smith) *hld up in midfield: clsd to chse ldrs over 3f out: chsd ldr over 2f out: led 2f out and sn rdn clr: eased towards fin: v easily* **1/1[1]**	65
-406	2	7	**Voice Of A Leader (IRE)**[38] 465 8-9-7 52 JoeyHaynes 6 (Paul Howling) *taken down early: hld up in last pair: hdwy to chse ldng pair over 2f out: rdn to chse wnr over 1f out: no ch but clr 2nd ins fnl f* **12/1**	54
0033	3	5	**Outlaw Torn (IRE)**[6] 983 10-9-0 45 (e) PhilipPrince 4 (Richard Guest) *taken down early: chsd ldrs tl wnt 2nd 5f out tl led wl over 3f out: rdn and hdd 2f out: 3rd and outpcd over 1f out: wknd* **8/1[3]**	37
0232	4	3 1/4	**Foxrush Take Time (FR)**[6] 984 4-9-0 45 (e) CallumShepherd 2 (Richard Guest) *taken down early: hld up in midfield: rdn over 2f out: struggling to qckn whn squeezed for room and jostling over 2f out: no ch after (jockey said gelding ran flat)* **15/8[2]**	31
-000	5	1	**Blue Rocks**[10] 914 5-9-9 57 GabrieleMalune(3) 5 (Lisa Williamson) *led tl 8f out: chsd ldr tl 5f out: rdn and losing pl whn jostling over 2f out: 4th and btn 2f out: wknd* **20/1**	41
000-	6	1 1/2	**Karam Albaari (IRE)**[108] 9159 11-9-5 50 (v) RossaRyan 1 (J R Jenkins) *s.i.s: hld up in last pair: forced to swtchd rt and effrt in 6th 2f out: no prog and wl btn over 1f out (jockey said horse was never travelling)* **10/1**	31
0-00	7	22	**Tabla**[22] 717 7-8-10 48 JoeBradnam(7) 7 (Lee Carter) *wd: hdwy to press ldr after 1f: led 8f out tl wl over 3f out: losing pl whn jostled over 2f out: sn bhd: t.o fnl f* **50/1**	

2m 3.65s (-2.95) **Going Correction** -0.05s/f (Stan) 7 Ran SP% **119.4**
Speed ratings (Par 101): **109,103,99,96,96 94,77**
CSF £16.29 TOTE £1.70: £1.10, £6.40; EX 10.70 Trifecta £42.00.
Owner The Affluence Partnership **Bred** Mrs Michelle Smith **Trained** Newmarket, Suffolk

FOCUS
This was solidly run and they finished well strung out. The winner has been rated back to his best.

1079 LADBROKES HOME OF THE ODDS BOOST H'CAP 5f 6y(P)
4:55 (4:55) (Class 6) (0-65,65) 3-Y-O £3,105 (£924) Stalls High

Form				RPR
-614	1		**Sister Of The Sign (IRE)**[18] 783 3-9-2 60 BarryMcHugh 2 (James Given) *mde all: restrained and set stdy gallop: pushed 2 l clr 2f out: a in command after: eased towards fin* **11/8[2]**	64

40-6 **2** 1 3/4 **Dandy Lad (IRE)**[14] [854] 3-9-4 **65**........................ FinleyMarsh(3) 1 63
(Richard Hughes) *taken down early and led to post: awkward leaving stalls: plld hrd and pressed wnr on inner and short of room over 2f: effrt over 1f out: sn swtchd rt and no imp fnl f* **8/15**[1]

59.62s (0.82) **Going Correction** -0.05s/f (Stan) **2** Ran SP% **107.3**
Speed ratings (Par 96): **91,88**
TOTE £1.60.
Owner The Cool Silk Partnership **Bred** Mrs Claire Doyle **Trained** Willoughton, Lincs

FOCUS
A tactical affair. A token figure has been given.
T/Plt: £3,431.70 to a £1 stake. Pool: £43,390.45 - 9.23 winning units T/Qpdt: £268.80 to a £1 stake. Pool: £3124.71 - 8.60 winning units **Steve Payne**

968 NEWCASTLE (A.W) (L-H)
Friday, March 8

OFFICIAL GOING: Tapeta: standard
Wind: Fresh, half against Weather: Rain from race 4 (7.00)

1080 BETWAY HEED YOUR HUNCH MAIDEN STKS — 1m 4f 98y (Tp)
5:20 (5:20) (Class 5) 3-Y-0+ £3,752 (£1,116; £557; £278) **Stalls** High

Form RPR

0-4 **1** **Seeusoon (IRE)**[44] [358] 3-8-5 0........................ DuranFentiman 3 67
(Andrew Balding) *t.k.h: trckd ldrs: pushed along to ld 2f out: hrd pressed fnl f: hld on wl towards fin* **4/11**[1]

56 **2** hd **Withoutdestination**[22] [723] 3-8-2 0..................(b) AaronJones(3) 2 66
(Marco Botti) *in tch: outpcd and edgd lft over 2f out: rallied to chse wnr over 1f out: disp ld fnl f: kpt on: hld nr fin* **20/1**

052- **3** 10 **Glacier Fox**[203] [6259] 4-9-13 65........................ PJMcDonald 6 54
(Tom Tate) *led at ordinary gallop: rdn and hdd 2f out: wknd ins fnl f* **2/1**[2]

5- **4** 1 **The Perch (IRE)**[21] [751] 4-9-1 39..................(b) GearoidBrouder(7) 5 47
(Patrick J McKenna, Ire) *pressed ldr: rdn and ev ch over 2f out: wknd over 1f out* **40/1**

0/ **5** 4 1/2 **Cryogenics (IRE)**[928] [5728] 5-9-7 0........................ RPWalsh(7) 7 44
(Kenny Johnson) *s.i.s: hld up: rdn over 2f out: no imp over 1f out* **500/1**

4 **6** 1 **Nine Elms (USA)**[7] [971] 4-9-10 0........................ TimClark(3) 1 43
(Roy Bowring) *in tch on ins: drvn and outpcd over 2f out: sn btn* **14/1**[3]

5-0 **7** 2 3/4 **Nicky Nook**[31] [608] 6-9-9 0........................ CamHardie 4 33
(Stella Barclay) *hld up: drvn and struggling over 2f out: sn wknd* **500/1**

2m 44.59s (3.49) **Going Correction** +0.175s/f (Slow) **7** Ran SP% **120.9**
WFA 3 from 4yo 23lb 4 from 5yo+ 1lb
Speed ratings (Par 103): **95,94,88,87,84 83,82**
CSF £13.96 TOTE £1.40: £1.10, £6.20; EX 10.90 Trifecta £15.70.
Owner P H Betts **Bred** Nafferty Stud **Trained** Kingsclere, Hants

FOCUS
An ordinary middle-distance maiden on standard Tapeta. The modest pace picked up notably over 4f out and the odds-on favourite won narrowly in game fashion with a break to the third.

1081 LADBROKES APPRENTICE H'CAP — 6f (Tp)
5:55 (5:55) (Class 6) (0-65,67) 3-Y-0
£3,105 (£924; £461; £400; £400; £400) **Stalls** Centre

Form RPR

05-0 **1** **Camachess (IRE)**[9] [918] 3-9-10 **60**........................ PhilDennis 9 67
(Philip McBride) *hld up bhd ldng gp: effrt and rdn over 1f out: led and edgd lft ins fnl f: rdn out* **7/1**[2]

-612 **2** 3/4 **Klopp**[7] [972] 3-9-12 **67**..................(h) KieranSchofield(5) 8 72
(Antony Brittain) *s.i.s: plld hrd in rr: effrt on far side of gp over 2f out: hdwy to chse wnr ins fnl f: kpt on fin* **2/5**[1]

0-63 **3** 1 1/4 **Firsteen**[42] [406] 3-8-12 **53**........................ AledBeech(5) 7 54
(Alistair Whillans) *trckd ldrs: effrt and rdn 2f out: kpt on ins fnl f: hld towards fin* **12/1**

0 **4** 1/2 **Ascot Dreamer**[15] [834] 3-8-9 **52**..................(bt) OliverStammers(7) 2 52
(David Brown) *w ldr: led 1/2-way to ins fnl f: drvn and one pce last 100yds* **16/1**

0516 **5** 4 1/2 **Geography Teacher (IRE)**[15] [834] 3-9-4 **57**........................ BenSanderson(3) 5 43
(Roger Fell) *hld up: rdn and effrt over 2f out: edgd lft: no imp over 1f out* **7/1**[2]

0-66 **6** 2 3/4 **Kyroc (IRE)**[18] [783] 3-9-1 **54**........................ TheodoreLadd(3) 6 32
(Susan Corbett) *led to 1/2-way: cl up tl rdn and wknd over 1f out* **100/1**

0-05 **7** hd **Platinum Coast (USA)**[41] [431] 3-8-6 **45**........................ AndrewBreslin(3) 1 22
(James Tate) *s.i.s: bhd: rdn over 2f out: sme late hdwy: nvr on terms* **8/1**[3]

050- **8** 1 **Medoras Childe**[177] [7176] 3-9-8 **58**........................ AaronJones 4 32
(Heather Main) *chsd ldrs tl outpcd and edgd lft over 2f out: sn wknd* **20/1**

000- **9** 1 1/4 **Champagne Clouds**[170] [7413] 3-8-13 **49**........................ BenRobinson 3 19
(Brian Ellison) *in tch: drvn and struggling over 2f out: sn btn* **25/1**

1m 12.68s (0.18) **Going Correction** +0.175s/f (Slow) **9** Ran SP% **130.7**
Speed ratings (Par 96): **105,104,102,101,95 92,91,90,88**
CSF £11.47 CT £47.12 TOTE £8.70: £2.80, £1.10, £2.50; EX 18.50 Trifecta £123.90.
Owner The Narc Partnership **Bred** Yeomanstown Stud **Trained** Newmarket, Suffolk

FOCUS
A modest 3yo sprint handicap for apprentice riders. The winning time was a fair one for the grade. The winner has been rated near her best.

1082 BETWAY CASINO H'CAP — 5f (Tp)
6:30 (6:30) (Class 4) (0-80,77) 4-Y-0+ £5,530 (£1,645; £822; £411; £400) **Stalls** Centre

Form RPR

4133 **1** **Another Angel (IRE)**[8] [953] 5-9-6 **76**........................ CamHardie 4 84
(Antony Brittain) *t.k.h early: mde all: rdn along over 1f out: clr ins fnl f: unchal* **4/5**[1]

0030 **2** 2 1/4 **Tommy G**[8] [953] 6-9-4 **77**........................ PhilDennis(3) 2 77
(Jim Goldie) *in tch: effrt and rdn 2f out: chsd (clr) wnr ins fnl f: kpt on: nt pce to chal* **4/1**[3]

1100 **3** nse **Deeds Not Words (IRE)**[21] [741] 8-8-13 **69**........................ JasonHart 3 69
(Tracy Waggott) *in tch: rdn and outpcd over 2f out: rallied ins fnl f: kpt on fin* **28/1**

532/ **4** 3/4 **Fair Cop**[582] [5574] 5-9-7 **77**........................ PJMcDonald 5 74
(Andrew Balding) *pressed ldr: rdn over 2f out: no ex and lost two pls ins fnl f* **5/2**[2]

-120 **5** 1/2 **Pea Shooter**[11] [907] 10-9-4 **77**........................ BenRobinson(3) 1 72
(Brian Ellison) *trckd ldrs: effrt and rdn 2f out: no ex ins fnl f* **14/1**

58.56s (-0.94) **Going Correction** +0.175s/f (Slow) **5** Ran SP% **114.2**
Speed ratings (Par 105): **112,108,108,107,106**
CSF £4.76 TOTE £1.80: £1.20, £1.90; EX 4.40 Trifecta £29.60.
Owner Antony Brittain **Bred** Yeomanstown Stud **Trained** Warthill, N Yorks

FOCUS
The feature contest was a fair little sprint handicap. The odds-on favourite only took 58.56 seconds to win it from the front towards the near rail.

1083 SUNRACING.CO.UK H'CAP — 1m 5y (Tp)
7:00 (7:00) (Class 6) (0-60,57) 4-Y-0+
£3,105 (£924; £461; £400; £400; £400) **Stalls** Centre

Form RPR

0-56 **1** **Insurplus (IRE)**[16] [808] 6-9-4 **57**........................ PhilDennis(3) 10 67
(Jim Goldie) *hld up: smooth hdwy on nr side of gp 2f out: led ent fnl f: shkn up and kpt on wl fnl 100yds* **6/1**[3]

50-3 **2** 1 1/2 **Lukoutoldmakezebak**[7] [969] 6-8-3 **46**..................(p) RPWalsh(7) 8 53
(David Thompson) *led after 1f and set decent gallop: rdn 2f out: hdd ent fnl f: kpt on same pce last 100yds* **11/4**[2]

3 2 **La Cumparsita (IRE)**[181] [7091] 5-8-9 **45**........................ JasonHart 6 48
(Tristan Davidson) *t.k.h: hld up in tch: smooth hdwy to press ldrs over 1f out: rdn and outpcd last 100yds* **2/1**[1]

55-4 **4** 2 **Don't Be Surprised**[59] [125] 4-9-3 **56**..................(h) BenRobinson(3) 5 54
(Seb Spencer) *hld up: drvn and outpcd over 2f out: rallied over 1f out: kpt on fnl f: nt pce to chal (jockey said gelding was never travelling)* **2/1**[1]

0-05 **5** 3 3/4 **Rioja Day (IRE)**[11] [611] 9-8-2 **45**..................(p) CoreyMadden(7) 4 35
(Jim Goldie) *led 1f: chsd ldrs: rdn over 2f out: wknd over 1f out* **50/1**

00-3 **6** 1/2 **Manomine**[16] [208] 10-8-5 **48**..................(b) GearoidBrouder(7) 9 37
(R K Watson, Ire) *hld up on nr side of gp: drvn and outpcd over 2f out: n.d after* **10/1**

00/0 **7** 1 1/2 **Whisper A Word (IRE)**[7] [971] 5-8-9 **45**........................ MirkoSanna 3 31
(Lucinda Egerton) *pressed ldr: rdn over 2f out: wknd over 1f out* **125/1**

0-04 **8** 1 1/4 **Deolali**[36] [501] 5-8-9 **45**........................ CamHardie 2 28
(Stella Barclay) *hld up: drvn and outpcd over 2f out: btn over 1f out* **33/1**

23-0 **9** 1 1/2 **Lord Rob**[7] [969] 8-8-12 **48**..................(p) CliffordLee 1 28
(David Thompson) *missed break: hld up: stdy hdwy over 3f out: rdn and wknd over 2f out* **20/1**

000/ **10** 8 **Circuit**[581] [5618] 5-8-4 **45**........................ AndrewBreslin(5) 7 7
(Wilf Storey) *missed break: bhd: struggling 3f out: sn btn (jockey said mare was slowly away)* **125/1**

1m 40.01s (1.41) **Going Correction** +0.175s/f (Slow) **10** Ran SP% **128.0**
Speed ratings (Par 101): **99,97,95,93,89 89,87,86,85,77**
CSF £24.82 CT £47.39 TOTE £7.70: £1.90, £1.60, £1.10; EX 34.40 Trifecta £105.00.
Owner Mr & Mrs G Grant & Partner **Bred** Patrick J Monahan **Trained** Uplawmoor, E Renfrews

FOCUS
A moderate handicap. The winning time was fair for the grade but they went quite hard up front playing into the hands of a hold-up horse in the winner. The second has been rated in line with the balance of his form here last year.

1084 LADBROKES HOME OF THE ODDS BOOST H'CAP — 7f 14y (Tp)
7:30 (7:30) (Class 6) (0-65,66) 3-Y-0
£3,105 (£924; £461; £400; £400; £400) **Stalls** Centre

Form RPR

60-5 **1** **Simba Samba**[32] [606] 3-8-3 **45**........................ DuranFentiman 7 55+
(Philip McBride) *hld up in tch: hdwy to ld over 1f out: rdn clr fnl f* **15/2**

-231 **2** 3 **Macs Blessings (IRE)**[31] [612] 3-9-0 **56**..................(p) LiamKeniry 6 58
(Stef Keniry) *hld up in tch: hdwy to chse wnr over 1f out: kpt on fnl f: nt pce to chal* **9/4**[2]

3-66 **3** 1 1/4 **Cheap Jack**[39] [461] 3-9-3 **66**........................ RPWalsh(7) 2 65
(Ronald Thompson) *led at ordinary gallop: rdn and hdd over 1f out: edgd lft and sn one pce* **4/1**[3]

014 **4** hd **Kodi Dream**[33] [585] 3-8-13 **60**..................(h[1]) BenSanderson(5) 4 58
(Roger Fell) *t.k.h: hld up: pushed along over 2f out: hdwy and edgd lft over 1f out: no imp fnl f* **2/1**[1]

0-20 **5** 1 3/4 **Klipperty Klopp**[9] [931] 3-9-4 **60**........................ CamHardie 5 54
(Antony Brittain) *cl up: effrt and ev ch briefly over 1f out: outpcd fnl f* **8/1**

-200 **6** 1 3/4 **Arriba De Toda (IRE)**[31] [612] 3-7-11 **46**..................(p[1]) KieranSchofield(7) 8 36
(Brian Ellison) *trckd ldrs: rdn over 2f out: edgd rt and wknd appr fnl f* **20/1**

03-0 **7** nk **Alfred The Grey (IRE)**[31] [612] 3-9-1 **60**........................ PhilDennis(3) 1 49
(Tracy Waggott) *dwlt: hld up: rdn over 2f out: no imp whn hmpd ins fnl f* **20/1**

000- **8** 1 3/4 **Fitzy**[169] [7462] 3-8-4 **49**........................ AaronJones(3) 9 34
(David Brown) *cl up: rdn along over 2f out: edgd lft and wknd over 1f out* **16/1**

1m 28.07s (1.87) **Going Correction** +0.175s/f (Slow) **8** Ran SP% **122.4**
Speed ratings (Par 96): **96,92,91,90,88 86,86,84**
CSF £26.67 CT £80.01 TOTE £9.30: £2.40, £1.10, £1.90; EX 33.50 Trifecta £175.30.
Owner PMRacing **Bred** J W Mitchell **Trained** Newmarket, Suffolk
■ Good Tyne Girl was withdrawn. Price at time of withdrawal 6-1. Rule 4 applies to board prices prior to withdrawal but not to SP bets - deduction 10p in the pound. New market formed
■ Stewards' Enquiry : Kieran Schofield two-day ban: careless riding (Mar 22-23)

FOCUS
A modest 3yo handicap. The time was no better than fair for the grade but the winner picked up strongly to win decisively up the seemingly favoured near rail. Straightforward form in behind the winner.

1085 BETWAY LIVE CASINO H'CAP — 5f (Tp)
8:00 (8:00) (Class 6) (0-60,55) 4-Y-0+
£3,105 (£924; £461; £400; £400; £400) **Stalls** Centre

Form RPR

43-0 **1** **Decision Maker (IRE)**[64] [43] 5-9-3 **54**........................ TimClark(3) 5 61
(Roy Bowring) *t.k.h: pressed ldr: led 1/2-way: rdn: edgd lft and r.o wl fnl f (trainers rep said regarding apparent improvement in form that that the gelding appreciated the return to Newcastle where it has run well in the past and benefited from a 2 month break)* **10/11**[1]

5006 **2** 1 1/2 **Windforpower (IRE)**[7] [973] 9-8-10 **47** ow1........................ BenRobinson(3) 4 49
(Tracy Waggott) *prom: effrt and chsd wnr over 1f out: kpt on fnl f: nt pce to chal* **7/2**[3]

0252 **3** 3/4 **Star Cracker (IRE)**[7] [973] 7-8-10 **47**..................(p) PhilDennis(3) 1 46
(Jim Goldie) *cl up: effrt and disp 2nd pl over 1f out to ins fnl f: one pce* **3/1**[2]

260- **4** 1/2 **Guiding Star**[148] [8131] 5-8-6 **47**..................(p) GearoidBrouder(7) 6 44
(Patrick J McKenna, Ire) *hld up: rdn and effrt over 1f out: no imp fnl f* **11/2**

060- **5** 1 1/2 **Ise Lodge Babe**[251] [4376] 4-8-4 **45**........................ RPWalsh(7) 7 37
(Ronald Thompson) *s.i.s: sn prom: rdn over 2f out: outpcd fr over 1f out* **100/1**

000/ **6** 3 1/4 **Climax**[865] [7579] 5-9-7 **55**........................ DuranFentiman 2 35
(Wilf Storey) *hld up: rdn over 2f out: wknd over 1f out* **50/1**

The Form Book Flat 2019, Raceform Ltd, Newbury, RG14 5SJ

0-00 **7** *11* **Spoken Words**[50] 279 10-8-8 **45**....................(p) NoelGarbutt(3) 3
(John David Riches) *led to 1/2-way: rdn and wknd wl over 1f out* **200/1**

1m 1.16s (1.66) **Going Correction** +0.175s/f (Slow) **7** Ran SP% **118.4**
Speed ratings (Par 101): **93,90,89,88,86 81,63**
CSF £4.92 CT £7.09 TOTE £2.00: £1.30, £2.00; EX 5.70 Trifecta £11.00.
Owner K Nicholls **Bred** Brian Miller **Trained** Edwinstowe, Notts

FOCUS
A moderate sprint handicap. The heavily backed odds-on favourite won readily towards the seemingly favoured near side in a modest time.
T/Plt: £19.20 to a £1 stake. Pool: £82,327.44 - 3,119.93 winning units T/Qpdt: £9.80 to a £1 stake. Pool: £9,668.97 - 723.98 winning units **Richard Young**

1086 - 1092a (Foreign Racing) - See Raceform Interactive

1031 KEMPTON (A.W) (R-H)

Saturday, March 9

OFFICIAL GOING: Polytrack: standard to slow
Wind: light to medium, across Weather: overcast

1093 RACING TV APPRENTICE H'CAP 6f (P)

5:30 (5:32) (Class 7) (0-50,50) 4-Y-O+ **£2,587** (£770; £384; £192) **Stalls** Low

Form RPR

00 **1** **Mr Potter**[3] 1032 6-9-5 **48**....................(v) SeamusCronin 2 55
(Richard Guest) *taken down early: chsd ldrs: effrt jst over 1f out: rdn and hdwy to ld 100yds out: r.o wl (trainer's rep said, as to the apparent improvement in form, the gelding had worn earplugs on it's previous run but they had been removed at the start on this occasion)* **5/1**[2]

-524 **2** *1 3/4* **Canimar**[24] 702 4-8-11 **45**....................(p) GavinAshton(5) 9 47
(Shaun Keightley) *t.k.h: led early: sn hdd and chsd ldrs: rdn to chal and edgd rt over 1f out: led ent fnl f: hdd and no ex 100yds out: sddle slipped (jockey his saddle slipped and that the filly hung right-handed n the straight)* **7/1**

5536 **3** *3/4* **Storm Lightning**[17] 809 10-8-11 **45**.................... GraceMcEntee(5) 7 46
(Mark Brisbourne) *pushed along leaving stalls: racd in last trio: effrt 2f out: hdwy u.p over 1f out: chsd ldrs ins fnl f: kpt on same pce and nt clrest of runs towards fin* **16/1**

-403 **4** *1/2* **Alligator**[17] 809 5-8-8 **45**....................(p) ElishaWhittington(8) 4 43
(Tony Carroll) *hld up in tch in midfield: nt clr run 2f out: hdwy u.p jst over 1f out: edgd rt and kpt on ins fnl f: nvr getting on terms w wnr* **7/1**

-520 **5** *1 1/4* **Dalness Express**[35] 553 6-8-12 **49**....................(t) KateLeahy(8) 12 44
(John O'Shea) *hld up in rr: pushed along and hdwy over 1f out: styd on ins fnl f: nvr trbld ldrs* **11/1**

-053 **6** *1 1/2* **Legal Mind**[36] 531 6-9-4 **50**....................(v[1]) TristanPrice(3) 3 40
(Emma Owen) *t.k.h: hld up in last trio: effrt on inner ent fnl 2f: drvn and hdwy over 1f out: keeping on but no threat to wnr whn nt clr run and hmpd ins fnl f: swtchd lft towards fin (jockey said horse was denied a clear run)* **11/2**[3]

1000 **7** *1* **Deer Song**[10] 919 6-9-3 **46**....................(b) KatherineBegley 8 33
(John Bridger) *pushed along leaving stalls: sn led and crossed to inner: rdn 2f out: sn drvn and hdd edgd rt ent fnl f: fdd fnl 100yds (jockey said gelding hung right-handed in the straight)* **40/1**

5-40 **8** *3/4* **Queen Of Kalahari**[22] 742 4-9-3 **49**....................(t) CierenFallon(3) 1 34
(Les Eyre) *in tch in midfield: edgd rt and unable qck u.p over 1f out: wknd ins fnl f (jockey said filly hung right-handed throughout)* **7/2**[1]

-400 **9** *1* **Toolatetodelegate**[17] 809 5-9-1 **49**....................(vt) SeanKirrane(5) 6 31
(Brian Barr) *in tch in midfield: unable qck and no imp over 1f out: wknd ins fnl f* **16/1**

-060 **10** *3* **Wotamadam**[23] 718 4-9-5 **48**....................(p[1]) ThoreHammerHansen 5 21
(Dean Ivory) *chsd ldrs: unable qck u.p and lost pl over 1f out: wknd ins fnl f* **9/1**

000- **11** *nk* **Noble Deed**[185] 6947 9-9-2 **45**....................(p) ScottMcCullagh 10 17
(Michael Attwater) *in tch in midfield on outer: lost pl u.p ent fnl 2f: bhd ins fnl f* **40/1**

1m 13.97s (0.87) **Going Correction** +0.15s/f (Slow) **11** Ran SP% **114.2**
Speed ratings (Par 97): **100,97,96,96,94 92,91,90,88,84 84**
CSF £38.73 CT £520.71 TOTE £5.30: £1.90, £2.90, £4.80; EX 48.30 Trifecta £333.50.
Owner A Turton, A Rhodes & Mrs Alison Guest **Bred** P Balding **Trained** Ingmanthorpe, W Yorks

FOCUS
A rock-bottom apprentice handicap in which only two of the 11 runners had been placed in their most recent outing. The pace was solid enough and the market got it spot on. The winner is entitled to rated to this level on his late 2018 form.

1094 32RED ON THE APP STORE NOVICE STKS 7f (P)

6:00 (6:03) (Class 5) 3-Y-O+ **£3,881** (£1,155; £577; £288) **Stalls** Low

Form RPR

1 **Nahham (IRE)** 4-10-0 0.................... SeanLevey 8 76
(Richard Hannon) *chsd ldr tl led after 2f: rdn over 1f out: sustained duel w rival ins fnl f: r.o wl u.p: jst prevailed* **7/2**[2]

-224 **2** *nse* **Derry Boy**[21] 761 3-8-12 72.................... EoinWalsh 2 70
(David Evans) *taken down early and led to post: broke wl: led for 2f: styd handy: effrt and ev ch jst ins fnl f: sustained duel w wnr after: r.o wl: jst hld* **11/10**[1]

00- **3** *1 1/2* **Azets**[232] 5169 3-8-12 0.................... MartinDwyer 5 66+
(Amanda Perrett) *stdd s: hld up in last quartet: squeezed through: hdwy and swtchd rt ent fnl 2f: chsd clr ldng trio over 1f out: clsng and swtchd lft ins fnl f: wnt 3rd and gng on strly towards fin* **7/2**[2]

5 **4** *nk* **Velvet Morn (IRE)**[22] 732 4-9-2 0.................... Pierre-LouisJamin(7) 9 66
(William Knight) *chsd ldrs: wnt 2nd over 4f out: rdn and ev ch over 1f out tl no ex jst ins fnl f: outpcd fnl 100yds and lost 3rd towards fin* **16/1**

6-5 **5** *4 1/2* **Lucky Lou (IRE)**[63] 78 3-8-4 0.................... WilliamCox(3) 6 48
(Ken Cunningham-Brown) *wnt lft s: t.k.h: chsd ldrs: rdn and outpcd over 1f out: wl hld 5th 1f out: plugged on* **14/1**[3]

0 **6** *1/2* **Sacred Warner (IRE)**[35] 554 3-8-12 0.................... HectorCrouch 7 52
(Clive Cox) *dwlt and swtchd rt sn after s: hld up towards rr: swtchd lft and effrt over 2f out: no threat to ldrs but styd on ins fnl f* **20/1**

0 **7** *1 1/2* **Storm Girl**[63] 78 3-8-7 0.................... CharlieBennett 1 43
(Michael Attwater) *rn green in midfield: swtchd rt and effrt ent fnl 2f: sn outpcd and wl hld 1f out* **100/1**

0-6 **8** *1 1/4* **Nefyn Beach (IRE)**[50] 289 3-8-0 0.................... GeorgiaDobie(7) 11 39
(Jo Hughes, France) *t.k.h: hld up in midfield: effrt jst over 2f out: no threat to ldrs and keeping on same pce whn swtchd rt 1f out* **33/1**

0 **9** *nk* **Risk Mitigation (USA)**[11] 913 3-8-12 0.................... PaddyMathers 3 43
(David Evans) *a towards rr: rdn 3f out: keeping on but no threat to ldrs whn swtchd rt over 1f out: kpt on* **50/1**

00 **10** *hd* **Angel Black (IRE)**[11] 913 3-8-12 0.................... LiamJones 4 43
(Shaun Keightley) *midfield: rdn over 2f out unable qck and lost pl over 1f out: wknd fnl f* **40/1**

11 *1 1/4* **Rifft (IRE)** 4-10-0 0.................... JoeyHaynes 10 45
(Lydia Richards) *a in rr: nvr involved* **66/1**

0- **12** *6* **Time To Rock**[71] 9732 4-10-0 0.................... KieranO'Neill 12 29
(John Bridger) *plld hrd: hld up in midfield: hdwy to chse ldrs after 2f: rdn over 2f out: lost pl and hung lft jst over 1f out: bhd and eased wl ins fnl f (jockey said gelding ran too free)* **200/1**

1m 27.66s (1.66) **Going Correction** +0.15s/f (Slow)
WFA 3 from 4yo 16lb **12** Ran SP% **119.7**
Speed ratings (Par 103): **96,95,94,93,88 88,86,85,84,84 83,76**
CSF £7.49 TOTE £3.90: £1.80, £1.10, £1.80; EX 9.70 Trifecta £24.50.
Owner Al Shaqab Racing **Bred** George Kent **Trained** East Everleigh, Wilts

FOCUS
Despite the size of the field, this wasn't a deep novice event with the runner-up having an official mark of 72, but a thrilling finish. The winner, second and fourth were up there throughout.

1095 100% PROFIT BOOST AT 32REDSPORT.COM H'CAP (DIV I) 1m 3f 219y(P)

6:30 (6:32) (Class 5) (0-75,77) 4-Y-O+

£3,752 (£1,116; £557; £400; £400; £400) **Stalls** Low

Form RPR

-032 **1** **Singing Sheriff**[18] 793 4-8-12 **66**.................... LiamKeniry 4 71
(Ed Walker) *chsd ldng trio: effrt to and clsd to chal 2f out: drvn over 1f out: sustained effrt ins fnl f to ld cl home* **11/4**[1]

14-2 **2** *nk* **Hackbridge**[14] 876 4-9-1 **72**....................(p) PaddyBradley(3) 7 76
(Pat Phelan) *chsd ldrs: swtchd lft and effrt over 1f out: kpt on wl u.p ins fnl f: snatched 2nd last stride* **7/1**

6-66 **3** *shd* **Surrey Blaze (IRE)**[21] 754 4-9-3 **74**.................... FinleyMarsh(3) 1 78
(Joseph Tuite) *chsd ldr tl rdn to ld 2f out drvn and hrd pressed over 1f out: battled on u.p tl hdd and rdr briefly stopped riding wl ins fnl f: lost 2nd last stride* **7/2**[3]

160- **4** *3/4* **Dangerous Ends**[87] 9505 5-9-7 **74**.................... CallumShepherd 9 77
(Brett Johnson) *stdd and dropped in bhd after s: hld up in last pair: effrt over 1f out: hdwy u.p 1f out: kpt on wl ins fnl f: nvr quite getting to ldrs* **12/1**

14-5 **5** *hd* **Galactic Spirit**[31] 617 4-9-6 **77**....................(p[1]) GabrieleMalune(3) 2 79
(Marco Botti) *t.k.h: hld up in tch in midfield: effrt over 1f out: chsd ldrs and nt enough room ins fnl f: kpt on same pce towards fin* **10/3**[2]

531/ **6** *3/4* **Music Man (IRE)**[948] 5035 9-9-6 **73**.................... CharlieBennett 8 74
(Hughie Morrison) *hld up in tch in midfield: effrt 2f out: kpt on same pce u.p ins fnl f* **25/1**

-120 **7** *hd* **Ice Canyon**[9] 945 5-9-2 **69**....................(h) EoinWalsh 6 70
(Mark Brisbourne) *stdd s: hld up in last pair: swtchd rt and hdwy on inner ent fnl 2f: chsd ldrs over 1f out tl no ex 1f out: outpcd ins fnl f* **15/2**

8 *26* **Bringthehousedown (IRE)**[307] 2462 5-9-4 **71**.................... DavidProbert 3 30
(Ron Hodges) *led tl rdn and hdd 2f out: sn dropped out u.p: bhd fnl f (jockey said gelding stopped quickly)* **12/1**

2m 38.12s (3.62) **Going Correction** +0.15s/f (Slow)
WFA 4 from 5yo+ 1lb **8** Ran SP% **115.5**
Speed ratings (Par 103): **93,92,92,92,92 91,91,74**
CSF £22.86 CT £68.59 TOTE £3.20: £1.40, £1.90, £1.70; EX 15.60 Trifecta £39.30.
Owner Robert Ng **Bred** Miss K Rausing **Trained** Upper Lambourn, Berks

■ Stewards' Enquiry : Finley Marsh 10-day ban: failing to take all reasonable and permissible measures to obtain the best possible placing (Mar 23, 25-31, Apr 1-2)

FOCUS
The first division of an ordinary middle-distance handicap in which a fair early pace had slowed considerably by halfway and the principals finished in a heap. The form may not be totally reliable as a result.

1096 100% PROFIT BOOST AT 32REDSPORT.COM H'CAP (DIV II) 1m 3f 219y(P)

7:00 (7:01) (Class 5) (0-75,75) 4-Y-O+

£3,752 (£1,116; £557; £400; £400; £400) **Stalls** Low

Form RPR

-143 **1** **Nylon Speed (IRE)**[21] 754 5-9-7 **75**....................(t) DavidProbert 1 83
(Alan King) *hld up wl in tch in last trio: clsd and swtchd rt ent fnl 2f: rdn to ld jst over 1f out: r.o wl ins fnl f* **11/4**[1]

0-22 **2** *3/4* **Dono Di Dio**[21] 754 4-8-13 **75**.................... ScottMcCullagh(7) 3 81
(Michael Madgwick) *t.k.h early: hld up in tch in rr: clsd and swtchd rt ent fnl 2f: hdwy u.p to chse wnr ins fnl f: r.o but a hld* **5/1**[3]

3-21 **3** *nse* **Double Legend (IRE)**[35] 560 4-8-6 **61**....................(b) MartinDwyer 7 67
(Amanda Perrett) *hld up wl in tch in last trio: clsd and nt rt swtchd 2f out: swtchd lft and hdwy ent fnl f: styd on wl u.p: nvr quite getting to wnr* **10/3**[2]

3311 **4** *1 3/4* **Berrahri (IRE)**[20] 780 8-9-5 **73**.................... KierenFox 5 76
(John Best) *led: rdn ent fnl 2f: hdd jst over 1f out: lost 2 pls ins fnl f and outpcd fnl 75yds* **12/1**

052- **5** *1 3/4* **Sauchiehall Street (IRE)**[108] 9179 4-9-3 **72**.................... RobHornby 4 72
(Noel Williams) *chsd ldr for 1f: styd handy: unable qck u.p over 1f out: outpcd 1f out: wl hld and plugged on same pce ins fnl f* **7/1**

444- **6** *2* **With Good Grace (IRE)**[126] 8824 4-9-0 **69**.................... PJMcDonald 2 66
(Charles Hills) *trckd ldrs on inner: wnt 2nd over 2f out and sn rdn to chal: unable qck over 1f out: wknd ins fnl f* **16/1**

5-60 **7** *7* **Tenedos**[17] 803 4-9-4 **73**....................(b[1]) KieranO'Neill 6 59
(Ed de Giles) *dwlt and pushed along early: hdwy to chse ldr after 1f tl over 2f out: sn lost pl u.p: bhd ins fnl f* **25/1**

21-3 **8** *9* **Involved**[42] 434 4-9-5 **74**.................... RobertWinston 9 46
(Daniel Kubler) *stdd s: t.k.h: in tch in midfield on outer: rdn and unable qck jst over 2f out: lost pl over 1f out: bhd ins fnl f (jockey said colt stopped quickly)* **6/1**

2m 34.45s (-0.05) **Going Correction** +0.15s/f (Slow)
WFA 4 from 5yo+ 1lb **8** Ran SP% **110.6**
Speed ratings (Par 103): **106,105,105,104,103 101,97,91**
CSF £15.57 CT £43.36 TOTE £3.30: £1.40, £1.50, £2.20; EX 18.50 Trifecta £55.20.
Owner Axom Lxxiv **Bred** Stiftung Gestut Fahrhof **Trained** Barbury Castle, Wilts

FOCUS
They didn't go a great pace here either, but the winning time was still 3.67sec quicker than the first division. The first three home were the last three turning in.

1097 32RED.COM H'CAP — 7f (P)
7:30 (7:30) (Class 3) (0-95,96) 4-Y-0+
£9,337 (£2,796; £1,398; £699; £349; £175) Stalls Low

Form — RPR

1-34 **1** **Sanaadh**[17] 805 6-9-5 **91**......(t) FrannyNorton 5 100+
(Michael Wigham) *hld up in tch: pushed along over 1f out: stl only 7th 1f out: str run u.p ins fnl f to ld towards fin* 3/1[1]

6-00 **2** ¾ **Love Dreams (IRE)**[16] 843 5-9-6 **92**......(b) PJMcDonald 6 99
(Mark Johnston) *chsd ldrs tl wnt 2nd over 5f out: rdn 2f out: sn drvn and kpt on to chal ins fnl f: nt quite match pce of wnr towards fin but snatched 2nd last strides* 7/1[3]

-320 **3** hd **Exchequer (IRE)**[17] 805 8-9-3 **89**......(p) SeanLevey 12 95
(Richard Guest) *chsd ldr tl led over 5f out: off side cheekpiece fell off at 1/2-way: rdn 2f out: drvn over 1f out: hdd and no ex towards fin: lost 2nd last strides* 20/1

421- **4** ½ **Lethal Lunch**[172] 7385 4-9-4 **90**......AdamKirby 2 95
(Clive Cox) *hld up in tch in midfield: swtchd rt and clsd 2f out: drvn to chse wnr ins fnl f: no ex wl ins fnl f: outpcd towards fin* 7/2[2]

360- **5** 1 **Donncha (IRE)**[267] 3828 8-8-13 **88**......BenRobinson(3) 7 90
(Seb Spencer) *hld up in tch in midfield: effrt and edgd rt 1f out: kpt on u.p ins fnl f* 25/1

-360 **6** nse **Swift Approval (IRE)**[15] 856 7-8-9 **81**......(h[1]) TomMarquand 1 83
(Stuart Williams) *chsd ldrs: effrt jst over 2f out: chsd ldrs and keeping on same pce whn nt clrest of runs wl ins fnl f: swtchd rt towards fin* 15/2

56-1 **7** 1 **Maksab (IRE)**[15] 856 4-8-9 **88**......ScottMcCullagh(7) 10 87
(Mick Channon) *t.k.h: led tl over 5f out: styd chsng ldrs: effrt u.p on inner over 1f out: no ex and wknd ins fnl f* 10/1

6-40 **8** 1 **Ultimate Avenue (IRE)**[21] 762 5-9-4 **90**......(h) StevieDonohoe 3 86
(David Simcock) *s.i.s: hld up in tch in rr: effrt on inner over 1f out: kpt on but nvr trbld ldrs (jockey said gelding was slowly away)* 25/1

615- **9** 2 **Taurean Star (IRE)**[281] 3330 6-9-5 **91**......RobHornby 4 82
(Ralph Beckett) *hld up in tch in last trio: effrt over 2f out: nvr threatened to get on terms* 7/1[3]

0066 **10** hd **Atletico (IRE)**[12] 909 7-9-2 **88**......EoinWalsh 9 78
(David Evans) *hld up in tch in last pair: effrt over 2f out: no imp and nvr threatened ldrs* 50/1

135- **11** 5 **War Glory (IRE)**[150] 8105 6-9-5 **96**......ThoreHammerHansen(5) 11 73
(Richard Hannon) *midfield on outer: clsd to chse ldrs 5f out: rdn over 2f out: lost pl over 1f out: bhd ins fnl f* 8/1

1m 24.47s (-1.53) **Going Correction** +0.15s/f (Slow) 11 Ran SP% 118.6
Speed ratings (Par 107): **114,113,112,112,111 111,110,108,106,106 100**
CSF £23.44 CT £369.12 TOTE £3.80: £1.40, £2.60, £5.20; EX 24.30 Trifecta £289.10.
Owner M Wigham, G D J Linder, S Hassiakos **Bred** Rabbah Bloodstock Limited **Trained** Newmarket, Suffolk

FOCUS
A decent handicap run at a strong pace in a good time. Solid form.

1098 32RED H'CAP — 6f (P)
8:00 (8:00) (Class 3) (0-90,90) 4-Y-0+
£9,337 (£2,796; £1,398; £699; £349; £175) Stalls Low

Form — RPR

-311 **1** **Treacherous**[21] 755 5-8-12 **81**......CallumShepherd 6 87
(Ed de Giles) *hld up in midfield: 4th and stl plenty to do whn swtchd lft over 1f out: chsd ldr and 4 l down ins fnl f: r.o wl u.p to ld cl home* 4/1[3]

0-36 **2** hd **Equitation**[19] 786 5-8-11 **80**......(t) SeanLevey 7 85
(Stuart Williams) *hld up in midfield: nt clr run over 1f out tl rdn and hdwy ins fnl f: r.o v strly and ev ch towards fin: snatched 2nd on post* 7/1

4-66 **3** nse **Erissimus Maximus (FR)**[34] 588 5-9-0 **83**......NicolaCurrie 5 88
(Amy Murphy) *chsd ldrs: effrt 2f out: rallied u.p ins fnl f: r.o strly and ev ch nr fin: lost 2nd on post* 20/1

044- **4** hd **Global Academy (IRE)**[256] 4215 4-9-2 **85**......DanielMuscutt 9 89
(Gay Kelleway) *led: wnt clr fr 1/2-way: 5 l clr and rdn 2f out: stl wl clr and drvn 1f out: tired and reduced advantage fnl 75yds: hdd and lost 3 pls cl home* 40/1

-630 **5** ¾ **Compas Scoobie**[3] 1036 6-8-3 **77**......ThoreHammerHansen(5) 10 79
(Stuart Williams) *stdd and dropped in after s: hld up in rr: hdwy u.p 1f out: styd on wl ins fnl f: nvr quite getting to ldrs* 16/1

16-2 **6** ½ **Little Boy Blue**[7] 981 4-8-10 **86**......(h) SeamusCronin(7) 4 86
(Bill Turner) *t.k.h: chsd ldr: rdn and 5 l down 2f out: keeping on ins fnl f: nt clr run and forced to eased cl home* 7/1

-114 **7** ½ **Choice Encounter**[21] 755 4-8-9 **78**......HollieDoyle 3 77
(Archie Watson) *prom in main gp: effrt in 3rd 2f out: kpt on ins fnl f: nt quite enough pce to threaten ldrs* 7/2[2]

14-0 **8** ½ **Roman River**[35] 563 4-9-7 **90**......TomMarquand 2 87
(Martin Smith) *hld up in last trio: effrt 2f out: swtchd lft and kpt on ins fnl f: nvr getting to ldrs* 3/1[1]

-046 **9** 3 **Foxy Forever (IRE)**[16] 837 9-9-1 **84**......(t) FrannyNorton 8 71
(Michael Wigham) *t.k.h: hld up in tch in midfield: effrt 2f out: nvr threatened to get on terms: plugged on ins fnl f* 25/1

1550 **10** ¾ **Kodiline (IRE)**[10] 922 5-8-1 **77**......GinaMangan(7) 11 62
(David Evans) *hld up towards rr: effrt over 1f out: kpt on ins fnl f but nvr involved* 50/1

36-1 **11** ½ **Doc Sportello (IRE)**[52] 254 7-9-3 **86**......RobertWinston 1 69
(Tony Carroll) *t.k.h: hld up in last trio: effrt u.p over 1f out: kpt on ins fnl f but nvr involved (jockey said gelding ran too free)* 11/1

1m 12.66s (-0.44) **Going Correction** +0.15s/f (Slow) 11 Ran SP% 119.4
Speed ratings (Par 107): **108,107,107,107,106 105,105,104,100,99 98**
CSF £31.41 CT £508.00 TOTE £3.60: £1.80, £3.00, £3.70; EX 41.20 Trifecta £488.00.
Owner Woodham Walter Partnership **Bred** P M Hicks **Trained** Ledbury, H'fords

FOCUS
A warm sprint handicap and an amazing spectacle, with a horse who looked to have an unassailable lead passing the furlong pole not even being placed.

1099 32RED CASINO H'CAP (LONDON MILE SERIES QUALIFIER) — 1m (P)
8:30 (8:32) (Class 4) (0-85,84) 4-Y-0+
£6,469 (£1,925; £962; £481; £400; £400) Stalls Low

Form — RPR

01-1 **1** **Merchant Of Venice**[32] 608 4-9-2 **79**......GeorgeWood 1 85+
(James Fanshawe) *trckd ldrs: effrt between rivals over 1f out: led ins fnl f: r.o wl whn pressed wl ins fnl f* 7/4[1]

-141 **2** ½ **Harbour Vision**[17] 801 4-8-10 **73**......PaddyMathers 7 78
(Derek Shaw) *stdd s: hld up in tch in rr: swtchd lft and effrt 2f out: hdwy u.p 1f out: wnt 2nd and pressing wnr wl ins fnl f: r.o but hld towards fin* 6/1

-642 **3** ½ **Margie's Choice (GER)**[24] 699 4-8-10 **73**......(v[1]) TomMarquand 2 77
(Michael Madgwick) *pressed ldr: drvn and ev ch over 1f out: unable qck and one pce wl ins fnl f* 12/1

2-21 **4** 1¼ **Oneovdem**[14] 886 5-8-9 **77**......TheodoreLadd(5) 3 78
(Tim Pinfield) *led: rdn and hrd pressed over 1f out: hdd ins fnl f: no ex and outpcd towards fin* 7/2[2]

3132 **5** 1¼ **Glory Of Paris (IRE)**[17] 812 5-9-7 **84**......LukeMorris 6 82
(Michael Appleby) *t.k.h: hld up wl in tch in midfield: nt clr run ent fnl 2f: effrt over 1f out: kpt on same pce fnl f (jockey said gelding ran too free)* 4/1[3]

3453 **6** nse **Scofflaw**[10] 922 5-9-2 **79**......(v) EoinWalsh 4 77
(David Evans) *t.k.h: wl in tch in midfield: effrt 2f out: unable qck over 1f out: kpt on same pce ins fnl f (jockey said gelding ran too free)* 9/2

-540 **7** 4½ **Mont Kinabalu (IRE)**[17] 812 4-8-9 **72**......KevinStott 5 60
(Kevin Ryan) *dwlt: hld up in tch in last pair: no imp over 1f out: wknd ins fnl f* 10/1

1m 39.46s (-0.34) **Going Correction** +0.15s/f (Slow) 7 Ran SP% 127.8
Speed ratings (Par 105): **107,106,106,104,103 103,98**
CSF £15.32 TOTE £2.80: £2.30, £2.20; EX 25.10 Trifecta £199.90.
Owner Mr & Mrs P Hopper, Mr & Mrs M Morris **Bred** Mr & Mrs P Hopper & Mr & Mrs M Morris **Trained** Newmarket, Suffolk
■ Stewards' Enquiry : Paddy Mathers two-day ban: used whip above the permitted level (Mar 23, 25)

FOCUS
A fair handicap, but they didn't go a great pace and those ridden handily were favoured. The winner was the one with scope for further improvement.
T/Plt: £55.70 to a £1 stake. Pool: £79,612.23 - 1,042.65 winning units T/Qpdt: £9.90 to a £1 stake. Pool: £12,662.50 - 942.62 winning units **Steve Payne**

1021 WOLVERHAMPTON (A.W) (L-H)
Saturday, March 9

OFFICIAL GOING: Tapeta: standard
Wind: Strong behind Weather: Overcast

1100 BETWAY LIVE CASINO CLAIMING STKS — 5f 21y (Tp)
1:30 (1:30) (Class 5) 4-Y-0+
£3,752 (£1,116; £557; £300) Stalls Low

Form — RPR

-634 **1** **Drakefell (IRE)**[12] 907 4-9-5 76......(b) SeamusCronin(7) 3 85
(Richard Hannon) *mde all: qcknd 1/2-way: pushed clr over 1f out: r.o wl* 7/4[2]

-024 **2** 4 **It Must Be Faith**[15] 849 9-9-1 73......(p) JaneElliott(3) 2 63
(Michael Appleby) *plld hrd and prom: rdn over 1f out: styd on to go 2nd ins fnl f: no ch w wnr (vet reported the gelding had lost its left fore shoe)* 8/1[3]

3015 **3** 1½ **Captain Lars (SAF)**[7] 987 9-9-7 84......(b) ThomasGreatrex(5) 4 65
(Archie Watson) *sn chsng wnr: shkn up over 1f out: edgd lft and no ex ins fnl f: b.b.v (vet reported the gelding had bled from the nose)* 4/6[1]

00-0 **4** 1¼ **Excel Mate**[8] 973 5-8-4 42......CierenFallon(7) 1 46
(Roy Bowring) *s.i.s: hld up: pushed along and outpcd wl over 2f out: kpt on ins fnl f* 50/1

59.92s (-1.98) **Going Correction** -0.10s/f (Stan) 4 Ran SP% 109.4
Speed ratings (Par 103): **109,102,100,98**
CSF £13.34 TOTE £3.50; EX 9.30 Trifecta £12.60.The winner was claimed by Mr A. Brittain for £12,000
Owner Des Anderson **Bred** D J Anderson **Trained** East Everleigh, Wilts

FOCUS
A fair little claiming sprint on standard Tapeta. There is a reported strong headwind down the back straight. The field hesitated slightly leaving the gates but the second-favourite soon went on and kicked clear from over 2f out in a commanding victory.

1101 SUNRACING.CO.UK LINCOLN TRIAL H'CAP — 1m 142y (Tp)
2:05 (2:05) (Class 2) (0-105,105) 4-Y-0+
£31,125 (£9,320; £4,660; £2,330; £1,165; £585) Stalls Low

Form — RPR

200- **1** **Zwayyan**[140] 8409 6-9-2 **97**......DavidProbert 4 103+
(Andrew Balding) *hld up: hdwy over 1f out: rdn to ld wl ins fnl f: r.o* 7/1[2]

1-24 **2** 1 **Breden (IRE)**[17] 800 9-9-3 **98**......RobertWinston 2 101
(Linda Jewell) *hld up: hdwy over 4f out: rdn to ld and hung rt over 1f out: hdd wl ins fnl f: styd on* 14/1

002- **3** ¾ **Third Time Lucky (IRE)**[131] 8695 7-9-3 **98**......PaulHanagan 1 99
(Richard Fahey) *hld up in tch: rdn and ev ch ins fnl f: styd on same pce towards fin* 14/1

06-4 **4** shd **Qaffaal (USA)**[56] 212 8-8-13 **94**......NathanEvans 9 95
(Michael Easterby) *broke wl: sn stdd and lost pl: shkn up and swtchd lft ins fnl f: sn rdn: r.o to go 4th nr fin* 40/1

-000 **5** shd **Aquarium**[9] 961 4-9-4 **99**......FrannyNorton 12 100
(Mark Johnston) *dwlt: hld up: hdwy over 1f out: sn rdn: r.o* 28/1

051- **6** hd **Masham Star (IRE)**[125] 8866 5-9-8 **103**......JoeFanning 10 103
(Mark Johnston) *chsd ldr after 1f: carried wd wl over 1f out: rdn and ev ch sn after: styd on same pce wl ins fnl f* 20/1

3-00 **7** nk **Ventura Knight (IRE)**[30] 637 4-9-2 **97**......PJMcDonald 11 96
(Mark Johnston) *s.i.s: hdwy over 6f out: shkn up and nt clr run over 1f out: styd on* 33/1

4-25 **8** nk **Goring (GER)**[14] 880 7-9-4 **99**......(v) CharlesBishop 3 98
(Eve Johnson Houghton) *prom: stdd and lost pl after 1f: swtchd rt and hdwy over 1f out: nt rch ldrs* 10/1[3]

1-13 **9** 1 **Pinnata (IRE)**[17] 805 5-9-0 **95**......(t) JamieSpencer 5 92
(Stuart Williams) *sn led: rdn: hung rt and hdd over 1f out: no ex ins fnl f* 7/2[1]

246- **10** 1 **Wahash (IRE)**[224] 5498 5-9-3 **98**......TomMarquand 13 92
(Richard Hannon) *stdd s: hld up: rdn over 1f out: nt rch ldrs* 16/1

05-3 **11** ½ **Silver Quartz**[33] 601 4-9-5 **100**......HollieDoyle 8 93
(Archie Watson) *trckd ldrs: racd keenly: shkn up over 2f out: nt clr run over 1f out: swtchd lft: no ex ins fnl f (jockey said gelding stopped quickly)* 7/2[1]

164- **12** 2 **Victory Bond**[108] 9173 6-9-3 **105**......CierenFallon(7) 6 94
(William Haggas) *hld up in tch: rdn over 1f out: wknd ins fnl f* 7/2[1]

1-13 **13** 1 3/4 **Pactolus (IRE)**[14] 879 8-9-4 104........................(t) BenCoen(5) 7 89
(Stuart Williams) *s.i.s: hdwy over 5f out: rdn on outer over 2f out: wknd over 1f out (trainer said gelding was unsuited by racing very wide without cover throughout)* **12/1**

1m 47.31s (-2.79) **Going Correction** -0.10s/f (Stan) 13 Ran SP% **128.8**
Speed ratings (Par 109): **108,107,106,106,106 106,105,105,104,103 103,101,100**
CSF £104.78 CT £923.02 TOTE £7.80: £1.90, £4.10, £3.30; EX 135.30 Trifecta £2120.80.
Owner King Power Racing Co Ltd **Bred** Newsells Park Stud & Cheveley Park Stud **Trained** Kingsclere, Hants

FOCUS
A good renewal of this handicap, a trial for the Lincoln at Doncaster later this month. They went an even gallop into the headwind down the back straight and the winning time was over two seconds outside of standard in quite a bunched finish. The second and third help set the level.

1102 FOLLOW SUN RACING ON TWITTER NOVICE STKS 1m 142y (Tp)
2:40 (2:40) (Class 5) 4-Y-O+ **£3,752** (£1,116; £557; £278) **Stalls** Low

Form RPR
03 **1** **Willy Sewell**[7] 979 6-8-11 0........................ TheodoreLadd(5) 4 79
(Michael Appleby) *mde virtually all: shkn up over 2f out: rdn over 1f out: jst hld on* **11/1**
1 **2** shd **Masked Identity**[16] 841 4-9-9 0........................ JoeFanning 5 86
(Kevin Frost) *a.p: chsd wnr over 5f out: shkn up and ev ch fr over 1f out: r.o* **2/1**[2]
5/3- **3** 1 3/4 **Harbour Breeze (IRE)**[296] 2783 4-9-2 0........................ DavidProbert 9 75+
(Lucy Wadham) *hld up: hdwy and hung lft fr over 1f out: nt rch ldrs* **5/6**[1]
/2-2 **4** 3 3/4 **Sarasota (IRE)**[11] 913 4-8-11 68........................ NicolaCurrie 3 62
(Jamie Osborne) *sn w wnr tl over 6f out: remained handy: rdn over 1f out: no ex ins fnl f* **11/2**[3]
6 **5** nk **Bawaader (IRE)**[16] 827 4-9-2 0........................ DanielMuscutt 6 66
(Ed Dunlop) *s.i.s: hdwy over 6f out: rdn over 1f out: no ex ins fnl f* **25/1**
423- **6** 1 1/4 **Nawar**[134] 8598 4-9-2 72........................ GeorgeWood 7 63
(Martin Bosley) *prom: rdn over 2f out: wknd ins fnl f* **16/1**
5- **7** 2 **Don't Fence Me In (IRE)**[101] 7680 4-8-11 0........................ TomMarquand 1 54
(Paul Webber) *prom: racd keenly: rdn over 2f out: wknd ins fnl f* **66/1**
6 **8** 6 **Bravantina**[8] 968 4-8-11 0........................ JasonHart 2 41
(Mark Walford) *hld up: nvr on terms* **100/1**
5/ **9** 1 3/4 **Muzaawel**[528] 7521 4-9-2 0........................ RossaRyan 10 42
(Ralph J Smith) *hld up: rdn over 2f out: n.d* **100/1**
00- **10** 3 **Carnage**[47] 9592 4-9-2 0........................ TrevorWhelan 8 35
(Nikki Evans) *prom: lost pl after 1f: rdn and wknd over 2f out* **100/1**

1m 49.36s (-0.74) **Going Correction** -0.10s/f (Stan) 10 Ran SP% **125.8**
Speed ratings (Par 103): **99,98,97,94,93 92,90,85,83,81**
CSF £36.15 TOTE £12.40: £2.20, £1.10, £1.20; EX 57.90 Trifecta £130.50.
Owner W Sewell **Bred** Cecil W Wardle & Mrs Janet E Wardle **Trained** Oakham, Rutland

FOCUS
A fair novice contest. The winning time was over two seconds slower than the previous Lincoln trial over this C&D off a modest initial pace. The third has been rated below his early 3yo figure.

1103 SUNRACING.CO.UK LADY WULFRUNA STKS (LISTED RACE) (ALL-WEATHER CHAMPIONSHIPS FAST-TRACK QUALIFIER) 7f 36y (Tp)
3:15 (3:15) (Class 1) 4-Y£28,355 (£10,750; £5,380; £2,680; £1,315; £Form) **Stalls** High

4-40 **1** **Above The Rest (IRE)**[58] 170 8-9-3 108........................(h) CliffordLee 1 110
(David Barron) *hld up: hdwy over 1f out: rdn to ld wl ins fnl f: r.o* **18/1**
11-1 **2** 1 **Island Of Life (USA)**[66] 30 5-8-12 101........................(tp) AndreaAtzeni 3 102
(William Haggas) *trckd ldrs: racd keenly: rdn over 1f out: r.o to go 2nd post* **7/1**[3]
300- **3** shd **Cardsharp**[154] 7977 4-9-3 107........................ JoeFanning 9 107
(Mark Johnston) *sn chsng ldr: rdn over 1f out: ev ch ins fnl f: kpt on* **10/1**
01-5 **4** nk **Arcanada (IRE)**[33] 601 6-9-3 108........................(p) RichardKingscote 7 106
(Tom Dascombe) *sn led: rdn over 1f out: edgd rt and hdd wl ins fnl f* **16/1**
61-1 **5** 1 1/4 **Documenting**[31] 623 6-9-3 101........................ JasonHart 4 107+
(Kevin Frost) *chsd ldrs: shkn up over 2f out: nt clr run fr over 1f out tl wl ins fnl f: nvr able to chal (jockey said gelding was denied a clear run inside the final furlong)* **5/2**[2]
5-12 **6** 3 **Apex King (IRE)**[14] 880 5-9-3 86........................ TrevorWhelan 2 94?
(David Loughnane) *s.i.s: hld up: rdn over 1f out: nvr nrr (jockey said gelding reared as the gates opened and was slowly away as a result)* **50/1**
6-21 **7** 1 1/4 **Oh This Is Us (IRE)**[14] 880 6-9-3 113........................ TomMarquand 8 91
(Richard Hannon) *hld up: rdn over 1f out: nvr on terms (trainer's rep said horse was unsuited by the Tapeta surface on this occasion)* **5/4**[1]
00-1 **8** 2 **Keystroke**[59] 136 7-9-3 105........................(t) AdamKirby 6 86
(Stuart Williams) *hld up: rdn over 1f out: wknd and eased ins fnl f* **10/1**

1m 26.25s (-2.55) **Going Correction** -0.10s/f (Stan) 8 Ran SP% **116.8**
Speed ratings (Par 111): **108,106,106,106,104 101,100,97**
CSF £139.32 TOTE £22.40: £5.00, £1.80, £3.10; EX 153.30 Trifecta £1032.90.
Owner Laurence O'Kane **Bred** J C Carr **Trained** Maunby, N Yorks

FOCUS
A good quality Listed contest. The pace really picked up in the final 4f and the winning time was nearly a second quicker than the following 3yo handicap over this C&D. The first two have been rated pretty much to form, while the sixth has been rated to his old best for now, but that looks a bit dubious.

1104 LADBROKES HOME OF THE ODDS BOOST H'CAP 7f 36y (Tp)
3:50 (3:50) (Class 4) (0-85,84) 3-Y-O
£5,530 (£1,645; £822; £411; £300; £300) **Stalls** High

Form RPR
2-31 **1** **Ballistic (IRE)**[45] 360 3-9-3 80........................(p) JasonHart 8 88
(David Loughnane) *led over 6f out: clr over 5f out tl over 2f out: rdn over 1f out: styd on wl* **5/1**[3]
450- **2** 2 3/4 **Howzer Black (IRE)**[154] 7988 3-9-1 78........................ TomMarquand 4 79
(Keith Dalgleish) *hld up: hdwy over 1f out: rdn to go 2nd ins fnl f: no ch w wnr* **11/1**
13-1 **3** 1/2 **Nubough (IRE)**[42] 431 3-9-7 84........................(h) RichardKingscote 2 83
(Charles Hills) *prom: nt clr run and lost pl 6f out: hdwy over 1f out: rdn and edgd lft ins fnl f: styd on* **5/4**[1]
11 **4** 2 3/4 **Dahawi**[21] 752 3-9-3 80........................ LukeMorris 7 72
(Hugo Palmer) *led: hdd over 6f out: chsd wnr who wnt clr over 5f out: tk clsr order over 2f out: rdn and hung lft fr over 1f out: lost 2nd and no ex ins fnl f* **10/3**[2]
411 **5** 2 3/4 **Bay Of Naples (IRE)**[11] 913 3-9-4 81........................ JoeFanning 3 65
(Mark Johnston) *chsd ldrs: rdn over 2f out: wknd fnl f* **6/1**
341- **6** nse **Gold At Midnight**[166] 7608 3-9-1 78........................ HollieDoyle 5 62
(William Stone) *hld up: shkn up over 2f out: nvr on terms* **25/1**

023- **7** 6 **Barasti Dancer (IRE)**[234] 5086 3-8-11 74........................ CliffordLee 6 42
(K R Burke) *chsd ldrs: rdn over 2f out: wknd over 1f out* **14/1**

1m 27.21s (-1.59) **Going Correction** -0.10s/f (Stan) 7 Ran SP% **117.3**
Speed ratings (Par 100): **105,101,101,98,95 94,88**
CSF £58.00 CT £109.34 TOTE £8.00: £3.40, £5.30; EX 82.40 Trifecta £233.80.
Owner K Sohi **Bred** Tally-Ho Stud **Trained** Tern Hill, Shropshire

FOCUS
A fairly decent 3yo handicap. The winner has done remarkably well to kick again in the straight after getting clear on the lead from a wide draw. The winning time was under a second slower than the previous C&D Listed contest. The second has been rated close to his 2yo form.

1105 BETWAY HEED YOUR HUNCH H'CAP 6f 20y (Tp)
4:25 (4:25) (Class 2) (0-105,105) 4£15,762 (£4,715; £2,357; £1,180; £587) **Stalls** Low

Form RPR
-515 **1** **Desert Doctor (IRE)**[21] 762 4-8-8 92........................ AndreaAtzeni 4 100
(Ed Walker) *s.i.s: hld up: hdwy and edgd rt over 1f out: rdn to ld wl ins fnl f: jst hld on* **7/2**[1]
2621 **2** hd **Merhoob (IRE)**[12] 909 7-9-2 100........................ LukeMorris 7 108+
(John Ryan) *prom: nt clr run and lost pl over 5f out: hdwy and nt clr run over 1f out: rdn and r.o wl ins fnl f* **11/2**[2]
000- **3** 1/2 **George Bowen (IRE)**[147] 8194 7-9-5 103........................(v) PaulHanagan 1 109
(Richard Fahey) *s.i.s: hdwy over 3f out: rdn over 1f out: r.o* **8/1**
3-02 **4** 1/2 **El Hombre**[12] 909 5-8-8 92........................ JoeFanning 9 96
(Keith Dalgleish) *s.i.s: hld up: shkn up over 1f out: r.o ins fnl f: nt rch ldrs* **13/2**[3]
-101 **5** 1/2 **Alsvinder**[21] 762 6-9-0 98........................(t) AdamKirby 2 101
(David O'Meara) *led: drvn over 2f out: hdd wl ins fnl f: no ex towards fin* **10/1**
2-43 **6** 1/2 **Raucous**[12] 909 6-9-0 98........................(tp) TomMarquand 5 99
(Robert Cowell) *s.i.s: hld up: hdwy on outer over 1f out: r.o: nt rch ldrs* **9/1**
1212 **7** 1 3/4 **Shamshon (IRE)**[16] 837 8-8-6 90........................ NicolaCurrie 3 85
(Stuart Williams) *trckd ldrs: rdn over 1f out: no ex ins fnl f* **7/1**
5032 **8** nse **Corinthia Knight (IRE)**[7] 987 4-9-7 105........................ EdwardGreatrex 6 100
(Archie Watson) *prom: racd keenly: rdn and nt clr run over 1f out: no ex ins fnl f* **13/2**[3]
00-1 **9** 4 1/2 **Zylan (IRE)**[16] 832 7-8-9 93........................(p) HollieDoyle 10 74
(Roger Fell) *chsd ldr: rdn over 2f out: nt clr run over 1f out: wknd ins fnl f* **22/1**
-224 **10** 8 **Foolaad**[34] 588 8-8-13 97........................(t) LewisEdmunds 8 52
(Roy Bowring) *chsd ldrs: hung rt and lost pl over 3f out: rdn on outer over 2f out: wknd wl over 1f out* **14/1**

1m 12.28s (-2.22) **Going Correction** -0.10s/f (Stan) 10 Ran SP% **118.0**
Speed ratings (Par 109): **107,106,106,105,104 104,101,101,95,85**
CSF £22.61 CT £148.70 TOTE £4.20: £1.50, £1.70, £3.00; EX 25.80 Trifecta £266.70.
Owner Mrs Fitri Hay **Bred** Skeaghmore Hill **Trained** Upper Lambourn, Berks

FOCUS
A good sprint handicap. The winning time compared quite favourably on the day and the close runner-up was a shade unlucky. The third has been rated close to his best, and the fifth close to form.

1106 BETWAY BEST FOR CHELTENHAM FESTIVAL OFFERS H'CAP 1m 1f 104y (Tp)
5:00 (5:00) (Class 4) (0-85,85) 4-Y-O+
£5,530 (£1,645; £822; £411; £300; £300) **Stalls** Low

Form RPR
-254 **1** **Fayez (IRE)**[17] 807 5-9-7 85........................ DavidNolan 6 91
(David O'Meara) *stdd s: hld up: hdwy over 1f out: rdn and r.o to ld wl ins fnl f* **15/2**
4-35 **2** nk **This Girl**[40] 460 4-8-13 77........................(p[1]) RichardKingscote 2 82
(Tom Dascombe) *s.i.s: sn chsng ldrs: rdn to go 2nd over 1f out: ev ch wl ins fnl f: r.o* **4/1**[3]
2212 **3** nk **Dommersen (IRE)**[9] 950 6-9-0 83........................ BenSanderson(5) 4 87
(Roger Fell) *awkward s: hld up: hdwy on outer over 2f out: hung rt over 1f out: rdn and edgd lft ins fnl f: r.o* **15/8**[1]
054- **4** 1/2 **Battalion (IRE)**[210] 6009 9-9-7 85........................ DougieCostello 8 88
(Jamie Osborne) *s.i.s: sn rcvrd to chse ldr: led over 2f out: rdn over 1f out: hdd and unable qck wl ins fnl f* **25/1**
10-5 **5** nk **Winged Spur (IRE)**[9] 950 4-9-3 81........................ JoeFanning 3 84
(Mark Johnston) *prom: rdn over 1f out: styd on* **9/1**
4541 **6** 1/2 **Thawry**[9] 950 4-8-8 72........................ CamHardie 5 74
(Antony Brittain) *s.i.s hld up: r.o ins fnl f: nt rch ldrs* **10/3**[2]
6-34 **7** 4 1/2 **Mr Minerals**[9] 952 5-8-12 76........................(t) RossaRyan 1 68
(Alexandra Dunn) *s.i.s: hld up: hdwy over 1f out: sn rdn: wknd wl ins fnl f* **10/1**
2/6 **8** 4 **Tommy Hallinan (IRE)**[9] 948 5-8-7 71 oh1........................ BarryMcHugh 7 55
(Marjorie Fife) *led: hdd over 2f out: wknd over 1f out* **33/1**

1m 59.68s (-1.12) **Going Correction** -0.10s/f (Stan) 8 Ran SP% **115.5**
Speed ratings (Par 105): **100,99,99,99,98 98,94,90**
CSF £37.93 CT £79.55 TOTE £9.00: £2.80, £1.70, £1.20; EX 40.40 Trifecta £147.40.
Owner Northern Lads & Nawton Racing **Bred** Miss Siobhan Ryan **Trained** Upper Helmsley, N Yorks
■ Stewards' Enquiry : Barry McHugh one-day ban: failure to ride to their draw (Mar 23)

FOCUS
A decent handicap. They finished in a bit of a heap off an initially slow gallop.
T/Plt: £3,710.50 to a £1 stake. Pool: £70,348.02 - 13.84 winning units T/Qpdt: £140.60 to a £1 stake. Pool: £7,201.22 - 37.90 winning units **Colin Roberts**

1107 - 1108a (Foreign Racing) - See Raceform Interactive

[996]MEYDAN (L-H)
Saturday, March 9

OFFICIAL GOING: Dirt: fast; turf: good

1109a MAHAB AL SHIMAAL SPONSORED BY EMIRATES SKYWARDS (GROUP 3) (DIRT) 6f (D)
12:00 3-Y-O+
£165,354 (£55,118; £27,559; £13,779; £8,267; £5,511)

RPR
1 **Drafted (USA)**[37] 512 5-9-0 110........................ PatDobbs 8 112
(Doug Watson, UAE) *mid-div: smooth prog 2 1/2f out: rdn to ld fnl 55yds* **15/8**[1]
2 nk **Nine Below Zero**[16] 842 4-9-0 98........................ AdriedeVries 5 111
(Fawzi Abdulla Nass, Bahrain) *mid-div: smooth prog 2 1/2f out: led 1f out: r.o but hdd fnl 55yds* **28/1**

3 *nk* **Tato Key (ARG)**[37] 512 4-9-0 109..............................(t) ShaneFoley 10 110
(David Marnane, Ire) *mid-div: chsd ldrs 2 1/2f out: ev ch 1 1/2f out: kpt on wl* **13/2**[3]
4 *3/4* **Comicas (USA)**[123] 8912 6-9-0 108..............................(b) WilliamBuick 3 108+
(Charlie Appleby) *s.i.s: nvr nr to chal but r.o wl fnl 1 1/2f: nrst fin* **10/1**
5 *1 1/2* **Switzerland (USA)**[23] 729 5-9-0 107..............................(t) MickaelBarzalona 2 103
(Steven Asmussen, U.S.A) *trckd ldr: led 3 1/2f out: hdd & wknd fnl f* **3/1**[2]
6 *1 1/4* **I Kirk (SWE)**[51] 280 5-9-0 110.............................. CarlosLopez 9 99
(Susanne Berneklint, Sweden) *wl away: trckd ldr tl wknd fnl 2f* **10/1**
7 *3 1/4* **Thammin**[15] 874 5-9-0 103.............................. JimCrowley 6 88
(M Al Mheiri, UAE) *nvr bttr than mid-div* **13/2**[3]
8 *hd* **Lansky (IRE)**[9] 960 4-9-0 95.............................. RoystonFfrench 1 88
(S bin Ghadayer, UAE) *a in rr* **33/1**
9 *5* **My Catch (IRE)**[15] 874 8-9-0 98.............................. SamHitchcott 7 72
(Doug Watson, UAE) *nvr nr to chal* **33/1**
10 *23* **Lavaspin**[23] 729 5-9-0 99..............................(b) RichardMullen 4
(S Seemar, UAE) *sn led: hdd & wknd 3 1/2f out* **11/1**

1m 11.66s (0.06) **Going Correction** +0.40s/f (Slow) **10 Ran SP% 122.3**
Speed ratings: **115,114,114,113,111 109,105,104,98,67**
CSF: 67.48; TRICAST: 306.38.
Owner Misty Hollow Farm **Bred** John Foster, Barbara Hooker & Field Commission Par **Trained** United Arab Emirates

FOCUS
TRAKUS (metres travelled compared to winner): 2nd -13, 3rd -3, 4th -5, 5th -11, 6th -4, 7th -9, 8th -11, 9th -5, 10th -7. A competitive Group 3 run at a solid, contested pace over a track that seemed faster than of late, but still slower than this time last year: 23.72 (400m from standing start), 23.00 (800m), with the late-closing winner to the line in 24.38. The level hangs on the second and fourth.

1110a AL BASTAKIYA SPONSORED BY EMIRATES.COM (LISTED RACE) (DIRT) 1m 1f 110y(D)
12:35 (12:35) 3-Y-O

£141,732 (£47,244; £23,622; £11,811; £7,086; £4,724)

RPR
1 **Divine Image (USA)**[16] 845 3-8-5 103.............................. BrettDoyle 3 107
(Charlie Appleby) *trckd ldr: n.m.r 2 1/2f out: r.o wl to ld fnl f: easily* **9/4**[1]
2 *7 1/4* **Superior (USA)**[44] 394 3-8-9 85.............................. ConnorBeasley 8 96
(A bin Harmash, UAE) *trckd ldr: led 3 1/2f out: hdd 1f out: kpt on wl: no ch w wnr* **33/1**
3 *1* **Manguzi (FR)**[44] 394 3-8-9 99.............................. FernandoJara 12 94
(A R Al Rayhi, UAE) *trckd ldr: ev ch 2 1/2f out: kpt on same pce fnl 2f* **6/1**[3]
4 *11 1/2* **Al Hayette (USA)**[16] 845 3-8-5 94.............................. FabriceVeron 6 67
(Ismail Mohammed) *mid-div: r.o same pce fnl 2 1/2f* **28/1**
5 *2* **Al Shamkhah (USA)**[16] 845 3-8-5 90..............................(b) RoystonFfrench 9 63
(S bin Ghadayer, UAE) *mid-div: r.o same pce fnl 2 1/2f* **66/1**
6 *1 1/4* **Red Cactus (USA)**[30] 636 3-8-9 93.............................. ElioneChaves 11 65
(Bent Olsen, Denmark) *nvr nr to chal but r.o fnl 2f* **50/1**
7 *3 1/4* **Tabarak (USA)**[30] 634 3-8-11 86 ow2.............................. AdriedeVries 14 60
(R Bouresly, Kuwait) *nvr nr to chal* **20/1**
8 *3/4* **Shanty Star (USA)**[9] 956 3-8-9 80.............................. BernardoPinheiro 2 57
(R Bouresly, Kuwait) *s.i.s: nvr bttr than mid-div* **40/1**
9 *1* **The Song Of John (USA)**[252] 3-8-9 93.............................. RichardMullen 4 55
(S Seemar, UAE) *sn led: hdd & wknd 3 1/2f out* **20/1**
10 *5 1/2* **Moshaher (USA)**[30] 636 3-8-9 91.............................. PatDobbs 5 44
(Doug Watson, UAE) *s.i.s: nvr bttr than mid-div* **8/1**
11 *nk* **Fintas**[30] 636 3-8-9 90..............................(b) ShaneKelly 7 43
(Richard Hughes) *nvr bttr than mid-div* **33/1**
12 *shd* **Grecko (ARG)**[44] 394 3-9-5 104..............................(t) FrankieDettori 10 37
(Kenneth McPeek, U.S.A) *trckd ldr tl wknd fnl 3f* **9/1**
13 *17* **Estihdaaf (USA)**[30] 636 3-8-9 106..............................(v) PatCosgrave 13 9
(Saeed bin Suroor) *nvr bttr than mid-div* **5/2**[2]
14 *9 1/2* **Tone Broke (CAN)**[44] 394 3-8-9 92..............................(bt) MickaelBarzalona 1
(Steven Asmussen, U.S.A) *nvr bttr than mid-div* **10/1**

1m 59.07s (0.27) **Going Correction** +0.40s/f (Slow) **14 Ran SP% 128.6**
Speed ratings: **114,108,107,98,96 95,93,92,91,87 86,86,73,65**
CSF: 94.67; TRICAST: 433.37.
Owner Godolphin **Bred** Peter Magnier **Trained** Newmarket, Suffolk

FOCUS
TRAKUS: 2nd +8, 3rd +21, 4th +9, 5th +22, 6th +19, 7th +16, 8th +8, 9th -1, 10th +18, 11th +11, 12th +14, 13th +31, 14th +8. This didn't look a strong race but the winner is pretty smart. The pace was solid: 25.56, 23.43, 24.24, 26.55 - the winner's final 400m split was 25.68.

1111a NAD AL SHEBA TURF SPRINT SPONSORED BY ARABIAN ADVENTURES (GROUP 3) (TURF) 6f
1:10 (1:10) 3-Y-O+

£165,354 (£55,118; £27,559; £13,779; £8,267; £5,511)

RPR
1 **Blue Point (IRE)**[23] 725 5-9-0 120.............................. WilliamBuick 9 123+
(Charlie Appleby) *mid-div: smooth prog 3 1/2f out: led 2f out: r.o wl: easily* **1/4**[1]
2 *3* **Ekhtiyaar**[16] 843 5-9-0 109.............................. JimCrowley 1 113
(Doug Watson, UAE) *mid-div: smooth prog 3f out: r.o wl fnl 2f but no ch w wnr* **6/1**[2]
3 *2 3/4* **Mazzini**[30] 639 6-9-0 106.............................. AdriedeVries 7 105
(Fawzi Abdulla Nass, Bahrain) *s.i.s: settled in rr: r.o fnl 2f: nrst fin* **11/1**[3]
4 *nse* **Riflescope (IRE)**[16] 843 6-9-0 95..............................(tp) RichardMullen 11 104
(S Seemar, UAE) *s.i.s: racd in rr: r.o fnl 2f: nrst fin* **80/1**
5 *1 3/4* **Ajwad**[7] 1000 6-9-0 96.............................. BernardoPinheiro 5 99
(R Bouresly, Kuwait) *trckd ldr: ev ch 3f out: r.o same pce fnl 2f* **100/1**
6 *1 3/4* **Gifted Master (IRE)**[112] 9127 6-9-0 112..............................(b) JamesDoyle 4 93
(Hugo Palmer) *a mid-div* **12/1**
7 *2 1/2* **Hit The Bid**[44] 393 5-9-0 110..............................(t) ChrisHayes 3 85
(D J Bunyan, Ire) *chsd ldrs tl wknd fnl f* **20/1**
8 *hd* **High On Life**[15] 874 8-9-0 100..............................(t) MickaelBarzalona 8 85
(S bin Ghadayer, UAE) *chsd ldrs tl wknd fnl 2 1/2f* **66/1**
9 *nse* **Portamento (IRE)**[23] 725 7-9-0 100.............................. FernandoJara 10 84
(A R Al Rayhi, UAE) *nvr bttr than mid-div* **100/1**
10 *1 3/4* **Faatinah (AUS)**[23] 725 6-9-0 111..............................(b) DaneO'Neill 6 79
(David A Hayes, Australia) *sn led: hdd & wknd 2f out* **33/1**
11 *12 1/2* **Log Out Island (IRE)**[16] 843 6-9-0 100..............................(bt) TadhgO'Shea 2 39
(S Seemar, UAE) *chsd ldrs tl wknd 3 1/2f out* **100/1**

1m 10.15s **11 Ran SP% 123.7**
CSF: 2.51; TRICAST: 8.25.
Owner Godolphin **Bred** Oak Lodge Bloodstock **Trained** Newmarket, Suffolk

FOCUS
This was a well-run sprint and the first four came from off the pace. No Trakus data. The fourth limits the level.

1112a BURJ NAHAAR SPONSORED BY EMIRATES HOLIDAYS (GROUP 3) (DIRT) 1m (D)
1:45 (1:45) 3-Y-O+

£165,354 (£55,118; £27,559; £13,779; £8,267; £5,511)

RPR
1 **Muntazah**[23] 726 6-9-0 111.............................. JimCrowley 1 119
(Doug Watson, UAE) *sn led: skipped clr 3f out: r.o wl: easily* **4/5**[1]
2 *10* **Good Curry (TUR)**[23] 729 7-9-0 108.............................. HalisKaratas 4 96
(Bayram Kocakaya, Turkey) *trckd ldr: r.o fnl 2 1/2f but no ch w wnr* **16/1**
3 *3/4* **Musawaat**[79] 9653 5-9-0 105..............................(v) AdriedeVries 11 94
(Fawzi Abdulla Nass, Bahrain) *mid-div: r.o fnl 2f but nvr able to chal* **40/1**
4 *nk* **Heavy Metal**[23] 726 9-9-0 109.............................. MickaelBarzalona 2 93
(S bin Ghadayer, UAE) *slowly away: nvr nr to chal but r.o fnl 2f* **4/1**[2]
5 *1 1/4* **Rodaini (USA)**[16] 842 5-9-0 101..............................(t) ConnorBeasley 9 90
(A bin Harmash, UAE) *chsd ldr: ev ch 3f out: wknd fnl f* **33/1**
6 *1 1/4* **Secret Ambition**[23] 726 6-9-0 106..............................(t) RichardMullen 10 88
(S Seemar, UAE) *a mid-div* **14/1**
7 *nk* **Ibn Malik (IRE)**[9] 957 6-9-0 105..............................(vt) DaneO'Neill 3 87
(M Al Mheiri, UAE) *chsd ldr tl wknd fnl 2f* **18/1**
8 *5* **Behavioral Bias (USA)**[23] 726 5-9-0 100..............................(bt) ChrisHayes 6 75
(S Seemar, UAE) *nvr nr to chal* **66/1**
9 *1/2* **Gm Hopkins**[9] 961 8-9-0 97..............................(t) AntonioFresu 8 74
(Jaber Ramadhan, Bahrain) *nvr bttr than mid-div* **40/1**
10 *6* **Axelrod (USA)**[73] 9711 4-9-0 114..............................(b) RoystonFfrench 5 60
(S bin Ghadayer, UAE) *nvr nr to chal* **13/2**[3]
11 *12 1/2* **Moqarrab (USA)**[16] 842 4-9-0 97.............................. BenCurtis 7 32
(M Al Mheiri, UAE) *nvr bttr than mid-div* **14/1**

1m 34.99s (-2.51) **Going Correction** +0.40s/f (Slow) **11 Ran SP% 122.7**
Speed ratings: **128,118,117,116,115 114,114,109,108,102 90**
CSF: 17.90; TRICAST: 348.30.
Owner Hamdan Al Maktoum **Bred** Shadwell Estate Co Ltd **Trained** United Arab Emirates

FOCUS
TRAKUS: 2nd +5, 3rd +10, 4th +12, 5th +10, 6th +1, 7th +2, 8th +2, 9th +7, 10th +3, 11th +6. An extraordinary performance from the winner who, on a track that hasn't been riding that fast, lowered the course record, set by the same trainer's One Man Band in the 2016 Godolphin Mile, by 0.22sec: 24.40, 22.31, 23.66, 24.62. Another pb from the winner rated in line with the best recent winners of this race.

1113a DUBAI CITY OF GOLD SPONSORED BY EMIRATES SKYCARGO (GROUP 2) (TURF) 1m 4f 11y
2:20 (2:20) 3-Y-O+

£141,732 (£47,244; £23,622; £11,811; £7,086; £4,724)

RPR
1 **Old Persian**[175] 7293 4-8-11 117.............................. WilliamBuick 2 113+
(Charlie Appleby) *trckd ldrs: n.m.r 3f out: r.o wl fnl 1 1/2f: led cl home* **4/6**[1]
2 *shd* **Racing History (IRE)**[16] 844 7-9-0 111..............................(v) ChristopheSoumillon 6 112
(Saeed bin Suroor) *sn led: rdn 3f out: r.o wl but hdd cl home* **4/1**[2]
3 *3* **Desert Encounter (IRE)**[147] 8228 7-9-0 118..............................(h) JimCrowley 8 107
(David Simcock) *mid-div: smooth prog 4f out: ev ch 2f out: r.o same pce fnl 1 1/2f* **12/1**
4 *nk* **Prince Of Arran**[90] 9473 6-9-0 112.............................. OisinMurphy 7 107
(Charlie Fellowes) *trckd ldr: ev ch 2 1/2f out: r.o same pce fnl 2f* **14/1**
5 *hd* **Sharpalo (FR)**[23] 730 7-9-0 103..............................(t) ConnorBeasley 4 106
(A bin Harmash, UAE) *settled in rr: chsd ldrs 2 1/2f out: wknd fnl f* **40/1**
6 *hd* **Marinaresco (SAF)**[16] 846 6-9-0 112..............................(b) BernardFayd'Herbe 9 106
(M F De Kock, South Africa) *nvr nr to chal but r.o fnl 2f: nrst fin* **33/1**
7 *1 1/2* **Spotify (FR)**[16] 844 5-9-0 112..............................(p) JamesDoyle 5 104
(Charlie Appleby) *a mid-div* **7/1**[3]
8 *hd* **Team Talk**[16] 844 6-9-0 109..............................(h) PatCosgrave 10 103
(Saeed bin Suroor) *a mid-div* **22/1**
9 *3 1/4* **Crowned Eagle**[124] 8883 5-9-0 110.............................. FrankieDettori 1 98
(Marco Botti) *nvr bttr than mid-div* **28/1**
10 *1 3/4* **Second Summer (USA)**[30] 638 7-9-0 100..............................(t) RoystonFfrench 3 95
(A R Al Rayhi, UAE) *a in rr* **100/1**

2m 32.68s **10 Ran SP% 121.0**
WFA 4 from 5yo+ 1lb
CSF: 3.49; TRICAST: 18.52.
Owner Godolphin **Bred** Godolphin **Trained** Newmarket, Suffolk

FOCUS
This proved tactical. They went no pace for much of the race, plenty were keen, and it developed into a dash up the straight. The early sectionals were 27.85, 26.49, 25.54, 25,89, before they scampered home in 23.81 and 23.10. TRAKUS: 2nd 0, 3rd +15, 4th +7, 5th +13, 6th +3, 7th +9, 8th +12, 9th +1, 10th +8. The second to sixth help set the level in a bunched finish.

1114a AL MAKTOUM CHALLENGE R3 SPONSORED BY EMIRATES AIRLINE (GROUP 1) (DIRT) 1m 2f (D)
2:55 (2:55) 3-Y-O+

£283,464 (£94,488; £47,244; £23,622; £14,173; £9,448)

RPR
1 **Capezzano (USA)**[37] 513 5-9-0 109..............................(h) MickaelBarzalona 9 119
(S bin Ghadayer, UAE) *wl away: sn led: kicked clr 3f out: r.o wl: easily* **9/2**[2]
2 *9 1/2* **Thunder Snow (IRE)**[126] 8849 5-9-0 122..............................(p) ChristopheSoumillon 2 100+
(Saeed bin Suroor) *trckd ldr: smooth prog 3f out: ev ch 1 1/2f out: wknd fnl 110yds* **4/5**[1]
3 *nk* **Dolkong (USA)**[9] 959 5-9-0 108.............................. OlivierDoleuze 6 99
(Simon Foster, Korea) *nvr nr to chal but r.o wl fnl 2f* **9/1**
4 *1 1/4* **New Trails (USA)**[30] 638 5-9-0 111..............................(t) ConnorBeasley 3 97
(A bin Harmash, UAE) *mid-div: r.o same pce fnl 2 1/2f* **15/2**[3]
5 *1 1/4* **Gronkowski (USA)**[105] 4-9-0 112..............................(b) RoystonFfrench 4 94
(S bin Ghadayer, UAE) *nvr nr to chal but r.o fnl 2 1/2f* **14/1**
6 *6 3/4* **Nordic Lights**[30] 637 4-9-0 109.............................. WilliamBuick 8 81
(Charlie Appleby) *trckd ldrs tl wknd 3f out* **12/1**
7 *2 1/2* **Logrado (ARG)**[243] 4-9-0 110..............................(t) AntonioFresu 1 76
(E Charpy, UAE) *nvr bttr than mid-div* **40/1**
8 *1 3/4* **Furia Cruzada (CHI)**[23] 728 7-8-9 100..............................(t) FrankieDettori 10 67
(E Charpy, UAE) *s.i.s: nvr bttr than mid-div* **50/1**
9 *27* **Montsarrat (IRE)**[15] 872 6-9-0 102..............................(b) XavierZiani 5 18
(S bin Ghadayer, UAE) *nvr bttr than mid-div* **50/1**

10 34 **Cosmo Charlie (USA)**[30] 638 5-9-0 109 .... PatDobbs 7
(Doug Watson, UAE) *trckd ldr tl wknd 4f out* **18/1**

2m 5.02s (0.32) **Going Correction** +0.40s/f (Slow) **10** Ran SP% **121.5**
Speed ratings: **114,106,106,105,104 98,96,95,73,46**
CSF: 8.74; TRICAST: 32.15.
Owner Sultan Ali **Bred** Darley **Trained** United Arab Emirates

FOCUS
TRAKUS: 2nd 0, 3rd +25, 4th +17, 5th +23, 6th +15, 7th +4, 8th +15, 9th +3, 10th +12. The winner made all through stretch, gradually slowing splits and the overall time was relatively ordinary. It looked a case that most of these were spent by trying to keep up down the back, and the runner-up, the only one to make a race of it into the straight, needed the run: 24.99 (from standing start), 23.66, 23.99, 25.94, 26.44. Another pb from the winner.

1115a JEBEL HATTA SPONSORED BY EMIRATES AIRLINE (GROUP 1) (TURF) 1m 1f
3:30 (3:30) 3-Y-O+
£188,976 (£62,992; £31,496; £15,748; £9,448; £6,299)

RPR
1 **Dream Castle**[44] 395 5-9-0 116 .... ChristopheSoumillon 9 116
(Saeed bin Suroor) *mid-div: smooth prog 2 1/2f out: led 1f out: r.o wl* **9/4**[2]
2 1 1/4 **Wootton (FR)**[16] 846 4-9-0 112 .... WilliamBuick 6 113
(Charlie Appleby) *mid-div: chsd ldrs 2 1/2f out: r.o wl fnl 1 1/2f but no ch w wnr* **11/10**[1]
3 2 3/4 **First Contact (IRE)**[16] 846 4-9-0 107 .... MickaelBarzalona 2 107
(Charlie Appleby) *sn led: kicked clr 2 1/2f out: hdd 1f out but r.o wl* **28/1**
4 1 1/4 **Century Dream (IRE)**[16] 846 5-9-0 115 ....(t) OisinMurphy 4 105
(Simon Crisford) *trckd ldrs: ev ch 2 1/2f out: r.o same pce fnl 1 1/2f* **13/2**[3]
5 nk **Loxley (IRE)**[154] 8011 4-9-0 112 .... JamesDoyle 10 104
(Charlie Appleby) *trckd ldr: ev ch 3f out: r.o same pce fnl 2f* **8/1**
6 1 1/4 **Majestic Mambo (SAF)**[245] 4701 4-9-0 113 .... BernardFayd'Herbe 1 101
(M F De Kock, South Africa) *trckd ldrs: ev ch 2 1/2f out: wknd fnl 1 1/2f* **40/1**
7 1 3/4 **Forest Ranger (IRE)**[147] 8191 5-9-0 113 .... TonyHamilton 7 98
(Richard Fahey) *nvr nr to chal* **20/1**
8 1/2 **Janoobi (SAF)**[16] 846 5-9-0 106 .... JimCrowley 3 97
(M F De Kock, South Africa) *nvr bttr than mid-div* **66/1**
9 4 **Muzdawaj**[16] 844 6-9-0 102 .... DaneO'Neill 5 88
(M Al Mheiri, UAE) *nvr nr to chal* **66/1**
10 7 3/4 **Blair House (IRE)**[44] 395 6-9-0 116 ....(b) BrettDoyle 8 72
(Charlie Appleby) *v.s.a: a in rr* **16/1**

1m 48.17s **10** Ran SP% **122.3**
CSF: 5.15; TRICAST: 53.36; PLACEPOT: £7.00 to a £1 stake. QUADPOT: £3.60 to a £1 stake.
Owner Godolphin **Bred** Darley **Trained** Newmarket, Suffolk

FOCUS
Rarely a strong Group 1, but the winner has been the form horse of the carnival and he is clearly much improved since being gelded. They went through in 25.53, 22.66, 23.69, 23.77 and finished in 12.52. TRAKUS: 2nd +2, 3rd -5, 4th -1, 5th -2, 6th -6, 7th -6, 8th -1, 9th -5, 10th -3.

1116 - 1126a (Foreign Racing) - See Raceform Interactive

SAINT-CLOUD (L-H)
Sunday, March 10

OFFICIAL GOING: Turf: heavy

1127a PRIX ALTIPAN (LISTED RACE) (4YO+) (TURF) 1m
1:52 4-Y-O+ **£23,423** (£9,369; £7,027; £4,684; £2,342)

RPR
1 **The Revenant**[121] 4-9-0 0 ....(h) Pierre-CharlesBoudot 6 112+
(F-H Graffard, France) **12/5**[1]
2 2 1/2 **Qualisaga (FR)**[26] 5-8-10 0 .... EddyHardouin 5 101
(Carina Fey, France) **18/5**[2]
3 hd **Jazz Melodie (FR)**[77] 9689 5-8-10 0 .... FabienLefebvre 2 101
(P De Chevigny, France) **18/5**[2]
4 5 **Zyzzyva (FR)**[26] 4-9-0 0 .... StephanePasquier 1 94
(Gavin Hernon, France) **23/5**
5 1 3/4 **Time For A Toot (IRE)**[124] 8914 4-8-10 0 .... MaximeGuyon 4 85
(Charles Hills) *chsd ldr on outside: drvn ins fnl 2 1/2f: hrd rdn but nt qckn 2f out: wknd fnl f* **43/5**
6 12 **Shamtee (IRE)**[225] 5514 4-9-0 0 .... MickaelBarzalona 3 62
(X Thomas-Demeaulte, France) **9/2**[3]

1m 47.23s (-0.27) **6** Ran SP% **119.3**
PARI-MUTUEL (all including 1 euro stake): WIN 3.40; PLACE 1.90, 2.20; SF 9.90.
Owner Al Asayl France **Bred** Al Asayl Bloodstock Ltd **Trained** France

1128 - 1138a (Foreign Racing) - See Raceform Interactive

1093
KEMPTON (A.W) (R-H)
Monday, March 11

OFFICIAL GOING: Polytrack: standard to slow
Wind: Fresh across Weather: Fine

1139 100% PROFIT BOOST AT 32REDSPORT.COM NOVICE STKS 5f (P)
5:00 (5:04) (Class 5) 3-Y-O+ **£3,881** (£1,155; £577; £288) **Stalls** Low

Form RPR
65-2 1 **Orange Blossom**[23] 752 3-8-10 70 .... BarryMcHugh 9 62
(James Given) *sn prom: chsd ldr 4f out: shkn up over 1f out: rdn and r.o to ld nr fin* **5/1**[3]
0- 2 hd **Show Me The Bubbly**[74] 9727 3-8-10 0 .... LiamJones 1 62
(John O'Shea) *s.i.s: hdwy over 1f out: swtchd lft ins fnl f: sn rdn: r.o: hung lft towards fin* **33/1**
00- 3 shd **Spirited Guest**[173] 7430 3-8-12 0 .... JaneElliott(3) 3 66
(George Margarson) *edgd lft s and stmbld sn after: hld up in tch: racd keenly: shkn up over 1f out: rdn and r.o ins fnl f: edgd rt nr fin* **9/2**[2]
3 4 shd **Brigadier**[23] 752 3-9-1 0 .... JoeFanning 7 66
(Robert Cowell) *s.i.s: sn rcvrd to ld: shkn up over 1f out: rdn and edgd lft ins fnl f: hdd nr fin* **7/2**[1]
42 5 3/4 **Rakastava (IRE)**[14] 908 3-9-1 0 .... CallumShepherd 2 63
(Mick Channon) *chsd ldrs: nt clr run fr over 1f out tl swtchd rt ins fnl f: r.o* **8/1**
5 6 hd **Physics (IRE)**[11] 943 3-9-1 0 ....(t) RaulDaSilva 6 63
(Paul Cole) *led early: chsd ldrs: pushed along 2f out: running on whn hmpd nr fin* **7/2**[1]
0- 7 1 1/2 **Sarsaparilla Kit**[89] 9497 3-8-10 0 .... OisinMurphy 5 52
(Stuart Williams) *s.i.s: hld up: nt clr run 4f out: shkn up over 1f out: nt trble ldrs* **7/1**
040- 8 nk **Te Amo Te Amo**[96] 9395 3-9-1 67 .... TomMarquand 4 56
(Simon Dow) *hmpd s: hld up: shkn up over 1f out: nt trble ldrs* **12/1**
6-3 9 5 **Spiritually**[46] 384 3-8-10 0 .... GeorgeWood 8 33
(Chris Wall) *dwlt: a in rr* **20/1**

1m 0.59s (0.09) **Going Correction** +0.025s/f (Slow) **9** Ran SP% **118.3**
Speed ratings (Par 103): **100,99,99,99,98 97,95,94,86**
CSF £149.09 TOTE £5.20: £1.60, £12.80, £2.80; EX 152.20 Trifecta £793.50.
Owner The Cool Silk Partnership **Bred** Whitsbury Manor Stud **Trained** Willoughton, Lincs
■ Stewards' Enquiry : Jane Elliott six-day ban: used whip in the incorrect place (Mar 25-30)

FOCUS
A modest 3yo novice sprint, but it resulted in a blanket finish. It's been rated around the fourth and fifth.

1140 BET AT RACINGTV.COM H'CAP (DIV I) 7f (P)
5:30 (5:32) (Class 6) (0-65,66) 3-Y-O
£3,105 (£924; £461; £400; £400; £400) **Stalls** Low

Form RPR
000- 1 **Run After Genesis (IRE)**[102] 9314 3-9-3 **60** ....(w) RossaRyan 3 68
(Brett Johnson) *hld up in tch: rdn over 1f out: styd on to ld wl ins fnl f: edgd rt towards fin* **12/1**
000- 2 nk **Strawberry Jack**[123] 8955 3-9-9 **66** ....(tp) OisinMurphy 13 73
(George Scott) *prom: chsd ldr over 5f out: led over 1f out: rdn and hdd wl ins fnl f: edgd rt towards fin* **20/1**
00-3 3 nk **Pentland Lad (IRE)**[17] 848 3-8-4 **47** ....(t) NicolaCurrie 10 53
(Charlie Fellowes) *s.i.s: swtchd rt sn after s: hld up: hdwy over 1f out: sn rdn: r.o: edgd lft towards fin* **4/1**[2]
45-5 4 hd **Lippy Lady (IRE)**[17] 855 3-8-8 **51** ....(h[1]) JFEgan 5 57
(Paul George) *hld up: hdwy 2f out: rdn and ev ch ins fnl f: eased whn n.m.r towards fin* **7/1**
5-04 5 2 **Remembering You (IRE)**[18] 841 3-9-4 **61** .... AdamKirby 4 62
(Clive Cox) *s.i.s: hld up: hdwy u.p over 1f out: styd on same wl ins fnl f* **12/1**
600- 6 1 1/4 **Monsieur Piquer (FR)**[171] 7476 3-9-9 **66** ....(w) CliffordLee 8 63
(K R Burke) *prom: outpcd over 2f out: styd on ins fnl f* **16/1**
50-2 7 3/4 **Bubbelah (IRE)**[19] 798 3-9-7 **64** .... JamieSpencer 7 60
(David Simcock) *s.i.s: hld up: shkn up over 2f out: styd on fr over 1f out: nt trble ldrs (trainer's rep said the gelding was outpaced and was unsuited by today's seven furlongs and may prefer further)* **2/1**[1]
43-0 8 1/2 **Molly Mai**[19] 798 3-9-7 **64** .... DavidProbert 1 58
(Philip McBride) *s.i.s: rcvrd to ld over 5f out: rdn: hung lft and hdd over 1f out: no ex ins fnl f* **11/2**[3]
65-6 9 1/2 **Nervous Nerys (IRE)**[12] 918 3-8-6 **49** .... LukeMorris 6 42
(Alex Hales) *hld up: hdwy u.p over 1f out: nt trble ldrs* **33/1**
4-00 10 1 **Maared (IRE)**[19] 802 3-9-0 **57** ....(b[1]) KieranO'Neill 2 47
(Luke McJannet) *plld hrd and prom: rdn and ev ch over 1f out: wknd ins fnl f* **50/1**
2036 11 4 **Lincoln Spirit**[11] 940 3-8-12 **55** ....(p[1]) CamHardie 9 35
(David O'Meara) *led: hdd over 5f out: chsd ldrs: rdn over 2f out: wknd over 1f out* **33/1**
4-22 12 1 **Pandora Star**[12] 931 3-8-13 **56** ....(v) JasonHart 12 33
(John Quinn) *prom: rdn over 2f out: wknd over 1f out* **20/1**
-064 13 3 1/4 **Drummer Jack (IRE)**[45] 400 3-8-11 **54** ....(bt) TomMarquand 11 23
(William Muir) *s.i.s: hld up: rdn over 2f out: wknd over 1f out* **10/1**

1m 25.46s (-0.54) **Going Correction** +0.025s/f (Slow) **13** Ran SP% **128.9**
Speed ratings (Par 96): **104,103,103,103,100 99,98,97,97,96 91,90,86**
CSF £244.57 CT £1191.51 TOTE £16.80: £5.00, £7.00, £2.90; EX 300.60 Trifecta £2369.20.
Owner Colin Westley **Bred** R Cantoni & G Benvenuto **Trained** Epsom, Surrey

FOCUS
The first of four successive races over 7f and the first division of a moderate handicap. It was messy in the early stages but produced another close finish. The second has been rated in line with his best 2yo form.

1141 BET AT RACINGTV.COM H'CAP (DIV II) 7f (P)
6:00 (6:03) (Class 6) (0-65,66) 3-Y-O
£3,105 (£924; £461; £400; £400; £400) **Stalls** Low

Form RPR
35-1 1 **Red Phoenix (IRE)**[17] 855 3-9-9 **66** .... JoeFanning 5 71+
(Mark Johnston) *chsd ldr tl over 5f out: remained handy: shkn up to ld over 2f out: rdn over 1f out: jst hld on* **7/2**[2]
0-51 2 nk **Simba Samba**[3] 1084 3-8-8 **51** 6ex .... NicolaCurrie 3 58+
(Philip McBride) *s.i.s: hld up: swtchd lft over 1f out: rdn and r.o wl ins fnl f: jst failed (jockey said gelding was slow into stride)* **1/1**[1]
3-51 3 1 **Rajman**[44] 437 3-9-6 **63** ....(h) LukeMorris 7 65
(Tom Clover) *chsd ldrs: shkn up over 2f out: styd on* **9/1**[3]
666- 4 nk **Es Que Magic (IRE)**[166] 7674 3-9-2 **59** .... LiamKeniry 4 60
(Alex Hales) *mid-div: hdwy over 2f out: chsd wnr over 1f out: sn rdn: styd on* **25/1**
00-0 5 nse **Cauthen (IRE)**[17] 855 3-8-12 **55** .... RobHornby 12 56
(Ken Cunningham-Brown) *s.i.s: hdwy over 4f out: rdn over 1f out: styd on* **66/1**
0-64 6 1 **Fast Endeavour**[12] 918 3-8-9 **52** .... AndreaAtzeni 11 50
(Ian Williams) *prom: hmpd over 5f out: rdn and ev ch over 2f out: styd on same pce ins fnl f* **20/1**
300- 7 shd **Havana Ooh Na Na**[166] 7674 3-9-0 **57** ....(p[1] w) CliffordLee 1 55
(K R Burke) *prom: rdn over 2f out: styd on same pce fnl f* **14/1**
6-36 8 1 **Nananita (IRE)**[44] 437 3-8-13 **56** .... LiamJones 6 52
(Mark Loughnane) *s.i.s: hld up: hdwy over 1f out: sn rdn: nt trble ldrs* **9/1**[3]
050- 9 1 **Free Gift**[102] 9314 3-9-9 **66** .... GeorgeDowning 9 59
(Tony Carroll) *dwlt: bhd: r.o ins fnl f: nvr nrr* **33/1**
0-60 10 nse **Tintern Spirit (IRE)**[37] 550 3-8-2 **45** .... RaulDaSilva 2 38
(Milton Bradley) *plld hrd and prom: stdd and lost pl over 5f out: hdwy over 1f out: no ex ins fnl f* **50/1**
003- 11 2 3/4 **Budaiya Fort (IRE)**[103] 9289 3-9-3 **60** .... OisinMurphy 8 46
(Robert Cowell) *sn led: rdn and hdd over 2f out: wknd ins fnl f* **12/1**
-522 12 1 **Sybil Grand**[16] 887 3-8-8 **51** ow1 ....(b) DavidProbert 10 34
(Katy Price) *plld hrd and prom: chsd ldr over 5f out tl rdn over 2f out: wknd ins fnl f* **16/1**

1m 26.93s (0.93) **Going Correction** +0.025s/f (Slow) **12** Ran SP% **127.5**
Speed ratings (Par 96): **95,94,93,93,93 91,91,90,89,89 86,85**
CSF £7.57 CT £32.20 TOTE £3.20: £1.40, £1.20, £1.80; EX 9.50 Trifecta £63.80.
Owner Sheikh Hamdan bin Mohammed Al Maktoum **Bred** Godolphin **Trained** Middleham Moor, N Yorks

FOCUS
The second leg of this handicap was run at a slow early pace and the time was 1.47secs slower than the first division. Ordinary form in behind the first two.

1142 32RED CASINO FILLIES' NOVICE STKS — 7f (P)
6:30 (6:31) (Class 5) 3-Y-O+ £3,881 (£1,155; £577; £288) Stalls Low

Form RPR

1 **Whisper Aloud** 3-8-11 0 ... OisinMurphy 5 68+
(Archie Watson) *s.i.s and hmpd s: rcvrd to ld over 6f out: rdn over 1f out: styd on* 5/2[1]

0 2 ½ **Gabriela Laura**[37] [556] 3-8-11 0 ... DavidProbert 3 66
(Clive Cox) *led early: remained w ldr: rdn over 1f out: styd on* 25/1

3 1 **Lady Schannell (IRE)** 3-8-11 0 ... TomMarquand 6 63+
(Marco Botti) *s.i.s and hmpd s: hld up: r.o ins fnl f: nt rch ldrs* 25/1

3-5 4 ½ **Lethal Lover**[44] [442] 3-8-11 0 ... HectorCrouch 10 62
(Clive Cox) *prom: racd keenly: rdn over 1f out: styd on* 8/1

0 5 nk **Canasta**[65] [78] 3-8-11 0 ... (h) GeorgeWood 12 61+
(James Fanshawe) *hld up in tch: shkn up over 1f out: styd on* 12/1

6 1 **Princesse Bassett (FR)** 3-8-11 0 ... NicolaCurrie 8 58+
(George Baker) *s.i.s: in rr: r.o ins fnl f: nt rch ldrs* 33/1

0-2 7 ¾ **Vegatina**[37] [556] 3-8-11 0 ... (t) NickyMackay 14 56+
(John Gosden) *prom: racd wd 2f: shkn up over 2f out: no ex ins fnl f (vet reported the filly had lost its right-hind shoe)* 3/1[2]

0- 8 ½ **Miss Enigma (IRE)**[240] [4926] 3-8-11 0 ... ShaneKelly 4 55
(Richard Hughes) *wnt lft s: plld hrd and prom: rdn over 1f out: no ex ins fnl f* 14/1

4 9 1¼ **Di Matteo**[20] [795] 3-8-8 0 ... GabrieleMalune(3) 7 52
(Marco Botti) *s.i.s: sn prom: rdn over 1f out: styng on whn nt clr run and swtchd lft ins fnl f (jockey said filly was denied a clear run)* 9/1

10 2¼ **Quemonda** 3-8-11 0 ... KieranO'Neill 1 46
(Ken Cunningham-Brown) *s.s: nvr on terms* 100/1

11 1 **Hooriya** 3-8-11 0 ... AndreaAtzeni 9 43
(Marco Botti) *s.i.s: sn pushed along in rr: n.d* 10/1

- 12 2½ **My Lady Claire** 3-8-11 0 ... LukeMorris 13 36
(Ed Walker) *s.s: rn wd turning for home: a in rr* 33/1

13 19 **Little Lady Luck** 3-8-6 0 ... DarraghKeenan(5) 11
(Denis Quinn) *s.i.s: a in rr* 100/1

0 P **Theban Air**[24] [733] 3-8-11 0 ... StevieDonohoe 2
(Lucy Wadham) *hld up in tch: cl up whn wnt wrong 3f out: sn p.u: dismntd over 1f out (jockey said filly lost its action rounding the home bend as a result of the interference)* 4/1[3]

1m 27.85s (1.85) **Going Correction** +0.025s/f (Slow) 14 Ran SP% 133.7
Speed ratings (Par 100): **90,89,88,87,87 86,85,84,83,80 79,76,55,**
CSF £82.01 TOTE £3.50: £1.60, £10.30, £8.30; EX 80.10 Trifecta £1549.80.
Owner Clipper Logistics **Bred** Lordship Stud **Trained** Upper Lambourn, W Berks
■ Stewards' Enquiry : Nicky Mackay five-day ban: interference & careless riding (Mar 25-29)

FOCUS
Some inexperienced fillies' in this novice stakes and the time was slower than the two earlier races over the trip. The winner made a nice debut. The form is rated around the fourth for now.

1143 32RED.COM H'CAP — 7f (P)
7:00 (7:00) (Class 4) (0-85,87) 4-Y-O+ £6,469 (£1,925; £962; £481; £400; £400) Stalls Low

Form RPR

1-31 1 **Glenn Coco**[46] [381] 5-9-4 82 ... (t) OisinMurphy 2 92
(Stuart Williams) *chsd ldrs: led over 1f out: rdn out* 3/1[1]

2353 2 1 **Areen Heart (FR)**[17] [856] 5-9-9 87 ... AdamKirby 10 94
(David O'Meara) *stdd s: hld up: hdwy over 1f out: rdn to chse wnr ins fnl f: styd on same pce towards fin* 10/1

/0-2 3 1¼ **Call Me Grumpy (IRE)**[18] [840] 5-8-11 75 ... (b) AndreaAtzeni 6 79
(Roger Varian) *hld up: r.o ins fnl f: nt rch ldrs* 7/2[2]

-516 4 1 **Fuwairt (IRE)**[17] [856] 7-8-11 80 ... CameronNoble(5) 1 81
(David Loughnane) *hld up in tch: rdn over 1f out: styd on same pce ins fnl f* 8/1

225- 5 ½ **Corazon Espinado (IRE)**[146] [8299] 4-9-9 87 ... TomMarquand 9 87
(Simon Dow) *sn chsng ldr: rdn and ev ch over 1f out: no ex ins fnl f* 10/1

230- 6 3¼ **Mamillius**[136] [8611] 6-9-1 79 ... NicolaCurrie 5 70
(George Baker) *chsd ldrs: rdn over 1f out: wknd ins fnl f (jockey said gelding hung left-handed throughout)* 6/1[3]

-324 7 2¼ **Roman Spinner**[23] [756] 4-9-1 79 ... (t) LukeMorris 7 64
(Rae Guest) *hld up: rdn over 2f out: nvr nrr* 8/1

3121 8 ½ **Portledge (IRE)**[11] [952] 5-9-7 85 ... (b) JamieSpencer 8 68
(James Bethell) *hld up: hdwy 2f out: sn rdn: wknd fnl f* 8/1

520- 9 4½ **Bungee Jump (IRE)**[159] [7910] 4-9-7 85 ... HectorCrouch 4 56
(Grace Harris) *led: clr over 4f out tl over 2f out: hdd over 1f out: wknd fnl f* 33/1

35-0 10 17 **Rosarno (IRE)**[19] [812] 5-8-9 73 ... JoeyHaynes 3
(Paul Howling) *hld up: pushed along 1/2-way: wknd over 2f out* 66/1

1m 24.4s (-1.60) **Going Correction** +0.025s/f (Slow) 10 Ran SP% 117.5
Speed ratings (Par 105): **110,108,107,106,105 102,99,98,93,74**
CSF £34.29 CT £113.53 TOTE £3.00: £1.30, £3.20, £1.70; EX 39.10 Trifecta £326.50.
Owner Miss Emily Stevens Partnership **Bred** Old Mill Stud And S C Williams **Trained** Newmarket, Suffolk

FOCUS
The best race on the card and a good competitive handicap run at a strong gallop. The time was not surprisingly over a second quicker than the fastest of the other three races over the trip. The second helps set the standard.

1144 32RED H'CAP — 1m 7f 218y(P)
7:30 (7:30) (Class 4) (0-80,82) 4-Y-O+ £6,469 (£1,925; £962; £481; £400; £400) Stalls Low

Form RPR

343 1 **Knight Crusader**[26] [696] 7-9-6 74 ... AdamKirby 5 85
(John O'Shea) *hld up: hdwy over 3f out: led over 2f out: rdn over 1f out: styd on u.p* 11/2[3]

144- 2 nk **Age Of Wisdom (IRE)**[18] [6908] 6-9-12 80 ... (p) HectorCrouch 9 90
(Gary Moore) *hld up: hdwy over 2f out: chsd wnr over 1f out: rdn and ev ch ins fnl f: styd on* 9/1

1323 3 2¾ **Elysees Palace**[19] [803] 5-9-13 81 ... (v[1]) LukeMorris 1 88
(Sir Mark Prescott Bt) *hld up: nt clr run over 2f out: hdwy over 1f out: rdn ins fnl f: styd on same pce* 9/4[1]

1-22 4 4½ **Houlton**[26] [700] 4-8-12 72 ... (tp) GabrieleMalune(3) 7 73
(Marco Botti) *chsd ldrs: rdn over 2f out: wknd wl ins fnl f* 5/2[2]

55-4 5 2¾ **Take Two**[45] [404] 10-9-4 72 ... DavidProbert 8 70
(Alex Hales) *hld up: shkn up over 2f out: hdwy over 1f out: wknd ins fnl f* 25/1

40-5 6 shd **Akavit (IRE)**[26] [700] 7-9-2 70 ... CallumShepherd 10 68
(Ed de Giles) *hld up: hdwy over 8f out: led over 2f out: sn rdn and hdd: wknd ins fnl f* 25/1

31-5 7 2¾ **The Way You Dance (IRE)**[23] [318] 7-9-3 71 ... (v) ShaneKelly 6 66
(Neil Mulholland) *hld up: hdwy over 3f out: rdn over 1f out: wknd ins fnl f* 25/1

60/6 8 15 **Shades Of Silver**[18] [833] 9-8-11 65 ... HollieDoyle 4 42
(Alexandra Dunn) *chsd ldrs: lost pl over 8f out: wknd over 3f out* 66/1

310- 9 nk **Gang Warfare**[176] [7337] 8-10-0 82 ... (tp) RossaRyan 2 58
(Alexandra Dunn) *led 1f: chsd ldr: rdn and ev ch over 2f out: wknd over 1f out* 33/1

3-01 10 31 **Galitello**[37] [566] 4-8-6 63 ... JoeFanning 3
(Mark Johnston) *led after 1f: clr 10f out tl over 6f out: hdd & wknd over 2f out (jockey said gelding stopped quickly)* 11/2[3]

3m 26.61s (-3.49) **Going Correction** +0.025s/f (Slow)
WFA 4 from 5yo+ 3lb 10 Ran SP% 116.1
Speed ratings (Par 105): **109,108,107,105,103 103,102,94,94,79**
CSF £49.27 CT £143.12 TOTE £6.90: £2.00, £2.40, £1.30; EX 61.10 Trifecta £178.90.
Owner S P Bloodstock **Bred** Steven & Petra Wallace **Trained** Elton, Gloucs

FOCUS
A fair staying handicap run at a sound gallop and they finished fairly strung out. A small pb from the second, with the winner rated in line with the better view of his previous effort.

1145 32RED ON THE APP STORE CLASSIFIED STKS (DIV I) — 1m 3f 219y(P)
8:00 (8:03) (Class 6) 4-Y-O+ £3,105 (£924; £461; £400; £400; £400) Stalls Low

Form RPR

0231 1 **Harry Callahan (IRE)**[37] [549] 4-9-0 50 ... (v) CallumShepherd 2 57
(Mick Channon) *chsd ldr tl over 9f out: remained handy: shkn up over 2f out: chsd ldr over 1f out: rdn to ld ins fnl f: styd on* 5/4[1]

4-04 2 1 **Schindlers Ark (USA)**[36] [589] 5-9-1 45 ... CharlieBennett 5 54
(Jane Chapple-Hyam) *sn led at stdy pce: qcknd over 2f out: rdn and hdd ins fnl f: kpt on* 9/1

-010 3 3 **Muraaqeb**[7] [1015] 5-9-1 46 ... (p) DavidProbert 9 49
(Milton Bradley) *hdwy to chse ldr over 9f out tl rdn over 1f out: no ex ins fnl f* 14/1

6-20 4 1½ **Gorham's Cave**[55] [245] 5-9-1 50 ... (h) HollieDoyle 11 47+
(Ali Stronge) *hld up: racd keenly: hdwy over 3f out: rdn over 1f out: styd on same pce fnl f (jockey said gelding ran too freely)* 9/1

625- 5 ¾ **Greenview Paradise (IRE)**[119] [6930] 5-9-1 48 ... HayleyTurner 1 46
(Jeremy Scott) *chsd ldrs: rdn over 2f out: styd on same pce fr over 1f out* 9/2[2]

50-3 6 1½ **Cottingham**[66] [62] 4-9-0 49 ... JasonHart 8 44
(Kevin Frost) *hld up: rdn over 2f out: nt trble ldrs* 11/2[3]

00-0 7 ½ **Ronni Layne**[18] [829] 5-9-1 45 ... (p) LukeMorris 4 42
(Louise Allan) *s.i.s: sn hld up in tch: rdn over 3f out: styd on same pce fnl 2f* 50/1

0-40 8 hd **Onda District (IRE)**[51] [321] 7-8-12 40 ... FinleyMarsh(3) 3 42
(Stella Barclay) *w ldr 1f: remained handy: rdn over 3f out: styd on same pce fnl 2f* 25/1

00-0 9 1 **Invisible Shadow**[60] [155] 4-9-0 39 ... (p[1]) LiamKeniry 10 41
(Alex Hales) *s.i.s: hld up: rdn over 2f out: nvr on terms* 66/1

030- 10 1¼ **Embankment**[102] [9319] 10-9-1 46 ... KierenFox 7 38
(Michael Attwater) *hld up: rdn over 2f out: n.d* 40/1

44-0 11 ¾ **Cloud Nine (FR)**[35] [593] 6-9-1 40 ... (b) TomMarquand 6 37
(Tony Carroll) *hld up: hdwy over 5f out: rdn and wknd over 1f out (jockey said mare hung right-handed under pressure)* 33/1

2m 35.23s (0.73) **Going Correction** +0.025s/f (Slow)
WFA 4 from 5yo+ 1lb 11 Ran SP% 117.4
Speed ratings (Par 101): **98,97,95,94,93 92,92,92,91,90 90**
CSF £13.00 TOTE £3.00: £2.10, £2.40, £1.60; EX 12.70 Trifecta £112.20.
Owner Chelsea Thoroughbreds- Dirty Harry **Bred** Corduff Stud **Trained** West Ilsley, Berks

FOCUS
The first leg of a low-grade classified stakes was steadily run and nothing got involved from off the pace. The winner has been rated similar to his recent win.

1146 32RED ON THE APP STORE CLASSIFIED STKS (DIV II) — 1m 3f 219y(P)
8:30 (8:31) (Class 6) 4-Y-O+ £3,105 (£924; £461; £400; £400; £400) Stalls Low

Form RPR

0440 1 **Murhib (IRE)**[24] [736] 7-9-1 44 ... (h) RichardKingscote 2 53
(Lydia Richards) *led 1f: chsd ldrs: rdn to ld over 1f out: styd on* 4/1[2]

4-02 2 1½ **First Call (FR)**[9] [983] 4-9-0 49 ... (p) StevieDonohoe 5 52
(Ian Williams) *chsd ldrs: lost pl over 10f out: hdwy over 2f out: sn shkn up: carried hd high ins fnl f: styd on to go 2nd nr fin* 13/8[1]

60-0 3 ½ **Sigrid Nansen**[20] [789] 4-9-0 50 ... (tp) RossaRyan 7 51
(Alexandra Dunn) *s.s: hld up: hdwy over 2f out: rdn to chse wnr over 1f out: styd on same pce and lost 2nd towards fin* 16/1

066/ 4 4 **Sir Dylan**[499] [8430] 10-9-1 46 ... (h) LiamKeniry 1 43
(Polly Gundry) *prom: lost pl after 1f: nt clr run over 2f out: swtchd lft: styd on ins fnl f (jockey said gelding was denied a clear run)* 16/1

0-05 5 nk **Chief Sittingbull**[40] [482] 6-9-1 48 ... (t[1]) KieranO'Neill 8 43
(Tony Carroll) *sn prom: chsd ldr over 8f out tl led over 2f out: rdn and hdd over 1f out: no ex ins fnl f* 8/1

0-04 6 nse **Passing Clouds**[26] [695] 4-8-11 44 ... GabrieleMalune(3) 3 44
(Michael Attwater) *hld up in tch: rdn over 2f out: styd on same pce fr over 1f out* 11/2[3]

-515 7 1¼ **Dolphin Village (IRE)**[9] [984] 9-9-1 47 ... (h) PaulMulrennan 9 41
(Shaun Harris) *hdwy to chse ldrs over 9f out: rdn and ev ch over 2f out: wknd fnl f* 6/1

-630 8 3¾ **Mr Frankie**[20] [792] 8-9-1 45 ... (p) EoinWalsh 6 35
(Roy Brotherton) *s.i.s: hld up: rdn over 2f out: nvr on terms* 20/1

00-0 9 35 **Late For The Sky**[38] [532] 5-8-12 41 ... FinleyMarsh(3) 4
(Stella Barclay) *s.i.s: sn prom: rdn and lost pl over 4f out: wknd over 3f out (jockey said mare was never travelling)* 50/1

6-00 10 7 **More Harry**[39] [504] 4-9-0 37 ... ShaneKelly 10
(Martin Smith) *s.i.s: rcvrd to ld after 1f: rdn and hdd over 2f out: wknd over 1f out: eased (jockey said gelding stopped quickly)* 50/1

2m 35.01s (0.51) **Going Correction** +0.025s/f (Slow)
WFA 4 from 5yo+ 1lb 10 Ran SP% 119.3
Speed ratings (Par 101): **99,98,97,95,94 94,93,91,68,63**
CSF £10.99 TOTE £4.00: £1.60, £2.10, £2.40; EX 13.00 Trifecta £140.10.
Owner The Murhib Partnership **Bred** A Stroud And J Hanly **Trained** Funtington, W Sussex

FOCUS
The second division of this classified contest was run just over a fifth of a second faster than the first. A pb from the winner.
T/Plt: £1,263.50 to a £1 stake. Pool: £76,680.19 - 44.30 winning units T/Qpdt: £13.20 to a £1 stake. Pool: £14,991.34 - 834.63 winning units **Colin Roberts**

1147a-1157a (Foreign Racing) - See Raceform Interactive

1067 SOUTHWELL (L-H)
Tuesday, March 12

OFFICIAL GOING: Fibresand: standard
Wind: Virtually nil changing to moderate across after race 3 Weather: Heavy cloud and rain

1158 SUNRACING.CO.UK H'CAP — 7f 14y(F)
1:45 (1:45) (Class 6) (0-60,62) 4-Y-O+
£3,105 (£924; £461; £300; £300; £300) Stalls Low

Form | | | | RPR
4-05 **1** **Fly True**[13] 926 6-8-9 **48** NickyMackay 2 59
(Ivan Furtado) *trckd ldrs: smooth hdwy on inner wl over 2f out: rdn to ld over 1f out: kpt on strly* **10/1**
-043 **2** 2 ½ **Joyful Dream (IRE)**[12] 941 5-8-7 **46** (e[1]) HollieDoyle 12 50
(John Butler) *trckd ldr: cl up over 3f out: rdn to ld over 2f out: sn jnd: drvn and hdd over 1f out: kpt on same pce u.p fnl f (jockey said mare hung left throughout; vet reported the mare lost its right hind shoe)* **8/1**[3]
304- **3** 1 ½ **Benjamin Thomas (IRE)**[126] 8897 5-9-4 **57** (v) JasonHart 3 57
(John Quinn) *in tch: pushed along 3f out: rdn to chse ldrs 2f out: drvn over 1f out: kpt on fnl f* **7/2**[1]
010- **4** 1 ½ **Port Soif**[105] 9278 5-9-1 **54** (p) PaulMulrennan 10 50
(Dianne Sayer) *chsd ldrs on outer: hdwy and wd st: rdn and ch 2f out: sn drvn and kpt on one pce* **16/1**
0665 **5** nse **Major Crispies**[17] 882 8-8-11 **57** RPWalsh(7) 11 53
(Ronald Thompson) *midfield: hdwy and wd st: rdn over 2f out: sn drvn and no imp appr fnl f* **25/1**
5416 **6** ¾ **Sooqaan**[19] 830 8-9-9 **62** (p) CamHardie 7 56
(Antony Brittain) *trckd ldrs: hdwy 3f out: cl up and rdn over 2f out: drvn wl over 1f out: sn wknd* **7/2**[1]
-343 **7** 3 **Hic Bibi**[27] 701 4-9-7 **60** (p[1]) TrevorWhelan 6 46
(David Loughnane) *led: rdn along 3f out: sn hdd: drvn 2f out and grad wknd (jockey said filly stopped quickly)* **11/2**[2]
50-0 **8** 2 ¼ **Big Amigo (IRE)**[42] 467 6-9-1 **54** EoinWalsh 5 34
(Ken Wingrove) *a towards rr (jockey said gelding hung both ways)* **20/1**
446- **9** 1 **Robben Rainbow**[186] 7035 5-9-2 **58** PhilDennis(3) 8 36
(Katie Scott) *chsd ldrs: hdwy 1/2-way: rdn along over 2f out: sn drvn and wknd (vet reported the gelding had bled from the nose)* **20/1**
620- **10** 2 ½ **My Valentino (IRE)**[180] 7219 6-8-10 **49** (e[1]) JamesSullivan 9 20
(Dianne Sayer) *dwlt and swtchd rt to outer after s: a towards rr* **33/1**
5-00 **11** 1 **Allleedsaren'Twe**[7] 1026 4-8-6 **48** JaneElliott(3) 1 17
(Shaun Harris) *a towards rr* **20/1**
-R03 **12** 45 **One More Chance (IRE)**[20] 814 4-9-2 **62** (b) MarkCrehan(7) 4
(Michael Appleby) *ref to r: a wl t.o (starter reported that the filly had refused to race; trainer was informed that any future similar behaviour from the filly may result in being reported to the Head Office of the BHA)* **7/2**[1]

1m 27.81s (-2.49) **Going Correction** -0.275s/f (Stan) **12** Ran SP% **129.2**
Speed ratings (Par 101): **103,100,98,96,96 95,92,89,88,85 84,33**
CSF £88.22 CT £353.44 TOTE £12.90: £3.60, £2.20, £1.80; EX 103.40 Trifecta £629.70.
Owner Stuart Dobb & Kate Dobb **Bred** The Kathryn Stud **Trained** Wiseton, Nottinghamshire

FOCUS
A moderate handicap.

1159 BETWAY HEED YOUR CHELTENHAM HUNCH H'CAP — 1m 4f 14y(F)
2:25 (2:25) (Class 5) (0-75,75) 4-Y-O+
£3,752 (£1,116; £557; £300; £300; £300) Stalls Low

Form | | | | RPR
-245 **1** **Champarisi**[20] 803 4-8-12 **66** SamJames 10 77
(Grant Tuer) *trckd ldrs: hdwy 3f out: sn chal in centre: slt ld wl over 1f out and sn rdn: hrd pressed and drvn ins fnl f: edgd lft and kpt on wl towards fin* **8/1**
0-01 **2** nk **Argus (IRE)**[19] 833 7-9-3 **75** ThoreHammerHansen(5) 5 85
(Alexandra Dunn) *led 1f: trckd ldr: effrt on inner to chal 3f out: led wl over 2f out: sn rdn and hdd wl over 1f out: drvn and ev ch ins fnl f: no ex towards fin* **3/1**[2]
5-66 **3** 3 ½ **Restive (IRE)**[12] 950 6-8-12 **65** (t) EoinWalsh 9 69
(Jim Goldie) *hld up towards rr: stdy hdwy over 4f out: chsd ldrs over 2f out: sn rdn to chse ldng pair: drvn over 1f out: kpt on same pce fnl f* **33/1**
0132 **4** 1 ¾ **Epitaph (IRE)**[13] 927 5-8-10 **63** (b) AndrewMullen 3 64
(Michael Appleby) *hld up towards rr: hdwy 5f out: wd st: rdn over 2f out: drvn to chse ldrs over 1f out: edgd lft ins fnl f: kpt on* **8/1**
2-42 **5** 1 ¼ **Second Page**[27] 704 5-9-0 **74** (b) SeamusCronin(7) 11 74
(Richard Hannon) *dwlt and in rr: hdwy over 3f out: rdn over 2f out: n.m.r and swtchd rt over 1f out: styng on whn sltly hmpd ins fnl f: n.d* **4/1**[3]
4-06 **6** 1 ¼ **High Command (IRE)**[13] 927 6-9-1 **68** BenCurtis 12 66
(Michael Appleby) *towards rr: hdwy over 3f out: rdn along wl over 2f out: styd on to chse ldrs over 1f out: sltly hmpd ins fnl f: n.d* **25/1**
-310 **7** ¾ **Star Ascending (IRE)**[20] 803 7-9-6 **73** JoeFanning 13 69
(Jennie Candlish) *trckd ldrs: hdwy over 3f out: rdn along over 2f out: sn wknd* **12/1**
102- **8** 2 **Earl Of Bunnacurry (IRE)**[23] 9625 5-8-13 **66** (t) KieranO'Neill 7 59
(Gavin Cromwell, Ire) *chsd ldrs on inner: pushed along after 3f: rdn along over 5f out: drvn wl over 2f out: grad wknd (jockey said gelding was never travelling)* **11/4**[1]
02-5 **9** 6 **Nietzsche**[12] 948 6-9-5 **75** (t) BenRobinson(3) 8 58
(Brian Ellison) *prom: cl up 1/2-way: rdn to dispute ld 3f out: drvn over 2f out: sn wknd* **8/1**
330- **10** 3 ¼ **Be Perfect (USA)**[143] 8414 10-9-8 **75** (p) JamesSullivan 6 53
(Ruth Carr) *led after 1f: pushed along 4f out: rdn over 3f out: hdd wl over 2f out: sn wknd* **25/1**
1-00 **11** 23 **Mouchee (IRE)**[10] 985 4-9-1 **69** (v) JoeyHaynes 1 11
(Michael Blake) *midfield: pushed along and lost pl 1/2-way: bhd fnl 3f* **50/1**
00-0 **12** 27 **Sonnetist**[62] 135 5-8-13 **66** (bt) StevieDonohoe 4
(Johnny Farrelly) *a towards rr: bhd fnl 3f (vet reported the gelding bled from the nose)* **25/1**
13 **3** **Black Noah**[53] 300 4-9-3 **71** TrevorWhelan 2
(Johnny Farrelly) *a in rr: bhd fnl 5f* **25/1**

2m 34.57s (-6.43) **Going Correction** -0.275s/f (Stan)
WFA 4 from 5yo+ 1lb **13** Ran SP% **133.0**
Speed ratings (Par 103): **110,109,107,106,105 104,104,102,98,96 81,63,61**
CSF £33.72 CT £813.99 TOTE £9.20: £2.30, £2.00, £11.50; EX 46.80 Trifecta £1589.80.
Owner Allerton Racing & G Tuer **Bred** Faisal Meshrf Alqahtani **Trained** Birkby, N Yorks

FOCUS
A fair handicap run at a sound gallop. The second has been rated as backing up his latest effort, and the third to last year's best.

1160 BETWAY BEST FOR CHELTENHAM FESTIVAL BETTING H'CAP — 6f 16y(F)
3:05 (3:05) (Class 4) (0-80,81) 4-Y-O+
£5,530 (£1,645; £822; £411; £300; £300) Stalls Low

Form | | | | RPR
2232 **1** **Crosse Fire**[19] 832 7-8-11 **69** (p) KieranO'Neill 3 75
(Scott Dixon) *cl up: pushed along over 3f out: wd st and rdn to take slt ld 2f out: drvn over 1f out: edgd lft ins fnl f: kpt on wl u.p towards fin* **5/1**[3]
-063 **2** nk **The Great Wall (USA)**[19] 832 5-9-9 **81** (b[1]) AndrewMullen 1 86
(Michael Appleby) *trckd ldrs: hdwy on inner and cl up over 3f out: rdn to chal 2f out: drvn over 1f out: ev ch tl no ex towards fin* **3/1**[2]
6113 **3** shd **Gentlemen**[10] 981 8-9-0 **79** (h) GraceMcEntee(7) 6 84
(Phil McEntee) *cl up on outer: wd st: rdn 2f out: sltly outpcd over 1f out: drvn ent fnl f: kpt on wl towards fin* **13/2**
03-3 **4** 5 **Global Exceed**[13] 928 4-8-12 **70** (p[1]) JoeFanning 4 59
(Robert Cowell) *chsd ldrs: pushed along and outpcd over 3f out: rdn wl over 2f out: n.d (trainer could offer no explanation for the gelding's performance)* **9/1**
60-0 **5** nk **Related**[19] 832 9-9-2 **74** (b) PaulMulrennan 5 62
(Paul Midgley) *dwlt: sn swtchd rt to outer: a outpcd in rr* **20/1**
-131 **6** 2 ¼ **Ballyquin (IRE)**[5] 1061 4-9-6 **81** 6ex JoshuaBryan(3) 2 62
(Andrew Balding) *slt ld: rdn along wl over 2f out: sn hdd: drvn wl over 1f out and sn wknd (trainer's rep said colt was unsuited by the fibresand surface)* **6/5**[1]

1m 14.61s (-1.89) **Going Correction** -0.275s/f (Stan) **6** Ran SP% **115.2**
Speed ratings (Par 105): **101,100,100,93,93 90**
CSF £20.97 TOTE £6.10: £2.80, £1.70; EX 15.90 Trifecta £82.20.
Owner Paul J Dixon & Darren Lucas **Bred** Dr A Gillespie **Trained** Babworth, Notts
■ Stewards' Enquiry : Kieran O'Neill two-day ban: used whip above the permitted level (Mar 26-27)

FOCUS
The pace was sound for this fair handicap. It's been rated around the first three to their recent form.

1161 BETWAY NOVICE STKS — 4f 214y(F)
3:45 (3:45) (Class 5) 3-Y-O+ £3,752 (£1,116; £557; £278) Stalls Centre

Form | | | | RPR
30- **1** **Lille**[160] 7896 3-8-3 0 (w) AndrewMullen 2 75
(Kevin Ryan) *mde most centre: rdn wl over 1f out: drvn ent fnl f: kpt on wl* **7/1**[3]
35- **2** 1 ¼ **Exalted Angel (FR)**[151] 8163 3-8-8 0 CliffordLee 3 75
(K R Burke) *dwlt: sn trcking ldrs: hdwy and cl up 1/2-way: rdn and ev ch whn edgd bdly lft ins fnl f: kpt on same pce* **10/11**[1]
54-2 **3** 2 ¾ **So Hi Speed (USA)**[19] 831 3-8-8 68 (p) JoeFanning 5 65
(Robert Cowell) *cl up: rdn along 2f out: kpt on same pce appr fnl f* **7/1**[3]
3 **4** ½ **Gupta**[19] 831 3-8-8 0 JamesSullivan 1 63
(David Brown) *cl up towards far side: rdn along 2f out: grad wknd* **12/1**
32 **5** 1 ½ **Olympic Spirit**[46] 408 3-8-8 0 BenCurtis 6 58
(David Barron) *racd towards stands' rail: chsd ldrs: rdn along wl over 1f out: sn one pce* **3/1**[2]
5 **6** 1 ¼ **Termonator**[19] 831 3-8-9 0 ow1 SamJames 7 54
(Grant Tuer) *racd nr stands' rail: towards rr: rdn along 2f out: n.d* **66/1**
032- **7** 5 **Coastal Drive**[155] 8063 4-9-7 63 KevinStott 4 41
(Paul Midgley) *chsd ldrs centre: rdn along over 2f out: sn wknd* **16/1**

58.0s (-1.70) **Going Correction** -0.275s/f (Stan)
WFA 3 from 4yo 13lb **7** Ran SP% **117.5**
Speed ratings (Par 103): **102,100,95,94,92 90,82**
CSF £14.46 TOTE £7.00: £2.90, £1.20; EX 21.40 Trifecta £78.80.
Owner Lille Partners **Bred** Cheveley Park Stud Ltd **Trained** Hambleton, N Yorks

FOCUS
A fair novice run at a solid pace. The second has been rated close to his debut figure, and the third and fourth close to their C&D latest.

1162 BETWAY BEST FOR CHELTENHAM FESTIVAL OFFERS H'CAP — 4f 214y(F)
4:25 (4:25) (Class 6) (0-65,71) 4-Y-O+
£3,105 (£924; £461; £300; £300; £300) Stalls Centre

Form | | | | RPR
54-2 **1** **Twentysvnthlancers**[19] 834 6-8-13 **57** PaulMulrennan 7 63
(Paul Midgley) *dwlt and in rr: hdwy in centre over 2f out: rdn to chse wnr over 1f out: styd on wl to ld nr fin* **10/1**
1201 **2** ½ **Warrior's Valley**[4] 1076 4-9-13 **71** 6ex (tp) LewisEdmunds 12 75
(David C Griffiths) *qckly away and led: clr towards centre over 2f out: rdn over 1f out: hung lft ins fnl f: hdd and no ex nr fin (jockey said gelding hung left)* **3/1**[1]
0-61 **3** 1 **Kath's Boy (IRE)**[13] 926 5-8-2 **53** (b) ElishaWhittington(7) 11 53
(Tony Carroll) *racd nr stands' rail: towards rr: hdwy wl over 1f out: sn rdn: kpt on fnl f* **8/1**[3]
400- **4** 2 ¼ **Socialites Red**[154] 8078 6-8-10 **54** (p) BenCurtis 6 46
(Scott Dixon) *racd centre: chsd ldr: rdn along 2f out: drvn over 1f out: grad wknd* **25/1**
0030 **5** 1 ½ **Always Amazing**[8] 1016 5-9-1 **59** PaddyMathers 2 46
(Derek Shaw) *racd towards far side: in tch: hdwy to chse ldrs 2f out: sn rdn and wknd over 1f out* **12/1**
0121 **6** nk **Spirit Power**[27] 707 4-9-8 **66** JasonHart 8 52
(Eric Alston) *prom centre: pushed along 1/2-way: rdn 2f out: sn drvn and btn* **3/1**[1]
056- **7** ½ **Rantan (IRE)**[164] 7783 6-9-7 **65** KevinStott 4 49
(Paul Midgley) *racd towards far side: dwlt and in rr tl styd on fr over 1f out: n.d* **8/1**[3]
410- **8** nse **Victors Lady (IRE)**[179] 7256 4-9-9 **67** JoeFanning 9 51
(Robert Cowell) *racd nr stands' rail: in tch: rdn along over 2f out: sn wknd* **6/1**[2]
0-20 **9** 1 ¾ **Cuppacoco**[40] 498 4-9-5 **63** JackGarritty 3 41
(Ann Duffield) *chsd ldrs centre: pushed along and edgd lft over 3f out: rdn and hung bdly lft to far rail over 2f out: sn outpcd (jockey said filly hung left)* **16/1**

-543 **10** *hd* **Bluella**[13] 926 4-8-2 **46** oh1 .... AndrewMullen 5 23
(Robyn Brisland) *dwlt: sn chsng ldrs centre: rdn along over 2f out: sn wknd* **25/1**

01-1 **11** *1 3/4* **Rockley Point**[25] 742 6-8-13 **60** ....(b) PhilDennis(3) 10 31
(Katie Scott) *racd nr stands' rail: sn outpcd and bhd* **8/1**[3]

58.03s (-1.67) **Going Correction** -0.275s/f (Stan) **11** Ran SP% **128.0**
Speed ratings (Par 101): **102,101,99,96,93 93,92,92,89,89 86**
CSF £43.76 CT £270.24 TOTE £11.60: £3.60, £1.30, £2.40; EX 56.10 Trifecta £365.50.
Owner Paul Williamson & Chris Priestley **Bred** Bucklands Farm & Stud Ltd **Trained** Westow, N Yorks

FOCUS
A strongly run handicap. Straightforward form, with the winner rated to the top end of his recent form, and the second and third to their marks.

1163 BETWAY APPRENTICE H'CAP 1m 4f 14y(F)
5:00 (5:00) (Class 6) (0-60,59) 4-Y-0+
£3,105 (£924; £461; £300; £300; £300) **Stalls** Low

Form RPR

0026 **1** **Going Native**[19] 829 4-8-6 **45** .... RhonaPindar(5) 14 58+
(Olly Williams) *chsd ldr: hdwy to ld over 4f out: rdn clr wl over 2f out: kpt on strly* **16/1**

42-3 **2** *5* **Siyahamba (IRE)**[40] 504 5-8-9 **45** .... HarryRussell(3) 7 49
(Bryan Smart) *dwlt and sn pushed along in rr: hdwy over 7f out: chsd ldrs over 4f out: rdn along over 3f out: drvn on inner wl over 1f out: kpt on wl fnl f* **7/2**[2]

4043 **3** *hd* **Break The Silence**[5] 1069 5-9-2 **52** .... CierenFallon(5) 3 56
(Scott Dixon) *hld up in midfield: hdwy over 4f out: chsd ldrs over 3f out: rdn over 2f out: drvn to chse wnr wl over 1f out: kpt on same pce* **11/2**

04-5 **4** *2* **Lean On Pete (IRE)**[47] 387 10-9-10 **57** .... RossTurner 6 57
(Ollie Pears) *trckd ldrs: pushed along and outpcd over 4f out: wd st: rdn along and hdwy on outer over 2f out: kpt on fnl f* **14/1**

00-0 **5** *1 1/4* **Esme Kate (IRE)**[37] 589 4-8-11 **45** ....(vt[1]) KieranSchofield 13 44
(Ivan Furtado) *set gd pce: pushed along and hdd over 4f out: chsd wnr and rdn along 3f out: drvn wl over 1f out: grad wknd* **50/1**

30-2 **6** *3/4* **Ipcress File**[5] 1070 4-8-9 **48** ....(p) GraceMcEntee(5) 9 46
(Scott Dixon) *chsd ldrs: rdn along over 3f out: wd st: drvn and kpt on same pce fnl 2f* **25/1**

3160 **7** *1 1/4* **Prerogative (IRE)**[10] 983 5-8-12 **50** ....(p) ElishaWhittington(5) 4 45
(Tony Carroll) *in rr tl hdwy over 3f out: rdn along and kpt on fnl 2f* **16/1**

3-00 **8** *3 3/4* **The Lock Master (IRE)**[26] 721 12-8-7 **45** ....(p) GavinAshton(5) 10 34
(Michael Appleby) *towards rr: effrt and sme hdwy on outer 1/2-way: rdn along over 4f out: n.d* **40/1**

405- **9** *1/2* **Amadeus (IRE)**[44] 6894 4-9-10 **58** .... ScottMcCullagh 5 47
(Gavin Cromwell, Ire) *hld up towards rr: pushed along over 5f out: rdn over 4f out: nvr a factor* **3/1**[1]

00-0 **10** *nk* **Let's Be Happy (IRE)**[67] 61 5-9-9 **59** .... AmeliaGlass(3) 8 47
(Mandy Rowland) *midfield: rapid hdwy to join ldrs after 4f: rdn along to chse ldng pair 4f out: drvn wl over 2f out: sn wknd* **50/1**

-050 **11** *1 3/4* **Elite Icon**[22] 782 5-8-9 **45** .... OliverStammers(3) 2 30
(Jim Goldie) *a towards rr* **33/1**

300- **12** *1* **Goldfox Girl**[120] 9033 4-8-12 **49** .... WilliamCarver(3) 12 34
(Robyn Brisland) *prom: rdn along over 5f out: wknd 4f out (vet reported the filly finished lame right fore)* **10/1**

06-4 **13** *1 1/4* **Pullman Brown (USA)**[11] 789 7-9-0 **47** .... SeamusCronin 1 29
(Philip Kirby) *hld up: hdwy 4f out: in tch and rdn along 3f out: drvn over 2f out: sn wknd* **4/1**[3]

000- **P** **Hilborough**[125] 8919 4-9-11 **59** ....(t) JonathanFisher 11
(Les Eyre) *midfield: rdn along 1/2-way: sn lost pl and hanging rt: p.u over 4f out (vet reported the gelding bled from the nose)* **33/1**

2m 38.07s (-2.93) **Going Correction** -0.275s/f (Stan)
WFA 4 from 5yo+ 1lb **14** Ran SP% **126.2**
Speed ratings (Par 101): **98,94,94,93,92 91,91,88,88,88 86,86,85,**
CSF £71.65 CT £366.02 TOTE £20.60: £3.80, £1.40, £2.40; EX 120.70 Trifecta £807.80.
Owner David L Bayliss **Bred** Newsells Park Stud **Trained** Market Rasen, Lincs

FOCUS
A modest handicap. It's been rated around the second and third.
T/Plt: £248.80 to a £1 stake. Pool: £55,012.54 - 161.35 winning units T/Qpdt: £20.50 to a £1 stake. Pool: £4,982.47 - 179.70 winning units **Joe Rowntree**

1100 WOLVERHAMPTON (A.W) (L-H)
Tuesday, March 12

OFFICIAL GOING: Tapeta: standard
Wind: Strong behind Weather: Fine

1164 LIKE SUN RACING ON FACEBOOK APPRENTICE H'CAP 7f 36y (Tp)
5:45 (5:45) (Class 5) (0-75,75) 4-Y-0+
£3,752 (£1,116; £557; £400; £400; £400) **Stalls** High

Form RPR

1111 **1** **Lion Hearted (IRE)**[22] 784 5-8-11 **72** .... MarkCrehan(7) 6 82+
(Michael Appleby) *prom: hmpd and lost pl over 6f out: hdwy on outer over 5f out: led over 4f out: rdn over 1f out: jst hld on* **10/11**[1]

0-00 **2** *hd* **Lefortovo (FR)**[55] 255 6-9-0 **75** ....(p) GeorgiaDobie(7) 7 84+
(Jo Hughes, France) *s.i.s: hld up: hdwy over 1f out: rdn to chse wnr ins fnl f: r.o wl* **6/1**[2]

26-3 **3** *3* **Saisons D'Or (IRE)**[25] 740 4-9-1 **72** .... SebastianWoods(3) 1 73
(Jedd O'Keeffe) *awkward s: racd keenly and sn prom: rdn and hung lft over 1f out: sn hung rt: styd on to go 3rd nr fin* **10/1**

-541 **4** *nk* **Gabrial The Tiger (IRE)**[19] 840 7-9-0 **71** .... ConnorMurtagh(3) 8 71
(Richard Fahey) *led: hdd over 4f out: remained handy: rdn over 1f out: styd on same pce ins fnl f* **14/1**

50-0 **5** *1/2* **Fire Diamond**[20] 812 6-9-2 **70** ....(p) JaneElliott 4 69
(Tom Dascombe) *hld up: rdn over 1f out: r.o ins fnl f: nt rch ldrs* **25/1**

5160 **6** *hd* **The British Lion (IRE)**[6] 1036 4-9-2 **70** .... FinleyMarsh 3 68
(Alexandra Dunn) *prom: rdn over 1f out: nt clr run and swtchd rt ins fnl f: styd on* **25/1**

4-42 **7** *1/2* **Kadrizzi (FR)**[47] 381 6-9-6 **74** ....(v) JackDuern 2 71
(Dean Ivory) *chsd ldrs: shkn up over 2f out: rn wd over 1f out: styd on same pce* **8/1**[3]

3-06 **8** *1* **Mutabaahy (IRE)**[8] 1016 4-9-4 **72** ....(h) WilliamCox 5 66
(Antony Brittain) *s.i.s: hld up: nvr nrr (jockey said gelding was awkward leaving the stalls and slowly into stride)* **16/1**

040- **9** *nk* **Shepherd's Purse**[125] 8924 7-9-2 **73** .... CameronNoble(3) 9 66
(David Loughnane) *plld hrd: wnt 2nd 6f out tl over 4f out: chsd wnr over 3f out tl rdn over 1f out: wknd ins fnl f* **20/1**

-051 **10** *1 1/4* **The Establishment**[21] 790 4-9-1 **72** ....(h) BenCoen(3) 11 62
(David Evans) *hld up: rdn over 2f out: n.d (trainer's rep said gelding had run flat)* **10/1**

11-5 **11** *nk* **Arlecchino's Leap**[14] 914 7-9-2 **73** .... ThomasGreatrex(3) 10 62
(Mark Usher) *hld up: shkn up over 2f out: n.d* **50/1**

-005 **12** *1* **Highly Sprung (IRE)**[19] 840 6-9-3 **71** .... ConorMcGovern 12 58
(Les Eyre) *s.i.s: hld up: n.d* **100/1**

1m 27.19s (-1.61) **Going Correction** -0.05s/f (Stan) **12** Ran SP% **123.9**
Speed ratings (Par 103): **107,106,103,103,102 102,101,100,100,98 98,97**
CSF £6.44 CT £39.96 TOTE £1.80: £1.30, £2.10, £2.90; EX 9.30 Trifecta £56.80.
Owner Slipstream Racing **Bred** Dowager Countess Harrington **Trained** Oakham, Rutland

FOCUS
The well-backed winner was a stone higher than for his last two wins but continues on the up. The third has been rated close to his recent form.

1165 LADBROKES HOME OF THE ODDS BOOST NOVICE STKS 1m 1f 104y (Tp)
6:15 (6:15) (Class 5) 3-Y-O £3,752 (£1,116; £557; £278) **Stalls** Low

Form RPR

2 **1** **Ragnar**[26] 723 3-9-2 0 .... CallumShepherd 7 76+
(Dominic Ffrench Davis) *led early: chsd ldrs: shkn up to ld ins fnl f: r.o wl* **3/1**[1]

3 **2** *3* **Ifreet (QA)**[55] 251 3-9-2 0 .... RossaRyan 6 69
(Richard Hannon) *s.i.s: sn prom: led over 4f out tl shkn up over 3f out: hung rt over 2f out: rdn to ld over 1f out: hdd ins fnl f: styd on same pce* **3/1**[1]

3 *1* **Follow A Dream (USA)** 3-8-11 0 .... KieranO'Neill 4 62+
(John Gosden) *prom: shkn up and carried hd high over 1f out: edgd lft and r.o ins fnl f* **3/1**[1]

4 *3/4* **Revamp (USA)** 3-9-2 0 .... ShaneKelly 1 65+
(David Simcock) *s.s: hld up: hdwy over 1f out: r.o wl: nt rch ldrs* **33/1**

0 **5** *1/2* **San Diaco (IRE)**[10] 979 3-9-2 0 .... JosephineGordon 8 64?
(Ed Dunlop) *sn led: hdd over 4f out: led again over 3f out: rdn and hdd over 1f out: no ex ins fnl f* **100/1**

5 **6** *5* **Teodora De Vega (IRE)**[21] 794 3-8-11 0 .... RichardKingscote 9 49
(Ralph Beckett) *chsd ldr after 1f tl over 4f out: shkn up over 3f out: outpcd fnl 2f* **6/1**[2]

7 *1 3/4* **Lock Seventeen (USA)**[161] 7883 3-9-2 0 .... StevieDonohoe 5 50
(Charlie Fellowes) *s.i.s: hld up: shkn up over 2f out: nt trble ldrs* **10/1**[3]

8 *nk* **Nathanielhawthorne** 3-8-13 0 .... AaronJones(3) 13 49
(Marco Botti) *unruly to post: s.s and awkwardly: in rr: rdn over 1f out: styd on ins fnl f* **33/1**

00 **9** *2 1/4* **Initial Approach (IRE)**[21] 795 3-8-11 0 .... CamHardie 11 40
(Alan Brown) *hld up: rdn over 3f out: n.d* **100/1**

0-4 **10** *nse* **Battle Of Pembroke (USA)**[12] 949 3-8-11 0 .... DylanHogan(5) 2 45
(David Simcock) *hld up: shkn up over 3f out: a in rr* **25/1**

4 **11** *3/4* **Tsarmina (IRE)**[8] 1019 3-8-11 0 .... EoinWalsh 12 38
(David Evans) *hdwy to go prom after 1f: rdn over 2f out: sn wknd* **66/1**

64 **12** *3 1/4* **Golden Grenade (FR)**[11] 967 3-9-2 0 .... GeorgeDowning 3 36
(Ian Williams) *hld up: pushed along over 3f out: wknd over 2f out* **100/1**

2m 2.03s (1.23) **Going Correction** -0.05s/f (Stan) **12** Ran SP% **112.6**
Speed ratings (Par 98): **92,89,88,87,87 82,81,81,79,79 78,75**
CSF £10.47 TOTE £3.50: £1.70, £1.20, £1.40; EX 11.30 Trifecta £41.60.
Owner Kingwood Stud Management Co Ltd **Bred** The National Stud **Trained** Lambourn, Berks

FOCUS
A fair novice and a nice performance from the winner. Muddling form. The winner has been rated in line with the better view of his debut effort.

1166 LADBROKES HOME OF THE ODDS BOOST H'CAP 1m 1f 104y (Tp)
6:45 (6:45) (Class 5) (0-75,75) 3-Y-O
£3,752 (£1,116; £557; £400; £400; £400) **Stalls** Low

Form RPR

506- **1** **Rock Up In Style**[162] 7837 3-9-0 **68** .... JoeFanning 9 73
(Mark Johnston) *sn prom: chsd ldr over 6f out: shkn up to ld over 1f out: rdn and edgd lft ins fnl f: styd on* **10/1**

0-24 **2** *1/2* **Barossa Red (IRE)**[19] 827 3-9-7 **75** .... DavidProbert 6 79
(Andrew Balding) *hld up: hdwy over 2f out: rdn and edgd lft ins fnl f: r.o* **5/2**[1]

04-3 **3** *shd* **Cabarita**[38] 556 3-9-4 **72** .... RichardKingscote 1 77+
(Ralph Beckett) *trckd ldrs: nt clr run and lost pl over 2f out: hdwy over 1f out: rdn and n.m.r wl ins fnl f: r.o* **7/2**[2]

0-00 **4** *3* **Gabriel The Giant (IRE)**[11] 966 3-8-6 **60** .... KieranO'Neill 5 57
(Ian Williams) *hmpd s: prom: racd keenly: rdn over 2f out: edgd lft and styd on same pce fnl f* **33/1**

533 **5** *1 1/2* **Al Daayen (FR)**[13] 930 3-8-3 **57** .... FrannyNorton 8 51
(Mark Johnston) *half-rrd s: sn prom: led 8f out: rdn and hdd over 1f out: wknd wl ins fnl f* **25/1**

5-46 **6** *3 1/2* **Ivory Charm**[20] 798 3-8-9 **63** .... PJMcDonald 2 50
(Richard Fahey) *broke wl enough: sn lost pl: rdn over 1f out: nt trble ldrs* **6/1**

046- **7** *3/4* **Smarter (IRE)**[103] 9308 3-9-0 **68** ....(b[1]) TomMarquand 3 53
(William Haggas) *s.i.s: hld up: rdn over 2f out: nvr nrr* **9/2**[3]

060- **8** *3/4* **Thermal (IRE)**[104] 9290 3-9-1 **69** .... RobHornby 7 53
(Martyn Meade) *broke wl: plld hrd: sn stdd and lost pl: rdn over 1f out: nt trble ldrs* **8/1**

002- **9** *5* **Swift Justice**[145] 8352 3-8-11 **65** ....(p) ShaneKelly 4 38
(Mark Loughnane) *edgd rt s: sn led: hdd 8f out: chsd ldrs: rdn over 2f out: wkng whn hung lft over 1f out (jockey said gelding hung left-handed)* **33/1**

2m 0.96s (0.16) **Going Correction** -0.05s/f (Stan) **9** Ran SP% **113.2**
Speed ratings (Par 98): **97,96,96,93,92 89,88,88,83**
CSF £34.01 CT £105.63 TOTE £10.30: £2.60, £1.60, £1.90; EX 50.50 Trifecta £189.30.
Owner Brian Yeardley **Bred** Bba 2010 Ltd **Trained** Middleham Moor, N Yorks

FOCUS
A fairly competitive affair. The winner has been rated back to his 2yo debut level.

1167 LADBROKES H'CAP 6f 20y (Tp)
7:15 (7:15) (Class 6) (0-60,60) 3-Y-O
£3,105 (£924; £461; £400; £400; £400) **Stalls** Low

Form RPR

5-01 **1** **Camachess (IRE)**[4] 1081 3-9-1 **57** .... PhilDennis(3) 3 67+
(Philip McBride) *a.p: shkn up to chse ldr over 1f out: led ins fnl f: r.o: comf* **2/1**[1]

0-01 **2** 1 ¾ **Global Acclamation**[38] 550 3-9-4 **57**............................(b) LiamKeniry 5 61
(Ed Dunlop) *led at stdy pce over 5f out: qcknd over 2f out: rdn over 1f out: hdd ins fnl f: styd on same pce* **6/1**

00-0 **3** shd **Awa Bomba**[34] 620 3-9-3 **56**............................ RichardKingscote 4 59+
(Tony Carroll) *hld up: shkn up over 1f out: nt clr run sn after: rdn: hung lft and r.o ins fnl f: nt rch ldrs* **9/2[3]**

0-00 **4** 1 ½ **Lysander Belle (IRE)**[38] 555 3-9-1 **54**............................ ShaneKelly 7 53
(Sophie Leech) *s.i.s: hld up: hdwy over 1f out: nt rch ldrs* **40/1**

1010 **5** nk **Deconso**[20] 813 3-9-3 **56**............................ HollieDoyle 2 55
(Christopher Kellett) *hld up in tch: nt clr run and lost pl over 4f out: hdwy over 1f out: sn rdn and edgd rt: styng on same pce whn carried lft wl ins fnl f* **4/1[2]**

06-0 **6** ¾ **Red Skye Delight (IRE)**[61] 156 3-9-5 **58**............................ KieranO'Neill 1 54
(Luke McJannet) *led: hdd over 5f out: chsd ldrs: shkn up: carried hd high and hung lft over 1f out: no ex ins fnl f* **12/1**

06-5 **7** ½ **Islay Mist**[43] 458 3-9-3 **59**............................(t[1]) GabrieleMalune(3) 6 53
(Amy Murphy) *hld up: rdn over 1f out: r.o ins fnl f: nvr nrr* **33/1**

6-03 **8** 3 ¼ **Oxygenic**[36] 605 3-8-10 **52**............................ ConorMcGovern(3) 9 37
(David O'Meara) *prom: racd keenly: shkn up over 1f out: sn wknd* **20/1**

-545 **9** ¾ **Gunnabedun (IRE)**[46] 406 3-8-12 **51**............................(p[1]) JoeFanning 10 34
(Iain Jardine) *chsd ldrs: lost off-side cheek piece over 4f out: ev ch on outer over 2f out: wkng whn nt clr run ins fnl f* **14/1**

6530 **10** ½ **Not So Shy**[13] 918 3-9-1 **54**............................ EoinWalsh 11 35
(David Evans) *plld hrd: jnd ldr 5f out: ev ch over 2f out: sn rdn: edgd rt and wknd fnl f* **50/1**

-355 **11** 10 **Spirit Of Lucerne (IRE)**[38] 550 3-9-4 **57**............................(p) OisinMurphy 12 8
(Phil McEntee) *s.i.s: hdwy on outer over 4f out: rdn over 2f out: wknd wl over 1f out* **16/1**

1m 14.51s (0.01) **Going Correction** -0.05s/f (Stan) **11** Ran SP% **118.1**
Speed ratings (Par 96): **97,94,94,92,92 91,90,86,85,84 71**
CSF £13.81 CT £49.49 TOTE £2.20: £1.10, £1.70, £2.70; EX 12.10 Trifecta £106.90.
Owner The Narc Partnership **Bred** Yeomanstown Stud **Trained** Newmarket, Suffolk

FOCUS
This was steadily run and turned into a dash up the straight. The second has been rated similar to his recent win.

1168 BETWAY BEST FOR CHELTENHAM FESTIVAL OFFERS NOVICE MEDIAN AUCTION STKS 6f 20y (Tp)
7:45 (7:45) (Class 6) 3-5-Y-O £3,105 (£924; £461; £230) Stalls Low

Form RPR

0 **1** **Pass The Vino (IRE)**[53] 306 3-9-0 0............................ TomMarquand 3 86
(Paul D'Arcy) *sn led at stdy pce: shkn up and qcknd over 2f out: rdn ins fnl f: r.o: eased nr fin* **9/4[2]**

11 **2** 4 **With Caution (IRE)**[15] 908 3-9-9 80............................ OisinMurphy 2 83
(James Tate) *prom: chsd wnr over 3f out: rdn over 1f out: no ex ins fnl f* **6/5[1]**

6 **3** 5 **Puzzle**[12] 943 3-9-0 0............................ ShaneKelly 1 59
(Richard Hughes) *s.i.s: hld up: hdwy 1/2-way: shkn up over 2f out: sn outpcd* **12/1**

4 nk **Sea Storm** 3-8-9 0............................ RobHornby 4 53+
(Martyn Meade) *s.i.s: hld up: racd keenly: hmpd over 2f out: hdwy over 1f out: nt trble ldrs (jockey said filly ran too freely)* **7/1**

22 **5** 1 **Plumette**[19] 841 3-8-9 0............................ PJMcDonald 5 50
(Richard Fahey) *prom: rdn whn hmpd over 2f out: wknd over 1f out (vet reported the filly lost its left hind shoe)* **5/1[3]**

6 ½ **Polaris Angel** 3-8-9 0............................ JasonHart 8 49
(Mark Walford) *s.i.s: pushed along early in rr: shkn up over 1f out: n.d* **50/1**

06 **7** 6 **Inverarity**[47] 388 3-8-11 0............................(p[1]) FinleyMarsh(3) 6 36
(Frank Bishop) *chsd wnr tl pushed along over 3f out: edgd lft over 2f out: wkng whn hung rt over 1f out (jockey said colt hung right-handed in the home straight)* **100/1**

6 **8** shd **Sharrabang**[19] 841 3-9-0 0............................ CamHardie 7 35
(Stella Barclay) *hld up: shkn up on outer over 2f out: sn wknd* **100/1**

1m 14.27s (-0.23) **Going Correction** -0.05s/f (Stan) **8** Ran SP% **117.0**
Speed ratings (Par 101): **99,93,87,86,85 84,76,76**
CSF £5.47 TOTE £3.40: £1.20, £1.02, £3.40; EX 5.60 Trifecta £29.80.
Owner Rowley Racing **Bred** Dr D Harron **Trained** Newmarket, Suffolk

FOCUS
They went a steady early gallop and few got into this, the market leaders having it between them from the turn in. The form has been rated at face value.

1169 BETWAY BEST FOR CHELTENHAM FESTIVAL BETTING H'CAP 1m 1f 104y (Tp)
8:15 (8:15) (Class 5) (0-75,76) 4-Y-O+ £3,752 (£1,116; £557; £400; £400; £400) Stalls Low

Form RPR

-004 **1** **Badenscoth**[12] 942 5-9-1 **67**............................ FrannyNorton 5 77
(Dean Ivory) *hld up: hdwy over 1f out: shkn up to ld and edgd lft wl ins fnl f: sn clr* **6/1[2]**

5353 **2** 2 ¾ **Ambient (IRE)**[11] 962 4-9-6 **72**............................ RichardKingscote 9 76
(Jane Chapple-Hyam) *sn led at stdy pce: qcknd over 2f out: rdn and hdd wl ins fnl f* **6/1[2]**

0-00 **3** 1 **Captain Pugwash (IRE)**[20] 803 5-9-2 **68**............................(v[1]) LiamKeniry 10 70
(Stef Keniry) *mid-div: swtchd rt and hdwy over 1f out: rdn and edgd lft ins fnl f: styd on same pce* **33/1**

/652 **4** nk **Stormy Blues**[41] 473 5-9-7 **73**............................(tp) DavidProbert 8 74
(Nigel Hawke) *sn prom: chsd ldr over 7f out: ev ch fr over 2f out: rdn over 1f out: no ex wl ins fnl f* **7/1[3]**

20-3 **5** 1 ½ **Lovely Approach**[19] 827 4-9-10 **76**............................ TomMarquand 7 74
(Hugo Palmer) *chsd ldrs: shkn up over 3f out: rdn and hung lft over 1f out: no ex ins fnl f* **5/2[1]**

02-4 **6** nk **Rubensian**[38] 559 6-8-13 **70**............................ DylanHogan(5) 2 67
(David Simcock) *s.i.s: hld up: shkn up over 1f out: rdn and r.o ins fnl f: nvr nrr* **12/1**

36-0 **7** nk **The Eagle's Nest (IRE)**[12] 942 5-9-2 **68**............................(t) RossaRyan 6 65
(Alexandra Dunn) *prom: rdn and hung lft fr over 1f out: no ex ins fnl f* **25/1**

10 **8** 1 ¾ **Manfadh (IRE)**[21] 793 4-9-3 **69**............................(h[1]) ShaneKelly 3 62
(Mark Brisbourne) *mid-div: pushed along over 4f out: n.d after* **10/1**

13-4 **9** hd **Mearing**[19] 833 4-9-4 **73**............................(p) JamieGormley(3) 11 65
(Iain Jardine) *s.s: hld up: nvr on terms (jockey said gelding was slowly away and hung left-handed)* **14/1**

21-5 **10** shd **Beatbybeatbybeat**[12] 951 6-9-3 **72**............................(v) WilliamCox(3) 12 64
(Antony Brittain) *hld up: plld hrd: rdn over 1f out: n.d* **25/1**

5-44 **11** nk **Rockwood**[12] 950 8-8-13 **65**............................(v) BarryMcHugh 4 57
(Karen McLintock) *hld up: rdn over 1f out: nvr on terms* **8/1**

320- **12** 4 ½ **Seek The Moon (USA)**[125] 8919 4-8-11 **63**............................ PJMcDonald 1 45
(Jedd O'Keeffe) *plld hrd and prom: rdn over 2f out: wknd over 1f out* **10/1[3]**

1m 59.11s (-1.69) **Going Correction** -0.05s/f (Stan) **12** Ran SP% **123.9**
Speed ratings (Par 103): **105,102,101,101,100 99,99,97,97,97 93,93**
CSF £43.09 CT £1128.22 TOTE £8.60: £2.80, £1.50, £10.00; EX 50.00 Trifecta £2099.70.
Owner Peter J Skinner **Bred** Peter J Skinner **Trained** Radlett, Herts

FOCUS
There wasn't much pace on early but they wound it up from a fair way out and the winner came from behind. Muddling form. It's been rated around the fourth.
T/Plt: £8.40 to a £1 stake. Pool: £76,694.46 - 6663.31 winning units T/Qpdt: £5.70 to a £1 stake. Pool: £9,560.60 - 1238.22 winning units **Colin Roberts**

1139 KEMPTON (A.W) (R-H)
Wednesday, March 13

OFFICIAL GOING: Polytrack: standard to slow
Wind: Strong against Weather: Fine

1170 32RED FILLIES' H'CAP 6f (P)
4:40 (4:40) (Class 5) (0-70,68) 3-Y-O £3,752 (£1,116; £557; £400; £400; £400) Stalls Low

Form RPR

-011 **1** **Camachess (IRE)**[1] 1167 3-8-13 **63** 6ex............................ PhilDennis(3) 1 69+
(Philip McBride) *wl away and a travelling wl bhd ldrs: cruised up wl over 1f out: sn to ld ent fnl f: sn in control: pushed out: easily* **4/6[1]**

0-03 **2** 1 ½ **Maisie Moo**[15] 913 3-9-0 **61**............................ HollieDoyle 12 60
(Shaun Keightley) *dropped into last fr wd draw: shkn up 2f out w a bit to do and wnt to inner: clsr ent fnl f where pushed along: tk 2nd 150yds out: kpt on: nvr nrr* **20/1**

-040 **3** 1 ½ **Zaula**[13] 943 3-8-13 **65**............................(b) ThomasGreatrex(5) 6 59
(Archie Watson) *racd in mid-div: rdn 2f out: kpt to ins fnl f to take 3rd nr fin* **20/1**

55-0 **4** ½ **Maid Millie**[70] 27 3-9-3 **64**............................ LukeMorris 2 56
(Robert Cowell) *in rr-div and niggled along at 1/2-way: rdn over 2f out on outer: styd on ent fnl f (vet said filly lost right hind shoe)* **10/1[3]**

4-14 **5** ½ **Halle's Harbour**[21] 813 3-8-10 **57**............................(v) JFEgan 9 48
(Paul George) *led: rdn 2f out: hdd ent fnl f: lost 2nd 150yds out: wknd qckly after (vet said filly lost right fore shoe)* **14/1**

-002 **6** hd **Grandee Daisy**[14] 918 3-8-1 **55** ow1............................(v) GeorgiaDobie(7) 3 45
(Jo Hughes, France) *half-rrd s: in rr-div: pushed along at 1/2-way: rdn wl over 2f out: no imp tl kpt on fnl f* **5/1[2]**

05-5 **7** ½ **Sepahi**[27] 720 3-9-2 **63**............................ DavidProbert 8 52
(Henry Spiller) *bhd ldr: rdn over 2f out: wknd over 1f out* **12/1**

5333 **8** 3 ¼ **Valley Belle (IRE)**[14] 918 3-8-10 **57**............................(v) JosephineGordon 10 35
(Phil McEntee) *w ldr: rdn 2f out: no ex and wknd sn after* **16/1**

6-45 **9** 1 ¾ **Starchant**[19] 854 3-9-6 **67**............................(h[1]) KieranO'Neill 4 40
(John Bridger) *in rr-div and t.k.h: effrt 2f out: sn wknd* **33/1**

1m 13.33s (0.23) **Going Correction** -0.025s/f (Stan) **9** Ran SP% **118.5**
Speed ratings (Par 95): **97,95,93,92,91 91,90,86,84**
CSF £20.87 CT £165.32 TOTE £1.50: £1.20, £3.70, £5.70; EX 18.40 Trifecta £229.50.
Owner The Narc Partnership **Bred** Yeomanstown Stud **Trained** Newmarket, Suffolk

FOCUS
Standard to slow Polytrack once more. Modest fillies' form.

1171 32RED CASINO NOVICE AUCTION STKS 7f (P)
5:10 (5:19) (Class 5) 3-Y-O £3,881 (£1,155; £577; £288) Stalls Low

Form RPR

1 **Munhamek** 3-9-0 0............................ SeanLevey 13 74
(Ivan Furtado) *mid-div: rdn 2f out: prog on outer over 1f out: kpt on wl to ld ins fnl f* **14/1**

3-3 **2** ¾ **Scorched Breath**[42] 477 3-8-13 0............................(t[1]) StevieDonohoe 4 70
(Charlie Fellowes) *bhd ldr: rdn 2f out on inner: ev ch over 1f out tl ins fnl f: stuck on to take 2nd 110yds out* **11/4[2]**

546- **3** ½ **Canford Dancer**[146] 8336 3-8-11 71............................ ShaneKelly 6 67
(Richard Hughes) *bhd ldr: rdn 2f out: led over 1f out: kpt on tl hdd ins fnl f and wknd nr fin* **4/1[3]**

33 **4** 1 ¼ **Tulloona**[21] 796 3-9-1 0............................ LukeMorris 12 68
(Tom Clover) *racd in mid-div: effrt 2f out: rn a bit green over 1f out: stuck on fnl f* **25/1**

5 ¾ **Sweet Celebration (IRE)** 3-8-5 0............................ GabrieleMalune(3) 2 59+
(Marco Botti) *hld up in rr: shkn up over 2f out w plenty to do: rdn wl over 1f out: kpt on wl on inner fnl f* **33/1**

54- **6** shd **The Dancing Poet**[140] 8543 3-9-0 0............................ EdwardGreatrex 8 64
(Ed Vaughan) *in rr-div: rdn 2f out: kpt on over 1f out* **12/1**

7 hd **May Sonic** 3-9-2 0............................ RichardKingscote 1 66+
(Charles Hills) *in rr-div: shkn up 2f out w plenty to do: travelled wl but nt qcknd and kpt on one pce (jockey said gelding was slowly away)* **7/4[1]**

8 ½ **Just Benjamin** 3-9-1 0............................ LiamJones 5 63
(William Haggas) *mid-div: rdn 2f out: kpt on* **14/1**

-662 **9** 2 **Stay Forever (FR)**[14] 930 3-8-10 67............................ DavidProbert 3 53
(Andrew Balding) *led: rdn 2f out: hdd over 1f out and wknd* **8/1**

0-3 **10** 1 ½ **Zorro's Girl**[11] 990 3-8-11 0............................ HollieDoyle 11 50
(Archie Watson) *cl up and t.k.h: effrt 2f out: sn wknd (jockey said filly ran green)* **40/1**

05 **11** ¾ **April Wine**[20] 841 3-8-10 0............................ RobHornby 14 47
(Clive Cox) *in rr-div: rdn 2f out: sn hld* **80/1**

12 2 ¼ **I'm Brian** 3-8-12 0............................ PaddyMathers 10 43
(Julia Feilden) *rr-div: effrt over 2f out: sn hld* **100/1**

1m 26.85s (0.85) **Going Correction** -0.025s/f (Stan) **12** Ran SP% **126.6**
Speed ratings (Par 98): **94,93,92,91,90 90,89,89,87,85 84,81**
CSF £55.03 TOTE £28.90: £4.20, £1.50, £1.80; EX 101.60 Trifecta £380.60.
Owner J C Fretwell **Bred** Shadwell Estate Company Limited **Trained** Wiseton, Nottinghamshire
■ Guiding Spirit was withdrawn, price at time of withdrawal 33/1. Rule 4 does not apply.

FOCUS
This ordinary event was delayed by several minutes, partly because Guiding Spirit (withdrawn) got loose down at the start.

1172 32RED H'CAP 1m 7f 218y(P)
5:45 (5:47) (Class 3) (0-95,91) 4-Y-O+ £9,337 (£2,796; £1,398; £699; £349; £175) Stalls Low

Form RPR

-132 **1** **Busy Street**[21] 799 7-9-5 **91**............................ MarkCrehan(7) 1 99
(Michael Appleby) *a cl up: pushed along over 2f out: rdn over 1f out: styd on wl ins fnl f to get up fnl strides* **11/2[3]**

/112 **2** *hd* **Ulster (IRE)**[15] 916 4-9-9 **91**........................ EdwardGreatrex 4 98
(Archie Watson) *led: pushed along 2f out: rdn over 1f out: kpt on wl tl one pce fnl 100yds and hdd last strides* **8/11**[1]

-000 **3** *1 3/4* **Addicted To You (IRE)**[28] 704 5-9-6 **85**..................(v) FrannyNorton 7 90
(Mark Johnston) *pushed along leaving stalls: settled in rr-div: impr to press ldr bef 1/2-way: niggled along and dropped off ldrs over 3f out: kpt on again fr over 1f out: styng on fnl f* **14/1**

2162 **4** *1 3/4* **Technological**[11] 980 4-9-7 **89**........................ DavidProbert 6 92
(George Margarson) *t.k.h: in rr-div: cl up and rdn 2f out: stuck on* **5/1**[2]

0553 **5** *1 3/4* **Alabaster**[11] 991 5-8-13 **78**........................(p) LukeMorris 3 79
(Sir Mark Prescott Bt) *mid-div: t.k.h wl over 3f out: smooth prog 3f out: nudged along 2f out: rdn over 1f out: plugged on (jockey said gelding hung right-handed)* **11/1**

65-0 **6** *10* **Baydar**[11] 980 6-9-6 **85**........................ StevieDonohoe 5 74
(Ian Williams) *in rr: rdn along wl over 3f out: sme prog over 2f out: no ex over 1f out* **33/1**

502- **7** *21* **Perfect Summer (IRE)**[55] 8807 9-8-7 **72**..................(p) KieranO'Neill 2 36
(Ian Williams) *in rr: pushed along wl over 3f out: no ex in st* **33/1**

2141 **8** *1 1/2* **Navajo Star (IRE)**[11] 991 5-8-5 **77**..................(v) WilliamCarver[(7)] 8 39
(Robyn Brisland) *cl up: rdn 3f out: no imp and wknd (jockey said mare stopped quickly)* **11/1**

3m 27.22s (-2.88) **Going Correction** -0.025s/f (Stan)
WFA 4 from 5yo+ 3lb 8 Ran SP% **119.2**
Speed ratings (Par 107): **106,105,105,104,103 98,87,87**
CSF £10.33 CT £53.98 TOTE £7.10: £1.70, £1.10, £2.50; EX 12.80 Trifecta £97.40.
Owner Khdrp & Martyn Elvin **Bred** Juddmonte Farms Ltd **Trained** Oakham, Rutland

FOCUS
A decent staying handicap.

1173 100% PROFIT BOOST AT 32REDSPORT.COM H'CAP (DIV I) 1m (P)
6:15 (6:17) (Class 6) (0-65,67) 3-Y-O
£3,105 (£924; £461; £400; £400; £400) **Stalls** Low

Form RPR

-522 **1** **Greyzee (IRE)**[20] 829 3-8-10 **53**........................ RobHornby 1 62+
(Rod Millman) *mde all: rdn 2f out: strly pressed over 1f: fnd plenty 1f out and in control fnl f* **11/4**[2]

004- **2** *2 1/4* **Image Of The Moon**[149] 8256 3-9-7 **64**........................ AdamKirby 10 68
(Shaun Keightley) *hld up in mid-div: shkn up over 2f out: rdn wl over 1f out on outer and edgd rt: chal and upsides ent fnl f: no ex 1f out: kpt on* **16/1**

00-0 **3** *2* **Hooflepuff (IRE)**[70] 27 3-8-13 **56**........................ LukeMorris 2 55
(Robert Cowell) *bhd ldr and t.k.h: rdn 2f out: briefly threatened over 1f out: stuck on one pce* **11/1**

31-4 **4** *3/4* **Torolight**[20] 825 3-9-10 **67**........................ ShaneKelly 7 66
(Richard Hughes) *bhd ldr and t.k.h: effrt 2f out: squeezed up bhd ldr over 1f out: kpt on again fnl f* **5/2**[1]

5-42 **5** *1/2* **Picture Poet (IRE)**[35] 614 3-9-5 **62**........................ DavidProbert 6 58
(Henry Spiller) *in rr: gng wl w plenty to do whn swtchd to outer over 2f out: rdn 2f out: pushed out fnl f* **8/1**

00-0 **6** *1/2* **Peruvian Summer (IRE)**[53] 316 3-9-3 **60**........................ JasonHart 8 55
(Kevin Frost) *slowly away: in rr: rdn 2f out on inner: kpt on fr over 1f out* **20/1**

0533 **7** *1 1/4* **Twpsyn (IRE)**[20] 841 3-9-10 **67**........................ EoinWalsh 3 59
(David Evans) *mid-div: rdn 2f out: kpt on fr over 1f out* **20/1**

0-04 **8** *1 1/4* **Moonlit Sea**[35] 615 3-9-9 **66**........................ OisinMurphy 11 55
(James Tate) *kpt wd fr wd draw and sn pressing ldr: shkn up wl over 1f out bhd ldr: gng okay whn short of room and squeezed up over 1f out: sn fdd* **13/2**[3]

-040 **9** *1 1/2* **Midnite Rendezvous**[40] 537 3-8-2 **45**........................ PaddyMathers 4 31
(Derek Shaw) *missed break and niggled along early in rr: effrt over 2f out: no imp* **100/1**

0-21 **10** *8* **Heatherdown (IRE)**[51] 341 3-8-9 **57**........................ CameronNoble[(5)] 5 25
(Ian Williams) *in rr-div: effrt over 2f out: nt qckn and plugged on* **9/1**

000- **11** *5* **Sussex Solo**[176] 7381 3-9-4 **61**..................(e[1]) KieranO'Neill 9 17
(Luke Dace) *pushed along early and a in rr* **50/1**

1m 39.19s (-0.61) **Going Correction** -0.025s/f (Stan) 11 Ran SP% **116.4**
Speed ratings (Par 96): **102,99,97,97,96 96,94,93,92,84 79**
CSF £43.37 CT £433.26 TOTE £3.50: £1.20, £3.50, £3.60; EX 59.10 Trifecta £373.00.
Owner David Little The Links Partnership **Bred** Barouche Stud Ireland Ltd **Trained** Kentisbeare, Devon

FOCUS
A very modest handicap, but it was the quicker division by 1.36sec.

1174 100% PROFIT BOOST AT 32REDSPORT.COM H'CAP (DIV II) 1m (P)
6:45 (6:47) (Class 6) (0-65,67) 3-Y-O
£3,105 (£924; £461; £400; £400; £400) **Stalls** Low

Form RPR

4-32 **1** **Lee Roy**[28] 698 3-9-10 **66**........................ KierenFox 5 71+
(Michael Attwater) *w ldr: rdn 2f out to ld: kpt on and in control 1f out: wknd fnl 150yds: hld on* **11/4**[1]

23-1 **2** *nk* **Dancing Jo**[61] 174 3-9-11 **67**........................ CharlesBishop 6 71
(Mick Channon) *in rr-div on outer: rdn 2f out and sltly outpcd on outer over 1f out: styd on wl fnl f to take 2nd fin: jst failed* **9/2**[3]

025- **3** *nk* **Mayfair Spirit (IRE)**[159] 7957 3-9-10 **66**..................(t) StevieDonohoe 8 69
(Charlie Fellowes) *racd in mid-div: rdn 2f out: no immediate imp over 1f out: stuck on wl fnl f to take 3rd nr fin* **7/2**[2]

-552 **4** *shd* **Shug**[19] 855 3-9-4 **60**........................ LiamKeniry 4 63
(Ed Walker) *bhd ldrs and keen at times: shkn up over 2f out: effrt and edgd rt over 1f out: tk 2nd 1f out: kpt on tl lost two plcd nr fin* **7/1**

60-3 **5** *3* **Bug Boy (IRE)**[61] 174 3-9-7 **63**........................(p) JFEgan 1 59
(Paul George) *bhd ldr: rdn 2f out: carried a bit rt wl over 1f out: swtchd out sn after: kpt on again fnl f* **6/1**

056 **6** *1 1/4* **Percy Alexander**[15] 913 3-9-1 **57**..................(v[1]) OisinMurphy 7 50
(James Tate) *s.s and hld up in rr: effrt over 2f out: kpt on one pce fr over 1f out* **7/1**

5044 **7** *3/4* **Bonneville (IRE)**[14] 931 3-8-3 **52**..................(p) OliverSearle[(7)] 2 44
(Rod Millman) *led: effrt wl over 2f out: hdd 2f out: fdd sn after* **20/1**

040- **8** *nk* **Another Approach (FR)**[119] 9050 3-9-6 **62**........................ NicolaCurrie 3 53
(George Baker) *s.s: sn in rr-div: plld hrd: effrt on inner 2f out: sme prog tl hmpd over 1f out: eased* **16/1**

0 **9** *2 1/2* **Chutzpah (IRE)**[46] 442 3-9-2 **58**........................ DavidProbert 11 43
(Mark Hoad) *hld up in rr: effrt wl over 2f out: no imp* **66/1**

60-0 **10** *3/4* **Breezing**[42] 476 3-8-11 **53**..................(b[1]) RobHornby 9 36
(Sylvester Kirk) *racd wd bhd ldrs: niggled along wl over 3f out: rdn wl over 2f out: wknd* **100/1**

1m 40.57s (0.77) **Going Correction** -0.025s/f (Stan) 10 Ran SP% **119.5**
Speed ratings (Par 96): **95,94,94,94,91 90,89,89,86,85**
CSF £15.61 CT £45.03 TOTE £3.40: £1.30, £1.80, £1.20; EX 14.40 Trifecta £45.50.
Owner Canisbay Bloodstock **Bred** Canisbay Bloodstock **Trained** Epsom, Surrey

FOCUS
This wasn't strongly run, with the time 1.36sec slower than the first division. It's been rated as straightforward, ordinary form.

1175 32RED ON THE APP STORE H'CAP (DIV I) 1m (P)
7:15 (7:16) (Class 6) (0-65,67) 4-Y-O+
£3,105 (£924; £461; £400; £400; £400) **Stalls** Low

Form RPR

211 **1** **Jai Hanuman (IRE)**[7] 1032 5-9-3 **61** 6ex..................(t) FrannyNorton 7 70+
(Michael Wigham) *mid-div: shkn up wl over 1f out and sltly outpcd: niggled along and tk clsr order 1f out: rdn to chal sn after and led 110yds out: sn in control: snug* **8/13**[1]

46-6 **2** *1* **Chikoko Trail**[54] 294 4-9-4 **62**..................(t[1]) HectorCrouch 1 66
(Gary Moore) *led: rdn 2f out: kpt on wl tl hdd 110yds out: stuck on* **12/1**

210- **3** *1 1/2* **Boxatricks (IRE)**[98] 9401 4-8-10 **54**........................ ShelleyBirkett 9 54
(Julia Feilden) *w ldr: rdn 2f out: kpt on wl tl one pce fnl f* **16/1**

1323 **4** *hd* **Bond Angel**[20] 830 4-9-2 **65**........................ KatherineBegley[(5)] 2 65
(David Evans) *bhd ldrs: rdn 2f out: chal over 1f out: dropped off ldng pair ins fnl f* **8/1**[3]

1114 **5** *2 1/4* **Naralsaif (IRE)**[6] 1060 5-8-12 **56**..................(v) PaddyMathers 8 51
(Derek Shaw) *in rr-div: rdn over 2f out and outpcd: styd on again ent fnl f* **11/2**[2]

/000 **6** *hd* **Sir George Somers (USA)**[16] 911 6-9-2 **60**..................(p) LiamKeniry 3 54
(Nigel Twiston-Davies) *in rr: effrt 2f out: nt qckn* **33/1**

-522 **7** *1* **Accomplice**[20] 828 5-9-5 **63**........................ FergusSweeney 4 55
(Michael Blanshard) *racd in mid-div: effrt 2f out: stuck on tl no ex 1f out: wknd qckly* **14/1**

1m 41.66s (1.86) **Going Correction** -0.025s/f (Stan) 7 Ran SP% **111.6**
Speed ratings (Par 101): **89,88,86,86,84 83,82**
CSF £8.88 CT £59.13 TOTE £1.30: £1.10, £6.00; EX 9.60 Trifecta £64.10.
Owner Ms I D Heerowa **Bred** Lynn Lodge Stud **Trained** Newmarket, Suffolk

FOCUS
This wasn't run at much of a gallop. The second and third set a straightforward level.

1176 32RED ON THE APP STORE H'CAP (DIV II) 1m (P)
7:45 (7:46) (Class 6) (0-65,66) 4-Y-O+
£3,105 (£924; £461; £400; £400; £400) **Stalls** Low

Form RPR

60-5 **1** **Lothario**[13] 942 5-9-7 **64**........................ MartinDwyer 3 72
(Dean Ivory) *racd in mid-div and t.k.h at times: effrt 2f out and swtchd to inner: chal ldr over 1f out: led jst ins fnl f: edgd lft fnl 100yds: comf* **3/1**[1]

0-52 **2** *1 3/4* **Baashiq (IRE)**[13] 942 5-9-9 **66**..................(p) LukeMorris 2 70
(Peter Hiatt) *bhd ldr: shkn up over 2f out and sn upsides: rdn 2f out and disp ld over 1f out: tk 2nd 110yds out: no ch w wnr* **7/2**[3]

2560 **3** *1/2* **False Id**[16] 910 6-8-13 **56**..................(b) DavidProbert 8 59
(David Loughnane) *hld up in rr: rdn 2f out: styd on wl fr over 1f out to take 3rd nr fin* **10/1**

5-46 **4** *nk* **My Town Chicago (USA)**[58] 239 4-9-5 **62**........................ JasonHart 4 64
(Kevin Frost) *led: rdn 2f out: kpt on being strly pressed either side fr over 1f out: hdd jst ins fnl f: lost 2nd 110yds out and 3rd sn after* **12/1**

44-0 **5** *3/4* **Silverturnstogold**[64] 125 4-9-3 **60**........................ TomMarquand 6 60
(Tony Carroll) *hld up in rr-div: clsr and rdn 2f out: plugged on fr over 1f out* **7/1**

-042 **6** *hd* **Stand N Deliver**[14] 925 5-9-2 **59**..................(v) AdamKirby 7 59
(Clive Cox) *bhd ldrs: effrt on outer over 2f out: kpt on tl one pce over 1f out* **10/3**[2]

0401 **7** *5* **Cold Fire (IRE)**[13] 940 6-9-0 **57**..................(v) KieranO'Neill 9 45
(Robyn Brisland) *racd in mid-div: rdn 2f out: no imp 2f out* **8/1**

000/ **8** *1 3/4* **Socks And Shares (IRE)**[665] 2727 6-8-9 **52**........................ PaddyMathers 1 36
(Derek Shaw) *in rr and t.k.h: rdn over 2f out: plugged on* **50/1**

500- **9** *7* **Imminent Approach**[146] 8349 4-9-5 **62**........................ EoinWalsh 5 30
(Tony Newcombe) *w ldr: rdn 3f out: no ex 2f out and wknd* **66/1**

1m 38.78s (-1.02) **Going Correction** -0.025s/f (Stan) 9 Ran SP% **114.1**
Speed ratings (Par 101): **104,102,101,101,100 100,95,93,86**
CSF £13.48 CT £90.98 TOTE £3.50: £1.40, £1.50, £2.90; EX 12.20 Trifecta £94.80.
Owner Michael & Heather Yarrow **Bred** J Troy, Mrs R Philipps & Highbury Stud **Trained** Radlett, Herts

FOCUS
Ordinary form, and the quicker division by 2.88sec. The second, third and fourth confirm a straightforward level in behind the winner.

1177 BET AT RACINGTV.COM H'CAP 7f (P)
8:15 (8:15) (Class 6) (0-65,63) 4-Y-O+
£3,105 (£924; £461; £400; £400; £400) **Stalls** Low

Form RPR

0511 **1** **Elusif (IRE)**[14] 924 4-9-1 **57**..................(v) HollieDoyle 4 64+
(Shaun Keightley) *w ldr: rdn 2f out: led over 1f out: stuck on wl fnl f: hld on post* **9/4**[1]

4631 **2** *nk* **Viola Park**[14] 925 5-9-2 **58**..................(p) DavidProbert 10 64
(Ronald Harris) *bhd ldrs: shkn up 2f out: rdn over 1f out: styd on wl ins fnl f between horses: tk 2nd last strides: jst failed* **11/1**

0-05 **3** *hd* **Flirtare (IRE)**[46] 439 4-9-3 **59**........................ OisinMurphy 8 64
(Amy Murphy) *racd in mid-div: shkn up over 2f out and swtchd to outer: rdn 2f out: styd on wl and tk 2nd ins fnl f: kpt on but lost 3rd last strides* **16/1**

/50- **4** *2 1/4* **Waqt (IRE)**[156] 8046 5-9-4 **60**........................ RossaRyan 11 60
(Alexandra Dunn) *bhd ldr: rdn 2f out: styd on one pce fnl f* **66/1**

-432 **5** *1 1/4* **Shamlan (IRE)**[43] 467 7-9-2 **58**..................(p) JasonHart 5 54
(Kevin Frost) *hld up in rr-div: effrt over 2f out: outpcd wl over 1f out: styd on wl fnl f* **11/1**

00-5 **6** *1 1/4* **Merdon Castle (IRE)**[14] 924 7-8-1 **48** ow3...... FayeMcManoman[(5)] 12 43
(Frank Bishop) *in rr: rdn 2f out on inner: keeping on steadily fr over 1f out: n.m.r and checked ins fnl f: plugged on fnl 100yds* **25/1**

3000 **7** *shd* **Independence Day (IRE)**[11] 982 6-9-6 **62**........................ JoeyHaynes 3 55
(Paul Howling) *in rr-div: shkn up 2f out: shuffled along fr over 1f out: nvr involved* **16/1**

050- **8** ½ **Captain Dion**[126] 8937 6-9-4 **63**................(p) GabrieleMalune(3) 2 55
(Ivan Furtado) *led: effrt 2f out: hdd wl over 1f out: kpt on and stl 2nd tl wknd qckly fr 1f out* **4/1**[2]

120- **9** ½ **Confrerie (IRE)**[99] 9387 4-9-2 **58**................ NicolaCurrie 7 48
(George Baker) *mid-div: rdn over 2f out and wnt to inner: briefly threatened for placings over 1f out: wknd fnl f* **10/1**

00-0 **10** nse **Showdance Kid**[20] 840 5-9-6 **62**................ CliffordLee 14 52+
(Kevin Frost) *hld up in rr-div: rdn over 2f out w plenty to do: styd on over 1f out: shuffled along and sme prog fnl f* **100/1**

4-54 **11** 1¼ **Qallaab (IRE)**[14] 919 4-9-3 **59**................(bt) AdamKirby 6 46
(Michael Appleby) *missed break and rdn leaving stalls: settled in rr: shuffled along w plenty to do fr 2f out: nvr involved (jockey said gelding was slowly away)* **14/1**

6215 **12** ¾ **Mochalov**[11] 982 4-8-13 **62**................ SeanKirrane(7) 1 47
(Jane Chapple-Hyam) *bhd ldr: shkn up over 2f out gng okay: styd on tl wknd v qckly fr 1f out* **7/1**[3]

-050 **13** 1¾ **Reignite**[14] 924 4-9-1 **57**................(h) EoinWalsh 13 37
(Emma Owen) *a in rr: sme effrt 2f out: no imp after* **33/1**

6-34 **14** 3¾ **The King's Steed**[20] 828 6-9-5 **61**................(bt) LukeMorris 9 32
(Shaun Lycett) *mid-div out wd: pushed along over 2f out: no ex and steadily wknd fr over 1f out (jockey said gelding hung left-handed)* **33/1**

1m 25.81s (-0.19) **Going Correction** -0.025s/f (Stan) **14** Ran SP% **119.7**
Speed ratings (Par 101): **100,99,99,96,95 94,93,93,92,92 91,90,88,84**
CSF £27.17 CT £338.96 TOTE £3.00: £1.50, £3.40, £4.20; EX 30.90 Trifecta £334.40.
Owner Simon Lockyer & Tim Clarke **Bred** Miss Y Jacques **Trained** Newmarket, Suffolk

FOCUS
This moderate handicap was run at a decent gallop. The first two won separate divisions of a C&D handicap on February 27th. The third has been rated near her best.
T/Plt: £21.00 to a £1 stake. Pool: £55,845.32 - 1,936.80 winning units T/Qpdt: £8.10 to a £1 stake. Pool: £11,066.66 - 1,003.61 winning units **Cathal Gahan**

1074 LINGFIELD (L-H)
Wednesday, March 13

OFFICIAL GOING: Polytrack: standard
Wind: Strong, across Weather: Light cloud, breezy

1178 LADBROKES HOME OF THE ODDS BOOST H'CAP 7f 1y(P)
1:55 (1:55) (Class 5) (0-75,75) 3-Y-O
£3,752 (£1,116; £557; £300; £300; £300) Stalls Low

Form RPR
2231 **1** **Shanghai Grace**[11] 978 3-9-0 **75**................ CierenFallon(7) 7 80+
(Charles Hills) *t.k.h: hld up in tch: hdwy on outer over 2f out: chsd ldrs and v wd bnd wl over 1f out: clsd u.p to chse ldr and hung lft ins fnl f: styd on wl to ld last strides* **7/4**[1]

46-5 **2** hd **Facethepuckout (IRE)**[53] 320 3-9-7 **75**................(p) AdamKirby 3 78
(John Ryan) *rousted along leaving stalls: sn prom: rdn to press ldr 2f out: drvn to ld ent fnl f: kpt on u.p: hdd last strides* **5/1**

2-56 **3** 2¼ **Fox Kasper (IRE)**[28] 698 3-9-5 **73**................(p¹) OisinMurphy 2 70
(Richard Hannon) *t.k.h: chsd ldr early: wl in tch in midfield after: effrt towards inner over 1f out: kpt on same pce ins fnl f* **11/4**[2]

2-05 **4** shd **Fiction Writer (USA)**[54] 289 3-9-5 **73**................ PJMcDonald 5 70
(Mark Johnston) *midfield on outer: hdwy to ld over 4f out: rdn ent fnl 2f: hdd ent fnl f: no ex and wknd fnl 100yds* **3/1**[3]

4-40 **5** 8 **Paddy's Pursuit (IRE)**[20] 841 3-9-2 **70**................ LiamJones 4 46
(Mark Loughnane) *sn led: hdd over 4f out: struggling u.p over 1f out: wknd fnl f* **33/1**

4421 **6** 2 **Axel Jacklin**[47] 401 3-9-1 **69**................ JoeyHaynes 1 39
(Paul Howling) *restless in stalls: broke wl: dropped to rr over 5f out: rdn over 4f out: wknd over 1f out* **12/1**

1m 23.9s (-0.90) **Going Correction** -0.175s/f (Stan) **6** Ran SP% **115.3**
Speed ratings (Par 98): **98,97,95,95,85 83**
CSF £11.54 TOTE £2.50: £2.60, £3.00; EX 10.50 Trifecta £22.90.
Owner Kangyu International Racing (HK) Limited **Bred** Wellsummers Stud **Trained** Lambourn, Berks

FOCUS
This looked reasonably competitive on paper, with just 6lb separating the six runners, but one or two of these proved a bit disappointing. The winner is the one on the upward curve right now but he very nearly blew it in the straight.

1179 BETWAY BEST FOR CHELTENHAM FESTIVAL BETTING H'CAP 6f 1y(P)
2:35 (2:35) (Class 6) (0-60,59) 4-Y-O+
£3,105 (£924; £461; £300; £300; £300) Stalls Low

Form RPR
5642 **1** **Tavener**[5] 1075 7-9-5 **58**................(p) AndreaAtzeni 6 66
(David C Griffiths) *sn led: rdn over 1f out: styd on wl ins fnl f: rdn out* **5/2**[1]

33-1 **2** ¾ **Spirit Of Zebedee (IRE)**[19] 857 6-9-4 **57**................(v) JasonHart 5 63
(John Quinn) *chsd ldrs: effrt 2f out: kpt on u.p to chse wnr ins fnl f: styd on but a hld towards fin* **7/1**[3]

-330 **3** ½ **Daring Guest (IRE)**[14] 920 5-9-2 **55**................(t¹) LukeMorris 3 59
(Tom Clover) *wl in tch in midfield: effrt ent fnl 2f: chsd ldrs ins fnl f: kpt on same pce fnl 100yds* **10/1**

4306 **4** nk **Knockout Blow**[14] 920 4-9-4 **57**................(v¹) CharlieBennett 12 60
(Jim Boyle) *wd early: midfield tl hdwy to press wnr 4f out: unable to match pce of wnr over 1f out: lost 2nd and kpt on same pce ins fnl f* **40/1**

54U- **5** shd **Falcao (IRE)**[265] 4040 7-9-4 **57**................(w) AdamKirby 8 60+
(John Butler) *awkward leaving stalls: t.k.h: hld up in midfield: effrt in 6th 2f out: hdwy u.p ins fnl f: nvr getting to ldrs* **3/1**[2]

-120 **6** 2 **Holdenhurst**[19] 857 4-9-0 **58**................ SeamusCronin(5) 4 55
(Bill Turner) *led early: sn hdd: chsd ldr tl 4f out: effrt 2f out: unable qck over 1f out: wknd ins fnl f* **12/1**

-003 **7** 1¾ **Little Miss Daisy**[14] 920 5-9-4 **57**................ MartinDwyer 11 49
(William Muir) *hld up in last trio: effrt over 1f out: kpt on ins fnl f: nvr trbld ldrs* **25/1**

-455 **8** ½ **Billyoakes (IRE)**[37] 596 7-9-5 **58**................(v¹) RichardKingscote 7 48
(Charlie Wallis) *dwlt: midfield: effrt 2f out: no imp over 1f out: wl hld and kpt on same pce ins fnl f (jockey said gelding anticipated the start and was slowly away)* **10/1**

5-44 **9** shd **Royal Mezyan (IRE)**[35] 626 8-9-6 **59**................ BenCurtis 10 49
(Henry Spiller) *hld up in last trio: effrt over 1f out: kpt on ins fnl f: nvr trbld ldrs* **14/1**

01-0 **10** ½ **Cuban Spirit**[42] 483 4-9-5 **58**................ DavidProbert 9 47
(Henry Candy) *t.k.h: effrt over 1f out: no imp and wknd ins fnl f* **8/1**

-020 **11** nk **Holy Tiber (IRE)**[5] 1075 4-9-6 **59**................ JoeyHaynes 1 47
(Paul Howling) *hld up in tch in midfield: effrt on inner over 1f out: no imp and wknd ins fnl f* **12/1**

0000 **12** ½ **Letmestopyouthere (IRE)**[14] 926 5-9-4 **57**................ HollieDoyle 2 43
(Archie Watson) *sn in rr and nvr travelling wl: rdn 3f out: swtchd rt and no hdwy over 1f out (jockey said gelding was never travelling)* **7/1**[3]

1m 10.56s (-1.34) **Going Correction** -0.175s/f (Stan) **12** Ran SP% **136.2**
Speed ratings (Par 101): **101,100,99,98,98 96,93,93,93,92 91,91**
CSF £24.45 CT £169.87 TOTE £3.60: £1.90, £2.50, £4.30; EX 19.20 Trifecta £145.80.
Owner Baker, Hensby, Longden, Baker **Bred** Car Colston Hall Stud **Trained** Bawtry, S Yorks

FOCUS
A big field so, as is nearly always the case on the 6f course around here, it paid to be have a good early position. The winner was given a positive ride, had all of his rivals in trouble by the home turn and had enough in the tank to finish the job. Straightforward form in behind the winner.

1180 BETWAY NOVICE STKS 6f 1y(P)
3:15 (3:15) (Class 5) 3-Y-O+
£3,752 (£1,116; £557) Stalls Low

Form RPR
322- **1** **Beat Le Bon (FR)**[137] 8630 3-8-9 **96**................ TomMarquand 1 87+
(Richard Hannon) *mde all: shkn up ent fnl 2f: lft wl clr bnd wl over 1f out: easily* **1/10**[1]

2 9 **Hey Ho Let's Go** 3-8-9 0................ DavidProbert 3 66+
(Clive Cox) *rn green thrght: chsd wnr: pushed along and ev ch over 2f out tl hung rt and v wd bnd wl over 1f out: no ch after (jockey said colt ran green and hung right-handed round the bend)* **6/1**[2]

06 **3** 8 **Fortunate Move**[22] 795 3-8-4 0................ PaddyMathers 2 28
(Richard Fahey) *a last: outpcd over 2f out: no ch after* **20/1**[3]

1m 11.07s (-0.83) **Going Correction** -0.175s/f (Stan) **3** Ran SP% **110.0**
Speed ratings (Par 103): **98,86,75**
CSF £1.35 TOTE £1.10; EX 1.30 Trifecta £1.10.
Owner Sullivan B'Stock/ Merriebelle Irish Farm **Bred** Gestut Zur Kuste Ag **Trained** East Everleigh, Wilts

FOCUS
You don't get many 96-rated horses running in novice races at this time of the year and Beat Le Bon only needed to show he was still in full working order to open his account, but there was also plenty to take from the effort of the runner-up.

1181 LIKE SUN RACING ON FACEBOOK H'CAP 7f 1y(P)
3:55 (3:55) (Class 2) (0-105,107) 4-Y£01,971 (£3,583; £1,791; £896; £446) Stalls Low

Form RPR
00-3 **1** **Cardsharp**[4] 1103 4-9-9 **107**................ JoeFanning 2 115
(Mark Johnston) *mounted in chute: chsd ldr tl led 5f out: hdd 3f out: shkn up ent fnl 2f: swtchd rt and clsd ent fnl f: led and reminders 100yds out: styd on wl* **5/2**[1]

1-02 **2** ¾ **Gallipoli (IRE)**[21] 805 6-8-7 **91**................(b) PaulHanagan 3 97
(Richard Fahey) *taken down early: broke wl: sn restrained and trckd ldrs: effrt over 1f out: clsd u.p to chse wnr ins fnl f: kpt on but a hld* **4/1**[3]

-126 **3** 2 **Apex King (IRE)**[4] 1103 5-7-9 **86**................ LauraCoughlan(7) 1 87
(David Loughnane) *awkward leaving stalls: t.k.h and clsd to chse ldrs over 5f out: switching out rt ent fnl f: kpt on same pce ins fnl f* **7/2**[2]

5241 **4** nse **Call Out Loud**[21] 807 7-8-2 **86** oh2................(vt) DavidEgan 4 86
(Michael Appleby) *sn led: hdd 5f out: chsd wnr tl led again 3f out: pushed along and 2 l clr ent fnl 2f: drvn and hdd 100yds out: no ex and wknd towards fin* **10/1**

4-10 **5** 3¼ **Salateen**[19] 869 7-9-5 **103**................(t) DavidNolan 5 95
(David O'Meara) *midfield tl dropped to last pair 5f out: effrt and stl plenty to do in 6th 2f out: no imp and nvr involved* **7/1**

0-03 **6** 3 **Main Street**[18] 880 4-8-12 **96**................(p¹) OisinMurphy 6 80
(David Elsworth) *s.i.s and sn swtchd lft: t.k.h: hld up in midfield: effrt ent fnl 2f: rdn and no hdwy over 1f out: wl hld and one pce ins fnl f* **4/1**[3]

2-30 **7** 1½ **Take The Helm**[61] 176 6-8-11 **95**................ MartinDwyer 7 75
(Brian Meehan) *swtchd lft after s: a towards rr: rdn over 2f out: no prog and nvr involved* **20/1**

1m 21.9s (-2.90) **Going Correction** -0.175s/f (Stan) **7** Ran SP% **117.1**
Speed ratings (Par 109): **109,108,105,105,102 98,96**
CSF £13.36 TOTE £2.60: £1.90, £1.80; EX 11.10 Trifecta £37.50.
Owner Sheikh Hamdan bin Mohammed Al Maktoum **Bred** Godolphin **Trained** Middleham Moor, N Yorks

FOCUS
A classy little handicap which looked a bit stop start to the eye, but they broke the track record so they can't have been hanging around for too long. The winner is proving a very tough little operator.

1182 BETWAY CASINO MEDIAN AUCTION MAIDEN STKS 1m 2f (P)
4:35 (4:35) (Class 6) 3-4-Y-O
£3,105 (£924; £461; £230) Stalls Low

Form RPR
0-3 **1** **Boutonniere (USA)**[47] 403 3-8-7 0................ OisinMurphy 3 76+
(Andrew Balding) *trckd ldrs: swtchd rt and effrt to chal over 1f out: rdn to ld jst ins fnl f: edgd lft u.p towards fin: hld on wl* **3/1**[3]

03- **2** hd **Emirates Empire (IRE)**[156] 8057 3-8-7 0................ AndreaAtzeni 2 76+
(Michael Bell) *w ldr tl led after 1f: rdn and hrd pressed over 1f out: hdd jst ins fnl f: kpt on wl: nudged lft and jst hld towards fin* **1/1**[1]

502- **3** 5 **Heart Of Soul (IRE)**[270] 3849 4-10-0 80................ BenCurtis 5 71
(Ian Williams) *chsd ldrs tl wnt 2nd over 7f out: effrt ent fnl 2f: 3rd and outpcd 1f out: wknd ins fnl f* **5/2**[2]

66 **4** 1 **Grange Walk (IRE)**[39] 562 4-9-11 0................ PaddyBradley(3) 6 69
(Pat Phelan) *hld up in midfield: nt clrest of runs on inner ent fnl 2f: effrt over 1f out: 4th and no imp fnl f* **50/1**

5 3½ **Clap Your Hands** 3-8-7 0................ CallumShepherd 7 57+
(David Simcock) *v.s.a: grad rcvrd: towards rr 1/2-way: nt clrest of runs and outpcd ent fnl 2f: pushed along over 1f out: no imp and wl hld fnl f (jockey said gelding was slowly away)* **25/1**

6 1¼ **Blue Beirut (IRE)** 3-8-7 0................ MartinDwyer 4 55
(William Muir) *dwlt and squeezed for room leaving stalls: sn off the pce in 7th and rdn along: clsd and in tch 1/2-way: last and rdn 3f out: nvr threatened ldrs* **25/1**

7 2¼ **Royal Born (IRE)** 3-8-7 0................ JoeFanning 8 50+
(Mark Johnston) *wd early and rn green: midfield: pushed along over 2f out: sn struggling: lost pl and bhd over 1f out* **10/1**

0- **8** ½ **Tattenhams**[116] 9132 3-7-11 0................ RhiainIngram(5) 1 44
(Adam West) *pushed along leaving stalls: led for 1f: chsd ldrs tl 4th and outpcd whn edgd lft ent fnl 2f: wknd fnl f* **100/1**

2m 4.49s (-2.11) **Going Correction** -0.175s/f (Stan)
WFA 3 from 4yo 21lb **8** Ran SP% **123.3**
Speed ratings (Par 101): **101,100,96,96,93 92,90,90**
CSF £6.87 TOTE £3.80: £1.10, £1.10, £1.30; EX 8.50 Trifecta £19.60.
Owner Miss A Nesser **Bred** Bhmfr Llc **Trained** Kingsclere, Hants

FOCUS
The front two pulled clear of a solid yardstick, albeit in receipt of a lot of weight, but there are reasons to think both can go on to be nice horses. The winner needed to survive a stewards enquiry. A clear step forward from the winner, and the race has been rated around the time, the second and the eighth.

1183 BETWAY BEST FOR CHELTENHAM FESTIVAL OFFERS H'CAP 1m 2f (P)
5:15 (5:15) (Class 6) (0-65,71) 4-Y-O+
£3,105 (£924; £461; £300; £300; £300) Stalls Low

Form RPR
-355 1 **Subliminal**[14] 923 4-9-0 **58**.............................. TomMarquand 8 64
(Simon Dow) *trckd ldrs: effrt ent fnl 2f: drvn to ld ent fnl f: drifted lft wl ins fnl f: all out (jockey said colt hung both ways under pressure)* **9/2**[2]

1641 2 *nk* **Arabic Culture (USA)**[8] 1024 5-9-13 **71** 6ex.................. SamJames 13 77+
(Grant Tuer) *hld up in tch in midfield: nt clr run and jostled jst over 2f out: hdwy to chse ldrs and nt clr run 1f out: gap sn opened and hdwy u.p to chal towards fin: r.o but nvr quite getting to wnr* **5/2**[1]

360- 3 ½ **Shufoog**[145] 7428 6-9-0 **65**........................... EllieMacKenzie(7) 2 69
(Mark Usher) *prom early: sn in tch in midfield: effrt to chse ldrs and bmpd ent fnl 2f: ev ch over 1f out: kpt on wl but unable qck wl ins fnl f* **16/1**

56-3 4 *hd* **Barrsbrook**[54] 295 5-9-6 **64**...........................(v) HectorCrouch 7 69
(Gary Moore) *hld up in tch in midfield: nt clr run jst over 2f out: swtchd rt: rdn and hdwy 2f out: ev ch u.p ins fnl f: unable qck towards fin* **6/1**[3]

20-4 5 ¾ **Sir Gnet (IRE)**[48] 386 5-9-5 **63**.......................(h) DanielMuscutt 12 66
(Ed Dunlop) *dropped in bhd after s: t.k.h: hld up in tch in rr: effrt 2f out: hdwy over 1f out: chsd ldrs but nvr enough room ins fnl f and unable to mount a chal* **14/1**

00-5 6 1¼ **Cherbourg (FR)**[57] 248 7-9-5 **63**.....................(p) RobertWinston 3 63
(Dr Jon Scargill) *hld up in tch in last quintet: nt clr run jst over 2f out: hdwy and swtchd rt ent fnl f: kpt on ins fnl f: nt rch ldrs* **16/1**

-034 7 1 **Natch**[27] 724 4-9-1 **59**...........................(p) CallumShepherd 11 57
(Michael Attwater) *wl in tch in midfield: hdwy to chse ldrs on outer 4f out: rdn to ld over 2f out: hdd ent fnl f: no ex and wknd wl ins fnl f* **7/1**

8 2 **Neff (GER)**[179] 4-8-11 **62**........................... RhysClutterbuck(7) 14 57
(Gary Moore) *wd early: hld up in rr: hdwy and v wd bnd 2f out: no imp and wl hld whn hung lft ins fnl f* **50/1**

3204 9 6 **Attain**[12] 965 10-8-10 **61**.. KateLeahy(7) 6 44
(Archie Watson) *s.i.s: a in rr: nvr involved (jockey said gelding was slowly away)* **10/1**

00 10 ¾ **Royal Goldie (IRE)**[42] 473 4-8-13 **60**...............(vt[1]) PaddyBradley(3) 10 42
(Lydia Richards) *wnt lft leaving stalls: hld up in tch in last quintet: shkn up ent fnl 2f: no imp over 1f out: wknd ins fnl f* **33/1**

43-2 11 1½ **Orobas (IRE)**[7] 1040 7-9-2 **60**...............................(v) GeorgeWood 1 39+
(Lucinda Egerton) *prom early: wl in tch in midfield: nt clr run and shuffled bk towards rr over 2f out: n.d after* **11/1**

5-60 12 2 **Sunbreak (IRE)**[23] 784 4-8-11 **62**......................... OliverStammers(7) 5 37
(Mark Johnston) *led for 2f: chsd ldr tl 6f out: losing pl whn jostled over 2f out: bhd fnl f* **11/1**

04-0 13 2¾ **Tebay (IRE)**[21] 801 4-9-7 **65**..................................... NickyMackay 9 35+
(Luke McJannet) *wd in midfield: hdwy to chse ldr 6f out tl lost pl u.p over 1f out: sn btn and eased ins fnl f* **33/1**

34-0 14 3¾ **Rainbow Jazz (IRE)**[63] 135 4-9-4 **62**......................(be) CharlieBennett 4 25
(Adam West) *pushed along leaving stalls: chsd ldrs tl led 8f out: rdn and hdd over 2f out: sn dropped out: bhd fnl f* **14/1**

2m 4.17s (-2.43) **Going Correction** -0.175s/f (Stan) **14 Ran SP% 132.2**
Speed ratings (Par 101): **102,101,101,101,100 99,98,97,92,91 90,89,86,83**
CSF £17.63 CT £182.33 TOTE £5.40: £2.00, £1.90, £6.80; EX 24.20 Trifecta £792.10.
Owner Mark McAllister **Bred** Juddmonte Farms (east) Ltd **Trained** Epsom, Surrey

FOCUS
A wide-open handicap on paper and it produced a busy finish with only a length separating the first four home. A minor pb from the second.
T/Plt: £8.00 to a £1 stake. Pool: £54,934.92 - 4,964.28 winning units T/Qpdt: £3.80 to a £1 stake. Pool: £3,211.12 - 625.24 winning units **Steve Payne**

1184 - 1191a (Foreign Racing) - See Raceform Interactive

1158 SOUTHWELL (L-H)
Thursday, March 14

OFFICIAL GOING: Fibresand: standard
Wind: Fresh, half behind Weather: Cloudy

1192 BETWAY CASINO H'CAP 6f 16y(F)
5:55 (5:55) (Class 6) (0-55,54) 4-Y-O+
£3,105 (£924; £461; £400; £400; £400) Stalls Low

Form RPR
046 1 **Marble Bar**[19] 882 4-9-0 **50**...........................(h) JamieGormley(3) 14 69
(Iain Jardine) *qckly away and mde all: pushed along and qcknd clr 1/2-way: rdn wl over 1f out: kpt on strly* **14/1**

-003 2 7 **Essential**[27] 742 5-8-13 **53**.....................................(b) MarkCrehan(7) 3 51
(Olly Williams) *midfield: hdwy on inner wl over 2f out: sn rdn: styd on to chse wnr appr fnl f: sn drvn and no imp (jockey said gelding was denied a clear run approximately 2 1/2f out)* **7/2**[2]

050- 3 1¼ **Fortinbrass (IRE)**[93] 9491 9-8-8 **48**........................ IzzyClifton(7) 2 42
(John Balding) *prom: rdn along wl over 2f out: drvn wl over 1f out: kpt on same pce* **33/1**

3124 4 ½ **Catapult**[9] 1021 4-9-0 **54**...............................(p) GavinAshton(7) 5 47+
(Shaun Keightley) *t.k.h: hld up in midfield and n.m.r after 1f: hdwy over 2f out: sn rdn: edgd lft over 1f out: kpt on (jockey said gelding anticipated the start and missed the break)* **13/8**[1]

2-00 5 2¾ **Poppy May (IRE)**[49] 379 5-9-3 **50**............................ BarryMcHugh 4 36
(James Given) *chsd ldrs: wd st: rdn along on outer over 2f out: drvn wl over 1f out: sn one pce* **10/1**

0040 6 ¾ **Diamond Pursuit**[9] 1026 4-8-13 **49**......................(p[1]) GabrieleMalune(3) 7 33
(Ivan Furtado) *prom: rdn along over 2f out: drvn wl over 1f out: sn one pce* **9/1**[3]

-003 7 1¼ **Dream Ally (IRE)**[29] 702 9-9-2 **49**............................... LukeMorris 13 29
(John Weymes) *sn chsng wnr: rdn along over 2f out: drvn wl over 1f out: grad wknd* **33/1**

5-54 8 *nk* **Polished Article**[29] 706 4-8-12 **48**........................ PhilDennis(3) 6 27
(Lawrence Mullaney) *towards rr: rdn along 1/2-way: kpt on fnl 2f: n.d (vet reported the filly was found to be lame on its right fore)* **40/1**

64-4 9 1¼ **Dark Confidant (IRE)**[38] 599 6-8-5 **45**.......................(p) EllaMcCain(7) 9 20
(Donald McCain) *a towards rr: wd st and bhd* **14/1**

2045 10 1½ **Divine Call**[15] 919 12-9-6 **53**.. FrannyNorton 8 24
(Charlie Wallis) *midfield and n.m.r after 1f: rdn along 1/2-way: sn outpcd and bhd* **10/1**

-005 11 1 **Henrietta's Dream**[14] 954 5-8-12 **45**............................(v) NathanEvans 1 13
(John Wainwright) *a in rr* **33/1**

60-5 12 ½ **Mountain Of Stars**[63] 166 4-8-12 **45**.............................(p) NickyMackay 12 11
(Suzzanne France) *chsd ldrs on outer: rdn along wl over 2f out: sn wknd* **25/1**

50/0 13 13 **Major Muscari (IRE)**[13] 973 11-8-12 **45**.....................(p) PaulMulrennan 11
(Shaun Harris) *rrd and dwlt s: a bhd (jockey said gelding jumped awkwardly from the stalls)* **66/1**

1m 14.31s (-2.19) **Going Correction** -0.30s/f (Stan) **13 Ran SP% 118.4**
Speed ratings (Par 101): **102,92,91,90,87 86,84,84,82,80 79,78,61**
CSF £58.86 CT £1676.52 TOTE £16.10: £3.60, £1.20, £7.10; EX 80.60 Trifecta £2987.50.
Owner The Twelve Munkys **Bred** The Earl Cadogan **Trained** Carruthterstown, D'fries & G'way
■ Stewards' Enquiry : Jamie Gormley one-day ban: failure to keep straight from the stalls (Mar 28)

FOCUS
The first fixture here under floodlights. A low grade handicap but the winner bolted up. The winner has been rated near his previous best.

1193 LADBROKES H'CAP 4f 214y(F)
6:30 (6:30) (Class 5) (0-75,75) 3-Y-O £3,752 (£1,116; £557; £400; £400) Stalls Centre

Form RPR
2-44 1 **Sandridge Lad (IRE)**[42] 506 3-9-7 **75**............................ StevieDonohoe 1 78
(John Ryan) *trckd ldrs: hdwy 1/2-way: rdn to ld 1 1/2f out: drvn ins fnl f: kpt on wl towards fin* **8/1**

60-1 2 ½ **Fair Alibi**[21] 831 3-9-2 **70**... JamesSullivan 4 71
(Tom Tate) *trckd ldrs: pushed along and outpcd after 2f: sn swtchd lft towards far side: rdn over 2f out: hdwy over 1f out: chsd wnr ins fnl f: kpt on wl towards fin* **6/4**[1]

2-12 3 1¼ **Key To Power**[22] 796 3-9-7 **75**...................................... JoeFanning 5 72
(Mark Johnston) *cl up: led 2f out: sn rdn: hdd 1 1/2f out: drvn and ev ch ent fnl f: kpt on same pce* **11/4**[2]

4-11 4 *nk* **Giacomo Casanova (IRE)**[24] 783 3-8-12 **66**............. AndrewMullen 3 62
(Kevin Ryan) *cl up: rdn wl over 1f out: ev ch appr fnl f: sn drvn and kpt on same pce* **4/1**[3]

-163 5 1½ **Swiss Chime**[20] 854 3-8-4 **58**..................................... KieranO'Neill 2 48
(Dean Ivory) *led: rdn along and hdd over 2f out: cl up: drvn over 1f out: sn wknd* **8/1**

58.04s (-1.66) **Going Correction** -0.30s/f (Stan) **5 Ran SP% 108.9**
Speed ratings (Par 98): **101,100,98,97,95**
CSF £20.16 TOTE £8.80: £5.80, £1.20; EX 20.70 Trifecta £72.40.
Owner John Stocker **Bred** D Phelan **Trained** Newmarket, Suffolk

FOCUS
They went a good gallop and the first two came from off the pace.

1194 BETWAY BEST FOR CHELTENHAM FESTIVAL OFFERS H'CAP 4f 214y(F)
7:00 (7:00) (Class 4) (0-80,80) 4-Y-O+
£5,530 (£1,645; £822; £411; £400; £400) Stalls Centre

Form RPR
2012 1 **Warrior's Valley**[2] 1162 4-8-12 **71** 6ex......................(tp) LewisEdmunds 1 81
(David C Griffiths) *sn swtchd rt and racd towards centre: mde all: rdn clr over 1f out: drvn out* **9/4**[1]

1-34 2 1 **Eternal Sun**[37] 610 4-9-0 **76**................................... GabrieleMalune(3) 7 82
(Ivan Furtado) *towards rr in centre: swtchd markedly lft to far rail after 1 1/2f: hdwy 2f out: sn rdn: styd on wl fnl f* **8/1**[3]

-136 3 ½ **Mininggold**[27] 743 6-8-4 **68**..................................(p) PaulaMuir(5) 6 72
(Michael Dods) *chsd ldrs centre: rdn along 2f out: chsd wnr ent fnl f: kpt on same pce* **9/1**

4042 4 ½ **Samovar**[7] 1072 4-8-11 **70**......................................(b) KieranO'Neill 12 72
(Scott Dixon) *racd towards stands' side: cl up: rdn along 2f out: edgd lft over 1f out: kpt on same pce* **25/1**

313- 5 1 **Casterbridge**[75] 9748 7-9-2 **75**................................ RachelRichardson 10 74
(Eric Alston) *chsd ldrs centre: rdn along 2f out: swtchd rt and drvn over 1f out: kpt on fnl f* **25/1**

61-6 6 *nk* **Arzaak (IRE)**[12] 981 5-9-6 **79**......................................(b) JoeFanning 2 77
(Charlie Wallis) *racd towards far side: prom: effrt 1/2-way: rdn to chal wl over 1f out: drvn and wknd ent fnl f* **10/1**

0131 7 ¾ **Tathmeen (IRE)**[17] 907 4-9-2 **75**...................................... CamHardie 5 70
(Antony Brittain) *racd centre: in rr: rdn along 1/2-way: swtchd lft 2f out: styd on u.p fnl f* **9/1**

5222 8 1½ **Something Lucky (IRE)**[13] 964 7-9-7 **80**............(v) AlistairRawlinson 9 70
(Michael Appleby) *in rr centre: rdn along: outpcd and bhd bef 1/2-way: sme late hdwy (jockey said gelding was outpaced and never travelling)* **6/1**[2]

-505 9 *nse* **Classic Pursuit**[22] 797 8-9-1 **79**...........................(b) TheodoreLadd(5) 13 68
(Michael Appleby) *racd nr stands' rail: a towards rr* **18/1**

06-0 10 *nse* **Dapper Man (IRE)**[14] 953 5-9-2 **75**................................... BenCurtis 11 64
(Roger Fell) *racd towards stands' rail: in tch: rdn along 1/2-way: sn outpcd* **20/1**

1351 11 1¼ **Point Zero (IRE)**[15] 928 4-8-10 **76** ow1....................(be) MarkCrehan(7) 3 61
(Michael Appleby) *racd centre: a towards rr* **20/1**

33-2 12 *nk* **Granny Roz**[15] 928 5-9-0 **73**....................................... PaulMulrennan 4 57
(Ray Craggs) *cl up centre: rdn along 2f out: wknd over 1f out* **14/1**

516- 13 7 **Desert Ace (IRE)**[159] 7994 8-9-4 **77**................................. KevinStott 14 35
(Paul Midgley) *racd towards stands' rail: a towards rr (jockey said gelding hung left)* **50/1**

57.5s (-2.20) **Going Correction** -0.30s/f (Stan) **13 Ran SP% 116.4**
Speed ratings (Par 105): **105,103,102,101,100 99,98,96,96,95 93,93,82**
CSF £17.47 CT £142.47 TOTE £3.70: £1.80, £1.90, £3.20; EX 26.80 Trifecta £178.60.
Owner N Davies, D Clarke & Eros **Bred** P Balding **Trained** Bawtry, S Yorks

FOCUS
A competitive sprint run at a good gallop.

1195 LIKE SUNRACING ON FACEBOOK MAIDEN STKS 7f 14y(F)
7:30 (7:30) (Class 5) 3-Y-O+ £3,752 (£1,116; £557; £278) Stalls Low

Form RPR
1 **Native Silver** 3-8-12 0... LukeMorris 11 75
(Robert Eddery) *dwlt and towards rr: hdwy and in tch 3f out: rdn along towards inner 2f out: styd on strly to ld last 100yds* **25/1**

2 1¼ **Lofty** 3-8-12 0.. LewisEdmunds 7 71
(David Barron) *dwlt: sn in tch: hdwy and wd st: chal over 2f out: rdn to ld 1 1/2f out: drvn and edgd rt ent fnl f: hdd last 100yds: kpt on same pce* **9/1**

3 1 1/4 **Battle Of Yarmouk (IRE)** 3-8-12 0 KevinStott 9 68
(Kevin Ryan) *cl up: wd st: rdn to ld over 2f out: hdd 1 1/2f out: sn drvn: kpt on same pce fnl f* 4/1[2]

63-6 4 1/2 **Mushaageb (IRE)**[48] 405 3-8-12 69 (b[1]) DavidEgan 1 67
(Roger Varian) *towards rr: hdwy on inner over 3f out: chsd ldrs 2f out: sn rdn and kpt on fnl f* 11/2[3]

3 5 2 1/4 **Creek Island (IRE)**[14] 943 3-8-12 0 JoeFanning 2 61
(Mark Johnston) *led: pushed along 3f out: rdn and hdd over 2f out: sn drvn and grad wknd* 5/2[1]

3 6 1/2 **Sense Of Direction**[60] 229 3-8-8 0 ow1 CliffordLee 10 56
(K R Burke) *cl up: wd st: rdn along over 2f out: sn edgd lft and grad wknd* 5/2[1]

05 7 4 **Zoom Out**[15] 930 3-8-7 0 FayeMcManoman(5) 5 49
(Nigel Tinkler) *chsd ldrs on inner: rdn along 3f out: wknd 2f out (jockey said her saddle slipped)* 100/1

600- 8 8 **Grayboy**[264] 4136 3-8-12 0 PaulMulrennan 13 29
(David Brown) *chsd ldrs on outer: rdn along and wd st: sn wknd* 33/1

00 9 2 3/4 **Half Bolly**[13] 971 3-8-12 0 JasonHart 4 21
(Mark Walford) *dwlt: a towards rr* 100/1

63- 10 3 **Kimberley Girl**[217] 5913 3-8-7 0 NathanEvans 3 9
(Michael Easterby) *a towards rr* 40/1

60 11 3 3/4 **Killer Queen**[21] 831 4-9-6 0 PhilDennis(3) 6 5
(David C Griffiths) *a towards rr* 100/1

12 14 **Nanning City (IRE)** 4-9-9 0 SeamusCronin(5) 8
(B A Murphy, Ire) *dwlt: a bhd* 50/1

0 13 35 **Fast'n Furious (GER)**[14] 949 3-8-12 0 AndrewMullen 12
(Adrian Nicholls) *dwlt: hdwy and in tch 4f out: rdn alo and wd st: sn wknd* 100/1

1m 29.15s (-1.15) **Going Correction** -0.30s/f (Stan)
WFA 3 from 4yo 16lb 13 Ran SP% 117.7
Speed ratings (Par 103): **94,92,91,90,88 87,82,73,70,67 62,46,6**
CSF £225.81 TOTE £31.10: £5.60, £4.30, £1.50; EX 332.20.
Owner Pamela Aitken & Julia Rayment **Bred** Scea Des Prairies **Trained** Newmarket, Suffolk

FOCUS
An ordinary maiden.

1196 BETWAY LIVE CASINO H'CAP 2m 102y(F)
8:00 (8:00) (Class 6) (0-65,65) 4-Y-0+
£3,105 (£924; £461; £400; £400; £400) Stalls Low

Form RPR

-202 1 **Tynecastle Park**[39] 589 6-8-13 59 DarraghKeenan(5) 4 65
(Robert Eddery) *cl up: led 3f out: rdn along 2f out: drvn and kpt on wl fnl f* 6/4[1]

05-0 2 2 1/2 **Amadeus (IRE)**[2] 1163 4-9-0 58 KieranO'Neill 2 63
(Gavin Cromwell, Ire) *rdn along s: slt ld: pushed along and hdd 3f out: rdn over 2f out: drvn* 12/1

3-36 3 3 1/2 **Galileo's Spear (FR)**[29] 700 6-9-8 63 (t) LukeMorris 5 63
(Sir Mark Prescott Bt) *trckd ldng pair: pushed along over 4f out: rdn over 3f out: drvn 2f out: kpt on same pce* 5/1[3]

33-6 4 10 **Di's Gift**[49] 387 10-8-10 56 (v) TheodoreLadd(5) 7 43
(Michael Appleby) *t.k.h: trckd ldrs: pushed along 4f out: rdn 3f out: sn drvn and one pce (jockey said gelding ran too freely)* 3/1[2]

3-10 5 2 1/4 **Katie Gale**[14] 947 9-9-10 65 (v) AndrewMullen 6 49
(Robyn Brisland) *towards rr: pushed along over 5f out: rdn 4f out: sn outpcd* 9/1

0-10 6 55 **Lady Makfi (IRE)**[9] 1022 7-9-2 57 (p) StevieDonohoe 3
(Johnny Farrelly) *towards rr: rdn along and outpcd 1/2-way: sn bhd (jockey said mare hung left throughout)* 16/1

00-2 7 9 **Hediddodinthe (IRE)**[41] 535 5-9-8 63 FrannyNorton 8
(Peter Winks) *trckd ldrs: pushed along over 5f out: rdn and wknd over 4f out: sn bhd (jockey said gelding was never travelling)* 16/1

3m 37.62s (-7.88) **Going Correction** -0.30s/f (Stan)
WFA 4 from 5yo+ 3lb 7 Ran SP% 111.1
Speed ratings (Par 101): **107,105,104,99,97 70,65**
CSF £19.74 CT £69.57 TOTE £3.20: £2.50, £3.20; EX 15.90 Trifecta £57.10.
Owner Robert Eddery **Bred** Fittocks Stud Ltd & Arrow Farm Stud **Trained** Newmarket, Suffolk

FOCUS
They didn't go a great gallop early on in this moderate staying handicap. The winner has been rated in line with the best of his hurdles/Flat form.

1197 SUNRACING.CO.UK H'CAP 1m 13y(F)
8:30 (8:30) (Class 5) (0-75,73) 4-Y-0+
£3,752 (£1,116; £557; £400; £400; £400) Stalls Low

Form RPR

0066 1 **Hammer Gun (USA)**[8] 1036 6-9-7 73 (v) PaddyMathers 5 82
(Derek Shaw) *dwlt and sn rdn along in rr: hdwy wl over 2f out: rdn and chsd ldng pair over 1f out: drvn and styd on gamely fnl f to ld last 110yds* 11/4[2]

2-30 2 1 **Tum Tum**[19] 886 4-9-1 70 (h) PhilDennis(3) 11 76
(Michael Herrington) *trckd ldrs: hdwy 3f out: cl up over 2f out: rdn to ld wl over 1f out: drvn ent fnl f: hdd and no ex last 100yds* 12/1

3021 3 4 **Baron Run**[21] 829 9-8-2 61 ow3 RhonaPindar(7) 8 58
(K R Burke) *cl up: led wl over 2f out: rdn and hdd wl over 1f out: kpt on same pce* 14/1

11-2 4 2 1/4 **Tagur (IRE)**[52] 5 5-9-2 73 (p) ThomasGreatrex(5) 7 65
(Kevin Ryan) *midfield: hdwy wl over 2f out: sn rdn: kpt on fnl f: n.d* 8/1[3]

104- 5 6 **Beverley Bullet**[128] 8898 6-9-2 68 (p) JoeFanning 2 46
(Lawrence Mullaney) *towards rr: rdn along and wd st: kpt on fnl 2f* 22/1

-000 6 1 3/4 **Muqarred (USA)**[49] 392 7-8-13 65 (p) BenCurtis 9 39
(Roger Fell) *chsd ldrs: rdn along 3f out: drvn over 2f out: sn wknd* 25/1

0-00 7 1 1/4 **Zaeem**[49] 386 10-8-12 64 JasonHart 1 35
(Ivan Furtado) *chsd ldrs: wd st: rdn along over 2f out: sn wknd* 66/1

30/4 8 3/4 **Annie Fior (IRE)**[8] 1048 5-8-3 62 SeanKirrane(7) 3 31
(B A Murphy, Ire) *chsd ldrs on inner: rdn along over 3f out: sn wknd* 33/1

1111 9 4 1/2 **Lion Hearted (IRE)**[2] 1164 5-8-13 72 MarkCrehan(7) 6 31
(Michael Appleby) *led: pushed along 3f out: sn hdd and rdn: sn wknd (trainer said gelding was outpaced and unsuited by the fibresand surface and added that the race may have also come too soon having raced 2 days previously; vet reported the gelding was treated for post-race heat stress)* 1/1[1]

530/ 10 8 **Satisfy (IRE)**[181] 7265 5-8-13 70 SeamusCronin(5) 4 10
(B A Murphy, Ire) *chsd ldng pair on inner: rdn along over 3f out: sn wknd* 28/1

1m 41.56s (-2.14) **Going Correction** -0.30s/f (Stan) 10 Ran SP% 118.2
Speed ratings (Par 103): **98,97,93,90,84 83,81,81,76,68**
CSF £32.81 CT £417.11 TOTE £4.90: £1.20, £4.80, £3.20; EX 39.90 Trifecta £287.60.

Owner A Flint **Bred** Her Majesty The Queen **Trained** Sproxton, Leics

FOCUS
This was well run and experience of the surface proved key.
T/Plt: £352.80 to a £1 stake. Pool: £87,056.27. 180.09 winning units. T/Qpdt: £63.80 to a £1 stake. Pool: £13,618.47. 157.85 winning units. **Joe Rowntree**

1027 CHANTILLY (R-H)
Thursday, March 14

OFFICIAL GOING: Polytrack: standard; turf: heavy

1198a PRIX DU BEAUVAISIS (MAIDEN) (UNRACED 3YO COLTS & GELDINGS) (ALL-WEATHER TRACK) (POLYTRACK) 1m (P)
1:15 3-Y-0 £11,261 (£4,504; £3,378; £2,252; £1,126)

RPR

1 **Singstreet (FR)** 3-9-2 0 AlexisBadel 6 78
(Mme M Bollack-Badel, France) 43/5

2 2 1/2 **Bizerta (FR)** 3-9-2 0 MickaelBarzalona 4 72
(A Fabre, France) *hld up towards rr: brought wd into st and hdwy 2f out: rdn and prog over 1f out: kpt on ins fnl f to take 2nd cl home* 5/2[1]

3 snk **Diaboleo (FR)** 3-9-2 0 MaximeGuyon 3 72
(F Head, France) *midfield on outer: pushed along to keep in tch over 3f out: rdn over 2f out: responded for press and prog fr 1 1/2f out: kpt on ins fnl f: nvr gng pce to chal wnr* 4/1[2]

4 hd **Fun Legend** 3-9-2 0 ChristopheSoumillon 2 71
(P Bary, France) 22/5[3]

5 8 **Woossett (FR)** 3-9-2 0 VincentCheminaud 1 53
(H-A Pantall, France) 113/10

6 nk **Ignacius Reilly** 3-9-2 0 BauyrzhanMurzabayev 5 52
(Vaclav Luka Jr, Czech Republic) 53/1

7 snk **Batbayar** 3-9-2 0 Pierre-CharlesBoudot 8 52
(A Fabre, France) 58/10

8 3 **Obsession For Gold (IRE)** 3-9-2 0 AntoineHamelin 10 45
(Mrs Ilka Gansera-Leveque) *slowly away: sn rcvrd to trck ldrs: rdn along 2f out: drvn and limited rspnse over 1f out: no ex ins fnl f* 148/10

9 1 1/4 **Top Space (USA)** 3-9-2 0 OlivierPeslier 9 42
(C Laffon-Parias, France) 196/10

10 12 **Wild Eagle (FR)** 3-9-2 0 TheoBachelot 7 15
(Vaclav Luka Jr, Czech Republic) 28/1

11 3 **Wolf Chop (FR)** 3-8-8 0 TomLefranc(8) 11 8
(C Boutin, France) 48/1

1m 39.19s 11 Ran SP% 118.9
PARI-MUTUEL (all including 1 euro stake): WIN 9.60; PLACE 2.60, 1.50, 1.90; DF 20.00;.
Owner Ecurie Noel Forgeard, EIRL Myriam Bollack-Badel & **Bred** M Bollack-Badel, N Forgeard & P Lamy **Trained** Lamorlaye, France

1199a PRIX MONTENICA (LISTED RACE) (3YO) (ALL-WEATHER TRACK) (POLYTRACK) 6f 110y(P)
2:35 3-Y-0 £24,774 (£9,909; £7,432; £4,954; £2,477)

RPR

1 **Transcendent (ITY)**[32] 683 3-9-2 0 ChristopheSoumillon 3 103
(F Chappet, France) 17/5[2]

2 shd **Sicilia**[178] 7372 3-8-13 0 OlivierPeslier 10 99
(C Laffon-Parias, France) 6/1[3]

3 1 1/2 **Vanilla Gold (IRE)**[88] 9570 3-8-13 0 StephanePasquier 9 95
(N Clement, France) 111/10

4 shd **Power Best (IRE)**[57] 3-9-2 0 (b) AndreaAtzeni 7 98
(G Botti, France) 99/10

5 3/4 **Wind Test**[228] 5532 3-9-2 0 CristianDemuro 12 96
(A Giorgi, Italy) 216/10

6 1/2 **Quiet Endeavour (IRE)**[12] 989 3-9-2 0 (p) HollieDoyle 11 94
(Archie Watson) *urged along leaving stalls to ld: hdd and rdn 2f out: drvn to chse ldr over 1f out: wknd ins fnl f* 147/10

7 2 **Kodyanna (IRE)**[138] 8629 3-8-13 0 TheoBachelot 5 85
(S Wattel, France) 174/10

8 2 **Big Brothers Pride (FR)**[149] 3-8-13 0 Pierre-CharlesBoudot 6 79
(F Rohaut, France) 13/5[1]

9 1/2 **Singing Tower (FR)**[121] 9045 3-8-13 0 SebastienMaillot 4 78
(N Clement, France) 59/1

10 2 1/2 **El Guanche (FR)**[40] 3-9-2 0 NicolasDeJulian 8 74
(Rama-Fernandez Blas, Spain) 193/10

11 3 1/2 **Strings Of Life**[88] 9570 3-8-13 0 MickaelBarzalona 2 61
(H-A Pantall, France) *settled in midfield: pushed along 2f out: rdn w limited rspnse over 1f out: heavily eased ins fnl f* 10/1

12 5 **No War (USA)**[70] 3-8-13 0 (p) Francois-XavierBertras 1 46
(F Rohaut, France) 23/1

1m 17.62s 12 Ran SP% 118.3
PARI-MUTUEL (all including 1 euro stake): WIN 4.40; PLACE 1.70, 2.00, 2.70; DF 16.20;.
Owner Antoine Gilibert, Ecurie Vivaldi & Fabrice Chappet **Bred** Antoine Gilibert, Ecurie Vivaldi & Fabrice Chappet **Trained** France

1200a PRIX RONDE DE NUIT (LISTED RACE) (3YO) (TURF) 5f 110y
3:50 3-Y-0 £24,774 (£9,909; £7,432; £4,954; £2,477)

RPR

1 **Tertius (FR)**[121] 9045 3-9-2 0 HugoJourniac 10 108
(M Nigge, France) 63/10

2 6 **Cigalera (FR)**[21] 3-8-13 0 TonyPiccone 4 85
(M Delcher Sanchez, France) 112/10

3 1 1/4 **Happy Odyssey (IRE)**[134] 8754 3-8-13 0 (p) StephanePasquier 5 81
(N Clement, France) 31/10[1]

4 1 1/4 **Milord's Song (FR)**[142] 8527 3-9-2 0 TheoBachelot 8 80
(S Wattel, France) 4/1[2]

5 nk **Pardon My French (IRE)**[197] 6704 3-9-2 0 BauyrzhanMurzabayev 6 79
(Vaclav Luka Jr, Czech Republic) 117/10

6 2 **Enough Said**[9] 1028 3-9-2 0 AntoineHamelin 7 72
(Matthieu Palussiere, France) 225/10

7 hd **Survoltee (GER)**[146] 3-8-13 0 CristianDemuro 2 69
(F Chappet, France) 152/10

8 nk **Tisona**[35] 3-8-13 0 EddyHardouin 1 68
(Matthieu Palussiere, France) 43/1

9 *nk* **Shumookhi (IRE)**[146] 8397 3-8-13 0........................... EdwardGreatrex 3 67
(Archie Watson) *sn front rnk: led: urged along 2f out: rdn and hdd 1 1/2f out: sn outpcd and wknd fnl f* **49/10**[3]

10 *dist* **We Go (FR)**[193] 6845 3-9-2 0.......................... Pierre-CharlesBoudot 9
(H-A Pantall, France) **57/10**

1m 11.86s (7.36) **10** Ran SP% **118.7**
PARI-MUTUEL (all including 1 euro stake): WIN 7.30; PLACE 2.40, 2.90, 1.90; DF 24.90.
Owner Mme Christa Zass **Bred** Mme C Zass **Trained** France

1201 - 1207a (Foreign Racing) - See Raceform Interactive

[1060] CHELMSFORD (A.W) (L-H)

Friday, March 15

OFFICIAL GOING: Polytrack: standard
Wind: Medium, Across Weather: Dry

1208 BET TOTEPLACEPOT AT TOTESPORT.COM AMATEUR RIDERS' H'CAP (DIV I) 6f (P)

4:40 (4:42) (Class 5) (0-70,71) 4-Y-O+
£4,991 (£1,548; £773; £400; £400; £400) **Stalls** Centre

Form RPR

0421 **1** **Zapper Cass (FR)**[14] 970 6-10-12 **68**........(v) MissSerenaBrotherton 10 75
(Michael Appleby) *taken down early: t.k.h: sn chsng ldr on outer: clr w ldr 1/2-way: tl led ent fnl 2f: kpt on u.p ins fnl f* **6/1**[3]

6311 **2** *3/4* **The Groove**[20] 883 6-10-6 **69**............................. MrPhilipThomas(7) 8 74
(David Evans) *midfield on outer: effrt over 1f out: hdwy u.p to chse wnr ins fnl f: kpt on wl but nvr quite getting to wnr* **7/1**

513- **3** *nse* **Caribbean Spring (IRE)**[85] 9634 6-9-12 **59**... MissRosieMargarson(5) 1 64
(George Margarson) *midfield: effrt on inner over 1f out: kpt on wl ins fnl f: nvr quite getting to wnr* **8/1**

11-4 **4** *3/4* **Poeta Brasileiro (IRE)**[10] 1023 4-10-10 **69**.......... MrJamesHarding(3) 3 71
(Seamus Durack) *midfield: effrt over 1f out: kpt on u.p ins fnl f: nvr quite enough pce to rch wnr* **11/4**[2]

10-4 **5** *1/2* **Vallarta (IRE)**[16] 928 9-10-1 **62**.......................... MissEmilyBullock(5) 5 63
(Ruth Carr) *taken down early: t.k.h: led: clr w wnr 1/2-way: hdd ent fnl 2f: unable to match pce of wnr over 1f out: wknd ins fnl f* **25/1**

4001 **6** *1 1/2* **Miracle Garden**[9] 1038 7-10-10 **71** 6ex..............(b) CharlieTodd(5) 4 67
(Ian Williams) *chsd ldrs: unable qck u.p over 1f out: kpt on same pce ins fnl f* **15/8**[1]

-354 **7** *nse* **Dotted Swiss (IRE)**[22] 824 4-10-10 **66**..........(b) MissBrodieHampson 7 62
(Archie Watson) *hld up in last pair: effrt over 1f out: keeping on whn nt clr run and swtchd lft ins fnl f: nvr getting on terms: nt clr run again and swtchd lft towards fin* **12/1**

0060 **8** *2 3/4* **Plucky Dip**[8] 1060 8-9-7 **56** oh11..........................(p) MrThomasMiles(7) 2 43
(John Ryan) *chsd ldrs: unable qck over 1f out: wknd ins fnl f* **50/1**

5002 **9** *5* **Hollander**[9] 1038 5-10-4 **63**............................(t) MissHannahWelch(3) 9 34
(Alexandra Dunn) *swtchd lft after s: a in rr* **33/1**

5300 **R** **Gold Hunter (IRE)**[17] 914 9-10-7 **70**........................... MrDannyKerr(7) 6
(Steve Flook) *v awkward as stalls opened and wnt sharply leaving stalls: tk no part* **16/1**

1m 13.46s (-0.24) **Going Correction** 0.0s/f (Stan) **10** Ran SP% **121.7**
Speed ratings (Par 103): **101,100,99,98,98 96,96,92,85,**
CSF £48.96 CT £352.63 TOTE £9.20: £2.50, £2.80, £2.00; EX 42.00 Trifecta £253.30.
Owner Stephen Louch **Bred** Arunas Cicenas **Trained** Oakham, Rutland
■ Stewards' Enquiry : Mr James Harding two-day ban: excessive use of whip (Mar 31, Apr 13)

FOCUS
The going was standard. Stalls 6f: Centre, Remainder: Inside. An ordinary sprint handicap run at a fair clip. The second and third have been rated to his recent form.

1209 BET TOTEPLACEPOT AT TOTESPORT.COM AMATEUR RIDERS' H'CAP (DIV II) 6f (P)

5:20 (5:22) (Class 5) (0-70,70) 4-Y-O+
£4,991 (£1,548; £773; £400; £400; £400) **Stalls** Centre

Form RPR

6- **1** **Gottardo (IRE)**[142] 8556 4-10-8 **69**............................... SophieSmith(5) 1 75
(Ed Dunlop) *hld up in last pair: effrt over 1f out: rdn and str run ins fnl f to ld last strides* **9/4**[1]

-060 **2** *hd* **Spenny's Lass**[8] 1061 4-9-12 **59**................................(p) CharlieTodd(5) 8 64
(John Ryan) *w ldr early: dropped to midfield over 3f out: clsd 2f out: ev ch 1f out: led wl ins fnl f: kpt on: hdd last strides* **16/1**

-631 **3** *hd* **Time To Reason (IRE)**[22] 823 6-10-10 **66**...........(p) MrSimonWalker 4 70
(Charlie Wallis) *midfield: swtchd lft and effrt to chal whn squeezed for room and bmpd over 1f out: rdn to ld 1f out: kpt on: hdd and no ex cl home* **11/4**[2]

001- **4** *1 1/4* **Winklemann (IRE)**[85] 9634 7-9-13 **62**...........(p) MissImogenMathias(7) 9 62
(John Flint) *taken down early: wd: midfield tl hdwy to chse ldr 4f out: drifted wd ent st: ev ch 1f out: no ex and wknd towards fin* **14/1**

060- **5** *1/2* **Zefferino**[135] 8733 5-10-2 **65**..............(t w) MissJenniferPahlman(7) 6 64
(Martin Bosley) *dwlt: towards rr: swtchd rt 4f out: hdwy and swtchd lft ins fnl f: kpt on but no threat to ldrs* **33/1**

0-32 **6** *1 1/2* **Lalania**[22] 824 4-10-12 **68**.. MrRossBirkett 5 62
(Stuart Williams) *led: sn hdd: midfield: clsd to chse ldrs whn swtchd rt 1f out: nt clr run sn after: no imp* **6/1**

3334 **7** *1 1/2* **Monumental Man**[11] 1016 10-11-0 **70**......................(p) MrAlexFerguson 7 59
(Jamie Osborne) *sn led: hdd over 4f out: rdn and struggling 2f out: wknd fnl f* **7/1**

6056 **8** *1 1/4* **National Glory (IRE)**[16] 928 4-11-0 **70**........(b[1]) MissBrodieHampson 3 55
(Archie Watson) *t.k.h: swtchd rt and hdwy to ld over 4f out: hung lft u.p over 1f out: ducked rt and hdd 1f out: wknd ins fnl f* **5/1**[3]

000- **9** *2 3/4* **Freddy With A Y (IRE)**[85] 9634 9-9-7 **56** oh8.......... MrDallonHolmes(7) 2 32
(J R Jenkins) *stdd and awkward leaving stalls: a bhd* **50/1**

1m 13.72s (0.02) **Going Correction** 0.0s/f (Stan) **9** Ran SP% **118.3**
Speed ratings (Par 103): **99,98,98,96,96 94,92,90,86**
CSF £41.60 CT £106.45 TOTE £3.20: £1.30, £7.80, £1.10; EX 37.90 Trifecta £142.70.
Owner The EDR Partnership **Bred** Mrs E J Stack **Trained** Newmarket, Suffolk
■ Stewards' Enquiry : Miss Brodie Hampson caution: careless riding

FOCUS
The second division of the amateur riders' handicap produced a thrilling finish, but the winner may have had more in hand than the narrow margin of victory suggested. The second and third have been rated close to their recent form.

1210 BET TOTEEXACTA AT TOTESPORT.COM H'CAP 5f (P)

6:00 (6:02) (Class 6) (0-55,55) 4-Y-O+
£3,105 (£924; £461; £400; £400; £400) **Stalls** Low

Form RPR

0-00 **1** **Precious Plum**[44] 483 5-9-7 **55**...........................(p) RichardKingscote 11 64
(Charlie Wallis) *taken down early: chsd ldr: rdn and ev ch over 1f out: led 100yds out: styd on wl and forged ahd towards fin* **20/1**

0103 **2** *1* **Red Stripes (USA)**[7] 1076 7-9-2 **55**.......................(b) SeamusCronin(5) 1 60
(Lisa Williamson) *led: rdn and hdd pressed over 1f out: hdd 100yds out: no ex and outpcd towards fin* **3/1**[2]

-051 **3** *3/4* **Atyaaf**[21] 848 4-9-7 **55**.. PaddyMathers 2 58
(Derek Shaw) *taken down early: wnt rt leaving stalls: sn rcvrd to chse ldrs and t.k.h over 4f out: drvn to press ldrs 1f out: kpt on same pce and no imp ins fnl f* **6/4**[1]

5-46 **4** *nse* **Coastal Cyclone**[27] 759 5-9-4 **52**..............................(v) TomMarquand 3 55
(Harry Dunlop) *hld up in rr of main gp: hdwy u.p to chse ldrs whn hung lft ins fnl f: kpt on towards fin* **9/2**[3]

0000 **5** *2 1/2* **Deer Song**[6] 1093 6-8-9 **48** ow2............................(v[1]) KatherineBegley(5) 6 42
(John Bridger) *rousted along early: in midfield: rdn over 2f out: drvn and no imp over 1f out: wl hld and one pce ins fnl f* **33/1**

2203 **6** *shd* **Pharoh Jake**[13] 986 11-8-8 **49**...................................... EllieMacKenzie(7) 8 42
(John Bridger) *wd: in tch in rr of main gp: effrt u.p over 1f out: no imp and wl hld ins fnl f* **16/1**

-120 **7** *2 1/4* **New Rich**[44] 484 9-8-11 **52**..................................(b) GeorgiaDobie(7) 5 37
(Eve Johnson Houghton) *sn outpcd in last and rdn: nvr involved* **14/1**

-531 **8** *1 1/2* **Hurricane Alert**[13] 986 7-9-0 **48**.. DavidEgan 7 28
(Mark Hoad) *taken down early: midfield: unable qck u.p over 1f out: wknd ins fnl f* **8/1**

59.58s (-0.62) **Going Correction** 0.0s/f (Stan) **8** Ran SP% **114.5**
Speed ratings (Par 101): **104,102,101,101,97 96,93,90**
CSF £79.71 CT £150.15 TOTE £21.90: £5.50, £1.30, £1.10; EX 77.10 Trifecta £156.30.
Owner Mrs Julia Hughes **Bred** Mrs J V Hughes **Trained** Ardleigh, Essex
■ Zipedeedodah was withdrawn. Price at time of withdrawal 20-1. Rule 4 does not apply

FOCUS
A modest sprint handicap. The second has been rated in line with his better recent form.

1211 BET TOTEQUADPOT AT TOTESPORT.COM H'CAP 5f (P)

6:30 (6:33) (Class 3) (0-95,91) 4-Y-O+ **£9,703** (£2,887; £1,443; £721) **Stalls** Low

Form RPR

-632 **1** **King Robert**[23] 797 6-8-13 **83**.. DavidEgan 1 92
(Charlie Wallis) *chsd ldrs on inner: swtchd out rt and effrt over 1f out: drvn to ld 1f out: r.o and in command wl ins fnl f: quite comf* **7/2**[2]

2220 **2** *1 1/4* **Something Lucky (IRE)**[1] 1194 7-8-5 **80**..............(v) TheodoreLadd(5) 3 84
(Michael Appleby) *restless in stalls: bhd: clsd and swtchd lft 1f out: r.o wl fnl 100yds: snatched 2nd last stride: no threat to wnr* **4/1**[3]

4-50 **3** *shd* **Verne Castle**[13] 987 6-9-7 **91**..(b[1]) FrannyNorton 8 95
(Michael Wigham) *chsd ldr: clsd to join ldr and hld together over 1f out: rdn 1f out: drvn and kpt on same pce ins fnl f: lost 2nd last stride (vet said gelding lost its right fore shoe)* **11/1**

5341 **4** *hd* **Primo's Comet**[15] 953 4-8-8 **81**... PhilDennis(3) 4 84
(Jim Goldie) *racd in last pair: rdn and clsd over 1f out: swtchd lft ins fnl f: kpt on wl but no threat to wnr* **5/1**

2120 **5** *1/2* **Shamshon (IRE)**[6] 1105 8-9-6 **90**................................. RichardKingscote 5 91
(Stuart Williams) *midfield: effrt over 1f out: kpt on u.p wl ins fnl f: nt enough pce to rch ldrs* **13/8**[1]

1-05 **6** *3/4* **You're Cool**[24] 791 7-8-10 **80**....................................(t) LewisEdmunds 9 78
(John Balding) *chsd ldrs on outer: effrt and unable qck over 1f out: kpt on same pce ins fnl f* **25/1**

004- **7** *3* **Bosham**[186] 7128 9-8-12 **82**..(bt) CamHardie 2 70
(Michael Easterby) *mounted in the chute and taken down early: led: rdn and hrd pressed over 1f out: hdd 1f out: no ex and wknd ins fnl f* **25/1**

40-6 **8** *2 1/4* **Green Door (IRE)**[41] 551 8-9-1 **85**.................................(v) LukeMorris 6 65
(Robert Cowell) *dwlt: t.k.h: sn rcvrd and in midfield: short of room and shuffled bk over 3f out: bhd over 1f out* **25/1**

59.27s (-0.93) **Going Correction** 0.0s/f (Stan) **8** Ran SP% **116.9**
Speed ratings (Par 107): **107,105,104,104,103 102,97,94**
CSF £17.88 CT £136.46 TOTE £4.40: £1.50, £1.10, £2.40; EX 17.10 Trifecta £79.90.
Owner Dab Hand Racing **Bred** Mrs P A Clark **Trained** Ardleigh, Essex

FOCUS
A decent sprint handicap which produced a decisive winner. The second has been rated to his recent 5f figures, with the fourth close to his recent form.

1212 BET TOTETRIFECTA AT TOTESPORT.COM NOVICE STKS 7f (P)

7:00 (7:01) (Class 4) 3-Y-O+ **£5,822** (£1,732; £865; £432) **Stalls** Low

Form RPR

4 **1** **Lestrade**[28] 733 3-8-12 0..(h) CallumShepherd 3 75+
(William Jarvis) *trckd ldrs on inner: swtchd out rt and effrt over 1f out: drvn and chalng ins fnl f: sn led and forged ahd towards fin* **6/4**[1]

0-22 **2** *1/2* **Assimilation (IRE)**[28] 733 3-8-12 75................................ LiamKeniry 7 73+
(Ed Walker) *chsd ldr tl led wl over 1f out: sn rdn: drvn and hdd ins fnl f: no ex and jst outpcd towards fin* **2/1**[2]

0002 **3** *5* **Middlescence (IRE)**[9] 1042 5-9-9 58....................(t) PoppyBridgwater(5) 8 65?
(Lucinda Egerton) *led: rdn and hdd wl over 1f out: sn drvn: 3rd and wknd ins fnl f* **16/1**

1- **4** *1 1/4* **Jack Berry House**[149] 8322 3-9-5 0..............................(t[1]) StevieDonohoe 5 63
(Charlie Fellowes) *dwlt: sn rcvrd and t.k.h in midfield: outpcd in 6th whn swtchd rt and wd ent fnl 2f: wnt 4th ins fnl f: kpt on but no threat to ldrs* **11/4**[3]

5 **5** *2 1/4* **I'm British**[13] 979 6-10-0 0..(h) RossaRyan 2 56
(Don Cantillon) *mounted on crse: midfield: rdn and outpcd over 2f out: no threat to ldrs after: wknd ins fnl f* **12/1**

0/0- **6** *5* **The Wire Flyer**[422] 252 4-10-0 0....................................(p[1]) DanielMuscutt 4 42
(John Flint) *midfield: rdn and outpcd over 2f out: wl btn 1f out: wknd fnl f* **100/1**

0/6 **7** *1 1/4* **One Last Hug**[15] 954 4-9-11 0... PhilDennis(3) 9 39
(Jim Goldie) *stdd s: hld up in rr: outpcd whn nt clr run and swtchd rt over 2f out: no threat to ldrs after* **50/1**

0 **8** *4 1/2* **Noel (IRE)**[22] 827 4-10-0-0 .... FergusSweeney 1 27
(Daniel Kubler) *a last trio: outpcd and rdn over 2f out: n.d after* **50/1**

0 **9** *6* **Aquarius Miracle**[58] 251 3-8-12 0 EoinWalsh 6 4
(George Scott) *stdd s: t.k.h: hld up in last trio: rdn over 3f out: outpcd over 2f out: wl bhd over 1f out* **33/1**

1m 26.26s (-0.94) **Going Correction** 0.0s/f (Stan)
WFA 3 from 4yo+ 16lb **9** Ran SP% **121.4**
Speed ratings (Par 105): **105,104,98,97,94 89,87,82,75**
CSF £5.01 TOTE £2.10: £1.10, £1.10, £5.70; EX 5.30 Trifecta £26.20.
Owner Clive Washbourn **Bred** Windmill Farm Partnership Ltd **Trained** Newmarket, Suffolk

FOCUS
A fair novice contest which saw the two principals draw clear. The winner is potentially useful. The third is the key to the form, and has been credited with running to his early form for now.

1213 BALLYMORE H'CAP 1m (P)
7:30 (7:32) (Class 4) (0-85,87) 4-Y-O+
£5,530 (£1,645; £822; £411; £400; £400) **Stalls** Low

Form RPR

32-2 **1** **Pride's Gold (USA)**[46] 460 4-9-10 **87** AdamKirby 11 95
(Simon Crisford) *chsd ldr: drvn to chal over 1f out: led 1f out: styd on wl: rdn out* **9/2**[2]

6515 **2** *1* **Samphire Coast**[16] 922 6-9-4 **81** (v) PaddyMathers 7 87
(Derek Shaw) *taken down early: hld up in midfield: effrt over 2f out: chsd ldrs 1f out: kpt on wl u.p ins fnl f: wnt 2nd towards fin (trainer said gelding had a breathing problem)* **7/1**[3]

0136 **3** *½* **Philamundo (IRE)**[23] 807 4-9-4 **81** (b) TomQueally 5 86
(Richard Spencer) *restrained after s: off the pce in last pair: clsd 4f out: hdwy u.p whn swtchd rt ins fnl f: styd on strly fnl 100yds: nt quite rch ldrs* **8/1**

-036 **4** *nk* **Glory Awaits (IRE)**[41] 548 9-8-8 **76** (b) DylanHogan(5) 9 80
(David Simcock) *led: rdn ent fnl 2f: hdd 1f out and kpt on same pce ins fnl f: lost 2 pls towards fin* **22/1**

-450 **5** *hd* **Brittanic (IRE)**[16] 922 5-8-12 **75** (p) StevieDonohoe 2 78
(David Simcock) *hld up in last trio: effrt over 2f out: hdwy u.p ins fnl f: styd on wl fnl 100yds: nt rch ldrs* **14/1**

-321 **6** *½* **Pheidippides**[14] 962 4-9-1 **78** (b) LukeMorris 3 80
(Tom Clover) *chsd ldrs: effrt over 1f out: no ex u.p ins fnl f: jst outpcd fnl 100yds* **5/2**[1]

1052 **7** *¾* **Florencio**[28] 734 6-9-9 **86** (p) DougieCostello 6 87
(Jamie Osborne) *in tch in midfield on inner: swtchd out rt and effrt over 1f out: no imp 1f out: wknd ins fnl f* **16/1**

0-02 **8** *3 ¼* **Key Player**[17] 915 4-9-7 **84** CharlesBishop 8 77
(Eve Johnson Houghton) *chsd ldrs: effrt in 4th 2f out: unable qck and btn whn sltly impeded jst ins fnl f: wknd fnl 100yds* **8/1**

0-20 **9** *½* **Intense Style (IRE)**[16] 922 7-9-2 **79** JosephineGordon 1 71
(Les Eyre) *t.k.h: hld up in tch in last quartet: effrt over 1f out: no imp and wl hld fnl f* **25/1**

0-60 **10** *1 ¾* **Able Jack**[41] 557 6-9-7 **84** RichardKingscote 10 72
(Stuart Williams) *midfield on outer: rdn over 2f out: unable qck and lost pl over 1f out: wknd fnl f* **7/1**[3]

300- **11** *15* **Sir Hamilton (IRE)**[91] 9532 4-9-9 **86** DavidProbert 4 39
(Luke McJannet) *slowly away: a in rr: bhd and eased wl ins fnl f (jockey said gelding was slowly away)* **12/1**

1m 38.48s (-1.42) **Going Correction** 0.0s/f (Stan) **11** Ran SP% **122.4**
Speed ratings (Par 105): **107,106,105,105,105 104,103,100,100,98 83**
CSF £37.82 CT £256.34 TOTE £8.60: £2.30, £2.20, £3.00; EX 51.30 Trifecta £212.20.
Owner Rabbah Racing **Bred** Rabbah Bloodstock Ltd **Trained** Newmarket, Suffolk

FOCUS
A fair handicap won in good style by the top weight. The second has been rated as running to his best, with the fourth close to his recent form.

1214 WAKE UP TO BENSON BBC ESSEX H'CAP (DIV I) 1m (P)
8:00 (8:05) (Class 6) (0-55,55) 4-Y-O+
£3,105 (£924; £461; £400; £400; £400) **Stalls** Low

Form RPR

0-45 **1** **Compass Point**[22] 829 4-9-6 **54** KieranO'Neill 6 63
(Robyn Brisland) *t.k.h: chsd ldr for 3f: wnt 2nd again over 1f out: led over 1f out: asserted and hung lft u.p ins fnl f: r.o wl* **5/1**[2]

-600 **2** *3* **Seaquinn**[22] 830 4-8-12 **46** oh1 KierenFox 2 48
(John Best) *hld up in tch in last pair: effrt and hdwy u.p over 1f out: styd on to snatch 2nd last strides: no threat to wnr* **20/1**

6330 **3** *nk* **Mans Not Trot (IRE)**[8] 1060 4-9-6 **54** (p) NicolaCurrie 3 55
(Jamie Osborne) *led: rdn and hdd over 1f out: unable to match pce of wnr and btn ins fnl f: lost 2nd last strides (jockey said gelding hung right-handed travelling up the home straight)* **8/1**[3]

-211 **4** *½* **Irish Times**[8] 1060 4-8-13 **52** DylanHogan(5) 1 52
(Henry Spiller) *trckd ldrs on inner and travelled strly: effrt over 1f out: unable qck u.p and one pce ins fnl f* **8/11**[1]

06-0 **5** *1 ¼* **Theydon Spirit**[50] 383 4-9-1 **49** MarcMonaghan 11 46
(Peter Charalambous) *dwlt: hld up in tch in last quartet: effrt over 1f out: sn swtchd rt and kpt on u.p ins fnl f: nvr trbld ldrs* **10/1**

0042 **6** *½* **Rising Sunshine (IRE)**[16] 924 6-8-12 **46** oh1 (vt) LukeMorris 10 42
(Milton Bradley) *taken down early: wl in tch in midfield: rdn and unable qck over 1f out: wl hld and one pce ins fnl f* **20/1**

3200 **7** *hd* **The Special One (IRE)**[8] 1060 6-9-7 **55** (h) JosephineGordon 4 51
(Phil McEntee) *hld up in tch in last quartet: effrt over 1f out: nvr threatened to get on terms: nt clrest of runs and one pce ins fnl f* **14/1**

130- **8** *¾* **Casey Banter**[168] 7730 4-9-3 **51** ShelleyBirkett 9 45
(Julia Feilden) *midfield on outer: no imp u.p over 1f out: wl hld ins fnl f* **33/1**

0-50 **9** *1 ¾* **Lesanti**[15] 941 5-8-9 **46** oh1 WilliamCox(3) 5 36
(Ed de Giles) *restrained sn after leaving stalls: hld up in rr: swtchd rt and effrt over 1f out: no prog: wknd ins fnl f* **40/1**

1-00 **10** *1 ¼* **Candesta (USA)**[40] 590 9-9-7 **55** (t) DanielMuscutt 8 42
(Julia Feilden) *dwlt: hld up in tch: hdwy u.p over 1f out: no ex and wknd ins fnl f* **33/1**

-065 **11** *4 ½* **Ertidaad (IRE)**[29] 719 7-8-13 **47** (v) EoinWalsh 12 28
(Emma Owen) *rousted along leaving stalls: hdwy to chse ldr 5f out: drvn and lost pl over 2f out: bhd and eased wl ins fnl f* **33/1**

1m 40.08s (0.18) **Going Correction** 0.0s/f (Stan) **11** Ran SP% **122.2**
Speed ratings (Par 101): **99,96,95,95,93 93,93,92,90,89 85**
CSF £105.12 CT £804.73 TOTE £7.00: £2.00, £5.30, £2.20; EX 114.80 Trifecta £648.00.
Owner Mrs Jackie Cornwell **Bred** Mrs J A Cornwell **Trained** Danethorpe, Notts

FOCUS
A low-grade handicap which saw the winner shed his maiden tag. A minor pb from the winner, with the second rated in line with her previous best.

1215 WAKE UP TO BENSON BBC ESSEX H'CAP (DIV II) 1m (P)
8:30 (8:32) (Class 6) (0-55,55) 4-Y-O+
£3,105 (£924; £461; £400; £400; £400) **Stalls** Low

Form RPR

4510 **1** **Amor Fati (IRE)**[8] 1060 4-9-4 **52** AdamKirby 9 60
(David Evans) *dwlt: hld up in tch: clsd and nt clr run 2f out: swtchd rt over 1f out: hdwy u.p 1f out: led 100yds out: r.o wl* **5/2**[1]

0-30 **2** *1 ¼* **Monsieur Fox**[16] 923 4-9-6 **54** RichardKingscote 4 59
(Lydia Richards) *wl in tch: effrt over 1f out: drvn and styd on to chal ins fnl f: no ex and outpcd by wnr fnl 50yds* **9/2**[3]

2203 **3** *2* **Sea Shack**[8] 1060 5-8-13 **54** (tp) ScottMcCullagh(7) 10 55
(Julia Feilden) *chsd ldr: rdn and ev ch over 1f out: led 1f out: hdd 100yds out: no ex and outpcd wl ins fnl f* **3/1**[2]

-600 **4** *¾* **Dukes Meadow**[29] 724 8-8-7 **46** oh1 RhiainIngram(5) 2 45
(Roger Ingram) *t.k.h: hld up in tch towards rr: effrt on inner over 1f out: chsd ldrs ins fnl f: no imp fnl 100yds* **20/1**

0440 **5** *½* **Malaysian Boleh**[16] 925 9-8-12 **46** oh1 (be) CallumShepherd 7 44
(Phil McEntee) *hld up in tch in midfield: rdn over 2f out: unable qck and no imp: no threat to ldrs but kpt on again ins fnl f* **14/1**

6020 **6** *½* **Admiral Rooke (IRE)**[10] 1021 4-9-0 **55** (p) MarkCrehan(7) 6 52
(Michael Appleby) *t.k.h: led: rdn and hrd pressed over 1f out: hdd 1f out: no ex and wknd ins fnl f* **10/1**

2165 **7** *1 ½* **Rapid Rise (IRE)**[10] 1026 5-9-0 **48** (p) LukeMorris 3 41
(Milton Bradley) *broke wl: hld up in tch in midfield: effrt 2f out: unable qck over 1f out: wknd ins fnl f* **16/1**

5000 **8** *¾* **Shovel It On (IRE)**[15] 941 4-8-12 **46** oh1 (b) RaulDaSilva 8 38
(Steve Flook) *midfield on outer: rdn over 3f out: unable qck over 1f out: wknd ins fnl f* **33/1**

1620 **9** *¾* **Diamond Reflection (IRE)**[24] 792 7-9-6 **54** (tp) RossaRyan 12 44
(Alexandra Dunn) *dwlt: hld up in tch towards rr: effrt and hung lft over 1f out: nvr involved (jockey said gelding was never travelling)* **16/1**

5-00 **10** *1 ¼* **Cooperess**[11] 1015 6-9-1 **49** DavidProbert 1 36
(Dai Burchell) *wl in tch in midfield: unable qck over 1f out and btn 1f out: wknd ins fnl f* **11/1**

/00- **11** *25* **Pocket Warrior**[281] 3526 8-8-13 **52** (p[1]) TheodoreLadd(5) 5
(Paul D'Arcy) *t.k.h: hld up in tch in midfield: swtchd rt and hdwy to chse ldrs over 4f out: rdn over 2f out: lost pl and btn over 1f out: bhd and eased ins fnl f* **12/1**

0-00 **12** *12* **Dunstall Dreamer**[50] 384 4-8-12 **46** oh1 KieranO'Neill 11
(Denis Quinn) *s.i.s: a outpcd in rr: eased over 1f out: t.o* **50/1**

1m 39.3s (-0.60) **Going Correction** 0.0s/f (Stan) **12** Ran SP% **125.0**
Speed ratings (Par 101): **103,101,99,99,98 98,96,95,95,93 68,56**
CSF £14.45 CT £37.55 TOTE £3.00: £1.50, £1.80, £1.60; EX 15.30 Trifecta £66.60.
Owner Mrs Catherine Gannon **Bred** Tony O'Meara **Trained** Pandy, Monmouths

FOCUS
Ordinary fare, but the winner did it nicely. The second has been rated near the balance of his better form.
T/Plt: £33.90 to a £1 stake. Pool: £58,235.11 - 1,251.43 winning units. T/Qpdt: £6.10 to a £1 stake. Pool: £11624.73 - 1,398.03 winning units. **Steve Payne**

1178 LINGFIELD (L-H)
Friday, March 15

OFFICIAL GOING: Polytrack: standard
Weather: Overcast

1216 LADBROKES HOME OF THE ODDS BOOST FILLIES' H'CAP 1m 1y(P)
2:20 (2:20) (Class 5) (0-70,69) 4-Y-O+
£3,752 (£1,116; £557; £300; £300; £300) **Stalls** High

Form RPR

020- **1** **Gainsay**[180] 7335 4-9-4 **66** RobHornby 2 73+
(Jonathan Portman) *hld up: pushed along and hdwy on outside wl over 1f out: led ins fnl f pushed out: comf* **6/1**[3]

-233 **2** *1 ½* **Dashing Poet**[43] 507 5-9-3 **65** DavidEgan 4 67
(Heather Main) *trckd ldrs: n.m.r and lost pl over 4f out: effrt whn nt clr run over 2f out to over 1f out: angled lft and kpt on wl fnl f to take 2nd nr fin: no ch w wnr* **9/4**[1]

43-6 **3** *hd* **Helfire**[7] 1075 6-8-8 **56** CharlieBennett 7 58
(Martin Bosley) *rn wout declared tongue tie: t.k.h: hld up in tch: hdwy on outside to ld over 1f out: hdd ins fnl f: kpt on same pce* **10/1**

600- **4** *nk* **Met By Moonlight**[170] 7661 5-9-5 **67** DavidProbert 5 68
(Ron Hodges) *walked to s: t.k.h: in tch: hdwy to ld 3f out: rdn and hdd over 1f out: rallied: one pce ins fnl f (jockey said mare ran too free in early stages)* **33/1**

205- **5** *hd* **Cheerfilly (IRE)**[177] 7427 5-9-5 **67** OisinMurphy 8 68
(Archie Watson) *s.i.s: sn cl up: effrt and rdn over 1f out: kpt on same pce ins fnl f* **5/2**[2]

500- **6** *nk* **Mississippi Miss**[150] 8298 5-8-7 **55** HollieDoyle 1 55
(Dr Jon Scargill) *hld up: effrt and pushed along on outside over 1f out: kpt on fnl f: nvr able to chal* **20/1**

3-30 **7** *3 ¾* **Mrs Benson (IRE)**[51] 364 4-9-4 **66** (h[1]) AdamKirby 9 57
(Michael Blanshard) *stdd and swtchd lft s: hld up: effrt and pushed along 2f out: sn no imp* **9/1**

23-3 **8** *1 ¾* **Golden Nectar**[15] 944 5-9-7 **69** LukeMorris 10 56
(Laura Mongan) *cl up: drvn along over 2f out: wknd fnl f* **13/2**

3156 **9** *8* **Rippling Waters (FR)**[22] 828 5-9-1 **63** (t[1]) DougieCostello 6 32
(Jamie Osborne) *t.k.h: led 2f: prom: nt clr run over 2f out: lost pl and rdn over 1f out: sn btn* **20/1**

4/0- **10** *20* **Beautiful Artist (USA)**[434] 78 4-9-3 **65** (p) KieranO'Neill 3
(Robyn Brisland) *cl up: led after 2f to 3f out: outpcd whn faltered ent st: sn eased (jockey said filly hung left-handed under pressure)* **50/1**

1m 37.9s (-0.30) **Going Correction** -0.075s/f (Stan) **10** Ran SP% **120.5**
Speed ratings (Par 100): **98,96,96,96,95 95,91,90,82,62**
CSF £19.80 CT £140.22 TOTE £8.00: £2.00, £1.80, £2.50; EX 23.60 Trifecta £182.30.
Owner Fillies First **Bred** Llety Farms **Trained** Upper Lambourn, Berks

FOCUS
Not particularly deep in terms of in-form contenders but the gallop looked an even one and there weren't any major hard-luck stories, although backers of the runner-up might feel she should have gone closer. The fourth has been rated close to the balance of her form.

1217 LIKE SUNRACING ON FACEBOOK NOVICE STKS 1m 1y(P)
3:00 (3:00) (Class 5) 3-Y-O+ **£3,752** (£1,116; £557; £278) **Stalls** High

Form RPR

1 **Train To Georgia (USA)** 3-8-8 0 OisinMurphy 8 74+
(Joseph Tuite) *hld up in tch: pushed along and rn green over 2f out: rallied over 1f out: edgd lft and led ins fnl f: pushed clr* **9/2**

06- 2 2 **Maqaadeer**[203] 6490 3-8-8 0 BenCurtis 5 69
(Ed Dunlop) *led 1f: pressed ldr: effrt and rdn 2f out: chsd wnr wl ins fnl f: r.o: nt pce to chal* **3/1**[3]

4- 3 ¾ **Dame Freya Stark**[296] 2973 3-8-3 0 JoeFanning 4 62
(Mark Johnston) *t.k.h: led after 1f: shkn up ent st: hdd ins fnl f: kpt on same pce* **9/4**[1]

00 4 4½ **Poor Auld Paddy**[9] 1033 3-8-8 0 DavidProbert 10 57
(David Elsworth) *trckd ldrs: drvn along over 2f out: outpcd fnl f* **33/1**

5 2½ **Osho** 3-8-8 0 (w) TomMarquand 7 51
(Richard Hannon) *trckd ldrs: drvn along 3f out: wknd over 1f out* **11/4**[2]

00- 6 nk **Confils (FR)**[172] 7613 3-8-3 0 KieranO'Neill 6 46
(George Baker) *hld up on ins: effrt and pushed along over 2f out: no imp fr over 1f out* **20/1**

00 7 3¼ **Whims Of Desire**[13] 979 3-8-3 0 LukeMorris 1 38
(Sir Mark Prescott Bt) *s.i.s: sn pushed along briefly in midfield: shkn up over 2f out: no imp whn edgd lft over 1f out: sn btn* **66/1**

50-0 8 3 **West Newton**[13] 979 3-8-8 0 EdwardGreatrex 9 36
(Roger Charlton) *sn pushed along in rr: struggling 3f out: nvr on terms (jockey said colt was never travelling)* **25/1**

505 9 nk **Hen (IRE)**[14] 967 3-8-3 0 NicolaCurrie 2 30
(Jamie Osborne) *s.i.s: hld up: rdn and outpcd over 2f out: sn btn* **66/1**

10 5 **Noverre Dancer (IRE)** 3-8-8 0 EoinWalsh 3 24
(Nick Littmoden) *slowly away: rn green in rr: struggling fr 3f out* **33/1**

1m 36.35s (-1.85) **Going Correction** -0.075s/f (Stan) **10 Ran SP% 118.1**
Speed ratings (Par 103): **106,104,103,98,96 95,92,89,89,84**
CSF £17.48 TOTE £4.80: £1.60, £1.30, £1.30; EX 21.60 Trifecta £77.60.
Owner Matt & Lauren Morgan **Bred** Edward A Seltzer & Beverly Anderson **Trained** Lambourn, Berks

FOCUS
No standout form contender in what was probably an ordinary novice event, but fair play to the winner who defied a major market drift pre-race and is clearly quite useful. The level is a bit fluid. The fourth has been rated similar to his previous efforts.

1218 SUN RACING CLAIMING STKS 7f 1y(P)
3:40 (3:40) (Class 6) 3-Y-O+ **£3,105** (£924; £461; £300; £300) **Stalls** Low

Form RPR

31-4 1 **Unforgiving Minute**[70] 56 8-10-0 85 JamesDoyle 3 67+
(John Butler) *trckd ldr: drvn to ld over 2f out: edgd lft over 1f out: kpt on wl fnl f* **1/2**[1]

0-2 2 2¼ **Upavon**[59] 247 9-9-11 84 AdamKirby 5 58+
(Tony Carroll) *stdd s: t.k.h and sn trcking ldrs: drvn over 2f out: rallied and chsd wnr ins fnl f: edgd lft: r.o* **7/1**[3]

1-21 3 1½ **Loyalty**[28] 734 12-9-9 86 (v) PaddyMathers 2 52+
(Derek Shaw) *t.k.h: led at stdy pce: hdd and rdn over 2f out: rallied: no ex and lost 2nd ins fnl f* **5/2**[2]

-000 4 4½ **Valentine Mist (IRE)**[15] 942 7-9-4 39 GeorgeWood 4 35
(James Grassick) *prom: drvn along over 2f out: wknd over 1f out* **100/1**

50-0 5 6 **High Language (IRE)**[11] 1017 5-9-8 90 DannyBrock 6 23
(Philip McBride) *s.i.s: hld up in tch: struggling wl over 2f out: sn btn* **25/1**

1m 25.38s (0.58) **Going Correction** -0.075s/f (Stan) **5 Ran SP% 112.6**
Speed ratings (Par 101): **93,90,88,83,76**
CSF £5.12 TOTE £1.50: £1.10, £1.80; EX 4.80 Trifecta £6.80.
Owner Power Geneva Ltd **Bred** Equine Breeding Limited **Trained** Newmarket, Suffolk

FOCUS
A result foretold by the market with the winner going off a very warm order despite the disadvantageous terms of this claimer. The fourth anchors the form.

1219 LADBROKES H'CAP 6f 1y(P)
4:20 (4:20) (Class 5) (0-75,77) 3-Y-O
£3,752 (£1,116; £557; £300; £300; £300) **Stalls** Low

Form RPR

332- 1 **Warning Fire**[147] 8369 3-9-2 70 JoeFanning 3 74
(Mark Johnston) *t.k.h early: trckd ldrs on ins: effrt and rdn over 1f out: led ins fnl f: edgd rt: kpt on wl* **4/1**[2]

1-30 2 ¾ **Klass Action (IRE)**[22] 838 3-9-7 75 (b[1]) LukeMorris 5 76
(Sir Mark Prescott Bt) *dwlt: sn pushed along and prom: effrt and rn wd bnd ent st: edgd lft and rallied fnl f: kpt on to take 2nd nr fin* **8/1**

03-1 3 hd **Distant Mirage**[41] 555 3-9-3 71 OisinMurphy 6 71
(James Tate) *trckd ldr: effrt and ev ch over 1f out to ins fnl f: sn pressing wnr: no ex and lost 2nd nr fin* **6/5**[1]

216- 4 ½ **Fizzy Feet (IRE)**[195] 6798 3-9-4 72 BenCurtis 4 70
(David Loughnane) *led: rdn along 2f out: hdd ins fnl f: kpt on same pce* **14/1**

2453 5 ½ **Beleaguerment (IRE)**[10] 1028 3-9-2 77 (b) Pierre-LouisJamin(7) 1 74
(Archie Watson) *dwlt: sn pushed along bhd ldng gp: stdy hdwy after 2f: drvn and effrt whn rn wd bnd ent st: kpt on fnl f: nrst fin* **9/2**[3]

10-0 6 hd **Kapono**[53] 342 3-9-8 76 GeorgeWood 2 72
(Amy Murphy) *in tch on ins: rdn over 2f out: effrt over 1f out: r.o same pce ins fnl f* **25/1**

000- 7 2¼ **Broughtons Flare (IRE)**[160] 7983 3-8-12 66 ow1 StevieDonohoe 8 55
(Philip McBride) *s.i.s: bhd: struggling wl over 2f out: rallied fnl f: nvr able to chal* **14/1**

410- 8 4 **Penarth Pier (IRE)**[193] 6882 3-8-10 71 MarkCrehan(7) 9 47
(Richard Hannon) *s.i.s: bhd: outpcd and detached over 2f out: sme late hdwy: nvr on terms* **20/1**

030- 9 72 **Maid From The Mist**[172] 7617 3-8-2 56 NicolaCurrie 7
(John Gallagher) *bhd: struggling 1/2-way: virtually p.u fnl 2f (jockey said filly was never travelling)* **66/1**

1m 10.38s (-1.52) **Going Correction** -0.075s/f (Stan) **9 Ran SP% 118.2**
Speed ratings (Par 98): **107,106,105,105,104 104,101,95,**
CSF £35.83 CT £60.59 TOTE £4.40: £1.90, £1.50, £1.30; EX 31.40 Trifecta £82.80.
Owner Sheikh Hamdan bin Mohammed Al Maktoum **Bred** Godolphin **Trained** Middleham Moor, N Yorks

FOCUS
A competitive little handicap run at what looked to the naked eye a decent gallop. Having said that, they finished in a bit of heap and it's hard to know exactly how strong the form is. The level is set around the third and fourth.

1220 BETWAY LIVE CASINO H'CAP 1m 4f (P)
5:00 (5:00) (Class 3) (0-95,97) 4-Y-O **£7,246** (£2,168; £1,084; £542; £270) **Stalls** Low

Form RPR

00-1 1 **Petite Jack**[20] 878 6-9-8 95 JamesDoyle 3 103+
(Neil King) *trckd ldrs on ins: shkn up to ld appr fnl f: drvn out* **5/2**[1]

1512 2 1¼ **Glan Y Gors (IRE)**[15] 948 7-8-5 78 (b[1]) KieranO'Neill 6 83
(David Thompson) *t.k.h: led: rdn over 2f out: hdd appr fnl f: kpt on same pce last 100yds* **10/1**

010- 3 1¾ **Fire Fighting (IRE)**[266] 4064 8-9-10 97 AdamKirby 1 99
(Mark Johnston) *hld up in tch: drvn and outpcd over 2f out: rallied fnl f: tk 3rd cl home* **7/1**

1153 4 hd **Fearsome**[11] 1017 5-9-1 91 JoshuaBryan(3) 7 93
(Nick Littmoden) *stdd in last pl: stdy hdwy 3f out: effrt and chsd ldng pair 1f out: sn one pce: lost 3rd cl home* **3/1**[2]

400- 5 1¾ **Paddyplex**[330] 1919 6-8-11 84 (w) JasonHart 4 83
(Karen McLintock) *pressed ldr to over 1f out: drvn and outpcd ins fnl f* **9/1**

-464 6 ¾ **Eddystone Rock (IRE)**[20] 878 7-9-0 87 KierenFox 2 85
(John Best) *dwlt: hld up: stdy hdwy over 3f out: drvn and outpcd on wd outside bnd ent st: n.d after* **4/1**[3]

150- 7 1 **Reverend Jacobs**[76] 7241 5-9-4 91 DavidProbert 5 87
(Alan King) *prom: stdy hdwy over 3f out: rdn and wknd over 1f out (jockey said gelding suffered interference rounding the final bend)* **7/1**

2m 34.2s (1.20) **Going Correction** -0.075s/f (Stan) **7 Ran SP% 117.7**
Speed ratings (Par 107): **93,92,91,90,89 89,88**
CSF £29.17 TOTE £3.00: £2.10, £5.90; EX 32.90 Trifecta £215.20.
Owner W Burn **Bred** Mrs Liz Nelson Mbe **Trained** Barbury Castle, Wilts

FOCUS
A decent handicap run at a sound gallop. Solid form for the grade. The winner has been rated to his old best, and the second to his recent form.

1221 LADBROKES HOME OF THE ODDS BOOST NOVICE STKS (PLUS 10 RACE) 1m 4f (P)
5:40 (5:40) (Class 5) 3-Y-O **£3,752** (£1,116; £557; £278) **Stalls** Low

Form RPR

21 1 **Cirque Royal**[29] 723 3-9-9 0 JamesDoyle 8 90+
(Charlie Appleby) *pressed ldr: led gng wl 3f out: pushed clr fr over 1f out: eased towards fin: readily* **5/6**[1]

5 2 7 **Blood Eagle (IRE)**[64] 156 3-9-2 0 RobHornby 3 72
(Andrew Balding) *trckd ldrs: rdn over 2f out: rallied and chsd (clr) wnr ins fnl f: nt pce to chal* **5/1**[3]

3 3 1½ **Allocator (FR)**[56] 299 3-9-2 0 SeanLevey 7 70
(Richard Hannon) *dwlt: t.k.h and sn prom on outside: pushed along and effrt 2f out: kpt on same pce ins fnl f* **3/1**[2]

32 4 ½ **Alpasu (IRE)**[21] 858 3-9-2 0 (t) EdwardGreatrex 1 69
(Archie Watson) *led to 3f out: rallied: lost 2nd ins fnl f: fdd* **11/1**

06 5 7 **Enyama (GER)**[21] 858 3-8-11 0 WilliamCarson 5 53
(Michael Attwater) *hld up: pushed along and outpcd over 2f out: rallied over 1f out: nvr able to chal* **100/1**

2 6 hd **Heavenly Tale (IRE)**[42] 518 3-8-11 0 OisinMurphy 2 52
(Ralph Beckett) *t.k.h: in tch: drvn and outpcd over 2f out: edgd rt and no imp over 1f out* **16/1**

7 hd **Message** 3-9-2 0 JoeFanning 4 57
(Mark Johnston) *slowly away: rn green in rr: shortlived effrt on outside over 3f out: struggling fnl 2f* **10/1**

0-5 7 dht **Surrey Breeze (IRE)**[21] 858 3-9-2 0 HollieDoyle 6 57
(Archie Watson) *t.k.h: hld up in tch: rdn and outpcd over 2f out: btn over 1f out* **66/1**

2m 30.81s (-2.19) **Going Correction** -0.075s/f (Stan) **8 Ran SP% 122.0**
Speed ratings (Par 98): **104,99,98,98,93 93,93,93**
WIN: 1.80 Cirque Royal; PL: 1.02 Cirque Royal 1.40 Allocator 1.90 Blood Eagle; EX: 6.70; CSF: 6.25; TF: 14.20 CSF £6.25 TOTE £1.80: £1.02, £1.90, £1.40; EX 6.70 Trifecta £14.20.
Owner Godolphin **Bred** Godolphin **Trained** Newmarket, Suffolk

FOCUS
This looked quite a competitive heat on paper but the market spoke firmly in favour of the Godolphin runner and he absolutely bolted up. The level is a bit fluid.
T/Plt: £11.80 to a £1 stake. Pool: £65,105.32 - 4,018.15 winning units. T/Qpdt: £4.60 to a £1 stake. Pool: £4,191.78 - 661.01 winning units. **Richard Young**

1222 - 1230a (Foreign Racing) - See Raceform Interactive

1164 WOLVERHAMPTON (A.W) (L-H)
Saturday, March 16

OFFICIAL GOING: Tapeta: standard
Wind: windy Weather: cold, rain

1231 SUN RACING H'CAP 1m 142y (Tp)
5:40 (5:40) (Class 6) (0-60,60) 4-Y-O+
£3,105 (£924; £461; £400; £400; £400) **Stalls** Low

Form RPR

00-1 1 **Citta D'Oro**[23] 835 4-9-6 60 (p) RobHornby 8 66
(James Unett) *hld up: pushed along and hdwy on outer over 2f out: drvn 1 1/2f out: rdn to ld jst ins fnl f: r.o wl* **7/2**[1]

0204 2 ½ **Aqua Libre**[19] 911 6-9-6 60 (p) JoeFanning 3 65
(Jennie Candlish) *t.k.h: led 1f: trckd ldrs whn hdd: pushed along in 4th 2f out: drvn to chal on inner 1 1/2f out: rdn and ev ch in 2nd ins fnl f: kpt on* **9/1**

-532 3 nse **Kilbaha Lady (IRE)**[12] 1015 5-9-3 60 RowanScott(3) 2 65+
(Nigel Tinkler) *hld up: effrt gng wl on inner 1 1/2f out: sn pushed along and looking for room: in clr and rdn fnl f: r.o wl: tk 3rd last stride* **8/1**

6535 4 nse **Pike Corner Cross (IRE)**[18] 912 7-9-2 56 LukeMorris 1 61
(Alastair Ralph) *mid-div: pushed along 2f out: drvn and effrt 1 1/2f out: briefly nt clr run over 1f out: swtchd and hdwy ins fnl f: sn rdn and r.o wl: nvr nrr* **16/1**

-235 5 1 **Big Bad Lol (IRE)**[28] 760 5-9-5 59 (p) LiamKeniry 7 62
(Ed Walker) *trckd ldrs: gng wl in 5th 2f out: angled out to chal 1 1/2f out: rdn fnl f: one pce* **7/1**

2-20 6 1 **Blessed To Empress (IRE)**[31] 701 4-9-6 60 NicolaCurrie 5 61
(Amy Murphy) *prom: led after 1f: pushed along in narrow ld 2f out: sn drvn: rdn over 1f out: hdd jst ins fnl f: wknd* **11/1**

4141 **7** ½ **Don't Do It (IRE)**[14] 984 4-8-11 **56**..........(v) TheodoreLadd(5) 6 55
(Michael Appleby) *hld up: drvn and swtchd to outer 1 1/2f out: sn rdn: kpt on fnl f* **4/1**[2]

1645 **8** 1 **Sharp Operator**[12] 1015 6-9-4 **58**..........(h) RichardKingscote 4 55
(Charlie Wallis) *hld up: drvn 1 1/2f out: one pce fnl f* **11/2**[3]

-203 **9** 1 ¾ **Classic Charm**[23] 828 4-9-5 **59**.......... RobertWinston 11 53
(Dean Ivory) *prom on outer: pushed along in 3rd 2f out: ev ch over 1f out: rdn and wknd fnl f* **10/1**

-006 **10** 2 **Rock Warbler (IRE)**[18] 914 6-9-3 **57**..........(e) PhilDennis 9 47
(Michael Mullineaux) *hld up: drvn over 2f out: reminders and wknd fnl f* **28/1**

10-0 **11** 2 ¼ **Adventureman**[18] 912 7-9-4 **58**..........(p) JamesSullivan 12 43
(Ruth Carr) *prom: drvn in cl 2nd 2f out: rdn and wknd over 1f out* **40/1**

61/0 **12** 1 ½ **Rock Island Line**[26] 784 5-9-2 **56**..........(p) DougieCostello 13 38
(Mark Walford) *slowly away: bhd: nvr a factor* **40/1**

600- **13** 17 **Palawan**[264] 4203 6-9-2 **59**.......... GabrieleMalune(3) 10 5
(Katy Price) *slowly away: bhd: hdwy 1/2-way: drvn over 2f out: sn wknd and dropped to rr: eased fnl f* **50/1**

1m 48.38s (-1.72) **Going Correction** -0.175s/f (Stan) **13** Ran SP% **124.8**
Speed ratings (Par 101): **100,99,99,99,98 97,97,96,94,93 91,89,74**
CSF £36.53 CT £256.12 TOTE £4.50: £2.10, £2.70, £2.80; EX 46.10 Trifecta £179.40.
Owner P S Burke **Bred** P & Mrs N Burke **Trained** Wolverhampton, West Midlands

FOCUS
An ordinary handicap but a competitive one. The second has been rated to her January C&D form.

1232 SUNRACING.CO.UK H'CAP 1m 142y (Tp)

6:15 (6:15) (Class 3) (0-95,94) 4-Y-O+ £7,246 (£2,168; £1,084; £542; £270) Stalls Low

Form RPR

1112 **1** nse **Executive Force**[10] 1031 5-9-4 **91**..........(p) FrannyNorton 6 98+
(Michael Wigham) *mid-div: pushed along 2f out: drvn and effrt 1 1/2f out: rdn and checked whn making hdwy ins fnl f: sn in clr: r.o wl last 100yds to cl on wnr: jst failed: fin 2nd: awrdd r* **7/2**[2]

112- **2** **Salute The Soldier (GER)**[105] 9358 4-9-7 **94**.......... AdamKirby 3 100+
(Clive Cox) *mid-div: hdwy into 3rd 3f out: drvn to ld 1 1/2f out: rdn and almost jnd 1f out: wandered in narrow ld fnl f: r.o wl to repel chalrs either side last 100yds: demoted to 2nd* **1/1**[1]

52-0 **3** nse **Gurkha Friend**[17] 929 7-9-2 **89**.......... JasonHart 2 95
(Karen McLintock) *disp ld tl hdd after 2f and chsd ldr: drvn 2f out: rdn and almost alongside wnr 1f out: r.o fnl f: jst hld by front two (jockey said gelding hung right-handed in the home straight)* **25/1**

4-12 **4** ½ **Tough Remedy (IRE)**[24] 800 4-8-11 **89**.......... AndrewBreslin(5) 10 94
(Keith Dalgleish) *hld up in rr: rdn and hdwy 1 1/2f out: r.o wl fnl f: nvr nrr* **10/1**

2455 **5** 1 ½ **Mythical Madness**[14] 988 8-8-12 **92**..........(b) CierenFallon(7) 5 94
(David O'Meara) *hld up: pushed along and hdwy into 4th on outer 2f out: sn drvn: rdn fnl f: no ex (vet reported the gelding sustained a wound to its left fore)* **20/1**

-251 **6** 1 ¼ **Illustrissime (USA)**[25] 793 6-8-9 **82**..........(p) JoeyHaynes 1 81
(Ivan Furtado) *hld up: drvn in 6th 2f out: rdn fnl f: no imp* **10/1**

1434 **7** ½ **Michele Strogoff**[18] 915 6-9-2 **89**.......... AlistairRawlinson 9 87
(Michael Appleby) *disp ld tl led on own after 2f: 3 l ld 3f out: rdn in 1 l ld 2f out: hdd 1 1/2f out: wknd fnl f* **13/2**[3]

-330 **8** nk **Ballard Down (IRE)**[24] 805 6-9-6 **93**..........(p[1]) DanielTudhope 8 90
(David O'Meara) *slowly away: bhd: drvn on outer over 2f out: sn rdn: no imp* **22/1**

-605 **9** 3 ¾ **Contrast (IRE)**[29] 740 5-8-5 **78**.......... CamHardie 4 67
(Michael Easterby) *hld up: drvn over 2f out: nvr involved* **50/1**

043- **10** 11 **Staplegrove (IRE)**[264] 4196 4-8-4 **77**.......... KieranO'Neill 7 42
(Philip Kirby) *chsd ldrs: pushed along in 4th 2f out: sn drvn and lost pl: dropped to last over 1f out* **50/1**

1m 46.48s (-3.62) **Going Correction** -0.175s/f (Stan) **10** Ran SP% **120.6**
Speed ratings (Par 107): **108,109,108,108,107 106,105,105,101,92**
CSF £7.21 CT £74.41 TOTE £4.20: £1.10, £1.40, £7.20; EX 9.90 Trifecta £172.50.
Owner Tugay Akman **Bred** Rabbah Bloodstock Limited **Trained** Newmarket, Suffolk

FOCUS
This was a well-run handicap and little separated the first three at the line. The fourth has been rated to form.

1233 LADBROKES HOME OF THE ODDS BOOST H'CAP 1m 4f 51y (Tp)

6:45 (6:45) (Class 5) (0-75,75) 3-Y-O
£3,752 (£1,116; £557; £400; £400; £400) Stalls Low

Form RPR

024- **1** **Caplin**[133] 8834 3-9-5 **73**.......... JoeFanning 4 79+
(Mark Johnston) *mde all: set mod gallop: qckng pce 3f out: pushed along in 1 l ld 2f out: drvn further clr over 1f out: rdn in 3 l ld fnl f: nvr in danger and pushed out nr fin* **3/1**[2]

3-12 **2** 1 ½ **Paradise Boy (FR)**[23] 836 3-9-7 **75**.......... RobHornby 6 78
(Andrew Balding) *hld up: pushed along in 5th 2f out: rdn in 4th 1f out: styd on into 2nd fnl f: nvr nr wnr* **7/1**

4-13 **3** ¾ **Albert Finney**[23] 826 3-9-7 **75**..........(h) KieranO'Neill 1 77
(John Gosden) *t.k.h: trckd wnr: pushed along in 3rd 2f out: reminder 1 1/2f out: rdn and wnt 2nd ent fnl f: one pce and lost 2nd last 100yds* **1/1**[1]

0-42 **4** 1 **Thunderoad**[18] 917 3-9-4 **72**.......... TomMarquand 5 72
(Marco Botti) *prom: drvn in 1 l 2nd 2f out: rdn over 1f out: wknd and lost two pls fr 1f out* **13/2**[3]

5-21 **5** 1 ¾ **Natsovia**[18] 917 3-9-3 **71**.......... NicolaCurrie 2 68
(Jamie Osborne) *hld up in rr: drvn 2f out: rdn fr over 1f out: no imp* **12/1**

0-20 **6** 1 ¼ **Time Immemorial (IRE)**[9] 1066 3-8-11 **65**..........(b) DavidEgan 3 60
(Roger Varian) *hld up: pushed along and reminder in 4th 3f out: sn drvn and lost pl: dropped to last over 1f out* **20/1**

2m 39.57s (-1.23) **Going Correction** -0.175s/f (Stan) **6** Ran SP% **113.3**
Speed ratings (Par 98): **97,96,95,94,93 92**
CSF £23.72 TOTE £3.80: £2.70, £3.00; EX 22.90 Trifecta £40.50.
Owner S R Counsell **Bred** Stuart Counsell **Trained** Middleham Moor, N Yorks

FOCUS
This was steadily run and the winner controlled the pace. The third and fourth have been rated close to their latest runs.

1234 LADBROKES EBF FILLIES' H'CAP 7f 36y (Tp)

7:15 (7:15) (Class 3) (0-90,87) 4-Y-O+ £10,396 (£3,111; £1,555; £778; £387) Stalls High

Form RPR

2-11 **1** **Tiger Eye (IRE)**[15] 963 4-9-3 **83**.......... GeorgeWood 3 94+
(James Fanshawe) *mid-div: pushed along in 3rd 2f out: hdwy to chal ldr 1 1/2f out: led over 1f out: drvn clr fnl f: comf* **11/10**[1]

-223 **2** 2 **Treasure Me**[16] 951 4-8-9 **82**..........(p) AledBeech(7) 7 85
(Charlie Fellowes) *chsd ldrs: drvn in 4th 2f out: rdn 1 1/2f out: r.o wl fnl f: tk 2nd nr fin* **11/2**[3]

0-50 **3** hd **Starlight Romance (IRE)**[24] 805 5-9-2 **87**.......... ConnorMurtagh(5) 6 90
(Richard Fahey) *hld up: pushed along in last 2f out: rdn on outer over 1f out: r.o wl fnl f: tk 3rd last stride* **12/1**

6-11 **4** shd **Toy Theatre**[16] 951 5-9-4 **87**.......... JaneElliott(3) 1 89
(Michael Appleby) *chsd ldr: drvn in 2 l 2nd 2f out: rdn in 3rd over 1f out: kpt on fnl f: lost 3rd last stride* **5/2**[2]

1130 **5** shd **Happy Escape**[28] 756 5-9-1 **81**.......... TomMarquand 5 83
(Tony Carroll) *bhd: pushed along 2f out: rdn and hdwy over 1f out: r.o fnl f: nvr nrr* **14/1**

10-3 **6** ¾ **Emily Goldfinch**[9] 1063 6-9-3 **83**..........(p) RossaRyan 8 83
(Phil McEntee) *trckd across fr wd draw to ld: drvn in 2 l ld 2f out: rdn and hdd over 1f out: wknd fnl f* **28/1**

0-03 **7** 2 **Sonnet Rose (IRE)**[31] 697 5-8-3 **68** oh1 ow1..........(bt) MartinDwyer 4 64
(Conrad Allen) *hld up: pushed along in 6th 2f out: rdn fnl f: no imp* **12/1**

4442 **8** 3 ¾ **Ventura Blues (IRE)**[16] 951 5-8-7 **73**..........(p) LukeMorris 2 57
(Alexandra Dunn) *hld up: drvn in 5th 2f out: sn rdn and wknd* **22/1**

1m 26.53s (-2.27) **Going Correction** -0.175s/f (Stan) **8** Ran SP% **121.4**
Speed ratings (Par 104): **105,102,102,102,102 101,99,94**
CSF £8.58 CT £52.26 TOTE £1.80: £1.10, £1.80, £2.70; EX 7.60 Trifecta £56.20.
Owner Qatar Racing Limited **Bred** Orpendale,Wynatt,Chelston & Daylesford **Trained** Newmarket, Suffolk
■ Stewards' Enquiry : Rossa Ryan two-day ban: interference & careless riding (Mar 30-31)

FOCUS
This was a soundly run handicap and the winner is nicely on the upgrade. The second has been rated close to form.

1235 BETWAY HEED YOUR HUNCH H'CAP 1m 5f 219y (Tp)

7:45 (7:45) (Class 6) (0-65,65) 4-Y-O+
£3,105 (£924; £461; £400; £400; £400) Stalls Low

Form RPR

3611 **1** **Singing The Blues (IRE)**[17] 923 4-9-7 **62**.......... RobHornby 11 70+
(Rod Millman) *chsd ldrs: pushed along and hdwy over 2f out: rdn to ld 1 1/2f out: 1 l ld 1f out: asserted fnl f: pushed out nr fin* **4/1**[3]

0-01 **2** 1 **Tour De Paris (IRE)**[24] 810 4-9-8 **63**..........(v) TomMarquand 7 70
(Alan King) *hld up: hdwy 1 1/2f out: drvn into 3rd 1f out: rdn and styd on into 2nd fnl f: no threat to wnr* **3/1**[1]

223/ **3** nk **Broughtons Admiral**[15] 7790 5-9-9 **62**..........(b) LukeMorris 1 66
(Alastair Ralph) *slowly away: in rr: drvn 3f out: rdn over 2f out: hdwy 1 1/2f out: styd on u.p fnl f: tk 3rd last 25yds* **9/2**

5-02 **4** 1 ¼ **Enmeshing**[11] 1022 6-9-12 **65**.......... RossaRyan 3 67
(Alexandra Dunn) *hld up: hdwy gng wl 2f out: drvn to chal 1 1/2f out: rdn in 1 l 2nd 1f out: no ex and lost two pls fnl f* **7/1**

-400 **5** 3 ¾ **Masters Apprentice (IRE)**[11] 1024 4-9-5 **60**.......... DavidEgan 12 59
(Sylvester Kirk) *chsd ldrs: drvn to ld 2f out: hdd 1 1/2f out: sn rdn and no ex* **22/1**

2-60 **6** 4 ½ **Strictly Art (IRE)**[16] 946 6-9-9 **65**..........(p) JoshuaBryan(3) 8 56
(Alan Bailey) *hld up: pushed along 2f out: rdn 1 1/2f out: kpt on fnl f (jockey said gelding was never travelling)* **20/1**

0-6P **7** 3 **Sark (IRE)**[29] 736 6-9-0 **53**.......... CharlesBishop 9 40
(David Evans) *mid-div: drvn 3f out: rdn 1 1/2f out: no imp* **28/1**

-352 **8** 3 **Rail Dancer**[17] 923 7-9-6 **59**..........(v) AdamKirby 2 41
(Shaun Keightley) *chsd ldrs: drvn in 5th 2f out: wknd over 1f out* **7/2**[2]

000- **9** 11 **Incus**[27] 9159 6-9-2 **55**.......... CallumShepherd 4 22
(Ed de Giles) *led: pushed along 4f out: rdn 3f out: hdd 2f out: sn wknd* **14/1**

1-05 **10** 6 **Handsome Bob (IRE)**[17] 927 4-9-10 **65**..........(v) JasonHart 13 26
(Keith Dalgleish) *chsd ldr: drvn in 2nd 3f out: rdn and wknd 1 1/2f out* **40/1**

13/0 **11** 1 ¼ **Dltripleseven (IRE)**[16] 947 6-9-2 **55**.......... WilliamCarson 10 12
(David W Drinkwater) *hld up: drvn 4f out: rdn in last over 2f out: no rspnse* **66/1**

3m 0.14s (-0.86) **Going Correction** -0.175s/f (Stan)
WFA 4 from 5yo+ 2lb **11** Ran SP% **121.1**
Speed ratings (Par 101): **95,94,94,93,91 88,87,85,79,75 74**
CSF £15.99 CT £57.68 TOTE £4.50: £1.90, £1.50, £2.20; EX 21.00 Trifecta £97.00.
Owner Rod Millman & Andy Smith **Bred** Lynn Lodge Stud **Trained** Kentisbeare, Devon

FOCUS
A modest affair but the winner is improving. The race has been rated a fraction positively.

1236 BETWAY MAIDEN STKS 6f 20y (Tp)

8:15 (8:15) (Class 5) 3-Y-O+ £3,752 (£1,116; £557; £278) Stalls Low

Form RPR

1 **Global Prospector (USA)** 3-9-1 **0**.......... AdamKirby 13 85+
(Clive Cox) *led after 1/2f: mde rest: 2 l ld 2f out: readily stretched into 3 l ld 1f out: in command and r.o wl fnl f: quite impressive* **3/1**[2]

0- **2** 3 ¼ **Moss Gill (IRE)**[299] 2909 3-9-1 **0**.......... JosephineGordon 11 72
(James Bethell) *chsd ldrs: pushed along in 3rd 2f out: rdn over 1f out: kpt on into 2nd fnl f: no ch w wnr* **16/1**

25- **3** ½ **Phosphor (IRE)**[141] 8606 3-9-1 **0**.......... RobHornby 5 70
(Martyn Meade) *chsd ldrs: pushed along in 4th 2f out: sn drvn: rdn 1f out: hung in bhd rival ins fnl f: sn stened and r.o to take 3rd nr fin* **5/6**[1]

2 **4** nk **Wise Words**[16] 954 3-8-10 **0**.......... FrannyNorton 12 64
(James Tate) *led 1/2f: chsd ldr whn hdd: pushed along in 2 l 2nd 2f out: rdn 1 1/2f out: no ex and lost two pls ins fnl f* **5/1**[3]

-23 **5** 4 ½ **Empty Promises**[19] 908 3-8-12 **0**.......... FinleyMarsh(3) 10 55
(Frank Bishop) *t.k.h: hld up: drvn 1 1/2f out: one pce fnl f* **33/1**

6 ½ **Victory Rose** 3-8-10 **0**.......... NicolaCurrie 9 48
(Luke McJannet) *hld up on outer: pushed along 2f out: kpt on fr over 1f out* **50/1**

00 **7** ½ **Frea**[57] 289 3-8-10 **0**.......... LukeMorris 7 46
(Harry Dunlop) *chsd ldrs: drvn in 5th 2f out: wknd over 1f out* **80/1**

6 **8** 1 ¼ **Easy Money (IRE)**[51] 384 4-9-9 **0**.......... BenSanderson(5) 4 51
(Roger Fell) *slowly away: bhd: drvn and reminder over 1f out: no imp (jockey said gelding ran too freely)* **33/1**

6-4 **9** 1 ½ **Ghost Buy (FR)**[50] 408 3-9-1 **0**..........(t[1]) JasonHart 2 43
(Ivan Furtado) *hld up: pushed along over 2f out: reminder over 1f out: no imp* **22/1**

10 1 **Arvensis** 3-8-10 **0**.......... CharlieBennett 3 34
(Hughie Morrison) *slowly away: bhd: reminder 1f out: no rspnse* **33/1**

11 ½ **Bannockburn (IRE)** 3-9-1 **0**.......... JoeFanning 8 38
(Keith Dalgleish) *slowly away: bhd: pushed along on outer over 2f out: no rspnse* **22/1**

12 *nk* **Lauberhorn Rocket (GER)**[336] 1811 4-10-0 0 .... KieranO'Neill 6 41
(Tim Vaughan) *bhd: pushed along over 2f out: rdn over 1f out: nvr involved* **50/1**

00 13 *3* **Doti**[16] 943 3-8-10 0 .... GeorgeWood 1 22
(Rod Millman) *t.k.h: mid-div: drvn and wknd 2f out* **100/1**

1m 12.81s (-1.69) **Going Correction** -0.175s/f (Stan) 13 Ran SP% **125.8**
WFA 3 from 4yo 13lb
Speed ratings (Par 103): **104,99,99,98,92 91,91,89,87,86 85,85,81**
CSF £45.86 TOTE £4.20: £1.70, £2.40, £1.10; EX 61.00 Trifecta £118.00.
Owner Dr Johnny Hon **Bred** Tada Nobutaka **Trained** Lambourn, Berks

FOCUS
A good performance from the winner, who drew clear to win nicely on his debut. The level is a bit fluid.
T/Plt: £20.20 to a £1 stake. Pool: £94,847.89 - 3,420.81 winning units T/Qpdt: £6.70 to a £1 stake. Pool: £11,109.92 - 1,214.08 winning units **Keith McHugh**

1237 - 1239a (Foreign Racing) - See Raceform Interactive

1127 SAINT-CLOUD (L-H)

Sunday, March 17

OFFICIAL GOING: Turf: heavy

1240a PRIX DE LA MARCHE (CLAIMER) (2YO) (TURF) 4f 110y
1:00 2-Y-O £10,360 (£4,144; £3,108; £2,072; £1,036)

RPR

1 **Throttle Control (IRE)** 2-8-11 0 .... AurelienLemaitre 5 60
(J-V Toux, France) **101/10**

2 *snk* **The Nile Song (FR)** 2-8-8 0 .... MickaelBarzalona 10 56
(Jane Soubagne, France) **57/10**[3]

3 *nse* **Wedding Proposal (FR)** 2-9-4 0 .... AntoineHamelin 2 66
(B De Montzey, France) **41/10**[1]

4 *nse* **Has D'Emra (FR)** 2-9-1 0 .... SylvainRuis 4 63
(C Plisson, France) **16/1**

5 *2 1/2* **Can't Hold Us (FR)** 2-8-11 0 .... JeromeMoutard(4) 1 53
(D Allard, France) **136/10**

6 *1 1/4* **Panthera Tigris** 2-8-5 0 .... GeorgiaDobie(3) 3 41
(Jo Hughes, France) *chsd ldrs on inner: outpcd and drvn 1/2-way: kpt on under hands and heels fnl f* **166/10**

7 *nk* **Captain Tatman (FR)** 2-9-4 0 .... TheoBachelot 11 50
(George Baker) *midfield towards centre of trck: outpcd and drvn 1/2-way: styd on ins fnl f: nvr in contention* **58/10**

8 *1 1/2* **Miss Tiche (IRE)** 2-8-11 0 .... CristianDemuro 12 37
(A Peraino, Italy) **89/10**

9 *5* **Gift Account** 2-8-11 0 .... AlexisBadel 8 17
(Mick Channon) *pressed ldrs: drvn and edgd rt 1 1/2f fr home: wknd fnl f* **11/2**[2]

10 *2 1/2* **Divergente (FR)** 2-8-8 0 .... AnthonyCrastus 9
(Jane Soubagne, France) **83/10**

11 *nse* **Kiastep (FR)** 2-8-9 0 .... QuentinPerrette(6) 7
(Mme E Vibert, France) **34/1**

12 *1 1/4* **Happy Pepite (FR)** 2-8-8 0 .... MickaelForest 6
(C Plisson, France) **38/1**

56.37s 12 Ran SP% **118.3**
PARI-MUTUEL (all including 1 euro stake): WIN 11.10; PLACE 2.40, 2.00, 1.90; DF 38.00.
Owner Jean-Vincent Toux **Bred** Killura Agri Limited **Trained** France

1241a PRIX CADET ROUSSEL (MAIDEN) (3YO COLTS & GELDINGS) (TURF) 1m
2:50 3-Y-O £13,513 (£5,135; £3,783; £2,162; £1,081; £810)

RPR

1 **Dave (FR)**[72] 3-9-2 0 .... MaximeGuyon 8 88
(Mme Pia Brandt, France) **32/5**[3]

2 *6* **Eagle Hunter**[275] 3819 3-9-2 0 .... Pierre-CharlesBoudot 6 74
(F-H Graffard, France) **6/4**[1]

3 *1 3/4* **Trentino (FR)**[16] 3-9-2 0 .... HugoJourniac 9 70
(M Nigge, France) **36/5**

4 *snk* **Top Max (FR)**[143] 3-9-2 0 .... OlivierPeslier 2 70
(H-A Pantall, France) **27/10**[2]

5 *4* **Awesomedude**[95] 9500 3-9-2 0 .... AntoineHamelin 5 61
(Mrs Ilka Gansera-Leveque) *dwlt sltly: racd keenly and hld up in fnl trio: plld way to front after 2f: drvn and hdd 2f out: wknd appr fnl f* **49/1**

6 *1 3/4* **Never Come Back (FR)** 3-9-2 0 .... GlenBraem 3 57
(M Nigge, France) **49/1**

7 *shd* **Vysotsky (FR)**[123] 9055 3-9-2 0 .... AurelienLemaitre 4 57
(L Gadbin, France) **78/10**

8 *7* **Il Decamerone (FR)**[109] 3-9-2 0 .... JeffersonSmith 1 40
(Elias Mikhalides, France) **183/10**

9 *13* **Fire At Midnight (FR)**[27] 3-9-2 0 .... EddyHardouin 7 11
(N Caullery, France) **183/10**

1m 50.61s (3.11) 9 Ran SP% **118.5**
PARI-MUTUEL (all including 1 euro stake): WIN 7.40; PLACE 2.10, 1.40, 2.00; DF 8.50.
Owner Mme Georges Sandor **Bred** Mat Daguzan-Garros **Trained** France

1242a PRIX LA CAMARGO (LISTED RACE) (3YO FILLIES) (TURF) 1m
3:25 3-Y-O £24,774 (£9,909; £7,432; £4,954; £2,477)

RPR

1 **Tifosa (IRE)**[23] 3-9-0 0 .... MaximeGuyon 4 108+
(Mme Pia Brandt, France) **3/1**[2]

2 *2* **Jet Setteuse (FR)**[139] 3-9-0 0 .... Francois-XavierBertras 6 103+
(F Rohaut, France) **8/5**[1]

3 *2 1/2* **Hold True**[137] 8754 3-9-0 0 .... CristianDemuro 3 97
(D Smaga, France) **42/10**[3]

4 *5* **Waldblumchen (GER)**[128] 3-9-0 0 .... MickaelBarzalona 1 86
(G Botti, France) **8/1**

5 *3 1/2* **Gospel**[141] 8648 3-9-0 0 .... AlexisBadel 2 77
(Mick Channon) *led: drvn whn pressed 2f out: hdd 1 1/2f fr home: wknd fnl f* **123/10**

6 *7* **Gina Bere (FR)**[22] 3-9-0 0 .... OlivierPeslier 7 61
(D Guillemin, France) **23/5**

1m 49.79s (2.29) 6 Ran SP% **119.2**
PARI-MUTUEL (all including 1 euro stake): WIN 4.00; PLACE 1.80, 1.70; SF 8.50.
Owner Ecurie Des Charmes **Bred** Corduff Stud & J Corcoran **Trained** France

1243a PRIX OMNIUM II (LISTED RACE) (3YO COLTS & GELDINGS) (TURF) 1m
4:00 3-Y-O £24,774 (£9,909; £7,432; £4,954; £2,477)

RPR

1 **Shaman (IRE)**[143] 3-9-2 0 .... MaximeGuyon 8 109+
(C Laffon-Parias, France) **31/10**[2]

2 *2* **Sagauteur (FR)**[150] 3-9-2 0 .... Francois-XavierBertras 1 104
(D Guillemin, France) **84/10**

3 *4* **Go To Hollywood (FR)**[127] 9007 3-9-2 0 .... JeromeCabre 2 95
(Y Barberot, France) **207/10**

4 *3/4* **Prince Hamlet (FR)**[153] 3-9-2 0 .... StephanePasquier 7 93
(M Delcher Sanchez, France) **5/2**[1]

5 *3/4* **Joe Francais (FR)**[135] 3-9-2 0 .... ChristopheSoumillon 6 92
(J-C Rouget, France) **33/10**[3]

6 *3 1/2* **It's All A Dream (FR)**[12] 3-9-2 0 .... AntoineHamelin 4 84
(Matthieu Palussiere, France) **14/1**

7 *8* **Trouville (FR)**[35] 683 3-9-2 0 .... CristianDemuro 3 65
(C Ferland, France) **36/5**

8 *3 1/2* **Sir George (FR)** 3-9-2 0 .... OlivierPeslier 5 57
(E Libaud, France) **107/10**

1m 49.56s (2.06) 8 Ran SP% **118.9**
PARI-MUTUEL (all including 1 euro stake): WIN 4.10; PLACE 1.80, 2.80, 4.20; DF 19.50.
Owner Wertheimer & Frere **Bred** Wertheimer Et Frere **Trained** Chantilly, France

1244a PRIX EXBURY (GROUP 3) (4YO+) (TURF) 1m 2f
4:35 4-Y-O+ £36,036 (£14,414; £10,810; £7,207; £3,603)

RPR

1 **Soleil Marin (IRE)**[12] 1030 5-9-0 0 .... Pierre-CharlesBoudot 7 114
(A Fabre, France) *midfield outside rival: 6th and drvn 2f out: clsd u.p ins fnl 1 1/2f: styd on wl to ld fnl 75yds: won gng away* **19/2**[3]

2 *1 1/4* **Magny Cours (USA)**[24] 4-9-0 0 .... MickaelBarzalona 4 111
(A Fabre, France) *towards rr on outer: hdwy 2f out: led ins fnl 1 1/2f: styd on under driving: hdd fnl 75yds: no ex* **51/10**[2]

3 *3* **Air Pilot**[134] 8837 10-9-0 0 .... ChristopheSoumillon 3 105
(Ralph Beckett) *led: hdd after 1f: chsd ldr on inner: 3rd and travelling wl 2 1/2f out: drvn and no immediate imp under 2f out: kpt on at same pce fnl f but no match for front pair* **23/10**[1]

4 *1* **Sacred Life (FR)**[130] 8945 4-9-0 0 .... (p) TheoBachelot 6 103
(S Wattel, France) *chsd ldr outside rival: drvn and tried to chal wl over 2f out: kpt on at one pce u.p* **51/10**[2]

5 *3/4* **Way To Paris**[11] 6-9-0 0 .... (p) CristianDemuro 8 102
(Andrea Marcialis, France) *dwlt: w.w in fnl pair: rdn 2f out: kpt on u.p fnl f: nt pce to ever be in contention* **97/10**

6 *1 1/4* **King Platin (FR)**[36] 7-9-0 0 .... StephanePasquier 2 99
(Mme C Barande-Barbe, France) *midfield on inner: drvn 2f out but no imp: kpt on same pce fnl f* **122/10**

7 *3/4* **Ficelle Du Houley (FR)**[131] 8914 4-8-10 0 .... JeromeCabre 1 94
(Y Barberot, France) *racd keenly: hld up towards rr: rdn and btn 1 1/2f out: nvr competitive* **196/10**

8 *shd* **Dolphin Vista (IRE)**[178] 7450 6-9-0 0 .... MaximeGuyon 9 97
(Ralph Beckett) *lft after 1f: kicked for home 2 1/2f out: hdd ins fnl 1 1/2f: wknd* **51/10**[2]

9 *2 1/2* **Tosen Gift (IRE)**[127] 9008 4-8-10 0 .... GregoryBenoist 5 88
(S Kobayashi, France) *w.w in fnl pair: drvn and no imp 2f out: wl hld fnl f* **113/10**

2m 17.29s (1.29) 9 Ran SP% **118.9**
PARI-MUTUEL (all including 1 euro stake): WIN 3.80 (coupled with Magny Cours); PLACE 2.70, 2.40, 1.60; DF 15.40.
Owner Godolphin SNC **Bred** Ecurie Peregrine SAS **Trained** Chantilly, France

1245a PRIX DE LA COTE D'AZUR (H'CAP) (4YO+) (TURF) 1m 4f
5:10 4-Y-O+ £11,711 (£4,450; £3,279; £1,873; £936; £702)

RPR

1 **Gipsy Song (FR)**[121] 4-9-5 0 .... VincentCheminaud 15 87
(M Delzangles, France) **93/10**[3]

2 *1* **Maratino (FR)**[23] 4-9-5 0 .... (b) MickaelBarzalona 5 86
(C Lotoux, France) **148/10**

3 *3* **Imago Jasius (FR)**[147] 6-9-6 0 .... MaximeGuyon 6 80
(F Monnier, France) **7/1**[1]

4 *3* **Changouro Basc (FR)**[15] 4-8-13 0 .... StephanePasquier 12 70
(Gianluca Bietolini, France) **148/10**

5 *nk* **Alliance A Vary (FR)**[151] 4-9-2 0 .... JeromeCabre 13 73
(M Brasme, France) **19/1**

6 *hd* **Kiunguja (FR)**[99] 4-8-6 0 .... MlleMickaelleMichel(3) 14 65
(C Plisson, France) **31/1**

7 *nk* **Great Tonio (FR)**[30] 5-9-1 0 .... ArnaudBourgeais 18 69
(N Leenders, France) **137/10**

8 *2* **Disco Flash (FR)**[23] 5-8-7 0 .... (b) AurelienLemaitre 1 58
(C Plisson, France) **29/1**

9 *nse* **Autocrat (FR)**[30] 5-9-3 0 .... IoritzMendizabal 3 68
(E Libaud, France) **134/10**

10 *hd* **Bleu Astral (FR)**[32] 7-9-0 0 .... MickaelForest 17 64
(Mme G Rarick, France) **193/10**

11 *1/2* **Nostalbowl (FR)**[94] 6-9-1 0 .... (p) AnthonyCrastus 4 65
(D & P Prod'Homme, France) **97/10**

12 *snk* **Aigle Teen (FR)**[113] 4-9-5 0 .... MickaelBerto 7 70
(S Dehez, France) **17/2**[2]

13 *12* **Saffo (IRE)**[72] 4-9-1 0 .... ChristopheSoumillon 11 47
(D Zarroli, Italy) **125/10**

14 *1* **Puelo (FR)**[36] 5-9-6 0 .... EddyHardouin 9 48
(Carina Fey, France) **34/1**

15 *3/4* **Vingtcoeurs (FR)**[121] 4-8-5 0 .... SylvainRuis 10 34
(C Plisson, France) **229/10**

16 *3/4* **Babel's Book (FR)**[23] 6-9-0 0 .... TonyPiccone 8 40
(Edouard Monfort, France) **99/10**

17 *12* **Flor De Seda (FR)**[180] 7412 4-9-6 0 .... TheoBachelot 2 29
(Jo Hughes, France) *prom: 5th and gng wl enough 1/2-way: drvn 3f out and began to lose pl: bhd whn eased ins fnl 2f* **28/1**

The Form Book Flat 2019, Raceform Ltd, Newbury, RG14 5SJ

18 2 **Cats On Trees (FR)**[141] [8661] 4-9-4 0........................(p) HugoJourniac 16 24
(L Gadbin, France) 155/10

2m 47.06s (6.66)
WFA 4 from 5yo+ 1lb 18 Ran SP% **118.0**
PARI-MUTUEL (all including 1 euro stake): WIN 10.30; PLACE 3.50, 5.10, 3.60; DF 103.60.
Owner Alain Louis-Dreyfus **Bred** A Louis-Dreyfus **Trained** France

1246 - 1263a (Foreign Racing) - See Raceform Interactive

[1216]LINGFIELD (L-H)

Friday, March 22

OFFICIAL GOING: Polytrack: standard
Wind: Quite fresh, half behind Weather: Dull

1264 LADBROKES HOME OF THE ODDS BOOST H'CAP 1m 1y(P)

2:10 (2:10) (Class 5) (0-75,75) 3-Y-O
£3,752 (£1,116; £557; £300; £300; £300) **Stalls** High

Form RPR

5-42 1 **On The Line (IRE)**[21] [966] 3-9-7 **75**........................(bt) JamesDoyle 3 83+
(Hugo Palmer) *hld up towards rr: taken to wd outside and rousted 3f out: gd prog to join ldrs 2f out: led over 1f out: sn: drvn clr* **9/2**[3]

4-01 2 3 **Little Rock (IRE)**[23] [930] 3-9-7 **75**........................ ShaneKelly 8 76+
(Richard Hughes) *hld up in midfield: pushed along over 2f out: prog over 1f out: r.o to take 2nd 100yds and fin to sme effect but no ch to threaten wnr* **14/1**

054- 3 2 **Prince Llyr (IRE)**[155] [8343] 3-9-2 **70**........................ DavidEgan 6 66
(Heather Main) *trckd ldr: rdn to ld over 2f out: hanging rt bnd sn after: hdd over 1f out and no ch w wnr after: lost 2nd last 100yds* **17/2**

3-12 4 ¾ **Dancing Jo**[9] [1174] 3-8-13 **67**........................ CharlesBishop 1 62
(Mick Channon) *trckd ldrs: rdn 2f out: nt qckn over 1f out: kpt on same pce fnl f* **10/3**[2]

3-25 4 dht **Redemptive**[51] [474] 3-8-11 **65**........................ HollieDoyle 9 60
(David Elsworth) *dropped in fr wd draw and hld up in last trio: pushed along over 2f out: swtchd rt over 1f out: styd on fnl f: nvr nrr* **20/1**

00-3 6 ½ **Azets**[13] [1094] 3-9-1 **69**........................ JasonWatson 2 63
(Amanda Perrett) *t.k.h early: trckd ldng pair to over 2f out: sn rdn and nt qckn: no prog over 1f out* **11/8**[1]

00-0 7 1½ **Sussex Solo**[9] [1173] 3-8-7 **61**........................ RaulDaSilva 4 51
(Luke Dace) *taken down early: led to over 2f out: wknd over 1f out* **80/1**

021- 8 1½ **Toybox**[165] [8040] 3-9-7 **75**........................ RobHornby 7 62
(Jonathan Portman) *racd on outer: chsd ldrs: rdn 2f out: wknd over 1f out* **12/1**

045- 9 ½ **Isle Of Wolves**[142] [8731] 3-9-6 **74**........................ CharlieBennett 10 59
(Jim Boyle) *hld up in last: lost tch over 3f out: kpt to inner and shkn up over 1f out: nvr in it* **28/1**

40-0 10 3 **Mitigator**[21] [966] 3-9-4 **72**........................ AdamKirby 5 51
(Lydia Pearce) *hld up in last trio: struggling over 2f out: sn no ch* **50/1**

1m 39.3s (1.10) **Going Correction** 0.0s/f (Stan) 10 Ran SP% **119.7**
Speed ratings (Par 98): **94,91,89,88,88 87,86,84,84,81**
WIN: 4.30 On The Line; PL: 3.20 Little Rock 1.50 On The Line 2.50 Prince Llyr; EX: 51.60; CSF: 63.45; TC: 536.68; TF: 501.90 CSF £63.45 CT £536.68 TOTE £4.30: £1.50, £3.20, £2.50; EX 51.60 Trifecta £501.90.
Owner V I Araci **Bred** Biddestone Stud Ltd **Trained** Newmarket, Suffolk

FOCUS
Reasonably competitive for the grade with a few of these lightly-raced and on the up. They steadied the pace up early on but James Doyle got the winner rolling down the outside a long way out and that momentum carried him clear in the straight. The second was a major eyecatcher.

1265 BETWAY H'CAP 6f 1y(P)

2:40 (2:40) (Class 6) (0-65,65) 4-Y-O+
£3,105 (£924; £461; £300; £300; £300) **Stalls** Low

Form RPR

3-12 1 **Spirit Of Zebedee (IRE)**[9] [1179] 6-8-13 **57**........................(v) JasonHart 2 67
(John Quinn) *fast away: mde virtually all: kicked 2 l clr wl over 1f out: drvn and kpt on wl fnl f* **3/1**[1]

60-0 2 1½ **Fiery Breath**[72] [144] 4-9-4 **62**........................(h[1]) DavidProbert 3 68
(Robert Eddery) *hld up in midfield gng wl: prog over 1f out: chsd clr wnr fnl f: kpt on but unable to chal* **16/1**

6421 3 ¾ **Tavener**[9] [1179] 7-9-6 **64** 6ex........................(p) AndreaAtzeni 1 67
(David C Griffiths) *unable to ld: chsd ldrs: shkn up over 2f out: effrt to dispute 2nd fnl f: kpt on but nvr able to chal* **4/1**[2]

5242 4 ½ **Canimar**[13] [1093] 4-7-9 **46** oh1........................(p) GavinAshton[(7)] 4 48
(Shaun Keightley) *in tch: prog out wd 1/2-way to chse ldrs over 2f out: rdn over 1f out: kpt on same pce fnl f (jockey said filly hung left-handed in the straight)* **12/1**

045- 5 1½ **Quick Recovery**[189] [7252] 4-9-3 **61**........................ CharlieBennett 7 58
(Jim Boyle) *chsd ldrs: rdn over 2f out: fdd fnl f* **14/1**

5-44 6 nk **Beepeecee**[16] [1037] 5-9-7 **65**........................(p) ShaneKelly 10 61
(Thomas Gallagher) *hld up in last trio: shkn up 2f out: kpt on steadily fr over 1f out: nvr nr ldrs* **10/1**

4U-5 7 2 **Falcao (IRE)**[9] [1179] 7-8-13 **57**........................ DavidEgan 8 47
(John Butler) *pressed wnr: nt qckn wl over 1f out: lost 2nd and wknd fnl f* **11/2**

60-0 8 1 **Red Invader (IRE)**[67] [236] 9-9-1 **59**........................(p) LiamKeniry 5 46
(John Butler) *awkward s: t.k.h and sn in midfield: rdn and no prog 2f out: no ch after* **5/1**[3]

52-1 9 ½ **At Your Service**[57] [383] 5-9-5 **63**........................ CallumShepherd 6 49
(Paul Howling) *hld up in last: pushed along over 2f out: kpt to inner in st: nvr in it (trainer's rep could offer no explanation for the gelding's performance)* **7/1**

00-0 10 nk **Noble Deed**[13] [1093] 9-8-2 **46** oh1........................(p) HollieDoyle 11 31
(Michael Attwater) *hld up: a in last trio: wd bnd 2f out: no ch after* **50/1**

4-04 11 76 **Nelson's Hill**[20] [990] 9-7-9 **46**........................ SophieRalston[(7)] 9
(William de Best-Turner) *racd on outer: chsd ldng pair to wl over 2f out: wknd rapidly: t.o and virtually p.u fnl f (jockey said gelding lost its action)* **66/1**

144- P **Catheadans Fury**[108] [9388] 5-9-1 **59**........................(t) GeorgeWood 12
(Martin Bosley) *hld up in rr: sme prog whn wnt v wd bnd 2f out: bhd after: p.u ins fnl f: dismntd (jockey said he felt the mare go amiss so he pulled the mare up)* **25/1**

1m 11.63s (-0.27) **Going Correction** 0.0s/f (Stan) 12 Ran SP% **126.2**
Speed ratings (Par 101): **101,99,98,97,95 94,92,90,90,89**
CSF £58.27 CT £188.12 TOTE £4.30: £1.90, £5.90, £1.40; EX 43.70 Trifecta £304.10.
Owner Malcolm Walker **Bred** N Hartery **Trained** Settrington, N Yorks

FOCUS
The start proved key here and Spirit Of Zebedee wasn't for catching. He's been rated close to his best, and the form is straightforward in behind.

1266 BETWAY CASINO H'CAP 5f 6y(P)

3:15 (3:15) (Class 6) (0-60,60) 4-Y-O+
£3,105 (£924; £461; £300; £300; £300) **Stalls** High

Form RPR

-042 1 **Fareeq**[17] [1021] 5-9-5 **58**........................(bt) RichardKingscote 7 68
(Charlie Wallis) *trckd ldng pair: rdn to ld jst ins fnl f: styd on wl and gng away at fin* **11/4**[1]

-062 2 1¾ **Prominna**[20] [986] 9-9-1 **54**........................(p[1]) DavidProbert 4 58
(Tony Carroll) *plld hrd early: in tch: clsd over 1f out: chsd wnr ins fnl f: outpcd last 100yds* **5/1**[3]

1104 3 ½ **Captain Ryan**[20] [986] 8-9-3 **56**........................(p) TrevorWhelan 8 58
(Geoffrey Deacon) *hld up in 6th: urged along 2f out: styd on fnl f to take 3rd last strides* **20/1**

4-05 4 hd **Avon Green**[29] [824] 4-9-7 **60**........................(b[1]) AdamKirby 3 61
(Joseph Tuite) *sltly s.i.s: towards rr: prog on inner wl over 1f out: chsd ldng pair ins fnl f: nvr able to chal and lost 3rd last strides* **7/1**

1206 5 ¾ **Holdenhurst**[9] [1179] 4-9-0 **58**........................ SeamusCronin[(5)] 1 56
(Bill Turner) *wl away: led but pressed: hdd 2f out: stl upsides 1f out: fdd* **4/1**[2]

0030 6 1 **Little Miss Daisy**[9] [1179] 5-9-4 **57**........................ TomMarquand 9 52
(William Muir) *chsd ldrs: rdn 1/2-way: lost pl u.p over 1f out: kpt on again nr fin* **14/1**

05-0 7 hd **Waneen (IRE)**[63] [298] 6-9-1 **54**........................(p) LiamKeniry 10 48
(John Butler) *wl in rr fr wdst draw: shkn up 2f out: kpt on fnl f: n.d* **7/1**

23-1 8 1¼ **Sandfrankskipsgo**[63] [298] 10-9-7 **60**........................ ShaneKelly 6 50
(Peter Crate) *pressed ldr: rdn to ld 2f out: hdd jst ins fnl f and wknd qckly* **13/2**

-020 9 2½ **Mr Gent (IRE)**[16] [1037] 4-9-5 **58**........................(p) JosephineGordon 5 39
(Ed Dunlop) *mostly in last and struggling fr 1/2-way: modest late prog* **25/1**

000- 10 2½ **Haveoneyerself (IRE)**[186] [7363] 4-9-3 **56**........................(p) DavidEgan 2 28
(John Butler) *a wl in rr: no ch over 1f out: plugged on* **33/1**

58.58s (-0.22) **Going Correction** 0.0s/f (Stan) 10 Ran SP% **119.9**
Speed ratings (Par 101): **101,98,97,97,95 94,93,91,87,83**
CSF £16.68 CT £234.40 TOTE £2.80: £1.50, £1.50, £4.60; EX 16.00 Trifecta £113.30.
Owner P E Axon **Bred** T J Cooper **Trained** Ardleigh, Essex

FOCUS
Not the strongest run sprint handicap, even for this grade. The winner was perfectly placed throughout and got a dream trip. He's been rated within 2lb of last year's best.

1267 BETWAY HEED YOUR HUNCH H'CAP 1m 4f (P)

3:50 (3:50) (Class 2) (0-100,101) 4-Y-O+**£11,971** (£3,583; £1,791; £896; £446) **Stalls** Low

Form RPR

22-6 1 **Maybe Today**[62] [310] 4-8-8 **85**........................(v[1]) DavidEgan 2 91
(Simon Crisford) *trckd ldr after 1f: shkn up to take narrow ld 2f out: kpt on wl and a holding on fnl f* **6/1**

10-3 2 ¾ **Fire Fighting (IRE)**[7] [1220] 8-9-7 **97**........................ AdamKirby 3 102
(Mark Johnston) *in tch in 5th but pushed along at times: rdn and nt clr run briefly wl over 1f out: drvn and styd on to take 2nd last 100yds: clsd on wnr but unable to chal* **4/1**[3]

00-4 3 1¾ **Amazing Red (IRE)**[18] [1017] 6-9-8 **98**........................ FrankieDettori 5 100
(Ed Dunlop) *trckd ldng trio: moved up on outer to chal ldng pair 2f out: rdn and nt qckn over 1f out: lost 2nd and one pce last 100yds* **3/1**[2]

14-2 4 ½ **Exceeding Power**[27] [878] 8-9-2 **92**........................ GeorgeWood 1 93
(Martin Bosley) *trckd ldr 1f: chsd ldng pair to over 2f out: stl cl up over 1f out: one pce fnl f* **8/1**

31-4 5 ¾ **Oasis Fantasy (IRE)**[16] [1031] 8-8-11 **87**........................ AndreaAtzeni 4 87
(David Simcock) *narrow ldr to 2f out: steadily fdd fr over 1f out* **9/1**

0-11 6 nk **Petite Jack**[7] [1220] 6-9-11 **101** 6ex........................ JamesDoyle 6 101
(Neil King) *hld up in last: tried to make prog on inner over 1f out but nowhere to go: hanging bdly lft after and nvr a threat (jockey said gelding had hung violently left-handed in behind runners to the point of being un-rideable)* **9/4**[1]

2m 30.37s (-2.63) **Going Correction** 0.0s/f (Stan)
WFA 4 from 5yo+ 1lb 6 Ran SP% **111.2**
Speed ratings (Par 109): **108,107,106,106,105 105**
CSF £29.05 TOTE £7.00: £3.20, £2.30; EX 24.20 Trifecta £132.70.
Owner Sheikh Juma Dalmook Al Maktoum **Bred** R Cantoni **Trained** Newmarket, Suffolk

FOCUS
A good little handicap but the gallop didn't look very strong and there were one or two hard luck stories as the field bunched up around the home turn, notably the runner-up.

1268 LADBROKES NOVICE STKS (PLUS 10 RACE) 1m 4f (P)

4:20 (4:20) (Class 5) 3-Y-O **£3,752** (£1,116; £557; £278) **Stalls** Low

Form RPR

042- 1 **Travel On**[149] [8549] 3-9-2 85........................ FrankieDettori 3 75+
(John Gosden) *hld up in tch: prog to ld over 4f out: stl green but pushed clr fr 2f out* **1/4**[1]

3 2 5 **Autumn Pride (IRE)**[22] [949] 3-9-2 0........................ JoeFanning 4 67+
(Mark Johnston) *trckd ldr: led 7f out to over 4f out: dropped to 3rd and shkn up 3f out: kpt on to take 2nd again ins fnl f: no ch w wnr* **4/1**[2]

3 3 ¾ **Thelonious**[21] [967] 3-9-2 0........................ JamesDoyle 2 66
(Michael Bell) *led at mod pce to 7f out: sn dropped to 3rd: shkn up to chse wnr 3f out: lft bhd fr 2f out: pushed along and lost 2nd ins fnl f* **10/1**[3]

4 1¼ **Flat Stone** 3-9-2 0........................ CallumShepherd 5 64
(Dominic Ffrench Davis) *dwlt: hld up in last: outpcd over 2f out: reminder on inner over 1f out: kpt on one pce* **33/1**

- 5 2 **Thinque Tank** 3-9-2 0........................ LiamKeniry 1 61
(Charlie Longsdon) *dwlt: in tch: outpcd over 2f out: no prog over 1f out* **66/1**

2m 33.14s (0.14) **Going Correction** 0.0s/f (Stan) 5 Ran SP% **113.5**
Speed ratings (Par 98): **99,95,95,94,93**
CSF £1.81 TOTE £1.20: £1.10, £1.60; EX 2.00 Trifecta £3.40.
Owner George Strawbridge **Bred** George Strawbridge **Trained** Newmarket, Suffolk

The Form Book Flat 2019, Raceform Ltd, Newbury, RG14 5SJ

FOCUS
No worries for the 85-rated Travel On despite the steady gallop and he was away and gone off the home turn.

1269 PLAY 4 TO SCORE AT BETWAY H'CAP 1m 2f (P)
4:55 (4:55) (Class 5) (0-75,77) 4-Y-O+
£3,752 (£1,116; £557; £300; £300; £300) **Stalls** Low

Form RPR
3-10 1 **Lunar Deity**[55] 429 10-8-12 **72** MarcoGhiani(7) 1 80
(Stuart Williams) *hld up in midfield: prog 2f out: shkn up to ld 1f out: styd on steadily and in command fnl f (trainer's rep could offer no explanation for the apparent improvement in form)* **33/1**
230- 2 1 1/2 **Stormingin (IRE)**[33] 8340 6-9-7 **74** HectorCrouch 8 79
(Gary Moore) *hld up towards rr: taken wd bnd 2f out and rdn: prog jst over 1f out: styd on wl to take 2nd nr fin* **11/1**
00-0 3 nk **Pendo**[22] 942 8-8-12 **65** KierenFox 4 69
(John Best) *trckd ldng pair: rdn 2f out: chal on inner jst over 1f out: chsd wnr fnl f but readily hld: lost 2nd nr fin* **20/1**
41-5 4 hd **Twist (IRE)**[23] 921 4-9-6 **73** AdamKirby 6 77
(Nicky Henderson) *trckd ldr: shkn up 2f out: rdn to chal jst over 1f out but nt qckn: kpt on again nr fin* **4/1[2]**
5-05 5 3/4 **Lacan (IRE)**[21] 962 8-9-7 **74** CallumShepherd 5 77
(Brett Johnson) *hld up towards rr: rdn 2f out: kpt on fr over 1f out but nvr able to threaten* **10/3[1]**
5221 6 nk **Magic Mirror**[22] 942 6-9-7 **74** (p) TomMarquand 7 76
(Mark Rimell) *trckd ldrs: rdn 2f out: nt qckn over 1f out: kpt on same pce after* **6/1**
1543 7 1 1/4 **Shyron**[16] 1040 8-9-10 **77** RobertWinston 10 76
(Lee Carter) *hld up in last pair: cajoled along fr 2f out: kpt on but nvr really in it* **14/1**
456- 8 2 **Kwanza**[120] 9209 4-8-10 **63** JoeFanning 2 58
(Mark Johnston) *v reluctant to enter stall: led: stl gng wl 2f out: hdd and folded rapidly 1f out (starter reported that the filly was unruly behind stalls; trainer was informed that the filly could not run until the day after passing a stalls test)* **8/1**
-065 9 3 1/2 **Presence Process**[20] 985 5-8-3 **63** SophieRalston(7) 9 51
(Pat Phelan) *racd wd: trckd ldrs: wd bnd 2f out and wknd (jockey said gelding lost its action)* **7/1**
242/ 10 2 1/4 **First Quest (USA)**[29] 8326 5-9-4 **71** CharlieBennett 3 55
(Jim Boyle) *a in last and nvr gng wl: lost tch over 3f out* **5/1[3]**

2m 5.23s (-1.37) **Going Correction** 0.0s/f (Stan) 10 Ran SP% **120.3**
Speed ratings (Par 103): **105,103,103,103,102 102,101,99,97,95**
CSF £366.95 CT £7287.59 TOTE £38.10: £6.10, £3.30, £5.70; EX 402.30 Trifecta £4968.60.
Owner W E Enticknap & Partner **Bred** Hermes Services Ltd **Trained** Newmarket, Suffolk

FOCUS
A wide open handicap but the gallop looked steady and this might not be particularly strong form. The winner is fully exposed but knows how to win, over a variety of trips.
T/Plt: £673.20 to a £1 stake. Pool: £73,829.05 - 80.05 winning units. T/Qpdt: £163.90 to a £1 stake. Pool: £8,846.75 - 39.93 winning units. **Jonathan Neesom**

1080 NEWCASTLE (A.W) (L-H)
Friday, March 22

OFFICIAL GOING: Tapeta: standard to slow
Wind: Fresh against Weather: Heavy cloud and rain

1270 LADBROKES H'CAP 1m 4f 98y (Tp)
5:30 (5:30) (Class 6) (0-65,67) 3-Y-O
£3,105 (£924; £461; £400; £400; £400) **Stalls** High

Form RPR
36-4 1 **Lord Lamington**[24] 917 3-9-7 **64** FrannyNorton 2 77
(Mark Johnston) *hld up towards rr: stdy hdwy 1/2-way: trckd ldrs over 3f out: swtchd rt and effrt 2f out: led wl over 1f out: sn clr: readily* **11/2[3]**
000- 2 7 **Rich Cummins**[92] 9637 3-8-13 **56** PJMcDonald 12 58
(Mark Johnston) *sn trcking ldr: cl up over 3f out: led wl over 2f out: rdn and hdd wl over 1f out: sn drvn and kpt on: no ch w wnr* **10/1**
06-2 3 nk **Tabou Beach Boy**[70] 183 3-8-13 **56** NathanEvans 1 58
(Michael Easterby) *bhd: swtchd rt to outer and hdwy over 3f out: chsd ldrs and rdn along over 2f out: sn hung lft to inner rail: styd on u.p fnl f: nrst fin* **13/2**
0-63 4 2 **Fanfaronade (USA)**[15] 1066 3-9-7 **64** KieranO'Neill 10 63
(John Gosden) *trckd ldrs: hdwy over 4f out: rdn along wl over 2f out: drvn wl over 1f out: kpt on one pce* **5/1[2]**
2212 5 8 **Colony Queen**[15] 1066 3-9-10 **67** DavidAllan 9 54
(James Tate) *hld up: hdwy and in tch 1/2-way: chsd ldrs over 3f out: rdn along over 2f out: drvn wl over 1f out: sn btn* **7/4[1]**
36-0 6 1 1/2 **Silk Island (IRE)**[30] 802 3-8-2 **45** CamHardie 8 29
(Michael Wigham) *hld up in rr: pushed along over 3f out: rdn over 2f out: plugged on: nvr nr ldrs* **33/1**
0400 7 3/4 **Midnite Rendezvous**[9] 1173 3-8-2 **45** PaddyMathers 6 28
(Derek Shaw) *hld up in rr: sme hdwy over 2f out: nvr nr ldrs* **80/1**
00-1 8 1/2 **Ginge N Tonic**[34] 765 3-8-3 **51** ThoreHammerHansen(5) 7 33
(Adam West) *led: pushed along over 3f out: rdn and hdd over 2f out: sn drvn and wknd* **5/1[2]**
0-50 9 11 **Freedom's Breath**[23] 931 3-8-2 **45** LukeMorris 5 11
(Michael Appleby) *a towards rr* **66/1**
00-0 10 hd **Russian Rum**[47] 585 3-8-6 **49** (v[1]) AndrewMullen 11 15
(James Given) *chsd ldng pair: rdn along 4f out: sn wknd* **33/1**
0-00 11 1/2 **George Hastings**[34] 765 3-7-13 **45** (p[1]) JamieGormley(3) 4 10
(K R Burke) *trckd ldrs: pushed along on inner over 5f out: rdn over 3f out: sn wknd* **50/1**
55-6 12 3/4 **Mendeleev**[30] 802 3-8-2 **45** (t[1]) JamesSullivan 3 9
(James Given) *a in rr* **40/1**

2m 44.85s (3.75) **Going Correction** +0.475s/f (Slow) 12 Ran SP% **120.5**
Speed ratings (Par 96): **106,101,101,99,94 93,92,92,85,85 84,84**
CSF £57.23 CT £372.22 TOTE £6.40: £1.90, £3.00, £2.00; EX 44.20 Trifecta £485.30.
Owner Netherfield House Stud **Bred** Newsells Park Stud **Trained** Middleham Moor, N Yorks

FOCUS
An ordinary 3yo middle-distance handicap on standard to slow Tapeta. The winning time confirmed that the track was riding slow and shouldn't be used to detract from the performance of the comprehensive winner.

1271 SUNRACING.CO.UK H'CAP 1m 5y (Tp)
6:00 (6:00) (Class 5) (0-75,75) 4-Y-O+
£3,752 (£1,116; £557; £400; £400; £400) **Stalls** Centre

Form RPR
-432 1 **Elixsoft (IRE)**[32] 784 4-8-11 **65** BenCurtis 13 74
(Roger Fell) *hld up towards rr: hdwy over 2f out: swtchd rt and chsd ldrs over 1f out: rdn to ld ins fnl f: kpt on strly* **5/1[3]**
-561 2 1 3/4 **Insurplus (IRE)**[14] 1083 6-8-8 **62** PhilDennis 3 67
(Jim Goldie) *hld up in rr: hdwy over 2f out: rdn over 1f out: styd on wl fnl f* **14/1**
4-50 3 3/4 **Street Poet (IRE)**[32] 784 6-8-8 **62** (p) JamesSullivan 8 65
(Michael Herrington) *trckd ldr: cl up 1/2-way: led 3f out: rdn wl over 1f out: drvn and hdd ins fnl f: kpt on same pce* **33/1**
000- 4 1 1/4 **Golden Guest**[114] 9285 5-8-13 **67** DanielTudhope 11 67
(Les Eyre) *hld up towards rr: hdwy over 2f out: chsd ldrs over 1f out: sn rdn and kpt on same pce* **20/1**
2110 5 1/2 **Cashel (IRE)**[22] 942 4-9-1 **69** AlistairRawlinson 9 68
(Michael Appleby) *trckd ldrs: hdwy over 2f out: rdn along over 1f out: sn drvn and no imp* **7/2[2]**
-112 6 nk **Porrima (IRE)**[30] 808 4-8-13 **67** AndrewMullen 5 66
(Ben Haslam) *fly-jmpd and dwlt s: in rr and sn swtchd rt to stands' side: in rr: hdwy over 2f out: rdn wl over 1f out: drvn and no imp fnl f (jockey said filly fly leapt leaving the stalls)* **15/2**
135- 7 2 1/2 **Zeshov (IRE)**[142] 8733 8-9-0 **68** (p) DavidAllan 10 61
(Rebecca Bastiman) *trckd ldng pair: hdwy and cl up 3f out: rdn along 2f out: grad wknd* **25/1**
6-50 8 2 **Seaborough (IRE)**[22] 950 4-8-11 **65** CliffordLee 7 53
(David Thompson) *midfield: pushed along and sme hdwy 3f out: rdn over 2f out: sn drvn and n.d* **50/1**
351- 9 1/2 **Gabrials Centurion (IRE)**[83] 9747 4-9-1 **69** PaulHanagan 12 56
(Richard Fahey) *chsd ldrs: pushed along over 2f out: rdn wl over 1f out: sn one pce* **7/1**
00-1 10 nse **International Law**[17] 1025 5-9-1 **69** CamHardie 6 56
(Antony Brittain) *trckd ldrs: hdwy and cl up 3f out: rdn along 2f out: sn drvn and btn* **9/4[1]**
U4/0 11 2 1/2 **Tarnhelm**[22] 952 4-8-10 **64** NathanEvans 1 45
(Wilf Storey) *a towards rr* **66/1**
236- 12 1 **Edgar Allan Poe (IRE)**[147] 8597 5-8-13 **67** LewisEdmunds 4 46
(Rebecca Bastiman) *chsd ldrs: rdn along wl over 2f out: sn wknd* **20/1**
2/60 13 2 3/4 **Tommy Hallinan (IRE)**[13] 1106 5-8-13 **67** (t) BarryMcHugh 2 40
(Marjorie Fife) *led: pushed along and hdd 3f out: sn rdn and wknd 2f out* **50/1**

1m 42.77s (4.17) **Going Correction** +0.475s/f (Slow) 13 Ran SP% **122.3**
Speed ratings (Par 103): **98,96,95,94,93 93,90,88,88,88 85,84,82**
CSF £68.35 CT £2187.63 TOTE £5.70: £1.70, £3.20, £8.20; EX 72.90 Trifecta £2484.50.
Owner Middleham Park Racing CXIII & Partner **Bred** Ciara Eglington **Trained** Nawton, N Yorks

FOCUS
An ordinary handicap. The winning third-favourite challenged towards the stands' rail from off the pace. The time was over six seconds outside of standard despite a fair tempo, confirming the Tapeta is riding on the slow side.

1272 LADBROKES HOME OF THE ODDS BOOST FILLIES' NOVICE STKS 7f 14y (Tp)
6:30 (6:30) (Class 5) 3-Y-O+
£3,752 (£1,116; £557; £278) **Stalls** Centre

Form RPR
22- 1 **Coastline (IRE)**[143] 8727 3-8-11 0 DavidAllan 9 69
(James Tate) *trckd ldrs: cl up 2f out: rdn over 1f out: kpt on wl to ld last 50yds* **9/4[2]**
10- 2 1/2 **Zofelle (IRE)**[146] 8648 3-9-4 0 BenCurtis 2 75
(Hugo Palmer) *t.k.h early: trckd ldrs: swtchd lft and hdwy over 1f out: rdn to take slt ld ins fnl f: hdd and no ex last 50yds* **5/4[1]**
3 3/4 **Paradise Papers** 3-8-11 0 LewisEdmunds 7 66
(David Barron) *hld up in rr: hdwy over 2f out: rdn over 1f out: styd on wl fnl f* **40/1**
4 1 **Hareem Queen (IRE)** 3-8-11 0 PJMcDonald 5 63
(K R Burke) *t.k.h: trckd ldr: cl up at 1/2-way: led wl over 2f out: rdn over 1f out: hdd ins fnl f: no ex last 100yds* **7/2[3]**
5 1 1/4 **Seraphim** 3-8-11 0 (t[1]) LukeMorris 8 60
(Marco Botti) *chsd ldrs: rdn wl over 1f out: sn drvn and kpt on one pce* **25/1**
53- 6 1/2 **Princess Palliser (IRE)**[154] 8385 3-8-11 0 KevinStott 3 58
(John Quinn) *chsd ldrs: rdn along 2f out: kpt on one pce (jockey said filly hung slightly left handed under pressure)* **11/1**
4 7 3/4 **Picture Your Dream**[32] 785 4-9-12 0 NathanEvans 6 61
(Seb Spencer) *hld up in rr: hdwy over 2f out: rdn wl over 1f out: kpt on fnl f* **66/1**
2 8 8 **Farrdhana**[35] 739 3-8-11 0 GrahamLee 1 35
(Bryan Smart) *led: jnd 1/2-way: rdn and hdd wl over 2f out: sn wknd* **25/1**
9 38 **Sophia's Princess** 3-8-8 0 GabrieleMalune(3) 4
(Ivan Furtado) *chsd ldrs: rdn along 3f out: sn wknd* **50/1**

1m 31.48s (5.28) **Going Correction** +0.475s/f (Slow) 9 Ran SP% **119.4**
WFA 3 from 4yo 15lb
Speed ratings (Par 100): **88,87,86,85,84 83,82,73,30**
CSF £5.44 TOTE £3.50: £1.20, £1.10, £8.30; EX 7.10 Trifecta £118.00.
Owner Sheikh Juma Dalmook Al Maktoum **Bred** Gerry Flannery Developments **Trained** Newmarket, Suffolk

FOCUS
A fair fillies' novice contest. They went a modest gallop and the second-favourite became the second consecutive winner on the straight track to challenge towards the stands' side.

1273 FOLLOW TOP TIPSTER TEMPLEGATE AT SUNRACING H'CAP 7f 14y (Tp)
7:00 (7:00) (Class 4) (0-80,81) 4-Y-O+
£5,530 (£1,645; £822; £411; £400; £400) **Stalls** Centre

Form RPR
00-5 1 **Tiercel**[49] 526 6-8-8 **67** PhilDennis 4 73+
(Rebecca Bastiman) *hld up in rr: hdwy wl over 1f out: str run ent fnl f: rdn to ld last 100yds: kpt on (trainer said regarding apparent improvement in form that the gelding benefited from the drop in trip from 1m to 7f; vet said gelding had bled from the nose)* **33/1**

-521 **2** ½ **Chosen World**[30] 808 5-8-13 **72**..............................(p) PaulMulrennan 5 77
(Julie Camacho) *t.k.h: trckd ldrs: hdwy 2f out: effrt and edgd rt over 1f out: rdn to chal and hung rt ent fnl f: sn drvn and kpt on (jockey said gelding ran too free)* **15/8**[1]

200- **3** *hd* **Sureyoutoldme (IRE)**[231] 5676 5-9-2 **75**.............................. JamesSullivan 11 79
(Ruth Carr) *trckd ldrs: hdwy towards stands' side 2f out: rdn over 1f out: kpt on u.p fnl f* **14/1**

510- **4** *hd* **Windsor Cross (IRE)**[216] 6293 4-9-2 **80**................ ConnorMurtagh(5) 2 83
(Richard Fahey) *hld up: hdwy and in tch over 2f out: rdn and nt clr run over 1f out: swtchd lft and drvn ent fnl f: kpt on wl towards fin* **12/1**

654- **5** *hd* **Outside Inside (IRE)**[286] 3592 4-9-4 **77**.......................... PJMcDonald 9 82+
(Mark Johnston) *in tch: hdwy to chse ldrs 2f out: rdn and n.m.r jst over 1f out: kpt on u.p fnl f (jockey said filly was denied a clear run)* **11/1**

2-03 **6** ½ **Confrontational (IRE)**[17] 1025 5-9-8 **81**......................(p) AndrewMullen 1 83
(Jennie Candlish) *trckd ldr: hdwy 2f out: rdn and ev ch ent fnl f: sn drvn and kpt on same pce* **6/1**[3]

006- **7** *nk* **Firmdecisions (IRE)**[181] 7540 9-9-3 **79**.................... RowanScott(3) 6 80
(Nigel Tinkler) *chsd ldrs: hdwy wl over 1f out: chal ent fnl f: ev ch tl drvn and no ex last 100yds* **12/1**

0-34 **8** *hd* **Mudawwan (IRE)**[45] 609 5-8-11 **70**...........................(tp) PaulHanagan 8 70
(James Bethell) *trckd ldrs: hdwy towards stands' side over 2f out: rdn to chse ldr over 1f out: drvn ent fnl f: kpt on same pce* **11/2**[2]

-645 **9** *shd* **Testa Rossa (IRE)**[30] 807 9-8-3 **69**.......................(b) CoreyMadden(7) 3 69
(Jim Goldie) *hld up in rr: effrt and sme hdwy nr stands' rail wl over 1f out: sn rdn and no imp* **12/1**

40-4 **10** *nk* **Alexandrakollontai (IRE)**[22] 951 9-9-4 **77**.................(b) CamHardie 7 76
(Alistair Whillans) *towards rr: pushed along over 3f out: rdn along wl over 2f out: n.d* **40/1**

06-0 **11** ½ **Logi (IRE)**[30] 812 5-9-1 **77**....................................(b) JamieGormley(3) 12 75
(Rebecca Bastiman) *led: pushed along 2f out: rdn over 1f out: drvn ent fnl f: hdd & wknd last 100yds* **12/1**

50- **12** *nk* **Irish Minister (USA)**[80] 8520 4-8-12 **71**.......................... CliffordLee 10 68
(David Thompson) *dwlt: sn chsng ldng pair: pushed along over 2f out: rdn wl over 1f out: hld whn n.m.r and hmpd over 1f out: bhd after* **22/1**

1m 30.19s (3.99) **Going Correction** +0.475s/f (Slow) **12** Ran SP% **120.0**
Speed ratings (Par 105): **96,95,95,94,94 94,93,93,93,93 92,92**
CSF £94.66 CT £993.31 TOTE £41.60: £7.60, £1.40, £3.80; EX 183.90 Trifecta £2402.50.
Owner Lets Be Lucky Racing 19 And Partner **Bred** Nawara Stud Co Ltd **Trained** Cowthorpe, N Yorks

FOCUS
The feature contest was a fair handicap. They finished bunched up and an outsider won centrally in a comparatively modest time for the grade.

1274 PLAY 4 TO SCORE AT BETWAY CLAIMING STKS 6f (Tp)
7:30 (7:30) (Class 6) 4-Y-0+
£3,105 (£924; £461; £400; £400; £400) **Stalls** Centre

Form RPR
1015 **1** **Alsvinder**[13] 1105 6-9-12 98...(t) DanielTudhope 9 90+
(David O'Meara) *mde all: rdn clr over 1f out: kpt on (trainer was informed that the horse could not run until the day after passing a stalls test)* **5/4**[1]

2610 **2** ¾ **Duke Cosimo**[20] 982 9-9-0 66.. PhilDennis 4 74
(Michael Herrington) *hld up towards rr: hdwy wl over 1f out: rdn to chse wnr ins fnl f: kpt on wl towards fin* **14/1**

4211 **3** 3¾ **Zapper Cass (FR)**[7] 1208 6-9-2 68........................(b) AlistairRawlinson 5 65+
(Michael Appleby) *trckd ldrs: hdwy 2f out: rdn over 1f out: drvn and edgd rt ent fnl f: kpt on same pce* **9/2**[3]

6322 **4** *nk* **Lucky Lodge**[24] 914 9-9-2 70...(v) CamHardie 1 64+
(Antony Brittain) *trckd ldrs on outer: hdwy over 2f out: rdn over 1f out: drvn and kpt on same pce fnl f* **8/1**

\- **5** 2½ **Tommycole**[90] 4-8-6 0 ow1.. RussellHarris(7) 6 53
(Susan Corbett) *dwlt and in rr: rdn along 2f out: kpt on fnl f* **200/1**

00-6 **6** 1½ **Bengali Boys (IRE)**[73] 127 4-9-4 83.............................. TonyHamilton 2 54
(Richard Fahey) *hld up in tch: hdwy over 2f out: rdn to chse wnr wl over 1f out: drvn and wknd ent fnl f* **4/1**[2]

320- **7** 2¼ **Searanger (USA)**[174] 7783 6-9-0 63................................ PJMcDonald 8 43
(Rebecca Menzies) *chsd ldrs: rdn along over 2f out: sn wknd* **33/1**

0-10 **8** 1¼ **Zylan (IRE)**[13] 1105 7-9-5 93.................................(p) BenSanderson(5) 3 49
(Roger Fell) *cl up: rdn along wl over 2f out: sn wknd* **8/1**

53-3 **9** 3¾ **Dories Delight (IRE)**[15] 1070 4-8-6 61.........................(p) TheodoreLadd(5) 7 25
(Scott Dixon) *chsd ldrs: rdn along wl over 2f out: sn wknd (jockey said gelding ran too free in the early stages; vet said that the gelding had lost its right hind shoe)* **66/1**

1m 14.23s (1.73) **Going Correction** +0.475s/f (Slow) **9** Ran SP% **116.4**
Speed ratings (Par 101): **107,106,101,100,97 95,92,90,85**
Alsvinder was claimer by P Kirby for £20,000. Bengali Boys was claimed by A. W. Carroll for £12,000. Tommycole was claimed by Olly Williams for £6,000. CSF £22.31 TOTE £2.00: £1.10, £2.40, £2.00; EX 26.50 Trifecta £86.80.
Owner F Gillespie **Bred** Northern Bloodstock Inc **Trained** Upper Helmsley, N Yorks

FOCUS
A good claiming sprint. The favourite made all towards the near side from a high draw and his winning time compared favourably on the night. The runner-up has been rated to his AW best from recent years.

1275 LADBROKES H'CAP 5f (Tp)
8:00 (8:00) (Class 6) (0-65,67) 3-Y-0
£3,105 (£924; £461; £400; £400; £400) **Stalls** Centre

Form RPR
4-20 **1** **Arishka (IRE)**[48] 550 3-9-4 **60**................................ KieranO'Neill 9 71+
(Daniel Kubler) *trckd ldr: cl up 1/2-way: led 2f out: rdn clr appr fnl f: kpt on strly (trainer said regarding apparent improvement in form that the gelding benefited from the drop back in trip from 6f to 5f and had settled better)* **8/1**

256- **2** 3¼ **Pinarella (FR)**[139] 8825 3-9-5 **61**................................ AndrewMullen 4 60
(Ben Haslam) *chsd ldrs: rdn along 2f out: drvn and kpt on fnl f* **8/1**

00-0 **3** *nk* **Kickham Street**[30] 813 3-9-7 **63**................................(h[1]) DanielTudhope 6 61
(John Quinn) *hld up in rr: hdwy 2f out: rdn over 1f out: drvn and kpt on fnl f* **9/2**[3]

460- **4** ½ **Tomahawk Ridge (IRE)**[156] 8314 3-9-3 **59**.......................... PJMcDonald 2 55
(John Gallagher) *dwlt and towards rr: hdwy over 3f out: rdn along to chse ldrs 2f out: drvn over 1f out: kpt on same pce* **10/1**

212 **5** ½ **Hanati (IRE)**[57] 388 3-9-10 **66**.. LukeMorris 1 60
(Simon Crisford) *prom: chsd wnr 2f out: sn rdn: drvn and kpt on same pce fnl f* **3/1**[1]

6141 **6** 7 **Sister Of The Sign (IRE)**[14] 1079 3-9-5 **61**.................... BarryMcHugh 3 30
(James Given) *led: jnd 1/2-way: rdn along and hdd 2f out: grad wknd* **13/2**

231 **7** ½ **Hanakotoba (USA)**[46] 605 3-9-11 **67**......................(t) LewisEdmunds 7 34
(Stuart Williams) *chsd ldrs: rdn along 2f out: sn drvn and grad wknd (jockey said filly ran flat)* **10/3**[2]

005- **8** 2½ **Nettie Honeyball**[141] 8777 3-8-0 **49** oh4.......................... IzzyClifton(7) 8 7
(Nigel Tinkler) *in tch: rdn along 2f out: sn outpcd* **100/1**

060- **9** 1½ **Equiano Perle**[288] 3514 3-9-0 **56**.....................(t[1] w) AlistairRawlinson 10 9
(Michael Appleby) *a towards rr* **25/1**

1m 1.37s (1.87) **Going Correction** +0.475s/f (Slow) **9** Ran SP% **115.7**
Speed ratings (Par 96): **104,98,98,97,96 85,84,80,78**
CSF £70.15 CT £327.50 TOTE £8.80: £2.40, £2.30, £2.70; EX 70.10 Trifecta £452.70.
Owner Crowd Racing & Diskovery Partnership Vi **Bred** John Malone **Trained** Lambourn, Berks

FOCUS
A modest 3yo sprint handicap. The decisive winner clocked a good comparative time for the grade. A clear pb from the winner, and straightforward form in behind her.
T/Plt: £216.50 to a £1 stake. Pool: £84,869.28 - 286.16 winning units. T/Qpdt: £10.50 to a £1 stake. Pool: £12,660.04 - 885.94 winning units. **Joe Rowntree**

1276 - 1284a (Foreign Racing) - See Raceform Interactive

1170 KEMPTON (A.W) (R-H)
Saturday, March 23

OFFICIAL GOING: Polytrack: standard to slow
Wind: Moderate, half behind Weather: Cloudy

1285 100% PROFIT BOOST AT 32REDSPORT.COM H'CAP 7f (P)
5:25 (5:28) (Class 5) (0-75,77) 3-Y-O
£3,752 (£1,116; £557; £400; £400; £400) **Stalls** Low

Form RPR
620- **1** **Oloroso (IRE)**[285] 3685 3-8-13 **70**................................ JoshuaBryan(3) 1 77+
(Andrew Balding) *hld up in last: gd prog on inner jst over 2f out: led jst over 1f out: edgd lft but styd on wl to draw clr* **7/1**[3]

540- **2** 2¼ **Lethal Missile (IRE)**[133] 9001 3-8-13 **67**.......................... HectorCrouch 10 68+
(Clive Cox) *dwlt: hld up in rr: shkn up 2f out: prog on wd outside over 1f out: styd on to take 2nd nr fin: no ch w wnr* **7/1**[3]

520- **3** ½ **Balata Bay**[135] 8955 3-8-11 **72**................................ LukeCatton(7) 6 72
(Richard Hannon) *hld up in midfield: shkn up on outer 2f out: prog over 1f out: disp 2nd ins fnl f: kpt on* **20/1**

651- **4** *hd* **Rambaldi (IRE)**[128] 9073 3-9-3 **71**................................ MarcMonaghan 12 70
(Marco Botti) *hld up in last trio: shkn up 2f out: prog on outer over 1f out: pressed for a pl ins fnl f: kpt on* **10/1**

555- **5** *shd* **Ventura Glory**[182] 7508 3-9-3 **71**.. RossaRyan 7 70
(Richard Hannon) *hld up in rr: rdn over 2f out: prog u.p over 1f out: kpt on to press for a pl last 75yds* **12/1**

415- **6** 1½ **Recuerdame (USA)**[211] 6484 3-9-0 **68**.............................. LouisSteward 4 63
(Simon Dow) *trckd ldrs: prog and cl up over 1f out: fdd ins fnl f* **8/1**

-622 **7** *nk* **Antonia Clara**[21] 990 3-8-13 **67**.. JamieSpencer 9 61
(Stuart Williams) *led: hdd jst over 1f out: wknd* **14/1**

6-52 **8** 1¼ **Facethepuckout (IRE)**[10] 1178 3-9-9 **77**.........................(v[1]) TomQueally 2 68
(John Ryan) *prom on inner: rdn 2f out: nt qckn over 1f out: wknd ins fnl f* **11/2**[2]

-032 **9** 1 **Maisie Moo**[10] 1170 3-8-8 **62**.. HollieDoyle 3 50
(Shaun Keightley) *hld up in midfield: shkn up 2f out: keeping on whn nt clr run over 1f out: no prog after (jockey said filly was denied a clear run)* **7/1**[3]

3-64 **10** 1 **Mushaageb (IRE)**[9] 1195 3-9-1 **69**...............................(b) AndreaAtzeni 8 54
(Roger Varian) *slowly away and rousted: then t.k.h and in midfield: rdn and nt looking a threat whn hmpd over 1f out: no ch after* **9/2**[1]

00-1 **11** 1½ **Love Your Work (IRE)**[16] 1067 3-9-0 **75**....................(b) RPWalsh(7) 13 56
(Adam West) *t.k.h: racd on outer: prom: chsd ldr jst over 2f out: edgd rt over 1f out: sn wknd qckly* **16/1**

5-10 **12** 6 **Greybychoice (IRE)**[17] 1035 3-9-6 **74**................................ EoinWalsh 11 39
(Nick Littmoden) *stdd s: t.k.h and sn trckd ldr: lost 2nd jst over 2f out: losing pl whn hmpd over 1f out: bhd fnl f* **40/1**

1m 25.96s (-0.04) **Going Correction** +0.05s/f (Slow) **12** Ran SP% **118.7**
Speed ratings (Par 98): **102,99,98,98,98 96,96,95,93,92 91,84**
CSF £55.49 CT £957.72 TOTE £6.80: £2.80, £3.50, £8.10; EX 70.10 Trifecta £959.20.
Owner Roger Hetherington & Jeremy Carey **Bred** Rathasker Stud **Trained** Kingsclere, Hants

FOCUS
The going was standard to slow. A competitive and interesting 3yo handicap with plenty of winners likely to come from it. Sound form rated around the third, fourth and fifth.

1286 32RED CASINO NOVICE STKS 6f (P)
6:00 (6:01) (Class 5) 4-Y-O+
£3,881 (£1,155; £577; £288) **Stalls** Low

Form RPR
54 **1** **Velvet Morn (IRE)**[14] 1094 4-8-11 0................................ AndreaAtzeni 6 69+
(William Knight) *mde all: stretched on jst over 2f out and sn 3 l ahd: kpt on wl fnl f: unchal* **15/2**[3]

5- **2** 1½ **Harry's Bar**[311] 2755 4-9-2 0.. GeorgeWood 4 68+
(James Fanshawe) *t.k.h early: trckd ldng pair: outpcd 2f out: shkn up to take 2nd fnl f: styd on but unable to chal* **10/11**[1]

3 ½ **Ghaith** 4-9-2 0...(h[1]) BenCurtis 2 66+
(Hugo Palmer) *hld up in last trio: shkn up and green over 2f out: no prog tl styd on fnl f to take 3rd last 75yds: nrst fin* **3/1**[2]

2-24 **4** 1 **Sarasota (IRE)**[14] 1102 4-8-11 66.. NicolaCurrie 7 58
(Jamie Osborne) *chsd wnr: outpcd 2f out: no imp after: lost 2nd fnl f and fdd* **8/1**

5 ½ **Magical Ride** 4-9-2 0...(h[1]) TomQueally 5 61
(Richard Spencer) *slowly away: rn green and detached in last early: shkn up over 2f out: kpt on one pce fr over 1f out* **12/1**

6006 **6** 2 **Mystical Moon (IRE)**[19] 1020 4-8-11 45............................ PhilDennis 1 50?
(David C Griffiths) *chsd ldrs: shkn up over 2f out: sn outpcd: wknd fnl f* **100/1**

7 2¼ **Vallachy** 4-9-2 0.. DavidEgan 3 48
(William Muir) *towards rr: rdn and no prog 2f out: wknd over 1f out (jockey said gelding hung left-handed up the straight)* **20/1**

1m 13.6s (0.50) **Going Correction** +0.05s/f (Slow) **7** Ran SP% **113.7**
Speed ratings (Par 103): **98,96,95,94,93 90,87**
CSF £14.66 TOTE £5.50: £2.20, £1.20; EX 16.90 Trifecta £48.80.
Owner Mrs Susie Hartley **Bred** Mrs J Norris **Trained** Angmering, W Sussex

The Form Book Flat 2019, Raceform Ltd, Newbury, RG14 5SJ

FOCUS
A novice which the market decided lay between two from powerful yards, but Andrea Atzeni had other ideas.

1287 32RED ON THE APP STORE FILLIES' NOVICE STKS (DIV I) 1m (P)
6:30 (6:31) (Class 5) 3-Y-O+ **£3,881** (£1,155; £577; £288) **Stalls Low**

Form				RPR
025-	1		**Star Of War (USA)**[162] 8151 3-8-10 82 .... SeanLevey 9	71+
			(Richard Hannon) *mde all: stl gng wl 2f out: shkn up and drew clr fnl f* **8/11**[1]	
5-	2	3	**Moneta**[175] 7775 3-8-10 0 .... RobHornby 6	64
			(Jonathan Portman) *chsd wnr 2f: wnt 2nd again jst over 2f out: rdn and outpcd fnl f* **9/1**[3]	
55-	3	3/4	**She's Apples (IRE)**[114] 9314 3-8-10 0 .... JasonWatson 5	62
			(Roger Charlton) *hld up in last: pushed along and prog on outer 2f out: tk 3rd fnl f: kpt on steadily* **5/2**[2]	
33	4	1	**Bequest**[19] 1020 3-8-10 0 .... DavidProbert 3	60
			(Ron Hodges) *hld up in 5th: pushed along 2f out: kpt on one pce and n.d* **16/1**	
0-6	5	hd	**Exoptable**[21] 979 3-8-7 0 .... GeorgiaCox(3) 8	59
			(William Haggas) *chsd wnr after 2f to jst over 2f out: pushed along and one pce after* **20/1**	
45	6	1	**Ripplet**[16] 1064 4-9-13 0 .... CharlieBennett 2	62
			(Hughie Morrison) *hld up in 6th: pushed along over 3f out: no real prog* **25/1**	
	7	1 1/4	**Thora (IRE)** 3-8-10 0 .... HarryBentley 10	54
			(Simon Dow) *s.i.s: sn rcvrd to chse ldng trio: shkn up and rn green over 2f out: steadily wknd* **33/1**	
50-	8	nk	**Mongolia**[171] 7904 3-8-10 0 .... TomMarquand 1	53
			(Richard Hannon) *hld up in last pair: pushed along over 2f out: no prog* **16/1**	

1m 42.71s (2.91) **Going Correction** +0.05s/f (Slow)
WFA 3 from 4yo 17lb 8 Ran SP% **119.8**
Speed ratings (Par 100): **87,84,83,82,82 81,79,79**
CSF £9.14 TOTE £1.60: £1.02, £2.10, £1.20; EX 9.20 Trifecta £16.00.
Owner M H Al Attiya **Bred** Jane Schosberg **Trained** East Everleigh, Wilts

FOCUS
The weaker looking division of a fillies' novice won decisively by the clear form choice. Time was nearly three seconds slower than the second division.

1288 32RED ON THE APP STORE FILLIES' NOVICE STKS (DIV II) 1m (P)
7:00 (7:01) (Class 5) 3-Y-O+ **£3,881** (£1,155; £577; £288) **Stalls Low**

Form				RPR
3-	1		**Madame Tantzy**[147] 8643 3-8-10 0 .... CharlesBishop 1	77+
			(Eve Johnson Houghton) *hld up in 5th: waiting for room briefly over 2f out: prog sn after: chsd ldr jst over 1f out: clsd fnl f: rdn to ld last 75yds: r.o wl and hld on* **11/10**[1]	
3-	2	hd	**Nooshin**[120] 9224 3-8-10 0 .... HayleyTurner 8	76+
			(Charles Hills) *t.k.h: trckd ldr 6f out: shkn up to ld 2f out: rdn fnl f: hdd last 75yds: r.o but jst hld* **7/2**[2]	
	3	6	**Scenesetter (IRE)** 3-8-10 0 .... HarryBentley 2	62+
			(Marco Botti) *hld up in last pair: shkn up over 2f out: prog over 1f out: tk modest 3rd ins fnl f: no ch but kpt on steadily* **8/1**[3]	
-6	4	1 1/4	**Lady Mascara**[73] 133 3-8-10 0 .... GeorgeWood 9	59
			(James Fanshawe) *hld up towards rr: shkn up over 2f out: sn outpcd: kpt on same pce over 1f out* **16/1**	
4-3	5	1 1/2	**Dame Freya Stark**[8] 1217 3-8-10 0 .... JoeFanning 5	56
			(Mark Johnston) *t.k.h: led over 6f out to 2f out: wknd fnl f* **7/2**[2]	
00	6	shd	**Watch And Learn**[35] 761 3-8-10 0 .... MartinDwyer 7	55+
			(Andrew Balding) *stdd s and detached in last: pushed along over 2f out: nvr in it but kpt on fnl f* **50/1**	
0	7	3/4	**Hooriya**[12] 1142 3-8-10 0 .... AndreaAtzeni 3	54
			(Marco Botti) *trckd ldng trio: pushed along over 3f out: wknd wl over 1f out* **25/1**	
00-	8	1	**Clubora (USA)**[171] 7906 3-8-10 0 .... TomMarquand 4	51
			(Richard Hannon) *led to over 6f out: rdn over 2f out: wknd over 1f out* **25/1**	

1m 39.81s (0.01) **Going Correction** +0.05s/f (Slow) 8 Ran SP% **118.7**
Speed ratings (Par 100): **101,100,94,93,92 91,91,90**
CSF £5.34 TOTE £2.00: £1.10, £1.20, £2.80; EX 6.60 Trifecta £25.50.
Owner Mrs R F Johnson Houghton **Bred** Mrs R F Johnson Houghton **Trained** Blewbury, Oxon

FOCUS
The second division of the fillies' novice looked better on paper and was run nearly 3 secs faster than the first. The first three home look useful.

1289 32RED/BRITISH STALLION STUDS EBF CONDITIONS STKS 7f (P)
7:30 (7:30) (Class 3) 4-Y-O+ **£9,337** (£2,796; £1,398; £699) **Stalls Low**

Form				RPR
11-0	1		**Crossing The Line**[80] 30 4-9-1 100 .... DavidProbert 3	105
			(Andrew Balding) *hld up in last: clsd towards inner 2f out: rdn to ld over 1f out: edgd lft sn after: hrd pressed fnl f: hld on wl* **5/1**[3]	
220-	2	hd	**Glendevon (USA)**[115] 9294 4-9-2 100 .... ShaneKelly 2	105
			(Richard Hughes) *hld up in 3rd: clsd to chal jst over 1f out: pressed wnr hrd fnl f: nt qckn and jst hld* **11/4**[2]	
0-31	3	3	**Cardsharp**[10] 1181 4-9-9 110 .... JoeFanning 1	110+
			(Mark Johnston) *trckd ldr: shkn up over 2f out: lost pl over 1f out: stl cl up but looked hld whn impeded jst ins fnl f: nt rcvr* **4/7**[1]	
/500	4	3	**Giogiobbo**[26] 909 6-9-6 95 ....(b) EoinWalsh 4	93
			(Nick Littmoden) *racd quite freely: led to over 1f out: steadily wknd* **50/1**	

1m 24.61s (-1.39) **Going Correction** +0.05s/f (Slow) 4 Ran SP% **108.9**
Speed ratings (Par 107): **109,108,105,101**
CSF £17.99 TOTE £5.10; EX 19.80 Trifecta £27.90.
Owner Sheikh Juma Dalmook Al Maktoum **Bred** Mrs F S Williams **Trained** Kingsclere, Hants
■ Stewards' Enquiry : David Probert caution: careless riding

FOCUS
A small field but a fairly tight contest and so it proved.

1290 32RED H'CAP 6f (P)
8:00 (8:00) (Class 4) (0-85,85) 4-Y-O+ **£6,469** (£1,925; £962; £481; £400; £400) **Stalls Low**

Form				RPR
200-	1		**Soldier's Minute**[162] 8167 4-9-5 83 .... JoeFanning 2	97
			(Keith Dalgleish) *trckd ldr: led over 1f out and dashed for home: clr fnl f: readily* **5/1**[3]	
3111	2	4	**Treacherous**[14] 1098 5-9-5 83 .... CallumShepherd 9	84
			(Ed de Giles) *trckd ldrs: shkn up wl over 1f out: no ch once wnr had gone but styd on to take 2nd last 75yds* **3/1**[1]	
44-4	3	1/2	**Global Academy (IRE)**[14] 1098 4-9-7 85 .... TomMarquand 8	85
			(Gay Kelleway) *led: hdd and outpcd over 1f out: one pce after and lost 2nd last 75yds* **10/1**	
310-	4	1 1/4	**Lightning Charlie**[147] 8641 7-9-7 85 .... JasonWatson 1	81
			(Amanda Perrett) *t.k.h: trckd ldrs: rdn over 2f out: sn outpcd: n.d over 1f out* **10/1**	
1140	5	2 1/4	**Choice Encounter**[14] 1098 4-8-13 77 .... HollieDoyle 6	65
			(Archie Watson) *hld up in last pair: sme prog on inner 2f out: no hdwy and btn over 1f out* **6/1**	
-534	6	1	**Reckless Endeavour (IRE)**[26] 909 6-9-4 82 .... JamieSpencer 5	67
			(David Barron) *towards rr: rdn and no rspnse over 2f out: wl btn over 1f out* **7/2**[2]	
5500	7	2 3/4	**Kodiline (IRE)**[14] 1098 5-8-4 75 .... GinaMangan(7) 10	51
			(David Evans) *a in last pair: shkn up and no prog over 2f out* **33/1**	
33-6	8	4	**Breaking Records (IRE)**[80] 19 4-9-7 85 ....(h) BenCurtis 7	49
			(Hugo Palmer) *sltly awkward s: nvr beyond midfield: rdn and struggling over 2f out: wknd (jockey said gelding was slowly away)* **11/2**	

1m 11.81s (-1.29) **Going Correction** +0.05s/f (Slow) 8 Ran SP% **114.7**
Speed ratings (Par 105): **110,104,104,102,99 98,94,89**
CSF £20.48 CT £144.67 TOTE £5.10: £2.00, £1.40, £2.50; EX 20.80 Trifecta £170.40.
Owner Weldspec Glasgow Limited **Bred** Rabbah Bloodstock Limited **Trained** Carluke, S Lanarks

FOCUS
A reasonable class 4 but the winner looks to be ahead of his mark after refinding his form. The winner has been rated back to his best, and could be rated a bit higher through the second and third.

1291 32RED.COM H'CAP 1m 3f 219y(P)
8:30 (8:30) (Class 4) (0-80,79) 4-Y-O+ **£6,469** (£1,925; £962; £481; £400; £400) **Stalls Low**

Form				RPR
1	1		**King's Advice**[21] 985 5-9-5 77 .... JoeFanning 12	87+
			(Mark Johnston) *led after 2f: mde rest: jnd over 2f out: shkn up and asserted wl over 1f out: pushed out firmly and nvr in any danger after* **1/1**[1]	
-300	2	2 1/4	**Thaqaffa (IRE)**[23] 945 6-9-6 78 ....(h) CharlesBishop 5	84
			(Amy Murphy) *chsd ldng quartet: rdn over 2f out: styd on over 1f out to take 2nd jst ins fnl f: no threat to wnr* **33/1**	
05-3	3	1	**Lawn Ranger**[23] 945 4-9-4 77 .... KierenFox 10	81
			(Michael Attwater) *chsd ldng trio: rdn over 2f out: kpt on fr over 1f out to take 3rd last 100yds* **7/1**[2]	
00-6	4	1 1/4	**Roar (IRE)**[67] 246 5-8-12 70 ....(w) DavidProbert 2	72
			(Ed de Giles) *chsd ldrs in 7th: rdn over 2f out: styd on over 1f out to take 4th nr fin* **20/1**	
1314	5	3/4	**Central City (IRE)**[30] 825 4-9-3 76 ....(p) KieranO'Neill 1	77
			(Ian Williams) *chsd ldng pair: rdn over 2f out: chsd wnr over 1f out to jst ins fnl f: wknd* **8/1**	
/12-	6	1/2	**Cubswin (IRE)**[98] 5335 5-9-6 78 .... HollieDoyle 9	78
			(Neil King) *hld up in last quartet: pushed along and wl off the pce over 2f out: styd on fnl f: nvr nrr* **20/1**	
4-55	7	nk	**Galactic Spirit**[14] 1095 4-9-4 77 ....(p) AndreaAtzeni 4	77
			(Marco Botti) *awkward s and rousted: sn in 9th: drvn and no prog wl over 2f out: modest late hdwy* **7/1**[2]	
000-	8	nse	**Gavlar**[143] 8735 8-9-7 79 ....(v) CallumShepherd 7	79
			(William Knight) *slowly away: hld up in last quartet: drvn over 2f out: styd on fnl f: nvr nrr* **25/1**	
2101	9	1 3/4	**Unit Of Assessment (IRE)**[35] 754 5-9-7 79 ....(vt) JasonWatson 11	76
			(William Knight) *led 2f: chsd wnr: chal and upsides over 2f out: btn off wl over 1f out: wknd sn after* **15/2**[3]	
-214	10	1	**Dutch Uncle**[49] 552 7-9-6 78 ....(p) JamieSpencer 8	73
			(Olly Murphy) *restrained s: hld up in last: pushed along over 2f out: modest late prog: nvr in it* **20/1**	
0-50	11	nk	**Gawdawpalin (IRE)**[45] 617 6-9-6 78 ....(t) DavidEgan 3	73
			(Sylvester Kirk) *nvr beyond midfield: rdn and dropped to rr over 2f out: no ch after* **33/1**	
40/6	12	2 3/4	**Corinthian**[25] 915 6-9-7 79 ....(v) EoinWalsh 6	70
			(Derek Shaw) *chsd ldrs in 6th: rdn over 3f out: lft bhd over 2f out: no ch after* **40/1**	
26-0	13	1 3/4	**El Borracho (IRE)**[23] 945 4-9-3 76 ....(h) TomMarquand 13	64
			(Simon Dow) *slowly away: hld up in last pair: rdn and no prog over 2f out* **16/1**	

2m 34.16s (-0.34) **Going Correction** +0.05s/f (Slow) 13 Ran SP% **130.2**
WFA 4 from 5yo+ 1lb
Speed ratings (Par 105): **103,101,100,100,99 99,98,98,97,97 96,95,93**
CSF £58.72 CT £198.73 TOTE £2.20: £1.30, £7.20, £2.20; EX 65.50 Trifecta £300.50.
Owner Saeed Jaber **Bred** Rabbah Bloodstock Limited **Trained** Middleham Moor, N Yorks

FOCUS
A big field but a clear favourite and he made it look easy. The second has been rated to his winter form and third to his recent efforts.
T/Plt: £105.00 to a £1 stake. Pool: £57,912.00 - 402.42 winning units T/Qpdt: £13.40 to a £1 stake. Pool: £12,449.38 - 683.83 winning units **Jonathan Neesom**

1264 LINGFIELD (L-H)
Saturday, March 23

OFFICIAL GOING: Polytrack: standard
Wind: light, across Weather: light cloud

1292 BETWAY H'CAP 1m 4f (P)
2:00 (2:00) (Class 5) (0-70,72) 4-Y-O+ **£3,752** (£1,116; £557; £300; £300; £300) **Stalls Low**

Form				RPR
00-3	1		**Sotomayor**[21] 985 4-9-0 63 .... TomMarquand 3	71+
			(Jane Chapple-Hyam) *hld up wl in tch in quartet: clsd over 2f out: chsng ldrs whn nt clr run and swtchd lft over 1f out: rdn and hdwy to ld ins fnl f: r.o wl* **6/1**	
0-45	2	1/2	**The Jean Genie**[16] 1065 5-9-7 69 .... HollieDoyle 2	75
			(William Stone) *t.k.h: chsd ldrs: switching rt and effrt ent fnl 2f: ev ch whn squeezed for room ent fnl f: kpt on wl but hld fnl 100yds* **12/1**	
52-5	3	nk	**Sauchiehall Street (IRE)**[14] 1096 4-9-8 71 .... RobHornby 9	76
			(Noel Williams) *niggled along early: hdwy to chse ldrs after 2f: effrt to press ldrs 2f out: led and hung lft over 1f out: hdd ins fnl f: kpt on but hld towards fin* **13/2**	

-441 **4** 2 ½ **Music Major**[29] 859 6-8-11 **59**..(p) LukeMorris 7 60
(Michael Attwater) *wl in tch in midfield: effrt ent fnl 2f: stdy on same pce u.p ins fnl f* **8/1**

0323 **5** ½ **Harbour Quay**[24] 927 5-9-2 **64**...................................... KieranO'Neill 8 64
(Robyn Brisland) *chsd ldrs: effrt over 2f out: rdn to ld 2f out: sn hdd and struggling to qckn whn squeezed for room ent fnl f: wknd ins fnl f* **11/2**[3]

1-31 **6** 1 ½ **Rakematiz**[28] 876 5-9-10 **72**..................................... CallumShepherd 6 70
(Brett Johnson) *hld up in tch in midfield: effrt jst over 2f out: swtchd rt and nt clr run over 1f: swtchd rt again 1f out: kpt on same pce and no imp ins fnl f (trainer said gelding ran flat)* **4/1**[2]

-052 **7** 1 ½ **Gendarme (IRE)**[29] 859 4-9-3 **66**....................................... RossaRyan 4 62
(Alexandra Dunn) *led: rdn and hdd 2f out: unable qck ent fnl f: wknd ins fnl f (jockey said gelding was never travelling)* **12/1**

16-0 **8** ½ **Outofthequestion**[35] 754 5-9-5 **67**.................................... DavidProbert 1 62
(Alan King) *hld up in tch towards rr: effrt over 2f out: edging lft and no imp u.p over 1f out: nvr threatened ldrs (jockey said gelding was never travelling)* **7/2**[1]

0- **9** ¾ **Ace Combat**[86] 9397 4-9-2 **72**.............................(w) ScottMcCullagh(7) 10 67
(Michael Madgwick) *stdd and dropped in after s: hld up in last pair: effrt over 2f out: no hdwy and wl hld over 1f out* **33/1**

111/ **10** 9 **Coorg (IRE)**[1150] 358 7-9-8 **70**....................................... LiamKeniry 5 49
(John Butler) *s.i.s: hld up in last pair: shkn up over 2f out: no prog and wknd over 1f out* **20/1**

2m 31.3s (-1.70) **Going Correction** -0.075s/f (Stan)
WFA 4 from 5yo+ 1lb **10** Ran SP% **119.4**
Speed ratings (Par 103): **102,101,101,99,99 98,97,97,96,90**
CSF £77.33 CT £489.27 TOTE £8.30: £2.60, £3.30, £2.60; EX 81.70 Trifecta £428.10.
Owner Madhi M M S Alteesi **Bred** Good Breeding **Trained** Dalham, Suffolk

FOCUS
A fair handicap.

1293 LADBROKES HOME OF THE ODDS BOOST NOVICE STKS 1m 1y(P)
2:35 (2:35) (Class 5) 3-Y-O **£3,752** (£1,116; £557; £278) **Stalls** High

Form RPR

4 **1** **Mohtarrif (IRE)**[21] 979 3-9-2 0.. MartinDwyer 4 78+
(Marcus Tregoning) *pushed along leaving stalls: t.k.h and sn chsng ldr: effrt to chal ent fnl 2f: rdn to ld over 1f out: styd on wl and a doing enough ins fnl f* **7/2**[3]

13- **2** 1 **Fields Of Athenry (USA)**[105] 9459 3-9-9 0.................... PJMcDonald 7 82+
(James Tate) *hld up in midfield: effrt to chse ldrs 2f out: drvn and hdwy to chse wnr ins fnl f: kpt on but nt enough pce to chal* **5/2**[2]

55- **3** nk **Ritchie Valens (IRE)**[240] 5391 3-9-2 0.............................. SeanLevey 8 74+
(Richard Hannon) *chsd ldrs on outer: effrt ent fnl 2f: kpt on u.p ins fnl f: nvr quite enough pce to rch wnr* **6/1**

13- **4** 3 ¼ **Metatron (IRE)**[127] 9104 3-9-9 0............................ RichardKingscote 1 74+
(Tom Dascombe) *led: clr 5f out tl rdn and pressed 2f out: hdd over 1f out: lost 2nd and wknd ins fnl f* **9/4**[1]

3 **5** 4 **Moftris**[21] 978 3-9-2 0... JamesDoyle 5 58
(William Haggas) *dwlt: rn green in rr: rdn and hung lft over 3f out: 6th and outpcd over 2f out: wl hld whn hung again lft over 1f out (jockey said colt hung left-handed throughout)* **11/2**

6 hd **Power Of You (IRE)** 3-8-9 0................................(t[1]) Pierre-LouisJamin(7) 6 57
(William Knight) *sn dropped to rr: rdn 4f out: outpcd over 2f out: n.d after* **50/1**

40 **7** 2 **Tsarmina (IRE)**[11] 1165 3-8-11 0.. EoinWalsh 3 48
(David Evans) *sn stdd and rn green in last pair: outpcd over 2f out: n.d after (jockey said filly ran green)* **100/1**

0-0 **8** nk **Miss Enigma (IRE)**[12] 1142 3-8-11 0.................................. ShaneKelly 2 47
(Richard Hughes) *t.k.h: chsd ldrs: pushed along over 2f out: sn outpcd and wknd over 1f out* **50/1**

1m 37.45s (-0.75) **Going Correction** -0.075s/f (Stan) **8** Ran SP% **116.1**
Speed ratings (Par 98): **100,99,98,95,91 91,89,88**
CSF £12.92 TOTE £4.20: £2.10, £1.20, £1.60; EX 13.40 Trifecta £55.60.
Owner Hamdan Al Maktoum **Bred** Shadwell Estate Company Limited **Trained** Whitsbury, Hants

FOCUS
The bare form looks just fair, but a few of these are open to plenty of improvement.

1294 SUN RACING NO1 RACING SITE H'CAP 1m 1y(P)
3:10 (3:10) (Class 3) (0-95,93) 4-Y-O+ **£7,246** (£2,168; £1,084; £542; £270) **Stalls** High

Form RPR

1122 **1** **Executive Force**[7] 1232 5-9-7 **93**.................................(p) FrannyNorton 1 101
(Michael Wigham) *rdn along leaving stalls: in tch in midfield: effrt and nt clrest of runs 2f out: hdwy u.p to chse ldr ins fnl f: r.o wl u.p to ld last strides* **7/2**[2]

4-21 **2** nk **Sha La La La Lee**[21] 988 4-9-1 **87**............................ RichardKingscote 5 94
(Tom Dascombe) *led: rdn wl over 1f out: drvn ins fnl f: hdd and no ex last strides* **9/4**[1]

245- **3** 1 ½ **Hateya (IRE)**[181] 7588 4-9-6 **92**.. JamesDoyle 9 96
(Jim Boyle) *wd early: hdwy to chse ldr and t.k.h 6f out: rdn and unable to match pce of ldr over 1f out: lost 2nd and one pce ins fnl f* **20/1**

3133 **4** hd **Nonios (IRE)**[17] 1031 7-9-1 **92**..(h) DylanHogan(5) 6 95
(David Simcock) *s.i.s: t.k.h: hld up in tch in rr: clsd but forced wd bnd 2f out: rdn and hdwy to chse ldrs 1f out: kpt on same pce ins fnl f* **14/1**

0146 **5** nk **Mr Scaramanga**[28] 880 5-9-2 **88**... AdamKirby 2 91
(Simon Dow) *in tch in midfield on inner: nt clr run 2f out: swtchd lft over 1f out: kpt on same pce and edgd rt ins fnl f* **8/1**

6-23 **6** shd **Insurgence**[21] 988 4-9-2 **88**..(p[1]) DanielMuscutt 7 90
(James Fanshawe) *hld up in tch in last trio: clsd and n.m.r bnd wl over 1f out: n.m.r tl swtchd lft ins fnl f: kpt on u.p but no threat to ldrs* **5/1**

3466 **7** hd **Come On Tier (FR)**[18] 1025 4-8-2 **74** oh1............................ LukeMorris 4 76
(David Simcock) *pressed ldr for 2f: styd handy: rdn ent fnl 2f: unable qck over 1f out: hung rt and wknd ins fnl f* **20/1**

0660 **8** 1 ¾ **Atletico (IRE)**[14] 1097 7-8-13 **85**..(v[1]) EoinWalsh 3 83
(David Evans) *hld up in tch in last pair: nt clr run over 1f out: swtchd lft 1f out: nt enough room and unable to cl ins fnl f: wl hld whn swtchd lft again towards fin (jockey said gelding was denied a clear run in the final furlong)* **33/1**

2212 **9** nse **Family Fortunes**[21] 988 5-8-11 **90**........................ ScottMcCullagh(7) 8 88
(Michael Madgwick) *in tch in midfield: effrt ent fnl 2f: unable qck over 1f out: wknd ins fnl f* **9/2**[3]

1m 36.48s (-1.72) **Going Correction** -0.075s/f (Stan) **9** Ran SP% **118.1**
Speed ratings (Par 107): **105,104,103,103,102 102,102,100,100**
CSF £11.78 CT £138.20 TOTE £3.80: £1.50, £1.40, £4.40; EX 12.90 Trifecta £193.70.
Owner Tugay Akman **Bred** Rabbah Bloodstock Limited **Trained** Newmarket, Suffolk

FOCUS
A useful, competitive handicap.

1295 BETWAY CASINO H'CAP 5f 6y(P)
3:45 (3:45) (Class 2) (0-105,106) 3-Y-O+ **£11,971** (£3,583; £1,791; £896; £446) **Stalls** High

Form RPR

340- **1** **Gold Filigree (IRE)**[162] 8165 4-9-1 **92**................................... ShaneKelly 5 101
(Richard Hughes) *chsd ldrs tl wnt 2nd 2f out: sn upsides ldrs: rdn to ld 1f out: drvn and kpt on ins fnl f* **20/1**

6212 **2** ½ **Merhoob (IRE)**[14] 1105 7-9-11 **102**.. AdamKirby 4 109+
(John Ryan) *dwlt: in rr: effrt over 1f out: clsd and swtchd lft 1f out: hdwy u.p to chse wnr ins fnl f: r.o wl but nvr quite getting to wnr* **10/3**[2]

0320 **3** 1 **Corinthia Knight (IRE)**[14] 1105 4-9-8 **104**............ ThomasGreatrex(5) 10 107
(Archie Watson) *dwlt: wd and pushed along early: dropped into midfield after 1f: effrt over 1f out: styd on wl ins fnl f: nt rch ldrs* **10/1**

-643 **4** shd **Gracious John (IRE)**[21] 987 6-9-8 **99**...................................... JFEgan 3 102
(David Evans) *t.k.h: hld up in midfield: effrt over 1f out: styd on wl ins fnl f: nt rch ldrs* **8/1**

-221 **5** nse **Royal Birth**[21] 987 8-9-11 **102**..(t) SeanLevey 9 105
(Stuart Williams) *t.k.h: in tch in midfield: effrt u.p but unable qck over 1f out: kpt on same pce ins fnl f* **8/1**

01-0 **6** nse **Doctor Sardonicus**[30] 837 8-10-1 **106**.................... RichardKingscote 8 109
(Tom Dascombe) *sn led: rdn ent fnl 2f: hdd 1f out: no ex and wknd towards fin* **20/1**

-332 **7** shd **Stone Of Destiny**[28] 892 4-9-13 **104**.................................. JamesDoyle 2 106+
(Andrew Balding) *dwlt: t.k.h: hld up in last trio: c wd and effrt wl over 1f out: styd on u.p ins fnl f: nt rch ldrs (jockey said gelding was slowly away and ran too free)* **11/4**[1]

00-3 **8** 1 **George Bowen (IRE)**[14] 1105 7-9-7 **103**...............(v) SebastianWoods(5) 7 102
(Richard Fahey) *racd in last trio: t.k.h 1/2-way: c wd bnd 2f out: sn swtchd lft: nvr enough room ins fnl f: eased towards fin: nvr trbld ldrs (jockey said gelding was denied a clear run)* **7/1**[3]

-503 **9** ½ **Verne Castle**[8] 1211 6-9-0 **91**..(b) FrannyNorton 6 88
(Michael Wigham) *t.k.h: chsd ldr tl 2f out: stl handy edgd lft over 1f out: rdn 1f out: no ex and wknd ins fnl f (jockey said gelding ran too free)* **16/1**

1-50 **10** ¾ **Shining Armor**[51] 511 3-7-12 **92**...................................... DarraghKeenan(5) 1 81
(John Ryan) *chsd ldrs: nt clr run on inner 2f out: effrt whn short of room briefly over 1f out: wknd ins fnl f* **10/1**

58.37s (-0.43) **Going Correction** -0.075s/f (Stan)
WFA 3 from 4yo+ 12lb **10** Ran SP% **118.1**
Speed ratings (Par 109): **100,99,97,97,97 97,97,95,94,93**
CSF £87.01 CT £734.17 TOTE £27.00: £6.60, £1.60, £3.40; EX 152.10 Trifecta £1247.70.
Owner Galloway,Lawrence,Merritt & Mrs Blake **Bred** Grangecon Holdings Ltd **Trained** Upper Lambourn, Berks

■ Stewards' Enquiry : Franny Norton caution: careless riding

FOCUS
A good, competitive sprint handicap but the winner did this surprisingly well.

1296 LADBROKES H'CAP 6f 1y(P)
4:20 (4:20) (Class 6) (0-65,65) 3-Y-O
£3,105 (£924; £461; £300; £300; £300) **Stalls** Low

Form RPR

5-42 **1** **Sundiata**[19] 1020 3-9-5 **63**.. RichardKingscote 6 71+
(Charles Hills) *in tch: clsd 2f out: swtchd lft over 1f out: pushed into ld 1f out: kpt on under hands and heels and holding runner-up cl home* **9/4**[1]

0-44 **2** hd **Sussudio**[19] 1020 3-8-13 **57**...(p) HarryBentley 11 65+
(Richard Spencer) *dwlt: dropped in sn after s: hld up in last pair: clsd over 2f out: drvn over 1f out: hdwy to chse wnr ins fnl f: str chal towards fin: hld cl home* **8/1**

2-21 **3** 1 ½ **Eye Of The Water (IRE)**[31] 813 3-8-12 **56**.................... DavidProbert 5 59
(Ronald Harris) *t.k.h: chsd ldrs: rdn to ld over 1f out: hdd 1f out: kpt on same pce ins fnl f* **5/1**[3]

40-4 **4** 1 ¼ **Your Mothers' Eyes**[52] 476 3-8-10 **59**.................... DarraghKeenan(5) 1 58
(Alan Bailey) *chsd ldrs: drvn and pressed ldrs over 1f out: no ex ins fnl f: wknd towards fin* **7/1**

0-54 **5** 1 ½ **Fox Happy (IRE)**[49] 554 3-9-5 **63**.. SeanLevey 3 58+
(Richard Hannon) *hld up in rr: sme prog jst over 2f out: swtchd rt over 1f out: kpt on ins fnl f: nvr trbld ldrs* **3/1**[2]

0-62 **6** 1 **Dandy Lad (IRE)**[15] 1079 3-9-6 **64**....................................(p) ShaneKelly 2 56
(Richard Hughes) *taken down early and led to s: w ldr tl led 2f out: sn drifted rt and hdd over 1f out: wknd ins fnl f* **20/1**

665- **7** 3 ¼ **Tarrzan (IRE)**[225] 5940 3-9-0 **58**.. PJMcDonald 4 40
(John Gallagher) *in tch in midfield: unable qck u.p and btn over 1f out: wknd ins fnl f* **33/1**

4-05 **8** 7 **Superseded (IRE)**[57] 412 3-9-6 **64**.................................. RobertWinston 7 25
(John Butler) *mde most tl 2f out: sn drifted rt and lost pl: wknd fnl f and eased towards fin* **12/1**

0360 **9** ½ **Lincoln Spirit**[12] 1140 3-8-9 **53**.....................................(p) LewisEdmunds 12 13
(David O'Meara) *taken down early and mounted in chute: in tch in midfield: rdn and lost pl over 2f out: bhd and eased wl ins fnl f* **25/1**

-366 **10** 1 ½ **Yfenni (IRE)**[26] 906 3-8-2 **46** oh1..................................(p[1]) LukeMorris 8 1
(Milton Bradley) *in tch in midfield tl shuffled bk to rr over 2f out: bhd and no rspnse to press 2f out: wl bhd and eased ins fnl f* **33/1**

03-0 **11** 2 ½ **Invincible Sea (IRE)**[23] 943 3-9-2 **60**.............................. CallumShepherd 9 8
(Linda Jewell) *chsd ldrs tl rdn and lost pl over 2f out: wl bhd and eased ins fnl f* **50/1**

1m 11.86s (-0.04) **Going Correction** -0.075s/f (Stan) **11** Ran SP% **120.2**
Speed ratings (Par 96): **97,96,94,93,91 89,85,76,75,73 70**
CSF £20.33 CT £86.92 TOTE £2.60: £1.40, £2.50, £1.90; EX 21.70 Trifecta £73.80.
Owner K Abdullah **Bred** Juddmonte Farms Ltd **Trained** Lambourn, Berks

FOCUS
A modest sprint handicap. The third has been rated close to his recent effort.

1297 BETWAY LIVE CASINO H'CAP 1m 2f (P)
4:55 (4:55) (Class 6) (0-60,61) 4-Y-O+
£3,105 (£924; £461; £300; £300; £300) **Stalls** Low

Form RPR

/66- **1** **Amaretto**[159] 8282 4-9-1 **54**......................................(v[1]) CharlieBennett 7 64+
(Jim Boyle) *chsd ldrs: wnt 2nd over 8f out tl over 6f out: styd handy tl clsd to press ldr ent fnl 2f: rdn to ld over 1f out: edgd rt ins fnl f: kpt on (trainer said, as to the apparent improvement in form, the gelding had benefited a break and the application of first-time visor)* **5/1**[3]

3551 **2** nk **Subliminal**[10] 1183 4-9-8 **61**.. TomMarquand 1 70+
(Simon Dow) *chsd ldrs: effrt over 1f out: chsd wnr and swtchd lft ins fnl f: kpt on u.p: nvr quite getting to wnr* **2/1**[1]

-021 **3** *4* **Tesorina (IRE)**[36] 736 4-9-4 **57**..............................(v) RichardKingscote 2 58
(William Knight) *led tl hdd and unable qck u.p over 1f out: wknd ins fnl f* **6/1**

6200 **4** *1* **Diamond Reflection (IRE)**[8] 1215 7-8-8 **52**(bt) ThoreHammerHansen(5) 9 52
(Alexandra Dunn) *awkward leaving stalls and slowly away: sn swtchd lft and hdwy into midfield: effrt to chse ldrs 2f out: unable qck over 1f out: wknd ins fnl f* **16/1**

-566 **5** *1 ½* **Hidden Dream (IRE)**[21] 984 4-8-10 **49**....................(p) FrannyNorton 11 46
(Christine Dunnett) *hld up in last quartet: nt clrest of runs over 2f out: hdwy u.p over 1f out: kpt on ins fnl f: nvr trbld ldrs* **20/1**

0-16 **6** *½* **Cold Harbour**[24] 923 4-9-1 **54**.................................(t) KieranO'Neill 14 50
(Robyn Brisland) *t.k.h: hld up in last quartet: carried lft and impeded ent fnl 2f: hdwy u.p over 1f out: kpt on ins fnl f: nvr trbld ldrs (jockey said gelding ran too free)* **9/2**[2]

5-00 **7** *3 ¾* **Golconda Prince (IRE)**[23] 941 5-9-1 **54**.................... WilliamCarson 4 43
(Mark Pattinson) *chsd ldr tl over 8f out: in tch in midfield: edgd lft and struggling to qckn ent fnl 2f: wknd over 1f out* **33/1**

344- **8** *nse* **Cat Royale (IRE)**[112] 9360 6-9-1 **54**...............................(p) LiamKeniry 10 42
(John Butler) *chsd ldrs: hdwy to chse ldr over 6f out tl over 2f out: sn u.p and lost pl over 1f out: wknd fnl f* **16/1**

056 **9** *1* **Oborne Lady (IRE)**[24] 921 6-9-0 **53**................................ RobHornby 8 40
(Seamus Mullins) *s.i.s: in rr: no hdwy u.p 2f out: nvr involved* **33/1**

650- **10** *2* **Widnes**[143] 8737 5-9-0 **58**..............................(vt w) DarraghKeenan(5) 6 41
(Alan Bailey) *taken down early: hld up in last quartet: effrt but stl plenty whn nt clr run and hmpd on inner ent fnl 2f: nvr involved* **8/1**

3-20 **11** *1* **Orobas (IRE)**[10] 1183 7-9-1 **59**......................(v) PoppyBridgwater(5) 5 40
(Lucinda Egerton) *t.k.h: hld up in tch in midfield: swtchd to outer 7f out: rdn and lost pl over 2f out: bhd over 1f out* **20/1**

2m 4.03s (-2.57) **Going Correction** -0.075s/f (Stan) **11** Ran SP% **120.7**
Speed ratings (Par 101): **107,106,103,102,101 101,98,98,97,95 94**
CSF £15.07 CT £62.25 TOTE £5.00: £1.40, £1.50, £1.90; EX 18.20 Trifecta £84.10.
Owner Allen B Pope **Bred** Razza Del Sole Societa Agricola Srl **Trained** Epsom, Surrey

FOCUS
A moderate handicap. It's been rated at something like face value.
T/Plt: £56.50 to a £1 stake. Pool: £83,188.52 - 1,074.01 winning units T/Qpdt: £8.60 to a £1 stake. Pool: £7,465.41 - 636.79 winning units **Steve Payne**

1298 - 1305a (Foreign Racing) - See Raceform Interactive

NAAS (L-H)

Sunday, March 24

OFFICIAL GOING: Yielding to soft (soft in places)

1306a NAAS RACECOURSE BUSINESS CLUB MADRID H'CAP (PREMIER HANDICAP) 7f

3:05 (3:09) 3-Y-O

£26,576 (£8,558; £4,054; £1,801; £900; £450)

RPR

1 **Never No More (IRE)**[161] 8238 3-9-7 **97**.................. DonnachaO'Brien 8 107+
(A P O'Brien, Ire) *sn chsd ldrs: 5th after 1f: gd prog fr 3f out to ld under 2f out: sn rdn and kpt on strly u.p to assert ins fnl 150yds* **8/1**[2]

2 *3 ¾* **Black Magic Woman (IRE)**[170] 7965 3-8-7 **83**..........(b[1]) ChrisHayes 4 82
(Jack W Davison, Ire) *disp ld: settled in 3rd after 1f: gng wl over 2f out and prog to dispute ld under 2f out: sn hdd but kpt on wl u.p tl no ex ins fnl 150yds* **16/1**

3 *1 ¼* **Crockford (IRE)**[16] 1121 3-8-4 **80**............................(t) WayneLordan 16 76+
(Joseph Patrick O'Brien, Ire) *hld up in rr: stl in rr under 3f out but gng wl: sn prog between horses and rdn 1 1/2f out: sn hung lft and bmpd w rival ent fnl f: kpt on to go 3rd cl home* **8/1**[2]

4 *½* **Wasntexpectingthat**[169] 7988 3-8-7 **83**........................... PaulHanagan 5 78
(Richard Fahey) *chsd ldrs in 6th mostly: rdn over 2f out and kpt on wl u.p to go 3rd ent fnl f: no ex and dropped to 4th cl home* **10/1**[3]

5 *¾* **Third World (IRE)**[214] 6431 3-8-8 **84**.............................. ConorHoban 10 77
(D K Weld, Ire) *mid-div: pushed along 2f out: kpt on wl u.p: bmpd w rivals 1f out: no ex ins fnl f and one pce* **8/1**[2]

6 *¾* **Copia Verborum (IRE)**[155] 8428 3-8-11 **87**................... KevinManning 7 78
(J S Bolger, Ire) *sn chsd ldrs in 4th: pushed along over 2f out but sn no ex and styd on same pce u.p: bmpd w rival 1f out: kpt on* **12/1**

7 *2 ¼* **Chicas Amigas (IRE)**[189] 7354 3-9-2 **92**............................ ShaneFoley 13 77
(Mrs John Harrington, Ire) *broke wl but sn restrained in rr of mid-div: pushed along under 3f out and sme prog on outer: no ex u.p ent fnl f and one pce* **16/1**

8 *nk* **Swissterious**[44] 667 3-9-8 **98**...................................... RonanWhelan 15 82
(Damian Joseph English, Ire) *sn towards rr: rdn over 2f out and sme prog u.p but nvr nr to chal* **25/1**

9 *nk* **San Andreas (IRE)**[147] 8668 3-9-10 **100**.............................. RyanMoore 1 83
(A P O'Brien, Ire) *in rr of mid-div: pushed along on far side over 2f out: short of room and sltly hmpd 1 1/2f out: fnd room 1f out and sme prog but nt hrd rdn* **4/1**[1]

10 *6* **Parkers Hill (IRE)**[283] 3797 3-8-7 **83**..........................(t[1]) NGMcCullagh 6 50
(J P Murtagh, Ire) *mid-div: rdn over 2f out but sn no imp and styd on same pce* **12/1**

11 *½* **Colfer Me (IRE)**[18] 1049 3-9-3 **98**............................(b) ShaneCrosse(5) 3 63
(Joseph Patrick O'Brien, Ire) *disp ld: trckd ldr in 2nd after 1f: pushed along to dispute ld again under 3f out: hdd under 2f out and sn no ex: wknd* **8/1**[2]

12 *½* **Engles Rock (IRE)**[191] 7262 3-8-1 **80** oh6.............. KillianLeonard(3) 12 44
(Mark Michael McNiff, Ire) *towards rr: rdn under 3f out but sn one pce and nvr nr to chal* **33/1**

13 *1 ¾* **Barend Boy**[156] 8387 3-7-11 **80** oh2..........................(t) AndrewSlattery(7) 2 39
(Richard John O'Brien, Ire) *disp ld and def ldr after 1f: pushed along whn chal under 3f out: hdd under 2f out and sn no ex u.p: wknd* **12/1**

14 *½* **Zander**[195] 7137 3-9-8 **98**... ColinKeane 14 56
(G M Lyons, Ire) *hld up in rr: pushed along under 3f out: hung lft u.p 2f out: sn no imp: nvr in contention* **8/1**[2]

15 *1* **Leagan Gaeilge (IRE)**[148] 8653 3-8-7 **83**........................ RoryCleary 9 38
(J S Bolger, Ire) *sn mid-div: rdn under 3f out but sn no ex u.p and wknd* **12/1**

16 *3 ¾* **Dandys Ocean (IRE)**[140] 8858 3-8-6 **85**...............(p[1]) TomMadden(3) 11 30
(Mrs John Harrington, Ire) *mid-div on outer: rdn over 2f out but sn no imp and grad wknd* **16/1**

1m 34.89s (7.39) **16** Ran SP% **139.9**
CSF £149.22 CT £1146.56 TOTE £10.10: £2.40, £4.10, £2.50, £3.00; DF 162.80 Trifecta £1562.10.
Owner Michael Tabor & Derrick Smith & Mrs John Magnier **Bred** Rjb Bloodstock **Trained** Cashel, Co Tipperary

FOCUS
This looked typically open on paper, but the Ballydoyle second-string proved much too good, suggesting this may have been a case of a Group horse running in a handicap. The runner-up performed with much credit in the circumstances. The level is set around the placed horses.

1307a LODGE PARK STUD IRISH EBF PARK EXPRESS STKS (GROUP 3) (F&M) 1m

3:40 (3:42) 3-Y-O+

£41,193 (£13,265; £6,283; £2,792; £1,396; £698)

RPR

1 **Normandel (FR)**[140] 8862 5-9-11 99.............................. KevinManning 9 98
(J S Bolger, Ire) *w.w in rr: hdwy under 3f out: impr between horses 2f out to sn dispute ld: rdn on terms ent fnl f and led 100yds out: kpt on wl far side cl home where strly pressed: jst hld on* **14/1**

2 *hd* **Hand On Heart (IRE)**[155] 8429 4-9-11 87........................ WayneLordan 5 98+
(J A Stack, Ire) *hld up towards rr: last 3f out: hdwy under 2f out where swtchd lft to chse ldrs 1f out where rdn: nt clr run and swtchd rt in 3rd wl ins fnl f: r.o wl to strly press wnr cl home: jst failed* **20/1**

3 *½* **Yulong Gold Fairy**[168] 8019 4-10-0 105............................ ShaneFoley 1 99
(D K Weld, Ire) *chsd ldrs: 4th into st: smooth hdwy travelling wl 2f: sn disp ld gng best: rdn on terms ins fnl f and hdd u.p 100yds out: hld by wnr cl home where dropped to 3rd* **6/4**[1]

4 *1 ½* **Ilex Excelsa (IRE)**[154] 8439 4-9-11 90.........................(p) ChrisHayes 6 93
(J A Stack, Ire) *led: pushed along 2f out and sn jnd: rdn and hdd over 1f out: sn no imp on ldrs u.p in 3rd and dropped to 4th wl ins fnl f* **20/1**

5 *2 ¼* **Fresnel**[30] 860 3-8-9 0... GaryHalpin 7 84
(Jack W Davison, Ire) *chsd ldrs: 3rd 1/2-way: drvn nr side over 2f out to chal briefly: no ex u.p in 4th over 1f out: one pce after* **20/1**

6 *2 ¾* **Delphinia (IRE)**[146] 8706 3-8-9 91................................. RyanMoore 2 78
(A P O'Brien, Ire) *cl up bhd ldr: 2nd 1/2-way: rdn over 2f out and sn wknd towards rr: kpt on again under hands and heels in 7th ins fnl f into mod 6th* **2/1**[2]

7 *2 ¼* **Ellthea (IRE)**[129] 9091 4-9-11 98.. WJLee 3 76
(J A Stack, Ire) *chsd ldrs: disp 5th gng wl into st: rdn 1 1/2f out and sn no ex u.p in 6th: wknd into mod 7th ins fnl f* **13/2**[3]

8 *2 ½* **Drombeg Dream (IRE)**[162] 8205 4-9-11 99....................... ColinKeane 4 71
(Augustine Leahy, Ire) *hld up towards rr: hdwy far side gng wl over 2f out to chse ldrs: sn pushed along and wknd 1 1/2f out: eased* **11/1**

9 *5 ½* **Rionach**[189] 7341 4-9-11 95..(h) LeighRoche 8 58
(M D O'Callaghan, Ire) *sltly awkward s: hld up in tch: disp 5th into st: drvn nr side over 2f out and sn wknd: eased* **12/1**

1m 49.31s (9.31) **9** Ran SP% **123.6**
WFA 3 from 4yo+ 17lb
CSF £266.79 TOTE £15.40: £2.20, £5.60, £1.02; DF 453.70 Trifecta £1600.50.
Owner Ballylinch Stud **Bred** Franklin Finance S A **Trained** Coolcullen, Co Carlow

FOCUS
Four-year-olds were in the majority, but the only five-year-old prevailed for the in-form Jim Bolger stable. Only two of the Classic generation involved, and neither made the first four. A pb from the second, while the fourth potentially limits the form.

1308a TOTE IRISH LINCOLNSHIRE (PREMIER H'CAP) 1m

4:10 (4:24) 4-Y-O+

£53,153 (£17,117; £8,108; £3,603; £1,801; £900)

RPR

1 **Karawaan (IRE)**[270] 4254 5-8-11 **83**.................................. ColinKeane 3 98+
(G M Lyons, Ire) *delayed s: chsd ldrs on inner: pushed along 2f out and prog to go 3rd: sltly bmpd rival: sn rdn and kpt on wl between horses to ld jst under 1f out: asserted fnl 150yds* **9/1**[3]

2 *2 ¾* **Trading Point (FR)**[290] 3510 5-8-12 **89**................ DonaghO'Connor(5) 4 98
(Damian Joseph English, Ire) *delayed s: chsd ldrs: prog over 2f out and led under 2f out: sn rdn: kpt on wl u.p but hdd jst under 1f out: no ex and one pce* **25/1**

3 *1 ¼* **Master Speaker (IRE)**[37] 748 9-9-1 **87**........................(t) RonanWhelan 6 93
(Adrian McGuinness, Ire) *delayed s: towards rr: gd prog fr 3f out on far side: rdn 2f out and kpt on wl to go 3rd 100yds out: nrst fin* **12/1**

4 *1 ¼* **Warnaq (IRE)**[88] 8859 5-9-2 **88**.................................... RobbieColgan 5 91
(Matthew J Smith, Ire) *delayed s: sn led: pushed along over 2f out: hdd under 2f out: kpt on strly u.p but no ex ent fnl f and one pce* **6/1**[1]

5 *1 ¼* **Crownthorpe**[153] 8487 4-9-0 **86**..................................(p) TonyHamilton 12 86
(Richard Fahey) *delayed s: towards rr: rdn over 2f out and prog on far side to go 5th ins fnl f: nrst fin* **10/1**

6 *½* **Tony The Gent (IRE)**[65] 305 6-8-5 **87**.................... JohnShinnick(10) 16 86
(G M Lyons, Ire) *delayed s: towards rr: pushed along on far side over 2f out: taken to centre of trck over 1f out and kpt on steadily but nvr nr to chal* **20/1**

7 *4 ½* **Honor Oak (IRE)**[107] 9453 7-9-0 **86**..................................... WJLee 1 75
(T Hogan, Ire) *delayed s: sn chsd ldrs: wnt 3rd over 2f out: bmpd sltly by rival under 2f out: sn rdn but no ex: kpt on same pce* **14/1**

8 *1* **Fastar (IRE)**[156] 8371 5-8-13 **85**............................... NGMcCullagh 9 71
(Gerard O'Leary, Ire) *delayed s: in rr of mid-div: rdn over 2f out and kpt on same pce u.p but nvr nr to chal* **16/1**

9 *½* **Ciao (IRE)**[9] 1224 4-8-13 **85** 7ex.................................(b) ChrisHayes 7 70
(Gavin Cromwell, Ire) *delayed s: hld up in rr: rdn and sme prog over 2f out: kpt on same pce u.p but no ex fr 1f out* **12/1**

10 *2 ¼* **Charcor (IRE)**[168] 8018 5-9-0 **86**.................................... ShaneFoley 11 66
(Mrs John Harrington, Ire) *delayed s: in rr: last 3f out: sn pushed along and kpt on steadily u.p but nvr nr to chal* **8/1**[2]

11 *1 ½* **Quizical (IRE)**[321] 2511 4-9-8 **94**................................... GaryHalpin 19 71
(Ms Sheila Lavery, Ire) *delayed s: towards rr on outer: rdn under 3f out and kpt on same pce: taken to far side ent fnl f and styd on steadily* **16/1**

12 *1 ½* **Society Red**[192] 7203 5-9-1 **92**............................ ConnorMurtagh(5) 8 65
(Richard Fahey) *delayed s: mid-div: pushed along over 2f out and sn taken to outer: rdn and no ex u.p: one pce* **25/1**

13 *¾* **Shatharaat (IRE)**[155] 8430 4-9-3 **89**.........................(t[1]) WayneLordan 2 61
(A Oliver, Ire) *delayed s: sn trckd ldr in 2nd: rdn over 2f out and sn no ex: wknd* **10/1**

14 *2 ½* **Marshall Jennings (IRE)**[168] 8019 7-9-9 **98**.............. TomMadden(3) 13 64
(Mrs John Harrington, Ire) *delayed s: chsd ldrs: rdn over 2f out and sn no ex u.p: grad wknd* **18/1**

15 *hd* **Insignia Of Rank (IRE)**[148] 8657 4-9-11 **97**................... GaryCarroll 17 62
(Joseph G Murphy, Ire) *delayed s: mid-div: rdn over 2f out and short of room briefly: kpt on same pce but nvr nr to chal* **14/1**

16 *nk* **Set In Stone (IRE)**[146] 8708 5-8-7 **86** .... AlanPersse(7) 15 51
(Andrew Hughes, Ire) *delayed s: in rr of mid-div on outer: rdn 3f out but sn no ex and one pce* **25/1**

17 *3* **Spiorad Saoirse**[144] 8749 4-9-0 **86** .... AJSlattery(7) 10 44
(Andrew Slattery, Ire) *delayed s: chsd ldrs: rdn over 2f out but sn no ex and wknd* **16/1**

18 *nk* **Aussie Valentine (IRE)**[30] 861 8-8-12 **91** ....(tp) GavinRyan(7) 20 48
(Adrian McGuinness, Ire) *delayed s: chsd ldrs: rdn 3f out but no imp and grad wknd* **12/1**

19 *26* **Calvados Spirit**[232] 5757 6-8-11 **83** .... PaulHanagan 18
(Richard Fahey) *delayed s: mid-div on outer: rdn under 3f out: sn no ex and wknd* **12/1**

20 *2 ½* **Theobald (IRE)**[51] 540 4-9-11 **97** .... KevinManning 14
(J S Bolger, Ire) *reshod bef s: delayed s: sn chsd ldrs: rdn in 3rd 3f out but sn no ex and wknd* **11/1**

1m 47.17s (7.17) **20** Ran SP% **145.2**
CSF £246.55 CT £1642.68 TOTE £11.00: £3.00, £8.50, £4.80, £1.60; DF 340.60 Trifecta £6201.00.
Owner David Spratt & Sean Jones & Mrs Lynne Lyons **Bred** D Phelan **Trained** Dunsany, Co Meath

FOCUS
Low numbers dominated, the first four all drawn six or lower. The first two had an identical profile as imports from Britain making a first Irish appearance. The third to the sixth help set the level.

1309a DEVOY STKS (LISTED RACE) 1m 2f
4:45 (4:48) 4-Y-O+

£23,918 (£7,702; £3,648; £1,621; £810; £405)

RPR

1 **Still Standing (IRE)**[181] 7635 4-9-5 97 .... ShaneFoley 6 100+
(Mrs John Harrington, Ire) *chsd ldrs: disp 4th fr bef 1/2-way: prog into 2nd travelling wl over 2f out: sn disp ld gng best and led over 1f out: extended advantage under hands and heels ins fnl f: easily* **9/4**[1]

2 *3 ½* **Hazel Bay (IRE)**[37] 750 4-9-0 0 .... ChrisHayes 2 85+
(D K Weld, Ire) *chsd ldrs: racd keenly: disp 4th fr bef 1/2-way: tk clsr order bhd ldrs gng wl in 3rd over 2f out: rdn over 1f out and impr into 2nd ins fnl f where no imp on wnr: kpt on same pce* **11/4**[2]

3 *1 ½* **Amedeo Modigliani (IRE)**[596] 5672 4-9-5 96 .... RyanMoore 8 87+
(A P O'Brien, Ire) *dwlt: settled towards rr: hdwy nr side over 2f out: rdn briefly disputing 3rd 1 1/2f out and no imp on wnr under hands and heels in 3rd wl ins fnl f: kpt on same pce* **11/4**[2]

4 *1 ¼* **Tiger Voice (FR)**[88] 1421 4-9-5 91 .... WayneLordan 1 84+
(Henry De Bromhead, Ire) *led: rdn and strly pressed tl 2f out: sn jnd and hdd over 1f out: wknd into 4th ins fnl f: jst hld 4th* **12/1**

5 *hd* **Satisfy (IRE)**[10] 1197 5-9-0 70 .... DeclanMcDonogh 7 79
(B A Murphy, Ire) *dwlt: settled in rr: prog far side over 2f out: sn pushed along and nt clr run briefly 1 1/2f out: sn rdn in 5th and no imp on ldrs: swtchd rt in 5th ins fnl f and kpt on nr fin: jst failed for 4th* **100/1**

6 *1 ¾* **Stellar Mass (IRE)**[161] 8242 6-9-5 106 .... KevinManning 5 81
(J S Bolger, Ire) *chsd ldrs: 3rd 1/2-way: drvn in 3rd 3f out and sn lost pl: no imp in 6th over 1f out: one pce fnl f* **5/1**[3]

7 *4 ¾* **Allez Kal (IRE)**[59] 2536 8-9-0 0 .... MarkGallagher 4 66
(James M Barcoe, Ire) *hld up towards rr: drvn in 7th bef st and struggling in rr over 2f out: kpt on one pce fnl 2f* **40/1**

8 *7* **Algo Rhythm**[146] 8709 4-9-0 0 .... LeighRoche 3 52
(D J Bunyan, Ire) *trckd ldr in 2nd: rdn in 2nd bef st and wknd qckly under 3f out* **66/1**

2m 25.76s (10.16) **8** Ran SP% **113.4**
CSF £8.54 TOTE £2.80: £1.20, £1.20, £1.60; DF 8.00 Trifecta £27.50.
Owner Mrs P K Cooper **Bred** D G Iceton **Trained** Moone, Co Kildare

FOCUS
No real strength-in-depth given that the third probably needed the run, but the winner is on the upgrade and should hold his own in Pattern company. The fifth, seventh and eighth hall potentially limit the form.

1310 - 1321a (Foreign Racing) - See Raceform Interactive

1086
JEBEL ALI (L-H)
Friday, March 22

OFFICIAL GOING: Dirt: fast

1322a SCHOOL TRANSPORT SERVICES (H'CAP) (DIRT) 1m (D)
10:45 (10:45) (65-90,84) 3-Y-O+ **£12,179** (£4,059; £2,232; £1,217; £608)

RPR

1 **Craving (IRE)**[20] 1001 4-9-10 **83** .... PatCosgrave 2 91
(Simon Crisford) *trckd ldrs: rdn to ld 1 1/2f out: r.o wl* **10/1**

2 *2 ¼* **Almoreb (IRE)**[8] 1205 5-9-11 **84** .... DaneO'Neill 6 87
(A R Al Rayhi, UAE) *mid-div: chsd ldrs 3f out: r.o wl fnl 2f* **14/1**

3 *nk* **Spirit Of Scotland (USA)**[8] 1202 5-9-0 **74** .... SPaiva 1 75
(R Bouresly, Kuwait) *mid-div: chsd ldrs 2f out: r.o wl fnl 1 1/2f* **13/2**[2]

4 *1 ¼* **Island Sound**[8] 1202 4-8-6 **67** ....(vt) AntonioFresu 7 64
(H Al Alawi, UAE) *slowly away: nvr nr to chal but r.o fnl 1 1/2f* **18/1**

5 *hd* **Kunani (USA)**[14] 1088 5-9-3 **77** ....(v) FabriceVeron 3 75
(M Al Mheiri, UAE) *mid-div: r.o same pce fnl 2 1/2f* **11/1**

6 *3* **Etisalat**[14] 1088 4-9-1 **75** ....(b) FernandoJara 13 66
(A R Al Rayhi, UAE) *a mid-div* **16/1**

7 *nk* **Almushref (USA)**[12] 1126 4-9-8 **82** ....(b) JimCrowley 4 72
(M Al Mheiri, UAE) *trckd ldrs: led 2 1/2f out: hdd & wknd 1 1/2f out* **7/2**[1]

8 *¾* **Invincible Strike (IRE)**[48] 572 8-9-1 **75** .... TadhgO'Shea 16 63
(S Seemar, UAE) *trckd ldrs tl wknd fnl 2f* **18/1**

9 *1 ½* **Treasured Times (IRE)**[12] 1126 5-9-1 **75** .... SzczepanMazur 14 60
(R Bouresly, Kuwait) *nvr nr to chal* **16/1**

10 *1 ¼* **Arroway (USA)**[14] 1088 4-9-1 **75** ....(b) XavierZiani 11 57
(S bin Ghadayer, UAE) *a mid-div* **12/1**

11 *2 ¼* **Untold Secret**[14] 1088 7-9-7 **81** .... RoystonFfrench 10 58
(S bin Ghadayer, UAE) *nvr bttr than mid-div* **12/1**

12 *3 ½* **Sa'ada (USA)**[12] 1126 4-9-4 **78** ....(h) ConnorBeasley 5 47
(A bin Harmash, UAE) *a in rr* **7/1**[3]

13 *2 ¼* **Glorious Poet**[8] 1202 6-8-8 **74** ....(h) SaeedAlMazrooei(6) 12 38
(S bin Ghadayer, UAE) *a in rr* **16/1**

14 *4 ½* **Denzille Lane (IRE)**[14] 1092 7-8-11 **72** ....(b) PatDobbs 15 24
(Doug Watson, UAE) *sn led: hdd & wknd 2 1/2f out* **20/1**

15 *shd* **Heraldic (USA)**[8] 1202 6-9-1 **75** ....(bt) RichardMullen 9 28
(S Seemar, UAE) *nvr bttr than mid-div* **7/1**[3]

1m 38.42s **15** Ran SP% **133.0**
CSF: 156.70; TRICAST: 1010.93.
Owner Sultan Ali **Bred** Lynn Lodge Stud **Trained** Newmarket, Suffolk

1323 - 1327a (Foreign Racing) - See Raceform Interactive

1292
LINGFIELD (L-H)
Monday, March 25

OFFICIAL GOING: Polytrack: standard
Wind: medium, against Weather: fine

1328 FOLLOW TOP TIPSTERS AT SUN RACING H'CAP 7f 1y(P)
2:30 (2:30) (Class 6) (0-58,58) 4-Y-O+

£3,105 (£924; £461; £300; £300; £300) **Stalls** Low

Form RPR

50-4 1 **Waqt (IRE)**[12] 1177 5-9-6 **58** .... RossaRyan 2 65
(Alexandra Dunn) *pushed along leaving stalls: trckd ldrs on inner: effrt to chal jst over 1f out: rdn to ld ins fnl f: sn hrd pressed: hld on wl towards fin* **11/2**[3]

0621 2 *hd* **Maazel (IRE)**[17] 1075 5-9-3 **55** .... RobertWinston 6 62+
(Lee Carter) *hld up in tch in midfield: clsd over 2f out: effrt and produced to chal ins fnl f: drvn and hld towards fin* **5/1**[2]

4325 3 *1 ½* **Shamlan (IRE)**[12] 1177 7-9-5 **57** ....(v[1]) JasonHart 8 60
(Kevin Frost) *w ldr: led u.p jst over 1f out: hdd ins fnl f: no ex and wknd towards fin* **6/1**

3625 4 *nse* **Dark Magic**[19] 1037 5-9-6 **58** ....(b) RobHornby 3 62
(Dean Ivory) *hld up in tch in midfield: clsd on inner over 1f out: chsd ldrs and kpt on ins fnl f* **7/2**[1]

0-P0 5 *¾* **Kafeel (USA)**[37] 760 8-9-5 **57** ....(v[1]) HectorCrouch 5 59
(Gary Moore) *chsd ldrs: nt clrst of runs over 1f out: swtchd rt and kpt on ins fnl f* **9/1**

20-0 6 *1 ½* **Confrerie (IRE)**[12] 1177 4-9-4 **56** ....(p[1]) NicolaCurrie 12 53
(George Baker) *hld up in tch in last trio: effrt over 2f out: swtchd rt jst over 1f out: kpt on ins fnl f: nvr trbld ldrs* **9/1**

0023 7 *½* **Middlescence (IRE)**[10] 1212 5-9-1 **58** ....(t) PoppyBridgwater(5) 11 54
(Lucinda Egerton) *pushed along leaving stalls: mde most tl hdd u.p over 1f out: no ex and wknd ins fnl f* **10/1**

00-0 8 *½* **Jupiter**[79] 86 4-9-6 **58** .... RichardKingscote 1 53
(Alexandra Dunn) *hld up in tch in last trio: pushed along over 1f out: kpt on ins fnl f: nvr trbld ldrs* **25/1**

10-0 9 *2* **Soaring Spirits (IRE)**[37] 760 9-9-6 **58** ....(v) FrannyNorton 4 48
(Dean Ivory) *in rr: pushed along 5f out: effrt and swtchd lft over 1f out: kpt on ins fnl f: nvr trbld ldrs* **16/1**

3064 10 *nk* **Knockout Blow**[12] 1179 4-9-4 **56** ....(v) CharlieBennett 7 45
(Jim Boyle) *in tch in midfield: effrt but v wd bnd 2f out: sn lost pl and edgd lft: wl hld fnl f* **10/1**

4550 11 *1 ¼* **Billyoakes (IRE)**[12] 1179 7-9-4 **56** ....(t[1]) LukeMorris 13 42
(Charlie Wallis) *sn prom: rdn and struggling to qckn ent fnl 2f: lost pl over 1f out: wknd fnl f* **25/1**

00-0 12 *8* **Formiga (IRE)**[20] 1021 4-9-4 **56** ....(vt) RaulDaSilva 10 22
(Seamus Durack) *in tch in midfield: swtchd rt and effrt on outer over 2f out: sn struggling: bhd and eased ins fnl f* **28/1**

1m 24.34s (-0.46) **Going Correction** -0.125s/f (Stan) **12** Ran SP% **123.8**
Speed ratings (Par 101): **97,96,95,95,94 92,91,91,89,88 87,78**
CSF £34.00 CT £179.60 TOTE £5.30: £2.10, £2.10, £2.60; EX 39.50 Trifecta £261.70.
Owner Helium Racing Ltd **Bred** Ennistown Stud **Trained** West Buckland, Somerset

FOCUS
A modest handicap run at a solid pace.

1329 SUNRACING.CO.UK H'CAP 7f 1y(P)
3:00 (3:00) (Class 5) (0-75,75) 4-Y-O+

£3,752 (£1,116; £557; £300; £300; £300) **Stalls** Low

Form RPR

5114 1 **First Link (USA)**[18] 1063 4-8-12 **66** .... NicolaCurrie 10 74+
(Jean-Rene Auvray) *t.k.h: chsd ldrs: nt clrst of runs 2f out: effrt over 1f out: styd on u.p to ld ins fnl f: r.o wl* **4/1**[2]

030- 2 *1* **Marshal Dan (IRE)**[129] 9094 4-9-3 **71** .... DavidEgan 9 76
(Heather Main) *in tch: effrt ent fnl 2f: hdwy to chse ldrs u.p 1f out: wnt 2nd and pressing wnr wl ins fnl f: styd on* **8/1**[3]

/05- 3 *½* **Gunmaker (IRE)**[145] 8748 5-9-0 **68** ....(w) JamesSullivan 8 72
(Ruth Carr) *t.k.h: hld up in tch towards rr: swtchd rt and effrt over 1f out: hdwy whn sltly impeded jst ins fnl f: r.o strly fnl 100yds* **16/1**

0242 4 *nk* **It Must Be Faith**[16] 1100 9-9-3 **71** ....(p) HayleyTurner 13 74
(Michael Appleby) *sn chsng ldr: ev ch over 1f out: unable qck u.p and one pce ins fnl f* **33/1**

-146 5 *shd* **Little Palaver**[37] 755 7-8-13 **74** ....(p) AmeliaGlass(7) 12 77
(Clive Cox) *chsd ldrs: rdn ent fnl 2f: kpt on same pce ins fnl f* **25/1**

-650 6 *shd* **Evening Attire**[33] 801 8-8-12 **66** .... HollieDoyle 4 68
(William Stone) *led: hrd drvn over 1f out: hdd ins fnl f: no ex and wknd towards fin* **12/1**

0-04 7 *1 ½* **Full Intention**[25] 944 5-9-2 **70** .... TomMarquand 5 68
(Lydia Pearce) *chsd ldrs: rdn ent fnl 2f: unable qck u.p 1f out: wknd wl ins fnl f* **14/1**

3-04 8 *nse* **Nezar (IRE)**[27] 914 8-9-2 **73** .... JackDuern(3) 6 71
(Dean Ivory) *hld up in rr: effrt and wd bnd 2f out: edgd lft over 1f out: styd on ins fnl f: nvr trbld ldrs* **14/1**

-340 9 *shd* **Mr Minerals**[16] 1106 5-9-6 **74** .... RossaRyan 11 72
(Alexandra Dunn) *in tch in midfield: clsd over 1f out: chsng ldrs u.p and nt clrest of runs ins fnl f: kpt on same pce* **25/1**

0-23 10 *nk* **Call Me Grumpy (IRE)**[14] 1143 5-9-6 **74** ....(bt) AndreaAtzeni 3 71
(Roger Varian) *hld up in tch towards rr: swtchd lft and effrt over 1f out: kpt on ins fnl f: nvr threatened ldrs: burst blood vessel (vet said gelding bled from the nose)* **2/1**[1]

-663 11 *hd* **Murdanova (IRE)**[33] 812 6-9-7 **75** .... JasonHart 14 72
(Ivan Furtado) *s.i.s: hdwy into midfield on outer after 2f: rdn 2f out: unable qck over 1f out: hld whn nt clr run ins fnl f: swtchd lft cl home* **14/1**

6524 12 *5* **Stormy Blues**[13] 1169 5-9-4 **72** ....(bt[1]) LukeMorris 7 55
(Nigel Hawke) *sn dropped to rr and bustled along early: no hdwy u.p over 1f out: wknd fnl f* **16/1**

200- 13 *6* **Perfect Symphony (IRE)**[159] 8315 5-9-0 **68** ....(h[1]) WilliamCarson 2 35
(Mark Pattinson) *a towards rr: no hdwy u.p over 1f out: sn wknd* **66/1**

30-6 14 *¾* **Blazed (IRE)**[24] 962 5-9-6 **74** ....(t) StevieDonohoe 1 39
(Ed Vaughan) *taken down early: dwlt and bustled along leaving stalls: in tch but a towards rr: no hdwy over 1f out: wknd fnl f* **8/1**[3]

1m 23.33s (-1.47) **Going Correction** -0.125s/f (Stan) **14** Ran SP% **127.1**
Speed ratings (Par 103): **103,101,101,100,100 100,99,98,98,98 98,92,85,84**
CSF £37.26 CT £485.84 TOTE £4.70: £1.70, £2.40, £4.20; EX 54.50 Trifecta £568.90.
Owner Stuart McPhee **Bred** Juddmonte Farms Inc **Trained** Calne, Wilts

FOCUS
The pace was sound for this fair handicap. It's been rated as ordinary form.

1330 BETWAY LIVE CASINO H'CAP — 1m 7f 169y(P)
3:30 (3:30) (Class 5) (0-75,77) 4-Y-0+
£3,752 (£1,116; £557; £300; £300; £300) **Stalls Low**

Form — RPR

012- **1** **Eden Rose**[139] 8910 4-9-7 **74** .... DavidEgan 9 — 91+
(Mick Channon) *in tch in midfield: clsd to trck ldrs wl over 3f out: pushed along and qcknd to ld 2f out: sn clr: eased towards fin: v easily* **4/1**[2]

5535 **2** *8* **Alabaster**[12] 1172 5-9-13 **77** .... (v[1]) LukeMorris 5 — 82
(Sir Mark Prescott Bt) *wnt rt and bmpd rival leaving stalls: chsd ldrs tl wnt 2nd wl over 3f out: drvn and ev ch 2f out: sn outpcd by wnr: wl hld but plugged on for clr 2nd after* **6/1**[3]

005- **3** *3 ½* **Jacob Cats**[143] 8807 10-9-12 **76** .... (v) OisinMurphy 3 — 77
(William Knight) *s.i.s and reminder sn after s: swtchd rt over 4f out: no imp u.p over 2f out: no ch w ldrs but plugged on into modest 3rd ins fnl f* **10/1**

0/ **4** *¾* **Hadfield (IRE)**[458] 8151 7-9-8 **72** .... (p) LiamKeniry 4 — 72
(Neil Mulholland) *midfield: swtchd rt and rdn over 4f out: sme prog over 2f out: sn struggling and outpcd: battling for wl hld 3rd fnl f: plugged on* **12/1**

-122 **5** *2 ½* **Atomic Jack**[23] 991 4-9-2 **69** .... NicolaCurrie 1 — 66
(George Baker) *led for 3f: chsd ldrs after tl 4th and outpcd 2f out: battling for wl hld 3rd over 1f out: wknd ins fnl f (jockey said gelding was never travelling)* **2/1**[1]

31/6 **6** *¾* **Music Man (IRE)**[16] 1095 9-9-8 **72** .... CharlieBennett 10 — 68
(Hughie Morrison) *midfield: rdn wl over 4f out: no imp and outpcd 2f out: sn wknd* **16/1**

0-10 **7** *2 ½* **Le Torrent**[23] 991 7-9-10 **74** .... TomMarquand 2 — 67
(Simon Dow) *midfield: effrt and sme hdwy u.p over 2f out: sn no imp and struggling 2f out: wknd over 1f out* **10/1**

-010 **8** *2 ¼* **Galitello**[14] 1144 4-8-10 **63** .... FrannyNorton 11 — 54
(Mark Johnston) *a towards rr: rdn over 4f out: sn struggling: no ch fnl 2f* **14/1**

0/60 **9** *4 ½* **Shades Of Silver**[14] 1144 9-8-12 **62** .... RossaRyan 12 — 47
(Alexandra Dunn) *a towards rr: rdn over 4f out: sn struggling: no ch 2f out* **66/1**

1410 **10** *1 ¼* **Navajo Star (IRE)**[12] 1172 5-9-6 **77** .... WilliamCarver[(7)] 13 — 60
(Robyn Brisland) *sn chsng ldrs: wnt 2nd after 4f tl led 6f out: rdn and hdd 2f out: sn outpcd: wknd over 1f out* **20/1**

345- **11** *18* **Methag (FR)**[128] 8613 6-9-3 **67** .... HectorCrouch 6 — 29
(Alex Hales) *bmpd leaving stalls: a in rr: lost tch and t.o 2f out (jockey said mare was never travelling)* **20/1**

42-5 **P** **Omotesando**[27] 916 9-9-2 **66** .... (p) RichardKingscote 8
(Oliver Greenall) *chsd ldr tl led after 3f: hdd 6f out: sn rdn and dropped out rapidly: bhd and eased 3f out: p.u and dismntd wl over 1f out (jockey said gelding stopped quickly)* **25/1**

3m 19.05s (-6.65) **Going Correction** -0.125s/f (Stan) — **12** Ran SP% **120.9**
WFA 4 from 5yo+ 3lb
Speed ratings (Par 103): **111,107,105,104,103 103,102,100,98,98 89,**
CSF £27.55 CT £229.99 TOTE £5.00: £1.70, £2.40, £2.70; EX 32.80 Trifecta £221.40.
Owner Jon and Julia Aisbitt **Bred** Jon And Julia Aisbitt **Trained** West Ilsley, Berks

FOCUS
A fair staying handicap. The second has been rated to his penultimate C&D form.

1331 BETWAY NOVICE STKS — 1m 4f (P)
4:00 (4:00) (Class 5) 4-Y-0+
£4,043 (£1,203; £601; £300) **Stalls Low**

Form — RPR

1 **1** **Gumball (FR)**[26] 921 5-9-8 0 .... (h) OisinMurphy 5 — 85+
(Philip Hobbs) *nudged leaving stalls: led for 2f: chsd ldr after tl effrt to chal 2f out: led ent fnl f: grad asserted u.p ins fnl f: styd on* **5/6**[1]

/3-2 **2** *1 ¼* **Allieyf**[24] 968 4-9-0 76 .... TomMarquand 8 — 76
(William Haggas) *styd wd early: prom tl led after 2f: rdn and hrd pressed 2f out: hdd ent fnl f: no ex and btn fnl 100yds* **9/4**[2]

33- **3** *4 ½* **Momtalik (USA)**[186] 7467 4-9-0 0 .... DaneO'Neill 3 — 69
(John Gosden) *bmpd sn after leaving stalls: in tch in midfield: chsd ldrs and effrt jst over 2f out: sn outpcd: wl hld and kpt on same pce fr over 1f out* **3/1**[3]

4 *2 ¾* **Made For You**[174] 7887 4-8-9 0 .... SeamusCronin[(5)] 1 — 64
(Olly Murphy) *chsd ldrs tl rdn and outpcd ent fnl 2f: wl hld and plugged on same pce fr over 1f out* **10/1**

6 **5** *4 ½* **Lawyersgunsn'money**[26] 921 4-9-0 0 .... FergusSweeney 4 — 57
(Roger Teal) *dwlt and short of room leaving stalls: hld up in tch: rdn and outpcd over 2f out: sn wl btn* **80/1**

4-0 **6** *1 ¼* **Sacred Sprite**[26] 921 4-8-9 0 .... JFEgan 2 — 50
(John Berry) *stdd s: t.k.h: hld up in last pair: rdn over 2f out: sn wl btn* **66/1**

56 **7** *1* **Dimmesdale**[40] 696 4-9-0 0 .... LiamJones 7 — 53
(John O'Shea) *racd in last pair: rdn and outpcd over 2f out: sn wl btn* **50/1**

5/0 **8** *2 ¾* **Muzaawel**[16] 1102 4-9-0 0 .... CharlesBishop 6 — 49
(Ralph J Smith) *wnt lft leaving stalls: chsd ldr for 2f: chsd ldr tl lost pl over 2f out: sn wl btn* **66/1**

2m 29.94s (-3.06) **Going Correction** -0.125s/f (Stan) — **8** Ran SP% **125.6**
WFA 4 from 5yo 1lb
Speed ratings (Par 103): **105,104,101,99,96 95,94,93**
CSF £3.50 TOTE £1.60: £1.10, £1.10, £1.30; EX 3.70 Trifecta £6.60.
Owner Terry Warner **Bred** J Gallorini, Mlle M Bilesimo Et Al **Trained** Withycombe, Somerset

FOCUS
An interesting novice dominated by the market leaders. The winner, fifth and sixth came here from the same Kempton race and have been rated similar.

1332 LADBROKES H'CAP — 1m 2f (P)
4:30 (4:30) (Class 6) (0-55,55) 3-Y-0
£3,105 (£924; £461; £300; £300; £300) **Stalls Low**

Form — RPR

0620 **1** **Vin D'Honneur (IRE)**[27] 917 3-9-7 **55** .... (p) OisinMurphy 12 — 62+
(Stuart Williams) *stmbld leaving stalls: hdwy to chse ldrs after 2f: led over 6f out: mde rest: rdn clr over 1f out: in command and kpt on ins fnl f: rdn out (trainer said, reg app imp in form, filly benefitted from being able to dominate on this occasion)* **17/2**

0440 **2** *1 ¾* **Bonneville (IRE)**[12] 1174 3-9-3 **51** .... (b) CharlesBishop 11 — 55
(Rod Millman) *hld up in tch in midfield: effrt ent fnl 2f: hdwy u.p ins fnl f: styd on to go 2nd towards fin: no threat to wnr* **8/1**

5335 **3** *1 ¼* **Al Daayen (FR)**[13] 1166 3-9-6 **54** .... FrannyNorton 14 — 55
(Mark Johnston) *midfield: stdy hdwy on outer to chse wnr over 4f out: rdn and unable to match pce of wnr over 1f out: kpt on same pce and lost 2nd towards fin* **16/1**

-510 **4** *½* **Lady Wolf**[18] 1066 3-9-4 **52** .... (p) RobHornby 4 — 52
(Rod Millman) *chsd ldrs: 4th and unable qck u.p 2f out: kpt on same pce ins fnl f* **17/2**

060- **5** *hd* **Parknacilla (IRE)**[95] 9636 3-9-0 **53** .... DylanHogan[(5)] 13 — 53
(Henry Spiller) *s.i.s: hld up in rr: nt clrest of runs over 2f out: rdn and hdwy over 1f out: r.o wl ins fnl f: nt rch ldrs (jockey said filly was never travelling in the early stages)* **25/1**

03-5 **6** *1 ¼* **Ignatius (IRE)**[59] 400 3-9-5 **53** .... KierenFox 2 — 51
(John Best) *hld up in tch in midfield: effrt over 2f out: unable qck over 1f out: kpt on same pce fnl f* **3/1**[1]

1325 **7** *1 ¼* **Chakrii (IRE)**[18] 1066 3-9-6 **54** .... RichardKingscote 9 — 50
(Henry Spiller) *s.i.s: hld up in rr: nt clrest of runs over 2f out: hdwy ent fnl f: nt clr run and swtchd rt ins fnl f: styd on but nvr threatened ldrs* **7/2**[2]

00 **8** *nk* **Chutzpah (IRE)**[12] 1174 3-9-5 **53** .... DavidEgan 10 — 48
(Mark Hoad) *in tch towards rr: effrt and wd ent fnl 2f: no imp and kpt on same pce fnl f* **25/1**

000- **9** *shd* **Ventura Island (FR)**[171] 7956 3-9-5 **53** .... TomMarquand 3 — 47
(Richard Hannon) *led for 1f: chsd ldrs: struggling to qckn u.p 2f out: wknd fnl f* **7/1**[3]

0-20 **10** *1 ¼* **Piccolita**[34] 795 3-9-3 **51** .... CharlieBennett 6 — 44
(Hughie Morrison) *midfield: rdn wl over 2f out: no imp whn nt clr run over 1f out: wknd ins fnl f* **33/1**

00-2 **11** *½* **Abenaki**[19] 1041 3-9-4 **52** .... DannyBrock 8 — 43
(Sheena West) *w ldr tl led after 1f: hdd over 6f out: chsd wnr tl over 4f out: rdn and struggling to qckn ent fnl 2f: wknd fnl f* **33/1**

-433 **12** *½* **Miss Green Dream**[37] 765 3-9-1 **49** .... ShelleyBirkett 1 — 39
(Julia Feilden) *hld up in midfield: effrt on inner over 1f out: nt clr run ins fnl f: wknd towards fin* **14/1**

000- **13** *21* **Inosanto**[208] 6681 3-9-4 **52** .... (h[1]) LukeMorris 7
(Robyn Brisland) *stdd after s: t.k.h: hld up towards rr: rdn and lost tch 2f out* **16/1**

600- **14** *6* **Monadante**[135] 8993 3-9-3 **51** .... JFEgan 5
(John Butler) *a towards rr: bhd over 2f out: sn lost tch* **14/1**

2m 6.26s (-0.34) **Going Correction** -0.125s/f (Stan) — **14** Ran SP% **130.6**
Speed ratings (Par 96): **96,94,93,93,93 92,91,90,90,89 89,88,72,67**
CSF £78.70 CT £1101.39 TOTE £10.00: £2.80, £3.10, £4.30; EX 97.30 Trifecta £1060.70.
Owner J W Parry **Bred** Mount Coote Stud **Trained** Newmarket, Suffolk

FOCUS
A modest handicap. A minor pb from the second.

1333 BETWAY AMATEUR RIDERS' H'CAP — 1m 2f (P)
5:00 (5:00) (Class 6) (0-60,62) 4-Y-0+
£2,994 (£928; £464; £300; £300; £300) **Stalls Low**

Form — RPR

-200 **1** **Orobas (IRE)**[2] 1297 7-10-13 **59** .... (v) MrSimonWalker 1 — 65
(Lucinda Egerton) *mde all: grad wnt clr fr 5f out: 7 l clr 3f out: rdn 2f out: tiring ins fnl f but nvr gng to be ct (trainer said, reg app imp in form, gelding benefitted from being able to dominate on this occasion)* **7/1**[3]

404- **2** *1 ¾* **Light Of Air (FR)**[68] 9585 6-10-9 **62** .... (b) MissKatyBrooks[(7)] 11 — 65
(Gary Moore) *dwlt: swtchd lft after s: hld up towards rr: hdwy into midfield and nt clr run over 2f out: hdwy over 1f out: chsd wnr ins fnl f: styd on but nvr getting on terms* **10/1**

0000 **3** *nk* **Clive Clifton (IRE)**[21] 1015 6-10-0 **46** oh1 .... (v) MissBeckyBrisbourne 7 — 48
(Mark Brisbourne) *hld up in rr on outer: effrt over 2f out: hdwy u.p to go 3rd ins fnl f: styd on but nvr getting wnr* **16/1**

1410 **4** *1 ¼* **Don't Do It (IRE)**[9] 1231 4-10-10 **56** .... (v) MissSerenaBrotherton 13 — 56
(Michael Appleby) *wd early: midfield: nt clr run over 2f out: effrt to chse clr wnr 2f out: kpt on but nvr threatened to get on terms: lost 2 pls ins fnl f* **5/2**[1]

2040 **5** *¾* **Attain**[12] 1183 10-10-13 **59** .... MissBrodieHampson 5 — 57+
(Archie Watson) *hld up towards rr: nt clr run over 2f out: rdn and hdwy over 1f out: styd on ins fnl f: nvr trbld ldrs* **7/1**[3]

1400 **6** *1 ¾* **Baasha**[28] 911 4-10-11 **62** .... (p) SophieSmith[(5)] 10 — 57
(Ed Dunlop) *hld up towards rr: nt clr run over 2f out: hdwy over 1f out: nvr getting on terms but kpt on ins fnl f* **8/1**

4-40 **7** *1 ¼* **Don't Cry About It (IRE)**[26] 923 4-10-1 **54** .... (bt) AlfieJordan[(7)] 3 — 47
(Ali Stronge) *t.k.h: prom in chsng gp: effrt to chse clr wnr over 2f out tl 2f out: plugged on same pce after* **9/1**

3-50 **8** *1 ½* **Dove Mountain (IRE)**[28] 910 8-10-5 **51** .... (tp) MrAlexFerguson 4 — 41
(Olly Murphy) *prom in chsng gp on inner: nt clr run over 2f out: swtchd rt and rdn over 1f out: nvr threatened and kpt on same pce fnl f* **15/2**

606/ **9** *shd* **Saga Sprint (IRE)**[463] 9278 6-9-7 **46** oh1 .... MrDallonHolmes[(7)] 8 — 36
(J R Jenkins) *wd thrght: prom in chsng gp: urged along 4f out: no imp and wl hld whn impeded jst over 1f out: wknd fnl f* **66/1**

-430 **10** *1 ½* **Tobacco Road (IRE)**[30] 876 9-10-13 **59** .... (t) MrRossBirkett 9 — 46
(Mark Pattinson) *hld up towards rr: effrt towards outer over 2f out: no imp and impeded over 1f out: wknd fnl f* **5/1**[2]

0 **11** *2 ½* **Vocal Heir (IRE)**[21] 602 7-9-7 **46** oh1 .... (b) MrLukeScott[(7)] 2 — 28
(Olly Murphy) *prom in chsng gp: wknd over 1f out* **25/1**

6-0 **12** *2* **Estibdaad (IRE)**[80] 58 9-9-12 **49** .... (bt[1]) MissMichelleBryant[(5)] 12 — 27
(Paddy Butler) *chsd wnr tl over 2f out: wknd over 1f out* **66/1**

501/ **13** *1* **Khismet**[529] 1234 6-10-7 **60** .... (p) MissImogenMathias[(7)] 6 — 36
(John Flint) *a towards rr: bhd fnl 3f* **33/1**

2m 6.3s (-0.30) **Going Correction** -0.125s/f (Stan) — **13** Ran SP% **127.9**
Speed ratings (Par 101): **96,94,94,93,92 91,90,89,89,87 85,84,83**
CSF £79.04 CT £1111.55 TOTE £6.30: £2.40, £2.50, £6.10; EX 63.30 Trifecta £828.60.
Owner Northern Belles **Bred** Ciaran Mac Ferran **Trained** Malton, N Yorks
■ Stewards' Enquiry : Miss Serena Brotherton five-day ban; careless riding (tba)

FOCUS
Not a strong race. The second and third have been rated near their recent figures.
T/Plt: £373.90 to a £1 stake. Pool: £94,729.39 - 184.94 winning units T/Qpdt: £62.30 to a £1 stake. Pool: £8,918.16 - 105.86 winning units **Steve Payne**

The Form Book Flat 2019, Raceform Ltd, Newbury, RG14 5SJ

1231 WOLVERHAMPTON (A.W) (L-H)

Monday, March 25

OFFICIAL GOING: Tapeta: standard
Wind: Fresh across Weather: Fine

1334 BETWAY LIVE CASINO H'CAP 1m 4f 51y (Tp)

5:15 (5:15) (Class 6) (0-55,55) 4-Y-0+
£3,105 (£924; £461; £400; £400; £400) Stalls Low

Form				RPR
543-	1		**Kirtling**[123] 9202 8-9-6 **55**....(t) JackMitchell 7 (Andi Brown) *s.i.s: hld up: racd keenly: swtchd rt over 2f out: hdwy on outer over 1f out: rdn to ld and hung lft wl ins fnl f: styd on* **6/1**[3]	62
005-	2	1	**Givepeaceachance**[110] 9406 4-8-12 **55**.... ScottMcCullagh(7) 5 (Denis Coakley) *chsd ldr 8f: remained handy: rdn over 1f out: led ins fnl f: sn hdd and unable qck* **17/2**	61
4-40	3	½	**Hussar Ballad (USA)**[35] 782 10-9-2 **51**.... CamHardie 9 (Antony Brittain) *chsd ldrs: rdn and ev ch ins fnl f: styd on same pce (vet said gelding lost it's right fore shoe)* **12/1**	56
6-00	4	hd	**Mac O'Polo (IRE)**[54] 482 5-9-4 **53**....(p) PaulMulrennan 10 (Donald McCain) *hld up: hdwy over 2f out: nt clr run over 1f out: rdn and edgd lft ins fnl f: styd on (jockey said gelding hung right-handed)* **50/1**	57
2106	5	½	**Ember's Glow**[28] 910 5-9-5 **54**.... EoinWalsh 8 (Mark Loughnane) *hld up: hdwy over 1f out: nt clr run ins fnl f: styd on* **8/1**	57
3-64	6	½	**Di's Gift**[11] 1196 10-9-5 **54**....(p1) AlistairRawlinson 1 (Michael Appleby) *sn prom: rdn over 2f out: styd on same pce ins fnl f* **16/1**	57
4-11	7	1	**Clearance**[40] 695 5-9-6 **55**.... AdamKirby 2 (Gary Moore) *hld up: nt clr run over 2f out: hdwy over 1f out: sn rdn: no ex wl ins fnl f* **13/8**[1]	58
-404	8	½	**Yasir (USA)**[15] 810 11-9-5 **54**.... DougieCostello 11 (Sophie Leech) *s.i.s hld up: nt clr run over 2f out: nvr nrr* **25/1**	54
-050	9	½	**Qayed (CAN)**[33] 810 4-9-3 **53**....(p) ShaneKelly 12 (Mark Brisbourne) *hld up in tch: chsd ldr 4f out: rdn to ld and hung lft over 1f out: hdd and no ex ins fnl f* **16/1**	53
0-00	10	3	**Lady Of York**[61] 363 5-9-5 **54**....(t1) JoeyHaynes 3 (Paul Howling) *led at stdy pce: qcknd over 2f out: rdn and hdd over 1f out: wknd ins fnl f* **33/1**	49
032	11	9	**Nice To Sea (IRE)**[28] 910 5-9-2 **51**....(p) DavidProbert 4 (Olly Murphy) *chsd ldrs: rdn and ev ch over 1f out: wknd ins fnl f (trainers' rep could offer no explanation for the poor performance)* **9/2**[2]	31
360-	12	24	**Scottsdale**[212] 6533 6-9-6 **55**....(p) TomQueally 6 (Peter Winks) *hld up: rdn and wknd over 2f out* **50/1**	

2m 41.23s (0.43) **Going Correction** -0.10s/f (Stan)
WFA 4 from 5yo+ 1lb **12 Ran SP% 122.4**
Speed ratings (Par 101): **94,93,93,92,92 92,91,91,90,88 82,66**
CSF £56.56 CT £603.31 TOTE £7.10: £2.40, £4.30, £2.60; EX 68.60 Trifecta £522.60.
Owner Faith Hope And Charity **Bred** L P R Partnership **Trained** Newmarket, Suffolk

FOCUS
A moderate middle-distance handicap on standard Tapeta. They went a muddling gallop and the third-favourite's winning time was over six seconds outside of standard. The third has been rated within 4lb of his recent best.

1335 BETWAY H'CAP 6f 20y (Tp)

5:45 (5:45) (Class 6) (0-55,55) 4-Y-0+
£3,105 (£924; £461; £400; £400; £400) Stalls Low

Form				RPR
4-41	1		**Krazy Paving**[26] 920 7-9-0 **53**....(b) MeganNicholls(5) 7 (Olly Murphy) *a.p: shkn up over 1f out: rdn ins fnl f: r.o to ld post* **11/1**	59
3303	2	nse	**Daring Guest (IRE)**[12] 1179 5-9-7 **55**....(bt) JackMitchell 4 (Tom Clover) *trckd ldrs: plld hrd: swtchd rt over 2f out: rdn ins fnl f: r.o* **10/3**[2]	61
620-	3	hd	**Wild Flower (IRE)**[143] 8795 7-8-13 **50**.... GaryMahon(3) 10 (Jimmy Fox) *led early: chsd ldr 5f out: rdn and hung lft over 1f out: styd on to ld nr fin: hdd post* **50/1**	55
226-	4	½	**Viking Way (IRE)**[115] 9328 4-8-11 **50**....(b) ConnorMurtagh(5) 6 (Olly Williams) *sn led: pushed clr over 1f out: rdn ins fnl f: hdd nr fin* **8/1**	54
5140	5	3¼	**Picks Pinta**[24] 973 8-8-6 **47**....(b) RPWalsh(7) 2 (John David Riches) *s.i.s: hld up: n.m.r over 5f out: rdn and r.o ins fnl f: nt trble ldrs* **22/1**	41+
0105	6	1¼	**Indian Affair**[20] 1021 9-9-7 **55**....(vt) DavidProbert 9 (Milton Bradley) *chsd ldrs: rdn over 1f out: styd on same pce* **16/1**	45
3504	7	hd	**Thorntoun Lady (USA)**[20] 1026 9-9-3 **51**.... AlistairRawlinson 13 (Jim Goldie) *hld up: r.o ins fnl f: nvr nrr* **20/1**	41
0513	8	nk	**Atyaaf**[10] 1210 4-9-7 **55**.... PaddyMathers 8 (Derek Shaw) *hld up: effrt over 1f out: no imp fnl f* **17/2**	44
00-3	9	4	**Compton Abbey**[54] 478 5-9-0 **48**....(vt) CallumShepherd 11 (Alexandra Dunn) *s.i.s: nvr nrr* **33/1**	25
5-04	10	1¼	**Filbert Street**[53] 503 4-9-6 **54**....(p) EoinWalsh 5 (Roy Brotherton) *s.i.s: hld up: plld hrd: nt clr run over 2f out: rdn and hung lft over 1f out: n.d (jockey said gelding ran too freely)* **28/1**	27
1/2-	11	5	**Mercury**[59] 420 7-9-7 **55**....(bt) AdamKirby 1 (Adrian Brendan Joyce, Ire) *chsd ldrs: nt clr run over 2f out: sn rdn and hung lft: wknd and eased fnl f (jockey said gelding moved poorly throughout)* **11/4**[1]	13+
2332	12	30	**Dodgy Bob**[20] 1026 6-9-1 **49**....(v) PhilDennis 3 (Michael Mullineaux) *s.i.s: pushed along early in rr: wknd and eased wl over 1f out (jockey said gelding got upset in the stalls and lost it's action in the home straight)* **5/1**[3]	

1m 13.85s (-0.65) **Going Correction** -0.10s/f (Stan) **12 Ran SP% 119.7**
Speed ratings (Par 101): **100,99,99,99,94 93,92,92,87,85 78,38**
CSF £45.32 CT £1828.86 TOTE £11.00: £3.40, £1.40, £18.20; EX 55.10 Trifecta £3823.30.
Owner All The Kings Horses & Aiden Murphy **Bred** Trebles Holford Farm Thoroughbreds **Trained** Wilmcote, Warks

FOCUS
A moderate sprint handicap, but an exciting three-way go resulted in a tight photo-finish, and the winning time was fair for the grade. The winner has been rated as repeating last year's level at this time of year.

1336 BETWAY CASINO NOVICE STKS 5f 21y (Tp)

6:15 (6:15) (Class 5) 3-Y-O+
£4,916 (£1,463; £731; £365) Stalls Low

Form				RPR
12-	1		**Top Breeze (IRE)**[109] 9427 3-9-9 0.... ShaneKelly 5 (Richard Hughes) *led: hdd over 3f out: chsd ldr: led again over 1f out: pushed out* **4/6**[1]	87+
	2	1½	**Sound Of Iona** 3-8-11 0.... PhilDennis 4 (Jim Goldie) *hld up: hdwy 1/2-way: chsd wnr fnl f: edgd rt: styd on same pce towards fin* **66/1**	70
-61	3	2½	**Major Blue**[47] 621 3-9-7 0.... AdamKirby 6 (James Eustace) *hld up: hdwy over 1f out: rdn to go 3rd wl ins fnl f: nt rch ldrs* **12/1**	71
33-	4	nk	**Rainbow Girl (IRE)**[262] 4613 3-8-11 0.... SeanLevey 3 (Richard Hannon) *chsd ldrs: rdn and ev ch over 1f out: no ex ins fnl f* **4/1**[2]	60
	5	1½	**Ginger Max** 3-9-2 0.... PaulHanagan 11 (Richard Fahey) *s.i.s: rn green in rr: hung rt 1/2-way: r.o ins fnl f (jockey said colt hung right-handed)* **11/2**[3]	60+
34	6	½	**Gupta**[13] 1161 3-9-2 0.... PaulMulrennan 9 (David Brown) *chsd ldrs: shkn up over 1f out: no ex fnl f* **22/1**	58
60	7	½	**Sharrabang**[13] 1168 3-9-2 0.... CamHardie 8 (Stella Barclay) *hld up in tch: rdn over 1f out: no ex fnl f* **100/1**	56
0	8	1	**Bannockburn (IRE)**[9] 1236 3-9-2 0.... JoeFanning 1 (Keith Dalgleish) *s.i.s: nvr on terms* **50/1**	52
56	9	hd	**Termonator**[13] 1161 3-9-2 0.... SamJames 7 (Grant Tuer) *hld up: shkn up 1/2-way: nvr on terms* **100/1**	52
505-	10	2½	**Seanjohnsilver (IRE)**[114] 9353 3-9-2 0....(t) CallumShepherd 2 (Declan Carroll) *s.i.s: a in rr (jockey said gelding jumped awkwardly leaving the stalls)* **18/1**	43
0-2	11	1¼	**Miaella**[60] 380 4-9-9 0.... JoeyHaynes 10 (Paul Howling) *chsd ldrs: led over 3f out: hdd over 1f out: wknd ins fnl f* **33/1**	38

1m 1.37s (-0.53) **Going Correction** -0.10s/f (Stan)
WFA 3 from 4yo 12lb **11 Ran SP% 121.1**
Speed ratings (Par 103): **100,97,93,93,90 89,89,87,87,83 81**
CSF £94.10 TOTE £1.40: £1.10, £9.70, £2.90; EX 61.50 Trifecta £639.90.
Owner Life's A Breeze **Bred** John Cullinan **Trained** Upper Lambourn, Berks

FOCUS
The feature race was a fair novice sprint contest. The odds-on favourite won well off a decent tempo. The winner has been rated in line with his previous runs.

1337 LADBROKES, HOME OF THE ODDS BOOST H'CAP 6f 20y (Tp)

6:45 (6:45) (Class 5) (0-70,72) 3-Y-O
£3,752 (£1,116; £557; £400; £400; £400) Stalls Low

Form				RPR
-221	1		**Second Collection**[21] 1020 3-9-1 **64**....(h) HollieDoyle 4 (Tony Carroll) *broke wl: sn lost pl and pushed along: swtchd rt: hdwy and nt clr run over 1f out: rdn to ld and edgd lft wl ins fnl f: r.o* **5/1**[2]	73+
6122	2	2	**Klopp**[17] 1081 3-9-5 **68**....(h) CamHardie 1 (Antony Brittain) *hld up in tch: swtchd rt over 1f out: nt clr run sn after: rdn and r.o to go 2nd nr fin* **15/2**[3]	70
04	3	½	**Ascot Dreamer**[17] 1081 3-7-11 **51** oh1.... AndrewBreslin(5) 9 (David Brown) *sn chsng ldr: led over 2f out: rdn and hdd wl ins fnl f* **25/1**	51
32-4	4	¾	**Griggy (IRE)**[28] 906 3-9-2 **65**.... AdamKirby 2 (John Butler) *chsd ldrs: rdn over 1f out: no ex wl ins fnl f* **5/1**[2]	63
243-	5	nse	**Friendly Advice (IRE)**[142] 8827 3-9-7 **70**.... PaulMulrennan 5 (Keith Dalgleish) *s.i.s: sn prom: rdn and edgd rt over 1f out: styd on same pce ins fnl f* **9/1**	67
3-13	6	nk	**Distant Mirage**[10] 1219 3-9-9 **72**....(p1) DavidAllan 3 (James Tate) *s.i.s: hld up: hdwy over 1f out: sn rdn: styd on same pce wl ins fnl f* **11/4**[1]	68
636-	7	1¾	**Molaaheth**[94] 9671 3-9-9 **72**.... SeanLevey 11 (Richard Hannon) *hld up: plld hrd: hdwy over 2f out: rdn and nt clr run over 1f out: wknd ins fnl f* **10/1**	63
16-4	8	nk	**Fizzy Feet (IRE)**[10] 1219 3-9-9 **72**....(p1) BenCurtis 6 (David Loughnane) *led: hdd over 2f out: rdn over 1f out: wknd wl ins fnl f* **8/1**	62
4216	9	14	**Axel Jacklin**[12] 1178 3-9-6 **69**.... JoeyHaynes 8 (Paul Howling) *broke wl enough: sn lost pl: shkn up 4f out: eased over 1f out* **100/1**	14
00-4	10	2½	**Evangeline Samos**[24] 972 3-8-13 **62**.... ShaneGray 7 (Kevin Ryan) *s.i.s: outpcd (jockey said filly was never travelling)* **20/1**	
55-4	11	17	**Invincible One (IRE)**[25] 943 3-9-4 **70**.... GaryMahon(3) 10 (Sylvester Kirk) *prom tl rdn and wknd over 2f out (jockey said he eased the gelding down in the straight as he felt the gelding did not feel right in it's action)* **20/1**	

1m 12.88s (-1.62) **Going Correction** -0.10s/f (Stan) **11 Ran SP% 116.3**
Speed ratings (Par 98): **106,103,102,101,101 101,98,98,79,76 53**
CSF £39.73 CT £869.07 TOTE £5.80: £2.00, £2.20, £4.90; EX 36.70 Trifecta £503.40.
Owner A A Byrne **Bred** Anthony Byrne **Trained** Cropthorne, Worcs

FOCUS
An ordinary 3yo handicap. One of the joint-second favourites won readily from off a decent pace in a good time. The second and third have been rated similar to their Newcastle latest.

1338 FOLLOW TOP TIPSTER TEMPLEGATE AT SUN RACING H'CAP 7f 36y (Tp)

7:15 (7:15) (Class 6) (0-65,65) 4-Y-O+
£3,105 (£924; £461; £400; £400; £400) Stalls High

Form				RPR
2630	1		**Grey Destiny**[32] 830 9-9-3 **62**....(p) CamHardie 12 (Antony Brittain) *s.i.s: hld up: hdwy on outer over 1f out: sn rdn and edgd lft: r.o to ld post (trainer could offer no explanation for the app imp in form other than the gelding may have been suited by the strong pace on this occasion)* **8/1**	69
0-00	2	shd	**De Little Engine (IRE)**[40] 701 5-9-3 **62**....(p) RossaRyan 10 (Alexandra Dunn) *led 1f: chsd ldr tl led again over 2f out: rdn over 1f out: hdd post* **16/1**	69
3001	3	1	**Peachey Carnehan**[20] 1021 5-9-4 **63**....(v) PhilDennis 7 (Michael Mullineaux) *chsd ldrs: rdn to go 2nd over 1f out: styd on* **9/1**	67

The Form Book Flat 2019, Raceform Ltd, Newbury, RG14 5SJ

5111 4 *1* **Elusif (IRE)**[12] 1177 4-9-2 **61**...............................(v) HollieDoyle 2 63
(Shaun Keightley) *sn pushed along: led 6f out: shkn up and hdd over 2f out: rdn over 1f out: styd on same pce wl ins fnl f (jockey said gelding ran too freely)* **7/4**[1]

00-0 5 *3/4* **Bouclier (IRE)**[56] 463 9-9-4 **63**.................................. DavidProbert 9 63
(James Unett) *hld up: hdwy u.p over 1f out: styd on* **20/1**

50-0 6 *nk* **Takeonefortheteam**[65] 315 4-9-3 **62**............................ EoinWalsh 8 61
(Mark Loughnane) *hld up: plld hrd: effrt and nt clr run over 1f out: r.o towards fin (jockey said gelding ran too freely)* **16/1**

112- 7 *3/4* **Agent Of Fortune**[130] 9077 4-9-5 **64**............................ AdamKirby 6 61
(Christine Dunnett) *chsd ldrs: rdn over 1f out: no ex ins fnl f* **10/3**[2]

-000 8 *3 3/4* **Makaarim**[25] 944 5-9-4 **63**...................................(h) TomQueally 3 51
(Seamus Durack) *hld up: a in rr* **18/1**

140- 9 *3/4* **Roaring Forties (IRE)**[147] 8697 6-9-5 **64**....................(p) DanielTudhope 5 50
(Rebecca Bastiman) *prom: shkn up over 2f out: rdn and wknd ins fnl f* **13/2**[3]

1m 28.16s (-0.64) **Going Correction** -0.10s/f (Stan) **9** Ran SP% **115.7**
Speed ratings (Par 101): **99,98,97,96,95 95,94,90,89**
CSF £125.23 CT £1180.60 TOTE £8.20: £2.10, £3.20, £2.30; EX 103.20 Trifecta £676.40.
Owner Antony Brittain **Bred** Northgate Lodge Stud Ltd **Trained** Warthill, N Yorks

FOCUS
A modest handicap. A C&D specialist got up late from off a decent gallop. The second has been rated near the best of his 2018 form.

1339 FOLLOW SUN RACING ON TWITTER H'CAP 1m 142y (Tp)
7:45 (7:45) (Class 6) (0-55,55) 4-Y-O+

£3,105 (£924; £461; £400; £400; £400) **Stalls** Low

Form RPR

0045 1 **Ubla (IRE)**[18] 1060 6-8-13 **55**....................................(e) SeanKirrane(7) 8 62
(Gay Kelleway) *hld up in tch: tk clsr order over 2f out: rdn to ld over 1f out: styd on u.p* **6/1**[3]

-260 2 *3/4* **Molten Lava (IRE)**[32] 829 7-9-4 **53**..............................(p) AdamKirby 2 58
(Steve Gollings) *chsd ldrs: rdn over 2f out: styd on* **8/1**

-504 3 *nk* **La Sioux (IRE)**[33] 814 5-9-3 **52**................................(b) PaulHanagan 6 57
(Richard Fahey) *led: hdd over 6f out: chsd ldrs: led over 1f out: sn rdn and hdd: kpt on* **11/2**[2]

-023 4 *1 1/2* **Final Attack (IRE)**[21] 1015 8-9-0 **52**......................(p) GabrieleMalune(3) 11 54
(Sarah Hollinshead) *s.i.s: hld up and bhd: pushed along over 5f out: hdwy and edgd lft fr over 1f out: nt rch ldrs (jockey said gelding was never travelling in the early stages)* **11/2**[2]

0032 5 *2 1/2* **Essential**[11] 1192 5-8-13 **53**....................................(b) ConnorMurtagh(5) 3 49
(Olly Williams) *prom: rdn over 1f out: styd on same pce fnl f* **10/1**

0-51 6 *8* **Seaforth (IRE)**[20] 1026 7-9-4 **53**.................................. HollieDoyle 5 33
(Adrian Wintle) *s.i.s: hld up: hdwy over 4f out: wknd over 1f out (jockey said gelding ran too freely)* **5/2**[1]

0-00 7 *1 1/2* **Cosmic Ray**[34] 792 7-9-3 **52**....................................(h) JoeFanning 12 28
(Les Eyre) *hld up: racd keenly: rdn over 2f out: nvr on terms* **40/1**

0-00 8 *2* **Big Amigo (IRE)**[13] 1158 6-9-2 **51**...............................(e) EoinWalsh 4 23
(Ken Wingrove) *hld up: drvn along over 3f out: n.d* **40/1**

000 9 *6* **Ainne**[25] 940 4-9-0 **52**..(bt) GaryMahon(3) 7 12
(Sylvester Kirk) *chsd ldrs: led over 3f out: rdn and hdd over 1f out: wknd fnl f* **28/1**

0206 10 *3 3/4* **Admiral Rooke (IRE)**[10] 1215 4-9-2 **51**...............(b[1]) AlistairRawlinson 9 3
(Michael Appleby) *plld hrd and sn prom: led over 6f out: hdd over 3f out: wknd and eased over 1f out* **10/1**

000- 11 *16* **Frank's Legacy**[108] 9441 5-9-6 **55**............................... TrevorWhelan 10
(Nikki Evans) *s.i.s: hld up: rdn and wknd over 3f out* **66/1**

1m 47.61s (-2.49) **Going Correction** -0.10s/f (Stan) **11** Ran SP% **112.7**
Speed ratings (Par 101): **107,106,106,104,102 95,94,92,86,83 69**
CSF £44.93 CT £214.40 TOTE £7.00: £3.00, £2.00, £2.10; EX 51.00 Trifecta £353.50.
Owner N Scandrett & Strictly Fun Racing Club **Bred** Tenuta Genzianella **Trained** Exning, Suffolk
■ Mans Not Trot was withdrawn. Price at time of withdrawal 8/1. Rule 4 applies to all bets - deduction 10p in the pound
■ Stewards' Enquiry : Gary Mahon £140 fine; change of boots after weighing out

FOCUS
A moderate handicap. The fourth favourite's winning time was fair for the grade. The second and third help set the level.
T/Jkpt: Not Won. T/Plt: £1,615.60 to a £1 stake. Pool: £99,640.18 - 45.02 winning units T/Qpdt: £80.10 to a £1 stake. Pool: £16,885.96 - 155.84 winning units **Colin Roberts**

1198 CHANTILLY (R-H)
Monday, March 25

OFFICIAL GOING: Polytrack: standard

1340a PRIX DU BOIS DE LA GRANDE MARE (CLAIMER) (3YO) (ALL-WEATHER TRACK) (POLYTRACK) 6f
1:55 3-Y-O **£12,162** (£4,864; £3,648; £2,432; £1,216)

RPR

1 **Big Boots (IRE)**[20] 1028 3-9-5 0.................................. ThierryThulliez 6 90
(F Rossi, France) **3/1**[2]

2 *5* **Pardon My French (IRE)**[11] 1200 3-8-11 0.................. TheoBachelot 8 66
(Vaclav Luka Jr, Czech Republic) **31/10**[3]

3 *1 1/4* **Amor Kethley**[33] 813 3-8-8 0.................................(p) MickaelBarzalona 4 59
(Amy Murphy) *wl into stride: led early: hdd after 1f but remained cl up: shkn up over 2f out: rdn to chse ldrs over 1f out: drvn and kpt on ins fnl f: no ch w wnr* **74/10**

4 *shd* **Enough Said**[11] 1200 3-8-11 0.................................. AntoineHamelin 2 62
(Matthieu Palussiere, France) *settled in midfield on inner: angled out 2f fr home: drvn to chal for 2nd and chsd clr ldr over 1f out: one pce ins fnl f* **15/1**

5 *2* **Lucky Bird (FR)**[40] 3-8-11 0.................................. AnthonyCrastus 5 55
(Louis Baudron, France) **17/1**

6 *1 1/4* **K Club (IRE)**[68] 261 3-8-11 0.............................. FrauRebeccaDanz(4) 3 55
(J Hirschberger, Germany) **12/1**

7 *1/2* **El Junco (FR)**[24] 3-9-1 0.................................. CristianDemuro 7 54
(Simone Brogi, France) **9/5**[1]

8 *14* **Islay Mist**[13] 1167 3-8-3 0.....................................(b[1]) ThomasTrullier(5) 1
(Amy Murphy) *trckd ldr: urged along 2f out: rdn and sn lost tch over 1f out: eased ins fnl f* **28/1**

1m 10.73s **8** Ran SP% **120.0**
PARI-MUTUEL (all including 1 euro stake): WIN 4.00; PLACE 1.80, 1.60, 2.10; DF 9.10.
Owner L Haegel **Bred** A Malone **Trained** France

1334 WOLVERHAMPTON (A.W) (L-H)
Tuesday, March 26

OFFICIAL GOING: Tapeta: standard
Wind: Light across Weather: Cloudy

1341 BETWAY LIVE CASINO H'CAP 1m 5f 219y (Tp)
5:00 (5:00) (Class 6) (0-65,65) 4-Y-O+

£3,105 (£924; £461; £400; £400; £400) **Stalls** Low

Form RPR

100- 1 **Ebqaa (IRE)**[125] 9179 5-9-11 **64**.................................. DavidProbert 10 70
(James Unett) *hld up in tch: racd keenly: chsd ldr 4f out: shkn up to ld over 1f out: rdn and edgd rt ins fnl f: styd on* **11/1**

4162 2 *nk* **Top Rock Talula (IRE)**[39] 736 4-8-11 **57**.............. ThomasGreatrex(5) 1 65
(Warren Greatrex) *led early: chsd ldrs: lost pl over 3f out: hdwy over 1f out: swtchd lft ins fnl f: r.o* **4/1**[2]

-403 3 *nk* **Hussar Ballad (USA)**[1] 1334 10-8-12 **51**......................... CamHardie 7 56
(Antony Brittain) *prom: lost pl over 10f out: hdwy over 2f out: rdn over 1f out: styd on* **4/1**[2]

20-0 4 *4* **Folies Bergeres**[21] 1024 4-9-5 **60**..............................(b) LukeMorris 8 62
(Grace Harris) *pushed along early in rr: hdwy over 4f out: rdn over 2f out: styd on same pce fr over 1f out* **66/1**

0/12 5 *1/2* **Geordielad**[34] 810 5-8-13 **52**................................ EdwardGreatrex 11 51
(Oliver Sherwood) *sn chsng ldrs: led 8f out: hdd 7f out: led again over 4f out: rdn and hdd over 1f out: no ex ins fnl f* **5/2**[1]

0062 6 *1/2* **Demophon**[26] 947 5-8-9 **48**.. RaulDaSilva 12 46
(Steve Flook) *prom: led after 1f: hdd 11f out: remained handy: rdn over 3f out: styd on same pce fr over 1f out* **14/1**

0-06 7 *13* **Seventii**[52] 549 5-8-2 **46**.................................. DarraghKeenan(5) 4 26
(Robert Eddery) *s.i.s: sn prom: rdn over 2f out: wknd over 1f out* **20/1**

060- 8 *18* **Midas Maggie**[87] 9751 4-8-2 **46** oh1..............................(p) WilliamCox(3) 2 3
(Philip Kirby) *s.i.s: nvr on terms (jockey said filly lugged left-handed throughout)* **50/1**

0-20 9 *10* **Hediddodinthe (IRE)**[12] 1196 5-9-9 **62**........................(p) HayleyTurner 13 3
(Peter Winks) *chsd ldrs: led over 8f out: sn hdd: led again 7f out: hdd over 4f out: sn rdn: wknd 3f out (jockey said gelding stopped quickly)* **33/1**

600/ 10 *13* **Guaracha**[603] 6835 8-9-7 **60**...................................... RossaRyan 9
(Alexandra Dunn) *broke wl: sn lost pl: n.d after* **100/1**

550- P **Big Sigh (IRE)**[158] 8386 5-9-12 **65**............................... JoeFanning 3
(John Mackie) *broke wl: sn lost pl: pushed along over 6f out: wknd over 5f out: p.u fnl 3f (jockey said gelding was never travelling)* **11/2**[3]

61-0 P **Brigadoon**[22] 481 12-9-12 **65**................................ RobertWinston 6
(Michael Appleby) *sn led: hdd after 1f: led again 11f out: hdd over 8f out: rdn over 4f out: sn wknd: p.u fnl 2f (jockey said gelding had no more to give)* **33/1**

3m 2.02s (1.02) **Going Correction** -0.075s/f (Stan)
WFA 4 from 5yo+ 2lb **12** Ran SP% **114.0**
Speed ratings (Par 101): **94,93,93,91,91 90,83,73,67,59 ,**
CSF £50.07 CT £208.85 TOTE £11.60: £3.50, £1.60, £2.00; EX 70.00 Trifecta £223.40.
Owner James Unett **Bred** Shadwell Estate Company Limited **Trained** Wolverhampton, West Midlands

FOCUS
An ordinary handicap, and a good ride won the day. A pb from the second.

1342 BETWAY CASINO H'CAP 5f 21y (Tp)
5:30 (5:30) (Class 5) (0-75,75) 4-Y-O+

£3,752 (£1,116; £557; £400; £400; £400) **Stalls** Low

Form RPR

-301 1 **Miracle Works**[32] 849 4-9-6 **74**.................................. TomMarquand 6 83
(Robert Cowell) *sn led: rdn over 1f out: drvn out* **11/2**[3]

006- 2 *nk* **Venturous (IRE)**[145] 8786 6-9-5 **73**.............................. SeanLevey 7 81
(David Barron) *hld up: hdwy over 1f out: rdn to chse wnr wl ins fnl f: r.o* **16/1**

4-10 3 *1 1/4* **Union Rose**[56] 471 7-9-5 **73**...................................(p) DavidProbert 9 76
(Ronald Harris) *sn chsng wnr: edgd lft over 3f out: shkn up and ev ch over 1f out: no ex wl ins fnl f* **16/1**

5252 4 *1 1/4* **Amazing Grazing (IRE)**[29] 907 5-9-7 **75**..................... DanielTudhope 8 74
(Rebecca Bastiman) *broke wl: lost pl after 1f: hdwy on outer over 1f out: r.o* **7/2**[2]

16-5 5 *1/2* **Nibras Again**[26] 953 5-9-6 **74**.................................. PaulMulrennan 3 71
(Paul Midgley) *chsd ldrs: hmpd over 3f out: rdn over 1f out: no ex ins fnl f* **8/1**

444- 6 *nk* **Sir Hector (IRE)**[335] 2068 4-9-2 **70**...................... RichardKingscote 10 66
(Charlie Wallis) *pushed along early in rr: shkn up over 1f out: rdn ins fnl f: nt trble ldrs* **16/1**

00-2 7 *nk* **Canford Bay (IRE)**[25] 970 5-9-4 **72**............................. CamHardie 11 67
(Antony Brittain) *s.i.s: swtchd lft sn after s: nt clr run 1f out: sn swtchd lft: styd on: nt trble ldrs (jockey said gelding was denied a clear run and hung left-handed)* **12/1**

045- 8 *3/4* **Patrick (IRE)**[158] 8382 7-8-10 **64**............................... BarryMcHugh 5 56
(Paul Midgley) *s.i.s: hld up: nt clr run over 1f out: nvr on terms* **16/1**

0510 9 *nk* **The Establishment**[14] 1164 4-9-4 **72**...............................(h) EoinWalsh 1 63
(David Evans) *s.i.s: nt clr run over 4f out: nvr on terms* **14/1**

3531 10 *1* **A Sure Welcome**[21] 1023 5-9-6 **74**..............................(b) LukeMorris 4 61
(John Spearing) *plld hrd and prom: hmpd over 3f out: hung rt 1/2-way: rdn over 1f out: edgd lft and no ex ins fnl f (jockey said gelding ran flat)* **3/1**[1]

-504 11 *2 1/4* **Van Gerwen**[25] 970 6-8-10 **64**...................................... JoeFanning 2 43
(Les Eyre) *chsd ldrs: n.m.r over 3f out: shkn up over 1f out: wknd fnl f* **20/1**

1m 0.31s (-1.59) **Going Correction** -0.075s/f (Stan) **11** Ran SP% **116.4**
Speed ratings (Par 103): **109,108,106,104,103 103,102,101,101,99 95**
CSF £88.77 CT £1324.36 TOTE £5.10: £1.50, £3.80, £4.80; EX 85.70 Trifecta £604.40.
Owner T W Morley **Bred** Worksop Manor Stud **Trained** Six Mile Bottom, Cambs
■ Stewards' Enquiry : David Probert two-day ban: interference & careless riding (Apr 9-10)
Sean Levey two-day ban: interference & careless riding (Apr 9-10)

FOCUS
It paid to be handy in this sprint. The second has been rated close to his 2018 turf form.

1343 BETWAY H'CAP — 1m 1f 104y (Tp)
6:00 (6:00) (Class 5) (0-70,70) 4-Y-0+
£3,752 (£1,116; £557; £400; £400; £400) Stalls Low

Form RPR

-614 1 **Anif (IRE)**[33] 835 5-8-7 63 .... GinaMangan(7) 7 73
(David Evans) *disp ld after 1f tl wnt on over 6f out: pushed clr 2f out: rdn and edgd lft ins fnl f: styd on wl* 3/1[1]

2 3 ¼ **Movie Star (GER)**[261] 4-9-1 64 .... (h[1]) OisinMurphy 12 67
(Amy Murphy) *trckd ldrs: racd keenly: rdn to go 2nd and hung lft wl ins fnl f: nt trble wnr* 18/1

3-40 3 1 **Bayston Hill**[31] 876 5-9-5 68 .... FergusSweeney 8 69
(Mark Usher) *disp ld after 1f tl settled into 2nd over 6f out: rdn over 2f out: no ex ins fnl f* 14/1

1242 4 nk **Zorawar (FR)**[25] 965 5-9-7 70 .... ShaneGray 5 70
(David O'Meara) *hld up: hdwy over 1f out: nt rch ldrs* 7/2[2]

4-34 5 1 ¾ **Iconic Girl**[25] 963 4-9-5 68 .... DavidProbert 11 65
(Andrew Balding) *hld up in tch: rdn over 1f out: styd on same pce* 5/1[3]

-003 6 ½ **Captain Pugwash (IRE)**[14] 1169 5-9-4 67 .... (v) LiamKeniry 3 63
(Stef Keniry) *hld up in tch: swtchd rt over 2f out: rdn over 1f out: styd on same pce* 13/2

63-6 7 2 ¼ **Ghazan (IRE)**[64] 344 4-9-2 65 .... JasonHart 9 56
(Kevin Frost) *hld up: shkn up over 1f out: nvr nrr* 14/1

1-50 8 1 **Beatbybeatbybeat**[14] 1169 6-9-7 70 .... (v) CamHardie 13 59
(Antony Brittain) *s.i.s: hld up: rdn over 1f out: n.d* 22/1

-000 9 2 ¼ **Tangramm**[35] 793 7-9-5 68 .... (p) RobertWinston 1 52
(Dean Ivory) *hld up: shkn up over 3f out: sme hdwy over 1f out: wknd fnl f* 10/1

00-0 10 1 ¼ **Jack Of Diamonds (IRE)**[31] 886 10-8-13 62 .... (p) HollieDoyle 2 43
(Roger Teal) *s.s: hld up: n.d* 66/1

6-00 11 ¾ **The Eagle's Nest (IRE)**[14] 1169 5-9-3 66 .... (t) RossaRyan 10 46
(Alexandra Dunn) *s.i.s: hld up: shkn up and hung lft over 1f out: n.d* 12/1

00-0 12 ¾ **Deadly Accurate**[57] 463 4-9-3 66 .... EoinWalsh 4 44
(Roy Brotherton) *led 1f: chsd ldrs: rdn over 2f out: wknd over 1f out* 150/1

1m 59.3s (-1.50) **Going Correction** -0.075s/f (Stan) **12 Ran SP% 119.1**
Speed ratings (Par 103): **103,100,99,98,97 96,94,94,92,90 90,89**
CSF £59.55 CT £670.00 TOTE £3.20: £1.10, £6.00, £4.30; EX 63.60 Trifecta £534.80.
Owner Dave & Emma Evans **Bred** Shadwell Estate Company Limited **Trained** Pandy, Monmouths

FOCUS
A modest affair dominated from the front. The winner has been rated close to his early 2018 form.

1344 LADBROKES HOME OF THE ODDS BOOST NOVICE MEDIAN AUCTION STKS — 1m 1f 104y (Tp)
6:30 (6:30) (Class 5) 3-Y-0
£3,752 (£1,116; £557; £278) Stalls Low

Form RPR

62- 1 **Dark Miracle (IRE)**[125] 9172 3-9-2 0 .... DanielMuscutt 6 66+
(Marco Botti) *mde all: set stdy pce tl qckn over 2f out: pushed clr over 1f out: comf* 1/2[1]

0 2 3 **Just Benjamin**[13] 1171 3-9-2 0 .... LiamJones 1 57+
(William Haggas) *a.p: racd keenly: rdn to chse wnr and edgd lft over 1f out: no imp fnl f* 7/2[2]

5- 3 2 ½ **Tribune**[276] 4126 3-9-2 0 .... BenCurtis 3 52
(Sylvester Kirk) *hld up: hdwy over 1f out: nt trble ldrs* 20/1

5 4 hd **Clap Your Hands**[13] 1182 3-9-2 0 .... CallumShepherd 4 51+
(David Simcock) *s.s: hld up: carried wd over 2f out: r.o ins fnl f: nt rch ldrs* 11/1

00 5 nse **Risk Mitigation (USA)**[17] 1094 3-9-2 0 .... TomMarquand 7 51
(David Evans) *hmpd s: prom: rdn over 2f out: hung lft over 1f out: styd on same pce* 25/1

00- 6 1 **Frenchmans Creek (IRE)**[105] 9490 3-9-2 0 .... RaulDaSilva 8 49
(Seamus Durack) *edgd lft s: chsd wnr after 1f: rdn over 2f out: lost 2nd over 1f out: wknd ins fnl f* 33/1

7 ½ **Peripherique** 3-8-11 0 .... LukeMorris 2 43
(James Eustace) *s.i.s: pushed along in rr: nt clr run and swtchd lft ins fnl f: n.d* 33/1

8 1 **Yellow Label (USA)** 3-9-2 0 .... OisinMurphy 5 46
(Andrew Balding) *s.s: in rr: shkn up over 3f out: hung rt over 2f out: n.d after (jockey said gelding hung right-handed)* 8/1[3]

2m 2.46s (1.66) **Going Correction** -0.075s/f (Stan) **8 Ran SP% 122.8**
Speed ratings (Par 98): **89,86,84,83,83 83,82,81**
CSF £2.72 TOTE £1.40: £1.10, £1.20, £4.50; EX 3.10 Trifecta £21.50.
Owner H Szabo **Bred** Selwood Bloodstock Ltd & R S Hoskins **Trained** Newmarket, Suffolk

FOCUS
Not a strong novice, and it might be that the winner didn't need to improve much on his previous effort to take it. Muddling form, and the fifth, sixth and seventh will ultimately decide the level.

1345 LADBROKES H'CAP — 1m 142y (Tp)
7:00 (7:00) (Class 4) (0-85,83) 3-Y-0
£5,530 (£1,645; £822; £411; £400; £400) Stalls Low

Form RPR

055- 1 **Prince Of Harts**[176] 7830 3-8-8 70 .... RobHornby 6 75+
(Rod Millman) *s.i.s: hld up and bhd: swtchd rt and hdwy on outer over 1f out: rdn to ld and edgd lft wl ins fnl f: r.o* 16/1

222 2 1 ½ **Assimilation (IRE)**[11] 1212 3-8-13 75 .... LiamKeniry 3 77
(Ed Walker) *hld up in tch: nt clr run over 2f out: rdn to ld ins fnl f: sn hdd and unable qck* 6/1[3]

43-1 3 ½ **Havana Rocket (IRE)**[63] 354 3-9-7 83 .... OisinMurphy 1 84
(Andrew Balding) *trckd ldrs: nt clr run over 2f out: led over 1f out: rdn and hdd ins fnl f: styd on same pce* 11/10[1]

155- 4 4 ½ **Self Assessment (IRE)**[164] 8195 3-9-6 82 .... BenCurtis 4 73
(K R Burke) *chsd ldr: led 2f out: rdn and hdd over 1f out: wknd wl ins fnl f* 10/1

6-32 5 5 **Wanaasah**[22] 1019 3-8-10 72 .... JasonHart 2 52
(David Loughnane) *led: shkn up and hdd 2f out: wknd ins fnl f* 13/2

201- 6 3 ¼ **Multamis (IRE)**[147] 8728 3-9-2 78 .... DaneO'Neill 5 51
(Owen Burrows) *chsd ldrs: shkn up on outer over 3f out: wknd wl over 1f out (trainer's rep said gelding had run flat)* 7/2[2]

1m 47.53s (-2.57) **Going Correction** -0.075s/f (Stan) **6 Ran SP% 112.4**
Speed ratings (Par 100): **108,106,106,102,97 94**
CSF £103.55 TOTE £18.10: £5.20, £2.50; EX 87.70 Trifecta £278.80.
Owner Perfect Match 2 **Bred** Harts Farm Stud **Trained** Kentisbeare, Devon

FOCUS
An interesting handicap and the unexposed winner enjoyed the smoothest trip. The second and third have been rated in line with the better view of their form, and the fourth to the balance of his form.

1346 SUN RACING NO1 RACING SITE NOVICE STKS — 7f 36y (Tp)
7:30 (7:30) (Class 5) 3-Y-0+
£3,752 (£1,116; £557; £278) Stalls High

Form RPR

1- 1 **Jackstar (IRE)**[343] 1873 3-9-6 0 .... RichardKingscote 2 86+
(Tom Dascombe) *chsd ldrs: shkn up to ld wl over 1f out: edgd lft ins fnl f: r.o wl* 8/11[1]

2 2 **Delta River** 4-9-7 0 .... GeorgiaDobie(7) 5 77+
(Jo Hughes, France) *hld up: plld hrd: hdwy over 1f out: r.o to go 2nd wl ins fnl f: no ch w wnr* 100/1

4 3 1 ¾ **Sea Storm**[14] 1168 3-8-13 0 .... RobHornby 9 62
(Martyn Meade) *chsd ldrs: shkn up over 2f out: ev ch wl over 1f out: styd on same pce fnl f* 20/1

4 nk **Bobby Shaft** 3-8-13 0 .... PaulHanagan 8 66+
(Richard Fahey) *s.i.s: hld up: hdwy and nt clr run over 1f out: nt rch ldrs* 28/1

5 2 ¼ **Oasis Prince** 3-8-13 0 .... JoeFanning 11 60+
(Mark Johnston) *s.i.s: in rr: pushed along 4f out: hung lft over 1f out: r.o towards fin* 18/1

4- 6 ¾ **Shamkha (IRE)**[152] 8577 3-8-8 0 .... FergusSweeney 7 53
(Richard Hannon) *hld up in tch: rdn over 2f out: wknd ins fnl f* 22/1

5-4 7 2 ¼ **Global Destination (IRE)**[26] 954 3-8-13 0 .... JosephineGordon 10 52
(Ed Dunlop) *hld up: shkn up over 1f out: nvr on terms* 28/1

44 8 ¾ **Cardano (USA)**[28] 913 3-8-13 0 .... StevieDonohoe 4 50
(Ian Williams) *hld up: shkn up whn nt clr run 1f out: nvr on terms* 100/1

0-2 9 1 **Soul Searching**[35] 795 3-8-8 0 .... OisinMurphy 1 43
(James Tate) *wnt prom over 5f out: rdn over 1f out: wknd ins fnl f* 9/2[2]

0 10 11 **Lauberhorn Rocket (GER)**[10] 1236 4-10-0 0 .... LiamKeniry 6 23
(Tim Vaughan) *hld up: n.d* 250/1

00- 11 5 **Kyllachy Princess**[181] 7675 3-8-8 0 .... BenCurtis 3
(David Loughnane) *led: rdn and hdd whn hmpd wl over 1f out: sn hung lft and wknd (jockey said filly hung left-handed throughout)* 100/1

P **River Dawn** 3-8-13 0 .... RaulDaSilva 12
(Paul Cole) *chsd ldr: shkn up and edgd rt over 2f out: sn ev ch: lost action jst over 1f out: sn p.u and dismntd (jockey said he felt the colt had lost its action and felt amiss)* 7/1[3]

1m 27.3s (-1.50) **Going Correction** -0.075s/f (Stan)
WFA 3 from 4yo 15lb **12 Ran SP% 113.2**
Speed ratings (Par 103): **105,102,100,100,97 96,94,93,92,79 74,**
CSF £148.89 TOTE £1.60: £1.10, £7.80, £4.20; EX 119.40 Trifecta £1548.30.
Owner Mrs Caroline Ingram **Bred** Skymarc Farm **Trained** Malpas, Cheshire

FOCUS
Probably not a strong novice but a pleasing return from the winner. The level is fluid.
T/Jkpt: Partly won. £39,109.10 to a £1 stake. Pool: £39,109.18 - 0.5 winning units. T/Plt: £659.70 to a £1 stake. Pool: £94,728.04 - 104.82 winning units T/Qpdt: £48.60 to a £1 stake. Pool: £15,109.72 - 230.01 winning units **Colin Roberts**

1240 SAINT-CLOUD (L-H)
Tuesday, March 26

OFFICIAL GOING: Turf: very soft

1347a PRIX FRANCOIS MATHET (LISTED RACE) (3YO) (TURF) — 1m 2f 110y
2:30 3-Y-0
£24,774 (£9,909; £7,432; £4,954; £2,477)

RPR

1 **Talk Or Listen (IRE)**[31] 3-8-13 0 .... StephanePasquier 4 104
(F Rossi, France) 123/10

2 nse **Surrey Thunder (FR)**[169] 8058 3-8-13 0 .... AlexisBadel 1 104
(Joseph Tuite) *wl into stride: disp ld early: settled to trck ldr: pushed through gap on rails to ld over 2f out: rdn to extend advantage over 1f out: drvn and strly chal ins fnl f: hdd on post* 18/1

3 3 **Argyron (IRE)**[147] 3-8-13 0 .... Pierre-CharlesBoudot 9 99
(A Fabre, France) 6/4[1]

4 3 **Pappalino (FR)**[135] 9027 3-9-3 0 .... CristianDemuro 7 97
(J Reynier, France) 14/1

5 shd **Famous Wolf (FR)**[18] 3-9-3 0 .... VincentCheminaud 12 97
(A Fabre, France) 39/10[2]

6 1 **Gritti (FR)**[238] 3-8-13 0 .... JulienAuge 8 91
(C Ferland, France) 11/1[3]

7 4 ½ **Marrakech Express (FR)**[16] 3-8-13 0 .... AntoineHamelin 11 82
(Laurent Loisel, France) 18/1

8 nk **Alabaa**[150] 8663 3-8-13 0 .... HugoJourniac 3 82
(L Gadbin, France) 18/1

9 4 **Bobydargent (FR)**[18] 3-9-0 0 ow1 .... OlivierPeslier 10 75
(J-P Gauvin, France) 19/1

10 ¾ **Falcon Run (FR)**[174] 3-8-13 0 .... AurelienLemaitre 5 73
(F Head, France) 14/1

11 13 **Bobesh** 3-8-13 0 .... MartinLaube 2 48
(Stepanka Myskova, Czech Republic) 126/1

12 1 ¼ **Beeswax (FR)**[39] 3-9-0 0 ow1 .... ChristopheSoumillon 6 47
(Gavin Hernon, France) 11/1[3]

2m 13.21s (-6.39) **12 Ran SP% 119.5**
PARI-MUTUEL (all including 1 euro stake): WIN 13.30; PLACE 2.50, 4.00, 1.40; DF 89.70.
Owner Patrick Dreux **Bred** T Darcy & V McCarthy **Trained** France

1349a PRIX DE MAUREPAS (CLAIMER) (4YO+) (TURF) — 1m
4:15 4-Y-0+
£8,558 (£3,423; £2,567; £1,711; £855)

RPR

1 **Ziveri (FR)**[12] 4-9-4 0 .... (b) ChristopheSoumillon 10 87
(F Rossi, France) 31/10[1]

2 3 **Flight To Dubai (IRE)**[41] 5-8-11 0 .... (p) MickaelBarzalona 5 73
(C Escuder, France) 63/10

3 snk **Wagram (FR)**[123] 4-8-9 0 .... MlleChloeHue(9) 11 80
(Hue & Lamotte D'Argy, France) 5/1[3]

4 nse **Nimr**[12] 6-9-1 .... Pierre-CharlesBoudot 1 77
(J Phelippon, France) 36/5

5 1 ¼ **Khochenko (FR)**[93] 4-9-4 0 .... HugoJourniac 8 77
(M Nigge, France) 19/5[2]

6 snk **Well Fleeced**[41] 7-9-2 0..........(p) StephanePasquier 3 74
(F Vermeulen, France) 6/1

7 1 **Menardais (FR)**[265] 10-8-10 0.......... JeremieMonteiro(8) 4 74
(N Caullery, France) 27/1

8 2 **Topmeup**[140] 8897 5-8-8..........(b) AlexisBadel 9 59
(Gay Kelleway) *settled towards rr: tk clsr order 3f out: urged along over 2f out: rdn to chse ldrs over 1f out: kpt on same pce fnl f* 16/1

9 2 **Bridport (IRE)**[501] 8725 4-9-1 0.......... MartinLaube 7 62
(Stepanka Myskova, Czech Republic) 120/1

10 4 **Favori Royal (FR)**[61] 384 4-9-4 0.......... VincentCheminaud 6 56
(E Lyon, France) 16/1

11 20 **Los Ojos (FR)**[152] 6-8-6 0..........(b1) BenjaminMarie(5) 2 3
(S Jeddari, France) 150/1

1m 40.76s (-6.74) **11 Ran SP% 118.9**
PARI-MUTUEL (all including 1 euro stake): WIN 4.10; PLACE 1.80, 2.20, 2.10; DF 10.60.
Owner Mme Caroline L'Abbe **Bred** Razza Della Sila **Trained** France

1348 - 1350a (Foreign Racing) - See Raceform Interactive

1285

KEMPTON (A.W) (R-H)

Wednesday, March 27

OFFICIAL GOING: Polytrack: standard to slow
Wind: Fine Weather: 1/2 against

1351 32RED CASINO MEDIAN AUCTION MAIDEN FILLIES' STKS 1m 2f 219y(P)
5:30 (5:34) (Class 6) 3-5-Y-O £3,105 (£924; £461; £230) Stalls Low

Form RPR

1 **Moment Of Hope (IRE)** 3-8-9 0 ow2.......... JamieSpencer 3 73+
(David Simcock) *s.i.s and niggled along: hld up in rr: shkn up and swtchd to outer wl over 2f out: rn green and cajoled along to take clsr order over 1f out: in tch and pushed along 1f out: led 150yds out: comf: gng on at fin* 5/4[1]

0-05 2 ½ **Vampish**[35] 814 4-10-0 69.......... AndreaAtzeni 7 71
(Philip McBride) *cl up bhd ldrs: rdn 2f out: kpt on wl between horses fr 1f out: styd on and tk 2nd 110yds out: nt get past snug wnr* 5/1[3]

4-33 3 1 **Bolt N Brown**[70] 259 3-8-7 63.......... JosephineGordon 4 65
(Gay Kelleway) *led: slowed tempo at 1/2-way: shkn up 3f out and increased pce: rdn over 2f out: stuck on tl hdd 150yds out: lost 2nd sn after* 6/1

6- 4 1½ **Luck Of Clover**[163] 8256 3-8-4 0.......... WilliamCox(3) 6 63
(Andrew Balding) *hld up in rr-div: shuffled along 2f out and prog over 1f out: pushed out to take 4th wl ins fnl f: nvr involved* 13/2

420- 5 2 **Ballet Red (FR)**[125] 9216 3-8-7 70.......... NicolaCurrie 9 59
(Harry Dunlop) *bhd ldr on inner: rdn over 2f out: ch over 1f out and kpt on wl tl wknd qckly wl ins fnl f* 7/2[2]

00 6 9 **Puzzle Cache**[28] 921 5-9-7 0..........(b) OliverSearle(7) 5 47
(Rod Millman) *racd in mid-div: rdn 2f out: nt qckn and pushed out fnl f* 125/1

6-35 7 ½ **Maria Magdalena (IRE)**[32] 884 3-8-4 67.......... AaronJones(3) 8 43
(Marco Botti) *sluggish s: pushed along fr wd drawn to sit on outer bhd ldr: rdn over 2f out: no ex over 1f out* 33/1

8 2½ **Annabelle Fritton (IRE)** 4-10-0 0.......... HectorCrouch 2 43
(Robyn Brisland) *hld up in rr-div: effrt over 2f out: no ex over 1f out (jockey said filly had an awkward gait)* 50/1

9 12 **Lovely Jubbly**[26] 4-9-11 0..........(t1) PaddyBradley(3) 1 23
(Pat Phelan) *s.i.s: a in last: struggling fr 2f out* 100/1

2m 22.45s (1.45) **Going Correction** 0.0s/f (Stan) **9 Ran SP% 117.6**
WFA 3 from 4yo+ 21lb
Speed ratings (Par 98): **98,97,96,95,94 87,87,85,76**
CSF £8.19 TOTE £2.00: £1.30, £1.60, £1.90; EX 8.70 Trifecta £26.40.
Owner Saeed Jaber **Bred** Rabbah Bloodstock Limited **Trained** Newmarket, Suffolk

FOCUS
An uncompetitive fillies' maiden opened the card on Polytrack once again described as 'standard to slow'. They seemed to go something of an uneven gallop.

1352 32RED ON THE APP STORE NOVICE STKS 1m (P)
6:00 (6:05) (Class 5) 3-Y-O+ £3,881 (£1,155; £577; £288) Stalls Low

Form RPR

4- 1 **Lehoogg**[189] 7431 3-8-11 0.......... AndreaAtzeni 12 79+
(Roger Varian) *w ldr: rdn jst over 2f out: qckndand led over 1f out: in control ent fnl f: rn green and wandered fnl 200yds: kpt on wl fnl 100yds whn pressed: comf* 9/4[1]

2 1¼ **Desert Lion** 3-8-11 0.......... OisinMurphy 9 75
(David Simcock) *bhd ldrs on outer: effrt 2f out: green and sltly outpcd over 1f out: fnd stride and qcknd ent fnl f: tk 2nd sn after: kpt on wl but no match for wnr cl home* 11/2

0-4 3 1¾ **Swiss Cheer (FR)**[21] 1033 3-8-11 0..........(h1) RobHornby 7 71
(Jonathan Portman) *racd in mid-div on inner: t.k.h at times particularly on bnd wl over 3f out: shkn up 2f out and prog swtchd to inner over 1f out: stuck on wl to take 3rd ins fnl f* 6/1

520- 4 nk **Glory**[195] 7201 3-8-11 78.......... TomMarquand 4 70
(Richard Hannon) *trckd ldr on inner: rdn over 2f out: kpt on wl and tk 2nd over 1f out: lost 2nd jst ins fnl f and dropped to 4th cl home* 5/2[2]

6- 5 3¾ **Dargel (IRE)**[186] 7531 3-8-11 0.......... HectorCrouch 5 62
(Clive Cox) *t.k.h in mid-div between horses for 2f: effrt on outer 2f out: pushed out fr 1f out (jockey said colt ran too free)* 5/1[3]

6 1 **Al Moataz (IRE)** 3-8-11 0.......... MarcMonaghan 8 59
(Marco Botti) *racd in mid-div: rdn over 2f out: kpt on one pce fr over 1f out* 25/1

7 2½ **Thunder And Light** 3-8-11 0.......... JamieSpencer 11 54
(Marco Botti) *hld up in rr-div on outer: shuffled along fr over 2f out: pleasing prog fr over 1f out* 20/1

8 shd **Mandocello (FR)** 3-8-11 0.......... CharlieBennett 10 53
(Rod Millman) *hld up in rr: shuffled along fr over 2f out: no prog* 66/1

0-6 9 1 **Tavus (IRE)**[49] 615 3-8-11 0.......... JasonWatson 6 51
(Roger Charlton) *led: rdn over 2f out: hdd over 1f out: wknd qckly sn after* 33/1

10 nk **Treble Clef** 4-10-0 0.......... KieranO'Neill 3 55
(Lee Carter) *bhd ldrs: lost pl over 3f out: no ex 2f out* 66/1

6 11 3 **Necoleta**[23] 1019 3-8-6 0.......... DavidEgan 1 38
(Sylvester Kirk) *slow to gather stride: a towards rr* 66/1

0-0 12 11 **Redemptress (IRE)**[57] 472 3-8-6 0.......... LiamJones 2 13
(John O'Shea) *racd in rr-div: pushed along 3f out: no ex sn after* 150/1

1m 40.02s (0.22) **Going Correction** 0.0s/f (Stan)
WFA 3 from 4yo 17lb **12 Ran SP% 122.4**
Speed ratings (Par 103): **98,96,95,94,90 89,87,87,86,86 83,72**
CSF £15.10 TOTE £3.30: £1.30, £2.50, £1.80; EX 24.80 Trifecta £115.40.
Owner Sheikh Ahmed Al Maktoum **Bred** P E Barrett **Trained** Newmarket, Suffolk

FOCUS
Just a fair novice event in which they didn't seem to go a great gallop.

1353 WISE BETTING AT RACINGTV.COM CLASSIFIED STKS (DIV I) 1m (P)
6:30 (6:34) (Class 6) 3-Y-O+ £3,105 (£924; £461; £400; £400; £400) Stalls Low

Form RPR

0062 1 **Dawn Commando**[21] 1032 4-10-0 46..........(b) AdamKirby 3 54
(Daniel Kubler) *mde most: pushed along leaving stalls and sn led: shkn up 2f out and qcknd 5 l clr over 1f out: in control and kidded along fnl f: ld reduced fnl 110yds* 13/8[1]

6344 2 1½ **Red Cossack (CAN)**[25] 983 8-10-0 45..........(b) RobertWinston 10 51
(Dean Ivory) *t.k.h in mid-div: rdn 2f out: tk 2nd over 1f out: clsd gap on idling wnr last 110yds (jockey said gelding ran too free)* 11/2[2]

30-0 3 3 **Casey Banter**[12] 1214 4-9-7 50.......... ScottMcCullagh(7) 5 44
(Julia Feilden) *bhd wnr: rdn over 2f out: lost 2nd over 1f out but styd on fnl f in 3rd* 15/2

-520 4 2¾ **Be Bold**[51] 594 7-10-0 45..........(b) DavidProbert 1 37
(Rebecca Bastiman) *hld up in rr-div on inner: gng okay whn trapped on heels fr over 2f out tl styd on between horses over 1f out: plugged on fnl f (jockey said gelding suffered interference early on)* 16/1

-050 5 nk **More Salutes (IRE)**[28] 925 4-10-0 48..........(p1) RobHornby 2 37
(Michael Attwater) *hld up in rr-div: rdn 2f out: kpt on one pce fr over 1f out* 6/1[3]

5306 6 1¾ **Sir Lancelott**[20] 1060 7-10-0 44..........(p) TomMarquand 9 33
(Adrian Nicholls) *bhd ldrs: rdn over 2f out and tk 3rd 2f out: plugged on at one pce fr over 1f out* 12/1

00-0 7 1½ **Push Back**[84] 27 3-8-11 48..........(p1) EoinWalsh 6 24
(George Scott) *s.s and pushed along to make rapid prog into mid-div: niggled along wl over 3f out: rdn over 2f out and kpt on one pce fr over 1f out* 14/1

000 8 ½ **Angel Black (IRE)**[18] 1094 3-8-11 50.......... JosephineGordon 11 23
(Shaun Keightley) *hld up in rr: nt handle bnd wl fr 4f out: wnt wd and dropped to 4 l 3f out: kpt on again past btn horses fr 2f out* 33/1

-000 9 hd **Isabella Red (IRE)**[32] 887 3-8-11 47.......... HectorCrouch 8 23
(David Evans) *in rr: rdn over 2f out: no imp over 1f out* 25/1

6-00 10 nk **Stay In The Light**[56] 479 4-10-0 44.......... KieranO'Neill 7 27
(Roger Ingram) *in rr-div on outer: rdn over 2f out w plenty to do: no imp over 1f out* 20/1

/-00 11 1½ **Twistsandturns (IRE)**[54] 531 8-9-7 38.......... MarkCrehan(7) 4 23
(Adrian Wintle) *bhd ldr on inner: rdn over 2f out: fdd over 1f out* 150/1

0005 12 14 **Herringswell (FR)**[27] 940 4-9-9 50..........(p) DylanHogan(5) 12
(Henry Spiller) *on outer of mid-div and t.k.h at times: pushed along over 2f out: wknd steadily fr 2f out (vet said filly was lame right hind)* 20/1

1m 38.9s (-0.90) **Going Correction** 0.0s/f (Stan)
WFA 3 from 4yo+ 17lb **12 Ran SP% 116.7**
Speed ratings (Par 101): **104,102,99,96,96 94,93,92,92,92 90,76**
CSF £9.15 TOTE £2.30: £1.70, £2.00, £2.10; EX 9.40 Trifecta £39.20.
Owner Andrew Stonehill **Bred** Brendan Boyle Bloodstock Ltd **Trained** Lambourn, Berks

FOCUS
The first division of a classified event restricted to horses rated 50 or less.

1354 WISE BETTING AT RACINGTV.COM CLASSIFIED STKS (DIV II) 1m (P)
7:00 (7:01) (Class 6) 3-Y-O+ £3,105 (£924; £461; £400; £400; £400) Stalls Low

Form RPR

060 1 **Capofaro**[40] 733 3-8-11 50.......... NicolaCurrie 10 52
(Jamie Osborne) *mde most: shkn up 2f out: rdn over 1f out: strly pressed in hd bobbing fin last 125yds: fnd more cl home* 5/1[2]

-000 2 ¾ **Sir Jamie**[51] 595 6-10-0 47..........(b) TomMarquand 6 55
(Tony Carroll) *s.s and hld up in last: shkn up over 2f out: rdn 2f out: rapid prog over 1f out on inner: c w str run to pressed wnr last 125yds in hd bobbing fin: no ex cl home* 9/2[1]

0300 3 5 **Cash N Carrie (IRE)**[34] 829 5-9-7 50..........(p) MarkCrehan(7) 4 44
(Michael Appleby) *hld up in rr-div: rdn 2f out: styd on to take modest 3rd last 150yds* 8/1

-300 4 1¾ **Woggle (IRE)**[21] 1032 4-10-0 47..........(p) TrevorWhelan 2 40
(Geoffrey Deacon) *bhd ldr: rdn bhd ldr 2f out: tk 3rd ent fnl f: plugged on but lost 3rd 150yds out* 13/2[3]

-464 5 1 **Gone With The Wind (GER)**[51] 595 8-10-0 43.....(p) WilliamCarson 5 43
(Rebecca Bastiman) *hld up in rr-div and t.k.h at times: trapped on heels fr 2f out tl shuffled along fr 1f out: sme prog after: can do bttr (jockey said gelding was denied a clear run)* 7/1

00-0 6 nk **Ramblow**[81] 80 6-10-0 49..........(tp) RossaRyan 7 37
(Alexandra Dunn) *cl up bhd ldrs: rdn over 2f out: sn one pce* 25/1

0-00 7 shd **Jack Louie**[27] 941 3-8-11 41.......... MartinDwyer 11 32
(Dean Ivory) *hld bhd ldr and t.k.h early: rdn over 2f out: stl 2nd wl over 1f out: dropped away sn after* 7/1

0-0 8 2¾ **Polly's Gold (IRE)**[75] 180 4-10-0 49..........(p) JFEgan 8 30
(Paul George) *cl up in mid-div on outer and t.k.h: rdn 2f out: plugged on (jockey said filly hung left-handed)* 13/2[3]

0-62 9 1½ **One Liner**[54] 532 5-10-0 45.......... LiamJones 9 27
(John O'Shea) *hld up in rr-div: rdn 2f out on wd outside: no imp (jockey said gelding was never travelling)* 5/1[2]

1m 40.55s (0.75) **Going Correction** 0.0s/f (Stan) **9 Ran SP% 118.1**
WFA 3 from 4yo+ 17lb
Speed ratings (Par 101): **96,95,90,88,87 87,87,84,82**
CSF £28.49 TOTE £3.70: £2.00, £1.70, £2.60; EX 25.00 Trifecta £181.50.
Owner Michael Buckley **Bred** Cheveley Park Stud Ltd **Trained** Upper Lambourn, Berks

FOCUS
Slower than the first division. The original favourite was weak but managed to defy market expectations.

1355 100% PROFIT BOOST AT 32REDSPORT.COM H'CAP 1m (P)
7:30 (7:31) (Class 5) (0-70,72) 4-Y-O+
£3,752 (£1,116; £557; £400; £400; £400) Stalls Low

Form RPR

00-0 **1** **Gossiping**[53] 557 7-9-7 **69** ShaneKelly 3 79+
(Gary Moore) *bhd ldr: shkn up 2f out and smooth prog over 1f out: rdn to ld ent fnl f: pushed out fnl 110yds: comf (trainer's rep said, regarding the apparent improvement in form, gelding benefitted from a drop-in grade, from Class 4 to Class 5 and that the gelding behaved better in the stalls and was then able to settle in the race)* **13/8**[1]

4-05 **2** 1 ½ **Silverturnstogold**[14] 1176 4-8-10 **58** TomMarquand 11 65
(Tony Carroll) *hld up in rr-div: prog over 2f out: rdn to chse ldrs 2f out: kpt on wl to take 2nd 150yds out: no match for wnr* **16/1**

0-51 **3** 1 ¾ **Lothario**[14] 1176 5-9-6 **68** MartinDwyer 6 71
(Dean Ivory) *hld up in mid-div: rdn 2f out: kpt on on inner over 1f out: styd on fnl f to take 3rd fnl 110yds but no match for front pair* **3/1**[2]

0255 **4** ¾ **Creek Harbour (IRE)**[26] 965 4-8-12 **67** (p[1]) GeorgeRooke(7) 1 68
(Richard Hughes) *led: rdn over 2f out: styd on over 1f out: hdd ent fnl f: fdd sn after* **8/1**

4/6- **5** 2 ¼ **Angel's Whisper (IRE)**[437] 229 4-9-3 **65** (h[1]) NicolaCurrie 8 61
(Amy Murphy) *s.s and in rr: rdn over 2f out: prog over 1f out: one pce fnl f (jockey said filly was slowly away)* **66/1**

0-0 **6** 1 ¼ **Militry Decoration (IRE)**[81] 91 4-9-7 **69** RobertWinston 12 62
(Dr Jon Scargill) *racd in rr-div: shuffled along fr 2f out: styd on fr over 1f out: nvr nrr* **25/1**

-522 **7** ½ **Baashiq (IRE)**[14] 1176 5-9-4 **66** (p) LukeMorris 10 58
(Peter Hiatt) *w ldr: rdn over 2f out: kpt on tl wknd over 1f out* **10/1**

446- **8** ¾ **Casina Di Notte (IRE)**[142] 8885 5-9-3 **72** (b) StefanoCherchi(7) 13 62
(Marco Botti) *racd in mid-div on outer: rdn 2f out: one pce fr over 1f out* **20/1**

235- **9** 2 ½ **Crystal Casque**[137] 8997 4-9-7 **69** OisinMurphy 2 54
(Rod Millman) *bhd ldrs: effrt over 2f out: plugged on fr over 1f out* **4/1**[3]

/0-0 **10** 2 ¾ **Fighting Temeraire (IRE)**[21] 1036 6-9-6 **68** RobHornby 9 46
(Dean Ivory) *t.k.h in mid-div on outer: effrt over 2f out: one pce after* **25/1**

1- **11** 2 ¼ **Less Of That (IRE)**[176] 7872 5-9-7 **69** DavidProbert 4 42
(Matthew Salaman) *hld up in rr: effrt over 2f out: no imp* **33/1**

144- **12** 9 **Roy Rocket (FR)**[206] 6841 9-8-13 **61** JFEgan 5 13
(John Berry) *in rr: rdn ovr 2f out: dropped away over 1f out: eased fnl f* **66/1**

1m 38.04s (-1.76) **Going Correction** 0.0s/f (Stan) **12** Ran SP% **127.6**
Speed ratings (Par 103): **108,106,104,104,101 100,100,99,96,94 91,82**
CSF £32.46 CT £82.01 TOTE £2.80: £1.40, £4.20, £1.50; EX 37.50 Trifecta £135.20.
Owner The Buckwell Partnership **Bred** Darley **Trained** Lower Beeding, W Sussex

FOCUS
A modest handicap taken apart by the easy, extremely well-backed winner.

1356 32RED.COM H'CAP 7f (P)
8:00 (8:01) (Class 4) (0-85,85) 4-Y-O+
£6,469 (£1,925; £962; £481; £400; £400) Stalls Low

Form RPR

0-02 **1** **Poetic Force (IRE)**[28] 922 5-9-7 **85** (t) GeorgeDowning 1 93
(Tony Carroll) *edgy hding to post: hld up in mid-div on inner: rdn 2f out: kpt on fr over 1f out to ld cl home: all out at fin* **11/4**[1]

1-41 **2** hd **Unforgiving Minute**[12] 1218 8-9-7 **85** AdamKirby 9 92
(John Butler) *hld up in mid-div on outer: rdn 2f out: kpt on wl ent fnl f chsng wnr: tk 2nd cl home: jst failed post* **7/1**

2414 **3** 1 ½ **Call Out Loud**[14] 1181 7-8-13 **84** (vt) MarkCrehan(7) 6 87
(Michael Appleby) *rdn leaving stalls and sn led: kicked for home 3f out: drifted to rail over 1f out and pack clsd: kpt on grittily tl hdd cl home* **4/1**[3]

-525 **4** 1 ½ **Human Nature (IRE)**[25] 981 6-8-13 **84** (t) MarcoGhiani(7) 4 83
(Stuart Williams) *mid-div: effrt over 2f out: no imp fnl f (jockey said he ran too free)* **10/1**

5-23 **5** ½ **Last Page**[40] 734 4-9-0 **78** TrevorWhelan 2 76
(David Loughnane) *s.s and hld up in rr-div: rdn 2f out: one pce (jockey said gelding ran in snatches)* **8/1**

25-5 **6** shd **Corazon Espinado (IRE)**[16] 1143 4-9-7 **85** TomMarquand 8 82
(Simon Dow) *bhd ldr: rdn 2f out: kpt on one pce (vet said colt lost right hind shoe)* **7/2**[2]

25-0 **7** nk **Rock Icon**[28] 922 6-8-9 **80** GeorgiaDobie(7) 3 76
(Jo Hughes, France) *hld up in last pair: rdn over 2f out: plugged on one pce* **20/1**

030- **8** 6 **The Gates Of Dawn (FR)**[137] 8999 4-9-3 **81** (t) NicolaCurrie 7 61
(George Baker) *hld up in last pair: effrt over 2f out: sn hld and pushed out* **12/1**

301- **9** 1 ½ **Folie Douze**[410] 659 4-8-12 **76** BenCurtis 5 52
(Henry Spiller) *racd in mid-div on outer: rdn over 2f out: hld over 1f out* **33/1**

1m 25.03s (-0.97) **Going Correction** 0.0s/f (Stan) **9** Ran SP% **117.0**
Speed ratings (Par 105): **105,104,103,101,100 100,100,93,91**
CSF £22.98 CT £77.38 TOTE £3.10: £1.50, £1.60, £1.80; EX 22.90 Trifecta £87.50.
Owner S J Barton **Bred** S J Macdonald **Trained** Cropthorne, Worcs

FOCUS
A trappy affair.

1357 32RED H'CAP 6f (P)
8:30 (8:30) (Class 4) (0-80,79) 4-Y-O+
£6,469 (£1,925; £962; £481; £400; £400) Stalls Low

Form RPR

-554 **1** **Global Tango (IRE)**[21] 1036 4-9-4 **76** (b[1]) JamieSpencer 3 87
(Charles Hills) *sn led and wnt lft first 150yds: set scorching pce tl given breather over 3f out: pressed whn kicked again wl over 1f out: kpt on ins fnl f to maintain advantage: fine ride* **5/2**[1]

-242 **2** 2 **Enthaar**[20] 1061 4-9-2 **74** (t) SeanLevey 10 79
(Stuart Williams) *racd in mid-div but in tch: clsr and rdn over 2f out: kpt on fr over 1f out: tk 2nd 100yds out* **5/1**[2]

-402 **3** hd **Madrinho (IRE)**[36] 790 6-9-0 **77** PoppyBridgwater(5) 11 81
(Tony Carroll) *awkward leaving stalls and hld up in rr: shkn up wl over 2f out: gd prog 2f out wnt to inner and rdn: kpt on wl to press for 2nd last strides (jockey said gelding was slowly away)* **11/1**

1405 **4** ½ **Choice Encounter**[4] 1290 4-9-5 **77** OisinMurphy 7 79
(Archie Watson) *racd in mid-div: rdn 2f out on outer: kpt on wl over 1f out: keeping on at fin: nvr nrr* **5/1**[2]

3213 **5** shd **Steelriver (IRE)**[23] 1016 9-8-10 **68** PhilDennis 2 70
(Michael Herrington) *racd in rr-div: shkn up over 2f out: rdn 2f out: kpt on wl ent fnl f to chal for a pl cl home: no ex last 50yds* **8/1**[3]

-253 **6** 2 **Cappananty Con**[20] 1061 5-9-0 **72** RichardKingscote 1 68
(Charlie Wallis) *bhd wnr: rdn over 2f out: styd on over 1f out bhd ldng pair: plugged on fnl f* **5/1**[2]

0-50 **7** 2 ¾ **Top Boy**[34] 832 9-9-1 **73** (v) PaddyMathers 5 60
(Derek Shaw) *chsd wnr: rdn over 2f out: chal over 1f out: styd on tl wknd ins fnl f* **20/1**

1050 **8** ¾ **Mont Kiara (FR)**[20] 1061 6-8-13 **71** TomMarquand 9 55
(Simon Dow) *in rr and outpcd: pushed along wl over 2f out: no imp over 1f out* **25/1**

-034 **9** 1 ¾ **Smokey Lane (IRE)**[35] 797 5-8-13 **78** GinaMangan(7) 4 57
(David Evans) *in last and outpcd: styd on past btn horses fr over 1f out* **14/1**

005- **10** 6 **Waqaas**[128] 9157 5-9-7 **79** FergusSweeney 8 39
(Mark Usher) *in rr-div and niggled along thrght to go pce: no ex 2f out* **12/1**

300R **11** 3 ½ **Gold Hunter (IRE)**[12] 1208 9-8-12 **70** RaulDaSilva 6 18
(Steve Flook) *bhd wnr: rdn over 2f out: struggling 2f out: wknd sn after* **50/1**

1m 11.75s (-1.35) **Going Correction** 0.0s/f (Stan) **11** Ran SP% **122.9**
Speed ratings (Par 105): **109,106,106,105,105 102,98,97,95,87 82**
CSF £15.16 CT £123.92 TOTE £3.60: £1.20, £2.20, £2.70; EX 25.60 Trifecta £225.10.
Owner Dr Johnny Hon **Bred** Ballycrighaun Stud **Trained** Lambourn, Berks

FOCUS
They were quickly strung out in this run-of-the-mill sprint handicap.
T/Plt: £13.20 to a £1 stake. Pool: £85,618.67 - 4715.39 winning units T/Qpdt: £4.30 to a £1 stake. Pool: £11,935.33 - 2018.78 winning units **Cathal Gahan**

1328 LINGFIELD (L-H)
Wednesday, March 27

OFFICIAL GOING: Polytrack: standard
Wind: Almost nil Weather: Cloudy

1358 LADBROKES HOME OF THE ODDS BOOST H'CAP 1m 1y(P)
2:00 (2:00) (Class 6) (0-65,66) 3-Y-O
£3,105 (£924; £461; £300; £300; £300) Stalls High

Form RPR

000- **1** **Dragon Sun**[154] 8548 3-9-7 **65** SeanLevey 4 78+
(Richard Hannon) *t.k.h early: trckd ldng pair: carried wd bnd 2f out: sn clsd and rdn to ld over 1f out: styd on wl* **3/1**[1]

04-2 **2** 1 **Image Of The Moon**[14] 1173 3-9-7 **65** AdamKirby 2 73
(Shaun Keightley) *trckd ldng pair tl wnt 2nd over 2f out: rdn to ld wl over 1f out: sn hdd: kpt on same pce u.p* **4/1**[2]

00-4 **3** 2 ½ **What Will Be (IRE)**[33] 855 3-9-1 **59** JamieSpencer 9 61+
(Olly Murphy) *dropped in fr wd draw and hld up in last quartet: stl there 2f out: nt clr run wl over 1f out and swtchd to inner: gd prog fnl f: tk 3rd last 75yds and r.o: too late (jockey said gelding was denied a clear run shortly after turning in)* **9/2**[3]

0-65 **4** 1 **Truckingby**[27] 949 3-9-2 **60** (b) JoeFanning 1 60
(Mark Johnston) *chsd ldrs disputing 5th: rdn over 2f out: kpt on and tk 3rd briefly ins fnl f: nvr gng pce to threaten* **20/1**

-334 **5** ¾ **Spirit Kingdom (USA)**[54] 524 3-9-0 **63** AndrewBreslin(5) 7 61
(Mark Johnston) *racd on outer: chsd ldrs tl lost pl suddenly and reminder after 3f: rdn wl over 2f out: modest late prog but nvr a factor* **16/1**

5524 **6** ½ **Shug**[14] 1174 3-9-3 **61** (p[1]) LiamKeniry 12 58
(Ed Walker) *dropped in fr wdst draw and hld up in last pair: stl there 2f out: prog jst over 1f out: rdn and styd on fnl f: nrst fin* **8/1**

-245 **7** 1 **Wall Of Sapphire (IRE)**[34] 826 3-9-8 **66** (b) EdwardGreatrex 5 61
(Hugo Palmer) *sn led: kicked on over 2f out: hdd wl over 1f out: wknd fnl f* **8/1**

0-06 **8** nk **Iris's Spirit**[49] 614 3-8-2 **46** oh1 HayleyTurner 3 40
(Tony Carroll) *nvr beyond midfield: outpcd and rdn over 2f out: no hdwy after* **50/1**

0-40 **9** 1 **Archdeacon**[20] 1066 3-8-8 **52** RobHornby 10 44
(Dean Ivory) *hld up in last pair: taken wd bnd 2f out: rdn and no great prog over 1f out* **10/1**

0000 **10** 1 **Jasmine B (IRE)**[20] 1066 3-8-3 **47** oh1 ow1 NicolaCurrie 6 36
(John Ryan) *hld up in last quartet: rdn and no prog 2f out* **66/1**

-513 **11** 2 ¼ **Rajman**[16] 1141 3-9-5 **63** (h) TomMarquand 11 47
(Tom Clover) *pressed ldr to over 2f out: edgd rt sn after: wknd rapidly wl over 1f out (jockey said colt ran too free)* **7/1**

00-0 **12** 1 **Freedreams**[21] 1034 3-8-3 **47** KieranO'Neill 8 29
(Tony Carroll) *chsd ldrs disputing 5th: rdn wl over 2f out: wknd wl over 1f out* **100/1**

1m 36.45s (-1.75) **Going Correction** -0.225s/f (Stan) **12** Ran SP% **122.1**
Speed ratings (Par 96): **99,98,95,94,93 93,92,91,90,89 87,86**
CSF £14.91 CT £55.75 TOTE £3.90: £1.50, £1.20, £2.60; EX 15.50 Trifecta £109.20.
Owner Mrs Fitri Hay **Bred** Rabbah Bloodstock Limited **Trained** East Everleigh, Wilts

FOCUS
This wasn't a bad 3yo handicap for the class. It's been rated as pretty good form for the grade.

1359 LADBROKES MEDIAN AUCTION MAIDEN FILLIES' STKS 1m 1y(P)
2:30 (2:30) (Class 6) 3-5-Y-O £3,105 (£924; £461; £230) Stalls High

Form RPR

322- **1** **Pytilia (USA)**[154] 8546 3-8-9 77 ShaneKelly 1 74+
(Richard Hughes) *led after 1f: mde rest: shkn up and drew clr over 1f out: ld dwindled nr fin but nt in danger* **10/11**[1]

2 1 ½ **Sashenka (GER)** 3-8-9 0 DavidEgan 5 70+
(Sylvester Kirk) *hld up in last pair: wl adrift 3f out: str prog on outer 2f out: r.o wl to take 2nd last 100yds and clsd on wnr nr fin* **25/1**

02 **3** 3 ¼ **Gabriela Laura**[16] 1142 3-8-9 0 DavidProbert 2 62
(Clive Cox) *led 1f: chsd wnr: rdn and nt qckn 2f out: sn outpcd: lost 2nd last 100yds* **4/1**[2]

4 ½ **Its Nice Tobe Nice** 3-8-9 0 EdwardGreatrex 8 61
(Archie Watson) *trckd ldrs: wnt 3rd 3f out: rdn and outpcd by wnr over 1f out: kpt on same pce after* **8/1**

5 1 ½ **Huddle** 3-8-9 0 CallumShepherd 10 57
(William Knight) *stdd s: hld up in last pair: lft bhd 3f out: sme prog over 1f out: shkn up and kpt on: nt wout promise* **20/1**

4 **6** *3* **Jazzy Card (IRE)**^{53} 547 3-8-6 0.................... WilliamCox$^{(3)}$ 7 51
(Linda Jewell) *in tch towards rr: outpcd and shkn up 3f out: no ch after* **100/1**

00- **7** *2 1/4* **Nyanga (IRE)**^{179} 7774 3-8-2 0.................... EllieMacKenzie$^{(7)}$ 3 45
(David Menuisier) *in tch: outpcd and pushed along 3f out: no ch after* **50/1**

8 *3 1/2* **Al Anaab (FR)** 3-8-9 0.................... TomMarquand 4 37
(Peter Chapple-Hyam) *dwlt sltly: in tch in rr: outpcd and shkn up 3f out: no ch after* **16/1**

40- **9** *3/4* **Croqueta (IRE)**^{110} 9442 3-8-9 0.................... SeanLevey 6 36
(Richard Hannon) *chsd ldng pair to 3f out: wknd qckly jst over 2f out* **20/1**

03- **10** *1 3/4* **Adena Star (IRE)**^{163} 8256 3-8-9 0.................... RobHornby 9 32
(Jonathan Portman) *in tch tl outpcd 3f out: no ch after: wknd over 1f out (jockey said filly moved poorly down the hill)* **6/1**^{3}

1m 36.31s (-1.89) **Going Correction** -0.225s/f (Stan) **10** Ran SP% **120.0**
Speed ratings (Par 98): **100,98,95,94,93 90,88,84,83,82**
CSF £37.31 TOTE £1.50: £1.10, £7.50, £1.40; EX 35.10 Trifecta £111.40.
Owner K Dhunjibhoy & Z Dhunjibhoy **Bred** Mike Pietrangelo **Trained** Upper Lambourn, Berks

FOCUS
Few got into this modest 3yo fillies' maiden.

1360 LADBROKES H'CAP — 7f 1y(P)
3:05 (3:05) (Class 4) (0-85,82) 3-Y-O
£5,530 (£1,645; £822; £411; £300; £300) **Stalls** Low

Form RPR

2311 **1** **Shanghai Grace**^{14} 1178 3-8-11 **79**.................... CierenFallon$^{(7)}$ 4 85
(Charles Hills) *hld up towards rr: prog 2f out: rdn to ld jst over 1f out: sn in command: styd on wl* **9/4**^{1}

006- **2** *2* **Pacino**^{166} 8161 3-9-1 **76**.................... JackGarritty 2 76
(Richard Fahey) *hld up in rr: effrt 2f out: swtchd rt jst over 1f out: r.o to take 2nd ins fnl f: no threat to wnr* **11/2**^{3}

50-2 **3** *nk* **Howzer Black (IRE)**^{18} 1104 3-9-4 **79**.................... TomMarquand 9 78
(Keith Dalgleish) *dropped in fr wd draw and hld up last of main gp: shkn up 2f out: prog jst over 1f out: styd on to take 3rd ins fnl f: pressed runner-up nr fin* **6/1**

631- **4** *3/4* **Harbour Spirit (FR)**^{99} 9601 3-9-6 **81**.................... ShaneKelly 6 78
(Richard Hughes) *prom: trckd ldr 1/2-way: poised to chal 2f out: rdn and no rspnse over 1f out: one pce after* **7/2**^{2}

402- **5** *1 1/2* **Usain Boat (IRE)**^{156} 8475 3-9-5 **80**.................... (h^{1}) JasonWatson 7 73
(George Scott) *trckd ldr to 1/2-way: rdn 2f out: one pce over 1f out (jockey said gelding hung right-handed throughout)* **25/1**

0-06 **6** *3/4* **Kapono**^{12} 1219 3-8-13 **74**.................... GeorgeWood 3 65
(Amy Murphy) *chsd ldrs: rdn 2f out: no prog on inner over 1f out: one pce after* **16/1**

210- **7** *1/2* **Azor Ahai**^{277} 4103 3-8-12 **80**.................... GeorgeBass$^{(7)}$ 8 70
(Mick Channon) *spd fr wd draw to ld: rdn 2f out: hdd & wknd jst over 1f out* **16/1**

231- **8** *1* **Deira Surprise**^{96} 9669 3-9-7 **82**.................... AdamKirby 5 69
(Hugo Palmer) *trckd ldrs on outer: rdn and nt qckn 2f out: lost pl fnl f (jockey said filly hung right-handed throughout)* **7/2**^{2}

5- **9** *17* **Champagne Marengo (IRE)**^{234} 5776 3-9-0 **75**......... StevieDonohoe 1 16
(Ian Williams) *immediately outpcd and detached in last: t.o (jockey said gelding was never travelling)* **25/1**

1m 23.11s (-1.69) **Going Correction** -0.225s/f (Stan) **9** Ran SP% **124.3**
Speed ratings (Par 100): **100,97,97,96,94 93,93,92,72**
CSF £16.67 CT £68.57 TOTE £3.00: £1.20, £2.20, £2.00; EX 16.50 Trifecta £97.00.
Owner Kangyu International Racing (HK) Limited **Bred** Wellsummers Stud **Trained** Lambourn, Berks

FOCUS
This modest handicap was run at a sound pace. The second, third and fourth have been rated close to form.

1361 BETWAY LIVE CASINO H'CAP — 1m 7f 169y(P)
3:35 (3:35) (Class 6) (0-55,55) 4-Y-O+
£3,105 (£924; £461; £300; £300; £300) **Stalls** Low

Form RPR

2455 **1** **Bird For Life**^{27} 947 5-8-13 **54**.................... (p) EllieMacKenzie$^{(7)}$ 13 63
(Mark Usher) *hld up in rr: stdy prog fr 3f out: led wl over 1f out: pushed clr and styd on wl* **7/1**

4-50 **2** *3 1/2* **Tilsworth Sammy**^{40} 731 4-8-12 **49**.................... KieranO'Neill 10 56
(J R Jenkins) *hld up towards rr: rdn and prog on outer 3f out: drvn to take 2nd over 1f out: kpt on but no ch w wnr* **10/1**

2311 **3** *3/4* **Harry Callahan (IRE)**^{16} 1145 4-8-13 **50**.................... (v) CallumShepherd 12 56
(Mick Channon) *trckd ldng pair: led wl over 2f out: rdn and hdd wl over 1f out: kpt on same pce* **7/4**^{1}

4 *nk* **Extreme Appeal (IRE)**^{23} 2098 7-9-4 **52**.................... (p) LiamKeniry 2 56
(Kelly Morgan) *hld up in midfield: gng wl enough but trapped on inner and lost pl 3f out: sn in rr: prog 2f out: drvn to take 4th 1f out: styd on but too late* **16/1**

25-5 **5** *3 1/2* **Greenview Paradise (IRE)**^{16} 1145 5-8-13 **47**.................... HayleyTurner 6 46
(Jeremy Scott) *hld up and sn in midfield: lost pl over 3f out and sn in rr: rdn on outer 2f out: styd on fnl f but no ch* **10/1**

44-0 **6** *3/4* **Planetoid (IRE)**^{63} 369 11-9-4 **52**.................... (b) RobHornby 7 50
(Suzi Best) *hld up: dropped to last pair 3f out: drvn and kpt on fr 2f out: nvr nrr but no ch* **14/1**

0041 **7** *3* **Sea's Aria (IRE)**^{21} 1044 8-8-13 **47**.................... DavidProbert 11 42
(Mark Hoad) *chsd ldng pair: rdn and lost pl wl over 2f out: steadily wknd* **16/1**

-042 **8** *shd* **Schindlers Ark (USA)**^{16} 1145 5-8-13 **47**.................... CharlieBennett 3 42
(Jane Chapple-Hyam) *mde most to wl over 2f out: sn btn (trainer's rep said gelding may have been unsuited by the longer trip having run over 1 mile 4 furlongs last time out)* **9/2**^{2}

-510 **9** *2 3/4* **Sweetest Smile (IRE)**^{27} 946 4-8-13 **50**.................... JoeFanning 4 43
(Ed de Giles) *w ldr to 3f out: nudged along and steadily dropped away* **5/1**^{3}

0-30 **10** *1 3/4* **Picture Painter (IRE)**^{36} 789 6-9-7 **55**.................... AdamKirby 5 44
(David Pipe) *urged along fr s and rn in snatches: drvn and rapid prog fr rr over 3f out to chal over 2f out: wknd qckly wl over 1f out* **8/1**

3/00 **11** *32* **Ditripleseven (IRE)**^{11} 1235 6-9-5 **53**.................... WilliamCarson 1 4
(David W Drinkwater) *v restless stalls: chsd ldng pair to 3f out: wknd rapidly: t.o* **66/1**

3m 21.17s (-4.53) **Going Correction** -0.225s/f (Stan)
WFA 4 from 5yo+ 3lb **11** Ran SP% **132.9**
Speed ratings (Par 101): **102,100,99,99,97 97,96,96,94,93 77**
CSF £85.30 CT £183.51 TOTE £10.40: £3.00, £3.40, £1.50; EX 98.00 Trifecta £361.10.
Owner The Mark Usher Racing Club **Bred** Mrs Robert Langton **Trained** Upper Lambourn, Berks

FOCUS
There was a fair pace on in this moderate staying handicap. It's been rated around the second and third at face value.

1362 BETWAY CASINO H'CAP — 1m 2f (P)
4:10 (4:10) (Class 6) (0-60,62) 4-Y-O+
£3,105 (£924; £461; £300; £300; £300) **Stalls** Low

Form RPR

0-45 **1** **Sir Gnet (IRE)**^{14} 1183 5-9-10 **62**.................... (h) DanielMuscutt 10 68
(Ed Dunlop) *hld up in last pair: pushed along and rapid prog on outer over 1f out: str run fnl f to ld last strides* **7/2**^{3}

-521 **2** *1/2* **Creative Talent (IRE)**^{23} 1015 7-9-6 **58**.................... TomMarquand 1 63
(Tony Carroll) *hld up in 7th: urged along 3f out and no prog: hdwy wl over 1f out: clsd qckly fnl f and upsides nr fin: jst outpcd* **2/1**^{2}

0213 **3** *nk* **Tesorina (IRE)**^{4} 1297 4-9-5 **57**.................... (v) RichardKingscote 5 61
(William Knight) *led: rdn 2f out: clung on to ld over 1f out tl swamped last strides* **7/4**^{1}

-600 **4** *hd* **Sunbreak (IRE)**^{14} 1183 4-9-2 **59**.................... (b^{1}) AndrewBreslin$^{(5)}$ 9 63
(Mark Johnston) *hld up in 6th: shkn up wl over 2f out: limited prog tl styd on wl fnl f: jst lacked pce of other fast fniers* **12/1**

-000 **5** *nk* **Altaira**^{27} 941 8-8-7 **45**.................... (p) DavidProbert 4 49
(Tony Carroll) *hld up in 8th: prog 3f out to chse ldr 2f out: drvn and tried to chal 1f out: no ex and lost pls ins fnl f* **33/1**

-600 **6** *1/2* **Nicky Baby (IRE)**^{51} 593 5-8-0 **45**.................... (b) SophieRalston$^{(7)}$ 11 48
(Dean Ivory) *tk fierce hold: trckd ldng pair: lost pl 2f out: urged along and kpt on fnl f but nt pce to chal* **33/1**

0-50 **7** *1 1/2* **The Celtic Machine**^{42} 695 4-8-7 **45**.................... CharlieBennett 7 45
(Pat Phelan) *trckd ldng pair: shkn up 3f out: lost pl on inner fr 2f out: fdd fnl f* **20/1**

4-00 **8** *nk* **Cloud Nine (FR)**^{16} 1145 6-8-7 **45**.................... (p) KieranO'Neill 6 44
(Tony Carroll) *chsd ldr: shkn up 3f out: lost 2nd 2f out: steadily fdd* **50/1**

00-0 **9** *1 1/2* **Ice Cool Cullis (IRE)**^{72} 239 4-8-7 **45**.................... (t^{1}) EoinWalsh 8 41
(Mark Loughnane) *dwlt: hld up in last pair: struggling in last 1/2-way and sn detached: stl same over 1f out: styd on quite wl fnl 150yds* **33/1**

46-0 **10** *hd* **Phobos**^{70} 250 4-9-0 **52**.................... RobHornby 3 48
(Michael Blanshard) *trckd ldrs in 5th: pushed along and lost pl over 2f out: fdd* **33/1**

-000 **11** *1 1/2* **Amy Kane**^{27} 940 5-8-0 **45**.................... (b^{1}) SeanKirrane$^{(7)}$ 2 38
(Jimmy Fox) *dwlt: hld up in last trio: urged along 3f out and no prog* **50/1**

2m 4.49s (-2.11) **Going Correction** -0.225s/f (Stan) **11** Ran SP% **120.1**
Speed ratings (Par 101): **99,98,98,98,97 97,96,96,94,94 93**
CSF £10.48 CT £15.96 TOTE £7.10: £1.30, £1.10, £1.70; EX 11.60 Trifecta £23.00.
Owner Quentin Zheng **Bred** Ecoutila Partnership **Trained** Newmarket, Suffolk

FOCUS
There was a tight finish to this ordinary handicap.

1363 BETWAY H'CAP — 1m 4f (P)
4:40 (4:40) (Class 5) (0-70,70) 4-Y-O+
£3,752 (£1,116; £557; £300; £300; £300) **Stalls** Low

Form RPR

-541 **1** **Power Home (IRE)**^{30} 910 5-8-13 **61**.................... CharlesBishop 9 67
(Denis Coakley) *hld up tl prog to trck ldr 7f out: shkn up to chal over 1f out: drvn ahd last 100yds* **11/2**^{2}

-032 **2** *1/2* **Make Good (IRE)**^{22} 1024 4-8-12 **61**.................... (bt) DavidProbert 2 66
(David Dennis) *nt that wl away: rcvrd to ld after 1f and dictated mod pce: rdn wl over 1f out: hdd last 100yds: nt qckn* **7/2**^{1}

6-64 **3** *3/4* **Famous Dynasty (IRE)**^{33} 859 5-8-13 **61**.................... RobHornby 1 65
(Michael Blanshard) *hld up towards rr: gng strly 3f out: prog to chse ldng trio over 1f out: nt qckn after but kpt on to take 3rd last strides* **7/1**^{3}

4602 **4** *1/2* **Smiley Bagel (IRE)**^{25} 985 6-9-6 **68**.................... RichardKingscote 4 71
(Ed Walker) *led 1f: styd prom: rdn over 2f out: chal over 1f out: nt qckn ins fnl f* **7/2**^{1}

026- **5** *nk* **Cheeky Rascal (IRE)**^{38} 8002 4-9-1 **69**.....(p) ThoreHammerHansen$^{(5)}$ 5 72
(Richard Hannon) *trckd ldr after 1f to 7f out: lost pl and urged along 3f out: kpt on again ins fnl f: nt pce to chal* **8/1**

0464 **6** *1/2* **Makambe (IRE)**^{25} 985 4-9-4 **67**.................... JoeyHaynes 10 69
(Paul Howling) *t.k.h early: hld up in last: prog on inner over 1f out: kpt on same pce ins fnl f* **10/1**

1-50 **7** *1/2* **The Way You Dance (IRE)**^{16} 1144 7-9-8 **70**.................... (v) ShaneKelly 6 71
(Neil Mulholland) *hld up in last trio: prog to chse ldrs over 4f out: drvn over 2f out: nt qckn wl over 1f out: fdd ins fnl f* **20/1**

04-5 **8** *4* **Luna Magic**^{40} 736 5-8-9 **57**.................... EoinWalsh 3 52
(Lydia Pearce) *n.m.r after 2f and dropped to rr: rdn 3f out: no prog and btn 2f out* **12/1**

0-50 **9** *3/4* **River Dart (IRE)**^{27} 947 7-9-1 **63**.................... SeanLevey 7 56
(Tony Carroll) *chsd ldrs: lost pl 5f out: dropped to last and u.p 3f out: no ch after* **16/1**

300- **10** *1/2* **Kings Inn (IRE)**^{27} 4220 5-8-13 **66**.................... (p) MeganNicholls$^{(5)}$ 8 59
(Paul Nicholls) *hld up: dropped to last trio sn after 1/2-way: rdn and no imp on ldrs 2f out: wknd fnl f (vet reported the gelding had bled from the nose)* **9/1**

2m 31.43s (-1.57) **Going Correction** -0.225s/f (Stan)
WFA 4 from 5yo+ 1lb **10** Ran SP% **120.9**
Speed ratings (Par 103): **96,95,95,94,94 94,93,91,90,90**
CSF £26.10 CT £140.61 TOTE £6.00: £2.30, £1.40, £3.60; EX 32.40 Trifecta £152.00.
Owner Poachers' Dozen **Bred** C Farrell **Trained** West Ilsley, Berks
■ Stewards' Enquiry : Megan Nicholls caution: careless riding

FOCUS
It paid to be handy in this ordinary handicap. It's been rated at face value around the first three.
T/Plt: £7.10 to a £1 stake. Pool: £75,068.78 - 7671.67 winning units T/Qpdt: £4.30 to a £1 stake. Pool: £6,163.54 - 1053.03 winning units **Jonathan Neesom**

1192 SOUTHWELL (L-H)
Wednesday, March 27

OFFICIAL GOING: Fibresand: standard
Wind: Moderate half behind Weather: Cloudy

1364 BETWAY CASINO H'CAP — 4f 214y(F)
2:20 (2:20) (Class 6) (0-60,62) 4-Y-O+
£3,105 (£924; £461; £300; £300; £300) **Stalls** Centre

Form RPR

212- **1** **Honey Gg**^{106} 9493 4-9-0 **60**.................... CianMacRedmond$^{(7)}$ 5 69
(Declan Carroll) *racd centre: mde all: rdn over 1f out: kpt on strly* **8/1**

1032 **2** 1½ **Red Stripes (USA)**^{12} 1210 7-8-11 **55**.................(b) SeamusCronin$^{(5)}$ 10 59
(Lisa Williamson) *racd towards stands' side: prom: rdn along to chse wnr wl over 1f out: drvn and kpt on same pce fnl f* **14/1**

4-21 **3** nk **Twentysvnthlancers**^{15} 1162 6-9-7 **60**.......................... PaulMulrennan 7 63
(Paul Midgley) *racd centre: trckd ldrs: hdwy over 2f out: rdn to chse wnr ent fnl f: sn drvn and kpt on same pce* **9/2^{2}**

000- **4** 1¼ **Scuzeme**^{190} 7392 5-9-8 **61**.. SamJames 8 59
(Phillip Makin) *dwlt and rr towards stands' side: rdn along over 2f out: kpt on wl fnl f* **12/1**

034- **5** nk **Lexington Place**^{148} 8725 9-9-7 **60**.. JamesSullivan 1 57
(Ruth Carr) *racd towards far side: trckd ldrs: hdwy over 2f out: rdn over 1f out: kpt on same pce fnl f* **16/1**

-613 **6** nk **Kath's Boy (IRE)**^{15} 1162 5-8-7 **53**......................(b) ElishaWhittington$^{(7)}$ 9 49
(Tony Carroll) *racd towards stands' side: towards rr: rdn along over 2f out: styd on fnl f* **6/1^{3}**

2-61 **7** ¾ **Furni Factors**^{26} 973 4-8-11 **57**.......................................(b) RPWalsh$^{(7)}$ 2 50
(Ronald Thompson) *dwlt and n.m.r towards far side: sn swtchd lft and pushed along to chse ldrs after 1 1/2f: rdn over 2f out: wknd wl over 1f out* **7/1**

-465 **8** 1¾ **Becker**^{39} 759 4-9-9 **62**.. LukeMorris 3 49
(Robert Cowell) *dwlt: racd towards far side: a towards rr* **5/2^{1}**

00-0 **9** 2¾ **Oriental Relation (IRE)**^{72} 236 8-9-6 **59**.............(b w) LewisEdmunds 4 36
(John Balding) *chsd ldrs centre: rdn along over 2f out: sn wknd (vet reported the gelding lost its left fore shoe)* **20/1**

0000 **10** ¾ **Independence Day (IRE)**^{14} 1177 6-9-7 **60**............(h^{1}) TonyHamilton 6 34
(Paul Howling) *a towards rr (vet reported the horse lost its right fore shoe)* **12/1**

58.65s (-1.05) **Going Correction** -0.125s/f (Stan) **10** Ran SP% **117.3**
Speed ratings (Par 101): **103,100,100,98,97 97,95,93,88,87**
CSF £114.06 CT £580.84 TOTE £8.20: £2.60, £3.00, £1.70; EX 88.60 Trifecta £285.50.

Owner The Commissioning Team **Bred** West Dereham Abbey Stud **Trained** Malton, N Yorks

FOCUS
A modest sprint handicap on standard Fibresand. The fifth-favourite successfully made all in a fair time for the grade. It's been rated at face value.

1365 BETWAY MAIDEN STKS 1m 4f 14y(F)
2:50 (2:50) (Class 5) 3-Y-O+ **£3,752** (£1,116; £557; £278) **Stalls** Low

Form RPR

1 **Ranch Hand** 3-8-6 0.. MartinDwyer 3 75+
(Andrew Balding) *green and pushed along in rr s: hdwy and in tch after 3f: trckd ldrs 4f out: hdwy on outer 3f out: rdn to chal over 1f out: edgd lft ent fnl f: drvn and styd on wl to ld last 50yds* **12/1**

02-3 **2** 1 **Heart Of Soul (IRE)**^{14} 1182 4-9-13 78.......................... PJMcDonald 6 76+
(Ian Williams) *trckd ldrs: hdwy over 3f out and sn cl up: slt ld 2f out and sn rdn: drvn ent fnl f: hdd and no ex last 50yds* **6/1^{3}**

2-4 **3** ½ **Escapability (IRE)**^{27} 945 4-9-13 80.......................... DougieCostello 4 75+
(Alan King) *trckd ldng pair: hdwy over 3f out: chal over 2f out: sn rdn: drvn and ev ch ent fnl f: kpt on same pce* **9/4^{1}**

23 **4** 5 **Ydra**^{33} 858 3-8-6 0.. BenCurtis 5 64
(Archie Watson) *cl up: slt ld after 1f: pushed along 4f out: rdn over 3f out: hdd 2f out: sn drvn and grad wknd* **11/4^{2}**

0-05 **5** 11 **Esme Kate (IRE)**^{15} 1163 4-9-8 41...........................(bt^{1}) PaddyMathers 2 44?
(Ivan Furtado) *slt ld 1f: prom: pushed along over 4f out: rdn over 3f out: sn wknd* **80/1**

324 **6** 1¼ **Alpasu (IRE)**^{12} 1221 3-8-6 76..(t^{1}) HollieDoyle 7 44
(Archie Watson) *reminders s and rdn along to chse ldrs: cl up after 2f: rdn along over 3f out: sn drvn and wknd* **11/4^{2}**

7 30 **Limited Reserve (IRE)**^{459} 7-10-0 0.................................... TonyHamilton 1
(Christian Williams) *s.i.s: a bhd: t.o fnl 4f* **20/1**

300- **8** 14 **Boffo (IRE)**^{207} 6818 4-9-13 0.. LukeMorris 8
(Ian Williams) *swtchd lft s: a bhd: t.o fnl 4f* **50/1**

2m 37.68s (-3.32) **Going Correction** -0.125s/f (Stan)
WFA 3 from 4yo 22lb 4 from 7yo 1lb **8** Ran SP% **114.0**
Speed ratings (Par 103): **106,105,105,101,94 93,73,64**
CSF £79.47 TOTE £11.80: £3.00, £1.80, £1.20; EX 88.10 Trifecta £405.60.

Owner Kingsclere Racing Club **Bred** Kingsclere Stud **Trained** Kingsclere, Hants

FOCUS
A fair middle-distance maiden. The cosy winning newcomer's time was nearly four seconds above standard from off a start-stop gallop. The third has been rated in line with his latest effort.

1366 BETWAY LIVE CASINO H'CAP 6f 16y(F)
3:25 (3:25) (Class 5) (0-75,74) 4-Y-O+ **£3,752** (£1,116; £557; £300; £300; £300) **Stalls** Low

Form RPR

461 **1** **Marble Bar**^{13} 1192 4-8-6 **62**.................................(h) JamieGormley$^{(3)}$ 3 76+
(Iain Jardine) *qckly away: mde all: rdn over 1f out: kpt on strly* **13/8^{1}**

0306 **2** 2 **Katheefa (USA)**^{26} 970 5-8-13 **66**................................ JamesSullivan 7 73
(Ruth Carr) *chsd ldrs: hdwy 1/2-way: rdn to chse wnr wl over 1f out: sn edgd lft: drvn and no imp fnl f* **12/1**

50-0 **3** 1¾ **Captain Dion**^{14} 1177 6-8-4 **60**..........................(p) GabrieleMalune$^{(3)}$ 6 61
(Ivan Furtado) *chsd ldrs on inner: rdn along 3f out: swtchd markedly rt over 2f out: sn drvn and kpt on fnl f* **10/1**

321 **4** 1½ **Crosse Fire**^{15} 1160 7-8-12 **70**...............................(p) TheodoreLadd$^{(5)}$ 8 67
(Scott Dixon) *chsd ldrs on outer: wd st: rdn over 2f out: drvn wl over 1f out: sn no imp* **10/3^{2}**

3510 **5** 3¾ **Point Zero (IRE)**^{13} 1194 4-9-7 **74**........................(be) AlistairRawlinson 4 59
(Michael Appleby) *chsd wnr: rdn along 3f out: drvn 2f out: grad wknd* **12/1**

5414 **6** 3¾ **Gabrial The Tiger (IRE)**^{15} 1164 7-8-12 **70**............ ConnorMurtagh$^{(5)}$ 2 43
(Richard Fahey) *in tch: rdn along wl over 2f out: sn drvn and n.d* **13/2^{3}**

6636 **7** ½ **Pearl Spectre (USA)**^{27} 944 8-8-8 **68**...................(v) GraceMcEntee$^{(7)}$ 1 39
(Phil McEntee) *dwlt: a in rr* **10/1**

220- **8** 4½ **Royal Connoisseur (IRE)**^{146} 8786 8-9-0 **67**................ PaulHanagan 5 24
(Richard Fahey) *dwlt: a in rr* **25/1**

1m 14.47s (-2.03) **Going Correction** -0.125s/f (Stan) **8** Ran SP% **111.9**
Speed ratings (Par 103): **108,105,103,101,96 91,90,84**
CSF £21.86 CT £146.55 TOTE £3.30: £1.10, £3.40, £2.40; EX 28.10 Trifecta £185.40.

Owner The Twelve Munkys **Bred** The Earl Cadogan **Trained** Carrutherstown, D'fries & G'way

FOCUS
A fair handicap. The clear favourite made all, eased-down in a decent time. The winner was backing up his latest effort, and the second has been rated to his recent form.

1367 SUNRACING.CO.UK H'CAP 1m 13y(F)
3:55 (3:55) (Class 4) (0-80,81) 4-Y-O+ **£5,530** (£1,645; £822; £411; £300; £300) **Stalls** Low

Form RPR

0661 **1** **Hammer Gun (USA)**^{13} 1197 6-9-7 **78**......................(v) PaddyMathers 11 85
(Derek Shaw) *towards rr: hdwy and wd st: chsd ldrs 2f out: sn rdn: drvn nr stands' rail ins fnl f: styd on wl to ld nr fin* **4/1^{1}**

-320 **2** hd **Mama Africa (IRE)**^{27} 951 5-8-13 **75**..................... PoppyBridgwater$^{(5)}$ 6 81
(David Barron) *led: rdn along 2f out: drvn and edgd rt ins fnl f: hdd and no ex nr fin* **10/1**

-542 **3** ½ **Majestic Moon (IRE)**^{19} 1074 9-8-13 **70**...............(p) ShelleyBirkett 10 75
(Julia Feilden) *cl up: chal 2f out: rdn over 1f out: drvn ins fnl f: kpt on same pce towards fin* **20/1**

1-24 **4** 2¾ **Tagur (IRE)**^{13} 1197 5-9-2 **73**..(p) TomEaves 5 72
(Kevin Ryan) *trckd ldrs: pushed along over 2f out: rdn wl over 1f out: drvn and kpt on same pce fnl f* **12/1**

2135 **5** nk **Master Diver**^{21} 1036 4-9-7 **78**.. LukeMorris 3 76
(Sir Mark Prescott Bt) *dwlt and swtchd rt sn after s: hdwy to chse ldrs over 3f out: rdn over 2f out: drvn wl over 1f out: kpt on same pce* **9/2^{2}**

30-6 **6** 1¼ **Noble Peace**^{70} 252 6-8-13 **70**..................................(b^{1}) TonyHamilton 12 65
(Lydia Pearce) *chsd ldng pair: rdn along and wd st: drvn 2f out: grad wknd* **33/1**

2-36 **7** 2¼ **Mr Carbonator**^{62} 390 4-8-7 **67**................................... JamieGormley$^{(3)}$ 2 57
(Philip Kirby) *in rr: hdwy over 2f out: sn rdn: kpt on appr fnl f: n.d* **8/1^{3}**

2033 **8** 2½ **Juanito Chico (IRE)**^{29} 915 5-9-6 **77**................................ PJMcDonald 1 61
(Stuart Williams) *chsd ldrs on inner: rdn along wl over 2f out: drvn and wknd 2f out* **8/1^{3}**

23-0 **9** 2 **Fingal's Cave (IRE)**^{84} 23 7-8-11 **68**.................................. KevinStott 4 48
(Philip Kirby) *trckd ldrs: rdn along wl over 2f out: sn wknd* **16/1**

04-5 **10** 2½ **Beverley Bullet**^{13} 1197 6-8-3 **67**..........................(p) KieranSchofield$^{(7)}$ 7 41
(Lawrence Mullaney) *a towards rr* **40/1**

0632 **11** 4½ **The Great Wall (USA)**^{15} 1160 5-9-10 **81**........................ LewisEdmunds 8 44
(Michael Appleby) *chsd ldrs on outer: rdn along 3f out: drvn and wknd over 2f out (trainer's rep said gelding was unsuited by the removal of headgear on this occasion)* **4/1^{1}**

5-00 **12** 3¾ **Rosarno (IRE)**^{16} 1143 5-8-13 **70**.................................... PaulMulrennan 9 25
(Paul Howling) *dwlt: a in rr* **66/1**

1m 42.03s (-1.67) **Going Correction** -0.125s/f (Stan) **12** Ran SP% **114.7**
Speed ratings (Par 105): **103,102,102,99,99 98,95,93,91,88 84,80**
CSF £41.34 CT £719.79 TOTE £5.80: £2.40, £3.40, £4.60; EX 42.30 Trifecta £475.60.

Owner A Flint **Bred** Her Majesty The Queen **Trained** Sproxton, Leics

FOCUS
The feature race was a fair handicap. One of the joint-favourites got up late in a modest comparative time on the day. It's been rated around the second and third.

1368 BETWAY HEED YOUR HUNCH H'CAP 6f 16y(F)
4:30 (4:30) (Class 6) (0-60,60) 4-Y-O+ **£3,105** (£924; £461; £300; £300; £300) **Stalls** Low

Form RPR

00-4 **1** **Socialites Red**^{15} 1162 6-8-9 **53**..............................(p) TheodoreLadd$^{(5)}$ 6 61
(Scott Dixon) *cl up: rdn to ld wl over 1f out: drvn ins fnl f: hld on gamely nr line* **10/1**

0030 **2** hd **Dream Ally (IRE)**^{13} 1192 9-8-7 **46**.. PhilDennis 2 53
(John Weymes) *trckd ldrs on inner: smooth hdwy and cl up over 2f out: rdn to chal over 1f out: drvn ins fnl f: ev ch tl no ex nr line* **25/1**

-352 **3** 1¼ **Liamba**^{42} 702 4-9-7 **60**.. DavidNolan 8 63
(David O'Meara) *led: rdn along and wd st: hdd wl over 1f out: sn drvn nr stands' rail and ev ch tl wknd last 100yds* **5/2^{1}**

50-3 **4** 1¼ **Fortinbrass (IRE)**^{13} 1192 9-8-1 **47**................................... IzzyClifton$^{(7)}$ 7 47
(John Balding) *chsd ldrs: rdn along 2f out: drvn over 1f out: kpt on same pce* **25/1**

2114 **5** shd **Gorgeous General**^{28} 926 4-8-13 **59**...................... WilliamCarver$^{(7)}$ 12 59
(Lawrence Mullaney) *in tch: hdwy to chse ldrs and wd st: rdn along nr stands' rail wl over 1f out: sn drvn and kpt on same pce* **9/2^{2}**

0-05 **6** ½ **Alba Del Sole (IRE)**^{28} 928 4-9-3 **59**................(p) GabrieleMalune$^{(3)}$ 4 57
(Ivan Furtado) *n.m.r after s and towards rr: hdwy over 2f out: rdn wl over 1f out: kpt on fnl f: nrst fin* **8/1**

0640 **7** 1½ **Jacob's Pillow**^{22} 1023 8-9-6 **59**.................................(p) LewisEdmunds 11 52
(Rebecca Bastiman) *prom: wd st: rdn along over 2f out: drvn wl over 1f out: grad wknd* **33/1**

650- **8** ½ **Meshardal (GER)**^{186} 7522 9-9-7 **60**................................ JamesSullivan 10 52
(Ruth Carr) *in tch: wd st: hdwy over 2f out: n.m.r and swtchd lft wl over 1f out: sn rdn and no imp* **13/2^{3}**

-064 **9** 1¼ **Blistering Dancer (IRE)**^{56} 478 9-8-7 **46** oh1............(v) PaulHanagan 1 34
(Tony Carroll) *a towards rr* **33/1**

-310 **10** ¾ **Elliot The Dragon (IRE)**^{28} 919 4-8-7 **46**.................... PaddyMathers 13 32
(Derek Shaw) *dwlt: a towards rr* **16/1**

4034 **11** 2¼ **Alligator**^{18} 1093 5-8-7 **46** oh1..(p) BenCurtis 9 25
(Tony Carroll) *chsd ldrs: wd st: rdn along 2f out: grad wknd* **9/1**

0-60 **12** 8 **Rizzle Dizzle**^{64} 356 4-9-5 **58**......................................(b^{1}) CamHardie 5 13
(Rebecca Menzies) *t.k.h: in tch whn n.m.r bnd after 2f: sn lost pl and bhd* **16/1**

0/00 **13** ¾ **Whisper A Word (IRE)**^{19} 1083 5-8-0 **46** oh1............ VictorSantos$^{(7)}$ 14
(Lucinda Egerton) *racd wd: in rr and wd st: a bhd* **100/1**

10-0 **14** 9 **Astrojewel**^{34} 830 4-9-4 **57**... PaulMulrennan 3
(Mark H Tompkins) *dwlt: a in rr* **25/1**

1m 15.84s (-0.66) **Going Correction** -0.125s/f (Stan) **14** Ran SP% **120.5**
Speed ratings (Par 101): **99,98,97,95,95 94,92,91,90,89 86,75,74,62**
CSF £248.08 CT £847.42 TOTE £10.00: £3.10, £6.90, £1.60; EX 306.90 Trifecta £1070.10.

Owner William A Robinson & Partners **Bred** Selwood, Hoskins & Trickledown **Trained** Babworth, Notts

FOCUS
A modest handicap. It paid to race relatively prominently off a tactical early gallop. The second has been rated as bettering this winter's form, but the third as below her good recent run behind the fifth.

1369 LIKE SUNRACING ON FACEBOOK AMATEUR RIDERS' H'CAP 1m 13y(F)
5:05 (5:05) (Class 6) (0-65,66) 4-Y-0+
£2,994 (£928; £464; £300; £300; £300) **Stalls Low**

Form RPR
60-5 **1** **Equidae**[35] 808 4-10-7 **65**...............(t) MrNathanSeery(7) 10 73
(Iain Jardine) *cl up: led after 2f: rdn along 2f out: drvn ent fnl f: edgd lft and kpt on wl towards fin (trainer said, as to the apparent improvement in form, the colt appreciated the fibresand surface)* **33/1**

10-4 **2** 1 1/4 **Port Soif**[15] 1158 5-10-1 **52**...............(p) MissEmmaSayer 3 57
(Scott Dixon) *trckd ldrs on inner: smooth hdwy 3f out: chal wl over 1f out: sn rdn and ev ch tl kpt on same pce last 75yds* **12/1**

0213 **3** 1/2 **Baron Run**[13] 1197 9-10-7 **58**............... MrSimonWalker 11 62
(K R Burke) *prom: cl up after 2f: rdn along 2f out: drvn over 1f out: kpt on same pce fnl f* **3/1**[1]

3234 **4** 1 1/2 **Bond Angel**[14] 1175 4-10-6 **64**............... MrPhilipThomas(7) 7 65+
(David Evans) *t.k.h: in rr whn hmpd after 2f: bhd tl gd hdwy 2f out: rdn over 1f out: kpt on wl fnl f (jockey said filly suffered interference in the back straight)* **9/2**[2]

13-3 **5** 2 3/4 **Caribbean Spring (IRE)**[12] 1208 6-10-3 **59**. MissRosieMargarson(5) 13 53+
(George Margarson) *in tch: hdwy over 3f out: wd st: chsd ldrs over 2f out: rdn wl over 1f out: kpt on one pce* **13/2**[3]

01-4 **6** 3/4 **Winklemann (IRE)**[12] 1209 7-10-3 **61**...............(p) MissImogenMathias(7) 1 53
(John Flint) *towards rr: swtchd rt to outer 1/2-way: wd st: hdwy nr stands' rail 2f out: rdn and kpt on fnl f* **16/1**

-446 **7** 4 1/2 **Red Touch (USA)**[26] 965 7-11-0 **65**...............(b) MissSerenaBrotherton 12 47
(Michael Appleby) *chsd ldrs: wd st: rdn along 2f out: grad wknd* **9/2**[2]

000- **8** 1/2 **Medici Moon**[167] 8134 5-10-8 **59**............... MrRossBirkett 8 40
(Richard Price) *cl up: pushed along 1/2-way: rdn over 3f out: sn wknd* **14/1**

-000 **9** nk **Zaeem**[13] 1197 10-10-0 **58**............... MissKayleighRayner(7) 2 38
(Ivan Furtado) *dwlt: hdwy to chse ldrs over 3f out: rdn along wl over 2f out: sn wknd* **33/1**

10 1 **Lafilia (GER)**[157] 4-11-1 **66**............... MissBrodieHampson 5 44
(Archie Watson) *led 2f: chsd ldrs: rdn along 3f out: sn wknd* **8/1**

200- **11** 2 3/4 **Mime Dance**[117] 9337 8-9-12 **54** ow2...............(e[1]) MrMatthewJohnson(5) 6 24
(John Butler) *midfield whn swtchd lft after 1f: swtchd rt to outer over 3f out: wd st: sn rdn and n.d* **33/1**

0/6- **12** 3 3/4 **Four Mile Beach**[262] 163 6-10-2 **60**............... MrHakanSensoy(7) 9 23
(Michael Chapman) *dwlt: a bhd* **100/1**

00-0 **13** 7 **Luduamf (IRE)**[76] 166 5-9-2 **46** oh1............... MrDallonHolmes(7) 14
(Michael Chapman) *dwlt: a bhd* **250/1**

1m 43.9s (0.20) **Going Correction** -0.125s/f (Stan) **13 Ran SP% 116.3**
Speed ratings (Par 101): **94,92,92,90,88 87,82,82,81,80 78,74,67**
CSF £372.61 CT £1605.94 TOTE £30.50: £9.30, £3.00, £1.70; EX 463.20 Trifecta £2882.50.
Owner I J Jardine **Bred** L J Vaessen **Trained** Carruthertown, D'fries & G'way
■ Stewards' Enquiry : Mr Matthew Johnson one-day ban: weighing in at 2lb overweight (Apr 13)

FOCUS
A modest amateur riders' handicap. An outsider became another winner on the card to benefit from getting on the lead early on. A minor pb from the winner.
T/Jkpt: Not won. T/Plt: £40.10 to a £1 stake. Pool: £77,619.82 - 1411.75 winning units T/Qpdt: £24.10 to a £1 stake. Pool: £7,361.19 - 225.74 winning units **Joe Rowntree**

1370a-1377a (Foreign Racing) - See Raceform Interactive

1208 CHELMSFORD (A.W) (L-H)
Thursday, March 28

OFFICIAL GOING: Polytrack: standard
Wind: Virtually nil Weather: Dry

1378 PONTLANDS PARK HOTEL H'CAP 1m (P)
5:30 (5:31) (Class 6) (0-60,62) 4-Y-0+
£3,105 (£924; £461; £400; £400; £400) **Stalls Low**

Form RPR
-451 **1** **Compass Point**[13] 1214 4-9-6 **59**............... PJMcDonald 6 65
(Robyn Brisland) *chsd ldrs: effrt to chse ldr jst over 1f out: hung lft u.p 1f out: styd on wl ins fnl f to ld cl home* **3/1**[1]

5101 **2** hd **Amor Fati (IRE)**[13] 1215 4-9-4 **57**............... AdamKirby 11 63
(David Evans) *hld up in tch in last trio: effrt ent fnl 2f: nt clrest of runs over 1f out: hdwy u.p to chse ldrs ins fnl f: swtchd rt and r.o strly towards fin: snatched 2nd last strides* **9/2**[2]

0320 **3** hd **Squire**[42] 724 8-9-7 **60**...............(tp) LukeMorris 2 65
(Marjorie Fife) *led: clr and rdn wl over 1f out: drvn 1f out: kpt on u.p: hdd and lost 2 pls cl home* **6/1**

5323 **4** 2 **Kilbaha Lady (IRE)**[12] 1231 5-9-5 **61**............... RowanScott(3) 5 61
(Nigel Tinkler) *in tch in midfield: nt clr run over 2f out: swtchd rt and effrt over 1f out: styd on ins fnl f: no threat to ldrs* **5/1**[3]

6004 **5** 3/4 **Dukes Meadow**[13] 1215 8-8-2 **46** oh1............... RhiainIngram(5) 9 45
(Roger Ingram) *stdd s: hld up in rr: swtchd rt and effrt over 1f out: styd on wl ins fnl f: nvr trbld ldrs* **33/1**

5220 **6** 1 **Accomplice**[15] 1175 5-9-9 **62**............... FergusSweeney 8 58
(Michael Blanshard) *stdd s: hld up in tch on last trio: effrt over 1f out: sme prog and nt clr run ins fnl f: hdwy and kpt on wl fnl 75yds: nvr trbld ldrs* **25/1**

04-3 **7** hd **Benjamin Thomas (IRE)**[16] 1158 5-9-3 **56**...............(v) JasonHart 4 52
(John Quinn) *in tch in midfield: effrt towards inner over 1f out: swtchd rt 1f out: kpt on ins fnl f* **6/1**

-206 **8** 3/4 **Blessed To Empress (IRE)**[12] 1231 4-9-6 **59**............... NicolaCurrie 7 53
(Amy Murphy) *chsd ldrs tl wnt 2nd 5f out tl 2f out: unable qck u.p and wknd ins fnl f* **8/1**

0600 **9** 1 1/2 **Plucky Dip**[13] 1208 8-8-0 **46** oh1............... LauraPearson(7) 10 37
(John Ryan) *in tch in midfield on outer: lost pl over 1f out: bhd ins fnl f* **50/1**

-464 **10** 1 1/2 **My Town Chicago (USA)**[15] 1176 4-9-8 **61**............... DougieCostello 3 48
(Kevin Frost) *plld hrd: chsd ldr tl 5f out: wnt 2nd again 2f out tl over 1f out: wknd ins fnl f (jockey said gelding ran too freely)* **8/1**

1m 40.13s (0.23) **Going Correction** -0.025s/f (Stan) **10 Ran SP% 119.4**
Speed ratings (Par 101): **97,96,96,94,93 92,92,91,90,88**
CSF £16.58 CT £79.71 TOTE £3.50: £1.60, £1.60, £2.70; EX 19.10 Trifecta £106.10.
Owner Mrs Jackie Cornwell **Bred** Mrs J A Cornwell **Trained** Danethorpe, Notts

FOCUS
Not much pace on early, but it picked up from the turn in.

1379 ANDERSON GROUP NOVICE STKS (PLUS 10 RACE) 1m (P)
6:00 (6:01) (Class 4) 3-Y-0
£5,530 (£1,645; £822; £411) **Stalls Low**

Form RPR
532- **1** **Fox Leicester (IRE)**[160] 8387 3-9-2 **81**............... SilvestreDeSousa 3 79+
(Andrew Balding) *mde all: pushed along and asserted over 1f out: wl in command fnl f: eased towards fin* **1/4**[1]

2 3 **King Shamardal** 3-9-2 **0**............... PJMcDonald 4 66+
(Mark Johnston) *rn in snatches and v green: mostly last: swtchd rt and effrt wl over 1f out: hanging lft and chsd clr wnr 1f out: stl hanging but kpt on ins fnl f: no threat to wnr* **3/1**[2]

0 **3** 5 **Obsession For Gold (IRE)**[14] 1198 3-9-2 **0**...............(bt[1]) PaddyMathers 1 55
(Mrs Ilka Gansera-Leveque) *plld hrd: chsd wnr: rdn to press wnr 2f out: hung lft and outpcd over 1f out: lost 2nd and wknd ins fnl f (jockey said gelding ran too freely)* **50/1**

450- **4** 1 **Rum Lad**[203] 6973 3-9-2 **68**...............(w) JasonHart 2 52
(Ivan Furtado) *t.k.h: in tch: rdn jst over 2f out: unable qck and outpcd over 1f out: wknd ins fnl f (jockey said gelding was slowly away)* **25/1**[3]

1m 39.86s (-0.04) **Going Correction** -0.025s/f (Stan) **4 Ran SP% 110.8**
Speed ratings (Par 100): **99,96,91,90**
CSF £1.40 TOTE £1.10; EX 1.60 Trifecta £6.40.
Owner King Power Racing Co Ltd **Bred** Marston Stud **Trained** Kingsclere, Hants

FOCUS
A walk in the park for the odds-on favourite.

1380 DG INTERNATIONAL H'CAP 5f (P)
6:30 (6:30) (Class 6) (0-60,60) 3-Y-0
£3,105 (£924; £461; £400; £400; £400) **Stalls Low**

Form RPR
5-50 **1** **Sepahi**[15] 1170 3-9-2 **60**...............(p[1]) DylanHogan(5) 2 65
(Henry Spiller) *sn in rr: hdwy u.p towards inner over 1f out: styd on to ld wl ins fnl f: gng away at fin* **5/1**[3]

6-30 **2** 1 1/4 **Secret Picnic (FR)**[29] 918 3-8-12 **51**...............(vt[1]) JasonHart 4 52
(John Quinn) *chsd ldr: clsd to press ldr after 1f: rdn and ev ch whn wnt rt over 1f out: stl ev ch tl no ex and outpcd wl ins fnl f* **2/1**[1]

-002 **3** nse **Sing Bertie (IRE)**[31] 906 3-8-7 **46**............... PaddyMathers 7 46
(Derek Shaw) *t.k.h: hld up in rr: racd awkwardly and hung rt bnd over 3f out: impeded and hung rt over 1f out: hdwy and ev ch ins fnl f: no ex and outpcd wl ins fnl f (jockey said gelding hung right-handed around the bend)* **6/1**

1635 **4** nk **Swiss Chime**[14] 1193 3-8-13 **57**............... MeganNicholls(5) 5 56
(Dean Ivory) *broke fast: led: pressed after 1f: rdn over 1f out: kpt on wl u.p tl hdd wl ins fnl f: no ex and outpcd wl ins fnl f* **5/1**[3]

00-0 **5** 1 1/4 **Champagne Clouds**[20] 1081 3-8-7 **46**...............(b[1]) CamHardie 6 41
(Brian Ellison) *restless in stalls: chsd ldrs: kpt on same pce u.p ins fnl f* **16/1**

000- **6** 1 **Two Faced**[87] 9771 3-8-9 **48**............... EoinWalsh 3 39
(Lydia Pearce) *midfield: rdn over 3f out: styd on same pce ins fnl f* **40/1**

53-0 **7** 4 **Milldean Panther**[69] 296 3-9-2 **55**...............(v[1]) DougieCostello 1 32
(Suzi Best) *bustled along in midfield: unable qck over 1f out: wknd ins fnl f (jockey said gelding lugged right-handed up the home straight)* **11/4**[2]

00-5 **8** 13 **Chocco Star (IRE)**[55] 520 3-9-5 **58**............... JoeyHaynes 8
(Paul Howling) *pressed ldrs on outer tl lost pl qckly over 1f out: fdd ins fnl f* **50/1**

1m 1.05s (0.85) **Going Correction** -0.025s/f (Stan) **8 Ran SP% 117.9**
Speed ratings (Par 96): **92,90,89,89,87 85,79,58**
CSF £15.98 CT £62.99 TOTE £4.70: £1.80, £1.10, £1.50; EX 17.60 Trifecta £85.00.
Owner Select-Racing-Club Co Uk & Partner **Bred** Mr & Mrs I Wilson **Trained** Newmarket, Suffolk
■ Stewards' Enquiry : Dylan Hogan two-day ban: misuse of whip (Apr 11-12)

FOCUS
Plenty of pace on and the winner and third came from the back of the field. The straightforward level is set around the second and third.

1381 MAYOR OF CHELMSFORD MAIDEN STKS 7f (P)
7:00 (7:01) (Class 4) 3-Y-0+
£5,530 (£1,645; £822; £411) **Stalls Low**

Form RPR
02- **1** **Rux Power**[238] 5653 3-8-8 **0**............... SilvestreDeSousa 1 77+
(Andrew Balding) *mde all: rdn and kicked clr over 1f out: in command ins fnl f: eased towards fin* **1/1**[1]

-322 **2** 3 1/2 **White Coat**[26] 979 3-8-13 **80**...............(t[1]) KieranO'Neill 12 70
(John Gosden) *t.k.h: hld up in tch in midfield: swtchd rt and effrt 2f out: hdwy to chse clr wnr and hung lft wl ins fnl f: kpt on but no ch w wnr* **13/8**[2]

35 **3** 1 3/4 **Creek Island (IRE)**[14] 1195 3-8-13 **0**............... PJMcDonald 3 65
(Mark Johnston) *restless in stalls: chsd ldrs: effrt on inner over 1f out: rn green and wandered rt 1f out: kpt on same pce ins fnl f* **10/1**

4 1/2 **Global Gift (FR)** 3-8-13 **0**............... JosephineGordon 8 64
(Ed Dunlop) *t.k.h: hld up in midfield: effrt wl over 1f out: kpt on same pce ins fnl f* **20/1**

5 **5** hd **Highest Mountain (FR)**[34] 868 3-8-13 **0**............... FrannyNorton 7 63
(Joseph Tuite) *chsd wnr: rdn and unable to match pce of wnr over 1f out: lost 2nd and wknd wl ins fnl f* **8/1**[3]

0- **6** 1 1/4 **Onebaba (IRE)**[146] 8803 3-8-13 **0**............... LouisSteward 11 60
(Michael Bell) *in tch in rr: hdwy and nt clrest runs over 1f out: kpt on same pce ins fnl f* **25/1**

55 **7** 1 1/2 **I'm British**[13] 1212 6-10-0 **0**...............(p[1]) RossaRyan 10 61
(Don Cantillon) *taken down early and mounted on crse: stdd s: hld up in rr of main gp: pushed along and sme hdwy over 1f out: nt clrest of runs and no imp ins fnl f* **100/1**

0- **8** 1/2 **Take It Down Under**[308] 3012 4-9-7 **0**............... StefanoCherchi(7) 5 60
(Amy Murphy) *in tch in midfield: effrt and nt clrest of runs over 1f out: kpt on same pce ins fnl f* **66/1**

9 4 1/2 **Broughtons Bear (IRE)** 3-8-13 **0**............... CamHardie 2 43
(Stuart Williams) *restless in stalls: a towards rr: nvr involved* **50/1**

0 **10** nse **Star Of Valour (IRE)**[27] 971 4-10-0 **0**...............(h[1]) DougieCostello 4 47
(David C Griffiths) *in tch in midfield: rdn and lost pl over 1f out: wknd fnl f* **66/1**

05-6 **11** 2 1/4 **Miss Communicate**[34] 855 3-8-8 **56**............... LukeMorris 13 31
(Lydia Pearce) *towards rr of main gp: rdn wl over 1f out: sn btn* **100/1**

12 6 **Mazmerize** 3-8-13 **0**............... EoinWalsh 6 20
(Christine Dunnett) *s.i.s: rn green and a towards rr (jockey said gelding ran green)* **125/1**

0-0 13 2 **Sarsaparilla Kit**[17] 1139 3-8-8 0 .... MartinDwyer 9 10
(Stuart Williams) *chsd ldrs on outer tl hung rt 2f out: sn bhd* **66/1**

1m 25.26s (-1.94) **Going Correction** -0.025s/f (Stan)
WFA 3 from 4yo+ 15lb **13** Ran SP% **126.1**
Speed ratings (Par 105): **110,106,104,103,103 101,100,99,94,94 91,84,82**
CSF £2.81 TOTE £1.80: £1.10, £1.10, £2.70; EX 3.40 Trifecta £15.40.
Owner King Power Racing Co Ltd **Bred** Cliveden Stud Ltd **Trained** Kingsclere, Hants

FOCUS
The market had this as a two-horse race but it proved very one-sided.

1382 GEPP SOLICITORS FILLIES' H'CAP 6f (P)
7:30 (7:30) (Class 4) (0-85,85) 4-Y-O+

£5,530 (£1,645; £822; £411; £400; £400) **Stalls** Centre

Form RPR
000- 1 **Puds**[133] 9084 4-9-3 **81** .... ShaneKelly 3 88
(Richard Hughes) *led for 2f: pressed ldr after tl rdn to ld 1f out: sn drvn: kpt on and nvr gng to be ct* **10/3**[3]
20-5 2 ¾ **Sweet And Dandy (IRE)**[76] 177 4-8-5 **69** .... KieranO'Neill 2 74+
(Luke McJannet) *dwlt and short of room leaving stalls: in tch in rr: nt clr run and swtchd rt over 1f out: hdwy ins fnl f: styd on wl ins fnl f to go 2nd towards fin: nvr getting to wnr* **25/1**
161- 3 nk **Indian Tygress**[156] 8498 4-9-7 **85** .... GeorgeWood 8 89+
(James Fanshawe) *in rr: swtchd lft after 1f: clsd: nt clr run and swtchd lft over 1f out: hdwy ins fnl f: styd in wl to 3rd nr fin: nvr getting to wnr* **2/1**[1]
0-36 4 ½ **Emily Goldfinch**[12] 1234 6-8-10 **81** ....(p) GraceMcEntee(7) 6 83
(Phil McEntee) *chsd ldr tl led after 2f: rdn over 1f out: hdd 1f out: keeping on same pce whn short of room wl ins fnl f: lost 2 pls towards fin* **16/1**
-321 5 nk **Chica De La Noche**[43] 697 5-8-2 **66** ....(p) LukeMorris 4 67
(Simon Dow) *chsd ldrs: rdn over 2f out: unable qck and outpcd over 1f out: rallied and kpt on u.p ins fnl f: nvr getting bk on terms w wnr* **8/1**
20-2 6 ½ **Rose Berry**[40] 755 5-9-6 **84** ....(h) SilvestreDeSousa 5 84
(Charlie Wallis) *taken down early: dwlt: sn in tch in midfield: shkn wl over 1f out: sn u.p: styd on ins fnl f: nvr getting on terms w wnr* **3/1**[2]
-030 7 nk **Sonnet Rose (IRE)**[12] 1234 5-8-3 **67** ow1........(bt) MartinDwyer 1 66
(Conrad Allen) *chsd ldrs: effrt and swtchd rt over 1f out: sn u.p and unable qck: kpt on ins fnl f wout threatening wnr (vet said mare lost it's right hind shoe)* **8/1**
0-25 8 18 **Peggy's Angel**[71] 254 4-8-8 **72** .... BarryMcHugh 7 13
(Marjorie Fife) *t.k.h: midfield and wd thrght: sn hdwy 1/2-way: lost pl over 1f out: bhd and eased ins fnl f* **20/1**

1m 11.97s (-1.73) **Going Correction** -0.025s/f (Stan) **8** Ran SP% **118.1**
Speed ratings (Par 102): **110,109,108,107,107 106,106,82**
CSF £79.85 CT £211.57 TOTE £4.00: £1.20, £6.70, £1.20; EX 92.00 Trifecta £631.30.
Owner N Martin **Bred** N Martin **Trained** Upper Lambourn, Berks
■ Stewards' Enquiry : Martin Dwyer caution; careless riding

FOCUS
It was an advantage to be handy here.

1383 KIDS INSPIRE CLASSIFIED STKS (DIV I) 6f (P)
8:00 (8:03) (Class 6) 3-Y-O+

£3,105 (£924; £461; £400; £400; £400) **Stalls** Centre

Form RPR
0066 1 **Mystical Moon (IRE)**[5] 1286 4-9-8 45 .... DougieCostello 6 54
(David C Griffiths) *wnt rt leaving stalls: chsd ldrs tl wnt 2nd over 3f out: led over 2f out: styd on wl ins fnl f: drvn out* **14/1**
-060 2 1½ **My Girl Maisie (IRE)**[27] 973 5-9-8 42........(e) PhilipPrince 2 50
(Richard Guest) *taken down early: chsd ldrs: wnt 2nd jst over 2f out: swtchd rt and effrt wl over 1f out: kpt on u.p but no imp ins fnl f* **14/1**
256 3 1¾ **Le Manege Enchante (IRE)**[57] 483 6-9-8 47........(v) PaddyMathers 8 44
(Derek Shaw) *bdly bmpd and rdr unbalanced leaving stalls: in rr: hdwy over 1f out: kpt on wl u.p ins fnl f: nvr getting to ldrs (jockey said gelding suffered interference shortly after the start)* **7/1**[3]
4405 4 ¾ **Malaysian Boleh**[13] 1215 9-9-1 42........(v) GraceMcEntee(7) 13 42+
(Phil McEntee) *towards rr on outer: pushed along over 2f out: swtchd lft over 1f out and nt clr run: swtchd lft again ins fnl f: r.o wl towards fin: nvr trbld ldrs (jockey said gelding was denied a clear run)* **16/1**
00-5 5 nse **Camino**[34] 848 6-9-3 38........ DylanHogan(5) 12 42
(Andi Brown) *wnt sltly lft leaving stalls: t.k.h: hld up in midfield: effrt and hemmed in over 1f out: hdwy 1f out: kpt on ins fnl f: nvr getting to ldrs* **50/1**
0-60 6 nk **Multitask**[28] 941 9-9-8 50........ AdamKirby 1 41
(Gary Moore) *in tch in midfield: effrt towards inner over 1f out: drvn and no imp ins fnl f* **11/4**[2]
0-60 7 1¼ **Melo Pearl**[28] 941 3-8-4 41........(b) AndrewBreslin(5) 4 33
(Mrs Ilka Gansera-Leveque) *t.k.h: hld up towards rr: effrt on inner and sme hdwy over 1f out: no imp ins fnl f* **14/1**
5205 8 nk **Dalness Express**[19] 1093 6-9-8 48........(t) LukeMorris 9 36
(John O'Shea) *bmpd and hmpd leaving stalls: towards rr: swtchd rt and effrt over 1f out: kpt on ins fnl f: nvr trbld ldrs* **10/1**
00- 9 1 **Rock In Society (IRE)**[113] 9415 4-9-5 43........ TimClark(3) 3 33
(John Butler) *t.k.h: wl in tch in midfield: effrt and edgd lft over 1f out: no imp ins fnl f (jockey said gelding ran too freely)* **5/2**[1]
00- 10 hd **Lady York (IRE)**[105] 9523 4-9-8 48........ FrannyNorton 10 33
(Charlie Wallis) *wnt sharply lft sn after s: chsd ldr tl over 3f out: unable qck u.p over 1f out: wknd ins fnl f* **20/1**
0525 11 shd **Roy's Legacy**[26] 986 10-9-8 45........ GeorgeWood 5 32
(Shaun Harris) *led tl rdn and hdd over 2f out: no ex u.p over 1f out: wknd ins fnl f and eased towards fin (jockey said horse moved poorly)* **14/1**
50-0 12 6 **Following Breeze (IRE)**[22] 1037 4-9-8 43........ CharlieBennett 7 14
(Jim Boyle) *bdly bmpd s: a towards rr and nvr gng wl* **50/1**

1m 13.32s (-0.38) **Going Correction** -0.025s/f (Stan)
WFA 3 from 4yo+ 13lb **12** Ran SP% **118.1**
Speed ratings (Par 101): **101,99,96,95,95 95,93,93,91,91 91,83**
CSF £181.83 TOTE £17.10: £4.50, £4.30, £2.20; EX 223.10 Trifecta £2138.00.
Owner Wentdale Limited And Partner **Bred** M Smith **Trained** Bawtry, S Yorks

FOCUS
A weak race, but the quicker of the two divisions.

1384 KIDS INSPIRE CLASSIFIED STKS (DIV II) 6f (P)
8:30 (8:30) (Class 6) 3-Y-O+

£3,105 (£924; £461; £400; £400; £400) **Stalls** Centre

Form RPR
-005 1 **Poppy May (IRE)**[14] 1192 5-9-8 48........ BarryMcHugh 8 57
(James Given) *hld up in tch in midfield: swtchd rt and effrt over 1f out: chsd ldrs ins fnl f: r.o wl to ld towards fin* **9/1**
043 2 ¾ **Ascot Dreamer**[3] 1337 3-8-4 50........ AndrewBreslin(5) 11 51+
(David Brown) *t.k.h: hld up in tch: effrt over 1f out: rdn and hdwy 1/2-way: rdn and hdwy to press ldr ent fnl f: sn led: hdd and no ex towards fin* **6/4**[1]
0-00 3 2 **Swendab (IRE)**[29] 920 11-9-8 50........(b) RossaRyan 13 49
(John O'Shea) *rousted along leaving stalls: sn led: rdn over 1f out: drvn and hdd 1f out: no ex: lost 2nd and outpcd towards fin* **33/1**
0536 4 nk **Legal Mind**[19] 1093 6-9-8 49........(v) AdamKirby 7 48
(Emma Owen) *rousted along early: chsd ldr tl over 4f out: effrt and swtchd rt over 1f out: kpt on same pce u.p ins fnl f* **6/1**[3]
2-40 5 hd **Soldier Blue (FR)**[36] 809 5-9-8 50........(v) CamHardie 12 48
(Brian Ellison) *s.i.s: hld up in last trio: effrt over 1f out: styd on wl ins fnl f: no threat to ldrs* **7/1**
-544 6 hd **Kyllukey**[29] 920 6-9-8 44........ FrannyNorton 10 47
(Charlie Wallis) *chsd ldrs: unable qck u.p over 1f out: kpt on same pce ins fnl f* **7/1**
2525 7 1 **Ever Rock (IRE)**[50] 620 3-8-9 49........ KieranO'Neill 3 40
(J S Moore) *towards rr: short of room and pushed along on inner over 3f out: clsd and swtchd lft over 1f out: no imp ins fnl f* **5/1**[2]
3505 8 ½ **Swiss Cross**[29] 920 12-9-1 50........(p) GraceMcEntee(7) 9 42
(Phil McEntee) *chsd ldrs: nt clr run over 1f out: nvr enough room and no imp fnl f* **20/1**
-500 9 1 **Speed Skater**[29] 918 3-8-9 49........ JoeyHaynes 1 35
(Amanda Perrett) *midfield: effrt on inner u.p over 1f out: no imp 1f out and wknd ins fnl f* **25/1**
U-00 10 1¼ **Lisnamoyle Lady (IRE)**[29] 920 4-9-8 40........(t[1]) PaddyMathers 6 36
(Martin Smith) *broke okay: sn rdn along and dropped to rr: nvr involved after* **25/1**
0/00 11 ½ **Major Muscari (IRE)**[14] 1192 11-9-8 41........(p) CharlieBennett 14 34
(Shaun Harris) *chsd ldrs: wnt 2nd over 4f out tl over 1f out: sn wknd* **100/1**

1m 13.58s (-0.12) **Going Correction** -0.025s/f (Stan)
WFA 3 from 4yo+ 13lb **11** Ran SP% **122.3**
Speed ratings (Par 101): **99,98,95,94,94 94,93,92,91,89 88**
CSF £22.75 TOTE £10.00: £2.40, £1.30, £8.40; EX 30.30 Trifecta £850.20.
Owner Team Given 1 **Bred** Mount Coote Stud **Trained** Willoughton, Lincs

FOCUS
The second division of a weak classified race, and the slower of the two legs by 0.26sec. The winner has been rated to her previous best.
T/Plt: £17.80 to a £1 stake. Pool: £85,845.27 - 3,511.10 winning units T/Qpdt: £10.80 to a £1 stake. Pool: £11,218.02 - 767.81 winning units **Steve Payne**

1341 WOLVERHAMPTON (A.W) (L-H)
Thursday, March 28

OFFICIAL GOING: Tapeta: standard
Wind: Almost nil Weather: Fine

1385 LADBROKES HOME OF THE ODDS BOOST H'CAP 7f 36y (Tp)
2:20 (2:20) (Class 6) (0-65,65) 3-Y-O

£3,105 (£924; £461; £300; £300; £300) **Stalls** High

Form RPR
00-0 1 **Havana Ooh Na Na**[17] 1141 3-8-11 **55**........(p) CliffordLee 5 60
(K R Burke) *led early: chsd ldr: shkn up over 2f out: rdn to ld wl ins fnl f: styd on* **12/1**
356- 2 ¾ **Moveonup (IRE)**[194] 7276 3-9-7 **65**........ HollieDoyle 3 68
(Gay Kelleway) *sn led: racd keenly: rdn and edgd rt over 1f out: hdd wl ins fnl f* **11/1**
66-4 3 1¾ **Es Que Magic (IRE)**[17] 1141 3-9-0 **58**........ DavidProbert 6 57
(Alex Hales) *hld up in tch: rdn over 1f out: edgd lft: styd on same pce ins fnl f* **8/1**
33-4 4 hd **French Twist**[64] 360 3-9-6 **64**........ JoeFanning 1 62
(Mark Johnston) *s.i.s: sn chsng ldrs: rdn over 1f out: no ex wl ins fnl f* **11/4**[1]
500- 5 nk **Coastguard Watch (FR)**[107] 9489 3-9-0 **58**........ OisinMurphy 9 56+
(Richard Hughes) *hld up: hdwy over 1f out: rdn and swtchd lft ins fnl f: styd on* **3/1**[2]
530- 6 3 **Schnapps**[191] 7390 3-9-6 **64**........ JackGarritty 4 54
(Jedd O'Keeffe) *chsd ldrs: pushed along 1/2-way: rdn over 2f out: hung lft fr over 1f out: styd on same pce (jockey said filly hung left-handed in the home straight)* **20/1**
5-04 7 3½ **Maid Millie**[15] 1170 3-9-4 **62**........(p[1]) LukeMorris 10 44
(Robert Cowell) *s.i.s: sn rcvrd into mid-div: pushed along 3f out: rdn over 1f out: wknd fnl f* **33/1**
-663 8 shd **Cheap Jack**[20] 1084 3-8-13 **64**........ RPWalsh(7) 2 45
(Ronald Thompson) *s.i.s: hld up: rdn over 2f out: nvr on terms* **7/1**[3]
403 9 ¾ **Dorchester**[54] 547 3-9-2 **63**........(h[1]) GabrieleMalune(3) 7 43
(Marco Botti) *s.i.s: pushed along 5f out: n.d* **11/1**
0403 10 2¾ **Zaula**[15] 1170 3-9-1 **64**........(b) ThomasGreatrex(5) 11 37
(Archie Watson) *s.i.s: wnt prom 6f out: rdn over 2f out: wknd over 1f out* **33/1**
0-35 11 nk **Divied (USA)**[31] 908 3-9-2 **60**........ AndrewMullen 8 32
(John Quinn) *hld up: shkn up over 2f out: bhd whn edgd lft fnl f* **20/1**

1m 28.14s (-0.66) **Going Correction** -0.15s/f (Stan) **11** Ran SP% **115.0**
Speed ratings (Par 96): **97,96,94,93,93 90,86,86,85,82 81**
CSF £126.26 CT £1115.41 TOTE £15.40: £3.50, £3.00, £2.20; EX 177.80 Trifecta £2706.60.
Owner The Havana Ooh Na Na Partnership **Bred** Mickley Stud & Lady Lonsdale **Trained** Middleham Moor, N Yorks

FOCUS
The presence of several handicap debutants from decent yards added some interest to this Class 6 event but none of them made any impact, which was disappointing. They appeared to go a reasonable gallop but nothing got in a blow from off the pace. The winner has been rated near last year's best.

1386 LADBROKES H'CAP 1m 4f 51y (Tp)
2:50 (2:50) (Class 4) (0-85,81) 3-Y-O

£5,530 (£1,645; £822; £411; £300; £300) **Stalls** Low

Form RPR
24-1 1 **Caplin**[12] 1233 3-9-3 **77**........ JoeFanning 2 87
(Mark Johnston) *mde all: set stdy pce tl qcknd 3f out: pushed clr fr over 1f out: comf* **6/4**[1]
-122 2 3 **Paradise Boy (FR)**[12] 1233 3-9-2 **76**........ RobHornby 3 81
(Andrew Balding) *prom: chsd wnr over 2f out: rdn and hung lft over 1f out: styd on same pce fnl f* **6/1**

-212 **3** *3/4* **Gantier**[35] 839 3-9-7 **81**...............................(b) KieranO'Neill 5 85
(John Gosden) *s.i.s: pushed along early in rr: rdn over 2f out: hdwy over 1f out: sn edgd lft: kpt on* **5/2**[2]

-213 **4** *2 3/4* **Water's Edge (IRE)**[35] 839 3-9-4 **78**.................... OisinMurphy 1 77
(James Tate) *chsd ldrs: shkn up whn nt clr run over 1f out: wknd ins fnl f* **4/1**[3]

653- **5** *14* **Hurricane Hero (FR)**[155] 8564 3-9-0 **74**.................... BenCurtis 6 51
(K R Burke) *chsd wnr tl rdn over 2f out: sn wknd* **16/1**

165- **6** *2 1/2* **Patchouli**[237] 5675 3-9-4 **78**.................... CharlesBishop 4 51
(Mick Channon) *hld up: pushed along over 4f out: wknd over 2f out (vet reported the filly lost its right fore shoe)* **25/1**

2m 36.24s (-4.56) **Going Correction** -0.15s/f (Stan) **6** Ran SP% **112.6**
Speed ratings (Par 100): **109,107,106,104,95 93**
CSF £11.22 TOTE £2.30: £1.60, £2.40; EX 10.00 Trifecta £24.00.
Owner S R Counsell **Bred** Stuart Counsell **Trained** Middleham Moor, N Yorks

FOCUS
A good little handicap but the pace slackened down the far side and the winner put this to bed with a smart change of gear around the home bend that immediately put his rivals in trouble.

1387 LADBROKES FILLIES' H'CAP — 1m 142y (Tp)
3:25 (3:25) (Class 5) (0-75,77) 4-Y-0+

£3,752 (£1,116; £557; £300; £300; £300) **Stalls** Low

Form — RPR

-006 **1** **Bell Heather (IRE)**[36] 814 6-8-7 **61**....................(p) DavidEgan 1 68
(Patrick Morris) *led at stdy pce tl hdd over 5f out: chsd ldr tl rdn to ld and hung lft over 1f out: drvn out* **14/1**

1-52 **2** *nk* **Yusra**[55] 516 4-9-6 **77**.................... GabrieleMalune(3) 2 83
(Marco Botti) *racd keenly in 2nd tl led over 5f out: rdn and hdd over 1f out: ev ch ins fnl f: r.o* **5/2**[1]

135 **3** *2 1/4* **Lady Alavesa**[21] 1063 4-9-5 **73**....................(p) JosephineGordon 7 74
(Gay Kelleway) *hld up: hdwy over 1f out: sn rdn and hung lft: styd on to go 3rd wl ins fnl f: nt rch ldrs (jockey said filly hung left-handed in the home straight)* **7/2**[3]

22-3 **4** *1 1/2* **Indiscretion (IRE)**[55] 516 4-9-7 **75**.................... RobHornby 4 73
(Jonathan Portman) *chsd ldrs: rdn over 2f out: styd on same pce ins fnl f* **5/1**

5 *1 1/2* **Dream World (IRE)**[199] 7139 4-8-11 **65**.................... LewisEdmunds 5 59
(Michael Appleby) *s.i.s: hld up: hdwy over 1f out: no ex wl ins fnl f* **12/1**

100- **6** *10* **Plansina**[85] 8379 4-9-4 **72**....................(h[1]) StevieDonohoe 3 44
(Tom Symonds) *hld up: rdn and wknd over 2f out* **100/1**

54-1 **7** *93* **American Endeavour (USA)**[36] 814 4-9-7 **75**........ MarcMonaghan 6
(Marco Botti) *trckd ldrs: shkn up over 2f out: sn wknd and eased: virtually p.u: b.b.v (vet reported the filly had bled from the nose)* **11/4**[2]

1m 48.36s (-1.74) **Going Correction** -0.15s/f (Stan) **7** Ran SP% **109.5**
Speed ratings (Par 100): **101,100,98,97,96 87,4**
CSF £45.03 TOTE £17.80: £6.70, £1.30; EX 54.30 Trifecta £166.00.
Owner Dr Marwan Koukash **Bred** Tinnakill Bloodstock & Joe Osborne **Trained** Prescot, Merseyside

FOCUS
An ordinary fillies handicap but it was another steadily run affair and the front two had it between them from a fair way out. It's hard to get excited about the form.

1388 BETWAY CASINO H'CAP — 6f 20y (Tp)
3:55 (3:55) (Class 3) (0-90,92) 3-Y-O **£7,246** (£2,168; £1,084; £542; £270) **Stalls** Low

Form — RPR

0-40 **1** **Reflektor (IRE)**[31] 909 6-10-0 **89**.................... RichardKingscote 7 97
(Tom Dascombe) *mde all: rdn over 1f out: styd on* **12/1**

3532 **2** *3/4* **Areen Heart (FR)**[17] 1143 5-9-13 **88**.................... DavidNolan 5 94+
(David O'Meara) *hld up: hdwy and nt clr run over 1f out: swtchd lft ins fnl f: r.o: nt rch wnr* **6/1**

-024 **3** *1/2* **El Hombre**[19] 1105 5-10-3 **92**.................... JoeFanning 3 96
(Keith Dalgleish) *a.p: swtchd rt and chsd wnr over 1f out: sn rdn: styd on same pce ins fnl f* **11/4**[1]

41-6 **4** *nk* **Fares Kodiac (IRE)**[35] 838 3-9-0 **88**....................(t[1]) AndreaAtzeni 9 87
(Marco Botti) *sn prom: chsd wnr over 4f out tl rdn over 1f out: styd on same pce ins fnl f* **9/2**[3]

022- **5** *3 1/4* **Punjab Mail**[161] 8337 3-8-3 **77**.................... DavidEgan 1 66
(Ian Williams) *stdd s: hld up: shkn up over 1f out: edgd lft and r.o ins fnl f: nvr nr to chal* **16/1**

-441 **6** *nse* **Sandridge Lad (IRE)**[14] 1193 3-8-6 **80**.................... BenCurtis 8 69
(John Ryan) *prom: rdn over 1f out: no ex ins fnl f (jockey said gelding ran too freely)* **16/1**

-500 **7** *1/2* **Shining Armor**[5] 1295 3-8-13 **92**.................... DarraghKeenan(5) 2 79
(John Ryan) *s.i.s: hld up: r.o ins fnl f: nvr nr to chal (jockey said gelding missed the break and was therefore unable to get a prominent position and was latterly denied a clear run turning into the home straight)* **8/1**

20-0 **8** *2* **Bungee Jump (IRE)**[17] 1143 4-9-8 **83**.................... HectorCrouch 6 68
(Grace Harris) *plld hrd in 2nd pl tl over 4f out: remained handy: rdn over 1f out: wknd ins fnl f* **50/1**

-113 **9** *2 1/2* **Coolagh Magic**[35] 838 3-8-7 **81**....................(p) PaulHanagan 4 54
(Richard Fahey) *chsd ldrs: nt clr run and lost pl after 1f: nt clr run wl over 3f out: sme hdwy over 1f out: nt clr run sn after: wknd ins fnl f (jockey said colt was never travelling)* **4/1**[2]

1m 13.33s (-1.17) **Going Correction** -0.15s/f (Stan) **9** Ran SP% **111.7**
WFA 3 from 4yo+ 13lb
Speed ratings (Par 107): **101,100,99,98,94 94,93,91,87**
CSF £78.36 CT £254.23 TOTE £13.40: £2.70, £1.90, £1.10; EX 84.10 Trifecta £257.20.
Owner David Lowe & Miss Amber Lowe **Bred** Hyde Park Stud & Paddy Conney **Trained** Malpas, Cheshire

FOCUS
Yet another race dominated by the pace and Reflektor got the perfect set up to repeat his C&D victory from last year. The front four came clear.

1389 BETWAY NOVICE STKS — 6f 20y (Tp)
4:30 (4:30) (Class 5) 3-Y-O+ **£3,752** (£1,116; £557; £278) **Stalls** Low

Form — RPR

43- **1** **Mawakib**[147] 8783 3-9-1 0.................... AndreaAtzeni 4 81+
(Roger Varian) *chsd ldr 1f: remained handy: wnt 2nd again over 1f out: rdn and r.o to ld nr fin* **1/1**[1]

226- **2** *1/2* **Ustath**[176] 7896 3-9-1 77.................... DaneO'Neill 7 79
(Owen Burrows) *led: shkn up and qcknd 2f out: rdn and hdd nr fin* **5/2**[2]

255- **3** *2 1/2* **Serengeti Song (IRE)**[189] 7462 3-9-1 76.................... BenCurtis 1 71
(K R Burke) *hld up in tch: shkn up and hung lft over 1f out: styd on same pce ins fnl f* **4/1**[3]

33- **4** *4 1/2* **Sarasota Bay**[164] 8279 3-8-10 0.................... KevinStott 3 52
(John Quinn) *prom: rdn over 2f out: no ex whn hung lft fnl f* **28/1**

00- **5** *3/4* **Antico Lady (IRE)**[292] 3581 3-8-10 0.................... AndrewMullen 2 49
(Brian Ellison) *s.s: r.o ins fnl f: nvr nrr* **66/1**

/ **6** *1 1/2* **Northern Queen (IRE)** 4-9-6 0....................(w) BenRobinson(3) 5 48
(Brian Ellison) *prom: chsd ldr 5f out tl rdn over 1f out: wknd ins fnl f* **20/1**

7 *25* **Reformed Character (IRE)** 3-9-1 0.................... HollieDoyle 6
(Lydia Pearce) *s.s: outpcd (jockey said colt ran greenly)* **66/1**

1m 12.82s (-1.68) **Going Correction** -0.15s/f (Stan)
WFA 3 from 4yo 13lb **7** Ran SP% **109.8**
Speed ratings (Par 103): **105,104,101,95,94 92,58**
CSF £3.29 TOTE £1.80: £1.10, £1.40; EX 3.70 Trifecta £7.80.
Owner Sheikh Ahmed Al Maktoum **Bred** Mrs J E Laws **Trained** Newmarket, Suffolk

FOCUS
Most of these look handicappers going forward but the front two, who finished clear, both cost plenty and represent powerful connections.

1390 PLAY 4 TO SCORE AT BETWAY H'CAP — 1m 1f 104y (Tp)
5:05 (5:05) (Class 6) (0-55,61) 4-Y-O+

£3,105 (£924; £461; £300; £300; £300) **Stalls** Low

Form — RPR

360- **1** **Kingfast (IRE)**[192] 7371 4-9-2 **50**.................... DavidEgan 5 56
(David Dennis) *chsd ldrs: wnt 2nd over 2f out: sn rdn: styd on to ld post* **11/1**

523- **2** *hd* **Optima Petamus**[172] 7599 7-9-1 **49**....................(p) PhilDennis 7 55
(Liam Bailey) *chsd ldrs: rdn over 1f out: ev ch ins fnl f: styd on* **20/1**

2033 **3** *shd* **Sea Shack**[13] 1215 5-8-12 **53**....................(tp) ScottMcCullagh(7) 13 58
(Julia Feilden) *chsd ldr after 1f tl led over 2f out: rdn over 1f out: hdd post* **12/1**

-036 **4** *3/4* **Herm (IRE)**[40] 760 5-9-4 **52**.................... HectorCrouch 6 56
(David Evans) *hld up: hdwy over 1f out: r.o u.p: nt rch ldrs* **11/1**

0-25 **5** *hd* **Zarkavon**[35] 835 5-8-7 **46**....................(p) FayeMcManoman(5) 12 51
(John Wainwright) *chsd ldrs: nt clr run and swtchd rt over 2f out: shkn up over 1f out: styd on* **40/1**

5603 **6** *2 1/4* **False Id**[15] 1176 6-9-7 **55**....................(b) DavidProbert 2 54
(David Loughnane) *dwlt: hld up: hdwy over 1f out: r.o* **9/1**

0234 **7** *nk* **Final Attack (IRE)**[3] 1339 8-9-1 **52**....................(p) GabrieleMalune(3) 10 51
(Sarah Hollinshead) *s.i.s: hld up: rdn and r.o ins fnl f: nt rch ldrs* **9/2**[2]

0-03 **8** *1/2* **Lady Of Authority**[37] 792 4-9-5 **53**....................(p[1]) HollieDoyle 8 51
(Richard Phillips) *hld up: rdn on outer over 1f out: styd on ins fnl f: nt trble ldrs* **11/2**[3]

0451 **9** *3/4* **Ubla (IRE)**[3] 1339 6-9-6 **61** 6ex....................(e) SeanKirrane(7) 4 57
(Gay Kelleway) *hld up: effrt whn nt clr run fr over 2f out tl over 1f out: styd on same pce fnl f (jockey said gelding was denied a clear run rounding the top bend)* **7/2**[1]

0020 **10** *3* **Captain Kissinger**[33] 887 4-8-9 **50**....................(v) GeorgiaDobie(7) 1 41
(Jo Hughes, France) *broke wl: racd keenly: sn stdd and lost pl: hdwy over 5f out: swtchd rt over 2f out: rdn and hung rt over 1f out: no ex fnl f* **14/1**

6-55 **11** *3 1/4* **Amity Island**[53] 590 4-8-13 **50**.................... BenRobinson(3) 9 35
(Ollie Pears) *hld up: rdn over 3f out: n.d* **14/1**

0005 **12** *2 1/4* **Blue Rocks**[20] 1078 5-9-2 **55**.................... SeamusCronin(5) 3 35
(Lisa Williamson) *led: rdn and hdd over 2f out: wknd over 1f out* **40/1**

1m 59.92s (-0.88) **Going Correction** -0.15s/f (Stan) **12** Ran SP% **113.1**
Speed ratings (Par 101): **97,96,96,96,95 93,93,93,92,89 86,84**
CSF £206.40 CT £2645.41 TOTE £11.40: £3.80, £4.30, £3.60; EX 182.70 Trifecta £3715.80.
Owner G Saville, G Brandrick & Partner **Bred** D Veitch & B Douglas **Trained** Hanley Swan, Worcestershire

FOCUS
A wide-open low-grade handicap that once again proved difficult for hold-up horses to make an impact - a theme that continued throughout the card. Straightforward form rated around those in behind the winner.
T/Jkpt: Not Won. T/Plt: £2,225.80 to a £1 stake. Pool: £79,734.07 - 26.15 winning units T/Qpdt: £85.20 to a £1 stake. Pool: £9,479.73 - 82.32 winning units **Colin Roberts**

1340 CHANTILLY (R-H)
Thursday, March 28

OFFICIAL GOING: Polytrack: standard

1391a PRIX DE LA STALLE DE PELAGIE (H'CAP) (4YO) (ALL-WEATHER TRACK) (POLYTRACK) — 6f 110y(P)
4:50 4-Y-O

£11,711 (£4,450; £3,279; £1,873; £936; £702)

RPR

1 **Gloria**[14] 4-9-4 0.................... ClementLecoeuvre 3 90
(Mme M Bollack-Badel, France) **9/2**

2 *1 1/4* **Royal Diplomat (IRE)**[16] 4-8-9 0....................(p) MaximeGuyon 5 77
(P Monfort, France) **41/10**[2]

3 *3* **Brian Ryan**[43] 4-9-1 0.................... DelphineSantiago(3) 1 77
(Andrea Marcialis, France) **43/10**[3]

4 *snk* **Vent Charlie (FR)**[266] 4597 4-8-7 0.................... JeffersonSmith 4 66
(P Fleurie, France) **114/1**

5 *snk* **Ayounor (FR)**[49] 4-8-9 0.................... AntoineCoutier 10 67
(T Mace, France) **20/1**

6 *nk* **Get Even**[166] 8252 4-9-4 0.................... TheoBachelot 2 76
(Jo Hughes, France) *settled in midfield: pushed along and hdwy 2f out: rdn to chse ldrs over 1f out: kpt on same pce fnl f* **44/5**

7 *nse* **Dancing Master (FR)**[27] 4-8-4 0.................... AnthonyCrastus 7 61
(J-V Toux, France) **22/1**

8 *1/2* **Kyvon Des Aigles (FR)**[14] 4-7-12 0 ow1.................... ThomasTrullier(3) 11 57
(Mme C Barande-Barbe, France) **13/1**

9 *hd* **Mont Plaza (FR)**[49] 4-9-6 0....................(b) Pierre-CharlesBoudot 8 75
(J Reynier, France) **13/5**[1]

10 *3/4* **Heptathlete (IRE)**[14] 4-9-3 0....................(p) TonyPiccone 6 70
(Mme B Jacques, France) **33/1**

11 *3* **Nimocis (FR)**[132] 4-9-1 0.................... SylvainRuis 9 60
(C Boutin, France) **18/1**

1m 17.17s **11** Ran SP% **120.0**
PARI-MUTUEL (all including 1 euro stake): WIN 5.50; PLACE 1.90, 1.70, 1.80; DF 11.20.
Owner Philippe Ezri **Bred** Gestut Gorlsdorf **Trained** Lamorlaye, France

[1358]LINGFIELD (L-H)

Friday, March 29

OFFICIAL GOING: Polytrack: standard

Wind: light, across Weather: fine

1392 SUNRACING.CO.UK H'CAP — 1m 1y(P)

2:00 (2:00) (Class 5) (0-75,77) 4-Y-O+

£3,752 (£1,116; £557; £300; £300; £300) **Stalls** High

Form | | | | RPR

-123 **1** **In The Red (IRE)**[23] 1036 6-9-9 **76**..............(p) AdamKirby 8 — 84
(Martin Smith) *mde virtually all: rdn 2f out: drvn over 1f out: kpt on and a holding on towards fin* — **9/4**[1]

1444 **2** *nk* **Dark Alliance (IRE)**[28] 962 8-9-3 **70**.............. OisinMurphy 9 — 77
(Mark Loughnane) *stdd s: hld up in tch: effrt and clsd ent fnl 2f: chsd wnr 1f out: styd on wl but nvr quite getting to wnr (vet said gelding had lost its right-fore shoe)* — **9/2**[3]

4-03 **3** *2 1/4* **Choral Music**[21] 1074 4-9-7 **74**.............. RobHornby 2 — 76
(John E Long) *in tch in midfield: effrt in 3rd 2f out: unable qck 1f out: wknd wl ins fnl f* — **11/1**

00-4 **4** *3/4* **Golden Guest**[7] 1271 5-8-7 **67**.............. CierenFallon(7) 4 — 67+
(Les Eyre) *in tch in last pair: rdn over 2f out: hdwy and hung lft 1f out: kpt on ins fnl f wout threatening wnr* — **11/2**

-356 **5** *1/2* **The Warrior (IRE)**[43] 722 7-9-6 **73**.............. LiamJones 3 — 72
(Lee Carter) *hld up in tch in last trio: effrt and n.m.r 2f out: swtchd lft and hdwy 1f out: kpt on wout threatening ldrs ins fnl f* — **4/1**[2]

6-40 **5** *dht* **Cuttin' Edge (IRE)**[29] 944 5-8-9 **62**.............. TomMarquand 5 — 61
(William Muir) *chsd ldrs tl wnt 2nd 6f out: rdn ent 2f out: lost 2nd 1f out and wknd ins fnl f* — **11/2**

350- **7** *3/4* **Duke Of North (IRE)**[158] 8488 7-8-5 **65**.............. IsobelFrancis(7) 6 — 63
(Jim Boyle) *s.i.s: hld up in rr: effrt wl over 1f out: rdn and styd on ins fnl f: nvr trbld ldrs (jockey said gelding was slowly away)* — **33/1**

/50- **8** *2* **Bin Daahir**[302] 3281 4-8-11 **71**.............. OwenLewis(7) 1 — 64
(Charles Hills) *awkward leaving stalls: chsd wnr for 2f: lost pl over 1f out: wknd ins fnl f* — **16/1**

1m 36.11s (-2.09) **Going Correction** -0.175s/f (Stan) — 8 Ran SP% **116.9**

Speed ratings (Par 103): **103,102,100,99,99 99,98,96**

WIN: 2.60 In The Red; PL: 1.10 In The Red 3.00 Choral Music 1.80 Dark Alliance; EX: 11.30; CSF: 12.92; TC: 92.49; TF: 65.90 CSF £12.92 CT £92.49 TOTE £2.60: £1.10, £1.80, £3.00; EX 11.30 Trifecta £65.90.

Owner Sunville Rail Limited **Bred** Airlie Stud **Trained** Newmarket, Suffolk

FOCUS

A fair handicap. The second has been rated close to his recent form.

1393 BETWAY CASINO H'CAP — 6f 1y(P)

2:30 (2:30) (Class 5) (0-70,70) 4-Y-O+

£3,752 (£1,116; £557; £300; £300; £300) **Stalls** Low

Form | | | | RPR

4322 **1** **Kraka (IRE)**[23] 1037 4-9-3 **66**..............(v) KieranO'Neill 1 — 75
(Christine Dunnett) *mde all: rdn wl over 1f out: sn edgd rt u.p: styd on wl: rdn out* — **3/1**[1]

-121 **2** *2* **Spirit Of Zebedee (IRE)**[7] 1265 6-9-1 **64** 6ex..............(v) JasonHart 9 — 67
(John Quinn) *chsd ldrs: effrt over 1f out: chsd wnr 1f out: kpt on but no imp* — **13/2**

4213 **3** *1/2* **Tavener**[7] 1265 7-8-12 **61**..............(p) AndreaAtzeni 11 — 62
(David C Griffiths) *sn pressing wnr: rdn ent fnl 2f: unable qck and lost 2nd 1f out: kpt on same pce ins fnl f (vet said gelding had lost its left-fore shoe)* — **6/1**

1062 **4** *3/4* **Aguerooo (IRE)**[25] 1016 6-9-7 **70**..............(tp) FrannyNorton 10 — 69+
(Charlie Wallis) *swtchd lft after s: hld up in rr of main gp: nt clr run on inner ent fnl 2f: swtchd rt 1f out: kpt on u.p ins fnl f* — **7/1**

450- **5** *1/2* **Swissal (IRE)**[171] 8086 4-9-5 **68**.............. LukeMorris 2 — 65
(David Dennis) *chsd ldr: rdn ent fnl 2f: drvn wl over 1f out: kpt on same pce ins fnl f* — **11/1**

3261 **6** *nk* **Real Estate (IRE)**[27] 982 4-9-7 **70**..............(p) CallumShepherd 7 — 66
(Michael Attwater) *hld up in rr of main gp: effrt and hdwy on inner over 1f out: no imp ins fnl f* — **5/1**[3]

7 *1 1/4* **Savitar (IRE)**[188] 7557 4-9-4 **67**..............(h[1]) CharlieBennett 4 — 59
(Jim Boyle) *s.i.s: sn detached in last: reminder at 1/2-way: clsd on to rr of field over 2f out: kpt on ins fnl f: nvr involved* — **25/1**

05-2 **8** *nk* **Qaaraat**[24] 1023 4-9-6 **69**.............. CamHardie 3 — 60
(Antony Brittain) *hld up in tch in midfield: effrt and no imp over 1f out: wl hld ins fnl f* — **7/2**[2]

600- **9** *10* **Ad Valorem Queen (IRE)**[289] 3746 4-8-11 **60**.............. JasonWatson 6 — 19
(William Knight) *wd: in tch in midfield: lost pl bnd wl over 1f out: bhd ins fnl f* — **25/1**

1m 10.21s (-1.69) **Going Correction** -0.175s/f (Stan) — 9 Ran SP% **120.0**

Speed ratings (Par 103): **104,101,100,99,99 98,96,96,83**

CSF £24.09 CT £110.76 TOTE £3.40: £1.30, £3.10, £2.00; EX 26.20 Trifecta £104.30.

Owner Team Kraka **Bred** Fontstown Stud **Trained** Hingham, Norfolk

FOCUS

It paid to be handy in this sprint handicap. The winner has been rated back to his early best.

1394 BETWAY H'CAP — 5f 6y(P)

3:05 (3:05) (Class 4) (0-85,87) 4-Y-O+

£5,530 (£1,645; £822; £411; £300; £300) **Stalls** High

Form | | | | RPR

6341 **1** **Drakefell (IRE)**[20] 1100 4-8-12 **77**..............(b) SeamusCronin(5) 5 — 85
(Antony Brittain) *mde all: rdn over 1f out: hld on wl u.p ins fnl f* — **9/2**[2]

0121 **2** *nk* **Warrior's Valley**[15] 1194 4-9-1 **75**..............(tp) LewisEdmunds 7 — 82
(David C Griffiths) *taken down early: chsd wnr: rdn over 1f out: ev ch ins fnl f: kpt on but hld towards fin* — **4/1**[1]

0153 **3** *1/2* **Captain Lars (SAF)**[20] 1100 9-9-7 **81**..............(b) OisinMurphy 2 — 86
(Archie Watson) *chsd ldrs: pressing ldng pair u.p ins fnl f: kpt on same pce cl home* — **8/1**

50-0 **4** *1/2* **George Dryden (IRE)**[38] 791 7-9-6 **80**.............. DavidEgan 1 — 83
(Charlie Wallis) *in tch in midfield: effrt over 1f out: chsd ldrs ins fnl f: kpt on but nvr quite getting on terms* — **7/1**

1310 **5** *1 1/4* **Tathmeen (IRE)**[15] 1194 4-9-1 **75**.............. CamHardie 4 — 76+
(Antony Brittain) *t.k.h: hld up in tch in midfield: effrt over 1f out: sn hung lft: clsd and nt clr run ins fnl f: swtchd rt towards fin (jockey said gelding was denied a clear run in the home straight and hung left-handed)* — **5/1**[3]

60-1 **6** *1 1/2* **Just That Lord**[38] 791 6-9-13 **87**.............. LukeMorris 8 — 81
(Michael Attwater) *chsd ldrs: unable qck u.p over 1f out: wknd ins fnl f* — **5/1**[3]

2202 **7** *1/2* **Something Lucky (IRE)**[14] 1211 7-9-6 **80**..............(v) AdamKirby 10 — 72
(Michael Appleby) *s.i.s: styd on ins fnl f: nvr trbld ldrs (jockey said gelding was slowly away)* — **7/1**

300- **8** *1/2* **Harrogate (IRE)**[174] 7994 4-8-13 **80**.............. IsobelFrancis(7) 9 — 70
(Jim Boyle) *restless in stalls: v.s.a: bhd: effrt and rdn over 1f out: nvr involved (trainer was informed that the gelding could not run until the day after passing a stalls test)* — **33/1**

3416 **9** *nk* **It's All A Joke (IRE)**[32] 907 4-8-9 **76**..............(b) Pierre-LouisJamin(7) 3 — 65
(Archie Watson) *squeezed for room after 1f: effrt on inner and sme prog over 1f out: wknd ins fnl f* — **8/1**

306- **10** *1 3/4* **Peggie Sue**[162] 8341 4-8-6 **71**.............. RhiainIngram(5) 6 — 54
(Adam West) *towards rr of main gp: hung rt: wd and lost pl bnd wl over 1f out: bhd ins fnl f (jockey said filly hung right-handed down the hill)* — **33/1**

57.66s (-1.14) **Going Correction** -0.175s/f (Stan) — 10 Ran SP% **124.6**

Speed ratings (Par 105): **102,101,100,99,97 95,94,93,93,90**

CSF £24.68 CT £147.14 TOTE £5.30: £1.90, £1.70, £3.40; EX 29.00 Trifecta £321.30.

Owner Northgate Racing **Bred** D J Anderson **Trained** Warthill, N Yorks

FOCUS

The third winner in a row on the card to make all, and nothing got into it from behind. The second has been rated in line with his recent effort.

1395 PLAY 4 TO SCORE AT BETWAY H'CAP — 1m 2f (P)

3:35 (3:35) (Class 4) (0-85,85) 4-Y-O+

£5,530 (£1,645; £822; £411; £300; £300) **Stalls** Low

Form | | | | RPR

250- **1** **El Ghazwani (IRE)**[153] 8642 4-9-5 **83**..............(t[1]) OisinMurphy 4 — 93
(Hugo Palmer) *trckd ldr tl pushed along and clsd to chal 2f out: rdn to ld jst over 1f out: styd on and c clr ins fnl f* — **6/5**[1]

440- **2** *3 1/4* **Hollywood Road (IRE)**[179] 7848 6-9-5 **83**.............. HectorCrouch 8 — 86
(Gary Moore) *in tch in midfield: outpcd over 2f out: rallied and kpt on u.p ins fnl f: wnt 2nd cl home: no threat to wnr* — **16/1**

0-45 **3** *hd* **Emenem**[41] 758 5-9-1 **79**.............. TomMarquand 2 — 82
(Simon Dow) *chsd ldng pair: rdn and outpcd over 2f out: rallied and kpt on u.p ins fnl f: no threat to wnr* — **4/1**[2]

-214 **4** *nk* **Oneovdem**[20] 1099 5-8-8 **77**.............. TheodoreLadd(5) 5 — 79
(Tim Pinfield) *led: rdn and kicked clr w wnr over 2f out: hdd jst over 1f out: sn outpcd: wknd wl ins fnl f and lost 2 pls nr fin* — **11/2**[3]

4-64 **5** *3* **Mickey (IRE)**[51] 623 6-9-7 **85**.............. RichardKingscote 6 — 81
(Tom Dascombe) *t.k.h: hld up in rr: outpcd over 2f out: n.d after* — **11/2**[3]

0-55 **6** *3* **Winged Spur (IRE)**[20] 1106 4-9-2 **80**.............. FrannyNorton 3 — 70
(Mark Johnston) *niggled along early: a towards rr: outpcd over 2f out: n.d after* — **14/1**

5416 **7** *hd* **Thawry**[20] 1106 4-8-8 **72**.............. CamHardie 1 — 62
(Antony Brittain) *bustled along early: midfield: outpcd over 2f out: rdn and no hdwy over 1f out: wknd* — **14/1**

2m 3.49s (-3.11) **Going Correction** -0.175s/f (Stan) — 7 Ran SP% **115.4**

Speed ratings (Par 105): **105,102,102,102,99 97,97**

CSF £23.76 CT £62.94 TOTE £2.10: £1.40, £8.40; EX 24.60 Trifecta £101.30.

Owner Hamad Rashed Bin Ghedayer **Bred** Longueville Bloodstock **Trained** Newmarket, Suffolk

FOCUS

Once again it was an advantage to race up with the pace. The second and third have been rated to their recent form for now.

1396 LADBROKES H'CAP — 1m 2f (P)

4:10 (4:10) (Class 5) (0-75,75) 3-Y-O

£3,752 (£1,116; £557; £300; £300; £300) **Stalls** Low

Form | | | | RPR

-133 **1** **Albert Finney**[13] 1233 3-9-7 **75**.............. KieranO'Neill 5 — 82
(John Gosden) *mde all: rdn ent fnl 2f: styd on u.p ins fnl f: rdn out* — **6/4**[1]

6-41 **2** *1 1/4* **Lord Lamington**[7] 1270 3-9-2 **70** 6ex.............. FrannyNorton 8 — 74
(Mark Johnston) *chsd wnr thrght: rdn ent fnl 2f: kpt on same pce and a hld fr over 1f out* — **6/4**[1]

00-0 **3** *3/4* **Spirit Of Angel (IRE)**[65] 359 3-8-6 **60**.............. HayleyTurner 3 — 62
(Marcus Tregoning) *in tch in 5th: rdn wl over 1f out: swtchd rt and styd on ins fnl f: wnt 3rd cl home: no threat to wnr* — **12/1**[3]

530- **4** *hd* **Chinese Alphabet**[158] 8467 3-9-0 **68**.............. AndreaAtzeni 6 — 70
(William Knight) *a same pl: rdn over 4f out: racd awkwardly bnd 2f out and sn hung lft: styd on ins fnl f: no threat to wnr (jockey said gelding hung left-handed in the straight)* — **5/1**[2]

56-0 **5** *nk* **Sarasota Star (IRE)**[75] 229 3-9-1 **69**..............(h[1]) JoeyHaynes 2 — 70
(Martin Keighley) *chsd ldng pair: unable qck u.p 1f out: kpt on same pce ins fnl f: lost 2 pls cl home* — **16/1**

050- **6** *12* **Alramz**[156] 8549 3-8-12 **66**.............. LiamJones 7 — 43
(Lee Carter) *dwlt: hld up in rr: rdn over 2f out: sn struggling and btn: bhd fnl f* — **50/1**

2m 4.13s (-2.47) **Going Correction** -0.175s/f (Stan) — 6 Ran SP% **112.2**

Speed ratings (Par 98): **102,101,100,100,100 90**

CSF £3.80 CT £15.01 TOTE £2.20: £1.10, £1.10; EX 4.10 Trifecta £20.10.

Owner Ms Rachel D S Hood **Bred** Ms Rachel Hood **Trained** Newmarket, Suffolk

■ Cromwell was withdrawn. Price at time of withdrawal 25-1. Rule 4 does not apply.

FOCUS

Another race in which the pace held up, albeit it was the front two in the market who dominated throughout. The third and fourth have been rated close to their maiden form.

1397 LADBROKES HOME OF THE ODDS BOOST FILLIES' NOVICE STKS — 1m 2f (P)

4:40 (4:40) (Class 5) 3-Y-O+

£3,752 (£1,116; £557; £278) **Stalls** Low

Form | | | | RPR

0- **1** **Kvetuschka**[146] 8832 3-8-8 0.............. LukeMorris 5 — 64
(Peter Chapple-Hyam) *chsd ldrs tl wnt 2nd over 6f out: rdn to ld over 1f out: hdd 100yds out: hung rt but battled bk to ld again towards fin* — **16/1**

2 *1/2* **Sadler's Soul (USA)** 3-8-8 0.............. OisinMurphy 3 — 63
(Archie Watson) *t.k.h: chsd ldrs: effrt to press ldng pair jst over 2f out: kpt on to ld 100yds out: rn green and hung rt in front: hdd towards fin* — **12/1**

3 *1/2* **Samstar** 3-8-8 0.............. FrannyNorton 7 — 62+
(Mark Johnston) *s.i.s and impeded sn after s: rn green and pushed along early: racd in last pair: nt clr run over 2f out: swtchd rt over 1f out: styd on strly ins fnl f: nvr quite getting to ldrs (jockey said filly suffered interference shortly after leaving the stalls)* — **9/1**

4 *3/4* **Cherries At Dawn (IRE)** 4-10-0 0..............(w) CallumShepherd 1 — 64
(Dominic Ffrench Davis) *in tch in midfield: effrt and drvn over 1f out: nt clrest of runs and swtchd rt ins fnl f: kpt on fnl 100yds* — **33/1**

0- **5** ½ **Spice Of Life**[143] 8888 3-8-8 0 .... HarryBentley 2 59
(Ralph Beckett) *led for 2f: chsd ldr tl over 6f out: rdn and struggling to qckn over 2f out: kpt on same pce fnl f* **10/3**[2]

0- **6** nk **Dear Miriam (IRE)**[153] 8647 3-8-8 0 .... DavidEgan 4 59
(Mick Channon) *hld up in tch in last trio: effrt and hdwy on inner over 1f out: kpt on but no imp ins fnl f* **7/2**[3]

3 **7** nk **Follow A Dream (USA)**[17] 1165 3-8-8 0 .... KieranO'Neill 8 58
(John Gosden) *t.k.h: w ldr tl led 8f out: rdn and hrd pressed 2f out: sn hdd: no ex and wknd wl ins fnl f* **5/4**[1]

53 **8** shd **Mi Manchi (IRE)**[21] 1077 3-8-5 0 .... AaronJones(3) 9 58
(Marco Botti) *in tch in midfield: effrt over 1f out: kpt on same pce and no imp ins fnl f* **50/1**

9 10 **Just A Minute** 4-10-0 0 .... RobHornby 10 42
(Jonathan Portman) *s.i.s: in tch in rr: pushed along jst over 2f out: sn outpcd and wknd* **50/1**

2m 6.53s (-0.07) **Going Correction** -0.175s/f (Stan) **9** Ran SP% **120.2**
WFA 3 from 4yo 20lb
Speed ratings (Par 100): **93,92,92,91,91 90,90,90,82**
CSF £192.97 TOTE £18.30: £3.60, £3.50, £3.10; EX 223.10 Trifecta £5462.30.
Owner Woodcote Stud Ltd **Bred** Woodcote Stud **Trained** Newmarket, Suffolk

FOCUS
No great pace on here and once again the winner raced handily. Muddling form.
T/Plt: £64.60 to a £1 stake. Pool: £58,372.79 - 903.13 winning units T/Qpdt: £27.70 to a £1 stake. Pool: £5,196.95 - 187.44 winning units **Steve Payne**

1270 NEWCASTLE (A.W) (L-H)
Friday, March 29

OFFICIAL GOING: Tapeta: standard to slow
Wind: Light, half against in races up to 1m and in over 3f of home straight in races on the round course Weather: Dry

1398 PLAY 4 TO SCORE AT BETWAY H'CAP — 1m 4f 98y (Tp)
5:55 (5:55) (Class 6) (0-65,67) 4-Y-O+
£3,105 (£924; £461; £400; £400; £400) **Stalls** High

Form — RPR

50-1 **1** **Echo (IRE)**[39] 782 4-9-4 60 ....(b) JackGarritty 10 69
(Jedd O'Keeffe) *pressed ldr: led over 4f out: shkn up and clr over 2f out: kpt on wl fnl f: unchal* **5/2**[1]

0-22 **2** 3 **Nevada**[39] 782 6-9-9 64 ....(p) AndrewMullen 5 68
(Steve Gollings) *missed break: t.k.h: hld up towards rr: drvn over 2f out: effrt whn n.m.r briefly over 1f out: rallied and chsd (clr) wnr last 30yds: r.o (jockey said gelding was slowly away)* **4/1**[2]

-412 **3** ¾ **Champagne Rules**[57] 495 8-9-7 67 .... ConnorMurtagh(5) 2 69
(Sharon Watt) *missed break: hld up: hdwy to chse (clr) wnr over 2f out: rdn and edgd rt over 1f out: no ex and lost 2nd last 30yds* **8/1**

-663 **4** ¾ **Restive (IRE)**[17] 1159 6-9-10 65 ....(t) PhilDennis 1 66
(Jim Goldie) *hld up: effrt over 2f out: kpt on fnl f: no imp* **10/1**

-022 **5** ½ **First Call (FR)**[18] 1146 4-8-7 49 ....(p) PaulHanagan 4 51
(Patrick Morris) *prom: effrt and pushed along over 2f out: kpt on same pce over 1f out* **11/1**

500- **6** ¾ **Up Ten Down Two (IRE)**[156] 8538 10-9-10 65 ....(t) NathanEvans 7 64
(Michael Easterby) *hld up in midfield: drvn and effrt over 2f out: one pce fr over 1f out* **15/2**[3]

626- **7** 4 **Mont Royal (FR)**[199] 7145 5-9-6 61 .... PaulMulrennan 11 54
(Ollie Pears) *hld up: rdn whn nt clr run over 2f out: no imp over 1f out* **20/1**

1455 **8** nse **Splash Of Verve (IRE)**[27] 983 7-8-9 50 .... PaddyMathers 3 43
(David Thompson) *hld up in tch: effrt and drvn along over 2f out: wknd fnl f* **11/1**

332- **9** 1½ **Nearly There**[104] 9555 6-8-9 55 ....(t) AndrewBreslin(5) 9 46
(Wilf Storey) *hld up: effrt on outside 3f out: sn no imp: btn over 1f out* **14/1**

3230 **10** nk **Hugoigo**[39] 782 5-7-13 47 oh1 ow1 .... CoreyMadden(7) 6 38
(Jim Goldie) *hld up: effrt on wd outside over 2f out: sn no imp and btn* **11/1**

0-00 **11** 44 **Adventureman**[13] 1231 7-9-1 56 ....(p) JamesSullivan 13
(Ruth Carr) *led and sn crossed to ins rail: hdd over 4f out: wknd wl over 2f out: t.o* **66/1**

60-0 **12** 14 **Midas Maggie**[3] 1341 4-8-1 46 oh1 ....(p) JamieGormley(3) 12
(Philip Kirby) *in tch: drvn and struggling 3f out: sn wknd: t.o* **40/1**

/0-0 **13** 13 **Judith Gardenier**[52] 607 7-8-2 46 oh1 ....(t[1]) GabrieleMalune(3) 8
(R Mike Smith) *prom tl drvn along and wknd fr wl over 2f out (jockey said mare weakened quickly turning into the home straight)* **80/1**

2m 40.9s (-0.20) **Going Correction** +0.35s/f (Slow) **13** Ran SP% **122.1**
WFA 4 from 5yo+ 1lb
Speed ratings (Par 101): **114,112,111,111,110 110,107,107,106,106 76,67,58**
CSF £11.76 CT £72.65 TOTE £3.30: £1.70, £1.80, £3.20; EX 13.30 Trifecta £59.90.
Owner Miss S E Hall & C Platts **Bred** Pat McCarthy **Trained** Middleham Moor, N Yorks
■ Stewards' Enquiry : Phil Dennis two-day ban: careless riding (Apr 12-13)

FOCUS
The early fractions for this modest handicap were fast, with the overall time 5.2sec outside the standard. The second, third and fourth help set the level.

1399 SUNRACING.CO.UK APPRENTICE H'CAP — 1m 5y (Tp)
6:30 (6:30) (Class 6) (0-65,71) 4-Y-O+
£3,105 (£924; £461; £400; £400; £400) **Stalls** Centre

Form — RPR

5612 **1** **Insurplus (IRE)**[7] 1271 6-9-7 62 .... PhilDennis 5 70
(Jim Goldie) *hld up: gd hdwy on nr side of gp over 1f out: led ins fnl f: rdn and r.o wl* **7/2**[1]

4321 **2** ¾ **Elixsoft (IRE)**[7] 1271 4-10-2 71 6ex .... BenSanderson 9 77
(Roger Fell) *hld up: hdwy on nr side of gp over 1f out: effrt and ev ch ins fnl f: kpt on: hdd nr fin* **7/2**[1]

-602 **3** nk **Corked (IRE)**[37] 814 6-9-3 58 .... RowanScott 2 64
(Alistair Whillans) *led in centre of gp: rdn over 1f out: hdd ins fnl f: kpt on same pce* **16/1**

64-0 **4** 1¾ **Midnight Vixen**[81] 120 5-9-2 57 .... SebastianWoods 12 59
(Ben Haslam) *t.k.h: cl up in centre of gp: effrt and rdn over 1f out: kpt on same pce ins fnl f* **40/1**

-254 **5** hd **Roman De Brut (IRE)**[24] 1025 7-9-7 62 .... GabrieleMalune 14 63
(Ivan Furtado) *prom in centre of gp: effrt and rdn over 1f out: ch ent fnl f: sn no ex* **11/2**[3]

-500 **6** hd **Gabrial's Kaka (IRE)**[24] 1025 9-9-7 62 .... ConnorMurtagh 8 63
(Patrick Morris) *in tch on far side of gp: effrt and rdn over 1f out: outpcd ins fnl f* **33/1**

20-6 **7** 1¼ **Celtic Artisan (IRE)**[39] 784 8-9-1 61 ....(bt) EllaMcCain(5) 13 59
(Rebecca Menzies) *hld up in midfield on nr side of gp: stdy hdwy over 2f out: rdn over 1f out: sn no ex* **16/1**

006- **8** ¾ **Jetstream (IRE)**[98] 9664 4-9-7 62 ....(t) JoshuaBryan 3 59
(Kerry Lee) *hld up: stdy hdwy on nr side of gp over 2f out: rdn and no imp over 1f out (jockey said gelding was denied a clear run approaching the final furlong)* **11/1**

000- **9** 1½ **Spirit Of Sarwan (IRE)**[101] 9593 5-9-8 63 ....(p) DannyRedmond 7 56
(Stef Keniry) *dwlt: hld up in centre of gp: drvn along over 2f out: no imp fr over 1f out* **40/1**

20-0 **10** ½ **Seek The Moon (USA)**[17] 1169 4-9-6 61 .... BenRobinson 6 53
(Jedd O'Keeffe) *plld hrd: sn prom on far side of gp: drvn along 2f out: wknd fnl f* **12/1**

5020 **11** ½ **Mossy's Lodge**[31] 912 6-9-3 58 ....(tp) PaulaMuir 1 49
(Rebecca Menzies) *t.k.h: cl up on far side of gp: drvn along over 2f out: wknd fnl f* **20/1**

5-50 **12** ½ **Hippeia (IRE)**[34] 886 4-9-9 64 .... AndrewBreslin 10 54
(Grant Tuer) *dwlt: t.k.h: hld up: effrt on far side of gp over 2f out: wknd over 1f out* **50/1**

5/1- **13** 1½ **Dreamofdiscovery (IRE)**[366] 1424 5-9-9 64 .... ConorMcGovern 11 51
(Julie Camacho) *dwlt: hld up on nr side of gp: stdy hdwy 1/2-way: rdn and outpcd whn nt clr run briefly over 1f out: sn btn* **9/2**[2]

300- **14** 17 **Sulafaat (IRE)**[304] 3207 4-9-2 57 .... HarrisonShaw 4 6
(Rebecca Menzies) *in tch on far side of gp: lost pl 1/2-way: struggling over 2f out: t.o (jockey said filly stumbled shortly after the start)* **20/1**

1m 42.97s (4.37) **Going Correction** +0.35s/f (Slow) **14** Ran SP% **125.1**
Speed ratings (Par 101): **92,91,90,89,89 88,87,86,85,84 84,83,82,65**
CSF £14.59 CT £186.88 TOTE £3.90: £1.40, £2.10, £4.10; EX 18.60 Trifecta £210.30.
Owner Mr & Mrs G Grant & Partner **Bred** Patrick J Monahan **Trained** Uplawmoor, E Renfrews

FOCUS
The early pace in this ordinary race was pretty sedate, but it picked up after a couple of furlongs.

1400 LADBROKES FILLIES' NOVICE STKS — 1m 5y (Tp)
7:00 (7:00) (Class 5) 3-Y-O+
£3,752 (£1,116; £557; £278) **Stalls** Centre

Form — RPR

1 **Robotique Danseur (FR)** 3-8-9 0 .... PJMcDonald 4 65+
(K R Burke) *in tch: smooth hdwy 2f out: shkn up to ld ins fnl f: edgd rt: kpt on wl towards fin* **9/2**[3]

0-3 **2** 1¼ **Elikapeka (FR)**[63] 405 3-8-9 0 .... KevinStott 3 62
(Kevin Ryan) *led at ordinary gallop: drvn along over 1f out: hdd ins fnl f: kpt on same pce* **16/1**

1- **3** nk **Astonished (IRE)**[112] 9445 4-10-5 0 .... DavidAllan 7 73+
(James Tate) *dwlt: plld hrd in rr: hdwy over 2f out: rdn and kpt on fnl f: nt pce to chal (jockey said filly ran too free)* **5/6**[1]

6 **4** ½ **Hikayah**[28] 971 3-8-10 0 ow1 ....(p[1]) RobbieDowney 10 61
(David O'Meara) *dwlt: hld up: rdn over 2f out: kpt on fnl f: nrst fin* **50/1**

55-3 **5** 2½ **Twiggy**[57] 501 5-9-9 45 .... BenRobinson(3) 2 59?
(Karen McLintock) *hld up in tch: drvn along over 2f out: no imp over 1f out* **50/1**

6 1½ **Under The Storm** 3-8-9 0 .... CliffordLee 1 50
(James Tate) *prom: rdn over 2f out: effrt over 1f out: wknd ins fnl f* **20/1**

00- **7** 1 **Nanjoe**[156] 8545 4-9-12 0 .... PhilDennis 8 53
(Jim Goldie) *hld up: drvn along over 2f out: sn no imp: btn fnl f* **250/1**

0 **8** ½ **Honey Bear (IRE)**[38] 795 3-8-9 0 .... AndrewMullen 6 47
(Mark Johnston) *dwlt: hld up: rdn and outpcd over 2f out: btn over 1f out* **40/1**

60 **9** 1¼ **Bravantina**[20] 1102 4-9-12 0 .... DougieCostello 9 49
(Mark Walford) *pressed ldr: drvn along over 2f out: wknd over 1f out* **250/1**

2- **10** 6 **Maid For Life**[176] 7932 3-8-9 0 ....(h) StevieDonohoe 5 29
(Charlie Fellowes) *plld hrd: hld up in tch: struggling over 2f out: sn btn (jockey said filly ran too free and hung right)* **2/1**[2]

1m 44.12s (5.52) **Going Correction** +0.35s/f (Slow) **10** Ran SP% **123.9**
WFA 3 from 4yo+ 17lb
Speed ratings (Par 100): **86,84,84,83,81 79,78,78,77,71**
CSF £65.96 TOTE £4.70: £1.30, £3.20, £1.20; EX 38.40 Trifecta £166.00.
Owner John Dance **Bred** Sahara Group Holdings **Trained** Middleham Moor, N Yorks
■ Oblate was withdrawn. Price at time of withdrawal 80-1. Rule 4 does not apply

FOCUS
Fair fillies' novice form, but the slowest of the three mile races on the card. Muddling form.

1401 FOLLOW TOP TIPSTER TEMPLEGATE AT SUNRACING H'CAP — 1m 5y (Tp)
7:30 (7:30) (Class 4) (0-85,87) 4-Y-O+
£5,530 (£1,645; £822; £411; £400; £400) **Stalls** Centre

Form — RPR

2122 **1** **Rey Loopy (IRE)**[37] 807 5-9-6 81 .... AndrewMullen 2 91+
(Ben Haslam) *stdd s: hld up: rdn and hdwy wl over 1f out: led ins fnl f: hld on wl cl home* **5/2**[1]

0-12 **2** shd **Trevithick**[66] 350 4-9-12 87 .... GrahamLee 7 96
(Bryan Smart) *led at ordinary gallop: rdn and hrd pressed over 1f out: hdd ins fnl f: rallied: hld nr fin* **4/1**[3]

6450 **3** 2 **Testa Rossa (IRE)**[7] 1273 9-8-1 69 .... CoreyMadden(7) 8 73
(Jim Goldie) *hld up: rdn over 2f out: hdwy over 1f out: chsd ldng pair ins fnl f: r.o* **20/1**

5152 **4** 1 **Samphire Coast**[14] 1213 6-9-7 82 ....(v) PaddyMathers 5 84
(Derek Shaw) *t.k.h: trckd ldrs: effrt and ev ch over 1f out: no ex ins fnl f* **5/1**

444- **5** 1¼ **Lawmaking**[183] 7705 6-9-11 86 ....(b) LiamKeniry 1 85
(Michael Scudamore) *hld up in tch: effrt and hdwy 2f out: wknd ins fnl f* **7/1**

331- **6** 1¼ **Thaayer**[119] 9327 4-9-6 81 ....(t) AlistairRawlinson 3 77
(Rebecca Menzies) *t.k.h: pressed ldr: rdn over 2f out: wknd over 1f out* **3/1**[2]

0-40 **7** 1¼ **Alexandrakollontai (IRE)**[7] 1273 9-8-11 77 ....(b) ConnorMurtagh(5) 6 70
(Alistair Whillans) *hld up: rdn and outpcd over 2f out: sn no imp: btn fnl f* **28/1**

022- **8** shd **Trinity Star (IRE)**[270] 4472 8-8-13 74 ....(v) PJMcDonald 4 67
(Karen McLintock) *prom: lost grnd over 2f out: sn struggling: btn over 1f out* **33/1**

1m 41.49s (2.89) **Going Correction** +0.35s/f (Slow) **8** Ran SP% **113.9**
Speed ratings (Par 105): **99,98,96,95,94 93,92,92**
CSF £12.42 CT £158.90 TOTE £2.90: £1.10, £1.40, £3.30; EX 10.50 Trifecta £73.50.
Owner Daniel Shapiro & Mrs C Barclay **Bred** Worldwide Partners **Trained** Middleham Moor, N Yorks

FOCUS
A fair handicap, in which the finish was fought out by a pair of track specialists. A small step forward from the second.

1402 BETWAY SPRINT H'CAP 5f (Tp)
8:00 (8:00) (Class 6) (0-55,55) 4-Y-O+
£3,105 (£692; £692; £400; £400; £400) **Stalls Centre**

Form RPR

424- 1 **Everkyllachy (IRE)**[158] 8482 5-9-4 55.................(v[1]) JamieGormley(3) 13 62
(Karen McLintock) *s.i.s: sn pushed along in rr in centre of crse: hdwy and swtchd to stands' rail over 1f out: sustained run to ld cl home* **2/1[1]**

6-55 2 shd **Angel Eyes**[25] 1020 4-8-5 46.................. RPWalsh(7) 4 53
(John David Riches) *led in centre of crse: drvn clr 2f out: hrd pressed fnl f: hdd cl home* **9/1**

4553 2 dht **Novabridge**[28] 973 11-8-12 46 oh1..................(b) CliffordLee 7 53
(Karen Tutty) *in tch in centre of gp: effrt and rdn over 1f out: disp ld wl ins fnl f: kpt on: hld cl home* **10/1**

000- 4 1 3/4 **Rock Hill (IRE)**[184] 7673 4-9-1 49.................. GrahamLee 9 50
(Paul Midgley) *midfield towards nr side of gp: drvn along 1/2-way: hdwy over 1f out: r.o ins fnl f* **16/1**

0-50 5 1/2 **Bahango (IRE)**[34] 882 7-8-12 51..................(p) ConnorMurtagh(5) 11 50
(Patrick Morris) *in tch on nr side of gp: chsd ldr gng wl 1/2-way: rdn over 1f out: no ex ins fnl f* **10/1**

541- 6 nk **The Bull (IRE)**[142] 8926 4-9-6 54..................(p) AndrewMullen 8 52
(Ben Haslam) *hld up towards far side of gp: rdn over 2f out: hdwy over 1f out: kpt on fnl f: nvr able to chal* **9/2[2]**

0062 7 2 1/2 **Windforpower (IRE)**[21] 1085 9-8-12 46.................. BenCurtis 5 35
(Tracy Waggott) *in tch towards far side of gp: drvn and outpcd over 2f out: no imp fr over 1f out* **8/1**

-066 8 1 **High Anxiety**[42] 742 5-8-7 46 oh1..................(b) AndrewBreslin(5) 10 31
(Andrew Crook) *hld up on nr side of gp: drvn and outpcd 1/2-way: rallied ins fnl f: no imp* **25/1**

2523 9 3/4 **Star Cracker (IRE)**[21] 1085 7-8-12 46.................. PJMcDonald 2 29
(Jim Goldie) *hld up towards far side of gp: rdn 2f out: nvr able to chal* **6/1[3]**

60-0 10 2 1/4 **Men United (FR)**[69] 322 6-8-5 46 oh1..................(b) AledBeech(7) 6 20
(Roy Bowring) *prom in centre of gp: drvn over 2f out: wknd over 1f out* **66/1**

00/6 11 hd **Climax**[21] 1085 5-9-4 52.................. NathanEvans 1 26
(Wilf Storey) *midfield on far side of gp: rdn over 2f out: wknd over 1f out* **100/1**

5430 12 9 **Bluella**[17] 1162 4-8-9 46 oh1..................(p[1]) BenRobinson(3) 3
(Robyn Brisland) *prom on far side of gp: rdn 1/2-way: wknd over 1f out (jockey said filly stopped quickly)* **25/1**

0-00 13 3/4 **Tina Teaspoon**[27] 986 5-8-12 46 oh1..................(h) PaddyMathers 12
(Derek Shaw) *hld up nr side: struggling over 2f out: btn over 1f out* **40/1**

000- 14 3 1/2 **Jean Excels**[137] 9036 4-8-12 46 oh1.................. LiamKeniry 14
(Roy Bowring) *unruly in paddock: midfield on nr side of gp: struggling 1/2-way: sn btn* **33/1**

1m 0.4s (0.90) **Going Correction** +0.35s/f (Slow) **14 Ran SP% 126.5**
Speed ratings (Par 101): **106,105,105,103,102 101,97,96,94,91 91,76,75,69**
PL: Angel Eyes 2.60, Novabridge 2.50; EX: E/AE 14.30, E/N 15.90; CSF: E/AN 10.65, E/N 11.92; TF: E/AE/N 81.79, E/N/AE 82.68 TOTE £3.00: £1.60.
Owner Ever Equine **Bred** Mrs T Mahon **Trained** Ingoe, Northumberland

FOCUS
A three-way photo to this low-grade sprint. The winner has been rated near the best of last year's form.

1403 BETWAY LIVE CASINO H'CAP 5f (Tp)
8:30 (8:30) (Class 5) (0-70,72) 4-Y-O+
£3,752 (£1,116; £557; £400; £400; £400) **Stalls Centre**

Form RPR

-343 1 **Gowanbuster**[39] 788 4-9-3 66..................(t) PaulMulrennan 9 75
(Susan Corbett) *mde all: rdn over 1f out: kpt on wl towards fin* **7/2[2]**

4013 2 1/2 **Jan Van Hoof (IRE)**[28] 970 8-9-7 70.................. BarryMcHugh 3 77
(Michael Herrington) *prom: effrt and shkn up over 1f out: effrt and pressed wnr ins fnl f: kpt on: hld nr fin (trainer was informed that the gelding could not run until the day after passing a stalls test)* **5/1[3]**

0-20 3 1 3/4 **Canford Bay (IRE)**[3] 1342 5-9-9 72.................. CliffordLee 8 73
(Antony Brittain) *t.k.h early: chsd ldrs: wnt 2nd 1/2-way to ins fnl f: sn one pce (jockey said gelding hung left)* **5/4[1]**

430- 4 1 1/2 **Loulin**[251] 5231 4-8-7 56.................. JamesSullivan 4 51
(Ruth Carr) *hld up in tch: drvn along 2f out: one pce fnl f* **8/1**

200- 5 1 3/4 **Danehill Desert (IRE)**[140] 8981 4-8-13 62..................(p) TonyHamilton 1 51
(Richard Fahey) *t.k.h: hld up in tch: rdn and outpcd 1/2-way: rallied fnl f: no imp* **20/1**

56-0 6 3/4 **Rantan (IRE)**[17] 1162 6-9-0 63.................. KevinStott 2 49
(Paul Midgley) *bhd and outpcd: drvn and hdwy over 1f out: kpt on steadily fnl f: nvr nrr (jockey said gelding hung right)* **14/1**

6630 7 3/4 **Haader (FR)**[31] 914 4-8-13 62..................(t) PaddyMathers 5 46
(Derek Shaw) *hld up bhd ldng gp: drvn along 1/2-way: no imp fr over 1f out: btn fnl f* **25/1**

0-00 8 hd **Orient Class**[29] 953 8-9-5 68.................. GrahamLee 6 51
(Paul Midgley) *chsd wnr to 1/2-way: cl up tl wknd fnl f* **22/1**

000- 9 3/4 **Jeffrey Harris**[142] 8928 4-8-12 61..................(h[1]) PhilDennis 7 41
(Jim Goldie) *s.i.s: bhd and outpcd: short-lived effrt over 1f out: btn fnl f* **33/1**

59.73s (0.23) **Going Correction** +0.35s/f (Slow) **9 Ran SP% 117.0**
Speed ratings (Par 103): **112,111,108,106,103 102,100,100,99**
CSF £20.40 CT £33.00 TOTE £4.60: £1.20, £1.60, £1.30; EX 15.10 Trifecta £48.10.
Owner Hassle-Free Racing **Bred** L Waugh **Trained** Otterburn, Northumberland

FOCUS
This was 0.67sec quicker than the previous Class 6 event. Not many got into it. The second has been rated back to form.

T/Jkpt: £16,263.30 to a £1 stake. Pool: £148,889.88 - 6.50 winning units T/Plt: £12.50 to a £1 stake. Pool: £103,066.41 - 5,978.19 winning units T/Qpdt: £6.30 to a £1 stake. Pool: £11,323.82 - 1,329.30 winning units **Richard Young**

1404 - 1411a (Foreign Racing) - See Raceform Interactive

DONCASTER (L-H)
Saturday, March 30

OFFICIAL GOING: Good (good to firm in places; 7.9)
Wind: Light across Weather: Fine & dry

1412 UNIBET CAMMIDGE TROPHY STKS (LISTED RACE) 6f 2y
1:50 (1:50) (Class 1) 3-Y-O+
£20,982 (£7,955; £3,981; £1,983; £995; £499) **Stalls Centre**

Form RPR

200- 1 **Invincible Army (IRE)**[252] 5213 4-9-8 112.................. PJMcDonald 9 116
(James Tate) *sn trcking ldr: cl up over 2f out: led over 1f out: sn rdn and kpt on wl fnl f* **4/1[2]**

201- 2 2 **Major Jumbo**[168] 8194 5-9-8 107.................. KevinStott 2 109
(Kevin Ryan) *led: pushed along and jnd 2f out: rdn and hdd over 1f out: drvn and kpt on wl fnl f* **15/2**

144- 3 3/4 **Equilateral**[162] 8397 4-9-8 104.................. AndreaAtzeni 6 106
(Charles Hills) *trckd ldrs: pushed along and sltly outpcd over 2f out: swtchd rt and rdn over 1f out: kpt on u.p fnl f* **11/4[1]**

100- 4 1/2 **Tis Marvellous**[196] 7290 5-9-8 104..................(t) AdamKirby 1 105
(Clive Cox) *chsd ldrs: rdn along over 2f out: drvn over 1f out: kpt on same pce* **11/1**

523- 5 4 1/2 **Arbalet (IRE)**[217] 6549 4-9-8 107..................(t) JamesDoyle 4 90
(Hugo Palmer) *trckd ldrs: pushed along wl over 2f out: sn rdn and grad wknd* **13/2**

3121 6 1 1/2 **Gorgeous Noora (IRE)**[35] 877 5-9-6 100.................. HollieDoyle 5 83
(Archie Watson) *towards rr: pushed along wl over 2f out: rdn and sme hdwy wl over 1f out: sn drvn and no imp* **16/1**

253- 7 8 **Eirene**[140] 9003 4-9-3 102.................. RobertWinston 7 55
(Dean Ivory) *hld up: a in rr* **8/1**

0/-4 8 4 1/2 **Mokarris (USA)**[56] 563 5-9-8 100.................. SilvestreDeSousa 8 45
(Simon Crisford) *t.k.h: trckd ldrs: pushed along over 2f out: sn rdn and wknd (vet said horse had bled from the nose)* **9/2[3]**

1m 11.63s (-1.07) **Going Correction** -0.10s/f (Good) **8 Ran SP% 115.3**
Speed ratings (Par 111): **103,100,99,98,92 90,80,74**
CSF £34.07 TOTE £5.00: £1.90, £2.00, £1.40; EX 38.20 Trifecta £101.40.
Owner Saeed Manana **Bred** Rabbah Bloodstock Limited **Trained** Newmarket, Suffolk

FOCUS
The first turf Flat meeting of the year and it was run on ground officially described as good, good to firm in places (GoingStick 7.9). All distances were as advertised. A strong renewal of this Listed contest and it was won in taking fashion by the highest rated horse in the line-up. The second has been rated close to form.

1413 UNIBET SPRING MILE H'CAP 1m (S)
2:25 (2:25) (Class 2) 4-Y-O+
£28,012 (£8,388; £4,194; £2,097; £1,048; £526) **Stalls Centre**

Form RPR

340- 1 **Petrus (IRE)**[154] 8649 4-9-5 91..................(p[1]) TomMarquand 3 102
(Brian Meehan) *trckd ldrs: effrt 2f out and sn pushed along to chal: rdn to ld over 1f out: drvn and edgd rt ins fnl f: hld on wl towards fin* **7/1[3]**

113- 2 1/2 **Exec Chef (IRE)**[164] 8331 4-9-4 90.................. JamesDoyle 10 100
(Jim Boyle) *hld up: hdwy over 2f out: trckd ldrs and n.m.r over 1f out: sn swtchd rt and rdn: styd on wl to chal ins fnl f: drvn and no ex towards fin (jockey said gelding was denied a clear run approximately 2f out)* **6/1[2]**

6-35 3 2 3/4 **Al Jellaby**[63] 441 4-9-3 89.................. AdamKirby 16 93
(Clive Cox) *cl up: rdn along 2f out: drvn and ev ch over 1f out: kpt on same pce* **15/2**

042- 4 3/4 **Dawaaleeb (USA)**[175] 7991 5-9-8 94..................(v) DavidAllan 8 96
(Les Eyre) *trckd ldng pair: rdn along 2f out: drvn and edgd lft ins fnl f: kpt on* **12/1**

645- 5 1/2 **Gulf Of Poets**[140] 9004 7-9-6 92.................. NathanEvans 7 93
(Michael Easterby) *trckd ldrs: pushed along and sltly outpcd over 2f out: swtchd lft and rdn ent fnl f: kpt on* **10/1**

45-0 6 hd **Calvados Spirit**[6] 1308 6-8-11 83.................. PaulHanagan 2 83
(Richard Fahey) *led: rdn along over 2f out: drvn and hdd over 1f out: grad wknd* **9/1**

4026 7 1 1/4 **Isomer (USA)**[42] 764 5-8-9 88..................(p) WilliamCarver(7) 13 85
(Andrew Balding) *hld up towards rr: hdwy 3f out: rdn along wl over 1f out: styng on whn n.m.r ins fnl f (jockey said gelding was denied a clear run in the final furlong)* **20/1**

13-1 8 3/4 **Rampant Lion (IRE)**[31] 922 4-9-1 87 5ex..........(p) SilvestreDeSousa 11 83
(William Jarvis) *t.k.h early: chsd ldrs: rdn along 2f out: drvn and edgd lft ent fnl f: sn wknd* **11/2[1]**

2541 9 1 **Fayez (IRE)**[21] 1106 5-9-6 92 5ex..................(p) DavidNolan 15 85
(David O'Meara) *dwlt and in rr: hdwy over 2f out: rdn and kpt on fnl f* **33/1**

000- 10 1 1/4 **Sands Chorus**[138] 9035 7-8-4 81..................(p[1]) TheodoreLadd(5) 4 71
(Scott Dixon) *dwlt and in rr: rapid hdwy on inner to chse ldrs after 2f: rdn along over 2f out: sn wknd (jockey said he was slow to remove the blindfold resulting in his horse being slow to start; jockey said gelding ran too free in the early stages)* **25/1**

113- 11 3/4 **Sod's Law**[162] 8371 4-8-12 84.................. PJMcDonald 14 73
(Hughie Morrison) *hld up: hdwy on outer 3f out: in tch and rdn 2f out: sn btn* **6/1[2]**

004- 12 nk **Brian The Snail (IRE)**[165] 8304 5-9-3 94.................. SeanDavis(5) 6 82
(Richard Fahey) *midfield: hdwy over 3f out: in tch and rdn along 2f out: sn btn* **14/1**

116- 13 1 **Detachment**[150] 8740 6-8-11 83.................. HayleyTurner 1 69
(Les Eyre) *hld up: hdwy on inner over 2f out: rdn along wl over 1f out: sn btn* **25/1**

-456 14 7 **Calling Out (FR)**[38] 800 8-9-5 96..................(p) DylanHogan(5) 5 66
(David Simcock) *midfield: rdn along over 3f out: sn wknd* **100/1**

000- 15 4 **Fake News**[115] 9414 4-8-6 78.................. HollieDoyle 9 38
(David Barron) *a towards rr* **25/1**

020- 16 26 **Robsdelight (IRE)**[154] 8635 4-8-7 79.................. JosephineGordon 12
(Gay Kelleway) *in tch on inner: rdn along 3f out: sn wknd* **33/1**

1m 37.5s (-2.70) **Going Correction** -0.10s/f (Good) **16 Ran SP% 124.8**
Speed ratings (Par 109): **109,108,105,105,104 104,103,102,101,100 99,99,98,91,87 61**
CSF £45.99 CT £349.14 TOTE £8.10: £2.40, £1.80, £2.20, £2.70; EX 62.90 Trifecta £380.90.
Owner G P M Morland **Bred** Timothy Nuttall **Trained** Manton, Wilts

FOCUS
It doesn't come much more open than this year's edition of the Spring Mile. The centre proved the place to be, as was the case in the opener, and two came clear off a sound pace. The winner has been rated back to his best.

1414 UNIBET DONCASTER MILE STKS (LISTED RACE) 1m (S)
3:00 (3:00) (Class 1) 4-Y-O+

£20,982 (£7,955; £3,981; £1,983; £995; £499) **Stalls** Centre

Form					RPR
401-	1		**Sharja Bridge**161 8409 5-9-0 110 — AndreaAtzeni 2 *(Roger Varian) hld up in tch: smooth hdwy 3f out: chal 2f out: rdn to ld 1 1/2f out: kpt on strly* **8/13**1		115+
132-	2	2	**Red Starlight**175 7978 4-8-9 100 — TomMarquand 1 *(Richard Hannon) trckd ldrs: hdwy to ld 2f out: sn jnd and rdn: hdd 1 1/2f out: drvn and kpt on fnl f* **9/2**2		104
560-	3	3 3/4	**Gabrial (IRE)**161 8407 10-9-0 107 — PaulHanagan 8 *(Richard Fahey) trckd ldrs: effrt and n.m.r 2f out: sn swtchd rt and rdn: kpt on fnl f (jockey said gelding got caught on the heels of a weakening runner approaching 2f out)* **10/1**		100
201/	4	nk	**Remarkable**567 6918 6-9-0 110 — (b) ShaneGray 7 *(David O'Meara) dwlt and in rr: hdwy on inner over 2f out: rdn over 1f out: kpt on fnl f* **12/1**		100
200-	5	5	**Hells Babe**175 7978 6-8-9 90 — LewisEdmunds 3 *(Michael Appleby) led: rdn along over 2f out: sn hdd: drvn and wknd wl over 1f out* **66/1**		83
200-	6	1	**Circus Couture (IRE)**161 8409 7-9-0 105 — JamesDoyle 4 *(Jane Chapple-Hyam) t.k.h: hld up in tch: swtchd rt to outer over 3f out: sn chsng ldrs: rdn to chal 2f out: sn drvn and wknd over 1f out* **13/2**3		86
1263	7	1/2	**Apex King (IRE)**17 1181 5-9-0 86 — TrevorWhelan 5 *(David Loughnane) cl up: rdn along over 2f out: sn drvn and wknd* **66/1**		85
524-	8	4 1/2	**King's Pavilion (IRE)**132 9150 6-9-0 91 — ConorMcGovern 9 *(Jason Ward) cl up: rdn along over 2f out: sn wknd* **25/1**		74
	9	1 1/2	**Givinitsum (SAF)**266 3-8-10 0 — EdwardGreatrex 6 *(Eve Johnson Houghton) t.k.h: trckd ldrs early: lost pl over 4f out: sn in rr (jockey said gelding ran too freely)* **20/1**		67

1m 36.65s (-3.55) **Going Correction** -0.10s/f (Good) **9 Ran SP% 121.8**
WFA 3 from 4yo+ 17lb
Speed ratings (Par 111): **113,111,107,106,101 100,100,95,94**
CSF £3.90 TOTE £1.40: £1.10, £1.50, £2.60; EX 3.90 Trifecta £19.40.
Owner Sheikh Mohammed Obaid Al Maktoum **Bred** Stiftung Gestut Fahrhof **Trained** Newmarket, Suffolk

FOCUS
A strong-looking renewal of this Listed contest and there was much to like about the way in which the odds-on favourite got the job done. It's been rated around the first two.

1415 UNIBET LINCOLN (HERITAGE H'CAP) 1m (S)
3:35 (3:35) (Class 2) 4-Y-O+

£62,250 (£18,640; £6,990; £6,990; £2,330; £1,170) **Stalls** Centre

Form					RPR
111-	1		**Auxerre (IRE)**171 8105 4-9-3 100 — (p) JamesDoyle 17 *(Charlie Appleby) sed wl and sn swtchd lft to centre: mde all: rdn clr wl over 1f out: kpt on strly* **5/2**1		114+
265-	2	2 1/4	**Kynren (IRE)**161 8409 5-9-1 98 — RobertWinston 22 *(David Barron) in tch: hdwy over 2f out: rdn to chse wnr ent fnl f: sn drvn and no imp towards fin* **9/2**2		105
-242	3	3/4	**Breden (IRE)**21 1101 9-9-2 99 — GrahamLee 14 *(Linda Jewell) in tch whn n.m.r after 150yds: t.k.h after: chsd ldrs: rdn wl over 1f out: kpt on fnl f* **40/1**		104
320-	3	dht	**Beringer**189 7532 4-8-13 96 — AndreaAtzeni 11 *(Alan King) n.m.r and hmpd after 150yds: in rr: hdwy 2f out: sn rdn: styd on wl fnl f* **9/1**3		101+
420-	5	1	**Ripp Orf (IRE)**154 8634 5-9-1 98 — HayleyTurner 9 *(David Elsworth) hld up towards rr: hdwy over 2f out: swtchd rt and rdn wl over 1f out: kpt on strly fnl f* **14/1**		101
1045	6	nk	**Another Batt (IRE)**37 843 4-9-5 107 — CameronNoble(5) 12 *(George Scott) midfield whn n.m.r and hmpd after 150yds: in rr after: swtchd lft to inner and hdwy 2f out: sn rdn: kpt on fnl f* **25/1**		109
00-1	7	3/4	**Zwayyan**21 1101 6-9-5 102 5ex — SilvestreDeSousa 1 *(Andrew Balding) in tch: hdwy to chse ldrs over 2f out: sn rdn and no imp appr fnl f* **10/1**		103
02-3	8	hd	**Third Time Lucky (IRE)**21 1101 7-9-1 98 — TonyHamilton 7 *(Richard Fahey) hld up: hdwy over 2f out: sn rdn and kpt on fnl f* **25/1**		98
46-0	9	nk	**Wahash (IRE)**21 1101 5-9-1 98 — TomMarquand 2 *(Richard Hannon) t.k.h: chsd ldrs: rdn along over 2f out: grad wknd* **33/1**		97
020-	10	1/2	**Waarif (IRE)**161 8409 6-9-0 100 — ConorMcGovern(3) 15 *(David O'Meara) towards rr tl styd on fnl 2f* **25/1**		98
5-30	11	shd	**Silver Quartz**21 1101 4-9-3 100 — EdwardGreatrex 20 *(Archie Watson) cl up: rdn along 2f out: drvn over 1f out: wknd ent fnl f* **33/1**		98
000-	12	4	**Raydiance**161 8409 4-9-1 98 — CliffordLee 13 *(K R Burke) chsd ldrs: rdn along over 2f out: grad wknd* **33/1**		87
365-	13	1/2	**Great Prospector (IRE)**126 9245 4-9-0 97 — PaulHanagan 19 *(Richard Fahey) midfield: pushed along over 2f out: sn rdn and n.d* **20/1**		85
-000	14	1 1/2	**Ventura Knight (IRE)**21 1101 4-9-1 98 — PJMcDonald 4 *(Mark Johnston) in tch: rdn along over 2f out: sn wknd* **25/1**		82
51-6	15	1 1/4	**Masham Star (IRE)**21 1101 5-9-1 103 — AndrewBreslin(5) 3 *(Mark Johnston) prom: rdn along wl over 2f out: sn wknd* **33/1**		84
0005	16	nk	**Aquarium**21 1101 4-9-5 102 — FrannyNorton 21 *(Mark Johnston) midfield: effrt on outer over 3f out: sn rdn along and wknd* **40/1**		83
100-	17	1 1/2	**Humbert (IRE)**161 8409 5-9-1 98 — (p) DavidNolan 5 *(David O'Meara) prom: rdn along wl over 2f out: sn wknd* **14/1**		75
000-	18	1	**Saltonstall**210 6829 5-9-3 100 — (t) RonanWhelan 18 *(Adrian McGuinness, Ire) trckd ldrs whn n.m.r after 150yds: t.k.h after: rdn along over 2f out: sn wknd (jockey said gelding stopped quickly)* **10/1**		75
520-	19	5	**South Seas (IRE)**161 8409 5-9-3 100 — JamieSpencer 16 *(Philip Kirby) dwlt: a in rr* **20/1**		63

1m 36.82s (-3.38) **Going Correction** -0.10s/f (Good) **19 Ran SP% 129.8**
Speed ratings (Par 109): **112,109,109,109,108 107,106,106,106,105 105,101,101,99,98 98,96,95,90**
WIN: 3.00 Auxerre; PL: 1.40 Auxerre 6.50 Breden 2.20 Kynren 3.10 Beringer; EX: 18.60; CSF: 10.55; TC: 48.20 197.40; TF: 433.80 97.20 CSF £10.55 CT £197.40 TOTE £3.00: £1.40, £2.20, £6.50; EX 18.60 Trifecta £433.80.
Owner Godolphin **Bred** Merriebelle Irish Farm Ltd **Trained** Newmarket, Suffolk

FOCUS
Again those drawn in the centre held an advantage, but this year's Lincoln proved one-way traffic. It was the quickest winning time since 2009 and the form is worth being positive about. Sound form rated around the third to his best.

1416 UNIBET BROCKLESBY CONDITIONS STKS (PLUS 10 RACE) 5f 3y
4:10 (4:10) (Class 3) 2-Y-O

£7,115 (£2,117; £1,058; £529) **Stalls** Centre

Form					RPR
	1		**Show Me Show Me** 2-9-3 0 — PaulHanagan 16 *(Richard Fahey) prom: pushed along to ld over 1f out: edgd lft ins fnl f: pressed 110yds out: rdn and kpt on wl* **11/4**1		83+
	2	3/4	**Strong Power (IRE)** 2-9-3 0 — HarryBentley 5 *(George Scott) midfield: pushed along and gd hdwy on outer over 1f out: rdn to chal 110yds out: kpt on but a hld* **4/1**2		79+
	3	1 1/4	**Zulu Zander (IRE)** 2-9-3 0 — AdamKirby 15 *(David Evans) prom: rdn 2f out: edgd lft over 1f out: kpt on same pce ins fnl f* **18/1**		75
	4	1 3/4	**Dorchester Dom (IRE)** 2-9-3 0 — LiamKeniry 4 *(David Evans) chsd ldrs on outer: pushed along whn checked sltly appr fnl f: kpt on ins fnl f* **33/1**		69+
	5	1 1/4	**Arasugar (IRE)** 2-8-12 0 — HollieDoyle 14 *(Seamus Mullins) led: rdn and hdd over 1f out: short of room appr fnl f: sn no ex* **100/1**		59
	6	1 3/4	**Birkenhead** 2-9-3 0 — CallumShepherd 6 *(Mick Channon) midfield: pushed along 2f out: one pce* **11/2**		58
	7	1 3/4	**Heer We Go Again** 2-9-3 0 — EoinWalsh 11 *(David Evans) dwlt: sn midfield: rdn along to chse ldrs 2f out: edgd lft over 1f out: sn wknd* **33/1**		51
	8	1 1/4	**Paddy Elliott (IRE)** 2-9-0 0 — BenRobinson(3) 9 *(Brian Ellison) hld up: pushed along 3f out: nvr threatened* **25/1**		47
	9	3 1/4	**Bendy Spirit (IRE)** 2-9-3 0 — TonyHamilton 8 *(Richard Fahey) chsd ldrs: pushed along 1/2-way: wknd appr fnl f* **14/1**		35
	10	1 1/2	**Dark Optimist (IRE)** 2-9-3 0 — CliffordLee 10 *(David Evans) dwlt: hld up: sn pushed along: nvr threatened* **25/1**		30
	11	1	**Coast Of Dubai (IRE)** 2-9-3 0 — KevinStott 1 *(Kevin Ryan) slowly away: sn rdn along in rr: minor late hdwy* **5/1**3		36+
	12	nse	**Victochop (FR)** 2-8-10 0 — WilliamCarver(7) 17 *(George Baker) midfield towards nr side: pushed along 1/2-way: wknd over 1f out* **33/1**		26
	13	1/2	**Prosecutor (IRE)** 2-8-12 0 — PaulMulrennan 7 *(Mark H Tompkins) midfield: lost pl 3f out: outpcd and sn towards rr* **50/1**		19
	14	1	**Hell Of A Joker** 2-8-12 0 — RyanWhile(5) 3 *(Bill Turner) prom: rdn 1/2-way: wknd over 1f out* **10/1**		21
	15	12	**Richard R H B (IRE)** 2-9-3 0 — TrevorWhelan 2 *(David Loughnane) v.s.a: a in rr (jockey said colt ran green and hung right)* **50/1**		+
	16	2 1/4	**Walton Thorns (IRE)** 2-9-3 0 — RobertWinston 12 *(Charles Hills) midfield: pushed along 1/2-way: bdly hmpd by faller appr fnl f and eased (jockey said colt was badly hampered by a faller)* **10/1**		
	F		**Anna Fallow** 2-8-5 0 — RPWalsh(7) 13 *(Ronald Thompson) chsd ldrs: pushed along 2f out: fell appr fnl f* **150/1**		

1m 0.35s (0.75) **Going Correction** -0.10s/f (Good) **17 Ran SP% 130.9**
Speed ratings (Par 96): **90,88,86,84,82 79,76,74,69,66 65,65,64,62,43 39,**
CSF £13.17 TOTE £2.90: £1.60, £2.00, £5.00; EX 16.70 Trifecta £222.50.
Owner Ontoawinner 8 And Partner 4 **Bred** Whitsbury Manor Stud **Trained** Musley Bank, N Yorks

FOCUS
The market often proves a good guide in this juvenile contest and that proved the case again. The first two home pulled clear and look above-average. It's been rated around the recent race average.

1417 32RED CASINO MAIDEN STKS 1m 2f 43y
4:45 (4:45) (Class 5) 3-Y-O

£3,752 (£1,116; £557; £278) **Stalls** Low

Form					RPR
244-	1		**Bangkok (IRE)**184 7699 3-9-5 88 — SilvestreDeSousa 7 *(Andrew Balding) prom: hdwy and cl up 4f out: led 3f out: rdn over 1f out: kpt on strly* **1/1**1		101
	2	1 1/4	**Telecaster** 3-9-5 0 — CharlieBennett 3 *(Hughie Morrison) hld up in midfield: hdwy 4f out: rdn along 2f out: chsd wnr over 1f out: drvn and kpt on fnl f* **20/1**		98+
	3	9	**Noble Music (GER)** 3-9-0 0 — HarryBentley 6 *(Ralph Beckett) hld up towards rr: hdwy 4f out: rdn along to chse ldrs on inner over 2f out: styd on same pce fnl f* **33/1**		75
6-	4	2 1/4	**Dubai Instinct**211 6752 3-9-5 0 — MartinDwyer 12 *(Brian Meehan) trckd ldrs: hdwy over 4f out: rdn along 3f out: drvn 2f out: kpt on one pce* **20/1**		76
3	5	1 1/4	**Ironclad**24 1033 3-9-5 0 — AdamKirby 17 *(Hugo Palmer) trckd ldrs: hdwy on outer 4f out: rdn along to chse ldng pair wl over 2f out: drvn: edgd lft and one pce fr wl over 1f out* **9/2**3		73
	6	3 1/4	**Just You Wait** 3-9-5 0 — JamesDoyle 5 *(Charlie Appleby) trckd ldrs: hdwy over 4f out: rdn along over 3f out: sn btn* **5/2**2		67
33	7	1 1/2	**Allocator (FR)**15 1221 3-9-5 0 — TomMarquand 1 *(Richard Hannon) led: rdn along 4f out: hdd 3f out: drvn over 2f out: sn wknd* **20/1**		64
	8	2 3/4	**Thomas Cubitt (FR)** 3-9-5 0 — HayleyTurner 10 *(Michael Bell) towards rr: sme hdwy over 3f out: sn rdn along: nvr nr ldrs* **40/1**		58
0	9	3/4	**Lock Seventeen (USA)**18 1165 3-9-5 0 — (v1) AndreaAtzeni 14 *(Charlie Fellowes) chsd ldr: rdn along 4f out: sn wknd* **66/1**		57
	10	3/4	**Star Guide (GER)** 3-9-5 0 — (h1) KevinStott 4 *(David Menuisier) a towards rr* **100/1**		55
	11	1 1/2	**Frequency Code (FR)** 3-9-5 0 — PJMcDonald 15 *(Jedd O'Keeffe) a towards rr* **33/1**		52
	12	3 1/2	**War Empress (IRE)** 3-9-0 0 — ShelleyBirkett 9 *(Julia Feilden) a towards rr* **100/1**		40
	13	5	**Soft Summer Rain** 3-9-0 0 — NathanEvans 8 *(Michael Easterby) dwlt: a in rr* **100/1**		30
60-	14	2	**Amber Rock (USA)**120 9323 3-9-5 0 — DavidAllan 11 *(Les Eyre) chsd ldrs: rdn along 4f out: sn wknd (jockey said gelding hung both ways in the straight)* **100/1**		31
	15	1/2	**Ho Whole Dream (IRE)** 3-9-5 0 — CamHardie 2 *(Michael Easterby) a towards rr* **100/1**		30
0	16	hd	**Black Kraken**30 949 3-9-5 0 — GrahamLee 13 *(Ben Haslam) a towards rr* **100/1**		30

The Form Book Flat 2019, Raceform Ltd, Newbury, RG14 5SJ

17 59 **Olivia On Green** 3-9-0 0 .... TrevorWhelan 16
(Ronald Thompson) *a towards rr* **150/1**
2m 8.93s (-3.37) **Going Correction** -0.10s/f (Good) **17** Ran SP% **127.5**
Speed ratings (Par 98): **109,108,100,99,98 95,94,92,91,90 89,86,82,81,80 80,33**
CSF £31.09 TOTE £1.90: £1.10, £4.60, £8.00; EX 26.60 Trifecta £517.50.
Owner King Power Racing Co Ltd **Bred** Barronstown Stud **Trained** Kingsclere, Hants
FOCUS
Always a fair 3yo maiden. It was run at a sound pace and two came well clear late on. The first two have been rated above the race standard.

1418 32RED.COM APPRENTICE H'CAP (ROUND 1 OF THE GO RACING IN YORKSHIRE FUTURE STARS SERIES) 1m 2f 43y
5:20 (5:20) (Class 5) (0-75,77) 4-Y-0+
£3,752 (£1,116; £557; £300; £300; £300) **Stalls** Low

Form RPR
3145 **1** **Central City (IRE)**[7] 1291 4-9-8 **76** ....(p) CameronNoble 6 86
(Ian Williams) *hld up: gd hdwy over 2f out: sn chsd ldrs: rdn to ld 1f out: styd on wl* **8/1**[3]
0254 **2** 2 ½ **Apache Blaze**[23] 1065 4-8-5 **62** ....(p[1]) SeamusCronin(3) 9 67
(Robyn Brisland) *trckd ldrs: rdn to ld over 2f out: hdd 1f out: no ex and edgd rt towards fin* **8/1**[3]
/26- **3** 1 ¼ **Consultant**[147] 8835 4-8-12 **71** .... WilliamCarver(5) 18 74
(Andrew Balding) *in tch towards outer: rdn and bit outpcd 2f out: styd on wl fnl f: wnt 3rd nr fin* **9/2**[1]
00-1 **4** shd **The Night King**[23] 1065 4-9-5 **73** ....(p) DarraghKeenan 17 75
(Mick Quinn) *midfield: pushed along and hdwy over 2f out: rdn to chse ldrs over 1f out: one pce ins fnl f: sltly impeded nr fin* **16/1**
6-16 **5** 1 **Cosmic Landscape**[30] 945 4-9-2 **75** .... CierenFallon(5) 12 75
(William Jarvis) *in tch: rdn over 2f out: one pce ins fnl f* **5/1**[2]
621/ **6** 1 ¾ **Miss Ranger (IRE)**[658] 3580 7-9-0 **68** .... BenSanderson 14 65
(Roger Fell) *hld up: rdn over 2f out: styd on fr appr fnl f: nvr threatened ldrs* **20/1**
044- **7** 2 ½ **Music Seeker (IRE)**[178] 7901 5-9-2 **75** ....(t w) CianMacRedmond(5) 4 67
(Declan Carroll) *prom: led over 3f out: rdn and hdd over 2f out: wknd over 1f out* **10/1**
220- **8** 1 ½ **Kannapolis (IRE)**[155] 8597 4-9-1 **72** .... JoshQuinn(3) 2 61
(Michael Easterby) *prom: rdn 3f out: wknd over 1f out* **8/1**[3]
-012 **9** ½ **Misu Pete**[30] 941 7-8-4 **63** ....(p) GeorgiaDobie(5) 15 51
(Mark Usher) *trckd ldrs: rdn over 3f out: wknd over 1f out* **20/1**
05-0 **10** hd **Sociologist (FR)**[65] 390 4-9-0 **68** ....(p) TheodoreLadd 13 55
(Scott Dixon) *nvr bttr than midfield (jockey said gelding hung right throughout)* **33/1**
6-65 **11** ¾ **God Willing**[44] 722 8-8-7 **68** ....(t) ZakWheatley(7) 10 54
(Declan Carroll) *hld up in midfield: rdn along 3f out: nvr threatened* **33/1**
-543 **12** 1 ¼ **Remmy D (IRE)**[30] 950 4-8-10 **69** .... CoreyMadden(5) 7 52
(Jim Goldie) *stdd s: hld up in rr: rdn along over 2f out: nvr threatened* **14/1**
6050 **13** nk **Contrast (IRE)**[14] 1232 5-8-13 **70** .... ScottMcCullagh(3) 5 53
(Michael Easterby) *hld up: rdn over 2f out: nvr threatened* **16/1**
340- **14** 1 ¾ **Dark Devil (IRE)**[159] 8476 6-9-9 **77** ....(p) ConnorMurtagh 16 56
(Richard Fahey) *hld up: hdwy into midfield 3f out: wknd over 1f out* **16/1**
004- **15** nk **Andok (IRE)**[144] 8900 5-9-7 **75** ....(p) SeanDavis 8 54
(Richard Fahey) *midfield: rdn 3f out: sn wknd* **14/1**
240- **16** 4 **Anchises**[171] 8102 4-9-0 **73** .... EllaMcCain(5) 3 44
(Rebecca Menzies) *hld up in midfield on inner: rdn along 3f out: sn btn* **25/1**
43-0 **17** 51 **Staplegrove (IRE)**[14] 1232 4-9-6 **74** .... GaryMahon 1
(Philip Kirby) *led: racd keenly: hdd over 3f out: hung lft and sn wknd: eased (jockey said gelding ran too free)* **25/1**
2m 9.93s (-2.37) **Going Correction** -0.10s/f (Good) **17** Ran SP% **131.4**
Speed ratings (Par 103): **105,103,102,101,101 99,97,96,96,95 95,94,94,92,92 89,48**
CSF £69.01 CT £336.03 TOTE £10.00: £2.80, £2.40, £1.80, £3.80; EX 83.80 Trifecta £688.90.
Owner Spencer Coomes **Bred** Mattock Stud **Trained** Portway, Worcs
FOCUS
A typically competitive race of its type, though a number of these never really figured. The second has been rated close to form.
T/Jkpt: £1,865.60 to a £1 stake. Pool: £14,084.51 - 5.36 winning units T/Plt: £16.10 to a £1 stake. Pool: £191,270.56 - 8,650.20 winning units T/Qpdt: £5.30 to a £1 stake. Pool: £13,184.17 - 1,809.02 winning units **Joe Rowntree & Andrew Sheret**

1351 KEMPTON (A.W) (R-H)
Saturday, March 30
OFFICIAL GOING: Polytrack: standard to slow
Wind: Light, across Weather: Fine, warm

1419 MATCHBOOK BETTING EXCHANGE EBF NOVICE STKS 1m 1f 219y(P)
1:35 (1:37) (Class 5) 3-Y-O **£4,916** (£1,463; £731; £365) **Stalls** Low

Form RPR
51- **1** **Living Legend (IRE)**[186] 7652 3-9-7 0 .... JoeFanning 6 89+
(Mark Johnston) *trckd ldr: shkn up to chal over 2f out: rdn to ld narrowly 1f out: edgd lft after then hung lft last 100yds: drvn and hld on wl (jockey said colt hung left-handed)* **5/1**[3]
1- **2** ¾ **Sucellus**[112] 9460 3-9-9 0 .... KieranO'Neill 5 89+
(John Gosden) *led: rdn whn pressed over 2f out: narrowly hdd 1f out: hung bdly lft after and nt qckn nr fin* **8/11**[1]
0- **3** 7 **Sawasdee (IRE)**[157] 8552 3-9-2 0 .... DavidProbert 3 68
(Andrew Balding) *chsd ldng pair: pushed along over 3f out: outpcd over 2f out: no ch after* **5/2**[2]
4 nk **J Gaye (IRE)** 3-8-11 0 .... LukeMorris 7 62
(Richard Phillips) *s.s: racd in last pair to 1/2-way: urged along 3f out: kpt on over 1f out to press for 3rd nr fin* **150/1**
545- **5** 2 ¾ **Island Jungle (IRE)**[152] 8700 3-9-2 76 .... FergusSweeney 4 62
(Mark Usher) *chsd ldng trio: pushed along over 3f out: outpcd over 2f out: wknd* **25/1**
6 **6** 10 ¼ **Blue Beirut (IRE)**[17] 1182 3-9-2 0 .... NicolaCurrie 2 41
(William Muir) *in tch: dropped to last pair 1/2-way and struggling: bhd fnl 2f* **66/1**
6 dht **King's Counsel** 3-9-2 0 ....(h[1]) TomQueally 1 41
(Daniel Kubler) *s.s: rn green and mostly in last: bhd fnl 2f* **50/1**
2m 6.5s (-1.50) **Going Correction** -0.10s/f (Stan) **7** Ran SP% **111.1**
Speed ratings (Par 98): **102,101,95,95,93 85,85**
CSF £8.68 TOTE £5.00: £2.70, £1.10; EX 10.20 Trifecta £16.60.
Owner Barbara & Alick Richmond **Bred** A Oliver **Trained** Middleham Moor, N Yorks

FOCUS
An interesting novice stakes, but looking to concern just three according to the market and two of them had it between them in the straight.

1420 MATCHBOOK MAGNOLIA STKS (LISTED RACE) 1m 1f 219y(P)
2:05 (2:06) (Class 1) 4-Y-O+
£25,519 (£9,675; £4,842; £2,412; £1,210; £607) **Stalls** Low

Form RPR
11-1 **1** **Mootasadir**[26] 1017 4-9-5 110 .... BenCurtis 4 116
(Hugo Palmer) *chsd ldng pair: rdn 3f out: drvn ahd over 1f out: hrd pressed 100yds out: kpt on wl after: tk a long time to pull up after r* **4/1**[2]
210- **2** ½ **Extra Elusive**[189] 7533 4-9-0 96 ....(h[1]) JasonWatson 9 110
(Roger Charlton) *hld up in last pair in strly run event: rdn 3f out: gd prog wl over 1f out: tk 2nd jst ins fnl f: clsd to chal 100yds out: nt qckn after* **20/1**
01-6 **3** 2 ¾ **Master The World (IRE)**[35] 879 8-9-3 107 ....(p) SeanLevey 6 108
(David Elsworth) *hld up in 7th but pushed along at times: drvn over 3f out: prog on inner 2f out: tk 3rd jst ins fnl f: no imp 100yds out: fdd after* **25/1**
013- **4** 2 ½ **Fabricate**[175] 8011 7-9-0 110 ....(p) DavidProbert 7 100
(Michael Bell) *hld up in 6th: rdn 3f out: clsd over 1f out: nvr able to threaten but tk 4th ins fnl f* **10/1**
64-0 **5** 1 **Victory Bond**[21] 1101 6-9-0 102 .... RichardKingscote 2 98
(William Haggas) *chsd ldng quartet but shoved along at various times; rdn 3f out: briefly threatened to cl over 1f out: sn no imp* **14/1**
-124 **6** 3 **Three Weeks (USA)**[31] 929 4-9-0 92 .... ShaneKelly 5 92
(David O'Meara) *stdd s: mostly in last: struggling 3f out: no ch after* **100/1**
-111 **7** ½ **Matterhorn (IRE)**[24] 1031 4-9-0 112 .... JoeFanning 1 91
(Mark Johnston) *led at str pce: hdd 2f out: sn wknd qckly* **5/6**[1]
203- **8** nk **Robin Of Navan (FR)**[147] 8838 6-9-0 107 .... GeraldMosse 10 90
(Harry Dunlop) *pressed ldr at str pce and led briefly after 1f: rdn to ld 2f out: hdd & wknd rapidly over 1f out* **33/1**
2-24 **9** 34 **Big Country (IRE)**[35] 879 6-9-0 109 ....(p) LukeMorris 8 22
(Michael Appleby) *chsd ldng trio: rdn over 3f out: wknd over 2f out: sn eased: t.o (jockey said gelding stopped quickly; trainers rep reported that the gelding made a noise)* **8/1**[3]
2m 3.03s (-4.97) **Going Correction** -0.10s/f (Stan) **9** Ran SP% **114.0**
Speed ratings (Par 111): **115,114,112,110,109 107,106,106,79**
CSF £78.87 TOTE £4.70: £1.30, £4.30, £4.50; EX 66.20 Trifecta £766.60.
Owner Sheikh Mohammed Bin Khalifa Al Maktoum **Bred** Essafinaat Ltd **Trained** Newmarket, Suffolk
FOCUS
A good Listed race that often falls to a major Newmarket yard and did so again. They went off pretty hard in front and the leaders paid for their earlier efforts in the straight. The time was 3.47 secs faster than the opening novice stakes and a tenth of a second off the course record. The third has been rated close to form.

1421 BETTER ODDS WITH MATCHBOOK H'CAP 6f (P)
2:40 (2:42) (Class 2) (0-105,102) 4-Y-O+
£15,562 (£4,660; £2,330; £1,165; £582; £292) **Stalls** Low

Form RPR
0-30 **1** **George Bowen (IRE)**[7] 1295 7-9-2 **102** ....(v) SebastianWoods(5) 2 111
(Richard Fahey) *trckd ldrs: clsd over 1f out: rdn to ld last 150yds: styd on wl: readily* **7/1**[2]
-436 **2** 1 ¼ **Raucous**[21] 1105 6-9-2 **97** ....(tp) RichardKingscote 5 102
(Robert Cowell) *wnt lft s: trckd ldrs on inner: rdn to chal jst over 1f out: chsd wnr last 150yds: kpt on same pce* **10/1**
5151 **3** ¾ **Desert Doctor (IRE)**[21] 1105 4-9-0 **95** .... GeraldMosse 8 98+
(Ed Walker) *hld up in last pair: prog 2f out: styd on wl to take 3rd nr fin: too late* **7/1**[2]
050- **4** 1 ¼ **Whitefountainfairy (IRE)**[217] 6522 4-8-10 **91** .... DavidProbert 6 90
(Andrew Balding) *impeded s: wl in rr: prog wl over 1f out: styd on fnl f to take 4th last strides* **10/1**
00-1 **5** hd **Soldier's Minute**[7] 1290 4-8-12 **93** .... JoeFanning 4 91
(Keith Dalgleish) *t.k.h: led 1f: trckd ldr: rdn to ld over 1f out: hdd & wknd last 150yds* **7/4**[1]
605- **6** ¾ **Moon Trouble (IRE)**[178] 7920 6-8-11 **92** .... AlistairRawlinson 3 88
(Michael Appleby) *taken down early: led after 1f: rdn and hdd over 1f out: wknd fnl f* **9/1**[3]
020- **7** 2 **Gilgamesh**[175] 7977 5-9-2 **97** .... LukeMorris 7 86
(George Scott) *sltly impeded s: racd awkwardly in last pair: nvr a factor but passed a few late on* **9/1**[3]
603- **8** 1 ½ **Aeolus**[155] 8594 8-9-3 **98** .... JamesSullivan 1 82
(Ruth Carr) *chsd ldrs on inner: rdn over 2f out: no prog over 1f out: wknd* **20/1**
050- **9** 1 ¼ **Pipers Note**[168] 8194 9-9-0 **95** .... JackGarritty 10 75
(Ruth Carr) *in tch towards rr: rdn and brief effrt over 2f out: sn no prog* **66/1**
06-0 **10** 1 ½ **Udontdodou**[60] 470 6-9-0 **95** .... PhilipPrince 11 71
(Richard Guest) *taken down early: chsd ldrs: lost pl 1/2-way: shkn up over 2f out: steadily wknd* **50/1**
064- **11** 4 ½ **Haddaf (IRE)**[172] 8083 4-8-13 **94** .... CharlesBishop 9 55
(Robert Cowell) *trapped out wd: nvr beyond midfield: wknd over 2f out* **22/1**
1m 10.9s (-2.20) **Going Correction** -0.10s/f (Stan) **11** Ran SP% **112.1**
Speed ratings (Par 109): **110,108,107,105,105 104,101,99,98,96 90**
CSF £68.02 CT £512.94 TOTE £6.50: £1.90, £2.90, £2.20; EX 65.60 Trifecta £258.70.
Owner M A Scaife **Bred** Kevin Blake **Trained** Musley Bank, N Yorks
■ Alwasmiya was withdrawn. Price at time of withdrawal 16/1. Rule 4 does not apply
FOCUS
A very good, competitive sprint handicap in which the principals came from off the pace. The form looks sound, with the second rated close to his recent form.

1422 MATCHBOOK BETTING PODCAST ROSEBERY H'CAP (LONDON MIDDLE DISTANCE SERIES QUALIFIER) 1m 2f 219y(P)
3:15 (3:17) (Class 2) (0-105,102) 4-Y-O+
£31,125 (£9,320; £4,660; £2,330; £1,165; £585) **Stalls** Low

Form RPR
-112 **1** **Forbidden Planet**[37] 825 4-8-8 **86** .... JasonWatson 1 98+
(Roger Charlton) *cl up disputing 3rd: clsd to ld 2f out and sn dashed clr: in n.d fnl f: rdn out* **4/1**[2]
43-4 **2** 2 ¾ **Pipes Of Peace (IRE)**[42] 758 5-9-0 **92** ....(t) TomQueally 11 97
(Seamus Durack) *hld up in 10th: prog and swtchd to outer 2f out: drvn and styd on wl fnl f to snatch 2nd last stride* **33/1**

244- **3** *hd* **Desert Wind (IRE)**260 4912 4-9-1 **93**.......................... StevieDonohoe 2 97
(Ed Vaughan) *wl in tch disputing 6th: prog over 2f out: chsd wnr over 1f out: no imp and lost 2nd last stride* **5/1**3

010- **4** *nse* **Island Brave (IRE)**197 7241 5-9-8 **100**.......................... DavidEgan 14 104
(Heather Main) *wl in tch disputing 6th: rdn over 2f out: styd on over 1f out to dispute 2nd pl fnl f tl last strides* **50/1**

160- **5** *2 1/4* **Soto Sizzler**169 8149 4-8-6 **84**.......................... LukeMorris 15 84
(William Knight) *hld up disputing 8th: drvn over 2f out: tried to cl over 1f out: one pce after* **20/1**

2-51 **6** *2 1/4* **Count Calabash (IRE)**42 758 5-9-10 **102**.......................... CharlesBishop 3 99
(Eve Johnson Houghton) *disp ld tl def advantage over 3f out: hdd 2f out: wknd jst over 1f out* **3/1**1

2-32 **7** *3* **Caspar The Cub (IRE)**42 758 4-9-2 **94**..........................(p) NicolaCurrie 16 85+
(Alan King) *dropped in fr wdst draw and hld up in last: sn a long way off the pce: prog on inner over 2f out: rchd midfield over 1f out but no ch: no hdwy after* **11/1**

13-2 **8** *1 3/4* **Kelly's Dino (FR)**26 1017 6-9-5 **97**..........................(p) BenCurtis 4 86
(K R Burke) *cl up disputing 3rd: rdn and nt qckn over 2f out: wknd over 1f out* **6/1**

2123 **9** *nk* **Dommersen (IRE)**21 1106 6-8-0 **83**.......................... PaulaMuir(5) 5 71
(Roger Fell) *dwlt: hld up in last trio and long way off the pce: pushed along and prog into midfield over 1f out: no ch and no hdwy after (trainer was informed that the gelding could not run until the day after passing a stalls test)* **20/1**

1-23 **10** *3/4* **Cosmeapolitan**35 878 6-9-4 **96**.......................... DavidProbert 13 83
(Alan King) *dropped in fr wd draw: hld up in rr and off the pce: shkn up over 2f out: no real prog* **16/1**

054- **11** *7* **Manjaam (IRE)**191 7472 6-8-13 **91**.......................... RichardKingscote 7 66
(Ian Williams) *hld up off the pce disputing 10th: rdn and no prog over 2f out: wknd* **25/1**

-365 **12** *3/4* **Lexington Law (IRE)**26 1017 6-8-12 **90**..........................(p) KieranO'Neill 10 64
(Alan King) *hld up wl off the pce in last trio: nvr a factor* **33/1**

0-32 **13** *5* **Fire Fighting (IRE)**8 1267 8-9-7 **99**.......................... JoeFanning 9 64
(Mark Johnston) *hld up off the pce disputing 10th: brief prog over 2f out: wknd qckly over 1f out* **20/1**

065- **14** *14* **Nayel (IRE)**245 5485 7-9-1 **93**..........................(p) RossaRyan 6 34
(Richard Hannon) *disp ld to over 3f out: wknd rapidly: t.o* **50/1**

540- **15** *8* **Alternative Fact**168 8192 4-9-3 **95**.......................... GeraldMosse 8 24
(Ed Dunlop) *hld up in 8th: wknd 3f out: eased and t.o* **25/1**

-122 **16** *3/4* **Star Of Southwold (FR)**43 737 4-8-9 **87**.......................... SeanLevey 12 14
(Michael Appleby) *chsd ldrs disputing 3rd: rdn and wknd rapidly over 3f out: t.o* **25/1**

2m 15.65s (-5.35) **Going Correction** -0.10s/f (Stan) course record **16** Ran SP% **125.8**
Speed ratings (Par 109): **118,116,115,115,114 112,110,109,108,108 103,102,99,88,83 82**
CSF £139.31 CT £694.78 TOTE £4.50: £1.50, £5.00, £1.90, £8.20; EX 163.80 Trifecta £1688.60.

Owner Kingwood Stud Management Co Ltd **Bred** David John Brown **Trained** Beckhampton, Wilts

FOCUS
A long established high-class handicap and very competitive on paper. However, the winner looked a class apart.

1423 WILL UNWIN HALF CENTURY NOVICE STKS 7f (P)

3:50 (3:51) (Class 4) 3-Y-O+ £6,469 (£1,925; £962; £481) **Stalls** Low

Form RPR

01- **1** **Daarik (IRE)**122 9283 3-9-6 0.......................... DaneO'Neill 5 90+
(John Gosden) *trckd ldng trio: cajoled along 2f out: clsd over 1f out: shkn up to ld last 150yds: styd on* **6/5**1

233- **2** *3/4* **Chatham House**140 9001 3-8-13 81.......................... SeanLevey 1 80
(Richard Hannon) *t.k.h: trckd ldng pair: wnt 2nd over 1f out and sn chalng: upsides jst ins fnl f: styd on but a hld* **5/2**2

32- **3** *1 1/4* **Global Warning**231 6017 3-8-13 0.......................... GeraldMosse 2 77
(Ed Dunlop) *led at mod pce: tried to go for home 2f out: shkn up over 1f out: hdd and one pce last 150yds* **11/2**3

4 *1 3/4* **Desire For Freedom (USA)** 3-8-8 0.......................... DavidEgan 3 67
(Roger Varian) *trckd ldng quartet: shkn up 2f out: kpt on one pce and no threat* **16/1**

1 **5** *1 1/4* **Eardley Road (IRE)**30 943 3-9-6 0.......................... HectorCrouch 8 76
(Clive Cox) *trckd ldr to over 1f out: steadily fdd* **11/2**3

5 **6** *2 1/4* **Osho**15 1217 3-8-13 0.......................... RossaRyan 4 62
(Richard Hannon) *hld up in rr: pushed along and brief prog 2f out: no hdwy over 1f out* **40/1**

7 *2 1/2* **George Formby** 3-8-13 0.......................... NicolaCurrie 7 56
(Hugo Palmer) *t.k.h early: hld up in rr: pushed along and outpcd 2f out: no prog after* **33/1**

8 *hd* **Farhhmoreexciting** 4-10-0 0.......................... JasonWatson 6 60
(David Elsworth) *s.s: a in last pair: outpcd over 2f out* **50/1**

05- **9** *3/4* **Antidote (IRE)**155 8600 3-8-13 0.......................... ShaneKelly 9 53
(Richard Hughes) *a in last pair: outpcd over 2f out* **66/1**

1m 27.46s (1.46) **Going Correction** -0.10s/f (Stan) **9** Ran SP% **119.5**
WFA 3 from 4yo 15lb
Speed ratings (Par 105): **87,86,84,82,81 78,75,75,74**
CSF £4.45 TOTE £1.80: £1.10, £1.20, £2.00; EX 4.90 Trifecta £12.10.
Owner Hamdan Al Maktoum **Bred** Knocktoran & Ballantines Racing Stud Ltd **Trained** Newmarket, Suffolk

FOCUS
Two previous winners and a useful maiden featured in this novice stakes, and it produced a decent finish between the trio.

1424 MATCHBOOK BEST VALUE EXCHANGE H'CAP 6f (P)

4:25 (4:26) (Class 4) (0-85,85) 3-Y-O £6,469 (£1,925; £962; £481; £300; £300) **Stalls** Low

Form RPR

2131 **1** **Probability (IRE)**44 720 3-9-0 **78**.......................... BenCurtis 3 84
(Archie Watson) *mde all: stl gng strly 2f out: shkn up over 1f out: pushed out fnl f and a in command* **8/1**

202- **2** *3/4* **Magical Wish (IRE)**210 6790 3-9-7 **85**.......................... RossaRyan 8 88+
(Richard Hannon) *chsd ldrs but trapped out wd: shkn up over 2f out: no prog tl styd on wl fnl f to take 2nd last strides (jockey said colt hung right-handed in the final furlong)* **12/1**

3352 **3** *nk* **Uncle Jerry**37 838 3-9-6 **84**..........................(b) ShaneKelly 1 86
(Richard Hughes) *dwlt: sn wl in tch: prog 2f out: chsd wnr jst over 1f out: styd on but a readily hld: lost 2nd last strides* **4/1**2

212- **4** *3/4* **Ginger Fox**155 8602 3-8-12 **76**.......................... JasonWatson 5 76+
(Ian Williams) *wl in rr: prog on inner fr 2f out: rdn to dispute 3rd ins fnl f: kpt on same pce after* **11/2**3

231- **5** *hd* **Welcoming (FR)**162 8369 3-9-3 **81**.......................... HectorCrouch 12 80
(Clive Cox) *chsd wnr: rdn 2f out: lost 2nd and one pce jst over 1f out* **8/1**

600- **6** *1/2* **Jungle Inthebungle (IRE)**168 8193 3-9-4 **82**.......................... CharlesBishop 6 79
(Mick Channon) *hld up wl in rr: pushed along 2f out: sme prog over 1f out: kpt on but nvr nr enough to chal* **12/1**

200- **7** *nk* **Fly The Nest (IRE)**299 3430 3-9-4 **82**.......................... DavidProbert 2 78
(Tony Carroll) *chsd ldrs on inner: cl enough wl over 1f out: nt qckn and wl hld fnl f (jockey said gelding hung left-handed in the final 2f)* **25/1**

4211 **8** *3/4* **Solar Park (IRE)**29 972 3-8-13 **77**.......................... JoeFanning 11 71+
(James Tate) *s.i.s: rapid prog on outer to chse ldng pair after 1f: rdn 2f out: wknd jst over 1f out* **9/1**

4-11 **9** *shd* **Liberation Day**37 838 3-9-1 **79**..........................(p) RichardKingscote 4 73
(Tom Dascombe) *hld up in midfield: shkn up 2f out: making no real prog whn nt clr run over 1f out: no hdwy fnl f* **7/2**1

10-0 **10** *1 1/2* **Walkman (IRE)**38 806 3-9-1 **79**..........................(p1) RaulDaSilva 7 68
(Mark Usher) *a towards rr: rdn and no prog 2f out* **20/1**

540- **11** *hd* **Goldino Bello (FR)**140 9006 3-9-0 **78**.......................... StevieDonohoe 9 66
(Harry Dunlop) *hld up in last pair: shkn up and no prog 2f out* **40/1**

041- **12** *3* **Absolute Dream (IRE)**162 8385 3-9-1 **79**.......................... JackGarritty 10 58
(Richard Fahey) *trapped out wd: nvr beyond midfield: rdn over 2f out: wknd wl over 1f out* **20/1**

1m 12.96s (-0.14) **Going Correction** -0.10s/f (Stan) **12** Ran SP% **121.0**
Speed ratings (Par 100): **96,95,94,93,93 92,92,91,91,89 88,84**
CSF £96.71 CT £453.52 TOTE £9.20: £2.70, £4.30, £1.40; EX 140.80 Trifecta £735.30.
Owner Mrs C Cashman **Bred** Marie & Mossy Fahy **Trained** Upper Lambourn, W Berks

FOCUS
This competitive sprint handicap was run over 2secs slower than the earlier Class 2 handicap over the trip. The progressive winner dictated the pace and made all.

1425 MATCHBOOK CASINO H'CAP 1m 3f 219y(P)

5:00 (5:00) (Class 4) (0-85,84) 4-Y-O+ £6,469 (£1,925; £962; £481; £300; £300) **Stalls** Low

Form RPR

220- **1** **Al Kout**148 8807 5-9-7 **84**.......................... DavidEgan 10 91
(Heather Main) *led after 2f: mde rest: shkn up 2f out: pressed fr over 1f out but kpt on steadily* **10/1**

1431 **2** *1/2* **Nylon Speed (IRE)**21 1096 5-9-1 **78**..........................(t) DavidProbert 4 84
(Alan King) *hld up towards rr: prog over 2f out: shkn up over 1f out: chsd wnr ins fnl f: styd on but nvr really able to chal* **9/4**2

234- **3** *nk* **Running Cloud (IRE)**77 9155 4-8-13 **77**..........................(v) LouisSteward 11 82
(Alan King) *hld up in last pair: stl there over 2f out: prog wl over 1f out: rdn and r.o fnl f to take 3rd last strides: too late* **14/1**

310- **4** *nk* **Flintrock (GER)**290 3738 4-9-0 **81**.......................... JoshuaBryan(3) 7 85
(Andrew Balding) *hld up towards rr: prog over 2f out: drvn to chse wnr on inner over 1f out: kpt on but a hld: lost 2 pls ins fnl f* **7/1**3

0211 **5** *3* **Ilhabela Fact**30 945 5-9-5 **82**.......................... KieranO'Neill 1 82
(Tony Carroll) *trckd ldrs: rdn over 2f out and sn disputing 2nd: no imp over 1f out: wknd fnl f* **15/8**1

5122 **6** *shd* **Glan Y Gors (IRE)**15 1220 7-9-2 **79**..........................(b) DaneO'Neill 6 79
(David Thompson) *trckd wnr after 3f: rdn over 2f out: nt qckn and lost pl over 1f out: wl btn fnl f* **14/1**

314- **7** *1 3/4* **Archimento**154 8642 6-9-7 **84**.......................... JasonWatson 8 81
(William Knight) *s.i.s and pushed along early: hld up in last pair: sme prog wl over 2f out: no hdwy wl over 1f out: fdd* **11/1**

144- **8** *3 1/2* **Panko (IRE)**138 5824 6-9-7 **84**.......................... ShaneKelly 2 76
(Alex Hales) *trckd ldrs: rdn and wknd over 2f out* **33/1**

-114 **9** *8* **Temur Khan**28 980 4-9-3 **81**.......................... GeorgeDowning 9 61
(Tony Carroll) *led 2f: styd prom tl wknd qckly wl over 2f out (jockey said gelding stopped quickly)* **20/1**

2m 33.43s (-1.07) **Going Correction** -0.10s/f (Stan)
WFA 4 from 5yo+ 1lb **9** Ran SP% **116.5**
Speed ratings (Par 105): **99,98,98,98,96 96,95,92,87**
CSF £33.15 CT £324.90 TOTE £11.90: £4.20, £1.20, £2.30; EX 37.80 Trifecta £263.00.
Owner John Rylands And Wetumpka Racing **Bred** Newsells Park Stud **Trained** Kingston Lisle, Oxon
■ Stewards' Enquiry : David Probert two-day ban: misuse of whip (Apr 13,15)

FOCUS
Another competitive handicap that produced a close finish.
T/Plt: £130.90 to a £1 stake. Pool: £87,434.63 - 487.54 winning units T/Qpdt: £26.30 to a £1 stake. Pool: £7,947.68 - 222.97 winning units **Jonathan Neesom**

1364 SOUTHWELL (L-H)

Saturday, March 30

OFFICIAL GOING: Fibresand: standard (watered)
Wind: light breeze Weather: mainly cloudy, quite cool

1426 FOLLOW TOP TIPSTER TEMPLEGATE AT SUNRACING H'CAP 7f 14y(F)

6:00 (6:00) (Class 5) (0-70,71) 4-Y-O+ £3,752 (£1,116; £557; £400; £400; £400) **Stalls** Low

Form RPR

214 **1** **Crosse Fire**3 1366 7-9-7 **70**..........................(p) PaddyMathers 8 79
(Scott Dixon) *prom: disp ld 1/2-way: drvn to ld on own 2f out: rdn in 3 l ld 1f out: kpt on wl fnl f* **4/1**2

4166 **2** *2 1/2* **Sooqaan**18 1158 8-8-12 **61**..........................(p) CamHardie 7 64
(Antony Brittain) *prom on outer: drvn in 3rd 3f out: rdn over 2f out: styd on u.p into 2nd fnl f* **9/1**

1431 **3** *1/2* **Thunder Buddy**37 830 4-9-0 **63**..........................(p) CliffordLee 2 64
(K R Burke) *mid-div: pushed along and lost pl over 3f out: sn drvn and dropped to last: rdn over 2f out: hdwy over 1f out: r.o into 3rd fnl f* **5/4**1

0261 **4** *1 1/2* **Going Native**18 1163 4-8-1 **56** oh2 ow1.......................... RhonaPindar(7) 5 54
(Olly Williams) *racd wd in rr: hdwy 1/2-way: rdn in mid-div over 2f out: one pce fr over 1f out: tk 4th nr fin* **15/2**

10/4 **5** *3/4* **Just For The Craic (IRE)**24 1038 4-9-0 **63**.......................... LiamKeniry 9 58
(Neil Mulholland) *led: jnd 1/2-way: hdd and rdn 2f out: 3 l 2nd 1f out: wknd fnl f* **33/1**

53-0 **6** *4 1/2* **Christmas Night**38 808 4-8-11 **63**.......................... BenRobinson(3) 1 47
(Ollie Pears) *trckd ldrs on inner: pushed along in 4th 3f out: rdn 2f out: sn wknd: eased fnl f* **16/1**

2042 **7** *shd* **Aqua Libre**14 1231 6-8-11 **60**..........................(p) AndrewMullen 3 43
(Jennie Candlish) *hld up: pushed along 3f out: rdn over 2f out: no imp and sn eased* **12/1**

The Form Book Flat 2019, Raceform Ltd, Newbury, RG14 5SJ

2424 **8** *2* **It Must Be Faith**[5] 1329 9-9-1 **71**.....................(p) MarkCrehan(7) 6 49
(Michael Appleby) *mid-div: pushed along 3f out: rdn over 2f out: wknd and dropped to last over 1f out* **7/1**[3]

1m 28.08s (-2.22) **Going Correction** -0.175s/f (Stan) **8** Ran SP% **115.2**
Speed ratings (Par 103): **105,102,101,99,99 93,93,91**
CSF £39.61 CT £69.19 TOTE £5.00: £1.70, £1.80, £1.10; EX 32.50 Trifecta £109.80.
Owner Paul J Dixon & Darren Lucas **Bred** Dr A Gillespie **Trained** Babworth, Notts

FOCUS
Mainly exposed performers in an ordinary handicap. The gallop was reasonable. The second has been rated close to his winter form.

1427 BETWAY CASINO NOVICE STKS 6f 16y(F)
6:30 (6:30) (Class 5) 3-Y-O+ **£3,752** (£1,116; £557; £278) **Stalls** Low

Form RPR
1 **Astro Jakk (IRE)** 3-8-10 0.....................ClifffordLee 6 69
(K R Burke) *chsd ldrs: pushed along and tk clsr order 1/2-way: prom whn shkn up 2f out: rdn in cl 2nd 1f out: r.o to ld 1/2f out: drvn clr nr fin* **3/1**[2]

4-23 **2** *1* **So Hi Speed (USA)**[18] 1161 3-8-10 67.....................PaddyMathers 1 66
(Robert Cowell) *unruly s and dismntd to enter stalls: prom: pushed along in 1/2 l 2nd 3f out: sn drvn: led 2f out: rdn in narrow ld 1f out: hdd 1/2f out: one pce* **7/4**[1]

420- **3** *nk* **Vikivaki (USA)**[294] 3581 3-8-5 81.....................LukeMorris 5 60
(Robert Cowell) *chsd ldrs: pushed along in 4th on outer 3f out: drvn over 2f out: sn rdn: 4th 1f out: kpt on into 3rd fnl f* **3/1**[2]

53 **4** *3 1/4* **Muhallab (IRE)**[30] 954 3-8-10 0.....................AndrewMullen 2 55
(Adrian Nicholls) *uns rdr on way to s: led: 1/2 l ld 3f out: drvn over 2f out: rdn and hdd 2f out: sn wknd: dropped to 4th fnl f (jockey said colt hung left throughout)* **11/2**[3]

0 **5** *15* **Opera Kiss (IRE)**[30] 954 3-8-5 0.....................PhilDennis 3 2
(Lawrence Mullaney) *slowly away and sn scrubbed along: drvn and wl bhd fr 1/2-way* **50/1**

60 **6** *3 1/4* **Easy Money (IRE)**[14] 1236 4-9-9 0.....................TonyHamilton 4
(Roger Fell) *slowly away: a bhd: drvn and lost tch 1/2-way* **10/1**

1m 15.21s (-1.29) **Going Correction** -0.175s/f (Stan)
WFA 3 from 4yo 13lb **6** Ran SP% **112.8**
Speed ratings (Par 103): **101,99,99,94,74 70**
CSF £8.79 TOTE £4.30: £2.10, £1.70; EX 9.10 Trifecta £29.10.
Owner John Dance **Bred** P Hyland & C & J McHale **Trained** Middleham Moor, N Yorks

FOCUS
A modest novice event in which the gallop was fair. It's been rated around the second.

1428 FOLLOW SUNRACING ON TWITTER H'CAP 1m 13y(F)
7:00 (7:00) (Class 3) (0-95,92) 4-Y-O+ **£7,439** (£2,213; £1,106; £553) **Stalls** Low

Form RPR
4612 **1** **Space Bandit**[31] 929 4-8-9 **87**.....................MarkCrehan(7) 4 96
(Michael Appleby) *prom: drvn over 2f out: rdn in 3rd 2f out: hdwy into cl 2nd 1f out: led 1/2f out: r.o wl* **5/2**[2]

2-11 **2** *3/4* **Weld Al Emarat**[31] 929 7-9-3 **88**.....................NathanEvans 2 95
(Michael Easterby) *trckd ldrs: pushed along over 2f out: sn drvn: rdn over 1f out: 3rd 1f out: r.o wl fnl f: tk 2nd nr fin but nvr a threat to wnr* **11/8**[1]

-123 **3** *nk* **Mister Music**[31] 929 10-8-7 **83**.....................PoppyBridgwater(5) 3 89
(Tony Carroll) *hld up: pushed along and hdwy on inner over 2f out: rdn to ld 2f out: narrow ld 1f out: hdd 1/2f out: no ex: lost 2nd nr fin* **9/1**

-100 **4** *2 3/4* **Zylan (IRE)**[8] 1274 7-9-7 **92**.....................(p) TonyHamilton 1 92
(Roger Fell) *led: pushed along in 2 l ld 3f out: drvn and hdd 2f out: sn rdn and wknd* **25/1**

6611 **5** *hd* **Hammer Gun (USA)**[3] 1367 6-8-12 **83** 5ex.....................(v) PaddyMathers 5 83
(Derek Shaw) *in rr: pushed along over 2f out: sn rdn: no imp* **7/2**[3]

1-12 **6** *2 1/2* **Showboating (IRE)**[79] 164 11-8-11 **82**.....................(p) LewisEdmunds 6 76
(John Balding) *hld up on outer: pushed along 1/2-way: drvn over 3f out: sn rdn and dropped to last* **20/1**

1m 41.33s (-2.37) **Going Correction** -0.175s/f (Stan) **6** Ran SP% **111.5**
Speed ratings (Par 107): **104,103,102,100,100 97**
CSF £6.24 TOTE £3.10: £1.50, £1.40; EX 6.70 Trifecta £31.90.
Owner Rod In Pickle Partnership **Bred** Newsells Park Stud **Trained** Oakham, Rutland
■ Stewards' Enquiry : Poppy Bridgwater three-day ban: weighing in at 2lbs or more overweight (Apr 13,15-16)

FOCUS
The feature event of the evening. A decent handicap in which the modest gallop, which only picked up turning for home, was a big factor in determining the outcome of the race.

1429 BETWAY LIVE CASINO H'CAP 2m 102y(F)
7:30 (7:30) (Class 6) (0-65,66) 4-Y-O+
£3,105 (£924; £461; £400; £400; £400) **Stalls** Low

Form RPR
2021 **1** **Tynecastle Park**[16] 1196 6-9-2 **62**.....................DarraghKeenan(5) 8 69
(Robert Eddery) *trckd ldrs: pushed along in 3rd 3f out: rdn into 2nd 2f out: led over 1f out: styd on wl fnl f* **5/4**[1]

/1-2 **2** *1* **Shine Baby Shine**[67] 99 5-9-8 **63**.....................(w) JackMitchell 2 69
(Philip Kirby) *hld up: effrt over 3f out: drvn on outer over 2f out: hdwy into 3rd over 1f out: sn rdn: tk 2nd 1f out: kpt on fnl f but a hld by wnr* **5/1**[3]

106 **3** *2* **Lady Makfi (IRE)**[16] 1196 7-9-1 **56**.....................AndrewMullen 11 59
(Johnny Farrelly) *hld up: hdwy 4f out: pushed along in 4th 3f out: rdn and hdwy to ld over 2f out: hdd over 1f out: no ex fnl f* **40/1**

-105 **4** *2* **Katie Gale**[16] 1196 9-9-1 **63**.....................WilliamCarver(7) 7 64
(Robyn Brisland) *mid-div: rdn over 2f out: styd on into 4th fnl f* **20/1**

-363 **5** *1/2* **Galileo's Spear (FR)**[16] 1196 6-9-7 **62**.....................(bt[1]) LukeMorris 1 62
(Sir Mark Prescott Bt) *t.k.h: trckd ldr: disp ld 3f out: drvn and hdd over 2f out: sn rdn and no ex (horse arrived at the start with a small amount of blood in its mouth, vet said the horse had bitten its tongue and was deemed fit to race)* **15/2**

-066 **6** *3/4* **High Command (IRE)**[18] 1159 6-9-11 **66**.....................(p[1]) AlistairRawlinson 9 66
(Michael Appleby) *hld up: rdn 3f out: one pce fr 2f out* **12/1**

7 *3/4* **Panatos (FR)**[52] 4-8-11 **62**.....................MarkCrehan(7) 4 63
(Alexandra Dunn) *hld up: rdn over 2f out: n.m.r and swtchd 2f out: one pce* **33/1**

/0-0 **8** *1/2* **Tsundoku (IRE)**[19] 619 8-8-0 **46** oh1.....................ThoreHammerHansen(5) 10 44
(Alexandra Dunn) *hld up: rdn over 2f out: no imp (jockey said mare hung left)* **50/1**

113/ **9** *4* **Fern Owl**[24] 1045 7-9-9 **64**.....................(b) LiamKeniry 6 57
(John Butler) *hld up: drvn 3f out: sn rdn and wknd* **7/2**[2]

00-0 **10** *32* **Incus**[14] 1235 6-8-12 **53**.....................CallumShepherd 5 8
(Ed de Giles) *led: drvn and jnd 3f out: sn rdn and hdd: wknd and dropped away* **33/1**

212- **11** *21* **Royal Flag**[159] 8480 9-9-8 **66**.....................BenRobinson(3) 12
(Brian Ellison) *mid-div: drvn and lost pl over 3f out: sn wl bhd (trainer said the gelding was unsuited by the fibresand surface)* **20/1**

4/0- **12** *53* **Free Bounty**[177] 286 6-9-7 **65**.....................TimClark(3) 3
(Clare Ellam) *hld up: drvn in last 1/2-way: sn lost tch: lame (vet said gelding was lame on its right fore)* **100/1**

3m 38.78s (-6.72) **Going Correction** -0.175s/f (Stan)
WFA 4 from 5yo+ 3lb **12** Ran SP% **123.6**
Speed ratings (Par 101): **109,108,107,106,106 105,105,105,103,87 76,50**
CSF £7.54 CT £179.08 TOTE £2.00: £1.10, £1.90, £11.20; EX 9.00 Trifecta £194.10.
Owner Robert Eddery **Bred** Fittocks Stud Ltd & Arrow Farm Stud **Trained** Newmarket, Suffolk

FOCUS
Just an ordinary gallop to a modest handicap. Straightforward form.

1430 LADBROKES H'CAP 6f 16y(F)
8:00 (8:00) (Class 6) (0-65,61) 3-Y-O
£3,105 (£924; £461; £400; £400; £400) **Stalls** Low

Form RPR
0-03 **1** **Awa Bomba**[18] 1167 3-9-4 **58**.....................JoeyHaynes 9 71+
(Tony Carroll) *mid-div on outer: hdwy into 3rd 3f out: pushed into ld 2f out: rdn in 2 l ld 1f out: kpt up to work and c further clr run-in* **4/1**[2]

2601 **2** *3 1/4* **Champagne Mondays**[24] 1043 3-8-11 **51**.....................(p) NicolaCurrie 8 54
(Scott Dixon) *prom: drvn in 1 1/2 l 2nd 3f out: rdn 2f out: chsd wnr 1f out: one pce fnl f* **6/1**

0105 **3** *3 1/2* **Deconso**[18] 1167 3-9-1 **55**.....................(t) HollieDoyle 7 48
(Christopher Kellett) *hld up: pushed along in 5th over 2f out: sn rdn: r.o into 3rd fnl f* **5/1**[3]

5165 **4** *2* **Geography Teacher (IRE)**[22] 1081 3-9-1 **55**.....................BenCurtis 3 42
(Roger Fell) *bhd: drvn over 3f out: sn rdn: kpt on fr 2f out: tk 4th last two strides* **5/2**[1]

404- **5** *nk* **Tizwotitiz**[152] 8699 3-9-7 **61**.....................(v) HayleyTurner 1 47
(Steph Hollinshead) *led: pushed along in 1 1/2 l ld 3f out: rdn and hdd 2f out: sn wknd* **10/1**

200- **6** *1/2* **Biscuit Queen**[185] 7666 3-8-11 **54**.....................BenRobinson(3) 4 38
(Brian Ellison) *hld up: drvn over 3f out: rdn on outer 2f out: one pce fnl f* **12/1**

0-00 **7** *1 1/4* **Showshutai**[32] 913 3-8-10 **50**.....................PaddyMathers 2 31
(Christopher Kellett) *in rr: drvn and adrift of pack 1/2-way: mod hdwy fnl f: nvr a factor* **20/1**

035- **8** *nk* **The Big House (IRE)**[181] 7806 3-9-0 **54**.....................PhilDennis 5 34
(Noel Wilson) *mid-div: drvn in 5th 3f out: sn rdn and wknd (vet said horse was a gelding and not a colt as published in the racecard)* **9/1**

03-0 **9** *4* **Budaiya Fort (IRE)**[19] 1141 3-9-4 **58**.....................LukeMorris 6 26
(Robert Cowell) *chsd ldrs: drvn in 4th 3f out: sn rdn and wknd* **16/1**

1m 15.41s (-1.09) **Going Correction** -0.175s/f (Stan) **9** Ran SP% **117.0**
Speed ratings (Par 96): **100,95,91,88,87 87,85,85,79**
CSF £28.67 CT £113.21 TOTE £4.30: £1.90, £1.40, £1.90; EX 27.60 Trifecta £67.70.
Owner Mrs Katie Morgan **Bred** Mr And Mrs L Norris **Trained** Cropthorne, Worcs

FOCUS
A decidedly ordinary handicap but a good gallop and a career-best effort from the winner, who had the race in the bag some way from home. The second has been rated to his mark.

1431 SUNRACING.CO.UK H'CAP 1m 13y(F)
8:30 (8:30) (Class 7) (0-50,50) 3-Y-O+ **£2,264** (£673; £336; £168) **Stalls** Low

Form RPR
1333 **1** **Limerick Lord (IRE)**[22] 1075 7-9-10 **50**.....................(p) ShelleyBirkett 13 58
(Julia Feilden) *prom: led over 3f out: pushed along in 1 l ld 3f out: drvn and reminder 2f out: sn 3 l clr: rdn in 1 l ld 1f out: kpt on wl fnl f* **4/1**[1]

4062 **2** *1 1/2* **Voice Of A Leader (IRE)**[22] 1078 8-9-10 **50**.....................(h) JoeyHaynes 10 55
(Paul Howling) *mid-div: hdwy on outer over 3f out: pushed along in 2nd 3f out: rdn in 3 l 2nd over 1f out: 1 l 2nd 1f out: no ex fnl f* **10/1**

2324 **3** *3 3/4* **Foxrush Take Time (FR)**[22] 1078 4-9-6 **46**.....................(e) PhilipPrince 11 42
(Richard Guest) *chsd ldrs: pushed along and lost pl over 3f out: sn drvn: rdn and kpt on fr 2f out: tk 3rd 1f out* **6/1**

0-32 **4** *1* **Lukoutoldmakezebak**[22] 1083 6-9-3 **46**.....................(p) JamieGormley(3) 5 40
(David Thompson) *hld up: drvn and hdwy on inner over 2f out: sn rdn: kpt on into 4th fnl f* **5/1**[3]

-003 **5** *1 1/4* **Puchita (IRE)**[26] 1018 4-9-5 **45**.....................CamHardie 6 36
(Antony Brittain) *chsd ldrs: drvn in 3rd 3f out: sn rdn and wknd* **16/1**

000- **6** *1/2* **Shakiah (IRE)**[211] 6759 4-9-6 **46**.....................PhilDennis 7 36
(Sharon Watt) *hld up: rdn and effrt on outer over 2f out: no ex fr over 1f out* **40/1**

0432 **7** *2 1/4* **Joyful Dream (IRE)**[18] 1158 5-9-6 **46**.....................(be[1]) HollieDoyle 4 30
(John Butler) *hld up: drvn over 2f out: rdn 2f out: no imp (jockey said mare was slowly away and was never travelling thereafter)* **9/2**[2]

500- **8** *3* **Hollywood Dream**[119] 9356 4-9-6 **46**.....................LiamKeniry 3 24
(Neil Mulholland) *mid-div: drvn 3f out: rdn and wknd over 2f out* **16/1**

-540 **9** *3/4* **Highwayman**[29] 969 6-9-6 **46**.....................(h) CliffordLee 1 22
(David Thompson) *dwlt in stall losing many l: bhd: drvn in last over 3f out: rdn and no ch fr over 2f out (jockey said gelding was slow to remove the blindfold, resulting in his horse being slow to start)* **9/1**

6-40 **10** *19* **Pullman Brown (USA)**[18] 1163 7-9-6 **46**.....................AndrewMullen 9
(Philip Kirby) *slowly away: bhd: drvn over 3f out: dropped away and eased over 2f out* **12/1**

-004 **11** *4* **Petra's Pony (IRE)**[26] 1018 4-9-10 **50**.....................(p[1]) CallumShepherd 14
(Brian Meehan) *trckd across fr wd draw to ld: rdn and hdd over 3f out: sn wknd and eased* **10/1**

1m 43.37s (-0.33) **Going Correction** -0.175s/f (Stan) **11** Ran SP% **119.2**
Speed ratings (Par 97): **94,92,88,87,86 86,83,80,80,61 57**
CSF £45.22 CT £204.99 TOTE £4.20: £2.10, £3.60, £1.60; EX 51.30 Trifecta £224.10.
Owner Steve Clarke & Partner **Bred** R N Auld **Trained** Exning, Suffolk

FOCUS
A very moderate handicap in which very few figured. The gallop was fair. It's been rated around the second.

T/Plt: £17.10 to a £1 stake. Pool: £88,730.01 - 3,767.06 winning units T/Qpdt: £6.70 to a £1 stake. Pool: £9,830.03 - 1,075.16 winning units **Keith McHugh**

1432 - 1433a (Foreign Racing) - See Raceform Interactive

NAVAN (L-H)

Saturday, March 30

OFFICIAL GOING: Good (yielding in places)

1434a CORK STKS (LISTED RACE) 5f 164y

2:50 (2:53) 3-Y-0+

£23,918 (£7,702; £3,648; £1,621; £810; £405)

RPR

1 **Sergei Prokofiev (CAN)**[148] 8818 3-9-0 111 DonnachaO'Brien 5 107
(A P O'Brien, Ire) *w.w towards rr: gd hdwy nr side 1 1/2f out: qckned wl to ld ins fnl f and rdn: kpt on wl clsng stages where strly pressed* 15/8[1]

2 *hd* **Chessman (IRE)**[6] 1305 5-9-7 95 OisinOrr 1 104+
(Richard John O'Brien, Ire) *dwlt and towards rr: last at 1/2-way: gd hdwy nr side 1 1/2f out to chse ldrs: r.o wl into 3rd ins fnl f and strly pressed wnr cl home where wnt 2nd: jst hld* 16/1

3 *nk* **Smash Williams (IRE)**[154] 8654 6-9-10 106 (t) KevinManning 8 106
(J S Bolger, Ire) *mid-div: hdwy after 1/2-way: rdn in 2nd over 1f out and disp ld briefly tl sn hdd: kpt on wl in cl 2nd and strly pressed wnr wl ins fnl f tl dropped to 3rd cl home* 6/1[2]

4 *3 1/4* **Urban Beat (IRE)**[195] 7340 4-9-7 101 NGMcCullagh 11 93
(J P Murtagh, Ire) *mid-div: tk clsr order and pushed along 1 1/2f out: sn rdn and no imp on wnr in 4th wl ins fnl f: kpt on same pce* 14/1

5 *hd* **Angelic Light (IRE)**[148] 8805 3-8-7 96 LeighRoche 13 87
(M D O'Callaghan, Ire) *mid-div early: hdwy between horses after 1/2-way: rdn in 6th 1f out and no imp on ldrs in 5th wl ins fnl f: kpt on same pce* 25/1

6 *1* **Soffia**[167] 8239 4-9-2 94 DeclanMcDonogh 9 84
(Edward Lynam, Ire) *cl up: disp ld bef 1/2-way: led narrowly fr 1/2-way: rdn over 1f out where jnd and sn hdd: sn no imp on ldrs u.p in 4th and wknd clsng stages* 8/1[3]

7 *1 1/4* **Son Of Rest**[161] 8405 5-9-7 111 (p[1]) ChrisHayes 2 85
(J A Stack, Ire) *hld up in rr of mid-div: n.m.r briefly after 1/2-way where tk clsr order: drvn into 7th ins fnl f where no imp on ldrs: kpt on same pce* 6/1[2]

8 *1/2* **Downforce (IRE)**[140] 9003 7-9-10 106 (v[1]) WJLee 10 86
(W McCreery, Ire) *hld up in rr of mid-div early: gng wl under 2f out where n.m.r and checked in rr: swtchd rt 1 1/2f out and r.o ins fnl f: nvr nrr* 20/1

9 *hd* **Primo Uomo (IRE)**[284] 3963 7-9-10 106 (t) RossCoakley 7 86
(Gerard O'Leary, Ire) *hooded to load: mid-div: n.m.r far side after 1/2-way where checked: swtchd rt in 13th 1 1/2f out and r.o (jockey said gelding got tight for space)* 20/1

10 *2 1/4* **Texas Rock (IRE)**[146] 8856 8-9-7 87 (p) RobbieColgan 4 75
(M C Grassick, Ire) *trckd ldrs: drvn and wknd 1 1/2f out* 50/1

11 *nk* **Swissterious**[6] 1306 3-8-9 95 BenCoen 16 71
(Damian Joseph English, Ire) *loaded wout rdr and on toes behand: chsd ldrs early: pushed along in mid-div after 1/2-way and sn no ex* 25/1

12 *3/4* **Gordon Lord Byron (IRE)**[140] 9003 11-9-7 106 SeamieHeffernan 15 72
(T Hogan, Ire) *trckd ldrs: almost on terms at 1/2-way: drvn and wknd fr under 2f out (trainer said gelding was found to be coughing post race)* 20/1

13 *1* **Medicine Jack**[167] 8239 5-9-10 101 (b) ColinKeane 3 72
(G M Lyons, Ire) *mid-div: pushed along far side after 1/2-way and no ex over 1f out: wknd and eased ins fnl f* 10/1

14 *4 3/4* **All The King's Men (IRE)**[162] 8397 3-8-12 98 MichaelHussey 14 54
(A P O'Brien, Ire) *sn led narrowly: pushed along and jnd bef 1/2-way: hdd fr 1/2-way and sn wknd qckly (jockey said colt was weakening when tight for room)* 16/1

15 *nk* **Fantasy (IRE)**[162] 8397 3-8-4 90 RoryCleary 6 45
(A P O'Brien, Ire) *trckd ldrs: pushed along disputing cl 2nd at 1/2-way and sn wknd qckly* 33/1

1m 12.35s
WFA 3 from 4yo+ 13lb **15 Ran SP% 128.9**
CSF £35.02 TOTE £2.40: £1.40, £5.30, £1.60; DF 40.60 Trifecta £213.20.
Owner Derrick Smith & Mrs John Magnier & Michael Tabor **Bred** Anderson Farms (Ontario) Inc
Trained Cashel, Co Tipperary

FOCUS
An informative sprint in all likelihood, the winner can only improve it would seem. The standard is set by the second and third.

1435 - 1439a (Foreign Racing) - See Raceform Interactive

1201

MEYDAN (L-H)

Saturday, March 30

OFFICIAL GOING: Dirt: fast; turf: good

1440a GODOLPHIN MILE SPONSORED BY MOHAMMED BIN RASHID AL MAKTOUM CITY-DISTRICT ONE (GROUP 2) (DIRT) 1m (D)

12:15 (12:15) 3-Y-0+

£708,661 (£236,220; £118,110; £59,055; £35,433; £23,622)

RPR

1 **Coal Front (USA)**[40] 5-9-0 112 JoseLOrtiz 12 117
(Todd Pletcher, U.S.A) *trckd ldrs: rdn 3f out: r.o wl fnl 1 1/2f: led nr line* 5/1[2]

2 *3/4* **Heavy Metal**[21] 1112 9-9-0 109 MickaelBarzalona 5 115
(S bin Ghadayer, UAE) *sn led: rdn clr 2f out: hdd cl home* 8/1[3]

3 *5 3/4* **Muntazah**[21] 1112 6-9-0 116 JimCrowley 6 102
(Doug Watson, UAE) *trckd ldrs: ev ch 2f out: r.o same pce fnl 1 1/2f* 10/11[1]

4 *shd* **Kimbear (USA)**[44] 726 5-9-0 106 PatDobbs 4 102
(Doug Watson, UAE) *s.i.s: settled in rr: r.o wl fnl 2f: nrst fin* 12/1

5 *2* **Secret Ambition**[21] 1112 6-9-0 104 (vt) RichardMullen 13 97
(S Seemar, UAE) *mid-div: r.o same pce fnl 2f* 33/1

6 *nk* **Musawaat**[21] 1112 5-9-0 105 (v) AdriedeVries 11 97
(Fawzi Abdulla Nass, Bahrain) *a in mid-div* 50/1

7 *1 1/4* **Logrado (ARG)**[21] 1114 4-9-0 109 (bt) AntonioFresu 9 94
(E Charpy, UAE) *nvr bttr than mid-div* 80/1

8 *2* **Ibn Malik (IRE)**[21] 1112 6-9-0 104 (v) TadhgO'Shea 7 89
(M Al Mheiri, UAE) *nvr bttr than mid-div* 66/1

9 *nk* **True Timber (USA)**[63] 445 5-9-0 111 JoelRosario 3 88
(Kiaran McLaughlin, U.S.A) *nvr nr to chal* 12/1

10 *1 1/4* **Nonkono Yume (JPN)**[41] 781 7-9-0 114 (t) JoaoMoreira 2 85
(Yukihiro Kato, Japan) *slowly away: nvr nr to chal* 28/1

11 *38* **Major Partnership (IRE)**[37] 847 4-9-0 102 (tp) OisinMurphy 1
(Saeed bin Suroor) *nvr nr to chal* 25/1

12 *37* **Good Curry (TUR)**[21] 1112 7-9-0 108 HalisKaratas 10
(Bayram Kocakaya, Turkey) *trckd ldr: ev ch 3f out: wknd fnl 1 1/2f* 33/1

1m 36.51s (-0.99) **Going Correction** +0.325s/f (Slow) **12 Ran SP% 113.4**
Speed ratings: **117,116,110,110,108 108,106,104,104,103 65,28**
CSF: 37.63; TRICAST: 60.24.
Owner Robert V LaPenta & Head Of Plains Partners LLC **Bred** Michael Edward Connelly **Trained** USA

FOCUS
Increased prize money for the Godolphin Mile, worth an extra $500,000 compared to the previous year. No Trakus data at the time of writing but the winner overcame a wide draw/trip to run down the second, who contested the pace before skipping clear in the straight whilst racing on the rail throughout.

1441a DUBAI GOLD CUP SPONSORED BY AL TAYER MOTORS (GROUP 2) (TURF) 2m

12:50 (12:50) 3-Y-0+

£708,661 (£236,220; £118,110; £59,055; £35,433; £23,622)

RPR

1 **Cross Counter**[144] 8911 4-8-9 117 WilliamBuick 9 118+
(Charlie Appleby) *trckd ldrs: rdn 2 1/2f out: led 1/2f out: comf* 7/4[1]

2 *1 1/4* **Ispolini**[30] 958 4-8-9 113 (t) BrettDoyle 6 117
(Charlie Appleby) *mid-div: smooth prog 4f out: led 3 1/2f out: r.o wl but hdd 1/2f out* 9/4[2]

3 *3* **Call The Wind**[25] 1030 5-9-1 115 AurelienLemaitre 2 114
(F Head, France) *mid-div: r.o fnl 2 1/2f but no ch w first two* 3/1[3]

4 *4* **Gold Mount**[41] 776 6-9-1 112 (t) RyanMoore 10 109
(Richard Gibson, Hong Kong) *nvr nr to chal but r.o fnl 2 1/2f* 25/1

5 *4 1/4* **Marinaresco (SAF)**[21] 1113 6-9-1 112 BernardFayd'Herbe 1 104
(M F De Kock, South Africa) *a mid-div* 33/1

6 *4 1/2* **Platinum Warrior (IRE)**[49] 4-8-9 111 (bt) ShaneFoley 4 98
(John W Sadler, U.S.A) *s.i.s: nvr nr to chal* 40/1

7 *1/2* **Sharpalo (FR)**[21] 1113 7-9-1 103 (t) ConnorBeasley 7 98
(A bin Harmash, UAE) *nvr bttr than mid-div* 50/1

8 *13 1/2* **Red Galileo**[30] 958 8-9-1 102 (p) PatCosgrave 3 82
(Saeed bin Suroor) *sn led: hdd & wknd 3 1/2f out* 25/1

9 *nk* **Prince Of Arran**[21] 1113 6-9-1 112 OisinMurphy 5 81
(Charlie Fellowes) *trckd ldr tl wknd 3 1/2f out* 14/1

10 *dist* **Team Talk**[21] 1113 6-9-1 108 (h) ChristopheSoumillon 8
(Saeed bin Suroor) *slowly away: mid-div tl wknd 4f out* 33/1

3m 19.0s (-5.50) **Going Correction** +0.15s/f (Good)
WFA 4 from 5yo+ 3lb **10 Ran SP% 116.8**
Speed ratings: **119,118,116,114,112 110,110,103,103,**
CSF: 5.43; TRICAST: 10.46.
Owner Godolphin **Bred** Godolphin **Trained** Newmarket, Suffolk

FOCUS
The front three came home in market order and the form looks pretty solid for the grade. No Trakus data available. The winner and fourth help set the level, with the third rated in line with the better view of his Cadran win.

1442a AL QUOZ SPRINT SPONSORED BY AZIZI DEVELOPMENTS (GROUP 1) (TURF) 6f

1:30 (1:30) 3-Y-0+

£944,881 (£314,960; £157,480; £78,740; £47,244; £31,496)

RPR

1 **Blue Point (IRE)**[21] 1111 5-9-0 119 WilliamBuick 8 124+
(Charlie Appleby) *trckd ldrs: rdn 1 1/2f out: led 1/2f out: comf* 4/6[1]

2 *1 1/4* **Belvoir Bay**[42] 6-8-9 111 FlavienPrat 7 115
(Peter Miller, U.S.A) *sn led: hdd 1/2f out but r.o wl* 66/1

3 *3/4* **Stormy Liberal (USA)**[36] 7-9-0 117 (t) JoelRosario 1 118
(Peter Miller, U.S.A) *trckd ldrs: ev ch 1 1/2f out: r.o same pce fnl 1f* 9/1

4 *4* **Viddora (AUS)**[35] 891 6-8-9 115 (t) JoeBowditch 12 100
(Lloyd Kennewell, Australia) *mid-div: r.o same pce fnl 2f* 25/1

5 *1/2* **The Right Man**[150] 8755 7-9-0 111 Francois-XavierBertras 5 103
(D Guillemin, France) *nvr nr to chal but r.o fnl 2f* 80/1

6 *nse* **Sands Of Mali (FR)**[161] 8405 4-9-0 118 OisinMurphy 2 103
(Richard Fahey) *trckd ldr: ev ch 1 1/2f out: wknd fnl 1f* 8/1[3]

7 *2 1/4* **Wishful Thinker (AUS)**[20] 1147 5-9-0 111 (b) AlexisBadel 13 96
(Richard Gibson, Hong Kong) *a in rr* 22/1

8 *nse* **Brave Smash (JPN)**[21] 1107 6-9-0 118 (bt) HughBowman 6 96
(Kris Lees, Australia) *trckd ldrs ev ch 2f out: wknd fnl 1 1/2f* 7/1[2]

9 *2 1/4* **Ekhtiyaar**[21] 1111 5-9-0 110 JimCrowley 10 89
(Doug Watson, UAE) *s.i.s: nvr bttr than mid-div* 11/1

10 *1/2* **Lost Treasure (IRE)**[147] 8842 4-9-0 112 RyanMoore 3 87
(A P O'Brien, Ire) *nvr bttr than mid-div* 33/1

11 *3/4* **Mazzini**[21] 1111 6-9-0 106 AdriedeVries 4 85
(Fawzi Abdulla Nass, Bahrain) *slowly away: a in rr* 50/1

12 *2 3/4* **Illustrious Lad (AUS)**[49] 7-9-0 111 AnthonyDarmanin 11 76
(Peter Gelagotis, Australia) *a in rr* 100/1

13 *3* **Caribou Club (USA)**[88] 5-9-0 112 (bt) JosephTalamo 9 66
(Thomas F Proctor, U.S.A) *a in rr* 33/1

1m 8.39s (-0.61) **Going Correction** +0.15s/f (Good) **13 Ran SP% 121.7**
Speed ratings: **110,108,107,102,101 101,98,98,95,94 93,89,85**
CSF: 94.26; TRICAST: 292.40.
Owner Godolphin **Bred** Oak Lodge Bloodstock **Trained** Newmarket, Suffolk

FOCUS
The early pace was not frenetic and as a result it paid to race handily. No sectional data available.

1443a UAE DERBY SPONSORED BY SAEED & MOHAMMED AL NABOODAH GROUP (GROUP 2) (DIRT) 1m 1f 110y(D)

2:05 (2:05) 3-Y-0

£1,181,102 (£393,700; £196,850; £98,425; £59,055; £39,370)

RPR

1 **Plus Que Parfait (USA)**[41] 3-9-0 113 (bt) JoseLOrtiz 4 110
(Brendan P Walsh, U.S.A) *mid-div: smooth prog 2 1/2f out: led 1f out: r.o wl* 25/1

2 *3/4* **Gray Magician (USA)**[42] 3-9-0 102 JoelRosario 8 109
(Peter Miller, U.S.A) *mid-div: smooth prog 2 1/2f out: r.o wl 1 1/2f out: nrst fin* 28/1

3 *nk* **Manguzi (FR)**[21] 1110 3-9-0 100 FernandoJara 14 108
(A R Al Rayhi, UAE) *trckd ldrs: led 1 1/2f out: hdd 1f out but r.o wl* 40/1

4 5 1/4 **Derma Louvre (JPN)**41 3-9-0 108............ Christophe-PatriceLemaire 5 97
(Hirofumi Toda, Japan) *nvr nr to chal but r.o wl fnl 2f: nrst fin* **12/1**
5 2 **Swift Rose (IRE)**37 845 3-8-9 102..................(p) PatCosgrave 13 88
(Saeed bin Suroor) *sn led: hdd 1 1/2f out: wknd fnl 1/2f* **22/1**
6 1 **Stubbins (USA)**28 3-9-0 102..(vt) FlavienPrat 12 91
(Doug O'Neill, U.S.A) *trckd ldr: ev ch 1 1/2f out: wknd fnl 1/2f* **11/1**
7 1/2 **Walking Thunder (USA)**51 636 3-9-0 105...............(h) FrankieDettori 1 90
(A bin Harmash, UAE) *trckd ldrs: ev ch 2 1/2f out: one pce fnl 1 1/2f* **7/2**2
8 4 **Superior (USA)**21 1110 3-9-0 101.............................(p) ConnorBeasley 7 82
(A bin Harmash, UAE) *nvr bttr than mid-div* **33/1**
9 3 1/4 **Van Beethoven (CAN)**24 1049 3-9-0 107....................... RyanMoore 11 75
(A P O'Brien, Ire) *slowly away: nvr nr to chal* **8/1**
10 1 1/2 **Razeena (CAN)**37 845 3-8-9 97... PatDobbs 9 67
(Doug Watson, UAE) *nvr bttr than mid-div* **33/1**
11 2 **Jahbath**24 1035 3-9-0 102.. JimCrowley 2 68
(William Haggas) *nvr bttr than mid-div* **13/2**3
12 nk **Al Hayette (USA)**21 1110 3-8-9 95............................... FabriceVeron 10 62
(Ismail Mohammed) *nvr nr to chal* **80/1**
13 6 3/4 **Divine Image (USA)**21 1110 3-8-9 109........................ WilliamBuick 6 49
(Charlie Appleby) *mid-div: rdn 3 1/2f out: n.m.r 3f out: wknd 2 1/2f out* **9/4**1
14 1 **Golden Jaguar (USA)**30 956 3-9-0 102....................(h) OisinMurphy 3 52
(A bin Harmash, UAE) *slowly away: a in rr* **12/1**

1m 58.41s (-0.39) **Going Correction** +0.325s/f (Slow) **14 Ran SP% 122.4**
Speed ratings: **114,113,113,108,107 106,106,102,100,99 97,97,91,91**
CSF: 577.73; TRICAST: 24,303.73.
Owner Imperial Racing LLC **Bred** Calloway Stables, Llc **Trained** USA

FOCUS
Again, no Trakus. An extra $500,000 was in the pot compared to 2018. Most of the local form had been substandard this season and the one-two were US raiders, with a Japanese runner in fourth. It's been rated around the balance of the winner, third and fifth.

1444a DUBAI GOLDEN SHAHEEN SPONSORED BY GULF NEWS (GROUP 1) (DIRT) 6f (Tp)
2:40 (2:40) 3-Y-O+
£1,181,102 (£393,700; £196,850; £98,425; £59,055; £39,370)

RPR
1 **X Y Jet (USA)**45 7-9-0 115..........................(bt) EmisaelJaramillo 2 121
(Jorge Navarro, U.S.A) *wl away: sn led: rdn 2 1/2f out: r.o wl: comf* **15/8**1
2 1 1/2 **Matera Sky (USA)**62 5-9-0 111.................................. YutakaTake 8 116
(Hideyuki Mori, Japan) *trckd ldr: ev ch 2f out: r.o wl* **33/1**
3 1/2 **Imperial Hint (USA)**42 6-9-0 120..............................(t) JoseLOrtiz 1 114+
(Luis Carvajal Jr, U.S.A) *trckd ldr: t.k.h: r.o wl fnl 1 1/2f: nrst fin* **7/2**3
4 1 1/4 **Promises Fulfilled (USA)**147 8845 4-9-0 117..........(t) RobbyAlbarado 3 110
(Dale Romans, U.S.A) *s.i.s: mid-div: r.o same pce fnl 2f* **3/1**2
5 1 **Drafted (USA)**21 1109 5-9-0 111...................................... PatDobbs 4 107+
(Doug Watson, UAE) *nvr nr to chal but r.o wl fnl 2f: nrst fin* **13/2**
6 2 **Fight Hero**77 226 8-9-0 104..(h) JoaoMoreira 9 101+
(Y S Tsui, Hong Kong) *nvr nr to chal* **50/1**
7 1 1/2 **Nine Below Zero**21 1109 4-9-0 110............................ AdriedeVries 6 96
(Fawzi Abdulla Nass, Bahrain) *nvr bttr than mid-div* **25/1**
8 1 3/4 **Switzerland (USA)**21 1109 5-9-0 106...................(tp) MickaelBarzalona 5 90
(Steven Asmussen, U.S.A) *bmpd at s: nvr nr to chal* **33/1**
9 4 1/2 **Tato Key (ARG)**21 1109 4-9-0 109.................................(t) ShaneFoley 7 76
(David Marnane, Ire) *a in rr* **16/1**

1m 10.75s (-0.85) **Going Correction** +0.325s/f (Slow) **9 Ran SP% 112.9**
Speed ratings: **118,116,115,113,112 109,107,105,99**
CSF: 73.56; TRICAST: 203.92.
Owner Rockingham Ranch & Gelfenstein Farm **Bred** Didier Plasencia **Trained** North America

FOCUS
Prize money was up $500,000. A race weakened by the mid-week withdrawal of Roy H, and the fourth missed the break, meaning the winner could do his own thing in front and the first three raced 1-2-3 more or less throughout. So, not as good or competitive a contest as had originally seemed the case.

1445a DUBAI TURF SPONSORED BY DP WORLD (GROUP 1) (TURF) 1m 1f (T)
3:20 (3:20) 3-Y-O+
£2,834,645 (£944,881; £472,440; £236,220; £141,732; £94,488)

RPR
1 **Almond Eye (JPN)**125 9270 4-8-9 124...(h) Christophe-PatriceLemaire 7 117+
(Sakae Kunieda, Japan) *mid-div: smooth prog 2 1/2f out: led 1f out: r.o wl* **6/5**1
2 1 1/4 **Vivlos (JPN)**111 9476 6-8-9 113.............................(h) MickaelBarzalona 4 114
(Yasuo Tomomichi, Japan) *mid-div: r.o wl fnl 1 1/2f but no ch w wnr: nrst fin* **22/1**
3 1/2 **Lord Glitters (FR)**161 8407 6-9-0 115......................... DanielTudhope 6 118
(David O'Meara) *settled in rr: smooth prog 3f out: r.o wl fnl 1 1/2f* **22/1**
4 4 1/4 **Deirdre (JPN)**34 5-8-9 113... JoaoMoreira 3 104
(Mitsuru Hashida, Japan) *settled in rr: r.o wl fnl 2f: nrst fin* **14/1**
5 hd **Without Parole**202 7105 4-9-0 116.......................(p) FrankieDettori 12 109
(John Gosden) *trckd ldr: ev ch 2f out: wknd fnl 1f* **16/1**
6 4 **Southern Legend (AUS)**41 776 6-9-0 116............................ ZacPurton 1 100
(C Fownes, Hong Kong) *a mid-div* **40/1**
7 hd **Century Dream (IRE)**21 1115 5-9-0 114.....................(t) OisinMurphy 11 100
(Simon Crisford) *sn led: hdd & wknd 1f out* **33/1**
8 1 **Majestic Mambo (SAF)**21 1115 4-9-0 113....................... AntonMarcus 5 98
(M F De Kock, South Africa) *s.i.s: nvr nr to chal* **100/1**
9 1 **Wootton (FR)**21 1115 4-9-0 114.................................... WilliamBuick 13 96
(Charlie Appleby) *trckd ldrs tl wknd fnl 1 1/2f* **12/1**
10 nk **Yulong Prince (SAF)**301 4-9-0 115................... BernardFayd'Herbe 10 95
(M F De Kock, South Africa) *s.i.s: nvr nr to chal* **100/1**
11 3/4 **I Can Fly**24 1048 4-8-9 116.. RyanMoore 8 88
(A P O'Brien, Ire) *s.i.s: nvr nr to chal* **15/2**3
12 2 1/2 **Mountain Hunter (USA)**30 961 5-9-0 110..................... PatCosgrave 9 88
(Saeed bin Suroor) *nvr bttr than mid-div* **100/1**
13 nse **Dream Castle**21 1115 5-9-0 117................... ChristopheSoumillon 2 88
(Saeed bin Suroor) *trckd ldrs tl wknd fnl 1 1/2f* **5/2**2

1m 46.78s (-2.32) **Going Correction** +0.15s/f (Good) **13 Ran SP% 123.1**
Speed ratings: **116,114,114,110,110 106,106,105,104,104 104,101,101**
CSF: 39.14; TRICAST: 427.38.
Owner Silk Racing Co Ltd **Bred** Northern Racing **Trained** Japan

FOCUS
A good performance from the winner, who outclassed her rivals despite running over a trip short of her optimum. No Trakus data available. The level is set around the second and third.

1446a LONGINES DUBAI SHEEMA CLASSIC (GROUP 1) (TURF) 1m 4f 11y(T)
4:00 (4:00) 3-Y-O+
£2,834,645 (£944,881; £472,440; £236,220; £141,732; £94,488)

RPR
1 **Old Persian**21 1113 4-8-13 117.. WilliamBuick 2 122
(Charlie Appleby) *mid-div: smooth prog 4f out: n.m.r 3f out: rdn to ld 1 1/2f out: r.o wl* **5/4**1
2 1 1/2 **Cheval Grand (JPN)**97 9691 7-9-0 119.......................... HughBowman 1 119
(Yasuo Tomomichi, Japan) *s.i.s: settled in rr: r.o wl fnl 2f: nrst fin* **20/1**
3 1/2 **Suave Richard (JPN)**34 5-9-0 121.................................. JoaoMoreira 7 118
(Yasushi Shono, Japan) *settled in rr: r.o wl fnl 2f: nrst fin* **11/1**
4 8 1/4 **Hunting Horn (IRE)**35 894 4-8-13 113.......................... WayneLordan 5 106
(A P O'Brien, Ire) *a mid-div* **50/1**
5 nse **Magic Wand (IRE)**63 444 4-8-8 114.................................. RyanMoore 3 101
(A P O'Brien, Ire) *trckd ldr tl wknd fnl 2f* **9/2**3
6 2 1/4 **Rey De Oro (JPN)**97 9691 5-9-0 123......... Christophe-PatriceLemaire 6 101
(Kazuo Fujisawa, Japan) *sn led: hdd & wknd 1 1/2f out* **11/4**2
7 1 3/4 **Racing History (IRE)**21 1113 7-9-0 113..........(v) ChristopheSoumillon 4 98
(Saeed bin Suroor) *nvr bttr than mid-div* **16/1**
8 2 1/4 **Desert Encounter (IRE)**21 1113 7-9-0 117..................(h) JimCrowley 8 95
(David Simcock) *s.i.s: a in rr* **25/1**

2m 27.17s (-4.63) **Going Correction** +0.15s/f (Good)
WFA 4 from 5yo+ 1lb **8 Ran SP% 114.1**
Speed ratings: **121,120,119,114,114 112,111,109**
CSF: 31.53; TRICAST: 196.70.
Owner Godolphin **Bred** Godolphin **Trained** Newmarket, Suffolk

FOCUS
They appeared to go a solid enough gallop and the winner showed himself to be well up to competing in the top middle-distance races this year. No Trakus data available. The level is set around the second and third.

1447a DUBAI WORLD CUP SPONSORED BY EMIRATES AIRLINE (GROUP 1) (DIRT) 1m 2f (D)
4:40 (4:40) 3-Y-O+
£5,669,291 (£1,889,763; £944,881; £472,440; £283,464; £188,976)

RPR
1 **Thunder Snow (IRE)**21 1114 5-9-0 122........(p) ChristopheSoumillon 11 119
(Saeed bin Suroor) *trckd ldr: rdn 3f out: led 1/2f out: r.o wl* **4/1**3
2 nse **Gronkowski (USA)**21 1114 4-9-0 111..........................(bt) OisinMurphy 7 119
(S bin Ghadayer, UAE) *trckd ldr: led 2f out: hdd 1/2f out but r.o wl* **28/1**
3 2 3/4 **Gunnevera (USA)**63 445 5-9-0 119......................(vt) EmisaelJaramillo 1 114
(Antonio Sano, U.S.A) *mid-div: r.o wl fnl 2f: nrst fin* **12/1**
4 1/2 **Pavel (USA)**56 5-9-0 115...(vt) JoelRosario 6 113
(Doug O'Neill, U.S.A) *mid-div: r.o same pce fnl 3f* **40/1**
5 shd **Audible (USA)**63 445 4-9-0 120... FlavienPrat 4 112
(Todd Pletcher, U.S.A) *mid-div: r.o wl fnl 2 1/2f: nrst fin* **12/1**
6 1 3/4 **Yoshida (JPN)**63 444 5-9-0 120...................................... JoseLOrtiz 10 109
(William Mott, U.S.A) *s.i.s: nvr nr to chal but r.o fnl 2 1/2f* **10/1**
7 2 1/2 **North America**51 638 7-9-0 118...................................(t) RichardMullen 3 104
(S Seemar, UAE) *wl away: sn led: hdd 2f out: wknd fnl 1 1/2f* **3/1**2
8 hd **Seeking The Soul (USA)**63 445 6-9-0 115.................(t) MikeESmith 5 103
(Dallas Stewart, U.S.A) *nvr bttr than mid-div* **8/1**
9 nk **Axelrod (USA)**21 1112 4-9-0 110..................................(b) RoystonFfrench 8 103
(S bin Ghadayer, UAE) *nvr bttr than mid-div* **66/1**
10 1 1/4 **New Trails (USA)**21 1114 5-9-0 111.............................(vt) ConnorBeasley 9 100
(A bin Harmash, UAE) *nvr bttr than mid-div* **50/1**
11 6 **Dolkong (USA)**21 1114 5-9-0 110.................................. OlivierDoleuze 12 88
(Simon Foster, Korea) *s.i.s: a in rr* **50/1**
12 17 **Capezzano (USA)**21 1114 5-9-0 118............................(h) MickaelBarzalona 2 54
(S bin Ghadayer, UAE) *trckd ldrs: n.m.r after 1f: wknd 3f out* **2/1**1

2m 3.87s (-0.83) **Going Correction** +0.325s/f (Slow) **12 Ran SP% 125.2**
Speed ratings: **116,115,113,113,113 111,109,109,109,108 103,90**
CSF: 121.92; TRICAST: 1,279.59; PLACEPOT: £365.70 to a £1 stake. Pool: £12,448.90 - 24.85 winning units. QUADPOT: £15.50 to a £1 stake. Pool: £1,317.20 - 62.80 winning units..
Owner Godolphin **Bred** Darley **Trained** Newmarket, Suffolk

FOCUS
Prize money was up $2M for a total purse of $12M. It wasn't a strong race form-wise but there were some solid, closely matched runners so it was competitive, with a thrilling finish, and Thunder Snow edged it to create a bit of history. Although not the most naturally talented winner in this race's 24-year history, he became the first horse to win it twice and is a good, thoroughly admirable campaigner. The anticipated speed duel between North America and Capezzano failed to materialise, and the pace looked to slacken early in the back straight, before the race really got going again into the final turn, so it paid to be close up. The second has been rated back to his Belmont Stakes level.

1347 SAINT-CLOUD (L-H)
Saturday, March 30

OFFICIAL GOING: Turf: good

1448a PRIX DU DEBUT (MAIDEN) (UNRACED 2YO) (TURF) 4f 110y
1:10 2-Y-O **£12,162** (£4,864; £3,648; £2,432; £1,216)

RPR
1 **Brand New Day (IRE)** 2-8-13 0.............................. AntoineHamelin 11 80
(Matthieu Palussiere, France) **61/10**3
2 nk **Kenway (FR)** 2-9-2 0... FranckBlondel 3 82
(F Rossi, France) **41/5**
3 3 1/2 **Charlemaine (IRE)** 2-9-2 0.. OlivierPeslier 2 68+
(Paul Cole) *prom: nudged along briefly bef 1/2-way: pushed along 1 1/2f out: r.o under hands and heels ins fnl f: nt match front pair* **42/10**2
4 1 1/4 **Galloon (FR)** 2-9-2 0... TheoBachelot 1 63
(Y Barberot, France) **17/1**
5 2 1/2 **Goldmembers (FR)** 2-9-2 0.. AlexandreGavilan 9 53
(D Guillemin, France) **12/5**1
6 2 **Digosville (FR)** 2-8-13 0.. CristianDemuro 10 42
(F-H Graffard, France) **32/5**
7 1 1/4 **Autumn (FR)** 2-9-2 0.. LukasDelozier 8 40
(Henk Grewe, Germany) **14/1**

8 1 1/4 **Milos (FR)** 2-8-13 0 Pierre-CharlesBoudot 6 32
(H-A Pantall, France) **61/10[3]**
9 3/4 **Picnic Boreal (FR)** 2-8-13 0 JeromeMoutard[(3)] 7 32
(D Allard, France) **31/1**
10 3 **Tinalixa (FR)** 2-8-13 0 SylvainRuis 4 17
(C Plisson, France) **39/1**
52.64s **10 Ran SP% 119.0**
PARI-MUTUEL (all including 1 euro stake): WIN 7.10; PLACE 2.50, 2.90, 2.10; DF 26.10.
Owner Mrs Theresa Marnane **Bred** Con Marnane **Trained** France

1449a PRIX DES LANDES (H'CAP) (4YO) (TURF) 1m
2:25 4-Y-O
£23,423 (£8,900; £6,558; £3,747; £1,873; £1,405)

RPR
1 **Billabong Cat (FR)**[45] 4-9-11 0 TonyPiccone 7 96
(F Vermeulen, France) **101/10**
2 3 **Qatar Bolt**[16] 4-8-13 0 OlivierPeslier 1 77
(H-A Pantall, France) **74/10**
3 snk **Land Of Mind**[16] 4-9-2 0 StephanePasquier 2 80
(M Delcher Sanchez, France) **66/10[3]**
4 hd **For Ever Fun (FR)**[16] 4-8-9 0 TheoBachelot 6 72
(L Gadbin, France) **10/1**
5 hd **Fairy Tale (IRE)**[107] 9584 4-9-4 0 Pierre-CharlesBoudot 17 81
(Gay Kelleway) *broke wl fr wd draw: prom: drvn to chse ldrs ins fnl 2f: styd on at same pce fnl f* **16/1**
6 nk **Irish Emperor (IRE)**[247] 4-9-3 0 MaximeGuyon 5 79
(Mme Pia Brandt, France) **13/2[2]**
7 2 1/2 **Hautot (FR)**[86] 4-9-1 0 AntoineHamelin 9 71
(Gerald Geisler, Germany) **35/1**
8 1 1/4 **Barodar (FR)**[16] 4-8-13 0 EddyHardouin 4 67
(T Lemer, France) **57/10[1]**
9 1 1/2 **Nosdargent (FR)**[107] 4-9-0 0 HugoJourniac 11 64
(D & P Prod'Homme, France) **14/1**
10 1 1/2 **El Indio (FR)**[130] 4-8-13 0 RonanThomas 15 60
(H-A Pantall, France) **39/1**
11 hd **Latinius (FR)**[46] 4-8-9 0 MlleMickaelleMichel 10 55
(J-M Beguigne, France) **15/1**
12 nse **Alets (FR)**[227] 4-8-10 0 IoritzMendizabal 18 56
(J Reynier, France) **26/1**
13 hd **Epouville (FR)**[46] 4-9-5 0 CristianDemuro 3 65
(F Vermeulen, France) **24/1**
14 5 **Moses (FR)**[130] 4-8-9 0 (p) ClementLecoeuvre 14 43
(Mario Hofer, Germany) **53/1**
15 1 1/2 **Park Tower (FR)**[127] 4-8-13 0 VincentCheminaud 12 44
(H-A Pantall, France) **16/1**
16 shd **Lorraynio (FR)**[16] 4-8-9 0 FranckBlondel 13 39
(C Lerner, France) **20/1**
17 10 **Vicopisano (FR)**[46] 4-9-3 0 (b) JackyNicoleau 8 24
(B Legros, France) **53/1**
18 nk **Unguja (FR)**[43] 4-8-10 0 AnthonyCrastus 16 17
(E Lyon, France) **46/1**
1m 39.47s (-8.03) **18 Ran SP% 119.7**
PARI-MUTUEL (all including 1 euro stake): WIN 11.10; PLACE 3.80, 3.10, 2.70; DF 49.30.
Owner Ecurie Ammonites Racing SAS **Bred** B Van Dalfsen & M Perret **Trained** France

1450a PRIX SUAVE DANCER (MAIDEN) (UNRACED 3YO COLTS & GELDINGS) (TURF) 1m 2f
3:00 3-Y-O **£11,261** (£4,504; £3,378; £2,252; £1,126)

RPR
1 **Rudimental (FR)** 3-9-2 0 GregoryBenoist 13 82
(C Lerner, France) **125/10**
2 nk **Ballet Russe (IRE)** 3-9-2 0 Pierre-CharlesBoudot 1 81
(A Fabre, France) *racd keenly: hld up towards rr on inner: sn plld way to chse ldng gp: restrained in midfield bef 1/2-way: clsd last 2f: r.o u.p fnl f: wnt 2nd cl home* **19/5[2]**
3 1/2 **Le Mont (FR)** 3-9-2 0 CristianDemuro 4 80
(P Bary, France) **19/10[1]**
4 4 1/2 **Kaiser Soze (FR)** 3-9-2 0 PierreBazire 2 71
(G Botti, France) **27/1**
5 1 3/4 **Boreas (IRE)** 3-9-2 0 StephanePasquier 9 68
(A Fabre, France) **39/10[3]**
6 2 **Strike Bomber (FR)** 3-9-2 0 TonyPiccone 12 64
(Andrea Marcialis, France) **38/1**
7 1 3/4 **Rock At The Park (FR)** 3-9-2 0 (p) VincentCheminaud 10 60
(H-A Pantall, France) **13/1**
8 snk **Suman (FR)** 3-9-2 0 TheoBachelot 5 60
(Rod Collet, France) **27/1**
9 1 **Daligar (FR)** 3-8-7 0 MlleMarieVelon[(9)] 7 58
(A De Royer-Dupre, France) **74/10**
10 1 1/4 **Lord Spirit (FR)** 3-8-13 0 AlexandreChesneau[(3)] 14 56
(T Castanheira, France) **83/1**
11 8 **Flight Command (FR)** 3-9-2 0 ClementLecoeuvre 3 40
(Mme M Bollack-Badel, France) **27/1**
12 10 **Hawk Cliff (FR)** 3-9-2 0 OlivierPeslier 11 20
(Jo Hughes, France) *dwlt: sn rcvrd to chse ldng gp on outer: 5th and drvn w 3f to run: sn lost pl: wl hld whn eased ins fnl f* **36/1**
2m 11.81s (-4.19) **12 Ran SP% 119.4**
PARI-MUTUEL (all including 1 euro stake): WIN 13.50; PLACE 2.50, 1.80, 1.30; DF 31.00.
Owner Ecurie Haras Du Cadran, Ecurie Patrick Klein & C & **Bred** Ecurie Haras Du Cadran, J-L Burgat & Ecurie Patric **Trained** France

1451a PRIX EDMOND BLANC (GROUP 3) (4YO+) (TURF) 1m
4:55 4-Y-O+ **£36,036** (£14,414; £10,810; £7,207; £3,603)

RPR
1 **The Revenant**[20] 1127 4-9-0 0 (h) OlivierPeslier 5 111
(F-H Graffard, France) *t.k.h: hld up in fnl trio: 3 l off pce and pushed along 2f out: styng on whn rdn ent fnl f: r.o to ld cl home* **3/1[3]**
2 hd **Graphite (FR)**[25] 1027 5-9-2 0 Pierre-CharlesBoudot 3 113
(A Fabre, France) *led: drvn over 2f out: r.o fnl f: hdd cl home* **9/5[1]**
3 snk **Lunch Lady**[97] 9689 4-8-10 0 MaximeGuyon 4 107
(F Head, France) *chsd ldr outside rival: drvn wl over 2f out and sn pressed ldr: rdn and nt qckn 1 1/2f out: styd on fnl f but nt quite match first two home* **23/5**
4 1 **Olmedo (FR)**[265] 4721 4-9-0 0 CristianDemuro 6 108
(J-C Rouget, France) *racd keenly: hld up in rr: drvn to cl 1 1/2f out: styd on ins fnl f: nt pce to get on terms w ldrs* **5/2[2]**
5 1 1/4 **Crown Walk**[175] 8006 4-8-13 0 VincentCheminaud 1 104
(H-A Pantall, France) *chsd ldr on inner: drvn to hold pl 2f out: n.m.r briefly 1 1/2f fr home: dropped away ins fnl f* **10/1**
6 3 1/2 **Schang (GER)**[153] 6-9-0 0 JaromirSafar 2 97
(P Vovcenko, Germany) *plld hrd: hld up in fnl pair: rdn but no imp 1 1/2f out: eased whn btn fnl f* **39/1**
1m 41.73s (-5.77) **6 Ran SP% 118.7**
PARI-MUTUEL (all including 1 euro stake): WIN 4.00; PLACE 2.00, 1.70; SF 11.00.
Owner Al Asayl France **Bred** Al Asayl Bloodstock Ltd **Trained** France
FOCUS
They went steady early and it resulted in a bit of a bunched finish.

1452 - 1456a (Foreign Racing) - See Raceform Interactive

[1412]DONCASTER (L-H)
Sunday, March 31

OFFICIAL GOING: Straight course - good to firm (good in places); round course - good (good to firm in places)
Wind: Moderate half behind Weather: Cloudy

1457 32RED.COM H'CAP 7f 6y
2:00 (2:00) (Class 4) (0-85,84) 4-Y-O+
£5,530 (£1,645; £822; £411; £400; £400) **Stalls** Centre

Form RPR
343- 1 **Right Action**[145] 8898 5-9-4 **81** SilvestreDeSousa 8 86
(Richard Fahey) *cl up: rdn to ld over 1f out: drvn out* **7/1[2]**
054- 2 1/2 **Saluti (IRE)**[160] 8472 5-9-4 **81** (w) OisinMurphy 19 85
(Paul Midgley) *cl up: effrt to chal wl over 1f out: sn rdn: ev ch ent fnl f: sn drvn and kpt on* **8/1[3]**
022- 3 1/2 **Queen's Sargent (FR)**[145] 8898 4-9-5 **82** ShaneGray 15 85
(Kevin Ryan) *trckd ldrs: hdwy over 2f out: rdn over 1f out: kpt on fnl f* **7/1[2]**
256- 4 nk **Queen Penn**[149] 8809 4-9-0 **77** (p) PaulHanagan 10 79
(Richard Fahey) *trckd ldrs: hdwy 3f out: cl up 2f out: sn rdn: drvn and kpt on same pce fnl f* **20/1**
413- 5 nk **Buccaneers Vault (IRE)**[152] 8719 7-9-2 **82** BenRobinson[(3)] 9 83
(Paul Midgley) *hld up in midfield: hdwy over 2f out: rdn wl over 1f out: kpt on fnl f* **33/1**
040- 6 1/2 **Proud Archi (IRE)**[141] 8999 5-9-5 **82** PaulMulrennan 1 82
(Michael Dods) *in tch on inner: hdwy to chse ldrs over 2f out: rdn wl over 1f out: kpt on same pce fnl f* **16/1**
/0-0 7 nk **Valley Of Fire**[88] 24 7-8-9 **72** (p) DavidAllan 20 71
(Les Eyre) *hld up towards rr: hdwy 2f out: rdn over 1f out: styd on wl fnl f* **50/1**
160- 8 shd **Start Time (IRE)**[162] 8415 6-9-2 **79** KevinStott 14 78
(Paul Midgley) *trckd ldrs: hdwy over 2f out: rdn and ev ch over 1f out: drvn ent fnl f: grad wknd* **16/1**
045- 9 shd **Theodorico (IRE)**[238] 5777 6-9-5 **82** BenCurtis 18 80
(David Loughnane) *led: rdn along over 2f out: drvn and hdd over 1f out: grad wknd* **16/1**
660- 10 3/4 **Magic City (IRE)**[162] 8415 10-8-4 **74** JoshQuinn[(7)] 4 70
(Michael Easterby) *dwlt and in rr tl styd on fnl 2f (jockey said gelding was denied a clear run in the closing stages)* **28/1**
260- 11 1/2 **Courtside (FR)**[155] 8640 4-9-3 **80** DanielTudhope 21 75
(David O'Meara) *hld up towards rr: hdwy over 2f out: rdn along and edgd lft over 1f out: sn no imp (jockey said gelding hung left from 3 furlongs out)* **13/2[1]**
1210 12 3/4 **Portledge (IRE)**[20] 1143 5-9-5 **82** (b) PJMcDonald 2 75
(James Bethell) *chsd ldrs: rdn along wl over 2f out: sn wknd* **14/1**
105- 13 1 **Explain**[162] 8415 7-8-12 **75** (p) JamesSullivan 3 65
(Ruth Carr) *in tch: pushed along 3f out: rdn over 2f out: edgd rt and wknd over 1f out* **33/1**
14 nk **First Response**[149] 8813 4-9-3 **80** TonyHamilton 12 69
(Linda Stubbs) *hld up in rr: hdwy over 2f out: rdn along and styng on whn n.m.r and hmpd jst over 1f out: bhd after* **33/1**
530- 15 hd **Highlight Reel (IRE)**[121] 9324 4-9-6 **83** LewisEdmunds 22 72
(Rebecca Bastiman) *in tch on outer: hdwy 3f out: rdn along over 2f out: sn wknd* **33/1**
4242 16 1 1/4 **Esprit De Corps**[31] 952 5-8-11 **74** AndreaAtzeni 7 60
(David Barron) *dwlt: a towards rr* **8/1[3]**
205- 17 3/4 **Prevent**[190] 7538 4-9-3 **80** JamesDoyle 17 63
(Ian Williams) *a towards rr* **10/1**
600- 18 nk **Mutafarrid (IRE)**[157] 8580 4-9-4 **81** GrahamLee 16 64
(Paul Midgley) *chsd ldrs: rdn along 3f out: sn wknd* **20/1**
2-10 19 nk **Capriolette (IRE)**[43] 756 4-9-4 **81** LiamKeniry 5 63
(Ed Walker) *in tch: rdn along 3f: wknd over 2f out* **14/1**
1m 24.08s (-2.32) **Going Correction** -0.175s/f (Firm) **19 Ran SP% 127.3**
Speed ratings (Par 105): **106,105,104,104,104 103,103,103,103,102 101,100,99,99,99 97,96,96,96**
CSF £57.29 CT £431.75 TOTE £6.20: £1.70, £2.50, £2.30, £4.10; EX 39.00 Trifecta £122.30.
Owner Middleham Park Racing LVII & Partner **Bred** Aunty Ifl **Trained** Musley Bank, N Yorks
FOCUS
All distances as advertised. The dry weather produced in fast going and resulted in a plethora of non-runners. The jockeys said the ground was on the quick side of good, which was backed up by the time. A fair handicap, but comprising a large field and very competitive, but it paid to race close to the pace.

1458 UNIBET NOVICE STKS 7f 6y
2:35 (2:35) (Class 5) 3-Y-O **£3,752** (£1,116; £557; £278) **Stalls** Centre

Form RPR
21- 1 **Fox Champion (IRE)**[159] 8496 3-9-9 0 SilvestreDeSousa 12 93
(Richard Hannon) *mde all: rdn along 2f out: drvn and edgd rt ent fnl f: kpt on wl towards fin* **9/4[1]**
36- 2 1/2 **Franz Kafka (IRE)**[156] 8608 3-9-2 0 KieranO'Neill 6 85
(John Gosden) *trckd ldrs: hdwy over 2f out: chsd ldng pair whn swtchd rt over 1f out: sn rdn: styd on to chal whn n.m.r jst ins fnl f: sn ev ch: kpt on* **11/4[2]**
1- 3 4 **Cool Exhibit**[313] 2956 3-9-9 0 (v[1]) OisinMurphy 9 81
(Simon Crisford) *prom: effrt and cl up 2f out: rdn over 1f out: hld whn carried sltly rt jst ins fnl f: kpt on same pce* **6/1**
4 3/4 **Double Honour** 3-9-2 0 PJMcDonald 11 72
(James Bethell) *dwlt: green and towards rr: hdwy 4f out: rdn along 2f out: styd on wl appr fnl f* **33/1**

5 1 1/2 **Kodi King (IRE)** 3-9-2 0 CliffordLee 3 68
(K R Burke) *cl up: rdn along over 2f out: drvn wl over 1f out: grad wknd* 25/1

6 1 3/4 **Country** 3-9-2 0 JamesDoyle 4 63
(William Haggas) *hld up towards rr: hdwy over 2f out: sn rdn and n.d* 7/2[3]

5 7 1 1/2 **Menina Atrevida**[30] 971 3-8-11 0 JasonHart 8 54
(Ivan Furtado) *dwlt: a towards rr* 66/1

2 8 1/2 **Conaglen**[41] 785 3-9-2 0 PaulHanagan 5 58
(James Bethell) *green in rr and pushed along 1/2-way: kpt on fnl 2f: nvr nr ldrs* 8/1

04 9 3 1/4 **Guiding Spirit (IRE)**[43] 752 3-9-2 0 AdamKirby 2 49
(Clive Cox) *chsd ldrs: rdn along wl over 2f out: sn wknd* 50/1

00- 10 4 **Preservation**[218] 6534 3-8-8 0 RowanScott(3) 1 33
(Jedd O'Keeffe) *a towards rr: outpcd and bhd fnl 2f* 100/1

1m 24.25s (-2.15) **Going Correction** -0.175s/f (Firm) **10** Ran SP% **116.3**
Speed ratings (Par 98): **105,104,99,99,97 95,93,93,89,84**
CSF £8.32 TOTE £2.70: £1.10, £1.10, £2.40; EX 10.40 Trifecta £25.30.
Owner King Power Racing Co Ltd **Bred** Con Marnane **Trained** East Everleigh, Wilts

FOCUS
A decent looking 3yo novice contest run just 0.17secs slower than the opening handicap. The market leaders had it between them in the last furlong.

1459 32RED H'CAP 6f 2y
3:10 (3:10) (Class 3) (0-95,95) 4-Y-0+ **£7,762** (£2,310; £1,154; £577) **Stalls** Centre

Form RPR

2240 1 **Foolaad**[22] 1105 8-9-7 95 (t) LiamKeniry 8 102
(Roy Bowring) *mde all: rdn and edgd lft over 1f out: drvn and edgd sltly rt wl ins fnl f: hld on gamely* 20/1

400- 2 shd **Danielsflyer (IRE)**[141] 9004 5-9-1 89 AndrewMullen 18 96
(Michael Dods) *in rr: hdwy 2f out: rdn over 1f out: str run ins fnl f: jst failed* 10/1

553- 3 hd **Jawwaal**[177] 7948 4-8-13 87 PaulMulrennan 5 93
(Michael Dods) *trckd ldrs: hdwy 2f out: rdn along and cl up whn sltly hmpd over 1f out: drvn and ev ch ins fnl f: kpt on* 14/1

500- 4 1/2 **Green Power**[177] 7950 4-9-7 95 AndreaAtzeni 6 100
(John Gallagher) *cl up: rdn along wl over 1f out: drvn and ev ch ent fnl f: sn edgd lft and kpt on* 12/1

020- 5 shd **Louie De Palma**[155] 8641 7-9-1 89 AdamKirby 13 93
(Clive Cox) *trckd ldrs: hdwy 2f out: rdn and ev ch over 1f out: drvn ins fnl f: kpt on same pce towards fin* 13/2[2]

305- 6 1 1/2 **Tommy Taylor (USA)**[169] 8194 5-9-7 95 TomEaves 17 95
(Kevin Ryan) *dwlt and in rr: gd hdwy 2f out: rdn over 1f out: kpt on wl fnl f: nrst fin* 10/1

140- 7 nk **Buridan (FR)**[237] 5800 4-9-4 92 RyanMoore 10 91
(Richard Hannon) *chsd ldrs: rdn along wl over 1f out: kpt on same pce fnl f* 7/1[3]

400- 8 1/2 **Naadirr (IRE)**[169] 8194 8-9-6 94 (v w) KevinStott 22 91
(Kevin Ryan) *dwlt: bhd and swtchd lft sn after s: hdwy 2f out: swtchd rt and rdn over 1f out: styd on wl towards fin* 12/1

220- 9 shd **Gabrial The Devil (IRE)**[191] 7481 4-9-1 89 PaulHanagan 2 86
(Richard Fahey) *in tch on inner: rdn along 2f out: kpt on same pce appr fnl f* 16/1

106- 10 1 3/4 **Captain Jameson (IRE)**[141] 8999 4-9-1 89 JasonHart 21 80
(John Quinn) *chsd ldrs towards outer: rdn along over 2f out: wknd over 1f out* 9/1

102- 11 3/4 **Von Blucher (IRE)**[156] 8594 6-9-3 91 (p) PJMcDonald 19 80
(Rebecca Menzies) *in tch on outer: hdwy wl over 2f out: rdn wl over 1f out: sn drvn and btn* 9/1

560- 12 1 **Ower Fly**[183] 7781 6-9-0 88 JamesSullivan 14 74
(Ruth Carr) *chsd ldrs: rdn along 2f out: sn wknd* 25/1

400- 13 1/2 **Quick Look**[155] 8632 6-8-12 86 NathanEvans 4 70
(Michael Easterby) *trckd ldrs on inner: rdn along over 2f out: sn wknd* 33/1

050- 14 1/2 **Upstaging**[155] 8641 7-8-10 84 (p) BarryMcHugh 7 66
(Noel Wilson) *chsd ldrs centre: rdn along 2f out: drvn and wknd over 1f out* 50/1

01-5 15 16 **How Far (IRE)**[66] 382 4-9-5 93 SilvestreDeSousa 11 24
(Simon Crisford) *in tch: rdn along wl over 2f out: sn wknd (jockey said colt was never travelling)* 6/1[1]

324- 16 2 1/4 **Boy In The Bar**[90] 9772 8-8-10 84 (p) JosephineGordon 3 8
(Ian Williams) *towards rr: rdn along 1/2-way: sn outpcd and bhd* 25/1

030- 17 1 **Penwortham (IRE)**[197] 7288 6-9-0 88 TonyHamilton 15 9
(Richard Fahey) *a in rr: bhd fr over 2f out* 50/1

1m 10.3s (-2.40) **Going Correction** -0.175s/f (Firm) **17** Ran SP% **125.6**
Speed ratings (Par 107): **109,108,108,107,107 105,105,104,104,102 101,99,99,98,77 74,72**
CSF £201.70 CT £3013.55 TOTE £24.70: £4.00, £3.60, £3.60, £3.70; EX 287.20 Trifecta £3800.20.
Owner K Nicholls **Bred** Darley **Trained** Edwinstowe, Notts
■ Stewards' Enquiry : Liam Keniry caution: careless riding

FOCUS
Another strong, very competitive, sprint handicap and it produced a blanket finish. Most of those involved were in the leading group throughout.

1460 UNIBET CONDITIONS STKS 1m 3f 197y
3:45 (3:45) (Class 2) 4-Y-0+ **£12,938** (£3,850; £1,924; £962) **Stalls** Low

Form RPR

500- 1 **Red Verdon (USA)**[112] 9473 6-9-5 110 (b) RyanMoore 1 107
(Ed Dunlop) *trckd ldng pair on inner: hdwy 2f out: rdn over 1f out: led jst ins fnl f: kpt on strly towards fin* 5/2[2]

0- 2 2 1/4 **Indianapolis (IRE)**[129] 9200 4-9-2 96 BarryMcHugh 3 102
(James Given) *hld up: hdwy on outer 3f out: swtchd lft wl over 1f out: sn rdn: drvn fnl f: kpt on wl towards fin* 50/1

25-0 3 nk **Crowned Eagle**[22] 1113 5-9-5 108 DanielMuscutt 6 103
(Marco Botti) *led: pushed along and qcknd over 3f out: rdn over 2f out: drvn over 1f out: hdd jst ins fnl f: kpt on same pce* 5/1[3]

/10- 4 nk **Willie John**[190] 7567 4-9-2 95 AndreaAtzeni 2 101
(Roger Varian) *trckd ldr: hdwy over 3f out: chal wl over 2f out: rdn along and edgd rt wl over 1f out: drvn and ev ch ent fnl f: kpt on same pce* 10/11[1]

040/ 5 3 **Tamleek (USA)**[606] 5525 5-9-3 98 DanielTudhope 4 95
(David O'Meara) *trckd ldng pair on outer: hdwy over 3f out: rdn along over 2f out: drvn wl over 1f out: grad wknd* 16/1

166- 6 7 **Sir Chauvelin**[197] 7285 7-9-5 106 PaulMulrennan 5 86
(Jim Goldie) *hld up in rr: pushed along over 3f out: rdn over 2f out: nvr a factor* 18/1

2m 34.88s (-1.72) **Going Correction** -0.175s/f (Firm)
WFA 4 from 5yo+ 1lb **6** Ran SP% **110.7**
Speed ratings (Par 109): **98,96,96,96,94 89**
CSF £76.58 TOTE £3.70: £1.80, £9.30; EX 63.90 Trifecta £192.10.
Owner The Hon R J Arculli **Bred** Liberty Road Stables **Trained** Newmarket, Suffolk
■ Stewards' Enquiry : Andrea Atzeni two-day ban: used whip in the incorrect place (Apr 15-16)

FOCUS
The going was officially Good, good to firm in places on the round course, so not quite as fast as the straight track. The feature race and a classy conditions stakes, but the market concerned only three.

1461 32RED CASINO H'CAP 1m 2f 43y
4:20 (4:20) (Class 4) (0-85,87) 4-Y-0+
£5,530 (£1,645; £822; £411; £400; £400) **Stalls** Low

Form RPR

600- 1 **Stonific (IRE)**[160] 8476 6-9-1 79 DanielTudhope 17 87
(David O'Meara) *stdd s and hld up in rr: hdwy over 2f out: swtchd rt to outer and str run to ld jst over 1f out: sn rdn and edgd lft: styd on* 14/1

360- 2 1 **Employer (IRE)**[173] 8095 4-9-3 81 PhilDennis 13 87
(Jim Goldie) *hld up in rr: hdwy over 2f out: nt clr run and swtchd rt over 1f out: rdn to chse wnr ins fnl f: sn drvn: edgd lft and kpt on same pce towards fin* 40/1

331- 3 1 1/4 **Hulcote**[212] 6755 4-9-5 83 AdamKirby 19 87
(Clive Cox) *in tch: hdwy over 2f out: nt clr run and hmpd over 1f out: sn swtchd rt and rdn: kpt on ins fnl f* 9/2[2]

066- 4 nk **Grandee (IRE)**[142] 8974 5-9-3 81 BenCurtis 2 84
(Roger Fell) *trckd clr ldr: hdwy on inner over 4f out: led 3f: rdn 2f out: sn drvn: hdd over 1f out: kpt on u.p fnl f* 6/1

004- 5 3/4 **Cote D'Azur**[145] 8899 6-9-9 87 DavidAllan 18 88
(Les Eyre) *hld up towards rr: hdwy 3f out: chsd ldrs 2f out: sn rdn and kpt on same pce fnl f* 25/1

202- 6 1/2 **Indomeneo**[186] 7672 4-9-2 85 SeanDavis(5) 8 85
(Richard Fahey) *trckd ldrs: hdwy 3f out: rdn along and n.m.r wl over 1f out: drvn and kpt on wl fnl f* 25/1

042- 7 1 3/4 **Shareef Star**[300] 3426 4-9-3 81 RyanMoore 9 78
(Sir Michael Stoute) *trckd ldrs on inner: effrt over 2f out: sn n.m.r and hmpd wl over 1f out: sn btn* 2/1[1]

410- 8 1 **Bacacarat (IRE)**[198] 7234 4-9-4 82 SilvestreDeSousa 14 77
(Andrew Balding) *trckd ldrs: hdwy 4f out: rdn along 3f out: drvn over 2f out: sn wknd* 11/2[3]

135- 9 1 1/4 **Mapped (USA)**[170] 8156 4-9-1 79 PJMcDonald 12 71
(Garry Moss) *chsd clr ldr: hdwy and cl up 4f out: rdn 3f out: drvn over 2f out: grad wknd* 22/1

320- 10 19 **Falmouth Light (FR)**[162] 8415 4-9-2 80 JoeFanning 5 34
(Iain Jardine) *plld hrd: sn led and clr: rdn along 4f out: hdd 3f out and sn wknd (jockey said gelding ran too free)* 14/1

200- 11 nk **Armandihan (IRE)**[160] 8476 5-9-6 84 (p) KevinStott 10 38
(Kevin Ryan) *trckd ldrs: hdwy 4f out: rdn along 3f out: sn drvn and wknd* 25/1

146- 12 6 **Delph Crescent (IRE)**[190] 7513 4-9-6 84 (p) PaulHanagan 15 26
(Richard Fahey) *chsd ldrs: rdn along over 3f out: sn wknd* 14/1

2m 8.44s (-3.86) **Going Correction** -0.175s/f (Firm) **12** Ran SP% **119.5**
Speed ratings (Par 105): **108,107,106,105,105 104,103,102,101,86 86,81**
CSF £491.81 CT £2910.87 TOTE £15.50: £3.90, £10.20, £1.70; EX 609.20 Trifecta £6325.50.
Owner Rasio Cymru 1 & Hurn Racing Club **Bred** Wertheimer & Frere **Trained** Upper Helmsley, N Yorks

FOCUS
This competitive handicap suffered from a mass of withdrawals. The early pace looked strong and the principals came from well back.

1462 UNIBET H'CAP 1m 2f 43y
4:55 (4:55) (Class 3) (0-95,83) 3-Y-O **£7,762** (£2,310; £1,154; £577) **Stalls** Low

Form RPR

021- 1 **Good Birthday (IRE)**[156] 8607 3-9-6 82 SilvestreDeSousa 8 89
(Andrew Balding) *hld up and bhd: stdy hdwy down wd outside 3f out: led 1 1/2f out: rdn and green ins fnl f: kpt on* 7/2[2]

6-11 2 1 3/4 **Red Bond (IRE)**[38] 826 3-9-2 78 OisinMurphy 4 81
(Keith Dalgleish) *sn led: rdn along over 2f out: drvn and hdd 1 1/2f out: kpt on wl u.p fnl f* 11/2

314- 3 3/4 **Guildhall**[163] 8372 3-9-2 78 HarryBentley 7 80
(Ralph Beckett) *hld up in tch: hdwy over 3f out: rdn along to chse ldrs 2f out: drvn over 1f out: kpt on fnl f* 10/3[1]

241- 4 3 1/4 **Mister Chiang**[101] 9637 3-9-3 79 FrannyNorton 2 74
(Mark Johnston) *chsd ldrs: rdn along wl over 2f out: drvn over 1f out: sn one pce* 11/2

426- 5 3 **Embrace The Moment (IRE)**[219] 6484 3-8-13 75 AndreaAtzeni 10 64
(Richard Hannon) *chsd ldr: rdn along 3f out: drvn over 2f out: sn wknd* 33/1

225- 6 2 3/4 **Venedegar (IRE)**[198] 7257 3-9-6 82 RyanMoore 6 66
(Ed Dunlop) *hld up in rr: hdwy 3f out: rdn along over 2f out: n.d* 5/1[3]

020- 7 1/2 **Al Suil Eile (FR)**[144] 8922 3-9-0 76 (t[1] w) JasonHart 5 59
(John Quinn) *chsd ldrs: rdn along 3f out: wknd 2f out* 18/1

316- 8 nk **Flying Dragon (FR)**[169] 8185 3-9-7 83 TomMarquand 1 65
(Richard Hannon) *dwlt and in rr: sme hdwy on inner 4f out: rdn along over 3f out: sn wknd* 9/1

254- 9 11 **Mrs Hoo (IRE)**[185] 7709 3-8-13 75 PaulHanagan 9 35
(Richard Fahey) *chsd ldrs: rdn along over 3f out: sn drvn and wknd* 25/1

2m 10.18s (-2.12) **Going Correction** -0.175s/f (Firm) **9** Ran SP% **114.8**
Speed ratings (Par 102): **101,99,99,96,94 91,91,91,82**
CSF £22.99 CT £68.71 TOTE £3.50: £1.10, £2.50, £1.90; EX 25.30 Trifecta £126.80.
Owner King Power Racing Co Ltd **Bred** Ecurie Normandie Pur Sang **Trained** Kingsclere, Hants

FOCUS
This decent 3yo handicap was run a fair bit slower than the preceding contest. That said, the form looks sound enough.

1463 32RED.COM AMATEUR RIDERS' H'CAP 1m 3f 197y
5:30 (5:30) (Class 5) (0-70,72) 4-Y-O+
£3,618 (£1,122; £560; £400; £400; £400) **Stalls** Low

Form RPR

4 1 **Extreme Appeal (IRE)**[4] 1361 7-9-7 56 oh4 (p) MissAntoniaPeck(7) 17 62
(Kelly Morgan) *prom: cl up over 4f out: rdn to ld 1 1/2f out: kpt on wl fnl f* 11/1

531- **2** ¾ **Cristal Spirit**[159] 8500 4-10-12 **69**.......................... MrSimonWalker 13 73
(George Baker) *midfield: reminders 4f out: rdn along 3f out: drvn over 1f out: fin strly* **7/2**[1]

4646 **3** *hd* **Makambe (IRE)**[4] 1363 4-10-3 **67**................ MissChelseaBanham(7) 18 70
(Paul Howling) *bhd: hdwy on outer 4f out: pushed along and edgd lft over 2f out: chsd ldrs: rdn along and hung lft over 1f out: ev ch ent fnl f: kpt on same pce* **12/1**

214- **4** *shd* **Grandscape**[144] 8936 4-10-9 **71**.......................... SophieSmith(5) 3 74
(Ed Dunlop) *hld up towards rr: hdwy on outer over 3f out: rdn along 2f out: chsd ldrs over 1f out: kpt on fnl f* **11/1**

1000 **5** *hd* **Belabour**[31] 946 6-10-6 **62**.......................... MissBeckyBrisbourne 11 65
(Mark Brisbourne) *bhd: hdwy on wd outside over 3f out: rdn along 2f out: styd on wl fnl f: nrst fin* **33/1**

/06- **6** ½ **Nabhan**[132] 7337 7-10-7 **70**...................(tp) MissJessicaLlewellyn(7) 19 72
(Bernard Llewellyn) *trckd ldrs: hdwy over 4f out: cl up 3f out: rdn and ev ch 2f out: grad wknd fnl f* **66/1**

2-52 **7** 2 **Country'N'Western (FR)**[27] 703 7-10-11 **72**.(h[1]) MrGeorgeEddery(5) 16 71
(Robert Eddery) *hld up towards rr: hdwy 4f out: chsd ldrs 3f out: rdn along over 2f out: drvn and hld whn n.m.r and hmpd over 1f out* **8/1**[2]

6-03 **8** 1½ **Gravity Wave (IRE)**[60] 481 5-10-3 **66**......(p[1]) MissImogenMathias(7) 23 63
(John Flint) *prom: led after 4f: rdn along 3f out: hdd 1 1/2f out: grad wknd* **20/1**

000- **9** 1½ **Place Des Vosges (IRE)**[152] 8726 4-9-13 **59**.......(t[1]) MrDavidTurner(3) 5 54
(David Menuisier) *midfield: hdwy to chse ldrs over 3f out: rdn along over 2f out: sn no imp* **20/1**

5-45 **10** 4½ **Take Two**[20] 1144 10-10-7 **70**.......................... MrJamieBrace(7) 12 57
(Alex Hales) *cl up: disp ld 3f out: rdn along over 2f out: wknd wl over 1f out* **12/1**

125- **11** 1¾ **Ascot Day (FR)**[145] 8894 5-10-5 **64**.................(p) MissHannahWelch(3) 6 48
(Bernard Llewellyn) *chsd ldrs: rdn along over 2f out: grad wknd* **9/1**[3]

-046 **12** 1½ **Butterfield (IRE)**[39] 810 6-9-8 **57**.......................... MissSarahBowen(7) 2 39
(Tony Carroll) *prom: pushed along over 5f out: rdn along 4f out: sn wknd* **10/1**

250- **13** 10 **Master Grey (IRE)**[174] 8054 4-10-4 **61**.......................... MrPatrickMillman 21 28
(Rod Millman) *trckd ldrs: hdwy and cl up over 4f out: rdn along 3f out: wknd over 2f out* **8/1**[2]

0405 **14** 9 **Attain**[6] 1333 10-10-3 **59**.......................... MissBrodieHampson 10 10
(Archie Watson) *in tch: rdn along over 3f out: sn wknd* **22/1**

20-3 **15** ½ **Punkawallah**[62] 457 5-10-5 **68**..................(p) MrTambyWelch(7) 1 19
(Alexandra Dunn) *a in rr (jockey said gelding was never travelling; vet reported the gelding had bled from the nose)* **20/1**

04-5 **16** 4½ **Luv U Whatever**[46] 703 9-10-11 **67**.......................... MissBeckySmith 20 10
(Marjorie Fife) *led 4f: chsd ldrs: rdn along and lost pl over 4f out: sn bhd* **12/1**

60-0 **17** 23 **Scottsdale**[6] 1334 6-9-7 **56** oh1.......................... MissLaurenSanders(7) 7
(Peter Winks) *a in rr: bhd fnl 4f* **100/1**

2m 34.81s (-1.79) **Going Correction** -0.175s/f (Firm) **17 Ran SP% 127.3**
WFA 4 from 5yo+ 1lb
Speed ratings (Par 103): **98,97,97,97,97 96,95,94,93,90 89,88,81,75,75 72,57**
CSF £47.11 CT £497.53 TOTE £11.50: £3.00, £1.10, £4.20, £2.60; EX 54.80 Trifecta £727.00.
Owner J R Weatherby **Bred** D Wachman & M Nolan **Trained** Witchcote, Leics
■ Stewards' Enquiry : Miss Becky Brisbourne seven-day ban (reduced from 14 on appeal): insufficient effort to obtain best possible placing (Apr 28-29, May 11, 28, Jun 1, 6-7)

FOCUS
A big field for this modest amateur riders' handicap and it appeared they went too quickly, as apart from the winner the principals came from well back. The level is set around the third and fourth.
T/Jkpt: Not won. T/Plt: £343.40 to a £1 stake. Pool: £136,771.55 - 290.68 winning units T/Qpdt: £148.10 to a £1 stake. Pool: £11494.57 - 57.40 winning units **Joe Rowntree**

1464 - 1474a (Foreign Racing) - See Raceform Interactive

1378

CHELMSFORD (A.W) (L-H)

Monday, April 1

OFFICIAL GOING: Polytrack: standard
Wind: light, across Weather: sunny and bright

1475 BET TOTEPLACEPOT AT TOTESPORT.COM FILLIES' NOVICE STKS 6f (P)
1:30 (1:30) (Class 4) 3-Y-O+ £5,757 (£1,713; £856; £428) **Stalls Centre**

Form RPR

225- **1** **Shorter Skirt**[206] 7024 3-8-11 78.......................... CharlesBishop 2 73
(Eve Johnson Houghton) *t.k.h: trckd ldr on inner: swtchd rt and effrt over 1f out: r.o u.p ins fnl f to ld fnl strides* **7/2**[2]

1 **2** *nk* **Fen Breeze**[40] 796 3-9-4 0.......................... OisinMurphy 3 79
(Rae Guest) *led: rdn over 1f out: drvn and kpt on ins fnl f: hdd fnl strides* **8/13**[1]

42- **3** 2 **Painted Dream**[133] 9151 3-8-11 0.......................... DavidProbert 5 65
(George Margarson) *hld up in tch: effrt towards inner over 1f out: rdn and kpt on ins fnl f: nvr enough pce to rch ldrs* **4/1**[3]

0-35 **4** ¾ **Alicia Darcy (IRE)**[31] 966 3-8-11 72.......................... BarryMcHugh 4 63
(James Given) *hld up in tch: effrt over 1f out: kpt on u.p ins fnl f: nt rch ldrs* **16/1**

0-2 **5** *nk* **Show Me The Bubbly**[21] 1139 3-8-11 0.......................... LiamJones 6 62
(John O'Shea) *chsd ldrs: effrt over 1f out: unable qck over 1f out: outpcd ins fnl f* **22/1**

6 24 **Wadah** 4-9-9 0.......................... DannyBrock 7
(J R Jenkins) *dwlt and wnt rt leaving stalls: sn rousted along and hdwy to go prom after 2f: hung rt and lost pl bnd 1/2-way: wl btn 2f out (jockey said filly hung right-handed)* **100/1**

7 *nk* **Jazzameer** 4-9-9 0.......................... WilliamCarson 1
(Matthew Salaman) *s.i.s: rn green in rr: lost tch over 2f out* **100/1**

1m 12.76s (-0.94) **Going Correction** -0.15s/f (Stan) **7 Ran SP% 116.4**
WFA 3 from 4yo 12lb
Speed ratings (Par 102): **100,99,96,95,95 63,63**
CSF £6.22 TOTE £3.70: £1.50, £1.10; EX 6.00 Trifecta £15.30.
Owner Hot To Trot Racing - Shorter Skirt **Bred** P T Tellwright **Trained** Blewbury, Oxon

FOCUS
A fair fillies' novice, with the right pair asserting late on.

1476 BET TOTESWINGER AT TOTESPORT.COM FILLIES' H'CAP 6f (P)
2:00 (2:00) (Class 5) (0-75,76) 3-Y-O £4,140 (£1,232; £615; £307; £300; £300) **Stalls Centre**

Form RPR

545- **1** **Shimmering Dawn (IRE)**[129] 9224 3-9-7 **73**.......................... OisinMurphy 1 81
(James Tate) *in tch: nt clr run ent fnl 2f: sn swtchd rt: hdwy u.p to ld and hung lft ins fnl f: r.o strly* **13/8**[2]

-421 **2** 2 **Sundiata**[9] 1296 3-9-3 **69**.......................... RichardKingscote 2 71+
(Charles Hills) *in rr: clsd and nt clr run over 1f out: gap opened and effrt jst ins fnl f: chsd clr wnr wl ins fnl f: r.o but no threat to wnr* **11/8**[1]

6220 **3** 2 **Antonia Clara**[9] 1285 3-8-13 **65**..................(t[1]) SilvestreDeSousa 7 60
(Stuart Williams) *w ldr tl led 1/2-way: rdn over 1f out: hdd ins fnl f: no ex: lost 2nd and wknd wl ins fnl f (jockey said filly jumped left-handed when leaving the stalls)* **6/1**[3]

3330 **4** 1¾ **Valley Belle (IRE)**[19] 1170 3-8-4 **56**..................(v) JosephineGordon 5 46
(Phil McEntee) *t.k.h early: hld up in tch: effrt over 1f out: hung lft and no prog ent fnl f: wknd ins fnl f* **25/1**

03-4 **5** *nk* **Diva D (IRE)**[40] 798 3-9-4 **70**.......................... JoeFanning 6 59
(Mark Johnston) *stdd s: t.k.h: hdwy to chse ldrs over 4f out: clsd to press ldr ent fnl 2f: struggling to qckn and sltly impeded jst ins fnl f: wknd fnl 150yds* **8/1**

60-0 **6** 17 **Equiano Perle**[10] 1275 3-7-13 **54** oh3..................(t) JaneElliott(3) 4
(Michael Appleby) *led tl 1/2-way: sn rdn and struggling: bhd fnl f* **66/1**

1m 12.26s (-1.44) **Going Correction** -0.15s/f (Stan) **6 Ran SP% 110.9**
Speed ratings (Par 95): **103,100,97,95,94 72**
CSF £4.10 TOTE £2.10: £1.30, £1.20; EX 4.00 Trifecta £10.20.
Owner Sheikh Juma Dalmook Al Maktoum **Bred** Cloneymore Farm Ltd **Trained** Newmarket, Suffolk

FOCUS
A modest fillies' handicap, but it was run at a good gallop and the winner did it nicely.

1477 BET TOTETRIFECTA AT TOTESPORT.COM H'CAP (DIV I) 7f (P)
2:35 (2:35) (Class 6) (0-55,55) 4-Y-O+ £3,493 (£1,039; £519; £300; £300; £300) **Stalls Low**

Form RPR

001 **1** **Mr Potter**[23] 1093 6-9-4 **52**..................(v) PhilipPrince 9 59
(Richard Guest) *taken down early: t.k.h: hld up in tch: clsd and swtchd rt ent fnl 2f: hdwy over 1f out: rdn to ld ins fnl f: r.o wl* **10/1**

4-65 **2** 1½ **Slipalongtrevaskis**[56] 594 6-8-12 **46** oh1..................(b) JoeyHaynes 3 49
(Paul Howling) *t.k.h: hld up in tch towards rr: clsd to trck ldrs ent fnl 2f: nudged lft and bmpd rival over 1f out: led 1f out: sn rdn: hung rt and hdd ins fnl f: outpcd towards fin* **8/1**[3]

-405 **3** *shd* **Kellington Kitty (USA)**[46] 717 4-8-12 **46**.......................... RossaRyan 1 49
(Mike Murphy) *chsd ldrs: ev ch u.p over 1f out: unable to match pce of wnr ins fnl f: one pce towards fin* **5/1**[2]

0-56 **4** ¾ **Merdon Castle (IRE)**[19] 1177 7-8-12 **46** oh1.......................... JoeFanning 8 47
(Frank Bishop) *in rr: effrt over 1f out: hdwy u.p 1f out: styd on ins fnl f: nt rch ldrs* **5/1**[2]

6212 **5** ½ **Maazel (IRE)**[7] 1328 5-9-0 **55**.......................... GeorgiaDobie(7) 7 57
(Lee Carter) *pushed along leaving stalls: in tch towards rr: clsd to chse ldrs and nt clr run over 1f out: swtchd lft ins fnl f: no imp fnl 100yds (jockey said gelding was denied a clear run)* **11/4**[1]

2424 **6** 1¾ **Canimar**[10] 1265 4-8-5 **46** oh1..................(p) GavinAshton(7) 10 41
(Shaun Keightley) *w ldr tl led and edgd lft over 1f out: no ex whn squeezed for room and hmpd ins fnl f: wknd towards fin* **8/1**[3]

2-50 **7** *shd* **Secret Lightning (FR)**[46] 719 7-9-0 **51**..................(v) JaneElliott(3) 4 48
(Michael Appleby) *hld up in midfield tl dropped to last pair 4f out: clsd and nt clr run over 1f out: gap opened and effrt 1f out: keeping on whn hmpd and snatched up 100yds out: no imp after (jockey said mare suffered interference one furlong out)* **14/1**

0306 **8** 5 **Little Miss Daisy**[10] 1266 5-9-7 **55**.......................... MartinDwyer 2 37
(William Muir) *chsd ldrs: rdn and lost pl over 2f out: bhd ins fnl f* **14/1**

-500 **9** ½ **Lesanti**[17] 1214 5-8-12 **46** oh1..................(b) LukeMorris 11 26
(Ed de Giles) *chsd ldrs: rdn over 2f out: lost pl and btn over 1f out: wknd fnl f* **33/1**

00-0 **10** *nse* **Pocket Warrior**[17] 1215 8-8-10 **49**..................(t) TheodoreLadd(5) 6 29
(Paul D'Arcy) *led tl rdn: hdd and bmpd over 1f out: sn outpcd and wknd ins fnl f* **33/1**

2000 **11** ¾ **The Special One (IRE)**[17] 1214 6-8-12 **53**..........(v[1]) GraceMcEntee(7) 5 31
(Phil McEntee) *bustled along early: midfield: effrt wd bnd 2f out: unable qck and no imp over 1f out: wknd fnl f* **10/1**

1m 26.73s (-0.47) **Going Correction** -0.15s/f (Stan) **11 Ran SP% 119.6**
Speed ratings (Par 101): **96,94,94,93,92 90,90,84,84,84 83**
CSF £89.18 CT £460.36 TOTE £12.30: £2.80, £2.90, £1.60; EX 131.10 Trifecta £1163.90.
Owner A Turton, A Rhodes & Mrs Alison Guest **Bred** P Balding **Trained** Ingmanthorpe, W Yorks

FOCUS
The first leg of a moderate handicap.

1478 BET TOTETRIFECTA AT TOTESPORT.COM H'CAP (DIV II) 7f (P)
3:05 (3:06) (Class 6) (0-55,55) 4-Y-O+ £3,493 (£1,039; £519; £300; £300; £300) **Stalls Low**

Form RPR

3 **1** **La Cumparsita (IRE)**[24] 1083 5-8-12 **46** oh1.......................... LukeMorris 5 53+
(Tristan Davidson) *chsd ldrs: effrt to chse ldr and swtchd rt 2f out: drvn to ld ent fnl f: edgd lft but kpt on wl ins fnl f* **2/1**[1]

0050 **2** 1 **Clement (IRE)**[33] 925 9-9-1 **49**..................(p) BarryMcHugh 1 53
(Marjorie Fife) *hld up in tch in last trio: swtchd rt and clsd over 1f out: clsd u.p to chse wnr wl ins fnl f: kpt on same pce after* **11/4**[2]

0602 **3** ¾ **My Girl Maisie (IRE)**[4] 1383 5-8-12 **46** oh1..................(e) PhilipPrince 6 48
(Richard Guest) *taken down early: chsd ldrs: effrt over 1f out: pressed wnr and hrd drvn ins fnl f: one pce: sn lost 2nd and edgd lft* **7/1**

4054 **4** ¾ **Malaysian Boleh**[4] 1383 9-8-5 **46** oh1..................(v) GraceMcEntee(7) 10 49+
(Phil McEntee) *in tch in midfield: clsd on outer bnd 2f out: stl hld together over 1f out: swtchd lft and effrt 1f out: carried lft and kpt on same pce ins fnl f* **11/1**

3450 **5** 1 **Caledonian Gold**[25] 1060 6-8-12 **46** oh1.......................... HectorCrouch 4 44
(Lisa Williamson) *taken down early and mounted in chute: in tch in midfield: effrt to chse ldrs over 1f out: keeping on same pce whn carried lft ins fnl f* **20/1**

-100 **6** *shd* **Cool Echo**[32] 941 5-9-4 **52**..................(p) DavidProbert 7 50
(J R Jenkins) *in tch in midfield: rdn over 2f out: kpt on same pce ins fnl f* **10/1**

0-20 **7** 2¼ **Percy Toplis**[33] 924 5-8-12 **46** oh1..................(p) EoinWalsh 3 39+
(Christine Dunnett) *hld up in last pair: shkn up and clsd jst over 1f out: nt clr run and hmpd ins fnl f: wknd towards fin* **14/1**

5050 **8** 6 **Swiss Cross**[4] 1384 12-9-2 **50**..................(be[1]) SilvestreDeSousa 8 26
(Phil McEntee) *rousted along leaving stalls: led after 2f: rdn over 1f out: sn hdd: wknd and eased ins fnl f* **5/1**[3]

600/ **9** 1½ **Lovely Acclamation (IRE)**[524] 8329 5-9-4 **52**.......................... WilliamCarson 9 24
(Matthew Salaman) *led and crossed over fr wd draw: hdd after 2f out: chsd ldr tl 2f out: losing pl whn hmpd over 1f out: wknd fnl f* **33/1**

The Form Book Flat 2019, Raceform Ltd, Newbury, RG14 5SJ

06/0 10 1 3/4 **Dream On Dreamer (IRE)**[12] 608 5-9-2 **55**....(t[1]) PoppyBridgwater[(5)] 2 23
(Lucinda Egerton) *sn in rr and nvr travelling wl: bhd fnl f* **50/1**

1m 26.75s (-0.45) **Going Correction** -0.15s/f (Stan) **10** Ran SP% **122.9**
Speed ratings (Par 101): **96,94,94,93,92 91,89,82,80,78**
CSF £7.85 CT £34.51 TOTE £2.80: £1.10, £1.50, £2.10; EX 10.20 Trifecta £44.80.
Owner Ben Greenslade, David McCrone & J Dixon **Bred** Highfort Stud **Trained** Irthington, Cumbria
■ Stewards' Enquiry : Luke Morris caution; careless riding

FOCUS
Little between this and the first division, with the time almost identical. The winner was well in on the previous season's peak Irish form.

1479 BET TOTEQUADPOT AT TOTESPORT.COM H'CAP 1m (P)
3:40 (3:42) (Class 5) (0-75,77) 4-Y-0+

£4,140 (£1,232; £615; £307; £300; £300) **Stalls** Low

Form RPR
235- 1 **Simoon (IRE)**[149] 8835 5-9-9 **77**.......................... OisinMurphy 2 85+
(Andrew Balding) *chsd ldrs: effrt on inner over 1f out: led 1f out: edgd rt but kpt on wl ins fnl f* **5/4**[1]

0364 2 3/4 **Glory Awaits (IRE)**[17] 1213 9-9-2 **75**..................(b) DylanHogan[(5)] 3 81
(David Simcock) *chsd ldr: rdn and ev ch over 1f out tl hung lft ins fnl f: kpt on same pce towards fin (vet said gelding lost it's left fore shoe)* **8/1**

164- 3 nk **Arctic Sea**[147] 8885 5-9-3 **71**.......................... RaulDaSilva 4 76
(Paul Cole) *in tch in midfield: swtchd rt and effrt over 1f out: kpt on to go 3rd wl ins fnl f: nvr getting to wnr* **12/1**

1105 4 1 1/4 **Cashel (IRE)**[10] 1271 4-9-0 **68**.......................... TomMarquand 8 70
(Michael Appleby) *hld up in tch: effrt jst over 2f out: swtchd lft over 1f out: chsd ldrs and kpt on same pce u.p ins fnl f* **10/1**

1412 5 1 **Harbour Vision**[23] 1099 4-9-6 **74**.......................... PaddyMathers 5 74
(Derek Shaw) *stdd after s: hld up in last pair: effrt jst over 2f out: edgd lft and styd on ins fnl f: nvr trbld ldrs* **7/2**[2]

6360 6 hd **Pearl Spectre (USA)**[5] 1366 8-9-0 **68**..................(v) NicolaCurrie 1 68
(Phil McEntee) *led: drifted rt and rdn over 1f out: hdd 1f out: jst getting outpcd whn squeezed for room wl ins fnl f: wknd towards fin* **20/1**

0330 7 1 **Juanito Chico (IRE)**[5] 1367 5-9-9 **77**..................(t) SilvestreDeSousa 6 74
(Stuart Williams) *t.k.h: hld up in tch: effrt over 2f out: unable qck u.p over 1f out: plugged on same pce ins fnl f* **6/1**[3]

115- 8 7 **Roof Garden**[145] 8918 4-9-0 **68**.......................... MarcMonaghan 7 49
(Mark H Tompkins) *dropped in bhd after s: hld up in rr: no hdwy u.p and wknd ins fnl f* **33/1**

1m 37.65s (-2.25) **Going Correction** -0.15s/f (Stan) **8** Ran SP% **116.5**
Speed ratings (Par 103): **105,104,103,102,101 101,100,93**
CSF £12.69 CT £85.21 TOTE £2.00: £1.10, £2.40, £2.90; EX 10.90 Trifecta £90.80.
Owner Lord Blyth **Bred** Lemington Grange Stud **Trained** Kingsclere, Hants

FOCUS
Ordinary handicap form, with the race working out perfectly for the favourite, who'd been well backed.

1480 BET TOTESCOOP6 AT TOTESPORT.COM H'CAP 1m (P)
4:10 (4:11) (Class 4) (0-80,78) 3-Y-O

£5,757 (£1,713; £856; £428; £300; £300) **Stalls** Low

Form RPR
410- 1 **Balladeer**[172] 8139 3-9-4 **75**.......................... HayleyTurner 4 79
(Michael Bell) *t.k.h: in tch in midfield: effrt to chal and edgd lft 1f out: led ins fnl f: r.o wl* **7/1**

1-26 2 1 **Whenapoet**[39] 826 3-8-6 **68**..................(p) TheodoreLadd[(5)] 5 70
(Michael Appleby) *sn led: rdn over 1f out: hdd ins fnl f: no ex and kpt on same pce wl ins fnl f* **20/1**

412 3 nk **Mustadun**[30] 978 3-9-7 **78**.......................... JoeFanning 1 81+
(Mark Johnston) *chsd ldr tl 1/2-way: styd handy: nt clr run over 1f out: rdn ent fnl f: nt clr run again ins fnl f: kpt on same pce towards fin* **9/2**[3]

06-2 4 hd **Maqaadeer**[17] 1217 3-9-1 **72**.......................... BenCurtis 3 73
(Ed Dunlop) *chsd ldrs: wnt 2nd 4f out: rdn to press ldr 2f out tl unable qck u.p 1f out: kpt on same pce ins fnl f* **9/4**[2]

421 5 nk **I'm Available (IRE)**[26] 1033 3-9-3 **74**.......................... OisinMurphy 2 75+
(Andrew Balding) *hld up in tch: nt clr run over 2f out: effrt u.p 1f out: n.m.r and bmpd ins fnl f: kpt on but nvr getting to wnr* **13/8**[1]

0-20 6 1/2 **Bubbelah (IRE)**[21] 1140 3-8-6 **63**.......................... LukeMorris 6 62
(David Simcock) *in tch in rr: swtchd rt and effrt over 1f out: wnt lft u.p and bmpd ins fnl f: kpt on fnl 100yds: nvr getting to wnr* **14/1**

1m 38.79s (-1.11) **Going Correction** -0.15s/f (Stan) **6** Ran SP% **111.0**
Speed ratings (Par 100): **99,98,97,97,97 96**
CSF £108.53 TOTE £8.30: £3.40, £8.40; EX 114.20 Trifecta £775.70.
Owner Mascalls Stud **Bred** Mascalls Stud **Trained** Newmarket, Suffolk

FOCUS
Bit of a turn up here in a muddling race, with around 2l covering the whole field at the line.

1481 BET TOTEEXACTA AT TOTESPORT.COM H'CAP 1m 2f (P)
4:45 (4:46) (Class 5) (0-70,72) 3-Y-O

£4,140 (£1,232; £615; £307; £300; £300) **Stalls** Low

Form RPR
2236 1 **Hypnos (IRE)**[25] 1066 3-8-12 **65**.......................... DylanHogan[(5)] 7 71
(David Simcock) *hld up in last pair: rdn and hdwy ent fnl 2f: str chal 1f out: r.o wl to ld last strides* **14/1**

046- 2 hd **Agent Basterfield (IRE)**[115] 9442 3-9-6 **68**.......................... OisinMurphy 9 73+
(Andrew Balding) *chsd ldrs: rdn over 2f out: styd on u.p to ld over 1f out: drvn and kpt on ins fnl f: hdd last strides* **5/1**[3]

-634 3 1 1/2 **Fanfaronade (USA)**[10] 1270 3-9-2 **64**..................(b[1]) NickyMackay 3 66
(John Gosden) *trckd ldrs: nt clr run over 1f out: swtchd lft and chsd ldrs 1f out: kpt on same pce u.p ins fnl f* **8/1**

025- 4 2 **Toro Dorado**[137] 9073 3-9-4 **66**..................(p[1]) DavidProbert 5 64
(Ed Dunlop) *awkward leaving stalls: hld up in tch: nt clr run 2f out: swtchd rt over 1f out: hdwy to chse ldrs and kpt on same pce ins fnl f* **16/1**

3-23 5 3 1/4 **Navadir (JPN)**[58] 567 3-9-7 **69**..................(t) TomMarquand 8 61
(Marco Botti) *stdd s: hld up in last pair: swtchd rt and effrt over 2f out: no imp over 1f out and wl hld fnl f* **16/1**

5221 6 1/2 **Greyzee (IRE)**[19] 1173 3-8-11 **59**.......................... SilvestreDeSousa 1 50
(Rod Millman) *led: rdn and hdd over 1f out: sn no ex and wknd ins fnl f* **7/4**[1]

653 7 4 1/2 **Shaleela's Dream**[28] 1019 3-9-6 **71**..................(p[1]) GabrieleMalune[(3)] 2 53
(Marco Botti) *midfield early: clsd to chse ldrs 7f out: nt clr run over 1f out: sn rdn and btn: wknd ins fnl f* **25/1**

06-1 8 1 1/2 **Rock Up In Style**[20] 1166 3-9-10 **72**.......................... JoeFanning 4 51
(Mark Johnston) *chsd ldr: rdn over 1f out: squeezed out and btn over 1f out: wknd ins fnl f* **4/1**[2]

654- 9 29 **Charmed Spirit**[152] 8731 3-9-4 **66**.......................... RobHornby 6
(Jonathan Portman) *in tch in midfield: rdn over 3f out: lost pl and bhd over 1f out* **10/1**

2m 6.2s (-2.40) **Going Correction** -0.15s/f (Stan) **9** Ran SP% **115.5**
Speed ratings (Par 98): **103,102,101,100,97 97,93,92,69**
CSF £82.45 CT £607.57 TOTE £18.90: £3.60, £1.70, £2.30; EX 130.40 Trifecta £1242.80.
Owner The Khat Partnership **Bred** Gigginstown House Stud **Trained** Newmarket, Suffolk

FOCUS
Those coming from off the pace came to the fore in what was a modest enough 3yo handicap. The market leaders did a bit too much up front.

1482 BUY TICKETS AT CHELMSFORDCITYRACECOURSE.COM H'CAP 1m 2f (P)
5:15 (5:16) (Class 5) (0-70,71) 4-Y-0+

£4,140 (£1,232; £615; £307; £300; £300) **Stalls** Low

Form RPR
-403 1 **Bayston Hill**[6] 1343 5-9-7 **68**..................(p[1]) NicolaCurrie 7 76
(Mark Usher) *led tl 7f out: chsd ldr: after tl rdn to chal ent fnl 2f: led over 1f out: kpt on wl ins fnl f: rdn out* **6/1**[3]

-220 2 nk **Gas Monkey**[25] 1065 4-9-1 **62**.......................... ShelleyBirkett 3 69
(Julia Feilden) *chsd ldrs early: in tch in midfield: clsd to chse ldrs over 2f out: swtchd rt and chsd wnr over 1f out: ev ch and edging towards wnr ins fnl f: hld towards fin* **7/4**[1]

440- 3 1 3/4 **Velvet Vision**[174] 8081 4-9-10 **71**.......................... OisinMurphy 6 75
(Mark H Tompkins) *hld up towards rr: hdwy on inner over 2f out: chsd ldng pair over 1f out: kpt on ins fnl f* **7/1**

4104 4 5 **Don't Do It (IRE)**[7] 1333 4-8-9 **56**..................(v) LukeMorris 4 50
(Michael Appleby) *chsd ldrs early: dropped to midfield 7f out: effrt 3f out: wnt modest 4th 1f out: no imp* **5/1**[2]

050- 5 1 1/2 **Roc Astrale (IRE)**[131] 9179 5-9-0 **68**.......................... GraceMcEntee[(7)] 5 59
(Phil McEntee) *hld up in last trio: clsd on outer bnd 2f out: hung lft and plugged on same pce ins fnl f (jockey said gelding hung left-handed)* **20/1**

3-40 6 nk **Princess Harley (IRE)**[54] 616 4-9-4 **65**.......................... CharlesBishop 1 55
(Mick Quinn) *in tch in midfield: effrt whn nt clr run and swtchd lft over 1f out: no threat to ldrs and kpt on same pce ins fnl f (jockey said filly was denied a clear run)* **12/1**

2001 7 1 3/4 **Orobas (IRE)**[7] 1333 7-8-10 **62** 4ex..................(v) PoppyBridgwater[(5)] 2 48
(Lucinda Egerton) *chsd ldrs: rdn and unable qck over 1f out: sn btn and wknd ins fnl f* **8/1**

-500 8 1 1/4 **Agent Gibbs**[63] 457 7-9-6 **67**..................(p) ShaneKelly 10 51
(John O'Shea) *chsd ldr tl 7f out: styd prom tl unable qck and edgd rt over 1f out: carried lft: impeded and wknd ins fnl f* **33/1**

3203 9 3 1/2 **Squire**[4] 1378 8-8-10 **60**..................(tp) JaneElliott[(3)] 9 37
(Marjorie Fife) *dwlt: hdwy to ld 7f out: rdn to chal ent fnl 2f: led and drvn over 1f out: kpt on wl ins fnl f: rdn out* **8/1**

01- 10 2 3/4 **Overtrumped**[234] 5969 4-9-2 **63**.......................... HayleyTurner 8 34
(Mike Murphy) *a in rr: rdn over 3f out: sn struggling and bhd over 1f out* **14/1**

2m 5.85s (-2.75) **Going Correction** -0.15s/f (Stan) **10** Ran SP% **124.1**
Speed ratings (Par 103): **105,104,103,99,98 97,96,95,92,90**
CSF £18.04 CT £80.64 TOTE £6.60: £1.90, £1.10, £2.50; EX 21.90 Trifecta £275.30.
Owner High Five Racing and Partners **Bred** Selwood Bloodstock & Mrs S Read **Trained** Upper Lambourn, Berks

FOCUS
Three pulled clear in this modest handicap. The winner had a good trip at head of the field.
T/Plt: £435.70 to a £1 stake. Pool: 68,797.04 - 115.25 winning units T/Qpdt: £228.10 to a 31 stake. Pool: £8,478.07 - 115.25 winning units **Steve Payne**

1398 NEWCASTLE (A.W) (L-H)
Monday, April 1

OFFICIAL GOING: Tapeta: standard
Wind: Moderate against Weather: Grey cloud

1483 BETWAY CASINO H'CAP 2m 56y (Tp)
5:45 (5:45) (Class 2) (0-105,102) 4-Y-0+ **£18,562** (£4,660; £2,330; £1,165; £582) **Stalls** Low

Form RPR
1-23 1 **Stargazer (IRE)**[59] 519 6-9-9 **102**.......................... RobertWinston 3 109
(Philip Kirby) *hld up in rr: smooth hdwy to trck ldrs over 2f out: swtchd rt and effrt to chal over 1f out: shkn up ins fnl f: pushed out to ld last 50yds* **10/3**[2]

-056 2 nk **Cosmelli (ITY)**[28] 1017 6-9-2 **95**..................(b) DanielMuscutt 1 101
(Gay Kelleway) *set stdy pce: hdd after 4f: prom: effrt over 2f out: rdn to take slt ld over 1f out: sn jnd and riven: hdd and no ex last 50yds* **18/1**

1321 3 1 3/4 **Busy Street**[19] 1172 7-8-9 **95** ow1.......................... MarkCrehan[(7)] 4 99
(Michael Appleby) *trckd ldrs: pushed along and sltly outpcd 3f out: rdn whn rdr lost rein and dropped whip 2f out: kpt on wl fnl f* **4/1**[3]

4-21 4 1 **Lucky Deal**[40] 799 4-9-1 **96**.......................... FrannyNorton 2 99
(Mark Johnston) *cl up on inner: led after 4f: sn jnd: hdd 5f out: cl up and rdn 3f out: led again briefly 2f out: sn drvn and hdd: kpt on same pce* **5/6**[1]

1323 5 6 **Loud And Clear**[32] 948 8-8-4 **83** oh1.......................... PhilDennis 5 79
(Jim Goldie) *hld up: hdwy to trck ldr after 5f: sn cl up: disp ld 1/2-way: slt ld 5f out: rdn along and qcknd over 3f out: drvn and hdd 2f out: sn wknd* **9/1**

3m 36.84s (1.84) **Going Correction** +0.10s/f (Slow)
WFA 4 from 6yo+ 2lb **5** Ran SP% **112.9**
Speed ratings (Par 109): **99,98,97,97,94**
CSF £46.34 TOTE £4.00: £1.80, £5.30; EX 30.00 Trifecta £112.30.
Owner Zoe Hassall & George Hassall & P Kirby **Bred** Chelston Ireland **Trained** East Appleton, N Yorks
■ Stewards' Enquiry : Daniel Muscutt two-day ban: careless riding (Apr 15-16)

FOCUS
The going was standard. \n\x\x Stalls: Straight - centre; 1m2f outside; 2m56yds inside\n\x\x Only five runners, but a competitive staying handicap with decent prize money on offer. They did not go a great gallop and the winner gained a small personal best.

1484 LADBROKES NOVICE STKS (PLUS 10 RACE) 1m 2f 42y (Tp)
6:15 (6:15) (Class 4) 3-Y-O **£5,530** (£1,645; £822; £411) **Stalls** High

Form RPR
1 **El Misk** 3-9-5 0.......................... KieranO'Neill 4 87+
(John Gosden) *dwlt: green and sn pushed along in rr: rdn along over 4f out: swtchd rt to outer over 3f out: hdwy to chse ldrs 2f out: chal over 1f out: led ins fnl f: kpt on wl towards fin* **8/11**[1]

2 1 **Rochester House (IRE)** 3-9-5 0 FrannyNorton 2 85+
(Mark Johnston) *trckd ldrs on inner: hdwy over 3f out: chal over 1f out: rdn to take slt ld briefly ent fnl f: sn hdd: kpt on* **22/1**

36- 3 1 1/4 **Purdey's Gift**[180] 7904 3-9-5 0 GrahamLee 5 82+
(Andrew Balding) *racd wd: trckd ldrs: hdwy and cl up over 3f out: led over 2f out: rdn over 1f out: drvn and hdd ent fnl f: kpt on same pce* **9/2**[3]

502- 4 7 **Coup De Gold (IRE)**[164] 8372 3-9-5 76 (h) JamesDoyle 1 68
(William Haggas) *led: pushed along over 3f out: rdn and hdd over 2f out: sn drvn and wknd* **15/8**[2]

05- 5 4 1/2 **Well Funded (IRE)**[174] 8091 3-9-0 0 PaulHanagan 3 54
(James Bethell) *sn trcking ldr: pushed along 4f out: rdn 3f out: sn outpcd* **100/1**

2m 10.28s (-0.12) **Going Correction** +0.10s/f (Slow) **5 Ran SP% 116.2**
Speed ratings (Par 100): **104,103,102,96,93**
CSF £18.94 TOTE £1.60: £1.10, £4.40; EX 12.70 Trifecta £38.80.
Owner Sheikh Mohammed Bin Khalifa Al Maktoum **Bred** Essafinaat Ltd **Trained** Newmarket, Suffolk

FOCUS
Some nicely-bred sorts fought out the finish of this novice event and the form may be useful. The first two were newcomers.

1485 LADBROKES HOME OF THE ODDS BOOST H'CAP 1m 5y (Tp)
6:45 (6:45) (Class 3) (0-90,86) 3-Y-O £9,056 (£2,695; £1,346; £673) **Stalls Centre**

Form RPR
506- 1 **Hesslewood (IRE)**[201] 7169 3-9-3 82 DanielTudhope 2 86
(James Bethell) *trckd ldrs: hdwy 3f out: rdn to chal jst over 1f out: led ins fnl f: kpt on wl towards fin* **14/1**[3]

-111 2 nk **Alkaamel**[37] 885 3-8-12 84 CierenFallon(7) 3 87
(William Haggas) *trckd ldr: effrt 2f out: rdn to chal over 1f out: slt ld ent fnl f: sn drvn and hdd: edgd rt and kpt on (two-day ban: used whip above permitted level (15-16 Apr))* **2/1**[2]

100- 3 nk **Loch Ness Monster (IRE)**[174] 8075 3-9-6 85 AlistairRawlinson 4 87
(Michael Appleby) *trckd ldrs: hdwy 3f out: chsd ldr 2f out: rdn and ev ch ent fnl f: sn drvn and kpt on* **28/1**

421 4 4 1/2 **Kinver Edge (USA)**[39] 827 3-9-7 86 JamesDoyle 5 78
(Charlie Appleby) *sn led at stdy pce: pushed along and qcknd 3f out: rdn and hdd over 1f out: sn drvn and btn* **4/9**[1]

332- 5 9 **Five Helmets (IRE)**[177] 7997 3-8-5 73 JamieGormley(3) 1 44
(Iain Jardine) *chsd ldng pair: pushed along and lost pl appr 1/2-way: sn bhd* **50/1**

1m 38.65s (0.05) **Going Correction** +0.10s/f (Slow) **5 Ran SP% 114.7**
Speed ratings (Par 102): **103,102,102,97,88**
CSF £43.74 TOTE £11.20: £4.40, £1.20; EX 37.10 Trifecta £146.60.
Owner Clarendon Thoroughbred Racing **Bred** Nesco II **Trained** Middleham Moor, N Yorks

FOCUS
With the hot favourite failing to perform to expectations, the winner cashed in on his reduced handicap mark to land a nice prize on his seasonal reappearance.

1486 LADBROKES H'CAP 7f 14y (Tp)
7:15 (7:15) (Class 6) (0-60,60) 3-Y-O
£3,105 (£924; £461; £400; £400; £400) **Stalls Centre**

Form RPR
03-3 1 **Blazing Dreams (IRE)**[55] 612 3-8-13 52 (p) AndrewMullen 3 59
(Ben Haslam) *trckd ldrs: hdwy over 2f out: rdn to ld 1 1/2f out: drvn out* **7/2**[2]

-633 2 3/4 **Firsteen**[24] 1081 3-8-13 52 GrahamLee 5 57
(Alistair Whillans) *hld up in tch: hdwy over 2f out: rdn over 1f out: chsd wnr ins fnl f: sn drvn and kpt on wl* **11/2**[3]

3-00 3 1/2 **Alfred The Grey (IRE)**[24] 1084 3-9-4 57 TomEaves 4 61
(Tracy Waggott) *dwlt and in rr: swtchd rt to stands' rail and hdwy over 2f out: rdn wl over 1f out: kpt on wl fnl f* **16/1**

0144 4 hd **Kodi Dream**[24] 1084 3-9-1 59 BenSanderson(5) 9 62
(Roger Fell) *towards rr: swtchd rt towards stands' side 2f out: sn rdn: styd on fnl f: nrst fin* **3/1**[1]

-205 5 nk **Klipperty Klopp**[24] 1084 3-9-6 59 CamHardie 8 62
(Antony Brittain) *cl up: led 4f out: rdn along over 2f out: drvn and hdd 1 1/2f out: kpt on same pce* **7/1**

400- 6 1/2 **She'Zanarab**[181] 7865 3-9-0 56 JamieGormley(3) 13 57
(Iain Jardine) *midfield: hdwy towards stands' side over 2f out: rdn wl over 1f out: kpt on same pce fnl f* **50/1**

050 7 1 1/4 **Zoom Out**[18] 1195 3-9-0 56 (t[1]) RowanScott(3) 14 54
(Nigel Tinkler) *hld up in rr: hdwy towards stands' side whn nt clr run and swtchd lft 2f out: sn rdn: styd on fnl f* **16/1**

535- 8 shd **Mi Laddo (IRE)**[189] 7624 3-9-3 56 (p[1]) JamesSullivan 2 54
(Oliver Greenall) *t.k.h early: in tch towards far side: hdwy over 2f out: sn rdn and no imp* **16/1**

050- 9 1 3/4 **Pageant Master (IRE)**[100] 9683 3-9-7 60 PaulMulrennan 11 53
(Mark H Tompkins) *trckd ldng pair: pushed along 3f out: rdn 2f out: grad wknd* **8/1**

204- 10 hd **Caramel Curves**[124] 9289 3-9-2 55 LewisEdmunds 7 48
(David Barron) *towards rr: pushed along 1/2-way: rdn over 2f out: sme late hdwy* **10/1**

040- 11 1/2 **Our Secret (IRE)**[166] 8323 3-8-13 52 PhilDennis 1 44
(Liam Bailey) *trckd ldrs towards far side: pushed along 3f out: rdn over 2f out: sn wknd* **66/1**

056- 12 nk **Jagerbond**[122] 9325 3-9-1 54 KevinStott 12 45
(Andrew Crook) *in tch: rdn along wl over 2f out: sn wknd* **8/1**

430- 13 1 3/4 **Smashing Lass (IRE)**[174] 8092 3-9-4 57 ShaneGray 6 43
(Ollie Pears) *led centre: hdd 4f out: cl up and rdn along 3f out: wknd over 2f out* **8/1**

0-06 14 1 **Cool Kitty**[70] 341 3-8-13 52 PJMcDonald 10 36
(Rebecca Menzies) *chsd ldrs: rdn along over 2f out: sn wknd* **25/1**

1m 28.74s (2.54) **Going Correction** +0.10s/f (Slow) **14 Ran SP% 142.5**
Speed ratings (Par 96): **89,88,87,87,87 86,85,84,82,82 82,81,79,78**
CSF £27.99 CT £258.54 TOTE £5.30: £2.30, £2.90, £6.40; EX 29.60 Trifecta £482.90.
Owner Champagne Charlies Club & B Haslam **Bred** Rory O'Brien **Trained** Middleham Moor, N Yorks

FOCUS
Ordinary fare, but the well-backed winner did it nicely. The runner-up gained a minor personal best.

1487 BETWAY H'CAP 6f (Tp)
7:45 (7:45) (Class 4) (0-80,81) 4-Y-O+
£5,530 (£1,645; £822; £411; £400; £400) **Stalls Centre**

Form RPR
-011 1 **Martineo**[34] 914 4-9-6 78 JamesDoyle 5 87+
(John Butler) *hld up in midfield: hdwy over 2f out and sn swtchd rt to stands' rail: rdn wl over 1f out: drvn and styd on wl fnl f to ld last 75yds: edgd lft nr fin* **7/4**[1]

3224 2 nk **Lucky Lodge**[10] 1274 9-8-5 70 (v) KieranSchofield(7) 14 78
(Antony Brittain) *prom: rdn to ld over 1f out: drvn ins fnl f: hdd last 75yds: hld whn bmpd nr line* **14/1**

1323 3 1 **Atholblair Boy (IRE)**[32] 952 6-9-4 81 FayeMcManoman(5) 11 86
(Nigel Tinkler) *hld up in tch: hdwy 2f out: rdn and ev ch ent fnl f: kpt on same pce towards fin* **5/1**[2]

4054 4 1/2 **Choice Encounter**[5] 1357 4-9-4 76 DanielTudhope 1 72
(Archie Watson) *prom: rdn along 2f out: sltly hmpd wl over 1f out: drvn and kpt on fnl f: fin 5th: plcd 4th* **8/1**[3]

6036 5 2 1/4 **Dirchill (IRE)**[32] 952 5-8-11 69 (b) CliffordLee 4 67
(David Thompson) *prom: hdwy to ld 2f out: sn rdn and hung bdly lft to far rail and hdd over 1f out: one pce after: fin 4th: disqualified and plcd 5th (jockey said gelding hung left)* **28/1**

6102 6 1/2 **Duke Cosimo**[10] 1274 9-8-9 67 PhilDennis 9 61
(Michael Herrington) *hld up in rr: hdwy 2f out: rdn over 1f out: styd on wl fnl f: nrst fin* **11/1**

000- 7 3/4 **Paddy Power (IRE)**[157] 8594 6-9-0 77 SeanDavis(5) 2 69
(Richard Fahey) *midfield: hdwy 2f out: rdn wl over 1f out: no imp fnl f* **8/1**[3]

5050 8 shd **Classic Pursuit**[18] 1194 8-9-5 77 (v) DavidNolan 12 69
(Stef Keniry) *chsd ldrs: rdn along 2f out: sn drvn and wknd* **100/1**

013- 9 nk **Manshood (IRE)**[104] 9596 6-9-4 76 (b) PJMcDonald 3 67
(Paul Midgley) *in tch: rdn along 2f out: grad wknd* **14/1**

4-45 10 nk **Chookie Dunedin**[42] 786 4-9-7 79 (h) PaulMulrennan 10 69
(Keith Dalgleish) *led: rdn along over 2f out: sn hdd & wknd* **9/1**

3115 11 hd **Epeius (IRE)**[31] 970 6-8-12 70 (v) AndrewMullen 7 59
(Ben Haslam) *a in rr* **14/1**

-060 12 1 **Mutabaahy (IRE)**[20] 1164 4-8-11 69 (h) CamHardie 8 55
(Antony Brittain) *dwlt: a in rr* **12/1**

566- 13 2 1/4 **Inviolable Spirit (IRE)**[153] 8717 4-8-12 70 PaulHanagan 6 49
(Richard Fahey) *chsd ldrs: rdn along over 2f out: sn wknd* **10/1**

4-12 14 3 1/2 **Inaam (IRE)**[58] 564 6-9-3 75 (h) KieranO'Neill 13 43
(John Butler) *t.k.h: hld up: a towards rr (trainer could offer no explanation for the poor form shown)* **16/1**

1m 11.09s (-1.41) **Going Correction** +0.10s/f (Slow) **14 Ran SP% 140.7**
Speed ratings (Par 105): **113,112,111,107,108 106,105,105,105,105 104,103,100,95**
CSF £36.84 CT £129.91 TOTE £3.10: £1.90, £5.80, £2.50; EX 51.50 Trifecta £213.10.
Owner Power Geneva Ltd **Bred** Saleh Al Homaizi & Imad Al Sagar **Trained** Newmarket, Suffolk

FOCUS
A fair sprint handicap won by an improving type. The second produced a sound effort on the pace as well.

1488 LADBROKES HOME OF THE ODDS BOOST H'CAP 6f (Tp)
8:15 (8:15) (Class 5) (0-70,72) 3-Y-O
£3,752 (£1,116; £557; £400; £400; £400) **Stalls Centre**

Form RPR
330- 1 **Bugler Bob (IRE)**[171] 8161 3-9-10 72 JasonHart 8 77
(John Quinn) *towards rr: hdwy 2f out: rdn over 1f out: str run fnl f to ld towards fin* **5/1**[3]

031- 2 3/4 **Magical Spirit (IRE)**[188] 7636 3-9-9 71 KevinStott 4 73
(Kevin Ryan) *t.k.h: trckd ldrs: hdwy 2f out: rdn to ld 1 1/2f out: drvn ins fnl f: hdd and no ex towards fin* **3/1**[2]

332- 3 nk **Tie A Yellowribbon**[182] 7836 3-9-6 68 DanielTudhope 10 69
(James Bethell) *t.k.h: prom: hdwy and cl up 2f out: rdn and ev ch ent fnl f: sn drvn and kpt on same pce* **5/1**[3]

050- 4 1/2 **Stallone (IRE)**[142] 9001 3-9-6 68 (p[1]) TomQueally 1 67
(Richard Spencer) *t.k.h: trckd ldr: hdwy and cl up 2f out: rdn wl over 1f out: drvn ent fnl f: kpt on same pce* **3/1**[2]

1222 5 1 **Klopp**[7] 1337 3-9-6 68 (h) CamHardie 6 64
(Antony Brittain) *t.k.h: trckd ldrs: hdwy wl over 1f out and sn rdn: drvn ent fnl f and kpt on same pce (jockey said filly ran too free)* **9/4**[1]

221- 6 2 1/4 **Primeiro Boy (IRE)**[168] 8261 3-9-2 69 ConnorMurtagh(5) 7 58
(Richard Fahey) *in rr: hdwy wl over 1f out: sn rdn and kpt on fnl f* **16/1**

3-30 7 3 3/4 **Harperelle**[27] 1023 3-9-3 65 AndrewMullen 5 42
(Alistair Whillans) *a in rr* **66/1**

-050 8 1 **Superseded (IRE)**[9] 1296 3-9-0 62 RobertWinston 3 36
(John Butler) *led: rdn along over 2f out: hdd wl over 1f out: sn wknd* **28/1**

650- 9 1 3/4 **Quanah (IRE)**[206] 7007 3-9-6 68 PaulMulrennan 9 36
(Mark H Tompkins) *plld hrd: hld up: a in rr (jockey said gelding ran too free)* **16/1**

1m 12.83s (0.33) **Going Correction** +0.10s/f (Slow) **9 Ran SP% 130.8**
Speed ratings (Par 98): **101,100,99,98,97 94,89,88,85**
CSF £23.44 CT £85.92 TOTE £6.80: £2.40, £1.10, £1.60; EX 24.40.
Owner Robert Houlton **Bred** Knocktartan House Stud **Trained** Settrington, N Yorks

FOCUS
A fair sprint handicap in which a slow early pace resulted in a few of the runners pulling hard. The winner did it nicely.
T/Jkpt: Not won T/Plt: £296.30 to a £1 stake. Pool: £96,187.57 - 236.95 winning units T/Qpdt: £28.60 to a £1 stake. Pool: £18,751.83 - 483.88 winning units **Joe Rowntree**

1391 CHANTILLY (R-H)
Monday, April 1

OFFICIAL GOING: Polytrack: standard; turf: good to soft

1489a PRIX DE LA BELLE CROIX (MAIDEN) (UNRACED 3YO) (TURF) 6f
2:35 3-Y-O £11,261 (£4,504; £3,378; £2,252; £1,126)

RPR
1 **Eraidah (FR)** 3-8-13 0 MickaelBarzalona 2 78
(H-F Devin, France) **26/5**

2 3/4 **Midnight Shine (FR)** 3-8-8 0 AugustinMadamet(8) 6 79
(A Fabre, France) *racd in fnl trio: pushed along and prog fr over 2f out: rdn ent fnl f: r.o clsng stages: nt quite match pce of wnr* **9/2**[3]

3 *nk* **Mubarmaj (FR)** 3-9-2 0 .... RonanThomas 7 78
(J E Hammond, France) *mid-div: pushed along and effrt 2f out: responded for press ins fnl f: r.o strly clsng stages: nrst fin* **15/1**
4 *1 ½* **Alkawthar (USA)** 3-8-13 0 .... MaximeGuyon 3 70
(Mme Pia Brandt, France) **14/5**[1]
5 *¾* **Danseur D'Argent (FR)** 3-8-13 0 .... TheoBachelot 4 67
(Jo Hughes, France) *qckly into stride: led: asked to qckn 2f out: hdd over 1f out: kpt on same pce ins fnl f* **21/1**
6 *hd* **Inner Charm** 3-8-13 0 .... AlexisBadel 8 67
(H-F Devin, France) **41/5**
7 *1 ¾* **Khanchaym (FR)** 3-8-13 0 .... ChristopheSoumillon 1 61
(M Delcher Sanchez, France) **69/10**
8 *4 ½* **Baahi (GER)** 3-9-2 0 .... VincentCheminaud 5 50
(J E Hammond, France) *mid-div: pushed along over 2f out: unable qck and wl btn ent fnl f: eased clsng stages* **33/10**[2]

1m 11.46s (0.06) **8** Ran SP% **118.2**
PARI-MUTUEL (all including 1 euro stake): WIN 6.20 PLACE 2.00, 1.80, 2.50 DF 20.40.
Owner Al Shaqab Racing **Bred** Al Shaqab Racing **Trained** France

1491a PRIX DES COMMERCANTS (H'CAP) (4YO+ FILLIES & MARES) (ALL-WEATHER TRACK) (POLYTRACK) 1m 1f 110y(P)

4:20 4-Y-0+
£11,711 (£4,450; £3,279; £1,873; £936; £702)

RPR
1 **Zoelola (FR)**[27] 5-9-0 0 .... GregoryBenoist 8 75
(Mme P Butel & J-L Beaunez, France) **31/10**[1]
2 *1 ½* **Calaconta (FR)**[24] 4-9-1 0 .... MickaelBerto 4 73
(S Dehez, France) **40/1**
3 *nk* **Selini Mou (IRE)**[24] 4-8-11 0 ....(p) MickaelBarzalona 2 68
(Georgios Alimpinisis, France) **10/1**
4 *shd* **Achillea (FR)**[27] 6-8-11 0 .... JimmyTastayre(4) 1 72
(M Le Forestier, France) **9/1**
5 *¾* **Marobob**[27] 5-8-9 0 ....(p) DelphineSantiago(4) 6 68
(R Le Dren Doleuze, France) **9/1**
6 *1 ¼* **Madiva (FR)**[60] 7-9-2 0 .... Pierre-CharlesBoudot 11 69
(Vaclav Luka Jr, Czech Republic) **77/10**[2]
7 *nk* **My Lovely One (FR)**[24] 4-8-10 0 .... AugustinMadamet(4) 5 66
(E Libaud, France) **52/1**
8 *nk* **Samba Pa Ti (IRE)**[20] 5-8-9 0 .... StephanePasquier 7 60
(Mlle E Schmitt, France) **9/1**
9 *1 ½* **Willow Tree (FR)**[172] 4-9-4 0 .... MaximeGuyon 14 66
(E Libaud, France) **14/1**
10 *¾* **Champagne Pink (FR)**[159] 5-9-2 0 .... ThomasTrullier(3) 13 66
(Vaclav Luka Jr, Czech Republic) **27/1**
11 *shd* **Sissi Doloise (FR)**[20] 5-8-11 0 .... ClementCadel 10 58
(A Bonin, France) **79/10**[3]
12 *nk* **Nelly (FR)**[129] 4-8-13 0 .... BayarsaikhanGanbat 3 59
(S Smrczek, Germany) **18/1**
13 *1 ½* **Flor De Seda (FR)**[15] 1245 4-9-6 0 .... TheoBachelot 12 63
(Jo Hughes, France) *led at stdy pce tl hdd after 3f: pushed along to chse clr ldr 2 1/2f out: rdn 1 1/2f out: sn no ex and grad wknd ins fnl f* **23/1**
14 *7* **Praleen (FR)**[171] 4-9-4 0 .... EddyHardouin 9 47
(P Nador, France) **17/2**

1m 58.24s **14** Ran SP% **120.7**
PARI-MUTUEL (all including 1 euro stake): WIN 4.10 PLACE 1.90, 9.00, 3.70 DF 44.80.
Owner Mme P Butel & J-L Beaunez & Mlle M Mullier **Bred** Mme P Butel **Trained** France

1490 - 1491a (Foreign Racing) - See Raceform Interactive

1392 LINGFIELD (L-H)

Tuesday, April 2

OFFICIAL GOING: Polytrack: standard
Wind: Fresh, across (towards stands) Weather: Overcast and drizzly becoming brighter, cold

1492 LADBROKES HOME OF THE ODDS BOOST H'CAP 5f 6y(P)

2:00 (2:00) (Class 5) (0-75,77) 3-Y-O
£3,752 (£1,116; £557; £300; £300; £300) **Stalls** High

Form RPR
6-40 1 **Fizzy Feet (IRE)**[8] 1337 3-9-5 72 .... TrevorWhelan 7 79
(David Loughnane) *trckd ldr: shkn up 2f out: rdn to ld 1f out: styd on wl: readily (jockey said filly hung left-handed under pressure)* **12/1**
26-1 2 *2* **Swiss Pride (IRE)**[31] 990 3-9-10 77 .... ShaneKelly 6 77
(Richard Hughes) *slowly away: t.k.h: hld up in last pair: prog over 1f out: shkn up to chse wnr fnl 100yds: no imp* **13/8**[1]
223- 3 *1 ¼* **Shining**[133] 9163 3-9-9 76 .... CharlieBennett 4 71
(Jim Boyle) *chsd ldng pair: shkn up over 2f out: nt qckn over 1f out: kpt on* **8/1**
30-1 4 *½* **Lille**[21] 1161 3-9-2 74 .... DylanHogan(5) 1 68
(Kevin Ryan) *led: rdn and hdd 1f out: wknd* **11/4**[2]
310 5 *½* **Hanakotoba (USA)**[11] 1275 3-9-0 67 ....(t) SilvestreDeSousa 5 59
(Stuart Williams) *chsd ldng trio: rdn 1/2-way: no prog and btn over 1f out: kpt on again ins fnl f* **11/1**
041- 6 *1 ¾* **Keyhaven**[189] 7657 3-9-4 71 .... GeorgeWood 2 56
(James Fanshawe) *hld up towards rr: rdn over 2f out: kpt on inner in st and no prog* **9/2**[3]
506- 7 *1* **Cookupastorm (IRE)**[170] 8231 3-9-6 73 .... TomQueally 3 55
(Richard Spencer) *mostly in last and nvr a factor: rdn and no prog 2f out* **16/1**

57.81s (-0.99) **Going Correction** -0.275s/f (Stan) **7** Ran SP% **116.0**
Speed ratings (Par 98): **96,92,90,90,89 86,84**
CSF £32.98 TOTE £13.00: £3.50, £1.40; EX 38.20 Trifecta £173.00.
Owner D Lowe & S Hoyland **Bred** Tipper House Stud J Troy & R Levitt **Trained** Tern Hill, Shropshire
■ Stewards' Enquiry : Trevor Whelan three-day ban: careless riding (Apr 16-18)

FOCUS
A fair sprint handicap. The winner was back to 5f and built on his 2yo form.

1493 LADBROKES NOVICE MEDIAN AUCTION STKS 5f 6y(P)

2:30 (2:30) (Class 5) 2-Y-O
£3,752 (£1,116; £557; £278) **Stalls** High

Form RPR
1 **Electric Ladyland (IRE)** 2-9-0 0 .... LukeMorris 10 75+
(Archie Watson) *gd spd fr wdst draw: mde all: shkn up over 1f out: styd on wl fnl f* **4/1**[3]
6 2 *2* **Birkenhead**[3] 1416 2-9-5 0 .... CallumShepherd 4 73
(Mick Channon) *chsd wnr: shkn up 2f out: styd on but no imp fnl f* **6/5**[1]
0 3 *1 ½* **Heer We Go Again**[3] 1416 2-9-5 0 .... AdamKirby 5 68
(David Evans) *pushed up on outer to dispute 2nd over 3f out: shkn up 2f out: wl hld in 3rd fr over 1f out but clr of rest* **5/2**[2]
4 *4* **Forced** 2-9-0 0 .... ShaneKelly 9 48+
(Richard Hughes) *racd on outer: chsd ldng trio 3f out: outpcd over 2f out: no imp after* **8/1**
5 *2 ½* **Bainne Dubh** 2-8-9 0 .... SeamusCronin(5) 6 41
(Bill Turner) *chsd ldng pair to over 3f out: wl outpcd whn bmpd over 2f out: no prog after* **33/1**
6 *1* **Hypochondriac** 2-8-7 0 .... GinaMangan(7) 3 36+
(David Evans) *dwlt: hld up in rr: outpcd whn nt clr run 1/2-way: no ch whn short of room wl over 1f out* **33/1**
7 *1 ¾* **Is She The One** 2-9-0 0 .... DannyBrock 7 29
(Philip McBride) *v s.i.s: rn green in rr: shkn up and no prog 2f out* **20/1**
0 8 *shd* **Victochop (FR)**[3] 1416 2-8-12 0 .... WilliamCarver(7) 1 36
(George Baker) *nvr beyond midfield: wl outpcd whn bmpd over 2f out: no prog* **20/1**
9 *7* **Lakeview (IRE)** 2-9-5 0 .... TrevorWhelan 2 9
(David Loughnane) *s.i.s: outpcd and a bhd (jockey said colt ran green and hung wide on bend)* **28/1**

58.05s (-0.75) **Going Correction** -0.275s/f (Stan) **9** Ran SP% **124.0**
Speed ratings (Par 92): **95,91,89,83,79 77,74,74,63**
CSF £9.41 TOTE £6.70: £1.90, £1.10, £1.20; EX 14.70 Trifecta £38.10.
Owner Miss Emily Asprey & Christopher Wright **Bred** Rathasker Stud **Trained** Upper Lambourn, W Berks
■ Stewards' Enquiry : Gina Mangan two-day ban: careless riding (Apr 16-17)

FOCUS
A good performance from the winner, who overcame lack of previous experience and a wide draw to beat a couple of rivals who weren't disgraced in the Brocklesby the other day. The juvenile course record was lowered by 0.06sec.

1494 BETWAY LIVE CASINO (S) STKS 1m 2f (P)

3:00 (3:00) (Class 6) 3-6-Y-O
£3,105 (£924; £461; £300; £300) **Stalls** Low

Form RPR
520- 1 **Cafe Espresso**[109] 9530 3-8-0 70 ....(p[1]) HollieDoyle 1 44+
(Archie Watson) *mde all: shkn up 2f out: rdn out and kpt on fnl f* **11/8**[2]
036- 2 *¾* **Glorious Dane**[109] 9530 3-8-0 70 .... ThoreHammerHansen(5) 3 48+
(Richard Hannon) *free to post: hld up in 3rd: chsd wnr 2f out: rdn and nt qckn over 1f out: kpt on but readily hld after* **4/6**[1]
0000 3 *½* **Shovel It On (IRE)**[18] 1215 4-9-10 41 ....(bt) RaulDaSilva 5 51
(Steve Flook) *hld up in last: prog jst over 2f out: chsd clr ldng pair over 1f out: drvn and clsd fnl f: kpt on but no imp nr fin* **66/1**
-00 4 *7* **Breezing**[20] 1174 3-8-0 48 ....(b) KieranO'Neill 2 28
(Sylvester Kirk) *chsd wnr: drvn 3f out: lost 2nd 2f out and sn wknd* **50/1**
-600 5 *2 ¾* **Claudine (IRE)**[34] 923 4-8-12 58 .... AmeliaGlass(7) 4 27
(Alexandra Dunn) *hld up in 4th: rdn wl over 2f out: wknd wl over 1f out* **20/1**[3]

2m 4.69s (-1.91) **Going Correction** -0.275s/f (Stan)
WFA 3 from 4yo 19lb **5** Ran SP% **110.3**
Speed ratings: **96,95,95,89,87**
CSF £2.60 TOTE £2.10: £1.20, £1.02; EX 2.70 Trifecta £12.50.The winner was bought in for £7,000. Glorious Dane was claimed by Mr Lee Bolingbroke for £7,000.
Owner Boadicea Bloodstock **Bred** Churchill Bloodstock Investments Ltd **Trained** Upper Lambourn, W Berks

FOCUS
It's hard to rate this form positively, with the lowly rated third finishing close up.

1495 LADBROKES HOME OF THE ODDS BOOST NOVICE STKS 1m 1y(P)

3:30 (3:30) (Class 5) 3-Y-O
£3,752 (£1,116; £557; £278) **Stalls** High

Form RPR
226- 1 **Sash**[111] 9500 3-9-3 82 .... AndreaAtzeni 6 76
(Amanda Perrett) *trckd ldr after 2f: chal 2f out: hung fire over 1f out: drvn and styd on fnl f to ld fnl 75yds* **8/13**[1]
2 *nk* **Doughan Alb** 3-9-3 0 .... SeanLevey 1 75
(Richard Hannon) *trckd ldr 2f: styd cl up: pushed along 3f out: renewed effrt on inner over 1f out: rdn to ld ins fnl f: hdd and no ex fnl 75yds* **16/1**
12 3 *½* **Moongazer**[27] 1033 3-9-5 0 .... RichardKingscote 7 76
(Charles Hills) *led: pressed 2f out: rdn and hdd 1f out: styd on same pce* **5/1**[3]
4- 4 *hd* **Dancingwithwolves (IRE)**[174] 8099 3-9-3 0 ....(h) DanielMuscutt 4 74
(Ed Dunlop) *t.k.h: trckd ldrs: rdn and tried to chal between rivals over 1f out: styd on same pce ins fnl f* **12/1**
1- 5 *¾* **Fragrant Belle**[213] 6803 3-9-3 0 .... HarryBentley 3 72
(Ralph Beckett) *hld up in midfield: pushed along and outpcd over 2f out: rdn and styd on fnl f: clsng at fin* **7/2**[2]
6 *2 ½* **Corncrake** 3-9-3 0 .... TomMarquand 9 66
(Richard Hannon) *a towards rr: rdn and outpcd 3f out: no prog after (jockey said colt was never travelling)* **16/1**
0 7 *2 ½* **Quemonda**[22] 1142 3-8-12 0 .... ShaneKelly 2 56
(Ken Cunningham-Brown) *s.s: a in last pair: rdn and no prog 3f out* **100/1**
-5 8 *3 ¾* **Thinque Tank**[11] 1268 3-9-3 0 .... CallumShepherd 8 52
(Charlie Longsdon) *dwlt: hld up in last: pushed along and lft bhd over 2f out* **66/1**

1m 35.61s (-2.59) **Going Correction** -0.275s/f (Stan) **8** Ran SP% **122.7**
Speed ratings (Par 98): **101,100,100,100,99 96,94,90**
CSF £15.82 TOTE £1.40: £1.10, £4.00, £1.20; EX 14.60 Trifecta £54.70.
Owner K Abdullah **Bred** Juddmonte Farms Ltd **Trained** Pulborough, W Sussex

FOCUS
The pace held up pretty well but they finished in a heap and it's just fair form.

1496 BETWAY H'CAP — 6f 1y(P)
4:00 (4:00) (Class 4) (0-80,82) 4-Y-O+
£5,530 (£1,645; £822; £411; £300; £300) **Stalls Low**

Form — RPR

5541 **1** **Global Tango (IRE)**[6] 1357 4-9-3 **81** 5ex.....(b) CierenFallon(7) 4 — 93
(Charles Hills) *chsd clr ldng pair: rdn to cl fr 2f out: led ins fnl f: drvn out* 6/4[1]

24-1 **2** 2 **Field Gun (USA)**[59] 548 4-9-6 **77**.....(t) AdamKirby 6 — 82
(Stuart Williams) *racd in 6th and off the pce: rdn 2f out: styd on wl fr over 1f out to take 2nd fnl 75yds: no threat to wnr* 11/4[2]

30-6 **3** ½ **Mamillius**[22] 1143 6-9-6 **77**..... ShaneKelly 1 — 80
(George Baker) *chsd clr ldrs: 4th and no imp over 2f out: hrd rdn and kpt on to take 3rd fnl 75yds* 5/1[3]

4-66 **4** 1½ **Zac Brown (IRE)**[32] 964 8-9-8 **82**.....(t) JoshuaBryan(3) 10 — 80+
(Charlie Wallis) *led at str pce and clr w one rival: drvn wl over 1f out: hdd & wknd ins fnl f* 25/1

-000 **5** 1 **Regulator (IRE)**[34] 922 4-9-6 **77**..... GeorgeWood 5 — 72
(Alexandra Dunn) *hld up in last trio and wl off the pce: shkn up on inner 2f out: kpt on steadily fnl f: nvr in it* 50/1

104- **6** nk **Big Lachie**[157] 8636 5-9-6 **77**..... AndrewMullen 7 — 71
(Mark Loughnane) *hld up in 8th and wl off the pce: rdn 2f out: sme prog over 1f out: no imp on ldrs ins fnl f* 33/1

2133 **7** 1½ **Tavener**[4] 1393 7-8-7 **64** oh1.....(p) MartinDwyer 2 — 53
(David C Griffiths) *wl off the pce in 7th: urged along and no prog over 2f out: nvr on terms* 12/1

5000 **8** 2¾ **Kodiline (IRE)**[10] 1290 5-8-9 **73**..... GinaMangan(7) 8 — 53
(David Evans) *awkward s and rdr nrly off: mostly in last and a wl off the pce (jockey said gelding ducked head at start which meant she was slow to remove blindfold)* 22/1

1-43 **9** hd **Red Alert**[41] 797 5-9-10 **81**.....(p) TomMarquand 11 — 61
(Tony Carroll) *outpcd in last trio and nvr a factor* 20/1

5460 **10** nk **Tan**[33] 953 5-9-7 **78**.....(p) AlistairRawlinson 3 — 57
(Michael Appleby) *w ldr at str pce and clr of the rest tl wknd over 1f out* 8/1

030- **11** 11 **Bahamian Sunrise**[146] 8934 7-9-6 **77**.....(b) SilvestreDeSousa 9 — 21
(John Gallagher) *chsd clr ldrs to 1/2-way: sn wknd: eased whn btn: t.o (jockey said gelding did not face kick back)* 33/1

1m 9.4s (-2.50) **Going Correction** -0.275s/f (Stan) — **11 Ran SP% 122.9**
Speed ratings (Par 105): **105,102,101,99,98 97,95,92,92,91 76**
CSF £5.34 CT £17.66 TOTE £2.40: £1.30, £1.30, £1.70; EX 8.20 Trifecta £25.50.
Owner Dr Johnny Hon **Bred** Ballycrighaun Stud **Trained** Lambourn, Berks

FOCUS
This was a well-run sprint handicap.

1497 BETWAY HEED YOUR HUNCH H'CAP — 1m 7f 169y(P)
4:30 (4:30) (Class 5) (0-70,67) 4-Y-O+
£3,752 (£1,116; £557; £300; £300; £300) **Stalls Low**

Form — RPR

5-22 **1** **Tin Fandango**[33] 946 4-9-3 **63**.....(p) JosephineGordon 7 — 71
(Mark Usher) *trckd ldr: clsd to ld 3f out: rdn 2f out: styd on steadily and in command fnl f* 12/1

6111 **2** 2 **Singing The Blues (IRE)**[17] 1235 4-9-6 **66**..... CharlesBishop 11 — 72
(Rod Millman) *t.k.h early: hld up bhd ldrs: pushed along and nt qckn 3f out: rallied over 1f out: styd on to take 2nd ins fnl f: unable to chal* 11/4[1]

364- **3** nk **Love To Breeze**[161] 8513 4-9-6 **66**.....(t¹) RichardKingscote 10 — 71
(Jonathan Portman) *hld up in last trio: swift prog 5f out to chse wnr wl over 2f out: nt qckn over 1f out w plenty of tail swishing: lost 2nd ins fnl f: kpt on* 13/2

0-43 **4** 1 **Knight Commander**[24] 810 6-8-12 **56**.....(t w) RaulDaSilva 2 — 60
(Steve Flook) *hld up in midfield: lost pl over 3f out: pushed along in 8th over 2f out: drvn and styd on over 1f out to take 4th fnl 75yds: nrst fin* 20/1

213- **5** 1¾ **Looking For Carl**[164] 8421 4-9-6 **66**..... AndrewMullen 8 — 68
(Mark Loughnane) *hld up in last pair: prog over 4f out: drvn to chse ldng trio over 2f out: nt qckn u.p over 1f out: fdd* 12/1

6243 **6** hd **Mood For Mischief**[28] 1024 4-9-2 **62**.....(p) HarryBentley 6 — 64
(Ed Walker) *mostly trckd ldng pair: nt qckn over 2f out: wl hld over 1f out and racd on inner: fdd fnl f* 3/1[2]

320- **7** 1 **Fitzwilly**[138] 9076 9-9-1 **66**..... ScottMcCullagh(7) 5 — 66
(Mick Channon) *hld up in 7th: pushed along over 4f out: lost pl over 3f out: n.d after: plugged on fnl f* 25/1

-464 **8** hd **Queen Of Paris**[33] 946 4-9-4 **64**.....(t) AndreaAtzeni 1 — 64
(William Knight) *dwlt: hld up in last pair: rdn and prog 3f out: rchd 6th 2f out: no hdwy after* 6/1[3]

22-6 **9** 6 **Whinging Willie (IRE)**[68] 385 10-9-9 **67**.....(v) HectorCrouch 4 — 60
(Gary Moore) *a in rr: shkn up and wknd 3f out: bhd over 1f out (vet said gelding struck into right fore)* 10/1

3033 **10** 12 **Highway One (USA)**[32] 965 5-9-4 **62**..... SilvestreDeSousa 9 — 41
(George Baker) *led and clr: hdd & wknd 3f out: eased whn no ch* 8/1

/40- **11** 56 **Everlasting Sea**[147] 8893 5-8-6 **50**.....(w) KieranO'Neill 3
(Stuart Kittow) *chsd ldrs tl wknd over 3f out: sn t.o (jockey said mare stopped quickly)* 50/1

3m 19.98s (-5.72) **Going Correction** -0.275s/f (Stan) — **11 Ran SP% 125.4**
WFA 4 from 5yo+ 2lb
Speed ratings (Par 103): **103,102,101,101,100 100,99,99,96,90 62**
CSF £47.35 CT £248.96 TOTE £13.20: £3.10, £1.20, £2.20; EX 56.80 Trifecta £620.80.
Owner M A Humphreys **Bred** Stuart & Sarah Matheson **Trained** Upper Lambourn, Berks

FOCUS
A modest affair.

1498 BETWAY CASINO APPRENTICE H'CAP — 1m 4f (P)
5:00 (5:00) (Class 6) (0-60,62) 4-Y-O+
£3,105 (£924; £461; £300; £300; £300) **Stalls Low**

Form — RPR

-524 **1** **Dream Magic (IRE)**[28] 1024 5-9-9 **62**.....(b¹) CameronNoble(3) 11 — 72
(Mark Loughnane) *t.k.h: trckd ldrs: led over 2f out and sn dashed clr: 5 l ahd 1f out: in n.d after* 9/2[2]

0-24 **2** 2¼ **Zamperini (IRE)**[34] 923 7-9-2 **59**..... RhysClutterbuck(7) 12 — 62
(Gary Moore) *hld up wl in rr: prog wl over 1f out: r.o to take 2nd fnl 100yds: fin strly but too late* 15/2

4050 **3** 2½ **Attain**[2] 1463 10-9-2 **59**..... KateLeahy(7) 2 — 58
(Archie Watson) *t.k.h: trckd ldrs: outpcd over 2f out: rdn and styd on over 1f out to take 3rd wl ins fnl f: n.d* 12/1

01-0 **4** ½ **Millie May**[76] 257 5-8-6 **47**..... ThoreHammerHansen(5) 4 — 45
(Jimmy Fox) *trckd ldr to 1/2-way: styd prom: chal 3f out: outpcd over 2f out: stl disputing 2nd ins fnl f: fdd* 20/1

2133 **5** 1½ **Tesorina (IRE)**[6] 1362 4-9-2 **57**.....(v) Pierre-LouisJamin(5) 3 — 54
(William Knight) *led to 3f out: sn outpcd by wnr: stl in 2nd pl jst ins fnl f: wknd* 5/1[3]

0322 **6** nk **Make Good (IRE)**[6] 1363 4-9-4 **61**.....(bt) CierenFallon(7) 10 — 57
(David Dennis) *s.s: sn chsd ldrs: outpcd on inner over 2f out: no hdwy over 1f out: fdd (trainer's rep had no explanation for the gelding's performance; jockey said gelding was slowly away)* 2/1[1]

4414 **7** ½ **Music Major**[10] 1292 6-9-4 **59**..... ScottMcCullagh(5) 9 — 54
(Michael Attwater) *hld up and mostly in last pair: outpcd over 2f out: kpt on fnl f but nvr any ch* 8/1

0650 **8** ½ **Presence Process**[11] 1269 5-9-11 **61**..... PaddyBradley 7 — 55
(Pat Phelan) *trckd ldrs early but sn in midfield: outpcd over 2f out: rdn and no prog on outer 2f out* 10/1

-005 **9** 2 **Sellingallthetime (IRE)**[55] 622 8-9-3 **60**.....(p) GeorgiaDobie(7) 8 — 51
(Mark Usher) *t.k.h: trckd ldrs: outpcd and lost pl 3f out: no ch after* 25/1

5150 **10** 7 **Dolphin Village (IRE)**[22] 1146 9-8-4 **47**.....(h) GavinAshton(7) 6 — 26
(Shaun Harris) *dwlt: t.k.h: hld up in last tl rapid prog to trck ldr 1/2-way: chal 3f out: sltly impeded over 2f out and wknd qckly* 18/1

2m 30.09s (-2.91) **Going Correction** -0.275s/f (Stan) — **10 Ran SP% 121.7**
Speed ratings (Par 101): **98,96,94,94,93 93,92,92,91,86**
CSF £40.15 CT £389.13 TOTE £5.70: £2.00, £2.30, £3.20; EX 46.00 Trifecta £461.60.
Owner Mrs C Loughnane **Bred** Paul V Jackson & Janet P Jackson **Trained** Rock, Worcs

FOCUS
This looked fairly competitive on paper but the winner, aided by first-time blinkers, came clear to score with ease.
T/Plt: £5.40 to a £1 stake. Pool: £87,084.00 - 11,736.66 winning units T/Qpdt: £2.40 to a £1 stake. Pool: £9,162.80 - 2,811.69 winning units **Jonathan Neesom**

MUSSELBURGH (R-H)
Tuesday, April 2

OFFICIAL GOING: Good to firm (good in places; 8.7)
Wind: Breezy, half against in approximately 4f of home straight Weather: Cloudy, bright

1499 WATCH RACING TV NOW NOVICE STKS (PLUS 10 RACE) — 5f 1y
2:15 (2:16) (Class 4) 2-Y-O
£4,787 (£1,424; £711; £355) **Stalls High**

Form — RPR

1 **Proper Beau** 2-9-5 0..... GrahamLee 6 — 81
(Bryan Smart) *early ldr: disp ld: regained ld 2f out: shkn up fnl f: kpt on wl cl home* 10/1

2 nk **Alminoor (IRE)** 2-9-5 0..... PJMcDonald 5 — 80
(Mark Johnston) *edgy in preliminaries: wnt rt s: sn led: hdd 2f out: styd w wnr: kpt on fnl f: hld cl home* 11/10[1]

3 7 **War Of Clans (IRE)** 2-9-5 0..... BenCurtis 2 — 55+
(K R Burke) *green in preliminaries: trckd ldrs: pushed along 2f out: outpcd fnl f* 10/1

4 1½ **Coast Ofalfujairah (IRE)** 2-9-5 0..... TomEaves 4 — 49+
(Kevin Ryan) *dwlt and carried rt s: hld up: effrt and pushed along whn nt clr run briefly over 1f out: sn no imp* 5/1[2]

5 nk **Mystic Knight (IRE)** 2-9-5 0..... DavidAllan 7 — 48
(Tim Easterby) *in tch: pushed along 1/2-way: no imp fr over 1f out* 20/1

6 1¼ **Baileys Freedom** 2-9-5 0..... EdwardGreatrex 1 — 44+
(Archie Watson) *prom on outside: drvn along 1/2-way: wknd fnl f* 11/2[3]

7 2½ **Gina D'Cleaner** 2-9-0 0..... PaulMulrennan 3 — 30+
(Keith Dalgleish) *carried rt s: bhd and outpcd: nvr on terms* 16/1

59.85s (0.15) **Going Correction** -0.05s/f (Good) — **7 Ran SP% 108.5**
Speed ratings (Par 94): **96,95,84,81,81 79,75**
CSF £19.39 TOTE £10.70: £4.80, £1.10; EX 25.10 Trifecta £113.30.
Owner Michael Moses & Terry Moses **Bred** The Aston House Stud **Trained** Hambleton, N Yorks

FOCUS
The return of Flat racing to Musselburgh in 2019, a meeting run on heavy 12 months earlier. All race distances as advertised.\n \n\x\x It paid to be near the stands' rail in this modest juvenile event and the first pair came clear.

1500 FOLLOW @RACINGTV ON TWITTER H'CAP — 1m 4f 104y
2:45 (2:45) (Class 6) (0-65,65) 4-Y-O+
£3,105 (£924; £461; £300; £300; £300) **Stalls Low**

Form — RPR

00-0 **1** **Sioux Frontier (IRE)**[38] 886 4-9-7 **65**..... LewisEdmunds 2 — 71
(Iain Jardine) *t.k.h: hld up on ins: stdy hdwy over 2f out: effrt and led over 1f out: rdn out fnl f* 14/1

15-5 **2** ½ **Pammi**[86] 101 4-8-10 **57** ow2..... JamieGormley(3) 9 — 62
(Jim Goldie) *hld up: hdwy on outside over 2f out: checked and edgd rt over 1f out: chsd wnr ins fnl f: r.o* 13/2

0500 **3** ½ **Elite Icon**[21] 1163 5-8-4 **48** oh1 ow2..... PhilDennis 5 — 51
(Jim Goldie) *hld up: pushed along and hdwy over 2f out: kpt on ins fnl f: nrst fin* 20/1

5053 **4** 2¼ **Sosian**[31] 984 4-8-2 **46** oh1.....(v) PaddyMathers 10 — 47
(Richard Fahey) *chsd clr ldr to 1/2-way: drvn along 3f out: rallied: one pce fr over 1f out* 7/1

400- **5** ½ **Fillydelphia (IRE)**[11] 8416 8-8-3 **47** oh1 ow1.....(h) RachelRichardson 4 — 46
(Liam Bailey) *hld up: rdn along over 3f out: outpcd over 2f out: r.o fnl f: nvr able to chal* 16/1

3-46 **6** 1¼ **Home Before Dusk**[28] 1022 4-9-7 **65**.....(p) ConnorBeasley 7 — 63
(Keith Dalgleish) *cl up in chsng gp: wnt 2nd and clsd on ldr 1/2-way: led over 2f out: hdd over 1f out: drvn and wknd ins fnl f* 3/1[2]

600- **7** ½ **Dutch Melody**[28] 9551 5-7-9 **46** oh1..... VictorSantos(7) 8 — 42
(Lucinda Egerton) *led and clr to 1/2-way: hdd over 2f out: rallied: wknd over 1f out* 200/1

402- **8** ¾ **Enemy Of The State (IRE)**[235] 5964 5-8-3 **47**..... NathanEvans 6 — 42
(Jason Ward) *t.k.h: in tch: pushed along and hdwy over 2f out: drifted lft u.p over 1f out: sn wknd (jockey said gelding hung left-handed in the straight)* 11/4[1]

-024 **9** *37* **Enmeshing**[17] 1235 6-9-6 **64** RossaRyan 3
(Alexandra Dunn) *prom: effrt and drvn along over 2f out: wknd over 1f out: eased whn btn fnl f* **9/2**[3]

2m 43.98s (-0.52) **Going Correction** -0.05s/f (Good) **9** Ran SP% **113.5**
Speed ratings (Par 101): **99,98,98,96,96 95,95,94,70**
CSF £99.93 CT £1817.08 TOTE £13.00: £3.30, £1.90, £4.70; EX 125.30 Trifecta £1664.40.
Owner Let's Be Lucky Racing 23 **Bred** P J Towell **Trained** Carrutherstown, D'fries & G'way

FOCUS
Thanks to Dutch Melody this moderate handicap was run at a decent pace. The consistent runner-up helps set the level.

1501 BORDERLESCOTT SPRINT TROPHY CONDITIONS STKS 5f 1y
3:15 (3:15) (Class 2) 4-Y-0+

£12,450 (£3,728; £1,864; £932; £466; £234) **Stalls** High

Form RPR

056- **1** **Tanasoq (IRE)**[175] 8083 6-9-2 94 GrahamLee 7 102
(Paul Midgley) *hld up: nt clr run over 2f out to over 1f out: effrt and led fnl 75yds: hld on wl* **12/1**

121- **2** *hd* **El Astronaute (IRE)**[171] 8215 6-9-6 106 JasonHart 6 105
(John Quinn) *propped as stall opened and wnt rt s: sn w ldr: rdn and led over 1f out: hdd fnl 75yds: edgd rt: r.o* **7/4**[1]

221- **3** *1 ½* **Tarboosh**[157] 8632 6-9-2 108 KevinStott 3 96
(Paul Midgley) *checked sn after s: sn prom: effrt and rdn over 1f out: ev ch ins fnl f: no ex fnl 75yds* **5/2**[2]

100- **4** *nk* **Royal Brave (IRE)**[161] 8503 8-9-2 91 DavidAllan 8 95
(Rebecca Bastiman) *hld up: nt clr run 2f out: effrt and angled rt over 1f out: kpt on ins fnl f* **25/1**

401- **5** *5* **Merry Banter**[178] 7994 5-8-11 85 PaulMulrennan 2 72
(Paul Midgley) *swtchd lft sn after s: led to over 1f out: drvn and wknd fnl f* **28/1**

112- **6** *3 ¼* **Captain Colby (USA)**[164] 8413 7-9-2 99 (w) BenRobinson 5 65
(Paul Midgley) *hld up: drvn along over 2f out: wknd over 1f out (vet said gelding lost left fore shoe)* **7/1**

2122 **7** *1 ½* **Merhoob (IRE)**[10] 1295 7-9-2 103 PaulHanagan 4 60
(John Ryan) *dwlt and blkd s: sn pushed along in rr: effrt and drvn 1/2-way: wknd over 1f out (jockey said gelding was short of room shortly after the start and was never travelling thereafter)* **5/1**[3]

600- **8** *7* **Longroom**[172] 8165 7-9-2 82 (t[1]) PhilDennis 1 35
(Noel Wilson) *missed break: hld up: effrt on outside 1/2-way: wknd wl over 1f out* **100/1**

58.95s (-0.75) **Going Correction** -0.05s/f (Good) **8** Ran SP% **110.1**
Speed ratings (Par 109): **104,103,101,100,92 87,85,74**
CSF £31.05 TOTE £12.80: £2.70, £1.20, £1.10; EX 38.30 Trifecta £144.20.
Owner F Brady & J S Morrison **Bred** Mountarmstrong Stud **Trained** Westow, N Yorks

FOCUS
Predictably this decent conditions sprint was run at a frantic pace and the first four pulled clear.

1502 RACINGTV.COM H'CAP 7f 33y
3:45 (3:48) (Class 3) (0-95,94) 4-Y-0+

£8,092 (£2,423; £1,211; £605; £302; £152) **Stalls** Low

Form RPR

100- **1** **Porth Swtan (IRE)**[168] 8299 4-9-2 89 JasonHart 2 97
(Garry Moss) *trckd ldrs: effrt and angled lft over 1f out: led ins fnl f: rdn out* **8/1**[2]

351- **2** *1* **Raselasad (IRE)**[216] 6670 5-9-2 89 BenCurtis 8 94
(Tracy Waggott) *led: rdn along over 1f out: hdd ins fnl f: kpt on same pce* **5/1**[1]

010- **3** *¾* **Hayadh**[157] 8634 6-9-3 90 DavidAllan 9 93
(Rebecca Bastiman) *chsd ldrs: drvn along over 2f out: r.o ins fnl f* **8/1**[2]

204- **4** *nk* **Three Saints Bay (IRE)**[169] 8265 4-9-7 94 DavidNolan 3 96
(David O'Meara) *hld up in tch: effrt and rdn on outside over 2f out: kpt on same pce ins fnl f* **9/1**

000- **5** *1 ½* **Fennaan (IRE)**[162] 8472 4-9-4 91 (h[1]) SamJames 11 89
(Phillip Makin) *hld up in midfield: effrt and pushed along 2f out: kpt on fnl f: nvr able to chal* **33/1**

5346 **6** *1 ½* **Reckless Endeavour (IRE)**[10] 1290 6-8-4 77 JoeFanning 7 71
(David Barron) *dwlt: hld up: pushed along over 2f out: hdwy and edgd rt over 1f out: sn no imp* **17/2**[3]

05-0 **7** *½* **Oriental Lilly**[43] 786 5-8-1 77 JamieGormley[(3)] 6 70
(Jim Goldie) *hld up on ins: rdn over 2f out: no imp over 1f out* **33/1**

6-10 **8** *1* **Saint Equiano**[34] 929 5-9-5 92 GrahamLee 5 82
(Keith Dalgleish) *chsd ldr: drvn over 2f out: wknd fnl f* **10/1**

000- **9** *5* **Lualiwa**[143] 9004 5-9-3 90 KevinStott 10 67
(Kevin Ryan) *dwlt: hld up: rdn and struggling 3f out: btn fnl 2f* **11/1**

311- **10** *10* **Alfred Richardson**[144] 8974 5-9-2 89 (b) ConnorBeasley 1 39
(John Davies) *s.i.s: nvr gng wl in rr: struggling fnl 3f* **11/1**

1m 26.86s (-2.14) **Going Correction** -0.05s/f (Good) **10** Ran SP% **91.1**
Speed ratings (Par 107): **110,108,108,107,105 104,103,102,96,85**
CSF £28.94 CT £142.78 TOTE £6.20: £2.10, £1.60, £2.40; EX 25.50 Trifecta £131.50.
Owner C H McGhie **Bred** Irish National Stud **Trained** Wynyard, Stockton-On-Tees
■ Love Dreams was withdrawn, price at time of withdrawal 5/2f. Rule 4 applies to all bets. Deduction of 25p in the pound.

FOCUS
This good-quality handicap was markedly weakened by the defection of Love Dreams. The sound pace held up and the winner gained a clear personal best on debut for Gary Moss.

1503 LIKE RACING TV ON FACEBOOK H'CAP 1m 5f 216y
4:15 (4:17) (Class 4) (0-80,82) 4-Y-0+

£5,692 (£1,694; £846; £423; £300; £300) **Stalls** Low

Form RPR

2451 **1** **Champarisi**[21] 1159 4-8-11 69 SamJames 3 75+
(Grant Tuer) *prom: rdn to ld over 2f out: sn hrd pressed: hld on wl fnl f* **5/2**[1]

4100 **2** *¾* **Navajo Star (IRE)**[8] 1330 5-9-6 77 (v) PJMcDonald 5 81
(Robyn Brisland) *hld up in tch: shkn up over 2f out: effrt and angled rt over 1f out: kpt on to take 2nd cl home: nt rch wnr (jockey said mare was denied a clear run inside the final furlong)* **12/1**

020- **3** *shd* **Akamanto (IRE)**[167] 8320 5-9-11 82 BenCurtis 8 86
(R Mike Smith) *pressed ldr: effrt and ev ch over 2f out to ins fnl f: hld and lost 2nd nr fin* **11/2**[2]

-331 **4** *1 ¾* **Cry Wolf**[33] 948 6-9-11 82 RossaRyan 6 84
(Alexandra Dunn) *hld up: stdy hdwy 3f out: effrt and ev ch over 1f out: edgd rt and one pce ins fnl f (jockey said gelding hung right-handed in the final furlong)* **13/2**

230- **5** *nk* **Four Kingdoms (IRE)**[197] 6417 5-8-7 69 AndrewBreslin[(5)] 2 70
(R Mike Smith) *t.k.h early: trckd ldrs: drvn along over 2f out: no ex fnl f* **12/1**

162- **6** *nk* **Maulesden May (IRE)**[169] 8267 6-8-13 70 JoeFanning 7 71
(Keith Dalgleish) *hld up: stdy hdwy on outside over 2f out: effrt and ev ch over 1f out: wknd ins fnl f* **11/2**[2]

510- **7** *2* **Sarvi**[24] 8130 4-8-10 71 JamieGormley[(3)] 1 70
(Jim Goldie) *s.i.s: bhd and detached: hdwy after 4f: rdn and outpcd over 2f out: sn btn* **10/1**

110- **8** *¾* **Dragon Mountain**[174] 8102 4-9-7 79 GrahamLee 4 77
(Keith Dalgleish) *led to over 2f out: rdn and wknd fnl f* **6/1**[3]

3m 4.14s (0.24) **Going Correction** -0.05s/f (Good)
WFA 4 from 5yo+ 1lb **8** Ran SP% **111.4**
Speed ratings (Par 105): **97,96,96,95,95 95,94,93**
CSF £32.53 CT £146.06 TOTE £3.00: £1.20, £3.20, £1.60; EX 29.30 Trifecta £156.90.
Owner Allerton Racing & G Tuer **Bred** Faisal Meshrf Alqahtani **Trained** Birkby, N Yorks

FOCUS
There was a sound pace on in this modest staying handicap. The form looks ordinary, however, with the runner-up still looking high in weights.

1504 EVERY RACE LIVE ON RACING TV H'CAP 7f 33y
4:45 (4:49) (Class 5) (0-75,75) 3-Y-O

£3,752 (£1,116; £557; £300; £300; £300) **Stalls** Low

Form RPR

254- **1** **City Tour**[143] 9001 3-9-5 73 JoeFanning 12 78+
(Mark Johnston) *prom: effrt on outside 2f out: hung rt fnl f: kpt on wl to ld cl home* **5/2**[1]

303- **2** *shd* **Lightning Attack**[165] 8374 3-9-6 74 (p) TonyHamilton 8 78
(Richard Fahey) *hld up in midfield: effrt on outside 2f out: hdwy and edgd rt fnl f: kpt on to take 2nd cl home: jst hld* **9/2**[2]

302- **3** *hd* **Staycation (IRE)**[160] 8532 3-8-13 67 DavidAllan 1 70
(Rebecca Bastiman) *led: rdn over 1f out: hung lft ins fnl f: hdd and no ex cl home* **25/1**

603- **4** *¾* **Call Him Al (IRE)**[137] 9095 3-8-2 61 SeanDavis[(5)] 3 62
(Richard Fahey) *trckd ldrs: effrt and disp 2nd pl over 1f out to ins fnl f: kpt on same pce towards fin* **12/1**

403- **5** *¾* **Spirit Of Lund (IRE)**[165] 8378 3-9-3 74 JamieGormley[(3)] 2 75+
(Iain Jardine) *hld up: pushed along 3f out: hdwy on ins over 1f out: cl 5th and keeping on wl whn no room and snatched up nr fin (jockey said gelding was denied a clear run approaching the winning line)* **8/1**

061- **6** *1 ¾* **Jackamundo (FR)**[196] 7390 3-9-5 73 KevinStott 4 68
(Declan Carroll) *hld up in midfield: effrt over 2f out: rdn and kpt on same pce fnl f* **5/1**[3]

636- **7** *1 ½* **Silver Dust (IRE)**[255] 5226 3-9-7 75 PaulHanagan 6 66
(Richard Fahey) *t.k.h: prom: effrt and rdn 2f out: edgd rt: one pce whn nt clr run briefly ins fnl f: sn btn* **17/2**

601- **8** *2 ½* **Uncle Norman (FR)**[155] 8692 3-8-6 60 (b) RachelRichardson 5 44
(Tim Easterby) *slowly away: hld up: rdn along 3f out: no imp whn edgd lft over 1f out: sn btn* **28/1**

446- **9** *1 ¼* **Iron Mike**[147] 8896 3-9-5 73 ConnorBeasley 7 54
(Keith Dalgleish) *midfield: drvn and effrt over 2f out: no imp over 1f out* **15/2**

63-0 **10** *1 ¼* **Kimberley Girl**[19] 1195 3-8-6 60 NathanEvans 9 37
(Michael Easterby) *hld up: drvn along over 3f out: btn fnl 2f* **50/1**

024- **11** *1* **Beechwood Izzy (IRE)**[138] 9085 3-9-7 75 PaulMulrennan 10 49
(Keith Dalgleish) *t.k.h: cl up: rdn over 2f out: wknd over 1f out* **20/1**

0-63 **12** *1 ½* **Popping Corks (IRE)**[61] 497 3-7-13 58 PaulaMuir[(5)] 11 28
(Linda Perratt) *s.i.s: bhd: stmbld sn after s: rdn over 3f out: edgd rt and wknd 2f out* **50/1**

1m 28.22s (-0.78) **Going Correction** -0.05s/f (Good) **12** Ran SP% **120.5**
Speed ratings (Par 98): **102,101,101,100,99 97,96,93,91,90 89,87**
CSF £12.73 CT £233.07 TOTE £3.20: £1.50, £1.60, £8.80; EX 15.10 Trifecta £210.90.
Owner Abdulla Al Mansoori **Bred** Jointsense Limited **Trained** Middleham Moor, N Yorks

FOCUS
A modest 3yo handicap that saw a bunched finish. The winner was backed as if he was well treated.

1505 JOIN RACING TV NOW H'CAP 5f 1y
5:15 (5:17) (Class 6) (0-65,65) 4-Y-0+

£3,105 (£924; £461; £300; £300; £300) **Stalls** High

Form RPR

011- **1** **Our Place In Loule**[184] 7811 6-9-7 65 (b) PaulHanagan 9 75+
(Noel Wilson) *trckd ldrs: led gng wl over 1f out: rdn and edgd rt ins fnl f: kpt on wl* **5/1**[3]

-060 **2** *1 ¾* **Gamesome (FR)**[36] 907 8-9-5 63 PaulMulrennan 1 65
(Paul Midgley) *dwlt and swtchd lft sn after s: hld up: effrt and angled rt over 1f out: chsd wnr ins fnl f: kpt on* **2/1**[1]

00-0 **3** *1 ½* **Jessie Allan (IRE)**[28] 1021 8-8-7 58 CoreyMadden[(7)] 3 54
(Jim Goldie) *hld up: rdn and hdwy over 1f out: kpt on ins fnl f* **40/1**

-600 **4** *1 ¼* **Astraea**[28] 1021 4-9-0 58 (b[1]) NathanEvans 4 50
(Michael Easterby) *dwlt: bhd and outpcd: hdwy on outside over 1f out: kpt on fnl f: no imp* **9/2**[2]

0055 **5** *shd* **Lord Of The Glen**[46] 743 4-9-6 64 (v) PhilDennis 2 55
(Jim Goldie) *hld up in tch: rdn over 2f out: one pce fr over 1f out* **11/2**

0-45 **6** *½* **Vallarta (IRE)**[18] 1208 9-9-3 61 JackGarritty 6 51
(Ruth Carr) *pressed ldr: drvn and ev ch briefly over 1f out: wknd ins fnl f* **9/2**[2]

0140 **7** *2 ½* **Foxy Boy**[41] 809 5-8-6 50 (b) RachelRichardson 8 31
(Rebecca Bastiman) *led against stands' rail to over 1f out: wknd fnl f* **7/1**

666- **8** *2 ½* **Economic Crisis (IRE)**[164] 8412 10-9-1 64 ConnorMurtagh[(5)] 5 36
(Alan Berry) *slowly away: sn prom: drvn along over 2f out: wknd over 1f out (jockey said mare was slowly away)* **25/1**

-000 **9** *3 ¼* **Camanche Grey (IRE)**[75] 277 8-7-13 50 VictorSantos[(7)] 7 10
(Lucinda Egerton) *missed break: bhd and sn swtchd rt: struggling 2f out: sn btn (jockey said he removed blindfold early and gelding was slowly away)* **40/1**

58.85s (-0.85) **Going Correction** -0.05s/f (Good) **9** Ran SP% **123.0**
Speed ratings (Par 101): **104,101,98,96,96 95,91,87,82**
CSF £16.34 CT £373.55 TOTE £5.70: £2.00, £1.10, £11.70; EX 22.70 Trifecta £396.60.
Owner Paver & Marwood Racing Limited **Bred** John And Susan Davis **Trained** Marwood, Co Durham
■ Stewards' Enquiry : Corey Madden two-day ban: careless riding (Apr 16-17)

FOCUS
An ordinary sprint handicap.
T/Jkpt: Not Won. T/Plt: £123.70 to a £1 stake. Pool: £78,936.96 - 465.64 winning units T/Qpdt: £7.20 to a £1 stake. Pool: £8,851.59 - 898.91 winning units **Richard Young**

[1385]WOLVERHAMPTON (A.W) (L-H)

Tuesday, April 2

OFFICIAL GOING: Tapeta: standard

Wind: Light behind Weather: Cloudy with sunny spells

1506 BETWAY CASINO H'CAP — 1m 1f 104y (Tp)

5:25 (5:25) (Class 6) (0-60,62) 4-Y-0+

£3,105 (£924; £461; £400; £400; £400) **Stalls** Low

Form — RPR

3630 **1** **King Oswald (USA)**[26] 1065 6-9-7 **58**..........(tp) LiamJones 5 — 66
(James Unett) *hld up in tch: nt clr run over 3f out: shkn up over 2f out: rdn to ld and hung lft ins fnl f: r.o* **6/1**

6036 **2** *2* **False Id**[5] 1390 6-9-4 **55**..........(b) DavidProbert 6 — 59
(David Loughnane) *s.s: hld up: hdwy wl over 1f out: shkn up to ld 1f out: rdn and hdd ins fnl f: styd on same pce (jockey said gelding was slowly away)* **9/2**[2]

5334 **3** *3/4* **Traveller (FR)**[29] 1015 5-9-7 **58**..........(t) CamHardie 2 — 61
(Antony Brittain) *pushed along and prom: lost pl after 1f: hdwy over 3f out: rdn over 1f out: nt clr run ins fnl f: styd on same pce* **11/2**[3]

5354 **4** *shd* **Pike Corner Cross (IRE)**[17] 1231 7-9-5 **56**.......... RobHornby 1 — 59
(Alastair Ralph) *chsd ldrs: rdn and ev ch over 1f out: styd on same pce ins fnl f* **4/1**[1]

-406 **5** *1/2* **Destinys Rock**[40] 835 4-9-10 **61**.......... OisinMurphy 7 — 63
(Mark Loughnane) *hld up: hdwy over 2f out: rdn to ld over 1f out: sn hdd: no ex wl ins fnl f* **9/2**[2]

0-00 **6** *1* **Art Of Swing (IRE)**[34] 923 7-9-5 **56**..........(p[1]) JackMitchell 8 — 56
(Lee Carter) *hld up: hdwy over 1f out: nt rch ldrs* **18/1**

-006 **7** *1 1/2* **Just Heather (IRE)**[33] 951 5-8-8 **45**..........(v) FrannyNorton 9 — 42
(John Wainwright) *prom: lost pl after 1f: hdwy over 1f out: no ex ins fnl f* **200/1**

34/ **8** *1/2* **Ursus Belle (IRE)**[11] 1280 4-9-1 **52**..........(p) StevieDonohoe 4 — 48
(John James Feane, Ire) *chsd ldr 3f: remained handy: shkn up and swtchd rt over 2f out: rdn over 1f out: edgd lft and no ex fnl f* **14/1**

-650 **9** *2 3/4* **Kodi Koh (IRE)**[58] 590 4-8-8 **48**.......... WilliamCox(3) 12 — 39
(Simon West) *sn prom: rdn on outer over 2f out: edgd lft and wknd over 1f out (jockey said filly hung right-handed)* **50/1**

000- **10** *1* **Jock Talk (IRE)**[147] 8906 5-8-1 **45**..........(h[1]) EllaMcCain(7) 3 — 34
(Patrick Morris) *led: rdn and hdd over 1f out: wknd ins fnl f* **80/1**

000- **11** *35* **Wasm**[229] 6184 5-9-1 **52**..........(w) JamesSullivan 11
(Ruth Carr) *hld up: rdn and wknd over 2f out: hung lft over 1f out* **20/1**

/36- **12** *4* **Diamond Avalanche (IRE)**[293] 3735 6-9-5 **56**.......... DanielTudhope 10
(Liam Bailey) *prom: chsd ldr over 6f out tl rdn over 2f out: wknd and eased over 1f out (jockey said gelding hung right-handed and stopped quickly. post-race examination failed to reveal any abnormalities)* **15/2**

2m 0.43s (-0.37) **Going Correction** -0.05s/f (Stan) — **12** Ran SP% **118.2**

Speed ratings (Par 101): **99,97,96,96,96 95,93,93,90,90 58,55**

CSF £32.50 CT £159.47 TOTE £6.80: £2.40, £1.80, £1.80; EX 34.20 Trifecta £203.70.

Owner M Watkinson & P Steadman **Bred** Darley **Trained** Wolverhampton, West Midlands

■ Stewards' Enquiry : Liam Jones two-day ban: careless riding (Apr 16-17)

FOCUS

This very ordinary handicap was run at a good initial clip. The second and third help set a straightforward level.

1507 BETWAY H'CAP — 5f 21y (Tp)

6:00 (6:00) (Class 5) (0-70,72) 4-Y-0+

£3,752 (£1,116; £557; £400; £400; £400) **Stalls** Low

Form — RPR

2113 **1** **Zapper Cass (FR)**[11] 1274 6-9-1 **71**..........(v) MarkCrehan(7) 1 — 79
(Michael Appleby) *pushed along early towards rr: swtchd rt 1/2-way: hdwy over 1f out: rdn and r.o to ld wl ins fnl f* **8/1**

000- **2** *1 3/4* **Foxtrot Knight**[181] 7903 7-9-2 **65**.......... JamesSullivan 5 — 67
(Ruth Carr) *n.m.r sn after s: in rr whn hmpd over 4f out: shkn up over 1f out: edgd lft and r.o ins fnl f: wnt 2nd post* **12/1**

-203 **3** *nk* **Canford Bay (IRE)**[4] 1403 5-9-9 **72**.......... CamHardie 8 — 73
(Antony Brittain) *trckd ldrs: shkn up to ld and hung lft over 1f out: rdn and hdd wl ins fnl f (jockey said gelding hung left-handed throughout)* **5/2**[1]

455- **4** *1 1/4* **Dandy's Beano (IRE)**[175] 8094 4-9-3 **71**.......... SebastianWoods(5) 4 — 68
(Kevin Ryan) *chsd ldrs: rdn over 1f out: no ex wl ins fnl f* **5/1**[3]

5434 **5** *nk* **Wiff Waff**[31] 982 4-9-7 **70**.......... OisinMurphy 9 — 65
(Stuart Williams) *in tch: lost pl and edgd lft over 4f out: hdwy and swtchd rt over 1f out: nt rch ldrs* **11/4**[2]

102- **6** *6* **David's Beauty (IRE)**[183] 7832 6-8-10 **59**..........(b) LiamJones 10 — 33
(Brian Baugh) *prom on outer: lost pl over 3f out: n.d after* **40/1**

-206 **7** *2 1/4* **Entertaining Ben**[40] 823 6-8-11 **60**..........(p) DavidProbert 7 — 26
(Amy Murphy) *led 1f: chsd ldr: pushed along 1/2-way: lost 2nd over 1f out: wknd ins fnl f* **25/1**

0316 **8** *hd* **Toni's A Star**[34] 926 7-8-8 **62**.......... PoppyBridgwater(5) 2 — 31
(Tony Carroll) *chsd ldrs: pushed along 1/2-way: nt clr run and lost all ch 1f out (jockey said mare was denied a clear run ins fnl f)* **12/1**

0-00 **9** *1* **Red Invader (IRE)**[11] 1265 9-8-3 **57**..........(p) DarraghKeenan(5) 3 — 18
(John Butler) *s.s: hmpd over 4f out: nvr on terms* **33/1**

20-0 **10** *3/4* **Krystallite**[28] 1023 6-8-8 **62**..........(b) TheodoreLadd(5) 6 — 21
(Scott Dixon) *led 4f out: rdn and hdd over 1f out: wknd ins fnl f (jockey said mare stopped quickly. post-race examination failed to reveal any abnormalities)* **18/1**

1m 0.47s (-1.43) **Going Correction** -0.05s/f (Stan) — **10** Ran SP% **112.9**

Speed ratings (Par 103): **109,106,105,103,103 93,90,89,88,86**

CSF £93.64 CT £313.62 TOTE £17.00: £1.60, £3.40, £1.90; EX 102.60 Trifecta £341.40.

Owner Stephen Louch **Bred** Arunas Cicenas **Trained** Oakham, Rutland

■ Stewards' Enquiry : Oisin Murphy four-day ban: careless riding (Apr 16-19)

FOCUS

The first five finished well clear in a sprint run at a good gallop. The winner was close to last yea's turf best.

1508 BETWAY LIVE CASINO H'CAP — 1m 4f 51y (Tp)

6:30 (6:30) (Class 5) (0-75,75) 4-Y-0+

£3,752 (£1,116; £557; £400; £400; £400) **Stalls** Low

Form — RPR

6412 **1** *shd* **Arabic Culture (USA)**[20] 1183 5-9-5 **73**.......... DanielTudhope 8 — 82
(Grant Tuer) *hld up: hdwy: nt clr run and swtchd rt over 1f out: chsd wnr and nt clr run ins fnl f: r.o wl: fin 2nd: awrdd the r* **13/8**[1]

0321 **2** **Singing Sheriff**[24] 1095 4-9-0 **68**.......... LiamKeniry 4 — 78+
(Ed Walker) *hld up in tch: racd keenly: led over 1f out: sn rdn and hung lft: hung rt ins fnl f: jst hld on: fin 1st: disqualified and plcd 2nd* **9/2**[3]

4160 **3** *2 3/4* **Thawry**[4] 1395 4-9-4 **72**.......... CamHardie 7 — 76
(Antony Brittain) *s.i.s: hld up: hdwy over 3f out: rdn over 1f out: styd on same pce ins fnl f* **12/1**

2 **4** *6* **Redemptorist (IRE)**[57] 598 4-9-2 **75**.......... SeamusCronin(5) 1 — 69
(Olly Murphy) *led 1f: chsd ldrs: rdn over 1f out: wknd ins fnl f* **4/1**[2]

-523 **5** *shd* **Spiritual Man (IRE)**[28] 1022 7-8-13 **67**.......... LukeMorris 3 — 60
(Jonjo O'Neill) *prom: racd keenly: wnt 2nd over 9f out: led 2f out: rdn and hdd over 1f out: edgd lft and wknd ins fnl f* **14/1**

3100 **6** *2 1/4* **Star Ascending (IRE)**[21] 1159 7-9-4 **72**..........(v) OisinMurphy 6 — 62
(Jennie Candlish) *led at stdy pce after 1f: shkn up and hdd 2f out: wknd fnl f* **9/1**

30-0 **7** *8* **Be Perfect (USA)**[21] 1159 10-9-4 **72**..........(p) JamesSullivan 9 — 49
(Ruth Carr) *prom: racd wd thrght: lost pl over 5f out: hdwy over 3f out: wknd over 1f out* **40/1**

1324 **8** *1 1/2* **Epitaph (IRE)**[21] 1159 5-8-8 **62**..........(b) DavidEgan 5 — 36
(Michael Appleby) *s.i.s: hld up: wknd over 2f out (jockey said gelding was never travelling)* **10/1**

2-5P **9** *hd* **Omotesando**[8] 1330 9-8-12 **66**..........(p) LiamJones 2 — 40
(Oliver Greenall) *hld up in tch: rdn over 3f out: wknd over 2f out* **66/1**

2m 38.21s (-2.59) **Going Correction** -0.05s/f (Stan) — **9** Ran SP% **113.7**

Speed ratings (Par 103): **105,106,104,100,100 98,93,92,92**

CSF £8.73 CT £62.99 TOTE £2.10: £1.30, £1.10, £3.80; EX 9.00 Trifecta £55.20.

Owner Grant Tuer **Bred** Darley **Trained** Birkby, N Yorks

FOCUS

This fair handicap looked to be run at a pretty steady pace, only really picking up as they approached the home turn. The time was respectable, however. The dead-heaters are on the upgrade.

1509 LADBROKES NOVICE STKS (PLUS 10 RACE) — 1m 4f 51y (Tp)

7:00 (7:00) (Class 5) 3-Y-O

£3,752 (£1,116; £557; £278) **Stalls** Low

Form — RPR

52 **1** **Blood Eagle (IRE)**[18] 1221 3-9-5 0.......... OisinMurphy 6 — 78
(Andrew Balding) *led 1f: racd keenly in 2nd tl led over 2f out: rdn over 1f out: r.o* **5/2**[2]

2- **2** *1* **Eagles By Day (IRE)**[174] 8108 3-9-5 0.......... DanielTudhope 3 — 76
(Michael Bell) *trckd ldrs: shkn up to chse wnr over 1f out: edgd lft: rdn ins fnl f: r.o* **1/2**[1]

3 *6* **Isolate (FR)** 3-9-5 0.......... RobHornby 4 — 67
(Martyn Meade) *unruly in stalls: s.s: hld up: hdwy over 1f out: styd on to go 3rd nr fin: nt trble ldrs (jockey said colt reared as stalls opened and as a result was slowly away)* **25/1**

0 **4** *nk* **Message**[18] 1221 3-9-5 0.......... FrannyNorton 2 — 66
(Mark Johnston) *hung rt almost thrght: led at stdy pce after 1f: shkn up and hdd over 2f out: no ex fnl f* **14/1**[3]

0 **5** *4* **Nathanielhawthorne**[21] 1165 3-9-5 0..........(h[1]) LukeMorris 5 — 60
(Marco Botti) *prom: shkn up over 3f out: wknd wl over 1f out* **40/1**

6 **6** *7* **Matilda Bay (IRE)**[38] 884 3-9-0 0.......... NicolaCurrie 1 — 44
(Jamie Osborne) *s.s: hld up and a in rr: outpcd fr over 3f out* **100/1**

2m 45.88s (5.08) **Going Correction** -0.05s/f (Stan) — **6** Ran SP% **109.2**

Speed ratings (Par 98): **81,80,76,76,73 68**

CSF £3.86 TOTE £3.10: £1.20, £1.10; EX 3.90 Trifecta £11.40.

Owner Mrs Fitri Hay **Bred** Directa Princess Partnership **Trained** Kingsclere, Hants

FOCUS

This novice event was very slowly run, the time 10.88 outside the standard. The form is hard to pin down.

1510 LADBROKES, HOME OF THE ODDS BOOST H'CAP — 1m 4f 51y (Tp)

7:30 (7:30) (Class 5) (0-70,71) 3-Y-O

£3,752 (£1,116; £557; £400; £400; £400) **Stalls** Low

Form — RPR

562 **1** **Withoutdestination**[25] 1080 3-9-1 **71**..........(b) StefanoCherchi(7) 7 — 78
(Marco Botti) *s.i.s: hld up: shkn up and hdwy to ld over 1f out: rdn and hung lft ins fnl f: r.o* **10/1**

66-0 **2** *nk* **Another Reason (IRE)**[39] 855 3-8-8 **57**.......... LukeMorris 8 — 63
(Olly Murphy) *trckd ldrs: rdn and ev ch fr over 1f out: edgd lft ins fnl f: r.o u.p* **14/1**

636- **3** *3 3/4* **Mondain**[136] 9131 3-9-8 **71**.......... FrannyNorton 6 — 71
(Mark Johnston) *chsd ldr: shkn up to ld wl over 1f out: rdn and hdd jst over 1f out: no ex wl ins fnl f* **13/8**[1]

046- **4** *3/4* **L'Un Deux Trois (IRE)**[155] 8682 3-9-7 **70**.......... HayleyTurner 2 — 69
(Michael Bell) *trckd ldrs: plld hrd: shkn up over 1f out: no ex ins fnl f* **11/4**[2]

000- **5** *8* **Queen's Soldier (GER)**[176] 8057 3-9-2 **65**.......... OisinMurphy 3 — 51
(Andrew Balding) *hld up: rdn over 2f out: hung lft over 1f out: wknd fnl f* **4/1**[3]

54-0 **6** *1 1/2* **Achaeus (GER)**[27] 1033 3-9-1 **64**.......... ShaneKelly 4 — 48
(Ed Dunlop) *led at stdy pce: qcknd over 3f out: rdn and hdd wl over 1f out: wknd fnl f* **25/1**

066- **7** *2 1/2* **Sea Art**[176] 8058 3-9-4 **67**..........(v[1]) JasonWatson 1 — 47
(William Knight) *hld up: shkn up over 3f out: wknd over 2f out* **12/1**

2m 39.48s (-1.32) **Going Correction** -0.05s/f (Stan) — **7** Ran SP% **112.1**

Speed ratings (Par 98): **102,101,99,98,93 92,90**

CSF £125.09 CT £341.68 TOTE £7.00: £4.60, £3.20; EX 49.90 Trifecta £213.70.

Owner Fabfive **Bred** Charles Cyzer **Trained** Newmarket, Suffolk

FOCUS

An interesting handicap for the grade of largely unexposed types, in which the first pair quickly drew clear.

1511 SUN RACING H'CAP — 1m 142y (Tp)

8:00 (8:00) (Class 5) (0-70,72) 4-Y-O+

£3,752 (£1,116; £557; £400; £400; £400) **Stalls** Low

Form — RPR

0-10 **1** **International Law**[11] 1271 5-9-6 **69**.......... CamHardie 1 — 77
(Antony Brittain) *hld up: hdwy over 1f out: rdn and r.o to ld towards fin (trainer rep could offer no explanation for the gelding's improved form other than he performs well at Wolverhampton)* **5/1**

306 **2** *1* **Energia Flavio (BRZ)**[35] 912 8-8-8 **57**..........(p) DavidEgan 8 — 63
(Patrick Morris) *s.i.s: hld up: hdwy to ld over 4f out: rdn over 1f out: hdd towards fin* **16/1**

0-05 **3** *nse* **Fire Diamond**[21] 1164 6-9-1 **67**..........(p) JaneElliott(3) 2 — 73
(Tom Dascombe) *s.i.s: hld up: hdwy over 1f out: r.o* **10/1**

520- **4** ¾ **Abushamah (IRE)**[152] 8780 8-8-10 **59** JamesSullivan 3 63
(Ruth Carr) *led 1f: chsd ldrs: lost pl over 5f out: hdwy over 2f out: nt clr run over 1f out: styd on* **40/1**

1-50 **5** 2¼ **Arlecchino's Leap**[21] 1164 7-9-7 **70** JasonWatson 4 69
(Mark Usher) *chsd ldrs: lost pl over 3f out: r.o towards fin* **14/1**

6-31 **6** ½ **Elenora Delight**[69] 364 4-9-7 **72** (t) MarcMonaghan 5 70
(Marco Botti) *led over 7f out: hdd 6f out: chsd ldrs: rdn and hung rt over 1f out: no ex ins fnl f* **3/1**[2]

-665 **7** hd **Decoration Of War (IRE)**[28] 1025 4-9-4 **67** LukeMorris 6 65
(Michael Appleby) *chsd ldrs: pushed along over 3f out: nt clr run over 1f out: styd on same pce fnl f* **9/2**[3]

4442 **8** 1½ **Dark Alliance (IRE)**[4] 1392 8-9-7 **70** ShaneKelly 7 64
(Mark Loughnane) *hld up: racd keenly: hdwy over 5f out: shkn up over 1f out: no ex fnl f* **9/4**[1]

000- **9** 5 **Mi Capricho (IRE)**[207] 7030 4-8-12 **61** (w) DavidProbert 9 44
(Keith Dalgleish) *chsd ldrs: led at stdy pce 6f out: hdd over 4f out: rdn over 1f out: wknd fnl f* **20/1**

1m 50.11s (0.01) **Going Correction** -0.05s/f (Stan) **9** Ran SP% **119.5**
Speed ratings (Par 103): **98,97,97,96,94 93,93,92,88**
CSF £82.96 CT £785.86 TOTE £5.70: £1.90, £3.80, £2.00; EX 78.20 Trifecta £411.30.
Owner John And Tony Jarvis And Partner **Bred** Ed's Stud Ltd **Trained** Warthill, N Yorks

FOCUS
Just modest form. There was no pace on in the first half of the race.
T/Plt: £266.40 to a £1 stake. Pool: £107,534.06 - 294.64 winning units T/Qpdt: £57.00 to a £1 stake. Pool: £14,842.22 - 192.65 winning units **Colin Roberts**

MAISONS-LAFFITTE (R-H)
Tuesday, April 2

OFFICIAL GOING: Turf: good to soft

1512a PRIX PLAY IT SAFE (MAIDEN) (3YO FILLIES) (TURF) 7f
1:25 3-Y-O **£11,261** (£4,504; £3,378; £2,252; £1,126)

RPR

1 **Simplicity (FR)**[21] 3-9-2 0 (b) CristianDemuro 1 83
(F Chappet, France) **13/10**[1]

2 1¼ **Dream With You (FR)**[40] 845 3-9-2 0 AurelienLemaitre 3 80
(N Caulley, France) **12/1**

3 2½ **Morning Basma (FR)**[204] 3-9-2 0 MaximeGuyon 6 73
(E J O'Neill, France) **23/5**[2]

4 3½ **Eternal Summer (FR)** 3-9-2 0 TheoBachelot 2 64
(Jean-Pierre Carvalho, Germany) **22/1**

5 2½ **What A Queen (FR)**[187] 7715 3-9-2 0 AntoineHamelin 11 57
(Matthieu Palussiere, France) **32/1**

6 1½ **Zalpa (USA)**[299] 3514 3-9-2 0 Pierre-CharlesBoudot 8 53
(H-A Pantall, France) *mid-div: racd in centre gp: pushed along over 3f out: limited rspnse and sn rdn: wl btn over 1f out: kpt on same pce clsng stages* **9/1**

7 shd **Lady's Maid (USA)** 3-8-11 MickaelBarzalona 7 48
(A Fabre, France) *dwlt s: bustled along early: racd in rr of centre gp: outpcd and pushed along over 1/2-way: modest prog fr 2f out: kpt on ins fnl f but nvr a factor* **10/1**

8 1¼ **Belladone Spirit (IRE)**[153] 3-9-2 0 ThierryThulliez 4 49
(J-M Baudrelle, France) **13/1**

9 ½ **Tencaratrubieslace (FR)**[125] 3-9-2 0 StephanePasquier 9 48
(M Delcher Sanchez, France) **31/5**[3]

10 7 **Cinquain** 3-8-11 0 IoritzMendizabal 10 24
(Jo Hughes, France) *racd towards rr of centre gp: outpcd and pushed along over 1/2-way: rdn 2f out: no imp and sn wl btn: eased ins fnl f* **59/1**

11 1 **La Mirada (FR)** 3-8-13 0 MlleCoraliePacaut(3) 5 26
(Mlle V Dissaux, France) **91/1**

12 14 **Ticolet (IRE)**[125] 3-9-2 0 TonyPiccone 12
(M Delcher Sanchez, France) **55/1**

1m 22.6s (-5.40) **12** Ran SP% **121.1**
PARI-MUTUEL (all including 1 euro stake): WIN 2.30 PLACE 1.20, 2.10, 1.60 DF 12.90 SF 12.90.
Owner Alain Jathiere & Khalifa Mohammed Al Attiyah **Bred** Khalifa Mohammed Al Attiyah **Trained** France

1419 KEMPTON (A.W) (R-H)
Wednesday, April 3

OFFICIAL GOING: Polytrack: standard to slow
Wind: Nil Weather: Fine

1513 100% PROFIT BOOST AT 32REDSPORT.COM EBF FILLIES' NOVICE STKS (PLUS 10 RACE) 5f (P)
4:40 (4:43) (Class 5) 2-Y-O **£3,881** (£1,155; £577; £288) **Stalls Low**

Form RPR

1 **Lady Kermit (IRE)** 2-9-0 0 EdwardGreatrex 10 89+
(Archie Watson) *sn led and set gd pce: shkn up 2f out: shot clr of field over 1f out: in command fnl f and nudged out: v easily* **1/1**[1]

2 6 **Bettys Hope** 2-9-0 0 OisinMurphy 9 67
(Rod Millman) *bhd ldr: rdn wl over 1f out: sn lft bhd: pushed out fnl f* **16/1**

3 3½ **Perfect Rose** 2-9-0 0 PJMcDonald 1 55
(Mark Johnston) *chsd ldr on inner: rdn 2f out: plugged on fnl f to hold 3rd* **2/1**[2]

4 shd **Bartat** 2-9-0 0 DavidEgan 2 54
(Mick Channon) *racd in mid-div and t.k.h: effrt wl over 1f out: kpt on fnl f* **7/1**[3]

5 1½ **Zampa Road (IRE)** 2-9-0 0 TomMarquand 3 49
(David Evans) *wnt lft leaving stalls: mid-div: scrubbed along over 2f out: styd on fnl f* **14/1**

6 3¼ **Swiss Bond** 2-9-0 0 RobertWinston 8 37
(J S Moore) *bucked leaving stalls: a towards rr* **50/1**

7 ¾ **Little Devil** 2-8-11 0 ow2 RyanWhile(5) 7 37
(Bill Turner) *towards rr and rn v green thrght: sme prog fnl f (jockey said filly hung left-handed in the bend)* **33/1**

8 ½ **Hollaback Girl** 2-9-0 0 TomQueally 5 33
(Richard Spencer) *hmpd s and in rr: rapid prog on outer over 2f out: rdn 2f out: no ex over 1f out* **16/1**

59.92s (-0.58) **Going Correction** -0.075s/f (Stan) **8** Ran SP% **119.2**
Speed ratings (Par 89): **101,91,85,85,83 78,76,76**
CSF £21.64 TOTE £2.00: £1.10, £3.10, £1.20; EX 20.50 Trifecta £52.30.
Owner Justin Dowley & Michael Pescod **Bred** Philip & Orla Hore **Trained** Upper Lambourn, W Berks

FOCUS
A juvenile fillies' novice contest with a field made up entirely by newcomers on standard to slow Polytrack. The strong favourite bolted up despite the widest available draw.

1514 RACINGTV.COM H'CAP (DIV I) 7f (P)
5:10 (5:11) (Class 6) (0-55,57) 3-Y-O
£3,105 (£924; £461; £400; £400; £400) **Stalls Low**

Form RPR

0-33 **1** **Pentland Lad (IRE)**[23] 1140 3-9-1 **49** (t) OisinMurphy 3 60
(Charlie Fellowes) *hld up in mid-div on inner: shkn up and smooth prog over 2f out: rdn 2f out: led ent fnl f: sn clr* **8/13**[1]

0-30 **2** 3½ **Zorro's Girl**[21] 1171 3-9-7 **55** (p[1]) HollieDoyle 8 57
(Archie Watson) *sn led: rdn over 2f out: kpt on wl tl hdd ent fnl f: sn lft bhd by wnr but styd on* **14/1**

0-00 **3** 4½ **Miss Enigma (IRE)**[11] 1293 3-9-9 **57** (b[1]) ShaneKelly 2 47
(Richard Hughes) *bhd ldrs and t.k.h: effrt 2f out: no imp tl kpt on being shuffled along fnl f* **10/1**

0-00 **4** 2 **Anglesey Penny**[72] 341 3-9-0 **48** ow1 RobertWinston 6 32
(J R Jenkins) *hld up in rr-div: rdn over 2f out: plugged on inner fr over 1f out* **100/1**

460- **5** ½ **Dragon Kuza**[253] 5298 3-9-6 **54** (h) AdamKirby 4 37
(Hugo Palmer) *bhd ldrs between horses: scrubbed along wl over 3f out: plugged on fr over 1f out* **7/2**[2]

646 **6** 1¼ **Fast Endeavour**[23] 1141 3-8-13 **50** (p) CameronNoble(3) 9 30
(Ian Williams) *w ldr: rdn 2f out: kpt on tl lost 3rd 1f out and wknd qckly* **8/1**[3]

00-0 **7** 2 **Sittin Handy (IRE)**[68] 406 3-9-5 **53** (p[1]) JoeFanning 10 27
(Mark Loughnane) *awkward leaving stalls: in rr: effrt over 2f out: no imp sn after* **22/1**

6-06 **8** 3¾ **Red Skye Delight (IRE)**[22] 1167 3-9-3 **56** DarraghKeenan(5) 7 20
(Luke McJannet) *mid-div on outer w no cover: effrt over 2f out: sn btn* **20/1**

00-0 **9** 7 **We Are All Dottie**[34] 940 3-8-7 **48** EllaBoardman(7) 5
(Pat Phelan) *in rr: c wd into st: rdn over 2f out: no imp fr 2f out* **80/1**

1m 26.58s (0.58) **Going Correction** -0.075s/f (Stan) **9** Ran SP% **122.3**
Speed ratings (Par 96): **93,89,83,81,81 79,77,73,65**
CSF £12.51 CT £58.15 TOTE £1.30: £1.10, £2.40, £2.60; EX 11.60 Trifecta £63.30.
Owner GG Thoroughbreds VIII **Bred** Yeomanstown Stud **Trained** Newmarket, Suffolk

FOCUS
The first division of a moderate 3yo handicap. The odds-on favourite came through from midfield to win easily. The winning time was marginally slower than the second division.

1515 RACINGTV.COM H'CAP (DIV II) 7f (P)
5:45 (5:46) (Class 6) (0-55,57) 3-Y-O
£3,105 (£924; £461; £400; £400; £400) **Stalls Low**

Form RPR

000- **1** **Gregorian Girl**[211] 6904 3-9-6 **57** JackDuern(3) 2 64
(Dean Ivory) *mde most: rdn 2f out: kpt on wl over 1f out: pressed fnl f but maintained advantage* **12/1**

0-05 **2** 1 **Cauthen (IRE)**[23] 1141 3-9-6 **54** RobHornby 1 58
(Ken Cunningham-Brown) *bhd ldrs: rdn 2f out: kpt on wl over 1f out: tried to cl on wnr ins fnl f but no ex cl home* **6/5**[1]

50-0 **3** 3 **Medoras Childe**[26] 1081 3-9-5 **53** (h[1]) DavidEgan 6 49
(Heather Main) *w wnr: rdn over 2f out: no imp on front two over 1f out but kpt on fnl f* **6/1**[3]

0-60 **4** 1¾ **Apron Strings**[35] 918 3-9-0 **48** KierenFox 3 39
(Michael Attwater) *bhd ldrs: rdn over 2f out: outpcd 2f out: styd on ent fnl f* **20/1**

0-60 **5** ½ **Nefyn Beach (IRE)**[25] 1094 3-9-7 **55** RobertWinston 5 45
(Jo Hughes, France) *stmbld and dipped leaving stalls: in rr: rdn 2f out: shuffled along over 1f out: nvr involved (jockey said filly ducked down leaving the stalls)* **9/2**[2]

-600 **6** 1½ **Tintern Spirit (IRE)**[23] 1141 3-8-12 **46** oh1 ShaneKelly 8 32
(Milton Bradley) *bhd ldrs: rdn over 2f out: one pce fr over 1f out* **33/1**

040- **7** 6 **Treasured Company (IRE)**[111] 9521 3-9-0 **48** PhilipPrince 9 18
(Richard Guest) *wnt lft leaving stalls: tk fierce hold in mid-div on outer: settled bttr after 3f: rdn over 2f out: no ex over 1f out* **6/1**[3]

006- **8** 1¼ **Secret Magic (IRE)**[103] 9670 3-9-3 **51** LiamJones 7 17
(Mark Loughnane) *hld up in rr: no imp over 1f out* **12/1**

0-00 **9** ¾ **Laguna Spirit**[40] 855 3-8-12 **46** CharlieBennett 10 10
(Pat Phelan) *hmpd s: t.k.h in rr: effrt over 2f out: no ex sn after* **33/1**

1m 26.06s (0.06) **Going Correction** -0.075s/f (Stan) **9** Ran SP% **118.2**
Speed ratings (Par 96): **96,94,91,89,88 87,80,78,78**
CSF £27.13 CT £101.26 TOTE £12.10: £3.50, £1.10, £1.80; EX 39.70 Trifecta £187.90.
Owner Skipsey, Franks & Roper And A Chapman **Bred** Shortgrove Manor Stud **Trained** Radlett, Herts

FOCUS
The second division of a moderate 3yo handicap. It paid to be prominent and the winning time was marginally quicker than the first division. The well-backed runner-up is rated in line with the best of his 2yo form.

1516 32RED CASINO H'CAP 7f (P)
6:15 (6:17) (Class 5) (0-75,76) 3-Y-O
£3,752 (£1,116; £557; £400; £400; £400) **Stalls Low**

Form RPR

20-3 **1** **Balata Bay**[11] 1285 3-8-11 **72** LukeCatton(7) 3 79+
(Richard Hannon) *hld up: clsr and shkn up 2f out: ct on heels over 1f: rdn ent fnl f: qcknd wl to ld nr fin* **8/1**[3]

253- **2** ¾ **Regular**[141] 9037 3-9-6 **74** JamesDoyle 2 77
(Michael Bell) *bhd ldrs: rdn 2f out: led over 1f out: kpt on tl hdd cl home* **9/4**[1]

003- **3** 1¾ **Canal Rocks**[161] 8553 3-8-13 **74** GeorgiaDobie(7) 9 72
(Henry Candy) *hld up in mid-div: shkn up and clsr over 2f out: rdn 2f out: kpt on wl fnl f* **8/1**[3]

-342 **4** ¾ **Adelante (FR)**[32] 993 3-9-5 **73** OisinMurphy 4 69
(George Baker) *hld up in mid-div: rdn 2f out: kpt on one pce (jockey said filly was denied a clear run)* **16/1**

3-32 **5** hd **Scorched Breath**[21] 1171 3-9-4 **72** (t) StevieDonohoe 1 67
(Charlie Fellowes) *mid-div on inner: rdn 2f out: kpt on wl and ev ch 1f out: no ex fnl f* **7/2**[2]

41-6 **6** 1¼ **Gold At Midnight**[25] 1104 3-9-7 **75** (p[1]) HollieDoyle 11 67
(William Stone) *w ldrs on outer: rdn 2f out: plugged on fr 1f out* **40/1**

536- **7** 2¾ **Crackin Dream (IRE)**[170] 8255 3-9-3 **71** .... AdamKirby 7 56
(Clive Cox) *in tch on inner: rdn 2f out: no imp over 1f out* **8/1**[3]

5-11 **8** 3¼ **Red Phoenix (IRE)**[23] 1141 3-9-3 **71** .... JoeFanning 12 47
(Mark Johnston) *bhd ldrs: rdn over 2f out: no ex over 1f out* **11/1**

00-0 **9** ½ **Broughtons Flare (IRE)**[19] 1219 3-8-9 **63** .... NicolaCurrie 5 38
(Philip McBride) *sluggish s: in rr-div: rdn over 2f out: no imp over 1f out (jockey said gelding suffered interference at the start and ran too free)* **16/1**

220- **10** nse **John Betjeman**[177] 8056 3-9-3 **76** .... (h[1]) RyanWhile(5) 8 50
(Bill Turner) *led: rdn over 2f out: hdd & wknd over 1f out* **33/1**

434- **11** 1¾ **Such Promise**[156] 8692 3-8-9 **63** .... DavidEgan 10 33
(Mike Murphy) *in rr: rdn over 2f out: sn hld* **20/1**

5330 **12** 1¼ **Twpsyn (IRE)**[21] 1173 3-8-4 **65** .... GinaMangan(7) 6 31
(David Evans) *wnt rt s and in rr: t.k.h: rdn over 2f out: sn hld (jockey said gelding jumped awkwardly)* **50/1**

30-3 **13** 11 **Four Mile Bridge (IRE)**[84] 134 3-9-2 **70** .... FergusSweeney 14 7
(Mark Usher) *t.k.h and a towards rr: no ex 2f out (jockey said gelding hung left-handed throughout)* **25/1**

1m 25.87s (-0.13) **Going Correction** -0.075s/f (Stan) **13 Ran SP% 122.4**
Speed ratings (Par 98): **97,96,94,93,93 91,88,84,84,84 82,80,68**
CSF £25.55 CT £161.71 TOTE £9.30: £2.90, £1.60, £2.70; EX 37.10 Trifecta £224.90.
Owner J R Shannon **Bred** J R Shannon **Trained** East Everleigh, Wilts

FOCUS
A fair 3yo handicap. The winner had to wait for a gap and quickened up nicely between horses in the final furlong. The winning time was marginally the quickest of the three 7f races on the card.

1517 32RED.COM NOVICE STKS 1m (P)
6:45 (6:49) (Class 5) 4-Y-O+
£3,881 (£1,155; £577; £288) **Stalls** Low

Form RPR

1- **1** **Canvassed (IRE)**[208] 7040 4-9-9 0 .... AndreaAtzeni 1 97+
(Roger Varian) *sltly reluctant to load: bhd ldr: shkn up wl over 1f: cruised upsides and led sn after: galloped clr fnl f and eased cl home: v impressive* **8/13**[1]

1/5- **2** 7 **Just Brilliant (IRE)**[349] 1929 4-9-9 0 .... JamesDoyle 8 81
(Peter Chapple-Hyam) *led: rdn 2f out: hdd jst over 1f out: sn lft bhd by wnr: plugged on for remote 2nd* **7/1**[3]

3/ **3** 1½ **I Can (IRE)**[497] 8888 4-9-2 0 .... TomQueally 4 71
(Henry Candy) *hld up in 6th and t.k.h at times: clsr whn shuffled along fr 2f out: tk 3rd over 1f out: kpt on fnl f: nvr involved* **16/1**

3/2- **4** 4½ **Ocala**[349] 1930 4-8-11 0 .... OisinMurphy 5 55
(Andrew Balding) *missed break: sn mde up grnd and pressed ldr: rdn over 2f out: plugged on in 4th fr over 1f out* **5/2**[2]

4 **5** nk **Captain Scott (IRE)**[33] 968 4-8-13 0 .... JaneElliott(3) 7 60
(Heather Main) *racd in 4th: rdn over 2f out: no ex over 1f out* **66/1**

00 **6** 18 **Noel (IRE)**[19] 1212 4-9-2 0 .... FergusSweeney 3 18
(Daniel Kubler) *racd in 5th: effrt over 2f out: sn hld and eased ent fnl f* **100/1**

0-0 **7** 3¾ **Time To Rock**[25] 1094 4-9-2 0 .... LiamJones 2 9
(John Bridger) *uns rdr bhd stalls: a in last: struggling fr 2f out* **200/1**

1m 38.18s (-1.62) **Going Correction** -0.075s/f (Stan) **7 Ran SP% 111.9**
Speed ratings (Par 103): **105,98,96,92,91 73,69**
CSF £5.65 TOTE £1.30: £1.10, £2.20; EX 5.70 Trifecta £24.60.
Owner Sheikh Mohammed Obaid Al Maktoum **Bred** Dayton Investments (breeding) Ltd **Trained** Newmarket, Suffolk

FOCUS
A decent novice contest. They didn't go much of an initial gallop but the impressive winner still clocked the second best comparative time on the card.

1518 32RED H'CAP (LONDON MIDDLE DISTANCE SERIES QUALIFIER) 2m 2f 219y(P)
7:15 (7:17) (Class 4) (0-80,82) 4-Y-O+
£6,469 (£1,925; £962; £481; £400; £400) **Stalls** Low

Form RPR

-222 **1** **Dono Di Dio**[25] 1096 4-8-10 **76** .... ScottMcCullagh(7) 7 84
(Michael Madgwick) *hld up in mid-div: shkn up over 2f out: rdn 2f out: styd on wl on outer ent fnl f: c home wl to grab ld last strides* **8/1**

5-33 **2** nk **Lawn Ranger**[11] 1291 4-9-4 **77** .... KierenFox 4 84
(Michael Attwater) *early spd: sn w ldr: tk up the running 4f out: kicked 3f out: styd on wl tl hdd last strides* **6/1**[3]

2216 **3** 2¼ **Magic Mirror**[12] 1269 6-9-1 **74** .... (p) TomMarquand 5 77
(Mark Rimell) *hld up in mid-div on inner: shkn up over 2f out: rdn 2f out: ev ch ent fnl f: no ex last 110yds* **10/1**

30-2 **4** nk **Valentino Dancer**[34] 945 4-9-1 **81** .... CierenFallon(7) 9 84
(Olly Murphy) *hld up in rr-div: effrt over 2f out: kpt on fnl f* **11/2**[2]

453- **5** nk **Framley Garth (IRE)**[163] 8476 7-9-1 **79** .... PaulaMuir(5) 8 81
(Liam Bailey) *hld up in rr: rdn over 2f out: outpcd over 1f out: shuffled along fnl f* **33/1**

-663 **6** 1½ **Surrey Blaze (IRE)**[25] 1095 4-9-2 **75** .... OisinMurphy 1 75
(Joseph Tuite) *bhd ldrs: rdn over 2f out: styd on wl and ev ch over 1f out: no ex ins fnl f and plugged on* **11/2**[2]

045- **7** 1½ **Rashdan (FR)**[159] 8596 4-9-7 **80** .... (p) JamesDoyle 10 79
(Hugo Palmer) *s.s: in rr: shkn up over 2f out: effrt 2f out: no imp on ldrs over 1f out: plugging on fnl f: eased last 110yds* **5/2**[1]

-515 **8** ¾ **Voi**[34] 945 5-8-13 **72** .... (t) MartinDwyer 11 68
(Conrad Allen) *racd in rr-div: effrt wl over 2f out: outpcd 2f tl styd on fr over 1f out: shuffled along after and styd on (vet reported the mare had been struck into on its left fore)* **20/1**

5-06 **9** 3 **Baydar**[21] 1172 6-9-9 **82** .... (p) StevieDonohoe 2 73
(Ian Williams) *in last: effrt over 3f out: sme prog over 2f out* **25/1**

1010 **10** 2¼ **Unit Of Assessment (IRE)**[11] 1291 5-9-6 **79** .... (vt) AdamKirby 6 66
(William Knight) *sn led: hdd 4f out: remained w ldr: rdn 3f out: no ex in 3rd over 1f and wknd qckly sn after* **15/2**

2/0- **11** 52 **Movie Set (USA)**[267] 2788 7-9-0 **80** .... SeanKirrane(7) 3
(Richard Spencer) *bhd ldrs: shkn up wl over 4f out and losing grnd: dropped to last over 2f out and eased: t.o* **33/1**

2m 19.17s (-1.83) **Going Correction** -0.075s/f (Stan) **11 Ran SP% 120.1**
Speed ratings (Par 105): **106,105,104,103,103 102,101,100,98,97 59**
CSF £54.13 CT £490.28 TOTE £9.60: £2.70, £2.00, £3.60; EX 44.80 Trifecta £343.90.
Owner Oliver Lodge **Bred** Newsells Park Stud **Trained** Denmead, Hants
■ Stewards' Enquiry : Scott McCullagh two-day ban: used whip above the permitted level (Apr 17-18)

FOCUS
The feature contest was a fair handicap. The fourth-favourite shot clear at the top of the straight from off a slightly muddling gallop but got collared close home.

1519 32RED ON THE APP STORE CLASSIFIED STKS (DIV I) 1m 2f 219y(P)
7:45 (7:48) (Class 6) 4-Y-O+
£3,105 (£924; £461; £400; £400; £400) **Stalls** Low

Form RPR

3113 **1** **Harry Callahan (IRE)**[7] 1361 4-9-0 50 .... (v) CallumShepherd 9 56
(Mick Channon) *mde most: rdn 2f out: strly pressed fr over 1f out tl asserted fnl 150yds* **4/7**[1]

0420 **2** 3¼ **Schindlers Ark (USA)**[7] 1361 5-9-0 47 .... (b) CharlieBennett 13 50
(Jane Chapple-Hyam) *bhd wnr: rdn over 2f out: chal wnr fr wl over 1f out: no ex last 150yds and wknd* **4/1**[2]

3004 **3** 1¾ **Woggle (IRE)**[7] 1354 4-9-0 47 .... (t[1]) TrevorWhelan 11 47+
(Geoffrey Deacon) *s.s and in rr: rdn on outer w plenty to do over 2f out: kpt on steadily fr over 1f out to take 3rd nr fin (jockey said filly was slowly away and hung left-handed)* **20/1**

3003 **4** nse **Cash N Carrie (IRE)**[7] 1354 5-9-0 50 .... (p) AlistairRawlinson 10 47
(Michael Appleby) *bhd ldr: rdn over 2f out: kpt on one pce tl lost 3rd nr fin* **12/1**[3]

04-0 **5** 2½ **River Rule**[89] 58 4-9-0 44 .... HollieDoyle 3 42
(Adrian Wintle) *racd in mid-div: rdn over 2f out: kpt on one pce* **33/1**

60-0 **6** ½ **John Caesar (IRE)**[36] 912 8-8-11 44 .... (p) RowanScott(3) 1 42
(Rebecca Bastiman) *racd in mid-div: rdn over 2f out: plugged on* **16/1**

60/2 **7** ½ **Ledbury (IRE)**[28] 1044 7-9-0 43 .... RobertWinston 4 41
(J R Jenkins) *racd in mid-div: one pce fr 2f out* **20/1**

30-0 **8** 1¼ **Embankment**[23] 1145 10-9-0 45 .... KierenFox 14 38
(Michael Attwater) *s.s and in rr: rdn over 2f out: plugged on one pce* **33/1**

000- **9** ¾ **Argent Bleu**[334] 2382 4-8-9 49 .... RhiainIngram(5) 2 37
(Roger Ingram) *bhd ldrs: rdn over 2f out: no ex over 1f out* **50/1**

0/0- **10** 2¾ **Shadow's Girl**[23] 2739 7-9-0 36 .... (p) StevieDonohoe 6 32
(Bernard Llewellyn) *racd in rr-div: rdn and hld over 2f out* **33/1**

-060 **11** 8 **Seventii**[8] 1341 5-8-9 46 .... DarraghKeenan(5) 7 18
(Robert Eddery) *hld up in rr-div: rdn wl over 2f out: one pce sn after* **20/1**

/00- **12** 4 **My Lord**[198] 7361 11-8-9 39 .... (p) ThoreHammerHansen(5) 12 10
(Paddy Butler) *racd in mid-div: no imp over 1f out and eased (jockey said gelding hung right-handed under pressure)* **100/1**

4-00 **13** 10 **Unsuspected Girl (IRE)**[60] 549 6-9-0 40 .... (tp) TomMarquand 8
(Milton Bradley) *racd in mid-div on outer: rdn over 3f out: no ex over 2f and eased over 1f out* **50/1**

2m 20.87s (-0.13) **Going Correction** -0.075s/f (Stan) **13 Ran SP% 125.2**
Speed ratings (Par 101): **100,97,96,96,94 94,93,92,92,90 84,81,74**
CSF £2.58 TOTE £1.40: £1.10, £1.40, £5.80; EX 3.90 Trifecta £29.40.
Owner Chelsea Thoroughbreds- Dirty Harry **Bred** Corduff Stud **Trained** West Ilsley, Berks

FOCUS
The first division of a moderate classified contest. The first two raced in those positions throughout.

1520 32RED ON THE APP STORE CLASSIFIED STKS (DIV II) 1m 2f 219y(P)
8:15 (8:17) (Class 6) 4-Y-O+
£3,105 (£924; £461; £400; £400; £400) **Stalls** Low

Form RPR

000- **1** **Hi There Silver (IRE)**[223] 6158 5-9-0 42 .... GeorgeWood 5 48
(Michael Madgwick) *hld up in rr-div: shkn up over 2f out: prog on outer over 1f out: rdn ins fnl f to ld nr fin* **33/1**

-046 **2** hd **Passing Clouds**[23] 1146 4-9-0 43 .... KierenFox 1 48
(Michael Attwater) *rdn leaving stalls to ld: clr ldr over 4f out: rdn 2f out: edgd lft w pack on heels over 1f out: fnd plenty tl hdd nr fin* **8/1**

0-03 **3** 1¾ **Sigrid Nansen**[23] 1146 4-9-0 48 .... (tp) RossaRyan 3 44
(Alexandra Dunn) *hld up in rr: shkn up over 2f out and prog: rdn 2f out: styd on wl fr over 1f out* **9/2**[3]

3-55 **4** ¾ **Born To Reason (IRE)**[75] 288 5-9-1 45 ow1 .... (v[1]) DougieCostello 2 44
(Kevin Frost) *racd in mid-div on inner: rdn over 2f out: kpt on tl no ex last 150yds* **12/1**

23-2 **5** ½ **Optima Petamus**[6] 1390 7-8-9 49 .... (p) PaulaMuir(5) 12 42
(Liam Bailey) *s.s: in rr: prog into rr-div sn after: rdn over 2f out: kpt on wl fr over 1f out (jockey said gelding ducked as the stalls opened)* **7/2**[2]

4401 **6** nse **Murhib (IRE)**[23] 1146 7-9-0 50 .... (h) RichardKingscote 14 42
(Lydia Richards) *hld up in mid-div: effrt over 2f out: plugged on fr over 1f out* **5/2**[1]

0-00 **7** ¾ **Loving Your Work**[75] 288 8-8-11 50 .... CameronNoble(3) 7 41
(Ken Cunningham-Brown) *racd in rr-div: rdn over 2f out: plugged on fr over 1f out* **25/1**

/0-6 **8** 2¼ **The Wire Flyer**[19] 1212 4-9-0 43 .... (p) DanielMuscutt 13 37
(John Flint) *hld up in rr-div: effrt over 2f out: one pce (jockey said gelding suffered interference approximately 1½ furlongs out)* **33/1**

0-00 **9** hd **Ronni Layne**[23] 1145 5-9-0 44 .... (p) HollieDoyle 8 36
(Louise Allan) *racd in mid-div: rdn over 2f out: no imp* **25/1**

-000 **10** hd **Allleedsaren'Twe**[22] 1158 4-9-0 46 .... KieranO'Neill 9 36
(Shaun Harris) *bhd ldrs: rdn over 2f out: no ex over 1f out* **50/1**

0103 **11** 1½ **Muraaqeb**[23] 1145 5-9-0 46 .... (p) TomMarquand 11 33
(Milton Bradley) *rdn along leaving stalls to sit w ldr: rdn 3f out: no ex and wknd* **7/1**

0650 **12** nse **Ertidaad (IRE)**[19] 1214 7-9-0 45 .... (b) EoinWalsh 4 33
(Emma Owen) *bhd ldrs: rdn over 2f out: hld sn after* **33/1**

/06- **13** 2¼ **Petrify**[184] 4902 9-9-0 47 .... (tp) StevieDonohoe 10 29
(Bernard Llewellyn) *missed break and a in rr* **66/1**

2m 20.71s (-0.29) **Going Correction** -0.075s/f (Stan) **13 Ran SP% 120.2**
Speed ratings (Par 101): **101,100,99,99,98 98,98,96,96,96 95,95,93**
CSF £268.48 TOTE £47.10: £9.70, £2.40, £2.00; EX 513.40 Trifecta £3494.90.
Owner Los Leader **Bred** Mrs Eleanor Commins **Trained** Denmead, Hants

FOCUS
The second division of a moderate classified contest. The winning time was slightly quicker.
T/Jkpt: Partly won. £19,296.70 to a £1 stake. T/Plt: £35.10 to a £1 stake. Pool: £65,510.94 - 1,361.80 winning units. T/Qpdt: £18.90 to a £1 stake. Pool: £11,160.09 - 435.43 winning units.
Cathal Gahan

[1426]SOUTHWELL (L-H)

Wednesday, April 3

OFFICIAL GOING: Fibresand: standard

Wind: Light across Weather: Fine & dry

1521 BETWAY SPRINT H'CAP 4f 214y(F)

2:20 (2:20) (Class 6) (0-65,66) 4-Y-0+

£3,105 (£924; £461; £300; £300; £300) **Stalls** Centre

Form RPR

0322 **1** **Red Stripes (USA)**[7] 1364 7-8-6 **55**........................(b) SeamusCronin(5) 7 62
(Lisa Williamson) *sn led in centre: rdn along 2f out: sn edgd lft towards far side: drvn ins fnl f: hld on gamely* **4/1**[2]

12-1 **2** *hd* **Honey Gg**[7] 1364 4-9-0 **65** 5ex............................ CianMacRedmond(7) 4 71
(Declan Carroll) *cl up centre: disp ld 1/2-way: rdn wl over 1f out: sn edgd lft towards far rail: ev ch and drvn ins fnl f: kpt on wl* **6/4**[1]

040- **3** *hd* **Rasheeq (IRE)**[185] 7808 6-9-8 **66**........................ LukeMorris 1 71
(Mohamed Moubarak) *racd towards far side: prom: rdn to chal over 1f out: drvn ins fnl f: sn ev ch: n.m.r and kpt on wl towards fin* **15/2**

-040 **4** *1 1/4* **Filbert Street**[9] 1335 4-8-10 **54**........................(p) EoinWalsh 2 55
(Roy Brotherton) *dwlt: sn rdn along and outpcd in rr towards far side: hdwy 2f out: swtchd rt and drvn over 1f out: kpt on wl fnl f: nrst fin (jockey said gelding jumped awkwardly from stalls)* **20/1**

300- **5** *nk* **Flying Foxy**[195] 7456 5-9-5 **63**........................(p[1]) HayleyTurner 5 63
(George Scott) *racd centre: chsd ldrs: rdn along wl over 1f out: drvn and kpt on same pce fnl f* **16/1**

2432 **6** *1 3/4* **Piazon**[35] 926 8-8-11 **62**........................(be) HarryRussell(7) 6 55
(Julia Brooke) *racd towards stands' side: in tch: rdn along over 2f out: sn drvn and btn* **8/1**

0-00 **7** *1/2* **Guardia Svizzera (IRE)**[79] 237 5-9-7 **65**........................(h) BenCurtis 3 57
(Roger Fell) *racd centre: chsd ldrs: rdn along 1/2-way: sn wknd* **6/1**[3]

/34- **8** *5* **Indian Tinker**[232] 6133 10-8-10 **61**........................(p) CierenFallon(7) 8 35
(Robert Cowell) *sn rdn along in rr: outpcd and bhd whn edgd bdly lft to far rail 2f out (jockey said gelding lost action upon pulling up; post-race examination failed to reveal any abnormalities)* **40/1**

59.83s (0.13) **Going Correction** -0.20s/f (Stan) 8 Ran SP% **110.2**
Speed ratings (Par 101): **91,90,90,88,87 85,84,76**
CSF £9.59 CT £38.25 TOTE £4.00: £1.10, £1.30, £3.10; EX 11.00 Trifecta £51.80.
Owner E H Jones (paints) Ltd **Bred** Tim Ahearn **Trained** Taporley, Wrexham

FOCUS
A modest handicap in which the pace was sound but those attempting to make ground from off the pace were at a disadvantage. The first three ended up against the far rail.

1522 BETWAY OFFICIAL GRAND NATIONAL BETTING PARTNER H'CAP 6f 16y(F)

2:55 (2:55) (Class 5) (0-70,69) 4-Y-0+

£3,752 (£1,116; £557; £300; £300; £300) **Stalls** Low

Form RPR

3062 **1** **Katheefa (USA)**[7] 1366 5-9-4 **66**........................ JamesSullivan 5 81
(Ruth Carr) *trckd ldng pair: hdwy to join ld on bit over 2f out: led wl over 1f out: rdn clr appr fnl f: kpt on strly* **7/2**[2]

0-50 **2** *4* **Rock Of Estonia (IRE)**[46] 755 4-9-0 **69**........................ CierenFallon(7) 7 71
(Charles Hills) *dwlt and towards rr: hdwy wl over 2f out: rdn to chse ldrs wl over 1f out: styd on u.p fnl f: tk 2nd towards fin* **8/1**[3]

4611 **3** *nk* **Marble Bar**[7] 1366 4-9-2 **67** 5ex........................(h) JamieGormley(3) 3 68
(Iain Jardine) *led: pushed along wl over 2f out: sn jnd and rdn: hdd wl over 1f out: sn drvn and kpt on same pce: lost 2nd towards fin* **4/6**[1]

41-4 **4** *1* **Global Melody**[92] 2 4-9-5 **67**........................ LukeMorris 4 65
(Phil McEntee) *chsd ldrs: hdwy over 2f out: rdn along wl over 1f out: kpt on same pce* **12/1**

6660 **5** *6* **Princely**[32] 982 4-9-5 **67**........................ EoinWalsh 6 46
(Tony Newcombe) *chsd ldrs: rdn along 3f out: sn wknd* **50/1**

0140 **6** *2 1/4* **Newstead Abbey**[30] 1016 9-9-1 **63**........................(p) PhilDennis 2 35
(Rebecca Bastiman) *dwlt: a in rr (jockey said gelding missed the break)* **28/1**

41-4 **7** *8* **Mr Strutter (IRE)**[90] 42 5-9-5 **67**........................ TomEaves 1 13
(Ronald Thompson) *chsd ldr: pushed along over 3f out: sn rdn and wknd: bhd and eased fr over 1f out* **16/1**

1m 14.05s (-2.45) **Going Correction** -0.20s/f (Stan) 7 Ran SP% **112.3**
Speed ratings (Par 103): **108,102,102,100,92 89,79**
CSF £29.68 TOTE £6.10: £1.80, £2.70; EX 25.80 Trifecta £56.00.
Owner Grange Park Racing XIV & Ruth Carr **Bred** Shadwell Farm LLC **Trained** Huby, N Yorks

FOCUS
A modest handicap in which \bKatheefa\p comprehensively reversed last week's course and distance placings with \bMarble Bar\p in a race that didn't take much winning. The gallop was sound throughout.

1523 BETWAY NOVICE MEDIAN AUCTION STKS 6f 16y(F)

3:25 (3:25) (Class 5) 3-4-Y-0 **£3,752** (£1,116; £557; £278) **Stalls** Low

Form RPR

1 **Inspired Thought (IRE)** 3-9-0 0........................ DanielTudhope 4 70+
(Archie Watson) *n.m.r s: sn trcking ldrs: smooth hdwy 3f out: cl up over 2f out: led wl over 1f out: pushed out* **6/4**[2]

2 **2** *1 1/4* **Lofty**[20] 1195 3-9-5 0........................ LewisEdmunds 1 70
(David Barron) *hld up in tch: hdwy over 2f out: rdn wl over 1f out: styd on fnl f* **1/1**[1]

60- **3** *hd* **Tease Maid**[163] 8483 3-9-0 0........................ JasonHart 5 64
(John Quinn) *cl up: led after 1f: pushed along and jnd wl over 2f out: rdn and hdd wl over 1f out: drvn and kpt on same pce fnl f* **33/1**

400- **4** *1 1/2* **Ollivander (IRE)**[163] 8474 3-9-5 67........................(p[1]) DavidNolan 2 65
(David O'Meara) *led 1f: chsd ldng pair: rdn along over 2f out: kpt on same pce* **12/1**[3]

5 *6* **Manzoni** 3-9-0 0........................ DylanHogan(5) 3 45
(Mohamed Moubarak) *n.m.r s: in tch: rdn along wl over 2f out: sn wknd* **33/1**

0- **6** *1/2* **Laura's Legacy**[242] 5746 3-9-0 0........................ DavidProbert 6 39
(Andrew Balding) *cl up: rdn along 3f out: sn wknd* **18/1**

- **7** *8* **Martha McEwan (IRE)** 3-9-0 0........................ BenCurtis 7 13
(David Barron) *dwlt: green and sn outpcd in rr* **33/1**

1m 14.96s (-1.54) **Going Correction** -0.20s/f (Stan) 7 Ran SP% **111.8**
Speed ratings (Par 103): **102,100,100,98,90 89,78**
CSF £3.11 TOTE £2.40: £1.10, £1.10; EX 3.60 Trifecta £22.70.
Owner Clipper Logistics **Bred** L Wright **Trained** Upper Lambourn, W Berks

FOCUS
No more than a fair maiden but the winner did it nicely and looks to have a future. The gallop was an ordinary one and the first four finished clear.

1524 BETWAY MARATHON H'CAP 2m 2f 98y(F)

3:55 (3:55) (Class 3) (0-90,90) 4-Y-0+

£9,337 (£2,796; £1,398; £699; £349; £175) **Stalls** Low

Form RPR

01-4 **1** **Mixboy (FR)**[24] 231 9-9-9 **90**........................ PaulMulrennan 5 98
(Keith Dalgleish) *trckd ldr: cl up 1/2-way: led 1m out: pushed along and wd st: rdn 2f out: kpt on strly fnl f* **5/1**[3]

0003 **2** *2 1/4* **Addicted To You (IRE)**[21] 1172 5-9-4 **85**........................(v) FrannyNorton 4 90
(Mark Johnston) *trckd ldrs: hdwy 4f out: chsd wnr and swtchd lft wl over 2f out: sn rdn: drvn wl over 1f out: no imp* **5/4**[1]

10-0 **3** *3 1/4* **Gang Warfare**[23] 1144 8-9-0 **81**........................(tp) RossaRyan 8 82
(Alexandra Dunn) *trckd ldrs: hdwy over 4f out: rdn along and wd st: drvn over 2f out: kpt on same pce* **25/1**

2-60 **4** *9* **Final Choice**[15] 991 6-7-11 **71** oh1........................(b) GavinAshton(7) 6 63
(Adam West) *dwlt and bhd: hdwy to take clsr order after 1m: chsd ldrs 6f out: rdn along over 4f out: drvn 3f out: sn one pce* **33/1**

-111 **5** *18* **Blazon**[34] 946 6-8-4 **71** oh1........................(p) LukeMorris 3 43
(Kim Bailey) *hld up in tch: hdwy over 6f out: chsd ldrs over 3f out: sn rdn: drvn over 2f out: sn wknd and eased (trainer's rep said, regarding the poor form shown, that gelding was unsuited by the fibresand surface on this occasion)* **7/4**[2]

154- **6** *95* **The Resdev Way**[147] 7518 6-8-12 **79**........................ GrahamLee 1
(Philip Kirby) *a in rr: bhd fr 1/2-way: t.o fnl 4f (jockey said gelding was never travelling)* **25/1**

/00- **P** **Claudio Monteverdi (IRE)**[321] 2800 6-9-3 **84**........................(bt[1]) HayleyTurner 2
(Adam West) *led: hdd 8f out: rdn along and lost pl over 6f out: lost action and bhd whn p.u over 4f out* **100/1**

4m 5.94s (-5.56) **Going Correction** -0.20s/f (Stan) 7 Ran SP% **109.1**
Speed ratings (Par 107): **104,103,101,97,89 47,**
CSF £10.66 CT £120.87 TOTE £4.90: £1.90, £1.20; EX 12.90 Trifecta £84.50.
Owner Paul & Clare Rooney **Bred** E A R L Jourdier **Trained** Carluke, S Lanarks

FOCUS
A decent handicap for the stayers - even allowing for the fact that \bBlazon\p underperformed. The gallop was reasonable and the first three came clear.

1525 BETWAY LIVE CASINO H'CAP 1m 3f 23y(F)

4:25 (4:25) (Class 5) (0-75,75) 4-Y-0+

£3,752 (£1,116; £557; £300; £300; £300) **Stalls** Low

Form RPR

0-35 **1** **Lovely Approach**[22] 1169 4-9-6 **74**........................ BenCurtis 5 84+
(Hugo Palmer) *prom: led 4f out: rdn over 2f out: drvn and kpt on strly fnl f* **6/4**[1]

4113 **2** *1 1/2* **Royal Cosmic**[47] 737 5-8-11 **70**........................ SeanDavis(5) 8 77
(Richard Fahey) *hld up in tch: hdwy over 3f out: rdn over 2f out: chsd wnr wl over 1f out: sn drvn and edgd lft ins fnl f: kpt on* **3/1**[2]

5 **3** *6* **Quila Saeda (GER)**[47] 739 5-8-2 **61** oh4........................ TheodoreLadd(5) 7 58
(Michael Appleby) *hld up in rr: hdwy over 3f out: wd st: rdn over 2f out: styd on u.p appr fnl f* **16/1**

412- **4** *5* **Just Wait (IRE)**[154] 8744 4-9-7 **75**........................ FrannyNorton 3 63
(Mark Johnston) *rdn along s and sn in tch: effrt over 4f out: sn pushed along: rdn over 3f out: sn drvn and plugged on one pce* **7/2**[3]

-600 **5** *6* **Tenedos**[25] 1096 4-9-1 **69**........................(b) RossaRyan 2 47
(Ed de Giles) *led 2f: cl up: rdn along over 3f out: drvn over 2f out: sn wknd* **12/1**

4-00 **6** *10* **Rainbow Jazz (IRE)**[21] 1183 4-8-7 **61** oh1........................(be) NickyMackay 1 22
(Adam West) *prom on inner: led after 2f: rdn along over 4f out: sn hdd: drvn 3f out and sn wknd* **25/1**

606/ **P** **Royal Sunday (FR)**[24] 3426 5-8-11 **65**........................ LukeMorris 4
(Alex Hales) *chsd ldrs: rdn along 5f out: lost pl wl over 3f out: bhd and p.u 2f out: fatally injured* **12/1**

2m 22.35s (-5.65) **Going Correction** -0.20s/f (Stan) 7 Ran SP% **112.3**
Speed ratings (Par 103): **112,110,106,102,98 91,**
CSF £5.89 CT £46.12 TOTE £2.20: £1.70, £1.40; EX 6.70 Trifecta £44.90.
Owner Dr Ali Ridha **Bred** Rabbah Bloodstock Limited **Trained** Newmarket, Suffolk

FOCUS
Not the most competitive of handicaps but an improved performance from the unexposed winner. The gallop was an ordinary one but the first two pulled clear in the last quarter mile.

1526 FOLLOW TOP TIPSTER TEMPLEGATE AT SUNRACING H'CAP 1m 13y(F)

4:55 (4:55) (Class 5) (0-75,77) 4-Y-0+

£3,752 (£1,116; £557; £300; £300; £300) **Stalls** Low

Form RPR

0006 **1** **Muqarred (USA)**[20] 1197 7-8-7 **61** oh1........................(p) BenCurtis 8 70
(Roger Fell) *cl up: chal 2f out: rdn to ld over 1f out: edgd lft ins fnl f: kpt on (trainer rep could offer no explanation for gelding's improvement in form)* **12/1**

5423 **2** *1 1/4* **Majestic Moon (IRE)**[7] 1367 9-9-2 **70**........................(p) ShelleyBirkett 2 76
(Julia Feilden) *trckd ldrs: hdwy 3f out: chsd ldng pair wl over 1f out: rdn ent fnl f: swtchd rt wl ins fnl f: styd on* **7/1**

5-20 **3** *hd* **Motajaasid (IRE)**[33] 962 4-9-6 **77**........................(t) FinleyMarsh(3) 4 82
(Richard Hughes) *cl up on inner: led 3f out: rdn 2f out: hdd over 1f out: sn drvn and kpt on same pce* **5/1**

2133 **4** *8* **Baron Run**[7] 1369 9-8-1 **62** oh3 ow1........................ RhonaPindar(7) 9 49
(K R Burke) *cl up: disp ld over 3f out: rdn along wl over 2f out: drvn wl over 1f out: sn wknd* **8/1**

62-1 **5** *hd* **Long Socks**[80] 232 5-8-12 **66**........................ DavidProbert 3 53
(Alan King) *hld up in tch: pushed along 1/2-way: rdn over 3f out: sn outpcd (jockey said gelding was never travelling)* **7/2**[1]

-302 **6** *hd* **Tum Tum**[20] 1197 4-9-5 **73**........................(h) PhilDennis 5 59
(Michael Herrington) *chsd ldrs: rdn along over 3f out: sn wknd* **4/1**[2]

3202 **7** *1/2* **Mama Africa (IRE)**[7] 1367 5-9-2 **75**........................ PoppyBridgwater(5) 6 60
(David Barron) *sn slt ld: rdn along and hdd 3f out: wknd over 2f out* **9/2**[3]

4460 **8** *1/2* **Red Touch (USA)**[7] 1369 7-8-11 **65**........................(b) LukeMorris 1 49
(Michael Appleby) *a in rr* **33/1**

1m 40.85s (-2.85) **Going Correction** -0.20s/f (Stan) 8 Ran SP% **111.3**
Speed ratings (Par 103): **106,104,104,96,96 96,95,95**
CSF £87.35 CT £470.58 TOTE £18.30: £3.80, £2.60, £1.90; EX 119.60 Trifecta £553.70.
Owner R G Fell **Bred** Shadwell Farm LLC **Trained** Nawton, N Yorks

FOCUS
An open handicap on paper but a race in which the three market leaders disappointed. The gallop was reasonable and the first three pulled clear. It can be rated around the runner-up's recent form.

1527 SUNRACING.CO.UK H'CAP 1m 13y(F)
5:25 (5:25) (Class 6) (0-55,55) 4-Y-O+
£3,105 (£924; £461; £300; £300; £300) **Stalls** Low

Form RPR

-000 1 **Atalanta Queen**[27] 1060 4-8-7 **46** oh1......................(v) SeamusCronin(5) 6 52
(Robyn Brisland) mde most: rdn wl over 1f out and sn edgd rt: drvn and hung bdly rt ins fnl f: hld on gamely towards fin (trainer said, regarding improvement in form, filly appreciated a return to fibresand surface) **50/1**

55-2 2 *hd* **Thecornishbarron (IRE)**[81] 210 7-8-12 **46**.................(w) TomEaves 14 52
(Brian Ellison) on outer: wd st: effrt 2f out: rdn wl over 1f out and sn carried rt: ev ch ins fnl f: drvn and n.m.r nr stands' rail: kpt on wl towards fin **12/1**

2602 3 *1 1/4* **Molten Lava (IRE)**[9] 1339 7-9-5 **53**.......................(p) FrannyNorton 1 56
(Steve Gollings) trckd ldrs on inner: hdwy over 2f out: rdn along wl over 1f out: styd on fnl f (jockey said gelding hung right) **6/1**[3]

0-42 4 *nk* **Port Soif**[7] 1369 5-8-13 **52**..(p) TheodoreLadd(5) 9 54
(Scott Dixon) cl up: chal 2f out: rdn whn carried rt over 1f out: drvn and ev ch whn n.m.r and hmpd ins fnl f: swtchd lft and one pce after **15/8**[1]

3-06 5 *2* **Luath**[59] 590 6-9-0 **48**.. NickyMackay 13 45
(Suzzanne France) cl up towards outer: rdn along 2f out: carried rt: drvn and ch over 1f out: hld whn n.m.r and hmpd ins fnl f **10/1**

00-0 6 *4* **War Of Succession**[41] 830 5-9-7 **55**................................ HayleyTurner 10 43
(Tony Newcombe) dwlt and bhd tl styd on fnl 2f: nrst fin **16/1**

00-0 7 *nk* **Mime Dance**[7] 1369 8-9-1 **52**..(e) TimClark(3) 5 39
(John Butler) chsd ldrs: rdn along over 2f out: sn one pce **50/1**

05-0 8 *3 1/2* **Lone Voice (IRE)**[34] 940 4-8-12 **46** oh1.............................. LukeMorris 8 25
(Tony Carroll) prom: rdn along 3f out: sn wknd **25/1**

005/ 9 *3 1/2* **Kathy**[620] 5161 4-8-12 **46** oh1....................................... PaddyMathers 12 17
(Scott Dixon) a towards rr **50/1**

3331 10 *nk* **Limerick Lord (IRE)**[4] 1431 7-9-6 **54** 4ex......................(p) ShelleyBirkett 7 25
(Julia Feilden) swtchd lft sn after s: a in rr (jockey said gelding was slowly away) **9/4**[2]

5646 11 *1* **Jeremy's Jet (IRE)**[28] 1032 8-8-12 **46**..........................(t) GeorgeDowning 11 14
(Tony Carroll) a in rr **20/1**

000- 12 *37* **Amy Blair**[228] 6287 6-9-5 **53**.. LiamKeniry 3
(Stef Keniry) a in rr: bhd fnl 2f **40/1**

1m 42.56s (-1.14) **Going Correction** -0.20s/f (Stan) **12** Ran SP% **119.4**
Speed ratings (Par 101): **97,96,95,95,93 89,88,85,81,81 80,43**
CSF £540.28 CT £4182.20 TOTE £86.80: £17.50, £3.50, £1.60; EX 2735.10 Trifecta £3735.90.
Owner Ferrybank Properties Limited **Bred** R T Dunne **Trained** Danethorpe, Notts

FOCUS
A very ordinary handicap in which the gallop was reasonable but those that attempted to make ground from off the pace were at a disadvantage.
T/Plt: £30.10 to a £1 stake. Pool: £66,967.07 - 1,622.02 winning units T/Qpdt: £7.30 to a £1 stake. Pool: £6,958.86 - 702.73 winning units **Joe Rowntree**

1528a-1530a (Foreign Racing) - See Raceform Interactive

LEOPARDSTOWN (L-H)
Wednesday, April 3
OFFICIAL GOING: Good to yielding changing to yielding after race 4 (5.00)

1531a SPIN 1038 HERITAGE STKS (LISTED RACE) 1m
5:00 (5:01) 4-Y-O+
£24,450 (£7,873; £3,729; £1,657; £828; £414)

RPR

1 **Imaging**[158] 8654 4-9-8 105.. OisinOrr 5 104+
(D K Weld, Ire) hld up: 7th 1/2-way: gng wl 2f out: sn pushed along and gd hdwy between horses 1 1/2f out to ld ent fnl f: sn rdn w narrow advantage and kpt on wl to assert clsng stages **3/1**[2]

2 *1/2* **Zihba (IRE)**[200] 7317 4-9-10 104...................................... ChrisHayes 7 104
(J A Stack, Ire) cl up and disp 2nd early: gng wl in cl 3rd into st: rdn bhd ldrs over 1f out and wnt 2nd ins fnl f: kpt on wl wout matching wnr clsng stages **10/1**

3 *1* **Surrounding (IRE)**[28] 1048 6-9-3 97...............................(t) RonanWhelan 8 95+
(M Halford, Ire) prom tl sn settled bhd ldrs: 5th after 1f: 6th bef 1/2-way: tk clsr order on outer over 2f out: rdn 1 1/2f out and kpt on u.p into 3rd nr fin: nt trble wnr **8/1**

4 *nk* **Amedeo Modigliani (IRE)**[10] 1309 4-9-5 96........................ RyanMoore 2 96
(A P O'Brien, Ire) dwlt: sn chsd ldrs: 3rd bef 1/2-way: tk clsr order bhd ldrs far side 2f out: nt clr run 1 1/2f out and lost pl: swtchd rt in 6th ins fnl f and r.o: nvr trbld ldrs **9/2**[3]

5 *1/2* **Verbal Dexterity (IRE)**[165] 8408 4-9-5 107.................... KevinManning 9 95
(J S Bolger, Ire) sn disp cl 2nd: 2nd 1/2-way: rdn in 2nd 1 1/2f out and led briefly over 1f out tl sn hdd: wknd in 3rd wl ins fnl f **11/8**[1]

6 *1/2* **Marshall Jennings (IRE)**[10] 1308 7-9-5 97......................... ShaneFoley 11 94+
(Mrs John Harrington, Ire) hld up: 8th 1/2-way: rdn nr side fr over 1f out and r.o into nvr threatening 6th nr fin **25/1**

7 *1 3/4* **Quizical (IRE)**[10] 1308 4-9-5 93...................................... RobbieColgan 4 90
(Ms Sheila Lavery, Ire) sn led: stl gng wl into st: rdn 1 1/2f out and sn hdd: wknd ins fnl f **25/1**

8 *1/2* **Sam Missile (IRE)**[264] 4891 6-9-5 90.............................. SeamieHeffernan 10 89
(Patrick J McKenna, Ire) dwlt and pushed along briefly in rr early: rdn and no imp under 2f out: kpt on one pce ins fnl f where swtchd rt nr fin **66/1**

9 *shd* **Harvestfortheworld (IRE)**[224] 6434 4-9-0 95...............(t[1]) LeighRoche 3 83
(J A Stack, Ire) mid-div: 5th bef 1/2-way: 6th 3f out: drvn 1 1/2f out where n.m.r briefly: rdn briefly and wknd ins fnl f **20/1**

1m 44.99s (1.19) **Going Correction** +0.40s/f (Good) **9** Ran SP% **119.4**
Speed ratings: **110,109,108,108,107 107,105,104,104**
CSF £31.89 TOTE £3.70: £1.20, £2.50, £2.10; DF 27.30 Trifecta £161.20.
Owner K Abdullah **Bred** Juddmonte Farms Ltd **Trained** Curragh, Co Kildare

FOCUS
Three horses with a rating in three figures in this nine-runner field, and two of them dominated. Dermot Weld has a fine record in this race and has now won it on six occasions since the highly talented Famous Name initiated a hat-trick in 2010.

1532 - 1542a (Foreign Racing) - See Raceform Interactive

1475
CHELMSFORD (A.W) (L-H)
Thursday, April 4
OFFICIAL GOING: Polytrack: standard
Wind: medium, behind Weather: overcast, showers

1543 £20 FREE BETS AT TOTESPORT.COM FILLIES' NOVICE STKS 1m (P)
6:00 (6:01) (Class 4) 3-Y-O+ **£5,530** (£1,645; £822; £411) **Stalls** Low

Form RPR

61- 1 **Diamond Oasis**[106] 9604 3-9-6 0.................................(h[1]) OisinMurphy 4 71+
(Saeed bin Suroor) s.i.s: hld up in tch: clsd over 2f out: swtchd rt and rdn over 1f out: led ins fnl f: r.o wl **10/11**[1]

5-1 2 *nk* **Yimkin (IRE)**[61] 556 3-9-6 0... JasonWatson 7 70
(Roger Charlton) led: rdn wl over 1f out: hdd and ins fnl f: kpt on wl but a jst hld after **2/1**[2]

00 3 *1 1/4* **Dusty Damsel**[33] 979 3-8-13 0.. RossaRyan 1 60
(Mike Murphy) t.k.h: chsd ldrs: effrt over 1f out: kpt on same pce u.p ins fnl f **25/1**

0- 4 *nk* **Grape Shot**[117] 9460 3-8-13 0.. SeanLevey 8 59
(Richard Hannon) t.k.h: pressed ldr: rdn ent fnl 2f: jst getting outpcd whn sltly squeezed for room ins fnl f: outpcd towards fin **50/1**

0- 5 *nk* **Mystiquestar (IRE)**[198] 7382 3-8-13 0...................(h[1]) AdamMcNamara 9 58+
(Roger Charlton) s.i.s: dropped in and hld up in rr: effrt and hung lft over 1f out: kpt on ins fnl f: nvr trbld ldrs **25/1**

6 *6* **Wareeda (IRE)** 3-8-13 0...(t[1]) TomMarquand 5 44
(Richard Hannon) rn green and a towards rr: bhd fnl 2f (jockey said filly ran green) **9/2**[3]

0 7 *3/4* **Al Anaab (FR)**[8] 1359 3-8-13 0.. LukeMorris 3 42
(Peter Chapple-Hyam) midfield: rdn and outpcd over 2f out: bhd over 1f out **100/1**

1m 41.7s (1.80) **Going Correction** -0.05s/f (Stan)
WFA 3 from 4yo 15lb **7** Ran SP% **114.5**
Speed ratings (Par 102): **89,88,87,87,86 80,80**
CSF £2.92 TOTE £1.70: £1.10, £1.40; EX 3.10 Trifecta £11.90.
Owner Godolphin **Bred** Godolphin **Trained** Newmarket, Suffolk

FOCUS
Only fair form on the face of it and the first five finished in a bit of a heap thanks to the muddling gallop but the winner's performance can be upgraded.

1544 TOTEPOOL CASHBACK CLUB AT TOTESPORT.COM H'CAP 1m (P)
6:30 (6:47) (Class 4) (0-85,86) 4-Y-O+ **£5,530** (£1,645; £822; £411; £400) **Stalls** Low

Form RPR

1110 1 **Lion Hearted (IRE)**[21] 1197 5-8-10 **78**.............................. MarkCrehan(7) 1 85
(Michael Appleby) t.k.h: trckd ldrs on inner: effrt over 1f out: drvn and clsd to ld ins fnl f: r.o wl **7/4**[1]

4-20 2 *3/4* **Intrepidly (USA)**[36] 922 5-9-4 **86**..............................(p) CierenFallon(7) 4 91
(Charlie Fellowes) s.i.s: sn pressing ldr and t.k.h: drvn and ev ch over 1f out: kpt on but unable qck wl ins fnl f **7/2**[3]

-600 3 *3/4* **Able Jack**[20] 1213 6-9-5 **80**.. SeanLevey 6 83
(Stuart Williams) t.k.h: hld up in tch in last pair: effrt jst over 1f out: chsd ldrs u.p 1f out: kpt on same pce ins fnl f **7/1**

4660 4 *nk* **Come On Tier (FR)**[12] 1294 4-8-12 **73**.............................. LukeMorris 2 75
(David Simcock) led and set stdy gallop: rdn over 1f out: hdd and drvn ins fnl f: kpt on same pce ins fnl f **8/1**

1524 5 *nk* **Samphire Coast**[6] 1401 6-9-7 **82**.................................(vt[1]) PaddyMathers 3 84
(Derek Shaw) broke wl: sn restrained and t.k.h in last pair: effrt and nt clr run over 1f out: swtchd rt ins fnl f: r.o towards fin **11/4**[2]

1m 42.92s (3.02) **Going Correction** -0.05s/f (Stan) **5** Ran SP% **108.9**
Speed ratings (Par 105): **82,81,80,80,79**
CSF £7.92 TOTE £2.30: £1.50, £1.90; EX 7.20 Trifecta £33.90.
Owner Slipstream Racing **Bred** Dowager Countess Harrington **Trained** Oakham, Rutland
■ Arabian Jazz was withdrawn. Price at time of withdrawal 33-1. Rule 4 does not apply.

FOCUS
A reasonable handicap which was delayed by over 15 minutes due to a horse bolting and crashing through the running rail. However the pace was slow to the home turn and this bare form isn't reliable.

1545 EXTRA PLACES AT TOTESPORT.COM H'CAP 1m 2f (P)
7:00 (7:10) (Class 2) (0-105,106) 4-Y-O+ **£12,938** (£3,850; £1,924; £962) **Stalls** Low

Form RPR

1334 1 **Nonios (IRE)**[12] 1294 7-8-9 **92**.......................................(h) DylanHogan(5) 8 101
(David Simcock) stdd and dropped in bhd after s: hld up in tch in rr: clsd on outer over 2f out: rdn to chal ent fnl f: r.o to ld towards fin **10/1**

0050 2 *hd* **Aquarium**[5] 1415 4-9-7 **99**.. FrannyNorton 6 107+
(Mark Johnston) bustled along leaving stalls: midfield: rdn over 2f out: nt clr run and shuffled bk over 1f out: swtchd rt and rallied u.p 1f out: ev ch wl ins fnl f: r.o (jockey said colt was denied a clear run) **6/1**

1221 3 *1/2* **Executive Force**[12] 1294 5-9-5 **97**......................................(p) JFEgan 3 104
(Michael Wigham) trckd ldrs: nt clrest of runs jst over 2f out: hdwy u.p to chal ent fnl f: led jst ins fnl f: hdd and no ex towards fin **11/4**[1]

26-1 4 *3* **Swiss Storm**[37] 915 5-9-0 **92**... DavidProbert 7 93
(Michael Bell) chsd ldr after 2f tl led 4f out: rdn over 1f out: hdd jst ins fnl f: no ex and wknd wl ins fnl f **5/1**

625- 5 *1* **Secret Art (IRE)**[187] 7758 9-9-2 **94**.................................... JamesDoyle 5 93
(William Knight) chsd ldr for 2f: styd prom: effrt over 2f out: unable qck u.p over 1f out: wknd ins fnl f **14/1**

610- 6 *2 1/4* **Pivoine (IRE)**[187] 7773 5-9-11 **106**...............................(v) JoshuaBryan(3) 1 101
(Andrew Balding) hld up in tch: short of room after 1f: nt clrest of runs over 2f out: effrt on inner over 1f out: no imp ins fnl f **7/2**[3]

-036 7 *3/4* **Main Street**[22] 1181 4-9-2 **94**.......................................(p) OisinMurphy 2 87
(David Elsworth) hld up in tch towards rr: effrt over 1f out: rdn and no imp fnl f **3/1**[2]

004- 8 *8* **Mutamaded (IRE)**[248] 5544 6-9-1 **93**................................ JamesSullivan 4 70
(Ruth Carr) led tl 4f out: lost pl over 1f out: bhd fnl f **33/1**

2m 3.93s (-4.67) **Going Correction** -0.05s/f (Stan) **8** Ran SP% **123.5**
Speed ratings (Par 109): **110,109,109,107,106 104,103,97**
CSF £73.71 CT £216.71 TOTE £12.40: £3.00, £2.40, £1.30; EX 75.50 Trifecta £213.50.
Owner Millingbrook Racing **Bred** Sheikh Sultan Bin Khalifa Al Nayhan **Trained** Newmarket, Suffolk
■ Stewards' Enquiry : J F Egan caution: careless riding

FOCUS
A couple of the market leaders disappointed but this was still a good quality handicap in which the pace was reasonable throughout. The winner and second came down the centre of the track in the closing stages and the first three pulled clear.

1546 IRISH LOTTO AT TOTESPORT.COM H'CAP 1m 2f (P)
7:30 (7:35) (Class 6) (0-55,56) 4-Y-O+
£3,105 (£924; £461; £400; £400; £400) **Stalls** Low

Form RPR
2031 1 **Arlecchino's Arc (IRE)**[33] 983 4-9-7 **55**..........(v) DavidProbert 11 61
(Mark Usher) *trckd ldrs: clsd and travelling strly jst over 2f out: rdn to chal over 1f out: led ins fnl f: styd on and hld on towards fin: rdn out* **11/4**[1]
6450 2 *nk* **Sharp Operator**[19] 1231 6-9-8 **56**..........(h) RichardKingscote 2 61
(Charlie Wallis) *wl in tch in midfield: clsd and swtchd rt 2f out: effrt to chse ldrs over 1f out: drvn ins fnl f: wnt 2nd and pressing wnr wl ins fnl f: r.o wl: nvr quite getting to wnr* **9/2**[3]
-410 3 *shd* **Mullarkey**[49] 724 5-9-7 **55**..........(t) KierenFox 9 60
(John Best) *in tch in midfield: clsd ent fnl 2f: chsd ldrs and drvn 1f out: r.o wl and pressing ldrs towards fin: nvr quite getting to wnr* **6/1**
5665 4 1 3/4 **Hidden Dream (IRE)**[12] 1297 4-8-13 **47**..........(p) FrannyNorton 5 49
(Christine Dunnett) *led: rdn and hrd pressed over 1f out: sn drvn and hdd ins fnl f: lost 2 pls and outpcd towards fin: eased cl home* **6/1**
-354 5 3 3/4 **Blyton Lass**[33] 984 4-9-3 **51**.......... BarryMcHugh 3 46
(James Given) *midfield: effrt jst over 1f out: kpt on but no imp ins fnl f* **4/1**[2]
0333 6 1 1/4 **Outlaw Torn (IRE)**[27] 1078 10-8-12 **46** oh1..........(e) PhilipPrince 1 38
(Richard Guest) *chsd ldrs: rdn over 2f out: unable qck over 1f out: wknd ins fnl f* **14/1**
134- 7 1 **Castle Talbot (IRE)**[206] 7125 7-9-6 **54**..........(p) LukeMorris 6 45
(Tom Clover) *bustled along leaving stalls: hld up in last trio: effrt over 2f out: drvn and kpt on same pce ins fnl f: nvr trbld ldrs* **20/1**
-400 8 1/2 **Lulu Star (IRE)**[33] 983 4-8-12 **53**..........(p[1]) ScottMcCullagh[(7)] 10 43
(Julia Feilden) *s.i.s: hld up in tch in rr: effrt and swtchd rt over 1f out: kpt on same pce ins fnl f: nvr trbld ldrs* **25/1**
566- 9 14 **Pollyissimo**[135] 9160 4-8-12 **51**.......... DylanHogan[(5)] 12 14
(Henry Spiller) *hld up in last trio: rdn and btn over 1f out: sn wknd* **33/1**
0/5- 10 22 **Ocean Spray**[219] 6648 4-8-5 **46** oh1.......... CierenFallon[(7)] 8
(Eugene Stanford) *midfield: rdn over 3f out: sn struggling and bhd over 1f out: t.o* **100/1**
4010 P **Cold Fire (IRE)**[22] 1176 6-9-7 **55**..........(v) KieranO'Neill 7
(Robyn Brisland) *chsd ldr tl wl over 1f out: sn eased and p.u ins fnl f: lame (vet said gelding was lame on it's left-fore leg)* **14/1**
2m 6.58s (-2.02) **Going Correction** -0.05s/f (Stan) **11 Ran SP% 119.3**
Speed ratings (Par 101): **100,99,99,98,95 94,93,93,81,64**
CSF £14.72 CT £69.94 TOTE £4.00: £1.60, £1.60, £1.80; EX 19.00 Trifecta £65.80.
Owner K Senior **Bred** Mrs Eithne Hamilton **Trained** Upper Lambourn, Berks

FOCUS
Not much to dwell on in an ordinary handicap. The gallop picked up turning for home and the first four pulled clear.

1547 BET IN PLAY AT TOTESPORT.COM H'CAP 5f (P)
8:00 (8:05) (Class 4) (0-85,87) 4-Y-O+
£5,530 (£1,645; £822; £411; £400; £400) **Stalls** Low

Form RPR
50-6 1 **Poyle Vinnie**[44] 791 9-9-7 **82**.......... JamesSullivan 1 90
(Ruth Carr) *wnt rt leaving stalls: trckd ldrs and travelled strly: clsd and upsides ldr over 1f out: shkn up to ld 1f out: sn rdn: edgd rt but doing enough ins fnl f: rdn out* **4/1**[1]
-056 2 1/2 **You're Cool**[20] 1211 7-9-4 **79**..........(t) LewisEdmunds 2 85
(John Balding) *wnt lft and bmpd leaving stalls: midfield: clsd over 1f out: hdwy u.p to chse wnr ins fnl f: kpt on wl but nvr quite getting to wnr* **7/1**
00-0 3 *nk* **Equimou**[93] 3 5-8-13 **79**.......... DarraghKeenan[(5)] 4 84
(Robert Eddery) *hld up in rr: clsd over 1f out: hdwy and rdn ins fnl f: chsd ldrs wl ins fnl f: styd on wl: nvr quite getting to ldrs* **12/1**
04-0 4 1 1/4 **Bosham**[20] 1211 9-9-5 **80**..........(bt) NathanEvans 3 81
(Michael Easterby) *led: rdn over 1f out: hdd 1f out: no ex u.p and wknd wl ins fnl f* **10/1**
1533 5 1/2 **Captain Lars (SAF)**[6] 1394 9-9-6 **81**..........(b) OisinMurphy 5 80
(Archie Watson) *midfield: effrt over 1f out: kpt on same pce ins fnl f* **5/1**[3]
-664 6 3/4 **Zac Brown (IRE)**[2] 1496 8-9-4 **82**..........(t) JoshuaBryan[(3)] 6 78
(Charlie Wallis) *in tch in midfield: effrt over 1f out: drvn 1f out: kpt on same pce and no imp ins fnl f* **6/1**
1-66 7 3/4 **Arzaak (IRE)**[21] 1194 5-9-3 **78**..........(b) DavidEgan 8 71
(Charlie Wallis) *in tch in last trio: swtchd rt and effrt over 1f out: kpt on ins fnl f: nvr trbld ldrs* **20/1**
1331 8 1/2 **Another Angel (IRE)**[27] 1082 5-9-5 **80**.......... CamHardie 9 72
(Antony Brittain) *pressed ldr tl unable qck over 1f out: wknd ins fnl f* **8/1**
3411 9 1 1/4 **Drakefell (IRE)**[6] 1394 4-9-2 **82** 5ex..........(b) SeamusCronin[(5)] 11 69
(Antony Brittain) *chsd ldrs but stuck on outer: rdn and lost pl over 1f out: wknd ins fnl f* **9/2**[2]
0420 10 1 3/4 **Dynamo Walt (IRE)**[44] 791 8-9-7 **82**..........(v) PaddyMathers 7 63
(Derek Shaw) *in rr: swtchd rt and effrt over 1f out: edgd lft and no imp 1f out: nvr involved* **14/1**
58.93s (-1.27) **Going Correction** -0.05s/f (Stan) **10 Ran SP% 121.0**
Speed ratings (Par 105): **108,107,106,104,103 102,101,100,98,95**
CSF £33.57 CT £260.49 TOTE £4.40: £1.40, £2.10, £5.10; EX 32.40 Trifecta £328.60.
Owner Formulated Polymer Products Ltd **Bred** Cecil And Miss Alison Wiggins **Trained** Huby, N Yorks

FOCUS
A useful handicap run at a decent gallop and this form should prove reliable.

1548 DOUBLE DELIGHT HAT-TRICK HEAVEN AT TOTESPORT.COM H'CAP 1m 6f (P)
8:30 (8:31) (Class 6) (0-60,59) 4-Y-O+
£3,105 (£924; £461; £400; £400; £400) **Stalls** Low

Form RPR
-200 1 **Heron (USA)**[48] 731 5-9-4 **56**..........(p) DanielMuscutt 11 64
(Brett Johnson) *hld up in midfield: clsd and nt clrest of runs jst over 2f out: hdwy and swtchd lft over 1f out: rdn and styd on to ld ins fnl f: sn wnt clr* **8/1**
1622 2 2 1/2 **Top Rock Talula (IRE)**[9] 1341 4-9-4 **57**.......... EdwardGreatrex 4 64
(Warren Greatrex) *trckd ldrs: clsd to press ldr ent fnl 2f: rdn to ld over 1f out: hdd and nt match pce of wnr ins fnl f* **2/1**[1]
4005 3 1 3/4 **Masters Apprentice (IRE)**[19] 1235 4-9-5 **58**.......... DavidEgan 1 62
(Sylvester Kirk) *chsd ldr for over 1f out: chsd ldrs but rn in snatches after: unable qck u.p and edgd rt 1f out: edgd lft and kpt on same pce ins fnl f* **3/1**[2]
-500 4 3/4 **Carvelas (IRE)**[36] 923 10-9-7 **59**.......... DavidProbert 3 61
(J R Jenkins) *stdd s: hld up in rr: clsd and nt clr run jst over 2f out: hdwy u.p 1f out: kpt on ins fnl f: no threat to ldrs* **20/1**
-430 5 4 **Normandy Blue**[35] 946 4-8-7 **46**.......... KieranO'Neill 10 44
(Louise Allan) *broke wl sn restrained to rr and t.k.h: rdn and gd hdwy on outer over 2f out: no imp whn hmpd 1f out: sn wknd* **20/1**
5224 6 1/2 **Banta Bay**[35] 947 5-8-10 **48**.......... JosephineGordon 5 44
(John Best) *chsd ldr after over 1f tl led over 3f out: rdn and hdd over 1f out: sn outpcd and wknd ins fnl f* **7/1**[3]
4033 7 *nk* **Hussar Ballad (USA)**[9] 1341 10-8-13 **51**.......... CamHardie 7 46
(Antony Brittain) *stdd s: hld up in tch towards rr: clsd over 2f out: no imp u.p and btn over 1f out: wknd ins fnl f* **12/1**
00-0 8 1 **Eurato (FR)**[15] 1024 9-9-3 **55**..........(v[1]) PaddyMathers 12 49
(Derek Shaw) *in tch in midfield: rdn 3f out: unable qck and btn over 1f out: wknd ins fnl f* **50/1**
1203 9 7 **Apex Predator (IRE)**[38] 910 4-9-3 **56**..........(bt) TomQueally 2 43
(Seamus Durack) *in tch in midfield: nt clrest of runs over 2f out: no hdwy over 1f out: wknd fnl f* **10/1**
-006 10 4 1/2 **Lazarus (IRE)**[20] 789 5-9-0 **52**..........(t) CharlesBishop 8 31
(Amy Murphy) *midfield: rdn briefly over 7f out: reminder over 5f out: lost pl and bhd over 2f out: wknd over 1f out (jockey said gelding was never travelling)* **8/1**
000- 11 *shd* **Cue's Folly**[122] 9383 4-8-6 **45**..........(b[1]) HollieDoyle 13 26
(Ed Dunlop) *mounted in the chute and taken down early: awkward leaving stalls and slowly away: wd thrght and rn in snatches: chsd ldrs after 2f tl over 2f out: sn dropped out: bhd fnl f* **33/1**
065- 12 18 **Oyster Card**[233] 6118 6-8-9 **47**..........(b[1]) LukeMorris 9 2
(Michael Appleby) *led tl over 3f out: lost pl u.p ent fnl 2f: bhd and eased ins fnl f: t.o (jockey said gelding stopped quickly)* **33/1**
3m 0.92s (-2.28) **Going Correction** -0.05s/f (Stan)
WFA 4 from 5yo+ 1lb **12 Ran SP% 127.2**
Speed ratings (Par 101): **104,102,101,101,98 98,98,97,93,91 91,80**
CSF £24.83 CT £64.12 TOTE £9.70: £2.90, £1.10, £1.60; EX 45.50 Trifecta £111.20.
Owner 01 Racing Partnership **Bred** Juddmonte Farms Inc **Trained** Epsom, Surrey

FOCUS
A moderate handicap but a decent gallop and the field were well strung out in the straight.
T/Plt: £17.20 to a £1 stake. Pool: £89,485.45. 3,791.55 winning units. T/Qpdt: £18.60 to a £1 stake. Pool: £11,745.72. 466.10 winning units. **Steve Payne**

[1521]SOUTHWELL (L-H)
Thursday, April 4

OFFICIAL GOING: Fibresand: standard
Wind: Strong, against Weather: Cloudy

1549 LADBROKES HOME OF THE ODDS BOOST H'CAP 7f 14y(F)
1:55 (1:55) (Class 6) (0-60,60) 3-Y-O
£3,105 (£924; £461; £300; £300; £300) **Stalls** Low

Form RPR
-135 1 **Sylviacliffs (FR)**[36] 931 3-9-1 **54**..........(p) BenCurtis 14 67+
(K R Burke) *sn chsng ldrs: led over 2f out: rdn clr fnl f* **6/1**[3]
50 2 4 1/2 **Act Of Magic (IRE)**[42] 829 3-8-12 **51**.......... KieranO'Neill 7 52
(Mohamed Moubarak) *sn pushed along and prom: nt clr run and lost pl over 5f out: hdwy over 4f out: rdn to chse wnr over 1f out: styd on same pce fnl f* **5/2**[1]
0-06 3 1/2 **Peruvian Summer (IRE)**[22] 1173 3-9-4 **57**.......... JackMitchell 8 57
(Kevin Frost) *chsd ldrs: rdn over 1f out: no ex fnl f* **10/1**
1-00 4 2 1/4 **Singe Du Nord**[36] 931 3-8-6 **50**..........(p) FayeMcManoman[(5)] 6 44
(Nigel Tinkler) *chsd ldrs: lost pl over 2f out: swtchd lft and hdwy over 1f out: no ex fnl f (jockey said filly never faced kickback)* **9/1**
0112 5 2 3/4 **Dolly Dupree**[28] 1067 3-8-12 **56**.......... TheodoreLadd[(5)] 12 43
(Paul D'Arcy) *hld up: racd wd tl over 4f out: wnt wd again over 2f out: nvr nrr* **9/2**[2]
060- 6 1/2 **Seafaring Girl (IRE)**[171] 8258 3-8-13 **52**.......... NicolaCurrie 13 37
(Mark Loughnane) *s.i.s: hld up: hdwy on outer 1/2-way: rdn over 2f out: wknd over 1f out* **66/1**
533- 7 1 **Lincoln Red**[154] 8777 3-8-10 **49**.......... RachelRichardson 10 32
(Olly Williams) *s.i.s: hdwy on outer 1/2-way: rdn over 1f out: wknd over 1f out* **16/1**
0-44 8 3/4 **Your Mothers' Eyes**[12] 1296 3-8-13 **57**.......... DarraghKeenan[(5)] 9 38
(Alan Bailey) *chsd ldrs: rdn over 1f out: sn wknd* **6/1**[3]
6-50 9 3 1/2 **Hua Hin (IRE)**[57] 620 3-9-7 **60**..........(t) SeanLevey 4 32
(Richard Hannon) *led 6f out: rdn and hdd over 2f out: wknd over 1f out* **14/1**
000- 10 3 **Zalmi Angel**[162] 8543 3-9-4 **57**.......... AndrewMullen 5 21
(Adrian Nicholls) *s.i.s: sn pushed along towards rr: nvr on terms* **50/1**
4502 11 4 **Thedevilinneville**[28] 1071 3-8-13 **52**.......... LukeMorris 3 6
(Adam West) *pushed along early in rr: rdn 1/2-way: wknd over 2f out* **20/1**
00-0 12 2 1/2 **Jungle Warfare (IRE)**[75] 316 3-9-4 **57**.......... RossaRyan 1 4
(Richard Hannon) *led 1f: chsd ldrs tl rdn and wknd wl over 2f out* **20/1**
060 13 6 **Tanzerin (IRE)**[33] 979 3-9-7 **60**.......... StevieDonohoe 2
(Charlie Fellowes) *s.i.s: sn outpcd* **25/1**
000- 14 15 **Slaithwaite (IRE)**[148] 8929 3-8-13 **57**.......... BenSanderson[(5)] 11
(Roger Fell) *s.i.s: sn outpcd: eased fnl 2f* **20/1**
1m 28.79s (-1.51) **Going Correction** -0.05s/f (Stan) **14 Ran SP% 128.5**
Speed ratings (Par 96): **106,100,100,97,94 94,92,92,88,84 80,77,70,53**
CSF £21.00 CT £164.33 TOTE £7.10: £2.40, £1.70, £2.90; EX 33.20 Trifecta £298.90.
Owner The Mount Racing Club & Mrs E Burke **Bred** P Lemarie & S A R L Ecurie Silgezam **Trained** Middleham Moor, N Yorks

FOCUS
A moderate handicap run at a sound pace with the field finishing well strung out. The winner was well paced off the home bend.

1550 SUNRACING.CO.UK MAIDEN STKS 1m 13y(F)
2:30 (2:30) (Class 5) 3-Y-O+ **£3,752** (£1,116; £557; £278) **Stalls** Low

Form RPR
533- 1 **Scat King (IRE)**[168] 8345 3-8-13 **76**.......... ShaneKelly 8 84
(Richard Hughes) *mde virtually all: rdn clr and edgd lft fr over 1f out: styd on wl* **11/4**[2]

-242 **2** 6 **Barossa Red (IRE)**[23] 1166 3-8-13 78........ DavidProbert 3 70
(Andrew Balding) *chsd ldrs: chsd wnr over 3f out: rdn over 1f out: sn outpcd* **6/4**[1]

3 **3** 11 **Battle Of Yarmouk (IRE)**[21] 1195 3-8-13 0........ KevinStott 5 45
(Kevin Ryan) *trckd ldrs: rdn over 3f out: wknd over 2f out* **3/1**[3]

32 **4** 2 1/4 **Ifreet (QA)**[23] 1165 3-8-13 0........ SeanLevey 9 40
(Richard Hannon) *chsd wnr over 4f: sn rdn: wknd over 2f out* **5/1**

5 2 3/4 **Warning Light**[183] 7915 4-9-9 0........ JosephineGordon 2 32
(Shaun Keightley) *prom: sn pushed along: lost pl over 5f out: n.d after* **66/1**

46 **6** shd **Nine Elms (USA)**[27] 1080 4-9-11 0........ TimClark[(3)] 1 37
(Roy Bowring) *s.i.s: hdwy over 4f out: rdn and wknd over 2f out (jockey said gelding was fractious in stalls)* **33/1**

7 2 1/2 **Beechwood James (FR)** 3-8-13 0........ RossaRyan 7 27
(Richard Hannon) *s.s: outpcd* **18/1**

0/5 **8** 7 **Cryogenics (IRE)**[27] 1080 5-9-7 0........ WilliamCarver[(7)] 10 15
(Kenny Johnson) *s.s: outpcd* **100/1**

05- **9** 8 **Sunbright (IRE)**[96] 9746 4-9-9 0........ AlistairRawlinson 11
(Michael Appleby) *s.s: a in rr (jockey said filly anticipated the start and as a result was slowly away and hung left-handed)* **100/1**

1m 40.9s (-2.80) **Going Correction** -0.05s/f (Stan)
WFA 3 from 4yo+ 15lb **9** Ran SP% **120.0**
Speed ratings (Par 103): **112,106,95,92,90 89,87,80,72**
CSF £7.61 TOTE £3.40: £1.10, £1.20, £1.40; EX 8.90 Trifecta £18.90.
Owner Jaber Abdullah **Bred** Lynch Bages Ltd & Longfield Stud **Trained** Upper Lambourn, Berks
■ Desai was withdrawn. Price at time of withdrawal 66-1. Rule 4 does not apply.

FOCUS
A fair maiden run at a decent pace and dominated by the market leaders.

1551 BETWAY OFFICIAL GRAND NATIONAL BETTING PARTNER H'CAP 4f 214y(F)
3:00 (3:00) (Class 5) (0-75,77) 4-Y-0+
£3,752 (£1,116; £557; £300; £300; £300) **Stalls** Centre

Form RPR

1363 **1** **Mininggold**[21] 1194 6-8-9 68........(p) PaulaMuir[(5)] 1 79
(Michael Dods) *w ldr tl led over 3f out: hdd 1/2-way: rallied to ld ins fnl f: r.o* **5/1**

1212 **2** 2 3/4 **Warrior's Valley**[6] 1394 4-9-7 75........(tp) LewisEdmunds 5 76
(David C Griffiths) *chsd ldrs: led 1/2-way: shkn up over 1f out: hdd and no ex ins fnl f* **6/4**[1]

6-00 **3** nk **Dapper Man (IRE)**[21] 1194 5-8-13 72........ BenSanderson[(5)] 3 72
(Roger Fell) *chsd ldrs: outpcd 1/2-way: rallied over 1f out: styd on* **12/1**

3535 **4** 2 3/4 **Jack The Truth (IRE)**[28] 1061 5-9-3 71........(p) LukeMorris 4 61
(George Scott) *hld up in tch: rdn over 1f out: wknd ins fnl f* **4/1**[3]

-342 **5** 1 1/2 **Eternal Sun**[21] 1194 4-9-6 77........ GabrieleMalune[(3)] 6 62
(Ivan Furtado) *s.i.s: hld up: rdn over 1f out: nt trble ldrs (jockey said filly was never travelling)* **10/3**[2]

5105 **6** 1/2 **Point Zero (IRE)**[8] 1366 4-9-6 74........(be) AlistairRawlinson 2 57
(Michael Appleby) *led: hdd over 3f out: rdn over 1f out: wknd fnl f* **14/1**

1m 1.52s (1.82) **Going Correction** -0.05s/f (Stan) **6** Ran SP% **114.1**
Speed ratings (Par 103): **83,78,78,73,71 70**
CSF £13.34 TOTE £5.60: £2.50, £1.10; EX 14.20 Trifecta £80.10.
Owner Mrs C E Dods **Bred** Mrs G S Rees **Trained** Denton, Co Durham

FOCUS
The pace was strong for this fair handicap.

1552 BETWAY H'CAP 6f 16y(F)
3:35 (3:35) (Class 4) (0-85,85) 4-Y-0+ **£5,530** (£1,645; £822; £411; £300) **Stalls** Low

Form RPR

2141 **1** **Crosse Fire**[5] 1426 7-8-10 74 4ex........(p) KieranO'Neill 4 81
(Scott Dixon) *led: rdn over 2f out: hdd over 1f out: rallied to ld ins fnl f: styd on* **15/8**[1]

-514 **2** shd **Saaheq**[33] 981 5-9-7 85........ AlistairRawlinson 5 92
(Michael Appleby) *a.p: chsd wnr over 4f out: rdn to ld over 1f out: hdd ins fnl f: styd on* **3/1**[3]

6113 **3** 4 **Marble Bar**[1] 1522 4-8-4 71 5ex........(h) JamieGormley[(3)] 2 65
(Iain Jardine) *s.i.s: swtchd rt sn after s: hdwy on outer over 3f out: rdn over 2f out: no ex fnl f* **5/2**[2]

310- **4** 1/2 **Mujassam**[135] 9162 7-9-0 78........(b) DanielTudhope 3 71
(David O'Meara) *hld up in tch: rdn over 2f out: no ex fr over 1f out* **8/1**

1133 **5** nk **Gentlemen**[23] 1160 8-9-1 79........(h) NicolaCurrie 1 71
(Phil McEntee) *chsd wnr tl over 4f: rdn over 2f out: sn outpcd* **6/1**

1m 14.82s (-1.68) **Going Correction** -0.05s/f (Stan) **5** Ran SP% **113.8**
Speed ratings (Par 105): **109,108,103,102,102**
CSF £8.14 TOTE £3.20: £2.80, £1.90; EX 8.30 Trifecta £18.80.
Owner Paul J Dixon & Darren Lucas **Bred** Dr A Gillespie **Trained** Babworth, Notts

FOCUS
A competitive handicap despite the small field.

1553 PLAY 4 TO SCORE AT BETWAY H'CAP 6f 16y(F)
4:15 (4:15) (Class 6) (0-55,58) 4-Y-0+
£3,105 (£924; £461; £300; £300; £300) **Stalls** Low

Form RPR

6-21 **1** **Jazz Legend (USA)**[28] 1071 6-9-5 53........ LiamKeniry 10 59
(Mandy Rowland) *led 5f out: rdn over 1f out: hung lft ins fnl f: jst hld on* **13/2**[3]

0-41 **2** nk **Socialites Red**[8] 1368 6-9-5 58 5ex........(p) TheodoreLadd[(5)] 5 63
(Scott Dixon) *led 1f: remained handy: rdn to chse wnr ins fnl f: r.o* **9/2**[2]

550- **3** 1/2 **Space War**[112] 9523 12-8-5 46........(t) JoshQuinn[(7)] 7 50
(Michael Easterby) *hld up: c stands' side over 2f out: r.o wl ins fnl f: nt rch ldrs* **8/1**

0 **4** 1 1/4 **Kris Black (IRE)**[6] 1405 6-8-13 47........(t) BenCurtis 12 47
(Kieran P Cotter, Ire) *prom: chsd wnr 1/2-way: rdn over 1f out: styd on same pce wl ins fnl f* **14/1**

0/30 **5** 3/4 **Intense Starlet (IRE)**[34] 973 8-8-9 46 oh1........(p) BenRobinson[(3)] 1 44
(Brian Ellison) *chsd ldrs: rdn over 2f out: no ex wl ins fnl f* **16/1**

0410 **6** 2 **Black Truffle (FR)**[50] 701 9-8-6 47........(p) EllieMacKenzie[(7)] 2 39
(Mark Usher) *broke wl enough: sn pushed along and lost pl: n.m.r wl over 4f out: styd on ins fnl f: nt trble ldrs* **20/1**

U-50 **7** nk **Falcao (IRE)**[13] 1265 7-9-7 55........(e[1]) KieranO'Neill 4 46
(John Butler) *s.i.s: sn prom: outpcd over 3f out: styd on u.p fr over 1f out* **5/2**[1]

6655 **8** 1/2 **Major Crispies**[23] 1158 8-9-6 54........ ShaneKelly 11 43
(Ronald Thompson) *s.i.s: sn drvn along: hdwy to go prom over 4f out: rdn and hung lft fr over 1f out: wknd ins fnl f (jockey said gelding hung left-handed)* **12/1**

0200 **9** 1 1/4 **Holy Tiber (IRE)**[22] 1179 4-9-9 57........(t) JoeyHaynes 6 42
(Paul Howling) *in rr: rdn over 4f out: n.d* **20/1**

0302 **10** hd **Dream Ally (IRE)**[8] 1368 9-8-12 46........ PhilDennis 9 31
(John Weymes) *prom: pushed along over 4f out: rdn: hung lft and wknd over 1f out (jockey said gelding was never travelling and hung left-handed up the home straight)* **13/2**[3]

510- **11** 1 3/4 **Ace Master**[139] 9099 11-9-1 52........(b) TimClark[(3)] 8 32
(Roy Bowring) *s.i.s and n.m.r s: bhd and swtchd wd sn after: c towards stands' side over 2f out: nvr on terms (jockey said gelding was slowly away)* **16/1**

0406 **12** 28 **Diamond Pursuit**[21] 1192 4-8-9 46........(t[1]) GabrieleMalune[(3)] 3
(Ivan Furtado) *in rr whn edgd lft wl over 4f out: bhd fr 1/2-way: eased over 1f out: b.b.v (jockey said filly bled from the nose)* **11/1**

1m 17.07s (0.57) **Going Correction** -0.05s/f (Stan) **12** Ran SP% **128.5**
Speed ratings (Par 101): **94,93,92,91,90 87,87,86,84,84 82,44**
CSF £39.08 CT £249.60 TOTE £6.00: £1.90, £1.80, £3.20; EX 30.00 Trifecta £618.90.
Owner Miss M E Rowland **Bred** Two Hearts Farm LLC & Four Legacy LLC **Trained** Lower Blidworth, Notts

FOCUS
A modest handicap.

1554 BETWAY LIVE CASINO H'CAP 4f 214y(F)
4:50 (4:50) (Class 7) (0-50,52) 3-Y-0+ **£1,940** (£577; £288; £144) **Stalls** Centre

Form RPR

5450 **1** **Gunnabedun (IRE)**[23] 1167 3-8-8 49........(b[1]) JamieGormley[(3)] 2 55
(Iain Jardine) *chsd ldrs: wnt 2nd over 3f out: led over 1f out: rdn out* **7/2**[2]

0/ **2** 1 3/4 **Tookiedoo (IRE)**[151] 8856 5-9-4 45........(t) BenCurtis 11 50+
(Kieran P Cotter, Ire) *prom: rdn and outpcd over 3f out: rallied and hung lft fr over 1f out: r.o to go 2nd wl ins fnl f: nt rch wnr* **14/1**

000- **3** 1 1/2 **Poppy Jag (IRE)**[148] 8935 4-9-7 48........ JackMitchell 3 47
(Kevin Frost) *chsd ldrs: rdn over 3f out: sn outpcd: hdwy over 1f out: styd on* **6/1**

00-0 **4** hd **Rock In Society (IRE)**[7] 1383 4-9-1 45........ TimClark[(3)] 4 44
(John Butler) *sn led: rdn and hdd over 1f out: no ex ins fnl f* **5/1**[3]

000- **5** 1/2 **Robbian**[114] 9493 8-8-13 45........ BenSanderson[(5)] 1 42
(Charles Smith) *chsd ldrs: sn pushed along: outpcd 3f: styd on fnl f* **33/1**

2060 **6** 1 1/4 **Admiral Rooke (IRE)**[10] 1339 4-9-10 51........(b) AlistairRawlinson 7 43
(Michael Appleby) *chsd ldrs: rdn over 1f out: styd on same pce* **3/1**[1]

-500 **7** 2 1/4 **Coiste Bodhar (IRE)**[42] 830 8-9-1 45........ JaneElliott[(3)] 6 29
(Scott Dixon) *led early: chsd ldrs: rdn and outpcd 1/2-way: n.d after* **17/2**

00-0 **8** 1 1/4 **Jean Excels**[6] 1402 4-9-4 45........(p[1]) LiamKeniry 10 25
(Roy Bowring) *stdd s: hld up: hdwy 1/2-way: rdn and edgd lft over 1f out: wknd fnl f* **25/1**

305- **9** shd **Groundworker (IRE)**[186] 7811 8-9-11 52........(t) PaulMulrennan 5 31
(Paul Midgley) *chsd ldrs: shkn up over 1f out: wknd fnl f* **8/1**

0-00 **10** 1/2 **Men United (FR)**[6] 1402 6-8-11 45........(v) AledBeech[(7)] 8 23
(Roy Bowring) *prom: rdn and lost pl 1/2-way: wknd over 1f out* **16/1**

000 **11** 3/4 **Doti**[19] 1236 3-8-7 45........(b[1]) NicolaCurrie 9 15
(Rod Millman) *sn outpcd* **20/1**

1m 1.54s (1.84) **Going Correction** -0.05s/f (Stan)
WFA 3 from 4yo+ 11lb **11** Ran SP% **123.9**
Speed ratings (Par 97): **83,80,77,77,76 74,71,69,68,68 66**
CSF £53.51 CT £302.70 TOTE £3.90: £1.60, £3.60, £2.70; EX 66.20 Trifecta £439.30.
Owner Davidson & Jardine **Bred** Rathasker Stud **Trained** Carruthерstown, D'fries & G'way

FOCUS
A weak contest.

1555 LADBROKES H'CAP 1m 4f 14y(F)
5:30 (5:30) (Class 6) (0-65,64) 3-Y-0
£3,105 (£924; £461; £300; £300; £300) **Stalls** Low

Form RPR

46-0 **1** **Smarter (IRE)**[23] 1166 3-9-7 64........ DanielTudhope 7 82+
(William Haggas) *hld up in tch on outer: led on bot over 3f out: shkn up and wnt readily clr fr over 1f out: easily* **5/2**[1]

4402 **2** 9 **Bonneville (IRE)**[10] 1332 3-8-3 51........(b) TheodoreLadd[(5)] 8 54
(Rod Millman) *hld up in tch on outer: lost pl over 9f out: hdwy over 7f out: chal over 3f out: rdn and outpcd fr over 1f out* **5/2**[1]

00-1 **3** 6 **Glutnforpunishment**[29] 1039 3-9-4 61........ EoinWalsh 6 54
(Nick Littmoden) *chsd ldrs: rdn over 4f out: sn outpcd: hdwy to go 3rd 2f out: no further prog* **14/1**

660- **4** 3 3/4 **Victoriano (IRE)**[155] 8732 3-9-1 63........(p[1]) ThomasGreatrex[(5)] 4 50
(Archie Watson) *s.i.s: sn pushed along to go prom: rdn over 6f out: outpcd over 4f out: n.d after (jockey said gelding was never travelling)* **5/1**[3]

0-60 **5** 3 3/4 **Munstead Moonshine**[49] 723 3-8-5 51........ WilliamCox[(3)] 2 32
(Andrew Balding) *s.i.s: hdwy 10f out: rdn and lost pl over 6f out: n.d after (jockey said filly was never travelling)* **16/1**

-654 **6** 9 **Truckingby**[8] 1358 3-9-3 60........(b) JoeFanning 3 27
(Mark Johnston) *sn chsng ldr: ev ch over 3f out: wknd wl over 1f out* **9/2**[2]

0-10 **7** 21 **Ginge N Tonic**[13] 1270 3-8-3 51........ ThoreHammerHansen[(5)] 1
(Adam West) *led: rdn and hdd over 3f out: wknd 2f out (jockey said gelding hung right-handed)* **9/1**

-000 **8** 9 **Gate City (USA)**[62] 537 3-8-5 48........(b[1]) AndrewMullen 5
(Adrian Nicholls) *sn pushed along in rr: rdn and lost tch over 5f out* **25/1**

2m 38.04s (-2.96) **Going Correction** -0.05s/f (Stan) **8** Ran SP% **118.4**
Speed ratings (Par 96): **107,101,97,94,92 86,72,66**
CSF £8.95 CT £72.10 TOTE £3.30: £1.80, £1.30, £3.10; EX 8.30 Trifecta £68.90.
Owner Sheikh Ahmed Al Maktoum **Bred** Roundhill Stud & C & M Murphy **Trained** Newmarket, Suffolk

FOCUS
Plenty of unexposed types in this fair handicap, and the winner was a complete revelation up in trip.

T/Plt: £36.00 to a £1 stake. Pool: £58,980.67. 1,193.77 winning units. T/Qpdt: £12.30 to a £1 stake. Pool: £4,884.06. 293.33 winning units. **Colin Roberts**

LEICESTER (R-H)

Friday, April 5

OFFICIAL GOING: Good (good to firm in places; 7.4)

Wind: Fresh half-behind Weather: Overcast

1556 BRITISH STALLION STUDS EBF NOVICE STKS 5f

2:00 (2:01) (Class 5) 2-Y-O £3,752 (£1,116; £557; £278) Stalls High

Form RPR

3 **1** **Zulu Zander (IRE)**[6] 1416 2-9-5 0 AdamKirby 2 81
(David Evans) *mde virtually all: shkn up over 1f out: r.o wl* **10/11**[1]

2 3 ¼ **Mr Fudge** 2-9-5 0 PaulHanagan 10 69
(Richard Fahey) *sn pushed along and prom: rdn and edgd rt over 1f out: wnt 2nd ins fnl f: nt rch wnr (jockey said colt ran green)* **6/1**[3]

3 2 ¼ **Danny Ocean (IRE)** 2-9-5 0 CliffordLee 11 61+
(K R Burke) *s.i.s: outpcd: r.o to go 3rd wl ins fnl f: nt trble ldrs* **10/1**

4 1 ¾ **Queens Road (IRE)** 2-8-9 0 RyanWhile(5) 12 50
(Bill Turner) *w wnr tl shkn up 2f out: rdn and edgd rt over 1f out: wknd wl ins fnl f* **50/1**

5 nk **Foad** 2-9-5 0 PJMcDonald 3 54
(Ed Dunlop) *s.i.s: hdwy 1/2-way: hung rt wl over 1f out: rdn and wknd ins fnl f* **5/1**[2]

6 5 **Sir Gordon** 2-9-5 0 GeorgeDowning 8 36
(Mick Channon) *s.i.s: outpcd: nvr nrr* **14/1**

7 nse **Six Gun** 2-9-5 0 EdwardGreatrex 9 36
(Archie Watson) *chsd ldrs: pushed along 1/2-way: hmpd over 1f out: wknd fnl f* **10/1**

8 nk **Es Que Pearl (IRE)** 2-9-0 0 RobHornby 1 30
(Rod Millman) *edgd rt s: chsd ldrs: pushed along over 3f out: wknd 2f out* **25/1**

9 ¾ **Never Said Nothing (IRE)** 2-9-2 0 BenRobinson(3) 5 32
(Brian Ellison) *s.i.s: outpcd* **50/1**

10 45 **Brown Eyes Blue (IRE)** 2-9-0 0 ShaneKelly 4
(J S Moore) *s.s: outpcd* **66/1**

1m 1.1s (-0.70) **Going Correction** 0.0s/f (Good) **10 Ran SP% 117.4**
Speed ratings (Par 92): **105,99,96,93,92 84,84,84,83,11**
CSF £6.63 TOTE £1.60: £1.10, £1.90, £2.30; EX 8.80 Trifecta £38.30.
Owner J A Wilcox **Bred** Oliver Donlon **Trained** Pandy, Monmouths

FOCUS
Race distances on the round course increased by 15yds. They were strung out from an early stage and plenty of these needed this first day at school. Zulu Zander had the benefit of a run under his belt and, despite a wide draw, made it count - although the form doesn't look up to much at this stage.

1557 BURTON OVERY (S) STKS 6f

2:30 (2:32) (Class 5) 3-Y-O

£3,752 (£1,116; £557; £300; £300; £300) Stalls High

Form RPR

225 **1** **Plumette**[24] 1168 3-8-9 68 PJMcDonald 9 66+
(Richard Fahey) *n.m.r sn after s: in rr: hdwy over 1f out: rdn and r.o to ld nr fin* **5/2**[2]

4535 **2** ½ **Beleaguerment (IRE)**[21] 1219 3-8-11 75 (b) Pierre-LouisJamin(7) 4 74
(Archie Watson) *chsd ldrs: led over 3f out: shkn up over 1f out: hdd nr fin* **9/4**[1]

232- **3** 2 ¼ **Mr Buttons (IRE)**[294] 3827 3-8-13 77 SeanDavis(5) 2 67
(Richard Fahey) *hld up in tch: shkn up over 3f out: chsd ldr 2f out: rdn: hung lft and ev ch over 1f out: styd on same pce ins fnl f* **5/2**[2]

-004 **4** 2 **Peters Pudding (IRE)**[70] 401 3-8-7 58 (b) GinaMangan(7) 1 57
(David Evans) *prom: chsd ldr over 3f out tl shkn up 2f out: no ex ins fnl f* **16/1**

-626 **5** nk **Dandy Lad (IRE)**[13] 1296 3-9-0 62 (b[1]) ShaneKelly 8 56
(Richard Hughes) *edgd lft s: hld up: plld hrd: hdwy over 3f out: nt clr run and lost pl over 2f out: r.o u.p ins fnl f* **20/1**

65-0 **6** ½ **Tarrzan (IRE)**[13] 1296 3-8-13 54 TheodoreLadd(5) 11 58
(John Gallagher) *led early: chsd ldrs: rdn over 1f out: styd on same pce fnl f* **66/1**

-500 **7** 1 ½ **Islay Mist**[11] 1340 3-8-10 56 (p) GabrieleMalune(3) 7 49
(Amy Murphy) *hld up: hdwy over 1f out: sn rdn: wknd wl ins fnl f* **40/1**

300- **8** ½ **Tigerinmytank**[171] 8307 3-8-9 55 BarryMcHugh 12 43
(John Holt) *chsd ldrs: rdn over 2f out: wknd over 1f out* **80/1**

00-5 **9** 1 ¼ **Coastguard Watch (FR)**[8] 1385 3-8-11 58 (p) FinleyMarsh(3) 14 45
(Richard Hughes) *hld up: rdn over 1f out: nvr trbld ldrs* **14/1**[3]

-004 **10** 2 **Lysander Belle (IRE)**[24] 1167 3-8-9 52 DavidProbert 5 34
(Sophie Leech) *s.i.s: hld up: hdwy over 1f out: sn rdn: wknd ins fnl f* **20/1**

06- **11** 2 **Little Anxious**[170] 8314 3-8-9 0 JohnFahy 13 28
(Grace Harris) *s.i.s: outpcd* **100/1**

320- **12** 30 **Solesmes**[227] 6387 3-9-3 63 EoinWalsh 3
(Tony Newcombe) *unruly in stalls: sn led: rdn and hdd over 3f out: wknd over 2f out* **33/1**

1m 12.87s (0.77) **Going Correction** 0.0s/f (Good) **12 Ran SP% 119.1**
Speed ratings (Par 98): **94,93,90,87,87 86,84,83,82,79 76,36**
CSF £8.04 TOTE £3.50: £1.70, £1.30, £1.10; EX 8.90 Trifecta £26.40.The winner was sold for £10,000.
Owner Titanium Racing Club **Bred** Whitsbury Manor Stud **Trained** Musley Bank, N Yorks
■ Chains Of Love was withdrawn. Price at time of withdrawal 11-2. Rule 4 applies to board prices prior to withdrawal, but not to SP bets - deduction 15p in the pound. New market formed.

FOCUS
Three horses dominated the betting in this seller and it was the same three that dominated the finish.

1558 KIBWORTH NOVICE STKS (PLUS 10 RACE) 1m 3f 179y

3:05 (3:05) (Class 3) 3-Y-O £9,703 (£2,887; £1,443; £721) Stalls Low

Form RPR

3- **1** **Technician (IRE)**[149] 8931 3-9-2 OisinMurphy 2 90
(Martyn Meade) *prom: led over 10f out: shkn up and qcknd over 2f out: styd on wl* **11/8**[1]

1-1 **2** 3 ¼ **Themaxwecan (IRE)**[85] 156 3-9-12 89 PJMcDonald 5 95
(Mark Johnston) *sn led: hdd over 10f out: chsd wnr: rdn over 2f out: styd on same pce ins fnl f* **9/4**[2]

622- **3** 8 **Fox Fearless**[183] 7942 3-9-2 80 BenCurtis 3 72
(K R Burke) *led early: chsd ldrs: rdn over 2f out: wknd fnl f* **8/1**

4 ¾ **Arthur Pendragon (IRE)** 3-9-2 0 CallumShepherd 8 71
(Brian Meehan) *hld up: hdwy 2f out: sn hung rt: wknd fnl f (jockey said colt hung right-handed in the final two furlongs)* **40/1**

1- **5** 3 ¼ **Landa Beach (IRE)**[161] 8608 3-9-8 0 DavidProbert 6 72
(Andrew Balding) *s.i.s: hdwy over 10f out: rdn whn hmpd wl over 1f out: sn wknd* **3/1**[3]

6 nk **Tidal Point (IRE)** 3-8-9 0 TobyEley(7) 7 65
(Steph Hollinshead) *s.i.s: hld up: shkn up over 2f out: n.m.r and wknd wl over 1f out* **150/1**

2m 34.47s (-0.53) **Going Correction** 0.0s/f (Good) **6 Ran SP% 112.1**
Speed ratings (Par 102): **101,98,93,93,90 90**
CSF £4.74 TOTE £2.30: £1.50, £1.90; EX 4.80 Trifecta £12.30.
Owner David Caddy **Bred** Barronstown Stud **Trained** Manton, Wilts

FOCUS
Add 15yds. A decent contest but one dominated by the winner who had all of his rivals in trouble halfway up the straight before seeing his race out strongly. He looks extremely useful at this stage.

1559 EVERARDS OF LEICESTERSHIRE H'CAP 1m 3f 179y

3:40 (3:42) (Class 3) (0-90,91) 4-Y-O+ £7,762 (£2,310; £1,154; £577) Stalls Low

Form RPR

4646 **1** **Eddystone Rock (IRE)**[21] 1220 7-9-2 85 AdamKirby 1 94
(John Best) *sn pushed along to chse ldrs: rdn and swtchd lft 2f out: r.o u.p to ld towards fin* **8/1**

603- **2** ½ **Mandalayan (IRE)**[178] 8081 4-9-1 84 RobHornby 12 92
(Jonathan Portman) *racd wd 4f: chsd ldr: rdn to ld over 1f out: hdd towards fin* **8/1**

110- **3** ½ **Rare Groove (IRE)**[175] 8164 4-9-4 87 PJMcDonald 9 94
(Jedd O'Keeffe) *prom: racd keenly: lost pl over 5f out: hdwy over 3f out: rdn to chse ldr over 1f out: sn ev ch: styd on* **6/1**[3]

1/1- **4** 5 **Showroom (FR)**[287] 4080 4-9-7 90 JoeFanning 3 89
(Mark Johnston) *sn led: shkn up and hdd over 1f out: wknd wl ins fnl f* **7/2**[2]

0-31 **5** 2 ¼ **Desert Ruler**[44] 803 6-9-2 85 JackGarritty 13 80
(Jedd O'Keeffe) *s.i.s: swtchd rt sn after s: hld up: styd on fr over 1f out: nt rch ldrs* **10/1**

520- **6** nk **Dagueneau (IRE)**[188] 7755 4-8-11 80 BenCurtis 7 75
(Ed Dunlop) *broke wl: sn lost pl: hdwy 1/2-way: outpcd over 2f out: n.d after* **25/1**

405- **7** 1 ½ **Inn The Bull (GER)**[275] 4522 6-8-13 82 TomMarquand 2 74
(Alan King) *stdd s: hld up: nt clr run over 2f out: n.d* **40/1**

13/- **8** hd **Michael's Mount**[356] 8076 6-8-13 82 RichardKingscote 8 74
(Ian Williams) *hld up: shkn up over 2f out: nvr on terms* **16/1**

222- **9** 1 ¼ **Petrastar**[199] 7378 4-8-13 82 JamesDoyle 5 73+
(Clive Cox) *s.i.s: sn chsng ldrs: shkn up whn hmpd and wknd over 1f out (jockey said gelding ran too freely)* **11/4**[1]

054- **10** ¾ **Amourice (IRE)**[154] 8807 4-9-4 87 (h) CharlieBennett 10 76
(Jane Chapple-Hyam) *s.i.s: hld up: hdwy on outer over 3f out: sn rdn: wknd wl over 1f out* **25/1**

50-0 **11** 18 **Reverend Jacobs**[21] 1220 5-9-7 90 DavidProbert 11 50
(Alan King) *s.i.s: hld up: rdn over 2f out: wknd and eased over 1f out* **16/1**

2m 32.84s (-2.16) **Going Correction** 0.0s/f (Good) **11 Ran SP% 116.4**
Speed ratings (Par 107): **107,106,106,103,101 101,100,100,99,98 86**
CSF £68.28 CT £414.26 TOTE £9.10: £2.30, £2.60, £1.60; EX 80.20 Trifecta £441.30.
Owner Curtis, Malt & Williams **Bred** Ballygallon Stud Limited **Trained** Oad Street, Kent
■ Stewards' Enquiry : Adam Kirby caution: careless riding

FOCUS
Add 15yds. Quite a competitive handicap on paper but fitness levels vary quite widely at this time of year and only three mattered in the final furlong.

1560 H.A.C. PIPELINE SUPPLIES H'CAP (DIV I) 7f

4:15 (4:19) (Class 4) (0-80,82) 4-Y-O+

£5,530 (£1,645; £822; £411; £300; £300) Stalls High

Form RPR

-221 **1** **Kupa River (IRE)**[32] 1016 5-8-13 71 (h) BenCurtis 6 80+
(Roger Fell) *trckd ldrs: racd keenly: led over 1f out: sn rdn: edgd rt ins fnl f: jst hld on* **3/1**[1]

145- **2** hd **Young John (IRE)**[141] 9070 6-9-5 77 RossaRyan 4 85
(Mike Murphy) *disp ld tl wnt on over 2f out: rdn and hdd over 1f out: nt clr run towards fin: styd on* **9/2**[2]

5166 **3** 2 ¾ **Custard The Dragon**[37] 929 6-9-6 78 (v) AndrewMullen 11 79
(John Mackie) *s.i.s: hld up: hdwy u.p and hung rt fr over 1f out: nt rch ldrs* **20/1**

50-0 **4** 1 ½ **Mighty Mac (IRE)**[46] 784 4-8-9 67 (p) LukeMorris 1 64
(Karen McLintock) *prom: rdn over 2f out: no ex ins fnl f* **33/1**

4536 **5** hd **Scofflaw**[27] 1099 5-9-6 78 (v) AdamKirby 5 74
(David Evans) *hld up: rdn over 1f out: nt trble ldrs* **9/2**[2]

15-2 **6** 4 ½ **The Lamplighter (FR)**[30] 1036 4-9-3 75 (t) NicolaCurrie 2 59
(George Baker) *hld up in tch: shkn up over 2f out: wknd fnl f* **9/2**[2]

5254 **7** ¾ **Human Nature (IRE)**[9] 1356 6-9-0 79 (t) MarcoGhiani(7) 7 61
(Stuart Williams) *disp ld tl over 2f out: sn rdn: wknd fnl f* **8/1**

3-11 **8** 53 **Astrospeed (IRE)**[36] 944 4-9-1 73 (h) GeorgeWood 9
(James Fanshawe) *s.i.s: hld up: shkn up and wknd over 2f out: eased (trainer's rep said gelding was unsuited by the ground (good, good to firm in places) on this occasion and would prefer a softer surface)* **6/1**[3]

1m 24.5s (-1.20) **Going Correction** 0.0s/f (Good) **8 Ran SP% 112.6**
Speed ratings (Par 105): **106,105,102,100,100 95,94,34**
CSF £16.03 CT £223.92 TOTE £3.70: £1.60, £1.50, £5.30; EX 16.20 Trifecta £197.40.
Owner Middleham Park Racing Lxxii & Partner **Bred** Airlie Stud & Mrs S Rogers **Trained** Nawton, N Yorks

FOCUS
Competitive enough for the grade, with plenty fit from the all-weather, and they appeared to go an even enough gallop. Two came clear.

1561 H.A.C. PIPELINE SUPPLIES H'CAP (DIV II) 7f

4:50 (4:53) (Class 4) (0-80,80) 4-Y-O+

£5,530 (£1,645; £822; £411; £300; £300) Stalls High

Form RPR

060- **1** **Candelisa (IRE)**[179] 8052 6-9-1 74 (t w) BenCurtis 9 83
(David Loughnane) *hld up in tch: shkn up to ld over 1f out: rdn and hdd ins fnl f: rallied to ld towards fin* **7/2**[2]

000- **2** hd **Electric Landlady (IRE)**[161] 8603 4-9-6 79 CharlesBishop 8 87
(Denis Coakley) *chsd ldrs: shkn up to ld ins fnl f: rdn and hdd towards fin* **7/1**

6506 **3** 3 ¼ **Evening Attire**[11] 1329 8-8-7 66 HollieDoyle 1 65
(William Stone) *led: rdn and hdd over 1f out: no ex ins fnl f (starter reported that the gelding was the subject of a third criteria failure; trainer was informed that the gelding could not run until the day after passing a stalls test)* **11/1**

125- **4** *shd* **Stealth Fighter (IRE)**[163] 8545 4-9-7 **80** .... JasonWatson 2 79
(Saeed bin Suroor) *chsd ldrs: rdn over 1f out: styd on same pce ins fnl f* **3/1**[1]

6305 **5** *3/4* **Compas Scoobie**[27] 1098 6-9-3 **76** .... TomMarquand 10 73
(Stuart Williams) *s.i.s: hld up: rdn over 2f out: styd on fnl f: nt pce to chal* **28/1**

6600 **6** *1/2* **Atletico (IRE)**[13] 1294 7-8-12 **71** .... EoinWalsh 11 67
(David Evans) *stmbld s: hld up: shkn up over 1f out: edgd lft and styd on ins fnl f: nt trble ldrs* **20/1**

413- **7** *nk* **Star Shield**[228] 6355 4-9-4 **77** .... DanielTudhope 7 72
(David O'Meara) *chsd ldrs: rdn and ev ch wl over 1f out: no ex ins fnl f* **6/1**[3]

314- **8** *5* **Coverham (IRE)**[179] 8046 5-8-11 **70** .... (p) LukeMorris 6 51
(James Eustace) *chsd ldrs: rdn over 2f out: wknd over 1f out* **20/1**

-420 **9** *1/2* **Kadrizzi (FR)**[24] 1164 6-9-5 **78** .... (p) AdamKirby 5 58
(Dean Ivory) *hld up: rdn over 2f out: wknd over 1f out* **10/1**

430- **10** *1/2* **Ragstone View (IRE)**[195] 7538 4-8-12 **71** .... (h[1]) DavidProbert 3 50
(Rod Millman) *s.i.s: hld up: rdn over 2f out: wknd over 1f out (jockey said gelding was never travelling)* **25/1**

06-0 **11** *3/4* **Firmdecisions (IRE)**[14] 1273 9-9-2 **78** .... RowanScott(3) 4 55
(Nigel Tinkler) *hld up: rdn over 2f out: wknd wl over 1f out (trainer could offer no explanation for the geldings performance)* **10/1**

1m 24.4s (-1.30) **Going Correction** 0.0s/f (Good) **11 Ran SP% 117.3**
Speed ratings (Par 105): **107,106,103,102,102 101,101,95,94,94 93**
CSF £26.46 CT £250.38 TOTE £4.30: £1.70, £2.10, £2.50; EX 29.00 Trifecta £195.00.
Owner Dewhurst & Swansbury **Bred** Prostock Ltd **Trained** Tern Hill, Shropshire

FOCUS
Not as competitive as the first division but it still featured one or two unexposed runners.

1562 BARKBY NOVICE STKS 7f
5:25 (5:26) (Class 5) 3-Y-O+ **£3,752** (£1,116; £557; £278) **Stalls High**

Form RPR

5 **1** **Oasis Prince**[10] 1346 3-9-0 **0** .... PJMcDonald 1 84
(Mark Johnston) *chsd ldr: shkn up over 2f out: rdn to ld ins fnl f: styd on wl* **7/4**[1]

0- **2** *1 3/4* **Dominus (IRE)**[161] 8606 3-9-0 **0** .... TomMarquand 2 79
(Brian Meehan) *led: rdn over 1f out: edgd lft and hdd ins fnl f: styd on same pce* **3/1**[2]

63- **3** *4 1/2* **Saikung (IRE)**[149] 8915 3-8-9 **0** .... JasonWatson 4 62
(Charles Hills) *trckd ldrs: plld hrd: shkn up over 2f out: no ex fnl f* **11/2**[3]

4 *2 1/4* **Noble Prospector (IRE)** 3-9-0 **0** .... PaulHanagan 12 61+
(Richard Fahey) *rrd s: bhd: hdwy over 2f out: nt trble ldrs* **12/1**

5 *1 1/4* **San Sebastian (IRE)** 3-9-0 **0** .... BenCurtis 6 58
(Ed Dunlop) *prom: rdn over 2f out: wknd over 1f out* **20/1**

0-0 **6** *2 3/4* **Take It Down Under**[8] 1381 4-10-0 **0** .... GeorgeWood 5 55
(Amy Murphy) *s.i.s: hld up: shkn up over 2f out: nt trble ldrs* **33/1**

00 **7** *1* **Sir Canford (IRE)**[30] 1034 3-9-0 **0** .... CharlesBishop 3 47
(Ali Stronge) *chsd ldrs: rdn over 2f out: wknd over 1f out* **100/1**

06 **8** *nse* **Sacred Warner (IRE)**[27] 1094 3-9-0 **0** .... HectorCrouch 13 47
(Clive Cox) *hld up: rdn over 2f out: hung rt over 1f out: n.d* **50/1**

4 **9** *1* **Jeanette May**[34] 978 3-8-9 **0** .... HollieDoyle 9 40
(William Stone) *hld up: shkn up and wknd over 2f out* **200/1**

10 *4 1/2* **Hat Yai (IRE)** 3-9-0 **0** .... JamesDoyle 7 32
(Andrew Balding) *s.s: hdwy over 4f out: rdn over 2f out: sn wknd* **11/2**[3]

11 *3 1/4* **Sandy Steve** 3-9-0 **0** .... RichardKingscote 11 24
(Stuart Williams) *sn pushed along in rr: hdwy over 4f out: wknd over 2f out* **33/1**

12 *3 3/4* **Best Haaf** 3-9-0 **0** .... AlistairRawlinson 10 14
(Michael Appleby) *hld up: wknd over 2f out* **66/1**

13 *18* **Mousquetaire (FR)** 3-8-7 **0** .... Pierre-LouisJamin(7) 8
(David Menuisier) *s.i.s: hdwy over 4f out: rdn 1/2-way: wknd over 2f out* **50/1**

1m 24.72s (-0.98) **Going Correction** 0.0s/f (Good) **13 Ran SP% 117.4**
WFA 3 from 4yo 14lb
Speed ratings (Par 103): **105,103,97,95,93 90,89,89,88,83 79,75,54**
CSF £6.26 TOTE £2.10: £1.10, £1.70, £1.50; EX 7.70 Trifecta £25.00.
Owner J David Abell **Bred** Highclere Stud And Floors Farming **Trained** Middleham Moor, N Yorks

FOCUS
Unlikely this is particularly strong novice form and nothing got into it from off the pace.

1563 SIMON DE MONTFORT H'CAP 1m 53y
5:55 (5:55) (Class 5) (0-70,70) 4-Y-O+ **£3,752** (£1,116; £557; £300; £300; £300) **Stalls Low**

Form RPR

100- **1** **Ventura Gold (IRE)**[132] 9252 4-9-1 **69** .... SeanDavis(5) 10 77
(Richard Fahey) *chsd ldrs on outer: shkn up over 2f out: rdn to ld over 1f out: styd on* **25/1**

3212 **2** *nk* **Elixsoft (IRE)**[7] 1399 4-9-2 **65** .... BenCurtis 9 72
(Roger Fell) *s.i.s: hld up: swtchd lft over 2f out: hdwy over 1f out: rdn to chse wnr and hung rt ins fnl f: styd on* **3/1**[2]

040- **3** *1 3/4* **Sir Roderic (IRE)**[169] 8350 6-9-7 **70** .... DanielMuscutt 7 73
(Rod Millman) *hld up: hdwy on outer over 1f out: sn rdn: styd on same pce towards fin* **11/1**

2332 **4** *1* **Dashing Poet**[21] 1216 5-9-2 **65** .... DavidEgan 5 66
(Heather Main) *prom: racd keenly: shkn up over 2f out: styd on same pce fnl f* **9/4**[1]

300- **5** *nk* **Oud Metha Bridge (IRE)**[121] 9397 5-9-4 **67** .... ShelleyBirkett 6 67
(Julia Feilden) *led 1f: racd keenly in 2nd: led over 2f out: rdn and hdd over 1f out: no ex ins fnl f (jockey said gelding ran too freely)* **7/1**

3-60 **6** *1 3/4* **Ghazan (IRE)**[10] 1343 4-9-2 **65** .... CliffordLee 1 61
(Kevin Frost) *trckd ldrs: rdn over 1f out: styd on same pce fnl f* **12/1**

000- **7** *2 1/4* **Art Echo**[115] 9494 6-9-7 **70** .... (tp) AndrewMullen 3 61
(John Mackie) *hld up: rdn over 1f out: nvr on terms* **25/1**

05-5 **8** *9* **Cheerfilly (IRE)**[21] 1216 5-9-7 **70** .... (b[1]) HollieDoyle 4 40
(Archie Watson) *s.i.s: rcvrd to ld after 1f: rdn and hdd over 2f out: wknd fnl f (jockey said mare stopped quickly)* **4/1**[3]

1m 46.28s (-0.02) **Going Correction** 0.0s/f (Good) **8 Ran SP% 112.0**
Speed ratings (Par 103): **100,99,97,96,96 94,92,83**
CSF £95.11 CT £716.48 TOTE £31.60: £5.80, £1.20, £2.00; EX 99.80 Trifecta £1141.50.
Owner Middleham Park Racing XLVIII & Partner **Bred** Michael Fennessy **Trained** Musley Bank, N Yorks

FOCUS
Add 15yds. A weak race featuring very few in-form horses. Two Middleham Park horses came clear in the closing stages to fight it out but it was the one returning from a layoff that came out on top.
T/Plt: £75.10 to a £1 stake. Pool: £51,987.16. - 504.81 winning units. T/Qpdt: £56.40 to a £1 stake. Pool: £3,648.88 - 47.87 winning units. **Colin Roberts**

[1506] WOLVERHAMPTON (A.W) (L-H)
Friday, April 5

OFFICIAL GOING: Tapeta: standard
Wind: Slight cross wind Weather: overcast

1565 BETWAY APPRENTICE H'CAP 6f 20y (Tp)
5:30 (5:30) (Class 6) (0-65,71) 4-Y-O+ **£3,105** (£924; £461; £400; £400; £400) **Stalls Low**

Form RPR

0661 **1** **Mystical Moon (IRE)**[8] 1383 4-8-7 **51** 5ex .... PhilDennis 2 56
(David C Griffiths) *trckd ldr: pushed along to chse ldr 2f out: drvn along 1f out: kpt on wl to ld fnl 75yds* **14/1**

3221 **2** *1/2* **Kraka (IRE)**[7] 1393 4-9-8 **71** 5ex .... (v) ScottMcCullagh(5) 8 75
(Christine Dunnett) *rdn fr stalls to ld after 1f: rdn and strly pressed by wnr over 1f out: drvn and hdd by wnr 75yds out: no ex* **1/1**[1]

4-00 **3** *3/4* **Mansfield**[39] 907 6-8-12 **59** .... DylanHogan(3) 6 62+
(Stella Barclay) *dwlt sltly and racd in rr: stl gng wl in rr whn short of room 2f out: sn rdn and mde quick prog over 1f out to go 5th: styng on wl under hands and heels whn short of room ins fnl f: fin w running lft* **8/1**[3]

061- **4** *shd* **Zebulon (IRE)**[170] 8321 5-9-7 **65** .... ConorMcGovern 7 66
(Ruth Carr) *restless in stalls: settled in midfield: niggled along whn sltly hmpd 1/2-way: drvn once in the clr over 1f out: styd on wl ins fnl f: nt rch front pair* **8/1**[3]

-400 **5** *1* **Mother Of Dragons (IRE)**[30] 1037 4-8-7 **58** .... (v) GraceMcEntee(7) 9 56
(Phil McEntee) *led briefly bef trcking new ldr after 1f: pushed along and swung wd off home bnd over 1f out: sn rdn and kpt on one pce fnl f* **50/1**

-461 **6** *1 1/4* **Bond Street Beau**[37] 919 4-8-11 **60** .... MarkCrehan(5) 5 54
(Philip McBride) *dwlt and racd in rr: rdn wl over 1f out: kpt on one pce fnl f: n.d* **7/1**[2]

620- **7** *2 3/4* **Wensley**[178] 8086 4-9-5 **63** .... (p) PaddyBradley 3 49
(Rebecca Bastiman) *racd keenly in 4th: v keen and short of room over 3f out: pushed along and little rspnse 2f out: sn rdn and plugged on one pce fnl f* **25/1**

623- **8** *1/2* **Poetic Principle (IRE)**[139] 9125 5-9-0 **65** .... AaronMackay(7) 10 49
(J S Moore) *racd keenly in midfield on the outer: pushed along and rn wd off home bnd: sn struggling* **20/1**

020- **9** *8* **Chickenfortea (IRE)**[178] 8077 5-9-0 **65** .... CierenFallon(7) 12 25
(Eric Alston) *v.s.a and detached early: mde rapid hdwy and field to take clsr order over 3f out: rdn and lost pl 2f out: wknd fnl f (jockey said gelding was slowly away)* **12/1**

022- **10** *2 1/2* **My Society (IRE)**[177] 8104 4-9-1 **59** .... (tp) WilliamCox 4 12
(David Dennis) *racd in rr of midfield on inner: pushed along over 2f out: rdn and lost pl over 1f out: wknd fnl f* **12/1**

1m 13.84s (-0.66) **Going Correction** -0.075s/f (Stan) **10 Ran SP% 117.3**
Speed ratings (Par 101): **101,100,99,99,97 96,92,91,81,77**
CSF £28.16 CT £134.56 TOTE £16.90: £3.50, £1.30, £2.80; EX 50.80 Trifecta £244.80.
Owner Wentdale Limited And Partner **Bred** M Smith **Trained** Bawtry, S Yorks

FOCUS
A decent apprentices' sprint handicap for the grade, with an unlikely pb from the winner.

1566 PLAY 4 TO SCORE AT BETWAY H'CAP 1m 1f 104y (Tp)
6:00 (6:00) (Class 5) (0-75,75) 4-Y-O+ **£3,752** (£1,116; £557; £400; £400; £400) **Stalls Low**

Form RPR

0041 **1** **Badenscoth**[24] 1169 5-9-6 **74** .... FrannyNorton 1 85+
(Dean Ivory) *settled in 4th: smooth hdwy gng wl 2f out: pushed along to ld 1f out: sn in command and pushed out* **2/1**[2]

46-0 **2** *3* **Casina Di Notte (IRE)**[9] 1355 5-9-1 **72** .... (b) AaronJones(3) 5 76
(Marco Botti) *trckd ldr: rdn along to chse ldr 2f out: sn drvn and outpcd by wnr 1f out: kpt on fnl f* **16/1**

-165 **3** *hd* **Cosmic Landscape**[6] 1418 4-9-0 **75** .... CierenFallon(7) 6 79
(William Jarvis) *led: rdn along and hdd by wnr 1f out: kpt on wl ins fnl f in battle for 2nd: no match for wnr* **6/4**[1]

60-4 **4** *2* **Dangerous Ends**[27] 1095 5-9-6 **74** .... (p) CallumShepherd 3 73
(Brett Johnson) *hld up: rdn along and unable qck 2f out: hung lft u.p over 1f out: snatched 4th ins fnl f* **10/1**

2-46 **5** *nse* **Rubensian**[24] 1169 6-8-9 **68** .... DylanHogan(5) 4 67
(David Simcock) *trckd ldng pair: pushed along and little rspnse 2f out: sn rdn and no imp over 1f out: one pce fnl f* **15/2**[3]

4505 **6** *1 1/4* **Brittanic (IRE)**[21] 1213 5-9-6 **74** .... StevieDonohoe 2 71
(David Simcock) *hld up in last: rdn and outpcd over 2f out: nvr on terms* **15/2**[3]

2m 0.51s (-0.29) **Going Correction** -0.075s/f (Stan) **6 Ran SP% 111.8**
Speed ratings (Par 103): **98,95,95,93,93 92**
CSF £30.29 TOTE £2.70: £1.10, £7.30; EX 20.30 Trifecta £86.80.
Owner Peter J Skinner **Bred** Peter J Skinner **Trained** Radlett, Herts

FOCUS
The early pace was not strong but they wound it up from a fair way out and the winner came from off the pace. The winner is rated close to his old best.

1567 LADBROKES HOME OF THE ODDS BOOST FILLIES' H'CAP 7f 36y (Tp)
6:30 (6:30) (Class 5) (0-70,72) 3-Y-O **£3,752** (£1,116; £557; £400; £400; £400) **Stalls High**

Form RPR

533- **1** **Isango**[176] 8138 3-9-8 **71** .... StevieDonohoe 2 76
(Charlie Fellowes) *mde all: pushed along to qckn tempo 2f out: rdn and 2 l clr 1f out: drvn and all out to hold on cl home* **3/1**[1]

01-0 **2** *shd* **Engrossed (IRE)**[77] 289 3-9-9 **72** .... RobHornby 9 76+
(Martyn Meade) *hld up in last: hdwy u.p arnd outside of field 2f out: sn rdn and wnt 3rd over 1f out: styd on wl fnl f: jst failed* **5/1**

3-00 **3** *1 1/4* **Molly Mai**[25] 1140 3-8-12 **61** .... JasonHart 4 62
(Philip McBride) *settled in midfield: effrt to cl u.p 2f out: sn drvn and kpt on wl fnl f: no ch w wnr* **4/1**[2]

0-06 **4** *2 1/2* **Symphony (IRE)**[63] 537 3-8-3 **52** .... LiamJones 3 46
(James Unett) *trckd wnr: rdn and outpcd by wnr 2f out: rdn and kpt on one pce fnl f (jockey said filly ran too freely)* **10/1**

333- **5** *1/2* **Arctic Spirit**[223] 6512 3-9-0 **70** .... CierenFallon(7) 8 63
(Ed Dunlop) *midfield on outer: rdn and unable qck 2f out: sn outpcd by front pair 1f out: plugged on* **9/2**[3]

100- **6** *1 3/4* **Lexington Palm (IRE)**[121] 9396 3-9-3 **66** .... SeanLevey 7 54
(Keith Dalgleish) *chsd wnr: drvn and reminders 2f out: hung lft u.p over 1f out: lost pl ins fnl f (jockey said filly hung left-handed in the home straight)* **25/1**

05-4 **7** *3* **Laxmi (IRE)**[35] 966 3-9-5 **68** .... CallumShepherd 10 69+
(Brian Meehan) *hld up in tch on inner: hdwy gng wl bhd runners 2f out: sn v short of room and hmpd: nt rcvr fnl f* **9/2**[3]

0-34 **8** *3 1/2* **Shesadabber**[39] 908 3-8-2 **51** oh4 .... PaddyMathers 6 22
(Brian Baugh) *hld up in rr: drvn and lost grnd qckly over 2f out: a in rr* **50/1**

1m 29.47s (0.67) **Going Correction** -0.075s/f (Stan) **8** Ran SP% **112.9**
Speed ratings (Par 95): **93,92,91,88,88 86,82,78**
CSF £17.80 CT £59.11 TOTE £5.00: £2.50, £2.10, £1.50; EX 16.10 Trifecta £82.60.
Owner A E Oppenheimer **Bred** Hascombe And Valiant Studs **Trained** Newmarket, Suffolk

FOCUS
A modest pace and the improved winner made all from a low draw.

1568 LADBROKES, HOME OF THE ODDS BOOST H'CAP 1m 1f 104y (Tp)
7:00 (7:00) (Class 4) (0-80,80) 3-Y-O

£5,530 (£1,645; £822; £411; £400; £400) **Stalls** Low

Form RPR

451- **1** **Noble Lineage (IRE)**[99] 9725 3-9-7 **80** .... OisinMurphy 6 90+
(James Tate) *hld up in tch in midfield: hdwy gng wl in 5th 2f out: swtchd lft and pushed along to chse ldr over 1f out: qcknd up wl to ld 100yds out: won gng away* **2/1**[2]

334- **2** *1 1/2* **Ballylemon (IRE)**[163] 8548 3-9-5 **78** .... ShaneKelly 4 83
(Richard Hughes) *trckd ldr: pushed along to ld 3f out: rdn and 2 l clr 2f out: sn pressed by wnr 1f out: kpt on but no match for wnr* **4/5**[1]

640- **3** *1 3/4* **Peckinpah (IRE)**[141] 9083 3-8-12 **71** .... DavidProbert 7 72
(Alan King) *racd in midfield: effrt to cl over 2f out: sn rdn and kpt on wl ins fnl f: no match for wnr* **16/1**[3]

644- **4** *2 3/4* **Fares Alpha (USA)**[140] 9104 3-9-1 **74** .... AndreaAtzeni 2 70
(Marco Botti) *racd in midfield: pushed along to chse ldr 2f out: sn drvn and little rspnse: wknd fnl f* **20/1**

6-15 **5** *6* **Gold Bere (FR)**[51] 698 3-9-3 **76** ....(p[1]) NicolaCurrie 5 59
(George Baker) *dwlt bdly and detached early: rdn along over 3f out and stl detached: plugged on passed btn rivals fnl f (jockey said gelding was never travelling)* **20/1**

042 **6** *1 3/4* **Copper Rose (IRE)**[29] 1064 3-9-0 **73** .... JoeFanning 1 52
(Mark Johnston) *racd in midfield on inner: pushed along 3f out: rdn and unable qck over 1f out: wknd fnl f* **40/1**

-563 **7** *1 3/4* **Fox Kasper (IRE)**[23] 1178 3-8-12 **71** ....(p) SeanLevey 3 47
(Richard Hannon) *led: rdn and hdd by rival 3f out: drvn 2f out: wknd qckly over 1f out* **28/1**

1m 58.18s (-2.62) **Going Correction** -0.075s/f (Stan) **7** Ran SP% **110.2**
Speed ratings (Par 100): **108,106,105,102,97 95,94**
CSF £3.55 CT £11.78 TOTE £2.80: £1.60, £1.10; EX 3.90 Trifecta £17.50.
Owner Saeed Manana **Bred** Rabbah Bloodstock Limited **Trained** Newmarket, Suffolk

FOCUS
A decent handicap for the grade. The pace was modest, but the form should hold up and the two market leaders filled the first two places.

1569 LADBROKES FILLIES' H'CAP 1m 4f 51y (Tp)
7:30 (7:30) (Class 5) (0-75,73) 4-Y-O+

£3,752 (£1,116; £557; £400; £400; £400) **Stalls** Low

Form RPR

-052 **1** **Vampish**[9] 1351 4-9-3 **69** .... AndreaAtzeni 2 75
(Philip McBride) *trckd ldr: effrt to chse ldr over 2f out: pushed along and 1 l down over 1f out: sn drvn and styd on wl to ld fnl 50yds: won gng away* **11/2**[3]

54- **2** *3/4* **French Riviera (FR)**[153] 4-9-6 **72** .... HarryBentley 3 77
(Ralph Beckett) *trckd ldr early: pushed along to ld 2f out: sn rdn and strly pressed by wnr 1f out: kpt on but hdd by wnr fnl 50yds* **7/2**[2]

/41- **3** *1* **Birch Grove (IRE)**[150] 8909 4-9-2 **73** .... DylanHogan[(5)] 4 76
(David Simcock) *hld up: effrt to chse wnr on outer over 2f out: sn rdn and hung lft in bhd wnr 1f out: kpt on* **6/4**[1]

134- **4** *1/2* **Sula Island**[35] 4680 5-9-5 **71** .... DavidProbert 1 72
(Alan King) *hld up in tch: rdn along and hdwy over 1f out: kpt on one pce fnl f* **12/1**

6-33 **5** *14* **Tappity Tap**[29] 1064 4-9-1 **67** ....(h) OisinMurphy 6 47
(Daniel Kubler) *led at a stdy pce: qckly hdd over 4f out and lost pl on inner: sn btn* **7/2**[2]

0-04 **6** *1* **Folies Bergeres**[10] 1341 4-8-8 **60** ....(b) LiamJones 5 38
(Grace Harris) *racd in midfield: hdwy arnd field to ld over 4f out: rdn along and hdd 2f out: wknd fnl f* **20/1**

2m 39.03s (-1.77) **Going Correction** -0.075s/f (Stan) **6** Ran SP% **112.3**
Speed ratings (Par 100): **102,101,100,100,91 90**
CSF £24.76 TOTE £4.90: £2.10, £2.60; EX 28.20 Trifecta £70.80.
Owner C M Budgett **Bred** Kirtlington Stud Ltd And C M Budgett **Trained** Newmarket, Suffolk

FOCUS
A muddling pace and it turned into something of a sprint. Very ordinary form.

1570 FOLLOW SUN RACING ON TWITTER NOVICE STKS 7f 36y (Tp)
8:00 (8:00) (Class 5) 3-4-Y-O **£3,752** (£1,116; £557; £278) **Stalls** High

Form RPR

0- **1** **Kodiac Lass (IRE)**[165] 8469 3-8-6 0 .... GabrieleMalune[(3)] 5 70
(Marco Botti) *hld up in tch: rdn along and gd prog over 1f out: drvn and r.o strly ins fnl f to ld fnl strides* **40/1**

30- **2** *nk* **Rhossili Down**[175] 8150 3-8-9 0 .... PJMcDonald 2 69
(Charles Hills) *disp str pce tl kicked on to ld 2f out: rdn and 1 l clr 1f out: all out whn hdd fnl strides* **5/4**[1]

0-6 **3** *shd* **Onebaba (IRE)**[8] 1381 3-9-0 0 .... LouisSteward 4 74
(Michael Bell) *trckd ldrs: pushed along 2f out: rdn and lugging in bhd ldr 1f out: styd on wl fnl f clsng all the way to line* **13/2**

4 *3 3/4* **Dabouk (IRE)** 3-9-0 0 .... CamHardie 1 64
(David O'Meara) *cl up in tch: pushed along over 2f out: rdn and outpcd over 1f out: one pce fnl f* **25/1**

66 **5** *3/4* **Charlie Arthur (IRE)**[48] 753 3-9-0 0 .... ShaneKelly 7 62+
(Richard Hughes) *hld up in rr: effrt to cl over 2f out: kpt on wl ins fnl f: nrst fin (jockey said colt hung left-handed)* **20/1**

1-6 **6** *1/2* **Roma Bangkok**[30] 1033 3-9-7 0 ....(t[1]) OisinMurphy 8 67
(Marco Botti) *disp ld tl rdn along 2 out: sn u.p and wknd ins fnl f* **9/4**[2]

7 *1/2* **Gonbutnotforgotten (FR)** 3-8-9 0 .... JasonHart 6 54
(Philip McBride) *dwlt and racd in rr: rdn along over 2f out: drvn and no imp over 1f out: nvr a factor* **66/1**

8 *8* **Gonzaga** 4-9-9 0 .... RachealKneller[(5)] 10 42
(James Bennett) *racd in tch on the outer: pushed along and unable qck 2f out: sn struggling and wknd over 1f out* **200/1**

9 *3 3/4* **A Hundred Echoes** 3-9-0 0 .... AndreaAtzeni 9 27
(Roger Varian) *dwlt and racd in rr: niggled along over 4f out: rdn and no imp 2f out: nvr a factor* **5/1**[3]

00 **10** *30* **Bannockburn (IRE)**[11] 1336 3-9-0 0 .... JoeFanning 3
(Keith Dalgleish) *dwlt and racd in rr: rdn and lost grnd over 4f out: sn t.o* **66/1**

1m 27.55s (-1.25) **Going Correction** -0.075s/f (Stan)
WFA 3 from 4yo 14lb **10** Ran SP% **119.7**
Speed ratings (Par 103): **104,103,103,99,98 97,97,88,83,49**
CSF £92.00 TOTE £38.90: £6.90, £1.10, £2.00; EX 149.80 Trifecta £1388.00.
Owner Heart Of The South Racing 107 & Partner **Bred** Tally-Ho Stud **Trained** Newmarket, Suffolk

FOCUS
They went hard up front and it suited the winner, who came from off the pace. The form is open to question.
T/Plt: £29.90 to a £1 stake. Pool: £65,881.03 - 1,606.75 winning units. T/Qpdt: £9.30 to a £1 stake. Pool: £7,498.92 - 591.25 winning units. **Mark Grantham**

1571 - (Foreign Racing) - See Raceform Interactive

1404
DUNDALK (A.W) (L-H)
Friday, April 5

OFFICIAL GOING: Polytrack: standard

1572a GREYHOUND RACING EVERY FRIDAY AND SATURDAY NIGHT AT DUNDALK CLAIMING RACE 1m 4f (P)
6:10 (6:10) 4-Y-O+ **£5,549** (£1,720; £819; £369; £144)

RPR

1 **Georgian Bay (IRE)**[21] 1223 9-8-4 73 ....(v) DaireDavis[(10)] 4 70+
(Thomas Coyle, Ire) *hld up in rr early: tk clsr order in 6th at 1/2-way: gng wl in 4th over 4f out: impr to ld under 2f out: rdn clr nr side 1f out and styd on wl: easily* **11/2**[3]

2 *7 1/2* **With A Start (IRE)**[30] 1051 4-10-0 72 .... SeamieHeffernan 8 73
(Denis Gerard Hogan, Ire) *prom tl sn hdd and settled bhd ldr in 2nd: clsr 2nd after 1/2-way: impr to ld under 3f out: rdn and hdd under 2f out: no imp on easy wnr ins fnl f: kpt on same pce* **9/1**

3 *1/2* **Black Label**[7] 1410 8-9-2 60 ....(v) ColinKeane 3 59
(Adrian McGuinness, Ire) *dwlt: hld up in 6 early: 5th 1/2-way: tk clsr order bhd ldrs over 4f out: rdn 2f out and no imp on easy wnr in 3rd ins fnl f where wandered sltly: kpt on same pce* **4/1**[2]

4 *15* **Swiss Cottage**[7] 1408 4-9-8 70 ....(b) RobbieColgan 6 42
(Karl Thornton, Ire) *chsd ldrs: 4th 1/2-way: pushed along in 6th over 4f out and no imp on ldrs u.p in 5th 2f out: one pce after: wnt remote 4th wl ins fnl f* **25/1**

5 *1 1/4* **Elysees Palace**[25] 1144 5-10-0 80 ....(b[1]) DeclanMcDonogh 7 45
(Sir Mark Prescott Bt) *dwlt sltly: reminder and pushed along to sn ld: over 3 l clr bef 1/2-way: reduced advantage after 1/2-way: pushed along and hdd w high hd carriage under 3f out: sn no ex and wknd: lame (jockey said his mount finished lame; vet said gelding was lame on his near fore leg)* **1/2**[1]

6 *1 1/2* **Multiviz**[242] 5509 6-9-7 44 ....(t) FrankHayes[(7)] 1 43
(S M Duffy, Ire) *towards rr thrght: last at 1/2-way: drvn and no imp in 6th over 2f out: wknd* **80/1**

7 *24* **Chateau Conti (FR)**[14] 1276 7-10-0 0 .... DonnachaO'Brien 9 4
(Joseph Patrick O'Brien, Ire) *chsd ldrs: 3rd 1/2-way: reminders bhd ldrs after 1/2-way and struggling in 5th under 5f out: wknd 3f out: eased in 7th over 2f out* **25/1**

8 *4 1/2* **Khawaatem (USA)**[7] 1408 4-9-4 0 .... RoryCleary 2
(Keith Henry Clarke, Ire) *chsd ldrs and disp 3rd early: dropped to 5th after 2f: pushed along in 7th bef 1/2-way and sn no imp u.p in rr 4f out: eased over 1f out* **66/1**

2m 34.81s (2.31) **Going Correction** +0.275s/f (Slow) **8** Ran SP% **122.5**
Speed ratings: **103,98,97,87,86 85,69,66**
CSF £52.63 TOTE £6.60: £2.70, £1.70, £1.60; DF 27.30 Trifecta £130.50.
Owner Rory Slevin **Bred** Old Carhue & Graeng Bloodstock **Trained** Batterstown, Co Meath

FOCUS
The winner had been in good form for Ado McGuinness and he carried that through on his first run for his new trainer.

1573a-1577a (Foreign Racing) - See Raceform Interactive

COMPIEGNE (L-H)
Friday, April 5

OFFICIAL GOING: Turf: very soft

1578a PRIX DE CLERMONT DE L'OISE (CLAIMER) (4YO) (TURF) 1m 2f
4:14 4-Y-O **£8,558** (£3,423; £2,567; £1,711; £855)

RPR

1 **Heroine (FR)**[147] 4-9-2 0 ....(b) MlleCoraliePacaut[(3)] 10 79
(J-C Rouget, France) **23/10**[1]

2 *1/2* **Taekwondo (FR)**[22] 4-9-5 0 .... MaximeGuyon 4 78
(Mme Pia Brandt, France) **11/2**[3]

3 *5* **Marcelle (FR)**[29] 1073 4-8-6 0 ....(p) AugustinMadamet[(5)] 11 60
(M Seror, France) **51/10**[2]

4 *1* **Aiseolas (IRE)**[29] 1073 4-8-8 0 .... StephanePasquier 9 55
(Gavin Hernon, France) **36/5**

5 *nse* **Debatable (IRE)**[149] 8936 4-8-11 0 .... MlleMickaelleMichel[(4)] 8 62
(Gay Kelleway) *sn front rnk: led: jnd and hdd after 5f: remained cl up: pushed along over 2f out: rdn along w limited rspnse over 1f out: no ex ins fnl f* **17/1**

6 *3/4* **Neige Eternelle (FR)**[22] 4-8-13 0 .... Pierre-CharlesBoudot 12 58
(H-A Pantall, France) **12/1**

7 *3 1/2* **O Fortuna (FR)**[43] 4-9-1 0 .... MickaelBarzalona 5 53
(Mme Pia Brandt, France) **13/1**

8 *4 1/2* **Magnetique (IRE)**[308] 4-8-11 0 .... AntoineHamelin 7 40
(J Parize, France) **87/10**

9 *6* **Dimanche A Bamako (FR)**[52] 4-8-10 0 .... TomLefranc[(8)] 6 35
(C Boutin, France) **150/1**

10 *2* **Laxxia (GER)**[170] 4-9-5 0 .... CristianDemuro 1 32
(M Nigge, France) **26/1**

11 *nse* **Ever Love (FR)**[10] 4-8-8 0 .... EddyHardouin 2 21
(C Boutin, France) **13/1**

12 *dist* **Magnet (FR)**[100] 4-8-8 0 .... DamienBoche[(8)] 3
(L Gadbin, France) **29/1**
2m 7.52s **12** Ran SP% **119.8**
PARI-MUTUEL (all including 1 euro stake): WIN 2.90; PLACE 1.70, 1.90, 1.80; DF 10.40.
Owner Gerard Augustin-Normand **Bred** Haras Du Logis Saint Germain **Trained** Pau, France

1579 - 1585a (Foreign Racing) - See Raceform Interactive

[1492] LINGFIELD (L-H)
Saturday, April 6

OFFICIAL GOING: Polytrack: standard
Wind: light breeze Weather: cloudy, cool

1586 LADBROKES HOME OF THE ODDS BOOST FILLIES' H'CAP 7f 1y(P)
2:00 (2:00) (Class 5) (0-70,71) 4-Y-0+
£3,752 (£1,116; £557; £300; £300; £300) **Stalls** Low

Form RPR

00-4 **1** **Met By Moonlight**[22] 1216 5-9-3 **66** .... DavidProbert 1 74
(Ron Hodges) *mde virtually all: pushed along in narrow ld 2f out: drvn in share of ld 1f out: rdn to regain ld ent fnl f: grad asserted and on top at fin* **7/1**[3]

006- **2** *3/4* **Diamond Lady**[97] 9764 8-9-1 **64** .... HollieDoyle 2 70
(William Stone) *chsd wnr: pushed along in cl 2nd 2f out: rdn and jnd issue 1f out: one pce as wnr asserted ins fnl f* **22/1**

3215 **3** *2* **Chica De La Noche**[9] 1382 5-9-2 **65** .... (p) AdamKirby 10 66+
(Simon Dow) *hld up: pushed along on outer 2f out: drvn 1 1/2f out: hdwy fnl f: rdn into 4th 1/2f out: r.o wl to take 3rd last few strides* **9/2**[2]

1141 **4** *nk* **First Link (USA)**[12] 1329 4-9-8 **71** .... NicolaCurrie 5 71
(Jean-Rene Auvray) *trckd ldrs: pushed along in 3rd 2f out: rdn over 1f out: no ex fnl f: lost 3rd last few strides (jockey said filly had no more to give)* **11/8**[1]

0300 **5** *1 1/4* **Sonnet Rose (IRE)**[9] 1382 5-8-9 **65** .... (bt) WilliamCarver[(7)] 9 61
(Conrad Allen) *mid-div: pushed into 4th 1f out: rdn and no ex fnl f* **12/1**

3-63 **6** *1* **Helfire**[22] 1216 6-8-6 **55** .... CharlieBennett 8 49
(Martin Bosley) *in rr: pushed along over 1f out: effrt and nt clr fnl f: nvr a threat (jockey said mare was denied a clear run inside the final furlong)* **10/1**

-244 **7** *1 3/4* **Sarasota (IRE)**[14] 1286 4-9-1 **64** .... (p[1]) JamesDoyle 7 53
(Jamie Osborne) *chsd ldrs: drvn in 4th 2f out: sn rdn and wknd* **7/1**[3]

040- **8** *1 1/4* **Gloweth**[166] 8488 4-9-0 **63** .... LiamKeniry 3 53+
(Stuart Kittow) *slowly away and chsd along: bhd: drvn 2f out: rdn over 1f out and no rspnse: no ch whn hmpd ins fnl f* **25/1**

0/0- **9** *3 3/4* **Conqueress (IRE)**[97] 9765 5-8-10 **59** .... JackMitchell 4 34
(Lydia Pearce) *mid-div: drvn 2f out: rdn and wknd fr 1 1/2f out* **50/1**

026- **10** *22* **More Than More (USA)**[115] 9501 4-9-7 **70** .... AndreaAtzeni 6
(James Fanshawe) *mid-div: drvn and reminder over 2f out: wknd and dropped to last 1 1/2f out: sn eased (jockey said filly stopped quickly)* **10/1**

1m 22.38s (-2.42) **Going Correction** -0.125s/f (Stan) **10** Ran SP% **121.3**
Speed ratings (Par 100): **108,107,104,104,103 101,99,98,94,69**
CSF £152.46 CT £802.67 TOTE £7.60: £1.90, £5.70, £1.90; EX 199.30 Trifecta £1901.70.
Owner P E Axon **Bred** John Frampton & Paul Frampton **Trained** Charlton Adam, Somerset
■ Stewards' Enquiry : William Carver two-day ban: interference & careless riding (Apr 20-21)

FOCUS
Just ordinary handicap form, even for this grade, but they went a decent gallop and there were no excuses for the beaten horses. The winner's best form bar her standout Bath win.

1587 LADBROKES NOVICE STKS 7f 1y(P)
2:35 (2:35) (Class 5) 3-Y-O **£3,752** (£1,116; £557; £278) **Stalls** Low

Form RPR

330- **1** **Mawsool (IRE)**[180] 8042 3-9-2 75 .... JimCrowley 5 70
(Ed Dunlop) *prom: pushed along to dispute ld 2f out: sn drvn: rdn to ld 1f out: strly pressed thrght fnl f: r.o wl: a jst holding runner-up* **6/4**[2]

41 **2** *hd* **Lestrade**[22] 1212 3-9-9 0 .... (h) JasonWatson 6 76
(William Jarvis) *hld up: drvn to chal 2f out: rdn in cl 2nd 1f out: r.o wl and persistent chal fnl f: jst hld* **8/11**[1]

20-0 **3** *1 3/4* **John Betjeman**[3] 1516 3-8-11 76 .... (p) RyanWhile[(5)] 1 64
(Bill Turner) *led: pushed along and jnd 2f out: rdn and hdd 1f out: one pce fnl f* **10/1**[3]

4 *1 3/4* **Potters Question** 3-8-13 0 .... GabrieleMalune[(3)] 2 60?
(Amy Murphy) *hld up: drvn 2f out: reminder 1 1/2f out: hung rt over 1f out: rdn fnl f: one pce* **33/1**

5 *1 3/4* **Dor's Diamond** 3-9-2 .... (h[1]) DavidProbert 4 55?
(Dean Ivory) *fractious at s: t.k.h: chsd ldrs: dropped to 4th over 2f out: sn drvn: reminder and wknd over 1f out* **33/1**

6 *10* **Glory Street** 3-8-11 0 .... SeamusCronin[(5)] 3 28
(Paddy Butler) *v reluctant to load: dwlt in stalls losing many l: bhd: latched on to pack bef 1/2-way: drvn on outer over 2f out: sn lost tch (starter reported that the colt was was reluctant to enter the stalls; trainer was informed that the colt could not run until the day after passing a stalls test)* **66/1**

1m 25.04s (0.24) **Going Correction** -0.125s/f (Stan) **6** Ran SP% **114.4**
Speed ratings (Par 98): **93,92,90,88,86 75**
CSF £2.97 TOTE £2.20: £1.30, £1.10; EX 3.00 Trifecta £4.60.
Owner Hamdan Al Maktoum **Bred** Shadwell Estate Company Limited **Trained** Newmarket, Suffolk

FOCUS
The betting had this down as a match and that's how it panned out, with just a head separating the market principals at the line. The form may not prove that solid.

1588 BETWAY LIVE CASINO H'CAP 1m 4f (P)
3:10 (3:10) (Class 4) (0-80,81) 4-Y-O+
£5,530 (£1,645; £822; £411; £300; £300) **Stalls** Low

Form RPR

0-31 **1** **Sotomayor**[14] 1292 4-8-8 **66** .... DavidEgan 6 74
(Jane Chapple-Hyam) *hld up: shkn up and hdwy on outer over 2f out: drvn and rn wd 1 1/2f out: rdn to ld 1f out: chal by runner-up ent fnl f: pushed along and qcknd clr last 150yds* **3/1**[2]

-453 **2** *1 1/2* **Emenem**[8] 1395 5-9-7 **79** .... TomMarquand 5 84
(Simon Dow) *trckd ldrs: drvn over 2f out: rdn over 1f out: hdwy to chal 1f out: cl 2nd ent fnl f: r.o but nt pce of wnr last 150yds* **13/8**[1]

153- **3** *3/4* **Saryshagann (FR)**[39] 9642 6-9-9 **81** .... AdamKirby 7 84
(David O'Meara) *t.k.h: prom: drvn to ld 2f out: rdn and hdd 1f out: one pce fnl f* **10/3**[3]

126- **4** *1/2* **Tiar Na Nog (IRE)**[136] 9175 7-9-1 **73** .... CharlesBishop 3 76
(Denis Coakley) *trckd ldrs: pushed along in 3rd 2f out: drvn and lost pl over 1f out: rdn fnl f: kpt on* **12/1**

3114 **5** *nk* **Berrahri (IRE)**[28] 1096 8-9-1 **73** .... KierenFox 2 75
(John Best) *led: drvn and hdd 2f out: sn rdn: wknd fnl f* **15/2**

0-66 **6** *1* **Noble Peace**[10] 1367 6-8-9 **67** .... (b) DavidProbert 1 68
(Lydia Pearce) *hld up: drvn in 6th 2f out: effrt on inner over 1f out: rdn and wknd fnl f (vet reported the gelding to be sore and have pus in its left-fore foot)* **14/1**

11/0 **7** *12* **Coorg (IRE)**[14] 1292 7-8-4 **67** .... DarraghKeenan[(5)] 4 48
(John Butler) *a in rr: pushed along and lost tch 3f out* **50/1**

2m 30.5s (-2.50) **Going Correction** -0.125s/f (Stan) **7** Ran SP% **114.3**
Speed ratings (Par 105): **103,102,101,101,100 100,92**
CSF £8.28 TOTE £3.90: £2.10, £1.50; EX 8.90 Trifecta £24.50.
Owner Madhi M M S Alteesi **Bred** Good Breeding **Trained** Dalham, Suffolk

FOCUS
Not a particularly competitive event with only two horses rated within 7lb of the ceiling for the grade. They went steady enough but that didn't prevent the patiently ridden horses swooping, and it was the pair that came widest into the straight that dominated the finish. The winner is rated back towards his best.

1589 BETWAY OFFICIAL GRAND NATIONAL BETTING PARTNER H'CAP 1m 2f (P)
3:45 (3:45) (Class 3) (0-90,90) 4-Y-O+ **£7,718** (£2,310; £1,155; £578; £287) **Stalls** Low

Form RPR

50-1 **1** **El Ghazwani (IRE)**[8] 1395 4-9-7 **90** .... (t) JamesDoyle 5 97
(Hugo Palmer) *chsd ldr: pushed along to dispute ld 2f out: drvn to ld over 1f out: rdn in 1 l ld ent fnl f: sn chal by runner-up: r.o wl and a holding on nr fin* **4/9**[1]

4555 **2** *nk* **Mythical Madness**[21] 1232 8-9-7 **90** .... (b) AdamKirby 4 96
(David O'Meara) *hld up: pushed along and hdwy into 3rd 2f out: drvn over 1f out: wnt 2nd ent fnl f: sn rdn to chal wnr: r.o wl but a hld* **12/1**[3]

250- **3** *1 3/4* **Sweet Charity**[199] 7426 4-8-7 **76** .... DavidEgan 3 79
(Denis Coakley) *hld up in last: pushed along and effrt on outer 1 1/2f out: rdn in 4th over 1f out: kpt on into 3rd fnl f* **6/1**[2]

4340 **4** *1* **Michele Strogoff**[21] 1232 6-9-5 **88** .... AlistairRawlinson 1 89
(Michael Appleby) *led: pushed along and qcknd pce 3f out: drvn and jnd 2f out: rdn and hdd over 1f out: wknd fnl f* **6/1**[2]

030- **5** *18* **Juneau (IRE)**[182] 7985 4-9-0 **83** .... FrannyNorton 2 48
(Mark Johnston) *chsd ldr: pushed along 3f out: lost pl over 2f out: dropped to last 1 1/2f out: kpt on: sn lost tch* **20/1**

2m 3.3s (-3.30) **Going Correction** -0.125s/f (Stan) **5** Ran SP% **110.3**
Speed ratings (Par 107): **108,107,106,105,91**
CSF £6.92 TOTE £1.30: £1.10, £2.30; EX 4.70 Trifecta £15.10.
Owner Hamad Rashed Bin Ghedayer **Bred** Longueville Bloodstock **Trained** Newmarket, Suffolk

FOCUS
A decent little contest despite the small field and it produced a good finish which ensured the short-priced favourite needed to dig deep. The winner built on his latest win.

1590 BETWAY H'CAP 5f 6y(P)
4:15 (4:15) (Class 6) (0-65,66) 4-Y-O+
£3,105 (£924; £461; £300; £300; £300) **Stalls** High

Form RPR

4323 **1** **Big Time Maybe (IRE)**[32] 1023 4-9-2 **66** .... (p) ScottMcCullagh[(7)] 3 72
(Michael Attwater) *mde all: pushed along in 1/2 l ld 2f out: rdn in 1 l ld 1f out: r.o wl fnl f* **3/1**[2]

0-05 **2** *3/4* **Come On Dave (IRE)**[59] 626 10-9-5 **62** .... (v) LiamKeniry 8 65
(John Butler) *prom: pushed along in 1/2 l 2nd 2f out: sn drvn: rdn in 1 l 2nd 1f out: kpt on fnl f but no imp on wnr* **3/1**[2]

0421 **3** *1/2* **Fareeq**[15] 1266 5-9-7 **64** .... (bt) DavidEgan 1 67
(Charlie Wallis) *chsd ldrs on inner: drvn in 3rd 2f out: rdn and n.m.r fnl f: kpt on (jockey said gelding was denied a clear run on the run to the line)* **5/2**[1]

0622 **4** *shd* **Prominna**[15] 1266 9-8-11 **54** .... (p) LukeMorris 6 55
(Tony Carroll) *hld up: drvn 2f out: wnt 4th 1f out: rdn fnl f: r.o* **7/1**[3]

2036 **5** *nse* **Pharoh Jake**[22] 1210 11-8-6 **49** .... LiamJones 4 50
(John Bridger) *chsd ldrs: drvn in 4th 2f out: dropped to 5th 1f out: rdn and kpt on fnl f* **14/1**

2-10 **6** *3/4* **At Your Service**[15] 1265 5-9-5 **62** .... JoeyHaynes 7 60
(Paul Howling) *bhd: drvn on outer 2f out: sme hdwy fnl f but nvr a threat* **10/1**

000- **7** *1 1/2* **Awsaaf**[159] 8689 4-9-0 **57** .... (h) FrannyNorton 10 50
(Michael Wigham) *hld up: drvn 2f out: no imp* **10/1**

1-3F **8** *3/4* **Mercers**[85] 179 5-9-2 **59** .... (p) JasonWatson 5 49
(Paddy Butler) *hld up: last 2f out: drvn on inner over 1f out: no imp* **16/1**

3-10 **9** *nk* **Sandfrankskipsgo**[15] 1266 10-9-2 **59** .... ShaneKelly 9 48
(Peter Crate) *slowly away: sn rcvrd to r in midfield on outer: rdn and wknd over 1f out (jockey said gelding jumped awkwardly from the stalls)* **25/1**

59.06s (0.26) **Going Correction** -0.125s/f (Stan) **9** Ran SP% **125.6**
Speed ratings (Par 101): **92,90,90,89,89 88,86,84,84**
CSF £13.82 CT £27.09 TOTE £4.50: £1.60, £1.50, £1.30; EX 16.00 Trifecta £48.70.
Owner Dare To Dream Racing **Bred** Joe Fogarty **Trained** Epsom, Surrey

FOCUS
A competitive sprint but one dominated by the pair that filled the first two places throughout.

1591 BETWAY HEED YOUR HUNCH H'CAP 1m 2f (P)
4:50 (4:50) (Class 6) (0-65,66) 4-Y-O+
£3,105 (£924; £461; £300; £300; £300) **Stalls** Low

Form RPR

2111 **1** **Jai Hanuman (IRE)**[24] 1175 5-9-8 **66** .... (t) FrannyNorton 4 74+
(Michael Wigham) *mid-div: pushed along and effrt on inner over 1f out: swtchd and hdwy ent fnl f: chal 1/2f out: drvn and r.o wl to ld last 25yds* **5/2**[2]

0-03 **2** *1/2* **Pendo**[15] 1269 8-9-6 **64** .... KierenFox 11 70
(John Best) *hld up in last: pushed along and hdwy on outer 1 1/2f out: rdn over 1f out: str run fnl f: ev ch 100yds out: kpt on into 2nd last few strides* **11/1**

5512 **3** *hd* **Subliminal**[14] 1297 4-9-7 **65** .... TomMarquand 2 71
(Simon Dow) *restless in stalls: trckd ldrs: pushed along in 4th 2f out: rdn to chal on inner over 1f out: led 1/2f out: hdd 25yds out: no ex: lost shoe (vet reported the colt had lost its right-fore shoe)* **5/4**[1]

000- **4** *1 1/4* **The Lords Walk**[162] 8613 6-8-12 **61** .... RyanWhile[(5)] 3 64
(Bill Turner) *trckd ldrs: pushed along in cl 3rd 2f out: drvn to ld 1 1/2f out: rdn in 1/2 l ld 1f out: hdd & wknd 1/2f out* **25/1**

-451 **5** *hd* **Sir Gnet (IRE)**[10] 1362 5-9-6 **64**........................(h) DanielMuscutt 7 67
(Ed Dunlop) *hld up: pushed along and effrt on outer 1 1/2f out: hdwy 1f out: rdn and r.o fnl f* **5/1**[3]

4-50 **6** *5* **Luna Magic**[10] 1363 5-8-12 **56**........................ JackMitchell 5 49
(Lydia Pearce) *hld up: nt clr run over 1f out: pushed along and kpt on fnl f (jockey said mare was denied a clear run)* **10/1**

-300 **7** *3 1/2* **Sunshineandbubbles**[42] 876 6-9-4 **62**..................(v) EdwardGreatrex 6 49
(Jennie Candlish) *mid-div: drvn in 5th 2f out: sn rdn and wknd* **40/1**

464- **8** *1 3/4* **Officer Drivel (IRE)**[326] 2739 8-8-13 **62**..................(h) SeamusCronin(5) 8 45
(Paddy Butler) *prom: disp ld 1/2-way: drvn and dropped to 1/2 l 2nd 2f out: wknd 1 1/2f out* **40/1**

6-62 **9** *1 1/2* **Chikoko Trail**[24] 1175 4-9-5 **63**..................(t) HectorCrouch 1 44
(Gary Moore) *led: jnd 1/2-way: led and drvn 2f out: hdd 1 1/2f out: wknd qckly and eased* **11/1**

2m 3.4s (-3.20) **Going Correction** -0.125s/f (Stan) **9** Ran SP% **124.2**
Speed ratings (Par 101): **107,106,106,105,105 101,98,97,95**
CSF £32.13 CT £50.39 TOTE £3.20: £1.50, £3.20, £1.10; EX 33.30 Trifecta £94.00.
Owner Ms I D Heerowa **Bred** Lynn Lodge Stud **Trained** Newmarket, Suffolk

FOCUS
Competitive enough for the grade and it produced a thrilling finish but Jai Hanuman would have been an unlucky loser had he not poked his head in front close home. He probably has more to offer.

1592 LADBROKES HOME OF THE ODDS BOOST NOVICE STKS 1m 2f (P)
5:45 (5:45) (Class 5) 3-Y-O **£3,752** (£1,116; £557; £278) **Stalls** Low

Form RPR

41- **1** **Mackaar (IRE)**[140] 9131 3-9-9 0........................ AndreaAtzeni 4 92
(Roger Varian) *prom: led after 1f: hdd after 3f: trckd ldr whn hdd: pushed along in 1/2 l 2nd 2f out: drvn to ld 1f out: drvn clr fnl f* **4/5**[1]

252- **2** *1 1/2* **Damon Runyon**[154] 8834 3-9-2 85........................(p) NickyMackay 1 82
(John Gosden) *racd in 3rd: hdwy to ld after 3f: drvn in 1/2 l ld 2f out: sn rdn: hdd 1f out: no ex fnl f* **11/10**[2]

0- **3** *3 1/2* **Starlight Red (IRE)**[128] 9315 3-8-11 0........................ LukeMorris 2 70
(Charles Hills) *led tl hdd after 1f: dropped to 3rd after 3f: drvn 2f out: rdn and one pce fnl f* **25/1**[3]

0 **4** *13* **Thora (IRE)**[14] 1287 3-8-11 0........................ TomMarquand 3 44
(Simon Dow) *a in rr: drvn over 2f out: sn lost tch: bit slipped through filly's mouth (jockey said the bit slipped through the mouth of the filly)* **50/1**

2m 5.99s (-0.61) **Going Correction** -0.125s/f (Stan) **4** Ran SP% **109.0**
Speed ratings (Par 98): **97,95,93,82**
CSF £1.97 TOTE £1.50; EX 1.80 Trifecta £2.70.
Owner Sheikh Ahmed Al Maktoum **Bred** Mrs H Varian **Trained** Newmarket, Suffolk

FOCUS
Effectively a match and although Mackaar had something to find on form, he was strong in the market and looks a horse who could prove Group-class this year. He showed improved form giving weight to the runner-up.
T/Plt: £9.10 to a £1 stake. Pool: £52,709.04 - 4,190.08 winning units T/Qpdt: £2.00 to a £1 stake. Pool: £4,358.10 - 1,548.78 winning units **Keith McHugh**

1565 WOLVERHAMPTON (A.W) (L-H)
Saturday, April 6

OFFICIAL GOING: Tapeta: standard
Wind: Light against Weather: Overcast

1593 LADBROKES HOME OF THE ODDS BOOST H'CAP 1m 1f 104y (Tp)
6:00 (6:00) (Class 6) (0-60,62) 3-Y-O
£3,105 (£924; £461; £400; £400; £400) **Stalls** Low

Form RPR

0566 **1** **Percy Alexander**[24] 1174 3-9-1 **54**........................(b[1]) PJMcDonald 2 62
(James Tate) *s.i.s: hld up: hdwy to ld over 1f out: drvn out* **7/1**

0-41 **2** *nk* **Mr Fox**[30] 1066 3-9-6 **59**........................ CallumShepherd 10 66
(Michael Attwater) *hld up: shkn up and hdwy over 1f out: rdn and ev ch ins fnl f: r.o* **6/1**

0-03 **3** *3 1/4* **Crazy Spin**[38] 931 3-8-8 **47**........................(p) KieranO'Neill 9 48
(Ivan Furtado) *chsd ldr: rdn over 3f out: ev ch over 1f out: styd on same pce ins fnl f* **16/1**

40-0 **4** *nse* **Another Approach (FR)**[24] 1174 3-9-6 **59**........................ NicolaCurrie 7 60
(George Baker) *s.i.s and hmpd s: hld up: rdn and r.o ins fnl f: nt rch ldrs (jockey said filly was denied a clear run just inside the 2 furlong marker)* **12/1**

000- **5** *nk* **Mukha Magic**[150] 8930 3-9-0 **60**........................(p[1]) SeanKirrane(7) 6 60
(Gay Kelleway) *s.i.s and hmpd s: hld up: hdwy on outer over 2f out: rdn over 1f out: sn edgd lft: nt clr run wl ins fnl f: styd on* **5/1**[2]

3353 **6** *1/2* **Al Daayen (FR)**[12] 1332 3-9-1 **54**........................ JoeFanning 4 53
(Mark Johnston) *chsd ldrs: rdn and ev ch over 1f out: edgd lft and no ex ins fnl f* **6/1**

206- **7** *1 3/4* **Highway Robbery**[173] 8277 3-8-7 **46** oh1........................ ShelleyBirkett 8 43
(Julia Feilden) *prom: pushed along over 3f out: nt clr run over 1f out: no ex ins fnl f* **33/1**

-213 **8** *hd* **Precision Prince (IRE)**[45] 802 3-9-9 **62**........................ EoinWalsh 3 60
(Mark Loughnane) *broke wl: sn stdd and lost pl: hld up: nt clr run over 2f out: rdn over 1f out: no ex ins fnl f (jockey said colt was denied a clear run 2 1/2 furlongs out)* **3/1**[1]

006- **9** *hd* **Florence Rose**[200] 7375 3-9-3 **56**........................ RobHornby 1 51
(Jonathan Portman) *prom: rdn and ev ch over 1f out: wknd ins fnl f* **20/1**

-000 **10** *2* **With Pride**[37] 940 3-8-7 **46** oh1........................(h[1]) HollieDoyle 5 37
(Neil Mulholland) *wnt rt s: sn led: hung rt wl over 1f out: rdn and hdd jst over 1f out: wknd ins fnl f (jockey said colt hung badly right-handed off the bend turning into the home straight)* **33/1**

400 **11** *nk* **Tsarmina (IRE)**[14] 1293 3-9-3 **56**........................ OisinMurphy 12 48
(David Evans) *hld up in tch: shkn up and nt clr run over 1f out: edgd lft and wknd ins fnl f* **33/1**

0-53 **12** *1* **Tails I Win (CAN)**[77] 319 3-9-6 **59**........................(h) BenCurtis 11 48
(Roger Fell) *s.i.s: hld up: rdn over 2f out: sn wknd (jockey said the saddle slipped)* **11/2**[3]

2m 1.25s (0.45) **Going Correction** -0.05s/f (Stan) **12** Ran SP% **125.3**
Speed ratings (Par 96): **96,95,92,92,92 92,90,90,90,88 88,87**
CSF £49.69 CT £659.24 TOTE £7.40: £2.20, £3.20, £4.80; EX 62.50 Trifecta £376.40.
Owner Saeed Manana **Bred** Rosyground Stud **Trained** Newmarket, Suffolk

FOCUS
A low-grade handicap that didn't appear to be run at a furious gallop, but those patiently ridden did best. The first two came clear.

1594 LADBROKES HOME OF THE ODDS BOOST NOVICE STKS 1m 142y (Tp)
6:30 (6:30) (Class 5) 3-Y-O **£3,752** (£1,116; £557; £278) **Stalls** Low

Form RPR

5- **1** **Flighty Almighty**[253] 5414 3-8-11 0........................ RichardKingscote 2 80+
(Tom Dascombe) *trckd ldrs: shkn up to ld and edgd rt 1f out: pushed out* **5/1**[2]

1 **2** *1 1/4* **Ebury**[31] 1034 3-9-9 0........................ OisinMurphy 4 89
(Martyn Meade) *s.i.s: racd keenly: hdwy to go 2nd over 7f out: led over 2f out: rdn and hung rt over 1f out: hdd 1f out: styd on same pce wl ins fnl f* **1/4**[1]

04- **3** *3 1/4* **Innocent (IRE)**[203] 7298 3-8-11 0........................ HarryBentley 5 70
(Ralph Beckett) *chsd ldrs: shkn up over 2f out: nt clr run over 1f out: no ex ins fnl f* **7/1**[3]

005- **4** *4* **El Picador (IRE)**[187] 7846 3-9-2 0........................ LouisSteward 1 66
(Sir Michael Stoute) *hld up: shkn up and edgd rt over 1f out: wknd ins fnl f* **18/1**

04- **5** *21* **Night Closure**[282] 4288 3-9-2 0........................ SeanLevey 3 20
(John Butler) *led: shkn up and hdd over 2f out: wknd over 1f out* **100/1**

1m 48.57s (-1.53) **Going Correction** -0.05s/f (Stan) **5** Ran SP% **115.4**
Speed ratings (Par 98): **104,102,100,96,77**
CSF £7.16 TOTE £6.10: £1.90, £1.10; EX 10.30 Trifecta £19.90.
Owner Chasemore Farm **Bred** Chasemore Farm **Trained** Malpas, Cheshire

FOCUS
A small novice in which the two fancied runners dominated, though the odds-on favourite didn't get things his own way. The winner built on his debut run and the short-priced second probably improved in defeat.

1595 BETWAY CASINO (S) H'CAP 6f 20y (Tp)
7:00 (7:00) (Class 6) (0-60,60) 4-Y-O+
£3,105 (£924; £461; £400; £400; £400) **Stalls** Low

Form RPR

30 **1** **Brockey Rise (IRE)**[32] 1021 4-9-3 **56**........................(b) OisinMurphy 8 63
(David Evans) *chsd ldrs: lost pl over 4f out: hdwy over 1f out: shkn up to ld wl ins fnl f: r.o* **5/1**[1]

0606 **2** *1 1/2* **Admiral Rooke (IRE)**[2] 1554 4-8-4 **48**........................(b) TheodoreLadd(5) 7 51
(Michael Appleby) *led: clr 1/2-way: rdn over 1f out: hung rt: hdd and no ex wl ins fnl f (jockey said gelding hung right-handed throughout)* **5/1**[1]

6300 **3** *hd* **Haader (FR)**[8] 1403 4-9-4 **57**........................(t) PaddyMathers 1 59
(Derek Shaw) *s.i.s: hld up: nt clr run over 2f out: hdwy over 1f out: rdn and r.o to go 3rd post: nt rch ldrs* **16/1**

5500 **4** *nse* **Billyoakes (IRE)**[12] 1328 7-9-1 **54**........................(p) RichardKingscote 9 56
(Charlie Wallis) *chsd ldrs: rdn over 2f out: styd on same pce wl ins fnl f* **5/1**[1]

050- **5** *1 1/4* **Mad Endeavour**[206] 7175 8-9-0 **53**........................(b) BenCurtis 3 51
(Stuart Kittow) *chsd ldrs: rdn over 1f out: styng on same pce whn edgd lft wl ins fnl f* **10/1**

-405 **6** *1/2* **Soldier Blue (FR)**[9] 1384 5-8-9 **48**........................(b[1]) TomEaves 5 45
(Brian Ellison) *s.i.s: hld up: nt clr run over 1f out: r.o ins fnl f: nvr nrr (jockey said the gelding ran onto heels exiting the back straight and he therefore briefly had to switch wide round the bend)* **6/1**[3]

0-20 **7** *1/2* **Carpet Time (IRE)**[82] 236 4-9-7 **60**........................ SeanLevey 2 55
(David Barron) *hld up in tch: rdn over 1f out: styd on same pce fnl f* **5/1**[1]

50-4 **8** *1* **Terri Rules (IRE)**[29] 1076 4-9-7 **60**........................(h[1]) ShelleyBirkett 10 56
(Julia Feilden) *s.i.s: hdwy over 1f out: styng on same pce whn nt clr run and eased wl ins fnl f (jockey said filly was slowly away)* **28/1**

20-3 **9** *3/4* **Wild Flower (IRE)**[12] 1335 7-8-12 **51**........................ KieranO'Neill 11 41
(Jimmy Fox) *chsd ldrs: hung lft fr over 4f out: rdn over 2f out: btn over 1f out (jockey said mare hung left-handed)* **11/2**[2]

003 **10** *2* **Swendab (IRE)**[9] 1384 11-8-10 **49**........................(b) RossaRyan 6 33
(John O'Shea) *s.i.s: nvr on terms* **18/1**

1m 13.62s (-0.88) **Going Correction** -0.05s/f (Stan) **10** Ran SP% **120.0**
Speed ratings (Par 101): **103,101,100,100,99 98,97,96,95,92**
CSF £30.81 CT £388.01 TOTE £6.10: £1.90, £2.80, £3.30; EX 36.60 Trifecta £353.10.There was no bid for the winner
Owner John Abbey & Emma Evans **Bred** P O'Rourke **Trained** Pandy, Monmouths

FOCUS
An open selling handicap sprint and they went a good clip. The winner is rated in line with the best of this year's form.

1596 BETWAY HEED YOUR HUNCH H'CAP 1m 5f 219y (Tp)
7:30 (7:30) (Class 3) (0-95,92) 4-Y-O+ **£7,439** (£2,213; £1,106; £553) **Stalls** Low

Form RPR

11 **1** **King's Advice**[14] 1291 5-8-13 **83**........................ JoeFanning 4 95+
(Mark Johnston) *led 1f: chsd ldr: shkn up over 1f out: led ins fnl f: r.o strly* **9/4**[2]

331- **2** *3* **Bartholomeu Dias**[168] 8419 4-9-7 **92**........................ OisinMurphy 5 99
(Charles Hills) *led at stdy pce after 1f: qcknd over 2f out: shkn up and hdd ins fnl f: styd on same pce* **11/4**[3]

1226 **3** *2 1/2* **Glan Y Gors (IRE)**[7] 1425 7-8-9 **79**........................(b) CliffordLee 2 82
(David Thompson) *hld up in tch: shkn up over 2f out: rdn: hung lft and no ex ins fnl f* **25/1**

1624 **4** *1 1/4* **Technological**[24] 1172 4-9-3 **88**........................ AdamKirby 3 90
(George Margarson) *hld up: effrt and nt clr run over 1f out: nt trble ldrs (jockey said colt was never travelling)* **10/1**

2-11 **5** *1/2* **Flaming Marvel (IRE)**[39] 916 5-9-7 **91**........................ DavidProbert 1 91
(James Fanshawe) *prom: racd keenly: rdn over 2f out: wknd ins fnl f (jockey said gelding ran too freely)* **11/8**[1]

3m 0.83s (-0.17) **Going Correction** -0.05s/f (Stan)
WFA 4 from 5yo+ 1lb **5** Ran SP% **112.5**
Speed ratings (Par 107): **98,96,94,94,93**
CSF £9.03 TOTE £3.20: £1.50, £1.40; EX 9.70 Trifecta £76.30.
Owner Saeed Jaber **Bred** Rabbah Bloodstock Limited **Trained** Middleham Moor, N Yorks

FOCUS
Despite the small numbers a good-quality staying contest in which the progressive winner recorded a hat-trick. Rather muddling form though.

1597 BETWAY H'CAP — 6f 20y (Tp)
8:00 (8:00) (Class 5) (0-75,76) 4-Y-O+

£3,752 (£1,116; £557; £400; £400; £400) **Stalls** Low

Form				RPR
06-2	**1**		**Venturous (IRE)**[11] 1342 6-9-8 **76**......SeanLevey 2	85
			(David Barron) *a.p: chsd ldr over 4f out: shkn up to ld over 1f out: rdn and edgd lft ins fnl f: r.o* **4/1**[3]	
/254	**2**	½	**Followthesteps (IRE)**[46] 790 4-9-7 **75**......(p[1]) AdamKirby 1	82
			(Ivan Furtado) *chsd ldr tl over 4f out: remained handy: rdn over 1f out: hung lft and chsd wnr ins fnl f: r.o u.p* **9/4**[1]	
2135	**3**	1 ¼	**Steelriver (IRE)**[10] 1357 9-8-13 **67**......PhilDennis 6	70
			(Michael Herrington) *hld up in tch: racd keenly: shkn up and swtchd lft over 1f out: r.o* **7/1**	
1131	**4**	1 ½	**Zapper Cass (FR)**[4] 1507 6-9-1 **76** 5ex......(v) MarkCrehan[(7)] 7	74
			(Michael Appleby) *plld hrd and sn prom: ct wd over 2f out: rdn over 1f out: styd on* **7/2**[2]	
3112	**5**	½	**The Groove**[22] 1208 6-8-6 **69**......GinaMangan[(7)] 10	66
			(David Evans) *broke wl: sn lost pl: hdwy over 3f out: rdn over 1f out: styd on* **12/1**	
6-14	**6**	½	**Bellevarde (IRE)**[86] 165 5-9-6 **74**......HollieDoyle 5	69
			(Richard Price) *led: rdn and hdd over 1f out: no ex ins fnl f* **22/1**	
0624	**7**	nk	**Aguerooo (IRE)**[8] 1393 6-9-2 **70**......(tp) RichardKingscote 11	64
			(Charlie Wallis) *broke wl: sn stdd and lost pl: r.o ins fnl f: nt rch ldrs* **14/1**	
301-	**8**	1	**Spirit Of Wedza (IRE)**[179] 8078 7-8-10 **71**......VictorSantos[(7)] 8	62
			(Julie Camacho) *s.i.s: hld up: plld hrd: shkn up over 1f out: nvr on terms* **50/1**	
0013	**9**	¾	**Peachey Carnehan**[12] 1338 5-8-9 **63**......(v) JamesSullivan 4	51
			(Michael Mullineaux) *s.i.s: pushed along early in rr: shkn up and hdwy over 1f out: eased whn btn ins fnl f* **14/1**	
5100	**10**	4 ½	**The Establishment**[11] 1342 4-9-3 **71**......(h) EoinWalsh 9	45
			(David Evans) *s.s: a in rr (jockey said the gelding boiled over in the preliminaries and was slowly away)* **18/1**	

1m 13.27s (-1.23) **Going Correction** -0.05s/f (Stan) **10 Ran SP% 118.1**
Speed ratings (Par 103): **106,105,103,101,101 100,99,98,97,91**
CSF £13.58 CT £61.55 TOTE £4.70: £1.70, £1.40, £1.90; EX 16.70 Trifecta £113.40.
Owner Laurence O'Kane/Harrowgate BloodstockLtd **Bred** John Doyle **Trained** Maunby, N Yorks

FOCUS
A competitive sprint and it paid to race prominently as there wasn't a great deal of early pace.

1598 BETWAY EBF NOVICE STKS — 5f 21y (Tp)
8:30 (8:30) (Class 5) 3-Y-O+ **£3,752** (£1,116; £557; £278) **Stalls** Low

Form				RPR
	1		**Tabaahy**[223] 6595 4-9-13 0......CamHardie 4	73+
			(David O'Meara) *hmpd s: hld up: hdwy over 1f out: shkn up to ld wl ins fnl f: r.o* **16/1**	
34	**2**	¾	**Brigadier**[26] 1139 3-9-2 0......JoeFanning 8	65
			(Robert Cowell) *sn w ldr: plld hrd: led over 3f out tl over 2f out: shkn up to ld ins fnl f: sn hdd: styd on* **11/2**[3]	
24	**3**	nk	**Wise Words**[21] 1236 3-8-11 0......OisinMurphy 2	59+
			(James Tate) *hmpd s: hld up: hdwy whn nt clr run and swtchd rt over 1f out: r.o ins fnl f: nt rch ldrs (jockey said filly was denied a clear run inside the final furlong)* **3/1**[2]	
3-	**4**	hd	**Alqaab**[273] 4647 4-9-13 0......JamesSullivan 7	68
			(Ruth Carr) *s.i.s: in rr: r.o ins fnl f: nt rch ldrs (jockey said gelding was slowly away)* **20/1**	
52-2	**5**	nse	**Glorious Emaraty (FR)**[84] 217 3-9-2 76......AdamKirby 6	63
			(Clive Cox) *trckd ldrs: rdn over 1f out: edgd rt ins fnl f: styd on* **8/11**[1]	
	6	1 ¼	**Crown Leah**[364] 1665 4-9-8 78......KieranO'Neill 5	59
			(Peter Charalambous) *wnt lft s: sn led: hdd over 3f out: led again 1/2-way: hdd and no ex ins fnl f* **20/1**	
6-40	**7**	½	**Ghost Buy (FR)**[21] 1236 3-9-2 62......(t[1]) SeanLevey 1	57
			(Ivan Furtado) *wnt rt s: chsd ldrs: rdn over 1f out: no ex wl ins fnl f* **33/1**	
	8	1	**Bedtime Bella (IRE)** 3-8-11 0......PJMcDonald 3	48
			(K R Burke) *hmpd s: in rr: shkn up over 1f out: nt trble ldrs* **8/1**	

1m 1.92s (0.02) **Going Correction** -0.05s/f (Stan) **8 Ran SP% 127.7**
WFA 3 from 4yo 11lb
Speed ratings (Par 103): **97,95,95,95,94 92,92,90**
CSF £108.43 TOTE £19.40: £3.10, £1.90, £1.50; EX 138.80 Trifecta £446.90.
Owner Rasio Cymru Racing 1 **Bred** Cheveley Park Stud Ltd **Trained** Upper Helmsley, N Yorks

FOCUS
A novice sprint in which plenty pulled hard in the early stages. They finished in a heap and the form's probably just modest.
T/Plt: £78.30 to a £1 stake. Pool: £68,394.46 - 636.91 winning units T/Qpdt: £26.30 to a £1 stake. Pool: £13,561.54 - 380.95 winning units **Colin Roberts**

1599 - (Foreign Racing) - See Raceform Interactive

[1528] LEOPARDSTOWN (L-H)
Saturday, April 6

OFFICIAL GOING: Soft (yielding in places)

1600a BALLYLINCH STUD "RED ROCKS" 2,000 GUINEAS TRIAL STKS (LISTED RACE) (C&G) — 7f
2:10 (2:12) 3-Y-O

£26,576 (£8,558; £4,054; £1,801; £900; £450)

			RPR
1		**Never No More (IRE)**[13] 1306 3-9-3 107......RyanMoore 1	109+
		(A P O'Brien, Ire) *settled bhd ldrs: 4th 1/2-way: swtchd rt 1 1/2f out: sn rdn and hdwy nr side to chal and led narrowly wl ins fnl f: kpt on wl to assert cl home: readily* **5/2**[2]	
2	½	**Madhmoon (IRE)**[203] 7314 3-9-6 115......ChrisHayes 6	111+
		(Kevin Prendergast, Ire) *towards rr early tl tk clsr order in 5th after 2f: clsr in 3rd bef 1/2-way: prog nr side 1 1/2f out: rdn to ld fr 1f out: sn strly pressed and hdd wl ins fnl f: kpt on wl wout matching wnr* **4/6**[1]	
3	2	**Could Be King**[168] 8428 3-9-3 102......RonanWhelan 8	102
		(John M Oxx, Ire) *sn trckd ldr: 2nd 1/2-way: effrt under 2f out: on terms briefly between horses over 1f out tl sn hdd: no imp on wnr u.p in 3rd wl ins fnl f: kpt on same pce* **10/1**[3]	
4	¾	**Wargrave (IRE)**[13] 1310 3-9-3 97......LeighRoche 3	100
		(J A Stack, Ire) *hooded to load: sltly awkward s: sn led: 1 l clr at 1/2-way: rdn and strly pressed 1 1/2f out: sn jnd and hdd fr 1f out: no ex and wknd into 4th ins fnl f* **12/1**	
5	¾	**The Irish Rover (IRE)**[196] 7534 3-9-3 105......SeamieHeffernan 2	98
		(A P O'Brien, Ire) *w.w in rr: last at 1/2-way: sme hdwy 2f out: rdn in 5th 1 1/2f out where edgd sltly lft and no imp on ldrs ins fnl f: kpt on nr fin* **22/1**	
6	5	**Copia Verborum (IRE)**[13] 1306 3-9-3 87......KevinManning 5	85
		(J S Bolger, Ire) *chsd ldrs: pushed along in 5th after 1/2-way and no ex u.p in 6th under 2f out: wknd: eased ins fnl f* **50/1**	
7	2 ¾	**San Andreas (IRE)**[13] 1306 3-9-3 100......DonnachaO'Brien 7	77
		(A P O'Brien, Ire) *got upset in stalls briefly: hld up towards rr: 6th 1/2-way: drvn after 1/2-way and no ex u.p nr side under 2f out: wknd and eased ins fnl f* **14/1**	

1m 32.01s (1.61) **7 Ran SP% 118.3**
CSF £4.73 TOTE £3.50: £1.30, £1.10; DF 6.70 Trifecta £19.10.
Owner Michael Tabor & Derrick Smith & Mrs John Magnier **Bred** Rjb Bloodstock **Trained** Cashel, Co Tipperary

FOCUS
It would be surprising if this race did not prove informative for the first set of Classics. The first two should go on to better this but the fourth limits the form.

1601a BALLYLINCH STUD "PRIORY BELLE" 1,000 GUINEAS TRIAL STKS (GROUP 3) (FILLIES) — 7f
2:45 (2:46) 3-Y-O

£34,549 (£11,126; £5,270; £2,342; £1,171; £585)

			RPR
1		**Lady Kaya (IRE)**[189] 7771 3-9-0 110......RobbieColgan 2	108+
		(Ms Sheila Lavery, Ire) *trckd ldrs early tl impr between horses to ld after 1f and mde rest: narrow ld at 1/2-way: extended advantage stl travelling wl under 2f out: pushed out ins fnl f: easily* **11/4**[1]	
2	2 ¼	**Happen (USA)**[161] 8651 3-9-0 84......(t) SeamieHeffernan 3	102+
		(A P O'Brien, Ire) *hld up in rr of mid-div: hdwy in 10th after 1/2-way to chse ldrs between horses over 1f out: drvn into 3rd ins fnl f and r.o wl into nvr threatening 2nd cl home: nt trble easy wnr* **16/1**	
3	hd	**Iridessa (IRE)**[176] 8148 3-9-3 113......DonnachaO'Brien 10	104
		(Joseph Patrick O'Brien, Ire) *chsd ldrs: tk clsr order bhd ldrs over 2f out: rdn in 2nd 1f out and no imp on easy wnr: dropped to 3rd cl home* **5/1**[3]	
4	½	**Zagitova (IRE)**[176] 8148 3-9-0 106......RyanMoore 6	100
		(A P O'Brien, Ire) *hld up in 6th early: drvn over 2f out and hdwy to dispute 3rd ins fnl f where no imp on easy wnr: kpt on same pce in 4th nr fin* **10/3**[2]	
5	¾	**Secret Thoughts (USA)**[254] 5407 3-9-0 93......WayneLordan 11	98
		(A P O'Brien, Ire) *wnt sltly rt s and sltly bmpd rival: mid-div: drvn nr side 2f out and sme hdwy 1f out: no imp on easy wnr ins fnl f: kpt on same pce in 5th nr fin* **14/1**	
6	2 ½	**Chicas Amigas (IRE)**[13] 1306 3-9-0 91......(p) ShaneFoley 7	91
		(Mrs John Harrington, Ire) *led narrowly tl hdd after 1f: cl 2nd at 1/2-way: rdn 2f out and sn no imp on easy wnr u.p in 3rd over 1f out: wknd ins fnl f* **16/1**	
7	¾	**Elleanthus (IRE)**[161] 8656 3-9-0 92......DeclanMcDonogh 1	89
		(Joseph Patrick O'Brien, Ire) *cl up bhd ldr early: 3rd after 1f: rdn bhd ldrs under 2f out and sn no ex u.p in 4th: wknd 1f out* **14/1**	
8	1	**Rainbow Moonstone (IRE)**[167] 8436 3-9-0 89......GaryHalpin 5	87
		(Joseph Patrick O'Brien, Ire) *mid-div: rdn in 9th under 2f out and no imp over 1f out: kpt on one pce ins fnl f* **33/1**	
9	½	**Harriet's Force (IRE)**[162] 8616 3-9-0 88......RonanWhelan 8	85
		(Keith Henry Clarke, Ire) *bmpd sltly s: in rr of mid-div for most: rdn and no imp towards rr 1 1/2f out: kpt on one pce ins fnl f* **50/1**	
10	shd	**Fire Fly (IRE)**[219] 6728 3-9-0 89......MichaelHussey 4	85
		(A P O'Brien, Ire) *dwlt: towards rr: pushed along and sme hdwy under 2f out: kpt on one pce ins fnl f* **16/1**	
11	1	**Viadera**[223] 6596 3-9-0 101......ColinKeane 13	82
		(G M Lyons, Ire) *dwlt and sltly awkward s: settled in mid-div: drvn over 2f out and sn no ex u.p: wknd and eased ins fnl f* **10/1**	
12	½	**Black Magic Woman (IRE)**[13] 1306 3-9-0 84......OisinOrr 9	81
		(Jack W Davison, Ire) *wnt sltly lft s and sltly bmpd rival: chsd ldrs: 3rd 1/2-way: pushed along bhd ldrs into st and no ex u.p under 2f out: wknd* **16/1**	
13	nk	**I Remember You (IRE)**[161] 8653 3-9-0 78......PBBeggy 12	80
		(A P O'Brien, Ire) *bmpd sltly s: a bhd: pushed along in rr under 2f out and no imp: kpt on one pce ins fnl f: nvr a factor* **40/1**	
14	hd	**Operatic Export (IRE)**[233] 6214 3-9-0 0......KevinManning 14	80
		(J S Bolger, Ire) *hld up: shkn up disputing 11th bef 1/2-way: rdn and no ex under 2f out: wknd: eased wl ins fnl f* **8/1**	

1m 31.14s (0.74) **14 Ran SP% 130.8**
CSF £54.44 TOTE £3.20: £1.50, £5.70, £2.10; DF 63.30 Trifecta £488.10.
Owner Joanne Lavery **Bred** John O'Connor **Trained** Summerhill, Co. Meath

FOCUS
A fine performance from the winner, confirming the impression she gave on occasion last year. The form makes plenty of sense.

1602a (Foreign Racing) - See Raceform Interactive

1603a P.W. MCGRATH MEMORIAL BALLYSAX STKS (GROUP 3) — 1m 2f
3:50 (3:51) 3-Y-O

£31,891 (£10,270; £4,864; £2,162; £1,081; £540)

			RPR
1		**Broome (IRE)**[181] 8025 3-9-3 112......RyanMoore 2	117+
		(A P O'Brien, Ire) *dwlt sltly and settled in rr: last at 1/2-way: tk clsr order stl in rr 3f out where pushed along: hdwy on outer fr over 2f out to ld nr side 1 1/2f out: drvn clr and styd on strly ins fnl f: easily* **5/2**[2]	
2	8	**Sovereign (IRE)**[161] 8656 3-9-3 103......SeamieHeffernan 3	101
		(A P O'Brien, Ire) *sn disp ld tl settled in cl 2nd after 1f: disp ld fr 4f out: led over 2f out tl rdn and hdd 1 1/2f out: sn no ch w easy wnr: kpt on same pce ins fnl f* **7/1**	
3	4	**Pythion (FR)**[188] 7818 3-9-3 0......ColinKeane 4	93
		(G M Lyons, Ire) *chsd ldrs: disp 3rd bef 1/2-way: mod 3rd at 1/2-way: clsr 3rd over 3f out: rdn bhd ldrs 2f out and no imp on easy wnr u.p in 3rd over 1f out: kpt on same pce* **12/1**	
4	5	**Sydney Opera House**[161] 8663 3-9-3 110......DonnachaO'Brien 5	83
		(A P O'Brien, Ire) *prom early tl sn settled bhd ldrs in 3rd: jnd for 3rd bef 1/2-way: mod 4th at 1/2-way: clsr 4th over 3f out: rdn bhd ldrs 1 1/2f out and sn no imp on easy wnr into 4th: eased ins fnl f* **9/2**[3]	
5	7	**Tankerville (USA)**[165] 8519 3-9-3 0......ChrisHayes 6	69
		(D K Weld, Ire) *w.w towards rr: mod 5th at 1/2-way: clsr 5th over 3f out: drvn nr side over 2f out and sn no ex in 5th: wknd: eased ins fnl f* **7/4**[1]	

6 16 **Guaranteed (IRE)**[161] 8656 3-9-6 107 (t) KevinManning 1 40
(J S Bolger, Ire) *led and disp: narrow advantage after 1f: jnd fr 4f out: drvn and hdd over 2f out: sn wknd qckly to rr: eased 1 1/2f out* **7/1**

2m 12.61s (0.91) **6** Ran SP% **115.8**
CSF £20.56 TOTE £2.20: £1.20, £3.20; DF 18.60 Trifecta £125.80.
Owner Michael Tabor & Derrick Smith & Mrs John Magnier **Bred** Epona Bloodstock Ltd **Trained** Cashel, Co Tipperary

FOCUS
A race run to suit the winner. The gallop was honest and, given a patient ride, he came from the rear to pick up the pieces and win going away. What he achieved here remains to be seen and quotes of 12-1 about him winning a Derby look skimpy at this juncture at least. The time was very good compared to the handicap.

1604 - 1619a (Foreign Racing) - See Raceform Interactive

CORK (R-H)

Sunday, April 7

OFFICIAL GOING: Good (good to yielding in places)

1620a BETVICTOR BET 5EURO GET 30EURO OFFER IRISH EBF NOBLESSE STKS (LISTED RACE) (F&M) 1m 4f

3:45 (3:46) 4-Y-0+

£31,891 (£10,270; £4,864; £2,162; £1,081; £540)

RPR

1 **Cimeara (IRE)**[255] 5410 4-9-5 102 DonnachaO'Brien 4 102
(Joseph Patrick O'Brien, Ire) *sn chsd ldr in 2nd: rdn to ld 2f out: edgd lft fnl 200yds: kpt on wl clsng stages* **7/1**[3]

2 ½ **Who's Steph (IRE)**[203] 7341 4-9-5 108 ColinKeane 3 101+
(G M Lyons, Ire) *chsd ldrs whn clipped heels and stmbld after 2f: 4th at 1/2-way: clsr in 3rd 2f out: disp 2nd ins fnl f: kpt on wl into 2nd cl home* **11/8**[1]

3 ½ **Warnaq (IRE)**[14] 1308 5-9-0 88 RobbieColgan 8 95
(Matthew J Smith, Ire) *led tl hdd 2f out: rallied wl fnl f: dropped to 3rd cl home* **7/1**[3]

4 1 **Hazel Bay (IRE)**[14] 1309 4-9-0 96 ChrisHayes 1 94
(D K Weld, Ire) *sn chsd ldrs in 3rd: pushed along in 4th under 2f out: kpt on same pce fnl f: no imp fnl 100yds* **6/1**[2]

5 1 **Jaega (IRE)**[176] 8202 4-9-0 97 ConorHoban 5 92
(D K Weld, Ire) *racd in mid-div: clsr under 2f out into 5th: no imp fnl 150yds: kpt on same pce* **11/1**

6 1¾ **Echo Park (IRE)**[170] 8399 4-9-0 91 ShaneFoley 9 90
(Mrs John Harrington, Ire) *racd towards rr: pushed along over 3f out: kpt on wl ins fnl f: nvr nrr* **7/1**[3]

7 nk **Tipitena**[174] 8291 4-9-0 0 WJLee 7 89
(W McCreery, Ire) *racd in mid-div: clsr on outer over 2f out in 6th: no imp ent fnl f: kpt on same pce* **33/1**

8 3¾ **Bongiorno (IRE)**[168] 8442 4-9-0 96 LeighRoche 2 83
(W McCreery, Ire) *chsd ldrs: 5th at 1/2-way: pushed along 3f out: wknd over 1f out* **12/1**

9 4½ **Chiavari (IRE)**[15] 8859 5-9-0 76 GaryHalpin 6 75
(Miss Ellmarie Holden, Ire) *sn in rr of mid-div: wknd towards rr 3f out: sn no ex* **100/1**

10 10 **Endless Tangent (IRE)**[160] 8711 4-9-0 73 NGMcCullagh 10 60
(John M Oxx, Ire) *a in rr: pushed along and detached over 2f out: nvr a factor* **100/1**

2m 35.67s (-12.23) **10** Ran SP% **114.8**
CSF £16.68 TOTE £6.30: £1.40, £1.02, £2.40; DF 14.40 Trifecta £228.20.
Owner Sun Bloodstock **Bred** J S Bolger **Trained** Owning Hill, Co Kilkenny

FOCUS
Two runners here with a three-figure rating. They took the first two placings, and the form looks solid enough despite the proximity in third of an 88-rated mare, with fourth and fifth supplying a healthy context.

1621 - 1624a (Foreign Racing) - See Raceform Interactive

LONGCHAMP (R-H)

Sunday, April 7

OFFICIAL GOING: Turf: good

1625a PRIX LA FORCE (GROUP 3) (3YO COLTS & GELDINGS) (TURF) 1m 1f

1:35 3-Y-0 £36,036 (£14,414; £10,810; £7,207; £3,603)

RPR

1 **Shaman (IRE)**[21] 1243 3-9-2 0 MaximeGuyon 7 111
(C Laffon-Parias, France) *racd keenly on outer: led after 1f: rdn and jnd 2f out: qcknd 2 l clr 1f out: hrd rdn and styd on wl ins fnl f: a doing enough* **7/5**[1]

2 nk **Rockemperor (IRE)**[43] 3-9-2 0 IoritzMendizabal 3 110+
(Simone Brogi, France) *broke wl: settled on inner in 5th: nt clr run 3f fr home: angled out and rdn w 2f to run: hrd drvn to chse ldr ins fnl f: jst hld* **13/1**

3 2 **Roman Candle**[165] 8564 3-9-2 0 MickaelBarzalona 6 106+
(A Fabre, France) *w.w in fnl pair: drvn 2f out but no immediate imp: styd on fr over 1f out: nt enough pce to get on terms w front two* **16/5**[2]

4 ½ **Veronesi (FR)**[31] 3-9-2 0 CristianDemuro 4 105
(J-C Rouget, France) *racd keenly in 4th: rdn but nt enough pce to chal 2f out: hrd rdn ins fnl f: styd on last 100yds to take 4th post: nvr nrr* **17/2**

5 nse **Sottsass (FR)**[163] 3-9-2 0 ChristopheSoumillon 1 105
(J-C Rouget, France) *chsd ldrs on inner: rdn 2f out: hrd rdn and unable to chal 1f out: styd on same pce: lost 4th last stride* **58/10**[3]

6 3 **Getchagetchagetcha**[32] 1035 3-9-2 0 TonyPiccone 2 99
(Clive Cox) *w.w in rr: drvn along 3f out: hrd rdn 2f out: kpt on ins fnl f: nvr in contention* **10/1**

7 1 **Urwald**[149] 3-9-2 0 Pierre-CharlesBoudot 5 97
(A Fabre, France) *chsd ldr on outer: stl 2nd ent st: rdn to join ldr briefly 2f out: sn hrd rdn and outpcd w 1f to run: wknd ins fnl f* **32/5**

1m 50.24s (-1.36) **7** Ran SP% **120.5**
PARI-MUTUEL (all including 1 euro stake): WIN 2.40; PLACE 1.70, 4.00; SF 15.90.
Owner Wertheimer & Frere **Bred** Wertheimer Et Frere **Trained** Chantilly, France

FOCUS
This comes out as 20lb quicker than the Prix Vanteau.

1626a PRIX VANTEAUX (GROUP 3) (3YO FILLIES) (TURF) 1m 1f

2:50 3-Y-0 £36,036 (£14,414; £10,810; £7,207; £3,603)

RPR

1 **Platane**[26] 3-9-0 0 MaximeGuyon 2 104+
(C Laffon-Parias, France) *chsd ldrs on outer: shkn up appr 2f out: drvn to ld 1 1/2f out: immediately jnd on inner by eventual runner-up: styd on strly and asserted last 100yds* **9/10**[1]

2 nk **Etoile (FR)**[57] 3-9-0 0 ChristopheSoumillon 5 104+
(J-C Rouget, France) *racd in midfield on inner: clsd to chse ldrs on inner after 3f: rdn to squeeze between horses and chal 2f out: jnd wnr ins fnl 1 1/2f: sustained chal u.p fnl f: nt match wnr fnl 100yds* **27/10**[2]

3 4½ **Lady Te (GER)**[13] 3-9-0 0 AlexisBadel 8 94
(Carina Fey, France) *sn chsd ldr: drvn to ld 2f out: hdd 1 1/2f fr home: sn hrd rdn styd on but readily outpcd by front two* **18/1**

4 1 **Alimnia (FR)**[15] 3-9-0 0 Pierre-CharlesBoudot 3 92
(F-H Graffard, France) *racd keenly: midfield: 5th and drvn bhd ldrs 2f out: styd on u.p ent fnl f: nt pce to trble ldrs* **54/10**[3]

5 1 **Suquitho (FR)**[21] 3-9-0 0 OlivierPeslier 4 90
(H-A Pantall, France) *dwlt: nudged along early towards rr: impr into midfield on inner at 1/2-way: drvn whn short of room briefly 2f out: kpt on u.p wout ever being in contention* **9/1**

6 nk **High Ball (FR)**[136] 3-9-0 0 TonyPiccone 7 89
(F Vermeulen, France) *slowly away: niggled along in rr: drvn 3f out: rdn and began to cl appr fnl f: styd on tl run flattened out last 100yds* **30/1**

7 2 **Fan Zone (FR)**[28] 1128 3-9-0 0 TheoBachelot 6 85
(B De Montzey, France) *sn towards rr: last whn drvn 2 1/2f out: hrd rdn and outpcd 2f out: kpt on ins fnl 150yds: nvr got involved* **22/1**

8 5 **Zighidi**[6] 3-9-0 0 JamesDoyle 1 75
(Frank Sheridan, Italy) *led: drvn 3f out: rdn and hdd 2f out: sn btn: eased ins fnl f* **63/1**

1m 51.69s (0.09) **8** Ran SP% **119.7**
PARI-MUTUEL (all including 1 euro stake): WIN 1.90; PLACE 1.10, 1.30, 2.00; DF 2.30.
Owner Wertheimer & Frere **Bred** Wertheimer & Frere **Trained** Chantilly, France

FOCUS
The first two finished clear, in a race that was considerably slower than the Prix la Force.

1627a PRIX ZARKAVA - FONDS EUROPEEN DE L'ELEVAGE (LISTED RACE) (4YO+ FILLIES & MARES) (TURF) 1m 2f 110y

3:25 4-Y-0+ £21,621 (£8,648; £6,486; £4,324; £2,162)

RPR

1 **Morgan Le Faye**[161] 8667 5-9-2 0 MickaelBarzalona 12 110
(A Fabre, France) *w.w in fnl pair: gng wl whn angled out and hemmed in briefly 2f out: smooth hdwy w 1 1/2f to run: led last 150yds: sn clr: easily* **21/10**[1]

2 2½ **Shahnaza (FR)**[162] 8665 4-9-2 0 ChristopheSoumillon 6 105
(A De Royer-Dupre, France) **23/10**[2]

3 1 **Lady Sidney (FR)**[56] 682 5-8-11 0 (b) MaximeGuyon 10 98
(R Le Dren Doleuze, France) **9/1**

4 2½ **Ficelle Du Houley (FR)**[21] 1244 4-8-11 0 CristianDemuro 8 94
(Y Barberot, France) **20/1**

5 1 **Duchess Of Danzig (GER)**[152] 8914 4-8-11 0 AlexisBadel 2 92
(H-F Devin, France) **25/1**

6 1½ **Magnolia Springs (IRE)**[249] 5610 4-9-2 0 TonyPiccone 7 94
(Eve Johnson Houghton) *sn chsng ldr: led after 2 1/2f: drvn whn pressed over 2f out: hdd ins fnl 2f: kpt on same pce u.p* **92/1**

7 2 **Cheshmeh (FR)**[25] 4-9-2 0 ClementLecoeuvre 1 90
(Henk Grewe, Germany) **31/1**

8 1 **Hermaphrodite (FR)**[183] 8014 4-8-11 0 Pierre-CharlesBoudot 4 83
(F-H Graffard, France) **31/5**[3]

9 ¾ **Amazing Lips (IRE)**[27] 4-8-11 0 IoritzMendizabal 9 82
(S Kobayashi, France) **15/1**

10 4½ **Wonder Of Lips (GER)**[23] 4-9-2 0 OlivierPeslier 3 78
(H-F Devin, France) **23/1**

11 2½ **Arusha (FR)**[27] 4-8-11 0 (p) TheoBachelot 5 68
(P Decouz, France) **51/1**

12 1 **Lady Athena (FR)**[217] 6846 4-8-11 0 StephanePasquier 11 67
(Y Durepaire, France) **12/1**

2m 9.21s (-0.99) **12** Ran SP% **119.3**
PARI-MUTUEL (all including 1 euro stake): WIN 3.10; PLACE 1.40, 1.40, 2.40; DF 3.90.
Owner Godolphin SNC **Bred** Dieter Burkle **Trained** Chantilly, France

1628a PRIX D'HARCOURT (GROUP 2) (4YO+) (TURF) 1m 2f

4:00 4-Y-0+ £66,756 (£25,765; £12,297; £8,198; £4,099)

RPR

1 **Ghaiyyath (IRE)**[197] 7567 4-9-0 0 WilliamBuick 1 122+
(Charlie Appleby) *mde all: 5 l clr by 1/2-way: drvn and drew further away 2f out: hrd drvn 1f out to maintain advantage: heavily eased cl home: impressive* **7/10**[1]

2 1½ **Soleil Marin (IRE)**[21] 1244 5-9-0 Pierre-CharlesBoudot 6 112+
(A Fabre, France) *w.w in last pl: stl in rr 4f out: drvn to improve on outer 2f out: hrd drvn to go 2nd 1 1/2f out: sn rdn and r.o fnl f: no ch w easy wnr* **43/5**

3 3½ **Intellogent (IRE)**[210] 7105 4-9-6 0 ChristopheSoumillon 2 111+
(F Chappet, France) *w.w in fnl pair: drvn whn nt clr run 3f out: hrd drvn 2f out: rdn and styd on to take 3rd ins fnl f: nvr on terms* **42/10**[2]

4 1 **Lucius Tiberius (IRE)**[176] 8191 4-9-0 JamesDoyle 7 103+
(Charlie Appleby) *chsd clr ldr: drvn 3f out: hrd drvn among those in pursuit 2f out: kpt on u.p: lost 3rd ins fnl f: no ex late on* **66/10**

5 ¾ **Volfango (IRE)**[50] 766 5-9-0 0 MaximeGuyon 3 102+
(F Vermeulen, France) *chsd ldr on inner: drvn 3f out: hrd drvn among those chsng ldr but no imp 2f out: kpt on same pce u.p* **32/5**[3]

6 hd **Nocturnal Fox (IRE)**[294] 3920 4-9-3 MickaelBarzalona 4 104+
(A Fabre, France) *chsd ldr: drvn but unable to reduce deficit 3f out: hrd drvn and lost pl 2f out: no ex ins fnl f* **17/1**

2m 2.87s (-1.13) **6** Ran SP% **120.7**
PARI-MUTUEL (all including 1 euro stake): WIN 1.10 (coupled with Nocturnal Fox, Lucius Tiberius & Soleil Marin); PLACE 1.10, 1.50; SF 4.70.
Owner Godolphin **Bred** Springbank Way Stud **Trained** Newmarket, Suffolk

FOCUS
Not easy form to peg given Ghaiyyath enjoyed a solo in front, but he's clearly still progressing.

1629 - 1630a (Foreign Racing) - See Raceform Interactive

SENONNES-POUANCE
Sunday, April 7

OFFICIAL GOING: Turf: soft

1631a PRIX DES FORETS (CONDITIONS) (4YO+) (TURF) 6f 110y
1:30 4-Y-O+ £5,180 (£2,072; £1,554; £1,036; £518)

RPR

1 **Brian Ryan**[10] 1391 4-9-3 0 MlleCoraliePacaut(3) 5
(Andrea Marcialis, France) 9/2[1]

2 1 **Toriano (FR)** 4-8-10 0 JeromeMoutard(4) 2
(Waldemar Hickst, Germany)

3 1/2 **Koukiboy (FR)**[318] 5-9-0 0 AlexandreRoussel 8
(F Foucher, France)

4 1 **Lefortovo (FR)**[26] 1164 6-9-3 0 ow1 JeromeCabre 9
(Jo Hughes, France)

5 2 1/2 **Lord Torranaga (FR)**[33] 1027 4-9-8 0 MathieuAndrouin 4
(Alain Couetil, France)

6 4 1/2 **Dusk Till Down (FR)**[201] 7412 4-8-6 0 MlleLucieOger(9) 6
(L Gadbin, France)

7 nk **Marsh Harbour (FR)**[326] 4-9-0 0 ArnaudBourgeais 3
(Mme Pia Brandt, France)

8 dist **Duke Bere (FR)**[94] 6-9-4 0 ChristopherGrosbois 1
(J Boisnard, France)

PARI-MUTUEL (all including 1 euro stake): WIN 5.40; PLACE 1.60, 1.70, 1.60.
Owner Torsten Raber **Bred** D Curran **Trained** France

1632 - 1641a (Foreign Racing) - See Raceform Interactive

REDCAR (L-H)
Monday, April 8

OFFICIAL GOING: Good (good to firm in places; 8.4)
Wind: light against Weather: overcast

1642 FLAT IS BACK AT REDCAR FILLIES' NOVICE STKS (PLUS 10 RACE) 5f
2:00 (2:01) (Class 5) 2-Y-O £3,752 (£1,116; £557; £278) Stalls Centre

Form RPR

1 **Exclusively** 2-9-0 0 OisinMurphy 10 80+
(Archie Watson) *prom: pushed along over 1f out: rdn to chal strly fnl f: r.o wl: led 75yds out* 11/10[1]

2 1 1/4 **Iva Go (IRE)** 2-9-0 0 DavidAllan 8 76+
(Tim Easterby) *led: rdn and pressed fnl f: kpt on wl but hdd 75yds out* 11/2[3]

3 3 1/4 **Bare All (IRE)** 2-9-0 0 BenCurtis 3 64+
(K R Burke) *in tch: sn pushed along: kpt on wl fnl f: wnt 3rd 100yds out: no ch w ldng pair* 9/1

4 3/4 **Leave Em Alone (IRE)** 2-9-0 0 JohnFahy 12 61+
(David Evans) *midfield: sn pushed along: kpt on wl fnl f* 80/1

5 3/4 **Lara Silvia** 2-8-11 0 JamieGormley(3) 11 58
(Iain Jardine) *trckd ldrs: rdn over 1f out: one pce* 100/1

6 1 1/4 **Lili Wen Fach (IRE)** 2-9-0 0 KieranO'Neill 1 54
(David Evans) *wnt lft s: hld up: sn pushed along: kpt on fr over 1f out* 40/1

7 2 3/4 **Great Dame (IRE)** 2-9-0 0 DanielTudhope 5 44+
(David O'Meara) *prom: hung lft fr early stage: rdn 2f out: wknd fnl f* 5/1[2]

8 nse **Flight Of Thunder (IRE)** 2-9-0 0 KevinStott 2 44+
(Kevin Ryan) *chsd ldrs: rdn along 1/2-way: wknd fnl f* 11/1

9 1 **Bankawi** 2-9-0 0 NathanEvans 13 40
(Michael Easterby) *chsd ldrs: wknd over 1f out* 100/1

10 3/4 **Azteca** 2-9-0 0 GrahamLee 7 38
(Bryan Smart) *dwlt: hld up: sn pushed along: nvr threatened* 25/1

11 6 **Grace Plunkett** 2-9-0 0 PaulHanagan 9 16
(Richard Spencer) *slowly away: a in rr* 16/1

12 3/4 **Lady Erimus** 2-9-0 0 ShaneGray 4 13
(Kevin Ryan) *a in rr* 33/1

13 1 3/4 **Stittenham** 2-9-0 0 PhilDennis 6 7
(Michael Easterby) *sn pushed along and a in rr* 100/1

59.54s (1.04) **Going Correction** +0.225s/f (Good) 13 Ran SP% 117.3
Speed ratings (Par 89): **100,98,92,91,90 88,84,83,82,81 71,70,67**
CSF £6.70 TOTE £2.10: £1.10, £1.80, £2.10; EX 9.30 Trifecta £33.10.
Owner Qatar Racing Limited **Bred** Newsells Park Stud **Trained** Upper Lambourn, W Berks

FOCUS
A fair juvenile fillies' novice contest with a field made up entirely by debutantes. The official going description was good, good to firm in places. The winning time concurred with that assessment and the right two horses came to the fore. The form is rated a bit better than the par for fillies' novice events in April.

1643 BECOME A REDCAR ANNUAL BADGEHOLDER NOVICE STKS 1m 2f 1y
2:30 (2:31) (Class 5) 3-4-Y-O £3,752 (£1,116; £557; £278) Stalls Low

Form RPR

22- 1 **Private Secretary**[152] 8931 3-8-9 0 KieranO'Neill 4 82+
(John Gosden) *in tch: pushed along and hdwy over 2f out: led appr fnl f: drvn ins fnl f: kpt on* 10/11[1]

5- 2 1/2 **Sinjaari (IRE)**[297] 3819 3-8-9 0 OisinMurphy 3 79+
(William Haggas) *trckd ldrs: pushed along 2f out: bit short of room appr fnl f and swtchd rt to outer: r.o wl fnl 110yds* 5/2[2]

5- 3 1 1/4 **Entrusting**[152] 8930 3-8-9 0 SilvestreDeSousa 8 76
(James Fanshawe) *led for 2f: prom: rdn to ld again 2f out: hdd appr fnl f: kpt on same pce* 4/1[3]

4 4 **Itchingham Lofte (IRE)** 3-8-9 0 LewisEdmunds 7 68+
(David Barron) *midfield: pushed along 2f out: kpt on wl fnl f* 66/1

5 1 3/4 **Smeaton (IRE)** 3-8-9 0 BenCurtis 2 65
(Roger Fell) *dwlt: sn in tch towards inner: rdn along over 2f out: kpt on same pce* 100/1

0-5 6 1 3/4 **Awesomedude**[22] 1241 3-8-9 0 PaddyMathers 12 61
(Mrs Ilka Gansera-Leveque) *midfield: pushed along 3f out: sn one pce* 80/1

7 6 **Royal Sands (FR)** 3-8-9 0 BarryMcHugh 13 49
(James Given) *trckd ldrs: rdn over 2f out: wknd over 1f out* 10/1

6/ 8 nk **Khazaf**[563] 7355 4-10-0 0 JamesSullivan 1 52
(Ruth Carr) *prom: racd keenly: led 8f out: pushed along and hdd 2f out: sn wknd* 100/1

0- 9 2 **Littlebitofmagic**[129] 9323 3-8-9 0 TomEaves 5 44
(Michael Dods) *nvr bttr than midfield* 100/1

6- 10 3/4 **Feebi**[167] 8502 3-8-4 0 DuranFentiman 10 38
(Chris Fairhurst) *hld up: nvr threatened* 150/1

11 hd **Basildon**[44] 4-9-11 0 BenRobinson(3) 6 47
(Brian Ellison) *dwlt: hld up in midfield: pushed along 3f out: wknd over 1f out* 66/1

12 4 **Two For Three (IRE)** 3-8-9 0 JasonHart 14 35
(Roger Fell) *hld up: nvr threatened* 125/1

13 4 **Yasmin From York** 3-8-4 0 CamHardie 9 22
(Brian Rothwell) *a towards rr* 250/1

0 14 60 **Put The Law On You (IRE)**[38] 968 4-10-0 0 PaulMulrennan 11
(Alistair Whillans) *a in rr: t.o fnl 4f* 200/1

2m 9.05s (2.15) **Going Correction** +0.225s/f (Good)
WFA 3 from 4yo 19lb 14 Ran SP% 119.6
Speed ratings (Par 103): **100,99,98,95,94 92,87,87,85,85 85,82,78,30**
CSF £3.31 TOTE £1.80: £1.10, £1.30, £1.10; EX 3.70 Trifecta £6.30.
Owner Denford Stud **Bred** Denford Stud Ltd **Trained** Newmarket, Suffolk

FOCUS
A fairly decent novice contest. It paid to race prominently from off a modest enough pace. The three horses at the head of the betting finished in market order, having raced in the first five turning for home. The winner didn't need to match last year's form.

1644 TOMMY SANDERSON IS 9 TODAY H'CAP 7f 219y
3:00 (3:01) (Class 4) (0-85,85) 4-Y-O+
£5,530 (£1,645; £822; £411; £300; £300) Stalls Centre

Form RPR

051- 1 **Give It Some Teddy**[184] 7991 5-9-2 80 DuranFentiman 9 87
(Tim Easterby) *in tch: trckd ldrs 3f out: rdn to ld ins fnl f: sn drvn: all out* 8/1

1221 2 nse **Rey Loopy (IRE)**[10] 1401 5-8-8 72 AndrewMullen 11 79+
(Ben Haslam) *hld up: drvn and hdwy over 1f out: chsd ldrs ins fnl f: r.o wl: jst failed* 7/1[3]

053- 3 1 **International Man**[163] 8635 4-8-7 76 ConnorMurtagh(5) 5 81
(Richard Fahey) *trckd ldrs: rdn to chal appr fnl f: kpt on same pce ins fnl f* 9/2[1]

136- 4 nk **Kripke (IRE)**[338] 2402 4-9-0 78 LewisEdmunds 12 82
(David Barron) *midfield: pushed along over 2f out: rdn ins fnl f: kpt on wl fnl 110yds* 20/1

000- 5 1 1/2 **Tadaawol**[160] 8717 6-8-13 82 BenSanderson(5) 13 83
(Roger Fell) *led: rdn and hdd over 1f out: no ex ins fnl f* 33/1

050- 6 nse **Strong Steps**[188] 7869 7-8-7 71 oh1 PhilDennis 3 72
(Jim Goldie) *hld up: racd quite keenly: rdn and kpt on fnl f: nrst fin* 25/1

10-4 7 1 3/4 **Windsor Cross (IRE)**[17] 1273 4-9-2 80 PaulHanagan 10 77
(Richard Fahey) *dwlt: hld up: pushed along over 2f out: swtchd rt ins fnl f: kpt on: nvr involved* 11/1

230- 8 hd **Intense Pleasure (IRE)**[354] 1933 4-8-9 73 JamesSullivan 7 71+
(Ruth Carr) *hld up: pushed along and hdwy in midfield: keeping on whn short of room 150yds out: no ch after: kpt on pushed out* 33/1

000- 9 3/4 **Alfa McGuire (IRE)**[233] 6314 4-9-7 85 SamJames 15 80
(Phillip Makin) *trckd ldrs: rdn over 2f out: wknd ins fnl f* 12/1

2-34 10 3/4 **Sheberghan (IRE)**[61] 625 4-9-4 82 (p) OisinMurphy 14 75
(Archie Watson) *prom: led over 1f out: rdn and edgd lft 1f out: sn hdd: wknd fnl 110yds* 8/1

5164 11 2 **Fuwairt (IRE)**[28] 1143 7-8-12 79 (p[1]) CameronNoble(3) 8 68
(David Loughnane) *hld up in rr: rdn and hdwy over 1f out: nvr threatened* 10/1

005- 12 3 **Vive La Difference (IRE)**[149] 8999 5-9-0 78 RachelRichardson 4 60
(Tim Easterby) *midfield: racd keenly: rdn over 2f out: sn wknd* 9/1

600- 13 3 3/4 **Brother McGonagall**[153] 8898 5-9-1 79 DavidAllan 16 53
(Tim Easterby) *midfield: rdn over 2f out: wknd over 1f out* 28/1

600- 14 3/4 **Royal Shaheen (FR)**[171] 8371 6-9-4 82 PaulMulrennan 1 54
(Alistair Whillans) *a towards rr* 25/1

3-31 15 1 1/2 **Helovaplan (IRE)**[52] 740 5-9-7 85 GrahamLee 2 54
(Bryan Smart) *trckd ldrs: rdn and outpcd 3f out: sn wknd* 5/1[2]

/40- 16 6 **Crown Vallary (FR)**[260] 5258 4-9-0 85 (h[1]) RhonaPindar(7) 6 41
(K R Burke) *trckd ldrs: racd keenly: wknd 2f out* 40/1

1m 38.37s (1.77) **Going Correction** +0.225s/f (Good) 16 Ran SP% 128.9
Speed ratings (Par 105): **100,99,98,98,97 97,95,95,94,93 91,88,84,84,82 76**
CSF £61.64 CT £295.21 TOTE £10.30: £2.30, £2.10, £1.60, £5.50; EX 89.40 Trifecta £750.10.
Owner Lee Bond **Bred** Usk Valley Stud **Trained** Great Habton, N Yorks

FOCUS
A decent handicap. Most of the principals came through from midfield or further back from off a solid enough gallop. The winner may have more to give.

1645 WATCH RACING TV IN STUNNING HD H'CAP 1m 2f 1y
3:30 (3:30) (Class 4) (0-85,86) 3-Y-O
£5,530 (£1,645; £822; £411; £300; £300) Stalls Centre

Form RPR

321- 1 **Sameem (IRE)**[195] 7637 3-9-5 81 DavidAllan 4 91
(James Tate) *mde all: pushed clr 2f out: rdn out ins fnl f: reduced advantage ins fnl f but nvr in danger* 3/1[1]

42-1 2 1 1/4 **Forest Of Dean**[39] 949 3-9-7 83 KieranO'Neill 6 91+
(John Gosden) *midfield: short of room over 2f out: plenty to do once swtchd rt over 1f out: wnt 2nd ins fnl f: kpt on wl but nvr getting to wnr* 3/1[1]

221- 3 3 **Red October (IRE)**[165] 8576 3-9-6 82 JamesDoyle 3 84
(Hugo Palmer) *trckd ldrs: rdn along 3f out: styd on same pce* 3/1[1]

146- 4 1 **Flint Hill**[171] 8377 3-9-2 78 PaulMulrennan 9 78
(Michael Dods) *midfield: rdn along and outpcd 3f out: styd on fr over 1f out* 25/1

2-64 5 4 **Curfewed (IRE)**[47] 804 3-8-7 69 CamHardie 8 62
(Tracy Waggott) *hld up in rr: pushed along and hdwy over 2f out: rdn over 1f out: wknd ins fnl f* 66/1

024- 6 1 1/2 **Artistic Language**[166] 8549 3-9-3 79 AndreaAtzeni 11 69
(Brian Meehan) *prom: rdn over 2f out: wknd over 1f out* 11/1[3]

140- 7 1 **Must See The Doc**[182] 8049 3-9-4 80 AndrewMullen 10 69
(Iain Jardine) *hld up: short of room on inner ins fnl f: nvr threatened* 40/1

333- 8 1 **One To Go**[156] 8834 3-8-9 71 RachelRichardson 7 58
(Tim Easterby) *hld up: rdn over 2f out: sn btn* 25/1

-412 **9** *3* **Harvey Dent**[46] 826 3-9-3 **79**............................ OisinMurphy 5 60
(Archie Watson) *trckd ldrs: rdn over 2f out: wknd over 1f out* **9/2**[2]
2m 6.76s (-0.14) **Going Correction** +0.225s/f (Good) **9** Ran SP% **113.1**
Speed ratings (Par 100): **109,108,105,104,101 100,99,98,96**
CSF £11.33 CT £27.82 TOTE £4.00: £1.30, £1.40, £1.50; EX 12.60 Trifecta £39.90.
Owner Sultan Ali **Bred** Rabbah Bloodstock Limited **Trained** Newmarket, Suffolk
FOCUS
A decent 3yo handicap. One of the co-favourites made all from a low draw in a time over two seconds quicker than the earlier C&D novice. The first four finished clear and quite a positive view has been taken of the form.

1646 RACING TV STRAIGHT MILE H'CAP (REDCAR STRAIGHT MILE SERIES QUALIFIER) 7f 219y
4:00 (4:02) (Class 4) (0-85,85) 3-Y-O
£5,530 (£1,645; £822; £411; £300; £300) **Stalls** Centre

Form RPR
601- **1** **Absolutio (FR)**[118] 9490 3-8-13 **77**....................(h) BenCurtis 2 87
(K R Burke) *mde all: rdn over 1f out: drvn and strly pressed ins fnl f: hld on gamely* **11/2**
-421 **2** *1* **On The Line (IRE)**[17] 1264 3-9-5 **83**....................(bt) JamesDoyle 3 91
(Hugo Palmer) *hld up in tch: pushed along over 2f out: hdwy over 1f out: rdn to chal strly ins fnl f: one pce towards fin* **10/3**[3]
613- **3** *5* **Reloaded (IRE)**[175] 8280 3-9-7 **85**.............................. OisinMurphy 7 82
(George Scott) *trckd ldrs: rdn along 2f out: drvn appr fnl f: sn wknd* **11/4**[2]
033- **4** *1 1/4* **Tucson**[129] 9323 3-8-11 **75**.............................. PJMcDonald 5 69
(James Bethell) *hld up in tch: rdn 2f out: wnt modest 4th post: nvr involved* **17/2**
3222 **5** *nse* **White Coat**[11] 1381 3-9-2 **80**....................(tp) KieranO'Neill 8 74
(John Gosden) *trckd ldrs: pushed along over 2f out: drvn over 1f out: wknd ins fnl f* **5/2**[1]
521- **6** *hd* **Amadeus Grey (IRE)**[248] 5675 3-9-7 **85**.............................. DavidAllan 4 79
(Tim Easterby) *trckd ldrs: rdn 2f out: wknd fnl f* **16/1**
001- **7** *12* **Gremoboy**[144] 9083 3-8-9 **73**.............................. DuranFentiman 6 40
(Tim Easterby) *trckd ldrs: rdn over 2f out: wknd over 1f out* **40/1**
005- **8** *1* **Here's Rocco (IRE)**[184] 7989 3-8-6 **70**.............................. AndrewMullen 1 35
(John Quinn) *slowly away: hld up: rdn over 2f out: wknd over 1f out* **40/1**
1m 39.47s (2.87) **Going Correction** +0.225s/f (Good) **8** Ran SP% **115.0**
Speed ratings (Par 100): **94,93,88,86,86 86,74,73**
CSF £24.34 CT £60.29 TOTE £6.80: £1.70, £1.50, £1.60; EX 28.10 Trifecta £97.70.
Owner S P C Woods **Bred** Jean-Pierre Dubois **Trained** Middleham Moor, N Yorks
FOCUS
Another decent 3yo handicap. The fourth-favourite gamely made all and his winning time was over a second slower than the older horses managed over this C&D earlier on. The form could possibly have been rated higher.

1647 WATCH IRISH RACING ON RACING TV H'CAP (DIV I) 1m 2f 1y
4:30 (4:31) (Class 5) (0-70,70) 4-Y-O+
£3,752 (£1,116; £557; £300; £300; £300) **Stalls** Low

Form RPR
3234 **1** **Kilbaha Lady (IRE)**[11] 1378 5-8-12 **64**....................(p[1]) RowanScott[(3)] 1 71
(Nigel Tinkler) *dwlt: sn in tch on inner: chsd ldrs 2f out: angled rt to outer over 1f out: rdn to ld 110yds out: drvn and kpt on* **7/1**[3]
50-0 **2** *1* **Bahkit (IRE)**[92] 102 5-8-13 **62**.............................. BenCurtis 10 67
(Philip Kirby) *prom: rdn to ld wl over 1f out: drvn fnl f: hdd 110yds out: one pce* **7/1**[3]
-500 **3** *nk* **Seaborough (IRE)**[17] 1271 4-8-11 **60**.............................. PJMcDonald 12 65+
(David Thompson) *hld up: hdwy on inner 2f out: sn chsd ldrs: short of room 150yds out tl 75yds out: kpt on (jockey said gelding was denied a clear run in final 1/2f)* **25/1**
-632 **4** *1 1/4* **Duke Of Alba (IRE)**[46] 835 4-8-11 **60**.............................. AndrewMullen 7 62
(John Mackie) *hld up in midfield: rdn over 2f out: sme hdwy over 1f out: edgd jst lft ins fnl f: swtchd rt 75yds out: styd on* **3/1**[1]
0 **5** *nk* **Lafilia (GER)**[12] 1369 4-9-0 **63**.............................. OisinMurphy 3 64
(Archie Watson) *led: rdn and hdd wl over 1f out: keeping on same pce in 3rd whn bmpd 110yds out: no ex* **16/1**
2424 **6** *1 3/4* **Zorawar (FR)**[13] 1343 5-9-7 **70**.............................. DanielTudhope 8 68+
(David O'Meara) *hld up: pushed along and hdwy 2f out: rdn ent fnl f: wknd fnl 110yds* **7/2**[2]
-650 **7** *4* **God Willing**[9] 1418 8-8-9 **65**....................(t) ZakWheatley[(7)] 6 55
(Declan Carroll) *midfield towards outer: rdn over 2f out: nvr threatened* **12/1**
050- **8** *6* **French Flyer (IRE)**[184] 7992 4-8-9 **58**.............................. LewisEdmunds 4 36
(Rebecca Bastiman) *trckd ldrs: rdn over 2f out: wknd over 1f out* **50/1**
3-00 **9** *7* **Lord Rob**[31] 1083 8-8-4 **56** oh10.............................. JamieGormley[(3)] 2 20
(David Thompson) *dwlt: sn midfield: rdn along 3f out: wknd 2f out* **80/1**
5633 **10** *1 3/4* **Channel Packet**[32] 1065 5-8-10 **66**....................(p) MarkCrehan[(7)] 11 26
(Michael Appleby) *trckd ldrs: rdn over 2f out: sn wknd* **15/2**
5430 **11** *2 1/4* **Remmy D (IRE)**[9] 1418 4-9-5 **68**.............................. PaulMulrennan 9 24
(Jim Goldie) *hld up: rdn over 3f out: sn btn* **9/1**
/1-0 **12** *2 3/4* **Dreamofdiscovery (IRE)**[10] 1399 5-9-0 **63**.............................. GrahamLee 5 13
(Julie Camacho) *trckd ldrs: rdn along over 3f out: wknd over 2f out* **25/1**
2m 7.49s (0.59) **Going Correction** +0.225s/f (Good) **12** Ran SP% **118.4**
Speed ratings (Par 103): **106,105,104,103,103 102,99,94,88,87 85,83**
CSF £53.72 CT £1168.11 TOTE £6.50: £2.30, £2.70, £10.90; EX 70.40 Trifecta £2817.00.
Owner The Dapper Partnership **Bred** Helen Lyons **Trained** Langton, N Yorks
FOCUS
The first-division of a modest handicap. The winning time was fair for the grade and over two seconds quicker than the later division. It's been rated as routine form.

1648 WATCH IRISH RACING ON RACING TV H'CAP (DIV II) 1m 2f 1y
5:00 (5:00) (Class 5) (0-70,68) 4-Y-O+
£3,752 (£1,116; £557; £300; £300; £300) **Stalls** Low

Form RPR
30-1 **1** **Mr Coco Bean (USA)**[67] 507 5-8-12 **59**.............................. PJMcDonald 7 67+
(David Barron) *in tch: chsd ldrs over 2f out: pushed along over 1f out: led ins fnl f: rdn and kpt on* **9/2**[2]
4123 **2** *1* **Champagne Rules**[10] 1398 8-9-1 **67**.............................. ConnorMurtagh[(5)] 10 72
(Sharon Watt) *prom: n.m.r and lost pl sltly over 1f out: nt in clr tl 110yds out: rdn and styd on wl: wnt 2nd towards fin (jockey said gelding hung right and was denied a clear run in final furlong)* **11/1**
060- **3** *3/4* **Maghfoor**[187] 7901 5-9-7 **68**.............................. JasonHart 6 72
(Eric Alston) *trckd ldrs: pushed along to ld 1f out: sn rdn: hdd ins fnl f: one pce: lost 2nd towards fin* **11/4**[1]
0036 **4** *1 3/4* **Captain Pugwash (IRE)**[13] 1343 5-9-5 **66**....................(b[1]) JoeFanning 8 67
(Stef Keniry) *prom: led 2f out: sn rdn: hdd 1f out: no ex fnl 110yds* **13/2**[3]
6634 **5** *nse* **Restive (IRE)**[10] 1398 6-9-2 **63**....................(t) PhilDennis 9 64
(Jim Goldie) *hld up in rr: hdwy on inner over 3f out: rdn over 2f out: one pce* **7/1**
120- **6** *1* **Acadian Angel (IRE)**[108] 9665 5-8-13 **60**.............................. KieranO'Neill 2 59
(Steph Hollinshead) *trckd ldrs: rdn along over 2f out: no ex fnl f* **10/1**
4/00 **7** *3/4* **Tarnhelm**[17] 1271 4-8-13 **60**.............................. NathanEvans 3 57
(Wilf Storey) *hld up: rdn over 2f out: sme hdwy over 1f out: kpt on: nvr threatened ldrs* **50/1**
5400 **8** *nk* **Highwayman**[9] 1431 6-8-4 **54** oh9.............................. JamieGormley[(3)] 5 51
(David Thompson) *midfield: rdn along 3f out: no imp* **25/1**
263- **9** *2 1/4* **Zealous (IRE)**[114] 9555 6-9-4 **65**.............................. DougieCostello 11 58
(Alistair Whillans) *led: rdn and hdd 2f out: sn wknd* **14/1**
240- **10** *1* **Dutch Coed**[164] 8597 7-8-4 **56**.............................. FayeMcManoman[(5)] 1 47
(Nigel Tinkler) *racd keenly in midfield: rdn over 2f out: wknd over 1f out (jockey said gelding ran too free)* **13/2**[3]
/06- **11** *1 3/4* **Gabriel's Oboe (IRE)**[247] 5755 4-9-1 **62**.............................. PaulHanagan 12 50
(Mark Walford) *midfield: rdn over 3f out: outpcd and sn btn* **50/1**
000- **12** *3 1/2* **Duke Of Yorkshire**[164] 8597 9-8-10 **64**.............................. RobertDodsworth[(7)] 4 46
(Tim Easterby) *hld up: rdn over 2f out: sn btn* **25/1**
2m 9.62s (2.72) **Going Correction** +0.225s/f (Good) **12** Ran SP% **119.7**
Speed ratings (Par 103): **98,97,96,95,95 94,93,93,91,90 89,86**
CSF £51.98 CT £162.08 TOTE £6.00: £2.00, £3.10, £2.00; EX 28.20 Trifecta £169.70.
Owner S Raines **Bred** Stewart Larkin Armstrong **Trained** Maunby, N Yorks
FOCUS
The potentially weaker second-division of a modest handicap and the second-favourite's winning time was significantly slower. The winner looks as if he can replicate his AW figures on turf.

1649 EVERY RACE LIVE ON RACING TV NOVICE MEDIAN AUCTION STKS 7f
5:30 (5:34) (Class 6) 3-4-Y-O **£3,234** (£962; £481; £240) **Stalls** Centre

Form RPR
1 **1** **Sandret (IRE)**[39] 954 3-9-7 0.............................. AndrewMullen 12 77
(Ben Haslam) *midfield: pushed along and hdwy fr 2f out: rdn appr fnl f: led 50yds out: edgd lft: kpt on* **20/1**
4 **2** *1/2* **Bobby Shaft**[13] 1346 3-9-0 0.............................. PaulHanagan 2 69
(Richard Fahey) *prom: keen early: rdn along to ld appr fnl f: drvn and edgd lft ins fnl f: hdd 50yds out: one pce* **7/4**[1]
3 *1 1/2* **Mina Velour** 3-8-9 0....................(h[1]) GrahamLee 13 60
(Bryan Smart) *hld up: racd keenly: pushed along and hdwy over 1f out: kpt on fnl f: wnt 3rd towards fin* **28/1**
03- **4** *nk* **Atalanta's Boy**[207] 7216 4-9-7 0....................(h) Pierre-LouisJamin[(7)] 1 69
(David Menuisier) *prom: pressed ldr over 3f out: rdn 2f out: sltly hmpd 75yds out: one pce and lost 3rd towards fin* **25/1**
5 *1 1/4* **Jet Set Go** 4-9-9 0.............................. NathanEvans 6 61
(Seb Spencer) *dwlt sltly: hld up: hdwy and chsd ldrs 4f out: rdn over 2f out: drvn over 1f out: one pce whn bmpd 25yds out* **66/1**
55-3 **6** *3 1/4* **Serengeti Song (IRE)**[11] 1389 3-9-0 75.............................. BenCurtis 4 53
(K R Burke) *led: racd keenly: rdn and hdd appr fnl f: wknd* **15/8**[2]
7 *hd* **International Guy (IRE)** 3-9-0 0.............................. TonyHamilton 3 52+
(Richard Fahey) *midfield: rdn over 2f out: kpt on same pce* **16/1**
3 **8** *3 1/2* **Paradise Papers**[17] 1272 3-8-9 0.............................. LewisEdmunds 9 38
(David Barron) *midfield: rdn over 2f out: wknd ins fnl f* **14/1**
00- **9** *1 1/2* **Jack Randall**[153] 8895 3-9-0 0.............................. DavidAllan 14 39
(Tim Easterby) *hld up: rdn over 2f out: nvr threatened* **66/1**
10 *1/2* **Parallel World (IRE)** 3-8-9 0.............................. HarrisonShaw[(5)] 5 38
(K R Burke) *trckd ldrs: rdn along 3f out: wknd over 1f out* **33/1**
0 **11** *nk* **George Formby**[9] 1423 3-9-0 0.............................. JackMitchell 8 37
(Hugo Palmer) *hld up: nvr threatened* **9/1**[3]
43- **12** *3/4* **Bumbledom**[220] 6757 3-9-0 0.............................. PaulMulrennan 7 35
(Michael Dods) *midfield: rdn over 2f out: sn wknd* **16/1**
13 *6* **Dream House** 3-9-0 0.............................. RachelRichardson 10 19
(Tim Easterby) *trckd ldrs: rdn over 2f out: wknd* **50/1**
1m 25.29s (-0.11) **Going Correction** +0.225s/f (Good)
WFA 3 from 4yo 14lb **13** Ran SP% **119.5**
Speed ratings (Par 101): **105,104,102,102,100 97,97,93,91,90 90,89,82**
CSF £53.08 TOTE £24.10: £4.50, £1.10, £8.90; EX 79.50 Trifecta £2243.30.
Owner Ben Haslam Racing Syndicate **Bred** Tally-Ho Stud **Trained** Middleham Moor, N Yorks
FOCUS
An ordinary novice auction contest. The favourite raced keenly into a prominent pitch and proved vulnerable to the penalised winner in the final furlong. The level is a bit fluid.
T/Plt: £24.00 to a £1 stake. Pool: £68,028.05 - 2,064 winning units T/Qpdt: £19.90 to a £1 stake. Pool: £5,445.16 - 201.77 winning units **Andrew Sheret**

WINDSOR (R-H)
Monday, April 8
OFFICIAL GOING: Good (good to firm in places; 8.4)
Wind: Almost nil Weather: Overcast

1650 STARSPORTS.BET H'CAP 5f 21y
2:20 (2:20) (Class 6) (0-65,65) 3-Y-O
£3,105 (£924; £461; £300; £300; £300) **Stalls** Centre

Form RPR
5250 **1** **Ever Rock (IRE)**[11] 1384 3-8-1 **52** oh4 ow1.............. LauraCoughlan[(7)] 9 59
(J S Moore) *towards rr early: prog on outer 1/2-way: clsd on ldrs over 1f out: shkn up to ld ins fnl f: pushed clr: readily* **20/1**
324- **2** *2* **Cobweb Catcher**[159] 8730 3-9-4 **62**....................(h) CharlesBishop 6 62
(Rod Millman) *disp ld and racd against nr side rail: rdn over 1f out: hdd ins fnl f: no ch w wnr after but clung on for 2nd* **7/2**[1]
160- **3** *hd* **Valentino Sunrise**[149] 9006 3-8-12 **63**.................. ScottMcCullagh[(7)] 12 62
(Mick Channon) *cl up bhd ldrs: rdn wl over 1f out: kpt on fnl f to press for 2nd nr fin* **11/2**[2]
0-05 **4** *nk* **Brother Bentley**[42] 906 3-8-9 **53**....................(p) DavidProbert 8 51
(Ronald Harris) *chsd ldrs: rdn 2f out: styd on ins fnl f to press for a pl nr fin* **10/1**
6-36 **5** *hd* **Urban Highway (IRE)**[65] 555 3-9-3 **61**.............................. TomMarquand 14 58
(Tony Carroll) *wl in rr: rdn and prog on wd outside over 2f out: kpt on fnl f: nt pce to chal* **10/1**
04-1 **6** *2 3/4* **The Defiant**[42] 906 3-8-11 **55**.............................. LukeMorris 10 42
(Paul Midgley) *t.k.h: hld up bhd ldrs: rdn and nt qckn over 1f out: wknd ins fnl f* **11/2**[2]
60-0 **7** *1/2* **Carla Koala**[63] 605 3-8-10 **54**.............................. HollieDoyle 11 40
(Natalie Lloyd-Beavis) *disp ld: edgd lft u.p over 1f out: wknd fnl f* **50/1**

30-0 **8** ¾ **Maid From The Mist**[24] 1219 3-8-10 **54**.................. JoeyHaynes 4 37
(John Gallagher) *outpcd after 1f and urged along in rr: nvr on terms w ldrs after* **33/1**

-450 **9** 1¼ **Starchant**[26] 1170 3-9-7 **65**.................. LiamJones 13 45
(John Bridger) *w ldng pair: u.p whn bmpd over 1f out: wknd sharply ins fnl f* **10/1**

6354 **10** hd **Swiss Chime**[11] 1380 3-8-7 **56**.................. MeganNicholls(5) 2 34
(Dean Ivory) *a towards rr: rdn and no prog 2f out* **8/1**[3]

000- **11** nk **Vena D'Amore (IRE)**[166] 8532 3-9-0 **61**.................. JackDuern(3) 5 38
(Dean Ivory) *hld up wl in rr: rdn and no prog over 1f out* **20/1**

3304 **12** ¾ **Valley Belle (IRE)**[7] 1476 3-8-5 **56**..................(v) GraceMcEntee(7) 3 30
(Phil McEntee) *chsd ldrs: rdn and no prog 2f out: wknd over 1f out* **16/1**

600- **13** 7 **Princess Florence (IRE)**[167] 8509 3-8-2 **51** oh1..... DarraghKeenan(5) 1
(John Ryan) *in tch tl wknd qckly 2f out: t.o* **33/1**

1m 0.51s (0.41) **Going Correction** +0.075s/f (Good) **13 Ran SP% 114.6**
Speed ratings (Par 96): **99,95,95,95,94 90,89,88,86,85 85,84,73**
CSF £77.72 CT £394.35 TOTE £21.30: £5.80, £1.70, £2.10; EX 125.80 Trifecta £973.50.
Owner Ever Equine & J S Moore **Bred** Tom Twomey **Trained** Upper Lambourn, Berks
■ Melya was withdrawn. Price at time of withdrawal 14-1. Rule 4 applies to all bets - deduction 5p in the pound

FOCUS
A bit of a turn-up in the first race of Windsor's season, with a 20/1 shot, fit from the AW, coming clear of the market leaders bunched up behind. A minor pb from the winner.

1651 DOWNLOAD THE STAR SPORTS APP NOW! EBF NOVICE STKS 5f 21y
2:50 (2:50) (Class 5) 2-Y-O £3,752 (£1,116; £557; £278) **Stalls** Centre

Form RPR

1 **Chasanda** 2-9-0 **0**.................. TomMarquand 7 69
(David Evans) *w ldr: rdn to ld wl over 1f out: drvn clr fnl f* **25/1**

2 2½ **Out Of Breath** 2-9-5 **0**.................. NicolaCurrie 9 65+
(Jamie Osborne) *dwlt and s.i.s: detached in last tl rdn and prog on outer 2f out: styd on to take 2nd last 100yds: no ch to threaten (jockey said colt ran green early)* **25/1**

3 ¾ **Champagne Supanova (IRE)** 2-9-5 **0**.................. TomQueally 4 62+
(Richard Spencer) *dwlt: t.k.h: hld up in rr: sme prog and shifted lft 1f out: styd on to take 3rd nr fin* **12/1**

4 1 **Gin Gembre (FR)** 2-9-5 **0**.................. CliffordLee 1 59
(K R Burke) *cl up bhd ldrs: shkn up and nt qckn over 1f out: one pce after* **5/1**[2]

5 ½ **Copacabana Dancer (IRE)** 2-9-5 **0**.................. JasonWatson 5 57
(Joseph Tuite) *mde most to wl over 1f out: fdd fnl f* **33/1**

6 ¾ **Lexington Quest (IRE)** 2-9-5 **0**.................. SeanLevey 6 54
(Richard Hannon) *chsd ldrs: rdn 2f out: wknd over 1f out: wl btn whn impeded sltly ins fnl f* **5/2**[1]

7 ¾ **Fact Or Fable (IRE)** 2-9-5 **0**.................. CallumShepherd 10 52
(J S Moore) *towards rr: rdn and no prog whn bmpd jst ins fnl f* **66/1**

8 3 **Good Times Too** 2-9-5 **0**.................. CharlesBishop 11 41
(Mick Channon) *w ldng pair: wkng whn sltly impeded jst ins fnl f* **8/1**[3]

9 ½ **Dover Light** 2-9-2 **0**.................. JackDuern(3) 8 39
(Dean Ivory) *t.k.h: hld up in rr: wknd qckly over 1f out* **66/1**

1m 1.96s (1.86) **Going Correction** +0.075s/f (Good) **9 Ran SP% 77.7**
Speed ratings (Par 92): **88,84,82,81,80 79,78,73,72**
CSF £174.18 TOTE £24.00: £4.30, £4.40, £1.80; EX 262.20 Trifecta £828.60.
Owner E A R Morgans **Bred** E A R Morgans **Trained** Pandy, Monmouths
■ Dorchester Dom was withdrawn. Price at time of withdrawal 11-10f. Rule 4 applies to all bets - deduction 45p in the pound

FOCUS
An inconclusive event after the odds-on favourite \bDorchester Dom\p played up before the start, got loose and was withdrawn, leaving what looked like the stable's second string to come home strongly. The form has a fluid look to it.

1652 CALL STAR SPORTS ON 08000 521 321 NOVICE STKS 1m 2f
3:20 (3:20) (Class 5) 3-Y-O £3,752 (£1,116; £557; £278) **Stalls** Centre

Form RPR

02- **1** **Days Of Glory (CAN)**[151] 8954 3-9-5 **0**.................. RossaRyan 2 83+
(Richard Hannon) *trckd ldrs: pushed along and prog to take 2nd over 2f out: clsd over 1f out: shkn up to ld ins fnl f: sn in command* **13/8**[1]

-5 **2** 2 **Will Of Iron**[90] 128 3-9-5 **0**.................. NickyMackay 5 79
(John Gosden) *chsd ldrs: reminders to take 3rd 2f out: shkn up and styd on fnl f to take 2nd last strides* **8/1**

5 **3** hd **Lumination**[33] 1033 3-9-5 **0**.................. RobHornby 9 79
(Martyn Meade) *led: kicked clr 3f out: rdn 2f out: hdd and one pce ins fnl f: lost 2nd last strides* **9/1**

56 **4** 3½ **Teodora De Vega (IRE)**[27] 1165 3-9-0 **0**.................. HarryBentley 8 67
(Ralph Beckett) *chsd ldrs: pushed along 4f out: outpcd over 2f out: kpt on* **20/1**

4 **5** ¾ **Global Falcon**[33] 1034 3-9-5 **0**.................. GeraldMosse 1 71
(Charles Hills) *settled in midfield: pushed along over 3f out: lost pl over 2f out: n.d after but kpt on fnl f* **9/4**[2]

00- **6** nk **London Eye (USA)**[168] 8467 3-9-5 **0**.................. RyanMoore 4 70+
(Sir Michael Stoute) *hld up in last quartet: nudged along 3f out: kpt on steadily fnl 2f: likely to do bttr* **7/1**[3]

0 **7** 3¼ **Yellow Label (USA)**[13] 1344 3-9-2 **0**.................. JoshuaBryan(3) 3 63+
(Andrew Balding) *stdd s: hld up in last pair: effrt on wd outside over 2f out: no great prog over 1f out* **50/1**

8 3 **All Right** 3-9-0 **0**.................. DavidProbert 6 52
(Henry Candy) *hld up in midfield: pushed along whn sltly impeded over 2f out: no prog after* **33/1**

0- **9** nk **Mystical Jadeite**[187] 7905 3-9-5 **0**.................. LiamJones 12 57
(Grace Harris) *in tch in midfield: shkn up whn hmpd and swtchd lft over 2f out: fdd over 1f out* **200/1**

40- **10** 3 **Smith (IRE)**[319] 3017 3-9-5 **0**.................. CharlesBishop 7 51
(Eve Johnson Houghton) *chsd ldrs: effrt 3f out: n.m.r against rail over 2f out: sn wknd* **20/1**

11 2¾ **Onedownunder** 3-9-5 **0**.................. NicolaCurrie 11 45
(Jonathan Portman) *sn struggling in last: nvr a factor (jockey said gelding ran green)* **66/1**

12 6 **Lexington Warlord** 3-9-5 **0**.................. SeanLevey 10 33
(Richard Hannon) *chsd ldr: urged along 4f out: lost 2nd and wknd rapidly over 2f out* **33/1**

2m 9.85s (0.85) **Going Correction** +0.075s/f (Good) **12 Ran SP% 121.8**
Speed ratings (Par 98): **99,97,97,94,93 93,91,88,88,85 83,78**
CSF £15.27 TOTE £2.90: £1.40, £2.30, £2.40; EX 15.60 Trifecta £75.50.
Owner Derrick Smith & Mrs John Magnier & Michael Tabor **Bred** J & J Everatt & A Everatt-Meeuse **Trained** East Everleigh, Wilts

FOCUS
A steadily-run novice that saw the well-backed favourite win comfortably. The bare form looks ordinary

1653 HAPPY 70TH BIRTHDAY NICK CHAPMAN H'CAP 1m 2f
3:50 (3:50) (Class 5) (0-70,70) 4-Y-O+
£3,752 (£1,116; £557; £300; £300; £300) **Stalls** Centre

Form RPR

42/0 **1** **First Quest (USA)**[17] 1269 5-9-5 **68**.................. CharlieBennett 12 76
(Jim Boyle) *chsd ldrs: prog to take 2nd 1/2-way: rdn to ld 2f out: hrd pressed after: drvn out and hld on* **20/1**

003- **2** nk **Simbirsk**[188] 7877 4-9-4 **67**.................. ShaneKelly 14 74
(John O'Shea) *chsd ldr to 1/2-way: styd v cl up: chal 2f out: pressed wnr hrd after: nt qckn nr fin* **25/1**

064- **3** hd **Highfaluting (IRE)**[130] 9312 5-9-2 **65**.................. LukeMorris 10 72
(James Eustace) *hld up in midfield: rdn and prog over 2f out: chsd ldng pair over 1f out: styd on and gaining at fin* **8/1**

664 **4** 1¾ **Grange Walk (IRE)**[26] 1182 4-8-13 **65**.................. PaddyBradley(3) 2 69
(Pat Phelan) *hld up in midfield: rdn wl over 2f out: prog wl over 1f out: tk 4th ins fnl f: nvr able to chal* **14/1**

0330 **5** 1¾ **Global Style (IRE)**[34] 1025 4-9-4 **67**.................. GeorgeDowning 5 67
(Tony Carroll) *hld up in midfield: rdn 3f out: kpt on fnl 2f but nvr gng pce to threaten* **9/2**[2]

000- **6** nk **Essenaitch (IRE)**[129] 9332 6-9-2 **65**.................. AdamKirby 15 64
(David Evans) *led: rdn and hdd 2f out: fdd* **10/3**[1]

2344 **7** 4½ **Bond Angel**[12] 1369 4-9-1 **64**.................. JasonWatson 16 54
(David Evans) *prom: rdn 3f out: wknd wl over 1f out* **9/1**

030- **8** 3¼ **Yamuna River**[103] 9510 4-9-2 **65**..................(p) CharlesBishop 4 49
(Chris Gordon) *nvr gng wl: drvn in rr 4f out: sme prog on wd outside 3f out: no hdwy fnl 2f* **25/1**

00-0 **9** 1½ **Enzo (IRE)**[95] 33 4-8-9 **58**.................. EoinWalsh 8 39
(John Butler) *hld up: last 4f out but gng bttr than sme: limited prog fnl 3f: nvr remotely involved (jockey said gelding ran too free)* **20/1**

4006 **10** 1 **Baasha**[14] 1333 4-8-12 **61**..................(b) DanielMuscutt 1 40
(Ed Dunlop) *nvr beyond midfield: rdn and no prog 3f out: wknd 2f out* **16/1**

0-60 **11** 8 **Face Like Thunder**[67] 507 4-9-2 **65**.................. LiamKeniry 3 28
(John Butler) *a towards rr: wknd over 2f out* **16/1**

225- **12** 6 **Pilot Wings (IRE)**[103] 9706 4-9-7 **70**.................. DavidProbert 6 21
(David Dennis) *chsd ldrs tl wknd qckly 3f out* **11/2**[3]

200- **13** nk **Camakasi (IRE)**[122] 9447 8-9-5 **68**.................. TomMarquand 13 18
(Ali Stronge) *s.v.s: detached in last: jst in tch at bk of field 4f out: sn rdn and wknd (jockey said gelding was slowly away)* **12/1**

453 **14** 3 **Sweet Nature (IRE)**[33] 1042 4-9-2 **65**.................. LiamJones 11 9
(Laura Mongan) *chsd ldrs tl wknd rapidly 3f out* **25/1**

00-0 **15** 1¾ **Brigand**[95] 45 4-8-5 **59**.................. DarraghKeenan(5) 7
(John Butler) *a wl in rr: nvr a factor* **50/1**

2m 8.7s (-0.30) **Going Correction** +0.075s/f (Good) **15 Ran SP% 126.9**
Speed ratings (Par 103): **104,103,103,102,100 100,96,94,93,92 85,81,80,78,77**
CSF £440.32 CT £4307.02 TOTE £22.40: £6.50, £7.90, £2.50; EX 818.00 Trifecta £2108.70.
Owner The Waterboys **Bred** Paul Tackett **Trained** Epsom, Surrey
■ Stewards' Enquiry : Shane Kelly two-day ban; misuse of whip (Apr 22-23)

FOCUS
A close finish with a quirky character holding off two handicap debutants. It paid to race prominently. The winner is perhaps the best guide to the form.

1654 WATCH THE £BETTINGPEOPLE VIDEOS STARSPORTSBET.CO.UK H'CAP 6f 12y
4:20 (4:20) (Class 3) (0-90,92) 4-Y-O+
£7,158 (£2,143; £1,071; £535; £267; £134) **Stalls** Centre

Form RPR

420- **1** **Diamond Dougal (IRE)**[163] 8632 4-9-7 **89**.................. CharlesBishop 2 96
(Mick Channon) *trckd ldrs: clsd over 1f out: rdn to ld ins fnl f: styd on* **4/1**[2]

-362 **2** ½ **Equitation**[30] 1098 5-8-13 **81**..................(t) SeanLevey 14 88
(Stuart Williams) *hld up in 8th: prog 2f out: nt clr run bhd ldrs jst over 1f out tl swtchd lft ins fnl f: r.o to take 2nd last 75yds: jst hld (jockey said gelding was denied a clear run inside the final furlong)* **6/1**

530- **3** 1¼ **Handytalk (IRE)**[175] 8259 6-8-10 **78**.................. DavidEgan 12 80
(Rod Millman) *w ldr: led wl over 1f out: hdd and no ex ins fnl f* **20/1**

035- **4** 1¾ **Private Matter**[171] 8370 5-9-2 **84**.................. DavidProbert 11 81
(Amy Murphy) *in tch on outer: rdn and tried to cl over 1f out: one pce after* **16/1**

200- **5** hd **Major Pusey**[194] 7661 7-8-11 **79**.................. JoeyHaynes 3 75
(John Gallagher) *led to wl over 1f out: fdd fnl f* **25/1**

100- **6** ½ **Embour (IRE)**[249] 5654 4-9-6 **88**.................. TomMarquand 7 82
(Richard Hannon) *trckd ldrs: shkn up 2f out: stl cl up over 1f out: fdd* **9/1**

211- **7** ¾ **Beyond Equal**[187] 7909 4-9-6 **88**.................. AdamKirby 6 80
(Stuart Kittow) *t.k.h: w ldr: stl upsides 2f out: fdd over 1f out* **11/4**[1]

10-4 **8** ¾ **Lightning Charlie**[16] 1290 7-9-2 **84**.................. JasonWatson 9 74
(Amanda Perrett) *dwlt: hld up in last pair: rdn against nr side rail 2f out: no great prog* **9/1**

000- **9** ¾ **Gabrial The Saint (IRE)**[198] 7510 4-9-5 **92**..................(w) SeanDavis(5) 10 80
(Richard Fahey) *hld up in last trio: shkn up and no real prog 2f out* **5/1**[3]

6-10 **10** 2¼ **Doc Sportello (IRE)**[30] 1098 7-9-4 **86**.................. GeorgeDowning 13 67
(Tony Carroll) *hld up in last quartet: shkn up and no prog 2f out: nvr in it* **50/1**

050- **11** ½ **Mostahel**[216] 6913 5-8-12 **80**.................. LukeMorris 1 59
(Paul Midgley) *cl up tl wknd wl over 1f out* **16/1**

1m 12.3s (0.20) **Going Correction** +0.075s/f (Good) **11 Ran SP% 120.0**
Speed ratings (Par 107): **101,100,98,96,96 95,94,93,92,89 88**
CSF £28.34 CT £444.39 TOTE £4.00: £1.40, £2.40, £6.30; EX 35.60 Trifecta £446.50.
Owner Insignia Racing (flag) **Bred** Con Marnane **Trained** West Ilsley, Berks
■ Stewards' Enquiry : Sean Levey two-day ban; misuse of whip (Apr 22-23)

FOCUS
A competitive handicap run at a good pace. The winner posted at least a minor best, with the second rated to his best.

1655 ROYAL WINDSOR HORSE SHOW H'CAP 1m 31y
4:50 (4:50) (Class 5) (0-75,77) 4-Y-O+
£3,752 (£1,116; £557; £300; £300; £300) **Stalls** Low

Form RPR

243- **1** **Mr Tyrrell (IRE)**[284] 4308 5-9-9 **77**.................. RyanMoore 9 83
(Richard Hannon) *dwlt: hld up in 7th: cajoled along to make prog over 2f out: urged into the ld jst ins fnl f: hrd rdn and jnd last 75yds: jst prevailed (vet said gelding lost it's left hind shoe)* **5/1**[3]

The Form Book Flat 2019, Raceform Ltd, Newbury, RG14 5SJ

4-22 **2** *nse* **Hackbridge**[30] 1095 4-9-2 **73**....................(v) PaddyBradley(3) 5 79
(Pat Phelan) *t.k.h: hld up in 6th: rdn 2f out: prog fnl f: jnd wnr last 75yds: jst pipped* **10/1**
20-1 **3** *1* **Gainsay**[24] 1216 4-9-1 **69**.................... RobHornby 12 73
(Jonathan Portman) *trckd ldr: led 2f out: rdn and hdd jst ins fnl f: one pce (vet said filly lost it's right fore shoe)* **17/2**
3565 **4** *½* **The Warrior (IRE)**[10] 1392 7-9-3 **71**....................(b) TomMarquand 11 74
(Lee Carter) *slowly away: hld up in last trio: rdn and prog 2f out: drvn and ch fnl f: nt qckn* **14/1**
-120 **5** *1* **Mr Mac**[38] 962 5-9-3 **71**.................... CharlesBishop 1 71
(Peter Hedger) *wl away: t.k.h and trckd ldng pair: rdn and no rspnse over 1f out: one pce after* **7/1**
4402 **6** *nse* **High Acclaim (USA)**[34] 1025 5-9-7 **75**....................(p) DavidProbert 6 75
(Roger Teal) *slowly away: sn wl in tch: rdn and nt qckn jst over 2f out: one pce after* **7/2**[1]
50-0 **7** *1¼* **Duke Of North (IRE)**[10] 1392 7-8-2 **63**.................... IsobelFrancis(7) 7 61
(Jim Boyle) *dwlt: hld up in detached last: pushed along over 2f out: kpt on steadily over 1f out: nvr involved (jockey said gelding was slowly away and ran too free early on)* **16/1**
-040 **8** *½* **Nezar (IRE)**[14] 1329 8-9-3 **71**.................... AdamKirby 4 67
(Dean Ivory) *hld up in last trio: pushed along over 2f out: limited hdwy over 1f out and nvr in it* **4/1**[2]
145- **9** *1¼* **Uther Pendragon (IRE)**[115] 9532 4-9-8 **76**..........(p) JosephineGordon 8 70
(J S Moore) *trckd ldng trio: lost pl wl over 1f out: fdd (jockey said gelding suffered interference in running)* **12/1**
-405 **10** *2½* **Cuttin' Edge (IRE)**[10] 1392 5-8-7 **61** oh1....................(b[1]) MartinDwyer 2 49
(William Muir) *plld hrd: sn led: hdd over 2f out: wknd over 1f out* **11/1**

1m 44.29s (-0.21) **Going Correction** +0.075s/f (Good) **10** Ran SP% **119.6**
Speed ratings (Par 103): **104,103,102,102,101 101,100,99,98,95**
CSF £55.63 CT £432.41 TOTE £4.10: £1.90, £3.20, £3.30; EX 25.30 Trifecta £167.20.
Owner Robert Tyrrell **Bred** Wardstown Stud Ltd **Trained** East Everleigh, Wilts

FOCUS
A tight handicap produced an appropriately tight finish with the first four fighting it out. The winner is rated in line with his previous best.

1656 FIRST FOR INDUSTRY JOBS VISIT STARRECRUITMENT.BET H'CAP 1m 31y
5:20 (5:20) (Class 5) (0-70,70) 3-Y-O
£3,752 (£1,116; £557; £300; £300; £300) **Stalls** Low

Form RPR
40-2 **1** **Lethal Missile (IRE)**[16] 1285 3-9-4 **69**.................... AdamKirby 1 76+
(Clive Cox) *chsd ldrs in 6th: rdn over 2f out: grad clsd over 1f out: drvn ahd ins fnl f: styd on* **6/4**[1]
-124 **2** *½* **Dancing Jo**[17] 1264 3-8-10 **68**.................... ScottMcCullagh(7) 6 74
(Mick Channon) *pressed ldng pair: rdn to chal 2f out: led jst over 1f out to ins fnl f: kpt on* **9/1**
056- **3** *2* **Perfecimperfection (IRE)**[131] 9290 3-9-0 **68**.......... GabrieleMalune(3) 9 71
(Marco Botti) *hld up in midfield: nt clr run and swtchd rt 2f out: tried to cl over 1f out: kpt on fnl f to take 3rd last stride (jockey said filly was denied a clear run)* **16/1**
266- **4** *nse* **Ventura Bay (IRE)**[152] 8929 3-8-11 **67**.................... SeanDavis(5) 14 68
(Richard Fahey) *led: hung lft bnd 5f out: hdd and fdd jst over 1f out (jockey said gelding ran slightly wide on the bend)* **10/1**
-640 **5** *1* **Mushaageb (IRE)**[16] 1285 3-9-2 **67**....................(p[1]) DavidEgan 8 66
(Roger Varian) *pressed ldr: carried lft bnd 5f out: lost 2nd over 1f out: fdd (jockey said gelding suffered interference on the bend)* **10/1**
446- **6** *2¼* **Petits Fours**[166] 8547 3-8-11 **69**.................... AledBeech(7) 12 63
(Charlie Fellowes) *hld up towards rr: shkn up over 2f out: nvr on terms but modest late prog* **33/1**
4113 **7** *1½* **Sir Ox (USA)**[54] 698 3-9-3 **68**....................(p) LukeMorris 5 59
(Robert Cowell) *hld up: n.m.r after 1f and dropped to last trio: rdn and modest prog over 2f out: wknd over 1f out* **7/1**[2]
003- **8** *½* **Dark Glory (IRE)**[172] 8336 3-9-4 **69**.................... MartinDwyer 3 59
(Brian Meehan) *t.k.h: hld up wl in rr: rdn and no prog 2f out: wknd over 1f out* **8/1**[3]
003- **9** *¾* **Jungle Juice (IRE)**[175] 8277 3-8-10 **68**.................... GeorgeBass(7) 10 56
(Mick Channon) *chsd ldrs: rdn over 2f out: wknd over 1f out* **25/1**
23-0 **10** *1¼* **Barasti Dancer (IRE)**[30] 1104 3-9-5 **70**.................... CliffordLee 2 57+
(K R Burke) *pressed ldrs on outer: rdn over 2f out: stl in tch over 1f out: sn wknd* **9/1**
5-0 **11** *2½* **Champagne Marengo (IRE)**[12] 1360 3-9-4 **69**.......... StevieDonohoe 7 49
(Ian Williams) *a in rr: bhd over 2f out* **50/1**
100- **12** *8* **Knockabout Queen**[215] 6948 3-9-2 **67**.................... CharlesBishop 11 29
(Dai Burchell) *s.v.s: a in rr: in tch over 2f out: sn wknd (jockey said filly ran too free)* **50/1**

1m 43.92s (-0.58) **Going Correction** +0.075s/f (Good) **12** Ran SP% **118.4**
Speed ratings (Par 98): **105,104,102,102,101 99,97,97,96,95 92,84**
CSF £15.03 CT £160.99 TOTE £2.40: £1.20, £2.60, £4.90; EX 16.20 Trifecta £179.60.
Owner B Allen, G Hill & N Wagland **Bred** J McGlynn & C Lyons **Trained** Lambourn, Berks
■ Stewards' Enquiry : Scott McCullagh four-day ban; misuse of whip (Apr 22-25)

FOCUS
The market saw only one winner of this moderate handicap, but it took the length of the straight for the favourite to get on top. The runner-up looks the key to the form.
T/Jkpt: Not Won. T/Plt: £11,654.70 to a £1 stake. Pool: £85,414.77 - 5.35 winning units T/Qpdt: £147.50 to a £1 stake. Pool: £10,689.96 - 53.60 winning units **Jonathan Neesom**

1489 CHANTILLY (R-H)
Monday, April 8

OFFICIAL GOING: Polytrack: standard; turf: good

1657a PRIX DU PREMIER PAS (MAIDEN) (UNRACED 2YO) (TURF) 5f
2:00 2-Y-O **£12,162** (£4,864; £3,648; £2,432; £1,216)

RPR
1 **My Love's Passion (FR)** 2-8-13 0.................... ChristopheSoumillon 7 84
(Y Barberot, France) **56/10**[3]
2 *1½* **Crew Dragon (FR)** 2-9-2 0.................... TonyPiccone 12 82
(M Delcher Sanchez, France) **10/1**
3 *½* **Ammobaby (FR)** 2-8-13 0.................... TheoBachelot 10 77
(H De Nicolay, France) **26/1**
4 *2½* **Run Like Hell (FR)** 2-8-13 0.................... MaximeGuyon 9 68
(Jane Soubagne, France) **51/10**[2]
5 *snk* **Mehanydream (FR)** 2-9-2 0.................... StephanePasquier 13 70
(C Boutin, France) **15/1**
6 *1½* **Miss Bassett (FR)** 2-8-13 0.................... AntoineWerle 3 62
(T Lemer, France) **19/1**
7 *3* **Diva Du Dancing (FR)** 2-8-13 0.................... Pierre-CharlesBoudot 6 51
(T Castanheira, France) **15/1**
8 *¾* **Bene Bene (FR)** 2-8-13 0.................... MlleCoraliePacaut(3) 14 52
(M Boutin, France) **20/1**
9 *nk* **Baileys Courage (FR)** 2-8-13 0.................... AurelienLemaitre 2 47
(J-V Toux, France) **31/1**
10 *hd* **Yomogi (FR)** 2-8-13 0.................... PierreBazire 4 47
(Hiroo Shimizu, France) **18/1**
11 *nse* **Gran Risa (IRE)** 2-8-13 0.................... CristianDemuro 8 47
(A Giorgi, Italy) **26/1**
12 *3½* **Lost In France (IRE)** 2-8-13 0.................... AntoineHamelin 11 34
(Matthieu Palussiere, France) **33/10**[1]
13 *1¼* **Rioviejo (FR)** 2-9-2 0.................... MickaelBarzalona 15 32
(X Thomas-Demeaulte, France) **84/10**
14 *1* **Look At Him** 2-9-2 0.................... Louis-PhilippeBeuzelin 1 29
(Jo Hughes, France) *wl into stride: disp ld early: pushed along over 3f out: rdn and outpcd 2f out: no ex over 1f out and kpt on one pce* **26/1**
15 *1½* **Adehaine (IRE)** 2-8-8 0....................(b[1]) JeremieMonteiro(8) 5 23
(N Caullery, France) **34/1**

58.14s (-0.16) **15** Ran SP% **119.1**
PARI-MUTUEL (all including 1 euro stake): WIN 6.60; PLACE 2.80, 3.50, 6.80; DF 45.50.
Owner Passion Racing Club **Bred** Pat Chedeville **Trained** France

1658a PRIX DU BOIS DE LA VIGNE (CLAIMER) (3YO FILLIES) (ALL-WEATHER TRACK) (POLYTRACK) 6f 110y(P)
4:20 3-Y-O **£8,558** (£3,423; £2,567; £1,711; £855)

RPR
1 **Capla Gilda**[55] 3-9-0 0.................... MlleLeaBails(8) 1 76
(Andrea Marcialis, France) **7/5**[1]
2 *hd* **Elieden (IRE)**[73] 401 3-8-11 0....................(p) AlexisBadel 11 64
(Gay Kelleway) *sn prom: settled in 2nd: shkn up over 2f out: rdn to chal over 1f out: drvn and upsides ins fnl f: ev ch fnl 100yds: jst failed* **11/1**
3 *½* **Million Dreams (FR)**[60] 3-8-11 0....................(p) JeromeMoutard(4) 8 67
(F-H Graffard, France) **31/1**
4 *2* **Philippine Cobra (FR)**[115] 3-9-3 0..............(p) AlexandreChesneau(5) 2 68
(G Botti, France) **14/1**
5 *nk* **Dolynska (FR)**[11] 3-8-6 0....................(p) ThomasTrullier(5) 5 56
(M Boutin, France) **55/1**
6 *hd* **Sandy Dream (FR)**[54] 3-9-2 0....................(b) MickaelBarzalona 10 61
(Mme R Philippon, France) **11/2**[3]
7 *1¼* **Aquilina**[54] 3-9-1 0.................... Pierre-CharlesBoudot 12 56
(F Rossi, France) **43/10**[2]
8 *1¼* **Hinemoa (FR)**[37] 993 3-8-6.................... MlleLauraGrosso(9) 9 52
(N Clement, France) *mid-div: angled out and asked for effrt over 2f fr home: unable qck* **84/10**
9 *1¾* **Florissante (FR)**[75] 3-8-11 0.................... IoritzMendizabal 3 43
(J Bertran De Balanda, France) **22/1**
10 *10* **La Miura (FR)**[55] 3-8-13 0.................... TeddyHautbois(5) 7 21
(T Castanheira, France) **49/1**
11 *2* **Hemera (FR)** 3-9-1 0....................(p) AntoineWerle 4 13
(T Lemer, France) **20/1**
12 *2* **Phaidra Jasmin (FR)**[232] 6336 3-8-11 0....................(b) TheoBachelot 6 3
(Mlle L Kneip, France) **49/1**

1m 17.89s **12** Ran SP% **119.6**
PARI-MUTUEL (all including 1 euro stake): WIN 2.40; PLACE 1.40, 3.00, 5.40; DF 12.60.
Owner Montgomery Motto **Bred** Alvediston Stud **Trained** France

PONTEFRACT (L-H)
Tuesday, April 9

OFFICIAL GOING: Good to firm (good in places; watered; 8.4)
Wind: Fresh against Weather: Sunny periods

1659 ROA OWNERS' JACKPOT H'CAP (DIV I) 1m 6y
2:00 (2:00) (Class 5) (0-70,72) 4-Y-O+
£5,175 (£1,540; £769; £384; £300; £300) **Stalls** Low

Form RPR
5400 **1** **Mont Kinabalu (IRE)**[31] 1099 4-9-6 **69**.................... TomEaves 6 76
(Kevin Ryan) *hld up towards rr: hdwy over 2f out: n.m.r and swtchd rt to outer over 1f out: rdn and styd on strly fnl f to ld last 50yds* **9/1**
64-3 **2** *½* **Arctic Sea**[8] 1479 5-9-8 **71**.................... PJMcDonald 7 77
(Paul Cole) *trckd ldrs: hdwy 2f out: swtchd rt and rdn to chal over 1f out: slt ld ins fnl f: sn drvn: hdd and no ex last 50yds* **11/4**[1]
0-60 **3** *1¾* **Celtic Artisan (IRE)**[11] 1399 8-8-12 **61**....................(bt) CamHardie 2 63
(Rebecca Menzies) *trckd ldrs on inner: pushed along over 3f out: outpcd over 2f out and sn rdn: styng on along inner whn n.m.r over 1f out: kpt on wl towards fin* **7/1**[2]
300- **4** *2¼* **Buckland Beau**[165] 8598 8-8-10 **66**.................... AledBeech(7) 11 63
(Charlie Fellowes) *trckd ldrs on outer: cl up 1/2-way: rdn to chal wl over 1f out: ev ch tl drvn and kpt on same pce fnl f* **25/1**
00 **5** *hd* **Star Of Valour (IRE)**[12] 1381 4-9-2 **65**....................(h) DougieCostello 1 62
(David C Griffiths) *led: pushed along over 3f out: rdn 2f out: drvn and hdd ins fnl f: grad wknd (jockey said gelding hung left in the final 3f)* **33/1**
310- **6** *¾* **Thornaby Nash**[196] 7641 8-8-8 **62**.................... ConnorMurtagh(5) 8 57
(Jason Ward) *trckd ldrs: hdwy 2f out: rdn over 1f out: kpt on same pce fnl f* **33/1**
150- **7** *2½* **Straight Ash (IRE)**[186] 7961 4-9-0 **66**.................... BenRobinson(3) 12 56
(Ollie Pears) *hld up in rr: hdwy 2f out: rdn over 1f out: kpt on fnl f* **33/1**
400- **8** *6* **Magwadiri (IRE)**[122] 9465 5-8-10 **59**.................... EoinWalsh 4 35
(Mark Loughnane) *dwlt: a towards rr* **16/1**
460- **9** *3½* **Quoteline Direct**[169] 8476 6-9-9 **72**....................(h) FrannyNorton 3 41
(Micky Hammond) *a towards rr* **7/1**[2]
20-2 **10** *1* **Billy Roberts (IRE)**[45] 886 6-9-5 **68**.................... JasonHart 10 34
(Richard Whitaker) *sn cl up on outer: disp ld over 3f out: rdn along 2f out: drvn and wknd over 1f out* **11/4**[1]
100- **11** *3½* **Pumaflor (IRE)**[196] 7640 7-8-12 **61**....................(p) AndrewMullen 9 20
(Philip Kirby) *in rr: hdwy on outer and in tch 1/2-way: rdn along 3f out: sn wknd* **33/1**

204- **12** *1* **Farhh Away**[263] 5162 4-9-7 **70**........................ PaulMulrennan 5 27
(Michael Dods) *wnt lft s: cl up: rdn along over 3f out: sn wknd* **8/1**[3]

1m 45.79s (-0.11) **Going Correction** -0.025s/f (Good) **12** Ran SP% **120.9**
Speed ratings (Par 103): **99,98,96,94,94 93,91,85,81,80 77,76**
CSF £33.03 CT £186.54 TOTE £9.70: £3.00, £1.50, £2.50; EX 42.50 Trifecta £258.40.
Owner JCG Chua & CK Ong 1 **Bred** Tally-Ho Stud **Trained** Hambleton, N Yorks

FOCUS
The watered ground was given as good to firm, good in places (GoingStick 8.4). Five of these had already run this season and four of them finished in the first five. The runner-up helps set the level.

1660 ROA OWNERS' JACKPOT H'CAP (DIV II) 1m 6y
2:30 (2:31) (Class 5) (0-70,72) 4-Y-O+
£5,175 (£1,540; £769; £384; £300; £300) **Stalls** Low

Form RPR
260- **1** **Casement (IRE)**[200] 6108 5-9-9 **72**........................ AlistairRawlinson 12 81
(Michael Appleby) *led 1f: trckd ldr: led again 2f out: rdn clr over 1f out: kpt on wl* **10/1**

-360 **2** *1 3/4* **Mr Carbonator**[13] 1367 4-8-8 **60**........................ JamieGormley(3) 8 65
(Philip Kirby) *hld up towards rr: hdwy on wd outside wl over 1f out: sn rdn: styd on wl fnl f* **11/2**[2]

-225 **3** *1 1/4* **Zodiakos (IRE)**[68] 507 6-9-3 **66**........................(p) BenCurtis 7 68
(Roger Fell) *trckd ldrs: hdwy over 2f out: rdn to chse wnr over 1f out: sn drvn and kpt on same pce* **10/3**[1]

616- **4** *hd* **Ascot Week (USA)**[112] 9593 5-9-3 **66**........................(v) JasonHart 10 68
(John Quinn) *hld up in tch: hdwy 2f out: rdn to chse ldrs and edgd lft over 1f out: drvn and kpt on fnl f* **16/1**

500- **5** *3/4* **Agar's Plough**[165] 8599 4-9-7 **70**........................ NathanEvans 9 70+
(Michael Easterby) *hld up in rr: hdwy on inner 2f out: nt clr run and swtchd rt over 1f out: swtchd wd to outer and rdn ent fnl f: kpt on wl towards fin* **12/1**

045- **6** *1/2* **Jo's Girl (IRE)**[169] 8476 4-9-7 **70**........................(h[1] w) DougieCostello 6 69
(Micky Hammond) *in tch: hdwy over 2f out: rdn along wl over 1f out: kpt on same pce fnl f* **8/1**

200- **7** *1 1/4* **Im Dapper Too**[157] 8828 8-9-0 **63**........................ SamJames 4 59
(John Davies) *trckd ldrs on inner: rdn along over 2f out: grad wknd* **25/1**

4-50 **8** *1/2* **Beverley Bullet**[13] 1367 6-9-4 **67**........................(p) JoeFanning 3 62
(Lawrence Mullaney) *trckd ldng pair on inner: pushed along 2f out: sn rdn and wknd* **15/2**

2030 **9** *4* **Squire**[8] 1482 8-8-9 **61**........................(tp) JaneElliott(3) 11 50
(Marjorie Fife) *cl up: led after 1f: rdn along and hdd 2f out: sn wknd (jockey said gelding missed the break)* **16/1**

-655 **10** *1 1/4* **Steal The Scene (IRE)**[40] 944 7-8-13 **62**........................ JackMitchell 5 46
(Kevin Frost) *a towards rr* **7/1**[3]

200- **11** *9* **Hitman**[196] 7640 6-9-6 **69**........................(w) DanielTudhope 2 33
(Rebecca Bastiman) *a towards rr* **10/1**

-200 **12** *4 1/2* **Hediddodinthe (IRE)**[14] 1341 5-8-7 **59**........................ WilliamCox(3) 1 13
(Peter Winks) *awkward and dwlt s: hdwy on inner and in tch over 4f out: rdn along 3f out: sn wknd (jockey said gelding was never travelling)* **66/1**

1m 44.51s (-1.39) **Going Correction** -0.025s/f (Good) **12** Ran SP% **116.8**
Speed ratings (Par 103): **105,103,102,101,101 100,99,98,94,93 84,80**
CSF £63.19 CT £229.67 TOTE £12.50: £3.20, £2.40, £1.70; EX 87.60 Trifecta £518.90.
Owner John Phelan **Bred** Mrs Clodagh McStay **Trained** Oakham, Rutland

FOCUS
The quicker of the two divisions by 1.28sec, and the winner has more to give for his new yard. The form could be rated a tad higher.

1661 BRITISH STALLION STUDS "HIGH-RISE" EBF NOVICE STKS (PLUS 10 RACE) 1m 4f 5y
3:00 (3:00) (Class 3) 3-Y-O
£9,337 (£2,796; £1,398) **Stalls** Low

Form RPR
2 **1** **Rochester House (IRE)**[8] 1484 3-9-5 0........................ FrannyNorton 1 80+
(Mark Johnston) *mde all: pushed along and qcknd 2f out: rdn clr over 1f out: kpt on strly* **11/8**[2]

24- **2** *3* **Rowland Ward**[215] 6995 3-9-5 0........................ HarryBentley 3 75
(Ralph Beckett) *dwlt: sn w ldng pair and t.k.h: trckd wnr after 4f: effrt 3f out: rdn along 2f out: drvn over 1f out: kpt on same pce* **8/11**[1]

0- **3** *4 1/2* **Nordano (GER)**[139] 9172 3-9-5 0........................ JoeFanning 2 68
(Mark Johnston) *cl up 4f: trckd ldng pair: pushed along over 3f out: rdn over 2f out: sn one pce* **14/1**[3]

2m 41.69s (0.59) **Going Correction** -0.025s/f (Good) **3** Ran SP% **106.7**
Speed ratings (Par 102): **97,95,92**
CSF £2.76 TOTE £2.00; EX 2.20 Trifecta £2.40.
Owner John Brown & Megan Dennis **Bred** Stall Ullmann **Trained** Middleham Moor, N Yorks

FOCUS
Just the three runners but the winner looks useful and one to keep on side. The race has been given a token rating to some extent.

1662 JOIN MORE THAN 8000 ROA MEMBERS H'CAP 6f
3:30 (3:31) (Class 3) (0-95,93) 3-Y-O
£7,470 (£2,236; £1,118; £559; £279; £140) **Stalls** Low

Form RPR
005- **1** **Ventura Ocean (IRE)**[185] 7987 3-8-11 **88**........................ SeanDavis(5) 7 94
(Richard Fahey) *towards rr: pushed along and hdwy over 2f out: rdn on wd outside to chse ldrs wl over 1f out: styd on to chal ins fnl f: sn drvn and edgd lft: led last 50yds* **8/1**

405- **2** *1/2* **Chapelli**[220] 6798 3-9-7 **93**........................ JamesDoyle 2 97
(Mark Johnston) *trckd ldr: effrt over 2f out: rdn to ld 1 1/2f out: drvn ins fnl f: hdd and no ex last 50yds* **13/2**[2]

114 **3** *1 1/4* **Dahawi**[31] 1104 3-8-7 **79**........................(t[1]) BenCurtis 6 79
(Hugo Palmer) *chsd ldrs: rdn along 2f out: drvn over 1f out: kpt on same pce* **8/1**

610- **4** *nk* **Wild Edric**[192] 7751 3-8-11 **83**........................ RichardKingscote 12 82
(Tom Dascombe) *sn led: rdn along over 2f out: hdd 1 1/2f out: sn drvn and kpt on same pce* **8/1**

21-3 **5** *3 1/2* **Edgewood**[39] 972 3-8-5 **77**........................ LukeMorris 11 65
(James Bethell) *trckd ldrs: rdn along over 2f out: drvn and wknd over 1f out* **8/1**

416- **6** *1/2* **Look Out Louis**[297] 3848 3-8-5 **77**........................ RachelRichardson 3 63
(Tim Easterby) *chsd ldrs: rdn along over 2f out: sn one pce* **25/1**

040- **7** *1 3/4* **Kinks**[178] 8193 3-9-5 **91**........................ SilvestreDeSousa 4 72+
(Mick Channon) *in rr: pushed along and swtchd rt to outer over 2f out: sn rdn and nvr a factor* **5/2**[1]

211- **8** *1* **Lorton**[185] 7983 3-8-13 **85**........................ PaulMulrennan 8 62
(Julie Camacho) *towards rr: rdn along over 2f out: n.d* **7/1**[3]

0-12 **9** *6* **Fair Alibi**[26] 1193 3-8-2 **74** oh1........................ JamesSullivan 1 32
(Tom Tate) *in tch: rdn along over 2f out: sn btn* **14/1**

610- **10** *1 1/2* **Carey Street (IRE)**[337] 2489 3-8-4 **76**........................ AndrewMullen 5 29
(John Quinn) *dwlt: a in rr* **28/1**

22-5 **11** *14* **Punjab Mail**[12] 1388 3-8-4 **76**........................ DavidEgan 10
(Ian Williams) *chsd ldrs: rdn along over 2f out: sn wknd* **25/1**

1m 16.47s (-0.63) **Going Correction** -0.025s/f (Good) **11** Ran SP% **116.7**
Speed ratings (Par 102): **103,102,100,100,95 94,92,91,83,81 62**
CSF £57.35 CT £440.64 TOTE £9.30: £2.70, £2.00, £2.40; EX 68.30 Trifecta £454.10.
Owner Middleham Park Racing Xix & Partner **Bred** Mrs Renata Coleman **Trained** Musley Bank, N Yorks

FOCUS
An open sprint handicap run at a decent pace. The first four finished clear.

1663 ENJOY RACEHORSE OWNERSHIP JAMAICAN FLIGHT H'CAP (ROUND 1 PONTEFRACT STAYERS' CHAMPIONSHIP) 2m 2f 2y
4:00 (4:00) (Class 5) (0-75,73) 4-Y-O+
£3,881 (£1,155; £577; £300; £300; £300) **Stalls** Low

Form RPR
636- **1** **Valkenburg**[35] 9721 4-9-0 **63**........................ JoeFanning 2 73
(Harriet Bethell) *trckd ldrs: pushed along and outpcd over 3f out: hdwy on inner 2f out: rdn to chse ldr over 1f out: kpt on wl u.p to chal ins fnl f: led nr fin* **10/1**[3]

120- **2** *hd* **So Near So Farhh**[169] 8480 4-9-1 **64**........................ SilvestreDeSousa 6 74
(Mick Channon) *prom: trckd ldr bef 1/2-way: led over 4f out: rdn clr wl over 1f out: jnd and drvn ins fnl f: kpt on gamely: hdd and no ex nr fin* **11/4**[1]

111- **3** *5* **Bailarico (IRE)**[46] 5661 6-9-7 **73**........................(p w) ThomasGreatrex(5) 11 75
(Warren Greatrex) *trckd ldrs: hdwy 5f out: cl up over 3f out: rdn along 2f out: drvn wl over 1f out: kpt on one pce* **11/4**[1]

54-6 **4** *11* **The Resdev Way**[6] 1524 6-9-3 **64**........................ KevinStott 8 55
(Philip Kirby) *in rr: hdwy over 4f out: rdn along 3f out: kpt on fnl 2f: nvr nr to chal* **12/1**

000/ **5** *8* **Strait Run (IRE)**[23] 7290 8-8-7 **54** oh4........................(tp) AndrewMullen 1 37
(Micky Hammond) *hld up in rr: hdwy 5f out: rdn along 3f out: kpt on u.p fnl 2f: n.d* **50/1**

0100 **6** *13* **Galitello**[15] 1330 4-8-13 **62**........................(b[1]) PJMcDonald 4 35
(Mark Johnston) *chsd ldr: cl up over 4f out: rdn along over 3f out: drvn over 2f out and sn wknd* **6/1**[2]

0-56 **7** *2* **Akavit (IRE)**[29] 1144 7-9-7 **68**........................ CallumShepherd 3 36+
(Ed de Giles) *hld up in rr: rapid hdwy on outer over 5f out: cl up 3f out: rdn along and ev ch over 2f out: sn drvn and wknd (jockey said gelding became tired and had no more to give in the final furlong)* **11/4**[1]

0-00 **8** *20* **Lots Ov (IRE)**[38] 984 5-8-7 **54** oh9........................ FrannyNorton 5
(John Wainwright) *midfield: rdn along over 5f out: sn outpcd and bhd* **100/1**

015- **9** *2 1/2* **Leodis (IRE)**[112] 6763 7-8-11 **58**........................ GrahamLee 9
(Micky Hammond) *in tch: pushed along 6f out: rdn over 5f out: outpcd and bhd fnl 3f* **25/1**

00-0 **10** *74* **Dutch Melody**[7] 1500 5-8-0 **54** oh9........................ VictorSantos(7) 7
(Lucinda Egerton) *led: rdn along over 5f out: hdd over 4f out: sn wknd* **100/1**

3m 59.73s (-7.97) **Going Correction** -0.025s/f (Good)
WFA 4 from 5yo+ 2lb **10** Ran SP% **118.9**
Speed ratings (Par 103): **109,108,106,101,98 92,91,82,81,48**
CSF £38.19 CT £99.42 TOTE £11.30: £2.80, £1.10, £1.60; EX 38.10 Trifecta £163.80.
Owner W A Bethell **Bred** Haddenham Stud Farm Ltd **Trained** Arnold, E Yorks

FOCUS
They finished well strung out in behind the first two in this marathon. The form's rated around the third to last year's level.

1664 SPONSORSHIP FOR ROA MEMBERS H'CAP 1m 2f 5y
4:30 (4:32) (Class 2) (0-105,100) 4-Y-O+
£15,562 (£4,660; £2,330; £1,165; £582; £292) **Stalls** Low

Form RPR
350- **1** **Aasheq (IRE)**[150] 9005 6-9-1 **94**........................ DavidAllan 3 102
(Tim Easterby) *trckd ldrs: cl up over 3f out: chal 2f out: rdn to take slt ld over 1f out: drvn ins fnl f: hld on wl towards fin* **13/2**

00-0 **2** *1/2* **Society Red**[16] 1308 5-8-11 **90**........................ PaulHanagan 2 97
(Richard Fahey) *led: rdn along and jnd over 2f out: hdd over 1f out: drvn and rallied gamely ins fnl f: ev ch tl no ex towards fin* **5/1**[3]

1451 **3** *3/4* **Central City (IRE)**[10] 1418 4-8-4 **83**........................(p) KieranO'Neill 7 88
(Ian Williams) *trckd ldrs: effrt to chse ldng pair over 2f out: rdn wl over 1f out: drvn and kpt on fnl f* **14/1**

050- **4** *2 1/2* **Mukhayyam**[154] 8899 7-8-2 **88**........................ RobertDodsworth(7) 10 88+
(Tim Easterby) *dwlt and in rr: hdwy over 4f out: rdn wl over 1f out: kpt on fnl f: nrst fin* **40/1**

-320 **5** *1 1/4* **Fire Fighting (IRE)**[10] 1422 8-9-6 **99**........................ PJMcDonald 5 97
(Mark Johnston) *n.m.r and hmpd s: in rr tl styd on fnl 2f* **16/1**

031- **6** *2 1/4* **Dukhan**[164] 8649 4-9-1 **94**........................ JamesDoyle 1 87
(Hugo Palmer) *trckd ldrs on inner: rdn over 2f out: sn btn* **11/10**[1]

406- **7** *67* **Mount Tahan (IRE)**[122] 9463 7-9-0 **93**........................(w) ShaneGray 8 +
(Kevin Ryan) *n.m.r s: trckd ldrs whn carried bdly wd bnd over 6f out: bhd after* **25/1**

200- **P** **Ayutthaya (IRE)**[178] 8198 4-8-13 **92**........................(w) KevinStott 4 +
(Kevin Ryan) *awkward in stalls and wnt rt s: trckd ldrs on inner whn rn v wd bnd over 6f out: bhd after: t.o whn p.u and dismntd wl over 1f out* **4/1**[2]

2m 12.17s (-2.83) **Going Correction** -0.025s/f (Good) **8** Ran SP% **116.5**
Speed ratings (Par 109): **103,102,102,100,99 97,43,**
CSF £39.59 CT £442.95 TOTE £8.70: £2.20, £1.90, £2.40; EX 40.90 Trifecta £200.00.
Owner Ryedale Partners No1 **Bred** Castlemartin Sky & Skymarc Farm **Trained** Great Habton, N Yorks

FOCUS
They didn't go that quick early and the pace held up. The first two are rated in line with last year's marks.

1665 A VOICE FOR RACEHORSE OWNERS NOVICE STKS 6f
5:00 (5:00) (Class 5) 3-Y-O
£3,881 (£1,155; £577; £288) **Stalls** Low

Form RPR
200- **1** **Rathbone**[185] 7988 3-9-5 87........................ TomEaves 4 88+
(Kevin Ryan) *trckd ldrs: hdwy on outer over 2f out: led over 1f out: rdn and edgd lft ent fnl f: kpt on wl* **13/8**[2]

0-36 **2** *2 3/4* **Amplify (IRE)**[34] 1035 3-9-5 86........................ TomMarquand 3 79
(Brian Meehan) *prom: rdn to chal wl over 1f out and ev ch: drvn ins fnl f: kpt on same pce* **4/1**[3]

422- **3** *nk* **Alfred Boucher**[181] 8106 3-9-5 82 .... TomQueally 2 78
(Henry Candy) *towards rr: hdwy wl over 2f out: rdn to chse ldrs over 1f out: drvn and kpt on fnl f* **5/4**[1]

0- **4** *1* **Abate**[286] 4251 3-9-5 0 .... AndrewMullen 10 75
(Adrian Nicholls) *led: rdn 2f out: hdd over 1f out: kpt on same pce fnl f* **40/1**

\- **5** *5* **Obee Jo (IRE)** 3-9-5 0 .... DavidAllan 1 59+
(Tim Easterby) *towards rr: hdwy over 2f out: styd on fr over 1f out: nrst fin* **10/1**

6 *17* **Luna Princess** 3-8-11 0 .... JaneElliott(3) 8
(Michael Appleby) *a towards rr: outpcd and bhd fnl 3f* **33/1**

03 **7** *1 1/4* **Obsession For Gold (IRE)**[12] 1379 3-9-5 0 ....(bt) PaddyMathers 7 1
(Mrs Ilka Gansera-Leveque) *chsd ldrs: rdn along over 2f out: sn wknd* **50/1**

8 *3/4* **Hawk In The Sky** 3-9-5 0 .... PhilDennis 9
(Richard Whitaker) *in tch: rdn along 1/2-way: sn outpcd* **50/1**

50 **9** *14* **Parker's Pride**[50] 785 3-9-2 0 .... JamieGormley(3) 6
(Brian Rothwell) *a in rr: wl bhd fr 1/2-way* **100/1**

1m 16.35s (-0.75) **Going Correction** -0.025s/f (Good) 9 Ran SP% **121.9**
Speed ratings (Par 98): **104,100,99,98,91 69,67,66,47**
CSF £9.08 TOTE £2.60: £1.10, £1.60, £1.10; EX 9.00 Trifecta £13.90.
Owner Mrs Angie Bailey **Bred** Whitsbury Manor Stud **Trained** Hambleton, N Yorks

FOCUS
Those with form set a decent standard in this novice. The race could be rated a bit better using the second and third but there a few concerns in behind.

1666 BENEFITS FOR ROA MEMBERS APPRENTICE H'CAP — 1m 4f 5y
5:30 (5:30) (Class 5) (0-75,75) 4-Y-O+
£3,881 (£1,155; £577; £300; £300; £300) Stalls Low

Form — RPR

0-64 **1** **Archive (FR)**[40] 948 9-9-6 69 .... BenRobinson 3 75
(Brian Ellison) *hld up in rr: stdy hdwy on inner wl over 2f out: rdn to chse ldrs over 1f out: chal ins fnl f: kpt on wl u.p to ld last 100yds* **8/1**

551- **2** *nk* **Sempre Presto (IRE)**[183] 8054 4-9-3 69 .... SebastianWoods(3) 10 76
(Richard Fahey) *trckd ldrs: gd hdwy on inner to ld 2f out: rdn over 1f out: jnd and drvn ins fnl f: hdd last 100yds: kpt on* **9/2**[2]

450- **3** *2 1/2* **Bit Of A Quirke**[49] 7993 6-9-3 69 .... ConnorMurtagh(3) 8 71
(Mark Walford) *hld up in rr: rapid hdwy on outer over 2f out: chal wl over 1f out: sn rdn and ev ch: drvn ent fnl f: grad wknd* **14/1**

530- **4** *1 1/2* **Kajaki (IRE)**[98] 6741 6-9-9 75 ....(p) ThomasGreatrex(3) 1 75
(Kevin Ryan) *trckd ldrs: cl up over 4f out: rdn along over 2f out: drvn and wknd over 1f out* **2/1**[1]

114- **5** *2 3/4* **Gemini**[162] 8684 4-9-2 70 .... MarkCrehan(5) 4 66
(John Quinn) *hld up: rapid hdwy to trck ldr 1/2-way: rdn along and outpcd 3f out: plugged on u.p fr over 1f out* **5/1**[3]

5-64 **6** *5* **Raashdy (IRE)**[43] 910 6-8-10 59 ow1 ....(p) FinleyMarsh 5 46
(Peter Hiatt) *prom: rdn along wl over 2f out: sn wknd* **16/1**

413- **7** *1/2* **Regal Mirage (IRE)**[213] 7074 5-9-9 75 .... DannyRedmond(3) 2 61
(Tim Easterby) *hld up: a towards rr* **5/1**[3]

146- **8** *1 1/2* **Low Profile**[227] 6536 4-9-8 71 ....(p) PhilDennis 6 56
(Rebecca Bastiman) *prom: cl up 3f out: rdn along over 2f out: sn drvn and wknd* **33/1**

4-50 **9** *6* **Luv U Whatever**[9] 1463 9-9-4 67 ....(t) JaneElliott 7 41
(Marjorie Fife) *sn led: pushed along over 3f out: rdn over 2f out: drvn and hdd 2f out: sn wknd* **33/1**

2m 41.46s (0.36) **Going Correction** -0.025s/f (Good) 9 Ran SP% **114.4**
Speed ratings (Par 103): **97,96,95,94,92 88,88,87,83**
CSF £43.44 CT £492.98 TOTE £9.50: £2.60, £1.80, £3.70; EX 41.20 Trifecta £822.40.
Owner Brian Ellison Racing Club **Bred** E A R L Elevages Des Loges & J Hanamy **Trained** Norton, N Yorks

FOCUS
An uneven gallop and those ridden with patience came to the fore. The winner is rated in line with his best domestic Flat form.
T/Jkpt: £252,124.71 to a £1 stake. Pool: £252,124.71 - 1.0 winning unit T/Plt: £77.20 to a £1 stake. Pool: £78,955.18 - 746.04 winning units T/Qpdt: £17.50 to a £1 stake. Pool: £5,528.38 - 232.66 winning units **Joe Rowntree**

1667 - 1674a (Foreign Racing) - See Raceform Interactive

1513 KEMPTON (A.W) (R-H)
Wednesday, April 10

OFFICIAL GOING: Polytrack: standard to slow
Wind: Fresh, across (towards stands) Weather: Fine

1675 32RED ON THE APP STORE H'CAP — 1m (P)
4:35 (4:38) (Class 6) (0-65,65) 4-Y-O+
£3,105 (£924; £461; £400; £400; £400) Stalls Low

Form — RPR

0-06 **1** **Takeonefortheteam**[16] 1338 4-9-2 60 .... EdwardGreatrex 4 67
(Mark Loughnane) *hld up in rr: rdn and prog over 2f out: sustained effrt to ld jst over 1f out: edgd lft and drvn out* **12/1**

-013 **2** *1 1/4* **Purple Paddy**[35] 1032 4-8-7 51 .... JohnFahy 11 55
(Jimmy Fox) *trckd ldrs on outer: rdn over 2f out: chal over 1f out: chsd wnr ins fnl f: no imp* **10/3**[1]

0-06 **3** *shd* **Militry Decoration (IRE)**[14] 1355 4-9-7 65 .... KierenFox 9 69
(Dr Jon Scargill) *prom: rdn over 2f out: stl cl up over 1f out: kpt on same pce fnl f* **8/1**

-040 **4** *hd* **Laqab (IRE)**[34] 1065 6-9-6 64 .... PaddyMathers 1 67
(Derek Shaw) *hld up towards rr: rdn over 2f out: prog wl over 1f out: kpt on fnl f but nvr able to chal* **10/1**

10-3 **5** *nse* **Boxatricks (IRE)**[28] 1175 4-8-9 53 .... ShelleyBirkett 5 56
(Julia Feilden) *hld up in last pair: prog over 2f out but lugged to inner and racd alone against rail after: kpt on but nvr quite able to chal (jockey said gelding hung right-handed under pressure)* **6/1**[3]

0-41 **6** *1/2* **Waqt (IRE)**[16] 1328 5-9-3 61 .... RossaRyan 10 63
(Alexandra Dunn) *sn led: drvn over 2f out: hdd jst over 1f out: fdd (jockey said gelding hung left-handed under presure)* **8/1**

-000 **7** *3/4* **The Eagle's Nest (IRE)**[15] 1343 5-9-2 63 ....(t[1]) JoshuaBryan(3) 6 63
(Alexandra Dunn) *sn pressed ldr: lost 2nd wl over 1f out: grad fdd* **12/1**

-446 **8** *nk* **Beepeecee**[19] 1265 5-9-6 64 ....(p) LiamKeniry 2 64
(Thomas Gallagher) *hld up in midfield: shkn up over 2f out: nt clr run briefly and swtchd lft: nt qckn after but kpt on same pce* **5/1**[2]

310- **9** *nk* **Topology**[137] 9248 6-8-9 60 .... WilliamCarver(7) 8 59
(Joseph Tuite) *hld up in last pair: stl there over 2f out: pushed along and kpt on steadily: nvr nrr* **16/1**

3-35 **10** *7* **Screaming Gemini (IRE)**[56] 705 5-9-6 64 .... JoeyHaynes 3 47
(Tony Carroll) *t.k.h early: hld up: urged along over 3f out: struggling over 2f out* **10/1**

000- **11** *4 1/2* **Fair Power (IRE)**[101] 9765 5-9-2 60 .... KieranO'Neill 12 33
(John Butler) *t.k.h and sn restrained in rr: rdn and no prog over 2f out: wknd* **40/1**

006- **12** *1 3/4* **Live Dangerously**[174] 8335 9-8-7 51 ....(p) LiamJones 7 20
(John Bridger) *prom tl wknd rapidly over 2f out (vet said gelding lost right fore shoe)* **50/1**

1m 39.8s **Going Correction** -0.075s/f (Stan) 12 Ran SP% **120.1**
Speed ratings (Par 101): **97,95,95,95,95 94,94,93,93,86 82,80**
CSF £52.45 CT £356.59 TOTE £17.10: £5.70, £1.20, £2.90; EX 78.70 Trifecta £1526.30.
Owner S & A Mares **Bred** G S Shropshire **Trained** Rock, Worcs
■ Stewards' Enquiry : Rossa Ryan two-day ban: careless riding (Apr 24-25)

FOCUS
A modest handicap on standard to slow Polytrack. The previous five renewals have gone to 4yos and that age-group completed a big odds trifecta from just four representatives. A compressed finish limits the form.

1676 BET AT RACINGTV.COM NOVICE MEDIAN AUCTION STKS (DIV I) — 7f (P)
5:10 (5:14) (Class 6) 3-5-Y-O
£3,105 (£924; £461; £230) Stalls Low

Form — RPR

10- **1** **Masaru**[230] 6455 3-9-7 0 .... TomMarquand 2 89
(Richard Hannon) *led 1f: sn in 3rd: chsd ldr over 2f out: rdn to chal over 1f out: drvn ahd last 100yds: styd on* **1/3**[1]

6-2 **2** *1/2* **You Little Ripper (IRE)**[75] 405 3-9-0 0 .... JohnFahy 8 81
(Peter Chapple-Hyam) *led after 1f and stretched field: rdn and pressed over 1f out: styd on but worn down last 100yds* **7/2**[2]

3 *nk* **Bighearted** 3-8-6 0 ....(h[1]) CameronNoble(3) 7 75
(Michael Bell) *sn trckd ldng trio: wnt 3rd wl over 1f out: shkn up and steadily clsd fnl f: jst unable to chal* **33/1**

4 *6* **Cristal Breeze (IRE)** 3-9-0 0 .... JamesDoyle 11 65
(William Haggas) *s.i.s: sn wl off the pce in rr: prog to take modest 5th over 2f out: n.d but kpt on steadily to take 4th last strides* **7/1**[3]

5 **5** *nk* **Huddle**[14] 1359 3-8-9 0 .... DavidEgan 9 59
(William Knight) *chsd ldr after 1f to over 2f out: wknd over 1f out: lost 4th last strides* **40/1**

00 **6** *5* **Storm Girl**[32] 1094 3-8-9 0 .... CharlieBennett 5 46
(Michael Attwater) *chsd ldrs but sn outpcd and pushed along: nvr on terms* **150/1**

0 **7** *1/2* **Circle Of Stars (IRE)**[77] 359 3-9-0 0 .... EdwardGreatrex 4 50
(Charlie Fellowes) *sn off the pce towards rr: nvr a factor* **14/1**

5-3 **8** *1/2* **Tribune**[15] 1344 3-8-11 0 .... GaryMahon(3) 10 48
(Sylvester Kirk) *sn outpcd in midfield: no prog fnl 2f* **66/1**

0- **9** *5* **Je M'En Fiche**[140] 9170 3-8-9 .... KieranO'Neill 3 30
(Patrick Chamings) *a in rr: bhd over 1f out* **100/1**

00 **10** *1* **George Formby**[2] 1649 3-9-0 0 .... JackMitchell 6 33
(Hugo Palmer) *t.k.h: hld up in last pair: pushed along over 2f out and no prog: bhd after (jockey said filly hung badly left-handed throughout)* **25/1**

11 *41* **Scarlet Red** 4-9-9 0 .... LiamKeniry 1
(Malcolm Saunders) *awkward s: t.k.h: green and hanging: a last: t.o (jockey said filly hung badly left-handed throughout)* **100/1**

1m 25.19s (-0.81) **Going Correction** -0.075s/f (Stan)
WFA 3 from 4yo 14lb 11 Ran SP% **129.8**
Speed ratings (Par 101): **101,100,100,93,92 87,86,86,80,79 32**
CSF £2.24 TOTE £1.20: £1.02, £1.30, £6.10; EX 2.90 Trifecta £31.20.
Owner Michael Daniels & Jonathan Palmer-Brown **Bred** Crossfields Bloodstock Ltd **Trained** East Everleigh, Wilts

FOCUS
The first division of a decent novice contest. The odds-on favourite gradually wore down the long-time leader in the second half of the straight. The winning time was fractionally slower than the later division, and the fifth and sixth help offer perspective.

1677 BET AT RACINGTV.COM NOVICE MEDIAN AUCTION STKS (DIV II) — 7f (P)
5:45 (5:45) (Class 6) 3-5-Y-O
£3,105 (£924; £461; £230) Stalls Low

Form — RPR

0 **1** **May Sonic**[28] 1171 3-9-0 0 .... RichardKingscote 4 79
(Charles Hills) *mde all: skipped clr 2f out: 5 l ahd 1f out: pushed out and ld dwindling qckly towards fin* **11/4**[2]

03- **2** *nk* **Characteristic (IRE)**[177] 8257 3-9-0 0 .... JackMitchell 2 78
(Tom Clover) *chsd ldng trio: rdn to chse clr wnr over 1f out and 5 l bhd: hanging rt but clsd qckly fnl f: jst too late* **5/4**[1]

3 *3 1/4* **Jadella Willfin (FR)** 3-8-9 0 .... TomMarquand 6 64+
(Richard Hannon) *hld up in midfield: pushed along over 2f out: styd on steadily after and tk 3rd last 100yds* **20/1**

1-4 **4** *1 1/4* **Jack Berry House**[26] 1212 3-9-7 0 ....(t) JamesDoyle 7 73
(Charlie Fellowes) *chsd wnr: outpcd 2f out: lost 2nd over 1f out: fdd* **9/2**[3]

5 *3* **Foxes Flyer (IRE)** 3-8-12 0 ow3 .... JamieJones(5) 5 61
(Luke McJannet) *chsd ldng quartet: outpcd over 2f out: nvr on terms after* **66/1**

-033 **6** *1* **Altar Boy**[40] 966 3-8-11 69 .... GaryMahon(3) 1 55
(Sylvester Kirk) *chsd ldng pair: rdn over 2f out: wknd over 1f out* **13/2**

6 **7** *4* **Power Of You (IRE)**[18] 1293 3-8-7 0 ....(t) Pierre-LouisJamin(7) 9 44
(William Knight) *racd wd in midfield: hung lft bnd 3f out and dropped to rr: no ch after* **50/1**

-0 **8** *3 1/2* **My Lady Claire**[30] 1142 3-8-9 0 .... DavidEgan 8 30
(Ed Walker) *a towards rr: lft bhd 2f out* **25/1**

0 **9** *2* **Arvensis**[25] 1236 3-8-9 0 .... CharlieBennett 3 24
(Hughie Morrison) *dwlt: sme prog into midfield 2f out but already outpcd: wknd over 1f out* **50/1**

10 *2* **For Richard** 3-9-0 0 .... KierenFox 10 24
(John Best) *dwlt: a in last pair and nvr a factor* **50/1**

11 *12* **Ideal Grace** 3-8-9 0 .... EdwardGreatrex 11
(Eve Johnson Houghton) *dwlt: rn green and a in last: t.o* **50/1**

1m 25.11s (-0.89) **Going Correction** -0.075s/f (Stan) 11 Ran SP% **120.6**
Speed ratings (Par 101): **102,101,97,96,93 91,87,83,81,78 65**
CSF £6.40 TOTE £4.00: £1.20, £1.10, £5.20; EX 7.80 Trifecta £93.00.
Owner Hills' Angels **Bred** Minster Stud **Trained** Lambourn, Berks

The Form Book Flat 2019, Raceform Ltd, Newbury, RG14 5SJ

FOCUS
The second division of a decent novice contest. The second-favourite made all and his winning time was fractionally quicker. Not many got into it. A slight step forward from the second.

1678 32RED CASINO H'CAP 7f (P)
6:15 (6:15) (Class 6) (0-60,61) 3-Y-O
£3,105 (£924; £461; £400; £400; £400) Stalls Low

Form RPR

-331 1 **Pentland Lad (IRE)**[7] [1514] 3-9-3 **55** 6ex........................(t) JamesDoyle 4 65+
(Charlie Fellowes) *trckd ldrs: prog 2f out: chal on inner over 1f out: drvn to ld jst ins fnl f: edgd lft but styd on* **8/11**[1]

-213 2 ¾ **Eye Of The Water (IRE)**[18] [1296] 3-9-4 **56**........................ RaulDaSilva 1 62
(Ronald Harris) *led 100yds: sn in 3rd: chsd ldr wl over 2f out: clsd over 1f out but wnr wnt past: rdn to take 2nd last 100yds: a hld* **5/1**[2]

-302 3 1 ¾ **Zorro's Girl**[7] [1514] 3-9-3 **55**................................(b[1]) HollieDoyle 11 57
(Archie Watson) *led after 100yds: tried to kick on over 2f out: hdd and one pce jst ins fnl f* **12/1**[3]

6-43 4 4 ½ **Es Que Magic (IRE)**[13] [1385] 3-9-6 **58**.............................. LukeMorris 8 48
(Alex Hales) *in tch in midfield: rdn to chse clr ldng trio 2f out: clr of rest but no imp over 1f out* **16/1**

0026 5 3 ¼ **Grandee Daisy**[28] [1170] 3-8-8 **53**...........................(v) EllieMacKenzie(7) 10 34
(Jo Hughes, France) *dwlt: wl in rr: tried to make prog arnd rivals bnd at 1/2-way: dropped to rr again 2f out: kpt on fnl f* **25/1**

6006 6 nk **Tintern Spirit (IRE)**[7] [1515] 3-8-7 **45**................................ DavidEgan 13 26
(Milton Bradley) *in tch: rdn over 2f out: nt enough pce to make real prog* **100/1**

550- 7 nk **Savoy Brown**[126] [9403] 3-9-9 **61**.. KierenFox 7 41
(Michael Attwater) *hld up wl in rr: urged along and passed a few fr 2f out: no ch* **20/1**

4030 8 ½ **Zaula**[13] [1385] 3-9-4 **61**..................................(b) ThomasGreatrex(5) 2 39
(Archie Watson) *dwlt: wl in rr: urged along and modest prog over 1f out: no hdwy after* **25/1**

500- 9 ½ **Approve The Dream (IRE)**[177] [8278] 3-9-7 **59**.............. ShelleyBirkett 14 36
(Julia Feilden) *chsd ldr after 1f to wl over 2f out: wknd* **66/1**

5-60 10 2 ¼ **Miss Communicate**[13] [1381] 3-9-3 **55**.................................. EoinWalsh 6 26
(Lydia Pearce) *a wl in rr: u.p and struggling 3f out* **66/1**

055- 11 2 **Cedar**[183] [8066] 3-9-6 **58**.. RobertHavlin 9 24
(Mohamed Moubarak) *nvr beyond midfield: wknd 2f out* **25/1**

-545 12 7 **Fox Happy (IRE)**[18] [1296] 3-9-4 **61**..................... ThoreHammerHansen(5) 3 9
(Richard Hannon) *towards rr: rdn and no prog over 2f out: nvr a factor* **5/1**[2]

1m 25.42s (-0.58) **Going Correction** -0.075s/f (Stan) **12** Ran SP% **125.1**
Speed ratings (Par 96): **100,99,97,92,88 87,87,87,86,83 81,73**
CSF £4.58 CT £29.59 TOTE £1.30: £1.02, £1.70, £2.70; EX 4.90 Trifecta £22.70.
Owner GG Thoroughbreds VIII **Bred** Yeomanstown Stud **Trained** Newmarket, Suffolk

FOCUS
A modest 3yo handicap. The odds-on favourite's winning time was approaching half-a-second slower than the previous two C&D novice contests. The form could be rated a bit higher, but for now the third has been rated as posting a similar effort to the previous week.

1679 100% PROFIT BOOST AT 32REDSPORT.COM H'CAP (DIV I) 1m 2f 219y(P)
6:45 (6:46) (Class 6) (0-55,57) 4-Y-O+
£3,105 (£924; £461; £400; £400; £400) Stalls Low

Form RPR

-633 1 **Iley Boy**[42] [923] 5-9-0 **55**..................................(p) CierenFallon(7) 9 60
(John Gallagher) *hld up in last quartet: prog on outer over 2f out: led over 1f out: pushed out firmly fnl f: jst hld on* **11/4**[1]

0003 2 hd **Shovel It On (IRE)**[8] [1494] 4-8-12 **46** oh1.......................(bt) RaulDaSilva 4 51
(Steve Flook) *in tch in midfield: rdn and prog 2f out: styd on to take 2nd ins fnl f: clsd on wnr fin: jst failed* **14/1**

4016 3 nk **Murhib (IRE)**[7] [1520] 7-9-2 **50**................................(h) RichardKingscote 8 54
(Lydia Richards) *prom: disp 2nd briefly over 2f out: styd cl up: drvn and kpt on fnl f but a hld* **7/2**[2]

3243 4 nk **Foxrush Take Time (FR)**[11] [1431] 4-8-12 **46** oh1..........(e) PhilipPrince 1 50
(Richard Guest) *chsd ldr 1f: styd prom: rdn to chse ldr over 2f out to wl over 1f out: kpt on u.p fnl f* **9/1**

04-4 5 1 ¾ **Goldslinger (FR)**[23] [38] 7-9-7 **55**..................................(t) HectorCrouch 2 56
(Gary Moore) *hld up in last quartet: pushed along over 2f out: prog to chse ldrs over 1f out: nvr nr enough to chal but kpt on fnl f* **9/2**[3]

-000 6 1 ½ **Golconda Prince (IRE)**[18] [1297] 5-9-0 **51**......................... JoshuaBryan(3) 6 49
(Mark Pattinson) *led: stretched on over 2f out: hdd over 1f out: wknd ins fnl f* **25/1**

4-60 7 2 **Far Cry**[85] [245] 6-9-0 **48**.. CharlieBennett 10 43
(Hughie Morrison) *nvr beyond midfield: rdn and no prog over 2f out: one pce after* **16/1**

-000 8 6 **Harbour Force (FR)**[55] [724] 5-8-13 **47**.............................. LiamKeniry 11 32
(Neil Mulholland) *s.i.s: rapid prog on outer to press ldr after 1f: lost 2nd 1/2-way: styd prom tl wknd qckly 2f out* **12/1**

00/0 9 16 **Guaracha**[15] [1341] 8-9-8 **56**.. EdwardGreatrex 5 13
(Alexandra Dunn) *hld up and mostly in last pair: pushed along and wknd over 2f out: t.o* **100/1**

500- 10 1 ¼ **Becky Sharp**[169] [8500] 4-9-9 **57**.. PatCosgrave 7 12
(Jim Boyle) *dwlt: prog fr rr to chse ldr 1/2-way: lost 2nd and wknd rapidly over 2f out: t.o* **6/1**

0-00 11 2 ½ **Mime Dance**[7] [1527] 8-9-0 **51**.......................................(p) TimClark(3) 3 2
(John Butler) *stdd s: t.k.h: hld up and mostly in last: rdn and wknd over 2f out: t.o* **50/1**

2m 20.59s (-0.41) **Going Correction** -0.075s/f (Stan) **11** Ran SP% **118.4**
Speed ratings (Par 101): **101,100,100,100,99 98,96,92,80,79 77**
CSF £43.56 CT £140.84 TOTE £3.30: £1.60, £3.10, £1.60; EX 37.50 Trifecta £123.30.
Owner J & L Wetherald - M & M Glover **Bred** C R Marks (Banbury) **Trained** Chastleton, Oxon

FOCUS
The first division of a moderate handicap, and straightforward, limited form. The favourite's winning time was comparatively modest in a bunched finish.

1680 100% PROFIT BOOST AT 32REDSPORT.COM H'CAP (DIV II) 1m 2f 219y(P)
7:15 (7:16) (Class 6) (0-55,56) 4-Y-O+
£3,105 (£924; £461; £400; £400; £400) Stalls Low

Form RPR

1030 1 **Muraaqeb**[7] [1520] 5-8-12 **46**..(p) LukeMorris 3 54
(Milton Bradley) *hld up in midfield: clsd smoothly over 2f out: led over 1f out: sn pressed: drvn and asserted fnl f* **12/1**

2004 2 1 ¼ **Diamond Reflection (IRE)**[18] [1297] 7-8-9 **50**..........(bt) AmeliaGlass(7) 6 56
(Alexandra Dunn) *hld up towards rr: smooth prog over 2f out: chal over 1f out: sn rdn to chse wnr: nt qckn and readily hld fnl f* **12/1**

-166 3 2 ¾ **Cold Harbour**[18] [1297] 4-9-5 **53**...................................(t) TomMarquand 9 54
(Robyn Brisland) *tried to ld but had to settle for 3rd pl early: wnt 2nd 4f out: rdn to ld 2f out: hdd and one pce over 1f out* **3/1**[1]

006 4 2 ¾ **Puzzle Cache**[14] [1351] 5-9-0 **48**..................................(b) RobHornby 8 45
(Rod Millman) *mostly in midfield: rdn and no prog over 2f out: kpt on over 1f out to take 4th last strides* **25/1**

1500 5 shd **Dolphin Village (IRE)**[8] [1498] 9-8-13 **47**.....................(h) JoeyHaynes 2 43
(Shaun Harris) *slowly away: hld up in last pair: prog over 2f out and looked a possible threat: rdn and no hdwy over 1f out* **20/1**

2423 6 ½ **Contingency Fee**[66] [589] 4-9-0 **55**.........................(p) GraceMcEntee(7) 10 51
(Phil McEntee) *won battle for ld but had to work hrd to do so: hdd 2f out: wknd over 1f out* **10/1**

4-00 7 ¾ **Shaji**[44] [910] 4-9-3 **56**.. PoppyBridgwater(5) 1 50
(David Bridgwater) *hld up in last pair: swtchd sharply lft over 2f out: hung lft after and ended towards nr side rail: plugged on over 1f out: no ch* **10/1**

-500 8 1 **The Celtic Machine**[14] [1362] 4-8-12 **46** oh1.................... CharlieBennett 4 39
(Pat Phelan) *mostly in midfield: tried to cl u.p over 2f out: no hdwy over 1f out: fdd* **16/1**

3336 9 ¾ **Outlaw Torn (IRE)**[6] [1546] 10-8-12 **46** oh1.....................(e) PhilipPrince 5 37
(Richard Guest) *chsd ldrs: rdn and no imp over 2f out: wknd over 1f out* **16/1**

-006 10 25 **Art Of Swing (IRE)**[8] [1506] 7-9-8 **56**.................................(p) RossaRyan 7 5
(Lee Carter) *a towards rr: struggling wl over 2f out: t.o* **11/2**[3]

60-1 11 ¾ **Kingfast (IRE)**[13] [1390] 4-9-3 **51**.. DavidEgan 12
(David Dennis) *tried to ld fr wdst draw but unable to: chsd ldng trio: wnt 3rd 4f out tl over 2f out: wknd rapidly: t.o* **4/1**[2]

-055 12 27 **Esme Kate (IRE)**[14] [1365] 4-8-12 **46** oh1.........................(bt) PaddyMathers 11
(Ivan Furtado) *tried to ld fr wdst draw but forced to chse ldr after 1f: wknd rapidly 4f out and wd after: t.o* **25/1**

2m 19.69s (-1.31) **Going Correction** -0.075s/f (Stan) **12** Ran SP% **118.2**
Speed ratings (Par 101): **105,104,102,100,100 99,99,98,97,79 79,59**
CSF £143.46 CT £544.57 TOTE £12.20: £3.60, £2.30, £1.30; EX 243.70 Trifecta £1088.60.
Owner E A Hayward **Bred** Peter Winkworth **Trained** Sedbury, Gloucs

FOCUS
The second division of a moderate handicap. The winning time was nearly a second quicker and it's not bad form for the grade.

1681 32RED H'CAP 1m 3f 219y(P)
7:45 (7:45) (Class 3) (0-95,97) 4-Y-O+
£9,337 (£2,796; £1,398; £699; £349; £175) Stalls Low

Form RPR

410- 1 **Collide**[158] [8837] 4-9-8 **96**...(t) JamesDoyle 2 102
(Hugo Palmer) *tk v t.k.h: trckd ldr 1f: styd cl up: dashed to inner 2f out and narrow ld over 1f out: rdn out and a jst holding on in sprint fin* **11/10**[1]

402- 2 hd **Al Hamdany (IRE)**[280] [4522] 5-9-5 **96**........................ GabrieleMalune(3) 5 101
(Marco Botti) *t.k.h: trckd ldr after 1f: rdn to ld briefly wl over 1f out: pressed wnr after: jst hld in sprint fin* **11/1**

2213 3 ¾ **Executive Force**[6] [1545] 5-9-9 **97**...................................(p) FrannyNorton 1 100
(Michael Wigham) *hld up in last pair: gng easily whn sprint sed 2f out: urged along and clsd to take 3rd ins fnl f: r.o but a jst too much to do* **11/4**[2]

4/ 4 ½ **Dalgarno (FR)**[693] 6-9-7 **95**.. JFEgan 3 98
(Jane Chapple-Hyam) *t.k.h: hld up: clsd on ldrs 5f out: shkn up over 2f out: tried to chal over 1f out but nt qckn: kpt on fnl f but a jst outpcd* **6/1**[3]

025- 5 1 ¼ **Noble Gift**[142] [9155] 9-8-13 **87**.. CallumShepherd 4 88
(William Knight) *led at mod pce: tried to stretch on over 2f out but limited rspnse: hdd and one pce wl over 1f out* **25/1**

242- 6 nse **Hyanna**[186] [7986] 4-8-13 **87**.. CharlesBishop 6 89
(Eve Johnson Houghton) *hld up in last pair: shkn up whn sprint s 2f out: one pce and nvr able to threaten* **8/1**

2m 36.24s (1.74) **Going Correction** -0.075s/f (Stan) **6** Ran SP% **111.9**
Speed ratings (Par 107): **91,90,90,90,89 89**
CSF £14.38 TOTE £1.40: £1.10, £3.30; EX 13.30 Trifecta £30.00.
Owner K Abdullah **Bred** Juddmonte Farms Ltd **Trained** Newmarket, Suffolk

FOCUS
The feature contest was a good middle-distance handicap. The favourite did well to edge this in an exciting final furlong from off a slow gallop. A compressed finish and not form to rely on too literally.

1682 32RED.COM H'CAP 6f (P)
8:15 (8:16) (Class 6) (0-65,67) 4-Y-O+
£3,105 (£924; £461; £400; £400; £400) Stalls Low

Form RPR

-253 1 **Secret Potion**[35] [1037] 5-9-5 **63**.. RobbieDowney 3 69
(Ronald Harris) *chsd ldrs: one of first rdn over 2f out: responded to press and tk 2nd fnl f: styd on dourly to ld nr fin* **7/2**[2]

4621 2 nk **Sir Ottoman (FR)**[35] [1037] 6-9-9 **67**..................................(tp) JasonHart 7 72
(Ivan Furtado) *led: rdn over 1f out: kpt on u.p but hdd nr fin* **9/4**[1]

005- 3 2 **Red Tycoon (IRE)**[225] [6657] 7-9-6 **64**.................................. HectorCrouch 5 63
(Ken Cunningham-Brown) *hld up in midfield: gng bttr than most 2f out: prog over 1f out: drvn to take 3rd ins fnl f: nt pce to chal* **16/1**

0-00 4 ½ **Noble Deed**[19] [1265] 9-8-7 **51** oh6..(p) KierenFox 4 49
(Michael Attwater) *chsd ldrs: rdn 2f out: kpt on but nvr gng pce to chal: tk 4th last stride* **50/1**

0-00 5 shd **Just An Idea (IRE)**[76] [383] 5-8-8 **57**..........................(b) RhiainIngram(5) 1 54
(Roger Ingram) *in tch in midfield: effrt on inner 2f out: nt qckn over 1f out: one pce fnl f* **33/1**

3432 6 hd **Secondo (FR)**[46] [883] 9-9-0 **63**..........................(v) PoppyBridgwater(5) 11 60
(Robert Stephens) *pressed ldr: rdn 2f out: nt qckn over 1f out: lost 2nd and one pce fnl f* **10/1**

500- 7 1 ¾ **Pastfact**[219] [6879] 5-9-7 **65**.. LiamKeniry 2 56
(Malcolm Saunders) *dwlt: hld up towards rr: shkn up 2f out: sme prog over 1f out but nvr threatened ldrs* **9/1**

-423 8 ½ **Mount Wellington (IRE)**[39] [982] 4-9-4 **67**...............(p) DylanHogan(5) 9 57
(Henry Spiller) *nvr beyond midfield: struggling on outer wl over 1f out* **13/2**[3]

4005 9 2 ¼ **Mother Of Dragons (IRE)**[5] [1565] 4-9-0 **58**............(v) CallumShepherd 8 41
(Phil McEntee) *chsd ldrs but trapped wd: wknd wl over 1f out* **16/1**

300- 10 3 ¼ **Jonnysimpson (IRE)**[203] [7421] 4-8-13 **57**........................ KieranO'Neill 10 30
(Lee Carter) *stdd s: dropped in fr wd draw and hld up in last pair: shkn up and no rspnse 2f out* **40/1**

The Form Book Flat 2019, Raceform Ltd, Newbury, RG14 5SJ

-000 **11** *5* **Our Man In Havana**[71] 468 4-8-10 **61**........................ CierenFallon(7) 6 19
(Richard Price) *dwlt: mostly in last: bhd over 1f out* **7/1**

1m 12.3s (-0.80) **Going Correction** -0.075s/f (Stan) **11** Ran SP% **117.0**
Speed ratings (Par 101): **102,101,98,98,98 97,95,94,91,87 80**
CSF £11.54 CT £110.17 TOTE £4.30: £1.70, £1.20, £4.10; EX 12.30 Trifecta £160.20.
Owner RHS Ltd, R Fox, P Charter **Bred** Llety Farms **Trained** Earlswood, Monmouths

FOCUS
A modest sprint handicap. The front two in the market came to the fore in a fair comparative winning time. The winner is rated in line with last year's best.
T/Jkpt: £10,000. 1 winning unit. T/Plt: £7.70 to a £1 stake. Pool: £59,151.42 - 5540.90 winning units T/Qpdt: £4.40 to a £1 stake. Pool: £10,453.74 - 1756.81 winning units **Jonathan Neesom**

1586 LINGFIELD (L-H)
Wednesday, April 10

OFFICIAL GOING: Polytrack: standard
Wind: medium, half against Weather: fine, chilly wind

1683 FOLLOW SUN RACING ON TWITTER H'CAP — 1m 1y(P)
2:20 (2:20) (Class 6) (0-55,55) 4-Y-0+
£3,105 (£924; £461; £300; £300; £300) **Stalls High**

Form RPR

0502 **1** **Clement (IRE)**[9] 1478 9-9-1 **49**........................(p) LukeMorris 11 58
(Marjorie Fife) *stdd after s: hld up in tch towards rr: clsd and wd bnd 2f out: rdn and hdwy to chse clr ldr jst ins fnl f: r.o wl to ld last strides* **6/1**[3]

-636 **2** *hd* **Helfire**[4] 1586 6-9-7 **55**........................ CharlieBennett 4 64
(Martin Bosley) *taken down early and led rdrless to post: trckd ldrs: effrt and qcknd to ld over 1f out: clr ins fnl f: kpt on u.p but hdd last strides* **5/2**[1]

0425 **3** *3 3/4* **Ahfad**[35] 1032 4-8-13 **47**........................(b) LiamKeniry 7 47
(Gary Moore) *rousted along leaving stalls: sn rcvrd and in tch in midfield: effrt over 1f out: kpt on but no threat to ldrs ins fnl f: snatched 3rd last strides* **9/1**

00-0 **4** *hd* **Ad Valorem Queen (IRE)**[12] 1393 4-9-0 **55**........ Pierre-LouisJamin(7) 8 55
(William Knight) *chsd ldrs tl wnt 2nd over 4f out: rdn and ev ch ent fnl 2f tl unable to match pce of wnr over 1f out: outpcd ins fnl f: lost 3rd last strides* **40/1**

0035 **5** *nk* **Puchita (IRE)**[11] 1431 4-8-12 **46** oh1........................(p[1]) CamHardie 1 46
(Antony Brittain) *hld up in tch in midfield: nt clr run and shuffled bk wl over 1f out: rallied and styd on u.p ins fnl f: no threat to ldrs* **12/1**

0-00 **6** *1* **Brecqhou Island**[41] 942 4-9-3 **54**........................ PaddyBradley(3) 12 51
(Mark Pattinson) *stdd after s: bhd: clsd over 2f out: swtchd rt jst ins fnl f: rdn and styd on fnl 150yds: nvr trbld ldrs* **33/1**

0002 **7** *nk* **Sir Jamie**[14] 1354 6-9-3 **51**........................(b) TomMarquand 2 47
(Tony Carroll) *hld up in tch in rr of main gp: effrt 2f out: kpt on u.p ins fnl f: nvr trbld ldrs* **5/1**[2]

0-06 **8** *1/2* **Ramblow**[14] 1354 6-8-6 **47**........................(vt[1]) AmeliaGlass(7) 6 42
(Alexandra Dunn) *led for 1f: chsd ldr tl over 4f out: unable qck over 1f out: wknd ins fnl f* **50/1**

5-43 **9** *2* **Three C's (IRE)**[55] 719 5-9-4 **52**........................(p) HollieDoyle 3 42
(Adrian Wintle) *midfield: unable qck over 1f out: wknd ins fnl f (jockey said gelding ran flat)* **5/1**[2]

-00 **10** *1* **Estibdaad (IRE)**[16] 1333 9-8-7 **46**..........(vt[1]) ThoreHammerHansen(5) 10 34
(Paddy Butler) *taken down early and led to post: led after 1f tl over 1f out: wknd ins fnl f* **33/1**

0-06 **P** **Confrerie (IRE)**[16] 1328 4-9-6 **54**........................(p) NicolaCurrie 9
(George Baker) *sn dropped to last pair: lost tch and eased over 1f out: t.o: p.u ins fnl f: dismntd (jockey said gelding was never travelling)* **5/1**[2]

1m 40.02s (1.82) **Going Correction** +0.175s/f (Slow) **11** Ran SP% **120.8**
Speed ratings (Par 101): **97,96,93,92,92 91,91,90,88,87**
CSF £21.51 CT £141.10 TOTE £6.40: £3.00, £1.10, £4.70; EX 27.00 Trifecta £248.80.
Owner T W Fife **Bred** P Kelly **Trained** Stillington, N Yorks

FOCUS
There was a fair pace on in this weak handicap. The first two finished clear and the form seems sound enough.

1684 LIKE SUN RACING ON FACEBOOK H'CAP — 7f 1y(P)
2:50 (2:50) (Class 5) (0-70,68) 4-Y-0+
£3,752 (£1,116; £557; £300; £300; £300) **Stalls Low**

Form RPR

242- **1** **Javelin**[159] 8797 4-9-4 **65**........................ MartinDwyer 5 74+
(William Muir) *chsd ldrs: effrt and clsd 2f out: hdwy to ld 1f out: sn rdn and r.o wl* **12/1**[3]

/34- **2** *1 1/4* **Rewaayat**[236] 6255 4-9-3 **64**........................ JimCrowley 9 70+
(Charles Hills) *t.k.h: hld up in midfield: effrt on outer over 1f out: hdwy u.p to chse wnr wl ins fnl f: no imp towards fin* **13/8**[1]

3-34 **3** *1* **Global Exceed**[29] 1160 4-9-7 **68**........................ JoeFanning 4 71
(Robert Cowell) *chsd ldr tl rdn to ld over 1f out: sn hdd and kpt on same pce ins fnl f* **25/1**

60-5 **4** *3/4* **Zefferino**[26] 1209 5-9-3 **64**........................(t) TomMarquand 7 65
(Martin Bosley) *hld up in tch in last trio: hdwy u.p and edgd lft 1f out: kpt on ins fnl f but no threat to ldrs* **12/1**[3]

6301 **5** *1/2* **Grey Destiny**[16] 1338 9-9-4 **65**........................(p) CamHardie 8 65
(Antony Brittain) *short of room and dropped to rr sn after s: hld up in rr: effrt over 1f out: swtchd lft and ins fnl f: kpt on but no threat to ldrs* **20/1**

1330 **6** *4 1/2* **Tavener**[8] 1496 7-9-1 **62**........................(p) LukeMorris 1 49
(David C Griffiths) *led: rdn ent fnl 2f: hdd over 1f out: fdd ins fnl f* **12/1**[3]

1606 **7** *2 1/2* **The British Lion (IRE)**[29] 1164 4-9-7 **68**........................(v[1]) RossaRyan 2 49
(Alexandra Dunn) *chsd ldr: effrt but unable qck over 1f out: fdd ins fnl f* **14/1**

21-3 **8** *1/2* **Garth Rockett**[74] 430 5-8-11 **65**........................(tp) CierenFallon(7) 3 44
(Mike Murphy) *mounted in chute and unruly on way to s: hld up in tch in midfield: effrt on inner 2f out: no hdwy u.p over 1f out: wknd ins fnl f (trainer said, regarding the poor form shown, that gelding boiled over in preliminares)* **2/1**[2]

01-5 **9** *12* **Wilson (IRE)**[85] 249 4-9-7 **68**........................(p) ShelleyBirkett 6 15
(Julia Feilden) *in tch in last trio: effrt 2f out: sn btn and bhd ins fnl f (jockey said gelding moved poorly)* **12/1**[3]

1m 26.15s (1.35) **Going Correction** +0.175s/f (Slow) **9** Ran SP% **117.5**
Speed ratings (Par 103): **97,96,96,95,95 89,87,86,72**
CSF £32.50 CT £506.59 TOTE £10.20: £2.90, £1.10, £4.30; EX 37.70 Trifecta £430.40.
Owner G O Leach & Mrs J M Leach **Bred** Dukes Stud & Overbury Stallions Ltd **Trained** Lambourn, Berks

FOCUS
It paid to be handy in this ordinary handicap. The first two can rate higher.

1685 LADBROKES HOME OF THE ODDS BOOST H'CAP — 7f 1y(P)
3:25 (3:25) (Class 4) (0-85,87) 3-Y-0
£5,530 (£1,645; £822; £411; £300; £300) **Stalls Low**

Form RPR

02-2 **1** **Magical Wish (IRE)**[11] 1424 3-9-8 **86**........................ TomMarquand 6 95+
(Richard Hannon) *chsd ldrs for 1f: in tch in midfield after: effrt 2f out: clsd to chal 1f out: sn led but strly pressed: sustained duel after: nudged and attempted to bite chalr ins fnl f: jst prevailed on the nod* **11/2**[3]

031- **2** *nse* **Attainment**[188] 7943 3-9-1 **79**........................ JamieSpencer 5 88+
(James Tate) *hld up in tch in last pair: hdwy over 1f out: str chal u.p jst ins fnl f: edgd sltly lft but r.o wl in sustained duel w wnr after: jst btn on the nod* **11/4**[1]

-520 **3** *3 1/2* **Facethepuckout (IRE)**[18] 1285 3-8-12 **76**........................(p) LukeMorris 7 76
(John Ryan) *sn chsng ldrs: effrt and rdn to ld over 1f out: sn hung lft and hdd jst ins fnl f: outpcd fnl 100yds* **22/1**

150- **4** *nse* **Buckingham (IRE)**[206] 7346 3-9-5 **83**........................(w) CharlesBishop 4 80
(Eve Johnson Houghton) *dwlt and bustled along early: in tch: effrt whn nt clr run and hmpd over 1f out: sn swtchd rt: kpt on but no threat to ldrs ins fnl f: fin 4th: plcd 5th* **16/1**

3111 **5** *1 1/4* **Shanghai Grace**[14] 1360 3-9-0 **85**........................ CierenFallon(7) 1 84
(Charles Hills) *in tch in midfield: nt clr run and swtchd lft over 1f out: wnt lft: squeezed for room and hmpd jst ins fnl f: swtchd rt: no ch w ldrs and pushed along after: fin 4th: disqualified and plcd 5th* **11/4**[1]

104- **6** *2 1/2* **Sir Victor (IRE)**[187] 7957 3-9-5 **83**........................ RichardKingscote 8 73
(Tom Dascombe) *sn in rr and nvr travelling: nvr involved* **7/1**

01-5 **7** *11* **Freedom And Wheat (IRE)**[96] 65 3-8-0 **69**..........(p[1]) RhiainIngram(5) 3 30+
(Mark Usher) *w ldr tl rdn to ld 2f out: sn hdd: unable qck whn squeezed for room and snatched up ins fnl f: nt rcvr and eased after* **16/1**

341- **8** *1 1/4* **Winter Light**[163] 8683 3-9-9 **87**........................ JimCrowley 2 45
(Richard Hughes) *led tl hdd and rdn 2f out: sn lost pl and bhd whn swtchd rt 1f out: eased* **4/1**[2]

1m 25.75s (0.95) **Going Correction** +0.175s/f (Slow) **8** Ran SP% **117.3**
Speed ratings (Par 100): **101,100,96,95,95 92,80,78**
CSF £21.65 CT £312.19 TOTE £5.20: £1.50, £1.30, £5.60; EX 24.20 Trifecta £355.60.
Owner Middleham Park Racing XXXV **Bred** Mrs B McCullagh **Trained** East Everleigh, Wilts

FOCUS
This feature 3yo handicap was run at an average pace and it got tight in the home straight. It looks decent form with the front pair clear.

1686 BETWAY CLASSIFIED CLAIMING STKS — 6f 1y(P)
3:55 (3:55) (Class 6) 3-Y-0+
£3,105 (£924; £461; £300; £300; £300) **Stalls Low**

Form RPR

1353 **1** **Steelriver (IRE)**[4] 1597 9-9-3 67........................ JasonHart 2 74
(Michael Herrington) *hld up in midfield: clsd and swtchd lft over 1f out: led 1f out: r.o wl* **10/3**[1]

4345 **2** *1 1/2* **Wiff Waff**[8] 1507 4-9-5 70........................ RichardKingscote 6 72
(Stuart Williams) *prom in chsng gp: chsd clr ldr over 2f out: rdn and clsd over 1f out: ev ch 1f out: unable to match pce of wnr ins fnl f* **6/1**

1125 **3** *shd* **The Groove**[4] 1597 6-8-10 69........................ GinaMangan(7) 3 69
(David Evans) *hld up in last pair: clsd over 2f out: rdn and clsd to chse ldrs whn swtchd lft 1f out: kpt on ins fnl f* **4/1**[3]

4240 **4** *nk* **It Must Be Faith**[11] 1426 9-8-9 70 ow1........................(p) MarkCrehan(7) 7 67
(Michael Appleby) *s.i.s: sn in midfield on outer: clsd to go prom in main gp over 2f out: hdwy and ev ch u.p 1f out: unable to match pce of wnr ins fnl f* **12/1**

40-0 **5** *5* **Shepherd's Purse**[29] 1164 7-9-0 70........................(p) LauraCoughlan(7) 5 57
(David Loughnane) *taken down early: bustled along leaving stalls: sn led and wnt clr: rdn over 1f out: hdd 1f out: edgd rt and wknd ins fnl f* **6/1**

2242 **6** *1/2* **Lucky Lodge**[9] 1487 9-9-7 70........................(v) CamHardie 4 56
(Antony Brittain) *led: sn hdd and chsd clr ldr: lost 2nd and rdn over 2f out: wknd ins fnl f* **7/2**[2]

1026 **7** *13* **Duke Cosimo**[9] 1487 9-9-3 67........................(p) GeorgeWood 1 13
(Michael Herrington) *s.i.s: a in rr: rdn 3f out: wl bhd ins fnl f (jockey said gelding was never travelling)* **13/2**

1m 12.6s (0.70) **Going Correction** +0.175s/f (Slow) **7** Ran SP% **114.9**
Speed ratings (Par 101): **102,100,99,99,92 92,74**
CSF £23.70 TOTE £1.90: £1.10, £5.40; EX 28.00 Trifecta £93.10.
Owner Mrs H Lloyd-Herrington **Bred** Kildaragh Stud **Trained** Cold Kirby, N Yorks

FOCUS
Not the worst claimer, the winner rated near his better recent form.

1687 LADBROKES FILLIES' H'CAP — 6f 1y(P)
4:30 (4:30) (Class 5) (0-70,71) 3-Y-0+
£3,752 (£1,116; £557; £300; £300; £300) **Stalls Low**

Form RPR

3210 **1** **Pink Flamingo**[36] 1023 3-8-6 **67**........................ CierenFallon(7) 7 70
(Michael Attwater) *in tch in midfield: effrt over 1f out: hdwy u.p to chal ins fnl f: led cl home and hld on* **25/1**

030- **2** *hd* **Kwela**[216] 6996 3-8-10 **71**........................ GeorgiaDobie(7) 3 74
(Eve Johnson Houghton) *in tch in midfield: clsd to chse ldrs whn nt clr run 1f out: bmpd: wnt between rivals and ev ch wl ins fnl f: jst hld cl home* **12/1**

334 **3** *nk* **Bequest**[18] 1287 3-8-8 **62**........................ HollieDoyle 5 63
(Ron Hodges) *chsd ldrs: str chal and edgd lft u.p ins fnl f: no ex cl home* **8/1**[3]

650- **4** *1/2* **Devils Roc**[186] 7983 3-8-9 **63**........................ RobHornby 2 63
(Jonathan Portman) *trckd ldrs: effrt to chal on inner over 1f out: rdn to ld 1f out: edgd rt ins fnl f: hdd and no ex towards fin* **3/1**[2]

2203 **5** *3/4* **Antonia Clara**[9] 1476 3-8-4 **65**........................(p[1]) MarcoGhiani(7) 11 62
(Stuart Williams) *in tch on outer: effrt over 1f out: edgd lft but kpt on ins fnl f: nvr trbld ldrs* **14/1**

036- **6** *1 1/4* **Miss Gargar**[144] 9133 3-8-13 **67**........................ NicolaCurrie 4 61
(Harry Dunlop) *in tch in midfield: effrt over 1f out: kpt on same pce and no imp ins fnl f* **33/1**

-442 **7** *1* **Sussudio**[18] 1296 3-8-7 **61**........................(p) MartinDwyer 6 52
(Richard Spencer) *stdd and swtchd lft sn after s: t.k.h: hld up in tch in last trio: effrt over 1f out: keeping on but no threat to ldrs whn nt clrest of runs ins fnl f* **3/1**[2]

U00- **8** *1 1/4* **My Law**[196] 7667 3-8-5 **66**........................ IsobelFrancis(7) 10 53
(Jim Boyle) *sn in resr: effrt over 1f out: swtchd rt ins fnl f: nvr involved* **66/1**

-054 **9** 3/4 **Avon Green**[19] 1266 4-9-3 **59**................(b) JoeFanning 9 50
(Joseph Tuite) *chsd ldr over 4f out: ev ch u.p over 1f out: struggling to qckn whn squeezed for room: hmpd and snatched up ins fnl f: nt rcvr* **20/1**

541 **10** 3 1/4 **Velvet Morn (IRE)**[18] 1286 4-10-0 **70**................ FrankieDettori 1 60+
(William Knight) *hld up in last trio: clsd on inner whn nt clr run 1f out: nvr any room after and eased ins fnl f (jockey said filly suffered interference on the first bend and was denied a clear run in the home straight)* **5/2**[1]

432- **11** 1 3/4 **Vino Rosso (IRE)**[170] 8483 3-8-8 **62**................ JosephineGordon 8 47
(Michael Blanshard) *led: rdn and hdd 1f out: struggling to qckn whn squeezed for room and snatched up ins fnl f: dropped to rr and eased* **33/1**

1m 13.98s (2.08) **Going Correction** +0.175s/f (Slow) 11 Ran SP% **120.0**
WFA 3 from 4yo 12lb
Speed ratings (Par 100): **93,92,92,91,90 89,87,86,85,80 78**
CSF £286.42 CT £2627.40 TOTE £26.30: £6.40, £3.50, £2.40; EX 349.80 Trifecta £3556.20.
Owner Dare To Dream Racing **Bred** Lowther Racing **Trained** Epsom, Surrey

FOCUS
A moderate fillies' sprint handicap that proved a rough race. The form has been rated with feet on the ground.

1688 LADBROKES HOME OF THE ODDS BOOST FILLIES' H'CAP 1m 2f (P)
5:00 (5:00) (Class 5) (0-75,73) 4-Y-O+
£3,752 (£1,116; £557; £300; £300; £300) **Stalls** Low

Form RPR

-452 **1** **The Jean Genie**[18] 1292 5-9-5 **71**................ JoeFanning 8 82
(William Stone) *chsd ldr tl clsd to ld and travelling strly 2f out: sn rdn and clr and in n.d 1f out: easily* **4/1**[3]

1353 **2** 4 1/2 **Lady Alavesa**[13] 1387 4-9-5 **71**................(p) JosephineGordon 6 73
(Gay Kelleway) *hld up in last pair: effrt in 5th and stl plenty to do 2f out: kpt on u.p to snatch 2nd last strides: no ch w wnr* **13/2**

-002 **3** nk **Jamaican Jill**[34] 1065 4-9-6 **72**................ MartinDwyer 1 73
(William Muir) *led: rdn and hdd 2f out: sn outpcd: wl hld and plugged on same pce ins fnl f: lost 2nd last strides* **4/1**[3]

000- **4** 1 1/2 **Colourfield (IRE)**[146] 9087 4-8-4 **63**................(w) AledBeech(7) 4 61
(Charlie Fellowes) *midfield: effrt in 4th ent fnl f: no imp and plugged on same pce ins fnl f* **25/1**

-500 **5** 8 **Beatbybeatbybeat**[15] 1343 6-9-2 **68**................(b[1]) CamHardie 2 50
(Antony Brittain) *midfield: u.p and no imp ent fnl 2f: wl btn over 1f out* **25/1**

5 **6** 2 **Dream World (IRE)**[13] 1387 4-8-11 **63**................ LewisEdmunds 5 41
(Michael Appleby) *chsd ldrs: hung lft over 2f out: hung lft again and wl btn over 1f out: wknd (jockey said filly hung badly left-handed)* **3/1**[1]

2542 **7** 5 **Apache Blaze**[11] 1418 4-8-7 **64**................(p) DarraghKeenan(5) 3 32
(Robyn Brisland) *chsd ldrs tl over 2f out: wl bhd ins fnl f* **7/2**[2]

6423 **8** 1 3/4 **Margie's Choice (GER)**[32] 1099 4-9-0 **73**................(v) ScottMcCullagh(7) 7 38
(Michael Madgwick) *stdd s: hld up in rr: effrt and plenty to do jst over 2f out: sn wl btn (jockey said filly was never travelling)* **7/1**

2m 5.22s (-1.38) **Going Correction** +0.175s/f (Slow) 8 Ran SP% **120.7**
Speed ratings (Par 100): **104,100,100,98,92 90,86,85**
CSF £31.92 CT £111.07 TOTE £4.50: £1.50, £1.70, £1.10; EX 26.70 Trifecta £105.00.
Owner Miss Caroline Scott **Bred** Whitley Stud **Trained** West Wickham, Cambs

FOCUS
This run-of-the-mill fillies' handicap fell apart from 3f out. A minor pb from the winner.

1689 LADBROKES NOVICE STKS (PLUS 10 RACE) 1m 4f (P)
5:35 (5:35) (Class 5) 3-Y-O **£3,752** (£1,116; £557; £278) **Stalls** Low

Form RPR

52- **1** **So High**[132] 9308 3-9-5 0................ FrankieDettori 4 81+
(John Gosden) *w ldr tl led over 10f out: rdn and qcknd 2f out: r.o and in command ins fnl f* **1/10**[1]

32 **2** 3 **Autumn Pride (IRE)**[19] 1268 3-9-5 0................ JoeFanning 2 76
(Mark Johnston) *led tl over 10f out: chsd wnr after: rdn jst over 2f out: kpt on same pce and hld ins fnl f* **14/1**[3]

4 **3** 8 **Revamp (USA)**[29] 1165 3-9-5 0................ JamieSpencer 3 64
(David Simcock) *stdd and dropped in bhd after s: t.k.h and hld up in last: wnt 3rd 3f out: rdn over 1f out: sn outpcd and btn: eased wl ins fnl f* **11/1**[2]

04 **4** 21 **Winter Snowdrop (IRE)**[33] 1077 3-8-7 0................ SeanKirrane(7) 1 25
(Julia Feilden) *chsd ldng pair tl dropped to last 3f out: sn rdn and wl btn* **100/1**

2m 34.32s (1.32) **Going Correction** +0.175s/f (Slow) 4 Ran SP% **106.9**
Speed ratings (Par 98): **94,92,86,72**
CSF £2.38 TOTE £1.10; EX 1.90 Trifecta £2.60.
Owner George Strawbridge & John R Hass **Bred** George Strawbridge **Trained** Newmarket, Suffolk

FOCUS
A fair little novice event, which predictably proved tactical. The runner-up is perhaps the key to the form.
T/Plt: £501.60 to a £1 stake. Pool: £75,089.56 - 109.27 winning units T/Qpdt: £86.60 to a £1 stake. Pool: £7,735.95 - 66.07 winning units **Steve Payne**

NOTTINGHAM (L-H)
Wednesday, April 10

OFFICIAL GOING: Good to firm (good in places; watered; 7.9)
Wind: Fresh half- behind Weather: Sunny spells

1690 INTRODUCING RACING TV NOVICE STKS 1m 75y
1:30 (1:34) (Class 5) 3-Y-O **£3,881** (£1,155; £577; £288) **Stalls** Centre

Form RPR

22- **1** **King Of Change**[144] 9131 3-9-5 0................ SeanLevey 5 95+
(Richard Hannon) *led early: chsd ldr: led over 2f out: rdn out* **3/1**[2]

42- **2** 2 1/2 **King Ademar (USA)**[168] 8548 3-9-5 0................ OisinMurphy 4 90
(Martyn Meade) *s.i.s: sn rcvrd to ld: shkn up and hdd over 2f out: no ex wl ins fnl f* **11/8**[1]

2- **3** 1 1/2 **Vasiliev**[132] 9315 3-9-5 0................ AdamKirby 1 87+
(Clive Cox) *s.i.s: sn pushed along to chse ldrs: shkn up over 2f out: rdn over 1f out: styd on same pce ins fnl f* **3/1**[2]

4 2 1/2 **Pondus** 3-9-5 0................ DanielMuscutt 14 81+
(James Fanshawe) *s.i.s: hld up: shkn up and styd on fnl 3f: wnt 4th wl ins fnl f: nt rch ldrs* **33/1**[3]

5 1/2 **Piper Arrow** 3-9-5 0................ PJMcDonald 9 80
(Andrew Balding) *prom: rdn over 3f out: styd on same pce fnl 2f* **33/1**[3]

0 **6** 13 **Mandocello (FR)**[14] 1352 3-9-5 0................ DanielTudhope 16 51
(Rod Millman) *s.i.s: shkn up over 4f out: nvr on terms* **100/1**

06- **7** 3 **Monsieur Lambrays**[168] 8552 3-9-5 0................ JackMitchell 6 44
(Tom Clover) *s.i.s: nvr on terms* **40/1**

5 **8** nse **So Hi Cardi (FR)**[37] 1019 3-9-0 0................ JasonWatson 12 39
(Roger Charlton) *hld up: shkn up over 4f out: nvr on terms* **50/1**

0 **9** nk **Thomas Cubitt (FR)**[11] 1417 3-9-5 0................ HayleyTurner 3 44
(Michael Bell) *s.i.s: hld up: n.d* **80/1**

00- **10** 23 **Cheng Gong**[182] 8109 3-9-5 0................ StevieDonohoe 15
(Tom Clover) *a in rr* **250/1**

0- **11** 1 3/4 **Deerfoot**[156] 8880 3-9-5 0................ DavidAllan 8
(Anthony Carson) *mid-div: pushed along 1/2-way: wknd over 4f out* **250/1**

0 **12** 1/2 **Reformed Character (IRE)**[13] 1389 3-9-5 0................ EoinWalsh 2
(Lydia Pearce) *mid-div: pushed along 1/2-way: wknd 4f out* **250/1**

1m 42.32s (-4.38) **Going Correction** -0.425s/f (Firm) 12 Ran SP% **105.8**
Speed ratings (Par 98): **104,101,100,97,97 84,81,80,80,57 55,55**
CSF £5.94 TOTE £2.70: £1.10, £1.10, £1.20; EX 6.50 Trifecta £12.60.
Owner Ali Abdulla Saeed **Bred** Rabbah Bloodstock Limited **Trained** East Everleigh, Wilts
■ Lethal Look and Mokammal were withdrawn. Prices at time of withdrawal 250-1 and 6-1. Rule 4 applies to all bets - deduction 10p in the pound.

FOCUS
Inner Track in use and distances as advertised. The going was given as good to firm, good in places (Going Stick 7.9). Few got into this, the market principals dominating throughout. It's been rated as a decent race.

1691 JOIN RACING TV NOW H'CAP 5f 8y
2:00 (2:03) (Class 4) (0-80,81) 3-Y-O
£6,469 (£1,925; £962; £481; £300; £300) **Stalls** High

Form RPR

302- **1** **Free Love**[134] 9276 3-8-10 **74**................ TheodoreLadd(5) 5 81
(Michael Appleby) *w ldrs: shkn up to ld 2f out: rdn out* **12/1**

324- **2** 2 **Khafooq**[169] 8509 3-8-13 **72**................ PJMcDonald 4 72
(Robert Cowell) *chsd ldrs: rdn over 1f out: no ex wl ins fnl f* **11/1**

201- **3** nk **True Hero**[189] 7896 3-9-4 **80**................ RowanScott(3) 3 79+
(Nigel Tinkler) *s.i.s: hld up: hdwy over 1f out: rdn and edgd lft ins fnl f: styd on same pce* **16/1**

145- **4** 1 **Typhoon Ten (IRE)**[228] 6541 3-9-8 **81**................ SeanLevey 8 76
(Richard Hannon) *s.i.s: pushed along 1/2-way: hdwy over 1f out: nt rch ldrs* **13/2**[3]

01-3 **5** 2 1/2 **Phoenix Star (IRE)**[63] 621 3-9-6 **79**................ SilvestreDeSousa 12 65
(Amy Murphy) *s.i.s: shkn up 1/2-way: styd on ins fnl f: nt trble ldrs* **10/1**

114- **6** hd **Enchanted Linda**[180] 8161 3-9-6 **79**................ OisinMurphy 1 64
(Richard Hannon) *w ldrs on outer 3f: shkn up over 1f out: wknd ins fnl f* **4/1**[1]

305- **7** shd **Baby Steps**[196] 7676 3-9-7 **80**................ BenCurtis 2 65
(David Loughnane) *sn chsng ldrs: pushed along 1/2-way: wknd over 1f out* **11/2**[2]

203- **8** 1 1/4 **Pink Iceburg (IRE)**[175] 8314 3-9-5 **78**................ ShaneKelly 7 59
(Richard Hughes) *racd keenly: w ldr tl led over 3f out: hdd 2f out: wknd fnl f: b.b.v (vet said gelding bled from the nose)* **12/1**

002- **9** 3/4 **Raypeteafterme**[158] 8827 3-8-12 **71**................ CallumShepherd 11 49
(Declan Carroll) *sn led: hdd over 3f out: edgd lft 1/2-way: wknd and eased fnl f (jockey said gelding had no more to give)* **22/1**

410- **10** 1 **Aloysius Lilius (IRE)**[194] 7720 3-8-12 **71**................ TomEaves 6 45
(Kevin Ryan) *hld up in tch: rdn over 1f out: sn wknd* **9/1**

4416 **11** 5 **Sandridge Lad (IRE)**[13] 1388 3-9-7 **80**................ StevieDonohoe 9 36
(John Ryan) *chsd ldrs: lost pl over 3f out: n.d after (trainer said gelding was unsuited by the undulating inner track on this occasion)* **40/1**

100- **12** 25 **Dark Shadow (IRE)**[189] 7899 3-9-5 **78**................ AdamKirby 10
(Clive Cox) *awkward s: sn pushed along in rr: outpcd fr over 3f out: eased over 1f out (jockey said gelding lost its action)* **8/1**

58.0s (-2.20) **Going Correction** -0.425s/f (Firm) 12 Ran SP% **115.3**
Speed ratings (Par 100): **100,96,96,94,90 90,90,88,87,85 77,37**
CSF £133.73 CT £2110.09 TOTE £13.30: £4.80, £3.30, £3.90; EX 134.80 Trifecta £2644.20.
Owner The North South Syndicate **Bred** Brendan Boyle Bloodstock Ltd **Trained** Oakham, Rutland

FOCUS
A competitive sprint handicap. The second has been rated to the balance of last year's better form.

1692 WATCH RACING TV NOW CONDITIONS STKS (PLUS 10 RACE) 5f 8y
2:30 (2:33) (Class 3) 3-Y-O **£9,337** (£2,796; £1,398; £699; £349) **Stalls** High

Form RPR

144- **1** **Garrus (IRE)**[165] 8629 3-8-12 95................ RyanMoore 3 105+
(Jeremy Noseda) *w ldr tl led 4f out: shkn up over 1f out: hung rt wl ins fnl f: pushed out* **13/8**[2]

450- **2** 1 1/4 **Pocket Dynamo (USA)**[159] 8818 3-9-4 106................(h) OisinMurphy 5 106
(Robert Cowell) *chsd ldrs: swtchd lft over 4f out: chsd wnr over 1f out: sn rdn and edgd lft: styd on same pce ins fnl f* **6/4**[1]

451- **3** 6 **Broken Spear**[180] 8163 3-9-0 94................(p) KevinStott 4 80
(Tony Coyle) *led 1f: remained handy: pushed along 1/2-way: rdn and hung lft over 1f out: wknd ins fnl f* **7/2**[3]

5000 **4** 2 **Shining Armor**[13] 1388 3-8-12 88................ SilvestreDeSousa 1 73
(John Ryan) *w ldrs to 1/2-way: rdn and hung lft over 1f out: sn wknd* **14/1**

416- **5** 11 **Mawde (IRE)**[284] 4405 3-8-2 79................ TheodoreLadd(5) 2 27
(Rod Millman) *w ldrs to 1/2-way: rdn and wknd over 1f out (jockey said filly stopped quickly)* **33/1**

57.01s (-3.19) **Going Correction** -0.425s/f (Firm) course record 5 Ran SP% **109.9**
Speed ratings (Par 102): **108,106,96,93,75**
CSF £4.43 TOTE £3.90: £2.60, £1.10; EX 4.70 Trifecta £7.60.
Owner Mrs Susan Roy **Bred** Mrs Max Morris **Trained** Newmarket, Suffolk

FOCUS
A nice performance from the winner, who beat the form horse a shade comfortably and set a new course record in the process. The front pair were well clear.

1693 BARRY HILLS FURTHER FLIGHT STKS (LISTED RACE) 1m 6f
3:05 (3:05) (Class 1) 4-Y-O+ **£22,684** (£8,600; £4,304; £2,144) **Stalls** Low

Form RPR

22-2 **1** **Elegiac**[34] 1062 4-9-0 104................ FrannyNorton 1 107
(Mark Johnston) *mde all: shkn up over 2f out: rdn and edgd rt fr over 1f out: styd on* **7/4**[2]

0-43 **2** 3/4 **Amazing Red (IRE)**[19] 1267 6-9-1 102................ PJMcDonald 4 104
(Ed Dunlop) *hld up: hdwy over 2f out: chsd wnr over 1f out: sn rdn: styd on* **16/1**[3]

130- **3** 3 3/4 **Pilaster**[172] 8406 4-8-9 108................ RyanMoore 2 97
(Roger Varian) *edgd rt s: trckd ldrs: shkn up and swtchd rt over 3f out: wnt 2nd over 2f out tl over 1f out: eased whn btn ins fnl f* **4/7**[1]

10-5 **4** *16* **Ravenous**[16] 735 8-9-1 75........ DanielMuscutt 3 78
(Luke Dace) *chsd wnr: ev ch wl over 2f out: sn lost 2nd: wknd over 1f out: eased fnl f* **100/1**

3m 1.58s (-4.82) **Going Correction** -0.425s/f (Firm)
WFA 4 from 6yo+ 1lb **4 Ran SP% 106.9**
Speed ratings (Par 111): **96,95,93,84**
CSF £19.22 TOTE £2.10; EX 14.00 Trifecta £13.10.
Owner S&d Richards, N Browne And I Boyce **Bred** Aston House Stud **Trained** Middleham Moor, N Yorks

FOCUS
With the favourite below form this didn't take a lot of winning. There's every chance the winner can rate higher.

1694 EVERY RACE LIVE ON RACING TV H'CAP — 1m 75y
3:35 (3:36) (Class 3) (0-95,95) 4-Y-0+ **£9,703** (£2,887; £1,443; £721) **Stalls** Centre

Form RPR

136- **1** **Rise Hall**[166] 8596 4-8-13 **87**........(b) OisinMurphy 10 96+
(Martyn Meade) *s.i.s: hld up: hdwy over 2f out: rdn: edgd lft and r.o to ld wl ins fnl f* **8/1**

103- **2** *2 1/4* **The Emperor Within (FR)**[153] 8957 4-9-5 **93**........ GeraldMosse 4 97
(Martin Smith) *chsd ldr: led over 2f out: rdn over 1f out: hdd wl ins fnl f: eased nr fin* **11/1**

211/ **3** *2 1/2* **Bowerman**[489] 9125 5-9-6 **94**........ AndreaAtzeni 6 93+
(Roger Varian) *s.i.s: hld up: hdwy over 2f out: edgd lft and styd on same pce ins fnl f: b.b.v (jockey said horse bled from the nose)* **5/2**[1]

35-0 **4** *1 1/4* **War Glory (IRE)**[32] 1097 6-9-1 **94**........ SeamusCronin(5) 11 90
(Richard Hannon) *chsd ldrs: rdn to go 2nd over 1f out: no ex ins fnl f* **25/1**

42-4 **5** *1/2* **Dawaaleeb (USA)**[11] 1413 5-9-6 **94**........(v) DavidAllan 12 89
(Les Eyre) *hld up: rdn over 3f out: styd on ins fnl f: nt rch ldrs* **10/1**

110- **6** *nk* **Knighted (IRE)**[186] 7991 4-9-3 **91**........ KevinStott 8 85
(Kevin Ryan) *chsd ldrs: rdn over 3f out: wknd fnl f* **10/1**

340- **7** *3 1/2* **Pastime**[280] 4525 5-8-2 **79**........ WilliamCox(3) 13 65
(Gay Kelleway) *sn pushed along and prom: rdn over 3f out: wknd over 1f out* **50/1**

100- **8** *2* **Qaysar (FR)**[293] 4028 4-9-7 **95**........ SeanLevey 3 77
(Richard Hannon) *hld up: rdn over 2f out: wknd fnl f* **6/1**[2]

236- **9** *3* **Kaeso**[186] 7991 5-9-0 **88**........ TomEaves 1 63
(Nigel Tinkler) *s.i.s: hld up: plld hrd: rdn over 2f out: sn wknd* **14/1**

/46- **10** *1* **Markazi (FR)**[194] 7722 5-9-3 **91**........(b) DanielTudhope 2 64
(David O'Meara) *sn led: rdn and hdd over 2f out: wknd over 1f out* **7/1**[3]

-645 **11** *1* **Mickey (IRE)**[12] 1395 6-8-6 **83**........(v) JaneElliott(3) 14 54
(Tom Dascombe) *hld up: a in rr* **40/1**

1325 **12** *1 3/4* **Glory Of Paris (IRE)**[32] 1099 5-8-10 **84**........ SilvestreDeSousa 9 51
(Michael Appleby) *dwlt: hld up: racd keenly: wknd 3f out (jockey said gelding ran too free)* **9/1**

1m 41.6s (-5.10) **Going Correction** -0.425s/f (Firm) course record **12 Ran SP% 117.9**
Speed ratings (Par 107): **108,105,103,102,101 101,97,95,92,91 90,88**
CSF £90.94 CT £285.62 TOTE £7.90: £2.70, £4.00, £1.80; EX 100.40 Trifecta £686.10.
Owner R C Bond **Bred** Bond Thoroughbred Corporation **Trained** Manton, Wilts

FOCUS
A good, competitive handicap, and the winner did it well. The pace was strong and it looks quite a deep race.

1695 RACINGTV.COM H'CAP — 1m 75y
4:10 (4:12) (Class 5) (0-75,77) 4-Y-0+
£3,881 (£1,155; £577; £300; £300; £300) **Stalls** Centre

Form RPR

6-33 **1** **Saisons D'Or (IRE)**[29] 1164 4-9-2 **70**........ JackGarritty 6 78
(Jedd O'Keeffe) *mde virtually all: rdn and edgd rt over 1f out: jst hld on* **13/2**[3]

060- **2** *shd* **Stringybark Creek**[172] 8415 5-9-3 **71**........ TrevorWhelan 4 79
(David Loughnane) *chsd ldrs: rdn and ev ch ins fnl f: styd on* **28/1**

3532 **3** *1 1/4* **Ambient (IRE)**[29] 1169 4-9-5 **73**........ AdamKirby 8 78
(Jane Chapple-Hyam) *chsd wnr: rdn and hung rt fr over 1f out: kpt on* **7/2**[1]

263- **4** *nk* **Where's Jeff**[198] 7601 4-9-7 **75**........ NathanEvans 2 79
(Michael Easterby) *hld up: racd keenly: rdn over 2f out: hdwy over 1f out: styd on* **6/1**[2]

0-00 **5** *3/4* **Fighting Temeraire (IRE)**[14] 1355 6-8-9 **63**........ FrannyNorton 7 66
(Dean Ivory) *prom: stdd and lost pl over 6f out: hdwy over 2f out: shkn up and carried rt fr over 1f out: styd on* **13/2**[3]

-656 **6** *1 1/2* **Me Too Nagasaki (IRE)**[42] 922 5-9-9 **77**........(t) OisinMurphy 1 76+
(Stuart Williams) *hld up: hdwy over 2f out: shkn up over 1f out: styd on same pce ins fnl f* **7/2**[1]

44-0 **7** *nk* **Music Seeker (IRE)**[11] 1418 5-8-13 **74**........(t) CianMacRedmond(7) 10 73
(Declan Carroll) *hld up: racd keenly: r.o ins fnl f: nvr nr to chal* **8/1**

35-0 **8** *7* **Zeshov (IRE)**[19] 1271 8-9-7 **75**........(p) DanielTudhope 5 58
(Rebecca Bastiman) *sn prom: rdn over 2f out: wknd fnl f* **16/1**

662- **9** *1* **Donnelly's Rainbow (IRE)**[190] 7871 6-8-2 **61**........ TheodoreLadd(5) 9 42
(Rebecca Bastiman) *s.i.s: hld up: wknd over 2f out* **12/1**

1m 42.67s (-4.03) **Going Correction** -0.425s/f (Firm) **9 Ran SP% 113.5**
Speed ratings (Par 103): **103,102,101,101,100 99,98,91,90**
CSF £160.19 CT £737.98 TOTE £6.30: £1.80, £8.00, £2.30; EX 123.00 Trifecta £835.90.
Owner The Fatalists **Bred** Mount Coote Stud & Knocktoran Stud **Trained** Middleham Moor, N Yorks

FOCUS
They went fairly steady early and those towards the fore stayed there. Straightforward form, with the first two rated to their best.

1696 FOLLOW @RACINGTV ON TWITTER H'CAP (DIV I) — 1m 2f 50y
4:40 (4:40) (Class 5) (0-75,77) 3-Y-O
£3,881 (£1,155; £577; £300; £300; £300) **Stalls** Low

Form RPR

053- **1** **Love So Deep (JPN)**[186] 7995 3-8-10 **64**........ BenCurtis 4 70+
(Jane Chapple-Hyam) *chsd ldr tl over 8f out: remained handy: rdn over 1f out: r.o u.p to ld towards fin* **16/1**

535- **2** *hd* **Buriram (IRE)**[180] 8157 3-9-6 **74**........ SilvestreDeSousa 7 80
(Ralph Beckett) *broke wl enough: sn stdd and lost pl: hdwy over 2f out: rdn to ld ins fnl f: edgd lft: hdd towards fin* **3/1**[2]

564- **3** *1/2* **Bo Samraan (IRE)**[168] 8550 3-9-9 **77**........ FrannyNorton 3 82
(Mark Johnston) *prom: chsd ldr over 8f out: led over 2f out: rdn over 1f out: hdd ins fnl f: unable qck towards fin* **2/1**[1]

035- **4** *4 1/2* **Valence**[163] 8682 3-9-2 **70**........ DanielMuscutt 9 67
(Ed Dunlop) *hld up: hdwy over 2f out: rdn over 1f out: styd on same pce fnl f (vet said gelding had a small amount of blood in its mouth due to the colt having bitten its tongue)* **25/1**

-024 **5** *4* **Smoki Smoka (IRE)**[48] 839 3-8-12 **69**........(p[1]) JaneElliott(3) 8 59
(Tom Dascombe) *led: rdn and hdd over 2f out: wknd fnl f* **16/1**

034- **6** *1 1/2* **Fares Poet (IRE)**[177] 8257 3-9-7 **75**........ GeraldMosse 2 62
(Marco Botti) *hld up: hdwy over 2f out: rdn and wknd over 1f out* **10/1**

45-0 **7** *nk* **Isle Of Wolves**[19] 1264 3-9-3 **71**........ ShaneKelly 10 58
(Jim Boyle) *hld up: shkn up over 3f out: nvr on terms* **22/1**

55-3 **8** *2* **She's Apples (IRE)**[18] 1287 3-9-0 **68**........ JasonWatson 6 51
(Roger Charlton) *prom: pushed along and lost pl over 4f out: wknd over 2f out* **4/1**[3]

004 **9** *12* **Poor Auld Paddy**[26] 1217 3-8-7 **61** oh1........ HayleyTurner 1 22
(David Elsworth) *hld up: hdwy over 6f out: rdn and wknd over 2f out* **16/1**

2m 10.52s (-2.88) **Going Correction** -0.425s/f (Firm) **9 Ran SP% 113.3**
Speed ratings (Par 98): **94,93,93,89,86 85,85,83,74**
CSF £62.62 CT £140.62 TOTE £17.70: £4.10, £1.40, £1.20; EX 93.10 Trifecta £342.90.
Owner Love So Deep Syndicate **Bred** Daylesford Stud **Trained** Dalham, Suffolk
■ Stewards' Enquiry : Ben Curtis two-day ban; misuse of whip (Apr 24-25)

FOCUS
Marginally the quicker of the two divisions. The winner can do better and the next two are credited with improvement.

1697 FOLLOW @RACINGTV ON TWITTER H'CAP (DIV II) — 1m 2f 50y
5:15 (5:18) (Class 5) (0-75,77) 3-Y-O
£3,881 (£1,155; £577; £300; £300; £300) **Stalls** Low

Form RPR

25-3 **1** **Mayfair Spirit (IRE)**[28] 1174 3-8-12 **66**........ StevieDonohoe 2 72
(Charlie Fellowes) *chsd ldrs: rdn over 1f out: led ins fnl f: styd on (ran without a tongue strap because it had come adrift on the way to the start and could not be re-fitted)* **9/2**[2]

305- **2** *1/2* **Cuban Sun**[146] 9083 3-8-11 **65**........ BarryMcHugh 4 70
(James Given) *led 2f: chsd ldr: shkn up to ld over 2f out: rdn and hdd ins fnl f: kpt on (vet was informed that the filly could not run until the day after passing a stalls test)* **40/1**

532- **3** *1 1/2* **Nabbeyl (IRE)**[123] 9460 3-9-9 **77**........ AndreaAtzeni 6 79
(Roger Varian) *chsd ldrs: lost pl over 5f out: hdwy over 2f out: rdn over 1f out: styd on* **11/10**[1]

042- **4** *1 3/4* **Silkstone (IRE)**[154] 8929 3-9-5 **73**........ AdamKirby 8 72
(Pam Sly) *hld up: pushed along and hdwy over 4f out: rdn over 2f out: styd on same pce ins fnl f* **5/1**[3]

663- **5** *shd* **Fantastic Ms Fox**[160] 8782 3-8-2 **61** oh1........ SeanDavis(5) 7 60
(Richard Fahey) *hld up: pushed along over 5f out: rdn over 2f out: nt pce to chal* **16/1**

226- **6** *5* **Startego**[160] 8782 3-9-7 **75**........ DanielTudhope 3 65
(Archie Watson) *chsd ldr: led 8f out: rdn and hdd over 2f out: wknd and eased fnl f* **9/1**

660- **7** *1 1/4* **Robert Fitzroy (IRE)**[161] 8738 3-9-3 **71**........ LouisSteward 1 59
(Michael Bell) *hld up: racd keenly: nvr on terms* **8/1**

2m 10.67s (-2.73) **Going Correction** -0.425s/f (Firm) **7 Ran SP% 111.9**
Speed ratings (Par 98): **93,92,91,90,89 85,84**
CSF £126.98 CT £322.43 TOTE £5.60: £2.70, £15.80; EX 141.00 Trifecta £338.50.
Owner J Soiza **Bred** Ringfort Stud Ltd **Trained** Newmarket, Suffolk

FOCUS
Slightly the slower of the two divisions, and it was the one who had the benefit of a previous run this season who came out on top. A minor pb from the winner as rated.
T/Plt: £68.00 to a £1 stake. Pool: £54,425.12 - 583.73 winning units T/Qpdt: £13.70 to a £1 stake. Pool: £3,930.93 - 211.35 winning units **Colin Roberts**

1698 - 1705a (Foreign Racing) - See Raceform Interactive

1512 MAISONS-LAFFITTE (R-H)
Wednesday, April 10

OFFICIAL GOING: Turf: good to soft

1706a PRIX IMPRUDENCE (GROUP 3) (3YO FILLIES) (TURF) — 7f
3:27 3-Y-O **£36,036** (£14,414; £10,810; £7,207; £3,603)

RPR

1 **Watch Me (FR)**[151] 9007 3-9-0 0........ ChristopheSoumillon 4 107
(F-H Graffard, France) *racd in fnl trio: asked for effrt between rivals 2f out: rdn to chal ent fnl f: r.o strly clsng stages: led fnl 50yds* **58/10**[3]

2 *snk* **Suphala (FR)**[207] 3-9-0 0........ Pierre-CharlesBoudot 5 107
(A Fabre, France) *disp early tl sn trckd ldr: pushed along to chse ldr 2f out: rdn 1 1/2f out: led narrowly ent fnl f: hrd pressed clsng stages: hdd fnl 50yds* **6/4**[1]

3 *1 1/2* **Jet Setteuse (FR)**[24] 1242 3-9-0 0........ Francois-XavierBertras 3 103
(F Rohaut, France) *mid-div: pushed along and effrt over 2f out: rdn 1 1/2f out: nt qckn w ldrs ent fnl f: kpt on but nt match pce of front pair* **36/5**

4 *hd* **Devant (FR)**[161] 8754 3-9-0 0........ OlivierPeslier 2 102
(H-A Pantall, France) *in tch: pushed along whn pce qcknd 2f out: rdn over 1f out: sltly hmpd ent fnl f: kpt on clsng stages: nvr trbld ldrs* **41/10**[2]

5 *3/4* **Vanilla Gold (IRE)**[27] 1199 3-9-0 0........ StephanePasquier 1 100
(N Clement, France) *disp early tl sn led at stdy pce: asked to qckn over 2f out: sn rdn: hdd over 1f out: no ex ins fnl f* **11/1**

6 *1/2* **Lucky Jolie (USA)**[194] 3-9-0 0........ MaximeGuyon 6 99
(A Fabre, France) *racd a little keenly: hld up in fnl pair: pushed along and effrt on outside of rivals 2f out: limited rspnse: kpt on same pce ins fnl f: n.d* **7/1**

7 *nk* **Pure Zen (FR)**[187] 7971 3-9-0 0........ AlexisBadel 7 98
(Gianluca Bietolini, France) *hld up in rr: pushed along and effrt on nr side rail 2f out: sltly short of racing room ent fnl f: kpt on same pce clsng stages: nvr threatened* **7/1**

1m 28.09s (0.09) **7 Ran SP% 119.8**
PARI-MUTUEL (all including 1 euro stake): WIN 6.80; PLACE 2.70, 1.70; SF 18.30.
Owner Alexander Tamagni & Mme R Vannod **Bred** Mme A Tamagni & Cocheese Bloodstock Anstalt **Trained** France

FOCUS
This can be an informative race at the start of a long season but it remains to be seen how good this running will be.

1707a PRIX DJEBEL (GROUP 3) (3YO COLTS & GELDINGS) (TURF) — 7f
4:02 3-Y-O **£36,036** (£14,414; £10,810; £7,207; £3,603)

RPR

1 **Munitions (USA)**[148] 9045 3-9-2 0........ MickaelBarzalona 4 113
(A Fabre, France) *racd in 2nd in nr side gp: pushed along to chal 2f out: led 1 1/2f out: sn rdn: hrd pressed ins fnl f: jst prevailed on line* **27/10**[1]

2 nse **Graignes (FR)**[164] 8668 3-9-2 0 CristianDemuro 2 113
(Y Barberot, France) *hld up in rr of nr side gp: pushed along and prog fr 2f out: rdn to press ldr ent fnl f: kpt on strly clsng stages: denied on line* **33/10**[2]

3 1 1/2 **Amilcar (IRE)**[141] 9167 3-9-2 0 Pierre-CharlesBoudot 3 109
(H-A Pantall, France) *led nr side gp: asked to qckn w overall ldr 2f out: sn u.p: kpt on gamely ins fnl f: nt match front pair* **47/10**

4 1/2 **Toijk (FR)**[220] 6845 3-9-2 0 HugoJourniac 1 108
(M Nigge, France) *racd in 3rd in nr side gp: pushed along 2f out: unable qck w ldrs: kpt on u.p ins fnl f: nvr gng pce to threaten* **79/10**

5 nk **Marie's Diamond (IRE)**[159] 8821 3-9-2 0 IoritzMendizabal 7 107
(Mark Johnston) *led centre gp and overall ldr: asked to qckn 2f out: rdn and hdd 1 1/2f out: grad wknd ins fnl f: no ex towards fin* **9/1**

6 3/4 **Pretty Boy (IRE)**[187] 7971 3-9-2 0 ChristopheSoumillon 5 105
(Mme Pia Brandt, France) *last of trio in centre gp: pushed along and effrt whn gps merged 2f out: rdn over 1f out: kpt on ins fnl f but n.d* **74/10**

7 8 **Harmless (FR)**[270] 4973 3-9-2 0 MaximeGuyon 6 83
(C Ferland, France) *trckd ldr in centre gp: struggling to go pce and pushed along over 2f out: dropped to rr 1 1/2f out: wl btn ent fnl f: eased clsng stages* **22/5**[3]

1m 25.57s (-2.43) 7 Ran SP% 119.5
PARI-MUTUEL (all including 1 euro stake): WIN 3.70; PLACE 2.10, 1.90; SF 15.50.
Owner Godolphin SNC **Bred** Winchell Thoroughbreds LLC **Trained** Chantilly, France

FOCUS
Much like the Prix Imprudence that preceded this contest, there have been good and ordinary runnings of this, so only time will tell which it turns out to be. They split into two groups early and the four that stayed stands' side filled the first four positions.

1708a PRIX JACQUES LAFFITTE (LISTED RACE) (4YO+) (TURF) 1m 1f
4:37 4-Y-O+ £23,423 (£9,369; £7,027; £4,684; £2,342)

RPR

1 **Danceteria (FR)**[154] 8945 4-9-0 0 MaximeGuyon 3 108+
(David Menuisier) *hld up towards rr of nrside gp: pushed along over 2f out: swtchd to centre of crse and hdwy over 1f out: rdn to chse ldr: drvn ins fnl f to chal: led cl home* **12/1**

2 hd **Mer Et Nuages (FR)**[321] 3041 4-9-4 0 Pierre-CharlesBoudot 8 112
(A Fabre, France) *towards rr of gp nrside early: impr between rivals 2f out: rdn to ld over 1f out: drvn and strly chal ins fnl f: hdd fnl strides* **6/4**[1]

3 3 **Mind Mapping (USA)**[154] 8945 4-9-0 0 MickaelBarzalona 6 102
(A Fabre, France) *trckd ldr nrside: pushed into ld 2f out: rdn and hdd over 1f out: kpt on same pce fnl f* **9/1**

4 1/2 **Aviateur (FR)**[177] 4-9-0 0 StephanePasquier 2 101
(A Kleinkorres, Germany) **18/1**

5 shd **Palmyre (FR)**[155] 8914 4-8-10 0 AlexisBadel 1 96
(H-F Devin, France) **13/1**

6 1/2 **Jazz Melodie (FR)**[31] 1127 5-8-10 0 FabienLefebvre 7 95
(P De Chevigny, France) **12/1**

7 2 1/2 **Vadavar (FR)**[29] 4-9-0 0 ChristopheSoumillon 11 94
(A De Royer-Dupre, France) **44/5**[3]

8 snk **Isole Canarie (IRE)**[150] 9025 4-9-1 0 (b[1]) AntoineHamelin 10 95
(Gavin Hernon, France) **28/1**

9 1/2 **Qualisaga (FR)**[23] 5-8-10 0 EddyHardouin 5 89
(Carina Fey, France) **83/10**[2]

10 7 **Watayouna (FR)**[268] 5035 4-9-1 0 OlivierPeslier 4 79
(F-H Graffard, France) **11/1**

11 3/4 **Broderie**[29] 4-8-10 0 VincentCheminaud 9 73
(H-A Pantall, France) *led gp down centre of crse: urged along and hdd 2f out: sn btn and eased over 1f out* **13/1**

12 10 **Replenish (FR)**[36] 1030 6-9-0 0 TheoBachelot 12 56
(S Cerulis, France) **41/1**

1m 50.25s (-4.45) 12 Ran SP% 120.1
PARI-MUTUEL (all including 1 euro stake): WIN 13.00; PLACE 3.40, 1.90, 1.90; DF 20.20.
Owner Clive Washbourn **Bred** Berend Van Dalfsen **Trained** Pulborough, W Sussex

1709a PRIX DE RUEIL (CLAIMER) (2YO) (TURF) 5f
5:45 2-Y-O £10,360 (£4,144; £3,108; £2,072; £1,036)

RPR

1 **Ask Me Not (IRE)** 2-9-4 0 AntoineHamelin 3 77
(Matthieu Palussiere, France) **9/5**[1]

2 shd **Miss Tiche (IRE)**[24] 1240 2-8-11 0 CristianDemuro 9 70
(G Botti, France) **18/1**

3 snk **Jolie (FR)** 2-8-8 0 DelphineSantiago(3) 8 69
(D Guillemin, France) **3/1**[2]

4 3 1/2 **Captain Tatman (FR)**[24] 1240 2-8-11 0 TheoBachelot 6 57
(George Baker) *dwlt: sn rcvrd to ld after 1f: pushed along 2f out: rdn and hdd over 1f out: kpt on one pce fnl f* **9/1**

5 snk **Panthera Tigris**[24] 1240 2-8-8 0 MickaelBarzalona 2 53
(Jo Hughes, France) *trckd ldrs nrside: shkn up 2f out: rdn w limited rspnse over 1f out: styd on same pce fnl f* **12/1**

6 hd **Can't Hold Us (FR)**[24] 1240 2-8-8 0 JeromeMoutard(3) 11 56
(D Allard, France) **25/1**

7 1 1/4 **Dalkelef (FR)** 2-8-9 0 ThomasTrullier(6) 4 55
(M Boutin, France) **26/5**[3]

8 hd **Proun (FR)** 2-7-13 0 MlleLeaBails(9) 10 47
(Andrea Marcialis, France) **22/1**

9 4 **Out Bound (IRE)** 2-9-1 0 AurelienLemaitre 5 40
(J-V Toux, France) **18/1**

10 10 **L'Ami De Baileys (FR)** 2-9-1 0 IoritzMendizabal 7 4
(J-V Toux, France) **14/1**

1m 1.46s 10 Ran SP% 119.9
PARI-MUTUEL (all including 1 euro stake): WIN 2.80; PLACE 1.40, 3.80, 1.50; DF 21.40.
Owner Mrs Theresa Marnane **Bred** A Marnane & J Halligan **Trained** France

[1543] CHELMSFORD (A.W) (L-H)
Thursday, April 11

OFFICIAL GOING: Polytrack: standard
Wind: Light, across Weather: Fine

1710 TRANSPARENT RECRUITMENT SOLUTIONS LTD APPRENTICE H'CAP 1m 2f (P)
2:00 (2:02) (Class 6) (0-60,62) 4-Y-0+
£3,105 (£924; £461; £300; £300; £300) Stalls Low

Form RPR

4511 1 **Compass Point**[14] 1378 4-9-6 62 SeamusCronin(3) 5 69
(Robyn Brisland) *chsd ldrs: clsd to trck ldrs and nt clr run over 1f out: rdn to chse ldr 1f out: led 100yds out: styd on: rdn out* **9/4**[1]

0503 2 1/2 **Attain**[9] 1498 10-8-11 57 KateLeahy(7) 7 62
(Archie Watson) *s.i.s: hld up in tch in last pair: clsd u.p over 1f out: styd on to press wnr towards fin: nvr quite getting on terms* **14/1**

1044 3 3/4 **Don't Do It (IRE)**[10] 1482 4-9-2 55 (v) TheodoreLadd 3 59
(Michael Appleby) *led over 8f out: rdn and hrd pressed over 1f out: hdd 100yds out: no ex and jst outpcd towards fin* **3/1**[2]

000- 4 nk **Foxy's Spirit**[24] 5978 4-8-4 46 oh1 ThoreHammerHansen(3) 6 49
(Clare Hobson) *broke wl and led early: dropped into midfield over 8f out: rdn 3f out: drifted to inner 2f out: n.m.r over 1f out: clsd to chse ldrs whn nt clr run and swtchd rt ins fnl f: kpt on towards fin* **100/1**

5004 5 1/2 **Carvelas (IRE)**[7] 1548 10-9-6 59 SeanDavis 10 61
(J R Jenkins) *stdd s: hld up in tch in last pair: effrt wd over 1f out: styd on wl u.p ins fnl f: nt rch ldrs* **20/1**

-500 6 nk **Chantresse (IRE)**[37] 1024 4-9-9 62 (p) ThomasGreatrex 2 64
(Mark Usher) *bustled along leaving stalls: chsd ldr over 8f out tl 6f out: rdn over 3f out: lost pl and swtchd rt 1f out: kpt on wl ins fnl f: nt rch ldrs* **8/1**

00-4 7 2 1/4 **The Lords Walk**[5] 1591 6-9-8 61 (p) RyanWhile 8 58
(Bill Turner) *in tch in midfield on outer: unable qck u.p over 1f out: wknd ins fnl f* **5/1**

6023 8 2 **Corked (IRE)**[13] 1399 6-9-7 60 DylanHogan 4 53
(Alistair Whillans) *led 9f out tl over 8f out: styd prom: jnd ldr 6f out tl unable qck over 1f out: wknd ins fnl f* **4/1**[3]

2m 8.63s (0.03) **Going Correction** +0.025s/f (Slow) 8 Ran SP% 116.0
Speed ratings (Par 101): **100,99,99,98,98 98,96,94**
CSF £36.10 CT £96.99 TOTE £2.80: £1.10, £2.90, £1.60; EX 25.40 Trifecta £84.10.
Owner Mrs Jackie Cornwell **Bred** Mrs J A Cornwell **Trained** Danethorpe, Notts

FOCUS
An ordinary handicap which played towards those ridden with a bit of patience. Straightforward form, rated around the second and third.

1711 BET TOTEEXACTA AT TOTESPORT.COM NOVICE STKS 1m 2f (P)
2:30 (2:30) (Class 4) 3-Y-O+ £5,530 (£1,645; £822; £411) Stalls Low

Form RPR

2- 1 **Derevo**[167] 8593 3-9-3 0 RyanMoore 4 78+
(Sir Michael Stoute) *chsd ldr: pushed along and clsd ent fnl 2f: rdn to ld over 1f out: styd on wl ins fnl f* **8/13**[1]

1- 2 1 1/4 **Kimblewick (IRE)**[148] 9049 3-9-5 0 RobertHavlin 3 77+
(John Gosden) *chsd ldng pair: effrt and clsd to press ldng pair 2f out: drvn and ev ch over 1f out: unable to match pce of wnr ins fnl f* **13/8**[2]

606- 3 3 1/2 **Mr Zoom Zoom**[124] 9460 3-9-3 0 EoinWalsh 1 68
(Luke McJannet) *stdd and awkward leaving stalls: hld up in tch in last: effrt on outer and wnt 3rd over 1f out: no imp whn rn green and hung lft 1f out: kpt on same pce ins fnl f* **40/1**

3 4 9 **Hendrix (IRE)**[69] 518 3-9-3 0 CharlieBennett 2 51
(Hughie Morrison) *led: pushed along ent fnl 2f: hdd over 1f out: sn dropped out: bhd and wknd ins fnl f* **25/1**[3]

2m 9.03s (0.43) **Going Correction** +0.025s/f (Slow) 4 Ran SP% 106.3
Speed ratings (Par 105): **99,98,95,88**
CSF £1.77 TOTE £1.50; EX 1.60 Trifecta £7.50.
Owner K Abdullah **Bred** Juddmonte Farms Ltd **Trained** Newmarket, Suffolk

FOCUS
Not a bad little novice. The 1-2 are likely to do a good deal better from here.

1712 BET TOTEQUADPOT AT TOTESPORT.COM FILLIES' H'CAP 6f (P)
3:05 (3:05) (Class 3) (0-95,92) 4-Y-0+ £8,409 (£2,502; £1,250; £625) Stalls Centre

Form RPR

0-26 1 **Rose Berry**[14] 1382 5-8-12 83 (h) SilvestreDeSousa 5 89
(Charlie Wallis) *mounted in chute and taken down early: stdd and dropped in bhd after s: swtchd rt and drvn wl over 1f out: chsd ldrs 1f out: str run to ld towards fin: eased cl home (jockey said mare hung left-handed under pressure)* **11/4**[2]

223- 2 3/4 **Goodnight Girl (IRE)**[203] 7465 4-9-7 92 RobHornby 2 96
(Jonathan Portman) *chsd ldr: clsd over 1f out: rdn to chal and hung lft 1f out: led ins fnl f: hdd and no ex towards fin (jockey said filly hung left-handed under pressure. Vet said filly lost it's left fore shoe)* **13/8**[1]

-364 3 1 1/2 **Emily Goldfinch**[14] 1382 6-8-2 80 (p) GraceMcEntee(7) 1 79
(Phil McEntee) *led: clr over 2f out: rdn over 1f out: hdd ins fnl f: no ex and wknd towards fin* **5/1**

0-52 4 3/4 **Sweet And Dandy (IRE)**[14] 1382 4-8-2 73 oh3 KieranO'Neill 4 70
(Luke McJannet) *chsd ldrs: effrt u.p over 1f out: kpt on same pce and no imp ins fnl f* **7/2**[3]

500- 5 3 1/2 **La Fortuna**[103] 9748 6-8-6 77 (t) DavidEgan 3 64
(Charlie Wallis) *dwlt: in tch: unable qck u.p over 1f out: wknd ins fnl f* **12/1**

1m 12.19s (-1.51) **Going Correction** +0.025s/f (Slow) 5 Ran SP% 111.3
Speed ratings (Par 104): **111,110,108,107,102**
CSF £7.77 TOTE £3.20: £1.70, £1.40; EX 8.40 Trifecta £25.10.
Owner Strawberry Fields Stud **Bred** Aljw Bloodstock **Trained** Ardleigh, Essex

FOCUS
This was a well-run sprint and the winner came from the back of the field. Limited fillies' form, with the winner rated to her best.

1713 WOODFORD RESERVE CARDINAL CONDITIONS STKS (PLUS 10 RACE) (THE ROAD TO THE KENTUCKY DERBY) 1m (P)
3:35 (3:37) (Class 2) 3-Y-O
£37,350 (£11,184; £5,592; £2,796; £1,398; £702) **Stalls** Low

Form RPR
152- **1** **Bye Bye Hong Kong (USA)**[196] 7702 3-9-5 107..... SilvestreDeSousa 1 109
(Andrew Balding) *chsd ldrs: swtchd rt and hdwy over 1f out: sn drvn and chalng: led jst ins fnl f: hld on wl towards fin* **7/2**[2]
2 *nk* **Antilles (USA)**[158] 8858 3-9-5 87.............................. SeamieHeffernan 8 108
(A P O'Brien, Ire) *in tch in last trio: swtchd lft after 1f: rdn ent fnl 3f: swtchd rt and hdwy on outer over 1f out: clsd to chse ldrs ins fnl f: styd on wl to press ldrs and go 2nd cl home* **33/1**
116- **3** *hd* **Dark Vision (IRE)**[208] 7292 3-9-5 111.............................. JamesDoyle 6 108
(Mark Johnston) *short of room sn after s and swtchd lft: in tch in last trio: clsd: swtchd rt and hdwy u.p over 1f out: wnt 2nd and pressing wnr ins fnl f: styd on wl but lost 2nd last strides* **6/1**[3]
4 *2 ½* **U S S Michigan (USA)**[41] 975 3-9-5 0.............................. RyanMoore 2 103
(A P O'Brien, Ire) *in tch in midfield: nt clrest of runs 2f out: hdwy u.p to chse ldrs 1f out: no imp ins fnl f: wknd towards fin* **15/8**[1]
316- **5** *2 ¼* **Certain Lad**[158] 8869 3-9-5 103.............................. CharlesBishop 3 98
(Mick Channon) *chsd ldr early: styd handy: effrt over 1f out: hung lft and unable qck ent fnl f: wknd ins fnl f (jockey said gelding hung left-handed up the home straight)* **8/1**
1-10 **6** *nse* **Barys**[36] 1049 3-9-5 100..............................(b) EdwardGreatrex 7 97
(Archie Watson) *chsd ldr over 6f out tl led ent fnl 2f: rdn over 1f out: hdd jst ins fnl f: sn btn and wknd fnl 100yds* **20/1**
24-1 **7** *1 ¼* **Fanaar (IRE)**[40] 989 3-9-5 99.............................. JimCrowley 4 96
(William Haggas) *w ldrs early: in tch in midfield: effrt over 1f out: unable qck whn hung lft and n.m.r 1f out: sn btn and wknd ins fnl f (jockey said gelding hung left-handed)* **7/2**[2]
01- **8** *10* **Shir Khan**[145] 9132 3-9-5 0.............................. OisinMurphy 5 73
(Paul Cole) *sn led: hdd and rdn ent fnl 2f: dropped out over 1f out: wl bhd ins fnl f* **25/1**
001- **9** *8* **Battle Of Waterloo (IRE)**[152] 8993 3-9-5 81.............................. AdamKirby 9 55
(John Ryan) *t.k.h: hld up in rr: swtchd lft over 1f out: effrt 2f out: sn btn and wl bhd ins fnl f* **100/1**

1m 36.9s (-3.00) **Going Correction** +0.025s/f (Slow) **9 Ran SP% 117.2**
Speed ratings (Par 104): **116,115,115,113,110 110,109,99,91**
CSF £114.33 TOTE £4.70: £1.60, £10.30, £1.90; EX 141.80 Trifecta £520.40.
Owner King Power Racing Co Ltd **Bred** WinStar Farm LLC **Trained** Kingsclere, Hants

FOCUS
Hard to imagine this will have any bearing on the Kentucky Derby itself, but a good race in itself. The form has been rated at something like face value, with the fifth and sixth rated near their respective levels.

1714 BET TOTETRIFECTA AT TOTESPORT.COM H'CAP 7f (P)
4:10 (4:12) (Class 4) (0-85,87) 4-Y-O+
£5,692 (£1,694; £846; £423; £300; £300) **Stalls** Low

Form RPR
1101 **1** **Lion Hearted (IRE)**[7] 1544 5-8-12 **83** 5ex.............................. MarkCrehan(7) 8 89
(Michael Appleby) *t.k.h: led tl 4f out: styd w ldr tl rdn to ld again and edgd lft over 1f out: styd on wl ins fnl f: all out cl home: gamely* **3/1**[2]
005- **2** *½* **Quick Breath**[168] 8578 4-8-11 **75**.............................. RichardKingscote 2 81
(Jonathan Portman) *chsd ldrs: nt clr run and swtchd rt over 1f out: chsd wnr wl ins fnl f: styd on and grad clsng towards fin: nvr quite getting to wnr* **5/2**[1]
-400 **3** *¾* **Ultimate Avenue (IRE)**[33] 1097 5-9-4 **87**..............................(h) DylanHogan(5) 6 90
(David Simcock) *hld up in rr: clsd and n.m.r over 1f out: wnt between horses to chse ldrs ins fnl f: styd on: nvr quite getting to ldrs* **9/1**
5245 **4** *hd* **Samphire Coast**[7] 1544 6-9-3 **81**..............................(vt) PaddyMathers 7 83
(Derek Shaw) *taken down early: t.k.h: hld up in tch towards rr: effrt u.p over 1f out: styd on ins fnl f: nvr quite getting to ldrs* **8/1**
-412 **5** *hd* **Unforgiving Minute**[15] 1356 8-9-8 **86**.............................. AdamKirby 5 88
(John Butler) *trckd ldrs: effrt over 1f out: kpt on u.p ins fnl f: nvr quite enough pce to get on terms w ldrs* **5/1**[3]
004- **6** *1* **Pettifogger (IRE)**[118] 9532 4-9-9 **87**..............................(h[1]) MarcMonaghan 4 86
(Marco Botti) *restless in stalls: stdd leaving stalls: t.k.h: hdwy to join ldr over 6f out: led 4f out: rdn and hdd over 1f out: lost 2nd and wknd ins fnl f* **10/1**
034- **7** *2 ¾* **Magical Effect (IRE)**[194] 7750 7-9-2 **80**.............................. OisinMurphy 1 72
(Ruth Carr) *take down early: t.k.h: hld up in tch: effrt on inner over 1f out: no ex and wknd ins fnl f* **9/1**
350- **8** *1 ¼* **Perfect Hustler (USA)**[201] 7540 4-9-7 **85**.............................. ShaneKelly 9 74
(Jeremy Noseda) *chsd ldrs on outer: rdn over 2f out: unable qck and lost pl over 1f out: wknd ins fnl f* **14/1**

1m 26.33s (-0.87) **Going Correction** +0.025s/f (Slow) **8 Ran SP% 117.1**
Speed ratings (Par 105): **105,104,103,103,103 101,98,97**
CSF £11.28 CT £60.11 TOTE £3.90: £1.30, £1.10, £3.20; EX 14.60 Trifecta £89.70.
Owner Slipstream Racing **Bred** Dowager Countess Harrington **Trained** Oakham, Rutland

FOCUS
This was steadily run in the early stages and resulted in a bunched finish. The winner could even do better again.

1715 BET TOTESWINGER AT TOTESPORT.COM H'CAP 7f (P)
4:40 (4:42) (Class 6) (0-60,62) 4-Y-O+
£3,105 (£924; £461; £300; £300; £300) **Stalls** Low

Form RPR
3430 **1** **Hic Bibi**[30] 1158 4-9-6 **59**.............................. DavidEgan 12 67
(David Loughnane) *led for 3f: styd prom: rdn to ld over 1f out: hld on wl u.p ins fnl f* **5/1**[3]
2000 **2** *hd* **Holy Tiber (IRE)**[7] 1553 4-9-4 **57**..............................(b[1]) JoeyHaynes 9 64
(Paul Howling) *dropped in after s: hld up in rr of main gp: pushed along over 1f out: hdwy over 1f out: ev ch ins fnl f: kpt on wl* **20/1**
4246 **3** *3 ¼* **Canimar**[10] 1477 4-8-0 **46** oh1..............................(p) GavinAshton(7) 2 45
(Shaun Keightley) *hld up in tch: effrt and swtchd rt wl over 1f out: chsd ldrs 1f out: kpt on same pce and no imp ins fnl f: snatched 3rd last strides* **9/1**
-340 **4** *hd* **The King's Steed**[29] 1177 6-9-6 **59**..............................(bt) SilvestreDeSousa 4 58
(Shaun Lycett) *chsd ldrs tl wnt 2nd 1/2-way: rdn to ld ent fnl 2f: drvn and hdd over 1f out: wknd ins fnl f: lost 3rd last strides* **9/2**[2]
0-05 **5** *2* **Mezmaar**[43] 925 10-9-2 **58**.............................. GaryMahon(3) 11 51
(Mark Usher) *taken down early: in tch: effrt u.p over 1f out: kpt on ins fnl f: nvr trbld ldrs* **10/1**
0200 **6** *shd* **Mr Gent (IRE)**[20] 1266 4-9-2 **55**..............................(b) RobertHavlin 8 48
(Ed Dunlop) *hld up towards rr of main gp: effrt over 1f out: kpt on ins fnl f: nvr trbld ldrs* **20/1**
3306 **7** *1 ¾* **Tavener**[1] 1684 7-9-9 **62**..............................(p) OisinMurphy 7 51
(David C Griffiths) *chsd ldrs: u.p and struggling over 2f out: wknd fnl f* **9/2**[2]
6312 **8** *½* **Viola Park**[29] 1177 5-9-7 **60**..............................(p) LukeMorris 6 47
(Ronald Harris) *chsd ldrs: outpcd over 2f out: rallied u.p and wnt lft 1f out: sn no prog and wknd ins fnl f* **4/1**[1]
-200 **9** *nse* **Percy Toplis**[10] 1478 5-8-7 **46** oh1..............................(v) KieranO'Neill 10 33
(Christine Dunnett) *in tch in midfield: lost pl u.p over 1f out: wknd ins fnl f* **25/1**
0230 **10** *1 ¾* **Middlescence (IRE)**[17] 1328 5-8-10 **56**..............................(t) VictorSantos(7) 15 39
(Lucinda Egerton) *pushed and wd early: led 5f out: rdn and hdd ent fnl 2f: lost pl over 1f out: wknd fnl f* **25/1**
040- **11** *1 ½* **Kingsley Klarion (IRE)**[141] 9177 6-9-3 **59**.............................. TimClark(3) 1 38
(John Butler) *short of room and dropped to rr sn after s: n.d* **11/1**
/00- **12** *16* **Out Of The Ashes**[448] 274 6-9-4 **57**.............................. StevieDonohoe 5
(Mohamed Moubarak) *sn bhd: nvr involved* **25/1**

1m 26.38s (-0.82) **Going Correction** +0.025s/f (Slow) **12 Ran SP% 121.5**
Speed ratings (Par 101): **105,104,101,100,98 98,96,95,95,93 92,73**
CSF £107.89 CT £882.49 TOTE £7.40: £2.40, £6.00, £2.50; EX 160.70 Trifecta £1648.60.
Owner Peter Onslow **Bred** Peter Onslow **Trained** Tern Hill, Shropshire
■ Stewards' Enquiry : Joey Haynes 12-day ban (6 days deferred for 2 months): misuse of whip (totting-up procedure) (Apr 26-May 7)

FOCUS
A moderate handicap, but it was well run. Sound form for the grade, with the winner rated to her best.

1716 BET TOTESCOOP6 AT TOTESPORT.COM H'CAP 5f (P)
5:15 (5:15) (Class 6) (0-55,59) 4-Y-O+
£3,105 (£924; £461; £300; £300; £300) **Stalls** Low

Form RPR
5446 **1** *shd* **Kyllukey**[14] 1384 6-8-12 **46** oh1.............................. DavidEgan 10 52
(Charlie Wallis) *short of room sn after s: hld up in tch towards rr: rdn and hdwy to chse ldrs 1f out: nt clr run ins fnl f: swtchd rt and styd on strly towards fin: jst hld: fin 2nd: awrdd r* **12/1**
5310 **2** **Hurricane Alert**[27] 1210 7-9-0 **48**.............................. JackMitchell 8 53
(Mark Hoad) *taken down early: chsd ldrs: effrt in 4th 2f out: clsd u.p to chal ins fnl f: r.o wl to ld towards fin: jst hld on: fin 1st: disqualified and plcd 2nd - caused interference* **12/1**
5130 **3** *hd* **Atyaaf**[17] 1335 4-9-6 **54**.............................. PaddyMathers 7 58
(Derek Shaw) *stdd s: t.k.h: hld up in tch in midfield: effrt u.p over 1f out: clsd to press ldrs and edgd lft ins fnl f: ev ch towards fin: styd on wl* **4/1**[2]
05 **4** *nk* **Zipedeedodah (IRE)**[90] 179 7-9-1 **49**.............................. OisinMurphy 3 52
(Joseph Tuite) *in tch in midfield: swtchd rt and effrt over 1f out: hdwy and ev ch whn edgd lft ins fnl f: sn led: hdd and lost 3 pls towards fin* **7/1**[3]
6062 **5** *shd* **Admiral Rooke (IRE)**[5] 1595 4-8-9 **48**..............................(b) TheodoreLadd(5) 1 50+
(Michael Appleby) *chsd ldrs: short of room on inner over 2f out: ev ch u.p and edgd rt ins fnl f: unable qck towards fin* **11/4**[1]
3221 **6** *1 ½* **Red Stripes (USA)**[8] 1521 7-9-6 **59** 4ex..............................(b) SeamusCronin(5) 4 56+
(Lisa Williamson) *led tl over 3f out: chsd ldr and edgd lft over 2f: rdn to ld again over 1f out: hdd ins fnl f: sn wknd* **4/1**[2]
5-00 **7** *2 ¾* **Waneen (IRE)**[20] 1266 6-9-4 **52**..............................(v) AdamKirby 11 39
(John Butler) *midfield: rdn and finding little whn swtchd rt over 1f out: no imp ins fnl f* **7/1**[3]
-060 **8** *2* **Dubai Elegance**[79] 356 5-9-7 **55**..............................(p) CallumShepherd 12 35
(Derek Shaw) *s.i.s: sn swtchd lft and in rr: styd on and swtchd lft ins fnl f: nvr involved* **20/1**
5250 **9** *nk* **Roy's Legacy**[14] 1383 10-8-12 **46** oh1.............................. CharlieBennett 6 25
(Shaun Harris) *a towards rr: nvr involved* **33/1**
0-55 **10** *2 ¼* **Camino**[14] 1383 6-8-12 **46** oh1.............................. ShaneKelly 5 17
(Andi Brown) *dwlt: midfield: effrt over 1f out: no prog: wknd ins fnl f* **25/1**
-506 **11** *15* **Shackled N Drawn (USA)**[40] 986 7-9-3 **51**..............................(v) CharlesBishop 9
(Peter Hedger) *nt that wl away: hdwy on outer to ld over 3f out: rdn and hdd over 1f out: sn dropped out: bhd and eased ins fnl f: burst blood vessel (vet said gelding bled from the nose)* **20/1**

1m 0.48s (0.28) **Going Correction** +0.025s/f (Slow) **11 Ran SP% 123.4**
Speed ratings (Par 101): **97,98,97,97,96 94,90,86,86,82 58**
TOTE £12.30: £3.80, £4.50, £2.40; EX 196.50 Trifecta £917.10.
Owner Mrs Hayley Wallis **Bred** Whatton Manor Stud **Trained** Ardleigh, Essex

FOCUS
A controversial finish to this low-grade sprint handicap. Very limited form.

1717 BUY TICKETS AT CHELMSFORDCITYRACECOURSE.COM CLASSIFIED STKS 1m (P)
5:50 (5:52) (Class 6) 4-Y-O+
£3,105 (£924; £461; £300; £300; £300) **Stalls** Low

Form RPR
6006 **1** **Nicky Baby (IRE)**[15] 1362 5-8-7 42..............................(b) SophieRalston(7) 7 51
(Dean Ivory) *t.k.h: mde all: rdn and forged clr over 1f out: edging lft but kpt on ins fnl f (jockey said gelding jumped left-handed leaving the stalls)* **25/1**
-050 **2** *1 ¼* **Imperial Act**[56] 717 4-9-0 45.............................. OisinMurphy 1 48
(Andrew Balding) *hld up in midfield: effrt and hdwy over 1f out: styd on to chse wnr wl ins fnl f: clsng at fin but nvr getting to wnr* **10/3**[1]
0-03 **3** *¾* **Casey Banter**[15] 1353 4-8-7 49.............................. SeanKirrane(7) 12 46
(Julia Feilden) *t.k.h: chsd wnr: rdn and unable to match pce of wnr over 1f out: kpt on same pce u.p and one pce ins fnl f: lost 2nd wl ins fnl f* **16/1**
0200 **4** *½* **Captain Kissinger**[14] 1390 4-8-7 49..............................(v) GeorgiaDobie(7) 13 45
(Jo Hughes, France) *t.k.h: chsd ldrs: rdn and unable qck w wnr over 1f out: kpt on same pce ins fnl f* **12/1**
6002 **5** *1 ¼* **Seaquinn**[27] 1214 4-9-0 45.............................. KierenFox 10 42
(John Best) *in tch in midfield: effrt ent fnl 2f: unable qck over 1f out: wl hld and kpt on same pce ins fnl f* **16/1**
5021 **6** *nk* **Clement (IRE)**[1] 1683 9-9-4 49..............................(p) LukeMorris 11 46
(Marjorie Fife) *t.k.h: hld up towards rr of main gp: effrt over 1f out: kpt on ins fnl f: nvr trbld ldrs* **4/1**[3]
3442 **7** *½* **Red Cossack (CAN)**[15] 1353 8-9-0 46..............................(b) ShaneKelly 3 41
(Dean Ivory) *impeded and stdd after s: t.k.h: hld up in rr of main gp: effrt on outer over 1f out: kpt on ins fnl f: nvr trbld ldrs* **7/2**[2]

0045 **8** 1 ½ **Dukes Meadow**[14] 1378 8-8-9 43 .... RhiainIngram(5) 9 37
(Roger Ingram) *in tch in midfield: effrt u.p over 1f out: unable qck and kpt on same pce ins fnl f* **25/1**

500- **9** ½ **Clary (IRE)**[134] 9286 9-9-0 45 .... (w) RichardKingscote 4 36
(Alistair Whillans) *impeded sn after s: midfield: effrt over 1f out: kpt on same pce and nvr threatened to get on terms* **12/1**

6000 **10** nk **Plucky Dip**[14] 1378 8-8-7 42 .... (p) LauraPearson(7) 8 35
(John Ryan) *midfield: rdn and unable qck over 1f out: wl hld and kpt on same pce ins fnl f* **40/1**

0-00 **11** ½ **Tha'ir (IRE)**[71] 481 9-9-0 50 .... (t) DannyBrock 5 34
(Philip McBride) *impeded and awkward sn after leaving stalls and sn detached in last: nvr involved (jockey said gelding reared at the stalls opened, causing the gelding to be slowly away and moved poorly in the early stages)* **7/1**

6500 **12** 1 **Ertidaad (IRE)**[8] 1520 7-9-0 45 .... (b) EoinWalsh 2 32
(Emma Owen) *chsd ldrs: u.p and unable qck over 2f out: wknd fnl f (jockey said gelding jumped right-handed from the stalls)* **33/1**

0034 **13** ¾ **Cash N Carrie (IRE)**[8] 1519 5-8-9 48 .... (v1) TheodoreLadd(5) 6 30
(Michael Appleby) *impeded sn after s: hld up in rr of main gp: effrt over 1f out: no hdwy and nvr involved (jockey said mare suffered interference at the start)* **12/1**

1m 40.51s (0.61) **Going Correction** +0.025s/f (Slow) **13 Ran SP% 125.7**
Speed ratings (Par 101): **97,95,95,94,93 92,92,90,90,90 89,88,87**
CSF £109.40 TOTE £51.50: £10.40, £1.70, £5.80; EX 282.10 Trifecta £1721.30.
Owner Mrs Doreen Carter **Bred** C Farrell **Trained** Radlett, Herts

FOCUS
A low-grade affair, and a steadily run one, the pace holding up well. Weak form.
T/Plt: £82.30 to a £1 stake. Pool: £52,187.31 - 462.43 winning units T/Qpdt: £23.90 to a £1 stake. Pool: £5,196.57 - 160.30 winning units **Steve Payne**

1483 NEWCASTLE (A.W) (L-H)

Thursday, April 11

OFFICIAL GOING: Tapeta: standard to slow
Wind: Breezy, across Weather: Fine

1718 BETWAY STAYERS H'CAP — 2m 56y (Tp)

5:30 (5:30) (Class 6) (0-60,58) 4-Y-0+
£3,105 (£924; £461; £400; £400; £400) **Stalls** Low

Form RPR

41 **1** **Extreme Appeal (IRE)**[11] 1463 7-9-5 55 4ex .... (p) GrahamLee 9 62
(Kelly Morgan) *hld up in midfield on outside: stdy hdwy over 3f out: chsd clr ldr and rdn over 2f out: led fnl 100yds: dwindling advantage cl home: jst lasted* **7/2**[1]

10-0 **2** nse **Urban Spirit (IRE)**[70] 504 5-9-2 52 .... DanielTudhope 4 59
(Lawrence Mullaney) *led: rdn clr over 2f out: hdd fnl 100yds: rallied cl home: jst hld* **10/1**[3]

000- **3** 3 ¼ **Misscarlett (IRE)**[148] 9054 5-8-12 48 .... PaulHanagan 10 51
(Philip Kirby) *trckd ldrs: effrt and disp 2nd pl over 2f out: rdn and one pce fr over 1f out* **11/1**

0-40 **4** 3 ¼ **Rock N'Stones (IRE)**[38] 589 8-9-0 50 .... PhilDennis 14 49
(Gillian Boanas) *hld up in midfield: drvn and outpcd over 3f out: rallied 2f out: kpt on fnl f: no imp* **80/1**

2300 **5** nk **Hugoigo**[13] 1398 5-8-2 45 .... (p) CoreyMadden(7) 5 44
(Jim Goldie) *hld up: pushed along 3f out: hdwy over 1f out: kpt on fnl f: nrst fin* **14/1**

-026 **6** 1 ¾ **Good Man (IRE)**[52] 782 6-8-9 48 .... (p) BenRobinson(3) 8 45
(Karen McLintock) *hld up towards rr: effrt and edgd lft over 2f out: drvn and no imp fr over 1f out* **7/1**[2]

30- **7** nk **Excalibur (POL)**[30] 6354 6-8-13 49 .... (p) PJMcDonald 3 45
(Micky Hammond) *midfield: drvn along over 5f out: rallied: no further imp fr 2f out* **40/1**

32-0 **8** 1 ½ **Nearly There**[13] 1398 6-9-5 55 .... (t) NathanEvans 11 50
(Wilf Storey) *in tch on outside: effrt and rdn over 2f out: wknd over 1f out* **18/1**

1065 **9** 4 ½ **Ember's Glow**[17] 1334 5-9-4 54 .... JoeFanning 6 43
(Mark Loughnane) *hld up: stdy hdwy over 3f out: drvn along and effrt over 2f out: wknd over 1f out* **7/1**[2]

0-01 **10** 2 ¼ **Rajapur**[35] 1068 6-8-12 48 .... (e) CliffordLee 7 34
(David Thompson) *hld up: rdn along over 3f out: no imp fr 2f out* **33/1**

0053 **11** 14 **Masters Apprentice (IRE)**[7] 1548 4-9-6 58 .... BenCurtis 13 30
(Sylvester Kirk) *cl up tl rdn and wknd over 2f out* **7/2**[1]

04-5 **12** 4 ½ **Dizoard**[20] 99 9-8-6 45 .... JamieGormley(3) 1 9
(Iain Jardine) *trckd ldrs: rdn along over 3f out: wknd over 2f out* **25/1**

222- **13** 5 **Canford Thompson**[173] 1035 6-9-2 52 .... (p) AndrewMullen 2 10
(Micky Hammond) *midfield on ins: struggling 3f out: sn btn* **28/1**

1-25 **14** 32 **Betancourt (IRE)**[32] 810 9-9-5 55 .... (p) LiamKeniry 12
(Stef Keniry) *hld up: rdn and outpcd over 4f out: sn struggling: t.o (jockey said gelding was never travelling and stopped quickly)* **7/1**[2]

3m 35.98s (0.98) **Going Correction** +0.175s/f (Slow)
WFA 4 from 5yo+ 2lb **14 Ran SP% 125.2**
Speed ratings (Par 101): **104,103,102,100,100 99,99,98,96,95 88,86,83,67**
CSF £40.53 CT £365.81 TOTE £4.30: £1.60, £3.50, £4.00; EX 52.30 Trifecta £580.70.
Owner J R Weatherby **Bred** D Wachman & M Nolan **Trained** Withcote, Leics

FOCUS
Standard to slow Tapeta. A very modest staying handicap run almost 10sec outside the standard. The 1-2 are afforded minor pbs.

1719 PLAY 4 TO SCORE AT BETWAY H'CAP — 1m 2f 42y (Tp)

6:00 (6:00) (Class 4) (0-85,85) 4-Y-0+
£5,530 (£1,645; £822; £411; £400; £400) **Stalls** High

Form RPR

66-4 **1** **Grandee (IRE)**[11] 1461 5-8-12 81 .... BenSanderson(5) 5 95
(Roger Fell) *prom: shkn up and hdwy to ld over 1f out: rdn clr fnl f* **9/4**[1]

2516 **2** 5 **Illustrissime (USA)**[26] 1232 6-9-4 82 .... (p) JasonHart 4 87
(Ivan Furtado) *reluctant to enter stalls: hld up: hdwy over 2f out: effrt and ev ch briefly over 1f out: sn chsng wnr: no imp fnl f* **8/1**[3]

230- **3** 2 ¾ **Addis Ababa (IRE)**[214] 7097 4-9-5 83 .... DanielTudhope 9 83
(David O'Meara) *pressed ldr: led 3f out: rdn: edgd lft and hdd over 1f out: sn outpcd* **9/4**[1]

60-2 **4** 4 ½ **Employer (IRE)**[11] 1461 4-9-3 81 .... PaulMulrennan 8 73
(Jim Goldie) *hld up: stdy hdwy 1/2-way: gng wl over 2f out: rdn and ev ch over 1f out: wknd ins fnl f* **3/1**[2]

055- **5** 1 **Zabeel Star (IRE)**[156] 8899 7-9-4 85 .... JamieGormley(3) 3 75
(Karen McLintock) *s.s: hld up: rdn and hdwy over 2f out: wknd fnl f* **10/1**

000/ **6** 2 **Apterix (FR)**[74] 3657 9-8-11 78 .... BenRobinson(3) 1 65
(Brian Ellison) *chsd ldrs tl rdn and wknd fr 2f out* **50/1**

210- **7** 3 ¾ **Double Reflection**[203] 7451 4-9-5 83 .... CliffordLee 7 63
(K R Burke) *led to 3f out: rdn and wknd 2f out* **18/1**

50-0 **8** 45 **Starplex**[46] 272 9-8-8 72 .... AndrewMullen 6
(Kenny Johnson) *hld up: struggling over 3f out: sn lost tch: t.o* **150/1**

2m 10.23s (-0.17) **Going Correction** +0.175s/f (Slow) **8 Ran SP% 114.6**
Speed ratings (Par 105): **107,103,100,97,96 94,91,55**
CSF £21.59 CT £44.13 TOTE £3.90: £1.10, £2.20, £1.40; EX 18.40 Trifecta £55.10.
Owner Nick Bradley Racing 12 & Sohi **Bred** Oak Hill Stud **Trained** Nawton, N Yorks
■ Irish Minister was withdrawn, price at time of withdrawal 50/1. Rule 4 does not apply.

FOCUS
Decent handicap form. They went a good initial gallop and the winner cashed in on a good mark.

1720 LADBROKES H'CAP — 7f 14y (Tp)

6:30 (6:30) (Class 5) (0-70,71) 3-Y-O
£3,752 (£1,116; £557; £400; £400; £400) **Stalls** Centre

Form RPR

025- **1** **Camber**[170] 8509 3-9-7 69 .... PaulHanagan 6 75
(Richard Fahey) *trckd ldrs: effrt in centre of gp over 1f out: led ins fnl f: drvn and hld on wl* **16/1**

00-2 **2** hd **Strawberry Jack**[31] 1140 3-9-7 69 .... (tp) HarryBentley 4 74
(George Scott) *led in centre of gp: rdn along over 1f out: edgd rt and hdd ins fnl f: rallied: hld nr fin* **7/1**

503- **3** ½ **Midnight In Havana**[164] 8698 3-8-9 57 .... GrahamLee 2 61
(Bryan Smart) *prom on far side of gp: effrt and rdn over 1f out: ev ch briefly ins fnl f: sn one pce* **25/1**

51-4 **4** 2 **Rambaldi (IRE)**[19] 1285 3-9-9 71 .... DanielMuscutt 10 70
(Marco Botti) *hld up in centre of gp: rdn and effrt over 1f out: kpt on ins fnl f: nt rch first three* **6/1**[3]

-136 **5** ½ **Distant Mirage**[17] 1337 3-9-9 71 .... JamieSpencer 3 69
(James Tate) *stdd and swtchd rt s: hld up in centre of gp: rdn: hdwy and edgd lft over 1f out: no further imp ins fnl f* **9/2**[2]

0-56 **6** 2 ½ **Fort Benton (IRE)**[71] 477 3-8-12 60 .... SeanLevey 1 52
(David Barron) *dwlt: hld up in centre of gp: effrt and swtchd to stands' side over 1f out: r.o ins fnl f: no imp* **66/1**

00-6 **7** ½ **She'Zanarab**[10] 1486 3-8-5 56 .... JamieGormley(3) 8 46
(Iain Jardine) *prom early: sn towards rr: effrt on far side of gp over 1f out: nvr able to chal* **33/1**

56-1 **8** 1 **Devil's Angel**[70] 500 3-9-7 69 .... PJMcDonald 9 57
(Jedd O'Keeffe) *t.k.h: in tch on nr side of gp: drvn over 2f out: wknd ins fnl f (vet said colt finished lame left fore)* **7/2**[1]

3-14 **9** nk **Rich Approach (IRE)**[57] 698 3-9-7 69 .... DanielTudhope 7 56
(James Bethell) *hld up on far side of gp: effrt and rdn 2f out: wknd fnl f* **7/2**[1]

1444 **10** ½ **Kodi Dream**[10] 1486 3-8-6 59 .... BenSanderson(5) 11 45
(Roger Fell) *t.k.h: in tch on nr side of gp: rdn over 2f out: wknd over 1f out* **10/1**

00-6 **11** 3 **Monsieur Piquer (FR)**[31] 1140 3-9-1 63 .... BenCurtis 5 41
(K R Burke) *pressed ldr in centre of gp: edgd rt over 2f out: rdn and wknd over 1f out* **12/1**

1m 27.77s (1.57) **Going Correction** +0.175s/f (Slow) **11 Ran SP% 120.4**
Speed ratings (Par 98): **98,97,97,94,94 91,90,89,89,88 85**
CSF £124.94 CT £2810.23 TOTE £18.60: £6.10, £2.80, £9.30; EX 98.70 Trifecta £2817.70.
Owner Highclere Thoroughbred Racing - Ganton **Bred** Dandy's Farm **Trained** Musley Bank, N Yorks

FOCUS
An interesting handicap, but it wasn't strongly run. A step forward from the winner.

1721 LADBROKES HOME OF THE ODDS BOOST H'CAP — 1m 5y (Tp)

7:00 (7:00) (Class 6) (0-60,60) 3-Y-O
£3,105 (£924; £461; £400; £400; £400) **Stalls** Centre

Form RPR

3-31 **1** **Blazing Dreams (IRE)**[10] 1486 3-9-5 58 6ex .... (p) AndrewMullen 8 64
(Ben Haslam) *hld up towards nr side of gp: rdn and hdwy wl over 1f out: edgd lft: led ins fnl f: kpt on wl* **8/1**

5-20 **2** nk **Lexikon**[43] 931 3-8-4 46 .... JamieGormley(3) 5 51
(Ollie Pears) *led in centre of gp: drvn along 2f out: hdd ins fnl f: rallied: hld cl home* **12/1**

0-43 **3** nk **What Will Be (IRE)**[15] 1358 3-9-6 59 .... JamieSpencer 14 63
(Olly Murphy) *hld up: effrt nr side of gp over 2f out: chsd ldrs over 1f out: r.o ins fnl f* **7/4**[1]

650- **4** 1 ¼ **Hector's Here**[113] 9612 3-9-3 56 .... JasonHart 9 58+
(Ivan Furtado) *dwlt: hld up in centre of gp: rdn and hdwy over 1f out: kpt on ins fnl f: nt pce to chal* **18/1**

2312 **5** 1 ¾ **Macs Blessings (IRE)**[34] 1084 3-9-3 56 .... (p) LiamKeniry 11 54
(Stef Keniry) *chsd ldr to over 1f out: drvn and no ex ins fnl f* **10/1**

0-01 **6** 2 **Havana Ooh Na Na**[14] 1385 3-9-7 60 .... (p) CliffordLee 6 53
(K R Burke) *chsd ldrs in centre of gp: drvn over 2f out: wknd ins fnl f* **11/1**

0-55 **7** ¾ **Robeam (IRE)**[65] 612 3-8-13 52 .... PaulHanagan 4 44
(Richard Fahey) *prom towards far side of gp: rdn over 2f out: fdd over 1f out* **7/1**[3]

56-0 **8** 1 ¼ **Jagerbond**[10] 1486 3-9-1 54 .... KevinStott 13 43
(Andrew Crook) *hld up in midfield on nr side of gp: drvn and outpcd over 2f out: n.d after* **40/1**

-512 **9** 1 **Simba Samba**[31] 1141 3-9-1 54 .... (t1) DuranFentiman 1 41
(Philip McBride) *in tch on far side of gp: drvn and effrt over 2f out: wknd over 1f out (jockey said gelding ran flat)* **4/1**[2]

0500 **10** nse **Zoom Out**[10] 1486 3-9-0 56 .... RowanScott(3) 2 43
(Nigel Tinkler) *hld up on far side of gp: drvn over 2f out: sn no imp* **14/1**

0-60 **11** 6 **Amourie**[89] 211 3-9-5 58 .... JamesSullivan 3 31
(Ray Craggs) *hld up on far side of gp: struggling and hung lft over 2f out: sn btn (jockey said filly hung left)* **66/1**

0-00 **12** hd **Somewhat Sisyphean**[41] 971 3-8-10 49 .... NathanEvans 12 22
(Wilf Storey) *slowly away: hld up: struggling over 2f out: nvr on terms* **100/1**

000- **13** 3 ¾ **Juals Spirit (IRE)**[287] 4297 3-8-7 46 .... CamHardie 10 11
(Brian Ellison) *prom in centre of gp: drvn and outpcd over 2f out: sn btn* **100/1**

00-0 **14** ¾ **Slaithwaite (IRE)**[7] 1549 3-9-4 57 .... BenCurtis 7 20
(Roger Fell) *hld up in centre of gp: struggling over 2f out: sn wknd* **50/1**

1m 40.98s (2.38) **Going Correction** +0.175s/f (Slow) **14 Ran SP% 124.9**
Speed ratings (Par 96): **95,94,94,93,91 89,88,87,86,86 80,80,76,75**
CSF £103.00 CT £253.86 TOTE £10.00: £2.70, £4.00, £1.50; EX 115.50 Trifecta £473.10.

Owner Champagne Charlies Club & B Haslam **Bred** Rory O'Brien **Trained** Middleham Moor, N Yorks

FOCUS
This modest handicap wasn't run at a strong gallop. The form seems straightforward.

1722 SUNRACING.CO.UK CLASSIFIED STKS 7f 14y (Tp)
7:30 (7:30) (Class 6) 3-Y-0+

£3,105 (£924; £461; £400; £400; £400) **Stalls** Centre

Form | | | | RPR
4-04 **1** **Midnight Vixen**[13] 1399 5-9-10 55..........................(p[1]) AndrewMullen 10 61
(Ben Haslam) *hld up in tch on nr side of gp: drvn and outpcd over 2f out: rallied over 1f out: led wl ins fnl f: kpt on wl* **7/1**

-000 **2** ½ **Adventureman**[13] 1398 7-9-10 55..........................(b) JamesSullivan 11 60
(Ruth Carr) *led in centre of gp: drvn along 2f out: hdd wl ins fnl f: kpt on same pce* **33/1**

1351 **3** 1 ¼ **Sylviacliffs (FR)**[7] 1549 3-9-2 54..........................(p) BenCurtis 9 58
(K R Burke) *cl up on far side of gp: effrt and ch over 1f out to ins fnl f: kpt on same pce fnl 100yds* **11/10**[1]

3036 **4** *shd* **Classy Cailin (IRE)**[37] 1026 4-9-10 50.......................... JoeFanning 8 56
(Mark Loughnane) *fly-jmpd s: hld up in centre of gp: hdwy and in tch over 1f out: drvn and one pce ins fnl f* **16/1**

0362 **5** *nk* **False Id**[9] 1506 6-9-10 54..........................(b) TrevorWhelan 4 56
(David Loughnane) *missed break: hld up and sn swtchd rt: drvn over 2f out: hdwy on nr side of gp over 1f out: kpt on fnl f: no imp* **6/1**[3]

560- **6** 1 ½ **Size Matters**[174] 8388 5-9-10 52..........................(w) JasonHart 12 52
(Mark Walford) *t.k.h: cl up in centre of gp: drvn along over 2f out: one pce appr fnl f* **11/1**

0-30 **7** *shd* **Magical Molly Joe**[71] 484 5-9-10 53..........................(h) SeanLevey 3 52
(David Barron) *hld up in centre of gp: hdwy and in tch over 1f out: no ex ins fnl f* **5/1**[2]

00-6 **8** 3 ½ **Biscuit Queen**[12] 1430 3-8-7 52.......................... BenRobinson[(3)] 5 38
(Brian Ellison) *prom on far side of gp: drvn along over 2f out: wknd fnl f (jockey said filly was never travelling)* **50/1**

0/60 **9** 1 ¼ **One Last Hug**[27] 1212 4-9-3 50.......................... CoreyMadden[(7)] 1 40
(Jim Goldie) *dwlt: hld up on nr side of gp: struggling over 2f out: sn btn* **25/1**

230- **10** ½ **Joyful Star**[174] 8381 9-9-10 55.......................... PaulHanagan 2 39
(Fred Watson) *bhd on far side of gp: struggling over 2f out: sn btn* **20/1**

6550 **11** 2 ½ **Major Crispies**[7] 1553 8-9-10 54.......................... TomEaves 13 32
(Ronald Thompson) *prom on nr side of gp: drvn along over 2f out: wknd over 1f out* **20/1**

005- **12** 1 ½ **Mosseyb (IRE)**[164] 8703 4-9-10 54..........................(w) GrahamLee 14 29
(Paul Midgley) *hld up on nr side of gp: struggling over 2f out: sn btn* **28/1**

1m 27.03s (0.83) **Going Correction** +0.175s/f (Slow)
WFA 3 from 4yo+ 14lb **12** Ran SP% **127.0**
Speed ratings (Par 101): **102,101,100,99,99 97,97,93,92,91 88,87**
CSF £232.24 TOTE £9.50: £2.20, £8.10, £1.30; EX 204.20 Trifecta £751.40.
Owner Ms Sara Humber **Bred** Wretham Stud **Trained** Middleham Moor, N Yorks
■ Easy Money was withdrawn, price at time of withdrawal 18/1. Rule 4 does not apply.

FOCUS
Very ordinary form, but straightforward enough.

1723 FOLLOW TOP TIPSTER TEMPLEGATE AT SUNRACING NOVICE STKS 7f 14y (Tp)
8:00 (8:00) (Class 5) 3-Y-0+ **£3,752** (£1,116; £557; £278) **Stalls** Centre

Form | | | | RPR
20 **1** **Conaglen**[11] 1458 3-9-0 0.......................... PJMcDonald 13 74+
(James Bethell) *in tch on nr side of gp: hdwy to ld over 1f out: sn rdn along: hld on wl fnl f* **6/1**[3]

1 **2** *hd* **Munhamek**[29] 1171 3-9-5 0.......................... SeanLevey 12 78+
(Ivan Furtado) *hld up: effrt nr side of gp to chse wnr over 1f out: kpt on wl fnl f: jst hld* **5/1**[2]

/62 **3** 3 ¾ **Scots Sonnet**[41] 971 5-10-0 0..........................(h) AlistairRawlinson 9 68+
(Jim Goldie) *dwlt: hld up on nr side of gp: pushed along and effrt over 1f out: chsd clr ldng pair wl ins fnl f: r.o* **33/1**

33- **4** *hd* **Alnasherat**[293] 4074 3-9-0 0.......................... HarryBentley 5 63+
(Sir Michael Stoute) *cl up on far side of gp: effrt and ev ch over 1f out: outpcd fnl f* **8/11**[1]

240- **5** 1 ¼ **Algaffaal (USA)**[189] 7940 4-9-11 79.......................... BenRobinson[(3)] 7 64
(Brian Ellison) *hld up on far side of gp: effrt and drvn along 2f out: no imp fnl f* **33/1**

34- **6** ½ **Bataar (IRE)**[132] 9323 3-9-0 0.......................... PaulHanagan 8 58
(Richard Fahey) *midfield in centre of gp: drvn along over 2f out: outpcd appr fnl f* **13/2**

7 ¾ **Siglo Six** 3-9-0 0..........................(h[1]) BenCurtis 1 56+
(Hugo Palmer) *dwlt: hld up in centre of gp: shkn up and stdy hdwy over 1f out: kpt on fnl f: nvr nrr* **20/1**

4- **8** 4 ½ **Gylo (IRE)**[134] 9283 3-9-0 0.......................... DanielTudhope 3 44
(David O'Meara) *prom on far side of gp: drvn along over 2f out: wknd over 1f out* **16/1**

000- **9** 1 **Pontecarlo Boy**[296] 3972 5-10-0 39..........................(w) PhilDennis 10 46
(Richard Whitaker) *led in centre of gp: drvn and hdd over 1f out: sn wknd* **250/1**

40 **10** *shd* **Picture Your Dream**[20] 1272 4-9-9 0.......................... NathanEvans 11 41
(Seb Spencer) *cl up in centre of gp: drvn and ev ch briefly over 1f out: wknd fnl f* **150/1**

00- **11** 2 ¾ **Lewis Slack**[292] 4109 3-9-0 0.......................... JackGarritty 6 33
(Jedd O'Keeffe) *bhd towards far side of gp: struggling over 2f out: sn btn* **50/1**

12 *11* **Corralejo (IRE)** 3-9-0 0.......................... CamHardie 4 4
(John Wainwright) *missed break: bhd in centre of gp: struggling wl over 2f out: wknd* **125/1**

13 2 ¾ **Fabulous View (FR)** 3-8-9 0.......................... JamesSullivan 2
(Ruth Carr) *hld up on nr side of gp: struggling 3f out: sn btn* **100/1**

1m 28.12s (1.92) **Going Correction** +0.175s/f (Slow)
WFA 3 from 4yo+ 14lb **13** Ran SP% **123.5**
Speed ratings (Par 103): **96,95,91,91,89 89,88,83,82,82 78,66,63**
CSF £36.16 TOTE £8.70: £2.20, £1.60, £6.00; EX 42.30 Trifecta £411.50.
Owner P Hibbert-Foy And Partners **Bred** Glebe Farm Stud **Trained** Middleham Moor, N Yorks

FOCUS
The first two, who came from the two highest stalls, pulled clear in this novice event. The pace was steady and the ninth holds down the form.
T/Jkpt: Not Won. T/Plt: £280.30 to a £1 stake. Pool: £89,510.92 - 233.05 winning units T/Qpdt: £67.80 to a £1 stake. Pool: £14,701.25 - 160.41 winning units **Richard Young**

1724 - (Foreign Racing) - See Raceform Interactive

[1675] KEMPTON (A.W) (R-H)
Friday, April 12

OFFICIAL GOING: Polytrack: standard to slow
Wind: Moderate, half behind Weather: Cloudy

1725 WISE BETTING AT RACINGTV.COM H'CAP (DIV I) 1m (P)
4:35 (4:40) (Class 6) (0-55,56) 3-Y-O

£3,105 (£924; £461; £400; £400; £400) **Stalls** Low

Form | | | | RPR
0-03 **1** **Medoras Childe**[9] 1515 3-9-5 53..........................(h) CharlesBishop 1 58
(Heather Main) *trckd ldrs gng wl: led wl over 1f out: sn rdn: styd on* **8/1**

6-00 **2** 2 **Power Of Life (USA)**[66] 612 3-9-1 52.......................... CameronNoble[(3)] 11 52
(Michael Bell) *trckd ldr on outer after 2f: rdn to chal over 2f out and sn upsides: nt qckn and chsd wnr after: no imp* **20/1**

50-0 **3** *hd* **Mongolia**[20] 1287 3-9-2 55.......................... SeamusCronin[(5)] 6 55
(Richard Hannon) *led 1f: steadily lost pl: rdn over 2f out: prog over 1f out: kpt on to battle for 2nd nr fin* **16/1**

0-03 **4** ¾ **Hooflepuff (IRE)**[30] 1173 3-9-7 55..........................(p[1]) LukeMorris 7 53
(Robert Cowell) *pushed along early in rr: rdn over 3f out: kpt on fnl 2f: nrst fin but nvr any ch* **5/2**[1]

-400 **5** 2 ½ **Archdeacon**[16] 1358 3-8-10 49.......................... MeganNicholls[(5)] 10 41
(Dean Ivory) *rousted early and dropped to last trio: rdn over 2f out: kpt on to take 5th nr fin: n.d* **6/1**[2]

0-60 **6** 1 **The Numismatist (IRE)**[43] 943 3-8-12 46..........................(t[1]) NicolaCurrie 8 36
(Jamie Osborne) *s.i.s: hld up in last: pushed along over 2f out: kpt on over 1f out: nvr nrr (jockey said colt was never travelling)* **12/1**

5-06 **7** *shd* **Freesia Gold (IRE)**[43] 941 3-9-3 51..........................(p[1]) KieranO'Neill 4 41
(Daniel Kubler) *led after 1f: edgd lft over 2f out: hdd wl over 1f out: sn wknd* **6/1**[2]

-050 **8** 1 ¼ **Platinum Coast (USA)**[35] 1081 3-8-12 46 oh1..........................(p[1]) JoeFanning 3 33
(James Tate) *dwlt: mostly in last trio: pushed along over 2f out: kpt on one pce after and n.d* **15/2**[3]

60-5 **9** 2 ¼ **Dragon Kuza**[9] 1514 3-8-13 54..........................(h) MarkCrehan[(7)] 9 36
(Hugo Palmer) *towards rr: pushed along and prog on outer to chse ldrs 3f out: drvn over 2f out: wknd wl over 1f out* **14/1**

00-6 **10** *11* **Frenchmans Creek (IRE)**[17] 1344 3-9-5 53.......................... AdamKirby 5 10
(Seamus Durack) *hld up in tch: pushed along sn after 1/2-way: wknd 3f out: t.o* **11/1**

3-00 **11** 1 **Invincible Sea (IRE)**[20] 1296 3-9-8 56.......................... LiamKeniry 2 10
(Linda Jewell) *chsd ldrs tl wknd qckly wl over 2f out: t.o (vet said filly was in season)* **40/1**

1m 40.15s (0.35) **Going Correction** -0.075s/f (Stan) **11** Ran SP% **115.8**
Speed ratings (Par 96): **95,93,92,92,89 88,88,87,84,73 72**
CSF £153.03 CT £2527.31 TOTE £9.10: £2.60, £6.50, £4.30; EX 191.70.
Owner Mr & Mrs D R Guest **Bred** Mr & Mrs James Main **Trained** Kingston Lisle, Oxon

FOCUS
Just a 0-55 and this looked the weaker of the two divisions.

1726 WISE BETTING AT RACINGTV.COM H'CAP (DIV II) 1m (P)
5:10 (5:13) (Class 6) (0-55,55) 3-Y-O

£3,105 (£924; £461; £400; £400; £400) **Stalls** Low

Form | | | | RPR
4450 **1** **Comeonfeeltheforce (IRE)**[55] 765 3-9-2 50..........................(t) PJMcDonald 6 55
(Lee Carter) *in tch in midfield: rdn and prog 2f out: drvn to chal fnl f: led last 75yds: styd on wl* **8/1**

0601 **2** ½ **Capofaro**[16] 1354 3-9-5 53.......................... NicolaCurrie 11 57
(Jamie Osborne) *t.k.h early: trckd ldr 2f: styd prom: rdn to cl over 2f out: led over 1f out: styd on but hdd last 75yds* **3/1**[2]

-604 **3** 1 ¼ **Apron Strings**[9] 1515 3-9-0 48.......................... KierenFox 2 49
(Michael Attwater) *prom: rdn over 2f out: tried to chal over 1f out: nt qckn and hld in 3rd ins fnl f* **16/1**

4640 **4** 2 ¼ **Margaret J**[51] 802 3-8-12 46 oh1..........................(p) LukeMorris 7 42
(Phil McEntee) *hld up in rr: drvn over 2f out: sme prog over 1f out: nvr on terms but kpt on fnl f* **16/1**

-052 **5** 1 ½ **Cauthen (IRE)**[9] 1515 3-9-3 54.......................... JoshuaBryan[(3)] 9 46
(Ken Cunningham-Brown) *trckd ldr after 2f: led 2f out: sn rdn and fnd nil: hdd over 1f out: wknd fnl f* **11/4**[1]

4000 **6** 1 ½ **Midnite Rendezvous**[21] 1270 3-8-12 46 oh1..........................(v[1]) EoinWalsh 4 35
(Derek Shaw) *dwlt: towards rr: rdn over 2f out: no prog tl kpt on ins fnl f* **66/1**

300- **7** *nk* **Sonnetina**[171] 8493 3-9-7 55.......................... CharlesBishop 10 43
(Denis Coakley) *restrained into rr: pushed along over 2f out: threatened to make prog wl over 1f out: sn no hdwy* **5/1**[3]

00-0 **8** *nk* **Nyanga (IRE)**[16] 1359 3-8-11 52..........................(t[1]) EllieMacKenzie[(7)] 3 40
(David Menuisier) *dwlt: sn in midfield: rdn over 2f out: no prog and btn over 1f out: fdd* **20/1**

0-00 **9** 1 ¼ **Sussex Solo**[21] 1264 3-9-7 55.......................... KieranO'Neill 1 40
(Luke Dace) *led to 2f out: wknd over 1f out* **8/1**

40-0 **10** 1 ¼ **Croqueta (IRE)**[16] 1359 3-8-12 53.......................... LukeCatton[(7)] 5 35
(Richard Hannon) *dwlt: a in rr: rdn and no prog over 2f out* **20/1**

006- **11** *11* **Milistorm**[123] 9484 3-9-5 53.......................... AdamKirby 8 9+
(Michael Blanshard) *rrd bdly s and slowly away: mostly in last: wknd over 2f out: t.o* **20/1**

1m 39.71s (-0.09) **Going Correction** -0.075s/f (Stan) **11** Ran SP% **118.1**
Speed ratings (Par 96): **97,96,95,93,91 90,89,89,88,86 75**
CSF £30.82 CT £390.25 TOTE £9.80: £3.00, £1.50, £3.50; EX 43.00 Trifecta £313.90.
Owner Kestonracingclub **Bred** Thomas & Seamus Whelan & David Harrison **Trained** Epsom, Surrey

FOCUS
Probably the stronger division (a bit quicker on the clock too) but still very modest fare.

1727 32RED H'CAP (LONDON MILE SERIES QUALIFIER) 1m (P)
5:40 (5:43) (Class 4) (0-85,87) 4-Y-O+

£6,469 (£1,925; £962; £481; £400; £400) **Stalls** Low

Form | | | | RPR
102- **1** **King's Slipper**[167] 8640 4-9-9 87.......................... AdamKirby 10 98+
(Clive Cox) *hld up off the pce in midfield: prog jst over 2f out: chsd clr ldr over 1f out: rdn and styd on wl fnl f to ld last 50yds: shade cleverly* **9/4**[1]

1631 **2** ¾ **Divine Messenger**[35] 1074 5-8-11 80..........................(p) SeamusCronin[(5)] 2 88
(Emma Owen) *led at str pce and spreadeagled field: pushed along 2f out: stl clr 1f out: tired and hdd last 50yds (bolted on the way to post)* **9/1**

1-11 **3** *nk* **Merchant Of Venice**[34] 1099 4-9-4 **82**............................ GeorgeWood 14 90+
(James Fanshawe) *hld up in rr and off the pce: rdn over 2f out: prog over 1f out: styd on wl fnl f and nrly snatched 2nd* **8/1**

-020 **4** *3 1/4* **Key Player**[28] 1213 4-9-5 **83**..............................(b[1]) CharlesBishop 13 83
(Eve Johnson Houghton) *chsd clr ldr and wl ahd of rest: rdn over 2f out: lost 2nd over 1f out: fdd* **25/1**

505- **5** *nk* **Medieval (IRE)**[161] 8809 5-9-7 **85**..............................(b) PJMcDonald 6 84
(Paul Cole) *chsd clr ldrs: rdn and nt qckn over 2f out: lost pl and sltly impeded over 1f out: kpt on again fnl f and nrly snatched 4th* **11/2**[3]

3466 **6** *hd* **Reckless Endeavour (IRE)**[10] 1502 6-8-11 **80**........ ConnorMurtagh[(5)] 4 79
(David Barron) *hld up towards rr and off the pce: effrt on inner over 2f out: kpt on but nvr a threat* **16/1**

24-5 **7** *2* **Jellmood**[98] 56 4-9-7 **85**..............................(t) ShaneKelly 5 79
(Chris Gordon) *a in midfield: rdn and no imp on clr ldrs over 2f out: btn after (briefly got loose in the Pre-Parade Ring; jockey said gelding hung left-handed throughout; coughing post-racevet said gelding was coughing post-race)* **33/1**

560- **8** *1/2* **Biotic**[168] 8598 8-8-4 **75**.............................. EllieMacKenzie[(7)] 9 68
(Rod Millman) *dwlt: mostly in last quartet and wl off the pce: shkn up over 2f out: kpt on fr over 1f out: nrst fin but no ch* **100/1**

-100 **9** *1/2* **Capriolette (IRE)**[12] 1457 4-9-3 **81**.............................. LiamKeniry 1 73
(Ed Walker) *chsd clr ldrs: rdn and no prog over 2f out: wknd over 1f out* **25/1**

331- **10** *hd* **Directory**[163] 8733 4-8-9 **73**.............................. LukeMorris 12 65
(James Eustace) *chsd clr ldng pair and wl ahd of rest: rdn over 2f out: wknd over 1f out* **16/1**

40-1 **11** *3/4* **La Maquina**[37] 1036 4-9-4 **82**..............................(t) NicolaCurrie 8 72
(George Baker) *s.s: hld up wl in rr: shkn up over 2f out: no real prog (jockey said gelding ran flat)* **5/1**[2]

216- **12** *1* **Sir Plato (IRE)**[186] 8061 5-9-0 **78**.............................. KieranO'Neill 11 66
(Rod Millman) *sn urged along and wl off the pce in rr: nvr a factor* **25/1**

5-00 **13** *24* **Rock Icon**[16] 1356 6-9-0 **78**.............................. PhilipPrince 3 10+
(Jo Hughes, France) *s.v.s: a bhd: t.o* **50/1**

154- **14** *12* **Dragons Voice**[161] 8806 5-9-4 **82**.............................. AndreaAtzeni 7
(David Menuisier) *chsd clr ldrs tl wknd rapidly 3f out: t.o (jockey said gelding stopped quickly)* **8/1**

1m 37.28s (-2.52) **Going Correction** -0.075s/f (Stan) **14 Ran SP% 124.2**
Speed ratings (Par 105): **109,108,107,104,104 104,102,101,101,101 100,99,75,63**
CSF £22.74 CT £151.71 TOTE £3.10: £1.40, £2.90, £2.50; EX 26.80 Trifecta £170.30.
Owner D B Clark & A R Bentall **Bred** Bugley Stud (last Slipper) Partnership **Trained** Lambourn, Berks

FOCUS
This looked a typically competitive London Mile Series Qualifier, but it was pretty unsatisfactory as they were strung out from an early stage, there was a desperate finish and many never looked like getting involved.

1728 32RED CASINO NOVICE STKS 6f (P)
6:15 (6:16) (Class 4) 3-Y-O+ **£6,469** (£1,925; £962; £481) **Stalls** Low

Form RPR

01- **1** **Intuitive (IRE)**[186] 8041 3-9-8 0.............................. PJMcDonald 2 84+
(James Tate) *hld up towards rr: prog over 2f out: clsd on ldrs over 1f out: rdn to ld 100yds out then hung lft: styd on* **7/4**[2]

42- **2** *3/4* **Moraawed**[132] 9354 3-9-2 0.............................. DaneO'Neill 3 76+
(Roger Varian) *dwlt and sltly impeded s: mostly in last trio: rdn and prog 2f out: clsd on ldrs and swtchd rt 1f out: chal last 100yds: styd on to take 2nd last strides* **11/8**[1]

5-2 **3** *hd* **Harry's Bar**[20] 1286 4-10-0 0.............................. GeorgeWood 9 78+
(James Fanshawe) *trckd ldr: led over 2f out: edgd lft 1f out: hdd and no ex last 100yds* **10/1**

3 **4** *3/4* **Ghaith**[20] 1286 4-10-0 0..............................(h) JamesDoyle 11 77
(Hugo Palmer) *prom: trckd ldr over 2f out: sn tried to chal but carried hd awkwardly and nt qckn: stl rt on terms ins fnl f: hld whn hmpd last 50yds* **14/1**

2 **5** *3* **Hey Ho Let's Go**[30] 1180 3-9-2 0.............................. AdamKirby 8 64
(Clive Cox) *in tch: shkn up and effrt over 2f out: no imp on ldrs over 1f out: one pce* **25/1**

6 *hd* **Somethingaboutjack (IRE)** 3-9-2 0.............................. CharlesBishop 5 63
(Eve Johnson Houghton) *dwlt: wl in rr: pushed along over 2f out: kpt on steadily after: sme promise* **33/1**

5 **7** *3 3/4* **Magical Ride**[20] 1286 4-10-0 0..............................(h) TomQueally 4 55
(Richard Spencer) *sn in last: pushed along 1/2-way: nvr a factor but passed wkng rivals over 1f out* **40/1**

305- **8** *nk* **Adam Tiler (USA)**[171] 8496 3-8-9 73.............................. CierenFallon[(7)] 7 51
(Robert Cowell) *chsd ldng pair: lost pl fr 2f out: wknd fnl f* **25/1**

43- **9** *2 1/4* **Came From The Dark (IRE)**[203] 7484 3-9-2 0.............................. AndreaAtzeni 10 44
(Ed Walker) *chsd ldrs on outer: shkn up over 2f out: wknd wl over 1f out* **6/1**[3]

50- **10** *nk* **Jailbreak (IRE)**[112] 9671 3-9-2 0.............................. ShaneKelly 1 44
(Richard Hughes) *chsd ldrs tl wknd over 2f out* **100/1**

405- **11** *28* **True Belief (IRE)**[153] 8993 3-9-2 78.............................. RossaRyan 6
(Brett Johnson) *racd v freely: led to over 2f out: wknd rapidly: t.o (jockey said gelding ran too free)* **33/1**

1m 11.4s (-1.70) **Going Correction** -0.075s/f (Stan)
WFA 3 from 4yo 12lb **11 Ran SP% 125.5**
Speed ratings (Par 105): **108,107,106,105,101 101,96,96,93,92 55**
CSF £4.60 TOTE £2.70: £1.10, £1.40, £2.10; EX 4.50 Trifecta £24.30.
Owner Sheikh Hamed Dalmook Al Maktoum **Bred** Domenico Fonzo & Maria Teresa Matouani **Trained** Newmarket, Suffolk

FOCUS
A bit of a messy finish, but the front four were clear and it looks novice form to be positive about.

1729 32RED.COM H'CAP 6f (P)
6:45 (6:45) (Class 4) (0-85,85) 3-Y-O **£6,469** (£1,925; £962; £440; £440; £400) **Stalls** Low

Form RPR

1311 **1** **Probability (IRE)**[13] 1424 3-9-4 **82**.............................. EdwardGreatrex 4 86
(Archie Watson) *mde all: shkn up over 1f out: 2 l ahd fnl f: rdn out and clung on* **7/1**[3]

616- **2** *1/2* **Tinto**[167] 8644 3-8-13 **77**.............................. JoeFanning 3 82+
(Amanda Perrett) *trckd ldng trio: effrt whn hmpd over 1f out: rdn and styd on fnl f to take 2nd last stride: jst too late* **7/1**[3]

122- **3** *hd* **Reticent Angel (IRE)**[119] 9533 3-9-3 **81**.............................. AdamKirby 6 83
(Clive Cox) *chsd wnr to over 2f out and again wl over 1f out: no imp tl clsd ins fnl f: kpt on nr fin but lost 2nd last stride* **12/1**

43-1 **4** *shd* **Mawakib**[15] 1389 3-9-1 **79**.............................. AndreaAtzeni 7 82
(Roger Varian) *dwlt and sltly impeded s: hld up in 6th: effrt on outer whn bmpd over 1f out: styd on ins fnl f: jst too late* **11/4**[2]

152- **4** *dht* **Converter (IRE)**[197] 7695 3-9-4 **82**.............................. JamesDoyle 2 84
(Mick Channon) *chsd ldng pair to over 2f out: sn rdn: kpt on and one of many clsng ins fnl f: a hld* **15/8**[1]

204- **6** *nk* **Thegreatestshowman**[204] 7454 3-9-1 **79**.............................. DougieCostello 1 80+
(Amy Murphy) *awkward s: sn in 5th: urged along over 1f out: grad clsd fnl f and rdn last 100yds: too late (jockey said gelding hung left-handed up the straight)* **10/1**

30-5 **7** *1* **Under Curfew**[69] 555 3-8-2 **66**.............................. KieranO'Neill 8 64
(Tony Carroll) *slowly away: hld up tl swift prog 3f out: chsd wnr over 2f out to wl over 1f out: lost pl fnl f and btn whn impeded nr fin* **33/1**

3523 **8** *hd* **Uncle Jerry**[13] 1424 3-8-13 **84**..............................(b) GeorgeRooke[(7)] 10 81
(Richard Hughes) *hld up in last pair fr wdst draw: effrt on outer whn nudged by rival over 1f out: kpt on but nvr pce to chal* **14/1**

413- **9** *3/4* **Be Like Me (IRE)**[171] 8496 3-9-1 **82**.............................. GabrieleMalune[(3)] 9 77
(Marco Botti) *hld up in last pair: pushed along and taken wdst of all 2f out: hung lft over 1f out and reminders: kpt on fnl f: nvr in it* **20/1**

155- **10** *2 1/2* **Autumn Splendour (IRE)**[114] 9605 3-9-7 **85**.............................. LukeMorris 5 72
(Milton Bradley) *dwlt: nvr bttr than midfield: rdn and struggling 2f out* **66/1**

1m 13.38s (0.28) **Going Correction** -0.075s/f (Stan) **10 Ran SP% 119.1**
Speed ratings (Par 100): **95,94,94,93,93 93,92,91,90,87**
CSF £55.44 CT £586.86 TOTE £5.90: £1.40, £2.00, £2.90; EX 63.00 Trifecta £706.50.
Owner Mrs C Cashman **Bred** Marie & Mossy Fahy **Trained** Upper Lambourn, W Berks

FOCUS
This 3yo sprint handicap was two seconds slower than the preceding novice event, which goes some way to explain the winner being able to make all and there was a bunched finish in behind.

1730 32RED ON THE APP STORE FILLIES' H'CAP 1m 3f 219y(P)
7:15 (7:18) (Class 5) (0-75,76) 3-Y-O **£3,752** (£1,116; £557; £400; £400; £400) **Stalls** Low

Form RPR

20-1 **1** **Cafe Espresso**[10] 1494 3-9-8 **76** 6ex..............................(b[1]) HollieDoyle 4 78
(Archie Watson) *trckd ldng trio: moved up to take 2nd 2f out: chal over 1f out: narrow ld fnl f: kpt on wl* **8/1**

344- **2** *nk* **Sapa Inca (IRE)**[215] 7099 3-9-6 **74**.............................. JoeFanning 2 77
(Mark Johnston) *trckd ldng pair: trapped over 2f out as wnr moved up: chsd ldng pair over 1f out: styd on wl fnl f: tk 2nd last stride but jst too late* **5/4**[1]

-325 **3** *hd* **Wanaasah**[17] 1345 3-9-3 **71**.............................. TrevorWhelan 6 73
(David Loughnane) *led: dictated stdy pce: sent for home 2f out: hrd pressed over 1f out: narrowly hdd fnl f: kpt on and upsides 75yds out: jst hld and lost 2nd last stride* **14/1**

220- **4** *2 1/2* **Little India (FR)**[170] 8565 3-9-7 **75**..............................(w) BenCurtis 3 73
(K R Burke) *chsd ldrs in 5th: effrt over 2f out: nt qckn over 1f out: one pce after* **6/1**[3]

0-44 **5** *1 1/2* **Mrs Meader**[36] 1064 3-8-11 **65**.............................. RobHornby 1 60
(Seamus Mullins) *hld up in last trio: nt qckn whn pce lifted over 2f out: nvr able to cl after* **33/1**

-235 **6** *1 1/4* **Navadir (JPN)**[11] 1481 3-9-1 **69**..............................(t) PJMcDonald 5 62
(Marco Botti) *hld up in last trio: pushed along over 2f out: nvr gng pce to make any impact on ldrs in r that turned into a sprint* **11/2**[2]

056- **7** *2 3/4* **Padmavati**[140] 9227 3-8-8 **62**..............................(h[1]) AndreaAtzeni 7 51
(Ed Walker) *stdd s: hld up in last: pushed along over 3f out: no prog and bhd 2f out (trainers rep could offer no explanation for the filly's performance)* **11/2**[2]

004- **8** *hd* **Riverina**[177] 8311 3-8-5 **59**.............................. LukeMorris 8 48
(Harry Dunlop) *trckd ldr to 2f out: losing pl whn impeded sn after: wknd* **16/1**

2m 35.33s (0.83) **Going Correction** -0.075s/f (Stan) **8 Ran SP% 116.1**
Speed ratings (Par 95): **94,93,93,92,91 90,88,88**
CSF £18.78 CT £143.19 TOTE £11.90: £2.00, £1.10, £2.40; EX 26.00 Trifecta £188.10.
Owner Boadicea Bloodstock **Bred** Churchill Bloodstock Investments Ltd **Trained** Upper Lambourn, W Berks

FOCUS
Unexposed sorts in this fair fillies handicap but, again, the bare result does not tell the whole story.

1731 £100 PROFIT BOOST AT 32REDSPORT.COM CLASSIFIED STKS (DIV I) 7f (P)
7:45 (7:45) (Class 6) 3-Y-O+ **£3,105** (£924; £461; £400; £400; £400) **Stalls** Low

Form RPR

000- **1** **Fantastic Flyer**[241] 6134 4-9-8 45.............................. MartinDwyer 1 54+
(Dean Ivory) *hld up in midfield: prog on inner over 2f out: led over 1f out: pushed clr sn after: comf* **6/1**[2]

00-0 **2** *3 1/4* **Only Ten Per Cent (IRE)**[57] 719 11-9-8 41........... AlistairRawlinson 7 46
(J R Jenkins) *dwlt: towards rr: prog on inner wl over 1f out: chsd wnr ins fnl f: kpt on but no imp* **50/1**

4320 **3** *nk* **Joyful Dream (IRE)**[13] 1431 5-9-8 46..............................(p) ShaneKelly 8 45
(John Butler) *trckd ldrs but n.m.r early: rdn and prog 2f out: disp 2nd fnl f: kpt on but no ch w wnr* **10/1**

000- **4** *2 3/4* **Poetic Motion**[142] 9170 3-8-8 50.............................. CharlieBennett 12 33+
(Jim Boyle) *tried to get across fr wd draw: in tch: wd in st: rdn and nt qckn 2f out: no ch after but styd on fnl f to take 4th last strides (jockey said filly hung left-handed throughout)* **8/1**

-U30 **5** *3/4* **Cristal Pallas Cat (IRE)**[36] 1060 4-9-3 48..............(h) RhiainIngram[(5)] 3 36
(Roger Ingram) *led but pressed: hdd wl over 1f out: fdd* **11/4**[1]

6023 **6** *shd* **My Girl Maisie (IRE)**[11] 1478 5-9-8 47..............................(e) PhilipPrince 2 36
(Richard Guest) *trckd ldng trio: prog to go 2nd over 2f out: led v briefly wl over 1f out: sn no ch w wnr: wknd fnl f* **6/1**[2]

4106 **7** *nk* **Black Truffle (FR)**[8] 1553 9-9-1 47..............................(p) EllieMacKenzie[(7)] 4 35
(Mark Usher) *trckd ldrs: pushed along and nt qckn 2f out: one pce and no imp after (jockey said gelding suffered interference approaching the first bend)* **7/1**[3]

-550 **8** *1/2* **Haraz (IRE)**[55] 760 6-9-3 44..............................(bt) ThoreHammerHansen[(5)] 10 34
(Paddy Butler) *hld up in rr: effrt over 2f out: modest prog over 1f out: no hdwy fnl f (jockey said gelding was never travelling)* **33/1**

0500 **9** *3 3/4* **Swiss Cross**[11] 1478 12-9-1 48..............................(p) GraceMcEntee[(7)] 6 24
(Phil McEntee) *pressed ldng pair on outer to over 2f out: wknd* **16/1**

1650 **10** *1/2* **Rapid Rise (IRE)**[28] 1215 5-9-8 46..............................(p) LukeMorris 11 23
(Milton Bradley) *detached in last most of way: passed a few late on: nvr a factor* **14/1**

050/ **11** 2 **Angelical Eve (IRE)**[534] 8345 5-9-8 40 TrevorWhelan 13 18
(Dai Williams) *hld up in last trio: pushed along over 2f out: no prog over 1f out: wknd* **100/1**

-040 **12** nk **Purbeck Gem**[67] 599 5-9-3 50 SeamusCronin(5) 5 17
(Robyn Brisland) *pressed ldr to over 2f out: wknd qckly* **6/1**[2]

0004 **13** 7 **Valentine Mist (IRE)**[28] 1218 7-9-8 45 GeorgeWood 9
(James Grassick) *towards rr: urged along sn after 1/2-way: wknd over 2f out* **66/1**

1m 25.42s (-0.58) **Going Correction** -0.075s/f (Stan)
WFA 3 from 4yo+ 14lb **13** Ran SP% **122.2**
Speed ratings (Par 101): **100,96,95,92,91 91,91,90,86,86 83,83,75**
CSF £289.28 TOTE £7.00: £2.30, £16.00, £2.90; EX 560.10 Trifecta £2624.00.
Owner Mrs K M Young **Bred** Gracelands Stud **Trained** Radlett, Herts
■ Stewards' Enquiry : Charlie Bennett four-day ban: careless riding (Apr 26-29)

FOCUS
Not form to dwell upon.

1732 £100 PROFIT BOOST AT 32REDSPORT.COM CLASSIFIED STKS (DIV II) 7f (P)
8:15 (8:18) (Class 6) 3-Y-O+
£3,105 (£924; £461; £400; £400; £400) **Stalls** Low

Form RPR

00 **1** **Ainne**[18] 1339 4-9-5 50 (t[1]) GaryMahon(3) 4 55
(Sylvester Kirk) *mostly chsd ldr: rdn to ld over 1f out: kpt on steadily fnl f* **8/11**[2]

0-04 **2** 1¼ **Rock In Society (IRE)**[8] 1554 4-9-5 43 (v[1]) TimClark(3) 10 52
(John Butler) *led: clr w wnr 2f out: hdd over 1f out: one pce* **25/1**

00-0 **3** ½ **Freddy With A Y (IRE)**[28] 1209 9-9-8 48 AlistairRawlinson 6 50
(J R Jenkins) *chsd ldrs: effrt to chse clr ldng pair over 2f out: kpt on over 1f out: nrst fin (jockey said gelding hung right-handed in the final 2f)* **33/1**

-000 **4** 1¼ **Jack Louie**[16] 1354 3-8-8 39 MartinDwyer 2 42
(Dean Ivory) *hld up in midfield: effrt over 2f out: chsd clr ldrs over 1f out: kpt on but n.d* **10/1**[3]

0544 **5** ¾ **Malaysian Boleh**[11] 1478 9-9-1 42 (v) GraceMcEntee(7) 7 45
(Phil McEntee) *hld up in rr: pushed along over 2f out: kpt on one pce over 1f out: n.d* **20/1**

23 **6** ½ **Tellovoi (IRE)**[36] 1071 11-9-8 46 (p) PhilipPrince 12 44
(Richard Guest) *chsd ldng trio to 3f out: sn outpcd: no imp fnl 2f* **16/1**

-600 **7** 1 **Burauq**[44] 920 7-9-8 39 (p) JackMitchell 1 41
(Milton Bradley) *hld up in rr: effrt over 2f out: plugged on over 1f out on inner: nvr a threat* **40/1**

5364 **8** 1½ **Legal Mind**[15] 1384 6-9-3 48 (v) SeamusCronin(5) 14 37
(Emma Owen) *wl in rr: struggling and wl off the pce over 2f out: kpt on for over 1f out* **25/1**

0621 **9** 3½ **Dawn Commando**[16] 1353 4-9-8 50 (b) AdamKirby 11 27
(Daniel Kubler) *dwlt: sn in last and urged along: stl last and gng nowhere over 2f out: modest prog over 1f out: no hdwy after (trainer said that the gelding missed the break and was unable to dominate)* **8/11**[1]

063/ **10** 4 **Q Cee**[534] 8345 6-9-1 50 CierenFallon(7) 9 17
(Eugene Stanford) *chsd ldng pair to over 2f out: wknd qckly* **14/1**

464- **11** 1¼ **Spirit Of Ishy**[210] 7247 4-9-8 42 BenCurtis 8 13
(Stuart Kittow) *chsd ldrs tl wknd u.p over 2f out* **33/1**

000 **12** 11 **Georgearthurhenry**[50] 827 3-8-8 48 GeorgeWood 5
(Amy Murphy) *dwlt: a wl in rr: t.o* **12/1**

1m 25.4s (-0.60) **Going Correction** -0.075s/f (Stan)
WFA 3 from 4yo+ 14lb **12** Ran SP% **119.1**
Speed ratings (Par 101): **100,98,98,96,95 95,94,92,88,83 82,69**
CSF £197.60 TOTE £9.80: £2.10, £8.40, £4.90; EX 373.90 Trifecta £1486.30.
Owner Sylvester Kirk **Bred** The Kathryn Stud **Trained** Upper Lambourn, Berks
■ Rising Sunshine was withdrawn. Price at time of withdrawal 14-1. Rule 4 applies to board prices prior to withdrawal but not to SP bets. Deduction 5p in the pound. New market formed

FOCUS
Very weak form with the favourite blowing out altogether.
T/Plt: £119.90 to a £1 stake. Pool: £60,153.99 - 366.20 winning units T/Qpdt: £10.30 to a £1 stake. Pool: £13,154.30 - 943.47 winning units **Jonathan Neesom**

NEWBURY (L-H)
Friday, April 12

OFFICIAL GOING: Soft (good to soft in places; 5.3)
Wind: Light behind Weather: Cloudy

1733 WEST BERKSHIRE BREWERY "NEWCOMERS" EBF MAIDEN STKS (PLUS 10 RACE) 5f 34y
2:00 (2:02) (Class 4) 2-Y-O **£6,469** (£1,925; £962; £481) **Stalls** Centre

Form RPR

1 **Highland Chief (IRE)** 2-9-5 0 RaulDaSilva 8 84+
(Paul Cole) *ly; sltly on toes; broke wl enough: sn lost pl: pushed along 1/2-way: hdwy 2f out: rdn to ld over 1f out: edgd lft ins fnl f: styd on* **16/1**

2 nk **Separate** 2-9-0 0 SeanLevey 3 78+
(Richard Hannon) *compact; w ldrs: led 2f out: shkn up and hdd over 1f out: edgd lft wl ins fnl f: styd on* **11/1**

3 1¾ **Chattanooga Boy (IRE)** 2-9-5 0 HarryBentley 2 77
(George Scott) *compact; looked wl; hld up in tch: shkn up and ev ch over 1f out: styd on same pce wl ins fnl f* **3/1**[3]

4 2½ **Klopp Of The Kop (IRE)** 2-9-5 0 AdamKirby 5 68+
(Clive Cox) *str; sltly on toes; chsd ldrs: shkn up 1/2-way: nt clr run over 1f out: rdn and hung rt ins fnl f: styd on same pce* **11/4**[2]

5 1¾ **Isobar Wind (IRE)** 2-9-5 0 DavidProbert 6 61
(David Evans) *str; chsd ldrs: pushed along 1/2-way: wknd ins fnl f* **16/1**

6 ¾ **Album (IRE)** 2-9-5 0 OisinMurphy 7 59
(Martyn Meade) *unfurnished; scope; prom: shkn up over 1f out: wknd ins fnl f* **9/4**[1]

7 ¾ **Barry Magoo** 2-9-5 0 CharlieBennett 4 56+
(Adam West) *leggy; led 3f: hmpd and wknd ins fnl f (jockey said colt hung right-handed)* **66/1**

8 ¾ **Show Me Heaven** 2-9-0 0 LukeMorris 1 48
(Bill Turner) *leggy; s.i.s: pushed along 1/2-way: wknd over 1f out* **33/1**

9 3½ **Littleton Hall (IRE)** 2-9-5 0 CallumShepherd 9 41
(Mick Channon) *leggy; s.i.s: a in rr: rdn and wknd over 1f out* **14/1**

1m 4.98s (3.48) **Going Correction** +0.525s/f (Yiel) **9** Ran SP% **113.6**
Speed ratings (Par 94): **93,92,89,85,82 81,80,79,73**
CSF £175.04 TOTE £14.80: £2.90, £2.10, £1.50; EX 102.30 Trifecta £584.30.
Owner Mrs Fitri Hay **Bred** Mrs Fitri Hay **Trained** Whatcombe, Oxon

FOCUS
After the first Adam Kirby said of the ground: "It's dead." Sean Levey agreed and added: "It's a bit sticky," while Harry Bentley said: "There's a bit of give, but it's no worse than good." No previous form in this juvenile event, in which the principals came down the centre of the track.

1734 DUBAI DUTY FREE H'CAP 5f 34y
2:35 (2:36) (Class 2) (0-110,103) 4-Y-O+
£15,562 (£4,660; £2,330; £1,165; £582; £292) **Stalls** Centre

Form RPR

200/ **1** **Stake Acclaim (IRE)**[517] 8738 7-9-5 **101** AdamKirby 4 111
(Dean Ivory) *looked wl; mde all: shkn up and qcknd over 1f out: drvn out* **25/1**

550- **2** 2¾ **Blue De Vega (GER)**[174] 8413 6-8-9 **91** PJMcDonald 1 91
(Robert Cowell) *bit bkward; prom: chsd wnr 2f out: sn rdn: no ex ins fnl f* **5/1**[3]

433- **3** ¾ **Kick On Kick On**[156] 8933 4-8-13 **95** (w) WilliamBuick 7 92
(Clive Cox) *hld up: racd keenly: hdwy over 1f out: sn rdn: styd on: nt rch ldrs* **4/1**[2]

500- **4** hd **Spoof**[188] 7974 4-9-2 **98** (h) AndreaAtzeni 3 95
(Charles Hills) *stdd s: plld hrd and sn prom: outpcd over 1f out: styd on ins fnl f* **12/1**

400- **5** 2½ **Ice Age (IRE)**[202] 7512 6-9-7 **103** CharlesBishop 6 91
(Eve Johnson Houghton) *chsd wnr 3f: wknd ins fnl f* **8/1**

05-6 **6** ½ **Moon Trouble (IRE)**[13] 1421 6-8-8 **90** (h[1]) SilvestreDeSousa 5 76+
(Michael Appleby) *looked wl; s.i.s: sn pushed along in rr: edgd lft and styd on ins fnl f: nvr nrr* **9/4**[1]

-440 **7** nk **Orvar (IRE)**[50] 837 6-9-1 **97** LukeMorris 2 82
(Paul Midgley) *looked wl; chsd ldrs tl rdn and wknd over 1f out* **14/1**

6434 **8** 9 **Gracious John (IRE)**[20] 1295 6-8-9 **91** OisinMurphy 8 43+
(David Evans) *on toes; sweating; awkward s: hld up: pushed along 1/2-way: wknd over 1f out* **5/1**[3]

1m 2.48s (0.98) **Going Correction** +0.525s/f (Yiel) **8** Ran SP% **113.4**
Speed ratings (Par 109): **113,108,107,107,103 102,101,87**
CSF £142.27 CT £621.33 TOTE £38.00: £7.20, £1.80, £1.40; EX 219.80 Trifecta £3498.90.
Owner M J Yarrow **Bred** G Devlin **Trained** Radlett, Herts

FOCUS
Good sprint handicap form. A fractional pb from the winner.

1735 COMPTON BEAUCHAMP ESTATES LTD SILVER BAR H'CAP 2m 2f
3:05 (3:05) (Class 2) (0-105,100) 4-Y-O+
£24,900 (£7,456; £3,728; £1,864; £932; £468) **Stalls** Low

Form RPR

100- **1** **Coeur Blimey (IRE)**[27] 6901 8-8-12 **86** DavidProbert 6 94
(Sue Gardner) *chsd ldr after 1f: led over 4f out: rdn over 2f out: styd on wl* **16/1**

050- **2** 2¾ **Coeur De Lion**[181] 8188 6-9-0 **88** (p) HollieDoyle 2 93
(Alan King) *looked wl; chsd ldr 1f: remained handy: chsd wnr over 3f out: rdn over 2f out: edgd lft ins fnl f: styd on same pce* **7/2**[2]

0/3- **3** hd **Who Dares Wins (IRE)**[336] 2596 7-9-12 **100** (p) TomMarquand 3 105
(Alan King) *hld up: rdn over 3f out: hdwy over 2f out: styd on* **8/1**

403/ **4** 5 **The Cashel Man (IRE)**[27] 3073 7-9-4 **92** (p) PJMcDonald 7 92
(Nicky Henderson) *hld up: rdn over 3f out: hdwy u.p over 1f out: edgd lft and no imp fnl f* **4/1**[3]

0-24 **5** 17 **Castlelyons (IRE)**[69] 558 7-9-1 **89** (h) CallumShepherd 1 72
(Robert Stephens) *hld up: rdn over 3f out: wknd over 2f out* **14/1**

104- **6** 50 **Medburn Cutler**[322] 3055 9-8-9 **83** (p) SilvestreDeSousa 5 16
(Peter Hedger) *led at stdy pce: shkn up and hdd over 4f out: wknd over 3f out: eased (jockey said gelding had no more to give)* **10/1**

12-2 **7** 2 **Festival Of Ages (USA)**[88] 238 5-9-10 **98** WilliamBuick 8 29
(Charlie Appleby) *looked wl; prom: rdn over 3f out: wknd over 2f out: eased (jockey said gelding stopped quickly)* **6/4**[1]

4m 9.54s (2.74) **Going Correction** +0.525s/f (Yiel) **7** Ran SP% **115.0**
Speed ratings (Par 109): **109,107,107,105,97 75,74**
CSF £71.68 CT £492.66 TOTE £19.50: £5.40, £2.10; EX 75.30 Trifecta £316.30.
Owner Keith Harris & Tom Gardner **Bred** J P King **Trained** Longdown, Devon
■ Stewards' Enquiry : William Buick one-day ban: failing to ride out (Apr 26)

FOCUS
Add 9yds to race distance. A decent staying handicap. A minor pb from the third.

1736 DUBAI DUTY FREE FULL OF SURPRISES H'CAP 7f (S)
3:40 (3:44) (Class 2) (0-100,96) 3-Y-O
£12,450 (£3,728; £1,864; £932; £466; £234) **Stalls** Centre

Form RPR

131- **1** **Happy Power (IRE)**[167] 8630 3-9-4 **93** SilvestreDeSousa 9 109+
(Andrew Balding) *looked wl; hld up: hdwy over 2f out: shkn up to ld over 1f out: pushed clr ins fnl f* **9/4**[1]

221- **2** 5 **Reeves**[168] 8592 3-8-9 **84** RaulDaSilva 7 87
(Robert Cowell) *prom: rdn over 2f out: sn outpcd: rallied over 1f out: styd on to go 2nd wl ins fnl f* **10/1**

46- **3** ½ **Tulfarris**[185] 8097 3-9-1 **90** StevieDonohoe 14 92
(Charlie Fellowes) *hld up: shkn up over 2f out: r.o ins fnl f: nt rch ldrs* **33/1**

413- **4** nk **Topical**[223] 6793 3-8-1 **81** ThoreHammerHansen(5) 1 82+
(Richard Hannon) *chsd ldrs: led over 3f out: rdn clr over 2f out: edgd rt and hdd over 1f out: no ex ins fnl f* **8/1**[3]

151- **5** nk **Sparklealot (IRE)**[180] 8232 3-8-11 **86** TrevorWhelan 5 86
(Ivan Furtado) *sltly on toes; w ldrs tl over 3f out: rdn over 2f out: styd on same pce fr over 1f out* **20/1**

112- **6** 1¾ **Shallow Hal**[153] 9006 3-9-0 **89** BenCurtis 6 85
(K R Burke) *looked wl; chsd ldrs: rdn over 2f out: wknd ins fnl f* **9/1**

400- **7** ¾ **Lihou**[153] 9006 3-8-6 **81** ow1 JohnFahy 4 75
(David Evans) *hld up: hdwy 1/2-way: rdn over 1f out: wknd ins fnl f* **33/1**

22-1 **8** 6 **Beat Le Bon (FR)**[30] 1180 3-9-7 **96** TomMarquand 8 75
(Richard Hannon) *looked wl; prom: rdn over 2f out: wknd over 1f out* **5/1**[2]

101- **9** 7 **Hackle Setter (USA)**[194] 7798 3-8-5 **80** DavidEgan 10 42
(Sylvester Kirk) *hld up: pushed along over 4f out: bhd fr 1/2-way* **40/1**

16-4 **10** 1¼ **Chairmanoftheboard (IRE)**[37] 1035 3-9-7 **96** AndreaAtzeni 12 54
(Mick Channon) *looked wl; hld up: bhd fr 1/2-way* **12/1**

30-4 **11** 1¼ **Wasntexpectingthat**[19] 1306 3-8-2 **82** SeanDavis(5) 2 37+
(Richard Fahey) *hld up: effrt whn hmpd over 2f out: sn wknd* **11/1**

336- **12** 1¾ **Tin Hat (IRE)**[149] 9051 3-8-4 **86** GeorgiaDobie(7) 11 37
(Eve Johnson Houghton) *hld up: bhd fr 1/2-way* **50/1**

115- **13** 4½ **Lincoln Park**[167] 8630 3-8-13 **88** DougieCostello 3 28
(Michael Appleby) *led to 1/2-way: wknd over 2f out* **20/1**

The Form Book Flat 2019, Raceform Ltd, Newbury, RG14 5SJ

102- **14** *17* **Blonde Warrior (IRE)**[223] 6791 3-9-5 94.......................... JamesDoyle 13
(Hugo Palmer) *hld up: wknd 4f out (jockey said colt stopped quickly)* 14/1

1m 28.21s (1.21) **Going Correction** +0.525s/f (Yiel) 14 Ran SP% **120.1**
Speed ratings (Par 104): **114,108,107,107,107 105,104,97,89,87 86,84,79,59**
CSF £23.15 CT £622.43 TOTE £3.30: £1.80, £2.80, £11.20; EX 26.90 Trifecta £672.20.
Owner King Power Racing Co Ltd **Bred** Yeomanstown Stud **Trained** Kingsclere, Hants

FOCUS
A classy 3yo handicap that looks certain to contain winners, with the favourite proving a class apart. The third has been rated to his mark.

1737 DUBAI DUTY FREE GOLF WORLD CUP BRITISH EBF CONDITIONS STKS (PLUS 10 RACE) 1m 2f
4:10 (4:13) (Class 3) 3-Y-O **£10,350** (£3,080; £1,539; £769) **Stalls** Low

Form RPR
10- **1** **King Ottokar (FR)**[167] 8633 3-9-2 0.......................... BenCurtis 3 107+
(Charlie Fellowes) *ly; a.p: chsd ldr over 2f out: led over 1f out: rdn and edgd lft ins fnl f: r.o* 14/1
120- **2** *1 ½* **Dashing Willoughby**[167] 8633 3-9-2 99.......................... OisinMurphy 10 104
(Andrew Balding) *athletic; pushed along early in rr: hdwy over 8f out: led over 7f out: rdn and hdd over 1f out: styd on* 12/1
1- **3** *3 ½* **Kaloor**[191] 7904 3-9-2 0.......................... JimCrowley 1 98
(Brian Meehan) *str; hld up: pushed along over 3f out: r.o ins fnl f: nt rch ldrs* 9/1[3]
1- **4** *1 ½* **Space Blues (IRE)**[156] 8931 3-9-2 0.......................... WilliamBuick 9 95+
(Charlie Appleby) *str; plld hrd: led early: remained handy: shkn up over 1f out: no ex fnl f* 11/8[1]
126- **5** *7* **Floating Artist**[197] 7702 3-9-2 102.......................... RossaRyan 7 82
(Richard Hannon) *sltly on toes; hld up: swtchd rt over 3f out: sn pushed along: styd on ins fnl f: nvr nrr* 40/1
12- **6** *hd* **Headman**[142] 9170 3-9-2 0.......................... JasonWatson 8 82
(Roger Charlton) *tall; str; looked wl; plld hrd and prom: stdd and lost pl over 7f out: shkn up over 2f out: wknd fnl f* 9/1[3]
110- **7** *1 ¾* **Turgenev**[167] 8633 3-9-5 102.......................... FrankieDettori 6 82
(John Gosden) *hld up: swtchd rt over 3f out: shkn up over 2f out: edgd lft and wknd fnl f* 9/4[2]
1- **8** *10* **Stormwave (IRE)**[191] 7905 3-9-2 0.......................... HarryBentley 11 61
(Ralph Beckett) *str; prom: chsd ldr over 7f out tl rdn over 2f out: wknd over 1f out* 20/1
1- **9** *20* **Power Of States (IRE)**[176] 8344 3-9-2 0.......................... JamesDoyle 4 25
(Hugo Palmer) *athletic; sn led: hdd over 7f out: rdn and wknd over 2f out (jockey said colt stopped quickly)* 25/1

2m 14.89s (5.19) **Going Correction** +0.525s/f (Yiel) 9 Ran SP% **118.3**
Speed ratings (Par 102): **100,98,96,94,89 89,87,79,63**
CSF £165.59 TOTE £14.00: £3.10, £2.70, £2.50; EX 197.40 Trifecta £1840.80.
Owner Mrs Susan Roy **Bred** E A R L Haras Du Quesnay **Trained** Newmarket, Suffolk

FOCUS
A classy conditions event contested by a number of bright prospects. A small step up from the second.

1738 MANSIONBET MAIDEN FILLIES' STKS (PLUS 10 RACE) (DIV I) 1m 2f
4:45 (4:51) (Class 4) 3-Y-O **£5,530** (£1,645; £822; £411) **Stalls** Low

Form RPR
6- **1** **Star Catcher**[113] 9637 3-9-0 0.......................... FrankieDettori 2 89+
(John Gosden) *athletic; racd keenly: led 1f: remained handy: led again over 3f out: pushed clr fnl f* 10/11[1]
2 **2** *4 ½* **Sashenka (GER)**[16] 1359 3-9-0 0.......................... DavidEgan 1 80
(Sylvester Kirk) *sltly on toes; chsd ldrs: chal over 3f out tl shkn up and hung lft over 2f out: no ex ins fnl f* 12/1
4- **3** *1 ¾* **Royal Star**[167] 8643 3-9-0 0.......................... JasonWatson 8 77
(Roger Charlton) *str; prom: racd keenly: rdn over 1f out: no ex fnl f* 7/2[2]
4 *13* **Happy Hiker (IRE)** 3-9-0 0.......................... (h[1]) HayleyTurner 4 54
(Michael Bell) *compact; hld up: shkn up over 4f out: rdn and hung lft over 2f out: nvr nrr* 50/1
0- **5** *1 ½* **Mrs Ivy**[210] 7249 3-9-0 0.......................... HarryBentley 6 51
(Ralph Beckett) *tall; hld up: shkn up over 5f out: nvr on terms* 33/1
6 *2 ½* **Brass (FR)** 3-9-0 0.......................... SeanLevey 5 46
(Paul Webber) *workmanlike; s.i.s: hld up: pushed along: hdwy and hung lft over 2f out: sn wknd* 66/1
7 *3 ¾* **Born Leader (FR)** 3-9-0 0.......................... RobertHavlin 3 40
(Hughie Morrison) *tall; hld up: hdwy over 3f out: wknd over 2f out* 8/1[3]
8 *5* **Lucy Lou (IRE)** 3-9-0 0.......................... JimCrowley 10 31
(Charles Hills) *athletic; sn pushed along and a in rr* 14/1
0- **9** *9* **Universal Song**[149] 9049 3-9-0 0.......................... RobHornby 9 14
(Seamus Mullins) *led 9f out tl over 3f out: wknd over 2f out* 200/1
3 **10** *13* **Samstar**[14] 1397 3-9-0 0.......................... FrannyNorton 11
(Mark Johnston) *workmanlike; chsd ldrs: rdn over 3f out: wknd over 2f out* 16/1
11 *3 ½* **Soloist (IRE)** 3-9-0 0.......................... JamesDoyle 7
(William Haggas) *str; sltly on toes; s.i.s: rdn and wknd over 3f out (starter reported that the filly was very reluctant to enter the stalls; trainer was informed that the filly could not run until the day after passing a stalls test)* 10/1

2m 15.88s (6.18) **Going Correction** +0.525s/f (Yiel) 11 Ran SP% **121.9**
Speed ratings (Par 97): **96,92,91,80,79 77,74,70,63,52 50**
CSF £14.92 TOTE £1.90: £1.10, £4.60, £1.40; EX 12.70 Trifecta £43.60.
Owner A E Oppenheimer **Bred** Hascombe And Valiant Studs **Trained** Newmarket, Suffolk

FOCUS
Division one of a maiden which has been won, amongst others, by Oaks winners Eswarah (2005) and Dancing Rain (2011). The bulk of the field came down the centre in the straight and the first three finished a long way clear. It was the quicker division by the best part of two seconds. The opening level is fluid.

1739 MANSIONBET MAIDEN FILLIES' STKS (PLUS 10 RACE) (DIV II) 1m 2f
5:20 (5:21) (Class 4) 3-Y-O **£5,530** (£1,645; £822; £411) **Stalls** Low

Form RPR
64- **1** **Katiesheidinlisa**[195] 7763 3-9-0 0.......................... RichardKingscote 5 83+
(Tom Dascombe) *athletic; looked wl; chsd ldrs: led over 2f out: shkn up over 1f out: pushed out* 11/2[3]
2 *2 ¾* **Sneaky Peek** 3-9-0 0.......................... OisinMurphy 6 78+
(Andrew Balding) *leggy; athletic; chsd ldr tl led over 2f out: sn hdd: edgd lft and styd on same pce ins fnl f* 5/1[2]
5- **3** *3* **Fabulist**[118] 9556 3-9-0 0.......................... FrankieDettori 1 73
(John Gosden) *str; s.i.s: sn hld up in tch: rdn over 1f out: no ex ins fnl f* 4/6[1]
0- **4** *1 ¾* **Tamachan**[209] 7298 3-9-0 0.......................... (h[1]) JasonWatson 4 70
(Roger Charlton) *compact; s.i.s: hld up: pushed along and hdwy over 2f out: styd on same pce fnl f* 16/1
3 **5** *3* **Scenesetter (IRE)**[20] 1288 3-9-0 0.......................... HarryBentley 7 64
(Marco Botti) *compact; chsd ldrs: rdn over 2f out: wknd over 1f out* 14/1
6- **6** *2 ½* **Spring Run**[167] 8647 3-9-0 0.......................... RobHornby 2 60
(Jonathan Portman) *workmanlike; sweating; s.i.s: hld up: shkn up over 2f out: nvr nrr* 12/1
0- **7** *8* **Relative Ease**[291] 4191 3-9-0 0.......................... TomMarquand 10 45
(J S Moore) *str; hld up: pushed along over 5f out: rdn and wknd over 2f out* 100/1
8 *1* **Lollipop Lady** 3-9-0 0.......................... CallumShepherd 8 43
(Brian Meehan) *workmanlike; s.i.s: hld up: rdn over 3f out: sn wknd* 25/1
04- **9** *nk* **Island Reel (IRE)**[116] 9590 3-9-0 0.......................... DavidEgan 9 43
(Heather Main) *tall; led: rdn and hdd over 2f out: sn wknd* 33/1
10 *25* **Flaming Red** 3-9-0 0.......................... DavidProbert 3
(Kevin Bishop) *angular; broke wl enough: sn lost pl: wknd over 3f out* 100/1

2m 17.75s (8.05) **Going Correction** +0.525s/f (Yiel) 10 Ran SP% **121.0**
Speed ratings (Par 97): **88,85,83,82,79 77,71,70,70,50**
CSF £33.89 TOTE £7.50: £1.50, £1.90, £1.10; EX 40.90 Trifecta £69.60.
Owner D R Passant & Hefin Williams **Bred** Glebe Farm Stud **Trained** Malpas, Cheshire

FOCUS
This was the slower division by 1.87sec, and it looks weaker form.

1740 COLN VALLEY STUD BRIDGET MAIDEN FILLIES' STKS (PLUS 10 RACE) (NEWCOMERS' RACE) 7f (S)
5:50 (5:54) (Class 4) 3-Y-O **£5,530** (£1,645; £822; £411) **Stalls** Centre

Form RPR
1 **Quick** 3-9-0 0.......................... TomMarquand 5 78
(Richard Hannon) *leggy; athletic; sltly on toes; prom: pushed along and lost pl 1/2-way: rallied over 1f out: r.o u.p to ld post* 25/1
2 *shd* **Millicent Fawcett** 3-9-0 0.......................... RobertHavlin 19 77+
(John Gosden) *athletic; hld up: hdwy over 4f out: swtchd rt 1/2-way: rdn to ld wl ins fnl f: hdd post* 5/1[2]
3 *¾* **Hotsy Totsy (IRE)** 3-9-0 0.......................... GeraldMosse 2 75
(Ed Walker) *str; looked wl; s.i.s: sn rcvrd to ld: hdd wl ins fnl f: kpt on* 33/1
4 *½* **Maggi Rockstar (IRE)** 3-9-0 0.......................... JosephineGordon 3 74+
(Paul D'Arcy) *str; s.i.s and hmpd s: hdwy on outer over 1f out: styd on* 40/1
5 *¾* **Farnham** 3-9-0 0.......................... DanielTudhope 15 72+
(Roger Varian) *str; s.s: hld up: racd keenly: swtchd rt 1/2-way: hdwy over 2f out: rdn over 1f out: styd on same pce ins fnl f* 13/8[1]
6 *nse* **La Voix Magique** 3-8-7 0.......................... TobyEley[(7)] 18 72
(Steph Hollinshead) *workmanlike; s.i.s: pushed along over 4f out: hdwy over 1f out: styd on* 100/1
7 *¾* **Mayfair Pompette (FR)** 3-9-0 0.......................... StevieDonohoe 10 70
(Charlie Fellowes) *str; unruly leaving stalls: pushed along towards rr: hdwy over 1f out: nt trble ldrs* 20/1
8 *6* **Roong Roong (IRE)** 3-9-0 0.......................... SilvestreDeSousa 8 55
(Richard Hannon) *str; chsd ldrs: rdn over 1f out: wknd ins fnl f* 7/1[3]
9 *2 ¾* **Aperitif** 3-9-0 0.......................... HayleyTurner 7 48
(Michael Bell) *workmanlike; bit on the leg; prom: racd keenly: rdn over 1f out: wknd fnl f* 25/1
10 *1 ¼* **Marlyn (IRE)** 3-9-0 0.......................... OisinMurphy 20 45+
(Martyn Meade) *unfurnished; prom: rdn over 1f out: wknd fnl f* 14/1
11 *nk* **Society Sweetheart (IRE)** 3-9-0 0.......................... CallumShepherd 11 44
(J S Moore) *workmanlike; s.i.s: pushed along in rr: nvr nrr* 150/1
12 *½* **Misty** 3-9-0 0.......................... HarryBentley 16 43+
(Ralph Beckett) *athletic; prom: pushed along 1/2-way: wknd over 1f out* 16/1
13 *½* **Alnaseem** 3-9-0 0.......................... JimCrowley 17 42+
(Owen Burrows) *str; s.i.s: sn prom: rdn and wknd over 1f out* 15/2
14 *3 ¼* **Zappiness (USA)** 3-9-0 0.......................... JackMitchell 1 33
(Peter Chapple-Hyam) *leggy; athletic; wnt lft s: a in rr* 33/1
15 *1 ¾* **Impressionable** 3-9-0 0.......................... DavidEgan 12 29
(Marco Botti) *athletic; looked wl; mid-div: pushed along and lost pl 1/2-way: n.d after* 50/1
16 *3* **Mooteram (IRE)** 3-8-7 0.......................... GeorgeBass[(7)] 9 22
(Mick Channon) *leggy; unfurnished; s.i.s: hdwy over 2f out: wknd over 1f out* 66/1
17 *3* **Aide Memoire (IRE)** 3-9-0 0.......................... DavidProbert 6 14
(David Elsworth) *tall; s.i.s: a in rr* 50/1
18 *1 ½* **Forever Mine** 3-9-0 0.......................... JasonWatson 4 10
(Eve Johnson Houghton) *str; edgd lft s: chsd ldrs: rdn and wknd over 2f out* 66/1
19 *8* **Be Together** 3-9-0 0.......................... FrankieDettori 14
(Charles Hills) *str; half-rrd s: sn prom: wknd over 2f out (jockey said filly stopped quickly)* 16/1

1m 31.49s (4.49) **Going Correction** +0.525s/f (Yiel) 19 Ran SP% **126.8**
Speed ratings (Par 97): **95,94,94,93,92 92,91,84,81,80 79,79,78,75,73 69,66,64,55**
CSF £139.90 TOTE £35.70: £8.30, £1.90, £10.30; EX 336.10 Trifecta £2430.70.
Owner Mrs J Wood **Bred** Brightwalton Bloodstock Ltd **Trained** East Everleigh, Wilts

FOCUS
A big field of unraced fillies, and something of a bunch finish with the first seven finishing clear.
T/Jkpt: Not Won. T/Plt: £1,217.90 to a £1 stake. Pool: £87,125.80 - 52.22 winning units T/Qpdt: £269.00 to a £1 stake. Pool: £7,470.81 - 20.55 winning units **Colin Roberts**

1448 SAINT-CLOUD (L-H)
Friday, April 12

OFFICIAL GOING: Turf: good

1741a PRIX DE LOUVECIENNES (CLAIMER) (3YO COLTS & GELDINGS) (TURF) 1m 2f
3:06 3-Y-O **£8,558** (£3,423; £2,567; £1,711; £855)

RPR
1 **Run Ashore (FR)**[90] 216 3-8-9 0.......................... (p) QuentinPerrette[(6)] 2 73
(M Nigge, France) 171/10
2 *hd* **Urlucc (IRE)**[50] 3-8-11 0.......................... (p) ClementLecoeuvre 1 69
(R Le Gal, France) 13/5[1]
3 *1* **Valentino (FR)** 3-9-4 0.......................... EddyHardouin 5 74
(Alex Fracas, France) 31/1

4 ¾ **Never Come Back (FR)**[26] 1241 3-9-4 0 GlenBraem 3 72
(M Nigge, France) **11/2**
5 3 **Pinaclouddown (IRE)**[214] 7141 3-9-1 0 MrDamienArtu 10 63
(J-Y Artu, France) **22/1**
6 hd **Aborigene (FR)**[234] 3-8-11 0 (b) ThibaultSpeicher 4 59
(Louis Baudron, France) **87/10**
7 ¾ **Seed Of Love (FR)**[33] 3-9-1 0 ChristopheSoumillon 7 61
(Simone Brogi, France) **53/10**[3]
8 1 **Kenzohope (FR)**[69] 3-8-11 0 (p) MaximeGuyon 9 55
(C Boutin, France) **49/10**[2]
9 5 ½ **Hawk Cliff (FR)**[13] 1450 3-9-4 0 Louis-PhilippeBeuzelin 6 51
(Jo Hughes, France) *wl into stride: disp ld early: settled in 2nd: sent on to ld 6f out: urged along and hdd 2f out: sn rdn w limited rspnse: wknd fnl f* **45/1**
10 8 **Clair Matin (FR)**[66] 3-8-11 0 (p) MatthiasLauron 8 28
(T Lemer, France) **54/10**
11 6 **Jamal (FR)**[169] 3-8-6 0 (b) JeremieMonteiro(5) 11 16
(R Le Dren Doleuze, France) **60/1**

2m 15.74s (-0.26) **11** Ran SP% **118.7**
PARI-MUTUEL (all including 1 euro stake): WIN 18.10; PLACE 5.30, 1.70, 6.20; DF 21.10.
Owner Mme Christa Zass **Bred** Team Hogdala Ab **Trained** France

1579 MEYDAN (L-H)
Friday, April 12

OFFICIAL GOING: Turf: good; dirt: fast

1742a AL TAYER MOTORS (MAIDEN) (TURF) 7f
3:30 (3:30) 3-Y-O+ **£21,153** (£7,051; £3,878; £2,115; £1,057)

RPR
1 **Jaarim (USA)**[41] 996 3-8-10 0 AdriedeVries 2 67
(Fawzi Abdulla Nass, Bahrain) *mid-div: smooth prog 2 1/2f out: rdn 1 1/2f out: led cl home* **13/2**[2]
2 ½ **Dark Thunder (IRE)**[35] 1090 3-8-10 77 (v) PatDobbs 10 66
(Doug Watson, UAE) *trckd ldr: led 2f out: r.o wl but hdd cl home* **6/4**[1]
3 nk **Rayig**[63] 677 3-8-10 72 (t) FernandoJara 6 65
(A R Al Rayhi, UAE) *mid-div: r.o wl fnl 1 1/2f: nrst fin* **20/1**
4 1 **Antimo**[7] 1579 6-9-6 0 (t) SzczepanMazur 13 63
(A Al Shemaili, UAE) *mid-div: r.o fnl 2f: nrst fin* **50/1**
5 1 ¾ **Miqyaas** 4-9-6 0 BernardoPinheiro 8 59
(R Bouresly, Kuwait) *sn led: hdd 2f out but r.o wl* **22/1**
6 ¾ **Ariette Du Rue (USA)**[21] 1326 3-8-6 0 RoystonFfrench 1 52
(A bin Harmash, UAE) *mid-div: r.o same pce fnl 2f* **12/1**
7 1 ¼ **Gypsy Moth (USA)**[29] 1201 5-9-6 0 (t) ConnorBeasley 14 53
(A bin Harmash, UAE) *a mid-div* **16/1**
8 ¾ **Muraahib (IRE)** 5-9-6 0 AAlajmi 16 51
(R Bouresly, Kuwait) *nvr nr to chal but r.o fnl 2f* **33/1**
9 ½ **Rule Of Honour**[29] 1201 4-9-6 0 (t) FabriceVeron 3 50
(Ismail Mohammed) *s.i.s: nvr bttr than mid-div* **16/1**
10 2 ¾ **Lady Snazz (USA)** 3-8-3 0 ow4 JoannaGrzybowska(7) 9 41
(S Seemar, UAE) *nvr nr to chal* **40/1**
11 ½ **Refulgence Star (IRE)**[69] 570 3-8-10 67 (v) RyanPowell 4 40
(S Seemar, UAE) *slowly away: nvr nr to chal* **10/1**
12 shd **Alda'iya (USA)**[78] 394 3-8-10 0 GeorgeBuckell 12 40
(Doug Watson, UAE) *nvr nr to chal* **66/1**
13 1 ½ **Dubai Canal** 3-8-10 0 RichardMullen 11 36
(S Seemar, UAE) *nvr bttr than mid-div* **9/1**
14 7 ¼ **Daltrey**[29] 1201 4-9-6 75 (t) AntonioFresu 5 17
(A R Al Rayhi, UAE) *trckd ldr tl wknd 2f out* **7/1**[3]
15 6 ¾ **Close Pass** 4-9-6 0 (t) TadhgO'Shea 7
(S Seemar, UAE) *nvr bttr than mid-div* **14/1**
16 8 ¾ **Playwriter (IRE)**[7] 1579 5-9-6 0 JRosales 15
(M Ibrahim, UAE) *nvr bttr than mid-div* **20/1**

1m 25.64s
WFA 3 from 4yo+ 14lb **16** Ran SP% **133.8**
CSF: 16.95.
Owner Fawzi Abdulla Nass **Bred** WinStar Farm LLC **Trained** Bahrain

1743a-1747a (Foreign Racing) - See Raceform Interactive

1748a LONGINES LA GRANDE CLASSIQUE COLLECTION (H'CAP) (TURF) 1m 1f
7:10 (7:10) (70-100,94) 3-Y-O+ **£24,358** (£8,119; £4,465; £2,435; £1,217)

RPR
1 **Carrington (FR)**[7] 1585 6-9-1 85 ConnorBeasley 6 90
(A bin Harmash, UAE) *s.i.s: mid-div: smooth prog 3f out: led 2f out: r.o wl* **25/1**
2 nk **Almoreb (IRE)**[7] 1583 5-9-5 89 FernandoJara 5 93
(A R Al Rayhi, UAE) *mid-div: chsd ldrs and ev ch 2 1/2f out: r.o wl fnl 1 1/2f: jst failed* **9/2**[1]
3 1 ¼ **Valcartier (IRE)**[41] 1000 5-9-4 88 (h) AdriedeVries 4 89
(Fawzi Abdulla Nass, Bahrain) *slowly away: nvr nr to chal but r.o wl fnl 2f: nrst fin* **9/2**[1]
4 3 ¼ **Mujeeb**[7] 1583 5-9-2 86 (p) AntonioFresu 8 81
(E Charpy, UAE) *mid-div: r.o same pce fnl 2 1/2f: nrst fin* **22/1**
5 ½ **Firnas**[7] 1583 6-9-6 90 (h) XavierZiani 13 84
(S bin Ghadayer, UAE) *mid-div: r.o same pce fnl 2f: nrst fin* **22/1**
6 ¾ **Mailshot (USA)**[41] 1000 5-9-3 87 JRosales 11 79
(S bin Ghadayer, UAE) *nvr nr to chal but r.o fnl 2 1/2f* **22/1**
7 1 **Tafaakhor (IRE)**[8] 5-9-1 90 SaeedAlMazrooei(5) 16 80
(A R Al Rayhi, UAE) *mid-div: r.o same pce fnl 2f* **20/1**
8 nk **Craving (IRE)**[21] 1322 4-9-4 88 RyanPowell 7 77
(Simon Crisford) *trckd ldr tl wknd fnl 2 1/2f* **13/2**[3]
9 1 ½ **Walk In The Sun (USA)**[28] 1230 4-9-11 94 RoystonFfrench 1 81
(S bin Ghadayer, UAE) *sn led: hdd & wknd 2f out* **11/2**[2]
10 1 **Bold Rex (SAF)**[21] 1324 5-9-5 89 BernardFayd'Herbe 3 73
(M F De Kock, South Africa) *trckd ldr tl wknd fnl 2 1/2f* **9/1**
11 9 ¾ **Flag Festival**[456] 164 4-9-0 84 (t) TadhgO'Shea 2 48
(S Seemar, UAE) *nvr bttr than mid-div* **14/1**
12 6 ½ **Bawaasil**[7] 1584 4-9-4 88 PatDobbs 9 38
(Doug Watson, UAE) *nvr bttr than mid-div* **9/1**
13 5 ½ **Mr Pommeroy (FR)**[97] 98 8-9-4 94 AdamMcLean(7) 12 34
(M Ramadan, UAE) *a in rr* **28/1**
14 4 ¾ **Broadcast (USA)**[43] 957 4-9-1 85 (t) RichardMullen 14 14
(S Seemar, UAE) *nvr bttr than mid-div* **25/1**
15 shd **Juthoor (IRE)**[7] 1583 4-9-3 87 (h) FabriceVeron 15 16
(E Charpy, UAE) *a in rr* **25/1**
P **Takatul (USA)**[21] 1324 6-9-5 89 BernardoPinheiro 10
(M Al Mheiri, UAE) *p.u 4f out* **14/1**

1m 50.39s **16** Ran SP% **131.2**
CSF: 131.02; TRICAST: 505.57.
Owner Saoud Raeisi/Masoud Mohamed **Bred** Sarl De Chambure Haras D'Etreham & Sarl Pontchartr **Trained** United Arab Emirates

1749 - (Foreign Racing) - See Raceform Interactive

1733 NEWBURY (L-H)
Saturday, April 13

OFFICIAL GOING: Good to soft (soft in places; 5.3)
Wind: fresh behind Weather: cloudy periods

1750 DUBAI DUTY FREE FINEST SURPRISE STKS (REGISTERED AS THE JOHN PORTER STAKES) (GROUP 3) 1m 4f
1:40 (1:40) (Class 1) 4-Y-O+

£34,026 (£12,900; £6,456; £3,216; £1,614; £810) **Stalls** Low

Form RPR
122- 1 **Marmelo**[158] 8911 6-9-0 117 GeraldMosse 3 117
(Hughie Morrison) *hld up: rdn and hdwy fr 2f out: sn edging lft: r.o ins fnl f: led towards fin: readily* **7/1**[3]
033- 2 1 **Aspetar (FR)**[169] 8610 4-9-0 105 JasonWatson 5 117
(Roger Charlton) *racd keenly: hld up: hdwy over 2f out: led over 1f out: sn rdn: kpt on but no ex whn hdd towards fin* **20/1**
061- 3 2 **Laraaib (IRE)**[189] 7975 5-9-3 112 JimCrowley 10 116
(Owen Burrows) *trckd ldrs: disp ld travelling strly over 2f out tl rdn over 1f out: kpt on same pce ins fnl f* **12/1**
202- 4 1 **Defoe (IRE)**[163] 8794 5-9-0 117 AndreaAtzeni 8 111
(Roger Varian) *prom: disp ld over 2f out: sn rdn: hdd over 1f out: keeping on at same pce in hld 3rd whn squeezed up fnl 100yds* **9/4**[2]
011- 5 2 ¾ **Young Rascal (FR)**[168] 8645 4-9-3 116 JamesDoyle 7 111
(William Haggas) *hld up: hdwy over 4f out: sn pushed along: rdn in cl 4th 2f out: wknd ins fnl f* **13/8**[1]
302- 6 2 ½ **Proschema (IRE)**[183] 8164 4-9-0 105 RichardKingscote 4 104
(Tom Dascombe) *in tch: rdn over 2f out: sn one pce* **10/1**
125- 7 6 **Communique (IRE)**[168] 8645 4-9-0 109 SilvestreDeSousa 9 95
(Mark Johnston) *led: rdn and hdd over 2f out: wknd over 1f out* **11/1**
515- 8 14 **Blakeney Point**[189] 7975 6-9-0 105 AdamMcNamara 1 73
(Roger Charlton) *trckd ldrs: rdn over 2f out: sn wknd* **40/1**
430/ U **Pilansberg**[44] 7502 7-9-0 108 (b) LukeMorris 6
(Mark Gillard) *stmbld bdly and uns rdr leaving stalls* **200/1**

2m 42.15s (4.15) **Going Correction** +0.425s/f (Yiel) **9** Ran SP% **114.2**
Speed ratings (Par 113): **103,102,101,100,98 96,92,83,**
CSF £126.16 TOTE £7.90: £2.00, £4.40, £3.10; EX 125.20 Trifecta £821.00.
Owner The Fairy Story Partnership & Aziz Kheir **Bred** Deepwood Farm Stud **Trained** East Ilsley, Berks

FOCUS
Add 10yds. The going had dried out a little since Friday's card. This looked a decent edition of this Group 3. As they'd been doing in round-course races the day before, they came down the middle in the home straight. The time was quite slow, 13.65sec outside standard. A big pb from the second, while the third has been rated as improving slightly.

1751 DUBAI DUTY FREE STKS (REGISTERED AS THE FRED DARLING STAKES) (GROUP 3) (FILLIES) 7f (S)
2:10 (2:13) (Class 1) 3-Y-O

£34,026 (£12,900; £6,456; £3,216; £1,614; £810) **Stalls** Centre

Form RPR
412- 1 **Dandhu**[197] 7734 3-9-0 105 GeraldMosse 6 107
(David Elsworth) *hld up in last trio: gd prog over 2f out: chal over 1f out: v narrow ld ins fnl f: jst hld on* **8/1**
511- 2 shd **Iconic Choice**[168] 8648 3-9-0 101 RichardKingscote 13 106
(Tom Dascombe) *hld up in midfield: rdn over 2f out: prog over 1f out: str run fnl f: tk 2nd last stride and jst failed* **7/1**[3]
233- 3 shd **So Perfect (USA)**[162] 8818 3-9-0 110 WayneLordan 1 106+
(A P O'Brien, Ire) *trckd ldr in pair towards far side: on terms whn c across 2f out: str chal over 1f out: w wnr ins fnl f: jst pipped nr fin and lost 2nd last stride* **9/2**[2]
123- 4 ¾ **Star Terms**[188] 8024 3-9-0 108 TomMarquand 11 104
(Richard Hannon) *prom: led main gp over 2f out and overall ldr over 1f out: sn hrd rdn: hdd and no ex ins fnl f* **8/1**
134- 5 4 ½ **Queen Jo Jo**[203] 7511 3-9-0 98 DanielTudhope 4 92
(Kevin Ryan) *prom in main gp: rdn 2f out: steadily fdd over 1f out* **20/1**
1- 6 nk **Modern Millie**[166] 8696 3-9-0 0 DavidEgan 5 92
(Mick Channon) *cl up bhd ldrs in main gp: shkn up 2f out: outpcd over 1f out: n.d after* **33/1**
033- 7 nse **Gypsy Spirit**[162] 8805 3-9-0 95 LukeMorris 7 92
(Tom Clover) *hld up in midfield: rdn and sme prog 2f out: no imp on ldrs over 1f out: kpt on* **66/1**
31- 8 1 ¼ **Muchly**[168] 8647 3-9-0 0 FrankieDettori 9 88
(John Gosden) *led main gp to over 2f out: wknd qckly fnl f* **9/1**
122- 9 3 ½ **Stay Classy (IRE)**[164] 8754 3-9-0 98 (h) TomQueally 8 80
(Richard Spencer) *stdd s: hld up in last trio: rdn over 2f out: hanging and racd awkwardly after: no significant prog* **20/1**
202- 10 nse **Roxy Art (IRE)**[204] 7490 3-9-0 87 RobertHavlin 3 80
(Ed Dunlop) *impeded s: wl in tch: shkn up 2f out: nt qckn and wknd over 1f out* **50/1**
256- 11 1 ½ **Dutch Treat**[197] 7734 3-9-0 95 DavidProbert 14 76
(Andrew Balding) *w ldrs tl rdn and wknd jst over 2f out* **25/1**
1- 12 1 ¼ **Dancing Vega (IRE)**[169] 8591 3-9-0 0 HarryBentley 16 73
(Ralph Beckett) *hld up in tch: rdn over 2f out: no prog and wknd over 1f out* **3/1**[1]
110- 13 3 ¼ **Yourtimeisnow**[197] 7734 3-9-0 102 AndreaAtzeni 2 65
(Roger Varian) *wnt rt s: overall ldr in pair towards far side: lost ld and wknd qckly over 1f out* **11/1**
116- 14 3 **Glass Slippers**[203] 7511 3-9-0 94 TomEaves 15 57
(Kevin Ryan) *hld up in last trio: shkn up and no prog over 2f out: wknd over 1f out (vet reported the filly lost both front shoes)* **66/1**
3-1 15 11 **Madame Tantzy**[21] 1288 3-9-0 0 CharlesBishop 12 30
(Eve Johnson Houghton) *chsd ldrs to over 2f out: wknd rapidly: t.o* **33/1**

1m 28.88s (1.88) **Going Correction** +0.425s/f (Yiel) **15** Ran SP% **120.4**
Speed ratings (Par 105): **106,105,105,104,99 99,99,97,93,93 92,90,87,83,71**
CSF £57.19 TOTE £9.70: £2.80, £2.30, £1.90; EX 69.80 Trifecta £391.60.

Owner The Dandhu Partnership **Bred** Barton Bloodstock **Trained** Newmarket, Suffolk

FOCUS

A competitive renewal of this event with a tight finish, the first four coming nicely clear. It's been 20 years since the winner of this trial - Wince - went on to land the 1000 Guineas, but the main contenders did their Classic prospects no harm.

1752 WATERSHIP DOWN STUD GREENHAM STKS (GROUP 3) (C&G) 7f (S)

2:40 (2:45) (Class 1) 3-Y-O

£39,697 (£15,050; £7,532; £3,752; £1,883; £945) **Stalls** Centre

Form RPR

211- **1** **Mohaather**[168] 8646 3-9-0 108 .... JimCrowley 8 114
(Marcus Tregoning) *cl up: led over 1f out: sn drifted rt: stened up ins fnl f and r.o wl: drifting lft towards fin: readily* **9/2**

315- **2** *¾* **Great Scot**[168] 8633 3-9-0 110 .... RichardKingscote 4 112
(Tom Dascombe) *in tch: rdn and stdy prog fr 2f out: sn hanging lft: bmpd into 4th fnl 130yds: r.o wl to chse wnr sn after but nt quite pce to chal* **4/1[3]**

11- **3** *2¼* **Urban Icon**[305] 3706 3-9-0 96 .... TomMarquand 7 107
(Richard Hannon) *trckd ldrs: rdn and ev ch briefly over 1f out: kpt on but nt pce of wnr sn after: lost 2nd fnl 120yds* **7/1**

121- **4** *1¾* **Hello Youmzain (FR)**[182] 8214 3-9-0 114 .... JamesDoyle 5 102
(Kevin Ryan) *prom: rdn and ev ch 2f out tl jst over 1f out: keeping on at same pce and hld whn hmpd fnl 130yds (vet reported the colt lost its right fore shoe)* **5/2[1]**

114- **5** *nse* **Boitron (FR)**[188] 8025 3-9-0 107 ....(w) SilvestreDeSousa 6 102
(Richard Hannon) *led: rdn and hdd over 1f out: kpt on same pce fnl f* **3/1[2]**

41-1 **6** *6* **No Nonsense**[99] 57 3-9-0 98 .... GeraldMosse 10 87
(David Elsworth) *in tch: effrt over 2f out: outpcd by ldrs over 1f out: no threat after* **20/1**

014- **7** *½* **Tailor Made**[173] 8477 3-9-0 89 .... StevieDonohoe 9 86
(Mohamed Moubarak) *hld up in last pair: rdn 2f out: nt pce to get on terms* **100/1**

310- **8** *21* **He'Zanarab (IRE)**[233] 6455 3-9-0 96 .... SeanLevey 3 33
(Richard Hannon) *slowly away: t.k.h: hld up last: rdn over 2f out: wknd over 1f out (jockey said colt ran too freely)* **33/1**

1m 26.89s (-0.11) **Going Correction** +0.425s/f (Yiel) **8 Ran SP% 112.9**
Speed ratings (Par 108): **117,116,113,111,111 104,104,80**
CSF £22.08 TOTE £5.60: £1.80, £1.50, £2.00; EX 23.60 Trifecta £87.40.
Owner Hamdan Al Maktoum **Bred** Mrs R F Johnson Houghton **Trained** Whitsbury, Hants

FOCUS

The incomparable Frankel won this in 2011 en route to the Guineas, and Newmarket runners-up Kingman and Barney Roy have won this since, as well as top sprinter Muhaarar. The absence of Too Darn Hot stripped this race of a layer of interest.

1753 MANSIONBET SPRING CUP H'CAP 1m (S)

3:15 (3:22) (Class 2) 4-Y-O+

£31,125 (£9,320; £4,660; £2,330; £1,165; £585) **Stalls** Centre

Form RPR

402- **1** **Chatez (IRE)**[112] 8649 8-9-4 99 .... WilliamBuick 3 109
(Alan King) *wl in tch: prog on wd outside over 2f out: rdn to chse ldr over 1f out: drvn to ld last 100yds: styd on wl* **16/1**

2 *nk* **Indeed**[215] 7142 4-8-11 92 .... CallumShepherd 17 101
(Dominic Ffrench Davis) *w ldrs: led over 2f in centre and sent for home: styd on fr over 1f out but hdd and hld last 100yds* **50/1**

013- **3** *2¼* **Borodin (IRE)**[203] 7509 4-8-10 91 .... PaddyMathers 2 95
(Richard Fahey) *wl in tch on outer: rdn over 2f out: hanging but tk 3rd jst ins fnl f: styd on same pce and no imp on ldng pair* **12/1**

544- **4** *1¾* **Greenside**[168] 8649 8-8-9 90 .... HarryBentley 5 91
(Henry Candy) *racd on outer: in tch: effrt over 2f out: prog whn nt clr run over 1f out: styd on ins fnl f to take 4th nr fin* **8/1**

026- **5** *¾* **Plutonian (IRE)**[161] 8837 5-9-7 102 .... SilvestreDeSousa 6 101
(Charles Hills) *racd on outer: mostly pressed ldr: upsides over 2f out: chsd new ldr after tl over 1f out: one pce* **25/1**

32-2 **6** *1¼* **Red Starlight**[14] 1414 4-9-5 100 .... TomMarquand 1 96
(Richard Hannon) *prom on outer: rdn over 2f out: fdd ins fnl f* **13/2[1]**

504- **7** *2½* **History Writer (IRE)**[162] 8809 4-8-10 91 ....(t) JasonWatson 9 82
(David Menuisier) *hld up wl in rr: stl in last trio over 2f out: taken to outer and gd prog after: rchd 7th fnl f but no ch: styd on wl nr fin* **14/1**

-332 **8** *8* **Pattie**[37] 1063 5-9-2 97 .... GeraldMosse 12 70+
(Mick Channon) *trckd ldrs: rdn over 2f out: sn lft bhd and btn* **50/1**

2-30 **9** *1¾* **Third Time Lucky (IRE)**[14] 1415 7-8-10 96 .... SeanDavis(5) 7 65
(Richard Fahey) *prom on outer: lost pl over 2f out: no ch over 1f out* **16/1**

030- **10** *¾* **George Of Hearts (FR)**[232] 6485 4-8-10 91 ....(w) ShaneKelly 8 59
(Richard Hughes) *nvr beyond midfield: shkn up whn nt clr run over 2f out: no prog after* **11/1**

110- **11** *2* **Ibraz**[273] 4949 4-8-12 93 .... JimCrowley 16 56+
(Roger Varian) *nvr beyond midfield: rdn over 2f out: wknd wl over 1f out* **7/1[2]**

350- **12** *1* **Bubble And Squeak**[137] 9280 4-8-9 90 .... LukeMorris 11 51
(Sylvester Kirk) *chsd ldrs towards outer: rdn and lost pl over 2f out: wl in rr over 1f out: plugged on again nr fin* **100/1**

00-6 **13** *hd* **Circus Couture (IRE)**[14] 1414 7-9-9 104 .... FrankieDettori 4 65
(Jane Chapple-Hyam) *nvr beyond midfield: rdn and lft bhd over 2f out* **25/1**

0456 **14** *nk* **Another Batt (IRE)**[14] 1415 4-9-10 105 .... OisinMurphy 14 65+
(George Scott) *rrd s: wl in rr: rdn over 2f out: nvr on terms* **16/1**

302- **15** *shd* **Escobar (IRE)**[175] 8409 5-9-8 103 ....(t) AdamKirby 13 63+
(David O'Meara) *hld up wl in rr: shkn up 3f out: modest prog 2f out but nvr a factor* **14/1**

20-5 **16** *nk* **Ripp Orf (IRE)**[14] 1415 5-9-2 97 .... SeanLevey 25 56+
(David Elsworth) *hld up wl in rr: shkn up and sme prog over 2f out: no ch and no hdwy over 1f out* **14/1**

-124 **17** *½* **Tough Remedy (IRE)**[28] 1232 4-8-3 89 .... AndrewBreslin(5) 18 47
(Keith Dalgleish) *in tch: rdn sn after 1/2-way: dropped to rr and wl btn over 2f out* **40/1**

00-0 **18** *1¾* **Raydiance**[14] 1415 4-8-9 95 .... HarrisonShaw(5) 23 49+
(K R Burke) *chsd ldrs and racd towards nr side: drvn wl over 2f out: sn wknd* **66/1**

1-60 **19** *5* **Masham Star (IRE)**[14] 1415 5-9-5 100 .... FrannyNorton 15 43
(Mark Johnston) *led to over 2f out: wknd qckly* **66/1**

45-5 **20** *¾* **Gulf Of Poets**[14] 1413 7-8-10 91 .... DavidEgan 27 32+
(Michael Easterby) *racd nrest to stands' rail: in tch tl wknd over 2f out* **25/1**

13-2 **21** *¾* **Exec Chef (IRE)**[14] 1413 4-9-0 95 .... PatCosgrave 19 35+
(Jim Boyle) *chsd ldrs: wknd u.str.p over 2f out* **15/2[3]**

260- **22** *3¾* **Fire Brigade**[154] 9004 5-8-13 94 .... JamieSpencer 24 25+
(Michael Bell) *s.i.s: mostly in last trio: rdn and no prog over 2f out* **28/1**

-145 **23** *1* **Chiefofchiefs**[49] 879 6-9-5 100 ....(p) JamesDoyle 26 29+
(Charlie Fellowes) *nvr beyond midfield: wknd wl over 2f out (jockey said gelding stopped quickly)* **20/1**

204- **24** *4* **Banditry (IRE)**[151] 8693 7-9-5 100 .... AndreaAtzeni 10 20+
(Ian Williams) *a wl in rr: eased whn no ch 2f out (jockey said gelding ran freely to post)* **100/1**

634- **25** *nk* **Wafy (IRE)**[225] 6754 4-8-10 91 .... RichardKingscote 22 11
(Charles Hills) *nvr beyond midfield: wknd over 2f out: eased over 1f out* **25/1**

00-0 **P** **Humbert (IRE)**[14] 1415 5-9-1 96 ....(p) DanielTudhope 21
(David O'Meara) *chsd ldrs: lost pl qckly wl over 2f out and sn heavily eased: p.u fnl f: lame (jockey said he pulled up as the gelding felt wrong; vet reported the gelding to be lame left fore)* **28/1**

1m 41.31s (1.41) **Going Correction** +0.425s/f (Yiel) **26 Ran SP% 140.8**
Speed ratings (Par 109): **109,108,106,104,103 102,100,92,90,89 87,86,86,86,86 85,85,83,78,77 77,73,72,68,68**
CSF £709.11 CT £9659.93 TOTE £16.70: £4.20, £13.00, £3.90, £3.40; EX 1762.90 Trifecta £5502.40.
Owner Mrs Peter Andrews **Bred** Colin Kennedy **Trained** Barbury Castle, Wilts

FOCUS

A typically wide-open Spring Cup. Those drawn low came out on top, with five of the first six home coming out of the six lowest stalls. Those five were among a group of seven to race separately from the main pack for the first furlong and a half or so.

1754 DUBAI DUTY FREE TENNIS CHAMPIONSHIPS MAIDEN STKS (PLUS 10 RACE) (DIV I) 1m (S)

3:50 (3:53) (Class 4) 3-Y-O

£5,530 (£1,645; £822; £411) **Stalls** Centre

Form RPR

1 **Fox Chairman (IRE)** 3-9-5 0 .... SilvestreDeSousa 4 98+
(Andrew Balding) *s.i.s: sn trcking ldrs: led 2f out: qcknd clr fnl f: comf* **15/8[1]**

05- **2** *4* **Migration (IRE)**[192] 7904 3-9-5 0 .... JasonWatson 13 86
(David Menuisier) *hld up: stdy prog fr 3f out: rdn 2f out: sn hung lft: r.o ins fnl f to go 2nd fnl 130yds but no threat to wnr* **25/1**

42- **3** *¾* **Just The Man (FR)**[122] 9499 3-9-5 0 .... AdamKirby 5 84
(Clive Cox) *led tl 2f out: sn rdn: kpt on same pce fnl f: lost 3rd fnl 130yds* **9/2[3]**

4 *1¾* **Fifth Position (IRE)** 3-9-5 0 .... AndreaAtzeni 1 80
(Roger Varian) *trckd ldrs: rdn 2f out: nt pce to chal but kpt on fnl f* **12/1**

5 *6* **Guandi (USA)** 3-9-5 0 .... RichardKingscote 10 66
(Tom Dascombe) *mid-div: stdy prog over 2f out: sn rdn: kpt on but nt pce to get on terms* **10/1**

0- **6** *¾* **Darwin Dream**[185] 8099 3-9-5 0 .... SeanLevey 11 64
(David Elsworth) *s.i.s: towards rr: kpt on steadily fnl 2f but nvr gng pce to get involved* **25/1**

7 *2¾* **Air Hair Lair (IRE)** 3-9-5 0 .... CharlesBishop 9 58
(Sheena West) *mid-div: rdn over 2f out: little imp: fdd ins fnl f* **100/1**

8 *1* **Michigan Blue (IRE)** 3-9-0 0 .... RossaRyan 6 51
(Richard Hannon) *rdn 3f out: nvr bttr than mid-div* **20/1**

00- **9** *1¼* **Tigerskin**[144] 9165 3-9-5 0 .... HarryBentley 3 53
(Ralph Beckett) *mid-div: rdn over 2f out: wknd over 1f out* **22/1**

10 *5* **Crystal Tribe (IRE)** 3-9-5 0 .... JamesDoyle 2 41
(William Haggas) *s.i.s: a towards rr* **3/1[2]**

05 **11** *16* **San Diaco (IRE)**[32] 1165 3-9-5 0 .... DanielMuscutt 8 5
(Ed Dunlop) *trckd ldrs tl wknd qckly 2f out* **66/1**

0- **12** *14* **Global Freedom**[144] 9165 3-9-5 0 ....(t w) GeraldMosse 7
(Ed Dunlop) *chsd ldrs tl over 2f out: sn wknd (jockey said colt hung left-handed; trainer said colt had a breathing problem)* **33/1**

13 *10* **Aleatoric (IRE)** 3-9-5 0 .... DannyBrock 12
(Martin Smith) *struggling in rr 1/2-way: t.o* **200/1**

1m 43.36s (3.46) **Going Correction** +0.425s/f (Yiel) **13 Ran SP% 117.5**
Speed ratings (Par 100): **99,95,94,92,86 85,83,82,80,75 59,45,35**
CSF £60.13 TOTE £2.50: £1.30, £5.00, £1.70; EX 51.70 Trifecta £245.40.
Owner King Power Racing Co Ltd **Bred** Manister House Stud **Trained** Kingsclere, Hants

FOCUS

Division one of this maiden saw a dominant winner. It was the slower division by 1.66sec and probably isn't strong form.

1755 DUBAI DUTY FREE TENNIS CHAMPIONSHIPS MAIDEN STKS (PLUS 10 RACE) (DIV II) 1m (S)

4:25 (4:27) (Class 4) 3-Y-O

£5,530 (£1,645; £822; £411) **Stalls** Centre

Form RPR

2- **1** **Raise You (IRE)**[203] 7536 3-9-5 0 .... OisinMurphy 11 99+
(Andrew Balding) *mde all: drifted rt fnl f: kpt on wl* **10/11[1]**

2 *6* **Ocean Paradise** 3-9-0 0 ....(h[1]) RichardKingscote 5 80
(Charles Hills) *trckd wnr thrght: rdn over 2f out: kpt on but nt pce to chal* **50/1**

3 *2¼* **Roseman (IRE)** 3-9-5 0 .... AndreaAtzeni 2 80+
(Roger Varian) *hld up towards rr: pushed along and hdwy over 2f out: wnt 3rd ent fnl f: kpt on* **9/2[3]**

53- **4** *¾* **Pour Me A Drink**[140] 9255 3-9-5 0 .... AdamKirby 1 78
(Clive Cox) *wnt rt s: mid-div: hdwy 3f out: rdn 2f out: kpt on same pce fnl f* **10/1**

5 *10* **Gold Stick (IRE)** 3-9-5 0 .... FrankieDettori 3 55+
(John Gosden) *slowly away and wnt lft: rn green: towards rr: stdy prog fr 2f out: kpt on fnl f wout ever threatening* **7/2[2]**

0- **6** *shd* **Light Up Our Stars (IRE)**[215] 7126 3-9-5 0 ....(w) DavidEgan 4 55
(Richard Hughes) *mid-div: hdwy fr 3f out: rdn and edgd rt over 1f out: fdd ins fnl f* **100/1**

7 *5* **City Wanderer (IRE)** 3-9-5 0 .... CharlesBishop 12 43
(Mick Channon) *mid-div: rdn over 2f out: wknd jst over 1f out* **66/1**

8 *9* **Global Rock (FR)** 3-9-5 0 .... GeraldMosse 10 23
(Ed Dunlop) *trckd ldrs tl wknd 2f out* **40/1**

9 *1* **Aql (IRE)** 3-9-5 0 .... JimCrowley 6 20
(Brian Meehan) *s.i.s: sn mid-div: wknd over 1f out* **20/1**

0- **10** *3¾* **Enhanced**[169] 8607 3-9-5 0 .... RobHornby 9 12
(Hughie Morrison) *s.i.s: a towards rr* **100/1**

11 *1¾* **Loch Laggan (IRE)** 3-9-5 0 .... JasonWatson 8 8
(David Menuisier) *chsd ldrs: rdn over 3f out: wknd over 2f out* **40/1**

12 *2¼* **Verify** 3-9-5 0 .... JamieSpencer 7 2
(Ed Walker) *s.i.s: a towards rr* **33/1**

1m 41.7s (1.80) **Going Correction** +0.425s/f (Yiel) **12 Ran SP% 119.9**
Speed ratings (Par 100): **108,102,99,99,89 88,83,74,73,70 68,66**
CSF £80.20 TOTE £1.70: £1.10, £9.70, £1.60; EX 57.80 Trifecta £239.20.
Owner J Palmer-Brown **Bred** Brucetown Farms Ltd **Trained** Kingsclere, Hants

FOCUS
This was the quicker division by 1.66sec. They finished well stretched out behind the all-the-way winner.

1756 DREWEATTS MAIDEN STKS (PLUS 10 RACE) 1m 3f
5:00 (5:02) (Class 3) 3-Y-O **£9,703** (£2,887; £1,443; £721) **Stalls** Low

Form RPR
-22 **1** **Majestic Dawn (IRE)**[38] 1034 3-9-5 0 DavidProbert 6 88
(Paul Cole) *mde all: styd on wl fnl f: unchal* **12/1**
2- **2** *6* **Pianissimo**[114] 9635 3-9-5 0 FrankieDettori 1 78
(John Gosden) *trckd wnr thrght: nudged along 5f out: rdn 3f out: nvr threatened to get on terms w wnr: styd on same pce* **8/13[1]**
3 *1* **Severance** 3-9-5 0 (h[1]) GeorgeDowning 5 76+
(Mick Channon) *s.i.s: last: stdy hdwy fr over 2f out: r.o ent fnl f: snatched 3rd cl home (vet reported the colt lost its right hind shoe)* **40/1**
4 *hd* **Space Walk** 3-9-5 0 JamesDoyle 4 76+
(William Haggas) *in tch: hdwy into 3rd 2f out: sn rdn: kpt on same pce fnl f: lost 3rd cl home* **10/3[2]**
5 *3 ¾* **Storting** 3-9-5 0 DavidEgan 7 70
(Mick Channon) *hld up: hdwy into 4th 2f out: sn rdn: fdd ins fnl f* **16/1**
0- **6** *10* **Kiefer**[221] 6899 3-9-5 0 CharlesBishop 2 54
(Eve Johnson Houghton) *trckd ldrs: rdn over 2f out: sn wknd* **9/1[3]**
7 *¾* **Doune Castle** 3-9-5 0 OisinMurphy 9 53
(Andrew Balding) *s.i.s: a in last pair* **16/1**
03- **8** *19* **State Of Affair (USA)**[148] 9105 3-9-5 0 JamieSpencer 3 22
(Ed Walker) *trckd ldrs: rdn 3f out: wknd 2f out* **20/1**

2m 29.27s (6.07) **Going Correction** +0.425s/f (Yiel) **8 Ran SP% 121.7**
Speed ratings (Par 102): **94,89,88,88,86 78,78,64**
CSF £21.27 TOTE £10.90: £1.90, £1.10, £7.30; EX 27.20 Trifecta £381.10.
Owner Green & Norman **Bred** Hall Of Fame Stud Ltd **Trained** Whatcombe, Oxon

FOCUS
Add 10yds. Fair maiden form. They came down the middle again once in line for home.

1757 DUBAI DUTY FREE MILLENNIUM MILLIONAIRE H'CAP 1m 2f
5:35 (5:35) (Class 3) (0-90,90) 4-Y-0+ **£7,762** (£2,310; £1,154; £577) **Stalls** Low

Form RPR
523- **1** **Lunar Jet**[94] 8112 5-9-0 **83** JamesDoyle 1 98
(John Mackie) *hld up towards rr: smooth prog towards far side fr 3f out: shkn up to ld over 1f out: sn drew clr: comf* **4/1[2]**
102- **2** *5* **Infanta Isabella**[169] 8609 5-8-12 **81** (t) NicolaCurrie 13 86
(George Baker) *trckd ldng pair: chal and upsides over 2f out to over 1f out: chsd wnr after but sn outpcd* **33/1**
00-0 **3** *1 ¼* **Sands Chorus**[14] 1413 7-8-4 **78** (p) TheodoreLadd[(5)] 6 81
(Scott Dixon) *mde most: rdn and hdd over 1f out: kpt on same pce (jockey said gelding hung right-handed)* **28/1**
44-5 **4** *1 ¼* **Lawmaking**[15] 1401 6-9-2 **85** (b) CallumShepherd 8 85
(Michael Scudamore) *hld up in last trio: gd prog over 3f out to join ldrs over 2f out: drvn and stl chalng over 1f out: one pce fnl f* **50/1**
025- **5** *½* **Frontispiece**[182] 8198 5-9-3 **86** WilliamBuick 3 85
(Amanda Perrett) *chsd ldrs: rdn and outpcd 2f out: n.d after: kpt on* **12/1**
10-5 **6** *hd* **Time For A Toot (IRE)**[34] 1127 4-9-1 **84** JimCrowley 19 83
(Charles Hills) *dropped in fr wd draw and hld up wl in rr: stdy prog 3f out: shkn up 2f out: no real hdwy after but kpt on* **25/1**
000- **7** *3* **Rayna's World (IRE)**[173] 8476 4-8-6 **80** SeanDavis[(5)] 10 73
(Philip Kirby) *hld up wl in rr: prog towards far side 3f out: nt rch ldrs 2f out: fdd fnl f* **50/1**
5-44 **8** *3* **C Note (IRE)**[71] 521 6-9-4 **87** (w) CharlesBishop 18 74
(Heather Main) *mostly chsd ldr to over 2f out: wknd u.p* **22/1**
/31- **9** *3 ¾* **Time Change**[331] 2787 4-9-1 **84** HarryBentley 7 63+
(Ralph Beckett) *chsd ldrs: rdn wl over 2f out: steadily wknd* **14/1**
/2-1 **10** *1* **Military Law**[101] 29 4-9-7 **90** OisinMurphy 14 67
(John Gosden) *trckd ldrs: racd towards nr side in st: cl up 3f out: rdn and lost pl over 2f out: steadily wknd* **3/1[1]**
625- **11** *3* **Moxy Mares**[197] 7729 4-8-12 **81** LiamJones 12 52
(Mark Loughnane) *nvr beyond midfield: rdn and no prog wl over 2f out: sn wl btn* **25/1**
406- **12** *nk* **Compton Mill**[162] 8808 7-8-11 **80** CharlieBennett 16 51
(Hughie Morrison) *hld up in rr: brought to nr side in st: no prog over 2f out: sn wknd* **40/1**
452- **13** *1* **Dream Machine (IRE)**[173] 8485 5-8-13 **82** SilvestreDeSousa 2 51
(Neil Mulholland) *wl in tch: rdn against far rail over 2f out: no prog and btn wl over 1f out: heavily eased (jockey said gelding hung left-handed)* **8/1**
516- **14** *¾* **New Show (IRE)**[254] 5648 4-9-4 **87** JamieSpencer 11 54
(Michael Bell) *wl in rr: rdn 4f out and racd towards nr side: struggling over 2f out* **8/1**
150- **15** *½* **Universal Command**[107] 9723 4-8-6 **82** WilliamCarver[(7)] 15 48
(Jack R Barber) *a towards rr: rdn and wknd wl over 2f out* **66/1**
640- **16** *¾* **Mushtaq (IRE)**[156] 8957 4-9-4 **87** RossaRyan 20 52
(Richard Hannon) *wl in tch: effrt towards nr side over 3f out: rdn and wknd over 2f out* **33/1**
/3-3 **17** *33* **Harbour Breeze (IRE)**[35] 1102 4-8-10 **79** DavidProbert 9
(Lucy Wadham) *hld up: effrt out wd 5f out: wknd 3f out: eased 2f out: t.o (jockey said colt ran too freely and hung right-handed)* **9/2[3]**
1363 **18** *28* **Philamundo (IRE)**[29] 1213 4-8-12 **81** (b) TomQueally 17
(Richard Spencer) *a in rr: wknd over 3f out: sn t.o* **40/1**

2m 12.05s (2.35) **Going Correction** +0.425s/f (Yiel) **18 Ran SP% 131.4**
Speed ratings (Par 107): **107,103,102,101,100 100,98,95,92,91 89,89,88,87,87 86,60,38**
CSF £145.89 CT £3388.76 TOTE £4.10: £1.20, £5.00, £8.30, £10.90; EX 155.60 Trifecta £2933.60.
Owner Ladas **Bred** Ladas **Trained** Church Broughton, Derbys

FOCUS
Add 10yds. A big-field handicap in which they raced down the middle in the straight. The pace appeared solid.

T/Plt: £1,196.80 to a £1 stake. Pool: £116,327.92 - 70.95 winning units T/Qpdt: £46.00 to a £1 stake. Pool: £14,771.29 - 237.42 winning units **Tim Mitchell & Jonathan Neesom**

THIRSK (L-H)
Saturday, April 13

OFFICIAL GOING: Good to firm
Wind: fresh half against Weather: Fine

1758 BRITISH EBF MAIDEN STKS (PLUS 10 RACE) (DIV I) 5f
2:00 (2:03) (Class 4) 2-Y-O **£4,851** (£1,443; £721; £360) **Stalls** Centre

Form RPR
1 **Xcelente** 2-9-5 0 JoeFanning 5 76
(Mark Johnston) *dwlt: sn trckd ldrs: pushed into ld over 1f out: kpt on wl* **3/1[2]**
03 **2** *2* **Heer We Go Again**[11] 1493 2-9-5 0 LiamKeniry 11 69
(David Evans) *led narrowly: rdn and hdd over 1f out: kpt on same pce (jockey said gelding hung left throughout)* **15/2**
0 **3** *hd* **Paddy Elliott (IRE)**[14] 1416 2-9-2 0 BenRobinson[(3)] 6 68
(Brian Ellison) *in tch: rdn to chse ldr appr fnl f: kpt on* **9/1**
4 *1* **Il Maestro (IRE)** 2-9-5 0 JasonHart 3 65
(John Quinn) *midfield: rdn and kpt on fnl f* **12/1**
5 *¾* **Kidda** 2-9-5 0 PaulHanagan 2 62+
(Richard Fahey) *slowly away: hld up in rr: sn pushed along and rn green: rdn and kpt on fnl f: nrst fin (jockey said colt was slowly away)* **9/4[1]**
6 *¾* **Cmon Cmon (IRE)** 2-9-2 0 RowanScott[(3)] 9 59
(Nigel Tinkler) *dwlt: hld up: sn pushed along: kpt on ins fnl f* **50/1**
3 **7** *½* **War Of Clans (IRE)**[11] 1499 2-9-5 0 CliffordLee 10 57
(K R Burke) *midfield on outside: rdn and hdwy over 1f out: wknd fnl 110yds* **6/1[3]**
8 *nk* **Congratulate** 2-9-0 0 JackGarritty 7 51
(Tim Easterby) *slowly away: hld up: sn pushed along: nvr threatened* **33/1**
9 *1* **Bezzas Lad (IRE)** 2-9-5 0 SamJames 4 53
(Phillip Makin) *pressed ldr: rdn 2f out: wknd fnl f* **20/1**
10 *1* **Road Rage (IRE)** 2-9-5 0 PaulMulrennan 8 49
(Michael Dods) *in tch: sn pushed along: wknd fnl f* **9/1**

1m 0.54s (1.14) **Going Correction** -0.175s/f (Firm) **10 Ran SP% 119.2**
Speed ratings (Par 94): **83,79,79,77,76 75,74,74,72,71**
CSF £26.05 TOTE £3.70: £1.70, £2.10, £3.10; EX 20.30 Trifecta £126.00.
Owner Jane Newett And Dougie Livingston **Bred** Hascombe & Valiant Stud Ltd **Trained** Middleham Moor, N Yorks

FOCUS
Mostly newcomers so no surprise these got strung out quite early with greenness an issue for many of these. The winner looks by no means the finished article either, but still won this with a fair bit in hand and he could be useful. The stalls were placed in the centre of the straight course but the field drifted towards the far rail. The level is fluid.

1759 BRITISH EBF MAIDEN STKS (PLUS 10 RACE) (DIV II) 5f
2:30 (2:33) (Class 4) 2-Y-O **£4,851** (£1,443; £721; £360) **Stalls** Centre

Form RPR
1 **Ventura Rebel** 2-9-5 0 PaulHanagan 3 78+
(Richard Fahey) *dwlt: hld up: sn pushed along: hdwy over 1f out: chsd ldrs whn swtchd lft ins fnl f: rdn and kpt on to ld towards fin* **11/4[2]**
2 *¾* **Jm Jackson (IRE)** 2-9-0 0 PJMcDonald 10 69
(Mark Johnston) *w ldr towards outer: rdn over 1f out: drvn ins fnl f: kpt on* **7/4[1]**
3 *nk* **Knightcap** 2-9-0 0 DavidAllan 6 68
(Tim Easterby) *trckd ldrs: pushed along to ld appr fnl f: drvn ins fnl f: no ex and hdd towards fin* **25/1**
5 **4** *2 ¼* **Bainne Dubh**[11] 1493 2-8-9 0 DylanHogan[(5)] 2 60
(Bill Turner) *prom: rdn and outpcd over 1f out: kpt on ins fnl f* **40/1**
5 *nk* **Dazzling Des (IRE)** 2-9-5 0 DavidNolan 9 64+
(David O'Meara) *chsd ldrs: pushed along to chal 2f out: rdn 1f out: no ex ins fnl f* **12/1**
6 *¾* **King Lenox** 2-9-2 0 RowanScott[(3)] 11 61
(Nigel Tinkler) *dwlt: hld up in tch: sn pushed along: kpt on ins fnl f* **66/1**
6 **7** *hd* **Baileys Freedom**[11] 1499 2-9-5 0 EdwardGreatrex 4 61
(Archie Watson) *led narrowly: rdn and hdd appr fnl f: wknd ins fnl f* **7/2[3]**
8 *3 ¼* **Must Dream** 2-9-5 0 CamHardie 5 49
(Seb Spencer) *slowly away: sn pushed along in rr: minor late hdwy* **50/1**
9 *shd* **Sparkling Breeze** 2-9-5 0 PaulMulrennan 7 49
(Michael Dods) *hld up: sn pushed along: wknd over 1f out* **25/1**
10 *2 ¼* **She's Easyontheeye (IRE)** 2-9-0 0 JasonHart 8 35
(John Quinn) *prom: pushed along and lost pl 1/2-way: rdn and wknd over 1f out* **10/1**
11 *1 ¼* **Miss Chilli** 2-9-0 0 NathanEvans 1 31
(Michael Easterby) *dwlt: hld up: sn pushed along: wknd over 1f out* **40/1**

1m 0.26s (0.86) **Going Correction** -0.175s/f (Firm) **11 Ran SP% 118.1**
Speed ratings (Par 94): **86,84,84,80,80 79,78,73,73,69 67**
CSF £7.52 TOTE £3.60: £1.50, £1.50, £4.20; EX 9.60 Trifecta £95.20.
Owner Middleham Park Racing LXXXI **Bred** Crossfields Bloodstock Ltd **Trained** Musley Bank, N Yorks

FOCUS
Very marginally quicker than the first division and the field tended to edge middle to stands' side this time. The winner overcame greenness to get up late in the day and looks a good bit better than the bare form. The level is very fluid.

1760 DEBBIE STEPHENSON BIRTHDAY CELEBRATION H'CAP 6f
3:05 (3:11) (Class 5) (0-75,75) 4-Y-0+
£4,398 (£981; £981; £327; £300; £300) **Stalls** Centre

Form RPR
060- **1** **Pennsylvania Dutch**[163] 8786 5-9-2 **70** (e[1] w) SamJames 12 84
(Kevin Ryan) *mde all: pushed along over 1f out: rdn and kpt on fnl f* **12/1**
-350 **2** *1 ¼* **Black Salt**[51] 832 5-8-13 **67** ow1 RobbieDowney 8 77
(David Barron) *hld up: pushed along and hdwy 2f out: rdn to chse ldr ins fnl f: kpt on* **5/1[1]**
234- **2** *dht* **Molls Memory**[169] 8611 4-9-6 **74** LiamKeniry 19 84
(Ed Walker) *trckd ldrs: rdn to chse ldr 1f out: kpt on* **6/1[2]**
421- **4** *2 ½* **Musharrif**[173] 8481 7-9-7 **75** DavidNolan 9 77
(Declan Carroll) *hld up: hdwy over 1f out: swtchd rt ent fnl f: sn rdn: kpt on same pce* **16/1**
005- **5** *1 ½* **Afandem (IRE)**[173] 8481 5-9-3 **71** DuranFentiman 6 68
(Tim Easterby) *midfield: pushed along and in tch over 1f out: kpt on same pce fnl f* **25/1**
6-00 **6** *½* **Logi (IRE)**[22] 1273 5-9-4 **75** (b) LewisEdmunds 10 68
(Rebecca Bastiman) *hld up: rdn over 2f out: kpt on ins fnl f* **14/1**

360- **7** 1 **I Know How (IRE)**[236] 6352 4-9-2 **70**.................... JasonHart 4 62+
(Julie Camacho) *hld up in rr: pushed along over 2f out: sme hdwy whn sltly short of room and swtchd lft 110yds out: kpt on: nrst fin* **16/1**
530- **8** 1 **Prestbury Park (USA)**[177] 8353 4-9-4 **72**..........(w) KevinStott 16 61
(Paul Midgley) *midfield: rdn 2f out: drvn ent fnl f: wknd fnl 110yds* **8/1**[3]
063/ **9** ½ **Mr Greenlight**[564] 7472 4-8-13 **67**.................... DavidAllan 15 55
(Tim Easterby) *slowly away: sn midfield: bit short of room over 1f out: sn pushed along: rdn and one pce fnl f* **33/1**
440- **10** 1½ **Cameo Star (IRE)**[176] 8383 4-9-0 **68**.................... PaulHanagan 5 51
(Richard Fahey) *midfield: rdn over 2f out: edgd lft and wknd ins fnl f* **10/1**
550- **11** 2½ **Rickyroadboy**[224] 6784 4-9-0 **68**.................... AndrewMullen 7 43
(Mark Walford) *prom: rdn over 2f out: wknd over 1f out* **28/1**
0364 **12** 1 **Dirchill (IRE)**[12] 1487 5-9-0 **68**..........(b) CliffordLee 2 40
(David Thompson) *1 of 3 to r far side: in tch: rdn over 2f out: outpcd and btn over 1f out* **9/1**
000- **13** nse **Kenny The Captain (IRE)**[134] 9324 8-9-1 **74**....... DannyRedmond(5) 14 45
(Tim Easterby) *in tch: pushed along and lost pl over 2f out: wknd over 1f out* **12/1**
-250 **14** ½ **Peggy's Angel**[16] 1382 4-8-11 **70**..........(h) FayeMcManoman(5) 20 40
(Marjorie Fife) *chsd ldrs: rdn 2f out: wknd over 1f out* **28/1**
1-40 **15** 2½ **Mr Strutter (IRE)**[10] 1522 5-9-1 **69**.................... KieranO'Neill 17 31
(Ronald Thompson) *slowly away: hld up: nvr threatened* **16/1**
006- **16** ¾ **Secretinthepark**[115] 9615 9-9-4 **72**.................... DaneO'Neill 18 31
(Michael Mullineaux) *v.s.a: a towards rr (jockey said the gelding dropped its head as he went to remove the blind, and it came away at the second attempt)* **25/1**
121- **17** 1¼ **Gullane One (IRE)**[268] 5135 4-8-13 **67**..........(t) RachelRichardson 3 22
(Tim Easterby) *1 of 3 to r far side: chsd ldrs: rdn over 2f out: wknd over 1f out* **12/1**
3-20 **18** 3½ **Granny Roz**[30] 1194 5-9-4 **72**..........(p[1]) JamesSullivan 1 16
(Ray Craggs) *1 of 3 to r far side: in tch: rdn over 2f out: sn wknd* **25/1**
50-0 **19** 3¼ **Rumshak (IRE)**[44] 953 4-9-7 **75**.................... PaulMulrennan 13 9
(Michael Dods) *prom: rdn over 2f out: sn wknd* **25/1**

1m 11.71s (-1.09) **Going Correction** -0.175s/f (Firm) **19** Ran SP% **133.8**
Speed ratings (Par 103): **100,98,98,95,93 92,91,89,89,87 83,82,82,81,78 77,75,70,66**
PL: MU 3.90, MM 1.50, BS 1.60, PD 4.10; EX: PD/MM 52.10, PD/BS 39.50; CSF: PD/MM 40.81, PD/BS 35.13; TC: PD/MM/BS 219.36, PD/BS/MM 214.70; TF: PD/MM/BS 321.60, PD/BS/MM 339.00; TOTE £15.20.
Owner K&J Bloodstock Ltd **Bred** Lael Stables **Trained** Hambleton, N Yorks

FOCUS
A big-field wide-open sprint handicap in which the field formed a peloton down the centre of the track. Nothing got in a blow on long-time leader Pennsylvania Dutch who returned with a bang. Straightforward form.

1761 SCOUTING FOR GIRLS @THIRSKRACES FRIDAY 16TH AUGUST H'CAP 1m 4f 8y
3:40 (3:44) (Class 3) (0-90,90) 4-Y-O+ **£9,703** (£2,887; £1,443; £721) **Stalls** High

Form RPR
111 **1** **King's Advice**[7] 1596 5-9-7 **90**.................... JoeFanning 8 96+
(Mark Johnston) *trckd ldrs: pushed along to ld 2f out: pressed 110yds out: rdn and kpt on* **6/5**[1]
030- **2** nk **Starcaster**[185] 8112 4-8-9 **78**.................... JackMitchell 9 85+
(Jedd O'Keeffe) *hld up in rr: hdwy on outside over 2f out: rdn over 1f out: edgd lft but sn chsd ldr: drvn to chal 110yds out: kpt on* **7/1**[3]
-315 **3** 4½ **Desert Ruler**[5] 1559 6-9-2 **85**.................... JackGarritty 10 84
(Jedd O'Keeffe) *hld up: pushed along and sme hdwy whn checked over 1f out: sn rdn: styd on to go 3rd fnl 110yds* **14/1**
124- **4** 1¼ **Benadalid**[222] 6873 4-9-3 **86**.................... MichaelStainton 1 84
(Chris Fairhurst) *trckd ldrs: rdn along 3f out: no ex ins fnl f* **10/1**
00-1 **5** ½ **Stonific (IRE)**[13] 1461 6-9-1 **84**.................... DavidNolan 4 80
(David O'Meara) *midfield: rdn over 2f out: one pce and nvr threatened* **8/1**
460- **6** 2¼ **Super Kid**[126] 9463 7-8-13 **82**..........(t) RachelRichardson 6 75
(Tim Easterby) *hld up: pushed along over 2f out: angled rt towards outer ent fnl f: nvr threatened* **50/1**
406- **7** ½ **Celestial Force (IRE)**[198] 7711 4-9-0 **83**.................... PJMcDonald 2 76
(Tom Dascombe) *led: rdn and hdd 2f out: sn wknd* **4/1**[2]
100- **8** 7 **Multellie**[168] 8631 7-9-3 **86**.................... DavidAllan 3 68
(Tim Easterby) *midfield: rdn along 3f out: wknd over 1f out* **40/1**
00-0 **9** hd **Armandihan (IRE)**[13] 1461 5-8-13 **82**..........(p) KevinStott 7 63
(Kevin Ryan) *prom: rdn over 2f out: wknd over 1f out* **20/1**

2m 31.45s (-8.55) **Going Correction** -0.175s/f (Firm) **9** Ran SP% **114.0**
Speed ratings (Par 107): **110,109,106,105,105 104,103,99,99**
CSF £9.79 CT £78.01 TOTE £1.70: £1.10, £2.50, £2.70; EX 9.60 Trifecta £69.70.
Owner Saeed Jaber **Bred** Rabbah Bloodstock Limited **Trained** Middleham Moor, N Yorks

FOCUS
Not a particularly deep race for the grade and the front two came clear. The well-backed market leader needed to work hard to maintain his winning run.

1762 RACING TV HOME OF BRITISH & IRISH RACING H'CAP 5f
4:15 (4:17) (Class 3) (0-95,90) 3-Y-O **£9,703** (£2,887; £1,443; £721) **Stalls** Centre

Form RPR
211- **1** **Leodis Dream (IRE)**[158] 8903 3-9-3 **86**.................... DavidNolan 7 91
(David O'Meara) *pressed ldr: led wl over 1f out: sn pushed along: drvn and wandered sltly ins fnl f: kpt on* **3/1**[1]
210- **2** nk **Princess Power (IRE)**[183] 8161 3-8-12 **81**.................... AndrewMullen 3 85
(Nigel Tinkler) *hld up: pushed along and hdwy over 1f out: drvn and kpt on wl fnl f* **14/1**
- **3** nk **Tenax (IRE)**[201] 7631 3-8-6 **80**.................... FayeMcManoman(5) 1 83
(Nigel Tinkler) *hld up: n.m.r over 1f out: sn pushed along: kpt on wl fnl 110yds: nrst fin* **28/1**
1130 **4** ¾ **Coolagh Magic**[16] 1388 3-8-12 **81**..........(v[1]) PaulHanagan 2 81
(Richard Fahey) *midfield: pushed along to chse ldr over 1f out: rdn 1f out: kpt on* **14/1**
0-41 **5** nk **Yolo Again (IRE)**[82] 342 3-9-2 **85**.................... DavidAllan 9 84
(Roger Fell) *chsd ldrs: rdn 2f out: one pce fnl f* **12/1**
410- **6** 3¼ **Three Card Trick**[183] 8161 3-9-1 **84**.................... KevinStott 5 71
(Kevin Ryan) *midfield: rdn over 2f out: wknd fnl f* **6/1**
043- **7** 1¼ **Triggered (IRE)**[183] 8161 3-9-7 **90**.................... LiamKeniry 4 73
(Ed Walker) *midfield: rdn along whn hmpd over 1f out: wknd ins fnl f* **11/2**[3]
102- **8** ½ **Mutawaffer (IRE)**[247] 5918 3-9-4 **87**..........(h) DaneO'Neill 6 68
(Charles Hills) *slowly away: veered bdly lft sn after s and bhd: hdwy and in tch w main field 2f out: rdn and hung lft over 1f out: wknd ins fnl f (jockey said gelding jumped awkwardly from the stalls)* **7/2**[2]
124- **9** ½ **Little Legs**[231] 6551 3-9-1 **87**.................... BenRobinson(3) 10 66
(Brian Ellison) *chsd ldrs towards outer: rdn over 2f out: wknd ins fnl f* **14/1**
210- **10** 6 **Que Amoro (IRE)**[189] 7988 3-9-1 **84**..........(p) PaulMulrennan 8 42
(Michael Dods) *led narrowly: rdn and hdd wl over 1f out: wknd* **7/1**

59.24s (-0.16) **Going Correction** -0.175s/f (Firm) **10** Ran SP% **120.5**
Speed ratings (Par 102): **94,93,93,91,91 86,84,83,82,72**
CSF £48.41 CT £1038.35 TOTE £3.50: £1.50, £4.20, £8.00; EX 60.90 Trifecta £1931.00.
Owner Andrew Kendall-Jones I **Bred** R & M Bloodstock **Trained** Upper Helmsley, N Yorks

FOCUS
Some potential improvers on show here and it was one of them, a handicap debutant, that got his 3yo career off to the perfect start.

1763 EBFSTALLIONS.COM MICHAEL FOSTER CONDITIONS STKS 7f
4:50 (4:51) (Class 3) 4-Y-O+
£9,337 (£2,796; £1,398; £699; £349; £175) **Stalls** Low

Form RPR
040- **1** **Vanbrugh (USA)**[156] 8965 4-9-2 105.................... DaneO'Neill 5 105
(Charles Hills) *hld up in tch: hdwy on outer 2f out: pushed along to ld appr fnl f: kpt on wl* **7/4**[1]
112- **2** 2¼ **Muntadab (IRE)**[161] 8838 7-9-6 107.................... GrahamLee 1 102
(Roger Fell) *led: rdn 2f out: hdd appr fnl f: kpt on but sn no ch w wnr* **11/4**[3]
024- **3** 2¾ **So Beloved**[161] 8838 9-9-2 107.................... DavidNolan 2 91
(David O'Meara) *dwlt: sn in tch: rdn 2f out: kpt on same pce* **15/8**[2]
03-0 **4** ½ **Aeolus**[14] 1421 8-9-2 97.................... JamesSullivan 6 90
(Ruth Carr) *hld up: pushed along and sme hdwy on inner 2f out: rdn over 1f out: one pce* **20/1**
400- **5** 8 **Florenza**[171] 8551 6-8-11 84.................... MichaelStainton 4 65
(Chris Fairhurst) *chsd ldrs on outer: rdn over 2f out: wknd appr fnl f* **33/1**
325- **6** 1¾ **Flying Pursuit**[157] 8933 6-9-6 103..........(p) RachelRichardson 3 70
(Tim Easterby) *prom: rdn over 2f out: wknd over 1f out* **14/1**

1m 23.74s (-3.86) **Going Correction** -0.175s/f (Firm) **6** Ran SP% **112.2**
Speed ratings (Par 107): **104,101,98,97,88 86**
CSF £6.97 TOTE £2.20: £1.20, £1.90; EX 7.40 Trifecta £13.40.
Owner K Abdullah **Bred** Juddmonte Farms Inc **Trained** Lambourn, Berks

FOCUS
A useful conditions race on paper but it was won easily by French recruit Vanbrugh who looks bound for Group races this summer.

1764 @THIRSKRACES NORTH YORKSHIRE CONFERENCE CENTRE NOVICE STKS 7f 218y
5:25 (5:28) (Class 5) 3-Y-O **£4,528** (£1,347; £673; £336) **Stalls** Low

Form RPR
1- **1** **Top Rank (IRE)**[112] 9683 3-9-7 0.................... PJMcDonald 8 83+
(James Tate) *trckd ldrs: chal 2f out: pushed along to ld appr fnl f: kpt on wl to assert fnl 110yds* **6/4**[1]
4-1 **2** 2 **Lehoogg**[17] 1352 3-9-9 0.................... JackMitchell 3 81
(Roger Varian) *prom: led over 2f out: rdn and pressed 2f out: hdd appr fnl f: kpt on* **3/1**[2]
5- **3** 6 **Beautiful Gesture**[196] 7774 3-8-11 0.................... CliffordLee 13 55
(K R Burke) *in tch: pushed along over 2f out: styd on to go 3rd 110yds out: no ch w ldng pair* **11/2**[3]
00- **4** 1¼ **George Ridsdale**[204] 7476 3-9-2 0.................... NathanEvans 14 57
(Michael Easterby) *trckd ldrs on outer: rdn and ev ch over 2f out: wknd fnl f* **66/1**
00- **5** nk **Happy Hannah (IRE)**[219] 6974 3-8-11 0.................... SamJames 2 51
(John Davies) *prom: trckd ldrs 5f out: rdn along 3f out: wknd fnl f* **100/1**
6 6 **Great Example** 3-9-2 0.................... JosephineGordon 4 43+
(Saeed bin Suroor) *in tch: sn pushed along: outpcd and btn over 3f out (jockey said colt hung left in the final 3 furlongs)* **3/1**[2]
7 1½ **Ghathanfar (IRE)** 3-9-2 0.................... RoystonFfrench 11 39
(Tracy Waggott) *dwlt: sn midfield: pushed along over 2f out: nvr threatened* **66/1**
8 2¼ **Voiceoftheemirates** 3-9-2 0.................... KevinStott 6 34
(Kevin Ryan) *v.s.a: in rr: rdn along and sme hdwy over 2f out: nvr involved* **20/1**
04- **9** ½ **Ritchie Star (IRE)**[155] 8975 3-9-2 0.................... AndrewMullen 12 33
(Ben Haslam) *hld up: nudged along over 2f out: nvr threatened* **50/1**
50- **10** 3 **Mo Emmad Ali (IRE)**[241] 6145 3-9-2 0.................... DougieCostello 1 26
(Kevin Ryan) *led: rdn and hdd over 2f out: sn wknd* **33/1**
11 3½ **Theatro (IRE)** 3-8-11 0.................... GrahamLee 15 13
(Jedd O'Keeffe) *hld up in midfield: sn pushed along: wknd over 2f out* **40/1**
12 ¾ **Gloryella** 3-8-11 0.................... JamesSullivan 9 11
(Ruth Carr) *dwlt: hld up: pushed along 4f out: nvr threatened* **100/1**
00 **13** 34 **Black Kraken**[14] 1417 3-9-2 0.................... PaulMulrennan 7
(Ben Haslam) *dwlt: hld up: bhd fnl 5f* **66/1**

1m 38.46s (-3.24) **Going Correction** -0.175s/f (Firm) **13** Ran SP% **123.9**
Speed ratings (Par 98): **98,96,90,88,88 82,80,78,78,75 71,70,36**
CSF £6.11 TOTE £2.30: £1.40, £1.20, £1.60; EX 6.50 Trifecta £18.60.
Owner Saeed Manana **Bred** Wicklow Bloodstock **Trained** Newmarket, Suffolk

FOCUS
They finished struing out all over Thirsk here and the front two had this between them from a long way out. They look the pair to concentrate on going forward.

1765 BOOK ONLINE FOR BEST TICKET PRICES @THIRSKRACES H'CAP 6f
5:55 (5:58) (Class 6) (0-60,60) 4-Y-O+
£3,126 (£930; £464; £300; £300; £300) **Stalls** Centre

Form RPR
500- **1** **Lucky Beggar (IRE)**[134] 9335 9-9-7 **60**.................... DavidAllan 11 73+
(David C Griffiths) *mde all: pushed clr appr fnl f: kpt on wl: comf* **6/1**[2]
00-4 **2** 2¼ **Sczueme**[17] 1364 5-9-6 **59**..........(h[1]) SamJames 19 65
(Phillip Makin) *dwlt hld up in midfield: pushed along and hdwy over 2f out: rdn to go 2nd ins fnl f: kpt on but nvr getting to wnr* **11/2**[1]
0-14 **3** ¾ **Ginger Jam**[57] 742 4-9-1 **59**.................... FayeMcManoman(5) 3 64+
(Nigel Tinkler) *dwlt: hld up: gng wl whn n.m.r 2f out: hdwy whn short of room again appr fnl f: kpt on to go 3rd towards fin (jockey said gelding was denied a clear run approaching 2 furlongs out)* **10/1**
-200 **4** ¾ **Carpet Time (IRE)**[7] 1595 4-9-5 **58**.................... PJMcDonald 6 60
(David Barron) *midfield: rdn appr fnl f: kpt on* **25/1**
0-03 **5** 2¼ **Milton Road**[39] 1021 4-9-3 **56**.................... LewisEdmunds 12 51
(Rebecca Bastiman) *chsd ldrs: rdn over 2f out: wknd fnl 110yds* **14/1**
-044 **6** 1¼ **Roaring Rory**[57] 738 6-9-2 **58**.................... JamieGormley(3) 16 49
(Ollie Pears) *dwlt: hld up: rdn over 2f out: sme hdwy over 1f out: nvr threatened ldrs* **12/1**
20-4 **7** nk **Kroy**[78] 410 5-8-13 **55**..........(p) BenRobinson(3) 18 45
(Ollie Pears) *midfield: pushed along 2f out: rdn appr fnl f: one pce* **20/1**

-200 **8** *3/4* **Cuppacoco**[32] 1162 4-9-5 **58**.................................. PaulMulrennan 9 46
(Ann Duffield) *prom: rdn over 2f out: wknd ins fnl f* **33/1**
-020 **9** *nk* **Scenery**[57] 738 4-9-5 **58**.................................. AlistairRawlinson 10 45
(Marjorie Fife) *chsd ldrs: rdn over 2f out: wknd fnl f* **16/1**
530- **10** *shd* **Cliff (IRE)**[158] 8902 9-8-10 **56**.................................. IzzyClifton(7) 1 43
(Nigel Tinkler) *midfield on outer: pushed along 2f out: wknd fnl f* **33/1**
0-03 **11** *3/4* **Jessie Allan (IRE)**[11] 1505 8-8-10 **56**.................................. CoreyMadden(7) 8 41
(Jim Goldie) *hld up: nvr threatened* **25/1**
50-0 **12** *shd* **Meshardal (GER)**[17] 1368 9-9-4 **57**.................................. JamesSullivan 17 41
(Ruth Carr) *hld up in midfield: angled rt 2f out: sn pushed along: nvr threatened* **8/1**[3]
46-0 **13** *nk* **Robben Rainbow**[32] 1158 5-9-4 **57**.................................. PhilDennis 7 40
(Katie Scott) *hld up: rdn over 2f out: sn btn* **28/1**
5-00 **14** *shd* **My Name Is Rio (IRE)**[81] 356 9-9-7 **60**.................................. KevinStott 2 43
(John Davies) *hld up in midfield: pushed along 2f out: nvr threatened* **20/1**
231- **15** *3 1/4* **Boudica Bay (IRE)**[214] 7144 4-9-2 **55**.................. RachelRichardson 14 28
(Eric Alston) *prom: rdn and hung lft over 1f out: sn wknd (jockey said filly hung left)* **8/1**[3]
0016 **16** *hd* **Miracle Garden**[29] 1208 7-9-6 **59**..................................(v) KieranO'Neill 13 32
(Ian Williams) *chsd ldrs: rdn over 2f out: wknd over 1f out (jockey said gelding was never travelling)* **9/1**
00-5 **17** *2* **Danehill Desert (IRE)**[15] 1403 4-9-7 **60**..................(p) PaulHanagan 4 27
(Richard Fahey) *chsd ldrs: rdn over 2f out: sn wknd* **10/1**

1m 12.03s (-0.77) **Going Correction** -0.175s/f (Firm) **17 Ran SP% 126.9**
Speed ratings (Par 101): **98,95,94,93,90 88,87,86,86,86 85,85,84,84,80 80,77**
CSF £36.44 CT £346.67 TOTE £6.20: £1.50, £2.10, £2.40, £5.60; EX 49.30 Trifecta £133.20.
Owner Eros Bloodstock **Bred** Mrs Cherry Faeste **Trained** Bawtry, S Yorks

FOCUS
A big field but not form to take too literally given the inconsistent nature of so many of these. The winner bolted up to be fair but it's hard to have too much confidence in him following up. Straightforward form in behind.
T/Plt: £35.00 to a £1 stake. Pool: £50,744.92 - 1,057.09 winning units T/Qpdt: £10.90 to a £1 stake. Pool: £3,862.74 - 261.40 winning units **Andrew Sheret**

1593 WOLVERHAMPTON (A.W) (L-H)

Saturday, April 13

OFFICIAL GOING: Tapeta: standard
Wind: Light against Weather: Sunny spells

1766 BETWAY AMATEUR RIDERS' H'CAP 6f 20y (Tp)

6:00 (6:00) (Class 5) (0-70,71) 4-Y-O+

£3,618 (£1,122; £560; £400; £400; £400) **Stalls Low**

Form RPR
3531 **1** **Steelriver (IRE)**[3] 1686 9-11-1 **71** 4ex.................. MrPatrickMillman 8 80
(Michael Herrington) *s.i.s: hld up: swtchd rt and hdwy over 2f out: rdn and hung lft over 1f out: styd on to ld wl ins fnl f* **3/1**[1]
0-02 **2** *1 1/4* **Fiery Breath**[22] 1265 4-10-2 **63**..................................(h) MrGeorgeEddery(5) 4 68
(Robert Eddery) *hld up in tch: lost pl over 3f out: hdwy over 1f out: r.o to go 2nd wl ins fnl f* **11/1**
6-1 **3** *1 1/2* **Gottardo (IRE)**[29] 1209 4-10-9 **70**.................................. SophieSmith(5) 1 71
(Ed Dunlop) *hld up: swtchd wd and pushed along on outer over 2f out: hdwy over 1f out: r.o to go towards fin: nt rch ldrs* **9/2**[3]
3540 **4** *1* **Dotted Swiss (IRE)**[29] 1208 4-10-8 **64**..........(b) MissBrodieHampson 11 62+
(Archie Watson) *sn led: pushed clr over 2f out: rdn: hdd and no ex wl ins fnl f* **14/1**
2235 **5** *3/4* **Bobby Joe Leg**[40] 1016 5-10-4 **65**..................(b) MissEmilyBullock(5) 2 61
(Ruth Carr) *s.i.s: sn pushed along in rr: hdwy over 1f out: nt trble ldrs* **6/1**
0-40 **6** *hd* **Terri Rules (IRE)**[7] 1595 4-10-2 **58**.................................. MrRossBirkett 9 53
(Julia Feilden) *s.i.s: hdwy over 3f out: rdn over 1f out: no ex ins fnl f* **50/1**
1253 **7** *1 1/2* **The Groove**[3] 1686 6-10-6 **69**.................................. MrPhilipThomas(7) 6 59
(David Evans) *led early: chsd ldrs: lost pl over 3f out: rdn and nt clr run over 1f out: wknd ins fnl f* **4/1**[2]
3-35 **8** *1* **Caribbean Spring (IRE)**[17] 1369 6-9-12 **59**. MissRosieMargarson(5) 12 46
(George Margarson) *broke wl enough: sn lost pl: racd wd: pushed along over 2f out: n.d after* **16/1**
20-0 **9** *1* **Searanger (USA)**[22] 1274 6-9-13 **62**.................. MrAndrewMcBride(7) 10 46
(Rebecca Menzies) *chsd ldrs: pushed along over 2f out: wknd fnl f* **33/1**
1-10 **10** *1 1/4* **Rockley Point**[32] 1162 6-10-4 **60**..................(b) MissAbbieMcCain 13 41
(Katie Scott) *chsd ldr 5f out: pushed along over 2f out: rdn: edgd lft and lost 2nd over 1f out: wknd ins fnl f* **33/1**
5200 **11** *1/2* **Bernie's Boy**[42] 981 6-11-0 **70**..................................(p) MrSimonWalker 5 49
(Phil McEntee) *chsd ldrs: pushed along over 2f out: wknd fnl f (starter reported that the gelding was the subject of a third criteria failure; trainer was informed that the gelding could not run until the day after passing a stalls test)* **11/2**
20-0 **12** *3/4* **Royal Connoisseur (IRE)**[17] 1366 8-10-2 **65**...... MrEireannCagney(7) 7 42
(Richard Fahey) *chsd ldrs: lost pl 5f out: n.d after* **28/1**

1m 14.5s **Going Correction** -0.025s/f (Stan) **12 Ran SP% 125.0**
Speed ratings (Par 103): **99.97,95,94,93 92,90,89,88,86 85,84**
CSF £39.17 CT £157.03 TOTE £4.30: £1.40, £3.20, £2.40; EX 46.30 Trifecta £171.70.
Owner Mrs H Lloyd-Herrington **Bred** Kildaragh Stud **Trained** Cold Kirby, N Yorks

FOCUS
It was standard on the Tapeta ahead of the opener in which those patiently ridden enjoyed the strong pace.

1767 BETWAY SPRINT H'CAP 5f 21y (Tp)

6:30 (6:30) (Class 5) (0-70,77) 4-Y-O+

£3,752 (£1,116; £557; £400; £400; £400) **Stalls Low**

Form RPR
2536 **1** **Cappananty Con**[17] 1357 5-9-4 **70**.................................. JoshuaBryan(3) 10 77
(Charlie Wallis) *hld up: hdwy over 1f out: r.o u.p to ld wl ins fnl f* **13/2**
34-5 **2** *hd* **Lexington Place**[17] 1364 9-8-7 **59**.................................. JaneElliott(3) 6 65
(Ruth Carr) *s.i.s: outpcd: swtchd rt ins fnl f: fin wl* **10/1**
0305 **3** *1* **Always Amazing**[32] 1162 5-8-8 **57**.................................. PaddyMathers 5 60
(Derek Shaw) *chsd ldrs: pushed along 1/2-way: hmpd wl over 1f out: sn rdn: r.o* **16/1**
02-6 **4** *nk* **David's Beauty (IRE)**[11] 1507 6-8-11 **60** ow2.........(b) ConnorBeasley 11 62
(Brian Baugh) *chsd ldrs: rdn over 1f out: styd on* **66/1**
1-44 **5** *nk* **Poeta Brasileiro (IRE)**[29] 1208 4-9-5 **68**.................................. RaulDaSilva 7 69
(Seamus Durack) *w ldr: shkn up to ld over 1f out: rdn and hdd wl ins fnl f* **5/1**[3]

1314 **6** *nk* **Zapper Cass (FR)**[7] 1597 6-9-7 **77**..................................(v) MarkCrehan(7) 1 76
(Michael Appleby) *chsd ldrs: swtchd rt wl over 1f out: sn rdn: styd on* **5/2**[1]
600- **7** *1* **Boundsy (IRE)**[176] 8382 5-9-4 **67**.................................. TonyHamilton 2 63
(Richard Fahey) *hld up: hdwy over 1f out: nt clr run ins fnl f: styng on whn short of room: eased towards fin* **9/2**[2]
3231 **8** *nk* **Big Time Maybe (IRE)**[7] 1590 4-9-0 **70**..................(p) ScottMcCullagh(7) 3 65
(Michael Attwater) *led: rdn and hdd over 1f out: no ex ins fnl f* **6/1**
0-00 **9** *7* **Rockies Spirit**[84] 317 4-9-7 **70**..................................(t[1]) LukeMorris 8 40
(Denis Quinn) *prom: lost pl after 1f: pushed along 1/2-way: wknd fnl f* **25/1**
1000 **10** *166* **The Establishment**[7] 1597 4-9-7 **70**..................................(h) EoinWalsh 4
(David Evans) *rrd s and lost all ch* **12/1**

1m 1.08s (-0.82) **Going Correction** -0.025s/f (Stan) **10 Ran SP% 119.0**
Speed ratings (Par 103): **105,104,103,102,102 101,100,99,88,**
CSF £71.16 CT £1006.20 TOTE £6.70: £2.10, £2.90, £4.90; EX 77.70 Trifecta £1812.60.
Owner Jim Biggane **Bred** Miss H Botterill & Mr D R Botterill **Trained** Ardleigh, Essex

FOCUS
There was plenty of pace for this open sprint handicap, and the race changed late on with those arriving late coming through in a bunched finish.

1768 SUN RACING H'CAP 7f 36y (Tp)

7:00 (7:00) (Class 5) (0-75,75) 4-Y-O+

£3,752 (£1,116; £557; £400; £400; £400) **Stalls High**

Form RPR
00-3 **1** **Sureyoutoldme (IRE)**[22] 1273 5-9-7 **75**.................................. JackGarritty 3 83
(Ruth Carr) *hld up in tch: shkn up over 1f out: rdn to ld wl ins fnl f: r.o* **8/1**
6630 **2** *1 1/4* **Murdanova (IRE)**[19] 1329 6-9-3 **74**..................(p) GabrieleMalune(3) 1 79
(Ivan Furtado) *hld up: hdwy 1/2-way: nt clr run over 1f out: swtchd rt ins fnl f: r.o to go 2nd nr fin* **7/2**[1]
30-2 **3** *nk* **Marshal Dan (IRE)**[19] 1329 4-9-3 **71**.................................. LukeMorris 7 75
(Heather Main) *a.p: chsd ldr over 5f out tl over 4f out: wnt 2nd again over 2f out: rdn to ld and hung lft over 1f out: hdd wl ins fnl f* **4/1**[2]
-200 **4** *nse* **Luis Vaz De Torres (IRE)**[44] 952 7-8-13 **72**......... ConnorMurtagh(5) 5 76
(Richard Fahey) *hld up: racd keenly: hdwy over 1f out: r.o* **8/1**
2426 **5** *1/2* **Lucky Lodge**[3] 1686 9-9-4 **72**..................................(b) CamHardie 6 75
(Antony Brittain) *led early: chsd ldrs: rdn over 1f out: styd on* **5/1**[3]
-421 **6** *2* **Muatadel**[54] 788 6-8-8 **67**..................................(p) BenSanderson(5) 8 65
(Roger Fell) *hld up in tch: racd keenly: lost pl over 4f out: rdn over 1f out: r.o ins fnl f* **8/1**
-002 **7** *3/4* **De Little Engine (IRE)**[19] 1338 5-8-10 **64**..................(p) GeorgeWood 10 60
(Alexandra Dunn) *chsd ldrs: rdn and nt clr run over 1f out: hung lft and no ex ins fnl f* **16/1**
0020 **8** *3/4* **Hollander**[29] 1208 5-8-7 **61**..................................(vt) HollieDoyle 4 55
(Alexandra Dunn) *hld up: rdn over 1f out: nt trble ldrs* **25/1**
4146 **9** *1* **Gabrial The Tiger (IRE)**[17] 1366 7-9-1 **69**.................. TonyHamilton 11 61
(Richard Fahey) *sn led: rdn and hdd over 1f out: wknd wl ins fnl f* **18/1**
-000 **10** *3/4* **Rosarno (IRE)**[17] 1367 5-8-11 **65**.................................. JoeyHaynes 9 55
(Paul Howling) *s.i.s: shkn up over 1f out: nvr nr to chal* **66/1**
021- **11** *1/2* **How Bizarre**[195] 7807 4-9-7 **75**.................................. DanielTudhope 12 63
(Liam Bailey) *hdwy on outer to go prom over 5f out: chsd ldr over 4f out tl hung rt over 2f out: wknd ins fnl f (jockey said gelding hung right-handed rounding the bend up the home straight)* **8/1**

1m 27.97s (-0.83) **Going Correction** -0.025s/f (Stan) **11 Ran SP% 119.8**
Speed ratings (Par 103): **103,101,101,101,100 98,97,96,95,94 94**
CSF £36.83 CT £135.26 TOTE £8.70: £2.80, £1.90, £1.70; EX 50.60 Trifecta £187.00.
Owner Michael Hill **Bred** Michael Downey & Roalso Ltd **Trained** Huby, N Yorks

FOCUS
An average handicap and another on the card where they went fast, suiting those coming from behind.

1769 SUN RACING TOP TIPS & PREVIEWS H'CAP 1m 142y (Tp)

7:30 (7:30) (Class 6) (0-60,60) 4-Y-O+

£3,105 (£924; £461; £400; £400; £400) **Stalls Low**

Form RPR
00-0 **1** **Medici Moon**[17] 1369 5-9-3 **56**..................................(p) RobHornby 3 62
(Richard Price) *chsd ldrs: pushed along over 3f out: rdn over 1f out: r.o to ld wl ins fnl f (trainer said, as to the apparent improvement in form, the gelding appreciated the return to the Tapeta surface and to Wolverhampton where he had ran well previously)* **20/1**
3343 **2** *nk* **Traveller (FR)**[11] 1506 5-9-5 **58**..................................(p[1]) CamHardie 4 63
(Antony Brittain) *disp ld tl settled into 2nd over 5f out: rdn to ld and hung rt over 1f out: hdd wl ins fnl f (jockey said gelding hung right-handed throughout)* **4/1**[1]
-460 **3** *nk* **Spiritual Star (IRE)**[44] 942 10-8-13 **59**............(t) Pierre-LouisJamin(7) 5 64
(Paul George) *hld up: hmpd over 2f out: hdwy and hung lft over 1f out: r.o* **8/1**
5006 **4** *nk* **Gabrial's Kaka (IRE)**[15] 1399 9-9-7 **60**.................................. PaddyMathers 11 64
(Patrick Morris) *s.i.s: hld up: hdwy over 1f out: nt clr run ins fnl f: r.o* **16/1**
4510 **5** *nse* **Ubla (IRE)**[16] 1390 6-8-11 **57**..................................(e) SeanKirrane(7) 10 61
(Gay Kelleway) *broke wl: stdd and lost pl after 1f: hdwy on outer over 2f out: rdn and ev ch ins fnl f: unable qck towards fin* **9/2**[2]
65-6 **6** *1* **Snooker Jim**[92] 180 4-8-10 **56**..................................(t[1]) TobyEley(7) 8 58
(Steph Hollinshead) *hld up: hdwy over 3f out: rdn over 1f out: no ex nr fin (jockey said gelding stopped quickly)* **10/1**
4-01 **7** *hd* **Our Manekineko**[46] 912 9-8-10 **49**..................................(bt) LukeMorris 9 50
(Stephen Michael Hanlon, Ire) *hld up: pushed along over 2f out: hdwy over 1f out: styd on u.p: nt rch ldrs* **6/1**[3]
20-4 **8** *1/2* **Abushamah (IRE)**[11] 1511 8-9-5 **58**.................................. JackGarritty 2 58
(Ruth Carr) *trckd ldrs: rdn over 1f out: no ex wl ins fnl f* **6/1**[3]
0200 **9** *2 3/4* **Mossy's Lodge**[15] 1399 6-8-11 **57**..................................(tp) EllaMcCain(7) 13 52
(Rebecca Menzies) *hood removed late: s.i.s: in rr whn hung rt over 2f out: r.o ins fnl f: nvr nrr* **20/1**
062 **10** *2 3/4* **Energia Flavio (BRZ)**[11] 1511 8-9-4 **57**..................................(p) DavidEgan 1 46
(Patrick Morris) *disp ld tl wnt on over 5f out: rdn and hdd over 1f out: hung rt and wknd ins fnl f* **6/1**[3]
00-6 **11** *4* **Mississippi Miss**[29] 1216 5-9-0 **53**.................................. GeorgeWood 12 33
(Dr Jon Scargill) *s.i.s: a in rr: rdn over 2f out: wknd fnl f* **16/1**
6005 **12** *1 1/2* **Claudine (IRE)**[11] 1494 4-8-8 **54**..................................(p[1]) AmeliaGlass(7) 6 31
(Alexandra Dunn) *sn prom: rdn and wknd over 2f out (jockey said filly hung left-handed throughout)* **50/1**

1m 49.82s (-0.28) **Going Correction** -0.025s/f (Stan) **12 Ran SP% 124.5**
Speed ratings (Par 101): **100,99,99,99,99 98,98,97,95,92 89,87**
CSF £101.44 CT £725.73 TOTE £22.30: £7.10, £1.60, £3.70; EX 148.80 Trifecta £921.10.
Owner The Cosimo Syndicate **Bred** G E Amey **Trained** Ullingswick, H'fords

FOCUS
A low-grade handicap and another come-from-behind winner. The likes of the second and fifth confirm the modest, straightforward level of the form.

1770 LADBROKES, HOME OF THE ODDS BOOST H'CAP 1m 4f 51y (Tp)
8:00 (8:00) (Class 6) (0-60,62) 3-Y-O

£3,105 (£924; £461; £400; £400; £400) Stalls Low

Form				RPR
6-02	1		**Another Reason (IRE)**[11] 1510 3-9-8 61 LukeMorris 8 (Olly Murphy) *hld up: hdwy over 2f out: rdn to ld and edgd lft ins fnl f: all out* 5/2[1]	67+
00-2	2	nk	**Rich Cummins**[22] 1270 3-9-2 55 JoeFanning 11 (Mark Johnston) *chsd ldrs: led over 2f out: rdn and hdd ins fnl f: styd on* 7/2[2]	61+
6-30	3	2 ¼	**Willkommen**[52] 802 3-8-9 55 (b) StefanoCherchi(7) 3 (Marco Botti) *chsd ldr tl wnt upsides over 7f out: led over 3f out: hdd over 2f out: rdn: edgd rt and ev ch over 1f out: styd on same pce ins fnl f* 28/1	57
-004	4	hd	**Gabrial The Giant (IRE)**[32] 1166 3-9-5 58 DavidEgan 9 (Patrick Morris) *hld up: hdwy over 5f out: rdn over 2f out: edgd lft fr over 1f out: nt clr run ins fnl f: styd on same pce* 14/1	60
4330	5	1	**Miss Green Dream**[19] 1332 3-8-2 48 SeanKirrane(7) 2 (Julia Feilden) *hld up: hdwy over 1f out: styd on same pce ins fnl f* 25/1	48
0-40	6	¾	**Oliver Hardy**[38] 1033 3-9-9 62 (t) RaulDaSilva 6 (Paul Cole) *hld up: rdn over 1f out: styd on ins fnl f: nt trble ldrs* 8/1[3]	61
5104	7	1 ¼	**Lady Wolf**[19] 1332 3-8-12 51 (p) RobHornby 10 (Rod Millman) *prom: rdn over 1f out: no ex ins fnl f* 14/1	48
-605	8	nk	**Munstead Moonshine**[9] 1555 3-8-9 48 (p[1]) MartinDwyer 5 (Andrew Balding) *s.i.s: hmpd sn after s: hld up: nvr nrr* 28/1	44
0-00	9	nk	**So I'm Told (IRE)**[59] 695 3-8-7 46 oh1 GeorgeWood 4 (Gary Moore) *s.i.s: hld up: rdn over 1f out: edgd lft ins fnl f: n.d* 5/2[1]	42
-530	10	1 ¾	**Tails I Win (CAN)**[7] 1593 3-9-1 59 (h) BenSanderson(5) 7 (Roger Fell) *hld up in tch: racd keenly: nt clr run and lost pl over 2f out: n.d after* 25/1	52
065	11	1 ½	**Enyama (GER)**[29] 1221 3-8-11 57 ScottMcCullagh(7) 1 (Michael Attwater) *sn led: hdd over 3f out: rdn over 2f out: wknd over 1f out* 50/1	48

2m 41.48s (0.68) **Going Correction** -0.025s/f (Stan) 11 Ran SP% 120.4
Speed ratings (Par 96): **96,95,94,94,93 93,92,91,91,90 89**
CSF £10.89 CT £201.19 TOTE £3.50: £1.20, £2.00, £7.60; EX 12.60 Trifecta £199.80.
Owner Olly Murphy Racing Club **Bred** Asterra Holdings Ltd **Trained** Wilmcote, Warks
■ Stewards' Enquiry : Rob Hornby four-day ban: interference & careless riding (Apr 27-30); one-day ban: failure to ride out (May 1)

FOCUS
Plenty made their handicap debut or tried a longer trip. They didn't go fast, but it was another patiently-ridden winner on the card.

1771 BETWAY MAIDEN STKS 1m 4f 51y (Tp)
8:30 (8:30) (Class 5) 3-Y-O+ £3,752 (£1,116; £557; £278) Stalls Low

Form				RPR
03-2	1		**Emirates Empire (IRE)**[31] 1182 3-8-7 76 DavidProbert 12 (Michael Bell) *sn prom: chsd ldr over 8f out: led and hung rt fr over 2f out: rdn out* 3/1[2]	81+
30-	2	4 ½	**Palladium**[157] 8930 3-8-7 0 RobHornby 10 (Martyn Meade) *s.i.s: hld up: hdwy over 5f out: rdn to chse wnr over 1f out: styd on same pce ins fnl f* 11/8[1]	72+
05	3	2 ½	**Nathanielhawthorne**[11] 1509 3-8-4 0 (h) AaronJones(3) 4 (Marco Botti) *hld up: hdwy and hung lft over 1f out: sn rdn: styd on to go 3rd wl ins fnl f* 50/1	68
6-4	4	1 ¾	**Luck Of Clover**[17] 1351 3-8-3 0 ow1 MartinDwyer 11 (Andrew Balding) *racd keenly in 2nd pl tl over 8f out: remained handy: rdn over 2f out: edgd lft over 1f out: wknd ins fnl f* 25/1	61
04	5	nk	**Message**[11] 1509 3-8-7 0 JoeFanning 7 (Mark Johnston) *hld up: shkn up over 2f out: styd on ins fnl f: nvr nrr* 11/1	65
340-	6	1 ¼	**Armed (IRE)**[204] 7491 4-10-0 80 TonyHamilton 3 (Phillip Makin) *prom: racd keenly: rdn over 2f out: hung lft and wknd over 1f out* 10/1	66+
3-22	7	nk	**Allieyf**[19] 1331 4-9-11 77 GeorgiaCox(3) 5 (William Haggas) *pushed along to ld: rdn and hdd over 2f out: wknd ins fnl f* 7/2[3]	65
66	8	3 ¼	**Blue Beirut (IRE)**[14] 1419 3-8-7 0 DavidEgan 9 (William Muir) *chsd ldrs: lost pl over 7f out: sn pushed along: rdn over 2f out: wknd over 1f out* 66/1	57
	9	4 ½	**Western Dixie (IRE)**[115] 5-9-9 0 ConnorBeasley 8 (Jennie Candlish) *s.i.s: nvr on terms* 100/1	47
	10	3	**And The New (IRE)**[20] 8-10-0 0 LukeMorris 2 (Johnny Farrelly) *s.s: outpcd (jockey said geldiing was slowly away)* 12/1	47
0	11	2 ½	**Sorbet**[59] 696 4-9-9 0 (w) GeorgeWood 1 (Lucy Wadham) *hld up: rdn and wknd over 2f out* 50/1	39

2m 38.65s (-2.15) **Going Correction** -0.025s/f (Stan)
WFA 3 from 4yo+ 21lb 11 Ran SP% 124.7
Speed ratings (Par 103): **106,103,101,100,99 99,98,96,93,91 90**
CSF £7.88 TOTE £3.60: £1.50, £1.50, £8.00; EX 9.10 Trifecta £489.90.
Owner Ahmad Al Shaikh **Bred** A Al Shaikh **Trained** Newmarket, Suffolk

FOCUS
An interesting maiden and the fancied runners came to the fore. The winner looked a nice sort in coming clear.
T/Plt: £133.80 to a £1 stake. Pool: £91,347.61 - 498.32 winning units T/Qpdt: £8.60 to a £1 stake. Pool: £13,603.06 - 1,160.42 winning units **Colin Roberts**

1772a-1775a (Foreign Racing) - See Raceform Interactive

1303 NAAS (L-H)
Saturday, April 13

OFFICIAL GOING: Good to yielding

1776a GLADNESS STKS (GROUP 3) 7f
4:00 (4:02) 3-Y-O+

£31,891 (£10,270; £4,864; £2,162; £1,081; £540)

			RPR
1		**Imaging**[10] 1531 4-9-7 105 OisinOrr 8 (D K Weld, Ire) *hld up: pushed along under 2f out: wnt 6th ent fnl f: styd on strly to ld fnl 50yds* 7/2[2]	106+
2	½	**No Needs Never (IRE)**[175] 8428 3-8-7 104 (t[1]) ShaneCrosse 6 (Joseph Patrick O'Brien, Ire) *racd in mid-div: clsr ent fnl f in 4th: styd on wl for press to press wnr in 2nd fnl 50yds* 8/1	100+
3	¾	**Le Brivido (FR)**[359] 1928 5-9-7 117 RyanMoore 9 (A P O'Brien, Ire) *rrd leaving stalls and slowly away: racd in rr tl prog appr fnl f in 8th: styd on strly fnl 100yds into 3rd on line: nrst fin* 5/2[1]	103+
4	hd	**Smash Williams (IRE)**[14] 1434 6-9-7 106 (t) KevinManning 3 (J S Bolger, Ire) *t.k.h early and settled off ldrs in 4th: 5th at 1/2-way: travelled wl 2f out in 3rd: rdn to dispute fnl 150yds: hdd fnl 50yds and dropped to 4th on line* 9/2[3]	102
5	hd	**Romanised (IRE)**[175] 8407 4-9-12 117 (t) WJLee 1 (K J Condon, Ire) *racd in mid-div: pushed along in 6th under 2f out: clsr ins fnl f where briefly short of room: kpt on wl clsng stages* 5/1	107+
6	¾	**Texas Rock (IRE)**[7] 1602 8-9-7 86 (p) RobbieColgan 5 (M C Grassick, Ire) *trckd ldr in 2nd: pushed along under 2f out: nt qckn fnl 150yds: wknd clsng stages* 50/1	100
7	¾	**Psychedelic Funk**[188] 8019 5-9-7 110 (b) ColinKeane 4 (G M Lyons, Ire) *led tl strly pressed and hdd fnl 150yds: wknd fnl 50yds* 8/1	98
8	1	**Nebo (IRE)**[189] 7990 4-9-7 100 RonanWhelan 2 (T Hogan, Ire) *chsd ldrs in 3rd: rdn and no imp ent fnl f: wknd* 33/1	95
9	8 ½	**Ellthea (IRE)**[20] 1307 4-9-4 97 ChrisHayes 7 (J A Stack, Ire) *a towards rr: pushed along and detached over 1f out: eased ins fnl f* 33/1	69

1m 28.25s (0.75)
WFA 3 from 4yo+ 14lb 9 Ran SP% 115.7
CSF £31.02 TOTE £4.50: £1.60, £2.70, £1.40; DF 32.00 Trifecta £111.00.
Owner K Abdullah **Bred** Juddmonte Farms Ltd **Trained** Curragh, Co Kildare

FOCUS
This was a top-notch renewal with last year's Irish 2,000 Guineas winner Romanised taking on last season's Jersey Stakes winner, Le Brivido. The gallop was generous thanks to Psychedelic Funk. The form is rated around the winner, second and fourth.

1777a ALLEGED STKS (GROUP 3) 1m 2f
4:35 (4:38) 4-Y-O+

£34,549 (£11,126; £5,270; £2,342; £1,171; £585)

			RPR
1		**Magical (IRE)**[161] 8848 4-9-5 122 RyanMoore 7 (A P O'Brien, Ire) *trckd ldrs in 4th: clsr traveling wl in 3rd under 2f out: led under hands and heels ent fnl f: shkn up to go clr fnl 100yds* 1/1[1]	121+
2	4 ½	**Flag Of Honour (IRE)**[167] 8667 4-9-8 117 SeamieHeffernan 6 (A P O'Brien, Ire) *trckd ldr in 2nd tl disp under 3f out: led 2f out tl hdd ent fnl f: sn no match for wnr: kpt on wl in clr 2nd* 12/1	115
3	4 ½	**Latrobe (IRE)**[125] 9473 4-9-8 115 DonnachaO'Brien 2 (Joseph Patrick O'Brien, Ire) *towards rr: pushed along over 2f out: 7th ent fnl f: styd on wl into 3rd cl home: nvr nrr* 6/1[3]	106+
4	½	**Still Standing (IRE)**[20] 1309 4-9-3 104 ShaneFoley 3 (Mrs John Harrington, Ire) *trckd ldrs in 3rd: pushed along in 4th over 2f out: no imp ent fnl f: kpt on same pce: dropped to 4th cl home* 7/1	100
5	1	**Hazapour (IRE)**[268] 5150 4-9-6 110 ChrisHayes 8 (D K Weld, Ire) *racd in mid-div: 5th at 1/2-way: pushed along and no imp appr fnl f: kpt on same pce* 12/1	101
6	1 ¼	**Stellar Mass (IRE)**[20] 1309 6-9-3 105 KevinManning 4 (J S Bolger, Ire) *racd in rr: pushed along in rr 2f out: kpt on ins fnl f: nvr on terms* 66/1	96
7	½	**Mustajeer**[160] 8862 6-9-3 111 (h) ColinKeane 1 (G M Lyons, Ire) *racd in mid-div: 6th at 1/2-way: pushed along over 2f out and sn no imp: one pce* 4/1[2]	95
8	1	**Success Days (IRE)**[175] 8429 7-9-3 105 (t) WJLee 5 (K J Condon, Ire) *sn led: strly pressed under 3f out and hdd 2f out: wknd fnl f* 20/1	93

2m 14.44s (-1.16) 8 Ran SP% 118.4
CSF £16.08 TOTE £1.70: £1.02, £3.30, £1.80; DF 11.30 Trifecta £56.20.
Owner Derrick Smith & Mrs John Magnier & Michael Tabor **Bred** Orpendale, Chelston & Wynatt **Trained** Cashel, Co Tipperary

FOCUS
Quality stuff with five of the eight runners rated 110 or higher. This was a strongly-run affair with Flag Of Honour taking on Success Days up front but Magical never came out of her comfort zone and destroyed them. The winner and fourth have been rated to their best.

1778 - 1779a (Foreign Racing) - See Raceform Interactive

1657 CHANTILLY (R-H)
Saturday, April 13

OFFICIAL GOING: Polytrack: standard; turf: good to soft

1780a PRIX SIGY (GROUP 3) (3YO) (TURF) 5f 110y
1:52 3-Y-O £36,036 (£14,414; £10,810; £7,207; £3,603)

			RPR
1		**Big Brothers Pride (FR)**[30] 1199 3-8-10 0 Pierre-CharlesBoudot 2 (F Rohaut, France) *mde all: kicked clr ins fnl 2f: wl on top last 150yds: v comf* 105/10	111+
2	4	**Happy Odyssey (IRE)**[30] 1200 3-8-10 0 StephanePasquier 5 (N Clement, France) *settled in fnl trio: drvn 1/2-way: hdwy 1 1/2f out: styd on to go 2nd last 80yds: no ch w wnr* 57/10[3]	98
3	1 ¼	**Kenbaio (FR)**[144] 9167 3-9-0 0 GregoryBenoist 3 (P Bary, France) *racd keenly: hld up in rr: began to cl and nt clr run 1 1/2f out: styd on ins fnl f: wnt 3rd post* 24/1	98
4	shd	**True Mason**[183] 8145 3-9-0 BenCurtis 4 (K R Burke) *trckd ldr: drvn to dispute 2nd ins rivals wl over 1 1/2f out: one pce u.p fnl f: lost 3rd post* 31/5	98
5	hd	**Ilanga (FR)**[33] 3-8-10 0 MaximeGuyon 7 (D Guillemin, France) *racd keenly: hld up towards rr: rdn to cl wl over 1f out: styd on ins fnl f: nvr trbld ldrs* 76/10	93
6	¾	**Barbill (IRE)**[52] 806 3-9-0 0 JFEgan 8 (Mick Channon) *cl up on outer: drvn but no imp under 2f out: sn rdn: grad lft bhd ins fnl f* 6/4[1]	94
7	2	**Vintage Brut**[182] 8193 3-9-0 0 (p) ChristopheSoumillon 6 (Tim Easterby) *chsd ldr: drvn and nt qckn w less than 2f to run: dropped away fr wl over 1f out* 41/10[2]	88
8	1 ¾	**Bravo Sierra**[199] 7690 3-8-10 0 VincentCheminaud 1 (A Fabre, France) *w.w in fnl trio on inner: tk clsr order after 1/2-way: sn rdn and no further imp: wknd fnl f* 13/1	78

1m 4.51s (0.01) 8 Ran SP% 119.9
PARI-MUTUEL (all including 1 euro stake): WIN 11.50; PLACE 3.20, 2.00, 4.50; DF 31.30.

Owner Kin Hung Kei & Qatar Racing Ltd **Bred** Ecurie Des Monceaux, Framont Limited & Beauregard **Trained** Sauvagnon, France

1781 - 1782a (Foreign Racing) - See Raceform Interactive

1607 RANDWICK (L-H)
Saturday, April 13

OFFICIAL GOING: Turf: good to soft changing to good after 4.50 race

1783a LONGINES QUEEN ELIZABETH STKS (GROUP 1) (3YO+) (TURF) 1m 2f
6:05 3-Y-O+
£1,345,027 (£417,127; £218,232; £99,447; £52,486; £22,099)

RPR

1 **Winx (AUS)**[21] 1299 7-9-0 0 .... HughBowman 9 115+
(Chris Waller, Australia) *settled in midfield: hdwy on outer 2 1/2f out: drvn along to ld 1 1/2f out: a in control after: comf* **1/16[1]**

2 *1 ½* **Kluger (JPN)**[7] 1610 7-9-4 0 .... TommyBerry 1 115
(Tomokazu Takano, Japan) **50/1**

3 *2 ½* **Hartnell**[7] 1610 8-9-4 0 .... KerrinMcEvoy 4 110
(James Cummings, Australia) *led 1f: trckd ldr: shkn up to chal 2f out: outpcd over 1f out: kpt on same pce fnl f: rdn out* **25/1[3]**

4 *2* **Happy Clapper (AUS)**[28] 8-9-4 0 ....(p) BlakeShinn 6 106
(Patrick Webster, Australia) **30/1**

5 *2 ½* **Shillelagh (NZ)**[7] 1610 7-9-0 0 .... BrentonAvdulla 2 97
(Chris Waller, Australia) **100/1**

6 *3* **Mask Of Time (IRE)**[14] 5-9-4 0 .... SamClipperton 7 95
(Ciaron Maher & David Eustace, Australia) **150/1**

7 *3 ½* **Danzdanzdance (AUS)**[21] 1300 4-9-0 0 .... OpieBosson 5 84
(Chris Gibbs & Michelle Bradley, New Zealand) **50/1**

8 *1 ¼* **Eminent (IRE)**[21] 1300 5-9-4 0 .... JamesMcDonald 3 86
(Sir Mark Todd) **20/1[2]**

9 *14 ½* **Harlem**[35] 1108 7-9-4 0 ....(b) JamieKah 8 57
(David A & B Hayes & Tom Dabernig, Australia) **80/1**

2m 2.54s **9 Ran SP% 112.7**

Owner Magic Bloodstock Racing, R G Treweeke & Mrs D N Ke **Bred** Fairway Thoroughbreds **Trained** Australia

FOCUS
The result everyone wanted, but Winx did not need to be at her best on her farewell appearance.

1784a SCHWEPPES SYDNEY CUP (GROUP 1 H'CAP) (3YO+) (TURF) 2m
6:50 3-Y-O+
£729,005 (£209,944; £107,734; £49,723; £24,861; £11,049)

RPR

1 **Shraaoh (IRE)**[7] 6-8-0 0 ....(t) JayFord 3 102
(Chris Waller, Australia) **11/1**

2 *½* **Vengeur Masque (IRE)**[7] 7-8-7 0 .... DamienOliver 15 108
(Michael Moroney, Australia) **30/1**

3 *1 ½* **Glory Days (NZ)**[35] 6-8-3 0 .... CoreyBrown 18 102
(Bill Thurlow, New Zealand) **16/1**

4 *1* **Rondinella (NZ)**[14] 1454 4-8-3 0 ow3 ....(b) SamClipperton 1 101
(Roger James & Robert Wellwood, New Zealand) **17/2[3]**

5 *1 ¼* **Doukhan (IRE)**[14] 1454 10-8-0 0 .... AndrewGibbons 2 97
(Kris Lees, Australia) **100/1**

6 *hd* **Gallic Chieftain (FR)**[7] 6-8-2 0 ....(bt) GlenBoss 7 98
(Archie Alexander, Australia) **17/1**

7 *½* **Patrick Erin (NZ)**[14] 1454 7-8-8 0 ....(b[1]) GlynSchofield 5 104
(Chris Waller, Australia) **70/1**

8 *shd* **Sound (GER)**[14] 1454 6-8-10 0 .... DamianLane 12 106
(Michael Moroney, Australia) **40/1**

9 *½* **Midterm**[21] 6-8-4 0 ....(b) JamieKah 9 99
(Liam Howley, Australia) **11/2[2]**

10 *1 ½* **Big Duke (IRE)**[14] 1454 7-8-7 0 .... BrentonAvdulla 20 100
(Kris Lees, Australia) **13/1**

11 *hd* **Top Of The Range (NZ)**[33] 5-8-0 0 ....(b) MichaelDee 16 93
(Michael Moroney, Australia) **150/1**

12 *hd* **Dubhe**[65] 635 4-8-4 0 ....(tp) KerrinMcEvoy 4 101
(Charlie Appleby) *settled towards rr: pushed along 4f out: no imp and rdn along 2f out: limited hdwy late on: nvr involved* **17/5[1]**

13 *shd* **Rodrico (AUS)**[7] 6-8-0 0 ....(b) JamesInnesJnr 10 93
(Bjorn Baker, Australia) **150/1**

14 *shd* **Zacada (NZ)**[7] 6-8-3 0 ....(b) KathyO'Hara 11 95
(Murray Baker & Andrew Forsman, New Zealand) **100/1**

15 *½* **Semari (NZ)**[7] 4-8-3 0 ow3 .... TimothyClark 6 95
(Trent Busuttin & Natalie Young, Australia) **60/1**

16 *hd* **Yogi (NZ)**[14] 1454 6-8-5 0 ....(b) CraigAWilliams 14 97
(Ciaron Maher & David Eustace, Australia) **9/1**

17 *1 ¼* **Red Cardinal (IRE)**[14] 1454 7-8-7 0 .... JasonCollett 17 97
(Kris Lees, Australia) **11/1**

18 *¾* **The Taj Mahal (IRE)**[7] 5-8-11 0 ....(bt) JamesMcDonald 8 100
(Liam Howley, Australia) **20/1**

19 *3* **Charles Road (AUS)**[7] 5-8-5 0 ....(bt) RobbieDolan 19 91
(Lance O'Sullivan & Andrew Scott, New Zealand) **14/1**

20 *1 ¼* **Brimham Rocks**[14] 1454 5-8-5 0 ....(b[1]) TommyBerry 13 89
(Chris Waller, Australia) **40/1**

3m 22.06s
WFA 4 from 5yo+ 2lb **20 Ran SP% 119.8**

Owner Mrs R Hillen, D M Ackery Et Al **Bred** Sunderland Holdings Inc **Trained** Australia

1785 - 1792a (Foreign Racing) - See Raceform Interactive

DUSSELDORF (R-H)
Sunday, April 14

OFFICIAL GOING: Turf: good

1793a KALKMANN FRUHJAHRS-MEILE (GROUP 3) (4YO+) (TURF) 1m
2:00 4-Y-O+ **£28,828** (£10,810; £5,405; £2,702; £1,801)

RPR

1 **Stormy Antarctic**[126] 9477 6-9-4 0 .... GeraldMosse 8 116
(Ed Walker) *settled in midfield: pushed along and hdwy over 2f out: rdn to ld 1f out: sn pressed: a doing enough* **1/2[1]**

2 *nk* **Madita (GER)**[150] 9091 4-8-8 0 .... BauyrzhanMurzabayev 4 106
(S Smrczek, Germany) *in rr of midfield: pushed along and hdwy 2f out: pressed ldr under 1f out: a jst hld: rdn out* **26/1**

3 *2 ½* **Degas (GER)**[80] 397 6-9-2 0 .... AdriedeVries 5 108
(Markus Klug, Germany) *towards rr: drvn along and tk clsr order over 1f out: wnt 3rd and rdn along under 1f out: no imp on ldng pair* **12/1[3]**

4 *3 ½* **Palace Prince (GER)**[57] 766 7-9-0 0 ....(p) FilipMinarik 3 98
(Jean-Pierre Carvalho, Germany) *midfield: drvn along 2f out: kpt on same pce: nvr a threat* **212/10**

5 *½* **Wonnemond (GER)**[168] 6-9-0 0 .... BayarsaikhanGanbat 9 97
(S Smrczek, Germany) *in fnl pair: rdn along under 2f out: styd on but nvr on terms w ldrs: rdn out* **42/10[2]**

6 *2* **Alinaro (GER)**[217] 7103 4-9-0 0 .... MirkoSanna 6 92
(Henk Grewe, Germany) *in fnl pair: effrt 2f out: plugged on: nvr on terms* **41/1**

7 *1 ¼* **Wetrov (FR)**[52] 4-8-11 0 .... MarcoCasamento 7 86
(R Rohne, Germany) *settled in 3rd: wnt 2nd turning in: shkn up and lost position under 2f out: wl hld fnl f* **52/1**

8 *¾* **Zargun (GER)**[142] 9239 4-8-11 0 ....(p) LukasDelozier 1 84
(Henk Grewe, Germany) *led: 5 l clr 1/2-way: shkn up 2f out: hdd 1f out: wknd fnl f* **173/10**

9 *41* **Los Campanos (GER)** 5-9-0 0 .... RenePiechulek 2
(Dr A Bolte, Germany) *trckd ldr: drvn along and lost position turning in: heavily eased over 1f out* **137/10**

1m 34.11s (-7.05) **9 Ran SP% 118.3**
PARI-MUTUEL (all including 10 euro stake): WIN 15 PLACE: 12, 25, 22, SF: 551.
Owner P K Siu **Bred** East Bloodstock Ltd **Trained** Upper Lambourn, Berks

1625 LONGCHAMP (R-H)
Sunday, April 14

OFFICIAL GOING: Turf: good

1794a PRIX DE FONTAINEBLEAU (GROUP 3) (3YO COLTS) (TURF) 1m
1:35 3-Y-O **£36,036** (£14,414; £10,810; £7,207; £3,603)

RPR

1 **Persian King (IRE)**[183] 8186 3-9-2 0 .... Pierre-CharlesBoudot 2 115+
(A Fabre, France) *led after 1/2f: drvn along 2f out and sn 2 l clr: drew further clr fnl f: drvn out: comf* **1/5[1]**

2 *5* **Epic Hero (FR)**[26] 3-9-2 0 .... MickaelBarzalona 1 103
(A Fabre, France) *sn settled in 3rd: shkn up 2f out: wnt 2nd but nt pce of wnr fnl 2f: jst hld 2nd* **9/1[3]**

3 *hd* **Duke Of Hazzard (FR)**[172] 8563 3-9-2 0 .... ChristopheSoumillon 3 103
(Paul Cole) *settled in 4th: effrt 2f out: kpt on wl and almost tk 2nd but no ch w easy wnr: rdn out* **32/5[2]**

4 *3* **Price Range (USA)**[138] 3-9-2 0 .... VincentCheminaud 5 96
(P Bary, France) *s.i.s: settled in last: shkn up 2f out: kpt on same pce: rdn out* **15/1**

5 *2* **Prince Hamlet (FR)**[28] 1243 3-9-2 0 .... TonyPiccone 4 92
(M Delcher Sanchez, France) *led 1/2f: settled in 2nd: drvn along and lost position under 2f out: wl hld in last fnl f* **14/1**

1m 36.41s (-1.99) **5 Ran SP% 119.8**
PARI-MUTUEL (all including 1 euro stake): WIN 1.10; PLACE 1.10, 1.10; SF 2.60.
Owner Godolphin SNC & Ballymore Thoroughbred Ltd **Bred** Dayton Investments (Breeding) Limited **Trained** Chantilly, France

FOCUS
A nice performance from the winner, and all five have been rated close to their marks.

1795a PRIX DE LA GROTTE (GROUP 3) (3YO FILLIES) (TURF) 1m
2:50 3-Y-O **£36,036** (£14,414; £10,810; £7,207; £3,603)

RPR

1 **Castle Lady (IRE)**[31] 3-9-0 0 .... MickaelBarzalona 6 110
(H-A Pantall, France) *disp ld 100yds: settled bhd ldrs: effrt 2f out: rdn to ld 175yds out: drew clr fnl 100yds: rdn out* **47/10[3]**

2 *1 ¾* **Imperial Charm**[162] 8833 3-9-0 0 .... AndreaAtzeni 3 106
(Simon Crisford) *led after 100yds: jnd after 1f: drvn along in front over 2f out: hdd 175yds out: sn rdn along but no ex: rdn out* **15/1**

3 *1* **Epistrophy (FR)**[26] 3-9-0 0 .... FabriceVeron 7 104
(S Kobayashi, France) *jnd ldr after 1f: drvn along in 2nd 2f out: rdn along and dropped to 3rd 1f out: kpt on wl fnl f: rdn out* **47/1**

4 *nk* **Cala Tarida**[172] 8562 3-9-0 0 .... GregoryBenoist 4 103+
(F Rossi, France) *disp ld 100yds: settled in rr of midfield: shkn up and hdwy fr 1 1/2f out: nvr rching ldrs* **9/1**

5 *snk* **Rocques (FR)**[189] 8024 3-9-0 0 .... Pierre-CharlesBoudot 8 103+
(F Chappet, France) *hld up in last: angled out and shkn up 1f out: styd on to go 5th cl home: rdn out* **9/1**

6 *shd* **Tifosa (IRE)**[28] 1242 3-9-0 0 .... MaximeGuyon 5 103
(Mme Pia Brandt, France) *towards rr: drvn along 2f out: rdn 1f out: styd on but nvr on terms w ldrs* **42/10[2]**

7 *snk* **Montviette (FR)**[172] 8562 3-9-0 0 .... CristianDemuro 2 102
(J-C Rouget, France) *in rr of midfield: shkn up 2f out: kpt on same pce: rdn out* **9/1**

8 *2* **Sicilia**[31] 1199 3-9-0 0 .... OlivierPeslier 1 98
(C Laffon-Parias, France) *trckd ldrs on inner: asked for effrt 1 1/2f out: kpt on tl dropping away cl home* **26/5**

9 *3 ½* **Lily's Candle (FR)**[163] 8819 3-9-0 0 .... AurelienLemaitre 9 90
(F Head, France) *midfield on outer: effrt 2f out: outpcd and rdn in last 1f out: wl hld fnl f* **13/5[1]**

1m 38.39s (-0.01) **9 Ran SP% 119.0**
PARI-MUTUEL (all including 1 euro stake): WIN 5.70; PLACE 2.70, 5.20, 8.40; DF 27.30.

Owner Godolphin SNC **Bred** Godolphin **Trained** France

FOCUS

They went fairly steady early and finished in a bit of a heap, the time being 1.98sec slower than the Fontainebleau, but the winner has been rated a bit above the race average.

1796a (Foreign Racing) - See Raceform Interactive

1797a PRIX NOAILLES (GROUP 3) (3YO) (TURF) 1m 2f 110y

4:35 3-Y-0 £36,036 (£14,414; £10,810; £7,207; £3,603)

RPR

1 **Slalom (FR)**[158] 3-9-2 0 MaximeGuyon 8 107+
(A Fabre, France) *w.w in fnl pair: angled out and drvn along 2f out: qcknd wl 1f out: led 100yds out: drew clr under hands and heels* 31/10[2]

2 2 1/2 **Syrtis**[195] [7853] 3-9-2 0 MickaelBarzalona 7 102+
(A Fabre, France) *settled in fnl pair: shkn up 1 1/2f out: hdwy to ld 175yds out: hdd 100yds out: nt pce of wnr cl home* 5/2[1]

3 1 **Surrey Thunder (FR)**[19] [1347] 3-9-2 0 OisinMurphy 9 100+
(Joseph Tuite) *midfield: shkn up to chal 2f out: outpcd by front pair fnl f: kpt on wl for 3rd: rdn out* 37/10[3]

4 1 **Joe Francais (FR)**[28] [1243] 3-9-2 0 CristianDemuro 5 98
(J-C Rouget, France) *trckd ldrs: shkn up over 2f out: chal 1f out: outpcd fnl f: rdn out* 10/1

5 1/2 **Soft Light (FR)**[29] 3-9-2 0 ChristopheSoumillon 3 97
(J-C Rouget, France) *in rr of midfield: drvn along turning in and gd hdwy to ld over 1f out: hdd 175yds out: no ex and dropped away fnl f* 53/10

6 3/4 **Life's A Breeze (IRE)**[20] 3-9-2 0 (p) AntoineHamelin 6 96
(R Le Gal, France) *in rr of midfield: tk clsr order 2f out: shkn up over 1f out: kpt on same pce: rdn out* 44/1

7 12 **Thyme White (FR)**[29] 3-9-2 0 IoritzMendizabal 4 73
(B De Montzey, France) *settled in 2nd: led 3f out: effrt 2f out: hdd over 1f out: qckly dropped away* 15/1

8 dist **Lone Peak (FR)**[211] 3-9-2 0 AurelienLemaitre 2
(F Head, France) *led: hdd 3f out and qckly dropped to last: wl hld fnl 2f* 15/2

2m 10.88s (0.68) **8 Ran SP% 119.4**

PARI-MUTUEL (all including 1 euro stake): WIN 4.10; PLACE 1.40, 1.30, 1.50; DF 4.90.

Owner Wertheimer & Frere **Bred** Wertheimer & Frere **Trained** Chantilly, France

FOCUS

They finished fairly well bunched and the sixth limits the form somewhat

1798a-1811a (Foreign Racing) - See Raceform Interactive

1659

PONTEFRACT (L-H)

Monday, April 15

OFFICIAL GOING: Good to firm (good in places; 8.2)

Wind: Moderate half against Weather: Fine & dry

1812 FARMER COPLEYS GFF FARM-SHOP OF-THE-YEAR 2019 EBF NOVICE STKS 5f 3y

2:20 (2:20) (Class 5) 2-Y-O £3,881 (£1,155; £577; £288) Stalls Low

Form RPR

2 1 **Alminoor (IRE)**[13] [1499] 2-9-5 0 DaneO'Neill 3 83
(Mark Johnston) *qckly away: mde all: rdn clr over 1f out: kpt on strly* 4/9[1]

0 2 4 1/2 **Bendy Spirit (IRE)**[16] [1416] 2-9-5 0 PaulHanagan 5 67
(Richard Fahey) *trckd ldrs on inner: hdwy 2f out: swtchd rt and chsd wnr wl over 1f out: sn rdn and no imp* 9/1[3]

3 3 1 **Danny Ocean (IRE)**[10] [1556] 2-9-5 0 CliffordLee 7 63+
(K R Burke) *chsd ldng pair on outer: pushed along 1/2-way: rdn and sltly outpcd 2f out: kpt on u.p fnl f* 7/2[2]

4 1 1/4 **Amnaa** 2-9-0 0 ConnorBeasley 6 54+
(Adrian Nicholls) *cl up: pushed along 1/2-way: rdn 2f out: grad wknd appr fnl f* 66/1

5 3/4 **Vardon Flyer** 2-9-5 0 NathanEvans 1 56
(Michael Easterby) *dwlt and in rr tl styd on fnl 2f* 40/1

6 6 **The Mystery Wizard** 2-9-5 0 DavidAllan 2 34
(Tim Easterby) *dwlt: a in rr* 33/1

7 3/4 **Manolith** 2-9-5 0 DanielTudhope 4 32+
(David O'Meara) *trckd ldrs: pushed along 2f out: hdwy and green whn n.m.r over 1f out: stmbld sltly and lost action jst ins fnl f: sn eased (jockey said colt lost it's action inside the final furlong)* 20/1

1m 4.76s (0.86) **Going Correction** +0.15s/f (Good) **7 Ran SP% 113.1**

Speed ratings (Par 92): **99,91,90,88,87 77,76**

CSF £5.11 TOTE £1.30: £1.10, £3.50; EX 5.40 Trifecta £8.60.

Owner Hamdan Al Maktoum **Bred** Mrs P K O'Rourke **Trained** Middleham Moor, N Yorks

FOCUS

With the weather remaining dry, there had been extensive watering. 10mm applied on Thursday on the entire track, between 3mm and 5mm on Friday and between 2 and 4mm over the final mile on Sunday morning. Despite this the going was changed to good to firm just after midday, and some jockeys were calling it firm after the first. All race distances were as advertised. An ordinary looking novice but a useful winner who was very professional. The third has been rated to his debut effort.

1813 NAPOLEONS CASINO BRADFORD H'CAP 1m 6y

2:50 (2:50) (Class 4) (0-85,87) 4-Y-O+ £6,469 (£1,925; £962; £481; £300; £300) Stalls Low

Form RPR

3- 1 **Hortzadar**[294] 4-9-6 81 DavidNolan 4 100
(David O'Meara) *hld up: hdwy 3f out: sn trcking ldrs: effrt to chal wl over 1f out: rdn to ld appr fnl f: sn clr: comf* 12/1

60-0 2 8 **Courtside (FR)**[15] [1457] 4-9-3 78 DanielTudhope 8 79
(David O'Meara) *trckd ldr: hdwy 3f out: rdn along 2f out: drvn over 1f out: kpt on same pce* 4/1[2]

46-0 3 hd **Delph Crescent (IRE)**[15] [1461] 4-9-7 82 (p) PaulHanagan 5 83
(Richard Fahey) *trckd ldrs: effrt on outer over 2f out and sn rdn along: drvn over 1f out: kpt on same pce* 7/1

3-00 4 1/2 **Staplegrove (IRE)**[16] [1418] 4-8-10 71 ConnorBeasley 3 70
(Philip Kirby) *led: rdn clr over 2f out: hdd appr fnl f: sn drvn and kpt on same pce* 33/1

04-5 5 3/4 **Cote D'Azur**[15] [1461] 6-9-11 86 DavidAllan 10 84
(Les Eyre) *hld up in rr: hdwy over 2f out: rdn along to chse ldrs over 1f out: kpt on same pce fnl f* 11/2[3]

060- 6 nk **Ghayyar (IRE)**[175] [8476] 5-9-1 76 (t) RachelRichardson 9 73
(Tim Easterby) *in tch: effrt on outer to chse ldrs over 2f out: sn rdn along and no imp* 20/1

6121 7 shd **Space Bandit**[16] [1428] 4-9-5 87 MarkCrehan(7) 1 84
(Michael Appleby) *trckd ldr on inner: pushed along over 2f out: rdn wl over 1f out: sn drvn: n.m.r and one pce* 2/1[1]

40-0 8 1 1/4 **Dark Devil (IRE)**[16] [1418] 6-8-8 74 (p) ConnorMurtagh(5) 2 68
(Richard Fahey) *trckd ldrs: rdn along over 2f out: drvn wl over 1f out: grad wknd* 13/2

203- 9 13 **Whitehall**[212] [7274] 4-9-3 78 (p[1]) SilvestreDeSousa 7 42
(Geoffrey Harker) *s.i.s and lost 6 l s: bhd: hdwy to join field 5f out: pushed along over 2f out: sn rdn and wknd (jockey said gelding was slowly away)* 16/1

1m 45.05s (-0.85) **Going Correction** +0.15s/f (Good) **9 Ran SP% 115.8**

Speed ratings (Par 105): **110,102,101,101,100 100,100,98,85**

CSF £59.76 CT £368.89 TOTE £12.80: £3.20, £1.40, £2.20; EX 66.10 Trifecta £457.00.

Owner Akela Construction Ltd **Bred** The Aston House Stud **Trained** Upper Helmsley, N Yorks

FOCUS

An open-looking Class 4 mile handicap turned into a rout by a useful French import. The second has been rated in line with his reappearance.

1814 RIU HOTELS AND RESORTS H'CAP 5f 3y

3:20 (3:22) (Class 2) (0-100,98) 4-Y-O+ £15,562 (£4,660; £2,330; £1,165; £582; £292) Stalls Low

Form RPR

5-65 1 **Mokaatil**[53] [837] 4-8-8 85 PJMcDonald 7 91
(Ian Williams) *hld up: hdwy on outer 2f out: rdn over 1f out: drvn to chal ins fnl f: led on line* 10/1

50-0 2 nse **Pipers Note**[16] [1421] 9-9-2 93 JackGarritty 5 99
(Ruth Carr) *hld up: hdwy on inner 2f out: n.m.r and swtchd rt over 1f out: rdn to chal ins fnl f: drvn to take slt ld fnl 40yds: hdd on line* 20/1

2401 3 nk **Foolaad**[15] [1459] 8-9-7 98 (t) DaneO'Neill 2 103
(Roy Bowring) *trckd ldng pair on inner: hdwy 2f out: chal over 1f out: rdn to ld ins fnl f: drvn and hdd fnl 40yds: kpt on* 5/2[1]

112- 4 2 1/4 **Sandra's Secret (IRE)**[296] [4113] 6-9-6 97 DavidAllan 1 94
(Les Eyre) *led: rdn along and jnd over 1f out: drvn and hdd ins fnl f: grad wknd* 10/1

000- 5 1/2 **Powerallied (IRE)**[205] [7510] 6-8-10 87 PaulHanagan 8 82
(Richard Fahey) *t.k.h: hld up: hdwy 2f out: rdn over 1f out: kpt on fnl f* 6/1

260- 6 hd **War Whisper (IRE)**[185] [8167] 6-8-6 83 JoeFanning 3 77
(Paul Midgley) *hld up in rr: hdwy 2f out: rdn over 1f out: kpt on fnl f* 11/2[3]

0-61 7 1 **Poyle Vinnie**[11] [1547] 9-8-8 85 JamesSullivan 4 76
(Ruth Carr) *t.k.h: trckd ldrs: hdwy 2f out: rdn and n.m.r over 1f out: sltly hmpd ent fnl f: one pce after* 5/1[2]

640- 8 4 **Leo Minor (USA)**[144] [9206] 5-8-10 87 SilvestreDeSousa 9 63
(Robert Cowell) *in tch: hdwy on outer to join ldrs over 2f out: rdn along wl over 1f out: wknd fnl f* 5/1[2]

530- 9 1 **Kodiac Express (IRE)**[194] [7911] 4-8-2 79 oh2 CamHardie 6 52
(Mike Murphy) *cl up: rdn along 2f out: drvn and wknd over 1f out* 40/1

1m 3.53s (-0.37) **Going Correction** +0.15s/f (Good) **9 Ran SP% 117.0**

Speed ratings (Par 109): **108,107,107,103,103 102,101,94,93**

CSF £187.60 CT £658.12 TOTE £11.00: £2.20, £4.10, £1.30; EX 254.90 Trifecta £2604.70.

Owner Midtech **Bred** Biddestone Stud **Trained** Portway, Worcs

■ Stewards' Enquiry : Jack Garritty three-day ban; careless riding (Apr 29-30,May 1)

FOCUS

A fiercely competitive sprint with the favourite swooped on late. The third looks the best guide to the level, rated close to his winning form in this race last year.

1815 INTO THE SKY PONTEFRACT MARATHON H'CAP (ROUND 2 OF THE PONTEFRACT STAYERS CHAMPIONSHIP 2019) 2m 5f 139y

3:50 (3:50) (Class 5) (0-70,72) 4-Y-O+ £5,175 (£1,540; £769; £384; £300; £300) Stalls Low

Form RPR

253- 1 **Rubenesque (IRE)**[12] [8480] 7-9-7 66 (t) JasonHart 3 73
(Tristan Davidson) *cl up: led after 1f: rdn clr 2f out: kpt on wl towards fin* 6/4[1]

0211 2 2 1/4 **Tynecastle Park**[16] [1429] 6-9-1 65 DarraghKeenan(5) 1 69
(Robert Eddery) *led 1f: trckd ldrs: hdwy 4f out: rdn along over 2f out: drvn to chse wnr ins fnl f: kpt on* 11/4[2]

3635 3 4 1/2 **Galileo's Spear (FR)**[16] [1429] 6-9-2 61 LukeMorris 2 61
(Sir Mark Prescott Bt) *hld up in rr: hdwy over 5f out: rdn along 4f out: drvn to chse wnr over 1f out: kpt on same pce u.p fnl f* 9/2[3]

- 4 12 **Brandy James (GER)**[23] [4230] 4-9-5 67 DaneO'Neill 4 53
(Harry Whittington) *prom: trckd wnr after 4f: cl up over 7f out: pushed along 3f out: rdn over 2f out: sn drvn and wknd* 5/1

/6-4 5 19 **Primogeniture (IRE)**[61] [703] 8-9-13 72 (t) JoeFanning 6 44
(Martin Keighley) *hld up: a in rr: outpcd and bhd fr over 2f out* 33/1

-606 6 13 **Strictly Art (IRE)**[30] [1235] 6-8-11 63 JessicaCooley(7) 5 23
(Alan Bailey) *chsd ldrs: rdn along over 3f out: sn wknd (vet said gelding lost it's right fore shoe)* 16/1

5m 4.09s (6.09) **Going Correction** +0.15s/f (Good)

WFA 4 from 6yo+ 3lb **6 Ran SP% 110.3**

Speed ratings (Par 103): **94,93,91,87,80 75**

CSF £5.60 TOTE £2.70: £1.20, £1.90; EX 6.50 Trifecta £15.50.

Owner Ben Greenslade & David McCrone **Bred** John Joseph Murphy **Trained** Irthington, Cumbria

FOCUS

A small field for this extreme staying contest but the well-backed favourite saw it out well under a fine ride. The second has been rated to his recent Southwell form.

1816 THANKS AND HAPPY RETIREMENT RICHARD PEMBERTON FILLIES' NOVICE STKS 6f

4:20 (4:23) (Class 5) 3-Y-O+ £3,881 (£1,155; £577; £288) Stalls Low

Form RPR

1 **Melrose Way** 3-8-11 0 GrahamLee 14 67+
(James Bethell) *dwlt and towards rr: hdwy 2f out: rdn over 1f out: styd on wl fnl f to ld last stride* 20/1

3- 2 shd **Texting**[137] [9306] 3-8-11 0 SilvestreDeSousa 9 66
(Mohamed Moubarak) *midfield: hdwy over 2f out: swtchd rt to outer and rdn over 1f out: str run ins fnl f: slt ld briefly towards fin: hdd last stride* 10/3[2]

622- 3 nk **Sophia Maria**[230] [6660] 3-8-11 69 PJMcDonald 10 65
(James Bethell) *in tch: hdwy 2f out: chsd ldrs over 1f out: rdn to chal ins fnl f: led last 75yds: hdd towards fin* 9/2[3]

/6 4 3/4 **Northern Queen (IRE)**[18] [1389] 4-9-6 0 BenRobinson(3) 1 66
(Brian Ellison) *sn led: rdn along 2f out: drvn over 1f out: hdd last 75yds: kpt on same pce* 12/1

5 1/2 **Grey Berry (IRE)** 3-8-11 0 DavidAllan 7 61
(Tim Easterby) *towards rr: hdwy over 2f out: rdn along on inner to chse ldrs over 1f out: kpt on fnl f* 33/1

0- **6** ½ **Reasoned (IRE)**[115] 9670 3-8-11 0 LukeMorris 6 59
(James Eustace) *trckd ldrs: hdwy and cl up over 2f out: rdn to chal over 1f out: ev ch ent fnl f: sn drvn and kpt on same pce* **25/1**

523- **7** 1¾ **Collect Call (IRE)**[168] 8683 3-8-11 80 CliffordLee 5 54
(K R Burke) *trckd ldrs: hdwy and cl up 3f out: rdn along to chal 2f out: drvn over 1f out: wknd fnl f* **11/4**[1]

3-3 **8** 2½ **Dream Chick (IRE)**[83] 354 3-8-11 0 KevinStott 11 46
(Kevin Ryan) *trckd ldrs: effrt and cl up on outer over 2f out: rdn along wl over 1f out: drvn and hld whn n.m.r jst ins fnl f: one pce after* **6/1**

9 7 **Lyons Lane** 3-8-11 0 PaulMulrennan 3 23
(Michael Dods) *chsd ldrs on inner: rdn along over 2f out: sn wknd* **13/2**

00-0 **10** 1 **Kyllachy Princess**[20] 1346 3-8-4 39 LauraCoughlan(7) 12 20
(David Loughnane) *cl up on outer: rdn along over 2f out: sn wknd* **125/1**

0660 **11** 19 **High Anxiety**[17] 1402 5-9-9 41 TonyHamilton 8
(Andrew Crook) *cl up: rdn along 3f out: sn wknd* **100/1**

05 **12** ½ **Opera Kiss (IRE)**[16] 1427 3-8-6 0 FayeMcManoman(5) 2
(Lawrence Mullaney) *a in rr (trainer said filly had a breathing problem)* **100/1**

13 1¼ **The Thorny Rose** 3-8-11 0 TomEaves 13
(Michael Dods) *dwlt: a bhd* **33/1**

- **14** 22 **Anythingispossible** 3-8-11 0 (h[1]) JasonHart 4
(Ivan Furtado) *sn outpcd and bhd* **25/1**

1m 18.69s (1.59) **Going Correction** +0.15s/f (Good)
WFA 3 from 4yo+ 12lb **14** Ran SP% **124.3**
Speed ratings (Par 100): **95,94,94,93,92 92,89,86,77,75 50,49,48,18**
CSF £84.94 TOTE £29.30: £6.20, £1.70, £2.00; EX 155.10 Trifecta £633.00.
Owner David W Armstrong **Bred** Highfield Farm Llp **Trained** Middleham Moor, N Yorks

FOCUS
A potentially interesting 3yo+ fillies' novice with a surprise but deserved winner. The second and third have been rated close to form.

1817 GOLDEN HORSERACING CLUB IS WITH ROBERT STEWART H'CAP (DIV I) 5f 3y

4:50 (4:52) (Class 5) (0-70,71) 4-Y-O+

£3,881 (£1,155; £577; £300; £300; £300) **Stalls** Low

Form RPR

-412 **1** **Socialites Red**[11] 1553 6-8-10 64 (p) TheodoreLadd(5) 3 73
(Scott Dixon) *prom: cl up over 2f out: led wl over 1f out: rdn clr ent fnl f: sn edgd rt: kpt on wl* **3/1**[1]

150- **2** 1¼ **Kibaar**[178] 8383 7-8-11 60 JamesSullivan 1 64+
(Ruth Carr) *hld up in rr: hdwy and nt clr run wl over 1f out: effrt ent fnl f: sn rdn to chse wnr last 150yds: no imp towards fin* **11/1**

0050 **3** 1¾ **Highly Sprung (IRE)**[34] 1164 6-9-7 70 DavidAllan 7 68
(Les Eyre) *hld up towards rr: hdwy over 2f out: rdn along on outer to chse ldrs over 1f out: drvn and kpt on fnl f* **9/2**[3]

052- **4** ½ **One Boy (IRE)**[182] 8268 8-9-0 63 (b) GrahamLee 9 59
(Paul Midgley) *hld up in rr: hdwy on outer wl over 1f out: sn rdn: styd on wl fnl f* **20/1**

3-01 **5** 1 **Decision Maker (IRE)**[38] 1085 5-8-5 57 WilliamCox(3) 5 49
(Roy Bowring) *cl up: rdn along 2f out: ev ch tl drvn and wknd ent fnl f* **8/1**

45-0 **6** 1½ **Patrick (IRE)**[20] 1342 7-8-12 61 BarryMcHugh 6 48
(Paul Midgley) *chsd ldrs: rdn along 2f out: sn drvn and wknd over 1f out* **7/2**[2]

1216 **7** nk **Spirit Power**[34] 1162 4-9-3 66 JasonHart 2 52
(Eric Alston) *chsd ldrs on inner: hdwy 2f out: rdn over 1f out: wknd ins fnl f* **13/2**

U40- **8** 8 **Suitcase 'N' Taxi**[166] 8742 5-9-8 71 RachelRichardson 4 28
(Tim Easterby) *chsd ldrs: rdn along 2f out: sn wknd (jockey said gelding was restless in the stalls)* **9/1**

005- **9** 5 **King Crimson**[132] 9393 7-9-0 68 DarraghKeenan(5) 8 7
(John Butler) *racd wd: sn led: rdn along 2f out: sn hdd & wknd* **25/1**

1m 4.24s (0.34) **Going Correction** +0.15s/f (Good) **9** Ran SP% **116.8**
Speed ratings (Par 103): **103,101,98,97,95 93,92,80,72**
CSF £37.42 CT £149.13 TOTE £3.70: £1.50, £3.30, £1.50; EX 40.60 Trifecta £193.90.
Owner William A Robinson & Partners **Bred** Selwood, Hoskins & Trickledown **Trained** Babworth, Notts

FOCUS
A solid class 5 sprint won by an in-form mare. The winner has been rated close to form.

1818 GOLDEN HORSERACING CLUB IS WITH ROBERT STEWART H'CAP (DIV II) 5f 3y

5:20 (5:21) (Class 5) (0-70,70) 4-Y-O+

£3,881 (£1,155; £577; £300; £300; £300) **Stalls** Low

Form RPR

6-50 **1** **Johnny Cavagin**[83] 356 10-9-0 63 (w) GrahamLee 1 75
(Paul Midgley) *trckd ldrs: hdwy 2f out: chal over 1f out: rdn to ld ins fnl f: kpt on strly* **7/2**[2]

003- **2** 1¼ **Super Julius**[16] 1433 5-8-13 62 (p) JoeFanning 3 69
(S Donohoe, Ire) *led: pushed along over 2f out: rdn wl over 1f out: sn jnd: drvn and hdd ins fnl f: kpt on* **7/2**[2]

1003 **3** 1¾ **Deeds Not Words (IRE)**[38] 1082 8-9-5 68 RoystonFfrench 7 69
(Tracy Waggott) *hld up in rr: hdwy on wd outside wl over 1f out: sn rdn: styd on wl fnl f* **25/1**

00-2 **4** 1 **Foxtrot Knight**[13] 1507 7-9-2 65 JamesSullivan 2 62
(Ruth Carr) *dwlt and hld up in rr: hdwy and n.m.r wl over 1f out: rdn to chse ldrs ent fnl f: sn drvn and no imp* **7/4**[1]

430- **5** hd **Round The Island**[157] 8981 6-9-6 69 PhilDennis 5 66
(Richard Whitaker) *in tch: hdwy 2f out: rdn and edgd lft over 1f out: kpt on fnl f* **14/1**

-213 **6** 1½ **Twentysvnthlancers**[19] 1364 6-8-11 60 PaulMulrennan 9 51
(Paul Midgley) *in tch: hdwy to chse ldrs over 2f out: rdn wl over 1f out: wknd fnl f* **12/1**[3]

6-24 **7** 4½ **Dandilion (IRE)**[53] 823 6-8-8 57 (t) LukeMorris 4 32
(Alex Hales) *prom: rdn along 2f out: sn drvn and wknd* **12/1**[3]

46-4 **8** shd **Skyva**[88] 277 4-8-5 57 (b[1]) BenRobinson(3) 6 32
(Brian Ellison) *dwlt: a towards rr (jockey said gelding ran onto heels 1f out)* **12/1**[3]

020- **9** 1¼ **B Fifty Two (IRE)**[242] 6181 10-9-2 70 (tp) HarrisonShaw(5) 8 40
(Marjorie Fife) *prom: effrt over 2f out: sn chal: rdn and wknd over 1f out* **33/1**

1m 4.11s (0.21) **Going Correction** +0.15s/f (Good) **9** Ran SP% **117.3**
Speed ratings (Par 103): **104,102,99,97,97 94,87,87,85**
CSF £16.52 CT £266.52 TOTE £4.30: £1.70, £1.10, £5.90; EX 17.40 Trifecta £244.60.
Owner A Bell **Bred** A Bell **Trained** Westow, N Yorks

FOCUS
Second division of the class 5 sprint won decisively by a well-backed 10yo. The third has been rated in line with his recent form for this yard and close to last year's turf form.

1819 BECOME A RACEHORSE OWNER AT THEGOLDENHORSE.CO.UK H'CAP 1m 6y

5:50 (5:52) (Class 5) (0-70,72) 3-Y-O

£3,881 (£1,155; £577; £300; £300; £300) **Stalls** Low

Form RPR

043- **1** **Conundrum**[175] 8474 3-9-6 69 JackGarritty 13 75+
(Jedd O'Keeffe) *trckd ldrs: hdwy on outer over 2f out: chal over 1f out: rdn to ld ins fnl f: kpt on* **11/2**[3]

050- **2** ¾ **Gennaro (IRE)**[186] 8139 3-9-1 64 (t[1]) JasonHart 1 68
(Ivan Furtado) *led: rdn along 2f out: drvn over 1f out: hdd ins fnl f: sn drvn and edgd rt last 100yds: kpt on* **8/1**

-645 **3** 1¾ **Curfewed (IRE)**[7] 1645 3-9-6 69 CamHardie 2 69
(Tracy Waggott) *in tch on inner: hdwy 2f out: chsd ldrs and swtchd rt over 1f out: n.m.r and swtchd rt again ins fnl f: kpt on wl towards fin* **11/2**[3]

600- **4** 1¼ **George Mallory**[160] 8896 3-9-7 70 TomEaves 12 67
(Kevin Ryan) *trckd ldr: hdwy and cl up over 2f out: rdn wl over 1f out: drvn ent fnl f: kpt on same pce* **8/1**

606- **5** 5 **High Contrast**[138] 9283 3-9-2 65 (h[1]) PJMcDonald 4 51
(K R Burke) *chsd ldrs: rdn along over 2f out: drvn over 1f out: grad wknd* **7/2**[1]

620- **6** 3¾ **Diviner (IRE)**[168] 8691 3-9-9 72 JoeFanning 8 49
(Mark Johnston) *chsd ldrs: rdn along 2f out: grad wknd* **10/1**

555- **7** 2¼ **Seven For A Pound (USA)**[192] 7956 3-9-2 65 TonyHamilton 9 37
(Richard Fahey) *a towards rr* **5/1**[2]

050- **8** 3½ **Highwaygrey**[191] 7989 3-9-1 64 DuranFentiman 5 28
(Tim Easterby) *dwlt: a towards rr* **66/1**

060- **9** hd **SDH Dream Team**[178] 8374 3-8-10 59 DavidAllan 11 22
(Tim Easterby) *a towards rr* **16/1**

006- **10** 7 **Straitouttacompton**[173] 8549 3-9-7 70 (p) LukeMorris 6 17
(Denis Quinn) *a towards rr* **16/1**

01-6 **11** 6 **The Meter**[102] 32 3-9-8 71 DanielTudhope 7 4
(Mohamed Moubarak) *t.k.h: chsd ldrs: pushed along 3f out: sn rdn and wknd over 2f out* **25/1**

1m 47.04s (1.14) **Going Correction** +0.15s/f (Good) **11** Ran SP% **118.1**
Speed ratings (Par 98): **100,99,97,96,91 87,85,81,81,74 68**
CSF £49.34 CT £259.86 TOTE £6.00: £1.70, £3.00, £2.10; EX 53.70 Trifecta £365.80.
Owner Highbeck Racing 2 **Bred** Mr & Mrs A E Pakenham **Trained** Middleham Moor, N Yorks

FOCUS
Probably a few winners to come out of this 3yo handicap but one with experience took the honours. The third has been rated as running his best race since his stable debut in December.
T/Plt: £45.10 to a £1 stake. Pool: £62,551.66 - 1012.21 winning units T/Qpdt: £12.30 to a £1 stake. Pool: £6,612.33 - 396.67 winning units **Joe Rowntree**

1650 WINDSOR (R-H)

Monday, April 15

OFFICIAL GOING: Good (good to firm in places; 8.1)
Wind: Moderate, half against Weather: Fine

1820 SEAN LEAHY MEMORIAL H'CAP 6f 12y

2:00 (2:01) (Class 6) (0-60,60) 4-Y-O+

£3,105 (£924; £461; £300; £300; £300) **Stalls** Centre

Form RPR

360- **1** **Incentive**[180] 8315 5-9-7 60 (p) BenCurtis 4 68
(Stuart Kittow) *racd against nr side rail: w ldrs: rdn over 2f out: kpt on u.p to chal fnl f: led nr fin* **6/1**[2]

302- **2** hd **Trotter**[175] 8484 5-9-4 57 AdamKirby 14 64
(Stuart Kittow) *racd on outer: pushed along in rr bef 1/2-way: prog u.p over 2f out: narrow ld over 1f out: hdd and nt qckn nr fin* **4/1**[1]

301 **3** ½ **Brockey Rise (IRE)**[9] 1595 4-9-7 60 (b) OisinMurphy 13 66
(David Evans) *racd on outer: chsd ldrs: rdn to cl 2f out: chal fnl f: nt qckn last 75yds* **8/1**[3]

3036 **4** 1 **Storm Melody**[40] 1037 6-9-7 60 (p) CharlesBishop 10 63
(Ali Stronge) *s.i.s: wl in rr: rdn 2f out: prog over 1f out: styd on wl fnl f: nrst fin* **6/1**[2]

630- **5** ½ **Lily Of Year (FR)**[180] 8318 4-8-10 56 ScottMcCullagh(7) 1 57+
(Denis Coakley) *taken down early: dwlt: wl in rr: stl there whn swtchd lft over 1f out: fin wl last 150yds: nvr nrr* **12/1**

-140 **6** ½ **Mooroverthebridge**[61] 701 5-9-3 59 FinleyMarsh(3) 15 59
(Grace Harris) *w ldrs towards outer: stl upsides over 1f out: fdd ins fnl f* **10/1**

4042 **7** hd **Fantasy Justifier (IRE)**[47] 920 8-9-3 56 (p) RaulDaSilva 7 55
(Ronald Harris) *t.k.h: trckd ldrs: rdn and nt qckn over 1f out: kpt on same pce fnl f* **11/1**

-066 **8** ¾ **Hello Girl**[41] 1023 4-9-4 57 FrannyNorton 16 54
(Dean Ivory) *mde most towards outer to over 1f out: fdd fnl f* **12/1**

45-5 **9** 1¼ **Quick Recovery**[24] 1265 4-9-7 60 PatCosgrave 9 53+
(Jim Boyle) *chsd ldrs: squeezed out after 2f: dropped to rr and urged along: effrt over 1f out: no imp on ldrs fnl f* **10/1**

000- **10** ¾ **Firenze Rosa (IRE)**[175] 8482 4-9-2 55 KieranO'Neill 6 46
(John Bridger) *disp ld tl wknd over 1f out* **22/1**

000- **11** nse **Arnoul Of Metz**[201] 7673 4-8-12 56 DylanHogan(5) 8 47
(Henry Spiller) *t.k.h: hld up bhd ldrs: rdn and fnd nil over 1f out: fdd* **33/1**

244- **12** ½ **Vincenzo Coccotti (USA)**[212] 7270 7-9-4 60 (p) JoshuaBryan(3) 2 49
(Ken Cunningham-Brown) *trckd ldrs: rdn 2f out: fdd* **12/1**

260- **13** 4 **Golden Footsteps (IRE)**[68] 9507 4-9-1 57 TimClark(3) 12 34
(Mark Gillard) *s.i.s: hld up in last trio: rdn and no prog over 2f out* **100/1**

1043 **14** shd **Captain Ryan**[24] 1266 8-9-2 55 (p) TrevorWhelan 11 32
(Geoffrey Deacon) *chsd ldrs: rdn 2f out: wknd qckly over 1f out (jockey said gelding stopped quickly)* **25/1**

100- **15** 1¾ **Mister Freeze (IRE)**[357] 2027 5-9-2 55 (vt) LiamKeniry 5 27
(Patrick Chamings) *chsd ldrs to 1/2-way: sn lost pl: wl in rr over 1f out* **66/1**

1m 14.41s (2.31) **Going Correction** 0.0s/f (Good) **15** Ran SP% **122.9**
Speed ratings (Par 101): **84,83,83,81,81 80,80,79,77,76 76,75,70,70,67**
CSF £29.29 CT £204.59 TOTE £7.50: £2.30, £2.10, £2.20; EX 43.80 Trifecta £340.50.
Owner Stuart Kittow **Bred** The Hon Mrs R Pease **Trained** Blackborough, Devon

FOCUS
Ben Curtis described the ground as being "on the quicker side but with a good covering of grass." A one-two for Stuart Kittow in this moderate sprint. Straightforward form, with the winner rated to her mark.

1821 EBF FILLIES' NOVICE AUCTION STKS (PLUS 10 RACE) 5f 21y
2:30 (2:37) (Class 5) 2-Y-O £3,752 (£1,116; £557; £278) Stalls Centre

Form RPR

1 **Lambeth Walk** 2-8-13 0 OisinMurphy 10 82+
(Archie Watson) *racd on outer: led 2f: pressed ldr: shkn up to ld again over 1f out: styd on wl* 4/5[1]

2 2 1/4 **Dr Simpson (FR)** 2-8-13 0 RichardKingscote 1 74+
(Tom Dascombe) *dwlt: racd against nr side rail: w ldrs: led after 2f: edgd lft and hdd over 1f out: kpt on one pce fnl f* 11/4[2]

3 1 1/4 **Maybellene (IRE)** 2-8-11 0 HarryBentley 12 67
(George Scott) *racd on outer: chsd ldrs: prog 2f out: shkn up to take 3rd fnl f: no ch w wnr* 25/1

4 1 1/4 **Dancing Leopard (IRE)** 2-8-11 0 BenCurtis 14 63+
(K R Burke) *difficult to load: dwlt: wl in rr on outer: prog over 1f out: kpt on same pce fnl f* 33/1

5 shd **Brazen Safa** 2-8-13 0 HayleyTurner 11 65
(Michael Bell) *chsd ldrs on outer: shkn up wl over 1f out: outpcd after* 12/1[3]

6 1 **Dreamy Rascal (IRE)** 2-8-12 0 TomMarquand 8 60+
(Richard Hannon) *t.k.h: in tch but rn green: hanging whn shkn up 2f out: kpt on same pce after* 14/1

7 nse **Crime Of Passion (IRE)** 2-9-0 0 NicolaCurrie 7 62
(Jamie Osborne) *trckd ldrs gng strly: shkn up over 1f out: wknd fnl f* 20/1

8 1 3/4 **Amber Road (IRE)** 2-8-11 0 SeanLevey 9 52
(Richard Hannon) *difficult to load: dwlt: wl in rr: pushed along 2f out: nvr in it but kpt on fnl f* 20/1

9 nk **Trouser The Cash (IRE)** 2-8-11 0 GabrieleMalune(3) 3 54+
(Amy Murphy) *pressed ldng pair tl wknd over 1f out* 66/1

0 10 1 1/2 **Little Devil**[12] 1513 2-8-10 0 (p[1]) KieranO'Neill 13 45
(Bill Turner) *dwlt: in tch tl wknd over 1f out* 100/1

11 1 3/4 **Daddies Diva** 2-8-10 0 RobHornby 6 39
(Rod Millman) *nvr bttr than midfield: rdn 2f out: wknd over 1f out* 66/1

12 2 1/4 **Whispering Leaves (IRE)** 2-8-12 0 HollieDoyle 2 33
(Clive Cox) *a in rr: nvr a factor* 16/1

13 1/2 **Port Noir** 2-8-5 0 RhiainIngram(5) 5 29
(Paul George) *dwlt: a in rr: nvr a factor* 66/1

14 2 1/4 **Twice As Likely** 2-8-11 0 ShaneKelly 4 22
(Richard Hughes) *s.s: ct up at bk of field over 3f out: no prog 2f out: wknd (jockey said filly was slowly away)* 66/1

1m 1.77s (1.67) **Going Correction** 0.0s/f (Good) 14 Ran SP% 125.7
Speed ratings (Par 89): **86,82,80,78,78 76,76,73,73,70 68,64,63,60**
CSF £2.73 TOTE £1.70: £1.10, £1.50, £7.70; EX 4.50 Trifecta £56.10.
Owner Blackbriar Racing **Bred** The Kathryn Stud **Trained** Upper Lambourn, W Berks

FOCUS
The two who dominated the market came to the fore in this ordinary novice. It's hard to rate the race higher.

1822 MPM FLOORING H'CAP 5f 21y
3:00 (3:03) (Class 4) (0-85,87) 4-Y-O+ £5,530 (£1,645; £822; £411; £300; £300) Stalls Centre

Form RPR

-146 1 **Bellevarde (IRE)**[9] 1597 5-8-10 73 HollieDoyle 8 81
(Richard Price) *w ldr: rdn 2f out: narrow ld ins fnl f: hld on wl* 25/1

060- 2 nk **The Daley Express (IRE)**[183] 8235 5-9-7 84 FrannyNorton 9 91+
(Ronald Harris) *hld up in rr: prog 2f out: swtchd lft over 1f out: r.o to press wnr last 75yds: jst hld* 7/1

00-1 3 nk **Puds**[18] 1382 4-9-7 84 ShaneKelly 7 90
(Richard Hughes) *mde most and racd against nr side rail: narrowly hdd ins fnl f: no ex nr fin* 7/1

2422 4 1 1/4 **Enthaar**[19] 1357 4-8-11 74 (t) OisinMurphy 12 75+
(Stuart Williams) *racd on outer: nt on terms w ldrs: rdn to cl 2f out: ch 1f out: one pce after* 4/1[1]

6321 5 nk **King Robert**[31] 1211 6-9-1 78 DavidEgan 6 78
(Charlie Wallis) *hld up in midfield: prog to press ldrs over 1f out: one pce ins fnl f* 9/2[2]

06-0 6 1/2 **Peggie Sue**[17] 1394 4-8-7 70 oh1 NicolaCurrie 4 68
(Adam West) *hld up in rr: stl gng wl 2f out: pushed along whn nt clr run jst ins fnl f: r.o last 100yds: nrst fin (jockey said filly was denied a clear run approaching the final 110yds)* 50/1

0340 7 1/2 **Smokey Lane (IRE)**[19] 1357 5-8-5 75 GinaMangan(7) 1 72
(David Evans) *sltly s.i.s: hld up in rr and racd against nr side rail: shkn up and n.m.r over 1f out: nvr any ch but styd on last 100yds* 16/1

200- 8 hd **Han Solo Berger (IRE)**[194] 7900 4-8-11 74 GeorgeWood 2 70
(Chris Wall) *chsd ldrs: rdn 2f out: nt qckn over 1f out: one pce after* 12/1

04-6 9 shd **Big Lachie**[13] 1496 5-8-13 76 RobertHavlin 10 73+
(Mark Loughnane) *hld up in last: prog 2f out: pushed along whn impeded over 1f out: kpt on fnl f but no ch* 10/1

3011 10 shd **Miracle Works**[20] 1342 4-9-2 79 TomMarquand 5 74
(Robert Cowell) *chsd ldrs: rdn 2f out: fdd fnl f* 12/1

32/4 11 1 **Fair Cop**[38] 1082 5-8-12 75 RobHornby 3 67
(Andrew Balding) *chsd ldrs 3f: steadily fdd* 5/1[3]

306- 12 2 1/4 **Harry Beau**[128] 9462 5-8-8 71 (v) JohnFahy 11 55
(David Evans) *racd on outer: dropped to rr over 3f out: nvr on terms after* 33/1

530- 13 4 **Pettochside**[171] 8612 10-9-10 87 JosephineGordon 13 56
(John Bridger) *taken steadily to post: racd on outer: nvr on terms w ldrs: wknd over 1f out* 33/1

1m 0.65s (0.55) **Going Correction** 0.0s/f (Good) 13 Ran SP% 121.9
Speed ratings (Par 105): **95,94,94,92,91 90,89,89,89,89 87,84,77**
CSF £190.93 CT £1386.39 TOTE £29.60: £5.50, £2.40, £2.50; EX 206.50 Trifecta £2118.40.
Owner Barry Veasey **Bred** Tally-Ho Stud **Trained** Ullingswick, H'fords
■ Stewards' Enquiry : Franny Norton caution; careless riding

FOCUS
The field finished pretty well bunched in what was a fair sprint. It's been rated around the winner and third.

1823 HORSE GUARDS GIN FESTIVAL 8TH JULY H'CAP 1m 2f
3:30 (3:30) (Class 4) (0-85,85) 3-Y-O £5,530 (£1,645; £822; £411; £300; £300) Stalls Low

Form RPR

614- 1 **Korcho**[171] 8590 3-8-12 76 CharlieBennett 1 84
(Hughie Morrison) *trckd ldrs: rdn jst over 2f out: no imp tl drvn between rivals to ld last 75yds: readily* 15/2

1331 2 1/2 **Albert Finney**[17] 1396 3-9-2 80 RobertHavlin 3 87
(John Gosden) *led: rdn 2f out: edgd lft fnl f: hdd and outpcd last 75yds* 4/1[3]

-012 3 2 1/4 **Little Rock (IRE)**[24] 1264 3-8-13 77 ShaneKelly 8 79
(Richard Hughes) *pressed ldr: pushed along and hanging lft 3f out: nt qckn and hld jst over 1f out: one pce and lost 2nd ins fnl f* 5/1

343- 4 1 3/4 **Gentle Look**[179] 8343 3-9-0 78 PatCosgrave 4 77
(Saeed bin Suroor) *trckd ldrs: rdn over 2f out: tried to chal over 1f out but nt qckn: fdd fnl f* 3/1[1]

661- 5 2 1/4 **The Pink'n**[183] 8233 3-9-1 79 RobHornby 7 73
(Seamus Mullins) *dwlt: hld up in last: rdn over 2f out: no great prog over 1f out and btn after* 25/1

13-2 6 5 **Fields Of Athenry (USA)**[23] 1293 3-9-6 84 RyanMoore 5 68
(James Tate) *t.k.h: hld up in 5th: shkn up 3f out: fnd little and btn 2f out: wknd* 10/3[2]

646- 7 2 1/4 **Greeley (IRE)**[171] 8590 3-9-0 78 OisinMurphy 6 58
(Rod Millman) *hld up in 6th: pushed along wl over 3f out: no prog over 2f out: sn wknd* 13/2

2m 7.95s (-1.05) **Going Correction** 0.0s/f (Good) 7 Ran SP% 113.7
Speed ratings (Par 100): **104,103,101,100,98 94,92**
CSF £36.84 CT £164.65 TOTE £8.20: £3.30, £2.80; EX 35.70 Trifecta £276.10.
Owner M Kerr-Dineen, M Hughes & W Eason **Bred** Jeremy Green And Sons **Trained** East Ilsley, Berks

FOCUS
A fair 3yo handicap that was run at a stop-start gallop and it paid to race handily. The third and fourth have been rated close to form.

1824 FOLLOW AT THE RACES ON TWITTER NOVICE STKS 1m 2f
4:00 (4:01) (Class 5) 3-Y-O £3,752 (£1,116; £557; £278) Stalls Low

Form RPR

2 1 **Telecaster**[16] 1417 3-9-2 0 OisinMurphy 8 101+
(Hughie Morrison) *led after 2f: mde rest: pushed along and drew rt away fr 2f out: impressive* 10/11[1]

2- 2 9 **Deal A Dollar**[124] 9500 3-9-2 0 RyanMoore 5 83
(Sir Michael Stoute) *chsd ldrs in 6th: pushed along 3f out: prog 2f out: tk 2nd fnl f and kpt on but no ch w wnr* 7/4[2]

3 1/2 **Future Investment** 3-9-2 0 HarryBentley 9 82
(Ralph Beckett) *chsd ldng trio: shkn up wl over 2f out: effrt to dispute 2nd fnl f: kpt on but no ch w wnr* 40/1

30- 4 3 **Navigate By Stars (IRE)**[205] 7539 3-8-11 0 RichardKingscote 11 71+
(Tom Dascombe) *hld up in 8th: shkn up wl over 2f out: styd on after to take 4th nr fin* 33/1

41- 5 nk **Ginistrelli (IRE)**[173] 8552 3-9-9 0 WilliamBuick 3 82
(Ed Walker) *led 2f: chsd wnr: lft bhd 2f out: lost 2nd and wknd fnl f* 8/1[3]

5- 6 4 **Suakin (IRE)**[163] 8832 3-8-11 0 RobertHavlin 1 62+
(John Gosden) *chsd ldrs in 5th: looked to be hanging lft bnd over 5f out: nudged along and no prog fnl 2f: nt disgracd* 14/1

-50 7 1 1/4 **Thinque Tank**[13] 1495 3-9-2 0 LiamKeniry 6 65+
(Charlie Longsdon) *hld up in 7th: nudged along 2f out: stuck bhd wkng rival over 1f out: no prog after: likely to do bttr* 100/1

21 8 2 1/4 **Ragnar**[34] 1165 3-9-9 0 CallumShepherd 4 67
(Daniele Camuffo) *chsd ldng pair tl wknd 2f out* 20/1

9 1 3/4 **Video Diva (IRE)** 3-8-11 0 GeorgeWood 14 52
(James Fanshawe) *hld up in 11th and wl off the pce: pushed along and passed two rivals 2f out: nvr a factor* 100/1

10 5 **Australis (IRE)** 3-9-2 0 DavidEgan 12 47
(Roger Varian) *dwlt: mostly in last pair: wl bhd 4f out: picked up 2f out and passed a few rivals after* 33/1

00- 11 nk **Bader**[189] 8058 3-9-2 0 SeanLevey 10 46
(Richard Hannon) *nvr bttr than disputing 9th: shkn up 3f out: no prog* 100/1

12 2 1/4 **Gustave Aitch (FR)** 3-9-2 0 ShaneKelly 7 42
(Sophie Leech) *nvr bttr than disputing 9th: shkn up 3f out: no prog and wknd over 1f out* 100/1

13 2 1/2 **Spirit Of Nicobar** 3-8-11 0 RobHornby 16 32
(Andrew Balding) *slowly away: a in last quintet and wl bhd* 50/1

14 10 **Fyodor** 3-9-2 0 KieranO'Neill 13 17
(Seamus Mullins) *dwlt: a in last trio and wl bhd: t.o* 150/1

66 15 16 **Matilda Bay (IRE)**[13] 1509 3-8-11 0 NicolaCurrie 2
(Jamie Osborne) *dwlt: a in last quintet and wl bhd: t.o* 100/1

0-0 16 9 **Poet Pete (IRE)**[89] 251 3-9-2 0 FergusSweeney 15
(Mark Usher) *a in last quintet and bhd: t.o* 100/1

2m 6.87s (-2.13) **Going Correction** 0.0s/f (Good) 16 Ran SP% 128.2
Speed ratings (Par 98): **108,100,100,98,97 94,93,91,90,86 86,84,82,74,61 54**
CSF £2.58 TOTE £1.80: £1.10, £1.10, £12.80; EX 3.40 Trifecta £62.00.
Owner Castle Down Racing **Bred** Meon Valley Stud **Trained** East Ilsley, Berks

FOCUS
A useful novice that had looked a match, but any potential duel between the two market leaders failed to materialise with the odds-on favourite running out a most impressive winner. This is a race that should produce plenty of decent winners. The second has been rated a bit below his debut figure, with the fourth and fifth close to their marks.

1825 DOM & GERI PERSONALISED WRAP H'CAP 1m 31y
4:30 (4:30) (Class 6) (0-65,65) 3-Y-O £3,105 (£924; £461; £300; £300; £300) Stalls Low

Form RPR

2450 1 **Wall Of Sapphire (IRE)**[19] 1358 3-8-12 65 GeorgiaDobie(7) 8 68
(Hugo Palmer) *hld up in midfield: prog on outer jst over 2f out: clsd on ldrs over 1f out: rdn to ld ins fnl f: kpt on wl* 13/2[2]

-254 2 hd **Redemptive**[24] 1264 3-9-4 64 HollieDoyle 10 67
(David Elsworth) *trckd ldrs: clsd to chal over 1f out: led briefly jst ins fnl f: kpt on but jst hld fnl 50yds* 7/1[3]

050- **3** ½ **Poet's Magic**[170] 8643 3-9-5 **65** RobHornby 1 66
(Jonathan Portman) *trckd ldng pair: rdn to chal over 1f out: upsides jst ins fnl f: nt qckn* **9/1**

0-60 **4** 1½ **Monsieur Piquer (FR)**[4] 1720 3-9-3 **63** (v[1]) BenCurtis 12 61
(K R Burke) *awkward s: t.k.h: hld up in rr: stl gng strly in rr over 2f out: gd prog to chse ldrs jst over 1f out: sn rdn and nt qckn* **7/1**[3]

544- **5** 2¼ **Shifting Gold (IRE)**[129] 9443 3-9-5 **65** OisinMurphy 6 58
(William Knight) *led: racd against nr side rail: hdd & wknd jst ins fnl f* **10/1**

6-55 **6** 1¼ **Lucky Lou (IRE)**[37] 1094 3-9-2 **62** DavidEgan 7 52
(Ken Cunningham-Brown) *t.k.h: trckd ldng pair: rdn 2f out: fnd nil and wknd over 1f out* **12/1**

664- **7** ½ **Sukalia**[230] 6653 3-9-4 **64** AdamKirby 14 53+
(Alan King) *hld up in rr: taken wd 3f out: rdn and no real prog over 2f out* **12/1**

0-35 **8** hd **Bug Boy (IRE)**[33] 1174 3-8-11 **62** (p) RhiainIngram(5) 11 51
(Paul George) *slowly away: hld up in last pair: taken to outer 3f out: sn rdn and no prog* **8/1**

00-1 **9** 1¼ **Run After Genesis (IRE)**[35] 1140 3-9-4 **64** RossaRyan 5 50
(Brett Johnson) *chsd ldrs but racd rather awkwardly: rdn over 2f out: no rspnse and wknd over 1f out (jockey said colt ran green)* **4/1**[1]

05-0 **10** ½ **Antidote (IRE)**[16] 1423 3-9-5 **65** ShaneKelly 9 50
(Richard Hughes) *pressed ldr to over 1f out: wknd qckly* **16/1**

000- **11** ½ **Sherella**[117] 9603 3-9-2 **62** AlistairRawlinson 2 46
(J R Jenkins) *hld up in rr: shkn up and no prog over 2f out* **50/1**

-040 **12** hd **Moonlit Sea**[33] 1173 3-9-1 **64** PaddyBradley(3) 4 48
(Pat Phelan) *stdd s: hld up in rr: detached in last 3f out: nvr in it but kpt on fnl f* **20/1**

036- **13** 3 **Summa Force (IRE)**[221] 6980 3-9-3 **63** SeanLevey 13 40
(Richard Hannon) *in tch in midfield: urged along wl over 3f out: wknd over 2f out* **14/1**

1m 44.76s (0.26) **Going Correction** 0.0s/f (Good) **13** Ran SP% **123.2**
Speed ratings (Par 96): **98,97,97,95,93 92,91,91,90,89 89,89,86**
CSF £53.28 CT £434.94 TOTE £7.50: £2.60, £2.20, £3.10; EX 56.20 Trifecta £474.50.
Owner Aziz Kheir **Bred** Charlie Brooks **Trained** Newmarket, Suffolk

FOCUS
Modest 3yo form. The race could be a shade better than rated.

1826 SKY SPORTS RACING VIRGIN 535 H'CAP — 1m 3f 99y
5:00 (5:01) (Class 6) (0-65,65) 4-Y-O+
£3,105 (£924; £461; £300; £300; £300) **Stalls** Low

Form RPR

113- **1** **Kirkland Forever**[179] 8338 5-8-12 **63** GeorgiaDobie(7) 7 71+
(Eve Johnson Houghton) *hld up towards rr: prog on wd outside 3f out: shkn up to ld wl over 1f out: kpt on steadily and in command fnl f* **8/1**

424- **2** 1¾ **Broad Appeal**[161] 8886 5-8-9 **60** TylerSaunders(7) 6 65+
(Jonathan Portman) *cl up: squeezed through on inner to ld over 2f out: hdd wl over 1f out: kpt on same pce after* **6/1**[3]

-030 **3** shd **Mobham (IRE)**[41] 1022 4-9-7 **65** AlistairRawlinson 15 70
(J R Jenkins) *hld up in last pair: prog on outer over 2f out: clsd on ldrs 1f out: kpt on same pce fnl f* **33/1**

-643 **4** 3 **Famous Dynasty (IRE)**[19] 1363 5-9-4 **62** RobHornby 10 62
(Michael Blanshard) *hld up towards rr: stl gng strly whn nt clr run over 2f out: prog and swtchd rt over 1f out: styd on but nt rch ldrs* **16/1**

25-0 **5** nk **Ascot Day (FR)**[15] 1463 5-9-5 **63** (p) RobertHavlin 14 63+
(Bernard Llewellyn) *chsd ldrs: drvn to chal 2f out: nt qckn wl over 1f out: fdd* **15/2**

0-0 **6** 2¾ **Ace Combat**[23] 1292 4-9-0 **65** ScottMcCullagh(7) 13 60
(Michael Madgwick) *chsd ldrs: rdn wl over 2f out: no prog and btn u.p over 1f out* **25/1**

0-63 **7** 1 **Vanity Vanity (USA)**[52] 859 4-9-2 **60** OisinMurphy 2 54
(Denis Coakley) *hld up in rr: urged along 3f out: kpt on against nr side rail fnl 2f but nvr a threat* **8/1**

2436 **8** 1 **Mood For Mischief**[13] 1497 4-9-2 **60** (p) LiamKeniry 9 52
(Ed Walker) *chsd ldrs: rdn over 3f out: lost pl u.p 2f out* **14/1**

2-53 **9** 1¾ **Sauchiehall Street (IRE)**[23] 1292 4-9-4 **62** AdamKirby 5 51
(Noel Williams) *trckd ldrs: lost pl after 5f and in midfield: effrt whn nt clr run over 2f out: no ch after* **5/1**[2]

00-5 **10** 3 **Zenith One (IRE)**[90] 246 4-9-4 **62** (t w) TomQueally 8 47
(Seamus Durack) *dwlt: hld up in last pair: rdn over 2f out: racd awkwardly and no real prog* **12/1**

66-1 **11** 2½ **Amaretto**[23] 1297 4-9-1 **59** (v) CharlieBennett 16 40
(Jim Boyle) *racd keenly: trckd ldng pair: chal gng strly over 3f out: wknd tamely over 2f out* **9/2**[1]

004- **12** 6 **The Secrets Out**[209] 7388 5-9-4 **62** SeanLevey 1 33
(Luke Dace) *trckd ldr: led 7f out: hdd & wknd qckly over 2f out* **10/1**

600- **13** ½ **Tuscan Pearl**[151] 9075 4-9-2 **60** JasonWatson 12 30
(William Knight) *hld up in rr: rdn and no prog 3f out: no ch after* **100/1**

00-0 **14** 18 **Boffo (IRE)**[19] 1365 4-9-2 **60** (v[1]) DavidEgan 3
(Ian Williams) *pushed up to ld: hdd 7f out: wknd qckly over 3f out: t.o* **33/1**

2m 27.06s (-2.64) **Going Correction** 0.0s/f (Good) **14** Ran SP% **123.2**
Speed ratings (Par 101): **109,107,107,105,105 103,102,101,100,98 96,92,91,78**
CSF £55.33 CT £1535.69 TOTE £8.00: £3.10, £2.70, £10.30; EX 69.90 Trifecta £2386.50.
Owner Mrs M Fairbairn & P Dean **Bred** Mrs M Fairbairn **Trained** Blewbury, Oxon

FOCUS
Fairly lowly form, but it was run at a good gallop and won by a progressive type.
T/Jkpt: Not Won. T/Plt: £167.20 to a £1 stake. Pool: £91,283.96 - 398.33 winning units T/Qpdt: £58.00 to a £1 stake. Pool: £8,558.55 - 109.12 winning units **Jonathan Neesom**

1706 MAISONS-LAFFITTE (R-H)
Monday, April 15

OFFICIAL GOING: Turf: good to soft

1827a PRIX MINCIO (CONDITIONS) (4YO+) (TURF) — 1m
2:35 4-Y-O+
£12,612 (£4,792; £3,531; £2,018; £1,009; £756)

RPR

1 **Buthela (FR)**[562] 7640 5-8-11 0 VincentCheminaud 5 91
(A Fabre, France) **11/10**[1]

2 nse **Sea Prose (FR)**[34] 4-8-8 0 AurelienLemaitre 3 87
(F Head, France) **12/5**[2]

3 1½ **Walec**[11] 7-8-10 0 JeremieMonteiro(8) 4 94
(N Caulley, France) **16/1**

4 nk **Fulminato (GER)**[194] 7929 5-8-11 0 TheoBachelot 2 86
(Dr A Bolte, Germany) **74/1**

5 ½ **Delta River**[20] 1346 4-8-8 0 MlleCoraliePacaut(3) 6 85
(Jo Hughes, France) *sn front rnk: led: urged along 2f out to hold advantage: rdn and hdd over 1f out: wknd ins fnl f* **38/1**

6 1¼ **Vilaro (FR)**[8] 6-9-2 0 Pierre-CharlesBoudot 9 87
(D Smaga, France) **54/10**[3]

7 nse **La Canche (FR)**[151] 9091 4-8-13 0 EddyHardouin 8 84
(Carina Fey, France) **15/1**

8 2 **Park Bloom (IRE)**[243] 6168 4-8-8 0 AlexisBadel 7 75
(H-F Devin, France) **15/1**

9 5½ **Caffe Macchiato (IRE)**[324] 3122 4-8-11 0 MaximeGuyon 1 65
(Mme Pia Brandt, France) **17/1**

1m 37.54s (-4.76) **9** Ran SP% **120.5**
PARI-MUTUEL (all including 1 euro stake): WIN 2.10; PLACE 1.20, 1.30, 2.10; DF 3.10.
Owner Al Shaqab Racing **Bred** Ecurie Des Monceaux **Trained** Chantilly, France

NEWMARKET (R-H)
Tuesday, April 16

OFFICIAL GOING: Good to firm (good in places; watered; 8.3)
Wind: Light, against Weather: Light cloud

1828 BET365 EUROPEAN BREEDERS' FUND FILLIES' MAIDEN STKS (PLUS 10 RACE) (DIV I) — 1m
1:15 (1:17) (Class 4) 3-Y-O
£6,469 (£1,925; £962; £481) **Stalls** High

Form RPR

23- **1** **Maqsad (FR)**[175] 8511 3-9-0 0 JimCrowley 1 96
(William Haggas) *has done wl; mde all: wnt clr w runner-up ent fnl 2f: rdn and sustained duel w runner-up fr over 1f out: narrow advantage wl ins fnl f: styd on* **6/4**[1]

3- **2** shd **Twist 'N' Shake**[255] 5749 3-9-0 0 FrankieDettori 9 95
(John Gosden) *compact; trckd ldrs tl clsd to trck wnr ent fnl 2f: sn clr w wnr and chalng: rdn and sustained duel fr over 1f out: styd on wl but jst hld towards fin* **2/1**[2]

6- **3** 9 **Artistic Streak**[164] 8832 3-9-0 0 RichardKingscote 10 75
(Tom Dascombe) *hld up in tch in midfield: effrt over 2f out: sn outpcd by ldng pair: wnt modest 3rd 1f out: no imp* **14/1**

4 1¼ **Venusta (IRE)** 3-9-0 0 SilvestreDeSousa 2 72
(Mick Channon) *leggy; hld up in last trio: effrt and swtchd rt 2f out: no ch w ldrs but kpt on steadily to go modest 4th ins fnl f* **33/1**

04- **5** ¾ **Inclyne**[186] 8150 3-9-0 0 OisinMurphy 6 70
(Andrew Balding) *athletic; chsd ldrs tl rdn and clsd to press wnr 3f out tl over 2f out: sn outpcd and btn whn drifted rt over 1f out: wknd ins fnl f (jockey said filly became unbalanced in dip)* **6/1**[3]

6 4 **Specialise** 3-9-0 0 AndreaAtzeni 4 61
(Roger Varian) *str; bit bakward; hld up in tch in midfield: shkn up 1/2-way: outpcd over 2f out: wl btn over 1f out* **25/1**

30- **7** 2¾ **Forty Four Sunsets (FR)**[109] 9730 3-9-0 0 TomMarquand 7 54
(Richard Hannon) *str; wnt lft s: hld up in midfield: rdn over 2f out: sn struggling and wl btn over 1f out* **100/1**

03- **8** hd **Beguiling Charm (IRE)**[145] 9205 3-9-0 0 GeraldMosse 8 54
(Ed Walker) *stdd s: hld up in last trio: effrt and outpcd over 2f out: wl btn over 1f out* **33/1**

2- **9** nk **Stagehand**[174] 8539 3-9-0 0 RyanMoore 3 53
(Charles Hills) *athletic; looked wl; awkward leaving stalls: sn rcvrd and chsd wnr: rdn over 3f out: lost pl 3f out and sn struggling: wknd over 1f out* **10/1**

10 1¼ **Tereshkova** 3-9-0 0 (h[1]) HayleyTurner 5 50
(Michael Bell) *workmanlike; stdd s: t.k.h: hld up in rr: effrt over 2f out: sn wl btn* **100/1**

1m 39.27s (0.87) **Going Correction** +0.125s/f (Good) **10** Ran SP% **115.1**
Speed ratings (Par 97): **100,99,90,89,88 84,82,81,81,80**
CSF £4.34 TOTE £2.40: £1.20, £1.20, £2.60; EX 6.00 Trifecta £37.10.
Owner Hamdan Al Maktoum **Bred** Dayton Investments Limited **Trained** Newmarket, Suffolk

FOCUS
Far side course. Stalls: All races stands' side. The watered ground was given as good to firm, good in places (Going Stick 8.3). The first two came well clear and this looks like form to rate positively. The level is a bit fluid.

1829 WEATHERBYS TBA H'CAP — 6f
1:50 (1:52) (Class 2) (0-100,97) 4-Y-O+ £16,172 (£4,812; £2,405; £1,202) **Stalls** High

Form RPR

324- **1** **Flavius Titus**[193] 7950 4-9-1 **91** AndreaAtzeni 2 100+
(Roger Varian) *chsd ldr in centre gp and prom overall: effrt to chal 2f out: led ins fnl f: kpt on gamely u.p* **8/1**[2]

030- **2** nk **Summerghand (IRE)**[185] 8194 5-9-7 **97** DanielTudhope 12 105
(David O'Meara) *looked wl; hld up towards rr of nr side gp: pushed along and clsd but nt clr run over 1f out: swtchd rt fr 1f out: hdwy to chse ldrs ins fnl f: r.o wl to go 2nd cl home (jockey said gelding was denied a clear run)* **8/1**[2]

00-4 **3** nk **Green Power**[16] 1459 4-9-5 **95** RyanMoore 14 102
(John Gallagher) *racd nr side and overall ldr: rdn and hrd pressed 2f out: hdd ins fnl f: kpt on wl but lost 2nd cl home* **7/1**[1]

201- **4** 1½ **Ice Lord (IRE)**[172] 8594 7-9-5 **95** RichardKingscote 15 97
(Chris Wall) *s.i.s: t.k.h: hld up in rr of nr side gp: clsd and nt clr run 2f out tl hdwy ins fnl f: kpt on (jockey said gelding was denied a clear run)* **16/1**

40-0 **5** 1¾ **Buridan (FR)**[16] 1459 4-9-1 **91** SeanLevey 1 88
(Richard Hannon) *led centre gp and chsd ldr overall: rdn and ev ch 2f out tl no ex jst ins fnl f: wknd fnl 100yds* **10/1**

242- **6** ½ **Blackheath**[195] 7909 4-8-8 **84** LukeMorris 11 79
(Ed Walker) *sltly on toes; in tch in midfield in nr side gp: effrt u.p over 2f out: unable qck over 1f out: wknd ins fnl f* **12/1**

1513 **7** ¾ **Desert Doctor (IRE)**[17] 1421 4-9-5 **95** GeraldMosse 9 88
(Ed Walker) *sltly on toes; t.k.h: hld up in midfield of nr side gp: nt clr run: swtchd rt and effrt over 1f out: no imp 1f out and kpt on same pce ins fnl f* **8/1**[2]

135- **8** ½ **Count Otto (IRE)**[193] 7950 4-9-0 **90** (h) JasonWatson 8 81
(Amanda Perrett) *in tch in nr side gp: effrt over 1f out: unable qck and no imp 1f out: wknd ins fnl f* **9/1**[3]

50-0 **9** *hd* **Burguillos**[90] 255 6-8-12 **88**.........................(t[1]) HarryBentley 10 78
(Stuart Williams) *s.i.s: hld up in rr of nr side gp: effrt over 1f out: kpt on u.p ins fnl f: nvr involved* **25/1**

02-0 **10** *nk* **Von Blucher (IRE)**[16] 1459 6-9-0 **90**.........................(p) PJMcDonald 6 79
(Rebecca Menzies) *stdd s: t.k.h: hld up in midfield in centre gp: effrt and no hdwy over 1f out: kpt on same pce ins fnl f: nvr involved* **20/1**

101- **11** *1* **Alemaratalyoum (IRE)**[179] 8371 5-9-6 **96**.........................(t[1]) JimCrowley 5 82
(Stuart Williams) *midfield in centre gp: unable qck over 1f out: wknd ins fnl f* **20/1**

460- **12** *nk* **Kimifive (IRE)**[206] 7510 4-9-0 **90**......................... OisinMurphy 3 75
(Joseph Tuite) *midfield in centre gp: clsd over 1f out: rdn and unable qck 1f out: wknd ins fnl f* **10/1**

020- **13** *3/4* **Normandy Barriere (IRE)**[185] 8194 7-9-6 **96**......................... WilliamBuick 4 79
(Nigel Tinkler) *bit bkward; a towards rr of centre gp: rdn 1/2-way: nvr involved* **11/1**

030- **14** *hd* **Zain Hana**[153] 9052 4-9-1 **91**......................... DanielMuscutt 13 73
(John Butler) *sweating; on toes; stmbld leaving stalls: in tch in nr side gp: effrt over 1f out: nt clr run ent fnl f: nt rcvr and wknd ins fnl f (jockey said filly stumbled leaving stalls)* **50/1**

05-6 **15** *2 1/4* **Tommy Taylor (USA)**[16] 1459 5-9-4 **94**......................... TomEaves 7 69
(Kevin Ryan) *sweating; restless in stalls: s.i.s: t.k.h: hld up in midfield of nr side gp: effrt whn pushed rt and impeded over 1f out: nt clr run 1f out: nt rcvr and wknd ins fnl f* **9/1[3]**

1m 12.57s (0.67) **Going Correction** +0.125s/f (Good) **15** Ran SP% **121.3**
Speed ratings (Par 109): **100,99,99,97,94 94,93,92,92,91 90,90,89,88,85**
CSF £67.28 CT £489.63 TOTE £8.60: £2.50, £3.30, £2.50; EX 89.90 Trifecta £677.80.

Owner Sheikh Mohammed Obaid Al Maktoum **Bred** Cheveley Park Stud Ltd **Trained** Newmarket, Suffolk

FOCUS
Official figures suggest this was a decent sprint handicap. Although there was no obvious bias, the winner was the only one of the bunch who raced more towards the centre of the track involved in the finish, potentially upgrading his effort slightly. It's been rated around the third.

1830 BET365 EUROPEAN FREE H'CAP (LISTED RACE) 7f
2:25 (2:25) (Class 1) 3-Y-O

£28,355 (£10,750; £5,380; £2,680; £1,345; £675) **Stalls** High

Form RPR

333- **1** **Shine So Bright**[206] 7534 3-9-3 **106**......................... SilvestreDeSousa 5 112
(Andrew Balding) *t.k.h: mde all: gng best over 2f out: pushed along and wnt clr wl over 1f out: r.o strly: readily* **5/2[2]**

200- **2** *1 3/4* **Space Traveller**[185] 8193 3-8-13 **102**......................... DanielTudhope 4 102
(Richard Fahey) *chsd ldrs: effrt to chse wnr over 2f out: unable to match pce of wnr wl over 1f out: wl hld but kpt on for clr 2nd ins fnl f* **10/1**

012- **3** *3 1/2* **Azano**[171] 8646 3-9-1 **104**.........................(t) FrankieDettori 3 95+
(John Gosden) *compact; hld up in tch: effrt over 2f out: no imp over 1f out: kpt on to go 3rd ins fnl f: no threat to wnr* **2/1[1]**

-300 **4** *1 3/4* **Victory Command (IRE)**[47] 956 3-9-0 **103**......................... RyanMoore 7 89
(Mark Johnston) *chsd wnr for 2f: styd prom: effrt over 2f out: unable to match pce of wnr and outpcd wl over 1f out: wl hld and plugged on same pce fnl f* **14/1**

611- **5** *4 1/2* **Arctic Sound**[201] 7702 3-9-7 **110**......................... JamesDoyle 1 84
(Mark Johnston) *hld up in last pair: effrt and clsd over 2f out: struggling and outpcd 2f out: sn wl btn and wknd fnl f* **9/2[3]**

324- **6** *3* **Dubai Dominion**[193] 7971 3-8-11 **100**......................... OisinMurphy 2 66
(Ed Vaughan) *in tch in midfield: effrt over 2f out: sn struggling and outpcd: wknd over 1f out* **11/1**

150- **7** *6* **Kuwait Currency (USA)**[171] 8633 3-9-2 **105**.........(t[1]) TomMarquand 6 54
(Richard Hannon) *str; looked wl; dwlt: t.k.h: sn rcvrd to go prom: chsd wnr after 2f tl over 2f out: sn lost pl and bhd over 1f out* **12/1**

1m 24.68s (-0.72) **Going Correction** +0.125s/f (Good) **7** Ran SP% **111.9**
Speed ratings (Par 106): **109,107,103,101,95 92,85**
CSF £25.74 TOTE £3.30: £1.60, £4.40; EX 22.70 Trifecta £83.40.

Owner King Power Racing Co Ltd **Bred** Miss K Rausing **Trained** Kingsclere, Hants

FOCUS
It's unlikely this will have much bearing on the Guineas, and it proved a rather uncompetitive affair, with the winner gifted an easy lead. The time was 1.09sec faster than the Nell Gwyn. A pb from the winner.

1831 BET365 FEILDEN STKS (LISTED RACE) 1m 1f
3:00 (3:02) (Class 1) 3-Y-O

£22,684 (£8,600; £4,304; £2,144; £1,076; £540) **Stalls** High

Form RPR

216- **1** **Kick On**[171] 8633 3-9-0 105......................... OisinMurphy 5 108
(John Gosden) *sweating; racd keenly: mde all: clr w runner-up over 1f out: styd on gamely u.p ins fnl f* **2/1[2]**

21- **2** *nk* **Walkinthesand (IRE)**[209] 7423 3-9-0 0......................... TomMarquand 1 107
(Richard Hannon) *sltly on toes; sweating; chsd ldrs: effrt to press wnr ent fnl 2f: clr w wnr and str chal over 1f out: kpt on wl u.p but a jst hld ins fnl f* **14/1**

135- **3** *4 1/2* **Boerhan**[185] 8186 3-9-0 98......................... JamesDoyle 2 97
(William Haggas) *str; looked wl; dwlt and pushed along early: hld up in tch: effrt over 2f out: chsd ldng pair and no imp whn edgd lft 1f out: wknd ins fnl f* **13/2[3]**

1- **4** *1* **Kadar (USA)**[222] 6988 3-9-0 0......................... DanielTudhope 7 95
(K R Burke) *unfurnished; scope; hld up in tch in last pair: effrt and rdn ent fnl 3f: outpcd ent fnl 2f: no threat to ldrs and plugged on same pce fr over 1f out* **7/1**

43-2 **5** *6* **Western Australia (IRE)**[41] 1049 3-9-0 110......................... RyanMoore 4 82
(A P O'Brien, Ire) *looked wl; pressed wnr tl unable qck u.p and outpcd ent fnl 2f: 4th and wl btn over 1f out: wknd fnl f* **6/4[1]**

323- **6** *10* **I'll Have Another (IRE)**[176] 8477 3-8-12 99......................... SilvestreDeSousa 3 58
(Mark Johnston) *looked wl; in tch: clsd to chse ldrs and u.p 3f out: lost pl qckly and bhd 2f out: wl bhd and eased off ins fnl f* **16/1**

1m 51.16s (0.06) **Going Correction** +0.125s/f (Good) **6** Ran SP% **111.7**
Speed ratings (Par 106): **104,103,99,98,93 84**
CSF £27.29 TOTE £2.90: £2.30, £3.90; EX 25.00 Trifecta £97.00.

Owner Qatar Racing Limited **Bred** Shutford Stud **Trained** Newmarket, Suffolk

FOCUS
This often goes to a classy performer, with Golden Horn in 2015 the stand out of a decent bunch, although it's worth noting that subsequent St Leger winner Kew Gardens was third last year. It was a good performance by the John Gosden colt but, by the time this race jumped off, there had to be a suspicion, judged on earlier events, that grabbing the stands' side rail under a positive ride was a benefit. The winner has been rated similar to his 2yo form, and the third close to form.

1832 LANWADES STUD NELL GWYN STKS (GROUP 3) (FILLIES) 7f
3:35 (3:37) (Class 1) 3-Y-O

£34,026 (£12,900; £6,456; £3,216; £1,614; £810) **Stalls** High

Form RPR

1- **1** **Qabala (USA)**[199] 7775 3-9-0 0......................... DavidEgan 7 110+
(Roger Varian) *sweating; dwlt: hld up in tch: pushed along and clsd 3f out: rdn to chse ldrs over 1f out: led ins fnl f: styd on strly and gng away at fin* **10/3[1]**

411- **2** *1 3/4* **Mot Juste (USA)**[186] 8146 3-9-0 103......................... AndreaAtzeni 6 104
(Roger Varian) *sltly on toes; looked wl; hld up in tch in midfield: effrt and clsd to chse ldrs over 2f out: rdn to ld over 1f out: hdd and one pce ins fnl f* **7/1**

002- **3** *3/4* **Angel's Hideaway (IRE)**[186] 8146 3-9-0 105......................... RobertHavlin 5 102+
(John Gosden) *restless in stalls: s.i.s: hld up in rr: hdwy and swtchd rt over 1f out: styd on to go 3rd wl ins fnl f: no threat to wnr* **9/2[3]**

110- **4** *1* **Look Around**[234] 6521 3-9-0 97......................... OisinMurphy 8 99
(Andrew Balding) *hld up in last pair: effrt over 1f out: rdn and hdwy 1f out: styd on wl ins fnl f to snatch 4th last stride: nvr trbld ldrs (vet said filly lost left fore shoe)* **16/1**

1-25 **5** *shd* **Nashirah**[75] 511 3-9-0 90......................... WilliamBuick 1 99
(Charlie Appleby) *t.k.h: hld up in tch towards rr: clsd over 2f out: chsng ldrs but no ex u.p 1f out: wknd ins fnl f* **10/1**

2-11 **6** *3 1/4* **Orchid Star**[60] 739 3-9-0 85......................... JamesDoyle 4 90
(Charlie Appleby) *compact; led and sn crossed to nr side rail: rdn and hdd over 1f out: no ex and wknd ins fnl f* **14/1**

153- **7** *3* **Main Edition (IRE)**[200] 7734 3-9-0 107......................... RyanMoore 9 82
(Mark Johnston) *looked wl; t.k.h: chsd ldr: rdn to press ldr over 2f out tl unable qck over 1f out: wknd ins fnl f* **4/1[2]**

331- **8** *shd* **Come On Leicester (IRE)**[182] 8306 3-9-0 94........ SilvestreDeSousa 10 82
(Richard Hannon) *t.k.h: hld up in tch in midfield: lost pl and bhd whn swtchd rt 2f out: no threat to ldrs after: plugged on ins fnl f* **20/1**

163- **9** *3/4* **Mistress Of Love (USA)**[164] 8836 3-9-0 86......................... DanielTudhope 2 80
(K R Burke) *hld up in tch in midfield: losing pl whn hmpd over 1f out: wknd ins fnl f (jockey said filly became unbalanced in the dip)* **40/1**

1- **10** *4* **Mercenary Rose (IRE)**[133] 9392 3-9-0 0......................... DavidProbert 11 69
(Paul Cole) *str; t.k.h: chsd ldrs tl 2f out: lost pl and btn over 1f out: wknd ins fnl f* **33/1**

213- **11** *2 1/2* **Sunday Star**[186] 8146 3-9-0 100......................... GeraldMosse 3 62
(Ed Walker) *t.k.h: chsd ldrs tl 2f out: sn btn and hung rt: bhd whn eased ins fnl f (jockey said filly hung right-handed)* **9/1**

1m 25.77s (0.37) **Going Correction** +0.125s/f (Good) **11** Ran SP% **115.5**
Speed ratings (Par 105): **102,100,99,98,97 94,90,90,89,85 82**
CSF £25.78 TOTE £4.30: £1.80, £2.20, £2.40; EX 26.50 Trifecta £141.40.

Owner H H Sheikh Mohammed Bin Khalifa Al Thani **Bred** Eutrophia Farm **Trained** Newmarket, Suffolk

FOCUS
The last winner of the Nell Gwyn to go on and win the Guineas was Speciosa in 2006, but this year's winner has every chance of emulating her. The time was 1.09sec slower than the Free Handicap, and, unlike that race in which the winner made all, it was the hold-up horses who came to the fore here. The second has been rated to the race average and the third close to form.

1833 BET365 BRITISH EBF MAIDEN FILLIES' STKS (PLUS 10 RACE) 5f
4:10 (4:10) (Class 4) 2-Y-O **£5,175** (£1,540; £769; £384) **Stalls** High

Form RPR

1 **Chasing Dreams** 2-9-0 0.........................(h[1]) WilliamBuick 6 95+
(Charlie Appleby) *athletic; looked wl; racd keenly: mde all: rdn and rn green jst over 1f out: asserted 1f out: r.o strly and drew clr ins fnl f: readily* **4/9[1]**

2 *5* **Good Vibes** 2-9-0 0......................... OisinMurphy 4 77+
(David Evans) *unfurnished; s.i.s: rn green but hdwy to chse wnr 3f out: pushed along and ev ch over 1f out: jst getting outpcd whn short of room 1f out: wl hld but stl clr 2nd ins fnl f* **12/1[3]**

3 *2 3/4* **Kemble (IRE)** 2-9-0 0......................... SeanLevey 1 67
(Richard Hannon) *leggy; athletic; wnt rt and flashing tail leaving stalls: in tch in rr: effrt to chse ldng pair wl over 1f out: sn no imp and wl hld fr over 1f out* **7/2[2]**

4 **4** *6* **Bartat**[13] 1513 2-9-0 0......................... SilvestreDeSousa 2 46
(Mick Channon) *workmanlike; chsd ldrs: effrt ent fnl 2f: sn outpcd: 4th and wknd fnl f* **12/1[3]**

5 **5** *8* **Arasugar (IRE)**[17] 1416 2-9-0 0......................... KieranO'Neill 5 17
(Seamus Mullins) *leggy; pressed wnr tl 3f out: sn rdn and steadily lost pl: bhd over 1f out* **25/1**

1m 0.09s (0.99) **Going Correction** +0.125s/f (Good) **5** Ran SP% **110.7**
Speed ratings (Par 91): **97,89,84,75,62**
CSF £7.10 TOTE £1.30: £1.10, £3.90; EX 6.30 Trifecta £11.50.

Owner Godolphin **Bred** Ors Bloodstock & Stanley House Stud **Trained** Newmarket, Suffolk

FOCUS
The market only wanted to know about one of these, and she got the job done after taking a while to hit top gear.

1834 BET365 EUROPEAN BREEDERS' FUND FILLIES' MAIDEN STKS (PLUS 10 RACE) (DIV II) 1m
4:45 (4:47) (Class 4) 3-Y-O **£6,469** (£1,925; £962; £481) **Stalls** High

Form RPR

1 **Lavender's Blue (IRE)** 3-9-0 0......................... RobertHavlin 9 88+
(Amanda Perrett) *athletic; gd walker; trckd ldrs: swtchd rt and nudged way between rivals over 1f out: rdn to ld jst ins fnl f: r.o strly and gng away at fin* **3/1[3]**

00- **2** *2 1/2* **Maamora (IRE)**[199] 7763 3-9-0 0......................... SilvestreDeSousa 8 82
(Simon Crisford) *str; sltly on toes; led: rdn over 1f out: hdd jst ins fnl f: no ex and outpcd by wnr fnl 100yds* **2/1[1]**

4- **3** *4 1/2* **Alandalos**[118] 9607 3-9-0 0......................... JimCrowley 5 72
(Charles Hills) *str; chsd ldr: ev ch but struggling to qckn whn nudged rt over 1f out: sn outpcd and wknd ins fnl f* **11/4[2]**

4 *6* **Tatweej** 3-9-0 0......................... DaneO'Neill 4 58
(Owen Burrows) *compact; chsd ldrs: pushed along and outpcd over 2f out: wl btn 4th and plugged on fr over 1f out* **6/1**

5 ½ **Plisken** 3-9-0 0....(h1) PatCosgrave 6 57
(Tom Clover) *unfurnished; scope; t.k.h: hld up in tch in midfield: rdn over 2f out: outpcd and wl hld in 5th over 1f out (jockey said filly ran too free)* **66/1**

0- **6** 3 **Dinah Washington (IRE)**175 8510 3-9-0 0.... LouisSteward 7 50
(Michael Bell) *leggy; hld up in last trio: effrt and outpcd over 2f out: wl btn 6th over 1f out* **33/1**

7 10 **Ximena** 3-9-0 0.... EoinWalsh 10 27
(Samuel Farrell, Ire) *ly; hld up in tch in last trio: effrt over 2f out: sn struggling and outpcd: wl btn over 1f out* **50/1**

8 6 **Rimmal (USA)** 3-9-0 0....(h1) JamieSpencer 1 13
(Jeremy Noseda) *leggy; sltly on toes; t.k.h: stdd into midfield sn after s: in tch: pushed along over 2f out: sn lost pl and no ch over 1f out* **14/1**

9 28 **Princess Juliana (IRE)** 3-9-0 0.... CallumShepherd 2
(Brian Meehan) *leggy; athletic; wnt rt leaving stalls and slowly away: hung rt thrght and a towards rr: lost tch 2f out: t.o (jockey said filly hung right-handed)* **25/1**

1m 39.68s (1.28) **Going Correction** +0.125s/f (Good) **9** Ran SP% **116.2**
Speed ratings (Par 97): **98,95,91,85,84 81,71,65,37**
CSF £9.26 TOTE £4.10: £1.30, £1.10, £2.00; EX 10.20 Trifecta £28.10.
Owner Benny Andersson **Bred** Chess Racing **Trained** Pulborough, W Sussex

FOCUS
The slower of the two divisions by 0.41sec, but the winner was well backed and value for an easier win. The opening level is fluid.

1835 BET365 H'CAP 1m 2f
5:20 (5:22) (Class 3) (0-95,95) 3-Y-O **£12,938** (£3,850; £1,924; £962) **Stalls** High

Form RPR

421- **1** **Solid Stone (IRE)**160 8923 3-8-11 **85**.... RyanMoore 1 93
(Sir Michael Stoute) *str; hld up wl in tch: effrt to chal 2f out: edgd lft u.p and led 1f out: styd on gamely u.p ins fnl f* **9/4**1

-311 **2** ½ **War Tiger (USA)**54 839 3-8-12 **86**.... TonyHamilton 5 93
(Richard Fahey) *athletic; mde most: shkn up ent fnl 2f: rdn and hdd 1f out: kpt on wl u.p but a jst hld ins fnl f* **3/1**2

311- **3** 2 ¾ **Never Do Nothing (IRE)**201 7712 3-8-9 **83**.... OisinMurphy 2 84
(Andrew Balding) *looked wl; pressed ldng pair: clsd and ev ch 3f out: unable qck u.p 1f out: wknd ins fnl f* **7/2**3

5-11 **4** 1 ¾ **Marhaban (IRE)**71 606 3-9-0 **88**.... WilliamBuick 3 86
(Charlie Appleby) *str; w ldr: rdn over 1f out: no ex 1f out: wknd ins fnl f* **3/1**2

102- **5** ½ **Mordred (IRE)**201 7700 3-9-7 **95**.... SeanLevey 4 92
(Richard Hannon) *sltly on toes; stdd s: hld up wl in tch: clsd and nt clr run 2f out: swtchd rt and effrt over 1f out: no imp* **11/1**

2m 6.93s (1.53) **Going Correction** +0.125s/f (Good) **5** Ran SP% **111.3**
Speed ratings (Par 102): **98,97,95,94,93**
CSF £9.38 TOTE £2.90: £1.60, £1.60; EX 9.00 Trifecta £25.50.
Owner Saeed Suhail **Bred** Epona Bloodstock Ltd **Trained** Newmarket, Suffolk

FOCUS
This has a mixed history but Group race performers have emerged from it, like Wigmore Hall, Main Sequence and Old Persian. A small field lined up but this might be smart form, with four of the field winning last time out, three of which had won their last two. Most of these had a chance inside the final furlong. The fifth has been rated close to form.
T/Jkpt: £3,688.50 to a £1 stake. Pool: £25,819.89 - 7.0 winning units T/Plt: £53.10 to a £1 stake. Pool: £128,181.28 - 1,760.28 winning units T/Qpdt: £13.40 to a £1 stake. Pool: £11,726.56 - 645.60 winning units **Steve Payne**

1766 WOLVERHAMPTON (A.W) (L-H)
Tuesday, April 16

OFFICIAL GOING: Tapeta: standard
Wind: Light against Weather: Overcast

1836 FOLLOW TOP TIPSTER TEMPLEGATE AT SUN RACING H'CAP 1m 142y (Tp)
5:45 (5:46) (Class 6) (0-60,60) 4-Y-O+
£3,105 (£924; £461; £400; £400; £400) **Stalls** Low

Form RPR

1012 **1** **Amor Fati (IRE)**19 1378 4-9-6 **59**.... NicolaCurrie 5 65
(David Evans) *broke wl: sn stdd and lost pl: hdwy over 1f out: r.o to ld nr fin* **11/4**1

0420 **2** nk **Aqua Libre**17 1426 6-9-6 **59**....(p) JoeFanning 13 64
(Jennie Candlish) *s.i.s: hdwy to chse ldr over 7f out: rdn to ld over 1f out: sn hung lft: hdd nr fin (trainer was informed that the mare could not run until the day after passing a stalls test)* **15/2**

00-0 **3** 1 **Captain Marmalade (IRE)**71 599 7-8-2 **46** oh1
ThoreHammerHansen(5) 12 49
(Jimmy Fox) *hld up: hdwy over 1f out: r.o* **100/1**

-324 **4** hd **Lukoutoldmakezebak**17 1431 6-8-7 **46**....(p) FrannyNorton 9 49
(David Thompson) *sn led at stdy pce: pushed along and qckned over 2f out: rdn and hdd over 1f out: carried lft ins fnl f: styd on same pce* **7/1**3

000- **5** nk **Highland Bobby**26 8054 4-9-5 **58**.... ShaneGray 11 60+
(David O'Meara) *hld up: plld hrd: rdn over 1f out: r.o ins fnl f: nt rch ldrs* **18/1**

3150 **6** 1 ½ **Arrowzone**43 1015 8-9-7 **60**....(b) JasonHart 10 59
(Kevin Frost) *prom: racd keenly: rdn over 1f out: edgd lft ins fnl f: styd on same pce* **10/1**

-255 **7** ½ **Zarkavon**19 1390 5-8-2 **46** oh1....(p) FayeMcManoman(5) 7 44
(John Wainwright) *hld up: hdwy over 5f out: hung rt on outer over 2f out: styd on same pce fnl f (jockey said mare hung right-handed throughout)* **12/1**

0200 **8** ¾ **Scenery**3 1765 4-9-5 **58**.... LukeMorris 6 54
(Marjorie Fife) *chsd ldrs: lost pl over 5f out: pushed along and hdwy over 1f out: sn rdn and edgd lft: nt clr run ins fnl f: styd on same pce* **14/1**

0064 **9** ¾ **Gabrial's Kaka (IRE)**3 1769 9-9-7 **60**.... PaddyMathers 8 55
(Patrick Morris) *s.i.s: hld up: shkn up over 2f out: nt clr run over 1f out: n.d* **13/2**2

0426 **10** 1 ¼ **Stand N Deliver**34 1176 5-9-5 **58**....(v) AdamKirby 3 50
(Clive Cox) *trckd ldrs: rdn over 1f out: nt clr run and no ex ins fnl f* **11/4**1

4645 **11** ½ **Gone With The Wind (GER)**20 1354 8-8-7 **46** oh1....(p) PhilDennis 1 37
(Rebecca Bastiman) *hmpd s: hld up in tch: shkn up over 2f out: wknd fnl f* **50/1**

1m 49.83s (-0.27) **Going Correction** -0.025s/f (Stan) **11** Ran SP% **122.6**
Speed ratings (Par 101): **100,99,98,98,98 97,96,95,95,94 93**
CSF £25.74 CT £1745.31 TOTE £3.40: £1.80, £2.50, £12.80; EX 33.70 Trifecta £3749.80.
Owner Mrs Catherine Gannon **Bred** Tony O'Meara **Trained** Pandy, Monmouths

FOCUS
An ordinary handicap but an improver did well to justify support from off the steady pace. Straightforward form.

1837 SUNRACING.CO.UK H'CAP 7f 36y (Tp)
6:15 (6:16) (Class 6) (0-55,55) 4-Y-O+
£3,105 (£924; £461; £400; £400; £400) **Stalls** High

Form RPR

-300 **1** **Magical Molly Joe**5 1722 5-9-3 **53**....(h) PJMcDonald 1 59
(David Barron) *hld up: hdwy over 1f out: hmpd 1f out: rdn to ld ins fnl f: styd on* **9/4**1

1145 **2** nk **Naralsaif (IRE)**34 1175 5-9-5 **55**....(v) PaddyMathers 10 60
(Derek Shaw) *hld up: plld hrd: hdwy on outer over 1f out: rdn and r.o to go 2nd wl ins fnl f: nt quite rch wnr* **8/1**

0216 **3** ½ **Clement (IRE)**5 1717 9-9-4 **50**....(v) LukeMorris 7 58
(Marjorie Fife) *hld up: rdn on outer over 1f out: r.o wl ins fnl f: nt rch ldrs* **7/1**3

200- **4** hd **Muraadef**213 7309 4-9-3 **53**.... JamesSullivan 8 56
(Ruth Carr) *hld up in tch: racd keenly: rdn and ev ch over 1f out: sn hung lft: styd on same pce ins fnl f* **10/1**

6611 **5** ½ **Mystical Moon (IRE)**11 1565 4-9-4 **54**.... PhilDennis 9 56
(David C Griffiths) *hld up: hdwy wl over 1f out: sn rdn: styd on same pce wl ins fnl f* **8/1**

1056 **6** hd **Indian Affair**22 1335 9-9-3 **53**....(vt) FrannyNorton 6 56
(Milton Bradley) *hld up: shkn up over 1f out: hdwy: nt clr run and swtchd lft ins fnl f: r.o* **25/1**

636/ **7** 2 ¼ **Bazzat (IRE)**826 166 6-8-11 **54**....(p) MarkCrehan(7) 5 50
(C Moore, Ire) *chsd ldr tl led wl over 1f out: rdn and hdd ins fnl f: no ex* **5/1**2

000- **8** nk **Prince Of Time**132 9415 7-8-11 **52**.... DylanHogan(5) 2 48
(Stella Barclay) *chsd ldrs: nt clr run over 1f out: no ex ins fnl f* **33/1**

-516 **9** ½ **Seaforth (IRE)**22 1339 7-9-0 **53**.... FinleyMarsh(3) 11 49
(Adrian Wintle) *hld up: running on whn hmpd ins fnl f: nt rcvr* **17/2**

0050 **10** ½ **Blue Rocks**19 1390 5-8-12 **53**....(b) SeamusCronin(5) 4 46
(Lisa Williamson) *led: rdn and hdd wl over 1f out: btn whn nt clr run wl ins fnl f* **18/1**

3060 **11** nk **Little Miss Daisy**15 1477 5-9-3 **53**.... NicolaCurrie 3 48
(William Muir) *hld up: hdwy over 1f out: nt clr run thrght fnl f: nvr able to chal (jockey said mare was denied a clear run in the home straight)* **14/1**

0-00 **12** 8 **Formiga (IRE)**22 1328 4-9-4 **54**....(t) RaulDaSilva 12 47+
(Seamus Durack) *prom: ev ch fr over 2f out tl rdn and hmpd 1f out: hmpd again and eased ins fnl f* **40/1**

1m 29.27s (0.47) **Going Correction** -0.025s/f (Stan) **12** Ran SP% **122.9**
Speed ratings (Par 101): **96,95,95,94,94 94,91,91,90,90 89,80**
CSF £21.21 CT £117.16 TOTE £2.60: £1.10, £2.60, £2.70; EX 20.70 Trifecta £133.70.
Owner Lee Woolams & Partner **Bred** Bambi Bloodstock **Trained** Maunby, N Yorks
■ Stewards' Enquiry : Franny Norton four-day ban: careless riding (Apr 30, May 1-3)

FOCUS
They went an uneven gallop and it was a rough race but the favourite overcame some trouble to score with some authority. Straightforward form.

1838 LADBROKES HOME OF THE ODDS BOOST FILLIES' NOVICE STKS 7f 36y (Tp)
6:45 (6:48) (Class 5) 3-Y-O+ **£3,752** (£1,116; £557; £278) **Stalls** High

Form RPR

0-1 **1** **Invitational**101 78 3-9-4 0.... JackMitchell 10 92+
(Roger Varian) *edgd rt s: hdwy to chse ldr over 5f out: led over 4f out: rdn clr whn hung lft over 1f out: styd on* **13/2**3

60- **2** 2 ¾ **Astrologer**125 9499 3-8-11 0.... RobbieDowney 5 77
(David O'Meara) *hld up: hdwy over 4f out: nt clr run and lost pl 1/2-way: hdwy on outer over 2f out: rdn to chse wnr over 1f out: styd on* **40/1**

01- **3** 1 ½ **Vivionn**210 7382 3-9-4 0.... DavidProbert 8 80
(Sir Michael Stoute) *stmbld s: hld up: hdwy 1/2-way: hmpd and lost pl over 2f out: styd on to go 3rd nr fin* **9/4**2

3-2 **4** nk **Nooshin**24 1288 3-8-11 0.... HayleyTurner 4 72
(Charles Hills) *plld hrd and prom: hung rt 1/2-way: hung lft fr over 2f out: rdn over 1f out: no ex (jockey said filly hung left and right-handed)* **1/1**1

41- **5** 1 ¾ **Sonja Henie (IRE)**153 9050 3-9-4 0.... DanielMuscutt 7 74
(Marco Botti) *sn led: hdd over 4f out: rdn over 2f out: wknd ins fnl f* **14/1**

40 **6** 3 ¼ **Di Matteo**36 1142 3-8-8 0.... AaronJones(3) 2 59
(Marco Botti) *s.i.s: hld up: shkn up over 2f out: nvr nrr* **33/1**

5-2 **7** 6 **Moneta**24 1287 3-8-11 0....(t1) RobHornby 1 42
(Jonathan Portman) *chsd ldrs: rdn over 2f out: sn wknd (vet said filly lost its right fore shoe)* **20/1**

8 2 ¼ **Jumeirah (IRE)** 3-8-11 0.... CharlesBishop 12 36
(Eve Johnson Houghton) *s.i.s and carried rt s: nvr on terms (jockey said filly was slowly away)* **100/1**

3 **9** 3 ¼ **Lady Schannell (IRE)**36 1142 3-8-11 0.... LukeMorris 9 28
(Marco Botti) *prom: hmpd over 2f out: sn wknd (jockey said filly lost its action)* **20/1**

U- **10** nk **Loveatfirstlight (IRE)**202 7676 3-8-4 0.... TobyEley(7) 6 27
(James Unett) *s.s and sn hung rt: outpcd (jockey said filly hung right-handed)* **100/1**

0 **11** ½ **Gonbutnotforgotten (FR)**11 1570 3-8-11 0.... JasonHart 3 25
(Philip McBride) *hld up: shkn up and wknd over 2f out* **25/1**

1m 27.43s (-1.37) **Going Correction** -0.025s/f (Stan) **11** Ran SP% **121.5**
Speed ratings (Par 100): **106,102,101,100,98 95,88,85,81,81 81**
CSF £236.36 TOTE £7.60: £1.80, £10.80, £1.10; EX 300.30 Trifecta £1098.30.
Owner Ziad A Galadari **Bred** Galadari Sons Stud Company Limited **Trained** Newmarket, Suffolk

FOCUS
There seemed to be quite a bit of depth in this decent novice event but the winner scored eased down under a positive ride. The third and fifth have been rated close to their wins.

1839 BETWAY CONDITIONS STKS 5f 21y (Tp)
7:15 (7:15) (Class 3) 4-Y-O+
£7,158 (£2,143; £1,071; £535; £267; £134) **Stalls** Low

Form RPR

3203 **1** **Corinthia Knight (IRE)**24 1295 4-9-6 103.... HollieDoyle 7 104
(Archie Watson) *sn w ldr: shkn up to ld over 1f out: rdn and edgd lft ins fnl f: r.o* **9/2**2

140- **2** 1 ¼ **Storm Over (IRE)**178 8413 5-9-6 92.... HarryBentley 3 99
(George Scott) *s.i.s: hld up: hdwy over 1f out: r.o to go 2nd post: nt rch wnr* **14/1**

-103 **3** shd **Tropics (USA)**54 837 11-9-6 104....(h) AdamKirby 2 99
(Dean Ivory) *chsd ldrs: rdn over 1f out: chsd wnr ins fnl f: styd on: lost 2nd post* **8/1**

-401 **4** *shd* **Reflektor (IRE)**[19] 1388 6-9-2 92.............................. RichardKingscote 5 94
(Tom Dascombe) *chsd ldrs: rdn over 1f out: styd on* **11/2**[3]

0-16 **5** *1* **Just That Lord**[18] 1394 6-9-2 87.............................. LukeMorris 1 91
(Michael Attwater) *led: hung rt over 1f out: sn rdn and hdd: styd on same pce ins fnl f (jockey said gelding hung right-handed in the home straight)* **16/1**

/16- **6** *nse* **Kyllang Rock (IRE)**[339] 2664 5-9-2 107.............................. PJMcDonald 6 91
(James Tate) *hld up: shkn up and hung lft fr over 1f out: nt pce to chal* **6/5**[1]

4340 **7** *½* **Gracious John (IRE)**[4] 1734 6-9-2 98.............................. TomMarquand 4 89
(David Evans) *prom: sn lost pl: outpcd 3f out: rdn over 1f out: r.o towards fin* **7/1**

(-1.90) **Going Correction** -0.025s/f (Stan) **7 Ran SP% 115.2**
Speed ratings (Par 107): **114,112,111,111,110 110,109**
CSF £62.06 TOTE £5.20: £2.50, £6.30; EX 59.50 Trifecta £254.40.
Owner Ontoawinner & Partner **Bred** Tally-Ho Stud **Trained** Upper Lambourn, W Berks

FOCUS
The leading contender didn't really fire in this conditions event but his main market rival knuckled down well to enhance his impressive AW strike-rate. The level is set around the second and fifth.

1840 BETWAY LIVE CASINO H'CAP — 2m 120y (Tp)
7:45 (7:45) (Class 4) (0-80,77) 4-Y-0+

£5,530 (£1,645; £822; £411; £400; £400) **Stalls Low**

Form RPR

310- **1** **Seinesational**[152] 9076 4-9-9 77..............................(v) DavidEgan 3 84
(William Knight) *chsd ldrs: nt clr run over 3f out: rdn to ld and edgd rt ins fnl f: styd on* **11/4**[2]

-434 **2** *nk* **Knight Commander**[14] 1497 6-8-7 59 oh3..............................(t) RaulDaSilva 7 65
(Steve Flook) *prom: lost pl 1/2-way: shkn up over 2f out: hdwy over 1f out: sn rdn: carried rt ins fnl f: styd on* **8/1**

5352 **3** *2* **Alabaster**[22] 1330 5-9-11 77..............................(v) LukeMorris 4 81
(Sir Mark Prescott Bt) *chsd ldr to 1/2-way: remained handy: wnt 2nd again over 2f out: led over 1f out: rdn and hdd ins fnl f: styd on same pce* **5/2**[1]

-520 **4** *1½* **Country'N'Western (FR)**[16] 1463 7-9-0 71.............. DarraghKeenan(5) 1 73
(Robert Eddery) *hld up: hdwy over 1f out: rdn ins fnl f: styd on same pce* **4/1**[3]

-414 **5** *1* **Lopes Dancer (IRE)**[55] 803 7-9-7 73.............................. JoeFanning 6 74
(Harriet Bethell) *led to 1/2-way: chsd ldr tl led again over 3f out: hdd over 1f out: no ex ins fnl f* **4/1**[3]

06/5 **6** *2¾* **Uncle Bernie (IRE)**[78] 457 9-8-13 68..................(p) GabrieleMalune(3) 5 66
(Sarah Hollinshead) *hld up: racd keenly: hdwy over 13f out: racd wd fr over 3f out: rdn and hung rt over 1f out: styd on same pce (jockey said gelding hung right-handed)* **20/1**

0 **7** *29* **Black Noah**[35] 1159 4-9-0 68.............................. DavidProbert 2 33
(Johnny Farrelly) *s.i.s: hld up: hdwy to ld 1/2-way: hdd over 3f out: rdn and wknd over 2f out: eased over 1f out (jockey said gelding ran too freely)* **20/1**

3m 39.93s (0.63) **Going Correction** -0.025s/f (Stan) **7 Ran SP% 115.9**
WFA 4 from 5yo+ 2lb
Speed ratings (Par 105): **97,96,95,95,94 93,79**
CSF £25.31 TOTE £4.50: £2.50, £3.00; EX 27.90 Trifecta £80.60.
Owner One Day Rodney Partnership **Bred** Fittocks Stud **Trained** Angmering, W Sussex
■ Stewards' Enquiry : David Egan two-day ban: careless riding (Apr 30, May 1)

FOCUS
They went a stop-start gallop in this staying handicap and there was a tight finish. The second has been rated up a bit on his recent effort.

1841 BETWAY H'CAP — 1m 1f 104y (Tp)
8:15 (8:16) (Class 6) (0-55,55) 4-Y-0+

£3,105 (£924; £461; £400; £400; £400) **Stalls Low**

Form RPR

-000 **1** **Tha'ir (IRE)**[5] 1717 9-9-2 50..............................(t) DannyBrock 6 57+
(Philip McBride) *hld up in tch: shkn up to ld ins fnl f: drvn out (trainer said regarding apparent improvement in form that the gelding had jumped better from the stalls on this occasion and had also appreciated the return to Wolverhampton where the gelding has performed well in the past)* **8/1**

4550 **2** *1¼* **Splash Of Verve (IRE)**[18] 1398 7-9-1 49.............................. FrannyNorton 7 54
(David Thompson) *hld up: swtchd rt and hdwy over 1f out: r.o: wnt 2nd nr fin* **15/2**

0225 **3** *nk* **First Call (FR)**[18] 1398 4-9-0 48..............................(p) DavidEgan 4 52
(Patrick Morris) *led: rdn over 1f out: hdd ins fnl f: styd on same pce (jockey said gelding hung right-handed in the final furlong)* **3/1**[1]

-554 **4** *2* **Born To Reason (IRE)**[13] 1520 5-8-12 46 oh1.........(b) DougieCostello 3 47
(Kevin Frost) *hld up: swtchd rt and hdwy over 1f out: sn rdn: styd on same pce wl ins fnl f* **20/1**

0364 **5** *shd* **Herm (IRE)**[19] 1390 5-9-3 51.............................. TomMarquand 12 51
(David Evans) *prom: chsd ldr over 7f out: rdn over 2f out: no ex wl ins fnl f* **15/2**

410- **6** *1¼* **Allux Boy (IRE)**[174] 8544 5-8-11 50..............(p) FayeMcManoman(5) 11 48
(Nigel Tinkler) *prom: rdn over 2f out: no ex ins fnl f* **14/1**

0622 **7** *½* **Voice Of A Leader (IRE)**[17] 1431 8-9-2 50..............................(h) JoeyHaynes 2 47
(Paul Howling) *s.i.s: hld up: swtchd rt and hdwy over 1f out: rdn: nt clr run and swtchd lft ins fnl f: nt trble ldrs* **11/1**

44-0 **8** *¾* **Cat Royale (IRE)**[24] 1297 6-9-5 53..............................(v) AdamKirby 5 49
(John Butler) *chsd ldr 1f: remained handy: shkn up 7f out: rdn over 1f out: wknd wl ins fnl f* **13/2**[2]

0006 **9** *hd* **Sir George Somers (USA)**[34] 1175 6-9-7 55..............(t[1]) LiamKeniry 9 50
(Nigel Twiston-Davies) *hld up: shkn up over 2f out: nvr nrr* **20/1**

2340 **10** *3¾* **Final Attack (IRE)**[19] 1390 8-9-0 51..............(p) GabrieleMalune(3) 1 39
(Sarah Hollinshead) *s.i.s: pushed along early in rr: rdn over 1f out: n.d* **17/2**

150- **11** *3* **Grasmere (IRE)**[152] 9072 4-8-13 52..............(t) DarraghKeenan(5) 10 34
(Alan Bailey) *hld up: shkn up over 2f out: n.d* **100/1**

302/ **12** *1½* **Eugenic**[541] 8261 8-9-1 49.............................. HayleyTurner 8 29
(Tracey Barfoot-Saunt) *chsd ldrs: shkn up over 2f out: wknd over 1f out* **100/1**

006/ **13** *13* **Penny Green**[855] 8341 5-8-9 50..............................(p) MarkCrehan(7) 13 5
(C Moore, Ire) *dwlt: hld up: wknd 3f out* **7/1**[3]

2m 0.17s (-0.63) **Going Correction** -0.025s/f (Stan) **13 Ran SP% 122.5**
Speed ratings (Par 101): **101,99,99,97,97 96,96,95,95,92 89,88,76**
CSF £66.62 CT £225.49 TOTE £10.10: £3.30, £3.00, £1.80; EX 68.80 Trifecta £273.30.
Owner P J McBride **Bred** Lodge Park Stud **Trained** Newmarket, Suffolk

FOCUS
The winner turned things around to land a gamble back on Tapeta. Straightforward form in behind the winner.
T/Plt: £238.20 to a £1 stake. Pool: £107,190.68 - 328.38 winning units T/Qpdt: £51.80 to a £1 stake. Pool: £14,132.06 - 201.57 winning units **Colin Roberts**

[1780] CHANTILLY (R-H)
Tuesday, April 16
OFFICIAL GOING: Polytrack: standard; turf: good to soft

1842a PRIX DE LA GOURSAULE (CLAIMER) (3YO) (TURF) — 6f
3:10 3-Y-0 **£10,360** (£4,144; £3,108; £2,072; £1,036)

RPR

1 **Powerful Sole**[19] 3-9-2 0.............................. MaximeGuyon 10 78
(Andrea Marcialis, France) **31/10**[2]

2 *1¾* **Tudo Bem (FR)**[14] 3-9-4 0.............................. EddyHardouin 2 75
(M Boutin, France) **14/1**

3 *hd* **Pardon My French (IRE)**[22] 1340 3-9-4 0.............................. TheoBachelot 7 74
(Vaclav Luka Jr, Czech Republic) **8/5**[1]

4 *1¼* **Grandee Daisy**[6] 1678 3-8-8 0..............................(v) RonanThomas 1 60
(Jo Hughes, France) *trckd ldrs on rail: urged along 2f out: rdn to chse ldrs over 1f out: kpt on ins fnl f* **18/1**

5 *2½* **Loquen (IRE)** 3-8-3 0.............................. MlleLeaBails(8) 6 55
(Andrea Marcialis, France) **86/1**

6 *hd* **Hamper (FR)**[360] 1997 3-8-11 0.............................. AlexisBadel 3 54
(P Adda, France) **15/1**

7 *2½* **Imotep (FR)**[158] 3-8-5 0.............................. MlleCoraliePacaut(3) 8 43
(M Boutin, France) **11/1**

8 *1¾* **Blury (ITY)**[350] 3-9-1 0.............................. CristianDemuro 4 45
(Andrea Marcialis, France) **13/1**

9 *hd* **Amor Kethley**[22] 1340 3-8-11 0..............................(p) MickaelBarzalona 9 40
(Amy Murphy) *trckd ldrs on outer: pushed along 2f out: rdn w limited rspnse over 1f out: wknd fnl f* **41/10**[3]

10 *1* **Velvet Vixen (IRE)**[71] 597 3-8-8 0..............(p) Louis-PhilippeBeuzelin 5 34
(Jo Hughes, France) *midfield: rowed along 2f out: rdn over 1f out: sn btn and grad lft bhd* **31/1**

1m 11.76s (0.36) **10 Ran SP% 120.4**
PARI-MUTUEL (all including 1 euro stake): WIN 4.10; PLACE 1.60, 2.50, 1.30; DF 28.40.
Owner Mme Janina Burger **Bred** Miss Harriet Loder **Trained** France

BEVERLEY (R-H)
Wednesday, April 17
OFFICIAL GOING: Good to firm (good in places; watered; 7.6)
Wind: Almost nil Weather: Sunny

1843 FIND PROMO CODES AT ACEODDS.COM EBF NOVICE AUCTION STKS (DIV I) — 5f
2:15 (2:19) (Class 5) 2-Y-0 **£4,032** (£1,207; £603; £302; £150) **Stalls Low**

Form RPR

62 **1** **Birkenhead**[15] 1493 2-9-1 0.............................. CallumShepherd 2 74
(Mick Channon) *disp ld: rdn over 1f out: r.o for press ins fnl f: nosed ahd post* **13/8**[1]

2 **2** *nse* **Bettys Hope**[14] 1513 2-8-10 0.............................. JoeFanning 1 69
(Rod Millman) *disp ld: rdn over 1f out: edgd lft and r.o for press ins fnl f: jst denied post* **9/4**[2]

3 *shd* **Birdie Bowers (IRE)** 2-9-3 0.............................. PaulMulrennan 3 75
(Michael Dods) *wnt sltly lft leaving stalls: chsd ldrs: rdn and swtchd lft over 1f out: r.o to press front two towards fin* **6/1**[3]

4 **4** *3½* **Leave Em Alone (IRE)**[9] 1642 2-8-11 0.............................. JohnFahy 6 57
(David Evans) *chsd ldrs: rdn over 2f out: hung rt over 1f out: rn green: no imp on front trio* **7/1**

5 *1¾* **Cock Robin** 2-9-4 0.............................. KevinStott 10 58+
(Kevin Ryan) *pushed along in midfield: rdn over 2f out: kpt on ins fnl f: nvr able to trble ldrs* **25/1**

6 *4* **The Ginger Bullet** 2-9-5 0.............................. PaulHanagan 11 44
(Richard Fahey) *pushed along and no bttr than midfield: rdn over 2f out: nvr able to get involved* **10/1**

7 *2* **Sassy Lassy (IRE)** 2-8-11 0.............................. TrevorWhelan 5 29
(David Loughnane) *sn pushed along: towards rr: nvr able to get on terms w ldrs (jockey said filly ran green)* **33/1**

8 *7* **Hovingham (IRE)** 2-8-12 0.............................. RowanScott(3) 7 8
(Nigel Tinkler) *pushed along and outpcd: a bhd* **100/1**

0 **9** *½* **Hell Of A Joker**[18] 1416 2-8-11 0..............................(p[1]) RyanWhile(5) 9 7
(Bill Turner) *w ldrs tl rdn 2f out: wknd over 1f out* **50/1**

10 *1½* **Chocoholic** 2-9-3 0.............................. GrahamLee 8 3
(Bryan Smart) *dwlt: rn green: pushed along and outpcd: a bhd* **20/1**

U **Tonquin Valley** 2-8-10 0.............................. KieranSchofield(7) 4
(Brian Ellison) *s.s: wnt erratically lft leaving stalls and uns rdr* **66/1**

1m 3.4s (0.50) **Going Correction** +0.15s/f (Good) **11 Ran SP% 120.7**
Speed ratings (Par 92): **102,101,101,96,93 86,83,72,71,69**
CSF £5.19 TOTE £3.00: £1.30, £1.30, £1.70; EX 6.40 Trifecta £28.80.
Owner M Channon **Bred** Mike Channon Bloodstock Limited **Trained** West Ilsley, Berks
■ Stewards' Enquiry : Callum Shepherd two-day ban: misuse of whip (May 1-2)

FOCUS
Quickish ground. Probably just ordinary form, but it was the quicker division by 1.39sec. The first three, who contested a tight finish clear of the rest, came out of the three lowest stalls. The first two have been rated as improving slightly.

1844 FIND PROMO CODES AT ACEODDS.COM EBF NOVICE AUCTION STKS (DIV II) — 5f
2:50 (2:50) (Class 5) 2-Y-0 **£4,032** (£1,207; £603; £302; £150) **Stalls Low**

Form RPR

1 **Rodnee Tee** 2-8-13 0.............................. ConorMcGovern(3) 3 71
(David O'Meara) *mde all: rdn over 1f out: all out towards fin* **14/1**

4 **2** *shd* **Gin Gembre (FR)**[9] 1651 2-9-5 0.............................. BenCurtis 2 74
(K R Burke) *chsd ldrs: effrt ent fnl 2f: wnt 2nd over 1f out: r.o for press ins fnl f: pressed wnr towards fin: jst hld* **5/4**[1]

6 **3** *½* **Lili Wen Fach (IRE)**[9] 1642 2-8-12 0.............................. JohnFahy 6 65
(David Evans) *w wnr: rdn 2f out: unable qck over 1f out and dropped to 3rd: rallied towards fin* **6/1**[3]

4 4 1/2 **Noddy Shuffle** 2-9-2 0 .... NathanEvans 4 53
(Michael Easterby) *midfield and drvn along: hdwy for press over 1f out: nvr able to trble front trio* **8/1**

5 3/4 **Puerto Sol (IRE)** 2-8-13 0 .... BenRobinson(3) 1 50+
(Brian Ellison) *towards rr and pushed along: hdwy u.p ins fnl f: edgd rt: kpt on towards fin* **12/1**

6 8 **Vodka Dawn (IRE)** 2-8-11 0 .... SamJames 7 16
(Phillip Makin) *chsd ldrs: rdn and edgd rt over 1f out: wknd ins fnl f* **25/1**

7 1 1/2 **Troubador (IRE)** 2-9-3 0 .... PaulMulrennan 5 17
(Michael Dods) *missed break: bhd and pushed along: nvr able to threaten* **4/1[2]**

8 hd **Jakodobro** 2-9-1 0 .... GrahamLee 9 14
(Bryan Smart) *in tch: rdn in midfield over 2f out: no imp over 1f out: wknd ins fnl f* **20/1**

9 1/2 **Nostalgic Air** 2-8-11 0 .... JamesSullivan 8 8
(Ruth Carr) *dwlt: outpcd and a bhd* **25/1**

10 6 **Comeatchoo (IRE)** 2-9-2 0 .... DavidAllan 10
(Tim Easterby) *w ldrs: rdn 2f out: wknd over 1f out* **50/1**

1m 4.79s (1.89) **Going Correction** +0.15s/f (Good) 10 Ran SP% **118.6**
Speed ratings (Par 92): **90,89,89,81,80 67,65,65,64,54**
CSF £31.44 TOTE £18.90: £3.20, £1.10, £1.90; EX 35.90 Trifecta £172.40.

Owner David Lumley & Partner 2 **Bred** Highclere Stud **Trained** Upper Helmsley, N Yorks

■ Stewards' Enquiry : Nathan Evans two-day ban: misuse of whip (May 1-2)

FOCUS
This was the slower division by 1.39sec. Again, a low draw proved advantageous. Modest form.

1845 FOLLOW US ON TWITTER @BEVERLEY_RACES H'CAP 1m 1f 207y
3:25 (3:31) (Class 4) (0-80,79) 3-Y-O **£5,418** (£1,621; £810; £405; £300) **Stalls** Low

Form RPR

553- **1** **Fraser Island (IRE)**[146] 9203 3-9-5 **77** .... JoeFanning 3 85+
(Mark Johnston) *prom: rdn and angled to outer over 2f out: led over 1f out: r.o and in command towards fin* **1/1[1]**

426- **2** 1 3/4 **Whiskey And Water**[222] 7039 3-8-11 **72** .... BenRobinson(3) 6 76
(Brian Ellison) *prom: led after 2f: rdn over 2f out: hdd over 1f out: no ex towards fin* **18/1**

231- **3** 2 1/4 **Gabrial The One (IRE)**[177] 8474 3-9-2 **79** .... SeanDavis(5) 1 80+
(Richard Fahey) *racd keenly: hld up in rr: effrt on inner whn nt clr run over 1f out and sn lost a little grnd: swtchd lft ins fnl f: styd on towards fin (jockey said gelding was denied a clear run approximately 1 1/2f out)* **11/4[2]**

0-31 **4** nk **Boutonniere (USA)**[35] 1182 3-9-2 **77** .... JoshuaBryan(3) 4 76
(Andrew Balding) *uns rdr and broke loose on way to s: led for 2f: chsd ldr after: rdn and chalng 2f out: ev ch tl ins fnl f: sn swtchd lft: wknd fnl 75yds* **11/4[2]**

344- **5** 1 **Hoffa**[194] 7960 3-8-12 **70** .... PaulMulrennan 5 67
(Michael Dods) *chsd ldrs: effrt on outer over 2f out: outpcd over 1f out: sn hung rt whn wl hld* **12/1[3]**

2m 7.61s (1.91) **Going Correction** +0.15s/f (Good) 5 Ran SP% **116.3**
Speed ratings (Par 100): **98,96,94,94,93**
CSF £20.40 TOTE £2.00: £1.30, £4.60; EX 16.30 Trifecta £42.70.

Owner A D Spence **Bred** Rockhart Trading Ltd, China Horse Club **Trained** Middleham Moor, N Yorks

FOCUS
This handicap was won in 2017 by champion stayer Stradivarius, and in 2015 by Antiquarium, who went on to win the Northumberland Plate. The latest running looked a decent little race. The runner-up has been rated in line with his second start.

1846 ARGRAIN LTD REMEMBERING LAURA BARRY H'CAP 7f 96y
4:00 (4:02) (Class 4) (0-80,79) 3-Y-O **£5,418** (£1,621; £810; £405; £300; £300) **Stalls** Low

Form RPR

06-2 **1** **Pacino**[21] 1360 3-9-5 **77** .... TonyHamilton 2 82
(Richard Fahey) *racd keenly: led early: trckd ldrs sn after: effrt to ld jst over 1f out: kpt on wl fnl f* **16/1**

10-0 **2** 3/4 **Azor Ahai**[21] 1360 3-9-5 **77** .... CallumShepherd 3 80
(Mick Channon) *racd keenly: sn led: rdn over 2f out: hung lft fr jst over 1f out and hdd: kpt on ins fnl f but a hld (jockey said gelding hung left-handed throughout)* **33/1**

31-2 **3** 1 **Attainment**[7] 1685 3-9-7 **79** .... DavidAllan 5 79+
(James Tate) *racd keenly: in tch: rdn over 2f out: unable qck: styd on towards fin: nt pce to chal* **7/4[1]**

20-1 **4** nk **Oloroso (IRE)**[25] 1285 3-9-3 **78** .... JoshuaBryan(3) 8 78+
(Andrew Balding) *racd keenly: hld up in rr: rdn over 2f out: hdwy over 1f out: styd on ins fnl f: one pce nr fin: nvr able to trble ldrs* **6/1**

54-1 **5** 1 1/2 **City Tour**[15] 1504 3-9-4 **76** .... JoeFanning 4 72
(Mark Johnston) *midfield: rdn over 2f out: wanted to lug rt fr over 1f out: kpt on ins fnl f: nvr able to chal* **11/4[2]**

240- **6** 1 1/2 **Stronsay (IRE)**[180] 8374 3-9-2 **74** .... GrahamLee 9 66
(Bryan Smart) *midfield: hdwy to chse ldr over 5f out: rdn over 2f out and chalng: lost 2nd over 1f out: fdd fnl 100yds* **25/1**

61-6 **7** 1/2 **Jackamundo (FR)**[15] 1504 3-9-0 **72** .... KevinStott 10 63
(Declan Carroll) *hld up: pushed along over 3f out: kpt on towards fin: nvr a threat* **16/1**

405- **8** 1 **Pearl Of Qatar**[208] 7497 3-8-7 **68** .... BenRobinson(3) 1 56
(Brian Ellison) *racd keenly towards rr: rdn over 2f out: hdwy over 1f out: no imp on ldrs: wknd fnl 75yds* **33/1**

215- **9** 1/2 **Axe Axelrod (USA)**[217] 7169 3-9-5 **77** .... PaulMulrennan 7 64
(Michael Dods) *chsd ldrs: rdn over 2f out: wknd over 1f out (jockey said colt lost its left hind shoe)* **20/1**

03-2 **10** 11 **Lightning Attack**[15] 1504 3-9-4 **76** .... (p) PaulHanagan 6 34
(Richard Fahey) *midfield: pushed along and lost pl over 3f out: bhd wl over 1f out (jockey said gelding ran too free)* **5/1[3]**

1m 34.16s (1.56) **Going Correction** +0.15s/f (Good) 10 Ran SP% **120.2**
Speed ratings (Par 100): **97,96,95,94,92 91,90,89,88,76**
CSF £456.02 CT £1389.22 TOTE £19.20: £3.90, £7.50, £1.10; EX 211.70 Trifecta £1958.20.

Owner Dr Marwan Koukash **Bred** Richard Kent **Trained** Musley Bank, N Yorks

FOCUS
A competitive handicap run at a reasonable gallop. The second has been rated close to his standout 2yo run.

1847 HAPPY 70TH BIRTHDAY MY SPECIAL MUM KATHIE H'CAP 5f
4:35 (4:35) (Class 3) (0-95,97) 4-Y-O+
£7,470 (£2,236; £1,118; £559; £279; £140) **Stalls** Low

Form RPR

3-06 **1** **Teruntum Star (FR)**[89] 297 7-9-6 **93** .... KevinStott 4 101
(Kevin Ryan) *w ldr: led jst over 2f out: rdn over 1f out: r.o ins fnl f* **5/1**

430- **2** 2 1/2 **Line Of Reason (IRE)**[172] 8632 9-9-7 **94** .... JoeFanning 8 93
(Paul Midgley) *stdd s: hld up: rdn and hdwy over 1f out: styd on to take 2nd towards fin: nt trble wnr* **6/1**

602- **3** 3/4 **Airshow**[205] 7609 4-8-10 **83** .... (h) LukeMorris 1 79
(Michael Appleby) *trckd ldrs: drvn to take 2nd over 1f out: hung rt and no imp on wnr ins fnl f: no ex and lost 2nd towards fin (jockey said gelding hung right-handed under pressure)* **9/4[1]**

2431 **4** 1/2 **Watchable**[47] 964 9-9-4 **91** .... (p) DavidNolan 6 86
(David O'Meara) *in tch: rdn over 2f out: chsd ldrs over 1f out: one pce ins fnl f (An enquiry was held to consider why David O'Meara, was running the gelding here on going described as Good to Firm (Good in Places), having declared the gelding a non-runner at Pontefract on 15 April 2019 on ground with the same official description. Tr* **3/1[2]**

243- **5** 7 **Wentworth Falls**[214] 7290 7-9-7 **94** .... DavidAllan 5 63
(Geoffrey Harker) *hld up: rdn 2f out: nvr got involved* **4/1[3]**

410- **6** 3/4 **Billy Dylan (IRE)**[207] 7527 4-8-12 **88** .... ConorMcGovern(3) 3 55
(David O'Meara) *led: hdd jst over 2f out: sn rdn: wknd over 1f out* **9/1**

1m 1.96s (-0.94) **Going Correction** +0.15s/f (Good) 6 Ran SP% **116.7**
Speed ratings (Par 107): **113,109,107,107,95 94**
CSF £35.22 CT £85.96 TOTE £6.10: £2.60, £2.90; EX 28.10 Trifecta £144.70.
Owner T A Rahman **Bred** Petra Bloodstock Agency **Trained** Hambleton, N Yorks

FOCUS
A good sprint handicap, run nearly a second inside the standard. The winner has been rated in line with his better 2018 form.

1848 WESTWOOD H'CAP 1m 4f 23y
5:10 (5:10) (Class 5) (0-75,75) 4-Y-O+
£4,284 (£1,282; £641; £320; £300; £300) **Stalls** Low

Form RPR

-641 **1** **Archive (FR)**[8] 1666 9-8-12 **69** .... BenRobinson(3) 1 77+
(Brian Ellison) *trckd ldrs: wnt 2nd over 2f out: rdn to ld over 1f out: styd on wl fnl 100yds* **3/1[1]**

114- **2** 2 1/4 **Flower Power**[169] 8718 8-9-1 **69** .... (p) DougieCostello 12 72
(Tony Coyle) *hld up in rr: hdwy on inner 2f out: plld out over 1f out: styd on ins fnl f: tk 2nd towards fin: nt trble wnr* **28/1**

0-00 **3** 1 1/4 **Be Perfect (USA)**[15] 1508 10-9-1 **69** .... (p) JamesSullivan 2 70
(Ruth Carr) *led: stdd pce after 4f: increased tempo 3f out: rdn over 2f out: hdd over 1f out: no ex fnl 100yds* **10/1**

560- **4** nk **Zihaam**[193] 8002 5-8-8 **67** .... BenSanderson(5) 4 67
(Roger Fell) *midfield: hdwy over 2f out: swtchd lft whn chsng ldrs over 1f out: one pce fnl 100yds* **6/1[3]**

-345 **5** hd **Iconic Girl**[22] 1343 4-8-12 **66** .... FrannyNorton 6 66
(Andrew Balding) *racd keenly: hld up: rdn over 2f out: hdwy over 1f out: styd on towards fin: nvr able to chal* **4/1[2]**

50-3 **6** 2 1/4 **Bit Of A Quirke**[8] 1666 6-9-1 **69** .... AndrewMullen 9 65
(Mark Walford) *midfield: rdn over 2f out: edgd rt u.p ins fnl f: no imp: eased towards fin* **7/1**

426- **7** 3 3/4 **Swansway**[176] 8507 6-8-10 **64** .... NathanEvans 7 54
(Michael Easterby) *midfield: lost pl over 7f out: in rr 6f out: rdn over 2f out: nvr a threat* **12/1**

12-4 **8** 1 **Just Wait (IRE)**[14] 1525 4-9-7 **75** .... JoeFanning 5 64
(Mark Johnston) *hld up: hdwy after 4f: sn prom and chsd ldr over 7f out: rdn and lost 2nd over 2f out: wknd over 1f out* **15/2**

0520 **9** 1 **Gendarme (IRE)**[25] 1292 4-8-12 **66** .... LukeMorris 8 53
(Alexandra Dunn) *hld up: hdwy and swtchd let over 7f out: midfield: rdn and lost pl over 3f out: n.d after* **20/1**

460- **10** 8 **Accessor (IRE)**[193] 7993 4-9-5 **73** .... PaulMulrennan 3 47
(Michael Dods) *midfield: impr to chse ldrs over 7f out: drvn and lost pl over 3f out: wknd over 2f out* **11/1**

104- **11** 1 **Airplane (IRE)**[168] 8743 4-8-11 **65** .... DuranFentiman 10 38
(Tim Easterby) *chsd ldr tl over 7f out: remained prom: rdn and wknd over 2f out* **28/1**

2m 40.23s (1.43) **Going Correction** +0.15s/f (Good) 11 Ran SP% **120.3**
Speed ratings (Par 103): **101,99,98,98,98 96,94,93,93,87 87**
CSF £99.48 CT £756.64 TOTE £3.70: £1.80, £5.70, £3.50; EX 79.80 Trifecta £819.70.
Owner Brian Ellison Racing Club **Bred** E A R L Elevages Des Loges & J Hanamy **Trained** Norton, N Yorks

FOCUS
Ordinary handicap form.

1849 RACING TV NOVICE STKS 1m 100y
5:40 (5:42) (Class 5) 4-Y-O+ **£4,140** (£1,232; £615; £307) **Stalls** Low

Form RPR

1 **Katinka (FR)**[212] 4-9-0 75 .... HollieDoyle 9 71
(Archie Watson) *chsd ldr: led over 2f out: rdn over 1f out: kpt on wl* **4/1[2]**

23 **2** 1 1/4 **Blindingly (GER)**[47] 971 4-9-5 0 .... AndrewMullen 5 73
(Ben Haslam) *chsd ldrs: rdn over 3f out: swtchd lft over 2f out: wnt 2nd over 1f out: no imp on wnr towards fin* **9/2[3]**

4-44 **3** 5 **Mount Ararat (IRE)**[63] 696 4-9-5 81 .... (p[1]) BenCurtis 4 63
(K R Burke) *racd keenly: led: rdn and hdd over 2f out: lost 2nd over 1f out: one pce u.p fnl f* **1/1[1]**

4 4 **Spiorad (IRE)**[196] 7915 4-9-5 0 .... ShaneGray 8 54
(David O'Meara) *hld up on outer: stdy hdwy over 3f out: rdn whn chsng ldrs over 2f out: no imp over 1f out and wl btn* **4/1[2]**

5 9 **Heavenly Secret (IRE)**[46] 4-9-5 0 .... (t[1]) DougieCostello 2 36
(Tony Coyle) *hld up: rdn over 3f out: nvr able to get on terms w ldrs* **40/1**

6 2 1/4 **Emerald Fox** 4-9-0 0 .... LukeMorris 3 26
(Robyn Brisland) *chsd ldrs: rdn over 3f out: wknd over 1f out* **11/1**

0-00 **7** 2 1/4 **Dutch Melody**[8] 1663 5-8-7 39 .... VictorSantos(7) 1 21
(Lucinda Egerton) *hld up: rdn over 3f out: nvr got involved* **150/1**

00-0 **8** 1 3/4 **Pontecarlo Boy**[6] 1723 5-9-5 39 .... JoeFanning 6 22
(Richard Whitaker) *midfield: rdn over 3f out: sn outpcd: wknd over 1f out* **66/1**

1m 47.47s (1.07) **Going Correction** +0.15s/f (Good) 8 Ran SP% **121.1**
Speed ratings (Par 103): **100,98,93,89,80 78,76,74**
CSF £23.71 TOTE £4.10: £1.10, £1.20, £1.10; EX 23.90 Trifecta £49.00.

Owner The Keg Partnership **Bred** D Krajnc, P Lazare Et Al **Trained** Upper Lambourn, W Berks

FOCUS

Little strength in depth to this older-horse novice event. The level is a bit fluid.

1850 RACING AGAIN NEXT THURSDAY FILLIES' H'CAP — 1m 100y

6:10 (6:11) (Class 5) (0-70,71) 4-Y-O+

£4,284 (£1,282; £641; £320; £300; £300) **Stalls** Low

Form RPR

066- **1** **Kylie Rules**[205] 7601 4-8-12 **60**.................................. JamesSullivan 3 78
(Ruth Carr) *midfield: rapid hdwy 3f out: led over 2f out: edgd rt over 1f out: r.o to draw clr ins fnl f: eased cl home* **13/2**

130- **2** *8* **Ideal Candy (IRE)**[205] 7603 4-9-9 **71**..............................(h) ShaneGray 4 72
(Karen Tutty) *led: rdn and hdd over 2f out: no ch w wnr fnl f* **9/2**[2]

003- **3** *1* **Shazzab (IRE)**[191] 8052 4-9-0 **62**.................................. PaulHanagan 1 61
(Richard Fahey) *chsd ldrs: rdn over 2f out: kpt on same pce u.p fnl f* **5/1**[3]

-400 **4** *1 ½* **Alexandrakollontai (IRE)**[19] 1401 9-9-2 **69**.........(b) ConnorMurtagh(5) 2 65
(Alistair Whillans) *hld up: rdn and hdwy on inner over 2f out: kpt on ins fnl f: nvr able to trble ldrs* **16/1**

500- **5** *1 ½* **Dominannie (IRE)**[165] 8830 6-8-3 **51** oh4 ow1............. AndrewMullen 6 44
(Ron Barr) *hld up: drvn over 2f out: hdwy over 1f out: one pce ins fnl f: nvr able to trble ldrs* **28/1**

20-6 **6** *6* **Acadian Angel (IRE)**[9] 1648 5-8-12 **60**....................... RoystonFfrench 8 40
(Steph Hollinshead) *in rr: rdn over 3f out: kpt on u.p over 1f out: nvr a threat* **16/1**

2122 **7** *2 ¼* **Elixsoft (IRE)**[12] 1563 4-9-6 **68**..................................(p[1]) BenCurtis 7 43
(Roger Fell) *midfield: rdn and wknd over 2f out* **9/4**[1]

2-54 **8** *hd* **Bubbly**[95] 202 4-9-1 **63**.................................. LukeMorris 10 38
(Mark Loughnane) *in tch: rdn 3f out: wknd over 2f out* **25/1**

000- **9** *9* **Roue De Charrette**[151] 9125 4-8-2 **50** oh4..................(p[1]) NathanEvans 11 6
(Geoffrey Harker) *midfield: rdn on outer over 3f out: on wd outside and wknd over 2f out* **66/1**

6/00 **10** *1 ½* **Dream On Dreamer (IRE)**[16] 1478 5-7-10 **51** ow1.(tp) VictorSantos(7) 5 4
(Lucinda Egerton) *chsd ldr tl rdn 3f out: hung lft over 2f out: sn wknd* **100/1**

0-13 **11** *¾* **Gainsay**[9] 1655 4-9-7 **69**.................................. NicolaCurrie 12 20
(Jonathan Portman) *chsd ldrs: cl up 3f out: rdn over 2f out: sn wknd* **9/2**[2]

1m 46.67s (0.27) **Going Correction** +0.15s/f (Good) **11 Ran SP% 118.7**

Speed ratings (Par 100): **104,96,95,93,92 86,83,83,74,73 72**

CSF £35.42 CT £143.73 TOTE £6.90: £2.10, £1.30, £2.40; EX 44.10 Trifecta £289.10.

Owner J A Knox and Mrs M A Knox **Bred** J A Knox **Trained** Huby, N Yorks

FOCUS

A modest fillies' handicap with a very easy winner. The second has been rated a bit below form on her reappearance.

T/Plt: £102.10 to a £1 stake. Pool: £56,711.85 - 405.29 winning units T/Qpdt: £53.00 to a £1 stake. Pool: £3,768.90 - 52.61 winning units **Darren Owen**

1828 NEWMARKET (R-H)

Wednesday, April 17

OFFICIAL GOING: Good to firm (good in places; watered; 7.8)

Wind: light, half against Weather: hazy sunshine

1851 BET365 H'CAP — 6f

1:50 (1:51) (Class 2) (0-100,98) 3-Y-O **£16,172** (£4,812; £2,405; £1,202) **Stalls** Low

Form RPR

12-1 **1** **Top Breeze (IRE)**[23] 1336 3-8-9 **86**.................................. ShaneKelly 6 93
(Richard Hughes) *sweating; mde all and crossed over to r against far rail: rdn ent fnl f: clr and styd on strly ins fnl f: rdn out* **15/2**[3]

126- **2** *1* **Yousini**[217] 7168 3-9-0 **91**..................................(w) TomEaves 3 95
(Kevin Ryan) *bmpd s: hld up in tch towards rr: clsd whn nt clr run and swtchd lft over 1f out: styd on wl ins fnl f to go 2nd wl ins fnl f: nvr getting to wnr* **16/1**

05-2 **3** *½* **Chapelli**[8] 1662 3-9-2 **93**.................................. JamesDoyle 2 95
(Mark Johnston) *looked wl; chsd wnr early: sn settled bk and in tch in midfield: effrt over 1f out: drvn and chsd wnr 1f out: kpt on but no imp: lost 2nd wl ins fnl f* **6/1**[2]

210- **4** *1* **Naughty Rascal (IRE)**[172] 8644 3-9-0 **91**....................... TomMarquand 9 90
(Richard Hannon) *looked wl; chsd ldr sn after s tl over 4f out: styd chsng ldrs: drvn over 1f out: unable qck and one pce ins fnl f* **8/1**

013- **5** *nse* **Breath Of Air**[172] 8629 3-9-2 **93**.................................. RyanMoore 1 92
(Charles Hills) *tall; hld up in tch in midfield: nt clr run against far rail over 1f out: effrt 1f out: kpt on but no real imp ins fnl f* **3/1**[1]

105- **6** *½* **Sheila's Showcase**[191] 8041 3-8-4 **81**.................................. DavidEgan 4 78+
(Denis Coakley) *wnt rt and bmpd rival leaving stalls: in tch in midfield: unable qck and outpcd over 1f out: rallied and kpt on u.p ins fnl f: nvr enough pce to threaten ldrs* **8/1**

-436 **7** *½* **Don Armado (IRE)**[46] 989 3-9-1 **92**....................(t) RichardKingscote 8 87
(Stuart Williams) *hld up in tch: effrt over 2f out: carried rt: squeezed for room and swtchd lft over 1f out: kpt on ins fnl f: no threat ldrs* **14/1**

232- **8** *1* **Moyassar**[168] 8741 3-9-7 **98**..................................(w) JimCrowley 7 90
(Richard Hannon) *looked wl; s.i.s: hld up in tch in rr: effrt 2f out: hdwy and edgd rt over 1f out: no ex 1f out: wknd ins fnl f* **6/1**[2]

240- **9** *1 ½* **Alfie Solomons (IRE)**[193] 7988 3-8-13 **90**....................... TomQueally 11 77
(Richard Spencer) *bit edgy; chsd ldrs tl hdwy to press wnr over 4f out: unable qck u.p over 1f out: lost 2nd 1f out and wknd ins fnl f* **12/1**

135- **10** *5* **Jack's Point**[155] 9045 3-9-6 **97**.................................. MartinDwyer 5 68
(William Muir) *a towards rr: struggling and rdn whn swtchd lft over 1f out: wl btn over 1f out: wknd* **25/1**

40-4 **11** *6* **Oberyn Martell**[55] 838 3-9-1 **92**.................................. CharlesBishop 10 44
(Eve Johnson Houghton) *chsd ldrs: rdn ent fnl 2f: losing pl whn squeezed for room and hmpd over 1f out: bhd fnl f* **16/1**

1m 12.62s (0.72) **Going Correction** +0.275s/f (Good) **11 Ran SP% 117.5**

Speed ratings (Par 104): **106,104,104,102,102 101,101,99,97,91 83**

CSF £120.49 CT £771.02 TOTE £7.80: £2.40, £4.50, £2.10; EX 127.80 Trifecta £1295.90.

Owner Life's A Breeze **Bred** John Cullinan **Trained** Upper Lambourn, Berks

FOCUS

Far side course. Stalls: far side. The watered ground (3mm applied after racing on Tuesday) was given as good to firm, good in places (Going Stick 7.8). As is often the case, racing against the far rail looked an advantage, and the winner's early pace to bag the lead proved crucial. The trend did not continue throughout the card, though. The second has been rated up a length on his 2yo form, with the fourth and fifth close to form.

1852 BET365 WOOD DITTON MAIDEN STKS (PLUS 10 RACE) — 1m

2:25 (2:34) (Class 3) 3-Y-O **£9,703** (£2,887; £1,443; £721) **Stalls** Low

Form RPR

1 **UAE Jewel** 3-9-5 0.................................. AndreaAtzeni 11 99+
(Roger Varian) *str; chsd ldr: clsd and upsides ldr 2f out: rdn to ld over 1f out: asserting whn edgd rt ins fnl f: r.o strly: v readily* **10/11**[1]

2 *5* **Al Hadeer (USA)** 3-9-5 0.................................. JimCrowley 2 87+
(William Haggas) *str; chsd ldrs: effrt ent fnl 2f: clr 3rd but outpcd over 1f out: no ch w wnr and kpt on same pce ins fnl f: snatched 2nd last strides* **6/1**[2]

3 *hd* **Mutaraffa (IRE)** 3-9-5 0..................................(h[1]) RichardKingscote 9 86
(Charles Hills) *tall; racd keenly: led: wandered rt and hdd over 1f out: no ex and wknd fnl 100yds: lost 2nd last strides* **33/1**

4 *6* **Desert Icon (FR)** 3-9-5 0.................................. JamesDoyle 5 72+
(William Haggas) *tall; ly; green and coltish; s.i.s: in rr: pushed along wl over 2f out: sme prog and swtchd lft 1f out: kpt on ins fnl f: nvr trbld ldrs* **12/1**

5 *nse* **Junooh (IRE)** 3-9-5 0.................................. RyanMoore 3 72+
(Sir Michael Stoute) *leggy; bit edgy; restless in stalls: t.k.h: hld up towards rr: pushed along over 2f out: sme prog whn nt clr run and swtchd lft 1f out: kpt on: nvr trbld ldrs (colt lost a right-fore shoe on the way to post and was re-shod at the start)* **20/1**

6 *2 ½* **Kung Fu** 3-9-5 0.................................. SilvestreDeSousa 1 66
(Simon Crisford) *str; dwlt: sn rcvrd and in tch in midfield: struggling and rdn 3f out: sn outpcd and wl btn 2f out: plugged on (jockey said colt was slowly away)* **12/1**

7 *1 ¾* **Samba Saravah (USA)** 3-9-5 0.................................. JasonWatson 6 62
(Jeremy Noseda) *athletic; gd walker; midfield: rdn over 2f out: sn outpcd and struggling: wl btn over 1f out: wknd ins fnl f* **33/1**

8 *3 ½* **Wild Animal** 3-9-5 0.................................. ChristopheSoumillon 8 54
(Saeed bin Suroor) *str; looked wl; chsd ldng trio: rdn over 2f out: sn struggling and outpcd: wl btn over 1f out: wknd* **7/1**[3]

9 *3* **Damlaj** 3-9-5 0.................................. DaneO'Neill 4 47
(Owen Burrows) *compact; midfield: rdn over 2f out: sn outpcd and wl btn over 1f out: wknd fnl f* **25/1**

10 *½* **Geomatrician (FR)** 3-9-5 0.................................. DavidProbert 7 46
(Andrew Balding) *str; s.i.s: rn green in rr and sn rdn along: nvr involved* **16/1**

11 *1 ¾* **Caesonia** 3-9-0 0.................................. JamieSpencer 12 37
(Charles Hills) *workmanlike; sltly on toes; stdd and dropped in after s: hld up towards rr: rdn 3f out: sn struggling and btn: wl bhd fnl f* **66/1**

12 *4 ½* **Inspirational (IRE)** 3-9-0 0.................................. DanielMuscutt 10 27
(Ed Dunlop) *workmanlike; bit on the leg; midfield: rdn over 2f out: sn struggling and lost pl: wl bhd ins fnl f* **100/1**

1m 39.51s (1.11) **Going Correction** +0.275s/f (Good) **12 Ran SP% 117.4**

Speed ratings (Par 102): **105,100,99,93,93 91,89,86,83,82 80,76**

CSF £5.68 TOTE £1.70: £1.10, £2.00, £8.30; EX 8.40 Trifecta £134.70.

Owner Sheikh Mohammed Obaid Al Maktoum **Bred** Highclere Stud & Ors Bloodstock **Trained** Newmarket, Suffolk

FOCUS

Some quality horses have emerged from this, with Mukhadram, awarded the race in 2012, sticking out as the best. However, the 2016 running was particularly strong with regards to depth, with subsequent Group 3 winner Sky Kingdom landing it, followed home by Muntahaa (third), Thundering Blue (fifth) and recent Australian Group 1 winner Shraaoh in sixth. That said, a lot of the other runnings have been fairly ordinary events. The opening level is set around the place averages.

1853 CONNAUGHT ACCESS FLOORING ABERNANT STKS (GROUP 3) — 6f

3:00 (3:07) (Class 1) 3-Y-O+

£34,026 (£12,900; £6,456; £3,216; £1,614; £810) **Stalls** Low

Form RPR

0-10 **1** **Keystroke**[39] 1103 7-9-7 104..................................(t) AdamKirby 7 112
(Stuart Williams) *sweating; dropped in bhd after s: off the pce in last pair: clsd 2f out: rdn and hdwy jst over 1f out: chsng ldrs and hung lft u.p ins fnl f: hung bk rt u.p but r.o wl to ld last strides* **66/1**

210- **2** *hd* **Yafta**[242] 6298 4-9-7 110.................................. JimCrowley 5 111+
(Richard Hannon) *off the pce in midfield: clsd 2f out: rdn and hdwy to chse ldrs 1f out: nt clr run and swtchd rt ins fnl f: r.o wl despite hanging lft to ld cl home: hdd last strides* **7/1**

024- **3** *nk* **Brando**[179] 8405 7-9-7 116.................................. TomEaves 6 110
(Kevin Ryan) *dropped in last trio: clsd 2f out: rdn to chse ldrs 1f out: str chal ins fnl f: kpt on to ld wl ins fnl f: hdd and lost 2 pls cl home* **15/8**[1]

44-3 **4** *1 ¾* **Equilateral**[18] 1412 4-9-7 104.................................. RyanMoore 3 104
(Charles Hills) *t.k.h: chsd ldng pair: swtchd lft and clsd to join ldrs over 1f out: rdn to jst over 1f out: drvn and hdd wl ins fnl f: short of room and wknd towards fin* **5/1**[3]

3-55 **5** *nse* **Sir Thomas Gresham (IRE)**[51] 909 4-9-7 99..........(t[1]) MartinDwyer 8 104
(Tim Pinfield) *chsd ldrs: rdn to ld over 1f out: sn hdd and one pce ins fnl f* **25/1**

55-6 **6** *2 ½* **Gifted Master (IRE)**[39] 1111 6-9-7 110..................................(b) JasonWatson 4 96
(Hugo Palmer) *pressed ldrs early but sn struggling to go pce and dropped to 4th: effrt 2f out: no imp: wl hld and plugged on same pce fnl f* **6/1**

600- **7** *5* **Time's Arrow (IRE)**[213] 7352 5-9-7 103.................................. DanielTudhope 2 80
(David O'Meara) *sn dropped to last pair and wl off the pce: effrt and clsd 2f out: no hdwy u.p over 1f out: wknd ins fnl f* **33/1**

260- **8** *4* **Dreamfield**[235] 6530 5-9-7 110.................................. JamesDoyle 1 67
(John Gosden) *led and set str gallop: rdn and hdd over 1f out: wknd ins fnl f* **11/4**[2]

1m 11.64s (-0.26) **Going Correction** +0.275s/f (Good) **8 Ran SP% 113.2**

Speed ratings (Par 113): **112,111,111,109,108 105,98,93**

CSF £462.75 TOTE £68.70: £11.50, £1.90, £1.10; EX 658.30 Trifecta £1797.60.

Owner GG Thoroughbreds XI **Bred** Cheveley Park Stud Ltd **Trained** Newmarket, Suffolk

FOCUS
The leaders went off too quick and the pace collapsed late on. The shock winner benefited from being held up last early on. The runner-up has been rated close to form, while the fifth helps set the standard.

1854 BET365 CRAVEN STKS (GROUP 3) (C&G) 1m
3:35 (3:39) (Class 1) 3-Y-O

£34,026 (£12,900; £6,456; £3,216; £1,614; £810) Stalls Low

Form RPR

1- **1** **Skardu**[201] 7736 3-9-0 0 .... JamesDoyle 1 112+
(William Haggas) *athletic; str; stdd after s: hld up in tch in last pair: clsd whn nt clr run and swtchd lft 2f out: rdn and hdwy to chal 1f out: led ins fnl f: edgd rt but hld on wl towards fin* **3/1**[2]

312- **2** *nk* **Momkin (IRE)**[236] 6476 3-9-0 90 .... MaximeGuyon 5 111
(Roger Charlton) *str; t.k.h: hld up in tch in midfield: clsd and nt clr run wl over 1f out: hdwy to press ldrs and n.m.r 1f out: ev ch and bmpd ins fnl f: kpt on wl but hld towards fin* **28/1**

1-1 **3** *1 ¾* **Set Piece**[99] 128 3-9-0 86 .... FrankieDettori 2 107
(Hugo Palmer) *ly; stdd s: hld up in tch in last pair: swtchd lft and clsd over 2f out: rdn and hdwy to chal jst over 1f out: led jst ins fnl f: sn hdd: edgd rt and no ex wl ins fnl f* **14/1**

11-4 **4** *¾* **Royal Marine (IRE)**[97] 169 3-9-0 113 .... ChristopheSoumillon 4 105+
(Saeed bin Suroor) *stdd s: t.k.h: hld up in midfield against far rail: effrt and forced to switch lft over 1f out: kpt on ins fnl f: nvr getting on terms w ldrs* **13/8**[1]

1- **5** *1 ½* **Zakouski**[147] 9170 3-9-0 0 .... WilliamBuick 10 102
(Charlie Appleby) *athletic; restless in stalls: chsd ldrs: ev ch u.p over 1f out tl no ex jst ins fnl f: wknd fnl 100yds* **7/2**[3]

251- **6** *1* **Watan**[170] 8690 3-9-0 105 .... RyanMoore 8 100
(Richard Hannon) *t.k.h: led: rdn and hrd pressed over 1f out: hdd jst ins fnl f: sn btn and wknd fnl 100yds* **12/1**

1-11 **7** *9* **Golden Spectrum**[53] 893 3-9-0 97 .... GeraldMosse 6 79
(Gay Kelleway) *athletic; t.k.h: hld up in tch in midfield: effrt over 2f out: sn struggling and outpcd wl over 1f out: wknd fnl f* **20/1**

1-1 **8** *1 ¼* **Jackstar (IRE)**[22] 1346 3-9-0 89 .... RichardKingscote 3 76
(Tom Dascombe) *str; t.k.h: chsd ldng pair: effrt over 2f out: sn struggling and outpcd over 1f out: wknd fnl f* **10/1**

1m 37.89s (-0.51) **Going Correction** +0.275s/f (Good) **8 Ran SP% 117.0**
Speed ratings (Par 108): **113,112,110,110,108 107,98,97**
CSF £78.70 TOTE £4.20: £1.30, £5.60, £2.50; EX 81.40 Trifecta £645.50.
Owner Abdulla Al Khalifa **Bred** Sheikh Abdulla Bin Isa Al-Khalifa **Trained** Newmarket, Suffolk

FOCUS
With Royal Marine not at his Group 1-winning best, the standard to aim at wasn't that high, but there were one or two promising performances, not least from the winner. The winner has been rated a bit below the race standard.

1855 ROSSDALES MAIDEN FILLIES' STKS (PLUS 10 RACE) 7f
4:10 (4:13) (Class 4) 3-Y-O £6,469 (£1,925; £962; £481) Stalls Low

Form RPR

3- **1** **Clerisy**[128] 9485 3-9-0 0 .... RyanMoore 10 80
(Sir Michael Stoute) *athletic; looked wl; racd in centre quintet: midfield overall: effrt to chse ldr over 1f out: styd on to ld 100yds out: hld on wl towards fin* **8/1**

2 *nk* **Gentlewoman (IRE)** 3-9-0 0 .... RobertHavlin 9 79
(John Gosden) *str; racd in centre quintet: stdd s: hld up in rr overall: effrt over 1f out: hdwy ins fnl f: wnt 2nd and pressing wnr wl ins fnl f: r.o wl* **10/1**

3 *1 ¾* **Ojooba** 3-9-0 0 .... JimCrowley 6 74
(Owen Burrows) *athletic; looked wl; racd in centre quintet: midfield overall: effrt to chse ldrs over 1f out: drvn and kpt on ins fnl f: wnt 3rd last strides* **2/1**[1]

4 *nk* **Aristocratic Lady (IRE)** 3-9-0 0 .... AndreaAtzeni 1 73
(Simon Crisford) *compact; t.k.h: racd far side and overall ldr: rdn over 1f out: hdd 100yds out: no ex and outpcd towards fin* **10/3**[3]

0- **5** *¾* **Thakaa (USA)**[128] 9485 3-9-0 0 .... DaneO'Neill 7 71
(Charles Hills) *str; sweating; on toes; racd far side: hld up in rr overall: swtchd lft and effrt over 1f out: styd on wl fnl 100yds: nvr trbld ldrs* **25/1**

223- **6** *shd* **Handmaiden**[176] 8512 3-9-0 85 .... FrankieDettori 12 70
(John Gosden) *led centre gp and chsd ldrs overall: effrt and unable qck over 1f out: kpt on same pce ins fnl f* **5/2**[2]

60- **7** *2* **Queen Of Burgundy**[153] 9068 3-9-0 0 .... JoeyHaynes 4 65
(Christine Dunnett) *leggy; racd far side: hld up in tch in midfield overall: effrt to chse ldrs and drvn over 1f out: no ex ins fnl f: wknd fnl 100yds* **150/1**

05- **8** *shd* **Pempie (IRE)**[147] 9170 3-9-0 0 .... DavidProbert 8 65
(Andrew Balding) *str; racd far side: in tch in midfield overall: effrt over 1f out: sn unable qck and wknd ins fnl f* **33/1**

0- **9** *5* **Secret Treaties**[176] 8512 3-9-0 0 .... HayleyTurner 2 51
(Christine Dunnett) *leggy; racd far side: t.k.h: w overall ldr tl unable qck and lost pl over 1f out: wknd fnl f* **150/1**

10 *4 ½* **Starlight** 3-9-0 0 .... JamieSpencer 11 39
(Michael Bell) *athletic; racd in centre quintet: hld up in rr: effrt over 2f out: sn struggling: bhd ins fnl f* **40/1**

11 *3 ¼* **Cala D'Or (IRE)** 3-9-0 0 .... EoinWalsh 3 30
(Samuel Farrell, Ire) *workmanlike; racd far side: t.k.h: chsd overall ldrs: rdn wl over 2f out: lost pl over 1f out: bhd ins fnl f* **100/1**

1m 28.43s (3.03) **Going Correction** +0.275s/f (Good) **11 Ran SP% 116.7**
Speed ratings (Par 97): **93,92,90,90,89 89,87,86,81,76 72**
CSF £79.06 TOTE £7.40: £2.30, £3.30, £1.10; EX 67.40 Trifecta £354.80.
Owner K Abdullah **Bred** Juddmonte Farms Ltd **Trained** Newmarket, Suffolk

FOCUS
This maiden has gone to fillies who have held their own in Pattern company in recent times, notably Grade 1 winner Sheikha Reika last year. The field split into two groups soon after the start and the finish suggested it was better to be in the bunch that came down the middle of the track than up against the rail, although it contained plenty of the more fancied horses. The winner has been rated a bit below par.

1856 BRITISH EBF BET365 "CONFINED" NOVICE STKS (PLUS 10 RACE) (HORSES WHICH HAVE RUN NO MORE THAN ONCE) 1m 2f
4:45 (4:46) (Class 4) 3-Y-O £6,469 (£1,925; £962; £481) Stalls Low

Form RPR

2- **1** **Jalmoud**[146] 9203 3-9-2 0 .... WilliamBuick 7 93+
(Charlie Appleby) *compact; mde all: rdn over 1f out: clr and in command ins fnl f: r.o strly* **15/8**[1]

2 *2* **Cape Cavalli (IRE)** 3-9-2 0 .... SilvestreDeSousa 6 88
(Simon Crisford) *str; in tch in midfield: rdn over 2f out: rn green and outpcd 2f out: rallied u.p 1f out: wnt 2nd wl ins fnl f: nvr getting to wnr but gng on wl at fin* **13/2**

1- **3** *1* **Eightsome Reel**[152] 9104 3-9-9 0 .... HayleyTurner 5 93
(Michael Bell) *str; broke wl: sn restrained into midfield and bmpd after 1f: effrt over 1f out: hdwy to chse ldrs over 1f out: nvr getting on terms w wnr but kpt on wl to go 3rd towards fin* **25/1**

4 *1 ¼* **Mons Star (IRE)** 3-9-2 0 .... ChristopheSoumillon 4 84
(Saeed bin Suroor) *str; coltish; chsd ldrs: bmpd after 1f: effrt to chse clr wnr over 1f out: no imp and lost 2 pls wl ins fnl f* **11/1**

1 **5** *5* **One Vision (IRE)**[101] 103 3-9-9 0 .... JamesDoyle 9 81
(Charlie Appleby) *compact; hld up in last trio: effrt and hung lft 2f out: no imp over 1f out: wl hld and plugged on same pce fnl f* **6/1**[3]

4- **6** *nk* **Vindolanda**[137] 9354 3-8-11 0 .... JamieSpencer 1 68
(Charles Hills) *athletic; hld up in last pair: effrt over 2f out: no imp over 1f out: wl hld and plugged on same pce fnl f* **33/1**

1 **7** *3 ¼* **El Misk**[16] 1484 3-9-9 0 .... FrankieDettori 8 73
(John Gosden) *str; sweating; chsd wnr tl 7f out: styd chsng ldrs: rdn to chse wnr jst over 2f out tl over 1f out: sn outpcd and btn: wknd ins fnl f (trainer's rep could offer no explanation for the colt's performance other than the colt stopped quickly)* **9/4**[2]

2 **8** *1 ¾* **Doughan Alb**[15] 1495 3-9-2 0 .... RyanMoore 3 63
(Richard Hannon) *athletic; chsd ldrs: wnt 2nd 7f out tl jst over 2f out: sn dropped out: wknd fnl f* **25/1**

6- **9** *2 ½* **Catch My Breath**[168] 8739 3-9-2 0 .... BrettDoyle 2 58
(John Ryan) *workmanlike; hld up in last pair: effrt over 2f out: no prog and sn outpcd: bhd fnl f* **100/1**

2m 8.47s (3.07) **Going Correction** +0.275s/f (Good) **9 Ran SP% 113.1**
Speed ratings (Par 100): **98,96,95,94,90 90,87,86,84**
CSF £13.76 TOTE £2.50: £1.30, £1.60, £4.80; EX 13.30 Trifecta £168.50.
Owner Godolphin **Bred** Godolphin **Trained** Newmarket, Suffolk

FOCUS
An interesting contest considering the race conditions, and they all came down the middle of the track. The level is a bit fluid.

1857 COATES & SEELY BLANC DE BLANCS H'CAP 1m
5:20 (5:23) (Class 4) (0-85,84) 3-Y-O

£7,762 (£2,310; £1,154; £577; £300; £300) Stalls Low

Form RPR

336- **1** **Aweedram (IRE)**[161] 8930 3-9-1 78 .... WilliamBuick 4 86
(Alan King) *athletic; sltly on toes; t.k.h: hld up wl in tch in midfield: effrt over 2f out: rdn to ld wl over 1f out: styd on wl ins fnl f: rdn out* **5/1**[2]

2 *¾* **Archaeology**[178] 8437 3-9-0 77 .... JamieSpencer 2 83
(Jedd O'Keeffe) *stdd s: hld up wl in tch in rr: clsd over 2f out: rdn to press wnr 1f out: kpt on but a hld ins fnl f* **14/1**

341- **3** *1* **Gallic**[180] 8377 3-9-6 83 .... GeraldMosse 7 87+
(Ed Walker) *t.k.h: hld up wl in tch towards rr: clsd to chse ldrs 2f out: kpt on same pce u.p ins fnl f* **12/1**

0050 **4** *¾* **Burj**[48] 956 3-9-7 84 .... (h) AdamKirby 12 86
(Saeed bin Suroor) *hld up wl in tch in midfield: effrt and clsd over 1f out: drvn and kpt on ins fnl f* **10/1**

541- **5** *¾* **Brian Epstein (IRE)**[198] 7845 3-9-7 84 .... TomMarquand 15 85
(Richard Hannon) *str; chsd ldrs: effrt to ld jst over 2f out: hdd wl over 1f out: unable qck and wknd ins fnl f* **5/1**[2]

041- **6** *2 ¼* **Karnavaal (IRE)**[181] 8345 3-9-5 82 .... JimCrowley 14 77+
(Sir Michael Stoute) *hld up wl in tch: clsd to chse ldrs 2f out: drvn and unable qck over 1f out: wknd ins fnl f* **11/4**[1]

7 *nse* **The Corporal (IRE)**[172] 8652 3-9-1 78 .... GeorgeWood 5 73
(Chris Wall) *t.k.h: chsd ldrs: shuffled bk and short of room 2f out: swtchd rt and tried to rally over 1f out: kpt on same pce ins fnl f* **66/1**

121- **8** *½* **Jem Scuttle (USA)**[144] 9256 3-8-11 74 .... (t) TomEaves 8 68
(Declan Carroll) *hld up wl in tch in rr: stmbld over 6f out: swtchd lft and effrt 2f out: sn hung rt: hdwy and stl hanging rt ins fnl f: nvr trbld ldrs (jockey said colt stumbled approaching six furlongs out)* **40/1**

044- **9** *4* **God Has Given**[191] 8057 3-8-13 76 .... RichardKingscote 13 61
(Ian Williams) *hld up wl in tch in rr: effrt 2f out: nvr getting on terms w ldrs and wl hld whn hung rt ins fnl f* **22/1**

55-4 **10** *1 ¼* **Self Assessment (IRE)**[22] 1345 3-9-3 80 .... CliffordLee 10 62
(K R Burke) *stmbld leaving stalls: sn rcvrd and prom: led over 6f out tl hdd jst over 2f out: sn outpcd: wknd f* **20/1**

31-4 **11** *1* **Harbour Spirit (FR)**[21] 1360 3-9-3 80 .... ShaneKelly 9 60
(Richard Hughes) *mounted on crse and taken down early: chsd ldrs: shuffled bk and short of room 2f out: no imp after and wl hld whn short of room and hmpd ins fnl f* **20/1**

521- **12** *nse* **Kamikaze Lord (USA)**[212] 7366 3-9-5 82 .... RyanMoore 3 62
(Jeremy Noseda) *t.k.h: led tl over 6f out: chsd ldrs tl 2f out: unable qck u.p over 1f out: wknd fnl f* **8/1**[3]

440- **13** *1* **Purbeck Hills (IRE)**[126] 9500 3-8-7 70 .... HarryBentley 6 47
(Richard Hannon) *wl in tch in midfield: pushed along wl over 2f out: sn struggling: wl hld whn short of room and impeded ins fnl f* **20/1**

1-66 **14** *hd* **Gold At Midnight**[14] 1516 3-8-10 73 .... (p) DavidProbert 1 50
(William Stone) *t.k.h: chsd ldrs tl 2f out: unable qck u.p over 1f out: wknd fnl f* **50/1**

1m 40.97s (2.57) **Going Correction** +0.275s/f (Good) **14 Ran SP% 119.1**
Speed ratings (Par 100): **98,97,96,95,94 92,92,91,87,86 85,85,84,84**
CSF £65.13 CT £806.22 TOTE £5.60: £2.10, £5.10, £2.50; EX 73.20 Trifecta £792.90.
Owner McNeill Family & Niall Farrell **Bred** Petra Bloodstock Agency Ltd **Trained** Barbury Castle, Wilts

FOCUS
An interesting handicap, in which the whole field came together more towards the far rail. There should be a few winners in the short term to come out of this. It's been rated around the fourth to his turf form and the fifth in line with his maiden form.

T/Plt: £113.10 to a £1 stake. Pool: £133,706.76 - 862.90 winning units T/Qpdt: £39.20 to a £1 stake. Pool: £11,988.98 - 226.06 winning units **Steve Payne**

[1549]SOUTHWELL (L-H)

Wednesday, April 17

OFFICIAL GOING: Fibresand: standard

1858 BETWAY LIVE CASINO H'CAP — 1m 4f 14y(F)

6:00 (6:00) (Class 6) (0-60,60) 4-Y-O+

£3,105 (£924; £461; £400; £400; £400) **Stalls Low**

Form — RPR

4236 **1** **Contingency Fee**[7] [1680] 4-8-9 **55**............(p) GraceMcEntee(7) 7 — 66
(Phil McEntee) *trckd ldrs: hdwy over 5f out: cl up 4f out: led wl over 2f out: rdn wl over 1f out: wandered ent fnl f: kpt on strly towards fin* **11/2**[2]

5-22 **2** 3 ¾ **Thecornishbarron (IRE)**[14] [1527] 7-8-9 **48**............CamHardie 3 — 52
(Brian Ellison) *prom: hdwy and cl up over 4f out: chal 3f out: rdn over 2f out: drvn and ch over 1f out: kpt on same pce u.p fnl f* **8/1**

2614 **3** 7 **Going Native**[18] [1426] 4-8-8 **54**............RhonaPindar(7) 6 — 48
(Olly Williams) *sn led: clr 7f out: pushed along and jnd over 4f out: rdn over 3f out: hdd wl over 2f out: sn drvn and grad wknd* **8/1**

0 **4** 1 ¼ **Panatos (FR)**[18] [1429] 4-9-6 **59**............RossaRyan 10 — 51
(Alexandra Dunn) *towards rr: hdwy 1/2-way: pushed along to chse ldrs 4f out: rdn over 3f out: sn drvn and no imp* **14/1**

4202 **5** 6 **Schindlers Ark (USA)**[14] [1519] 5-8-9 **48**............CharlieBennett 9 — 29
(Jane Chapple-Hyam) *prom on outer: pushed along 5f out: rdn 4f out: sn drvn and outpcd* **8/1**

53 **6** 3 ¼ **Quila Saeda (GER)**[14] [1525] 5-8-13 **57**............TheodoreLadd(5) 11 — 33
(Michael Appleby) *in rr: hdwy over 3f out: rdn along wl over 2f out: kpt on: nvr nr ldrs (vet said mare finished lame left fore)* **7/1**[3]

255- **7** 3 ¾ **Motahassen (IRE)**[168] [8745] 5-9-5 **58**............JasonHart 4 — 28
(Declan Carroll) *sn pushed along to chse ldrs: rdn over 4f out: sn wknd* **11/4**[1]

4600 **8** ½ **Red Touch (USA)**[14] [1526] 7-9-7 **60**............(v) AlistairRawlinson 5 — 29
(Michael Appleby) *in tch: rdn along over 4f out: sn outpcd (jockey said gelding had no more to give)* **25/1**

-526 **9** 5 **Mundersfield**[46] [991] 5-9-2 **60**............(h) DylanHogan(5) 8 — 21
(David Simcock) *chsd ldrs: rdn along over 5f out: sn wknd and bhd (vet said mare lost it's left fore shoe)* **14/1**

0-60 **10** 12 **Zahraani**[74] [562] 4-8-11 **50**............KieranO'Neill 2
(J R Jenkins) *prom on inner: rdn along over 5f out: sn wknd and bhd* **33/1**

00-0 **11** 4 ½ **Place Des Vosges (IRE)**[17] [1463] 4-9-4 **57**............(t[1]) PJMcDonald 12
(David Menuisier) *a in rr: bhd fnl 3f* **10/1**

0-00 **12** 1 ½ **Let's Be Happy (IRE)**[36] [1163] 5-9-1 **57**............WilliamCox(3) 1
(Mandy Rowland) *dwlt: a bhd (jockey said mare was slowly away and never travelling)* **50/1**

640- **13** 14 **Intermodal**[126] [9510] 5-9-0 **58**............(p[1]) HarrisonShaw(5) 13
(Julia Brooke) *in tch: effrt to chse ldrs on outer 1/2-way: rdn along 5f out: sn lost pl and bhd fnl 3f* **33/1**

/6-0 **P** **Four Mile Beach**[14] [1369] 6-9-2 **55**............RachelRichardson 14
(Michael Chapman) *a in rr: bhd whn lost action and p.u 5f out* **150/1**

2m 38.97s (-2.03) **Going Correction** -0.05s/f (Stan) **14 Ran SP% 122.7**
Speed ratings (Par 101): **104,101,96,96,92 89,87,87,83,75 72,71,62,**
CSF £48.37 CT £360.45 TOTE £6.70: £2.70, £1.10, £3.80; EX 48.20 Trifecta £319.80.
Owner M Hall **Bred** Whitwell Bloodstock **Trained** Newmarket, Suffolk

FOCUS
Absolutely desperate stuff with most of the field tailed off by the home turn. The gallop looked strong and they were strung out from an early stage.

1859 SUNRACING.CO.UK H'CAP — 1m 13y(F)

6:30 (6:31) (Class 5) (0-75,77) 4-Y-O+

£3,752 (£1,116; £557; £400; £400; £400) **Stalls Low**

Form — RPR

3440 **1** **Bond Angel**[9] [1653] 4-8-5 **64**............TheodoreLadd(5) 9 — 75
(David Evans) *dwlt: in tch and swtchd rt to outer after 2f: hdwy and cl up 1/2-way: wd st: led over 2f out: sn rdn: drvn over 1f out: kpt on strly fnl f* **15/2**[2]

4232 **2** 3 **Majestic Moon (IRE)**[14] [1526] 9-9-2 **70**............(p) ShelleyBirkett 3 — 74
(Julia Feilden) *trckd ldrs: hdwy 3f out: swtchd rt to outer and rdn 2f out: drvn to chse wnr ins fnl f: no imp towards fin* **9/1**

0061 **3** 1 ½ **Muqarred (USA)**[14] [1526] 7-8-10 **64**............(p) GrahamLee 8 — 65
(Roger Fell) *trckd ldrs: swtchd rt towards outer after 2f: pushed along 3f out: wd st: sn rdn and edging lft: drvn and kpt on fnl f* **9/1**

10-4 **4** nk **Mujassam**[13] [1552] 7-9-7 **75**............(b) DanielTudhope 4 — 75
(David O'Meara) *slt ld 2f: cl up: rdn over 2f out and ev ch tl drvn over 1f out and grad wknd* **9/1**

2020 **5** 2 ½ **Mama Africa (IRE)**[14] [1526] 5-9-4 **75**............JaneElliott(3) 7 — 69
(David Barron) *cl up: slt ld after 2f: rdn along 3f out: hdd over 2f out: sn drvn and grad wknd* **20/1**

0404 **6** nk **Laqab (IRE)**[7] [1675] 6-8-10 **64**............PaddyMathers 5 — 58
(Derek Shaw) *dwlt and in rr: hdwy towards inner wl over 2f out: sn rdn: kpt on u.p fr over 1f out (vet said gelding lost it's left hind shoe)* **14/1**

3602 **7** ½ **Mr Carbonator**[8] [1660] 4-8-9 **66**............JamieGormley(3) 1 — 58
(Philip Kirby) *cl up on inner: pushed along over 3f out: rdn wl over 2f out: sn drvn and grad wknd* **8/1**[3]

60-1 **8** 7 **Casement (IRE)**[8] [1660] 5-9-9 **77** 5ex............AlistairRawlinson 10 — 53
(Michael Appleby) *cl up: pushed along over 3f out: sn rdn and btn over 2f out (trainers' rep said gelding would be better suited by a turf track)* **3/1**[1]

-244 **9** ½ **Tagur (IRE)**[21] [1367] 5-8-13 **72**............(p) ThomasGreatrex(5) 2 — 47
(Kevin Ryan) *chsd ldrs: rdn along over 3f out: sn wknd* **10/1**

3642 **10** 11 **Glory Awaits (IRE)**[16] [1479] 9-9-2 **75**............(b) DylanHogan(5) 11 — 25
(David Simcock) *t.k.h: swtchd lft after s and towards rr: rdn along 4f out: sn outpcd (jockey said gelding had no more to give)* **8/1**[3]

4313 **11** 7 **Thunder Buddy**[18] [1426] 4-8-2 **63**............(p) RhonaPindar(7) 6
(K R Burke) *trckd ldrs: swtchd rt to outer after 2f: rdn along wl over 3f out: sn outpcd and bhd (enq held into running and riding of the gelding which having jumped level was switched wide down the back straight and soon lost ground under tender handling to finish last of eleven, beaten by 33 1/2 lengths. Vet said gelding was slightly lame on its l* **15/2**[2]

1m 41.71s (-1.99) **Going Correction** -0.05s/f (Stan) **11 Ran SP% 121.3**
Speed ratings (Par 103): **107,104,102,102,99 99,98,91,91,80 73**
CSF £75.70 CT £637.04 TOTE £2.60: £1.02, £4.40, £4.70; EX 105.10 Trifecta £1360.50.
Owner M W Lawrence **Bred** R C Bond **Trained** Pandy, Monmouths
■ Stewards' Enquiry : Rhona Pindar £140 fine; failure to report reason for poor performance

FOCUS
This looked quite competitive for the grade and the pace looked quite strong. The second has been rated to his recent form.

1860 BETWAY H'CAP — 4f 214y(F)

7:00 (7:01) (Class 4) (0-85,85) 4-Y-O+

£5,530 (£1,645; £822; £411; £400; £400) **Stalls Centre**

Form — RPR

-410 **1** **Midnight Malibu (IRE)**[73] [588] 6-9-7 **85**............RachelRichardson 6 — 93
(Tim Easterby) *trckd ldrs towards centre: hdwy 2f out: rdn over 1f out: chal ent fnl f: sn drvn: kpt on wl to ld last 75yds* **8/1**

003- **2** nk **Jabbarockie**[193] [7994] 6-9-0 **78**............JasonHart 4 — 85
(Eric Alston) *racd centre: prom: effrt 2f out: sn chal: rdn to ld ent fnl f and sn edgd rt: drvn and hdd last 75yds: kpt on* **15/8**[1]

3631 **3** 1 **Mininggold**[13] [1551] 6-8-4 **73**............(p) PaulaMuir(5) 8 — 76
(Michael Dods) *racd towards stands' rail: chsd ldr: rdn along 2f out: drvn over 1f out: kpt on same pce fnl f* **5/1**[2]

053- **4** ¾ **Show Palace**[161] [8934] 6-8-11 **75**............ConnorBeasley 2 — 76
(Jennie Candlish) *racd towards far side: in tch: hdwy 2f out: rdn wl over 1f out: styd on wl fnl f* **12/1**

2122 **5** ½ **Warrior's Valley**[13] [1551] 4-8-12 **76**............(tp) PhilDennis 7 — 75
(David C Griffiths) *racd towards centre: led: rdn along wl over 1f out: hdd ent fnl f: sn n.m.r and wknd* **11/2**[3]

460- **6** 2 ¼ **Only Spoofing (IRE)**[146] [9206] 5-8-9 **78**............SeanDavis(5) 1 — 69+
(Jedd O'Keeffe) *dwlt and bhd tl sme late hdwy (jockey said gelding missed the break)* **5/1**[2]

0424 **7** 1 **Samovar**[34] [1194] 4-8-7 **71** oh2............(b) KieranO'Neill 5 — 58
(Scott Dixon) *racd centre: cl up: rdn along 2f out: drvn and hung lft over 1f out: sn wknd* **9/1**

0500 **8** 9 **Classic Pursuit**[16] [1487] 8-8-11 **75**............(b) LiamKeniry 3 — 30
(Stef Keniry) *dwlt: a bhd (jockey said gelding missed the break)* **28/1**

1m 0.18s (0.48) **Going Correction** -0.05s/f (Stan) **8 Ran SP% 115.8**
Speed ratings (Par 105): **94,93,91,90,89 86,84,70**
CSF £23.77 CT £85.58 TOTE £9.10: £2.10, £1.60, £2.20; EX 35.70 Trifecta £157.20.
Owner D A West & Partner **Bred** Kabansk Ltd & Rathbarry Stud **Trained** Great Habton, N Yorks
■ Stewards' Enquiry : Jason Hart caution; careless riding

FOCUS
A warm sprint handicap featuring some proper Fibresand specialists. The winner has been rated to her best since last winter, with the second pretty much to form.

1861 BETWAY CASINO H'CAP — 1m 6f 21y(F)

7:30 (7:31) (Class 6) (0-65,65) 4-Y-O+

£3,105 (£924; £461; £400; £400; £400) **Stalls Low**

Form — RPR

5-55 **1** **Greenview Paradise (IRE)**[21] [1361] 5-8-3 **46** oh1............KieranO'Neill 14 — 55
(Jeremy Scott) *trckd ldrs: hdwy on inner over 3f out: led briefly over 2f out: sn rdn and cl up: drvn over 1f out: rallied gamely to ld again wl ins fnl f: hld on wl towards fin* **17/2**

2 nse **Loose Chippings (IRE)**[242] [6319] 5-8-1 **47** oh1 ow1(h) GabrieleMalune(3) 10 — 55
(Ivan Furtado) *hld up: hdwy 5f out: str run on outer over 3f out: slt ld 2f out and sn rdn: drvn over 1f out: hdd narrowly wl ins fnl f: kpt on gamely* **25/1**

3104 **3** 7 **Seasearch**[49] [927] 4-9-2 **63**............(p) JoshuaBryan(3) 6 — 65
(Andrew Balding) *hld up and bhd: stdy hdwy 5f out: chsd ldrs and rdn along 3f out: styd on to chse ldng pair over 1f out: sn drvn and no imp* **11/4**[1]

0666 **4** 1 ½ **High Command (IRE)**[18] [1429] 6-9-1 **63**............(v[1]) TheodoreLadd(5) 11 — 62
(Michael Appleby) *dwlt: hdwy and in tch on outer after 3f: cl up 5f out: chal 3f out: sn rdn: drvn and kpt on one pce fnl 2f* **6/1**[2]

060- **5** 1 ½ **Dew Pond**[28] [8718] 7-8-13 **56**............(b) RachelRichardson 1 — 53
(Tim Easterby) *towards rr tl styd on fnl 3f: nvr a factor* **25/1**

3235 **6** 14 **Harbour Quay**[25] [1292] 5-9-0 **62**............SeamusCronin(5) 3 — 42
(Robyn Brisland) *cl up: led over 4f out: rdn along 3f out: sn hdd & wknd* **11/4**[1]

13/0 **7** ¾ **Fern Owl**[18] [1429] 7-9-4 **61**............(v[1]) LiamKeniry 8 — 40
(John Butler) *dwlt: hdwy to join ldrs after 3f: rdn along on outer over 4f out: drvn over 3f out: sn wknd* **16/1**

00-5 **8** ¾ **Bertie Moon**[104] [40] 9-8-0 **48**............(p) RhiainIngram(5) 12 — 26
(Tony Forbes) *cl up: led 6f out: rdn along and hdd over 4f out: wknd over 3f out* **80/1**

3- **9** 1 ¾ **Magic Sea (IRE)**[19] [1410] 4-8-9 **58**............DylanHogan(5) 4 — 35
(Sarah Dawson, Ire) *a towards rr* **8/1**[3]

5100 **10** 1 **Sweetest Smile (IRE)**[21] [1361] 4-8-2 **49**............JaneElliott(3) 5 — 25
(Ed de Giles) *a in rr (jockey said filly hung badly left. Vet said filly was lame on it's right hind)* **25/1**

456 **11** 7 **Ripplet**[25] [1287] 4-9-4 **62**............CharlieBennett 9 — 30
(Hughie Morrison) *prom: cl up 6f out: rdn along over 3f out: sn wknd* **9/1**

-500 **12** 41 **Luv U Whatever**[8] [1666] 9-9-3 **65**............(t) HarrisonShaw(5) 2
(Marjorie Fife) *led: rdn along and hdd 6f out: sn wknd (vet said gelding suffered from mild heat stress)* **33/1**

000- **13** 46 **Melanna (IRE)**[316] [3444] 8-8-3 **46** oh1............CamHardie 7
(Stella Barclay) *a in rr* **100/1**

/6-6 **14** 11 **Unonothinjonsnow**[73] [589] 5-8-1 **49** oh1 ow3(e[1]) FayeMcManoman(5) 13
(Frank Bishop) *chsd ldrs: rdn along and lost pl 1/2-way: sn bhd (jockey said gelding was never travelling)* **50/1**

3m 7.9s (-0.40) **Going Correction** -0.05s/f (Stan)
WFA 4 from 5yo+ 1lb **14 Ran SP% 123.8**
Speed ratings (Par 101): **99,98,94,94,93 85,84,84,83,82 78,55,29,22**
CSF £211.74 CT £746.80 TOTE £8.20: £2.30, £8.30, £1.60; EX 203.40 Trifecta £1114.90.
Owner Friends From Insurance **Bred** Senza Rete Partnership **Trained** Brompton Regis, Somerset
■ Stewards' Enquiry : Gabriele Malune £140 fine; changed boots after weighing out

FOCUS
Fairly modest stuff but the galloped looked honest. The front two, who came clear, were both thoroughly exposed maidens coming into this which puts the form into perspective.

1862 BETWAY HEED YOUR HUNCH NOVICE STKS — 6f 16y(F)

8:00 (8:01) (Class 5) 3-Y-O+

£3,752 (£1,116; £557; £278) **Stalls Low**

Form — RPR

1 **1** **Inspired Thought (IRE)**[14] [1523] 3-8-12 **0**............DanielTudhope 1 — 77
(Archie Watson) *trckd ldrs: smooth hdwy 3f out: led 2f out: rdn along wl over 1f out: drvn and edgd lft ins fnl f: kpt on wl towards fin* **13/8**[1]

1 **2** ¾ **Astro Jakk (IRE)**[18] [1427] 3-9-5 **0**............PJMcDonald 7 — 82
(K R Burke) *cl up on outer: hdwy to chal 2f out: rdn and edgd lft over 1f out: drvn and ev ch ins fnl f: no ex towards fin* **7/2**[3]

0- **3** *6* **Sapphire Jubilee**[267] 5319 3-8-4 0 ..... JamieGormley(3) 5 52
(Ollie Pears) *cl up: led 3f out: rdn and hdd 2f out: kpt on same pce fr over 1f out* **125/1**

305- **4** *3 ¾* **Sense Of Belonging (FR)**[208] 7477 3-8-12 78 ..... KevinStott 3 46
(Kevin Ryan) *sn slt ld: pushed along over 3f out: sn rdn and hdd: grad wknd (vet said gelding was struck into on the inside of it's right hind)* **9/4**[2]

2- **5** *¾* **Parion**[305] 3855 3-8-2 0 ..... SeanDavis(5) 2 39
(Richard Fahey) *chsd ldrs: rdn along and outpcd over 3f out: kpt on u.p fr wl over 1f out* **9/2**

6 **6** *7* **Luna Princess**[8] 1665 3-8-4 0 ..... JaneElliott(3) 6 18
(Michael Appleby) *chsd ldrs: rdn along and outpcd fr 1/2-way* **66/1**

-5 **7** *14* **Tommycole**[26] 1274 4-9-4 0 ..... TheodoreLadd(5) 4
(Olly Williams) *in tch: rdn along and outpcd fr 1/2-way (jockey said gelding didn't face the kickback)* **33/1**

1m 15.84s (-0.66) **Going Correction** -0.05s/f (Stan)
WFA 3 from 4yo 11lb 7 Ran SP% **114.5**
Speed ratings (Par 103): **102,101,93,88,87 77,59**
CSF £7.81 TOTE £2.90: £2.40, £1.10; EX 8.40 Trifecta £140.90.
Owner Clipper Logistics **Bred** L Wright **Trained** Upper Lambourn, W Berks

FOCUS
This looked quite a useful little novice event and the front two, who came clear, are probably quite nice horses in the making. The level is fluid.

1863 LADBROKES H'CAP 6f 16y(F)
8:30 (8:33) (Class 6) (0-60,61) 3-Y-O
£3,105 (£924; £461; £400; £400; £400) Stalls Low

Form RPR

560 **1** **Termonator**[23] 1336 3-9-5 57 ..... SamJames 11 67
(Grant Tuer) *in tch: hdwy on outer to chse ldrs and wd st: rdn 2f out: str run ent fnl f: styd on wl to ld last 100yds (trainer said, reg app imp in form, colt was suited by a step up in trip and benefited from what was a weaker contest in his opinion)* **17/2**

600 **2** *1 ¼* **Sharrabang**[23] 1336 3-9-4 56 ..... CamHardie 8 62
(Stella Barclay) *slt ld: hdd over 3f out: cl up: rdn to ld 1 1/2f out: drvn ins fnl f: hdd and no ex last 100yds* **50/1**

0- **3** *3 ¾* **Slainte (IRE)**[18] 1432 3-8-10 53 ..... DylanHogan(5) 9 48
(Sarah Dawson, Ire) *cl up: led over 3f out: rdn over 2f out: hdd 1 1/2f out: sn drvn: kpt on same pce* **10/1**

4501 **4** *1* **Gunnabedun (IRE)**[13] 1554 3-8-12 53 ..... (b) JamieGormley(3) 3 45
(Iain Jardine) *prom: effrt on inner 3f out: rdn and ev ch wl over 1f out: drvn appr fnl f and kpt on same pce* **7/1**

0-46 **5** *2 ½* **Atwaar**[55] 831 3-8-7 50 ..... FayeMcManoman(5) 2 35
(Charles Smith) *towards rr: hdwy on inner 3f out: rdn over 2f out: kpt on appr fnl f: nrst fin* **16/1**

0320 **6** *nk* **Maisie Moo**[25] 1285 3-9-9 61 ..... TonyHamilton 5 45
(Shaun Keightley) *hld up in rr: wd st: hdwy 2f out: kpt on fnl f: nrst fin* **6/1**[3]

3-00 **7** *¾* **Milldean Panther**[20] 1380 3-9-0 52 ..... PJMcDonald 6 33
(Suzi Best) *in rr: rdn along over 3f out: wd st: drvn 2f out: plugged on* **9/1**

1053 **8** *¾* **Deconso**[18] 1430 3-9-2 54 ..... (t) HollieDoyle 4 33
(Christopher Kellett) *chsd ldrs: rdn along 3f out: wknd over 2f out* **9/2**[2]

9 *¾* **Scarlet Skis**[222] 7046 3-9-7 59 ..... (p[1]) LiamKeniry 7 36
(Stef Keniry) *in tch: hdwy to chse ldrs 3f out: sn rdn and wknd 2f out* **33/1**

6012 **10** *3 ¼* **Champagne Mondays**[18] 1430 3-8-13 51 ..... (p) NicolaCurrie 10 18
(Scott Dixon) *chsd ldrs: rdn along and wd st: drvn and wknd over 2f out (jockey said gelding had no more to give)* **3/1**[1]

364- **11** *6* **Superstition**[252] 5853 3-8-13 58 ..... GeorgiaDobie(7) 12 7
(Eve Johnson Houghton) *a in rr: wd st and bhd* **14/1**

1m 16.95s (0.45) **Going Correction** -0.05s/f (Stan) 11 Ran SP% **117.0**
Speed ratings (Par 96): **95,93,88,87,83 83,82,81,80,75 67**
CSF £347.57 CT £4244.89 TOTE £9.90: £2.80, £13.50, £4.50; EX 258.50 Trifecta £2419.10.
Owner E Tuer **Bred** E Tuer **Trained** Birkby, N Yorks

FOCUS
One or two possible improvers in an otherwise uninspiring contest even for this grade. The the first three home were all making their handicap debuts.
T/Plt: £627.50 to a £1 stake. Pool: £79,748.64 - 92.77 winning units T/Qpdt: £55.10 to a £1 stake. Pool: £11,007.20 - 147.75 winning units **Joe Rowntree**

1864 - 1878a (Foreign Racing) - See Raceform Interactive

1710 CHELMSFORD (A.W) (L-H)
Thursday, April 18

OFFICIAL GOING: Polytrack: standard
Wind: virtually nil Weather: fine and sunny

1879 £20 FREE BETS AT TOTESPORT.COM NOVICE AUCTION STKS (PLUS 10 RACE) 5f (P)
5:25 (5:25) (Class 4) 2-Y-O
£5,530 (£1,645; £822; £411) Stalls Low

Form RPR

5 **1** **Copacabana Dancer (IRE)**[10] 1651 2-9-4 0 ..... JasonWatson 2 69
(Joseph Tuite) *chsd ldr tl rdn to ld over 1f out: edgd lft briefly but sn clr: in command ins fnl f: r.o wl* **5/1**[3]

2 *1 ½* **What A Business (IRE)** 2-9-4 0 ..... NicolaCurrie 9 64+
(Jamie Osborne) *pushed lft leaving stalls: hld up towards rr: clsd and swtchd rt jst over 1f out: sltly impeded and edgd out rt again ins fnl f: r.o wl to go 2nd towards fin* **25/1**

3 *1* **Gracie's Girl** 2-8-12 0 ..... LiamJones 6 54+
(Michael Appleby) *short of room leaving stalls: towards rr: switching rt and hdwy 2f out: hung lft but clsd to chse clr wnr whn wnt rt jst ins fnl f: stl hanging lft and no imp after: lost 2nd towards fin* **25/1**

4 *½* **Red Maharani** 2-9-0 0 ..... BarryMcHugh 11 54
(James Given) *sn bhd and wd: detached in last 1/2-way: prog 1f out: styd on v strly ins fnl f: nt rch ldrs* **33/1**

0 **5** *¾* **Is She The One**[16] 1493 2-8-10 0 ..... DannyBrock 10 48
(Philip McBride) *wnt lft leaving stalls: t.k.h: hld up in rr: effrt over 1f out: hdwy ent fnl f: sltly impeded impeded jst ins fnl f: kpt on wl: nvr trbld ldrs* **33/1**

6 *nse* **Lexi The One (IRE)** 2-9-1 0 ..... PaddyMathers 3 52
(Richard Fahey) *squeezed for room leaving stalls: sn rcvrd and in tch in midfield: rdn ent fnl 2f: swtchd rt over 1f out: keeping on same pce and no threat to wnr whn carried lft and hmpd ins fnl f* **9/1**

7 *½* **The Lazy Monkey (IRE)** 2-9-0 0 ..... SilvestreDeSousa 7 50
(Mark Johnston) *midfield: pushed along over 3f out: effrt on outer over 1f out: sltly impeded jst ins fnl f: kpt on: nvr trbld ldrs* **2/1**[2]

8 *1 ½* **Frida Kahlo (IRE)** 2-8-12 0 ..... HollieDoyle 1 42
(Archie Watson) *led: hdd and hung lft over 1f out: wknd ins fnl f* **15/8**[1]

9 *2 ¾* **Craigburn** 2-9-3 0 ..... LukeMorris 5 37
(Tom Clover) *wnt rt leaving stalls: chsd ldrs: rdn over 3f out: struggling to qckn whn squeezed for room jst over 1f out: sn btn and wknd ins fnl f (jockey said colt suffered interference approaching the final furlong)* **16/1**

5 **10** *3 ¼* **Zampa Road (IRE)**[15] 1513 2-8-13 0 ..... KieranO'Neill 4 32
(David Evans) *chsd ldrs: u.p and struggling to qckn whn squeezed for room and hmpd jst over 1f out: sn btn and wknd fnl f* **14/1**

1m 1.28s (1.08) **Going Correction** -0.175s/f (Stan) 10 Ran SP% **120.9**
Speed ratings (Par 94): **84,81,80,79,78 77,77,74,70,65**
CSF £127.42 TOTE £6.50: £2.30, £5.40, £4.70; EX 151.00 Trifecta £1966.90.
Owner Alan & Christine Bright **Bred** Mount Coote Estates **Trained** Lambourn, Berks
■ Stewards' Enquiry : Liam Jones two-day ban; careless riding (May 2-3)

FOCUS
An informative contest and encouragement can be gleaned from the first four home. The level is fluid but looks ordinary.

1880 TOTEPOOL CASHBACK CLUB AT TOTESPORT.COM H'CAP 7f (P)
6:00 (6:03) (Class 5) (0-75,76) 4-Y-O+
£5,175 (£1,540; £769; £400; £400; £400) Stalls Low

Form RPR

-040 **1** **Full Intention**[24] 1329 5-9-1 69 ..... (p) JackMitchell 14 77
(Lydia Pearce) *in tch in midfield on outer: effrt to cl over 1f out: chsd clr ldr and hung lft 1f out: stl edging lft but r.o wl to ld towards fin* **10/1**

14-0 **2** *shd* **Coverham (IRE)**[13] 1561 5-9-1 69 ..... (p) LukeMorris 2 76
(James Eustace) *midfield and bustled along early: rdn and clsd over 1f out: nt clrest of runs ent fnl f: hung lft but styd on ins fnl f: str chal towards fin: jst hld* **7/1**[3]

05-3 **3** *1* **Gunmaker (IRE)**[24] 1329 5-8-13 67 ..... JackGarritty 13 71
(Ruth Carr) *wl in tch in midfield: clsd to trck ldrs 2f: led over 1f out: sn rdn clr but hung lft: drvn ins fnl f: hdd and lost 2 pls towards fin* **4/1**[1]

1-12 **4** *1 ¼* **Chloellie**[64] 697 4-9-3 71 ..... DavidProbert 15 72
(J R Jenkins) *in tch in midfield: effrt and pushed rt over 1f out: kpt on u.p ins fnl f: nt enough pce to rch ldrs* **8/1**

105- **5** *1 ¼* **Kafoo**[377] 1633 6-8-4 61 oh4 ..... (v) WilliamCox(3) 7 58
(Michael Appleby) *chsd ldr tl over 5f out: styd prom: effrt whn n.m.r and swtchd rt over 1f out: kpt on same pce ins fnl f* **50/1**

3606 **6** *½* **Pearl Spectre (USA)**[17] 1479 8-8-11 65 ..... (v) NicolaCurrie 4 64+
(Phil McEntee) *in tch in midfield: effrt whn nt clr run and swtchd rt jst over 1f out: kpt on ins fnl f: no threat to ldrs* **7/1**[3]

6060 **7** *nk* **The British Lion (IRE)**[8] 1684 4-9-0 68 ..... RobertHavlin 1 63
(Alexandra Dunn) *restless in stalls and briefly dismntd: in tch in midfield: effrt on inner over 1f out: kpt on same pce and no imp ins fnl f* **14/1**

0005 **8** *1 ¾* **Regulator (IRE)**[16] 1496 4-9-7 75 ..... RossaRyan 11 65
(Alexandra Dunn) *chsd ldrs: effrt over 1f out: short of room and swtchd lft jst over 1f out: no hdwy u.p and wknd ins fnl f (jockey said gelding was denied a clear run)* **16/1**

-120 **9** *½* **Inaam (IRE)**[17] 1487 6-9-7 75 ..... (h) KieranO'Neill 5 64
(John Butler) *in tch in midfield: effrt over 1f out: hung lft and no imp ins fnl f* **20/1**

330- **10** *3 ¼* **Dark Side Dream**[140] 9305 7-9-3 76 ..... ThoreHammerHansen(5) 6 56
(Charlie Wallis) *led tl over 2f out: unable qck and edgd lft ent fnl f: wknd ins fnl f* **8/1**

0000 **11** *1* **Kodiline (IRE)**[16] 1496 5-8-10 71 ..... GinaMangan(7) 9 49
(David Evans) *last pair: pushed along 4 out: effrt on inner over 1f out: no real imp: nvr involved* **25/1**

2404 **12** *1 ½* **It Must Be Faith**[8] 1686 9-8-12 69 ..... (p) JaneElliott(3) 10 43
(Michael Appleby) *chsd ldrs tl wnt 2nd over 5f out: led over 2f out: hdd over 1f out: sn struggling u.p: wknd ins fnl f* **14/1**

01-0 **13** *hd* **Folie Douze**[22] 1356 4-8-13 72 ..... DylanHogan(5) 8 45
(Henry Spiller) *a towards rr: nvr involved* **50/1**

3005 **14** *½* **Sonnet Rose (IRE)**[12] 1586 5-8-9 63 ..... (bt) MartinDwyer 3 35
(Conrad Allen) *a towards rr: rdn over 3f out: hung lft and no hdwy over 1f out: bhd ins fnl f (jockey said mare was never travelling)* **5/1**[2]

3-30 **15** *3 ¼* **Golden Nectar**[34] 1216 5-9-0 68 ..... LiamJones 12 31
(Laura Mongan) *sn towards rr and nvr gng wl: nvr involved and bhd ins fnl f* **20/1**

1m 25.29s (-1.91) **Going Correction** -0.175s/f (Stan) 15 Ran SP% **129.5**
Speed ratings (Par 103): **103,102,101,100,98 98,97,95,95,91 90,88,88,88,84**
CSF £79.29 CT £344.62 TOTE £10.30: £3.50, £2.60, £1.80; EX 106.80 Trifecta £568.70.
Owner Killarney Glen & Lydia Pearce **Bred** Springcombe Park Stud **Trained** Newmarket, Suffolk

FOCUS
This looked competitive beforehand and it produced tight finish.

1881 IRISH LOTTO AT TOTESPORT.COM H'CAP 7f (P)
6:30 (6:31) (Class 3) (0-90,91) 4-Y-O+ £9,703 (£2,887; £1,443; £721) Stalls Low

Form RPR

-311 **1** **Glenn Coco**[38] 1143 5-9-3 86 ..... (t) PJMcDonald 9 93
(Stuart Williams) *chsd ldr tl over 4f out: rdn over 1f out: ev ch 1f out: sustained effrt u.p to ld 50yds out: styd on* **3/1**[3]

531- **2** *¾* **Qaroun**[199] 7847 4-9-5 88 ..... RyanMoore 3 93
(Sir Michael Stoute) *hld up in tch in midfield: effrt and hdwy over 1f out: ev ch 1f out: drvn ins fnl f: disputing 2nd and keeping on same pce and hld whn lft 2nd cl home* **2/1**[1]

100- **3** *1* **Rogue**[197] 7910 4-9-8 91 ..... RossaRyan 6 93
(Alexandra Dunn) *led: hrd pressed over 2f out: rdn over 1f out: hdd 1f out: kpt on same pce after and hld whn lft 3rd cl home* **50/1**

600- **4** *hd* **Salt Whistle Bay (IRE)**[178] 8487 5-8-13 82 ..... JackMitchell 10 84
(Rae Guest) *hld up in tch towards rr: effrt on outer over 1f out: kpt on ins fnl f but no threat to ldrs: lft 4th cl home* **12/1**

50-4 **5** *2 ¾* **Whitefountainfairy (IRE)**[19] 1421 4-9-7 90 ..... SilvestreDeSousa 1 84
(Andrew Balding) *chsd ldrs: effrt on inner over 1f out: no ex u.p jst ins fnl f: wknd fnl 100yds: lft 5th cl home (trainers' rep said filly may have been unsuited by the Standard going after running on Standard-to-Slow at Kempton last time out)* **9/4**[2]

605- **6** *1* **Mountain Rescue (IRE)**[135] 9390 7-9-1 84 ..... LukeMorris 2 76
(Michael Attwater) *in tch in midfield: effrt over 1f out: unable qck and wl hld whn lft 6th and bdly hmpd clsd home* **66/1**

6-10 **7** *½* **Maksab (IRE)**[40] 1097 4-8-11 87 ..... ScottMcCullagh(7) 7 77
(Mick Channon) *s.i.s: in tch towards rr: effrt u.p over 1f out: no imp ins fnl f: lft 7th cl home* **8/1**

6006 **8** *1* **Atletico (IRE)**[13] 1561 7-8-4 80 ..... GinaMangan(7) 5 68
(David Evans) *uns rdr bef s: rrd as stalls opened and slowly away: bhd: effrt jst over 1f out: sn hung rt and no real imp wl btn whn lft 8th and bdly hmpd cl home* **50/1**

The Form Book Flat 2019, Raceform Ltd, Newbury, RG14 5SJ

30-0 **9** *1 3/4* **Penwortham (IRE)**[18] 1459 6-8-13 **82**................ PaddyMathers 4 65
(Richard Fahey) *hld up in tch in last trio: effrt over 1f out: no imp and nvr involved: lft 9th cl home* **40/1**

1335 **F** **Gentlemen**[14] 1552 8-8-9 **78**.................................(h) NicolaCurrie 8
(Phil McEntee) *midfield on outer: clsd to chse ldr over 4f out: ev ch over and u.p over 1f out: led 1f out: hdd 50yds: keeping on but hld whn lost action: stmbld and fell nr fin (fatally injured)* **25/1**

1m 24.99s (-2.21) **Going Correction** -0.175s/f (Stan) 10 Ran SP% **119.6**
Speed ratings (Par 107): **105,104,103,102,99 98,97,96,94,**
CSF £9.44 CT £251.85 TOTE £3.70: £1.10, £1.20, £18.10; EX 12.40 Trifecta £246.80.
Owner Miss Emily Stevens Partnership **Bred** Old Mill Stud And S C Williams **Trained** Newmarket, Suffolk

FOCUS
A good quality handicap, although the race was marred by a horrible incident shortly before the line.

1882 EXTRA PLACES AT TOTESPORT.COM H'CAP — 1m 2f (P)
7:00 (7:07) (Class 4) (0-85,87) 4-Y-O+
£5,530 (£1,645; £822; £411; £400; £400) **Stalls** Low

Form RPR

131- **1** **Lexington Empire**[204] 7681 4-9-5 **79**........................ DanielMuscutt 3 92
(David Lanigan) *in tch in midfield: wnt 3rd and travelling strly over 1f out: sn rdn and readily asserted: hung lft but drew wl clr ins fnl f: eased towards fin: v easily* **15/8[1]**

3300 **2** *4 1/2* **Juanito Chico (IRE)**[17] 1479 5-9-0 **74**..........................(t) PJMcDonald 4 78
(Stuart Williams) *stdd and short of room leaving stalls: effrt in centre over 1f out: edging lft but kpt on ins fnl f to go 2nd wl ins fnl f: no ch w wnr* **8/1**

3404 **3** *3/4* **Michele Strogoff**[12] 1589 6-9-13 **87**..................... AlistairRawlinson 5 89
(Michael Appleby) *taken down early: led: rdn ent fnl 2f: hdd over 1f out and immediately outpcd by wnr: lost 2nd wl ins fnl f* **4/1[3]**

0-14 **4** *1 1/2* **The Night King**[19] 1418 4-8-13 **73**.............................. PatCosgrave 7 72
(Mick Quinn) *hld up in tch: nt clr run over 2f out: effrt and bmpd over 1f out: no imp and barging match w rival 1f out: wl hld and plugged on same pce after* **9/4[2]**

053- **5** *1 3/4* **Sea Tide**[273] 5132 5-8-13 **73**... LiamJones 6 69
(Laura Mongan) *swtchd rt leaving stalls: hdwy to chse ldr 8f out: effrt ent fnl 2f: edgd rt and unable qck over 1f out: wknd ins fnl f* **33/1**

3216 **6** *3/4* **Pheidippides**[34] 1213 4-9-4 **78**..(b) LukeMorris 8 72
(Tom Clover) *hld up in midfield: rdn over 3f out: struggling to qckn whn edgd lft and bmpd rival over 1f out: no imp and wl hld whn barging w rival 1f out: wknd ins fnl f* **8/1**

30-5 **7** *16* **Juneau (IRE)**[12] 1589 4-9-7 **81**.................................... FrannyNorton 2 43
(Mark Johnston) *chsd ldr for 2f: styd ldrs tl outpcd u.p over 1f out: bhd ins fnl f* **14/1**

2m 4.56s (-4.04) **Going Correction** -0.175s/f (Stan) 7 Ran SP% **117.4**
Speed ratings (Par 105): **109,105,104,103,102 101,88**
CSF £18.53 CT £55.44 TOTE £2.60: £1.70, £3.20; EX 17.20 Trifecta £83.60.
Owner Middleham Park XXV,Ms Delaney & Black **Bred** Cheveley Park Stud Ltd **Trained** Newmarket, Suffolk
■ Shareef Star was withdrawn. Price at time of withdrawal 4-7. Rule 4 applies only to board prices prior to withdrawal - deduction 60p in the pound. New market formed.

FOCUS
The late withdrawal of odds-on favourite Shareef Dancer completely changed the look of this handicap.

1883 BET IN PLAY AT TOTESPORT.COM H'CAP — 5f (P)
7:30 (7:33) (Class 6) (0-60,59) 4-Y-O+
£3,105 (£924; £461; £400; £400; £400) **Stalls** Low

Form RPR

0625 **1** **Admiral Rooke (IRE)**[7] 1716 4-8-5 **48**...................(b) TheodoreLadd(5) 2 61+
(Michael Appleby) *trckd ldrs on inner and travelled strly: swtchd rt and waiting for gap over 1f out: rdn to ld 1f out: r.o strly and drew clr fnl f: v readily* **7/2[1]**

3053 **2** *3 1/4* **Always Amazing**[5] 1767 5-9-5 **57**................................ PaddyMathers 7 59
(Derek Shaw) *hld up in midfield: effrt and swtchd lft over 1f out: pressed ldrs and drvn 1f out: wnt 2nd but nvr matching pce of wnr ins fnl f* **5/1[2]**

0602 **3** *1/2* **Spenny's Lass**[34] 1209 4-9-7 **59**..................................(p) BrettDoyle 9 59
(John Ryan) *bmpd s: towards rr: swtchd lft and hdwy 1f out: styd on u.p ins fnl f: no ch w wnr* **6/1[3]**

-440 **4** *1/2* **Royal Mezyan (IRE)**[36] 1179 8-9-0 **57**......................... DylanHogan(5) 11 55
(Henry Spiller) *bhd: effrt on outer ent fnl 2f: styd wl on ins fnl f: nvr trbld ldrs* **14/1**

-001 **5** *1/2* **Precious Plum**[34] 1210 5-9-7 **59**........................(p) SilvestreDeSousa 12 55
(Charlie Wallis) *broke fast fr wd draw and w ldr: rdn over 1f out: no ex 1f out: wknd ins fnl f* **7/2[1]**

4505 **6** *nk* **Caledonian Gold**[17] 1478 6-8-7 **45**............................... KieranO'Neill 1 40
(Lisa Williamson) *taken down early and led to post: led on inner: rdn over 1f out: hdd 1f out: no ex and wknd ins fnl f* **16/1**

000- **7** *1/2* **Racquet**[192] 8063 6-9-1 **53**.. JackGarritty 3 46
(Ruth Carr) *chsd ldrs: rdn over 1f out: unable qck 1f out: wknd ins fnl f* **11/1**

1-26 **8** *1* **Alaskan Bay (IRE)**[90] 298 4-9-3 **55**............................ DavidProbert 8 45
(Rae Guest) *wnt rt s: midfield: effrt over 1f out: no imp and one pce ins fnl f* **14/1**

0600 **9** *nk* **Dubai Elegance**[7] 1716 5-9-3 **55**.................................(p) EoinWalsh 6 44
(Derek Shaw) *taken down early: hld up in rr: clsd and nt clr run over 1f out: nvr trbld ldrs* **33/1**

510- **10** *1/2* **Good Business (IRE)**[201] 7762 5-9-7 **59**..................... RobertHavlin 5 46
(Henry Spiller) *in rr: effrt on inner over 1f out: nvr getting on terms and wl btn ins fnl f* **22/1**

0540 **11** *2* **Avon Green**[8] 1687 4-9-7 **59**.....................................(b) JasonWatson 4 39
(Joseph Tuite) *chsd ldrs on outer: unable qck over 1f out: wknd ins fnl f* **10/1**

0000 **12** *1/2* **Independence Day (IRE)**[22] 1364 6-9-7 **59**...............(h) JoeyHaynes 10 37
(Paul Howling) *midfield on outer: rdn over 2f out: outpcd over 1f out and bhd ins fnl f* **14/1**

59.55s (-0.65) **Going Correction** -0.175s/f (Stan) 12 Ran SP% **126.0**
Speed ratings (Par 101): **98,92,92,91,90 89,89,87,87,86 83,82**
CSF £21.92 CT £108.74 TOTE £4.20: £1.70, £2.50, £2.10; EX 29.20 Trifecta £159.30.
Owner Slipstream Racing **Bred** William J Kennedy **Trained** Oakham, Rutland
■ Stewards' Enquiry : Brett Doyle two-day ban; misuse of whip (May 2-3)

FOCUS
This looked wide open on paper but was taken apart by long standing maiden Admiral Rooke.

1884 DOUBLE DELIGHT HAT-TRICK HEAVEN AT TOTESPORT.COM H'CAP — 1m 5f 66y(P)
8:00 (8:01) (Class 5) (0-75,77) 3-Y-O
£5,175 (£1,540; £769; £400) **Stalls** Low

Form RPR

-412 **1** **Lord Lamington**[20] 1396 3-9-7 **75**.............................. FrannyNorton 4 84
(Mark Johnston) *chsd ldng pair: clsd to ld over 2f out: pushed along over 1f out: in command and styd on wl ins fnl f: comf* **2/1[2]**

2 *3* **Tigray (USA)**[41] 1119 3-9-0 **68**............................... AlistairRawlinson 3 72
(Michael Appleby) *stdd s: hld up in rr: pushed along 4f out: swtchd rt and clsd 3f out: pressing ldr 2f out: unable qck ent fnl f: hld and kpt on same pce ins fnl f* **16/1**

225- **3** *4 1/2* **Surrey Warrior (USA)**[147] 9203 3-9-9 **77**.....................(b[1]) HollieDoyle 1 74
(Archie Watson) *led tl hdd wl over 2f out: unable qck whn short of room wl over 1f out: wl hld 3rd and kpt on same pce fnl f* **4/1[3]**

0-41 **4** *4 1/2* **Seeusoon (IRE)**[41] 1080 3-9-4 **72**......................... SilvestreDeSousa 2 63
(Andrew Balding) *pressed ldr tl led wl over 2f out: sn hdd and unable qck: wl btn 4th and hung lft ins fnl f (jockey said colt hung left-handed)* **5/6[1]**

2m 51.17s (-2.43) **Going Correction** -0.175s/f (Stan) 4 Ran SP% **113.8**
Speed ratings (Par 98): **100,98,95,92**
CSF £22.30 TOTE £2.80; EX 18.40 Trifecta £53.00.
Owner Netherfield House Stud **Bred** Newsells Park Stud **Trained** Middleham Moor, N Yorks

FOCUS
Only a small field but two of these got racing from an early stage and it played right into the hands of the patiently ridden Lord Lamington.

1885 BUY TICKETS AT CHELMSFORDCITYRACECOURSE.COM FILLIES' H'CAP — 1m 2f (P)
8:30 (8:30) (Class 4) (0-85,84) 3-Y-O
£5,530 (£1,645) **Stalls** Low

Form RPR

621- **1** **Mehdaayih**[177] 8511 3-9-7 **84**.. RobertHavlin 1 97
(John Gosden) *chsd ldr tl swtchd rt and pushed into ld over 1f out: wnt clr fr over 1f out: r.o strly* **1/4[1]**

0-11 **2** *14* **Cafe Espresso**[6] 1730 3-8-13 **76** 6ex..........................(b) HollieDoyle 3 61
(Archie Watson) *led tl hdd and rdn over 2f out: sn outpcd and wl btn over 1f out* **9/4[2]**

2m 3.81s (-4.79) **Going Correction** -0.175s/f (Stan) 2 Ran SP% **110.8**
Speed ratings (Par 97): **112,100**
TOTE £1.10.
Owner Emirates Park Pty Ltd **Bred** Rabbah Bloodstock Limited **Trained** Newmarket, Suffolk

FOCUS
A disappointing turn out for this fillies' only handicap, though it appeared genuinely run and the winner could be anything. The winning time was furlong for furlong, the quickest on the card.
T/Plt: £221.70 to a £1 stake. Pool: £68,985.84. 227.13 winning units. T/Qpdt: £10.10 to a £1 stake. Pool: £13,693.04. 996.95 winning units. **Steve Payne**

1851 NEWMARKET (R-H)
Thursday, April 18

OFFICIAL GOING: Good to firm (good in places; watered; 7.7)
Wind: Light, against Weather: Fine

1886 ALEX SCOTT MAIDEN STKS (C&G) (PLUS 10 RACE) — 7f
1:50 (2:01) (Class 4) 3-Y-O
£6,469 (£1,925; £962; £481) **Stalls** Low

Form RPR

1 **Far Above (IRE)** 3-9-0 0..................................... PJMcDonald 12 90+
(James Tate) *str; hld up: hdwy over 4f out: shkn up and edgd rt fr over 1f out: led 1f out: pushed out* **11/8[1]**

36-2 **2** *hd* **Franz Kafka (IRE)**[18] 1458 3-9-0 82.......................... FrankieDettori 3 89
(John Gosden) *str; hld up in tch: rdn over 1f out: r.o* **13/8[2]**

223- **3** *3 1/2* **Qutob (IRE)**[187] 8196 3-9-0 80.................................... JimCrowley 5 80
(Charles Hills) *sn led: rdn and hdd 1f out: no ex wl ins fnl f* **8/1[3]**

4 *1/2* **Joyful Mission (USA)** 3-9-0 0.................................. RyanMoore 15 79+
(Sir Michael Stoute) *str; sltly on toes; s.i.s: hld up: shkn up over 1f out: r.o ins fnl f: nt rch ldrs* **25/1**

04- **5** *shd* **Entertaining (IRE)**[112] 9725 3-9-0 0...................... SilvestreDeSousa 6 78
(Richard Hannon) *s.i.s: sn prom: lost pl 5f out: swtchd rt over 4f out: pushed along and hdwy over 2f out: styd on* **50/1**

23- **6** *1 1/2* **Greek Kodiac (IRE)**[167] 8804 3-9-0 0.......................... PatCosgrave 10 74
(Mick Quinn) *chsd ldrs: rdn over 1f out: no ex fnl f* **20/1**

32- **7** *shd* **Sassoon**[121] 9601 3-9-0 0.. RaulDaSilva 4 74
(Paul Cole) *str; chsd ldr: rdn over 1f out: no ex fnl f* **20/1**

4 **8** *4 1/2* **Global Gift (FR)**[21] 1381 3-9-0 0.................................. GeraldMosse 9 62
(Ed Dunlop) *compact; hld up in tch: racd keenly: rdn and wknd over 1f out* **33/1**

- **9** *2 1/2* **Lost In Alaska (USA)** 3-9-0 0.................................... JasonWatson 8 55
(Jeremy Noseda) *str; chsd ldrs: rdn over 2f out: wknd fnl f* **66/1**

0 **10** *shd* **Sandy Steve**[13] 1562 3-9-0 0..................................... DanielMuscutt 1 55
(Stuart Williams) *workmanlike; hld up: shkn up over 2f out: nvr on terms* **200/1**

0 **11** *2 1/4* **Broughtons Bear (IRE)**[21] 1381 3-9-0 0.................. StevieDonohoe 14 49
(Stuart Williams) *workmanlike; hld up: shkn up over 2f out: edgd rt over 1f out: n.d* **200/1**

12 *1 1/4* **Rum Baba** 3-9-0 0.. WilliamBuick 16 45
(Charlie Fellowes) *str; on toes; coltish; sn pushed along in rr: n.d* **28/1**

13 *1* **Mohareb** 3-9-0 0... HarryBentley 7 43
(Saeed bin Suroor) *unfurnished; bit bkward; s.i.s: sn in tch: racd keenly: n.m.r and lost pl 6f out: shkn up over 2f out: wknd over 1f out* **20/1**

56- **14** *3/4* **Global Quality**[206] 7612 3-9-0 0................................... DavidProbert 13 41
(Charles Hills) *str; hld up: a in rr* **100/1**

1m 27.14s (1.74) **Going Correction** +0.40s/f (Good) 14 Ran SP% **121.3**
Speed ratings (Par 100): **106,105,101,101,101 99,99,94,91,91 88,87,86,85**
CSF £3.25 TOTE £2.20: £1.10, £1.20, £2.20; EX 4.30 Trifecta £16.50.
Owner Sheikh Rashid Dalmook Al Maktoum **Bred** Mohamed Abdul Malik **Trained** Newmarket, Suffolk
■ Dutch Story was withdrawn. Price at time of withdrawal 100-1. Rule 4 does not apply.

FOCUS
Far side course used. Stalls: far side. 3mm of water was added following racing the previous day but Frankie Dettori, having ridden in the opener, confirmed it was still good to firm and with there being a headwind it would likely have getting quicker as the meeting progressed. Not a terribly strong edition of the race, they raced down the centre and the market leaders dominated. It's been rated as an up-to-standard renewal, with the third close to form.

1887 MONTAZ RESTAURANT BRITISH EBF NOVICE STKS (PLUS 10 RACE) 5f
2:25 (2:30) (Class 4) 2-Y-O **£5,175** (£1,540; £769; £384) **Stalls** Low

Form RPR

1 **Well Of Wisdom** 2-9-5 0 WilliamBuick 8 88+
(Charlie Appleby) *compact; hld up: racd keenly: hdwy 1/2-way: shkn up over 1f out: r.o to ld nr fin* **5/1[3]**

2 *1/2* **Electrical Storm** 2-9-5 0 RyanMoore 2 86+
(Saeed bin Suroor) *athletic; s.i.s: hld up: nt clr run and swtchd lft 1/2-way: hdwy and swtchd rt over 1f out: r.o to ld wl ins fnl f: hdd nr fin* **7/1**

3 *1 1/2* **City Walk (IRE)** 2-9-5 0 PatCosgrave 5 81+
(Saeed bin Suroor) *str; dwlt: racd keenly: hdwy over 3f out: rdn and swtchd lft over 1f out: styd on same pce wl ins fnl f* **12/1**

2 **4** *hd* **Strong Power (IRE)**[19] 1416 2-9-5 0 HarryBentley 4 80
(George Scott) *athletic; led: rdn over 1f out: edgd lft and hdd wl ins fnl f: no ex towards fin* **2/1[1]**

5 *1/2* **Millionaire Waltz** 2-9-5 0 RaulDaSilva 7 78+
(Paul Cole) *str; hld up: hdwy over 1f out: styd on same pce wl ins fnl f* **33/1**

6 *1 1/4* **Full Verse (IRE)** 2-9-5 0 JamesDoyle 6 74
(Charlie Appleby) *str; chsd ldr: rdn over 1f out: no ex wl ins fnl f* **9/4[2]**

6 **7** *12* **Lexington Quest (IRE)**[10] 1651 2-9-5 0 SeanLevey 3 31
(Richard Hannon) *compact; s.i.s: sn chsng ldrs: pushed along 1/2-way: wknd over 1f out* **20/1**

8 *3* **Percy Green (IRE)** 2-9-5 0 BenCurtis 1 20
(K R Burke) *workmanlike; bit on the leg; prom over 3f* **22/1**

1m 1.4s (2.30) **Going Correction** +0.40s/f (Good) 8 Ran SP% **113.0**
Speed ratings (Par 94): **97,96,93,93,92 90,71,66**
CSF £37.50 TOTE £5.00: £1.70, £2.00, £2.00; EX 27.40 Trifecta £137.10.
Owner Godolphin **Bred** Godolphin **Trained** Newmarket, Suffolk

FOCUS
This looked a quality race featuring some some well-bred juveniles and it was the unraced brigade who came to the fore over those with experience. It's been rated in line with the recent race average.

1888 BRITISH EBF BET365 CONDITIONS STKS (PLUS 10 RACE) 7f
3:00 (3:02) (Class 3) 3-Y-O **£9,703** (£2,887; £1,443; £721) **Stalls** Low

Form RPR

21-1 **1** **Fox Champion (IRE)**[18] 1458 3-9-9 90 SilvestreDeSousa 3 103
(Richard Hannon) *compact; racd far side: mde all: shkn up over 1f out: rdn and edgd lft ins fnl f: styd on: 1st of 4 in gp* **5/2[2]**

632- **2** *1 1/4* **Double Kodiac (IRE)**[185] 8255 3-9-6 85 WilliamBuick 6 97
(Simon Crisford) *led centre trio: shkn up over 2f out: rdn and edgd rt ins fnl f: styd on: 1st of 3 in gp* **25/1**

413- **3** *2 1/4* **Almufti**[173] 8646 3-9-6 93 JamesDoyle 2 91
(Hugo Palmer) *compact; sweating; racd far side: chsd ldrs: chsd wnr 2f out: rdn over 1f out: nt clr run and swtchd rt ins fnl f: sn lost 2nd: styd on same pce: 2nd of 4 in gp* **4/1[3]**

1- **4** *2* **Almashriq (USA)**[134] 9411 3-9-6 0 JimCrowley 5 86
(John Gosden) *ly; looked wl; dwlt: racd centre: hld up: hdwy and edgd rt over 2f out: rdn over 1f out: no ex ins fnl f: 2nd of 3 in gp* **11/8[1]**

3-13 **5** *2* **Havana Rocket (IRE)**[23] 1345 3-9-6 83 DavidProbert 1 80
(Andrew Balding) *racd far side: s.i.s: shkn up and swtchd lft over 2f out: nt trble ldrs: 3rd of 4 in gp* **20/1**

215- **6** *1/2* **Dirty Rascal (IRE)**[173] 8646 3-9-9 95 TomMarquand 7 82
(Richard Hannon) *racd centre: chsd ldr: rdn over 1f out: wknd ins fnl f: last of 3 in gp* **10/1**

01-0 **7** *5* **Battle Of Waterloo (IRE)**[7] 1713 3-9-6 81 LukeMorris 4 65
(John Ryan) *racd far side: chsd wnr tl rdn over 2f out: wknd over 1f out: last of 4 in gp* **100/1**

1m 27.6s (2.20) **Going Correction** +0.40s/f (Good) 7 Ran SP% **109.4**
Speed ratings (Par 102): **103,101,99,96,94 93,88**
CSF £52.93 TOTE £2.80: £1.40, £7.70; EX 49.90 Trifecta £153.60.
Owner King Power Racing Co Ltd **Bred** Con Marnane **Trained** East Everleigh, Wilts

FOCUS
Not the deepest of conditions races, but a progressive winner. They races in two groups with just three racing away from the rail more towards the centre. The second is the key to the form, but it's been rated around the third and fifth.

1889 COATES & SEELY BRUT RESERVE H'CAP 1m
3:35 (3:35) (Class 2) (0-100,98) 4-Y-O+ **£16,172** (£4,812; £2,405; £1,202) **Stalls** Low

Form RPR

20-3 **1** **Beringer**[19] 1415 4-9-5 96 AndreaAtzeni 2 104+
(Alan King) *looked wl; hld up: hdwy over 1f out: rdn to ld ins fnl f: r.o* **4/1[2]**

/11- **2** *hd* **Power Of Darkness**[295] 4259 4-8-12 89 (w) HayleyTurner 5 96+
(Marcus Tregoning) *dwlt: hld up: racd keenly: hdwy over 1f out: swtchd lft ins fnl f: rdn and r.o wl* **7/1**

613- **3** *1* **Sawwaah**[167] 8809 4-9-2 93 JimCrowley 3 98
(Owen Burrows) *looked wl; chsd ldr tl led over 2f out: rdn over 1f out: hdd ins fnl f: styd on same pce towards fin* **9/4[1]**

/45- **4** *nk* **Thrave**[166] 8837 4-9-0 91 HarryBentley 1 95
(Henry Candy) *chsd ldrs: ev ch fr over 1f out tl ins fnl f: styd on same pce towards fin* **11/2[3]**

2423 **5** *2* **Breden (IRE)**[19] 1415 9-9-7 98 JamesDoyle 7 98
(Linda Jewell) *hld up: shkn up over 2f out: hdwy over 1f out: edgd lft and styd on same pce wl ins fnl f* **9/1**

3456 **6** *1* **Bedouin's Story**[49] 960 4-9-4 95 (h) JasonWatson 8 92
(Saeed bin Suroor) *hld up: shkn up over 3f out: rdn over 1f out: nt clr run wl ins fnl f: nt trble ldrs* **6/1**

256- **7** *4 1/2* **Exhort**[187] 8192 4-9-4 95 RyanMoore 4 82
(Richard Fahey) *led over 5f: wknd fnl f* **16/1**

110- **8** *1* **Protected Guest**[192] 8060 4-9-1 92 TomQueally 6 77
(George Margarson) *chsd ldrs: rdn: hung rt and wknd over 1f out* **25/1**

1m 39.88s (1.48) **Going Correction** +0.40s/f (Good) 8 Ran SP% **112.7**
Speed ratings (Par 109): **108,107,106,106,104 103,99,98**
CSF £30.88 CT £76.07 TOTE £4.70: £1.50, £2.10, £1.30; EX 16.40 Trifecta £40.20.
Owner L Field, B Cognet, N Farrell, J Spack **Bred** Aiden Murphy **Trained** Barbury Castle, Wilts
■ Stewards' Enquiry : Andrea Atzeni six-day ban; misuse of whip (May 2-7)

FOCUS
A very useful handicap and another example of Alan King's burgeoning Flat talents.

1890 BET365 EARL OF SEFTON STKS (GROUP 3) 1m 1f
4:10 (4:12) (Class 1) 4-Y-O+
£34,026 (£12,900; £6,456; £3,216; £1,614; £810) **Stalls** Low

Form RPR

102- **1** **Zabeel Prince (IRE)**[202] 7735 6-9-0 111 AndreaAtzeni 2 120
(Roger Varian) *looked wl; broke wl: sn stdd and lost pl: hld up: swtchd lft over 2f out: hdwy wl over 1f out: shkn up to ld 1f out: edgd rt ins fnl f: r.o wl* **9/2[1]**

52-0 **2** *2 3/4* **Forest Ranger (IRE)**[40] 1115 5-9-0 112 TonyHamilton 10 114
(Richard Fahey) *sweating; sn prom: chsd ldr over 2f out: rdn and ev ch over 1f out: styd on same pce ins fnl f* **13/2[3]**

110- **3** *1* **Mustashry**[166] 8846 6-9-5 115 DaneO'Neill 11 117
(Sir Michael Stoute) *bit bkward; s.i.s: hld up: hdwy over 2f out: rdn over 1f out: styd on same pce fnl f* **10/1**

634- **4** *2* **Elarqam**[245] 6196 4-9-0 111 (w) JimCrowley 6 108
(Mark Johnston) *led over 5f: shkn up over 2f out: outpcd over 1f out: r.o towards fin* **9/2[1]**

4-13 **5** *1/2* **First Nation**[56] 844 5-9-0 109 JamesDoyle 7 107
(Charlie Appleby) *s.i.s: hld up: shkn up over 2f out: nt trble ldrs* **15/2**

-033 **6** *hd* **First Contact (IRE)**[40] 1115 4-9-0 108 WilliamBuick 8 106
(Charlie Appleby) *looked wl; w ldr tl led over 3f out: rdn and hdd over 1f out: wknd ins fnl f (jockey said gelding hung left-handed from half way out)* **5/1[2]**

03-0 **7** *1* **Robin Of Navan (FR)**[19] 1420 6-9-0 105 RyanMoore 3 104
(Harry Dunlop) *chsd ldrs: led over 1f out: sn shkn up and hdd: wknd wl ins fnl f* **33/1**

0-60 **8** *2 1/2* **Circus Couture (IRE)**[5] 1753 7-9-0 104 JFEgan 1 99
(Jane Chapple-Hyam) *hld up: rdn over 1f out: wknd ins fnl f* **50/1**

41-0 **9** *9* **Vintager**[56] 844 4-9-0 112 AdamKirby 5 80
(Charlie Appleby) *chsd ldrs: rdn over 2f out: wknd over 1f out (trainer said gelding ran flat)* **9/2[1]**

130- **10** *26* **Fajjaj (IRE)**[250] 6011 4-9-0 109 FrankieDettori 4 25
(Hugo Palmer) *sweating; chsd ldrs: pushed along over 3f out: wknd over 2f out (jockey said gelding stopped quickly)* **25/1**

1m 52.43s (1.33) **Going Correction** +0.40s/f (Good) 10 Ran SP% **114.1**
Speed ratings (Par 113): **110,107,106,104,104 104,103,101,93,70**
CSF £32.50 TOTE £5.50: £1.80, £1.30, £3.70; EX 33.30 Trifecta £206.80.
Owner Sheikh Mohammed Obaid Al Maktoum **Bred** Roundhill Stud **Trained** Newmarket, Suffolk

FOCUS
Rock-solid Group 3 form with the right horses coming to the fore and an impressive winner. It's been rated around the second and third.

1891 BET365 H'CAP 7f
4:45 (4:45) (Class 2) (0-105,105) 4-Y-O+ **£16,172** (£4,812; £2,405; £1,202) **Stalls** Low

Form RPR

4-12 **1** **Mubtasim (IRE)**[49] 960 5-9-7 105 (h) WilliamBuick 5 114
(Charlie Appleby) *mde all: shkn up over 1f out: rdn and edgd rt ins fnl f: styd on* **5/2[1]**

-231 **2** *1* **On The Warpath**[49] 960 4-9-3 101 JamesDoyle 2 107
(Charlie Appleby) *looked wl; chsd wnr: rdn and ev ch over 1f out: styd on same pce wl ins fnl f* **5/2[1]**

413- **3** *1 3/4* **Presidential (IRE)**[159] 8999 5-8-7 91 oh1 BenCurtis 11 92+
(Roger Fell) *s.i.s: hld up: swtchd rt and hdwy over 1f out: styd on same pce towards fin* **16/1**

112- **4** *1/2* **Game Player (IRE)**[195] 7948 4-8-7 91 oh2 AndreaAtzeni 7 91
(Roger Varian) *hmpd s: sn hld up in tch: rdn over 1f out: styd on same pce ins fnl f* **13/2[2]**

010- **5** *nse* **Hajjam**[184] 8304 5-8-11 95 JimCrowley 6 95
(David O'Meara) *edgd lft s: hld up: hdwy over 1f out: nt rch ldrs* **20/1**

103- **6** *shd* **Betty F**[238] 6459 4-9-1 99 FrankieDettori 9 99
(Jeremy Noseda) *hld up: hdwy over 2f out: rdn over 1f out: styd on same pce ins fnl f* **12/1**

20-0 **7** *2 1/2* **Gilgamesh**[19] 1421 5-8-12 96 (p) HarryBentley 4 89
(George Scott) *hld up in tch: rdn and edgd rt over 1f out: no ex ins fnl f* **10/1[3]**

016- **8** *4 1/2* **Zap**[208] 7525 4-8-8 97 SeanDavis[(5)] 3 78
(Richard Fahey) *hld up: rdn over 2f out: wknd over 1f out* **11/1**

2-26 **9** *3 1/2* **Cenotaph (USA)**[75] 563 7-7-7 105 RyanMoore 1 76
(Jeremy Noseda) *hld up in tch: lost pl over 3f out: wknd over 1f out* **14/1**

003- **10** *10* **Rufus King**[168] 8768 4-9-1 99 PJMcDonald 8 43
(Mark Johnston) *hmpd s: sn chsng wnr: rdn over 2f out: wknd over 1f out* **20/1**

1m 26.67s (1.27) **Going Correction** +0.40s/f (Good) 10 Ran SP% **117.7**
Speed ratings (Par 109): **108,106,104,104,104 104,101,96,92,80**
CSF £7.90 CT £78.77 TOTE £3.00: £1.30, £1.50, £4.80; EX 9.90 Trifecta £80.00.
Owner Godolphin **Bred** Mrs Natasha Drennan **Trained** Newmarket, Suffolk

FOCUS
Another race where they pretty much raced in two groups and the winner made all more down the centre. A one-two for Godolphin. A pb from the winner.

1892 BARONS CAMBRIDGE BMW H'CAP 5f
5:20 (5:20) (Class 3) (0-95,94) 4-Y-O+ **£12,938** (£3,850; £1,924; £962) **Stalls** Low

Form RPR

1225 **1** **Ornate**[54] 877 6-9-7 94 PhilDennis 5 103
(David C Griffiths) *edgd lft s: sn led: shkn up over 1f out: rdn ins fnl f: jst hld on* **10/1**

4-00 **2** *hd* **Roman River**[40] 1098 4-9-1 88 GeraldMosse 11 96+
(Martin Smith) *looked wl; hld up: racd keenly: hdwy over 1f out: chsd wnr ins fnl f: r.o* **6/1[3]**

320- **3** *1* **Open Wide (USA)**[215] 7290 5-9-6 93 (b w) AndreaAtzeni 12 98
(Amanda Perrett) *hld up: r.o ins fnl f: nt rch ldrs* **5/1[2]**

600- **4** *1 1/2* **Abel Handy (IRE)**[173] 8632 4-9-2 89 JamesDoyle 1 88
(Declan Carroll) *sltly on toes; w wnr tl pushed along 1/2-way: rdn over 1f out: styd on same pce ins fnl f* **5/2[1]**

64-0 **5** *1* **Haddaf (IRE)**[19] 1421 4-9-0 92 SeanDavis[(5)] 2 88
(Robert Cowell) *hld up: shkn up 1/2-way: r.o ins fnl f: nt rch ldrs* **25/1**

1205 **6** *hd* **Shamshon (IRE)**[34] 1211 8-8-7 80 oh1 HarryBentley 9 75
(Stuart Williams) *hld up: rdn over 1f out: r.o towards fin: nt trble ldrs* **8/1**

0-03 **7** *1/2* **Equimou**[14] 1547 5-8-8 86 DarraghKeenan[(5)] 3 79
(Robert Eddery) *chsd ldrs: rdn over 1f out: no ex ins fnl f* **16/1**

200- **8** *3/4* **Soie D'Leau**[201] 7766 7-9-7 94 (w) TonyHamilton 10 84
(Linda Stubbs) *looked wl; prom: rdn and edgd rt over 1f out: no ex ins fnl f* **25/1**

530- **9** *nk* **Move In Time**[194] 7994 11-9-0 **87**.................... DougieCostello 6 76
(Paul Midgley) *bit bkward; s.i.s: hld up: hdwy 1/2-way: outpcd fr over 1f out* **20/1**

600- **10** *1 1/2* **Quench Dolly**[173] 8641 5-8-11 **89**.................... TheodoreLadd(5) 8 73
(John Gallagher) *chsd ldrs: rdn over 1f out: wknd ins fnl f* **16/1**

015- **11** *8* **Consequences (IRE)**[168] 8784 4-8-10 **83**.................... WilliamBuick 7 38
(Ian Williams) *s.i.s: hld up: wknd over 1f out (jockey said gelding lost it's action into the dip)* **15/2**

1m 0.55s (1.45) **Going Correction** +0.40s/f (Good) **11** Ran SP% **115.7**
Speed ratings (Par 107): **104,103,102,99,98 97,96,95,95,92 80**
CSF £65.94 CT £340.68 TOTE £9.50: £2.80, £2.30, £2.10; EX 72.40 Trifecta £462.50.
Owner Kings Road Racing Partnership **Bred** Cheveley Park Stud Ltd **Trained** Bawtry, S Yorks

FOCUS
A very useful handicap that looked wide open beforehand and so it proved. The winner has been rated as finding a bit on his AW form.
T/Plt: £39.30 to a £1 stake. Pool: £121,461.45. 2,252.29 winning units. T/Qpdt: £10.80 to a £1 stake. Pool: £10,616.30. 722.78 winning units. **Colin Roberts**

RIPON (R-H)
Thursday, April 18

OFFICIAL GOING: Good (good to firm in places; 8.5)
Wind: Light, half against Weather: Fine

1893 MANDALE HOMES AT JUNIPER GROVE RIPON EBF NOVICE STKS 5f
2:15 (2:16) (Class 5) 2-Y-O
£3,881 (£1,155; £577; £288) **Stalls** High

Form RPR

0 **1** **Great Dame (IRE)**[10] 1642 2-9-0 0.................... DanielTudhope 1 79+
(David O'Meara) *led after 1f: mde rest: pushed clr over 1f out: kpt on wl* **9/1**

2 *2 3/4* **Infinite Grace** 2-9-0 0.................... CamHardie 9 69+
(David O'Meara) *hld up: sn pushed along: hdwy over 1f out: chsd ldr ent fnl f: kpt on* **16/1**

3 *1/2* **Hurstwood** 2-9-5 0.................... DavidAllan 8 72+
(Tim Easterby) *s.i.s: hld up in rr: sn pushed along: stl plenty to do appr fnl f: r.o wl: wnt 3rd fnl 50yds* **6/1**

3 **4** *3* **Bare All (IRE)**[10] 1642 2-9-0 0.................... CliffordLee 3 56+
(K R Burke) *wnt rt s: chsd ldrs towards outer: rdn 1/2-way: wknd ins fnl f* **9/4**[1]

5 *3 1/4* **Stone Princess (IRE)** 2-8-11 0.................... BenRobinson(3) 7 44
(Brian Ellison) *chsd ldrs: hung rt fr early stage: pushed along 1/2-way: wknd fnl f* **28/1**

0 **6** *1/2* **Lakeview (IRE)**[16] 1493 2-9-5 0.................... DavidEgan 5 48
(David Loughnane) *led for 1f: w ldr: rdn 2f out: wknd appr fnl f* **33/1**

7 *1/2* **Good Night Mr Tom (IRE)** 2-9-5 0.................... JoeFanning 4 46
(Mark Johnston) *wnt sltly rt s: chsd ldrs: rdn along and losing pl whn n.m.r over 1f out: sn wknd* **10/3**[3]

8 *1 1/4* **Warily** 2-9-5 0.................... PaulHanagan 2 41+
(Richard Fahey) *s.i.s and carried rt s: hld up on outer: sn pushed along: wknd fnl f* **3/1**[2]

1m 0.33s (0.93) **Going Correction** -0.15s/f (Firm) **8** Ran SP% **115.4**
Speed ratings (Par 92): **86,81,80,76,70 70,69,67**
CSF £137.49 TOTE £8.60: £2.20, £3.30, £2.00; EX 124.60 Trifecta £494.60.
Owner Nick Bradley Racing 7 And Partner 2 **Bred** Mark Salmon **Trained** Upper Helmsley, N Yorks
■ Stewards' Enquiry : David Egan two-day ban; careless riding (May 2-3)

FOCUS
The rail on the bend from the back straight to the home straight was dolled out by 6 yards, adding about 12 yards to races on the round course. A good race for trainer David O'Meara, who had the first two home. The level is hard to pin down.

1894 MANDALE HOMES THE AWARD WINNING HOUSEBUILDER H'CAP 6f
2:50 (2:50) (Class 5) (0-75,77) 3-Y-O
£4,075 (£1,212; £606; £303; £300; £300) **Stalls** High

Form RPR

640- **1** **Lady Calcaria**[171] 8696 3-8-11 **65**.................... DuranFentiman 2 71
(Tim Easterby) *swtchd rt sn after s and chsd ldr on far side (1 of 2 who racd there): rdn to ld ent fnl f: kpt on wl* **40/1**

02-3 **2** *1* **Staycation (IRE)**[16] 1504 3-9-1 **69**.................... DavidAllan 3 72
(Rebecca Bastiman) *1 of 2 who racd far side: overall ldr: drvn and hdd 1f out: kpt on* **7/1**

25-3 **3** *1 3/4* **Fume (IRE)**[90] 289 3-9-5 **73**.................... DanielTudhope 8 70+
(James Bethell) *dwlt: hld up stands' side: pushed along and hdwy over 2f out: led gp 1f out: rdn and kpt on wl: 1st of 12 in gp* **7/1**

363- **4** *shd* **Arletta Star**[180] 8411 3-8-9 **63**.................... NathanEvans 11 60+
(Tim Easterby) *hld up stands' side: pushed along and n.m.r wl over 1f out: hdwy appr fnl f: rdn and kpt on wl: 2nd of 12 in gp* **18/1**

4212 **5** *1 1/4* **Sundiata**[17] 1476 3-9-2 **70**....................(p[1]) RichardKingscote 12 63
(Charles Hills) *led stands' side gp: prom overall: rdn and hung rt over 2f out: hdd in gp 1f out: no ex: 3rd of 12 in gp (jockey said filly hung right)* **7/2**[1]

220- **6** *2 1/2* **Hard Solution**[224] 6973 3-9-2 **70**.................... DavidNolan 9 55
(David O'Meara) *prom stands' side: rdn 2f out: no ex fnl f: 4th of 12 in gp* **16/1**

32-3 **7** *2* **Tie A Yellowribbon**[17] 1488 3-9-0 **68**.................... PaulHanagan 6 47
(James Bethell) *chsd ldrs stands' side: rdn over 2f out: wknd ins fnl f: 5th of 12 in gp* **6/1**[3]

656- **8** *1* **Parisean Artiste (IRE)**[274] 5079 3-8-8 **69**.................... GeorgiaDobie(7) 10 44
(Eve Johnson Houghton) *hld up stands' side: sn pushed along: sme late hdwy: 6th of 12 in gp* **14/1**

060- **9** *nk* **Mark's Choice (IRE)**[181] 8374 3-9-7 **75**.................... JamesSullivan 13 50
(Ruth Carr) *chsd ldrs stands' side: rdn over 2f out: wknd fnl f: 7th of 12 in gp* **12/1**

610- **10** *1/2* **Cotubanama**[206] 7617 3-9-9 **77**.................... CharlesBishop 1 50
(Mick Channon) *dwlt: swtchd lft sn after s: hld up in rr stands' side: hld up: nvr threatened: 8th of 12 in gp* **20/1**

5 **11** *hd* **Dancing Mountain (IRE)**[48] 972 3-8-6 **60**.................... DavidEgan 5 32
(Roger Fell) *chsd ldrs towards outer stands' side: rdn over 2f out: wknd fnl f: 9th of 12 in gp* **28/1**

30-1 **12** *hd* **Bugler Bob (IRE)**[17] 1488 3-9-8 **76**.................... JasonHart 7 48
(John Quinn) *midfield stands' side: rdn over 2f out: wknd fnl f: 10 of 12 in gp* **9/2**[2]

13 *nk* **Fox Hill**[176] 8555 3-8-9 **63**.................... RachelRichardson 4 34
(Eric Alston) *chsd ldrs stands' side: wknd over 1f out: 11th of 12 in gp* **33/1**

320- **14** *1* **Jill Rose**[190] 8107 3-8-13 **67**.................... CamHardie 14 34
(Richard Whitaker) *chsd ldrs stands' side: rdn over 2f out: wknd over 1f out* **33/1**

1m 11.14s (-1.36) **Going Correction** -0.15s/f (Firm) **14** Ran SP% **121.7**
Speed ratings (Par 98): **103,101,99,99,97 94,91,90,89,89 88,88,88,86**
CSF £293.08 CT £2296.30 TOTE £62.70: £14.40, £2.50, £2.90; EX 487.10 Trifecta £1853.20.
Owner Ontoawinner 10 & Partner **Bred** Lady Juliet Tadgell **Trained** Great Habton, N Yorks

FOCUS
The two that decided to go to the inside rail were the two that seemingly found the faster strip of ground. The second helps set the standard and has been rated in line with his latest effort.

1895 PPR FOUNDATION H'CAP 6f
3:25 (3:26) (Class 4) (0-80,82) 4-Y-O+
£5,692 (£1,694; £846; £423; £300; £300) **Stalls** High

Form RPR

024- **1** **Bossipop**[152] 9135 6-9-8 **81**....................(b) DavidAllan 1 88
(Tim Easterby) *racd far side: mde all: rdn over 1f out: drvn ins fnl f: all out* **9/1**[3]

540- **2** *nk* **Zumurud (IRE)**[219] 7147 4-9-3 **76**.................... DanielTudhope 8 82
(Rebecca Bastiman) *trckd ldrs stands' side: rdn over 1f out: drvn to ld gp 75yds out: kpt on: 1st of 9 in gp* **25/1**

040/ **3** *1/2* **Cartmell Cleave**[921] 7186 7-9-7 **80**.................... JamesSullivan 6 84
(Ruth Carr) *hld up stands' side: hdwy over 1f out: rdn ins fnl f: kpt on wl: 2nd of 9 in gp* **18/1**

120- **4** *3/4* **Redrosezorro**[180] 8415 5-8-10 **69**....................(h) RachelRichardson 13 71
(Eric Alston) *led stands' side gp: prom overall: rdn 2f out: hdd in gp 75yds out: one pce: 3rd of 9 in gp* **11/1**

00-0 **5** *nk* **Paddy Power (IRE)**[17] 1487 6-9-2 **75**.................... PaulHanagan 2 76
(Richard Fahey) *in tch far side: pushed along to chse ldr over 1f out: rdn and kpt on: 2nd of 4 in grnd* **4/1**[2]

040- **6** *1/2* **Mr Orange (IRE)**[178] 8481 6-9-5 **78**.................... KevinStott 11 78
(Paul Midgley) *chsd ldrs stands' side: rdn 2f out: kpt on: bit short of room towards fin: 4th of 9 in gp* **14/1**

2211 **7** *1 1/2* **Kupa River (IRE)**[13] 1560 5-8-10 **74**....................(h) BenSanderson(5) 12 69
(Roger Fell) *dwlt: sn chsd ldrs stands' side: rdn over 1f out: sn one pce: 5th of 9 in gp* **2/1**[1]

600- **8** *nk* **Penny Pot Lane**[160] 8977 6-8-8 **67**.................... LewisEdmunds 5 61
(Richard Whitaker) *hld up far side: nvr threatened: 3rd of 4 in gp* **25/1**

120- **9** *1 1/2* **Daffy Jane**[221] 7102 4-9-4 **82**.................... FayeMcManoman(5) 4 71
(Nigel Tinkler) *chsd ldr far side: wknd over 1f out: last of 4 in gp* **12/1**

6/0- **10** *1* **Eccleston**[455] 285 8-9-4 **77**.................... GrahamLee 9 63
(Paul Midgley) *nvr bttr than midfield stands' side: 6th of 9 in gp* **33/1**

60-0 **11** *6* **Indian Pursuit (IRE)**[97] 187 6-8-7 **66**....................(v) AndrewMullen 7 32
(John Quinn) *chsd ldrs stands' side: rdn over 2f out: wknd over 1f out: 7th of 9 in gp* **33/1**

600- **12** *nk* **Music Society (IRE)**[185] 8259 4-9-4 **77**.................... CamHardie 10 43
(Tim Easterby) *hld up stands' side: nvr threatened: 8th of 9 in gp* **12/1**

006- **13** *5* **Mr Wagyu (IRE)**[173] 8635 4-9-4 **77**....................(v) JasonHart 3 27
(John Quinn) *dwlt: swtchd lft sn after s to r stands' side: a towards rr* **9/1**[3]

1m 10.93s (-1.57) **Going Correction** -0.15s/f (Firm) **13** Ran SP% **122.6**
Speed ratings (Par 105): **104,103,102,101,101 100,98,98,96,95 87,86,80**
CSF £225.17 CT £4027.25 TOTE £6.30: £2.20, £11.50, £5.70; EX 256.40 Trifecta £1631.40.
Owner Ambrose Turnbull **Bred** Lady Whent **Trained** Great Habton, N Yorks

FOCUS
A decent handicap, but the majority were making their seasonal reappearance, meaning the form may not be reliable. They split into two groups once again. The second has been rated to his Pontefract win.

1896 KIRBY THOMAS SPONSORED DEBBY SHIPPAM MEMORIAL H'CAP (FOR THE RIPON SILVER BOWL) 1m 1f 170y
4:00 (4:02) (Class 3) (0-95,94) 4-Y-O+
£8,715 (£2,609; £1,304; £652; £326; £163) **Stalls** Low

Form RPR

412- **1** **Epaulement (IRE)**[180] 8419 4-9-7 **94**.................... RichardKingscote 1 103
(Tom Dascombe) *mde all: pushed along over 2f out: pressed over 1f out: rdn and kpt on wl* **15/8**[1]

030- **2** *1/2* **Poet's Prince**[240] 6382 4-9-3 **90**.................... JoeFanning 4 98
(Mark Johnston) *trckd ldrs: pushed along over 2f out: rdn to chal over 1f out: kpt on but a hld* **17/2**

120- **3** *1* **Everything For You (IRE)**[159] 9005 5-9-6 **93**....................(p w) KevinStott 11 99
(Kevin Ryan) *hld up: pushed along and hdwy on outside over 2f out: rdn to chse ldrs appr fnl f: edgd rt: kpt on* **8/1**

P00- **4** *1 3/4* **Anythingtoday (IRE)**[187] 8198 5-9-4 **91**.................... DanielTudhope 9 93
(David O'Meara) *hld up: pushed along and hdwy over 2f out: rdn to chse ldrs appr fnl f: no ex fnl 50yds* **10/1**

0-02 **5** *3 1/4* **Society Red**[9] 1664 5-9-3 **90**.................... PaulHanagan 8 86
(Richard Fahey) *midfield: rdn along over 2f out: in tch whn n.m.r 1f out: wknd (jockey said gelding became unbalanced on the undulations)* **13/2**[2]

04-0 **6** *3/4* **Mutamaded (IRE)**[14] 1545 6-9-4 **91**.................... JamesSullivan 6 85
(Ruth Carr) *in tch: rdn along and outpcd over 3f out: no threat after* **7/1**[3]

00-P **7** *1/2* **Ayutthaya (IRE)**[9] 1664 4-9-5 **92**.................... TomEaves 3 85
(Kevin Ryan) *prom: rdn over 2f out: wknd over 1f out* **14/1**

000- **8** *6* **Mooltazem (IRE)**[163] 8899 5-9-1 **88**.................... PaulMulrennan 7 69
(Michael Dods) *slowly away: a towards rr* **20/1**

045- **9** *5* **Appointed**[183] 8331 5-8-8 **81**....................(t) RachelRichardson 2 52
(Tim Easterby) *prom: rdn along over 3f out: wknd over 2f out* **11/1**

24-0 **10** *2* **King's Pavilion (IRE)**[19] 1414 6-9-1 **91**.................... ConorMcGovern(3) 5 57
(Jason Ward) *hld up in midfield: rdn 3f out: sn wknd* **20/1**

2m 1.05s (-3.55) **Going Correction** -0.15s/f (Firm) **10** Ran SP% **115.9**
Speed ratings (Par 107): **109,108,107,106,103 103,102,98,94,92**
CSF £18.19 CT £100.89 TOTE £2.30: £1.20, £2.70, £2.70; EX 17.80 Trifecta £159.30.
Owner Deva Racing Epaulette Partnership **Bred** Mrs Vanessa Hutch **Trained** Malpas, Cheshire
■ Scottish Summit was withdrawn. Price at time of withdrawal 25-1. Rule 4 does not apply.

FOCUS
This race distance was increased by 12yds, making it 1m1f 182yds. The favourite dominated in this and made every yard of the running. The second has been rated to his 3yo best.

1897 RIPON "COCK O' THE NORTH" H'CAP 1m
4:35 (4:38) (Class 3) (0-90,86) 3-Y-O
£8,715 (£2,609; £1,304; £652; £326; £163) **Stalls** Low

Form RPR

003- **1** **Divinity**[187] 8195 3-9-7 **86**.................... CliffordLee 1 92
(K R Burke) *mde all: clr over 4f out: rdn over 1f out: kpt on: unchal* **10/1**[3]

The Form Book Flat 2019, Raceform Ltd, Newbury, RG14 5SJ

1112 **2** *1* **Alkaameel**[17] 1485 3-8-13 **85**............ CierenFallon(7) 3 89
(William Haggas) *trckd ldrs: pushed along to chse ldr 2f out: kpt on but nvr getting to wnr* **4/1**[1]

06-1 **3** *¾* **Hesslewood (IRE)**[17] 1485 3-9-5 **84**............ DanielTudhope 9 86
(James Bethell) *trckd ldrs: pushed along over 2f out: rdn over 1f out: kpt on* **4/1**[1]

145- **4** *3 ½* **Two Blondes (IRE)**[186] 8232 3-9-7 **86**............ CharlesBishop 2 80
(Mick Channon) *prom: rdn over 3f out: wknd fnl f* **7/1**[2]

420- **5** *½* **Irv (IRE)**[187] 8195 3-8-10 **75**............ GrahamLee 4 68
(Micky Hammond) *hld up in midfield on inner: rdn along over 2f out: kpt on ins fnl f: nvr threatened* **33/1**

4123 **6** *2* **Mustadun**[17] 1480 3-8-13 **78**............ JoeFanning 5 66
(Mark Johnston) *hld up: nvr threatened* **10/1**[3]

13-4 **7** *shd* **Metatron (IRE)**[26] 1293 3-9-5 **84**............ RichardKingscote 6 72
(Tom Dascombe) *hld up in rr: rdn over 2f out: nvr threatened* **10/1**[3]

213- **8** *2 ¼* **Ideological (IRE)**[153] 9106 3-9-4 **83**............ DavidEgan 8 66
(Roger Varian) *midfield on inner: rdn over 2f out: wknd fnl f* **4/1**[1]

345- **9** *½* **Garrison Commander (IRE)**[152] 9122 3-8-3 **75**...... GeorgiaDobie(7) 10 57
(Eve Johnson Houghton) *midfield: pushed along over 3f out: sn wknd* **12/1**

105- **10** *nk* **Off Piste**[201] 7779 3-9-0 **79**............(t) DavidAllan 7 60
(Tim Easterby) *dwlt: hld up: pushed along over 2f out: nvr threatened* **12/1**

1m 39.23s (-1.77) **Going Correction** -0.15s/f (Firm) **10** Ran SP% **118.1**
Speed ratings (Par 102): **102,101,100,96,96 94,94,91,91,91**
CSF £50.50 CT £195.06 TOTE £12.40: £3.50, £1.50, £1.80; EX 51.50 Trifecta £277.80.
Owner Cheveley Park Stud **Bred** Cheveley Park Stud Ltd **Trained** Middleham Moor, N Yorks

FOCUS
This race distance was increased by 12yds, making it 1m 12yds. This looked a strong 3yo only handicap, and it was run at a good gallop thanks to the winner.

1898 PULSE 1 AND PULSE 2 NOVICE STKS (PLUS 10 RACE) 1m 4f 10y
5:10 (5:11) (Class 5) 3-Y-O **£3,881** (£1,155; £577; £288) **Stalls** Centre

Form RPR

24- **1** **Sir Ron Priestley**[226] 6899 3-9-5 0............ JoeFanning 4 91+
(Mark Johnston) *pressed ldr: led over 2f out: pushed clr over 1f out: kpt on* **4/9**[1]

04- **2** *6* **Babbo's Boy (IRE)**[174] 8607 3-9-5 0............(w) DanielTudhope 1 84+
(Michael Bell) *trckd ldrs on inner: stl gng wl whn short of room 2f out tl over 1f out: no ch w wnr after but kpt on to take 2nd ins fnl f* **9/2**[2]

4 **3** *3 ½* **Arthur Pendragon (IRE)**[13] 1558 3-9-5 0............ CallumShepherd 2 76
(Brian Meehan) *led narrowly: rdn along and hdd over 2f out: sn edgd rt: wknd ins fnl f* **9/1**

3- **4** *7* **Global Express**[197] 7905 3-9-5 0............ DavidEgan 5 65
(Ed Dunlop) *midfield: pushed along to chse ldrs over 3f out: wknd over 1f out* **7/1**[3]

6 **5** *7* **Tidal Point (IRE)**[13] 1558 3-9-5 0............ RoystonFfrench 6 54
(Steph Hollinshead) *trckd ldrs: wknd over 3f out* **50/1**

6 *8* **Night Fury** 3-8-12 0............ MarkCrehan(7) 7 41
(Michael Appleby) *dwlt: hld up: rn wd on bnd 5f out: sn wknd* **33/1**

0 **7** *35* **Two For Three (IRE)**[10] 1643 3-9-5 0............ JasonHart 3
(Roger Fell) *hld up: rdn over 4f out: wknd and bhd* **50/1**

2m 34.49s (-1.81) **Going Correction** -0.15s/f (Firm) **7** Ran SP% **116.8**
Speed ratings (Par 98): **100,96,93,89,84 79,55**
CSF £3.03 TOTE £1.40: £1.10, £2.00; EX 2.90 Trifecta £9.00.
Owner Paul Dean **Bred** Mascalls Stud **Trained** Middleham Moor, N Yorks

FOCUS
This race distance was increased by 12yds, making it 1m4f 22yds. The favourite did it nicely but the second found trouble in running. The second has been rated as improving in line with his 2yo form, and the third as finding a bit on his debut run.

1899 MANDALE HOMES AT ROKESBY PLACE PICKHILL APPRENTICE H'CAP (YORKSHIRE FUTURE STARS SERIES) 5f
5:45 (5:45) (Class 4) (0-80,81) 4-Y-O+
£5,692 (£1,694; £846; £423; £300; £300) **Stalls** High

Form RPR

2033 **1** **Canford Bay (IRE)**[16] 1507 5-9-3 **71**............ KieranSchofield 12 81
(Antony Brittain) *racd towards stands' side: pressed ldr: led 2f out: rdn over 1f out: kpt on wl* **15/2**

6-55 **2** *1* **Nibras Again**[23] 1342 5-9-5 **73**............ TobyEley 3 79+
(Paul Midgley) *hld up towards centre: pushed along and hdwy 2f out: edgd lft over 1f out: rdn to chse ldr appr fnl f: kpt on (jockey said gelding hung left from 2 1/2f out)* **9/1**

561- **3** *2 ½* **Wrenthorpe**[162] 8934 4-9-2 **76**............(p) HarryRussell(6) 11 73
(Bryan Smart) *racd stands' side: led narrowly: rdn and hdd 2f out: one pce fnl f* **9/2**[1]

50-2 **4** *1 ½* **Bowson Fred**[86] 353 7-9-9 **80**............(w) JoshQuinn(3) 10 72
(Michael Easterby) *prom stands' side: rdn 1/2-way: no ex fnl f* **8/1**

400- **5** *1* **Sheepscar Lad (IRE)**[188] 8167 5-9-2 **80**............ IzzyClifton(10) 6 68
(Nigel Tinkler) *hld up: pushed along 1/2-way: kpt on fnl f: nvr threatened* **17/2**

-003 **6** *nk* **Dapper Man (IRE)**[14] 1551 5-9-9 **77**............ Pierre-LouisJamin 2 64
(Roger Fell) *1 of 2 to r far side: sn outpcd: edgd lft towards main gp over 1f out: kpt on fnl f: nvr threatened* **7/1**[3]

4600 **7** *1 ½* **Tan**[16] 1496 5-9-8 **76**............ MarkCrehan 7 58
(Michael Appleby) *hld up towards centre: rdn along 1/2-way: nvr threatened* **9/1**

4110 **8** *1* **Drakefell (IRE)**[14] 1547 4-9-11 **79**............(b) SeamusCronin 9 57
(Antony Brittain) *chsd ldrs: rdn along 3f out: wknd over 1f out* **14/1**

151- **9** *hd* **Machree (IRE)**[133] 9432 4-9-5 **81**............ CianMacRedmond(8) 5 59
(Declan Carroll) *hld up towards centre: nvr threatened* **7/1**[3]

060- **10** *hd* **Bahuta Acha**[222] 7057 4-9-6 **80**............(p) LauraCoughlan(6) 8 57
(David Loughnane) *dwlt: hld up: sn pushed along: nvr involved* **33/1**

000- **11** *9* **East Street Revue**[154] 9084 6-9-7 **78**............(b) RobertDodsworth(3) 1 22
(Tim Easterby) *1 of 2 to r far side: a outpcd and bhd main gp* **13/2**[2]

58.32s (-1.08) **Going Correction** -0.15s/f (Firm) **11** Ran SP% **119.5**
Speed ratings (Par 105): **102,100,96,94,92 91,89,87,87,87 72**
CSF £74.57 CT £349.37 TOTE £6.80: £2.30, £3.20, £2.10; EX 86.00 Trifecta £759.20.
Owner Northgate Racing **Bred** R McCulloch **Trained** Warthill, N Yorks

FOCUS
Probably just a fair handicap for apprentice jockeys. Early on, there were three groups and going towards the inside rail didn't work out. The winner has been rated as finding a bit on his AW form.
T/Plt: £1,684.20 to a £1 stake. Pool: £66,609.51. 28.87 winning units. T/Qpdt: £42.30 to a £1 stake. Pool: £8,968.93. 156.56 winning units. **Andrew Sheret**

1900 - 1907a (Foreign Racing) - See Raceform Interactive

CHOLET (R-H)
Thursday, April 18

OFFICIAL GOING: Turf: good

1908a PRIX DU CREDIT AGRICOLE DE CHOLET (CONDITIONS) (4YO) (TURF) 1m 2f 110y
1:42 4-Y-O **£7,207** (£2,882; £2,162; £1,441; £720)

RPR

1 **Sensazione Poy** 4-9-3 0............ PierreBazire 1 77
(G Botti, France) **147/10**

2 *2* **Tranquil Storm (IRE)**[36] 4-8-10 0............ FranckBlondel 2 66
(Gavin Hernon, France) **48/10**[3]

3 *½* **Debatable (IRE)**[13] 1578 4-8-10 0............ ClementLecoeuvre 10 65
(Gay Kelleway) *prom: pushed along to chse ldrs over 2f out: rdn 1 1/2f out: kpt on ins fnl f: nt pce to chal eventual wnr* **63/10**

4 *hd* **Antisana**[22] 4-8-10 0............ SoufianeSaadi 8 65
(H-A Pantall, France) *racd in mid-div: asked to improve 3f out: prog on nr side rail fr 1 1/2f out: r.o strly ins fnl f: nrst fin* **47/10**[2]

5 *2* **Destinata**[240] 4-8-10 0............ AnthonyCrastus 5 61
(Mme Pia Brandt, France) **14/1**

6 *nk* **Rebel Queen (FR)**[35] 4-8-10 0............(b) AlexandreRoussel 12 60
(P Monfort, France) **54/10**

7 *hd* **Philosophy (FR)**[22] 4-9-0 0............ ArnaudBourgeais 7 64
(N Leenders, France) **33/1**

8 *1 ½* **L'Improviste (FR)**[178] 4-9-2 0............ MlleMarylineEon(3) 3 66
(Alain Couetil, France) **31/10**[1]

9 *¾* **Hygrove Dan (FR)**[23] 4-8-11 0............ DamienBoche(8) 9 65
(L Gadbin, France) **10/1**

10 *6* **Tchapalo (FR)**[179] 4-9-0 0............ YoannBarille 11 48
(N Leenders, France) **68/1**

11 *½* **Piccolo Ristretto (FR)** 4-9-0 0............ FabienLefebvre 4 47
(Louisa Carberry, France) **29/1**

12 *15* **Pearl Fly (FR)** 4-8-10 0............ AnthonyBernard 6 15
(J Jouin, France) **94/1**

2m 10.46s **12** Ran SP% **119.4**
PARI-MUTUEL (all including 1 euro stake): WIN 15.70 PLACE 4.40, 2.10, 2.30 DF 55.50.
Owner Giulio Spozio **Bred** Scuderia Blueberry SRL **Trained** France

BATH (L-H)
Friday, April 19

OFFICIAL GOING: Good to firm (firm in places; 8.7)
Wind: virtually nil Weather: warm

1909 BETWAY NOVICE STKS (PLUS 10 RACE) 5f 160y
1:50 (2:08) (Class 4) 3-Y-O **£5,013** (£1,491; £745; £372) **Stalls** Centre

Form RPR

024- **1** **The Cruising Lord**[189] 8145 3-9-2 **98**............ JFEgan 1 83
(Michael Attwater) *a.p: led after 2f: rdn clr ent fnl f: r.o wl* **5/2**[2]

304- **2** *6* **Bluebell Time (IRE)**[226] 6928 3-8-11 **59**............ MartinDwyer 3 58
(Malcolm Saunders) *led for 2f: prom: outpcd by wnr ent fnl f but kpt on* **40/1**

1 **3** *2 ½* **Global Prospector (USA)**[34] 1236 3-9-9 0............ AdamKirby 5 62
(Clive Cox) *wnt to s early and had to wait 20 minutes after r delayed: chsd ldrs: rdn 2f out: sn one pce (jockey said colt boiled over in the preliminaries)* **1/2**[1]

55 **4** *3 ¾* **Highest Mountain (FR)**[22] 1381 3-9-2 0............ FrannyNorton 2 43
(Joseph Tuite) *prom tl rdn over 2f out: wknd jst over 1f out* **9/1**[3]

0-6 **5** *4* **Laura's Legacy**[16] 1523 3-8-11 0............ LiamKeniry 4 24
(Andrew Balding) *chsd ldrs: rdn over 2f out: sn wknd* **50/1**

1m 9.37s (-1.73) **Going Correction** -0.175s/f (Firm) **5** Ran SP% **109.6**
Speed ratings (Par 100): **104,96,92,87,82**
CSF £54.28 TOTE £2.90: £1.20, £4.90; EX 36.60 Trifecta £80.70.
Owner Mrs M S Teversham **Bred** Mrs Monica Teversham **Trained** Epsom, Surrey

FOCUS
A good little 3yo novice contest on ground officially described as good to firm, firm in places. The second-favourite won readily from his inside draw and the winning time concurred with that ground assessment. The runner-up is the key to the form.

1910 HEED YOUR HUNCH CONDITIONS STKS (PLUS 10 RACE) 5f 10y
2:20 (2:35) (Class 2) 2-Y-O
£12,450 (£3,728; £1,864; £932; £466; £234) **Stalls** Centre

Form RPR

31 **1** **Zulu Zander (IRE)**[14] 1556 2-9-6 0............ AdamKirby 4 81
(David Evans) *mde all: r.o wl: readily* **10/11**[1]

6 **2** *1 ¾* **Album (IRE)**[7] 1733 2-9-2 0............ DaneO'Neill 1 71
(Martyn Meade) *slowly away: sn rousted along to chse wnr: rdn 2f out: kpt on but nt gng pce to chal* **5/1**[3]

3 *¾* **Don't Joke** 2-9-2 0............ FrannyNorton 5 68
(Mark Johnston) *trckd wnr: rdn over 2f out: kpt on but nt pce to chal* **9/4**[2]

0 **4** *1 ½* **Dark Optimist (IRE)**[20] 1416 2-9-2 0............(h[1]) HarryBentley 2 63
(David Evans) *trckd ldrs: rdn 3f out: one pce fnl 2f* **14/1**

0 **5** *1 ¼* **Fact Or Fable (IRE)**[11] 1651 2-9-2 0............ CallumShepherd 6 58
(J S Moore) *chsd ldrs: rdn over 2f out: nt pce to threaten: fdd ins fnl f (vet reported gelding lost its right fore shoe)* **33/1**

6 *4* **Contract Kid (IRE)** 2-9-2 0............ ShaneKelly 3 44
(Mark Loughnane) *s.i.s: in last but in tch and sn pushed along: nvr gng pce to get on terms* **33/1**

1m 1.9s (-0.10) **Going Correction** -0.175s/f (Firm) **6** Ran SP% **112.4**
Speed ratings (Par 98): **93,90,89,86,84 78**
CSF £6.12 TOTE £1.60: £1.10, £2.20; EX 4.40 Trifecta £12.10.
Owner J A Wilcox **Bred** Oliver Donlon **Trained** Pandy, Monmouths

FOCUS
A decent juvenile conditions sprint contest. The odds-on favourite made all in ready enough fashion. It's not sure if the winner had to improve.

1911 VALUE RATER RACING CLUB IS FREE H'CAP — 1m 3f 137y
2:55 (3:11) (Class 2) (0-100,94) 3-Y-O

£31,125 (£9,320; £4,660; £2,330; £1,165; £585) **Stalls** Low

Form | | | | RPR
51-1 **1** **Living Legend (IRE)**[20] 1419 3-8-13 **86** .... FrannyNorton 5 96
(Mark Johnston) *trckd ldrs tl lost pl after 3f: in last pair: rdn and hdwy fr over 2f out: tk narrow advantage ins fnl f: kpt on wl: hld on* 4/1[3]
421- **2** *shd* **Pablo Escobarr (IRE)**[205] 7659 3-9-6 **93** ....(t) CharlesBishop 1 102
(William Haggas) *pressed ldr: rdn to ld over 1f out: narrowly hdd ins fnl f: kpt on wl: jst hld* 7/2[2]
312- **3** *6* **Fearless Warrior (FR)**[177] 8550 3-8-11 **84** .... HarryBentley 7 83
(Ralph Beckett) *s.i.s: last: rdn and stdy prog fnl 2f: kpt on to snatch 3rd fnl strides: improve* 9/2
011- **4** *nk* **West End Charmer (IRE)**[184] 8311 3-9-7 **94** .... AdamKirby 3 92
(Mark Johnston) *led: rdn and hdd over 1f out: no ex ins fnl f: lost 3rd fnl strides* 3/1[1]
521 **5** *5* **Blood Eagle (IRE)**[17] 1509 3-8-5 **78** .... HayleyTurner 4 68
(Andrew Balding) *hld up in last pair: hdwy over 2f out: sn rdn: nvr threatened: fdd fnl f* 5/1
210- **6** *4 ½* **Just Hubert (IRE)**[177] 8550 3-8-10 **83** .... MartinDwyer 6 66
(William Muir) *trckd ldr: rdn over 2f out: wknd over 1f out* 25/1
32-1 **7** *11* **Robert L'Echelle (IRE)**[105] 66 3-8-3 **76** .... KieranO'Neill 2 40
(Hughie Morrison) *slowly away: sn trcking ldrs: rdn 3f out: wknd over 2f out* 13/2

2m 25.84s (-4.96) **Going Correction** -0.175s/f (Firm) 7 Ran SP% **119.3**
Speed ratings (Par 104): **109,108,104,104,101 98,91**
CSF £19.53 TOTE £4.30: £2.00, £2.50; EX 14.10 Trifecta £74.50.
Owner Barbara & Alick Richmond **Bred** A Oliver **Trained** Middleham Moor, N Yorks

FOCUS
5 yards added. A fairly good 3yo middle-distance handicap. Two horses towards the head of the betting fought out an exciting final furlong and the winning time dipped under standard. This form looks pretty solid.

1912 BETWAY H'CAP — 1m
3:30 (3:47) (Class 2) 4-Y-O+

£31,125 (£9,320; £4,660; £2,330; £1,165; £585) **Stalls** Low

Form | | | | RPR
40-1 **1** **Petrus (IRE)**[20] 1413 4-9-7 **97** ....(p) MartinDwyer 14 105
(Brian Meehan) *mid-div: hdwy over 2f out: sn rdn: str chal ins fnl f: led fnl stride* 5/1[3]
12-1 **2** *shd* **Salute The Soldier (GER)**[34] 1232 4-9-5 **95** .... AdamKirby 13 103
(Clive Cox) *trckd ldrs: rdn to chal 2f out: led ent fnl f: kpt on: hdd fnl stride* 7/2[1]
6-00 **3** *1* **Wahash (IRE)**[20] 1415 5-9-6 **96** .... SeanLevey 12 102
(Richard Hannon) *trckd ldrs: chal over 2f out: rdn to ld over 1f out: hdd ent fnl f: kpt on but no ex fnl 120yds* 8/1
0-10 **4** *¾* **Zwayyan**[20] 1415 6-9-7 **100** .... JoshuaBryan(3) 8 104
(Andrew Balding) *hld up towards rr: hdwy over 2f out: sn rdn: kpt on fnl f but nt pce to threaten* 6/1
4325 **5** *1* **Mr Top Hat**[52] 915 4-8-12 **88** .... HarryBentley 9 90
(David Evans) *led: rdn and hdd over 1f out: kpt on tl no ex fnl 120yds* 12/1
5-04 **6** *hd* **War Glory (IRE)**[9] 1694 6-8-13 **94** .... SeamusCronin(5) 11 95
(Richard Hannon) *hld up towards rr: rdn wl over 2f out: little imp tl hdwy over 1f out: kpt on fnl f* 12/1
20-0 **7** *1 ¼* **Waarif (IRE)**[20] 1415 6-9-5 **98** .... ConorMcGovern(3) 6 96
(David O'Meara) *s.i.s: in last pair: rdn whn swtchd rt over 1f out: kpt on fnl f bet nvr any threat* 9/2[2]
3-10 **8** *1 ¼* **Rampant Lion (IRE)**[20] 1413 4-8-10 **86** ....(p) CallumShepherd 7 81
(William Jarvis) *s.i.s: sn mid-div: hdwy over 2f out: sn rdn: fdd ins fnl f* 16/1
45-0 **9** *¾* **Uther Pendragon (IRE)**[11] 1655 4-7-7 **76** ....(p) IsobelFrancis(7) 2 70
(J S Moore) *trckd ldrs tl outpcd over 2f out: no threat after* 50/1
-656 **10** *2 ¼* **Sea Fox (IRE)**[48] 988 5-8-8 **84** .... JohnFahy 3 73
(David Evans) *rousted along leaving s: sn trcking ldr: rdn wl over 2f out: sn wknd* 25/1
200- **11** *2 ¼* **Tricorn (IRE)**[181] 8409 5-9-10 **100** .... JamesSullivan 10 83
(Ruth Carr) *a towards rr* 25/1
21-6 **12** *9* **Ghayadh**[44] 1031 4-8-12 **88** ....(t) NicolaCurrie 5 51
(Stuart Williams) *hld up towards rr: hung rt thrght: sme prog in centre over 2f out: wknd over 1f out (jockey said gelding hung badly right handed)* 20/1

1m 38.04s (-3.66) **Going Correction** -0.175s/f (Firm) 12 Ran SP% **118.1**
Speed ratings (Par 109): **111,110,109,109,108 107,106,105,104,102 100,91**
CSF £21.68 CT £126.80 TOTE £5.30: £2.10, £1.60, £2.90; EX 16.20 Trifecta £214.00.
Owner G P M Morland **Bred** Timothy Nuttall **Trained** Manton, Wilts
■ Mythical Madness was withdrawn. Price at time of withdrawal 20-1. Rule 4 does not apply
■ Stewards' Enquiry : Adam Kirby two-day ban: misuse of the whip (TBC)

FOCUS
5 yards added. A good handicap. The third-favourite nabbed the market leader right on the line from off the pace. Solid form.

1913 WHITSBURY MANOR STUD / BRITISH EBF LANSDOWN STKS (LISTED RACE) (F&M) — 5f 10y
4:05 (4:21) (Class 1) 3-Y-O+

£31,190 (£11,825; £5,918; £2,948; £1,479; £742) **Stalls** Centre

Form | | | | RPR
161- **1** **Queen Of Desire (IRE)**[213] 7403 4-9-2 89 .... JackMitchell 1 96
(Roger Varian) *in tch: squeezed through gap over 1f out: led ent fnl f: kpt on wl: rdn out* 11/4[1]
40-1 **2** *½* **Gold Filigree (IRE)**[27] 1295 4-9-2 95 .... ShaneKelly 10 95
(Richard Hughes) *trckd ldrs: rdn wl over 1f out: kpt on ins fnl f: wnt 2nd towards fin* 7/1
200- **3** *nk* **Heartwarming**[174] 8629 3-8-6 92 .... JosephineGordon 5 90
(Clive Cox) *stdd s: plld hrd: led after 2f: rdn over 1f out: sn edging rt: hdd ent fnl f: kpt on but hld fnl 120yds* 7/1
114- **4** *nk* **Blame Roberta (USA)**[200] 7851 3-8-6 87 .... HayleyTurner 4 89
(Robert Cowell) *trckd ldrs: rdn wl over 1f out: kpt on ins fnl f: no ex nring fin* 14/1
26-0 **5** *½* **Shumookhi (IRE)**[36] 1200 3-8-6 100 ....(p¹) HarryBentley 9 87
(Archie Watson) *led for 2f: rdn over 2f out: no ex ins fnl f* 9/2[3]
-261 **6** *¾* **Rose Berry**[8] 1712 5-9-2 83 ....(h) JamesSullivan 6 88
(Charlie Wallis) *hld up: rdn over 1f out: kpt on fnl f but nt pce to get involved* 25/1
110- **7** *½* **Ocelot**[148] 9206 5-9-2 81 .... DougieCostello 2 86
(Robert Cowell) *hld up: rdn 2f out: kpt on fnl f but nt pce to get on terms* 33/1
31-0 **8** *1* **Come On Leicester (IRE)**[3] 1832 3-8-6 94 ....(h¹) KieranO'Neill 7 79
(Richard Hannon) *s.i.s: towards rr: rdn 2f out: kpt on fnl f but nt pce to get on terms* 13/2
2- **9** *3* **One Last Night (IRE)**[143] 4-9-2 95 .... SeanLevey 3 86
(Robert Cowell) *racd keenly: cl up: nt clr run briefly over 1f out: sn rdn: keeping on at same pce whn stmbld jst ins fnl f (jockey said filly stumbled a furlong out)* 7/2[2]

1m 0.4s (-1.60) **Going Correction** -0.175s/f (Firm)
WFA 3 from 4yo+ 10lb 9 Ran SP% **118.9**
Speed ratings (Par 111): **105,104,103,103,102 101,100,98,94**
CSF £23.47 TOTE £3.30: £1.60, £1.60, £2.80; EX 17.50 Trifecta £137.30.
Owner Clipper Logistics **Bred** Southacre Bloodstock **Trained** Newmarket, Suffolk

FOCUS
The feature contest was a Listed sprint for fillies and mares. The favourite had to force her way into an attacking position on the inside and gamely saw off her challengers once on the lead about 1f out. The form's ordinary by Listed standards.

1914 DRIBUILD GROUP H'CAP — 1m 3f 137y
4:35 (4:50) (Class 4) (0-85,86) 4-Y-O+

£5,322 (£1,593; £796; £398; £300; £300) **Stalls** Low

Form | | | | RPR
532- **1** **Hareeq**[184] 8320 4-9-5 **81** ....(p¹) ShaneKelly 10 93
(Richard Hughes) *trckd ldrs: rdn to ld over 1f out: kpt on strly: rdn out* 8/1
133- **2** *3 ½* **Bayshore Freeway (IRE)**[251] 5992 4-9-10 **86** .... FrannyNorton 2 92
(Mark Johnston) *led: rdn and hdd over 1f out: styd on same pce fnl f* 5/2[1]
40-2 **3** *1* **Hollywood Road (IRE)**[21] 1395 6-9-7 **83** .... HectorCrouch 8 87
(Gary Moore) *in tch: rdn and hdwy over 2f out: styd on fnl f* 5/1[3]
3314 **4** *1 ¼* **Cry Wolf**[17] 1503 6-9-3 **82** .... JoshuaBryan(3) 5 84
(Alexandra Dunn) *in tch: smooth hdwy over 2f out: chal over 1f out: sn rdn and hld: fdd ins fnl f* 14/1
112- **5** *3 ½* **Jacbequick**[113] 7600 8-9-3 **82** ....(v) FinleyMarsh(3) 11 78
(David Pipe) *in tch: rdn over 2f out: hdwy over 1f out: nt pce to get on terms: fdd fnl 120yds* 10/1
6 *4* **Meagher's Flag (IRE)**[246] 6216 4-9-0 **81** ....(t) MeganNicholls(5) 1 72
(Paul Nicholls) *racd keenly: prom: rdn over 2f out: sn wknd* 8/1
22-0 **7** *hd* **Petrastar**[14] 1559 4-9-4 **80** .... AdamKirby 4 69
(Clive Cox) *racd keenly: trckd ldrs: rdn 3f out: wknd over 1f out* 4/1[2]
100- **8** *26* **Hell Of A Lady**[141] 9318 5-7-9 **64** oh16 .... IsobelFrancis(7) 7 10
(Johnny Farrelly) *s.i.s: detached in last: struggling 4f out: nvr on terms: t.o (jockey said mare was slowly away)* 66/1
/05- **9** *2 ¼* **Rossetti**[211] 7455 11-8-2 **64** oh1 ....(h) KieranO'Neill 3 7
(Natalie Lloyd-Beavis) *hld up in last pair: struggling 5f out: nvr on terms: t.o* 66/1

2m 27.81s (-2.99) **Going Correction** -0.175s/f (Firm) 9 Ran SP% **106.2**
Speed ratings (Par 105): **102,99,99,98,95 93,93,75,74**
CSF £22.80 CT £71.35 TOTE £8.10: £2.50, £1.20, £1.50; EX 24.40 Trifecta £86.00.
Owner Rashed Al Daban **Bred** Normandie Stud Ltd **Trained** Upper Lambourn, Berks
■ Given Choice was withdrawn. Price at time of withdrawal 11-2. Rule 4 applies to all bets - deduction 15p in the pound

FOCUS
5 yards added. A decent middle-distance handicap. The easy winner's time was nearly two seconds slower than the earlier 3yo handicap over this C&D. Improvement from the winner, the third and fourth helping with the standard.

1915 INSPIRE RACING CLUB H'CAP — 5f 10y
5:05 (5:21) (Class 4) (0-85,85) 4-Y-O+

£5,322 (£1,593; £796; £398; £300; £300) **Stalls** Centre

Form | | | | RPR
60-2 **1** **The Daley Express (IRE)**[4] 1822 5-9-6 **84** .... FrannyNorton 4 91+
(Ronald Harris) *mid-diviion: hdwy over 2f out: sn rdn: kpt on strly ins fnl f: led cl home* 5/4[1]
1-21 **2** *nk* **Acclaim The Nation (IRE)**[80] 471 6-9-7 **85** ....(p) TomEaves 9 91
(Eric Alston) *led: rdn over 1f out: kpt on wl: hdd cl home* 6/1[3]
6-26 **3** *1* **Little Boy Blue**[41] 1098 4-9-2 **85** ....(h) RyanWhile(5) 1 87
(Bill Turner) *unsettled stalls: trckd ldr: rdn 2f out: kpt on ins fnl f* 9/1
0-00 **4** *1 ¼* **Bungee Jump (IRE)**[22] 1388 4-8-11 **80** .... MeganNicholls(5) 5 78
(Grace Harris) *mid-div: hdwy over 2f out: ch whn rdn over 1f out: kpt on same pce fnl f* 12/1
430- **5** *1* **Delagate This Lord**[205] 7661 5-8-12 **76** .... JFEgan 7 70
(Michael Attwater) *squeezed up and lost pl sn after s: in last pair: sn pushed along: kpt on fnl f but nt pce to get involved (jockey said gelding suffered interference leaving the stalls)* 9/2[2]
004- **6** *1* **Powerful Dream (IRE)**[200] 7829 6-8-7 **71** oh3 ....(p) RaulDaSilva 3 62
(Ronald Harris) *trckd ldrs: rdn and ch over 1f out: no ex fnl f* 33/1
-103 **7** *2* **Union Rose**[24] 1342 7-8-9 **73** ....(p) KieranO'Neill 10 57
(Ronald Harris) *trckd ldrs: rdn and ch over 1f out: wknd fnl f* 8/1
256- **8** *1 ¼* **Waseem Faris (IRE)**[146] 9247 10-9-1 **82** .... CameronNoble(3) 6 61
(Ken Cunningham-Brown) *a towards rr* 16/1
520- **9** *7* **Secretfact**[169] 8784 6-8-13 **77** ....(h) ShaneKelly 8 31
(Malcolm Saunders) *a towards rr* 20/1

1m 0.16s (-1.84) **Going Correction** -0.175s/f (Firm) 9 Ran SP% **119.3**
Speed ratings (Par 105): **107,106,104,102,101 99,96,94,83**
CSF £9.56 CT £50.39 TOTE £1.90: £1.10, £2.00, £2.30; EX 8.20 Trifecta £27.80.
Owner The W H O Society **Bred** Allevamento Ficomontanino Srl **Trained** Earlswood, Monmouths

FOCUS
A decent sprint handicap. The clear favourite won this race for the second consecutive year in a good comparative time. Straightforward form.

T/Plt: £35.30 to a £1 stake. Pool: £72,543.60 - 1,496.33 winning units. T/Qpdt: £6.80 to a £1 stake. Pool: £7,484.29 - 809.95 winning units. **Tim Mitchell**

1683 LINGFIELD (L-H)
Friday, April 19

OFFICIAL GOING: Polytrack: standard
Weather: warm and sunny

1916 SUN RACING ALL-WEATHER CHAMPIONSHIPS APPRENTICE H'CAP 7f 1y(P)
1:30 (1:36) (Class 2) (0-100,98) 4-Y-O+
£31,125 (£9,320; £4,660; £2,330; £1,165; £585) Stalls Low

Form				RPR
-250	1		**Goring (GER)**41 1101 7-9-4 97 ...(v) GeorgiaDobie(7) 14 (Eve Johnson Houghton) *a handy: pushed along to chse ldng pair over 1f out: drvn and styd on wl to ld fnl 50yds* **14/1**	106
4362	2	½	**Raucous**20 1421 6-9-6 97 ...(tp) CierenFallon(5) 2 (Robert Cowell) *trckd ldr early: rdn along to chse ldr 2f out: drvn and led 1f out: kpt on wl fnl f but hdd and no match for wnr fnl 50yds* **9/1**	104
5004	3	1¾	**Giogiobbo**27 1289 6-9-3 92 ...(t1) DylanHogan(3) 9 (Nick Littmoden) *racd keenly in tch early: sn settled: pushed along to chse ldr 2f out: rdn and kpt on wl fnl f: no match for wnr* **50/1**	94
-022	4	hd	**Gallipoli (IRE)**37 1181 6-9-3 92 ...(b) SeanDavis(3) 8 (Richard Fahey) *racd in rr of midfield: rdn along and outpcd 3f out: stdy hdwy u.p fr over 1f out: kpt on* **6/1**	94+
-021	5	nk	**Poetic Force (IRE)**23 1356 5-8-12 87 ...(t) PoppyBridgwater(3) 5 (Tony Carroll) *trckd ldr: rdn along and unable qck 2f out: sn drvn and one pce appr fnl f: kpt on* **9/1**	88
3203	6	shd	**Exchequer (IRE)**41 1097 8-9-0 89 ...(p) DarraghKeenan(3) 12 (Richard Guest) *broke wl to ld fr wd draw: rdn along and hdd 1f out: wknd ins fnl f* **16/1**	90
16-5	7	½	**Breathless Times**58 805 4-9-12 98 ...(t) CameronNoble 6 (Roger Charlton) *settled in midfield: effrt to cl over 2f out: sn rdn and kpt on one pce ins fnl f* **7/2**1	97
-212	8	hd	**Sha La La La Lee**27 1294 4-9-4 90 ... JaneElliott 10 (Tom Dascombe) *dwlt and racd in rr: rdn along and sltly detached in last 2f out: kpt on passed btn horses fnl f (jockey said gelding was slowly away)* **5/1**2	89+
-533	9	½	**Suzi's Connoisseur**49 964 8-8-13 85 ...(b) PaddyBradley 13 (Jane Chapple-Hyam) *hld up in last trio: stl in rr but gng wl over 2f out: rdn and no immediate imp over 1f out: one pce fnl f* **20/1**	82
1011	10	hd	**Lion Hearted (IRE)**8 1714 5-8-9 86 5ex ... MarkCrehan(5) 7 (Michael Appleby) *dwlt sltly and pushed along to r midfield: effrt 2f out: rdn and no imp over 1f out: no ex fnl f (trainer said gelding was unsuited by the tight bend at lingfield)* **11/2**3	83
1465	11	nse	**Mr Scaramanga**27 1294 5-8-9 88 ... LeviWilliams(7) 11 (Simon Dow) *racd in last trio: niggled along 4f out: rdn on inner 2f out: unable qck 1f out: one pce fnl f* **20/1**	85
-503	12	½	**Starlight Romance (IRE)**34 1234 5-8-11 86 ... ConnorMurtagh(3) 4 (Richard Fahey) *settled wl on inner in midfield: pushed along to maintain position over 2f out: sn rdn and wknd fnl f* **10/1**	81

1m 24.15s (-0.65) **Going Correction** -0.025s/f (Stan) 12 Ran SP% 121.7
Speed ratings (Par 109): **102,101,99,99,98 98,98,97,97,97 97,96**
CSF £134.76 CT £6133.97 TOTE £20.10: £5.10, £3.20, £19.00; EX 163.70 Trifecta £2542.10.
Owner G C Stevens **Bred** Westminster Race Horses Gmbh **Trained** Blewbury, Oxon
■ Apex King and Philamundo were withdrawn. Prices at time of withdrawal 6-1 and 20-1 respectively. Rule 4 applies to bets placed prior to withdrawal but not to SP bets - deduction 10p in the pound. New market formed

FOCUS
A competitive handicap in which it didn't pay to be too far off the pace. The form's rated around the runner-up.

1917 BETWAY ALL-WEATHER MARATHON CHAMPIONSHIPS CONDITIONS STKS 1m 7f 169y(P)
2:00 (2:05) (Class 2) 4-Y-O+
£93,375 (£27,960; £13,980; £6,990; £3,495; £1,755) Stalls Low

Form				RPR
4-32	1		**Watersmeet**77 519 8-9-5 103 ... JoeFanning 7 (Mark Johnston) *dwlt but sn rcvrd to r in midfield: smooth hdwy to chse ldrs 2f out: c wdst of all of home bnd: rdn to ld jst over 1f out: hung bdly lft handed in clsng stages but sn in command: comf* **7/1**2	109
1-11	2	2¼	**Amade (IRE)**43 1062 5-9-5 109 ...(b) ChristopheSoumillon 5 (G Botti, France) *settled in midfield: stdy hdwy to go 2nd over 2f out: pushed along to ld briefly wl over 1f out: rdn and hdd by wnr over 1f out: carried lft by wnr ins fnl f: swtchd rt and kpt on but no ch* **4/6**1	105
51-2	3	1¾	**Spark Plug (IRE)**62 757 8-9-5 99 ...(p) TomMarquand 8 (Brian Meehan) *racd in midfield: pushed along 6f out: effrt to chse ldrs 2f out: rdn and kpt on fr over 1f out* **9/1**3	103
3-43	4	nk	**Higher Power**43 1062 7-9-5 102 ... DavidProbert 11 (James Fanshawe) *trckd ldr: led gng wl over 2f out: rdn along and hdd wl over 1f out: one pce ins fnl f* **12/1**	103
1534	5	nk	**Fearsome**35 1220 5-9-5 90 ... EoinWalsh 6 (Nick Littmoden) *hld up in last pair: rdn along 2f out: sn drvn and mde late hdwy passed rivals ins fnl f* **50/1**	102
1-14	6	1	**Aircraft Carrier (IRE)**43 1062 4-9-3 100 ...(p) StevieDonohoe 4 (John Ryan) *hld up in last: rdn and no imp 2f out: kpt on one pce fnl f* **7/1**2	103
-034	7	nk	**Lord George (IRE)**77 519 6-9-5 102 ...(p) DanielMuscutt 9 (James Fanshawe) *racd in midfield: rdn along to chse wnr over 1f out: no imp and one pce fnl f (jockey said gelding hung right handed)* **33/1**	101
-116	8	½	**Petite Jack**28 1267 6-9-5 100 ... JamesDoyle 10 (Neil King) *trckd ldr: short of room on inner over 2f out: swtchd off heels and rdn over 1f out: kpt on one pce fnl f* **16/1**	100+
-653	9	27	**Battle Of Marathon (USA)**63 440 7-9-5 84 ... BrettDoyle 3 (John Ryan) *settled wl in 4th: rdn and lost pl 4f out: sn t.o: eased fnl f (jockey said the surcingle snapped)* **66/1**	68
-213	10	7	**Stamford Raffles**48 980 6-9-5 92 ... RichardKingscote 1 (Jane Chapple-Hyam) *led at a stdy tempo: rdn along and hdd over 2f out: wknd fr over 1f out* **16/1**	60

3m 21.74s (-3.96) **Going Correction** -0.025s/f (Stan)
WFA 4 from 5yo+ 2lb 10 Ran SP% 120.8
Speed ratings (Par 109): **108,106,106,105,105 105,105,104,91,87**
CSF £12.39 CT £47.82 TOTE £7.70: £2.10, £1.10, £2.30; EX 15.40 Trifecta £81.50.
Owner J Barson **Bred** Stetchworth & Middle Park Studs **Trained** Middleham Moor, N Yorks

FOCUS
This was steadily run and turned into a bit of a dash for home. The winner is rated back to his best but the runner-up couldn't match his Chelmsford latest form.

1918 LADBROKES ALL-WEATHER FILLIES' AND MARES' CHAMPIONSHIPS CONDITIONS STKS 7f 1y(P)
2:30 (2:35) (Class 2) 4-Y-O+
£93,375 (£27,960; £13,980; £6,990; £3,495; £1,755) Stalls Low

Form				RPR
115-	1		**Heavenly Holly (IRE)**117 9689 4-9-0 94 ... RyanMoore 12 (Hugo Palmer) *mde all: effrt to qckn tempo over 2f out and sn 2 l clr: rdn out ins fnl f and a doing enough* **9/1**	98
1-12	2	1	**Island Of Life (USA)**41 1103 5-9-0 101 ...(tp) JamesDoyle 7 (William Haggas) *settled wl in midfield: stl gng wl shuffled bk towards rr 2f out: swtchd rt off heels and rdn over 1f out: styd on strly ins fnl f: nt rch wnr* **9/2**2	95+
22-	3	½	**Silvery Mist (FR)**18 4-9-0 93 ... StephanePasquier 8 (F Chappet, France) *hld up in rr: pushed along wl over 2f out: swtchd rt and c wdst of all over 1f out: drvn and kpt on wl ins fnl f* **11/1**	94+
00/	4	nk	**Cry Baby (IRE)**25 5-9-1 88 ow1 ...(p) ChristopheSoumillon 9 (Y Barberot, France) *racd promly in 4th: pushed along to chse wnr 2f out: rdn and kpt on one pce ins fnl f* **25/1**	94
1-01	5	½	**Crossing The Line**27 1289 4-9-0 100 ... DavidProbert 3 (Andrew Balding) *racd in rr of midfield on inner: pushed along over 2f out: swtchd lft to far rail and rdn along over 1f out: one pce fnl f* **9/2**2	92+
3320	6	hd	**Pattie**6 1753 5-9-0 97 ... JoeFanning 4 (Mick Channon) *trckd wnr: rdn along to chse wnr 2f out: sn one pce and no ex ins fnl f* **20/1**	91
2232	7	½	**Treasure Me**34 1234 4-9-0 82 ...(v1) StevieDonohoe 5 (Charlie Fellowes) *racd keenly in 3rd: effrt to chse wnr 2f out: sn rdn and unable qck over 1f out: no ex fnl f* **40/1**	90
1216	8	½	**Gorgeous Noora (IRE)**20 1412 5-9-0 99 ... HollieDoyle 1 (Archie Watson) *racd in midfield: bmpd along over 2f out: swtchd rt off home bnd over 1f out: sn rdn and little imp 1f out: one pce fnl f* **6/1**3	89
15-1	9	½	**Clon Coulis (IRE)**43 1063 5-9-0 101 ...(h) JamieSpencer 10 (David Barron) *dwlt and racd in last pair: rdn and no imp 2f out: a towards rr (jockey said mare reared as the stalls opened and was slowly away; vet reported mare lost her right-fore shoe)* **7/1**	87
1-21	10	¾	**Castle Hill Cassie (IRE)**81 460 5-9-0 100 ... AndrewMullen 11 (Ben Haslam) *racd in tch in midfield: rdn along over 2f out: hung lft u.str.p over 1f out: one pce fnl f* **12/1**	85
-114	11	1¼	**Toy Theatre**34 1234 5-9-0 87 ... TomMarquand 6 (Michael Appleby) *racd in midfield: rdn along and outpcd over 1f out: sn struggling: wknd fnl f* **33/1**	82
251-	12	hd	**Rasima**169 8769 4-9-0 102 ... DavidEgan 2 (Roger Varian) *hld up in last pair: rdn and no imp over 2f out: nvr on terms (jockey said filly was slowly away. vet reported filly had a mild cough)* **7/2**1	81

1m 25.16s (0.36) **Going Correction** -0.025s/f (Stan) 12 Ran SP% 125.4
Speed ratings (Par 96): **96,94,94,93,93 93,92,92,91,90 89,88**
CSF £50.29 CT £475.11 TOTE £10.20: £3.10, £2.50, £2.90; EX 66.20 Trifecta £946.20.
Owner Hunscote Stud Limited **Bred** Hunscote Stud **Trained** Newmarket, Suffolk

FOCUS
A pretty tight race on the ratings, and it was stolen from the front. The bare form is compromised by the fourth and the seventh.

1919 BETWAY ALL-WEATHER SPRINT CHAMPIONSHIPS CONDITIONS STKS 6f 1y(P)
3:05 (3:08) (Class 2) 4-Y-O+
£93,375 (£27,960; £13,980; £6,990; £3,495; £1,755) Stalls Low

Form				RPR
51-1	1		**Kachy**76 563 6-9-5 112 ... RichardKingscote 8 (Tom Dascombe) *broke v smartly and mde all: effrt to qckn tempo over 2f out and sn 4 l clr: pushed out ins fnl f: easily* **4/9**1	119+
-301	2	3¼	**George Bowen (IRE)**20 1421 7-9-5 106 ...(v) DavidNolan 2 (Richard Fahey) *racd in midfield: effrt to cl 2f out: swtchd rt and rdn over 1f out: styd on wl fnl f for clr 2nd* **10/1**	108
1220	3	2	**Merhoob (IRE)**17 1501 7-9-5 103 ... JamesDoyle 4 (John Ryan) *hld up: pushed along over 2f out: rdn and styd on wl ins fnl f to snatch 3rd fnl strides* **20/1**	102
-406	4	nk	**Alfredo Arcano (IRE)**14 1574 5-9-5 104 ...(t) OisinOrr 3 (David Marnane, Ire) *racd promly in 4th: effrt to go 2nd and chse wnr 2f out: sn rdn and nt match pce of wnr: kpt on one pce fnl f* **16/1**	101
5322	5	¾	**Areen Heart (FR)**22 1388 5-9-5 89 ... RobbieDowney 7 (David O'Meara) *hld up: rdn and little imp 2f out: swtchd lft and mde hdwy u.p over 1f out: kpt on* **66/1**	98
2-16	6	3	**Encore D'Or**55 877 7-9-5 108 ... LukeMorris 10 (Robert Cowell) *slowly away and racd in rr: rdn and hung lft over 1f out: kpt on one pce fnl f* **33/1**	89
403-	7	1	**Forza Capitano (FR)**45 1029 4-9-5 107 ... VincentCheminaud 5 (H-A Pantall, France) *racd in midfield: rdn along and outpcd by wnr 2f out: one pce fnl f* **13/2**2	85
2215	8	3	**Royal Birth**27 1295 8-9-5 101 ...(t) TomMarquand 6 (Stuart Williams) *hld up and racd keenly at times: rdn along and no imp over 1f out: nvr able to chal* **33/1**	76
0151	9	4	**Alsvinder**28 1274 6-9-5 98 ...(t) DanielTudhope 11 (Philip Kirby) *racd in midfield: pushed along and lost pl 2f out: wknd fnl f* **66/1**	63
3320	10	1½	**Stone Of Destiny**27 1295 4-9-5 104 ... DavidProbert 9 (Andrew Balding) *trckd wnr early: rdn along and lost pl off home bnd over 1f out: wknd fnl f (jockey said gelding stopped quickly)* **20/1**	58
201-	11	½	**Encrypted**153 9127 4-9-5 106 ... RyanMoore 1 (Hugo Palmer) *chsd wnr: rdn and unable to match pce of wnr 2f out: wknd over 1f out: eased fnl 100yds* **7/1**3	57

1m 9.55s (-2.35) **Going Correction** -0.025s/f (Stan) 11 Ran SP% 128.4
Speed ratings (Par 109): **114,109,107,106,105 101,100,96,90,88 88**
CSF £6.54 CT £58.96 TOTE £1.40: £1.10, £2.60, £4.20; EX 10.10 Trifecta £65.50.
Owner David Lowe **Bred** Denniff Farms Ltd **Trained** Malpas, Cheshire

FOCUS
This proved very straightforward for the favourite once he showed his customary speed from the stalls to get the lead from stall 8. The runner-up was close to form with the fifth limiting the form to some extent.

1920 LADBROKES 3 YEAR OLD ALL-WEATHER CHAMPIONSHIPS CONDITIONS STKS 6f 1y(P)
3:40 (3:42) (Class 2) 3-Y-O

£93,375 (£27,960; £13,980; £6,990; £3,495; £1,755) Stalls Low

Form RPR

0-21 1 **Transcendent (ITY)**[36] 1199 3-9-5 100............... ChristopheSoumillon 8 105+
(F Chappet, France) *hld up in rr of midfield: smooth hdwy on outer of field over 1f out: pushed into ld fnl 100yds: mostly hands and heels and jst prevailed* 11/4[1]

211- 2 shd **Deputise**[132] 9461 3-9-5 94............................... JamesDoyle 4 104
(William Haggas) *racd in midfield: clsd on inner gng wl over 2f out: rdn between rivals to ld over 1f out: sn drvn and hdd by wnr 100yds out: battle all the way to the line: jst failed* 9/2[2]

-225 3 4 ½ **James Street (IRE)**[80] 470 3-9-5 89........................ RyanMoore 6 89
(Hugo Palmer) *hld up: niggled along in rr 3f out: rdn and responded wl to press over 1f out: kpt on wl to snatch 3rd wl ins fnl f: no ch w front pair* 8/1

-415 4 hd **Yolo Again (IRE)**[6] 1762 3-9-0 85.......................... DavidEgan 1 84
(Roger Fell) *trckd ldr: effrt to chse ldr 2f out: sn drvn and unable qck over 1f out: kpt on one pce fnl f* 50/1

11-0 5 shd **Concierge (IRE)**[55] 893 3-9-5 99......................... WilliamBuick 7 88
(George Scott) *hld up in last: drvn along and forced wd off home bnd wl over 1f out: kpt on wl ins fnl f* 7/1

6-31 6 ½ **Charming Kid**[91] 306 3-9-5 99............................... DavidNolan 12 87
(Richard Fahey) *racd in midfield: rdn along 2f out: u.p whn short of room over 1f out: kpt on* 8/1

6112 7 1 ½ **Deep Intrigue**[48] 989 3-9-5 97............................ DanielTudhope 11 82
(Mark Johnston) *trckd ldr: rdn to chse ldr over 2f out: briefly short of room 1f out: no ex fnl f* 5/1[3]

1-64 8 1 **Fares Kodiac (IRE)**[22] 1388 3-9-5 87.......................(t) TomMarquand 9 79
(Marco Botti) *settled in 4th: rdn as pce qcknd 2f out and no imp: one pce ins fnl f* 33/1

0004 9 1 ¼ **Shining Armor**[9] 1692 3-9-5 88.............................. LukeMorris 10 75
(John Ryan) *racd in midfield: pushed along 2f out: effrt to cl whn nt clr run over 1f out: nt rcvr* 50/1

-546 10 1 ½ **Quiet Endeavour (IRE)**[36] 1199 3-9-5 93....................(b[1]) HollieDoyle 2 70
(Archie Watson) *pushed along to ld early: rdn along and hdd by rivals over 1f out: sn btn and wknd fnl f* 8/1

4160 11 5 **Sandridge Lad (IRE)**[9] 1691 3-9-5 80......................... StevieDonohoe 5 54
(John Ryan) *racd in midfield: pushed along and struggling 2f out: sn bhd* 100/1

-063 P **You Never Can Tell (IRE)**[48] 989 3-9-5 91................(b[1]) TomQueally 3
(Richard Spencer) *broke slowly: p.u qckly after 1f* 20/1

1m 11.14s (-0.76) **Going Correction** -0.025s/f (Stan) 12 Ran SP% 120.0
Speed ratings (Par 104): **104,103,97,97,97 96,94,93,91,89 83,**
CSF £14.40 CT £90.37 TOTE £3.00: £1.20, £2.20, £2.80; EX 16.60 Trifecta £106.80.
Owner Antoine Gilibert **Bred** Antoine Gilibert, Ecurie Vivaldi & Fabrice Chappet **Trained** France

FOCUS
This was a well-run race and the first two finished nicely clear. The third and fourth help with the level.

1921 BETWAY EASTER CLASSIC ALL-WEATHER MIDDLE DISTANCE CHAMPIONSHIPS CONDITIONS STKS 1m 2f (P)
4:15 (4:16) (Class 2) 4-Y-O+

£124,500 (£37,280; £18,640; £9,320; £4,660; £2,340) Stalls Low

Form RPR

1110 1 **Matterhorn (IRE)**[20] 1420 4-9-5 112......................... JoeFanning 4 121
(Mark Johnston) *trckd ldr: cruised into the ld gng wl 2f out: sn rdn and readily asserted: pushed out whn wl in command fnl f: impressive* 9/2[2]

1-11 2 7 **Wissahickon (USA)**[55] 879 4-9-5 117.................... FrankieDettori 8 107
(John Gosden) *hld up: effrt on outer to cl on wnr over 2f out: sn rdn and unable to match pce of wnr over 1f out: drifted lft under hands and heels ins fnl f* 1/3[1]

-130 3 ¾ **Pactolus (IRE)**[41] 1101 8-9-5 104..........................(t) RichardKingscote 2 105
(Stuart Williams) *trckd ldr in 3rd: rdn along and qckly outpcd by wnr 2f out: kpt on wl u.p ins fnl f* 40/1

10-3 4 1 ¼ **Roc Angel (FR)**[22] 5-9-5 0............................ ChristopheSoumillon 6 103
(F Chappet, France) *hld up: rdn and unable qck 2f out: kpt on one pce ins fnl f* 25/1

4-05 5 ½ **Victory Bond**[20] 1420 6-9-5 100..............................(b) JamesDoyle 7 102
(William Haggas) *settled in midfield: drvn along and no imp 2f out: kpt on one pce fnl f* 16/1

-132 6 1 ½ **Court House (IRE)**[55] 879 4-9-5 107........................ RobertHavlin 1 99
(John Gosden) *pushed along to ld early: rdn and hdd by wnr 2f out: wknd fr 1f out* 7/1[3]

2133 7 4 ½ **Executive Force**[9] 1681 5-9-5 97..........................(p) ConnorBeasley 5 90
(Michael Wigham) *hld up in rr: rdn and outpcd over 2f out: a in rr (trainer said gelding did not face the kickback on this occasion)* 25/1

1-63 8 1 ½ **Master The World (IRE)**[20] 1420 8-9-5 107..................(p) RyanMoore 3 87
(David Elsworth) *racd in midfield: rdn along and lost pl 2f out: wknd fnl f* 10/1

2m 1.09s (-5.51) **Going Correction** -0.025s/f (Stan) 8 Ran SP% 130.8
Speed ratings (Par 109): **121,115,114,113,113 112,108,107**
CSF £7.28 CT £74.42 TOTE £6.20: £1.40, £1.02, £14.60; EX 9.30 Trifecta £168.10.
Owner Sheikh Hamdan bin Mohammed Al Maktoum **Bred** Barronstown Stud **Trained** Middleham Moor, N Yorks

FOCUS
Something of a turn-up here, with the winner bouncing back to his best and the favourite below par. The form could be rated a length better.

1922 SUN RACING ALL-WEATHER MILE CHAMPIONSHIPS CONDITIONS STKS 1m 1y(P)
4:45 (4:46) (Class 2) 4-Y-O+

£93,375 (£27,960; £13,980; £6,990; £3,495; £1,755) Stalls High

Form RPR

-210 1 **Oh This Is Us (IRE)**[41] 1103 6-9-5 113..................... TomMarquand 8 115+
(Richard Hannon) *hld up: effrt to cl over 2f out: c wd in home st and rdn over 1f out: clsd qckly to ld 110yds out: styd on wl* 5/1[2]

412- 2 ¾ **Indyco (FR)**[45] 1027 4-9-5 101.......................... VincentCheminaud 6 113
(H-A Pantall, France) *hld up: hdwy u.p 2f out: sn rdn and ev ch 1f out: kpt on but unable to match pce of wnr ins fnl f* 4/1[1]

20-2 3 2 ½ **Glendevon (USA)**[27] 1289 4-9-5 100............................ RyanMoore 5 108
(Richard Hughes) *racd in tch in 4th: rdn and unable qck 2f out: drvn and kpt on wl for press to snatch 3rd fnl strides* 8/1

-105 4 shd **Salateen**[37] 1181 7-9-5 102.......................................(tp) DavidNolan 2 107
(David O'Meara) *chsd ldr: rdn upsides ldr 2f out: drvn to ld over 1f out: hdd by wnr 110yds out and no ex: lost 3rd fnl strides* 33/1

1-11 5 nk **Keyser Soze (IRE)**[58] 805 5-9-5 105......................... TomQueally 11 107+
(Richard Spencer) *dwlt and racd in last: pushed along and rn wd off home bnd wl over 1f out: kpt on wl ins fnl f* 5/1[2]

1-15 6 1 **Documenting**[41] 1103 6-9-5 103................................. JamesDoyle 1 104
(Kevin Frost) *racd in midfield: effrt over 2f out: sn rdn and no imp over 1f out: kpt on one pce fnl f* 5/1[2]

5-22 7 ½ **Straight Right (FR)**[87] 351 5-9-5 107.......................(h) DavidProbert 3 103
(Andrew Balding) *racd in midfield: bmpd along over 2f out: snatched up and short of room over 1f out: rdn but unable to rcvr ins fnl f* 8/1

-401 8 ½ **Above The Rest (IRE)**[41] 1103 8-9-5 108...................(h) CliffordLee 9 102
(David Barron) *hld up: rdn along in last 2f out: plugged on one pce against far rail ins fnl f* 16/1

1-54 9 ½ **Arcanada (IRE)**[41] 1103 6-9-5 107........................(p) RichardKingscote 4 101
(Tom Dascombe) *led at a str pce: rdn and strly pressed by rival 2f out: drvn and hdd over 1f out: wknd ins fnl f* 6/1[3]

-313 10 shd **Cardsharp**[27] 1289 4-9-5 110..................................... JoeFanning 10 101
(Mark Johnston) *racd in midfield: rdn along and outpcd 2f out: u.p whn bdly hmpd 1f out: nt rcvr* 8/1

-300 11 6 **Silver Quartz**[20] 1415 4-9-5 98....................................(t[1]) LukeMorris 7 87
(Archie Watson) *trckd ldr: pushed along 3f out: drvn along and lost pl over 1f out: wknd fnl f (trainer said gelding had a breathing problem)* 33/1

1m 35.26s (-2.94) **Going Correction** -0.025s/f (Stan) 11 Ran SP% 129.4
Speed ratings (Par 109): **113,112,109,109,109 108,107,107,106,106 100**
CSF £28.17 CT £166.33 TOTE £5.90: £2.10, £1.80, £2.90; EX 43.10 Trifecta £364.00.
Owner Team Wallop **Bred** Herbertstown House Stud **Trained** East Everleigh, Wilts

FOCUS
This was run at a strong gallop and suited those challenging late. The time was good and the form looks pretty solid.
T/Plt: £80.10 to a £1 stake. Pool: £154,792.33 - 1,409.80 winning units. T/Qpdt: £6.00 to a £1 stake. Pool: £16,751.69 - 2,064.39 winning units. **Mark Grantham**

1718 NEWCASTLE (A.W) (L-H)
Friday, April 19

OFFICIAL GOING: Tapeta: standard
Wind: Breezy, half behind in races on the straight course and in over 3f of home straight in races on the Weather: Sunny, warm

1923 LADBROKES HOME OF THE ODDS BOOST FILLIES' CONDITIONS STKS (PLUS 10 RACE) 5f (Tp)
1:40 (1:43) (Class 2) 2-Y-O

£12,938 (£3,850; £1,924; £962) Stalls Centre

Form RPR

1 1 **Lady Kermit (IRE)**[16] 1513 2-9-1 .... PaulMulrennan 6 90+
(Archie Watson) *mde all: shkn up and clr over 1f out: pushed out ins fnl f: comf* 1/4[1]

2 1 ¾ **Mighty Spirit (IRE)** 2-8-12 .... PJMcDonald 10 81+
(Richard Fahey) *dwlt: rn green in rr: hdwy nr side of gp over 1f out: chsd (clr) wnr ins fnl f: clsng at fin: bttr for r (jockey said filly reared as the stalls opened)* 10/1[3]

3 1 ¼ **Stars In The Night (IRE)** 2-8-12 .... KevinStott 5 76+
(Kevin Ryan) *hld up towards rr: hdwy over 2f out: effrt and chsd (clr) wnr briefly appr fnl f: sn one pce* 14/1

1 4 3 ¾ **Chasanda**[11] 1651 2-9-1 .... CamHardie 7 66
(David Evans) *t.k.h: chsd wnr to appr fnl f: sn drvn and outpcd* 17/2[2]

5 1 **Mia Diva** 2-8-12 .... JasonHart 1 59
(John Quinn) *trckd ldrs: rdn over 2f out: outpcd over 1f out: sn btn* 16/1

6 1 ¾ **Macho Touch (IRE)** 2-8-12 .... BenCurtis 3 53
(K R Burke) *t.k.h: in tch: effrt and edgd rt over 1f out: wknd fnl f* 10/1[3]

7 nk **Penmellyn (IRE)** 2-8-12 ....(h[1]) SamJames 2 52
(Phillip Makin) *midfield on outside: rdn over 2f out: wknd over 1f out* 80/1

8 5 **Moneyball** 2-8-12 .... TonyHamilton 4 34
(Keith Dalgleish) *dwlt: bhd: struggling over 2f out: sn btn* 40/1

9 4 ½ **Siena Bay** 2-8-12 .... DavidAllan 9 18
(Tim Easterby) *prom tl rdn and wknd fr 2f out* 33/1

10 6 **Northern Grace** 2-8-12 .... BenRobinson 8
(Brian Ellison) *bhd and sn outpcd: struggling 1/2-way: sn btn* 50/1

59.73s (0.23) **Going Correction** +0.125s/f (Slow) 10 Ran SP% 129.8
Speed ratings (Par 95): **103,100,98,92,90 87,87,79,72,62**
CSF £5.20 TOTE £1.20: £1.02, £1.90, £3.40; EX 5.00 Trifecta £25.90.
Owner Justin Dowley & Michael Pescod **Bred** Philip & Orla Hore **Trained** Upper Lambourn, W Berks

FOCUS
Standard Polytrack. This decent and quite valuable novice event went to the short-priced favourite, in a time 1.73sec slower than the standard. The winner looks a live Queen Mary candidate.

1924 LADBROKES NOVICE STKS (PLUS 10 RACE) 5f (Tp)
2:10 (2:13) (Class 3) 3-Y-O

£9,703 (£2,887; £1,443; £721) Stalls Centre

Form RPR

3- 1 **Lufricia**[200] 7844 3-8-11 .... AndreaAtzeni 8 86+
(Roger Varian) *prom: wnt 2nd 1/2-way: rdn to ld over 1f out: pushed out: idled nr fin* 7/1[3]

31- 2 1 ¼ **Rocket Action**[148] 9207 3-9-8 .... GeraldMosse 6 90
(Robert Cowell) *in tch: effrt and pushed along over 1f out: chsd wnr ins fnl f: kpt on fin* 9/4[2]

35-2 3 2 **Exalted Angel (FR)**[38] 1161 3-9-2 75.........................(p[1]) BenCurtis 4 77
(K R Burke) *led: rdn: edgd rt and hdd over 1f out: lost 2nd and outpcd ins fnl f* 11/1

51- 4 2 ¾ **Aplomb (IRE)**[186] 8279 3-9-1 .... GianlucaSanna(7) 10 73
(William Haggas) *dwlt: hld up: pushed along and hdwy 2f out: kpt on fnl f: nt pce to chal* 8/1

20- 5 2 **Skeetah**[189] 8163 3-8-11 .... JasonHart 3 55
(John Quinn) *plld hrd: chsd ldr to 1/2-way: rdn and wknd over 1f out* 80/1

5 6 1 ¼ **Kodi King (IRE)**[19] 1458 3-9-2 .... LewisEdmunds 5 55
(K R Burke) *hld up in tch: pushed along and outpcd over 2f out: sn n.d: btn over 1f out* 18/1

7 *hd* **Show Me A Sunset** 3-9-2 .... TonyHamilton 11 55
(Richard Fahey) *chsd ldrs: pushed along over 2f out: wknd over 1f out* **11/8**[1]

0- 8 *¾* **Shall We Begin (IRE)**[246] 6178 3-8-11 .... NathanEvans 1 47
(Michael Easterby) *s.i.s: bhd and outpcd: hung lft 1/2-way: nvr on terms* **100/1**

2 9 *2* **Sound Of Iona**[25] 1336 3-8-11 .... PhilDennis 9 40
(Jim Goldie) *dwlt: hld up: shkn up 2f out: sn btn* **22/1**

325 10 *2 ¼* **Olympic Spirit**[38] 1161 3-9-2 70 .... PJMcDonald 7 37
(David Barron) *bhd: outpcd and hung lft 1/2-way: sn btn* **50/1**

11 *26* **Piccupaprosecco** 3-8-11 .... PaddyMathers 2
(Derek Shaw) *dwlt: sn t.o* **100/1**

58.78s (-0.72) **Going Correction** +0.125s/f (Slow) **11** Ran SP% **119.6**
Speed ratings (Par 102): **110,108,104,100,97 95,94,93,90,86 45**
CSF £23.24 TOTE £6.20: £1.70, £1.30, £2.80; EX 19.70 Trifecta £106.40.
Owner Sheikh Mohammed Obaid Al Maktoum **Bred** Serge Boucheron **Trained** Newmarket, Suffolk

FOCUS
Fairly useful novice form, rated around the third.

1925 SUNRACING.CO.UK H'CAP 7f 14y (Tp)
2:45 (2:47) (Class 4) (0-80,80) 3-Y-0+
£6,727 (£2,002; £1,000; £500; £300; £300) **Stalls** Centre

Form RPR

32-3 1 **Global Warning**[20] 1423 3-8-12 **77** .... GeraldMosse 5 87+
(Ed Dunlop) *hld up in midfield on far side of gp: hdwy to ld over 1f out: rdn clr fnl f* **3/1**[1]

5212 2 *3 ¼* **Chosen World**[28] 1273 5-9-7 **73** ....(p) PaulMulrennan 10 79
(Julie Camacho) *taken early to post: prom on nr side of gp: effrt and ev ch briefly over 1f out: sn edgd lft and chsng wnr: kpt on fnl f: nt pce to chal* **6/1**[2]

430- 3 *1* **Chaplin Bay (IRE)**[182] 8388 7-9-9 **75** .... JackGarritty 7 78
(Ruth Carr) *hld up on far side of gp: rdn and hdwy over 1f out: kpt on ins fnl f: nt pce to chal* **13/2**[3]

520- 4 *1 ½* **Twin Appeal (IRE)**[164] 8898 8-10-0 **80** .... ShaneGray 1 79
(Karen Tutty) *led on far side of gp to over 1f out: rallied: outpcd ins fnl f* **33/1**

4503 5 *nk* **Testa Rossa (IRE)**[21] 1401 9-8-9 **68** ....(b) CoreyMadden(7) 8 66
(Jim Goldie) *prom in centre of gp: drvn and outpcd over 2f out: rallied fnl f: no imp* **20/1**

5365 6 *nk* **Scofflaw**[14] 1560 5-9-11 **77** ....(v) CamHardie 9 75
(David Evans) *prom on nr side of gp: drvn along over 2f out: one pce fr over 1f out* **14/1**

320- 7 *3 ¼* **Desert Lantern (USA)**[187] 8232 3-8-13 **78** .... PJMcDonald 2 62
(Mark Johnston) *in tch on far side of gp: outpcd and hung lft over 2f out: sme late hdwy: nvr rchd ldrs* **10/1**

6121 8 *shd* **Insurplus (IRE)**[21] 1399 6-9-0 **66** .... PhilDennis 6 55
(Jim Goldie) *hld up in centre of gp: rdn over 2f out: sme hdwy over 1f out: nvr rchd ldrs* **14/1**

51-5 9 *1 ¾* **Dubai Acclaim (IRE)**[107] 19 4-9-3 **74** .... SebastianWoods(5) 14 58
(Richard Fahey) *taken early to post: cl up on nr side of gp: ev ch over 2f out to over 1f out: sn wknd* **8/1**

0 10 *hd* **First Response**[19] 1457 4-9-11 **77** .... TonyHamilton 4 60
(Linda Stubbs) *dwlt: bhd on far side of gp: rdn along over 2f out: sn n.d: btn over 1f out* **14/1**

003- 11 *3 ½* **Our Charlie Brown**[171] 8717 5-9-4 **70** .... DavidAllan 3 44
(Tim Easterby) *cl up towards far side of gp: effrt and ev ch briefly over 1f out: sn wknd* **14/1**

015- 12 *4 ½* **Etikaal**[121] 9615 5-9-2 **68** .... SamJames 11 30
(Grant Tuer) *dwlt: bhd in centre of gp: drvn and outpcd over 2f out: sn btn* **14/1**

0-51 13 *10* **Tiercel**[28] 1273 6-9-4 **70** .... LewisEdmunds 12 5
(Rebecca Bastiman) *hld up on nr side of gp: rdn over 2f out: sn wknd* **14/1**

1m 26.7s (0.50) **Going Correction** +0.125s/f (Slow)
WFA 3 from 4yo+ 13lb **13** Ran SP% **120.5**
Speed ratings (Par 105): **102,98,97,95,95 94,91,90,88,88 84,79,68**
CSF £19.67 CT £112.15 TOTE £4.40: £2.10, £1.70, £2.50; EX 24.20 Trifecta £102.00.
Owner Dr Johnny Hon **Bred** Mrs Elizabeth Grundy **Trained** Newmarket, Suffolk

FOCUS
Fair handicap form, with an improved effort from the winner.

1926 LADBROKES BURRADON STKS (LISTED RACE) 1m 5y (Tp)
3:20 (3:21) (Class 1) 3-Y-O
£56,710 (£21,500; £10,760; £5,360; £2,690; £1,350) **Stalls** Centre

Form RPR

132- 1 **Fox Power (IRE)**[175] 8590 3-9-2 95 .... SilvestreDeSousa 7 106
(Richard Hannon) *pressed ldr: led over 2f out: rdn and hrd pressed fnl f: kpt on strly last 100yds* **7/1**[3]

01-1 2 *1 ¼* **Daarik (IRE)**[20] 1423 3-9-2 90 .... JimCrowley 9 103
(John Gosden) *trckd ldrs: effrt and ev ch over 1f out to ins fnl f: one pce last 100yds* **5/2**[1]

1- 3 *hd* **Bayroot (IRE)**[179] 8467 3-9-2 0 .... AndreaAtzeni 3 102
(Roger Varian) *hld up: rdn over 2f out: hdwy on far side of gp over 1f out: kpt on fnl f: nrst fin* **15/2**

40-5 4 *1 ¼* **Marie's Diamond (IRE)**[9] 1707 3-9-2 108 .... PJMcDonald 6 99
(Mark Johnston) *midfield: drvn over 2f out: hdwy over 1f out: one pce ins fnl f* **8/1**

3-11 5 *¾* **Creationist (USA)**[77] 523 3-9-2 86 .... JasonWatson 1 97
(Roger Charlton) *midfield: drvn along over 2f out: effrt over 1f out: sn no imp* **11/1**

433- 6 *½* **Pogo (IRE)**[201] 7799 3-9-2 97 .... PaulMulrennan 12 96
(Charles Hills) *hld up: rdn and outpcd over 2f out: rallied over 1f out: kpt on fnl f: no imp* **66/1**

226- 7 *1 ¾* **Dark Jedi (IRE)**[194] 8025 3-9-2 100 .... BenCurtis 2 92
(Charles Hills) *prom: drvn along over 2f out: wknd over 1f out* **14/1**

1- 8 *½* **Magic J (USA)**[213] 7398 3-9-2 0 .... PatCosgrave 11 91
(Ed Vaughan) *hld up: rdn over 2f out: hdwy over 1f out: no further imp ins fnl f* **9/2**[2]

61- 9 *3* **Dark Lochnagar (USA)**[172] 8700 3-9-2 0 .... GeraldMosse 4 84
(Keith Dalgleish) *dwlt: hld up: struggling over 2f out: btn and eased fnl f* **80/1**

12 10 *3 ¼* **Ebury**[13] 1594 3-9-2 0 .... RobHornby 5 76
(Martyn Meade) *led to over 2f out: wknd over 1f out* **9/1**

11- 11 *13* **Antagonize**[271] 5241 3-9-2 85 .... GrahamLee 8 47
(Bryan Smart) *dwlt: plld hrd: hld up: struggling over 2f out: sn btn (jockey said colt ran too free)* **16/1**

1m 39.03s (0.43) **Going Correction** +0.125s/f (Slow) **11** Ran SP% **115.7**
Speed ratings (Par 106): **102,100,100,99,98 98,96,95,92,89 76**
CSF £24.33 TOTE £6.80: £2.50, £1.50, £2.20; EX 26.10 Trifecta £204.20.
Owner King Power Racing Co Ltd **Bred** Diomed Bloodstock Ltd **Trained** East Everleigh, Wilts

FOCUS
The third running of this event, and the second to have Listed status. Last year's winner Gronkowski has gone on to finish second in both the Belmont Stakes and the Dubai World Cup. The field tacked over to the stands' side before halfway and the form looks pretty sound, with the time two and a half seconds slower than the standard. The winner continues to progress, and the level is set around the sixth.

1927 BETWAY LIVE CASINO H'CAP 1m 4f 98y (Tp)
3:55 (3:55) (Class 2) (0-100,100) 4-Y-O **£54,986** (£16,362; £8,177; £4,088) **Stalls** High

Form RPR

31-2 1 **Bartholomeu Dias**[13] 1596 4-9-1 **94** .... AndreaAtzeni 5 103
(Charles Hills) *cl up: led over 3f out: rdn over 1f out: r.o wl fnl f* **18/1**

1121 2 *½* **Forbidden Planet**[20] 1422 4-8-9 **93** .... ThomasGreatrex(5) 14 101+
(Roger Charlton) *dwlt and swtchd lft s: hld up and bhd: smooth hdwy on outside 3f out: rdn 2f out: chsd wnr last 100yds: kpt on fin* **3/1**[1]

311- 3 *hd* **Baghdad (FR)**[302] 4029 4-9-5 **98** .... PJMcDonald 10 106+
(Mark Johnston) *hld up: hdwy 3f out: rdn and in tch over 1f out: kpt on ins fnl f* **7/1**

-123 4 *½* **Desert Fire (IRE)**[50] 961 4-9-7 **100** .... PatCosgrave 3 107
(Saeed bin Suroor) *trckd ldrs: wnt 2nd over 2f out to last 100yds: kpt on same pce* **7/2**[2]

02-2 5 *1 ½* **Al Hamdany (IRE)**[9] 1681 5-9-3 **96** .... GeraldMosse 6 100
(Marco Botti) *t.k.h in midfield: effrt and hdwy wl over 1f out: rdn and one pce ins fnl f* **22/1**

130- 6 *nk* **Shailene (IRE)**[216] 7285 4-8-12 **94** .... WilliamCox(3) 13 98+
(Andrew Balding) *hld up towards rr: stdy hdwy whn nt clr run briefly over 2f out: sn rdn: rallied fnl f: nrst fin* **28/1**

152- 7 *2 ¼* **Buzz (FR)**[151] 9155 5-9-6 **99** .... CharlieBennett 4 99
(Hughie Morrison) *hld up in tch: rdn along over 2f out: outpcd fr over 1f out* **16/1**

510- 8 *½* **Lady Bergamot (FR)**[195] 7986 5-8-13 **92** .... GeorgeWood 8 92
(James Fanshawe) *hld up on ins: stdy hdwy whn n.m.r briefly over 2f out: rdn over 1f out: sn no imp* **25/1**

10-4 9 *nk* **Island Brave (IRE)**[20] 1422 5-9-0 **100** .... ScottMcCullagh(7) 12 99
(Heather Main) *in tch on outside: rdn over 2f out: wknd over 1f out* **6/1**

101- 10 *½* **Big Kitten (USA)**[148] 9204 4-8-12 **91** .... JimCrowley 9 89
(William Haggas) *t.k.h early: hld up: smooth hdwy on outside 3f out: rdn 2f out: wknd appr fnl f* **5/1**[3]

12- 11 *12* **Ashington**[237] 6515 4-8-11 **90** ....(p) JasonHart 7 69
(John Quinn) *midfield: rdn and outpcd whn n.m.r over 2f out: sn btn* **40/1**

130- 12 *¾* **Daawy (IRE)**[148] 9200 5-8-10 **89** .... BenCurtis 1 67
(Roger Fell) *trckd ldrs: rdn over 2f out: sn wknd* **66/1**

004/ 13 *6* **Seamour (IRE)**[548] 7115 8-9-0 **96** .... BenRobinson(3) 11 64
(Brian Ellison) *hld up: rdn and struggling 3f out: sn btn* **66/1**

/1-4 14 *17* **Showroom (FR)**[14] 1559 4-8-11 **90** .... SilvestreDeSousa 2 32
(Mark Johnston) *led to over 3f out: wknd and eased fr over 2f out (jockey said gelding moved poorly throughout)* **20/1**

2m 39.71s (-1.39) **Going Correction** +0.125s/f (Slow) **14** Ran SP% **123.6**
Speed ratings (Par 109): **109,108,108,108,107 107,105,105,104,104 96,96,92,80**
CSF £69.16 CT £436.91 TOTE £24.00: £5.10, £1.60, £2.70; EX 114.90 Trifecta £561.70.
Owner P K Siu **Bred** Newsells Park Stud **Trained** Lambourn, Berks

FOCUS
A hot handicap, and pretty solid form. A pb from the winner with the fifth helping with the standard.

1928 LADBROKES HOME OF THE ODDS BOOST H'CAP 1m 4f 98y (Tp)
4:25 (4:26) (Class 4) (0-85,81) 3-Y-O **£6,727** (£2,002; £1,000; £500; £300) **Stalls** High

Form RPR

2123 1 **Gantier**[22] 1386 3-9-6 **81** ....(b) JimCrowley 5 88
(John Gosden) *hld up in tch: hdwy on outside 3f out: led and hrd pressed over 1f out: drvn out fnl f* **5/2**[2]

6-01 2 *½* **Smarter (IRE)**[15] 1555 3-9-3 **78** .... BenCurtis 3 84
(William Haggas) *prom: hdwy on outside over 2f out: effrt and ev ch over 1f out: kpt on fnl f: hld nr fin* **3/1**[3]

64-3 3 *2 ¾* **Bo Samraan (IRE)**[9] 1696 3-9-2 **77** .... PJMcDonald 2 79
(Mark Johnston) *led: rdn over 2f out: edgd rt and hdd over 1f out: sn outpcd* **7/4**[1]

330 4 *7* **Allocator (FR)**[20] 1417 3-9-2 **77** .... RossaRyan 1 68
(Richard Hannon) *t.k.h: chsd ldrs: outpcd and edgd lft over 2f out: n.d after* **12/1**

22-3 5 *¾* **Fox Fearless**[14] 1558 3-9-3 **78** ....(p[1]) SilvestreDeSousa 4 67
(K R Burke) *pressed ldr: rdn along and outpcd over 2f out: sn struggling* **15/2**

2m 43.92s (2.82) **Going Correction** +0.125s/f (Slow) **5** Ran SP% **109.4**
Speed ratings (Par 100): **95,94,92,88,87**
CSF £10.14 TOTE £2.70: £1.90, £1.70; EX 9.00 Trifecta £14.80.
Owner K Abdullah **Bred** Juddmonte Farms Ltd **Trained** Newmarket, Suffolk

FOCUS
This was over 4sec slower than the preceding Class 2 handicap. The form makes sense.

1929 PLAY 4 TO SCORE AT BETWAY H'CAP 5f (Tp)
4:55 (4:55) (Class 4) (0-85,87) 3-Y-O+
£6,727 (£2,002; £1,000; £500; £300; £300) **Stalls** Centre

Form RPR

5-00 1 **Oriental Lilly**[17] 1502 5-9-3 **74** .... JamieGormley(3) 6 83
(Jim Goldie) *bhd: pushed along 1/2-way: gd hdwy nr side over 1f out: led ins fnl f: kpt on wl* **6/1**[3]

-665 2 *¾* **Landing Night (IRE)**[73] 610 7-9-4 **72** ....(tp) PJMcDonald 13 78
(Rebecca Menzies) *hld up on nr side of gp: rdn and hdwy over 1f out: ev ch briefly ins fnl f: sn chsng wnr: r.o* **18/1**

3310 3 *½* **Another Angel (IRE)**[15] 1547 5-9-5 **80** .... KieranSchofield(7) 4 84
(Antony Brittain) *prom on far side of gp: drvn along over 2f out: rallied: kpt on ins fnl f* **5/1**[2]

-123 4 *nse* **Key To Power**[36] 1193 3-8-6 **75** .... AndrewBreslin(5) 8 75
(Mark Johnston) *led in centre of gp: rdn and hrd pressed over 1f out: hdd ins fnl f: one pce* **14/1**

141- 5 *hd* **Burford Brown**[192] 8096 4-9-12 **80** .... GeraldMosse 11 83
(Robert Cowell) *in tch on nr side of gp: hdwy to dispute ld over 1f out to last 100yds: sn no ex* **3/1**[1]

3105 **6** 1 **Tathmeen (IRE)**[21] 1394 4-9-7 **75** CamHardie 1 75
(Antony Brittain) *hld up on far side of gp: rdn over 2f out: effrt over 1f out: no imp ins fnl f* **7/1**

0132 **7** ½ **Jan Van Hoof (IRE)**[21] 1403 8-9-3 **71** BarryMcHugh 2 69
(Michael Herrington) *hld up in midfield on far side of gp: effrt and edgd rt over 1f out: no ex ins fnl f* **13/2**

100- **8** ¾ **Henley**[189] 8165 7-10-5 **87** BenCurtis 7 82
(Tracy Waggott) *chsd ldrs in centre of gp: rdn 2f out: wknd ins fnl f* **16/1**

000- **9** 2 ¾ **Marietta Robusti (IRE)**[224] 7017 4-9-5 **73** JackGarritty 9 58
(Stella Barclay) *midfield in centre of gp: drvn over 2f out: wknd over 1f out* **100/1**

4200 **10** 3 ½ **Dynamo Walt (IRE)**[15] 1547 8-9-12 **80** (v) PaddyMathers 5 53
(Derek Shaw) *dwlt: bhd in centre of gp: rdn along after 2f: nvr rchd ldrs* **20/1**

24-0 **11** ½ **Little Legs**[6] 1762 3-9-6 **87** BenRobinson(3) 10 54
(Brian Ellison) *cl up on nr side of gp tl rdn and wknd over 1f out (jockey said filly stopped quickly)* **8/1**

420- **12** 10 **Bashiba (IRE)**[184] 8333 8-9-6 **77** RowanScott(3) 3 12
(Nigel Tinkler) *bhd and outpcd in centre of gp: struggling bef 1/2-way: sn btn (jockey said gelding was never travelling)* **28/1**

59.35s (-0.15) **Going Correction** +0.125s/f (Slow)
WFA 3 from 4yo+ 10lb **12** Ran SP% **119.9**
Speed ratings (Par 105): **106,104,104,103,103 102,101,100,95,90 89,73**
CSF £107.55 CT £593.95 TOTE £7.40: £2.50, £5.10, £2.50; EX 107.70 Trifecta £607.10.
Owner Johnnie Delta Racing **Bred** Johnnie Delta Racing **Trained** Uplawmoor, E Renfrews

FOCUS
There was a bunch finish to this fair sprint, which was run at a good clip. The winner add to her good C&D record off a good mark.
T/Jkpt: Not Won. T/Plt: £14.20 to a £1 stake. Pool: £95,103.79 - 4,858.05 winning units. T/Qpdt: £8.70 to a £1 stake. Pool: £8,668.92 - 732.94 winning units. **Richard Young**

BRIGHTON (L-H)
Saturday, April 20

OFFICIAL GOING: Good to firm (watered; 9.9)
Wind: slight cross breeze Weather: warm and sunny

1930 STARSPORTS.BET H'CAP 5f 215y
4:45 (4:45) (Class 5) (0-70,72) 4-Y-O+
£3,752 (£1,116; £557; £400; £400; £400) **Stalls** Centre

Form RPR

06-2 **1** **Diamond Lady**[14] 1586 8-9-6 **69** ShaneKelly 2 81
(William Stone) *mde all: effrt to qckn tempo and sn 3 l clr over 2f out: wl in command 1f out: pushed out fnl f* **4/1**[2]

2616 **2** 2 ¼ **Real Estate (IRE)**[22] 1393 4-9-4 **70** (p) PaddyBradley(3) 4 75
(Michael Attwater) *trckd wnr in 3rd: wnt 2nd gng wl over 1f out: sn rdn to chse wnr 1f out: kpt on fnl f but nt rch wnr (vet reported colt lost its left-fore shoe)* **6/1**

4326 **3** 1 ½ **Secondo (FR)**[10] 1682 9-8-6 **60** (v) PoppyBridgwater(5) 3 60
(Robert Stephens) *racd in midfield: effrt to chse wnr in 4th 2f out: rdn along 1f out: kpt on one pce fnl f* **9/2**[3]

1212 **4** 1 **Spirit Of Zebedee (IRE)**[22] 1393 6-8-13 **62** (v) LiamKeniry 8 59
(John Quinn) *chsd wnr: rdn and outpcd by wnr 2f out: one pce ins fnl f* **11/2**

0560 **5** hd **National Glory (IRE)**[36] 1209 4-8-12 **68** (b) Pierre-LouisJamin(7) 1 64
(Archie Watson) *dwlt bdly and racd in rr: hdwy on outer over 3f out: rdn and unable qck 2f out: kpt on fnl f* **6/1**

50-5 **6** 2 **Swissal (IRE)**[22] 1393 4-8-10 **66** (p) CierenFallon(7) 6 56
(David Dennis) *hld up: rdn and outpcd over 2f out: one pce fnl f: nvr able to chal* **3/1**[1]

-3F0 **7** 9 **Mercers**[14] 1590 5-8-9 **58** (b) JasonWatson 7 19
(Paddy Butler) *stdy to post: racd in midfield: niggled along 1/2-way: rdn and hung rt u.p 2f out: sn btn and wknd fnl f* **25/1**

-22 **8** 20 **Upavon**[36] 1218 9-9-9 **72** JFEgan 5
(Tony Carroll) *s.v.s and qckly detached: nt persevered w (jockey said gelding reared and hit his head as the stalls opened)* **8/1**

1m 7.12s (-3.98) **Going Correction** -0.525s/f (Hard) course record **8** Ran SP% **122.1**
Speed ratings (Par 103): **105,102,100,98,98 95,83,57**
CSF £30.28 CT £115.72 TOTE £4.40: £1.70, £2.10, £1.50; EX 27.30 Trifecta £158.20.
Owner Miss Caroline Scott **Bred** Mickley Stud **Trained** West Wickham, Cambs

FOCUS
A bright, warm evening and a decent pace for this modest sprint handicap, where the winner made all in a new 6f track record time. Winning jockey Shane Kelly reported the ground to be "riding quick and a little bit rough, which was a little bit disappointing."

1931 STARSPORTS.BET / EBF MAIDEN STKS 5f 60y
5:20 (5:20) (Class 5) 2-Y-O **£3,752** (£1,116; £557; £278) **Stalls** Centre

Form RPR

3 **1** **Charlemaine (IRE)**[21] 1448 2-9-5 RaulDaSilva 6 73+
(Paul Cole) *trckd ldr in 3rd: effrt to chse ldr 2f out: rdn to ld 1f out: rdn out ins fnl f* **9/4**[2]

2 1 ¾ **Beignet (IRE)** 2-9-0 TomMarquand 5 62
(Richard Hannon) *chsd ldr: pushed along to ld 2f out: rdn and hdd by wnr 1f out: kpt on fnl f but unable to match pce of wnr* **7/2**[3]

6 **3** 1 **Hypochondriac**[18] 1493 2-9-0 HectorCrouch 2 58
(David Evans) *hld up: pushed along over 2f out: rdn 1f out: kpt on promisingly wl ins fnl f* **22/1**

2 **4** 1 ¾ **Out Of Breath**[12] 1651 2-9-5 NicolaCurrie 3 57
(Jamie Osborne) *racd in 4th: pushed along and outpcd over 2f out: sn rdn 1f out: kpt on one pce fnl f (jockey said colt was never travelling)* **6/4**[1]

0 **5** 1 **Good Times Too**[12] 1651 2-9-5 CharlesBishop 4 53
(Mick Channon) *led: rdn along and hdd 2f out: hung lft handed u.p whn wkng ins fnl f* **12/1**

6 6 **Ivor** 2-9-5 RossaRyan 7 32
(Richard Hannon) *restless in stalls: dwlt and racd in last: c wd u.p 3f out: rdn and drifted rt 2f out: nvr able to land a blow* **14/1**

7 ¾ **Spiritulist** 2-9-5 JasonWatson 1 29
(David Evans) *hld up: rdn and outpcd over 2f out: nvr able to get on terms* **25/1**

1m 0.65s (-2.35) **Going Correction** -0.525s/f (Hard) **7** Ran SP% **115.5**
Speed ratings (Par 92): **97,94,92,89,88 78,77**
CSF £10.89 TOTE £3.00: £1.60, £2.10; EX 11.00 Trifecta £105.10.
Owner P F I Cole Ltd **Bred** Haras Du Mont Dit Mont **Trained** Whatcombe, Oxon

FOCUS
The official ground was changed to good to firm, firm in places after a track record in the first race. They went a decent pace and they finished quite well strung out. The form should hold up.

1932 DOWNLOAD THE STAR SPORTS APP NOW! H'CAP 6f 210y
5:50 (5:50) (Class 4) (0-80,79) 4-Y-O+
£5,530 (£1,645; £822; £411; £400; £400) **Stalls** Centre

Form RPR

0-63 **1** **Mamillius**[18] 1496 6-9-5 **77** PatCosgrave 2 86
(George Baker) *trckd ldng pair: encouraged along to take clsr order 3f out: rdn and led wl over 1f out: kpt rt up to work ins fnl f: a doing enough* **2/1**[1]

316- **2** 1 ¾ **Dream Catching (IRE)**[200] 7880 4-8-13 **78** WilliamCarver(7) 5 82
(Andrew Balding) *s.i.s and racd in last early as a result: hdwy arnd field 3f out: sn rdn to chse wnr over 1f out: kpt on ins fnl f but unable to match pce of wnr (jockey said gelding was slowly away)* **4/1**[2]

020- **3** 3 **Crystal Deauville (FR)**[147] 9247 4-9-3 **75** (h[1]) ShaneKelly 6 71
(Gay Kelleway) *led and racd keenly: rdn along to maintain short ld 2f out: hdd by wnr and drifted lft u.p over 1f out: kpt on one pce ins fnl f* **14/1**

140- **4** 2 ¾ **Kachumba**[197] 7948 4-8-5 **70** CierenFallon(7) 4 59
(Rae Guest) *hld up: making stdy hdwy under hands and heels whn short of room against far rail over 1f out: nt rcvr and one pce fnl f* **5/1**

142- **5** ½ **Blanchefleur (IRE)**[180] 8487 4-8-13 **76** ThoreHammerHansen(5) 7 63
(Richard Hannon) *racd in midfield: rdn along and outpcd over 2f out: drvn and no imp 1f out: no ex (trainer's rep said the filly was unsuited by the undulations and camber of brighton)* **9/2**[3]

3643 **6** 2 ½ **Emily Goldfinch**[9] 1712 6-9-0 **79** (p) GraceMcEntee(7) 3 60
(Phil McEntee) *chsd ldr early: rdn along and outpcd 3f out: drvn over 1f out: wknd fnl f* **8/1**

-343 **7** 2 ¾ **Global Exceed**[10] 1684 4-8-9 **67** (p) RaulDaSilva 1 40
(Robert Cowell) *hld up: rdn along and lost pl 1/2-way: sn bhd (trainer's rep said the gelding was unsuited by the good to firm, firm in places going and would prefer an easier surface)* **10/1**

1m 20.03s (-3.77) **Going Correction** -0.525s/f (Hard) course record **7** Ran SP% **115.1**
Speed ratings (Par 105): **100,98,94,91,90 88,84**
CSF £10.29 TOTE £2.50: £1.70, £2.80; EX 12.50 Trifecta £85.00.
Owner The Mamillius Partnership **Bred** East Bloodstock & Mr S Graham **Trained** Chiddingfold, Surrey

FOCUS
Fairly competitive for the grade and the pace was true.

1933 CALL STAR SPORTS ON 08000 521 321 H'CAP 6f 210y
6:20 (6:21) (Class 6) (0-65,65) 4-Y-O+
£3,105 (£924; £461; £400; £400; £400) **Stalls** Centre

Form RPR

0020 **1** **De Little Engine (IRE)**[7] 1768 5-9-5 **63** (p) RossaRyan 3 71
(Alexandra Dunn) *settled wl in midfield: hdwy u.p to chse ldr 2f out: str run between rivals to ld jst ins fnl f: styd on wl* **14/1**

2060 **2** 1 ¼ **Blessed To Empress (IRE)**[23] 1378 4-8-11 **58** GabrieleMalune(3) 1 63
(Amy Murphy) *trckd runaway ldr: rdn to chse wnr 2f out: led briefly over 1f out: sn drvn and hdd by wnr jst ins fnl f: no ex* **4/1**[3]

600- **3** ½ **N Over J**[134] 9441 4-9-0 **58** (v) JasonWatson 5 61
(William Knight) *racd in rr of midfield: pushed along and outpcd 3f out: sn rdn and little imp 2f out: kpt on wl ins fnl f* **11/2**

00-0 **4** 1 **Perfect Symphony (IRE)**[26] 1329 5-9-4 **65** PaddyBradley(3) 6 66
(Mark Pattinson) *settled wl in 3rd: hdwy u.p to chse ldr over 2f out: rdn and ev ch on outer over 1f out: one pce fnl f* **28/1**

2125 **5** 1 **Maazel (IRE)**[19] 1477 5-8-12 **56** DannyBrock 2 54
(Lee Carter) *dwlt and racd in rr: attempting to cl on rail whn bdly hmpd by rival over 3f out: rdn along 2f out: kpt on fnl f* **10/1**

4234 **6** 2 ¼ **Rivas Rob Roy**[43] 1075 4-8-11 **55** HectorCrouch 8 47
(John Gallagher) *hld up: rdn 3f out: drvn 2f out: nvr on terms* **5/2**[1]

554 **7** 6 **Creek Harbour (IRE)**[24] 1355 4-9-7 **65** (b[1]) ShaneKelly 7 41
(Richard Hughes) *t.k.h to post: led and racd keenly: plld 5 l clr 1/2-way: rdn and reduced advantage 2f out: hdd wl over 1f out: wknd fnl f* **7/2**[2]

5445 **8** 3 ¼ **Malaysian Boleh**[8] 1732 9-8-2 **46** oh1 (v) RaulDaSilva 4 13
(Phil McEntee) *racd in rr: keen and hmpd rival wl over 3f out whn hanging lft: sn rdn: nvr on terms* **12/1**

0505 **9** 10 **More Salutes (IRE)**[24] 1353 4-8-2 **46** (p) LukeMorris 9
(Michael Attwater) *hld up: pushed along in rr 1/2-way: rdn and no rspnse over 2f out: wknd fnl f (jockey said colt moved poorly)* **16/1**

1m 19.78s (-4.02) **Going Correction** -0.525s/f (Hard) course record **9** Ran SP% **119.0**
Speed ratings (Par 101): **101,99,99,97,96 94,87,83,72**
CSF £71.41 CT £357.86 TOTE £14.50: £3.80, £1.90, £2.30; EX 42.30 Trifecta £452.60.
Owner Equinox Racing & Team Dunn **Bred** Glenvale Stud **Trained** West Buckland, Somerset

FOCUS
A genuine pace for a modest handicap.

1934 WATCH THE £BETTINGPEOPLE VIDEOS STARSPORTSBET.CO.UK H'CAP 1m 1f 207y
6:50 (6:50) (Class 5) (0-75,78) 4-Y-O+
£3,752 (£1,116; £557; £400; £400; £400) **Stalls** High

Form RPR

4521 **1** **The Jean Genie**[10] 1688 5-9-10 **78** RichardKingscote 2 85
(William Stone) *trckd ldr: clsd gng wl 2f out: rdn along to ld over 1f out: drvn ins fnl f and styd on wl: a doing enough* **6/4**[1]

060- **2** ½ **Grapevine (IRE)**[192] 8102 6-9-0 **75** CierenFallon(7) 5 81
(Charles Hills) *slow into stride and racd in rr: hdwy on outer to go 4th 4f out: rdn along to chse wnr over 1f out: drifted lft u.p but styd on wl ins fnl f: nt rch wnr* **13/8**[2]

30-2 **3** 1 ½ **Stormingin (IRE)**[29] 1269 6-9-6 **74** HectorCrouch 7 77
(Gary Moore) *racd in 3rd on inner: niggled along 3f out: rdn to chse wnr over 1f out: drvn and ev ch 1f out: kpt on one pce fnl f* **9/2**[3]

620- **4** 1 **Last Enchantment (IRE)**[105] 7754 4-9-5 **73** ShaneKelly 1 74
(Neil Mulholland) *led: rdn along and strly pressed by wnr 2f out: hdd by wnr over 1f out: wknd ins fnl f* **18/1**

44-0 **5** 1 ½ **Roy Rocket (FR)**[24] 1355 9-8-13 **67** JFEgan 3 65
(John Berry) *hld up: smooth hdwy onto heels of ldng gp wl over 2f out: pushed along and no immediate rspnse over 1f out: sn rdn and unable qck 1f out: kpt on one pce* **14/1**

600- **6** 13 **Lyn's Secret (IRE)**[136] 9400 4-8-12 **66** (h[1]) LiamJones 6 38
(Seamus Mullins) *hld up: rdn and outpcd 3f out: sn bhd and struggling* **33/1**

00-0 **7** *9* **Camakasi (IRE)**[12] 1653 8-8-13 **67**.............................. TomMarquand 4 21
(Ali Stronge) *dwlt bdly and detached: a in rr (jockey said gelding was slowly away)* **25/1**

1m 59.07s (-5.93) **Going Correction** -0.525s/f (Hard) **7** Ran SP% **115.0**
Speed ratings (Par 103): **102,101,100,99,98 88,80**
CSF £4.28 TOTE £2.40: £1.40, £1.20; EX 4.80 Trifecta £11.20.

Owner Miss Caroline Scott **Bred** Whitley Stud **Trained** West Wickham, Cambs

FOCUS
Due to a false patch of ground, the start was moved forward 11 yards. A fair handicap and a generous pace. The market spoke correctly.

1935 FIRST FOR INDUSTRY JOBS VISIT STARRECRUITMENT.BET CLASSIFIED STKS — 1m 1f 207y
7:20 (7:21) (Class 6) 3-Y-O+

£3,105 (£924; £461; £400; £400; £400) Stalls High

Form — RPR

2361 **1** **Contingency Fee**[3] 1858 4-9-10 54..............(p) GraceMcEntee(7) 8 65
(Phil McEntee) *trckd ldrs tl led 5f out: effrt to qckn tempo and c centre of trck over 2f out: drvn and strly pressed by rival 1f out: kpt on wl and a doing enough fnl f* **3/1**[1]

0-03 **2** *nk* **Mongolia**[8] 1725 3-8-9 55.............................. RossaRyan 6 56
(Richard Hannon) *disp ld for 3f then trckd ldr: niggled along 4f out: effrt to chse wnr on outer 2f out: sn rdn and ev ch 1f out: kpt on wl but nt rch wnr fnl f* **5/1**

00-0 **3** *1 1/4* **Miss Havana**[99] 183 3-8-2 53.............................. GeorgiaDobie(7) 5 54
(Eve Johnson Houghton) *racd in rr of midfield: hdwy u.p 3f out: rdn 2f out: drvn and styd on wl fnl f: nt rch ldng pair* **8/1**

3536 **4** *7* **Al Daayen (FR)**[14] 1593 3-8-9 53..............(b[1]) JFEgan 9 41
(Mark Johnston) *racd in midfield: rdn along and outpcd by wnr 3f out: drvn 1f out: no ex fnl f (jockey said filly ran too free and hung left-handed)* **15/2**

410- **5** *1 1/4* **Rocksette**[157] 9054 5-9-12 55.............................. HectorCrouch 4 41
(Gary Moore) *dwlt sltly and racd in rr: effrt to cl on ldrs 3f out: pushed along and no immediate imp 2f out: sn rdn and kpt on one pce fnl f* **9/2**[3]

6331 **6** *1 1/2* **Iley Boy**[10] 1679 5-9-8 58..............(p) CierenFallon(7) 7 42
(John Gallagher) *hld up: stl in rr whn hmpd 3f out: rdn 2f out: kpt on one pce fnl f* **7/2**[2]

02-0 **7** *2 1/2* **Kenoughty (FR)**[57] 855 3-8-9 51..............(p) ShaneKelly 1 31
(Richard Hughes) *racd in midfield in tch: drvn along to chse wnr over 2f out: wknd fr 1f out* **10/1**

00-4 **8** *10* **Foxy's Spirit**[9] 1710 4-9-12 44.............................. LukeMorris 3 15
(Clare Hobson) *disp ld for 3f then trckd pce: rdn along and no imp over 2f out: wknd fnl f* **33/1**

5500 **9** *8* **Haraz (IRE)**[8] 1731 6-9-12 43..............(bt) JasonWatson 11
(Paddy Butler) *hld up in rr: drvn and no rspnse on outer over 2f out: nvr on terms* **50/1**

-000 **10** *9* **Estibdaad (IRE)**[10] 1683 9-9-12 39..............(t) TomMarquand 2
(Paddy Butler) *disp ld for 3f on inner then trckd ld: rdn and lost pl 3f out: sn bhd* **80/1**

534- **11** *15* **Triple First**[215] 7362 5-9-12 53.............................. LiamJones 10
(Seamus Mullins) *racd in midfield on outer: pushed along 4f out: rdn and lost pl 2f out: sn detached* **18/1**

1m 58.99s (-6.01) **Going Correction** -0.525s/f (Hard)
WFA 3 from 4yo+ 17lb **11** Ran SP% **125.4**
Speed ratings (Par 101): **103,102,101,96,95 93,91,83,77,70 58**
CSF £19.61 TOTE £3.60: £1.80, £2.10, £2.90; EX 24.20 Trifecta £137.70.

Owner M Hall **Bred** Whitwell Bloodstock **Trained** Newmarket, Suffolk

■ Stewards' Enquiry : Georgia Dobie four-day ban: misuse of the whip and careless riding (May 6-9)

FOCUS
The start was moved forward 11 yards. A low-grade handicap where the first two came down the stands' side. The first three drew clear of the remainder. Solid form for the grade.

1936 STREAMLINE TAXIS 01273 202020 H'CAP — 7f 211y
7:50 (7:50) (Class 6) (0-65,65) 4-Y-O+

£3,105 (£924; £461; £400; £400; £400) Stalls Centre

Form — RPR

645- **1** **Junoesque**[170] 8780 5-8-11 55..............(p) HectorCrouch 5 62
(John Gallagher) *led for 2f then trckd new ldr: effrt to chse clr ldr over 2f out: qckly clsd margin to ld over 1f out: drvn out ins fnl f* **9/4**[1]

60-0 **2** *1 1/4* **Khazix (IRE)**[101] 145 4-8-8 55.............................. WilliamCox(3) 2 59
(Daniele Camuffo) *settled in midfield: pushed along to chse clr ldr over 2f out: drvn to chse wnr 1f out: kpt on but a hld by wnr fnl f* **17/2**

0-00 **3** *nse* **Duke Of North (IRE)**[12] 1655 7-8-11 62.............................. IsobelFrancis(7) 6 66
(Jim Boyle) *hld up: hdwy u.p on outer over 2f out: rdn and wnt 3rd over 1f out: styd on wl fnl f: nt rch front pair (jockey said gelding hung left-handed)* **9/2**[3]

-101 **4** *3* **Lunar Deity**[29] 1269 10-9-0 65.............................. MarcoGhiani(7) 4 63+
(Stuart Williams) *sed awkwardly and racd in last: pushed along in last 4f out: rdn and no immediate rspnse over 2f out: kpt on passed btn horses fnl f (jockey said gelding was slowly away)* **10/3**[2]

0-10 **5** *3 1/4* **With Approval (IRE)**[94] 250 7-8-12 56..............(p) LukeMorris 1 46
(Laura Mongan) *rdn along fr stalls to chse ldr: drvn to chse clr ldr over 2f out: lost pl over 1f out: plugged on fnl f* **17/2**

0000 **6** *1 3/4* **The Special One (IRE)**[19] 1477 6-8-7 51..............(h) LiamJones 10 38
(Phil McEntee) *racd in rr of midfield: hdwy u.p 3f out: rdn and ev ch 2f out: sltly unbalanced over 1f out: one pce fnl f* **12/1**

56 **7** *2* **Zephyros (GER)**[54] 911 8-9-0 63..............(b[1]) PoppyBridgwater(5) 7 45
(David Bridgwater) *trckd wnr early tl led after 2f: sn 6 l clr over 3f out: rdn and reduced advantage 2f out: hdd by wnr over 1f out: wknd ins fnl f (jockey said gelding ran too free)* **8/1**

3F6- **8** *nse* **Iballisticvin**[242] 6374 6-8-12 63.............................. RhysClutterbuck(7) 8 45
(Gary Moore) *racd in midfield: pushed along 1/2-way: rdn and little rspnse wl over 2f out: nvr on terms* **16/1**

1m 32.91s (-3.99) **Going Correction** -0.525s/f (Hard) **8** Ran SP% **117.8**
Speed ratings (Par 101): **98,96,96,93,90 88,86,86**
CSF £23.19 CT £81.44 TOTE £2.60: £1.10, £3.10, £2.20; EX 20.20 Trifecta £114.40.

Owner The Juniper Racing Club Ltd **Bred** Adweb Ltd **Trained** Chastleton, Oxon

FOCUS
Not a strong race for the grade and won by a course specialist. The pace was solid.
T/Plt: £53.70 to a £1 stake. Pool: £53,924.94 - 732.54 winning units T/Qpdt: £11.40 to a £1 stake. Pool: £9,763.31 - 633.03 winning units **Mark Grantham**

1725 KEMPTON (A.W) (R-H)
Saturday, April 20

OFFICIAL GOING: Polytrack: standard to slow

1937 RTV/BRITISH STALLION STUDS EBF NOVICE STKS (PLUS 10 RACE) — 5f (P)
1:25 (1:26) (Class 4) 2-Y-O

£5,822 (£1,732; £865; £432) Stalls Low

Form — RPR

1 **1** **Electric Ladyland (IRE)**[18] 1493 2-9-3 0.............................. LukeMorris 6 77
(Archie Watson) *mde all: shkn up 2f out: rdn over 1f out: kpt on wl fnl f: pushed out last 100yds* **11/8**[2]

0 **2** *1 1/2* **Littleton Hall (IRE)**[8] 1733 2-9-5 0.............................. CallumShepherd 1 73
(Mick Channon) *bhd wnr: rdn wl over 1f out: styd on fnl f* **16/1**

3 *1* **Audio** 2-9-5 0.............................. TomMarquand 3 69
(Richard Hannon) *w wnr on outer: nudged along fr 1/2-way: effrt wl over 1f out: styd on fnl f* **15/2**[3]

4 *1/2* **Dark Of Night (IRE)** 2-9-5 0.............................. PatCosgrave 5 67+
(Saeed bin Suroor) *bdly missed break: mde up grnd and on terms at 1/2-way on outer: rdn wl over 1f out: no ex fnl f (jockey said colt was slowly away)* **1/1**[1]

5 *1 1/4* **Ride And Prejudice** 2-9-0 0.............................. ShelleyBirkett 4 58
(Julia Feilden) *hld up: shuffled along fr over 1f out: nvr involved (vet reported filly lost its right fore shoe)* **50/1**

1m 1.6s (1.10) **Going Correction** -0.075s/f (Stan) **5** Ran SP% **111.7**
Speed ratings (Par 94): **88,85,84,83,81**
CSF £20.39 TOTE £2.20: £1.20, £4.90; EX 14.30 Trifecta £38.80.

Owner Miss Emily Asprey & Christopher Wright **Bred** Rathasker Stud **Trained** Upper Lambourn, W Berks

FOCUS
This was decided soon after the start.

1938 BET AT RACINGTV.COM H'CAP — 5f (P)
2:00 (2:00) (Class 2) (0-100,101) 4-Y-O+

£15,562 (£4,660; £2,330; £1,165; £582; £292) Stalls Low

Form — RPR

320- **1** **Cowboy Soldier (IRE)**[243] 6361 4-8-11 87.............................. LukeMorris 9 98
(Robert Cowell) *cl up bhd ldrs on outer: shkn up over 1f out: prog and rdn ent fnl f: led 150yds out: kpt on wl* **20/1**

0-13 **2** *1 1/4* **Puds**[5] 1822 4-8-1 84.............................. GeorgeRooke(7) 7 90
(Richard Hughes) *hld up in rr: effrt on outer over 1f out: kpt on wl ent fnl f and tk 2nd cl home* **11/2**[2]

4-43 **3** *1 1/4* **Global Academy (IRE)**[28] 1290 4-8-8 84..............(p) SilvestreDeSousa 6 86
(Gay Kelleway) *led: rdn over 1f out: hdd 150yds out and lost 2nd sn after* **7/2**[1]

0460 **4** *hd* **Foxy Forever (IRE)**[42] 1098 9-8-6 82..............(bt) JFEgan 2 83
(Michael Wigham) *hld up in mid-div: rdn over 1f out: plugged on fnl f (vet reported gelding lost its right fore shoe)* **16/1**

2150 **5** *nk* **Royal Birth**[1] 1919 8-9-11 101..............(t) OisinMurphy 5 101
(Stuart Williams) *hld up: swtchd to outer at 1/2-way: effrt over 1f out trying to edge out: nt qckn last 150yds* **7/2**[1]

6-00 **6** *1/2* **Udontdodou**[21] 1421 6-9-0 90.............................. GeraldMosse 8 88
(Richard Guest) *bhd ldr on outer: rdn wl over 1f out: one pce fnl f* **25/1**

400- **7** *1/2* **Tomily (IRE)**[137] 9391 5-9-7 97.............................. TomMarquand 1 93
(Richard Hannon) *bhd ldr on inner: rdn over 1f out: nt qckn fnl f* **10/1**

50-2 **8** *3/4* **Blue De Vega (GER)**[8] 1734 6-9-1 91.............................. PJMcDonald 4 84
(Robert Cowell) *rr-div on inner: pushed along over 1f out and sltly ct on heels: no imp fnl f: nvr involved (jockey said gelding was denied a clear run)* **7/2**[1]

-144 **9** *1 1/4* **Outrage**[61] 786 7-9-3 93..............(b) KieranO'Neill 3 82
(Daniel Kubler) *sluggish s and a bhd: plugged on fnl f* **8/1**[3]

58.69s (-1.81) **Going Correction** -0.075s/f (Stan) **9** Ran SP% **116.7**
Speed ratings (Par 109): **111,109,107,106,106 105,104,103,101**
CSF £127.28 CT £486.64 TOTE £20.20: £3.70, £2.20, £1.50; EX 154.20 Trifecta £609.60.

Owner Mrs Fitri Hay **Bred** Rockfield Farm **Trained** Six Mile Bottom, Cambs

FOCUS
Unusually for this track, the first two came three wide around the turn.

1939 RACING TV FILLIES' CONDITIONS STKS (PLUS 10 RACE) — 1m (P)
2:35 (2:37) (Class 2) 3-Y-O

£15,562 (£4,660; £2,330; £1,165; £582; £292) Stalls Low

Form — RPR

332- **1** **El Gumryah (IRE)**[189] 8177 3-8-12 83.............................. AndreaAtzeni 4 91
(Simon Crisford) *edgy bhd stalls: wl away and mde all: pressed whn rdn 2f out: qcknd up wl over 1f out: edgd rt ins fnl f: styd on wl* **20/1**

02-1 **2** *3/4* **Rux Power**[23] 1381 3-9-2 82.............................. SilvestreDeSousa 3 93
(Andrew Balding) *hld up in last pair: shkn up over 2f out and prog on outer: rdn 2f out: outpcd tl kpt on fnl f and tk 2nd cl home* **9/2**[3]

31- **3** *1/2* **Rainbow Heart (IRE)**[178] 8546 3-9-2 0.............................. OisinMurphy 2 92
(William Haggas) *t.k.h gng to post and overshot s by 4f: bhd ldrs and plld hrd: rdn 2f out: chsd wnr over 1f out: no ex wl ins fnl f and lost 2nd cl home* **3/1**[2]

1- **4** *3 3/4* **Nausha**[175] 8643 3-9-2 0.............................. DavidEgan 1 83
(Roger Varian) *w wnr and t.k.h: rdn 2f out: fdd over 1f out* **5/6**[1]

20-5 **5** *hd* **Gospel**[34] 1242 3-9-2 89.............................. RyanMoore 7 83
(Mick Channon) *s.s and in last pair: rdn 2f out: kpt on one pce* **33/1**

155- **6** *3/4* **Canton Queen (IRE)**[175] 8629 3-9-2 93.............................. TomMarquand 5 81
(Richard Hannon) *in last pair: kpt on one pce bhd early tl tk clsr order after 3f: rdn 2f out: no imp (jockey said filly hung left-handed throughout)* **12/1**

1m 38.36s (-1.44) **Going Correction** -0.075s/f (Stan) **6** Ran SP% **113.1**
Speed ratings (Par 101): **104,103,102,99,98 98**
CSF £105.63 TOTE £20.20: £6.20, £2.00; EX 69.10 Trifecta £305.60.

Owner H H SH Nasser Bin Hamad Al Khalifa **Bred** Lynch-Bages & Rhinestone Bloodstock **Trained** Newmarket, Suffolk

FOCUS
A tactical affair, dominated by the winner from the front. The first two improved but the level of the form looks fluid.

1940 RACING TV CONDITIONS STKS (C&G) (PLUS 10 RACE) 1m (P)
3:10 (3:10) (Class 2) 3-Y-O

£15,562 (£4,660; £2,330; £1,165; £582; £292) Stalls Low

Form RPR

1- **1** **Name The Wind**[205] 7694 3-9-2 0 PJMcDonald 2 100+
(James Tate) *racd in mid-div on inner: gng wl whn shkn up and prog angling to outer fr 2f out: rdn on outer over 1f out: kpt on wl and pressed ldr fr 1f out: stuck on and led last strides* **2/1**[2]

1- **2** *shd* **Senza Limiti (IRE)**[199] 7906 3-9-2 0 OisinMurphy 4 99+
(William Haggas) *bhd ldr on outer and t.k.h: rdn wl over 1f out and led jst ins fnl f: kpt on wl in narrow ld tl hdd last strides: gng on after post and difficult to pull up* **6/5**[1]

311- **3** *2 1/2* **Riviera Nights**[203] 7779 3-9-5 91 RyanMoore 5 96
(Richard Hannon) *led: rdn 2f out: hdd jst ins fnl f and lost 2nd briefly after: one pce* **12/1**

216- **4** *1/2* **Leroy Leroy**[181] 8462 3-9-2 94 SilvestreDeSousa 7 92
(Richard Hannon) *racd in mid-div: rdn over 2f out: ev ch over 1f out and kpt on: no ex and plugged on one pce fnl f* **12/1**

-213 **5** *1 3/4* **Target Zone**[45] 1035 3-9-2 94 DavidProbert 3 88
(David Elsworth) *t.k.h bhd ldr on inner: settled bttr by 1/2-way: effrt 2f out: one pce fr over 1f out (jockey said colt hung left-handed throughout)* **7/1**[3]

6-40 **6** *8* **Chairmanoftheboard (IRE)**[8] 1736 3-9-2 94 CallumShepherd 6 70
(Mick Channon) *hld up in last pair: rdn over 2f out: one pce* **25/1**

7 *2 1/4* **Juan De Valdes** 3-8-9 0 JosephineGordon 1 57
(Shaun Keightley) *hld up in last pair: rdn over 2f out: one pce* **66/1**

1m 37.5s (-2.30) **Going Correction** -0.075s/f (Stan) 7 Ran SP% **112.0**
Speed ratings (Par 104): **108,107,105,104,103 95,92**
CSF £4.52 TOTE £2.60: £1.20, £1.70; EX 5.40 Trifecta £31.90.
Owner Sheikh Rashid Dalmook Al Maktoum **Bred** Hungerford Park Stud & Al Shaqab Racing **Trained** Newmarket, Suffolk

FOCUS
This was steadily run and developed into a bit of a dash. The winner did well to come from behind.

1941 RACING TV SNOWDROP FILLIES' STKS (LISTED RACE) 1m (P)
3:45 (3:45) (Class 1) 4-Y-0+

£25,519 (£9,675; £4,842; £2,412; £1,210; £607) Stalls Low

Form RPR

425- **1** **Agrotera (IRE)**[204] 7732 4-9-0 102 GeraldMosse 5 106
(Ed Walker) *ponied arnd paddock and to s: t.k.h bhd ldrs on inner: rdn wl over 1f out: led 1f out: styd on wl fnl f* **7/2**[1]

335- **2** *1* **Preening**[240] 6459 4-9-0 97 DavidProbert 6 104
(James Fanshawe) *hld up in rr-div: shkn up and prog gng wl over 2f out w a bit to do: rdn 2f out: styng on wl fnl f* **10/1**[3]

221- **3** *3/4* **Rawdaa**[196] 7985 4-9-0 96 RyanMoore 2 102+
(Sir Michael Stoute) *hld up in rr: shkn up and swtchd to outer over 2f out: rdn 2f out w a bit to do: kpt on strly fnl f to take 3rd cl home: nvr nrr* **9/2**[2]

052- **4** *1* **Shenanigans (IRE)**[161] 9002 5-9-0 96 AndreaAtzeni 11 100
(Roger Varian) *early ldr: sn chsd ldrs: rdn 2f out and led over 1f out: hdd 1f out: plugged on tl lost 3rd cl home* **10/1**[3]

-111 **5** *3/4* **Tiger Eye (IRE)**[35] 1234 4-9-0 91 OisinMurphy 1 98
(James Fanshawe) *hld up in rr-div: effrt w plenty to do 2f out: nt clrest run wl over 1f out: pushed out ent fnl f* **7/2**[1]

024- **6** *1/2* **Savaanah (IRE)**[181] 8449 4-9-0 95 SilvestreDeSousa 10 97
(Roger Charlton) *racd in mid-div: rdn over 2f out: plugged on* **20/1**

206- **7** *1 1/4* **Dancing Brave Bear (USA)**[213] 7432 4-9-0 95 StevieDonohoe 3 94
(Ed Vaughan) *hld up in rr-div: rdn 2f out: kpt on one pce* **20/1**

166- **8** *2* **Anna Nerium**[181] 8448 4-9-0 108 TomMarquand 7 90
(Richard Hannon) *racd in mid-div: pushed along wl over 3f out: rdn over 2f out: stuck on one pce fr over 1f out* **10/1**[3]

330- **9** *1/2* **Queen Of Time**[161] 9002 5-9-0 98 HarryBentley 13 88
(Henry Candy) *cl up bhd ldrs: rdn 2f out: sn one pce* **20/1**

004- **10** *1* **Vivianite (IRE)**[176] 8618 4-9-0 92 LukeMorris 9 86
(Archie Watson) *cl up bhd ldrs: rdn 2f out: outpcd and plugged on over 1f out* **33/1**

261- **11** *1* **Shepherd Market (IRE)**[213] 7445 4-9-3 96 AdamKirby 14 87
(Clive Cox) *w ldr: rdn 2f out: ev ch wl over 1f out: fnd nil and wknd* **40/1**

1- **12** *1 1/4* **Daddy's Daughter (CAN)**[166] 8881 4-9-0 0 (w) MartinDwyer 4 81
(Dean Ivory) *hld up in last: shuffled along w plenty to do over 2f out: nvr involved* **20/1**

111- **13** *nse* **Contrive (IRE)**[138] 9384 4-9-0 91 DavidEgan 8 81
(Roger Varian) *early spd: settled in mid-div: rdn 2f out: kpt on tl wknd 1f out* **16/1**

1-3 **14** *1 1/4* **Astonished (IRE)**[22] 1400 4-9-0 0 PJMcDonald 12 78
(James Tate) *led after 2f: rdn 2f out: hdd over 1f out: wknd qckly* **20/1**

1m 37.01s (-2.79) **Going Correction** -0.075s/f (Stan) 14 Ran SP% **125.0**
Speed ratings (Par 108): **110,109,108,107,106 106,104,102,102,101 100,99,98,97**
CSF £36.58 TOTE £4.20: £1.70, £3.10, £1.70; EX 35.70 Trifecta £199.90.
Owner B E Nielsen **Bred** Bjorn Nielsen **Trained** Upper Lambourn, Berks
■ Stewards' Enquiry : David Probert two-day ban: careless riding (May 6-7)

FOCUS
They went a solid gallop and this looks reliable form for the grade.

1942 WISE BETTING AT RACINGTV.COM H'CAP 6f (P)
4:15 (4:16) (Class 2) (0-105,104) 4-Y-0+

£15,562 (£4,660; £2,330; £1,165; £582; £292) Stalls Low

Form RPR

00-6 **1** **Embour (IRE)**[12] 1654 4-8-4 87 MartinDwyer 1 94
(Richard Hannon) *hld up towards rr on inner: shkn up 2f out and clsr whn rdn over 1f out: kpt on wl and led jst ins fnl f: strly pressed last 110yds but kpt finding* **12/1**

100- **2** *nse* **Vibrant Chords**[239] 6485 6-9-1 98 RyanMoore 4 104
(Henry Candy) *racd in 4th: rdn 2f out: kpt on and ev ch 1f out: pressed wnr last 110yds but unable to get past* **14/1**

2036 **3** *1/2* **Exchequer (IRE)**[1] 1916 8-8-6 89 (p) PhilipPrince 2 93
(Richard Guest) *led for 2f: sn bhd ldr: rdn 2f out: stuck on wl on outer fr over 1f out and ch last 110yds: no ex last strides* **5/1**[3]

61-3 **4** *shd* **Indian Tygress**[23] 1382 4-8-2 85 DavidEgan 5 89
(James Fanshawe) *hld up in rr: rdn 2f out: gd prog over 1f out: keeping on last 150yds but no ex* **5/2**[1]

4600 **5** *shd* **Victory Wave (USA)**[51] 960 5-8-13 96 (h) OisinMurphy 7 100
(Saeed bin Suroor) *racd in 3rd: shkn up over 2f out: rdn 2f out: outpcd over 1f out: kpt on again fnl f and styng on at fin* **8/1**

5411 **6** *1 1/4* **Global Tango (IRE)**[18] 1496 4-8-5 88 (b) SilvestreDeSousa 8 88
(Charles Hills) *s.s and rousted along leaving stalls to ld after 2f: build up 4 l ld by 1/2-way: rdn 2f out: hdd jst ins fnl f: wknd last 150yds (jockey said gelding hung left-handed throughout)* **9/2**[2]

00-0 **7** *3/4* **Naadirr (IRE)**[20] 1459 8-8-9 92 (v) JamieSpencer 3 89
(Kevin Ryan) *hld up in rr: angled to inner and rdn 2f out: kpt on tl no ex 1f out: one pce fnl f* **20/1**

00-4 **8** *hd* **Tis Marvellous**[21] 1412 5-9-7 104 (t) AdamKirby 10 101
(Clive Cox) *towards rr: rdn on outer 2f out: nt qckn over 1f out: nt clr run 1f out: pushed out fnl f* **13/2**

1112 **9** *3 1/4* **Treacherous**[28] 1290 5-8-2 85 oh2 LukeMorris 6 71
(Ed de Giles) *hld up towards rr: rdn 2f out: one pce after* **11/1**

1m 11.01s (-2.09) **Going Correction** -0.075s/f (Stan) 9 Ran SP% **115.3**
Speed ratings (Par 109): **110,109,109,109,109 107,106,106,101**
CSF £164.37 CT £952.15 TOTE £12.80: £3.80, £4.30, £1.80; EX 159.00 Trifecta £1408.70.
Owner Sullivanb'Stock,Ruxleyholdings,Mrs Doyle **Bred** Carpet Lady Partnership **Trained** East Everleigh, Wilts

FOCUS
They went a good gallop but finished in a heap.

1943 RACING TV QUEEN'S PRIZE H'CAP 1m 7f 218y(P)
4:50 (4:50) (Class 2) (0-100,101) 4-Y-0+

£15,562 (£4,660; £2,330; £1,165; £582; £292) Stalls Low

Form RPR

12-1 **1** **Eden Rose**[26] 1330 4-8-9 85 DavidEgan 3 96+
(Mick Channon) *bhd ldrs: impr 6f out to ld: kicked for home over 3f out: kpt on wl fr over 1f out: galloped on fnl f* **3/1**[2]

232- **2** *1 1/4* **Sharja Silk**[201] 7838 4-8-7 83 AndreaAtzeni 5 91+
(Roger Varian) *bhd ldrs: tk clsr order bef first winning post to ld: hdd 6f out and remained w wnr: rdn 3f out: kpt on wl but unable to get past fr over 1f out* **9/4**[1]

514/ **3** *5* **Fibonacci**[101] 5-8-8 82 DavidProbert 2 84
(Alan King) *cl up: rdn to chse ldng pair over 3f out: plugged on but no ch w ldng pair* **33/1**

0562 **4** *hd* **Cosmelli (ITY)**[19] 1483 6-9-9 97 (b) DanielMuscutt 10 99
(Gay Kelleway) *led: hdd after first winning post: remained handy: rdn over 3f out: plugged on one pce* **25/1**

0- **5** *1 3/4* **Cliffs Of Dooneen (IRE)**[188] 8242 4-9-11 101 HarryBentley 8 101
(Ralph Beckett) *hld up in rr-div: prog over 4f out: rdn over 3f out: kpt on one pce fr over 1f out* **14/1**

14-0 **6** *3 1/2* **Archimento**[21] 1425 6-8-10 84 SilvestreDeSousa 7 80
(William Knight) *hld up in rr: in last over 4f out: rdn over 3f out: kpt on past btn rivals fr 2f out* **25/1**

00-0 **7** *nk* **Gavlar**[28] 1291 8-8-0 81 oh4 (v) GeorgiaDobie(7) 1 76
(William Knight) *hld up in rr: rdn 3f out: plugged on one pce* **25/1**

111- **8** *1* **What A Welcome**[197] 7952 5-9-12 100 JoeyHaynes 6 94
(Patrick Chamings) *rrd s and plld hrd in snatches thrght: rdn over 3f out: no ex over 2f out* **15/2**

3-61 **9** *1 1/2* **Cayirli (FR)**[77] 558 7-9-3 91 FergusSweeney 11 83
(Seamus Durack) *bhd ldrs: rdn over 3f out and outpcd: plugged on fr over 1f out* **12/1**

003- **10** *2* **Polish**[216] 7337 4-8-7 83 PJMcDonald 9 73
(Roger Charlton) *in rr: pushed along over 4f out: no prog fr over 2f out* **6/1**[3]

262- **11** *3* **Never Surrender (IRE)**[197] 7952 5-8-11 85 JamieSpencer 4 71
(Charles Hills) *hld up in mid-div: rdn over 3f out: no imp sn after* **12/1**

3m 29.86s (-0.24) **Going Correction** -0.075s/f (Stan)
WFA 4 from 5yo+ 2lb 11 Ran SP% **118.4**
Speed ratings (Par 109): **97,96,93,93,92 91,91,90,89,88 87**
CSF £9.72 CT £184.25 TOTE £4.20: £1.50, £1.20, £7.60; EX 12.40 Trifecta £136.20.
Owner Jon and Julia Aisbitt **Bred** Jon And Julia Aisbitt **Trained** West Ilsley, Berks

FOCUS
They went fairly steady early and it didn't pay to be too far off the pace. The first two finished nicely clear, though.
T/Plt: £690.80 to a £1 stake. Pool: £57,841.27 - 61.12 winning units T/Qpdt: £124.60 to a £1 stake. Pool: £5,036.32 - 29.90 winning units **Cathal Gahan**

[1499] MUSSELBURGH (R-H)
Saturday, April 20

OFFICIAL GOING: Good (good to firm in places; 8.4)
Wind: Light, half against in sprints and in 4f of home straight in races on the round course Weather: Sunny, warm

1944 SILVER ARROW H'CAP 7f 33y
1:50 (1:50) (Class 3) (0-95,97) 4-Y-0+

£12,450 (£3,728; £1,864; £932; £466; £234) Stalls Low

Form RPR

04-4 **1** **Three Saints Bay (IRE)**[18] 1502 4-9-7 93 DanielTudhope 3 106
(David O'Meara) *trckd ldrs: smooth hdwy to ld over 1f out: drvn clr fnl f* **6/1**[3]

10-3 **2** *4 1/2* **Hayadh**[18] 1502 6-9-3 89 DavidAllan 4 90
(Rebecca Bastiman) *prom: rdn over 2f out: hdwy to chse (clr) wnr ins fnl f: kpt on: no imp* **11/2**[2]

532- **3** *1 1/4* **Commander Han (FR)**[207] 7647 4-9-4 90 KevinStott 6 88
(Kevin Ryan) *midfield: drvn along over 2f out: hdwy and hung rt over 1f out: kpt on ins fnl f: nt pce to chal* **17/2**

060- **4** *2* **Lake Volta (IRE)**[189] 8194 4-9-11 97 JoeFanning 5 89
(Mark Johnston) *dwlt: hld up: rdn and hung rt over 2f out: kpt on fnl f to take 4th nr fin: nvr able to chal (jockey said gelding anticipated the start)* **13/2**

51-2 **5** *1/2* **Raselasad (IRE)**[18] 1502 5-9-3 89 RoystonFfrench 10 80
(Tracy Waggott) *led: sn crossed to ins rail and stdd gallop: rdn and hdd over 1f out: rallied: wknd ins fnl f* **13/2**

04-0 **6** *2 3/4* **Brian The Snail (IRE)**[21] 1413 5-9-6 92 PaulHanagan 8 75
(Richard Fahey) *s.i.s: sn pushed along in rr: rdn whn checked 3f out: nvr on terms (jockey said gelding was hampered by the fall of Porth Swtan)* **8/1**

60-0 **7** *7* **Ower Fly**[20] 1459 6-9-1 87 JamesSullivan 9 52
(Ruth Carr) *pressed ldr: rdn along over 2f out: wknd over 1f out* **25/1**

311- **8** *11* **Parys Mountain (IRE)**[165] 8898 5-9-2 **88**..................(h) PaulMulrennan 2 23
(Tim Easterby) *s.i.s: bhd and outpcd: struggling whn checked 3f out: sn btn (jockey said gelding was hampered by the fall of porth swtan)* **14/1**

00-1 **F** **Porth Swtan (IRE)**[18] 1502 4-9-6 **92**.................................. JasonHart 1
(Garry Moss) *in tch: rdn along whn broke down fatally 3f out* **5/2**[1]

320- **U** **Garrick**[294] 4395 5-9-1 **87**.................................. RachelRichardson 7
(Tim Easterby) *hld up on ins: shkn up whn checked and uns rdr 3f out* **33/1**

1m 27.21s (-1.79) **Going Correction** +0.075s/f (Good) **10** Ran SP% **120.0**
Speed ratings (Par 107): **113,107,106,104,103 100,92,79, ,**
CSF £40.24 CT £286.31 TOTE £6.00: £1.90, £2.40, £3.50; EX 34.50 Trifecta £394.90.
Owner Gary Douglas **Bred** Epona Bloodstock Ltd **Trained** Upper Helmsley, N Yorks

FOCUS
All distances as advertised. A race marred by the horrible injury suffered by Porth Swtan. They went a good gallop but the race was over as a contest when Three Saints Bay swept to the front over a furlong out. He gave the second and fifth a much bigger beating than over C&D latest.

1945 ROYAL MILE H'CAP — 1m 2y
2:25 (2:25) (Class 2) (0-100,89) 3-Y-O

£18,675 (£5,592; £2,796; £1,398; £699; £351) **Stalls** Low

Form RPR

1-33 **1** **Coolagh Forest (IRE)**[86] 391 3-8-12 **80**........................ PaulHanagan 3 86
(Richard Fahey) *prom: drvn and outpcd 3f out: rallied wl over 1f out: kpt on wl fnl f to ld cl home* **13/2**[3]

421 **2** *nk* **Reggae Runner (FR)**[63] 761 3-9-0 **82**............................ JoeFanning 1 87
(Mark Johnston) *t.k.h early: pressed ldr: rdn to ld over 1f out: kpt on: hdd cl home* **11/4**[1]

612- **3** *1 ½* **Politicise (IRE)**[194] 8057 3-9-3 **85**................................ DanielTudhope 6 87+
(William Haggas) *s.i.s: hld up: effrt on outside over 2f out: sn rdn: hdwy to chse ldng pair ins fnl f: r.o* **11/4**[1]

15-0 **4** *1 ¼* **Lincoln Park**[8] 1736 3-9-4 **86**.. DougieCostello 5 85
(Michael Appleby) *t.k.h: led: rdn and hdd over 1f out: no ex ins fnl f (jockey said colt hung left on the bend)* **16/1**

4212 **5** *2* **On The Line (IRE)**[12] 1646 3-9-5 **87**..................(bt) JackMitchell 2 81
(Hugo Palmer) *s.i.s: hld up: effrt and angled lft over 2f out: rdn and edgd lft over 1f out: sn no imp* **3/1**[2]

0-23 **6** *1 ¾* **Howzer Black (IRE)**[24] 1360 3-8-6 **79**.................. SeanDavis(5) 4 69
(Keith Dalgleish) *prom: effrt and rdn over 2f out: hung lft over 1f out: sn wknd* **9/1**

21-6 **7** *7* **Amadeus Grey (IRE)**[12] 1646 3-9-2 **84**........................ DavidAllan 7 58
(Tim Easterby) *chsd ldrs: drvn along over 2f out: wknd over 1f out* **14/1**

1m 39.68s (-0.32) **Going Correction** +0.075s/f (Good) **7** Ran SP% **114.2**
Speed ratings (Par 104): **104,103,102,100,98 97,90**
CSF £24.66 CT £60.52 TOTE £6.40: £2.70, £1.70; EX 26.70 Trifecta £126.80.
Owner Alan Harte **Bred** Leaf Stud **Trained** Musley Bank, N Yorks

FOCUS
Not a strong race for the grade, with the highest-rated runner competing off a mark of 87 despite this being open to horses rated up to 100. They went a gallop and the winner, who is rated just 80, needed every yard of the mile to get on top. The positive side of the form is that the front three are all fairly unexposed. The form may limit the form.

1946 SCOTTISH SPRINT CUP H'CAP — 5f 1y
3:00 (3:01) (Class 2) 4-Y-O+

£31,125 (£9,320; £4,660; £2,330; £1,165; £585) **Stalls** High

Form RPR

5142 **1** **Saaheq**[16] 1552 5-8-3 **85**.. HollieDoyle 15 94
(Michael Appleby) *prom on nr side of gp: rdn to ld over 1f out: kpt on wl fnl f* **11/2**[1]

553- **2** *¾* **Final Venture**[203] 7766 7-9-7 **103**................................ PaulMulrennan 17 109
(Paul Midgley) *led against stands' rail: rdn and hdd over 1f out: rallied: kpt on fnl f: hld towards fin* **10/1**

-651 **3** *1 ¾* **Mokaatil**[5] 1814 4-8-3 **90** 5ex.................................. AndrewBreslin(5) 10 90
(Ian Williams) *midfield towards nr side of gp: drvn along 1/2-way: hdwy to chse ldng pair over 1f out: kpt on fnl f: nt pce to chal* **10/1**

441- **4** *1 ¾* **Copper Knight (IRE)**[164] 8933 5-9-4 **100**..................(t) DavidAllan 8 93
(Tim Easterby) *bhd and sn pushed along in centre of gp: hdwy and looking for room over 1f out: kpt on fnl f: nrst fin* **10/1**

30-2 **5** *nk* **Line Of Reason (IRE)**[3] 1847 9-8-12 **94**...................... ConnorBeasley 5 86
(Paul Midgley) *bhd and outpcd in centre of gp: hdwy over 1f out: kpt on fnl f: nrst fin* **9/1**[3]

3414 **6** *½* **Primo's Comet**[36] 1211 4-7-11 **82** oh1.................. JamieGormley(3) 12 73
(Jim Goldie) *bhd and outpcd towards stands' rail: nt clr run and swtchd to wd outside fr over 1f out: kpt on ins fnl f: no imp (jockey said gelding hung left)* **10/1**

010- **7** *hd* **A Momentofmadness**[196] 7974 6-9-8 **104**..............(h) DanielTudhope 7 94
(Charles Hills) *dwlt: sn pushed along in midfield towards outside of gp: effrt and prom over 1f out: kpt on same pce ins fnl f (jockey said gelding missed the break)* **7/1**[2]

00-4 **8** *¾* **Royal Brave (IRE)**[18] 1501 8-8-9 **91**........................ RoystonFfrench 11 78
(Rebecca Bastiman) *midfield against stands' rail: rdn over 2f out: nt clr run briefly over 1f out: kpt on fnl f: no imp* **10/1**

00-0 **9** *2 ¼* **Gabrial The Saint (IRE)**[12] 1654 4-8-3 **90**...................... SeanDavis(5) 4 69
(Richard Fahey) *dwlt: bhd and sn pushed along in centre of gp: drvn along 1/2-way: kpt on fnl f: n.d* **25/1**

060- **10** *½* **Harome (IRE)**[241] 6425 5-8-9 **91**.................................. BenCurtis 14 68
(Roger Fell) *prom in centre of gp: drvn along 1/2-way: wknd fnl f* **16/1**

1-60 **11** *2 ½* **Marnie James**[86] 393 4-9-3 **106**..................(t) ScottMcCullagh(7) 9 74
(Iain Jardine) *in tch in centre of gp: drvn along 1/2-way: n.m.r over 1f out: sn wknd* **33/1**

12-6 **12** *2 ½* **Captain Colby (USA)**[18] 1501 7-8-13 **98**.................. BenRobinson(3) 6 57
(Paul Midgley) *sn drvn along in midfield in centre of gp: outpcd 1/2-way: n.d* **14/1**

5000 **13** *¾* **Classic Pursuit**[3] 1860 8-8-1 **83** oh2 ow1...............(b) AndrewMullen 16 40
(Stef Keniry) *slowly away: bhd and outpcd on nr side of gp: nvr on terms* **80/1**

510- **14** *¾* **Eeh Bah Gum (IRE)**[210] 7527 4-8-7 **89**........................ RachelRichardson 3 43
(Tim Easterby) *spd on outside of gp tl wknd fr over 1f out: hld whn checked ins fnl f* **25/1**

0-15 **15** *1* **Soldier's Minute**[21] 1421 4-8-11 **93**.................................. JoeFanning 1 48
(Keith Dalgleish) *midfield on far side of gp: drvn along 1/2-way: wknd over 1f out: eased whn no ch ins fnl f* **12/1**

003- **16** *½* **Savalas (IRE)**[207] 7639 4-9-2 **98**.................................. TomEaves 2 46
(Kevin Ryan) *in tch on far side of gp: struggling over 2f out: sn btn* **6/1**[2]

58.79s (-0.91) **Going Correction** +0.075s/f (Good) **16** Ran SP% **124.5**
Speed ratings (Par 109): **110,108,106,103,102 101,101,100,96,96 92,88,86,85,84 83**
CSF £58.60 CT £552.47 TOTE £6.40: £3.30, £2.90, £2.70, £2.60; EX 64.40 Trifecta £899.90.
Owner The Horse Watchers **Bred** Cliveden Stud Ltd **Trained** Oakham, Rutland

FOCUS
A competitive sprint handicap on paper but those drawn high had a clear edge up the rail and very few got into this, especially from the single-figure stalls. Everything went to plan for the well-backed winner who provided trainer Michael Appleby with a third success in the race. The form is rated a round thew runner-up to last year's best.

1947 QUEEN'S CUP STKS (A HERITAGE H'CAP) — 1m 5f 216y
3:35 (3:35) (Class 2) 4-Y-O+

£62,250 (£18,640; £9,320; £4,660; £2,330; £1,170) **Stalls** Low

Form RPR

223- **1** **Austrian School (IRE)**[197] 7951 4-9-5 **102**........................ JoeFanning 14 114
(Mark Johnston) *sn trcking ldr: led 3f out: pushed clr fr 2f out: readily* **4/1**[1]

1122 **2** *6* **Ulster (IRE)**[38] 1172 4-8-10 **93**.. HollieDoyle 6 97
(Archie Watson) *t.k.h early: trckd ldrs: effrt and chsd wnr over 2f out: rdn and hung rt over 1f out: kpt on fnl f: nt pce to chal* **4/1**[1]

3-42 **3** *hd* **Pipes Of Peace (IRE)**[21] 1422 5-8-10 **92**.......................(t) TomEaves 1 95
(Seamus Durack) *hld up in midfield: effrt whn nt clr run over 2f out: hdwy and angled lft wl over 1f out: kpt on fnl f: nrst fin* **15/2**[3]

-214 **4** *1* **Lucky Deal**[19] 1483 4-8-13 **96**.. FrannyNorton 10 98+
(Mark Johnston) *s.i.s: hld up: rdn over 4f out: hdwy on wd outside 2f out: kpt on fnl f: nvr able to chal* **11/1**

003- **5** *1 ¼* **Making Miracles**[161] 8995 4-9-1 **98**................................ AndrewMullen 5 98+
(Mark Johnston) *dwlt: hld up towards rr: drvn along over 3f out: hdwy wl over 1f out: kpt on fnl f: no imp* **8/1**

3-20 **6** *nk* **Kelly's Dino (FR)**[21] 1422 6-9-0 **96**...............................(p) BenCurtis 4 96
(K R Burke) *in tch: effrt and drvn along over 2f out: kpt on same pce fnl f* **11/2**[2]

66-6 **7** *1 ½* **Sir Chauvelin**[20] 1460 7-9-10 **106**................................ DanielTudhope 2 104
(Jim Goldie) *stdd s: hld up: hdwy whn n.m.r briefly 2f out: sn rdn along: no imp fnl f* **20/1**

050- **8** *nk* **Eye Of The Storm (IRE)**[189] 8188 9-8-0 **87**..................... SeanDavis(5) 7 84
(Keith Dalgleish) *in tch: effrt and drvn along 3f out: wknd over 1f out* **25/1**

300- **9** *nk* **Mirsaale**[245] 4390 9-8-10 **92**.................................(p) JamesSullivan 3 89
(Keith Dalgleish) *hld up: effrt and pushed along over 2f out: no imp fr over 1f out* **16/1**

220- **10** *1 ¾* **Hochfeld (IRE)**[161] 9005 5-9-2 **103**.............................. AndrewBreslin(5) 12 97
(Mark Johnston) *in tch: drvn along 3f out: wknd over 1f out* **9/1**

46-4 **11** *1* **Tor**[106] 61 5-8-5 **90**.. JamieGormley(3) 9 83
(Iain Jardine) *hld up: rdn along 3f out: nvr on terms* **25/1**

320- **12** *hd* **Fire Jet (IRE)**[185] 8332 6-8-5 **87**.................................. RoystonFfrench 11 80
(John Mackie) *hld up: outpcd wl over 2f out: sn btn* **28/1**

500- **13** *11* **My Reward**[238] 6550 7-9-4 **100**.. DavidAllan 8 77
(Tim Easterby) *led 1f: cl up tl rdn and wknd wl over 1f out* **50/1**

110- **14** *12* **Artarmon (IRE)**[190] 8149 4-8-7 **90**................................(v) PaulHanagan 13 51
(Michael Bell) *t.k.h: pressed ldr: led after 1f to 3f out: rdn and wknd 2f out* **16/1**

3m 0.01s (-3.89) **Going Correction** +0.075s/f (Good)
WFA 4 from 5yo+ 1lb **14** Ran SP% **123.3**
Speed ratings (Par 109): **114,110,110,109,109 109,108,107,107,106 106,106,99,92**
CSF £17.74 CT £120.21 TOTE £4.50: £1.90, £1.50, £2.20; EX 24.60 Trifecta £134.60.
Owner Dr J Walker **Bred** G O'Brien **Trained** Middleham Moor, N Yorks

FOCUS
A highly competitive renewal but Joe Fanning stole this with an injection of pace early in the home straight and he had this sewn up a long way out aboard the admirably consistent Austrian School. He built on last season's form.

1948 LIKE RACING TV ON FACEBOOK H'CAP — 1m 208y
4:05 (4:10) (Class 4) (0-85,87) 4-Y-O+

£5,692 (£1,694; £846; £423; £300; £300) **Stalls** Low

Form RPR

00-1 **1** **Ventura Gold (IRE)**[15] 1563 4-8-6 **73**............................ SeanDavis(5) 3 79
(Richard Fahey) *mde all at modest gallop: hrd pressed and rdn over 1f out: edgd lft ins fnl f: hld on wl cl home* **4/1**[3]

4001 **2** *hd* **Mont Kinabalu (IRE)**[11] 1659 4-8-12 **74**.............................. TomEaves 2 79+
(Kevin Ryan) *hld up: rdn over 2f out: hdwy and swtchd lft over 1f out: chsd wnr last 50yds: kpt on: jst hld* **3/1**[2]

205- **3** *1 ¼* **Jacob Black**[187] 8263 8-8-11 **73**..................................(p) JoeFanning 4 74
(Keith Dalgleish) *t.k.h early: prom: smooth hdwy and ev ch over 1f out to ins fnl f: rdn: one pce and lost 2nd last 50yds* **5/1**

5-00 **4** *shd* **Zeshov (IRE)**[10] 1695 8-8-11 **73**..............................(p) LewisEdmunds 1 74
(Rebecca Bastiman) *trckd ldrs: rdn along and n.m.r over 2f out and over 1f out: kpt on same pce ins fnl f* **12/1**

240- **5** *4* **Mulligatawny (IRE)**[183] 8371 6-9-7 **83**.........................(p) BenCurtis 5 75
(Roger Fell) *cl up: drvn along over 2f out: rallied: wknd fnl f* **2/1**[1]

005- **6** *6* **Brilliant Vanguard (IRE)**[323] 3325 6-9-6 **87**............. BenSanderson(5) 6 66
(Kevin Ryan) *stdd and swtchd rt s: hld up: rdn over 2f out: wknd appr fnl f* **9/1**

1m 54.42s (1.32) **Going Correction** +0.075s/f (Good) **6** Ran SP% **112.7**
Speed ratings (Par 105): **97,96,95,95,92 86**
CSF £16.46 TOTE £4.60: £2.20, £1.80; EX 13.90 Trifecta £49.20.
Owner Middleham Park Racing XLVIII & Partner **Bred** Michael Fennessy **Trained** Musley Bank, N Yorks

FOCUS
Not the most competitive of Class 4 handicaps and it was run at a steady enough gallop but it threw up a cracking finish and Ventura Gold dug deep into his reserves to follow up his Leicester win. The form has been rated cautiously.

1949 FOLLOW @RACINGTV ON TWITTER (S) STKS — 1m 4f 104y
4:40 (4:43) (Class 4) 4-Y-O+ **£5,692** (£1,694; £846; £423; £300) **Stalls** Low

Form RPR

204/ **1** **Clayton**[36] 1569 10-9-2 96....................................(t) HollieDoyle 2 74
(Archie Watson) *mde all at stdy gallop: rdn along and edgd lft 2f out: edgd rt and kpt on strly fnl f* **6/5**[1]

00/6 **2** *3* **Apterix (FR)**[9] 1719 9-8-13 75.................................... BenRobinson(3) 5 69
(Brian Ellison) *pressed wnr: ev ch over 4f out to over 2f out: one pce whn hung rt over 1f out (jockey said gelding hung right in the home straight)* **9/1**

04-0 **3** *8* **Andok (IRE)**[21] 1418 5-9-1 74.......................................(p) SeanDavis(5) 6 61
(Richard Fahey) *hld up in tch: drvn over 4f out: chsd clr ldng pair over 2f out: no imp over 1f out* **6/1**[3]

050- **4** *3* **Hayward Field (IRE)**[144] 9271 6-9-2 47.............................. ConnorBeasley 3 52
(Noel Wilson) *t.k.h: hld up in tch: outpcd over 2f out: edgd rt and btn over 1f out* **33/1**

250- **5** 3 1/2 **Grand Inquisitor**[36] 9534 7-9-2 **86**.. BenCurtis 4 47
(Ian Williams) *chsd ldrs to over 2f out: rdn and wknd over 1f out* **13/8**[2]

2m 45.12s (0.62) **Going Correction** +0.075s/f (Good) **5** Ran SP% **110.8**
Speed ratings (Par 105): **100,98,92,90,88**
CSF £12.33 TOTE £1.80: £1.20, £3.60; EX 9.70 Trifecta £22.80.There was no bid for the winner
Owner Marco Polo **Bred** G Reed **Trained** Upper Lambourn, W Berks

FOCUS
Stronger than many sellers with the winner rated 96, although it has been almost three years since he's been seen in this sphere so it was anyone's guess whether he was still worthy of that sort of mark. The runner-up is rated 21lb inferior and was carrying the same weight, so Clayton didn't need to run to his mark to win. The form is limited by the fourth.

1950 RACINGTV.COM H'CAP (DIV I) 5f 1y
5:15 (5:18) (Class 5) (0-75,77) 4-Y-O+
£4,398 (£1,309; £654; £327; £300; £300) **Stalls** High

Form RPR

03-2 **1** **Super Julius**[5] 1818 5-8-8 **62**..(p) BenCurtis 1 70
(S Donohoe, Ire) *mde all: sn crossed over to ins rail: rdn: hrd pressed and edgd rt ins fnl f: kpt on wl cl home* **5/2**[1]

004- **2** 3/4 **Suwaan (IRE)**[143] 9288 5-9-1 **69**.. JamesSullivan 7 74
(Ruth Carr) *in tch: hdwy over 1f out: hdwy to and ev ch whn carried hd high and carried sltly rt ins fnl f: nt go past* **9/2**[3]

1-04 **3** 1 3/4 **Gold Stone**[51] 953 4-9-4 **72**.. ShaneGray 9 71
(Kevin Ryan) *sn rdn along towards rr: hdwy over 1f out: chsd ldng pair ins fnl f: kpt on: nt pce to chal* **6/1**

00-0 **4** hd **Jeffrey Harris**[22] 1403 4-8-7 **61** oh2..(h) PhilDennis 8 59
(Jim Goldie) *dwlt: bhd: effrt on outside over 2f out: kpt on same pce ins fnl f* **20/1**

060- **5** 3/4 **Kinloch Pride**[183] 8383 7-8-10 **64**..(p) PaulHanagan 3 60
(Noel Wilson) *pressed ldr: drvn over 1f out: fdd ins fnl f* **12/1**

-450 **6** 1 3/4 **Chookie Dunedin**[19] 1487 4-9-9 **77**.. ConnorBeasley 2 66
(Keith Dalgleish) *in tch on outside: drvn along over 2f out: wknd ins fnl f* **3/1**[2]

0555 **7** 2 **Lord Of The Glen**[18] 1505 4-8-4 **61**.. JamieGormley(3) 4 43
(Jim Goldie) *chsd ldrs: drvn along 1/2-way: wknd over 1f out* **17/2**

0-00 **8** 1/2 **Rumshak (IRE)**[7] 1760 4-9-0 **73**..(t[1]) PaulaMuir(5) 10 53
(Michael Dods) *dwlt: bhd and pushed along: hung rt over 1f out: nvr on terms* **12/1**

-000 **9** 36 **Orient Class**[22] 1403 8-9-1 **69**.. GrahamLee 6
(Paul Midgley) *t.k.h: trckd ldrs tl lost pl wl over 1f out: sn eased (vet reported gelding was lame left fore)* **14/1**

59.4s (-0.30) **Going Correction** +0.075s/f (Good) **9** Ran SP% **123.4**
Speed ratings (Par 103): **105,103,101,100,99 96,93,92,35**
CSF £15.27 CT £64.58 TOTE £3.20: £1.20, £1.80, £2.00; EX 15.00 Trifecta £71.70.
Owner S Donohoe **Bred** T R G Vestey **Trained** Cootehill Road, Co. Cavan
■ Amazing Grazing was withdrawn. Price at time of withdrawal 3/1. Rule 4 applies to board prices prior to withdrawal - deduction 25p in the pound. New market formed

FOCUS
Not many in-form horses in here and not a particularly strong contest even for this grade. The first two were both well in on last season's form.

1951 RACINGTV.COM H'CAP (DIV II) 5f 1y
5:45 (5:51) (Class 5) (0-75,75) 4-Y-O+
£4,398 (£1,309; £654; £327; £300; £300) **Stalls** High

Form RPR

60-1 **1** **Pennsylvania Dutch**[7] 1760 5-9-2 **75**..(e) SeanDavis(5) 3 83
(Kevin Ryan) *dwlt: hld up: hdwy on outside over 2f out: led 1f out: rdn and edgd rt ins fnl f: r.o* **3/1**[1]

400- **2** 3/4 **Burmese Blazer (IRE)**[143] 9281 4-8-6 **63**..(h) BenRobinson(3) 4 68
(Jim Goldie) *dwlt: bhd: hdwy and swtchd rt over 1f out: effrt and pressed wnr ins fnl f: kpt on: hld nr fin* **7/1**

3431 **3** 1 **Gowanbuster**[22] 1403 4-9-0 **68**..(t) PaulMulrennan 1 69
(Susan Corbett) *led: rdn and hdd over 1f out: kpt on same pce ins fnl f* **11/2**[3]

11-1 **4** nk **Our Place In Loule**[18] 1505 6-9-5 **73**..(b) PaulHanagan 8 73
(Noel Wilson) *in tch: pushed along over 2f out: effrt whn nt clr run and swtchd rt ent fnl f: kpt on: no imp (jockey said gelding was denied a clear run approaching the final furlong)* **11/2**[3]

1 **5** shd **Tabaahy**[14] 1598 4-9-6 **74**.. DanielTudhope 9 74
(David O'Meara) *cl up: ev ch and rdn over 1f out: kpt on same pce ins fnl f* **7/2**[2]

540/ **6** 3/4 **Lathom**[512] 8927 6-9-2 **70**.. GrahamLee 2 67+
(Paul Midgley) *prom: smooth hdwy to ld briefly over 1f out: rdn and outpcd ins fnl f* **12/1**

66-0 **7** 1/2 **Economic Crisis (IRE)**[18] 1505 10-8-7 **61**.. JamesSullivan 7 56
(Alan Berry) *prom: n.m.r over 2f out and over 1f out: btn ins fnl f* **33/1**

000- **8** 1 1/2 **Havana Go**[150] 9182 4-8-7 **61**.. JoeFanning 6 51
(Keith Dalgleish) *bhd and outpcd: struggling 1/2-way: nvr on terms* **8/1**

030- **9** 8 **Super Florence (IRE)**[193] 8077 4-8-12 **69**.. JamieGormley(3) 5 30
(Iain Jardine) *t.k.h: trckd ldrs: rdn over 2f out: wknd over 1f out* **16/1**

59.87s (0.17) **Going Correction** +0.075s/f (Good) **9** Ran SP% **118.1**
Speed ratings (Par 103): **101,99,98,97,97 96,95,93,80**
CSF £25.20 CT £111.88 TOTE £4.10: £1.60, £1.90, £1.60; EX 23.40 Trifecta £79.60.
Owner K&J Bloodstock Ltd **Bred** Lael Stables **Trained** Hambleton, N Yorks

FOCUS
More competitive than the first division with four last-time-out winners in the line-up but it wasn't the cleanest race and one or two didn't get the rub of the green. The winner was still on a good mark after his Thirsk win.
T/Plt: £64.10 to a £1 stake. Pool: £103,587.65 - 1,178.16 winning units T/Qpdt: £7.40 to a £1 stake. Pool: £9,259.16 - 924.57 winning units **Richard Young**

1690 NOTTINGHAM (L-H)
Saturday, April 20

OFFICIAL GOING: Good to firm (good in places; watered)
Wind: Fine Weather: Nil

1952 UK MEDS DIRECT APPRENTICE H'CAP 5f 8y
4:30 (4:35) (Class 6) (0-65,67) 4-Y-O+
£3,234 (£962; £481; £400; £400; £400) **Stalls** Centre

Form RPR

610- **1** **Major Valentine**[201] 7829 7-9-5 **64**.. KateLeahy(7) 9 71
(John O'Shea) *hld up: hdwy 1/2-way: edgd lft ins fnl f: r.o to ld post* **16/1**

0602 **2** hd **Gamesome (FR)**[18] 1505 8-9-9 **64**.. ConnorMurtagh(3) 8 70
(Paul Midgley) *hld up: hdwy and swtchd lft over 1f out: rdn to ld ins fnl f: hdd post* **3/1**[2]

0-04 **3** 2 **Pearl Noir**[44] 1071 9-9-0 **55**..(b) TheodoreLadd(3) 3 54
(Scott Dixon) *w ldr tl led 2f out: rdn and hdd 1f out: styd on same pce ins fnl f* **14/1**

-464 **4** 1 1/4 **Coastal Cyclone**[36] 1210 5-8-13 **51**..(v) MitchGodwin 1 46
(Harry Dunlop) *chsd ldrs: ev ch 1f out: edgd rt and no ex ins fnl f (jockey said gelding hung right under pressure)* **10/1**

0562 **5** hd **You're Cool**[16] 1547 7-9-0 **59**..(t) IzzyClifton(7) 4 53
(John Balding) *led 3f: sn rdn: hmpd and no ex ins fnl f* **5/1**[3]

442- **6** 2 **Paco Escostar**[182] 8417 4-9-7 **62**.. DannyRedmond(3) 6 49
(Julie Camacho) *chsd ldrs: led 1f out: hdd ins fnl f: sn hung rt and wknd* **8/1**

0600 **7** 1 **Mutabaahy (IRE)**[19] 1487 4-9-10 **67**..(h) KieranSchofield(5) 7 50+
(Antony Brittain) *s.s: outpcd (jockey said gelding reared as the stalls opened)* **5/2**[1]

56-6 **8** 2 **Teepee Time**[91] 322 6-9-3 **55**..(b) JaneElliott 2 31
(Michael Mullineaux) *prom: lost pl and rdn 1/2-way: wknd over 1f out* **33/1**

00-5 **9** 1 1/4 **Flying Foxy**[17] 1521 5-9-2 **61**..(p) JessicaCooley(7) 11 32
(George Scott) *s.i.s: hdwy 1/2-way: rdn and wknd over 1f out* **14/1**

0030 **10** 3/4 **Swendab (IRE)**[14] 1595 11-8-7 **50** oh3..(b) AledBeech(5) 5 19
(John O'Shea) *s.i.s: sn pushed along in rr: rdn and lost pl over 3f out: n.d after (jockey said gelding was never travelling)* **33/1**

59.7s (-0.50) **Going Correction** -0.20s/f (Firm) **10** Ran SP% **115.5**
Speed ratings (Par 101): **96,95,92,90,90 86,85,82,80,78**
CSF £63.23 CT £713.56 TOTE £15.80: £4.70, £1.40, £3.70; EX 72.20 Trifecta £598.60.
Owner Pete Smith **Bred** J R Salter **Trained** Elton, Gloucs

FOCUS
The going was good to firm, good in places (GoingStick: 7.8). Races were run on the inner track with the rail out 2yds on the home bend, adding 6yds to distances on the round course. An ordinary apprentice sprint handicap to start in which they raced centre-to-far side. The winning time was 1.2sec outside standard.

1953 SOIZA FAMILY NOVICE STKS 5f 8y
5:05 (5:10) (Class 5) 2-Y-O
£4,140 (£1,232; £615; £307) **Stalls** Centre

Form RPR

1 **Temple Of Heaven** 2-9-5 0.. SeanLevey 4 85+
(Richard Hannon) *prom: jnd ldrs over 3f out: shkn up over 1f out: r.o to ld nr fin* **11/4**[2]

2 1/2 **Dylan De Vega** 2-9-5 0.. TonyHamilton 7 83+
(Richard Fahey) *w ldr tl rdn to ld and hung lft wl over 1f out: hdd nr fin* **14/1**

5 **3** 5 **Isobar Wind (IRE)**[8] 1733 2-9-5 0.. KieranO'Neill 1 65
(David Evans) *wnt lft s: sn w ldrs: pushed along 1/2-way: no ex fnl f* **9/1**

4 1 1/4 **Making History (IRE)** 2-9-5 0.. HayleyTurner 2 61+
(Saeed bin Suroor) *s.i.s: pushed along over 3f out: rdn 1/2-way: nt trble ldrs* **11/8**[1]

3 **5** 2 3/4 **Champagne Supanova (IRE)**[12] 1651 2-9-5 0.. TomQueally 5 51
(Richard Spencer) *dwlt: racd keenly: hdwy over 3f out: rdn over 1f out: hung lft and wknd ins fnl f* **9/1**

5 **6** 1 1/2 **Foad**[15] 1556 2-9-5 0.. JimCrowley 6 45
(Ed Dunlop) *led: rdn and hdd wl over 1f out: sn wknd* **9/2**[3]

7 9 **Zain Storm (FR)** 2-9-5 0.. PaddyMathers 3 13
(John Butler) *sn outpcd (trainer's rep said colt was unsuited by the undulating track)* **50/1**

59.65s (-0.55) **Going Correction** -0.20s/f (Firm) **7** Ran SP% **115.6**
Speed ratings (Par 92): **96,95,87,85,80 78,64**
CSF £39.67 TOTE £3.60: £1.60, £5.10; EX 41.50 Trifecta £157.00.
Owner Rockcliffe Stud **Bred** Highclere Stud & Jake Warren Ltd **Trained** East Everleigh, Wilts

FOCUS
An interesting 2yo contest with newcomers from the yards responsible for the last two winners of the race providing a stirring finish. The winning time was fractionally faster than the older horses in the opener and they raced up the middle.

1954 LEAFLABS H'CAP 5f 8y
5:35 (5:36) (Class 5) (0-70,70) 3-Y-O
£4,204 (£1,251; £625; £400; £400; £400) **Stalls** Centre

Form RPR

-201 **1** **Arishka (IRE)**[29] 1275 3-9-5 **68**.. KieranO'Neill 11 72
(Daniel Kubler) *chsd ldrs: shkn up 1/2-way: rdn and hung lft ins fnl f: r.o to ld nr fin* **7/1**[3]

105 **2** nk **Hanakotoba (USA)**[18] 1492 3-8-9 **65**..(t) MarkCrehan(7) 9 68
(Stuart Williams) *led: rdn and hung lft ins fnl f: hdd nr fin* **10/1**

1-55 **3** 1 1/4 **One One Seven (IRE)**[61] 783 3-8-8 **57**.. CamHardie 10 55
(Antony Brittain) *s.i.s: sn prom: rdn and hung lft fr over 1f out: styd on to go 3rd post* **8/1**

24-2 **4** nk **Cobweb Catcher**[12] 1650 3-8-13 **62**..(h) RobHornby 7 60
(Rod Millman) *w ldrs: rdn and ev ch fr over 1f out tl carried lft wl ins fnl f: lost 3rd post* **3/1**[1]

053- **5** 2 1/4 **Amazing Alba**[210] 7519 3-9-6 **69**.. RobbieDowney 1 58
(Michael Dods) *plld hrd: w ldr 1f: remained handy: rdn over 1f out: no ex ins fnl f* **5/1**[2]

0-03 **6** hd **Kickham Street**[29] 1275 3-8-13 **62**..(h) TonyHamilton 8 50
(John Quinn) *s.i.s: hld up: effrt and n.m.r over 1f out: nt clr run ins fnl f: nt trble ldrs* **8/1**

330- **7** 7 **Murqaab**[224] 7082 3-9-7 **70**.. DavidNolan 5 33
(David O'Meara) *prom: hmpd and lost pl over 4f out: rdn over 1f out: wknd fnl f* **5/1**[2]

55-0 **8** 1 1/2 **Cedar**[10] 1678 3-7-12 **54**..(v[1]) SaraDelFabbro(7) 2 12
(Mohamed Moubarak) *in tch: lost pl over 3f out: n.d after* **28/1**

20-0 **9** 1/2 **Teodula (IRE)**[93] 274 3-8-10 **64**.. DylanHogan(5) 3 20
(Henry Spiller) *s.s: pushed along 1/2-way: wknd over 1f out (vet reported filly was lame on its right fore)* **33/1**

410- **10** 6 **Legal Tender (IRE)**[183] 8368 3-9-0 **70**..(h) HarryRussell(7) 6 4
(Bryan Smart) *plld hrd: jnd ldrs 4f out tl pushed along 1/2-way: rdn: hung lft and wknd over 1f out* **16/1**

59.57s (-0.63) **Going Correction** -0.20s/f (Firm) **10** Ran SP% **114.4**
Speed ratings (Par 98): **97,96,94,94,90 90,78,76,75,66**
CSF £73.31 CT £430.73 TOTE £5.90: £2.20, £3.00, £2.40; EX 91.10 Trifecta £627.30.
Owner Crowd Racing & Diskovery Partnership Vi **Bred** John Malone **Trained** Lambourn, Berks

FOCUS
A modest 3yo sprint handicap and few got into it, with those that raced handily holding away. They started up the centre, though the principals edged towards the far side late on. It was marginally the fastest of the three races over the trip.

1955 JARROD MARSLAND 50TH BIRTHDAY H'CAP 1m 75y
6:05 (6:22) (Class 4) (0-80,80) 4-Y-O+
£7,762 (£2,310; £1,154; £577; £400; £400) Stalls Centre

Form RPR
3002 1 **Juanito Chico (IRE)**[2] 1882 5-9-1 74...........(t) JimCrowley 1 83
(Stuart Williams) *chsd ldrs: led 2f out: rdn clr fr over 1f out: eased nr fin* 2/1[1]
400- 2 5 **Mutarakez (IRE)**[233] 6711 7-9-3 76........... JackGarritty 6 74
(Ruth Carr) *s.i.s: hld up: hdwy over 2f out: rdn to chse wnr fnl f: styng on same pce whn hung lft wl ins fnl f (jockey said gelding hung both ways in the straight)* 20/1
-036 3 hd **Confrontational (IRE)**[29] 1273 5-9-7 80...........(p) TomQueally 4 77
(Jennie Candlish) *led: rdn and hdd 2f out: hung rt fr over 1f out: styd on same pce ins fnl f (jockey said gelding hung right)* 7/1
0- 4 1 3/4 **Kenstone (FR)**[177] 8580 6-9-0 80...........(p) MarkCrehan(7) 7 73
(Adrian Wintle) *chsd ldr: ev ch 2f out: sn rdn: no ex fnl f* 14/1
400- 5 3 1/4 **Kharbetation (IRE)**[196] 7993 6-9-6 79........... DavidNolan 5 65
(David O'Meara) *hld up: rdn over 3f out: nvr trbld ldrs* 5/1[3]
43-1 6 5 **Mr Tyrrell (IRE)**[12] 1655 5-9-7 80........... SeanLevey 3 54
(Richard Hannon) *prom: rdn over 3f out: wknd over 1f out* 5/1[3]
212/ 7 1 **Lady Of Aran (IRE)**[528] 8671 4-9-6 79........... HayleyTurner 2 51
(Charlie Fellowes) *hld up: plld hrd: hdwy 1/2-way: rdn and ev ch 2f out: wknd fnl f* 7/2[2]

1m 42.78s (-3.92) **Going Correction** -0.20s/f (Firm) 7 Ran SP% **112.8**
Speed ratings (Par 105): **111,106,105,104,100 95,94**
CSF £41.88 TOTE £2.70: £1.50, £5.40; EX 34.00 Trifecta £392.00.
Owner Tony Verrier **Bred** Miss Catherine Monaghan **Trained** Newmarket, Suffolk
FOCUS
Add 6yds to race distance. A fair handicap, taken apart by the favourite.

1956 CASTLE BEAUTY MAIDEN STKS 1m 2f 50y
6:35 (6:57) (Class 5) 3-Y-O £4,528 (£1,347; £673; £336) Stalls Low

Form RPR
6-4 1 **Dubai Instinct**[21] 1417 3-9-5 0........... CallumShepherd 7 88
(Brian Meehan) *mde virtually all: qcknd over 3f out: rdn over 2f out: edgd lft ins fnl f: styd on wl (trainer's rep was asked why they were running the colt on going described as good to firm, good in places having been declared a non-runner at nottingham 10th april on going with the same description. trainer's rep stated, following its run at doncaster* 7/1
2 1 3/4 **First In Line** 3-9-5 0........... RobertHavlin 1 84
(John Gosden) *s.i.s: sn prom: shkn up over 3f out: styd on to go 2nd ins fnl f: nt rch wnr* 13/8[1]
3 1 3/4 **Aktau** 3-9-5 0........... CharlieBennett 3 81
(Roger Varian) *s.i.s: sn chsng ldrs: shkn up and outpcd over 3f out: rdn and hung lft over 2f out: styd on to go 3rd nr fin* 20/1
34- 4 3/4 **Alhaazm**[129] 9499 3-9-5 0........... JimCrowley 5 79
(Sir Michael Stoute) *w wnr tl settled into 2nd over 7f out: rdn over 2f out: hung lft over 1f out: no ex ins fnl f* 2/1[2]
5 5 **Munaazil (IRE)** 3-9-5 0........... DaneO'Neill 8 69
(Roger Varian) *s.i.s: hld up: outpcd over 3f out: n.d after* 9/1
6- 6 10 **Memphis Bleek**[211] 7476 3-9-5 0........... TrevorWhelan 6 49
(Ivan Furtado) *hld up: hdwy over 3f out: wknd wl over 1f out* 50/1
54- 7 7 **Top Top (IRE)**[151] 9165 3-8-12 0........... TristanPrice(7) 11 35
(Sir Michael Stoute) *s.i.s: hld up and bhd: shkn up over 3f out: sn wknd (jockey said colt reared as the stalls opened)* 6/1[3]
0 8 6 **Lexington Warlord**[12] 1652 3-9-5 0........... SeanLevey 9 23
(Richard Hannon) *prom: lost pl over 8f out: shkn up and wknd over 3f out* 100/1

2m 12.15s (-1.25) **Going Correction** -0.20s/f (Firm) 8 Ran SP% **115.9**
Speed ratings (Par 98): **97,95,94,93,89 81,76,71**
CSF £18.99 TOTE £7.70: £2.20, £1.10, £3.10; EX 28.70 Trifecta £221.10.
Owner Araam **Bred** Car Colston Hall Stud **Trained** Manton, Wilts
■ Boreas Duke, Platform Nineteen and Thelonious were withdrawn. Prices at time of withdrawal 80/1, 66/1 and 33/1 respectively. Rule 4 does not apply
FOCUS
Add 6yds to race distance. An interesting maiden with several top yards represented, though quite extraordinary with the Michael Bell pair Platform Nineteen and Thelonious both running loose beforehand and being withdrawn, whilst Boreas Duke was also withdrawn after breaking out of the front of the stalls. The order didn't change much once the race started and again those that were handy were favoured.

1957 DS DERBY SALON H'CAP 1m 2f 50y
7:05 (7:20) (Class 6) (0-60,62) 3-Y-O
£3,493 (£1,039; £519; £400; £400; £400) Stalls Low

Form RPR
3-56 1 **Ignatius (IRE)**[26] 1332 3-9-0 51........... KierenFox 6 58
(John Best) *mde all: rdn over 1f out: edgd lft ins fnl f: styd on gamely* 5/1[2]
064- 2 3/4 **Hummdinger (FR)**[207] 7653 3-9-8 62........... FinleyMarsh(3) 4 68+
(Alan King) *plld hrd and prom: shkn up over 3f out: rdn and ev ch ins fnl f: styd on* 3/1[1]
-210 3 3/4 **Heatherdown (IRE)**[38] 1173 3-9-6 57...........(p[1]) RobertHavlin 9 61
(Ian Williams) *hld up: hdwy over 3f out: rdn ins fnl f: styd on: nt clr run towards fin* 14/1
6546 4 1 1/4 **Truckingby**[16] 1555 3-9-7 58...........(b) JimCrowley 3 60
(Mark Johnston) *chsd ldrs: rdn over 2f out: styd on same pce fnl f* 7/1[3]
2130 5 1 1/4 **Precision Prince (IRE)**[14] 1593 3-9-8 62........... CameronNoble(3) 11 61
(Mark Loughnane) *hld up in tch: rdn over 2f out: sn outpcd: styd on ins fnl f* 7/1[3]
06-0 6 nse **Red Archangel (IRE)**[99] 174 3-9-6 57...........(h) TomQueally 12 56
(Richard Spencer) *s.i.s: hld up: rdn and hung lft over 2f out: nt rch ldrs* 28/1
-033 7 nk **Crazy Spin**[14] 1593 3-8-10 47...........(p) KieranO'Neill 2 46
(Ivan Furtado) *chsd wnr: rdn over 2f out: lost 2nd over 1f out: no ex ins fnl f* 15/2
3300 8 nk **Twpsyn (IRE)**[17] 1516 3-9-4 62........... GinaMangan(7) 1 60
(David Evans) *s.i.s: hld up: racd keenly: effrt and nt clr run over 2f out: swtchd rt over 1f out: styd on ins fnl f: nt rch ldrs* 20/1
000- 9 nk **Bumblekite**[161] 9000 3-8-7 51........... TobyEley(7) 8 49
(Steph Hollinshead) *s.i.s: hld up: hdwy over 4f out: rdn and nt clr run over 1f out: no ex ins fnl f* 50/1
033- 10 2 **Jazz Hands (IRE)**[177] 8575 3-9-0 51........... TonyHamilton 15 45
(Richard Fahey) *broke wl: sn stdd and lost pl: hld up: racd keenly: nt trble ldrs* 5/1[2]
2006 11 1/2 **Arriba De Toda (IRE)**[43] 1084 3-8-8 45...........(p) CamHardie 13 38
(Brian Ellison) *hld up: hdwy u.p over 2f out: wknd over 1f out* 40/1
000- 12 1 1/2 **Nabvutika (IRE)**[143] 9291 3-9-1 55........... TimClark(3) 5 45
(John Butler) *s.i.s: hld up: rdn over 3f out: nvr on terms (jockey said filly ran too freely)* 40/1

2m 15.03s (1.63) **Going Correction** -0.20s/f (Firm) 12 Ran SP% **116.8**
Speed ratings (Par 96): **85,84,83,82,81 81,81,81,81,79 79,77**
CSF £18.96 CT £198.41 TOTE £7.00: £2.10, £1.50, £4.50; EX 28.10 Trifecta £475.70.
Owner Keaveney & Butcher **Bred** Lisieux Stud **Trained** Oad Street, Kent
FOCUS
Add 6yds to race distance. A moderate 3yo handicap run at a modest pace and another race won from the front. The winning time was almost three seconds slower than the maiden.

1958 DARREN'S 50TH BIRTHDAY CELEBRATION CLASSIFIED STKS 1m 2f 50y
7:35 (7:43) (Class 6) 4-Y-O+
£3,363 (£1,001; £500; £400; £400; £400) Stalls Low

Form RPR
000 1 **Cosmic Ray**[26] 1339 7-9-0 50...........(h) DaneO'Neill 13 56
(Les Eyre) *mde all: racd freely: clr whn hung rt over 4f out: rdn over 1f out: unchal (regarding the apparent improved form shown, trainer's rep said the gelding was suited by a return to turf)* 9/2[2]
550- 2 2 1/4 **Bambajee (FR)**[154] 9134 6-8-9 45........... TheodoreLadd(5) 10 52
(Tim Pinfield) *chsd wnr tl over 7f out: lost grnd on ldng pair over 6f out: hdwy to go 2nd over 1f out: no ch w wnr* 16/1
03-0 3 3 1/4 **Telekinetic**[94] 257 4-9-0 49........... ShelleyBirkett 11 46
(Julia Feilden) *hdwy to chse wnr over 7f out: rdn over 2f out: lost 2nd over 1f out: no ex fnl f* 33/1
0-00 4 hd **Perceived**[60] 792 7-9-0 49...........(p) CamHardie 6 45+
(Antony Brittain) *hld up in tch: lost grnd on ldrs over 6f out: rdn over 2f out: styd on fr over 1f out* 7/1
0064 5 6 **Puzzle Cache**[10] 1680 5-9-0 47...........(b) RobHornby 14 34
(Rod Millman) *chsd ldrs: lost grnd over 6f out: rdn over 3f out: styd on ins fnl f* 10/1
3-25 6 3 **Optima Petamus**[17] 1520 7-9-0 49...........(t[1]) JackGarritty 4 28+
(Liam Bailey) *s.i.s: hld up: nvr on terms* 5/2[1]
-550 7 2 **Amity Island**[23] 1390 4-8-9 48........... ConnorMurtagh(5) 12 24+
(Ollie Pears) *hld up: nvr on terms* 8/1
0043 8 5 **Woggle (IRE)**[17] 1519 4-9-0 45...........(t[1]) TrevorWhelan 15 15+
(Geoffrey Deacon) *hld up: rdn over 3f out: n.d* 20/1
001 9 1 1/2 **Ainne**[8] 1732 4-8-12 51...........(tp) GaryMahon(3) 8 13
(Sylvester Kirk) *prom: lost pl 8f out: nt clr run over 3f out: n.d after* 6/1[3]
0-00 10 hd **Jack Of Diamonds (IRE)**[25] 1343 10-9-0 50...........(p) MarkCrehan 1 12+
(Roger Teal) *s.s: hld up: hdwy u.p over 3f out: sn wknd* 33/1
0-60 11 18 **The Wire Flyer**[17] 1520 4-9-0 43...........(p) TomQueally 16
(John Flint) *hld up in tch: lost pl whn hung rt home turn: sn wknd* 16/1
006 12 nk **Noel (IRE)**[17] 1517 4-9-0 44........... KieranO'Neill 5
(Daniel Kubler) *s.i.s: in rr: bhd fr 1/2-way* 25/1

2m 10.75s (-2.65) **Going Correction** -0.20s/f (Firm) 12 Ran SP% **120.0**
Speed ratings (Par 101): **102,100,97,97,92 90,88,84,83,83 68,68**
CSF £71.18 TOTE £5.40: £2.10, £7.50, £4.10; EX 75.10 Trifecta £1243.10.
Owner Mrs Melissa Anne Cooke **Bred** Winterbeck Manor Stud **Trained** Catwick, N Yorks
FOCUS
Add 6yds to race distance. A rock-bottom classified event in which the winner dominated throughout and was never in any danger on a track where pace was key. It was the fastest time of the three races over the trip on the night.
T/Plt: £718.00 to a £1 stake. Pool: £42,868.93 - 43.58 winning units T/Qpdt: £35.20 to a £1 stake. Pool: £7,100.07 - 148.93 winning units **Colin Roberts**

1959 - 1966a (Foreign Racing) - See Raceform Interactive

1858 SOUTHWELL (L-H)
Sunday, April 21

OFFICIAL GOING: Fibresand: standard
Wind: negligible Weather: sunny and very warm

1967 SW AND AT DARBY MEMORIAL H'CAP 7f 14y(F)
2:05 (2:07) (Class 6) (0-55,54) 4-Y-O+
£3,105 (£924; £461; £400; £400; £400) Stalls Low

Form RPR
-051 1 **Fly True**[40] 1158 6-9-7 54........... NickyMackay 9 63
(Ivan Furtado) *mid-div on inner: rdn and hdwy 2f out: cl up 1f out: led 1/2f out: r.o wl* 7/2[2]
31 2 3/4 **La Cumparsita (IRE)**[20] 1478 5-9-3 50........... JasonHart 2 57
(Tristan Davidson) *trckd ldrs: drvn 3f out: rdn and hdwy over 2f out: led over 1f out: hdd 1/2f out: no ex* 11/4[1]
1-46 3 1 **I Am Dandy (IRE)**[65] 738 4-9-4 51...........(t w) PaulHanagan 14 55
(James Ewart) *hld up: plenty to do 3f out: pushed along over 2f out: rdn and hdwy 2f out: sn drifted lft: wnt 4th ent fnl f: kpt on to take 3rd last 100yds* 7/1
50-0 4 1 1/2 **Maureb (IRE)**[80] 502 7-9-6 53...........(p) DougieCostello 4 53
(Tony Coyle) *led: drvn in narrow ld 2f out: rdn and hdd over 1f out: wknd fnl f* 20/1
50-3 5 2 **Space War**[17] 1553 12-8-6 46...........(t) JoshQuinn(7) 3 41
(Michael Easterby) *mid-div: drvn 2f out: reminder over 1f out: kpt on under hand riding fnl f* 10/1
5204 6 1/2 **Be Bold**[25] 1353 7-8-12 45...........(b) LewisEdmunds 8 38
(Rebecca Bastiman) *chsd ldrs: drvn 2f out: rdn over 1f out: one pce fnl f* 33/1
00-6 7 1 1/2 **Shakiah (IRE)**[22] 1431 4-8-12 45........... PhilDennis 12 34
(Sharon Watt) *prom: drvn 3f out: lost pl 2f out: rdn over 1f out: no ex* 25/1
5500 8 hd **Major Crispies**[10] 1722 8-9-2 49...........(p) TomEaves 10 38
(Ronald Thompson) *chsd ldrs on outer: drvn 2f out: rdn over 1f out: no ex fnl f* 28/1
36 9 3/4 **Tellovoi (IRE)**[9] 1732 11-8-12 45...........(p) PhilipPrince 6 32
(Richard Guest) *bhd: drvn 3f out: no imp* 11/1
0325 10 nse **Essential**[27] 1339 5-9-0 52...........(b) ConnorMurtagh(5) 13 39
(Olly Williams) *chsd ldrs: pushed along and ev ch 3f out: rdn 2f out: sn wknd* 5/1[3]
/000 11 6 **Major Muscari (IRE)**[24] 1384 11-8-12 45...........(p) BenCurtis 11 16
(Shaun Harris) *bhd: rdn over 2f out: nvr a factor* 100/1
3203 12 1 1/4 **Joyful Dream (IRE)**[9] 1731 5-8-13 46...........(p) LiamKeniry 7 13
(John Butler) *mid-div: drvn and lost pl over 3f out: sn wknd* 14/1

000- **13** *3* **Another Situation (USA)**[122] 9648 4-9-0 **47** .... BarryMcHugh 1 6
(John Mackie) *a bhd: lost shoe (vet reported the filly lost its right fore shoe)* **28/1**

-060 **14** *5* **Ramblow**[11] 1683 6-8-12 **45** ....(tp) RossaRyan 5
(Alexandra Dunn) *a bhd* **33/1**

1m 29.84s (-0.46) **Going Correction** -0.05s/f (Stan) **14** Ran SP% **124.5**
Speed ratings (Par 101): **100,99,98,96,94 93,91,91,90,90 83,82,78,73**
CSF £12.96 CT £69.09 TOTE £4.10: £1.60, £1.60, £2.70; EX 16.30 Trifecta £64.40.
Owner Stuart Dobb & Kate Dobb **Bred** The Kathryn Stud **Trained** Wiseton, Nottinghamshire
■ Stewards' Enquiry : Nicky Mackay seven-day ban: used whip above the permitted level (May 5-11)

FOCUS
A moderate if competitive handicap to start and a fine performance from a mare in form who clearly likes it here. She was the only one to come up the inside rail.

1968 TOALSBET EBF NOVICE STKS 4f 214y(F)
2:35 (2:37) (Class 5) 2-Y-O **£3,752** (£1,116; £557; £278) **Stalls** Centre

Form RPR

1 **Littledidyouknow (IRE)** 2-9-0 **0** .... LukeMorris 2 64
(Archie Watson) *mde all: drvn and almost jnd by runner-up 2f out: rdn in narrow ld 1f out: rn green but r.o wl to assert fnl f* **10/3**[3]

0 **2** *1 ¼* **Hollaback Girl**[18] 1513 2-8-7 **0** .... SeanKirrane(7) 5 60
(Richard Spencer) *slowly away: sn rcvrd to chse ldrs: hdwy and almost upsides wnr 2f out: shkn up and ev ch 1f out: rdn and no ex fnl f* **16/1**

3 *1 ¾* **Constitutional (IRE)** 2-9-5 **0** .... BenCurtis 1 62+
(K R Burke) *rrd up in stalls and slowly away: sn rcvrd to be prom 1/2-way: pushed along 2f out: rdn in cl 3rd over 1f out: no ex fnl f* **5/2**[2]

4 *5* **Ambyfaeirvine (IRE)** 2-9-5 **0** .... JasonHart 4 40
(Ivan Furtado) *prom: pushed along 1/2-way: rdn and wknd 2f out* **9/2**

5 *1 ½* **Mumsbirthdaygirl (IRE)** 2-9-0 **0** .... EoinWalsh 6 30
(Mark Loughnane) *prom on stands' side: rdn 1/2-way: wknd 2f out* **33/1**

5 **6** *4* **Mystic Knight (IRE)**[19] 1499 2-9-5 **0** .... DavidAllan 3 20
(Tim Easterby) *prom: pushed along and lost pl after 2f: drvn over 2f out: sn dropped away* **2/1**[1]

1m 1.93s (2.23) **Going Correction** -0.05s/f (Stan) **6** Ran SP% **112.0**
Speed ratings (Par 92): **80,78,75,67,64 58**
CSF £47.85 TOTE £4.30: £2.30, £6.50; EX 40.20 Trifecta £195.60.
Owner El Jefe **Bred** Rathasker Stud **Trained** Upper Lambourn, W Berks

FOCUS
A modest novice event with the first three pulling well clear of the other trio.

1969 TOALSBET.COM CLAIMING STKS 6f 16y(F)
3:05 (3:08) (Class 5) 3-Y-O+ **£3,752** (£1,116; £557; £400; £400; £400) **Stalls** Low

Form RPR

-500 **1** **Falcao (IRE)**[17] 1553 7-9-5 **53** .... LiamKeniry 6 62
(John Butler) *mde all: pushed along over 2f out: rdn in 1/2 l ld 1f out: kpt on resolutely to repel rivals ins fnl f* **25/1**

000- **2** *½* **Inexes**[166] 8891 7-10-0 **74** ....(p) JasonHart 3 70
(Ivan Furtado) *bhd: drvn 3f out: rdn and hdwy 2f out: 3rd ent fnl f: clsd on wnr in 2nd 1/2f out: r.o but hld last 100yds* **5/1**

32-3 **3** *nk* **Mr Buttons (IRE)**[16] 1557 3-8-12 **73** .... PaulHanagan 9 61
(Richard Fahey) *prom: cl up and rdn 2f out: 1/2 l 2nd 1f out: kpt on fnl f: lost 2nd last 100yds* **3/1**[3]

6320 **4** *1 ½* **The Great Wall (USA)**[25] 1367 5-10-0 **81** ....(v[1]) AlistairRawlinson 5 64
(Michael Appleby) *mid-div: rdn over 2f out: kpt on fnl f (jockey said gelding was never travelling)* **2/1**[1]

5335 **5** *3 ¼* **Captain Lars (SAF)**[17] 1547 9-9-7 **80** ....(b) LukeMorris 4 47
(Archie Watson) *chsd ldrs on inner: rdn 2f out: no imp* **9/4**[2]

2463 **6** *9* **Canimar**[10] 1715 4-8-8 **44** ....(p) GavinAshton(7) 8 14
(Shaun Keightley) *bhd: drvn 2f out: no imp* **33/1**

4-05 **7** *1* **Westfield Wonder**[77] 587 4-8-12 **41** .... RPWalsh(7) 1 15
(Ronald Thompson) *in rr: detached fr rest and rdn 3f out: nvr a factor* **100/1**

0/00 **8** *10* **Whirl Me Round**[50] 982 5-9-0 **58** ....(v[1]) SeamusCronin(5) 10
(Robyn Brisland) *unruly ent stalls: slowly away: sn prom on outer: drvn 3f out: sn rdn and wknd* **20/1**

1m 16.81s (0.31) **Going Correction** -0.05s/f (Stan) **8** Ran SP% **118.3**
WFA 3 from 4yo+ 11lb
Speed ratings (Par 103): **95,94,93,91,87 75,74,60**
CSF £144.18 TOTE £27.20: £5.00, £1.80, £1.20; EX 208.00 Trifecta £1521.40.Mr Buttons was claimed by Mr R. W. Stubbs for £8,000
Owner Power Geneva Ltd **Bred** Castleton Lyons & Kilboy Estate **Trained** Newmarket, Suffolk

FOCUS
A wide range of abilities in this claimer with 40lb separating the highest and lowest rated horses on official figures, but is often happens in races like this official ratings can go out of the window.

1970 NOTTINGHAM CITY TRANSPORT NOVICE AUCTION STKS 7f 14y(F)
3:35 (3:37) (Class 5) 3-Y-O **£3,752** (£1,116; £557; £278) **Stalls** Low

Form RPR

0 **1** **Parallel World (IRE)**[13] 1649 3-8-12 **0** .... JonathanFisher(7) 4 74
(K R Burke) *prom: drvn in 3 l 2nd 3f out: clsd on ldr and reminder 2f out: rdn and ev ch over 1f out: cl 2nd 1/2f out: r.o wl to ld last few strides* **16/1**

2- **2** *shd* **Cape Victory (IRE)**[137] 9411 3-9-5 **0** .... PJMcDonald 6 73
(James Tate) *slowly away: hld up on outer: drvn and hdwy over 2f out: rdn to chal over 1f out: led narrowly ins fnl f: r.o: hdd last few strides* **1/3**[1]

00-4 **3** *1 ¼* **Ollivander (IRE)**[18] 1523 3-9-5 **65** ....(p) DavidNolan 1 70
(David O'Meara) *led: pushed along in 3 l ld 3f out: drvn in reduced ld 2f out: rdn 1f out: hdd ins fnl f: no ex last 100yds* **7/1**[3]

40- **4** *19* **Chance Of Glory (FR)**[212] 7494 3-9-5 **0** .... JoeFanning 2 20
(Mark Johnston) *chsd ldrs: drvn in 3rd 3f out: dropped to 4th 2f out: sn rdn and wknd* **6/1**[2]

03- **5** *9* **Baby Maureb (IRE)**[251] 6092 3-9-0 **0** .... KevinStott 5
(Tony Coyle) *hld up: rdn in 5th 3f out: wknd 2f out* **33/1**

0- **6** *28* **Secret Footsteps (IRE)**[184] 8378 3-9-0 **0** ....(h w) HarrisonShaw(5) 3
(K R Burke) *dwlt: bhd: drvn and lost tch 4f out: eased whn no ch over 2f out: sddle slipped (vet reported the gelding was suffering from post-race heat stress)* **25/1**

1m 29.46s (-0.84) **Going Correction** -0.05s/f (Stan) **6** Ran SP% **114.5**
Speed ratings (Par 98): **102,101,100,78,68 36**
CSF £22.98 TOTE £16.90: £5.00, £1.10; EX 33.50 Trifecta £81.80.
Owner Ontoawinner, SDH Project Services Ltd 1 **Bred** Tally-Ho Stud **Trained** Middleham Moor, N Yorks
■ Stewards' Enquiry : David Nolan caution: careless riding

FOCUS
An uncompetitive novice auction event and a bit of a turn up.

1971 TOALSBET CASINO H'CAP 2m 102y(F)
4:10 (4:14) (Class 4) (0-80,80) 4-Y-O+ **£6,404** (£1,905; £952; £476; £400; £400) **Stalls** Low

Form RPR

4511 **1** **Champarisi**[19] 1503 4-8-13 **72** .... SamJames 7 81+
(Grant Tuer) *rrd up in stalls but broke wl enough: hld up: hdwy 6f out: led 4f out: jnd 3f out: pushed into ld 2f out: rdn in 1 l ld 1f out: strly pressed fnl f: hld on wl* **3/1**[2]

6664 **2** *nk* **High Command (IRE)**[4] 1861 6-8-1 **63** ....(b) TheodoreLadd(5) 3 70
(Michael Appleby) *mid-div: pushed along and hdwy 2f out: rdn over 1f out: chal wnr ins fnl f: r.o: hld nr fin* **9/1**

45-0 **3** *3 ¼* **Rashdan (FR)**[18] 1518 4-9-5 **78** ....(b) JackMitchell 6 83
(Hugo Palmer) *chsd ldrs: pushed along in 4th 3f out: drvn to chal 2f out: sn rdn: one pce fnl f* **9/2**[3]

1002 **4** *4* **Navajo Star (IRE)**[19] 1503 5-9-7 **78** ....(v) PJMcDonald 1 76
(Robyn Brisland) *trckd ldrs: hdwy to dispute ld on inner 3f out: drvn and hdd 2f out: sn rdn: no ex* **14/1**

011- **5** *2 ½* **Bodacious Name (IRE)**[143] 8480 5-9-0 **71** .... JasonHart 9 66
(John Quinn) *bhd: drvn 3f out: rdn 2f out: effrt over 1f out: no ex and eased fnl f* **25/1**

0-03 **6** *5* **Gang Warfare**[18] 1524 8-9-9 **80** ....(bt) RossaRyan 4 69
(Alexandra Dunn) *hld up on outer: tk clsr order 4f out: drvn in 3rd 3f out: rdn and wknd over 2f out* **20/1**

/ **7** *14* **Nelson Road (IRE)**[15] 7049 6-8-5 **62** .... JoeFanning 2 35
(Tristan Davidson) *prom: lost pl and drvn 4f out: sn lost tch: eased 2f out: lame (vet reported the gelding was lame on its right fore and was treated for post-race heat stress)* **11/10**[1]

6005 **8** *½* **Tenedos**[18] 1525 4-8-7 **66** ....(be) BarryMcHugh 5 40
(Ed de Giles) *led: hdd 4f out: lost grnd qckly: wl bhd whn eased 2f out* **50/1**

3/0- **9** *66* **Deep Resolve (IRE)**[32] 9657 8-8-4 **61** oh1 ....(b) LukeMorris 8
(Barry Leavy) *hld up: rdn and dropped to last 6f out: sn lost tch and heavily eased* **66/1**

3m 40.74s (-4.76) **Going Correction** -0.05s/f (Stan) **9** Ran SP% **119.5**
WFA 4 from 5yo+ 2lb
Speed ratings (Par 105): **109,108,107,105,103 101,94,94,61**
CSF £29.58 CT £122.99 TOTE £4.00: £1.50, £2.00, £1.50; EX 36.80 Trifecta £115.10.
Owner Allerton Racing & G Tuer **Bred** Faisal Meshrf Alqahtani **Trained** Birkby, N Yorks

FOCUS
A fair staying handicap and a game performance by the winner.

1972 TOALSBET APP H'CAP 1m 4f 14y(F)
4:45 (4:47) (Class 5) (0-70,72) 3-Y-O **£3,752** (£1,116; £557; £400; £400; £400) **Stalls** Low

Form RPR

2 **1** **Tigray (USA)**[3] 1884 3-9-5 **68** .... AlistairRawlinson 7 75
(Michael Appleby) *hld up: tk clsr order 3f out: pushed into 2nd 2f out: rdn to ld over 1f out: narrow ld ent fnl f: r.o wl: asserted nr fin* **9/4**[2]

53-5 **2** *¾* **Hurricane Hero (FR)**[24] 1386 3-9-8 **71** ....(p[1]) BenCurtis 6 77
(K R Burke) *led: pushed along in 1 l ld 3f out: rdn 2f out: hdd over 1f out: cl 2nd ent fnl f: kpt on wl but hld nr fin* **8/1**[3]

36-3 **3** *9* **Mondain**[19] 1510 3-9-7 **70** .... JoeFanning 2 62
(Mark Johnston) *trckd ldr: drvn over 3f out: rdn in 3rd 2f out: sn wknd* **11/10**[1]

304- **4** *nk* **Swerved (IRE)**[233] 6757 3-9-1 **64** .... ShaneGray 5 55
(Ollie Pears) *prom: pushed along in 2nd 3f out: drvn and dropped to 4th 2f out: reminders over 1f out and ins fnl f: wknd* **20/1**

052- **5** *41* **Archies Lad**[148] 9243 3-9-2 **65** .... PaulHanagan 1
(Richard Fahey) *racd in 4th: rdn and lost pl over 5f out: sn lost tch* **11/1**

030- **6** *¾* **Simon's Smile (FR)**[149] 9227 3-9-4 **67** .... CliffordLee 4
(K R Burke) *in rr: rdn and lost tch over 5f out (jockey said gelding was never travelling)* **10/1**

2m 37.95s (-3.05) **Going Correction** -0.05s/f (Stan) **6** Ran SP% **111.7**
Speed ratings (Par 98): **108,107,101,101,73 73**
CSF £19.60 TOTE £3.10: £1.70, £3.50; EX 17.80 Trifecta £31.20.
Owner Honestly Racing **Bred** Flaxman Holdings Ltd **Trained** Oakham, Rutland

FOCUS
An ordinary 3yo handicap contested by six maidens, none of whom had experience of racing on Fibresand.

1973 TOALSBET WORLD LOTTERIES H'CAP 6f 16y(F)
5:15 (5:18) (Class 6) (0-65,67) 4-Y-O+ **£3,105** (£924; £461; £400; £400; £400) **Stalls** Low

Form RPR

-502 **1** **Ticks The Boxes (IRE)**[77] 587 7-7-9 **46** .... KieranSchofield(7) 12 57
(Brian Ellison) *mid-div on outer: pushed along to take clsr order 3f out: drvn to chal 2f out: rdn into ld 1 1/2f out: 1 l ld 1f out: rdn clr fnl f* **10/3**[1]

4121 **2** *3* **Socialites Red**[6] 1817 6-9-6 **64** 5ex ....(p) TheodoreLadd(5) 1 66
(Scott Dixon) *led: 1/2 l ld 3f out: strly pressed 2f out: drvn and hdd 1 1/2f out: sn rdn: kpt on fnl f* **8/1**

1-44 **3** *2* **Global Melody**[18] 1522 4-9-7 **65** .... BenCurtis 7 61
(Phil McEntee) *prom: 1/2 l 2nd 3f out: rdn and ev ch 2f out: lost grnd on ldrs over 1f out: kpt on for 3rd fnl f* **13/2**

1145 **4** *nk* **Gorgeous General**[25] 1368 4-9-1 **59** .... JackMitchell 6 54
(Lawrence Mullaney) *prom: drvn over 3f out: rdn in 4th 2f out: one pce fnl f* **7/1**

40-3 **5** *2 ¼* **Rasheeq (IRE)**[18] 1521 6-9-8 **66** .... LukeMorris 2 54
(Mohamed Moubarak) *mid-div: drvn on inner 3f out: rdn 2f out: one pce* **12/1**

0-03 **6** *hd* **Captain Dion**[25] 1366 6-8-12 **59** ....(vt) GabrieleMalune(3) 8 47
(Ivan Furtado) *bhd: rdn on stands' side 2f out: kpt on past btn rivals fr over 1f out* **4/1**[2]

6-13 **7** *1 ¼* **The Golden Cue**[77] 586 4-8-12 **63** .... TobyEley(7) 9 47
(Steph Hollinshead) *hld up: pushed along 3f out: rdn 2f out: no imp (jockey said gelding was never travelling)* **14/1**

56-0 **8** *2 ½* **Stoneyford Lane (IRE)**[100] 187 5-9-4 **62** ....(p) RoystonFfrench 10 39
(Steph Hollinshead) *hld up: drvn 3f out: rdn 2f out: no imp* **33/1**

-500 **9** *¾* **Hippeia (IRE)**[23] 1399 4-8-11 **60** .... AndrewBreslin(5) 3 34
(Grant Tuer) *hld up: drvn 3f out: sn rdn: no imp (jockey said filly hung right in the back straight)* **33/1**

1114 **10** 2 1/4 **Elusif (IRE)**[27] 1338 4-9-3 **61**........ HollieDoyle 4 29
(Shaun Keightley) *slowly away: sn pushed along in rr: drvn 3f out: rdn 2f out: nvr involved (jockey said gelding was never travelling)* **11/2**[3]

310- **11** 1/2 **Danish Duke (IRE)**[166] 8902 8-8-7 **51**........ JamesSullivan 11 17
(Ruth Carr) *slowly away: bhd on outer: hdwy after 2f: drvn in 6th 3f out: rdn and wknd 2f out* **20/1**

030- **12** 1/2 **Fumbo Jumbo (IRE)**[201] 7867 6-9-9 **67**........ LewisEdmunds 5 32
(Rebecca Bastiman) *mid-div: lost pl 1/2-way: drvn and dropped to last 2f out* **33/1**

1m 16.18s (-0.32) **Going Correction** -0.05s/f (Stan) **12** Ran SP% **123.4**
Speed ratings (Par 101): **100,96,93,92,89 89,88,84,83,80 80,79**
CSF £30.65 CT £168.92 TOTE £3.90: £1.90, £2.10, £3.10; EX 27.00 Trifecta £224.90.
Owner Kristian Strangeway **Bred** John B Hughes **Trained** Norton, N Yorks

FOCUS
A modest sprint handicap to end with. The market proved a useful guide.
T/Plt: £118.30 to a £1 stake. Pool: £61,796.27 - 381.25 winning units T/Qpdt: £21.10 to a £1 stake. Pool: £5,520.99 - 192.81 winning units **Keith McHugh**

[1782]RANDWICK (L-H)
Saturday, April 20

OFFICIAL GOING: Turf: good

1974a SCHWEPPES ALL AGED STKS (GROUP 1) (2YO+) (TURF) 7f
6:35 2-Y-0+
£192,817 (£62,983; £32,044; £15,469; £7,734; £3,314)

RPR

1 **Pierata (AUS)**[14] 1609 4-9-4 0........(b) TommyBerry 9 115
(Gregory Hickman, Australia) **16/5**[2]

2 1/2 **Osborne Bulls (AUS)**[14] 1609 5-9-4 0........ HughBowman 1 114
(James Cummings, Australia) *in rr of midfield: shkn up 2f out: gd hdwy on inner to chal 110yds out: hld fnl 1/2f: rdn out* **9/5**[1]

3 1/2 **Siege Of Quebec (AUS)**[14] 1610 4-9-4 0........(bt) TimothyClark 10 112
(Gai Waterhouse & Adrian Bott, Australia) **40/1**

4 *shd* **Champagne Cuddles (AUS)**[14] 1609 4-9-0 0........(b) BrentonAvdulla 2 108
(Bjorn Baker, Australia) **18/1**

5 *hd* **Manuel (AUS)**[21] 5-9-4 0........(t) BlakeShinn 6 111
(Tony McEvoy, Australia) **18/1**

6 1 **Le Romain (AUS)**[14] 1610 6-9-4 0........(b[1]) JamesMcDonald 13 109
(Kris Lees, Australia) **6/1**[3]

7 *shd* **Fierce Impact (JPN)**[35] 5-9-4 0........ JasonCollett 5 108
(Matthew A Smith, Australia) **100/1**

8 *nk* **D'bai (IRE)**[86] 397 5-9-4 0........(bt) KerrinMcEvoy 8 108
(Charlie Appleby) *in rr of midfield: drvn along 2 1/2f out: rdn in midfield 1f out: kpt on same pce: rdn out* **7/1**

9 1/2 **Naantali (NZ)**[29] 4-9-0 0........ MarkZahra 4 102
(Ciaron Maher & David Eustace, Australia) **19/1**

10 *nk* **Siren's Fury (AUS)**[7] 5-9-0 0........ AdamHyeronimus 7 102
(Jason Coyle, Australia) **150/1**

11 1 1/2 **Malaguerra (AUS)**[56] 889 7-9-4........(vt) SamClipperton 12 101
(Peter Gelagotis, Australia) **25/1**

12 *nk* **Youngstar (AUS)**[165] 8911 4-9-0 0........ CoreyBrown 11 97
(Chris Waller, Australia) **30/1**

13 1/2 **Lanciato (NZ)**[43] 6-9-4 0........(t) JoshuaParr 3 99
(Mark Newnham, Australia) **25/1**

1m 20.64s **13** Ran SP% **116.8**

Owner G D Hickman, R W Wilson Et Al **Bred** Hobartville Stud **Trained** Australia

FOCUS
A bunch finish to this Grade 1.

[1642]REDCAR (L-H)
Monday, April 22

OFFICIAL GOING: Good to firm (firm in places; watered; 8.7)
Wind: light across Weather: fine

1975 WATCH RACING TV IN STUNNING HD NOVICE STKS 7f 219y
1:55 (1:57) (Class 5) 3-Y-0+ **£4,528** (£1,347; £673; £336) **Stalls** Centre

Form RPR

6 **1** **Country**[22] 1458 3-9-5 0........ DanielTudhope 1 86+
(William Haggas) *trckd ldr: led on bit over 2f out: nudged clr fnl f: easily* **1/2**[1]

4-4 **2** 3 3/4 **Dancingwithwolves (IRE)**[20] 1495 3-9-5 0........(h) DanielMuscutt 9 72
(Ed Dunlop) *trckd ldr: racd quite keenly: rdn over 2f out: kpt on same pce* **7/1**[2]

33- **3** *shd* **Fragrant Dawn**[179] 8577 3-9-0 0........ PaulHanagan 7 67
(Charles Hills) *led: rdn and hdd over 2f out: one pce* **7/1**[2]

4 **4** 3/4 **Dabouk (IRE)**[17] 1570 3-9-5 0........ DavidNolan 6 70
(David O'Meara) *chsd ldrs: rdn and bit outpcd over 2f out: kpt on fnl f* **10/1**[3]

5 5 **Stone Cougar (USA)** 3-9-0 0........ PJMcDonald 2 54
(Mark Johnston) *hld up: pushed along 5f out: rdn over 2f out: nvr threatened* **10/1**[3]

0 **6** 1/2 **Ghathanfar (IRE)**[9] 1764 3-9-5 0........ RoystonFfrench 8 57
(Tracy Waggott) *hld up in tch: pushed along over 2f out: wknd ins fnl f* **100/1**

00- **7** 1 1/4 **Jimmy Greenhough (IRE)**[167] 8896 3-9-5 0........ TonyHamilton 4 55
(Richard Fahey) *dwlt: a outpcd towards rr* **40/1**

1m 38.47s (1.87) **Going Correction** +0.075s/f (Good) **7** Ran SP% **113.3**
Speed ratings (Par 103): **93,89,89,88,83 82,81**
CSF £4.61 TOTE £1.40: £1.10, £2.40; EX 5.00 Trifecta £14.50.
Owner Sheikh Ahmed Al Maktoum **Bred** Godolphin **Trained** Newmarket, Suffolk

FOCUS
This novice featured lightly-raced potential improvers but though the winner scored in good style it is hard to know the value of the form. The runner-up is rated close to his AW latest.

1976 REMEMBERING SUSAN RUSHBY H'CAP 5f 217y
2:30 (2:35) (Class 5) (0-75,76) 4-Y-0+
£3,840 (£1,142; £571; £300; £300; £300) **Stalls** Centre

Form RPR

000- **1** **Galloway Hills**[194] 8101 4-9-13 **76**........ SamJames 1 85
(Phillip Makin) *mde all: pushed along 2f out: rdn and strly pressed ins fnl f: kpt on wl* **15/2**

1150 **2** 3/4 **Epeius (IRE)**[21] 1487 6-9-6 **69**........(v) AndrewMullen 9 76
(Ben Haslam) *s.i.s: hld up: rdn and gd hdwy appr fnl f: chal ins fnl f: kpt on same pce* **12/1**

4216 **3** 2 **Muatadel**[9] 1768 6-9-4 **67**........(p) BenCurtis 3 68
(Roger Fell) *dwlt: sn midfield: rdn and hdwy to chse ldr 1f out: kpt on same pce (gelding anticipated the start and accelerated the gate at the same moment as the race had been started. Being satisfied that it was not caused through a faulty action of the starting stalls, no further action was taken)* **7/2**[1]

05-5 **4** 3 1/4 **Afandem (IRE)**[9] 1760 5-9-6 **69**........(p[1]) DuranFentiman 6 59
(Tim Easterby) *midfield: rdn and hdwy 2f out: chal appr fnl f: wknd ins fnl f* **6/1**

32-0 **5** *nk* **Coastal Drive**[41] 1161 4-8-13 **62**........ KevinStott 2 51
(Paul Midgley) *trckd ldrs: rdn over 2f out: outpcd and btn over 1f out* **12/1**

540- **6** 3/4 **Ventura Secret (IRE)**[164] 8981 5-8-10 **64**........ PaulaMuir[(5)] 7 51
(Michael Dods) *trckd ldrs: rdn and along 3f out: sn lost pl and btn: edgd lft fnl f* **25/1**

0621 **7** 2 1/2 **Katheefa (USA)**[19] 1522 5-9-1 **64**........ JackGarritty 10 43
(Ruth Carr) *hld up: rdn over 2f out: nvr threatened* **11/2**[3]

40-5 **8** 2 1/4 **Ninjago**[58] 883 9-9-2 **65**........ PaulMulrennan 8 37
(Paul Midgley) *trckd ldrs: rdn over 2f out: wknd over 1f out* **14/1**

61-4 **9** 1 **Zebulon (IRE)**[17] 1565 5-9-2 **65**........ JamesSullivan 5 33
(Ruth Carr) *prom: rdn over 2f out: sn wknd* **5/1**[2]

6/ **10** 2 **Eldelbar (SPA)**[219] 5-9-7 **70**........(h[1]) ConnorBeasley 4 32
(Geoffrey Harker) *hld up: rdn 3f out: sn wknd (jockey said gelding hung right in the closing stages)* **10/1**

1m 11.52s (-0.28) **Going Correction** +0.075s/f (Good) **10** Ran SP% **115.3**
Speed ratings (Par 103): **108,107,104,100,99 98,95,92,90,88**
CSF £92.32 CT £380.13 TOTE £7.00: £2.10, £3.70, £1.60; EX 108.10 Trifecta £591.00.
Owner P J Makin **Bred** Rosyground Stud **Trained** Easingwold, N Yorks

FOCUS
Mainly exposed sorts in this sprint handicap in which the winner made all but the placed horses came from the back. The winner was back to his early 3yo form.

1977 JOIN RACING TV NOW H'CAP 7f
3:05 (3:14) (Class 4) (0-85,86) 4-Y-0+
£6,339 (£1,886; £942; £471; £300; £300) **Stalls** Centre

Form RPR

3-1 **1** **Hortzadar**[7] 1813 4-9-8 **86** 5ex........ DanielTudhope 7 95+
(David O'Meara) *trckd ldr: pushed along to ld over 1f out: rdn out fnl 110yds* **4/7**[1]

146- **2** 1 1/4 **Amplification (USA)**[184] 8415 4-9-0 **78**........ PaulMulrennan 3 84
(Michael Dods) *hld up: pushed along and hdwy over 1f out: rdn to chse ldr 110yds out: kpt on* **8/1**[3]

00-5 **3** 1 1/2 **Tadaawol**[14] 1644 6-8-12 **81**........ BenSanderson[(5)] 8 83
(Roger Fell) *led: rdn over 2f out: hdd over 1f out: one pce ins fnl f (vet said gelding lost its right fore shoe)* **5/1**[2]

3233 **4** 2 1/4 **Athollblair Boy (IRE)**[21] 1487 6-8-12 **81**........ FayeMcManoman[(5)] 5 77
(Nigel Tinkler) *trckd ldr: rdn 2f out: no ex ins fnl f* **16/1**

05-0 **5** 1 1/2 **Explain**[22] 1457 7-8-9 **73**........(p) JamesSullivan 4 65
(Ruth Carr) *hld up: rdn over 2f out: kpt on ins fnl f: nvr threatened* **12/1**

00-0 **6** 1/2 **Brother McGonagall**[14] 1644 5-8-13 **77**........ DavidAllan 6 67
(Tim Easterby) *midfield: rdn and outpcd over 2f out: kpt on ins fnl f* **25/1**

13-5 **7** 1 1/2 **Buccaneers Vault (IRE)**[22] 1457 7-9-3 **81**........ KevinStott 9 67
(Paul Midgley) *midfield: rdn over 2f out: wknd ins fnl f* **9/1**

0-00 **8** 12 **Starplex**[11] 1719 9-8-6 **77**........ RPWalsh[(7)] 2 31
(Kenny Johnson) *in tch: rdn 3f out: sn wknd and bhd* **100/1**

1m 25.2s (-0.20) **Going Correction** +0.075s/f (Good) **8** Ran SP% **119.8**
Speed ratings (Par 105): **104,102,100,98,96 96,94,80**
CSF £6.71 CT £15.10 TOTE £1.30: £1.10, £1.70, £1.80; EX 6.30 Trifecta £24.20.
Owner Akela Construction Ltd **Bred** The Aston House Stud **Trained** Upper Helmsley, N Yorks

■ Pettifogger was withdrawn. Price at time of withdrawal 11/1. Rule 4 applies to all bets struck prior to withdrawal. Deduction - 5p in the pound. New market formed

FOCUS
A race in which the winner had plenty in hand on ratings with his penalty following his easy Pontefract win seven days earlier. The pace was ordinary and those who raced up close up were favoured. The third helps with the level.

1978 MARKET CROSS JEWELLERS H'CAP 5f 217y
3:40 (3:42) (Class 3) (0-90,90) 4-Y-0+ **£9,703** (£2,887; £1,443; £721) **Stalls** Centre

Form RPR

054- **1** **The Armed Man**[192] 8167 6-8-8 **82**........ PaulaMuir[(5)] 2 89
(Chris Fairhurst) *prom: pushed along to ld ins fnl f: kpt on* **11/2**[3]

54-2 **2** 1 1/4 **Saluti (IRE)**[22] 1457 5-8-13 **82**........ KevinStott 4 85
(Paul Midgley) *led: rdn and hdd ins fnl f: one pce* **6/5**[1]

344- **3** 1 **Seen The Lyte (IRE)**[234] 6739 4-8-10 **82**........ RowanScott[(3)] 3 82
(Nigel Tinkler) *slowly away: sn hld up in tch: rdn along and hung lft over 2f out: kpt on fnl f (jockey said filly missed the break)* **25/1**

34-0 **4** *nse* **Magical Effect (IRE)**[11] 1714 7-8-9 **78**........ JamesSullivan 6 78
(Ruth Carr) *hld up: rdn 2f out: kpt on fnl 110yds: nvr threatened ldrs* **15/2**

033- **5** *nk* **John Kirkup**[181] 8501 4-8-11 **80**........ ConnorBeasley 5 79
(Michael Dods) *trckd ldr: racd quite keenly: rdn over 2f out: no ex ins fnl f* **8/1**

543- **6** 2 **Muscika**[181] 8503 5-9-7 **90**........ DanielTudhope 7 82
(David O'Meara) *chsd ldr: rdn 2f out: hung lft and wknd fnl f* **10/3**[2]

1m 11.46s (-0.34) **Going Correction** +0.075s/f (Good) **6** Ran SP% **110.6**
Speed ratings (Par 107): **109,107,106,105,105 102**
CSF £12.25 TOTE £5.90: £2.00, £1.40; EX 13.50 Trifecta £151.30.
Owner Mrs C A Arnold **Bred** C W Fairhurst **Trained** Middleham, N Yorks

FOCUS
A six-runner 0-90 6f handicap run at just an ordinary gallop. The form is no more than fair for the grade.

1979 GRACE CHAPMAN DESIGNED TODAY'S RACECARD COVER H'CAP (DIV I) 7f 219y
4:15 (4:18) (Class 6) (0-65,66) 3-Y-O

£3,493 (£1,039; £519; £300; £300; £300) **Stalls** Centre

Form RPR
-202 1 **Lexikon**[11] 1721 3-8-1 **48** .... JamieGormley(3) 8 55
(Ollie Pears) *mde all: rdn over 2f out: hung lft over 1f out: ended up on fair rail: hld on towards fin* 9/1
00-0 2 nk **Fitzy**[45] 1084 3-8-2 **46** .... (p[1]) JamesSullivan 7 52
(David Brown) *hld up: rdn over 2f out: short of room wl over 1f out: sn hdwy: chsd ldr ins fnl f: kpt on wl to chal towards fin* 50/1
400- 3 2 ¾ **Kensington Art**[208] 7667 3-9-8 **66** .... TonyHamilton 2 66
(Richard Fahey) *hld up in midfield: rdn along over 2f out: bit short of room and swtchd rt over 1f out: kpt on ins fnl f: wnt 3rd towards fin* 3/1[2]
060- 4 1 ¼ **Spiritual Boy (IRE)**[138] 9411 3-9-3 **61** .... DanielTudhope 3 58
(David O'Meara) *hld up: pushed along and hdwy 2f out: rdn and hung lft over 1f out: one pce ins fnl f* 6/1
540- 5 4 ½ **Early Edition (IRE)**[195] 8092 3-9-3 **61** .... BenCurtis 10 48
(Roger Fell) *prom: rdn over 2f out: hung lft over 1f out: sn wknd* 33/1
550- 6 1 ¼ **Juniors Fantasy (IRE)**[291] 4566 3-8-12 **56** .... DavidAllan 9 40
(Tim Easterby) *chsd ldrs: rdn over 2f out: wknd over 1f out* 28/1
000- 7 nk **Ransomed Dreams (USA)**[157] 9104 3-9-8 **66** .... LiamKeniry 4 49
(Ed Walker) *trckd ldrs: rdn over 2f out: wknd over 1f out* 5/1[3]
0-56 8 2 ¾ **Just Once**[52] 977 3-9-1 **59** .... RoystonFfrench 6 38
(Mrs Ilka Gansera-Leveque) *trckd ldrs: rdn over 2f out: losing pl whn hmpd over 1f out: wknd* 20/1
6405 9 hd **Mushaageb (IRE)**[14] 1656 3-9-7 **65** .... (b) JackMitchell 1 41
(Roger Varian) *hld up: rdn over 2f out: wknd fnl f* 5/2[1]
-003 10 2 **Alfred The Grey (IRE)**[21] 1486 3-9-0 **58** .... TomEaves 5 30
(Tracy Waggott) *slowly away: hld up: rdn and hdwy over 2f out: wknd over 1f out* 11/1

1m 38.58s (1.98) **Going Correction** +0.075s/f (Good) 10 Ran SP% 116.0
Speed ratings (Par 96): **93,92,89,88,84 82,82,79,79,77**
CSF £388.76 CT £1696.27 TOTE £6.20: £1.90, £9.60, £1.20; EX 266.80 Trifecta £3296.30.
Owner Mrs S D Pearson **Bred** Burns Farm Stud **Trained** Norton, N Yorks

FOCUS
The first division of a 0-65 handicap for three-year-olds which featured several lightly-raced sorts making their handicap debuts. There was a fair bit of trouble so the form may not work out quite as expected. The third is rated to his 2yo form.

1980 GRACE CHAPMAN DESIGNED TODAY'S RACECARD COVER H'CAP (DIV II) 7f 219y
4:50 (4:52) (Class 6) (0-65,66) 3-Y-O

£3,493 (£1,039; £519; £300; £300; £300) **Stalls** Centre

Form RPR
046- 1 **Anna Bunina (FR)**[208] 7667 3-9-3 **61** .... JackGarritty 4 71+
(Jedd O'Keeffe) *trckd ldrs: rdn to ld over 1f out: strly pressed fnl f: edgd rt: hld on wl* 7/2[2]
4440 2 nk **Kodi Dream**[11] 1720 3-8-9 **58** .... BenSanderson(5) 7 67
(Roger Fell) *hld up: pushed along and hdwy over 1f out: rdn to chal strly fnl f: kpt on (vet said gelding lost its left hind shoe)* 9/1
-311 3 3 ½ **Blazing Dreams (IRE)**[11] 1721 3-9-3 **61** .... (p) AndrewMullen 3 63
(Ben Haslam) *dwlt: hld up: pushed along and hdwy over 1f out: sn chsd ldrs: n.m.r ins fnl f and swtchd lft: drvn and one pce fnl 110yds* 4/1[3]
25-4 4 3 ¼ **Toro Dorado**[21] 1481 3-9-7 **65** .... (b) DanielTudhope 1 59
(Ed Dunlop) *wnt lft s: sn trckd ldrs: rdn over 2f out: ev ch over 1f out: hung lft appr fnl f: wknd fnl 110yds* 7/4[1]
404- 5 8 **Lady Lavinia**[208] 7674 3-9-3 **61** .... NathanEvans 8 36
(Michael Easterby) *hld up in tch: tk str hold: rdn and hdwy to ld 2f out: hdd over 1f out: sn wknd* 12/1
600- 6 1 ¾ **Northern Footsteps**[234] 6757 3-7-13 **46** oh1 .... JamieGormley(3) 6 17
(Ollie Pears) *prom: rdn over 2f out: wknd over 1f out* 40/1
400- 7 shd **Myklachi (FR)**[166] 8922 3-9-8 **66** .... DavidNolan 9 37
(David O'Meara) *sn led: rdn over 2f out: hdd 2f out: wknd over 1f out* 14/1
060- 8 6 **Separable**[207] 7707 3-8-11 **55** .... (b[1]) RachelRichardson 5 12
(Tim Easterby) *prom: rdn over 2f out: wknd over 1f out* 14/1

1m 38.87s (2.27) **Going Correction** +0.075s/f (Good) 8 Ran SP% 112.1
Speed ratings (Par 96): **91,90,87,83,75 74,74,68**
CSF £33.10 CT £129.44 TOTE £4.50: £1.70, £2.80, £1.10; EX 33.40 Trifecta £126.80.
Owner Highbeck Racing 3 **Bred** Dermot Cantillon **Trained** Middleham Moor, N Yorks

FOCUS
The second division of a 0-65 handicap for three-year-olds over a mile. The pace was ordinary, several pulled hard and the first four were well clear. The winner can do better from here.

1981 RACINGTV.COM H'CAP 1m 7f 217y
5:25 (5:29) (Class 6) (0-65,66) 4-Y-O+

£3,493 (£1,039; £519; £300; £300; £300) **Stalls** Low

Form RPR
0-11 1 **Echo (IRE)**[24] 1398 4-10-0 **66** .... (b) JackGarritty 5 75
(Jedd O'Keeffe) *midfield: smooth hdwy on outer 3f out: rdn to chal 2f out: drvn into narrow ld 1f out: styd on wl* 4/1[3]
/16- 2 1 **Divin Bere (FR)**[59] 9400 6-9-13 **66** .... (t[1] w) JamieGormley(3) 3 72
(Iain Jardine) *trckd ldrs: rdn over 2f out: chal strly over 1f out: one pce fnl 50yds* 3/1[2]
-460 3 3 **Highway Robber**[63] 782 6-8-4 **45** .... (t) PaulaMuir(5) 2 47
(Wilf Storey) *trckd ldrs: pushed along to ld 3f out: rdn and strly pressed 2f out: hdd 1f out: no ex ins fnl f* 16/1
4-64 4 nk **The Resdev Way**[13] 1663 6-9-12 **62** .... KevinStott 9 64
(Philip Kirby) *hld up in rr: hdwy 3f out: rdn 2f out: drvn to chal over 1f out: no ex ins fnl f* 7/1
/20- 5 11 **Russian Royale**[26] 5827 9-9-3 **53** .... (p) PJMcDonald 4 42
(Micky Hammond) *midfield: rdn over 2f out: sn btn* 25/1
411 6 ½ **Extreme Appeal (IRE)**[11] 1718 7-9-9 **59** .... (p) GrahamLee 8 47
(Kelly Morgan) *hld up: wnt a little in snatches: rdn over 3f out: sn btn* 2/1[1]
300- 7 2 ¼ **Wadacre Gigi**[146] 9271 4-8-9 **47** .... FrannyNorton 7 35
(Mark Johnston) *midfield: pushed along 9f out: rdn and outpcd over 3f out: nvr involved* 8/1
6606 8 15 **Prince Consort (IRE)**[51] 983 4-8-7 **45** .... (p) NathanEvans 1 15
(John Wainwright) *led: rdn and hdd 3f out: sn wknd (jockey said gelding hung right in the final furlong)* 80/1
06-3 9 16 **Unique Company (IRE)**[46] 1068 4-8-7 **45** .... (p[1]) JamesSullivan 6
(David Thompson) *prom: rdn over 4f out: sn wknd (jockey said gelding hung right in the straight)* 80/1

3m 33.07s (-0.63) **Going Correction** +0.075s/f (Good)
WFA 4 from 6yo+ 2lb 9 Ran SP% 114.1
Speed ratings (Par 101): **104,103,102,101,96 96,94,87,79**
CSF £16.09 CT £168.18 TOTE £3.40: £1.40, £1.40, £3.90; EX 16.60 Trifecta £155.80.
Owner Miss S E Hall & C Platts **Bred** Pat McCarthy **Trained** Middleham Moor, N Yorks

FOCUS
A 0-65 staying handicap run at a fair gallop in which the first four finished clear. The third helps guide the level.

1982 LIKE RACING TV ON FACEBOOK H'CAP 5f 217y
6:00 (6:01) (Class 6) (0-60,61) 3-Y-O

£3,493 (£1,039; £519; £300; £300; £300) **Stalls** Centre

Form RPR
0432 1 **Ascot Dreamer**[25] 1384 3-8-12 **51** .... LewisEdmunds 5 63
(David Brown) *chsd ldrs: rdn 2f out: led jst ins fnl f: kpt on* 4/1[1]
33-0 2 1 ½ **Lincoln Red**[18] 1549 3-8-8 **47** .... PhilDennis 14 54
(Olly Williams) *chsd ldrs on outer: rdn 2f out: ev ch ent fnl f: kpt on* 20/1
505- 3 hd **Frosted Lass**[180] 8542 3-9-0 **53** .... BenCurtis 9 59
(David Barron) *prom: rdn 2f out: chal strly over 1f out: one pce ins fnl f* 10/1
60-4 4 2 ¼ **Tomahawk Ridge (IRE)**[31] 1275 3-9-4 **57** .... PJMcDonald 7 57
(John Gallagher) *prom: rdn to ld narrowly over 1f out: hdd jst ins fnl f: sn no ex* 9/2[2]
0-60 5 nk **She'Zanarab**[11] 1720 3-8-12 **54** .... JamieGormley(3) 11 53
(Iain Jardine) *dwlt: sn chsd ldrs: rdn over 2f out: one pce* 33/1
640- 6 nk **Newgate Angel**[180] 8542 3-8-12 **51** .... (p) AndrewMullen 1 49
(Tony Coyle) *midfield: rdn over 2f out: chsd ldrs over 1f out: one pce* 22/1
02-6 7 1 ¼ **You Little Beauty**[81] 501 3-8-7 **46** .... (t[1]) FrannyNorton 10 41
(Ann Duffield) *chsd ldrs: outpcd and n.m.r over 2f out: kpt on ins fnl f* 16/1
000- 8 1 **Ey Up Its Mick**[175] 8699 3-9-4 **57** .... (p) DougieCostello 6 48
(Tony Coyle) *hld up: rdn over 2f out: kpt on ins fnl f: nvr threatened* 14/1
0-05 9 nse **Champagne Clouds**[25] 1380 3-8-7 **49** oh1 ow3 .... (b) BenRobinson(3) 15 40
(Brian Ellison) *prom: rdn 3f out: wknd ins fnl f* 40/1
-302 10 nse **Secret Picnic (FR)**[25] 1380 3-8-12 **51** .... (vt) JasonHart 3 42
(John Quinn) *trckd ldrs: rdn over 2f out: hung lft over 1f out: sn btn* 15/2[3]
600- 11 ¾ **Furyan**[216] 7390 3-9-5 **61** .... RowanScott(3) 4 50
(Nigel Tinkler) *dwlt: hld up: sn pushed along: nvr threatened* 12/1
5246 12 ½ **Shug**[26] 1358 3-9-7 **60** .... (p) LiamKeniry 12 47
(Ed Walker) *hld up: nvr threatened* 9/1
500- 13 5 **Raquelle (IRE)**[259] 5791 3-8-11 **50** .... DavidAllan 2 22
(Tim Easterby) *led: rdn and hdd over 1f out: sn wknd* 11/1
006- 14 ¾ **Se Green**[203] 7836 3-8-8 **47** .... RachelRichardson 16 17
(Tim Easterby) *midfield: rdn over 2f out: sn btn* 33/1
-025 15 5 **Joey Boy (IRE)**[54] 918 3-9-6 **59** .... (b) ShaneGray 13 14
(Kevin Ryan) *a in rr (jockey said gelding was never travelling)* 12/1

1m 12.72s (0.92) **Going Correction** +0.075s/f (Good) 15 Ran SP% 122.7
Speed ratings (Par 96): **100,98,97,94,94 93,92,90,90,90 89,89,82,81,74**
CSF £91.91 CT £785.16 TOTE £4.10: £1.90, £6.00, £3.70; EX 83.50 Trifecta £1082.90.
Owner Ron Hull **Bred** Usk Valley Stud **Trained** Averham Park, Notts

FOCUS
A moderate handicap, but the form is rated slightly on the positive side.
T/Jkpt: £15,384.60 to a £1 stake. Pool: £97,508.39 - 4.50 winning units T/Plt: £83.50 to a £1 stake. Pool: £41,676.52 - 364.18 winning units T/Qpdt: £9.90 to a £1 stake. Pool: £5,069.20 - 375.25 winning units **Andrew Sheret**

1836 WOLVERHAMPTON (A.W) (L-H)
Monday, April 22

OFFICIAL GOING: Tapeta: standard
Wind: Light breeze, against in home straight Weather: Overcast with occasional hazy sunshine, warm

1983 FRUIT SHOOT APPRENTICE H'CAP 1m 1f 104y (Tp)
2:10 (2:11) (Class 6) (0-65,64) 4-Y-O+

£3,105 (£924; £461; £300; £300; £300) **Stalls** Low

Form RPR
3625 1 **False Id**[11] 1722 6-8-10 **56** .... (b) LauraCoughlan(3) 11 63
(David Loughnane) *hld up: hdwy on outer over 2f out: rdn in 3rd 1 1/2f out: led ins fnl f: r.o wl* 13/2
-606 2 1 **Ghazan (IRE)**[17] 1563 4-9-4 **61** .... (t[1]) ThoreHammerHansen 10 66
(Kevin Frost) *chsd ldrs: tk clsr order 3f out: pushed into 2nd over 2f out: rdn to ld 1 1/2f out: hdd ins fnl f: kpt on* 6/1[3]
-503 3 2 ¾ **Street Poet (IRE)**[31] 1271 6-9-5 **62** .... (p) KatherineBegley 7 62
(Michael Herrington) *chsd ldr: led 3f out: pushed along in 1 l ld 2f out: rdn and hdd 1 1/2f out: no ex fnl f (gelding sustained a laceration to its right shoulder en route to the racecourse; having been examined by the vet upon arrival, the gelding was deemed fit to race)* 7/2[1]
4515 4 1 ¼ **Sir Gnet (IRE)**[16] 1591 5-9-7 **64** .... (h) CierenFallon 1 62
(Ed Dunlop) *hld up: pushed along on inner 2f out: swtchd to centre and drvn 1 1/2f out: sn rdn: r.o fnl f: tk 4th nr fin* 9/2[2]
10-0 5 ½ **Topology**[12] 1675 6-8-13 **59** .... WilliamCarver(3) 5 56
(Joseph Tuite) *mid-div: pushed along 2f out: reminder and wandered briefly 1 1/2f out: rdn into 4th fnl f: no ex and lost 4th nr fin* 8/1
0-00 6 1 ½ **Perfect Soldier (IRE)**[88] 386 5-8-11 **59** .... GavinAshton(5) 2 53
(Shaun Keightley) *chsd ldrs: pushed along 2f out: wknd fnl f* 16/1
/00- 7 3 **Wedding Breakfast (IRE)**[276] 5168 5-8-13 **59** .... GeorgiaDobie(3) 9 47
(Stella Barclay) *slowly away: bhd: pushed along over 2f out: rdn over 1f out: kpt on fnl f (jockey said mare was slowly away)* 66/1
453- 8 4 ½ **Rock On Bertie (IRE)**[233] 6787 4-8-8 **51** .... (p) RobertDodsworth 4 30
(Derek Shaw) *t.k.h: led: pushed along and hdd 3f out: sn wknd* 40/1
3432 9 ½ **Traveller (FR)**[9] 1769 5-9-1 **58** .... (t[1]) KieranSchofield 13 37
(Antony Brittain) *prom: drvn 3f out: rdn and lost pl over 2f out: wknd (jockey said gelding ran flat)* 9/2[2]
0-00 10 5 **Cookie Ring (IRE)**[83] 465 8-8-2 **50** oh5 .... (t w) ElishaWhittington(5) 12 19
(Liam Bailey) *hld up: drvn over 2f out: sn rdn and wknd* 66/1
5032 11 nk **Attain**[11] 1710 10-8-9 **57** .... KateLeahy(5) 6 25
(Archie Watson) *mid-div: pushed along and lost pl 3f out: wknd (jockey said gelding ran flat)* 10/1

0060 **12** *11* **Just Heather (IRE)**[20] [1506] 5-8-4 **50** oh5....................(v) EllaMcCain(3) 3
(John Wainwright) *hld up: last 3f out: sn drvn and lost tch* **80/1**
2m 1.23s (0.43) **Going Correction** -0.025s/f (Stan) **12** Ran SP% **118.9**
Speed ratings (Par 101): **97,96,93,92,92 90,88,84,83,79 78,69**
CSF £45.08 CT £160.97 TOTE £7.70: £2.10, £2.20, £1.80; EX 57.10 Trifecta £272.00.
Owner Alex Percy **Bred** N E Poole And George Thornton **Trained** Tern Hill, Shropshire
FOCUS
An ordinary handicap, and the pace picked up a fair way out. Straightforward form.

1984 FRUIT SHOOT NOVICE MEDIAN AUCTION STKS 1m 142y (Tp)
2:45 (2:45) (Class 6) 3-5-Y-O **£3,105** (£924; £461; £230) **Stalls** Low

Form RPR
5 **1** **Liliofthelamplight (IRE)**[47] [1034] 3-8-12 0.................. JoeFanning 3 75
(Mark Johnston) *chsd ldr: pushed along in 1/2 l 2nd 2f out: sn drvn: rdn 1f out: sustained chal thrght fnl f: led last two strides* **11/1**[3]
41- **2** *nk* **Sunset Flash (IRE)**[151] [9205] 3-9-5 0.......................... StevieDonohoe 5 81
(David Lanigan) *led: qcknd pce over 3f out: pushed along in 1/2 l ld 2f out: drvn in narrow ld 1 1/2f out: sn rdn: strly pressed thrght fnl f: hdd last two strides* **5/6**[1]
0 **3** *11* **Fields Of Dreams**[60] [836] 3-9-3 0................................ JasonWatson 4 56
(Roger Charlton) *trckd ldrs: pushed along and lost grnd on ldrs 3f out: drvn in 7 l 3rd 2f out: one pce fnl 2f* **14/1**
6- **4** *1 ¼* **Song Without End (IRE)**[227] [7023] 3-9-3 0.........(h[1]) RichardKingscote 2 53
(Sir Michael Stoute) *hld up: pushed along in 5th 3f out: wnt distant 4th 2f out: sn drvn: no imp* **11/8**[2]
5 *14* **Katie O'Hara (IRE)**[169] [8855] 3-8-12 0.......................... EoinWalsh 1 19
(Samuel Farrell, Ire) *t.k.h: trckd ldrs: lost pl as pce qcknd over 3f out: wkng whn n.m.r over 2f out: sn lost tch (jockey said filly ran green)* **100/1**
6 *6* **Melwood** 3-9-3 0.. CamHardie 6 11
(Antony Brittain) *dwlt: sn mde up lost grnd: hld up: drvn in rr 3f out: sn lost tch* **28/1**
1m 50.9s (0.80) **Going Correction** -0.025s/f (Stan) **6** Ran SP% **116.1**
Speed ratings (Par 101): **95,94,84,83,71 66**
CSF £21.86 TOTE £7.90: £2.90, £1.10; EX 22.20 Trifecta £89.80.
Owner Garrett J Freyne **Bred** L Montgomery **Trained** Middleham Moor, N Yorks
FOCUS
This was steadily run and turned into a bit of a dash to the line. It's hard to pin down the form.

1985 FRUIT SHOOT FILLIES' H'CAP 7f 36y (Tp)
3:20 (3:21) (Class 5) (0-75,77) 3-Y-O
£3,752 (£1,116; £557; £300; £300; £300) **Stalls** High

Form RPR
3424 **1** **Adelante (FR)**[19] [1516] 3-8-11 **72**.......................... CierenFallon(7) 3 81
(George Baker) *mid-div: hdwy over 2f out: pushed into 3rd 2f out: drvn to chal 1 1/2f out: led ins fnl f: pushed out and gng away nr fin* **12/1**
61-1 **2** *1 ¼* **Diamond Oasis**[18] [1543] 3-9-9 **77**.......................... (h) OisinMurphy 7 83
(Saeed bin Suroor) *chsd ldr: pushed along in 2 l 2nd 2f out: drvn to ld 1 1/2f out: rdn and hdd ins fnl f: no ex fnl 100yds* **15/8**[1]
5-40 **3** *2 ½* **Laxmi (IRE)**[17] [1567] 3-9-0 **68**.......................... CallumShepherd 1 67
(Brian Meehan) *hld up: pushed along 2f out: drvn in 4th 1f out: r.o into 3rd last 1/2 f* **12/1**
344- **4** *nk* **Gleeful**[181] [8512] 3-9-5 **73**.......................... AndreaAtzeni 4 71
(Roger Varian) *hld up in rr: pushed along 2f out: reminder on outer 1 1/2f out: rdn fnl f: kpt on* **2/1**[2]
632- **5** *2 ¼* **Evolutionary (IRE)**[159] [9050] 3-9-5 **73**.......................... TomMarquand 2 65
(James Tate) *led: pushed along over 2f out: 2 l ld 2f out: rdn and hdd 1 1/2f out: wknd fnl f* **5/1**[3]
041- **6** *½* **Chasing The Rain**[174] [8727] 3-9-6 **74**.......................... CliffordLee 6 65
(K R Burke) *slowly away: bhd: pushed along 2f out: sn drvn: reminder in 5th 1f out: wknd fnl f* **9/1**
02-0 **7** *16* **Annecy**[68] [698] 3-9-7 **75**.......................... StevieDonohoe 5 23
(David Simcock) *chsd ldrs: pushed along in 3rd 3f out: drvn and lost pl 2f out: dropped to last over 1f out: sn eased (jockey said filly stopped quickly)* **25/1**
1m 28.14s (-0.66) **Going Correction** -0.025s/f (Stan) **7** Ran SP% **114.0**
Speed ratings (Par 95): **102,100,97,97,94 94,75**
CSF £34.80 TOTE £10.40: £3.60, £1.80; EX 53.30 Trifecta £489.40.
Owner Adams And Baker **Bred** Christopher Richard Hirst **Trained** Chiddingfold, Surrey
FOCUS
Just a fair handicap, the winner and third having already shown their hands to an extent. The time was sound.

1986 FRUIT SHOOT H'CAP 7f 36y (Tp)
3:55 (3:55) (Class 6) (0-60,60) 4-Y-O+
£3,105 (£924; £461; £300; £300; £300) **Stalls** High

Form RPR
4640 **1** **My Town Chicago (USA)**[25] [1378] 4-9-7 **60**.......................... CliffordLee 8 67
(Kevin Frost) *mde all: pushed along in 2 l ld 2f out: rdn 1 1/2f out: 1 l ld 1f out: ld diminished in fnl f but kpt on resolutely to repel rivals: lost shoe (vet said gelding had lost its left hind shoe)* **10/1**
3523 **2** *½* **Liamba**[26] [1368] 4-9-7 **60**.......................... CamHardie 9 66
(David O'Meara) *chsd wnr: drvn in 2 l 2nd 2f out: sn rdn: r.o u.p fnl f: a hld* **8/1**
-003 **3** *1 ½* **Mansfield**[17] [1565] 6-9-1 **59**.......................... DylanHogan(5) 7 61
(Stella Barclay) *hld up: pushed along and hdwy on outer 2f out: rdn in share of 3rd 1f out: kpt on fnl f: secured 3rd on line* **13/2**[3]
-416 **4** *shd* **Waqt (IRE)**[12] [1675] 5-9-7 **60**.......................... RossaRyan 3 62
(Alexandra Dunn) *chsd ldrs: drvn in 3rd 2f out: rdn in share of 3rd 1f out: r.o fnl f: lost 3rd on line* **7/1**
0620 **5** *hd* **Energia Flavio (BRZ)**[9] [1769] 8-9-2 **55**.......................... (v[1]) DavidEgan 2 56
(Patrick Morris) *hld up: drvn on outer 1 1/2f out: kpt on fnl f (jockey said gelding hung left-handed in the home straight)* **9/1**
010- **6** *3* **Rockesbury**[137] [9428] 4-9-0 **60**.......................... (b) LauraCoughlan(7) 10 54
(David Loughnane) *stmbld leaving stalls: prom: cl 3rd 3f out: drvn and lost pl over 2f out: sn rdn: no ex (jockey said gelding stumbled leaving the stalls)* **14/1**
1452 **7** *½* **Naralsaif (IRE)**[6] [1837] 5-9-2 **55**.......................... (v) PaddyMathers 5 48
(Derek Shaw) *hld up: pushed along 3f out: sn drvn: rdn 1 1/2f out: no imp* **11/4**[1]
3120 **8** *1* **Viola Park**[11] [1715] 5-9-7 **60**.......................... (p) DavidProbert 4 50
(Ronald Harris) *mid-div: pushed along 2f out: rdn over 1f out: wknd and eased fnl f* **6/1**[2]
0000 **9** *5* **Makaarim**[28] [1338] 5-9-6 **59**.......................... (h) TomQueally 11 37
(Seamus Durack) *slowly away: bhd: pushed along 3f out: rdn on outer 1 1/2f out: nvr a factor* **33/1**

0000 **10** *4 ½* **Our Man In Havana**[12] [1682] 4-9-5 **58**.......................... LukeMorris 1 25
(Richard Price) *mid-div: drvn 3 out: lost pl and struggling whn hmpd over 2f out: sn rdn and bhd* **40/1**
3253 **11** *6* **Shamlan (IRE)**[28] [1328] 7-9-0 **56**.......................... (b) JoshuaBryan(3) 6 8
(Kevin Frost) *a bhd (jockey said gelding was slowly into stride and never travelling)* **8/1**
1m 28.55s (-0.25) **Going Correction** -0.025s/f (Stan) **11** Ran SP% **120.1**
Speed ratings (Par 101): **100,99,97,97,97 93,93,92,86,81 74**
CSF £89.57 CT £569.51 TOTE £12.60: £4.10, £2.70, £2.50; EX 80.20 Trifecta £285.30.
Owner J T Stimpson **Bred** Godolphin **Trained** Newcastle-under-Lyme, Staffs
FOCUS
A modest handicap in which the pace held up.

1987 BRITVIC H'CAP 5f 21y (Tp)
4:30 (4:31) (Class 6) (0-55,55) 4-Y-O+
£3,105 (£924; £461; £300; £300; £300) **Stalls** Low

Form RPR
-000 **1** **Red Invader (IRE)**[20] [1507] 9-9-7 **55**.......................... (p) OisinMurphy 1 62
(John Butler) *chsd ldrs: gng wl in 3rd 2f out: pushed along to chal on inner 1 1/2f out: led and rdn 1f out: forged clr fnl f (trainer said, regarding the apparent improvement in form, that gelding settled better in the preliminaries on this occasion)* **4/1**[2]
-505 **2** *1 ¼* **Bahango (IRE)**[24] [1402] 7-8-10 **49**.......................... ThomasGreatrex(5) 3 52
(Patrick Morris) *led: 1/2 l ld 2f out: rdn over 1f out: hdd 1f out: kpt on fnl f* **7/1**
1303 **3** *¾* **Atyaaf**[11] [1716] 4-9-6 **54**.......................... PaddyMathers 2 54
(Derek Shaw) *mid-div: drvn 2f out: rdn over 1f out: hdwy fnl f: r.o: snatched 3rd on line* **7/2**[1]
000- **4** *shd* **Raffle King (IRE)**[193] [8131] 5-9-6 **54**.......................... CamHardie 7 53
(Ruth Carr) *rrd and uns rdr gng out on to crse: chsd ldr: drvn in 1/2 l 2nd 2f out: sn rdn: dropped to 3rd 1f out: one pce fnl f: lost 3rd on line* **9/2**[3]
0430 **5** *1 ½* **Captain Ryan**[7] [1820] 8-9-7 **55**.......................... (t[1]) TrevorWhelan 4 49
(Geoffrey Deacon) *chsd ldrs: pushed along in 5th 2f out: rdn over 1f out: nt qckn fnl f* **12/1**
54 **6** *¾* **Zipedeedodah (IRE)**[11] [1716] 7-8-7 **48**.......................... WilliamCarver(7) 8 39
(Joseph Tuite) *mid-div: hdwy into 4th 2f out: drvn and lost pl over 1f out: rdn fnl f: no ex* **10/1**
4462 **7** *1 ¾* **Kyllukey**[11] [1716] 6-9-0 **48**.......................... DavidEgan 11 33
(Charlie Wallis) *hld up on outer: drvn 2f out: reminders over 1f out: no imp* **4/1**[2]
066- **8** *1 ¼* **Glyder**[187] [8334] 5-9-0 **48**.......................... LukeMorris 9 29
(John Holt) *bhd: drvn 2f out: rdn fnl f: no imp* **33/1**
0020 **9** *½* **Fuel Injection**[87] [411] 8-8-12 **46**.......................... (b) BarryMcHugh 6 25
(Ruth Carr) *bhd: drvn 2f out: no ch fr over 1f out* **20/1**
206- **10** *2 ½* **John Joiner**[165] [8961] 7-8-9 **50**.......................... GavinAshton(7) 10 20
(Shaun Keightley) *slowly away: a in rr* **25/1**
1m 1.9s **Going Correction** -0.025s/f (Stan) **10** Ran SP% **121.2**
Speed ratings (Par 101): **99,97,95,95,93 92,89,87,86,82**
CSF £32.77 CT £104.75 TOTE £4.10: £2.20, £2.40, £1.70; EX 36.50 Trifecta £145.00.
Owner Power Geneva Ltd **Bred** Tally-Ho Stud **Trained** Newmarket, Suffolk
FOCUS
An ordinary sprint in which those held up struggled to get involved. Limited form in behind the winner.

1988 PEPSI MAX H'CAP 1m 4f 51y (Tp)
5:05 (5:05) (Class 5) (0-70,70) 4-Y-O+
£3,752 (£1,116; £557; £300; £300; £300) **Stalls** Low

Form RPR
430- **1** **Raven's Raft (IRE)**[152] [9179] 4-8-3 **59**.......................... LauraCoughlan(7) 8 66
(David Loughnane) *chsd ldrs: pushed along in 3rd over 2f out: hdwy into 3 l 2nd 2f out: rdn 1 1/2f out: clsd on ldr 1f out: led 1/2f out: sn clr* **33/1**
2 *1* **Lost History (IRE)**[55] [7469] 6-9-4 **70**.......................... JaneElliott(3) 10 75
(John Spearing) *chsd ldrs: drvn on outer over 2f out: hdwy and rdn in 3rd 1 1/2f out: r.o fnl f: tk 2nd fnl 100yds* **50/1**
00-1 **3** *¾* **Ebqaa (IRE)**[27] [1341] 5-9-4 **67**.......................... DavidProbert 9 71+
(James Unett) *hld up: pushed along 2f out: drvn and hdwy on outer 1 1/2f out: sn rdn: r.o u.p fnl f: tk 3rd last stride (jockey said mare hung left-handed throughout)* **13/2**
5411 **4** *hd* **Power Home (IRE)**[26] [1363] 5-9-1 **64**.......................... OisinMurphy 5 68
(Denis Coakley) *chsd ldrs: pushed along in 5th 2f out: rdn over 1f out: r.o fnl f: denied for 3rd last stride* **5/1**[3]
5241 **5** *½* **Dream Magic (IRE)**[20] [1498] 5-9-3 **69**.......................... (b) CameronNoble(3) 2 72
(Mark Loughnane) *led: 3 l ld 2f out: drvn 1 1/2f out: sn rdn: 1 l ld 1f out: hdd 1/2f out: no ex* **3/1**[1]
1232 **6** *5* **Champagne Rules**[14] [1648] 8-9-0 **68**.......................... ConnorMurtagh(5) 7 63
(Sharon Watt) *hld up: pushed along on inner over 2f out: drvn 1 1/2f out: sn rdn: no imp* **9/2**[2]
646 **7** *4* **Raashdy (IRE)**[13] [1666] 6-8-8 **57**.......................... (p) LukeMorris 6 46
(Peter Hiatt) *mid-div: drvn 2f out: nt clr run 1 1/2f out: rdn fnl f: no imp* **20/1**
050- **8** *2 ½* **Boychick (IRE)**[156] [1723] 6-9-5 **68**.......................... RichardKingscote 3 53
(Mark Loughnane) *hld up: pushed along and effrt 1 1/2f out: no further prog* **25/1**
21-2 **9** *nk* **Para Mio (IRE)**[108] [61] 4-9-5 **68**.......................... (t) TomQueally 4 52
(Seamus Durack) *hld up: pushed along: nt clr run and dropped to rr over 2f out: sn rdn: no imp* **8/1**
0240 **10** *1 ½* **Enmeshing**[20] [1500] 6-9-0 **63**.......................... RossaRyan 1 45
(Alexandra Dunn) *bhd: effrt on outer over 2f out: drvn 1 1/2f out: sn rdn: no ex (jockey said gelding was slowly away and stopped quickly)* **8/1**
660- **11** *4* **Collodi (GER)**[17] [8936] 10-9-4 **67**.......................... HayleyTurner 11 42
(Conor Dore) *mid-div: drvn and lost pl over 2f out: wknd* **33/1**
2 **12** *nk* **Movie Star (GER)**[27] [1343] 4-9-1 **64**.......................... (h) TomMarquand 12 39
(Amy Murphy) *prom on outer: drvn in 2nd 3f out: sn rdn and lost pl: eased and dropped to last ins fnl f* **10/1**
2m 39.77s (-1.03) **Going Correction** -0.025s/f (Stan) **12** Ran SP% **120.9**
Speed ratings (Par 103): **102,101,100,100,100 97,94,92,92,91 88,88**
CSF £1136.39 CT £11458.08 TOTE £53.00: £11.50, £16.90, £2.10; EX 446.60.
Owner Jamie Rocke **Bred** Timmy & Michael Hillman **Trained** Tern Hill, Shropshire

FOCUS
A modest handicap that produced a surprise exacta. It's rated as ordinary form.

1989 FRUIT SHOOT NOVICE STKS 1m 4f 51y (Tp)
5:35 (5:35) (Class 5) 4-Y-O+ £3,752 (£1,116; £557; £278) Stalls Low

Form RPR
21/ 1 **Setting Sail**[572] 7503 4-9-9 0 WilliamBuick 5 100+
(Charlie Appleby) *prom: cl 2nd 3f out: eased into ld over 2f out: pushed into 3 l ld 1f out: readily drew further clr ins fnl f: easily* **10/11**[1]
14- 2 6 **Charles Kingsley**[113] 9766 4-9-9 0 JoeFanning 1 88
(Mark Johnston) *trckd ldrs: pushed into 3rd 2f out: drvn to chse wnr 1 1/2f out: 3 l 2nd 1f out: no ch w wnr: dismntd after fin* **7/1**
2-32 3 2 **Heart Of Soul (IRE)**[26] 1365 4-9-2 78 RichardKingscote 4 78
(Ian Williams) *chsd ldrs: pushed along 3f out: rdn into 3rd over 1f out: one pce fnl f* **7/2**[3]
0- 4 5 **Motaraabet**[329] 3159 4-9-2 0 DaneO'Neill 9 70
(Owen Burrows) *led: drvn and hdd over 2f out: sn rdn and dropped to 3rd: wknd into 4th appr fnl f* **11/4**[2]
5 7 **Le Musee (FR)**[38] 6-9-2 0 RossaRyan 2 58+
(Nigel Hawke) *hld up: drvn in distant 7th over 2f out: kpt on past btn rivals fnl 2f* **16/1**
45 6 1 1/4 **Captain Scott (IRE)**[19] 1517 4-9-2 0 DavidEgan 3 57
(Heather Main) *mid-div: drvn in 5th 3f out: sn wknd* **40/1**
65 7 hd **Lawyersgunsn'money**[28] 1331 4-9-2 0 DavidProbert 7 56
(Roger Teal) *hld up: drvn in 6th over 2f out: wknd* **80/1**
8 8 **Och Aye**[48] 4-8-11 0 AndrewBreslin(5) 8 44
(Mark Johnston) *in rr: drvn 5f out: nvr a factor* **50/1**
9 4 **Barrier Reef (IRE)**[345] 2668 4-9-2 0 KieranO'Neill 6 37
(Tim Vaughan) *hld up: drvn and lost tch 4 out* **66/1**
5/5- 10 37 **Samson's Reach**[8] 8373 6-9-2 0 (p) LukeMorris 10
(Richard Price) *hld up: drvn and reminders 4f out: sn lost tch* **80/1**

2m 37.2s (-3.60) **Going Correction** -0.025s/f (Stan) 10 Ran SP% **128.0**
Speed ratings (Par 103): **111,107,105,102,97 96,96,91,88,64**
CSF £9.99 TOTE £1.60: £1.10, £2.30, £1.10; EX 9.00 Trifecta £21.40.
Owner Godolphin **Bred** Godolphin **Trained** Newmarket, Suffolk

FOCUS
They finished well strung out here and the form looks strong for the grade. It was sound run.
T/Plt: £1,306.10 to a £1 stake. Pool: £62,194.18 - 34.76 winning units T/Qpdt: £326.30 to a £1 stake. Pool: £5,248.49 - 11.90 winning units **Keith McHugh**

1990 - 2001a (Foreign Racing) - See Raceform Interactive

STRASBOURG
Monday, April 22

OFFICIAL GOING: Turf: good to soft

2002a PRIX DU CREA (CONDITIONS) (4YO) (TURF) 1m 2f
5:00 4-Y-O £5,180 (£2,072; £1,554; £1,036; £518)

RPR
1 **Plain Beau**[150] 4-9-8 0 ValentinSeguy 7
(Mme Conny Whitfield, France) **61/10**[1]
2 2 1/2 **Moonracer (FR)**[211] 7587 4-9-11 0 CyrilleStefan 3
(S Smrczek, Germany)
3 4 **Quantum Love (GER)** 4-8-7 0 FrauTamaraHofer(3) 8
(Frau J Mayer, Germany)
4 2 1/2 **Menuetto**[37] 4-8-10 0 SoufianeSaadi 13
(H-A Pantall, France)
5 6 **Abiona (GER)**[278] 4-9-5 0 PatrickGibson 6
(Frau S Steinberg, Germany)
6 2 1/2 **Griffone (FR)**[117] 4-9-8 0 Louis-PhilippeBeuzelin 12
(J D Hillis, Germany)
7 hd **Earl (GER)** 4-9-0 0 (p) RodrigoOlechea-Rodriguez 4
(Lennart Hammer-Hansen, Germany)
8 5 **Miss Sixtina (FR)** 4-8-10 0 MickaelBerto 2
(J Parize, France)
9 1 **Zampano (FR)** 4-9-0 0 YoussefEchariaa 9
(A Kleinkorres, Germany)
10 8 **Great America (IRE)**[182] 8492 4-9-1 0 MlleZoePfeil(6) 1
(F Bossert, France)
11 nk **Global Hope (IRE)**[328] 3213 4-9-0 0 GeraldMosse 11
(Gay Kelleway)
12 dist **Grise Magicienne (FR)** 4-8-5 0 DamienBoutet(5) 5
(Gerard Aidant, France)
13 15 **Kranachberg (FR)** 4-8-7 0 MlleLauraGrosso(7) 10
(J D Hillis, Germany)

2m 7.06s 13 Ran SP% **14.1**
PARI-MUTUEL (all including 1 euro stake): WIN 7.10; PLACE 2.80, 1.60, 3.40; DF 6.00.
Owner Anton-Robert Baechler **Bred** Dominic J Burke **Trained** France

LES LANDES
Monday, April 22

OFFICIAL GOING: Turf: firm

2003a LE VERTE RUE ASSOCIATES H'CAP (TURF) 1m 4f
3:05 (3:05) (0-65,0) 3-Y-O+ £1,780 (£640; £380)

RPR
1 **Gabster (IRE)**[238] 6-10-6 0 PaddyAspell
(K Kukk, Jersey) *trckd ldrs: rdn fr over 3f out: styd on to ld 1f out: idled in front: all out* **11/4**[2]
2 hd **Rainbow Lad (IRE)**[62] 789 6-10-5 0 (p) MissSerenaBrotherton
(Michael Appleby) *trckd ldrs: hdwy to go 2nd after 3f: shkn up to ld 3f out: hdd 1f out: kpt on again cl home: jst failed* **4/7**[1]
3 10 **Safira Menina**[238] 7-10-12 0 MrFrederickTett
(Mrs A Malzard, Jersey) *hld up: 5th and outpcd 4f out: kpt on one pce to go 3rd 1f out* **4/1**
4 4 **Fourni (IRE)**[344] 10-9-4 0 ow2 VictoriaMalzard
(Mrs A Malzard, Jersey) *hld up in rr: clipped heels turn over 7f out: outpcd 4f out: kpt on to take remote 4th cl home* **20/1**
5 nse **Grey Panel (FR)**[238] 11-9-6 0 TimClark
(T Le Brocq, Jersey) *sn trckd ldrs: rdn over 3f out: sn wknd* **3/1**[3]
6 nk **Jackblack**[167] 8887 7-10-9 0 DaveCrosse
(K Kukk, Jersey) *led: rdn and hdd 3f out: wknd fr 2f out* **13/2**
7 40 **Rainbow Charlie**[238] 8-8-5 0 oh14 DarraghKeogh
(Mrs A Corson, Jersey) *taken wd: bhd fr 1/2-way: t.o* **22/1**
8 1/2 **Little Lotte (IRE)**[365] 6-9-9 0 ow6 (p) MorganRaine
(Mrs A Corson, Jersey) *bhd fr 1/2-way: t.o* **10/1**

2m 50.0s 8 Ran SP% **166.9**

Owner Lavender Racing Club **Bred** T Whitehead **Trained** Jersey

2004a BLOODSTOCK ADVISORY SERVICE H'CAP (TURF) 1m 100y
4:50 (4:50) (0-55,0) 3-Y-O+ £1,780 (£640; £380)

RPR
1 **Honcho (IRE)**[344] 2690 7-10-12 0 VictoriaMalzard
(Mrs A Malzard, Jersey) *mde all: pressed for ld fr 5f out to 2f out: rdn clr fnl f* **5/1**[3]
2 8 **William Booth (IRE)**[253] 6081 5-10-10 0 (v) MrWillPettis
(Mrs C Gilbert, Jersey) *t.k.h: trckd ldrs: wnt 2nd and ev ch 2f out: one pce* **11/1**
3 nk **Drummer Jack (IRE)**[42] 1140 3-10-2 0 ow6 DaveCrosse
(K Kukk, Jersey) *hld up: kpt on to take 3rd 1f out: nt rch ldrs* **5/1**[3]
4 2 **Cash N Carrie (IRE)**[11] 1717 5-10-4 0 MissSerenaBrotherton
(Michael Appleby) *trckd ldr: lost pl fr 4f out: btn fr 2f out* **13/8**[1]
5 5 **Kalani Rose**[238] 5-9-6 0 (b) MorganRaine
(Mrs A Corson, Jersey) *trckers ldrs: rushed up to press ldr 5f out to 2f out: wknd rapidly* **12/1**
U **Brown Velvet**[589] 7-10-9 0 MissCPrichard
(Mrs C Gilbert, Jersey) *trckd ldrs: 5th and drvn whn bdly hmpd and uns rdr bnd 2f out* **9/4**[2]
F **Koshi**[238] 4-10-1 0 PaddyAspell
(K Kukk, Jersey) *hld up: hdwy to chse ldrs 4f out: 4th and drvn whn unbalanced and fell bnd 2f out* **9/4**[2]

Owner Sheik A Leg Racing **Bred** Paul Hancock **Trained** St Ouen, Jersey

1916 LINGFIELD (L-H)
Tuesday, April 23

OFFICIAL GOING: Polytrack: standard
Wind: virtually nil Weather: overcast

2005 CHOICE TRAINING H'CAP 1m 1y(P)
4:55 (4:55) (Class 5) (0-75,74) 4-Y-O+ £3,752 (£1,116; £557; £300; £300; £300) Stalls High

Form RPR
340- 1 **Here's Two**[179] 8611 6-9-0 67 JasonWatson 8 74
(Ron Hodges) *w ldrs early: sn settled bk to chse ldrs: effrt ent fnl 2f: hdwy u.p to ld ins fnl f: r.o strly* **14/1**
500- 2 1 1/2 **Dreaming Of Paris**[187] 8339 5-9-5 72 JoeFanning 11 76
(Patrick Chamings) *w ldr and travelled strly: effrt and qcknd to ld over 1f out: hdd ins fnl f: kpt on but no match for wnr* **9/1**
23-6 3 nk **Nawar**[45] 1102 4-9-3 70 (t[1] w) AdamKirby 2 73
(Martin Bosley) *hld up in tch in midfield: n.m.r: swtchd rt and effrt over 1f out: styd on wl ins fnl f: nvr getting to wnr* **8/1**[3]
000- 4 shd **She Believes (IRE)**[132] 9505 4-9-6 73 LiamKeniry 7 76
(Sylvester Kirk) *in tch in midfield: effrt jst over 2f out: kpt on ins fnl f: nt enough pce to rch ldrs* **16/1**
4-32 5 1/2 **Arctic Sea**[14] 1659 5-9-5 72 RaulDaSilva 6 74
(Paul Cole) *led: rdn ent fnl 2f: drvn and hdd over 1f out: no ex and outpcd ins fnl f* **5/4**[1]
5654 6 1/2 **The Warrior (IRE)**[15] 1655 7-9-1 70 ow1 (b) PaddyBradley(3) 9 71
(Lee Carter) *s.i.s and bustled along early: styd wd early and racd in last quartet: effrt and swtchd rt over 1f out: styd on ins fnl f: nvr trbld ldrs (jockey said gelding was slowly away)* **10/1**
4420 7 1 3/4 **Dark Alliance (IRE)**[21] 1511 8-9-4 71 JimCrowley 1 67
(Mark Loughnane) *t.k.h early: chsd ldrs: nt clr run on inner 2f out: effrt over 1f out: unable qck 1f out: wknd ins fnl f* **6/1**[2]
/00- 8 3 1/4 **Connaught Ranger (IRE)**[220] 7300 4-9-7 74 ShaneKelly 4 63
(Denis Coakley) *stdd sn after s: hld up in last quartet: effrt over 2f out: swtchd rt 1f out: nvr trbld ldrs* **8/1**[3]
02-1 9 1 1/2 **Weloof (FR)**[95] 295 5-8-13 66 KieranO'Neill 10 52
(John Butler) *stdd after s: hld up in tch in last quartet: swtchd to outer over 3f out: effrt bnd 2f out: no imp and wknd ins fnl f* **8/1**[3]
64-0 10 3/4 **Officer Drivel (IRE)**[17] 1591 8-8-7 60 oh1 (h) KierenFox 5 44
(Paddy Butler) *stdd after s: t.k.h: hld up in rr: nvr involved (jockey said gelding ran too free)* **66/1**

1m 37.61s (-0.59) **Going Correction** -0.025s/f (Stan) 10 Ran SP% **125.2**
Speed ratings (Par 103): **101,99,99,99,98 98,96,93,91,90**
CSF £143.14 CT £1133.68 TOTE £20.30: £4.50, £3.10, £2.20; EX 176.00 Trifecta £1805.40.
Owner K Corcoran, C E Weare, R J Hodges **Bred** D R Tucker **Trained** Charlton Adam, Somerset

FOCUS
A modest handicap and it paid to race handily. A length pb from the winner.

2006 DOWNLOAD THE STAR SPORTS APP NOW! (S) STKS 1m 1y(P)
5:25 (5:25) (Class 6) 3-Y-O+ £3,105 (£924; £461; £300; £300) Stalls High

Form RPR
6604 1 **Come On Tier (FR)**[19] 1544 4-9-7 71 JimCrowley 2 62+
(David Simcock) *broke wl: mde all: rdn and kicked clr over 1f out: r.o wl and a doing enough ins fnl f* **5/4**[1]
-055 2 1 1/4 **Lacan (IRE)**[32] 1269 8-9-7 74 TomMarquand 6 59+
(Brett Johnson) *hld up in tch in rr: effrt ent fnl 2f: chsd wnr u.p 1f out: kpt on but a hld ins fnl f* **7/4**[2]
5000 3 2 3/4 **Haraz (IRE)**[3] 1935 6-9-7 43 JasonWatson 4 53
(Paddy Butler) *chsd ldrs tl wnt 2nd over 2f out: drvn and unable to match pce of wnr over 1f out: 3rd and kpt on same pce ins fnl f* **66/1**
5430 4 12 **Shyron**[32] 1269 8-9-12 76 (v) AdamKirby 3 30
(Lee Carter) *hld up in tch: effrt in 3rd ent fnl 2f: fnd nil and btn 4th over 1f out: eased towards fin* **11/4**[3]

-064 **5** *33* **Lord Digby**[47] 1070 4-9-7 25..(b) LiamKeniry 5
(Adam West) *sn w wnr: lost pl qckly and short of room over 2f out: wl bhd and eased ins fnl f: t.o* **100/1**

1m 38.05s (-0.15) **Going Correction** -0.025s/f (Stan)
WFA 3 from 4yo+ 14lb **5** Ran SP% **110.0**
Speed ratings (Par 101): **99,97,95,83,50**
CSF £3.74 TOTE £2.00: £1.20, £1.30; EX 4.00 Trifecta £24.30.The winner was sold to Mr Lee Carter for £10,600. Lacan was claimed for £7,000 by Mr Michael Bell.
Owner Genting Casinos Uk Limited **Bred** T De La Heronniere Et Al **Trained** Newmarket, Suffolk

FOCUS
Little got into this, the winning favourite receiving a good ride from the front, and the 4l third carried a rating of just 43.

2007 STARSPORTS.BET H'CAP 1m 1y(P)
5:55 (5:58) (Class 6) (0-60,60) 3-Y-O
£3,105 (£924; £461; £300; £300; £300) **Stalls** High

Form RPR
6012 **1** **Capofaro**[11] 1726 3-9-2 **55**.. NicolaCurrie 6 64
(Jamie Osborne) *sn led and mde rest: rdn and kicked clr over 1f out: r.o wl and a doing enough ins fnl f* **5/1**[2]

4501 **2** *1 1/4* **Comeonfeelthefource (IRE)**[11] 1726 3-8-8 **54**.......(t) GeorgiaDobie[(7)] 11 60
(Lee Carter) *t.k.h: chsd ldrs: wnt 2nd 3f out tl over 2f out: rdn and lft chsng clr wnr wl over 1f out: styd on u.p ins fnl f but nvr getting on terms w wnr* **7/1**

5-54 **3** *1 1/2* **Lippy Lady (IRE)**[43] 1140 3-9-0 **53**.......................................(h) JFEgan 7 56
(Paul George) *in tch in midfield: effrt to chse ldrs jst over 2f out: 3rd and drvn over 1f out: kpt on ins fnl f but no threat to wnr* **5/1**[2]

-040 **4** *4* **Maid Millie**[26] 1385 3-9-6 **59**......................................(v[1]) JoeFanning 9 52+
(Robert Cowell) *s.i.s: prog into midfield on outer 5f out: wnt 2nd over 2f out tl wd and lost pl bnd wl over 1f out: wl hld 4th and hung lft ins fnl f* **20/1**

403- **5** *1/2* **Temujin (IRE)**[178] 8638 3-9-0 **60**.................................. CierenFallon[(7)] 2 52+
(Charles Hills) *hld up in tch in midfield: effrt in 5th ent fnl 2f: no imp over 1f out: pushed lft and kpt on same pce ins fnl f* **10/3**[1]

060 **6** *nk* **Sacred Warner (IRE)**[18] 1562 3-9-3 **56**.............................. AdamKirby 8 48+
(Clive Cox) *hld up in tch towards rr: effrt 2f out: nt clr run over 1f out: sme hdwy u.p whn short of room ins fnl f: nvr trbld ldrs* **8/1**

-504 **7** *nk* **Trouble Shooter (IRE)**[47] 1066 3-8-10 **48** ow1..........(p) ShaneKelly 12 40+
(Shaun Keightley) *bhd: sme prog over 1f out: kpt on same pce u.p and no imp ins fnl f* **6/1**[3]

0-00 **8** *2* **Croqueta (IRE)**[11] 1726 3-8-11 **50**............................... SeanLevey 4 36+
(Richard Hannon) *towards rr: u.p and no imp over 1f out: nvr involved* **33/1**

00-0 **9** *1/2* **Clubora (USA)**[31] 1288 3-9-1 **54**................................ TomMarquand 5 39
(Richard Hannon) *in tch in midfield: effrt and unable qck 2f out: no threat to ldrs after: keeping in same pce whn nudged lft ins fnl f* **16/1**

0040 **10** *3 1/2* **Poor Auld Paddy**[13] 1696 3-9-5 **58**.............................. JasonWatson 3 35+
(David Elsworth) *a in rr: effrt ent fnl 2f: no prog and nvr involved (jockey said colt lost its action in the final furlong)* **10/1**

00-0 **11** *1 1/2* **Supreme Chance**[88] 400 3-8-7 **46** oh1......................... KieranO'Neill 10 20
(Michael Blanshard) *midfield: rdn over 2f out: outpcd and btn over 1f out: bhd ins fnl f* **100/1**

4030 **12** *2 3/4* **Dorchester**[26] 1385 3-9-6 **59**.......................................(p[1]) HarryBentley 1 26
(Marco Botti) *taken down early and led to post: dwlt: sn rcvrd and chsd ldr tl 3f out: u.p and losing pl 2f out: bhd ins fnl f* **14/1**

1m 38.09s (-0.11) **Going Correction** -0.025s/f (Stan) **12** Ran SP% **124.6**
Speed ratings (Par 96): **99,97,96,92,91 91,91,89,88,85 83,80**
CSF £41.65 CT £193.71 TOTE £5.60: £2.50, £2.40, £1.60; EX 39.20 Trifecta £77.20.
Owner Michael Buckley **Bred** Cheveley Park Stud Ltd **Trained** Upper Lambourn, Berks

FOCUS
A moderate 3yo handicap and another race in which little got involved from off the pace, the winner making all.

2008 DOWNLOAD THE STAR SPORTS APP NOW! H'CAP 6f 1y(P)
6:25 (6:27) (Class 4) (0-85,85) 3-Y-O
£5,530 (£1,645; £822; £411; £300; £300) **Stalls** Low

Form RPR
33-4 **1** **Alnasherat**[12] 1723 3-9-0 **78**.............................. RichardKingscote 2 84+
(Sir Michael Stoute) *w ldr: rdn to ld jst over 1f out: r.o wl ins fnl f* **15/8**[1]

13-0 **2** *1* **Be Like Me (IRE)**[11] 1729 3-9-4 **82**.............................. HarryBentley 6 84
(Marco Botti) *t.k.h: hld up in tch in midfield: effrt on outer ent fnl 2f: chsd wnr ins fnl f: kpt on wl but a hld* **8/1**

010- **3** *1 1/4* **Motagally**[192] 8193 3-9-4 **82**.. JimCrowley 4 80+
(Charles Hills) *t.k.h: chsd ldrs: effrt 2f out: no ex ins fnl f: wknd towards fin* **7/2**[3]

040- **4** *1/2* **Prairie Spy (IRE)**[222] 7198 3-9-5 **83**................................. JoeFanning 1 79
(Mark Johnston) *niggled along in midfield early: effrt to chse ldrs ent fnl 2f: outpcd over 1f out: keeping on but no threat to wnr whn nt clr run and swtchd lft cl home* **9/1**

3111 **5** *1* **Probability (IRE)**[11] 1729 3-9-7 **85**................................ BenCurtis 3 78
(Archie Watson) *broke wl: led but pestered: hdd u.p jst over 1f out: lost 2nd and wknd ins fnl f (jockey said filly ran flat)* **3/1**[2]

00-6 **6** *2* **Jungle Inthebungle (IRE)**[24] 1424 3-9-3 **81**............... TomMarquand 7 68
(Mick Channon) *dwlt and swtchd lft sn after s: effrt and clsd jst over 2f out: outpcd and btn over 1f out: wknd ins fnl f* **10/1**

010- **7** *9* **Aegean Mist**[139] 9396 3-8-8 **72**..................................... KieranO'Neill 5 30
(John Bridger) *sn dropped to last pair: effrt over 2f out: sn struggling and outpcd: wknd fnl f* **66/1**

1m 11.48s (-0.42) **Going Correction** -0.025s/f (Stan) **7** Ran SP% **113.7**
Speed ratings (Par 100): **101,99,98,97,96 93,81**
CSF £17.65 CT £48.19 TOTE £2.90: £1.40, £3.60; EX 15.30 Trifecta £57.10.
Owner Mohamed Obaida **Bred** Rabbah Bloodstock Limited **Trained** Newmarket, Suffolk

FOCUS
A decent 3yo sprint won by a progressive sort. The second is rated in line with her Wolverhampton win.

2009 CALL STAR SPORTS ON 08000 521 321 NOVICE STKS 6f 1y(P)
6:55 (6:55) (Class 5) 3-Y-O+ **£3,752** (£1,116; £557; £278) **Stalls** Low

Form RPR
1- **1** **Habub (USA)**[210] 7648 4-10-2 0.. JimCrowley 2 88+
(Owen Burrows) *mde all: wnt clr 2f out: sn clr and in command: easily* **1/4**[1]

0 **2** *5* **Gonzaga**[18] 1570 4-9-4 0... RachealKneller[(5)] 4 65
(James Bennett) *chsd ldrs on inner: effrt to dispute 2nd but wnr clr over 1f out: kpt on same pce to go 2nd ins fnl f but no imp on wnr* **66/1**

14- **3** *shd* **Maid Of Spirit (IRE)**[231] 6905 4-9-11 0.............................. AdamKirby 8 67
(Clive Cox) *t.k.h: chsd ldrs tl clsd to join wnr over 4f out: outpcd by wnr and rdn 2f out: lost wl hld 2nd and kpt on same pce ins fnl f* **4/1**[2]

56 **4** *1 3/4* **Physics (IRE)**[43] 1139 3-8-12 0....................................... RaulDaSilva 6 56
(Paul Cole) *t.k.h: w wnr tl over 4f out: styd chsng ldrs: nt clr run ent fnl 2f: effrt over 1f out: wl hld 4th and kpt on same pce ins fnl f* **5/1**[3]

05-0 **5** *2 3/4* **True Belief (IRE)**[11] 1728 3-8-12 70............................ TomMarquand 7 48
(Brett Johnson) *taken down early: slowly away and awkward leaving stalls: t.k.h in rr: clsd and in tch on outer over 4f out: outpcd 2f out: wl hld after (jockey said gelding was slowly away and ran too free)* **33/1**

40-2 **6** *3/4* **Turquoise Friendly**[81] 520 3-8-12 70.............................. KieranO'Neill 5 45
(Robert Cowell) *t.k.h: hld up in tch in midfield: clsd 1/2-way: hung rt: wd and lost pl bnd wl over 1f out: wl btn fnl f (jockey said gelding hung right-handed)* **8/1**

0 **7** *3/4* **Farhhmoreexciting**[24] 1423 4-9-9 0.............................. JasonWatson 3 46
(David Elsworth) *s.i.s: pushed along early and rn green: clsd and in tch over 4f out: outpcd 2f out: wl btn after* **16/1**

00 **8** *5* **Arvensis**[13] 1677 3-8-7 0.. CharlieBennett 1 22
(Hughie Morrison) *mounted in chute and taken down early: s.i.s: pushed along and rn green early: clsd and in tch over 4f out: outpcd 2f out: sn bhd* **66/1**

1m 12.12s (0.22) **Going Correction** -0.025s/f (Stan)
WFA 3 from 4yo 11lb **8** Ran SP% **139.6**
Speed ratings (Par 103): **101,94,94,91,88 87,86,79**
CSF £57.72 TOTE £1.20: £1.02, £31.30, £1.10; EX 46.60 Trifecta £221.00.
Owner Hamdan Al Maktoum **Bred** Summer Wind Farm **Trained** Lambourn, Berks

FOCUS
An ordinary novice in terms of depth, but a potentially smart winner. A surprise second but the form is taken at face value.

2010 WATCH THE #BETTINGPEOPLE VIDEOS STARSPORTSBET.CO.UK H'CAP 5f 6y(P)
7:25 (7:25) (Class 6) (0-65,65) 4-Y-O+
£3,105 (£924; £461; £300; £300; £300) **Stalls** High

Form RPR
4402 **1** **Majorette**[46] 1076 5-9-3 **61**.. TrevorWhelan 4 67
(Brian Barr) *dwlt: in tch: clsd into midfield over 2f out: effrt to chse ldrs 1f out: styd on u.p to ld wl ins fnl f: sn in command* **9/2**

3101 **2** *1* **Hurricane Alert**[12] 1716 7-7-12 **49**................................ AledBeech[(7)] 2 51
(Mark Hoad) *taken down early: sn led on inner: rdn over 1f out: kpt on wl u.p tl hdd and no ex wl ins fnl f* **10/1**

4213 **3** *hd* **Fareeq**[17] 1590 5-9-6 **64**.......................................(bt) RichardKingscote 5 66
(Charlie Wallis) *w ldrs: rdn and ev ch over 1f out: kpt on wl u.p tl unable to match pce of wnr wl ins fnl f* **11/4**[1]

5404 **4** *shd* **Dotted Swiss (IRE)**[10] 1766 4-9-0 **63**...............(b) ThomasGreatrex[(5)] 10 64
(Archie Watson) *towards rr on outer: hdwy u.p 1f out: edgd lft and styd on wl ins fnl f: nvr getting to wnr* **4/1**[3]

200- **5** *1 3/4* **Ghepardo**[182] 8497 4-9-7 **65**..(t[1]) TomMarquand 3 60
(Patrick Chamings) *in tch: effrt on inner over 1f out: no ex ins fnl f: wknd towards fin* **12/1**

0365 **6** *3/4* **Pharoh Jake**[17] 1590 11-8-5 **49**..................................... KieranO'Neill 8 41
(John Bridger) *led: sn hdd and dropped to midfield: effrt 2f out: kpt on same pce and no imp whn sltly impeded ins fnl f* **16/1**

-052 **7** *1/2* **Come On Dave (IRE)**[17] 1590 10-9-6 **64**......................(b) LiamKeniry 6 55
(John Butler) *taken down early: dwlt and awkward leaving stalls: hld up in rr: effrt over 1f out: nvr involved* **7/2**[2]

-100 **8** *2 1/2* **Sandfrankskipsgo**[17] 1590 10-9-0 **58**................................ ShaneKelly 9 40
(Peter Crate) *w ldrs tl unable qck and outpcd jst over 1f out: wknd ins fnl f* **20/1**

58.7s (-0.10) **Going Correction** -0.025s/f (Stan) **8** Ran SP% **114.5**
Speed ratings (Par 101): **99,97,97,96,94 92,92,88**
CSF £48.02 CT £145.33 TOTE £5.50: £1.70, £2.80, £1.40; EX 34.60 Trifecta £122.10.
Owner Chris Clark & Daisy Hitchins **Bred** M Pennell **Trained** Longburton, Dorset
■ Stewards' Enquiry : Thomas Greatrex caution: careless riding

FOCUS
Moderate sprinting form.

2011 FIRST FOR INDUSTRY JOBS VISIT STARRECRUITMENT.BET H'CAP 1m 4f (P)
7:55 (7:55) (Class 6) (0-65,66) 3-Y-O
£3,105 (£924; £461; £300; £300; £300) **Stalls** Low

Form RPR
1-44 **1** **Torolight**[41] 1173 3-9-10 **66**.. ShaneKelly 5 74+
(Richard Hughes) *sltly impeded leaving stalls: midfield: swtchd rt and quick move to press ldr 3f out: rdn and qcknd to ld 2f out: hung lft ent fnl f: kpt on and a doing enough after* **2/1**[2]

0-22 **2** *3/4* **Rich Cummins**[10] 1770 3-9-2 **58**..................................... JoeFanning 6 65
(Mark Johnston) *chsd ldrs tl led 3f out: sn clr w wnr: hdd and unable to match pce of wnr 2f out: edgd lft over 1f out: sltly impeded and swtchd rt 1f out: styd on ins fnl f but nvr quite getting bk to wnr (jockey said gelding hung left-handed)* **13/8**[1]

600- **3** *4 1/2* **Brooklyn Boy**[124] 9637 3-9-5 **61**..................................... JimCrowley 8 61
(Harry Dunlop) *hld up in last pair: hdwy over 2f out: cl 3rd 2f out: sn outpcd: wl hld and kpt on same pce ins fnl f* **3/1**[3]

06-0 **4** *3 1/4* **Highway Robbery**[17] 1593 3-7-10 **45**..................(p[1]) SophieRalston[(7)] 4 40
(Julia Feilden) *chsd ldr tl 3f out: stl cl enough in 4th 2f out: sn outpcd u.p: wknd ins fnl f* **20/1**

00-6 **5** *1* **Moon Artist (FR)**[66] 765 3-8-3 **45**................................ KieranO'Neill 1 38
(Michael Blanshard) *chsd ldrs tl outpcd ent fnl 2f: wl hld after and wknd ins fnl f* **25/1**

-100 **6** *5* **Ginge N Tonic**[19] 1555 3-8-8 **50**..............................(p) NicolaCurrie 2 35
(Adam West) *led tl 3f out: sn rdn and outpcd jst over 2f out: wl btn over 1f out* **12/1**

50-6 **7** *nk* **Alramz**[25] 1396 3-9-4 **63**.. PaddyBradley[(3)] 3 48
(Lee Carter) *s.i.s: a in rr: outpcd over 2f out: sn u.p and no rspnse: bhd ins fnl f* **50/1**

530 **8** *6* **Mi Manchi (IRE)**[25] 1397 3-9-3 **62**................................ AaronJones[(3)] 7 37
(Marco Botti) *in last trio: outpcd over 2f out: sn wl btn and bhd fnl f* **16/1**

2m 31.75s (-1.25) **Going Correction** -0.025s/f (Stan) **8** Ran SP% **120.6**
Speed ratings (Par 96): **103,102,99,97,96 93,93,89**
CSF £5.92 CT £9.29 TOTE £3.00: £1.30, £1.10, £1.30; EX 5.60 Trifecta £16.00.
Owner D A Thorpe **Bred** Bobble Barn Stud **Trained** Upper Lambourn, Berks

FOCUS
The two market leaders dominated in the straight and look a progressive pair.
T/Plt: £67.70 to a £1 stake. Pool: £54,379.52 - 585.89 winning units T/Qpdt: £7.40 to a £1 stake. Pool: £8,796.51 - 875.53 winning units **Steve Payne**

1983 **WOLVERHAMPTON (A.W)** (L-H)
Tuesday, April 23

OFFICIAL GOING: Tapeta: standard
Wind: Light against Weather: Overcast

2012 FRUIT SHOOT APPRENTICE H'CAP 1m 142y (Tp)
5:10 (5:10) (Class 6) (0-55,55) 4-Y-O+
£3,105 (£924; £461; £300; £300; £300) **Stalls** Low

Form RPR
3303 1 **Mans Not Trot (IRE)**[39] 1214 4-9-5 **53**..................(p) MeganNicholls 13 60
(Brian Barr) *racd keenly: sn w ldr tl shkn up over 3f out: rdn over 1f out: r.o to ld nr fin* **22/1**
0001 2 *hd* **Tha'ir (IRE)**[7] 1841 9-8-13 **46**.................. ScottMcCullagh(3) 7 57
(Philip McBride) *chsd ldrs: rdn over 1f out: r.o* **7/4**[1]
0002 3 *½* **Adventureman**[12] 1722 7-9-7 **55**..................(b) ConnorMurtagh 2 61
(Ruth Carr) *led: rdn over 1f out: hdd nr fin* **15/2**[3]
0333 4 *2 ½* **Sea Shack**[26] 1390 5-9-2 **53**..................(t) ThoreHammerHansen(3) 5 53
(Julia Feilden) *stmbld s: hld up in tch: rdn over 1f out: edgd lft ins fnl f: styd on same pce* **5/2**[2]
000- 5 *1 ¼* **Ronnie The Rooster**[171] 8830 5-9-5 **53**..................(w) SeanDavis 6 51
(Les Eyre) *chsd ldrs: pushed along over 3f out: rdn over 1f out: styd on same pce ins fnl f* **25/1**
050- 6 *nse* **Majeste**[147] 9278 5-9-2 **50**.................. DannyRedmond 8 48
(Rebecca Bastiman) *hld up: shkn up over 2f out: styd on: nt rch ldrs* **20/1**
40-2 7 *nk* **Captain Peaky**[47] 1060 6-8-12 **46**.................. PaulaMuir 11 44
(Liam Bailey) *prom: hmpd sn after s: rdn over 1f out: styd on same pce ins fnl f* **8/1**
6460 8 *1* **Jeremy's Jet (IRE)**[20] 1527 8-8-12 **46** oh1..................(t) PoppyBridgwater 4 43
(Tony Carroll) *s.i.s: hld up: effrt and nt clr run over 1f out: nt trble ldrs (jockey said gelding was continually denied a clear run in the home straight)* **14/1**
410- 9 *½* **Silk Mill Blue**[165] 8979 5-9-2 **50**.................. SebastianWoods 9 44
(Richard Whitaker) *awkward s: hmpd sn after: hld up: rdn over 2f out: hdwy over 1f out: no ex ins fnl f* **25/1**
000- 10 *1 ¼* **Billiebrookedit (IRE)**[147] 9278 4-8-13 **50**.................. TobyEley(3) 3 41
(Steph Hollinshead) *bmpd s: hld up: pushed along over 3f out: nvr on terms (jockey said gelding was never travelling and hung left-handed on the home turn)* **22/1**
-620 11 *1* **One Liner**[27] 1354 5-8-5 **46** oh1..................(b) KateLeahy(7) 1 35
(John O'Shea) *s.i.s: sn pushed along and a in rr* **25/1**
000- 12 *10* **Quiet Moment (IRE)**[26] 4740 5-9-0 **48**..................(t) HarrisonShaw 10 16
(Maurice Barnes) *s.i.s: a in rr* **66/1**

1m 50.03s (-0.07) **Going Correction** -0.075s/f (Stan) **12 Ran SP% 121.0**
Speed ratings (Par 101): **97,96,96,94,93 93,92,91,91,90 89,80**
CSF £58.04 CT £349.95 TOTE £18.70: £4.90, £1.10, £2.00; EX 104.60 Trifecta £727.10.
Owner Miss Daisy Hitchins **Bred** Tally-Ho Stud **Trained** Longburton, Dorset
■ Stewards' Enquiry : Connor Murtagh two-day ban: used whip above the permitted level (May 7-8)
Megan Nicholls two-day ban: interference & careless riding (May 5, 7)

FOCUS
The winner and third appeared to do plenty in the early stages and looked vulnerable to the closers, but only the favourite was able to throw down a challenge, and he came up just short. Later races on the card would show that being on the pace was a big advantage.

2013 FRUIT SHOOT H'CAP 6f 20y (Tp)
5:40 (5:40) (Class 6) (0-55,57) 4-Y-O+
£3,105 (£924; £461; £300; £300; £300) **Stalls** Low

Form RPR
230- 1 **Olaudah**[183] 8473 5-9-2 **53**.................. DavidProbert 5 61+
(Henry Candy) *mde all: shkn up and edgd lft fr over 1f out: rdn ins fnl f: styd on* **10/1**
0051 2 *1 ¼* **Poppy May (IRE)**[26] 1384 5-9-2 **53**.................. BarryMcHugh 1 57
(James Given) *prom: nt clr run over 2f out: rdn and hung rt over 1f out: r.o to go 2nd nr fin* **11/1**
5004 3 *nk* **Billyoakes (IRE)**[17] 1595 7-9-3 **54**..................(p) DavidEgan 2 57
(Charlie Wallis) *chsd wnr to 1/2-way: rdn to go 2nd again and nt clr run over 1f out: styd on: lost 2nd nr fin* **8/1**
160- 4 *1 ¼* **Cupid's Arrow (IRE)**[147] 9273 5-9-3 **54**.................. JackGarritty 7 54
(Ruth Carr) *chsd ldrs: wnt 2nd 1/2-way tl shkn up and edgd rt over 1f out: styd on same pce ins fnl f* **11/1**
5160 5 *½* **Seaforth (IRE)**[7] 1837 7-8-13 **53**.................. FinleyMarsh(3) 4 51
(Adrian Wintle) *hld up: rdn over 1f out: r.o ins fnl f: nt rch ldrs* **10/1**
41-6 6 *nk* **The Bull (IRE)**[25] 1402 4-9-3 **54**..................(p) AndrewMullen 9 51+
(Ben Haslam) *hld up: pushed along 1/2-way: rdn over 1f out: r.o ins fnl f: nvr nrr* **9/1**
11 7 *hd* **Krazy Paving**[29] 1335 7-8-13 **55**..................(b) MeganNicholls(5) 6 52
(Olly Murphy) *hdwy over 4f out: shkn up over 2f out: styd on same pce fnl f* **5/1**[2]
606- 8 *1* **Ingleby Molly (IRE)**[175] 8721 4-8-13 **55**.................. SebastianWoods(5) 10 49
(Jason Ward) *chsd ldrs: rdn over 2f out: no ex fnl f* **16/1**
30-4 9 *2 ¾* **Loulin**[25] 1403 4-9-3 **54**.................. JamesSullivan 11 39+
(Ruth Carr) *rrd s and bhd: nvr nrr (jockey said gelding reared as the stalls opened and as a result was slowly away)* **15/2**[3]
00-0 10 *1* **Tiger Lyon (USA)**[59] 882 4-9-4 **55**..................(w) PaulMulrennan 13 37
(John Butler) *stdd s: hld up: plld hrd: nvr on terms (jockey said gelding hung right-handed)* **16/1**
0640 11 *shd* **King Of Rooks**[55] 919 6-9-3 **54**.................. RobertHavlin 3 36
(Henry Spiller) *hld up: rdn over 1f out: n.d* **9/2**[1]
0000 12 *¾* **Breathoffreshair**[64] 788 5-9-3 **54**..................(t) PhilipPrince 8 34
(Richard Guest) *s.i.s: a in rr* **16/1**

1m 13.9s (-0.60) **Going Correction** -0.075s/f (Stan) **12 Ran SP% 120.2**
Speed ratings (Par 101): **101,99,98,97,96 96,95,94,90,89 89,88**
CSF £116.94 CT £934.98 TOTE £11.40: £4.40, £2.90, £2.90; EX 111.00 Trifecta £1221.50.
Owner A Davis **Bred** D R Tucker **Trained** Kingston Warren, Oxon

FOCUS
Few got into this, the pace holding up well. The runner-up is rated to her latest form.

2014 BRITVIC H'CAP 1m 5f 219y (Tp)
6:10 (6:11) (Class 6) (0-55,55) 4-Y-O+
£3,105 (£924; £461; £300; £300; £300) **Stalls** Low

Form RPR
-551 1 **Greenview Paradise (IRE)**[6] 1861 5-9-2 **45**.................. DaneO'Neill 2 55
(Jeremy Scott) *chsd ldrs: pushed along over 3f out: nt clr run over 2f out: rdn over 1f out: styd on to ld post* **5/2**[1]
1131 2 *nse* **Harry Callahan (IRE)**[20] 1519 4-9-4 **53**..................(v) CallumShepherd 7 59
(Mick Channon) *a.p: chsd ldr over 12f out: wnt upsides over 5f out: led 3f out: sn pushed along: rdn over 1f out: edgd rt ins fnl f: hdd post* **11/4**[2]
4040 3 *1 ¼* **Yasir (USA)**[29] 1334 11-9-5 **53**.................. DougieCostello 4 57
(Sophie Leech) *s.s: hld up: nt clr run fr over 2f out tl over 1f out: r.o to go 3rd nr fin: nt rch ldrs (jockey said gelding was denied a clear run until approaching the final furlong)* **12/1**
0500 4 *½* **Qayed (CAN)**[29] 1334 4-9-2 **51**..................(p) PaulMulrennan 11 55
(Mark Brisbourne) *led early: chsd ldrs: shkn up to go 2nd over 2f out: sn rdn: lost 2nd ins fnl f: styd on same pce* **11/1**
0320 5 *4* **Nice To Sea (IRE)**[29] 1334 5-8-12 **51**..................(b[1]) SeanDavis(5) 5 48
(Olly Murphy) *hld up: pushed along and hdwy on outer over 2f out: rdn over 1f out: edgd lft and no ex fnl f* **14/1**
60/0 6 *2 ½* **Beau Knight**[69] 700 7-9-0 **53**.................. SebastianWoods(5) 12 46
(Alexandra Dunn) *chsd ldrs: rdn over 2f out: wknd fnl f* **80/1**
400- 7 *1 ¾* **Kerrera**[178] 8650 6-9-6 **54**.................. DavidProbert 9 45
(Paul Webber) *s.i.s: hld up: rdn and hung rt over 2f out: wkng whn hung rt fnl f (jockey said mare hung right-handed under pressure)* **10/1**
0-00 8 *½* **Eurato (FR)**[19] 1548 9-9-2 **50**..................(v) PaddyMathers 1 40
(Derek Shaw) *hld up: rdn over 4f out: n.d* **40/1**
0/00 9 *8* **Guaracha**[13] 1679 8-9-4 **52**.................. RobertHavlin 13 35
(Alexandra Dunn) *hdwy into mid-div over 11f out: rdn over 2f out: wknd and eased over 1f out (jockey said gelding hung badly left-handed)* **100/1**
0330 10 *¾* **Hussar Ballad (USA)**[19] 1548 10-9-4 **52**.................. CamHardie 3 30+
(Antony Brittain) *s.i.s: sn rcvrd to ld at stdy pce: pushed along and hdd 3f out: wknd over 1f out* **11/2**[3]
0/5- 11 *18* **Highcastle (IRE)**[374] 1801 4-9-6 **55**.................. JohnFahy 6 9
(Henry Oliver) *hld up: rdn over 4f out: wknd over 3f out* **33/1**

3m 2.52s (1.52) **Going Correction** -0.075s/f (Stan)
WFA 4 from 5yo+ 1lb **11 Ran SP% 110.0**
Speed ratings (Par 101): **92,91,91,90,88 87,86,85,81,80 70**
CSF £8.49 CT £59.59 TOTE £3.40: £1.90, £1.10, £2.90; EX 9.30.
Owner Friends From Insurance **Bred** Senza Rete Partnership **Trained** Brompton Regis, Somerset

FOCUS
Three of the first four raced in the first four positions virtually throughout. The winner more than backed up her Southwell win.

2015 PEPSI MAX H'CAP 7f 36y (Tp)
6:40 (6:40) (Class 3) (0-90,90) 4-Y-O- **£7,246** (£2,168; £1,084; £542; £270) **Stalls** High

Form RPR
102- 1 **Margub**[217] 7385 4-9-2 **85**.................. DaneO'Neill 2 102
(Marcus Tregoning) *mde all: rdn clr over 1f out: comf* **7/2**[1]
214- 2 *3 ½* **Elerfaan (IRE)**[293] 4538 5-9-1 **84**.................. LewisEdmunds 3 91+
(Rebecca Bastiman) *chsd ldrs: shkn up and swtchd rt over 1f out: wnt 2nd ins fnl f: no ch w wnr* **15/2**
0-31 3 *2 ¼* **Sureyoutoldme (IRE)**[10] 1768 5-8-9 **78**.................. JamesSullivan 5 79
(Ruth Carr) *hdwy over 4f out: rdn and edgd rt over 1f out: styd on same pce fnl f* **11/2**[3]
-545 4 *1 ½* **Robero**[55] 929 7-8-13 **82**..................(e) DavidProbert 4 79
(Gay Kelleway) *chsd ldrs: chsd wnr 1/2-way: rdn over 1f out: wknd ins fnl f* **11/2**[3]
250- 5 *¾* **Humble Gratitude**[228] 7018 4-9-1 **84**.................. DavidEgan 8 79
(Ian Williams) *s.i.s: sn prom: lost pl over 4f out: n.d after* **16/1**
000- 6 *½* **Lamloom (IRE)**[209] 7660 5-9-7 **90**.................. DavidNolan 1 84
(David O'Meara) *racd keenly in 2nd pl to 1/2-way: rdn over 1f out: wknd fnl f* **5/1**[2]
4666 7 *3 ¼* **Reckless Endeavour (IRE)**[11] 1727 6-8-8 **77**..................(b[1]) AndrewMullen 10 62
(David Barron) *s.i.s: hld up: plld hrd: hung rt almost thrght: swtchd rt over 4f out: wknd over 2f out: eased (jockey said gelding hung badly right-handed and was virtually unsteerable)* **13/2**
6115 8 *hd* **Hammer Gun (USA)**[24] 1428 6-8-11 **80**..................(v) PaddyMathers 9 64
(Derek Shaw) *s.s: hdwy on outer over 2f out: rdn and wknd over 1f out* **20/1**
600- 9 *3 ¼* **Ghalib (IRE)**[306] 4032 7-8-13 **85**.................. RowanScott(3) 7 60
(Rebecca Bastiman) *hld up: ct wd fnl 5f: carried rt and wknd over 2f out* **25/1**
0/0- 10 *4* **Quixote (GER)**[326] 3320 9-8-11 **87**..................(t) TobyEley(7) 6 52
(James Unett) *s.s: a in rr (jockey said horse was slowly away and hung right-handed throughout)* **50/1**

1m 26.51s (-2.29) **Going Correction** -0.075s/f (Stan) **10 Ran SP% 111.2**
Speed ratings (Par 107): **110,106,103,101,100 100,96,96,92,88**
CSF £27.78 CT £135.17 TOTE £3.80: £1.70, £2.20, £1.70; EX 27.10 Trifecta £88.40.
Owner Hamdan Al Maktoum **Bred** Mrs P D Gray And H Farr **Trained** Whitsbury, Hants

FOCUS
A comfortable success for the favourite, who was another on the card to show that being on the pace was the place to be. The form is taken at something like face value.

2016 J2O H'CAP 7f 36y (Tp)
7:10 (7:11) (Class 6) (0-60,60) 3-Y-O
£3,105 (£924; £461; £300; £300; £300) **Stalls** High

Form RPR
-016 1 **Havana Ooh Na Na**[12] 1721 3-9-6 **59**..................(p) CliffordLee 6 71
(K R Burke) *mde all: rdn clr fnl f: r.o wl* **9/2**[1]
-440 2 *3 ¼* **Your Mothers' Eyes**[19] 1549 3-8-11 **55**..................(p[1]) DarraghKeenan(5) 8 59
(Alan Bailey) *prom: chsd wnr over 5f out: rdn over 1f out: sn outpcd* **7/1**
00-5 3 *¾* **Antico Lady (IRE)**[26] 1389 3-9-0 **56**.................. BenRobinson(3) 3 58
(Brian Ellison) *hld up: hdwy over 1f out: nt rch ldrs* **6/1**[2]
644- 4 *2* **Liam's Lass (IRE)**[158] 9103 3-9-3 **56**.................. RobHornby 7 53
(Pam Sly) *hld up: hdwy u.p over 1f out: swtchd rt ins fnl f: nt rch ldrs* **12/1**
2055 5 *nk* **Klipperty Klopp**[22] 1486 3-9-5 **58**.................. CamHardie 2 55
(Antony Brittain) *chsd ldrs: rdn over 2f out: wknd ins fnl f* **9/1**
-012 6 *½* **Global Acclamation**[42] 1167 3-9-7 **60**..................(b) RobertHavlin 1 55
(Ed Dunlop) *wnt lft s: hld up: hdwy over 1f out: wknd ins fnl f* **6/1**[2]

-063 **7** *nk* **Peruvian Summer (IRE)**[19] 1549 3-9-3 **56**.................. JackMitchell 12 51
(Kevin Frost) *hld up: styng on whn nt clr run towards fin* **13/2**[3]

35-0 **8** *1* **Mi Laddo (IRE)**[22] 1486 3-9-1 **54**.................. DavidNolan 11 46
(Oliver Greenall) *s.i.s: hld up: rdn over 1f out: nt trble ldrs* **18/1**

000- **9** *2 1/2* **Rock N Roll Queen**[175] 8727 3-9-7 **60**.................. FrannyNorton 5 46
(John Mackie) *chsd wnr tl over 5f out: remained handy: rdn over 2f out: wknd fnl f (vet reported the filly lost its left hind shoe)* **25/1**

-566 **10** *4 1/2* **Fort Benton (IRE)**[12] 1720 3-9-5 **58**.................. LewisEdmunds 9 33
(David Barron) *s.i.s: hld up: effrt on outer whn nt clr run over 2f out: sn wknd* **9/1**

406- **11** *1 1/2* **I'm Billy Murphy (IRE)**[206] 7778 3-9-4 **60**.................. RowanScott(3) 4 31
(Nigel Tinkler) *prom: rdn and hung rt over 2f out: sn wknd (jockey said gelding hung right-handed under pressure)* **14/1**

0044 **12** *nse* **Peters Pudding (IRE)**[18] 1557 3-8-12 **58**........(b) ElishaWhittington(7) 10 29
(Lisa Williamson) *hld up: a in rr (vet reported the gelding finished lame on its left hind)* **66/1**

1m 28.14s (-0.66) **Going Correction** -0.075s/f (Stan) **12** Ran SP% **117.5**
Speed ratings (Par 96): **100,96,95,93,92 92,91,90,87,82 81,80**
CSF £35.02 CT £195.00 TOTE £4.70: £1.80, £2.80, £2.30; EX 40.80 Trifecta £215.80.
Owner The Havana Ooh Na Na Partnership **Bred** Mickley Stud & Lady Lonsdale **Trained** Middleham Moor, N Yorks

FOCUS
Another winner to make all on a day when it paid to be up there. He's going the right way, but this is only modest form.

2017 PEPSI MAX EBF FILLIES' NOVICE STKS 1m 4f 51y (Tp)
7:40 (7:40) (Class 5) 3-Y-O+ **£3,752** (£1,116; £557; £278) **Stalls** Low

Form RPR

030- **1** **Eesha My Flower (USA)**[131] 9522 3-8-8 73.................. DavidEgan 2 72
(Marco Botti) *prom: lft 2nd briefly over 5f out: chsd ldr over 3f out: shkn up to ld over 1f out: sn edgd lft: rdn and wandered ins fnl f: styd on* **13/2**

4 **2** *1/2* **Cherries At Dawn (IRE)**[25] 1397 4-10-0.................. CallumShepherd 9 73
(Dominic Ffrench Davis) *hld up: hdwy over 2f out: rdn to chse wnr ins fnl f: r.o* **18/1**

0- **3** *2 3/4* **Goscote**[211] 7616 4-10-0.................. DavidProbert 3 69
(Henry Candy) *hld up: hdwy over 2f out: styd on to go 3rd wl ins fnl f* **22/1**

4 *1 1/4* **Local Affair** 3-8-8.................. JackMitchell 8 64
(Simon Crisford) *racd keenly: prom: wnt 2nd 9f out: lft in ld over 5f out: rdn and hdd over 1f out: no ex ins fnl f* **4/1**[2]

30 **5** *7* **Samstar**[11] 1738 3-8-8.................. FrannyNorton 5 53
(Mark Johnston) *s.i.s: pushed along and rcvrd to chse ldr after 1f: lost 2nd 9f out: remained handy: drvn along over 6f out: wnt 2nd again 5f out tl pushed along over 3f out: wknd over 2f out* **6/1**[3]

5-6 **6** *2 1/4* **Suakin (IRE)**[8] 1824 3-8-9 ow1.................. RobertHavlin 4 50
(John Gosden) *led: hung lft and hdd over 5f out: sn lost pl and shkn up: rdn over 2f out: nt run on* **10/11**[1]

3- **7** *4* **Dubawi Meeznah (IRE)**[236] 6718 4-9-9.................. SeanDavis(5) 6 46
(David Simcock) *prom: lost pl after 1f: hdwy over 4f out: rdn: hung rt and wknd over 2f out* **9/1**

0 **P** **Western Dixie (IRE)**[10] 1771 5-10-0.................. AndrewMullen 7
(Jennie Candlish) *hld up: plld hrd: hmpd after 1f: hdwy over 9f out: hung rt and lost pl over 7f out: p.u over 6f out (jockey said mare hung badly right-handed and was virtually unsteerable)* **100/1**

2m 39.12s (-1.68) **Going Correction** -0.075s/f (Stan)
WFA 3 from 4yo+ 20lb **8** Ran SP% **120.6**
Speed ratings (Par 100): **102,101,99,99,94 92,90,**
CSF £115.89 TOTE £7.60: £1.50, £4.30, £4.10; EX 134.00 Trifecta £1232.30.
Owner K Sohi & Partner **Bred** Calumet Farm **Trained** Newmarket, Suffolk

FOCUS
Just an ordinary novice. The winner set the standard and is rated close to that.

2018 FRUIT SHOOT FILLIES' NOVICE STKS 1m 142y (Tp)
8:10 (8:11) (Class 5) 3-Y-O+ **£3,752** (£1,116; £557; £278) **Stalls** Low

Form RPR

1- **1** **Nearooz**[193] 8150 3-9-4 0.................. DavidEgan 7 85+
(Roger Varian) *trckd ldrs: racd keenly: shkn up to ld 1f out: edgd lft ins fnl f: r.o* **11/10**[1]

35- **2** *2 1/4* **New Jazz (USA)**[262] 5749 3-8-11 0.................. RobertHavlin 11 73+
(John Gosden) *a.p: chsd ldr over 6f out: shkn up and ev ch fr over 1f out tl styd on same pce wl ins fnl f* **9/4**[2]

0-0 **3** *1 3/4* **Sweet Poem**[80] 556 3-8-4 0.................. AmeliaGlass(7) 5 69
(Clive Cox) *chsd ldr: led 7f out: sn edgd lft: rdn and hdd 1f out: no ex ins fnl f* **80/1**

6 **4** *1/2* **Under The Storm**[25] 1400 3-8-11 0.................. CliffordLee 8 68+
(James Tate) *s.i.s: hld up: hmpd 7f out: hdwy over 1f out: r.o: nt rch ldrs* **16/1**

-64 **5** *1* **Lady Mascara**[31] 1288 3-8-11 0.................. GeorgeWood 9 66+
(James Fanshawe) *s.i.s: hld up: shkn up and hdwy over 1f out: r.o: nt rch ldrs* **25/1**

5 **6** *3/4* **Seraphim**[32] 1272 3-8-11 0..................(t) DavidProbert 1 64
(Marco Botti) *chsd ldrs: rdn over 1f out: no ex ins fnl f* **10/1**[3]

7 *1/2* **Jaidaa** 3-8-11 0.................. JackMitchell 10 63+
(Simon Crisford) *hld up: hmpd 7f out: styd on ins fnl f: nvr nrr* **10/1**[3]

6- **8** *4 1/2* **Masai Spirit**[171] 8833 3-8-11 0.................. DannyBrock 4 53
(Philip McBride) *sn pushed along to ld: hdd 7f out: hmpd sn after: remained handy: rdn over 1f out: wknd fnl f* **66/1**

64 **9** *1* **Hikayah**[25] 1400 3-8-11 0..................(p) CamHardie 3 51
(David O'Meara) *prom: hmpd 7f out: lost pl over 5f out: sn drvn along: edgd lft and wknd over 1f out* **50/1**

10 *2 3/4* **Taaldara (IRE)** 3-8-11 0.................. PaulMulrennan 13 45
(Ben Haslam) *s.s: nvr on terms* **66/1**

3-5 **11** *1* **Aigiarne (IRE)**[63] 795 3-8-11 0.................. HectorCrouch 6 43
(Clive Cox) *plld hrd and prom: hmpd and lost pl 7f out: hdwy on outer over 5f out: wknd over 1f out* **20/1**

2 **12** *1 1/4* **Sadler's Soul (USA)**[25] 1397 3-8-11 0..................(p[1]) AndrewMullen 2 40
(Archie Watson) *s.i.s: hld up: nt clr run over 7f out: nvr on terms* **25/1**

0 **13** *28* **Fabulous View (FR)**[12] 1723 3-8-11 0.................. JamesSullivan 12
(Ruth Carr) *hdwy 7f out: wknd over 2f out: eased over 1f out* **100/1**

1m 49.04s (-1.06) **Going Correction** -0.075s/f (Stan) **13** Ran SP% **122.1**
Speed ratings (Par 100): **101,99,97,97,96 95,95,91,90,87 86,85,60**
CSF £3.30 TOTE £2.10: £1.10, £1.30, £20.10; EX 4.90 Trifecta £316.00.
Owner Sheikh Ahmed Al Maktoum **Bred** Godolphin **Trained** Newmarket, Suffolk
■ Stewards' Enquiry : Amelia Glass two-day ban: interference & careless riding (Apr 26, May 7)

FOCUS
The market principals dominated came to the fore in this fillies' novice. The third is the key to this form.

T/Jkpt: Not won. T/Plt: £514.40 to a £1 stake. Pool: £64,563.77 - 91.61 winning units T/Qpdt: £45.20 to a £1 stake. Pool: £9,232.90 - 150.91 winning units **Colin Roberts**

YARMOUTH (L-H)
Tuesday, April 23

OFFICIAL GOING: Good to firm (good in places; watered; 7.7)
Wind: breezy Weather: sunny; 15 degrees

2019 HAVEN SEASHORE HOLIDAY H'CAP 1m 3y
1:30 (1:30) (Class 6) (0-65,62) 4-Y-O+
£3,105 (£924; £461; £300; £300; £300) **Stalls** Centre

Form RPR

0-06 **1** **Take It Down Under**[18] 1562 4-9-3 **58**..................(t[1]) SilvestreDeSousa 4 75+
(Amy Murphy) *mde all: gng best 2f out: clr over 1f out: unchal (jockey said gelding hung right-handed)* **5/2**[1]

650- **2** *4 1/2* **Sussex Girl**[159] 9072 5-8-12 **53**.................. OisinMurphy 5 58
(John Berry) *last away: bhd: rdn and stdy hdwy fnl 2f: wnt 2nd ins fnl f: no ch w wnr* **5/2**[1]

510- **3** *1 1/4* **Spanish Mane (IRE)**[124] 9638 4-9-3 **58**.................. ShelleyBirkett 8 60
(Julia Feilden) *t.k.h pressing wnr: rdn 2f out: sn outpcd by him: lost mod 2nd ins fnl f (jockey said filly ran too freely)* **11/1**

2000 **4** *1 3/4* **Percy Toplis**[12] 1715 5-8-4 **45**..................(p) LukeMorris 2 43
(Christine Dunnett) *midfield: rdn over 3f out: fnd nthing and wl hld after* **14/1**

600- **5** *nk* **Hi Ho Silver**[169] 8886 5-8-13 **54**.................. GeorgeWood 6 51
(Chris Wall) *pressed ldrs: rdn over 2f out: one pce and sn btn* **9/2**[2]

0000 **6** *1* **Rosarno (IRE)**[10] 1768 5-9-7 **62**.................. JoeyHaynes 7 57
(Paul Howling) *bhd and sn rdn: sme hdwy 3f out: btn over 2f out* **20/1**

2150 **7** *7* **Mochalov**[41] 1177 4-9-6 **61**.................. CharlieBennett 1 40
(Jane Chapple-Hyam) *t.k.h in rr early: j. path after 2f: rdn 1/2-way: struggling fnl 3f (jockey said gelding jumped the path approx 5 1/2f out)* **8/1**[3]

/0-0 **8** *3/4* **Conqueress (IRE)**[17] 1586 5-9-0 **55**.................. CharlesBishop 3 32
(Lydia Pearce) *cl up: rdn 1/2-way: wknd over 2f out* **12/1**

1m 36.37s (-1.83) **Going Correction** -0.30s/f (Firm) **8** Ran SP% **113.9**
Speed ratings (Par 101): **97,92,91,89,89 88,81,80**
CSF £8.40 CT £55.61 TOTE £4.30: £1.10, £1.40, £2.10; EX 9.40 Trifecta £52.90.
Owner The Champagne Club **Bred** Windmill Bloodstock Investments **Trained** Newmarket, Suffolk

FOCUS
This was Yarmouth's opening Flat meeting of 2019 and clerk of the course Richard Aldous said: 'I'm not happy with the ground as we've not had enough rain and it's not as green as usual in April.' Riders were complimentary about the going afterwards, though.\n\x\x They went down the centre at a fair pace in this moderate handicap. Straightforward form in behind the winner.

2020 EBF STALLIONS MAIDEN FILLIES' STKS (PLUS 10 RACE) 5f 42y
2:00 (2:00) (Class 5) 2-Y-O **£3,752** (£1,116; £557; £278) **Stalls** Centre

Form RPR

1 **Companion** 2-9-0 0.................. SilvestreDeSousa 1 75+
(Mark Johnston) *cl up: rdn and wnt 2nd wl over 1f out: sustained chal fnl f: duelled for ld last 100yds: won on nod* **4/1**[2]

2 *shd* **Quiet Place (IRE)** 2-9-0 0.................. OisinMurphy 2 75+
(Saeed bin Suroor) *led: rdn over 1f out: jnd 100yds out: kpt on wl: jst pipped* **6/1**[3]

3 *1 1/2* **Endless Joy** 2-9-0 0.................. DanielTudhope 4 69+
(Archie Watson) *t.k.h pressing ldr: drvn and outpcd over 1f out: a hld after* **4/6**[1]

4 *1/2* **Allez Sophia (IRE)** 2-9-0 0.................. CharlesBishop 5 67+
(Eve Johnson Houghton) *plld hrd in rr: effrt and rdn 2f out: styd on wl ins fnl f: promising* **6/1**[3]

5 *11* **Luna Wish** 2-9-0 0.................. TomQueally 6 28
(George Margarson) *wnt rt s: rn green and a outpcd* **50/1**

6 *3/4* **Kelinda Dice** 2-9-0 0.................. PatCosgrave 3 25
(Mick Quinn) *cl up: rdn 1/2-way: wknd 2f out: eased ins fnl f* **40/1**

1m 1.01s (-0.89) **Going Correction** -0.30s/f (Firm) **6** Ran SP% **113.0**
Speed ratings (Par 89): **95,94,92,91,74 72**
CSF £27.53 TOTE £3.90: £1.80, £2.40; EX 21.50 Trifecta £47.70.
Owner The Duchess Of Roxburghe **Bred** Floors Farming, Whitley & Newbyth Studs **Trained** Middleham Moor, N Yorks

FOCUS
Again the centre was favoured in this interesting 2yo fillies' maiden, full of newcomers. The front four created quite nice impressions.

2021 JOHN KEMP 4 X 4 CENTRE OF NORWICH H'CAP 1m 2f 23y
2:35 (2:37) (Class 5) (0-70,72) 3-Y-O
£3,752 (£1,116; £557; £300; £300; £300) **Stalls** Low

Form RPR

53-1 **1** **Love So Deep (JPN)**[13] 1696 3-9-6 **69**.................. SilvestreDeSousa 7 78
(Jane Chapple-Hyam) *pressed ldr: rdn to ld wl over 2f out: styd on gamely after* **10/3**[2]

46-2 **2** *1 1/4* **Agent Basterfield (IRE)**[22] 1481 3-9-7 **70**.................. OisinMurphy 8 76
(Andrew Balding) *3rd or 4th tl rdn to chse wnr wl over 2f out: no imp thrght fnl f* **5/2**[1]

044- **3** *3* **Lucipherus (IRE)**[136] 9459 3-9-9 **72**..................(t[1]) GeraldMosse 3 72
(Marco Botti) *t.k.h: settled in 3rd or 4th: rdn and outpcd by ldng pair over 1f out* **16/1**

050- **4** *1/2* **Swiss Peak**[182] 8509 3-9-0 **63**.................. JamieSpencer 5 62+
(Michael Bell) *stdd in rr: plld hrd: last home turn: hdwy over 2f out: kpt on ins fnl f: nt rch ldrs* **25/1**

500- **5** *1* **Homesick Boy (IRE)**[167] 8931 3-9-3 **66**.................. DanielMuscutt 2 63
(Ed Dunlop) *t.k.h in midfield: rdn 3f out: wl hld whn n.m.r 1f out* **33/1**

443 **6** *nk* **Kingdom Of Dubai (FR)**[64] 785 3-9-5 **68**.................. AndreaAtzeni 1 64
(Roger Varian) *led: drvn 4f out: hdd wl over 2f out: sn lost pl* **9/2**[3]

0-36 **7** *3/4* **Azets**[32] 1264 3-9-4 **67**.................. MartinDwyer 4 62
(Amanda Perrett) *midfield: rdn 3f out: racing awkwardly and edging lft whn making no imp fr over 2f out* **8/1**

006- **8** *1 1/2* **Manton Warrior (IRE)**[183] 8474 3-9-5 **68**.................. StevieDonohoe 6 60
(Charlie Fellowes) *a bhd: rdn and btn over 2f out* **5/1**

2361 **9** *3/4* **Hypnos (IRE)**[22] 1481 3-9-0 **68**..................(p[1]) DylanHogan(5) 9 58
(David Simcock) *stdd s: t.k.h in rr: rdn and btn over 2f out* **14/1**

2m 7.21s (-1.59) **Going Correction** -0.30s/f (Firm) **9** Ran SP% **116.9**
Speed ratings (Par 98): **94,93,90,90,89 89,88,87,86**
CSF £12.28 CT £115.51 TOTE £3.80: £1.40, £1.80, £3.90; EX 12.10 Trifecta £105.50.
Owner Love So Deep Syndicate **Bred** Daylesford Stud **Trained** Dalham, Suffolk

FOCUS
Probably not a bad 3yo handicap for the class. It was run at a sound pace and two came clear. The form makes some sense.

2022 PALM COURT HOTEL OF YARMOUTH H'CAP — 1m 2f 23y
3:05 (3:05) (Class 4) (0-85,85) 4-Y-0+ £5,530 (£1,645; £822; £411; £300) Stalls Low

Form	Pos	Btn	Horse / Details	Jockey	RPR
25-4	1		**Stealth Fighter (IRE)**[18] 1561 4-9-1 79 (Saeed bin Suroor) *2nd tl led over 2f out: sn rdn clr: styd on strly fnl f* **5/1**	PatCosgrave 2	94
3341	2	6	**Nonios (IRE)**[19] 1545 7-9-2 85 (David Simcock) *t.k.h in last pair: effrt over 2f out: rdn to chse wnr who was already clr over 1f out: no imp* **8/1**	(h) DylanHogan(5) 1	88
221-	3	1 3/4	**Mainsail Atlantic (USA)**[132] 9509 4-9-4 82 (James Fanshawe) *t.k.h: 3rd tl chsd wnr over 2f out: rdn and lost 2nd over 1f out: sn wknd* **3/1[3]**	DanielMuscutt 5	82
134-	4	1 1/4	**Hamlul (FR)**[217] 7399 4-9-7 85 (Sir Michael Stoute) *dwlt and rdn: in last pair: effrt on outer 3f out: no rspnse and wl hld after* **9/4[1]**	RyanMoore 3	82
551-	5	12	**Monoxide**[167] 8920 4-9-5 83 (Martyn Meade) *led tl over 2f out: fdd rapidly: t.o and eased ins fnl f: b.b.v (vet said gelding bled from the nose)* **5/2[2]**	OisinMurphy 4	56

2m 4.61s (-4.19) **Going Correction** -0.30s/f (Firm) 5 Ran SP% **112.1**
Speed ratings (Par 105): **104,99,97,96,87**
CSF £39.56 TOTE £5.40: £2.60, £3.10; EX 38.90 Trifecta £84.90.
Owner Godolphin **Bred** B Kennedy & Mrs Ann Marie Kennedy **Trained** Newmarket, Suffolk

FOCUS
This feature handicap proved a tactical affair. The market 1-2 were disappointing but the winner impressed, and the form is taken at face value.

2023 EASTERN POWER SYSTEMS OF NORWICH NOVICE STKS — 1m 3y
3:35 (3:36) (Class 5) 3-Y-0 £3,752 (£1,116; £557; £278) Stalls Centre

Form	Pos	Btn	Horse / Details	Jockey	RPR
12-	1		**King Of Comedy (IRE)**[168] 8895 3-9-9 0 (John Gosden) *handy: effrt and urged along over 1f out: led ins fnl f: in command cl home: bit in hand* **4/6[1]**	FrankieDettori 13	101+
	2	3/4	**Land Of Legends (IRE)** 3-9-2 0 (Saeed bin Suroor) *prom: rdn to ld over 1f out: hdd ins fnl f: kpt on but wnr too str cl home: wl clr of rest* **10/1[3]**	PatCosgrave 7	92+
	3	8	**Edaraat** 3-9-2 0 (Roger Varian) *chsd ldrs: drvn and outpcd over 2f out: rallied ins fnl f and fin strly to snatch mod 3rd: promising* **11/1**	RyanMoore 4	74+
0-	4	shd	**Fujaira King (USA)**[208] 7699 3-9-2 0 (Roger Varian) *t.k.h: prom: cl 4th and rdn over 1f out: nt qckn ins fnl f: jst lost 3rd* **18/1**	AndreaAtzeni 6	74
1-3	5	1	**Cool Exhibit**[23] 1458 3-9-9 0 (Simon Crisford) *led: drvn and hdd over 1f out: sn lost pl* **11/2[2]**	(v) OisinMurphy 5	78
	6	nse	**Dr Jekyll (IRE)** 3-9-2 0 (David Simcock) *s.s: t.k.h and wl in rr: hdwy over 2f out: wnt lft after: fin strly: promising* **10/1[3]**	JamieSpencer 12	71+
34-	7	shd	**Knowing**[204] 7846 3-9-2 0 (James Fanshawe) *chsd ldrs tl rdn and btn 2f out* **50/1**	GeorgeWood 3	71+
	8	3 1/4	**Military Tactic (IRE)** 3-9-2 0 (Saeed bin Suroor) *nvr bttr than midfield: btn 2f out* **20/1**	HayleyTurner 9	64
0	9	1 1/2	**Crystal Tribe (IRE)**[10] 1754 3-9-2 0 (William Haggas) *outpcd fnl 3f* **18/1**	JamesDoyle 11	60+
0	10	8	**I'm Brian**[41] 1171 3-9-2 0 (Julia Feilden) *s.s: t.o* **150/1**	DanielMuscutt 16	42
	11	1/2	**Sendeed (IRE)** 3-9-2 0 (Saeed bin Suroor) *chsd ldrs over 5f: t.o* **25/1**	JosephineGordon 14	41
	12	6	**Raha** 3-8-11 0 (Julia Feilden) *dwlt: nvr on terms: bdly t.o* **200/1**	ShelleyBirkett 2	22
0	13	4	**Best Haaf**[18] 1562 3-9-2 0 (Michael Appleby) *struggling fr 1/2-way: bdly t.o* **100/1**	AlistairRawlinson 1	18
0	14	nk	**Mazmerize**[26] 1381 3-9-2 0 (Christine Dunnett) *plld hrd: spd to 1/2-way: bdly t.o* **200/1**	StevieDonohoe 10	17

1m 34.15s (-4.05) **Going Correction** -0.30s/f (Firm) 14 Ran SP% **125.6**
Speed ratings (Par 98): **108,107,99,99,98 98,98,94,93,85 84,78,74,74**
CSF £8.88 TOTE £1.50: £1.10, £2.70, £3.50; EX 10.30 Trifecta £61.90.
Owner Lady Bamford **Bred** Lady Bamford **Trained** Newmarket, Suffolk

FOCUS
A decent 3yo novice event in which two pulled nicely clear. Improved form from the smart winner.

2024 THANKS JAN LEEDER AND BEST WISHES H'CAP — 6f 3y
4:05 (4:07) (Class 5) (0-75,77) 3-Y-0 £3,752 (£1,116; £557; £300; £300; £300) Stalls Centre

Form	Pos	Btn	Horse / Details	Jockey	RPR
0111	1		**Camachess (IRE)**[41] 1170 3-9-0 68 (Philip McBride) *trckd ldrs: wnt 2nd 1/2-way: led gng strly 1f out: hld on wl: readily* **6/1**	PhilDennis 6	74+
262-	2	3/4	**Sirius Slew**[243] 6448 3-9-6 74 (Alan Bailey) *towards rr: rdn and hdwy over 1f out: chal ins fnl f: carried lft: no imp fnl 100yds* **20/1**	(b) JoeyHaynes 1	77
660-	3	1	**Mykindofsunshine (IRE)**[251] 6159 3-9-6 74 (Clive Cox) *stdd s: rdn and hdwy over 1f out: 3rd and hld fnl 100yds* **7/1**	GeraldMosse 7	74
-302	4	1 1/4	**Klass Action (IRE)**[39] 1219 3-9-7 75 (Sir Mark Prescott Bt) *led: set modest pce: rdn 2f out: hdd 1f out: edgd lft and sn btn (caution; careless riding)* **9/2[3]**	(b) LukeMorris 8	71
2110	5	2	**Solar Park (IRE)**[24] 1424 3-9-9 77 (James Tate) *prom tl rdn over 1f out: wknd ins fnl f* **3/1[2]**	RyanMoore 4	66
11-	6	hd	**Airwaves**[117] 9727 3-9-7 75 (Martyn Meade) *stdd s: towards rr: rdn and struggling 2f out* **7/4[1]**	OisinMurphy 2	64
2160	7	21	**Axel Jacklin**[29] 1337 3-8-13 67 (Paul Howling) *cl up tl rdn 1/2-way: lost pl rapidly: t.o and eased* **33/1**	JamieSpencer 3	

1m 11.05s (-1.55) **Going Correction** -0.30s/f (Firm) 7 Ran SP% **114.0**
Speed ratings (Par 98): **98,97,95,94,91 91,63**
CSF £104.70 CT £853.83 TOTE £5.60: £3.10, £6.70; EX 84.80 Trifecta £500.40.
Owner The Narc Partnership **Bred** Yeomanstown Stud **Trained** Newmarket, Suffolk

FOCUS
Another fair handicap for the class. There was just an ordinary pace on. The winner looks capable of better again.

2025 INJURED JOCKEYS FUND H'CAP — 5f 42y
4:35 (4:36) (Class 5) (0-70,72) 4-Y-0+ £3,752 (£1,116; £557; £300; £300; £300) Stalls Centre

Form	Pos	Btn	Horse / Details	Jockey	RPR
640-	1		**Grandfather Tom**[174] 8742 4-9-7 70 (Robert Cowell) *prom: rdn to ld over 2f out: urged along and hld on wl cl home* **6/1**	LukeMorris 2	77
3452	2	nk	**Wiff Waff**[13] 1686 4-9-6 69 (Stuart Williams) *towards rr: 5th and effrt 1f out: drvn and str run after: jst hld cl home* **2/1[1]**	OisinMurphy 4	75
313-	3	1 1/4	**Princess Keira (IRE)**[166] 8960 4-8-12 61 (Mick Quinn) *prom: rdn and w wnr 1f out: nt qckn after* **11/2**	PatCosgrave 3	63
-406	4	hd	**Terri Rules (IRE)**[10] 1766 4-8-9 58 (Julia Feilden) *dwlt and lost 6 l at s: pushed along and hdwy over 1f out: no imp fnl 100yds (jockey said filly was slowly away)* **9/1**	ShelleyBirkett 1	59
0050	5	1 1/2	**Mother Of Dragons (IRE)**[13] 1682 4-8-7 56 oh1 (Phil McEntee) *rdn and outpcd 1/2-way: sme prog ins fnl f: n.d* **9/2[2]**	(v) JosephineGordon 6	51
1056	6	1 1/2	**Point Zero (IRE)**[19] 1551 4-9-4 72 (Michael Appleby) *taken down early: led at str pce tl rdn and hdd over 2f out: sn lost pl* **9/1**	(b) TheodoreLadd(5) 7	62
44-6	7	7	**Sir Hector (IRE)**[28] 1342 4-9-2 68 (Charlie Wallis) *sn pushed along: lost tch over 2f out: sn remote: eased (jockey said gelding was never travelling)* **5/1[3]**	JoshuaBryan(3) 5	33

1m 0.01s (-1.89) **Going Correction** -0.30s/f (Firm) 7 Ran SP% **117.9**
Speed ratings (Par 103): **103,102,100,100,97 95,84**
CSF £19.34 TOTE £6.90: £3.60, £1.60; EX 19.60 Trifecta £86.00.
Owner J Sargeant **Bred** J Sargeant **Trained** Six Mile Bottom, Cambs

FOCUS
They ended up stands' side in this moderate sprint handicap. The winner is rated around last year's C&D form.
T/Plt: £247.80 to a £1 stake. Pool: £51,698.90 - 152.29 winning units T/Qpdt: £85.50 to a £1 stake. Pool: £5,116.67 - 44.25 winning units **Iain Mackenzie**

1578 COMPIEGNE (L-H)
Tuesday, April 23

OFFICIAL GOING: Turf: good

2026a PRIX DE SAINT-CREPIN (CLAIMER) (4YO+) (TURF) — 1m 4f
4:20 4-Y-0+ £8,558 (£3,423; £2,567; £1,711; £855)

Pos	Btn	Horse / Details	Jockey	RPR
1		**Power Euro (IRE)**[255] 7-9-4 0 (Henk Grewe, Germany) **92/10**	AntoineHamelin 5	72
2	1	**Lodi (FR)**[26] 5-9-5 0 (L Rovisse, France) **27/10[1]**	StephanePasquier 8	71
3	1 1/4	**Island Song (IRE)**[40] 5-7-13 0 (Andrea Marcialis, France) **19/5[3]**	MlleLeaBails(9) 3	58
4	1 1/2	**Zatorius (GER)**[61] 4-8-13 0 ow2 (S Cerulis, France) **10/1**	(p) ChristopheSoumillon 4	62
5	nk	**Vienna Woods (FR)**[14] 5-8-8 0 (Y Barberot, France) **37/10[2]**	(p) MaximeGuyon 7	55
6	nk	**Temple Boy (FR)**[88] 7-8-11 0 (J Phelippon, France) **77/10**	AlexisBadel 6	58
7	1 1/4	**Cape Greco (USA)**[80] 548 4-9-4 0 (Jo Hughes, France) *settled to trck ldrs: pushed along 2f out: rdn and ev ch over 1f out: drvn and no ex ins fnl f* **11/1**	TheoBachelot 9	64
8	3/4	**Full Spirit (FR)**[28] 4-8-13 0 (J-M Lefebvre, France) **17/1**	(b) AlexandreChesneau(3) 10	60
9	12	**Heart Ahead (IRE)**[88] 5-8-11 0 (J D Hillis, Germany) **65/1**	Louis-PhilippeBeuzelin 2	35
10	8	**Serenu (FR)**[961] 6178 9-9-4 0 (A Sagot, France) **18/1**	FabriceVeron 1	29

2m 37.19s 10 Ran SP% **120.2**
PARI-MUTUEL (all including 1 euro stake): WIN 10.20; PLACE 2.50, 1.80, 1.80; DF 20.20.
Owner Rennstall Darboven **Bred** Gestut Idee **Trained** Germany

TOULOUSE
Tuesday, April 23

OFFICIAL GOING: Turf: good

2027a PRIX F.B.A. - AYMERI DE MAULEON (LISTED RACE) (3YO) (TURF) — 1m
12:25 3-Y-0 £24,774 (£9,909; £7,432; £4,954; £2,477)

Pos	Btn	Horse / Details	Jockey	RPR
1		**Sagauteur (FR)**[37] 1243 3-9-0 0 (D Guillemin, France) **21/10[1]**	OlivierPeslier 4	97
2	1/2	**Quindio (FR)**[43] 3-9-0 0 (X Thomas-Demeaulte, France) **18/5[3]**	MickaelBarzalona 1	96
3	3/4	**Got Wind**[25] 3-8-10 0 (C Ferland, France) **16/5[2]**	JulienAuge 2	90
4	hd	**Concello (IRE)**[178] 8648 3-8-10 0 (Archie Watson) *urged along leaving stalls to ld: pushed along to extend ld over 2f out: rdn and hdd over 1f out: drvn and kpt on ins fnl f* **23/1**	(p) HollieDoyle 5	90
5	hd	**Likala (FR)**[196] 8097 3-8-10 0 (J-C Rouget, France) **89/10**	HugoJourniac 7	90
6	snk	**Tilett**[25] 3-8-10 0 (F Rohaut, France) **47/10**	Francois-XavierBertras 6	89
7	snk	**Kanderas**[26] 3-9-0 0 (H-A Pantall, France) **9/1**	AurelienLemaitre 3	93

1m 39.3s (-4.00) 7 Ran SP% **119.6**
PARI-MUTUEL (all including 1 euro stake): WIN 3.10; PLACE 1.90, 2.00; SF 9.10.
Owner Pegase Bloodstock **Bred** C Mahoney **Trained** France

FOCUS A bunch finish.

2028a (Foreign Racing) - See Raceform Interactive

2029a PRIX DU HARAS DES GRANGES - PRIX CARAVELLE (LISTED RACE) (3YO FILLIES) (TURF) 1m 2f 110y

1:42 3-Y-O **£24,774** (£9,909; £7,432; £4,954; £2,477)

RPR

1 **Volskha (FR)**[23] 3-8-11 0 ..... IoritzMendizabal 8 94
(Simone Brogi, France) **8/1**

2 *nse* **Paramount (FR)**[225] 3-8-11 0 ..... JulienAuge 7 94
(C Ferland, France) **13/2**[3]

3 *¼* **Queendara (FR)**[46] 3-8-11 0 ..... AlexandreGavilan 4 93
(D Guillemin, France) **20/1**

4 *¼* **Lidena (FR)** 3-8-11 0 ..... Jean-BernardEyquem 9 93
(J-C Rouget, France) **12/1**

5 *1* **Bonnoeil (FR)**[172] 3-8-11 0 ..... AnthonyCrastus 5 91
(Jane Soubagne, France) **11/1**

6 *1 ¼* **Samothrace (FR)**[28] 3-8-11 0 ..... MickaelBarzalona 6 89
(F-H Graffard, France) **13/1**

7 *¼* **Suquitho (FR)**[16] 1626 3-8-11 0 ..... AurelienLemaitre 11 88
(H-A Pantall, France) **77/10**

8 *shd* **Lucky Lycra (IRE)**[47] 3-8-11 0 ..... Francois-XavierBertras 10 88
(F Rohaut, France) **51/10**[2]

9 *nse* **Norathir (FR)** 3-8-13 0 ow2 ..... OlivierPeslier 2 90
(D De Watrigant, France) **3/1**[1]

10 *2 ½* **Paravent**[34] 3-8-11 0 ..... MickaelForest 3 83
(F Rohaut, France) **36/5**

11 *4 ½* **Izvestia (IRE)**[212] 7586 3-8-11 0 ..... (p) HollieDoyle 12 75
(Archie Watson) *wl into stride: sn front rnk: settled in 2nd: pushed along to dispute ld 2f out: rdn over 1f out: wknd and eased ins fnl f* **38/1**

2m 14.0s **11** Ran SP% **120.0** PARI-MUTUEL (all including 1 euro stake): WIN 9.00; PLACE 3.00, 3.20, 5.20; DF 23.70.
Owner Alain Jathiere **Bred** A Jathiere **Trained** France

EPSOM (L-H)

Wednesday, April 24

OFFICIAL GOING: Round course - good (good to firm in places); straight course - good to firm (good in places) (watered; 7.5)
Wind: Medium to strong, across Weather: Overcast

2030 INVESTEC ASSET FINANCE H'CAP 5f

2:10 (2:10) (Class 3) (0-95,96) 4-Y-O+
£12,450 (£3,728; £1,864; £932; £466; £234) **Stalls** High

Form RPR

-165 1 **Just That Lord**[8] 1839 6-8-13 **82** ..... LukeMorris 6 90
(Michael Attwater) *sltly on toes; chsd ldr: clsd and upsides over 1f out: rdn to ld ins fnl f: sn drvn: a jst holding on cl home* **5/1**[3]

500- 2 *nk* **Dark Shot**[194] 8165 6-8-8 **82** ..... (p) TheodoreLadd(5) 9 89
(Scott Dixon) *in tch in midfield: clsd to chse ldng pair over 1f out: swtchd rt 1f out: styd on and chalng wl ins fnl f: clsng at fin but a jst hld* **4/1**[1]

01-5 3 *2 ¼* **Merry Banter**[22] 1501 5-9-2 **85** ..... PaulMulrennan 1 84
(Paul Midgley) *taken down early: broke fast to ld and crossed to r against stands' rail: rdn and jnd over 1f out: hdd ins fnl f: no ex and wknd towards fin* **9/1**

2056 4 *1* **Shamshon (IRE)**[6] 1892 8-8-10 **79** ..... HarryBentley 10 74
(Stuart Williams) *looked wl; midfield: clsd over 1f out: chsd ldrs and kpt on same pce u.p ins fnl f* **9/2**[2]

050- 5 *¾* **Duke Of Firenze**[179] 8632 10-9-1 **84** ..... DavidAllan 7 77
(David C Griffiths) *in rr: hdwy over 1f out: styd on same pce and no imp ins fnl f* **5/1**[3]

20-4 6 *½* **Harry Hurricane**[53] 987 7-8-13 **82** ..... (p) NicolaCurrie 2 73
(George Baker) *bhd: sme prog ins fnl f: nt clr run ins fnl f: nvr trbld ldrs (jockey said gelding was denied a clear run)* **10/1**

30-0 7 *½* **Bahamian Sunrise**[22] 1496 7-8-7 **76** oh1 ..... (b) SilvestreDeSousa 8 65
(John Gallagher) *chsd ldrs tl unable qck u.p over 1f out: wknd ins fnl f (jockey said gelding hung right-handed)* **8/1**

0316 8 *1 ¾* **Boom The Groom (IRE)**[53] 987 8-9-7 **90** ..... TomMarquand 5 73
(Tony Carroll) *looked wl; taken down early: racd in last trio: swtchd lft and pushed along 2f out: no imp and wl hld fnl f* **10/1**

4101 9 *hd* **Midnight Malibu (IRE)**[7] 1860 6-9-7 **90** 5ex ..... RachelRichardson 3 72
(Tim Easterby) *midfield: unable qck over 1f out: wknd ins fnl f* **16/1**

000- 10 *6* **Cox Bazar (FR)**[141] 9391 5-9-13 **96** ..... (w) JasonHart 4 56
(Ivan Furtado) *taken down early: chsd ldrs tl 2f out: sn lost pl and bhd ins fnl f (jockey said gelding was unsuited by Epsom and would prefer a flatter track; vet reported the gelding lost its right fore shoe)* **25/1**

54.87s (-0.43) **Going Correction** -0.15s/f (Firm) **10** Ran SP% **120.5**
Speed ratings (Par 107): **97,96,92,91,90 89,88,85,85,75**
CSF £26.30 CT £183.72 TOTE £5.40: £1.90, £1.80, £3.10; EX 28.30 Trifecta £214.90.
Owner Mrs M S Teversham **Bred** Mrs Monica Teversham **Trained** Epsom, Surrey

FOCUS
Rail movements added 27yds to all races except this opener. The 5f track was riding quicker than the round course and this good sprint handicap was run in a time 0.23sec inside the standard. They raced on the stands' side and Harry Bentley called it "good ground" and Like Morris "just on the quick side of good".

2031 INVESTEC BLUE RIBAND TRIAL (LISTED RACE) 1m 2f 17y

2:45 (2:45) (Class 1) 3-Y-O
£28,355 (£10,750; £5,380; £2,680; £1,345; £675) **Stalls** Low

Form RPR

23- 1 **Cape Of Good Hope (IRE)**[207] 7770 3-9-1 106 ..... RyanMoore 1 107
(A P O'Brien, Ire) *off the pce in midfield: clsd and wl in tch over 3f out: effrt to chse ldr over 1f out: kpt on u.p to ld wl ins fnl f: edgd rt and hld on cl home* **4/1**[3]

211- 2 *½* **Cap Francais**[207] 7765 3-9-1 90 ..... GeraldMosse 3 106
(Ed Walker) *quite str; sweating; coltish; t.k.h: hld up off the pce: clsd and wl in tch over 3f out: hdwy to chse ldrs over 1f out: edgd lft and swtchd rt ins fnl f: wnt 2nd and pressing wnr towards fin* **5/1**

10-0 3 *¾* **Turgenev**[12] 1737 3-9-1 102 ..... FrankieDettori 5 104
(John Gosden) *looked wl; chsd clr ldng pair: clsd and trcking ldrs over 3f out: led 2f out: sn edgd lft and rdn: drvn ins fnl f: hdd and no ex wl ins fnl f* **11/4**[2]

41-1 4 *6* **Mackaar (IRE)**[18] 1592 3-9-1 92 ..... AndreaAtzeni 2 92
(Roger Varian) *athletic; off the pce in midfield: effrt over 2f out: sn struggling and outpcd over 1f out: wknd ins fnl f* **11/1**

254- 5 *2 ¾* **Arthur Kitt**[173] 8821 3-9-1 109 ..... RichardKingscote 7 87
(Tom Dascombe) *stmbld bdly leaving stalls: racd off the pce in last pair: effrt over 2f out: no rspnse and wl btn over 1f out (jockey said colt stumbled leaving the stalls)* **9/4**[1]

102- 6 *2 ¾* **Massam**[165] 8994 3-9-1 93 ..... FrannyNorton 4 81
(Mark Johnston) *sweating; coltish; racd keenly: w ldr and sn clr: led over 7f out tl out: sn btn: bhd ins fnl f* **25/1**

21-1 7 *7* **Sameem (IRE)**[16] 1645 3-9-1 87 ..... OisinMurphy 6 67
(James Tate) *quite tall; led and sn clr w rival: hdd over 7f out but stl clr w ldr: rdn over 2f out: sn lost pl: bhd fnl f* **9/1**

2m 6.28s (-3.72) **Going Correction** -0.15s/f (Firm) **7** Ran SP% **116.3**
Speed ratings (Par 106): **108,107,107,102,100 97,92**
CSF £24.88 TOTE £4.00: £2.10, £3.10; EX 22.80 Trifecta £90.20.
Owner Mrs John Magnier & Michael Tabor & Derrick Smith **Bred** Hveger Syndicate **Trained** Cashel, Co Tipperary

FOCUS
Add 27yds. The second running of this event since it was elevated to Listed status. Cracksman won it in 2017 before finishing third in the Derby, while Dee Ex Bee, third last year, went one better in the Classic. The two leaders were ignored by the rest of the field for the first half of the race, and the first three finished clear in what looked a worthwhile early Derby trial. The time was a respectable 1.28sec outside standard.

2032 INVESTEC CORPORATE & INVESTMENT BANKING GREAT METROPOLITAN H'CAP 1m 4f 6y

3:20 (3:23) (Class 3) (0-95,96) 4-Y-O+
£12,450 (£3,728; £1,864; £932; £466; £234) **Stalls** Centre

Form RPR

60-5 1 **Soto Sizzler**[25] 1422 4-8-9 **83** ..... OisinMurphy 11 94
(William Knight) *looked wl; in tch in midfield: effrt to press ldrs 2f out: led u.p 1f out: r.o strly and drew clr ins fnl f: readily* **11/4**[1]

6461 2 *3 ¼* **Eddystone Rock (IRE)**[19] 1559 7-9-0 **88** ..... JamesDoyle 13 93
(John Best) *hld up in midfield: effrt 2f out: styd on wl ins fnl f: wnt 2nd towards fin: no threat to wnr* **6/1**

2-61 3 *½* **Maybe Today**[33] 1267 4-9-1 **89** ..... (v) SilvestreDeSousa 9 93
(Simon Crisford) *chsd ldr: reminders and rdn 4f out: ev ch u.p 2f out: led jst over 1f out: sn hdd: edgd lft and nt match pce of wnr ins fnl f: lost 2nd towards fin (jockey said filly hung left-handed)* **9/2**[2]

4532 4 *nk* **Emenem**[18] 1588 5-8-7 **81** oh2 ..... DavidEgan 3 85
(Simon Dow) *chsd ldrs: rdn to chal ent fnl 2f: led over 1f out: sn hdd: no ex and one pce ins fnl f* **10/1**

065- 5 *2 ¼* **Medalla De Oro**[155] 9164 5-8-8 **82** ..... LukeMorris 8 82
(Tom Clover) *led: hrd pressed and u.p 2f out: hdd over 1f out: wknd ins fnl f* **16/1**

54-0 6 *1 ¾* **Manjaam (IRE)**[25] 1422 6-9-1 **89** ..... RichardKingscote 6 86
(Ian Williams) *midfield: effrt over 2f out: no imp and wl hld over 1f out* **8/1**

320- 7 *¾* **Not So Sleepy**[30] 9463 7-9-8 **96** ..... (t) RyanMoore 10 92
(Hughie Morrison) *stdd after s: hld up wl off the pce in last pair: effrt and swtchd rt wl over 2f out: nvr getting on terms and wl hld whn edgd lft ins fnl f* **5/1**[3]

500- 8 *2 ¾* **Guns Of Leros (USA)**[161] 9053 6-9-0 **88** ..... (v[1]) HectorCrouch 2 80
(Gary Moore) *dwlt: sn rcvrd and racd in midfield: rdn and outpcd over 2f out: wl btn and pushed lft ins fnl f* **20/1**

3205 9 *7* **Fire Fighting (IRE)**[15] 1664 8-9-8 **96** ..... WilliamBuick 12 77
(Mark Johnston) *looked wl; sn dropped to rr and wl off the pce: nvr travelling and nvr involved* **10/1**

-314 10 *6* **Noble Expression**[77] 622 4-8-1 **82** ..... (v) IsobelFrancis(7) 4 53
(Jim Boyle) *chsd ldrs tl 3f out: sn lost pl and wl btn (jockey said gelding was never travelling)* **50/1**

06-0 11 *1* **Mount Tahan (IRE)**[15] 1664 7-9-5 **93** ..... ShaneGray 7 62
(Kevin Ryan) *taken down early: stdd s: hld up in midfield: short-lived effrt 3f out: sn dropped out and wl btn* **28/1**

0/3- 12 *88* **West Drive (IRE)**[26] 5369 6-8-12 **86** ..... ShaneKelly 14
(Gary Moore) *a in last trio: bhd 4f out: lost tch and eased fnl 2f: t.o (jockey said gelding was never travelling)* **33/1**

2m 35.89s (-4.91) **Going Correction** -0.15s/f (Firm) **12** Ran SP% **124.1**
Speed ratings (Par 107): **110,107,107,107,105 104,104,102,97,93 92,34**
CSF £19.53 CT £75.92 TOTE £3.20: £1.80, £1.80, £1.90; EX 20.30 Trifecta £125.00.
Owner I J Heseltine **Bred** D A Yardy **Trained** Angmering, W Sussex

FOCUS
Add 27yds. Not many became involved from off the pace in this decent handicap.

2033 INVESTEC CITY AND SUBURBAN H'CAP 1m 2f 17y

3:55 (3:57) (Class 2) (0-105,107) 4-Y-O+
£31,125 (£9,320; £4,660; £2,330; £1,165; £585) **Stalls** Low

Form RPR

220- 1 **Mountain Angel (IRE)**[193] 8192 5-8-12 **96** ..... AndreaAtzeni 5 106+
(Roger Varian) *looked wl; hld up in tch in midfield: effrt to chse ldrs and swtchd rt over 1f out: styd on to ld wl ins fnl f: r.o wl* **7/2**[2]

0502 2 *1 ½* **Aquarium**[20] 1545 4-9-2 **100** ..... FrannyNorton 11 107
(Mark Johnston) *t.k.h: hld up in tch in midfield: clsd whn nt clr run and swtchd lft jst over 2f out: chsd ldrs and swtchd rt ins fnl f: r.o wl to go 2nd cl home* **14/1**

50-1 3 *½* **Aasheq (IRE)**[15] 1664 6-8-12 **96** ..... DavidAllan 2 102
(Tim Easterby) *chsd ldr for over 1f: styd chsng ldrs tl clsd to join ldr jst over 2f out: rdn over 1f out: drvn to ld 100yds out: sn hdd and one pce: lost 2nd cl home* **12/1**

5552 4 *1 ¼* **Mythical Madness**[18] 1589 8-8-8 **92** ..... (v) SilvestreDeSousa 6 96
(David O'Meara) *led: jnd and rdn jst over 2f out: drvn over 1f out: hdd 100yds out: no ex and wknd towards fin* **14/1**

04-4 5 *1 ¾* **Lucius Tiberius (IRE)**[17] 1628 4-9-4 **102** ..... WilliamBuick 12 102
(Charlie Appleby) *ly; in tch in midfield: effrt over 2f out: nvr getting on terms w ldrs and kpt on same pce ins fnl f* **7/1**

600- 6 *¾* **Wingingit (IRE)**[165] 9002 5-8-8 **92** ..... OisinMurphy 4 91
(Andrew Balding) *taken down early: hld up in last trio: effrt over 2f out: swtchd rt over 1f out: styd on ins fnl f: nvr trbld ldrs* **25/1**

/12- 7 *½* **Mildenberger**[342] 2796 4-9-9 **107** ..... JamesDoyle 1 105
(Mark Johnston) *looked wl; slipped as stalls opened and slowly away: racd in last pair: niggled along over 4f out: swtchd rt over 3f out: no imp and looked wl btn over 2f out: hdwy 1f out: styd on ins fnl f: nvr trbld ldrs (jockey said colt slipped leaving the stalls)* **10/3**[1]

62- **8** 1 1/4 **Mazzuri (IRE)**194 8174 4-8-8 **92** .... JasonWatson 3 87
(Amanda Perrett) *chsd ldng trio tl 2f out: sn u.p and lost pl over 1f out: wknd ins fnl f* **22/1**

226- **9** hd **Crossed Baton**252 6175 4-9-7 **105** .... (w) FrankieDettori 9 100
(John Gosden) *looked wl; chsd ldrs: wnt 2nd over 10f out tl jst over 2f out: outpcd over 1f out: wknd ins fnl f* **5/1**3

44-3 **10** 8 **Desert Wind (IRE)**25 1422 4-8-9 **93** .... StevieDonohoe 13 72
(Ed Vaughan) *midfield tl dropped to rr 4f out: bhd fnl 3f (trainer's rep said colt was unsuited by Epsom and would prefer a flatter track)* **11/2**

04-0 **11** 2 **Banditry (IRE)**11 1753 7-9-0 **98** .... (h) JimCrowley 8 73
(Ian Williams) *taken down early: v.s.a: a towards rr (jockey said gelding was slowly away)* **40/1**

2m 6.65s (-3.35) **Going Correction** -0.15s/f (Firm) 11 Ran SP% **121.5**
Speed ratings (Par 109): **107,105,105,104,103 102,102,101,100,94 92**
CSF £52.45 CT £545.28 TOTE £4.00: £1.40, £3.30, £4.00; EX 56.10 Trifecta £424.90.

Owner Ziad A Galadari **Bred** Yeomanstown Stud **Trained** Newmarket, Suffolk

FOCUS
Add 27yds. A valuable and classy handicap.

2034 INVESTEC WEALTH NOVICE STKS 1m 113y
4:25 (4:26) (Class 4) 3-4-Y-O

£6,469 (£1,925; £962; £481) **Stalls** Low

Form RPR

353- **1** **Le Don De Vie**202 7933 3-9-5 81 .... OisinMurphy 5 92
(Andrew Balding) *looked wl; mde all: rdn over 1f out: battled on wl u.p and a jst holding chalr ins fnl f* **10/3**3

4- **2** nk **Casanova**151 9255 3-9-5 0 .... FrankieDettori 6 91
(John Gosden) *quite str; chsd wnr: ev ch 2f out: rdn over 1f out: sustained chal u.p ins fnl f: a jst hld* **5/2**2

23- **3** 3 1/2 **Current Option (IRE)**180 8607 3-9-5 0 .... JamesDoyle 4 84+
(William Haggas) *str; ly; looked wl; t.k.h: hld up in midfield: wnt 3rd 3f out: clsd to press ldrs over 1f out: sn rdn and fnd little: wknd ins fnl f (jockey said colt ran too free)* **1/1**1

05- **4** 8 **Turntable**146 9315 3-9-5 0 .... SilvestreDeSousa 3 67
(Simon Crisford) *quite str; t.k.h: hld up in last pair: effrt 2f out: sn outpcd and edgd lft: wknd fnl f* **11/1**

06-3 **5** nk **Mr Zoom Zoom**13 1711 3-9-5 72 .... EoinWalsh 1 66
(Luke McJannet) *stdd s: hld up in tch in last pair: effrt and hung lft 2f out: sn btn* **40/1**

6- **6** 8 **Fancy Dress (IRE)**203 7897 3-9-0 0 .... HarryBentley 2 44
(Ralph Beckett) *workmanlike; chsd ldrs tl 3f out: sn struggling: bhd 2f out: wknd* **25/1**

1m 44.67s (-1.73) **Going Correction** -0.15s/f (Firm) 6 Ran SP% **116.3**
Speed ratings (Par 105): **101,100,97,90,90 83**
CSF £12.69 TOTE £4.30: £2.10, £1.80; EX 12.70 Trifecta £24.50.

Owner Mick and Janice Mariscotti **Bred** Miss K Rausing **Trained** Kingsclere, Hants

FOCUS
Add 27yds. Decent form from the first three, who finished clear.

2035 INVESTEC PRIVATE BANKING H'CAP 1m 113y
5:00 (5:00) (Class 4) (0-80,81) 3-Y-O

£6,469 (£1,925; £962; £481; £300; £300) **Stalls** Low

Form RPR

01-6 **1** **Multamis (IRE)**29 1345 3-9-5 **78** .... JimCrowley 7 85
(Owen Burrows) *hld up in tch in midfield: effrt and hdwy u.p 2f out: swtchd lft and pressed ldrs 1f out: drvn to ld ins fnl f: r.o* **16/1**

2114 **2** 1 **Spirit Warning**60 885 3-9-7 **80** .... OisinMurphy 6 85
(Andrew Balding) *in tch in midfield: effrt to chse ldr over 2f out: str chal over 1f out: rdn to ld 1f out: hdd and one pce ins fnl f* **7/2**1

10-1 **3** 1/2 **Balladeer**23 1480 3-9-5 **78** .... HayleyTurner 9 82
(Michael Bell) *compact; taken down early: chsd ldrs: effrt ent fnl 2f: pressing ldrs and kpt on u.p ins fnl f* **11/2**3

145- **4** 1 1/2 **Majestic Mac**198 8056 3-9-3 **76** .... CharlieBennett 10 77
(Hughie Morrison) *dwlt: hld up in rr of main gp: effrt on outer over 2f out: hdwy over 1f out: styd on ins fnl f: nt rch ldrs* **8/1**

04-6 **5** hd **Sir Victor (IRE)**14 1685 3-9-8 **81** .... RichardKingscote 5 81
(Tom Dascombe) *led: rdn and hrd pressed over 1f out: hdd 1f out: no ex and wknd ins fnl f* **9/1**

532- **6** 3/4 **Gin Palace**114 9771 3-9-1 **74** .... CharlesBishop 3 72
(Eve Johnson Houghton) *hld up in tch in midfield: nudged lft jst over 2f out: nt clr run and swtchd rt over 1f out: kpt on ins fnl f (jockey said gelding was denied a clear run)* **12/1**

5-00 **7** hd **Isle Of Wolves**14 1696 3-8-2 **68** .... IsobelFrancis(7) 4 66
(Jim Boyle) *stdd after s: hld up in last trio: effrt and hung lft over 1f out: kpt on ins fnl f: nvr trbld ldrs* **25/1**

025- **8** 5 **Barbarosa (IRE)**210 7668 3-9-2 **75** .... (h1) TomMarquand 11 61
(Brian Meehan) *dropped in bhd after s: off the pce in last pair: effrt over 2f out: nvr involved* **7/1**

4115 **9** 1 3/4 **Bay Of Naples (IRE)**46 1104 3-9-6 **79** .... JoeFanning 8 61
(Mark Johnston) *quite str; chsd ldr tl over 2f out: lost pl and btn whn pushed lft 1f out: wknd ins fnl f* **10/1**

15-6 **10** 4 **Recuerdame (USA)**32 1285 3-8-8 **67** .... SilvestreDeSousa 2 40
(Simon Dow) *looked wl; chsd ldrs tl lost pl ent fnl 2f: sn btn and bhd ins fnl f (jockey said gelding became unbalanced in the straight)* **5/1**2

45-5 **11** 1 1/2 **Island Jungle (IRE)**25 1419 3-9-0 **73** .... FergusSweeney 1 43
(Mark Usher) *sn detached in last: nvr involved (jockey said gelding was slowly away)* **20/1**

032- **12** 13 **Winter Gleam (IRE)**206 7798 3-8-12 **71** .... HarryBentley 12 11
(William Knight) *midfield tl dropped to rr over 2f out: sn bhd* **10/1**

1m 44.47s (-1.93) **Going Correction** -0.15s/f (Firm) 12 Ran SP% **128.2**
Speed ratings (Par 100): **102,101,100,99,99 98,98,93,92,88 87,75**
CSF £77.22 CT £369.89 TOTE £20.10: £4.80, £1.60, £2.40; EX 83.40 Trifecta £1579.00.

Owner Hamdan Al Maktoum **Bred** Rathasker Stud **Trained** Lambourn, Berks

FOCUS
Add 27yds. Fairly useful handicap form. The first two are both sons of Charm Spirit.

T/Jkpt: Not Won. T/Plt: £90.20 to a £1 stake. Pool: £98,154.70 - 793.92 winning units T/Qpdt: £23.50 to a £1 stake. Pool: £9,599.70 - 301.64 winning units **Steve Payne**

2036 - 2050a (Foreign Racing) - See Raceform Interactive

1843
BEVERLEY (R-H)
Thursday, April 25

OFFICIAL GOING: Good to firm (good in places; 7.6)
Wind: Light across Weather: Cloudy with heavy showers

2051 RACING AGAIN ON MONDAY 6 MAY FILLIES' NOVICE AUCTION STKS (PLUS 10 RACE) (DIV I) 5f
1:40 (1:40) (Class 5) 2-Y-O

£4,032 (£1,207; £603; £302; £150) **Stalls** Low

Form RPR

2 **1** **Iva Go (IRE)**17 1642 2-9-0 0 .... DavidAllan 2 73
(Tim Easterby) *mde all: rdn ent fnl f: hld on wl towards fin* **2/9**1

0 **2** nk **Azteca**17 1642 2-9-0 0 .... GrahamLee 1 72
(Bryan Smart) *trckd ldrs on inner: hdwy 2f out: swtchd lft and rdn to chse wnr ent fnl f: kpt on wl towards fin* **20/1**

4 **3** 3/4 **Amnaa**10 1812 2-9-0 0 .... ConnorBeasley 3 69
(Adrian Nicholls) *chsd wnr: rdn along 1 1/2f out: drvn and kpt on same pce fnl f* **6/1**2

4 2 1/2 **Mecca's Hot Steps** 2-9-0 0 .... PaulMulrennan 8 60+
(Michael Dods) *towards rr: hdwy 2f out: sn rdn: kpt on fnl f* **8/1**3

5 1 1/4 **Insania** 2-9-0 0 .... PJMcDonald 10 56+
(K R Burke) *in tch on outer: rdn along and sltly outpcd over 2f out: kpt on fnl f* **10/1**

6 3 1/2 **Classy Lady** 2-8-11 0 .... BenRobinson(3) 4 43
(Ollie Pears) *green: s.i.s and bhd tl styd on fnl 2f (jockey said filly was restless in stalls)* **66/1**

0 **7** 7 **Siena Bay**6 1923 2-9-0 0 .... DuranFentiman 7 18
(Tim Easterby) *a towards rr* **66/1**

0 **8** 3 **She's Easyontheeye (IRE)**12 1759 2-9-0 0 .... JasonHart 5 7
(John Quinn) *t.k.h: chsd ldrs: rdn along 2f out: sn wknd* **25/1**

9 9 **My Dream Of You (IRE)** 2-9-0 0 .... KevinStott 6
(Tony Coyle) *chsd ldrs: rdn along 2f out: sn wknd* **25/1**

1m 3.49s (0.59) **Going Correction** +0.20s/f (Good) 9 Ran SP% **131.8**
Speed ratings (Par 89): **103,102,101,97,95 89,78,73,59**
CSF £14.95 TOTE £1.10: £1.02, £4.80, £1.50; EX 13.40 Trifecta £39.20.

Owner B Valentine & Partner **Bred** Enliven Partnership **Trained** Great Habton, N Yorks

FOCUS
A modest juvenile fillies' novice event in which a low draw was a big help. The winner is rated a bit below her debut.

2052 RACING AGAIN ON MONDAY 6 MAY FILLIES' NOVICE AUCTION STKS (PLUS 10 RACE) (DIV II) 5f
2:15 (2:15) (Class 5) 2-Y-O

£4,032 (£1,207; £603; £302; £150) **Stalls** Low

Form RPR

1 **Baileys In Bloom (FR)** 2-9-0 0 .... PaulHanagan 8 70+
(Richard Fahey) *wnt bdly lft s: sn swtchd rt to inner and in rr: hdwy 2f out: rdn to chse ldrs ent fnl f: styd on wl to ld last 50yds* **14/1**

2 1/2 **Ruby Wonder** 2-9-0 0 .... DanielTudhope 4 68
(David O'Meara) *led: rdn over 1f out: hung bdly lft ins fnl f: hdd and no ex last 50yds (jockey said filly ran green and hung left)* **14/1**

3 **3** nk **Maybellene (IRE)**10 1821 2-9-0 0 .... HarryBentley 3 67
(George Scott) *trckd ldng pair: swtchd lft and hdwy 2f out: rdn to chal over 1f out: drvn and ev ch ins fnl f: kpt on* **2/1**1

4 1 1/2 **Callipygian** 2-9-0 0 .... BarryMcHugh 9 62
(James Given) *carried bdly lft s: sn swtchd rt to inner and in rr: hdwy wl over 1f out: rdn and kpt on fnl f* **50/1**

3 **5** 2 1/4 **Knightcap**12 1759 2-9-0 0 .... DavidAllan 1 54
(Tim Easterby) *trckd ldrs: swtchd lft and hdwy over 1f out: sn chal and ev ch whn carried lft and hmpd ins fnl f: swtchd rt and one pce after* **3/1**2

3 **6** 2 1/2 **Gracie's Girl**7 1879 2-9-0 0 .... AlistairRawlinson 6 45
(Michael Appleby) *cl up: rdn along wl over 1f out: wkng and hld whn hmpd ins fnl f* **12/1**

0 **7** 2 1/2 **Flight Of Thunder (IRE)**17 1642 2-9-0 0 .... KevinStott 7 36
(Kevin Ryan) *towards rr: effrt and in tch 2f out: sn rdn and wknd* **11/2**

0 **8** 9 **The Lazy Monkey (IRE)**7 1879 2-9-0 0 .... JoeFanning 5 3
(Mark Johnston) *chsd ldrs on outer: rdn along over 2f out: sn wknd* **4/1**3

1m 3.7s (0.80) **Going Correction** +0.20s/f (Good) 8 Ran SP% **116.7**
Speed ratings (Par 89): **101,100,99,97,93 89,85,71**
CSF £189.74 TOTE £12.00: £3.40, £3.70, £1.10; EX 119.60 Trifecta £827.10.

Owner G R Bailey Ltd (Baileys Horse Feeds) **Bred** S A R L Haras Des Trois Chapelles **Trained** Musley Bank, N Yorks

FOCUS
This second division of the fillies' novice was another modest affair. The form's rated a shade negatively.

2053 BEVERLEY ANNUAL BADGEHOLDERS H'CAP 5f
2:50 (2:57) (Class 5) (0-75,75) 4-Y-O+

£4,032 (£1,207; £603; £302; £300; £300) **Stalls** Low

Form RPR

06-0 **1** **Secretinthepark**12 1760 9-9-4 **72** .... (b) TomEaves 4 80
(Michael Mullineaux) *trckd ldr: hdwy to ld wl over 1f out: rdn ent fnl f: sn jnd and drvn: edgd lft last 100yds: kpt on* **33/1**

-501 **2** hd **Johnny Cavagin**10 1818 10-8-13 **67** 4ex .... GrahamLee 10 74
(Paul Midgley) *trckd ldrs: hdwy wl over 1f out: chsd wnr ent fnl f: sn rdn to chal: ev ch whn carried sltly lft ins fnl 100yds: kpt on* **4/1**2

30-0 **3** 4 **Prestbury Park (USA)**12 1760 4-9-3 **71** .... KevinStott 7 64
(Paul Midgley) *trckd ldrs: hdwy 1 1/2f out: chsd ldng pair ent fnl f: sn rdn and kpt on same pce* **9/2**3

21-4 **4** 2 3/4 **Musharrif**12 1760 7-9-6 **74** .... DavidNolan 11 57
(Declan Carroll) *towards rr: hdwy 1/2-way: rdn along wl over 1f out: kpt on fnl f* **9/2**3

001- **5** 1 **Seamster**169 8935 12-8-4 **65** .... (t) LauraCoughlan(7) 3 44
(David Loughnane) *towards rr: hdwy 2f out: sn rdn and kpt on fnl f* **9/1**

4160 **6** 1/2 **It's All A Joke (IRE)**27 1394 4-9-0 **75** .... (b) Pierre-LouisJamin(7) 2 53
(Archie Watson) *chsd ldrs: rdn along wl over 1f out: sn drvn and one pce* **10/1**

20-0 **7** 1 1/4 **Wensley**20 1565 4-8-7 **61** .... (p) PhilDennis 6 34
(Rebecca Bastiman) *a in rr* **25/1**

6313 **8** 1 **Mininggold**8 1860 6-9-0 **73** .... (p) PaulaMuir(5) 1 42
(Michael Dods) *chsd ldrs on inner: rdn along and n.m.r 2f out: sn wknd (jockey said mare suffered interference shortly after leaving stalls)* **3/1**1

The Form Book Flat 2019, Raceform Ltd, Newbury, RG14 5SJ

4-04 **9** *5* **Bosham**[21] 1547 9-8-11 **65**..(bt) NathanEvans 9 16
(Michael Easterby) *qckly away: led and sn swtchd rt to inner rail: rdn along 2f out: sn hdd & wknd* **11/1**

6400 **10** *11* **Jacob's Pillow**[29] 1368 8-8-12 **66**..............................(b[1]) LewisEdmunds 8
(Rebecca Bastiman) *a in rr* **20/1**

1m 2.78s (-0.12) **Going Correction** +0.20s/f (Good) **10** Ran SP% **120.3**
Speed ratings (Par 103): **108,107,101,96,95 94,92,90,82,65**
CSF £163.06 CT £751.43 TOTE £36.70: £7.40, £1.80, £1.70; EX 276.60 Trifecta £1586.80.
Owner Mia Racing **Bred** Mia Racing **Trained** Alpraham, Cheshire

FOCUS
There was a 7min delay to this modest sprint handicap, in which it paid to be handy.

2054 ALAN MCGUINNESS AND ROBIN LUNNESS MEMORIAL H'CAP 7f 96y
3:20 (3:21) (Class 3) (0-90,90) 3-Y-O

£7,470 (£2,236; £1,118; £559; £279; £140) **Stalls** Low

Form RPR

123- **1** **Motafaawit (IRE)**[236] 6791 3-9-7 **90**.......................... JimCrowley 5 101
(Richard Hannon) *hld up in tch: hdwy on outer over 2f out: effrt over 1f out: rdn to chal ent fnl f: sn drvn and edgd rt: kpt on wl to ld nr fin* **4/1**[3]

123- **2** *shd* **King Of Tonga (IRE)**[223] 7233 3-9-0 **83**.......................... PaulHanagan 2 93
(Richard Fahey) *trckd ldng pair: hdwy and cl up on inner over 2f out: rdn to take slt ld over 1f out: drvn ins fnl f: sn edgd lft: hdd and no ex nr fin* **11/4**[2]

304- **3** *5* **James Watt (IRE)**[201] 7988 3-9-3 **86**.......................... HayleyTurner 4 83
(Michael Bell) *trckd ldrs: hdwy over 2f out: rdn and ev ch over 1f out: drvn whn n.m.r jst ins fnl f: sn one pce* **11/2**

32-5 **4** *3/4* **Five Helmets (IRE)**[24] 1485 3-7-13 **71**.......................... JamieGormley(3) 6 66
(Iain Jardine) *stdd s: hld up and bhd: hdwy over 2f out: rdn wl over 1f out: styd on wl fnl f: nrst fin* **33/1**

34-1 **5** *hd* **Nefarious (IRE)**[96] 320 3-9-1 **84**.......................... BenCurtis 3 79
(Henry Candy) *in tch: hdwy to chse ldrs over 2f out: rdn wl over 1f out: sn drvn and btn* **5/2**[1]

306- **6** *2 1/4* **Kuwait Station (IRE)**[198] 8075 3-9-3 **86**.......................... DavidNolan 1 75
(David O'Meara) *led: rn wd bnd after 3f: rdn along over 2f out: drvn and hdd over 1f out: sn wknd (jockey said gelding hung left throughout)* **7/1**

046- **7** *1 3/4* **I Am A Dreamer**[194] 8195 3-8-12 **81**.......................... JoeFanning 7 65
(Mark Johnston) *cl up whn carried wd bnd after 3f: rdn along over 2f out: wknd wl over 1f out* **10/1**

1m 34.32s (1.72) **Going Correction** +0.20s/f (Good) **7** Ran SP% **115.2**
Speed ratings (Par 102): **98,97,92,91,91 88,86**
CSF £15.67 TOTE £4.10: £2.70, £1.40; EX 14.90 Trifecta £52.40.
Owner Hamdan Al Maktoum **Bred** Shadwell Estate Company Limited **Trained** East Everleigh, Wilts

FOCUS
This feature 3yo handicap was run at a frantic pace and it's solid form.

2055 RACING TV H'CAP 7f 96y
3:55 (3:55) (Class 5) (0-70,72) 3-Y-O **£4,032** (£1,207; £603; £302; £300) **Stalls** Low

Form RPR

00-1 **1** **Dragon Sun**[29] 1358 3-9-9 **72**.......................... SeanLevey 2 77+
(Richard Hannon) *trckd ldrs on inner: hdwy over 2f out: swtchd lft and effrt to chal over 1f out: rdn to rake slt ld ent fnl f: sn drvn and kpt on* **11/8**[1]

0-22 **2** *nk* **Strawberry Jack**[14] 1720 3-9-8 **71**..............................(tp) BenCurtis 1 75
(George Scott) *cl up: led over 4f out: jnd and rdn over 1f out: hdd narrowly and drvn ent fnl f: kpt on gamely tl no ex towards fin* **11/4**[3]

346- **3** *5* **Defence Treaty (IRE)**[166] 9001 3-9-7 **70**.......................... DanielTudhope 4 61
(Richard Fahey) *trckd ldrs: hdwy on outer over 2f out: chsd ldng pair and rdn over 1f out: sn drvn and kpt on same pce* **5/2**[2]

50-0 **4** *10* **Quanah (IRE)**[24] 1488 3-9-2 **65**.......................... JFEgan 3 30
(Mark H Tompkins) *slt ld: hdd over 4f out: cl up: rdn along wl over 2f out: grad wknd* **40/1**

10-3 **5** *4 1/2* **Port Of Leith (IRE)**[82] 561 3-9-9 **72**.......................... JoeFanning 5 25
(Mark Johnston) *chsd ldng pair on outer: pushed along over 3f out: rdn wl over 2f out: sn wknd* **8/1**

1m 34.88s (2.28) **Going Correction** +0.20s/f (Good) **5** Ran SP% **110.9**
Speed ratings (Par 98): **95,94,88,77,72**
CSF £5.54 TOTE £2.20: £1.10, £1.60; EX 5.20 Trifecta £9.50.
Owner Mrs Fitri Hay **Bred** Rabbah Bloodstock Limited **Trained** East Everleigh, Wilts

FOCUS
This interesting little 3yo handicap was run at a muddling pace.

2056 RAPID LAD H'CAP 1m 1f 207y
4:25 (4:26) (Class 5) (0-70,71) 4-Y-O+

£4,032 (£1,207; £603; £302; £300; £300) **Stalls** Low

Form RPR

52-3 **1** **Glacier Fox**[48] 1080 4-9-2 **65**.......................... JamesSullivan 3 71
(Tom Tate) *mde all: rdn wl over 1f out: drvn and edgd lft ins fnl f: kpt on wl: rdr dropped rein towards fin* **9/1**

00-5 **2** *1/2* **Agar's Plough**[16] 1660 4-9-6 **69**.......................... NathanEvans 5 74
(Michael Easterby) *trckd ldrs: hdwy over 2f out: rdn to chal ent fnl f: sn ev ch: drvn and kpt on same pce towards fin* **9/2**[2]

40-3 **3** *1 1/4* **Velvet Vision**[24] 1482 4-9-8 **71**.......................... JFEgan 2 74
(Mark H Tompkins) *t.k.h early: prom: pushed along 2f out: rdn over 1f out: drvn and kpt on same pce fnl f* **11/2**[3]

110- **4** *1 1/2* **Whatwouldyouknow (IRE)**[140] 9431 4-9-4 **67**.......................... PhilipPrince 4 67
(Richard Guest) *hld up in tch: hdwy over 2f out: rdn wl over 1f out: kpt on fnl f* **7/1**

340- **5** *1/2* **Thorntoun Care**[169] 8936 8-9-4 **67**.......................... ShaneGray 8 66
(Karen Tutty) *in rr: hdwy over 2f out: sn rdn: kpt on fnl f* **28/1**

005 **6** *1 1/4* **Star Of Valour (IRE)**[16] 1659 4-9-0 **63**..............................(h) DougieCostello 9 59
(David C Griffiths) *prom: rdn along on outer over 2f out: sn wknd* **16/1**

4246 **7** *2 3/4* **Zorawar (FR)**[17] 1647 5-9-5 **68**..............................(p) DanielTudhope 6 59
(David O'Meara) *trckd ldrs: hdwy over 3f out: cl up 2f out: sn rdn: drvn and wknd ent fnl f* **3/1**[1]

335- **8** *10* **Never Be Enough**[192] 8267 4-9-7 **70**..............................(h[1]) TomEaves 7 74
(Keith Dalgleish) *hld up in rr: hdwy over 2f out: rdn to chse ldrs over 1f out: ev ch ins fnl f whn lost action and virtually p.u (jockey said filly lost action but on pulling up it was evident the hood had slipped and was covering the filly's eyes)* **12/1**

26-0 **9** *1/2* **Mont Royal (FR)**[27] 1398 5-8-9 **58**..............................(p) JoeFanning 1 28
(Ollie Pears) *dwlt and towards rr: hdwy on outer 3f out: sn chsng ldrs: rdn along 2f out: sn wknd* **9/2**[2]

2m 8.54s (2.84) **Going Correction** +0.20s/f (Good) **9** Ran SP% **116.3**
Speed ratings (Par 103): **96,95,94,93,93 92,89,81,81**
CSF £49.58 CT £247.33 TOTE £8.00: £2.10, £1.90, £1.80; EX 46.90 Trifecta £212.10.
Owner T T Racing **Bred** Winterbeck Manor Stud **Trained** Tadcaster, N Yorks

FOCUS
This moderate handicap was run at a stop-start tempo.

2057 WESTWOOD H'CAP 1m 100y
4:55 (4:55) (Class 4) (0-80,82) 4-Y-O+

£5,418 (£1,621; £810; £405; £300; £300) **Stalls** Low

Form RPR

66-1 **1** **Kylie Rules**[8] 1850 4-8-7 **66** 5ex.......................... JamesSullivan 8 76+
(Ruth Carr) *hld up towards rr: smooth hdwy on outer over 2f out: led 1 1/2f out: sn rdn clr and edgd rt to inner rail: kpt on* **15/8**[1]

051- **2** *1 1/2* **Placebo Effect (IRE)**[146] 9326 4-8-8 **70**.......................... BenRobinson(3) 1 75
(Ollie Pears) *trckd ldrs: effrt 2f out: rdn along and n.m.r over 1f out: chsd wnr ins fnl f: kpt on wl towards fin (jockey said gelding was denied a clear run)* **16/1**

20-0 **3** *1 3/4* **Kannapolis (IRE)**[26] 1418 4-8-12 **71**.......................... NathanEvans 2 72
(Michael Easterby) *bhd and niggled along after 2f: jnd field 1/2-way: effrt on outer wl over 2f out: rdn along over 1f out: sn drvn and kpt on fnl f* **4/1**[2]

356- **4** *4* **Autretot (FR)**[199] 8050 4-9-9 **82**.......................... DanielTudhope 7 74
(David O'Meara) *led: pushed along 3f out: rdn over 2f out: hdd 1 1/2f out: sn drvn and kpt on one pce* **11/2**[3]

40-6 **5** *nk* **Proud Archi (IRE)**[25] 1457 5-9-7 **80**.......................... PaulMulrennan 4 71
(Michael Dods) *trckd ldrs: hdwy 3f out and sn cl up: rdn along over 2f out: drvn over 1f out: kpt on one pce* **8/1**

0-40 **6** *1* **Windsor Cross (IRE)**[17] 1644 4-9-1 **79**..............................(p) ConnorMurtagh(5) 5 68
(Richard Fahey) *hld up: a towards rr* **16/1**

53-3 **7** *3 1/4* **International Man**[17] 1644 4-8-12 **76**.......................... SeanDavis(5) 6 57
(Richard Fahey) *chsd ldrs: rdn along over 2f out: sn drvn and wknd over 1f out* **6/1**

60-2 **8** *7* **Stringybark Creek**[15] 1695 5-8-7 **73**.......................... LauraCoughlan(7) 9 38
(David Loughnane) *chsd ldr on outer: pushed along wl over 2f out: rdn wl over 1f out and sn wknd (jockey said gelding stopped quickly)* **17/2**

1m 47.45s (1.05) **Going Correction** +0.20s/f (Good) **8** Ran SP% **117.9**
Speed ratings (Par 105): **102,100,98,94,94 93,90,83**
CSF £36.47 CT £113.34 TOTE £2.70: £1.20, £4.80, £1.50; EX 49.60 Trifecta £169.20.
Owner J A Knox and Mrs M A Knox **Bred** J A Knox **Trained** Huby, N Yorks

FOCUS
There was a fair pace on in this modest handicap.

2058 WHISTLEJACKETS CRAFT ALE BAR NOVICE AUCTION STKS 1m 100y
5:25 (5:27) (Class 5) 3-Y-O **£4,140** (£1,232; £461; £461) **Stalls** Low

Form RPR

51 **1** **Oasis Prince**[20] 1562 3-9-9 0.......................... JoeFanning 4 84+
(Mark Johnston) *set stdy pce: pushed along and qcknd over 2f out: rdn over 1f out: kpt on strly* **4/7**[1]

0 **2** *1 1/4* **International Guy (IRE)**[17] 1649 3-9-2 0.......................... TonyHamilton 2 72
(Richard Fahey) *sn trcking wnr: hdwy and cl up 2f out: rdn over 1f out: drvn and kpt on fnl f* **20/1**

3 *1/2* **Osmosis**[181] 8616 3-8-11 75.......................... BenCurtis 3 66
(Jason Ward) *trckd ldng pair on inner: swtchd lft and effrt 2f out: rdn over 1f out: drvn and kpt on fnl f* **14/1**[3]

240- **3** *dht* **Kingson (IRE)**[208] 7765 3-9-2 77.......................... PaulHanagan 1 71
(Richard Fahey) *hld up in rr: hdwy over 2f out: rdn along to chse ldrs on inner over 1f out: kpt on towards fin* **7/4**[2]

1m 52.75s (6.35) **Going Correction** +0.20s/f (Good) **4** Ran SP% **111.4**
Speed ratings (Par 98): **76,74,74,74**
CSF £11.84 TOTE £1.40; EX 12.60 Trifecta £17.20.
Owner J David Abell **Bred** Highclere Stud And Floors Farming **Trained** Middleham Moor, N Yorks

FOCUS
Not a bad little 3yo novice event.
T/Plt: £48.10 to a £1 stake. Pool: £58,155.06 - 881.14 winning units T/Qpdt: £14.40 to a £1 stake. Pool: £5,767.82 - 294.44 winning units **Joe Rowntree**

1879 CHELMSFORD (A.W) (L-H)
Thursday, April 25

OFFICIAL GOING: Polytrack: standard
Wind: light, half behind Weather: dry

2059 BET TOTEPLACEPOT AT TOTESPORT.COM H'CAP 1m 6f (P)
5:30 (5:30) (Class 5) (0-75,77) 4-Y-O+

£5,433 (£1,617; £808; £404; £300; £300) **Stalls** Low

Form RPR

-224 **1** **Houlton**[45] 1144 4-9-6 **71**..............................(tp) RyanMoore 1 81
(Marco Botti) *chsd ldr for 4f: styd chsng ldrs tl wnt 2nd again over 2f out: swtchd rt and effrt to chal over 1f out: carried rt but led ins fnl f: r.o wl* **3/1**[2]

1112 **2** *1 3/4* **Singing The Blues (IRE)**[23] 1497 4-9-2 **67**.......................... OisinMurphy 6 75
(Rod Millman) *led: rdn and hrd pressed over 1f out: hung rt and hdd ins fnl f: no ex* **5/2**[1]

211- **3** *1 1/2* **The Pinto Kid (FR)**[161] 9075 4-9-12 **77**..............................(t) GeorgeWood 4 83
(James Fanshawe) *hld up in tch in midfield: clsd and nt clrest of runs jst over 2f out: hdwy to chse ldng pair wl over 1f out: styd on same pce and no imp ins fnl f* **3/1**[2]

14-4 **4** *7* **Grandscape**[25] 1463 4-9-7 **72**.......................... RobertHavlin 3 68
(Ed Dunlop) *stdd s: hld up in tch in last trio: clsd and nt clr run ent fnl 2f: effrt over 1f out: no ch w ldng trio but kpt on to snatch modest 4th cl home* **10/1**

431- **5** *1/2* **Press Gang**[45] 8650 6-9-4 **68**.......................... JamieSpencer 8 62
(Harry Fry) *in tch in midfield: effrt 3f out: sn u.p and outpcd wl over 1f out: wl hld after and lost modest 4th cl home* **16/1**

213- **6** *1 1/4* **Jumping Cats**[176] 8735 4-9-6 **71**.......................... JackMitchell 7 65
(Chris Wall) *hld up in tch in last trio: rdn over 3f out: struggling and outpcd wl over 1f out: wl btn after* **5/1**[3]

0- **7** *3/4* **Valse Au Taillons (FR)**[45] 4031 6-9-4 **68**.......................... DavidProbert 5 60
(Johnny Farrelly) *hld up in tch in rr: effrt wl over 1f out: sn u.p and outpcd: wl btn after* **33/1**

50-5 **8** *12* **Roc Astrale (IRE)**[24] 1482 5-8-9 **66**.......................... GraceMcEntee(7) 9 41
(Phil McEntee) *chsd ldrs tl clsd to press ldr after 4f: lost pl u.p over 2f out: wl bhd fnl f* **33/1**

3m 0.25s (-2.95) **Going Correction** -0.125s/f (Stan)
WFA 4 from 5yo+ 1lb **8** Ran SP% **116.1**
Speed ratings (Par 103): **103,102,101,97,96 96,95,88**
CSF £11.16 CT £22.97 TOTE £3.60: £1.40, £1.20, £1.70; EX 11.80 Trifecta £44.10.
Owner Fabfive **Bred** Deerfield Farm **Trained** Newmarket, Suffolk

The Form Book Flat 2019, Raceform Ltd, Newbury, RG14 5SJ

FOCUS
Few got into this.

2060 BET TOTEEXACTA AT TOTESPORT.COM MAIDEN STKS 6f (P)
6:00 (6:02) (Class 3) 3-Y-O+ **£8,086** (£2,406; £1,202; £601) **Stalls** Centre

Form RPR

- 1 **Jubiloso** 3-8-12 0 RyanMoore 4 87+
(Sir Michael Stoute) *midfield and niggled along early: swtchd lft and hdwy on inner over 1f out: chal 1f out: led ins fnl f and sn drew clr under hands heels riding: impressive* **11/4**[2]

0-2 2 2 3/4 **Dominus (IRE)**[20] 1562 3-9-3 0 TomMarquand 3 81
(Brian Meehan) *led: rdn and drifted rt wl over 1f out: drvn ent fnl f: hdd and nt match pce of wnr ins fnl f* **8/1**[3]

2- 3 hd **Hero Hero (IRE)**[166] 9001 3-9-3 0 SilvestreDeSousa 1 80
(Andrew Balding) *t.k.h: trckd ldrs on inner: swtchd rt and effrt to chse ldr wl over 1f out: 3rd and hrd drvn 1f out: unable qck and one pce fnl f* **4/6**[1]

2-0 4 1 1/2 **Maid For Life**[27] 1400 3-8-12 0 (h) OisinMurphy 5 71
(Charlie Fellowes) *stdd s: t.k.h: hld up wl in tch in midfield: effrt and carried rt over 1f out: kpt on same pce ins fnl f* **33/1**

56- 5 4 1/2 **Invincible Larne (IRE)**[192] 8279 3-9-3 0 CharlesBishop 7 61
(Mick Quinn) *styd wd early: chsd ldr tl wl over 1f out: unable qck and sn drifted rt: wknd fnl f* **100/1**

6 1/2 **Ice Cave (IRE)** 3-9-3 0 PatCosgrave 6 60
(Saeed bin Suroor) *dwlt and swtchd rt after s: in tch in last pair: unable qck and hung lft over 1f out: wknd fnl f* **9/1**

50 7 hd **Magical Ride**[13] 1728 4-10-0 0 (h) TomQueally 2 62
(Richard Spencer) *sn dropped to rr: shkn up over 1f out: sn outpcd and wknd ins fnl f* **100/1**

1m 12.09s (-1.61) **Going Correction** -0.125s/f (Stan)
WFA 3 from 4yo 11lb 7 Ran SP% **112.7**
Speed ratings (Par 107): **105,101,101,99,93 92,92**
CSF £23.13 TOTE £3.50: £1.60, £2.60; EX 17.70 Trifecta £37.70.
Owner K Abdullah **Bred** Juddmonte Farms Ltd **Trained** Newmarket, Suffolk

FOCUS
A good performance from the winner on her debut, coming from behind to beat a couple of rivals with fair form in the book.

2061 BET TOTEQUADPOT AT TOTESPORT.COM H'CAP 6f (P)
6:30 (6:30) (Class 3) (0-95,97) 4-Y-O+ **£9,703** (£2,887; £1,443; £721) **Stalls** Centre

Form RPR

12-1 1 **Walk On Walter (IRE)**[54] 981 4-9-5 **90** (h) RobHornby 2 100
(Jonathan Portman) *mde all: rdn over 1f out: styd on wl ins fnl f and a doing enough* **2/1**[1]

3225 2 nk **Areen Heart (FR)**[6] 1919 5-9-4 **89** AdamKirby 1 98
(David O'Meara) *trckd ldrs on inner: effrt to chse wnr over 1f out: drvn ins fnl f: kpt on u.p but a hld (jockey said whip broke inside the final furlong)* **9/4**[2]

-006 3 1 3/4 **Udontdodou**[5] 1938 6-9-5 **90** JamieSpencer 8 93
(Richard Guest) *stdd after s: t.k.h: hld up wl in tch in rr: effrt on inner 1f out: r.o to go 3rd 50yds out: no threat to ldrs* **9/1**

40-2 4 1/2 **Storm Over (IRE)**[9] 1839 5-9-7 **92** HarryBentley 5 94
(George Scott) *pushed rt leaving stalls: hld up in tch: effrt over 1f out: kpt on same pce u.p ins fnl f* **8/1**[3]

030- 5 1 **Vegas Boy (IRE)**[180] 8641 4-9-2 **87** NicolaCurrie 4 86
(Jamie Osborne) *wnt rt leaving stalls: sn chsng wnr tl unable qck over 1f out: wknd ins fnl f* **14/1**

3215 6 1 1/2 **King Robert**[10] 1822 6-9-2 **87** LukeMorris 3 81
(Charlie Wallis) *chsd ldrs: rdn ent fnl 2f: unable qck under over 1f out: wknd ins fnl f* **10/1**

06-0 7 nk **Captain Jameson (IRE)**[25] 1459 4-8-12 **88**(p[1]) ThoreHammerHansen(5) 6 81
(John Quinn) *t.k.h: wd and wl in tch in midfield: unable qck over 1f out: kpt on same pce u.p ins fnl f* **12/1**

/66- 8 3/4 **Lahore (USA)**[320] 3597 5-9-12 **97** SamJames 7 87
(Phillip Makin) *stdd s: t.k.h: hld up in tch: effrt over 1f out: kpt on same pce and no imp u.p ins fnl f* **14/1**

1m 11.97s (-1.73) **Going Correction** -0.125s/f (Stan) 8 Ran SP% **115.3**
Speed ratings (Par 107): **106,105,103,102,101 99,98,97**
CSF £6.76 CT £31.02 TOTE £2.30: £1.10, £1.10, £2.90; EX 6.30 Trifecta £45.60.
Owner Philip Simpson **Bred** Sandro Garavelli **Trained** Upper Lambourn, Berks

FOCUS
The pace was controlled by the winner and he only faced one serious rival up the straight.

2062 BETSI CONDITIONS STKS 6f (P)
7:00 (7:01) (Class 2) 4-Y-O+ **£16,172** (£4,812; £2,405; £1,202) **Stalls** Centre

Form RPR

220- 1 **Dream Of Dreams (IRE)**[187] 8405 5-9-2 109 RyanMoore 1 110
(Sir Michael Stoute) *hld up in tch: effrt and hdwy on inner over 1f out: r.o u.p to ld wl ins fnl f: r.o strly: readily* **6/4**[1]

032- 2 1 1/4 **Hey Jonesy (IRE)**[166] 9003 4-9-2 107 (p w) KevinStott 5 106
(Kevin Ryan) *sn led: rdn and drifted rt over 1f out: sn hrd pressed and drvn: hdd and unable to match pce of wnr wl ins fnl f* **11/4**[2]

53-0 3 1 1/4 **Eirene**[26] 1412 4-9-1 100 JamesDoyle 2 101
(Dean Ivory) *hld up in tch in rr: effrt over 1f out: hdwy whn swtchd rt and bmpd rival ins fnl f: r.o wl to go 3rd towards fin: no threat to wnr* **9/2**[3]

1033 4 1/2 **Tropics (USA)**[9] 1839 11-9-6 104 (h) AdamKirby 3 104
(Dean Ivory) *t.k.h: trckd ldrs on inner: rdn and clsd over 1f out: ev ch 1f out tl no ex and outpcd wl ins fnl f: lost 3rd towards fin* **12/1**

511- 5 1 1/4 **Baron Bolt**[215] 7512 6-9-6 108 LukeMorris 4 100
(Paul Cole) *hld up in tch: effrt on outer over 1f out: keeping on but no imp whn bmpd ins fnl f: wl hld and one pce after* **16/1**

621- 6 1/2 **Foxtrot Lady**[223] 7254 4-9-1 102 DavidProbert 7 94
(Andrew Balding) *chsd ldr tl over 4f out: u.p over 1f out: struggling and jst getting outpcd whn bmpd ins fnl f: wl hld and one pce after* **8/1**

340- 7 4 **Rock On Baileys**[194] 8190 4-9-1 99 (p) SilvestreDeSousa 6 81
(Amy Murphy) *stdd and sltly impeded leaving stalls: sn rcvrd and chse ldr over 4f out: rdn to press ldr over 1f out: unable qck and struggling whn edgd lft and bmpd ins fnl f: nt rcvr and bhd after* **25/1**

1m 11.52s (-2.18) **Going Correction** -0.125s/f (Stan) 7 Ran SP% **113.4**
Speed ratings (Par 109): **109,107,105,105,103 102,97**
CSF £5.64 TOTE £1.90: £1.20, £1.80; EX 6.20 Trifecta £18.60.
Owner Saeed Suhail **Bred** Prostock Ltd **Trained** Newmarket, Suffolk

FOCUS
A decent sprint, and as with the previous races on the card it was an advantage to stick to the inside.

2063 BET TOTETRIFECTA AT TOTESPORT.COM H'CAP 6f (P)
7:30 (7:31) (Class 6) (0-65,65) 3-Y-O
£3,105 (£924; £461; £300; £300; £300) **Stalls** Centre

Form RPR

603- 1 **Spirit Of May**[147] 9307 3-9-6 **64** JasonWatson 9 71
(Roger Teal) *mde all: rdn over 1f out: hrd pressed and all out towards fin: jst hld on* **14/1**

3311 2 shd **Pentland Lad (IRE)**[15] 1678 3-9-4 **62** (t) OisinMurphy 2 69
(Charlie Fellowes) *t.k.h: trckd ldrs: swtchd rt and effrt to chse wnr over 1f out: edgd lft but sustained effrt ins fnl f: clsng towards fin: jst hld (jockey said gelding hung left-handed under pressure)* **1/1**[1]

2035 3 2 1/2 **Antonia Clara**[15] 1687 3-8-12 **63** (p) MarcoGhiani(7) 3 62
(Stuart Williams) *wnt rt s: t.k.h: sn rcvrd to chse ldrs: effrt in 3rd over 1f out: no imp and btn wl ins fnl f* **7/1**[3]

60-3 4 1 1/2 **Tease Maid**[22] 1523 3-9-6 **64** KevinStott 7 59
(John Quinn) *wl in tch in midfield: swtchd lft and effrt over 1f out: chsd ldng trio and no imp ins fnl f: eased cl home* **8/1**

0-40 5 3 3/4 **Evangeline Samos**[31] 1337 3-9-2 **60** JamieSpencer 12 43+
(Kevin Ryan) *stdd s: hld up in rr: c wd bnd wl over 1f out: hdwy over 1f out: styd on to go modest 5th wl ins fnl f: nvr trbld ldrs* **25/1**

40-0 6 2 **Te Amo Te Amo**[45] 1139 3-9-7 **65** TomMarquand 11 42
(Simon Dow) *chsd wnr: rdn over 2f out: lost pl over 1f out and btn 5th 1f out: wknd ins fnl f* **20/1**

7 nk **Sweet Forgetme Not (IRE)**[32] 1304 3-8-7 **51** EoinWalsh 10 28
(Samuel Farrell, Ire) *s.i.s: towards rr: effrt over 1f out: nvr trbld ldrs* **50/1**

00-6 8 1 **Two Faced**[28] 1380 3-8-2 **46** oh1 HollieDoyle 5 20
(Lydia Pearce) *wnt rt s: racd in last trio: effrt and swtchd lft over 1f out: nvr involved (jockey said filly suffered interference at the start)* **66/1**

032 9 1/2 **Temple Of Wonder (IRE)**[62] 854 3-9-6 **64** (h) LukeMorris 1 36
(Charlie Wallis) *midfield: shkn up 4f out: no hdwy u.p and hung lft over 1f out: wl btn 1f after* **14/1**

00-0 10 3/4 **Vena D'Amore (IRE)**[17] 1650 3-8-13 **57** JoeyHaynes 6 27
(Dean Ivory) *squeezed for room leaving stalls: a towards rr: nvr involved* **33/1**

2-44 11 3 3/4 **Griggy (IRE)**[31] 1337 3-9-6 **64** AdamKirby 4 23
(John Butler) *wnt rt s: t.k.h: hld up in tch in midfield: 6th and rdn over 2f out: sn struggling and btn over 1f out: bhd ins fnl f (trainers' rep could offer no explanation for the poor performance)* **4/1**[2]

1m 12.48s (-1.22) **Going Correction** -0.125s/f (Stan) 11 Ran SP% **121.9**
Speed ratings (Par 96): **103,102,99,97,92 89,89,88,87,86 81**
CSF £28.51 CT £123.38 TOTE £14.20: £3.70, £1.10, £2.10; EX 51.10 Trifecta £267.20.
Owner Mrs Carol Borras **Bred** R P Phillips **Trained** Lambourn, Berks

FOCUS
The early pace wasn't strong and it paid to be up there.

2064 BET TOTESCOOP6 AT TOTESPORT.COM H'CAP 1m (P)
8:00 (8:01) (Class 4) (0-85,86) 4-Y-O+
£5,692 (£1,694; £846; £423; £300; £300) **Stalls** Low

Form RPR

/50- 1 **Itsakindamagic**[147] 9309 5-9-3 **81** OisinMurphy 6 86
(Ismail Mohammed) *t.k.h: trckd ldrs: effrt to chal over 1f out: drvn ins fnl f: awkward hd carriage: kpt on u.p to ld last strides* **7/1**[3]

540- 2 hd **Top Mission**[205] 7870 5-9-7 **85** RyanMoore 9 89
(Marco Botti) *hld up in last pair: swtchd rt and effrt wd wl over 1f out: hung lft but clsd jst over 1f out: styd on strly and ev ch towards fin: wnt 2nd last stride* **6/1**[2]

140- 3 nse **Labrega**[268] 5588 4-9-8 **86** (h[1]) JamesDoyle 8 90
(Hugo Palmer) *in tch in midfield: effrt over 1f out: clsng to chse ldrs and hung lft ins fnl f: ev ch towards fin: wnt 3rd last stride* **10/1**

100- 4 shd **Letsbe Avenue (IRE)**[199] 8061 4-9-1 **79** RossaRyan 2 83
(Richard Hannon) *led: rdn and jnd over 1f out: kpt on wl u.p: hdd and lost 3 pls last strides* **10/1**

10-0 5 nk **Bacacarat (IRE)**[25] 1461 4-9-3 **81** SilvestreDeSousa 3 84
(Andrew Balding) *t.k.h: hld up in tch in midfield: effrt over 1f out: hrd drvn ins fnl f: kpt on* **7/4**[1]

2454 6 2 **Samphire Coast**[14] 1714 6-9-2 **80** (vt) PaddyMathers 1 78
(Derek Shaw) *broke wl but sn pushed along: midfield whn short of room and restrained bk towards rr over 6f out: effrt on inner over 1f out: kpt on same pce u.p ins fnl f* **6/1**[2]

420- 7 1 3/4 **Oh It's Saucepot**[211] 7664 5-9-2 **80** GeorgeWood 4 74
(Chris Wall) *hld up in tch in midfield: effrt and unable qck over 1f out: kpt on ins fnl f: no threat to ldrs* **11/1**

-000 8 shd **Rock Icon**[13] 1727 6-8-5 **76** GeorgiaDobie(7) 5 70
(Jo Hughes, France) *v.s.a: sn rcvrd and clsd onto bk of field and t.k.h over 6f out: effrt and hung lft over 1f out: kpt on ins fnl f: nvr trbld ldrs (jockey said gelding was slowly away)* **25/1**

6003 9 1 **Able Jack**[21] 1544 6-9-1 **79** HarryBentley 7 71
(Stuart Williams) *chsd ldr tl over 1f out: unable qck and outpcd 1f out: wknd ins fnl f* **10/1**

1m 38.45s (-1.45) **Going Correction** -0.125s/f (Stan) 9 Ran SP% **116.9**
Speed ratings (Par 105): **102,101,101,101,101 99,97,97,96**
CSF £49.13 CT £423.33 TOTE £8.40: £2.20, £2.00, £2.60; EX 47.80 Trifecta £279.80.
Owner Sheikh Juma Dalmook Al Maktoum **Bred** Newsells Park & Mr & Mrs Flannigan **Trained** Newmarket, Suffolk

FOCUS
The early pace wasn't strong, they quickened from the turn in and finished in a heap.

2065 BET TOTESWINGER AT TOTESPORT.COM H'CAP 7f (P)
8:30 (8:31) (Class 4) (0-80,80) 4-Y-O+
£5,692 (£1,694; £846; £423; £300; £300) **Stalls** Low

Form RPR

4125 1 **Harbour Vision**[24] 1479 4-9-1 **74** PaddyMathers 7 80
(Derek Shaw) *niggled along and dropped to last pair over 5f out: swtchd rt and effrt over 1f out: edgd lft u.p and r.o wl to ld towards fin* **5/1**[3]

-524 2 1/2 **Sweet And Dandy (IRE)**[14] 1712 4-8-11 **70** EoinWalsh 4 75
(Luke McJannet) *wl in tch in midfield: effrt to ld u.p over 1f out: hdd 1f out: kpt on u.p to ld again wl ins fnl f: hdd and no ex towards fin* **16/1**

05-2 3 1/2 **Quick Breath**[14] 1714 4-9-3 **76** RichardKingscote 1 80
(Jonathan Portman) *trckd ldrs: swtchd lft and effrt to chal over 1f out: led and hung rt 1f out: hdd and no ex wl ins fnl f* **5/4**[1]

3210 **4** 1/2 **Blame Culture (USA)**[50] 1036 4-9-7 **80** DavidProbert 6 82
(George Margarson) *hld up in tch in rr: hdwy over 1f out: chsd ldrs whn nt clr run: hmpd and swtchd lft ins fnl f: kpt on towards fin* **9/2**[2]

040- **5** 3/4 **Regimented (IRE)**[251] 6240 4-9-5 **78** RossaRyan 5 78
(Richard Hannon) *hld up in tch: effrt over 2f out: clsd: nt clr run and swtchd rt over 1f out: chsng ldrs whn squeezed for room ins fnl f: nvr enough room and kpt on same pce wl ins fnl f (jockey said colt was denied a clear run)* **7/1**

6066 **6** nk **Pearl Spectre (USA)**[7] 1880 8-8-7 **66** oh1 (v) NicolaCurrie 3 65
(Phil McEntee) *wnt lft leaving stalls: led: sn hdd: restrained and swtchd rt 6f out: swtchd rt and effrt over 1f out: kpt on u.p: no imp towards fin* **10/1**

1411 **7** 11 **Crosse Fire**[21] 1552 7-9-2 **75** (p) KieranO'Neill 8 45
(Scott Dixon) *t.k.h: mde most tl rdn and hdd over 1f out: sn btn: wknd and bhd fnl f* **25/1**

200/ **8** 5 **Mulzim**[569] 7709 5-9-0 **73** TomMarquand 2 29
(Mike Murphy) *sltly impeded leaving stalls: t.k.h: hdwy to join ldr after 6f out: rdn and ev ch over 1f out: sn btn and wl bhd ins fnl f (jockey said gelding ran too free)* **20/1**

1m 25.26s (-1.94) **Going Correction** -0.125s/f (Stan) **8** Ran SP% **115.4**
Speed ratings (Par 105): **106,105,104,104,103 103,90,84**
CSF £78.94 CT £158.69 TOTE £6.00: £1.70, £4.00, £1.10; EX 103.00 Trifecta £256.50.
Owner New Vision Bloodstock **Bred** Newsells Park Stud **Trained** Sproxton, Leics

FOCUS
There was competition for the lead and this set up for the closers.

2066 BUY TICKETS AT CHELMSFORDCITYRACECOURSE.COM CLASSIFIED STKS 6f (P)
9:00 (9:00) (Class 6) 3-Y-O+

£3,105 (£924; £461; £300; £300; £300) **Stalls** Centre

Form RPR

60 **1** **Tellovoi (IRE)**[4] 1967 11-9-7 45 (p) PhilipPrince 9 51
(Richard Guest) *t.k.h: hld up in midfield: effrt but stl plenty to do over 1f out: hdwy u.p and edgd lft 1f out: str run fnl 100yds: led last stride* **12/1**

4620 **2** hd **Kyllukey**[3] 1987 6-9-7 48 RichardKingscote 1 50
(Charlie Wallis) *chsd ldrs: effrt ent fnl 2f: kpt on to chse wnr ins fnl f: styd on u.p to ld cl home: hdd last strides* **4/1**[2]

-042 **3** 1/2 **Rock In Society (IRE)**[13] 1732 4-9-4 47 (v) TimClark(3) 7 49
(John Butler) *led: rdn over 1f out: drvn and kpt on ins fnl f: hdd and lost 2 pls cl home* **9/1**

-652 **4** hd **Slipalongtrevaskis**[24] 1477 6-9-7 46 (b) JoeyHaynes 2 48
(Paul Howling) *hld up in midfield: swtchd rt and effrt over 1f out: clsd u.p to chse ldrs ins fnl f: styd on: nvr quite getting to ldrs* **6/1**[3]

6251 **5** hd **Admiral Rooke (IRE)**[7] 1883 4-9-7 48 (b) TheodoreLadd(5) 11 53
(Michael Appleby) *t.k.h: sn chsng ldr: rdn over 1f out: unable qck and kpt on same pce u.p and lost 3 pls ins fnl f (jockey said gelding ran too free)* **11/4**[1]

4053 **6** 2 1/2 **Kellington Kitty (USA)**[24] 1477 4-9-7 46 RossaRyan 8 40
(Mike Murphy) *chsd ldr briefly: styd prom: rdn ent fnl 2f: unable qck u.p 1f out: kpt on same pce ins fnl f* **9/1**

563 **7** 2 1/4 **Le Manege Enchante (IRE)**[28] 1383 6-9-7 47 (v) PaddyMathers 6 33
(Derek Shaw) *midfield: swtchd rt and effrt over 1f out: unable qck and btn fnl f* **12/1**

606- **8** 1 1/4 **Navarra Princess (IRE)**[131] 9560 4-9-7 49 (t) HollieDoyle 3 30
(Don Cantillon) *wnt rt leaving stalls: sn in rr: swtchd rt and rdn wl over 2f out: nvr getting on terms and btn whn hung lft 1f out* **7/1**

5220 **9** hd **Sybil Grand**[45] 1141 3-8-10 49 NicolaCurrie 4 26
(Katy Price) *midfield tl dropped towards rr wl over 3f out: no imp whn carried lft 1f out (jockey said filly suffered interference on the bend)* **20/1**

060- **10** 4 1/2 **Power Seeker (IRE)**[299] 4403 3-8-10 50 RobHornby 14 13
(Rod Millman) *a outpcd in rr* **16/1**

00-0 **11** 12 **All Or Nothin (IRE)**[106] 139 10-9-7 38 (p) CallumShepherd 5
(Paddy Butler) *a towards rr: no hdwy over 1f out: bhd and eased fnl f (jockey said gelding lost it's aciton)* **66/1**

1m 12.45s (-1.25) **Going Correction** -0.125s/f (Stan)
WFA 3 from 4yo+ 11lb **11** Ran SP% **121.0**
Speed ratings (Par 101): **103,102,102,101,101 98,95,93,93,87 71**
CSF £61.32 TOTE £13.50: £3.50, £1.70, £2.90; EX 51.00 Trifecta £755.20.
Owner R C Guest **Bred** Whisperview Trading Ltd **Trained** Ingmanthorpe, W Yorks
■ Stewards' Enquiry : Tim Clark two-day ban; misuse of whip (May 9-10)

FOCUS
A low-grade affair, but it was a competitive one, and there was little in it between the first five at the line.
T/Plt: £27.50 to a £1 stake. Pool: £69,312.34 - 1,837.42 winning units T/Qpdt: £8.60 to a £1 stake. Pool: £9,758.55 - 832.96 winning units **Steve Payne**

2067 - 2074a (Foreign Racing) - See Raceform Interactive

1457
DONCASTER (L-H)
Friday, April 26

OFFICIAL GOING: Good (watered; 8.2)
Wind: strong against Weather: Cloudy

2075 SKY SPORTS RACING SKY 415 H'CAP 1m 2f 43y
1:40 (1:41) (Class 4) (0-85,85) 3-Y-O

£5,530 (£1,645; £822; £411; £300; £300) **Stalls** High

Form RPR

2-12 **1** **Forest Of Dean**[18] 1645 3-9-7 **85** RobertHavlin 8 99
(John Gosden) *sn trckd ldr: hdwy to ld wl over 2f out: rdn clr 1 1/2f out: styd on strly* **7/4**[1]

55-3 **2** 3 1/4 **Ritchie Valens (IRE)**[34] 1293 3-8-12 **76** SeanLevey 2 83
(Richard Hannon) *sltly hmpd s and t.k.h early: trckd ldng pair on inner: effrt and n.m.r 2f out: sn swtchd rt and rdn to chse wnr: drvn ins fnl f: no imp towards fin* **11/1**

02-1 **3** 4 1/2 **Days Of Glory (CAN)**[18] 1652 3-9-6 **84** RossaRyan 7 82
(Richard Hannon) *hld up in tch: hdwy on outer 3f out: pushed along over 2f out: rdn wl over 1f out: kpt on same pce* **7/2**[2]

312- **4** shd **Felix**[196] 8166 3-9-7 **85** (t) JamieSpencer 1 82
(Sir Michael Stoute) *hld up towards rr: hdwy on outer 3f out: rdn along 2f out: sn chsng ldrs: kpt on same pce fnl f* **4/1**[3]

616- **5** 3/4 **Billy No Mates (IRE)**[216] 7508 3-9-6 **84** PaulMulrennan 10 80
(Michael Dods) *hld up in rr: hdwy on inner 3f out: rdn along 2f out: styd on wl fnl f: nrst fin* **20/1**

55-3 **6** 1 1/2 **Cormier (IRE)**[65] 804 3-8-7 **71** AndrewMullen 3 64
(Stef Keniry) *hmpd s and t.k.h after: chsd ldrs: rdn along wl over 2f out: grad wknd* **20/1**

-262 **7** 4 1/2 **Whenapoet**[25] 1480 3-8-4 **68** (p) LiamJones 4 52
(Michael Appleby) *wnt bdly rt s: sn led: pushed along over 3f out: rdn and hdd wl over 2f out: sn drvn and wknd* **33/1**

041- **8** 2 1/2 **War Eagle (IRE)**[176] 8782 3-8-13 **77** JasonHart 9 56
(Ian Williams) *hld up: a in rr* **25/1**

25-6 **9** nse **Venedegar (IRE)**[26] 1462 3-9-3 **81** (b[1]) BenCurtis 6 60
(Ed Dunlop) *t.k.h early: in tch: rdn along over 3f out: wknd over 2f out* **12/1**

613- **10** 1 3/4 **Spencers Son (IRE)**[175] 8796 3-8-12 **76** DanielMuscutt 5 51
(Richard Spencer) *hld up in tch: effrt and sme hdwy 3f out: rdn along over 2f out: sn wknd* **16/1**

2m 12.07s (-0.23) **Going Correction** +0.30s/f (Good) **10** Ran SP% **116.8**
Speed ratings (Par 100): **110,107,103,103,103 101,98,96,96,94**
CSF £21.54 CT £63.12 TOTE £2.20: £1.10, £2.80, £1.60; EX 18.30 Trifecta £125.80.
Owner HRH Princess Haya Of Jordan **Bred** Car Colston Hall Stud **Trained** Newmarket, Suffolk

FOCUS
Add 6yds. There was 9mm of rain on Wednesday and 3mm on Thursday, leaving the ground good all round (GoingStick 8.2). They didn't go that quick early and the winner settled matters with a turn of foot. Sound form.

2076 SKY SPORTS RACING VIRGIN 535 H'CAP 7f 6y
2:15 (2:15) (Class 5) (0-70,70) 4-Y-O+

£3,752 (£1,116; £557; £300; £300; £300) **Stalls** High

Form RPR

1150 **1** **Hammer Gun (USA)**[3] 2015 6-8-13 **62** (v) PaddyMathers 17 70
(Derek Shaw) *t.k.h: hld up and bhd: stdy hdwy over 2f out: chsd ldrs jst over 1f out: rdn and styd on strly fnl f to ld nr line* **8/1**

360- **2** hd **Tukhoom (IRE)**[128] 9614 6-9-5 **68** TomEaves 1 75
(Michael Herrington) *dwlt and hld up in rr: gd hdwy over 2f out: rdn and styd on wl to chal ins fnl f: sn drvn and ev ch: kpt on (starter reported the gelding was the subject of a third criteria failure; trainer was informed that the gelding could not run until the day after passing a stalls test)* **8/1**

0-40 **3** hd **Abushamah (IRE)**[13] 1769 8-8-8 **57** JamesSullivan 13 63
(Ruth Carr) *hld up in rr: swtchd lft to inner and hdwy 3f out: effrt 2f out: chal over 1f out: sn rdn: led ins fnl f: sn drvn and edgd rt: hdd nr line* **10/1**

26-0 **4** 1 1/4 **Somewhere Secret**[108] 125 5-8-4 **60** (p) LauraCoughlan(7) 14 63
(Michael Mullineaux) *prom: cl up over 2f out: rdn to ld over 1f out: drvn and hdd ins fnl f: n.m.r and kpt on* **12/1**

-005 **5** 2 1/4 **Fighting Temeraire (IRE)**[16] 1695 6-8-12 **61** MartinDwyer 6 58
(Dean Ivory) *dwlt: sn led: pushed along 2f out: rdn and hdd over 1f out: cl up and drvn ent fnl f: n.m.r and grad wknd* **4/1**[1]

03-4 **6** hd **Atalanta's Boy**[18] 1649 4-8-11 **67** (h) Pierre-LouisJamin(7) 11 63
(David Menuisier) *trckd ldrs: hdwy over 2f out: rdn and ev ch whn edgd lft ent fnl f: hld whn hmpd last 150yds* **11/2**[2]

005- **7** 1 **Rebel State (IRE)**[142] 9410 6-8-3 **59** (p) OwenPayton(7) 8 53
(Jedd O'Keeffe) *in rr: hdwy 2f out: swtchd rt and rdn over 1f out: kpt on fnl f* **16/1**

011- **8** nse **Redarna**[197] 8133 5-9-6 **69** GrahamLee 10 63
(Dianne Sayer) *in tch: hdwy to chse ldrs 3f out: rdn along wl over 1f out: wkng and hld whn n.m.r jst ins fnl f* **12/1**

0/0- **9** 1 1/2 **The Stalking Moon (IRE)**[214] 7627 5-9-5 **68** AndrewMullen 7 58
(Adrian Nicholls) *midfield: hdwy at 1/2-way: rdn along to chse ldrs 2f out: n.m.r appr fnl f: one pce after* **40/1**

000- **10** 1 1/4 **Dasheen**[210] 7727 6-9-4 **67** (p) ShaneGray 15 53
(Karen Tutty) *a towards rr* **28/1**

0-00 **11** 2 3/4 **Royal Connoisseur (IRE)**[13] 1766 8-8-9 **63** SebastianWoods(5) 16 42
(Richard Fahey) *a towards rr* **25/1**

0-00 **12** 3 **Brigand**[18] 1653 4-8-7 **56** KieranO'Neill 12 27
(John Butler) *prom: rdn along wl over 2f out: sn wknd* **80/1**

00-0 **13** 1 3/4 **Art Echo**[21] 1563 6-9-2 **65** (tp) BenCurtis 9 31
(John Mackie) *prom: rdn along wl over 2f out: wknd wl over 1f out* **10/1**

0-00 **14** 2 **Valley Of Fire**[26] 1457 7-9-7 **70** (p) DavidAllan 4 31
(Les Eyre) *trckd ldrs on inner: rdn along 3f out: wknd 2f out* **13/2**[3]

1m 28.01s (1.61) **Going Correction** +0.30s/f (Good) **14** Ran SP% **121.4**
Speed ratings (Par 103): **102,101,101,100,97 97,96,96,94,92 89,86,84,82**
CSF £69.31 CT £675.69 TOTE £9.00: £3.30, £2.40, £3.00; EX 94.30 Trifecta £1528.00.
Owner A Flint **Bred** Her Majesty The Queen **Trained** Sproxton, Leics

FOCUS
The leaders got racing soon enough here and the race set up for the closers to pounce late. The first three raced in the last three positions early on. The second has been rated similar to last year's C&D reappearance.

2077 SKY SPORTS RACING SKY 415 FILLIES' NOVICE STKS 6f 2y
2:50 (2:50) (Class 5) 3-Y-O+ **£3,752** (£1,116; £557; £278) **Stalls** High

Form RPR

1 **Archer's Dream (IRE)** 3-8-10 0 GeorgeWood 3 90
(James Fanshawe) *trckd ldrs: hdwy and cl up 2f out: rdn to ld appr fnl f: kpt on strly towards fin* **16/1**

2 1 1/4 **Tapisserie** 3-8-10 0 PaulHanagan 10 86
(William Haggas) *green and towards rr: hdwy 2f out: rdn over 1f out: styd on wl fnl f: tk 2nd on line* **12/1**

13- **3** shd **Shades Of Blue (IRE)**[310] 3995 3-9-3 0 AdamKirby 9 93
(Clive Cox) *chsd ldrs: pushed along 2f out: rdn to chse wnr ent fnl f: sn drvn and kpt on same pce: lost 2nd nr line* **1/2**[1]

4 **4** 2 3/4 **Hareem Queen (IRE)**[35] 1272 3-8-10 0 PJMcDonald 8 77
(K R Burke) *trckd ldng pair: hdwy 2f out: rdn over 1f out: n.m.r and swtchd lft ins fnl f: kpt on* **11/2**[3]

3- **5** 2 3/4 **Mrs Discombe**[267] 5655 3-8-10 0 FrannyNorton 7 68
(Mick Quinn) *prom: rdn along over 2f out: grad wknd* **10/1**

022- **6** 2 1/4 **Time For Bed (IRE)**[202] 7983 3-8-10 76 SeanLevey 2 61
(Richard Hannon) *led: rdn along 2f out: drvn and hdd appr fnl f: sn wknd (jockey said filly hung right in the final stages)* **4/1**[2]

6 **7** 11 **Wadah**[25] 1475 4-9-0 0 GinaMangan(7) 5 29
(J R Jenkins) *towards rr: rdn along 1/2-way: sn outpcd* **150/1**

00- **8** 3/4 **Swiss Miss**[354] 2485 3-8-10 0 RoystonFfrench 6 23
(John Gallagher) *a in rr (jockey said filly jumped awkwardly from the stalls)* **100/1**

0 **9** 7 **Forever Mine**[14] 1740 3-8-10 0 MartinDwyer 4
(Eve Johnson Houghton) *a in rr* **50/1**

1m 13.94s (1.24) **Going Correction** +0.30s/f (Good)
WFA 3 from 4yo 11lb **9** Ran SP% **128.3**
Speed ratings (Par 100): **103,101,101,97,93 90,76,75,65**
CSF £206.30 TOTE £26.80: £4.70, £3.30, £1.02; EX 275.80 Trifecta £600.90.
Owner Fred Archer Racing - Wheel Of Fortune **Bred** Ms Anne Coughlan **Trained** Newmarket, Suffolk

FOCUS
This looked a good novice. The first two look particularly promising. It's been rated around the second to the race standard.

2078 NAPOLEONS CASINO & RESTAURANT SHEFFIELD H'CAP — 6f 2y
3:25 (3:26) (Class 3) (0-90,90) 3-Y-O — **£7,762** (£2,310; £1,154; £577) Stalls High

Form — RPR
42-2 1 **Moraawed**[14] 1728 3-8-11 **80** ... DaneO'Neill 11 — 92+
(Roger Varian) *hld up in rr: gd hdwy on wd outside wl over 1f out: str run ent fnl f: edgd lft and styd on wl last 100yds to ld nr line* **11/4**[1]
221- 2 *hd* **Dazzling Dan (IRE)**[167] 9000 3-9-6 **89** ... AdamKirby 6 — 100
(Pam Sly) *led: rdn and qcknd clr wl over 1f out: drvn and edgd lft last 100yds: hdd nr line* **6/1**[3]
315- 3 2 3/4 **Hafeet Alain (IRE)**[264] 5769 3-8-11 **80** ... AndrewMullen 1 — 82
(Adrian Nicholls) *dwlt: sn in tch on inner: pushed along and hdwy over 2f out: rdn to chse wnr jst ins fnl f: sn drvn and kpt on same pce* **16/1**
40-0 4 3/4 **Kinks**[17] 1662 3-9-7 **90** ... FrannyNorton 5 — 90
(Mick Channon) *chsd ldrs: rdn along wl over 1f out: drvn ent fnl f: grad wknd* **16/1**
-362 5 1/2 **Amplify (IRE)**[17] 1665 3-9-0 **83** ... CallumShepherd 9 — 81
(Brian Meehan) *chsd ldrs: rdn along wl over 1f out: grad wknd* **22/1**
13-4 6 1 **Topical**[14] 1736 3-8-12 **81** ... PatDobbs 12 — 76
(Richard Hannon) *midfield: pushed along over 2f out: sn rdn and n.d* **4/1**[2]
440- 7 2 1/2 **Jean Valjean**[135] 9498 3-8-7 **76** oh4 ... (h) NicolaCurrie 13 — 63
(Richard Spencer) *dwlt and bhd tl sme late hdwy (jockey said gelding was outpaced early)* **28/1**
214- 8 *shd* **Fastman (IRE)**[195] 8193 3-9-5 **88** ... DavidNolan 4 — 75
(David O'Meara) *midfield: rdn along 1/2-way: wknd fnl 2f* **10/1**
1143 9 3/4 **Dahawi**[17] 1662 3-8-10 **79** ... (t) BenCurtis 14 — 63
(Hugo Palmer) *in tch: rdn along over 2f out: sn wknd* **11/1**
10-2 10 2 **Princess Power (IRE)**[13] 1762 3-8-11 **83** ... RowanScott(3) 8 — 61
(Nigel Tinkler) *chsd ldrs: rdn along over 2f out: sn wknd* **14/1**
134- 11 1/2 **Excelled (IRE)**[192] 8306 3-8-13 **82** ... (h) DanielMuscutt 10 — 58
(James Fanshawe) *chsd ldrs: rdn along wl over 2f out: sn drvn and wknd* **20/1**
12-4 12 2 1/4 **Ginger Fox**[27] 1424 3-8-7 **76** ... JasonHart 2 — 45
(Ian Williams) *dwlt and in rr: sme hdwy over 3f out: rdn along wl over 2f out and sn outpcd* **14/1**
256- 13 1 1/4 **Constant**[181] 8630 3-9-1 **84** ... CamHardie 7 — 49
(David O'Meara) *chsd ldr: rdn along over 2f out: sn wknd* **25/1**

1m 13.4s (0.70) **Going Correction** +0.30s/f (Good) — **13 Ran SP% 119.9**
Speed ratings (Par 102): **107,106,103,102,101 100,96,96,95,92 92,89,87**
CSF £17.73 CT £234.63 TOTE £3.10: £1.50, £2.00, £6.00; EX 18.70 Trifecta £282.20.
Owner Hamdan Al Maktoum **Bred** Whitsbury Manor Stud **Trained** Newmarket, Suffolk

FOCUS
A fine performance from the winner to catch the runner-up, who looked to have done enough when quickening clear of the bunch. The second has been rated as progressing in line with his good maiden win.

2079 WATCH SKY SPORTS RACING SKY 415 H'CAP — 5f 3y
3:55 (3:57) (Class 4) (0-85,85) 4-Y-O+ — **£5,530** (£1,645; £822; £411; £300; £300) Stalls High

Form — RPR
420- 1 **Boundary Lane**[273] 5440 4-8-10 **74** ... GrahamLee 11 — 83
(Julie Camacho) *chsd ldrs: hdwy over 2f out: rdn to ld ent fnl f: sn jnd and drvn: kpt on wl towards fin* **14/1**
540- 2 *shd* **Zamjar**[199] 8094 5-8-11 **80** ... SeanDavis(5) 6 — 88
(Robert Cowell) *hld up towards rr: hdwy 2f out: rdn to chse ldrs over 1f out: chal ins fnl f: sn drvn and ev ch tl no ex towards fin* **16/1**
500- 3 1 3/4 **Signore Piccolo**[182] 8612 8-8-12 **76** ... (p) TrevorWhelan 8 — 78
(David Loughnane) *hld up towards rr: hdwy 2f out: chsd ldrs over 1f out: swtchd lft and rdn ins fnl f: ev ch tl drvn and one pce towards fin* **10/1**
1056 4 1 **Tathmeen (IRE)**[7] 1929 4-8-11 **75** ... CamHardie 4 — 73
(Antony Brittain) *towards rr: hdwy 2f out: sn swtchd lft and rdn wl over 1f out: kpt on wl fnl f* **9/1**[3]
0331 5 *shd* **Canford Bay (IRE)**[8] 1899 5-8-0 **71** ... KieranSchofield(7) 10 — 69+
(Antony Brittain) *chsd ldr: hdwy to ld wl over 1f out: sn clr: rdn and hdd ent fnl f: sn one pce* **9/4**[1]
13-0 6 1 1/4 **Manshood (IRE)**[25] 1487 6-8-11 **75** ... (b) PatDobbs 3 — 68
(Paul Midgley) *towards rr: hdwy on inner and rdn along 2f out: kpt on fnl f* **10/1**
16-0 7 2 1/2 **Desert Ace (IRE)**[43] 1194 8-8-13 **77** ... KevinStott 5 — 61
(Paul Midgley) *dwlt: a towards rr* **25/1**
002- 8 *hd* **Requinto Dawn (IRE)**[178] 8719 4-8-8 **79** ... RussellHarris(7) 7 — 63
(Richard Fahey) *in tch: hdwy to chse ldrs 2f out: sn rdn: n.m.r and wknd appr fnl f* **9/1**[3]
20-0 9 1 1/2 **Bashiba (IRE)**[7] 1929 8-8-10 **77** ... RowanScott(3) 1 — 55
(Nigel Tinkler) *a in rr* **16/1**
410- 10 *hd* **Hawaam (IRE)**[170] 8934 4-9-2 **80** ... BenCurtis 2 — 57
(Roger Fell) *chsd ldng pair: rdn along wl over 2f out: sn drvn and wknd* **4/1**[2]
610- 11 2 1/4 **Angel Force (IRE)**[202] 7994 4-8-10 **74** ... (b) DavidAllan 9 — 43
(David C Griffiths) *qckly away: led and sn clr: rdn along 2f out: sn hdd & wknd* **20/1**
455- 12 1/2 **Robot Boy (IRE)**[280] 5192 9-9-7 **85** ... (w) PJMcDonald 14 — 53
(Marjorie Fife) *chsd ldrs: rdn along over 2f out: sn wknd* **33/1**

1m 0.69s (1.09) **Going Correction** +0.30s/f (Good) — **12 Ran SP% 118.9**
Speed ratings (Par 105): **103,102,100,98,98 96,92,91,89,89 85,84**
CSF £214.24 CT £2368.88 TOTE £15.90: £4.00, £4.80, £2.70; EX 205.00 Trifecta £2537.40.
Owner David W Armstrong **Bred** Highfield Farm Llp **Trained** Norton, N Yorks

FOCUS
They went a good early gallop and the majority of those involved in the finish had been held up off the pace. The third has been rated similar to his reappearance figures the last two years.

2080 WATCH SKY SPORTS RACING VIRGIN 535 H'CAP — 2m 109y
4:25 (4:26) (Class 4) (0-85,85) 4-Y-O+ — **£5,530** (£1,645; £822; £411; £300; £300) Stalls Low

Form — RPR
045- 1 **Handiwork**[177] 8743 9-9-6 **82** ... (p) PJMcDonald 13 — 90
(Steve Gollings) *hld up towards rr: swtchd rt to outer and hdwy 3f out: chsd ldrs over 1f out: sn rdn: styd on wl to ld last 100yds* **10/1**
612- 2 3/4 **Carnwennan (IRE)**[177] 8735 4-9-0 **78** ... StevieDonohoe 1 — 85
(Charlie Fellowes) *trckd ldrs on inner: hdwy over 3f out: led 2f out: rdn over 1f out: drvn and hdd last 100yds: kpt on same pce* **9/2**[2]
365- 3 *shd* **October Storm**[344] 2800 6-9-0 **76** ... GrahamLee 9 — 82
(Mick Channon) *hld up towards rr: hdwy on outer over 3f out: chsd ldrs 2f out: rdn over 1f out and ev ch: drvn ent fnl f: kpt on same pce last 100yds* **10/1**
11-3 4 3 1/2 **Bailarico (IRE)**[17] 1663 6-8-6 **73** ... (p) ThomasGreatrex(5) 5 — 75
(Warren Greatrex) *hld up in rr: hdwy on outer 3f out: rdn along 2f out: drvn over 1f out and kpt on same pce* **5/1**[3]
335- 5 3/4 **Groveman**[26] 9204 4-9-1 **79** ... JamieSpencer 2 — 80
(Jedd O'Keeffe) *trckd ldrs: hdwy over 3f out: rdn along over 2f out: drvn wl over 1f out: sn one pce* **11/4**[1]
4144 6 *nk* **Moon Of Baroda**[52] 1022 4-8-12 **76** ... (b) DaneO'Neill 4 — 77
(Charles Hills) *in tch: hdwy 4f out: pushed along 3f out: rdn over 2f out: sn no imp* **17/2**
0032 7 1 1/2 **Addicted To You (IRE)**[23] 1524 5-9-9 **85** ... (v) FrannyNorton 10 — 84
(Mark Johnston) *awkward s: sn trcking ldrs: pushed along over 4f out: rdn 3f out: sn drvn and wknd* **8/1**
12-0 8 3/4 **Royal Flag**[27] 1429 9-7-11 **66** ... KieranSchofield(7) 12 — 65
(Brian Ellison) *hld up: a in rr* **33/1**
305- 9 2 **Stone The Crows**[182] 8595 5-9-8 **84** ... (p) TomEaves 8 — 80
(Iain Jardine) *led: rdn along 3f out: hdd 2f out and sn wknd* **16/1**
450- 10 2 1/2 **Iolani (GER)**[89] 7074 7-8-7 **69** ... JamesSullivan 11 — 63
(Dianne Sayer) *a in rr* **50/1**
000- 11 12 **Stormin Tom (IRE)**[188] 8414 7-9-3 **79** ... RachelRichardson 3 — 59
(Tim Easterby) *trckd ldr: hdwy 3f out: rdn along over 2f out: sn wknd* **33/1**
20-6 12 4 1/2 **Dagueneau (IRE)**[21] 1559 4-9-1 **79** ... (b) BenCurtis 7 — 54
(Ed Dunlop) *trckd ldrs: pushed along 4f out: rdn 3f out: sn wknd (vet reported the gelding lost its right hind shoe)* **16/1**

3m 44.39s (3.99) **Going Correction** +0.30s/f (Good) — **12 Ran SP% 120.9**
WFA 4 from 5yo+ 2lb
Speed ratings (Par 105): **102,101,101,99,99 99,98,98,97,95 89,87**
CSF £55.11 CT £475.73 TOTE £14.50: £3.30, £2.50, £3.00; EX 85.40 Trifecta £702.70.
Owner C Johnstone **Bred** The Queen **Trained** Scamblesby, Lincs

FOCUS
Add 6yds. A competitive staying handicap, but the result was the same as the previous two editions. A small pb from the second, with the third rated in line with his handicap best.

2081 SKY SPORTS RACING SKY 415 FILLIES' H'CAP — 6f 2y
5:00 (5:03) (Class 5) (0-70,72) 4-Y-O+ — **£3,752** (£1,116; £557; £300; £300; £300) Stalls High

Form — RPR
56 1 **Dream World (IRE)**[16] 1688 4-8-8 **60** ... SeanDavis(5) 4 — 68
(Michael Appleby) *hld up: hdwy 1/2-way: sn trcking ldrs: effrt on outer 2f out: rdn to ld appr fnl f and sn hung rt: drvn and kpt on wl fnl f* **7/1**
2500 2 3/4 **Peggy's Angel**[13] 1760 4-9-1 **67** ... (h) FayeMcManoman(5) 7 — 72
(Marjorie Fife) *trckd ldrs: hdwy over 2f out: rdn over 1f out: styd on and ch ins fnl f: kpt on same pce towards fin* **33/1**
140- 3 1/2 **Lethal Angel**[127] 9640 4-9-6 **67** ... AdamKirby 9 — 70
(Stuart Williams) *hld up: hdwy on outer over 2f out: rdn and edgd lft over 1f out: drvn and ch ins fnl f: kpt on same pce towards fin* **13/2**[3]
560- 4 1/2 **Praxedis**[175] 8797 4-8-9 **56** ... GeorgeWood 11 — 59
(James Fanshawe) *hld up in rr: hdwy on outer 2f out: effrt whn hmpd and stmbld over 1f out: sn swtchd rt and rdn: kpt on fnl f (jockey said filly was denied a clear run approximately 2 furlongs out)* **9/2**[2]
00-0 5 *shd* **Penny Pot Lane**[8] 1895 6-6-9 **67** ... LewisEdmunds 3 — 68
(Richard Whitaker) *hld up: hdwy wl over 1f out: rdn and kpt on fnl f* **10/1**
50-0 6 3/4 **Tundra**[65] 801 5-9-7 **68** ... KieranO'Neill 6 — 67
(Anthony Carson) *prom: cl up 2f out: rdn and ev ch over 1f out: drvn and n.m.r appr fnl f: one pce after* **12/1**
-056 7 1 **Alba Del Sole (IRE)**[30] 1368 4-8-10 **57** ... (p) JasonHart 1 — 52+
(Ivan Furtado) *chsd ldrs: pushed along 2f out: rdn over 1f out: sn drvn and kpt on same pce* **7/2**[1]
000- 8 3/4 **Supaulette (IRE)**[168] 8980 4-9-1 **62** ... (bt) DavidAllan 8 — 55
(Tim Easterby) *a towards rr (jockey said filly was denied a clear run)* **16/1**
630- 9 3/4 **Red Allure**[167] 9003 4-7-11 **51** oh3 ow2 ... LauraCoughlan(7) 5 — 42
(Michael Mullineaux) *cl up: slt ld after 2f: rdn along 2f out: drvn and hdd appr fnl f: hld whn hmpd sn after and wknd* **16/1**
6115 10 1 3/4 **Mystical Moon (IRE)**[10] 1837 4-8-7 **54** ... PhilDennis 10 — 39
(David C Griffiths) *chsd ldrs: rdn along 2f out: wknd over 1f out* **12/1**
01-1 11 1 1/2 **Turanga Leela**[87] 468 5-9-11 **72** ... (b) StevieDonohoe 2 — 52
(John Mackie) *lef 2f: cl up on inner: rdn along to dispute ld over 1f out: drvn and cl up whn hmpd ent fnl f: wknd qckly after* **7/1**

1m 15.0s (2.30) **Going Correction** +0.30s/f (Good) — **11 Ran SP% 117.9**
Speed ratings (Par 100): **96,95,94,93,93 92,91,90,89,86 84**
CSF £210.21 CT £1595.20 TOTE £7.60: £2.60, £9.00, £2.00; EX 257.30 Trifecta £2296.70.
Owner Rod In Pickle Partnership **Bred** Miss L Cronin & Mrs U Lawler **Trained** Oakham, Rutland

FOCUS
A messy race. The pack was squeezed from both sides in the final 2f, causing several to be hampered. The second has been rated close to her one effort of note over the winter.
T/Plt: £216.20 to a £1 stake. Pool: £79,581.67 - 268.60 winning units T/Qpdt: £34.10 to a £1 stake. Pool: £7,636.14 - 165.67 winning units **Joe Rowntree**

SANDOWN (R-H)
Friday, April 26

OFFICIAL GOING: Good to firm (good in places; rnd, 7.9, spr 7.3)
Wind: Moderate, half against Weather: Fine, becoming overcast

2082 BET365 ESHER CUP H'CAP — 1m
1:50 (1:52) (Class 2) (0-100,91) 3-Y-O — **£15,562** (£4,660; £2,330; £1,165; £582; £292) Stalls Low

Form — RPR
10-1 1 **Masaru**[16] 1676 3-9-7 **91** ... RyanMoore 5 — 100
(Richard Hannon) *t.k.h: trckd ldng trio: rdn and clsd to ld over 1f out: in command fnl f but ld dwindled sharply last strides* **9/1**
05-2 2 1/2 **Migration (IRE)**[13] 1754 3-8-12 **82** ... AndreaAtzeni 11 — 90+
(David Menuisier) *slowly away: wl off the pce in last: stl only 8th and rdn over 1f out: gd prog fnl f: r.o to take 2nd nr fin: jst too late* **6/1**[3]
00-3 3 1 **Loch Ness Monster (IRE)**[25] 1485 3-9-1 **85** ... AlistairRawlinson 10 — 91
(Michael Appleby) *sltly awkward s: off the pce in last pair: rdn and prog on outer over 2f out: edgd rt over 1f out: styd on to take 2nd briefly last 75yds: nvr able to chal* **16/1**
32-1 4 1 1/2 **Fox Leicester (IRE)**[29] 1379 3-8-11 **81** ... SilvestreDeSousa 9 — 83
(Andrew Balding) *racd wd early: led after 1f and maintained str pce: hdd over 1f out: wknd ins fnl f* **5/2**[1]

21-2 **5** ½ **Reeves**[14] 1736 3-9-1 **85** .... RaulDaSilva 1 86
(Robert Cowell) *hld up in rr: prog on inner over 2f out: rdn and cl up jst over 1f out: no ex* **13/2**

4212 **6** 2¾ **Reggae Runner (FR)**[6] 1945 3-8-12 **82** .... JoeFanning 7 77
(Mark Johnston) *led at str pce but hdd after 1f: pressed ldr: upsides over 2f out to over 1f out: wknd* **9/2**[2]

332- **7** ¾ **Starfighter**[240] 6688 3-8-4 **74** .... DavidEgan 6 67
(Ed Walker) *t.k.h: wl in tch: rdn to chse ldrs over 2f out: wknd over 1f out* **14/1**

150- **8** 3¾ **Red Bravo (IRE)**[225] 7201 3-8-13 **83** .... WilliamBuick 4 67
(Charles Hills) *hld up in midfield: rdn to chse ldrs 2f out: no prog over 1f out: sn wknd* **16/1**

22-5 **9** 27 **Ours Puissant (IRE)**[62] 893 3-9-6 **90** .... (p[1]) JamesDoyle 2 12
(Hugo Palmer) *pressed ldrs to 3f out: wknd rapidly: eased over 1f out: t.o (jockey said colt lost its action 2 ½ furlongs out)* **12/1**

412 **10** 10 **Lestrade**[20] 1587 3-8-10 **80** .... (h) JasonWatson 8
(William Jarvis) *v free to post: t.k.h: hld up: wknd rapidly 2f out: t.o (jockey said colt boiled over in the preliminaries and ran freely to post)* **14/1**

1m 43.94s (0.64) **Going Correction** +0.15s/f (Good) **10** Ran SP% **117.2**
Speed ratings (Par 104): **102,101,100,99,98 95,95,91,64,54**
CSF £62.45 CT £879.23 TOTE £8.80: £2.80, £1.90, £5.20; EX 64.80 Trifecta £1229.30.
Owner Michael Daniels & Jonathan Palmer-Brown **Bred** Crossfields Bloodstock Ltd **Trained** East Everleigh, Wilts

FOCUS
Distance increased by 25yds. Traditionally a good handicap, but the leaders, who included the first two in the betting, went too fast and it set up for the closers. Perhaps doubts over the form, therefore.

2083 BET365 GORDON RICHARDS STKS (GROUP 3) 1m 1f 209y
2:25 (2:25) (Class 1) 4-Y-0+
£39,697 (£15,050; £7,532; £3,752; £1,883; £945) **Stalls** Low

Form RPR

222- **1** **Crystal Ocean**[188] 8408 5-9-0 125 .... RyanMoore 5 123+
(Sir Michael Stoute) *trckd ldr after 1f: led 2f out: pushed along firmly and drew clr over 1f out: v readily* **5/6**[1]

010- **2** 2¼ **Knight To Behold (IRE)**[202] 8011 4-9-0 116 .... (p) OisinMurphy 1 117
(Harry Dunlop) *led after 100yds: rdn and hdd 2f out: no ch w wnr but styd on and clr of rest* **15/2**[3]

10-2 **3** 3½ **Extra Elusive**[27] 1420 4-9-0 106 .... (h) JasonWatson 6 110
(Roger Charlton) *taken down early: hld up in last trio: shkn up 3f out: edgd lft over 2f out: drvn and kpt on one pce to take 3rd strides* **20/1**

13-4 **4** nk **Fabricate**[27] 1420 7-9-0 107 .... (p) JamesDoyle 4 109
(Michael Bell) *broke wl: led but hdd after 100yds and restrained bhd ldrs: rdn over 2f out: chsd ldng pair after but sn lft bhd: lost 3rd last strides* **16/1**

501- **5** 1½ **Trais Fluors**[52] 1030 5-9-0 109 .... Pierre-CharlesBoudot 2 106
(A Fabre, France) *trckd ldrs: shkn up over 2f out: no prog and fdd over 1f out* **10/3**[2]

10-6 **6** ½ **Pivoine (IRE)**[22] 1545 5-9-0 104 .... (b) SilvestreDeSousa 7 105
(Andrew Balding) *hld up in last: rdn and no prog over 2f out: one pce and no ch after* **28/1**

120- **7** 5 **Thundering Blue (USA)**[152] 9270 6-9-3 118 .... AndreaAtzeni 3 98
(David Menuisier) *hld up in last trio: shkn up and no prog over 2f out: bhd over 1f out* **14/1**

2m 7.8s (-2.40) **Going Correction** +0.15s/f (Good) **7** Ran SP% **110.2**
Speed ratings (Par 113): **115,113,110,110,108 108,104**
CSF £7.19 TOTE £1.50: £1.10, £2.70; EX 8.20 Trifecta £50.10.
Owner Sir Evelyn De Rothschild **Bred** Southcourt Stud **Trained** Newmarket, Suffolk

FOCUS
Distance increased by 25yds. In theory a stronger race than a year ago, it was run at a nice gallop and saw an impressive performance from the favourite. The winner has been rated 4lb off his best, with the third to his AW latest.

2084 BET365 CLASSIC TRIAL (GROUP 3) 1m 1f 209y
3:00 (3:00) (Class 1) 3-Y-O
£39,697 (£15,050; £7,532; £3,752; £1,883; £945) **Stalls** Low

Form RPR

44-1 **1** **Bangkok (IRE)**[27] 1417 3-9-1 88 .... SilvestreDeSousa 4 108+
(Andrew Balding) *hld up in 5th: swift prog on outer to ld over 1f out and sn 2 l clr: pushed out: decisively* **10/11**[1]

3-1 **2** 1¼ **Technician (IRE)**[21] 1558 3-9-1 0 .... OisinMurphy 2 104+
(Martyn Meade) *trckd ldng pair: nt clr run 2f out and swtchd lft: stl hemmed in and no room tl fnl f: styd on wl to take 2nd nr fin* **11/2**[2]

341- **3** ½ **Persian Moon (IRE)**[208] 7799 3-9-1 102 .... JoeFanning 5 103
(Mark Johnston) *trckd ldr: shkn up to ld over 2f out: rdn and hdd over 1f out: sn outpcd: lost 2nd nr fin* **7/1**

42-1 **4** 2½ **Travel On**[35] 1268 3-9-1 85 .... FrankieDettori 7 98
(John Gosden) *trckd ldng trio: shkn up over 2f out: cl enough over 1f out: wknd fnl f* **7/1**

1- **5** ½ **Alfaatik**[127] 9635 3-9-1 0 .... (b[1]) JimCrowley 6 97
(John Gosden) *s.s: racd in last and stl green: urged along over 3f out and detached: fnlly r.o over 1f out: fin to sme effect* **6/1**[3]

50-0 **6** 7 **Kuwait Currency (USA)**[10] 1830 3-9-1 105 .... (t) TomMarquand 1 83
(Richard Hannon) *led: rdn and hdd over 2f out: wknd qckly over 1f out* **28/1**

2m 9.43s (-0.77) **Going Correction** +0.15s/f (Good) **6** Ran SP% **110.5**
Speed ratings (Par 108): **109,108,107,105,105 99**
CSF £6.09 TOTE £1.50: £1.10, £2.30; EX 5.90 Trifecta £21.50.
Owner King Power Racing Co Ltd **Bred** Barronstown Stud **Trained** Kingsclere, Hants

FOCUS
Distance increased by 25yds. It can't be said this was a strong edition of the race and the runner-up looked unlucky. The first two can be rated much the best of these. The level looks a bit fluid, with the second, fourth and fifth all rated big improvers. The third has been rated close to form.

2085 BET365 MILE (GROUP 2) 1m
3:35 (3:35) (Class 1) 4-Y-O+
£56,710 (£21,500; £10,760; £5,360; £2,690; £1,350) **Stalls** Low

Form RPR

100- **1** **Beat The Bank**[138] 9476 5-9-1 116 .... SilvestreDeSousa 8 116
(Andrew Balding) *t.k.h: trckd ldr after 2f: rdn 2f out and no immediate rspnse: rallied over 1f out: drvn ahd jst ins fnl f: kpt on wl* **7/4**[1]

01-1 **2** ½ **Sharja Bridge**[27] 1414 5-9-1 111 .... AndreaAtzeni 7 115
(Roger Varian) *trckd ldng trio: clsd to chal jst over 1f out: drvn to chse wnr ins fnl f: styd on but a readily hld* **7/4**[1]

133- **3** 1 **Regal Reality**[210] 7735 4-9-1 109 .... RyanMoore 4 113
(Sir Michael Stoute) *slowly away: hld up in 6th: pushed along and prog on outer 2f out: briefly chal 1f out: one pce last 150yds (vet reported the colt lost its right fore shoe)* **7/1**[2]

324- **4** ¾ **Suedois (FR)**[244] 6549 8-9-1 115 .... DanielTudhope 3 111
(David O'Meara) *trckd ldr 2f: styd cl up: effrt to ld over 1f out: hdd and fdd jst ins fnl f* **11/1**

012- **5** 1¾ **Mitchum Swagger**[154] 9239 7-9-1 109 .... HarryBentley 5 107
(Ralph Beckett) *hld up in 5th: shkn up and nt qckn over 2f out: one pce and no imp on ldrs after* **20/1**

2101 **6** 2¾ **Oh This Is Us (IRE)**[7] 1922 6-9-1 113 .... TomMarquand 6 101
(Richard Hannon) *hld up in last: shkn up and no rspnse over 2f out: nvr a factor* **8/1**[3]

-104 **7** 4 **Zwayyan**[7] 1912 6-9-1 100 .... (v[1]) RobHornby 2 91
(Andrew Balding) *led: rdn and hdd over 1f out: wknd qckly fnl f* **40/1**

1m 43.23s (-0.07) **Going Correction** +0.15s/f (Good) **7** Ran SP% **111.9**
Speed ratings (Par 115): **106,105,104,103,102 99,95**
CSF £4.45 CT £14.24 TOTE £2.50: £1.40, £1.30; EX 5.20 Trifecta £26.70.
Owner King Power Racing Co Ltd **Bred** A S Denniff **Trained** Kingsclere, Hants

FOCUS
Distance increased by 25yds. The pacemaker didn't really do his job, setting a steady enough gallop early, although the pace increased from a fair way out. Rock-solid Group 2 form, with the second rated to form.

2086 BET365 H'CAP 5f 10y
4:05 (4:08) (Class 2) (0-100,93) 3-Y-O
£12,450 (£3,728; £1,864; £932; £466; £234) **Stalls** Low

Form RPR

11-1 **1** **Leodis Dream (IRE)**[13] 1762 3-9-4 **90** .... DanielTudhope 4 96
(David O'Meara) *taken down early: disp ld tl led 2f out: drvn and edgd lft 1f out: edgd rt ins fnl f: hrd pressed nr fin: jst hld on* **15/8**[1]

104- **2** hd **Kurious**[175] 8805 3-9-6 **92** .... DavidProbert 11 97
(Henry Candy) *chsd ldrs: rdn over 1f out: sltly checked ins fnl f: r.o last 100yds: tk 2nd nr fin and jst failed* **7/2**[2]

640- **3** hd **Pass The Gin**[202] 7988 3-8-7 **79** .... RobHornby 5 83+
(Andrew Balding) *hld up in last pair: rapid prog jst over 1f out: pushed along and clsd on wnr nr fin: nt qckn last strides* **25/1**

502- **4** nk **Recon Mission (IRE)**[187] 8437 3-9-7 **93** .... (h) TomMarquand 3 96
(Tony Carroll) *disp ld to 2f out: drvn over 1f out: stl pressed wnr ins fnl f: kpt on but lost 2 pls nr fin* **16/1**

013- **5** 1½ **Dancing Warrior**[207] 7851 3-9-3 **89** .... AndreaAtzeni 12 87
(William Knight) *chsd ldrs on outer: rdn 2f out: prog 1f out: tried to cl fnl f but one pce last 100yds* **10/1**

02-0 **6** ¾ **Mutawaffer (IRE)**[13] 1762 3-8-13 **85** .... JimCrowley 6 80
(Charles Hills) *walked to post: racd against rail: chsd ldrs: rdn over 1f out: one pce and no imp fnl f* **9/1**

16-5 **7** nk **Mawde (IRE)**[16] 1692 3-8-7 **79** .... DavidEgan 10 73
(Rod Millman) *wl in rr: rdn and hanging 2f out: styd on over 1f out on outer: nvr nrr* **50/1**

22-3 **8** 2¼ **Reticent Angel (IRE)**[14] 1729 3-8-9 **81** .... HollieDoyle 7 75
(Clive Cox) *hld up and steadily swtchd to r against rail: effrt over 1f out: keeping on but no ch whn short of room 100yds out* **14/1**

110- **9** 2¼ **Prince Of Rome (IRE)**[196] 8145 3-9-2 **88** .... (t) ShaneKelly 8 66
(Richard Hughes) *chsd ldrs: rdn 2f out: no prog over 1f out: fdd fnl f* **20/1**

110- **10** 2¾ **Good Luck Fox (IRE)**[225] 7201 3-9-4 **90** .... SilvestreDeSousa 1 76
(Richard Hannon) *racd against rail: disp ld to 2f out: wkng whn short of room 100yds out: eased* **8/1**[3]

0-40 **11** 1½ **Oberyn Martell**[9] 1851 3-9-6 **92** .... CharlesBishop 2 54
(Eve Johnson Houghton) *a towards rr: pushed along and no prog over 1f out* **16/1**

410- **12** 7 **Michaels Choice**[192] 8296 3-8-6 **78** .... JasonWatson 9 15
(William Jarvis) *stmbld s: a in last and nvr a factor (jockey said gelding stumbled badly leaving the stalls and was never travelling thereafter)* **16/1**

1m 1.6s (0.30) **Going Correction** +0.15s/f (Good) **12** Ran SP% **122.1**
Speed ratings (Par 104): **103,102,102,101,99 98,97,94,90,86 83,72**
CSF £7.96 CT £129.54 TOTE £2.70: £1.30, £1.70, £7.90; EX 12.10 Trifecta £193.40.
Owner Andrew Kendall-Jones I **Bred** R & M Bloodstock **Trained** Upper Helmsley, N Yorks

FOCUS
A typical 5f sprint for the track, with plenty having their chance and a few not getting a run. The fourth has been rated in line with his Irish form.

2087 NORDOFF ROBBINS SIR GEORGE MARTIN MEMORIAL FILLIES' NOVICE STKS (PLUS 10 RACE) 1m 1f 209y
4:35 (4:39) (Class 4) 3-Y-O **£6,469** (£1,925; £962; £481) **Stalls** Low

Form RPR

51- **1** **Sparkle Roll (FR)**[209] 7763 3-9-7 0 .... OisinMurphy 5 93+
(John Gosden) *trckd ldng pair after 3f: clsd to ld wl over 2f out: looked ill at ease on grnd and cajoled along: kpt on wl enough and in command fnl f* **13/8**[1]

5- **2** 2 **King Power**[181] 8643 3-9-0 0 .... SilvestreDeSousa 10 82
(Andrew Balding) *trckd ldr: rdn to chal over 2f out: styd on but no imp on wnr over 1f out* **9/4**[2]

34- **3** ½ **Scentasia**[163] 9048 3-9-0 0 .... TomMarquand 11 81
(Ismail Mohammed) *hld up in last trio early: rchd midfield 4f out: prog wl over 2f out: shkn up to chse clr ldng pair wl over 1f out: styd on wl fnl f: nrst fin* **25/1**

4 hd **Sea Of Faith (IRE)** 3-9-0 0 .... JamesDoyle 9 81+
(William Haggas) *s.s: detached in last early: stl in last pair jst over 2f out: gd prog over 1f out: pushed along and r.o fnl f: encouraging debut* **4/1**[3]

0-5 **5** 8 **Mystiquestar (IRE)**[22] 1543 3-9-0 0 .... (h) JasonWatson 1 65
(Roger Charlton) *hld up in midfield: shkn up over 2f out: nvr on terms w ldrs and modest 5th fnl f* **33/1**

6 nk **La Lune** 3-9-0 0 .... DavidProbert 3 64+
(Henry Candy) *dwlt: hld up in last trio: pushed along over 2f out: sme prog over 1f out: nvr on terms* **66/1**

7 1¼ **Motivate Me (FR)** 3-9-0 0 .... AndreaAtzeni 8 62
(Roger Varian) *towards rr: rdn over 2f out: nvr a factor but kpt on fnl f* **14/1**

6- **8** nk **Seeing Red (IRE)**[172] 8880 3-9-0 0 .... JimCrowley 2 61
(Amanda Perrett) *nvr beyond midfield: shkn up and no prog over 2f out: wl btn over 1f out* **40/1**

6- **9** 6 **Nantucket (IRE)**[163] 9050 3-9-0 0 .... RyanMoore 4 49
(Sir Michael Stoute) *t.k.h: chsd ldng pair 3f: prom to over 2f out: wknd qckly* **12/1**

3- **10** *1* **Monogamy**[181] 8647 3-9-0 0 .... RobHornby 7 47
(Martyn Meade) *racd freely: led and stretched field: hdd wl over 2f out: sn wknd qckly* **25/1**

0 **11** *¾* **Born Leader (FR)**[14] 1738 3-9-0 0 .... RichardKingscote 6 46
(Hughie Morrison) *chsd ldrs to over 2f out: wknd* **50/1**

2m 11.27s (1.07) **Going Correction** +0.15s/f (Good) 11 Ran SP% 119.7
Speed ratings (Par 97): **101,99,99,98,92 92,91,90,86,85 84**
CSF £5.11 TOTE £2.30: £1.10, £1.60, £5.50; EX 6.80 Trifecta £59.70.
Owner Kin Hung Kei, Qatar Racing & L Dassault **Bred** Mme Aliette Forien & Mr Gilles Forien **Trained** Newmarket, Suffolk

FOCUS
Distance increased by 25yds. Often a good-quality fillies' event, the first four pulled 8l clear and there might have been a couple of smart performers on show. The winner has been rated in line with the race average, including the penalty, and the third in line with her debut run.

2088 BET365.COM H'CAP — 1m 1f 209y
5:05 (5:08) (Class 3) (0-95,89) 3-Y-O
£12,450 (£3,728; £1,864; £932; £466; £234) Stalls Low

Form — RPR

22-1 **1** **Private Secretary**[18] 1643 3-9-1 83 .... FrankieDettori 3 97+
(John Gosden) *hld up in midfield: prog on inner 2f out: rdn to ld 1f out: styd on wl and drew away last 100yds: readily* **3/1**[1]

313- **2** *2 ¼* **Lariat**[196] 8166 3-9-0 82 .... DavidProbert 6 91
(Andrew Balding) *mde most: kicked on over 2f out: hdd 1f out: styd on same pce* **16/1**

061- **3** *2* **Zuba**[179] 8682 3-8-7 75 .... AndreaAtzeni 1 80
(Amanda Perrett) *w ldr 3f: styd prom: effrt 2f out: rdn and one pce over 1f out* **16/1**

41-3 **4** *½* **New King**[106] 156 3-9-6 88 .... OisinMurphy 2 92+
(John Gosden) *slowly away: hld up in last pair: pushed along over 2f out: stdy prog over 1f out: nvr a threat but styd on fnl f* **9/2**[3]

621- **5** *3 ¼* **Big Baby Bull (IRE)**[182] 8590 3-9-7 89 .... TomMarquand 7 87
(Richard Hannon) *trckd ldr after 3f: shkn up to chal 3f out: lost 2nd over 1f out: wknd qckly* **14/1**

55-1 **6** *hd* **Prince Of Harts**[31] 1345 3-8-7 75 .... DavidEgan 5 72
(Rod Millman) *in tch: prog to trck ldrs 4f: rdn over 2f out: hanging and nt qckn: steadily lost grnd* **8/1**

526- **7** *2 ¾* **James Park Woods (IRE)**[161] 9104 3-9-1 83 .... HarryBentley 4 75
(Ralph Beckett) *t.k.h: chsd ldrs: shkn up wl over 2f out: no prog and wknd over 1f out* **12/1**

156- **8** *1 ¼* **Layaleena (IRE)**[196] 8148 3-9-2 84 .... JimCrowley 9 73
(Sir Michael Stoute) *broke on terms but heavily restrained into last: pushed along 2f out: nvr in it and no ch whn reminder fnl f (jockey said the filly failed to pick up)* **5/1**

51-1 **9** *shd* **Noble Lineage (IRE)**[21] 1568 3-9-4 86 .... RyanMoore 8 75
(James Tate) *t.k.h: hld up in midfield: shkn up and no prog over 2f out: wknd over 1f out* **7/2**[2]

2m 11.53s (1.33) **Going Correction** +0.15s/f (Good) 9 Ran SP% 119.3
Speed ratings (Par 102): **100,98,96,96,93 93,91,90,90**
CSF £54.11 CT £675.35 TOTE £3.40: £1.50, £4.70, £4.80; EX 60.10 Trifecta £494.80.
Owner Denford Stud **Bred** Denford Stud Ltd **Trained** Newmarket, Suffolk

FOCUS
Distance increased by 25yds. A useful 3yo handicap, it paid to race handily as there wasn't much pace on and several failed to settle. It's been rated around the race averages.
T/Jkpt: £869.50 to a £1 stake. Pool: £14,084.51 - 11.50 winning units T/Plt: £22.40 to a £1 stake. Pool: £115,353.75 - 3,745.70 winning units T/Qpdt: £3.30. to a £1 stake. Pool: £10,473.63 - 2,337.98 winning units **Jonathan Neesom**

2089 - (Foreign Racing) - See Raceform Interactive

1827 MAISONS-LAFFITTE (R-H)
Friday, April 26

OFFICIAL GOING: Turf: good to soft

2090a PRIX DE BETHEMONT (CLAIMER) (3YO) (TURF) — 6f
2:32 3-Y-O
£8,558 (£3,423; £2,567; £1,711; £855)

RPR

1 **Trois Mille (FR)**[18] 3-8-13 0 .... MlleMarieVelon(6) 3 80
(F Rossi, France) **63/10**[3]

2 *4* **Philippine Cobra (FR)**[6] 3-8-10 0 ....(p) AlexandreChesneau(6) 2 64
(G Botti, France) **17/1**

3 *2* **Capla Gilda**[18] 1658 3-9-1 0 .... MlleLeaBails(9) 9 66
(Andrea Marcialis, France) **41/10**[2]

4 *nk* **Moonlight In Japan (FR)**[18] 3-9-2 0 ....(b) MickaelBarzalona 1 57
(Andrea Marcialis, France) **10/1**

5 *½* **Velvet Vixen (IRE)**[10] 1842 3-8-11 0 .... Louis-PhilippeBeuzelin 7 50
(Jo Hughes, France) *broke wl: disp ld early: pushed along and outpcd over 2f out: rdn to chse ldrs over 1f out: kpt on same pce fnl f* **58/1**

6 *2* **Frelene (FR)**[29] 3-8-13 0 .... ChristopheSoumillon 11 46
(C Lerner, France) **69/10**

7 *3 ½* **Captain Lancelot (FR)**[18] 3-8-9 0 ....(b) ThomasTrullier(6) 4 36
(F Chappet, France) **73/10**

8 *nk* **Addicted Love (FR)**[133] 3-8-8 0 .... MaximeGuyon 6 28
(F Foucher, France) **33/10**[1]

9 *1 ¼* **Hit The Track Jack**[277] 3-8-4 0 .... JeremieMonteiro(7) 8 27
(N Caullery, France) **41/1**

10 *snk* **Imotep (FR)**[10] 1842 3-9-1 0 .... StephanePasquier 12 31
(M Boutin, France) **10/1**

11 *1 ¼* **Storm Katy (FR)**[73] 3-8-3 0 .... SimoneGarau(5) 13 20
(M Boutin, France) **65/1**

12 *snk* **Division (FR)**[55] 3-8-8 0 ....(b) JeromeMoutard(3) 10 23
(J-M Baudrelle, France) **97/1**

13 *5 ½* **Adirondack (IRE)**[18] 3-8-11 0 .... TonyPiccone 5 5
(F Chappet, France) **40/1**

14 *20* **Nonaynevernomore (IRE)**[16] 3-9-1 0 ....(b) AntoineHamelin 14
(Matthieu Palussiere, France) **19/1**

1m 10.31s (-3.09) 14 Ran SP% 119.1
PARI-MUTUEL (all including 1 euro stake): WIN 7.30; PLACE 2.50, 4.40, 2.00; DF 44.60.
Owner L Haegel **Bred** P Boudengen **Trained** France

2091a PRIX CRICKET BALL (MAIDEN) (3YO) (TURF) — 6f
4:14 3-Y-O
£11,261 (£4,504; £3,378; £2,252; £1,126)

RPR

1 **Midnight Shine (FR)**[25] 1489 3-8-8 0 .... AugustinMadamet(8) 8 92
(A Fabre, France) *pushed along early: settled bhd ldrs: urged along over 2f out: rdn between rivals to chal over 1f out: drvn into ld ins fnl f: kpt on wl* **19/10**[1]

2 *1 ½* **Alkawthar (USA)**[25] 1489 3-8-13 0 .... MaximeGuyon 7 85
(Mme Pia Brandt, France) **59/10**

3 *1 ¼* **Dream With You (FR)**[24] 1512 3-8-13 0 .... AurelienLemaitre 1 81
(N Caullery, France) **37/10**[2]

4 *3* **Spanish Miss (IRE)**[16] 3-8-13 0 .... ChristopheSoumillon 5 71
(M Delcher Sanchez, France) **9/2**[3]

5 *nk* **Dream Life (FR)**[250] 6336 3-8-13 0 .... VincentCheminaud 2 70
(J-P Dubois, France) **19/1**

6 *6* **Belladone Spirit (IRE)**[24] 1512 3-8-7 0 ....(b[1]) ThomasTrullier(6) 10 51
(J-M Baudrelle, France) **12/1**

7 *1 ¼* **Danseur D'Argent (FR)**[25] 1489 3-8-13 0 .... TheoBachelot 3 47
(Jo Hughes, France) *settled midfield: rowed along 2f out: rdn w limited rspnse over 1f out: wknd and eased ins fnl f* **18/1**

8 *¾* **Fire At Midnight (FR)**[18] 3-8-8 0 ....(p) JeremieMonteiro(8) 6 47
(N Caullery, France) **22/1**

9 *¾* **La Mirada (FR)**[24] 1512 3-8-9 0 .... JeromeMoutard(4) 9 42
(Mlle V Dissaux, France) **63/1**

10 *1 ¾* **Inner Charm**[25] 1489 3-8-13 0 .... StephanePasquier 4 36
(H-F Devin, France) **12/1**

1m 10.17s (-3.23) 10 Ran SP% 120.0
PARI-MUTUEL (all including 1 euro stake): WIN 2.90; PLACE 1.30, 1.60, 1.40; DF 6.80.
Owner Godolphin SNC **Bred** E Puerari & Oceanic Bloodstock Inc **Trained** Chantilly, France

2091a (Foreign Racing) - See Raceform Interactive

2075 DONCASTER (L-H)
Saturday, April 27

OFFICIAL GOING: Good (watered; 8.2)
Wind: Strong half against Weather: Cloudy

2092 SKY SPORTS RACING SKY 415 H'CAP — 1m 3f 197y
5:10 (5:12) (Class 4) (0-80,81) 4-Y-O+
£5,530 (£1,645; £822; £411; £400; £400) Stalls Low

Form — RPR

512- **1** **Get Back Get Back (IRE)**[136] 9502 4-9-6 79 ....(w) AdamKirby 12 89+
(Clive Cox) *hld up in midfield: pushed along 4f out: hdwy on outer 2f out: rdn to chal ent fnl f: sn led and edgd lft: styd on* **11/2**[2]

0-64 **2** *1* **Roar (IRE)**[35] 1291 5-8-11 70 .... BarryMcHugh 9 77
(Ed de Giles) *trckd ldrs: smooth hdwy 3f out: cl up 2f out: rdn to ld appr fnl f: sn drvn: hdd ins fnl f: kpt on* **12/1**

2-50 **3** *1 ¾* **Nietzsche**[21] 1159 6-8-11 73 ....(t) BenRobinson(3) 13 78
(Brian Ellison) *hld up: hdwy 3f out: rdn to chse ldrs over 1f out: drvn and kpt on fnl f* **13/2**

0100 **4** *nk* **Unit Of Assessment (IRE)**[24] 1518 5-8-12 78(vt) Pierre-LouisJamin(7) 6 82
(William Knight) *trckd ldrs: hdwy over 2f out: rdn and ch over 1f out: hld whn n.m.r ent fnl f: kpt on same pce after* **33/1**

000- **5** *nse* **Ingleby Hollow**[35] 8414 7-9-3 76 ....(t) RobbieDowney 3 80
(David O'Meara) *hld up towards rr: hdwy on inner 3f out: rdn wl over 1f out: styd on and ch ent fnl f: sn drvn and kpt on same pce* **12/1**

3002 **6** *2 ¼* **Thaqaffa (IRE)**[35] 1291 6-9-8 81 ....(h) KevinStott 16 81
(Amy Murphy) *trckd ldrs: hdwy on outer to ld 3f out: rdn wl over 1f out: hdd and drvn appr fnl f: kpt on one pce* **25/1**

3-45 **7** *1 ¼* **Native Fighter (IRE)**[21] 737 5-9-5 78 .... JackGarritty 4 76
(Jedd O'Keeffe) *in tch: pushed along 3f out: rdn 2f out: plugged on one pce appr fnl f* **20/1**

60-3 **8** *½* **Maghfoor**[19] 1648 5-8-9 68 .... JasonHart 11 66
(Eric Alston) *stdd s: hld up: a towards rr* **14/1**

615- **9** *1 ¾* **Nuits St Georges (IRE)**[180] 8702 4-9-0 73 .... TomEaves 10 68
(David Menuisier) *trckd ldr: cl up 4f out: rdn along 3f out: wknd 2f out* **20/1**

3211 **10** *½* **Singing Sheriff**[25] 1508 4-8-13 72 .... LiamKeniry 15 66
(Ed Walker) *hld up in midfield: swtchd rt to outer and sme hdwy 3f out: pushed along over 2f out: sn rdn and n.d* **7/1**

165- **11** *1 ¼* **Blazing Saddles**[304] 4260 4-9-7 80 .... HarryBentley 2 72
(Ralph Beckett) *trckd ldrs: hdwy over 3f out: rdn along over 2f out: sn wknd* **9/1**

120- **12** *½* **Swordbill**[16] 8610 4-9-1 74 ....(p) LukeMorris 14 65
(Ian Williams) *a in rr* **33/1**

4312 **13** *¾* **Nylon Speed (IRE)**[28] 1425 5-9-7 80 ....(t) DavidProbert 5 70
(Alan King) *trckd ldrs: effrt 3f out and sn pushed along rdn 2f out: sn btn* **5/1**[1]

-060 **14** *5* **Baydar**[24] 1518 6-9-2 78 ....(p) CameronNoble(3) 7 60
(Ian Williams) *a in rr* **6/1**[3]

2263 **15** *15* **Glan Y Gors (IRE)**[21] 1596 7-9-6 79 ....(p) RoystonFfrench 1 37
(David Thompson) *led: rdn along and hdd 3f out: sn drvn and wknd* **50/1**

-000 **16** *8* **Starplex**[5] 1977 9-8-11 77 .... RPWalsh(7) 8 22
(Kenny Johnson) *a towards rr* **80/1**

2m 36.0s (-0.60) **Going Correction** +0.175s/f (Good) 16 Ran SP% 126.7
Speed ratings (Par 105): **101,100,99,98,98 97,96,96,95,94 93,93,93,89,79 74**
CSF £67.53 CT £454.41 TOTE £5.60: £1.80, £3.30, £2.10, £8.90; EX 71.40 Trifecta £781.10.
Owner Paul & Clare Rooney **Bred** Castlefarm Stud **Trained** Lambourn, Berks

FOCUS
A light shower overnight failed to alter the going and the runners raced into a fairly strong headwind in the straight but the times on the night suggest the ground was a bit slower than the official. Rail movements added 6yds to all races on the round course. Mainly exposed performers on show in an open handicap. The gallop was sound and this form should prove reliable. The third has been rated to last year's Flat form, and the fourth to his recent improved AW form.

2093 SKY SPORTS RACING VIRGIN 535 EBF MAIDEN STKS — 5f 3y
5:45 (5:47) (Class 5) 2-Y-O
£3,752 (£1,116; £557; £278) Stalls High

Form — RPR

1 **Iva Reflection (IRE)** 2-9-2 0 .... JaneElliott(3) 2 80+
(Tom Dascombe) *cl up: slt ld 1/2-way: rdn along and edgd rt over 1f out: drvn ent fnl f: sn edgd sltly lft: kpt on gamely towards fin* **16/1**

The Form Book Flat 2019, Raceform Ltd, Newbury, RG14 5SJ

2 *nk* **Taxiwala (IRE)** 2-9-5 0 .... LukeMorris 3 79
(Archie Watson) *trckd ldrs on outer: hdwy and cl up 2f out: rdn to chal and edgd rt over 1f out: drvn and ev ch whn edgd rt ins fnl f: no ex towards fin* **2/1**[1]
3 *½* **Galactic Glow (IRE)** 2-9-5 0 .... DavidProbert 4 77
(William Jarvis) *trckd ldrs: pushed along: n.m.r and sltly outpcd over 1f out: sn rdn and kpt on fnl f* **2/1**[1]
4 *nk* **Ocasio Cortez (IRE)** 2-9-0 0 .... SeanLevey 9 71
(Richard Hannon) *chsd ldrs: hdwy 2f out: rdn and edgd lft over 1f out: kpt on same pce fnl f* **8/1**[3]
5 *¾* **Dragon Command** 2-9-5 0 .... HarryBentley 10 73+
(George Scott) *green hld up towards rr: hdwy over 2f out: rdn along whn nt clr run 1 1/2f out: styd on wl fnl f* **9/1**
6 *1 ¾* **Irish Eileen** 2-9-0 0 .... NathanEvans 8 62
(Michael Easterby) *slt ld: hdd 1/2-way: sn rdn and grad wknd* **33/1**
7 *7* **Purple Empress** 2-9-0 0 .... TrevorWhelan 6 37
(Ivan Furtado) *dwlt: a in rr (jockey said filly was slowly away, ran green and hung left)* **20/1**
8 *3 ½* **Red Reflection (IRE)** 2-9-5 0 .... JackGarritty 1 29
(Richard Fahey) *wnt lft s: a in rr* **13/2**[2]

1m 2.68s (3.08) **Going Correction** +0.175s/f (Good) 8 Ran SP% **114.7**
Speed ratings (Par 92): **82,81,80,80,79 76,65,59**
CSF £48.62 TOTE £17.50: £3.20, £1.40, £1.30; EX 66.60 Trifecta £210.90.
Owner British Racing Club **Bred** Michael O'Mahony **Trained** Malpas, Cheshire

FOCUS
A field of newcomers but, although the pace was reasonable, the first five home finished in a heap and this form is unlikely to be anything out of the ordinary. The opening level is fluid, but it looks a lesser renewal.

2094 MORLEY GLASS & GLAZING MAIDEN STKS 7f 6y
6:15 (6:18) (Class 4) 3-Y-O+ £5,530 (£1,645; £822; £411) Stalls High

Form RPR
2- 1 **Jalaad (IRE)**[205] 7941 4-10-0 0 .... AdamKirby 12 92+
(Saeed bin Suroor) *prom: hdwy to ld 3f out: pushed along 2f out: jnd: rdn and edgd lft ent fnl f: kpt on strly* **6/1**[3]
24- 2 *2 ¼* **Lyndon B (IRE)**[183] 8606 3-9-1 0 .... HarryBentley 16 81
(George Scott) *stmbld sltly s: in tch: hdwy on outer over 2f out: rdn to chse ldrs over 1f out: kpt on wl fnl f* **10/1**
3 *1 ½* **Alkaraama (USA)** 3-9-1 0 .... DavidProbert 8 77+
(Sir Michael Stoute) *hld up in tch: gd hdwy 3f out: chal over 1f out: rdn ent fnl f: kpt on same pce* **10/1**
2- 4 *1* **Jabalaly (IRE)**[295] 4613 3-9-1 0 .... RobertHavlin 7 74
(Ed Dunlop) *in tch: hdwy 2f out: swtchd rt and rdn 1f out: kpt on wl towards fin* **10/1**
- 5 *1 ½* **Destination** 3-9-1 0 .... JamesDoyle 3 70
(William Haggas) *chsd ldrs: hdwy over 2f out: rdn along wl over 1f out: kpt on same pce* **6/4**[1]
6- 6 *3 ¾* **Stormbomber (CAN)**[162] 9103 3-9-1 0 .... LiamKeniry 9 60
(Ed Walker) *towards rr: hdwy 2f out: pushed along over 1f out: kpt on fnl f: nrst fin* **66/1**
33-2 7 *nk* **Chatham House**[28] 1423 3-9-1 81 .... SeanLevey 14 59
(Richard Hannon) *prom: rdn along over 2f out: sn drvn and wknd* **3/1**[2]
8 *2 ¾* **Secretarial (IRE)** 3-8-10 0 .... SilvestreDeSousa 17 47+
(Tim Easterby) *dwlt and bhd: hdwy 2f out: kpt on fnl f: nrst fin (jockey said filly ran green)* **22/1**
4-0 9 *shd* **Gylo (IRE)**[16] 1723 3-9-1 0 .... RobbieDowney 6 52
(David O'Meara) *towards rr: hdwy 2f out: rdn along over 1f out: n.d* **80/1**
10 *1 ¾* **Brutalab** 3-9-1 0 .... JackGarritty 13 47
(Tim Easterby) *dwlt and towards rr: sme hdwy 1/2-way: rdn along over 2f out: n.d* **100/1**
50 11 *2 ¼* **Menina Atrevida**[27] 1458 3-8-10 0 .... JasonHart 4 36
(Ivan Furtado) *led: hdd 3f out: sn rdn and wknd* **100/1**
0 12 *2* **Royal Sands (FR)**[19] 1643 3-9-1 0 .... BarryMcHugh 1 35
(James Given) *prom: rdn along 3f out: sn wknd* **50/1**
06- 13 *2 ¾* **Khaan**[166] 9032 4-10-0 0 .... LukeMorris 10 33
(Michael Appleby) *t.k.h: chsd ldrs: rdn along wl over 2f out: sn wknd (jockey said colt hung left)* **150/1**
14 *½* **Harry's Ridge (IRE)** 4-10-0 0 .... TomEaves 5 32
(Eric Alston) *s.i.s: a bhd* **40/1**
6- 15 *½* **Bagatino**[200] 8068 3-9-1 0 .... KevinStott 15 25
(Declan Carroll) *in tch: rdn along 3f out: sn wknd* **100/1**
16 *2* **Doncaster Star** 4-9-6 0 .... JaneElliott(3) 11 20
(Ivan Furtado) *a towards rr* **66/1**

1m 28.09s (1.69) **Going Correction** +0.175s/f (Good)
WFA 3 from 4yo 13lb 16 Ran SP% **123.2**
Speed ratings (Par 105): **97,94,92,91,89 85,85,82,81,79 77,75,71,71,70 68**
CSF £63.41 TOTE £6.30: £2.00, £2.30, £3.20; EX 54.40 Trifecta £313.20.
Owner Godolphin **Bred** Ballinacurra Stud Ltd **Trained** Newmarket, Suffolk

FOCUS
A wide range of ability on show but a useful effort from the winner in a race where the performances of the third and the sixth caught the eye. The gallop was fair and the first five pulled a few lengths clear. It's been rated around the second and fourth to their previous efforts.

2095 SWITCHED ON SOLUTIONS GROUP H'CAP 1m 2f 43y
6:45 (6:46) (Class 3) (0-95,97) 4-Y-O+ £7,762 (£2,310; £1,154; £577) Stalls High

Form RPR
/11- 1 **Fujaira Prince (IRE)**[324] 3497 5-9-1 88 .... AndreaAtzeni 3 99
(Roger Varian) *trckd ldrs: hdwy 3f out and sn cl up: led 2f out: rdn clr appr fnl f: comf* **11/8**[1]
500- 2 *3* **Mistiroc**[122] 8198 8-9-5 92 .... (v) JasonHart 10 97
(John Quinn) *in tch: hdwy wl over 2f out: rdn over 1f out: drvn and kpt on wl fnl f* **40/1**
-353 3 *½* **Al Jellaby**[28] 1413 4-9-2 89 .... (h[1]) AdamKirby 14 93
(Clive Cox) *trckd ldr: hdwy 4f out: led over 3f out: rdn along and hdd 2f out: chsd wnr and drvn over 1f out: kpt on same pce* **12/1**
114- 4 *nk* **Autumn War (IRE)**[212] 7697 4-9-0 87 .... DavidProbert 6 90+
(Charles Hills) *hld up in rr: hdwy 3f out: rdn along 2f out: styd on wl fnl f: nrst fin (jockey said colt was slowly away)* **20/1**
23-1 5 *5* **Lunar Jet**[14] 1757 5-9-4 91 .... JamesDoyle 9 84
(John Mackie) *towards rr: t.k.h and hmpd after 1 1/2f: hdwy on inner: 3f out: rdn along to chse ldrs wl over 1f out: kpt on same pce fnl f* **5/1**[2]
106- 6 *shd* **Finniston Farm**[182] 8631 4-9-10 97 .... RichardKingscote 12 90
(Tom Dascombe) *hld up: hdwy on outer over 3f out: rdn along to chse ldrs 2f out: sn drvn and kpt on same pce* **8/1**[3]
65-0 7 *2* **Nayel (IRE)**[28] 1422 7-8-11 91 .... (p) LukeCatton(7) 11 80
(Richard Hannon) *hld up towards rr: sme hdwy wl over 2f out: swtchd lft to inner wl over 1f out: kpt on: n.d (jockey said horse was slowly away)* **50/1**
-112 8 *1* **Weld Al Emarat**[28] 1428 7-8-10 83 .... NathanEvans 13 70
(Michael Easterby) *hld up: a towards rr* **14/1**
313- 9 *shd* **Awake My Soul (IRE)**[172] 8899 10-9-7 94 .... JamesSullivan 8 81
(Tom Tate) *trckd ldrs: hdwy and cl up over 3f out: rdn along wl over 2f out: sn wknd* **25/1**
4513 10 *¾* **Central City (IRE)**[18] 1664 4-8-10 83 .... (p) LukeMorris 7 69
(Ian Williams) *in tch: pushed along over 3f out: rdn and wknd wl over 2f out* **20/1**
52-0 11 *1 ¾* **Speed Company (IRE)**[94] 368 6-8-9 82 .... MartinDwyer 2 64
(Ian Williams) *s.i.s: a bhd* **33/1**
40-0 12 *nse* **Alternative Fact**[28] 1422 4-9-5 92 .... RobertHavlin 5 74
(Ed Dunlop) *a towards rr* **25/1**
02-6 13 *9* **Indomeneo**[27] 1461 4-8-11 84 .... SilvestreDeSousa 1 48
(Richard Fahey) *trckd ldrs on inner: rdn along 3f out: wknd 2f out* **10/1**
105- 14 *10* **Gossip Column (IRE)**[238] 6785 4-9-4 91 .... PaddyMathers 4 35
(Ian Williams) *led: rdn along 4f out: hdd over 3f out: sn wknd* **33/1**

2m 10.25s (-2.05) **Going Correction** +0.175s/f (Good) 14 Ran SP% **120.8**
Speed ratings (Par 107): **107,104,104,103,99 99,98,97,97,96 95,95,88,80**
CSF £86.32 CT £519.79 TOTE £2.30: £1.40, £13.70, £2.80; EX 101.40 Trifecta £1803.50.
Owner Sheikh Mohammed Obaid Al Maktoum **Bred** Rabbah Bloodstock Limited **Trained** Newmarket, Suffolk

FOCUS
Add 6yds to the official distance. A decent quality handicap won by a progressive sort who looks potentially smart. The gallop was sound and the first four finished clear. The third has been rated to form.

2096 SKY SPORTS RACING H'CAP 1m 3f 197y
7:15 (7:17) (Class 5) (0-75,76) 3-Y-O £3,752 (£1,116; £557; £400; £400; £400) Stalls Low

Form RPR
24-2 1 **Rowland Ward**[18] 1661 3-9-7 75 .... HarryBentley 7 85+
(Ralph Beckett) *hld up: hdwy 3f out: chsd ldrs 2f out: rdn along on inner to chal over 1f out: drvn to ld last 110yds: styd on wl* **9/2**[2]
004- 2 *1 ¼* **Beechwood Jude (FR)**[186] 8502 3-9-2 70 .... ConnorBeasley 12 77
(Keith Dalgleish) *hld up in rr: hdwy 3f out: chsd ldrs wl over 1f out: sn rdn and slt ld appr fnl f: drvn and edgd lft ins fnl f: hdd last 110yds: kpt on same pce* **50/1**
44-2 3 *2 ½* **Sapa Inca (IRE)**[15] 1730 3-9-7 75 .... JoeFanning 5 78+
(Mark Johnston) *led: pushed along over 2f out: rdn wl over 1f out: hdd appr fnl f: hld whn n.m.r ins fnl f: kpt on same pce* **4/1**[1]
30-2 4 *1 ½* **Palladium**[14] 1771 3-9-5 73 .... RobHornby 11 74
(Martyn Meade) *trckd ldrs: pushed along over 2f out: drvn wl over 1f out: kpt on one pce* **4/1**[1]
30-4 5 *1 ½* **Chinese Alphabet**[29] 1396 3-9-0 68 .... CharlesBishop 13 66
(William Knight) *t.k.h: chsd ldr: cl up 1/2-way: rdn along over 2f out: grad wknd (jockey said gelding hung left throughout)* **12/1**
63-5 6 *1 ½* **Fantastic Ms Fox**[17] 1697 3-8-5 59 .... PaddyMathers 10 55
(Richard Fahey) *t.k.h early: chsd ldrs: rdn along 3f out: drvn over 2f out: grad wknd* **20/1**
24-6 7 *2 ¼* **Artistic Language**[19] 1645 3-9-8 76 .... (p[1]) SilvestreDeSousa 3 68
(Brian Meehan) *trckd ldrs on inner: pushed along 3f out: rdn 2f out: sn btn* **8/1**[3]
-325 8 *9* **Debbonair (IRE)**[60] 917 3-9-0 68 .... JamesDoyle 8 46
(Hugo Palmer) *hld up: a towards rr* **8/1**[3]
46-4 9 *2 ¾* **Flint Hill**[19] 1645 3-9-8 76 .... PaulMulrennan 6 49
(Michael Dods) *trckd ldrs: pushed along 4f out: rdn 3f out: sn wknd* **17/2**
35-4 10 *5* **Valence**[17] 1696 3-9-1 69 .... DanielMuscutt 9 34
(Ed Dunlop) *chsd ldrs on outer: rdn along over 3f out: sn wknd* **20/1**
100- 11 *1 ¾* **Major Snugfit**[185] 8550 3-9-1 69 .... NathanEvans 1 32
(Michael Easterby) *trckd ldrs: rdn along over 3f out: sn wknd* **66/1**
-424 12 *8* **Thunderoad**[42] 1233 3-9-4 72 .... (p[1]) AndreaAtzeni 2 22
(Marco Botti) *a towards rr* **14/1**

2m 36.37s (-0.23) **Going Correction** +0.175s/f (Good) 12 Ran SP% **118.3**
Speed ratings (Par 98): **99,98,96,95,94 93,92,86,84,80 79,74**
CSF £224.56 CT £980.97 TOTE £5.30: £2.10, £14.00, £1.90; EX 289.90 Trifecta £1400.70.
Owner H H Sheikh Mohammed Bin Khalifa Al Thani **Bred** Al Shahania Stud **Trained** Kimpton, Hants

FOCUS
Add 6yds to the official distance. A fair handicap featuring several unexposed sorts and one run at a decent gallop. This form should work out.

2097 SKY SPORTS RACING V!RGIN 535 FILLIES' H'CAP 7f 6y
7:45 (7:46) (Class 4) (0-85,87) 4-Y-O+ £5,530 (£1,645; £822; £411; £400; £400) Stalls High

Form RPR
00-5 1 **Florenza**[14] 1763 6-9-5 82 .... MichaelStainton 8 89
(Chris Fairhurst) *led 1f: cl up: rdn along to ld again over 2f out: drvn and edgd lft over 1f out: edgd lft ins fnl f: hld on wl towards fin* **7/2**[2]
101- 2 *nk* **Agincourt (IRE)**[190] 8379 4-9-2 79 .... ShaneGray 7 85
(David O'Meara) *trckd ldrs: smooth hdwy over 2f out: rdn to chal over 1f out: drvn and ev ch whn edgd lft ins fnl f: kpt on* **11/1**
1126 3 *2 ¼* **Porrima (IRE)**[36] 1271 4-8-3 66 .... (p[1]) AndrewMullen 1 66
(Ben Haslam) *dwlt: hld up in rr: hdwy 3f out: chsd ldrs 2f out: effrt whn n.m.r and swtchd lft over 1f out: sn rdn and kpt on same pce* **5/1**
42-1 4 *6* **Javelin**[17] 1684 4-8-7 70 .... MartinDwyer 5 54
(William Muir) *t.k.h early: trckd ldrs: pushed along over 2f out: rdn whn n.m.r over 1f out: one pce after* **8/1**
212- 5 *2 ¼* **Excellent Times**[294] 4668 4-9-10 87 .... DavidAllan 2 65
(Tim Easterby) *racd wd: hld up in rr: effrt and hdwy over 2f out: rdn wl over 1f out: sn wknd* **8/1**
110- 6 *7* **Silca Mistress**[117] 9772 4-9-7 84 .... AdamKirby 4 43
(Clive Cox) *racd wd: prom: pushed along 3f out: rdn over 2f out: sn wknd* **9/2**[3]
060- 7 *14* **Dance Teacher (IRE)**[209] 7801 5-9-4 81 .... SilvestreDeSousa 6 2
(Shaun Keightley) *cl up: led after 1f: pushed along 3f out: sn rdn and hdd: wknd wl over 1f out (trainer could offer no explanation for the mare's poor performance)* **11/4**[1]

1m 27.29s (0.89) **Going Correction** +0.175s/f (Good) 7 Ran SP% **114.3**
Speed ratings (Par 102): **101,100,98,91,88 80,64**
CSF £39.85 CT £191.10 TOTE £3.90: £2.20, £4.70; EX 40.50 Trifecta £139.00.
Owner 980 Racing **Bred** 980 Racing **Trained** Middleham, N Yorks

FOCUS
A fair handicap for fillies and one in which the gallop was sound throughout. The field split but the two that raced in the centre finished well beaten. The winner has been rated to her late 2018 form.

2098 WATCH SKY SPORTS RACING SKY 415 H'CAP 6f 2y
8:15 (8:17) (Class 5) (0-70,72) 3-Y-O

£3,752 (£1,116; £557; £400; £400; £400) **Stalls High**

Form RPR
244- **1** **Socru (IRE)**[180] 8691 3-9-4 **67**........................ NathanEvans 6 75
(Michael Easterby) *trckd ldrs: effrt 2f out: rdn to chal over 1f out: led jst ins fnl f: drvn out* **7/1**[1]

36-0 **2** 1 1/4 **Molaaheth**[33] 1337 3-9-7 **70**........................(t[1]) SeanLevey 7 74
(Richard Hannon) *hld up towards rr: smooth hdwy 1/2-way: chsd ldrs 2f out: rdn to chal ent fnl f and ev ch: sn drvn and kpt on* **10/1**

216- **3** 3/4 **Epona**[190] 8368 3-9-6 **69**........................ ConnorBeasley 2 71
(Keith Dalgleish) *trckd ldrs: hdwy wl over 1f out: rdn ent fnl f: kpt on wl towards fin* **10/1**

53-6 **4** 1/2 **Princess Palliser (IRE)**[36] 1272 3-9-4 **67**........................ JasonHart 8 67
(John Quinn) *midfield: pushed along over 2f out: rdn wl over 1f out: styng on whn sltly hmpd jst ins fnl f: kpt on* **20/1**

5-36 **5** 1 **Serengeti Song (IRE)**[19] 1649 3-9-4 **72**........................(h[1]) HarrisonShaw(5) 3 69
(K R Burke) *hld up towards rr: hdwy on inner 2f out: rdn over 1f out: kpt on fnl f* **8/1**[2]

-613 **6** 3/4 **Major Blue**[33] 1336 3-9-9 **72**........................ HollieDoyle 10 66
(James Eustace) *trckd ldrs: hdwy 2f out and sn cl up: rdn to ld narrowly jst over 1f out: hdd and drvn jst ins fnl f: wknd (vet reported the gelding lost its right hind shoe)* **7/1**[1]

410- **7** hd **Timetodock**[180] 8699 3-9-1 **64**........................(b) DavidAllan 4 58
(Tim Easterby) *chsd ldr: cl up 1/2-way: rdn along over 2f out: grad wknd fr over 1f out* **16/1**

00-0 **8** 1 1/2 **Furyan**[5] 1982 3-8-9 **61**........................ RowanScott(3) 5 50
(Nigel Tinkler) *dwlt and in rr: rdn along over 2f out: styd on u.p appr fnl f: nrst fin* **40/1**

141- **9** 2 1/2 **House Deposit**[180] 8699 3-9-7 **70**........................(t) KevinStott 1 51
(Declan Carroll) *hld up in rr: hdwy 2f out: rdn over 1f out: no imp fnl f (jockey said gelding lugged left onto heels)* **14/1**

36-0 **10** 1 1/4 **Crackin Dream (IRE)**[24] 1516 3-9-5 **68**........................(b[1]) AdamKirby 13 45
(Clive Cox) *chsd ldrs: rdn along over 2f out: sn drvn and wknd* **8/1**[2]

05-0 **11** 1 1/4 **Pearl Of Qatar**[10] 1846 3-8-12 **64**........................(b[1]) BenRobinson(3) 9 37
(Brian Ellison) *in tch: hdwy to chse ldrs over 2f out: sn rdn and wknd* **20/1**

50-4 **12** hd **Rum Lad**[30] 1379 3-9-2 **65**........................(t[1]) SilvestreDeSousa 12 37
(Ivan Furtado) *led: rdn along over 2f out: drvn and hdd jst over 1f out: wknd* **9/1**[3]

242- **13** 1/2 **Dancing Rave**[180] 8696 3-9-3 **69**........................ ConorMcGovern(3) 15 40
(David O'Meara) *towards rr: effrt and sme hdwy on outer over 2f out: sn rdn along and wknd* **8/1**[2]

-354 **14** 9 **Alicia Darcy (IRE)**[26] 1475 3-9-6 **69**........................ BarryMcHugh 14 11
(James Given) *a towards rr* **16/1**

232- **15** 7 **Master Matt**[186] 8509 3-9-8 **71**........................ LukeMorris 11
(Denis Quinn) *in tch: pushed along wl over 2f out: sn rdn and wknd (jockey said colt stopped quickly)* **12/1**

1m 14.56s (1.86) **Going Correction** +0.175s/f (Good) **15 Ran SP% 124.6**
Speed ratings (Par 98): **94,92,91,90,89 88,88,86,82,81 79,79,78,66,57**
CSF £75.52 CT £717.56 TOTE £7.90: £2.50, £3.90, £4.00; EX 90.60 Trifecta £769.70.
Owner Winter Blackburn Lm Syn Cram Mb Sh & Sh **Bred** Miss Jill Finegan **Trained** Sheriff Hutton, N Yorks

FOCUS
A run of the mill handicap in which the gallop was sound throughout. The field raced in the centre of the course. The third and fourth have been rated close to form.
T/Plt: £181.00 to a £1 stake. Pool: £66,726.28 - 269 winning units T/Qpdt: £86.60 to a £1 stake. Pool: £8,258.77 - 70.50 winning units **Joe Rowntree**

HAYDOCK (L-H)
Saturday, April 27

OFFICIAL GOING: Good to soft changing to soft after race 1 (1.30)
Wind: windy, against in home straight Weather: overcast, light rain

2099 PLAY 4 TO SCORE AT BETWAY NOVICE STKS (PLUS 10 RACE) 1m 3f 175y
1:30 (1:33) (Class 3) 3-Y-O £9,703 (£2,887; £1,443; £721) **Stalls Centre**

Form RPR
3 **1** **Severance**[14] 1756 3-9-2 0........................(h) GeorgeDowning 4 89
(Mick Channon) *t.k.h: prom: plld way into ld after 3f: mde rest: gng wl in 7 l ld 4f out: shkn up 3f out: drvn in 5 l ld 2f out: rdn over 1f out: c further clr fnl f: pushed out nr fin* **6/1**

2 7 **Make My Day (IRE)** 3-9-2 0........................ RobertHavlin 7 78
(John Gosden) *sweating: mid-div: hdwy into 3rd over 3f out: sn pushed along: drvn into 2nd over 1f out: reminder and kpt on fnl f: nvr nr wnr* **4/1**[3]

65 **3** 5 **Tidal Point (IRE)**[9] 1898 3-9-2 0........................ RoystonFfrench 8 70
(Steph Hollinshead) *hld up: pushed along over 2f out: reminder in 5th 1f out: kpt on steadily into 3rd fnl f* **100/1**

1- **4** 1 **Great Bear**[162] 9105 3-9-8 0........................ JasonWatson 5 74
(Roger Charlton) *chsd ldrs: pushed along in 4th 3f out: drvn and reminder 2f out: one pce fnl f* **7/2**[2]

2- **5** 1 1/4 **Apparate**[183] 8608 3-9-2 0........................ DavidEgan 2 66
(Roger Varian) *unruly s and v reluctant to load: t.k.h: chsd ldrs: hdwy into 7 l 2nd 4f out: drvn 3f out: reminder in 5 l 2nd 2f out: drvn and lost pl 1f out: sn wknd (trainer's rep said that the rider lost an iron leaving the stalls, when the colt jumped awkwardly and that after running too freely)* **4/7**[1]

0 **6** 7 **Soft Summer Rain**[28] 1417 3-8-4 0........................ JoshQuinn(7) 9 50
(Michael Easterby) *in rr: pushed along 3f out: sn drvn: no imp* **125/1**

0-3 **7** 1 1/4 **Nordano (GER)**[18] 1661 3-9-2 0........................ FrannyNorton 3 53
(Mark Johnston) *led: hdd after 3f: chsd ldr whn hdd: lost pl 4f out: sn drvn and wknd* **20/1**

8 5 **Ozark** 3-8-11 0........................ GrahamLee 1 40
(Jennie Candlish) *hld up: drvn over 2f out: no imp* **100/1**

00- **9** 1 3/4 **Moor Top**[248] 6412 3-9-2 0........................ AndrewMullen 6 42
(Jennie Candlish) *restless in stalls: hld up: reminders 2f out: no rspnse* **125/1**

2m 40.14s (6.84) **Going Correction** +0.575s/f (Yiel) **9 Ran SP% 128.5**
Speed ratings (Par 102): **100,95,92,91,90 85,85,81,80**
CSF £33.10 TOTE £10.60: £1.50, £1.30, £15.50; EX 55.20 Trifecta £2044.00.
Owner J Turner & The Megsons **Bred** Highclere Stud & Hmh Management **Trained** West Ilsley, Berks

FOCUS
All races run on the stands' side home straight. Add 25yds. With Storm Hannah blowing through, there was plenty of rain overnight and on raceday, and there was a headwind in the straight. It looked tough going in the opener, and Franny Norton, Andrew Mullen and Robert Havlin all called the ground soft, while David Egan said it was testing. It's hard to gauge the level of the form.

2100 BETWAY OLD BOSTON H'CAP 7f 37y
2:05 (2:06) (Class 2) 4-Y-O+

£28,012 (£8,388; £4,194; £2,097; £1,048; £526) **Stalls Low**

Form RPR
110- **1** **Safe Voyage (IRE)**[189] 8409 6-9-8 **103**........................ JasonHart 14 114
(John Quinn) *hld up on outer: hdwy to trck ldrs 2f out: rdn to dispute ld 1f out: led 1/2f out: sn clr* **8/1**

012- **2** 1 1/4 **Ptarmigan Ridge**[183] 8611 5-8-7 **88**........................ DavidEgan 11 96
(Richard Hughes) *chsd ldrs: pushed into ld 1 1/2f out: rdn and jnd 1f out: hdd 1/2f out: no ex* **5/1**[1]

65-0 **3** 1 3/4 **Great Prospector (IRE)**[28] 1415 4-8-13 **94**........................ PaulHanagan 4 97
(Richard Fahey) *mid-div: hdwy gng wl 3f out: ev ch 2f out: drvn in 3rd 1f out: rdn fnl f: one pce* **7/1**[3]

24-3 **4** hd **So Beloved**[14] 1763 9-9-10 **105**........................(h) DavidNolan 13 108
(David O'Meara) *hld up: drvn to chse ldrs over 1f out: rdn in 4th fnl 1f: no ex* **16/1**

-003 **5** 3 3/4 **Wahash (IRE)**[8] 1912 5-9-1 **96**........................ SeanLevey 1 89
(Richard Hannon) *trckd ldrs: pushed along and cl up 2f out: sn rdn and lost pl: no ex fnl f* **5/1**[1]

060- **6** 2 3/4 **Burnt Sugar (IRE)**[202] 8029 7-9-9 **104**........................ BenCurtis 9 90
(Roger Fell) *hld up: pushed along and effrt 2f out: reminders and one pce fnl f* **16/1**

000- **7** 1 1/4 **Golden Apollo**[217] 7512 5-9-2 **97**........................ RachelRichardson 10 80
(Tim Easterby) *mid-div on outer: pushed along and hdwy 3f out: sn drvn and wknd* **33/1**

221- **8** 1/2 **Lord Oberon**[168] 9004 4-9-0 **95**........................ CliffordLee 12 76
(K R Burke) *hld up: drvn 3f out: reminder over 1f out: no imp* **6/1**[2]

502- **9** 3/4 **Cold Stare (IRE)**[168] 9004 4-8-13 **94**........................ JamesDoyle 6 74
(David O'Meara) *hld up: pushed along and hdwy 3f out: drvn and cl enough 2f out: rdn and wknd over 1f out* **7/1**[3]

300- **10** shd **Growl**[203] 7977 7-8-11 **97**........................ ConnorMurtagh(5) 2 76
(Richard Fahey) *trckd ldrs: rdn and wknd over 1f out* **12/1**

323- **11** 1 1/4 **Shady McCoy (USA)**[168] 9004 9-9-5 **100**........................ RichardKingscote 8 76
(Ian Williams) *slowly away: bhd: last 4f out: pushed along 2f out: no imp* **16/1**

-600 **12** 1 3/4 **Masham Star (IRE)**[14] 1753 5-9-1 **96**........................ PJMcDonald 3 67
(Mark Johnston) *led: disp ld after 3f: pushed along and hdd 3f out: drvn 2f out: sn rdn and wknd* **8/1**

6-00 **13** 1/2 **Double Up**[65] 843 8-8-11 **92**........................(t) JasonWatson 5 62
(Ian Williams) *prom: disp ld after 3f: led 3f out: drvn 2f out: rdn and hdd 1 1/2f out: sn dropped away* **50/1**

03-0 **14** 11 **Rufus King**[9] 1891 4-9-3 **98**........................ FrannyNorton 7 40
(Mark Johnston) *bhd: drvn 2f out: dropped to last over 1f out* **25/1**

1m 31.29s (-0.11) **Going Correction** +0.575s/f (Yiel) **14 Ran SP% 128.9**
Speed ratings (Par 109): **112,110,108,108,104 100,99,98,98,97 96,94,93,81**
CSF £50.56 CT £316.12 TOTE £10.90: £3.70, £2.20, £2.70; EX 111.50 Trifecta £562.60.
Owner Ross Harmon **Bred** Schneider Adolf **Trained** Settrington, N Yorks

FOCUS
A good competitive handicap.

2101 BETWAY H'CAP 1m 37y
2:40 (2:42) (Class 5) (0-75,75) 3-Y-O

£4,851 (£1,443; £721; £360; £300; £300) **Stalls Low**

Form RPR
53-4 **1** **Pour Me A Drink**[14] 1755 3-9-7 **75**........................ PJMcDonald 10 84
(Clive Cox) *hld up in midfield: hdwy over 2f out: rdn and disp ld over 1f out: led ins fnl f: styd on wl* **7/2**[1]

455- **2** 1/2 **Ouzo**[185] 8548 3-9-3 **71**........................ SeanLevey 17 79
(Richard Hannon) *hld up: hdwy 3f out: effrt and slt ld over 1f out to ins fnl f: kpt on: hld nr fin* **6/1**[2]

440 **3** shd **Cardano (USA)**[32] 1346 3-8-8 **62**........................ DavidEgan 8 70
(Ian Williams) *hld up: shkn up 1/2-way: hdwy and disp ld over 1f out to ins fnl f: edgd lft: kpt on same pce towards fin* **20/1**

66-4 **4** 2 1/2 **Ventura Bay (IRE)**[19] 1656 3-8-7 **66**........................ ConnorMurtagh(5) 7 68
(Richard Fahey) *led: rdn over 2f out: hdd over 1f out: no ex ins fnl f* **9/1**

253- **5** 2 **Snow Storm (IRE)**[172] 8888 3-9-6 **74**........................ HectorCrouch 12 72
(Saeed bin Suroor) *hld up: hdwy over 2f out: rdn and ev ch over 1f out: wknd ins fnl f* **9/1**

456- **6** 2 **Euro No More (IRE)**[200] 8091 3-8-13 **67**........................ GrahamLee 3 60
(Keith Dalgleish) *midfield: lost pl after 3f: rdn over 3f out: kpt on fr over 1f out: nvr able to chal* **50/1**

005- **7** 2 3/4 **Junior Rip (IRE)**[121] 9725 3-8-7 **61**........................ JasonWatson 16 48
(Roger Charlton) *hld up: hdwy and prom over 2f out: hung lft and wknd over 1f out* **20/1**

425 **7** dht **Rakastava (IRE)**[47] 1139 3-8-13 **67**........................ GeorgeDowning 6 54
(Mick Channon) *t.k.h early in rr: rdn along 3f out: hdwy over 1f out: nvr rchd ldrs* **33/1**

400- **9** 9 **Frankadore (IRE)**[199] 8108 3-9-5 **73**........................ RichardKingscote 14 39
(Tom Dascombe) *s.i.s: sn cl up: rdn over 2f out: hung lft and wknd wl over 1f out* **7/1**

21-0 **10** 1 1/2 **Jem Scuttle (USA)**[10] 1857 3-9-4 **72**........................(t) DavidNolan 13 35
(Declan Carroll) *prom tl rdn and lost pl over 2f out: sn struggling* **14/1**

015- **11** 2 1/4 **Our Rodney (IRE)**[177] 8774 3-8-9 **70**........................ EllaMcCain(7) 9 27
(Donald McCain) *in tch: drvn and outpcd over 2f out: sn btn* **33/1**

-321 **12** 4 1/2 **Lee Roy**[45] 1174 3-9-0 **68**........................ KierenFox 4 15
(Michael Attwater) *midfield: struggling 3f out: btn fnl 2f: lost shoe (trainer's rep said colt was unsuited by the soft going and would prefer a quicker surface; vet reported the colt lost its right hind shoe)* **12/1**

55-5 **13** 6 **Ventura Glory**[35] 1285 3-8-11 **70**........................ SeamusCronin(5) 11
(Richard Hannon) *cl up tl rdn and wknd over 2f out* **14/1**

03-4 **14** 1 1/4 **Call Him Al (IRE)**[25] 1504 3-8-7 **61**........................ PaulHanagan 2
(Richard Fahey) *prom: rdn over 3f out: wknd over 2f out (jockey said gelding hung left and the bit slipped through the gelding's mouth)* **14/1**

03-5 **15** 1 **Spirit Of Lund (IRE)**[25] 1504 3-9-7 **75**........................ AndrewMullen 1
(Iain Jardine) *dwlt: bhd: struggling 3f out: sn btn (jockey said gelding suffered interference in the back straight)* **13/2**[3]

1m 48.93s (4.03) **Going Correction** +0.575s/f (Yiel) **15 Ran SP% 127.4**
Speed ratings (Par 98): **102,101,101,98,96 94,92,92,83,81 79,74,68,67,66**
CSF £22.95 CT £397.03 TOTE £4.10: £2.10, £2.60, £10.00; EX 29.20 Trifecta £918.20.
Owner Paul & Clare Rooney **Bred** Wood Hall Stud **Trained** Lambourn, Berks

FOCUS
Plenty of unexposed runners here, and the first three were making their handicap debuts.

2102 BETWAY BRITISH EBF FILLIES' NOVICE STKS (PLUS 10 RACE) (DIV I) 1m 37y
3:15 (3:17) (Class 5) 3-Y-O £4,851 (£1,443; £721; £360) Stalls Low

Form RPR
1 **Search For Light (IRE)** 3-9-0 0 PatCosgrave 6 81
(Saeed bin Suroor) *slowly away: sn rcvrd to go prom: pushed into ld 2f out: rdn in 1/2 l ld ent fnl f: almost jnd by runner-up 1/2f out: drifted lft and bmpd rival: r.o: jst hld on* **5/1**[3]
55- 2 shd **Thanks Be**[193] 8295 3-9-0 0 (h[1]) StevieDonohoe 7 80
(Charlie Fellowes) *mid-div: hdwy into 3rd 3f out: drvn 2f out: rdn to chal wnr ent fnl f: almost alongside 1/2f out: bmpd as wnr drifted lft: r.o: jst hld* **11/1**
3 3 **Tabassor (IRE)** 3-9-0 0 JamesDoyle 1 73
(Charles Hills) *trckd ldrs: pushed along in 4th 2f out: reminder over 1f out: drvn into 3rd ins fnl f: nt pce of first two* **16/1**
4 ½ **Orchidia (IRE)** 3-9-0 0 JasonWatson 4 72
(Roger Charlton) *hld up: pushed along 2f out: drvn and rn green over 1f out: kpt on under hand riding fnl f* **16/1**
5 hd **Moll Davis (IRE)** 3-9-0 0 EoinWalsh 3 71
(George Scott) *hld up: pushed along and hdwy over 2f out: reminder 1 1/2f out: kpt on under hand riding fnl f* **25/1**
61- 6 4 **Dashed**[172] 8896 3-9-7 0 DavidEgan 8 69
(Roger Varian) *led: narrow ld 3f out: drvn and hdd 2f out: rdn over 1f out: sn wknd* **6/5**[1]
4 7 3½ **Maggi Rockstar (IRE)**[15] 1740 3-9-0 0 JosephineGordon 5 54
(Paul D'Arcy) *mid-div: pushed along in 5th 3f out: wkng whn reminder 2f out* **8/1**
0-6 8 2¼ **Dinah Washington (IRE)**[11] 1834 3-9-0 0 LouisSteward 9 49
(Michael Bell) *bhd and sn detached fr pack: jnd rest of runners over 4f out: drvn over 2f out: reminders over 1f out: no imp* **66/1**
9 10 **Sibylline** 3-8-9 0 DylanHogan(5) 12 26
(David Simcock) *bhd: drvn 3f out: no ch fr 2f out* **50/1**
1 10 ½ **Robotique Danseur (FR)**[29] 1400 3-9-7 0 PJMcDonald 2 32
(K R Burke) *mid-div: pushed along 3f out: drvn 2f out: wknd over 1f out: eased fnl f (trainer's rep could offer no explanation for the filly's performance, other than it may have been unsuited by the soft going, having only ever raced on an all-weather surface previously)* **9/2**[2]
1m 49.94s (5.04) **Going Correction** +0.575s/f (Yiel) **10 Ran SP% 118.8**
Speed ratings (Par 95): **97,96,93,93,93 89,85,83,73,72**
CSF £58.84 TOTE £5.70: £1.70, £2.60, £3.20; EX 53.70 Trifecta £400.30.
Owner Godolphin **Bred** Godolphin **Trained** Newmarket, Suffolk
■ Stewards' Enquiry : Stevie Donohoe caution: careless riding

FOCUS
The faster of the two divisions by 1.28sec. The second has been rated in line with her debut run for now.

2103 BETWAY BRITISH EBF FILLIES' NOVICE STKS (PLUS 10 RACE) (DIV II) 1m 37y
3:45 (3:52) (Class 5) 3-Y-O £4,851 (£1,443; £721; £360) Stalls Low

Form RPR
6 1 **La Voix Magique**[15] 1740 3-9-0 0 FrannyNorton 8 82
(Steph Hollinshead) *hld up: hdwy to chse ldrs 2f out: drvn to chal and n.m.r over 1f out: in clr and led ent fnl f: rdn clr last 1/2 f* **16/1**
634- 2 3 **I Am Magical**[255] 6152 3-9-0 76 StevieDonohoe 9 75
(Charlie Fellowes) *chsd ldrs: pushed along in 4th 2f out: rdn over 1f out: hdwy into 2nd 1/2f out: kpt on: nt pce of wnr* **11/2**[3]
0- 3 2¼ **Infuse (IRE)**[203] 7981 3-9-0 0 JasonWatson 12 70
(Roger Charlton) *chsd ldr: shkn up 2f out: drvn and wandered over 1f out: kpt on fnl f: tk 3rd nr fin* **3/1**[2]
1- 4 nk **Conga**[232] 7015 3-9-7 0 SamJames 11 76
(Kevin Ryan) *led: pushed along in 1 l ld 2f out: rdn in narrow ld 1f out: hdd ent fnl f: sn wknd* **8/1**
4-6 5 2¼ **Shamkha (IRE)**[32] 1346 3-9-0 0 FergusSweeney 6 64
(Richard Hannon) *hld up: pushed along 3f out: reminders 1 1/2f out: no imp* **28/1**
21- 6 hd **Listen To The Wind (IRE)**[177] 8771 3-9-7 0 JamesDoyle 5 70
(William Haggas) *trckd ldrs: pushed along in 3rd 2f out: drvn 1f out: no ex fnl f* **13/8**[1]
7 20 **Universal Effect** 3-9-0 0 (h[1]) JackMitchell 10 17
(David Lanigan) *bhd: pushed along and no ch fr 2f out* **25/1**
8 4 **Nespola** 3-9-0 0 DavidEgan 4 8
(Roger Varian) *hld up: drvn and wknd over 2f out* **13/2**
0 9 17 **Mooteram (IRE)**[15] 1740 3-9-0 0 GeorgeDowning 3
(Mick Channon) *slowly away: bhd: drvn and lost tch over 3f out* **50/1**
1m 51.22s (6.32) **Going Correction** +0.575s/f (Yiel) **9 Ran SP% 118.1**
Speed ratings (Par 95): **91,88,85,85,83 83,63,59,42**
CSF £101.54 TOTE £16.10: £2.70, £1.70, £1.50; EX 94.30 Trifecta £438.60.
Owner Ray Bailey And Steph Hollinshead **Bred** Ray Bailey **Trained** Upper Longdon, Staffs

FOCUS
This was the slower of the two divisions, although conditions were not getting any better. The level is a bit fluid, and the second and fourth could back the form being rated a bit higher on face value.

2104 BETWAY STUBSHAW CROSS H'CAP 1m 2f 100y
4:20 (4:22) (Class 4) (0-80,81) 4-Y-O+
£7,115 (£2,117; £1,058; £529; £300; £300) Stalls Centre

Form RPR
046- 1 **Lord Of The Rock (IRE)**[55] 8476 7-9-9 81 GrahamLee 15 89
(Lawrence Mullaney) *pressed ldr: led over 1f out: edgd lft u.p ins fnl f: hld on wl towards fin* **14/1**
320- 2 nk **Chingachgook**[48] 6147 4-9-0 72 ConnorBeasley 10 79
(Tristan Davidson) *prom: effrt and ev ch over 1f out to ins fnl f: kpt on: hld nr fin* **11/2**[3]
4-00 3 1¼ **Music Seeker (IRE)**[17] 1695 5-8-8 73 (t) CianMacRedmond(7) 1 78
(Declan Carroll) *chsd ldrs: effrt and ch over 1f out: kpt on same pce ins fnl f* **11/1**
0-03 4 nk **Sands Chorus**[14] 1757 7-9-1 78 (p) TheodoreLadd(5) 9 82
(Scott Dixon) *led: rdn over 2f out: hdd over 1f out: kpt on same pce ins fnl f* **7/1**
53-3 5 nk **Saryshagann (FR)**[21] 1588 6-9-9 81 DavidNolan 5 84+
(David O'Meara) *hld up: nt clr run over 2f out to over 1f out: kpt on fnl f: nvr able to chal* **8/1**
654- 6 ¾ **William Hunter**[145] 9382 7-9-5 77 JasonWatson 11 79
(Alan King) *s.i.s: sn midfield: nt clr run over 2f out: effrt wl over 1f out: no imp fnl f* **14/1**
45-0 7 3½ **Appointed**[9] 1896 5-9-6 78 (t) RachelRichardson 8 73
(Tim Easterby) *hld up: hdwy and prom over 2f out: edgd lft and wknd over 1f out* **25/1**
-352 8 hd **This Girl**[49] 1106 4-9-6 78 (p) RichardKingscote 3 73
(Tom Dascombe) *hld up in midfield: effrt on outside over 2f out: wknd over 1f out* **11/4**[1]
10-3 9 ½ **Tamreer**[57] 968 4-9-6 78 (h) BenCurtis 17 72
(Roger Fell) *hld up: hdwy to chse ldrs over 3f out: rdn and outpcd 2f out: sn btn* **14/1**
40-0 10 6 **Anchises**[28] 1418 4-8-13 71 StevieDonohoe 14 54
(Rebecca Menzies) *dwlt: hld up: shortlived effrt 3f out: sn struggling: btn fnl 2f* **66/1**
264- 11 4 **Rake's Progress**[192] 8320 5-9-7 79 DavidEgan 2 54
(Heather Main) *trckd ldrs: lost pl wl over 2f out: sn struggling* **10/3**[2]
2m 21.07s (4.47) **Going Correction** +0.575s/f (Yiel) **11 Ran SP% 122.4**
Speed ratings (Par 105): **105,104,103,103,103 102,99,99,99,94 91**
CSF £92.89 CT £903.22 TOTE £14.40: £3.70, £2.30, £3.20; EX 137.40 Trifecta £1408.70.
Owner Geoff & Sandra Turnbull **Bred** Geoff & Sandra Turnbull **Trained** Great Habton, N Yorks

FOCUS
Add 8yds. A pretty open handicap. The second has been rated similar to his effort here last year.

2105 BETWAY EDGE GREEN H'CAP 1m 37y
4:50 (4:53) (Class 2) (0-105,104) 4-Y-O+
£20,231 (£6,058; £3,029; £1,514; £757; £380) Stalls Low

Form RPR
022- 1 **Mordin (IRE)**[210] 7773 5-9-3 100 (p) PatCosgrave 13 111
(Simon Crisford) *mid-div: pushed along 2f out: drvn to ld on stands' rail over 1f out: rdn clr fnl f* **7/2**[2]
213- 2 2½ **Ledham (IRE)**[193] 8299 4-8-6 89 DavidEgan 9 94
(Sir Michael Stoute) *hld up: hdwy to trck ldrs 3f out: pushed along 2f out: sn drvn: rdn to chse wnr 1f out: kpt on fnl f* **5/1**[3]
513- 3 1¼ **Just Hiss**[180] 8695 6-8-7 90 (p) RachelRichardson 4 92
(Tim Easterby) *led: rdn and hdd 2f out: kpt on wl fnl f* **20/1**
10-6 4 1½ **Knighted (IRE)**[17] 1694 4-8-7 90 AndrewMullen 12 89
(Kevin Ryan) *prom: rdn and cl up 2f out: wknd fnl f* **11/1**
02-1 5 1 **Chatez (IRE)**[14] 1753 8-9-7 104 JasonWatson 6 100
(Alan King) *mid-div: chsd ldrs 3f out: rdn and effrt over 2f out: no ex fr over 1f out* **5/2**[1]
-046 6 3 **War Glory (IRE)**[8] 1912 6-8-9 92 FergusSweeney 10 81
(Richard Hannon) *chsd ldrs: hdwy on stands' side to ld 2f out: rdn and hdd over 1f out: wknd fnl f* **20/1**
600- 7 1¼ **Borderforce (FR)**[182] 8634 6-8-9 92 GrahamLee 11 79
(George Baker) *hld up: pushed along 3f out: rdn over 1f out: no imp* **18/1**
60-3 8 ¾ **Gabrial (IRE)**[28] 1414 10-9-7 104 PaulHanagan 7 89
(Richard Fahey) *hld up: pushed along over 2f out: sn rdn: no imp* **12/1**
02-0 9 3 **Escobar (IRE)**[14] 1753 5-9-5 102 (t) DavidNolan 2 80
(David O'Meara) *hld up: drvn 2f out: rdn over 1f out: no imp* **5/1**[3]
-230 10 6 **Cosmeapolitan**[28] 1422 6-8-13 96 NicolaCurrie 1 60
(Alan King) *slowly away: bhd: nvr a factor (jockey said gelding was never travelling)* **18/1**
6- 11 2¾ **New Look (FR)**[240] 4-7-12 88 RobertDodsworth(7) 3 46
(Tim Easterby) *a bhd* **33/1**
1m 48.16s (3.26) **Going Correction** +0.575s/f (Yiel) **11 Ran SP% 123.1**
Speed ratings (Par 109): **106,103,102,100,99 96,95,94,91,85 83**
CSF £22.03 CT £324.15 TOTE £4.50: £1.70, £1.80, £5.70; EX 21.70 Trifecta £370.10.
Owner Abdullah Saeed Al Naboodah **Bred** Bernard Cooke **Trained** Newmarket, Suffolk

FOCUS
A good handicap and unsurprisingly the quickest of the five races run over the trip on the card. The second has been rated similar to his autumn AW form.

2106 BETWAY HEED YOUR HUNCH H'CAP 1m 37y
5:25 (5:28) (Class 5) (0-70,70) 4-Y-O+
£4,851 (£1,443; £721; £360; £300; £300) Stalls Low

Form RPR
500- 1 **Bristol Missile (USA)**[199] 8113 5-9-0 60 (w) PatCosgrave 17 71+
(Richard Price) *hld up: gd hdwy 2f out: pushed into ld 1f out: rdn clr fnl f: pushed out nr fin: comf* **10/1**
0061 2 2¼ **Bell Heather (IRE)**[30] 1387 6-9-3 63 (p) DavidEgan 12 68
(Patrick Morris) *chsd ldr: trckd across to stands' rail to ld 3f out: drvn and hdd 1f out: rdn fnl f: no ex* **9/1**
440- 3 6 **Gamesters Icon**[186] 8507 4-9-4 64 GrahamLee 5 55
(Oliver Greenall) *chsd ldrs: pushed along in 3rd 3f out: rdn over 1f out: kpt on fnl f* **10/1**
00-0 4 ½ **Spirit Of Sarwan (IRE)**[29] 1399 5-8-10 61 (p) BenSanderson(5) 9 51
(Stef Keniry) *hld up: rdn and hdwy over 2f out: 5th 1f out: kpt on into 4th fnl f* **50/1**
03-3 5 ¾ **Shazzab (IRE)**[10] 1850 4-9-1 61 (p) PaulHanagan 16 49
(Richard Fahey) *mid-div: pushed along on stands' rail 3f out: rdn over 1f out: one pce fnl f* **8/1**
00- 6 1¼ **Milan Reef (IRE)**[166] 9029 4-9-0 60 JosephineGordon 13 45
(David Loughnane) *led after 2f: hdd 3f out: rdn and lost pl over 2f out: no ex* **20/1**
0-11 7 2¾ **Citta D'Oro**[42] 1231 4-9-2 62 (p) LiamJones 11 41
(James Unett) *hld up: pushed along and n.m.r 3f out: drvn over 2f out: sn rdn: no imp* **15/2**[3]
-004 8 2¼ **Staplegrove (IRE)**[12] 1813 4-9-10 70 SamJames 7 44
(Philip Kirby) *mid-div: pushed along 3f out: sn drvn: no imp* **20/1**
2163 9 9 **Magic Mirror**[24] 1518 6-9-1 61 (p) PJMcDonald 1 14
(Mark Rimell) *mid-div: pushed along to chse ldrs 3f out: sn drvn and wknd* **7/2**[1]
0640 10 3¼ **Gabrial's Kaka (IRE)**[11] 1836 9-8-13 59 AdamMcNamara 6 5
(Patrick Morris) *bhd: pushed along 3f out: rdn and wknd over 2f out (jockey said gelding was never travelling)* **16/1**
400- 11 ¾ **Lagenda**[150] 9285 6-9-7 67 DavidNolan 3 11
(Liam Bailey) *hld up: drvn 3f out: rdn and wknd over 2f out* **6/1**[2]
-061 12 ½ **Takeonefortheteam**[17] 1675 4-9-3 63 NicolaCurrie 4 6
(Mark Loughnane) *slowly away: bhd: pushed along and effrt 3f out: rdn and wknd over 2f out (jockey said gelding was unsuited by the soft ground and would prefer a quicker surface)* **12/1**
0364 13 9 **Captain Pugwash (IRE)**[19] 1648 5-9-0 65 (b) DylanHogan(5) 10
(Stef Keniry) *led 2f: chsd ldrs whn hdd: drvn and lost pl 3f out: sn rdn and wknd* **10/1**

1054 **14** *16* **Cashel (IRE)**[26] 1479 4-9-7 **67**.................................... AlistairRawlinson 2
(Michael Appleby) *mid-div: drvn and dropped away over 3f out (jockey said gelding was never travelling)* **10/1**

1m 49.09s (4.19) **Going Correction** +0.575s/f (Yiel) **14** Ran SP% **130.8**
Speed ratings (Par 103): **102,99,93,93,92 91,88,86,77,74 73,72,63,47**
CSF £103.53 CT £976.23 TOTE £11.50: £3.80, £3.30, £3.40; EX 100.00 Trifecta £1859.20.
Owner Mrs K Oseman **Bred** Kenneth L Ramsey & Sarah K Ramsey **Trained** Ullingswick, H'fords

FOCUS
The first two finished nicely clear and the winner looks improved for a wind operation. The second has been rated to her recent AW form.
T/Plt: £26,649.60 to a £1 stake. Pool: £91,265.90 - 2.50 winning units T/Qpdt: £732.60 to a £1 stake. Pool: £8,999.13 - 9.09 winning units **Keith McHugh & Richard Young**

1556 LEICESTER (R-H)
Saturday, April 27

OFFICIAL GOING: Good to firm (good on the bends; watered; 7.8)
Wind: Blustery Weather: Overcast

2107 DESFORD H'CAP 6f
1:40 (1:42) (Class 4) (0-80,82) 4-Y-O+
£5,530 (£1,645; £822; £411; £300; £300) **Stalls High**

Form RPR

-235 **1** **Last Page**[31] 1356 4-8-12 **77**....................................(h[1]) LauraCoughlan(7) 3 86
(David Loughnane) *s.i.s: sn pushed along in rr: hdwy over 1f out: r.o to ld wl ins fnl f* **7/1**

6-00 **2** *1 1/4* **Firmdecisions (IRE)**[22] 1561 9-9-4 **76**.................... SilvestreDeSousa 10 81
(Nigel Tinkler) *mid-div: lost pl over 4f out: hdwy over 1f out: rdn to ld ins fnl f: sn hdd: styd on same pce* **12/1**

3400 **3** *2* **Smokey Lane (IRE)**[12] 1822 5-9-1 **73**............................ HarryBentley 5 72
(David Evans) *mid-div: hdwy 1/2-way: sn rdn: styd on to go 3rd nr fin* **5/1**[2]

4-60 **4** *1/2* **Big Lachie**[12] 1822 5-9-2 **74**.................................... GeraldMosse 4 71
(Mark Loughnane) *hld up: hdwy 2f out: rdn to chse ldr and edgd lft over 1f out: ev ch ins fnl f: styd on same pce* **6/1**[3]

5310 **5** *hd* **A Sure Welcome**[32] 1342 5-9-2 **74**..............................(b) LiamKeniry 9 70
(John Spearing) *led: rdn over 1f out: hdd and no ex ins fnl f* **12/1**

-500 **6** *1 3/4* **Top Boy**[31] 1357 9-8-13 **71**....................................(v) PaddyMathers 7 62
(Derek Shaw) *in rr and pushed along over 4f out: hdwy over 1f out: styd on same pce wl ins fnl f* **25/1**

4224 **7** *5* **Enthaar**[12] 1822 4-9-2 **74**....................................(t) JimCrowley 2 49
(Stuart Williams) *mid-div: hung rt fr 1/2-way: hdwy over 2f out: rdn over 1f out: nt clr run sn after: wknd ins fnl f* **9/2**[1]

4023 **8** *nk* **Madrinho (IRE)**[31] 1357 6-9-0 **77**........................ PoppyBridgwater(5) 16 51
(Tony Carroll) *s.i.s: swtchd rt over 2f out: hdwy over 1f out: nt trble ldrs (jockey said gelding was never travelling)* **12/1**

-004 **9** *hd* **Bungee Jump (IRE)**[8] 1915 4-9-3 **78**...................... MeganNicholls(3) 1 51
(Grace Harris) *prom: chsd ldr over 4f out: rdn over 2f out: lost 2nd over 1f out: wknd ins fnl f (jockey said filly took a false step approximately 2 furlongs out)* **17/2**

200- **10** *1 3/4* **Englishman**[232] 7013 9-9-6 **78**.................................... ShaneKelly 13 46
(Milton Bradley) *hld up in tch: rdn over 2f out: wknd over 1f out* **50/1**

30-3 **11** *1/2* **Handytalk (IRE)**[19] 1654 6-9-6 **78**........................... AndreaAtzeni 14 44
(Rod Millman) *chsd ldrs: rdn and lost pl over 2f out: n.d after (jockey said gelding hung right-handed under pressure)* **10/1**

2212 **12** *1/2* **Kraka (IRE)**[22] 1565 4-9-0 **72**..............................(v) KieranO'Neill 15 36
(Christine Dunnett) *prom: rdn over 2f out: wknd over 1f out (jockey said gelding was never travelling)* **12/1**

30-0 **13** *1 1/2* **The Gates Of Dawn (FR)**[31] 1356 4-9-7 **79**..............(p[1]) NicolaCurrie 11 39
(George Baker) *prom: rdn 1/2-way: wknd over 1f out (jockey said gelding stopped quickly)* **33/1**

00R0 **14** *hd* **Gold Hunter (IRE)**[31] 1357 9-8-9 **67**........................ RaulDaSilva 12 26
(Steve Flook) *chsd ldrs: rdn 1/2-way: wknd wl over 1f out* **40/1**

24-0 **15** *7* **Boy In The Bar**[27] 1459 8-9-7 **82**........................(p) CameronNoble(3) 6 19
(Ian Williams) *s.s and rdr lost iron leaving stalls: outpcd (jockey said he lost his iron leaving the stalls)* **20/1**

1m 11.59s (-0.51) **Going Correction** -0.05s/f (Good) **15** Ran SP% **128.0**
Speed ratings (Par 105): **101,99,96,96,95 93,86,86,86,83 83,82,80,80,70**
CSF £88.66 CT £481.33 TOTE £8.60: £2.80, £3.50, £3.00; EX 114.10 Trifecta £1022.70.
Owner Philip G Harvey **Bred** Philip Graham Harvey **Trained** Tern Hill, Shropshire

FOCUS
A fairly decent sprint handicap on ground officially described as good to firm, good on the bends. The pack raced towards the stands' side but the first two horses home challenged towards the far side in the final furlong. The winning time concurred with the going assessment, although there were some loose patches on top.

2108 BIRSTALL NOVICE STKS (PLUS 10 RACE) 5f
2:15 (2:15) (Class 4) 2-Y-O **£3,946** (£1,174; £586; £293) **Stalls High**

Form RPR

3 **1** **Chattanooga Boy (IRE)**[15] 1733 2-9-5 0.......................... HarryBentley 7 72
(George Scott) *hmpd s: trckd ldrs: rdn to ins fnl f: hung rt: jst hld on* **13/8**[1]

032 **2** *shd* **Heer We Go Again**[14] 1758 2-9-5 0.............................. JimCrowley 5 72
(David Evans) *led: rdn and hdd ins fnl f: styd on* **7/1**

0 **3** *1/2* **Richard R H B (IRE)**[28] 1416 2-9-5 0........................ TrevorWhelan 1 70
(David Loughnane) *s.i.s: hdwy over 3f out: jnd ldr 1/2-way: rdn and ev ch fr over 1f out: unable qck nr fin (jockey said colt ran green)* **40/1**

4 *3* **Mr Kodi (IRE)** 2-9-5 0.. JFEgan 4 59
(David Evans) *sn prom and pushed along: rdn 1/2-way: styd on same pce fnl f* **20/1**

5 *nk* **Gobi Sunset** 2-9-5 .... SilvestreDeSousa 9 58+
(Mark Johnston) *edgd rt s: prom: pushed along and lost pl 4f out: n.d after* **15/8**[2]

6 *3 1/4* **Bravo Faisal (IRE)** 2-9-5 0.. TonyHamilton 6 46
(Richard Fahey) *s.s: sn hung rt and pushed along: nvr on terms* **5/1**[3]

0 **7** *2* **Grace Plunkett**[19] 1642 2-9-0 0................................ TomMarquand 3 34
(Richard Spencer) *chsd ldrs: rdn 1/2-way: wknd over 1f out* **25/1**

1m 1.61s (-0.19) **Going Correction** -0.05s/f (Good) **7** Ran SP% **113.1**
Speed ratings (Par 94): **99,98,98,93,92 87,84**
CSF £13.10 TOTE £1.90: £1.50, £2.60; EX 9.40 Trifecta £156.10.
Owner W J and T C O Gredley **Bred** Rathbarry Stud **Trained** Newmarket, Suffolk

FOCUS
A fair juvenile novice sprint. The favourite got up late to edge an exciting three-way go in the final furlong in a photo-finish. The opening level is fluid.

2109 EBF STALLIONS KING RICHARD III STKS (LISTED RACE) 7f
2:45 (2:45) (Class 1) 4-Y-O+
£34,026 (£12,900; £6,456; £3,216; £1,614; £810) **Stalls High**

Form RPR

530- **1** **Hey Gaman**[189] 8407 4-9-2 113.................................... FrankieDettori 2 116
(James Tate) *mde all: rdn and edgd lft over 1f out: styd on wl: comf* **9/4**[1]

310- **2** *2 1/4* **Larchmont Lad (IRE)**[265] 5780 5-9-2 110..................(p) JamieSpencer 6 109
(Joseph Tuite) *chsd ldrs: lost pl over 4f out: sn pushed along: rdn over 1f out: r.o to go 2nd nr fin: no ch w wnr* **14/1**

3130 **3** *hd* **Cardsharp**[8] 1922 4-9-2 109... WilliamBuick 4 108
(Mark Johnston) *w wnr tl over 4f out: remained handy: rdn over 2f out: edgd lft over 1f out: styd on same pce ins fnl f* **7/1**

124- **4** *nk* **Laugh A Minute**[168] 9003 4-9-2 107........................... AndreaAtzeni 1 108
(Roger Varian) *hld up in tch: racd keenly: rdn over 1f out: styd on same pce ins fnl f* **9/2**[3]

100- **5** *2 1/4* **Eqtidaar (IRE)**[231] 7062 4-9-2 112.............................. JimCrowley 3 102
(Sir Michael Stoute) *s.i.s: racd keenly: hdwy over 4f out: rdn over 1f out: wknd ins fnl f* **11/4**[2]

431- **6** *1 1/4* **Donjuan Triumphant (IRE)**[168] 9003 6-9-5 112...... SilvestreDeSousa 5 101
(Andrew Balding) *s.i.s: racd keenly and hdwy over 5f out: shkn up over 2f out: styd on same pce fr over 1f out* **9/2**[3]

1m 22.27s (-3.43) **Going Correction** -0.05s/f (Good) **6** Ran SP% **113.0**
Speed ratings (Par 111): **117,114,114,113,111 109**
CSF £32.41 TOTE £2.80: £1.50, £6.00; EX 26.90 Trifecta £150.90.
Owner Sultan Ali **Bred** Rabbah Bloodstock Limited **Trained** Newmarket, Suffolk

FOCUS
A good-quality renewal of the feature Listed contest. The favourite went over towards the far-side rail and won readily from the front in under standard time. The winner has been rated in line with the better view of his form, and the second close to form, while the fourth helps set the standard.

2110 ASHBY MAGNA H'CAP 1m 3f 179y
3:25 (3:25) (Class 3) (0-90,89) 3-Y-O **£7,439** (£2,213; £1,106; £553) **Stalls Low**

Form RPR

1-1 **1** **Moonlight Spirit (IRE)**[57] 967 3-9-4 86........................ WilliamBuick 2 101
(Charlie Appleby) *chsd ldr who wnt clr 10f out: tk clsr order over 4f out: led over 3f out: pushed clr 2f out: easily* **5/6**[1]

52-1 **2** *9* **So High**[17] 1689 3-9-7 **89**.. FrankieDettori 5 92
(John Gosden) *hld up and bhd: hdwy over 3f out: shkn up to chse wnr over 2f out: rdn: hung rt and styd on same pce fr over 1f out: eased ins fnl f* **5/2**[2]

521- **3** *8* **Cape Islay (FR)**[171] 8932 3-9-4 **86**........................ SilvestreDeSousa 1 73
(Mark Johnston) *chsd ldrs: rdn and ev ch wl over 2f out: wknd wl over 1f out* **7/2**[3]

3253 **4** *hd* **Wanaasah**[15] 1730 3-8-4 **72**....................................(p[1]) KieranO'Neill 3 59
(David Loughnane) *led: clr 10f out tl c bk to the field over 4f out: hdd over 3f out: wknd over 2f out* **25/1**

2m 32.73s (-2.27) **Going Correction** -0.05s/f (Good) **4** Ran SP% **109.2**
Speed ratings (Par 102): **105,99,93,93**
CSF £3.24 TOTE £1.50; EX 3.00 Trifecta £4.90.
Owner Godolphin **Bred** Godolphin **Trained** Newmarket, Suffolk

FOCUS
15 yards added. A decent 3yo middle-distance handicap. The pace slowed before the home straight but the well-backed, odds-on favourite quickened up tellingly over 2f out in an impressive victory thereafter.

2111 QUORN H'CAP (DIV I) 1m 2f
3:55 (3:56) (Class 6) (0-60,60) 4-Y-O+
£3,169 (£943; £471; £300; £300; £300) **Stalls Low**

Form RPR

0-40 **1** *hd* **The Lords Walk**[16] 1710 6-9-1 **59**..............................(p) RyanWhile(5) 3 68
(Bill Turner) *hld up: hdwy over 3f out: chsd ldr over 1f out: sn rdn: ev ch ins fnl f: hmpd nr fin: r.o: fin 2nd: plcd 1st* **10/1**

4103 **2** **Mullarkey**[23] 1546 5-9-3 **56**....................................(t) KieranO'Neill 9 65
(John Best) *chsd ldrs: led over 2f out: rdn over 1f out: hung rt nr fin: all out: fin 1st: plcd 2nd* **6/1**[3]

0-10 **3** *2 3/4* **Kingfast (IRE)**[17] 1680 4-8-12 **51**............................ TomMarquand 5 55
(David Dennis) *chsd ldrs: rdn over 2f out: hung rt over 1f out: swtchd lft ins fnl f: styd on to go 3rd towards fin* **14/1**

3221 **4** *1* **Affluence (IRE)**[39] 1078 4-9-7 **60**............................(p) DannyBrock 16 62
(Martin Smith) *hld up: hdwy over 4f out: jnd ldr over 2f out: shkn up and ev ch over 1f out: sn rdn and hung rt: styd on same pce fnl f* **6/1**[3]

0443 **5** *3/4* **Don't Do It (IRE)**[16] 1710 4-9-1 **54**....................(v) SilvestreDeSousa 13 55
(Michael Appleby) *hld up in tch: rdn over 2f out: styd on u.p to dispute 3rd wl ins fnl f: no ex towards fin* **5/1**[2]

3544 **6** *1 1/4* **Pike Corner Cross (IRE)**[25] 1506 7-9-3 **56**................ TomQueally 2 55
(Alastair Ralph) *hld up in tch: nt clr run and outpcd over 2f out: rallied u.p over 1f out: styd on same pce ins fnl f* **14/1**

1600 **7** *1* **Prerogative (IRE)**[46] 1163 5-8-3 **49**..............(p) ElishaWhittington(7) 17 45
(Tony Carroll) *hld up: pushed along over 4f out: hdwy on outer over 1f out: no imp ins fnl f* **25/1**

512- **8** *3 3/4* **Lucky's Dream**[47] 9769 4-9-7 **60**................................ AndreaAtzeni 1 50
(Ian Williams) *chsd ldrs: rdn over 3f out: wknd over 1f out* **4/1**[1]

0032 **9** *2 1/2* **Shovel It On (IRE)**[17] 1679 4-8-8 **47**......................(bt) RaulDaSilva 14 32
(Steve Flook) *s.s: hld up: rdn over 3f out: n.d* **14/1**

0600 **10** *nk* **Seventii**[24] 1519 5-8-7 **46** oh1.. JFEgan 15 31
(Robert Eddery) *s.s: hld up: hdwy u.p over 2f out: wknd over 1f out* **50/1**

50-0 **11** *1/2* **French Flyer (IRE)**[19] 1647 4-9-2 **55**.......................... LewisEdmunds 12 39
(Rebecca Bastiman) *hld up: plld hrd: rdn over 1f out: nvr on terms* **33/1**

43-1 **12** *3 3/4* **Kirtling**[33] 1334 8-9-5 **58**......................................(t) ShaneKelly 7 37+
(Andi Brown) *s.s: hld up: nt clr run fr over 2f out tl swtchd lft over 1f out: n.d (jockey said gelding was denied a clear run)* **12/1**

0-01 **13** *1 1/4* **Medici Moon**[14] 1769 5-9-1 **54**..............................(p) RobHornby 4 29
(Richard Price) *chsd ldr tl led over 6f out: rdn and hdd over 2f out: wknd over 1f out* **16/1**

0006 **14** *11* **Golconda Prince (IRE)**[17] 1679 5-9-2 **58**................ JoshuaBryan(3) 8 13
(Mark Pattinson) *led: hdd over 6f out: chsd ldr: ev ch 3f out: sn rdn and wknd* **25/1**

00-0 **15** *nk* **Matravers**[112] 85 8-9-2 **55**...................................... GeorgeWood 6 9+
(Martin Keighley) *s.s: a in rr: wknd over 2f out (jockey said gelding was slowly away)* **66/1**

0060 **16** 1 1/4 **Baasha**[19] 1653 4-9-6 **59**............(v1) JamieSpencer 11 11
(Ed Dunlop) *hld up: racd keenly: rdn over 3f out: wknd over 2f out* **20/1**
2m 9.48s (0.28) **Going Correction** -0.05s/f (Good) **16** Ran SP% **126.8**
Speed ratings (Par 101): **95,96,93,92,92 91,90,87,85,85 84,81,80,72,71 70**
CSF £66.92 CT £870.74 TOTE £11.90: £2.70, £1.80, £4.20, £2.10; EX 70.50 Trifecta £629.00.
Owner Mrs J V Wilkinson **Bred** Aston House Stud **Trained** Sigwells, Somerset

FOCUS
15 yards added. The first division of a modest handicap. The front two fought out a ding-dong battle in the final furlong and, as the first past the post bumped the runner-up close home, the placings were reversed.

2112 QUORN H'CAP (DIV II) 1m 2f
4:30 (4:32) (Class 6) (0-60,60) 4-Y-0+
£3,169 (£943; £471; £300; £300; £300) **Stalls** Low

Form RPR
6251 **1** **False Id**[5] 1983 6-8-10 **56**............(b) LauraCoughlan(7) 9 69+
(David Loughnane) *s.i.s: hld up: plld hrd: hdwy on outer over 5f out: led over 4f out: rdn clr fr over 2f out* **11/4**[1]
-506 **2** 6 **Luna Magic**[21] 1591 5-9-2 **55**............(h) BrettDoyle 12 57
(Lydia Pearce) *hld up: hdwy over 3f out: rdn over 2f out: styd on to go 2nd nr fin* **8/1**
6654 **3** 1/2 **Hidden Dream (IRE)**[23] 1546 4-8-8 **47**............(p) KieranO'Neill 3 48
(Christine Dunnett) *chsd ldrs: rdn over 2f out: chsd wnr who was clr over 1f out: lost 2nd nr fin* **15/2**
6500 **4** 1 **Kodi Koh (IRE)**[25] 1506 4-8-0 **46** oh1............ GeorgiaDobie(7) 15 45
(Simon West) *hld up: plld hrd: hdwy and hung rt fr over 3f out: nt trble ldrs (jockey said filly hung right-handed under pressure)* **20/1**
4300 **5** 1 3/4 **Tobacco Road (IRE)**[33] 1333 9-9-2 **58**............(t) JoshuaBryan(3) 16 54
(Mark Pattinson) *hld up: styd on appr fnl f: nvr nrr* **12/1**
6023 **6** shd **Molten Lava (IRE)**[24] 1527 7-9-0 **53**............(p) PatDobbs 14 49
(Steve Gollings) *s.i.s: hdwy to ld over 7f out: hdd over 4f out: chsd wnr who sn wnt clr tl lost 2nd over 1f out: wknd ins fnl f* **5/1**[2]
065- **7** 2 **Pivello**[149] 9312 4-9-1 **54**............(w) GeorgeWood 2 46
(Tom Clover) *chsd ldrs: lost pl over 5f out: n.d after* **14/1**
0-06 **8** 6 **John Caesar (IRE)**[24] 1519 8-8-7 **46** oh1............(tp) JFEgan 10 27
(Rebecca Bastiman) *chsd ldrs: rdn over 2f out: sn wknd* **33/1**
0-62 **9** 3 1/2 **Ejabah (IRE)**[51] 1068 5-8-4 **46** oh1............ NoelGarbutt(3) 13 21
(Charles Smith) *led: hdd over 7f out: rdn and wknd over 2f out* **100/1**
40-0 **10** 3 1/2 **Dutch Coed**[19] 1648 7-9-2 **55**............ LewisEdmunds 11 24
(Nigel Tinkler) *s.i.s: rdn over 3f out: a in rr* **9/1**
0-00 **11** 2 1/2 **Faraway Fields (USA)**[57] 962 4-9-0 **60**............ JessicaCooley(7) 5 24
(Peter Hiatt) *s.i.s: hld up: a in rr* **28/1**
-160 **12** 17 **My Brother Mike (IRE)**[70] 754 5-9-5 **58**............ TonyHamilton 1
(Kevin Frost) *hld up: rdn over 3f out: a in rr (trainer's rep could offer no explanation for the gelding's performance)* **6/1**[3]
53-0 **13** 4 1/2 **Rock On Bertie (IRE)**[5] 1983 4-8-12 **51**............(p) PaddyMathers 4
(Derek Shaw) *plld hrd and prom: lost pl over 3f out: sn bhd* **14/1**
2m 9.65s (0.45) **Going Correction** -0.05s/f (Good) **13** Ran SP% **123.7**
Speed ratings (Par 101): **96,91,90,90,88 88,86,82,79,76 74,60,57**
CSF £25.18 CT £156.18 TOTE £3.50: £2.20, £3.00, £2.60; EX 26.80 Trifecta £203.40.
Owner Alex Percy **Bred** N E Poole And George Thornton **Trained** Tern Hill, Shropshire
■ Stewards' Enquiry : Laura Coughlan two-day ban: used whip above the permitted level (May 11, 13)

FOCUS
15 yards added. The second division of a modest handicap. The favourite stormed clear towards the top of the straight and wasn't for catching thereafter. The winning time was only marginally slower. The winner has been rated back to his best.

2113 LUTTERWORTH NOVICE STKS 1m 2f
5:00 (5:02) (Class 5) 3-Y-O
£3,752 (£1,116; £557; £278) **Stalls** Low

Form RPR
52- **1** **Laafy (USA)**[193] 8302 3-9-2 0............ PatDobbs 7 85
(Sir Michael Stoute) *s.i.s: rcvrd to chse ldr after 1f: led over 1f out: hdd 1f out: rallied to ld wl ins fnl f: r.o* **7/2**[3]
1-2 **2** 3/4 **Sucellus**[28] 1419 3-9-9 0............ FrankieDettori 6 91
(John Gosden) *trckd ldrs: rdn to ld 1f out: hdd and unable qck wl ins fnl f* **4/5**[1]
6 **3** 2 1/4 **Just You Wait**[28] 1417 3-9-2 0............ WilliamBuick 4 79
(Charlie Appleby) *led at stdy pce after 1f: shkn up and qcknd over 2f out: hdd over 1f out: styd on same pce ins fnl f* **9/4**[2]
0-0 **4** 2 1/4 **Enhanced**[14] 1755 3-9-2 0............ GeorgeWood 5 75
(Hughie Morrison) *hld up: hdwy over 2f out: edgd rt over 1f out: nt trble ldrs* **100/1**
5 8 **Mithmaar (IRE)** 3-9-2 0............ DaneO'Neill 1 59
(Mark Johnston) *led 1f: chsd ldrs: rdn over 3f out: wknd over 1f out* **28/1**
00 **6** 1 **Yellow Label (USA)**[19] 1652 3-9-2 0............ RobHornby 2 57
(Andrew Balding) *s.i.s: hld up: a in rr* **66/1**
0 **7** 7 **Lollipop Lady**[15] 1739 3-8-11 0............(p1) CallumShepherd 3 38
(Brian Meehan) *s.i.s: hld up: rdn over 2f out: sn wknd* **100/1**
2m 11.57s (2.37) **Going Correction** -0.05s/f (Good) **7** Ran SP% **115.5**
Speed ratings (Par 98): **88,87,85,83,77 76,71**
CSF £6.94 TOTE £4.10: £1.80, £1.10; EX 7.80 Trifecta £13.50.
Owner Salem Bel Obaida **Bred** Michael Edward Connelly **Trained** Newmarket, Suffolk

FOCUS
15 yards added. A decent 3yo novice contest. The winning time was comparatively slow off a modest gallop but still plenty of promise on show. The fourth has been rated a big improver and could be the key to the form.

2114 PEATLING PARVA H'CAP 7f
5:35 (5:37) (Class 5) (0-75,80) 3-Y-O
£3,752 (£1,116; £557; £300; £300; £300) **Stalls** High

Form RPR
432- **1** **Ramesses**[214] 7637 3-9-0 **68**............ TonyHamilton 2 77+
(Richard Fahey) *s.i.s: hdwy over 4f out: chsd ldr and hung rt over 1f out: rdn to ld ins fnl f: r.o* **3/1**[1]
001- **2** 1/2 **John Clare (IRE)**[180] 8691 3-9-2 **70**............ JohnFahy 3 77
(Pam Sly) *w ldrs: led 5f out: rdn over 1f out: hdd ins fnl f: styd on* **7/1**
430- **3** 3 1/2 **Wild Hope**[217] 7508 3-9-6 **74**............ PatDobbs 11 72
(Kevin Ryan) *chsd ldrs: rdn over 1f out: styd on same pce ins fnl f* **10/1**
20-4 **4** 3/4 **Glory**[31] 1352 3-9-8 **76**............ TomMarquand 5 72
(Richard Hannon) *s.i.s: sn prom: outpcd over 4f out: hdwy u.p over 1f out: styd on same pce ins fnl f* **15/2**
0-50 **5** 2 3/4 **Under Curfew**[15] 1729 3-8-9 **63**............ BrettDoyle 13 51
(Tony Carroll) *hld up: plld hrd early: hdwy 1/2-way: rdn over 1f out: wknd ins fnl f* **20/1**
454- **6** 3/4 **Reconnaissance**[200] 8067 3-9-3 **71**............ WilliamBuick 15 57
(Tom Clover) *s.i.s: outpcd: styd on towards fin: nvr nrr (jockey said gelding was never travelling)* **16/1**
052- **7** nse **Solfeggio (IRE)**[176] 8796 3-9-3 **71**............(h1) GeorgeWood 9 57
(Chris Wall) *s.i.s and hmpd s: shkn up over 2f out: nvr on terms* **33/1**
30-1 **8** 2 3/4 **Mawsool (IRE)**[21] 1587 3-9-7 **75**............ DaneO'Neill 8 54
(Ed Dunlop) *hmpd s: sn chsng ldrs: rdn 1/2-way: wknd over 1f out* **12/1**
44-0 **9** 3/4 **God Has Given**[10] 1857 3-9-3 **74**............ GabrieleMalune(3) 12 50
(Ian Williams) *hld up: shkn up 1/2-way: nvr nr to chal* **25/1**
00-0 **10** 1/2 **Knockabout Queen**[19] 1656 3-8-7 **64**............ MeganNicholls(3) 4 39
(Dai Burchell) *in rr and pushed along over 4f out: hdwy over 1f out: wknd fnl f (jockey said filly jumped awkwardly when leaving the stalls)* **40/1**
0-02 **11** nk **Azor Ahai**[10] 1846 3-9-12 **80**............ CallumShepherd 1 54
(Mick Channon) *w ldrs tl pushed along over 2f out: rdn and hung lft over 1f out: wknd ins fnl f (jockey said gelding hung left-handed under pressure)* **9/2**[2]
2242 **12** 1 1/4 **Derry Boy**[49] 1094 3-9-4 **72**............ JFEgan 6 43
(David Evans) *led 2f: rdn 1/2-way: wknd over 1f out (jockey said gelding was never travelling)* **11/2**[3]
225- **13** 1/2 **Miss Elsa**[195] 8231 3-8-12 **73**............ GeorgiaDobie(7) 14 43
(Eve Johnson Houghton) *prom: racd keenly: lost pl over 3f out: n.d after* **25/1**
064- **14** 2 3/4 **Elsie Violet (IRE)**[175] 8833 3-8-10 **64**............ LewisEdmunds 7 26
(Robert Eddery) *edgd lft s: hld up: bhd fr 1/2-way* **28/1**
1m 24.24s (-1.46) **Going Correction** -0.05s/f (Good) **14** Ran SP% **126.8**
Speed ratings (Par 98): **106,105,101,100,97 96,96,93,92,91 91,90,89,86**
CSF £23.27 CT £203.39 TOTE £4.00: £2.00, £2.40, £2.90; EX 27.50 Trifecta £188.60.
Owner Sir Robert Ogden **Bred** Sir Robert Ogden **Trained** Musley Bank, N Yorks

FOCUS
A fair 3yo handicap. The winning time compared quite favourably on the day and the favourite battled on well to prevail. The third has been rated close to form.
T/Plt: £117.20 to a £1 stake. Pool: £49,513.93 - 308.23 winning units T/Qpdt: £31.70 to a £1 stake. Pool: £3,603.63 - 84.12 winning units **Colin Roberts**

1893 RIPON (R-H)
Saturday, April 27

OFFICIAL GOING: Good to firm (good in places) changing to good after race 1 (1.45)
Wind: Fresh across Weather: showers

2115 MANDALE HOMES AT ROKESBY PLACE PICKHILL EBF NOVICE AUCTION STKS (PLUS 10 RACE) 5f
1:45 (1:45) (Class 4) 2-Y-O
£4,851 (£1,443; £721; £360) **Stalls** High

Form RPR
0 **1** **Manolith**[12] 1812 2-9-1............ DanielTudhope 1 76
(David O'Meara) *prom: rdn over 1f out: drvn into narrow ld 110yds out: kpt on* **16/1**
1 **2** 1/2 **Rodnee Tee**[10] 1844 2-9-2............ ConorMcGovern(3) 8 78
(David O'Meara) *led narrowly: rdn and hdd appr fnl f: remained chalng: kpt on: edgd rt towards fin* **4/1**[2]
621 **3** 1 1/4 **Birkenhead**[10] 1843 2-9-3............ DavidProbert 2 72
(Mick Channon) *pressed ldr: rdn into narrow ld appr fnl f: sn drvn: hdd 110yds out: no ex and hld in 3rd whn short of room nr fin* **4/6**[1]
4 3/4 **It's Been Noted** 2-9-0............ JaneElliott(3) 6 69
(Tom Dascombe) *in tch: pushed along 1/2-way: rdn and kpt on ins fnl f* **20/1**
5 2 **Holloa** 2-8-12............ DuranFentiman 9 57+
(Tim Easterby) *chsd ldrs: pushed along 1/2-way: no ex ins fnl f* **33/1**
0 **6** 3 **Sparkling Breeze**[14] 1759 2-8-13............ PaulMulrennan 10 47
(Michael Dods) *chsd ldrs: rdn along 1/2-way: wknd ins fnl f* **28/1**
7 3/4 **Harswell (IRE)** 2-9-1............ PhilDennis 4 46
(Liam Bailey) *dwlt: sn chsd ldrs: wknd fnl f* **33/1**
8 1 **Two Hearts** 2-8-11............ JamesSullivan 7 39
(Grant Tuer) *dwlt: hld up: pushed along and rn green: sme late hdwy whn short of room nr fin* **50/1**
9 3 1/4 **Baileys Prayer (FR)** 2-8-10............ SeanDavis(5) 3 31
(Richard Fahey) *hld up: sn pushed along: wknd over 1f out* **6/1**[3]
10 1/2 **Ice Skate** 2-8-10............ DavidAllan 5 24
(Tim Easterby) *v.s.a and wl bhd: sme late hdwy (jockey said filly was slowly away)* **25/1**
1m 0.44s (1.04) **Going Correction** +0.075s/f (Good) **10** Ran SP% **120.1**
Speed ratings (Par 94): **94,93,91,90,86 82,80,79,74,73**
CSF £74.84 TOTE £19.20: £3.40, £1.30, £1.10; EX 44.50 Trifecta £173.70.
Owner York Thoroughbred Racing **Bred** Selwood Bloodstock Ltd & R S Hoskins **Trained** Upper Helmsley, N Yorks
■ Stewards' Enquiry : Conor McGovern two-day ban: interference & careless riding (May 11, 13)

FOCUS
There were two previous winners in this novice event but overall it was probably just an average contest. The ground was good. The third has been rated similar to his recent efforts.

2116 WATCH SKY SPORTS RACING IN HD H'CAP 1m
2:20 (2:20) (Class 3) (0-90,90) 4-Y-O+
£8,715 (£2,609; £1,304; £652; £326; £163) **Stalls** Low

Form RPR
212- **1** **New Graduate (IRE)**[190] 8373 4-9-7 **90**............ DavidAllan 4 112+
(James Tate) *trckd ldrs: pushed along to ld 2f out: sn qckd clr: eased towards fin: impressive* **5/4**[1]
36-0 **2** 5 **Kaeso**[17] 1694 5-8-13 **87**............ FayeMcManoman(5) 12 94
(Nigel Tinkler) *hld up: pushed along and hdwy to go 2nd appr fnl f: kpt on but no ch w wnr* **16/1**
5410 **3** 1/2 **Fayez (IRE)**[28] 1413 5-9-5 **88**............ RobbieDowney 6 94
(David O'Meara) *s.i.s: hld up in rr: rdn along and hdwy on outer 2f out: chsd (clr) ldr appr fnl f: kpt on* **16/1**
26-5 **4** 3/4 **Crownthorpe**[34] 1308 4-8-11 **85**............ SeanDavis(5) 5 89
(Richard Fahey) *dwlt sltly: hld up: n.m.r 3f out: pushed along and hdwy over 1f out: kpt on ins fnl f* **4/1**[2]
412- **5** 1 1/2 **Garden Oasis**[292] 4754 4-8-13 **82**............ JackGarritty 15 83
(Tim Easterby) *in tch: swtchd lft to outside 2f out: sn rdn along: no ex fnl 110yds* **33/1**
30-0 **6** 1 1/4 **Highlight Reel (IRE)**[27] 1457 4-8-12 **81**............ PhilDennis 3 79
(Rebecca Bastiman) *in tch: angled lft 2f out: bit short of room over 1f out: rdn appr fnl f: no ex fnl 110yds* **40/1**

143- **7** 6 **Al Barg (IRE)**[322] 3600 4-9-3 **86**.........(b) RossaRyan 8 70
(Richard Hannon) *trckd ldrs: rdn to chal over 2f out: wknd over 1f out*
14/1

46-0 **8** 2 3/4 **Markazi (FR)**[17] 1694 5-9-6 **89**.........(b) DanielTudhope 16 67
(David O'Meara) *trckd ldrs on outer: rdn 3f out: edgd rt over 1f out: wknd*
10/1

00-0 **9** 1 1/4 **Lualiwa**[25] 1502 5-9-4 **87**.........(p) TomEaves 10 62
(Kevin Ryan) *led: rdn and hdd over 2f out: sn wknd*
40/1

-100 **10** 2 1/4 **Saint Equiano**[25] 1502 5-9-7 **90**......... JoeFanning 9 60
(Keith Dalgleish) *prom: rdn into narrow ld over 2f out: hdd 2f out: sn wknd (jockey said gelding had no more to give)*
20/1

35-0 **11** 3/4 **Mapped (USA)**[27] 1461 4-8-5 **77**......... JamieGormley(3) 11 45
(Iain Jardine) *hld up: nvr threatened*
20/1

550- **12** nk **Radio Source (IRE)**[199] 8112 4-8-9 **78**......... DuranFentiman 7 45
(Tim Easterby) *hld up: nvr threatened*
50/1

6-14 **13** 3 **Swiss Storm**[23] 1545 5-9-7 **90**......... DavidProbert 13 50
(Michael Bell) *midfield: rdn over 2f out: wknd over 1f out*
15/2[3]

114- **14** 2 **Big Storm Coming**[252] 6291 9-9-5 **88**......... DougieCostello 14 44
(John Quinn) *midfield: rdn over 2f out: sn wknd*
33/1

1m 39.37s (-1.63) **Going Correction** +0.075s/f (Good) **14 Ran SP% 126.0**
Speed ratings (Par 107): **111,106,105,104,103 102,96,93,92,89 89,88,85,83**
CSF £24.67 CT £257.93 TOTE £2.20: £1.30, £4.70, £4.30; EX 22.00 Trifecta £189.60.
Owner Saeed Manana **Bred** Rabbah Bloodstock Limited **Trained** Newmarket, Suffolk

FOCUS
Add 12yds. This looked a competitive handicap run at a good gallop, and it produced a wide-margin winner who is likely to hold his own in Pattern company. The third has been rated close to his recent AW form, with the second not far below his best.

2117 CELEBRATING PIPERS NOTE H'CAP — 6f
2:55 (2:57) (Class 2) (0-105,105) 4-Y-O+
£12,450 (£3,728; £1,864; £932; £466; £234) **Stalls** High

Form | | | | RPR

250- **1** **Reputation (IRE)**[186] 8503 6-8-6 **90**......... BarryMcHugh 13 102
(Ruth Carr) *dwlt and wnt sltly rt s: sn trckd ldrs stands' side: rdn along to ld ent fnl f: kpt on wl to draw clr*
16/1

20-1 **2** 3 **Diamond Dougal (IRE)**[19] 1654 4-8-8 **92**......... DavidProbert 7 94
(Mick Channon) *midfield stands' side: hdwy 2f out: rdn over 1f out: kpt on to go 2nd 110yds out: kpt on but no ch w wnr: 2nd of 9 in gp*
6/1[1]

026- **3** 1 **Staxton**[196] 8194 4-9-3 **101**......... DavidAllan 11 100
(Tim Easterby) *led stands' side gp and overall ldr: rdn over 1f out: hdd ent fnl f: sn drvn: lost 2nd 110yds out: no ex: 3rd of 9 in gp*
7/1[2]

3000 **4** 1/2 **Intisaab**[65] 843 8-9-7 **105**.........(p) RobbieDowney 5 103
(David O'Meara) *hld up far side: pushed along and hdwy over 1f out: kpt on to ld gp 50yds: 1st of 6 in gp*
20/1

012- **5** 1 1/4 **Gin In The Inn (IRE)**[197] 8167 6-7-11 **86**......... SeanDavis(5) 2 80
(Richard Fahey) *chsd ldrs far side: rdn to ld gp wl over 1f out: hdd in gp 50yds out: one pce: 2nd of 6 in gp*
17/2

00-5 **6** 1 1/2 **Ice Age (IRE)**[15] 1734 6-9-4 **102**......... CharlesBishop 3 91
(Eve Johnson Houghton) *prom far side: led gp over 2f out: rdn and hdd in gp over 1f out: no ex ins fnl f: 3rd of 6 in gp*
8/1

0-05 **7** 1 1/2 **Buridan (FR)**[11] 1829 4-8-4 **88**......... MartinDwyer 9 72
(Richard Hannon) *chsd ldrs stands' side: rdn 2f out: wknd ins fnl f: 4th of 9 in gp*
15/2[3]

25-6 **8** 3/4 **Flying Pursuit**[14] 1763 6-8-13 **102**.........(p) DannyRedmond(5) 15 84
(Tim Easterby) *pressed ldr stands' side: rdn 2f out: wknd ins fnl f: 5th of 9 in gp*
33/1

300- **9** shd **Arecibo (FR)**[223] 7353 4-9-2 **100**.........(v[1]) DanielTudhope 10 81
(David O'Meara) *hld up in tch stands' side: n.m.r over 2f out: pushed along and hdwy to briefly chse ldrs appr fnl f: wknd ins fnl f: 6th of 9 in gp*
16/1

0-02 **10** 3/4 **Pipers Note**[12] 1814 9-8-11 **95**......... JamesSullivan 4 74
(Ruth Carr) *hld up in tch far side: rdn over 2f out: no imp: 4th of 6 in gp*
11/1

530- **11** 1/2 **Roundhay Park**[224] 7290 4-8-9 **93**......... TomEaves 8 70
(Nigel Tinkler) *hld up stands' side: short of room 2f out and swtchd rt: nvr threatened: 7th of 9 in gp*
20/1

20-0 **12** 1 1/2 **Normandy Barriere (IRE)**[11] 1829 7-8-7 **96**......... FayeMcManoman(5) 6 68
(Nigel Tinkler) *hld up far side: nvr threatened: 5th of 6 in gp*
25/1

010- **13** 1 1/4 **Lucky Lucky Man (IRE)**[204] 7950 4-7-13 **88**......... AndrewBreslin(5) 12 56
(Richard Fahey) *slowly away: hld up on outside of stands' side gp: isolated centre fr over 2f out: edgd further rt over 1f out: nvr threatened: 8th of 9 in gp*
25/1

-061 **14** 1/2 **Teruntum Star (FR)**[10] 1847 7-9-1 **99**......... KevinStott 14 66
(Kevin Ryan) *chsd ldrs stands' side: rdn over 2f out: wknd over 1f out: last of 9 in gp*
15/2[3]

12-4 **15** 33 **Sandra's Secret (IRE)**[12] 1814 6-8-12 **96**......... JoeFanning 1
(Les Eyre) *led far side gp: hdd in gp over 2f out: sn wknd: eased (trainer said mare was lame in front)*
9/1

1m 10.98s (-1.52) **Going Correction** +0.075s/f (Good) **15 Ran SP% 122.2**
Speed ratings (Par 109): **113,109,107,107,105 103,101,100,100,99 98,96,94,94,50**
CSF £102.17 CT £769.59 TOTE £19.40: £5.40, £2.40, £3.00; EX 136.40 Trifecta £1361.60.
Owner Fulbeck Horse Syndicate Ltd **Bred** Moyns Park Estate And Stud Ltd **Trained** Huby, N Yorks

FOCUS
A competitive srpint in which they split into two groups with the top six in the draw going far side. Unlike the sprints at the previous meeting, the winner came from the stands' side group. The second has been rated close to his Windsor win.

2118 VISIT ATTHERACES.COM H'CAP — 2m
3:30 (3:32) (Class 2) (0-105,98) 4-Y-O+
£15,562 (£4,660; £2,330; £1,165; £582; £292) **Stalls** High

Form | | | | RPR

03-5 **1** **Making Miracles**[7] 1947 4-9-7 **98**......... JoeFanning 3 107
(Mark Johnston) *pressed ldr: pushed along 3f out: rdn 2f out: led jst ins fnl f: drvn and styd on*
11/10[1]

2144 **2** 1 **Lucky Deal**[7] 1947 4-9-0 **96**......... AndrewBreslin(5) 7 104
(Mark Johnston) *hld up: rdn and hdwy 3f out: drvn to chal 2f out: styd on in 2nd fnl 110yds*
6/1[3]

505- **3** 2 1/4 **Yabass (IRE)**[274] 5416 4-9-1 **92**.........(t) HollieDoyle 2 97
(Archie Watson) *led narrowly: rdn over 2f out: hdd jst ins fnl f: sn no ex*
11/2[2]

660- **4** 4 1/2 **Northwest Frontier (IRE)**[196] 8197 5-9-1 **90**.........(b) DougieCostello 8 90
(Micky Hammond) *trckd ldrs: keen early: rdn along over 3f out: outpcd and btn over 1f out*
28/1

00-0 **5** 1 3/4 **Mirsaale**[7] 1947 9-9-1 **90**.........(p) JamesSullivan 6 88
(Keith Dalgleish) *hld up: rdn 3f out: no imp*
12/1

50-0 **6** shd **Eye Of The Storm (IRE)**[7] 1947 9-8-3 **83**......... SeanDavis(5) 4 80
(Keith Dalgleish) *midfield: rdn 3f out: no imp*
6/1[3]

6-40 **7** 6 **Tor**[7] 1947 5-8-9 **87**......... JamieGormley(3) 5 77
(Iain Jardine) *sn trckd ldrs: rdn 4f out: wknd over 1f out*
20/1

3m 30.43s (-1.97) **Going Correction** +0.075s/f (Good) **7 Ran SP% 107.5**
WFA 4 from 5yo+ 2lb
Speed ratings (Par 109): **107,106,105,103,102 102,99**
CSF £7.00 CT £20.20 TOTE £1.80: £1.50, £2.50; EX 6.00 Trifecta £18.30.
Owner Acorn, Brown, Parker & Scott **Bred** Cheveley Park Stud Ltd **Trained** Middleham Moor, N Yorks

■ My Reward was withdrawn. Price at time of withdrawal 14-1. Rule 4 applies to all bets - deduction 5p in the pound.

FOCUS
Add 12yds. Quite a competitive staying handicap but it was run at a modest gallop and it favoured those who raced close to the pace. The second has been rated to his best, and the third as running a small pb, in line with the better view of his Queen's Vase form.

2119 M.C.H. HUTCHINSON MEMORIAL H'CAP — 1m 4f 10y
4:00 (4:01) (Class 2) (0-110,106) 4-Y-O+
£15,562 (£4,660; £2,330; £1,165; £582; £292) **Stalls** Centre

Form | | | | RPR

1111 **1** **King's Advice**[14] 1761 5-8-10 **95**......... JoeFanning 5 102+
(Mark Johnston) *midfield: pushed along to chse ldr 2f out: edgd rt over 1f out: rdn to ld 110yds out: styd on*
4/5[1]

040- **2** 1 **Frankuus (IRE)**[161] 9126 5-9-1 **100**.........(b) DanielTudhope 1 105
(David O'Meara) *led: rdn 2f out: drvn ins fnl f: hdd 110yds out: one pce*
7/1[3]

-312 **3** hd **Claire Underwood (IRE)**[66] 803 4-7-11 **87** oh3......... SeanDavis(5) 7 91
(Richard Fahey) *hld up: rdn over 3f out: styd on fnl f: wnt 3rd towards fin*
11/1

50-4 **4** nk **Mukhayyam**[18] 1664 7-8-0 **88**.........(p) JamieGormley(3) 2 92
(Tim Easterby) *trckd ldrs: rdn over 2f out: kpt on same pce*
15/2

5-03 **5** 1/2 **Crowned Eagle**[27] 1460 5-9-7 **106**......... DanielMuscutt 3 109
(Marco Botti) *prom: rdn over 2f out: bit outpcd whn short of room over 1f out: one pce ins fnl f (jockey said gelding became unbalanced on the undulations in the home straight)*
9/2[2]

4-06 **6** 1 1/4 **Mutamaded (IRE)**[9] 1896 6-8-4 **89**......... JamesSullivan 6 90
(Ruth Carr) *hld up: rdn over 2f out: one pce and nvr threatened*
20/1

2m 34.81s (-1.49) **Going Correction** +0.075s/f (Good) **6 Ran SP% 111.1**
Speed ratings (Par 109): **107,106,106,106,105 104**
CSF £6.88 TOTE £1.50: £1.20, £2.80; EX 7.30 Trifecta £29.60.
Owner Saeed Jaber **Bred** Rabbah Bloodstock Limited **Trained** Middleham Moor, N Yorks

FOCUS
Add 12yds. This might prove muddling form for the pace wasn't that strong and the whole field closed up in the final furlong so only around three lengths covered the six at the line. The third has been rated to her best.

2120 MANDALE HOMES THE AWARD WINNING HOUSEBUILDER NOVICE STKS (PLUS 10 RACE) — 1m 1f 170y
4:35 (4:39) (Class 4) 3-Y-O
£5,822 (£1,732; £865; £432) **Stalls** Low

Form | | | | RPR

1-3 **1** **Eightsome Reel**[10] 1856 3-9-9 0......... HayleyTurner 6 94+
(Michael Bell) *dwlt: sn trckd ldr: jnd ldr gng wl 2 out: pushed along to ld over 1f out: kpt on: cosily*
2/1[2]

5 **2** 1 1/2 **Storting**[14] 1756 3-9-2 0......... CharlesBishop 4 82+
(Mick Channon) *trckd ldrs: pushed along over 2f out: swtchd lft over 1f out: wnt 2nd jst ins fnl f: rdn and hung rt: kpt on but nvr getting to wnr*
8/1[3]

43- **3** 8 **Asad (IRE)**[172] 8895 3-9-2 0......... PaulMulrennan 3 66
(Simon Crisford) *trckd ldr: led 7f out: rdn and jnd 2f out: hdd over 1f out: wknd fnl f*
10/11[1]

0- **4** 3 1/2 **Platform Nineteen (IRE)**[183] 8608 3-9-2 0......... CliffordLee 2 59
(Michael Bell) *hld up: sn pushed along: nvr threatened*
33/1

01- **5** 3 1/4 **Sky Cross (IRE)**[263] 5822 3-9-9 0......... JoeFanning 1 59
(Mark Johnston) *led: keen early and hung lft: hdd 7f out: trckd ldr: rdn over 2f out: wknd over 1f out (jockey said colt hung left-handed)*
12/1

6 1 3/4 **Tanaawol** 3-8-11 0......... AndrewBreslin(5) 5 49
(Mark Johnston) *hld up: rdn over 3f out: wknd over 1f out*
28/1

2m 5.75s (1.15) **Going Correction** +0.075s/f (Good) **6 Ran SP% 110.9**
Speed ratings (Par 100): **100,98,92,89,87 85**
CSF £17.32 TOTE £2.30: £1.20, £2.50; EX 13.60 Trifecta £29.30.
Owner The Queen **Bred** The Queen **Trained** Newmarket, Suffolk

FOCUS
Add 12yds. They finished well strung out in this novice event in which the first two finished well clear. The pace was fair. The level is a bit fluid.

2121 MANDALE HOMES AT JUNIPER GROVE RIPON H'CAP — 5f
5:05 (5:06) (Class 4) (0-85,82) 3-Y-O
£5,692 (£1,694; £846; £423; £300; £300) **Stalls** High

Form | | | | RPR

60-0 **1** **Mark's Choice (IRE)**[9] 1894 3-8-12 **73**......... JamesSullivan 6 78
(Ruth Carr) *hld up: pushed along and hdwy 2f out: angled lft over 1f out: squeezed through gap 1f out: rdn and kpt on wl: led nr fin*
12/1

10-0 **2** nk **Aloysius Lilius (IRE)**[17] 1691 3-8-8 **69**.........(p[1]) ShaneGray 2 73
(Kevin Ryan) *dwlt: sn trckd ldrs: rdn to ld narrowly appr fnl f: sn drvn: kpt on but hdd towards fin*
12/1

1234 **3** 1 **Key To Power**[8] 1929 3-8-9 **75**......... AndrewBreslin(5) 1 75
(Mark Johnston) *sltly awkward s: midfield on outer: rdn and hdwy to chal strly appr fnl f: no ex towards fin*
13/2[3]

14-6 **4** 3/4 **Enchanted Linda**[17] 1691 3-9-3 **78**......... HollieDoyle 4 76
(Richard Hannon) *prom: rdn to ld narrowly over 2f out: hdd appr fnl f: one pce ins fnl f (jockey said filly hung left-handed)*
9/2[2]

1-42 **5** 1/2 **Wedding Date**[96] 342 3-9-6 **81**......... RossaRyan 7 77
(Richard Hannon) *dwlt: hld up: rdn over 2f out: swtchd rt ent fnl f: edgd rt and kpt on: nrst fin*
9/2[2]

130- **6** 2 **Autumn Flight (IRE)**[199] 8107 3-8-13 **74**......... DavidAllan 9 63
(Tim Easterby) *led narrowly: hdd over 2f out: rdn 2f out: bit outpcd whn sltly short of room jst ins fnl f: no ex (jockey said gelding suffered interference in the final furlong)*
11/1

01-3 **7** 2 3/4 **True Hero**[17] 1691 3-9-2 **80**......... RowanScott(3) 3 59
(Nigel Tinkler) *prom: rdn 2f out: wknd fnl f*
11/4[1]

016- **8** 3/4 **On The Stage**[199] 8107 3-9-7 **82**......... CliffordLee 8 58
(K R Burke) *hld up: rdn and sme hdwy 2f out: short of room over 1f out: wknd*
9/1

10-0 9 10 **Lovin (USA)**[65] 838 3-9-7 **82**........ DanielTudhope 5 22
(David O'Meara) *hld up: rdn over 2f out: wknd over 1f out: eased* **12/1**

59.9s (0.50) **Going Correction** +0.075s/f (Good) 9 Ran SP% **117.8**
Speed ratings (Par 100): **99,98,96,95,94 91,87,86,70**
CSF £147.67 CT £1030.22 TOTE £16.00: £2.80, £3.50, £2.20; EX 150.90 Trifecta £1980.60.
Owner Cragg Wood Racing **Bred** Northern Bloodstock Agency Ltd **Trained** Huby, N Yorks

FOCUS
A competitive 5f handicap though with just 2.5l covering the first five home the form may not be anything special. The winner has been rated back to the level of his Nottingham win, the second to his late 2yo form and the third close to her recent AW form.
T/Plt: £25.20 to a £1 stake. Pool: £59,881.23 - 1728.64 winning units T/Qpdt: £11.10 to a £1 stake. Pool: £13,060.22 - 1566.85 winning units **Andrew Sheret**

2012 WOLVERHAMPTON (A.W) (L-H)
Saturday, April 27

OFFICIAL GOING: Tapeta: standard
Wind: strong, behind Weather: showers, breezy

2122 JOHN SYLVESTER MANN'S STAG APPRENTICE H'CAP 6f 20y (Tp)
5:30 (5:31) (Class 5) (0-70,72) 4-Y-0+
£3,752 (£1,116; £557; £400; £400; £400) **Stalls Low**

Form RPR

24-1 1 **Everkyllachy (IRE)**[29] 1402 5-8-6 **58**........(v) ThoreHammerHansen(3) 3 67
(Karen McLintock) *chsd ldrs: n.m.r 2f out: sn chalng: rdn to ld 1f out: styd on wl: rdn out* **8/1**

4265 2 3/4 **Lucky Lodge**[14] 1768 9-9-4 **70**........(v) KieranSchofield(3) 4 77
(Antony Brittain) *prom: pressed ldr over 3f out tl led 2f out: sn hrd pressed and u.p: hdd 1f out: kpt on but a hld after* **5/1**[2]

4044 3 2 **Dotted Swiss (IRE)**[4] 2010 4-9-0 **63**........(b) ThomasGreatrex 7 64
(Archie Watson) *wl in tch: clsd and chsng ldrs and rdn 2f out: 3rd and kpt on same pce ins fnl f (starter reported that the filly was the subject of a third criteria failure; trainer was informed that the filly could not run until the day after passing a stalls test)* **5/1**[2]

5361 4 3/4 **Cappananty Con**[14] 1767 5-9-4 **72**........ WilliamCarver(5) 8 70
(Charlie Wallis) *awkward leaving stalls and slowly away: sn swtchd sharply lft and hld up in rr: clsd over 3f out: hdwy u.p 1f out: edgd lft and styd on ins fnl f: nvr trbld ldrs* **9/2**[1]

0033 5 1 1/4 **Mansfield**[5] 1986 6-8-7 **59**........(p[1]) TobyEley(3) 12 53
(Stella Barclay) *taken down early: hld up in tch towards rr on outer: effrt and v wd bnd wl over 1f out: hdwy 1f out: styd on ins fnl f: nvr trbld ldrs (jockey said gelding hung left-handed)* **7/1**[3]

0-00 6 1 1/4 **Red Cymbal**[22] 1574 4-8-11 **65**........(bt) StephenMooney(5) 11 55
(Anthony McCann, Ire) *midfield: effrt and swtchd lft over 1f out: kpt on but no imp ins fnl f* **20/1**

00-0 7 1/2 **Boundsy (IRE)**[14] 1767 5-9-2 **65**........ SebastianWoods 10 54
(Richard Fahey) *taken down early: in tch: short of room sn after s: effrt over 1f out: no imp whn squeezed for room and swtchd lft ins fnl f* **9/1**

2531 8 hd **Secret Potion**[17] 1682 5-8-13 **65**........ ScottMcCullagh(3) 1 53
(Ronald Harris) *pressed ldr tl over 3f out: rdn and lost pl over 2f out: wl hld fnl f* **12/1**

-445 9 4 1/2 **Poeta Brasileiro (IRE)**[14] 1767 4-8-13 **67**........ AaronMackay(5) 9 41
(Seamus Durack) *in tch in midfield on outer: hdwy to chse ldrs over 2f out: unable qck over 1f out: wknd ins fnl f* **9/1**

030- 10 1 **Alfie's Angel (IRE)**[180] 8704 5-8-10 **62**........ SeamusCronin(3) 2 32
(Milton Bradley) *led tl 2f out: sn outpcd and btn: fdd and eased wl ins fnl f* **40/1**

441- 11 7 **Cosmic Chatter**[248] 6410 9-8-13 **62**........(p) ConnorMurtagh 5 10
(Ruth Carr) *in tch: squeezed for room and dropped to rr over 3f out: bhd fnl 2f* **50/1**

1m 13.16s (-1.34) **Going Correction** -0.175s/f (Stan) 11 Ran SP% **112.0**
Speed ratings (Par 103): **101,100,97,96,94 93,92,92,86,84 75**
CSF £44.54 CT £219.18 TOTE £8.00: £2.70, £1.70, £2.30; EX 54.60 Trifecta £406.80.
Owner Ever Equine & Self Preservation Society **Bred** Mrs T Mahon **Trained** Ingoe, Northumberland

FOCUS
A run-of-the-mill sprint handicap in which the ability to secure a handy early position proved crucial.

2123 BRAD FURNISS 18TH BIRTHDAY NOVICE STKS 5f 21y (Tp)
6:00 (6:00) (Class 5) 3-Y-0+ £3,752 (£1,116; £557; £278) **Stalls Low**

Form RPR

26-2 1 **Ustath**[30] 1389 3-9-2 77........ JimCrowley 3 81
(Owen Burrows) *t.k.h: trckd ldr tl led travelling strly 2f out: pushed clr over 1f out: r.o strly: v easily* **1/5**[1]

2 6 **Casarubina (IRE)** 3-8-6 0........(t[1]) DarraghKeenan(5) 2 54
(Nick Littmoden) *t.k.h: hld up wl in tch in midfield: swtchd rt and effrt wl over 1f out: chsd clr wnr over 1f out: hung rt and one pce ins fnl f (jockey said filly hung right-handed in the home straight)* **80/1**

3 3/4 **Fairy Fast (IRE)**[113] 70 3-8-11 0........ CamHardie 6 52
(David O'Meara) *wnt rt s: hld up wl in tch in midfield: effrt in 3rd but wnr clr over 1f out: wl hld: carried rt and one pce ins fnl f* **40/1**

235- 4 3 1/2 **Finch Hatton**[200] 8073 3-9-2 71........ RaulDaSilva 5 44
(Robert Cowell) *bustled along early: chsd ldrs tl wd and lost pl bnd wl over 1f out: no ch and plugged on same pce after* **9/2**[2]

41- 5 1 1/2 **Gifted Zebedee (IRE)**[351] 2614 3-9-7 0........(p[1] w) NickyMackay 4 44
(Luke McJannet) *taken down early: led tl rdn and hdd 2f out: lost pl over 1f out: wknd fnl f* **33/1**

0- 6 1 **Mithayel Style (FR)**[186] 8512 3-8-6 0........ ThomasGreatrex(5) 1 30
(Peter Chapple-Hyam) *s.i.s: a in last pair: rn green: hung lft and wknd over 1f out* **28/1**

0- 7 7 **Ingenium (IRE)**[149] 9306 3-8-11 0........ ShaneKelly 7 5
(David O'Meara) *wnt rt s: rn green and in rr thrght* **25/1**[3]

1m 0.68s (-1.22) **Going Correction** -0.175s/f (Stan) 7 Ran SP% **115.4**
Speed ratings (Par 103): **102,92,91,85,83 81,70**
CSF £45.09 TOTE £1.10: £1.30, £6.50; EX 52.40 Trifecta £293.70.
Owner Hamdan Al Maktoum **Bred** Cheveley Park Stud Ltd **Trained** Lambourn, Berks

FOCUS
No depth to this novice event and it says a fair bit about his rivals that Ustath was sent off 1-5 despite having been beaten on all four starts.

2124 NORTHWOOD CASTINGS LTD - SPECIALISTS IN ALUMINIUM PRODUCTS H'CAP 1m 1f 104y (Tp)
6:30 (6:32) (Class 5) (0-75,76) 4-Y-0+
£3,752 (£1,116; £557; £400; £400; £400) **Stalls Low**

Form RPR

-255 1 **Global Art**[84] 552 4-9-8 **76**........ GeraldMosse 9 86
(Ed Dunlop) *s.i.s: rcvrd and hdwy to chse ldrs 8f out: effrt to press ldrs 3f out: led jst over 2f out: clr and styd on wl ins fnl f: comf* **10/3**[2]

16- 2 2 1/4 **Paco's Prince**[334] 3177 4-9-4 **72**........ EoinWalsh 8 77
(Nick Littmoden) *hld up in midfield: effrt wl over 2f out: kpt on to chse clr wnr ins fnl f: nvr a threat* **28/1**

2545 3 3 1/4 **Roman De Brut (IRE)**[29] 1399 7-8-3 **62**........ ThoreHammerHansen(5) 3 60
(Ivan Furtado) *s.i.s: swtchd rt and hdwy into midfield 7f out: clsd to press ldr over 3f out: chsd wnr but unable to match his pce jst over 2f out: lost 2nd and wknd ins fnl f* **7/2**[3]

4200 4 nk **Kadrizzi (FR)**[22] 1561 6-9-5 **73**........ TomQueally 4 71
(Dean Ivory) *hld up in midfield: outpcd and rdn over 2f out: no ch w wnr but kpt on ins fnl f* **7/1**

-505 5 3 1/4 **Arlecchino's Leap**[25] 1511 7-8-11 **68**........ GaryMahon(3) 6 59
(Mark Usher) *hld up in last pair: rdn and outpcd over 2f out: n.d after* **10/1**

6-02 6 1 1/2 **Casina Di Notte (IRE)**[22] 1566 5-8-9 **70**........(b) StefanoCherchi(7) 7 58
(Marco Botti) *sn led: hung rt and hdd bnd over 7f out: led again over 5f out tl jst over 2f out: sn btn (jockey said gelding attempted to duck right-handed approaching the bend past the winning line on the final circuit)* **2/1**[1]

/35- 7 12 **Bleu Et Noir**[216] 4956 8-9-0 **68**........(h) KieranO'Neill 2 31
(Tim Vaughan) *awkward leaving stalls and stdd leaving stalls: hld up in rr: bhd fnl 2f* **22/1**

156- 8 26 **Acker Bilk (IRE)**[218] 5907 5-9-7 **75**........(p) FrannyNorton 1
(Ronald Harris) *w ldr tl lft in ld over 5f out: hdd over 5f out: lost pl rapidly over 3f out: wl bhd and eased fnl 2f: t.o (jockey said gelding hung badly left-handed)* **20/1**

1m 58.45s (-2.35) **Going Correction** -0.175s/f (Stan) 8 Ran SP% **112.8**
Speed ratings (Par 103): **103,101,98,97,94 93,82,59**
CSF £89.75 CT £343.62 TOTE £3.40: £1.10, £4.40, £1.40; EX 49.30 Trifecta £299.60.
Owner Dr Johnny Hon **Bred** Manor Farm Stud & J E Rose **Trained** Newmarket, Suffolk
■ Stewards' Enquiry : Thore Hammer Hansen caution: careless riding

FOCUS
Modest stuff and they finished well strung out. The winner was well on top in the final furlong.

2125 GM TREBLE LTD H'CAP 1m 1f 104y (Tp)
7:00 (7:01) (Class 5) (0-70,71) 3-Y-0
£3,752 (£1,116; £557; £400; £400; £400) **Stalls Low**

Form RPR

-600 1 **Emma Point (USA)**[72] 727 3-9-6 **69**........(h) JasonWatson 6 75
(Marco Botti) *chsd ldrs tl wnt 2nd and pressing ldr over 7f out: rdn to ld jst over 1f out: edgd rt 1f out: hld on wl ins fnl f: drvn out* **11/1**

-550 2 3/4 **Robeam (IRE)**[16] 1721 3-8-2 **51** oh1........ CamHardie 9 55
(Richard Fahey) *short of room and impeded sn after s: racd in last pair: clsd on inner and nt clr run wl over 1f out: hdwy over 1f out: wnt 2nd and pressing wnr ins fnl f: kpt on but hld fnl 50yds* **18/1**

4-22 3 3/4 **Image Of The Moon**[31] 1358 3-9-7 **70**........ FrannyNorton 5 72
(Shaun Keightley) *t.k.h early: hld up in midfield: clsd to trck ldrs over 4f out: effrt and chsd wnr wl over 1f out: struggling to qckn whn shifted rt and sltly impeded 1f out: 3rd and kpt on same pce ins fnl f* **4/1**[2]

410- 4 1 1/2 **Firewater**[187] 8474 3-8-11 **65**........(p) SebastianWoods(5) 7 64
(Richard Fahey) *hld up in midfield: effrt jst over 2f out: swtchd rt jst over 1f out: swtchd rt again and sltly impeded ins fnl f: styd on wl u.p fnl 100yds: no threat to ldrs* **16/1**

46-3 5 3/4 **Canford Dancer**[45] 1171 3-9-7 **70**........ ShaneKelly 1 68
(Richard Hughes) *wnt lft s: sn rcvrd to ld and t.k.h: rdn and hdd jst over 2f out: unable qck and wknd wl ins fnl f* **6/1**

52-1 6 nk **Hermocrates (FR)**[110] 122 3-9-1 **69**........ ThoreHammerHansen(5) 11 66
(Richard Hannon) *midfield: clsd to chse ldrs over 4f out: effrt jst over 2f out: unable qck and edgd lft over 1f out: wl hld and kpt on same pce ins fnl f* **7/2**[1]

2125 7 nk **Colony Queen**[36] 1270 3-9-4 **67**........ JamieSpencer 3 63
(James Tate) *hld up in midfield: effrt whn nt clr run and swtchd rt over 1f out: kpt on ins fnl f: nvr trbld ldrs* **9/2**[3]

1242 8 1 **Dancing Jo**[19] 1656 3-9-1 **71**........ ScottMcCullagh(7) 2 65
(Mick Channon) *led: hdd after 2f: chsd ldrs after: effrt 2f out: struggling to qckn whn short of room 1f out: wknd ins fnl f* **13/2**

6530 9 3/4 **Shaleela's Dream**[26] 1481 3-9-6 **69**........ GeraldMosse 8 62
(Marco Botti) *racd in last trio: effrt over 1f out: no imp and nvr involved* **10/1**

5-00 10 4 1/2 **Champagne Marengo (IRE)**[19] 1656 3-9-2 **65**........ StevieDonohoe 12 48
(Ian Williams) *sn bhd: clsd and in tch over 4f out: bhd over 1f out* **100/1**

2m 0.85s (0.05) **Going Correction** -0.175s/f (Stan) 10 Ran SP% **117.6**
Speed ratings (Par 98): **92,91,90,89,88 88,88,87,86,82**
CSF £191.16 CT £933.06 TOTE £12.40: £3.60, £3.30, £2.20; EX 124.00 Trifecta £1002.70.
Owner R Bruni **Bred** Waymore Llc **Trained** Newmarket, Suffolk

FOCUS
One or two potential improvers in here making their handicap debuts, and although they failed to fire, the winner is at least still fairly unexposed. The pace slackened noticeably down the far side and the winner had them all stacked up when kicking off the home turn. It has to go down as a tactically astute ride form Jason Watson.

2126 WEATHERBYS STALLION BOOK H'CAP 1m 4f 51y (Tp)
7:30 (7:31) (Class 3) (0-90,90) 4-Y-0 **£7,246** (£2,168; £1,084; £542; £270) **Stalls Low**

Form RPR

601- 1 **Crystal King**[193] 8309 4-9-0 **83**........ JimCrowley 8 94+
(Sir Michael Stoute) *hld up in last trio: effrt in 4th 2f out: clsd and pressing ldrs 1f out: led 100yds out: hung lft but sn asserted: r.o wl* **15/8**[2]

134- 2 1 3/4 **Sleeping Lion (USA)**[252] 6306 4-9-6 **89**........(h[1]) JamieSpencer 6 96+
(James Fanshawe) *stdd s: hld up in rr: swtchd rt and effrt in 5th 2f out: hung lft and swtchd rt over 1f out: clsd but stl hanging and swtchd rt again ins fnl f: styd on to go 2nd last strides* **5/4**[1]

05-0 3 nk **Inn The Bull (GER)**[22] 1559 6-8-11 **80**........ JasonWatson 5 86
(Alan King) *midfield: wnt 3rd wl over 2f out: clsd u.p and chalng 1f out: led ins fnl f: hdd and one pce fnl 100yds: lost 2nd last strides* **8/1**

630/ **4** 2 ½ **All Set To Go (IRE)**[21] 1880 8-9-4 **90**.........................(t) JoshuaBryan(3) 3 92
(Kevin Frost) *chsd ldrs tl wnt 2nd 9f out: rdn and unable to match pce of ldr over 2f out: rallied to press ldrs again 1f out: no ex and wknd ins fnl f* **33/1**

240- **5** 2 ½ **Throckley**[175] 4895 8-8-9 **78** ow1.........................(t) ShaneKelly 7 76
(Sophie Leech) *led after 1f: rdn and kicked 3 l 2f out: hdd ins fnl f: sn btn and wknd* **66/1**

3650 **6** ½ **Lexington Law (IRE)**[28] 1422 6-9-5 **88**.........................(p) CallumShepherd 4 85
(Alan King) *t.k.h: hld up in last trio: nt clr run jst over 2f out: nvr trbld ldrs* **7/1**[3]

6530 **7** 4 ½ **Battle Of Marathon (USA)**[8] 1917 7-9-1 **84**.........................(p) BrettDoyle 1 74
(John Ryan) *midfield: rdn 2f out: no prog and wl btn fnl f* **25/1**

100- **8** nk **Dr Richard Kimble (IRE)**[16] 7518 4-8-13 **82**......................... FrannyNorton 2 73
(Mark Johnston) *led for 1f: chsd ldr tl 9f out: rdn and unable qck over 2f out: wl btn and bhd ins fnl f* **14/1**

2m 35.92s (-4.88) **Going Correction** -0.175s/f (Stan) **8 Ran SP% 117.8**
Speed ratings (Par 107): **109,107,107,105,104 103,100,100**
CSF £4.68 CT £13.43 TOTE £2.70: £1.10, £1.10, £2.00; EX 5.50 Trifecta £16.10.
Owner Sir Evelyn De Rothschild **Bred** Southcourt Stud **Trained** Newmarket, Suffolk

FOCUS
This was all about two standout contenders who have a good deal more scope as 4yo's this year, and they came to the fore from off the pace despite this turning into quite a steadily run affair.

2127 HEREFORD ALLOYS UK LTD WITH MATTHEW GREEN H'CAP 1m 4f 51y (Tp)
8:00 (8:01) (Class 6) (0-55,61) 4-Y-O+
£3,105 (£924; £461; £400; £400; £400) Stalls Low

Form RPR

3611 **1** **Contingency Fee**[7] 1935 4-9-6 **61**.........................(p) GraceMcEntee(7) 8 69
(Phil McEntee) *midfield: hdwy on outer after 2f: chsd ldr over 8f out tl led 5f out: 4 l clr and rdn 2f out: kpt on and nvr in danger after: eased wl ins fnl f* **7/2**[2]

-030 **2** 1 ¾ **Lady Of Authority**[30] 1390 4-8-11 **52**......................... GeorgiaDobie(7) 6 56+
(Richard Phillips) *hld up in midfield: nt clr run over 3f out tl hdwy to go 3rd but stl plenty to do over 1f out: chsd clr wnr ins fnl f: styd on wl but nvr threatening wnr* **12/1**

0650 **3** 2 ¼ **Ember's Glow**[16] 1718 5-9-6 **54**......................... EoinWalsh 2 54+
(Mark Loughnane) *short of room leaving stalls: hld up in last trio: nt clr run 3f out: hdwy over 1f out: styd on wl to go 3rd ins fnl f: no threat to wnr* **12/1**

00 **4** 4 **Lauberhorn Rocket (GER)**[32] 1346 4-9-4 **52**......................... KieranO'Neill 11 46
(Tim Vaughan) *hld up in midfield: effrt to go prom in chsng gp but ldrs clr over 2f out: kpt on but no imp* **50/1**

2030 **5** ¾ **Apex Predator (IRE)**[23] 1548 4-9-7 **55**.........................(bt) TomQueally 5 48
(Seamus Durack) *wnt lft s: chsd ldrs: effrt to chse clr wnr 3f out: no imp: lost 2nd and wknd ins fnl f* **12/1**

402- **6** 8 **Broctune Red**[220] 7419 4-9-4 **52**......................... PhilDennis 12 32
(Gillian Boanas) *towards rr: hung rt bnd over 7f out: effrt wd and hung rt bnd 2f out: wl btn after* **40/1**

055- **7** 2 **Jaycols Star**[108] 8319 4-9-3 **51**......................... DougieCostello 1 28
(Tim Vaughan) *led tl over 9f out: styd prom in chsng gp: nt clr run over 2f out: no ch after* **33/1**

600- **8** 1 **Kenmare River**[91] 7161 4-9-5 **53**.........................(w) CallumShepherd 9 28
(Tim Vaughan) *stdd s: hld up in rr: nvr involved* **100/1**

9 10 **Jazzy J (IRE)**[10] 1870 4-9-5 **53**.........................(t) ShaneKelly 3 12
(Anthony McCann, Ire) *bmpd leaving stalls: midfield: effrt and prom in chsng gp over 2f out: wknd over 1f out* **13/2**[3]

1312 **10** 4 ½ **Harry Callahan (IRE)**[4] 2014 4-8-12 **53**.........................(v) ScottMcCullagh(7) 7 5
(Mick Channon) *chsd ldr tl led over 9f out: hdd 5f out: lost 2nd 3f out and sn dropped out: dismntd sn after fin: lame (vet reported the gelding finished lame on its left fore)* **7/4**[1]

0301 **11** 6 **Muraaqeb**[17] 1680 5-9-1 **49**.........................(p) FrannyNorton 10
(Milton Bradley) *midfield tl lost pl over 3f out: bhd fnl 2f: eased fnl f: t.o* **8/1**

33-4 **12** 25 **Filament Of Gold (USA)**[86] 504 8-9-0 **51**.........................(b) GaryMahon(3) 4
(Roy Brotherton) *bmpd leaving stalls: midfield: hmpd and lost pl after 1f out: a towards rr: lost tch 2f out: eased: t.o* **25/1**

2m 37.84s (-2.96) **Going Correction** -0.175s/f (Stan) **12 Ran SP% 118.3**
Speed ratings (Par 101): **102,100,99,96,96 90,89,88,82,79 75,58**
CSF £42.96 CT £460.57 TOTE £3.80: £1.60, £3.60, £3.60; EX 42.40 Trifecta £373.60.
Owner M Hall **Bred** Whitwell Bloodstock **Trained** Newmarket, Suffolk
■ Stewards' Enquiry : Scott McCullagh three-day ban: interference & careless riding (May 11, 13-14)

FOCUS
Reasonably competitive for the grade and they went a good gallop. The winner is on a roll and completed the hat-trick in style.

2128 FOLLOW US ON TWITTER @WOLVESRACES NOVICE STKS 1m 142y (Tp)
8:30 (8:34) (Class 5) 3-Y-O+
£3,752 (£1,116; £557; £278) Stalls Low

Form RPR

3- **1** **Muraad (IRE)**[161] 9122 3-8-13 0......................... JimCrowley 13 89
(Owen Burrows) *hld up in tch in midfield: effrt to chse ldr 2f out: chal u.p and carried rt ins fnl f: styd on wl to ld last strides* **6/4**[1]

432- **2** hd **Emirates Knight (IRE)**[154] 9254 3-8-13 **79**......................... DavidEgan 10 88
(Roger Varian) *chsd ldng pair: swtchd rt and hdwy to ld over 2f out: clr w wnr and hung rt ins fnl f: hdd last strides* **9/4**[2]

3- **3** 11 **Dubai Philosopher (FR)**[185] 8543 3-8-13 0......................... JamieSpencer 12 64
(Michael Bell) *hld up in midfield: effrt and hdwy over 2f out: chsd clr ldng pair 2f out: no imp and wknd ins fnl f* **13/2**[3]

4 1 ¾ **Better Than Ever (IRE)** 3-8-10 0......................... AaronJones(3) 2 60
(Marco Botti) *hld up in midfield: nt clr run: effrt and swtchd rt jst over 2f out: no imp over 1f out* **50/1**

5 shd **Mutadaawel (IRE)**[29] 1408 4-10-7 0.........................(h) ShaneKelly 7 70
(Anthony McCann, Ire) *chsd ldng trio: effrt over 2f out: outpcd and wl hld over 1f out: wknd ins fnl f* **28/1**

12- **6** 3 ¼ **One Cool Daddy (USA)**[385] 1656 4-10-7 0......................... FrannyNorton 9 63
(Dean Ivory) *hld up off the pce in midfield: clsd whn swtchd rt and carried rt jst over 2f out: no imp and wl btn over 1f out* **12/1**

0-0 **7** 2 **Global Freedom**[14] 1754 3-8-13 0......................... StevieDonohoe 11 48
(Ed Dunlop) *swtchd lft after s: a bhd* **100/1**

8 3 **Desert Mission (IRE)** 3-8-8 0......................... JackMitchell 8 37
(Simon Crisford) *midfield but nvr terms: wl btn over 1f out* **25/1**

0- **9** 1 ½ **Basilisk (USA)**[183] 8600 3-8-13 0......................... JasonWatson 3 38
(Roger Charlton) *s.i.s: in last trio: hung bdly rt bnd over 7f out: a bhd after and stl hanging (jockey said gelding hung badly right-handed)* **10/1**

0 **10** 2 **Barrier Reef (IRE)**[5] 1989 4-10-0 0......................... KieranO'Neill 5 37
(Tim Vaughan) *last trio: pushed rt bnd over 7f out: nvr involved* **200/1**

- **11** 1 ¼ **Test Valley (IRE)**[48] 4-9-9 0......................... KatherineBegley(5) 1 34
(Tracey Barfoot-Saunt) *tk keen hdwy to ld over 7f out: rdn and hdd over 2f out: sn btn and fdd fnl f* **200/1**

0-50 **12** 7 **Lope De Loop (IRE)**[5] 1020 4-9-9 45.........................(t) EoinWalsh 4 14
(Aytach Sadik) *led tl over 7f out: styd w ldr: rdn over 2f out: sn btn: fdd fnl f* **200/1**

1m 46.98s (-3.12) **Going Correction** -0.175s/f (Stan)
WFA 3 from 4yo 15lb **12 Ran SP% 112.6**
Speed ratings (Par 103): **106,105,96,94,94 91,89,87,85,83 82,76**
CSF £4.37 TOTE £2.20: £1.30, £1.10, £1.20; EX 5.10 Trifecta £16.10.
Owner Hamdan Al Maktoum **Bred** Knocktoran, A Mouknass, Ecurie Pandora **Trained** Lambourn, Berks

FOCUS
Probably not a bad little novice for the track, with the front two coming eleven lengths clear in the closing stages. Both could prove above average.
T/Plt: £91.60 to a £1 stake. Pool: £65,356.07 - 520.46 winning units T/Qpdt: £38.60 to a £1 stake. Pool: £8,513.96 - 162.86 winning units **Steve Payne**

2129 - 2137a (Foreign Racing) - See Raceform Interactive

SALISBURY (R-H)
Sunday, April 28

OFFICIAL GOING: Good to firm (8.3)
Wind: light against Weather: overcast with sunny periods

2138 BYERLEY STUD FILLIES' CONDITIONS STKS (PLUS 10 RACE) 5f
2:00 (2:03) (Class 3) 2-Y-O
£9,703 (£2,887; £1,443; £721) Stalls Low

Form RPR

2 **1** **Good Vibes**[12] 1833 2-8-12 0......................... HarryBentley 5 81
(David Evans) *trckd ldr: kpt on wl but drifting lft ins fnl f: led cl home (jockey said filly hung left-handed)* **11/2**[3]

1 **2** nk **Exclusively**[20] 1642 2-9-2 0......................... HollieDoyle 7 84
(Archie Watson) *led after 1f: rdn over 1f out: kpt on fnl f: hdd cl home* **8/15**[1]

54 **3** 3 ¾ **Bainne Dubh**[15] 1759 2-8-7 0......................... ThoreHammerHansen(5) 3 66
(Bill Turner) *led for 1f: trckd ldrs: rdn 2 out: kpt on same pce* **66/1**

4 ¾ **Aroha (IRE)** 2-8-9 0......................... CallumShepherd 1 60+
(Brian Meehan) *uns rdr gng to s and galloped loose: trckd ldrs: rdn 2f out: kpt on same pce* **33/1**

5 2 ¼ **Love Love** 2-8-9 0......................... SilvestreDeSousa 9 52+
(Richard Hannon) *wnt lft s: chsd ldrs after 2f: sn rdn: nt pce to chal: fdd ins fnl f* **3/1**[2]

6 3 **She's A Diamond** 2-8-9 0......................... DavidEgan 2 41
(Mick Channon) *s.i.s: in last pair but in tch: effrt over 2f out: wknd fnl f* **25/1**

7 ½ **Birkie Queen (IRE)** 2-8-9 0......................... KieranO'Neill 8 40
(J S Moore) *chsd ldrs: rdn 2f out: sn hld: wknd fnl f* **100/1**

1m 1.41s (0.91) **Going Correction** -0.15s/f (Firm) **7 Ran SP% 114.9**
Speed ratings (Par 93): **86,85,79,78,74 69,69**
CSF £9.10 TOTE £7.30: £2.80, £1.10; EX 9.30 Trifecta £118.60.
Owner Paul & Clare Rooney **Bred** Whitsbury Manor Stud **Trained** Pandy, Monmouths

FOCUS
All distances as advertised. An informative event, in which the first two pulled nicely clear. The level is fluid.

2139 BYERLEY STUD NOVICE STKS (C&G) (DIV I) 6f 213y
2:30 (2:32) (Class 5) 3-Y-O
£5,110 (£1,520; £759; £379) Stalls Low

Form RPR

5- **1** **Oxted**[169] 9000 3-9-0 0......................... DavidProbert 6 80
(Roger Teal) *led for 1f: prom: led wl over 1f out: sn rdn clr: readily* **25/1**

51- **2** 2 ¼ **The Night Watch**[148] 9354 3-9-7 0......................... JamesDoyle 9 81
(William Haggas) *led after 1f: rdn and hdd wl over 1f out: kpt on but nt pce of wnr* **11/4**[2]

3 nse **After John** 3-9-0 0......................... CallumShepherd 10 74+
(Mick Channon) *s.i.s: in last pair: hdwy fr 2f out: swtchd lft and r.o ins fnl f: nrly snatched 2nd* **33/1**

363- **4** ¾ **Voltaic**[206] 7943 3-9-0 **79**.........................(t[1]) RaulDaSilva 2 72
(Paul Cole) *trckd ldng pair: rdn 2f out: kpt on same pce fnl f* **7/1**[3]

2- **5** ½ **Real Smooth (IRE)**[177] 8803 3-9-0 0.........................(w) TomMarquand 3 70
(Richard Hannon) *hld up: swtchd lft over 2f out: sn rdn: kpt on but nt pce to threaten* **10/11**[1]

6 1 **Recondite (IRE)** 3-9-0 0......................... HarryBentley 5 68
(Ralph Beckett) *hld up: hdwy over 2f out: rdn over 1f out: one pce fnl f* **12/1**

7 3 **Immoral (IRE)** 3-9-0 0......................... DavidEgan 4 60
(Ed Walker) *in tch: rdn over 2f out: nt pce to threaten: fdd ins fnl f* **33/1**

30- **8** 9 **Gambon (GER)**[233] 7008 3-9-0 0......................... CharlesBishop 7 35
(Eve Johnson Houghton) *prom: rdn over 2f out: sn hung lft: wknd fnl f (jockey said gelding hung left-handed)* **14/1**

60- **9** ½ **Bartimaeus (IRE)**[127] 9683 3-9-0 0......................... ShaneKelly 1 34
(Denis Coakley) *in tch: effrt over 2f out: wknd over 1f out* **66/1**

55- **10** 6 **Scottish Blade (IRE)**[193] 8322 3-9-0 0......................... JimCrowley 8 18
(Charles Hills) *trckd ldrs: rdn over 2f out: sn wknd* **33/1**

1m 26.9s (-1.80) **Going Correction** -0.15s/f (Firm) **10 Ran SP% 120.1**
Speed ratings (Par 98): **104,101,101,100,99 98,95,85,84,77**
CSF £93.25 TOTE £38.40: £5.70, £1.20, £8.40; EX 176.20 Trifecta £2774.20.
Owner Homecroft Wealth And Partners **Bred** Homecroft Wealth Racing **Trained** Lambourn, Berks

FOCUS
It paid to race handily in this first division of this novice contest.

2140 BYERLEY STUD NOVICE STKS (C&G) (DIV II) 6f 213y
3:00 (3:02) (Class 5) 3-Y-O
£5,110 (£1,520; £759; £379) Stalls Low

Form RPR

1 **Biometric** 3-9-0 0......................... HarryBentley 4 72
(Ralph Beckett) *trckd ldrs: tk narrow advantage 2f out: kpt on wl fnl f: rdn out* **10/3**[3]

15 **2** hd **Songkran (IRE)**[72] 733 3-9-7 0......................... SilvestreDeSousa 2 78
(David Elsworth) *a.p: led over 2f out: sn rdn and hdd: kpt on gamely w ev ch: jst hld* **6/4**[1]

5- **3** 1 ¾ **Jilbaab**[219] 7484 3-9-0 0......................... JimCrowley 5 66
(Brian Meehan) *sn led: rdn whn hdd over 2f out: kpt on same pce fnl f* **9/4**[2]

6-5 **4** ½ **Dargel (IRE)**[32] 1352 3-9-0 0......................... DaneO'Neill 3 65
(Clive Cox) *little slowly away: in tch: rdn and hdwy over 1f out: drifted lft but kpt on ins fnl f: nt pce to get on terms* **8/1**

56 **5** *2 ¼* **Osho**[29] 1423 3-9-0 0 .... SeanLevey 6 59
(Richard Hannon) *prom tl rdn over 2f out: kpt on same pce fr over 1f out* **14/1**

0- **6** *5* **Keith**[172] 8931 3-9-0 0 .... CharlesBishop 1 45
(Rod Millman) *chsd ldrs: rdn over 2f out: wknd over 1f out* **33/1**

0- **7** *1* **Aiguillette**[207] 7906 3-9-0 0 .... HectorCrouch 7 43
(Gary Moore) *hld up: rdn over 2f out: little imp: wknd fnl f* **50/1**

000- **8** *14* **Dark Impulse (IRE)**[237] 6880 3-9-0 34 .... KieranO'Neill 8
(John Bridger) *in tch tl rdn 3f out: sn wknd* **100/1**

9 *1 ¼* **Purple Tommy** 3-9-0 0 .... JohnFahy 9
(Jimmy Fox) *wnt lft and slowly away: a bhd* **50/1**

1m 27.78s (-0.92) **Going Correction** -0.15s/f (Firm) **9** Ran SP% **119.5**
Speed ratings (Par 98): **99,98,96,96,93 87,86,70,69**
CSF £9.02 TOTE £3.20: £1.10, £1.20, £1.30; EX 9.40 Trifecta £20.80.
Owner K Abdullah **Bred** Juddmonte Farms Ltd **Trained** Kimpton, Hants

FOCUS
This looked the stronger of the two divisions on paper but the winning time, which was 0.88secs slower, fails to back that up.

2141 JOIN THE BYERLEY RACING CLUB H'CAP 1m 1f 201y
3:35 (3:35) (Class 4) (0-80,82) 3-Y-O
£5,757 (£1,713; £856; £428; £400; £400) **Stalls** Low

Form RPR

5-31 **1** **Mayfair Spirit (IRE)**[18] 1697 3-8-12 69 .... (t) StevieDonohoe 9 75
(Charlie Fellowes) *mid-div: hdwy over 5f out: chal wl over 2f out: rdn to ld narrowly ent fnl f: kpt on gamely: rdn out* **5/1**[3]

5-43 **2** *shd* **Htilominlo**[53] 1034 3-9-1 72 .... (t) SilvestreDeSousa 4 77
(Sylvester Kirk) *trckd ldr: chalng whn carried lft 3f out: tk narrow advantage 2f out: narrowly hdd ent fnl f: kpt on w ev ch: jst hld* **7/1**

61-5 **3** *2 ¼* **The Pink'n**[13] 1823 3-9-6 77 .... JamesDoyle 12 77
(Seamus Mullins) *s.i.s: in last pair: rdn over 2f out: hdwy over 1f out: styd on wl fnl f: snatched 3rd fnl stride* **20/1**

14-3 **4** *hd* **Guildhall**[28] 1462 3-9-7 78 .... HarryBentley 11 78
(Ralph Beckett) *trckd ldrs: hmpd 3f out: sn rdn: styd on ins fnl f: snatched 4th cl home* **9/4**[1]

26-1 **5** *nk* **Sash**[26] 1495 3-9-11 82 .... JimCrowley 3 81
(Amanda Perrett) *trckd ldrs: sltly hmpd 3f out: sn rdn: styd on same pce ins fnl f: lost 2 pls cl home* **7/2**[2]

35-3 **6** *2 ¼* **Cromwell**[52] 1067 3-8-5 62 .... RaulDaSilva 2 57
(Luke Dace) *mid-div: rdn and hdwy over 2f out: disputing 4th ent fnl f: no ex fnl 120yds* **33/1**

23-2 **7** *nk* **Air Force Amy**[51] 1077 3-9-4 75 .... CallumShepherd 10 69
(Mick Channon) *mid-div: rdn and hdwy over 2f out: sn chsng ldrs: one pce fnl f* **11/1**

22-1 **8** *7* **Pytilia (USA)**[32] 1359 3-9-6 77 .... ShaneKelly 5 57
(Richard Hughes) *led: jinked lft 3f out: sn rdn: hdd 2f out: wknd fnl f* **8/1**

40-0 **9** *½* **Purbeck Hills (IRE)**[11] 1857 3-8-10 67 .... HollieDoyle 1 46
(Richard Hannon) *mid-div: rdn over 2f out: wknd fnl f* **16/1**

000- **10** *6* **Crackaway (FR)**[164] 9074 3-9-2 73 .... (p[1]) HectorCrouch 8 40
(Harry Dunlop) *a towards rr* **40/1**

2m 10.17s (-0.33) **Going Correction** -0.15s/f (Firm) **10** Ran SP% **117.6**
Speed ratings (Par 100): **95,94,93,92,92 90,90,85,84,79**
CSF £39.38 CT £648.88 TOTE £6.10: £2.20, £2.50, £4.60; EX 44.90 Trifecta £453.90.
Owner J Soiza **Bred** Ringfort Stud Ltd **Trained** Newmarket, Suffolk

FOCUS
With five handicap debutants involved, this featured plenty of potential improvers.

2142 BRITISH EBF BYERLEY STUD MAIDEN STKS (PLUS 10 RACE) 1m 4f 5y
4:05 (4:07) (Class 4) 3-Y-O £6,727 (£2,002; £1,000; £500) **Stalls** Low

Form RPR

2-2 **1** **Eagles By Day (IRE)**[26] 1509 3-9-5 0 .... DanielTudhope 7 97+
(Michael Bell) *trckd ldrs: led travelling strly 3f out: nudged clr ent fnl f: v easily* **9/4**[2]

0-6 **2** *7* **Kiefer**[15] 1756 3-9-5 0 .... CharlesBishop 14 81
(Eve Johnson Houghton) *hld up towards rr: hdwy over 2f out: swtchd lft whn cl 3rd over 1f out: sn rdn: styd on go 2nd towards fin but no ch w easy wnr* **25/1**

3 **3** *nk* **Isolate (FR)**[26] 1509 3-9-5 0 .... SilvestreDeSousa 11 80
(Martyn Meade) *prom: led after 4f: hdd 3f out: sn rdn and hld: styd on same pce fnl f: lost 2nd towards fin* **14/1**

4 **4** *6* **Space Walk**[15] 1756 3-9-5 0 .... (t[1]) JamesDoyle 1 71
(William Haggas) *trckd ldrs: rdn 3f out: one pce fnl 2f* **5/4**[1]

5 *4 ½* **Johnny Kidd** 3-9-2 0 .... JoshuaBryan(3) 10 64
(Andrew Balding) *mid-div: rdn and edgd rt 3f out: styd on same pce fnl 2f* **20/1**

4-3 **6** *9* **Royal Star**[16] 1738 3-9-0 0 .... JasonWatson 12 44
(Roger Charlton) *led for 4f: trckd ldr: rdn and ev ch briefly 3f out: sn hld: wknd 2f out* **4/1**[3]

0 **7** *2 ¼* **Doune Castle**[15] 1756 3-9-5 0 .... DavidProbert 5 46
(Andrew Balding) *wnt lft s: mid-div: rdn over 3f out: wknd 2f out* **33/1**

8 *2 ½* **Moghram (IRE)** 3-9-5 0 .... JimCrowley 6 42
(Marcus Tregoning) *mid-div: rdn over 3f out: wknd over 2f out* **16/1**

0-0 **9** *8* **Universal Song**[16] 1738 3-9-0 0 .... HollieDoyle 2 24
(Seamus Mullins) *mid-div: rdn 3f out: wknd 2f out* **150/1**

4 **10** *22* **Flat Stone**[37] 1268 3-9-5 0 .... CallumShepherd 13
(Daniele Camuffo) *s.i.s: a twards rr: eased whn btn over 1f out* **50/1**

0 **11** *2 ½* **Fyodor**[13] 1824 3-9-5 0 .... KieranO'Neill 9
(Seamus Mullins) *a towards rr* **150/1**

0 **12** *34* **Flaming Red**[16] 1739 3-8-7 0 .... (p[1]) Pierre-LouisJamin(7) 8
(Kevin Bishop) *nvr travelling: a bhd: t.o* **150/1**

2m 33.7s (-3.90) **Going Correction** -0.15s/f (Firm) **12** Ran SP% **123.3**
Speed ratings (Par 100): **107,102,102,98,95 89,87,85,80,65 64,41**
CSF £64.84 TOTE £3.00: £1.10, £5.80, £2.10; EX 77.10 Trifecta £827.10.
Owner Clipper Logistics **Bred** Mrs Vanessa Hutch **Trained** Newmarket, Suffolk

FOCUS
This had quite a competitive look to it beforehand but it was taken apart by the impressive Eagles By Day.

2143 BYERLEY STUD "CITY BOWL" H'CAP 1m 6f 44y
4:40 (4:40) (Class 3) (0-95,95) 4-Y-O+
£14,006 (£4,194; £2,097; £1,048; £524; £263) **Stalls** Far side

Form RPR

11 **1** **Gumball (FR)**[34] 1331 5-8-13 86 .... SilvestreDeSousa 93+
(Philip Hobbs) *set decent pce: mde all: styd on wl: pushed out* **9/4**[2]

342- **2** *1 ½* **Scaramanga (IRE)**[28] 8081 4-8-8 85 .... MeganNicholls(3) 90
(Paul Nicholls) *trckd ldrs: rdn 2f out: sn chsng wnr: styd on but a being hld* **15/8**[1]

130- **3** *shd* **Reshoun (FR)**[144] 9399 5-9-8 95 .... (p) JamesDoyle 100
(Ian Williams) *hld up: hdwy 2f out: sn rdn: styd on to press for 2nd ins fnl 100yds: nvr threatening to get on terms w wnr* **12/1**

300- **4** *4* **Mancini**[205] 7952 5-9-5 92 .... RichardKingscote 91
(Jonathan Portman) *sweating: trckd wnr: rdn to chal over 3f out: styd on same pce fnl 2f* **7/1**

/50- **5** *7* **Quloob**[281] 5212 5-9-8 95 .... (w) JimCrowley 84
(Owen Burrows) *trckd ldrs: rdn over 3f out: wknd over 1f out* **9/2**[3]

10-4 **6** *19* **Flintrock (GER)**[29] 1425 4-8-8 82 .... DavidProbert 46
(Andrew Balding) *nt really travelling in last pair: rdn over 3f out: nvr any imp: eased whn btn over 1f out (jockey said colt was never travelling)* **11/1**

3m 0.66s (-5.94) **Going Correction** -0.15s/f (Firm)
WFA 4 from 5yo+ 1lb **6** Ran SP% **112.3**
Speed ratings (Par 107): **110,109,109,106,102 91**
CSF £6.89 TOTE £2.90: £1.50, £1.50; EX 7.40 Trifecta £43.20.
Owner Terry Warner **Bred** J Gallorini, Mlle M Bilesimo Et Al **Trained** Withycombe, Somerset

FOCUS
Not many runners but this looks solid staying handicap form.

2144 BYERLEY STUD FILLIES' H'CAP 6f 213y
5:10 (5:12) (Class 3) (0-90,90) 3-Y-O £9,056 (£2,695; £1,346; £673) **Stalls** Low

Form RPR

413- **1** **Ice Gala**[183] 8648 3-9-5 88 .... JamesDoyle 8 98
(William Haggas) *a.p: led 2f out: edgd rt whn bmpd ent fnl f: sn rdn: kpt on wl* **9/4**[1]

25-1 **2** *3 ½* **Star Of War (USA)**[36] 1287 3-8-13 82 .... SeanLevey 2 83
(Richard Hannon) *trckd ldrs: rdn whn swtchd lft 2f out: lft chsng wnr ent fnl f: kpt on* **7/1**

324- **3** *1* **Heritage**[198] 8151 3-9-1 84 .... DaneO'Neill 7 82
(Clive Cox) *trckd ldrs: rdn over 2f out: lft disputing 2nd ent fnl f: kpt on same pce fnl 120yds* **8/1**

416- **4** *1 ¼* **Sufficient**[219] 7487 3-8-9 78 .... (h) HollieDoyle 1 80+
(Rod Millman) *led: rdn and hdd 2f out: stl ev ch whn drifted lft ent fnl f and bdly hmpd: kpt on fnl 120yds but no ch after* **20/1**

126- **5** *nk* **Strict Tempo**[204] 7988 3-9-1 84 .... DavidProbert 4 78
(Andrew Balding) *hld up in last pair: hdwy over 1f out: sn rdn: kpt on but nt pce to get on terms* **6/1**[3]

10-2 **6** *1 ¼* **Zofelle (IRE)**[37] 1272 3-9-4 87 .... RichardKingscote 3 77
(Hugo Palmer) *trckd ldrs but tight for room on inner early: rdn over 2f out: chalng for 3rd whn sltly hmpd ent fnl f: kpt on same pce* **10/1**

454- **7** *1 ¼* **Impulsion (IRE)**[183] 8648 3-9-5 88 .... DavidEgan 5 75
(Roger Varian) *mid-div: tight for room and lost pl over 4f out: rdn and sme prog over 2f out but nvr gng pce to get bk on terms (jockey said filly suffered interference 4 1/2f out)* **4/1**[2]

31-0 **8** *1 ¼* **Deira Surprise**[32] 1360 3-8-13 82 .... SilvestreDeSousa 9 66
(Hugo Palmer) *trckd ldrs: rdn over 2f out: wknd ent fnl f* **12/1**

350- **9** *1 ¾* **No Way Jose (IRE)**[211] 7771 3-9-7 90 .... TomMarquand 10 69
(Brian Meehan) *mid-div: rdn and nt clrest of runs over 2f out: wknd ent fnl f* **28/1**

10-0 **10** *4 ½* **Cotubanama**[10] 1894 3-8-2 76 .... TheodoreLadd(5) 11 43
(Mick Channon) *hld up towards rr: rdn over 2f out: little imp: wknd over 1f out* **33/1**

010- **11** *1 ½* **Porcelain Girl (IRE)**[211] 7776 3-8-9 81 .... CameronNoble(3) 6 44
(Michael Bell) *awkwardly away: a towards rr* **33/1**

1m 27.19s (-1.51) **Going Correction** -0.15s/f (Firm) **11** Ran SP% **119.5**
Speed ratings (Par 99): **102,98,96,95,95 93,92,90,88,83 81**
CSF £17.92 CT £110.17 TOTE £3.10: £1.30, £2.70, £3.50; EX 19.30 Trifecta £125.40.
Owner Cheveley Park Stud **Bred** Cheveley Park Stud Ltd **Trained** Newmarket, Suffolk

FOCUS
This got quite messy when the winner and eventual fifth had a significant coming together around 2f from home.

2145 BYERLEY STUD H'CAP (FOR LADY AMATEUR RIDERS) 6f 213y
5:40 (5:44) (Class 6) (0-65,65) 4-Y-O+
£3,306 (£1,025; £512; £400; £400; £400) **Stalls** Low

Form RPR

500- **1** **Fieldsman (USA)**[137] 9507 7-10-2 63 .... MissSarahBowen(5) 7 71
(Tony Carroll) *disp ld tl edgd ahd over 2f out: strly chal ent fnl f: kpt on wl cl home* **9/2**[1]

0000 **2** *nk* **Letmestopyouthere (IRE)**[46] 1179 5-9-12 54(p) MissBrodieHampson 14 61
(Archie Watson) *mid-div: rdn and hdwy fr 2f out: kpt on wl ins fnl f: wnt 2nd towards fin* **5/1**[2]

1-46 **3** *nk* **Winklemann (IRE)**[32] 1369 7-9-10 59 .... (p) MissImogenMathias(7) 6 65
(John Flint) *towards rr: hdwy over 3f out: str chal over 1f out: kpt on w ev ch tl no ex towards fin* **8/1**

034- **4** *7* **Champagne Bob**[195] 8284 7-10-1 62 .... SophieSmith(5) 8 50
(Richard Price) *trckd ldrs: rdn over 2f out: kpt on same pce fnl f* **16/1**

0-04 **5** *2 ¼* **Perfect Symphony (IRE)**[8] 1933 5-10-7 63 .... MissSerenaBrotherton 5 45
(Mark Pattinson) *prom: rdn and ev ch 2f out: no ex ent fnl f* **10/1**

4644 **6** *1 ¼* **Coastal Cyclone**[8] 1952 5-9-1 50 .... (b[1]) MissRachelDavies(7) 16 29
(Harry Dunlop) *prom: hld whn drifting rt over 2f out: kpt on ins fnl f* **20/1**

450- **7** *½* **Masquerade Bling (IRE)**[181] 8694 5-9-13 60 MissMillieWonnacott(5) 10 38
(Neil Mulholland) *trckd ldrs: rdn over 2f out: fdd fnl f* **20/1**

2163 **8** *hd* **Clement (IRE)**[12] 1837 9-9-11 53 .... (v) MissBeckySmith 1 30
(Marjorie Fife) *midfield: trckd ldrs over 4f out: fdd fnl f* **8/1**

455- **9** *nk* **Hedging (IRE)**[181] 8694 5-9-12 61 .... (p) MissNykeSchilder(7) 4 38
(Eve Johnson Houghton) *hld up towards rr: hdwy over 2f out: nvr threatened: fdd fnl f* **14/1**

0-56 **10** *½* **Swissal (IRE)**[8] 1930 4-10-6 65 .... (p) MissLillyPinchin(3) 9 40
(David Dennis) *disp ld tl rdn over 2f out: wknd fnl f* **16/1**

0300 **11** *1 ¼* **Squire**[19] 1660 8-10-3 59 .... (tp) MissJoannaMason 13 31
(Marjorie Fife) *nvr bttr than mid-div* **14/1**

0132 **12** *¾* **Purple Paddy**[18] 1675 4-9-4 51 .... MissAntoniaPeck(5) 17 21
(Jimmy Fox) *mid-div: rdn over 2f out: little imp* **13/2**[3]

35-6 **13** *1* **Imbucato**[88] 484 5-9-3 52 .... MissEmmaWilkinson(7) 15 19
(Tony Carroll) *prom early: chsng ldrs and u.p over 3f out: wknd 2f out* **33/1**

600- **14** *1 ¼* **Who Told Jo Jo (IRE)**[164] 9080 5-9-5 54 .... MissMatildaBlundell(7) 3 18
(Joseph Tuite) *towards rr: hdwy over 3f out: wknd over 1f out* **40/1**

The Form Book Flat 2019, Raceform Ltd, Newbury, RG14 5SJ

0-00 **15** 2 1/2 **Tuscany (IRE)**[62] 911 5-9-5 **54**........................ MsSophieCarter(7) 11 12
(Grace Harris) *mid-div tl wknd 2f out* **100/1**

321- **16** 1/2 **Edge (IRE)**[181] 8688 8-10-0 **63**....................(b) MissJessicaLlewellyn(7) 18 19
(Bernard Llewellyn) *slowly away: a towards rr* **20/1**

000/ **17** 14 **Machiavelian Storm (IRE)**[501] 9218 7-8-12 **45**(t w) MissRosieMargarson(5) 2
(Richard Mitchell) *bhd fnl 3f* **66/1**

60-0 **18** 1 3/4 **Golden Footsteps (IRE)**[13] 1820 4-9-5 **50**..(b[1]) MissHannahWelch(3) 12
(Mark Gillard) *trckd ldrs tl 4f out: sn wknd (vet said filly was struck into left-hind leg)* **100/1**

1m 28.52s (-0.18) **Going Correction** -0.15s/f (Firm) **18 Ran SP% 127.7**
Speed ratings (Par 101): **95,94,94,86,83 82,81,81,81,80 79,78,77,75,72 72,56,54**
CSF £24.83 CT £189.03 TOTE £5.30: £1.60, £2.40, £2.70, £2.80; EX 37.40 Trifecta £182.70.
Owner Sf Racing Club **Bred** H Sexton, S Sexton & Silver Fern Farm **Trained** Cropthorne, Worcs

FOCUS
The first three came clear in this low grade finale. The winner has been rated to the best of last year's form.
T/Plt: £31.50 to a £1 stake. Pool: £81,381.12 - 1,880.87 winning units T/Qpdt: £7.80 to a £1 stake. Pool: £7,387.00 - 699.49 winning units **Tim Mitchell**

WETHERBY (L-H)
Sunday, April 28

OFFICIAL GOING: Good (7.4)
Wind: Moderate behind Weather: Cloudy

2146 SMURFIT KAPPA INSPIREPAC NOVICE STKS (DIV I) 7f
2:15 (2:18) (Class 5) 3-Y-O+ £4,851 (£1,443; £721; £360) Stalls Low

Form RPR

420- **1** **Irreverent**[173] 8895 3-9-1 **82**.................................... PaulHanagan 9 77
(Richard Fahey) *trckd ldrs: hdwy on outer 3f out: rdn to chal over 1f out: slt ld ins fnl f: kpt on wl towards fin* **5/2[3]**

53-2 **2** 3/4 **Regular**[25] 1516 3-9-1 **78**.................................... PJMcDonald 3 75
(Michael Bell) *led: pushed along over 2f out: rdn wl over 1f out: edgd rt and drvn ent fnl f: sn hdd: kpt on same pce* **9/4[2]**

3 1 3/4 **Stoney Lane** 4-10-0 **0**.................................... PhilDennis 1 75
(Richard Whitaker) *trckd ldrs: hdwy on inner wl over 1f out: sn n.m.r: squeezed through and ev ch jst ins fnl f: sn rdn and kpt on same pce* **66/1**

2225 **4** 1 1/4 **White Coat**[20] 1646 3-9-1 **78**..........................(tp) RobertHavlin 7 67
(John Gosden) *t.k.h early: trckd ldrs: hdwy 3f out: sn cl up: rdn wl over 1f out: drvn ent fnl f: wknd* **2/1[1]**

020- **5** nk **Ellheidi (IRE)**[187] 8509 3-8-10 **75**.................................... BenCurtis 5 61
(K R Burke) *cl up: disp ld over 2f out: rdn along wl over 1f out: drvn and hld whn n.m.r ent fnl f: kpt on one pce* **13/2**

00 **6** 1 1/2 **Circle Of Stars (IRE)**[18] 1676 3-9-1 **0**.................................... KevinStott 6 62
(Charlie Fellowes) *chsd ldrs: pushed along and sltly outpcd over 2f out: sn rdn and kpt on fnl f* **25/1**

5 **7** hd **Heavenly Secret (IRE)**[11] 1849 4-10-0 **0**..............(t) DougieCostello 10 67?
(Tony Coyle) *hld up in tch: effrt and sme hdwy on outer over 2f out: sn rdn and no imp* **100/1**

-0 **8** 5 **Martha McEwan (IRE)**[25] 1523 3-8-10 **0**.................................... LewisEdmunds 2 43
(David Barron) *in tch: rdn along over 2f out: sn wknd* **100/1**

600- **9** nse **Magic Ship (IRE)**[215] 7643 4-10-0 **39**.................................... PaulMulrennan 4 53?
(John Norton) *a in rr* **250/1**

0- **10** 3 **The Mekon**[360] 2348 4-10-0 **0**.................................... JackGarritty 12 45
(Noel Wilson) *dwlt and wnt rt s: a bhd (jockey said filly gelding left-handed)* **200/1**

0 **11** 15 **Sophia's Princess**[37] 1272 3-8-7 **0**..........................(t[1]) GabrieleMalune(3) 11
(Ivan Furtado) *a outpcd and bhd* **150/1**

1m 29.29s (2.09) **Going Correction** +0.20s/f (Good) **11 Ran SP% 114.9**
WFA 3 from 4yo 13lb
Speed ratings (Par 103): **96,95,93,91,91 89,89,83,83,80 63**
CSF £8.31 TOTE £3.30: £1.20, £1.10, £10.50; EX 8.30 Trifecta £390.60.
Owner Mr & Mrs N Wrigley **Bred** Mr & Mrs N Wrigley **Trained** Musley Bank, N Yorks

FOCUS
It paid to be handy in this modest novice event.

2147 SMURFIT KAPPA INSPIREPAC NOVICE STKS (DIV II) 7f
2:45 (2:49) (Class 5) 3-Y-O+ £4,851 (£1,443; £721; £360) Stalls Low

Form RPR

1 **Trinity Lake** 3-9-1 **0**.................................... DavidNolan 1 74
(Declan Carroll) *trckd ldng pair on inner: swtchd rt and hdwy 2f out: rdn to ld ent fnl f: kpt on strly* **12/1**

40 **2** 1 **Global Gift (FR)**[10] 1886 3-9-1 **0**..........................(h[1]) PJMcDonald 11 71
(Ed Dunlop) *wnt rt s and towards rr: gd hdwy over 2f out: rdn over 1f out: styd on strly fnl f* **10/1**

32- **3** 3/4 **Brandy Spirit**[166] 9037 3-9-1 **0**.................................... NathanEvans 4 69
(Michael Easterby) *t.k.h early: trckd ldrs: hdwy and cl up 2f out: rdn along over 1f out: drvn and kpt on same pce fnl f* **7/2[3]**

5 **4** 3/4 **Grey Berry (IRE)**[13] 1816 3-8-10 **0**.................................... DavidAllan 7 62
(Tim Easterby) *trckd ldr: hdwy and cl up over 2f out: rdn along over 1f out: kpt on same pce fnl f* **14/1**

15 **5** 1 1/4 **Eardley Road (IRE)**[29] 1423 3-9-8 **0**.................................... AdamKirby 10 71
(Clive Cox) *towards rr: hdwy on outer over 2f out: rdn along wl over 1f out: sn chsng ldrs: kpt on fnl f* **5/2[2]**

00- **6** 1/2 **The Rutland Rebel (IRE)**[184] 8592 3-9-1 **0**.................................... GrahamLee 5 62
(Micky Hammond) *towards rr: hdwy wl over 2f out: sn pushed along: rdn wl over 1f out: kpt on fnl f* **40/1**

2 **7** nk **King Shamardal**[31] 1379 3-9-1 **0**.................................... JoeFanning 3 61
(Mark Johnston) *led: pushed along and jnd over 2f out: rdn wl over 1f out: hdd ent fnl f and sn wknd* **9/4[1]**

R56 **8** 1 **Desai**[69] 785 5-10-0 **0**.................................... JackGarritty 2 64
(Noel Wilson) *trckd ldrs: hdwy over 2f out: rdn over 1f out: wknd fnl f (jockey said gelding was briefly denied a clear run approaching 2f out)* **100/1**

9 2 **Power Player** 3-9-1 **0**.................................... BenCurtis 8 53
(K R Burke) *a towards rr* **25/1**

04-0 **10** 13 **Royal Rattle**[87] 501 4-10-0 **44**.................................... PaulMulrennan 9 23
(John Norton) *prom: rdn along wl over 2f out: sn wknd* **150/1**

11 1 **Pandora's Minder** 3-8-3 **0**.................................... VictorSantos(7) 6 11
(Lucinda Egerton) *a in rr* **250/1**

1m 29.66s (2.46) **Going Correction** +0.20s/f (Good) **11 Ran SP% 113.3**
WFA 3 from 4yo+ 13lb
Speed ratings (Par 103): **93,91,91,90,88 88,87,86,84,69 68**
CSF £117.73 TOTE £14.20: £3.20, £2.60, £1.60; EX 125.90 Trifecta £470.80.
Owner Dreams **Bred** Juddmonte Farms (east) Ltd **Trained** Malton, N Yorks

FOCUS
This second division of the novice event was 0.43secs slower than the first.

2148 RACINGTV.COM FILLIES' NOVICE STKS 1m 2f
3:20 (3:20) (Class 5) 3-Y-O+ £4,851 (£1,443; £721; £360) Stalls Centre

Form RPR

2- **1** **Fanny Logan (IRE)**[187] 8511 3-8-11 **0**.................................... RobertHavlin 10 84
(John Gosden) *sn cl up: led 3f out: pushed clr wl over 1f out: rdn and kpt on fnl f* **2/7[1]**

2 1 3/4 **Inference** 3-8-11 **0**.................................... NickyMackay 4 80
(John Gosden) *hld up and bhd: stdy hdwy 4f out: chsd ldrs and swtchd rt over 2f out: rdn and chsd wnr ent fnl f: kpt on same pce* **6/1[3]**

4 **3** 2 1/2 **Happy Hiker (IRE)**[16] 1738 3-8-11 **0**.................................... HayleyTurner 5 75
(Michael Bell) *trckd ldrs: hdwy over 3f out: rdn to chse wnr 2f out: drvn over 1f out: kpt on same pce* **16/1**

22- **4** 2 1/2 **Dorah**[193] 8329 3-8-11 **0**.................................... LukeMorris 9 70
(Archie Watson) *led: pushed along 4f out: rdn and hdd 3f out: drvn over 2f out and grad wknd* **4/1[2]**

0 **5** 6 **War Empress (IRE)**[29] 1417 3-8-11 **0**.................................... ShelleyBirkett 3 58
(Julia Feilden) *hld up in rr: pushed along and sme hdwy 3f out: sn rdn and n.d* **150/1**

4- **6** nk **Tarbeyah (IRE)**[202] 8055 4-10-0 **0**.................................... PJMcDonald 6 60
(Kevin Frost) *nvr bttr than midfield* **20/1**

0 **7** 3 1/4 **Soloist (IRE)**[16] 1738 3-8-11 **0**.................................... LiamJones 8 51
(William Haggas) *a towards rr* **20/1**

8 4 **Kostantina** 3-8-11 **0**.................................... RachelRichardson 7 43
(Olly Williams) *a towards rr* **50/1**

30 **9** 8 **Paradise Papers**[20] 1649 3-8-11 **0**.................................... LewisEdmunds 11 27
(David Barron) *prom: pushed along 4f out: rdn 3f out: sn wknd* **40/1**

6-0 **10** 6 **Feebi**[20] 1643 3-8-11 **0**.................................... MichaelStainton 2 15
(Chris Fairhurst) *chsd ldng pair: rdn along on inner 4f out: wknd 3f out* **125/1**

0 **11** 3/4 **Yasmin From York**[20] 1643 3-8-11 **0**.................................... CamHardie 1 13
(Brian Rothwell) *in tch: chsd ldrs 1/2-way: rdn along 4f out: sn wknd* **200/1**

2m 9.44s (0.14) **Going Correction** +0.20s/f (Good) **11 Ran SP% 133.8**
WFA 3 from 4yo 17lb
Speed ratings (Par 100): **107,105,103,101,96 96,93,90,84,79 78**
CSF £3.61 TOTE £1.20: £1.10, £1.50, £3.50; EX 3.90 Trifecta £24.80.
Owner HH Sheikha Al Jalila Racing **Bred** Godolphin **Trained** Newmarket, Suffolk
■ Stewards' Enquiry : Nicky Mackay two-day ban: careless riding (13-14 May)

FOCUS
This wasn't a bad fillies' novice contest.

2149 WETHERBYRACING.CO.UK H'CAP 5f 110y
3:50 (3:51) (Class 4) (0-80,80) 3-Y-O £6,727 (£2,002; £1,000; £500; £400; £400) Stalls High

Form RPR

325- **1** **Roulston Scar (IRE)**[169] 9006 3-9-4 **77**.................................... TomEaves 1 86
(Kevin Ryan) *mde all: rdn wl over 1f out: drvn and kpt on wl fnl f* **7/1**

04-6 **2** 1 1/2 **Thegreatestshowman**[16] 1729 3-9-6 **79**.................................... DougieCostello 8 83
(Amy Murphy) *hld up on outer: hdwy over 2f out: chsd ldrs and rdn over 1f out: drvn and kpt on fnl f* **9/2[3]**

16-6 **3** nk **Look Out Louis**[19] 1662 3-9-2 **75**.................................... DavidAllan 2 78
(Tim Easterby) *cl up: rdn along over 2f out: drvn over 1f out: kpt on same pce fnl f* **6/1**

-120 **4** 2 1/2 **Fair Alibi**[19] 1662 3-8-13 **72**.................................... JamesSullivan 7 66
(Tom Tate) *hld up in rr: hdwy 2f out: rdn over 1f out: kpt on fnl f* **18/1**

05-0 **5** 1/2 **Baby Steps**[18] 1691 3-9-5 **78**.................................... BenCurtis 6 71
(David Loughnane) *chsd ldrs: rdn along on inner 2f out: drvn and wknd over 1f out* **4/1[2]**

32-1 **6** 1 3/4 **Warning Fire**[44] 1219 3-9-0 **73**.................................... JoeFanning 10 60
(Mark Johnston) *chsd ldrs on wd outside: rdn along over 2f out: wknd wl over 1f out* **7/2[1]**

1304 **7** 1 1/4 **Coolagh Magic**[15] 1762 3-9-7 **80**..........................(p) TonyHamilton 5 63
(Richard Fahey) *dwlt: a in rr* **8/1**

215- **8** 1 3/4 **Sylvia's Mother**[164] 9085 3-9-2 **75**..........................(b) PaulMulrennan 4 52
(Joseph Tuite) *prom: rdn along over 2f out: sn drvn and wknd* **33/1**

106- **9** 3/4 **Diamonique**[202] 8049 3-9-3 **76**.................................... ConnorBeasley 3 50
(Keith Dalgleish) *chsd ldrs: rdn along over 2f out: sn wknd* **16/1**

1m 6.98s (1.18) **Going Correction** +0.20s/f (Good) **9 Ran SP% 112.4**
Speed ratings (Par 100): **100,98,97,94,93 91,89,87,86**
CSF £37.21 CT £200.00 TOTE £7.20: £2.20, £1.80, £2.00; EX 37.60 Trifecta £228.80.
Owner K&J Bloodstock Ltd **Bred** Epona Bloodstock Ltd **Trained** Hambleton, N Yorks

FOCUS
This modest handicap was run at a fair pace.

2150 D M KEITH: SKODA, SEAT & HONDA H'CAP 1m 6f
4:25 (4:27) (Class 5) (0-70,68) 3-Y-O £5,433 (£1,617; £808; £404; £400; £400) Stalls Low

Form RPR

032- **1** **Moon King (FR)**[185] 8575 3-8-13 **60**.................................... JosephineGordon 1 71
(Ralph Beckett) *hld up towards rr: hdwy on wd outside over 2f out: rdn and edgd rt and lft over 1f out: str run to ld ins fnl f: sn clr* **10/1**

46-4 **2** 4 **L'Un Deux Trois (IRE)**[26] 1510 3-9-7 **68**.................................... HayleyTurner 10 73
(Michael Bell) *cl up: led after 3f: pushed along 3f out: rdn 2f out: clr over 1f out: hdd ins fnl f: kpt on same pce* **3/1[2]**

05-5 **3** 5 **Well Funded (IRE)**[27] 1484 3-8-8 **55**.................................... PaulHanagan 12 53
(James Bethell) *in tch: hdwy over 3f out: chsd ldrs 2f out: rdn to chse ldr over 1f out: sn drvn and kpt on one pce* **12/1**

6-23 **4** 1 3/4 **Tabou Beach Boy**[37] 1270 3-8-9 **56**.................................... NathanEvans 7 52
(Michael Easterby) *in tch: hdwy over 3f out: rdn along to chse ldrs 2f out: sn drvn and no imp* **8/1[3]**

33-0 **5** 2 1/2 **One To Go**[20] 1645 3-9-7 **68**.................................... DavidAllan 3 60
(Tim Easterby) *prom: effrt 3f out: rdn along to chse ldr 2f out: sn drvn and wknd appr fnl f* **9/1**

044- **6** 1 1/2 **Sinndarella (IRE)**[178] 8782 3-8-3 **50**.................................... JamesSullivan 11 40
(Sarah Hollinshead) *a towards rr* **50/1**

-222 **7** 7 **Rich Cummins**[5] 2011 3-8-11 **58**.................................... JoeFanning 4 38
(Mark Johnston) *trckd ldrs on inner: hdwy 3f out: rdn along 2f out: drvn and wknd over 1f out* **11/8[1]**

500- **8** 3/4 **Magrevio (IRE)**[191] 8372 3-9-4 **65**.................................... GrahamLee 2 44
(Liam Bailey) *led 3f: chsd ldr: rdn along over 3f out: sn wknd* **66/1**

000- **9** *15* **New Expo (IRE)**[164] 9074 3-8-2 **49** oh2.......................... ShelleyBirkett 9 7
(Julia Feilden) *towards rr: sme hdwy 1/2-way: rdn along over 4f out: sn outpcd and bhd (trainer's rep said gelding was unsuited by the good ground and would prefer a faster surface)* **66/1**

00-4 **10** *17* **Velvet Vista**[83] 598 3-8-7 **54**.......................... BenCurtis 6
(Mark H Tompkins) *a in rr* **33/1**

000- **11** *153* **Our Boy Zeus (IRE)**[211] 7778 3-8-2 **49** oh4.................. AndrewMullen 5
(Micky Hammond) *a in rr: bhd 1/2-way: t.o fnl 4f* **150/1**

3m 5.69s (-1.31) **Going Correction** +0.20s/f (Good) **11 Ran SP% 113.5**
Speed ratings (Par 98): **111,108,105,104,103 102,98,98,89,79**
CSF £38.34 CT £367.74 TOTE £8.50: £2.20, £1.30, £3.70; EX 36.50 Trifecta £255.60.
Owner What Asham Partnership **Bred** Rashit Shaykhutdinov **Trained** Kimpton, Hants

FOCUS
An ordinary 3yo staying handicap.

2151 EVERY RACE LIVE ON RACING TV H'CAP — 7f
4:55 (4:57) (Class 4) (0-80,80) 4-Y-0+

£6,727 (£2,002; £1,000; £500; £400; £400) **Stalls** Low

Form RPR

-331 **1** **Saisons D'Or (IRE)**[18] 1695 4-9-0 **73**.......................... JackGarritty 12 84
(Jedd O'Keeffe) *trckd ldrs: hdwy to ld 2f out: sn rdn: drvn and kpt on wl fnl f* **7/1**

231- **2** *1* **Shawaamekh**[218] 7521 5-9-3 **76**..........................(t) DavidNolan 10 84
(Declan Carroll) *trckd ldrs: hdwy 3f out: chal 2f out: sn rdn and ev ch tl drvn ins fnl f and kpt on same pce towards fin* **6/1**[2]

2110 **3** *1 1/4* **Kupa River (IRE)**[10] 1895 5-8-10 **74**..........................(h) BenSanderson(5) 11 79
(Roger Fell) *in tch: hdwy on outer wl over 2f out: rdn to chse ldrs over 1f out: drvn and kpt on same pce fnl f* **8/1**

20-4 **4** *1 3/4* **Twin Appeal (IRE)**[9] 1925 8-9-2 **75**.......................... ShaneGray 7 75
(Karen Tutty) *chsd ldrs: rdn along and sltly outpcd 2f out: kpt on u.p fnl f* **14/1**

6302 **5** *nk* **Murdanova (IRE)**[15] 1768 6-9-1 **74**..........................(p) DaleSwift 4 73
(Ivan Furtado) *trckd ldrs on inner: hdwy 3f out: rdn along 2f out: sn drvn and kpt on one pce* **16/1**

060- **6** *2 1/4* **Roller**[169] 8999 6-9-5 **78**.......................... NathanEvans 2 71
(Michael Easterby) *hld up in rr: hdwy over 2f out: styd on fnl f: nrst fin* **13/2**[3]

45-0 **7** *1 3/4* **Theodorico (IRE)**[28] 1457 6-9-7 **80**.......................... BenCurtis 8 68
(David Loughnane) *cl up: slt ld 3f out: rdn and hdd 2f out: grad wknd* **4/1**[1]

360- **8** *2 3/4* **Final Frontier (IRE)**[128] 9661 6-8-13 **72**.......................... JamesSullivan 6 53
(Ruth Carr) *hld up: a towards rr* **20/1**

300- **9** *nse* **Yorbelucky**[199] 8135 4-8-13 **72**..........................(w) PJMcDonald 13 53
(Ian Williams) *a in rr* **14/1**

05-0 **10** *2* **Prevent**[28] 1457 4-9-5 **78**.......................... PaulMulrennan 5 53
(Ian Williams) *a in rr* **33/1**

100- **11** *13* **Rose Marmara**[211] 7780 6-8-10 **74**..........................(tp) ConnorMurtagh(5) 3 14
(Brian Rothwell) *led: rdn along 3f out: sn hdd & wknd* **80/1**

1m 27.81s (0.61) **Going Correction** +0.20s/f (Good) **11 Ran SP% 99.4**
Speed ratings (Par 105): **104,102,101,99,99 96,94,91,91,89 74**
CSF £34.53 CT £179.34 TOTE £6.00: £2.30, £1.70, £2.30; EX 37.10 Trifecta £184.70.
Owner The Fatalists **Bred** Mount Coote Stud & Knocktoran Stud **Trained** Middleham Moor, N Yorks
■ Pastime was withdrawn. Price at time of withdrawal 9-2. Rule 4 applies to all bets - deduction 15p in the pound

2152 ROYAL PIGEON RACING ASSOCIATION H'CAP — 1m
5:25 (5:25) (Class 6) (0-60,61) 3-Y-0

£3,568 (£1,061; £530; £400; £400; £400) **Stalls** Low

Form RPR

-045 **1** **Remembering You (IRE)**[48] 1140 3-9-5 **59**.......................... AdamKirby 7 66+
(Clive Cox) *hld up in tch: hdwy 3f out: chal 2f out: sn rdn and slt ld wl over 1f out: drvn and edgd lft ins fnl f: kpt on wl towards fin* **11/2**[3]

50-4 **2** *3/4* **Hector's Here**[17] 1721 3-9-2 **56**.......................... DaleSwift 2 61
(Ivan Furtado) *hld up in rr: hdwy on inner wl over 2f out: rdn to chal over 1f out: ev ch ent fnl f: sn drvn and kpt on same pce towards fin* **3/1**[1]

046- **3** *nk* **Lincoln Tale (IRE)**[190] 8411 3-9-4 **58**.......................... DavidNolan 5 63
(David O'Meara) *hld up in rr: hdwy on outer over 2f out: rdn to chse ldrs over 1f out: kpt on fnl f* **10/1**

00-0 **4** *2 3/4* **Jack Randall**[20] 1649 3-9-3 **57**.......................... DavidAllan 4 56
(Tim Easterby) *trckd ldrs on inner: hdwy and cl up 3f out: disp ld over 2f out and sn rdn: drvn over 1f out and kpt on same pce* **8/1**

0030 **5** *3 1/2* **Alfred The Grey (IRE)**[6] 1979 3-9-4 **58**.......................... TomEaves 11 49
(Tracy Waggott) *trckd ldrs: hdwy 3f out: led 2f out: sn rdn: drvn and hdd: grad wknd appr fnl f* **22/1**

-604 **6** *2 1/4* **Monsieur Piquer (FR)**[13] 1825 3-9-2 **61**..........................(p1) HarrisonShaw(5) 3 47
(K R Burke) *trckd ldrs: hdwy on inner 3f out: sn cl up: rdn along 2f out: sn drvn and wknd* **7/1**

664- **7** *nse* **Burnage Boy (IRE)**[188] 8475 3-9-3 **57**.......................... GrahamLee 6 43
(Micky Hammond) *a towards rr* **16/1**

00-4 **8** *3 1/2* **George Ridsdale**[15] 1764 3-9-3 **57**.......................... NathanEvans 1 35
(Michael Easterby) *led: rdn along over 2f out: drvn wl over 1f out: sn hdd & wknd (jockey said gelding hung right-handed)* **9/2**[2]

040- **9** *2 1/4* **Dragons Will Rise (IRE)**[214] 7666 3-9-3 **57**.......................... PaulMulrennan 9 30
(Micky Hammond) *dwlt: a in rr* **25/1**

01-0 **10** *1/2* **Uncle Norman (FR)**[26] 1504 3-9-5 **59**..........................(b) RachelRichardson 8 31
(Tim Easterby) *t.k.h: cl up: rdn along wl over 2f out: sn wknd* **14/1**

0600 **11** *17* **Tanzerin (IRE)**[24] 1549 3-9-3 **57**.......................... KevinStott 10
(Charlie Fellowes) *cl up: rdn along 3f out: sn wknd* **25/1**

1m 43.54s (1.94) **Going Correction** +0.20s/f (Good) **11 Ran SP% 115.9**
Speed ratings (Par 96): **98,97,96,94,90 88,88,84,82,82 65**
CSF £21.36 CT £160.41 TOTE £7.10: £1.10, £1.70, £3.80; EX 27.90 Trifecta £175.10.
Owner Phillip Cove & Gb Horseracing **Bred** Thomas Hassett **Trained** Lambourn, Berks
■ Stewards' Enquiry : Dale Swift four-day ban: used whip above permitted level (13-16 May)

FOCUS
This was a tight-looking 3yo handicap. The opening level is fluid, but the second has been rated as improving slightly on his Newcastle effort last time out.

2153 RACING AGAIN ON TUESDAY 7TH MAY H'CAP — 5f 110y
5:55 (5:55) (Class 6) (0-60,60) 4-Y-0+

£3,568 (£1,061; £530; £400; £400; £400) **Stalls** High

Form RPR

4301 **1** **Hic Bibi**[17] 1715 4-9-4 **57**.......................... BenCurtis 6 70
(David Loughnane) *racd wd: cl up: hdwy 2f out: rdn to ld wl over 1f out: clr ent fnl f: kpt on strly* **5/2**[1]

5311 **2** *3 3/4* **Steelriver (IRE)**[15] 1766 9-9-4 **57**.......................... PhilDennis 5 58
(Michael Herrington) *trckd ldrs: hdwy over 2f out: sn ev ch: drvn over 1f out: kpt on same pce* **9/2**[3]

0446 **3** *2* **Roaring Rory**[15] 1765 6-9-0 **56**..........................(p) JamieGormley(3) 8 50
(Ollie Pears) *in rr: hdwy 2f out: rdn over 1f out: kpt on wl fnl f* **9/1**

-143 **4** *nk* **Ginger Jam**[15] 1765 4-9-1 **59**.......................... FayeMcManoman(5) 1 52
(Nigel Tinkler) *hld up: hdwy on inner over 2f out: swtchd rt and rdn to chse ldrs over 1f out: sn drvn and no imp* **3/1**[2]

-116 **5** *2 1/2* **Santafiora**[89] 468 5-9-4 **57**.......................... PaulMulrennan 10 42
(Julie Camacho) *towards rr: hdwy over 2f out: rdn to chse ldrs wl over 1f out: sn drvn and kpt on one pce* **10/1**

011 **6** *1/2* **Mr Potter**[27] 1477 6-9-3 **56**..........................(v) PhilipPrince 3 39
(Richard Guest) *chsd ldng pair: rdn along over 2f out: drvn over 1f out: grad wknd* **20/1**

50-2 **7** *3* **Kibaar**[13] 1817 7-9-7 **60**.......................... JamesSullivan 9 33
(Ruth Carr) *in tch: hdwy 1/2-way: sn chsng ldrs: rdn 2f out: sn drvn and btn (jockey said gelding ran too free)* **15/2**

0-00 **8** *1* **Oriental Relation (IRE)**[32] 1364 8-9-3 **56**..........................(bt) LewisEdmunds 4 26
(John Balding) *led: rdn 2f out: hdd wl over 1f out: grad wknd* **50/1**

5400 **9** *2 3/4* **Avon Green**[10] 1883 4-9-3 **56**.......................... JoeFanning 2 17
(Joseph Tuite) *chsd ldrs: rdn along over 2f out: drvn wl over 1f out: sn wknd* **33/1**

-240 **10** *2 1/4* **Dandilion (IRE)**[13] 1818 6-9-2 **55**..........................(t) LukeMorris 7 8
(Alex Hales) *a towards rr* **33/1**

1m 7.29s (1.49) **Going Correction** +0.20s/f (Good) **10 Ran SP% 115.2**
Speed ratings (Par 101): **98,93,90,89,86 85,81,80,76,73**
CSF £13.22 CT £86.00 TOTE £3.30: £1.40, £1.50, £3.20; EX 15.20 Trifecta £111.60.
Owner Peter Onslow **Bred** Peter Onslow **Trained** Tern Hill, Shropshire

FOCUS
They went a routine sort of pace in this moderate sprint handicap. The second sets the level.
T/Jkpt: Not Won. T/Plt: £75.70 to a £1 stake. Pool: £78,089.95 - 752.49 winning units T/Qpdt: £15.50 to a £1 stake. Pool: £7,257.66 - 346.15 winning units **Joe Rowntree**

2154 - 2155a (Foreign Racing) - See Raceform Interactive

1432 NAVAN (L-H)
Sunday, April 28

OFFICIAL GOING: Yielding

2156a COMMITTED STKS (LISTED RACE) — 5f 164y
3:10 (3:10) 3-Y-0

£25,247 (£8,130; £3,851; £1,711; £855; £427)

RPR

1 **Inverleigh (IRE)**[205] 7965 3-9-3 100.......................... DonaghO'Connor 3 106
(G M Lyons, Ire) *dwlt and pushed along briefly in rr early: hdwy between horses 1 1/2f out to chse ldrs: rdn to ld nr side ins fnl f and styd on wl to assert clsng stages* **6/1**

2 *1 3/4* **The Irish Rover (IRE)**[22] 1600 3-9-3 105.......................... RyanMoore 5 100
(A P O'Brien, Ire) *w.w: tk clsr order fr 2f out: rdn in 3rd ins fnl f and no imp on wnr u.p in 2nd nr fin: jst hld 2nd* **5/2**[1]

3 *nse* **Cava (IRE)**[301] 4438 3-8-12 100.......................... SeamieHeffernan 2 95+
(Joseph Patrick O'Brien, Ire) *w.w: gng wl bhd ldrs far side 2f out: nt clr run 1/2f out and sn outpcd: sn dropped to 9th: rdn and r.o ins fnl f into 3rd nr fin: jst failed for 2nd: nrst fin* **4/1**[2]

4 *hd* **Rainbow Moonstone (IRE)**[22] 1601 3-8-12 89.......................... DeclanMcDonogh 9 94
(Joseph Patrick O'Brien, Ire) *mid-div nr side: rdn under 2f out and sme hdwy over 1f out: no imp on wnr in 4th nr fin: kpt on same pce* **16/1**

5 *1* **Eclipse Storm**[8] 1962 3-9-3 91.......................... ConorMaxwell 7 96
(J A Stack, Ire) *chsd ldrs nr side: impr to dispute ld 1 1/2f out and sn led: rdn and hdd ins fnl f: wknd clsng stages* **25/1**

6 *nk* **Chicago May (IRE)**[189] 8437 3-8-12 90.......................... ColinKeane 8 90
(G M Lyons, Ire) *sn led nr side tl jnd bef 1/2-way and sn hdd: pushed along 2f out and sn no ex bhd ldrs: one pce ins fnl f* **5/1**[3]

7 *2* **San Andreas (IRE)**[22] 1600 3-9-3 99.......................... DonnachaO'Brien 6 88
(A P O'Brien, Ire) *dwlt: sn chsd ldrs: pushed along in 2nd under 2f out and s no ex u.p bhd ldrs: wknd 1f out* **10/1**

8 *2 1/4* **Gustavus Weston (IRE)**[189] 8438 3-9-3 92.......................... GaryCarroll 4 81
(Joseph G Murphy, Ire) *prom tl sn hdd and settled bhd ldr early: disp ld bef 1/2-way and sn led narrowly: jnd 1 1/2f out and sn hdd: wknd far side ins fnl f* **14/1**

9 *2 1/2* **Chestnut Express (IRE)**[221] 7437 3-8-12 78..........................(t) ChrisHayes 10 68
(D J Bunyan, Ire) *towards rr: rdn and no imp nr side 1 1/2f out: one pce after* **33/1**

10 *7* **Chicas Amigas (IRE)**[22] 1601 3-8-12 93..........................(p) ShaneFoley 1 45
(Mrs John Harrington, Ire) *chsd ldrs: pushed along far side after 1/2-way and sn no ex u.p: wknd ins fnl f where n.m.r briefly and eased* **6/1**

1m 14.04s **10 Ran SP% 122.2**
CSF £22.49 TOTE £5.80: £1.90, £1.40, £1.80; DF 22.20 Trifecta £85.30.
Owner Mrs A G Kavanagh & Michael Downey **Bred** Miss Hannah Patterson **Trained** Dunsany, Co Meath

FOCUS
An up-to-standard Listed sprint for three-year-olds saw an impressive win for an improving colt making his seasonal debut. The standard hangs on the fourth, fifth and sixth.

2157a IRISH STALLION FARMS EBF SALSABIL STKS (LISTED RACE) (FILLIES) — 1m 2f
3:40 (3:40) 3-Y-0

£31,891 (£10,270; £4,864; £2,162; £1,081; £540)

RPR

1 **Pink Dogwood (IRE)**[203] 8024 3-9-0 104.......................... RyanMoore 5 99+
(A P O'Brien, Ire) *w.w: 7th 1/2-way: tk clsr order gng wl on outer fr 2f out: drvn to ld 1f out and kpt on wl under hands and heels ins fnl f: readily* **4/5**[1]

2 *1/2* **Encapsulation (IRE)**[10] 1901 3-9-0 0.......................... ColinKeane 4 98
(Noel Meade, Ire) *hld up towards rr: tk clsr order gng wl over 2f out: pushed along in 8th under 2f out and prog on outer to chal in cl 2nd ins fnl f where rdn: kpt on wl wout matching wnr* **16/1**

3 *1 1/4* **Tarnawa (IRE)**[25] 1528 3-9-0 98.......................... ChrisHayes 1 95
(D K Weld, Ire) *chsd ldrs: 4th 1/2-way: n.m.r on inner bhd ldrs briefly under 2f out: sn rdn in 4th and impr into 3rd ins fnl f where no imp on ldrs: kpt on same pce* **4/1**[2]

The Form Book Flat 2019, Raceform Ltd, Newbury, RG14 5SJ

4 nk **Fresnel**[35] 1307 3-9-0 0 .... GaryHalpin 3 94
(Jack W Davison, Ire) *chsd ldrs: 5th 1/2-way: n.m.r briefly fr 2f out and sn dropped to 7th briefly: rdn in 5th ins fnl f and kpt on same pce into 4th nr fin where no imp on ldrs* **40/1**

5 3 **Altair (IRE)**[93] 417 3-9-0 0 .... DonnachaO'Brien 6 88
(Joseph Patrick O'Brien, Ire) *dwlt: in rr: rdn 2f out and impr into 7th ent fnl f: kpt on under hands and heels into nvr threatening 5th on line* **14/1**

6 shd **Credenza (IRE)**[196] 8241 3-9-0 96 .... SeamieHeffernan 9 88
(A P O'Brien, Ire) *broke wl to ld: rdn over 2f out and hdd u.p 1f out: no ex and wknd into 5th ins fnl f: denied 5th on line* **16/1**

7 ½ **Trethias**[210] 7813 3-9-0 97 .... ShaneFoley 2 87
(Mrs John Harrington, Ire) *mid-div: 6th 1/2-way: pushed along under 3f out and n.m.r on inner 2f out: checked and dropped towards rr briefly over 1f out: rdn and kpt on again ins fnl f: nvr trbld ldrs* **8/1**

8 2¼ **Sovereigns Bright (IRE)**[15] 1778 3-9-0 79 .... RobbieColgan 7 83
(Ms Sheila Lavery, Ire) *sn chsd ldrs: 3rd 1/2-way: rdn bhd ldrs 2f out and sn no ex: wknd over 1f out* **50/1**

9 2¼ **Harriet's Force (IRE)**[22] 1601 3-9-0 88 .... ShaneBKelly 8 78
(Keith Henry Clarke, Ire) *hld up towards rr: 8th 1/2-way: rdn 2f out and no imp u.p nr side over 1f out: one pce after* **66/1**

10 4½ **Chablis (IRE)**[187] 8517 3-9-0 0 .... WayneLordan 10 69
(A P O'Brien, Ire) *cl up bhd ldr: 2nd 1/2-way: drvn bhd ldr over 2f out and wknd 1 1/2f out* **6/1**[3]

2m 15.31s (-0.49) **10 Ran SP% 125.3**
CSF £19.43 TOTE £1.60: £1.02, £3.70, £1.10; DF 16.00 Trifecta £73.20.
Owner Derrick Smith & Mrs John Magnier & Michael Tabor **Bred** Sweetmans Bloodstock **Trained** Cashel, Co Tipperary

FOCUS
A smooth win on seasonal debut for one of the leading Oaks fancies and she can build on this with that classic in mind. They seemed to go steadily early on but quickened from the top of the straight and the front two came from the rear. The time was poor compared with the 3yo handicap and the second, fourth and eighth potentially limit the form.

2158a SEQUENCE EVENTS VINTAGE CROP STKS (GROUP 3) 1m 6f
4:15 (4:15) 4-Y-0+
£33,513 (£10,810; £5,135; £2,297; £1,162; £594)

RPR

1 **Master Of Reality (IRE)**[175] 8860 4-9-3 99 .... WayneLordan 5 110
(Joseph Patrick O'Brien, Ire) *pushed along to sn ld: over 1 l clr at 1/2-way: reduced advantage after 1/2-way: stl gng wl 3f out: rdn 1 1/2f out and sn hdd narrowly: regained narrow advantage ins fnl f and kpt on wl nr fin: all out* **33/1**

2 nk **Mustajeer**[15] 1777 6-9-4 110 ....(h) ColinKeane 2 109
(G M Lyons, Ire) *prom tl sn settled bhd ldrs early: 7th 1/2-way: hdwy 3f out: sn swtchd lft and rdn in 3rd over 2f out: impr to ld narrowly over 1f out tl hdd narrowly ins fnl f: kpt on wl wout matching wnr* **12/1**

3 ¾ **Southern France (IRE)**[197] 8188 4-9-3 111 .... DonnachaO'Brien 9 109
(A P O'Brien, Ire) *sweated up befhand: sn trckd ldr in 2nd: strly pressed wnr over 2f out: sn pushed along and lost pl: rdn in 3rd over 1f out and no imp on ldrs clsng stages: kpt on* **2/1**[2]

4 ¾ **Twilight Payment (IRE)**[19] 1674 6-9-4 109 ....(p) KevinManning 4 107
(J S Bolger, Ire) *prom tl sn settled bhd ldrs: 4th 1/2-way: disp 4th 4f out: rdn bhd ldrs under 3f out: u.p in 4th 1 1/2f out: kpt on ins fnl f: nvr trbld ldrs* **7/1**[3]

5 4½ **Capri (IRE)**[154] 9270 5-9-4 118 .... RyanMoore 7 101
(A P O'Brien, Ire) *w.w in mid-div: 6th 1/2-way: pushed along and tk clsr order fr 3f out: rdn in 5th under 2f out and no imp on ldrs 1f out: one pce under hands and heels ins fnl f* **5/4**[1]

6 ½ **Brazos (USA)**[19] 1674 5-9-4 97 ....(b) RobbieColgan 3 100
(John Joseph Murphy, Ire) *dwlt and pushed along towards rr early: 8th 1/2-way: pushed along bef st and struggling u.p in 9th over 2f out: sme hdwy into 6th ins fnl f: kpt on one pce* **33/1**

7 5½ **Cimeara (IRE)**[21] 1620 4-9-3 102 .... SeamieHeffernan 6 93
(Joseph Patrick O'Brien, Ire) *dwlt and in rr early: 5th 1/2-way: disp 4th 4f out: pushed along in 5th over 3f out and sn no ex: wknd over 2f out* **14/1**

8 1½ **Nakeeta**[173] 8911 8-9-4 105 ....(t) RonanWhelan 1 90
(Iain Jardine) *hld up towards rr: last at 1/2-way: pushed along over 3f out and no imp on ldrs u.p in 6th briefly under 2f out: sn wknd* **25/1**

9 9½ **Whirling Dervish**[19] 1674 4-9-3 100 ....(p) ShaneFoley 8 78
(Mrs John Harrington, Ire) *chsd ldrs: 3rd 1/2-way: niggled along in 3rd over 4f out: rdn bhd ldrs over 3f out and sn no ex: wknd over 2f out* **11/1**

3m 10.24s (-4.76) **9 Ran SP% 122.7**
WFA 4 from 5yo+ 1lb
CSF £392.21 TOTE £21.20: £10.70, £3.50, £1.02; DF 760.70 Trifecta £2381.10.
Owner Lloyd J Williams **Bred** March Thoroughbreds **Trained** Owning Hill, Co Kilkenny

FOCUS
A huge shock in this Group 3 staying event with the winner showing much improved form on his first start since being gelded. It's been rated around the balance of the second and sixth.

2159 - 2160a (Foreign Racing) - See Raceform Interactive

CAPANNELLE (R-H)
Sunday, April 28

OFFICIAL GOING: Turf: good

2161a PREMIO REGINA ELENA SHADWELL (GROUP 3) (3YO FILLIES) (GRANDE COURSE) (TURF) 1m
3:30 3-Y-0
£63,063 (£27,747; £15,135; £7,567)

RPR

1 **Fullness Of Life (IRE)**[196] 8245 3-8-11 0 .... GeraldMosse 7 99
(A Botti, Italy) *settled towards rr: tk clsr order and rdn along 2f out: hdwy to ld 150yds out: r.o wl* **15/8**[1]

2 1½ **Intense Battle (IRE)** 3-8-11 0 .... DarioDiTocco 2 96
(Marco Gasparini, Italy) *hld up in midfield: shkn up and hdwy 2f out: led over 1f out: hdd 150yds out: kpt on: rdn out* **174/10**

3 nk **Dehara (IRE)**[224] 3-8-11 0 ....(t) ChristianDiNapoli 12 95
(Rinaldo Boccardelli, Italy) *w.w towards rr: drvn along and hdwy on outer over 2f out: rdn 1f out and r.o wl: nvr getting to wnr* **39/1**

4 hd **Must Be Late (IRE)**[189] 8465 3-8-11 0 .... CarloFiocchi 5 95
(A Botti, Italy) *disp ld 2f: settled bhd ldrs: rdn along under 3f out: hdwy to ld under 2f out: hdd over 1f out: kpt on* **4/1**[3]

5 snk **Miss Moon (FR)**[189] 8465 3-8-11 0 .... DarioVargiu 3 94
(A Botti, Italy) *sn cl up: drvn along to press ldr over 2f out: rdn in 2nd over 1f out: no ex and lost position fnl f* **15/8**[1]

6 hd **Lamaire (IRE)**[22] 3-8-11 0 .... SilvanoMulas 4 94
(Riccardo Santini, Italy) *disp ld 2f: trckd ldr: effrt 2f out: kpt on: nt pce to chal* **91/10**

7 1½ **Bridge Battlango (IRE)**[343] 3-8-11 0 ....(t) PasqualeBorrelli 8 90
(Pierpaolo Sbariggia, Italy) *in rr of midfield: shkn up 2f out: kpt on wl but nvr on terms* **136/1**

8 nk **Cielo D'Irlanda (IRE)** 3-8-11 0 .... SalvatoreBasile 13 90
(D Grilli, Italy) *settled towards rr: rdn along in last 2f out: sme late hdwy but n.d* **21/1**

9 1¼ **Greach (IRE)**[196] 8245 3-8-11 0 ....(t) MarioSanna 1 87
(Sergio Dettori, Italy) *hld up in midfield: drvn along and briefly threatened 2f out: outpcd fnl f* **8/1**

10 1½ **Verde E Rosa (IRE)**[22] 3-8-11 0 .... FabioBranca 11 83
(Nicolo Simondi, Italy) *midfield: rdn over 2f out: kpt on same pce* **43/20**[2]

11 2½ **New Queen**[136] 9522 3-8-11 0 ....(t) AntonioFresu 6 78
(L Bietolini, Italy) *hld up in midfield: shkn up over 2f out: sn outpcd: plugged on same pce* **48/1**

12 1¼ **Crisaff's Queen**[168] 3-8-11 0 ....(t) SamueleDiana 9 75
(Agostino Affe', Italy) *midfield: rdn along 2f out: sn outpcd: eased fnl f* **202/10**

13 6 **Stone Tornado**[22] 3-8-11 0 .... AndreaAtzeni 10 61
(A Botti, Italy) *led after 2f: pushed along under 4f out: pressed and rdn along over 2f out: hdd under 2f out: qckly dropped away* **13/2**

1m 35.9s (-3.90) **13 Ran SP% 175.6**
PARI-MUTUEL (all including 1 euro stake): WIN 2.88; PLACE 4.03, 6.30, 10.12; DF 208.26.
Owner Scuderia New Age Srl **Bred** Allevamenot La Nuova Sbarra S R L **Trained** Italy

2162a PREMIO PARIOLI SHADWELL (GROUP 3) (3YO COLTS) (GRANDE COURSE) (TURF) 1m
4:45 3-Y-0
£63,063 (£27,747; £15,135; £7,567)

RPR

1 **Out Of Time (ITY)**[21] 3-9-2 0 .... AndreaAtzeni 7 102
(A Botti, Italy) *w.w towards rr: clsd fr 2f out: sustained run to ld fnl 75yds: sn asserted: readily* **57/10**[3]

2 1¼ **Mission Boy**[22] 3-9-2 0 .... CarloFiocchi 5 99
(A Botti, Italy) *a.p: rdn to chse ldr fr 1 1/2f out: jst abt to hd ldr whn passed by eventual wnr fnl 75yds: no ex cl home* **9/10**[1]

3 hd **Pensiero D'Amore (IRE)**[140] 3-9-2 0 .... DarioVargiu 8 99
(A Botti, Italy) *a cl up on outer: led 2f out: rdn over 1f out: styd on u.p: hdd fnl 75yds: kpt on gamely* **27/4**

4 6 **Gates Of Horn (IRE)**[188] 8474 3-9-2 0 .... FabioBranca 9 85
(P Riccioni, Italy) *hld up in fnl trio: rdn and began to cl ins fnl 2f: wnt 4th ent fnl f: nvr anywhere nr ldrs* **28/1**

5 3 **Zoman (ITY)**[22] 3-9-2 0 ....(t) SilvanoMulas 4 78
(Grizzetti Galoppo SRL, Italy) *disp ld: pressed ldr fr 1/2-way: led 2 1/2f out: hdd 2f out: sn wknd: wl hld fnl f* **35/1**

6 nse **Malibu Roan (USA)**[175] 8864 3-9-2 0 ....(t) SamueleDiana 2 78
(Agostino Affe', Italy) *w.w in rr: styd on fr over 1f out: nvr trbld ldrs* **51/1**

7 nk **Saga Timgad (FR)**[166] 9044 3-9-2 0 .... GiuseppeErcegovic 1 77
(Francesco Santella, Italy) *hld up in fnl trio: rdn and no imp 2f out: wl hld fnl f* **241/10**

8 2 **Foot Of King (IRE)**[168] 3-9-2 0 ....(t) FrankieDettori 3 73
(Endo Botti, Italy) *racd keenly: hld up bhd front rnk: rdn and wknd ins fnl 1 1/2f* **9/1**

9 6½ **Boitron (FR)**[15] 1752 3-9-2 0 .... RossaRyan 6 58
(Richard Hannon) *sweated up: disp ld early: led but pressed fr 1/2-way: drvn and hdd over 2 1/2f out: sn btn* **9/4**[2]

1m 34.9s (-4.90) **9 Ran SP% 133.4**
PARI-MUTUEL (all including 1 euro stake): WIN 6.72; PLACE 1.62, 1.13, 1.67; DF 4.20.
Owner Scuderia Del Giglio Sardo Srl **Bred** Rz Del Velino Srl **Trained** Italy

KREFELD (R-H)
Sunday, April 28

OFFICIAL GOING: Turf: good

2163a RENNEN UM DEN PREIS DER SWK STADTWERKE KREFELD - DR. BUSCH-MEMORIAL (GROUP 3) (3YO) (TURF) 1m 110y
3:40 3-Y-0
£28,828 (£10,810; £5,405; £2,702; £1,801)

RPR

1 **Winterfuchs (GER)**[218] 7564 3-9-2 0 .... SibylleVogt 9 106
(Carmen Bocskai, Germany) *hld up in rr: gained 2 pls over 1/2-way: pushed along and prog on inner fr 2f out: disp ld over 1f out: led jst ins fnl f: kpt on strly* **104/10**

2 nk **Moonlight Man (GER)**[196] 8247 3-9-2 0 .... AdriedeVries 3 105
(Markus Klug, Germany) *hld up towards rr on inner: swtchd lft and pushed along 2f out: rdn 1 1/2f out: kpt on into 2nd ins fnl f: nt quite rch wnr* **104/10**

3 nk **King (GER)**[196] 3-9-2 0 .... RenePiechulek 4 105
(C J M Wolters, Holland) *qckly into stride: led: asked to qckn over 2f out: sn rdn: hdd jst ins fnl f: kpt on gamely but nt match wnr* **31/5**[3]

4 3¼ **Sibelius (GER)**[175] 8869 3-9-2 0 .... MaximPecheur 6 98
(Markus Klug, Germany) *mid-div: effrt between rivals over 2f out: rdn 1 1/2f out: unable qck w ldrs: kpt on same pce ins fnl f* **131/10**

5 nk **Noble Moon (GER)**[196] 8247 3-9-2 0 .... FilipMinarik 2 97
(P Schiergen, Germany) *mid-div: asked for effrt over 2f out: sme prog between rivals fr 1 1/2f out: kpt on but nvr threatened* **12/5**[1]

6 shd **Barys**[17] 1713 3-9-2 0 ....(b) JackMitchell 5 97
(Archie Watson) *trckd ldr on outer: pushed along and effrt over 2f out: rdn and ev ch 1 1/2f out: sn no ex and wknd fnl f* **166/10**

7 1¾ **Man On The Moon (GER)**[196] 8247 3-9-2 0 .... MartinSeidl 7 93
(Markus Klug, Germany) *racd in fnl trio: pushed along over 2f out: rdn 1 1/2f out: limited rspnse: kpt on one pce fr over 1f out: n.d* **102/10**

8 ¾ **Nubbel (GER)**[210] 3-9-2 0 .... JiriPalik 8 91
(Markus Klug, Germany) *hld up in fnl pair: dropped to rr over 1/2-way: outpcd and pushed along 2 1/2f out: swtchd lft and rdn 1 1/2f out: no imp: kpt on same pce* **35/1**

9 1 **Hot Team (IRE)**[201] 8097 3-9-2 0 ....(b[1]) PatCosgrave 1 89
(Hugo Palmer) *in tch on inner: pushed along and effrt 2f out: rdn 1 1/2f out: grad wknd fnl f: no ex* **3/1**[2]

10 *2 1/2* **Lacento (IRE)** 3-9-2 0 BauyrzhanMurzabayev 10 83
(A Wohler, Germany) *in tch on outer: unable to go w ldrs whn pce qcknd over 2f out: sn struggling: wknd fr 1 1/2f out* **106/10**

1m 44.7s (-1.90) **10** Ran SP% **118.9**
PARI-MUTUEL (all including 1 euro stake): WIN 11.40 PLACE 3.00, 2.90, 2.60 SF 61.50.
Owner Gestut Ravensberg **Bred** Gestut Ravensberg **Trained** Germany

2164 - 2166a (Foreign Racing) - See Raceform Interactive

1794

LONGCHAMP (R-H)

Sunday, April 28

OFFICIAL GOING: Turf: good to soft

2167a PRIX ALLEZ FRANCE LONGINES (GROUP 3) (4YO+ FILLIES & MARES) (TURF) 1m 2f

2:50 4-Y-O+ **£36,036** (£14,414; £10,810; £7,207; £3,603)

RPR

1 **Morgan Le Faye**[21] 1627 5-8-10 0 MickaelBarzalona 10 110+
(A Fabre, France) *hld up towards rr: nudged along and prog fr over 2f out: pushed along to chal ent fnl f: sn led: in command fnl 110yds: gng away at fin* **7/10**[1]

2 *2* **Tosen Gift (IRE)**[42] 1244 4-8-10 0 FabriceVeron 5 106
(S Kobayashi, France) *in tch: asked to improve 2 1/2f out: disp ld 2f out: led 1 1/2f out: hrd pressed and rdn ent fnl f: sn hdd: kpt on clsng stages* **42/1**

3 *3/4* **Shahnaza (FR)**[21] 1627 4-8-10 0 ChristopheSoumillon 4 105
(A De Royer-Dupre, France) *racd in fnl pair: pushed along 2f out: prog to chse ldng pair ent fnl f: kpt on fnl 110yds: nt pce to chal* **19/5**[2]

4 *2* **Lunch Lady**[29] 1451 4-8-10 0 MaximeGuyon 8 101
(F Head, France) *mid-div: pushed along and effrt over 2f out: sn rdn: disp 3rd ent fnl f: kpt on same pce clsng stages: nvr threatened* **79/10**[3]

5 *4* **Watayouna (FR)**[18] 1708 4-8-10 0 RonanThomas 1 93
(F-H Graffard, France) *mid-div on inner: asked to improve 2f out: limited rspnse: edgd lft whn rdn 1 1/2f out: r.o and sme modest prog ins fnl f* **45/1**

6 *hd* **Qualisaga (FR)**[18] 1708 5-8-10 0 AntoineCoutier 6 92
(Carina Fey, France) *disp early tl sn led: asked to qckn whn chal over 2f out: hdd 1 1/2f out: grad wknd ins fnl f: no ex* **41/1**

7 *snk* **Lady Sidney (FR)**[21] 1627 5-8-10 0 (b) OlivierPeslier 9 92
(R Le Dren Doleuze, France) *cl up: pressed ldr over 2f out: unable qck w ldrs 1 1/2f out: rdn over 1f out: kpt on same pce clsng stages* **14/1**

8 *1 1/4* **Dramatic Queen (USA)**[178] 8770 4-8-10 0 WilliamBuick 3 89
(William Haggas) *disp early tl sn trckd ldr on inner: pushed along 2 1/2f out: sn struggling to go pce: rdn 1 1/2f out: no imp and wknd clsng stages* **83/10**

9 *nk* **Bella Bolide (FR)**[27] 5-8-10 0 CyrilleStefan 2 89
(M Brasme, France) *racd in fnl trio: outpcd and pushed along 2 1/2f out: no imp whn drvn 1 1/2f out: one pce fnl f* **96/1**

10 *4* **Sully (FR)**[43] 4-8-10 0 CristianDemuro 7 81
(Rod Collet, France) *a towards rr: pushed along over 2f out: no rspnse and sn btn: eased cl home* **38/1**

2m 4.43s (0.43) **10** Ran SP% **118.8**
PARI-MUTUEL (all including 1 euro stake): WIN 1.70 PLACE 1.10, 3.20, 1.40 DF 16.70.
Owner Godolphin SNC **Bred** Dieter Burkle **Trained** Chantilly, France

FOCUS
The first two have been rated to form.

2168a PRIX GANAY (GROUP 1) (4YO+) (TURF) 1m 2f 110y

3:25 4-Y-O+ **£154,432** (£61,783; £30,891; £15,432; £7,729)

RPR

1 **Waldgeist**[140] 9473 5-9-2 0 Pierre-CharlesBoudot 1 124+
(A Fabre, France) *settled in 3rd: angled out and pushed along 2f out: prog to chal over 1f out: led ent fnl f: r.o strly fnl 110yds: readily* **17/5**[2]

2 *4 1/2* **Study Of Man (IRE)**[203] 8026 4-9-2 0 StephanePasquier 3 116
(P Bary, France) *disp early: trckd ldr after 2f: pushed along to chse ldr 2f out: rdn 1 1/2f out: kpt on into 2nd fnl 50yds: nt match for wnr* **69/10**[3]

3 *shd* **Ghaiyyath (IRE)**[21] 1628 4-9-2 0 WilliamBuick 4 115
(Charlie Appleby) *disp early: led after 2f: asked to qckn over 2f out: hrd pressed over 1f out: sn hdd: kpt on gamely ins fnl f: lost 2nd fnl 50yds* **1/2**[1]

4 *1 3/4* **Soleil Marin (IRE)**[21] 1628 5-9-2 0 MickaelBarzalona 2 112
(A Fabre, France) *hld up in fnl pair: asked to improve over 2f out: rdn 1 1/2f out: unable qck w ldrs: kpt on ins fnl f: n.d* **13/1**

5 *7* **Intellogent (IRE)**[21] 1628 4-9-2 0 ChristopheSoumillon 5 99
(F Chappet, France) *hld up in rr: outpcd and pushed along over 2f out: sn btn: kpt on same pce fr over 1f out: eased cl home* **71/10**

2m 9.07s (-1.13) **5** Ran SP% **121.5**
PARI-MUTUEL (all including 1 euro stake): WIN 4.40 PLACE 7.50, 12.00 DF 22.00.
Owner Gestut Ammerland & Newsells Park **Bred** The Waldlerche Partnership **Trained** Chantilly, France

FOCUS
Despite the small field, this looked a decent contest.

2169a PRIX DE BARBEVILLE (GROUP 3) (4YO+) (TURF) 1m 7f 110y

4:00 4-Y-O+ **£36,036** (£14,414; £10,810; £7,207; £3,603)

RPR

1 **Holdthasigreen (FR)**[27] 1490 7-9-7 0 TonyPiccone 1 115
(B Audouin, France) *cl up: led after 3f: drvn along over 2f out: kpt on wl: pressed fnl 110yds: a holding on: drvn out* **21/10**[2]

2 *1 1/4* **Way To Paris**[42] 1244 6-9-1 0 CristianDemuro 2 108+
(Andrea Marcialis, France) *hld up towards rr: tk clsr order 1/2-way: travelling wl and nt clr run 2f out: sn drvn along and hdwy: rdn along in 2nd 1f out: a hld: rdn out* **16/1**

3 *4* **Called To The Bar (IRE)**[27] 1490 5-9-3 0 MaximeGuyon 8 105
(Mme Pia Brandt, France) *sn cl up on outer: shkn up 2f out: outpcd and dropped to 4th 1f out: battled bk to go 3rd fnl strides: no ch w front 2: rdn out* **7/5**[1]

4 *hd* **Mahoe (FR)**[27] 1490 4-9-0 0 OlivierPeslier 5 105
(A Junk, France) *led 3f: hdd and settled bhd ldrs: shkn up and hdwy to go 3rd 1f out: sn outpcd by front 2: lost 3rd fnl strides* **9/1**

5 *1 1/4* **Line Des Ongrais (FR)**[27] 1490 8-8-11 0 (p) MorganDelalande 7 97
(P Chemin & C Herpin, France) *towards rr shkn up and gradual hdwy fr 2 1/2f out: clst fin: nvr on terms w ldrs* **57/1**

6 *1/2* **Libello (IRE)**[27] 1490 6-9-1 0 ChristopheSoumillon 3 100
(C Boutin, France) *settled in midfield: effrt 2f out: kpt on same pce: nvr a threat* **12/1**

7 *3 1/2* **Nocturnal Fox (IRE)**[21] 1628 4-9-4 0 VincentCheminaud 6 103
(A Fabre, France) *settled in rr of midfield: relegated to last 1/2-way: effrt over 2f out: no imp and wl hld fnl 2f* **12/1**

8 *3* **Lillian Russell (IRE)**[27] 1490 4-8-10 0 MickaelBarzalona 4 92
(H-A Pantall, France) *cl up early: trckd ldr: drvn along over 2f out: sn dropped away: eased fnl f* **68/10**[3]

3m 22.41s (0.91)
WFA 4 from 5yo+ 1lb **8** Ran SP% **119.7**
PARI-MUTUEL (all including 1 euro stake): WIN 3.10; PLACE 1.10, 1.70, 1.10; DF 22.00.
Owner Jean Gilbert **Bred** J Gilbert & C Le Lay **Trained** France

2170a PRIX DES MIRAMIONES (H'CAP) (4YO) (TURF) 1m

5:10 4-Y-O **£8,558** (£3,423; £2,567; £1,711; £855)

RPR

1 **Hoquilebo (FR)**[40] 4-9-5 0 (p) Pierre-CharlesBoudot 11 69
(T Castanheira, France) **63/10**[2]

2 *1* **Minnehaha (FR)**[15] 4-8-5 0 MlleLeaBails(6) 6 59
(A Schouteet, Belgium) **21/1**

3 *snk* **Mirrii Yanan (IRE)**[40] 4-9-0 0 FabienLefebvre 5 62
(Carla O'Halloran, France) **36/1**

4 *1 1/2* **Espionne (FR)**[18] 4-9-3 0 TonyPiccone 16 61
(H De Nicolay, France) **66/10**[3]

5 *hd* **Vinaccia (IRE)**[40] 4-9-0 0 (p) ChristopheSoumillon 1 58
(C Lerner, France) **5/2**[1]

6 *hd* **Gossipe (FR)**[163] 4-8-13 0 MathieuPelletan 9 56
(J-L Pelletan, France) **21/1**

7 *hd* **Okiam Des Mottes (FR)**[12] 4-9-6 0 MickaelBerto 12 63
(P Lenogue, France) **18/1**

8 *1/2* **Hopalong Cassidy (FR)**[144] 4-9-3 0 FabriceVeron 17 59
(D & P Prod'Homme, France) **49/1**

9 *3/4* **Captain Kissinger**[17] 1717 4-9-2 0 (b) MickaelBarzalona 18 56
(Jo Hughes, France) *bustled along to ld: asked to qckn over 2f out: sn rdn: hdd ent fnl f: grad wknd clsng stages: no ex* **13/1**

10 *1 3/4* **Descouvrir Baileys (FR)**[40] 4-9-5 0 IoritzMendizabal 4 55
(J-V Toux, France) **9/1**

11 *hd* **Espaldinha (FR)**[15] 4-8-6 0 (b) ThomasTrullier(3) 13 44
(Mme M Bollack-Badel, France) **18/1**

12 *2* **Queen Of Style (IRE)**[47] 4-9-1 0 MarcNobili 10 46
(Rod Collet, France) **12/1**

13 *1 1/4* **Interstellaire (FR)**[106] 4-8-10 0 RonanThomas 15 38
(Mme B Jacques, France) **76/1**

14 *1 1/2* **Vadlana (FR)**[21] 4-9-5 0 (p) AurelienLemaitre 3 44
(Mlle B Renk, France) **5/1**

15 *6 1/2* **Crystal Blanc (FR)**[123] 4-9-3 0 JeffersonSmith 2 27
(Guillaume Courbot, France) **108/1**

16 *3* **Amiral Chop (FR)**[78] 4-8-9 0 CyrilleStefan 7 12
(C Boutin, France) **43/1**

17 *snk* **Hiva'Oa (FR)**[184] 4-8-5 0 SebastienJust(3) 14 10
(T Poche, France) **177/1**

18 *10* **Faunus D'Emra (FR)**[93] 4-9-4 0 MorganDelalande 8
(T Poche, France) **116/1**

1m 40.06s (1.66) **18** Ran SP% **120.5**
PARI-MUTUEL (all including 1 euro stake): WIN 7.30 PLACE 3.50, 6.10, 9.90 DF 58.10.
Owner David Dahan **Bred** P Lamy & S Lamy **Trained** France

2171 - 2181a (Foreign Racing) - See Raceform Interactive

LYON PARILLY (R-H)

Saturday, April 27

OFFICIAL GOING: Turf: very soft

2182a PRIX DE RILLIEUX-LA-PAPE (H'CAP) (4YO+) (TURF) 6f 156y

2:32 4-Y-O+ **£8,108** (£3,243; £2,432; £1,621; £810)

RPR

1 **Vive L'Ami (GER)**[20] 7-8-9 0 (p) FrankPanicucci 6 70
(Christina Bucher, Switzerland) **134/10**

2 *nk* **Canouville (FR)**[114] 4-9-4 0 (b) AurelienLemaitre 9 78
(Mlle Y Vollmer, France) **20/1**

3 *1* **Get Even**[30] 1391 4-9-4 0 AntoineHamelin 10 75
(Jo Hughes, France) *a.p on outer: 5th and drvn 2 1/2f out: styd on u.p fr 1 1/2f out: wnt 1 l 2nd 100yds out: nvr quite on terms and run flattened out cl home* **17/2**

4 *nk* **Chef Oui Chef (FR)**[14] 9-8-8 0 (p) SebastienMaillot 5 64
(M Boutin, France) **63/10**

5 *nk* **Ultim'Reve (FR)**[254] 4-8-11 0 FranckForesi 8 66
(F Foresi, France) **52/1**

6 *2 1/2* **Toriano (FR)**[20] 1631 4-8-13 0 TheoBachelot 2 61
(Waldemar Hickst, Germany) **16/5**[2]

7 *17* **Mojo Boy (FR)**[25] 4-8-9 0 (p) MaximeGuyon 1 6
(Gerald Geisler, Germany) **61/10**[3]

8 *1 3/4* **Nimocis (FR)**[11] 4-8-10 0 TonyPiccone 3 2
(C Boutin, France) **15/1**

9 *2 1/2* **L'Optimiste (FR)**[73] 6-9-6 0 (b) MlleMarieVelon(4) 4 8
(J Parize, France) **44/5**

10 *shd* **Joplin (GER)**[158] 5-9-7 0 ChristopheSoumillon 7 5
(D Fechner, Germany) **27/10**[1]

1m 29.39s **10** Ran SP% **119.2**
PARI-MUTUEL (all including 1 euro stake): WIN 14.40; PLACE 4.00, 5.30, 3.10; DF 99.10.
Owner Frau Sandra Lony & Gerhard Moser **Bred** Gestut Auenquelle **Trained** Switzerland

1923 **NEWCASTLE (A.W)** (L-H)

Monday, April 29

OFFICIAL GOING: Tapeta: standard

Wind: Breezy, half behind in races on the straight course and in over 3f of home straight in races on the Weather: Cloudy, bright

2183 WATCH SKY SPORTS RACING ON SKY 415 H'CAP — 6f (Tp)

2:20 (2:21) (Class 6) (0-65,65) 4-Y-O+

£3,105 (£924; £461; £300; £300; £300) **Stalls** Centre

Form — RPR

0-40 **1** **Kentuckyconnection (USA)**[97] 356 6-8-12 **63**...... HarryRussell(7) 10 72
(Bryan Smart) *hld up: hdwy nr side of gp over 1f out: led wl ins fnl f: pushed out* **9/1**[3]

0-42 **2** 3/4 **Scuzeme**[16] 1765 5-9-3 **61**......(h) SamJames 11 68
(Phillip Makin) *led on nr side of gp: rdn along over 1f out: edgd lft and hdd wl ins fnl f: kpt on same pce cl home* **7/2**[2]

1454 **3** 3 **Gorgeous General**[8] 1973 4-9-1 **59**...... DanielTudhope 7 57
(Lawrence Mullaney) *prom on far side of gp: rdn over 2f out: kpt on ins fnl f: nt rch first two* **12/1**

34-2 **4** hd **Rewaayat**[19] 1684 4-9-7 **65**...... DaneO'Neill 14 62
(Charles Hills) *t.k.h: prom on nr side of gp: effrt and edgd lft over 1f out: outpcd ins fnl f* **5/4**[1]

-100 **5** 2 1/4 **Rockley Point**[16] 1766 6-9-2 **60**......(b) PhilDennis 6 50
(Katie Scott) *cl up on far side of gp: rdn along over 2f out: wknd ins fnl f* **33/1**

0-00 **6** shd **Meshardal (GER)**[16] 1765 9-8-10 **54**......(p) JamesSullivan 3 44
(Ruth Carr) *in tch in centre of gp: drvn along over 2f out: one pce fnl f* **22/1**

3015 **7** 1/2 **Grey Destiny**[19] 1684 9-9-6 **64**......(p) CamHardie 1 53+
(Antony Brittain) *stdd s: hld up on far side of gp: rdn 1/2-way: kpt on fnl f: nvr rchd ldrs* **22/1**

00-0 **8** nk **Poyle George Two**[116] 45 4-8-11 **58**...... RowanScott(3) 5 46
(John Hodge) *hld up on far side of gp: drvn along over 3f out: sme hdwy over 1f out: nvr rchd ldrs* **100/1**

0-40 **9** hd **Kroy**[16] 1765 5-8-7 **54**......(p) BenRobinson(3) 9 41
(Ollie Pears) *hld up in centre of gp: drvn and outpcd over 2f out: rallied ins fnl f: n.d (jockey said he was unable to ride out to the line on the gelding as he was caught on heels)* **11/1**

531- **10** 3/4 **Tadaany (IRE)**[131] 9617 7-8-9 **53**......(p) AndrewMullen 4 38
(Ruth Carr) *in tch on nr side of gp: rdn along over 2f out: wknd fnl f* **22/1**

0260 **11** 1 1/4 **Duke Cosimo**[19] 1686 9-9-7 **65**...... JasonHart 13 46
(Michael Herrington) *hld up in centre of gp: drvn along and outpcd over 2f out: sn btn* **12/1**

00-5 **12** 2 3/4 **Pretty Passe**[94] 410 5-9-0 **58**...... PaulHanagan 8 31
(Martin Todhunter) *midfield in centre of gp: drvn and outpcd wl over 2f out: sn btn* **33/1**

2000 **13** 1 1/4 **Cuppacoco**[16] 1765 4-9-3 **61**......(v1) JoeFanning 12 30
(Ann Duffield) *cl up in centre of gp tl rdn and wknd over 1f out* **14/1**

6-06 **14** 2 **Rantan (IRE)**[31] 1403 6-9-3 **61**...... KevinStott 2 24
(Paul Midgley) *bhd in centre of gp: struggling 1/2-way: nvr on terms* **33/1**

1m 11.88s (-0.62) **Going Correction** +0.125s/f (Slow) **14** Ran SP% **129.9**
Speed ratings (Par 101): **109,108,104,103,100 100,99,99,99,98 96,92,91,88**
CSF £41.03 CT £405.30 TOTE £9.60: £3.30, £1.50, £4.00; EX 57.40 Trifecta £454.00.
Owner Woodcock Electrical Limited **Bred** Turner Breeders LLC **Trained** Hambleton, N Yorks

FOCUS
A modest sprint in which the short-priced favourite disappointed. The principals came from the front half of the field. The form makes sense with the first two clear.

2184 WATCH SKY SPORTS RACING 535 NOVICE STKS — 5f (Tp)

2:50 (2:54) (Class 5) 2-Y-O **£3,752** (£1,116; £557; £278) **Stalls** Centre

Form — RPR

1 **Strive For Glory (USA)** 2-9-0 0...... SeanDavis(5) 2 72+
(Robert Cowell) *t.k.h: sn led: rdn and hdd over 1f out: rallied ins fnl f: regained ld cl home* **15/2**[2]

0 **2** shd **Bezzas Lad (IRE)**[16] 1758 2-9-5 0...... SamJames 6 72
(Phillip Makin) *trckd ldrs: hdwy to ld over 1f out: rdn ins fnl f: hdd cl home* **14/1**[3]

3 1 1/4 **Keep Busy (IRE)** 2-9-0 0...... JasonHart 3 63
(John Quinn) *sn pushed along and rn green in rr: hdwy after 2f: effrt and rdn over 1f out: one pce wl ins fnl f* **18/1**

4 1/2 **Dutch Decoy** 2-9-5 0...... PaulHanagan 4 69+
(Richard Fahey) *s.i.s: sn prom: effrt and rn green over 1f out: kpt on same pce ins fnl f (jockey said colt hung both ways)* **4/9**[1]

5 **5** 3 **Puerto Sol (IRE)**[12] 1844 2-9-2 0...... BenRobinson(3) 1 55
(Brian Ellison) *early ldr: pressed wnr: rdn and ev ch over 1f out: wknd ins fnl f* **25/1**

1m 0.96s (1.46) **Going Correction** +0.125s/f (Slow) **5** Ran SP% **96.8**
Speed ratings (Par 92): **93,92,90,90,85**
CSF £57.77 TOTE £4.70: £2.10, £3.00; EX 39.00 Trifecta £83.90.
Owner T W Morley **Bred** Michael Feuerborn & Amy Feuerborn **Trained** Six Mile Bottom, Cambs
■ Good Night Mr Tom was withdrawn. Price at time of withdrawal 5/1. Rule 4 applies to all bets - deduction 15p in the £

FOCUS
Ordinary juvenile form with the red-hot favourite, whose task appeared to have been made easier with the late withdrawal of market rival Good Night Mr Tom, disappointing.

2185 PARKLANDS DRIVING RANGE H'CAP — 1m 4f 98y (Tp)

3:20 (3:20) (Class 5) (0-75,75) 4-Y-O+

£3,752 (£1,116; £557; £300; £300; £300) **Stalls** High

Form — RPR

6411 **1** **Archive (FR)**[12] 1848 9-8-10 **67**...... BenRobinson(3) 3 73
(Brian Ellison) *trckd ldrs: effrt and wnt 2nd over 1f out: led ins fnl f: hld on wl towards fin* **11/2**[3]

4145 **2** nk **Lopes Dancer (IRE)**[13] 1840 7-9-5 **73**...... JoeFanning 5 78
(Harriet Bethell) *chsd ldr: led over 2f out: edgd rt and hdd ins fnl f: rallied: hld towards fin* **4/1**[2]

000- **3** nk **Archippos**[18] 9156 6-9-7 **75**......(b1) PJMcDonald 2 80
(Philip Kirby) *hld up in midfield: rdn over 2f out: gd hdwy over 1f out: kpt on fnl f: hld nr fin* **11/1**

1132 **4** nk **Royal Cosmic**[26] 1525 5-8-12 **71**...... SeanDavis(5) 10 75
(Richard Fahey) *hld up in midfield: effrt and hung lft over 2f out: hdwy over 1f out: kpt on fnl f: no ex towards fin (jockey said mare hung left in the home straight)* **4/1**[2]

33-3 **5** 3 1/2 **Momtalik (USA)**[35] 1331 4-9-4 **72**......(b1) DaneO'Neill 4 71
(John Gosden) *t.k.h early: hld up in tch: rdn over 2f out: hdwy over 1f out: one pce whn short of room ins fnl f: sn btn* **11/4**[1]

1603 **6** 1 **Thawry**[27] 1508 4-9-4 **72**...... CamHardie 6 70
(Antony Brittain) *hld up on ins: drvn along wl over 2f out: hdwy over 1f out: no imp fnl f* **11/2**[3]

-003 **7** 9 **Be Perfect (USA)**[12] 1848 10-9-1 **69**......(p) JamesSullivan 7 51
(Ruth Carr) *led: rdn and hdd over 2f out: wknd wl over 1f out (jockey said gelding ran flat)* **16/1**

44U- **8** nk **Searching (IRE)**[243] 6668 7-8-13 **70**...... ConorMcGovern(3) 1 52
(Karen Tutty) *t.k.h: prom tl rdn and wknd over 2f out* **28/1**

104- **9** 3 1/2 **Question Of Faith**[166] 7866 8-9-7 **75**...... PaulHanagan 8 51
(Martin Todhunter) *slowly away: bhd: struggling over 4f out: sn btn* **33/1**

033/ **10** 25 **Aislabie (FR)**[799] 7993 6-8-7 **61** oh1...... RachelRichardson 9
(Jason Ward) *hld up: rdn and struggling 4f out: btn and eased fnl 2f* **28/1**

2m 43.75s (2.65) **Going Correction** +0.125s/f (Slow) **10** Ran SP% **121.5**
Speed ratings (Par 103): **96,95,95,95,93 92,86,86,83,67**
CSF £28.56 CT £241.18 TOTE £6.10: £1.70, £1.60, £3.00; EX 32.00 Trifecta £752.80.
Owner Brian Ellison Racing Club **Bred** E A R L Elevages Des Loges & J Hanamy **Trained** Norton, N Yorks

FOCUS
A competitive handicap run at a steady gallop and it produced a cracking four-way finish. The form is rated around the runner-up to his recent best.

2186 BORDER MINSTREL H'CAP — 1m 2f 42y (Tp)

3:55 (3:55) (Class 4) (0-85,85) 4-Y-O+

£5,530 (£1,645; £822; £411; £300; £300) **Stalls** High

Form — RPR

3-30 **1** **Harbour Breeze (IRE)**[16] 1757 4-9-1 **79**...... GrahamLee 4 89
(Lucy Wadham) *cl up: led after 4f: mde rest: rdn over 1f out: hrd pressed fnl f: kpt on wl* **4/1**[3]

30-3 **2** hd **Addis Ababa (IRE)**[18] 1719 4-9-4 **82**...... DanielTudhope 8 91
(David O'Meara) *led 4f: pressed wnr: effrt and rdn 2f out: ev ch ins fnl f: kpt on: hld nr fin* **11/4**[2]

55-5 **3** 3 1/2 **Zabeel Star (IRE)**[18] 1719 7-9-5 **83**...... JasonHart 2 85
(Karen McLintock) *missed break: hld up: effrt over 2f out: sn rdn: hdwy to chse clr ldng pair ins fnl f: kpt on: no imp* **16/1**

00-0 **4** 1 1/2 **Alfa McGuire (IRE)**[21] 1644 4-9-4 **82**...... SamJames 7 81
(Phillip Makin) *t.k.h early: chsd ldrs: effrt and chsd clr ldng pair wl over 1f out to ins fnl f: no ex* **8/1**

0-30 **5** 2 **Tamreer**[2] 2104 4-9-0 **78**......(h) DaneO'Neill 3 73
(Roger Fell) *hld up in tch: rdn along over 2f out: wknd ins fnl f* **16/1**

0-24 **6** nk **Employer (IRE)**[18] 1719 4-9-2 **80**...... PhilDennis 1 74
(Jim Goldie) *hld up: stdy hdwy gng wl over 2f out: rdn fnl f: no imp* **14/1**

60-6 **7** 3 1/4 **Super Kid**[16] 1761 7-9-2 **80**......(t) RachelRichardson 6 68
(Tim Easterby) *hld up: rdn and outpcd over 2f out: sn n.d: btn over 1f out* **16/1**

221- **8** 7 **Merweb (IRE)**[131] 9614 4-8-11 **75**...... DavidEgan 5 49
(Heather Main) *hld up in midfield: hdwy to chse ldrs 1/2-way: drvn over 2f out: wknd over 1f out (trainer said colt may have needed the run after a 131 day break)* **9/4**[1]

460- **9** 2 **Diodorus (IRE)**[346] 2804 5-9-7 **85**......(p) PJMcDonald 9 55
(Karen McLintock) *hld up in tch: drvn and outpcd over 2f out: sn wknd* **14/1**

2m 10.64s (0.24) **Going Correction** +0.125s/f (Slow) **9** Ran SP% **119.5**
Speed ratings (Par 105): **104,103,101,99,98 98,95,89,88**
CSF £16.06 CT £161.70 TOTE £5.80: £1.40, £1.40, £4.80; EX 20.70 Trifecta £237.00.
Owner B J Painter **Bred** Gestut Zur Kuste Ag **Trained** Newmarket, Suffolk

FOCUS
A fair handicap won by an unexposed type. It paid to race handily and there is a slight doubt over the form.

2187 MASTERDEBONAIR.COM H'CAP — 1m 5y (Tp)

4:25 (4:26) (Class 3) (0-95,94) 4-Y-O+ **£7,439** (£2,213; £1,106; £553) **Stalls** Centre

Form — RPR

11/3 **1** **Bowerman**[19] 1694 5-9-7 **94**...... DavidEgan 3 109+
(Roger Varian) *trckd ldrs: smooth hdwy to ld over 1f out: shkn up and sn qckd clr: eased nr fin: readily* **11/8**[1]

1240 **2** 2 1/4 **Tough Remedy (IRE)**[16] 1753 4-9-2 **89**...... PJMcDonald 4 94
(Keith Dalgleish) *hld up: outpcd over 2f out: sn angled lft: hdwy over 1f out: kpt on fnl f to take 2nd nr fin: no ch w wnr* **7/2**[2]

-122 **3** nk **Trevithick**[31] 1401 4-9-2 **89**...... GrahamLee 8 93
(Bryan Smart) *led tl rdn and hdd over 1f out: chsd wnr: no ex and lost 2nd nr fin* **9/2**[3]

121- **4** 3/4 **Bobby K (IRE)**[160] 9164 4-9-3 **90**......(p) RobertHavlin 1 93
(Simon Crisford) *hld up in tch: stdy hdwy over 2f out: drvn along over 1f out: kpt on same pce ins fnl f* **7/1**

000- **5** hd **Nicholas T**[184] 8634 7-8-5 **85**...... CoreyMadden(7) 7 87
(Jim Goldie) *dwlt and wnt lft s: t.k.h: hld up: effrt on outside over 2f out: rdn over 1f out: no ex ins fnl f* **22/1**

3300 **6** 3 **Ballard Down (IRE)**[44] 1232 6-9-4 **91**......(p) DavidNolan 5 86
(David O'Meara) *slowly away: hld up: drvn and outpcd over 2f out: sn n.d* **14/1**

2-03 **7** shd **Gurkha Friend**[44] 1232 7-9-0 **90**...... BenRobinson(3) 6 85
(Karen McLintock) *reluctant to leave paddock: pressed ldr: drvn and ev ch over 2f out: wknd over 1f out* **10/1**

/00- **8** 12 **Moonlightnavigator (USA)**[369] 2069 7-8-12 **85**...... JasonHart 2 52
(John Quinn) *prom: drvn and outpcd over 3f out: btn fnl 2f* **100/1**

1m 38.08s (-0.52) **Going Correction** +0.125s/f (Slow) **8** Ran SP% **116.1**
Speed ratings (Par 107): **107,104,104,103,103 100,100,88**
CSF £6.40 CT £16.82 TOTE £2.80: £1.90, £1.10, £1.30; EX 7.70 Trifecta £23.10.
Owner Paul Smith **Bred** Cheveley Park Stud Ltd **Trained** Newmarket, Suffolk

FOCUS
One-way traffic in this decent handicap, the favourite winning tidily. This was a smart effort and the form looks solid.

2188 MAVEN RESTAURANT & BAR NOW OPEN NOVICE STKS — 1m 5y (Tp)

5:00 (5:03) (Class 5) 3-Y-O+ **£3,752** (£1,116) **Stalls** Centre

Form — RPR

1- **1** **Lord North (IRE)**[192] 8387 3-9-7 0...... RobertHavlin 3 92+
(John Gosden) *reluctant to enter stalls: mde all: clr after 2f: v easily* **1/6**[1]

2 11 **Neesaan** 3-8-9 0 .... GrahamLee 1 55+
(Simon Crisford) *dwlt: chsd wnr: pushed along and outpcd after 2f: n.d after* 7/2[2]

1m 39.49s (0.89) **Going Correction** +0.125s/f (Slow)
WFA 3 from 4yo 14lb 2 Ran SP% **107.9**
Speed ratings (Par 103): **100,89**
TOTE £1.10.
Owner HH Sheikh Zayed bin Mohammed Racing **Bred** Godolphin **Trained** Newmarket, Suffolk
FOCUS
Just the two left and it proved little more than a canter for the 1-6 favourite. He could be smart but it's hard to know what he achieved here.

2189 MISSNEWCASTLE.COM H'CAP 5f (Tp)
5:30 (5:32) (Class 6) (0-55,54) 4-Y-O+
£3,105 (£924; £461; £300; £300; £300) Stalls Centre

Form RPR
5230 1 **Star Cracker (IRE)**[31] 1402 7-8-12 **45** ....(p) PhilDennis 9 52
(Jim Goldie) *mde all on nr side of gp: rdn over 1f out: edgd lft ins fnl f: kpt on wl* 13/2
000- 2 1 1/4 **Someone Exciting**[135] 9555 6-8-11 **49** .... HarrisonShaw(5) 8 52
(David Thompson) *in tch in centre of gp: rdn over 2f out: hdwy over 1f out: chsd wnr ins fnl f: r.o* 20/1
05-0 3 1 **Groundworker (IRE)**[25] 1554 8-9-3 **50** ....(t) DavidNolan 2 49
(Paul Midgley) *chsd ldrs on far side of gp: hdwy and ev ch over 1f out: lost 2nd and no ex ins fnl f* 12/1
105- 4 hd **Brendan (IRE)**[194] 8321 6-8-9 **49** .... CoreyMadden(7) 4 47+
(Jim Goldie) *bhd in centre of gp: outpcd 1/2-way: gd hdwy fnl f: nrst fin* 5/1[3]
506- 5 1 1/2 **Oriental Splendour (IRE)**[208] 7895 7-8-13 **46** ......(p w) JamesSullivan 7 39
(Ruth Carr) *hld up in tch on far side of gp: effrt and drvn along 2f out: one pce fnl f* 5/1[3]
20 6 nk **Dream Ally (IRE)**[25] 1553 9-8-9 **49** .... JonathanFisher(7) 10 41
(John Weymes) *cl up in centre of gp: rdn over 2f out: no ex fnl f* 9/1
00-0 7 nk **Racquet**[11] 1883 6-9-2 **52** .... ConorMcGovern(3) 5 43
(Ruth Carr) *pressed ldr in centre of gp: drvn along over 2f out: outpcd over 1f out* 4/1[2]
6-40 8 1 3/4 **Skyva**[14] 1818 4-9-4 **54** ....(b) BenRobinson(3) 6 38
(Brian Ellison) *s.i.s: bhd in centre of gp: struggling over 2f out: n.d after (jockey said gelding missed the break)* 3/1[1]
0/60 9 3/4 **Climax**[31] 1402 5-8-8 **48** ....(h[1]) ElishaWhittington(7) 11 30
(Wilf Storey) *prom on nr side of gp: rdn over 2f out: wknd over 1f out* 66/1
0-50 10 12 **Mountain Of Stars**[46] 1192 4-8-12 **45** ....(b[1]) RobertHavlin 3
(Suzzanne France) *bhd on far side of gp: struggling over 2f out: sn btn* 14/1

59.77s (0.27) **Going Correction** +0.125s/f (Slow) 10 Ran SP% **122.3**
Speed ratings (Par 101): **102,100,98,98,95 95,94,91,90,71**
CSF £132.27 CT £1584.05 TOTE £6.90: £2.40, £6.10, £4.60; EX 119.80 Trifecta £1712.30.
Owner G E Adams & J S Goldie **Bred** James Mc Claren **Trained** Uplawmoor, E Renfrews
FOCUS
A lowly sprint and the winner made all. Routine low-grade form.
T/Plt: £247.40 to a £1 stake. Pool: £51,828.95 - 152.92 winning units T/Qpdt: £4.80 to a £1 stake. Pool: £6,501.27 - 983.29 winning units **Richard Young**

1967 SOUTHWELL (L-H)
Monday, April 29

OFFICIAL GOING: Fibresand: standard
Wind: virtually nil Weather: Cloudy

2190 MAY BANK HOLIDAY RACECOURSE ANTIQUES FAIR H'CAP 7f 14y(F)
2:10 (2:13) (Class 6) (0-55,56) 3-Y-O
£3,105 (£924; £461; £300; £300; £300) Stalls Low

Form RPR
0630 1 **Peruvian Summer (IRE)**[6] 2016 3-9-8 **56** .... JackMitchell 12 67+
(Kevin Frost) *sn cl up: led 2f out: rdn clr ent fnl f: kpt on strly* 11/8[1]
3023 2 3 **Zorro's Girl**[19] 1678 3-9-7 **55** ....(b) HollieDoyle 11 58
(Archie Watson) *led: pushed along and hdd 2f out: sn rdn: drvn and edgd lft ins fnl f: kpt on same pce* 9/4[2]
40-0 3 1 1/4 **Treasured Company (IRE)**[26] 1515 3-8-12 **46** ....(e[1]) PhilipPrince 4 46
(Richard Guest) *towards rr: hdwy on inner 3f out: chsd ldrs 2f out: rdn over 1f out: swtchd rt and drvn ins fnl f: kpt on* 16/1
5400 4 3 1/2 **Amliba**[63] 906 3-9-3 **51** ....(h[1]) RobbieDowney 1 42
(David O'Meara) *trckd ldrs: effrt over 2f out: sn rdn: drvn and no imp fr over 1f out* 22/1
0-60 5 1/2 **Biscuit Queen**[18] 1722 3-9-2 **50** ....(b[1]) TomEaves 2 39
(Brian Ellison) *in tch: hdwy to chse ldrs over 2f out: swtchd rt wl over 1f out: sn drvn and one pce* 12/1[3]
00-0 6 2 3/4 **Juals Spirit (IRE)**[18] 1721 3-8-5 **46** oh1 ....(p[1]) KieranSchofield(7) 13 28
(Brian Ellison) *dwlt and in rr: wd st: rdn along and hdwy over 2f out: plugged on fnl f (jockey was slow to remove blindfold and explained that it had became stuck on the filly's headgear and took a second attempt to remove it)* 50/1
060- 7 5 **Oofy Prosser (IRE)**[152] 9292 3-9-6 **54** .... LukeMorris 10 23
(Harry Dunlop) *in tch: rdn along 3f out: sn wknd* 16/1
063 8 2 1/2 **Fortunate Move**[47] 1180 3-9-0 **53** .... ConnorMurtagh(5) 9 16
(Richard Fahey) *chsd ldrs: rdn along 3f out: sn wknd* 25/1
00-0 9 6 **Princess Florence (IRE)**[21] 1650 3-8-12 **46** ....(p[1]) LiamKeniry 8
(John Ryan) *trckd ldng pair: pushed along 1/2-way: rdn 3f out: sn wknd* 33/1
30-0 10 1 **Smashing Lass (IRE)**[28] 1486 3-9-7 **55** .... ShaneGray 6
(Ollie Pears) *a in rr* 12/1[3]
-000 11 1 1/4 **Showshutai**[30] 1430 3-8-13 **47** .... AlistairRawlinson 3
(Christopher Kellett) *bhd fr 1/2-way* 20/1
0-00 12 1 1/2 **Quarto Cavallo**[93] 437 3-9-4 **52** ....(b[1]) RoystonFfrench 7
(Adam West) *s.i.s: a bhd (jockey said filly reared at the stalls opened and was slowly away as a result)* 50/1

1m 30.13s (-0.17) **Going Correction** -0.075s/f (Stan) 12 Ran SP% **119.8**
Speed ratings (Par 96): **97,93,92,88,87 84,78,75,69,67 66,64**
CSF £3.95 CT £32.57 TOTE £2.20: £1.20, £1.40, £3.40; EX 5.90 Trifecta £49.60.
Owner J T Stimpson **Bred** Ballylinch Stud **Trained** Newcastle-under-Lyme, Staffs
FOCUS
A very moderate 3yo handicap. The favourite readily saw off the second-favourite from over 1f out, with the runner-up rated similar to recent Kempton starts.

2191 BRITISH EBF NOVICE MEDIAN AUCTION STKS (PLUS 10 RACE) 4f 214y(F)
2:40 (2:40) (Class 4) 2-Y-O
£4,787 (£1,424; £711; £355) Stalls Centre

Form RPR
1 1 **Littledidyouknow (IRE)**[8] 1968 2-9-5 0 .... LukeMorris 7 79
(Archie Watson) *racd centre: mde all: rdn and wandered over 1f out: drvn and edgd lft ins fnl f: kpt on wl* 7/2[2]
22 2 1 1/4 **Bettys Hope**[12] 1843 2-8-8 0 .... TheodoreLadd(5) 3 68
(Rod Millman) *racd towards far side: trckd wnr: hdwy 2f out and sn ev ch: rdn over 1f out: kpt on same pac e fnl f* 11/10[1]
3 2 **Elevate Her (IRE)** 2-8-13 0 .... HollieDoyle 8 61
(Richard Spencer) *racd towards stands' side: chsd wnr: ev ch 1 1/2f out: sn rdn and kpt on same pce fnl f* 16/1
02 4 3 **Bendy Spirit (IRE)**[14] 1812 2-9-4 0 .... TonyHamilton 4 55+
(Richard Fahey) *towards rr: pushed along 1/2-way: rdn and hdwy wl over 1f out: kpt on fnl f* 9/2[3]
4 5 1/2 **Ambyfaeirvine (IRE)**[8] 1968 2-9-1 0 .... GabrieleMalune(3) 9 53
(Ivan Furtado) *racd towards stands' side: chsd ldrs: rdn along 2f out: kpt on one pce (jockey said colt hung badly left)* 40/1
0 6 1/2 **Never Said Nothing (IRE)**[24] 1556 2-9-4 0 .... TomEaves 2 51
(Brian Ellison) *racd far side: in rr: rdn along 1/2-way: kpt on fnl f* 33/1
63 7 1 1/2 **Lili Wen Fach (IRE)**[12] 1844 2-8-13 0 .... LiamKeniry 6 41
(David Evans) *chsd ldrs: rdn along 2f out: sn edgd lft and wknd* 9/1
0 8 1 **Prosecutor (IRE)**[30] 1416 2-8-13 0 .... JFEgan 1 37
(Mark H Tompkins) *racd towards far side: chsd ldrs: rdn along 1/2-way: sn wknd* 22/1
9 hd **Mist In The Valley** 2-8-13 0 .... LewisEdmunds 5 37+
(David Brown) *dwlt: a in rr* 66/1

1m 0.98s (1.28) **Going Correction** -0.075s/f (Stan) 9 Ran SP% **115.1**
Speed ratings (Par 94): **86,84,80,76,75 74,72,70,70**
CSF £7.47 TOTE £3.00: £1.10, £1.30, £3.90; EX 8.90 Trifecta £106.40.
Owner El Jefe **Bred** Rathasker Stud **Trained** Upper Lambourn, W Berks
■ Stewards' Enquiry : Luke Morris two day ban; misuse of whip (May 13-14)
FOCUS
The feature contest was an ordinary juvenile novice sprint. The second-favourite defied a penalty from the front in gutsy fashion.

2192 SOUTHWELL RACECOURSE JOULES CLOTHING SALE 24TH JULY NOVICE STKS 1m 13y(F)
3:10 (3:13) (Class 5) 3-Y-O+ £3,752 (£1,116; £557; £278) Stalls Low

Form RPR
1 **Alexander James (IRE)** 3-8-11 0 .... JamieGormley(3) 9 91
(Iain Jardine) *cl up: led over 4f out: pushed clr over 2f out: unchal* 33/1
56- 2 13 **Chance**[297] 4604 3-9-0 0 .... JackMitchell 2 61
(Simon Crisford) *led: hdd over 4f out: rdn along wl over 2f out: sn drvn and kpt on: no ch w wnr* 9/4[2]
5 3 1 3/4 **Piper Arrow**[19] 1690 3-8-11 0 .... WilliamCox(3) 6 57
(Andrew Balding) *chsd ldng pair: rdn along wl over 2f out: sn drvn and kpt on one pce* 2/1[1]
1 4 6 **Native Silver**[46] 1195 3-9-7 0 .... LukeMorris 3 50
(Robert Eddery) *in tch: rdn along 1/2-way: plugged on fnl 3f: n.d* 5/1[3]
5 3 **Grazeon Roy** 3-9-0 0 .... RobbieDowney 11 36
(John Quinn) *in rr: pushed along on outer 3f out: swtchd lft and hdwy over 2f out: styd on appr fnl f* 66/1
1 6 nk **Lennybe**[53] 1070 3-9-5 0 .... LewisEdmunds 12 41
(David Brown) *chsd ldrs: rdn along over 3f out: drvn over 2f out: sn outpcd (jockey said gelding hung left)* 6/1
4 7 1 1/4 **Potters Question**[23] 1587 3-8-11 0 .... GabrieleMalune(3) 5 33
(Amy Murphy) *a towards rr* 66/1
8 1 1/4 **Unplugged (IRE)** 3-9-0 0 .... LiamKeniry 8 30
(Andrew Balding) *dwlt: in tch on outer: rdn along over 3f out: sn outpcd* 28/1
00 9 10 **Farhhmoreexciting**[6] 2009 4-10-0 0 .... HayleyTurner 10 11
(David Elsworth) *a in rr* 50/1
/0- 10 1 1/4 **Reedway (IRE)**[273] 5553 6-9-9 0 .... SeamusCronin(5) 7 8
(Robyn Brisland) *a towards rr* 66/1
0 11 nk **And The New (IRE)**[16] 1771 8-10-0 0 .... RossaRyan 4 7
(Johnny Farrelly) *a bhd* 66/1
43 12 49 **Revamp (USA)**[19] 1689 3-9-0 0 .... TomEaves 1
(David Simcock) *in tch on inner: pushed along and lost pl 1/2-way: sn bhd (trainers' rep said gelding didn't face the kickback on this occasion)* 16/1

1m 40.65s (-3.05) **Going Correction** -0.075s/f (Stan)
WFA 3 from 4yo+ 14lb 12 Ran SP% **115.3**
Speed ratings (Par 103): **112,99,97,91,88 87,86,85,75,74 73,24**
CSF £102.87 TOTE £32.80: £6.80, £1.10, £1.60; EX 178.70 Trifecta £386.50.
Owner James Property Ltd **Bred** Churchtown House Stud **Trained** Carrutherstown, D'fries & G'way
FOCUS
A fair novice contest. One of the newcomers defied big odds to turn this race into a procession in a good comparative from an always prominent pitch. This run could potentially have been rated in the high 90s at face value.

2193 VIST ATTHERACES.COM H'CAP 1m 13y(F)
3:45 (3:45) (Class 5) (0-75,75) 4-Y-O+
£3,752 (£1,116; £418; £418; £300; £300) Stalls Low

Form RPR
-053 1 **Fire Diamond**[27] 1511 6-9-0 **68** ....(p) RichardKingscote 6 82
(Tom Dascombe) *hld up: hdwy 3f out: cl up over 2f out: sn led: rdn over 1f out: kpt on strly* 8/1
4401 2 5 **Bond Angel**[12] 1859 4-8-10 **69** .... TheodoreLadd(5) 3 72
(David Evans) *in tch: hdwy and wd st: rdn along towards stands' side 2f out: drvn and kpt on fnl f* 9/4[1]
6566 3 1 1/4 **Me Too Nagasaki (IRE)**[19] 1695 5-9-7 **75** ....(t) AlistairRawlinson 4 75
(Stuart Williams) *cl up: rdn along 3f out: drvn 2f out: kpt on same pce* 5/1[3]
0613 3 dht **Muqarred (USA)**[12] 1859 7-8-6 **63** ....(p) JamieGormley(3) 1 63
(Roger Fell) *chsd ldrs on inner: pushed along and outpcd over 3f out: kpt on u.p fnl 2f* 7/2[2]
2322 5 3 3/4 **Majestic Moon (IRE)**[12] 1859 9-9-1 **69** ....(p) ShelleyBirkett 5 60
(Julia Feilden) *cl up on outer: wd st: ev ch over 2f out: sn rdn and grad wknd* 7/2[2]

1662 **6** 2 ¼ **Sooqaan**[30] 1426 8-8-4 **61**...............................(p) WilliamCox(3) 2 47
(Antony Brittain) *slt ld: rdn along 3f out: hdd 2f out: sn wknd (jockey said gelding stopped quickly)* **14/1**

50-0 **7** 28 **Reshaan (IRE)**[67] 835 4-8-7 **61**...............................(t[1]) LukeMorris 7
(Alexandra Dunn) *dwlt: in tch: rdn along over 4f out: outpcd fnl 3f (jockey was gelding was never travelling)* **66/1**

1m 41.98s (-1.72) **Going Correction** -0.075s/f (Stan) **7** Ran SP% **111.2**
Speed ratings (Par 103): **105,100,98,98,95 92,64**
PL: M 3.00, MTN; 2.60; TF: FD/BA/M £40.30, FD/BA/MTN £68.40 CSF £24.92 TOTE £5.30: £3.50, £1.80; EX 28.30.
Owner John Brown **Bred** John Brown **Trained** Malpas, Cheshire

FOCUS
A fair handicap. The winning time was nearly 1.5 seconds slower than the previous C&D novice contest. The winner is rated back to his best.

2194 SOUTHWELL RACECOURSE JOULES CLOTHING SALE 24TH JULY H'CAP 6f 16y(F)

4:15 (4:23) (Class 5) (0-70,72) 4-Y-O+
£3,752 (£1,116; £557; £300; £300; £300) **Stalls** Low

Form RPR
6210 **1** **Katheefa (USA)**[7] 1976 5-9-9 **72**...............................TomEaves 3 86+
(Ruth Carr) *cl up: pushed ahd wl over 1f out: rdn clr ent fnl f: easily* **2/1**[1]

1212 **2** 3 ½ **Socialites Red**[8] 1973 6-8-8 **62**...............................(p) TheodoreLadd(5) 10 63
(Scott Dixon) *slt ld: rdn along and hdd 2f out: sn drvn: kpt on: no ch w wnr* **5/1**[2]

6212 **3** 2 ¾ **Sir Ottoman (FR)**[19] 1682 6-9-2 **68**...............................(tp) GabrieleMalune(3) 6 60
(Ivan Furtado) *chsd ldng pair: rdn along 2f out: sn drvn and kpt on one pce* **5/1**[2]

0-35 **4** 2 ¼ **Rasheeq (IRE)**[8] 1973 6-9-3 **66**...............................LukeMorris 5 51
(Mohamed Moubarak) *hmpd s: sn chsng ldrs: wd st: rdn along wl over 2f out: sn one pce* **14/1**

0-05 **5** 1 ¾ **Shepherd's Purse**[19] 1686 7-9-4 **67**............................... TrevorWhelan 4 46
(David Loughnane) *sltly hmpd s: in tch: rdn along 1/2-way: n.d* **6/1**[3]

5001 **6** nk **Falcao (IRE)**[8] 1969 7-8-3 **53**...............................(t) DarraghKeenan(5) 1 35
(John Butler) *chsd ldrs on inner: rdn along over 2f out: sn one pce* **8/1**

-130 **7** 2 ¼ **The Golden Cue**[8] 1973 4-8-7 **63**...............................TobyEley(7) 9 34
(Steph Hollinshead) *sltly hmpd and stmbld s: a towards rr (jockey said gelding stumbled leaving the stalls and was never travelling)* **11/1**

01-2 **8** 14 **Pushkin Museum (IRE)**[93] 439 8-9-1 **64**...............................LiamKeniry 7
(John Butler) *hmpd s: a towards rr* **20/1**

1m 16.24s (-0.26) **Going Correction** -0.075s/f (Stan) **8** Ran SP% **111.8**
Speed ratings (Par 103): **98,93,89,86,84 83,80,62**
CSF £11.36 CT £41.99 TOTE £2.50: £1.10, £1.90, £2.10; EX 11.20 Trifecta £45.20.
Owner Grange Park Racing XIV & Ruth Carr **Bred** Shadwell Farm LLC **Trained** Huby, N Yorks

FOCUS
An ordinary sprint handicap. After an earlier false start, the clear favourite won easily in a good comparative time. The runner-up is a solid marker.

2195 SKY SPORTS RACING SKY 415 NOVICE MEDIAN AUCTION STKS 1m 3f 23y(F)

4:45 (4:48) (Class 5) 3-5-Y-O **£3,752** (£1,116; £557; £278) **Stalls** Low

Form RPR
1 **1** **Ranch Hand**[33] 1365 3-8-9 0...............................WilliamCarver(7) 7 89
(Andrew Balding) *trckd ldr: cl up 1/2-way: led 3f out: rdn clr and edgd lft to far rail wl over 1f out: kpt on strly* **10/11**[1]

22- **2** 12 **Say The Word**[182] 8682 3-8-9 0...............................JackMitchell 4 66
(Simon Crisford) *led: pushed along and hdd 3f out: rdn over 2f out: sn drvn and kpt on same pce: no ch w wnr* **11/8**[2]

0 **3** ¾ **Spirit Of Nicobar**[14] 1824 3-8-4 0...............................HayleyTurner 5 55
(Andrew Balding) *trckd ldng pair over 5f out: rdn along over 3f out: sn drvn and kpt on one pce* **40/1**

4 14 **Kalaya (IRE)** 3-8-1 0...............................JaneElliott(3) 3 31
(Archie Watson) *dwlt and in rr: hdwy and in tch 1/2-way: rdn along over 4f out: sn outpcd (jockey said filly was slowly away)* **28/1**

5 4 ½ **Tadasana** 3-8-4 0...............................LukeMorris 1 24
(Archie Watson) *trckd ldng pair: pushed along 1/2-way: rdn over 4f out: sn outpcd and bhd* **16/1**[3]

6 **6** 4 **Night Fury**[11] 1898 3-8-4 0...............................TheodoreLadd(5) 6 22
(Michael Appleby) *a in rr: t.o fnl 3f* **33/1**

0 **7** 12 **Annabelle Fritton (IRE)**[33] 1351 4-9-4 0...............................SeamusCronin(5) 2
(Robyn Brisland) *a in rr: t.o fnl 3f* **150/1**

2m 24.8s (-3.20) **Going Correction** -0.075s/f (Stan) **7** Ran SP% **109.9**
WFA 3 from 4yo 19lb
Speed ratings (Par 103): **108,99,98,88,85 82,73**
CSF £2.11 TOTE £1.70: £1.20, £1.10; EX 2.50 Trifecta £13.20.
Owner Kingsclere Racing Club **Bred** Kingsclere Stud **Trained** Kingsclere, Hants

FOCUS
A fair middle-distance novice contest. The odds-on favourite devoured this opposition, once on the lead on the far rail in the straight, in the quickest comparative time on the card. He improved from his debut win.

2196 FOLLOW AT THE RACES ON TWITTER H'CAP 1m 4f 14y(F)

5:20 (5:20) (Class 6) (0-55,55) 4-Y-O+
£3,105 (£924; £461; £300; £300; £300) **Stalls** Low

Form RPR
06-3 **1** **Thahab Ifraj (IRE)**[18] 160 6-8-12 **46** oh1...............................RossaRyan 5 51
(Alexandra Dunn) *towards rr: hdwy and in tch 1/2-way: chsd ldng pair over 3f out: rdn to chse wnr wl over 1f out: kpt on wl u.p to chal ins fnl f: led nr fin (trainer said, reg app imp in form, gelding stripped fitter from it's reappearance run over fences and appeared to be suited by a return to the fibresand surface)* **14/1**

2 **2** nk **Loose Chippings (IRE)**[12] 1861 5-9-1 **52**...............................(h) GabrieleMalune(3) 6 57
(Ivan Furtado) *trckd ldr: cl up over 4f out: led 3f out: rdn clr 2f out: drvn and jnd ins fnl f: hdd and no ex nr fin* **2/1**[1]

2-32 **3** 7 **Siyahamba (IRE)**[48] 1163 5-8-12 **46** oh1...............................RoystonFfrench 8 40
(Bryan Smart) *in rr: hdwy 5f out: rdn along to chse ldrs 3f out: drvn 2f out: kpt on same pce* **8/1**

6143 **4** 1 ¾ **Going Native**[12] 1858 4-8-12 **53**...............................RhonaPindar(7) 2 45
(Olly Williams) *led: jnd and pushed along 4f out: rdn and hdd 3f out: sn drvn and grad wknd* **7/1**[3]

5 2 **Dharma Rain (IRE)**[35] 8944 4-9-7 **55**...............................(t[1]) RichardKingscote 3 44
(Clare Hobson) *in rr: hdwy 4f out: rdn along 3f out: plugged on u.p fnl 2f: nvr rching ldrs* **25/1**

4-54 **6** 22 **Lean On Pete (IRE)**[48] 1163 10-9-2 **55**...............................ConnorMurtagh(5) 11 8
(Ollie Pears) *chsd ldrs: rdn along and outpcd 5f out: kpt on fnl 2f* **14/1**

-543 **7** ½ **Caracas**[74] 721 5-8-12 **49**...............................JoshuaBryan(3) 1 1
(Kevin Frost) *chsd ldrs on inner: rdn along 5f out: sn drvn and outpcd fr over 3f out* **18/1**

-222 **8** ½ **Thecornishbarron (IRE)**[12] 1858 7-9-0 **48**...............................TomEaves 10
(Brian Ellison) *trckd ldrs: chsd ldng pair over 4f out: rdn along over 3f out: sn drvn and wknd* **10/3**[2]

-010 **9** 1 ¼ **Rajapur**[18] 1718 6-9-0 **48**...............................(e) DannyBrock 14
(David Thompson) *rdn along s and sn chsng ldrs on wd outside: rdn along 5f out: wknd 4f out* **50/1**

0-50 **10** 4 ½ **Bertie Moon**[12] 1861 9-8-7 **46** oh1...............................(p) RhiainIngram(5) 7
(Tony Forbes) *chsd ldrs: rdn along 5f out: sn outpcd* **40/1**

05/0 **11** 1 **Kathy**[26] 1527 4-8-9 **46** oh1...............................(p[1]) JaneElliott(3) 9
(Scott Dixon) *a towards rr* **125/1**

330- **12** 19 **Tilsworth Lukey**[174] 8910 6-9-6 **54**............................... AlistairRawlinson 13
(J R Jenkins) *a towards rr* **25/1**

063 **13** shd **Lady Makfi (IRE)**[30] 1429 7-9-7 **55**...............................LukeMorris 4
(Johnny Farrelly) *chsd ldrs: rdn along 5f out: wknd 4f out (jockey said mare had no more to give)* **14/1**

0-26 **14** 6 **Ipcress File**[48] 1163 4-8-8 **47**...............................(p) TheodoreLadd(5) 12
(Scott Dixon) *a bhd* **25/1**

2m 39.9s (-1.10) **Going Correction** -0.075s/f (Stan) **14** Ran SP% **122.0**
Speed ratings (Par 101): **100,99,95,93,92 77,77,77,76,73 72,60,60,56**
CSF £40.58 CT £257.12 TOTE £18.70: £5.10, £1.40, £2.10; EX 67.40 Trifecta £522.90.
Owner The Dunnitalls **Bred** P G Lyons **Trained** West Buckland, Somerset

FOCUS
A moderate middle-distance handicap. The favourite lost out late on after racing in the teeth off a strong gallop, with the pace collapsing to a degree in the home straight. The winner's hurdles form suggests he can do a bit better than this.
T/Plt: £5.50 to a £1 stake. Pool: £57,039.94 - 7,455.04 winning units T/Qpdt: £2.90 to a £1 stake. Pool: £4,830.93 - 1,213.30 winning units **Joe Rowntree**

1758 THIRSK (L-H)

Monday, April 29

OFFICIAL GOING: Good (good to firm in places; watered)
Wind: Virtually nil Weather: fine

2197 RACINGTV.COM H'CAP 6f

5:05 (5:08) (Class 6) (0-60,62) 3-Y-O
£3,398 (£1,011; £505; £300; £300; £300) **Stalls** Centre

Form RPR
040- **1** **Aghast**[242] 6721 3-9-4 **57**...............................KevinStott 3 66+
(Kevin Ryan) *hld up centre: pushed along and hdwy 2f out: rdn to ld 1f out: kpt on* **11/1**

00-0 **2** 1 ½ **Ey Up Its Mick**[7] 1982 3-9-4 **57**...............................(b[1]) DougieCostello 6 59
(Tony Coyle) *chsd ldrs centre: rdn to chal appr fnl f: kpt on* **16/1**

05-0 **3** shd **Seanjohnsilver (IRE)**[35] 1336 3-9-4 **57**...............................(t) CamHardie 10 59
(Declan Carroll) *in tch stands' side: rdn and hdwy 2f out: chal 1f out: kpt on* **13/2**[3]

2-60 **4** 1 ½ **You Little Beauty**[7] 1982 3-8-7 **46**...............................HollieDoyle 16 43
(Ann Duffield) *hld up stands' side: pushed along 3f out: rdn and hdwy over 1f out: kpt on fnl f* **7/1**

000- **5** shd **Josiebond**[226] 7305 3-9-1 **57**...............................RowanScott(3) 15 54
(Rebecca Bastiman) *hld up stands' side: rdn over 2f out: hdwy over 1f out: kpt on* **40/1**

40-0 **6** 1 **Our Secret (IRE)**[28] 1486 3-8-5 **49**...............................AndrewBreslin(5) 17 43
(Liam Bailey) *dwlt: hld up: sn pushed along: hung lft to centre 3f out: kpt on fnl f* **33/1**

003- **7** 1 ½ **The Grey Zebedee**[196] 8261 3-9-4 **57**...............................(p) DavidAllan 5 46
(Tim Easterby) *racd centre: led narrowly: rdn 2f out: hdd 1f out: wknd ins fnl f* **10/1**

3-00 **8** 1 ¼ **Kimberley Girl**[27] 1504 3-9-4 **57**...............................NathanEvans 9 43
(Michael Easterby) *chsd ldrs centre: rdn and bit outpcd over 2f out: plugged on fnl f* **14/1**

600- **9** 1 ½ **Slieve Donard**[182] 8699 3-8-11 **50**...............................(b) ShaneGray 19 31
(Noel Wilson) *prom stands' side: rdn 2f out: wknd fnl f* **50/1**

35-0 **10** 2 **The Big House (IRE)**[30] 1430 3-8-12 **51**...............................AndrewMullen 4 26
(Noel Wilson) *hld up centre: nvr threatened* **16/1**

05-0 **11** 2 ¾ **Lethal Laura**[94] 406 3-8-7 **46**...............................(b[1]) JoeFanning 11 13
(James Given) *hld up centre: sn pushed along: minor late hdwy: nvr threatened* **20/1**

00-0 **12** nk **Tigerinmytank**[24] 1557 3-8-13 **52**...............................AndrewElliott 2 18
(John Holt) *in tch centre: rdn over 2f out: hung lft and wknd over 1f out* **33/1**

2-62 **13** nse **Willow Brook**[88] 497 3-9-3 **56**...............................(h) PaulMulrennan 8 22
(Julie Camacho) *chsd ldrs centre: rdn over 2f out: wknd over 1f out* **10/1**

-300 **14** 2 ¾ **Harperelle**[28] 1488 3-9-2 **60**...............................SebastianWoods(5) 7 18
(Alistair Whillans) *racd centre: a towards rr* **25/1**

15 5 **Montalvan (IRE)**[187] 8555 3-9-9 **62**...............................BenCurtis 1 5+
(Roger Fell) *pressed ldr centre: rdn over 2f out: wknd over 1f out* **11/2**[1]

534 **16** 1 ¼ **Muhallab (IRE)**[30] 1427 3-9-5 **58**...............................(v[1]) TadhgO'Shea 13
(Adrian Nicholls) *dwlt: sn prom stands' side: rdn over 2f out: wknd over 1f out: eased (jockey said colt hung right)* **6/1**[2]

-666 **17** 2 ½ **Kyroc (IRE)**[52] 1081 3-8-4 **50**...............................RussellHarris(7) 14
(Susan Corbett) *chsd ldrs stands' side: wknd 2f out* **25/1**

500- **18** 2 ¼ **Justice Shallow (FR)**[192] 8368 3-8-2 **46** oh1...............................PaulaMuir(5) 12
(Alan Berry) *midfield stands' side: rdn 3f out: sn wknd* **100/1**

006- **19** 6 **Pritty Livvy**[153] 9276 3-8-7 **46** oh1...............................DuranFentiman 18
(Noel Wilson) *chsd ldrs stands' side: wknd 2f out* **80/1**

1m 12.47s (-0.33) **Going Correction** -0.20s/f (Firm) **19** Ran SP% **125.4**
Speed ratings (Par 96): **94,92,91,89,89 88,86,84,82,80 76,76,75,72,65 63,60,57,49**
CSF £162.34 CT £1288.28 TOTE £14.40: £3.90, £4.80, £2.90, £2.30; EX 204.10 Trifecta £1518.40.
Owner Manor Farm Stud & John Rose **Bred** Manor Farm Stud (Rutland) **Trained** Hambleton, N Yorks

FOCUS
All distances as advertised. A low-grade sprint handicap in which the principals raced across the track. Improvement from both the winner and second.

2198 CLIFF STUD THIRSK HUNT CUP THIS SATURDAY NOVICE STKS 7f 218y

5:40 (5:43) (Class 5) 3-Y-O+ **£3,881** (£1,155; £577; £288) **Stalls** Low

Form RPR
12 **1** **Munhamek**[18] 1723 3-9-5 0...............................AndrewMullen 6 88
(Ivan Furtado) *prom: pushed along over 2f out: led over 1f out: sn drvn: kpt on* **9/2**[2]

2 1 **Hamish** 3-9-0 0 DanielTudhope 5 80+
(William Haggas) *dwlt: hld up in tch: pushed along and hdwy 2f out: wnt 2nd 110yds out: kpt on wl* **11/2**[3]

4 **3** 2 **Noble Prospector (IRE)**[24] 1562 3-9-0 0 PaulHanagan 3 76
(Richard Fahey) *hld up: pushed along and hdwy on outer over 2f out: rdn over 1f out: one pce ins fnl f* **12/1**

2 **4** 1 1/4 **Desert Lion**[33] 1352 3-9-0 0 JoeFanning 2 73
(David Simcock) *trckd ldrs: pushed along 3f out: rdn over 1f out: edgd lft 1f out: wknd fnl 110yds* **10/11**[1]

5-3 **5** 1 1/4 **Beautiful Gesture**[16] 1764 3-8-9 0 BenCurtis 1 65
(K R Burke) *led: rdn over 2f out: hdd over 1f out: wknd ins fnl f* **13/2**

6- **6** 17 **Transpennine Gold**[145] 9411 3-9-0 0 PaulMulrennan 4 31
(Michael Dods) *trckd ldrs: rdn over 3f out: wknd over 2f out* **80/1**

1m 38.25s (-3.45) **Going Correction** -0.20s/f (Firm) **6 Ran SP% 108.2**
Speed ratings (Par 103): **109,108,106,104,103 86**
CSF £26.38 TOTE £4.60: £2.30, £2.20; EX 22.80 Trifecta £96.50.
Owner J C Fretwell **Bred** Shadwell Estate Company Limited **Trained** Wiseton, Nottinghamshire

FOCUS
One or two interesting sorts contested this novice stakes but it went to the previous winner, who improved again.

2199 "IRISH DAY" @THIRSKRACES SATURDAY 18TH MAY MAIDEN AUCTION STKS 6f
6:10 (6:11) (Class 6) 3-Y-O **£3,234** (£962; £481; £240) **Stalls** Centre

Form RPR

-5 **1** **Obee Jo (IRE)**[20] 1665 3-9-2 0 DavidAllan 3 72+
(Tim Easterby) *prom: pushed along to ld over 1f out: rdn ins fnl f: jnd 50yds out: hld on wl* **7/2**[2]

2 shd **In Trutina** 3-8-9 0 HollieDoyle 1 67+
(Archie Watson) *dwlt: green and outpcd in rr tl gd hdwy on outer over 1f out: rdn and edgd lft ins fnl f: jnd ldr 50yds out: kpt on* **3/1**[1]

56-2 **3** 1 1/2 **Pinarella (FR)**[38] 1275 3-8-10 61 AndrewMullen 10 61
(Ben Haslam) *midfield: rdn along over 2f out: hdwy and chsd ldrs 1f out: kpt on* **4/1**[3]

0-6 **4** 1/2 **Reasoned (IRE)**[14] 1816 3-8-11 0 RyanTate 4 61
(James Eustace) *trckd ldrs: rdn 2f out: kpt on ins fnl f* **12/1**

0 **5** 1 3/4 **Mea Culpa (IRE)**[60] 954 3-9-0 0 PaulMulrennan 2 58
(Julie Camacho) *dwlt: hld up: racd keenly: pushed along and sme hdwy appr fnl f: kpt on (vet said gelding lost it's right hind shoe)* **28/1**

6 1/2 **Sharp Breath** 3-8-5 0 RussellHarris(7) 7 55
(Richard Fahey) *slowly away: hld up in midfield: rdn 2f out: edgd lft: kpt on fnl f* **18/1**

0 **7** 1 1/4 **Dream House**[21] 1649 3-9-5 0 DuranFentiman 8 58
(Tim Easterby) *prom: rdn over 1f out: already wkng whn short of room ins fnl f* **50/1**

4420 **8** hd **Sussudio**[19] 1687 3-8-10 61 (p) BenCurtis 9 48
(Richard Spencer) *midfield: rdn over 2f out: no imp* **5/1**

9 1 1/4 **Followme Followyou (IRE)** 3-8-13 0 JoeFanning 11 48
(Mark Johnston) *s.i.s: hld up: hdwy and chsd ldrs 3f out: rdn 2f out: wknd fnl f* **8/1**

10 3/4 **Torque Of The Town (IRE)** 3-9-0 0 NathanEvans 6 46
(Noel Wilson) *led: rdn and hdd over 1f out: wknd* **66/1**

5 **11** nk **Manzoni**[26] 1523 3-8-10 0 SeanDavis(5) 12 47
(Mohamed Moubarak) *trckd ldrs: rdn 2f out: wknd fnl f* **33/1**

1m 12.9s (0.10) **Going Correction** -0.20s/f (Firm) **11 Ran SP% 117.8**
Speed ratings (Par 96): **91,90,88,88,85 85,83,83,81,80 80**
CSF £14.11 TOTE £4.10: £1.60, £1.50, £1.80; EX 19.20 Trifecta £81.70.
Owner Mrs Joanne Boxcer & Partner **Bred** Tally-Ho Stud **Trained** Great Habton, N Yorks
■ Stewards' Enquiry : Hollie Doyle caution; careless riding

FOCUS
This 3yo sprint maiden was run 0.43 secs slower than the earlier handicap. The form looks ordinary, although the first two should improve. The third helps pin an ordinary level.

2200 SCOUTING FOR GIRLS - LIVE @THIRSKRACES FRIDAY 16TH AUGUST H'CAP 7f 218y
6:40 (6:42) (Class 5) (0-70,71) 3-Y-O **£4,075** (£1,212; £606; £303; £300; £300) **Stalls** Low

Form RPR

350- **1** **Joe The Beau**[199] 8166 3-9-7 **70** NathanEvans 2 76
(Michael Easterby) *trckd ldrs on inner: rdn over 2f out: chal appr fnl f: drvn to ld 110yds out: kpt on* **11/1**

50-0 **2** 1 **Highwaygrey**[14] 1819 3-8-12 **61** DavidAllan 10 65
(Tim Easterby) *dwlt: hld up: n.m.r 3f out: rdn along and hdwy 2f out: swtchd rt appr fnl f: sn chsd ldrs: kpt on* **66/1**

-222 **3** 1/2 **Strawberry Jack**[4] 2055 3-9-8 **71** (tp) BenCurtis 6 74
(George Scott) *led: rdn over 2f out: drvn and hdd 110yds out: sn no ex* **3/1**[1]

56-3 **4** 1 **Perfecimperfection (IRE)**[21] 1656 3-9-5 **68** PJMcDonald 9 69
(Marco Botti) *prom: rdn over 2f out: no ex fnl 75yds* **4/1**[2]

340- **5** hd **Chains Of Love (IRE)**[229] 7169 3-9-7 **70** (p) CliffordLee 14 70
(K R Burke) *dwlt: sn swtchd lft to inner: hld up in rr: rdn along over 2f out: hdwy over 1f out: kpt on ins fnl f: nrst fin* **28/1**

00-4 **6** 3/4 **George Mallory**[14] 1819 3-9-6 **69** KevinStott 5 67
(Kevin Ryan) *prom: rdn over 2f out: no ex ins fnl f* **9/2**[3]

353 **7** hd **Creek Island (IRE)**[32] 1381 3-9-5 **68** JoeFanning 13 66
(Mark Johnston) *midfield: rdn over 2f out: edgd lft 1f out: kpt on: nvr threatened ldrs* **10/1**

4501 **8** 1/2 **Wall Of Sapphire (IRE)**[14] 1825 3-9-5 **68** HollieDoyle 7 65
(Hugo Palmer) *hld up: rdn and sme hdwy on outer 2f out: nvr threatened ldrs* **11/2**

034- **9** 1 **Mecca's Gift (IRE)**[223] 7390 3-9-2 **65** PaulMulrennan 16 59
(Michael Dods) *chsd ldrs on outer: rdn along over 2f out: wknd ins fnl f* **25/1**

024- **10** 3 1/4 **Dancing Speed (IRE)**[262] 5946 3-9-7 **70** DanielTudhope 11 57
(Marjorie Fife) *trckd ldrs: briefly short of room over 2f out: sn rdn along: wknd fnl f* **33/1**

244- **11** 2 1/2 **Northern Lyte**[192] 8378 3-9-5 **68** LewisEdmunds 4 49
(Nigel Tinkler) *s.i.s: sn midfield: rdn over 2f out: wknd over 1f out* **28/1**

605- **12** 12 **Play It By Ear (IRE)**[182] 8698 3-9-1 **67** JamieGormley(3) 3 21
(Iain Jardine) *midfield: pushed along and lost pl 5f out: wknd and bhd fnl 2f* **20/1**

5-00 **13** 6 **Al Mortajaz (FR)**[80] 677 3-9-4 **67** AndrewMullen 12 7
(Adrian Nicholls) *trckd ldrs: rdn 3f out: wknd 2f out* **66/1**

1m 38.95s (-2.75) **Going Correction** -0.20s/f (Firm) **13 Ran SP% 117.4**
Speed ratings (Par 98): **105,104,103,102,102 101,101,100,99,96 94,82,76**
CSF £595.57 CT £2796.76 TOTE £12.00: £4.00, £9.70, £1.30; EX 777.60 Trifecta £1026.20.
Owner B Padgett Racing **Bred** Mill House Stud **Trained** Sheriff Hutton, N Yorks

FOCUS
A modest but competitive handicap run 0.70 secs slower than the earlier novice stakes over the trip. The form looks sound.

2201 LIKE RACING TV ON FACEBOOK H'CAP 6f
7:10 (7:13) (Class 4) (0-85,85) 4-Y-O+ **£5,692** (£1,694; £846; £423; £300; £300) **Stalls** Centre

Form RPR

0-11 **1** **Pennsylvania Dutch**[9] 1951 5-8-11 **80** (e) SeanDavis(5) 7 89
(Kevin Ryan) *half-rrd s and bit slowly away: sn in midfield: rdn and hdwy over 1f out: drvn to ld 110yds out: kpt on wl* **9/2**[2]

61-3 **2** 1 1/4 **Wrenthorpe**[11] 1899 4-8-6 **77** ow1 (p) HarryRussell(7) 8 82
(Bryan Smart) *led: rdn over 1f out: hdd 110yds out: kpt on* **15/2**

00-5 **3** 1 1/4 **Sheepscar Lad (IRE)**[11] 1899 5-8-9 **78** FayeMcManoman(5) 9 79
(Nigel Tinkler) *trckd ldrs: racd keenly: pushed along 2f out: rdn and kpt on same pce fnl f* **10/1**

320- **4** 3/4 **Orion's Bow**[158] 9206 8-9-3 **81** (t) DavidAllan 12 80
(Tim Easterby) *trckd ldrs: chal over 1f out: rdn and no ex ins fnl f* **14/1**

310- **5** 1/2 **Dark Defender**[220] 7481 6-9-2 **83** RowanScott(3) 3 80
(Rebecca Bastiman) *in tch on outer: rdn 2f out: drvn and kpt on fnl f* **33/1**

1004 **6** shd **Zylan (IRE)**[30] 1428 7-8-7 **76** (p) BenSanderson(5) 4 73
(Roger Fell) *prom: rdn over 2f out: no ex fnl f* **16/1**

0000 **7** 1/2 **Kodiline (IRE)**[11] 1880 5-8-0 **71** oh2 GinaMangan(7) 1 66
(David Evans) *outpcd in rr tl kpt on fnl f (jockey said gelding hung right throughout)* **50/1**

564- **8** nk **Dalton**[185] 8594 5-9-6 **84** (p) GrahamLee 13 78
(Julie Camacho) *hld up: rdn along 2f out: kpt on fnl 110yds: nvr threatened* **6/1**[3]

420- **9** nse **Black Isle Boy (IRE)**[135] 9564 5-9-4 **82** DanielTudhope 15 76
(David O'Meara) *hld up: rdn along 2f out: nvr threatened* **7/2**[1]

50-0 **10** nse **Mostahel**[21] 1654 5-8-13 **77** KevinStott 2 71
(Paul Midgley) *slowly away: hld up: drvn over 1f out: kpt on fnl f: nvr threatened* **33/1**

00-0 **11** 1 1/2 **Quick Look**[29] 1459 6-9-7 **85** NathanEvans 5 80
(Michael Easterby) *in tch: pushed along and sltly outpcd 2f out: hmpd over 1f out: swtchd rt appr fnl f: hmpd again ins fnl f: no ch after (jockey said gelding was denied a clear run in the final furlong)* **11/1**

50-0 **12** 3/4 **Upstaging**[29] 1459 7-9-4 **82** (p) BarryMcHugh 14 69
(Noel Wilson) *midfield: rdn over 2f out: wknd ins fnl f* **33/1**

06-0 **13** nk **Mr Wagyu (IRE)**[11] 1895 4-8-11 **75** (v) JasonHart 6 61
(John Quinn) *prom: rdn over 2f out: wknd fnl f* **33/1**

00-0 **14** 2 1/2 **Kenny The Captain (IRE)**[16] 1760 8-8-9 **73** RachelRichardson 10 51
(Tim Easterby) *trckd ldrs: rdn 3f out: wknd over 1f out* **25/1**

1m 11.8s (-1.00) **Going Correction** -0.20s/f (Firm) **14 Ran SP% 114.0**
Speed ratings (Par 105): **98,96,94,93,93 92,92,91,91,91 89,88,88,84**
CSF £33.20 CT £318.31 TOTE £5.40: £2.20, £2.70, £2.60; EX 31.20 Trifecta £191.30.
Owner K&J Bloodstock Ltd **Bred** Lael Stables **Trained** Hambleton, N Yorks

FOCUS
The feature race and the time was clearly the fastest of the three races over the trip on the evening. The form looks fairly sound, with the winner rated back to his old best.

2202 @THIRSKRACES CONFERENCE CENTRE H'CAP 1m 4f 8y
7:40 (7:50) (Class 6) (0-65,65) 4-Y-O+ **£3,398** (£1,011; £505; £300; £300; £300) **Stalls** High

Form RPR

020- **1** **Buckland Boy (IRE)**[181] 8722 4-9-7 **65** (p) StevieDonohoe 3 75
(Charlie Fellowes) *midfield on inner: angled rt to outer over 2f out: sn hdwy: rdn to ld appr fnl f: drvn and styd on* **8/1**[3]

6324 **2** 1 1/4 **Duke Of Alba (IRE)**[21] 1647 4-9-2 **60** JoeFanning 10 68
(John Mackie) *in tch: pushed along and hdwy over 2f out: rdn to chal over 1f out: styd on* **11/4**[1]

-222 **3** hd **Nevada**[31] 1398 6-9-7 **65** (p) PJMcDonald 12 72
(Steve Gollings) *trckd ldrs: rdn over 2f out: styd on fnl f* **7/2**[2]

00-5 **4** 3 3/4 **Highland Bobby**[13] 1836 4-8-13 **57** (h) ShaneGray 16 59
(David O'Meara) *slowly away: hld up in rr: rdn along and hdwy on outside over 2f out: styd on ins fnl f* **20/1**

1006 **5** 1 3/4 **Star Ascending (IRE)**[27] 1508 7-9-1 **64** (p) SeanDavis(5) 15 62
(Jennie Candlish) *hld up in midfield: rdn and sme hdwy over 2f out: styd on same pce* **33/1**

55-0 **6** 3/4 **Motahassen (IRE)**[12] 1858 5-8-13 **57** CamHardie 1 54
(Declan Carroll) *led: rdn over 2f out: hdd appr fnl f: wknd ins fnl f* **14/1**

U50- **7** 1/2 **The Fiddler**[193] 8347 4-8-9 **53** DavidAllan 7 50
(Chris Wall) *hld up: pushed along and hdwy on inner over 2f out: no further imp fnl f* **14/1**

04-0 **8** 3 1/4 **Airplane (IRE)**[12] 1848 4-9-6 **64** RachelRichardson 9 56
(Tim Easterby) *prom: rdn over 2f out: wknd over 1f out* **40/1**

500- **9** 1/2 **Point Of Honour (IRE)**[181] 8718 4-8-11 **55** JamesSullivan 2 46
(Ruth Carr) *midfield: pushed along over 2f out: nvr threatened* **18/1**

600- **10** 2 3/4 **Zig Zag (IRE)**[58] 8416 6-9-0 **58** (p) TonyHamilton 6 43
(Philip Kirby) *in tch: rdn over 2f out: wknd over 1f out* **25/1**

5123 **11** 3/4 **Subliminal**[23] 1591 4-9-7 **65** GrahamLee 17 50
(Simon Dow) *prom: rdn over 3f out: wknd over 1f out (jockey said colt hung left in the final 5f)* **8/1**[3]

3240 **12** 3 **Epitaph (IRE)**[27] 1508 5-8-11 **60** (v) TheodoreLadd(5) 5 39
(Michael Appleby) *hld up: rdn over 2f out: nvr threatened* **14/1**

600 **13** hd **Bravantina**[31] 1400 4-8-11 **55** JasonHart 14 35
(Mark Walford) *midfield: rdn over 3f out: wknd over 1f out* **66/1**

06-0 **14** shd **Gabriel's Oboe (IRE)**[21] 1648 4-8-13 **57** DougieCostello 13 37
(Mark Walford) *midfield: rdn over 7f out: lost pl 5f out: wknd 3f out* **100/1**

441- **15** 13 **Richard Strauss (IRE)**[120] 8718 5-8-12 **56** KevinStott 8 14
(Philip Kirby) *a in rr* **16/1**

2m 35.56s (-4.44) **Going Correction** -0.20s/f (Firm) **15 Ran SP% 118.7**
Speed ratings (Par 101): **106,105,105,102,101 100,100,98,98,96 95,93,93,93,84**
CSF £27.74 CT £93.83 TOTE £7.10: £2.10, £2.80, £1.90; EX 31.10 Trifecta £70.10.
Owner P S McNally **Bred** Thomas Hassett **Trained** Newmarket, Suffolk

FOCUS
A moderate middle-distance handicap but a couple of progressive sorts filled the first two placings. The form is rated around the second and third.

2203 FOLLOW @THIRSKRACES ON TWITTER H'CAP 7f
8:10 (8:18) (Class 6) (0-65,65) 4-Y-O+
£3,398 (£1,011; £505; £300; £300; £300) **Stalls** Low

Form | | | | RPR
10-6 1 **Thornaby Nash**[20] [1659] 8-8-12 **61**..........(b) SebastianWoods(5) 7 70
(Jason Ward) *prom: rdn 2f out: drvn to ld 125yds out: kpt on* **10/1**
0060 2 1 1/4 **Atletico (IRE)**[11] [1881] 7-9-7 **65**..........(v) BenCurtis 3 71+
(David Evans) *trckd ldrs: rdn along 2f out: bit short of room and squeezed through gap 1f out: sn chal: kpt on* **11/2[2]**
3-06 3 1 1/4 **Christmas Night**[30] [1426] 4-9-0 **61**.......... BenRobinson(3) 11 64
(Ollie Pears) *prom: rdn over 2f out: led over 1f out: sn drvn: hdd 125yds out: edgd rt and one pce* **12/1**
410- 4 1 1/4 **Sfumato**[182] [8705] 5-9-7 **65**.......... AndrewMullen 10 64
(Adrian Nicholls) *trckd ldrs: rdn over 2f out: one pce fnl f* **12/1**
62-0 5 shd **Donnelly's Rainbow (IRE)**[19] [1695] 6-9-0 **58**.......... LewisEdmunds 8 57+
(Rebecca Bastiman) *dwlt: hld up in midfield: rdn along and hdwy 2f out: kpt on fnl f* **14/1**
20-0 6 nk **Chickenfortea (IRE)**[24] [1565] 5-9-6 **64**.......... JasonHart 4 62
(Eric Alston) *led: rdn and hdd over 1f out: no ex ins fnl f* **16/1**
00-0 7 1 1/4 **Im Dapper Too**[20] [1660] 8-9-3 **61**.......... SamJames 16 56
(John Davies) *in tch on outer: rdn over 2f out: outpcd over 1f out: no threat after* **12/1**
040- 8 hd **Mywayistheonlyway (IRE)**[213] [7728] 6-9-7 **65**..........(w) PJMcDonald 2 59
(Grant Tuer) *dwlt: sn midfield: rdn over 2f out: no imp* **8/1[3]**
205- 9 nk **Naples Bay**[192] [8389] 5-9-6 **64**.......... PhilDennis 14 58
(Katie Scott) *hld up: pushed along 2f out: kpt on fnl f: nvr threatened* **16/1**
230- 10 nk **Kodicat (IRE)**[145] [9416] 5-9-5 **63**.......... DougieCostello 15 56+
(Kevin Ryan) *hld up: pushed along 2f out: swtchd rt and sme hdwy 1f out: one pce ins fnl f* **25/1**
05-3 11 1/2 **Proceeding**[102] [275] 4-9-4 **62**.......... CamHardie 5 54
(Tracy Waggott) *hld up towards inner: nvr threatened* **16/1**
400- 12 1 **Billy Wedge**[202] [8096] 4-9-2 **60**.......... RoystonFfrench 12 49
(Tracy Waggott) *hld up: nvr threatened* **20/1**
0-50 13 1/2 **Ninjago**[7] [1976] 9-9-7 **65**..........(v) PaulMulrennan 6 53
(Paul Midgley) *in tch: rdn to chse ldrs over 2f out: wknd appr fnl f* **25/1**
40-0 14 shd **Roaring Forties (IRE)**[35] [1338] 6-9-4 **62**..........(p) DanielTudhope 1 49
(Rebecca Bastiman) *midfield: rdn along 2f out: wknd fnl f* **20/1**
056- 15 7 **Forever A Lady (IRE)**[218] [7583] 6-9-6 **64**..........(v[1]) TonyHamilton 9 33
(Keith Dalgleish) *midfield on outer: rdn over 2f out: wknd over 1f out* **25/1**
000- 16 6 **Ebbisham (IRE)**[159] [9182] 6-9-5 **63**..........(p) JoeFanning 13 17
(John Mackie) *dwlt: hld up: rdn over 2f out: sn btn* **9/2[1]**

1m 26.29s (-1.31) **Going Correction** -0.20s/f (Firm) **16** Ran SP% **122.2**
Speed ratings (Par 101): **99,97,96,94,94 94,92,92,92,91 91,90,89,89,81 74**
CSF £58.94 CT £696.45 TOTE £11.40: £3.50, £2.10, £3.70, £4.20; EX 86.00 Trifecta £1068.90.
Owner Ingleby Bloodstock Limited **Bred** Dave Scott **Trained** Sessay, N Yorks

FOCUS
Another moderate contest in which it paid to race close to the pace. The first four were in the first five places throughout. The winner hasn't rated higher since 2015.
T/Jkpt: Not Won. T/Plt: £164.90 to a £1 stake. Pool: £50,186.41 - 222.12 winning units. T/Qpdt: £11.30 to a £1 stake. Pool: £8,183.80 - 532.87 winning units. **Andrew Sheret**

[1820] WINDSOR (R-H)
Monday, April 29

OFFICIAL GOING: Good (good to firm in places; 7.5)
Wind: Almost nil Weather: Fine but cloudy

2204 ZUPERMAN AUTOMOTIVE H'CAP 6f 12y
4:55 (4:56) (Class 5) (0-70,72) 3-Y-O
£3,752 (£1,116; £557; £300; £300; £300) **Stalls** Centre

Form | | | | RPR
000- 1 **Tone The Barone**[213] [7736] 3-8-6 **55**..........(t) SilvestreDeSousa 11 64+
(Stuart Williams) *trckd ldrs on outer: rdn to ld over 1f out: styd on wl: readily (trainer said, regarding apparent improvement in form, that gelding was having his first run in a handicap and has been gelded since it's last run)* **4/1[2]**
-365 2 1 1/4 **Urban Highway (IRE)**[21] [1650] 3-8-11 **60**.......... PatDobbs 7 65
(Tony Carroll) *hld up in midfield: prog 2f out: rdn to chse wnr fnl f: styd on and drew clr of rest but no imp last 100yds* **18/1**
00-0 3 3 **My Law**[19] [1687] 3-8-6 **62**.......... IsobelFrancis(7) 4 57
(Jim Boyle) *hld up in rr: nudged along 2f out: prog over 1f out: reminders and r.o fnl f to take 3rd nr fin* **66/1**
0-03 4 hd **John Betjeman**[23] [1587] 3-9-4 **72**..........(p) RyanWhile(5) 10 67
(Bill Turner) *racd on outer: mde most to over 1f out: outpcd after* **20/1**
30-2 5 nk **Kwela**[19] [1687] 3-9-2 **72**.......... GeorgiaDobie(7) 1 66
(Eve Johnson Houghton) *dwlt sltly: in rr and racd against nr side rail: nvr on terms but kpt on fr over 1f out: nvr nrr* **9/1[3]**
60-3 6 1/2 **Valentino Sunrise**[21] [1650] 3-8-7 **63**.......... GeorgeBass(7) 3 55
(Mick Channon) *w ldrs and towards nr side: stl gng wl 2f out: rdn and fdd over 1f out* **14/1**
3112 7 nk **Pentland Lad (IRE)**[4] [2063] 3-8-13 **62**..........(t[1]) JasonWatson 5 53
(Charlie Fellowes) *w ldrs: u.p over 2f out: nt qckn over 1f out: fdd* **13/8[1]**
-100 8 3/4 **Greybychoice (IRE)**[37] [1285] 3-8-12 **68**..........(b[1]) JessicaCooley(7) 2 57
(Nick Littmoden) *awkward s: mostly in last trio: kpt on towards nr side fnl f: nvr nrr* **50/1**
32-0 9 nk **Vino Rosso (IRE)**[19] [1687] 3-8-11 **60**.......... CallumShepherd 12 48
(Michael Blanshard) *in tch on outer: prog to chse ldrs over 2f out: wknd over 1f out* **33/1**
330- 10 1 1/2 **Cracking Speed (IRE)**[208] [7899] 3-9-6 **69**..........(t) KieranO'Neill 9 52
(Richard Hannon) *w ldrs to 1/2-way: rdn over 2f out: wknd wl over 1f out* **14/1**
42-3 11 3/4 **Painted Dream**[28] [1475] 3-9-7 **70**.......... OisinMurphy 15 51
(George Margarson) *chsd ldrs on outer: rdn 2f out: wknd over 1f out* **10/1**
035- 12 1 1/2 **Molly Blake**[123] [9727] 3-9-2 **65**.......... AdamKirby 8 41
(Clive Cox) *nvr beyond midfield: rdn and no prog 2f out: wknd over 1f out* **10/1**
1-50 13 nk **Freedom And Wheat (IRE)**[19] [1685] 3-9-4 **67**..........(v) FergusSweeney 14 42
(Mark Usher) *racd on wd outside: w ldr: led briefly 1/2-way: hung lft 2f out and wknd (jockey said gelding hung left-handed throughout)* **22/1**
-660 14 6 **Gold At Midnight**[12] [1857] 3-9-7 **70**..........(p) DavidProbert 6 26
(William Stone) *w ldrs to 1/2-way: wknd qckly over 2f out (jockey said filly suffered interference)* **20/1**
050- 15 21 **Ragstone Cowboy (IRE)**[187] [8553] 3-9-3 **66**.......... ShaneKelly 13
(Murty McGrath) *rel to r: a wl bhd: eased whn no ch fnl f: t.o (jockey said gelding was slowly away)* **66/1**

1m 12.11s (0.01) **Going Correction** -0.025s/f (Good) **15** Ran SP% **126.6**
Speed ratings (Par 98): **98,96,92,92,91 91,90,89,89,87 86,84,83,75,47**
CSF £71.85 CT £4255.91 TOTE £5.80: £2.00, £6.00, £21.10; EX 100.60 Trifecta £1892.40.
Owner B Piper And Partner **Bred** Ors Bloodstock & Stanley House Stud **Trained** Newmarket, Suffolk

FOCUS
20 yards were added to the 6.30, 7.00, 7.30 and 8.00 race distances due to the bend and bottom rail being moved in by 3 yards. Just a modest sprint handicap, but a progressive winner. The main action came out in the centre of the track and the time, on quickish ground, was 1.91sec outside the standard.

2205 BRITISH EBF NOVICE STKS (PLUS 10 RACE) 5f 21y
5:25 (5:26) (Class 4) 2-Y-O
£4,787 (£1,424; £711; £355) **Stalls** Centre

Form | | | | RPR
1 **Emten (IRE)** 2-9-0.......... NicolaCurrie 9 76+
(Jamie Osborne) *dwlt: racd wdst of all: chsd ldrs after 2f: clsd 2f out: shkn up to ld jst over 1f out: styd on wl* **5/1[3]**
2 1 1/4 **Top Buck (IRE)** 2-9-5.......... OisinMurphy 10 77
(Brian Meehan) *pressed ldng pair: rdn and upsides over 1f out: one pce fnl f* **9/1**
3 1 1/4 **Port Winston (IRE)** 2-9-5.......... DavidProbert 8 72
(Alan King) *pressed ldr: upsides over 1f out: outpcd fnl f* **9/1**
4 nk **Imperial Command (IRE)** 2-9-5.......... SilvestreDeSousa 3 71+
(Jonjo O'Neill) *towards rr and struggling to go the pce: styd on over 1f out: nrst fin* **14/1**
5 1/2 **I'm Digby (IRE)** 2-9-5.......... ShaneKelly 1 70+
(Richard Hughes) *chsd ldrs against nr side rail: rdn 2f out: no prog over 1f out: outpcd fnl f* **16/1**
53 6 1 1/4 **Isobar Wind (IRE)**[9] [1953] 2-9-5.......... AdamKirby 6 65
(David Evans) *led and racd against nr side rail: rdn and hdd jst over 1f out: wknd* **4/1[2]**
7 1/2 **Jim 'N' Tomic (IRE)** 2-9-5.......... CallumShepherd 5 63
(Dominic Ffrench Davis) *chsd ldrs: rdn sn after 1/2-way: hanging and green over 1f out: wknd* **12/1**
8 3/4 **Kuwait Direction (IRE)** 2-9-5.......... TomMarquand 7 61+
(Richard Hannon) *dwlt: urged along and reminder early: a struggling in rr* **13/8[1]**
0 9 2 **Brown Eyes Blue (IRE)**[24] [1556] 2-9-0..........(b[1]) KieranO'Neill 2 48
(J S Moore) *towards rr: pushed along bef 1/2-way: no prog* **50/1**
10 11 **Come On Girl** 2-9-0.......... TomQueally 4 9
(Jennie Candlish) *s.v.s: a wl bhd: t.o (jockey said filly was slowly away)* **50/1**

1m 0.67s (0.57) **Going Correction** -0.025s/f (Good) **10** Ran SP% **118.9**
Speed ratings (Par 94): **94,92,90,89,88 86,85,84,81,63**
CSF £50.52 TOTE £5.10: £1.60, £1.60, £2.90; EX 54.30 Trifecta £366.00.
Owner Melbourne 10 Racing **Bred** Rathasker Stud **Trained** Upper Lambourn, Berks

FOCUS
All five previous winners of this have gone on to show smart form, including last year's scorer Emaraaty Ana who landed the Gimcrack. Again the centre of the track was the place to be. The first three came out of the three highest stalls.

2206 CHRIS DANIEL BIRTHDAY H'CAP 5f 21y
6:00 (6:01) (Class 5) (0-70,70) 4-Y-O+
£3,752 (£1,116; £557; £300; £300; £300) **Stalls** Centre

Form | | | | RPR
643- 1 **Coronation Cottage**[332] [3306] 5-9-1 **64**.......... PatCosgrave 15 73
(Malcolm Saunders) *mde all: racd on outer fr wdst draw: shkn up and decisive advantage over 1f out: unchal* **20/1**
356- 2 1 1/4 **Essaka (IRE)**[194] [8315] 7-8-3 **59**.......... SophieRalston(7) 7 64+
(Tony Carroll) *dwlt: t.k.h and hld up in rr: moved to nr side rail and prog 2f out: rdn and r.o to take 2nd ins fnl f: unable to chal* **16/1**
1406 3 1 1/4 **Mooroverthebridge**[14] [1820] 5-8-7 **59**.......... MeganNicholls(3) 13 59
(Grace Harris) *chsd ldrs on outer: rdn to dispute 2nd over 1f out to ins fnl f: one pce* **5/1[2]**
0-0 4 hd **Awsaaf**[23] [1590] 4-8-7 **56** oh1..........(h) FrannyNorton 8 55
(Michael Wigham) *prom: rdn to dispute 2nd over 1f out to ins fnl f: one pce* **9/2[1]**
0660 5 1 1/4 **Hello Girl**[14] [1820] 4-8-7 **56** oh1.......... MartinDwyer 14 51
(Dean Ivory) *racd towards outer: mostly chsd wnr to over 1f out: fdd fnl f* **10/1**
046- 6 3/4 **Porto Ferro (IRE)**[122] [9733] 5-9-5 **68**.......... KieranO'Neill 5 60
(John Bridger) *chsd ldrs: rdn and no prog over 1f out* **11/2[3]**
00-0 7 1/2 **Firenze Rosa (IRE)**[14] [1820] 4-8-1 **57** oh5 ow1.......... GeorgiaDobie(7) 3 47
(John Bridger) *in tch: rdn and no imp on ldrs over 1f out* **12/1**
5-0P 8 nk **Look Surprised**[72] [763] 6-9-3 **66**.......... DavidProbert 1 55+
(Roger Teal) *hld up towards rr: pushed along 2f out: kpt on same pce fnl f: nvr in it* **6/1**
2-00 9 nk **Midnight Guest (IRE)**[82] [626] 4-9-0 **63**..........(v) TomMarquand 6 51
(David Evans) *t.k.h: hld up in rr: rdn and no prog 2f out: n.d after* **40/1**
300- 10 1 **Ladweb**[136] [9529] 9-9-4 **70**..........(w) CameronNoble(3) 4 55
(John Gallagher) *dwlt: wl in rr: no real prog over 1f out* **12/1**
0/45 11 1/2 **Just For The Craic (IRE)**[30] [1426] 4-8-13 **62**.......... ShaneKelly 2 45
(Neil Mulholland) *prom and racd against nr side rail: wknd over 1f out (jockey said gelding took a false step approaching 2f out)* **14/1**
2-00 12 1 3/4 **Vimy Ridge**[55] [1023] 7-8-13 **69**..........(t) JessicaCooley(7) 12 45
(Alan Bailey) *a in rr and nvr a factor (jockey said gelding hung right-handed)* **16/1**
4-60 13 nk **Sir Hector (IRE)**[6] [2025] 4-9-5 **68**.......... AdamKirby 9 43
(Charlie Wallis) *dwlt: a wl in rr: rdn and no prog 2f out* **12/1**
00-0 14 5 **Ballesteros**[109] [161] 10-8-0 **56** oh4.......... SeanKirrane(7) 10 13
(Emma Owen) *chsd ldrs to 1/2-way: wknd qckly* **33/1**
500- 15 3/4 **Jaganory (IRE)**[194] [8315] 7-8-7 **56** oh2..........(p) NicolaCurrie 11 11
(Christopher Mason) *a towards rr: wknd over 1f out* **33/1**

59.73s (-0.37) **Going Correction** -0.025s/f (Good) **15** Ran SP% **128.2**
Speed ratings (Par 103): **101,99,97,96,94 93,92,92,91,90 89,86,86,78,76**
CSF £317.42 CT £1908.82 TOTE £24.80: £6.50, £5.30, £2.30; EX 532.70 Trifecta £1088.80.
Owner Pat Hancock & Eric Jones **Bred** Eric Jones, Pat Hancock **Trained** Green Ore, Somerset

FOCUS
Ordinary sprint handicap form. The winner was close to her 3yo level.

2207 WINDSOR & ETON BREWERY H'CAP — 1m 2f
6:30 (6:33) (Class 4) (0-80,81) 4-Y-0+
£5,530 (£1,645; £822; £411; £300; £300) **Stalls Low**

Form — RPR

560- **1** **He's Amazing (IRE)**[202] 8081 4-9-7 **80**........................ OisinMurphy 9 91
(Ed Walker) *sn chsd ldr: chal 3f out: hanging lft but drvn to ld wl over 1f out: styd on wl fnl f (jockey said gelding hung both ways under pressure)* **5/1**[3]

510- **2** *2* **Allegiant (USA)**[202] 8069 4-8-13 **72**........................ SilvestreDeSousa 7 79
(Stuart Williams) *in tch: rdn 3f out: prog u.p towards outer 2f out: styd on to take 2nd fnl f: no imp on wnr* **5/1**[3]

2-43 **3** *hd* **Escapability (IRE)**[33] 1365 4-9-4 **77**........................ TomMarquand 8 83
(Alan King) *in tch: pushed along over 3f out: prog u.p on outer over 2f out: styd on to dispute 2nd fnl f: no imp on wnr* **3/1**[2]

4026 **4** *2* **High Acclaim (USA)**[21] 1655 5-9-1 **74**........................(p) JasonWatson 6 76
(Roger Teal) *s.s and rousted: sn in tch: prog 1/2-way to jnd ldrs 4f out: rdn to ld 3f out: hdd wl over 1f out: wknd fnl f (jockey said gelding was slowly away)* **14/1**

456- **5** *nse* **Follow Intello (IRE)**[178] 8798 4-8-13 **72**........................ TomQueally 3 74
(Chris Wall) *s.s and pushed along early: mostly in last pair: shkn up over 2f out: kpt on fnl f: n.d (jockey said gelding was slowly away)* **20/1**

330- **6** *nk* **Junderstand**[225] 7336 4-9-2 **75**........................ DavidProbert 2 76
(Alan King) *dwlt: hld up in last pair: pushed along over 2f out: nvr in it but kpt on steadily fnl f* **14/1**

/5-2 **7** *1* **Just Brilliant (IRE)**[26] 1517 4-9-8 **81**........................ AndreaAtzeni 4 80
(Peter Chapple-Hyam) *racd freely: led to 3f out: wknd u.p over 1f out* **9/4**[1]

-010 **8** *1 3/4* **New Agenda**[71] 780 7-9-3 **76**........................ PatDobbs 1 72
(Paul Webber) *trckd ldrs: stl gng strly 3f out: rdn 2f out: wknd tamely* **12/1**

0/5- **9** *12* **Perfect Cracker**[469] 240 11-9-7 **80**........................ AdamKirby 5 52
(Patrick Chamings) *in tch: wknd over 2f out: t.o* **50/1**

2m 7.33s (-1.67) **Going Correction** -0.025s/f (Good) **9** Ran SP% **116.9**
Speed ratings (Par 105): **105,103,103,101,101 101,100,99,89**
CSF £30.61 CT £88.22 TOTE £5.80: £1.80, £1.80, £1.50; EX 38.70 Trifecta £159.20.
Owner Eight Investment Holdings Ltd **Bred** Paget Bloodstock **Trained** Upper Lambourn, Berks

FOCUS
Distances increased by 20y to 1m 2f 20y. Fairly useful handicap form, taken at face value.

2208 ROBUSTO HOUSE MAIDEN STKS — 1m 2f
7:00 (7:01) (Class 5) 3-Y-0+
£3,752 (£1,116; £557; £278) **Stalls Low**

Form — RPR

5-2 **1** **Sinjaari (IRE)**[21] 1643 3-8-11........................ OisinMurphy 1 90+
(William Haggas) *trckd ldng pair: shkn up to ld over 1f out: styd on strly and drew clr fnl f* **11/10**[1]

23- **2** *2 1/2* **Global Heat (IRE)**[195] 8302 3-8-11........................ JasonWatson 11 85
(Saeed bin Suroor) *trckd ldr to 4f out: styd cl up: chal and upsides 2f out to over 1f out: styd on but outpcd by wnr* **3/1**[2]

5-3 **3** *2* **Entrusting**[21] 1643 3-8-11........................ SilvestreDeSousa 6 81
(James Fanshawe) *prom: trckd ldr 4f out: rdn to ld briefly wl over 1f out: outpcd fnl f* **11/2**[3]

32- **4** *1 1/2* **Durston**[173] 8930 3-8-11........................ JamieSpencer 4 78
(David Simcock) *wl in tch: pushed along to chse ldrs over 2f out: reminders over 1f out: outpcd but kpt on* **8/1**

5 *1 3/4* **Norma** 3-8-6........................ GeorgeWood 2 70+
(James Fanshawe) *hld up in midfield: wl in tch 3f out: outpcd and pushed along over 2f out: styd on steadily over 1f out* **40/1**

0- **6** *1/2* **Najib (IRE)**[156] 9254 3-8-11........................ CallumShepherd 13 74
(Saeed bin Suroor) *hld up towards rr: prog to chse ldrs 4f out: rdn and rt on terms 2f out: wknd qckly fnl f* **50/1**

7 *2 1/4* **Thounder (FR)**[28] 5-10-0........................ HectorCrouch 12 72+
(Gary Moore) *hld up in rr: 12th 1/2-way: nvr on terms but styd on quite takingly over 1f out* **66/1**

52- **8** *1/2* **Horatio Star**[292] 4805 4-10-0........................ MartinDwyer 5 71
(Brian Meehan) *led: rdn and hdd wl over 1f out: hung lft and wknd* **66/1**

30- **9** *3* **Calculation**[237] 6899 3-8-11........................ AndreaAtzeni 3 62
(Sir Michael Stoute) *chsd ldrs: pushed along wl over 3f out: wknd 2f out* **10/1**

33 **10** *3/4* **Thelonious**[38] 1268 3-8-11........................ LouisSteward 9 61+
(Michael Bell) *hld up in last quartet: pushed along 3f out: nvr in it but kpt on over 1f out* **66/1**

6 **11** *3/4* **Corncrake**[27] 1495 3-8-11........................ TomMarquand 7 59
(Richard Hannon) *hld up and sn in last: urged along 4f out: nvr in it but passed a few fr 2f out (jockey said colt was never travelling)* **50/1**

-52 **12** *3/4* **Will Of Iron**[21] 1652 3-8-11........................ NickyMackay 8 58
(John Gosden) *a towards rr: rdn and no prog 4f out* **14/1**

0 **13** *nse* **Samba Saravah (USA)**[12] 1852 3-8-11........................ HarryBentley 14 57
(Jeremy Noseda) *in tch in midfield: shkn up and wknd over 2f out* **100/1**

14 *8* **Lyrical Waters** 3-8-11........................ CharlesBishop 16 41
(Eve Johnson Houghton) *a wl in rr: t.o* **100/1**

15 *8* **Zaydanides (FR)**[368] 7-9-11........................ GaryMahon(3) 10 28
(Tim Pinfield) *a wl in rr: hung lft over 3f out and sn bhd: t.o* **100/1**

16 *1* **Pour Joie**[70] 4-10-0........................ DavidProbert 15 26
(Ian Williams) *c out of stall slowly: prog after 3f to chse ldrs: hung lft 3f out: wknd rapidly: t.o (jockey said gelding hung left-handed throughout)* **100/1**

2m 8.38s (-0.62) **Going Correction** -0.025s/f (Good)
WFA 3 from 4yo+ 17lb **16** Ran SP% **129.7**
Speed ratings (Par 103): **101,99,97,96,94 94,92,92,89,89 88,88,87,81,75 74**
CSF £4.55 TOTE £2.00: £1.20, £1.10, £1.90; EX 5.90 Trifecta £18.50.
Owner Mohammed Jaber **Bred** Dr T Purcell & Mr P Purcell **Trained** Newmarket, Suffolk

FOCUS
Distances increased by 20y to 1m 2f 20y. Winners should emerge from this maiden, which was a second slower than the preceding Class 4 handicap. The second, third and fourth were close to their marks.

2209 FOLLOW AT THE RACES ON TWITTER H'CAP — 1m 3f 99y
7:30 (7:30) (Class 4) (0-85,85) 4-Y-0+
£5,530 (£1,645; £822; £411; £300; £300) **Stalls Low**

Form — RPR

16-0 **1** **New Show (IRE)**[16] 1757 4-9-7 **85**........................(b[1]) JamieSpencer 7 90
(Michael Bell) *hld up in last pair: prog on wd outside over 2f out: drvn and clsd fnl f: led last 100yds: styd on wl* **6/1**

440- **2** *3/4* **C'Est No Mour (GER)**[185] 8595 6-9-0 **78**........................ GeraldMosse 6 82
(Peter Hedger) *t.k.h: hld up in last trio: clsd over 2f out: rdn to ld jst over 1f out: hdd and rdr dropped whip 100yds out: kpt on* **11/2**[3]

34-3 **3** *1/2* **Running Cloud (IRE)**[30] 1425 4-9-1 **79**........................(v) TomMarquand 3 82
(Alan King) *slowly away: hld up in last: rdn over 2f out: clsd on ldrs over 1f out but nvr a clr run: styd on to take 3rd nr fin* **12/1**

654- **4** *3/4* **Perfect Illusion**[180] 8736 4-9-4 **82**........................ OisinMurphy 2 84
(Andrew Balding) *t.k.h: trckd ldrs: rdn over 2f out: chal over 1f out and stl on terms jst ins fnl f: no ex* **4/1**[1]

651- **5** *3/4* **Persian Sun**[135] 9553 4-9-4 **82**........................ AndreaAtzeni 5 82
(Simon Crisford) *trckd ldr: rdn to ld 2f out: hdd jst over 1f out: fdd* **11/2**[3]

501- **6** *3 1/4* **Victory Chime (IRE)**[201] 8102 4-9-3 **81**........................ HarryBentley 4 76
(Ralph Beckett) *led: tried to kick on 3f out and styd against nr side rail: hdd 2f out: wknd over 1f out* **5/1**[2]

2115 **7** *1 1/4* **Ilhabela Fact**[30] 1425 5-9-4 **82**........................ AdamKirby 1 75
(Tony Carroll) *trckd ldrs: lost pl and rdn over 2f out: wknd over 1f out* **7/1**

26-4 **8** *1 1/4* **Tiar Na Nog (IRE)**[23] 1588 7-8-8 **72**........................ JasonWatson 8 63
(Denis Coakley) *trckd ldrs: rdn 3f out: no prog 2f out: wknd over 1f out* **7/1**

2m 27.06s (-2.64) **Going Correction** -0.025s/f (Good) **8** Ran SP% **114.4**
Speed ratings (Par 105): **108,107,107,106,106 103,102,101**
CSF £38.77 CT £382.84 TOTE £7.60: £2.10, £2.20, £2.40; EX 46.60 Trifecta £430.20.
Owner Edward J Ware **Bred** Rabbah Bloodstock Limited **Trained** Newmarket, Suffolk

FOCUS
Race distance increased by 20y to 1m 3f 119y. A fair handicap in which the first three came from the rear. The bare form is ordinary if sound.

2210 SKY SPORTS RACING VIRGIN 535 NOVICE STKS — 1m 31y
8:00 (8:02) (Class 5) 3-Y-0 **£3,752** (£1,116; £557; £278) **Stalls Low**

Form — RPR

14- **1** **Lady Madison (IRE)**[214] 7695 3-9-5 0........................ ShaneKelly 4 89+
(Richard Hughes) *led 2f: trckd ldr: led again 2f out gng easily: hanging lft but rdn clr fnl f* **7/2**[2]

32- **2** *3 3/4* **Durrell**[217] 7623 3-9-3 0........................(h[1]) DanielMuscutt 13 76
(James Fanshawe) *trckd ldng pair: rdn over 2f out: chsd wnr over 1f out: sn easily outpcd* **15/8**[1]

3 *2 1/4* **Noble Fox** 3-9-3 0........................ AdamKirby 12 71
(Clive Cox) *hld up disputing 7th: shkn up over 2f out: styd on over 1f out to take 3rd nr fin* **16/1**

6- **4** *nk* **Rachel Zane (IRE)**[172] 8954 3-8-12 0........................(h[1]) OisinMurphy 9 65
(Hugo Palmer) *trckd ldng pair: shkn up over 2f out: outpcd over 1f out* **6/1**[3]

0 **5** *1 1/2* **Air Hair Lair (IRE)**[16] 1754 3-9-3 0........................ CharlesBishop 11 67
(Sheena West) *chsd ldrs: shkn up over 2f out: outpcd over 1f out* **25/1**

6 *1 1/2* **Trust Me (IRE)** 3-9-3 0........................ MartinDwyer 10 63+
(Dean Ivory) *plld way to ld after 2f: hdd 2f out: wknd over 1f out* **20/1**

6- **7** *1 1/4* **Illywhacker (IRE)**[250] 6418 3-9-3 0........................ HectorCrouch 2 60
(Gary Moore) *a abt same pl: shkn up over 2f out: sn lft bhd* **33/1**

0-4 **8** *nk* **Grape Shot**[25] 1543 3-8-12 0........................ TomMarquand 8 55
(Richard Hannon) *hld up disputing 7th: shkn up and fdd over 2f out* **20/1**

9 *3 1/2* **Kasuku** 3-8-12 0........................ HarryBentley 7 47
(Ralph Beckett) *dwlt: a towards rr: shkn up and no prog over 2f out* **7/1**

10 *3/4* **Molotov (IRE)** 3-9-3 0........................ NicolaCurrie 3 50
(Jamie Osborne) *dwlt: rn green and wl in rr* **15/2**

46 **11** *3/4* **Jazzy Card (IRE)**[33] 1359 3-8-12 0........................ CallumShepherd 1 43
(Linda Jewell) *nvr bttr than midfield: shkn up and wknd over 2f out* **100/1**

12 *nk* **Bayaanaat**[196] 8285 3-9-3 0........................ KieranO'Neill 6 47
(Peter Hiatt) *s.v.s: mostly in last: nudged along and no prog over 2f out (jockey said gelding was slowly away)* **66/1**

3 **13** *3* **William McKinley**[90] 472 3-9-3 0........................ GeraldMosse 5 41
(Ali Stronge) *dwlt: a wl in rr* **25/1**

1m 44.37s (-0.13) **Going Correction** -0.025s/f (Good) **13** Ran SP% **124.1**
Speed ratings (Par 98): **99,95,93,92,91 89,88,88,84,83 83,82,79**
CSF £10.04 TOTE £4.60: £1.30, £1.40, £4.70; EX 14.80 Trifecta £120.60.
Owner M Clarke, P Munnelly & D Waters **Bred** Rockfield Farm **Trained** Upper Lambourn, Berks

FOCUS
Race distance increased by 20y to 1m 51y. A nice performance from the winner of this novice event. The form is taken at face value.
T/Plt: £1,119.80 to a £1 stake. Pool: £68,267.30 - 44.50 winning units. T/Qpdt: £36.80 to a £1 stake. Pool: £11,755.56 - 236.25 winning units. **Jonathan Neesom**

2122 WOLVERHAMPTON (A.W) (L-H)
Monday, April 29

OFFICIAL GOING: Tapeta: standard
Wind: Light against Weather: Fine

2211 SEE MADNESS HERE ON 30TH AUGUST H'CAP — 5f 21y (Tp)
2:00 (2:00) (Class 6) (0-60,60) 3-Y-0
£3,105 (£924; £461; £300; £300; £300) **Stalls Low**

Form — RPR

-003 **1** **Miss Enigma (IRE)**[26] 1514 3-8-13 **55**........................(b) FinleyMarsh(3) 1 60
(Richard Hughes) *edgd rt s: mde all: rdn over 1f out: styd on (trainers' rep said, reg app imp in form, filly benefitted from the drop down in trip)* **11/2**[3]

0440 **2** *1* **Wye Bother (IRE)**[66] 848 3-8-7 **46** oh1........................(t) FrannyNorton 6 47
(Milton Bradley) *chsd ldrs: edgd lft 1/2-way: rdn to chse wnr ins fnl f: r.o (jockey said filly hung left-handed down the back straight)* **33/1**

0023 **3** *1/2* **Sing Bertie (IRE)**[32] 1380 3-8-7 **46**........................ PaddyMathers 5 47+
(Derek Shaw) *hld up: nt clr run over 3f out and 1/2-way: hdwy over 1f out: r.o to go 3rd wl ins fnl f: nt rch ldrs* **4/1**[2]

6002 **4** *2* **Sharrabang**[12] 1863 3-9-2 **60**........................ DylanHogan(5) 3 55
(Stella Barclay) *s.i.s and hmpd s: in rr: nt clr run and swtchd rt 1/2-way: hdwy over 1f out: styd on* **7/2**[1]

0500 **5** *1* **Superseded (IRE)**[28] 1488 3-9-6 **59**........................(b[1]) JosephineGordon 8 48
(John Butler) *s.i.s: sn pushed along and rcvrd to chse wnr 4f out: rdn and ev ch over 1f out: hung rt and no ex ins fnl f* **9/1**

-030 **6** *1/2* **Oxygenic**[48] 1167 3-8-12 **51**........................ SeanLevey 7 39
(David O'Meara) *prom: lost pl 4f out: nt clr run and swtchd rt over 1f out: r.o towards fin* **7/1**

3660 **7** *hd* **Yfenni (IRE)**[37] 1296 3-8-0 **46** oh1........................ AmeliaGlass(7) 11 32
(Milton Bradley) *hdwy over 3f out: pushed along 1/2-way: rdn over 1f out: styng on same pce whn hung rt fnl f* **50/1**

-054 **8** *hd* **Brother Bentley**[21] 1650 3-8-13 **52**........................(p) RaulDaSilva 10 38
(Ronald Harris) *hmpd s: in rr: rdn over 1f out: nvr on terms* **7/1**

5-60 **9** *7* **North Korea (IRE)**[68] 813 3-9-4 **57**.............................. LiamJones 9 17
(Brian Baugh) *wnt rt s: towards rr whn hmpd over 4f out: n.d after* **25/1**

1416 **10** *3 ¾* **Sister Of The Sign (IRE)**[38] 1275 3-9-7 **60**.................. BarryMcHugh 2 7+
(James Given) *edgd rt s: sn chsng ldrs: nt clr run 1/2-way: wknd over 1f out* **13/2**

3-00 **11** *3* **Spring Holly (IRE)**[63] 906 3-8-0 **46** oh1......................(t[1]) AledBeech(7) 4
(Milton Bradley) *prom: hmpd and lost pl over 3f out: hmpd again 1/2-way: sn wknd* **100/1**

1m 2.47s (0.57) **Going Correction** +0.025s/f (Slow) **11** Ran SP% **115.7**
Speed ratings (Par 96): **96,94,93,90,88 88,87,87,76,70 65**
CSF £175.13 CT £818.63 TOTE £5.50: £2.50, £7.50, £1.70; EX 105.00 Trifecta £922.80.
Owner Sir Martyn Arbib & Everett Partnership **Bred** Flaxman Stables Ireland Ltd **Trained** Upper Lambourn, Berks
■ Stewards' Enquiry : Josephine Gordon caution; careless riding

FOCUS
This weak 3yo sprint handicap looked wide open. The winner is rated back to his previous best.

2212 BLACK COUNTRY FILLIES' H'CAP 6f 20y (Tp)
2:30 (2:30) (Class 5) (0-70,70) 3-Y-O
£3,752 (£1,116; £557; £300; £300; £300) **Stalls** Low

Form RPR

406 **1** **Di Matteo**[13] 1838 3-9-0 **63**...................................... DanielMuscutt 4 70
(Marco Botti) *s.i.s: sn prom: shkn up to ld 1f out: rdn and edgd lft wl ins fnl f: styd on* **14/1**

2211 **2** *¾* **Second Collection**[35] 1337 3-9-7 **70**..........................(h) TomMarquand 6 75
(Tony Carroll) *s.i.s: pushed along in rr early: hdwy over 1f out: rdn to chse wnr ins fnl f: styd on* **6/4**[1]

040- **3** *2 ¼* **Abanica**[166] 9049 3-9-5 **68**.......................................(p[1]) JimCrowley 7 66
(Amanda Perrett) *prom: chsd ldr over 4f out: led over 1f out: sn rdn: hung lft and hdd: no ex ins fnl f* **7/1**

03-0 **4** *1 ½* **Jungle Juice (IRE)**[21] 1656 3-9-3 **66**............................. FrannyNorton 8 59
(Mick Channon) *broke wl: sn stdd and lost pl: shkn up over 2f out: hdwy and nt clr run over 1f out: rdn and hung lft ins fnl f: nt run on* **6/1**[2]

2-30 **5** *1 ¼* **Tie A Yellowribbon**[11] 1894 3-9-5 **68**...................(p[1]) JosephineGordon 2 60
(James Bethell) *prom: pushed along and lost pl over 4f out: nt clr run and swtchd rt over 1f out: nt trble ldrs (jockey said filly was denied a clear run at the top of the home straight)* **13/2**[3]

33-4 **6** *2* **Rainbow Girl (IRE)**[35] 1336 3-9-7 **70**............................ SeanLevey 3 53
(Richard Hannon) *led early: chsd ldrs: rdn over 1f out: wknd ins fnl f* **15/2**

3-45 **7** *1 ¾* **Diva D (IRE)**[28] 1476 3-9-5 **68**...............................(b[1]) StevieDonohoe 5 45
(Mark Johnston) *sn led: rdn and hdd over 1f out: wknd ins fnl f* **9/1**

00-6 **8** *1 ¾* **Lexington Palm (IRE)**[24] 1567 3-8-9 **63**..................... BenSanderson(5) 1 34
(Keith Dalgleish) *s.i.s: sn pushed along in rr: nvr on terms* **50/1**

1m 14.21s (-0.29) **Going Correction** +0.025s/f (Slow) **8** Ran SP% **110.5**
Speed ratings (Par 95): **102,101,98,96,94 91,89,87**
CSF £33.19 CT £156.39 TOTE £12.90: £2.70, £1.20, £2.20; EX 35.80 Trifecta £277.20.
Owner C J Murfitt & Partner **Bred** Pantile Stud **Trained** Newmarket, Suffolk

FOCUS
The first two dominated the finish of this modest 3yo fillies' handicap. The third looks the best guide.

2213 SKY SPORTS RACING VIRGIN 535 H'CAP 1m 4f 51y (Tp)
3:00 (3:06) (Class 6) (0-60,62) 3-Y-O
£3,105 (£924; £461; £300; £300; £300) **Stalls** Low

Form RPR

000- **1** **Gold Arch**[156] 9255 3-9-3 **56**.. StevieDonohoe 9 66+
(David Lanigan) *s.i.s: hdwy to chse ldrs over 10f out: wnt 2nd over 2f out: led wl over 1f out: sn rdn: edgd lft ins fnl f: r.o (trainer said, reg app imp in form, gelding benfitted from the step up in trip and had been gelding since it's last run)* **5/2**[1]

-303 **2** *2* **Willkommen**[16] 1770 3-8-9 **55**..................................(b) StefanoCherchi(7) 7 60
(Marco Botti) *sn prom: rdn over 3f out: chsd wnr and carried lft ins fnl f: styd on same pce* **5/1**[3]

5050 **3** *hd* **Hen (IRE)**[45] 1217 3-9-5 **58**.. AdamMcNamara 5 63
(Jamie Osborne) *got loose on the way to post: hld up: hdwy over 1f out: styd on* **25/1**

0-13 **4** *¾* **Glutnforpunishment**[25] 1555 3-9-7 **60**.............................. EoinWalsh 6 63
(Nick Littmoden) *plld hrd and prom: stdd and lost pl over 10f out: hdwy on outer over 3f out: rdn over 1f out: sn hung lft: styd on same pce ins fnl f* **11/2**

3250 **5** *1* **Chakrii (IRE)**[35] 1332 3-8-9 **53**..................................(p) DylanHogan(5) 4 55
(Henry Spiller) *s.i.s: hld up: hdwy over 1f out: styd on same pce wl ins fnl f* **6/1**

0044 **6** *5* **Gabrial The Giant (IRE)**[16] 1770 3-8-13 **57**................ ThomasGreatrex(5) 8 51
(Patrick Morris) *chsd ldr tl led over 3f out: hdd wl over 1f out: sn rdn: wkng whn hmpd ins fnl f (vet said gelding lost both it's left and right fore shoes)* **4/1**[2]

0-00 **7** *3 ¾* **Half Full**[83] 612 3-8-4 **50**.. JoshQuinn(7) 1 38
(Michael Easterby) *chsd ldrs: rdn over 3f out: wknd over 1f out* **25/1**

00-0 **8** *7* **Ventura Island (FR)**[35] 1332 3-8-11 **50**.......................(p[1]) SeanLevey 2 27
(Richard Hannon) *led: rdn and hdd over 3f out: wknd over 1f out* **8/1**

0006 **9** *5* **Midnite Rendezvous**[17] 1726 3-8-7 **46** oh1..................(v) PaddyMathers 3 15
(Derek Shaw) *hld up in tch: racd keenly: lost pl 4f out: rdn over 2f out: sn wknd* **100/1**

2m 43.54s (2.74) **Going Correction** +0.025s/f (Slow) **9** Ran SP% **114.7**
Speed ratings (Par 96): **91,89,89,89,88 85,82,77,74**
CSF £14.84 CT £248.09 TOTE £3.70: £1.60, £1.70, £5.70; EX 18.90 Trifecta £253.10.
Owner Ventura Racing (ga), M Delaney & I Black **Bred** Trinity Park Stud **Trained** Newmarket, Suffolk

FOCUS
This moderate 3yo handicap was run at something of an uneven pace and the field finished quite compressed. The winner should progress.

2214 GRAND THEATRE WOLVERHAMPTON FILLIES' H'CAP 1m 4f 51y (Tp)
3:30 (3:31) (Class 5) (0-75,74) 4-Y-O+
£3,752 (£1,116; £557; £300; £300; £300) **Stalls** Low

Form RPR

314- **1** **Point In Time (IRE)**[143] 9447 4-9-7 **74**........................... StevieDonohoe 1 79
(Mark Usher) *prom: lost pl over 8f out: nt clr run over 2f out: hdwy over 1f out: rdn and r.o to ld nr fin* **8/1**

34-4 **2** *nse* **Sula Island**[24] 1569 5-9-0 **70**....................................... FinleyMarsh(3) 4 75
(Alan King) *prom: shkn up over 3f out: rdn to ld and hung lft fr 1f out: hdd nr fin* **11/2**

41-3 **3** *¾* **Birch Grove (IRE)**[24] 1569 4-9-0 **72**............................ DylanHogan(5) 3 75
(David Simcock) *hld up: hdwy and nt clr run over 2f out: swtchd rt over 1f out: nt clr run ins fnl f: r.o* **10/3**[3]

0521 **4** *½* **Vampish**[24] 1569 4-9-4 **71**.. JimCrowley 6 73
(Philip McBride) *led: hdd over 9f out: remained handy: swtchd rt wl over 2f out: led 2f out: rdn and hdd 1f out: styng on same pce whn hmpd ins fnl f* **11/4**[1]

0-13 **5** *5* **Ebqaa (IRE)**[7] 1988 5-8-13 **66**.. LiamJones 2 60
(James Unett) *s.i.s: sn pushed along in rr: hdwy to ld at stdy pce over 9f out: shkn up and qcknd over 3f out: rdn and hdd 2f out: wknd ins fnl f* **3/1**[2]

14-5 **6** *9* **Gemini**[20] 1666 4-9-2 **69**... SeanLevey 5 49
(John Quinn) *chsd ldr: rdn over 3f out: lost 2nd over 2f out: wknd over 1f out* **11/1**

2m 40.11s (-0.69) **Going Correction** +0.025s/f (Slow) **6** Ran SP% **109.6**
Speed ratings (Par 100): **103,102,102,102,98 92**
CSF £47.18 TOTE £4.70: £3.60, £3.50; EX 33.40 Trifecta £191.60.
Owner Gaf Racing **Bred** John O'Connor **Trained** Upper Lambourn, Berks
■ Stewards' Enquiry : Finley Marsh caution; careless riding

FOCUS
This run-of-the-mill fillies' handicap proved tactical and it saw a tight finish. The winner is rated to form.

2215 STAY AT THE WOLVERHAMPTON HOLIDAY INN H'CAP 7f 36y (Tp)
4:05 (4:07) (Class 6) (0-60,60) 4-Y-O+
£3,105 (£924; £461; £300; £300; £300) **Stalls** High

Form RPR

0600 **1** **Little Miss Daisy**[13] 1837 5-9-0 **53**................................. SeanLevey 11 59+
(William Muir) *hld up in tch: rdn over 1f out: led and edgd lft wl over 1f out: styd on wl* **28/1**

10-6 **2** *1 ½* **Rockesbury**[7] 1986 4-9-0 **60**............................(p) LauraCoughlan(7) 7 62
(David Loughnane) *chsd ldrs: rdn and ev ch ins fnl f: styd on same pce* **7/2**[2]

664- **3** *hd* **Bigshotte**[152] 9293 4-9-7 **60**.......................................(t w) EoinWalsh 1 62
(George Scott) *led at stdy pce: shkn up and qcknd over 2f out: rdn over 1f out: hdd and unable qck wl ins fnl f* **14/1**

0-00 **4** *3 ½* **Showdance Kid**[47] 1177 5-9-0 **60**......................... ScottMcCullagh(7) 9 53
(Kevin Frost) *chsd ldrs: rdn over 1f out: no ex ins fnl f* **20/1**

4603 **5** *½* **Spiritual Star (IRE)**[16] 1769 10-8-13 **59**..........(t) Pierre-LouisJamin(7) 12 51+
(Paul George) *s.i.s: hld up: rdn over 1f out: r.o ins fnl f: nvr nrr* **8/1**

0-05 **6** *hd* **Bouclier (IRE)**[35] 1338 9-9-7 **60**...................................... LiamJones 8 52+
(James Unett) *hld up: rdn over 2f out: r.o ins fnl f: nvr nrr* **3/1**[1]

0566 **7** *2 ½* **Indian Affair**[13] 1837 9-8-13 **52**................................(vt) RaulDaSilva 10 37+
(Milton Bradley) *hld up: rdn over 2f out: nvr on terms* **22/1**

00-4 **8** *1 ½* **Muraadef**[13] 1837 4-8-8 **52**.. ThomasGreatrex(5) 6 34+
(Ruth Carr) *s.i.s: hld up: shkn up over 1f out: nvr nr to chal* **5/1**[3]

5 **9** *2 ½* **Warning Light**[25] 1550 4-9-4 **57**................................ JosephineGordon 2 33+
(Shaun Keightley) *s.i.s: in rr: pushed along over 4f out: nvr on terms* **14/1**

6004 **10** *4 ½* **Astraea**[27] 1505 4-8-10 **56**...(b) JoshQuinn(7) 3 21
(Michael Easterby) *prom: edgd rt sn after s: rdn over 2f out: wknd wl over 1f out (vet said filly lost it's right fore shoe)* **20/1**

2530 **11** *1 ¼* **Shamlan (IRE)**[7] 1986 7-8-12 **56**............................... DylanHogan(5) 5 18+
(Kevin Frost) *hld up: pushed along over 4f out: n.d* **10/1**

00-0 **12** *5* **Another Situation (USA)**[8] 1967 4-8-8 **47**..............(p[1]) PaddyMathers 4
(John Mackie) *hmpd sn after s: hld up: hdwy 1/2-way: rdn and wknd over 2f out: b.b.v (vet said filly bled from the nose)* **66/1**

1m 29.17s (0.37) **Going Correction** +0.025s/f (Slow) **12** Ran SP% **116.2**
Speed ratings (Par 101): **98,96,96,92,91 91,88,86,83,78 77,71**
CSF £115.73 CT £1499.64 TOTE £28.10: £4.60, £2.50, £3.00; EX 157.30 Trifecta £2136.30.
Owner Mrs J M Muir **Bred** Hungerford Park Stud **Trained** Lambourn, Berks

FOCUS
Another wide-open looking handicap. The first four stole a march turning for home. The winner is rated to the best of this year's form.

2216 COME TO LADIES DAY - 31ST AUGUST NOVICE MEDIAN AUCTION STKS 1m 142y (Tp)
4:35 (4:37) (Class 6) 3-Y-O
£3,105 (£924; £461; £230) **Stalls** Low

Form RPR

3- **1** **Sea Sculpture**[228] 7215 3-9-5 0.................................... JosephineGordon 6 73+
(Andrew Balding) *s.i.s: sn pushed along in rr: hdwy over 1f out: r.o to ld wl ins fnl f: comf* **6/1**[2]

5- **2** *1* **Risaala (IRE)**[143] 9443 3-9-0 0... LiamJones 3 66
(Charles Hills) *chsd ldrs: rdn over 2f out: led ins fnl f: edgd lft and sn hdd: styd on same pce* **25/1**

2- **3** *1 ½* **Mokammal**[195] 8305 3-9-5 0.. JimCrowley 4 68
(Sir Michael Stoute) *led: rdn and hdd over 1f out: styd on same pce ins fnl f* **2/5**[1]

0-60 **4** *nk* **Frenchmans Creek (IRE)**[17] 1725 3-9-5 50....................... RaulDaSilva 7 67?
(Seamus Durack) *w ldr: rdn over 2f out: led over 1f out: hdd ins fnl f: styd on same pce* **100/1**

5 **5** *½* **Sweet Celebration (IRE)**[47] 1171 3-9-0 0..................... DanielMuscutt 5 62
(Marco Botti) *chsd ldrs: lost pl 7f out: hdwy and nt clr run over 1f out: styng on whn nt clr run wl ins fnl f* **16/1**

4- **6** *1* **Poetic Era**[187] 8547 3-8-9 0.. DylanHogan(5) 2 59
(David Simcock) *stdd s: hld up: effrt and nt clr run over 1f out: nvr trbld ldrs* **12/1**[3]

7 *hd* **Eddie Cochran (IRE)** 3-9-5 0... SeanLevey 1 63
(Richard Hannon) *chsd ldrs: pushed along 4f out: rdn over 2f out: no ex fnl f* **14/1**

1m 49.03s (-1.07) **Going Correction** +0.025s/f (Slow) **7** Ran SP% **110.8**
Speed ratings (Par 96): **105,104,102,102,102 101,101**
CSF £116.96 TOTE £6.90: £2.20, £5.30; EX 61.00 Trifecta £126.30.
Owner Kingsclere Racing Club **Bred** Kingsclere Stud **Trained** Kingsclere, Hants

FOCUS
There was a turn-up in this modest 3yo novice event. The form looks the key to the form and the winner looks sure to do better.

2217 HAPPY RETIREMENT LESLEY GROSS AMATEUR RIDERS' H'CAP 2m 120y (Tp)
5:10 (5:11) (Class 6) (0-65,65) 4-Y-O+
£2,994 (£928; £464; £300; £300; £300) **Stalls** Low

Form RPR

/1-1 **1** **Grey Mist**[38] 99 5-10-11 **62**.................................(h) MrPatrickMillman 2 70
(Karen McLintock) *chsd ldrs: rdn to go 2nd on outer over 2f out: hung rt over 1f out: flashed tail and led ins fnl f: drvn out* **11/10**[1]

1/00 **2** 2 ½ **Coorg (IRE)**[23] 1588 7-10-11 **65**........................ MissAliceHaynes(3) 1 70
(John Butler) *w ldr tl led 14f out: rdn and edgd rt over 1f out: hdd ins fnl f: styd on same pce* **40/1**

-030 **3** 2 **Gravity Wave (IRE)**[29] 1463 5-10-6 **64**..........(p) MissImogenMathias(7) 4 67
(John Flint) *broke wl: sn lost pl: hld up: hdwy over 1f out: styd on to go 3rd wl ins fnl f: nt rch ldrs* **7/1**[3]

00-6 **4** nk **Up Ten Down Two (IRE)**[31] 1398 10-10-12 **63**.(t) MissJoannaMason 11 65
(Michael Easterby) *prom: rdn over 2f out: styd on same pce ins fnl f* **9/2**[2]

4551 **5** 1 ¼ **Bird For Life**[33] 1361 5-10-2 **60**........................(p) MrCiaranJones(7) 3 61
(Mark Usher) *s.i.s: hld up: hdwy 1/2-way: lost pl 6f out: styd on fr over 1f out* **7/1**[3]

-400 **6** 2 ½ **Angel Gabrial (IRE)**[55] 1022 10-10-8 **59**..............(p[1]) MrSimonWalker 12 57
(Patrick Morris) *chsd ldrs: lost pl over 12f out: hdwy over 5f out: rdn over 1f out: wknd ins fnl f* **40/1**

451- **7** ¾ **St Andrews (IRE)**[194] 8319 6-10-9 **60**..................(v) MissEmmaTodd 10 57
(Gillian Boanas) *s.i.s: hld up: hdwy u.p over 1f out: nt trble ldrs* **20/1**

40-2 **8** 1 ¼ **Party Royal**[91] 457 9-10-9 **60**................................(p) MrDavidDunsdon 9 55
(Nick Gifford) *hld up: shkn up over 3f out: nvr on terms* **33/1**

05 **9** 1 **Lafilia (GER)**[21] 1647 4-10-9 **62**........................ MissBrodieHampson 13 58
(Archie Watson) *led: hdd 14f out: chsd ldr tl rdn over 2f out: wknd fnl f* **20/1**

20-0 **10** 4 ½ **Fitzwilly**[27] 1497 9-10-9 **65**........................ MissNellMcCann(5) 5 54
(Mick Channon) *hld up: hdwy on outer 12f out: rdn and wknd over 2f out* **14/1**

240/ **11** 4 **Consortium (IRE)**[767] 1330 7-11-0 **65**....................(p) MrAlexEdwards 8 49
(Alastair Ralph) *chsd ldrs: lost pl 1/2-way: hdwy over 4f out: wknd over 1f out* **40/1**

6/56 **12** 39 **Uncle Bernie (IRE)**[13] 1840 9-10-6 **64**................(p) MrSeanHawkins(7) 7 1+
(Sarah Hollinshead) *s.s: hld up: sddle slipped 13f out and rdr unable to help: rn wd over 10f out: lost tch fnl 6f (jockey said saddle slipped shortly after the start)* **40/1**

3m 41.9s (2.60) **Going Correction** +0.025s/f (Slow)
WFA 4 from 5yo+ 2lb **12** Ran SP% **119.7**
Speed ratings (Par 101): **94,92,91,91,91 89,89,89,88,86 84,66**
CSF £71.56 CT £219.98 TOTE £1.90: £1.10, £13.00, £2.30; EX 29.70 Trifecta £278.00.
Owner Brian Chicken & Equiname Ltd **Bred** David Jamison Bloodstock And G Roddick **Trained** Ingoe, Northumberland

FOCUS
A moderate staying handicap, confined to amateur riders. The winner's on a roll and his form has been working out.
T/Plt: £981.50 to a £1 stake. Pool: £52,329.71 - 38.92 winning units T/Qpdt: £310.10 to a £1 stake. Pool: £4,736.18 - 11.30 winning units **Colin Roberts**

2218 - 2220a (Foreign Racing) - See Raceform Interactive

[1772]NAAS (L-H)
Monday, April 29

OFFICIAL GOING: Good to yielding (yielding in places)

2221a WOODLANDS STKS (LISTED RACE) 5f
6:20 (6:22) 3-Y-O+

£23,918 (£7,702; £3,648; £1,621; £810; £405)

RPR

1 **Urban Beat (IRE)**[30] 1434 4-9-9 100........................ ShaneFoley 1 102+
(J P Murtagh, Ire) *broke wl to ld briefly tl sn hdd and settled bhd ldrs: 4th 2f out: drvn into 2nd 1f out and sn on terms: rdn to ld narrowly wl ins fnl f: kpt on wl* **9/4**[1]

2 nk **Soffia**[30] 1434 4-9-4 93........................ DeclanMcDonogh 4 96
(Edward Lynam, Ire) *cl up: cl 2nd at 1/2-way: led gng wl under 2f out: drvn and extended advantage briefly over 1f out tl jnd and hdd u.p ins fnl f: kpt on wl: a hld by wnr* **4/1**[3]

3 ½ **Primo Uomo (IRE)**[30] 1434 7-9-9 106........................(t) NGMcCullagh 3 99+
(Gerard O'Leary, Ire) *w.w in 7th early: tk clsr order and disp 5th 2f out: n.m.r briefly between horses ins fnl f where wnt 3rd: r.o wl clsngs stages: nrst fin* **7/2**[2]

4 1 ¼ **Ardhoomey (IRE)**[282] 5234 7-9-12 107........................(t) ColinKeane 7 98+
(G M Lyons, Ire) *trckd ldrs: disp 5th 2f out: sn pushed along and no imp on ldrs u.p ins fnl f: kpt on same pce in 4th nr fin* **6/1**

5 1 ¾ **Tammy Wynette (IRE)**[26] 1534 4-9-4 70........................(v) WJLee 2 83
(W McCreery, Ire) *w.w towards rr: pushed along and tk clsr order over 1f out: no imp on ldrs u.p disputing 6th wl ins fnl f: kpt on to snatch 5th on line* **14/1**

6 hd **Intense Romance (IRE)**[205] 7974 5-9-7 104........................ ConnorBeasley 8 86
(Michael Dods) *trckd ldrs tl led after 1f: narrow advantage at 1/2-way: sn pushed along and hdd u.p under 2f out: no ex in 3rd ins fnl f: wknd clsng stages: denied 5th on line* **7/1**

7 hd **Nitro Boost (IRE)**[15] 1788 3-8-8 86........................ LeighRoche 10 78
(W McCreery, Ire) *sn trckd ldr in 2nd: drvn in 3rd 2f out and no ex u.p in 4th ent fnl f: wknd* **28/1**

8 1 ½ **Medicine Jack**[30] 1434 5-9-12 100........................(b) GaryCarroll 9 84
(G M Lyons, Ire) *w.w in rr: rdn 2f out and no imp u.p in 8th ent fnl f: kpt on one pce: nvr a factor* **16/1**

9 1 ½ **Blyton**[199] 8161 3-8-13 92........................ RoryCleary 6 72
(Luke Comer, Ire) *trckd ldrs early: pushed along bef 1/2-way and no ex over 2f out: wknd* **33/1**

1m 0.46s (-1.54)
WFA 3 from 4yo+ 10lb **9** Ran SP% **118.7**
CSF £11.74 TOTE £2.60: £1.20, £1.30, £1.50; DF 11.50 Trifecta £39.30.
Owner Fitzwilliam Racing **Bred** Shane Quigley **Trained** Coolaghknock Glebe,Co Kildare

FOCUS
There will be better Listed sprints run this season, but the winner had to improve to show that he belonged in this company and he certainly seems to. The first two and the fifth had the favoured rail, and the second is the best guide.

2222 - 2225a (Foreign Racing) - See Raceform Interactive

BORDEAUX LE BOUSCAT (R-H)
Monday, April 29

OFFICIAL GOING: Turf: very soft

2226a HANDICAP DE BORDEAUX (4YO+) (TURF) 1m
12:50 4-Y-O+

£23,423 (£8,900; £6,558; £3,747; £1,873; £1,405)

RPR

1 **Ascot Angel (FR)**[135] 9567 5-9-6 0........................ MickaelBarzalona 13 88
(X Thomas-Demeaulte, France) **8/1**[3]

2 1 ½ **Qatar Bolt**[30] 1449 4-9-0 0........................ OlivierPeslier 6 79
(H-A Pantall, France) **43/10**[1]

3 hd **Shielding (USA)**[25] 5-9-5 0........................ Jean-BernardEyquem 3 84
(S Labate, France) **19/1**

4 shd **Larno (FR)**[25] 5-9-1 0........................ SylvainRuis 15 79
(M Boutin, France) **33/1**

5 nk **Rebel Lightning (IRE)**[25] 6-9-1 0........................(b) StephanePasquier 16 79
(P Monfort, France) **23/5**[2]

6 1 **Good Smash (FR)**[422] 7-9-0 0........................ JulienAuge 10 75
(F Pardon, France) **15/1**

7 nk **Rizzichop (FR)**[188] 7-9-4 0........................ IoritzMendizabal 1 79
(O Trigodet, France) **14/1**

8 shd **Pastichop (FR)**[137] 5-9-2 0........................ AntoineHamelin 12 76
(C Gourdain, France) **14/1**

9 ½ **El Indio (FR)**[30] 1449 4-8-13 0........................ RonanThomas 4 72
(H-A Pantall, France) **36/1**

10 3 ½ **Land Of Mind**[30] 1449 4-9-3 0........................ TonyPiccone 11 68
(M Delcher Sanchez, France) **15/1**

11 nk **Beyond My Dreams (IRE)**[17] 4-9-3 0........................(b) SoufianeSaadi 9 68
(H-A Pantall, France) **19/1**

12 4 **Park Tower (FR)**[30] 1449 4-9-0 0........................ VincentCheminaud 7 55
(H-A Pantall, France) **40/1**

13 1 **Cazaline (FR)**[157] 4-8-13 0........................ AnthonyCrastus 14 52
(M Delaplace, France) **18/1**

14 ½ **Barodar (FR)**[30] 1449 4-9-0 0........................ MatthiasLauron 2 52
(T Lemer, France) **17/1**

15 5 **Falco Delavilliere (FR)**[32] 4-9-3 0........................ MaximeGuyon 5 43
(R Avial Lopez, Spain) **14/1**

16 5 **Fairy Tale (IRE)**[30] 1449 4-9-5 0........................ Pierre-CharlesBoudot 8 34
(Gay Kelleway) *prom: struggling to go pce and lost position over 3f out: wknd qckly and sn btn over 2f out: eased over 1f out* **43/5**

1m 40.7s **16** Ran SP% **119.7**
PARI-MUTUEL (all including 1 euro stake): WIN 9.00; PLACE 3.30, 2.20, 5.00; DF 19.90.
Owner Ecurie Antonio Caro **Bred** Mme G Forien **Trained** France

[1930]BRIGHTON (L-H)
Tuesday, April 30

OFFICIAL GOING: Good to firm (watered; 9.2)
Wind: virtually nil Weather: cloudy with sunny spells

2227 CELEBRATING 80 YEARS OF COLIN MURPHY H'CAP 5f 60y
1:50 (1:50) (Class 4) (0-85,84) 4-Y-O+

£5,530 (£1,645; £822; £411; £300; £300) **Stalls** Centre

Form RPR

0564 **1** **Shamshon (IRE)**[6] 2030 8-9-1 **78**........................ JasonWatson 4 84
(Stuart Williams) *dwlt sltly and racd in rr: smooth hdwy on outer to chse ldr 2f out: effrt on outer to ld wl ins fnl f: rdn out* **4/1**[2]

0-46 **2** nk **Harry Hurricane**[6] 2030 7-9-5 **82**........................(p) JoeFanning 1 87
(George Baker) *racd keenly in midfield: stl gng wl on inner 2f out: effrt against far rail once gap appeared over 2f out: drvn and styd on wl ins fnl f: nt rch wnr* **7/2**[1]

-263 **3** ½ **Little Boy Blue**[11] 1915 4-9-2 **84**........................(h) RyanWhile(5) 5 87
(Bill Turner) *led or disp ld tl rdn along and strly pressed by wnr 1f out: kpt on but hdd by wnr wl ins fnl f* **7/2**[1]

234- **4** 2 ¼ **Jack Taylor (IRE)**[133] 9596 4-9-0 **77**........................(b) ShaneKelly 2 75
(Richard Hughes) *led or disp ld tl pushed along and unable qck 1f out: rdn and no ex fnl f* **11/2**[3]

6000 **5** 1 **Tan**[12] 1899 5-8-10 **73**........................ LiamJones 6 65
(Michael Appleby) *racd promly in 3rd: pushed along to chse ldr 2f out: sn rdn and unable qck over 1f out: wknd fnl f* **8/1**

-660 **6** 3 **Arzaak (IRE)**[26] 1547 5-8-13 **76**........................(b) BenCurtis 3 57
(Charlie Wallis) *hld up in tch: rdn along and outpcd over 1f out: wknd fnl f* **12/1**

20-3 **7** 2 ¼ **Crystal Deauville (FR)**[10] 1932 4-8-8 **74**........................(p) WilliamCox(3) 7 48
(Gay Kelleway) *sltly s.i.s and racd in rr: pushed along to get clsr over 2f out: rdn on outer and no imp 2f out: wknd fnl f (jockey said gelding was slowly away)* **7/1**

1m 0.83s (-2.17) **Going Correction** -0.35s/f (Firm) **7** Ran SP% **111.1**
Speed ratings (Par 105): **103,102,101,98,96 91,88**
CSF £17.27 TOTE £3.90: £2.20, £1.60; EX 18.50 Trifecta £9.90.
Owner T W Morley & Regents Racing **Bred** Stonethorn Stud Farms Ltd **Trained** Newmarket, Suffolk

FOCUS
The bend was moved out 3yds, adding that amount to all races. This fair sprint handicap was run at a strong pace and they stuck to the stands' side. Straightforward form.

2228 JIM LONG BIRTHDAY CELEBRATION/ EBF NOVICE AUCTION STKS 5f 60y
2:25 (2:25) (Class 5) 2-Y-O

£3,752 (£1,116; £557; £278) **Stalls** Centre

Form RPR

5 **1** **Brazen Safa**[15] 1821 2-8-10........................ HayleyTurner 5 71
(Michael Bell) *trckd ldr in 3rd: pushed along to chse ldr over 2f out: rdn and led wl ins fnl f: styd on wl* **9/4**[2]

2 nk **Rose Of Kildare (IRE)** 2-8-6........................ JoeFanning 3 69+
(Mark Johnston) *dwlt sltly and racd in rr: effrt to chse ldrs 2f out: clsng qckly whn short of room 1f out: kpt on wl but unable to get to wnr* **16/1**

3 **3** *nk* **Audio**[10] 1937 2-9-2 .... TomMarquand 4 75
(Richard Hannon) *trckd ldr: effrt to cl on ldr 2f out: rdn to ld over 1f out: ev ch whn hdd by wnr wl ins fnl f: no ex* **13/8**[1]

4 *hd* **Miss Matterhorn** 2-8-6 .... MartinDwyer 6 64
(Eve Johnson Houghton) *racd in midfield and a little green at times: swtchd rt off heels and effrt to chse wnr 2f out: rdn and kpt on wl fnl f* **9/1**

51 **5** *7* **Copacabana Dancer (IRE)**[12] 1879 2-9-5 .... JasonWatson 7 53
(Joseph Tuite) *broke wl and led: rdn along and hdd by rival over 1f out: wknd ins fnl f* **6/1**[3]

60 **6** *2 1/2* **Baileys Freedom**[17] 1759 2-8-11 .... ThomasGreatrex(5) 1 41
(Archie Watson) *racd in midfield: pushed along 1/2-way: rdn and no imp over 1f out: nvr on terms* **14/1**

7 *1 3/4* **Escape To Oz** 2-8-3 .... WilliamCox(3) 2 25
(Anthony Carson) *hld up: pushed along and green 2f out: hung lft u.p over 1f out: wknd fnl f* **40/1**

8 *3/4* **Village Rock (IRE)** 2-8-13 .... ShaneKelly 8 29
(Richard Hughes) *dwlt and racd in rr: rdn in last over 2f out: hung bdly rt u.p over 1f out: nvr a factor (jockey said colt hung right-handed)* **10/1**

1m 1.73s (-1.27) **Going Correction** -0.35s/f (Firm) 8 Ran SP% **117.2**
Speed ratings (Par 92): **96,95,95,94,83 79,76,75**
CSF £38.43 TOTE £2.50: £1.10, £2.70, £1.90; EX 32.60 Trifecta £110.50.
Owner Ontoawinner 9 And Partner **Bred** Biddestone Stud Ltd **Trained** Newmarket, Suffolk

FOCUS
Add 3yds. A 2yo novice event in which previous experience counted for plenty and it saw a tight finish. The ratings have a fluid look to them.

2229 PAULINE & DAVE SMART DIAMOND ANNIVERSARY H'CAP 1m 3f 198y
2:55 (2:55) (Class 5) (0-75,77) 3-Y-O **£3,752** (£1,116; £557; £300) **Stalls** Centre

Form RPR

6-22 **1** **Agent Basterfield (IRE)**[7] 2021 3-9-2 **70** .... DavidProbert 2 83
(Andrew Balding) *mde all: shkn up to readily draw clr 2f out: pushed out and in clr command fnl f: easily* **6/5**[1]

32-3 **2** *13* **Nabbeyl (IRE)**[20] 1697 3-9-9 **77** .... (p[1]) JackMitchell 3 69
(Roger Varian) *trckd wnr: pushed along to chse wnr over 2f out: rdn and sn wl bhd easy wnr: kpt on in battle for remote 2nd fnl f* **15/8**[2]

20-4 **3** *1* **Little India (FR)**[18] 1730 3-9-6 **74** .... BenCurtis 1 65
(K R Burke) *settled wl in 3rd: effrt to chse wnr 2f out and readily outpcd: kpt on one pce fnl f* **14/1**

322 **4** *15* **Autumn Pride (IRE)**[20] 1689 3-9-7 **75** .... JoeFanning 4 57
(Mark Johnston) *dwlt bdly and racd in last: effrt to cl on rivals 3f out: sn rdn and outpcd over 2f out: nvr on terms* **4/1**[3]

2m 29.06s (-6.94) **Going Correction** -0.35s/f (Firm) 4 Ran SP% **106.9**
Speed ratings (Par 98): **109,100,99,89**
CSF £3.64 TOTE £1.80; EX 3.10 Trifecta £10.30.
Owner Philip Fox & Partner **Bred** Premier Bloodstock **Trained** Kingsclere, Hants

FOCUS
Add 3yds. A modest little 3yo handicap that proved one-way traffic. It's not easy to gauge how much the winner improved.

2230 BRITISH EBF PREMIER FILLIES' H'CAP 1m 1f 207y
3:25 (3:26) (Class 3) (0-90,87) 4-Y-O+
£12,450 (£3,728; £1,864; £932; £466; £234) **Stalls** High

Form RPR

240- **1** **Ashazuri**[160] 9168 5-8-2 **68** .... (h) NicolaCurrie 6 73
(Jonathan Portman) *trckd ldr: effrt to chse ldr 2f out: rdn and ev ch 1f out: styd on wl to ld cl home* **13/2**

10-0 **2** *1/2* **Double Reflection**[19] 1719 4-9-2 **82** .... BenCurtis 1 86
(K R Burke) *led at stdy pce: effrt to qckn tempo over 2f out and drifted into centre of trck: sn rdn and briefly led 1f out: kpt on but hdd by wnr cl home* **5/1**[3]

50-0 **3** *nse* **Bubble And Squeak**[17] 1753 4-9-7 **87** .... PatDobbs 7 91
(Sylvester Kirk) *hld up in last pair: effrt to cl 2f out: rdn and c wdst of all 1f out: styd on wl fnl f: nt rch wnr* **7/1**

50-3 **4** *1/2* **Sweet Charity**[24] 1589 4-8-9 **75** .... JasonWatson 3 78
(Denis Coakley) *trckd ldr: rdn along and ev ch upsides ldr over 1f out: kpt on one pce fnl f* **2/1**[1]

321- **5** *3* **Geetanjali (IRE)**[223] 7427 4-8-10 **76** .... (p) HayleyTurner 5 73
(Michael Bell) *racd in midfield: pushed along over 2f out: rdn and hung lft against far rail over 1f out: one pce fnl f* **9/2**[2]

-556 **6** *14* **Winged Spur (IRE)**[32] 1395 4-8-13 **79** .... JoeFanning 4 48
(Mark Johnston) *dwlt bdly and racd in last: pushed along in last over 2f out: sn rdn and nvr on terms (jockey said filly anticipated the start and hit the gate which caused the filly to be slowly away)* **9/2**[2]

2m 0.31s (-4.69) **Going Correction** -0.35s/f (Firm) 6 Ran SP% **112.2**
Speed ratings (Par 104): **104,103,103,103,100 89**
CSF £37.68 TOTE £8.90: £3.80, £2.90; EX 37.10 Trifecta £448.50.
Owner RWH Partnership **Bred** G Wickens And J Homan **Trained** Upper Lambourn, Berks

FOCUS
Add 3yds. A modest fillies' handicap run at a steady pace. This time the main action was nearer the stands' side.

2231 THOROUGHLY GOOD H'CAP 7f 211y
3:55 (3:56) (Class 6) (0-60,61) 4-Y-O+
£3,105 (£924; £461; £300; £300; £300) **Stalls** Centre

Form RPR

4164 **1** **Waqt (IRE)**[8] 1986 5-9-7 **60** .... RossaRyan 12 67
(Alexandra Dunn) *racd in midfield: effrt to cl on ldrs over 2f out: rdn along to ld 2f out: drvn 1f out: kpt on wl* **8/1**

4502 **2** *1 1/4* **Sharp Operator**[26] 1546 6-9-4 **57** .... (h) BenCurtis 13 61
(Charlie Wallis) *hld up in rr of midfield: gd hdwy to chse wnr 2f out: rdn over 1f out: kpt on fnl f but unable to match wnr* **5/1**[2]

-105 **3** *1* **With Approval (IRE)**[10] 1936 7-9-2 **55** .... (p) LiamJones 8 57
(Laura Mongan) *trckd ldr early: pushed along to ld 3f out: rdn along and hdd by wnr 2f out: kpt on one pce fr 1f out* **25/1**

-06P **4** *1* **Confrerie (IRE)**[20] 1683 4-9-1 **54** .... FergusSweeney 6 54
(George Baker) *settled wl in midfield: effrt to chse wnr 2f out: rdn and no imp 1f out: one pce fnl f* **8/1**

0-02 **5** *1/2* **Khazix (IRE)**[10] 1936 4-8-13 **55** .... WilliamCox(3) 3 53+
(Daniele Camuffo) *racd in tch in 3rd: effrt to chse wnr 2f out: sn rdn and drifted lft u.p 1f out: no ex fnl f* **6/1**[3]

2511 **6** *1* **False Id**[3] 2112 6-9-1 **56** .... (b) LauraCoughlan(7) 10 57+
(David Loughnane) *t.k.h to post: v.s.a and r detached in last: rdn to cl on main field over 2f out: rn past btn rivals ins fnl f (jockey said gelding was slowly away)* **11/8**[1]

6-00 **7** *4 1/2* **Phobos**[34] 1362 4-8-10 **49** .... HayleyTurner 11 35
(Michael Blanshard) *racd in midfield: rdn along and unable qck 2f out: sn outpcd and no ex fnl f* **33/1**

0-04 **8** *2* **Solveig's Song**[61] 940 7-9-2 **55** .... (p) NicolaCurrie 4 36
(Steve Woodman) *dwlt and racd in last trio: rdn 2f out: nvr able to get on terms* **33/1**

4202 **9** *3 1/2* **Aqua Libre**[14] 1836 6-9-8 **61** .... (p) JoeFanning 5 34
(Jennie Candlish) *led: pushed along and hdd 3f out: wknd ins fnl f* **6/1**[3]

0000 **10** *10* **Amy Kane**[34] 1362 5-8-7 **46** oh1 .... (b) RoystonFfrench 2
(Jimmy Fox) *slowly away and racd in last trio: a bhd (jockey said mare was slowly away and jumped awkwardly)* **100/1**

0-00 **11** *14* **Following Breeze (IRE)**[33] 1383 4-8-0 **46** oh1 .... IsobelFrancis(7) 9
(Jim Boyle) *racd in tch in 4th: pushed along and ev ch on the outer over 2f out: sn lost pl qckly and eased ins fnl f* **100/1**

1m 34.11s (-2.79) **Going Correction** -0.35s/f (Firm) 11 Ran SP% **121.3**
Speed ratings (Par 101): **99,97,96,95,95 94,89,87,84,74 60**
CSF £47.80 CT £989.03 TOTE £7.70: £2.00, £1.70, £5.20; EX 40.20 Trifecta £686.30.
Owner Helium Racing Ltd **Bred** Ennistown Stud **Trained** West Buckland, Somerset

FOCUS
Add 3yds. This moderate handicap was run at a decent pace and the second sets the standard. Straightforward form.

2232 ROSENA COATES BIRTHDAY CELEBRATION H'CAP 6f 210y
4:25 (4:26) (Class 5) (0-75,75) 4-Y-O+ **£3,752** (£1,116; £557; £300; £300) **Stalls** Centre

Form RPR

140- **1** **He's Our Star (IRE)**[202] 8111 4-9-1 **69** .... TomMarquand 2 73
(Ali Stronge) *mde all: pushed along to maintain short ld 2f out: rdn and strly pressed by rivals either side 1f out: drvn and kpt on strly fnl f* **11/8**[1]

024- **2** *1* **Bbob Alula**[220] 7538 4-9-2 **75** .... (t) RyanWhile(5) 3 76
(Bill Turner) *trckd wnr in 3rd: clsd gng wl 2f out: swtchd lft and rdn to chse wnr 1f out: kpt on wl but no match for wnr fnl f* **7/2**[3]

0600 **3** *1/2* **The British Lion (IRE)**[12] 1880 4-8-11 **65** .... (t[1]) RossaRyan 1 65
(Alexandra Dunn) *trckd wnr: rdn upsides wnr and ev ch over 1f out: kpt on fnl f but nt match wnr* **5/2**[2]

530 **4** *1 1/2* **Sweet Nature (IRE)**[22] 1653 4-8-9 **63** .... LiamJones 4 59?
(Laura Mongan) *settled in 4th: rdn along and little imp 2f out: one pce fnl f* **20/1**

1-50 **5** *hd* **Wilson (IRE)**[20] 1684 4-8-12 **66** .... (p) RoystonFfrench 5 61
(Julia Feilden) *hld up and racd a little freely in last: effrt to cl 2f out: sn rdn and no imp 1f out: no ex fnl f* **11/2**

1m 24.56s (0.76) **Going Correction** -0.35s/f (Firm) 5 Ran SP% **113.0**
Speed ratings (Par 103): **81,79,79,77,77**
CSF £6.80 TOTE £2.00: £1.80, £1.60; EX 7.20 Trifecta £14.60.
Owner Mrs Jayne French & Mrs Jacqueline Pilling **Bred** Irish National Stud **Trained** Eastbury, Berks

FOCUS
Add 3yds. All of these lined up with something to prove. The runner-up is rated to form.

2233 CARE FOR VETERANS APPRENTICE H'CAP 1m 1f 207y
5:00 (5:02) (Class 6) (0-65,66) 4-Y-O+
£3,105 (£924; £461; £300; £300; £300) **Stalls** High

Form RPR

10/- **1** **Seaborn (IRE)**[505] 7253 5-8-10 **58** .... (w) WilliamCarver(7) 7 68
(Patrick Chamings) *settled wl in 3rd: pushed along a fair way off ldng pair over 2f out: clsd qckly u.p to ld over 1f out: styd on wl* **9/1**

04-2 **2** *1 1/4* **Light Of Air (FR)**[36] 1333 6-9-0 **62** .... (b) LouisGaroghan(7) 3 70
(Gary Moore) *hld up in rr of midfield: effrt to cl on ldrs over 2f out: rdn and hung lft to far rail over 1f out: kpt on wl fnl f* **5/1**[2]

0-06 **3** *7* **War Of Succession**[27] 1527 5-8-10 **58** .... JessicaCooley(7) 9 53
(Tony Newcombe) *racd in midfield: rdn 2f out: pushed along and no imp 2f out: sn rdn and unable qck over 1f out: one pce fnl f* **9/1**

4-05 **4** *2* **Roy Rocket (FR)**[10] 1934 9-9-6 **66** .... KatherineBegley(5) 5 57
(John Berry) *hld up in last: effrt to cl over 2f out: rdn and no immediate imp over 1f out: kpt on fnl f* **6/1**[3]

34-0 **5** *2 1/4* **Castle Talbot (IRE)**[26] 1546 7-8-12 **60** .... (b) GianlucaSanna(7) 6 47
(Tom Clover) *hld up in rr of midfield: rdn and no imp 2f out: one pce fnl f* **10/1**

1014 **6** *1/2* **Lunar Deity**[10] 1936 10-9-1 **63** .... MarcoGhiani(7) 2 49+
(Stuart Williams) *led: jnd by rival and qcknd tempo over 4f out: clr w rival 3f out: sn rdn and hdd by rival 2f out: wknd fnl f* **3/1**[1]

465 **7** *1 1/4* **Rubensian**[25] 1566 6-9-0 **62** .... GraceMcEntee(7) 1 45
(David Simcock) *chsd ldr early: effrt to press ldr over 4f out and sn clr w rival: rdn along and hdd by wnr over 1f out: sn btn and wknd fnl f* **7/1**

-003 **8** *1* **Duke Of North (IRE)**[10] 1936 7-9-0 **62** .... IsobelFrancis(7) 8 43
(Jim Boyle) *racd in midfield: effrt to cl on clr ldrs 3f out: sn rdn and no imp 2f out: plugged on (jockey said gelding ran flat)* **5/1**[2]

0320 **9** *1/2* **Attain**[8] 1983 10-8-9 **57** .... KateLeahy(7) 4 37
(Archie Watson) *racd in rr of midfield: rdn along and lost pl 3f out: sn in rr and struggling* **22/1**

2m 1.34s (-3.66) **Going Correction** -0.35s/f (Firm) 9 Ran SP% **118.6**
Speed ratings (Par 101): **100,99,93,91,90 89,88,87,87**
CSF £54.98 CT £425.08 TOTE £12.90: £3.70, £1.80, £2.80; EX 81.80 Trifecta £877.00.
Owner Ian Beach **Bred** Michael Fennessy **Trained** Baughurst, Hants

FOCUS
Add 3yds. A moderate handicap, confined to apprentice riders, that looked wide open. The first two finished clear with the runner-up the best guide.
T/Plt: £119.80 to a £1 stake. Pool: £55,496.28 - 337.94 winning units T/Qpdt: £46.90 to a £1 stake. Pool: £3,724.09 - 58.75 winning units **Mark Grantham**

2059 CHELMSFORD (A.W) (L-H)
Tuesday, April 30

OFFICIAL GOING: Polytrack: standard
Wind: virtually nil Weather: dry

2234 £20 FREE BETS AT TOTESPORT.COM CLASSIFIED STKS 1m 2f (P)
5:15 (5:19) (Class 6) 4-Y-O+
£3,105 (£924; £461; £300; £300; £300) **Stalls** Low

Form RPR

3010 **1** **Muraaqeb**[3] 2127 5-9-0 **49** .... (p) AdamMcNamara 13 52
(Milton Bradley) *hld up towards rr: effrt 3f out: hdwy u.p jst over 1f out: styd on to chse ldr wl ins fnl f: led last strides (trainer's rep could offer no explanation for the gelding's improved form, except that the gelding may have benefited from the recent run at Wolverhampton)* **6/1**[2]

-000 **2** *nk* **Ronni Layne**[27] 1520 5-9-0 43...(b) MartinDwyer 7 51
(Louise Allan) *t.k.h: hld up in midfield: effrt 2f out: hdwy u.p to ld 1f out: kpt on: hdd last strides* **20/1**

-564 **3** *1 1/2* **Merdon Castle (IRE)**[29] 1477 7-8-9 45.................... SeamusCronin(5) 4 49
(Frank Bishop) *hld up in midfield: clsd and travelling wl whn nt clr run over 1f out: sn swtchd rt and hdwy u.p: chsd ldr briefly 100yds out: 3rd and kpt on same pce towards fin* **12/1**

3545 **4** *1* **Blyton Lass**[26] 1546 4-9-0 50... LukeMorris 15 48+
(James Given) *dwlt and swtchd lft after s: hld up towards rr: clsd whn nt clr run over 1f out: swtchd lft and squeezed through jst ins fnl f: chsd ldrs and kpt on same pce fnl 100yds* **9/2[1]**

506- **5** *1* **Turnbury**[70] 6065 8-9-0 47...(p w) TrevorWhelan 2 45
(Nikki Evans) *bustled along early: in tch in midfield: effrt and hdwy on inner over 1f out: chsd ldrs 1f out: kpt on same pce u.p ins fnl f* **33/1**

6-05 **6** *nk* **Theydon Spirit**[46] 1214 4-9-0 47.................................. MarcMonaghan 8 44
(Peter Charalambous) *chsd ldr: upsides ldr and travelling strly over 2f out: rdn to ld over 1f out: hdd 1f out: no ex and wknd ins fnl f* **9/2[1]**

2434 **7** *1* **Foxrush Take Time (FR)**[20] 1679 4-9-0 45..................(e) LiamKeniry 6 42
(Richard Guest) *taken down early: t.k.h: chsd ldrs: effrt in 3rd ent fnl 2f: swtchd rt and drvn over 1f out: unable qck and one pce fnl f* **9/2[1]**

005- **8** *1 1/2* **Hidden Stash**[167] 9047 5-9-0 49.....................................(p) ShaneKelly 12 39
(William Stone) *sn chsng ldrs: unable qck u.p over 1f out: wknd ins fnl f* **20/1**

0050 **9** *nk* **Herringswell (FR)**[34] 1353 4-8-7 48.......................... LauraPearson(7) 1 40
(Henry Spiller) *hld up in last quartet: clsd and nt clr run over 1f out: kpt on same pce ins fnl f* **20/1**

3360 **10** *1/2* **Outlaw Torn (IRE)**[20] 1680 10-9-0 42..........................(e) PhilipPrince 3 38
(Richard Guest) *taken down early: led: rdn ent fnl 2f: hdd over 1f out: no ex and wknd ins fnl f* **10/1**

3-50 **11** *shd* **Sea Tea Dea**[90] 482 5-8-11 43...................................... FinleyMarsh(3) 5 38
(Adrian Wintle) *wl in tch in midfield: unable qck and lost pl over 1f out: wknd ins fnl f* **20/1**

0-40 **12** *2 1/4* **Foxy's Spirit**[10] 1935 4-8-9 44...................... ThoreHammerHansen(5) 9 33
(Clare Hobson) *bmpd leaving stalls: hld up in tch in midfield: effrt u.p but no imp whn sltly impeded over 1f out: wl btn fnl f* **8/1[3]**

-000 **13** *2 1/2* **Happy Ending (IRE)**[70] 789 4-8-9 47...................... RhiainIngram(5) 14 29
(Seamus Mullins) *swtchd lft after s: hld up in rr: effrt over 1f out: no hdwy and nvr involved* **33/1**

000- **14** *29* **Outrath (IRE)**[256] 6236 9-9-0 45..................................(vt w) EoinWalsh 10
(Suzi Best) *jostled and hmpd leaving stalls: a in rr: eased fnl f: t.o (jockey said gelding was never travelling)* **50/1**

66-0 **15** *3 1/4* **Pollyissimo**[26] 1546 4-8-9 48..................................(v) DarraghKeenan(5) 11
(Henry Spiller) *bmpd leaving stalls: hdwy on outer to chse ldrs over 8f out: lost pl and hung rt 3f out: bhd fnl 2f: eased: t.o* **33/1**

2m 7.43s (-1.17) **Going Correction** -0.125s/f (Stan) **15** Ran SP% **126.6**
Speed ratings (Par 101): **99,98,97,96,95 95,94,93,93,93 93,91,89,66,63**
CSF £127.94 TOTE £6.30: £2.20, £6.10, £4.60; EX 132.60 Trifecta £2785.40.
Owner E A Hayward **Bred** Peter Winkworth **Trained** Sedbury, Gloucs

FOCUS
As usual the surface was lightly decompacted and gallop master finished to two inches. The going was standard.\n\x\x It was tight at the top of the market between the first four. The first three home challenged late wide of the pack. Pretty lowly form.

2235 TOTEPOOL CASHBACK CLUB AT TOTESPORT.COM H'CAP 7f (P)

5:45 (5:49) (Class 6) (0-55,55) 4-Y-O+

£3,105 (£924; £461; £300; £300; £300) **Stalls** Low

Form RPR

00-1 **1** **Fantastic Flyer**[18] 1731 4-9-6 **54**.. MartinDwyer 10 63+
(Dean Ivory) *chsd ldrs: rdn to ld over 1f out: kpt on ins fnl f: eased towards fin* **9/2[2]**

1630 **2** *1/2* **Clement (IRE)**[2] 2145 9-9-2 **53**..............................(v) MeganNicholls(3) 4 58
(Marjorie Fife) *t.k.h: hld up towards rr: nt clrest of runs over 1f out: hdwy ent fnl f: styd on wl to go 2nd wl ins fnl f: clsng on eased wnr nr fin* **9/2[2]**

5056 **3** *1 3/4* **Caledonian Gold**[12] 1883 6-8-10 **47** oh1 ow1.............. FinleyMarsh(3) 2 47
(Lisa Williamson) *taken down early and led to post: chsd ldrs: effrt and pressing ldrs whn carried lft over 1f out: wnt 2nd briefly ins fnl f: 3rd and one pce fnl 75yds* **20/1**

601 **4** *1* **Tellovoi (IRE)**[5] 2066 11-9-1 **49** 4ex.......................................(p) PhilipPrince 12 47
(Richard Guest) *taken down early: chsd ldrs: effrt on outer over 1f out: edgd lft and kpt on same pce u.p ins fnl f* **4/1[1]**

25-4 **5** *3/4* **Locommotion**[97] 365 7-9-7 **55**.. LukeMorris 13 51
(Matthew Salaman) *dwlt: t.k.h: hld up in last quartet: effrt on inner and shifting rt over 1f out: kpt on same pce ins fnl f* **12/1**

1006 **6** *3/4* **Cool Echo**[29] 1478 5-9-2 **50**..(p) DavidProbert 11 44
(J R Jenkins) *hld up in tch in last quintet: effrt on outer over 1f out: styd on ins fnl f: nvr trbld ldrs* **14/1**

-005 **7** *1 1/4* **Just An Idea (IRE)**[20] 1682 5-9-2 **55**.......................(b) RhiainIngram(5) 8 46
(Roger Ingram) *t.k.h: w ldr tl led ent fnl 2f: hdd and hung lft u.p over 1f out: wknd ins fnl f* **25/1**

000- **8** *1/2* **Stand Firm (IRE)**[194] 8347 4-9-5 **53**....................................... ShaneKelly 9 42
(Robert Cowell) *in tch in midfield: reminder over 3f out: effrt on inner whn carried rt over 1f out: kpt on same pce u.p and no imp ins fnl f* **9/1[3]**

2000 **9** *nk* **Scenery**[14] 1836 4-9-0 **55**..(p) AmeliaGlass(7) 5 44
(Marjorie Fife) *hld up in tch: travelling strly 2f out: shkn up over 1f out: sn hung lft and fnd little: wl hld ins fnl f* **10/1**

0000 **10** *3 1/4* **Plucky Dip**[19] 1717 8-8-5 **46** oh1..............................(p) LauraPearson(7) 6 26
(John Ryan) *sn in rr: effrt over 1f out: nvr getting on terms and wl hld whn nt clr run and swtchd rt 1f out* **16/1**

6400 **11** *4 1/2* **King Of Rooks**[7] 2013 6-9-6 **54**..................................(v[1]) RobbieDowney 3 24
(Henry Spiller) *hld up in tch in midfield: effrt ent fnl 2f: struggling to qckn whn squeezed for room and hmpd over 1f out: no ch after* **10/1**

00-0 **12** *10* **Out Of The Ashes**[19] 1715 6-9-0 **53**.........................(b) SeamusCronin(5) 1
(Mohamed Moubarak) *led: rdn and hdd ent fnl 2f: lost pl over 1f out: bhd ins fnl f* **10/1**

003/ **13** *9* **Bullseye Bullet**[590] 7196 4-9-2 **50**..........................(p) JosephineGordon 7
(Mark Usher) *squeezed for room leaving stalls: a in rr: wl bhd fnl f: t.o* **40/1**

1m 26.01s (-1.19) **Going Correction** -0.125s/f (Stan) **13** Ran SP% **124.9**
Speed ratings (Par 101): **101,100,98,97,96 95,94,93,93,89 84,72,62**
CSF £25.76 CT £394.03 TOTE £4.90: £2.10, £2.10, £6.40; EX 22.20 Trifecta £298.60.
Owner Mrs K M Young **Bred** Gracelands Stud **Trained** Radlett, Herts
■ Stewards' Enquiry : Amelia Glass two-day ban; careless riding (May 3,14)

FOCUS
Just a moderate handicap but the form looks reliable with the top three in the market in the first four. The form is rated around the second.

2236 EXTRA PLACES AT TOTESPORT.COM NOVICE MEDIAN AUCTION STKS 7f (P)

6:20 (6:21) (Class 4) 3-5-Y-O **£5,530** (£1,645; £822; £411) **Stalls** Low

Form RPR

51- **1** **San Carlos**[131] 9636 3-9-8 0... ShaneKelly 6 86+
(Shaun Keightley) *chsd ldrs: clsd and effrt to chal over 1f out: rdn to ld ins fnl f: styd on strly* **9/2**

41- **2** *1 3/4* **Carnival Rose**[144] 9442 3-9-3 0...................................... GeorgeWood 7 76
(James Fanshawe) *t.k.h: chsd ldrs: wnt 2nd 5f out: pushed along to chal 2f out: ev ch u.p over 1f out tl no ex ins fnl f: kpt on same pce fnl 100yds* **3/1[2]**

60-2 **3** *nk* **Astrologer**[14] 1838 3-8-10 78....................................... RobbieDowney 8 68
(David O'Meara) *t.k.h: sn led: rdn and hrd pressed ent fnl 2f: drvn over 1f out: hdd and one pce ins fnl f* **4/1[3]**

3 **4** *1 3/4* **Bighearted**[20] 1676 3-8-7 0.....................................(h) CameronNoble(3) 1 64
(Michael Bell) *broke fast: sn hdd and chsd ldr for 2f: styd handy and t.k.h: effrt in 4th and swtchd rt over 1f out: no imp and hung lft ins fnl f* **6/4[1]**

66- **5** *3* **Leo Davinci (USA)**[171] 8993 3-9-1 0.................................... EoinWalsh 3 61+
(George Scott) *stdd s: hld up in last trio: pushed along and effrt over 1f out: no threat to ldrs but kpt on under hands and heels riding ins fnl f (jockey said regarding running and riding that his instructions were to make sure the gelding settled and to ride him as he found him. He added that the gelding settled adequately and he was happy with his position in the early stages and on entering the* **18/1**

5 **6** *1/2* **Dor's Diamond**[24] 1587 3-9-1 0......................................(h) MartinDwyer 5 59
(Dean Ivory) *t.k.h: hld up in tch in midfield: effrt over 1f out: sn hung lft and btn* **50/1**

7 *1* **Torochica** 3-8-10 0.. JosephineGordon 4 52
(John Best) *s.i.s: sn wnt rt and pushed along in rr: n.d* **33/1**

60 **8** *1 1/4* **Power Of You (IRE)**[20] 1677 3-8-8 0.................(t) Pierre-LouisJamin(7) 9 53
(William Knight) *t.k.h: hld up in last trio: effrt over 1f out: no imp and nvr involved* **50/1**

40 **9** *1 1/2* **Jeanette May**[25] 1562 3-8-10 0.. DavidProbert 2 44
(William Stone) *t.k.h: hld up in tch in midfield: u.p and outpcd over 1f out: wknd fnl f* **100/1**

1m 26.35s (-0.85) **Going Correction** -0.125s/f (Stan) **9** Ran SP% **116.3**
Speed ratings (Par 105): **99,97,96,94,91 90,89,88,86**
CSF £18.35 TOTE £5.80: £1.50, £1.40, £1.30; EX 22.40 Trifecta £72.90.
Owner Mrs C C Regalado-Gonzalez **Bred** Hall Of Fame Stud Ltd **Trained** Newmarket, Suffolk

FOCUS
The pace was decent as the first four in the betting pulled clear, with the previous winners dominating. The first two both improved.

2237 IRISH LOTTO AT TOTESPORT.COM H'CAP 7f (P)

6:55 (6:56) (Class 4) (0-80,82) 4-Y-O+

£5,692 (£1,694; £846; £423; £300; £300) **Stalls** Low

Form RPR

2-14 **1** **Javelin**[3] 2097 4-8-12 **70**... MartinDwyer 3 78
(William Muir) *bmpd sn after s: hld up in tch: effrt and hdwy to chse ldr over 1f out: str run to ld wl ins fnl f: gng away at fin* **9/2**

0666 **2** *1* **Pearl Spectre (USA)**[5] 2065 8-8-7 **65** oh2.....................(v) LukeMorris 6 70
(Phil McEntee) *led: rdn wl over 1f out: sn drvn: hdd and one pce wl ins fnl f* **20/1**

442- **3** *nk* **Dourado (IRE)**[198] 8236 5-9-10 **82**.................................. DavidProbert 1 86
(Patrick Chamings) *dropped in bhd after s: hld up in tch in rr: effrt and swtchd rt wl over 1f out: chsd ldrs: edgd lft and kpt on ins fnl f (jockey said horse hung left-handed in the straight)* **7/2[2]**

00-4 **4** *4* **Salt Whistle Bay (IRE)**[12] 1881 5-9-9 **81**......................... JackMitchell 2 74
(Rae Guest) *hld up in tch: effrt on inner over 1f out: no imp u.p 1f out: wknd ins fnl f* **4/1[3]**

4-12 **5** *1 1/4* **Field Gun (USA)**[28] 1496 4-9-5 **77**..............................(t) DanielMuscutt 5 67
(Stuart Williams) *edging lft after s: sn chsng ldr: rdn: lost 2nd and unable qck over 1f out: wknd ins fnl f* **9/4[1]**

45-2 **6** *12* **Young John (IRE)**[25] 1560 6-9-7 **79**.................................. RossaRyan 4 37
(Mike Murphy) *squeezed for room sn after s: swtchd rt and hdwy to chse ldrs on outer 5f out: rdn over 1f out: sn btn: bhd and eased ins fnl f* **5/1**

1m 25.5s (-1.70) **Going Correction** -0.125s/f (Stan) **6** Ran SP% **112.6**
Speed ratings (Par 105): **104,102,102,97,96 82**
CSF £74.27 TOTE £5.00: £2.70, £6.60; EX 87.20 Trifecta £380.20.
Owner G O Leach & Mrs J M Leach **Bred** Dukes Stud & Overbury Stallions Ltd **Trained** Lambourn, Berks

FOCUS
This was a tighter handicap on RPR than the official ratings suggested, with the two bottom-weights fighting out the finish off a good pace and just holding off the top-weight. The runner-up is rated in line with recent form.

2238 BET IN PLAY AT TOTESPORT.COM H'CAP 7f (P)

7:25 (7:28) (Class 6) (0-65,66) 3-Y-O

£3,105 (£924; £461; £300; £300; £300) **Stalls** Low

Form RPR

250- **1** **Filles De Fleur**[167] 9049 3-9-7 **65**.................................... HarryBentley 11 72+
(George Scott) *dwlt: in rr: c wd and effrt wl over 1f out: hdwy whn sltly impeded over 1f out: str run ins fnl f: hung lft but led towards fin: sn eased* **14/1**

3040 **2** *3/4* **Valley Belle (IRE)**[22] 1650 3-8-9 **53**........................ JosephineGordon 13 58
(Phil McEntee) *chsd ldrs: effrt to ld over 1f out: kpt on u.p ins fnl f: hdd and no ex towards fin* **20/1**

160- **3** *3/4* **In The Cove (IRE)**[130] 9669 3-9-7 **65**................................ RossaRyan 4 68
(Richard Hannon) *in tch in midfield on inner: nt clr run ent fnl 2f: swtchd rt and hdwy over 1f out: chsd ldrs and kpt on ins fnl f* **5/1[2]**

00-1 **4** *3 1/4* **Gregorian Girl**[27] 1515 3-9-5 **63**.................................... RobertHavlin 9 58
(Dean Ivory) *led and grad crossed over 1f to inner: rdn and hdd over 1f out: no ex and wknd ins fnl f* **8/1**

50-0 **5** *1 1/2* **Jailbreak (IRE)**[18] 1728 3-8-10 **54**..........................(b[1]) ShaneKelly 7 45
(Richard Hughes) *chsd ldrs: rdn 3f out: unable qck and btn over 1f out: wknd ins fnl f* **8/1**

030- **6** *hd* **Purgatory**[175] 8890 3-9-3 **61**... GeorgeWood 12 51
(Chris Wall) *hld up towards rr: effrt over 1f out: nvr threatened to get on terms and carried rt ins fnl f* **9/1**

040- 7 3/4 **Legend Island (FR)**[168] 9037 3-9-4 **62** .... LiamKeniry 2 51
(Ed Walker) *hld up towards rr: nt clr run over 2f out: effrt and hung lft over 1f out: hung rt u.p and sme hdwy 1f out: nvr trbld ldrs* **9/1**

0-00 8 2 1/4 **Mitigator**[39] 1264 3-9-7 **65** .... BrettDoyle 8 47
(Lydia Pearce) *pushed along leaving stalls: midfield on outer: rdn over 2f out: unable qck and btn 1f out: wknd ins fnl f* **28/1**

254- 9 5 **Mohogany**[203] 8074 3-9-5 **63** ....(p) LukeMorris 3 34
(Tom Clover) *chsd ldrs: effrt over 2f out: unable qck over 1f out: btn whn eased wl ins fnl f* **7/1**[3]

00-0 10 hd **Sherella**[15] 1825 3-9-1 **59** .... DavidProbert 10 28
(J R Jenkins) *dwlt: a towards rr: rdn whn nt clr run and swtchd rt over 1f out: nvr involved* **50/1**

0000 11 1 1/4 **Isabella Red (IRE)**[34] 1353 3-7-9 **46** oh1 ....(p[1]) ElishaWhittington(7) 5 12
(Lisa Williamson) *hld up in midfield: rdn and outpcd over 1f out: wknd fnl f* **50/1**

606- 12 1 1/4 **Mr Spirit (IRE)**[183] 8692 3-9-5 **66** .... GabrieleMalune(3) 6 28
(Marco Botti) *wl in tch in midfield: effrt jst over 2f out: unable qck u.p and lost pl over 1f out: wknd ins fnl f* **85/40**[1]

406- 13 2 1/2 **Little Tipple**[220] 7548 3-8-5 **49** .... NicolaCurrie 1 5
(John Ryan) *a in rr: bhd fnl f* **50/1**

1m 26.43s (-0.77) **Going Correction** -0.125s/f (Stan) 13 Ran SP% **124.1**
Speed ratings (Par 96): **99,98,97,93,91 91,90,88,82,82 80,79,76**
CSF £275.96 CT £1661.25 TOTE £18.40: £6.40, £7.70, £2.10; EX 382.40 Trifecta £1755.50.
Owner A Watson & B Malyon **Bred** Alan Watson & Brett Malyon **Trained** Newmarket, Suffolk

FOCUS
Another 7f race where the advantage went to those delivering a late challenge out wide, even though it looked an easy pace. The second is the best guide.

2239 DOUBLE DELIGHT HAT-TRICK HEAVEN AT TOTESPORT.COM H'CAP 2m (P)
8:00 (8:03) (Class 5) (0-75,76) 4-Y-O+

£5,433 (£1,617; £808; £404; £300; £300) **Stalls Low**

Form RPR

105- 1 **Dazzling Rock (IRE)**[181] 8735 4-9-10 **75** .... HarryBentley 4 83
(Ralph Beckett) *mde all: pushed along ent fnl 2f: drvn and hrd pressed over 1f out: edgd rt and bmpd ins fnl f: styd on wl ins fnl f: hld on cl home* **9/2**[3]

6-31 2 nk **True Destiny**[61] 947 4-9-2 **67** .... AdamMcNamara 2 74+
(Roger Charlton) *hld up in tch: effrt and swtchd rt wl over 1f out: effrt to chal and hung lft ent fnl f: stl hung lft u.p ins fnl f: kpt on but jst hld towards fin* **9/2**[3]

3523 3 3/4 **Alabaster**[14] 1840 5-9-13 **76** ....(v) LukeMorris 5 82
(Sir Mark Prescott Bt) *wl in tch: trckd ldrs and nt clr run over 2f out: swtchd rt and effrt wl over 1f out: sn chalng and drvn: ev ch whn bmpd ins fnl f: no ex and outpcd towards fin* **4/1**[2]

-012 4 6 **Tour De Paris (IRE)**[45] 1235 4-8-13 **64** ....(v) TomMarquand 6 65
(Alan King) *stdd s: t.k.h: hld up in tch: rdn over 3f out: shifted rt and unable qck u.p wl over 1f out: wl hld fnl f* **5/2**[1]

-221 5 1/2 **Tin Fandango**[28] 1497 4-9-2 **67** ....(p) JosephineGordon 1 67
(Mark Usher) *wl in tch in midfield tl lost pl and rdn 5f out: dropped to last over 3f out: swtchd rt wl over 1f out: no threat to ldrs and plugged on same pce after* **9/2**[3]

0626 6 14 **Demophon**[35] 1341 5-8-7 **56** oh8 .... RaulDaSilva 7 37
(Steve Flook) *chsd wnr: rdn 4f out: lost pl wl over 1f out: wl btn and eased ins fnl f* **25/1**

-604 7 15 **Final Choice**[27] 1524 6-8-12 **68** ....(v) TobyEley(7) 8 31
(Adam West) *v.s.a and rousted along early: hdwy to chse ldrs 11f out: rdn 6f out: dropped to last over 2f out: sn bhd (jockey said gelding was never travelling)* **20/1**

3m 25.96s (-4.04) **Going Correction** -0.125s/f (Stan) 7 Ran SP% **111.7**
WFA 4 from 5yo+ 2lb
Speed ratings (Par 103): **105,104,104,101,101 94,86**
CSF £23.67 CT £84.77 TOTE £4.50: £2.70, £2.80; EX 22.70 Trifecta £102.20.
Owner Pickford Hill P'Ship, Late R Roberts **Bred** Pigeon Park Stud **Trained** Kimpton, Hants

FOCUS
After a decent early pace three were left battling it out, but they came close together and the result may have been affected. The third looks the best guide.

2240 CELEBRATE APRIL'S HERO MICHAEL ORR CLASSIFIED STKS 1m (P)
8:30 (8:33) (Class 6) 3-Y-O+

£3,105 (£924; £461; £300; £300; £300) **Stalls Low**

Form RPR

0502 1 **Imperial Act**[19] 1717 4-9-7 47 .... OisinMurphy 8 58
(Andrew Balding) *trckd ldrs and travelled strly: trckd ldr 2f out: rdn to ld jst over 1f out: r.o strly: v readily* **5/2**[1]

0061 2 3 **Nicky Baby (IRE)**[19] 1717 5-9-0 49 ....(b) SophieRalston(7) 14 51
(Dean Ivory) *t.k.h: chsd ldrs: effrt to ld 2f out: hdd jst over 1f out: kpt on but no match for wnr ins fnl f* **8/1**[3]

-606 3 nk **The Numismatist (IRE)**[18] 1725 3-8-7 44 .... NicolaCurrie 15 47+
(Jamie Osborne) *hld up in midfield: swtchd rt and effrt over 1f out: hdwy to chse ldrs and hung lft ins fnl f: r.o strly but no threat to wnr* **12/1**

-033 4 2 3/4 **Casey Banter**[19] 1717 4-9-0 47 .... MarcoGhiani(7) 3 45
(Julia Feilden) *stdd s: hld up in rr: swtchd rt and sme hdwy over 1f out: swtchd lft ent fnl f: styd on wl but no threat to ldrs* **6/1**[2]

6220 5 3/4 **Voice Of A Leader (IRE)**[14] 1841 8-9-7 49 ....(p) LiamKeniry 7 43
(Paul Howling) *taken down early: t.k.h: hld up in tch in midfield: effrt to chse clr ldng pair jst over 1f out: drvn and no imp: hung lft and wknd ins fnl f* **10/1**

-060 6 1 1/2 **Freesia Gold (IRE)**[18] 1725 3-8-7 49 ....(p) KieranO'Neill 10 36
(Daniel Kubler) *wnt lft s: midfield: effrt u.p over 1f out: no imp and wknd ins fnl f* **14/1**

2-00 7 3/4 **Kenoughty (FR)**[10] 1935 3-8-0 49 ....(b[1]) GeorgeRooke(7) 9 34
(Richard Hughes) *hld up in rr: swtchd lft and effrt over 1f out: styd on ins fnl f: nvr trbld ldrs* **11/1**

000 8 3 1/2 **Chutzpah (IRE)**[36] 1332 3-8-4 50 .... WilliamCox(3) 4 26
(Mark Hoad) *a towards rr: swtchd rt and effrt over 1f out: plugged on to pass btn horses ins fnl f: n.d* **16/1**

60-0 9 nk **Exousia**[54] 1066 3-8-7 42 ....(t[1]) BrettDoyle 5 26
(Henry Spiller) *shifted lft leaving stalls: sn chsng ldrs: nt clr run ent fnl 2f: unable qck over 1f out: wknd ins fnl f* **33/1**

0-50 10 1 1/4 **Dragon Kuza**[18] 1725 3-8-0 50 ....(b[1]) GeorgiaDobie(7) 6 23
(Hugo Palmer) *t.k.h: hld up in midfield: nt clr run ent fnl 2f: swtchd rt and effrt over 1f out: no imp and wl hld fnl f (jockey said gelding ran too free)* **6/1**[2]

00-0 11 nk **Haabis (USA)**[115] 80 6-9-7 49 .... DavidProbert 11 26
(Patrick Chamings) *hld up in midfield: unable qck and btn over 1f out: wknd ins fnl f* **16/1**

34-0 12 8 **Triple First**[10] 1935 5-9-2 50 .... RhiainIngram(5) 2 9
(Seamus Mullins) *s.i.s: nvr travelling and a towards rr* **28/1**

-000 13 5 **Milldean Panther**[13] 1863 3-8-7 50 .... EoinWalsh 1
(Suzi Best) *midfield tl dropped towards rr after 2f: in rr and rdn wl over 1f out: sn btn* **33/1**

5-00 14 4 **Cedar**[10] 1954 3-8-7 50 ....(b[1]) LukeMorris 12
(Mohamed Moubarak) *w ldr tl over 2f out: sn lost pl and wknd over 1f out: bhd ins fnl f* **40/1**

010 15 2 1/2 **Ainne**[10] 1958 4-9-4 50 ....(tp) GaryMahon(3) 13
(Sylvester Kirk) *led tl rdn and hdd 2f out: lost pl over 1f out: bhd ins fnl f* **14/1**

1m 38.56s (-1.34) **Going Correction** -0.125s/f (Stan)
WFA 3 from 4yo+ 14lb 15 Ran SP% **130.2**
Speed ratings (Par 101): **101,98,97,94,94 92,91,88,88,86 86,78,73,69,67**
CSF £23.31 TOTE £2.60: £1.40, £2.60, £4.60; EX 16.80 Trifecta £251.30.
Owner A M Balding **Bred** The Victrix Ludorum Partnership **Trained** Kingsclere, Hants

FOCUS
Just modest fayre but it was run in a good time with recent C&D form between the first two proving a key factor. The winner is rated back to last year's better form.
T/Jkpt: Not won. T/Plt: £824.10 to a £1 stake. Pool: £50,759.61 - 44.96 winning units T/Qpdt: £76.70 to a £1 stake. Pool: £7,903.99 - 76.22 winning units **Steve Payne**

2183 NEWCASTLE (A.W) (L-H)
Tuesday, April 30

OFFICIAL GOING: Tapeta: standard
Wind: Breezy, half behind in races on the straight course and in over 3f of home straight in races on the Weather: Overcast, dry

2241 WATCH SKY SPORTS RACING ON SKY 415 APPRENTICE H'CAP 1m 5y (Tp)
4:45 (4:49) (Class 6) (0-60,60) 4-Y-O+

£3,105 (£924; £461; £300; £300; £300) **Stalls Centre**

Form RPR

656- 1 **She's Royal**[178] 8830 4-8-13 **57** .... HarryRussell(5) 6 65
(Bryan Smart) *hld up in midfield on nr side of gp: hdwy over 2f out: rdn to ld over 1f out: r.o wl fnl f* **8/1**

64-1 2 1 1/2 **Betty Grable (IRE)**[108] 210 5-8-4 **48** .... RhonaPindar(5) 14 53
(Wilf Storey) *chsd ldrs in centre of gp: effrt and drifted lft over 1f out: chsd wnr ins fnl f: kpt on same pce towards fin* **7/1**

0355 3 3/4 **Puchita (IRE)**[20] 1683 4-8-4 **46** oh1 ....(p) KieranSchofield(3) 12 49
(Antony Brittain) *led 2f in centre of gp: chsd ldr: regained ld over 2f out: rdn: edgd rt and hdd over 1f out: kpt on same pce ins fnl f* **14/1**

05-0 4 1/2 **Rebel State (IRE)**[4] 2076 6-8-13 **59** ....(p) OwenPayton(7) 3 61
(Jedd O'Keeffe) *t.k.h: hld up on far side of gp: effrt and hdwy over 1f out: kpt on ins fnl f: nt pce to chal* **6/1**[3]

5-35 5 nk **Twiggy**[32] 1400 5-8-9 **48** .... BenSanderson 2 50
(Karen McLintock) *hld up in centre of gp: effrt and swtchd rt over 2f out: edgd lft ins fnl f: kpt on same pce* **9/1**

3/0- 6 nse **Ishebayorgrey (IRE)**[46] 1223 7-9-2 **60** ....(h) EllaMcCain(5) 5 61
(Iain Jardine) *t.k.h: hld up in centre of gp: stdy hdwy gng wl 2f out: rdn last 150yds: no imp* **3/1**[1]

20-0 7 3 1/4 **Jennies Gem**[89] 501 6-8-7 **46** oh1 .... HarrisonShaw 9 40
(Ollie Pears) *cl up on far side of gp tl rdn and wknd over 1f out* **33/1**

00-0 8 nk **Clary (IRE)**[19] 1717 9-8-2 **46** oh1 .... CianMacRedmond(5) 10 40
(Alistair Whillans) *hld up in centre of gp: drvn along over 2f out: no imp fr over 1f out* **50/1**

-000 9 4 1/2 **Lord Rob**[22] 1647 8-8-2 **46** oh1 .... GavinAshton(5) 7 30
(David Thompson) *dwlt: hld up on nr side of gp: outpcd over 2f out: n.d after* **40/1**

050- 10 1 1/4 **Ingleby Angel (IRE)**[210] 7871 10-8-11 **50** ow2 .... SebastianWoods 11 31
(Fred Watson) *prom in centre of gp tl rdn and wknd over 1f out* **20/1**

036- 11 nk **Odds On Oli**[123] 9735 4-8-12 **56** .... RussellHarris(5) 4 36
(Richard Fahey) *dwlt: hld up on far side of gp: drvn and outpcd over 2f out: sn btn: lost front shoe (vet said gelding lost its right front shoe)* **7/1**

-041 12 nk **Midnight Vixen**[19] 1722 5-9-3 **56** ....(p) ConnorMurtagh 1 36
(Ben Haslam) *hld up on far side of gp: rdn and outpcd over 2f out: sn btn* **5/1**[2]

00-0 13 5 **Nanjoe**[32] 1400 4-8-4 **48** .... CoreyMadden(5) 8 17
(Jim Goldie) *hld up on nr side of gp: struggling over 2f out: sn btn* **28/1**

00-0 14 12 **Wasm**[28] 1506 5-8-8 **47** .... PaulaMuir 13
(Ruth Carr) *missed break: hdwy on nr side of gp and led after 2f: hdd over 3f out: wknd fnl 2f* **16/1**

1m 39.62s (1.02) **Going Correction** +0.15s/f (Slow) 14 Ran SP% **130.2**
Speed ratings (Par 101): **100,98,97,97,96 96,93,93,88,87 87,87,82,70**
CSF £65.29 CT £821.48 TOTE £10.60: £3.90, £2.70, £4.60; EX 107.70 Trifecta £1579.70.
Owner Smart, Moody, Hogan, **Bred** M A L Evans **Trained** Hambleton, N Yorks

FOCUS
A modest apprentice riders' handicap, and straightforward form.

2242 WATCH SKY SPORTS RACING ON VIRGIN 535 H'CAP 7f 14y (Tp)
5:20 (5:20) (Class 4) (0-85,84) 4-Y-O+

£5,530 (£1,645; £822; £411; £300; £300) **Stalls Centre**

Form RPR

40-5 1 **Algaffaal (USA)**[19] 1723 4-8-9 **75** .... BenRobinson(3) 6 83
(Brian Ellison) *prom: drvn along over 2f out: rallied and chal over 1f out: led ins fnl f: kpt on strly* **14/1**

/01- 2 1/2 **Glengarry**[203] 8095 6-9-6 **83** .... ConnorBeasley 7 90
(Keith Dalgleish) *t.k.h: hld up in tch: smooth hdwy over 2f out: led and rdn over 1f out: hdd ins fnl f: kpt on: hld nr fin* **11/2**[3]

30-3 3 1 **Chaplin Bay (IRE)**[11] 1925 7-8-11 **74** .... JamesSullivan 2 78
(Ruth Carr) *chsd ldrs: drvn and outpcd wl over 1f out: rallied ins fnl f: r.o* **9/1**

1663 4 nk **Custard The Dragon**[25] 1560 6-9-5 **82** ....(v) PJMcDonald 5 85
(John Mackie) *hld up: rdn over 2f out: hdwy over 1f out: kpt on same pce wl ins fnl f* **11/2**[3]

2004 5 3/4 **Luis Vaz De Torres (IRE)**[17] 1768 7-8-8 **71** ....(h) PaulHanagan 1 72
(Richard Fahey) *cl up: drvn and ev ch over 2f out: no ex ins fnl f* **16/1**

2122 6 3/4 **Chosen World**[11] 1925 5-8-11 **74** ....(p) PaulMulrennan 3 73
(Julie Camacho) *led or disp ld to over 1f out: drvn and outpcd fnl f* **3/1**[2]

2300 7 nk **Middlescence (IRE)**[19] 1715 5-8-0 **70** oh17 .... VictorSantos(7) 8 69?
(Lucinda Egerton) *led or disp ld to over 1f out: sn no ex* **250/1**

2212 **8** *hd* **Rey Loopy (IRE)**[22] 1644 5-9-7 **84** .... AndrewMullen 4 82
(Ben Haslam) *hld up: rdn over 2f out: shortlived effrt over 1f out: sn no imp (jockey said gelding was denied a clear run in the final furlong)* **7/4**[1]

1m 26.85s (0.65) **Going Correction** +0.15s/f (Slow) **8** Ran SP% **115.1**
Speed ratings (Par 105): **102,101,100,99,99 98,97,97**
CSF £88.97 CT £749.25 TOTE £13.90: £3.50, £1.60, £2.20; EX 95.20 Trifecta £448.50.
Owner Ian & Tom Pallas & Mrs D F Robe **Bred** WinStar Farm LLC **Trained** Norton, N Yorks

FOCUS
A fairly decent handicap. The seventh suggests the form may not be entirely reliable.

2243 PARKLANDS MINI GOLF NOVICE MEDIAN AUCTION STKS 6f (Tp)
5:55 (5:55) (Class 5) 3-5-Y-O **£3,752** (£1,116; £557; £278) **Stalls** Centre

Form RPR
22- **1** **Pendleton**[183] 8698 3-9-5 .... PaulMulrennan 1 81+
(Michael Dods) *t.k.h: pressed ldr: rdn to ld over 1f out: kpt on strly fnl f* **5/2**[2]

6-22 **2** *½* **You Little Ripper (IRE)**[20] 1676 3-9-5 79 .... PaulHanagan 6 78
(Peter Chapple-Hyam) *led to over 1f out: rallied: kpt on same pce ins fnl f* **8/15**[1]

0- **3** *4 ½* **Delachance (FR)**[179] 8803 3-9-5 .... TomEaves 3 64
(David Simcock) *t.k.h: hld up in last pl: effrt and pushed along over 2f out: chsd clr ldng pair ins fnl f: kpt on: nvr nrr* **9/1**[3]

4 *¾* **Senorita Grande (IRE)** 3-9-0 .... JasonHart 2 56
(John Quinn) *s.i.s: hld up in tch: pushed along over 2f out: one pce fr over 1f out* **50/1**

5 *1 ½* **Gunnison** 3-9-5 .... DavidNolan 4 56
(Richard Fahey) *chsd ldrs: rdn over 2f out: rallied: outpcd ins fnl f* **16/1**

0 **6** *18* **Pandora's Minder**[2] 2147 3-8-7 .... VictorSantos(7) 5
(Lucinda Egerton) *missed break: sn chsng ldrs: rdn over 3f out: wknd over 2f out* **250/1**

1m 13.06s (0.56) **Going Correction** +0.15s/f (Slow) **6** Ran SP% **112.0**
Speed ratings (Par 103): **102,101,95,94,92 68**
CSF £4.13 TOTE £4.40: £1.50, £1.10; EX 5.50 Trifecta £10.80.
Owner David W Armstrong **Bred** Highfield Farm Llp **Trained** Denton, Co Durham

FOCUS
A fair novice contest. The odds-on favourite was outstayed by his main market rival in a comparatively modest time. The first two came clear, with the runner-up close to form.

2244 EQUINE PRODUCTS H'CAP 1m 2f 42y (Tp)
6:30 (6:31) (Class 6) (0-65,67) 4-Y-O+
£3,105 (£924; £461; £300; £300; £300) **Stalls** High

Form RPR
-004 **1** **Perceived**[10] 1958 7-8-7 **51** oh3 ....(p) CamHardie 11 57
(Antony Brittain) *trckd ldr: rdn to ld over 1f out: kpt on wl fnl f* **11/1**

56-0 **2** *1 ¾* **Kwanza**[39] 1269 4-9-3 **61** .... PJMcDonald 4 64
(Mark Johnston) *led at ordinary gallop: rdn and hdd over 1f out: kpt on same pce ins fnl f* **10/1**

223- **3** *nk* **Majestic Stone (IRE)**[242] 6746 5-8-4 **51** oh2 .... JamieGormley(3) 9 53
(Julie Camacho) *t.k.h: chsd ldrs: rdn and outpcd over 2f out: rallied to chse ldng pair ins fnl f: r.o* **7/1**[3]

16-4 **4** *nk* **Ascot Week (USA)**[21] 1660 5-9-7 **65** ....(v) JasonHart 1 66
(John Quinn) *plld hrd in tch: checked and lost grnd after 1f: effrt u.p over 2f out: kpt on same pce ins fnl f* **6/1**[2]

0-02 **5** *1 ¾* **Bahkit (IRE)**[22] 1647 5-9-6 **64** .... PaulHanagan 10 62
(Philip Kirby) *chsd ldrs: effrt and rdn over 2f out: no ex ins fnl f (jockey said gelding ran too free)* **9/4**[1]

00-0 **6** *2 ¾* **Island Flame (IRE)**[113] 120 6-8-12 **56** .... DavidAllan 2 49
(Les Eyre) *t.k.h: prom: rdn over 2f out: outpcd over 1f out* **28/1**

4300 **7** *1* **Remmy D (IRE)**[22] 1647 4-9-8 **66** .... PhilDennis 7 58
(Jim Goldie) *slowly away: hld up: pushed along and hdwy over 2f out: kpt on fnl f: nvr able to chal (jockey said gelding was slowly away)* **7/1**[3]

000- **8** *hd* **Hillgrove Angel (IRE)**[197] 8267 7-8-5 **56** .... CoreyMadden(7) 8 47
(Jim Goldie) *hld up: stdy hdwy over 2f out: shkn up and no imp over 1f out* **16/1**

-000 **9** *¾* **Dutch Melody**[13] 1849 5-8-0 **51** oh6 .... VictorSantos(7) 5 41
(Lucinda Egerton) *hld up on ins: outpcd over 3f out: rallied 2f out: sn no imp* **100/1**

/000 **10** *2 ¼* **Tarnhelm**[22] 1648 4-8-12 **56** .... NathanEvans 3 42
(Wilf Storey) *t.k.h in midfield: effrt on outside over 2f out: wknd wl over 1f out (jockey said filly ran too free)* **25/1**

63-0 **11** *4 ½* **Zealous (IRE)**[22] 1648 6-9-6 **64** .... GrahamLee 12 42
(Alistair Whillans) *t.k.h: hld up in midfield: effrt over 2f out: sn wknd: lost front shoe (vet said gelding lost its left front shoe)* **12/1**

21/6 **12** *¾* **Miss Ranger (IRE)**[31] 1418 7-9-4 **67** .... BenSanderson(5) 13 43
(Roger Fell) *s.i.s: bhd: struggling and edgd lft over 2f out: nvr on terms* **8/1**

550- **13** *10* **Inflexiball**[94] 5280 7-8-10 **54** .... AndrewMullen 14 12
(John Mackie) *prom tl drvn and lost pl over 2f out: sn btn* **40/1**

54-0 **14** *3 ½* **Born In Thorne**[63] 913 6-9-3 **61** ....(t[1]) DavidNolan 6 13
(Ivan Furtado) *hld up towards rr: struggling over 3f out: sn btn* **28/1**

2m 12.04s (1.64) **Going Correction** +0.15s/f (Slow) **14** Ran SP% **126.3**
Speed ratings (Par 101): **99,97,97,97,95 93,92,92,91,90 86,85,77,75**
CSF £117.27 CT £846.84 TOTE £10.70: £2.70, £2.70, £2.60; EX 123.00 Trifecta £1757.40.
Owner Antony Brittain **Bred** J A E Hobby **Trained** Warthill, N Yorks

FOCUS
A modest handicap. The winning time was over six seconds above standard and it paid to race prominently. The runner-up is the best guide.

2245 BORDER MINSTREL PUB NOVICE STKS 1m 2f 42y (Tp)
7:05 (7:05) (Class 5) 3-Y-O+ **£3,752** (£1,116; £557; £278) **Stalls** High

Form RPR
31- **1** **Surfman**[174] 8930 3-9-4 0 .... JimCrowley 3 101+
(Roger Varian) *t.k.h early: mde all: qcknd clr on bit fr 3f out: v easily* **1/8**[1]

0 **2** *14* **Frequency Code (FR)**[31] 1417 3-8-11 0 .... PJMcDonald 5 66
(Jedd O'Keeffe) *s.i.s: hld up: outpcd over 3f out: rallied to chse (clr) wnr over 1f out: kpt on fnl f: no imp* **18/1**[3]

0 **3** *½* **Theatro (IRE)**[17] 1764 3-8-6 0 .... AndrewMullen 1 60
(Jedd O'Keeffe) *prom: drvn and outpcd over 4f out: rallied and disp modest 2nd pl over 1f out: no imp fnl f* **66/1**

4 *6* **Persian Beauty (IRE)** 3-8-6 0 .... PaulHanagan 4 48
(Simon Crisford) *dwlt: hld up in tch: effrt and rdn over 2f out: wknd over 1f out* **5/1**[2]

5 **5** *½* **Smeaton (IRE)**[22] 1643 3-8-11 0 .... GrahamLee 6 52
(Roger Fell) *t.k.h: prom on outside: chsd wnr over 4f out to over 1f out: sn wknd* **33/1**

6 *7* **Shamitsar**[35] 5-10-0 0 .... ConnorBeasley 2 41
(Ray Craggs) *hld up in tch: drvn and outpcd 3f out: btn fnl 2f* **66/1**

00 **7** *8* **Put The Law On You (IRE)**[22] 1643 4-9-9 0 ....(v[1]) ConnorMurtagh(5) 7 25
(Alistair Whillans) *pressed ldr to over 4f out: wknd fr 3f out* **150/1**

2m 9.63s (-0.77) **Going Correction** +0.15s/f (Slow)
WFA 3 from 4yo+ 17lb **7** Ran SP% **117.4**
Speed ratings (Par 103): **109,97,97,92,92 86,80**
CSF £5.21 TOTE £1.10: £1.10, £2.60; EX 4.90 Trifecta £92.80.
Owner P Winkworth **Bred** Peter Winkworth **Trained** Newmarket, Suffolk

FOCUS
A fair novice contest. The long odds-on favourite made all with ridiculous ease in a time nearly 2.5 seconds quicker than the previous C&D handicap. He's clearly smart but it's hard to pin down the form.

2246 RAMSIDE HALL HOTEL & SPA H'CAP 1m 5y (Tp)
7:40 (7:43) (Class 4) (0-80,78) 4-Y-O+
£5,530 (£1,645; £822; £411; £300; £300) **Stalls** Centre

Form RPR
3026 **1** **Tum Tum**[27] 1526 4-9-1 **72** ....(h) TomEaves 5 80
(Michael Herrington) *mde all in nr side gp: rdn over 1f out: kpt on wl fnl f* **9/1**[3]

04-0 **2** *¾* **Farhh Away**[21] 1659 4-8-10 **67** ....(p[1]) ConnorBeasley 4 73+
(Michael Dods) *hld up in nr side gp: outpcd and drvn over 2f out: hdwy over 1f out: chsd wnr ins fnl f: clsng at fin* **20/1**

1220 **3** *½* **Elixsoft (IRE)**[13] 1850 4-9-1 **72** ....(p) GrahamLee 10 77
(Roger Fell) *hld up in tch in nr side gp: pushed along over 1f out: rallied ins fnl f: kpt on* **9/1**[3]

-342 **4** *¾* **Newmarket Warrior (IRE)**[98] 355 8-8-9 **69** ....(p) JamieGormley(3) 6 72
(Iain Jardine) *prom in nr side gp: effrt and rdn over 1f out: no ex ins fnl f* **12/1**

322- **5** *1 ¼* **Kingdom Brunel**[188] 8545 4-9-2 **73** ....(w) DanielTudhope 3 74
(David O'Meara) *dwlt: sn chsng fair side ldrs: swtchd to nr side gp over 5f out: effrt and rdn 2f out: outpcd fnl f* **6/4**[1]

5035 **6** *¾* **Testa Rossa (IRE)**[11] 1925 9-8-3 **67** ....(b) CoreyMadden(7) 1 66
(Jim Goldie) *spd far side tl rdn and outpcd fr over 1f out* **9/1**[3]

232 **7** *hd* **Blindingly (GER)**[13] 1849 4-9-4 **75** ....(p[1]) AndrewMullen 8 73
(Ben Haslam) *cl up nr side gp tl rdn and outpcd over 1f out: sn btn* **9/2**[2]

1210 **8** *1 ¼* **Insurplus (IRE)**[11] 1925 6-8-8 **65** .... PhilDennis 2 60
(Jim Goldie) *chsd far side ldr: drvn and outpcd over 2f out: btn over 1f out* **10/1**

00 **9** *1 ¼* **Intense Style (IRE)**[46] 1213 7-9-7 **78** .... PaulHanagan 9 71
(Les Eyre) *hld up nr side gp: drvn and outpcd over 2f out: hung lft and wknd over 1f out (jockey said gelding hung left in the final 3f)* **33/1**

30-0 **10** *9* **Intense Pleasure (IRE)**[22] 1644 4-9-5 **76** .... JamesSullivan 7 48
(Ruth Carr) *hld up: rdn and struggling over 2f out: sn btn* **14/1**

1m 39.62s (1.02) **Going Correction** +0.15s/f (Slow) **10** Ran SP% **119.3**
Speed ratings (Par 105): **100,99,98,98,96 96,95,94,93,84**
CSF £175.26 CT £1705.63 TOTE £13.00: £2.90, £6.70, £2.70; EX 170.20 Trifecta £2413.20.
Owner Mrs H Lloyd-Herrington **Bred** Jeremy Green And Sons **Trained** Cold Kirby, N Yorks

FOCUS
A fair handicap. The clear favourite belatedly joined the bigger stands' side group but was never really travelling with much conviction. The runner-up looks the best guide.

2247 IMPECCABLE PIG INN, SEDGEFIELD H'CAP 6f (Tp)
8:15 (8:16) (Class 5) (0-75,75) 4-Y-O+
£3,752 (£1,116; £557; £300; £300; £300) **Stalls** Centre

Form RPR
4313 **1** **Gowanbuster**[10] 1951 4-9-0 **68** ....(t) PJMcDonald 4 80
(Susan Corbett) *mde all: shkn up and clr appr fnl f: kpt on strly: unchal* **10/3**[2]

5-33 **2** *2 ¾* **Gunmaker (IRE)**[12] 1880 5-8-13 **67** .... JamesSullivan 2 70
(Ruth Carr) *hld up bhd ldng gp: effrt whn nt clr run and swtchd lft over 1f out: chsd wnr wl ins fnl f: kpt on: nt pce to chal (jockey said gelding was denied a clear run 2f out)* **3/1**[1]

2652 **3** *hd* **Lucky Lodge**[3] 2122 9-9-2 **70** ....(v) CamHardie 1 73
(Antony Brittain) *chsd wnr: rdn along 2f out: lost 2nd wl ins fnl f: one pce* **4/1**[3]

0000 **4** *2 ¼* **Camanche Grey (IRE)**[28] 1505 8-8-0 **61** oh16 .... VictorSantos(7) 7 56
(Lucinda Egerton) *taken down early and t.k.h to post: prom: rdn over 2f out: one pce fnl f* **200/1**

-314 **5** *nse* **Avenue Of Stars**[71] 788 6-8-12 **66** ....(v) JasonHart 6 61
(Karen McLintock) *in tch: rdn along 2f out: outpcd fnl f* **6/1**

60-0 **6** *1* **I Know How (IRE)**[17] 1760 4-9-0 **68** ....(p[1]) PaulMulrennan 5 60
(Julie Camacho) *t.k.h: prom: rdn along 2f out: outpcd fnl f* **15/2**

/623 **7** *1 ½* **Scots Sonnet**[19] 1723 5-9-4 **72** ....(h) AlistairRawlinson 3 59
(Jim Goldie) *hld up: drvn and outpcd over 2f out: n.d after* **7/1**

4-40 **8** *1 ¼* **Russian Realm**[68] 832 9-9-7 **75** .... GrahamLee 8 58
(Paul Midgley) *s.i.s: hld up: rdn and outpcd over 2f out: sn btn* **9/1**

1m 11.88s (-0.62) **Going Correction** +0.15s/f (Slow) **8** Ran SP% **117.1**
Speed ratings (Par 103): **110,106,106,103,103 101,99,98**
CSF £14.20 CT £41.02 TOTE £4.50: £1.80, £1.50, £1.40; EX 16.10 Trifecta £58.00.
Owner Hassle-Free Racing **Bred** L Waugh **Trained** Otterburn, Northumberland

FOCUS
A fair sprint handicap. The second-favourite put this field to the sword from the front in the best comparative time on the card. This rated a personal best from him.
T/Plt: £453.80 to a £1 stake. Pool: £46,742.57 - 75.18 winning units T/Qpdt: £27.00 to a £1 stake. Pool: £7,323.82 - 200.22 winning units **Richard Young**

1952 NOTTINGHAM (L-H)
Tuesday, April 30

OFFICIAL GOING: Good to soft (6.6)
Wind: Almost nil Weather: Overcast

2248 INTRODUCING RACING TV FILLIES' NOVICE STKS (PLUS 10 RACE) 5f 8y
1:30 (1:30) (Class 5) 2-Y-O **£3,881** (£1,155; £577; £288) **Stalls** High

Form RPR
1 **Lady Fanditha (IRE)** 2-9-0 0 .... AdamKirby 5 74
(Clive Cox) *chsd ldrs: shkn up 1/2-way: rdn to ld ins fnl f: r.o* **5/2**[1]

0 **2** *1 ¼* **Daddies Diva**[15] 1821 2-9-0 0 .... CharlieBennett 2 70
(Rod Millman) *chsd ldr: rdn to ld and hung lft over 1f out: hdd ins fnl f: styd on same pce* **100/1**

3 *nk* **Flippa The Strippa (IRE)** 2-9-0 0........................ RichardKingscote 6 68+
(Charles Hills) *s.i.s: swtchd lft and hdwy 1/2-way: shkn up over 1f out: carried lft: styd on same pce ins fnl f* **16/1**

2 4 *2* **Beignet (IRE)**[10] 1931 2-9-0 0........................ SeanLevey 9 61
(Richard Hannon) *led: rdn: edgd lft and hdd over 1f out: no ex ins fnl f* **7/2[3]**

5 *1/2* **Maisie Ellie (IRE)** 2-8-11 0........................ MeganNicholls(3) 3 59
(Paul George) *hdwy over 3f out: shkn up over 1f out: no ex ins fnl f* **20/1**

6 *3/4* **Internationalangel (IRE)** 2-9-0 0........................ TonyHamilton 4 60+
(Richard Fahey) *sn pushed along in rr: r.o towards fin: nvr nrr* **3/1[2]**

02 7 *shd* **Hollaback Girl**[9] 1968 2-9-0 0........................ OisinMurphy 7 56
(Richard Spencer) *s.i.s: hld up: swtchd lft and hdwy over 1f out: no ex ins fnl f* **10/1**

8 *nk* **Bacchalot (IRE)** 2-8-9 0........................ SeamusCronin(5) 8 55+
(Richard Hannon) *s.i.s: rn green in rr: r.o ins fnl f: nvr nrr* **16/1**

9 *1/2* **Apache Bay** 2-9-0 0........................ JasonHart 10 53
(John Quinn) *chsd ldrs: shkn up over 1f out: wknd fnl f* **12/1**

10 *5* **Flashy Flyer** 2-9-0 0........................ CharlesBishop 1 35
(Dean Ivory) *s.i.s: sn pushed along in rr: bhd fr 1/2-way* **25/1**

1m 1.09s (0.89) **Going Correction** -0.10s/f (Good) **10 Ran SP% 113.9**
Speed ratings (Par 89): **88,86,85,82,81 80,80,79,78,70**
CSF £280.90 TOTE £3.00: £1.50, £10.90, £3.60; EX 172.90 Trifecta £1257.50.
Owner Peter Ridgers **Bred** Tally-Ho Stud **Trained** Lambourn, Berks

FOCUS
Inner track used. All distances as advertised. The going was given as good to soft (Going Stick 6.6). It's hard to know what the form is worth, with the 100-1 outsider finishing second but the well-backed winner seemingly well regarded.

2249 JOIN RACING TV NOW NOVICE STKS (DIV I) 1m 75y
2:00 (2:01) (Class 5) 3-Y-O **£3,881** (£1,155; £577; £288) **Stalls** Centre

Form RPR

4 1 **Fifth Position (IRE)**[17] 1754 3-9-2 0........................ AndreaAtzeni 3 91+
(Roger Varian) *led: shkn up over 2f out: hdd over 1f out: rallied to ld nr fin* **9/2[3]**

1-4 2 *hd* **Space Blues (IRE)**[18] 1737 3-9-9 0........................ WilliamBuick 5 98
(Charlie Appleby) *chsd wnr: shkn up to ld over 1f out: rdn ins fnl f: hdd nr fin* **1/3[1]**

53- 3 *5* **Rhythmic Intent (IRE)**[174] 8930 3-9-2 0........................ RichardKingscote 9 79
(Stuart Williams) *chsd ldrs: shkn up over 2f out: styd on same pce fr over 1f out* **7/2[2]**

\- 4 *1* **My Style (IRE)** 3-9-2 0........................ CharlesBishop 10 77
(Eve Johnson Houghton) *prom: lost pl over 6f out: hdwy over 2f out: rdn over 1f out: styd on same pce* **50/1**

5 *nse* **Sincerity** 3-8-11 0........................ GeorgeWood 8 72+
(James Fanshawe) *s.i.s: in rr: shkn up over 2f out: styd on fr over 1f out: nt trble ldrs (jockey said filly was slowly away)* **16/1**

00 6 *7* **Thomas Cubitt (FR)**[20] 1690 3-9-2 0........................ LouisSteward 6 61
(Michael Bell) *s.i.s: rdn over 2f out: n.d* **100/1**

0- 7 *1/2* **Queen Of Mayfair**[153] 9290 3-8-11 0........................ RobertHavlin 7 54
(John Gosden) *hld up: plld hrd early: rdn over 2f out: n.d* **7/1**

8 *3 1/2* **Holy Hymn (IRE)**[88] 544 3-9-2 0........................ CliffordLee 2 51
(Kevin Frost) *chsd ldrs: pushed along over 4f out: wknd wl over 1f out* **66/1**

0-0 9 *10* **Relative Ease**[18] 1739 3-8-11 0........................ CallumShepherd 4 23
(J S Moore) *hld up: racd keenly: shkn up over 3f out: wknd over 2f out* **125/1**

1m 46.08s (-0.62) **Going Correction** -0.10s/f (Good) **9 Ran SP% 139.0**
Speed ratings (Par 98): **99,98,93,92,92 85,85,81,71**
CSF £7.88 TOTE £7.10: £1.50, £1.10, £1.20; EX 16.60 Trifecta £33.70.
Owner Sheikh Mohammed Obaid Al Maktoum **Bred** Philip & Jane Myerscough & B & C Equine **Trained** Newmarket, Suffolk

FOCUS
Marginally the slower of the two divisions, but the first two finished nicely clear and had a good battle. It was 3lb slower than division two but rates as good form.

2250 JOIN RACING TV NOW NOVICE STKS (DIV II) 1m 75y
2:35 (2:36) (Class 5) 3-Y-O **£3,881** (£1,155; £577; £288) **Stalls** Centre

Form RPR

3 1 **Roseman (IRE)**[17] 1755 3-9-3 0........................ AndreaAtzeni 7 87+
(Roger Varian) *sn led: shkn up over 2f out: wnt readily clr fr over 1f out* **1/5[1]**

42- 2 *5* **Deebee**[195] 8327 3-9-3 0........................ KevinStott 5 75
(Declan Carroll) *prom: chsd wnr over 6f out: rdn over 1f out: sn outpcd: eased wl ins fnl f* **3/1[2]**

06 3 *5* **Mandocello (FR)**[20] 1690 3-9-3 0........................ CharlieBennett 9 64
(Rod Millman) *led early: sn stdd and lost pl: r.o ins fnl f: wnt 3rd towards fin: nvr nr to chal* **33/1**

0 4 *2 1/4* **Hat Yai (IRE)**[25] 1562 3-9-3 0........................ SilvestreDeSousa 6 58
(Andrew Balding) *sn racing keenly in 2nd pl: lost 2nd over 6f out: remained handy: rdn over 2f out: wknd over 1f out* **7/1[3]**

5 *4 1/2* **Skerryvore** 3-9-3 0........................ DanielMuscutt 10 48
(James Fanshawe) *broke wl: sn stdd and lost pl: shkn up over 2f out: nvr nr to chal* **10/1**

0 6 *3 3/4* **Society Sweetheart (IRE)**[18] 1740 3-8-12 .... CallumShepherd 1 34
(J S Moore) *s.i.s: hld up: shkn up over 2f out: nvr nr to chal* **50/1**

0 7 *7* **Starlight**[13] 1855 3-8-5 0........................ JoeBradnam(7) 4 18
(Michael Bell) *prom over 3f* **50/1**

8 *3* **Heart In Havana** 3-9-3 0........................ NathanEvans 8 16
(Michael Easterby) *hld up: a in rr* **33/1**

1m 45.87s (-0.83) **Going Correction** -0.10s/f (Good) **8 Ran SP% 139.7**
Speed ratings (Par 98): **100,95,90,87,83 79,72,69**
CSF £2.03 TOTE £1.10: £1.02, £1.10, £7.30; EX 1.90 Trifecta £13.40.
Owner Sheikh Mohammed Obaid Al Maktoum **Bred** Knocktoran Stud **Trained** Newmarket, Suffolk

FOCUS
The time was 0.21sec faster than the first division and they finished well strung out behind the odds-on favourite. He showed very useful form, but the race lacks depth.

2251 #GORACINGGREEN FILLIES' H'CAP 1m 75y
3:05 (3:06) (Class 5) (0-75,77) 3-Y-O
£3,881 (£1,155; £577; £300; £300; £300) **Stalls** Centre

Form RPR

4215 1 **I'm Available (IRE)**[29] 1480 3-9-6 **74**........................ OisinMurphy 2 91
(Andrew Balding) *sn led: shkn up and qckd over 2f out: wnt readily clr fr over 1f out* **15/8[1]**

250- 2 *8* **King's Girl**[196] 8296 3-9-1 **69**........................ RichardKingscote 4 68
(Sir Michael Stoute) *prom: racd keenly: shkn up to chse wnr over 1f out: no imp* **11/2[3]**

230- 3 *nk* **I'lletyougonow**[235] 7007 3-9-6 **74**........................ WilliamBuick 8 72+
(Mick Channon) *hld up: plld hrd: shkn up over 2f out: r.o ins fnl f: wnt 3rd nr fin* **10/1**

322- 4 *1* **Al Messila**[146] 9395 3-9-3 **71**........................(w) SeanLevey 7 67
(Richard Hannon) *chsd ldrs: stdd and lost pl over 6f out: hdwy and edgd lft over 2f out: sn rdn: styd on same pce fr over 1f out* **15/2**

004- 5 *1/2* **Tartlette**[188] 8546 3-8-9 **63**........................ CharlieBennett 6 58
(Hughie Morrison) *s.i.s: hld up: swtchd rt and effrt over 2f out: nt trble ldrs* **28/1**

436- 6 *1/2* **Arctic Fox**[193] 8387 3-9-4 **72**........................ TonyHamilton 1 65
(Richard Fahey) *hld up: plld hrd: rdn over 3f out: hdwy over 2f out: no ex fnl f* **14/1**

202- 7 *1 3/4* **Mary Somerville**[180] 8771 3-9-9 **77**........................ RobertHavlin 5 66
(John Gosden) *s.i.s: hld up: shkn up over 2f out: nvr on terms (jockey said filly was restless in the stalls and missed the break)* **9/2[2]**

33-1 8 *3* **Isango**[25] 1567 3-9-7 **75**........................ StevieDonohoe 3 57
(Charlie Fellowes) *chsd ldrs: rdn over 2f out: wknd fnl f* **11/1**

6-30 9 *9* **Hanbury Dreams**[69] 798 3-8-8 **62**........................ GeorgeWood 9 24
(Tom Clover) *led early: chsd wnr over 6f out: rdn over 2f out: wknd over 1f out* **66/1**

230- 10 *6* **Nostrovia (IRE)**[189] 8509 3-9-7 **75**........................ AdamKirby 11 23
(Richard Spencer) *plld hrd and prom: rdn and wknd over 2f out* **25/1**

20-0 11 *1* **Desert Lantern (USA)**[11] 1925 3-9-3 **76**........................ AndrewBreslin(5) 10 22
(Mark Johnston) *hld up: rdn over 3f out: sn wknd* **33/1**

1m 45.84s (-0.86) **Going Correction** -0.10s/f (Good) **11 Ran SP% 115.9**
Speed ratings (Par 95): **100,92,91,90,90 89,87,84,75,69 68**
CSF £11.34 CT £83.07 TOTE £2.20: £1.10, £2.20, £3.50; EX 12.90 Trifecta £107.30.
Owner George Strawbridge **Bred** George Strawbridge **Trained** Kingsclere, Hants

FOCUS
This proved very straightforward for the favourite, who got to set her own pace out in front, but still impressed in quickening right away in the straight. The time was quick.

2252 BRITISH STALLION STUDS EBF FILLIES' H'CAP 1m 75y
3:35 (3:36) (Class 3) (0-90,92) 4-Y-O+ **£16,172** (£4,812; £2,405; £1,202) **Stalls** Centre

Form RPR

350- 1 **Daddies Girl (IRE)**[171] 8999 4-8-13 **83**........................ TheodoreLadd(5) 4 92
(Rod Millman) *hld up: rn wd over 4f out: hdwy over 2f out: led over 1f out: rdn and edgd lft ins fnl f: r.o* **8/1**

45-3 2 *1* **Hateya (IRE)**[38] 1294 4-9-13 **92**........................ PatCosgrave 3 99
(Jim Boyle) *hld up: hdwy over 2f out: rdn and ev ch over 1f out: styd on same pce wl ins fnl f* **11/1**

122- 3 *2 1/4* **Black Lotus**[211] 7848 4-8-12 **77**........................ WilliamBuick 5 79
(Chris Wall) *s.i.s: hld up: hdwy over 2f out: rdn and ev ch over 1f out: no ex ins fnl f* **8/1**

0-56 4 *hd* **Time For A Toot (IRE)**[17] 1757 4-9-3 **82**........................ RichardKingscote 10 83
(Charles Hills) *prom: rdn and ev ch over 1f out: no ex ins fnl f* **13/2[3]**

56-4 5 *1 1/4* **Queen Penn**[30] 1457 4-8-6 **76**........................(p) SeanDavis(5) 1 74
(Richard Fahey) *s.i.s: hld up: swtchd lft and hdwy over 1f out: no ex ins fnl f* **10/1**

-522 6 *2* **Yusra**[33] 1387 4-8-13 **78**........................ AndreaAtzeni 9 72
(Marco Botti) *chsd ldr: led over 2f out: rdn and hdd over 1f out: wknd ins fnl f* **12/1**

106- 7 *2 1/4* **Existential (IRE)**[195] 8331 4-9-7 **86**........................ AdamKirby 2 75
(Clive Cox) *hld up in tch: nt clr run and lost pl over 3f out: n.d after* **7/2[1]**

052- 8 *3 1/4* **Madeleine Bond**[178] 8835 5-9-2 **81**........................ OisinMurphy 6 62
(Henry Candy) *chsd ldrs: rdn over 2f out: wknd over 1f out* **5/1[2]**

6-30 9 *nk* **Villette (IRE)**[61] 945 5-9-5 **84**........................ CharlesBishop 8 65
(Dean Ivory) *sn led: rdn and hdd over 2f out: wknd ins fnl f* **9/1**

1140 10 *2 1/4* **Toy Theatre**[11] 1918 5-9-4 **86**........................ JaneElliott(3) 7 61
(Michael Appleby) *chsd ldrs: rdn over 2f out: wkng whn hmpd over 1f out* **20/1**

1m 44.99s (-1.71) **Going Correction** -0.10s/f (Good) **10 Ran SP% 114.3**
Speed ratings (Par 104): **104,103,100,100,99 97,95,91,91,89**
CSF £90.39 CT £726.06 TOTE £10.00: £2.30, £3.20, £2.00; EX 93.30 Trifecta £1599.00.
Owner Daddies Girl Partnership **Bred** William Blake **Trained** Kentisbeare, Devon
■ Stewards' Enquiry : Sean Davis two-day ban; careless riding (May 14-15)

FOCUS
The leaders went off too quick and it paid to be held up in this fillies' handicap. The winner is rated in line with last summer's form.

2253 LIKE RACING TV ON FACEBOOK FILLIES' H'CAP 1m 2f 50y
4:05 (4:07) (Class 5) (0-75,75) 3-Y-O
£3,881 (£1,155; £577; £300; £300; £300) **Stalls** Low

Form RPR

05-2 1 **Cuban Sun**[20] 1697 3-8-13 **67**........................ BarryMcHugh 2 76+
(James Given) *led over 8f out: rdn and flashed tail fr over 1f out: wnt clr wl ins fnl f* **10/1**

021- 2 *2 1/4* **Queen Constantine (GER)**[174] 8929 3-8-13 **72**........................ SeanDavis(5) 7 76
(William Jarvis) *hld up: hdwy over 1f out: r.o go 2nd wl ins fnl f: no ch w wnr* **8/1**

65-6 3 *1 3/4* **Patchouli**[33] 1386 3-9-0 **75**........................ ScottMcCullagh(7) 12 75+
(Mick Channon) *hld up on outer: rdn over 2f out: r.o ins fnl f: wnt 3rd nr fin* **20/1**

300- 4 *1/2* **Amorously (IRE)**[131] 9637 3-9-1 **69**........................ SeanLevey 8 68
(Richard Hannon) *chsd ldrs: wnt 2nd over 2f out: rdn over 1f out: wknd towards fin* **16/1**

666- 5 *1 1/2* **Eesha's Smile (IRE)**[158] 9226 3-9-6 **74**........................ SilvestreDeSousa 14 70
(Ivan Furtado) *led: hdd over 8f out: chsd wnr tl rdn over 2f out: wknd ins fnl f* **12/1**

30-4 6 *1* **Navigate By Stars (IRE)**[15] 1824 3-9-2 **70**........................ RichardKingscote 5 64
(Tom Dascombe) *s.i.s: hld up: rdn over 3f out: styd on appr fnl f: nvr nrr* **4/1[1]**

46-6 7 *1 3/4* **Petits Fours**[22] 1656 3-8-13 **67**........................(h[1]) WilliamBuick 13 58
(Charlie Fellowes) *broke wl: stdd and lost pl over 8f out: rdn and hung lft over 1f out: nt trble ldrs* **20/1**

020- 8 *hd* **Arctic Ocean (IRE)**[167] 9049 3-9-1 **69**........................ OisinMurphy 1 59
(Sir Michael Stoute) *hld up: hdwy over 5f out: wknd 2f out* **9/2[2]**

64-0 9 *nk* **Sukalia**[15] 1825 3-8-8 **62**........................ CallumShepherd 10 52
(Alan King) *s.i.s: hld up: hdwy over 2f out: wknd fnl f* **33/1**

036- 10 *1 1/2* **Tasman Sea**[166] 9068 3-9-4 **72**........................ HollieDoyle 9 59
(Archie Watson) *prom: pushed along over 4f out: wknd over 1f out* **25/1**

060- 11 *1 1/4* **Rainbow Spirit**[189] 8511 3-8-10 **64** ow1........................(h[1]) StevieDonohoe 11 48
(Ed Dunlop) *s.s: nvr on terms* **66/1**

025- **12** *3* **Say Nothing**[153] 9291 3-9-6 **74** .... AdamKirby 4 52
(Hughie Morrison) *hld up in tch: rdn and wknd over 2f out* **15/2**[3]
644- **13** *½* **Guroor**[137] 9530 3-9-7 **75** .... (h[1]) AndreaAtzeni 3 52
(Marco Botti) *hld up: rdn over 4f out: wknd over 2f out* **8/1**
523- **14** *1 ¼* **Canavese**[237] 6941 3-9-2 **70** .... CharlesBishop 6 45
(Eve Johnson Houghton) *hld up: rdn over 3f out: sn wknd* **20/1**

2m 13.98s (0.58) **Going Correction** -0.10s/f (Good) **14** Ran SP% **117.4**
Speed ratings (Par 95): **93,91,89,89,88 87,86,85,85,84 83,81,80,79**
CSF £77.17 CT £1576.39 TOTE £9.50: £2.60, £2.60, £7.20; EX 72.90 Trifecta £1166.90.
Owner C G Rowles Nicholson **Bred** Limestone Stud **Trained** Willoughton, Lincs
FOCUS
The second and third came through late but for much of this race few got competitive, the fourth being the only two to seriously challenge the winner. The runner-up helps with the standard.

2254 BET AT RACINGTV.COM H'CAP — 1m 6f
4:35 (4:35) (Class 4) (0-80,80) 4-Y-O+
£6,469 (£1,925; £962; £481; £300; £300) **Stalls** Low

Form RPR
522- **1** **Orin Swift (IRE)**[198] 8230 5-9-6 **78** .... RichardKingscote 1 85
(Jonathan Portman) *led 1f: chsd ldrs: led again over 3f out: shkn up over 2f out: rdn out* **3/1**[2]
3431 **2** *¾* **Knight Crusader**[50] 1144 7-9-6 **78** .... AdamKirby 9 83
(John O'Shea) *hld up: shkn up over 5f out: hdwy u.p over 2f out: styd on to go 2nd nr fin* **16/1**
446- **3** *½* **Really Super**[186] 4130 5-9-0 **72** .... SilvestreDeSousa 8 76
(Amy Murphy) *chsd ldr over 12f out: rdn over 2f out: styd on same pce ins fnl f* **15/2**[3]
36-1 **4** *nk* **Valkenburg**[21] 1663 4-8-3 **67** .... SeanDavis(5) 6 70+
(Harriet Bethell) *prom: lost pl over 10f out: pushed along over 8f out: rdn and outpcd over 4f out: r.o ins fnl f* **14/1**
0/0- **5** *5* **Steaming (IRE)**[364] 2245 5-9-3 **75** .... HarryBentley 10 71
(Ralph Beckett) *chsd ldrs: rdn over 2f out: wknd ins fnl f* **33/1**
40-3 **6** *nk* **Champagne Champ**[9] 291 7-9-7 **79** .... (bt) OisinMurphy 2 75
(Rod Millman) *s.i.s: sn pushed along to go prom: rdn: carried hd high and lost pl wl over 3f out: styd on ins fnl f (trainer said gelding was unsuited by being unable to dominate and resent being crowded)* **6/4**[1]
403- **7** *3 ½* **Midnight Wilde**[182] 8716 4-9-7 **80** .... GeraldMosse 7 72
(John Ryan) *hld up: hdwy over 6f out: wknd over 2f out: eased over 1f out (jockey said gelding had no more to give)* **14/1**
321/ **8** *shd* **Remember The Man (IRE)**[118] 6-9-1 **73** .... WilliamBuick 4 64
(Michael Bell) *led after 1f: rdn and hdd over 3f out: wknd over 1f out* **12/1**
14-2 **9** *12* **Flower Power**[13] 1848 8-8-12 **70** .... (p) DougieCostello 5 44
(Tony Coyle) *hld up: rdn over 3f out: wknd wl over 1f out* **16/1**
6-00 **10** *10* **Outofthequestion**[38] 1292 5-8-12 **70** .... CallumShepherd 3 30
(Alan King) *hld up: rdn over 3f out: wknd wl over 1f out* **28/1**

3m 7.94s (1.54) **Going Correction** -0.10s/f (Good)
WFA 4 from 5yo+ 1lb **10** Ran SP% **115.9**
Speed ratings (Par 105): **91,90,90,90,87 87,85,85,78,72**
CSF £49.94 CT £332.21 TOTE £4.30: £1.70, £2.70, £2.00; EX 51.10 Trifecta £249.90.
Owner Laurence Bellman **Bred** Northern Bloodstock Agency Ltd **Trained** Upper Lambourn, Berks
FOCUS
A fair staying contest, but a bit muddling and the form is rated cautiously.

2255 RACING TV PROFITS RETURNED TO RACING H'CAP — 5f 8y
5:10 (5:11) (Class 4) (0-85,82) 3-Y-O
£6,469 (£1,925; £962; £481; £300; £300) **Stalls** High

Form RPR
02-1 **1** **Free Love**[20] 1691 3-9-1 **81** .... TheodoreLadd(5) 6 90
(Michael Appleby) *chsd ldrs: led and hung lft fr over 1f out: rdn out* **5/2**[1]
-3 **2** *1 ¾* **Tenax (IRE)**[17] 1762 3-9-1 **81** .... FayeMcManoman(5) 2 83
(Nigel Tinkler) *s.i.s: hdwy over 1f out: r.o to go 2nd wl ins fnl f: no ch w wnr* **4/1**[3]
2343 **3** *2 ½* **Key To Power**[3] 2121 3-8-9 **75** .... AndrewBreslin(5) 4 68
(Mark Johnston) *led: rdn and hdd over 1f out: hung lft and no ex ins fnl f* **5/1**
52-4 **4** *3 ½* **Converter (IRE)**[18] 1729 3-9-7 **82** .... WilliamBuick 5 62
(Mick Channon) *chsd ldrs: rdn 1/2-way: wknd over 1f out* **7/2**[2]
24-2 **5** *¾* **Khafooq**[20] 1691 3-8-6 **72** .... SeanDavis(5) 3 50
(Robert Cowell) *chsd ldr: hung lft 1/2-way: rdn and ev ch over 1f out: wknd ins fnl f* **4/1**[3]
010- **6** *2 ¾* **Red Saree (IRE)**[211] 7836 3-9-1 **76** .... (h) AdamKirby 1 44
(Michael Wigham) *s.i.s: a in rr: wknd over 1f out* **20/1**

59.6s (-0.60) **Going Correction** -0.10s/f (Good) **6** Ran SP% **112.2**
Speed ratings (Par 100): **100,97,93,87,86 82**
CSF £12.75 TOTE £2.80: £1.60, £1.60; EX 12.60 Trifecta £46.20.
Owner The North South Syndicate **Bred** Brendan Boyle Bloodstock Ltd **Trained** Oakham, Rutland
FOCUS
They finished well strung out here and the winner looks a much-improved filly this year. A decent race for the grade.
T/Plt: £146.20 to a £1 stake. Pool: £44,563.22 - 222.46 winning units T/Qpdt: £38.30 to a £1 stake. Pool: £6,306.27 - 121.80 winning units **Colin Roberts**

2019 YARMOUTH (L-H)
Tuesday, April 30

OFFICIAL GOING: Good (good to firm in places; watered; 7.4)
Wind: light breeze Weather: overcast early; sunny from race four; 11 degrees

2256 HAVEN SEASHORE HOLIDAY PARK H'CAP — 1m 3y
2:15 (2:16) (Class 6) (0-65,66) 4-Y-O+
£3,105 (£924; £461; £300; £300; £300) **Stalls** Centre

Form RPR
00-5 **1** **Oud Metha Bridge (IRE)**[25] 1563 5-9-1 **66** .... SeanKirrane(7) 8 73
(Julia Feilden) *cl up: wnt 2nd 3f out: rdn to ld ins fnl f: a gng wl after: pushed out* **9/2**[2]
00-4 **2** *nk* **Buckland Beau**[21] 1659 8-9-0 **65** .... AledBeech(7) 11 71
(Charlie Fellowes) *towards rr: hdwy in 4th over 2f out: rdn and sustained chal fnl f: kpt on wl to go 2nd fnl 75yds: a jst hld by wnr* **9/1**[3]
-061 **3** *1* **Take It Down Under**[7] 2019 4-9-3 **63** 5ex .... (t) GeorgiaDobie(7) 4 67
(Amy Murphy) *led and t.k.h: rdn 2f out: hdd ins fnl f: wkng whn lost 2nd 75yds out (jockey said gelding hung right-handed up the home straight)* **5/6**[1]
-350 **4** *2 ¾* **Screaming Gemini (IRE)**[20] 1675 5-9-4 **62** .... LukeMorris 9 60
(Tony Carroll) *bhd: shkn up after 3f: hrd rdn and hdwy to go 4th ins fnl f: racing awkwardly and nvr looked like landing a blow (vet said gelding lost its left fore shoe)* **28/1**
0-35 **5** *1 ½* **Boxatricks (IRE)**[20] 1675 4-8-9 **53** .... ShelleyBirkett 13 47
(Julia Feilden) *bhd: hdwy 3f out: tried to chal alone on stands' rails 2f out: rdn and no ex over 1f out (jockey said gelding hung right-handed)* **16/1**
00-0 **6** *¾* **Fair Power (IRE)**[20] 1675 5-9-0 **58** .... KieranO'Neill 7 51
(John Butler) *t.k.h and prom: rdn 2f out: btn over 1f out* **25/1**
033- **7** *1 ½* **Comporta**[157] 9253 4-9-1 **59** .... (b[1]) TomQueally 2 48
(Ismail Mohammed) *t.k.h: chsd ldrs: drvn over 2f out: sn btn* **10/1**
0-00 **8** *¾* **Enzo (IRE)**[22] 1653 4-9-0 **58** .... LiamKeniry 12 45
(John Butler) *t.k.h pressing ldrs: drvn and wknd 2f out (jockey said gelding failed to pick up when asked at 2f out)* **20/1**
650- **9** *3 ¾* **Harvest Ranger**[222] 7460 5-8-7 **51** oh6 .... (v) EoinWalsh 6 30
(Michael Appleby) *cl up: hrd drvn over 2f out: lost pl v tamely* **28/1**
0004 **10** *3 ¾* **Percy Toplis**[7] 2019 5-8-2 **51** oh6 .... (b) RhiainIngram(5) 3 21
(Christine Dunnett) *cl up: drvn over 2f out: fnd nil: wl btn over 1f out* **40/1**
000- **11** *nk* **Make On Madam (IRE)**[218] 7627 7-9-2 **60** .... LewisEdmunds 5 29
(Les Eyre) *midfield: rdn and wknd 3f out* **28/1**
0-00 **12** *6* **Astrojewel**[34] 1368 4-8-11 **55** .... (h[1]) JFEgan 1 11
(Mark H Tompkins) *wnt lft s: nvr bttr than midfield: rdn and labouring 3f out: t.o* **66/1**
00-0 **13** *18* **Magwadiri (IRE)**[21] 1659 5-8-7 **56** .... DylanHogan(5) 10 +
(Mark Loughnane) *lost abt 20 l at s: in tch by 1/2-way but no hope of rcvry: t.o and eased over 1f out (jockey said gelding was slowly away)* **16/1**

1m 36.85s (-1.35) **Going Correction** -0.075s/f (Good) **13** Ran SP% **126.5**
Speed ratings (Par 101): **103,102,101,98,97 96,95,94,90,86 86,80,62**
CSF £43.83 CT £69.10 TOTE £5.60: £1.30, £2.50, £1.10; EX 37.70 Trifecta £86.10.
Owner In It To Win Partnership **Bred** Rabbah Bloodstock Limited **Trained** Exning, Suffolk
■ Stewards' Enquiry : Sean Kirrane four-day ban: misuse of whip (May 14-17)
FOCUS
Modest sprinting form. The winner basically ran to his previous best turf figure.

2257 RACING WELFARE MAIDEN STKS (PLUS 10 RACE) — 5f 42y
2:45 (2:46) (Class 4) 2-Y-O
£4,787 (£1,424; £711; £355) **Stalls** Centre

Form RPR
1 **Fleeting Princess** 2-9-0 0 .... RyanMoore 2 73+
(Jeremy Noseda) *t.k.h and cl up: rdn 1/2-way: led over 1f out: pushed out cl home: readily* **8/13**[1]
2 *1* **Taste The Nectar (USA)** 2-9-0 0 .... LukeMorris 4 69
(Robert Cowell) *unruly in paddock: missed break and swished tail: green and t.k.h: sn pressing ldrs: rdn 1/2-way: wnt 2nd over 1f out: a hld ins fnl f but kpt on pleasingly: promising* **14/1**
3 **3** *1 ½* **Don't Joke**[11] 1910 2-9-5 0 .... FrankieDettori 5 69
(Mark Johnston) *pressed ldr: rdn 1/2-way: 3rd and no imp fnl f but kpt on* **9/4**[2]
4 *2 ½* **Dark Side Division** 2-9-5 0 .... BrettDoyle 3 60
(John Ryan) *in last pair: rdn 1/2-way: btn wl over 1f out* **33/1**
35 **5** *1* **Champagne Supanova (IRE)**[10] 1953 2-9-5 0 .... JamieSpencer 1 56
(Richard Spencer) *led: rdn 2f out: hdd over 1f out: racd awkwardly and sn lost pl* **8/1**[3]

1m 1.9s **Going Correction** -0.075s/f (Good) **5** Ran SP% **113.4**
Speed ratings (Par 94): **97,95,93,89,87**
CSF £11.30 TOTE £1.30: £1.10, £4.10; EX 8.40 Trifecta £15.60.
Owner Mrs Susan Roy **Bred** Aspire Stallions & Bloodstock Ltd **Trained** Newmarket, Suffolk
FOCUS
The two fillies' came to the fore in what looked an average juvenile maiden. The initial ratings will be very fluid.

2258 WEATHERBYS GLOBAL STALLIONS APP NOVICE STKS (PLUS 10 RACE) — 1m 3f 104y
3:15 (3:15) (Class 3) 3-Y-O
£9,703 (£2,887; £1,443; £721) **Stalls** Low

Form RPR
04-2 **1** **Babbo's Boy (IRE)**[12] 1898 3-9-2 79 .... RyanMoore 4 84
(Michael Bell) *2nd tl led over 2f out: sn almost jnd: rdn over 1f out: led fnl 75yds and battled on wl* **15/8**[2]
1 **2** *nk* **Questionare**[57] 1019 3-9-8 0 .... (t) FrankieDettori 3 89
(John Gosden) *dropped out in last pair: hdwy on outer 3f out: rdn and pressed wnr clly 2f out tl fnl 75yds: remained w ev ch tl outbattled nr fin* **7/4**[1]
21 **3** *6* **Rochester House (IRE)**[21] 1661 3-9-8 0 .... JFEgan 1 79
(Mark Johnston) *led: drvn and hdd over 2f out: sn lost tch w ldng pair* **3/1**[3]
03- **4** *1 ½* **Vexed**[181] 8738 3-9-2 0 .... JamieSpencer 2 72
(David Simcock) *t.k.h and stdd in 3rd pl: rdn and outpcd over 2f out: sn wl btn: eased cl home* **6/1**

2m 25.68s (-2.12) **Going Correction** -0.075s/f (Good) **4** Ran SP% **110.4**
Speed ratings (Par 102): **104,103,99,98**
CSF £5.65 TOTE £2.50; EX 5.80 Trifecta £13.70.
Owner Amo Racing Limited **Bred** Lynch Bages & Camas Park Stud **Trained** Newmarket, Suffolk
FOCUS
A fair novice run at an okay gallop and the two pulled clear. The form makes sense.

2259 GROSVENOR CASINO OF GREAT YARMOUTH H'CAP — 1m 2f 23y
3:45 (3:49) (Class 5) (0-70,72) 4-Y-O+
£3,752 (£1,116; £557; £300; £300; £300) **Stalls** Low

Form RPR
2202 **1** **Gas Monkey**[29] 1482 4-9-2 **63** .... (h[1]) ShelleyBirkett 5 72
(Julia Feilden) *trckd ldrs: effrt and squeezed through 2f out: led wl over 1f out: sn rdn and edgd rt but readily drew clr and in command fnl f* **3/1**[2]
/05- **2** *2* **Nasee**[188] 8534 4-9-0 **61** .... (p[1]) JamieSpencer 2 66
(Ed Vaughan) *cl up: drvn 3f out: outpcd 2f out: kpt on again to go 2nd ins fnl f: no ch w wnr* **11/4**[1]
5062 **3** *hd* **Luna Magic**[3] 2112 5-8-6 **55** .... (h) BrettDoyle 4 60
(Lydia Pearce) *2nd or 3rd tl rdn and lost pl over 3f out: kpt on again ins fnl f but no match for wnr* **7/2**[3]
-144 **4** *¾* **The Night King**[12] 1882 4-9-11 **72** .... TomQueally 6 75
(Mick Quinn) *dropped out last for 6f out: effrt on outer 3f out: rdn and tried to chal wl over 1f out: no ex ins fnl f* **13/2**
-032 **5** *¾* **Pendo**[24] 1591 8-9-4 **65** .... KierenFox 7 67
(John Best) *plld hrd on outside: prog after 3f: 2nd home turn: led 3f out tl rdn and hdd wl over 1f out: lost pl tamely ins fnl f (jockey said gelding ran too freely)* **7/1**

623- **6** 3¼ **Go Fox**[160] 9168 4-9-7 **68**...............................(h) KieranO'Neill 8 63
(Tom Clover) *t.k.h in rr: drvn 3f out: carried hd high and fnd nthing and sn btn* **8/1**

316- **7** 76 **Right About Now (IRE)**[189] 8513 5-9-6 **67**...............(b) LewisEdmunds 1
(Charlie Wallis) *led: rdn and hdd 3f out: sn bhd: t.o and virtually p.u: lame (jockey said gelding stopped quickly; vet said gelding was lame on its right fore)* **10/1**

2m 8.36s (-0.44) **Going Correction** -0.075s/f (Good) 7 Ran SP% **119.9**
Speed ratings (Par 103): **98,96,96,95,95 92,31**
CSF £12.58 CT £30.41 TOTE £3.40: £3.20, £1.80; EX 14.40 Trifecta £43.90.
Owner Newmarket Equine Tours Racing Club **Bred** Julia Feilden **Trained** Exning, Suffolk

FOCUS
The right horses came to the fore in this modest handicap. Ordinary form, the winner finding a bit for the hood.

2260 RIVERSIDE RENTAL LADIES OF HORNING H'CAP 7f 3y
4:15 (4:17) (Class 3) (0-95,95) 4-Y-0+ £7,246 (£2,168; £1,084; £542) **Stalls** Centre

Form RPR

60-4 **1** **Lake Volta (IRE)**[10] 1944 4-9-7 **95**.................................... RyanMoore 1 100
(Mark Johnston) *mde all: rdn 2f out: fnd plenty to assert ins fnl f* **4/6**[1]

126- **2** 1¾ **Whinmoor**[207] 7950 4-9-0 **91**.................................... RowanScott(3) 5 91
(Nigel Tinkler) *disp 2nd: rdn 2f out: tried to chal ins fnl f: wl hld fnl 100yds: game effrt* **6/1**[3]

0 **3** 3¾ **Givinitsum (SAF)**[31] 1414 3-9-3 **93**.................................... FrankieDettori 2 81
(Eve Johnson Houghton) *disp 2nd tl drvn wl over 2f out: fdd over 1f out* **10/1**

0-00 **4** 6 **Burguillos**[14] 1829 6-9-0 **88**.............................(t) JamieSpencer 3 62
(Stuart Williams) *a last: rdn over 2f out: fnd nil: sn struggling* **11/4**[2]

1m 23.82s (-1.28) **Going Correction** -0.075s/f (Good)
WFA 3 from 4yo+ 13lb 4 Ran SP% **110.0**
Speed ratings (Par 107): **104,102,97,90**
CSF £5.22 TOTE £1.30; EX 4.60 Trifecta £12.30.
Owner Sheikh Hamdan bin Mohammed Al Maktoum **Bred** Godolphin **Trained** Middleham Moor, N Yorks

FOCUS
Just the four of them but still a decent little handicap. The winner is rated close to his best.

2261 SKY SPORTS RACING SKY 415 FILLIES' H'CAP 7f 3y
4:50 (4:51) (Class 5) (0-70,72) 4-Y-0+
£3,752 (£1,116; £557; £300; £300; £300) **Stalls** Centre

Form RPR

561 **1** **Dream World (IRE)**[4] 2081 4-9-4 **65** 5ex................ JoshuaBryan(3) 1 75+
(Michael Appleby) *last early: hdwy on outer 2f out: pushed ahd fnl 120yds: sn clr* **13/8**[1]

0050 **2** 2¼ **Sonnet Rose (IRE)**[12] 1880 5-9-0 **61**.........................(bt) NickyMackay 6 65
(Conrad Allen) *cl up: led gng wl 3f out: rdn over 1f out: hdd and outpcd fnl 120yds* **5/1**[2]

/6-5 **3** 1½ **Angel's Whisper (IRE)**[34] 1355 4-9-1 **62**...............(h) LewisEdmunds 3 62
(Amy Murphy) *lost 5 l s: towards rr: swtchd rt sharply 3f out: rdn and effrt over 1f out: unable to chal* **8/1**

12-0 **4** 2 **Agent Of Fortune**[36] 1338 4-9-2 **63**.................................... KieranO'Neill 4 58
(Christine Dunnett) *chsd ldrs: rdn over 2f out: btn over 1f out* **5/1**[2]

41-0 **5** 4½ **Rotherhithe**[54] 1061 4-9-2 **68**.................................... DylanHogan(5) 2 50
(Henry Spiller) *taken down early: awkward leaving stalls: led: rdn and hdd 3f out: lost pl wl over 1f out* **10/1**

-316 **6** 27 **Elenora Delight**[28] 1511 4-9-4 **72**...............................(t) StefanoCherchi(7) 5
(Marco Botti) *2nd tl pushed along 1/2-way: sn fdd: t.o over 1f out* **6/1**[3]

10-3 **F** **Spanish Mane (IRE)**[7] 2019 4-8-11 **58**.................................... ShelleyBirkett 8
(Julia Feilden) *t.k.h: chsd ldrs and handy tl n.m.r and fell wl over 1f out (clipped heels)* **15/2**

1m 24.52s (-0.58) **Going Correction** -0.075s/f (Good) 7 Ran SP% **117.7**
Speed ratings (Par 100): **100,97,95,93,88 57,**
CSF £10.60 CT £51.25 TOTE £2.30: £1.70, £2.30; EX 10.80 Trifecta £56.60.
Owner Rod In Pickle Partnership **Bred** Miss L Cronin & Mrs U Lawler **Trained** Oakham, Rutland

FOCUS
Having started centre-field the action unfolded towards the stands' side, the favourite getting well on top late. She backed up her Doncaster win in this uncompetitive race.

2262 DRIFTERS FISH AND CHIP ALL EVENTS H'CAP 1m 3y
5:25 (5:40) (Class 6) (0-55,56) 3-Y-0
£3,105 (£924; £461; £300; £300; £300) **Stalls** Centre

Form RPR

502 **1** **Act Of Magic (IRE)**[26] 1549 3-9-3 **51**.................................... KieranO'Neill 11 57
(Mohamed Moubarak) *cl up: hrd drvn over 2f out: led over 1f out: holding rivals after* **7/2**[1]

00-0 **2** 1 **Approve The Dream (IRE)**[20] 1678 3-9-4 **55**............. JoshuaBryan(3) 6 59
(Julia Feilden) *led: rdn and hdd over 1f out: hld by wnr after but kpt on wl* **16/1**

00-0 **3** ½ **Nabvutika (IRE)**[10] 1957 3-9-3 **51**.................................... TomQueally 1 54
(John Butler) *bhd: last at 1/2-way: rdn and hdwy on stands' rail 1f out: fin wl: too much to do* **22/1**

60-5 **4** 1 **Parknacilla (IRE)**[36] 1332 3-9-0 **53**.................................... DylanHogan(5) 10 53
(Henry Spiller) *missed break: towards rr: rdn and effrt wl over 1f out: wnt 3rd briefly but nt qckn ins fnl f* **5/1**[2]

605- **5** nk **Kahina (IRE)**[175] 8890 3-9-1 **56**...............................(p[1]) GeorgiaDobie(7) 12 56
(Hugo Palmer) *t.k.h: prom: pushed along 2f out: outpcd over 1f out* **15/2**[3]

-002 **6** 3 **Power Of Life (USA)**[18] 1725 3-8-11 **52**.......................... SaraDelFabbro(7) 7 45
(Michael Bell) *t.k.h: prom: pushed along 2f out: btn over 1f out* **5/1**[2]

0-02 **7** shd **Fitzy**[8] 1979 3-8-12 **46**...............................(p) LewisEdmunds 9 38
(David Brown) *nvr bttr than midfield: rdn and btn wl over 1f out* **7/2**[1]

000- **8** 1¾ **Laura Louise (IRE)**[216] 7668 3-9-3 **54**.......................... RowanScott(3) 8 42
(Nigel Tinkler) *missed break: a bhd* **28/1**

-004 **9** hd **Tunky**[84] 612 3-9-4 **52**.................................... JFEgan 2 40
(James Given) *cl up: rdn 3f out: wknd 2f out* **10/1**

5364 **10** 1¾ **Al Daayen (FR)**[10] 1935 3-9-3 **51**.............................(b) TadhgO'Shea 5 35
(Mark Johnston) *missed break: sn racing freely on outer: rdn 2f out: fnd nil: eased ins fnl f* **12/1**

1m 38.09s (-0.11) **Going Correction** -0.075s/f (Good) 10 Ran SP% **120.0**
Speed ratings (Par 96): **97,96,95,94,94 91,91,89,89,87**
CSF £65.25 CT £1114.97 TOTE £4.60: £1.60, £5.90, £7.50; EX 64.00 Trifecta £731.30.
Owner The Mojito Partnership **Bred** Mr & Mrs W Evans **Trained** Newmarket, Suffolk
■ Stewards' Enquiry : Kieran O'Neill two-day ban: misuse of whip (May 14-15)

FOCUS
Moderate 3yo form, with the pace slow. Not form to dwell on.
T/Plt: £30.00 to a £1 stake. Pool: £47,271.49 - 1148.27 winning units T/Qpdt: £18.40 to a £1 stake. Pool: £3,362.46 - 134.83 winning units **Iain Mackenzie**

1842 CHANTILLY (R-H)
Tuesday, April 30

OFFICIAL GOING: Polytrack: standard; turf: soft

2263a PRIX DU VIADUC DE COMMELLES (CLAIMER) (2YO) (TURF) 5f
10:55 2-Y-0 £12,162 (£4,864; £3,648; £2,432; £1,216)

RPR

1 **Jolie (FR)**[20] 1709 2-8-8 0.................................... MaximeGuyon 3 73+
(Andrea Marcialis, France) **13/10**[1]

2 3 **Jayadeeva (FR)** 2-8-11 0.................................... CristianDemuro 7 65
(A Giorgi, Italy) **43/5**

3 hd **My Premier County (FR)** 2-9-1 0.........................(p) ClementLecoeuvre 2 68
(Matthieu Palussiere, France) **24/1**

4 nk **Panthera Tigris**[20] 1709 2-8-8 0.........................(b[1]) MickaelBarzalona 9 60
(Jo Hughes, France) *led centre gp and overall ldr: pushed along whn gps merged wl over 2f out: hdd 1 1/2f out: kpt on u.p ins fnl f* **12/1**

5 3 **Lost In France (IRE)**[22] 1657 2-8-11 0.................................... AntoineHamelin 6 52
(Matthieu Palussiere, France) **76/10**[3]

6 2 **Lalacelle (FR)** 2-8-5 0.................................... MlleCoraliePacaut(3) 4 42
(M Boutin, France) **43/10**[2]

7 ½ **Night Of The Opera (IRE)** 2-8-3 0.................................... MllePerrineCheyer(8) 1 43
(Matthieu Palussiere, France) **27/1**

8 1¼ **Captain Tatman (FR)**[20] 1709 2-8-11 0.................................... IoritzMendizabal 5 39
(M Krebs, France) **89/10**

9 1¼ **Illumina** 2-8-6 0.................................... ThomasTrullier(5) 10 34
(Gavin Hernon, France) **14/1**

10 20 **Look At Him**[22] 1657 2-9-4 0.........................(b[1]) TheoBachelot 8
(Jo Hughes, France) *bustled along early in centre gp: outpcd and in rr whn gps merged wl over 2f out: sn wl btn: eased fnl f* **28/1**

1m 0.02s (1.72) 10 Ran SP% **119.9**
PARI-MUTUEL (all including 1 euro stake): WIN 2.30 PLACE 1.30, 2.20, 4.70 DF 7.70.
Owner Torsten Raber **Bred** E Ciampi & P Nataf **Trained** France

2264a PRIX DE LA FU MADAME (CLAIMER) (4YO) (ALL-WEATHER TRACK) (POLYTRACK) 1m 2f 110y(P)
12:25 4-Y-0 £8,558 (£3,423; £2,567; £1,711; £855)

RPR

1 **Sensazione Poy**[12] 1908 4-8-13 0.................................... AlexandreChesneau(5) 5 77
(G Botti, France) **27/10**[1]

2 4 **Katie Or (FR)**[228] 4-8-13 0.................................... ChristopheSoumillon 12 64
(F Vermeulen, France) **33/10**[2]

3 hd **Neige Eternelle (FR)**[25] 1578 4-9-0 ow1........ Pierre-CharlesBoudot 14 65
(H-A Pantall, France) **10/1**

4 1 **Montgaroult (FR)**[47] 4-8-11 0.................................... DelphineSantiago(4) 8 64
(B De Montzey, France) **11/2**[3]

5 ¾ **Cape Greco (USA)**[7] 2026 4-9-4 0.................................... TheoBachelot 9 66
(Jo Hughes, France) *mid-div: pushed along and effrt on outer fr 3f out: rdn 1 1/2f out: limited rspnse: kpt on ins fnl f but nvr in contention* **44/5**

6 3½ **Tremont (FR)**[14] 4-9-5 0.................................... VincentCheminaud 11 60
(D De Waele, France) **20/1**

7 snk **Fakir Bere (FR)**[14] 4-8-11 0.........................(p) CristianDemuro 4 52
(P Adda, France) **17/1**

8 ¾ **Ever Love (FR)**[12] 4-8-8 0.................................... AnthonyCrastus 6 47
(C Boutin, France) **10/1**

9 ¾ **Tutti (FR)**[125] 4-8-7 0.................................... TristanBaron(1) 13 46
(D De Waele, France) **84/1**

10 3½ **Forbidden City (FR)**[74] 4-8-10 0.................................... DylanVanBelleghem(6) 10 47
(S Cerulis, France) **13/1**

11 2 **Sea Weed (FR)**[247] 6604 4-8-8 0.........................(b) AurelienLemaitre 2 35
(G Doleuze, France) **31/1**

12 5 **Forban Du Large (FR)**[76] 4-8-6 0.................................... DamienBoutet(5) 1 29
(Xavier Hondier, France) **94/1**

13 ¾ **Grise Magicienne (FR)**[8] 2002 4-8-5 0.................................... MlleLauraGrosso(6) 3 28
(Gerard Aidant, France) **105/1**

14 5½ **Mapocho (FR)**[15] 4-8-9 0.................................... MlleCrystalMiette(9) 15 24
(Frederic Lamotte D'Argy, France) **103/1**

15 ½ **Pepito (IRE)**[138] 4-8-8 0.................................... JeromeMoutard(3) 16 16
(Tania Filipa Vieira Teixeira, France) **144/1**

2m 12.13s 15 Ran SP% **119.5**
PARI-MUTUEL (all including 1 euro stake): WIN 3.70 PLACE 1.60, 1.60, 2.20 DF 7.10.
Owner Giulio Spozio **Bred** Scuderia Blueberry SRL **Trained** France

2265a PRIX DE MONGRESIN (CLAIMER) (3YO) (TURF) 1m 2f
1:07 3-Y-0 £12,162 (£4,864; £3,648; £2,432; £1,216)

RPR

1 **Balgees Time (FR)**[18] 3-8-8 0.................................... CristianDemuro 10 72
(A Schutz, France) **48/10**[3]

2 2 **Bigmouth (FR)**[31] 3-8-6 0.................................... JimmyTastayre(5) 2 71
(M Le Forestier, France) **17/2**

3 ¾ **Mirabelle (FR)**[53] 3-8-8 0.................................... MaximeGuyon 3 67
(C Laffon-Parias, France) **13/5**[1]

4 snk **Attirance (FR)** 3-8-4 0.................................... ThomasTrullier(7) 7 69
(N Clement, France) **6/1**

5 ½ **Dassom (IRE)**[12] 3-8-6 0.................................... AlexandreChesneau(5) 9 68
(G Botti, France) **22/5**[2]

6 snk **Winman In Grey (FR)**[188] 3-8-6 0.................................... MlleMarieTrublet(9) 6 72
(Y Barberot, France) **29/1**

7 ¾ **Trent (HUN)**[125] 3-7-13 0.................................... MllePerrineCheyer(9) 5 63
(Z Hegedus, Hungary) **116/1**

8 3½ **Zerano (FR)**[38] 3-8-11 0.................................... VincentCheminaud 8 59
(H-A Pantall, France) **76/10**

9 1¾ **Lovely Miss (FR)**[50] 3-8-8 0.........................(p) TonyPiccone 12 53
(H De Nicolay, France) **84/10**

10 2½ **Cinquain**[28] 1512 3-8-8 0.................................... Louis-PhilippeBeuzelin 11 48
(Jo Hughes, France) *led after 2f: asked to qckn whn chal 2 1/2f out: sn hdd: grad wknd fr 2f out: no ex fnl f* **67/1**

11 hd **Save You (FR)** 3-8-3 0.................................... MlleOphelieThiebaut(8) 1 51
(J-Y Artu, France) **84/1**

12 1 ¾ **Giving Wings (FR)**[12] 3-8-11 0 AntoineHamelin 4 47
(Matthieu Palussiere, France) 63/1

2m 7.57s (2.77) 12 Ran SP% 119.0
PARI-MUTUEL (all including 1 euro stake): WIN 5.80 PLACE 1.80, 2.40, 1.70 DF 19.90.
Owner Jaber Abdullah **Bred** S A S U Ecurie Normandie Pur Sang **Trained** France

2266a PRIX DE L'HEMICYCLE (CONDITIONS) (4YO+) (ALL-WEATHER TRACK) (POLYTRACK) 1m 1f 110y(P)
1:42 4-Y-O+

£12,612 (£4,792; £3,531; £2,018; £1,009; £756)

RPR

1 **Apollo Flight (FR)**[14] 4-8-11 0 TheoBachelot 9 89
(L Gadbin, France) 22/5[2]

2 3 **Aydon Castle (IRE)**[23] 4-8-4 0 AugustinMadamet(7) 3 83
(A Fabre, France) *racd a little keenly: led on inner: hdd over 1/2-way: pushed along over 2f out: kpt on in clr 2nd ins fnl f: no ch w wnr* 12/5[1]

3 4 **Replenish (FR)**[20] [1708] 6-9-6 0 VincentCheminaud 1 84
(S Cerulis, France) 36/5

4 snk **Teenage Gal (IRE)**[14] 4-8-13 0 StephanePasquier 7 76
(Gavin Hernon, France) 9/2[3]

5 snk **Park Bloom (IRE)**[15] [1827] 4-8-8 0 (p) MickaelBarzalona 6 71
(H-F Devin, France) 77/10

6 ¾ **Wooden (FR)**[232] [7142] 4-8-11 0 (b) Pierre-CharlesBoudot 11 72
(Y Durepaire, France) 56/10

7 nk **Perfect Pitch (GER)** 5-8-10 0 CyrilleStefan 10 71
(S Smrczek, Germany) 20/1

8 2 ½ **Turn Of Luck (IRE)**[101] [309] 4-9-0 0 (p) MickaelBerto 4 70
(I Endaltsev, Czech Republic) 26/1

9 2 ½ **Idle Wheel (FR)**[301] 7-8-6 0 ThomasTrullier(5) 8 61
(F-X Belvisi, France) 23/1

10 snk **Alonso Cano (IRE)**[107] [232] 4-8-11 0 (b) Louis-PhilippeBeuzelin 2 61
(Jo Hughes, France) *t.k.h: towards rr of mid-div: struggling to go pce and pushed along 3f out: no imp and grad wknd fr 2f out* 62/1

1m 56.48s 10 Ran SP% 119.2
PARI-MUTUEL (all including 1 euro stake): WIN 5.40 PLACE 1.70, 1.50, 2.00 DF 7.50.
Owner Mrs Waltraut Spanner **Bred** Mrs W Spanner **Trained** France

ASCOT (R-H)
Wednesday, May 1

OFFICIAL GOING: Good to firm (good in places; watered; str 8.3, rnd 7.9)
Wind: Almost nil, becoming moderate against last two races Weather: Cloudy

2267 IRISH THOROUGHBRED MARKETING ROYAL ASCOT TWO-YEAR-OLD TRIAL CONDITIONS STKS (PLUS 10 RACE) 5f
2:15 (2:15) (Class 2) 2-Y-O £9,056 (£2,695; £1,346; £673) **Stalls** Centre

Form RPR

1 1 **Ventura Rebel**[18] [1759] 2-9-5 0 PaulHanagan 4 95
(Richard Fahey) *athletic; pushed along after 2f and struggling to stay in tch: sed to stay on over 1f out: clsd qckly fnl f to ld fnl 75yds: won gng away* 20/1

2 1 **Lady Pauline (USA)**[26] 2-9-0 0 (bt) JohnRVelazquez 6 86
(Wesley A Ward, U.S.A) *str; led: stl gng easily 2f out w rest hrd at work: shkn up fnl f: hdd and no ex fnl 75yds* 4/11[1]

6 3 ½ **Full Verse (IRE)**[13] [1887] 2-9-2 0 WilliamBuick 5 87
(Charlie Appleby) *sltly on toes; sweating; trckd ldng pair: pushed along 1/2-way: rdn to chse ldr wl over 1f out: kpt on but nvr able to chal: lost 2nd fnl 100yds* 7/2[2]

311 4 5 **Zulu Zander (IRE)**[12] [1910] 2-9-8 0 OisinMurphy 2 75
(David Evans) *compact; chsd ldr to wl over 1f out: wknd* 14/1[3]

5 1 ¾ **Can't Stop Now (IRE)** 2-9-2 0 AdamKirby 3 62+
(Clive Cox) *ly; a last: outpcd and pushed along after 2f: nvr a factor* 20/1

1m 0.49s (-0.21) **Going Correction** +0.025s/f (Good) 5 Ran SP% 111.7
Speed ratings (Par 99): **102,100,99,91,88**
CSF £29.45 TOTE £20.80: £3.60, £1.10; EX 39.50 Trifecta £87.20.
Owner Middleham Park Racing LXXXI **Bred** Crossfields Bloodstock Ltd **Trained** Musley Bank, N Yorks

FOCUS
Straight course divided in two with rail down the middle from 1m start to beyond winning post. Far side used for this meeting. This may not be overly strong form, with the favourite clearly running below expectations. The form has been rated around the recent averages for the race.

2268 NAAS RACECOURSE ROYAL ASCOT TRIALS DAY BRITISH EBF FILLIES' CONDITIONS STKS (PLUS 10 RACE) 7f 213y(R)
2:50 (2:51) (Class 3) 3-Y-O £9,703 (£2,887; £1,443; £721) **Stalls** Centre

Form RPR

31-0 1 **Muchly**[18] [1751] 3-9-3 92 FrankieDettori 6 102
(John Gosden) *sweating; mde all: set stdy pce tl past 1/2-way: stretched on over 2f out: hrd pressed fnl 100yds: jst hld on* 9/1

1- 2 shd **Queen Power (IRE)**[201] [8151] 3-9-3 0 SilvestreDeSousa 3 101+
(Sir Michael Stoute) *str; t.k.h: hld up in tch: rdn over 2f out: prog to chse wnr over 1f out: grad clsd fnl f: jst failed* 11/8[1]

1-6 3 3 **Modern Millie**[18] [1751] 3-9-3 0 DavidEgan 5 94
(Mick Channon) *unfurnished; t.k.h: trckd wnr 3f and again briefly wl over 1f out: outpcd fnl f* 20/1

15- 4 nk **Hidden Message (USA)**[201] [8146] 3-9-3 0 OisinMurphy 9 93+
(William Haggas) *str; sweating; t.k.h: hld up in last trio: lot to do 2f out: prog over 1f out: drvn and styd on fnl f: nrly snatched 3rd* 5/1[3]

324- 5 3 **Model Guest**[215] [7734] 3-9-0 96 (p) LukeMorris 10 83
(George Margarson) *chsd ldrs: rdn over 2f out: wandered u.p over 1f out and outpcd: wknd fnl f* 33/1

020- 6 2 ½ **Ajrar**[186] [8648] 3-9-3 89 SeanLevey 7 81
(Richard Hannon) *chsd wnr after 3f to wl over 1f out: wknd* 50/1

41- 7 1 ¼ **Baba Ghanouj (IRE)**[154] [9290] 3-9-3 0 GeraldMosse 2 78
(Ed Walker) *t.k.h: hld up in last trio: effrt 2f out: sn no prog* 6/1

1- 8 2 ¼ **Fashion's Star (IRE)**[222] [7490] 3-9-3 0 JasonWatson 1 73
(Roger Charlton) *athletic; plld hrd: hld up in last: nt clr run 2f out: no prog and eased fnl f* 9/2[2]

-1 9 14 **Quick**[19] [1740] 3-9-3 0 TomMarquand 4 40
(Richard Hannon) *restless in stalls: t.k.h: hld up in midfield: wknd over 2f out: t.o* 33/1

1m 42.69s (2.09) **Going Correction** +0.025s/f (Good) 9 Ran SP% 113.8
Speed ratings (Par 100): **90,89,86,86,83 81,79,77,63**
CSF £20.92 TOTE £10.10: £2.20, £1.20, £3.30; EX 28.40 Trifecta £235.90.
Owner 5 Hertford Street Racing Club **Bred** Highclere Stud **Trained** Newmarket, Suffolk

FOCUS
An unsatisfactory contest with there being a very steady pace and the winner dictated. This looks bit better than the usual race standard, with a bigger field than usual too. The winner reversed Newbury form with the third.

2269 LONGINES SAGARO STKS (GROUP 3) (A GOLD CUP TRIAL) 1m 7f 209y
3:25 (3:25) (Class 1) 4-Y-O+

£34,026 (£12,900; £6,456; £3,216; £1,614; £810) **Stalls** Centre

Form RPR

243- 1 **Dee Ex Bee**[181] [8794] 4-9-1 112 WilliamBuick 5 113+
(Mark Johnston) *looked wl; trckd ldr after 2f: pushed along 4f out: led wl over 2f out: rdn and asserted over 1f out: styd on strly and pushed out fnl 150yds* 11/8[1]

61-6 2 3 ¼ **Raymond Tusk (IRE)**[67] [894] 4-9-6 111 JamieSpencer 7 114
(Richard Hannon) *looked wl; trckd ldng pair: rdn to chse wnr 2f out: no imp after: kpt on same pce* 20/1

613- 3 ¾ **Cleonte (IRE)**[200] [8188] 6-9-2 101 SilvestreDeSousa 6 108
(Andrew Balding) *hld up in last: prog over 2f out on outer: rdn wl over 1f out: chsd ldng pair fnl f: styd on same pce after* 11/1

12-2 4 1 ¾ **Verdana Blue (IRE)**[18] [921] 7-8-13 92 OisinMurphy 2 103
(Nicky Henderson) *trckd ldng pair: waiting for a gap over 2f out: rdn over 1f out: styd on same pce and nvr able to threaten* 7/2[3]

/22- 5 7 **Danehill Kodiac (IRE)**[356] [2582] 6-9-2 112 SeanLevey 4 98
(Richard Hannon) *t.k.h: trckd ldr 2f: sn hld up in last trio: shkn up wl over 2f out and no prog: wknd over 1f out* 16/1

230- 6 6 **Weekender**[186] [8645] 5-9-2 114 FrankieDettori 1 90
(John Gosden) *led: hdd wl over 2f out: nudged along and wknd wl over 1f out* 11/4[2]

-432 7 3 ¼ **Amazing Red (IRE)**[21] [1693] 6-9-2 102 PJMcDonald 3 86
(Ed Dunlop) *hld up in last trio: shkn up and no prog wl over 2f out: wknd over 1f out* 50/1

3m 24.97s (-8.33) **Going Correction** +0.025s/f (Good)
WFA 4 from 5yo+ 1lb 7 Ran SP% 111.9
Speed ratings (Par 113): **118,116,116,115,111 108,107**
CSF £30.27 TOTE £2.30: £1.60, £5.60; EX 22.90 Trifecta £154.20.
Owner Sheikh Hamdan bin Mohammed Al Maktoum **Bred** Godolphin **Trained** Middleham Moor, N Yorks

FOCUS
Although Weekender disappointed this still rates strong form, with the winner quite impressive and now looking a major Gold Cup contender. He didn't need to match his Derby form. The pace appeared a good one.

2270 MERRIEBELLE STABLE COMMONWEALTH CUP TRIAL STKS (REGISTERED AS THE PAVILION STAKES) (GROUP 3) 6f
3:55 (3:59) (Class 1) 3-Y-O

£45,368 (£17,200; £8,608; £3,220; £3,220; £1,080) **Stalls** Centre

Form RPR

11- 1 **Calyx**[316] [3962] 3-9-1 115 FrankieDettori 5 118+
(John Gosden) *on toes; sweating; taken steadily to post: rrd sltly s: hld up in tch: swift move to ld wl over 1f out and qcknd clr: pushed out: impressive* 1/3[1]

1-16 2 4 **No Nonsense**[18] [1752] 3-9-1 98 GeraldMosse 3 102
(David Elsworth) *hld up in last: rdn and prog wl over 1f out: styd on to take 2nd fnl 75yds: no ch w wnr* 33/1

446- 3 ½ **Konchek**[221] [7534] 3-9-1 104 (w) AdamKirby 4 100
(Clive Cox) *looked wl; plld hrd: hld up in last pair: rdn 2f out: prog over 1f out: styd on to take 3rd last strides* 14/1

50-2 4 hd **Pocket Dynamo (USA)**[21] [1692] 3-9-1 106 (h) JamesDoyle 6 100
(Robert Cowell) *taken steadily to post: t.k.h: hld up bhd ldng pair: chal 2f out: chsd wnr over 1f out but readily outpcd: lost pls fnl 75yds* 12/1[3]

120- 4 dht **Signora Cabello (IRE)**[214] [7771] 3-8-12 114 OisinMurphy 2 97
(John Quinn) *trckd ldrs: shkn up 2f out: lost pl over 1f out: one pce after* 12/1[3]

24-1 6 ½ **The Cruising Lord**[12] [1909] 3-9-1 98 JFEgan 7 98
(Michael Attwater) *mde most to wl over 1f out: outpcd and one pce after* 50/1

220- 7 shd **Well Done Fox**[180] [8818] 3-9-1 107 SilvestreDeSousa 1 98
(Richard Hannon) *looked wl; t.k.h: trckd ldr: chal 2f out: sn outpcd by wnr: one pce and lost pls ins fnl f* 9/1[2]

1m 12.48s (-1.22) **Going Correction** +0.025s/f (Good) 7 Ran SP% 112.0
Speed ratings (Par 109): **109,103,103,102,102 102,101**
CSF £15.21 TOTE £1.20: £1.10, £8.00; EX 12.70 Trifecta £55.30.
Owner K Abdullah **Bred** Juddmonte Farms Ltd **Trained** Newmarket, Suffolk

FOCUS
A race that revolved around the returning Calyx and he put on a show.He rates a potential top sprinter. They raced centre-field.

2271 ASCOT SHOP PARADISE STKS (A QUEEN ANNE STAKES TRIAL) (LISTED RACE) 1m (S)
4:25 (4:30) (Class 1) 4-Y-O+

£20,982 (£7,955; £3,981; £1,983; £995; £499) **Stalls** Centre

Form RPR

230- 1 **Zaaki**[249] [6547] 4-9-0 108 FrankieDettori 6 117
(Sir Michael Stoute) *c out of stall slowly: hld up in last: gd prog jst over 2f out: rdn to ld jst over 1f out: edgd lft and hrd pressed fnl f: mainly pushed out and a holding on* 9/1

230/ 2 nk **Barney Roy**[557] [8233] 5-9-0 117 WilliamBuick 5 116
(Charlie Appleby) *sltly on toes; trckd ldrs: wnt 2nd over 3f out: led wl over 1f out gng strly but sn pressed: rdn and hdd jst over 1f out: edgd lft but fought on wl: a hld* 6/4[1]

3-00 3 3 **Robin Of Navan (FR)**[13] [1890] 6-9-0 105 OisinMurphy 3 109
(Harry Dunlop) *hld up towards rr: gng strly but nt clr run over 2f out tl swtchd lft wl over 1f out: prog to take 3rd fnl f: styd on but no imp on ldng pair fnl 100yds (jockey said horse was denied a clear run)* 25/1

511- 4 4 ½ **Tabarrak (IRE)**[207] [7990] 6-9-3 110 DaneO'Neill 2 102
(Richard Hannon) *hld up in tch: clsd over 2f out: on terms and rdn wl over 1f out: wknd sn after* 20/1

1-1 **5** 3 ¾ **Canvassed (IRE)**[28] 1517 4-9-0 97 .... DavidEgan 7 90
(Roger Varian) *str; taken down early: trckd ldrs: disp 2nd over 3f to 2f out: wknd over 1f out* **6/1**[3]

0336 **6** ¾ **First Contact (IRE)**[13] 1890 4-9-3 108 .... JamesDoyle 4 92
(Charlie Appleby) *led: rdn over 2f out: hdd & wknd wl over 1f out* **10/1**

-600 **7** 2 ¼ **Circus Couture (IRE)**[13] 1890 7-9-0 100 .... JFEgan 8 84
(Jane Chapple-Hyam) *hld up in rr: rdn 1/2-way: sn struggling and btn over 2f out* **66/1**

011- **8** 2 ¾ **Wadilsafa**[224] 7424 4-9-3 112 .... JimCrowley 1 80
(Owen Burrows) *sweating; chsd ldr: rdn over 3f out: sn lost pl and wknd (jockey said colt hung left-handed)* **9/4**[2]

1m 39.13s (-2.27) **Going Correction** +0.025s/f (Good) **8** Ran SP% **114.2**
Speed ratings (Par 111): **112,111,108,104,100 99,97,94**
CSF £22.66 TOTE £8.90: £2.20, £1.20, £4.40; EX 29.30 Trifecta £299.30.
Owner Ahmad Alotaibi **Bred** Miss K Rausing **Trained** Newmarket, Suffolk

FOCUS
A strong Listed race. They raced down the centre of the track and two pulled clear late on, ending up stands' side. The winner improved, with the second 8lb off his old best.

2272 ASCOT SUPPORTS RACING CHARITIES H'CAP 5f

5:00 (5:03) (Class 4) (0-85,87) 4-Y-0+

£6,727 (£2,002; £1,000; £500; £300; £300) **Stalls** Centre

Form RPR

41-5 **1** **Burford Brown**[12] 1929 4-9-2 80 .... JamesDoyle 9 91
(Robert Cowell) *trckd ldrs: clsd to ld wl over 1f out: drvn and pressed fnl f: hld on wl* **10/1**

105- **2** ½ **Daschas**[236] 7013 5-9-2 80 .... (t) OisinMurphy 10 89
(Stuart Williams) *trckd ldrs: rdn to chse wnr over 1f out: chal ins fnl f: styd on but hld nr fin* **7/2**[1]

66-0 **3** *nk* **Gnaad (IRE)**[104] 278 5-8-5 74 .... DarraghKeenan(5) 11 82
(Alan Bailey) *awkward s: sn in midfield: gng bttr than most 2f out: trckd ldrs over 1f out: rdn to chse ldng pair fnl f: styd on but nt qckn* **20/1**

211/ **4** 1 ¾ **Indian Raj**[629] 5837 5-8-12 76 .... JimCrowley 4 78+
(Stuart Williams) *looked wl; dwlt: hld up in last pair: prog over 1f out: rdn and styd on to take 4th fnl 100yds: nvr nrr* **6/1**[3]

2020 **5** 1 ½ **Something Lucky (IRE)**[33] 1394 7-8-11 75 .... (v) GeraldMosse 3 71
(Michael Appleby) *chsd ldrs: rdn 2f out: cl up over 1f out: fdd ins fnl f* **14/1**

210- **6** *nse* **Our Oystercatcher**[175] 8934 5-8-8 75 .... FinleyMarsh(3) 2 71
(Mark Pattinson) *w ldr at str pce and clr of rest: lost pl over 1f out and wandered u.p: fdd grad* **16/1**

120- **7** 1 ½ **Iconic Knight (IRE)**[201] 8165 4-9-2 80 .... AdamKirby 1 71
(Ed Walker) *sltly awkward s: hld up in last pair: modest prog over 1f out: shkn up and kpt on fnl f: nvr in it* **11/2**[2]

2540 **8** ¾ **Human Nature (IRE)**[26] 1560 6-8-13 77 .... (t) SeanLevey 13 65
(Stuart Williams) *nvr beyond midfield: rdn and no prog jst over 2f out: n.d after* **16/1**

00-0 **9** ½ **Tomily (IRE)**[11] 1938 5-9-4 87 .... SeamusCronin(5) 7 73
(Richard Hannon) *taken down early: hld up towards rr: pushed along 2f out: dropped to last over 1f out: passed a few nr fin but nvr in it* **8/1**

406- **10** 1 **Rio Ronaldo (IRE)**[210] 7911 7-9-5 83 .... RossaRyan 6 66
(Mike Murphy) *dwlt: hld up in last trio: shkn up and modest prog over 1f out: no hdwy fnl f* **33/1**

0-04 **11** 1 **George Dryden (IRE)**[33] 1394 7-9-1 79 .... DavidEgan 12 58
(Charlie Wallis) *nvr beyond midfield: rdn and no prog 2f out: wl btn after* **12/1**

40-0 **12** ½ **Leo Minor (USA)**[16] 1814 5-9-7 85 .... (p) WilliamBuick 5 62
(Robert Cowell) *sweating; a towards rr: rdn and no prog 2f out: wknd jst over 1f out (jockey said gelding hung right-handed)* **10/1**

210- **13** 7 **Glamorous Rocket (IRE)**[167] 9084 4-9-0 78 .... TomMarquand 8 30
(Christopher Mason) *led and clr w one rival: hdd & wknd rapidly wl over 1f out: t.o* **33/1**

1m 0.41s (-0.29) **Going Correction** +0.025s/f (Good) **13** Ran SP% **118.0**
Speed ratings (Par 105): **103,102,101,98,96 96,94,92,92,90 88,88,76**
CSF £43.32 CT £535.20 TOTE £8.30: £3.00, £1.80, £6.80; EX 51.10 Trifecta £755.70.
Owner The Ever Hopefuls **Bred** Poulton Stud **Trained** Six Mile Bottom, Cambs

FOCUS
A decent sprint won by a progressive and unexposed sprinting type. They went a proper good gallop and pace held out.

2273 MANNY MERCER APPRENTICE H'CAP 1m (S)

5:35 (5:39) (Class 4) (0-85,86) 4-Y-0+

£6,727 (£2,002; £1,000; £500; £300; £300) **Stalls** Centre

Form RPR

160- **1** **Enigmatic (IRE)**[180] 8806 5-9-4 85 .... DarraghKeenan(3) 5 94
(Alan Bailey) *looked wl; racd towards far side: cl up: clsd over 2f out: rdn to ld over 1f out: hrd pressed fnl f: hld on wl but swvd sharply lft last strides* **14/1**

5323 **2** *nk* **Ambient (IRE)**[21] 1695 4-8-8 72 .... RowanScott 3 80
(Jane Chapple-Hyam) *racd towards far side: hld up in tch: prog over 2f out: chsd wnr jst over 1f out: str chal fnl f: drew away fr rest but jst hld* **20/1**

05-5 **3** 4 **Medieval (IRE)**[19] 1727 5-9-5 83 .... (t[1]) CameronNoble 13 82+
(Paul Cole) *looked wl; hld up in midfield: rdn and prog over 2f out: chsd ldng pair fnl f: no imp but did much the best of those drawn high* **9/1**[3]

026- **4** 2 **Kingston Kurrajong**[159] 9228 6-8-7 76 .... Pierre-LouisJamin(5) 8 70
(William Knight) *trckd ldrs: rdn and nt qckn over 2f out: styd on over 1f out: tk 4th ins fnl f: no threat to ldrs* **20/1**

0260 **5** *nk* **Isomer (USA)**[32] 1413 5-9-8 86 .... (p) JoshuaBryan 2 80
(Andrew Balding) *hld up towards rr: rdn over 2f out: prog over 1f out: styd on fnl f: nvr nrr (jockey said gelding was never travelling)* **10/1**

60-1 **6** 1 **Candelisa (IRE)**[26] 1561 6-8-9 78 .... (p) LauraCoughlan(5) 1 69
(David Loughnane) *racd towards far side: pressed ldr: led over 3f out: hdd & wknd over 1f out* **6/1**[2]

-203 **7** 2 ¾ **Motajaasid (IRE)**[28] 1526 4-8-13 77 .... (t) FinleyMarsh 4 62
(Richard Hughes) *awkward s: sn chsd ldrs towards far side: rdn and nt qckn over 2f out: one pce and nvr on terms after* **20/1**

60-0 **8** *nk* **Biotic**[19] 1727 8-8-2 73 .... OliverSearle(7) 6 57
(Rod Millman) *s.s: racd towards far side: detached in last: rdn and no prog 2f out: styd on over 1f out: gng on at fin* **50/1**

0215 **9** ½ **Poetic Force (IRE)**[12] 1916 5-8-9 76 .... (t) PoppyBridgwater(3) 17 59
(Tony Carroll) *hld up towards nr side: nvr on terms w ldrs: shkn up and kpt on one pce fnl 2f* **10/1**

-113 **10** ½ **Merchant Of Venice**[19] 1727 4-9-1 84 .... ScottMcCullagh(5) 18 66
(James Fanshawe) *looked wl; racd towards nr side: nvr on terms: no real ch whn hmpd over 2f out: kpt on* **11/2**[1]

6560 **11** *nk* **Sea Fox (IRE)**[12] 1912 5-9-0 81 .... DylanHogan(3) 15 62
(David Evans) *chsd ldrs: u.p sn after 1/2-way: no prog* **25/1**

0204 **12** *nk* **Key Player**[19] 1727 4-8-10 81 .... (p[1]) GeorgiaDobie(7) 7 62
(Eve Johnson Houghton) *chsd ldrs towards far side: rdn and fdd over 2f out* **16/1**

00-4 **13** 1 **Letsbe Avenue (IRE)**[6] 2064 4-8-10 79 .... SeamusCronin(5) 12 57
(Richard Hannon) *chsd ldrs: rdn wl over 2f out: steadily wknd* **12/1**

1414 **14** *nse* **First Link (USA)**[25] 1586 4-8-2 71 oh1 .... ThoreHammerHansen(5) 11 49
(Jean-Rene Auvray) *mde most in centre to over 3f out: wknd over 2f out* **12/1**

2104 **15** 1 ½ **Blame Culture (USA)**[6] 2065 4-8-10 74 .... JaneElliott 16 49
(George Margarson) *racd towards nr side: hld up in rr: gng wl enough 3f out: no prog after* **20/1**

16-0 **16** *hd* **Sir Plato (IRE)**[19] 1727 5-8-10 77 .... ThomasGreatrex(3) 14 51
(Rod Millman) *nvr on terms w ldrs: struggling in rr 3f out* **25/1**

5/6- **17** *shd* **Mandarin (GER)**[342] 3038 5-9-5 83 .... GabrieleMalune 20 57
(Ian Williams) *dwlt: racd towards nr side: a in rr: nvr a factor* **20/1**

05-6 **18** 2 ¼ **Mountain Rescue (IRE)**[13] 1881 7-9-3 81 .... PaddyBradley 10 50
(Michael Attwater) *chsd ldrs to 1/2-way: wknd wl over 2f out* **50/1**

0021 **19** 7 **Juanito Chico (IRE)**[11] 1955 5-9-3 81 .... (t) GaryMahon 9 34
(Stuart Williams) *prom: u.p over 3f out: sn wknd: bhd fnl f* **14/1**

040- **20** 5 **Pour La Victoire (IRE)**[199] 8236 9-8-10 81 .... ElishaWhittington(7) 19 22
(Tony Carroll) *racd towards nr side: nvr on terms: last and wkng 2f out: t.o* **66/1**

1m 40.66s (-0.74) **Going Correction** +0.025s/f (Good) **20** Ran SP% **129.4**
Speed ratings (Par 105): **104,103,99,97,97 96,93,93,92,92 92,91,90,90,89 89,88,86,79,74**
CSF £276.08 CT £2734.04 TOTE £17.70: £4.70, £5.10, £2.70, £5.40; EX 298.50 Trifecta £4951.00.
Owner Trevor Milner **Bred** Stonepark Farms **Trained** Newmarket, Suffolk

FOCUS
This had the look of a wide-open handicap, but two managed to put a few lengths between themselves and the rest. A length pb from the winner. Those racing towards the far side of the group were seemingly favoured.
T/Jkpt: Not Won. T/Plt: £20.10 to a £1 stake. Pool: £93,386.69 - 3,375.72 winning units T/Qpdt: £14.70 to a £1 stake. Pool: £8,260.27 - 413.13 winning units **Jonathan Neesom**

1909 BATH (L-H)

Wednesday, May 1

OFFICIAL GOING: Good to firm (firm in places; 9.1)
Wind: Light across Weather: Overcast but dry

2274 VALUE RATER RACING CLUB IS FREE H'CAP 5f 160y

4:50 (4:50) (Class 4) (0-85,84) 3-Y-O

£5,530 (£1,645; £822; £411; £300; £300) **Stalls** Centre

Form RPR

00-0 **1** **Dark Shadow (IRE)**[21] 1691 3-9-0 77 .... HectorCrouch 4 83
(Clive Cox) *hld up: hdwy over 1f out: led jst ins fnl f: readily* **8/1**

16-2 **2** *nk* **Tinto**[19] 1729 3-9-3 80 .... RobertHavlin 5 85
(Amanda Perrett) *trckd ldrs: led over 1f out: sn rdn: led over 1f out: hdd jst ins fnl f: kpt on but a being hld (jockey said gelding took a false step 1f out)* **5/2**[1]

52-5 **3** 2 ½ **Champion Brogie (IRE)**[112] 142 3-8-12 75 .... NicolaCurrie 1 72
(J S Moore) *hld up: hdwy but nt clrest of runs 2f out: r.o ins fnl f: wnt 3rd fnl 100yds (jockey said gelding was denied a clear run 1 1/2f out)* **8/1**

2-30 **4** ½ **Reticent Angel (IRE)**[5] 2086 3-9-4 81 .... (p) DavidProbert 2 76
(Clive Cox) *hld up: hdwy 2f out: sn rdn: kpt on ins fnl f but nt pce to threaten* **7/2**[2]

513- **5** ½ **Whataguy**[308] 4258 3-9-4 84 .... MeganNicholls(3) 6 77
(Paul Nicholls) *broke wl: led: drifted lft whn hdd over 1f out: no ex ins fnl f (jockey said gelding hung left-handed)* **4/1**[3]

36-0 **6** 2 **Tin Hat (IRE)**[19] 1736 3-9-7 84 .... MartinDwyer 3 74
(Eve Johnson Houghton) *trckd ldrs: snatched up after 1f: nt clr run and hmpd jst over 1f out: no ch after* **11/2**

55-0 **7** 3 ½ **Autumn Splendour (IRE)**[19] 1729 3-9-5 82 .... (p) RobHornby 7 57
(Milton Bradley) *little slowly away: sn trcking ldr: rdn over 2f out: wknd ent fnl f* **66/1**

1m 10.47s (-0.63) **Going Correction** -0.075s/f (Good) **7** Ran SP% **109.9**
Speed ratings (Par 101): **101,100,97,96,95 93,88**
CSF £26.12 TOTE £11.60: £3.50, £1.10; EX 30.00 Trifecta £183.70.
Owner J Goddard **Bred** Redpender Stud Ltd **Trained** Lambourn, Berks

FOCUS
The going was good to firm, firm in places. The first two pulled clear in this sprint handicap but there were a few hard luck stories. The time was 0.97 seconds slower than standard. The winner is rated in line with his Sandown win.

2275 LET'S PLAY "FOUR FROM THE TOP" / BRITISH EBF NOVICE MEDIAN AUCTION STKS 5f 10y

5:25 (5:26) (Class 5) 2-Y-O

£4,075 (£1,212; £606; £303) **Stalls** Centre

Form RPR

1 **Silver Start** 2-9-0 .... RichardKingscote 6 74+
(Charles Hills) *trckd ldr: chal gng best 2f out: led ent fnl f: qcknd clr: comf* **4/1**[2]

2 2 ¼ **Rockingham Jill** 2-9-0 .... FrannyNorton 5 66+
(Jo Hughes, France) *outpcd early: hdwy 2f out: nt clr run bhd ldrs over 1f out: sn swtchd rt: checked again ins fnl f: r.o fnl 120yds: wnt 2nd nring fin: improve (jockey said filly was denied a clear run; vet said filly finished lame on it's right hind)* **22/1**

44 **3** 1 **Bartat**[15] 1833 2-9-0 .... GeorgeDowning 7 62
(Mick Channon) *led: rdn and hdd ent fnl f: no ex fnl 120yds* **10/1**

4 *shd* **Royal Ambition (IRE)** 2-9-5 .... HectorCrouch 8 67+
(Clive Cox) *s.i.s: outpcd early: hdwy over 2f out: rdn in 3rd whn stmbld sltly jst ins fnl f: kpt on same pce* **6/1**[3]

24 **5** 3 ¾ **Out Of Breath**[11] 1931 2-9-5 .... NicolaCurrie 1 53
(Jamie Osborne) *outpcd early: sme hdwy over 2f out: nt pce to get on terms: wknd ins fnl f (jockey said colt was never travelling)* **13/8**[1]

0 **6** 1 ¾ **Spiritulist**[11] 1931 2-9-5 .... DavidProbert 2 47
(David Evans) *chsd ldrs: rdn 2f out: wknd ins fnl f* **33/1**

7 2 ¾ **Amazon Princess** 2-9-0 .... JackMitchell 4 32
(Archie Watson) *chsd ldrs: hung lft u.p over 1f out: sn wknd* **4/1**[2]

8 2 **Storm Wings (IRE)** 2-9-0 .... CharlieBennett 3 25
(Jo Hughes, France) *s.i.s: a outpcd in last: nvr on terms* **50/1**

1m 2.8s (0.80) **Going Correction** -0.075s/f (Good) **8** Ran SP% **110.7**
Speed ratings (Par 93): **90,86,84,84,78 75,71,68**
CSF £78.05 TOTE £5.20: £1.20, £5.50, £2.80; EX 73.90 Trifecta £353.50.
Owner R J Tufft **Bred** R J Tufft **Trained** Lambourn, Berks

FOCUS
They leader set a good pace in this novice and a newcomer was impressive. It;s likely that this lacked depth.

2276 "AROUND THE PADDOCK" AT VALUERATER.CO.UK H'CAP 5f 160y
6:00 (6:00) (Class 6) (0-65,67) 3-Y-O

£3,105 (£924; £461; £300; £300; £300) **Stalls** Centre

Form RPR

50-4 1 **Devils Roc**[21] 1687 3-9-4 **62**.......... RobHornby 6 71+
(Jonathan Portman) *chsd ldrs: rdn to chal wl over 1f out: led ins fnl f: won gng away: comf* **5/2**[1]

3343 2 1 **Bequest**[21] 1687 3-9-4 **62**.......... DavidProbert 2 68
(Ron Hodges) *sn led: rdn over 1f out: hdd ins fnl f: kpt on but no ex fnl 100yds* **11/4**[2]

3 4 **Man Of The Sea (IRE)**[189] 8555 3-9-4 **62**..........(tp) HectorCrouch 9 55
(Neil Mulholland) *trckd ldrs: rdn and ev ch over 1f out: no ex ins fnl f* **14/1**

04-2 4 1 **Bluebell Time (IRE)**[12] 1909 3-9-4 **67**.......... KatherineBegley(5) 1 57
(Malcolm Saunders) *sn trcking ldrs: rdn over 2f out: kpt on same pce fr over 1f out* **4/1**[3]

36-6 5 nk **Miss Gargar**[21] 1687 3-9-6 **64**.......... RichardKingscote 12 53
(Harry Dunlop) *trckd ldrs in centre: rdn 2f out: edgd lft over 1f out: one pce fnl f* **12/1**

-234 6 2 **Kadiz (IRE)**[69] 831 3-9-1 **62**..........(p) MeganNicholls(3) 10 44
(Paul George) *in tch: rdn over 2f out: nt quite pce to get on terms: fdd ins fnl f* **8/1**

20-0 7 2 ¾ **Solesmes**[26] 1557 3-9-1 **59**.......... JackMitchell 5 32
(Tony Newcombe) *hld up: hdwy 2f out: sn rdn: nt pce to chal: wknd ent fnl f* **33/1**

2501 8 ½ **Ever Rock (IRE)**[23] 1650 3-8-8 **57**.......... RhiainIngram(5) 7 28+
(J S Moore) *hld up: swtchd rt whn nt clr run over 2f out: sn rdn: nt pce to get on terms: wknd ent fnl f (trainer said was unsuited by the going and the 10lb rise in the weights)* **8/1**

06-0 9 1 **Little Anxious**[26] 1557 3-7-9 **46** oh1.......... KeelanBaker(7) 11 14
(Grace Harris) *hld up: effrt in centre over 2f out: little imp: wknd ent fnl f* **50/1**

0066 10 6 **Tintern Spirit (IRE)**[21] 1678 3-7-11 **46** oh1..........(t[1]) RachealKneller(5) 4
(Milton Bradley) *prom tl rdn over 2f out: wknd over 1f out* **50/1**

1m 10.42s (-0.68) **Going Correction** -0.075s/f (Good) **10** Ran SP% **118.7**
Speed ratings (Par 97): **101,99,94,93,92 89,86,85,84,76**
CSF £9.64 CT £80.44 TOTE £4.50: £2.00, £1.10, £3.40; EX 11.20 Trifecta £84.40.
Owner Roc Steady Partnership **Bred** Petches Farm Ltd **Trained** Upper Lambourn, Berks

FOCUS
The two market leaders pulled clear in this sprint handicap. The winner reversed Lingfield form with the second.

2277 FREE TIPS FROM "SANDSTORM" AT VALUERATER.CO.UK H'CAP 1m
6:30 (6:30) (Class 6) (0-65,66) 3-Y-O+

£3,105 (£924; £461; £300; £300; £300) **Stalls** Low

Form RPR

063- 1 **Freckles**[154] 9293 4-9-5 **60**.......... TylerSaunders(7) 13 71+
(Marcus Tregoning) *awkwardly away: in last pair: hdwy in centre fr over 2f out: led jst ins fnl f: r.o wl: readily* **9/2**[2]

110- 2 2 ¼ **Princess Way (IRE)**[181] 8781 5-9-6 **59**..........(v) RhiainIngram(5) 7 63
(Paul George) *led: set decent pce: rdn over 1f out: hdd jst ins fnl f: kpt on but nt pce of wnr* **8/1**

623- 3 1 ½ **Johni Boxit**[17] 7614 4-10-0 **62**..........(p) TrevorWhelan 12 63
(Brian Barr) *in tch: rdn over 2f out: kpt on to go 3rd ins fnl f but nt pce to chal* **33/1**

363- 4 1 **Aye Aye Skipper (IRE)**[167] 9078 9-9-2 **50**.......... RobertHavlin 10 48
(Ken Cunningham-Brown) *little slowly away: sn mid-div: rdn over 2f out: little imp tl styd on fnl f: snatched 4th cl home* **16/1**

2206 5 hd **Accomplice**[34] 1378 5-9-13 **61**.......... RobHornby 8 59
(Michael Blanshard) *trckd ldr: rdn over 2f out: ev ch over 1f out tl ent fnl f: no ex fnl 120yds* **5/1**[3]

0-45 6 1 **Brockagh Cailin**[105] 250 4-9-11 **59**.......... JackMitchell 11 54
(J S Moore) *s.i.s: bhd: stdy prog fnl 2f but nvr gng pce to get involved* **17/2**

40-0 7 nse **Gloweth**[25] 1586 4-9-12 **60**.......... MartinDwyer 4 55
(Stuart Kittow) *nvr really travelling in midfield: struggling in rr 3f out: styd on fr over 1f out: n.d* **7/2**[1]

10-5 8 ½ **Rocksette**[11] 1935 5-9-5 **53**.......... HectorCrouch 5 47
(Gary Moore) *nvr bttr than midfield* **11/2**

320- 9 2 **Mister Musicmaster**[205] 8046 10-10-4 **66**.......... DavidProbert 2 56
(Ron Hodges) *mid-div: rdn over 2f out: little imp: wknd ins fnl f* **12/1**

02-0 10 shd **Swift Justice**[50] 1166 3-9-3 **64**..........(v) RichardKingscote 9 50
(Mark Loughnane) *prom tl rdn over 3f out: wknd over 1f out* **16/1**

02/0 11 ¾ **Eugenic**[15] 1841 8-8-11 **45**.......... FrannyNorton 6 33
(Tracey Barfoot-Saunt) *trckd ldrs: rdn over 2f out: wknd ent fnl f (jockey said gelding hung left-handed)* **33/1**

000- 12 11 **Anonymous Blonde**[253] 6387 3-8-11 **58**.......... NicolaCurrie 1 17
(David Evans) *a towards rr (trainers' rep said filly would prefer a slower surface)* **50/1**

1m 39.64s (-2.06) **Going Correction** -0.075s/f (Good)
WFA 3 from 4yo+ 13lb **12** Ran SP% **121.4**
Speed ratings (Par 101): **107,104,103,102,102 101,101,100,98,98 97,86**
CSF £41.05 CT £1094.04 TOTE £5.90: £2.20, £3.10, £7.30; EX 49.70 Trifecta £2383.70.
Owner John & Heather Raw **Bred** Heather Raw **Trained** Whitsbury, Hants

FOCUS
Add 4yds. The pace was strong and the unexposed winner scored with authority from some way back. Pretty straightforward form in behind.

2278 ANDERSONS WASTE H'CAP 1m 6f
7:00 (7:00) (Class 3) (0-90,91) 4-Y-O+ **£7,439** (£2,213; £1,106; £553) **Stalls** Centre

Form RPR

33-2 1 **Bayshore Freeway (IRE)**[12] 1914 4-9-4 **86**.......... FrannyNorton 4 94
(Mark Johnston) *mde all: strly chal fr 2f out: shkn up and styd on wl to assert fnl f* **1/2**[1]

3-55 2 2 ½ **Seafarer (IRE)**[60] 980 5-9-9 **91**..........(b) MartinDwyer 2 95
(Marcus Tregoning) *trckd ldrs: rdn for str chal 2f out tl ent fnl f: styd on* **9/2**[2]

3144 3 4 ½ **Cry Wolf**[12] 1914 6-8-13 **81**.......... RobertHavlin 3 79
(Alexandra Dunn) *trckd wnr tl rdn over 2f out: sn one pce* **7/1**[3]

504- 4 1 ½ **Machine Learner**[186] 8631 6-9-4 **89**..........(v) MeganNicholls(3) 1 85
(Joseph Tuite) *racd keenly: trckd ldng trio: rdn over 1f out: edgd lft: nt pce to threaten* **9/1**

3m 4.08s (-2.02) **Going Correction** -0.075s/f (Good) **4** Ran SP% **107.3**
Speed ratings (Par 107): **102,100,98,97**
CSF £3.02 TOTE £1.30; EX 2.80 Trifecta £5.80.
Owner Kingsley Park Owners Club **Bred** Lynch Bages Ltd **Trained** Middleham Moor, N Yorks

FOCUS
Add 4yds. The hot favourite had to work quite hard but eventually forged clear in this staying handicap. A weak race but the winner is generally progressive.

2279 READ "GROUP 1 GRIFF" AT VALUERATER.CO.UK H'CAP 1m 3f 137y
7:35 (7:35) (Class 6) (0-65,67) 4-Y-O+

£3,105 (£924; £461; £300; £300; £300) **Stalls** Low

Form RPR

1122 1 **Singing The Blues (IRE)**[6] 2059 4-9-9 **67**.......... RobHornby 1 78
(Rod Millman) *trckd ldrs: rdn to ld 2f out: in command fnl f: kpt on gamely* **2/1**[1]

-340 2 1 **Francophilia**[55] 1065 4-9-8 **66**.......... FrannyNorton 3 75
(Mark Johnston) *mid-div: rdn and hdwy 2f out: chsd wnr ent fnl f: edgd lft: styd on but a being hld* **11/4**[2]

5200 3 2 **Gendarme (IRE)**[14] 1848 4-9-7 **65**.......... RossaRyan 10 71
(Alexandra Dunn) *trckd ldrs: rdn to chse wnr 2f out tl ent fnl f: styd on same pce* **16/1**

0-06 4 2 ¾ **Barca (USA)**[58] 1015 5-8-13 **57**..........(p[1]) MartinDwyer 8 59
(Marcus Tregoning) *hld up: hdwy in centre over 2f out: sn rdn: styd on into 4th fnl f but nt pce to get on terms* **6/1**[3]

5000 5 ¾ **Agent Gibbs**[30] 1482 7-9-7 **65**.......... RobertHavlin 2 66
(John O'Shea) *trckd ldr: rdn and ev ch over 2f out tl over 1f out: no ex fnl 120yds* **10/1**

3226 6 6 **Make Good (IRE)**[29] 1498 4-9-4 **62**..........(bt) DavidProbert 11 53
(David Dennis) *s.i.s: sn rousted along in midfield: rdn 3f out: nvr threatened: wknd ent fnl f* **8/1**

00-0 7 ¾ **Kings Inn (IRE)**[35] 1363 5-9-4 **65**.......... MeganNicholls(3) 5 55
(Paul Nicholls) *hld up: outpcd 3f out: styng on but no ch whn hmpd ent fnl f* **10/1**

30-0 8 5 **Yamuna River**[13] 1653 4-9-5 **63**..........(b) DaneO'Neill 9 45
(Chris Gordon) *sn led: rdn and hdd 2f out: sn wknd* **25/1**

2m 28.12s (-2.68) **Going Correction** -0.075s/f (Good) **8** Ran SP% **113.3**
Speed ratings (Par 101): **105,104,103,101,100 96,96,92**
CSF £7.38 CT £63.50 TOTE £2.40: £1.10, £1.90, £4.00; EX 8.20 Trifecta £65.40.
Owner Rod Millman & Andy Smith **Bred** Lynn Lodge Stud **Trained** Kentisbeare, Devon

FOCUS
Add 4yds. The two market leaders dominated this middle-distance handicap. The winner transferred his AW progression back to turf.

2280 FOLLOW US ON TWITTER @VALUERATER NOVICE STKS 1m
8:10 (8:12) (Class 5) 3-Y-O+ **£3,752** (£1,116; £557; £278) **Stalls** Low

Form RPR

1 1 **Nahham (IRE)**[53] 1094 4-10-2 0.......... SeamusCronin(5) 8 83+
(Richard Hannon) *trckd ldr: led 2f out: sn rdn: kpt on wl fnl f* **2/1**[2]

2 1 **Aegeus (USA)** 3-9-1 0.......... RobertHavlin 7 69+
(Amanda Perrett) *in tch: trckd ldrs 3f out: rdn to chse wnr ent fnl f: kpt on but a being hld* **4/1**[3]

32-0 3 4 ½ **Sassoon**[13] 1886 3-9-1 75.......... DavidProbert 9 59
(Paul Cole) *trckd ldrs: rdn over 2f out: nt pce to mount chal: kpt on ins fnl f* **5/4**[1]

-0 4 hd **Test Valley (IRE)**[4] 2128 4-9-9 0.......... KatherineBegley(5) 3 62
(Tracey Barfoot-Saunt) *s.i.s: in last pair: rdn over 2f out: hdwy over 1f out: styd on ins fnl f: wnt 4th cl home* **150/1**

00- 5 ½ **Double Coffee**[198] 8257 3-8-10 0.......... CharlieBennett 2 52
(Peter Hiatt) *led: rdn and hdd 2f out: kpt on tl no ex and lost 2 pls cl home* **150/1**

6 3 **Haadef** 3-9-1 0.......... DaneO'Neill 11 50
(Brian Meehan) *dwlt: towards rr: effrt over 2f out: nvr threatened: wknd ent fnl f* **5/1**

00- 7 3 ¼ **Sari Mareis**[181] 8771 3-8-10 0.......... RobHornby 1 38
(Denis Coakley) *dwlt: a towards rr* **33/1**

060- 8 nk **Lily Jean**[205] 8062 4-9-9 35.......... MartinDwyer 5 40?
(Stuart Kittow) *s.i.s: in last pair: hdwy 3f out: sn rdn: wknd ent fnl f* **66/1**

0 9 2 ¾ **Jazzameer**[30] 1475 4-9-4 0.......... RachealKneller(5) 12 34
(Matthew Salaman) *in tch: rdn 3f out: wknd over 1f out* **150/1**

1m 41.86s (0.16) **Going Correction** -0.075s/f (Good)
WFA 3 from 4yo 13lb **9** Ran SP% **120.9**
Speed ratings (Par 103): **96,95,90,90,89 86,83,83,80**
CSF £11.13 TOTE £2.60: £1.10, £1.50, £1.10; EX 11.90 Trifecta £20.10.
Owner Al Shaqab Racing **Bred** George Kent **Trained** East Everleigh, Wilts

FOCUS
Add 4yds. A well-bred 4yo stayed on well to defy a penalty and make it 2-2. The bare form is hard to gauge though.
T/Plt: £215.50 to a £1 stake. Pool: £52,503.35 - 177.80 winning units T/Qpdt: £10.00 to a £1 stake. Pool: £7,367.69 - 542.84 winning units **Tim Mitchell**

2227 BRIGHTON (L-H)
Wednesday, May 1

OFFICIAL GOING: Good to firm (watered; 8.9)
Wind: Light, half behind Weather: Overcast

2281 SKY SPORTS RACING ON SKY 415 H'CAP 5f 60y
4:35 (4:35) (Class 5) (0-70,69) 3-Y-O

£3,752 (£1,116; £557; £300; £300; £300) **Stalls** Centre

Form RPR

2101 1 **Pink Flamingo**[21] 1687 3-9-7 **69**.......... HarryBentley 2 75
(Michael Attwater) *trckd ldrs: effrt and ev ch u.p over 1f out: led 1f out: r.o wl* **13/8**[1]

106- **2** 3/4 **All Back To Mine**[204] 8067 3-9-1 **63**........................ JasonWatson 1 66
(Joseph Tuite) *awkward leaving stalls and dwlt: hld up in tch: short of room after 1f: effrt 2f out: drvn over 1f out: styd on to chse wnr ins fnl f: nvr getting to wnr* **5/1**[3]

5-06 **3** 2 **Tarrzan (IRE)**[26] 1557 3-8-6 **54**........................ LiamJones 4 50
(John Gallagher) *in tch: short of room after 1f: effrt 2f out: drvn over 1f out: kpt on ins fnl f: wnt 3rd towards fin: nvr enough pce to threaten wnr* **11/1**

4500 **4** 1/2 **Starchant**[23] 1650 3-9-0 **62**........................ ShaneKelly 3 56
(John Bridger) *s.i.s: swtchd rt and hdwy to ld after 1f: hrd pressed and drvn over 1f out: hdd 1f out: no ex: lost 2nd and wknd ins fnl f* **15/2**

1052 **5** 3/4 **Hanakotoba (USA)**[11] 1954 3-8-13 **68**........................(t) MarcoGhiani(7) 5 60
(Stuart Williams) *led for 1f: chsd ldr: effrt and ev ch u.p over 1f out: no ex ins fnl f: wknd towards fin* **9/4**[2]

3550 **6** *dist* **Spirit Of Lucerne (IRE)**[50] 1167 3-8-7 **55**........................(be[1]) HollieDoyle 6
(Phil McEntee) *stirrup leather broke sn after s and plld out wd: sn t.o and virtually p.u after (jockey said her right stirrup leather snapped)* **20/1**

1m 3.03s (0.03) **Going Correction** -0.075s/f (Good) **6** Ran SP% **110.4**
Speed ratings (Par 99): **96,94,91,90,89**
CSF £9.82 TOTE £2.00: £1.10, £2.20; EX 7.60 Trifecta £82.30.
Owner Dare To Dream Racing **Bred** Lowther Racing **Trained** Epsom, Surrey

FOCUS
The course had been watered to the tune of 6mm since the preceding day's action but was still genuine 'good to firm' ground. With the rails slightly out, 4yds were added to all races. \n\x\x A messy, modest sprint, rated through the second.

2282 EBF MAIDEN AUCTION STKS — 5f 60y
5:10 (5:16) (Class 5) 2-Y-O — **£4,032** (£1,207; £603; £302; £150) **Stalls** Centre

Form RPR

1 **Lady Quickstep (IRE)** 2-8-2........................ WilliamCox(3) 7 76+
(Gay Kelleway) *chsd ldr: hung rt over 1f out: racing against stands' rail and led jst ins fnl f: r.o strly and drew clr: readily (jockey said filly hung right-handed throughout)* **16/1**

2 4 **Paper Star** 2-8-7........................ HollieDoyle 3 64
(Archie Watson) *led: rdn over 1f out: hdd jst ins fnl f: sn brushed aside by wnr: hld on for 2nd cl home* **13/8**[1]

3 *nk* **Bushtucker Trial (IRE)** 2-9-0........................ HayleyTurner 2 70
(Michael Bell) *wl in tch: effrt wl over 1f out: wnt 3rd and swtchd rt ins fnl f: no ch w wnr but kpt on towards fin* **11/4**[2]

4 2 **Champagne Highlife (GER)** 2-8-13........................ CharlesBishop 9 62
(Eve Johnson Houghton) *wl in tch: chsd ldrs and effrt wl over 1f out: unable qck 1f out: wknd ins fnl f* **10/3**[3]

5 3 1/2 **Butterfly Pose (IRE)** 2-8-7........................ LiamJones 4 44
(J S Moore) *v.s.a and green early: cl and in tch over 3f out: no hdwy u.p over 1f out: wl btn fnl f* **40/1**

0 **6** 3/4 **Craigburn**[13] 1879 2-8-12........................ LukeMorris 6 46
(Tom Clover) *chsd ldrs tl lost pl u.p over 1f out: wknd ins fnl f* **33/1**

7 5 **Constanzia** 2-8-11 ow1........................ AdamMcNamara 5 28
(Jamie Osborne) *sn outpcd and pushed along: nvr involved* **13/2**

1m 3.05s (0.05) **Going Correction** -0.075s/f (Good) **7** Ran SP% **112.4**
Speed ratings (Par 93): **96,89,89,85,80 79,71**
CSF £41.21 TOTE £21.40: £5.20, £2.00; EX 44.30 Trifecta £165.30.
Owner Premier Thoroughbred R, The Glitter Ball **Bred** Thomas Smullen **Trained** Exning, Suffolk
■ Is She The One was withdrawn, price at time of withdrawal 16/1. Rule 4 does not apply.

FOCUS
Add 4yds. A typical maiden auction. The winner scooted up the stands' rail and the time was very close to the preceding class 5 3yo handicap over the same distance.

2283 SKY SPORTS RACING VIRGIN 535 H'CAP — 1m 3f 198y
5:45 (5:45) (Class 6) (0-55,55) 4-Y-O+ — **£3,105** (£924; £461; £300; £300; £300) **Stalls** Centre

Form RPR

-105 **1** **Tigerfish (IRE)**[65] 910 5-9-4 **52**........................(p) HollieDoyle 4 64
(William Stone) *chsd ldr tl led 5f out: rdn and kicked clr jst over 2f out: in n.d over 1f out: eased towards fin* **7/2**[2]

-033 **2** 9 **Sigrid Nansen**[28] 1520 4-8-12 **46**........................(tp) LukeMorris 6 44
(Alexandra Dunn) *dwlt: hld up in tch in rr: hdwy 5f out: rdn and effrt over 2f out: wnt 2nd but wnr kicking clr 2f out: no imp and wandered over 1f out: plugged on* **15/2**

00-1 **3** 3/4 **Hi There Silver (IRE)**[28] 1520 5-8-12 **46**........................ GeorgeWood 8 42
(Michael Madgwick) *in tch in midfield: clsd 5f out: rdn to go prom over 2f out: sn outpcd and no ch w wnr whn edgd rt over 1f out: plugged on same pce fnl f* **14/1**

4-45 **4** *hd* **Goldslinger (FR)**[21] 1679 7-9-6 **54**........................(t) ShaneKelly 9 50
(Gary Moore) *in tch in midfield: effrt jst over 2f out: sn outpcd: hrd drvn and no imp over 1f out: no ch but plugged on ins fnl f to go modest 3rd towards fin* **3/1**[1]

300- **5** 1 1/2 **Buxlow Belle (FR)**[204] 8072 4-8-9 **46** oh1........................(h) WilliamCox(3) 12 40
(David Menuisier) *hld up in tch: rdn 4f out: swtchd rt over 2f out: sn outpcd and wl hld over 1f out: plugged on into modest 4th towards fin* **9/1**

600- **6** 2 3/4 **Woofie (IRE)**[184] 8686 7-8-13 **47**........................ LiamJones 13 36
(Laura Mongan) *led tl 5f out: drvn and outpcd jst over 1f out: wl btn over 1f out: wknd ins fnl f* **25/1**

005- **7** 2 3/4 **Approaching Menace**[189] 8530 4-8-5 **46** oh1........................ SophieRalston(7) 5 31
(Amy Murphy) *mounted on the crse and taken down early: in rr: pushed along 5f out: nvr threatened to get involved after: wl btn over 1f out* **15/2**

00-0 **8** 4 **Becky Sharp**[21] 1679 4-9-5 **53**........................ PatDobbs 10 31
(Jim Boyle) *in tch: chsd ldrs 8f out: rdn over 2f out: sn outpcd and wl btn over 1f out: wknd* **10/1**

0/00 **9** 32 **Singer In The Sand (IRE)**[24] 736 4-8-12 **46** oh1........................ FergusSweeney 3
(Pat Phelan) *trckd ldrs: effrt 3f out: sn struggling and wl btn 2f out: eased fnl f: t.o* **40/1**

545- **10** 15 **Artic Nel**[197] 7833 5-8-13 **47**........................ AdamMcNamara 7
(Ian Williams) *nvr travelling wl: in tch tl dropped to rr and struggling 5f out: t.o over 2f out: eased (jockey said mare was never travelling)* **7/1**[3]

000- **R** **Duhr (IRE)**[10] 8765 5-9-6 **54**........................(p[1]) CharlesBishop 2
(Ralph J Smith) *ref to r* **28/1**

2m 34.32s (-1.68) **Going Correction** -0.075s/f (Good) **11** Ran SP% **118.7**
Speed ratings (Par 101): **102,96,95,95,94 92,90,88,66,56**
CSF £29.80 CT £332.46 TOTE £7.40: £2.30, £1.90, £3.40; EX 19.20 Trifecta £133.50.
Owner Miss Caroline Scott **Bred** Swordlestown Little **Trained** West Wickham, Cambs

FOCUS
Add 4yds. Moderate fare and the winner proved comfortably the best, turning this into a procession. The rating could underestimate this performance.

2284 GREAT BRITISH GIN FESTIVAL 20TH JULY NOVICE AUCTION STKS — 1m 1f 207y
6:15 (6:15) (Class 6) 3-Y-O — **£3,105** (£924; £461) **Stalls** High

Form RPR

02 **1** **Just Benjamin**[36] 1344 3-9-3........................ LiamJones 2 79+
(William Haggas) *stdd after s: trckd rivals: rdn 3f out: chalng whn hung lft over 1f out: led 1f out: styd on strly and in command 100yds out* **5/2**[2]

22 **2** 3 **Sashenka (GER)**[19] 1738 3-8-10........................ LiamKeniry 1 66
(Sylvester Kirk) *t.k.h: led and dictated stdy gallop: rdn over 2f out: drvn over 1f out: hdd 1f out: no ex and btn fnl 100yds* **4/7**[1]

0- **3** 3 3/4 **Flying Moon (GER)**[187] 8608 3-9-5........................ LukeMorris 4 68?
(Jonathan Portman) *pressed ldr: rdn and ev ch over 2f out tl no ex 1f out: sn outpcd: eased wl ins fnl f* **11/2**[3]

2m 4.89s (-0.11) **Going Correction** -0.075s/f (Good) **3** Ran SP% **107.6**
Speed ratings (Par 97): **97,94,91**
CSF £4.47 TOTE £2.90; EX 4.30 Trifecta £2.80.
Owner Ian and Christine Beard **Bred** Mrs J M Quy **Trained** Newmarket, Suffolk

FOCUS
Add 4yds. Despite this having just three runners and being a class 6, it's probably okay form.

2285 ANTIQUES COLLECTABLES VINTAGE FAIR 5 MAY H'CAP — 6f 210y
6:50 (6:50) (Class 5) (0-75,78) 3-Y-O — **£3,752** (£1,116; £557; £300; £300) **Stalls** Centre

Form RPR

3-00 **1** **Barasti Dancer (IRE)**[23] 1656 3-9-0 **67**........................ ShaneKelly 7 72
(K R Burke) *chsd ldrs: effrt to chal over 2f out: lft in ld 2f out: hung lft over 1f out: hrd pressed ins fnl f: hld on wl cl home* **11/1**

4241 **2** *hd* **Adelante (FR)**[9] 1985 3-9-6 **78** 6ex........................ SebastianWoods(5) 5 82+
(George Baker) *in tch in 4th: clsd to press ldrs whn squeezed for room: hmpd and stmbld over 2f out: rallied to chse wnr over 1f out: ev ch whn n.m.r: intimidated and hit rail ins fnl f: kpt on wl: jst hld* **2/1**[2]

560- **3** 9 **Daniel Dravot**[184] 8691 3-8-11 **64**........................ HarryBentley 3 44
(Michael Attwater) *stdd and awkward after leaving stalls: in rr: effrt over 2f out: hung lft but chsd clr ldng pair jst over 1f out: no imp and wl hld after (jockey said gelding hung left-handed under pressure)* **14/1**

300- **4** 5 **Tanqeeb**[205] 8042 3-9-9 **76**........................(b[1]) JasonWatson 4 42
(Owen Burrows) *sn pressing ldr: bmpd after 1f out: ev ch whn edgd lft and bmpd over 2f out: lost pl and wl btn over 1f out: wknd fnl f (jockey said gelding hung left-handed throughout)* **9/2**[3]

544- **5** *hd* **Hello Bangkok (IRE)**[153] 9306 3-9-7 **74**........................ SilvestreDeSousa 2 40
(Andrew Balding) *led: edgd rt and bmpd after 1f: rdn: edgd rt and bmpd over 2f out: sn hdd: lost pl and wl btn over 1f out: wknd fnl f (jockey said filly hung both ways)* **11/8**[1]

1m 23.57s (-0.23) **Going Correction** -0.075s/f (Good) **5** Ran SP% **108.6**
Speed ratings (Par 99): **98,97,87,81,81**
CSF £32.35 TOTE £13.00: £3.70, £1.10; EX 34.30 Trifecta £113.30.
Owner Ontoawinner 9 & Mrs E Burke **Bred** Declan Whelan **Trained** Middleham Moor, N Yorks

FOCUS
Add 4yds. A true pace in this eventful 3yo handicap but it was a rough race with the runner-up looking unlucky.

2286 RUM & REGGAE FESTIVAL 20 JULY H'CAP — 6f 210y
7:25 (7:25) (Class 6) (0-60,60) 4-Y-O+ — **£3,105** (£924; £461; £300; £300; £300) **Stalls** Centre

Form RPR

0602 **1** **Blessed To Empress (IRE)**[11] 1933 4-9-5 **58**........................ SilvestreDeSousa 6 65
(Amy Murphy) *t.k.h: chsd ldrs: swtchd rt and effrt jst over 2f out: hrd drvn and chsd ldr ins fnl f: r.o to ld last strides* **11/10**[1]

1255 **2** *hd* **Maazel (IRE)**[11] 1933 5-9-2 **55**........................ LiamJones 7 61
(Lee Carter) *hld up in tch in midfield: swtchd lft and clsd over 2f out: rdn to chal over 1f out: led 1f out: edgd rt ins fnl f: hdd last strides (jockey said gelding hung right-handed)* **7/1**

5000 **3** 1 3/4 **Swiss Cross**[19] 1731 12-8-7 **46** oh1........................(p) HollieDoyle 2 47
(Phil McEntee) *sn pushed up to ld: rdn over 1f out: hdd 1f out: no ex and lost 2nd ins fnl f: one pce* **28/1**

-053 **4** *nse* **Flirtare (IRE)**[49] 1177 4-9-7 **60**........................(t[1]) CharlesBishop 8 61
(Amy Murphy) *broke fast: sn hdd but styd pressing ldr: rdn and ev ch over 2f out: edgd lft over 1f out: no ex ins fnl f: one pce* **9/2**[3]

2346 **5** 2 **Rivas Rob Roy**[11] 1933 4-9-1 **54**........................ JasonWatson 3 50
(John Gallagher) *chsd ldrs: impeded and hit rail over 4f out: effrt over 2f out: sn pressing ldrs tl no ex 1f out: wknd ins fnl f* **7/2**[2]

6500 **6** 1 3/4 **Rapid Rise (IRE)**[19] 1731 5-8-7 **46** oh1........................(p) RaulDaSilva 9 37
(Milton Bradley) *in rr: rdn 3f out: kpt on ins fnl f: nvr trbld ldrs* **40/1**

0200 **7** *nse* **Hollander**[18] 1768 5-9-1 **59**........................(bt[1]) SebastianWoods(5) 10 50
(Alexandra Dunn) *dwlt and bustled along leaving stalls: in tch: effrt over 2f out: unable qck over 1f out: wknd* **25/1**

223- **8** 2 **Harlequin Rose (IRE)**[195] 8335 5-8-7 **46**........................(v) HayleyTurner 11 31
(Patrick Chamings) *a towards rr: rdn over 2f out: no hdwy and bhd ins fnl f* **11/1**

1m 22.91s (-0.89) **Going Correction** -0.075s/f (Good) **8** Ran SP% **118.6**
Speed ratings (Par 101): **102,101,99,99,97 95,95,93**
CSF £10.08 CT £143.70 TOTE £1.90: £1.10, £2.20, £4.40; EX 12.10 Trifecta £142.30.
Owner White Diamond Racing Partnership 1 **Bred** Liam Butler & Churchtown House Stud **Trained** Newmarket, Suffolk
■ Stewards' Enquiry : Hollie Doyle caution; careless riding

FOCUS
Add 4yds. A very modest handicap, but straightforward form.

2287 INJURED JOCKEYS FUND H'CAP — 5f 215y
7:55 (7:56) (Class 6) (0-55,56) 4-Y-O+ — **£3,105** (£924; £461; £300; £300; £300) **Stalls** Centre

Form RPR

00-0 **1** **Who Told Jo Jo (IRE)**[3] 2145 5-9-6 **54**........................ JasonWatson 6 63
(Joseph Tuite) *hld up in rr: hdwy in centre 2f out: chalng and hung lft over 1f out: led jst ins fnl f: styd on wl ins fnl f (jockey said gelding hung left-handed)* **7/2**[2]

2065 **2** *nk* **Holdenhurst**[40] 1266 4-9-3 **56**........................ RyanWhile(5) 4 64
(Bill Turner) *wl in tch in midfield: clsd on inner over 2f out: rdn to ld over 1f out: hdd jst ins fnl f: n.m.r and kpt on wl towards fin: a jst hld* **7/2**[2]

616- **3** 5 **Cool Strutter (IRE)**[191] 8473 7-9-3 **51**........................(p) LukeMorris 12 43
(John Spearing) *broke fast: led: rdn 2f out: drvn and hdd over 1f out: sltly impeded 1f out: outpcd by ldng pair but hung on for 3rd ins fnl f* **7/1**[3]

0-03 **4** *nk* **Red Snapper**[86] 596 4-8-12 **46** oh1..............................(p) HollieDoyle 10 37
(William Stone) *chsd ldr: ev ch u.p over 1f out: sltly impeded 1f out: outpcd by ldng pair and battling for 3rd ins fnl f* **12/1**

-004 **5** *½* **Noble Deed**[21] 1682 9-8-12 **46** oh1..............................(p) HarryBentley 11 35
(Michael Attwater) *chsd ldrs: unable qck u.p over 1f out: wl hld and plugged on same pce fnl f* **18/1**

0505 **6** *1* **Mother Of Dragons (IRE)**[8] 2025 4-9-7 **55**..........(v) SilvestreDeSousa 5 41
(Phil McEntee) *in tch in last quartet: swtchd rt and effrt over 2f out: no imp over 1f out and nvr getting on terms w ldrs: wl hld fnl f* **15/8[1]**

6000 **7** *nk* **Burauq**[19] 1732 7-8-12 **46** oh1..............................(p) RaulDaSilva 9 31
(Milton Bradley) *chsd ldrs: unable qck u.p and lost pl over 1f out: wknd ins fnl f* **25/1**

0220 **8** *1* **Baby Gal**[86] 594 5-8-12 **46**..............................(b) ShaneKelly 7 28
(Roger Ingram) *dwlt: in tch towards rr: hdwy to chse ldrs and rdn over 2f out: unable qck and outpcd whn hung lft 1f out: wknd ins fnl f* **12/1**

0000 **9** *3¾* **Major Muscari (IRE)**[10] 1967 11-8-9 **46** oh1.............. WilliamCox(3) 2 16
(Shaun Harris) *dwlt: t.k.h: hld up in tch towards rr: no hdwy u.p over 1f out: bhd ins fnl f* **66/1**

1m 10.71s (-0.39) **Going Correction** -0.075s/f (Good) **9 Ran SP% 117.7**
Speed ratings (Par 101): **99,98,91,91,90 89,89,87,82**
CSF £16.58 CT £82.18 TOTE £4.00: £1.40, £1.30, £2.10; EX 19.60 Trifecta £96.20.
Owner Felstead Court Flyers **Bred** James And Joe Brannigan **Trained** Lambourn, Berks

FOCUS
Add 4yds. The front two came clear in this moderate sprint, with a stewards' enquiry leaving the placings unaltered.
T/Plt: £104.30 to a £1 stake. Pool: £41,846.91 - 292.72 winning units T/Qpdt: £36.50 to a £1 stake. Pool: £5,391.49 - 109.05 winning units **Steve Payne**

1812 PONTEFRACT (L-H)

Wednesday, May 1

OFFICIAL GOING: Good to firm (good in places; watered; 8.1)
Wind: Virtually nil

2288 WILLIAM HILL SUPPORTS THE NORTHERN RACING COLLEGE EBF NOVICE STKS (PLUS 10 RACE) 5f 3y

2:25 (2:26) (Class 4) 2-Y-O **£5,175** (£1,540; £769; £384) **Stalls** Low

Form RPR

5 **1** **Kidda**[18] 1758 2-9-2 0.. TonyHamilton 1 78
(Richard Fahey) *dwlt: sn pushed along to take slt ld after 1f: rdn along wl over 1f out: drvn ins fnl f: hld on wl towards fin* **4/1[2]**

1 **2** *nk* **Xcelente**[18] 1758 2-9-8 0.. JoeFanning 2 83
(Mark Johnston) *slt ld: hdd after 1f and cl up: effrt 2f out: rdn over 1f out: drvn ins fnl f: kpt on towards fin* **4/9[1]**

3 *3* **River Of Kings (IRE)** 2-9-2 0.. ConnorBeasley 6 66+
(Keith Dalgleish) *trckd ldrs: pushed along over 2f out: rdn over 1f out: kpt on fnl f* **33/1**

4 **4** *1½* **Il Maestro (IRE)**[18] 1758 2-9-2 0.. JasonHart 7 61
(John Quinn) *chsd ldng pair: rdn along wl over 1f out: grad wknd fnl f* **8/1[3]**

5 *1½* **Corndavon Lad (IRE)** 2-9-2 0.. JackGarritty 5 55+
(Richard Fahey) *green and towards rr: swtchd rt and sme hdwy 2f out: rdn over 1f out: kpt on same pce* **33/1**

U **6** *3¾* **Tonquin Valley**[14] 1843 2-8-13 0.. BenRobinson(3) 3 42
(Brian Ellison) *dwlt: a towards rr* **100/1**

0 **7** *6* **Barry Magoo**[19] 1733 2-8-9 0.. TobyEley(7) 4 20
(Adam West) *a in rr (jockey said colt was never travelling and ran green)* **33/1**

1m 3.87s (-0.03) **Going Correction** -0.125s/f (Firm) **7 Ran SP% 110.2**
Speed ratings (Par 95): **95,94,89,87,84 78,69**
CSF £5.76 TOTE £4.70: £2.20, £1.10; EX 6.40 Trifecta £49.70.
Owner Nick Bradley Racing 36 & Partner **Bred** Jane Allison **Trained** Musley Bank, N Yorks

FOCUS
The first two, who were drawn on the inside, dominated this fair event. The race average helps with the ratings.

2289 TRUSTEES OF THE NORTHERN RACING COLLEGE/BRITISH EBF MAIDEN STKS 1m 2f 5y

3:00 (3:03) (Class 5) 3-Y-O **£4,528** (£1,347; £673; £336) **Stalls** Low

Form RPR

4 **1** **Desert Icon (FR)**[14] 1852 3-9-5.. DanielTudhope 7 87+
(William Haggas) *cl up: led wl over 1f out: sn clr: readily* **30/100[1]**

2 *1¼* **Selino** 3-9-5.. DanielMuscutt 1 82
(James Fanshawe) *dwlt and towards rr: hdwy 1/2-way: trckd ldrs 3f out: rdn along 2f out: chsd wnr ins fnl f: kpt on* **14/1**

3-4 **3** *3¾* **Global Express**[13] 1898 3-9-5.. PaulMulrennan 3 76
(Ed Dunlop) *sn trcking ldr: hdwy to ld 3f out: rdn along 2f out: sn hdd and drvn: wknd fnl f* **5/1[2]**

5 **4** *6* **Stone Cougar (USA)**[9] 1975 3-9-0.. JoeFanning 5 58
(Mark Johnston) *trckd ldrs: pushed along over 4f out: rdn wl over 2f out: sn one pce* **14/1**

0- **5** *½* **Jeweller**[229] 7257 3-9-5.. LouisSteward 8 62
(Sir Michael Stoute) *hld up towards rr: hdwy 3f out: rdn along wl over 1f out: n.d* **14/1**

0-6 **6** *1¼* **Darwin Dream**[18] 1754 3-9-5.. GrahamLee 2 59
(David Elsworth) *towards rr: pushed along 7f out: reminders 1/2-way: plugged on fnl 2f (jockey said gelding ran green)* **6/1[3]**

0 **7** *9* **Voiceoftheemirates**[18] 1764 3-9-5.. KevinStott 6 41
(Kevin Ryan) *dwlt and towards rr: hdwy 1/2-way and in tch: rdn along over 3f out: sn outpcd* **20/1**

00 **8** *35* **Two For Three (IRE)**[13] 1898 3-9-0.. BenSanderson(5) 4
(Roger Fell) *led: rdn along and hdd 3f out: sn wknd* **100/1**

2m 14.29s (-0.71) **Going Correction** -0.125s/f (Firm) **8 Ran SP% 133.6**
Speed ratings (Par 99): **97,96,93,88,87 86,79,51**
CSF £10.02 TOTE £1.30: £1.10, £3.10, £1.40; EX 6.70 Trifecta £27.30.
Owner Sheikh Juma Dalmook Al Maktoum **Bred** Ecurie Des Charmes **Trained** Newmarket, Suffolk

FOCUS
There wasn't much depth to this maiden, but the first two are promising. The third helps with the standard.

2290 DONCASTER EQUINE COLLEGE H'CAP 1m 2f 5y

3:35 (3:36) (Class 5) (0-70,70) 4-Y-O+
£4,528 (£1,347; £673; £336; £300; £300) **Stalls** Low

Form RPR

4100 **1** **Regular Income (IRE)**[55] 1065 4-8-13 **69**......................(b) TobyEley(7) 5 80
(Adam West) *dwlt and reminders in rr: hdwy 4f out: chsd ldrs 2f out: rdn over 1f out and sn edgd lft: drvn and styd on wl fnl f to ld nr fin* **6/1[3]**

30-2 **2** *nk* **Ideal Candy (IRE)**[14] 1850 4-9-7 **70**.. ShaneGray 1 80
(Karen Tutty) *led: qckned clr over 2f out: rdn jst over 1f out: drvn ins fnl f: hdd and no ex towards fin* **2/1[1]**

0-36 **3** *5* **Bit Of A Quirke**[14] 1848 6-9-5 **68**.. AndrewMullen 4 68
(Mark Walford) *trckd ldrs: effrt to chse ldr 3f out: rdn along 2f out: drvn over 1f out: kpt on same pce u.p fnl f* **9/2[2]**

055- **4** *2* **Frankster (FR)**[205] 8053 6-9-1 **64**..............................(tp) GrahamLee 3 60
(Micky Hammond) *hld up towards rr: hdwy over 4f out: chsd ldng pair over 2f out: sn rdn: drvn over 1f out: kpt on same pce* **16/1**

5003 **5** *18* **Seaborough (IRE)**[23] 1647 4-8-13 **62**.. CliffordLee 7 22
(David Thompson) *chsd ldrs: rdn along over 3f out: sn one pce* **8/1**

00-5 **6** *3* **Ronnie The Rooster**[8] 2012 5-7-13 **53**.. SeanDavis(5) 2 7
(Les Eyre) *towards rr: sme hdwy over 4f out: rdn along 3f out: n.d (jockey said gelding was never travelling)* **20/1**

506- **7** *14* **Metronomic (IRE)**[176] 8900 5-8-4 **53**..............................(h[1]) CamHardie 10
(Peter Niven) *trckd ldr: pushed along 4f out: rdn 3f out: sn drvn and wknd* **50/1**

45-6 **8** *14* **Jo's Girl (IRE)**[22] 1660 4-9-5 **68**..............................(h) DougieCostello 8
(Micky Hammond) *hld up towards rr: sme hdwy 4f out: rdn along 3f out: sn outpcd* **8/1**

1/00 **9** *28* **Rock Island Line**[46] 1231 5-8-3 **52**.. JoeFanning 9
(Mark Walford) *in tch: rdn along over 3f out: sn wknd* **11/1**

050- **10** *14* **Verdigris (IRE)**[183] 8722 4-9-3 **66**.. JamesSullivan 6
(Ruth Carr) *trckd ldrs: pushed along 4f out: sn rdn and wknd (jockey said filly lost it's action)* **12/1**

2m 12.25s (-2.75) **Going Correction** -0.125s/f (Firm) **10 Ran SP% 116.7**
Speed ratings (Par 103): **106,105,101,100,85 83,72,60,38,27**
CSF £18.35 CT £59.97 TOTE £7.70: £2.20, £1.30, £1.90; EX 23.70 Trifecta £93.50.
Owner Ian & Amanda Maybrey And Partners **Bred** Garrett O'Neill **Trained** Epsom, Surrey

FOCUS
This ordinary handicap was run at a good gallop and was 2sec quicker than the preceding maiden. The first four finished a mile clear and the form's rated around the runner-up.

2291 ZILCO TRAINING RANGE SUPPORTS THE NORTHERN RACING COLLEGE H'CAP 1m 6y

4:10 (4:10) (Class 4) (0-80,80) 4-Y-O+
£7,762 (£2,310; £1,154; £577; £300; £300) **Stalls** Low

Form RPR

36-4 **1** **Kripke (IRE)**[23] 1644 4-9-5 **78**.. BenCurtis 4 88+
(David Barron) *hld up in tch: pushed along and hdwy 3f out: rdn along to chse ldrs 2f out: drvn to chal ins fnl f: styd on wl to ld fnl 75yds* **7/4[1]**

0-10 **2** *1½* **Casement (IRE)**[14] 1859 5-9-5 **78**.. AlistairRawlinson 7 84
(Michael Appleby) *led: hdd over 5f out and cl up: led again over 2f out: rdn over 1f out: drvn ins fnl f: hdd and no ex fnl 75yds* **3/1[2]**

-443 **3** *1* **Mount Ararat (IRE)**[14] 1849 4-8-9 **75**.. JonathanFisher(7) 2 79
(K R Burke) *t.k.h early: trckd ldng pair: hdwy 3f out: effrt wl over 1f out and sn rdn: keeping on whn n.m.r jst ins fnl f: kpt on same pce after* **5/1[3]**

60-0 **4** *2* **Quoteline Direct**[22] 1659 6-8-12 **71**..............................(h) PaulMulrennan 3 70
(Micky Hammond) *trckd ldrs: pushed along over 3f out: rdn over 2f out: kpt on same pce* **33/1**

00-2 **5** *¾* **Mutarakez (IRE)**[11] 1955 7-9-2 **75**.. JamesSullivan 6 73
(Ruth Carr) *hld up and detached in rr: tk clsr order over 3f out: n.m.r on inner over 2f out and again 1 1/2f out: sn swtchd rt: swtchd lft again and rdn appr fnl f: no imp* **6/1**

00-0 **6** *3½* **Royal Shaheen (FR)**[23] 1644 6-9-7 **80**..............................(v) GrahamLee 1 70
(Alistair Whillans) *reminders s: chsd along and cl up on inner: led over 5f out: rdn along and hdd over 2f out: sn wknd* **17/2**

0500 **7** *5* **Contrast (IRE)**[32] 1418 5-8-8 **67**.. CamHardie 5 45
(Michael Easterby) *dwlt: a in rr* **14/1**

1m 44.01s (-1.89) **Going Correction** -0.125s/f (Firm) **7 Ran SP% 112.5**
Speed ratings (Par 105): **104,102,101,99,98 95,90**
CSF £6.85 TOTE £2.20: £1.20, £2.90; EX 7.90 Trifecta £32.00.
Owner Harrowgate Bloodstock Ltd **Bred** J Shanahan **Trained** Maunby, N Yorks

FOCUS
They went a reasonable gallop in this fair handicap. The form is best rated around the second.

2292 LADBROKES SUPPORTING THE NORTHERN RACING COLLEGE H'CAP 6f

4:45 (4:46) (Class 4) (0-80,82) 4-Y-O+
£7,762 (£2,310; £1,154; £577; £300; £300) **Stalls** Low

Form RPR

0503 **1** **Highly Sprung (IRE)**[16] 1817 6-8-13 **69**.. JoeFanning 1 77
(Les Eyre) *trckd ldng pair: hdwy on inner and cl up over 2f out: led wl over 1f out: sn rdn: drvn and kpt on strly fnl f* **4/1[3]**

160- **2** *2* **Cale Lane**[190] 8501 4-9-4 **74**.. DavidAllan 4 75
(Julie Camacho) *led: rdn along 2f out: hdd wl over 1f out: sn drvn: kpt on* **7/2[2]**

40-6 **3** *2¾* **Mr Orange (IRE)**[13] 1895 6-9-7 **77**..............................(p) KevinStott 3 69
(Paul Midgley) *awkward s and towards rr: pushed along 1/2-way: rdn 2f out: kpt on fnl f* **10/3[1]**

30-5 **4** *2* **Round The Island**[16] 1818 6-8-11 **67**.. PhilDennis 2 52
(Richard Whitaker) *trckd ldrs: hdwy 2f out: rdn over 1f out: kpt on same pce (jockey said gelding ran too freely)* **9/2**

44-3 **5** *1* **Seen The Lyte (IRE)**[9] 1978 4-9-7 **82**..............(h[1]) FayeMcManoman(5) 5 64
(Nigel Tinkler) *chsd ldrs on outer: rdn along 2f out: wknd over 1f out* **11/1**

2122 **6** *1¼* **Socialites Red**[2] 2194 6-8-8 **69**..............................(p) TheodoreLadd(5) 6 47
(Scott Dixon) *cl up: rdn along over 2f out: sn drvn and wknd* **7/2[2]**

1m 16.04s (-1.06) **Going Correction** -0.125s/f (Firm) **6 Ran SP% 114.0**
Speed ratings (Par 105): **102,99,95,93,91 90**
CSF £18.66 TOTE £3.50: £2.40, £2.20; EX 24.10 Trifecta £80.00.
Owner A Turton & Dr V Webb **Bred** Patrick J Moloney **Trained** Catwick, N Yorks

FOCUS
Modest sprint form, and a race which only really concerned two. The winner could be rated higher on last year's best.

2293 NORTHERN RACING COLLEGE H'CAP 6f
5:15 (5:19) (Class 5) (0-75,76) 3-Y-O

£3,881 (£1,155; £577; £300; £300; £300) Stalls Low

Form RPR
105- 1 Gale Force Maya[212] 7836 3-8-13 64 PaulMulrennan 4 69
(Michael Dods) hld up towards rr: hdwy over 2f out: chsd ldrs and swtchd rt to outer jst over 1f out: sn rdn and str run on wd outside in fnl f to ld towards fin 33/1
2-32 2 ½ Staycation (IRE)[13] 1894 3-9-7 72 (p) DavidAllan 9 75
(Rebecca Bastiman) led: pushed along 2f out: rdn over 1f out: drvn ins fnl f: hdd and no ex towards fin 7/1
40-1 3 1 Lady Calcaria[13] 1894 3-9-6 71 DuranFentiman 1 71
(Tim Easterby) trckd ldng pair: hdwy 2f out: chsd ldr over 1f out: rdn and ev ch ent fnl f: sn drvn and kpt on same pce 2/1[1]
4321 4 1 ¼ Ascot Dreamer[9] 1982 3-8-6 57 6ex JamesSullivan 2 53
(David Brown) trckd ldrs: hdwy over 2f out: rdn wl over 1f out: drvn and kpt on same pce ins fnl f 5/1[2]
20-6 5 2 ¼ Hard Solution[13] 1894 3-9-1 66 (p[1]) DanielTudhope 3 55
(David O'Meara) trckd ldr: hdwy over 2f out and sn pushed along: rdn wl over 1f out: drvn appr fnl f: wknd 11/2[3]
0-10 6 5 Bugler Bob (IRE)[13] 1894 3-9-11 76 (p[1]) JasonHart 8 49
(John Quinn) chsd ldrs: rdn along over 2f out: sn wknd 15/2
5-33 7 3 Fume (IRE)[13] 1894 3-9-7 72 (p[1]) GrahamLee 10 35
(James Bethell) a towards rr (trainer said gelding appeared not to face the first time application of cheek-pieces) 7/1
21-6 8 nk Primeiro Boy (IRE)[30] 1488 3-8-13 69 ConnorMurtagh(5) 6 31
(Richard Fahey) in tch: rdn along over 2f out: sn wknd 14/1
-405 9 7 Evangeline Samos[6] 2063 3-8-9 60 (p[1]) ShaneGray 7
(Kevin Ryan) a bhd 25/1

1m 15.92s (-1.18) **Going Correction** -0.125s/f (Firm) 9 Ran SP% 115.6
Speed ratings (Par 99): **102,101,100,98,95 88,84,84,74**
CSF £247.68 CT £689.60 TOTE £35.20: £11.20, £2.70, £1.30; EX 134.40 Trifecta £1672.60.
Owner Frank Lowe **Bred** Mrs J Imray **Trained** Denton, Co Durham

FOCUS
Limited sprint form, although it was slightly quicker than the preceding Class 4 handicap. The runner-up helps with the standard.

2294 GO RACING IN YORKSHIRE FUTURE STARS APPRENTICE H'CAP (ROUND 3) 5f 3y
5:50 (5:51) (Class 5) (0-75,76) 4-Y-O+

£3,881 (£1,155; £577; £300; £300; £300) Stalls Low

Form RPR
6-06 1 Peggie Sue[16] 1822 4-9-1 69 TobyEley 1 81
(Adam West) trckd ldrs: gd hdwy on inner 1/2-way: chsd ldr wl over 1f out: swtchd rt and rdn to chal ent fnl f: styd on wl to ld fnl 100yds 7/1[3]
50-0 2 2 ½ Rickyroadboy[18] 1760 4-8-10 67 HarryRussell(3) 2 70
(Mark Walford) led: rdn clr 2f out: jnd and drvn ent fnl f: hdd and no ex fnl 100yds 10/1
0-24 3 1 ½ Foxtrot Knight[16] 1818 7-8-8 65 EllaMcCain(3) 3 63
(Ruth Carr) dwlt and towards rr: hdwy on inner 2f out: sn chsng ldrs: rdn to chse ldng pair ins fnl f: sn no imp 11/4[1]
1-44 4 2 ¼ Musharrif[6] 2053 7-8-13 74 ZakWheatley(7) 4 64
(Declan Carroll) chsd ldrs: rdn along 2f out: drvn over 1f out: kpt on fnl f 9/2[2]
0033 5 1 ½ Deeds Not Words (IRE)[16] 1818 8-8-13 67 JonathanFisher 5 51+
(Tracy Waggott) dwlt and towards rr: effrt whn carried wd bnd 2f out: sn swtchd lft to inner and rdn: kpt on u.p fnl f: nrst fin 12/1
5040 6 1 Van Gerwen[36] 1342 6-9-2 73 JessicaCooley(3) 10 54
(Les Eyre) prom: rdn along 2f out: grad wknd 25/1
55-4 7 shd Dandy's Beano (IRE)[29] 1507 4-8-10 69 RhonaPindar(5) 7 49
(Kevin Ryan) t.k.h: cl up: rdn along and wd st: wknd over 1f out 8/1
-552 8 ½ Nibras Again[13] 1899 5-9-2 75 CianMacRedmond(5) 8 53
(Paul Midgley) chsd ldrs: rdn along 2f out: sn one pce 9/2[2]
3146 9 1 ¼ Zapper Cass (FR)[18] 1767 6-9-8 76 (b) KieranSchofield 9 50
(Michael Appleby) a towards rr 16/1
52-4 10 5 One Boy (IRE)[16] 1817 8-8-5 62 (b) RussellHarris(3) 6 18
(Paul Midgley) chsd ldrs: rdn along over 2f out: wd st and wknd 25/1
20-0 11 8 B Fifty Two (IRE)[16] 1818 10-8-10 67 (tp) WilliamCarver(3) 11
(Marjorie Fife) a towards rr 50/1

1m 2.71s (-1.19) **Going Correction** -0.125s/f (Firm) 11 Ran SP% 119.0
Speed ratings (Par 103): **104,100,97,94,91 90,89,89,87,79 66**
CSF £74.35 CT £215.43 TOTE £8.50: £1.90, £3.80, £1.20; EX 60.80 Trifecta £235.10.
Owner West Racing Partnership **Bred** Sean Gollogly **Trained** Epsom, Surrey

FOCUS
A real draw race this, with the first five home coming out of the inside five stalls, in ascending order. The winner is rated in line with her Sandown win last year.
T/Plt: £15.20 to a £1 stake. Pool: £46,922.09 - 2,250.79 winning units T/Qpdt: £11.40 to a £1 stake. Pool: £3,391.58 - 218.85 winning units **Joe Rowntree**

2190 SOUTHWELL (L-H)
Wednesday, May 1

OFFICIAL GOING: Fibresand: standard
Wind: Nil Weather: Cloudy

2295 SKY SPORTS RACING SKY 415 H'CAP 4f 214y(F)
12:00 (12:01) (Class 6) (0-55,59) 4-Y-O+

£3,105 (£924; £461; £300; £300; £300) Stalls Centre

Form RPR
0001 1 Red Invader (IRE)[9] 1987 9-9-11 59 4ex (b) StevieDonohoe 1 69
(John Butler) sn chsng ldrs: led over 1f out: rdn and edgd lft ins fnl f: r.o 5/1[3]
0404 2 1 ¾ Filbert Street[28] 1521 4-9-3 51 (p) BenCurtis 2 55
(Roy Brotherton) s.i.s: sn pushed along in rr: hdwy u.p over 1f out: wnt 2nd ins fnl f: nt rch wnr (jockey said gelding missed the break) 9/2[2]
26-4 3 2 ½ Viking Way (IRE)[37] 1335 4-8-11 50 (b) ConnorMurtagh(5) 4 45
(Olly Williams) chsd ldrs: rdn over 1f out: no ex ins fnl f 7/2[1]
31-0 4 shd Boudica Bay (IRE)[18] 1765 4-9-7 55 RachelRichardson 11 49
(Eric Alston) prom: pushed along 1/2-way: rdn and edgd lft over 1f out: styd on same pce fnl f 8/1
000- 5 ¾ Optimickstickhill[132] 9648 4-8-7 46 oh1 (b) TheodoreLadd(5) 7 38
(Scott Dixon) led: hdd over 3f out: rdn over 1f out: styd on same pce 25/1
5052 6 2 ¾ Bahango (IRE)[9] 1987 7-8-10 49 (v) ThomasGreatrex(5) 9 31
(Patrick Morris) w ldr tl led over 3f out: rdn and hdd over 1f out: wknd ins fnl f 13/2
-066 7 ½ Tilsworth Rose[68] 848 5-8-12 46 oh1 (b) RaulDaSilva 10 26
(J R Jenkins) s.i.s: outpcd 50/1
00-3 8 ½ Poppy Jag (IRE)[27] 1554 4-8-12 46 JasonHart 3 24
(Kevin Frost) chsd ldrs: pushed along and lost pl over 3f out: n.d after 10/1
0-04 9 nk Maureb (IRE)[10] 1967 7-9-5 53 (p) DougieCostello 5 30
(Tony Coyle) prom: pushed along over 3f out: sn lost pl 6/1
60-5 10 nk Ise Lodge Babe[54] 1085 4-8-5 46 oh1 RPWalsh(7) 6 22
(Ronald Thompson) in rr: rdn: edgd rt and wknd 1/2-way 80/1
-000 11 9 Tina Teaspoon[33] 1402 5-8-12 46 oh1 (h) PaddyMathers 8
(Derek Shaw) chsd ldrs: shkn up 1/2-way: wknd over 1f out 50/1

59.91s (0.21) **Going Correction** 0.0s/f (Stan) 11 Ran SP% 113.9
Speed ratings (Par 101): **98,95,91,91,89 85,84,83,83,82 68**
CSF £26.24 CT £85.59 TOTE £5.00: £2.90, £1.80, £1.10; EX 33.00 Trifecta £112.60.
Owner Power Geneva Ltd **Bred** Tally-Ho Stud **Trained** Newmarket, Suffolk

FOCUS
A moderate sprint, which produced an easy winner. Straightforward form in behind.

2296 SKY SPORTS RACING VIRGIN 535 H'CAP 4f 214y(F)
12:30 (12:30) (Class 5) (0-70,72) 3-Y-O+

£3,752 (£1,116; £557; £300; £300; £300) Stalls Centre

Form RPR
4240 1 Samovar[14] 1860 4-9-12 68 (b) PaddyMathers 4 77
(Scott Dixon) s.i.s: sn chsng ldrs: drvn along 1/2-way: styd on u.p to ld wl ins fnl f 6/1
2-12 2 ½ Honey Gg[28] 1521 4-9-2 65 CianMacRedmond(7) 7 72
(Declan Carroll) chsd ldrs: led 1/2-way: rdn and hdd wl ins fnl f 3/1[2]
0566 3 1 ¼ Point Zero (IRE)[8] 2025 4-9-11 72 (be) TheodoreLadd(5) 2 75
(Michael Appleby) w ldrs: led over 3f out: hdd 1/2-way: sn rdn: styd on same pce wl ins fnl f 9/2[3]
-443 4 ½ Global Melody[10] 1973 4-9-9 65 (p[1]) BenCurtis 5 66
(Phil McEntee) sn outpcd: drvn along 1/2-way: r.o u.p ins fnl f: nt rch ldrs 2/1[1]
-400 5 ¾ Ghost Buy (FR)[25] 1598 3-8-11 62 (t) TrevorWhelan 1 56
(Ivan Furtado) s.i.s: outpcd: rdn over 1f out: r.o ins fnl f: nt rch ldrs 12/1
00-0 6 3 Marietta Robusti (IRE)[12] 1929 4-9-11 72 DylanHogan(5) 3 59
(Stella Barclay) chsd ldrs: rdn 1/2-way: hung lft over 1f out: wknd fnl f 50/1
554- 7 4 ½ Lydiate Lady[182] 8742 7-9-11 67 JasonHart 8 38
(Eric Alston) led: hdd over 3f out: rdn 1/2-way: wknd over 1f out 10/1
060/ 8 23 Rio Glamorous[1074] 2503 6-8-12 54 oh2 (t) PhilipPrince 6
(Roy Bowring) s.i.s: outpcd 50/1

59.32s (-0.38) **Going Correction** 0.0s/f (Stan)
WFA 3 from 4yo+ 9lb 8 Ran SP% 111.5
Speed ratings (Par 103): **103,102,100,99,98 93,86,49**
CSF £23.10 CT £86.83 TOTE £6.90: £1.50, £1.10, £1.50; EX 24.30 Trifecta £92.10.
Owner Paul J Dixon And The Chrystal Maze Ptn **Bred** Paul Dixon & Crystal Maze Partnership **Trained** Babworth, Notts

FOCUS
A decent contest for the level at the track. The winner cashed in on a drop in grade.

2297 ADVERTISER LADIES DAY H'CAP 1m 13y(F)
1:00 (1:01) (Class 5) (0-75,73) 4-Y-O+

£3,752 (£1,116; £557; £300; £300; £300) Stalls Low

Form RPR
31-0 1 Directory[19] 1727 4-9-7 73 RyanTate 6 84
(James Eustace) prom: chsd ldr over 3f out: shkn up to ld 2f out: rdn clr fnl f 17/2
1334 2 4 Baron Run[28] 1526 9-8-0 59 ow2 RhonaPindar(7) 7 61
(K R Burke) led 7f out: hdd 2f out: styd on same pce fnl f 9/1
4012 3 ½ Bond Angel[2] 2193 4-8-12 69 TheodoreLadd(5) 3 70+
(David Evans) s.i.s: in rr: nt clr run over 3f out: hdwy over 1f out: nvr nrr 5/2[1]
6133 4 5 Muqarred (USA)[2] 2193 7-8-11 63 (p) BenCurtis 8 52
(Roger Fell) prom: rdn on outer over 3f out: wknd over 1f out 11/4[2]
3225 5 1 ½ Majestic Moon (IRE)[2] 2193 9-9-3 69 (p) RoystonFfrench 1 55
(Julia Feilden) chsd ldrs: rdn and nt clr run over 3f out: sn outpcd: styd on ins fnl f 6/1
0-44 6 1 ½ Mujassam[14] 1859 7-9-7 73 (b) DavidNolan 2 55
(David O'Meara) led early: chsd ldrs: rdn over 3f out: wknd over 1f out 5/1[3]
0-00 7 6 Blacklooks (IRE)[57] 1025 4-9-3 69 (p) TrevorWhelan 5 38
(Ivan Furtado) s.s: bhd and swtchd wd 6f out: sme hdwy u.p 2f out: wknd over 1f out (jockey said gelding was never travelling; vet said gelding was lame right hind) 33/1
224- 8 27 Flora Tristan[200] 8179 4-8-10 65 (h) GabrieleMalune(3) 4
(Ivan Furtado) sn led: hdd 7f out: chsd ldr tl rdn over 3f out: wknd and eased over 2f out (jockey said filly stopped quickly; vet said filly was stiff behind) 33/1

1m 42.38s (-1.32) **Going Correction** 0.0s/f (Stan) 8 Ran SP% 112.6
Speed ratings (Par 103): **106,102,101,96,95 93,87,60**
CSF £78.42 CT £246.55 TOTE £8.80: £2.40, £2.80, £1.20; EX 87.10 Trifecta £501.50.
Owner Blue Peter Racing 16 **Bred** Juddmonte Farms Ltd **Trained** Newmarket, Suffolk

FOCUS
They went a decent gallop here but nothing could get in a blow from off the pace. The form is rated around the second to recent C&D form.

2298 SOUTHWELL GOLF CLUB CLASSIFIED STKS 7f 14y(F)
1:30 (1:32) (Class 6) 4-Y-O+

£3,105 (£924; £461; £300; £300; £300) Stalls Low

Form RPR
0001 1 Atalanta Queen[28] 1527 4-8-9 49 (v) SeanKirrane(7) 6 57
(Robyn Brisland) led: hdd over 4f out: chsd ldr: rdn over 1f out: styd on to ld wl ins fnl f: hung rt nr fin 14/1
5021 2 nk Ticks The Boxes (IRE)[10] 1973 7-8-13 46 KieranSchofield(7) 5 61
(Brian Ellison) chsd ldrs: nt clr run and lost pl 5f out: hdwy over 3f out: rdn and edgd lft over 1f out: r.o 4/5[1]

000- **3** 1¼ **Cliff Bay (IRE)**[133] 9616 5-8-11 47....................(p) SeanDavis(5) 10 53
(Keith Dalgleish) *chsd ldrs: led over 4f out: rdn over 1f out: hdd wl ins fnl f: hmpd nr fin* **7/2**[2]

4060 **4** 2¼ **Diamond Pursuit**[27] 1553 4-8-13 45.................... GabrieleMalune(3) 12 47
(Ivan Furtado) *racd wd: hld up: hdwy over 2f out: sn rdn: styd on* **33/1**

6014 **5** ½ **Tellovoi (IRE)**[1] 2235 11-9-6 45....................(p) PhilipPrince 9 50
(Richard Guest) *sn pushed along in rr: rdn over 3f out: r.o ins fnl f: nt rch ldrs* **12/1**[3]

0000 **6** 1¼ **Plucky Dip**[1] 2235 8-8-9 40....................(p) LauraPearson(7) 4 43
(John Ryan) *sn pushed along in rr: hdwy over 1f out: no ex ins fnl f* **20/1**

5000 **7** 3¾ **Major Crispies**[10] 1967 8-9-2 49....................(p) AndrewElliott 8 33
(Ronald Thompson) *prom: hmpd and lost pl after 1f: n.d after* **20/1**

0-04 **8** ¾ **Excel Mate**[53] 1100 5-9-2 42.................... StevieDonohoe 3 31
(Roy Bowring) *plld hrd and prom: swtchd rt 5f out: rdn over 2f out: wknd fnl f (jockey said mare ran too free)* **33/1**

00-0 **9** 8 **Prince Of Time**[15] 1837 7-8-11 49.................... DylanHogan(5) 1 10
(Stella Barclay) *chsd ldrs: pushed along over 4f out: rdn 1/2-way: wknd over 1f out* **33/1**

5000 **10** *nk* **Ertidaad (IRE)**[20] 1717 7-9-2 42....................(v) EoinWalsh 2 9
(Emma Owen) *broke wl: sn rdn and lost pl: n.d after* **40/1**

0-02 **11** 1 **Only Ten Per Cent (IRE)**[19] 1731 11-9-2 45.................... AlistairRawlinson 11 7
(J R Jenkins) *prom: swtchd lft 6f out: lost pl over 4f out: rdn and wknd over 2f out* **33/1**

-050 **12** 2 **Westfield Wonder**[10] 1969 4-8-9 41.................... RPWalsh(7) 14
(Ronald Thompson) *sn prom: lost pl over 4f out: rdn and wknd over 2f out* **100/1**

0-02 **13** 1¼ **Kavora**[70] 809 4-8-13 46.................... AaronJones(3) 7
(Micky Hammond) *s.i.s: sn bhd* **25/1**

1m 30.27s (-0.03) **Going Correction** 0.0s/f (Stan) **13** Ran SP% **120.7**
Speed ratings (Par 101): **100,99,98,95,95 93,89,88,79,79 77,75,74**
CSF £23.67 TOTE £16.70: £3.50, £1.10, £1.70; EX 37.80 Trifecta £172.40.
Owner Ferrybank Properties Limited **Bred** R T Dunne **Trained** Danethorpe, Notts

FOCUS
A couple of in-form contenders in a reasonable race for the grade, but once again it was hard for the hold-up horses to get involved despite the gallop looking sound. The winner found a bit on her recent course win.

2299 VISITSOUTHWELL.COM H'CAP 1m 13y(F)
2:00 (2:01) (Class 5) (0-75,76) 3-Y-O
£3,752 (£1,116; £557; £300; £300; £300) **Stalls** Low

Form RPR

0-10 **1** **Love Your Work (IRE)**[39] 1285 3-9-7 **74**.................... RoystonFfrench 1 81
(Adam West) *s.i.s: outpcd: hdwy u.p over 1f out: r.o to ld wl ins fnl f (trainer said, reg app imp in form, gelding benefitted from being gelded and appreciated the return to Southwell)* **6/1**[3]

0-43 **2** 1 **Ollivander (IRE)**[10] 1970 3-8-9 **65**....................(p) ConorMcGovern(3) 4 70
(David O'Meara) *chsd ldr tl led over 3f out: rdn over 1f out: hung rt and hdd wl ins fnl f* **7/1**

6-05 **3** 2¼ **Sarasota Star (IRE)**[33] 1396 3-9-1 **68**.................... TomQueally 5 68
(Martin Keighley) *s.i.s: racd wd in bk st: hdwy over 4f out: chsd ldr over 2f out: sn rdn and hung lft: styd on same pce ins fnl f* **10/1**

-054 **4** 1¾ **Fiction Writer (USA)**[49] 1178 3-8-13 **71**.................... AndrewBreslin(5) 6 67
(Mark Johnston) *sn pushed along to chse ldrs: outpcd over 3f out: rdn over 2f out: styd on ins fnl f* **7/2**[2]

044- **5** 1 **Natty Night**[187] 8608 3-9-9 **76**.................... BenCurtis 3 70
(William Muir) *prom: outpcd over 4f out: hdwy over 3f out: rdn over 1f out: wknd fnl f* **11/4**[1]

3513 **6** 18 **Sylviacliffs (FR)**[20] 1722 3-8-3 **63**....................(p) RhonaPindar(7) 7 15
(K R Burke) *s.i.s: sn prom: rdn over 2f out: wknd over 1f out (jockey said filly missed the break)* **6/1**[3]

50-2 **7** 12 **Gennaro (IRE)**[16] 1819 3-8-13 **66**....................(t) TrevorWhelan 2
(Ivan Furtado) *led over 4f: sn rdn: wknd over 2f out (jockey said gelding stopped quickly)* **7/1**

1m 43.75s (0.05) **Going Correction** 0.0s/f (Stan) **7** Ran SP% **111.6**
Speed ratings (Par 99): **99,98,95,94,93 75,63**
CSF £44.03 TOTE £6.90: £3.10, £3.10; EX 40.80 Trifecta £254.80.
Owner Flawless Racing Limited **Bred** Gerard Mullins **Trained** Epsom, Surrey

FOCUS
A run of the mill Class 5 handicap but it threw up a quite remarkable performance from Love Your Work. The form's rated around the second.

2300 ATTHERACES.COM H'CAP 4f 214y(F)
2:35 (2:35) (Class 6) (0-55,53) 3-Y-O
£3,105 (£924; £461; £300; £300; £300) **Stalls** Centre

Form RPR

5014 **1** **Gunnabedun (IRE)**[14] 1863 3-9-4 **53**....................(b) JamieGormley(3) 8 59
(Iain Jardine) *s.i.s: outpcd: swtchd lft 1/2-way: hdwy u.p and edgd lft over 1f out: r.o to ld nr fin* **7/4**[1]

0040 **2** *nk* **Lysander Belle (IRE)**[26] 1557 3-9-6 **52**.................... StevieDonohoe 1 54
(Sophie Leech) *w ldrs: led 4f out: rdn over 1f out: sn hung rt: hdd nr fin* **6/1**[3]

400 **3** 2¼ **Purely Prosecco**[65] 908 3-8-13 **45**.................... PaddyMathers 2 39
(Derek Shaw) *w ldrs: racd keenly: rdn: edgd rt and ev ch over 1f out: no ex ins fnl f* **25/1**

0-65 **4** 1½ **Laura's Legacy**[12] 1909 3-8-13 **45**.................... JosephineGordon 7 34
(Andrew Balding) *chsd ldrs: outpcd over 3f out: rdn over 1f out: styd on ins fnl f* **8/1**

40-6 **5** *shd* **Newgate Angel**[9] 1982 3-9-5 **51**....................(p) DavidNolan 10 39
(Tony Coyle) *prom: rdn 1/2-way: edgd lft and no ex ins fnl f* **8/1**

00-0 **6** 3¾ **Raquelle (IRE)**[9] 1982 3-9-4 **50**.................... RachelRichardson 3 25
(Tim Easterby) *chsd ldrs: rdn: edgd lft and nt clr run over 1f out: wknd ins fnl f (jockey said saddle slipped)* **16/1**

0-00 **7** 2½ **Carla Koala**[23] 1650 3-9-2 **51**.................... AaronJones(3) 4 17
(Natalie Lloyd-Beavis) *led 1f: remained handy tl rdn and wknd over 1f out* **14/1**

000- **8** ½ **Remission**[250] 6468 3-9-3 **49**.................... EoinWalsh 9 13
(Derek Shaw) *sn pushed along in rr: hdwy u.p 1/2-way: wknd wl over 1f out (trainer said gelding was unsuited by the fibresand surface)* **50/1**

3020 **9** 1½ **Secret Picnic (FR)**[9] 1982 3-9-5 **51**....................(t) RobbieDowney 5 9
(John Quinn) *s.i.s: outpcd* **7/2**[2]

1m 0.2s (0.50) **Going Correction** 0.0s/f (Stan) **9** Ran SP% **113.4**
Speed ratings (Par 97): **96,95,91,89,89 83,79,78,76**
CSF £12.33 CT £189.33 TOTE £2.20: £1.30, £1.50, £6.10; EX 11.70 Trifecta £209.40.
Owner Davidson & Jardine **Bred** Rathasker Stud **Trained** Carruthorstown, D'fries & G'way

FOCUS
A weak handicap on paper but it turned into quite an attritional test for a sprint and Gunnabedun finished like a train to get up late. Routine form in behind.

2301 SOUTHWELLTRADERS.CO.UK MAIDEN STKS 1m 4f 14y(F)
3:10 (3:11) (Class 5) 3-Y-O+
£3,752 (£1,116; £557; £278) **Stalls** Low

Form RPR

0- **1** **Hiroshima**[189] 8549 3-8-9.................... BrettDoyle 8 76
(John Ryan) *sn pushed along to chse ldrs: wnt 2nd over 5f out: led over 2f out: rdn and hung rt over 1f out: styd on strly* **3/1**[2]

2 6 **Trailboss (IRE)**[75] 4-10-0.................... StevieDonohoe 7 71
(Ed Vaughan) *s.s: hdwy over 10f out: rdn to chse wnr 2f out: carried rt over 1f out: sn swtchd lft: no ex ins fnl f* **4/1**

06 **3** 7 **Soft Summer Rain**[4] 2099 3-7-11.................... RobertDodsworth(7) 5 50+
(Michael Easterby) *s.i.s: hld up: pushed along over 4f out: styd on to go 3rd ins fnl f: nt trble ldrs* **33/1**

0-50 **4** 1¾ **Roc Astrale (IRE)**[6] 2059 5-9-7 66....................(vt[1]) GraceMcEntee(7) 3 54
(Phil McEntee) *jnd ldr after 1f: led over 8f out: hdd over 2f out: sn rdn: hung rt and wknd over 1f out* **14/1**

4 **5** 5 **Itchingham Lofte (IRE)**[23] 1643 3-8-9.................... LewisEdmunds 4 44
(David Barron) *plld hrd: w ldr 1f: remained handy: rdn over 2f out: wknd over 1f out* **7/4**[1]

6 15 **Constraint** 3-8-4.................... JosephineGordon 1 15
(Andrew Balding) *s.i.s: outpcd: sme hdwy over 6f out: wknd over 5f out* **7/2**[3]

60- **7** 42 **E Si Si Muove (IRE)**[281] 5321 7-10-0.................... AndrewElliott 2
(Andrew Crook) *led: hdd over 8f out: rdn and wknd over 4f out* **100/1**

8 5 **Can Can Nights** 3-8-4.................... RachelRichardson 6
(Olly Williams) *s.s: outpcd: hdwy over 6f out: rdn and wknd over 4f out* **50/1**

2m 39.42s (-1.58) **Going Correction** 0.0s/f (Stan)
WFA 3 from 4yo+ 19lb **8** Ran SP% **116.1**
Speed ratings (Par 103): **105,101,96,95,91 81,53,50**
CSF £15.63 TOTE £5.20: £1.90, £1.20, £5.40; EX 13.50 Trifecta £199.40.
Owner G Smith-Bernal **Bred** Mrs P A Cave **Trained** Newmarket, Suffolk

FOCUS
This looked pretty weak on paper but the winner could easily be above average and there was some promise from the runner-up, too. The first pair were clear.
T/Plt: £68.00 to a £1 stake. Pool: £38,692.80 - 414.88 winning units T/Qpdt: £37.70 to a £1 stake. Pool: £4,996.79 - 98.06 winning units **Colin Roberts**

2302 - 2309a (Foreign Racing) - See Raceform Interactive

MUNICH (L-H)
Wednesday, May 1

OFFICIAL GOING: Turf: good

2310a PFERDEWETTEN.DE - BAVARIAN CLASSIC (GROUP 3) (3YO) (TURF) 1m 2f
3:05 3-Y-O
£28,828 (£10,810; £5,405; £2,702; £1,801)

RPR

1 **Django Freeman (GER)**[199] 8247 3-9-2 0.................... LukasDelozier 5 103
(Henk Grewe, Germany) *prom: pushed along and prog fr over 2f out: disp ld 1 1/2f out: led jst ins fnl f: kpt on strly clsng stages: gng away at fin* **9/5**[1]

2 1½ **Quest The Moon (GER)**[192] 8462 3-9-2 0.................... PatCosgrave 1 100
(Frau S Steinberg, Germany) *in tch on inner: pushed along whn pce qcknd over 2f out: prog to ld narrowly over 1 1/2f out: hdd jst ins fnl f: kpt on but nt match pce of wnr clsng stages* **37/10**[3]

3 1¼ **Dschingis First (GER)**[178] 8869 3-9-2 0.................... AdriedeVries 7 98
(Markus Klug, Germany) *hld up in rr after 2f: asked to improve over 2f out: rdn 1 1/2f out: responded for press ins fnl f: r.o strly: snatched 3rd last stride* **61/10**

4 *hd* **Amiro (GER)** 3-9-2 0....................(b) AlexanderPietsch 3 98
(M Figge, Germany) *led at stdy pce: asked to qckn over 2f out: u.p and sn hdd over 1 1/2f out: kpt on gamely ins fnl f: lost 3rd last stride* **234/10**

5 ¾ **Accon (GER)**[178] 8869 3-9-2 0.................... JiriPalik 6 96
(Markus Klug, Germany) *midfield on outer: sltly outpcd and pushed along 2 1/2f out: rdn 2f out: kpt on outside rivals: nt pce to chal* **149/10**

6 *nk* **Beam Me Up (GER)** 3-9-2 0.................... MartinSeidl 2 95
(Markus Klug, Germany) *hld up in fnl trio: pushed along and effrt on inner over 2f out: disp 1 1/2f out: no ex ins fnl f: wknd fnl 110yds* **93/10**

7 2 **Enjoy The Moon (IRE)** 3-9-2 0.................... FilipMinarik 4 91
(P Schiergen, Germany) *midfield on inner: dropped to fnl pair over 1/2-way: struggling to go pce 2 1/2f out: rdn 2f out: no imp: passed btn rival ins fnl f* **154/10**

8 3 **Quian (GER)**[213] 3-9-2 0.................... AndraschStarke 8 85
(P Schiergen, Germany) *cl up: pushed along to chse ldr 2 1/2f out: rdn 2f out: grad wekeaned fr 1 1/2f out: eased cl home* **7/2**[2]

2m 12.61s (3.64) **8** Ran SP% **119.5**
PARI-MUTUEL (all including 1 euro stake): WIN 2.80 PLACE 1.50, 1.60, 2.00 SF 7.90.
Owner Hedge Baumgarten Holschbach **Bred** Stiftung Gestut Fahrhof **Trained** Germany

1741 SAINT-CLOUD (L-H)
Wednesday, May 1

OFFICIAL GOING: Turf: good

2311a PRIX PENTHESILEE (CLAIMER) (LADY AMATEURS) (3YO) (TURF) 1m 2f 110y
1:00 3-Y-O
£8,558 (£3,423; £2,567; £1,711; £855)

RPR

1 **El Ingrato (FR)**[17] 3-9-7 0.................... MlleDianaLopezLeret 4 65
(M Delcher Sanchez, France) **17/10**[1]

2 3 **Gold Bere (FR)**[26] 1568 3-9-11 0....................(p) MlleBarbaraGuenet 9 63
(George Baker) *sn front rnk: settled in 2nd: pushed along and briefly chal 2f out: rdn to chse ldr over 1f out: kpt on but a being hld ins fnl f* **17/5**[2]

3 2 **Blackpearlsecrete (FR)**[16] 3-9-4 0....................(b) FrauBeritWeber 1 52
(S Cerulis, France) **18/1**

4 3 **Rue Dauphine (FR)**[83] 3-8-10 0.................... MlleMeganePeslier(5) 8 43
(Artus Adeline De Boisbrunet, France) **9/1**

5 *nse* **Tequila Boom Boom (FR)**[19] 3-9-1 0....................(p) MissMelaniePlat 6 43
(Mlle M-L Mortier, France) **18/5**[3]
6 *3* **Kenfaro (FR)**[78] 3-9-8 0....................(b) MlleSolangeGourdain 2 45
(Yannick Fouin, France) **53/10**
7 *8* **Eleven One (FR)**[182] 8753 3-9-4 0....................(p) MlleLaraLeGeay 7 25
(Gianluca Bietolini, France) **31/1**
8 *3* **Tour De Magie (IRE)**[13] 3-9-4 0................(b) MmeMelissaBoisgontier 5 20
(Mlle J Soudan, France) **23/1**
2m 13.09s (-6.51) **8** Ran SP% **119.9**
PARI-MUTUEL (all including 1 euro stake): WIN 2.70; PLACE 1.60, 1.70, 3.50; DF 3.70.
Owner Sunday Horses Club S L **Bred** Sunday Horses Club S.L And M Delcher Sanchez **Trained** France

2312a PRIX PENELOPE (GROUP 3) (3YO FILLIES) (TURF) 1m 2f 110y
1:35 3-Y-O **£36,036** (£14,414; £10,810; £7,207)

RPR
1 **Cartiem (FR)**[32] 3-9-0 0.................... CristianDemuro 4 102+
(J-C Rouget, France) *sn trcking ldr: keen early: urged along to chse ldr 2f out: rdn and clsng over 1f out: drvn ins fnl f to ld fnl 25yds* **21/10**[3]
2 *nk* **Phoceene (FR)**[52] 1128 3-9-0 0.................... ChristopheSoumillon 1 101
(F Rossi, France) *led: pushed along and qcknd 2f out: rdn to maintain advantage over 1f out: drvn ins fnl f: hdd fnl 25yds* **19/10**[2]
3 *3/4* **Romanciere (IRE)**[212] 7853 3-9-0 0.................... MaximeGuyon 5 100+
(A Fabre, France) *hld up in rr: hdwy over 2f out: rdn to chse ldrs over 1f out: drvn and kpt on ins fnl f* **6/5**[1]
4 *3* **Agnes (FR)**[30] 3-9-0 0.................... YutakaTake 3 94
(Mlle J Soudan, France) *settled in 3rd: shkn up over 2f out: rdn along over 1f out: no ex ins fnl f* **11/1**
2m 16.14s (-3.46) **4** Ran SP% **120.5**
PARI-MUTUEL (all including 1 euro stake): WIN 3.10; PLACE 1.50, 1.50; SF 6.20.
Owner J L Tepper, G Augustin-Normand & Ecurie Des Charme **Bred** R Shaykhutdinov, Haras Du Mezeray S A & C Clement **Trained** Pau, France

2313a PRIX DU MUGUET (GROUP 2) (4YO+) (TURF) 1m
3:25 4-Y-O+ **£66,756** (£25,765; £12,297; £8,198; £4,099)

RPR
1 **Plumatic**[207] 8012 5-9-0 0.................... VincentCheminaud 5 113+
(A Fabre, France) *hld up in rr: urged along over 2f out: rdn and gd hdwy over 1f out: drvn ins fnl f to ld fnl 50yds* **28/1**
2 *nk* **Olmedo (FR)**[32] 1451 4-9-0 0.................... CristianDemuro 3 113
(J-C Rouget, France) *tk v t.k.h early: trckd ldrs: settled in 2nd: pushed into ld 1 1/2f out: drvn ins fnl f: hdd fnl 50yds* **23/5**
3 *3/4* **Mer Et Nuages (FR)**[21] 1708 4-9-0 0.................... Pierre-CharlesBoudot 6 111
(A Fabre, France) *trckd ldrs in 3rd: pushed along 2f out: rdn and hdwy over 1f out: drvn and kpt on ins fnl f* **17/5**[3]
4 *2 1/2* **Tornibush (IRE)**[206] 8029 5-9-0 0.................... OlivierPeslier 2 105
(P Decouz, France) *disp ld early: settled to trck ldrs: rowed along over 2f out: rdn over 1f out: kpt on same pce fnl f* **10/1**
5 *snk* **Graphite (FR)**[32] 1451 5-9-0 0.................... MickaelBarzalona 1 108+
(A Fabre, France) *settled in midfield: urged along 2f out: hdwy against rails whn short of room over 1f out: nvr rcvrd* **5/1**
6 *snk* **Polydream (IRE)**[206] 8029 4-9-3 0.................... MaximeGuyon 8 108
(F Head, France) *towards rr early: shkn up 2f out: rdn to chse ldrs over 1f out: no ex ins fnl f* **31/10**[2]
7 *8* **Ostilio**[207] 8012 4-9-3 0.................... AndreaAtzeni 4 89
(Simon Crisford) *disp ld early: sent on to ld after 1f: pushed along 2f out: sn rdn and btn: eased ins fnl f* **3/1**[1]
1m 37.97s (-9.53) **7** Ran SP% **119.2**
PARI-MUTUEL (all including 1 euro stake): WIN 3.60; PLACE 2.70, 1.80, 1.60; DF 28.00.
Owner Wertheimer & Frere **Bred** Wertheimer Et Frere **Trained** Chantilly, France

2314a PRIX GREFFULHE (GROUP 2) (3YO COLTS & FILLIES) (TURF) 1m 2f 110y
4:35 3-Y-O **£66,756** (£25,765; £12,297; £8,198; £4,099)

RPR
1 **Roman Candle**[24] 1625 3-9-2 0.................... MickaelBarzalona 5 106+
(A Fabre, France) *sn prom: settled in 2nd: pushed along over 2f out: rdn to chse ldr over 1f out: drvn upsides ins fnl f: kpt on u.p to ld fnl 50yds* **11/5**[2]
2 *nk* **Pappalino (FR)**[36] 1347 3-9-2 0.................... CristianDemuro 4 105
(J Reynier, France) *led: qcknd over 2f out: rdn to hold advantage over 1f out: drvn and strly chal ins fnl f: hdd fnl 50yds* **11/1**
3 *3* **Starmaniac**[32] 3-9-2 0.................... MaximeGuyon 1 100
(C Laffon-Parias, France) *hld up in rr: urged along and hdwy over 2f out: rdn over 1f out: kpt on but unable to get to front two ins fnl f* **6/5**[1]
4 *3/4* **Goya Senora (FR)**[32] 3-9-2 0.................... JeromeCabre 2 98
(Y Barberot, France) *trckd ldrs: rdn along 2f out: drvn over 1f out: kpt on same pce fnl f* **66/10**
5 *3 1/2* **Sound Of Victory (IRE)**[30] 3-9-2 0.................... ChristopheSoumillon 3 92
(P Bary, France) *t.k.h early: settled in 4th: rowed along over 2f out: rdn w limited rspnse over 1f out: no ex fnl f* **18/5**[3]
2m 12.55s (-7.05) **5** Ran SP% **119.9**
PARI-MUTUEL (all including 1 euro stake): WIN 3.20; PLACE 2.10, 4.90; SF 22.90.
Owner Godolphin SNC **Bred** Ecurie Melanie, Ecurie Haras Du Cadran & A Von Gun **Trained** Chantilly, France

FOCUS
This event has been brought forward a week from its old spot in the calendar. The winner score with a bit to spare.

1631 SENONNES-POUANCE
Wednesday, May 1

OFFICIAL GOING: Turf: very soft

2315a PRIX DU DOCTEUR GUY JALLOT (MAIDEN) (2YO) (TURF) 6f
3:20 2-Y-O **£5,630** (£2,252; £1,689; £1,126; £563)

RPR
1 **Havana Bere (FR)** 2-8-13 0.................... ChristopherGrosbois 5 72
(J Boisnard, France) **13/10**[1]
2 *1 3/4* **Stelvio (FR)** 2-8-13 0.................... JeromeMoutard(3) 4 69
(A Giorgi, Italy)
3 *1 3/4* **Fact Or Fable (IRE)**[12] 1910 2-9-2 0.................... HugoJourniac 1 64
(J S Moore) *disp tl trckd ldr after 1f: pushed along on outer 2 1/2f out: prog to ld narrowly jst under 2f out: hdd over 1f out: kpt on same pce ins fnl f*
4 *2 1/2* **Trentatre (FR)** 2-8-13 0.................... AlexandreRoussel 3 54
(Simone Brogi, France)
5 *shd* **Hystery Bere (FR)** 2-8-13 0....................(p) MlleMarylineEon(3) 2 56
(J Boisnard, France)

Owner J Boisnard **Bred** Sas Regnier & San Gabriel Inv. Inc. **Trained** France

2234 CHELMSFORD (A.W) (L-H)
Thursday, May 2

OFFICIAL GOING: Polytrack: standard
Wind: Light, across Weather: Cloudy with sunny spells

2316 BET TOTEPLACEPOT AT TOTESPORT.COM EBF NOVICE STKS (PLUS 10 RACE) 5f (P)
5:45 (5:46) (Class 4) 2-Y-O **£5,822** (£1,732; £865; £432) **Stalls** Low

Form RPR
1 1 **Lambeth Walk**[17] 1821 2-9-3 0.................... OisinMurphy 2 82+
(Archie Watson) *edgd rt s: led early: chsd ldr: carried wd 3f out: shkn up over 1f out: edgd rt ins fnl f: r.o to ld nr fin* **4/6**[1]
2 *nk* **Praxeology (IRE)** 2-9-5 0.................... RyanMoore 3 81
(Mark Johnston) *pushed along to chse ldrs: lft in ld 1/2-way: rdn ins fnl f: hdd nr fin* **6/4**[2]
02 3 *9* **Littleton Hall (IRE)**[12] 1937 2-9-5 0.................... CallumShepherd 1 49
(Mick Channon) *sn led: hung rt 3f out: hdd 1/2-way: sn outpcd (jockey said colt hung badly right-handed)* **12/1**[3]
4 *13* **Star's Daughter** 2-9-0 0.................... JamieSpencer 4
(Ed Dunlop) *s.i.s: outpcd* **33/1**
1m 0.64s (0.44) **Going Correction** -0.175s/f (Stan) **4** Ran SP% **110.6**
Speed ratings (Par 95): **89,88,74,53**
CSF £2.00 TOTE £1.40; EX 2.60 Trifecta £2.60.
Owner Qatar Racing & David Howden **Bred** The Kathryn Stud **Trained** Upper Lambourn, W Berks

FOCUS
A good battle between the market leaders.

2317 BET TOTEEXACTA AT TOTESPORT.COM H'CAP 1m 6f (P)
6:20 (6:20) (Class 4) (0-85,80) 3-Y-O **£8,668** (£2,579; £1,289; £644; £300) **Stalls** Low

Form RPR
3-21 1 **Emirates Empire (IRE)**[19] 1771 3-9-7 **80**.................... JamieSpencer 3 93+
(Michael Bell) *sn led: shkn up and qcknd clr over 2f out: edgd rt over 1f out: eased towards fin* **13/8**[1]
21 2 *6* **Tigray (USA)**[11] 1972 3-9-1 **74** 6ex.................... AlistairRawlinson 2 78
(Michael Appleby) *chsd ldrs: shkn up over 3f out: rdn over 1f out: styd on same pce* **12/1**
-012 3 *3/4* **Smarter (IRE)**[13] 1928 3-9-7 **80**.................... JamesDoyle 4 83
(William Haggas) *hld up: pushed along over 4f out: rn wd 3f out: sn rdn: hdwy and hung lft over 1f out: styd on same pce* **3/1**[3]
5621 4 *3 1/4* **Withoutdestination**[30] 1510 3-9-3 **76**....................(b) OisinMurphy 1 74
(Marco Botti) *s.i.s: hld up: pushed along over 5f out: outpcd fr over 2f out* **8/1**
4121 5 *1/2* **Lord Lamington**[14] 1884 3-9-7 **80**.................... RyanMoore 5 78
(Mark Johnston) *led early: chsd wnr: rdn over 2f out: wknd fnl f* **5/2**[2]
3m 0.43s (-2.77) **Going Correction** -0.175s/f (Stan) **5** Ran SP% **110.5**
Speed ratings (Par 101): **100,96,96,94,94**
CSF £19.94 TOTE £2.20: £1.50, £3.40; EX 14.30 Trifecta £49.90.
Owner Ahmad Al Shaikh **Bred** A Al Shaikh **Trained** Newmarket, Suffolk

FOCUS
This was dominated by the favourite from the front, winning as he pleased. The third has been rated to form.

2318 BET TOTEQUADPOT AT TOTESPORT.COM H'CAP 6f (P)
6:55 (6:57) (Class 6) (0-65,66) 3-Y-O+
£3,428 (£1,020; £509; £300; £300; £300) **Stalls** Centre

Form RPR
600- 1 **Desert Fox**[161] 9211 5-10-0 **65**.................... RossaRyan 11 72
(Mike Murphy) *hld up: shkn up and hdwy over 1f out: rdn and hung lft ins fnl f: styd on to ld nr fin* **7/1**[3]
3032 2 *1/2* **Daring Guest (IRE)**[38] 1335 5-9-5 **56**....................(bt) OisinMurphy 10 62
(Tom Clover) *hld up in tch: shkn up over 1f out: rdn to ld wl ins fnl f: hdd nr fin* **8/1**
5063 3 *nse* **Evening Attire**[27] 1561 8-9-8 **64**.................... KatherineBegley(5) 2 69
(William Stone) *chsd ldrs: led over 3f out: rdn and edgd rt over 1f out: hdd wl ins fnl f* **4/1**[1]
6U5- 4 *1* **Diva Star**[196] 8340 4-9-10 **61**....................(t) JamieSpencer 3 63
(Rae Guest) *s.i.s: hld up: hdwy on outer over 1f out: r.o* **10/1**
1150 5 *1 3/4* **Mystical Moon (IRE)**[6] 2081 4-9-3 **54**.................... DougieCostello 9 51
(David C Griffiths) *led 1f: lost pl over 4f out: hdwy u.p over 1f out: r.o (jockey said filly lugged left-handed up the home straight.)* **16/1**
0-54 6 *1* **Zefferino**[22] 1684 5-9-11 **62**....................(t) GeorgeWood 13 56
(Martin Bosley) *s.i.s: pushed along early in rr: r.o ins fnl f: nt rch ldrs* **16/1**
3430 7 *1 1/4* **Global Exceed**[12] 1932 4-9-8 **66**....................(v[1]) CierenFallon(7) 8 56
(Robert Cowell) *pushed along and prom: lost pl 5f out: styd on ins fnl f* **12/1**
6023 8 *1/2* **Spenny's Lass**[14] 1883 4-9-8 **59**....................(p) BrettDoyle 4 48
(John Ryan) *pushed along to chse ldrs: rdn over 1f out: no ex ins fnl f* **8/1**
2515 9 *hd* **Admiral Rooke (IRE)**[7] 2066 4-9-7 **58**....................(b) AlistairRawlinson 7 46
(Michael Appleby) *racd keenly: prom towards outer: rdn over 1f out: no ex ins fnl f* **9/1**
-300 10 *nk* **Charlie Alpha (IRE)**[87] 597 5-8-4 **46** oh1....................(b) RhiainIngram(5) 6 33
(Roger Ingram) *prom: chsd ldr 3f out tl rdn over 1f out: no ex ins fnl f* **33/1**
-050 11 *2 1/4* **Lambrini Lullaby**[59] 1020 4-8-10 **47** oh1 ow1.................... CallumShepherd 1 28
(Lisa Williamson) *s.s: nvr on terms* **66/1**
06- 12 *2* **Nautical Haven**[123] 9769 5-10-0 **65**.................... TomQueally 5 40
(Suzi Best) *chsd ldrs: rdn over 1f out: wknd fnl f* **6/1**[2]
6313 13 *1/2* **Time To Reason (IRE)**[48] 1209 6-10-1 **66**....................(p) RichardKingscote 14 39
(Charlie Wallis) *led 5f out: hdd over 3f out: rdn over 1f out: wknd fnl f* **8/1**
1m 12.21s (-1.49) **Going Correction** -0.175s/f (Stan) **13** Ran SP% **123.1**
Speed ratings (Par 101): **102,101,101,99,97 96,94,93,93,93 90,87,86**
CSF £64.10 CT £268.62 TOTE £7.90: £2.80, £2.90, £2.30; EX 78.40 Trifecta £473.00.

Owner Rogerson, Lemon, Cooper & Arlotte **Bred** C Rogerson & G Parsons **Trained** Westoning, Beds

FOCUS

There was competition for the lead and they went a good pace here.

2319 TOTEPOOL CHELMER FILLIES' STKS (LISTED RACE) 6f (P)

7:25 (7:26) (Class 1) 3-Y-O

£31,190 (£11,825; £5,918; £2,948; £1,479; £742) **Stalls** Centre

Form | | | | RPR

25-3 **1** **Isaan Queen (IRE)**[106] 261 3-9-0 86 ..... OisinMurphy 6 100
(Archie Watson) *hld up: hdwy over 3f out: rdn and r.o to ld post* **28/1**

5-23 **2** *nse* **Chapelli**[15] 1851 3-9-0 95 ..... RyanMoore 1 99
(Mark Johnston) *led early: trckd ldrs: shkn up to ld 1f out: rdn and edgd rt ins fnl f: hdd post* **8/1**

11- **3** *½* **Red Impression**[159] 9246 3-9-0 96 ..... JasonWatson 14 97+
(Roger Charlton) *stdd s: hld up: hdwy on outer over 1f out: rdn and hung lft ins fnl f: r.o* **5/2**[1]

212- **4** *1* **Royal Intervention (IRE)**[278] 5455 3-9-0 99 ..... GeraldMosse 2 94
(Ed Walker) *s.i.s: sn rcvrd to ld: rdn and hdd 1f out: styd on same pce* **7/2**[2]

321- **5** *1* **Lady Aria**[216] 7718 3-9-0 98 ..... JamesDoyle 10 93
(Michael Bell) *hld up: swtchd rt and hdwy on outer over 1f out: sn rdn and edgd lft: styng on whn hmpd wl ins fnl f* **12/1**

6 *1 ¼* **Beau Warrior (IRE)**[27] 1576 3-9-0 93 ..... RonanWhelan 3 89
(Adrian McGuinness, Ire) *chsd ldrs: rdn over 1f out: looked hld whn hmpd wl ins fnl f* **6/1**[3]

12 **7** *1 ½* **Fen Breeze**[31] 1475 3-9-0 0 ..... NickyMackay 5 82
(Rae Guest) *s.s: hld up: rdn over 1f out: styd on ins fnl f: nt trble ldrs* **33/1**

4154 **8** *shd* **Yolo Again (IRE)**[13] 1920 3-9-0 85 ..... JimmyQuinn 11 82
(Roger Fell) *hld up: plld hrd: styd on u.p ins fnl f: nt trble ldrs* **66/1**

14-4 **9** *shd* **Blame Roberta (USA)**[13] 1913 3-9-0 92 ..... HayleyTurner 8 81
(Robert Cowell) *chsd ldr after 1f: rdn over 2f out: no ex ins fnl f* **40/1**

02-0 **10** *1 ¾* **Roxy Art (IRE)**[19] 1751 3-9-0 87 ..... RichardKingscote 7 76
(Ed Dunlop) *hld up: hdwy over 3f out: rdn over 1f out: no ex ins fnl f: nt clr run towards fin* **40/1**

-255 **11** *1 ½* **Nashirah**[16] 1832 3-9-0 98 ..... WilliamBuick 9 71
(Charlie Appleby) *chsd ldrs: rdn over 1f out: wknd fnl f* **6/1**[3]

31- **12** *½* **Raheeb (IRE)**[154] 9306 3-9-0 0 ..... JimCrowley 13 69
(Owen Burrows) *s.i.s: hld up: plld hrd: n.d* **33/1**

3-1 **13** *5* **Lufricia**[13] 1924 3-9-0 0 ..... DavidEgan 4 53
(Roger Varian) *plld hrd and sn prom: nt clr run and lost pl over 3f out: hdwy over 1f out: wknd fnl f (vet said filly lost left fore shoe)* **8/1**

1m 11.61s (-2.09) **Going Correction** -0.175s/f (Stan) **13** Ran SP% **125.0**
Speed ratings (Par 104): **106,105,105,103,102 100,98,98,98,96 94,93,87**
CSF £239.06 TOTE £33.20: £7.00, £2.20, £1.40; EX 231.70 Trifecta £1572.70.
Owner C R Hirst **Bred** Con Harrington **Trained** Upper Lambourn, W Berks
■ Stewards' Enquiry : Jason Watson caution: careless riding

FOCUS

A competitive Listed race and a tight finish. The second helps set the standard, and the likes of the eighth fit.

2320 TOTETRIFECTA AT TOTESPORT.COM H'CAP 1m 2f (P)

7:55 (7:56) (Class 2) (0-105,95) 4-Y-O+ **£12,938** (£3,850; £1,924; £962) **Stalls** Low

Form | | | | RPR

5524 **1** **Mythical Madness**[8] 2033 8-9-4 92 ..... (v) DanielTudhope 3 101
(David O'Meara) *w ldr 1f: remained handy: shkn up over 2f out: rdn to ld wl ins fnl f: styd on* **10/1**

01-0 **2** *hd* **Big Kitten (USA)**[13] 1927 4-9-2 90 ..... JamesDoyle 5 99
(William Haggas) *prom: chsd ldr 8f out tl led over 2f out: rdn and hdd wl ins fnl f: styd on* **5/2**[2]

0-11 **3** *2 ½* **El Ghazwani (IRE)**[26] 1589 4-9-5 93 ..... (t) OisinMurphy 6 97
(Hugo Palmer) *prom: rdn over 1f out: styd on same pce ins fnl f* **3/1**[3]

3412 **4** *1* **Nonios (IRE)**[9] 2022 7-9-1 94 ..... (h) DylanHogan[(5)] 7 96
(David Simcock) *hld up: shkn up and hdwy over 1f out: rdn ins fnl f: styd on same pce* **8/1**

4560 **5** *½* **Calling Out (FR)**[33] 1413 8-9-5 93 ..... (b[1]) JamieSpencer 8 94
(David Simcock) *s.s: hld up: r.o u.p ins fnl f: nvr nrr* **66/1**

5-00 **6** *1 ¼* **North Face (IRE)**[91] 514 4-9-7 95 ..... (t[1]) GeraldMosse 1 93
(Marco Botti) *s.s: hld up: rdn over 1f out: n.d* **16/1**

25-5 **7** *1 ¾* **Secret Art (IRE)**[28] 1545 9-9-4 92 ..... TomQueally 2 87
(Gary Moore) *stdd s: hld up: rdn over 1f out: n.d* **25/1**

30-2 **8** *1 ¼* **Poet's Prince**[14] 1896 4-9-4 92 ..... RyanMoore 4 84
(Mark Johnston) *led: shkn up and hdd over 2f out: wknd ins fnl f (trainers rep could offer no explanation for gelding's performance)* **2/1**[1]

2m 4.28s (-4.32) **Going Correction** -0.175s/f (Stan) **8** Ran SP% **118.3**
Speed ratings (Par 109): **110,109,107,107,106 105,104,103**
CSF £36.63 CT £96.89 TOTE £12.20: £2.60, £1.30, £1.40; EX 48.00 Trifecta £167.40.
Owner J C G Chua **Bred** Highbank Stud Llp **Trained** Upper Helmsley, N Yorks

FOCUS

A decent handicap, and the winner gained reward for his consistency these past few months. The winner has been rated to his winter best.

2321 BET TOTESWINGER AT TOTESPORT.COM NOVICE STKS 1m 2f (P)

8:25 (8:28) (Class 4) 3-Y-O+ **£5,822** (£1,732; £865; £432) **Stalls** Low

Form | | | | RPR

6- **1** **Duckett's Grove (USA)**[223] 7488 3-9-5 0 ..... GeraldMosse 1 94+
(Ed Walker) *w ldr 1f: remained handy: rdn over 1f out: r.o to ld wl ins fnl f* **8/1**

00-2 **2** *shd* **Maamora (IRE)**[16] 1834 3-8-8 80 ..... DavidEgan 4 82
(Simon Crisford) *sn led: qcknd over 2f out: rdn over 1f out: hdd wl ins fnl f* **4/1**[2]

6 **3** *2 ½* **Great Example**[19] 1764 3-8-13 0 ..... (h[1]) OisinMurphy 7 82
(Saeed bin Suroor) *awkward s: rcvrd to chse ldr after 1f: rdn and hung lft over 1f out: styd on same pce ins fnl f* **6/1**[3]

2-1 **4** *2* **Derevo**[21] 1711 3-9-5 0 ..... RyanMoore 9 84+
(Sir Michael Stoute) *hdwy over 7f out: shkn up over 2f out: edgd lft and no ex ins fnl f* **8/11**[1]

1-2 **5** *1* **Ramsbury**[107] 242 4-10-6 0 ..... JamieSpencer 3 83
(Charlie Fellowes) *s.i.s and hmpd s: hld up: shkn up over 1f out: nt rch ldrs* **8/1**

1-5 **6** *½* **Landa Beach (IRE)**[27] 1558 3-9-5 0 ..... WilliamBuick 2 81
(Andrew Balding) *edgd rt s: prom: sn pushed along: lost pl after 1f: rdn over 1f out: nt trble ldrs* **12/1**

4- **7** *5* **Almokhtaar (USA)**[166] 9123 3-8-13 0 ..... JimCrowley 5 65
(Owen Burrows) *awkward s: sn prom: racd keenly: rdn and wknd over 1f out* **20/1**

8 *23* **Emojie**[34] 5-9-11 0 ..... PaddyBradley[(3)] 8 20
(Jane Chapple-Hyam) *hld up: racd keenly: rdn over 3f out: sn wknd* **100/1**

2m 4.85s (-3.75) **Going Correction** -0.175s/f (Stan)
WFA 3 from 4yo+ 15lb **8** Ran SP% **127.9**
Speed ratings (Par 105): **108,107,105,104,103 103,99,80**
CSF £44.90 TOTE £9.20: £2.20, £1.50, £1.60; EX 63.90 Trifecta £293.70.
Owner P K Siu **Bred** Silver Springs Stud, Llc **Trained** Upper Lambourn, Berks

FOCUS

An interesting novice, but they didn't go much of a gallop and it was an advantage to be prominent. It's been rated around the second.

2322 BET TOTESCOOP6 AT TOTESPORT.COM H'CAP 1m 2f (P)

8:55 (8:57) (Class 6) (0-65,65) 3-Y-O

£3,428 (£1,020; £509; £300; £300; £300) **Stalls** Low

Form | | | | RPR

0-03 **1** **Spirit Of Angel (IRE)**[34] 1396 3-9-3 61 ..... MartinDwyer 6 66
(Marcus Tregoning) *s.i.s: hdwy over 8f out: swtchd rt over 1f out: sn rdn: styd on u.p to ld nr fin* **7/4**[1]

5661 **2** *nk* **Percy Alexander**[26] 1593 3-9-1 59 ..... (b) OisinMurphy 5 63
(James Tate) *chsd ldr after 1f: led 2f out: rdn over 1f out: hdd nr fin* **3/1**[2]

640- **3** *½* **Crimean Queen**[300] 4620 3-8-13 64 ..... (h) AledBeech[(7)] 2 67+
(Charlie Fellowes) *hld up: hdwy over 1f out: r.o* **12/1**

-425 **4** *1 ¾* **Picture Poet (IRE)**[50] 1173 3-8-12 61 ..... DylanHogan[(5)] 7 61
(Henry Spiller) *hld up: hdwy over 1f out: styd on same pce ins fnl f* **16/1**

412 **5** *2 ¼* **Mr Fox**[26] 1593 3-9-5 63 ..... CallumShepherd 3 59
(Michael Attwater) *chsd ldrs: lost pl over 8f out: hdwy over 1f out: sn rdn: no ex ins fnl f* **3/1**[2]

5-30 **6** *1* **Tribune**[22] 1676 3-8-10 61 ..... CierenFallon[(7)] 4 55
(Sylvester Kirk) *s.i.s: sn chsng ldrs: rdn over 2f out: wknd ins fnl f* **11/1**

003 **7** *5* **Dusty Damsel**[28] 1543 3-9-7 65 ..... RossaRyan 8 49
(Mike Murphy) *plld hrd: sn led: hdd 2f out: wknd ins fnl f (jockey said filly ran too freely in the early stages)* **7/1**[3]

2m 7.91s (-0.69) **Going Correction** -0.175s/f (Stan) **7** Ran SP% **120.8**
Speed ratings (Par 97): **95,94,94,92,91 90,86**
CSF £7.88 CT £49.16 TOTE £2.70: £1.60, £1.80; EX 12.50 Trifecta £66.30.
Owner Owenstown Stud & M P N Tregoning **Bred** Owenstown Stud **Trained** Whitsbury, Hants

FOCUS

A modest affair, and the early pace wasn't strong.

T/Plt: £141.50 to a £1 stake. Pool: £50,188.60. 258.89 winning units. T/Qpdt: £30.00 to a £1 stake. Pool: £8,741.08. 214.96 winning units. **Colin Roberts**

1944 MUSSELBURGH (R-H)

Thursday, May 2

OFFICIAL GOING: Good to firm (good in places; 8.8)

Wind: Breezy, half behind in sprints and in approximately 4f of home straight in races on the round course Weather: Overcast

2323 EBF NOVICE MEDIAN AUCTION STKS 1m 4f 104y

1:15 (1:15) (Class 5) 3-Y-O+ **£3,881** (£1,155; £577) **Stalls** Low

Form | | | | RPR

1 **Alright Sunshine (IRE)**[63] 4-10-0 0 ..... JoeFanning 3 91+
(Keith Dalgleish) *trckd ldrs: led 4f out: shkn up and clr over 2f out: v easily (vet reported the gelding lost its left hind shoe)* **2/5**[1]

26-2 **2** *6* **Whiskey And Water**[15] 1845 3-8-6 74 ..... BenRobinson[(3)] 2 73+
(Brian Ellison) *pressed ldr: carried lft bnd after 2f: rdn and carried lft bnd 4f out: sn chsng wnr: no imp fr over 2f out (jockey said gelding hung left on the bends)* **5/1**[3]

3-52 **3** *22* **Hurricane Hero (FR)**[11] 1972 3-8-9 71 ..... (p) BenCurtis 1 38
(K R Burke) *t.k.h: led: hung lft bnd after 2f: hung lft and hdd bnd 4f out: sn hdd & wknd* **9/2**[2]

2m 44.05s (-0.45) **Going Correction** +0.075s/f (Good)
WFA 3 from 4yo 19lb **3** Ran SP% **106.3**
Speed ratings (Par 103): **104,100,85**
CSF £2.63 TOTE £1.20; EX 2.70 Trifecta £3.40.
Owner Paul & Clare Rooney **Bred** Peter & Hugh McCutcheon **Trained** Carluke, S Lanarks

FOCUS

Add 7yds. This proved very one-sided. The time, on quickish ground, was 5.5sec outside standard. The second has been rated close to form.

2324 FOLLOW @RACINGTV ON TWITTER H'CAP 5f 1y

1:45 (1:45) (Class 6) (0-60,62) 4-Y-O+

£3,105 (£924; £461; £300; £300; £300) **Stalls** High

Form | | | | RPR

6- **1** **Bahlwan**[34] 1405 4-8-4 46 oh1 ..... (t) KillianLeonard[(3)] 12 57
(Denis Gerard Hogan, Ire) *cl up: effrt and disp ld over 1f out: led ent fnl f: drvn out* **9/2**[1]

-552 **2** *1 ½* **Angel Eyes**[34] 1402 4-8-2 48 ..... RPWalsh[(7)] 4 54
(John David Riches) *led: rdn and hdd ent fnl f: rallied: one pce last 75yds* **16/1**

120- **3** *¾* **Mr Shelby (IRE)**[55] 1120 5-9-2 55 ..... (p) BenCurtis 1 58
(S Donohoe, Ire) *trckd ldrs: effrt and drvn over 1f out: kpt on same pce ins fnl f* **11/1**

60-5 **4** *hd* **Kinloch Pride**[12] 1950 7-9-6 62 ..... (p) JamieGormley[(3)] 8 65
(Noel Wilson) *trckd ldrs: rdn along 2f out: kpt on same pce ins fnl f* **5/1**[2]

605- **5** *1 ¾* **Corton Lass**[276] 5546 4-8-7 46 oh1 ..... BarryMcHugh 3 42
(Keith Dalgleish) *t.k.h: hld up on outside of gp: hdwy and hung rt over 1f out: kpt on fnl f: no imp* **40/1**

404- **6** *shd* **Thornaby Princess**[214] 7811 8-8-7 46 oh1 ..... (p) PhilipPrince 6 42
(Jason Ward) *hld up: effrt on outside of gp over 1f out: no further imp ins fnl f* **20/1**

5550 **7** *¾* **Lord Of The Glen**[12] 1950 4-9-5 58 ..... (b) PhilDennis 2 51+
(Jim Goldie) *bhd: pushed along 1/2-way: kpt on fnl f: nvr rchd ldrs* **22/1**

30- **8** *1* **Pavlichenko (IRE)**[34] 1405 4-8-7 46 oh1 ..... (bt) JoeFanning 11 36
(John James Feane, Ire) *t.k.h: cl up: rdn over 1f out: wknd ins fnl f* **8/1**

000- **9** *1 ½* **Kodimoor (IRE)**[153] 9330 6-8-7 46 ..... (v[1]) ShaneGray 10 30
(Mark Walford) *in tch: rdn along over 2f out: wknd fnl f* **8/1**

4-52 **10** *nk* **Lexington Place**[19] 1767 9-9-7 60 ..... JamesSullivan 14 54+
(Ruth Carr) *dwlt: sn prom: rdn and outpcd over 1f out: hld whn short of room ins fnl f (jockey said gelding was denied a clear run approaching the final furlong)* **7/1**[3]

1400 **11** ½ **Foxy Boy**[30] 1505 5-8-9 **48** .... DavidAllan 7 32
(Rebecca Bastiman) hld up towards rr: rdn and hung rt 2f out: sn outpcd: hld whn short of room briefly ins fnl f (jockey said gelding hung right) **12/1**

2136 **12** nk **Twentysvnthlancers**[17] 1818 6-9-6 **59** .... KevinStott 13 39
(Paul Midgley) slowly away: bhd and outpcd: nvr on terms (jockey said gelding missed the break) **5/1**[2]

/305 **13** shd **Intense Starlet (IRE)**[28] 1553 8-8-6 **48** oh1 ow2....(tp) BenRobinson(3) 9 28
(Brian Ellison) bhd and sn pushed along: struggling 2f out: sn btn **28/1**

59.2s (-0.50) **Going Correction** +0.075s/f (Good) **13** Ran SP% **123.1**
Speed ratings (Par 101): **107,104,103,103,100 100,98,97,94,94 93,93,93**
CSF £76.33 CT £790.36 TOTE £6.00: £2.30, £3.40, £3.30; EX 107.40 Trifecta £1013.80.
Owner Platinum Thoroughbred Racing Club **Bred** Glebe Stud, J F Dean & Lady Trenchard **Trained** Cloughjordan, Co Tipperary

FOCUS
Low-grade sprinting form. Not much got into it from the rear.

2325 BOOGIE IN THE MORNING H'CAP — 1m 208y
2:15 (2:19) (Class 6) (0-65,64) 3-Y-O
£3,105 (£924; £461; £300; £300; £300) **Stalls** Low

Form RPR

33-0 **1** **Jazz Hands (IRE)**[12] 1957 3-8-7 **50** .... BarryMcHugh 8 55
(Richard Fahey) pressed ldr: led over 2f out: sn hrd pressed: hld on wl fnl f **6/1**[3]

0 **2** nk **Bellepower (IRE)**[25] 1618 3-8-6 **49** ....(p) BenCurtis 2 53
(John James Feane, Ire) t.k.h: trckd ldrs: effrt and swtchd rt over 2f out: sn pressing wnr: kpt on fnl f: hld nr fin **11/10**[1]

5464 **3** ¾ **Truckingby**[12] 1957 3-9-1 **58** .... JoeFanning 1 61
(Mark Johnston) dwlt: sn midfield: effrt over 2f out: chsd ldrs over 1f out: kpt on same pce ins fnl f **4/1**[2]

036 **4** ¾ **Three Castles**[63] 949 3-8-12 **55** .... ConnorBeasley 5 56
(Keith Dalgleish) missed break: hld up: rdn over 2f out: hdwy over 1f out: kpt on fnl f: nvr rchd ldrs **14/1**

0060 **5** nse **Arriba De Toda (IRE)**[12] 1957 3-7-13 **45** .... JamieGormley(3) 4 46
(Brian Ellison) in tch: effrt on outside over 2f out: hung rt over 1f out: no ex ins fnl f **22/1**

000- **6** 2¾ **Royal Countess**[188] 8591 3-8-7 **50** .... PhilDennis 3 45
(Lucy Normile) t.k.h: hld up: rdn over 2f out: outpcd fr over 1f out **80/1**

7 9 **Born Fighting (IRE)**[14] 1903 3-8-9 **52** .... RoystonFfrench 6 28
(Andrew Hughes, Ire) led at ordinary gallop: j. path after 100yds: rdn and hdd over 2f out: wknd over 1f out **25/1**

300- **8** 20 **Be Proud (IRE)**[166] 9130 3-8-12 **55** .... JamesSullivan 9
(R Mike Smith) hld up on outside: rdn and outpcd over 2f out: hung rt and wknd over 1f out **14/1**

04-6 **9** 8 **Lethal Guest**[115] 122 3-9-4 **64** .... BenRobinson(3) 7
(Ollie Pears) chsd ldrs tl rdn and wknd qckly over 1f out **9/1**

1m 55.0s (1.90) **Going Correction** +0.075s/f (Good) **9** Ran SP% **114.7**
Speed ratings (Par 97): **94,93,93,92,92 89,81,64,57**
CSF £12.68 CT £29.72 TOTE £6.30: £1.80, £1.10, £1.70; EX 15.20 Trifecta £55.20.
Owner Mike Browne & Mrs Dee Howe **Bred** Golden Vale Stud **Trained** Musley Bank, N Yorks

FOCUS
Add 7yds. A lowly handicap. The ratings shouldn't be far out.

2326 MACROBERTS LLP H'CAP — 1m 4f 104y
2:45 (2:45) (Class 5) (0-75,75) 4-Y-O+
£3,752 (£1,116; £557; £300; £300; £300) **Stalls** Low

Form RPR

0/62 **1** **Apterix (FR)**[12] 1949 9-9-4 **75** .... BenRobinson(3) 3 80
(Brian Ellison) led: jnd after 3f: rdn and hdd over 2f out: rallied fr over 1f out: regained ld ins fnl f: gamely **4/1**[2]

400- **2** ½ **Sebastian's Wish (IRE)**[24] 9608 6-9-2 **70** .... JamesSullivan 2 74
(Keith Dalgleish) hld up in tch: hdwy over 3f out: led over 2f out: hung rt and hdd ins fnl f: no ex **22/1**

023- **3** nk **Tomorrow's Angel**[107] 9553 4-8-8 **65** .... JamieGormley(3) 5 68
(Iain Jardine) hld up: rdn along 3f out: hdwy over 1f out: cl 3rd and keeping on whn n.m.r nr fin **5/1**[3]

62-6 **4** 1¼ **Maulesden May (IRE)**[30] 1503 6-9-2 **70** .... JoeFanning 6 71
(Keith Dalgleish) hld up: stdy hdwy over 2f out: effrt and pushed along over 1f out: one pce fnl f **5/1**[3]

30-4 **5** ¾ **Kajaki (IRE)**[23] 1666 6-9-6 **74** ....(p) TomEaves 4 74
(Kevin Ryan) chsd ldrs: rdn over 3f out: rallied: effrt 2f out: outpcd fnl f **11/4**[1]

30-5 **6** 2½ **Four Kingdoms (IRE)**[30] 1503 5-9-0 **68** .... BenCurtis 7 64
(R Mike Smith) hld up in tch: drvn and effrt over 2f out: wknd fnl f (jockey said gelding hung left throughout) **4/1**[2]

166- **7** ¾ **Golden Jeffrey (SWI)**[8] 7150 6-8-11 **70** ....(p) ConnorMurtagh(5) 1 65
(Iain Jardine) t.k.h: chsd ldrs: hdwy to dispute ld after 3f to 5f out: rdn and wknd over 2f out **10/1**

2m 44.73s (0.23) **Going Correction** +0.075s/f (Good) **7** Ran SP% **113.4**
Speed ratings (Par 103): **102,101,101,100,100 98,97**
CSF £76.62 TOTE £4.80: £2.10, £6.00; EX 76.60 Trifecta £362.90.
Owner Brian Ellison Racing Club **Bred** Joel Chaignon **Trained** Norton, N Yorks

FOCUS
Add 7yds. A bunched finish to this modest handicap. The second has been rated to last year's form and the third to her mark.

2327 WATCH RACING TV NOW H'CAP — 5f 1y
3:15 (3:17) (Class 6) (0-60,58) 3-Y-O
£3,105 (£924; £461; £300; £300; £300) **Stalls** High

Form RPR

4-16 **1** **The Defiant**[24] 1650 3-9-4 **55** .... KevinStott 1 66+
(Paul Midgley) mde all: sn crossed to stands' rail fr outside draw: clr over 1f out: pushed out fnl f: readily **5/2**[1]

05-0 **2** 2 **Brahma Kamal**[73] 785 3-8-9 **46** .... JoeFanning 5 50
(Keith Dalgleish) chsd wnr: rdn 2f out: kpt on fnl f: nt pce to chal **8/1**

-630 **3** 4½ **Popping Corks (IRE)**[30] 1504 3-9-2 **56** .... BenRobinson(3) 8 44
(Linda Perratt) bhd and sn outpcd: hdwy over 1f out: kpt on fnl f: no ch w first two **11/1**

00-0 **4** nk **Slieve Donard**[3] 2197 3-8-13 **50** ....(b) ShaneGray 4 37
(Noel Wilson) chsd ldrs: rdn over 2f out: edgd rt over 1f out: sn outpcd **13/2**

5 ½ **De Latour**[41] 1277 3-9-2 **58** ....(b) SebastianWoods(5) 7 43
(Jason Ward) prom: effrt and drvn along 1/2-way: outpcd fnl f **7/2**[2]

-605 **6** nse **She'Zanarab**[10] 1982 3-9-0 **54** .... JamieGormley(3) 3 39
(Iain Jardine) dwlt: bhd and outpcd: effrt over 2f out: rdn and no imp over 1f out (jockey said filly was slowly away) **5/1**[3]

060- **7** 6 **Frank's Law**[220] 7596 3-9-7 **58** ....(p[1]) ConnorBeasley 6 21
(Keith Dalgleish) dwlt: bhd and outpcd: struggling fr 1/2-way **15/2**

00- **8** 7 **Liberty Diva (IRE)**[190] 8542 3-8-8 **45** .... JamesSullivan 2
(Alan Berry) sn bhd and outpcd: struggling 1/2-way: nvr on terms **80/1**

59.55s (-0.15) **Going Correction** +0.075s/f (Good) **8** Ran SP% **113.2**
Speed ratings (Par 97): **104,100,93,93,92 92,82,71**
CSF £22.81 CT £184.70 TOTE £2.80: £1.60, £2.70, £2.20; EX 27.60 Trifecta £116.70.
Owner Joe And Frank Brady **Bred** Frank Brady **Trained** Westow, N Yorks

FOCUS
This was 0.35sec slower than the earlier handicap in this grade for older sprinters.

2328 EVERY RACE LIVE ON RACING TV H'CAP (DIV I) — 7f 33y
3:50 (3:51) (Class 6) (0-60,62) 4-Y-O+
£3,105 (£924; £461; £300; £300; £300) **Stalls** Low

Form RPR

345- **1** **Colour Contrast (IRE)**[203] 8133 6-8-6 **47** ....(b) JamieGormley(3) 7 55
(Iain Jardine) hld up in tch: smooth hdwy over 2f out: led on bit over 1f out: rdn ins fnl f: hld on wl cl home **6/1**[2]

530- **2** nk **Caesar's Comet (IRE)**[23] 1670 5-9-7 **62** ....(b) KillianLeonard(3) 3 69
(Denis Gerard Hogan, Ire) midfield on ins: stdy hdwy over 2f out: effrt and drvn along over 1f out: pressed wnr ins fnl f: kpt on: hld nr fin **6/4**[1]

060- **3** 2¼ **Crazy Tornado (IRE)**[221] 7580 6-9-6 **58** ....(h) ConnorBeasley 1 59
(Keith Dalgleish) led: rdn over 2f out: hdd over 1f out: kpt on same pce and lost 2nd ins fnl f **7/1**[3]

6-00 **4** 4 **Robben Rainbow**[19] 1765 5-9-4 **56** .... PhilDennis 4 47
(Katie Scott) hld up towards rr: rdn over 2f out: hdwy over 1f out: no imp fnl f **12/1**

2046 **5** 2½ **Be Bold**[11] 1967 7-9-0 **52** ....(b) DavidAllan 9 36
(Rebecca Bastiman) pressed ldrs: rdn over 2f out: wknd over 1f out **8/1**

2- **6** 2½ **Downtown Diva (IRE)**[15] 1866 4-8-12 **50** ....(be[1]) JoeFanning 10 28
(Adrian Paul Keatley, Ire) s.i.s: t.k.h in rr: rdn over 2f out: sn no imp **6/1**[2]

00-0 **7** 2¼ **Quiet Moment (IRE)**[9] 2012 5-8-10 **48** ....(t) TomEaves 8 20
(Maurice Barnes) dwlt: hld up: rdn and outpcd over 2f out: n.d after **66/1**

-456 **8** 3¼ **Vallarta (IRE)**[30] 1505 9-9-7 **59** .... JamesSullivan 5 26
(Ruth Carr) t.k.h: trckd ldrs: pushed along whn short of room and lost pl 2f out: sn btn **8/1**

046- **9** 7 **Bareed (USA)**[174] 8979 4-8-6 **47** ow2........................(h[1]) BenRobinson(3) 2
(Linda Perratt) slowly away: bhd: struggling 1/2-way: nvr on terms **14/1**

000- **10** 1½ **Tom's Anna (IRE)**[153] 9336 9-8-0 **45** .... RPWalsh(7) 11
(Sean Regan) hld up on outside: drvn and struggling over 2f out: sn btn **66/1**

000- **11** 22 **Palavicini Run (IRE)**[203] 8134 6-8-7 **45** .... ShaneGray 6
(Linda Perratt) pressed ldr: lost pl over 3f out: sn wknd: t.o **80/1**

1m 29.04s (0.04) **Going Correction** +0.075s/f (Good) **11** Ran SP% **121.9**
Speed ratings (Par 101): **102,101,99,94,91 88,86,82,74,72 47**
CSF £15.93 CT £69.56 TOTE £7.00: £1.80, £1.80, £2.30; EX 22.50 Trifecta £128.40.
Owner Kildonan Gold Racing **Bred** J P Keappock **Trained** Carrutherstown, D'fries & G'way
■ Stewards' Enquiry : Killian Leonard three-day ban: interference & careless riding (tba)

FOCUS
Add 7yds. Pretty moderate form, but the quicker division by 0.63sec.

2329 EVERY RACE LIVE ON RACING TV H'CAP (DIV II) — 7f 33y
4:25 (4:29) (Class 6) (0-60,60) 4-Y-O+
£3,105 (£924; £461; £300; £300; £300) **Stalls** Low

Form RPR

00-0 **1** **Mi Capricho (IRE)**[30] 1511 4-9-3 **56** .... JoeFanning 5 62
(Keith Dalgleish) pressed ldr: led and hrd pressed fr over 2f out: kpt on gamely u.p fnl f **12/1**

-035 **2** nk **Milton Road**[19] 1765 4-9-2 **55** .... DavidAllan 7 60
(Rebecca Bastiman) trckd ldrs: smooth hdwy and ev ch over 2f out: sn rdn: kpt on fnl f: hld nr fin **11/4**[2]

20-0 **3** nk **My Valentino (IRE)**[7] 1158 6-8-9 **48** ....(bt) JamesSullivan 6 52
(Dianne Sayer) s.i.s: hld up: pushed along over 2f out: hdwy over 1f out: n.m.r briefly ins fnl f: r.o **10/1**

/1-0 **4** ½ **Ahundrednotout**[101] 347 5-9-6 **59** ....(p) BenCurtis 9 62
(John James Feane, Ire) hld up in tch: effrt and rdn over 2f out: hung rt over 1f out: kpt on ins fnl f (jockey said gelding hung right under pressure) **9/4**[1]

30-0 **5** hd **Joyful Star**[21] 1722 9-8-13 **52** .... KevinStott 3 55
(Fred Watson) hld up in midfield: effrt whn nt clr run and swtchd lft over 1f out: r.o wl fnl f: nrst fin **16/1**

5040 **6** 1 **Thorntoun Lady (USA)**[38] 1335 9-8-10 **49** .... PhilDennis 4 49
(Jim Goldie) trckd ldrs: effrt and drvn along over 2f out: kpt on same pce fnl f **10/1**

-463 **7** 2½ **I Am Dandy (IRE)**[11] 1967 4-8-12 **51** ....(t) RoystonFfrench 8 45
(James Ewart) s.i.s: bhd: rdn over 2f out: hdwy over 1f out: kpt on fnl f: no imp **6/1**[3]

5000 **8** 1 **Hippeia (IRE)**[11] 1973 4-9-7 **60** ....(t[1]) TomEaves 2 51
(Grant Tuer) led to over 2f out: rdn and wknd over 1f out **20/1**

634- **9** 1 **Retirement Beckons**[262] 6085 4-8-7 **46** oh1........................(h) ShaneGray 1 34
(Linda Perratt) s.i.s: bhd: drvn along over 2f out: nvr rchd ldrs **16/1**

1405 **10** 5 **Picks Pinta**[38] 1335 8-8-1 **47** ....(b) RPWalsh(7) 11 22
(John David Riches) midfield on outside: drvn over 2f out: wknd over 1f out **20/1**

66-0 **11** 8 **Let Right Be Done**[91] 501 7-8-6 **48** oh1 ow2.......(b) BenRobinson(3) 10 3
(Linda Perratt) hld up: drvn along over 2f out: sn wknd **25/1**

1m 29.67s (0.67) **Going Correction** +0.075s/f (Good) **11** Ran SP% **122.7**
Speed ratings (Par 101): **99,98,98,97,97 96,93,92,91,85 76**
CSF £45.88 CT £361.40 TOTE £13.00: £3.80, £1.10, £3.30; EX 50.50.
Owner Charles Jones **Bred** Leslie Laverty **Trained** Carluke, S Lanarks

FOCUS
Add 7yds. The slower division by 0.63sec, and a tight finish. Ordinary form.

2330 RACINGTV.COM H'CAP — 1m 208y
5:00 (5:03) (Class 6) (0-65,65) 4-Y-O+
£3,105 (£924; £461; £300; £300; £300) **Stalls** Low

Form RPR

5043 **1** **La Sioux (IRE)**[38] 1339 5-8-12 **61** .... SebastianWoods(5) 4 70
(Richard Fahey) trckd ldrs: effrt and rdn 2f out: led ins fnl f: kpt on strly **5/1**[2]

001 **2** ½ **Cosmic Ray**[12] 1958 7-8-10 **54**........................(h) JoeFanning 9 62+
(Les Eyre) *t.k.h: cl up on outside: led gng wl over 2f out: rdn and hdd ins fnl f: kpt on same pce* **11/8**[1]

624- **3** *nk* **Jackhammer (IRE)**[150] 9278 5-8-6 **50**........................(bt) JamesSullivan 7 57
(Dianne Sayer) *t.k.h: hld up: hdwy to chse ldrs over 1f out: kpt on ins fnl f* **20/1**

6/0- **4** *3* **Spark Of War (IRE)**[370] 2108 4-9-7 **65**........................ ConnorBeasley 5 66
(Keith Dalgleish) *hld up on ins: effrt over 2f out: kpt on fnl f: nvr able to chal* **9/1**

36-0 **5** *8* **Edgar Allan Poe (IRE)**[41] 1271 5-9-7 **65**........................ DavidAllan 1 50
(Rebecca Bastiman) *hld up in tch: effrt and cl up over 2f out: rdn and wknd over 1f out* **5/1**[2]

6345 **6** *hd* **Restive (IRE)**[24] 1648 6-9-4 **62**........................ PhilDennis 6 47
(Jim Goldie) *hld up: effrt on outside over 2f out: wknd over 1f out* **11/2**[3]

302- **7** ¾ **Remember Rocky**[203] 8130 10-8-13 **62**...............(p) ConnorMurtagh(5) 3 46
(Lucy Normile) *in tch: lost grnd after 3f: rdn over 3f out: sn n.d* **33/1**

023- **8** 1 ¾ **Haymarket**[298] 4707 10-8-12 **56**........................(t[1]) BenCurtis 2 36
(R Mike Smith) *led to over 2f out: sn rdn and wknd* **25/1**

0-10 **9** *10* **Foxy Lady**[71] 814 4-9-2 **60**........................(p) ShaneGray 8 20
(Kevin Ryan) *prom: drvn and outpcd 3f out: struggling fnl 2f* **25/1**

1m 54.46s (1.36) **Going Correction** +0.075s/f (Good) **9 Ran SP% 116.2**
Speed ratings (Par 101): **97,96,96,93,86 86,85,84,75**
CSF £11.82 CT £127.45 TOTE £5.80: £1.40, £1.50, £6.10; EX 14.90 Trifecta £187.90.
Owner Mrs Una Towell **Bred** P J Towell **Trained** Musley Bank, N Yorks

FOCUS
Add 7yds. Another very ordinary handicap. Straightforward form.
T/Plt: £114.40 to a £1 stake. Pool: £34,563.37. 220.5 winning units. T/Qpdt: £16.30 to a £1 stake. Pool: £4,687.77. 212.42 winning units. **Richard Young**

1975 REDCAR (L-H)
Thursday, May 2

OFFICIAL GOING: Good to firm (8.4)
Wind: light against Weather: cloudy, showers after 3rd

2331 RACING TV CLUB DAY HERE TODAY (S) STKS 5f
1:55 (1:58) (Class 5) 2-Y-O
£3,752 (£1,116; £557; £300; £300; £300) **Stalls** Centre

Form RPR

1 **Gold Venture (IRE)** 2-8-7 0........................ HollieDoyle 2 64
(Archie Watson) *prom: pushed into ld 1f out: rdn and kpt on* **10/3**[2]

63 **2** *2* **Hypochondriac**[12] 1931 2-8-8 0 ow1........................ CliffordLee 7 58
(David Evans) *s.i.s: hld up: rdn and hdwy over 1f out: kpt on to go 2nd fnl 50yds* **5/2**[1]

0 **3** ½ **Frida Kahlo (IRE)**[14] 1879 2-8-7 0........................(b[1]) AndrewMullen 4 55
(Archie Watson) *led: drvn and hdd 1f out: hung lft and one pce* **11/1**

05 **4** *3* **Is She The One**[14] 1879 2-8-4 0........................ NoelGarbutt(3) 5 44
(Philip McBride) *trckd ldrs: rdn 2f out: no ex fnl f* **9/1**

0 **5** *3* **Six Gun**[27] 1556 2-8-12 0........................ PaulMulrennan 13 39
(Archie Watson) *chsd ldrs: rdn over 2f out: wknd over 1f out* **6/1**

6 **6** *1* **Vodka Dawn (IRE)**[15] 1844 2-8-2 0........................ SeanDavis(5) 9 30
(Phillip Makin) *trckd ldrs: rdn over 2f out: sn outpcd and btn* **33/1**

7 *hd* **Tiny Titan** 2-8-7 0........................ PJMcDonald 11 29
(Richard Fahey) *dwlt: sn in tch: rdn over 2f out: outpcd over 1f out* **5/1**[3]

6 **8** *4* **She's A Diamond**[4] 2138 2-8-7 0........................ PaulHanagan 12 15
(Mick Channon) *slowly away: hld up: nvr threatened (jockey said filly missed the break and was never travelling)* **12/1**

0 **9** 2 ¼ **Jakodobro**[15] 1844 2-8-12 0........................ GrahamLee 6 12
(Bryan Smart) *dwlt: hld up: nvr threatened* **40/1**

1m 0.77s (2.27) **Going Correction** +0.20s/f (Good) **9 Ran SP% 114.0**
Speed ratings (Par 93): **89,85,85,80,75 73,73,67,63**
CSF £11.91 TOTE £4.10: £1.70, £1.20, £2.30; EX 14.40 Trifecta £84.40.The winner was bought in for £9,500. Hypocondriac was claimed by Mr Claes Bjorling for £6,000.
Owner Saxon Thoroughbreds **Bred** Gearoid Cahill **Trained** Upper Lambourn, W Berks

FOCUS
A juvenile seller in which the field was reduced by almost a third due to withdrawals the day before and the majority of the field were fillies, and they dominated. The jockeys reported the going was much as the official description.

2332 FOLLOW @RACINGTV ON TWITTER FILLIES' NOVICE STKS 5f 217y
2:25 (2:30) (Class 5) 3-Y-O+ **£3,881** (£1,155; £577; £288) **Stalls** Centre

Form RPR

3 **1** **Mina Velour**[24] 1649 3-9-0 0........................(h) GrahamLee 11 64
(Bryan Smart) *prom: pushed along to ld over 1f out: rdn fnl f: wandered and kpt on* **7/2**[2]

55- **2** *nk* **Leopardina (IRE)**[160] 9225 3-9-0 0........................ SamJames 6 63
(David Simcock) *trckd ldrs: pushed along over 2f out: rdn to chal appr fnl f: kpt on* **16/1**

3 1 ¾ **Mendamay** 3-9-0 0........................ DuranFentiman 5 58
(Tim Easterby) *midfield: pushed along to chse ldr over 1f out: rdn 1f out: no ex fnl 50yds* **100/1**

4 *nse* **Raspberry** 3-9-0 0........................ HollieDoyle 4 58
(Olly Williams) *outpcd in rr tl kpt on wl fr over 1f out* **125/1**

0 **5** *hd* **The Thorny Rose**[17] 1816 3-8-9 0........................ PaulaMuir(5) 1 57
(Michael Dods) *midfield: rdn over 2f out: kpt on fnl f* **100/1**

6 ½ **Royal Welcome** 3-9-0 0........................ CliffordLee 12 55
(James Tate) *chsd ldrs: rdn and outpcd over 2f out: kpt on ins fnl f* **6/4**[1]

0 **7** ¾ **Bedtime Bella (IRE)**[26] 1598 3-9-0 0........................ PJMcDonald 3 53
(K R Burke) *rrd s: sn midfield: rdn and outpcd over 2f out: kpt on ins fnl f (jockey said filly was slowly away and missed the break)* **14/1**

0 **8** *hd* **Impressionable**[20] 1740 3-9-0 0........................ DaneO'Neill 8 52
(Marco Botti) *dwlt: hld up: pushed along over 2f out: kpt on ins fnl f: eased nr fin (jockey said filly hung badly right in the closing stages resulting in him being unable to ride out to the line)* **40/1**

2-5 **9** *4* **Parion**[15] 1862 3-8-9 0........................ SeanDavis(5) 2 40
(Richard Fahey) *prom: rdn over 2f out: wknd ins fnl f* **9/2**[3]

6- **10** ¾ **Saltie Girl**[247] 6660 3-9-0 0........................ LewisEdmunds 9 37
(David Barron) *midfield: rdn over 2f out: wknd fnl f* **25/1**

20-3 **11** ¾ **Vikivaki (USA)**[33] 1427 3-9-0 **75**........................(v[1]) PatCosgrave 10 35
(Robert Cowell) *led: rdn over 2f out: hdd over 1f out: wknd* **7/1**

0 **12** *6* **Rimmal (USA)**[16] 1834 3-9-0 0........................(h) PaulHanagan 7 16
(Jeremy Noseda) *hld up: wknd and bhd fnl 2f* **50/1**

1m 13.22s (1.42) **Going Correction** +0.20s/f (Good) **12 Ran SP% 116.5**
Speed ratings (Par 100): **102,101,99,99,98 98,97,97,91,90 89,81**
CSF £53.64 TOTE £3.60: £1.10, £3.10, £21.00; EX 47.60 Trifecta £3135.50.
Owner P Sutherland **Bred** Whatton Manor Stud **Trained** Hambleton, N Yorks

FOCUS
The only one with real experience set a fair standard in this 3yo fillies' novice, but she was outpointed, suggesting the form is not too bad. The second has been rated as improving a bit on her AW form.

2333 RACING TV PROFITS RETURNED TO RACING H'CAP 7f 219y
2:55 (2:56) (Class 4) (0-80,81) 3-Y-O
£5,692 (£1,694; £846; £423; £300; £300) **Stalls** Centre

Form RPR

43-4 **1** **Gentle Look**[17] 1823 3-9-7 **77**........................ PatCosgrave 6 85
(Saeed bin Suroor) *mde: 2 l up and gng wl 2f out: pushed along over 1f out: rdn out ins fnl f: kpt on wl* **4/1**[3]

25-1 **2** 1 ½ **Camber**[21] 1720 3-9-2 **72**........................ PaulHanagan 1 77
(Richard Fahey) *hld up: pushed along over 3f out: hdwy and chsd ldr over 1f out: rdn and kpt on* **5/1**

43-1 **3** 2 ¼ **Conundrum**[17] 1819 3-9-4 **74**........................ JackGarritty 4 74
(Jedd O'Keeffe) *trckd ldr: rdn along over 2f out: sn one pce* **9/4**[1]

1-35 **4** *nk* **Edgewood**[23] 1662 3-9-6 **76**........................ GrahamLee 2 75
(James Bethell) *dwlt: hld up: pushed along and sme hdwy over 1f out: rdn and one pce fnl f* **11/2**

631 **5** 1 ½ **Solar Heights (IRE)**[61] 979 3-9-6 **76**........................ PJMcDonald 5 72
(James Tate) *in tch: rdn along over 2f out: sn no imp* **7/2**[2]

143- **6** 3 ¾ **Over The Guns (IRE)**[212] 7875 3-9-6 **76**........................(b) CliffordLee 8 63
(K R Burke) *trckd ldrs: rdn over 2f out: wknd fnl f* **18/1**

1m 38.96s (2.36) **Going Correction** +0.20s/f (Good) **6 Ran SP% 110.3**
Speed ratings (Par 101): **96,94,92,91,90 86**
CSF £22.82 CT £50.90 TOTE £4.10: £2.30, £2.70; EX 23.40 Trifecta £47.50.
Owner Godolphin **Bred** Godolphin **Trained** Newmarket, Suffolk

FOCUS
The feature contest and a fair handicap with four last-time-out scorers. However, none of them could cope with the all-the-way winner. The third and fourth have been rated close to form.

2334 WATCH IRISH RACING ON RACING TV NOVICE MEDIAN AUCTION STKS 7f
3:25 (3:26) (Class 6) 3-Y-O **£3,557** (£1,058; £529; £264) **Stalls** Centre

Form RPR

4 **1** **Cristal Breeze (IRE)**[22] 1676 3-9-2 0........................ PaulHanagan 1 84+
(William Haggas) *led narrowly: pushed along and hdd narrowly over 1f out: edgd rt and led again appr fnl f: kpt on wl to draw clr* **5/4**[1]

63 **2** 4 ½ **Puzzle**[51] 1168 3-9-2 0........................ GrahamLee 4 72
(Richard Hughes) *trckd ldrs: rdn along over 2f out: kpt on to go 2nd fnl 75yds: no ch w wnr* **16/1**

22 **3** 1 ¾ **Lofty**[29] 1523 3-9-2 0........................ LewisEdmunds 5 67
(David Barron) *pressed ldr: drvn into narrow ld over 1f out: sn edgd rt: hdd appr fnl f: sn no ex: lost 2nd fnl 75yds (jockey said gelding hung right)* **7/2**[3]

1- **4** 1 ¾ **Myrmidons (IRE)**[208] 7989 3-9-9 0........................ PaulMulrennan 7 70
(Michael Dods) *hld up: rdn along and sn outpcd: styd on fnl f: nvr involved* **7/1**

1 **5** *nse* **Melrose Way**[17] 1816 3-9-4 0........................ PJMcDonald 3 65
(James Bethell) *trckd ldrs: rdn over 2f out: wknd ins fnl f (jockey said filly was never travelling)* **3/1**[2]

6 *12* **Freshfield Ferris** 3-8-8 0........................ ConorMcGovern(3) 2 27
(Brian Rothwell) *slowly away: a towards rr* **200/1**

1m 26.24s (0.84) **Going Correction** +0.20s/f (Good) **6 Ran SP% 110.5**
Speed ratings (Par 97): **103,97,95,93,93 80**
CSF £22.12 TOTE £2.30: £1.60, £4.70; EX 21.00 Trifecta £70.70.
Owner G & M Roberts, Green, Savidge & Whittal-Williams **Bred** Mrs K Prendergast **Trained** Newmarket, Suffolk

FOCUS
Quite an interesting 3yo novice contest but ultimately the favourite ran out a clear-cut winner.

2335 WATCH RACING TV IN STUNNING HD CLAIMING STKS 1m 2f 1y
4:00 (4:00) (Class 5) 3-Y-O+
£3,752 (£1,116; £557; £300; £300; £300) **Stalls** Low

Form RPR

04/1 **1** **Clayton**[12] 1949 10-9-12 96........................(t) HollieDoyle 4 78
(Archie Watson) *mde all: drvn and strly pressed over 1f out: kpt on wl* **2/5**[1]

4-03 **2** 1 ¾ **Andok (IRE)**[12] 1949 5-9-5 72........................(p) SeanDavis(5) 1 72
(Richard Fahey) *prom: rdn over 2f out: kpt on* **5/1**[3]

6-43 **3** ½ **Guvenor's Choice (IRE)**[85] 625 4-9-12 74...............(t w) CliffordLee 6 73
(K R Burke) *prom: drvn to chal strly over 1f out: no ex fnl 110yds* **9/2**[2]

26/0 **4** 2 ¼ **Graphite (IRE)**[73] 784 5-9-10 63........................(v[1]) PJMcDonald 2 67
(Geoffrey Harker) *trckd ldrs: rdn over 2f out: kpt on same pce* **25/1**

6500 **5** *5* **God Willing**[24] 1647 8-9-10 62........................(t) PaulMulrennan 7 58
(Declan Carroll) *midfield: rdn over 2f out: no imp* **8/1**

4000 **6** *3* **Highwayman**[24] 1648 6-9-9 47........................ AndrewMullen 3 51
(David Thompson) *hld up: rdn along over 2f out: nvr threatened ldrs* **50/1**

050/ **7** *7* **Jackman**[589] 7271 5-9-6 36........................(t[1]) DuranFentiman 5 35
(Lee James) *hld up in midfield: rdn along 3f out: wknd* **150/1**

6-30 **8** *2* **Unique Company (IRE)**[10] 1981 4-9-3 38........................ RowanScott(3) 9 31
(David Thompson) *a towards rr* **150/1**

00-0 **9** *4* **Pumaflor (IRE)**[23] 1659 7-9-2 59........................(p) PaulaMuir(5) 8 24
(Philip Kirby) *in tch: rdn along over 3f out: sn wknd* **40/1**

2m 7.75s (0.85) **Going Correction** +0.20s/f (Good) **9 Ran SP% 127.0**
Speed ratings (Par 103): **104,102,102,100,96 94,88,86,83**
CSF £3.62 TOTE £1.40: £1.10, £1.50, £1.50; EX 4.10 Trifecta £11.40.Guvenor's Choice was claimed by Marjorie Fife for £10,000.
Owner Marco Polo **Bred** G Reed **Trained** Upper Lambourn, W Berks

FOCUS
A wide range of abilities in this claimer and only three counted in the market. As expected they filled the first three places.

2336 EVERY RACE LIVE ON RACING TV H'CAP 1m 2f 1y
4:35 (4:37) (Class 5) (0-75,77) 3-Y-O
£3,752 (£1,116; £557; £300; £300; £300) **Stalls** Low

Form RPR

322- **1** **Dancin Boy**[195] 8378 3-9-9 **77**........................ AndrewMullen 4 84
(Michael Dods) *trckd ldr: rdn to ld 2f out: styd on wl to draw clr* **7/1**

30-6 **2** 3 ½ **Simon's Smile (FR)**[11] 1972 3-8-13 **67**........................(p[1]) CliffordLee 6 67
(K R Burke) *led: rdn and edgd rt over 2f out: hdd 2f out: styd on same pce* **40/1**

33-4 **3** 3/4 **Tucson**[24] [1646] 3-9-6 **74**........................ PJMcDonald 5 73
(James Bethell) *trckd ldrs: rdn over 3f out: outpcd over 2f out: styd on fnl f* **10/3**[3]

6-24 **4** *hd* **Maqaadeer**[31] [1480] 3-9-4 **72**........................(b[1]) DaneO'Neill 2 70
(Ed Dunlop) *s.i.s: hld up: pushed along and hdwy on outer over 2f out: rdn over 1f out: one pce ins fnl f* **11/4**[1]

03-0 **5** *hd* **State Of Affair (USA)**[19] [1756] 3-9-7 **75**........................ PaulHanagan 1 73
(Ed Walker) *midfield: pushed along over 3f out: hdwy and chsd ldrs over 2f out: rdn and one pce fnl f* **3/1**[2]

46-0 **6** 6 **Iron Mike**[30] [1504] 3-9-2 **70**........................ PaulMulrennan 8 56
(Keith Dalgleish) *dwlt: midfield on outer: trckd ldrs over 4f out: rdn 3f out: wknd over 1f out* **16/1**

000- **7** 4 1/2 **Agravain**[208] [7987] 3-8-6 **60**........................ DuranFentiman 9 37
(Tim Easterby) *hld up: rdn over 2f out: sn wknd* **50/1**

6-10 **8** 5 **Rock Up In Style**[31] [1481] 3-8-13 **72**........................ AndrewBreslin[(5)] 7 39
(Mark Johnston) *prom: rdn 3f out: wknd over 1f out* **12/1**

44-4 **9** *shd* **Fares Alpha (USA)**[27] [1568] 3-9-4 **72**........................(h[1]) GrahamLee 3 39
(Marco Botti) *hld up in midfield: rdn over 3f out: wknd 2f out* **8/1**

2m 7.9s (1.00) **Going Correction** +0.20s/f (Good) **9 Ran SP% 116.3**
Speed ratings (Par 99): **104,101,100,100,100 95,91,87,87**
CSF £231.24 CT £1100.92 TOTE £5.40: £1.90, £10.60, £1.30; EX 112.50 Trifecta £1022.50.
Owner R R D Saunders **Bred** Patrick & Simon Trant **Trained** Denton, Co Durham
■ Stewards' Enquiry : P J McDonald caution: careless riding

FOCUS
A fairly competitive 3yo handicap run 0.15secs slower than the preceding claimer. The top weight scored decisively. Ordinary form, with the third, fourth and fifth rated close to their marks.

2337 GO RACING AT THIRSK THIS SATURDAY H'CAP 7f 219y
5:10 (5:10) (Class 6) (0-65,65) 3-Y-O
£3,493 (£1,039; £519; £300; £300; £300) **Stalls Centre**

Form RPR

4402 **1** **Kodi Dream**[10] [1980] 3-8-9 **58**........................ BenSanderson[(5)] 14 70+
(Roger Fell) *dwlt: hld up: pushed along and gd hdwy over 2f out: led over 1f out: kpt on wl to draw clr* **7/2**[2]

-466 **2** 4 **Ivory Charm**[51] [1166] 3-9-2 **60**........................ PJMcDonald 8 62
(Richard Fahey) *trckd ldrs: rdn 2f out: chal over 1f out: kpt on same pce ins fnl f* **8/1**[3]

3125 **3** 1 1/2 **Macs Blessings (IRE)**[21] [1721] 3-8-7 **56**........................(p) SeanDavis[(5)] 2 55
(Stef Keniry) *hld up in midfield: rdn and hdwy over 2f out: chal over 1f out: no ex fnl 110yds* **14/1**

03-3 **4** 3 1/4 **Midnight In Havana**[21] [1720] 3-9-0 **58**........................ GrahamLee 5 50
(Bryan Smart) *chsd ldrs: rdn along over 2f out: outpcd over 1f out: plugged on ins fnl f* **3/1**[1]

00-0 **5** *nse* **Zalmi Angel**[28] [1549] 3-8-3 **54**........................ LauraCoughlan[(7)] 1 45
(Adrian Nicholls) *prom: rdn to ld over 2f out: hdd over 1f out: wknd ins fnl f* **80/1**

-206 **6** 1 3/4 **Bubbelah (IRE)**[31] [1480] 3-9-4 **62**........................ PatCosgrave 12 49
(David Simcock) *midfield: rdn over 2f out: no imp* **8/1**[3]

1654 **7** 1 **Geography Teacher (IRE)**[33] [1430] 3-8-9 **53**........................ HollieDoyle 7 38
(Roger Fell) *midfield: rdn over 2f out: no imp* **33/1**

060- **8** 1 **Angel Sarah (IRE)**[271] [5754] 3-8-7 **51**........................ PaulHanagan 3 34
(Richard Fahey) *hld up: rdn over 2f out: nvr involved* **18/1**

5000 **9** 3/4 **Zoom Out**[21] [1721] 3-8-5 **52**........................(t) RowanScott[(3)] 4 33
(Nigel Tinkler) *hld up: pushed along over 2f out: nvr threatened* **12/1**

6332 **10** 1 1/2 **Firsteen**[31] [1486] 3-8-10 **54**........................ LewisEdmunds 10 32
(Alistair Whillans) *s.i.s: sn midfield: rdn over 2f out: wknd over 1f out* **12/1**

3-30 **11** 2 3/4 **Dream Chick (IRE)**[17] [1816] 3-9-7 **65**........................ AndrewMullen 9 36
(Kevin Ryan) *trckd ldrs: rdn over 2f out: wknd over 1f out* **33/1**

000- **12** 2 3/4 **Langholm (IRE)**[322] [3782] 3-8-11 **55**........................ PaulMulrennan 15 20
(Declan Carroll) *led and racd keenly: rdn and hdd over 2f out: sn wknd* **10/1**

00-5 **13** 1 **Happy Hannah (IRE)**[19] [1764] 3-8-4 **51**........................ ConorMcGovern[(3)] 11 14
(John Davies) *w ldr: rdn over 2f out: wknd over 1f out* **22/1**

303- **14** 1/2 **Highjacked**[185] [8699] 3-8-7 **51**........................ SamJames 6 13
(John Davies) *prom: rdn over 2f out: wknd over 1f out: eased* **20/1**

1m 39.26s (2.66) **Going Correction** +0.20s/f (Good) **14 Ran SP% 122.1**
Speed ratings (Par 97): **94,90,88,85,85 83,82,81,80,79 76,73,72,72**
CSF £30.34 CT £368.70 TOTE £3.70: £1.50, £2.90, £4.70; EX 38.60 Trifecta £363.70.
Owner Nick Bradley Racing 29 & Partner **Bred** Whatcote Farm Stud **Trained** Nawton, N Yorks

FOCUS
This moderate handicap was run 0.30 secs slower than the earlier feature contest.
T/Plt: £51.70 to a £1 stake. Pool: £50,162.35. 707.09 winning units. T/Qpdt: £12.80 to a £1 stake. Pool: £4,414.39. 254.62 winning units. **Andrew Sheret**

2138

SALISBURY (R-H)
Thursday, May 2

OFFICIAL GOING: Good to firm (8.4)
Wind: Light, against Weather: Sunny periods with showers

2338 WILLIAM HILL LEADING RACECOURSE BOOKMAKER BRITISH EBF NOVICE STKS (PLUS 10 RACE) 5f
4:55 (4:57) (Class 4) 2-Y-O
£5,110 (£1,520; £759; £379) **Stalls Low**

Form RPR

1 **Firepower (FR)** 2-9-5 0........................ AdamKirby 8 81+
(Clive Cox) *trckd ldrs: led ent fnl f: drifted lft and running green: readily* **5/6**[1]

2 1/2 **When Comes Here (IRE)** 2-9-5 0........................ DavidProbert 7 79
(Andrew Balding) *chsd ldrs: swtchd lft to chal ent fnl f: kpt on but a being hld* **10/1**

04 **3** 3/4 **Dark Optimist (IRE)**[13] [1910] 2-9-5 0........................(h) JFEgan 4 76
(David Evans) *s.i.s: racd in last trio: hdwy over 1f out: r.o fnl f: wnt 3rd fnl 100yds* **16/1**

4 1 3/4 **Falconidae (IRE)** 2-9-0 0........................ SeanLevey 5 65
(Richard Hannon) *prom: led 2f out: rdn and hdd ent fnl f: sn no ex* **5/1**[3]

5 4 1/2 **Goodwood Rebel (IRE)** 2-9-5 0........................ HarryBentley 6 54
(Ralph Beckett) *s.i.s: rn green: sn rousted along in last pair: sme late prog but nvr any threat* **4/1**[2]

6 3 **Secret Cecil (FR)** 2-9-5 0........................ RobertHavlin 3 43
(Joseph Tuite) *chsd ldrs: effrt but nt clrest of runs over 2f out: nt pce to chal: no ex fnl f* **25/1**

55 **7** 1 3/4 **Arasugar (IRE)**[16] [1833] 2-9-0 0........................ RobHornby 2 31
(Seamus Mullins) *led tl rdn 2f out: sn hld: wknd fnl f* **12/1**

8 27 **Twentyonered** 2-9-0 0........................ RyanWhile[(5)] 1
(Grace Harris) *dwlt bdly and v green: a bhd (jockey said colt ran greenly)* **80/1**

1m 2.55s (2.05) **Going Correction** +0.10s/f (Good) **8 Ran SP% 119.0**
Speed ratings (Par 95): **87,86,85,82,75 70,67,24**
CSF £11.56 TOTE £1.50: £1.10, £2.80, £3.50; EX 10.60 Trifecta £55.20.
Owner Mrs Michelle Morgan **Bred** Mme Mise Soledad De Moratalla **Trained** Lambourn, Berks

FOCUS
No rain for the past five days and the going was good to firm with a reading of 8.4. An interesting 2yo contest with an odds-on favourite just getting the job done.

2339 WILLIAM HILL RETAIL BOOKMAKER OF THE YEAR H'CAP 6f
5:25 (5:32) (Class 5) (0-75,75) 3-Y-O+
£4,075 (£1,212; £606; £303; £300; £300) **Stalls Low**

Form RPR

0-00 **1** **Air Of York (IRE)**[103] [315] 7-9-0 **61**........................(p) StevieDonohoe 12 70
(John Flint) *hld up in last pair: swtchd lft over 2f out: rdn and gd hdwy over 1f out: r.o strly fnl f: led fnl 40yds* **66/1**

2530 **2** 1/2 **The Groove**[19] [1766] 6-9-0 **68**........................ GinaMangan[(7)] 3 75
(David Evans) *mid-div: travelling wl 2f out: qcknd up over 1f out: led fnl 120yds: hdd fnl 40yds: nt pce of wnr* **7/1**[2]

35-0 **3** 2 3/4 **Crystal Casque**[36] [1355] 4-9-1 **67**........................ TheodoreLadd[(5)] 10 65
(Rod Millman) *trckd ldrs: rdn over 2f out: kpt on but nvr quite pce to chal* **15/2**[3]

40-3 **4** 1/2 **Sir Roderic (IRE)**[27] [1563] 6-9-9 **70**........................ DanielMuscutt 7 67
(Rod Millman) *slowly away: towards rr: rdn and stdy prog fr over 2f out: kpt on fnl f but nvr gng pce to get on terms* **6/1**[1]

510- **5** *hd* **Cent Flying**[230] [7252] 4-9-5 **66**........................(t) TomMarquand 1 62
(William Muir) *prom: rdn to ld 2f out: hdd fnl 120yds: kpt on but no ex* **20/1**

1465 **6** 1/2 **Little Palaver**[38] [1329] 7-9-5 **73**........................(p) AmeliaGlass[(7)] 8 67
(Clive Cox) *led tl rdn 2f out: kpt on same pce fnl f* **10/1**

660- **7** 1/2 **Field Of Vision (IRE)**[188] [8612] 6-9-11 **72**........................(p) RobertHavlin 4 65
(John Flint) *hld up towards rr: hdwy 2f out: sn rdn: kpt on fnl f* **16/1**

-034 **8** *nk* **John Betjeman**[3] [2204] 3-8-10 **72**........................(p) RyanWhile[(5)] 13 61
(Bill Turner) *prom: rdn 2f out: sn one pce* **8/1**

06-0 **9** 3/4 **Harry Beau**[17] [1822] 5-9-7 **68**........................(v) HarryBentley 11 57
(David Evans) *nvr bttr than mid-div* **16/1**

05-3 **10** 1/2 **Red Tycoon (IRE)**[22] [1682] 7-9-2 **63**........................ PatDobbs 18 53
(Ken Cunningham-Brown) *s.i.s: towards rr: travelling strly over 2f out: making gd hdwy whn bdly hmpd over 1f out: sn rdn: kpt on fnl f but nt pce to get involved* **20/1**

60-1 **11** 1 1/4 **Incentive**[17] [1820] 5-9-2 **63**........................(p) LiamKeniry 16 47
(Stuart Kittow) *mid-div: rdn whn drifted rt over 1f out: nvr any real imp on ldrs* **20/1**

2-40 **12** *nse* **Spring Romance (IRE)**[56] [1061] 4-10-0 **75**........................ AdamKirby 6 59
(Dean Ivory) *mid-div: shkn up 3f out: nvr any imp* **12/1**

214- **13** 2 **The Lacemaker**[161] [9211] 5-9-4 **70**........................ DarraghKeenan[(5)] 2 47
(Simon Earle) *in tch: rdn over 2f out: wknd fnl f* **66/1**

00-0 **14** *hd* **Pastfact**[22] [1682] 5-9-1 **62**........................ JosephineGordon 9 39
(Malcolm Saunders) *s.i.s: a towards rr (jockey said gelding reared as stalls opened and was slowly away as result)* **25/1**

0-41 **15** 6 **Met By Moonlight**[26] [1586] 5-9-9 **70**........................ DavidProbert 14 27
(Ron Hodges) *trckd ldrs: rdn 2f out: hld whn hmpd over 1f out: wknd* **7/1**[2]

603- **16** 1 3/4 **Bounty Pursuit**[154] [9317] 7-9-6 **70**........................ MitchGodwin[(3)] 5 22
(Michael Blake) *prom tl wknd 2f out* **12/1**

-146 **17** 1 3/4 **Black Medick**[62] [966] 3-9-1 **75**........................ MeganNicholls[(3)] 15 18
(Laura Mongan) *mid-div: rdn whn bdly hmpd over 1f out: no ch after and eased* **66/1**

1m 15.24s (0.74) **Going Correction** +0.10s/f (Good) **17 Ran SP% 121.0**
WFA 3 from 4yo+ 10lb
Speed ratings (Par 103): **99,98,94,94,93 93,92,92,91,90 88,88,85,85,77 75,73**
CSF £457.47 CT £4027.91 TOTE £81.30: £12.80, £2.00, £2.30, £1.80; EX 727.10 Trifecta £3118.60.
Owner Mrs Lynn Cullimore **Bred** Hugh Ryan **Trained** Kenfig Hill, Bridgend

FOCUS
A competitive and wide open six furlong class 5 with a gamble foiled.

2340 FOLLOW @WILLHILLRACING ON TWITTER FILLIES' NOVICE STKS (PLUS 10 RACE) 6f 213y
5:55 (6:04) (Class 5) 3-Y-O
£4,787 (£1,424; £711; £355) **Stalls Low**

Form RPR

3 **1** **Hotsy Totsy (IRE)**[20] [1740] 3-8-12 0........................ LiamKeniry 3 89
(Ed Walker) *travelled wl thrght: trckd ldrs: led over 1f out: qcknd clr fnl f: easily* **12/1**

22- **2** 5 **Alhakmah (IRE)**[258] [6244] 3-8-12 0........................ SeanLevey 1 75
(Richard Hannon) *led: rdn and hdd over 1f out: kpt on but nt pce of wnr fnl f* **13/8**[1]

41- **3** 1/2 **She's Got You**[143] [9484] 3-9-5 0........................ RobertHavlin 4 81
(John Gosden) *s.i.s: sn in tch: rdn to chse wnr 2f out: sn drifted lft: kpt on same pce fnl f* **5/2**[2]

-0 **4** 3/4 **Marlyn (IRE)**[20] [1740] 3-8-12 0........................ RobHornby 9 72
(Martyn Meade) *in tch: rdn to chse ldrs 2f out: kpt on same pce fnl f* **16/1**

2- **5** *hd* **Neon Sea (FR)**[154] [9306] 3-8-12 0........................ PatDobbs 13 71+
(Sir Michael Stoute) *s.i.s: towards rr: pushed along and stdy prog fr 2f out: kpt on nicely fnl f* **8/1**[3]

0- **6** 2 **Manana Chica (IRE)**[329] [3501] 3-8-12 0........................ HectorCrouch 17 66
(Clive Cox) *mid-div: rdn over 1f out: kpt on fnl f but nt pce to get on terms* **125/1**

0 **7** *hd* **Mayfair Pompette (FR)**[20] [1740] 3-8-12 0........................ StevieDonohoe 16 65+
(Charlie Fellowes) *towards rr of midfield: hdwy fr 3f out: rdn 2f out: chal for hld 5th ent fnl f: kpt on same pce* **8/1**[3]

-00 **8** 3/4 **My Lady Claire**[22] [1677] 3-8-12 0........................ JackMitchell 11 63
(Ed Walker) *s.i.s: towards rr: pushed along over 2f out: hdwy over 1f out: kpt on fnl f but nvr gng pce to get involved* **125/1**

6- **9** 3/4 **Sweet Jemima (USA)**[309] [4250] 3-8-12 0........................ HarryBentley 7 61
(William Muir) *mid-div: rdn and sme prog over 2f out: fdd fnl f (vet said filly lost left hind shoe)* **100/1**

0 **10** 1/2 **Tereshkova**[16] [1828] 3-8-5 0........................(h) SaraDelFabbro[(7)] 18 60
(Michael Bell) *s.i.s: towards rr: rdn and hdwy over 1f out: kpt on fnl f but nvr any danger* **100/1**

0 **11** *nk* **Jumeirah (IRE)**[16] [1838] 3-8-12 0........................ CharlesBishop 5 59
(Eve Johnson Houghton) *s.i.s: towards rr: sme prog over 1f out but nvr threatening to get on terms* **100/1**

00 **12** 2 1/4 **Quemonda**[30] [1495] 3-8-7 0........................ ThomasGreatrex[(5)] 12 53
(Ken Cunningham-Brown) *mid-div: rdn over 2f out: wknd ins fnl f* **150/1**

The Form Book Flat 2019, Raceform Ltd, Newbury, RG14 5SJ

0 **13** *5* **Michigan Blue (IRE)**[19] 1754 3-8-12 0 .... TomMarquand 8 39
(Richard Hannon) *towards rr of midfield: outpcd 2f out: nvr bk on terms (jockey said filly was never travelling)* **40/1**

03- **14** *1 1/4* **Mrs Worthington (IRE)**[230] 7253 3-8-12 0 .... AdamMcNamara 6 36
(Jonathan Portman) *racd keenly: prom: rdn over 2f out: wknd over 1f out (jockey said filly ran too freely)* **50/1**

55- **15** *3 1/2* **Miss Liberty Belle (AUS)**[166] 9133 2-8-12 0 .... DavidProbert 15 27
(William Jarvis) *trckd ldrs: rdn over 2f out: wknd ent fnl f* **50/1**

6 **16** *1* **Princesse Bassett (FR)**[52] 1142 3-8-12 0 .... FergusSweeney 2 24
(George Baker) *s.i.s: a towards rr* **66/1**

43 **17** *2* **Any Smile (IRE)**[72] 795 3-8-12 0 .... LouisSteward 14 18
(Michael Bell) *a towards rr* **66/1**

0-1 **18** *2 1/2* **Kodiac Lass (IRE)**[27] 1570 3-9-2 0 .... GabrieleMalune(3) 10 19
(Marco Botti) *chsd ldrs: struggling over 3f out: sn wknd (trainers rep said, regarding performance that the fill y was unsuited by the Good to Firm going on this occasion, and would prefer a slower surface)* **40/1**

1m 28.12s (-0.58) **Going Correction** +0.10s/f (Good) **18** Ran SP% **119.5**
Speed ratings (Par 96): **107,101,100,99,99 97,97,96,95,94 94,91,86,84,80 79,77,74**
CSF £30.22 TOTE £13.30: £3.00, £1.20, £1.40; EX 41.30 Trifecta £85.60.

Owner D Ward **Bred** Ringfort Stud **Trained** Upper Lambourn, Berks

FOCUS
A deep-looking 3yo fillies' novice with a taking winner. The second has been rated a bit below her 2yo form, with the third similar to her Wolverhampton win.

2341 WILLIAM HILL EXTRA PLACES EVERY DAY H'CAP 1m 1f 201y
6:30 (6:34) (Class 6) (0-60,60) 3-Y-O

£3,493 (£1,039; £519; £300; £300; £300) **Stalls** Low

Form RPR

000- **1** **Seascape (IRE)**[180] 8832 3-9-7 **60** .... DavidProbert 11 67+
(Henry Candy) *mid-div: hdwy 3f out: sn rdn: r.o wl ins fnl f: led towards fin* **9/1**[3]

600- **2** *1* **Catch The Cuban**[166] 9123 3-9-3 **56** ....(t[1]) CharlieBennett 9 61
(Colin Tizzard) *mid-div: hdwy over 3f out: tk narrow advantage and rdn 2f out: kpt on but no ex whn hdd towards fin* **14/1**

6-06 **3** *1 1/2* **Red Archangel (IRE)**[12] 1957 3-9-3 **56** ....(h) AdamKirby 4 58
(Richard Spencer) *mid-div: hdwy 3f out: rdn for str chal 2f out: ev ch ent fnl f: no ex fnl 120yds* **11/1**

-556 **4** *3/4* **Lucky Lou (IRE)**[17] 1825 3-9-7 **60** ....(h[1]) PatDobbs 1 61
(Ken Cunningham-Brown) *mid-div: hdwy over 2f out: rdn and edgd rt fr wl over 1f out: kpt on ins fnl f: snatched 4th cl home* **14/1**

-145 **5** *nk* **Warrior Display (IRE)**[75] 765 3-9-7 **60** ....(p) StevieDonohoe 12 60
(Bernard Llewellyn) *trckd ldrs: hung rt 3f out: led over 2f out: sn rdn and hdd 2f out: kpt on w ev ch tl no ex fnl 120yds* **33/1**

30-0 **6** *1 3/4* **Forty Four Sunsets (FR)**[16] 1828 3-9-3 **56** .... SeanLevey 2 53
(Richard Hannon) *mid-div: hdwy over 2f out: sn rdn: kpt on ins fnl f but nt pce to threaten* **9/1**[3]

0-04 **7** *3/4* **Another Approach (FR)**[26] 1593 3-9-5 **58** .... RobertHavlin 6 54
(George Baker) *hld up towards rr: rdn and stdy prog fr over 2f out but nvr gng pce to get involved* **9/2**[2]

560- **8** *shd* **Duke Of Dunabar**[146] 9444 3-9-3 **56** .... TomMarquand 8 51
(Roger Teal) *hld up towards rr: rdn over 2f out: styd on fnl f: n.d* **16/1**

000- **9** *1 1/4* **Delta Bravo (IRE)**[178] 8880 3-9-4 **57** ....(w) JosephineGordon 5 50
(J S Moore) *sn outpcd and bhd: prog to latch on to main gp over 2f out: fdd ins fnl f* **33/1**

000- **10** *4 1/2* **Lucky Circle**[228] 7333 3-9-2 **55** .... JFEgan 13 39
(David Evans) *a towards rr* **66/1**

040- **11** *2 1/4* **Goodwood Sonnet (IRE)**[160] 9227 3-9-6 **59** .... HarryBentley 14 39+
(William Knight) *led for over 1f: trckd ldr: struggling whn sltly hmpd over 2f out: wknd over 1f out* **9/4**[1]

006- **12** *1 3/4* **Arbuckle**[285] 5208 3-9-3 **56** .... DanielMuscutt 7 33
(Michael Madgwick) *mid-div: rdn over 2f out: wknd over 1f out* **100/1**

000- **13** *1* **Grandad's Legacy**[181] 8796 3-9-7 **60** .... CharlesBishop 10 35+
(Ali Stronge) *plld hrd: led after 1f: rdn and hdd over 2f out: sn wknd (jockey said colt ran too freely)* **16/1**

56-0 **14** *7* **Padmavati**[20] 1730 3-9-6 **59** .... LiamKeniry 3 21
(Ed Walker) *trckd ldrs: rdn over 2f out: sn wknd* **14/1**

2m 11.16s (0.66) **Going Correction** +0.10s/f (Good) **14** Ran SP% **117.4**
Speed ratings (Par 97): **101,100,99,98,98 96,96,96,95,91 89,88,87,81**
CSF £123.29 CT £1403.79 TOTE £8.00: £3.60, £2.50, £3.10; EX 168.60 Trifecta £2122.50.

Owner Robert Allcock **Bred** Robert Allcock **Trained** Kingston Warren, Oxon

FOCUS
A decent 3yo fillies' handicap.

2342 WILLIAM HILL H'CAP 1m 4f 5y
7:05 (7:06) (Class 4) (0-85,86) 4-Y-O+ **£5,692** (£1,694; £846; £423; £300) **Stalls** Low

Form RPR

42-6 **1** **Hyanna**[22] 1681 4-9-11 **86** .... CharlesBishop 1 93
(Eve Johnson Houghton) *trckd ldr: str chal fr 3f out: sn rdn: led ent fnl f: styd on wl: drvn out* **7/2**[2]

2221 **2** *1* **Dono Di Dio**[29] 1518 4-8-11 **79** .... ScottMcCullagh(7) 2 84
(Michael Madgwick) *fly-leapt leaving stalls: last of the 5: tk clsr order 6f out: rdn 3f out: styd on ins fnl f: snatched 2nd fnl strides* **7/1**

03-2 **3** *hd* **Mandalayan (IRE)**[27] 1559 4-9-11 **86** .... RobHornby 6 91
(Jonathan Portman) *led: rdn whn strly chal fr 3f out: hdd ent fnl f: styd on: lost 2nd fnl strides* **9/4**[1]

120- **4** *1 1/2* **Lissitzky (IRE)**[173] 8995 4-9-7 **82** .... AdamKirby 5 84
(Andrew Balding) *trckd ldrs: rdn to chse ldng pair wl over 2f out: styd on same pce fnl f* **13/2**[3]

06-3 **5** *8* **Mary Elise (IRE)**[113] 135 4-8-4 **65** .... RaulDaSilva 3 54
(Michael Blake) *racd in 4th tl dropped to last but stl in tch 6f out: rdn 3f out: sn one pce* **33/1**

2m 38.47s (0.87) **Going Correction** +0.10s/f (Good) **5** Ran SP% **81.8**
Speed ratings (Par 105): **101,100,100,99,93**
CSF £13.41 TOTE £3.20: £1.90, £2.00; EX 14.10.

Owner G C Vibert **Bred** Al-Baha Bloodstock **Trained** Blewbury, Oxon

FOCUS
A small field but plenty of good recent form and a progressive winner. The second has been rated to her AW latest, and the third similar to Leicester.

2343 WILLIAM HILL BETTING TV H'CAP 1m 4f 5y
7:35 (7:38) (Class 6) (0-65,65) 3-Y-O

£3,493 (£1,039; £519; £300; £300; £300) **Stalls** Low

Form RPR

040- **1** **Green Etoile**[200] 8233 3-9-6 **64** .... DavidProbert 1 71+
(Alan King) *mid-div: rdn whn swtchd lft over 2f out: hdwy over 1f out: str run ins fnl f: led fnl stride* **8/1**

4022 **2** *hd* **Bonneville (IRE)**[28] 1555 3-8-3 **52** ....(b) TheodoreLadd(5) 14 59
(Rod Millman) *led: drvn 3 l clr 2f out: styd on but no ex whn collared fnl stride* **5/1**[2]

6-44 **3** *1 3/4* **Luck Of Clover**[19] 1771 3-9-4 **65** .... WilliamCox(3) 7 69
(Andrew Balding) *in tch: rdn to chse ldrs over 2f out: kpt on same pce ins fnl f* **8/1**

66-0 **4** *3/4* **Sea Art**[30] 1510 3-9-7 **65** ....(v) AdamKirby 5 68
(William Knight) *trckd ldr: rdn to chal 3f out tl over 2f out: styd on same pce* **10/1**

0-02 **5** *hd* **Brinkleys Katie**[57] 1039 3-8-8 **52** ....(p[1]) JFEgan 3 55
(Paul George) *mid-div: making hdwy whn hung rt and tched rails over 3f out: sn swtchd lft: kpt on but nt pce to threaten (jockey said filly hung right-handed)* **28/1**

-445 **6** *2* **Mrs Meader**[20] 1730 3-9-5 **63** .... RobHornby 4 63
(Seamus Mullins) *mid-div: rdn and hdwy over 2f out: kpt on but nt pce to threaten* **25/1**

004- **7** *1/2* **Blowing Dixie**[133] 9635 3-9-3 **61** .... AdamMcNamara 11 60
(Roger Charlton) *s.i.s: towards rr: hdwy over 3f out: sn rdn: styd on same pce fnl f* **6/1**[3]

04-0 **8** *1 1/4* **Riverina**[20] 1730 3-8-11 **55** ....(h[1]) HectorCrouch 13 52
(Harry Dunlop) *hld up towards rr: hdwy over 3f out: sn rdn: nt pce to get on terms fnl f* **50/1**

0-20 **9** *2 1/2* **Abenaki**[38] 1332 3-8-5 **49** .... KierenFox 10 42
(Sheena West) *mid-div: rdn over 3f out: little imp: wknd fnl f* **50/1**

00-6 **10** *1* **Confils (FR)**[48] 1217 3-9-4 **62** .... FergusSweeney 12 54
(George Baker) *hld up towards rr: hdwy over 3f out: sn rdn: nvr threatened: wknd fnl f* **20/1**

00 **11** *1 3/4* **Lock Seventeen (USA)**[33] 1417 3-9-2 **60** ....(v) StevieDonohoe 6 49
(Charlie Fellowes) *slowly away: nvr travelling: a towards rr* **7/1**

05-0 **12** *hd* **Loch Lady**[99] 370 3-9-1 **59** .... HarryBentley 9 48
(Ralph Beckett) *trckd ldrs: rdn over 2f out: wknd over 1f out* **10/3**[1]

0-65 **13** *6* **Moon Artist (FR)**[9] 2011 3-8-2 **46** oh1 .... RaulDaSilva 2 26
(Michael Blanshard) *trckd ldr: rdn wl over 2f out: wknd over 1f out (trainer said filly had a breathing problem)* **25/1**

2m 38.58s (0.98) **Going Correction** +0.10s/f (Good) **13** Ran SP% **117.7**
Speed ratings (Par 97): **100,99,98,98,98 96,96,95,93,93 92,91,87**
CSF £43.26 CT £333.43 TOTE £8.90: £3.00, £1.30, £3.00; EX 46.90 Trifecta £455.20.

Owner Simon Munir & Isaac Souede **Bred** Saxtead Livestock & Newsells Park Stud **Trained** Barbury Castle, Wilts

FOCUS
An open middle-distance handicap with another late swooping winner.

2344 WILLIAMHILL.COM BEST ODDS GUARANTEED H'CAP 1m 6f 44y
8:10 (8:10) (Class 6) (0-60,60) 4-Y-O+

£3,493 (£1,039; £519; £300; £300; £300) **Stalls** Far side

Form RPR

0560 **1** **Oborne Lady (IRE)**[40] 1297 6-8-9 **48** .... RobHornby 57
(Seamus Mullins) *trckd ldrs: led over 2f out: styd on strly: rdn out* **12/1**

440- **2** *2 3/4* **Vlannon**[103] 7371 4-8-12 **51** .... LiamKeniry 57
(Michael Madgwick) *trckd ldrs: rdn over 2f out: chsd wnr over 1f out: styd on but a being comf hld* **10/1**

13-3 **3** *3/4* **Percy Prosecco**[34] 946 4-9-7 **60** .... AdamKirby 65
(Noel Williams) *mid-div: hdwy over 3f out: rdn to chse ldrs over 2f out: styd on but nt pce to get on terms w wnr* **9/2**[2]

320- **4** *shd* **Earthly (USA)**[148] 9409 5-8-13 **52** ....(tp) StevieDonohoe 56
(Bernard Llewellyn) *hld up towards rr: rdn and hdwy fr 2f out: drifting rt ent fnl f: styd on same pce* **14/1**

50-0 **5** *nk* **Master Grey (IRE)**[32] 1463 4-9-7 **60** .... CharlesBishop 69
(Rod Millman) *hld up towards rr: hdwy fr 2f out: rdn and styd on ins fnl f but nvr gng pce to threaten* **7/2**[1]

64- **6** *2 1/2* **Prince Charmin' (IRE)**[41] 9721 6-9-5 **58** ....(tp) DavidProbert 58
(Tim Vaughan) *mid-div: rdn over 2f out: hdwy over 1f out: tight for room ent fnl f: sn no ex* **11/2**[3]

520- **7** *1 1/2* **Calvinist**[126] 9721 6-9-5 **58** ....(p) JackMitchell 56
(Kevin Frost) *mid-div: rdn and hdwy 2f out: hld whn tight for room ent fnl f: fdd* **12/1**

-031 **8** *1/2* **Thresholdofadream (IRE)**[76] 731 4-9-2 **55** .... PatDobbs 54
(Amanda Perrett) *hld up towards rr: hdwy over 3f out: rdn over 2f out: nt pce to get on terms: fdd fnl f* **7/1**

-502 **9** *1 1/2* **Tilsworth Sammy**[36] 1361 4-8-12 **51** .... TomMarquand 48
(J R Jenkins) *mid-div tl outpcd 3f out: no threat after* **10/1**

0050 **10** *6* **Sellingallthetime (IRE)**[30] 1498 8-9-0 **56** ....(v) GaryMahon(3) 44
(Mark Usher) *trckd ldrs: led over 4f out: rdn and hdd over 2f out: wknd jst over 1f out* **25/1**

-046 **11** *10* **Folies Bergeres**[27] 1569 4-9-3 **56** ....(b) TrevorWhelan 32
(Grace Harris) *trckd ldrs: rdn over 3f out: sn btn (jockey said filly stopped quickly)* **40/1**

4560 **12** *11* **Ripplet**[15] 1861 4-9-7 **60** .... CharlieBennett 22
(Hughie Morrison) *racd keenly: led: hdd over 4f out: sn btn (jockey said filly ran too freely)* **16/1**

3m 7.68s (1.08) **Going Correction** +0.10s/f (Good) **12** Ran SP% **120.7**
Speed ratings (Par 101): **100,98,98,97,97 96,95,95,94,90 85,78**
CSF £128.95 CT £632.25 TOTE £13.30: £2.90, £3.30, £2.00; EX 170.90 Trifecta £890.30.

Owner Simon & Christine Prout **Bred** A Mulligan **Trained** Wilsford-Cum-Lake, Wilts

FOCUS
A competitive flag-started staying contest with the Millman's unlucky again.
T/Jkpt: Not won. T/Plt: £131.40 to a £1 stake. Pool: £49,412.11. 274.50 winning units. T/Qpdt: £37.10 to a £1 stake. Pool: £5,854.21. 116.69 winning units. **Tim Mitchell**

2295 SOUTHWELL (L-H)

Thursday, May 2

OFFICIAL GOING: Fibresand: standard

Wind: Moderate, behind Weather: Cloudy and heavy wintery showers

2345 SKY SPORTS RACING SKY 415 H'CAP — 1m 3f 23y(F)

2:05 (2:05) (Class 6) (0-65,66) 4-Y-0+

£3,105 (£924; £461; £300; £300; £300) **Stalls** Low

Form RPR

1663 **1** **Cold Harbour**[22] 1680 4-8-10 **53**.....................(t) NicolaCurrie 8 60
(Robyn Brisland) *trckd ldrs: hdwy 4f out: chal over 2f out: rdn to ld wl over 1f out: hung lft jst ins fnl f: drvn and kpt on wl towards fin* **7/1[3]**

22 **2** 1 ¼ **Loose Chippings (IRE)**[3] 2196 5-8-9 **52**................ SilvestreDeSousa 6 57
(Ivan Furtado) *cl up 1/2-way: pushed along wl over 2f out: rdn and hdd wl over 1f out: carried sltly lft and n.m.r ent fnl f: sn drvn and kpt on* **4/5[1]**

1434 **3** 1 ½ **Going Native**[3] 2196 4-8-10 **53**.............................. RachelRichardson 3 56
(Olly Williams) *cl up: rdn along 3f out: sltly outpcd and swtchd lft wl over 1f out: sn drvn and rdr ct up in reins: n.m.r on inner and rallied ins fnl f: kpt on same pce* **12/1**

-251 **4** 2 ½ **Love Rat**[57] 1040 4-9-7 **64**..(v) KieranO'Neill 1 63
(Scott Dixon) *chsd ldrs: rdn along and outpcd over 4f out: styd on u.p to chse ldrs 2f out: sn drvn and no imp fnl f* **12/1**

6111 **5** 11 **Contingency Fee**[5] 2127 4-9-2 **66** 5ex..................(p) GraceMcEntee(7) 5 47
(Phil McEntee) *hld up: hdwy over 7f out: cl up over 4f out: rdn along* **7/2[2]**

653- **6** 3 ½ **Decima (IRE)**[156] 8391 5-9-0 **64**............................ JoshQuinn(7) 7 39
(Michael Easterby) *bhd tl styd on fr over 2f out: nt rch ldrs* **50/1**

000 **7** 2 ¼ **Sunshineandbubbles**[26] 1591 6-8-12 **60**...........(p w) HarrisonShaw(5) 9 32
(Jennie Candlish) *in tch: pushed along over 4f out: rdn wl over 3f out: sn wknd* **33/1**

433- **8** 18 **Billy Ruskin**[156] 9272 4-9-9 **66**..(w) DougieCostello 2 9
(Kevin Ryan) *led: rdn along and hdd 1/2-way: chsd ldrs tl wknd over 3f out (vet reported the gelding lost its left fore shoe)* **25/1**

00-6 **9** 2 ½ **Lyn's Secret (IRE)**[12] 1934 4-9-5 **62**...............................(h) ShaneKelly 4
(Seamus Mullins) *in tch: rdn along 1/2-way: sn lost pl and bhd (jockey said filly had no more to give)* **100/1**

2m 25.87s (-2.13) **Going Correction** -0.15s/f (Stan) 9 Ran SP% **115.4**
Speed ratings (Par 101): **101,100,99,97,89 86,85,71,70**
CSF £12.83 CT £68.47 TOTE £8.20: £1.90, £1.02, £2.60; EX 17.70 Trifecta £84.20.
Owner Mrs Jackie Cornwell And Mrs Jo Brisland **Bred** Exors Of The Late Mrs Liz Nelson **Trained** Danethorpe, Notts

FOCUS
Only a modest event but it did feature some in-form horses. The first four finished well clear. A minor pb from the winner, with the third rated near her better recent form.

2346 ATTHERACES.COM CLAIMING STKS — 1m 13y(F)

2:35 (2:35) (Class 6) 4-Y-0+

£3,105 (£924; £461; £300; £300; £300) **Stalls** Low

Form RPR

0205 **1** **Mama Africa (IRE)**[15] 1859 5-9-0 73.............................. JaneElliott(3) 1 56+
(David Barron) *cl up on inner: hdwy 3f out: rdn to ld in centre 2f out: drvn ins fnl f: hld on gamely* **4/1[3]**

1233 **2** nk **Mister Music**[33] 1428 10-9-9 85........................ PoppyBridgwater(5) 6 66+
(Tony Carroll) *dwlt and towards rr: hdwy on inner wl over 2f out: styd nr far rail: rdn over 1f out: ev ch ins fnl f: kpt on* **10/11[1]**

1334 **3** shd **Muqarred (USA)**[1] 2297 7-9-10 63..........................(b) SilvestreDeSousa 3 62+
(Roger Fell) *cl up: chal on outer 3f out: cl up and rdn 2f out: drvn and ev ch ins fnl f: no ex towards fin* **7/2[2]**

5544 **4** 1 ¾ **Born To Reason (IRE)**[16] 1841 5-8-10 43..................... WilliamCarver(7) 5 51
(Kevin Frost) *hld up in rr: hdwy and wd st: sn chsng ldrs: rdn along and cl up wl over 1f out: drvn and one pce fnl f* **50/1**

3204 **5** 4 ½ **The Great Wall (USA)**[11] 1969 5-10-0 81................... AlistairRawlinson 2 52
(Michael Appleby) *led: rdn along over 3f out: drvn and hdd 2f out: sn wknd* **7/1**

00-0 **6** 38 **Majestic Man (IRE)**[59] 462 6-9-0 38.................................... DannyBrock 4
(Ronald Thompson) *dwlt: sn chsng ldrs: rdn along 1/2-way: sn outpcd and bhd (jockey said gelding was never travelling)* **200/1**

1m 42.88s (-0.82) **Going Correction** -0.15s/f (Stan) 6 Ran SP% **109.6**
Speed ratings (Par 101): **98,97,97,95,91 53**
CSF £7.66 TOTE £5.10: £2.10, £1.10; EX 12.00 Trifecta £18.70.
Owner Harrowgate Bloodstock Ltd **Bred** G J King **Trained** Maunby, N Yorks

■ Stewards' Enquiry : Poppy Bridgwater 15-day ban: used whip above the permitted level (May 16-31)

FOCUS
Not many runners but they served up a thrilling finish.

2347 SKY SPORTS RACING SKY 415 NOVICE STKS — 1m 13y(F)

3:05 (3:06) (Class 5) 4-Y-0+

£3,752 (£1,116; £557; £278) **Stalls** Low

Form RPR

12 **1** **Masked Identity**[54] 1102 4-9-9 .... ShaneKelly 3 67+
(Kevin Frost) *cl up: slt ld after 2f: rdn over 1f out: kpt on wl fnl f* **5/6[1]**

0 **2** 1 ½ **Basildon**[24] 1643 4-9-2 .... CamHardie 2 57
(Brian Ellison) *chsd ldng pair: pushed along and sltly outpcd over 3f out: rdn and hdwy over 2f out: drvn and kpt on wl fnl f: tk 2nd nr line* **25/1[3]**

-50 **3** nk **Tommycole**[15] 1862 4-9-2 .... RachelRichardson 1 56
(Olly Williams) *slt ld 2f: cl up on inner: rdn along 3f out: drvn to chal over 1f out: ev ch 1f out: no ex last 100yds: lost 2nd nr line* **125/1**

0- **4** 1 ½ **Fox Mafia (IRE)**[320] 3867 4-9-2 .... SilvestreDeSousa 4 53
(Andrew Balding) *dwlt: green and sn pushed along: hdwy on outer over 3f out: rdn to chse ldng pair 2f out: drvn over 1f out: kpt on one pce* **11/10[2]**

1m 42.6s (-1.10) **Going Correction** -0.15s/f (Stan) 4 Ran SP% **106.8**
Speed ratings (Par 103): **99,97,97,95**
CSF £15.31 TOTE £1.60; EX 8.00 Trifecta £27.40.
Owner D S Lovatt **Bred** Cheveley Park Stud Ltd **Trained** Newcastle-under-Lyme, Staffs

FOCUS
Not much strength in depth here and a cosy win for the market leader, although his main market rival was disappointing.

2348 VISITSOUTHWELL.COM H'CAP — 7f 14y(F)

3:35 (3:35) (Class 4) (0-80,77) 4-Y-0+

£5,530 (£1,645; £822; £411; £300; £300) **Stalls** Low

Form RPR

-502 **1** **Rock Of Estonia (IRE)**[29] 1522 4-8-13 **69**......................... NicolaCurrie 7 82
(Charles Hills) *trckd ldrs in wd outside: hdwy and wd st: sn chsng ldng pair: rdn to ld wl over 1f out: clr ins fnl f: kpt on strly* **6/1**

4110 **2** 4 ½ **Crosse Fire**[7] 2065 7-9-7 **77**...(p) KieranO'Neill 8 78
(Scott Dixon) *cl up on outer: slt ld over 4f out: wd st: rdn and hdd narrowly 2f out: drvn over 1f out: kpt on same pce fnl f* **5/1[3]**

2420 **3** nse **Esprit De Corps**[32] 1457 5-9-3 **73**.. ShaneKelly 5 74
(David Barron) *cl up: rdn to ld 2f out: sn hdd and drvn: kpt on same pce fnl f* **11/2**

51/- **4** 9 **Furzig**[487] 9465 4-9-7 **77**... TonyHamilton 2 54
(Richard Fahey) *prom: rdn along and outpcd 1/2-way: kpt on u.p fr wl over 1f out* **12/1**

00-0 **5** 2 ¼ **Sword Exceed (GER)**[89] 548 5-9-5 **75**..................(w) SilvestreDeSousa 1 45
(Ivan Furtado) *a towards rr (jockey said gelding hung left under pressure)* **9/2[2]**

1355 **6** nk **Master Diver**[36] 1367 4-9-7 **77**..(v[1]) LukeMorris 4 47
(Sir Mark Prescott Bt) *dwlt and sn rdn along: hdwy to chse ldrs 1/2-way: rdn over 2f out: drvn and edgd lft wl over 1f out: sn btn (trainer's rep could offer no explanation for the gelding's performance)* **3/1[1]**

00-2 **7** 3 ¼ **Inexes**[11] 1969 7-9-4 **74**...(p) DougieCostello 3 35
(Ivan Furtado) *slt ld: hdd over 4f out: cl up: rdn along 3f out: drvn over 2f out: sn wknd* **8/1**

1m 28.26s (-2.04) **Going Correction** -0.15s/f (Stan) 7 Ran SP% **108.3**
Speed ratings (Par 105): **105,99,99,89,86 86,82**
CSF £31.82 CT £153.07 TOTE £6.30: £2.90, £3.20; EX 30.60 Trifecta £145.30.
Owner Kangyu Int Racing (HK) Ltd & F Ma **Bred** Colin Kennedy **Trained** Lambourn, Berks

FOCUS
This looked open beforehand but this fair handicap became processional in the home straight.

2349 SOUTHWELL GOLF CLUB H'CAP — 7f 14y(F)

4:10 (4:12) (Class 6) (0-65,66) 4-Y-0+

£3,105 (£924; £461; £300; £300; £300) **Stalls** Low

Form RPR

0212 **1** **Ticks The Boxes (IRE)**[1] 2298 7-7-13 **50** 4ex......... KieranSchofield(7) 1 58+
(Brian Ellison) *chsd ldrs on inner: rdn along to chal over 2f out: led wl over 1f out: drvn and kpt on wl fnl f* **13/8[1]**

5232 **2** ½ **Liamba**[10] 1986 4-9-2 **60**... DavidNolan 12 67
(David O'Meara) *cl up: rdn to take narrow ld briefly 2f out: sn hdd and drvn: ev ch ent fnl f: kpt on same pce last 75yds* **7/2[2]**

6626 **3** 4 ½ **Sooqaan**[3] 2193 8-9-3 **61**...(p) CamHardie 9 56
(Antony Brittain) *trckd ldrs: hdwy 3f out: rdn along to chse ldng pair 2f out: sn drvn and no imp fnl f* **7/1[3]**

400- **4** 1 ½ **Spinart**[185] 8697 6-9-8 **66**...(e[1]) ShaneKelly 8 57
(Pam Sly) *in tch: hdwy and wd st: chsd ldrs 2f out: rdn and edgd lft over 1f out: kpt on same pce* **25/1**

3130 **5** hd **Thunder Buddy**[15] 1859 4-9-0 **63**.................................(p) HarrisonShaw(5) 4 53
(K R Burke) *bhd: hdwy on inner 3f out: rdn along 2f out: styd on u.p fnl f: nrst fin* **8/1**

60-6 **6** 7 **Size Matters**[21] 1722 5-8-7 **51**.. LukeMorris 10 22
(Mark Walford) *chsd ldrs: rdn along wl over 2f out: sn drvn and one pce* **25/1**

00-0 **7** hd **Mister Freeze (IRE)**[17] 1820 5-9-2 **60**..............................(vt) KieranO'Neill 6 31
(Patrick Chamings) *a in rr* **33/1**

6401 **8** 2 **My Town Chicago (USA)**[10] 1986 4-9-4 **65** 5ex......... JoshuaBryan(3) 2 30
(Kevin Frost) *led: rdn along 3f out: sn hdd & wknd (vet reported the gelding lost its right hind shoe)* **9/1**

-400 **9** 1 **Mr Strutter (IRE)**[19] 1760 5-9-7 **65**................................... AndrewElliott 7 28
(Ronald Thompson) *a in rr* **40/1**

-600 **10** 2 ¼ **Face Like Thunder**[24] 1653 4-9-2 **60**...............................(b[1]) DannyBrock 3 17
(John Butler) *a in rr* **66/1**

30-6 **11** 6 **Sebastiano Ricci (IRE)**[106] 250 4-8-13 **57**......(w) SilvestreDeSousa 11
(Mark Loughnane) *racd wd: a in rr (jockey said gelding had no more to give)* **11/1**

/0-0 **12** 12 **Beautiful Artist (USA)**[48] 1216 4-8-11 **60**................. SeamusCronin(5) 5
(Robyn Brisland) *dwlt: sn swtchd rt to outer: a bhd* **66/1**

1m 28.19s (-2.11) **Going Correction** -0.15s/f (Stan) 12 Ran SP% **118.3**
Speed ratings (Par 101): **106,105,100,98,98 90,90,87,86,84 77,63**
CSF £6.48 CT £31.07 TOTE £2.80: £1.10, £1.30, £2.50; EX 7.80 Trifecta £28.90.
Owner Kristian Strangeway **Bred** John B Hughes **Trained** Norton, N Yorks

FOCUS
Only a moderate affair and two of the form horses, who were up with the pace throughout, pulled clear of the rest.

2350 ADVERTISER LADIES DAY H'CAP — 1m 13y(F)

4:45 (4:48) (Class 6) (0-55,61) 3-Y-0+

£3,105 (£924; £461; £300; £300; £300) **Stalls** Low

Form RPR

0121 **1** **Capofaro**[9] 2007 3-9-6 **61** 6ex....................................... NicolaCurrie 8 70+
(Jamie Osborne) *mde all: rdn and hung lft over 1f out: clr ins fnl f: kpt on strly* **2/1[1]**

-065 **2** 3 ¾ **Luath**[29] 1527 6-9-4 **46**...(p) ShaneKelly 12 49+
(Suzzanne France) *racd wd: reminders s: hdwy to chse ldrs 1/2-way: rdn over 2f out: drvn and ch over 1f out: kpt on same pce* **12/1**

424 **3** 3 ¼ **Port Soif**[29] 1527 5-9-10 **52**...(p) KieranO'Neill 10 48
(Scott Dixon) *trckd ldrs: hdwy 3f out: sn chsng wnr: rdn over 2f out: drvn over 1f out: kpt on one pce* **9/2[2]**

0330 **4** 4 **Crazy Spin**[12] 1957 3-8-0 **46**..............................(p) ThoreHammerHansen(5) 2 30
(Ivan Furtado) *chsd ldrs on inner: rdn along 3f out: sn outpcd* **6/1**

0232 **5** 3 ¼ **Zorro's Girl**[3] 2190 3-9-0 **55**..(b) LukeMorris 13 31
(Archie Watson) *chsd ldrs: rdn along and wd st: sn drvn and wknd (jockey said filly ran flat)* **5/1[3]**

6-00 **6** 4 **Jagerbond**[21] 1721 3-8-9 **50**...(p[1]) CamHardie 14 17
(Andrew Crook) *racd wd: in tch: rdn along to chse ldrs: wd st: sn drvn and wknd 2f out* **25/1**

05-0 **7** 2 **Sunbright (IRE)**[28] 1550 4-8-10 **45**............................... WilliamCarver(7) 4 10
(Michael Appleby) *bhd: wd st: sn rdn and nvr a factor* **16/1**

The Form Book Flat 2019, Raceform Ltd, Newbury, RG14 5SJ

4-00 **8** *5* **Cat Royale (IRE)**[16] 1841 6-9-10 **52**....(be[1]) DannyBrock 5 6
(John Butler) *chsd ldrs: rdn along wl over 3f out: sn outpcd (jockey said gelding had no more to give)* **9/1**

060- **9** *5* **Debbi's Dream**[192] 8478 4-9-3 **45**.... AndrewElliott 9
(Ronald Thompson) *a in rr* **100/1**

60-6 **10** *2 3/4* **Seafaring Girl (IRE)**[28] 1549 3-8-9 **50**.... SilvestreDeSousa 7
(Mark Loughnane) *chsd ldrs: rdn along 3f out: sn wknd (jockey said filly stopped quickly)* **16/1**

-000 **11** *9* **Mr Wing (IRE)**[88] 587 4-8-10 **45**....(v) VictorSantos(7) 6
(John Wainwright) *a bhd* **250/1**

1m 42.08s (-1.62) **Going Correction** -0.15s/f (Stan)
WFA 3 from 4yo+ 13lb **11** Ran SP% **117.2**
Speed ratings (Par 101): **102,98,95,91,87 83,81,76,71,69 60**
CSF £28.69 CT £99.70 TOTE £2.70: £1.70, £3.70, £1.30; EX 22.10 Trifecta £113.20.
Owner Michael Buckley **Bred** Cheveley Park Stud Ltd **Trained** Upper Lambourn, Berks

FOCUS
An easy win for the market leader in a race where they came home at long intervals. His win made it a treble on the day for his jockey.

2351 SKY SPORTS RACING VIRGIN 535 APPRENTICE H'CAP 1m 6f 21y(F)
5:15 (5:16) (Class 5) (0-70,72) 4-Y-0+
£3,752 (£1,116; £557; £300; £300; £300) **Stalls** Low

Form RPR

130- **1** **Aphaea**[32] 7030 4-8-13 **63**.... MarcoGhiani(5) 4 78
(Michael Easterby) *hld up in tch: rn wd bnd over 1m out: hdwy over 4f out: chsd ldrs over 2f out: rdn to ld over 1f out: sn clr: styd on strly* **6/1**[3]

6642 **2** *10* **High Command (IRE)**[11] 1971 6-8-13 **61**....(b) GraceMcEntee(3) 1 62
(Michael Appleby) *slt ld 6f: cl up on inner: effrt to chal over 3f out: sn disputing ld: rdn wl over 2f out: drvn wl over 1f out: kpt on same pce* **7/2**[2]

1043 **3** *5* **Seasearch**[15] 1861 4-9-3 **62**....(p) WilliamCarver 6 56
(Andrew Balding) *hld up towards rr: pushed along 5f out: rdn over 3f out: drvn 2f out: plugged on fnl f: n.d (jockey said gelding was never travelling)* **2/1**[1]

5204 **4** *1/2* **Country'N'Western (FR)**[16] 1840 7-9-11 **70**.... JessicaCooley 3 63
(Robert Eddery) *cl up: slt ld 1/2-way: hdd narrowly over 4f out: led again over 3f out and sn rdn along: drvn 2f out: hdd over 1f out: sn wknd* **16/1**

0-00 **5** *3 1/2* **Blame Me Forever (USA)**[70] 616 4-9-3 **67**....(b) StefanoCherchi(5) 5 55
(Don Cantillon) *cl up: slt ld on outer after 6f: hdd 1/2-way: cl up and led again over 4f out: rdn along and hdd over 3f out: sn wknd* **25/1**

1054 **6** *3/4* **Katie Gale**[33] 1429 9-9-0 **62**....(v) SeanKirrane(3) 7 49
(Robyn Brisland) *chsd ldrs: rdn along over 4f out: sn outpcd and bhd* **6/1**[3]

000/ **7** *27* **Discay**[49] 2659 10-9-13 **72**.... EllaMcCain 2 22
(Philip Kirby) *a in rr: outpcd and bhd fnl 3f* **40/1**

3m 4.55s (-3.75) **Going Correction** -0.15s/f (Stan) **7** Ran SP% **112.6**
Speed ratings (Par 103): **104,98,95,95,93 92,77**
CSF £26.34 TOTE £5.60: £2.60, £1.60; EX 33.00 Trifecta £96.10.
Owner M W Easterby **Bred** Worksop Manor Stud **Trained** Sheriff Hutton, N Yorks

FOCUS
They went a decent early clip and the winner was held up well off it before picking up the pieces in the home straight.
T/Plt: £18.00 to a £1 stake. Pool: £50,173.56. 2,031.19 winning units. T/Qpdt: £10.90 to a £1 stake. Pool: £3,943.80. 266.77 winning units. **Joe Rowntree**

2352 - (Foreign Racing) - See Raceform Interactive

CHEPSTOW (L-H)
Friday, May 3

OFFICIAL GOING: Good (good to firm in places; 6.6)
Wind: Slight across Weather: Sunny spells

2353 MARKETING STOP - THE DIRECT MARKETING SPECIALISTS H'CAP 1m 4f
1:45 (1:45) (Class 5) (0-75,75) 4-Y-0+
£3,752 (£1,116; £557; £300; £300; £300) **Stalls** High

Form RPR

04-0 **1** **Carp Kid (IRE)**[102] 346 4-8-12 **69**....(p) FinleyMarsh(3) 4 81
(John Flint) *led to 5f out: remained prom: rdn to ld again over 2f out: r.o wl* **10/1**[3]

13-1 **2** *3 3/4* **Kirkland Forever**[18] 1826 5-8-6 **67**.... GeorgiaDobie(7) 9 73
(Eve Johnson Houghton) *hld up: hdwy 5f out: rdn to chse wnr over 1f out: no imp and hld fnl f* **2/1**[1]

5-05 **3** *1/2* **Ascot Day (FR)**[18] 1826 5-8-8 **62**.... LukeMorris 6 67
(Bernard Llewellyn) *midfield: hdwy to press ldr 4f out: drvn and ev ch over 2f out: kpt on same pce* **7/1**[2]

504- **4** *1 1/2* **Cacophonous**[199] 8309 4-9-5 **73**.... JasonWatson 11 76
(David Menuisier) *s.i.s: hdwy on outer to go prom after 2f: rdn and sltly outpcd over 3f out: kpt on fnl 2f* **7/1**[2]

1-0 **5** *6* **Less Of That (IRE)**[37] 1355 5-8-8 **67**.... RachealKneller(5) 7 60
(Matthew Salaman) *hld up: hdwy 4f out: rdn over 2f out: fdd fnl f* **40/1**

53-5 **6** *1 1/2* **Sea Tide**[15] 1882 5-9-3 **71**.... LiamJones 8 62
(Laura Mongan) *dwlt: t.k.h and sn in midfield: hdwy to ld 5f out: rdn over 3f out: hdd over 2f out: wknd appr fnl f* **20/1**

0303 **7** *7* **Mobham (IRE)**[18] 1826 4-8-11 **65**.... FergusSweeney 10 44
(J R Jenkins) *s.i.s: in rr: rdn and sme prog 4f out: no ch fnl 3f* **14/1**

62-2 **8** *3 3/4* **White Turf (IRE)**[97] 435 4-9-4 **72**.... RobHornby 5 45
(Alastair Ralph) *chsd ldrs: rdn 4f out and sn lost pl: wknd 2f out* **25/1**

-500 **9** *5* **River Dart (IRE)**[37] 1363 7-8-13 **67**.... TomMarquand 2 32
(Tony Carroll) *trckd ldrs: rdn and lost pl over 3f out: sn wknd* **20/1**

26-3 **10** *4* **Consultant**[34] 1418 4-9-3 **71**.... DavidProbert 3 30
(Andrew Balding) *t.k.h: prom 2f: sn in midfield: rdn and dropped to rr 5f out: no ch fnl 3f: eased over 1f out (jockey said gelding had stopped quickly; trainer could offer no explanation for the gelding's performance)* **2/1**[1]

2m 35.37s (-4.93) **Going Correction** -0.25s/f (Firm) **10** Ran SP% **123.2**
Speed ratings (Par 103): **106,103,103,102,98 97,92,90,86,84**
CSF £30.86 CT £160.26 TOTE £12.30: £3.10, £1.20, £2.00; EX 43.80 Trifecta £221.20.
Owner Jack Racing **Bred** Acorn Stud **Trained** Kenfig Hill, Bridgend

FOCUS
The ground looked to be riding just on the quick side. Pretty modest form but a pb from the winner.

2354 PETE SMITH SPECIALIST CARS COLEFORD NOVICE STKS 1m 2f
2:15 (2:18) (Class 5) 3-Y-0+
£3,752 (£1,116; £557; £278) **Stalls** High

Form RPR

1 **Aloe Vera** 3-8-8 0.... JosephineGordon 5 82+
(Ralph Beckett) *s.i.s: in rr: stl a lot to do 5f out: hdwy on outer fr 4f out: rdn 3f out: r.o to ld fnl 75yds: cosily* **8/1**

4- **2** *nk* **Maiden Castle**[142] 9500 3-8-13 0.... HayleyTurner 16 86
(Henry Candy) *prom: led gng wl jst over 1f out: sn rdn: kpt on: hdd fnl 75yds* **11/2**[3]

02- **3** *3 3/4* **Wedding Blue**[184] 8739 3-8-13 0.... DavidProbert 10 78
(Andrew Balding) *trckd ldr: led 3f out: rdn over 2f out: hdd jst over 1f out: one pce and lost 2nd ins fnl f* **5/2**[1]

5/ **4** *2 1/2* **Flying Tiger (IRE)**[62] 7805 6-10-0 0.... TomMarquand 13 74
(Nick Williams) *sme way off pce in midfield: clsd 4f out: sn rdn: styd on fnl 2f: nt rch ldrs* **7/1**

03- **5** *3/4* **Culture (FR)**[181] 8840 3-8-13 0.... NicolaCurrie 3 72
(George Baker) *chsd ldrs: rdn 2f out: sn edgd sltly rt: lost 3rd 1f out: no ex* **50/1**

45 **6** *4 1/2* **Global Falcon**[25] 1652 3-8-13 0.... CallumShepherd 15 63
(Charles Hills) *midfield: rdn over 2f out: styd on steadily but nvr able to threaten ldrs* **12/1**

04- **7** *1/2* **Baasem (USA)**[177] 8930 3-8-13 0.... DaneO'Neill 12 62
(Owen Burrows) *led to 3f out: sn rdn: wknd appr fnl f* **3/1**[2]

8 *2* **Sherwood Forrester** 3-8-10 0.... MeganNicholls(3) 11 58
(Paul George) *in tch in midfield: rdn 4f out: sn no ch w ldrs* **66/1**

0- **9** *3* **Admirals Bay (GER)**[142] 9500 3-8-13 0.... RobHornby 8 52
(Andrew Balding) *towards rr: rdn over 4f out: modest late prog* **16/1**

10 *1/2* **Storm Eleanor** 3-8-8 0.... JFEgan 9 46
(Hughie Morrison) *sme way off pce in midfield: shkn up over 3f out: kpt on steadily* **50/1**

11 *1 3/4* **Dancing Lilly** 4-9-4 0.... RachealKneller(5) 14 43
(Matthew Salaman) *a towards rr (jockey said filly ran green)* **50/1**

12 *hd* **Bambys Boy**[462] 8-10-0 0.... LiamKeniry 1 48
(Neil Mulholland) *s.s: bhd: modest late prog* **40/1**

41- **13** *shd* **Manorah (IRE)**[155] 9315 3-9-1 0.... LukeMorris 2 48
(Roger Varian) *chsd ldrs: drvn 3f out: wknd over 1f out* **8/1**

14 *3/4* **Miss Harriett** 3-8-5 0.... WilliamCox(3) 7 40
(Stuart Kittow) *in tch in midfield: rdn 4f out: wknd over 2f out* **100/1**

0- **15** *7* **Vakilita (IRE)**[181] 8833 3-8-8 0.... MartinDwyer 6 26
(Andrew Balding) *hld up: a in rr* **33/1**

16 *73* **Indian Harbour**[21] 6-10-0 0.... FergusSweeney 4
(Sue Gardner) *s.i.s and a in rr: t.o fnl 3f* **66/1**

2m 5.34s (-7.46) **Going Correction** -0.25s/f (Firm)
WFA 3 from 4yo+ 15lb **16** Ran SP% **132.5**
Speed ratings (Par 103): **114,113,110,108,108 104,104,102,100,99 98,98,98,97,91 33**
CSF £54.80 TOTE £11.40: £2.90, £2.10, £2.10; EX 78.00 Trifecta £219.80.
Owner Miss K Rausing **Bred** Miss K Rausing **Trained** Kimpton, Hants

FOCUS
A fair novice that saw a taking first effort from the winning filly. She's sure to do better.

2355 AQS - A QUALITY CLEANING SERVICE H'CAP 1m 14y
2:45 (2:49) (Class 5) (0-70,71) 3-Y-0
£3,752 (£1,116; £557; £300; £300; £300) **Stalls** Centre

Form RPR

060- **1** **Lady Reset**[178] 8888 3-9-4 **65**.... RossaRyan 10 74
(David Evans) *w ldrs: shkn up over 2f out: led wl over 1f out: drvn clr fnl f: eased cl home (trainer said, as to the apparent improvement in form, the filly had strengthened up over the winter break)* **20/1**

000- **2** *2 3/4* **Lonicera**[141] 9522 3-8-12 **59**.... DavidProbert 4 62
(Henry Candy) *plld hrd: a.p: led narrowly over 2f out: sn rdn: hdd wl over 1f out: outpcd by wnr fnl f* **9/1**

054- **3** *1 3/4* **Akwaan (IRE)**[177] 8922 3-9-10 **71**.... DaneO'Neill 7 70
(Simon Crisford) *trckd ldrs: rdn over 2f out: kpt on same pce fnl f* **9/4**[1]

60-0 **4** *1 1/4* **Potenza (IRE)**[72] 813 3-8-1 **55**.... LauraCoughlan(7) 1 51
(Stef Keniry) *s.s: towards rr: shkn up and hdwy on outer 3f out: rdn 2f out: kpt on fnl f* **14/1**

0-30 **5** *3* **Four Mile Bridge (IRE)**[30] 1516 3-9-7 **68**.... FergusSweeney 9 57
(Mark Usher) *s.i.s: in rr: rdn 3f out: stl last 1f out: modest late prog* **40/1**

44-5 **6** *3/4* **Shifting Gold (IRE)**[18] 1825 3-9-2 **63**.... LukeMorris 3 50
(William Knight) *towards rr: rdn over 4f out: no imp on ldrs fnl 2f* **16/1**

220- **7** *3 3/4* **Elegant Love**[140] 9530 3-9-6 **67**.... JFEgan 6 46
(David Evans) *chsd ldrs: rdn 3f out: sn lost pl (jockey said filly was unsuited by the undulating track)* **9/2**[3]

-403 **8** *3 1/4* **Laxmi (IRE)**[11] 1985 3-9-7 **68**.... CallumShepherd 8 39
(Brian Meehan) *prom: rdn over 2f out: wknd over 1f out* **5/1**

50-3 **9** *8* **Poet's Magic**[18] 1825 3-9-5 **66**.... RobHornby 5 19
(Jonathan Portman) *led: rdn 3f out: hdd over 2f out: wknd qckly over 1f out (jockey said the filly was unsuited by the undulating track)* **3/1**[2]

1m 34.52s (-1.48) **Going Correction** -0.25s/f (Firm) **9** Ran SP% **120.4**
Speed ratings (Par 99): **97,94,92,91,88 87,83,80,72**
CSF £194.26 CT £579.59 TOTE £24.10: £6.40, £2.80, £1.40; EX 271.20 Trifecta £1232.50.
Owner R S Brookhouse **Bred** R S Brookhouse **Trained** Pandy, Monmouths

FOCUS
Moderate 3yo form, the winner pulled away late near to the stands' rail. Surprise improvement from the winner.

2356 PTL - PORTABLETOILETSLIMITED.COM FILLIES' H'CAP 7f 16y
3:15 (3:18) (Class 5) (0-75,77) 3-Y-0
£3,752 (£1,116; £557; £300; £300; £300) **Stalls** Centre

Form RPR

2251 **1** **Plumette**[28] 1557 3-9-1 **68**.... TrevorWhelan 3 71
(David Loughnane) *trckd ldrs: led gng wl over 1f out: sn drvn: r.o* **8/1**

0-00 **2** *1 1/2* **Cotubanama**[5] 2144 3-9-2 **76**.... ScottMcCullagh(7) 1 74
(Mick Channon) *s.i.s: hld up: hdwy on outer over 3f out: rdn over 2f out: wnt 2nd 1f out: kpt on but a hld by wnr* **16/1**

63-3 **3** *1/2* **Saikung (IRE)**[28] 1562 3-9-2 **69**.... JasonWatson 6 66
(Charles Hills) *s.i.s: t.k.h in rr: rdn and hdwy over 2f out: kpt on same pce fnl f* **5/2**[1]

5-20 **4** *1 3/4* **Moneta**[17] 1838 3-8-13 **66**.... RobHornby 2 58
(Jonathan Portman) *cl up: led 3f out: sn rdn: hdd over 1f out: no ex fnl f* **14/1**

023- **5** *1 3/4* **Shellebeau (IRE)**[199] 8295 3-9-4 **74** MeganNicholls(3) 5 61
(Paul Nicholls) *hld up: rdn and clsd over 2f out: kpt on same pce fnl f* **11/2**

3-54 **6** *3* **Lethal Lover**[53] 1142 3-8-13 **66** JosephineGordon 8 45
(Clive Cox) *uns rdr and rn loose on way to post: cl up: rdn over 2f out: wknd over 1f out* **5/1**[3]

533- **7** *1/2* **Knightshayes**[199] 8306 3-9-10 **77** JFEgan 7 55
(Paul George) *stmbld sltly leaving stalls: midfield: rdn and wkng whn n.m.r 2f out (jockey said the filly was unsuited by the undulating track; vet reported that the filly lost its right fore shoe)* **3/1**[2]

500- **8** *6* **Shaffire**[191] 8533 3-8-11 **64** RossaRyan 9 26
(Joseph Tuite) *plld hrd in midfield: rdn over 2f out: wknd wl over 1f out* **18/1**

600- **9** *12* **Yes Can Do (USA)**[181] 8832 3-8-8 **61** (h[1]) DavidProbert 4
(Ed Dunlop) *t.k.h: led to 3f out: sn rdn: wknd over 1f out (jockey said the saddle slipped)* **20/1**

1m 23.53s (-0.37) **Going Correction** -0.25s/f (Firm) **9 Ran SP% 119.3**
Speed ratings (Par 96): **92,90,89,87,85 82,81,74,61**
CSF £129.03 CT £418.60 TOTE £8.80: £1.80, £4.10, £1.40; EX 133.60 Trifecta £722.70.
Owner Jamie Rocke **Bred** Whitsbury Manor Stud **Trained** Tern Hill, Shropshire

FOCUS
Modest fillies' form, rated at face value through the runner-up.

2357 COUNTY MARQUEES H'CAP — 6f 16y
3:50 (3:57) (Class 6) (0-60,60) 3-Y-O
£3,105 (£924; £461; £300; £300; £300) **Stalls** Centre

Form RPR

0540 **1** **Brother Bentley**[4] 2211 3-8-13 **52** (b[1]) JasonWatson 6 58
(Ronald Harris) *midfield towards centre: hdwy 1/2-way: rdn to ld 2f out: r.o* **6/1**[2]

04-5 **2** *1 1/2* **Tizwotitiz**[34] 1430 3-9-0 **60** TobyEley(7) 8 62
(Steph Hollinshead) *led to post: t.k.h: chsd ldrs in centre: rdn 2f out: wnt 2nd over 1f out: r.o fnl f (jockey said gelding hung right-handed under pressure)* **12/1**

-145 **3** *nk* **Halle's Harbour**[51] 1170 3-9-3 **56** (v) LukeMorris 1 57
(Paul George) *s.s: in rr towards far side: rdn along and hdwy over 3f out: chsd ldrs 2f out: kpt on fnl f* **11/1**

-340 **4** *hd* **Shesadabber**[28] 1567 3-8-7 **47** oh1 JFEgan 12 46
(Brian Baugh) *prom on stands' side: led over 2f out: sn hdd: kpt on u.p* **50/1**

00-0 **5** *1/2* **Dark Poet**[105] 289 3-9-1 **57** WilliamCox(3) 11 56
(Clive Cox) *chsd ldrs stands' side: rdn 2f out: kpt on same pce* **6/1**[2]

000 **6** *3/4* **Frea**[48] 1236 3-8-11 **50** RaulDaSilva 13 46
(Harry Dunlop) *towards rr on stands' side: rdn and hdwy over 2f out: nt clr run briefly over 1f out: r.o ins fnl f* **16/1**

050- **7** *1/2* **Maktay**[133] 9671 3-8-7 **51** PoppyBridgwater(5) 5 46
(David Bridgwater) *racd towards far side: led over 1f: remained prom: rdn 2f out: unable qck fnl f* **25/1**

64-0 **8** *3/4* **Superstition**[16] 1863 3-8-9 **55** (p[1]) GeorgiaDobie(7) 14 48
(Eve Johnson Houghton) *t.k.h: chsd ldrs on stands' side: rdn 2f out: kpt on same pce* **16/1**

2132 **9** *1 1/2* **Eye Of The Water (IRE)**[23] 1678 3-9-7 **60** DavidProbert 15 48
(Ronald Harris) *towards rr on stands' side: rdn over 2f out: n.m.r and swtchd rt early ins fnl f: sme late prog (jockey said gelding hung left-handed; trainer said the gelding was unsuited by the going (good, good to firm in places) and would prefer a slower surface)* **5/4**[1]

000- **10** *2 1/2* **Andies Armies**[183] 8777 3-8-10 **52** FinleyMarsh(3) 4 33
(Lisa Williamson) *racd far side: s.i.s: sn rcvrd: led over 4f out: rdn and hdd over 2f out: wknd over 1f out* **66/1**

0126 **11** *1 1/2* **Global Acclamation**[10] 2016 3-9-7 **60** (b) LiamKeniry 3 36
(Ed Dunlop) *chsd ldrs far side: rdn over 2f out: sn wknd* **9/1**[3]

0-00 **12** *6* **Magnetic (IRE)**[97] 437 3-8-13 **52** (b[1]) JosephineGordon 2 10
(J S Moore) *prom on far side: rdn 3f out: wknd 2f out* **50/1**

6600 **13** *2 1/2* **Yfenni (IRE)**[4] 2211 3-8-7 **47** oh1 NicolaCurrie 9
(Milton Bradley) *prom in centre over 2f: sn lost pl: bhd fnl 2f (trainer's rep said filly was unsuited by the undulating track)* **33/1**

1m 10.8s (-0.70) **Going Correction** -0.25s/f (Firm) **13 Ran SP% 123.0**
Speed ratings (Par 97): **94,92,91,91,90 89,89,88,86,82 80,72,69**
CSF £71.46 CT £707.49 TOTE £7.60: £1.70, £4.10, £3.00; EX 99.40 Trifecta £1950.50.
Owner Ridge House Stables Ltd **Bred** Leslie Scadding **Trained** Earlswood, Monmouths
■ Sybil Grand was withdrawn. Price at time of withdrawal 12/1. Rule 4 applies to all bets - deduction 5p in the pound.

FOCUS
A competitive but low-grade sprint. The field initially split but came back together at halfway.

2358 CSP - CARING SAFE PROFESSIONAL H'CAP — 5f 16y
4:25 (4:27) (Class 5) (0-75,76) 4-Y-O+
£3,752 (£1,116; £557; £300; £300; £300) **Stalls** Centre

Form RPR

2/40 **1** **Fair Cop**[18] 1822 5-9-6 **72** (p[1]) DavidProbert 6 83+
(Andrew Balding) *cl up: led after 2f: shkn up over 1f out: sn in command: rdn out fnl f* **3/1**[1]

1030 **2** *1 1/2* **Union Rose**[14] 1915 7-9-7 **73** (p) JasonWatson 3 79
(Ronald Harris) *chsd ldrs tl rdn and sltly outpcd 1/2-way: swtchd rt 1f out: r.o: wnt 2nd nr fin but no ch w wnr* **4/1**[3]

10-1 **3** *1/2* **Major Valentine**[13] 1952 7-8-8 **67** KateLeahy(7) 1 71
(John O'Shea) *hld up: shkn up and hdwy 2f out: edgd lft 1f out: sn chsng wnr and rdn: no imp and lost 2nd nr fin* **5/1**

01-5 **4** *2 1/4* **Seamster**[8] 2053 12-8-6 **65** (t) LauraCoughlan(7) 7 61
(David Loughnane) *s.i.s: chsd along in rr: rdn and hdwy 1/2-way: disp 2nd 1f out: outpcd fnl f* **7/1**

04-6 **5** *1/2* **Powerful Dream (IRE)**[14] 1915 6-9-1 **67** (p) RaulDaSilva 5 61
(Ronald Harris) *hld up in tch: rdn 2f out: r.o fnl f: nt rch ldrs* **8/1**

52-6 **6** *2 1/4* **Justice Lady (IRE)**[64] 953 6-9-10 **76** LukeMorris 4 62
(Robert Cowell) *t.k.h: chsd ldrs: rdn 2f out: disp 2nd 1f out: wknd fnl f* **7/2**[2]

440- **7** *hd* **Silverrica (IRE)**[264] 6062 9-8-10 **67** KatherineBegley(5) 2 52
(Malcolm Saunders) *t.k.h: trckd ldrs: rdn 2f out: wknd fnl f* **22/1**

110- **8** *10* **Quantum Dot (IRE)**[238] 7017 8-9-6 **72** (b) CallumShepherd 8 21
(Ed de Giles) *led 2f: sn rdn: wknd 2f out: eased fnl f (jockey said gelding stopped quickly)* **20/1**

58.04s (-1.36) **Going Correction** -0.25s/f (Firm) **8 Ran SP% 116.6**
Speed ratings (Par 103): **100,97,96,93,92 88,88,72**
CSF £15.60 CT £58.34 TOTE £3.90: £2.40, £1.30, £1.90; EX 16.20 Trifecta £113.20.
Owner J C Smith **Bred** Littleton Stud **Trained** Kingsclere, Hants

FOCUS
Ordinary sprinting form. The winner has potential to do better.

2359 NETWORK PRODUCTIONS H'CAP — 2m
5:00 (5:03) (Class 6) (0-65,65) 4-Y-O+
£3,105 (£924; £461; £300; £300; £300) **Stalls** High

Form RPR

04 **1** **Panatos (FR)**[16] 1858 4-9-1 **57** RossaRyan 9 64
(Alexandra Dunn) *mde all: rdn 3f out: edgd lft ins fnl f: styd on wl* **5/1**[3]

/05- **2** *2* **Three Star General**[23] 8312 6-9-4 **62** (b) FinleyMarsh(3) 11 65
(David Pipe) *rousted along early and chsd wnr after 2f: lost 2nd 1/2-way: rdn along 5f out: drvn and disp 2nd over 2f out: hung lft ins fnl f: sn in def 2nd but hld by wnr (jockey said gelding was slowly away)* **15/8**[1]

0-00 **3** *3/4* **Fitzwilly**[4] 2217 9-9-3 **65** ScottMcCullagh(7) 2 67
(Mick Channon) *trckd ldrs: chsd wnr 4f out: rdn and lost 2nd over 2f out: styd on fnl f* **4/1**[2]

-5P0 **4** *1/2* **Omotesando**[31] 1508 9-9-5 **63** (b[1]) MeganNicholls(3) 13 64
(Oliver Greenall) *hld up: hdwy 4f out: drvn and disp 2nd over 2f out tl no ex ins fnl f* **10/1**

000- **5** *1 3/4* **Mustaaqeem (USA)**[165] 8312 7-9-2 **60** (b) WilliamCox(3) 4 59
(Bernard Llewellyn) *chsd ldrs tl lost pl 1/2-way: rdn on outer 4f out: styd on fnl 2f: no threat to ldrs* **25/1**

456/ **6** *2* **Norab (GER)**[563] 7832 8-9-10 **65** (b) LiamKeniry 10 62
(Bernard Llewellyn) *hld up: hdwy to chse ldrs 4f out: rdn 3f out: wknd fnl f* **25/1**

0/0- **7** *1 1/4* **Late Shipment**[19] 6126 8-9-8 **63** (p) TrevorWhelan 3 58
(Nikki Evans) *midfield: rdn 4f out: lost pl over 2f out: styd on again fnl f* **25/1**

4305 **8** *7* **Normandy Blue**[29] 1548 4-9-2 **58** CallumShepherd 7 47
(Louise Allan) *hld up: rdn over 3f out: no hdwy* **12/1**

0 **9** *1 3/4* **Sin Sin (IRE)**[9] 923 5-9-1 **56** HayleyTurner 6 41
(Nigel Hawke) *chsd ldrs: rdn over 3f out: sn wknd* **16/1**

4640 **10** *8* **Queen Of Paris**[31] 1497 4-9-8 **64** (vt[1]) JasonWatson 5 41
(William Knight) *s.i.s: sn in midfield: hdwy to trck wnr 1/2-way: rdn and lost 2nd 4f out: wknd over 2f out (jockey said filly was never travelling)* **6/1**

3m 35.42s (-6.68) **Going Correction** -0.25s/f (Firm)
WFA 4 from 5yo+ 1lb **10 Ran SP% 119.9**
Speed ratings (Par 101): **106,105,104,104,103 102,101,98,97,93**
CSF £14.88 CT £39.78 TOTE £5.80: £1.60, £1.90, £1.40; EX 17.70 Trifecta £63.00.
Owner Helium Racing Ltd **Bred** Appapays Racing Club **Trained** West Buckland, Somerset

FOCUS
A weak staying handicap, but the right horses at least came to the fore. Straightforward form, the winner entitled to win this on his French figures.
T/Jkpt: Not won T/Plt: £251.60 to a £1 stake. Pool: £65,642.85 - 190.40 winning units T/Qpdt: £42.10 to a £1 stake. Pool: £7,060.48 - 123.98 winning units **Richard Lowther**

2005 LINGFIELD (L-H)
Friday, May 3

OFFICIAL GOING: Good to firm (good in places) changing to good (good to firm in places) after race 1 (1.35)
Wind: Fine Weather: nil

2360 CH CONSTRUCTION BUILDING FIRST INISH H'CAP — 1m 2f
1:35 (1:35) (Class 4) (0-80,75) 4-Y-O+
£5,530 (£1,645; £822; £411; £300; £300) **Stalls** Low

Form RPR

00-4 **1** **She Believes (IRE)**[10] 2005 4-9-1 **73** GaryMahon(3) 4 79
(Sylvester Kirk) *cl bhd ldrs on outer: shkn up wl over 2f out to take clsr order: rdn to ld 2f out: kpt on wl fnl f* **6/1**

-213 **2** *1/2* **Narjes**[69] 876 5-8-9 **71** (h) SophieRalston(7) 3 76
(Laura Mongan) *cl up bhd ldrs on inner: shkn up 2f out: outpcd over 1f out: sn rdn and swtchd off rail: styd on wl between horses last 150yds to snatch 2nd post: too much to do* **6/1**

041- **3** *hd* **Sudona**[192] 8514 4-9-5 **74** JamesDoyle 1 79
(Hugo Palmer) *hld up in 5th: shkn up wl over 2f out: tk clsr order and ev ch whn rdn over 2f out: tk 2nd 1f out: kpt on tl lost 2nd post* **11/4**[1]

461- **4** *3/4* **My Boy Sepoy**[229] 7331 4-9-6 **75** OisinMurphy 2 78
(Stuart Williams) *narrow ldr on inner: hdd over 3f out: rdn 2f out: kpt on one pce fnl f* **7/2**[2]

50-3 **5** *nse* **King Of The Sand (IRE)**[70] 86 4-9-2 **71** HectorCrouch 6 74
(Gary Moore) *pressed ldr on outer: shkn up and led over 3f out: rdn 3f out: hdd 2f out: plugged on* **9/2**[3]

2/01 **6** *10* **First Quest (USA)**[25] 1653 5-9-3 **72** CharlieBennett 5 55
(Jim Boyle) *sluggish s: in last and nvr travelling: nudged along at 1/2-way: rdn over 3f out: wl hld 2f out and plugged on (jockey said gelding hung left-handed throughout)* **5/1**

2m 7.08s (-5.12) **Going Correction** -0.225s/f (Firm) **6 Ran SP% 112.3**
Speed ratings (Par 105): **111,110,110,109,109 101**
CSF £40.05 TOTE £7.10: £3.20, £2.90; EX 31.90 Trifecta £134.00.
Owner Miss A Jones **Bred** Ringfort Stud **Trained** Upper Lambourn, Berks

FOCUS
Add 4yds. An open handicap on paper and they finished in a bit of a heap so probably not form to get too excited about, although one or two might still have more to offer this year. The winner built on her latest AW run.

2361 9TH BARRY GURR MEMORIAL MAIDEN FILLIES' STKS — 1m 2f
2:05 (2:12) (Class 5) 3-Y-O+
£3,752 (£1,116; £557; £278) **Stalls** Low

Form RPR

26- **1** **Bella Vita**[241] 6898 3-8-13 **0** CharlesBishop 3 78+
(Eve Johnson Houghton) *trckd ldrs: shkn up to cl over 2f out: rdn 2f out in 3rd to chse clr ldr: styd on wl fnl f and wore down ldr cl home: gng on at fin* **7/1**

0- **2** *3/4* **Shrewdness**[188] 8643 3-8-13 **0** JamesDoyle 6 77+
(William Haggas) *led: shkn up over 3f out to ld by 5 l 2f out: sn rdn: kpt on tl no ex fnl f and wore cl home* **7/1**

4 **3** *4* **J Gaye (IRE)**[34] 1419 3-8-13 **0** RobertHavlin 13 69
(Richard Phillips) *in tch in mid-div: shkn up 3f out and clsr over 2f out: cajoled along in 5th fr 2f out: kpt on wl to take 3rd nr fin* **33/1**

4 *3/4* **Libbretta**[74] 4-9-7 **0** EllieMacKenzie(7) 2 68
(John E Long) *reluctant to load: trckd ldrs: rdn over 2f out: kpt on wl over 1f out to chse clr ldr: one pce fnl f and lost 3rd cl home* **100/1**

The Form Book Flat 2019, Raceform Ltd, Newbury, RG14 5SJ

	5	2 3/4	**Dubious Affair (IRE)** 3-8-13 0 ColmO'Donoghue 8	62+

(Sir Michael Stoute) *hld up in rr-div: rdn w plenty to do 3f out: shuffled along and kpt on w promise fr over 1f out to take 5th fnl strides* **6/1**[3]

3- **6** nk **Summer Flair (IRE)**[192] 8510 3-8-13 0 WilliamBuick 9 61
(Charlie Appleby) *in tch bhd ldrs on outer: sltly awkward on bnd into st: pushed along 3f out: rdn in 4th over 2f out to chse clr ldr: no ex ent fnl f: lost 5th fnl strides* **8/11**[1]

6-6 **7** 8 **Spring Run**[21] 1739 3-8-6 0 TylerSaunders(7) 7 45
(Jonathan Portman) *in last: effrt 3f out w plenty to do: kpt on inner fr 2f out and shaped wl* **50/1**

0 **8** 1 1/2 **Just A Minute**[35] 1397 4-10-0 0 AdamMcNamara 4 43
(Jonathan Portman) *spooked by rival bhd stalls and uns rdr: racd in rr-div: effrt over 2f out: no ex* **100/1**

9 3 **Mousebird (IRE)** 3-8-13 0 CharlieBennett 10 36
(Hughie Morrison) *hld up in last pair: shuffled along w plenty to do wl over 3f out: styd on past btn horses fr 2f out* **50/1**

10 1/2 **Persepone** 3-8-13 0 OisinMurphy 12 35
(Hugo Palmer) *missed break and lost 10 l s: grad mde up grnd and clsr in mid-div 5f out: shuffled along fr over 3f out: can do bttr (jockey said filly was slowly away)* **11/2**[2]

0 **11** 1 **Video Diva (IRE)**[18] 1824 3-8-13 0 GeorgeWood 14 33
(James Fanshawe) *racd in mid-div on inner: rdn over 2f out: one pce* **40/1**

00 **12** 5 **Lollipop Lady**[6] 2113 3-8-8 0 (p) ThomasGreatrex(5) 1 23
(Brian Meehan) *reluctant to load: racd in rr-div: niggled along at 1/2-way: rdn wl over 3f out: no imp* **66/1**

20 **13** 4 1/2 **Sadler's Soul (USA)**[10] 2018 3-8-13 0 (p) HollieDoyle 11 14
(Archie Watson) *a in rr: no imp over 3f out (jockey said filly stopped quickly)* **33/1**

2m 6.87s (-5.33) **Going Correction** -0.225s/f (Firm)
WFA 3 from 4yo+ 15lb **13 Ran SP% 128.3**
Speed ratings (Par 100): **112,111,108,107,105 105,98,97,95,94 93,89,86**
CSF £57.32 TOTE £8.10: £2.00, £2.00, £7.70; EX 75.40 Trifecta £4007.70.
Owner Mrs Heather Raw **Bred** Shoreham Stud **Trained** Blewbury, Oxon
■ Onomatopeia was withdrawn. Price at time of withdrawal 100/1. Rule 4 does not apply

FOCUS
Add 4yds. A bit of an unsatisfactory start to this maiden with a few playing up behind the gates and leaving some of these standing in the starting stalls for over six minutes. The gallop looked no more than steady and the well-backed market leader proved a bit disappointing, so the race probably isn't particularly strong, but, as ever in these types of races, there was promise from several. The first three home had all had a run.

2362 BRITISH STALLION STUDS EBF NOVICE STKS (PLUS 10 RACE) 4f 217y
2:35 (2:39) (Class 4) 2-Y-O **£6,301** (£1,886; £943; £472; £235) **Stalls** Centre

Form RPR
24 **1** **Strong Power (IRE)**[15] 1887 2-9-5 HarryBentley 1 84
(George Scott) *mde all: tacked across to rail after 1f: shkn up 2f out: rdn over 1f out: pressed ins fnl f: asserted fnl 100yds* **4/6**[1]

2 1 1/4 **Illusionist (GER)** 2-9-5 OisinMurphy 2 80
(Archie Watson) *carried lft s: sn w ldr on outer: rdn wl over 1f out: pressed wnr fnl 150yds: no ex cl home (jockey said colt stumbled leaving the stalls)* **5/2**[2]

3 9 **Misty Grey (IRE)** 2-9-5 AdamKirby 4 47
(Mark Johnston) *a in 3rd: rdn over 2f out: lft bhd ent fnl f: plugged on* **7/1**[3]

4 3 1/2 **Sea Of Cool (IRE)** 2-9-5 SilvestreDeSousa 3 35
(John Ryan) *wnt lft s: a in 4th: rdn over 2f out: plugged on* **12/1**

5 2 3/4 **Ask Siri (IRE)** 2-9-0 KieranO'Neill 5 20
(John Bridger) *in last and struggling after 1f: sme prog fr over 1f out (jockey said filly hung right-handed)* **66/1**

58.11s (-0.59) **Going Correction** -0.225s/f (Firm) **5 Ran SP% 110.2**
Speed ratings (Par 95): **95,93,78,73,68**
CSF £2.57 TOTE £1.70: £1.30, £1.50; EX 2.60 Trifecta £4.50.
Owner Abdulla Al Mansoori **Bred** Tally-Ho Stud **Trained** Newmarket, Suffolk

FOCUS
This turned into a shootout between Strong Power and Illusionist, with the pair a long way clear of the rest. Both look useful but it's hard to pin down the level of the form.

2363 JOHN LIFTON MEMORIAL H'CAP 7f
3:05 (3:07) (Class 3) (0-90,89) 4-Y-O **£7,246** (£2,168; £1,084; £542; £270) **Stalls** Centre

Form RPR
12-4 **1** **Game Player (IRE)**[15] 1891 4-9-6 **89** JackMitchell 4 102+
(Roger Varian) *trckd ldr: shkn up 2f out: drvn over 1f out: rdn to ld jst ins fnl f: hands and heels fnl 150yds and jst doing enough: easily at fin* **11/8**[1]

04-6 **2** 1 1/2 **Pettifogger (IRE)**[22] 1714 4-9-2 **85** (h) ShaneKelly 6 92
(Marco Botti) *sn led: increased advantage to 3 l at 1/2-way: pack clsd over 2f out: rdn 2f out: hdd jst ins fnl f: kpt on but no ch w wnr* **14/1**

320- **3** 5 **Graphite Storm**[174] 8999 5-9-6 **89** AdamKirby 5 83
(Clive Cox) *dwlt: in last pair: sltly ct on heels fr 2f out tl ent fnl f: fnd little whn rdn* **9/2**[2]

266- **4** 1 3/4 **Charles Molson**[183] 8768 8-9-3 **86** OisinMurphy 3 75
(Patrick Chamings) *dwlt: in last pair: effrt on wd outer over 2f out: plugged on* **17/2**

112- **5** 1 **Diocles Of Rome (IRE)**[123] 9772 4-9-2 **85** HarryBentley 1 71
(Ralph Beckett) *trckd ldr on outer: rdn over 2f out: no ex fnl f* **5/1**[3]

-100 **6** 2 **Maksab (IRE)**[15] 1881 4-9-3 **86** SilvestreDeSousa 2 67
(Mick Channon) *bhd ldr: rdn over 2f out: one pce over 1f out* **9/2**[2]

1m 21.3s (-3.00) **Going Correction** -0.225s/f (Firm) **6 Ran SP% 112.3**
Speed ratings (Par 107): **108,106,100,98,97 95**
CSF £21.94 TOTE £1.70: £1.20, £7.40; EX 17.90 Trifecta £65.20.
Owner Sheikh Mohammed Obaid Al Maktoum **Bred** Mrs Cherry Faeste **Trained** Newmarket, Suffolk

FOCUS
One or two potential improvers in here, including the well-backed winner, and he opened his account for the season with a bit in hand. The runner-up is rated to recent form.

2364 EVE MANNING 21ST BIRTHDAY H'CAP 7f
3:35 (3:38) (Class 4) (0-85,87) 3-Y-O
£5,530 (£1,645; £822; £411; £300; £300) **Stalls** Centre

Form RPR
50-5 **1** **Buckingham (IRE)**[23] 1685 3-9-4 **81** CharlesBishop 10 86
(Eve Johnson Houghton) *on inner pressing ldr: rdn 2f out: sltly checked 2f out: led jst ins fnl f: kpt on wl* **16/1**

352- **2** 3/4 **Al Mureib (IRE)**[179] 8880 3-9-7 **84** AdamKirby 11 87
(Saeed bin Suroor) *on inner trcking ldrs: effrt over 2f out: outpcd over 1f out and lost pl: kpt on again ins fnl f to take 2nd on post: gng on at fin* **15/8**[1]

3-13 **3** shd **Nubough (IRE)**[55] 1104 3-9-7 **84** JimCrowley 8 87
(Charles Hills) *one off rail and narrowly led: rdn over 2f out: edgd rt 2f out: hdd jst ins fnl f: kpt on but lost 2nd post* **4/1**[2]

1-00 **4** nk **Battle Of Waterloo (IRE)**[15] 1888 3-8-9 **79** CierenFallon(7) 4 81
(John Ryan) *dropped out in rr and wnt to inner: shkn up w a bit to do ent fnl f on rail and sltly ct on heels: rdn 1f out and fin w a flourish last 150yds to grab 4th (jockey said gelding ran too free in the early stages and was denied a clear run in the final furlong)* **33/1**

120- **5** 1 1/4 **Sir Busker (IRE)**[188] 8644 3-9-2 **79** JamesDoyle 7 78
(William Knight) *racd in mid-div: rdn over 2f out: kpt on* **8/1**

0-31 **6** 1 1/2 **Balata Bay**[30] 1516 3-8-8 **78** LukeCatton(7) 6 73
(Richard Hannon) *early pce and t.k.h: sn in rr-div: effrt over 2f out wdst of all: no ex fnl f* **16/1**

0-14 **7** shd **Oloroso (IRE)**[16] 1846 3-8-12 **78** JoshuaBryan(3) 2 72
(Andrew Balding) *dropped out in rr and carried to rail after 1f: effrt angling to outer over 2f out: plugged on fnl f (jockey said gelding was denied a clear run)* **7/1**[3]

522- **8** hd **Wiretap (FR)**[192] 8502 3-9-3 **80** OisinMurphy 5 74
(David Simcock) *racd in rr-div: shuffled along fr over 2f out: nt qckn* **7/1**[3]

100- **9** 4 **Indian Sounds (IRE)**[212] 7899 3-9-10 **87** WilliamBuick 3 70
(Mark Johnston) *trckd ldrs on outer: squeezed along to hold pl 4f out: pushed along over 2f out: no ex over 1f out: eased last 150yds* **16/1**

05-6 **10** 11 **Sheila's Showcase**[16] 1851 3-9-4 **81** ShaneKelly 9 34
(Denis Coakley) *in rr-div: dropped to last over 3f out: sn hld (jockey said colt was unsuited by the undulations at Lingfield in the early part of the race which caused the colt to become unbalanced)* **9/1**

1m 22.52s (-1.78) **Going Correction** -0.225s/f (Firm) **10 Ran SP% 121.5**
Speed ratings (Par 101): **101,100,100,99,98 96,96,96,91,79**
CSF £48.28 CT £154.63 TOTE £15.80: £3.70, £1.20, £2.60; EX 68.70 Trifecta £363.70.
Owner The Buckingham Partnership **Bred** Mrs Louise Quinn **Trained** Blewbury, Oxon

FOCUS
Four of these were having their first run since being gelded, including the runner-up. The winner came up the rail but one or two in behind caught the eye and look the ones to focus on going forward.

2365 PATRICIA'S HAPPINESS MAGNET H'CAP 7f
4:10 (4:10) (Class 5) (0-70,72) 4-Y-O+
£3,752 (£1,116; £557; £300; £300; £300) **Stalls** Centre

Form RPR
2153 **1** **Chica De La Noche**[27] 1586 5-9-3 **65** (p) AdamKirby 4 73
(Simon Dow) *early pce: sn trckd ldrs: clsd over 2f out: rdn between horses to ld 2f out: styd on wl* **9/2**[3]

30-0 **2** 3/4 **Ragstone View (IRE)**[28] 1561 4-9-7 **69** (h) CharlesBishop 2 75
(Rod Millman) *t.k.h for 2f in mid-div: rdn 2f out: kpt on wl fr 1f out take 2nd 110yds out: nt get to wnr* **11/1**

40-4 **3** 1 1/4 **Kachumba**[13] 1932 4-9-6 **68** SilvestreDeSousa 9 71
(Rae Guest) *hld up bhd ldrs on inner: clung to inner and rdn over 2f out: briefly threatened jst ins fnl f: no ex and lost 2nd fnl 110yds* **2/1**[1]

0-60 **4** 2 3/4 **Blazed (IRE)**[39] 1329 5-9-9 **71** (t) HarryBentley 5 66
(Ed Vaughan) *racd in rr-div: clsr whn effrt 2f out: styd on but nt pce of ldng trio* **3/1**[2]

0 **5** nk **Savitar (IRE)**[35] 1393 4-9-2 **64** (h) CharlieBennett 1 58
(Jim Boyle) *racd along in centre tl c across to press ldrs after 2f: rdn 2f out: plugged on fr over 1f out* **8/1**

500- **6** 2 1/4 **Flying Sakhee**[182] 8801 6-8-7 **55** oh7 KieranO'Neill 7 43
(John Bridger) *t.k.h early in rr on outer: squeezed along 4f out: rdn over 2f out: briefly threatened over 1f out: wknd ent fnl f* **25/1**

4230 **7** nk **Margie's Choice (GER)**[23] 1688 4-9-10 **72** (v) GeorgeWood 8 60
(Michael Madgwick) *led on inner: rdn over 2f out: hdd 2f out and one pce* **10/1**

300- **8** 5 **Good Luck Charm**[142] 9504 10-9-4 **66** HectorCrouch 6 40
(Gary Moore) *a towards rr: rdn in last over 2f out: pushed out fnl f* **25/1**

-500 **9** 10 **Archie (IRE)**[69] 886 7-9-0 **69** (vt w) CierenFallon(7) 3 16
(Brian Barr) *bhd ldrs on outer: effrt over 2f out: sn outpcd: eased fnl f* **14/1**

1m 23.73s (-0.57) **Going Correction** -0.225s/f (Firm) **9 Ran SP% 119.4**
Speed ratings (Par 103): **94,93,91,88,88 85,85,79,68**
CSF £54.63 CT £129.35 TOTE £4.50: £1.10, £3.30, £1.60; EX 57.10 Trifecta £219.70.
Owner Robert Moss **Bred** Horizon Bloodstock Limited **Trained** Epsom, Surrey

FOCUS
A modest affair won by a mare who had been in good form on the all-weather. She found a bit on that form.

2366 MRS ZOE MORTON TO BE NOVICE STKS 7f
4:45 (4:46) (Class 5) 3-Y-O+ **£3,752** (£1,116; £557; £278) **Stalls** Centre

Form RPR
3 **1** **Mutaraffa (IRE)**[16] 1852 3-9-5 (h) JimCrowley 3 93
(Charles Hills) *mde all: rdn 2f out: pressed tl asserted fnl 150yds* **13/8**[2]

4 **2** 5 **Aristocratic Lady (IRE)**[16] 1855 3-9-0 SilvestreDeSousa 4 74
(Simon Crisford) *bhd ldrs on outer: shkn up and upsides whn rdn 2f out: kpt on wl tl no ex fnl 150yds* **11/8**[1]

44- **3** 1/2 **Jaleel**[219] 7675 3-9-5 JackMitchell 1 78
(Roger Varian) *trckd ldrs: rdn over 2f out: in 3rd and outpcd wl over 1f out: shuffled along fr 1f out despite keeping on wl* **9/2**[3]

53- **4** 4 1/2 **Take Fright**[289] 5079 3-9-0 OisinMurphy 7 61
(Hugo Palmer) *bhd wnr: rdn 3f out: no imp and pushed out ent fnl f* **7/1**

5 2 1/2 **Lope Athena** 3-9-0 HarryBentley 5 54
(Stuart Williams) *hld up: rdn 3f out: no imp 2f out: pushed out* **25/1**

00 **6** 10 **Sandy Steve**[15] 1886 3-9-5 AdamKirby 2 32
(Stuart Williams) *a in rr: effrt 3f out: no imp* **50/1**

0-0 **7** nk **Deerfoot**[23] 1690 3-9-5 RyanTate 6 31
(Anthony Carson) *a in rr: effrt 3f out: no imp* **100/1**

1m 23.24s (-1.06) **Going Correction** -0.225s/f (Firm) **7 Ran SP% 117.7**
Speed ratings (Par 103): **97,91,90,85,82 71,70**
CSF £4.43 TOTE £2.20: £1.30, £1.30; EX 4.30 Trifecta £8.40.
Owner Hamdan Al Maktoum **Bred** Messrs Mark Hanly & James Hanly **Trained** Lambourn, Berks

FOCUS
Not much depth to this and they finished strung out but the winner could be quite useful and the runner-up will be winning races, too.
T/Plt: £449.50 to a £1 stake. Pool: £57,429.34 - 93.25 winning units T/Qpdt: £4.80 to a £1 stake. Pool: £7,597.46 - 1,153.27 winning units **Cathal Gahan**

2323 **MUSSELBURGH** (R-H)

Friday, May 3

OFFICIAL GOING: Good (good to firm in places; 9.1)

Wind: Breezy, half against in sprints and in approximately 4f of home straight in races on the round cours Weather: Overcast

2367 QUEST PRECISION ENGINEERING EBF NOVICE STKS (PLUS 10 RACE) 5f 1y
1:55 (1:55) (Class 4) 2-Y-O £4,787 (£1,424; £711; £355) Stalls High

Form RPR

0 1 **Harswell (IRE)**[6] 2115 2-9-5 0 DanielTudhope 2 72
(Liam Bailey) *pressed ldr: rdn to ld over 1f out: edgd lft ins fnl f: hld on wl cl home* 12/1

2 *nk* **Glasvegas (IRE)** 2-9-0 0 SeanDavis(5) 5 71+
(Keith Dalgleish) *dwlt: bhd and outpcd: hdwy over 1f out: chsd wnr ins fnl f: clsng at fin (jockey said colt was slowly away)* 5/1[3]

5 3 ¾ **Lara Silvia**[25] 1642 2-8-11 0 JamieGormley(3) 1 64
(Iain Jardine) *led to over 1f out: rallied: kpt on ins fnl f (jockey said filly ran green)* 10/3[2]

4 7 **Main Reef** 2-9-5 0 JoeFanning 4 43
(Mark Johnston) *noisy and green in paddock: dwlt: rn green and sn pushed along in tch: rdn 1/2-way: wknd over 1f out* 4/6[1]

5 3 **Hot Heir (IRE)** 2-9-0 0 ShaneGray 3 27
(Noel Wilson) *hung rt thrght: chsd ldrs: rdn over 2f out: drifted rt and wknd over 1f out* 33/1

1m 0.84s (1.14) **Going Correction** +0.05s/f (Good) 5 Ran SP% **110.4**
Speed ratings (Par 95): **92,91,90,79,74**
CSF £65.47 TOTE £13.10: £2.80, £2.50; EX 79.20 Trifecta £227.70.
Owner Harswell Thoroughbred Racing **Bred** Tally-Ho Stud **Trained** Middleham, N Yorks

FOCUS
The going was given as good, good to firm in places (Going Stick 9.1). The rail on the bottom bend was out 2yds, adding 7yds to all races of 7f plus. An ordinary novice but the winner took a nice step forward.

2368 CORE (OIL AND GAS) H'CAP 5f 1y
2:25 (2:27) (Class 4) (0-85,87) 4-Y-O+
£5,692 (£1,694; £846; £423; £300; £300) Stalls High

Form RPR

00-4 1 **Abel Handy (IRE)**[15] 1892 4-9-10 **87** DavidNolan 12 98
(Declan Carroll) *mde all against stands' rail: rdn over 1f out: kpt on wl fnl f* 9/4[1]

4604 2 1 ¼ **Foxy Forever (IRE)**[13] 1938 9-9-4 **81** (bt) ConnorBeasley 10 87
(Michael Wigham) *trckd ldrs: effrt and wnt 2nd over 1f out: kpt on ins fnl f* 10/1

2524 3 1 ½ **Amazing Grazing (IRE)**[38] 1342 5-8-12 **75** (e) LewisEdmunds 3 76
(Rebecca Bastiman) *bhd and sn pushed along: hdwy over 1f out: kpt on fnl f: nrst fin* 10/1

00-2 4 ¾ **Burmese Blazer (IRE)**[13] 1951 4-7-13 **65** (h) JamieGormley(3) 5 63
(Jim Goldie) *t.k.h: hld up: hdwy on outside and in tch over 1f out: one pce ins fnl f* 15/2[3]

50-5 5 ½ **Duke Of Firenze**[9] 2030 10-9-7 **84** DavidAllan 2 80
(David C Griffiths) *hld up: rdn and hdwy over 1f out: kpt on fnl f: nvr able to chal* 12/1

60-6 6 2 **War Whisper (IRE)**[18] 1814 6-9-5 **82** JoeFanning 11 71
(Paul Midgley) *in tch: effrt and rdn over 1f out: wknd ins fnl f (vet reported the gelding lost its right hind shoe)* 12/1

3-21 7 *nk* **Super Julius**[13] 1950 5-8-5 **68** ow1 (p) BenCurtis 6 59
(S Donohoe, Ire) *midfield: drvn along over 1f out: wknd ins fnl f (jockey said gelding was denied a clear run inside the final furlong)* 7/1[2]

0036 8 *hd* **Dapper Man (IRE)**[15] 1899 5-8-7 **75** (b) BenSanderson(5) 8 62
(Roger Fell) *w wnr to over 1f out: rdn and wknd fnl f* 10/1

4506 9 *shd* **Chookie Dunedin**[13] 1950 4-8-7 **75** SeanDavis(5) 1 62
(Keith Dalgleish) *hld up on outside: effrt and drvn along 2f out: wknd fnl f* 25/1

1-14 10 5 **Our Place In Loule**[13] 1951 6-8-10 **73** (b) PaulHanagan 9 42
(Noel Wilson) *dwlt: sn prom: rdn along 2f out: wknd fnl f* 14/1

00-0 11 3 **East Street Revue**[15] 1899 6-8-13 **76** (b) DuranFentiman 7 34
(Tim Easterby) *s.i.s: bhd and outpcd: nvr on terms* 20/1

1510 12 3 **Alsvinder**[14] 1919 6-9-6 **83** (t) DanielTudhope 4 30
(Philip Kirby) *prom on outside: drvn and struggling over 2f out: btn over 1f out (vet reported the gelding lost its right hind shoe)* 25/1

59.64s (-0.06) **Going Correction** +0.05s/f (Good) 12 Ran SP% **116.8**
Speed ratings (Par 105): **102,100,97,96,95 92,91,91,91,83 78,73**
CSF £23.97 CT £187.59 TOTE £3.10: £2.90, £3.30, £2.90; EX 25.70 Trifecta £202.60.
Owner F Gillespie **Bred** Mr & Mrs G Middlebrook **Trained** Malton, N Yorks

FOCUS
The first two raced on the stands' rail. The winner will still be on a good mark after this based on his 2yo form.

2369 WEATHERBYS STALLION BOOK H'CAP 1m 208y
2:55 (2:56) (Class 4) (0-85,84) 3-Y-O+
£5,692 (£1,694; £846; £423; £300; £300) Stalls Low

Form RPR

-331 1 **Coolagh Forest (IRE)**[13] 1945 3-9-2 **84** PaulHanagan 2 93
(Richard Fahey) *t.k.h: trckd ldrs: squeezed through to ld 2f out: rdn clr fnl f: eased nr fin* 8/11[1]

1236 2 6 **Mustadun**[15] 1897 3-8-9 **77** JoeFanning 4 73
(Mark Johnston) *led: rdn and hdd 2f out: sn no ch w easy wnr* 3/1[2]

-004 3 2 ½ **Zeshov (IRE)**[13] 1948 8-9-5 **73** (p) DanielTudhope 1 66
(Rebecca Bastiman) *hld up in tch: stdy hdwy over 2f out: rdn and hung lft over 1f out: no imp fnl f* 7/1[3]

106- 4 3 **Royal Regent**[213] 7870 7-9-9 **77** PhilDennis 5 64
(Lucy Normile) *dwlt: sn cl up: rdn and ev ch over 2f out: wknd over 1f out* 33/1

65-0 5 *nk* **Set In Stone (IRE)**[26] 1619 5-9-11 **82** RowanScott(3) 3 68
(Andrew Hughes, Ire) *dwlt: in tch: drvn and effrt over 2f out: wknd over 1f out* 18/1

60-6 6 5 **Ghayyar (IRE)**[18] 1813 5-9-6 **74** (t) RachelRichardson 6 50
(Tim Easterby) *dwlt: in tch on outside: effrt over 2f out: rdn and wknd over 1f out* 9/1

1m 52.84s (-0.26) **Going Correction** +0.05s/f (Good)
WFA 3 from 5yo+ 14lb 6 Ran SP% **113.6**
Speed ratings (Par 105): **103,97,95,92,92 88**
CSF £3.23 TOTE £1.60: £1.10, £2.20; EX 4.10 Trifecta £8.40.
Owner Alan Harte **Bred** Leaf Stud **Trained** Musley Bank, N Yorks

FOCUS
Add 7yds. They went a fairly steady early gallop. The two 3yos in the line-up finished 1-2 and the winner impressed, although there wasn't much depth.

2370 JACKSON BOYD - MORE THAN JUST H'CAP 1m 4f 104y
3:25 (3:25) (Class 3) (0-95,93) 4-Y-O-£9,372 (£2,831; £1,433; £734; £384) Stalls Low

Form RPR

3123 1 **Claire Underwood (IRE)**[6] 2119 4-8-7 **84** SeanDavis(5) 3 91
(Richard Fahey) *dwlt: sn led: mde rest at modest gallop: rdn along and hrd pressed fr 2f out: kpt on wl fnl f* 9/4[2]

20-3 2 1 ¼ **Everything For You (IRE)**[15] 1896 5-9-7 **93** (p) KevinStott 6 98
(Kevin Ryan) *in tch: effrt on outside over 2f out: chsd wnr fnl f: kpt on* 13/8[1]

356- 3 *hd* **Theglasgowwarrior**[162] 9200 5-9-3 **89** AlistairRawlinson 2 94
(Jim Goldie) *hld up in tch: smooth hdwy over 3f out: effrt and ev ch over 1f out: kpt on fnl f: hld towards fin* 5/1[3]

633- 4 2 ¼ **Aiya (IRE)**[328] 3620 4-8-9 **81** (h) DavidAllan 1 82
(Tim Easterby) *t.k.h: trckd ldrs: wnt 2nd over 4f out: effrt and ev ch over 1f out: no ex ins fnl f* 18/1

10-0 5 12 **Dragon Mountain**[31] 1503 4-8-6 **78** (p[1]) JoeFanning 4 60
(Keith Dalgleish) *t.k.h: early ldr: pressed wnr to over 4f out: rdn and wknd fnl 2f* 11/1

00-0 R **Mooltazem (IRE)**[15] 1896 5-9-0 **86** PaulMulrennan 5
(Michael Dods) *ref to r* 9/1

2m 42.0s (-2.50) **Going Correction** +0.05s/f (Good) 6 Ran SP% **109.1**
Speed ratings (Par 107): **110,109,109,107,99**
CSF £5.91 TOTE £2.80: £1.40, £1.40; EX 6.60 Trifecta £17.80.
Owner Parker Partnership **Bred** Sindjara Partnership **Trained** Musley Bank, N Yorks

FOCUS
Add 7yds. This was run at an ordinary early gallop and the winner was able to save something in front. The third seems the best guide.

2371 WEATHERBYS GLOBAL STALLIONS APP H'CAP 7f 33y
4:00 (4:01) (Class 4) (0-80,78) 3-Y-O £5,692 (£1,694; £846; £423; £300) Stalls Low

Form RPR

340- 1 **Smile A Mile (IRE)**[244] 6813 3-9-4 **75** JoeFanning 1 81
(Mark Johnston) *t.k.h early: cl up: wnt 2nd over 2f out: rdn and led 1f out: kpt on wl* 5/1

40-6 2 1 ½ **Stronsay (IRE)**[16] 1846 3-9-1 **72** GrahamLee 5 74
(Bryan Smart) *led at ordinary gallop: rdn and hdd 1f out: rallied: one pce last 75yds* 3/1[2]

-236 3 1 ¼ **Howzer Black (IRE)**[13] 1945 3-9-2 **78** (p) SeanDavis(5) 4 77
(Keith Dalgleish) *t.k.h: hld up in tch: rdn and hdwy 2f out: kpt on same pce ins fnl f (jockey said gelding ran too free)* 11/2

34-6 4 1 **Bataar (IRE)**[22] 1723 3-9-1 **72** PaulHanagan 6 68
(Richard Fahey) *pressed ldr to over 2f out: rdn and outpcd fr over 1f out* 5/2[1]

63-4 5 1 ½ **Arletta Star**[15] 1894 3-8-4 **61** NathanEvans 3 53
(Tim Easterby) *hld up in tch: effrt on outside over 2f out: wknd over 1f out* 10/3[3]

1m 28.82s (-0.18) **Going Correction** +0.05s/f (Good) 5 Ran SP% **108.7**
Speed ratings (Par 101): **103,101,99,98,97**
CSF £19.39 TOTE £3.00: £2.80, £3.80; EX 21.20 Trifecta £77.40.
Owner Sheikh Hamdan bin Mohammed Al Maktoum **Bred** Godolphin **Trained** Middleham Moor, N Yorks

FOCUS
Add 7yds. The winner deserves credit as the second very much had the run of things here. The form's rated around the second and third.

2372 CALUM LOGAN - HAPPY 30TH BIRTHDAY RACE H'CAP 7f 33y
4:35 (4:37) (Class 5) (0-75,75) 4-Y-O+
£3,752 (£1,116; £557; £300; £300; £300) Stalls Low

Form RPR

1103 1 **Kupa River (IRE)**[5] 2151 5-9-6 **74** (h) BenCurtis 4 84
(Roger Fell) *t.k.h: trckd ldrs: rdn to ld over 1f out: kpt on wl fnl f* 7/4[1]

0-00 2 1 ½ **Roaring Forties (IRE)**[4] 2203 6-8-8 **62** (p) ConnorBeasley 8 67
(Rebecca Bastiman) *stdd fr wd draw: hld up: effrt and hdwy over 1f out: chsd wnr ins fnl f: kpt on: nt pce to chal* 16/1

21-0 3 2 **How Bizarre**[20] 1768 4-9-6 **74** DavidNolan 1 74
(Liam Bailey) *mde most tl rdn: edgd lft and hdd over 1f out: no ex fnl f* 20/1

13-0 4 *hd* **Star Shield**[28] 1561 4-9-7 **75** DanielTudhope 3 74
(David O'Meara) *hld up in tch: hdwy whn nt clr run over 1f out: kpt on steadily fnl f: nvr nrr (jockey said gelding was denied a clear run from 2 furlongs out to the final furlong)* 7/2[2]

03-0 5 1 ¼ **Our Charlie Brown**[14] 1925 5-9-0 **68** DavidAllan 5 64
(Tim Easterby) *prom: effrt and ev ch over 1f out: wknd ins fnl f* 9/1

05-3 6 2 ½ **Jacob Black**[13] 1948 8-9-5 **73** (p) JoeFanning 7 62
(Keith Dalgleish) *hld up in tch: effrt and ev ch over 1f out: wknd fnl f* 4/1[3]

1-45 7 10 **Smugglers Creek (IRE)**[101] 356 5-8-8 **65** (p) JamieGormley(3) 2 27
(Iain Jardine) *disp ld to over 2f out: rdn and wknd over 1f out* 10/1

66-0 8 16 **Inviolable Spirit (IRE)**[32] 1487 4-8-9 **68** SeanDavis(5) 6
(Richard Fahey) *slowly away and nvr gng wl in detached last: no ch fr 1/2-way: eased fnl 2f (jockey said gelding stumbled leaving the stalls and was never travelling thereafter)* 10/1

1m 27.79s (-1.21) **Going Correction** +0.05s/f (Good) 8 Ran SP% **117.4**
Speed ratings (Par 103): **108,106,104,103,102 99,88,69**
CSF £34.06 CT £437.75 TOTE £2.60: £1.20, £4.00, £5.20; EX 26.60 Trifecta £303.10.
Owner Middleham Park Racing Lxxii & Partner **Bred** Airlie Stud & Mrs S Rogers **Trained** Nawton, N Yorks

FOCUS
Add 7yds. The leaders took each other on and it was run at a good gallop.

2373 CENTRAL TAXIS APP H'CAP 1m 5f 216y
5:10 (5:12) (Class 6) (0-60,62) 4-Y-0+
£3,105 (£924; £461; £300; £300; £300) Stalls Low

Form | | | | RPR
5003 1 **Elite Icon**[31] 1500 5-9-0 48 ... PhilDennis 1 56
(Jim Goldie) *hld up in tch: effrt and rdn 3f out: hdwy 2f out: led ins fnl f: styd on wl* 15/2
00- 2 ¾ **Frame Rate**[42] 8267 4-9-2 53 ... JamieGormley(3) 11 61
(Iain Jardine) *prom: drvn and outpcd over 3f out: rallied and edgd rt over 1f out: chsd wnr ins fnl f: r.o (jockey said gelding was never travelling)* 6/1[3]
60-5 3 ½ **Dew Pond**[16] 1861 7-9-5 53 ...(bt) RachelRichardson 7 59
(Tim Easterby) *hld up: smooth hdwy to ld over 2f out: rdn and hdd ins fnl f: kpt on same pce* 4/1[1]
044- 4 7 **Eyreborn (IRE)**[213] 7872 5-8-6 45 ...(p) SeanDavis(5) 6 41
(Keith Dalgleish) *hld up: rdn and outpcd over 4f out: swtchd lft and rallied wl over 1f out: kpt on: nvr rchd ldrs* 20/1
00-5 5 1¼ **Torch**[73] 789 6-8-11 52 ...(vt[1]) HarryRussell(7) 10 46
(Laura Morgan) *fly-jmpd s: hld up towards rr: rdn and outpcd over 3f out: hdwy over 1f out: nrst fin* 14/1
40-0 6 1¼ **Palermo (IRE)**[72] 810 5-9-4 52 ...(t) ConnorBeasley 8 44
(Michael Wigham) *pressed ldr: clr of rest after 5f: led over 3f out to over 2f out: wknd fnl f* 10/1
000- 7 1½ **Wise Coco**[163] 7038 6-8-6 45 ... AndrewBreslin(5) 9 35
(Alistair Whillans) *dwlt: bhd: rdn along over 4f out: no imp fr 2f out* 66/1
00-5 8 9 **Fillydelphia (IRE)**[31] 1500 8-8-6 45 ...(p[1]) PaulaMuir(5) 3 22
(Liam Bailey) *hld up on ins: pushed along over 4f out: shortlived effrt over 2f out: sn wknd* 16/1
02-0 9 5 **Enemy Of The State (IRE)**[31] 1500 5-8-6 47 ...(p) JoshQuinn(7) 5 17
(Jason Ward) *dwlt: hld up: drvn and outpcd over 3f out: hung rt: btn fnl 2f* 15/2
1006 10 6 **Galitello**[24] 1663 4-10-0 62 ...(b) JoeFanning 4 24
(Mark Johnston) *t.k.h: led: clr w one other after 5f: hdd over 3f out: wknd over 2f out (jockey said gelding stopped quickly)* 5/1[2]
534/ 11 18 **About Glory**[245] 8396 5-9-2 55 ... ConnorMurtagh(5) 2
(Iain Jardine) *in tch: lost pl over 3f out: sn struggling: t.o (trainer said gelding had a breathing problem)* 6/1[3]

3m 4.12s (0.22) **Going Correction** +0.05s/f (Good) **11** Ran SP% **116.7**
Speed ratings (Par 101): **101,100,100,96,95 94,94,88,86,82 72**
CSF £51.63 CT £207.61 TOTE £7.10: £1.90, £2.40, £1.90; EX 63.20 Trifecta £343.20.
Owner Johnnie Delta Racing **Bred** C A Cyzer **Trained** Uplawmoor, E Renfrews

FOCUS
Add 7yds. The leaders went off quickly and it set up for a closer. Straightforward form.
T/Plt: £175.60 to a £1 stake. Pool: £41,754.04 - 173.53 winning units T/Qpdt: £9.40 to a £1 stake. Pool: £4,403.84 - 343.48 winning units **Richard Young**

2241
NEWCASTLE (A.W) (L-H)
Friday, May 3

OFFICIAL GOING: Tapeta: standard
Wind: light across Weather: fine

2374 PERSPECTIVE (NORTH EAST) LTD H'CAP 1m 2f 42y (Tp)
5:50 (5:50) (Class 4) (0-85,83) 4-Y-0+
£5,530 (£1,645; £822; £411; £400; £400) Stalls High

Form | | | | RPR
42-0 1 **Shareef Star**[33] 1461 4-9-5 81 ... RyanMoore 4 91+
(Sir Michael Stoute) *dwlt and briefly rousted along: hld up in tch: pushed along and hdwy to chal 2f out: drvn into narrow ld jst ins fnl f: styd on to assert fnl 110yds* 8/11[1]
6-03 2 1½ **Delph Crescent (IRE)**[18] 1813 4-9-0 81 ...(p) SebastianWoods(5) 7 88
(Richard Fahey) *prom: pushed along to ld over 2f out: rdn and strly pressed 2f out: hdd jst ins fnl f: one pce fnl 110yds* 14/1
5/0- 3 1¾ **Regal Director (IRE)**[377] 1964 4-8-13 75 ... PatCosgrave 5 79
(Simon Crisford) *trckd ldrs: pushed along over 2f out: rdn over 1f out: kpt on same pce* 6/1[3]
142- 4 5 **Archie Perkins (IRE)**[209] 7993 4-8-6 71 ... RowanScott(3) 3 65
(Nigel Tinkler) *s.i.s: sn trckd ldrs on outer: rdn over 2f out: wknd ins fnl f (jockey said gelding hung right-handed)* 25/1
06-0 5 1¾ **Celestial Force (IRE)**[20] 1761 4-9-4 80 ...(h[1]) PJMcDonald 2 70
(Tom Dascombe) *hld up: rdn and sme hdwy 3f out: hung repeatedly lft: wknd fnl f (jockey said gelding hung left-handed in the home straight)* 11/4[2]
640- 6 18 **Casima**[269] 5824 4-8-12 74 ...(p[1]) TonyHamilton 6 28
(Philip Kirby) *led: rdn and hdd over 2f out: wknd and eased* 66/1

2m 10.24s (-0.16) **Going Correction** +0.10s/f (Slow) **6** Ran SP% **110.9**
Speed ratings (Par 105): **104,102,101,97,96 81**
CSF £12.57 TOTE £1.60: £1.10, £4.10; EX 10.70 Trifecta £29.60.
Owner Saeed Suhail **Bred** Haras Du Logis St Germain **Trained** Newmarket, Suffolk

FOCUS
A six-runner handicap which featured a lightly-raced odds-on favourite. The pace was fair and the first three were clear. The form's rated around the runner-up.

2375 SHOUT DIGITAL FOR INNOVATION NOVICE STKS 1m 2f 42y (Tp)
6:25 (6:25) (Class 5) 3-Y-O
£3,752 (£1,116; £557; £278) Stalls High

Form | | | | RPR
1 **Kashagan** 3-9-2 0 ... PaulMulrennan 2 76+
(Archie Watson) *trckd ldr: pushed along over 1f out: rdn 1f out: kpt on to ld nr fin* 7/1[2]
2-2 2 hd **Deal A Dollar**[18] 1824 3-9-2 0 ... RyanMoore 5 75+
(Sir Michael Stoute) *led at stdy pce: pushed along and pressed 2f out: rdn 1 l up 1f out: drvn ins fnl f: hung lft and one pce fnl 110yds: hdd nr fin* 1/8[1]
3 1½ **Big Daddy Kane** 3-9-2 0 ... DanielMuscutt 1 72+
(Marco Botti) *hld up in tch: hdwy 2f out: pushed along to chse ldr over 1f out: rdn ins fnl f: one pce fnl 110yds* 7/1[2]
4 3½ **Second Sight** 3-9-2 0 ...(v[1]) StevieDonohoe 3 65
(Charlie Fellowes) *trckd ldr: rdn to chal 2f out: wknd ins fnl f* 20/1[3]
0 5 12 **Gloryella**[20] 1764 3-8-11 0 ... JamesSullivan 4 36
(Ruth Carr) *stdd s: hld up in tch: pushed along over 2f out: wknd over 1f out* 66/1

2m 15.6s (5.20) **Going Correction** +0.10s/f (Slow) **5** Ran SP% **120.1**
Speed ratings (Par 99): **83,82,81,78,69**
CSF £9.38 TOTE £11.30: £1.80, £1.10; EX 15.90 Trifecta £24.00.
Owner Nurlan Bizakov **Bred** Hesmonds Stud Ltd **Trained** Upper Lambourn, W Berks

FOCUS
A hard race to assess with a long odds-on favourite taken on by three newcomers and a filly who had finished soundly beaten on her only previous start. The pace was very slow, and though there was no fluke about the result, the form as a whole should be treated with a degree of caution.

2376 ADVANTEX H'CAP 1m 2f 42y (Tp)
6:55 (6:59) (Class 6) (0-60,60) 4-Y-0+
£3,105 (£924; £461; £400; £400; £400) Stalls High

Form | | | | RPR
5004 1 **Kodi Koh (IRE)**[6] 2112 4-8-4 46 oh1 ... RowanScott(3) 13 52
(Simon West) *hld up in midfield on outer: pushed along and hdwy 2f out: rdn to chse ldr appr fnl f: styd on to ld towards fin* 14/1
5502 2 nk **Splash Of Verve (IRE)**[17] 1841 7-8-10 49 ... PJMcDonald 12 54
(David Thompson) *midfield: smooth hdwy 2f out: pushed into ld over 1f out: rdn and edgd rt ins fnl f: drvn and one pce fnl 110yds: hdd towards fin* 3/1[1]
2550 3 nk **Zarkavon**[17] 1836 5-8-7 46 oh1 ...(p) JamesSullivan 11 51
(John Wainwright) *hld up in midfield: pushed along over 2f out: rdn and gd hdwy appr fnl f: kpt on wl* 22/1
00-0 4 2 **Sulafaat (IRE)**[35] 1399 4-9-0 53 ...(p) CamHardie 2 54
(Rebecca Menzies) *trckd ldrs: rdn over 2f out: styd on same pce* 50/1
0000 5 1 **Tarnhelm**[3] 2244 4-9-3 56 ...(h[1]) NathanEvans 7 56
(Wilf Storey) *hld up: hdwy on wd outside fr 5f out: led 3f out: sn rdn: hdd over 1f out: no ex ins fnl f* 14/1
0-60 6 ½ **Shakiah (IRE)**[12] 1967 4-8-8 47 oh1 ow1 ... SamJames 6 46
(Sharon Watt) *rrd s and slowly away: hld up in rr: rdn over 2f out: styd on fr over 1f out: nrst fin (jockey said filly reared as the stalls opened and was slowly away)* 14/1
0-00 7 1½ **Prancing Oscar (IRE)**[95] 462 5-9-6 59 ...(p) PaulMulrennan 4 55+
(Ben Haslam) *prom: rdn over 2f out: wknd fnl f* 11/1
00-4 8 1¾ **Colourfield (IRE)**[23] 1688 4-9-7 60 ...(t[1]) StevieDonohoe 9 53
(Charlie Fellowes) *prom: rdn 3f out: wknd fnl f* 9/2[2]
550- 9 2½ **Doon Star**[269] 5821 4-9-2 55 ... AlistairRawlinson 3 43
(Jim Goldie) *hld up: rdn over 2f out: nvr threatened* 33/1
0534 10 hd **Sosian**[31] 1500 4-8-7 46 oh1 ...(v) BarryMcHugh 10 34
(Richard Fahey) *midfield: rdn over 2f out: wknd over 1f out* 9/2[2]
550 11 5 **I'm British**[36] 1381 6-9-6 59 ... GrahamLee 1 38
(Don Cantillon) *trckd ldrs: rdn over 2f out: wknd over 1f out* 6/1[3]
034- 12 4 **Itsupforgrabsnow (IRE)**[133] 9660 4-8-2 46 oh1 ...(h) TheodoreLadd(5) 14 18
(Susan Corbett) *led: tk str hold: rdn and hdd 3f out: wknd (jockey said filly ran too free)* 22/1

2m 11.65s (1.25) **Going Correction** +0.10s/f (Slow) **12** Ran SP% **117.6**
Speed ratings (Par 101): **99,98,98,96,96 95,94,93,91,90 86,83**
CSF £53.36 CT £947.49 TOTE £14.60: £4.20, £1.50, £5.30; EX 54.80 Trifecta £477.70.
Owner Wild West Racing **Bred** Ringfort Stud **Trained** Middleham Moor, N Yorks

FOCUS
A low-grade handicap with not many coming into it in the best of form so it didn't take that much winning. The second and third help pin a straightforward level. The gallop was fair.

2377 ASTRAL NOVICE STKS 5f (Tp)
7:30 (7:32) (Class 5) 3-Y-0+
£3,752 (£1,116; £557; £278) Stalls Centre

Form | | | | RPR
1 **Lady In France** 3-8-11 0 ... DanielTudhope 4 70+
(K R Burke) *trckd ldrs: pushed along 2f out: edgd lft but led 110yds out: kpt on pushed out* 11/4[2]
0-2 2 ½ **Moss Gill (IRE)**[48] 1236 3-9-2 0 ... PJMcDonald 3 73+
(James Bethell) *prom: pushed along over 1f out: rdn into narrow ld ins fnl f: edgd lft and hdd 110yds out: kpt on same pce* 4/6[1]
0-3 3 2¼ **Sapphire Jubilee**[16] 1862 3-8-8 0 ... BenRobinson(3) 2 60
(Ollie Pears) *led: rdn over 1f out: hdd ins fnl f: no ex fnl 110yds* 25/1
0- 4 2½ **Kodiac Dancer (IRE)**[399] 1486 3-8-11 0 ... GrahamLee 6 51
(Julie Camacho) *hld up: pushed along over 2f out: kpt on ins fnl f* 14/1
3-4 5 ½ **Alqaab**[27] 1598 4-9-11 0 ... JamesSullivan 5 58
(Ruth Carr) *trckd ldrs: rdn over 1f out: wknd ins fnl f (gelding arrived at the start with blood in its mouth, having bitten its tongue. The gelding then semi-reared and landed on its hind quarters, unseating the rider behind the stalls. Having been examined by the Veterinary Surgeon and Doctor at the start,* 7/1[3]
4- 6 21 **Lady Steps**[309] 4281 3-8-11 0 ... AlistairRawlinson 7
(Jim Goldie) *sn outpcd in rr: t.o 1/2-way* 50/1

59.28s (-0.22) **Going Correction** +0.10s/f (Slow)
WFA 3 from 4yo 9lb **6** Ran SP% **111.6**
Speed ratings (Par 103): **105,104,100,96,95 62**
CSF £4.87 TOTE £3.10: £1.40, £1.10; EX 6.30 Trifecta £25.90.
Owner Clipper Logistics **Bred** Whitsbury Manor Stud **Trained** Middleham Moor, N Yorks

FOCUS
Not a strong sprint novice though most of them were lightly-raced and unexposed sorts. The third looks the key to the form.

2378 NEWCASTLE INTERNATIONAL AIRPORT H'CAP 7f 14y (Tp)
8:00 (8:01) (Class 3) (0-95,97) 3-Y-0+ £9,703 (£2,887; £1,443; £721) Stalls Centre

Form | | | | RPR
101- 1 **Dubai Legacy (USA)**[295] 4855 3-9-1 95 ... PatCosgrave 3 101+
(Saeed bin Suroor) *trckd ldrs: rdn 2f out: hung lft but led narrowly over 1f out: hld on drvn out* 5/6[1]
312- 2 ½ **Glorious Lover (IRE)**[279] 5459 3-9-3 97 ... GeraldMosse 6 101+
(Ed Walker) *hld up in tch: rdn along 2f out: carried lft but hdwy over 1f out: chal 1f out: drvn and kpt on* 4/1[2]
600- 3 nk **What's The Story**[216] 7773 5-10-0 96 ...(p) PaulMulrennan 7 103+
(Keith Dalgleish) *hld up: pushed along over 1f out: sme hdwy 1f out: r.o wl fnl 110yds: nrst fin* 7/1[3]
10-5 4 1¼ **Hajjam**[15] 1891 5-9-12 94 ... DavidNolan 5 98
(David O'Meara) *in tch: rdn 2f out: hdwy and chal 1f out: no ex and edgd lft fnl 110yds* 11/1
0224 5 1¼ **Gallipoli (IRE)**[14] 1916 6-9-5 92 ...(b) SeanDavis(5) 2 92
(Richard Fahey) *wnt lft s: led: rdn over 2f out: hdd over 1f out: keeping on same pce whn hmpd 50yds out* 8/1
002- 6 2½ **Hyperfocus (IRE)**[197] 8346 5-9-7 89 ... DavidAllan 4 83
(Tim Easterby) *prom: rdn 2f out: wknd ins fnl f* 25/1

030- 7 ½ **Citron Major**[210] [7949] 4-9-7 **89** AndrewMullen 1 81
(Nigel Tinkler) *hmpd s: sn prom racing keenly: rdn over 2f out: wknd fnl f* **25/1**
(jockey said gelding ran too free)

1m 26.16s (-0.04) **Going Correction** +0.10s/f (Slow) **7** Ran SP% **114.2**
WFA 3 from 4yo+ 12lb
Speed ratings (Par 107): **104,103,103,101,100 97,96**
CSF £4.40 TOTE £1.40: £1.30, £2.30; EX 3.50 Trifecta £32.60.
Owner Godolphin **Bred** Godolphin **Trained** Newmarket, Suffolk

FOCUS
A competitive and interesting handicap with most either in good form or lightly-raced improvers. The two three-year-olds were the first two home in a race run at a decent gallop. The form's rated around the third and fourth.

2379 VISIT NORTH EAST ENGLAND H'CAP 6f (Tp)
8:30 (8:31) (Class 5) (0-70,73) 4-Y-0+
£3,752 (£1,116; £557; £400; £400; £400) **Stalls** Centre

Form RPR

1502 1 **Epeius (IRE)**[11] [1976] 6-9-6 **69** (v) AndrewMullen 4 80
(Ben Haslam) *dwlt: hld up in rr: pushed along and gd hdwy over 1f out: led ins fnl f: edgd lft: rdn and kpt on* **5/1**[3]

3131 2 1 **Gowanbuster**[3] [2247] 4-9-10 **73** 5ex (t) PaulMulrennan 10 80
(Susan Corbett) *led: pushed along over 1f out: hdd ins fnl f: rdn and one pce* **9/4**[1]

3640 3 nk **Dirchill (IRE)**[20] [1760] 5-9-4 **67** (b) PJMcDonald 9 73
(David Thompson) *chsd ldr: rdn 2f out: kpt on* **10/1**

4-11 4 2½ **Everkyllachy (IRE)**[6] [2122] 5-8-4 **58** (v) ThoreHammerHansen(5) 1 56
(Karen McLintock) *midfield: rdn 2f out: hdwy and chsd ldrs appr fnl f: no ex ins fnl f* **11/4**[2]

1-40 5 1 **Zebulon (IRE)**[11] [1976] 5-9-2 **65** JamesSullivan 8 60
(Ruth Carr) *dwlt: hld up: pushed along over 1f out: rdn and no imp fnl f* **14/1**

1320 6 nk **Jan Van Hoof (IRE)**[14] [1929] 8-9-7 **70** BarryMcHugh 5 64
(Michael Herrington) *hld up: pushed along and hdwy over 1f out: rdn and wknd fnl 110yds* **11/2**

025- 7 5 **Bibbidibobbidiboo (IRE)**[164] [9161] 4-9-7 **70** TomEaves 3 48
(Ann Duffield) *chsd ldr: rdn over 2f out: wknd over 1f out* **28/1**

30-0 8 ¾ **Gift In Time (IRE)**[67] [907] 4-9-7 **70** (t[1]) DavidAllan 6 45
(Paul Collins) *chsd ldr: rdn over 2f out: wknd over 1f out* **50/1**

0-00 9 21 **Indian Pursuit (IRE)**[15] [1895] 6-9-2 **65** (v) JasonHart 7
(John Quinn) *midfield: rdn along and lost pl 2f out: wknd and bhd over 1f out* **33/1**

1m 12.15s (-0.35) **Going Correction** +0.10s/f (Slow) **9** Ran SP% **113.6**
Speed ratings (Par 103): **106,104,104,100,99 99,92,91,63**
CSF £16.13 CT £106.95 TOTE £4.00: £1.40, £1.40, £3.10; EX 16.40 Trifecta £112.70.
Owner Ben Haslam Racing Syndicate **Bred** Mrs Dolores Gleeson **Trained** Middleham Moor, N Yorks

FOCUS
A decent sprint handicap with several coming into it in decent form. The pace was fair and the winner came from last to beat the long-time leader. A length pb from the winner.

2380 THAT'S WHY I FLY FROM NEWCASTLE H'CAP 5f (Tp)
9:00 (9:02) (Class 5) (0-75,74) 3-Y-O
£3,752 (£1,116; £557; £400; £400; £400) **Stalls** Centre

Form RPR

243 1 **Wise Words**[27] [1598] 3-9-1 **68** PJMcDonald 5 82
(James Tate) *in tch: pushed along and hdwy to chse ldr appr fnl f: led 110yds out: rdn and kpt on* **7/2**[2]

11 2 1¾ **Inspired Thought (IRE)**[16] [1862] 3-9-7 **74** DanielTudhope 6 83
(Archie Watson) *trckd ldr: led 2f out: sn pushed along: hdd 110yds out: rdn and one pce* **10/11**[1]

2225 3 3 **Klopp**[32] [1488] 3-9-1 **68** (h) CamHardie 2 67
(Antony Brittain) *dwlt and sltly hmpd s: sn trckd ldr: racd quite keenly: rdn over 1f out: no ex ins fnl f* **4/1**[3]

30-0 4 2¼ **Murqaab**[13] [1954] 3-9-0 **67** (v[1]) DavidNolan 4 59
(David O'Meara) *dwlt: hld up: rdn over 1f out: no imp* **18/1**

02-0 5 6 **Raypeteafterme**[23] [1691] 3-9-3 **70** TomEaves 1 43
(Declan Carroll) *led: rdn and hdd 2f out: sn wknd* **11/1**

400- 6 2½ **Heartstring**[164] [9163] 3-8-5 **63** SeanDavis(5) 3 28
(Ann Duffield) *wnt lft s: hld up: hung repeatedly lft: wknd over 1f out* **33/1**

59.42s (-0.08) **Going Correction** +0.10s/f (Slow) **6** Ran SP% **111.1**
Speed ratings (Par 99): **104,101,96,92,83 79**
CSF £6.94 TOTE £4.00: £1.90, £1.40; EX 7.90 Trifecta £19.50.
Owner Sheikh Rashid Dalmook Al Maktoum **Bred** Ropsley Bloodstock Llp **Trained** Newmarket, Suffolk

FOCUS
An interesting 5f handicap for three-year-olds with the finish being dominated by the two least exposed runners. They finished quite well strung out and the winner improved.
T/Plt: £7.30 to a £1 stake. Pool: £52,124.87 - 5,201.92 winning units T/Qpdt: £5.40 to a £1 stake. Pool: £7,607.04 - 1,028.13 winning units **Andrew Sheret**

2381 - 2389a (Foreign Racing) - See Raceform Interactive

2089 MAISONS-LAFFITTE (R-H)
Friday, May 3

OFFICIAL GOING: Turf: soft

2390a PRIX DES ALLUETS LE ROI (CLAIMER) (3YO) (TURF) 1m
12:50 3-Y-O
£8,558 (£3,423; £2,567; £1,711; £855)

RPR

1 **Tosen Shauna (IRE)**[53] 3-8-9 0 AlexandreChesneau(4) 11 84
(S Kobayashi, France) **5/2**[1]

2 7 **Altropasso**[15] 3-8-6 0 ThomasTrullier(5) 10 66
(A Giorgi, Italy) **78/10**

3 snk **Tosen Ciara (IRE)**[85] 3-8-8 0 GregoryBenoist 3 63
(S Kobayashi, France) **36/1**

4 ¾ **Deep State (IRE)**[44] 3-9-4 0 VincentCheminaud 6 71
(H-A Pantall, France) **7/1**

5 hd **Fire Of Beauty (FR)** 3-8-9 0 AugustinMadamet(6) 2 67
(Mlle J Soudan, France) **22/1**

6 nk **Gallia D'Emra (IRE)**[29] 3-8-8 0 JeromeClaudic 9 60
(Remy Nerbonne, France) **75/1**

7 ¾ **Elieden (IRE)**[25] [1658] 3-8-8 0 (p) AlexisBadel 1 58
(Gay Kelleway) *sn front rnk: settled bhd ldrs: pushed along 2f out: rdn to chse ldr over 1f out: wknd ins fnl f* **53/10**[3]

8 1¾ **Queen Morny (FR)**[70] 3-9-1 0 Pierre-CharlesBoudot 5 61
(H-A Pantall, France) **58/10**

9 ½ **Grandee Daisy**[17] [1842] 3-9-1 0 (b) RonanThomas 7 60
(Jo Hughes, France) *settled in midfield: tk clsr order on outer 3f out: rowed along over 2f out: rdn w limited rspnse over 1f out: no ex ins fnl f* **16/1**

10 1½ **Millesime (IRE)**[25] 3-8-5 0 MlleCoraliePacaut(3) 12 49
(J-C Rouget, France) **22/5**[2]

11 18 **Ticolet (IRE)**[31] [1512] 3-8-11 0 MathieuPelletan(4) 8 15
(M Delcher Sanchez, France) **71/1**

12 20 **Mineche (FR)** 3-8-6 0 (p) MohammedLyesTabti(5) 4
(N Milliere, France) **66/1**

1m 43.14s (0.84) **12** Ran SP% **118.7**
PARI-MUTUEL (all including 1 euro stake): WIN 3.20; PLACE 1.50, 2.50, 6.90; DF 10.50.
Owner Takaya Shimakawa **Bred** Mrs E Thompson **Trained** France

2391a PRIX DE BRUNOY (CLAIMER) (AMATEUR RIDERS) (4YO+) (TURF) 1m
1:58 4-Y-O+
£7,207 (£2,882; £2,162; £1,441; £720)

RPR

1 **Scribner Creek (IRE)**[15] 6-10-3 0 MissSerenaBrotherton(4) 4 79
(R Le Gal, France) **47/10**[3]

2 3 **Seqania**[17] 4-10-0 0 (p) FrauBeritWeber(3) 11 68
(Mario Hofer, Germany) **7/1**

3 2 **Carry Out (FR)**[18] 7-10-7 0 MlleBarbaraGuenet(3) 8 71
(D Allard, France) **22/5**[2]

4 nk **Galouska (FR)**[63] 4-9-6 0 MlleMeganePeslier(8) 9 60
(D Smaga, France) **10/1**

5 ½ **Sandoside (FR)**[295] 8-9-10 0 MlleCamilleColletVidal(7) 3 62
(C Boutin, France) **20/1**

6 ½ **Romantic Pur (FR)**[29] 7-10-0 0 MlleLaraLeGeay(3) 2 61
(Mlle B Renk, France) **17/2**

7 1½ **Flor De Seda (FR)**[32] [1491] 4-10-4 0 MrFrederickTett(3) 6 61
(Jo Hughes, France) *wl into stride: settled in 3rd: pushed along and dropped to midfield over 2f out: rdn over 1f out: kpt on same pce fnl f* **33/1**

8 1¼ **Admiral Thrawn (IRE)**[20] 4-10-11 0 MrFlorentGuy 7 62
(Andrea Marcialis, France) **14/5**[1]

9 2 **Cheries Amours (FR)**[214] 5-10-0 0 MrThomasGuineheux 10 47
(S Cerulis, France) **21/1**

10 snk **Iron Spirit (FR)**[80] 9-10-0 0 (p) MmeMelissaBoisgontier(3) 1 49
(J Phelippon, France) **9/1**

11 3 **Magicienmake Myday**[118] [115] 8-10-3 0 (p) MrThibaudMace 5 42
(H De Nicolay, France) **29/1**

1m 45.03s (2.73) **11** Ran SP% **120.1**
PARI-MUTUEL (all including 1 euro stake): WIN 5.70; PLACE 1.80, 1.90, 1.80; DF 20.10.
Owner Marc-Elie Uzan **Bred** Holborn Trust Co **Trained** France

2392a PRIX DU BUISSON RICHARD (CLAIMER) (3YO) (TURF) 5f 110y
4:14 3-Y-O
£10,360 (£4,144; £3,108; £2,072; £1,036)

RPR

1 **Tudo Bem (FR)**[17] [1842] 3-9-4 0 ChristopheSoumillon 1 76
(M Boutin, France) **8/5**[1]

2 3½ **Blury (ITY)**[17] [1842] 3-8-11 0 CristianDemuro 5 57
(Andrea Marcialis, France) **76/10**

3 1 **Loquen (IRE)**[17] [1842] 3-8-6 0 AugustinMadamet(5) 8 54
(Andrea Marcialis, France) **19/1**

4 nk **Velvet Vixen (IRE)**[7] [2090] 3-8-8 0 Louis-PhilippeBeuzelin 7 50
(Jo Hughes, France) *Quickly into stride: led and crossed to rails: urged along 2f out: rdn and hdd over 1f out: kpt on ins fnl f* **14/1**

5 nk **Belladone Spirit (IRE)**[7] [2091] 3-8-9 0 (b) ThomasTrullier(6) 4 56
(J-M Baudrelle, France) **11/2**[3]

6 snk **Mudeer (IRE)**[11] 3-9-4 0 PierreBazire 2 59
(G Botti, France) **29/10**[2]

7 1¼ **Hit The Track Jack**[7] [2090] 3-8-4 0 JeremieMonteiro(7) 6 47
(N Caullery, France) **24/1**

8 hd **Oh Say Can You See (FR)**[263] [6113] 3-9-1 0 ClementLecoeuvre 3 51
(Matthieu Palussiere, France) **47/1**

9 snk **Enough Said**[23] 3-9-4 0 AntoineHamelin 9 53
(Matthieu Palussiere, France) *chsd ldr on outer: virtually upsides after 2f: drvn and hdd over 1 1/2f out: wknd fnl f* **9/1**

1m 4.89s (-2.41) **9** Ran SP% **118.9**
PARI-MUTUEL (all including 1 euro stake): WIN 2.60; PLACE 1.30, 2.70, 3.00; DF 11.90.
Owner M Boutin **Bred** M Boutin & Mme C Sineux **Trained** France

2092 DONCASTER (L-H)
Saturday, May 4

OFFICIAL GOING: Good (8.1)
Wind: Moderate across Weather: Cloudy

2393 SKY SPORTS RACING SKY 415 H'CAP 6f 2y
5:15 (5:17) (Class 3) (0-90,90) 4-Y-0+ **£7,762** (£2,310; £1,154; £577) **Stalls** Centre

Form RPR

4314 1 **Watchable**[17] [1847] 9-9-7 **90** (p) DanielTudhope 9 98
(David O'Meara) *mde all: rdn wl over 1f out: drvn and edgd lft jst ins fnl f: kpt on wl towards fin* **9/2**[2]

53-3 2 ½ **Jawwaal**[34] [1459] 4-9-5 **88** PaulMulrennan 4 94
(Michael Dods) *trckd ldrs: hdwy and cl up 2f out: rdn to chal jst over 1f out: drvn and ev ch ins fnl f: no ex towards fin* **3/1**[1]

0-61 3 ½ **Embour (IRE)**[14] [1942] 4-9-6 **89** RossaRyan 8 93
(Richard Hannon) *in tch: pushed along and sltly outpcd 1/2-way: hdwy 2f out: sn rdn and styd on wl fnl f* **5/1**[3]

11-0 4 ¾ **Beyond Equal**[26] [1654] 4-9-5 **88** BenCurtis 5 90
(Stuart Kittow) *t.k.h: cl up: rdn along 2f out: drvn and n.m.r ent fnl f: kpt on same pce* **11/2**

100- 5 ½ **Wahoo**[224] [7510] 4-9-5 **88** ConnorBeasley 7 88
(Michael Dods) *cl up: rdn along over 2f out: sn drvn along and outpcd: kpt on fnl f* **11/1**

43-6 6 3½ **Muscika**[12] [1978] 5-9-6 **89** (v) RobbieDowney 1 78
(David O'Meara) *chsd ldrs: rdn along bef 1/2-way: sn outpcd and bhd* **8/1**

10-0 **7** 4 ½ **Lucky Lucky Man (IRE)**[7] 2117 4-8-12 **86**............. ConnorMurtagh(5) 2 61
(Richard Fahey) *a in rr (jockey said gelding was slowly into stride)* **20/1**
4-00 **8** *nk* **Boy In The Bar**[7] 2107 8-8-13 **82**............................(p) GeorgeDowning 3 56
(Ian Williams) *a in rr (jockey said gelding was slowly into stride)* **40/1**
0-00 **9** 4 **Naadirr (IRE)**[14] 1942 8-9-7 **90**....................................(v) JamieSpencer 6 51
(Kevin Ryan) *dwlt: awkward and wnt lft s: a in rr (jockey said gelding jumped awkwardly from the stalls and was never travelling)* **7/1**
1m 11.2s (-1.50) **Going Correction** 0.0s/f (Good) **9** Ran SP% **114.4**
Speed ratings (Par 107): **110,109,108,107,107 102,96,95,90**
CSF £18.21 CT £69.64 TOTE £5.20: £2.00, £1.60, £1.90; EX 20.00 Trifecta £95.20.
Owner Hambleton Xxxix P Bamford Roses Partners **Bred** Cheveley Park Stud Ltd **Trained** Upper Helmsley, N Yorks
FOCUS
A competitive 6f handicap with all the runners capable performers on their day. The pace was fair but not many got into it. The second has been rated as improving a bit on his C&D latest, with the third close to his AW latest.

2394 PPIWISE.COM DEADLINE EBF NOVICE STKS 5f 3y
5:50 (5:50) (Class 5) 2-Y-O **£3,752** (£1,116; £557) **Stalls** Centre

Form RPR
1 **Apollinaire** 2-9-5 0.. KevinStott 1 80
(Ralph Beckett) *qckly away: mde all: rdn over 1f out: drvn and edgd rt ins fnl f: hld on wl towards fin* **7/1**[3]
2 *nk* **Light Angel** 2-9-5 0.. KieranO'Neill 2 79
(John Gosden) *dwlt: green and in rr: pushed along and hdwy 1/2-way: rdn to chse wnr over 1f out: chal ins fnl f and ev ch tl no ex towards fin* **1/1**[1]
3 3 **Royal Council (IRE)** 2-9-5 0.. DavidAllan 3 68+
(James Tate) *chsd wnr: rdn along wl over 1f out: drvn and wknd fnl f* **6/5**[2]
1m 0.51s (0.91) **Going Correction** 0.0s/f (Good) **3** Ran SP% **108.0**
Speed ratings (Par 93): **92,91,86**
CSF £14.02 TOTE £5.50; EX 10.90 Trifecta £7.60.
Owner Adc Bloodstock **Bred** Adc Bloodstock **Trained** Kimpton, Hants
FOCUS
Just three newcomers contested this juvenile novice so it is impossible to get a handle on the form. The early pace was moderate so it developed into a sprint from halfway with the winner having the run of the race. The opening level is guessy.

2395 ELAINE BROWN AND FRIENDS H'CAP 1m (S)
6:20 (6:21) (Class 3) (0-90,90) 3-Y-O **£7,762** (£2,310; £1,154; £577) **Stalls** Centre

Form RPR
2 **1** **Archaeology**[17] 1857 3-8-11 **80**.. JamieSpencer 7 87
(Jedd O'Keeffe) *dwlt and wnt lft s: hld up in rr: swtchd to inner and hdwy 3f out: trckd ldrs 2f out: rdn to chal ins fnl f: led last 100yds: edgd rt and kpt on* **4/1**[2]
46-3 **2** ½ **Tulfarris**[22] 1736 3-9-7 **90**.. StevieDonohoe 5 95
(Charlie Fellowes) *hld up towards rr: hdwy 3f out: chsd ldrs 2f out: rdn and slt ld ent fnl f: drvn and hdd last 100yds: kpt on* **4/1**[2]
01-1 **3** 1 ½ **Absolutio (FR)**[26] 1646 3-9-0 **83**.....................................(h) BenCurtis 2 85
(K R Burke) *led: rdn along over 2f out: drvn and hdd 1 1/2f out: kpt on u.p fnl f* **5/1**[3]
4-12 **4** *nk* **Lehoogg**[21] 1764 3-8-11 **80**... CharlesBishop 4 81
(Roger Varian) *trckd ldrs: hdwy 3f out: rdn to ld briefly 1 1/2f out: drvn and hdd ent fnl f: kpt on same pce* **9/4**[1]
453- **5** 1 **Rangali Island (IRE)**[164] 9170 3-8-0 **74**.......................... SeanDavis(5) 6 73
(David Simcock) *bmpd s: hld up in tch: hdwy 2f out: rdn over 1f out: no imp fnl f* **12/1**
021- **6** ¾ **Romola**[228] 7383 3-8-13 **82**... DavidAllan 1 79
(Sir Michael Stoute) *trckd ldrs on inner: hdwy 3f out: sn cl up: rdn and ev ch over 1f out: sn drvn and wknd* **8/1**
521- **7** 3 **Triple Distilled**[234] 7162 3-8-7 **81**......................... FayeMcManoman(5) 8 71
(Nigel Tinkler) *trckd ldr: pushed along 3f out: rdn 2f out: sn wknd* **33/1**
030- **8** ¾ **Production**[189] 8644 3-8-13 **82**.. RossaRyan 3 71
(Richard Hannon) *trckd ldrs: pushed along 3f out: rdn over 2f out: sn wknd* **20/1**
1m 37.65s (-2.55) **Going Correction** 0.0s/f (Good) **8** Ran SP% **113.9**
Speed ratings (Par 103): **112,111,110,109,108 107,104,104**
CSF £20.23 CT £81.22 TOTE £4.50: £1.70, £1.70, £1.80; EX 20.60 Trifecta £85.60.
Owner Quantum **Bred** Callipygian Bloodstock **Trained** Middleham Moor, N Yorks
FOCUS
An interesting handicap for three-year-olds featuring several lightly-raced potential improvers but though many of these should be winning this season this was a slowly-run affair and therefore unlikely to prove the most reliable of guides. The first two have both been rated as improving on their good reappearance runs, with the fourth, fifth and sixth close to their maiden/novice form.

2396 ALAN WOOD PLUMBING AND HEATING H'CAP 6f 2y
6:50 (6:52) (Class 2) (0-105,100) 3-Y-O+
£12,450 (£3,728; £1,864; £932; £466; £234) **Stalls** Centre

Form RPR
053- **1** **Sir Maximilian (IRE)**[358] 2597 10-9-6 **92**............................... BenCurtis 6 101
(Ian Williams) *trckd ldrs: hdwy 2f out: rdn over 1f out: drvn to ld ins fnl f: kpt on wl towards fin* **33/1**
43-5 **2** *nk* **Wentworth Falls**[17] 1847 7-9-7 **93**.................................. ConnorBeasley 8 101
(Geoffrey Harker) *hld up towards rr: hdwy 2f out: styng on whn n.m.r ins fnl f: rdn and squeezed through to chal last 75yds: ev ch: no ex nr fin* **11/1**
5-60 **3** 1 ½ **Tommy Taylor (USA)**[18] 1829 5-9-5 **91**.............................(v¹) TomEaves 1 94
(Kevin Ryan) *racd towards far side: qckly away and clr: pushed along 2f out: rdn over 1f out: sn drvn: hdd ins fnl f: kpt on same pce* **12/1**
43-0 **4** ½ **Triggered (IRE)**[21] 1762 3-8-2 **89**..................................... SeanDavis(5) 7 88
(Ed Walker) *chsd ldng pair: hdwy 2f out: sn rdn: drvn ent fnl f: kpt on same pce* **12/1**
456- **5** *hd* **Get Knotted (IRE)**[190] 8594 7-9-9 **95**...........................(p) PaulMulrennan 4 96
(Michael Dods) *midfield: effrt and hdwy on inner 2f out: sn rdn: styd on fnl f: nrst fin* **10/1**
120- **6** *nse* **Royal Residence**[204] 8167 4-8-12 **84**.................................... DavidAllan 13 85
(James Tate) *towards rr: hdwy over 2f out: rdn wl over 1f out: swtchd lft ent fnl f: kpt on towards fin* **5/1**[2]
4013 **7** *nk* **Foolaad**[19] 1814 8-9-13 **99**...(t) RobertWinston 2 99
(Roy Bowring) *racd centre: chsd clr ldr: rdn along wl over 1f out: wknd ent fnl f* **8/1**[3]
30-0 **8** 3 **Roundhay Park**[7] 2117 4-9-3 **92**..................................... RowanScott(3) 5 82
(Nigel Tinkler) *in tch on inner: hdwy over 2f out: rdn wl over 1f out: sn wknd* **10/1**
3-04 **9** 3 ½ **Aeolus**[21] 1763 8-9-10 **96**.. JamesSullivan 9 75
(Ruth Carr) *a towards rr* **11/1**
2-00 **10** ¾ **Von Blucher (IRE)**[18] 1829 6-9-3 **89**...........................(p) PJMcDonald 14 66
(Rebecca Menzies) *chsd ldrs on outer: rdn along wl over 2f out: sn wknd* **14/1**
2-60 **11** 1 **Captain Colby (USA)**[14] 1946 7-9-7 **96**.......................... BenRobinson(3) 3 69
(Paul Midgley) *chsd ldrs: rdn along wl over 2f out: sn wknd (jockey said gelding stopped quickly)* **20/1**
00-2 **12** 2 ¼ **Danielsflyer (IRE)**[34] 1459 5-9-5 **91**.................................. AndrewMullen 10 57
(Michael Dods) *a towards rr (trainer could offer no explanation for the gelding's perfomance, other than this appeared to be a more competitive race)* **7/2**[1]
00-0 **13** 5 **Time's Arrow (IRE)**[17] 1853 5-10-0 **100**............................ DanielTudhope 12 50
(David O'Meara) *dwlt: a in rr* **25/1**
1m 11.27s (-1.43) **Going Correction** 0.0s/f (Good)
WFA 3 from 4yo+ 10lb **13** Ran SP% **118.4**
Speed ratings (Par 109): **109,108,106,105,105 105,105,101,96,95 94,91,84**
CSF £353.20 CT £4708.61 TOTE £41.70: £10.00, £3.30, £3.80; EX 562.00 Trifecta £3418.60.
Owner Paul Wildes **Bred** Holborn Trust Co **Trained** Portway, Worcs
FOCUS
A field of exposed sprinters but several had been in good form so the form should prove solid. The second has been rated as running as well as ever, with the third close to his C&D reappearance.

2397 ARTEX LTD NOVICE STKS 6f 2y
7:20 (7:23) (Class 5) 3-Y-O+ **£3,752** (£1,116; £557; £278) **Stalls** Centre

Form RPR
1 **Nahaarr (IRE)** 3-8-13 0.. GeorgiaCox(3) 4 77+
(William Haggas) *trckd ldrs: hdwy to ld 2f out: rdn over 1f out: drvn and edgd rt ins fnl f: kpt on wl towards fin* **14/1**
12 **2** *nk* **Astro Jakk (IRE)**[17] 1862 3-9-9 0.. PJMcDonald 2 83
(K R Burke) *trckd ldr: hdwy and cl up over 2f out: rdn over 1f out: ev ch: drvn ins fnl f: kpt on* **8/1**[2]
3 1 ½ **Fashion Stakes (IRE)** 3-8-11 0.. RobertHavlin 5 66+
(Jeremy Noseda) *towards rr: pushed along wl over 2f out: rdn and hdwy wl over 1f out: styd on wl fnl f* **11/10**[1]
6 **4** *nse* **Somethingaboutjack (IRE)**[22] 1728 3-9-2 0.............. CharlesBishop 3 71
(Eve Johnson Houghton) *dwlt and towards rr: hdwy over 2f out: sn rdn: kpt on fnl f* **9/1**[3]
5 1 ½ **Tipperary Jack (USA)** 3-9-2 0.. KieranO'Neill 8 66
(John Best) *t.k.h: hld up: hdwy 2f out: sn rdn along and no imp* **28/1**
0-2 **6** 2 **Barritus**[113] 178 4-9-12 0... PatCosgrave 6 63
(George Baker) *led: pushed along 1/2-way: rdn and hdd 2f out: sn wknd* **33/1**
01 **7** *shd* **May Sonic**[24] 1677 3-9-0 0.. CierenFallon(7) 7 64
(Charles Hills) *midfield: rdn along over 2f out: n.d* **8/1**[2]
5 **8** 2 **Jet Set Go**[26] 1649 4-9-7 0.. NathanEvans 9 51
(Seb Spencer) *chsd ldrs: rdn along wl over 2f out: sn wknd* **40/1**
5 **9** 1 **Ginger Max**[40] 1336 3-9-2 0.. PaulHanagan 10 50
(Richard Fahey) *wnt rt s: a in rr (jockey said colt hung right)* **8/1**[2]
1- **10** 10 **Heath Charnock**[157] 9282 3-9-9 0..................................... PaulMulrennan 1 25
(Michael Dods) *a towards rr (trainer's rep said colt was unsuited by the going (good) and would prefer a softer surface; vet reported the colt had lost its left hind shoe)* **8/1**[2]
1m 12.37s (-0.33) **Going Correction** 0.0s/f (Good)
WFA 3 from 4yo 10lb **10** Ran SP% **117.6**
Speed ratings (Par 103): **102,101,99,99,97 94,94,92,90,77**
CSF £119.82 TOTE £8.90: £2.80, £2.40, £1.20; EX 59.10 Trifecta £321.50.
Owner Sheikh Ahmed Al Maktoum **Bred** Rossenarra Bloodstock Limited **Trained** Newmarket, Suffolk
FOCUS
A potentially interesting novice event featuring three previous AW winners and a well supported debutant. However, it was another newcomer who took the spoils and with less than four lengths covering the first five the form may not be anything out of the ordinary. The runner-up has been rated similar to his AW form.

2398 HAPPY 40TH BIRTHDAY DARREN TOMLINSON H'CAP 1m 6f 115y
7:50 (7:51) (Class 4) (0-85,86) 4-Y-O+
£5,530 (£1,645; £822; £411; £400; £400) **Stalls** Low

Form RPR
013- **1** **Mugatoo (IRE)**[166] 9152 4-9-7 **81**....................................... JamieSpencer 2 95+
(David Simcock) *dwlt and hld up in rr: smooth hdwy wl over 2f out: trckd ldrs wl over 1f out: swtchd to inner and led on bit ent fnl f: v easily* **4/1**[2]
000- **2** 1 ¼ **Blue Rambler**[77] 9503 9-9-7 **81**.................................. GeorgeDowning 8 85
(Tony Carroll) *cl up: led after 3f: rdn along 3f out: hdd wl over 2f out: cl up: drvn and ev ch over 1f out: kpt on u.p fnl f: no ch w wnr* **25/1**
146- **3** 2 **Pirate King**[239] 7009 4-9-12 **86**.. BenCurtis 3 88
(Harry Dunlop) *trckd ldrs: hdwy on inner over 3f out: led wl over 2f out: sn rdn: drvn and hdd ent fnl f: kpt on same pce* **7/1**
-450 **4** 2 ½ **Native Fighter (IRE)**[7] 2092 5-9-2 **76**............................. JackGarritty 6 74
(Jedd O'Keeffe) *hld up in tch: hdwy 3f out: rdn along and outpcd 2f out: kpt on u.p fnl f (jockey said gelding hung left in the home straight)* **7/2**[1]
0024 **5** ½ **Navajo Star (IRE)**[13] 1971 5-9-4 **78**..........................(v) PJMcDonald 7 75
(Robyn Brisland) *trckd ldrs: effrt on outer 3f out: rdn along 2f out: sn drvn and one pce* **8/1**
10-1 **6** 2 **Seinesational**[18] 1840 4-9-6 **80**....................................(v) PatCosgrave 4 75
(William Knight) *trckd ldng pair: hdwy on outer and cl up 3f out: rdn along over 2f out: sn drvn and wknd* **9/2**[3]
2241 **7** 4 **Houlton**[9] 2059 4-9-2 **76**..(tp) DanielMuscutt 5 65
(Marco Botti) *cl up: pushed along 3f out: rdn over 2f out: sn wknd* **7/2**[1]
410- **8** *shd* **Tapis Libre**[217] 7782 11-9-5 **79**... NathanEvans 1 67
(Jacqueline Coward) *led 3f: trckd ldng pair: hdwy to chal 3f out: rdn along over 2f out: sn drvn and wknd* **28/1**
100- **9** 13 **Ice Galley (IRE)**[31] 8901 6-8-6 **66**....................................... JimmyQuinn 9 36
(Philip Kirby) *a in rr* **20/1**
3m 10.6s (-1.00) **Going Correction** 0.0s/f (Good) **9** Ran SP% **118.3**
Speed ratings (Par 105): **102,101,100,98,98 97,95,95,88**
CSF £101.15 CT £688.02 TOTE £4.00: £2.10, £6.50, £2.60; EX 89.20 Trifecta £453.80.
Owner Mrs Marcella Burns & Partners **Bred** Frau N Bscher **Trained** Newmarket, Suffolk
■ Stewards' Enquiry : George Downing two-day ban: used whip above the permitted level (May 19-20)

FOCUS
Add 6yds. Mainly exposed sorts in this staying handicap which was run at an ambling gallop. It was won in great style by the least experienced horse but overall the form might not be strong for the grade. The second is possibly the key to the level.

2399 WATCH SKY SPORTS RACING SKY 415 FILLIES' H'CAP — 1m 3f 197y
8:20 (8:21) (Class 4) (0-85,85) 3-Y-O+

£5,530 (£1,645; £822; £411; £400; £400) **Stalls** Low

Form | | | | RPR
64-1 **1** **Katiesheidinlisa**[22] 1739 3-8-1 **80**................ JaneElliott(3) 4 89+
(Tom Dascombe) *trckd ldrs: hdwy 3f out: led 2f out: rdn over 1f out: kpt on strly* **2/1**[1]

5150 **2** 2 3/4 **Voi**[31] 1518 5-8-7 **71**................(t) CierenFallon(7) 5 76
(Conrad Allen) *hld up in rr: hdwy on outer 3f out: chsd ldrs wl over 1f out: sn rdn: styd on to chse wnr ins fnl f: no imp* **10/1**

314- **3** nk **Quicksand (IRE)**[166] 9152 4-9-11 **82**................ PJMcDonald 6 86
(Hughie Morrison) *trckd ldrs: hdwy 3f out: cl up 2f out: sn rdn: drvn over 1f out and kpt on same pce* **11/4**[2]

234- **4** 3 **Aussie View (IRE)**[224] 7517 3-8-9 **85**................ JoeFanning 7 82
(Mark Johnston) *trckd ldr: hdwy and cl up 3f out: rdn along over 2f out: drvn wl over 1f out and sn wknd* **11/2**[3]

54-0 **5** 1 3/4 **Amourice (IRE)**[29] 1559 4-10-0 **85**................(h) PaulMulrennan 2 81
(Jane Chapple-Hyam) *trckd ldrs: hdwy 4f out: rdn along 3f out: sn wknd* **8/1**

301- **6** 3 **Miss Latin (IRE)**[246] 6744 4-9-6 **77**................ JamieSpencer 3 69
(David Simcock) *hld up in rr: hdwy 4f out: chsd ldrs 3f out: sn rdn and btn* **15/2**

51-2 **7** 1 1/2 **Sempre Presto (IRE)**[25] 1666 4-8-13 **70**................ PaulHanagan 1 59
(Richard Fahey) *led: pushed along 4f out: rdn 3f out: drvn and hdd 2f out: sn wknd (trainer's rep could offer no explanation for the filly's performance)* **12/1**

2m 36.84s (0.24) **Going Correction** 0.0s/f (Good)
WFA 3 from 4yo+ 19lb — 7 Ran SP% **115.0**
Speed ratings (Par 102): **99,97,96,94,93 91,90**
CSF £23.13 TOTE £2.90: £2.10, £4.40; EX 23.90 Trifecta £79.20.
Owner D R Passant & Hefin Williams **Bred** Glebe Farm Stud **Trained** Malpas, Cheshire

FOCUS
Add 6yds. A 1m4f handicap for fillies and mares run at an ordinary gallop. The winner is an interesting prospect. It's been rated as straightforward form, with the second close to form.
T/Plt: £661.20 to a £1 stake. Pool: £55,961.76 - 61.78 winning units T/Qpdt: £41.80 to a £1 stake. Pool: £9,138.57 - 161.43 winning units **Joe Rowntree**

GOODWOOD (R-H)
Saturday, May 4

OFFICIAL GOING: Good (good to firm in places; watered; 7.7)
Wind: Strong Cross Wind Weather: Overcast with sunny spells

2400 DOUBLE TRIGGER H'CAP — 1m 6f
1:35 (1:36) (Class 5) (0-75,74) 4-Y-O+

£5,433 (£1,617; £808; £404; £300; £300) **Stalls** Low

Form | | | | RPR
312- **1** **Rydan (IRE)**[127] 9731 8-9-5 **72**................(v) LiamKeniry 9 82
(Gary Moore) *hld up: clsd gng wl on heels of main gp over 2f out: qcknd up wl whn gap appeared on outer over 1f out: styd on strly to ld 100yds out: won gng away* **8/1**

1145 **2** 2 **Berrahri (IRE)**[28] 1588 8-9-5 **72**................ KierenFox 1 79
(John Best) *led: pushed along to maintain short ld 2f out: rdn and hdd by wnr 100yds out: kpt on but no match for wnr* **12/1**

041/ **3** 4 1/2 **Shambra (IRE)**[128] 7220 5-8-12 **65**................(h) JasonWatson 10 66
(Lucy Wadham) *racd in tch in 3rd: rdn and unable qck 2f out: kpt on one pce for remote 3rd ins fnl f* **7/1**[3]

31-2 **4** hd **Cristal Spirit**[34] 1463 4-9-3 **70**................(p) HarryBentley 2 70+
(George Baker) *pushed along early in rr: effrt in rr wl over 2f out: rdn an styd on wl passed btn horses ins fnl f (jockey said gelding was denied a clear run)* **7/2**[1]

541- **5** nse **Sassie (IRE)**[170] 9076 4-9-6 **73**................ LukeMorris 8 74+
(Sylvester Kirk) *hld up: stl gng wl in rr over 2f out: denied clr run wl over 1f out: effrt whn nt clr run again 1f out: styd on wl once in the clr (jockey said filly was denied a clear run)* **9/1**

0/4- **6** nk **Harmonise**[174] 8808 5-9-1 **68**................ HectorCrouch 14 68
(Sheena West) *trckd ldr: rdn along to chse ldr 2f out: upsides and ev ch over 1f out: wknd ins fnl f* **14/1**

340- **7** 1 **Hatsaway (IRE)**[165] 9159 8-8-13 **69**................ PaddyBradley(3) 5 68
(Pat Phelan) *hld up: hdwy on outer over 2f out: rdn and hung rt u.p over 1f out: one pce fnl f* **16/1**

05-3 **8** 1/2 **Jacob Cats**[40] 1330 10-9-7 **74**................(v) CallumShepherd 12 72
(William Knight) *dwlt and racd in rr: rdn along in rr over 2f out: nvr on terms* **14/1**

052- **9** 1 1/2 **Give Him Time**[76] 9505 8-9-5 **72**................(t) DavidProbert 13 68
(Nick Gifford) *hld up: pushed along 3f out: sn rdn and little rspnse: a in rr* **16/1**

64-3 **10** 1 **Love To Breeze**[32] 1497 4-9-0 **67**................(t) JosephineGordon 4 65+
(Jonathan Portman) *racd in midfield: effrt to cl 3f out: pushed along whn short of room and snatched up over 1f out: no ex fnl f* **7/1**[3]

-346 **11** shd **Ezanak (IRE)**[95] 469 6-9-4 **71**................(v[1]) AlistairRawlinson 11 65
(Michael Appleby) *settled in 4th: rdn along and outpcd 2f out: sn drvn and no imp: wknd fnl f* **25/1**

-213 **12** 8 **Double Legend (IRE)**[56] 1096 4-8-10 **63**................(b) FrannyNorton 7 47
(Amanda Perrett) *racd in midfield: niggled along 3f out: sn rdn and no imp 2f out: wknd fnl f (trainer's rep could offer no explanation for the poor form shown)* **9/2**[2]

-500 **13** 20 **The Way You Dance (IRE)**[38] 1363 7-9-2 **69**................(v) ShaneKelly 6 24
(Neil Mulholland) *racd in tch in midfield: rdn along and lost pl qckly 2f out: eased fnl f* **33/1**

3m 2.76s (-0.94) **Going Correction** +0.075s/f (Good) — 13 Ran SP% **126.1**
Speed ratings (Par 103): **105,103,101,101,101 100,100,100,99,98 98,94,82**
CSF £106.25 CT £723.75 TOTE £9.40: £2.70, £4.10, £2.80; EX 152.20 Trifecta £1634.30.
Owner Jacobs Construction Ltd Partnership **Bred** R Coffey **Trained** Lower Beeding, W Sussex

FOCUS
Stalls: Straight: stands side; Round Course: inside, except 1m4f: outside. This was run at a steady pace and those up with the pace looked likely to have it between them as they stretched out in the home straight, until the winner swooped late. It's been rated around the second to his best over the past year.

2401 UNIBET EBF DAISY WARWICK FILLIES' STKS (LISTED RACE) — 1m 3f 218y
2:05 (2:07) (Class 1) 4-Y-O+

£28,355 (£10,750; £5,380; £2,680; £1,345; £675) **Stalls** High

Form | | | | RPR
314- **1** **Enbihaar (IRE)**[211] 7951 4-9-0 **97**................ DaneO'Neill 3 105+
(John Gosden) *led after 1f and mde rest: effrt to qckn tempo whn pressed by rival 2f out: rdn and asserted wl again ins fnl f* **11/4**[2]

112- **2** 1 3/4 **Klassique**[189] 8664 4-9-0 **102**................ HarryBentley 5 102+
(William Haggas) *racd keenly in midfield: smooth hdwy on outer to chse wnr 2f out: rdn and ev ch 1f out: nt enough pce to match wnr fnl f* **10/11**[1]

62-0 **3** 4 1/2 **Mazzuri (IRE)**[10] 2033 4-9-0 **90**................ JasonWatson 2 95
(Amanda Perrett) *racd keenly in midfield: pushed along to chse wnr 3f out: sn rdn and unable qck 2f out: kpt on one pce fnl f* **20/1**

100- **4** 1/2 **Lorelina**[175] 9005 6-9-0 **96**................ DavidProbert 7 94
(Andrew Balding) *hld up: rdn along in rr 2f out: kpt on fnl f but n.d* **14/1**

310- **5** 3/4 **Crystal Moonlight**[210] 7986 4-9-0 **88**................ PatDobbs 1 93
(Sir Michael Stoute) *racd in midfield: effrt to chse ldng pair 2f out: rdn and unable qck over 1f out: one pce fnl f* **10/1**[3]

1-10 **6** 3 1/4 **Plait**[83] 682 4-9-0 **94**................ LouisSteward 4 88
(Michael Bell) *led for 1f then trckd wnr: rdn along and outpcd over 2f out: wknd fnl f* **16/1**

00-6 **7** 4 **Wingingit (IRE)**[10] 2033 5-9-0 **89**................ FrannyNorton 6 81
(Andrew Balding) *stood stl in stalls and gave away 20 l at s: ct up w main gp 1/2-way: rdn and sn btn over 2f out (jockey said mare was reluctant to race)* **12/1**

2m 40.44s (0.84) **Going Correction** +0.075s/f (Good) — 7 Ran SP% **113.1**
Speed ratings (Par 108): **100,98,95,95,95 92,90**
CSF £5.46 TOTE £3.50: £1.80, £1.10; EX 5.90 Trifecta £43.70.
Owner Hamdan Al Maktoum **Bred** Haras Du Mezeray **Trained** Newmarket, Suffolk

FOCUS
The winner was allowed an easy lead and duly made the most of it as the two market leaders came clear in an event that lacked depth. Muddling form, but the third has been rated as running as well as ever.

2402 UNIBET H'CAP — 7f
2:40 (2:40) (Class 2) (0-100,101) 4-Y-O+

£31,125 (£9,320; £4,660; £2,330; £1,165; £585) **Stalls** Low

Form | | | | RPR
60-0 **1** **Kimifive (IRE)**[18] 1829 4-8-13 **88**................ ShaneKelly 5 99
(Joseph Tuite) *hld up in rr of midfield: hdwy on outer 2f out: rdn and styd on wl to ld wl ins fnl f: won gng away* **20/1**

002 **2** 1 **Love Dreams (IRE)**[56] 1097 5-9-4 **93**................(b) FrannyNorton 6 101
(Mark Johnston) *led: rdn along to maintain 2 l ld over 1f out: drvn and hdd by wnr wl ins fnl f: no ex* **4/1**[2]

31-2 **3** 3 1/2 **Qaroun**[16] 1881 4-8-13 **88**................ DavidProbert 10 87
(Sir Michael Stoute) *racd in midfield: pushed along to chse ldr 2f out: sn rdn and readily outpcd by wnr 1f out: one pce fnl f* **5/1**[3]

2630 **4** 1 **Apex King (IRE)**[35] 1414 5-8-4 **86**................ LauraCoughlan(7) 1 82
(David Loughnane) *trckd ldr: rdn along and ev ch over 1f out: one pce fnl f* **7/1**

2501 **5** 1/2 **Goring (GER)**[15] 1916 7-8-8 **90**................(v) GeorgiaDobie(7) 8 85
(Eve Johnson Houghton) *hld up: effrt on outer over 2f out: rdn and little imp 1f out: kpt on fnl f* **12/1**

0-45 **6** 1 3/4 **Whitefountainfairy (IRE)**[16] 1881 4-8-9 **87**................ WilliamCox(3) 7 77
(Andrew Balding) *racd in midfield: effrt to chse ldr 2f out: sn rdn and unable qck over 1f out: one pce after* **12/1**

543- **7** 2 **Manton Grange**[140] 9564 6-8-8 **83**................(tp) JosephineGordon 4 67
(George Baker) *hld up in rr: rdn and no imp 2f out: kpt on one pce fnl f (jockey said gelding lost its back end rounding the first bend)* **10/1**

5-66 **8** 2 1/4 **Moon Trouble (IRE)**[22] 1734 6-8-13 **88**................ AlistairRawlinson 3 66
(Michael Appleby) *dwlt and sn rcvrd to r in 4th: rdn and little rspnse 2f out: grad wknd fr 1f out* **8/1**

3-00 **9** 3 3/4 **Rufus King**[7] 2100 4-9-7 **96**................ JFEgan 9 64
(Mark Johnston) *hld up: hung rt on to rail and bdly hmpd rival over 4f out: sn rdn and a bhd* **33/1**

4-41 **10** nk **Three Saints Bay (IRE)**[14] 1944 4-9-12 **101**................ HarryBentley 2 73
(David O'Meara) *trckd ldr in 3rd: rdn along and unable qck 2f out: wknd fnl f (trainer's rep could offer no explanation for the gelding's performance)* **11/4**[1]

35-0 **11** 54 **Count Otto (IRE)**[18] 1829 4-9-0 **89**................(b) JasonWatson 11
(Amanda Perrett) *hld up in last: bdly hmpd by rival on rail over 4f out and sn detached as a result: eased whn btn (jockey said gelding suffered interference in running)* **16/1**

1m 24.77s (-1.93) **Going Correction** +0.075s/f (Good) — 11 Ran SP% **125.0**
Speed ratings (Par 109): **114,112,108,107,107 105,102,100,96,95 33**
CSF £104.67 CT £492.56 TOTE £28.80: £6.00, £1.40, £1.90; EX 191.50 Trifecta £1057.00.
Owner Richard J Gurr **Bred** Miss Annmarie Burke **Trained** Lambourn, Berks

FOCUS
An open handicap. The pace was not that strong and it saw a 20-1 shot peg back the long-time leader. The stewards looked at interference on the first bend between Rufus King, who was keen and edged right, and Count Otto, but it was deemed accidental. The second has been rated in line with his recent form for now.

2403 FARMER, BUTCHER, CHEF H'CAP — 5f
3:15 (3:15) (Class 3) (0-95,94) 4-Y-O **£9,451** (£2,829; £1,414; £708; £352) **Stalls** High

Form | | | | RPR
-132 **1** **Puds**[14] 1938 4-8-13 **86**................ ShaneKelly 10 95+
(Richard Hughes) *hld up in rr: hdwy to chse ldrs 2f out: waited for gap to appear between rivals 1f out: rdn and qcknd up wl to ld post* **8/1**

054- **2** nse **Just Glamorous (IRE)**[161] 9247 6-8-7 **83**................ CameronNoble(3) 2 91
(Grace Harris) *broke smartly and led: rdn to maintain advantage 1f out: drvn fnl f and hdd by wnr on post* **14/1**

-462 **3** 1/2 **Harry Hurricane**[4] 2227 7-8-8 **81**................(p) JosephineGordon 4 87
(George Baker) *trckd ldr: effrt to chse ldr 2f out: rdn and ev ch 1f out: kpt on fnl f* **7/1**[3]

0-20 **4** 1/2 **Blue De Vega (GER)**[14] 1938 6-9-4 **91**................ LukeMorris 6 95
(Robert Cowell) *racd in rr of midfield: pushed along and outpcd 2f out: drvn and styd on wl fnl f* **12/1**

20-3 **5** *nk* **Open Wide (USA)**[16] 1892 5-9-6 **93**..............................(b) PatDobbs 8 99+
(Amanda Perrett) *hld up in last: clsd gng wl 2f out: snatched up whn short of room 1f out: rdn once gap appeared ins fnl f and styd on wl (jockey said gelding was denied a clear run)* **15/2**

0-21 **6** *1 3/4* **The Daley Express (IRE)**[15] 1915 5-9-0 **87**.................. FrannyNorton 1 84
(Ronald Harris) *racd in tch: effrt to chse ldr on outer over 1f out: rdn and ev ch fnl f: no ex* **11/4**[1]

00-0 **7** *2* **Quench Dolly**[16] 1892 5-8-13 **86**........................ HarryBentley 5 76
(John Gallagher) *hld up in rr of midfield: drvn along and no imp 2f out: one pce fnl f* **11/1**

012- **8** *1 1/2* **Mountain Peak**[224] 7527 4-9-1 **88**........................ LiamKeniry 3 72
(Ed Walker) *racd in midfield: rdn and ev ch over 1f out: one pce fnl f* **8/1**

505- **9** *2 1/2* **Helvetian**[148] 9446 4-9-3 **90**........................ CallumShepherd 7 65
(Mick Channon) *chsd ldr: rdn and lost pl appr fnl f: one pce after* **14/1**

30-0 **10** *1 1/4* **Pettochside**[19] 1822 10-8-11 **84**........................ HollieDoyle 11 55
(John Bridger) *hld up: rdn and no imp 2f out: one pce fnl f* **16/1**

33-3 **11** *1/2* **Kick On Kick On**[22] 1734 4-9-7 **94**........................ HectorCrouch 9 63
(Clive Cox) *racd in midfield: pushed along 2f out: rdn whn hmpd by rival over 1f out: nt rcvr* **11/2**[2]

57.43s (-0.67) **Going Correction** +0.075s/f (Good) **11** Ran SP% **123.8**
Speed ratings (Par 107): **108,107,107,106,105 103,99,97,93,91 90**
CSF £120.27 CT £850.02 TOTE £8.40: £2.70, £4.00, £2.30; EX 222.00 Trifecta £2480.70.
Owner N Martin **Bred** N Martin **Trained** Upper Lambourn, Berks

FOCUS
A competitive handicap that looked like the front-runners would prevail until the winner made a late swoop and edged it on the line. Solid form, with the second rated in line with last year's form, the third to his recent efforts and the fifth to form.

2404 CONQUEROR FILLIES' STKS (LISTED RACE) 1m
3:45 (3:45) (Class 1) 3-Y-O+
£28,355 (£10,750; £5,380; £2,680; £1,345; £675) **Stalls** Low

Form RPR

226- **1** **Awesometank**[203] 8191 4-9-7 106........................ PatDobbs 5 103+
(William Haggas) *trckd ldr: upsides ldr gng wl 2f out: pushed along to ld 1f out: sn drvn and styd on wl* **11/4**[1]

66-0 **2** *hd* **Anna Nerium**[14] 1941 4-9-7 107........................ DaneO'Neill 6 102+
(Richard Hannon) *racd in midfield: dropped to last but gng wl 3f out: swtchd off heels on outer and rdn to chse wnr over 1f out: styd on strly fnl f: nt rch wnr* **4/1**[3]

04-0 **3** *1 1/4* **Vivianite (IRE)**[14] 1941 4-9-7 92........................ HollieDoyle 1 99
(Archie Watson) *led: rdn along whn strly pressed by wnr 2f out: drvn and hdd by wnr 1f out: kpt on for press ins fnl f* **11/1**

1115 **4** *3/4* **Tiger Eye (IRE)**[14] 1941 4-9-7 94........................ GeorgeWood 2 97
(James Fanshawe) *racd in tch in 3rd: rdn along and briefly outpcd by ldng pair 2f out: r.o wl ins fnl f but a hld* **7/2**[2]

30-0 **5** *3 3/4* **Queen Of Time**[14] 1941 5-9-7 96........................ JasonWatson 8 88
(Henry Candy) *hld up: effrt on outer over 2f out: sn rdn and little rspnse: wknd fnl f* **9/2**

550- **6** *4* **Jet Streaming (IRE)**[199] 8313 5-9-7 88........................ ShaneKelly 3 79
(Samuel Farrell, Ire) *hld up: rdn along and unable qck 2f out: sn outpcd and bhd fnl f* **25/1**

114- **7** *27* **Akvavera**[184] 8769 4-9-7 94........................ HarryBentley 4 17
(Ralph Beckett) *rrd as stalls opened and racd keenly: rdn and lost pl 2f out: eased whn btn fnl f (jockey said filly ran too free)* **6/1**

1m 37.88s (-1.32) **Going Correction** +0.075s/f (Good) **7** Ran SP% **113.5**
Speed ratings (Par 108): **109,108,107,106,103 99,72**
CSF £13.79 TOTE £3.20: £1.90, £2.10; EX 12.40 Trifecta £110.40.
Owner Lee Yuk Lun Alan **Bred** Eminent Kind Ltd **Trained** Newmarket, Suffolk
■ Stewards' Enquiry : Hollie Doyle four-day ban: used whip above the permitted level (May 19-22)

FOCUS
Though the market was relatively open, two stood out on ratings and they finished one-two, with the front-running favourite holding off a fast-finishing challenger. The second has been rated back to form.

2405 SUSSEX ROOF GARDEN NOVICE STKS 7f
4:20 (4:24) (Class 4) 3-Y-O+ **£5,175** (£1,540; £769; £384) **Stalls** Low

Form RPR

0-22 **1** **Dominus (IRE)**[9] 2060 3-9-5 80........................(h[1]) JasonWatson 4 82
(Brian Meehan) *wnt lft at stalls and sltly hmpd runner-up: mde all: effrt to qckn temp over 2f out: rdn whn strly pressed by rival 1f out: drvn out: jst prevailed* **9/4**[2]

23-3 **2** *nk* **Qutob (IRE)**[16] 1886 3-9-5 80........................ DaneO'Neill 5 81
(Charles Hills) *hmpd by wnr leaving stalls and wnt lft as a result giving away several l: racd keenly in last: rdn patiently and clsd on wnr gng wl over 1f out: rdn and styd on wl fnl f: nvr quite getting to wnr* **6/5**[1]

0 **3** *5* **City Wanderer (IRE)**[21] 1755 3-9-5 0........................ CallumShepherd 1 68
(Mick Channon) *trckd wnr: effrt to chse wnr 2f out: sn rdn and unable qck over 1f out: one pce fnl f* **8/1**

4 *1* **Confab (USA)** 3-9-5 0........................ HarryBentley 2 65
(George Baker) *hld up: swtchd rt off heels over 1f out sn rdn and kpt on fnl f: no ch w front pair* **16/1**

43- **5** *2 1/4* **Deference**[164] 9171 3-9-5 0........................ PatDobbs 3 59
(Amanda Perrett) *settled wl in 3rd: rdn to chse wnr 2f out: sn drvn and fnd little: wknd fnl f* **9/2**[3]

1m 26.66s (-0.04) **Going Correction** +0.075s/f (Good) **5** Ran SP% **111.4**
Speed ratings (Par 105): **103,102,96,95,93**
CSF £5.44 TOTE £2.90: £1.50, £1.10; EX 4.80 Trifecta £20.90.
Owner G P M Morland & J W Edgedale **Bred** Morgan Cahalan **Trained** Manton, Wilts

FOCUS
A closely-matched contest on ratings and in the betting, and so it proved with the front two battling it out and pulling clear. It's been rated around them.

2406 LONG VIEW H'CAP (DIV I) 1m 1f 197y
4:55 (4:57) (Class 5) (0-75,77) 3-Y-O
£5,433 (£1,617; £808; £404; £300; £300) **Stalls** Low

Form RPR

006- **1** **Dreamweaver (IRE)**[168] 9123 3-8-10 **64**........................ LiamKeniry 5 71+
(Ed Walker) *settled wl in midfield: clsd under hands and heels 2f out: rdn and gd hdwy to ld wl ins fnl f: styd on wl* **10/1**

00-6 **2** *2* **London Eye (USA)**[26] 1652 3-9-4 **72**........................ PatDobbs 4 75+
(Sir Michael Stoute) *racd keenly in midfield: effrt to cl on outer over 2f out: sn rdn and tk a while to pick up: styd on wl fnl f: no ch w wnr* **3/1**[1]

-000 **3** *1 1/2* **Isle Of Wolves**[10] 2035 3-8-12 **66**........................ CharlieBennett 8 68
(Jim Boyle) *racd promly: wnt 2nd gng wl 4f out: rdn to ld 2f out: drvn 1f out: kpt on but hdd by wnr wl ins fnl f* **10/1**

-360 **4** *1* **Azets**[11] 2021 3-8-9 **63**........................(b[1]) HarryBentley 3 63
(Amanda Perrett) *racd promly in 4th: rdn to chse ldr over 1f out: drvn and ev ch 1f out: one pce fnl f* **4/1**[2]

-561 **5** *nse* **Ignatius (IRE)**[14] 1957 3-8-3 **56** oh1 ow1........................ JosephineGordon 2 57
(John Best) *trckd ldr: niggled along on inner 5f out: pushed along 2f out: rdn and ev ch appr fnl f: one pce fnl f (jockey said gelding hung left-handed up the straight)* **8/1**

0123 **6** *1 1/4* **Little Rock (IRE)**[19] 1823 3-9-9 **77**........................ ShaneKelly 9 74
(Richard Hughes) *hld up: stl gng wl enough in rr wl over 2f out: rdn to cl and immediately short of room over 1f out: kpt on once in clr (trainer could offer no explanation for the gelding's performance)* **9/2**[3]

06-0 **7** *1* **Monsieur Lambrays**[24] 1690 3-9-6 **74**........................ LukeMorris 10 69
(Tom Clover) *restrained in last: pushed along in rr 3f out: sme minor late hdwy* **12/1**

334- **8** *1* **Slade King (IRE)**[202] 8233 3-9-5 **73**........................ HectorCrouch 1 66
(Gary Moore) *racd in midfield: niggled along 4f out: rdn over 2f out: wknd fnl f* **9/1**

204- **9** *1 1/4* **Extreme Force (IRE)**[162] 9227 3-9-7 **75**........................(w) DavidProbert 6 66
(Jonjo O'Neill) *hld up: rdn along and no imp 3f out: a in rr* **25/1**

0426 **10** *2 3/4* **Copper Rose (IRE)**[29] 1568 3-9-3 **71**........................ FrannyNorton 7 56
(Mark Johnston) *led: rdn along and hdd 2f out: wknd fnl f* **20/1**

2m 9.22s (0.32) **Going Correction** +0.075s/f (Good) **10** Ran SP% **118.8**
Speed ratings (Par 99): **101,99,99,98,98 97,96,95,94,92**
CSF £40.92 CT £318.29 TOTE £14.90: £3.70, £1.60, £3.10; EX 54.90 Trifecta £393.80.
Owner Mrs Olivia Hoare **Bred** Mrs Olivia Hoare **Trained** Upper Lambourn, Berks

FOCUS
The race opened up in the straight and two hold-up horses came late past the leaders. Muddling form, but the third, fourth and fifth have been rated close to their latest efforts.

2407 LONG VIEW H'CAP (DIV II) 1m 1f 197y
5:30 (5:30) (Class 5) (0-75,75) 3-Y-O
£5,433 (£1,617; £808; £404; £300; £300) **Stalls** Low

Form RPR

630- **1** **Takumi (IRE)**[226] 7446 3-9-5 **73**........................ JackMitchell 1 84+
(Roger Varian) *hld up: smooth hdwy onto heels of ldrs 2f out: waited for gap between rivals over 1f out: qcknd up wl to ld 1f out: rdn and styd on strly ins fnl f* **9/4**[1]

-432 **2** *1/2* **Htilominlo**[6] 2141 3-9-1 **72**........................ GaryMahon[(3)] 3 82+
(Sylvester Kirk) *racd in midfield: effrt to cl on ldrs and drifted lft over 2f out: sn rdn and hung rt handed 1f out: styd on wl ins fnl f: nt rch wnr* **7/2**[3]

00-5 **3** *4* **Queen's Soldier (GER)**[32] 1510 3-8-9 **63**........................ FrannyNorton 5 65
(Andrew Balding) *hld up: pushed along on outer 3f out: kpt wd and rdn over 1f out: one pce fnl f (jockey said gelding hung left-handed in the straight)* **11/1**

200- **4** *3* **Limelighter**[198] 8336 3-9-1 **69**........................ KierenFox 7 65
(Sheena West) *led: nudged along to maintain short ld 3f out: rdn and hdd 2f out: kpt on one pce fnl f* **33/1**

5-36 **5** *shd* **Cromwell**[6] 2141 3-8-8 **62**........................ RaulDaSilva 2 58
(Luke Dace) *racd in tch: rdn along to ld narrowly 2f out: sn drvn and hdd by wnr 1f out: one pce fnl f* **16/1**

055- **6** *1* **Young Merlin (IRE)**[156] 9308 3-9-7 **75**........................ JasonWatson 4 69
(Roger Charlton) *trckd ldr: rdn and ev ch whn almost upsides 2f out: fdd ins fnl f* **9/1**

305- **7** *1 1/4* **Twenty Years On**[185] 8732 3-8-11 **65**........................ ShaneKelly 9 56
(Richard Hughes) *racd in tch: rdn along and outpcd 3f out: wknd fr wl over 1f out* **14/1**

40-3 **8** *7* **Peckinpah (IRE)**[29] 1568 3-9-3 **71**........................ DavidProbert 6 48
(Alan King) *hld up and racd keenly: rdn along and outpcd over 2f out: sn bhd (jockey said gelding ran too free)* **5/2**[2]

21-0 **9** *5* **Toybox**[43] 1264 3-9-6 **74**........................ AdamMcNamara 8 41
(Jonathan Portman) *racd in rr of midfield: rdn along 3f out: sn struggling: nvr on terms* **20/1**

2m 10.23s (1.33) **Going Correction** +0.075s/f (Good) **9** Ran SP% **120.1**
Speed ratings (Par 99): **97,96,93,91,90 90,89,83,79**
CSF £10.99 CT £72.96 TOTE £3.00: £1.50, £1.50, £3.20; EX 11.90 Trifecta £134.30.
Owner China Horse Club International Limited **Bred** Irish National Stud **Trained** Newmarket, Suffolk

FOCUS
This looked as competitive as the first division. The early pace was slower, with the first two pulling clear.
T/Plt: £86.50 to a £1 stake. Pool: £81,130.32 - 684.29 winning units T/Qpdt: £21.40 to a £1 stake. Pool: £7,547.03 - 259.82 winning units **Mark Grantham**

[1886] NEWMARKET (R-H)
Saturday, May 4

OFFICIAL GOING: Good to firm (good in places) changing to good after race 2 (2.20)
Wind: Strong behind Weather: Showers

2408 SPRING LODGE STKS (H'CAP) (FORMERLY THE SUFFOLK STAKES) 1m 1f
1:50 (1:51) (Class 2) 3-Y-O+
£31,125 (£9,320; £4,660; £2,330; £1,165; £585) **Stalls** Centre

Form RPR

333- **1** **Elector**[206] 8105 4-8-7 **93**........................ JoeFanning 9 101
(Sir Michael Stoute) *looked wl; a.p: chsd ldr over 7f out: shkn up over 1f out: rdn and r.o to ld wl ins fnl f: edgd lft nr fin* **9/1**

641- **2** *nk* **Jazeel (IRE)**[218] 7738 4-8-4 **90**........................ AntonioFresu 2 97
(Jedd O'Keeffe) *hld up: pushed along and hdwy over 2f out: rdn over 1f out: r.o to go 2nd nr fin* **12/1**

1-00 **3** *1/2* **Vintager**[16] 1890 4-9-10 **110**........................ WilliamBuick 6 116
(Charlie Appleby) *chsd ldrs: led over 2f out: rdn over 1f out: hdd wl ins fnl f* **8/1**

3-20 **4** *nk* **Exec Chef (IRE)**[21] 1753 4-8-9 **95**........................ OisinMurphy 7 100
(Jim Boyle) *looked wl; sn chsng ldr: lost 2nd over 7f out: remained handy: shkn up: outpcd and nt clr run over 1f out: swtchd lft: r.o ins fnl f* **9/1**

/14- **5** *3/4* **Al Muffrih (IRE)**[331] 3518 4-8-5 **91**........................ SilvestreDeSousa 5 95
(William Haggas) *free to post: led: plld hrd: rdn and hdd over 2f out: styd on same pce wl ins fnl f* **9/4**[1]

10-0 **6** *1* **Ibraz**[21] 1753 4-8-7 **93**........................ DavidEgan 1 94
(Roger Varian) *chsd ldrs: rdn and ev ch over 1f out: no ex wl ins fnl f* **7/1**[3]

11-2 **7** *1 3/4* **Power Of Darkness**[16] 1889 4-8-5 **91**............................ HayleyTurner 4 89
(Marcus Tregoning) *s.i.s: hld up: plld hrd: pushed along and hdwy over 2f out: sn rdn: no ex ins fnl f (jockey said gelding ran too free)* **7/2**[2]

5022 **8** *nse* **Aquarium**[10] 2033 4-9-1 **101**.. PJMcDonald 10 98
(Mark Johnston) *looked wl; s.s: hld up: hdwy over 2f out: rdn and nt clr run over 1f out: styd on same pce* **11/1**

344- **9** *9* **First Sitting**[220] 7662 8-9-6 **106**................................ RichardKingscote 3 84
(Chris Wall) *hld up: rdn over 2f out: sn wknd* **33/1**

343/ **10** *1 1/2* **Max Zorin (IRE)**[722] 2569 5-9-0 **100**.............................. RobHornby 8 74
(Andrew Balding) *prom: rdn over 2f out: sn wknd* **25/1**

1m 50.67s (-0.43) **Going Correction** +0.20s/f (Good) **10** Ran SP% **119.4**
Speed ratings (Par 109): **109,108,108,108,107 106,104,104,96,95**
CSF £113.91 CT £934.74 TOTE £10.10: £2.80, £4.40, £2.50; EX 149.80 Trifecta £579.90.

Owner The Queen **Bred** The Queen **Trained** Newmarket, Suffolk

■ Stewards' Enquiry : Antonio Fresu two-day ban: used whip above the permitted level (May 19-20)

FOCUS
Stands' side course used. Stalls: centre. Showers resulted in the ground easing slightly, but feedback about the surface was positive, with William Buick saying: "It's good ground out there but a bit blustery." while Oisin Murphy described it as: "Lovely racing ground." Traditionally a strong handicap, they went just an average gallop and plenty had their chance, with any one of six being in with a shot at the furlong pole. The third's July course win last year could be rated this high.

2409 ZOUSTAR PALACE HOUSE STKS (GROUP 3) 5f

2:20 (2:22) (Class 1) 3-Y-O+

£34,026 (£12,900; £6,456; £3,216; £1,614; £810) **Stalls** Centre

Form RPR

321- **1** **Mabs Cross**[209] 8028 5-9-10 112........................ PaulMulrennan 10 117
(Michael Dods) *s.i.s: hld up: pushed along 1/2-way: hdwy over 1f out: rdn and r.o to ld post (vet reported the mare lost its left fore shoe)* **6/1**[3]

4-34 **2** *nk* **Equilateral**[17] 1853 4-9-6 106................................ OisinMurphy 2 112
(Charles Hills) *looked wl; s.i.s: hdwy 4f out: led on bit over 1f out: rdn ins fnl f: hdd post* **11/2**[2]

01-2 **3** *1 3/4* **Major Jumbo**[35] 1412 5-9-6 107.............................. JamieSpencer 11 106
(Kevin Ryan) *prom: rdn over 1f out: edgd rt ins fnl f: styd on* **8/1**

10-1 **4** *1/2* **Sergei Prokofiev (CAN)**[35] 1434 3-9-0 111................... RyanMoore 9 103+
(A P O'Brien, Ire) *s.i.s: hld up: shkn up over 1f out: r.o to go 4th nr fin: nt rch ldrs* **6/4**[1]

251 **5** *1/2* **Ornate**[16] 1892 6-9-6 98....................................... PhilDennis 6 102
(David C Griffiths) *w ldr to 1/2-way: rdn over 1f out: styng on same pce whn hmpd ins fnl f* **40/1**

21-2 **6** *shd* **El Astronaute (IRE)**[32] 1501 6-9-6 106........................ JasonHart 3 102
(John Quinn) *led: racd keenly: rdn and hdd over 1f out: edgd lft ins fnl f: styd on same pce* **12/1**

105- **7** *1 1/4* **Judicial (IRE)**[224] 7535 7-9-6 108...........................(h) GrahamLee 5 97
(Julie Camacho) *hld up: hdwy 1/2-way: rdn over 1f out: styd on same pce ins fnl f* **12/1**

21-3 **8** *2 1/4* **Tarboosh**[32] 1501 6-9-6 108.................................... KevinStott 7 89
(Paul Midgley) *chsd ldrs: rdn and ev ch over 1f out: hmpd and wknd ins fnl f* **16/1**

-555 **9** *2 1/4* **Sir Thomas Gresham (IRE)**[17] 1853 4-9-6 101..........(t) MartinDwyer 8 81
(Tim Pinfield) *hld up: pushed along 1/2-way: nt trble ldrs* **20/1**

-166 **10** *2 1/4* **Encore D'Or**[15] 1919 7-9-6 103................................ JimCrowley 1 73
(Robert Cowell) *prom: rdn over 1f out: sn wknd* **33/1**

61-1 **11** *10* **Queen Of Desire (IRE)**[15] 1913 4-9-3 97.................... DanielTudhope 4 34
(Roger Varian) *chsd ldrs to 1/2-way (trainer said filly was unsuited by the ground (good to firm, good in places) and would prefer a faster surface)* **25/1**

58.67s (-0.43) **Going Correction** +0.20s/f (Good)
WFA 3 from 4yo+ 9lb **11** Ran SP% **116.0**
Speed ratings (Par 113): **111,110,107,106,106 105,103,100,96,93 77**
CSF £36.70 TOTE £6.60: £2.10, £1.70, £2.50; EX 42.60 Trifecta £255.70.

Owner David W Armstrong **Bred** Highfield Farm Llp **Trained** Denton, Co Durham

FOCUS
The going was changed to good all round after this race. They went a strong gallop and it was an advantage to be ridden with some patience. The second has been rated as running as well as ever, and the third to his 5f fast ground best.

2410 ROARING LION JOCKEY CLUB STKS (GROUP 2) 1m 4f

2:55 (2:57) (Class 1) 4-Y-O+

£56,710 (£21,500; £10,760; £5,360; £2,690; £1,350) **Stalls** Centre

Form RPR

25-0 **1** **Communique (IRE)**[21] 1750 4-9-1 108.................. SilvestreDeSousa 6 117
(Mark Johnston) *looked wl; mde all: clr over 9f out tl over 7f out: qcknd over 2f out: rdn and edgd lft ins fnl f: styd on* **12/1**

02-4 **2** *1 1/4* **Defoe (IRE)**[21] 1750 5-9-1 116................................ DavidEgan 1 115
(Roger Varian) *chsd ldrs: lost pl over 9f out: shkn up and hdwy over 3f out: rdn to chse wnr over 1f out: styd on* **7/2**[2]

12-0 **3** *2 1/4* **Mildenberger**[10] 2033 4-9-1 107............................. WilliamBuick 7 111
(Mark Johnston) *looked wl; prom: chsd wnr over 10f out: rdn over 2f out: lost 2nd over 1f out: styd on same pce ins fnl f* **13/2**

322- **4** *2* **Coronet**[196] 8406 5-8-12 115................................ FrankieDettori 2 105
(John Gosden) *trckd ldrs: racd keenly: rdn over 2f out: no ex ins fnl f* **5/4**[1]

00-1 **5** *8* **Red Verdon (USA)**[34] 1460 6-9-1 110........................(b) RyanMoore 3 95
(Ed Dunlop) *s.s: hld up: rdn and wknd over 1f out* **20/1**

11-5 **6** *1 3/4* **Young Rascal (FR)**[21] 1750 4-9-1 116....................... JamesDoyle 5 93
(William Haggas) *s.i.s: hld up: hdwy over 4f out: shkn up over 3f out: wknd over 1f out (trainer could offer no explanation for the colt's performance)* **5/1**[3]

210- **7** *7* **Maid Up**[231] 7293 4-8-12 105................................. RobHornby 4 78
(Andrew Balding) *chsd ldrs: rdn over 3f out: wknd wl over 1f out* **33/1**

2m 33.49s (0.99) **Going Correction** +0.20s/f (Good) **7** Ran SP% **112.1**
Speed ratings (Par 115): **104,103,101,100,95 93,89**
CSF £51.36 TOTE £14.60: £5.20, £2.40; EX 58.30 Trifecta £227.20.

Owner Sheikh Hamdan bin Mohammed Al Maktoum **Bred** Godolphin **Trained** Middleham Moor, N Yorks

FOCUS
Distance increased by 12yds. A bit of a turn up here with the pace a steady one and the winner making all. It's been rated a bit cautiously.

2411 QIPCO 2000 GUINEAS STKS (GROUP 1) (BRITISH CHAMPIONS SERIES) (C&F) 1m

3:35 (3:38) (Class 1) 3-Y-O

£297,018 (£112,606; £56,355; £28,073; £14,088; £7,070) **Stalls** Centre

Form RPR

21- **1** **Magna Grecia (IRE)**[189] 8633 3-9-0 113................ DonnachaO'Brien 17 121
(A P O'Brien, Ire) *looked wl; racd stands' side: chsd ldr: rdn to ld overall over 1f out: r.o wl: 1st of 3 in gp* **11/2**[2]

22-1 **2** *2 1/2* **King Of Change**[24] 1690 3-9-0 92.............................. SeanLevey 19 115
(Richard Hannon) *str; looked wl; racd stands' side: hld up in tch: rdn to chse wnr ins fnl f: r.o: 2nd of 3 in gp* **66/1**

1-1 **3** *1 3/4* **Skardu**[17] 1854 3-9-0 109.. JamesDoyle 3 111+
(William Haggas) *looked wl; racd centre: hld up: hdwy over 2f out: rdn and edgd rt over 1f out: r.o to ld his gp nr fin: 1st of 16 in gp* **8/1**

1-2 **4** *hd* **Madhmoon (IRE)**[28] 1600 3-9-0 115.............................. ChrisHayes 1 111+
(Kevin Prendergast, Ire) *compact; racd centre: hld up in tch: rdn and ev ch over 2f out: outpcd over 1f out: r.o ins fnl f: 2nd of 16 in gp* **7/1**[3]

11- **5** *hd* **Ten Sovereigns (IRE)**[217] 7772 3-9-0 120....................... RyanMoore 5 110+
(A P O'Brien, Ire) *looked wl; racd centre: chsd ldr: led that gp 2f out: rdn over 1f out: styd on same pce wl ins fnl f: hdd his gp nr fin: 3rd of 16 in gp* **9/4**[1]

33-1 **6** *1/2* **Shine So Bright**[18] 1830 3-9-0 112..................... SilvestreDeSousa 18 109
(Andrew Balding) *racd stands' side: led his gp tl overall ldr over 3f out: rdn and hdd over 1f out: styd on same pce ins fnl f: last of 3 in gp* **16/1**

16-1 **7** *1/2* **Kick On**[18] 1831 3-9-0 107....................................... OisinMurphy 9 108
(John Gosden) *looked wl; racd centre: chsd ldrs: led over 2f out: sn hdd: rdn over 1f out: styd on same pce: 4th of 16 in gp* **16/1**

11-3 **8** *3/4* **Urban Icon**[21] 1752 3-9-0 106................................ TomMarquand 10 106
(Richard Hannon) *racd centre: hld up: hdwy over 5f out: rdn over 2f out: styd on same pce fnl f: 5th of 16 in gp* **33/1**

15-2 **9** *1/2* **Great Scot**[21] 1752 3-9-0 111............................. RichardKingscote 6 105
(Tom Dascombe) *hld up: pushed along and hdwy over 2f out: rdn over 1f out: styd on same pce: 6th of 16 in gp* **25/1**

12-2 **10** *1 1/4* **Momkin (IRE)**[17] 1854 3-9-0 108......................... SeamieHeffernan 7 102
(Roger Charlton) *racd centre: hld up: nt clr run over 2f out: hdwy over 1f out: styd on: nt trble ldrs: 7th of 16 in gp* **33/1**

12-3 **11** *nk* **Azano**[18] 1830 3-9-0 104.......................................(t) RobertHavlin 15 101
(John Gosden) *led centre over 5f: sn rdn: wknd over 1f out: 8th of 16 in gp* **66/1**

16-3 **12** *4 1/2* **Dark Vision (IRE)**[23] 1713 3-9-0 109.......................... JoeFanning 16 91
(Mark Johnston) *racd centre: chsd ldrs: rdn over 3f out: wknd wl over 1f out: 9th of 16 in gp* **40/1**

1-44 **13** *3 3/4* **Royal Marine (IRE)**[17] 1854 3-9-0 113.........(h[1]) ChristopheSoumillon 11 82
(Saeed bin Suroor) *racd centre: hld up: hdwy u.p over 2f out: wknd wl over 1f out: 10th of 16 in gp* **16/1**

1-13 **14** *1 3/4* **Set Piece**[17] 1854 3-9-0 104...................................(t[1]) JimCrowley 4 78
(Hugo Palmer) *s.i.s: racd centre: hld up: hdwy over 2f out: rdn and wknd over 1f out: 11th of 16 in gp* **40/1**

112- **15** *1* **Advertise**[203] 8187 3-9-0 119................................. FrankieDettori 8 76
(Martyn Meade) *on toes; racd centre: hld up: shkn up over 3f out: wknd wl over 1f out: 12th of 16 in gp (jockey said colt was never travelling)* **11/1**

11- **16** *4 1/2* **Al Hilalee**[259] 6324 3-9-0 0.................................... WilliamBuick 12 66
(Charlie Appleby) *on toes; racd centre: hld up: hdwy u.p over 2f out: wknd wl over 1f out: 13th of 16 in gp* **8/1**

0341 **17** *8* **Sporting Chance**[65] 956 3-9-0 103............................ PatCosgrave 14 47
(Simon Crisford) *racd centre: chsd ldrs: rdn over 3f out: wkng whn hung rt wl over 1f out 14th of 16 in gp* **100/1**

315- **18** *2* **Emaraaty Ana**[217] 7772 3-9-0 110.............................. DavidEgan 2 43
(Kevin Ryan) *racd alone towards far side and overall ldr over 4f: sn jnd centre gp: wknd wl over 1f out: 15th of 16 in gp* **66/1**

1-1 **19** *1 3/4* **Name The Wind**[14] 1940 3-9-0 99............................. PJMcDonald 13 39
(James Tate) *racd centre: hld up: rdn over 3f out: sn wknd: last of 16 in gp* **66/1**

1m 36.84s (-1.56) **Going Correction** +0.20s/f (Good) **19** Ran SP% **128.4**
Speed ratings (Par 113): **115,112,110,110,110 109,109,108,108,106 106,102,98,96,95 91,83,81,79**
CSF £360.33 CT £3014.47 TOTE £6.00: £2.40, £21.20, £2.70; EX 521.40 Trifecta £4340.10.

Owner Smith/Mrs Magnier/Tabor/Flaxman Stables **Bred** Woodnook Farm Pty Ltd **Trained** Cashel, Co Tipperary

FOCUS
From the first five in the betting over the winter, only Ten Sovereigns made it to the start, and with a stamina query over him the race had an open look to it. Given the big field, a decision was made not to have a false rail, and with the stalls in the centre the expectation was that the field would split. Three came stands' side while the rest raced up the centre, and it turned out that the stands' rail was a big advantage. The winner has been rated in line with the more recent winners, while there's a case for the centre group being rated 3-4lb higher.

2412 HAVANA GOLD H'CAP 6f

4:10 (4:14) (Class 2) (0-100,98) 3-Y-O **£16,172** (£4,812; £2,405; £1,202) **Stalls** Centre

Form RPR

32-0 **1** **Moyassar**[17] 1851 3-9-7 **98**....................................... JimCrowley 9 110
(Richard Hannon) *looked wl; trckd ldrs: shkn up and qcknd to ld over 1f out: sn hung rt: r.o (jockey said colt hung right-handed)* **10/1**

3-14 **2** *2 1/2* **Mawakib**[22] 1729 3-8-2 **79**.. DavidEgan 6 83
(Roger Varian) *athletic; hld up: hdwy over 2f out: rdn and ev ch over 1f out: styd on same pce ins fnl f* **10/1**

04-3 **3** *3/4* **James Watt (IRE)**[9] 2054 3-8-8 **85**.......................... HayleyTurner 2 87
(Michael Bell) *hld up in tch: rdn and ev ch over 1f out: styd on same pce ins fnl f* **25/1**

2-10 **4** *1 3/4* **Beat Le Bon (FR)**[22] 1736 3-9-4 **95**............................ RyanMoore 1 91
(Richard Hannon) *dwlt: hld up: rdn: edgd rt and r.o ins fnl f: nt rch ldrs* **9/2**[2]

13-3 **5** *3/4* **Almufti**[16] 1888 3-9-2 **93**... JamesDoyle 3 87
(Hugo Palmer) *chsd ldrs: led over 2f out: rdn and hdd over 1f out: no ex ins fnl f* **12/1**

01-1 **6** *1 1/4* **Intuitive (IRE)**[22] 1728 3-8-10 **87**......................... PJMcDonald 8 77
(James Tate) *str; hld up: hdwy 1/2-way: rdn over 1f out: no ex* **4/1**[1]

4360 **7** *2 1/4* **Don Armado (IRE)**[17] 1851 3-9-0 **91**.....................(t) PatCosgrave 5 73
(Stuart Williams) *broke wl: sn lost pl: pushed along over 4f out: rallied over 1f out: hung lft and wknd ins fnl f* **33/1**

10-0 **8** *nk* **He'Zanarab (IRE)**[21] 1752 3-9-3 **94**..........................(h[1]) TomMarquand 12 75
(Richard Hannon) *edgd rt s: sn led: hdd over 2f out: wknd ins fnl f* **33/1**

021- **9** *3* **Cool Reflection (IRE)**[208] 8042 3-8-6 **83**..........(t[1] w) SilvestreDeSousa 7 55
(Paul Cole) *hld up: rdn over 2f out: wknd over 1f out* **16/1**

1-05 **10** *½* **Concierge (IRE)**[15] 1920 3-9-6 **97**..............................(p[1]) OisinMurphy 10 67
(George Scott) *hld up: rdn over 2f out: wknd over 1f out* **12/1**

210- **11** *6* **Louis Treize (IRE)**[233] 7201 3-8-6 **83**.................... NicolaCurrie 11 34
(Richard Spencer) *s.i.s: plld hrd and sn prom: rdn and wknd over 1f out (jockey said colt ran too free and stopped quickly)* **7/1**

1-10 **12** *1 ¼* **Jackstar (IRE)**[17] 1854 3-8-13 **90**.......................... RichardKingscote 4 37
(Tom Dascombe) *looked wl; chsd ldrs: rdn over 2f out: stmbld and wknd over 1f out: eased (jockey said colt stumbled approximately 2 furlongs out)* **6/1**[3]

1m 12.19s (0.29) **Going Correction** +0.20s/f (Good) **12** Ran SP% **114.1**
Speed ratings (Par 105): **106,102,101,99,98 96,93,93,89,88 80,78**
CSF £100.08 CT £2428.97 TOTE £11.40: £3.20, £2.80, £6.20; EX 110.80 Trifecta £1123.10.
Owner Hamdan Al Maktoum **Bred** Cheveley Park Stud Ltd **Trained** East Everleigh, Wilts
■ Princes Des Sables was withdrawn. Price at time of withdrawal 16/1. Rule 4 does not apply

FOCUS
A useful 3yo sprint that saw a smart effort from the winner, who defied a mark of 98 with a bit in hand. The second and third have been rated close to form, and in line with the bottom expected level for this race.

2413 LIGHTNING SPEAR NEWMARKET STKS (LISTED RACE) (C&G) 1m 2f
4:45 (4:47) (Class 1) 3-Y-O **£28,355** (£10,750; £5,380; £2,680) **Stalls** Centre

Form RPR

1 **1** **UAE Jewel**[17] 1852 3-9-0 0.. DavidEgan 2 112+
(Roger Varian) *looked wl; trckd ldr: racd keenly: led 3f out: shkn up and hung rt 2f out: rdn out* **8/11**[1]

21-2 **2** *¾* **Walkinthesand (IRE)**[18] 1831 3-9-0 106.......................... RyanMoore 1 108
(Richard Hannon) *sweating; on toes; s.i.s: racd keenly and sn prom: rdn to chse wnr over 1f out: r.o* **11/4**[2]

41-3 **3** *3* **Persian Moon (IRE)**[8] 2084 3-9-0 102.................... SilvestreDeSousa 3 102
(Mark Johnston) *led: shkn up and hdd 3f out: nt clr run 2f out: sn rdn: styng on same pce whn hung lft ins fnl f* **6/1**[3]

110- **4** *27* **Beatboxer (USA)**[217] 7770 3-9-0 97..............................(w) FrankieDettori 4 48
(John Gosden) *hld up: shkn up and wknd over 2f out* **11/1**

2m 6.02s (0.62) **Going Correction** +0.20s/f (Good) **4** Ran SP% **107.2**
Speed ratings (Par 107): **105,104,102,80**
CSF £2.91 TOTE £1.70; EX 2.80 Trifecta £4.80.
Owner Sheikh Mohammed Obaid Al Maktoum **Bred** Highclere Stud & Ors Bloodstock **Trained** Newmarket, Suffolk

FOCUS
This was steadily run and turned into a bit of a test of speed. The second and third have been rated close to form.

2414 QATAR RACING WELFARE H'CAP 1m
5:20 (5:20) (Class 2) (0-105,101) 3-Y-O **£16,172** (£4,812; £2,405; £1,202) **Stalls** Centre

Form RPR

33-6 **1** **Pogo (IRE)**[15] 1926 3-9-0 **94**...................................... OisinMurphy 4 106
(Charles Hills) *chsd ldrs in centre tl gps merged 1/2-way: nt clr run 2f out: sn swtchd rt: shkn up and ld ins fnl f: rdn out* **14/1**

1122 **2** *1 ¼* **Alkaamel**[16] 1897 3-8-6 **86**.. ChrisHayes 2 95
(William Haggas) *racd centre tl gps merged 1/2-way: hld up: hdwy over 2f out: led and hung lft over 1f out: rdn and hdd ins fnl f: styd on same pce* **8/1**[3]

2-14 **3** *2 ¼* **Fox Leicester (IRE)**[8] 2082 3-8-3 **83** oh1 ow1........ SilvestreDeSousa 10 87
(Andrew Balding) *tall; looked wl; racd stands' side: chsd ldr: led overall 2f out: sn rdn and edgd lft: hdd over 1f out: no ex ins fnl f* **15/8**[1]

41-5 **4** *2* **Brian Epstein (IRE)**[17] 1857 3-8-4 **84**.......................... MartinDwyer 1 83
(Richard Hannon) *racd centre tl gps merged 1/2-way: chsd ldrs: led over 2f out: sn rdn and hdd: edgd lft over 1f out: no ex fnl f* **8/1**[3]

16-4 **5** *3 ½* **Leroy Leroy**[14] 1940 3-9-0 **94**...................................... RyanMoore 7 85
(Richard Hannon) *racd stands' side: trckd ldrs: racd keenly: lost pl over 4f out: hdwy over 2f out: rdn over 1f out: wknd ins fnl f* **13/2**[2]

16-5 **6** *½* **Certain Lad**[23] 1713 3-9-0 **101**.............................. ScottMcCullagh(7) 5 91
(Mick Channon) *slipped over coming out to the crse: overall ldr in centre tl gps merged 1/2-way: hdd over 3f out: sn rdn: wknd fnl f* **10/1**

02-0 **7** *4* **Blonde Warrior (IRE)**[22] 1736 3-8-13 **93**.......................... JamesDoyle 9 74
(Hugo Palmer) *led stands' side gp: overall ldr over 3f out tl rdn over 2f out: hmpd wl over 1f out: sn wknd* **12/1**

3004 **8** *1 ¼* **Victory Command (IRE)**[18] 1830 3-9-2 **96**........................ JoeFanning 6 74
(Mark Johnston) *racd centre tl gps merged 1/2-way: chsd ldrs: rdn over 3f out: wknd over 2f out* **9/1**

02-5 **9** *nk* **Mordred (IRE)**[18] 1835 3-9-0 **94**.................................. SeanLevey 3 71
(Richard Hannon) *racd centre tl gps merged 1/2-way: s.i.s: hdwy 1/2-way: rdn and wknd over 2f out* **16/1**

2-31 **10** *9* **Global Warning**[15] 1925 3-8-6 **86**.................................. DavidEgan 8 43
(Ed Dunlop) *racd stands' side: hld up: rdn and wknd over 2f out* **10/1**

1m 37.64s (-0.76) **Going Correction** +0.20s/f (Good) **10** Ran SP% **118.8**
Speed ratings (Par 105): **111,109,107,105,102 101,97,96,95,86**
CSF £123.34 CT £317.51 TOTE £15.50: £3.80, £2.20, £1.30; EX 134.10 Trifecta £744.30.
Owner Gary And Linnet Woodward **Bred** Thomas Foy **Trained** Lambourn, Berks
■ Stewards' Enquiry : Silvestre De Sousa three-day ban: interference & careless riding (May 19-21)

FOCUS
A useful 3yo handicap, they raced in two groups until halfway and it was the low-drawn runners, racing more down the centre, who came out on top. It's been rated in line with the race standard.
T/Jkpt: Not Won. T/Plt: £2,611.20 to a £1 stake. Pool: £173,239.46 - 48.43 winning units T/Qpdt: £143.10 to a £1 stake. Pool: £14,707.23 - 76.03 winning units **Colin Roberts**

2197 THIRSK (L-H)
Saturday, May 4

OFFICIAL GOING: Good (good to firm in places)
Wind: fairly strong half against Weather: overcast

2415 NEW CHESTNUT ROOM @THIRSKRACES IDEAL WEDDING VENUE NOVICE AUCTION STKS 5f
2:00 (2:01) (Class 5) 2-Y-O **£3,881** (£1,155; £577; £288) **Stalls** Centre

Form RPR

5 **1** **Insania**[9] 2051 2-8-11 0.. CliffordLee 2 72+
(K R Burke) *trckd ldrs: rdn and edgd lft 2f out: led appr fnl f: continued to edge lft but kpt on wl* **3/1**[2]

2 *2 ¼* **Dandizette (IRE)** 2-8-11 0.............................. AndrewMullen 13 64
(Adrian Nicholls) *dwlt: sn prom: rdn into narrow ld over 1f out: hdd appr fnl f: kpt on same pce* **25/1**

01 **3** *¾* **Manolith**[7] 2115 2-9-8 0.. DavidNolan 11 72
(David O'Meara) *prom: rdn over 2f out: no ex towards fin* **7/2**[3]

4 *¾* **Royal Lightning** 2-8-11 0.................................. BarryMcHugh 10 58
(James Given) *midfield: pushed along over 2f out: sme hdwy 1f out: r.o wl fnl 110yds* **33/1**

5 **5** *1* **Stone Princess (IRE)**[16] 1893 2-8-8 0.................... BenRobinson(3) 12 55
(Brian Ellison) *led: rdn and hdd over 1f out: no ex ins fnl f* **50/1**

0 **6** *nk* **Comeatchoo (IRE)**[17] 1844 2-9-2 0.............................. DavidAllan 4 59
(Tim Easterby) *midfield: pushed along and hdwy over 1f out: kpt on fnl f* **50/1**

6 **7** *2 ½* **The Ginger Bullet**[17] 1843 2-9-2 0.............................. PaulHanagan 3 50
(Richard Fahey) *in tch: pushed along over 2f out: sn one pce* **7/1**

8 *¾* **Itwouldberudenotto** 2-9-2 0.............................. TonyHamilton 6 47
(Richard Fahey) *dwlt: hld up: sn pushed along: sme late hdwy: nvr involved* **20/1**

3 **9** *2 ½* **Birdie Bowers (IRE)**[17] 1843 2-9-2 0.............................. TomEaves 1 38
(Michael Dods) *wnt lft s: sn chsd ldrs on outer: rdn over 2f out: wknd over 1f out (jockey said colt slipped leaving the stalls)* **7/4**[1]

5 **10** *1 ½* **Mumsbirthdaygirl (IRE)**[13] 1968 2-8-11 0.................... JamesSullivan 7 28
(Mark Loughnane) *in tch: sn pushed along: wknd over 1f out* **50/1**

11 *nk* **Not Another Word** 2-8-8 0.................................. RowanScott(3) 9 26
(Nigel Tinkler) *a towards rr* **50/1**

12 *5* **Bob's Oss (IRE)** 2-9-2 0.. DougieCostello 5 13
(John Quinn) *wnt bdly lft s: a in rr* **40/1**

59.57s (0.17) **Going Correction** -0.10s/f (Good) **12** Ran SP% **117.9**
Speed ratings (Par 93): **94,90,89,88,86 85,81,80,76,74 73,65**
CSF £79.11 TOTE £4.20: £1.40, £6.50, £1.20; EX 83.20 Trifecta £288.60.
Owner Titanium Racing Club **Bred** Grovewood Stud **Trained** Middleham Moor, N Yorks

FOCUS
The going was good, good to firm in places with Clerk of the course James Sanderson saying: "It's not dissimilar to when we raced here on Monday. It's not been drying weather and we've probably had 2/2.5mm of rain since then, which has held the ground." Stalls - Straight course: Centre. Round course: Inside. 1m4f: Stands' side. A fair juvenile contest which produced a decisive winner. A step up from the winner.

2416 SCOUTING FOR GIRLS - LIVE @THIRSKRACES FRIDAY 16TH AUGUST H'CAP 6f
2:30 (2:31) (Class 4) (0-80,81) 4-Y-O+
£5,692 (£1,694; £846; £423; £300; £300) **Stalls** Centre

Form RPR

0-05 **1** **Paddy Power (IRE)**[16] 1895 6-9-1 **74**.......................... PaulHanagan 11 84
(Richard Fahey) *midfield: smooth hdwy 2f out: pushed into ld 1f out: sn rdn ¾ l up: edgd lft and hld on towards fin* **6/1**[3]

-221 **2** *nk* **Equiano Springs**[75] 786 5-8-13 **72**.......................... AndrewMullen 2 81
(Tom Tate) *led narrowly: rdn 2f out: hdd 1f out: kpt on* **4/1**[2]

2334 **3** *1 ¾* **Athollblair Boy (IRE)**[12] 1977 6-9-2 **80**.................... FayeMcManoman(5) 10 83
(Nigel Tinkler) *hld up: n.m.r 2f out and swtchd rt: squeezed through gap ins fnl f: r.o wl: wnt 3rd towards fin* **11/1**

00-1 **4** *½* **Galloway Hills**[12] 1976 4-9-7 **80**.............................. SamJames 8 82
(Phillip Makin) *prom: rdn 2f out: kpt on same pce fnl f: lost 3rd towards fin* **7/2**[1]

6-01 **5** *1 ¼* **Secretinthepark**[9] 2053 9-9-5 **78**..............................(b) AdamKirby 3 76
(Michael Mullineaux) *prom: rdn over 2f out: no ex fnl 110yds* **16/1**

40/3 **6** *½* **Cartmell Cleave**[16] 1895 7-9-8 **81**.............................. JamesSullivan 13 77
(Ruth Carr) *hld up: pushed along and hdwy over 2f out: rdn to chse ldrs appr fnl f: no ex fnl 110yds* **7/1**

-043 **7** *hd* **Gold Stone**[14] 1950 4-8-13 **72**.................................. TomEaves 5 68
(Kevin Ryan) *w ldr: rdn 2f out: wknd fnl 110yds* **16/1**

40-2 **8** *½* **Zumurud (IRE)**[16] 1895 4-9-5 **78**.............................. DavidAllan 9 72
(Rebecca Bastiman) *hld up: pushed along over 2f out: kpt on ins fnl f: nvr threatened* **14/1**

33-5 **9** *3 ¾* **John Kirkup**[12] 1978 4-9-1 **79**.............................. PaulaMuir(5) 12 61
(Michael Dods) *hld up: pushed along over 2f out: wknd ins fnl f* **8/1**

02-0 **10** *2 ½* **Requinto Dawn (IRE)**[8] 2079 4-9-5 **78**..........................(p) TonyHamilton 6 52
(Richard Fahey) *midfield: rdn over 2f out: wknd fnl f* **25/1**

0545 **11** *¾* **Choice Encounter**[33] 1487 4-8-11 **75**.................. ThomasGreatrex(5) 7 47
(Archie Watson) *hld up in midfield: pushed along over 2f out: edgd lft over 1f out and wknd* **25/1**

/0-0 **12** *1 ¼* **Eccleston**[16] 1895 8-9-1 **74**.................................. DougieCostello 1 42
(Paul Midgley) *midfield: rdn over 2f out: wknd over 1f out* **28/1**

225- **13** *3 ½* **Shortbackandsides (IRE)**[207] 8077 4-8-6 **67**.................. DuranFentiman 4 23
(Tim Easterby) *chsd ldrs: rdn over 2f out: sn lost pl: wknd over 1f out* **33/1**

1m 11.41s (-1.39) **Going Correction** -0.10s/f (Good) **13** Ran SP% **121.0**
Speed ratings (Par 105): **105,104,102,101,99 99,99,98,93,90 89,87,82**
CSF £29.28 CT £273.63 TOTE £5.70: £1.70, £1.40, £4.00; EX 37.30 Trifecta £339.50.
Owner M Scaife & R A Fahey **Bred** Yeguada De Milagro Sa **Trained** Musley Bank, N Yorks

FOCUS
An exciting finish to a competitive sprint handicap. The second has improved 5lb on the AW since he last ran on turf and has been rated in line with that.

2417 IRISH DAY @THIRSKRACES SATURDAY 18TH MAY MAIDEN STKS 1m 4f 8y
3:05 (3:14) (Class 5) 3-Y-O+ **£4,528** (£1,347; £673; £336) **Stalls** High

Form RPR

36-2 **1** **Glorious Dane**[32] 1494 3-8-4 69.............................. SeanDavis(5) 6 57
(Stef Keniry) *trckd ldr: pushed into ld 2f out: rdn out fnl 110yds* **10/11**[1]

3- **2** *1* **Sweet Marmalade (IRE)**[62] 3925 4-9-4 0.......... FayeMcManoman(5) 5 52
(Lawrence Mullaney) *in tch: pushed along over 2f out: rdn to chse ldr over 1f out: styd on* **8/1**[3]

-600 **3** *4 ½* **Zahraani**[17] 1858 4-10-0 48.. AdamKirby 1 50
(J R Jenkins) *in tch: pushed along over 4f out: n.m.r over 1f out: styd on same pce fnl f* **22/1**

4 *½* **Nineteenrbo'Malley** 7-9-7 0.............................. SeanKirrane(7) 4 49
(Robyn Brisland) *v.s.a: hld up in rr: pushed along and hdwy 2f out: kpt on fnl f* **50/1**

4- **5** *6* **Tajdeed (IRE)**[271] 5797 4-10-0 0.. DougieCostello 2 40
(Michael Appleby) *led: rdn and hdd 2f out: wknd over 1f out* **7/4**[2]

6 *11* **Queen Emily** 3-8-4 0 .... PaddyMathers 3 15
(Conor Dore) *galloped loose befhand: slowly away: hld up: rdn over 3f out: sn wknd* **20/1**

2m 40.41s (0.41) **Going Correction** -0.10s/f (Good) **6** Ran SP% **110.9**
WFA 3 from 4yo+ 19lb
Speed ratings (Par 103): **94,93,90,90,86 78**
CSF £8.60 TOTE £1.80: £1.10, £2.60; EX 7.30 Trifecta £35.60.
Owner L Bolingbroke, Mersey Racing, P Molony **Bred** Tareq Al Mazeedi **Trained** Middleham, N Yorks

FOCUS
A moderate maiden. Very shaky form.

2418 DARREN (STREET) BARRETT 2ND WEDDING H'CAP 7f
3:40 (3:43) (Class 5) (0-70,71) 3-Y-0+
£4,075 (£1,212; £606; £303; £300; £300) **Stalls** Low

Form RPR

00-0 **1** **Supaulette (IRE)**[8] 2081 4-9-6 **62** .... (bt) DavidAllan 8 72
(Tim Easterby) *in tch: pushed along and hdwy 2f out: rdn to chal strly jst ins fnl f: kpt on: led nr fin* **22/1**

404- **2** *shd* **Knowing Glance (IRE)**[189] 8635 4-9-8 **69** .... SeanDavis(5) 13 78
(Richard Fahey) *trckd ldrs: rdn along to ld over 1f out: drvn and strly pressed jst ins fnl f: kpt on but hdd towards fin* **7/1**[3]

/0-0 **3** *1 3/4* **The Stalking Moon (IRE)**[8] 2076 5-9-7 **63** .... AndrewMullen 10 67+
(Adrian Nicholls) *dwlt: sn midfield: pushed along and hdwy 2f out: rdn to chal 1f out: no ex fnl 110yds* **28/1**

4-02 **4** *1 3/4* **Coverham (IRE)**[16] 1880 5-10-1 **71** .... (p) RyanTate 15 71
(James Eustace) *hld up: rdn and hung lft 2f out: kpt on ins fnl f: nvr trbld ldrs* **5/1**[2]

-140 **5** *1/2* **Rich Approach (IRE)**[23] 1720 3-9-0 **68** .... AndrewElliott 4 62+
(James Bethell) *hld up in rr: rdn along 3f out: swtchd rt to wd outside 2f out: kpt on fnl f* **18/1**

506- **6** *1* **Uncle Charlie (IRE)**[247] 6711 5-9-12 **68** .... TomEaves 12 64
(Ann Duffield) *midfield: rdn and hdwy to chse ldrs over 1f out: wknd ins fnl f* **16/1**

3-00 **7** *1/2* **Fingal's Cave (IRE)**[38] 1367 7-9-10 **66** .... (p) TonyHamilton 6 60
(Philip Kirby) *chsd ldrs: rdn over 2f out: wknd ins fnl f* **33/1**

15-0 **8** *3/4* **Etikaal**[15] 1925 5-9-10 **66** .... SamJames 11 58
(Grant Tuer) *hld up in rr: rdn over 2f out: sme late hdwy: nvr threatened* **33/1**

6-04 **9** *nk* **Somewhere Secret**[8] 2076 5-9-2 **58** .... (p) AdamKirby 1 49
(Michael Mullineaux) *midfield: rdn along over 2f out: sme hdwy whn bit short of room ins fnl f: nvr involved* **7/1**[3]

40-6 **10** *nk* **Ventura Secret (IRE)**[12] 1976 5-9-1 **62** .... PaulaMuir(5) 7 53
(Michael Dods) *hld up in midfield: rdn along over 2f out: nvr involved* **12/1**

22-3 **11** *1* **Sophia Maria**[19] 1816 3-8-8 **69** .... CierenFallon(7) 5 53
(James Bethell) *racd on inner: nvr bttr than midfield* **9/1**

20-4 **12** *1/2* **Redrosezorro**[16] 1895 5-9-12 **68** .... (h) RachelRichardson 3 54
(Eric Alston) *led narrowly: rdn over 2f out: hdd over 1f out: wknd ins fnl f* **8/1**

00-0 **13** *3/4* **Hitman**[25] 1660 6-9-11 **67** .... LewisEdmunds 2 51
(Rebecca Bastiman) *hld up: nvr threatened* **28/1**

000- **14** *3/4* **Miss Sheridan (IRE)**[201] 8263 5-10-0 **70** .... NathanEvans 9 52
(Michael Easterby) *chsd ldrs: rdn over 3f out: wknd over 1f out* **40/1**

0363 **15** *2 1/2* **Exchequer (IRE)**[14] 1942 8-9-10 **69** .... (p) BenRobinson(3) 14 45
(Richard Guest) *pressed ldr on outer: rdn over 2f out: wknd over 1f out (jockey said gelding stopped quickly)* **4/1**[1]

1m 26.35s (-1.25) **Going Correction** -0.10s/f (Good) **15** Ran SP% **121.2**
WFA 3 from 4yo+ 12lb
Speed ratings (Par 103): **103,102,100,98,98 97,96,95,95,95 93,93,92,91,88**
CSF £160.34 CT £4332.51 TOTE £22.70: £5.30, £2.60, £6.70; EX 226.30 Trifecta £1667.30.
Owner Ambrose Turnbull & Partner **Bred** Dr Noel Cogan & Patrick Williams **Trained** Great Habton, N Yorks

FOCUS
A bob of heads at the end of a competitive handicap which suited the hold-up horses. Sound form. The second ran his best race last year first time out, and he's been rated to that level for now.

2419 CLIFF STUD THIRSK HUNT CUP H'CAP 7f 218y
4:15 (4:20) (Class 2) (0-100,97) 4-Y-0+
£24,900 (£7,456; £3,728; £1,864; £932; £468) **Stalls** Low

Form RPR

0-32 **1** **Hayadh**[14] 1944 6-8-12 **88** .... LewisEdmunds 10 97
(Rebecca Bastiman) *trckd ldrs: rdn 2f out: chal strly 1f out: drvn into narrow ld 110yds out: kpt on wl* **14/1**

32-3 **2** *3/4* **Commander Han (FR)**[14] 1944 4-8-13 **89** .... (p) TomEaves 16 96
(Kevin Ryan) *led: rdn and strly pressed fr 2f out: hdd 110yds out* **14/1**

00-5 **3** *3/4* **Nicholas T**[5] 2187 7-8-6 **85** .... JamieGormley(3) 6 90+
(Jim Goldie) *dwlt: hld up: rdn and hdwy on outer 2f out: kpt on wl fnl f: wnt 3rd post* **12/1**

13-3 **4** *nse* **Borodin (IRE)**[21] 1753 4-9-1 **91** .... PaddyMathers 15 96+
(Richard Fahey) *trckd ldrs: pushed along over 2f out: lugged lft but abt to chal whn collided w rival appr fnl f: drvn and hung lft ins fnl f: kpt on same pce* **9/4**[1]

00-5 **5** *1 1/4* **Fennaan (IRE)**[32] 1502 4-8-13 **89** .... (h) SamJames 14 91
(Phillip Makin) *in tch: rdn over 2f out: kpt on ins fnl f* **11/1**

0-00 **6** *1 1/4* **Waarif (IRE)**[15] 1912 6-9-4 **97** .... ConorMcGovern(3) 1 96
(David O'Meara) *midfield: rdn over 2f out: kpt on fnl f* **11/1**

2-45 **7** *nk* **Dawaaleeb (USA)**[24] 1694 5-8-9 **92** .... (v) CierenFallon(7) 7 91
(Les Eyre) *midfield: rdn and sme hdwy on wd outside over 2f out: kpt on same pce fnl f* **7/1**[3]

4-00 **8** *1/2* **King's Pavilion (IRE)**[16] 1896 6-8-13 **89** .... JimmyQuinn 5 87
(Jason Ward) *dwlt: hld up: pushed along over 2f out: swtchd lft over 1f out: sn hdwy: rdn and kpt on ins fnl f: nvr trbld ldrs (jockey said gelding reared slightly as the stalls opened causing the gelding to be slowly away)* **50/1**

20-U **9** *1 1/4* **Garrick**[14] 1944 5-8-9 **85** .... RachelRichardson 11 80
(Tim Easterby) *hld up: rdn over 2f out: nvr threatened* **40/1**

-202 **10** *hd* **Intrepidly (USA)**[30] 1544 5-8-10 **86** .... (p) StevieDonohoe 9 80
(Charlie Fellowes) *dwlt: hld up in rr: rdn along over 2f out: sme late hdwy: nvr threatened* **20/1**

334- **11** *shd* **Firmament**[140] 9557 7-9-5 **95** .... DavidNolan 3 89
(David O'Meara) *in tch: rdn over 2f out: wknd fnl f* **20/1**

00-4 **12** *3/4* **Anythingtoday (IRE)**[16] 1896 5-9-1 **91** .... (p) CamHardie 13 83
(David O'Meara) *hld up in midfield: rdn over 2f out: no imp* **20/1**

1-25 **13** *2 1/4* **Raselasad (IRE)**[14] 1944 5-8-12 **88** .... RoystonFfrench 12 75
(Tracy Waggott) *prom: rdn over 2f out: edgd rt and collided w rival appr fnl f: wknd* **20/1**

000- **14** *1 1/2* **Baraweez (IRE)**[208] 8044 9-8-12 **91** .... BenRobinson(3) 2 75
(Brian Ellison) *midfield: rdn over 2f out: sn outpcd and btn* **33/1**

02-1 **15** *1* **King's Slipper**[22] 1727 4-9-1 **91** .... AdamKirby 8 72
(Clive Cox) *midfield: rdn along over 2f out: wknd over 1f out (trainer's rep could offer no explanation for the gelding's performance)* **4/1**[2]

11-0 **16** *2 1/4* **Parys Mountain (IRE)**[14] 1944 5-8-12 **88** .... (h) DavidAllan 4 64
(Tim Easterby) *in tch on inner: rdn over 2f out: wknd over 1f out (vet reported the gelding had been struck into, right fore and lost its right fore shoe)* **25/1**

1m 37.49s (-4.21) **Going Correction** -0.10s/f (Good) **16** Ran SP% **131.2**
Speed ratings (Par 109): **117,116,115,115,114 112,112,112,110,110 110,109,107,106,105 102**
CSF £188.67 CT £2558.69 TOTE £16.60: £2.90, £3.20, £3.60, £1.30; EX 166.90 Trifecta £2589.10.
Owner Miss Rebecca Bastiman **Bred** Ashbrittle Stud **Trained** Cowthorpe, N Yorks

FOCUS
A typically-competitive renewal of this valuable handicap. Last year's runner-up saw it out well to go one better. The winner has been rated similar to when second in this last year, when the race was run at Wetherby.

2420 BRITISH STALLION STUDS EBF MAIDEN FILLIES' STKS 7f
4:50 (4:53) (Class 4) 3-Y-0+
£6,469 (£1,925; £962; £481) **Stalls** Low

Form RPR

30-4 **1** **Material Girl**[116] 126 3-8-7 72 .... (p) SeanKirrane(7) 5 74
(Richard Spencer) *trckd ldrs: rdn to ld over 1f out: kpt on* **9/2**[3]

3-24 **2** *1 1/2* **Nooshin**[18] 1838 3-9-0 77 .... PaulHanagan 3 70
(Charles Hills) *prom: rdn into narrow ld 2f out: hdd over 1f out: no ex fnl 75yds* **8/11**[1]

5- **3** *nk* **Shaqwar**[281] 5436 3-9-0 0 .... TomEaves 1 69
(Kevin Ryan) *led: rdn and hdd 2f out: sn drvn: no ex fnl 75yds* **5/2**[2]

06- **4** *2 1/4* **Hunterwali**[264] 6083 3-8-9 0 .... PaulaMuir(5) 2 63
(Michael Dods) *trckd ldrs: rdn over 2f out: outpcd over 1f out: kpt on ins fnl f (jockey said filly hung left-handed)* **50/1**

0-00 **5** *7* **Kyllachy Princess**[19] 1816 3-9-0 39 .... TrevorWhelan 4 44
(David Loughnane) *trckd ldrs: rdn over 2f out: wknd over 1f out (jockey said filly hung left-handed in the home straight)* **100/1**

00- **6** *3 3/4* **Keska**[311] 4250 3-9-0 0 .... TonyHamilton 6 34
(Richard Fahey) *hld up: pushed along 3f out: nvr threatened* **25/1**

7 *23* **Hasili Filly** 3-9-0 0 .... AndrewMullen 7
(Noel Wilson) *dwlt: hld up: pushed along 3f out: wknd and bhd fnl 2f* **40/1**

1m 26.28s (-1.32) **Going Correction** -0.10s/f (Good) **7** Ran SP% **113.9**
Speed ratings (Par 102): **103,101,100,98,90 86,59**
CSF £8.26 TOTE £4.30: £1.60, £1.20; EX 10.10 Trifecta £16.80.
Owner Miss Lauren Cunningham **Bred** Cheveley Park Stud Ltd **Trained** Newmarket, Suffolk

FOCUS
Not the strongest of maidens and the winner used her experience to good effect. Weak form.

2421 JOIN RACING TV NOW H'CAP 5f
5:25 (5:26) (Class 4) (0-85,86) 3-Y-0+
£5,692 (£1,694; £846; £423; £300; £300) **Stalls** Centre

Form RPR

265- **1** **Makanah**[210] 7994 4-9-9 **80** .... PaulHanagan 9 91
(Julie Camacho) *midfield: pushed along and hdwy over 1f out: led ins fnl f: kpt on wl* **7/1**

0-24 **2** *1 1/2* **Bowson Fred**[16] 1899 7-9-8 **79** .... NathanEvans 3 85
(Michael Easterby) *w ldr: rdn 2f out: kpt on ins fnl f but no ch w wnr* **11/2**[3]

03-2 **3** *1 1/4* **Jabbarockie**[17] 1860 6-9-9 **80** .... JackGarritty 8 81
(Eric Alston) *led narrowly: rdn 2f out: hdd ins fnl f: no ex fnl 110yds* **3/1**[1]

4146 **4** *nk* **Primo's Comet**[14] 1946 4-9-7 **81** .... JamieGormley(3) 7 81
(Jim Goldie) *hld up: rdn 2f out: kpt on fnl f: nrst fin* **9/2**[2]

0-00 **5** *hd* **Bashiba (IRE)**[8] 2079 8-8-10 **74** .... (t) IzzyClifton(7) 12 73
(Nigel Tinkler) *in tch: rdn and hdwy to chal appr fnl f: no ex fnl 50yds* **28/1**

560- **6** *1 1/4* **Excessable**[189] 8632 6-9-10 **81** .... RachelRichardson 5 76
(Tim Easterby) *chsd ldrs: rdn 2f out: edgd lft and no ex fnl 110yds* **12/1**

6652 **7** *1/2* **Landing Night (IRE)**[15] 1929 7-8-12 **74** .... (tp) AndrewBreslin(5) 6 67
(Rebecca Menzies) *hld up: rdn and hung lft over 1f out: n.m.r ent fnl f: sme late hdwy: nvr threatened* **12/1**

3103 **8** *hd* **Another Angel (IRE)**[15] 1929 5-9-9 **80** .... CamHardie 11 72
(Antony Brittain) *chsd ldrs: rdn 2f out: wknd ins fnl f* **14/1**

55-0 **9** *hd* **Robot Boy (IRE)**[8] 2079 9-9-5 **81** .... HarrisonShaw(5) 4 73
(Marjorie Fife) *dwlt: hld up: sme late hdwy: nvr threatened (jockey said gelding was slowly away)* **28/1**

00-0 **10** *3/4* **Henley**[15] 1929 7-10-1 **86** .... RoystonFfrench 1 75
(Tracy Waggott) *chsd ldrs: rdn over 2f out: wknd ins fnl f* **20/1**

1-35 **11** *1 1/2* **Phoenix Star (IRE)**[24] 1691 3-8-11 **77** .... (p[1]) LewisEdmunds 2 56
(Amy Murphy) *dwlt: hld up: nvr threatened (jockey said gelding was slowly away)* **12/1**

6-00 **12** *3* **Desert Ace (IRE)**[8] 2079 8-9-4 **75** .... DougieCostello 10 48
(Paul Midgley) *hld up: nvr threatened* **25/1**

10-6 **13** *nk* **Billy Dylan (IRE)**[17] 1847 4-9-12 **86** .... (p) ConorMcGovern(3) 13 58
(David O'Meara) *prom: rdn 2f out: wknd over 1f out (jockey said gelding ran too free)* **20/1**

58.74s (-0.66) **Going Correction** -0.10s/f (Good) **13** Ran SP% **121.1**
WFA 3 from 4yo+ 9lb
Speed ratings (Par 105): **101,98,96,96,95 93,93,92,92,91 88,83,83**
CSF £42.34 CT £147.17 TOTE £8.10: £2.20, £1.80, £1.90; EX 48.20 Trifecta £191.00.
Owner Axom Lxxi **Bred** Y E Mullin & Theobalds Stud **Trained** Norton, N Yorks

FOCUS
A fair sprint handicap in which the fancied horses fought out the finish. The winner looks worth following. The second has been rated to his recent AW form, with the third a bit below and the fourth pretty much to form.

T/Plt: £132.80 to a £1 stake. Pool: £51,646.04 - 283.81 winning units T/Qpdt: £20.60 to a £1 stake. Pool: £4,091.61 - 146.41 winning units **Andrew Sheret**

2422 - 2424a (Foreign Racing) - See Raceform Interactive

[2388]CHURCHILL DOWNS (L-H)

Saturday, May 4

OFFICIAL GOING: Dirt: fast changing to sloppy (sealed) after 9.28 race; turf: firm changing to good after 8.37 race

2425a KENTUCKY DERBY PRESENTED BY WOODFORD RESERVE (GRADE 1) (3YO) (MAIN TRACK) (DIRT) — 1m 2f (D)

11:50 3-Y-O **£1,464,566** (£472,440; £236,220; £1,181,102; £70,866)

RPR

1 1 3/4 **Country House (USA)**[20] 1799 3-9-0 0..........(b) FlavienPrat 19 117
(William Mott, U.S.A) *in tch in midfield: hdwy on outer fr over 3f out: pushed wd 2 1/2f out: sn chsng ldrs: rdn over 2f out: drvn and ev ch under 2f out: stl chalng wl ins fnl f: no ex fnl 100yds: fin 2nd: plcd 1st* **65/1**

2 3/4 **Code Of Honor (USA)**[35] 1452 3-9-0 0.......... JohnRVelazquez 12 116
(Claude McGaughey III, U.S.A) *in tch in midfield on inner: hdwy fr over 3f out: rdn 2 1/2f out: led briefly over 2f out: sn hdd: kpt on wl: fin 3rd: plcd 2nd* **144/10**

3 3/4 **Tacitus (USA)**[28] 1612 3-9-0 0.......... JoseLOrtiz 9 114+
(William Mott, U.S.A) *towards rr: rdn and hdwy into midfield 3f out: briefly nt clr run 2 1/2f out: drvn and kpt on fr 1 1/2f out: nrst fin: fin 4th: plcd 3rd* **58/10[3]**

4 hd **Improbable (USA)**[20] 1799 3-9-0 0.......... IradOrtizJr 6 114
(Bob Baffert, U.S.A) *in tch: briefly nt clr run over 2f out: sn rdn and swtchd towards outside: drvn and kpt on fr over 1f out: fin 5th: plcd 4th* **4/1[1]**

5 1/2 **Game Winner (USA)**[27] 1629 3-9-0 0.......... JoelRosario 15 113+
(Bob Baffert, U.S.A) *pushed lft and hmpd leaving stalls: towards rr: stdy hdwy on wd outside fr over 3f out: rdn under 3f out: drvn and kpt on wl fr 1 1/2f out: nrst fin: fin 6th: plcd 5th* **68/10**

6 hd **Master Fencer (JPN)**[34] 3-9-0 0.......... JulienRLeparoux 14 112+
(Koichi Tsunoda, Japan) *hung rt leaving stalls: sn bhd: rdn 2 1/2f out: styd on strly ins fnl f: nrst fin: fin 7th: plcd 6th* **59/1**

7 1/2 **War Of Will (USA)**[42] 3-9-0 0.......... TylerGaffalione 2 111
(Mark Casse, Canada) *trckd ldrs: chsd ldr under 3f out: sltly hmpd and carried rt 2 1/2f out: sn dropped to 4th and rdn: rallied and ev ch 1 1/2f out: drvn and no ex fnl f: wknd fnl 100yds: fin 8th: plcd 7th* **167/10**

8 3/4 **Plus Que Parfait (USA)**[35] 1443 3-9-0 0..........(b) RicardoSantanaJr 10 110
(Brendan P Walsh, U.S.A) *towards rr of midfield: rdn and gd hdwy on inner fr 2 1/2f out: nt clr whn chsng ldrs over 2f out: drvn and wknd steadily fnl f: fin 9th: plcd 8th* **57/1**

9 3 1/4 **Win Win Win (USA)**[28] 1615 3-9-0 0.......... JulianPimentel 13 103
(Michael Trombetta, U.S.A) *towards rr: nt clr run appr 2f out: rdn and kpt on steadily fr under 2f out: nvr in contention: fin 10th: plcd 9th* **168/10**

10 3/4 **Cutting Humor (USA)**[41] 3-9-0 0..........(b) MikeESmith 11 102
(Todd Pletcher, U.S.A) *towards rr of midfield: hdwy on wd outside appr 3f out: sltly hmpd 2 1/2f out: sn rdn: wknd steadily fr under 2f out: fin 11th: plcd 10th* **241/10**

11 2 **By My Standards (USA)**[42] 3-9-0 0.......... GabrielSaez 4 98
(W Bret Calhoun, U.S.A) *dwlt: towards rr: rdn and sme hdwy fr over 3f out: wknd over 1f out: fin 12th: plcd 11th* **188/10**

12 3 1/2 **Vekoma (USA)**[28] 1615 3-9-0 0.......... JavierCastellano 7 91
(George Weaver, U.S.A) *in tch tl lost pl qckly 3f out: sn struggling: fin 13th: plcd 12th* **168/10**

13 nk **Bodexpress (USA)**[35] 1452 3-9-0 0.......... ChrisLanderos 20 90
(Gustavo Delgado, U.S.A) *trckd ldrs: rdn 3f out: sltly outpcd whn nt clr run and hmpd under 3f out: sn wl btn: fin 14th: plcd 13th* **71/1**

14 hd **Tax (USA)**[28] 1612 3-9-0 0.......... JuniorAlvarado 3 90
(Danny Gargan, U.S.A) *towards rr of midfield: rdn and effrt on inner 2 1/2f out: wknd fr 1 1/2f out: eased ins fnl f: fin 15th: plcd 14th* **36/1**

15 1 1/2 **Roadster (USA)**[27] 1629 3-9-0 0.......... FlorentGeroux 16 87
(Bob Baffert, U.S.A) *a towards rr: fin 16th: plcd 15th* **116/10**

16 1 1/2 **Long Range Toddy (USA)**[20] 1799 3-9-0 0.......... JonKentonCourt 17 84
(Steven Asmussen, U.S.A) *chsd ldr: rdn 3f out: hung rt and lost pl 2 1/2f out: sn btn: fin 17th: plcd 16th* **55/1**

17 **Maximum Security (USA)**[35] 1452 3-9-0 0.......... LuisSaez 8 121+
(Jason Servis, U.S.A) *mde virtually all: hung rt and impeded rivals 2 1/2f out: sn rdn: hdd briefly over 2f out: sn rallied and regained ld: drvn and kpt on gamely fr under 2f out: kpt on strly and in command fnl 100yds: fin 1st: plcd 17th* **9/2[2]**

18 nse **Spinoff (USA)**[42] 3-9-0 0.......... ManuelFranco 18 84
(Todd Pletcher, U.S.A) *midfield towards outer: rdn over 3f out: losing pl whn nt clr run and sltly hmpd 3f out: sn struggling* **52/1**

19 8 1/4 **Gray Magician (USA)**[35] 1443 3-9-0 0.......... DraydenVanDyke 5 67
(Peter Miller, U.S.A) *towards rr: rdn and hdwy into midfield on inner 2 1/2f out: wknd 1 1/2f out* **34/1**

2m 3.93s (2.74) **19** Ran SP% **121.6**

PARI-MUTUEL (all including 2 unit stake): WIN 132.40; PLACE (1-2) 56.60, 15.20; SHOW (1-2-3) 24.60, 9.80, 5.60; SF 3,009.60.

Owner Mrs J V Shields Jr, E J M McFadden Jr & LNJ Foxwoo **Bred** Austin Paul **Trained** USA

FOCUS

This looked an ordinary Kentucky Derby in form terms but there was nothing ordinary about the conclusion as, for the first time in the race's 145-year history, the first past the post was disqualified for interference, and the wait for the result to become official lasted over 20 minutes. Lukewarm morning line favourite Omaha Beach was withdrawn during the week, replaced by Bodexpress (one of the horses who was hampered), and Haikal was also taken out, so the race was one shy of a full field. It poured with rain, so the track was sloppy (sealed). The opening split was rapid but the gallop slowed enough to avoid a pace meltdown: 22.31 (2f), 24.31 (4f), 25.88 (6f), 26.13 (8f), 25.33 (line).

[2165]LONGCHAMP (R-H)

Saturday, May 4

OFFICIAL GOING: Turf: soft

2426a PRIX DE L'AVRE (LISTED RACE) (3YO) (TURF) — 1m 4f

1:35 3-Y-O **£24,774** (£9,909; £7,432; £4,954; £2,477)

RPR

1 **Jalmoud**[17] 1856 3-9-2 0.......... OlivierPeslier 5 100+
(Charlie Appleby) *disp ld fr stalls: hdd after 1f and chsd ldr: pushed along 2 1/2f fr home: styd on under driving 1 1/2f out: sustained run fnl f: led last strides* **23/10[2]**

2 hd **Soft Light (FR)**[20] 1797 3-9-2 0.......... CristianDemuro 1 100
(J-C Rouget, France) *trckd ldng pair: shkn up and prog 2f out: rdn to chal appr fnl f: led narrowly 100yds out: hdd cl home* **54/10**

3 1/2 **Khagan (IRE)**[30] 3-9-2 0.......... MickaelBarzalona 4 99
(A Fabre, France) *settled in fnl trio abt 6 l off pce: drvn 3f out: hdwy w 1 1/2f to run: styd on ins fnl f: nt quite pce to chal* **19/10[1]**

4 nk **Psara**[19] 3-8-13 0.......... AlexisBadel 2 96
(H-F Devin, France) **33/10[3]**

5 hd **Pedro Cara (FR)**[33] 3-9-2 0.......... TonyPiccone 3 98
(M Delcher Sanchez, France) **15/2**

6 3/4 **Apadanah (GER)**[16] 3-8-13 0.......... AntoineHamelin 6 94
(Waldemar Hickst, Germany) **27/1**

2m 39.6s (9.20) **6** Ran SP% **119.0**

PARI-MUTUEL (all including 1 euro stake): WIN 1.50 (coupled with Khagan); PLACE 2.50, 3.30; SF 18.40.

Owner Godolphin **Bred** Godolphin **Trained** Newmarket, Suffolk

FOCUS

Potentially limited form with 2l covering the lot.

2427a (Foreign Racing) - See Raceform Interactive

2428a PRIX D'HEDOUVILLE (GROUP 3) (4YO+) (TURF) — 1m 4f

3:25 4-Y-O+ **£36,036** (£14,414; £10,810; £7,207; £3,603)

RPR

1 **Petit Fils (FR)**[27] 4-9-0 0.......... TheoBachelot 6 110
(J-P Gauvin, France) *mde all: drvn for home 1 1/2f out: styd on fnl f: a jst holding runner-up* **93/10**

2 hd **Folamour**[39] 1348 4-9-0 0.......... MaximeGuyon 2 109
(A Fabre, France) *missed break and lost 5 l: qckly rcvrd grnd to chse ldng trio: drvn to chse ldr w under 1 1/2f to run: styd on ins fnl f: nvr quite on terms* **31/10[1]**

3 2 **Nagano Gold**[20] 1796 5-9-0 0.......... GregoryBenoist 4 106+
(Vaclav Luka Jr, Czech Republic) *w.w in rr: hdwy over 1 1/2f out: styd on ins fnl f: nt rch front pair* **4/1[3]**

4 1 3/4 **Royal Julius (IRE)**[70] 894 6-9-0 0.......... CristianDemuro 8 103
(J Reynier, France) *hld up in fnl pair: rowed along but no immediate prog 2f out: styd on fnl f: n.d* **63/10**

5 1 **Aspetar (FR)**[21] 1750 4-9-0 0.......... Pierre-CharlesBoudot 3 102
(Roger Charlton) *w.w in fnl trio: tk clsr order 1/2-way: effrt on inner 2f out to chse ldng gp: sn rdn: outpcd ins fnl f* **7/2[2]**

6 2 **Gyllen (USA)**[262] 6175 4-9-4 0.......... MickaelBarzalona 5 102
(A Fabre, France) *settled in midfield: drvn 2f out: sn rdn and no prog: nvr in contention* **5/1**

7 3/4 **Caravagio (FR)**[20] 1796 6-9-0 0..........(p) MathieuAndrouin 1 97
(Alain Couetil, France) *chsd ldr on inner: n.m.r over 1 1/2f out: sn rdn and btn* **38/1**

8 hd **Tiberian (FR)**[20] 1796 7-9-0 0.......... OlivierPeslier 7 97
(Alain Couetil, France) *cl up on outer: 2nd and drvn wl over 1 1/2f out: wknd fnl f* **9/1**

2m 38.41s (8.01) **8** Ran SP% **119.3**

PARI-MUTUEL (all including 1 euro stake): WIN 10.30; PLACE 2.50, 1.70, 1.80; DF 12.70.

Owner Mathieu Offenstadt **Bred** M Offenstadt, S Fargeon & Rod Collet **Trained** France

2429a PRIX DU PONT AU CHANGE (CONDITIONS) (4YO+) (TURF) — 1m

4:05 4-Y-O+

£12,612 (£4,792; £3,531; £2,018; £1,009; £756)

RPR

1 **Skalleti (FR)**[37] 4-9-3 0.......... MaximeGuyon 7 101
(J Reynier, France) **27/10[2]**

2 2 **Young Fire (FR)**[18] 4-9-0.......... AurelienLemaitre 3 93
(F Head, France) **36/5[3]**

3 hd **Buthela (FR)**[19] 1827 5-8-9 0.......... AugustinMadamet(8) 6 96
(A Fabre, France) **13/10[1]**

4 hd **Walec**[19] 1827 7-8-6 0.......... JeremieMonteiro(8) 10 92
(N Caullery, France) **12/1**

5 3/4 **Ego Dancer (FR)**[165] 4-8-5 0.......... JeremyMoisan(5) 1 86
(M Delzangles, France) **42/1**

6 1 1/2 **Fulminato (GER)**[19] 1827 5-9-0 0.......... RenePiechulek 4 87
(Dr A Bolte, Germany) **35/1**

7 snk **Caffe Macchiato (IRE)**[19] 1827 4-9-0 0..........(b) MickaelBarzalona 9 87
(Mme Pia Brandt, France) **31/1**

8 1/2 **The Emperor Within (FR)**[24] 1694 4-9-0 0.......... GeraldMosse 5 85
(Martin Smith) *broke wl and led: hdd after 3f but remained a cl 2nd: drvn to chal 2f out: wknd fnl f* **11/1**

9 2 **Royal Town (FR)**[229] 4-9-3 0.......... RadekKoplik 8 84
(Z Koplik, Czech Republic) **54/1**

10 hd **Miracle Des Aigles (FR)**[37] 6-9-0 0.......... ThierryThulliez 2 80
(Mme C Barande-Barbe, France) **14/1**

11 snk **Bagel (FR)**[193] 6-9-0 0.......... RonanThomas 12 80
(J E Hammond, France) **23/1**

12 20 **Kool And The Gang (IRE)**[188] 9-9-0 0.......... CyrilleStefan 11 34
(J Albrecht, Czech Republic) **103/1**

1m 42.8s (4.40) **12** Ran SP% **120.6**

PARI-MUTUEL (all including 1 euro stake): WIN 3.70; PLACE 1.50, 1.70, 1.20; DF 14.20.

Owner Jean-Claude Seroul **Bred** Guy Pariente Holding **Trained** France

2430 - 2432a (Foreign Racing) - See Raceform Interactive

HAMILTON (R-H)

Sunday, May 5

OFFICIAL GOING: Good to firm (8.9)

Wind: Light, half behind in sprints and in over 4f of home straight in races on the round course Weather: Overcast, dry

2433 TOP CAT WINDOW BLINDS H'CAP — 5f 7y

1:30 (1:32) (Class 5) (0-70,70) 4-Y-0+

£4,787 (£1,424; £711; £400; £400; £400) **Stalls** Centre

Form				RPR
01-0	**1**		**Spirit Of Wedza (IRE)**[29] 1597 7-9-0 **70**....................... VictorSantos(7) 8 (Julie Camacho) *prom: rdn to ld over 1f out: kpt on wl fnl f* **9/2**[2]	80
40/6	**2**	¾	**Lathom**[15] 1951 6-9-5 **68**....................... GrahamLee 7 (Paul Midgley) *dwlt: hld up: hdwy 2f out: rdn to chse wnr ins fnl f: kpt on: hld nr fin* **10/3**[1]	75
-500	**3**	2¾	**Leeshaan (IRE)**[73] 834 4-8-2 **51**....................... NathanEvans 10 (Rebecca Bastiman) *dwlt: hld up: effrt and rdn over 1f out: kpt on to take 3rd towards fin: nt rch first two* **12/1**	48
30-0	**4**	½	**Super Florence (IRE)**[15] 1951 4-9-0 **66**..............(h) JamieGormley(3) 3 (Iain Jardine) *prom: effrt and ev ch over 1f out: chsd wnr to ins fnl f: outpcd and lost 3rd towards fin* **12/1**	62
2216	**5**	½	**Red Stripes (USA)**[24] 1716 7-8-0 **56**..............(b) KieranSchofield(7) 9 (Lisa Williamson) *w ldrs: rdn along 1/2-way: outpcd fnl f* **16/1**	50
0-04	**6**	2¼	**Jeffrey Harris**[15] 1950 4-8-10 **59**..............(h) PhilDennis 6 (Jim Goldie) *hld up bhd ldng gp: rdn along 1/2-way: no imp over 1f out* **8/1**	45
/04-	**7**	½	**Bronze Beau**[352] 2807 12-8-8 **62**..............(tp) FayeMcManoman(5) 5 (Linda Stubbs) *mde most to over 1f out: wknd ins fnl f* **33/1**	46
30-0	**8**	nk	**Fumbo Jumbo (IRE)**[14] 1973 6-9-2 **65**....................... LewisEdmunds 2 (Rebecca Bastiman) *dwlt: bhd: rdn 1/2-way: nvr rchd ldrs* **12/1**	48
6-00	**9**	1½	**Economic Crisis (IRE)**[15] 1951 10-8-4 **58**.............. ConnorMurtagh(5) 4 (Alan Berry) *w ldrs to over 2f out: rdn and wknd over 1f out* **14/1**	35
306-	**10**	½	**Arnold**[216] 7839 5-8-13 **62**..............(h) TomEaves 1 (Ann Duffield) *hld up: effrt on outside over 2f out: wknd over 1f out* **11/2**[3]	38
00-0	**11**	½	**Havana Go**[15] 1951 4-8-4 **58**....................... SeanDavis(5) 11 (Keith Dalgleish) *towards rr: struggling over 2f out: btn over 1f out* **8/1**	32

59.27s (-1.13) **Going Correction** -0.125s/f (Firm) **11 Ran SP% 117.4**

Speed ratings (Par 103): **104,102,98,97,96 93,92,91,89,88 87**

CSF £19.83 CT £169.76 TOTE £4.80: £1.50, £1.70, £4.80; EX 14.10 Trifecta £335.10.

Owner Owners Group 005 **Bred** N Hartery **Trained** Norton, N Yorks

FOCUS

All distances as advertised. It was good to firm ground ahead of the opener, a sprint handicap featuring several previous winners. The first two in the betting came clear and they came down the middle.

2434 HAMILTON PARK RACECOURSE NEW HOTEL TANGERINE TREES CONDITIONS STKS (PLUS 10 RACE) — 5f 7y

2:05 (2:05) (Class 2) 3-Y-O **£18,675** (£5,592; £2,796; £1,398) **Stalls** Centre

Form				RPR
166-	**1**		**Semoum (USA)**[216] 7851 3-9-9 **94**..............(w) JackMitchell 4 (Roger Varian) *mde all: pushed along over 1f out: kpt on strly fnl f* **2/1**[1]	99
103-	**2**	2	**Secret Venture**[226] 7479 3-9-2 **93**....................... DanielTudhope 1 (Kevin Ryan) *trckd ldrs: effrt and pressed wnr over 1f out: kpt on same pce ins fnl f (vet said colt lost its right fore shoe)* **5/2**[2]	85
31-2	**3**	nk	**Rocket Action**[16] 1924 3-9-6 **88**....................... PJMcDonald 5 (Robert Cowell) *pressed wnr to over 1f out: drvn and one pce ins fnl f (vet said colt was found to be lame right hind post race)* **4/1**	88
11-2	**4**	18	**Deputise**[16] 1920 3-9-9 **101**....................... PaulHanagan 3 (William Haggas) *sprawled s: in tch: outpcd and hung rt over 1f out: btn and eased fnl f (jockey said colt slipped leaving the stalls and stumbled coming down the hill resulting in it losing its action)* **11/4**[3]	26

59.79s (-0.61) **Going Correction** -0.125s/f (Firm) **4 Ran SP% 108.6**

Speed ratings (Par 105): **99,95,95,66**

CSF £7.18 TOTE £3.20; EX 9.30 Trifecta £18.00.

Owner H H SH Nasser Bin Hamad Al Khalifa **Bred** Godolphin & Summer Wind Equine **Trained** Newmarket, Suffolk

FOCUS

The feature event featured some interesting 3yo's, though past winners didn't achieve much at a higher level subsequently, bar Mecca's Angel in 2014. The positions remained the same throughout.

2435 HAMPTON BY HILTON OPENING THIS SUMMER BUTTONHOOK H'CAP — 1m 5f 16y

2:35 (2:43) (Class 3) (0-95,92) 4-Y-O+

£13,695 (£4,100; £2,050; £1,025; £512; £257) **Stalls** Low

Form				RPR
10-3	**1**		**Rare Groove (IRE)**[30] 1559 4-9-3 **88**....................... PJMcDonald 3 (Jedd O'Keeffe) *trckd ldrs: led over 2f out: pushed clr fnl f: readily* **5/4**[1]	98+
14-2	**2**	2¼	**Charles Kingsley**[13] 1989 4-9-2 **87**....................... AndrewMullen 2 (Mark Johnston) *led: rdn and hdd over 2f out: rallied: kpt on fnl f: nt pce of wnr* **9/4**[2]	92
22-5	**3**	1¼	**Jabbaar**[92] 558 6-9-0 **88**....................... JamieGormley(3) 6 (Iain Jardine) *hld up: rdn along over 2f out: hung rt over 1f out: kpt on fnl f: nrst fin* **9/1**	91
53-5	**4**	½	**Framley Garth (IRE)**[32] 1518 7-8-1 **77**....................... PaulaMuir(5) 7 (Liam Bailey) *prom: rdn along 3f out: edgd rt and one pce fr over 1f out* **14/1**	79
3235	**5**	2¾	**Loud And Clear**[34] 1483 8-8-9 **80**....................... PhilDennis 5 (Jim Goldie) *hld up: rdn and outpcd over 2f out: sme late hdwy: nvr rchd ldrs* **25/1**	78
660-	**6**	½	**Carbon Dating (IRE)**[135] 9677 7-8-7 **81**....................... RowanScott(3) 1 (Andrew Hughes, Ire) *t.k.h: hld up in tch: rdn and outpcd over 2f out: btn over 1f out* **18/1**	78
0-06	**7**	2¼	**Eye Of The Storm (IRE)**[8] 2118 9-8-5 **81**....................... SeanDavis(5) 4 (Keith Dalgleish) *pressed ldr: rdn over 3f out: wknd fr 2f out* **15/2**[3]	75
330/	**8**	11	**Shrewd**[568] 8038 9-9-7 **92**....................... TomEaves 8 (Iain Jardine) *hld up in last pl: outpcd and shkn up over 3f out: sn btn* **40/1**	70

2m 47.83s (-6.87) **Going Correction** -0.125s/f (Firm) **8 Ran SP% 115.2**

Speed ratings (Par 107): **114,112,111,111,109 109,108,101**

CSF £4.17 CT £15.59 TOTE £2.10: £1.10, £1.20, £1.70; EX 5.00 Trifecta £25.90.

Owner John Dance **Bred** Pier House Stud **Trained** Middleham Moor, N Yorks

FOCUS

A fair staying handicap in which the last four winners won or placed next time out. The first two were strong in the market, including the winner who came clear. The went a sensible gallop.

2436 FOLLOW US ON TWITTER @HAMILTONPARKRC H'CAP — 1m 3f 15y

3:10 (3:15) (Class 5) (0-70,72) 4-Y-O+

£4,787 (£1,424; £711; £400; £400; £400) **Stalls** Low

Form				RPR
0-01	**1**		**Sioux Frontier (IRE)**[33] 1500 4-9-7 **68**....................... LewisEdmunds 3 (Iain Jardine) *hld up in midfield on ins: effrt over 2f out: hdwy to ld wl ins fnl f: kpt on wl* **8/1**	77
531-	**2**	nk	**Makawee (IRE)**[240] 7030 4-9-10 **71**....................... DanielTudhope 8 (David O'Meara) *hld up in midfield on outside: drvn and effrt over 2f out: led briefly ins fnl f: kpt on: hld nr fin* **9/4**[1]	79
220-	**3**	1½	**Granite City Doc**[247] 6741 6-8-10 **62**....................... PaulaMuir(5) 12 (Lucy Normile) *t.k.h early: prom: smooth hdwy to ld 3f out: rdn: edgd rt and hdd ins fnl f: r.o same pce* **8/1**	67+
-466	**4**	nk	**Home Before Dusk**[33] 1500 4-8-11 **63**....................... SeanDavis(5) 7 (Keith Dalgleish) *hld up on outside: effrt over 2f out: chsd ldrs over 1f out: kpt on same pce ins fnl f* **14/1**	68
633-	**5**	1½	**Donnachies Girl (IRE)**[141] 9551 6-8-12 **62**....................... RowanScott(3) 10 (Alistair Whillans) *hld up: effrt and rdn over 2f out: edgd rt over 1f out: kpt on fnl f: no imp* **8/1**	64
5-52	**6**	2½	**Pammi**[33] 1500 4-8-6 **56**....................... JamieGormley(3) 1 (Jim Goldie) *cl up: drvn and led briefly over 3f out: rdn and outpcd over 1f out: btn ins fnl f* **5/1**[3]	54
	7	3	**Go Guarantor**[9] 3224 5-8-3 **50** oh4 ow1..............(bt) AndrewMullen 11 (R Mike Smith) *slowly away: bhd and detached: rdn 4f out: kpt on fr 2f out: nvr rchd ldrs* **66/1**	43
60-4	**8**	½	**Zihaam**[18] 1848 5-9-0 **66**..............(p) BenSanderson(5) 2 (Roger Fell) *dwlt: sn pushed along and prom: drvn along 3f out: wknd over 1f out* **9/2**[2]	58
434-	**9**	1½	**Bogardus (IRE)**[147] 8079 8-9-4 **65**....................... PhilDennis 6 (Liam Bailey) *t.k.h: hld up towards rr: drvn along over 2f out: wknd over 1f out* **33/1**	55
632-	**10**	¾	**Corton Lad**[234] 7223 9-9-8 **72**..............(tp) BenRobinson(3) 9 (Keith Dalgleish) *led or disp ld to over 3f out: rdn and wknd over 1f out* **16/1**	60
-055	**11**	2½	**Rioja Day (IRE)**[9] 1083 9-8-2 **49** oh4..............(p) NathanEvans 4 (Jim Goldie) *led or disp ld to over 3f out: wknd fnl 2f* **50/1**	33

2m 23.15s (-2.35) **Going Correction** -0.125s/f (Firm) **11 Ran SP% 117.9**

Speed ratings (Par 103): **103,102,101,101,100 98,96,96,94,94 92**

CSF £26.17 CT £153.66 TOTE £10.30: £2.90, £1.80, £2.90; EX 33.50 Trifecta £242.10.

Owner Let's Be Lucky Racing 23 **Bred** P J Towell **Trained** Carrutherstown, D'fries & G'way

FOCUS

An open handicap featuring mainly exposed types. They went only a steady pace, but that didn't stop the winner swooping late up the inside.

2437 TOP CAT - SCOTLAND'S PREMIER WINDOW BLINDS H'CAP — 6f 6y

3:45 (3:51) (Class 4) (0-80,80) 4-Y-O+ **£6,727** (£2,002; £1,000; £500; £400) **Stalls** Centre

Form				RPR
100-	**1**		**Zig Zag Zyggy (IRE)**[30] 1574 4-9-2 **78**....................... RowanScott(3) 4 (Andrew Hughes, Ire) *dwlt: sn cl up: rdn to ld over 1f out: edgd lft ins fnl f: kpt on wl* **10/1**	87
0302	**2**	½	**Tommy G**[58] 1082 6-9-3 **76**....................... DanielTudhope 2 (Jim Goldie) *led: rdn and hdd over 1f out: rallied: hld nr fin* **4/1**[3]	83
-006	**3**	3¼	**Logi (IRE)**[22] 1760 5-8-12 **74**..............(b) JamieGormley(3) 3 (Rebecca Bastiman) *cl up: rdn over 1f out: outpcd ins fnl f* **7/2**[2]	71
340-	**4**	¾	**Sharp Defence (USA)**[6] 2220 5-9-2 **80**....................... SeanDavis(5) 5 (Richard John O'Brien, Ire) *prom: rdn and outpcd over 1f out: btn ins fnl f* **1/1**[1]	75
3-50	**5**	3	**Buccaneers Vault (IRE)**[13] 1977 7-9-7 **80**....................... KevinStott 1 (Paul Midgley) *dwlt: hld up in tch: rdn and outpcd over 1f out: sn btn* **8/1**	65

1m 11.51s (-1.19) **Going Correction** -0.125s/f (Firm) **5 Ran SP% 112.4**

Speed ratings (Par 105): **102,101,97,96,92**

CSF £48.04 TOTE £8.50: £3.00, £1.80; EX 27.10 Trifecta £110.30.

Owner Thistle Bloodstock Limited **Bred** Thistle Bloodstock Limited **Trained** Kells, Co Kilkenny

FOCUS

A small sprint handicap won by the rank outsider, who came there more towards the middle.

2438 RACING TV HD ON SKY 426 MAIDEN STKS — 1m 68y

4:20 (4:21) (Class 5) 3-Y-O+ **£4,787** (£1,424; £711; £355) **Stalls** Low

Form				RPR
	1		**Southern Rock (IRE)**[198] 3-9-1 0....................... DanielTudhope 3 (David O'Meara) *mde all: pushed along 2f out: drew clr fnl f: comf* **7/2**[2]	74+
2	**2**	4½	**Al Hadeer (USA)**[18] 1852 3-9-1 0....................... DaneO'Neill 4 (William Haggas) *t.k.h: prom on outside: hdwy to chse wnr after 2f: effrt and rdn wl over 1f out: outpcd fnl f (jockey said colt stopped quickly)* **1/12**[1]	64+
	3	½	**Clovenstone** 3-9-1 0....................... GrahamLee 6 (Alistair Whillans) *s.i.s: hld up: pushed along over 2f out: hdwy to chse ldng pair ins fnl f: no imp* **33/1**	63
05-	**4**	1¾	**God Of Dreams**[206] 8129 3-8-12 0....................... JamieGormley(3) 2 (Iain Jardine) *chsd ldrs: drvn over 2f out: edgd rt and outpcd over 1f out* **33/1**	58
	5	8	**Seenit Doneit Next (IRE)** 3-8-7 0....................... RowanScott(3) 7 (Andrew Hughes, Ire) *s.i.s: hld up: drvn and outpcd over 2f out: sn btn* **16/1**[3]	35
050-	**6**	8	**Geyser**[193] 8541 3-8-10 38....................... ConnorMurtagh(5) 1 (Barry Murtagh) *chsd wnr 2f: prom tl rdn and wknd over 2f out* **66/1**	22

1m 46.03s (-2.37) **Going Correction** -0.125s/f (Firm) **6 Ran SP% 127.8**

Speed ratings (Par 103): **106,101,101,99,91 83**

CSF £4.87 TOTE £9.40: £1.10, £1.10; EX 13.70 Trifecta £51.60.

Owner Middleham Park Racing VI And Partner **Bred** Godolphin **Trained** Upper Helmsley, N Yorks

FOCUS

A lop-sided maiden in the betting, but a shock result with the long odds-on jolly getting turned over. The winner made all at his own pace.

2439 RACING TV PROFITS RETURNED TO RACING H'CAP — 1m 68y

4:55 (4:55) (Class 5) (0-70,71) 4-Y-O+

£4,787 (£1,424; £711; £400; £400; £400) **Stalls** Low

Form				RPR
3-40	**1**		**Mearing**[54] 1169 4-9-5 **71**..............(p) JamieGormley(3) 1 (Iain Jardine) *missed break: hld up: effrt and swtchd lft 2f out: hung lft and led ent fnl f: kpt on wl* **4/1**[3]	78

2253 **2** *nk* **Zodiakos (IRE)**[26] 1660 6-9-2 **65**.........................(p) BenCurtis 7 71
(Roger Fell) *cl up: led over 2f out: rdn and hdd ent fnl f: edgd lft: r.o: hld nr fin* **11/4**[2]
50-6 **3** *1 1/4* **Majeste**[12] 2012 5-8-9 **58**......................... LewisEdmunds 4 61
(Rebecca Bastiman) *hld up on ins: pushed along over 2f out: hdwy over 1f out: r.o ins fnl f* **9/1**
50-6 **4** *1/2* **Strong Steps**[27] 1644 7-9-7 **70**......................... DanielTudhope 2 72
(Jim Goldie) *trckd ldrs: effrt and rdn 2f out: nt qckn fnl f* **13/8**[1]
000- **5** *nk* **Pudding Chare (IRE)**[206] 8133 5-8-7 **56** oh1..............(t) AndrewMullen 3 57
(R Mike Smith) *led to over 2f out: rdn and outpcd over 1f out* **25/1**
455- **6** *1* **Chinese Spirit (IRE)**[180] 8900 5-8-12 **64**................. BenRobinson(3) 8 63
(Linda Perratt) *s.i.s: sn prom: effrt over 2f out: rdn and ev ch over 1f out: no ex ins fnl f* **14/1**
0-04 **7** *hd* **Spirit Of Sarwan (IRE)**[8] 2106 5-8-5 **59** ow1........(p) BenSanderson(5) 6 57
(Stef Keniry) *missed break: hld up: drvn along over 2f out: edgd lft: kpt on fnl f: no imp* **7/1**

1m 46.83s (-1.57) **Going Correction** -0.125s/f (Firm) **7 Ran SP% 117.8**
Speed ratings (Par 103): **102,101,100,99,99 98,98**
CSF £16.19 CT £93.95 TOTE £4.60: £2.30, £1.80; EX 17.70 Trifecta £99.50.
Owner Let's Be Lucky Racing 14 **Bred** Clive Dennett **Trained** Carruthertown, D'fries & G'way
■ Stewards' Enquiry : Ben Curtis two-day ban: used whip above permitted level (May 19-20); caution: careless riding

FOCUS
An ordinary handicap in which the winner came down the middle of the straight during the final few furlongs.
T/Plt: £59.50 to a £1 stake. Pool: £69,507.16 - 852.72 winning units T/Qpdt: £8.00 to a £1 stake. Pool: £6,745.78 - 623.96 winning units **Richard Young**

2408 NEWMARKET (R-H)

Sunday, May 5

OFFICIAL GOING: Good (good to firm in places; ovr 8.1, stand 8.1, ctr 8.4, far 7.9)
Wind: Strong tail wind Weather: Overcast, windy

2440 QATAR RACING H'CAP 1m 4f
1:50 (1:53) (Class 2) (0-105,102) 4-Y-O+
£31,125 (£9,320; £4,660; £2,330; £1,165; £585) **Stalls** Centre

Form RPR
11-3 **1** **Baghdad (FR)**[16] 1927 4-9-8 **100**......................... SilvestreDeSousa 6 108+
(Mark Johnston) *on toes; racd in midfield: effrt on outer to cl on ldr 2f out: rdn and gd hdwy to ld 100yds out: styd on wl* **9/4**[1]
131- **2** *1/2* **Corelli (USA)**[156] 9333 4-9-3 **95**..................(t) FrankieDettori 10 102
(John Gosden) *str; gd-bodied; looked wl; trckd ldr for 2f then led: pushed along to maintain short ld 2f out: rdn and hdd by wnr fnl 100yds: kpt on* **7/1**[3]
414- **3** *hd* **Koeman**[267] 5990 5-8-13 **91**......................... DavidEgan 7 97
(Mick Channon) *racd in midfield: hdwy u.p 2f out: rdn and styd on wl ins fnl f: nrst fin* **20/1**
2050 **4** *nk* **Fire Fighting (IRE)**[11] 2032 8-9-2 **94**......................... AdamKirby 9 99
(Mark Johnston) *hld up in last: pushed along 4f out: rdn and mde gd late hdwy ins fnl f: nrst fin* **33/1**
121- **5** *2* **Spirit Ridge**[208] 8081 4-9-0 **92**......................... JimCrowley 8 94
(Amanda Perrett) *tall; athletic; settled wl in 4th: pushed along and outpcd over 3f out: sn rdn and no immediate rspnse: kpt on one pce fnl f* **10/3**[2]
30-6 **6** *nk* **Shailene (IRE)**[16] 1927 4-9-1 **93**......................... OisinMurphy 2 95
(Andrew Balding) *trckd ldr: rdn and ev ch 2f out: sn outpcd and jst kpt on one pce fnl f* **7/1**[3]
20-0 **7** *1/2* **Hochfeld (IRE)**[15] 1947 5-9-9 **101**......................... JoeFanning 4 102
(Mark Johnston) *led for 2f then trckd ldr: niggled along 4f out: rdn and outpcd 3f out: kpt on again for press fr 1f out* **9/1**
6-01 **8** *1 3/4* **New Show (IRE)**[6] 2209 4-8-12 **90** 5ex..................(v[1]) JamieSpencer 1 88
(Michael Bell) *hld up in last pair: rdn along and little rspnse 3f out: nvr able to get on terms* **12/1**
120- **9** *3 3/4* **Melting Dew**[254] 6501 5-9-10 **102**......................... RyanMoore 5 94
(Sir Michael Stoute) *racd in midfield: rdn along and lost pl 3f out: sn bhd* **11/1**

2m 34.08s (1.58) **Going Correction** +0.125s/f (Good) **9 Ran SP% 112.6**
Speed ratings (Par 109): **99,98,98,98,97 96,96,95,92**
CSF £17.89 CT £244.07 TOTE £2.70: £1.30, £1.60, £4.90; EX 10.90 Trifecta £162.90.
Owner Mohammed Bin Hamad Khalifa Al Attiya **Bred** S C E A Haras De Saint Pair Et Al **Trained** Middleham Moor, N Yorks

FOCUS
Stands' side course. Stalls: centre. The going was given as good, good to firm in places (GoingStick 8.1. Stands' side 8.1; Centre 8.4; Far side 7.9) but the consensus from those involved in the opener was that it was good to firm, David Egan saying: "It's nice, quick ground." and Frankie Dettori adding: "Good to firm." Add 12yds. A good handicap, but the early pace wasn't that strong and they finished in a bit of a heap.

2441 CHARM SPIRIT DAHLIA STKS (GROUP 2) (F&M) 1m 1f
2:20 (2:36) (Class 1) 4-Y-O+ **£56,710** (£21,500; £10,760; £5,360; £2,690) **Stalls** Centre

Form RPR
114- **1** **Worth Waiting**[231] 7349 4-9-0 105......................... JamesDoyle 2 111
(David Lanigan) *trckd ldr: qcknd wl to ld over 3f out: rdn and in command over 1f out: kpt on wl ins fnl f* **3/1**[2]
532- **2** *1* **Nyaleti (IRE)**[182] 8867 4-9-0 109......................... JoeFanning 3 109
(Mark Johnston) *led: pushed along and hdd by wnr over 3f out: rdn and outpcd over 2f out: kpt on wl again for press ins fnl f* **11/2**
445- **3** *3 1/4* **Billesdon Brook**[211] 7982 4-9-0 115......................... SeanLevey 6 102
(Richard Hannon) *hld up in last and racd a little keenly: rdn and outpcd by wnr over 2f out: late hdwy into 3rd wl ins fnl f* **7/2**[3]
316- **4** *nse* **Veracious**[211] 7982 4-9-0 110......................... RyanMoore 4 102+
(Sir Michael Stoute) *looked wl; settled wl bhd ldr: effrt under hands and heels to chse wnr over 2f out: unable to match pce of wnr 1f out: pushed out fnl f* **5/4**[1]
51-0 **5** *3* **Rasima**[16] 1918 4-9-0 102......................... DavidEgan 1 95
(Roger Varian) *settled in 4th: rdn along and outpcd 3f out: sn dropped to last and wknd fnl f (vet said filly lost its right fore shoe)* **16/1**

1m 51.27s (0.17) **Going Correction** +0.125s/f (Good) **5 Ran SP% 112.9**
Speed ratings (Par 115): **104,103,100,100,97**
CSF £19.14 TOTE £3.50: £1.70, £2.50; EX 18.60 Trifecta £41.70.
Owner Saif Ali **Bred** Whatton Manor Stud **Trained** Newmarket, Suffolk

FOCUS
Run at an ordinary gallop, no more, the first two home were in the front pair from an early stage. They raced centre-field.

2442 LONGHOLES H'CAP 6f
2:55 (3:04) (Class 2) 4-Y-O+
£31,125 (£9,320; £4,660; £2,330; £1,165; £585) **Stalls** Centre

Form RPR
2312 **1** **On The Warpath**[17] 1891 4-9-3 **102**......................... WilliamBuick 5 115
(Charlie Appleby) *led gp on far side and travelled wl: qcknd to ld overall over 2f out: sn in command 1f out: pushed out fnl f: comf* **9/4**[1]
30-2 **2** *3* **Summerghand (IRE)**[19] 1829 5-9-1 **100**......................... DavidNolan 4 103
(David O'Meara) *racd in rr: hdwy u.p 2f out: rdn and styd on wl in battle for 2nd ins fnl f* **6/1**[3]
24-1 **3** *shd* **Flavius Titus**[19] 1829 4-8-10 **95**......................... DavidEgan 7 98
(Roger Varian) *trckd ldr: effrt to chse wnr over 2f out: sn rdn and kpt on wl fr 1f out: jst lost out in battle for 2nd* **5/1**[2]
300- **4** *1 3/4* **Victory Angel (IRE)**[191] 8594 5-8-8 **93**......................... HarryBentley 8 90
(Robert Cowell) *on toes; hld up in nrside gp: smooth hdwy to chse wnr over 2f out: rdn and drifted rt u.p over 1f out: one pce fnl f* **18/1**
010- **5** *2* **Gunmetal (IRE)**[225] 7512 6-9-5 **104**......................... JoeFanning 3 95
(David Barron) *trckd wnr: pushed along and outpcd by wnr 2f out: rdn and styd on one pce fnl f* **8/1**
0043 **6** *1* **Giogiobbo**[16] 1916 6-8-7 **92**..................(tp) EoinWalsh 2 80
(Nick Littmoden) *trckd wnr: rdn along and outpcd over 2f out: one pce fnl f* **50/1**
140- **7** *2* **Hart Stopper**[194] 8503 5-8-3 **88**..................(t) HayleyTurner 10 69
(Stuart Williams) *hld up in rr of nrside gp: rdn and detached 3f out: sme late hdwy passed btn rivals* **40/1**
5-66 **8** *1 1/4* **Gifted Master (IRE)**[18] 1853 6-9-10 **109**..................(b) JamesDoyle 9 86
(Hugo Palmer) *led tl rdn along and hdd over 2f out: wknd fr over 1f out (jockey said gelding stopped quickly)* **7/1**
141- **9** *1/2* **Lady Dancealot (IRE)**[180] 8892 4-8-3 **88** ow1......... SilvestreDeSousa 6 64
(David Elsworth) *racd in midfield: rdn along and outpcd over 2f out: plugged on one pce fnl f* **7/1**
4-05 **10** *1/2* **Haddaf (IRE)**[17] 1892 4-8-5 **90**......................... RaulDaSilva 11 64
(Robert Cowell) *hld up: rdn and no imp over 2f out: sn wknd and bhd* **25/1**

1m 10.66s (-1.24) **Going Correction** +0.125s/f (Good) **10 Ran SP% 111.3**
Speed ratings (Par 109): **113,109,108,106,103 102,99,98,97,96**
CSF £14.56 CT £57.77 TOTE £2.80: £1.50, £2.00, £1.20; EX 13.70 Trifecta £46.50.
Owner Godolphin **Bred** Sahara Group & Eurowest Bloodstock **Trained** Newmarket, Suffolk

FOCUS
They split into two groups of five and raced slightly apart up the centre of the track. The first two came from the far-side group, and there was a clear-cut winner.

2443 QIPCO 1000 GUINEAS STKS (GROUP 1) (BRITISH CHAMPIONS SERIES) (FILLIES) 1m
3:35 (3:39) (Class 1) 3-Y-O
£283,550 (£107,500; £53,800; £26,800; £13,450; £6,750) **Stalls** Centre

Form RPR
122- **1** **Hermosa (IRE)**[189] 8668 3-9-0 110......................... WayneLordan 4 113
(A P O'Brien, Ire) *mde all: niggled along to maintain short ld over 2f out: rdn over 1f out: drvn and responded generously to press ins fnl f: drvn out* **14/1**
26-1 **2** *1* **Lady Kaya (IRE)**[29] 1601 3-9-0 110......................... RobbieColgan 8 111+
(Ms Sheila Lavery, Ire) *trckd wnr and travelled strly thrght: effrt to cl on wnr over 1f out: drvn and ev ch fnl f: kpt on but unable to match wnr clsng stages* **11/1**
1-1 **3** *nk* **Qabala (USA)**[19] 1832 3-9-0 109......................... DavidEgan 6 110+
(Roger Varian) *looked wl; hld up in rr of midfield: hdwy u.p 3f out: swtchd wdst of all and rdn wl over 1f out: styd on wl fnl f: nt rch wnr* **7/2**[1]
02-3 **4** *hd* **Angel's Hideaway (IRE)**[19] 1832 3-9-0 105......................... RobertHavlin 7 109
(John Gosden) *settled wl in tch: pushed along and almost upsides wnr 2f out: rdn and ev ch 1f out: kpt on one pce* **33/1**
311- **5** *3/4* **Fairyland (IRE)**[218] 7771 3-9-0 112......................... FrankieDettori 1 108
(A P O'Brien, Ire) *looked wl; racd in midfield: effrt to chse wnr wl over 2f out: drvn along over 1f out: no ex fnl f* **15/2**
014- **6** *nk* **Just Wonderful (USA)**[184] 8819 3-9-0 111......................... RyanMoore 15 107
(A P O'Brien, Ire) *looked wl; hld up in rr: hdwy under hands and heels between rivals 3f out: rdn and wandered u.p over 1f out: kpt on wl fnl f: nrst fin* **13/2**[3]
11-2 **7** *nk* **Iconic Choice**[22] 1751 3-9-0 107......................... RichardKingscote 9 106
(Tom Dascombe) *racd in midfield: drvn and reminders 3f out: wandered arnd u.str.p 2f out: kpt on fnl f* **25/1**
31-3 **8** *shd* **Iridessa (IRE)**[29] 1601 3-9-0 112......................... DonnachaO'Brien 3 106
(Joseph Patrick O'Brien, Ire) *str; trckd wnr: rdn along to chse wnr over 2f out: kpt on one pce ins fnl f* **6/1**[2]
10-4 **9** *3 1/2* **Look Around**[19] 1832 3-9-0 98......................... OisinMurphy 10 98
(Andrew Balding) *racd in rr of midfield: pushed along 1/2-way: drvn and no imp 2f out: wknd fnl f* **33/1**
12-1 **10** *nk* **Dandhu**[22] 1751 3-9-0 108......................... GeraldMosse 14 97
(David Elsworth) *restrained in last: minor hdwy u.p 3f out: sn rdn and little rspnse: kpt on passed btn horses fnl f* **16/1**
23-4 **11** *2* **Star Terms**[22] 1751 3-9-0 107......................... JamesDoyle 5 93
(Richard Hannon) *trckd wnr: drvn along and outpcd over 2f out: wknd fnl f* **14/1**
61- **12** *1 1/2* **Garrel Glen**[193] 8547 3-9-0 0......................... JFEgan 13 89
(Mark H Tompkins) *racd keenly in rr: rdn and outpcd 3f out: nvr on terms* **100/1**
11-2 **13** *nk* **Mot Juste (USA)**[19] 1832 3-9-0 103......................... WilliamBuick 2 89
(Roger Varian) *racd promly: pushed along and lost pl 3f out: hmpd and lost grnd over 2f out: sn bhd and struggling* **16/1**
111- **14** *1/2* **Skitter Scatter (USA)**[231] 7343 3-9-0 114......................... RonanWhelan 11 87
(John M Oxx, Ire) *leggy; settled wl in tch: rdn and little rspnse 3f out: sn lost pl (jockey said filly stopped quickly)* **7/1**
031- **15** *nk* **Fleeting (IRE)**[234] 7199 3-9-0 106......................... SeamieHeffernan 12 87
(A P O'Brien, Ire) *racd in midfield: rdn along and lost pl over 3f out: sn bhd* **20/1**

1m 36.89s (-1.51) **Going Correction** +0.125s/f (Good) **15 Ran SP% 123.0**
Speed ratings (Par 110): **112,111,110,110,109 109,109,109,105,105 103,101,101,100,100**
CSF £154.34 CT £670.75 TOTE £16.00: £4.30, £4.20, £1.70; EX 202.50 Trifecta £1448.30.
Owner Michael Tabor & Derrick Smith & Mrs John Magnier **Bred** Beauty Is Truth Syndicate **Trained** Cashel, Co Tipperary

FOCUS
An open edition of the race, they went a decent clip courtesy of the winner yet finished in a bit of a bunch, suggesting there weren't any superstars on show. Little got into it from off the pace, as can be the case in a fast-ground Guineas, and those racing prominently more towards the far side of the group were seen to best effect.

2444 HOT STREAK MAIDEN STKS (PLUS 10 RACE) 5f
4:10 (4:10) (Class 3) 2-Y-O £7,762 (£2,310; £1,154; £577) Stalls Centre

Form RPR

1 **Threat (IRE)** 2-9-5 0 ... TomMarquand 1 96+
(Richard Hannon) *str; trckd ldr: effrt to ld 2f out: sn rdn and drifted lft u.p: wl on top 1f out and pushed out fnl f* 10/1[3]

2 2 2 1/4 **Electrical Storm**[17] 1887 2-9-5 0 ... RyanMoore 2 88
(Saeed bin Suroor) *trckd ldr: pushed along to chse wnr 2f out: sn rdn and unable to match pce of wnr 1f out: kpt on* 2/5[1]

3 3 1/4 **Path Of Thunder (IRE)** 2-9-5 0 ... WilliamBuick 3 78+
(Charlie Appleby) *compact; dwlt sltly and rn green: pushed along in rr 1/2-way: mde sme late hdwy under hands and heels fnl f: bttr for run* 10/3[2]

4 10 **Spanish Angel (IRE)** 2-9-5 0 ... OisinMurphy 4 40
(Andrew Balding) *leggy; led: rdn along and hdd by wnr 2f out: wknd fnl f* 22/1

59.9s (0.80) **Going Correction** +0.125s/f (Good) 4 Ran SP% 107.9
Speed ratings (Par 97): **98,94,89,73**
CSF £15.19 TOTE £9.40; EX 15.50 Trifecta £18.20.

Owner Cheveley Park Stud **Bred** La Lumiere Partnership **Trained** East Everleigh, Wilts

FOCUS
Just the four runners but an interesting little maiden, and the winner impressed in getting off the mark first time out.

2445 TWEENHILLS PRETTY POLLY STKS (LISTED RACE) (FILLIES) 1m 2f
4:45 (4:46) (Class 1) 3-Y-O
£28,355 (£10,750; £5,380; £2,680; £1,345; £675) Stalls Centre

Form RPR

23-1 1 **Maqsad (FR)**[19] 1828 3-9-0 92 ... JimCrowley 4 111+
(William Haggas) *looked wl; hld up: clsd travelling strly to ld over 2f out: readily asserted and sn clr over 1f out: nudged out: easily* 5/4[1]

140- 2 5 **Shambolic (IRE)**[190] 8663 3-9-0 100 ... FrankieDettori 1 101
(John Gosden) *led: rdn along and readily brushed aside by wnr 2f out: kpt on one pce for remote 2nd ins fnl f* 4/1[3]

23-6 3 4 **I'll Have Another (IRE)**[19] 1831 3-9-3 97 ... SilvestreDeSousa 5 96
(Mark Johnston) *trckd ldr: rdn to chal over 2f out: sn readily outpcd by wnr: wknd fnl f* 12/1

21- 4 11 **Lady Adelaide (IRE)**[172] 9048 3-9-0 0 ... JasonWatson 7 71
(Roger Charlton) *racd in midfield: rdn and outpcd 3f out: plugged on for poor remote 4th* 8/1

0- 5 1/2 **Mona Lisa's Smile (USA)**[192] 8583 3-9-0 76 ... RyanMoore 3 70
(A P O'Brien, Ire) *hld up: pushed along 4f out: rdn and readily outpcd 3f out: sn bhd* 20/1

641- 6 4 **Shagalla**[169] 9130 3-9-0 75 ... (b) DavidEgan 2 62
(Roger Varian) *trckd ldr: rdn and lost pl 3f out: sn struggling and bhd 2f out* 33/1

1- 7 20 **Clematis (USA)**[157] 9314 3-9-0 0 ... JamesDoyle 6 22
(Charles Hills) *str; hld up: smooth hdwy to chal 3f out: rdn and lost pl 2f out: heavily eased fnl f (jockey said filly stopped quickly; post-race examination during routine testing, revealed the filly to be very tired and to have recovered slowly)* 7/2[2]

2m 5.23s (-0.17) **Going Correction** +0.125s/f (Good) 7 Ran SP% 113.2
Speed ratings (Par 104): **105,101,97,89,88 85,69**
CSF £6.35 TOTE £2.10: £1.50, £2.10; EX 6.90 Trifecta £31.70.

Owner Hamdan Al Maktoum **Bred** Dayton Investments Limited **Trained** Newmarket, Suffolk

FOCUS
They finished well strung out behind the impressive winner, who proved a class or two above her rivals.

2446 QIPCO SUPPORTING BRITISH RACING H'CAP 1m 2f
5:20 (5:20) (Class 3) (0-95,96) 3-Y-O £12,938 (£3,850; £1,924; £962) Stalls Centre

Form RPR

103- 1 **Nayef Road (IRE)**[193] 8550 3-9-9 **96** ... SilvestreDeSousa 5 107
(Mark Johnston) *trckd ld for 1f then mde rest: effrt to extend ld 2f out: pushed along to ld by 4 l 1f out: pushed out fnl f: comf* 9/4[1]

53-1 2 5 **Fraser Island (IRE)**[18] 1845 3-8-10 **83** ... JoeFanning 2 84
(Mark Johnston) *settled in 3rd: drvn along to chse ldr over 2f out: kpt on wl enough u.p fnl f but no match for wnr* 3/1[3]

11-3 3 3 **Never Do Nothing (IRE)**[19] 1835 3-8-10 **83** ... OisinMurphy 1 78
(Andrew Balding) *looked wl; led for 1f then trckd wnr: effrt to chse wnr over 2f out: rdn and no imp over 1f out: one pce fnl f* 11/4[2]

01-0 4 2 1/2 **Shir Khan**[24] 1713 3-8-13 **86** ... RaulDaSilva 3 76
(Paul Cole) *hld up in last pair in tch: rdn and outpcd by wnr over 2f out: sn drvn and no imp 1f out: kpt on* 10/1

313- 5 13 **Aspire Tower (IRE)**[176] 8994 3-9-1 **88** ... JimCrowley 4 52
(Steve Gollings) *hld up: effrt to cl in last 3f out: sn rdn and little rspnse 2f out: wknd fnl f* 9/2

2m 4.91s (-0.49) **Going Correction** +0.125s/f (Good) 5 Ran SP% 109.7
Speed ratings (Par 103): **106,102,99,97,87**
CSF £9.18 TOTE £3.10: £1.60, £1.80; EX 9.00 Trifecta £16.40.

Owner Mohamed Obaida **Bred** B V Sangster **Trained** Middleham Moor, N Yorks

FOCUS
Traditionally a good 3yo handicap, but there was little depth to it this time around. Still, it was a smart effort from the 96-rated winner.

T/Jkpt: Part won. £44,984.30 to a £1 stake. Pool: £63,358.24 - 0.50 winning units. T/Plt: £799.40 to a £1 stake. Pool: £169,988.28 - 155.23 winning units T/Qpdt: £109.60 to a £1 stake. Pool: £15,777.05 - 106.46 winning units **Mark Grantham**

2447 - 2450a (Foreign Racing) - See Raceform Interactive

1667 GOWRAN PARK (R-H)
Sunday, May 5

OFFICIAL GOING: Yielding (good in places)

2451a IRISH STALLION FARMS EBF VICTOR MCCALMONT MEMORIAL STKS (LISTED RACE) (F&M) 1m 1f 100y
3:55 (3:55) 3-Y-O+ £29,234 (£9,414; £4,459; £1,981; £990)

RPR

1 **Who's Steph (IRE)**[28] 1620 4-9-9 108 ... ColinKeane 5 109+
(G M Lyons, Ire) *cl up tl sn led and mde rest: over 1 l clr at 1/2-way: stl travelling wl over 2f out and sn extended advantage: in command under hands and heels far side ent fnl f: eased nr fin: v easily* 2/7[1]

2 8 **Moteo (IRE)**[196] 8439 4-9-9 93 ... NGMcCullagh 2 91
(John M Oxx, Ire) *hld up bhd ldrs in 4th: impr into 3rd after 1/2-way: drvn into st and no imp on easy wnr u.p nr side under 2f out: impr into mod 2nd ins fnl f and kpt on one pce* 10/1[3]

3 1 3/4 **Credenza (IRE)**[7] 2157 3-8-9 96 ... MichaelHussey 3 85
(A P O'Brien, Ire) *led briefly tl sn hdd and settled bhd ldr in 2nd: rdn in 2nd over 3f out and no imp on easy wnr u.p nr side 1 1/2f out: dropped to mod 3rd ins fnl f and kpt on one pce* 4/1[2]

4 3 **Shekiba (IRE)**[15] 1961 4-9-9 92 ... GaryCarroll 4 81
(Joseph G Murphy, Ire) *w.w in rr of quintet: sme hdwy nr side 2f out: sn rdn in 4th and no imp on easy wnr u.p nr side 1 1/2f out: one pce fnl f* 20/1

5 3 1/2 **Coeur D'amour (IRE)**[574] 7859 4-9-9 97 ... WJLee 6 74
(Madeleine Tylicki, Ire) *chsd ldrs in 3rd tl dropped to 4th after 1/2-way: pushed along over 2f out and sn no imp on easy wnr in rr: wknd* 25/1

2m 3.24s (-3.76) 5 Ran SP% 115.5
WFA 3 from 4yo+ 14lb
CSF £4.84 TOTE £1.20: £1.02, £3.80; DF 3.30 Trifecta £6.60.
Owner George Strawbridge **Bred** Patrick Headon **Trained** Dunsany, Co Meath

FOCUS
A facile victory for the favourite as she proved way too good for these rivals.

2452 - 2454a (Foreign Racing) - See Raceform Interactive

1990 COLOGNE (R-H)
Sunday, May 5

OFFICIAL GOING: Turf: good

2455a CARL JASPERS-PREIS (FORMERLY THE GERLING-PREIS) (GROUP 2) (4YO+) (TURF) 1m 4f
3:40 4-Y-O+ £36,036 (£13,963; £7,207; £3,603; £2,252)

RPR

1 **French King**[71] 894 4-9-0 0 ... OlivierPeslier 3 112
(H-A Pantall, France) *racd keenly: led under restraint tl hdd after 1f: remained cl up tl shuffled bk 3 1/2f fr home: qckly rcvrd grnd in st: drvn to chal 2f out: led ent fnl 1 1/2f and styd on: drvn out* 29/10[1]

2 3/4 **Be My Sheriff (GER)**[14] 5-9-0 0 ... FilipMinarik 7 111
(Henk Grewe, Germany) *led after 1f: c towards' stands' side st w all but one of the field: drvn whn chal 2f out: hdd ent fnl 1 1/2f: styd on gamely but a hld by wnr* 41/10[3]

3 3/4 **Windstoss (GER)**[165] 5-9-2 0 ... AdriedeVries 5 112
(Markus Klug, Germany) *w.w in rr: shkn up and hdwy over 2f out: chsd ldng pair into fnl f: no further imp last 125yds* 5/1

4 1 3/4 **Alounak (FR)**[14] 4-9-0 0 ... AntoineHamelin 4 107
(Waldemar Hickst, Germany) *racd keenly: restrained in share of 2nd: outpcd and rousted along 2 1/2f fr home: styd on again over 1f out: run flattened out fnl 100yds* 7/2[2]

5 2 3/4 **Colomano**[308] 4444 5-9-0 0 ... MartinSeidl 1 102
(Markus Klug, Germany) *racd in fnl pair: rdn to cl 2 1/2f out: nt more prog last 1 1/2f* 97/10

6 nk **Walsingham (GER)**[196] 8463 5-9-2 0 ... AndraschStarke 6 104
(P Schiergen, Germany) *racd in midfield on outer: rdn and one pce 2f out: nvr in contention* 41/10[3]

7 24 **Khan (GER)**[35] 5-9-4 0 ... (p) MichaelCadeddu 2 68
(Henk Grewe, Germany) *settled midfield on inner: prog to chse ldr 3 1/2f out: styd alone on ins rail turning into home st: lost tch u.p ins fnl 2f* 171/10

2m 31.62s (-1.28) 7 Ran SP% 118.6
PARI-MUTUEL (all including 10 euro stake): WIN 39 PLACE: 24, 28; SF: 16.60.
Owner H H Sheikh Abdulla Bin Khalifa Al Thani **Bred** Umm Qarn Farms **Trained** France

2456 - 2467a (Foreign Racing) - See Raceform Interactive

2274 BATH (L-H)
Monday, May 6

OFFICIAL GOING: Firm (9.3)
Wind: light across Weather: sunny periods

2468 EMPIRE FIGHTING CHANCE H'CAP 1m 3f 137y
2:15 (2:15) (Class 6) (0-65,65) 4-Y-O+
£3,105 (£924; £461; £300; £300; £300) Stalls Low

Form RPR

2003 1 **Gendarme (IRE)**[5] 2279 4-9-7 **65** ... (b[1]) RossaRyan 6 72
(Alexandra Dunn) *trckd ldr: upsides and travelling strly 3f out: led wl over 1f out: drifted lft: kpt on wl: rdn out* 9/4[1]

0005 2 1 1/2 **Agent Gibbs**[5] 2279 7-9-7 **65** ... (p) ShaneKelly 1 70
(John O'Shea) *sn led: rdn and hdd wl over 1f out: swtchd rt: styd on same pce* 4/1[2]

0460 3 3 1/4 **Butterfield (IRE)**[36] 1463 6-8-10 **54** ... (p[1]) FrannyNorton 9 53
(Tony Carroll) *trckd ldrs: rdn 3f out: styd on same pce fnl 2f* 4/1[2]

1-04 4 1/2 **Millie May**[34] 1498 5-8-3 **47** ... JimmyQuinn 7 46
(Jimmy Fox) *in tch: rdn over 2f out: styd on fr over 1f out but nt pce to get on terms* 12/1

560 5 1 1/2 **Dimmesdale**[42] 1331 4-9-0 **58** ... LiamJones 4 54
(John O'Shea) *hld up towards rr: rdn over 2f out: little imp tl styd on ins fnl f* 18/1

400/ **6** *1 ¼* **Cougar Kid (IRE)**[15] 4967 8-7-13 **46** oh1......................(p) JaneElliott(3) 2 40
(John O'Shea) *hld up towards rr: rdn over 2f out: styd on fnl f: nvr trbld ldrs* **12/1**

460- **7** *hd* **General Brook (IRE)**[232] 7328 9-9-4 **65**..........................(h) WilliamCox(3) 8 59
(John O'Shea) *trckd ldrs: rdn over 2f out: fdd fnl f* **16/1**

-504 **8** *2 ¾* **Roc Astrale (IRE)**[5] 2301 5-8-10 **61**......................(tp) GraceMcEntee(7) 3 50
(Phil McEntee) *hld up: racing keenly and hdwy into midfield after 4f: rdn over 2f out: wknd over 1f out (jockey said gelding clipped heels approximately 1 mile out)* **5/1**[3]

400- **9** *34* **Another Go (IRE)**[14] 9687 6-9-2 **60**.................................. DavidProbert 5
(Ralph J Smith) *in tch: slipped leaving bk st: rdn 3f out: wknd qckly (jockey said gelding slipped entering the final bend)* **25/1**

2m 28.56s (-2.24) **Going Correction** -0.15s/f (Firm) 9 Ran SP% **117.8**
Speed ratings (Par 101): **101,100,97,97,96 95,95,93,71**
CSF £11.46 CT £34.16 TOTE £3.40: £2.50, £1.40, £1.60; EX 10.90 Trifecta £42.30.

Owner Helium Racing Ltd **Bred** Gillian, Lady Howard De Walden **Trained** West Buckland, Somerset

FOCUS
The rail was out between the 4f and 3f marker. An ordinary handicap, run at a sound pace. Only two mattered from a long way out. Add 5yds.

2469 CB PROTECTION NOVICE MEDIAN AUCTION STKS (PLUS 10 RACE) 5f 10y
2:50 (2:52) (Class 4) 2-Y-O **£4,787** (£1,424; £711; £355) **Stalls** Centre

Form RPR
0322 **1** **Heer We Go Again**[9] 2108 2-9-5 0..............................(v1) RossaRyan 6 75
(David Evans) *mde all: kpt on wl: unchal* **6/5**[1]

4 **2** *4* **Forced**[34] 1493 2-9-0 0.. ShaneKelly 1 56
(Richard Hughes) *sn trcking wnr: rdn over 2f out: kpt on but nt pce to chal* **3/1**[2]

3 *4 ½* **Perregrin** 2-9-5 0.. FrannyNorton 2 44+
(Mark Johnston) *outpcd in last pair after 1f: hdwy over 1f out: chsd ldng pair ent fnl f but nt pce to get on terms* **8/1**

0 **4** *2 ¾* **Show Me Heaven**[24] 1733 2-8-9 0.......................... RyanWhile(5) 3 30+
(Bill Turner) *s.i.s: outpcd in last: kpt on into 4th ent fnl f: n.d* **25/1**

5 **5** *6* **Ride And Prejudice**[16] 1937 2-9-0 0.......................... HectorCrouch 5 8
(Julia Feilden) *chsd wnr: rdn over 2f out: wknd over 1f out* **22/1**

3 **6** *½* **Elevate Her (IRE)**[7] 2191 2-9-0 0.......................... NicolaCurrie 7 6
(Richard Spencer) *chsd wnr: rdn over 2f out: wknd over 1f out* **7/2**[3]

1m 2.04s (0.04) **Going Correction** -0.15s/f (Firm) 6 Ran SP% **112.0**
Speed ratings (Par 95): **93,86,79,75,65 64**
CSF £5.00 TOTE £2.10: £1.60, £1.60; EX 5.70 Trifecta £17.30.

Owner Power Geneva Ltd & Partner **Bred** Dalwhinnie Bloodstock **Trained** Pandy, Monmouths

FOCUS
A modest 2yo novice event.

2470 F45 BATH TRAINING GUARANTEED RESULTS H'CAP 1m 2f 37y
3:25 (3:25) (Class 4) (0-85,82) 3-Y-O **£5,387** (£1,612; £806; £403; £300) **Stalls** Low

Form RPR
103- **1** **Sky Defender**[187] 8732 3-9-7 **82**.............................. FrannyNorton 4 87
(Mark Johnston) *led: narrowly hdd over 2f out: sn rdn: led jst over 1f out: styd on wl to assert ins fnl f* **11/8**[1]

04-5 **2** *2* **Entertaining (IRE)**[18] 1886 3-9-1 **76**.......................... SeanLevey 5 78
(Richard Hannon) *trckd wnr: tk narrow advantage over 2f out: sn rdn: hdd jst over 1f out: styd on but no ex ins fnl f* **7/2**[2]

46-0 **3** *5* **Greeley (IRE)**[21] 1823 3-9-0 **75**.......................... RobHornby 3 66
(Rod Millman) *trckd ldrs: rdn 3f out: kpt on fnl 2f but nt pce to chal* **11/2**

210 **4** *½* **Ragnar**[21] 1824 3-9-4 **79**.. JasonWatson 2 69
(Daniele Camuffo) *trckd ldrs: rdn 3f out: kpt on fnl 2f but nt pce to chal* **5/1**

-314 **5** *½* **Boutonniere (USA)**[19] 1845 3-9-2 **77**.......................... DavidProbert 1 66
(Andrew Balding) *trckd ldrs: rdn over 2f out: kpt on same pce* **9/2**[3]

2m 8.69s (-2.41) **Going Correction** -0.15s/f (Firm) 5 Ran SP% **114.6**
Speed ratings (Par 101): **103,101,97,97,96**
CSF £6.83 TOTE £2.20: £2.00, £2.30; EX 6.90 Trifecta £24.10.

Owner Hamad Rashed Bin Ghedayer **Bred** Rabbah Bloodstock Limited **Trained** Middleham Moor, N Yorks

FOCUS
Not a bad little 3yo handicap. Add 5yds. The form is possibly a bit better than rated.

2471 F45 BATH 8 WEEK CHALLENGE H'CAP 1m 2f 37y
4:00 (4:00) (Class 5) (0-70,70) 4-Y-O+
£3,752 (£1,116; £557; £300; £300; £300) **Stalls** Low

Form RPR
03-2 **1** **Simbirsk**[28] 1653 4-9-7 **70**.. ShaneKelly 7 75
(John O'Shea) *chsd ldrs: led over 2f out: sn rdn: kpt on wl and a holding on fnl f* **3/1**[2]

300- **2** *nk* **Champs De Reves**[227] 7491 4-9-6 **69**.......................... DavidProbert 1 73
(Michael Blake) *in tch: hdwy over 2f out: sn rdn: kpt on fnl f and clsng on wnr at fin but a being hld* **4/1**[3]

560 **3** *5* **Zephyros (GER)**[16] 1936 8-8-12 **61**.......................... JimmyQuinn 3 55
(David Bridgwater) *in tch: hdwy over 2f out: sn rdn: kpt on same pce fr over 1f out* **11/2**

0000 **4** *5* **The Eagle's Nest (IRE)**[26] 1675 5-8-6 **55**............(tp) JosephineGordon 6 39
(Alexandra Dunn) *s.i.s: sn chsng ldrs: rdn over 2f out: nt quite pce to chal: fdd fnl f* **9/2**

1115 **5** *7* **Contingency Fee**[4] 2345 4-8-11 **67**......................(p) GraceMcEntee(7) 8 37
(Phil McEntee) *pressed ldr tl rdn over 2f out: wknd over 1f out* **2/1**[1]

6200 **6** *19* **One Liner**[13] 2012 5-7-13 **51** oh6.............................. JaneElliott(3) 2
(John O'Shea) *led: rdn and hdd over 2f out: wknd over 1f out* **28/1**

2m 7.63s (-3.47) **Going Correction** -0.15s/f (Firm) 6 Ran SP% **115.3**
Speed ratings (Par 103): **107,106,102,98,93 77**
CSF £15.86 CT £62.09 TOTE £2.80: £1.60, £2.00; EX 17.70 Trifecta £57.60.

Owner S G Martin And The Cross Racing Club **Bred** Exors Of The Late Sir Eric Parker **Trained** Elton, Gloucs

FOCUS
This run-of-mill handicap was run at a fair gallop and all six held a chance of sorts in the home straight. Add 5yds. The winner has been rated in line with the better view of his 3yo form.

2472 F45 BATH GROUP TRAINING, LIFE CHANGING H'CAP 1m
4:35 (4:35) (Class 4) (0-80,80) 4-Y-O+
£5,322 (£1,593; £796; £398; £300; £300) **Stalls** Low

Form RPR
3-16 **1** **Mr Tyrrell (IRE)**[16] 1955 5-9-7 **80**.. SeanLevey 1 91
(Richard Hannon) *trckd ldrs: led wl over 1f out: rdn clr fnl f: comf (trainer's rep said regarding apparent improvement in form that the gelding may have been affected by banging its head in the stalls at Nottingham)* **6/1**

0-30 **2** *6* **Handytalk (IRE)**[9] 2107 6-9-3 **76**..............................(b1) RobHornby 5 73
(Rod Millman) *chsd ldrs: rdn over 2f out: kpt on to chse wnr ent fnl f: a being comf hld* **13/2**

303- **3** *½* **Cogital**[182] 8885 4-8-11 **70**..............................(h) RichardKingscote 3 66
(Amanda Perrett) *hld up: hdwy over 2f out: sn rdn: kpt on fr over 1f out but nvr gng pce to get on terms: wnt 3rd jst ins fnl f* **15/8**[1]

2144 **4** *1 ¾* **Oneovdem**[38] 1395 5-9-4 **77**.. MartinDwyer 4 69
(Tim Pinfield) *pressed ldr: rdn over 2f out: kpt on tl no ex ent fnl f* **5/1**[3]

20-0 **5** *2 ½* **Mister Musicmaster**[5] 2277 10-8-7 **66**.......................... DavidProbert 2 52
(Ron Hodges) *hld up: effrt over 2f out: nt pce to threaten: fdd fnl f* **12/1**

3656 **6** *4 ½* **Scofflaw**[17] 1925 5-9-2 **75**..............................(b1) RossaRyan 6 51
(David Evans) *racd freely: led: 4 l clr 3f out: rdn and hdd wl over 1f out: sn wknd (jockey said gelding ran too freely)* **11/4**[2]

1m 38.71s (-2.99) **Going Correction** -0.15s/f (Firm) 6 Ran SP% **113.4**
Speed ratings (Par 105): **108,102,101,99,97 92**
CSF £43.23 TOTE £4.50: £2.40, £3.80; EX 43.70 Trifecta £146.20.

Owner Robert Tyrrell **Bred** Wardstown Stud Ltd **Trained** East Everleigh, Wilts

FOCUS
They didn't hang around in this modest handicap. Add 5yds.

2473 F45 BATH NO CONTRACT REQUIRED H'CAP 5f 10y
5:10 (5:11) (Class 6) (0-65,69) 4-Y-O+
£3,105 (£924; £461; £300; £300; £300) **Stalls** Centre

Form RPR
000- **1** **Spanish Star (IRE)**[185] 8802 4-9-2 **59**.......................... LiamKeniry 2 70
(Patrick Chamings) *s.i.s: in last trio: hdwy over 2f out: rdn to chal ent fnl f: led fnl 100yds: r.o* **14/1**

4-65 **2** *1 ½* **Powerful Dream (IRE)**[3] 2358 6-9-10 **67**..................(p) JasonWatson 5 73
(Ronald Harris) *in tch: hdwy over 2f out: sn rdn: led over 1f out: kpt on but no ex whn hdd fnl 100yds* **3/1**[2]

2-64 **3** *5* **David's Beauty (IRE)**[23] 1767 6-9-1 **58**..................(b) RobHornby 11 46
(Brian Baugh) *prom: rdn and ev ch over 1f out: no ex ent fnl f* **6/1**

0-00 **4** *½* **Tally's Song**[74] 834 6-8-2 **45**..............................(p) JimmyQuinn 6 31
(Grace Harris) *towards rr: rdn 2f out: prog ent fnl f: kpt on to go 4th fnl 120yds* **50/1**

000- **5** *1* **Aquadabra (IRE)**[196] 8482 4-8-8 **51**.......................... NicolaCurrie 1 33
(Christopher Mason) *chsd ldrs: rdn and ev ch over 1f out: no ex fnl f* **33/1**

-000 **6** *1 ¼* **Midnight Guest (IRE)**[7] 2206 4-9-6 **63**.......................... RossaRyan 4 41
(David Evans) *in tch: rdn over 2f out: nt pce to threaten* **16/1**

43-1 **7** *1 ½* **Coronation Cottage**[7] 2206 5-9-12 **69** 5ex.................... PatCosgrave 12 41
(Malcolm Saunders) *s.i.s: sn trcking ldrs: rdn over 2f out: wknd over 1f out (trainer said that the race may have come too soon for the mare having run 7 days previously)* **9/4**[1]

4064 **8** *nk* **Terri Rules (IRE)**[13] 2025 4-9-0 **57**.......................... HectorCrouch 9 28
(Julia Feilden) *s.i.s: a towards rr (trainer was informed that the filly could not run until the day after passing a stalls test)* **10/1**

2133 **9** *nk* **Fareeq**[13] 2010 5-9-7 **64**..............................(bt) RichardKingscote 8 34
(Charlie Wallis) *trckd ldrs: rdn over 2f out: wknd over 1f out* **9/1**

-605 **10** *hd* **Fethiye Boy**[62] 1023 5-9-3 **60**.......................... DavidProbert 7 29
(Ronald Harris) *led: rdn and hdd over 1f out: sn wknd (jockey said gelding hung right-handed)* **11/2**[3]

1m 1.25s (-0.75) **Going Correction** -0.15s/f (Firm) 10 Ran SP% **122.0**
Speed ratings (Par 101): **100,97,89,88,87 85,82,82,81,81**
CSF £58.56 CT £299.13 TOTE £13.70: £3.20, £1.50, £2.50; EX 105.10 Trifecta £839.80.

Owner Shirley Symonds & Fred Camis **Bred** David Webb **Trained** Baughurst, Hants

FOCUS
This teed up for the closers.

2474 AVON VALLEY CLEANING AND RESTORATION H'CAP 5f 160y
5:45 (5:45) (Class 6) (0-65,67) 3-Y-O
£3,105 (£924; £461; £300; £300; £300) **Stalls** Centre

Form RPR
0-25 **1** **Show Me The Bubbly**[35] 1475 3-9-12 **67**.......................... LiamJones 7 74
(John O'Shea) *in tch: hdwy over 2f out: tk narrow advantage over 1f out: strly pressed thrght fnl f: jst hld on* **12/1**

-400 **2** *shd* **Thegreyvtrain**[70] 906 3-8-9 **50**.......................... NicolaCurrie 6 57
(Ronald Harris) *led for over 1f: prom: rdn for str chal fr 2f out: ev ch thrght fnl f: jst hld* **25/1**

565- **3** *2* **Glamorous Crescent**[201] 8314 3-8-9 **50**.......................... JimmyQuinn 3 50
(Grace Harris) *s.i.s: bhd: hdwy 2f out: sn rdn: r.o wl fnl f but no threat to front pair (jockey said filly reared in the stalls)* **25/1**

3432 **4** *1 ¼* **Bequest**[5] 2276 3-9-7 **62**.. DavidProbert 9 58
(Ron Hodges) *trckd ldrs: rdn and ev ch over 1f out: cl 3rd but hld whn briefly tight for room ent fnl f: sn no ex* **6/4**[1]

5401 **5** *½* **Brother Bentley**[3] 2357 3-9-3 **58** 6ex..............................(b) JasonWatson 5 52
(Ronald Harris) *last pair: rdn and hdwy over 1f out: kpt on fnl f but nvr any threat* **9/2**[3]

-600 **6** *2 ¼* **North Korea (IRE)**[7] 2211 3-9-2 **57**.......................... LiamKeniry 4 44
(Brian Baugh) *trckd ldrs: rdn over 2f out: wknd ent fnl f* **20/1**

320 **7** *½* **Temple Of Wonder (IRE)**[11] 2063 3-9-7 **62**..........(p1) RichardKingscote 2 47
(Charlie Wallis) *in tch: outpcd 3f out: no threat after* **10/1**

4-24 **8** *¾* **Cobweb Catcher**[16] 1954 3-9-6 **61**.......................... RobHornby 1 44
(Rod Millman) *led after 1f: rdn and hdd over 1f out: sn wknd* **5/2**[2]

1m 11.2s (0.10) **Going Correction** -0.15s/f (Firm) 8 Ran SP% **116.0**
Speed ratings (Par 97): **93,92,90,88,87 84,84,83**
CSF £258.86 CT £7165.45 TOTE £12.80: £3.20, £5.70, £6.80; EX 145.20 Trifecta £2644.60.

Owner A Cooke And The Cross Racing Club **Bred** D J And Mrs Deer **Trained** Elton, Gloucs

FOCUS
A moderate 3yo sprint handicap.
T/Plt: £96.10 to a £1 stake. Pool: £59,738.45 - 453.61 winning units. T/Qpdt: £49.20 to a £1 stake. Pool: £4,590.57 - 69.00 winning units. **Tim Mitchell**

2051 BEVERLEY (R-H)

Monday, May 6

OFFICIAL GOING: Good (good to soft in places; 6.9)
Wind: Moderate half behind Weather: Cloudy and raining

2475 KIPLINGCOTES NOVICE MEDIAN AUCTION STKS (DIV I) 5f
1:55 (1:59) (Class 5) 2-Y-O £4,140 (£1,232; £615; £307) Stalls Low

Form RPR
2 1 **Dylan De Vega**[16] 1953 2-9-5 0.............................. TonyHamilton 4 88+
(Richard Fahey) *trckd ldr: cl up 1/2-way: rdn to ld and jinked sharply lft jst over 1f out: styd on wl fnl f* 4/5[1]

2 2 3 **Ruby Wonder**[11] 2052 2-9-0 0.............................. DanielTudhope 10 69
(David O'Meara) *trckd ldrs: hdwy 2f out: rdn over 1f out: chsd wnr ins fnl f: kpt on same pce* 11/2[3]

02 3 1 **Azteca**[11] 2051 2-9-0 0.............................. GrahamLee 1 65
(Bryan Smart) *led: jnd and rdn along wl over 1f out: hdd appr fnl f: sn drvn and kpt on same pce* 4/1[2]

6 4 2 1/4 **King Lenox**[23] 1759 2-9-5 0.............................. SilvestreDeSousa 8 62
(Nigel Tinkler) *midfield: hdwy 2f out: rdn over 1f out: styd on fnl f: nrst fin* 11/1

5 1/2 **Speed Dating (FR)** 2-9-5 0.............................. BenCurtis 9 61+
(K R Burke) *towards rr: hdwy 2f out: rdn over 1f out: kpt on fnl f* 18/1

6 3 1/4 **South Light (IRE)** 2-9-0 0.............................. CamHardie 2 44
(Antony Brittain) *chsd ldrs: rdn along 2f out: wknd over 1f out* 40/1

7 1 1/2 **Loolabelle** 2-9-0 0.............................. DavidAllan 7 38
(Tim Easterby) *nvr bttr than midfield* 20/1

8 1 3/4 **Geepower (IRE)** 2-9-2 0.............................. BenRobinson(3) 5 37
(Brian Ellison) *a in rr* 22/1

9 3 1/4 **Susie Javea** 2-9-0 0.............................. ShaneGray 6 20
(Ollie Pears) *a in rr* 80/1

10 27 **Scotch Corner (IRE)** 2-9-5 0.............................. PhilDennis 3
(David C Griffiths) *green s.i.s: a outpcd and bhd fr 1/2-way* 50/1

1m 3.8s (0.90) **Going Correction** +0.30s/f (Good) **10 Ran SP% 119.3**
Speed ratings (Par 93): **104,99,97,94,93 88,85,82,77,34**
CSF £5.42 TOTE £1.70: £1.10, £1.70, £1.40; EX 6.40 Trifecta £12.70.
Owner Smarden Thoroughbreds **Bred** Mrs H J Fitzsimons & Mr S Bradley **Trained** Musley Bank, N Yorks

FOCUS
A dry run up to a meeting staged on goodish ground. Not much in the way of strength in depth but fair form from the winner, who should make further progress. The pace was sound and the newcomers never figured. The second helps set a straightforward level.

2476 KIPLINGCOTES NOVICE MEDIAN AUCTION STKS (DIV II) 5f
2:30 (2:33) (Class 5) 2-Y-O £4,140 (£1,232; £615; £307) Stalls Low

Form RPR
2 1 **Infinite Grace**[18] 1893 2-9-0 0.............................. DanielTudhope 9 71+
(David O'Meara) *trckd ldrs: hdwy 2f out: rdn to ld ent fnl f: drvn out* 4/1[2]

2 1 1/4 **Doncaster Rosa** 2-9-0 0.............................. JasonHart 2 67
(Ivan Furtado) *towards rr: hdwy on inner 2f out: chsd ldrs over 1f out: swtchd lft and drvn ins fnl f: kpt on wl to take 2nd nr line* 25/1

2 3 hd **Mr Fudge**[31] 1556 2-9-5 0.............................. PaulHanagan 3 71
(Richard Fahey) *cl up on inner: rdn to ld briefly over 1f out: hdd ent fnl f: sn drvn and kpt on same pce* 11/10[1]

4 1 1/4 **Yarrow Gate** 2-9-0 0.............................. PaulMulrennan 4 61+
(Michael Dods) *chsd ldrs: hdwy wl over 1f out: rdn and edgd rt ent fnl f: kpt on* 8/1

5 2 1/2 **Blitzle** 2-9-0 0.............................. TomEaves 6 52
(Ollie Pears) *slt ld: pushed along and hdd over 1f out: rdn ent fnl f: grad wknd* 20/1

6 4 1/2 **Van Dijk** 2-9-5 0.............................. CamHardie 8 41
(Antony Brittain) *dwlt: a towards rr* 25/1

023 7 hd **Littleton Hall (IRE)**[4] 2316 2-9-5 0.............................. BenCurtis 1 40
(Mick Channon) *chsd ldrs on inner: rdn along 2f out: sn drvn and wknd (jockey said colt ran too free)* 5/1[3]

0 8 2 **Lady Erimus**[28] 1642 2-9-0 0.............................. ShaneGray 7 28
(Kevin Ryan) *dwlt: a in rr* 50/1

9 25 **Champagne Victory (IRE)** 2-8-11 0.............................. BenRobinson(3) 5
(Brian Ellison) *chsd ldrs: rdn along over 2f out: wknd and hung rt wl over 1f out: sn eased and bhd (jockey said filly hung left throughout so felt it prudent to ease)* 16/1

1m 4.66s (1.76) **Going Correction** +0.30s/f (Good) **9 Ran SP% 115.7**
Speed ratings (Par 93): **97,95,94,92,88 81,81,77,37**
CSF £99.37 TOTE £3.90: £1.50, £5.60, £1.10; EX 102.50 Trifecta £432.20.
Owner K Nicholson **Bred** Kevin Nicholson **Trained** Upper Helmsley, N Yorks

FOCUS
Division two of a run-of-the mill median auction event. The pace was sound and the performances of the runner-up and fourth caught the eye. The opening level is fluid.

2477 BEVERLEY ANNUAL BADGEHOLDERS H'CAP 5f
3:05 (3:09) (Class 5) (0-70,72) 3-Y-O £4,032 (£1,207; £603; £302; £300; £300) Stalls Low

Form RPR
43-5 1 **Friendly Advice (IRE)**[42] 1337 3-9-6 69.............................. JoeFanning 8 74+
(Keith Dalgleish) *towards rr: swtchd to outer and rdn over 1f out: hdwy ent fnl f: sn edgd rt: kpt on wl to ld nr fin* 4/1[1]

4-25 2 hd **Kyllachy Warrior (IRE)**[101] 408 3-9-6 69.............................. DanielTudhope 12 73
(Lawrence Mullaney) *trckd ldrs: hdwy to ld 1 1/2f out: drvn ins fnl f: hdd and no ex nr line* 20/1

10-0 3 2 **Timetodock**[9] 2098 3-8-13 62..............................(b) DavidAllan 7 59
(Tim Easterby) *trckd ldrs: hdwy 2f out: swtchd rt and rdn over 1f out: ev ch ent fnl f: sn drvn and kpt on same pce* 5/1[2]

460- 4 2 3/4 **Baldwin (IRE)**[227] 7478 3-9-2 70.............................. SeanDavis(5) 3 57
(Kevin Ryan) *hld up: hdwy to chse ldrs wl over 1f out: rdn and kpt on fnl f* 6/1[3]

53-5 5 nk **Amazing Alba**[16] 1954 3-9-4 67..............................(h[1]) PaulMulrennan 6 53
(Michael Dods) *chsd ldrs: rdn along wl over 1f out: drvn appr fnl f: grad wknd* 9/1

20-5 6 1 1/2 **Skeetah**[17] 1924 3-9-9 72.............................. JasonHart 4 53
(John Quinn) *prom on inner: rdn along 2f out: wknd over 1f out* 10/1

-553 7 nk **One One Seven (IRE)**[16] 1954 3-8-7 56.............................. CamHardie 9 36
(Antony Brittain) *in tch on outer: hdwy 1/2-way: rdn along wl over 1f out: sn no imp* 10/1

5-00 8 1/2 **Pearl Of Qatar**[9] 2098 3-8-9 61..............................(b) BenRobinson(3) 5 39
(Brian Ellison) *towards rr: niggled along over 2f out: effrt and nt clr run wl over 1f out: sn rdn and n.d* 12/1

0 9 2 1/2 **Montalvan (IRE)**[7] 2197 3-8-13 62.............................. BenCurtis 2 31
(Roger Fell) *in tch on inner: effrt and n.m.r 2f out: rdn and n.m.r over 1f out: n.d* 15/2

200- 10 1 1/2 **Swiss Connection**[242] 6973 3-9-7 70.............................. GrahamLee 1 33
(Bryan Smart) *a towards rr* 6/1[3]

000- 11 8 **Sambucca Spirit**[188] 8714 3-8-2 51 oh6..............................(w) JamesSullivan 10
(Paul Midgley) *a towards rr on outer (jockey said gelding lost its action in the closing stages)* 50/1

2-05 12 3 1/2 **Raypeteafterme**[3] 2380 3-9-7 70..............................(b[1]) TomEaves 11
(Declan Carroll) *slt ld: rdn along 2f out: sn hdd & wknd* 22/1

1m 3.19s (0.29) **Going Correction** +0.30s/f (Good) **12 Ran SP% 123.9**
Speed ratings (Par 99): **109,108,105,101,100 98,97,96,92,90 77,72**
CSF £92.46 CT £428.46 TOTE £5.30: £1.90, £5.40, £1.70; EX 99.50 Trifecta £858.40.
Owner A R M Galbraith **Bred** A R M Galbraith **Trained** Carluke, S Lanarks

FOCUS
An ordinary handicap in which the gallop was sound and the first two deserve credit for pulling a couple of lengths clear close home. The second has been rated in line with his AW form, and the third similar to his latest.

2478 LECONFIELD H'CAP 7f 96y
3:40 (3:42) (Class 5) (0-70,67) 4-Y-O+ £4,284 (£1,282; £641; £320; £300; £300) Stalls Low

Form RPR
-403 1 **Abushamah (IRE)**[10] 2076 8-8-12 58.............................. JamesSullivan 7 66
(Ruth Carr) *mde all: pushed along and qcknd clr over 2f out: rdn over 1f out: jnd and drvn ins fnl f: kpt on wl towards fin* 3/1[2]

40-0 2 nk **Cameo Star (IRE)**[23] 1760 4-9-2 67.............................. ConnorMurtagh(5) 3 74
(Richard Fahey) *trckd ldng pair on inner: hdwy 2f out: swtchd lft and rdn over 1f out: styd on to chal ins fnl f: ev ch tl drvn and no ex towards fin* 4/1[3]

50-0 3 3 1/2 **Straight Ash (IRE)**[27] 1659 4-9-2 65.............................. BenRobinson(3) 5 63
(Ollie Pears) *trckd wnr: pushed along and sltly outpcd jst over 2f out: rdn wl over 1f out: drvn and kpt on fnl f* 6/1

2163 4 2 **Muatadel**[14] 1976 6-9-6 66..............................(p) BenCurtis 6 59
(Roger Fell) *trckd ldrs: hdwy over 2f out: rdn wl over 1f out: sn drvn and no imp fnl f* 9/4[1]

00-0 5 2 1/4 **Dasheen**[10] 2076 6-9-5 65..............................(p) RachelRichardson 2 52
(Karen Tutty) *hld up towards rr: effrt and sme hdwy over 2f out: rdn wl over 1f out: n.d* 8/1

0130 6 shd **Peachey Carnehan**[30] 1597 5-9-2 62..............................(v) PhilDennis 8 49
(Michael Mullineaux) *hld up: a towards rr* 18/1

010- 7 1 3/4 **Relight My Fire**[209] 8088 9-8-9 62.............................. RobertDodsworth(7) 1 44
(Tim Easterby) *chsd ldrs: rdn along 2 1/2f out: sn wknd* 14/1

1m 34.55s (1.95) **Going Correction** +0.30s/f (Good) **7 Ran SP% 113.1**
Speed ratings (Par 103): **100,99,95,93,90 90,88**
CSF £15.05 CT £65.65 TOTE £2.90: £1.70, £2.30; EX 13.80 Trifecta £75.70.
Owner Grange Park Racing VIII & Mrs R Carr **Bred** Shadwell Estate Company Limited **Trained** Huby, N Yorks

FOCUS
A modest handicap in which the gallop was steady and those held up were at a disadvantage. The first two pulled clear in the last furlong. The winner has been rated in line with his form since last May.

2479 BRIAN DIXON MEMORIAL H'CAP 1m 1f 207y
4:15 (4:16) (Class 4) (0-80,82) 4-Y-O+ £5,418 (£1,621; £810; £405; £300; £300) Stalls Low

Form RPR
63-4 1 **Where's Jeff**[26] 1695 4-9-1 74.............................. NathanEvans 1 83
(Michael Easterby) *trckd ldng pair: hdwy on inner to ld 1 1/2f out: sn rdn: drvn and kpt on wl fnl f* 10/3[3]

-034 2 2 1/4 **Sands Chorus**[9] 2104 7-8-13 77..............................(p) TheodoreLadd(5) 4 81
(Scott Dixon) *led: rdn along 2f out: edgd lft and hdd 1 1/2f out: sn drvn: kpt on wl u.p fnl f (trainer was informed that the gelding could not run until the day after passing a stalls test)* 9/4[1]

0-11 3 nk **Ventura Gold (IRE)**[16] 1948 4-8-12 76.............................. SeanDavis(5) 6 79
(Richard Fahey) *trckd ldrs: hdwy to chse ldr 2f out: rdn over 1f out and ev ch: drvn and kpt on same pce fnl f* 10/1

244- 4 3 1/4 **Breathable**[234] 7234 4-8-10 69.............................. RachelRichardson 3 66
(Tim Easterby) *hld up in rr: hdwy 2f out: rdn over 1f out: kpt on fnl f* 14/1

00-5 5 3 **Kharbetation (IRE)**[16] 1955 6-9-4 77..............................(h[1]) DavidNolan 5 68
(David O'Meara) *hld up in tch: effrt and sme hdwy over 2f out: sn rdn and btn* 9/1

46-0 6 3/4 **Low Profile**[27] 1666 4-8-11 70..............................(p) PhilDennis 2 59
(Rebecca Bastiman) *chsd ldrs: rdn along over 2f out: sn wknd* 33/1

0-04 7 1 3/4 **Alfa McGuire (IRE)**[7] 2186 4-9-9 82.............................. SamJames 7 68
(Phillip Makin) *chsd ldr: rdn along wl over 2f out: sn wknd (jockey said the gelding was restless in the stalls; jockey said that the gelding had reared in the stalls and slipped onto its hind quarters but having quickly regained its footing, he liaised with the Starters, and had no concerns over the gelding's pa* 3/1[2]

00-0 8 49 **Dr Richard Kimble (IRE)**[9] 2126 4-9-7 80.............................. JoeFanning 8
(Mark Johnston) *a in rr: bhd and eased fnl 2f (jockey said gelding was never travelling)* 12/1

2m 7.96s (2.26) **Going Correction** +0.30s/f (Good) **8 Ran SP% 115.2**
Speed ratings (Par 105): **103,101,100,98,95 95,93,54**
CSF £11.38 CT £65.99 TOTE £3.30: £1.20, £1.30, £2.50; EX 13.50 Trifecta £48.00.
Owner A G Pollock, Golden Ratio & J Sissons **Bred** Lucky 5 Partnership & Stittenham Racing **Trained** Sheriff Hutton, N Yorks

FOCUS
A fair handicap featuring mainly exposed sorts but another muddling gallop and this suited the prominent racers. It's been rated around the second and third to their recent form.

2480 RACING TV H'CAP 1m 100y
4:50 (4:52) (Class 4) (0-85,85) 4-Y-O+ £6,553 (£1,961; £980; £490; £300; £300) Stalls Low

Form RPR
6-54 1 **Crownthorpe**[9] 2116 4-9-1 84.............................. SeanDavis(5) 1 95
(Richard Fahey) *hld up towards rr: hdwy on inner over 2f out: trckd ldrs and n.m.r wl over 1f out: sn swtchd lft and rdn: styd on to ld last 100yds: sn clr* 9/4[1]

203- **2** *3* **Storm Ahead (IRE)**[187] 8740 6-8-11 **75**............................(b) DavidAllan 3 79
(Tim Easterby) *trckd ldr: effrt on inner to chal 2f out: rdn over 1f out: slt ld appr fnl f: sn drvn: hdd last 100yds: kpt on same pce* **6/1**

-534 **3** *2 1/4* **Enzemble (IRE)**[68] 922 4-9-0 **78**.................. SilvestreDeSousa 8 77
(James Fanshawe) *trckd ldng pair: effrt and cl up on outer 3f out: chal 2f out: sn rdn: drvn and ev ch over 1f out: kpt on same pce* **7/2**[2]

030- **4** *3/4* **Club Wexford (IRE)**[226] 7514 8-8-12 **81**.................. BenSanderson(5) 7 78+
(Roger Fell) *hld up in tch: hdwy on outer 3f out: rdn along to chse ldrs 2f out: drvn over 1f out: sn one pce* **20/1**

600- **5** *2* **Poet's Dawn**[178] 8974 4-9-3 **81**.................................. RachelRichardson 5 74
(Tim Easterby) *led: rdn along over 2f out: drvn over 1f out: hdd appr fnl f: wknd* **20/1**

0012 **6** *3 1/4* **Mont Kinabalu (IRE)**[16] 1948 4-8-12 **76**.......................... TomEaves 6 61
(Kevin Ryan) *hld up in rr: sme hdwy 2f out: sn rdn along and nvr a factor* **15/2**

-100 **7** *1 1/4* **Rampant Lion (IRE)**[17] 1912 4-9-4 **82**..................(p) JoeFanning 2 64
(William Jarvis) *in tch: pushed along 3f out: rdn over 2f out: sn drvn and wknd* **4/1**[3]

00-0 **8** *9* **Ghalib (IRE)**[13] 2015 7-9-4 **82**.................................. DanielTudhope 9 44
(Rebecca Bastiman) *chsd ldrs: rdn along wl over 2f out: sn wknd* **25/1**

506- **9** *23* **London Protocol (FR)**[191] 8634 6-9-7 **85**..................(p) BenCurtis 10
(John Mackie) *stmbld s: a in rr: bhd fnl 2f (jockey said gelding stumbled badly leaving the stalls)* **20/1**

1m 47.81s (1.41) **Going Correction** +0.30s/f (Good) 9 Ran SP% **117.2**
Speed ratings (Par 105): **104,101,98,98,96 92,91,82,59**
CSF £15.38 CT £46.64 TOTE £3.40: £1.30, £1.90, £1.60; EX 16.50 Trifecta £55.70.
Owner Richard Fahey Ebor Racing Club Ltd **Bred** Mrs Sheila Oakes **Trained** Musley Bank, N Yorks

FOCUS
Mainly exposed performers in a reasonable handicap. The pace was fair. The winner has been rated in line with his best.

2481 HOLDERNESS PLATE FILLIES' NOVICE STKS 1m 1f 207y
5:25 (5:28) (Class 5) 3-Y-O+ **£4,284** (£1,282; £641; £320; £159) **Stalls** Low

Form RPR

14- **1** **Mannaal (IRE)**[184] 8836 3-9-4 0.................................. SilvestreDeSousa 5 73+
(Simon Crisford) *trckd ldr: hdwy and cl up 3f out: led over 2f out and sn rdn: kpt on wl u.p fnl f* **5/6**[1]

2 *1 3/4* **Illumined (IRE)** 3-8-11 0.. KieranO'Neill 1 62+
(John Gosden) *green and slowly away: in rr: hdwy and hung lft bnd over 3f out: sn trcking ldrs: rdn to chse wnr jst over 1f out: green and edgd rt ins fnl f: sn no imp* **6/4**[2]

5- **3** *1 1/2* **Maktabba**[191] 8647 3-8-11 0.. DaneO'Neill 6 59+
(William Haggas) *trckd ldrs: hdwy 3f out: rdn along 2f out: drvn over 1f out: kpt on same pce* **11/2**[3]

400- **4** *7* **Bob's Girl**[186] 8773 4-9-12 43...(h) PhilDennis 2 46
(Michael Mullineaux) *trckd ldng pair: pushed along 3f out: rdn and outpcd over 2f out: plugged on fnl f* **125/1**

-620 **5** *8* **Ejabah (IRE)**[9] 2112 5-9-7 34.. BenSanderson(5) 3 30
(Charles Smith) *led: pushed along over 3f out: sn jnd and rdn: hdd over 2f out and sn wknd* **200/1**

6-00 **6** *18* **Trulove**[101] 411 6-9-7 41.. SeanDavis(5) 4
(John David Riches) *in tch: rdn along wl over 2f out: sn outpcd* **200/1**

2m 11.22s (5.52) **Going Correction** +0.30s/f (Good)
WFA 3 from 4yo+ 15lb 6 Ran SP% **111.7**
Speed ratings (Par 100): **89,87,86,80,74 60**
CSF £2.33 TOTE £1.50: £1.10, £1.20; EX 2.50 Trifecta £3.20.
Owner Sheikh Ahmed Al Maktoum **Bred** Godolphin **Trained** Newmarket, Suffolk

FOCUS
An uncompetitive race in which the winner didn't have to improve to defy a penalty. The gallop was steady to the home turn and the fourth was flattered by her proximity. The fourth and fifth limit the level.

2482 BURTON CONSTABLE PLATE APPRENTICE H'CAP 7f 96y
6:00 (6:00) (Class 6) (0-65,67) 3-Y-O **£3,105** (£924; £461; £300; £300; £300) **Stalls** Low

Form RPR

-003 **1** **Molly Mai**[31] 1567 3-9-8 **61**.. DylanHogan 12 68
(Philip McBride) *wnt lft s: midfield: hdwy on outer over 2f out: chsd ldrs over 1f out: rdn to chse clr ldr ent fnl f: styd on strly to ld last 50yds* **15/2**

5601 **2** *1 1/2* **Termonator**[19] 1863 3-9-11 **64**.. AndrewBreslin 4 67
(Grant Tuer) *in rr: hdwy and nt clr run wl over 1f out: swtchd rt and rdn ent fnl f: swtchd lft and kpt on strly last 100yds* **7/1**

2021 **3** *1/2* **Lexikon**[14] 1979 3-9-1 **54**.. ConnorMurtagh 2 56+
(Ollie Pears) *led and set str pce: sn clr: rdn along jst over 1f out: drvn ins fnl f: hdd last 50yds: no ex* **4/1**[2]

00-3 **4** *nk* **Kensington Art**[14] 1979 3-9-12 **65**.. SeanDavis 5 66
(Richard Fahey) *in rr: hdwy on wd outside over 2f out: rdn wl over 1f out: drvn and kpt on fnl f (jockey said gelding missed the break)* **11/4**[1]

000- **5** *1/2* **Neileta**[240] 7072 3-9-2 **55**.. DannyRedmond 7 55
(Tim Easterby) *hld up towards rr: hdwy wl over 2f out: chsd ldrs whn n.m.r and rdn over 1f out: kpt on fnl f* **33/1**

34-0 **6** *1 1/4* **Mecca's Gift (IRE)**[7] 2200 3-9-12 **65**.. PaulaMuir 10 62+
(Michael Dods) *towards rr: rdn along and hdwy 2f out: n.m.r over 1f out: sn swtchd lft to outer and fin wl* **8/1**

0-05 **7** *1 1/2* **Zalmi Angel**[4] 2337 3-9-1 **54**.. LauraCoughlan 11 47
(Adrian Nicholls) *chsd clr ldr: rdn along over 2f out: drvn over 1f out: grad wknd* **16/1**

0-00 **8** *4 1/2* **Furyan**[9] 2098 3-9-1 **57**.. IzzyClifton(3) 3 39
(Nigel Tinkler) *nvr bttr than midfield* **25/1**

50-4 **9** *1/2* **Stallone (IRE)**[35] 1488 3-9-11 **67**..................................(v[1]) SeanKirrane(3) 8 48
(Richard Spencer) *chsd ldrs on outer: hung lft and rn wd bnd 4f out: rdn along wl over 2f out: sn drvn and wknd (jockey said gelding hung left in the final 4 1/2f)* **5/1**[3]

300- **10** *7* **Supreme Dream**[201] 8323 3-8-13 **55**.. HarryRussell(3) 1 19
(Ollie Pears) *chsd ldng pair: rdn along on inner over 2f out: wknd wl over 1f out* **20/1**

360- **11** *1/2* **Good Looker (IRE)**[222] 7666 3-9-0 **56**.. ZakWheatley(3) 6 19
(Tony Coyle) *in tch: rdn along wl over 2f out: sn wknd* **20/1**

40-5 **12** *5* **Early Edition (IRE)**[14] 1979 3-9-5 **58**..................................(p) BenSanderson 9 9
(Roger Fell) *chsd ldrs: rdn along 3f out: sn wknd* **25/1**

1m 36.89s (4.29) **Going Correction** +0.30s/f (Good) 12 Ran SP% **124.7**
Speed ratings (Par 97): **87,85,84,84,83 82,80,75,74,66 66,60**
CSF £57.68 CT £251.38 TOTE £8.60: £2.70, £2.30, £1.80; EX 70.70 Trifecta £253.20.
Owner The Ten Fools & A Horse Partnership **Bred** Rosyground Stud **Trained** Newmarket, Suffolk

FOCUS
A decent gallop to this modest handicap and the form should work out. The winner has been rated to last year's turf best.

T/Plt: £15.50 to a £1 stake. Pool: £61,261.99 - 2,884.68 winning units. T/Qpdt: £10.60 to a £1 stake. Pool: £4,523.83 - 314.80 winning units. **Joe Rowntree**

2204 WINDSOR (R-H)
Monday, May 6

OFFICIAL GOING: Good (7.2)
Wind: Moderate, behind Weather: cloudy

2483 WATCH SKY SPORTS RACING VIRGIN 535 APPRENTICE TRAINING SERIES H'CAP (RACING EXCELLENCE INITATIVE) 6f 12y
2:00 (2:07) (Class 5) (0-70,71) 4-Y-O+ **£3,752** (£1,116; £557; £300; £300; £300) **Stalls** Centre

Form RPR

6162 **1** **Real Estate (IRE)**[16] 1930 4-9-7 **70**..................................(p) CierenFallon 12 74
(Michael Attwater) *cl up bhd ldrs: swtchd sharply lft jst over 2f out: rdn over 1f out: clsd to ld last 50yds: kpt on (jockey said colt hung both ways)* **10/3**[1]

2050 **2** *nk* **Dalness Express**[39] 1383 6-8-7 **56** oh10..................................(bt[1]) AledBeech 9 59
(John O'Shea) *chsd ldr: clsd fnl f: upsides 75yds out: jst outpcd* **50/1**

5605 **3** *nse* **National Glory (IRE)**[16] 1930 4-9-3 **66**..................(b) Pierre-LouisJamin 10 69
(Archie Watson) *led: racd against rail fr 1/2-way and sent for home over 2f out: clr over 1f out: hdd and no ex last 50yds* **8/1**

130- **4** *2* **Born To Finish (IRE)**[258] 6393 6-9-5 **71**.. AmeliaGlass(3) 4 68
(Ed de Giles) *hld up in last quartet: prog to chse ldrs 2f out: nt clr run briefly over 1f out: styd on to take 4th ins fnl f: unable to chal* **7/1**

4063 **5** *1 1/2* **Mooroverthebridge**[7] 2206 5-8-5 **59**.. KeelanBaker(5) 2 51
(Grace Harris) *hld up in midfield: prog to chse ldrs over 1f out: styd on same pce fnl f (jockey said mare jumped awkwardly leaving the stalls)* **13/2**[3]

1140 **6** *1/2* **Elusif (IRE)**[15] 1973 4-8-5 **59**.. GavinAshton(5) 13 49
(Shaun Keightley) *hld up in last pair and wl off the pce: pushed along over 1f out: styd on wl last 150yds: nvr nrr* **10/1**

420- **7** *nse* **Kinglami**[217] 7829 10-9-0 **68**.. KateLeahy(5) 7 58
(John O'Shea) *chsd ldrs: pushed along 2f out: no prog and btn over 1f out* **33/1**

44-0 **8** *nse* **Vincenzo Coccotti (USA)**[21] 1820 7-8-5 **59**..................(p) GeorgeRooke(5) 3 49
(Ken Cunningham-Brown) *cl up bhd ldrs: carried sharply lft jst over 2f out: sn rdn: styd wl in tch tl fdd fnl f* **12/1**

46-6 **9** *nk* **Porto Ferro (IRE)**[7] 2206 5-9-2 **68**.. GeorgiaDobie(3) 6 57
(John Bridger) *wl in tch towards outer: carried lft 2f out: rdn and no imp on ldrs over 1f out* **7/2**[2]

0-00 **10** *1 1/2* **Soaring Spirits (IRE)**[42] 1328 9-8-7 **63**.. LukeBacon(7) 5 47
(Dean Ivory) *nvr beyond midfield: rdn and no prog 2f out* **33/1**

000- **11** *6* **Another Boy**[184] 8839 6-8-11 **67**.. CharlotteBennett(7) 1 32
(Ralph Beckett) *sltly awkward s: a wl in rr: bhd fnl f (vet said gelding bled from the nose)* **8/1**

000- **12** *1/2* **Aegean Legend**[172] 9079 4-8-7 **56** oh6.. TobyEley 11 19
(John Bridger) *stdd s: hld up in last pair and wl off the pce: nvr any prog: bhd fnl f (jockey said gelding was never travelling)* **40/1**

453- **13** *2 3/4* **Spot Lite**[203] 8253 4-8-3 **59**.. OliverSearle(7) 8 14
(Rod Millman) *chsd ldrs on wd outside to 1/2-way: sn lost pl: bhd fnl f* **16/1**

1m 12.35s (0.25) **Going Correction** -0.05s/f (Good) 13 Ran SP% **126.3**
Speed ratings (Par 103): **96,95,95,92,90 90,90,90,89,87 79,79,75**
CSF £191.37 CT £999.04 TOTE £3.90: £1.50, £13.70, £2.60; EX 199.10 Trifecta £1123.90.
Owner Christian Main **Bred** Rabbah Bloodstock Limited **Trained** Epsom, Surrey
■ Stewards' Enquiry : Cieren Fallon three-day ban: careless riding (May 20-22)

FOCUS
Little got into this from off the pace, with the first three home in the leading trio throughout. The third has been rated to his best since February.

2484 PHIL RENDELL FORTY-THIRTEENTH BIRTHDAY H'CAP 6f 12y
2:35 (2:37) (Class 4) (0-85,84) 4-Y-O+ **£5,530** (£1,645; £822; £411; £300; £300) **Stalls** Centre

Form RPR

-663 **1** **Erissimus Maximus (FR)**[58] 1098 5-9-0 **84**..................(b) CierenFallon(7) 8 93
(Amy Murphy) *mde virtually all: rdn 2f out: edgd lft fr over 1f out: hotly pressed fnl f: hld on wl* **8/1**

42-6 **2** *3/4* **Blackheath**[20] 1829 4-9-7 **84**.. LiamKeniry 4 91
(Ed Walker) *hld up towards rr: shkn up and prog over 1f out: chal and nudged by wnr ins fnl f: nt qckn nr fin* **4/1**[2]

336- **3** *1/2* **Wiley Post**[201] 8333 6-9-1 **78**..................................(b) TomMarquand 11 83
(Tony Carroll) *cl up on outer: rdn to take 2nd wl over 1f out and sn chalng: nt qckn ins fnl f and lost 2nd sn after* **16/1**

02-0 **4** *nk* **Grey Galleon (USA)**[121] 91 5-8-5 **75**..................(p) AmeliaGlass(7) 7 79
(Clive Cox) *hld up in rr: prog on wd outside over 1f out: urged along to cl fnl f: one pce last 100yds (vet said gelding was treated for post-race ataxia)* **16/1**

6-21 **5** *2 1/4* **Diamond Lady**[16] 1930 8-8-13 **76**.. HollieDoyle 5 73
(William Stone) *w ldrs to 2f out: fdd jst over 1f out* **7/1**[3]

0-00 **6** *1 1/2* **Bahamian Sunrise**[12] 2030 7-8-3 **73**.. AledBeech(7) 6 65
(John Gallagher) *w ldrs to 1/2-way: nt qckn 2f out: fdd fnl f* **33/1**

35-4 **7** *shd* **Private Matter**[28] 1654 5-9-6 **83**..................................(h) DavidEgan 3 75
(Amy Murphy) *mostly in last: racd alone against nr side rail fr 1/2-way: nvr on terms but kpt on ins fnl f (trainer said gelding was unsuited by the going, which was officially described as Good, and would prefer a softer surface)* **10/1**

5-23 **8** *1* **Harry's Bar**[24] 1728 4-9-1 **78**.. OisinMurphy 9 67
(James Fanshawe) *dwlt: t.k.h and sn trckd ldrs: rdn and nt qckn wl over 1f out: no imp after* **6/4**[1]

015- **9** *3/4* **Delilah Park**[149] 9462 5-8-8 **71**.. GeorgeWood 1 57
(Chris Wall) *hld up: prog to chse ldrs 1/2-way: wknd fnl f* **22/1**

00-0 **10** *hd* **Englishman**[9] 2107 9-8-13 **76**.. LukeMorris 2 61
(Milton Bradley) *a towards rr: rdn and no prog over 2f out* **20/1**

00-0 **11** *1 1/2* **Harrogate (IRE)**[38] 1394 4-8-8 **78**.. IsobelFrancis(7) 10 59
(Jim Boyle) *t.k.h: w wnr to 2f out: wknd (jockey said gelding hung left-handed in the home straight)* **33/1**

1m 11.37s (-0.73) **Going Correction** -0.05s/f (Good) 11 Ran SP% **119.5**
Speed ratings (Par 105): **102,101,100,99,96 94,94,93,92,92 90**
CSF £38.90 CT £513.51 TOTE £9.50: £2.50, £1.50, £4.80; EX 46.80 Trifecta £1197.70.
Owner P Venner **Bred** Derek Clee **Trained** Newmarket, Suffolk

The Form Book Flat 2019, Raceform Ltd, Newbury, RG14 5SJ

FOCUS
A fair sprint and again it paid to be up with the pace. The third helps set the level.

2485 WATCH SKY SPORTS RACING IN HD H'CAP — 1m 3f 99y
3:10 (3:10) (Class 5) (0-75,77) 3-Y-O
£3,752 (£1,116; £557; £300; £300; £300) Stalls Low

Form					RPR
336-	1		**Summer Moon**[165] 9203 3-9-10 77	PJMcDonald 6	90+
			(Mark Johnston) *mde virtually all: shkn up and wl in command 2f out: pushed out* **9/4**[1]		
6-35	2	5	**Mr Zoom Zoom**[12] 2034 3-9-3 70	RobertHavlin 7	73
			(Luke McJannet) *hld up in rr: effrt over 3f out: rdn to chse wnr wl over 1f out: no imp* **9/1**		
2-16	3	7	**Hermocrates (FR)**[9] 2125 3-9-2 69	TomMarquand 5	60
			(Richard Hannon) *chsd wnr but rarely on the bridle: drvn 4f out: lost 2nd and wknd wl over 1f out* **10/1**		
64-2	4	2	**Hummdinger (FR)**[16] 1957 3-8-12 65	JamieSpencer 8	53
			(Alan King) *c out of stall slowly: hld up in detached last: effrt and reminders over 2f out: no significant inroads after* **7/2**[3]		
44-3	5	3	**Lucipherus (IRE)**[13] 2021 3-9-4 71	(t) DavidEgan 2	54
			(Marco Botti) *chsd ldrs: rdn to dispute 2nd 3f out to 2f out: wknd* **7/1**		
004-	6	28	**Pop The Cork**[163] 9256 3-9-1 68	LukeMorris 3	3
			(Jonjo O'Neill) *hld up in tch: hung v bdly lft bnd 6f out: sn t.o (jockey said colt hung badly left-handed throughout)* **16/1**		
00-0	7	32	**Tigerskin**[23] 1754 3-8-9 62	HarryBentley 1	
			(Ralph Beckett) *chsd ldrs: rdn 5f out: wknd rapidly wl over 3f out: t.o (trainer's rep said colt had a breathing problem)* **11/4**[2]		

2m 27.73s (-1.97) **Going Correction** -0.05s/f (Good) 7 Ran SP% **117.1**
Speed ratings (Par 99): **105,101,96,94,92 72,49**
CSF £24.13 CT £171.74 TOTE £2.90: £2.00, £4.30; EX 19.70 Trifecta £104.60.
Owner The Originals **Bred** Miss K Rausing **Trained** Middleham Moor, N Yorks

FOCUS
Add 20yds. One key non-runner and a second favourite who ran poorly, so this probably didn't take a whole deal of winning, but the well-backed favourite hammered his field. The second has been rated in line with his AW form.

2486 SKY SPORTS RACING ON SKY 415 H'CAP — 1m 2f
3:45 (3:45) (Class 4) (0-85,85) 4-Y-O+
£5,530 (£1,645; £822; £411; £300; £300) Stalls Low

Form					RPR
-332	1		**Lawn Ranger**[33] 1518 4-9-1 79	KierenFox 2	87
			(Michael Attwater) *trckd ldr: led over 6f out: shkn up and pressed 2f out: rdn to assert fnl f: on top at fin* **4/1**[2]		
4650	2	1 ½	**Mr Scaramanga**[17] 1916 5-9-5 83	OisinMurphy 5	88
			(Simon Dow) *led to over 6f out: pressed wnr: stl upsides 2f out: rdn and one pce jst over 1f out* **8/1**		
60-2	3	¾	**Grapevine (IRE)**[16] 1934 6-8-6 77	CierenFallon(7) 4	81
			(Charles Hills) *t.k.h early: trckd ldrs: rdn to cl 2f out: chal over 1f out: one pce fnl f* **5/2**[1]		
140-	4	1	**Zzoro (IRE)**[196] 8486 6-9-1 79	PatDobbs 3	81
			(Amanda Perrett) *hld up in rr but in tch: chsd ldrs over 2f out and reminder sn after: nt qckn over 1f out: styd on same pce fnl f* **5/1**		
4-55	5	1 ½	**Cote D'Azur**[21] 1813 6-9-6 84	LukeMorris 1	83
			(Les Eyre) *stdd and sltly awkward s: rcvrd to chse ldng pair after 4f: hanging lft fr 4f out: nt qckn over 2f out: fdd over 1f out* **9/2**[3]		
54-0	6	6	**Dragons Voice**[24] 1727 5-9-4 82	DavidEgan 6	69
			(David Menuisier) *hld up in rr but in tch: urged along 4f out: steadily wknd* **6/1**		
5/	7	99	**Mahari (IRE)**[406] 3450 6-9-7 85	RobertHavlin 7	
			(Kerry Lee) *in tch to 1/2-way: sn wknd: virtually p.u over 2f out (vet said gelding had bled from the nose)* **16/1**		

2m 7.1s (-1.90) **Going Correction** -0.05s/f (Good) 7 Ran SP% **114.7**
Speed ratings (Par 105): **105,103,103,102,101 96,17**
CSF £35.20 CT £94.74 TOTE £4.30: £2.20, £4.10; EX 39.90 Trifecta £244.90.
Owner Canisbay Bloodstock **Bred** Jacqueline Doyle **Trained** Epsom, Surrey
■ Navajo War Dance was withdrawn. Price at time of withdrawal 25/1. Rule 4 does not apply

FOCUS
Add 20yds. No great gallop on here and, once again, it paid to race up on the speed. They headed centre-field this time. Ordinary form, with the third rated to his latest.

2487 GEMS H'CAP — 1m 31y
4:20 (4:20) (Class 3) (0-95,93) 4-Y-O £7,246 (£2,168; £1,084; £542; £270) Stalls Low

Form					RPR
44-4	1		**Greenside**[23] 1753 8-9-4 90	HarryBentley 6	99
			(Henry Candy) *hld up in 6th: pushed along 3f out: prog 2f out and sn clsd on ldrs: rdn to ld ins fnl f: styd on wl and won gng away* **11/8**[1]		
6000	2	1 ¾	**Masham Star (IRE)**[9] 2100 5-9-7 93	PJMcDonald 8	99
			(Mark Johnston) *sn trckd ldr: rdn to ld 2f out: hdd and one pce ins fnl f: jst hld on for 2nd* **6/1**[3]		
410-	3	hd	**Lush Life (IRE)**[186] 8769 4-9-5 91	JamieSpencer 7	96
			(Jamie Osborne) *awkward s: hld up in last: rdn and prog on outer 2f out: drvn and styd on fnl f: nrly snatched 2nd* **7/2**[2]		
5-56	4	1 ½	**Corazon Espinado (IRE)**[40] 1356 4-8-11 83	OisinMurphy 3	85
			(Simon Dow) *led at decent pce: rdn and hdd 2f out: wknd fnl f (jockey said colt hung left-handed round the bend)* **7/1**		
065-	5	1 ¾	**Elysium Dream**[226] 7541 4-8-11 83	TomMarquand 5	81
			(Richard Hannon) *hld up in rr: last and pushed along over 2f out: passed a few fnl f: nvr in it* **20/1**		
4-50	6	nk	**Jellmood**[24] 1727 4-8-11 83	(t) CharlesBishop 1	80
			(Chris Gordon) *t.k.h: hld up in midfield: rdn over 2f out: wknd over 1f out (jockey said gelding hung badly left-handed)* **25/1**		
011/	7	3	**I'vegotthepower (IRE)**[670] 4491 5-9-2 88	CallumShepherd 2	78
			(Brian Meehan) *prom: shkn up over 3f out: wknd wl over 1f out* **20/1**		
40-2	8	2 ¾	**Top Mission**[11] 2064 5-8-13 85	DavidEgan 4	69
			(Marco Botti) *chsd ldrs: rdn over 2f out: sn wknd* **7/1**		

1m 42.45s (-2.05) **Going Correction** -0.05s/f (Good) 8 Ran SP% **117.0**
Speed ratings (Par 107): **108,106,106,104,102 102,99,96**
CSF £10.14 CT £24.80 TOTE £2.10: £1.10, £2.10, £1.40; EX 10.50 Trifecta £43.90.
Owner Clayton, Frost, Kebell & Turner **Bred** Lordship Stud **Trained** Kingston Warren, Oxon

FOCUS
Add 20yds. A useful handicap, run at a decent clip, and they again headed down the centre. The second has been rated as matching last year's turf handicap best.

2488 VISIT ATTHERACES.COM NOVICE STKS — 1m 31y
4:55 (4:57) (Class 5) 3-4-Y-O
£3,752 (£1,116; £557; £278) Stalls Low

Form					RPR
0-	1		**Davydenko**[242] 6994 3-9-1	LouisSteward 10	86+
			(Sir Michael Stoute) *hld up in 7th: shkn up and prog wl over 2f out: clsd to ld jst ins fnl f: pushed out: readily* **12/1**		
4-	2	1 ¼	**Birdcage Walk**[215] 7897 3-8-10	(h[1]) TomMarquand 1	77
			(Hugo Palmer) *prom: rdn over 2f out: hanging lft but prog to ld briefly 1f out: outpcd by wnr last 100yds (jockey said colt hung left-handed in the final furlong)* **16/1**		
21	3	2 ¼	**Sparkle In His Eye**[101] 405 3-9-8	OisinMurphy 4	84
			(William Haggas) *trckd ldrs: shkn up to chal 2f out: one pce fnl f (vet said colt lost its right hind shoe)* **3/1**[2]		
6	4	nk	**Specialise**[20] 1828 3-8-10	DavidEgan 12	72+
			(Roger Varian) *hld up in rr: pushed along over 2f out: styd on steadily over 1f out: nvr nrr and shaped w promise* **28/1**		
03-	5	½	**Tammooz**[158] 9308 3-9-1	JackMitchell 3	75+
			(Roger Varian) *slowest out of the gate: hld up in rr: pushed along over 2f out: hanging and stl green but styd on steadily over 1f out: shaped w promise* **20/1**		
3-	6	1	**To The Moon**[284] 5386 3-8-10	RobertHavlin 2	68
			(John Gosden) *trckd ldrs: shkn up over 2f out: nt qckn and no imp on ldrs after* **10/11**[1]		
4-	7	½	**Desert Land (IRE)**[229] 7430 3-9-1	JamieSpencer 9	72
			(David Simcock) *t.k.h: led after 2f out: edgd lft over 2f out: hdd & wknd 1f out* **7/1**[3]		
	8	9	**Forbidden Dance** 3-8-10	CharlieBennett 5	46
			(Hughie Morrison) *hld up wl in rr: wl adrift 3f out: pushed along over 2f out: nvr in it but fin quite wl* **50/1**		
3/3	9	nse	**I Can (IRE)**[33] 1517 4-10-0	LukeMorris 7	54
			(Henry Candy) *t.k.h: led 2f: trckd ldr: hanging lft u.p and wknd qckly 2f out* **16/1**		
0	10	2	**Misty**[24] 1740 3-8-10	HarryBentley 11	42
			(Ralph Beckett) *chsd ldrs but sn pushed along: steadily wknd over 2f out* **40/1**		
	11	2 ½	**Storm Approaching** 3-8-10	GeorgeWood 14	36
			(James Fanshawe) *nvr beyond midfield: pushed along and wknd over 2f out (jockey said filly ran green)* **50/1**		
	12	35	**Prime Approach (IRE)** 3-9-1	PJMcDonald 8	
			(Brett Johnson) *a wl bhd: t.o* **100/1**		
	13	25	**Heldtoransom** 3-8-10	(h[1]) CallumShepherd 13	
			(Joseph Tuite) *rn v green and sn t.o* **100/1**		

1m 43.2s (-1.30) **Going Correction** -0.05s/f (Good)
WFA 3 from 4yo 13lb 13 Ran SP% **125.9**
Speed ratings (Par 103): **104,102,100,100,99 98,98,89,89,87 84,49,24**
CSF £187.00 TOTE £15.50: £3.20, £5.00, £1.30; EX 252.50 Trifecta £1666.10.
Owner Cheveley Park Stud **Bred** Cheveley Park Stud Ltd **Trained** Newmarket, Suffolk

FOCUS
Add 20yds. A fair novice, they headed centre-field in the straight and, having got racing a fair way out, it was a changing picture late. The third has been rated as building on his Newcastle win.

2489 FOLLOW AT THE RACES ON TWITTER H'CAP — 5f 21y
5:30 (5:30) (Class 5) (0-70,72) 3-Y-O
£3,752 (£1,116; £557; £300; £300; £300) Stalls Centre

Form					RPR
0-44	1		**Tomahawk Ridge (IRE)**[14] 1982 3-8-7 56	PJMcDonald 1	64
			(John Gallagher) *mde all: hung lft 2f out: jnd over 1f out: stened out and styd on wl to assert fnl f* **4/1**[2]		
2011	2	1	**Arishka (IRE)**[16] 1954 3-9-9 72	RobertWinston 8	76
			(Daniel Kubler) *mostly trckd wnr: chal and upsides over 1f out: rdn and fnd little fnl f: readily hld last 100yds* **3/1**[1]		
0-36	3	1 ¾	**Valentino Sunrise**[7] 2204 3-8-7 63	GeorgeBass(7) 7	61
			(Mick Channon) *wl in tch: chsd ldng pair and cl up 2f out: sltly impeded over 1f out: one pce fnl f* **5/1**[3]		
0-06	4	nk	**Te Amo Te Amo**[11] 2063 3-8-12 61	TomMarquand 9	58
			(Simon Dow) *towards rr: rdn and prog 2f out: chsd ldng trio jst over 1f out: kpt on same pce* **12/1**		
400-	5	1 ¾	**Mayfair Madame**[243] 6933 3-9-2 65	DavidEgan 3	56
			(Stuart Kittow) *trckd ldrs: styd towards nr side rail in st: nt on terms over 1f out* **14/1**		
56-5	6	nk	**Invincible Larne (IRE)**[11] 2060 3-9-7 70	CharlesBishop 4	60
			(Mick Quinn) *s.s: prog fr rr 1/2-way: shkn up and no imp on ldrs over 1f out* **9/1**		
5-05	7	nk	**True Belief (IRE)**[13] 2009 3-9-4 67	(h[1]) JackMitchell 10	55
			(Brett Johnson) *taken down early: hld up in last: effrt on outer 2f out: nvr rchd ldrs* **14/1**		
10-0	8	4	**Aegean Mist**[13] 2008 3-9-7 70	HollieDoyle 6	44
			(John Bridger) *disp 2nd pl to 1/2-way: wknd wl over 1f out* **12/1**		
0-26	9	1 ¼	**Turquoise Friendly**[13] 2009 3-9-4 67	LukeMorris 2	37
			(Robert Cowell) *in tch: styd against nr side rail fr 1/2-way: struggling fnl 2f (jockey said gelding hung right-handed throughout)* **16/1**		
35-4	10	½	**Finch Hatton**[9] 2123 3-9-5 68	RaulDaSilva 5	36
			(Robert Cowell) *sn pushed along: nvr on terms: wl btn fnl 2f* **5/1**[3]		

59.76s (-0.34) **Going Correction** -0.05s/f (Good) 10 Ran SP% **122.9**
Speed ratings (Par 99): **100,98,95,95,92 91,91,84,82,82**
CSF £17.46 CT £65.01 TOTE £5.00: £1.80, £1.60, £1.80; EX 23.50 Trifecta £60.90.
Owner Max Europe Limited **Bred** Kilmoney Cottage Stud **Trained** Chastleton, Oxon

FOCUS
The right horses came to the fore in this modest sprint. The winner has been rated back to his early 2yo form.

T/Jkpt: Not won. T/Plt: £377.40 to a £1 stake. Pool: £90,529.29 - 175.09 winning units. T/Qpdt: £31.10 to a £1 stake. Pool: £8,077.91 - 191.76 winning units. **Jonathan Neesom**

2490 - (Foreign Racing) - See Raceform Interactive

CURRAGH (R-H)

Monday, May 6

OFFICIAL GOING: Straight course - yielding; round course - good to yielding

2491a FIRST FLIER STKS (LISTED RACE) 5f

2:25 (2:28) 2-Y-O

£23,918 (£7,702; £3,648; £1,621; £810; £405) **Stalls** Centre

RPR

1 **Ickworth (IRE)**[38] 1404 2-8-12 0 ... WJLee 4 98
(W McCreery, Ire) *on toes befhand: cl up: 2nd 1/2-way: impr travelling wl to ld narrowly 1 1/2f out: rdn clr ins fnl f and kpt on wl: comf* **8/1**[3]

2 2 1/4 **King Neptune (USA)**[19] 1864 2-9-3 0 ... RyanMoore 2 95
(A P O'Brien, Ire) *broke wl to ld narrowly: pushed along after 1/2-way and hdd narrowly u.p 1 1/2f out: no imp on easy wnr ins fnl f: kpt on same pce* **2/5**[1]

3 1/2 **In The Present (USA)**[23] 1772 2-8-12 0 ... ShaneFoley 6 88
(Mrs John Harrington, Ire) *chsd ldrs: 5th 1/2-way: n.m.r bhd horses after 1/2-way: sn swtchd rt and rdn into 3rd ins fnl f where no imp on easy wnr: kpt on same pce to jst hold 3rd* **11/2**[2]

4 shd **American Lady (IRE)**[11] 2067 2-8-12 0 ... ChrisHayes 7 88
(J A Stack, Ire) *w.w: sn in rr: swtchd rt bhd horses 1f out and r.o far side into 4th wl ins fnl f: jst failed for 3rd: nrst fin* **25/1**

5 1 3/4 **Moments Linger (IRE)**[31] 1571 2-8-12 0 ... KevinManning 1 81
(J S Bolger, Ire) *cl up early tl sn settled bhd ldrs: racd keenly: cl 3rd at 1/2-way: drvn after 1/2-way and no imp on wnr u.p in 3rd over 1f out: one pce fnl f* **12/1**

6 nk **Kocasandra (IRE)**[7] 2218 2-8-12 0 ... GaryHalpin 5 80
(J P Murtagh, Ire) *on toes befhand: chsd ldrs: 4th 1/2-way: pushed along bhd horses under 2f out: rdn and no imp on ldrs over 1f out: kpt on one pce in 6th wl ins fnl f* **33/1**

7 4 1/2 **Ampeson**[11] 2067 2-9-3 0 ... OisinOrr 3 69
(Richard John O'Brien, Ire) *w.w on outer in 6th early: tk clsr order after 1/2-way: rdn 1 1/2f out and sn no ex: wknd to rr ins fnl f* **33/1**

1m 2.2s (1.80) **Going Correction** +0.45s/f (Yiel) 7 Ran SP% **115.3**
Speed ratings: **103,99,98,98,95 95,87**
CSF £11.89 TOTE £8.50: £2.60, £1.02; DF 14.60 Trifecta £44.00.

Owner Godolphin **Bred** Godolphin **Trained** Rathbride, Co Kildare

FOCUS
There were some promising juveniles in here and three of the seven had already won. The winner made her rivals look quite ordinary.

2492a COOLMORE CHURCHILL IRISH EBF TETRARCH STKS (LISTED RACE) 7f

3:00 (3:03) 3-Y-O

£30,563 (£9,842; £4,662; £2,072; £1,036; £518)

RPR

1 **Shelir (IRE)**[37] 1437 3-9-3 0 ... ChrisHayes 10 101+
(D K Weld, Ire) *mid-div: 5th 1/2-way: pushed along fr 3f out and hdwy nr side 1f out where sltly impeded: r.o u.p to ld wl ins fnl f and styd on wl* **8/1**

2 1 1/4 **Eclipse Storm**[8] 2156 3-9-3 96 ... ConorMaxwell 1 98+
(J A Stack, Ire) *mid-div: 6th 1/2-way: n.m.r bhd horses fr over 2f out: rdn in 6th ent fnl f and r.o between horses into nvr nrr 2nd fnl stride* **33/1**

3 shd **Flash Gordon (IRE)**[23] 1774 3-9-3 0 ... ShaneFoley 6 97
(Mrs John Harrington, Ire) *led and disp early: cl 2nd after 2f: disp cl 2nd at 1/2-way: pushed along after 1/2-way: rdn over 1f out and disp ld briefly far side ins fnl f tl sn hdd: no ex in 2nd cl home: denied 2nd fnl stride* **15/2**

4 3/4 **Piano Solo (FR)**[37] 1437 3-9-3 0 ... WJLee 4 95
(K J Condon, Ire) *hld up towards rr: 8th at 1/2-way: prog far side to chse ldrs 1 1/2f out where rdn: disp 3rd u.p briefly ins fnl f: no imp on wnr in 4th nr fin* **20/1**

5 hd **I Am Superman (IRE)**[7] 2222 3-9-3 101 ... LeighRoche 3 94
(M D O'Callaghan, Ire) *chsd ldrs: disp 2nd at 1/2-way: impr gng wl nr side to chal on terms over 2f out: led narrowly under 2f out: sn rdn and hung lft over 1f out: jnd and hdd ins fnl f: wknd into 5th cl home (jockey said that his mount pulled his near fore shoe)* **11/8**[1]

6 1 3/4 **Limit Long**[16] 1964 3-9-3 82 ... KevinManning 8 89
(D J Bunyan, Ire) *sn led and disp: narrow advantage after 2f: rdn over 2f out and sn hdd: no ex u.p bhd ldrs over 1f out: sn wknd* **25/1**

7 3/4 **U S S Michigan (USA)**[25] 1713 3-9-3 101 ... DonnachaO'Brien 7 87+
(A P O'Brien, Ire) *hld up towards rr early: last at 1/2-way: rdn into 8th fr 2f out and wnt nvr threatening 7th ins fnl f: kpt on* **4/1**[2]

8 4 1/2 **Gloves Lynch**[167] 9167 3-9-3 98 ... DeclanMcDonogh 2 75
(Gordon Elliott, Ire) *led and disp early tl sn settled bhd ldrs in 3rd: disp cl 2nd at 1/2-way: pushed along far side 2f out and wknd over 1f out where rdn: eased nr fin* **25/1**

9 2 1/2 **Major Reward (IRE)**[7] 2222 3-9-3 83 ... GeraldMosse 9 69
(Adrian Paul Keatley, Ire) *w.w in rr: tk clsr order bef 1/2-way: 7th at 1/2-way: rdn 3f out and no ex u.p nr side 2f out: wknd: eased ins fnl f* **50/1**

10 1 **Antilles (USA)**[25] 1713 3-9-3 106 ... RyanMoore 5 66
(A P O'Brien, Ire) *hld up in 7th early: rdn in 9th fr 1/2-way and no imp u.p far side 2f out: eased wl ins fnl f* **9/2**[3]

1m 26.84s (1.84) **Going Correction** +0.45s/f (Yiel) 10 Ran SP% **120.5**
Speed ratings: **107,105,105,104,104 102,101,96,93,92**
CSF £244.82 TOTE £9.70: £2.10, £8.40, £1.40; DF 386.70 Trifecta £2593.60.

Owner H H Aga Khan **Bred** H H The Aga Khan's Studs Sc **Trained** Curragh, Co Kildare

FOCUS
A good performance from the winner, who appears to be learning and improving with each start. The beaten favourite may be better going left-handed than on a straight course.

2493a COOLMORE GLENEAGLES IRISH EBF ATHASI STKS (GROUP 3) (F&M) 7f

3:35 (3:38) 3-Y-O+

£42,522 (£13,693; £6,486; £2,882; £1,441; £720)

RPR

1 **Happen (USA)**[30] 1601 3-8-11 101 ... (t) RyanMoore 6 99+
(A P O'Brien, Ire) *in rr and pushed along briefly early: last at 1/2-way: pushed along over 2f out and prog nr side into 8th over 1f out: rdn and r.o wl into 3rd wl ins fnl f and led nr side fnl stride* **11/4**[2]

2 shd **Dan's Dream**[211] 8019 4-9-9 107 ... RonanWhelan 9 102+
(Mick Channon) *hld up towards rr: 8th 1/2-way: prog nr side over 2f out: rdn into 2nd over 1f out and kpt on wl u.p to dispute ld cl home tl hdd fnl stride* **15/2**

3 nk **Rionach**[43] 1307 4-9-9 94 ... LeighRoche 8 101
(M D O'Callaghan, Ire) *led and disp: narrow advantage over 2f out stl gng wl: extended advantage over 1f out: sn rdn and strly pressed nr fin where jnd and hdd: dropped to 3rd fnl strides* **33/1**

4 1 1/4 **Hand On Heart (IRE)**[43] 1307 4-9-9 97 ... ChrisHayes 2 98
(J A Stack, Ire) *hooded to load: sn settled in mid-div: disp 5th at 1/2-way: drvn under 2f out and no imp on ldr in 7th over 1f out: rdn and r.o into nvr threatening 4th nr fin: nvr trbld ldrs* **10/1**

5 nk **Foxtrot Liv**[218] 7813 3-8-11 102 ... WJLee 10 93
(P Twomey, Ire) *chsd ldrs: 3rd 1/2-way: drvn in 2nd briefly 1 1/2f out and no imp on ldr in 4th ins fnl f where n.m.r briefly far side: no ex u.p nr fin where dropped to 5th* **9/4**[1]

6 1/2 **Titanium Sky (IRE)**[33] 1532 3-8-11 0 ... OisinOrr 5 92
(D K Weld, Ire) *mid-div: disp 5th at 1/2-way: pushed along and tk clsr order bhd ldrs nr side under 2f out: rdn into 3rd briefly ins fnl f tl sn no ex: wknd into 6th nr fin* **6/1**[3]

7 1 3/4 **Drombeg Dream (IRE)**[11] 2069 4-9-9 101 ... ShaneFoley 4 91
(Augustine Leahy, Ire) *chsd ldrs: pushed along in 4th fr 1/2-way and no imp on ldr in 5th 1f out: wknd: eased nr fin* **20/1**

8 4 1/2 **Indian Blessing**[197] 8445 5-9-12 106 ... GeraldMosse 1 82
(Ed Walker) *w.w: 9th 1/2-way: rdn in 8th and no ex under 2f out: eased nr fin* **8/1**

9 2 **I Remember You (IRE)**[30] 1601 3-8-11 82 ... SeamieHeffernan 3 70
(A P O'Brien, Ire) *led and disp: pushed along in cl 2nd over 2f out and no ex u.p 1 1/2f out: wknd: eased in 9th nr fin* **25/1**

10 9 1/2 **Luceita (IRE)**[248] 6776 4-9-9 0 ... KevinManning 7 48
(J S Bolger, Ire) *mid-div: disp 5th at 1/2-way: sn pushed along and wknd to rr 2f out: eased fr over 1f out* **16/1**

1m 26.72s (1.72) **Going Correction** +0.45s/f (Yiel)
WFA 3 from 4yo+ 12lb 10 Ran SP% **121.1**
Speed ratings: **108,107,107,106,105 105,103,98,95,84**
CSF £24.33 TOTE £2.80: £1.20, £2.20, £6.20; DF 21.40 Trifecta £406.40.
Owner Mrs John Magnier & Michael Tabor & Derrick Smith **Bred** Orpendale/Chelston/Wynatt **Trained** Cashel, Co Tipperary

FOCUS
The winner got there in the nick of time, with the 12lb she received from the second and third proving crucial at the death. Ryan Moore's mount touched 249-1 in running on Betfair.

2494a COOLMORE HIGHLAND REEL IRISH EBF MOORESBRIDGE STKS (GROUP 2) 1m 2f

4:10 (4:12) 4-Y-O+ **£69,099** (£22,252; £10,540; £4,684)

RPR

1 **Magical (IRE)**[23] 1777 4-9-3 122 ... RyanMoore 3 112+
(A P O'Brien, Ire) *chsd ldr: clsr 2nd bef 1/2-way: hdwy gng best to ld over 1f out: pushed out ins fnl f: nt extended: comf* **2/9**[1]

2 1 1/2 **Flag Of Honour (IRE)**[23] 1777 4-9-6 117 ... SeamieHeffernan 1 111+
(A P O'Brien, Ire) *led and sn clr: over 3 l clr after 1f: reduced advantage bef 1/2-way: rdn 1 1/2f out and sn hdd: no imp on wnr in 2nd ins fnl f where swtchd lft: kpt on same pce to hold 2nd* **5/1**[2]

3 nk **The King (IRE)**[205] 8202 4-9-3 107 ... (t[1]) ShaneFoley 4 107
(Mrs John Harrington, Ire) *dwlt and rrd leaving gate: in rr: last at 1/2-way: pushed along over 3f out and tk clsr order nr side under 2f out: rdn into 3rd over 1f out and no imp on wnr ins fnl f: kpt on same pce* **33/1**

4 nk **Latrobe (IRE)**[23] 1777 4-9-3 114 ... DonnachaO'Brien 2 106
(Joseph Patrick O'Brien, Ire) *hld up bhd ldrs in 3rd: clsr 3rd bef 1/2-way: pushed along fr 3f out and lost pl over 1f out where rdn briefly: no imp on wnr and kpt on same pce between horses wl ins fnl f* **10/1**[3]

2m 12.19s (0.69) **Going Correction** +0.45s/f (Yiel) 4 Ran SP% **110.5**
Speed ratings: **115,113,113,113**
CSF £1.88 TOTE £1.10; DF 1.90 Trifecta £9.70.
Owner Derrick Smith & Mrs John Magnier & Michael Tabor **Bred** Orpendale, Chelston & Wynatt **Trained** Cashel, Co Tipperary

FOCUS
The winner had already confirmed her superiority over two of these rivals, Flag Of Honour and Latrobe, but was extremely convincing in victory again here. Jessica Harrington can be proud of The King's effort. Seamie Heffernan ensured this was a decent test from the front aboard a proven stayer. The third and fourth have been rated in line with their recent figures.

2495- 2497a (Foreign Racing) - See Raceform Interactive

2352 CHANTILLY (R-H)

Monday, May 6

OFFICIAL GOING: Polytrack: standard; turf: soft

2498a PRIX DES LILAS (LISTED RACE) (3YO FILLIES) (TURF) 1m

2:35 3-Y-O **£24,774** (£9,909; £7,432; £4,954; £2,477)

RPR

1 **Obligate**[178] 3-9-0 0 ... Pierre-CharlesBoudot 1 105+
(P Bary, France) **23/5**[2]

2 3 1/2 **Pure Zen (FR)**[26] 1706 3-9-0 0 ... MaximeGuyon 9 97
(Gianluca Bietolini, France) **56/10**[3]

3 1 **Gypsy Spirit**[23] 1751 3-9-0 0 ... JamesDoyle 4 95
(Tom Clover) *wl into stride: trckd ldrs in 3rd: impr to briefly chal ldr 2f out: rdn and outpcd over 1f out: kpt on ins fnl f* **12/1**

4 5 **Simplicity (FR)**[34] 1512 3-9-0 0 ... (b) CristianDemuro 3 84
(F Chappet, France) **41/5**

5 4 **Mythic (FR)**[173] 9055 3-9-0 0.............................. OlivierPeslier 10 74
(A De Royer-Dupre, France) **12/1**
6 2 **Olympe (FR)**[48] 3-9-0 0.............................. ChristopheSoumillon 7 70
(J-C Rouget, France) **11/10**[1]
7 10 **Etruria**[23] 3-9-0 0.............................. VincentCheminaud 6 47
(A Fabre, France) *dwlt: hld up towards rr of midfield: pushed along over 2f out: rdn but fnd little over 1f out: heavily eased ins fnl f* **9/1**
8 5 1/2 **Houesville (FR)**[20] 3-9-0 0.............................. MickaelBerto 2 34
(C Lerner, France) **32/1**
1m 39.22s (1.22) **8 Ran SP% 119.9**
PARI-MUTUEL (all including 1 euro stake): WIN 5.60; PLACE 2.10, 2.40, 3.50; DF 14.30.
Owner K Abdullah **Bred** Juddmonte Farms Ltd **Trained** Chantilly, France

2499a PRIX DE GUICHE (GROUP 3) (3YO COLTS & GELDINGS) (TURF) 1m 1f
3:10 3-Y-O **£36,036** (£14,414; £10,810; £7,207; £3,603)

RPR
1 **Flop Shot (FR)**[55] 3-9-2 0.............................. MaximeGuyon 1 109+
(A Fabre, France) *settled in 4th in tch w ldrs: drvn to chse ldr over 2f out: led 1 1/2f out: styd on strly fnl f: won easing down* **105/10**
2 3 **Syrtis**[22] 1797 3-9-2 0.............................. Pierre-CharlesBoudot 6 103
(A Fabre, France) *a cl up on outer: clsd smoothly to ld more than 2f out: sn drvn and hdd 1 1/2f fr home: kpt on u.p fnl f but no match for wnr* **11/10**[1]
3 1 1/4 **Savvy Nine (FR)**[239] 7106 3-9-2 0.............................. JamesDoyle 2 100
(William Haggas) *trckd ldr: n.m.r between horses 2f out: swtchd outside rivals and rdn 1 1/2f out: kpt on without having pce to trble ldrs* **71/10**[3]
4 1/2 **Famous Wolf (FR)**[41] 1347 3-9-2 0.............................. VincentCheminaud 4 99
(A Fabre, France) *hld up in rr: tk clsr order over 2f out: nt clr run w 1 1/2f to run: sn in clr but unable to change gear: kpt on at same pce* **14/1**
5 3 **Toijk (FR)**[26] 1707 3-9-2 0.............................. HugoJourniac 3 93
(M Nigge, France) *t.k.h: hld up in fnl pair: last wl over 1f out: kpt on for press fnl f but nvr in contention* **18/1**
6 6 **Tel Aviv (FR)**[41] 3-9-2 0.............................. CristianDemuro 7 80
(Andrea Marcialis, France) *t.k.h: hld up in fnl trio: hrd rdn and short-lived effrt 2f out: sn no further imp: wknd fnl f* **78/10**
7 10 **Makmour (FR)**[37] 3-9-2 0.............................. ChristopheSoumillon 5 59
(J-C Rouget, France) *led: hdd more than 2f out: wl hld in last whn eased ins fnl f* **13/5**[2]
1m 52.55s (1.45) **7 Ran SP% 119.7**
PARI-MUTUEL (all including 1 euro stake): WIN 11.50; PLACE 3.40, 1.50; SF 21.80.
Owner Wertheimer & Frere **Bred** Wertheimer & Frere **Trained** Chantilly, France

L'ANCRESSE
Monday, May 6
OFFICIAL GOING: Turf: firm

2500a GRC DERBY H'CAP (TURF) 1m 4f
2:15 (2:20) 3-Y-O+ **£1,800** (£750; £450)

RPR
1 **Herm (IRE)**[20] 1841 5-9-13 0.............................. PhilipPrince 36
(David Evans) *hld up: rdn to ld over 1f out: drvn out* **1/2**[1]
2 1 1/2 **Gabster (IRE)**[14] 2003 6-10-11 0 ow1.............................. KieronEdgar 46
(K Kukk, Jersey) *trckd ldr: wnt on 4f out: no ex whn hdd over 1f out* **Evs**[2]
3 24 **Little Lotte (IRE)**[14] 2003 6-9-2 0..............................(b) DarraghKeogh
(Mrs A Corson, Jersey) *bolted bef s; led: hdd 4f out: sn wknd* **9/2**[3]

Owner Trevor Gallienne **Bred** Mountarmstrong Stud **Trained** Pandy, Monmouths

2501a GRC "ECLIPSE" H'CAP (TURF) 1m 2f
2:50 (2:54) 3-Y-O+ **£1,800** (£750; £450)

RPR
1 **Twpsyn (IRE)**[16] 1957 3-9-9 0.............................. PhilipPrince 51
(David Evans) *trckd ldr: rdn along fr 1/2-way: wnt on 2f out: drvn out* **1/3**[1]
2 1 **Hard To Handel**[14] 7-10-12 0.............................. VictoriaMalzard 52
(Mrs A Malzard, Jersey) *led: hdd 2f out: kpt on one pce* **7/4**[2]
3 6 **Carrera**[288] 9-8-10 0 oh9 ow5.............................. DarraghKeogh 10
(Mrs A Malzard, Jersey) *a last: outpcd fr 3f out* **4/1**[3]

Owner Rob Emmanuelle, T Burns & P D Evans **Bred** Rathasker Stud **Trained** Pandy, Monmouths

2502a BETWAY H'CAP (TURF) 2m
3:25 (3:25) 3-Y-O+ **£3,100** (£1,200; £700)

RPR
1 **Rainbow Lad (IRE)**[14] 2003 6-8-11 0.............................. MissSerenaBrotherton 50
(Michael Appleby) *trckd ldr: rdn to ld over 1f out: drvn clr: fin lame* **4/6**[1]
2 4 1/2 **Barwick**[14] 5264 11-10-12 0..............................(p) VictoriaMalzard 74
(Mrs A Malzard, Jersey) *led: hdd over 1f out: no ex* **5/4**[2]
3 13 **Jackblack**[14] 2003 7-8-10 0.............................. PhilipPrince 30
(K Kukk, Jersey) *hld up: outpcd 1/2-way: sn btn* **7/2**[3]
4 20 **Rainbow Charlie**[14] 2003 8-8-10 0 oh43 ow5.............................. DarraghKeogh 8
(Mrs A Corson, Jersey) *trckd ldrs: outpcd 1/2-way: sn t.o* **16/1**

Owner Michael Appleby **Bred** Rathbarry Stud **Trained** Oakham, Rutland

2503a "ROSS GOWER GROUP" H'CAP (TURF) 6f
4:00 (4:00) 3-Y-O+ **£1,800** (£750; £450)

RPR
1 **It Must Be Faith**[18] 1880 9-10-12 0..............................(p) MissSerenaBrotherton 54
(Michael Appleby) *trckd ldr: wnt on over 3f out: hdd wl over 1f out: gamely rallied to ld again last few strides* **6/4**[2]
2 hd **Doctor Parkes**[267] 6079 13-10-10 0.............................. MrFrederickTett 51
(Natalie Lloyd-Beavis) *led to over 3f out: rdn & wnt on again wl over 1f out: no ex whn hdd last few strides* **5/2**[3]
3 3 **Haats Off**[61] 1043 3-9-13 0.............................. VictoriaMalzard 37
(Brian Barr) *chsd ldrs thrght: outpcd fr 1/2-way* **8/1**
4 1 **Toolatetodelegate**[58] 1093 5-9-7 0..............................(tp) DarraghKeogh 21
(Brian Barr) *bhd: outpcd fr 1/2-way: kpt on one pce late* **4/1**
5 40 **Brockey Rise (IRE)**[21] 1820 4-10-7 0..............................(b) PhilipPrince
(David Evans) *trckd ldrs: hung rt turn after 1f: sn t.o: virtually p.u cl home* **1/2**[1]

Owner Mick Appleby Racing **Bred** Matthew Sharkey & Newsells Park Stud Ltd **Trained** Oakham, Rutland

2504a "HUNSCOTE STUD" H'CAP (TURF) 1m
4:35 (4:35) (0-70,0) 3-Y-O+ **£1,800** (£750; £450)

RPR
1 **Amor Fati (IRE)**[20] 1836 4-10-12 0.............................. PhilipPrince 65
(David Evans) *trckd ldr: wnt on 4f out: rdn clr over 1f out: easily* **1/5**[1]
2 2 **Mendacious Harpy (IRE)**[267] 6080 8-8-13 0.............................. DarraghKeogh 33
(Mrs A Malzard, Jersey) *hld up: wnt 2nd & chsd wnr fr 3f out but a hld* **3/1**[2]
3 6 **Coastguard Watch (FR)**[31] 1557 3-9-6 0.............................. MrFrederickTett 36
(Natalie Lloyd-Beavis) *led to 4f out: sn outpcd* **6/1**[3]

Owner Mrs Catherine Gannon **Bred** Tony O'Meara **Trained** Pandy, Monmouths

[2146] WETHERBY (L-H)
Tuesday, May 7
OFFICIAL GOING: Good changing to good to soft after race 1 (1.50)
Wind: Light across Weather: Cloudy with sunny period heavy showers later

2505 FOLLOW @RACINGTV ON TWITTER NOVICE STKS 1m 2f
1:50 (1:51) (Class 5) 3-Y-O+ **£4,528** (£1,347; £673; £336) **Stalls** Centre

Form RPR
5 1 **Gold Stick (IRE)**[24] 1755 3-8-13 0.............................. RobertHavlin 8 84+
(John Gosden) *trckd ldrs: cl up 3f out: led jst over 2f out: rdn clr over 1f out: kpt on wl* **6/4**[1]
0 2 3 1/2 **Australis (IRE)**[22] 1824 3-8-13 0.............................. DavidEgan 9 76+
(Roger Varian) *hld up in tch: pushed along and sltly outpcd over 4f out: swtchd to outer and rdn along over 3f out: hdwy over 2f out: sn chsng ldrs: kpt on u.p fnl f* **8/1**
3 2 1/4 **Stone Mason (IRE)** 3-8-13 0.............................. JasonWatson 7 71
(Roger Charlton) *trckd ldrs: hdwy 3f out: sn cl up: rdn along and ev ch 2f out: drvn wl over 1f out: kpt on same pce* **5/2**[2]
4 3/4 **Walk It Talk It** 3-8-8 0..............................(h[1]) GeorgeWood 10 64+
(Chris Wall) *green and in rr: hdwy over 3f out: chsd ldrs 2f out: kpt on wl fnl f* **28/1**
5 3 1/2 **Kenica (IRE)** 3-8-2 0 ow1.............................. RhonaPindar(7) 11 57
(K R Burke) *chsd ldrs: pushed along 3f out: rdn 2f out: styd on fnl f* **28/1**
6 5 **Triple Genius (IRE)** 3-8-13 0.............................. DanielMuscutt 6 49
(Ed Dunlop) *midfield on inner: pushed along 4f out: hdwy over 2f out: sn rdn: plugged on fnl f* **25/1**
0-5 7 1 1/2 **Spice Of Life**[39] 1397 3-8-8 0.............................. HarryBentley 1 41
(Ralph Beckett) *led: hdd over 7f out: prom: pushed along 4f out: cl up and rdn over 2f out: drvn wl over 1f out: grad wknd* **7/1**[3]
8 1 3/4 **Stormin Norman**[34] 4-10-0 0.............................. GrahamLee 3 43
(Micky Hammond) *a towards rr* **33/1**
9 4 1/2 **Jesse Jude (IRE)**[232] 6-10-0 0.............................. AndrewElliott 5 33
(Simon West) *s.i.s: a bhd* **66/1**
0- 10 3 **Mullion Dreams**[360] 2660 5-9-11 0.............................. JamieGormley(3) 13 26
(James Ewart) *a in rr* **250/1**
0 11 9 **Loch Laggan (IRE)**[24] 1755 3-8-13 0.............................. PJMcDonald 14 4
(David Menuisier) *prom: trckd ldr 7f out: rdn along over 3f out: sn drvn and wknd* **16/1**
12 nk **The Retriever (IRE)**[22] 4-10-0 0.............................. PaulMulrennan 12 4
(Micky Hammond) *cl up: led over 7f out: pushed along over 3f out: sn rdn and hdd over 2f out: sn wknd* **150/1**
2m 10.31s (1.01) **Going Correction** +0.325s/f (Good) **12 Ran SP% 114.3**
WFA 3 from 4yo+ 15lb
Speed ratings (Par 103): **109,106,104,103,101 97,95,94,90,88 81,80**
CSF £13.13 TOTE £2.10: £1.30, £1.80, £1.40; EX 13.20 Trifecta £40.40.
Owner The Queen **Bred** Godolphin **Trained** Newmarket, Suffolk

FOCUS
There'd been around 7mm of rain since the previous day and the clerk of the course felt the ground was 'just on the slow side of good.' After riding in the opener Robert Havlin and Jason Watson called the ground 'good to soft', while George Wood felt it was 'soft.' Not a strong novice in terms of depth, but the right horses came to the fore and the favourite won readily. The level is fluid.

2506 100% RACING TV PROFITS RETURNED TO RACING NOVICE STKS (DIV I) 7f
2:20 (2:23) (Class 5) 3-Y-O+ **£4,528** (£1,347; £673; £336) **Stalls** Low

Form RPR
-5 1 **Destination**[10] 2094 3-9-2 0.............................. DanielTudhope 3 89+
(William Haggas) *trckd ldrs: hdwy 3f out: cl up 2f out: rdn to ld ent fnl f: kpt on wl* **5/2**[2]
51- 2 1 3/4 **Boston George (IRE)**[200] 8378 3-9-7 0.............................. JoeFanning 9 89
(Keith Dalgleish) *trckd ldrs: hdwy on outer 3f out: chal wl over 1f out: sn rdn and ev ch: drvn and kpt on fnl f* **8/1**
6-22 3 1 1/2 **Franz Kafka (IRE)**[19] 1886 3-9-2 86.............................. RobertHavlin 10 80
(John Gosden) *trckd ldng pair: cl up 3f out: sn led: jnd and rdn wl over 1f out: drvn and hdd ent fnl f: one pce* **1/2**[1]
0 4 6 **Followme Followyou (IRE)**[8] 2199 3-8-11 0.............................. PJMcDonald 8 59
(Mark Johnston) *in tch: pushed along 1/2-way: rdn wl over 2f out: styd on appr fnl f* **25/1**
420- 5 3 1/4 **Dream Of Honour (IRE)**[178] 9006 3-9-2 78.............................. DavidAllan 11 55
(Tim Easterby) *cl up: rdn along over 2f out: drvn wl over 1f out: grad wknd* **7/1**[3]
0 6 3/4 **Caesonia**[20] 1852 3-8-11 0.............................. JasonWatson 7 48
(Charles Hills) *led: rdn along 3f out: sn hdd and grad wknd* **40/1**
7 3 3/4 **Ripon Spa** 3-9-2 0.............................. JackGarritty 4 43
(Jedd O'Keeffe) *bhd: pushed along over 3f out: rdn wl over 2f out: kpt on appr fnl f* **25/1**
00 8 5 **Broughtons Bear (IRE)**[19] 1886 3-9-2 0.............................. StevieDonohoe 1 29
(Stuart Williams) *a in rr* **150/1**

0 **9** 1 3/4 **Harry's Ridge (IRE)**[10] 2094 4-10-0 0 .... TomEaves 5 29
(Eric Alston) *dwlt: a towards rr* **100/1**

0 **10** 2 1/2 **Corralejo (IRE)**[26] 1723 3-9-2 0 .... PaulMulrennan 6 18
(John Wainwright) *a in rr* **200/1**

50 **11** 1/2 **Heavenly Secret (IRE)**[9] 2146 4-10-0 0 .... (t) DougieCostello 2 21
(Tony Coyle) *a towards rr (vet said gelding was lame on its left-fore)* **66/1**

1m 27.83s (0.63) **Going Correction** +0.325s/f (Good)
WFA 3 from 4yo 12lb **11** Ran SP% **132.6**
Speed ratings (Par 103): **109,107,105,98,94 93,89,83,81,79 78**
CSF £25.47 TOTE £4.00: £1.10, £1.90, £1.10; EX 32.80 Trifecta £49.30.
Owner Cheveley Park Stud **Bred** Cheveley Park Stud Ltd **Trained** Newmarket, Suffolk

FOCUS
The going was changed to good to soft prior to this contest. The first leg of a fair novice and the right three pulled clear. The third has been rated a bit below form.

2507 100% RACING TV PROFITS RETURNED TO RACING NOVICE STKS (DIV II) 7f

2:50 (2:52) (Class 5) 3-Y-O+ **£4,528** (£1,347; £673; £336) **Stalls** Low

Form RPR

3 **1** **Stoney Lane**[9] 2146 4-10-0 0 .... PhilDennis 9 79
(Richard Whitaker) *cl up: led 2f out: rdn clr jst over 1f out: edgd lft ins fnl f: kpt on (vet said gelding had lost its left hind shoe)* **16/1**

4- **2** nk **Be More**[220] 7774 3-8-11 0 .... OisinMurphy 1 69
(Andrew Balding) *trckd ldng pair on inner: pushed along and sltly outpcd wl over 2f out: rdn wl over 1f out: chsd wnr and swtchd rt ins fnl f: kpt on wl towards fin* **2/1**[1]

3 1 1/2 **Assembled** 3-9-2 0 .... PatCosgrave 3 70
(Hugo Palmer) *trckd ldrs: hdwy 3f out: rdn along 2f out: drvn over 1f out: kpt on same pce* **11/1**

21- **4** 1/2 **Duneflower (IRE)**[195] 8539 3-9-4 0 .... RobertHavlin 8 71+
(John Gosden) *dwlt and in rr: pushed along on inner 3f out: hdwy over 2f out: rdn and kpt on fnl f: nrst fin (jockey said filly was slowly away)* **9/4**[2]

5 **5** 1/2 **Grazeon Roy**[8] 2192 3-9-2 0 .... JasonHart 7 68
(John Quinn) *trckd ldrs: pushed along 3f out: rdn 2f out: kpt on u.p fnl f (vet said gelding sustained a would to left hind)* **50/1**

42-2 **6** 1 1/4 **Deebee**[7] 2250 3-9-2 0 .... KevinStott 6 64
(Declan Carroll) *hld up towards rr: hdwy on wd outside over 2f out: rdn along wl over 1f out: kpt on fnl f* **9/2**[3]

00- **7** 1 1/2 **Alexandria**[182] 8909 4-9-9 0 .... StevieDonohoe 11 59?
(Charlie Fellowes) *a towards rr* **100/1**

8 1/2 **Lucky Number** 3-9-2 0 .... DanielTudhope 2 59
(William Haggas) *s.i.s: a in rr (jockey said gelding missed the break)* **10/1**

44 **9** nk **Dabouk (IRE)**[15] 1975 3-9-2 0 .... DavidNolan 4 58
(David O'Meara) *set stdy pce: pushed along and qcknd 3f out: hdd and rdn 2f out: sn drvn and wknd* **20/1**

00 **10** 1/2 **Dream House**[8] 2199 3-9-2 0 .... RachelRichardson 5 57
(Tim Easterby) *a towards rr* **100/1**

1m 29.97s (2.77) **Going Correction** +0.325s/f (Good)
WFA 3 from 4yo 12lb **10** Ran SP% **114.3**
Speed ratings (Par 103): **97,96,94,94,93 92,90,90,89,89**
CSF £46.87 TOTE £17.30: £3.20, £1.10, £2.60; EX 62.20 Trifecta £683.70.
Owner R M Whitaker **Bred** Hellwood Stud Farm **Trained** Scarcroft, W Yorks

FOCUS
The lesser of the two divisions and, with there being little pace on, it proved difficult to make ground. The runners ended up centre-to-stands' side. The second has been rated in line with her debut form.

2508 RACINGTV.COM H'CAP 5f 110y

3:20 (3:25) (Class 5) (0-75,75) 4-Y-O+

£4,075 (£1,212; £606; £303; £300; £300) **Stalls** High

Form RPR

3-06 **1** **Manshood (IRE)**[11] 2079 6-9-4 73 .... (b) OisinMurphy 8 84
(Paul Midgley) *hld up in rr: hdwy on wd outside 2f out: rdn over 1f out: qcknd to ld ent fnl f: kpt on strly* **7/1**

1-10 **2** 3 **Turanga Leela**[11] 2081 5-9-2 71 .... (b) StevieDonohoe 9 72
(John Mackie) *cl up: chal 2f out and sn rdn: drvn and ev ch ent fnl f: kpt on same pce* **16/1**

6520 **3** 1 1/4 **Landing Night (IRE)**[3] 2421 7-9-5 74 .... (tp) PJMcDonald 10 71
(Rebecca Menzies) *hld up in tch: hdwy over 2f out: chal wl over 1f out: ev ch: rdn and edgd lft appr fnl f: kpt on same pce* **13/2**[3]

0406 **4** nk **Van Gerwen**[6] 2294 6-9-4 73 .... DavidAllan 6 69
(Les Eyre) *led: rdn along 2f out: hdd and drvn wl over 1f out: kpt on u.p fnl f* **17/2**

15 **5** hd **Tabaahy**[17] 1951 4-9-5 74 .... DanielTudhope 7 69
(David O'Meara) *trckd ldrs: hdwy to ld over 1f out: rdn and hdd ent fnl f: sn drvn and kpt on same pce* **13/2**[3]

-444 **6** 1 **Musharrif**[6] 2294 7-9-4 73 .... DavidNolan 1 64
(Declan Carroll) *in tch on inner: rdn along 2f out: sn drvn and one pce* **6/1**[2]

5243 **7** 1 **Amazing Grazing (IRE)**[4] 2368 5-9-6 75 .... (e) LewisEdmunds 5 63
(Rebecca Bastiman) *a towards rr* **11/4**[1]

125- **8** 4 **Case Key**[202] 8315 6-9-3 72 .... AlistairRawlinson 4 46
(Michael Appleby) *chsd ldng pair: rdn along 2f out: sn wknd* **14/1**

53-4 **9** 2 1/4 **Show Palace**[20] 1860 6-9-5 74 .... JoeFanning 3 41
(Jennie Candlish) *t.k.h: a towards rr (jockey said gelding ran too free)* **10/1**

1m 7.17s (1.37) **Going Correction** +0.325s/f (Good) **9** Ran SP% **112.3**
Speed ratings (Par 103): **103,99,97,96,96 95,94,88,85**
CSF £106.48 CT £567.64 TOTE £7.10: £2.40, £4.30, £2.50; EX 102.70 Trifecta £597.80.
Owner Taylor's Bloodstock Ltd **Bred** John McEnery **Trained** Westow, N Yorks
■ Casterbridge was withdrawn. Price at time of withdrawal 22/1. Rule 4 does not apply.

FOCUS
A modest sprint and they once again headed down the centre, with the winner drawing clear nearest the stands' side. The winner has been rated to his AW win last November.

2509 WATCH RACING TV IN STUNNING HD H'CAP 1m

3:55 (3:56) (Class 5) (0-75,77) 4-Y-O+

£4,075 (£1,212; £606; £303; £300; £300) **Stalls** Low

Form RPR

2532 **1** **Zodiakos (IRE)**[2] 2439 6-8-11 65 .... (p) BenCurtis 7 73
(Roger Fell) *sn led: mde most: rdn over 1f out: drvn ins fnl f: hld on wl* **9/2**[2]

31-2 **2** 3/4 **Shawaamekh**[9] 2151 5-9-8 76 .... (t) DavidNolan 9 82
(Declan Carroll) *hld up in midfield: hdwy over 2f out: rdn to chse wnr ent fnl f: sn drvn and ev ch: no ex last 50yds* **2/1**[1]

0-51 **3** 1/2 **Equidae**[41] 1369 4-8-10 67 .... (t) JamieGormley(3) 12 72
(Iain Jardine) *trckd wnr: effrt and cl up over 2f out: rdn wl over 1f out: drvn ent fnl f: kpt on same pce* **11/1**

05-0 **4** 1/2 **Vive La Difference (IRE)**[29] 1644 5-9-8 76 .... DavidAllan 14 80
(Tim Easterby) *hld up towards rr: gd hdwy over 2f out: rdn to chse ldrs over 1f out: kpt on fnl f* **11/1**

1-50 **5** 1/2 **Dubai Acclaim (IRE)**[18] 1925 4-9-4 72 .... TonyHamilton 13 75
(Richard Fahey) *towards rr: hdwy 3f out: rdn along to chse ldrs wl over 1f out: kpt on same pce fnl f* **20/1**

/2-4 **6** nk **Ocala**[34] 1517 4-9-9 77 .... OisinMurphy 11 79
(Andrew Balding) *chsd ldrs: rdn along 2f out: drvn over 1f out: kpt on same pce* **5/1**[3]

11-0 **7** 1 1/4 **Redarna**[11] 2076 5-9-1 69 .... GrahamLee 5 68
(Dianne Sayer) *chsd ldrs on inner: rdn along over 2f out: sn drvn and no imp fnl f* **14/1**

00-0 **8** 1 **Ebbisham (IRE)**[8] 2203 6-8-9 63 .... (v[1]) PJMcDonald 10 60
(John Mackie) *trckd ldrs: pushed along 3f out: rdn 2f out: sn drvn and grad wknd* **28/1**

-126 **9** nk **Showboating (IRE)**[38] 1428 11-9-4 72 .... (p) LewisEdmunds 4 68
(John Balding) *hld up: hdwy over 2f out: rdn wl over 1f out: kpt on fnl f* **33/1**

4546 **10** 3 1/4 **Samphire Coast**[12] 2064 6-9-0 68 .... (v) TomEaves 15 57
(Derek Shaw) *dwlt: a towards rr (vet said gelding ran without tongue strap because it had become adrift on the way to start and could not be re-fitted)* **22/1**

5-60 **11** hd **Jo's Girl (IRE)**[6] 2290 4-9-0 68 .... (t[1]) DougieCostello 2 56
(Micky Hammond) *a towards rr* **33/1**

0000 **12** 9 **Starplex**[10] 2092 9-8-9 70 .... RPWalsh(7) 6 38
(Kenny Johnson) *a in rr* **100/1**

04R- **13** 1 **Duck Egg Blue (IRE)**[213] 7993 5-9-2 75 .... PaulaMuir(5) 1 40
(Liam Bailey) *s.i.s: a in rr (jockey said mare was slowly away)* **40/1**

000- **14** 21 **Khitaamy (IRE)**[272] 5880 5-8-8 62 .... (w) ShaneGray 3
(Tina Jackson) *cl up: rdn along on inner 3f out: sn wknd: bhd and eased fr over 1f out* **80/1**

650- **15** 4 1/2 **Coviglia (IRE)**[140] 9593 5-8-12 66 .... NathanEvans 8
(Jacqueline Coward) *chsd ldrs on outer: rdn along 3f out: sn wknd and bhd whn eased fr over 1f out* **14/1**

1m 42.27s (0.67) **Going Correction** +0.325s/f (Good) **15** Ran SP% **121.3**
Speed ratings (Par 103): **109,108,107,107,106 106,105,104,103,100 100,91,90,69,64**
CSF £12.64 CT £96.80 TOTE £5.60: £1.80, £1.20, £3.50; EX 16.40 Trifecta £117.60.
Owner C Varley & R G Fell **Bred** Brian Walsh **Trained** Nawton, N Yorks

FOCUS
Modest form and another race where the winner made most. Little happened in the last 2f. The second has been rated similar to his 7f latest here.

2510 JOIN RACING TV NOW H'CAP 7f

4:25 (4:27) (Class 4) (0-85,86) 3-Y-O

£5,692 (£1,694; £846; £423; £300; £300) **Stalls** Low

Form RPR

314- **1** **Mr Diamond (IRE)**[206] 8189 3-8-11 75 .... TonyHamilton 3 82
(Richard Fahey) *hld up towards rr: hdwy wl over 2f out: chsd ldrs over 1f out: rdn ent fnl f: sn swtchd rt and chal: led last 100yds: edgd rt and kpt on* **12/1**

11-0 **2** 1/2 **Lorton**[28] 1662 3-9-5 83 .... PaulMulrennan 7 88
(Julie Camacho) *hld up towards rr: gd hdwy 3f out: chsd ldrs 2f out: rdn to take slt ld ent fnl f: sn drvn: hdd last 100yds: kpt on* **14/1**

051- **3** 1/2 **Artistic Rifles (IRE)**[210] 8075 3-8-12 76 .... OisinMurphy 11 79+
(Charles Hills) *trckd ldrs: hdwy over 2f out: sn chal: rdn to ld 1 1/2f out: drvn and hdd ent fnl f: hld whn n.m.r last 100yds* **9/4**[1]

14-0 **4** 3 **Fastman (IRE)**[11] 2078 3-9-8 86 .... DanielTudhope 2 81
(David O'Meara) *trckd ldrs: hdwy over 2f out: rdn along wl over 1f out: sn drvn and no imp fnl f* **4/1**[2]

1-00 **5** 1 3/4 **Jem Scuttle (USA)**[10] 2101 3-8-6 70 .... (t) ShaneGray 1 60
(Declan Carroll) *in tch: rdn along over 2f out: kpt on fnl f* **20/1**

360- **6** 2 1/4 **Kolossus**[207] 8161 3-8-11 75 .... ConnorBeasley 12 59
(Michael Dods) *dwlt and swtchd lft s: t.k.h in rr: hdwy on wd outside over 2f out: rdn wl over 1f out: sn no imp* **14/1**

040- **7** 2 1/4 **Evie Speed (IRE)**[220] 7776 3-8-13 77 .... JackGarritty 4 55
(Jedd O'Keeffe) *prom on inner: hdwy and cl up 3f out: disp ld 2f out: sn rdn: drvn over 1f out: sn wknd* **17/2**

06-6 **8** 1 1/4 **Kuwait Station (IRE)**[12] 2054 3-9-6 84 .... DavidNolan 5 59
(David O'Meara) *in tch: pushed along 3f out: rdn over 2f out: sn wknd* **14/1**

01-0 **9** hd **Gremoboy**[29] 1646 3-8-4 68 .... DuranFentiman 8 42
(Tim Easterby) *a towards rr* **33/1**

45-4 **10** 2 **Two Blondes (IRE)**[19] 1897 3-9-7 85 .... (v) BenCurtis 9 54
(Mick Channon) *chsd ldr: rdn along over 2f out: sn wknd (jockey said gelding hung left-handed)* **7/1**[3]

06-5 **11** 8 **High Contrast**[22] 1819 3-8-2 66 oh3 .... (h) AndrewMullen 10 13
(K R Burke) *led: rdn along over 2f out: drvn and hdd 1 1/2f out: sn wknd* **28/1**

11-6 **12** 6 **Airwaves**[14] 2024 3-8-10 74 .... (b[1]) RobHornby 6 5
(Martyn Meade) *a in rr (jockey said filly did not appreciate the blinkers were applied for the first-time)* **16/1**

1m 28.14s (0.94) **Going Correction** +0.325s/f (Good) **12** Ran SP% **118.5**
Speed ratings (Par 101): **107,106,105,102,100 97,95,93,93,91 82,75**
CSF £164.77 CT £525.38 TOTE £9.80: £2.80, £3.70, £1.50; EX 113.90 Trifecta £546.80.
Owner Amie Canham I **Bred** Mel Roberts & R A Fahey **Trained** Musley Bank, N Yorks

FOCUS
Run at a good gallop, the pace didn't hold up this time and the closers were seen to best effect. It's been rated as standard form for now.

2511 EVERY RACE LIVE ON RACING TV H'CAP 1m 6f

4:55 (4:57) (Class 5) (0-70,71) 3-Y-O

£4,075 (£1,212; £606; £303; £300; £300) **Stalls** Low

Form RPR

32-1 **1** **Moon King (FR)**[9] 2150 3-9-6 66 6ex .... HarryBentley 6 72+
(Ralph Beckett) *hld up: hdwy on outer 3f out: rdn along over 2f out: styd on u.p to ld 1f out: kpt on wl towards fin* **8/15**[1]

0-30 **2** 2 1/4 **Nordano (GER)**[10] 2099 3-9-5 65 .... PJMcDonald 7 68
(Mark Johnston) *trckd ldrs: hdwy over 2f out: rdn to ld briefly over 1f out: drvn and hdd ent fnl f: kpt on* **12/1**

3 nk **Nobel Joshua (AUT)**[12] 2073 3-9-5 65 .... RobbieDowney 3 67
(Denis Gerard Hogan, Ire) *trckd ldrs: effrt over 2f out: rdn and ev ch over 1f out: kpt on same pce fnl f* **16/1**

0-00 **4** *1 ¼* **West Newton**[53] 1217 3-9-4 **64**....................(p[1]) JasonWatson 2 65
(Roger Charlton) *trckd ldr: cl up 4f out: slt ld over 2f out: sn rdn: hdd over 1f out: drvn and kpt on same pce fnl f* **25/1**

06- **5** *1 ½* **Earl Of Harrow**[190] 8700 3-9-7 **67**.................... JoeFanning 4 66
(Mick Channon) *hld up in rr: hdwy on inner 3f out: chal 2f out: rdn and ev ch over 1f out: drvn and wknd fnl f* **6/1**[2]

-000 **6** *3* **Champagne Marengo (IRE)**[10] 2125 3-8-12 **58**....(p) StevieDonohoe 5 52
(Ian Williams) *trckd ldrs: pushed along 3f out: rdn over 2f out: sn wknd* **66/1**

234 **7** *8* **Ydra**[41] 1365 3-9-11 **71**....................(b[1]) BenCurtis 1 54
(Archie Watson) *set stdy pce: pushed along and qcknd over 3f out: rdn and hdd jst over 2f out: wknd* **8/1**[3]

3m 15.13s (8.13) **Going Correction** +0.325s/f (Good) 7 Ran SP% **109.5**
Speed ratings (Par 99): **89,87,87,86,85 84,79**
CSF £7.38 TOTE £1.50: £1.20, £3.00; EX 6.60 Trifecta £34.10.
Owner What Asham Partnership **Bred** Rashit Shaykhutdinov **Trained** Kimpton, Hants

FOCUS
Little gallop on here and it took the favourite a while to assert as a result. Muddling form, but the winner has been rated as backing up his latest C&D win.

2512 DON'T MISS LADIES DAY - 30TH MAY H'CAP 1m 2f
5:25 (5:26) (Class 6) (0-65,65) 4-Y-0+

£3,737 (£1,112; £555; £300; £300; £300) **Stalls** Centre

Form RPR

3640 **1** **Captain Pugwash (IRE)**[10] 2106 5-9-3 **63**....................(v) LiamKeniry 1 69
(Stef Keniry) *mde all: rdn along 2f out: drvn ins fnl f: hld on gamely* **16/1**

5420 **2** *½* **Apache Blaze**[27] 1688 4-8-12 **63**.................... SeamusCronin(5) 5 68
(Robyn Brisland) *trckd ldrs: effrt over 2f out: rdn to chse wnr 1 1/2f out: drvn ins fnl f: kpt on* **7/2**[2]

/6-0 **3** *½* **Lucy's Law (IRE)**[78] 784 5-9-3 **63**.................... AndrewMullen 3 67
(Tom Tate) *trckd ldrs on inner: hdwy 3f out: rdn along over 2f out: drvn over 1f out: kpt on u.p fnl f* **12/1**

0035 **4** *¾* **Seaborough (IRE)**[6] 2290 4-9-2 **62**....................(p[1]) ConnorBeasley 4 65
(David Thompson) *hld up in rr: hdwy wl over 2f out: rdn along wl over 1f out: styd on fnl f: nrst fin* **9/1**

40-5 **5** *2 ½* **Thorntoun Care**[12] 2056 8-9-5 **65**.................... ShaneGray 2 63
(Karen Tutty) *dwlt and bhd tl styd on fnl 2f: nrst fin* **8/1**

325- **6** *1* **Move In Faster**[261] 6334 4-9-5 **65**.................... PaulMulrennan 9 62
(Michael Dods) *in tch: rdn along over 2f out: sn no imp* **14/1**

0-11 **7** *1* **Mr Coco Bean (USA)**[29] 1648 5-9-2 **62**.................... PJMcDonald 6 57+
(David Barron) *trckd ldng pair: hdwy to chse wnr over 4f out: cl up 3f out: sn ev ch: rdn 2f out: sn btn* **9/4**[1]

460- **8** *3 ½* **Pinchpoint (IRE)**[204] 8283 4-9-4 **64**....................(h) StevieDonohoe 10 52
(John Butler) *a towards rr* **33/1**

340- **9** *2 ½* **Rebel Cause (IRE)**[249] 6771 6-9-5 **65**.................... RoystonFfrench 7 49
(John Holt) *chsd ldrs: rdn along over 3f out: sn wknd* **20/1**

6-44 **10** *1* **Ascot Week (USA)**[7] 2244 5-9-5 **65**....................(v) JasonHart 11 47
(John Quinn) *rdn along sn after s: a in rr* **15/2**[3]

2m 15.6s (6.30) **Going Correction** +0.325s/f (Good) 10 Ran SP% **113.8**
Speed ratings (Par 101): **87,86,86,85,83 82,82,79,77,76**
CSF £69.78 CT £708.25 TOTE £17.50: £4.40, £1.50, £2.30; EX 89.00 Trifecta £693.10.
Owner Miss A Jones **Bred** Ardrums House Stud **Trained** Middleham, N Yorks

FOCUS
Moderate enough form and another winner on the card to make all.
T/Jkpt: £58,084.20 to a £1 stake. Pool: £81,808.75 - 1.00 winning units. T/Plt: £28.20 to a £1 stake. Pool: £63,047.99 - 1,631.11 winning units. T/Qpdt: £31.20 to a £1 stake. Pool: £4,628.23 - 109.59 winning units. **Joe Rowntree**

2211 WOLVERHAMPTON (A.W) (L-H)
Tuesday, May 7

OFFICIAL GOING: Tapeta: standard
Wind: Light against Weather: OVERCAST

2513 SKY SPORTS RACING SKY 415 H'CAP 1m 142y (Tp)
6:00 (6:00) (Class 6) (0-55,55) 4-Y-0+

£3,105 (£924; £461; £300; £300; £300) **Stalls** Low

Form RPR

10-6 **1** **Allux Boy (IRE)**[21] 1841 5-8-11 **50**....................(p) FayeMcManoman(5) 9 60
(Nigel Tinkler) *prom: chsd ldr over 2f out: led ins fnl f: pushed out* **11/2**[3]

220/ **2** *2 ¼* **Pushaq (IRE)**[20] 1867 6-9-0 **55**....................(t) StephenMooney(7) 8 60
(Anthony McCann, Ire) *prom: chsd ldr over 3f out: led over 2f out: rdn and hdd ins fnl f: styd on same pce* **4/1**[2]

0-03 **3** *1 ½* **Captain Marmalade (IRE)**[21] 1836 7-8-7 **46** ThoreHammerHansen(5) 6 48
(Jimmy Fox) *s.s: hld up: hdwy over 1f out: sn rdn: styd on: nt rch ldrs (jockey said gelding missed the break)* **10/1**

0041 **4** *hd* **Perceived**[7] 2244 7-9-4 **52** 4ex....................(p) CamHardie 13 54
(Antony Brittain) *s.i.s: sn hld up in tch: rdn over 2f out: styd on* **7/2**[1]

300- **5** *½* **Master Poet**[246] 6211 4-9-4 **52**.................... HectorCrouch 12 53
(Gary Moore) *led 1f: remained handy: rdn over 2f out: hung lft fr over 1f out: no ex wl ins fnl f* **11/1**

6302 **6** *4* **Clement (IRE)**[7] 2235 9-9-5 **53**....................(v) LukeMorris 10 45
(Marjorie Fife) *s.i.s: hld up: rdn over 2f out: styd on ins fnl f: nvr nrr* **9/1**

-000 **7** *1 ¾* **Cooperess**[53] 1215 6-8-10 **47** ow1....................(p[1]) FinleyMarsh(3) 7 36
(Adrian Wintle) *hld up: hdwy over 1f out: nt trble ldrs (jockey said mare moved poorly)* **22/1**

216- **8** *1 ¼* **Coachella (IRE)**[181] 8917 5-9-7 **55**.................... CallumShepherd 5 41
(Ed de Giles) *sn pushed along and prom: rdn over 2f out: wknd over 1f out* **12/1**

4-00 **9** *1* **Officer Drivel (IRE)**[14] 2005 8-9-2 **55**....................(bt) ThomasGreatrex(5) 1 39
(Paddy Butler) *hld up: shkn up over 1f out: n.d* **33/1**

0-00 **10** *4 ½* **Jupiter**[43] 1328 4-9-7 **55**....................(p[1]) RossaRyan 4 29
(Alexandra Dunn) *w ldrs: led over 5f out: rdn and hdd over 2f out: wknd fnl f* **18/1**

-023 **11** *19* **Blue Harmony**[82] 718 4-8-13 **47**....................(p) FrannyNorton 2
(Michael Blake) *w ldr: led over 7f out: hdd over 5f out: rdn over 2f out: sn wknd (jockey said filly stopped quickly; vet said filly had lost its right hind shoe)* **12/1**

000- **12** *11* **Ravenhoe (IRE)**[218] 7835 6-9-0 **55**.................... AidenSmithies(7) 11
(Mark Johnston) *s.i.s: racd wd and sn pushed along in rr: wknd over 2f out* **40/1**

1m 49.99s (-0.11) **Going Correction** +0.10s/f (Slow) 12 Ran SP% **115.4**
Speed ratings (Par 101): **104,102,100,100,100 96,94,93,92,88 72,62**
CSF £26.38 CT £214.68 TOTE £5.40: £2.00, £2.00, £2.70; EX 27.20 Trifecta £241.10.
Owner M Webb **Bred** Victor Stud Bloodstock Ltd **Trained** Langton, N Yorks

FOCUS
Not many got into this weak handicap. The winner stood out like a saw thumb cruising into contention in behind the leaders, before putting his seal on the race in the straight. The third has been rated close to his latest.

2514 HOTEL & CONFERENCING AT WOLVERHAMPTON RACECOURSE CLAIMING STKS 7f 36y (Tp)
6:30 (6:31) (Class 5) 4-Y-0+

£3,752 (£1,116; £557; £300; £300; £300) **Stalls** High

Form RPR

3006 **1** **Ballard Down (IRE)**[8] 2187 6-9-7 **91**....................(v) CamHardie 5 78+
(David O'Meara) *s.i.s: hld up: racd keenly: rdn over 1f out: str run to ld towards fin* **9/2**[3]

-055 **2** *1 ¼* **Shepherd's Purse**[8] 2194 7-8-12 **67**.................... TrevorWhelan 7 66+
(David Loughnane) *plld hrd and prom: wnt 2nd over 5f out: rdn over 1f out: led ins fnl f: edgd rt: hdd towards fin* **11/1**

3025 **3** *1 ¾* **Murdanova (IRE)**[9] 2151 6-8-13 **74**............(p) ThoreHammerHansen(5) 6 68+
(Ivan Furtado) *led: rdn over 1f out: hdd ins fnl f: styd on same pce* **3/1**[2]

5-26 **4** *1 ¼* **The Lamplighter (FR)**[32] 1560 4-8-10 **77**....................(t) CierenFallon(7) 2 64+
(George Baker) *prom: lost pl over 5f out: rdn and edgd lft over 1f out: kpt on ins fnl f* **9/2**[3]

-213 **5** *hd* **Loyalty**[53] 1218 12-8-13 **85**....................(v) PaddyMathers 4 59+
(Derek Shaw) *prom: rdn over 1f out: no ex wl ins fnl f* **11/1**

4125 **6** *1* **Unforgiving Minute**[26] 1714 8-9-7 **85**.................... KieranO'Neill 3 65+
(John Butler) *chsd ldrs: rdn over 2f out: edgd lft and no ex ins fnl f* **9/4**[1]

0460 **7** *1 ¾* **Brother In Arms (IRE)**[74] 848 5-8-9 **43**.................... FrannyNorton 8 48
(Tony Carroll) *s.i.s: hld up: racd wd: bhd fr 1/2-way* **100/1**

1m 28.22s (-0.58) **Going Correction** +0.10s/f (Slow) 7 Ran SP% **109.8**
Speed ratings (Par 103): **107,105,103,102,101 100,98**
.Ballard Down was claimed by Mr D. Pipe for £15000\n\x\x Shepherd's Purse was claimed by Mrs Ruth A. Carr for £6000
Owner Thoroughbred British Racing **Bred** D Harron, Ederidge Ltd & Glenvale Stud **Trained** Upper Helmsley, N Yorks

FOCUS
Reasonably competitive for the grade and they went what looked an even enough gallop. It looked open going into the closing stages but the winner mowed them down late on. The seventh anchors the form.

2515 HELLERMANNTYTON/ELECTRIC CENTRE H'CAP 5f 21y (Tp)
7:00 (7:01) (Class 5) (0-75,77) 4-Y-0+

£3,752 (£1,116; £557; £300; £300; £300) **Stalls** Low

Form RPR

3614 **1** **Cappananty Con**[10] 2122 5-9-2 **72**.................... JoshuaBryan(3) 4 81
(Charlie Wallis) *broke wl: sn stdd and lost pl: hdwy over 1f out: shkn up: edgd lft and r.o to ld wl ins fnl f* **4/1**[3]

2310 **2** *1 ½* **Big Time Maybe (IRE)**[24] 1767 4-8-10 **70**..........(p) ScottMcCullagh(7) 2 74
(Michael Attwater) *racd freely: prom: rdn and ev ch wl ins fnl f: styd on same pce* **12/1**

3105 **3** *nk* **A Sure Welcome**[10] 2107 5-9-7 **74**....................(b) LukeMorris 5 77+
(John Spearing) *hld up: pushed along 1/2-way: hdwy over 1f out: nt clr run and swtchd rt ins fnl f: r.o: nt rch ldrs* **5/2**[1]

5-20 **4** *½* **Qaaraat**[39] 1393 4-9-2 **69**.................... CamHardie 6 70
(Antony Brittain) *sn w ldr: led wl over 1f out: rdn and hdd wl ins fnl f: no ex towards fin (jockey said gelding ran too free)* **4/1**[3]

5006 **5** *5* **Top Boy**[10] 2107 9-9-1 **68**....................(v) PaddyMathers 8 51
(Derek Shaw) *s.i.s: towards rr: pushed along and hung rt 1/2-way: sn outpcd* **8/1**

2101 **6** *1 ¾* **Katheefa (USA)**[8] 2194 5-9-10 **77** 5ex.................... JamesSullivan 3 54
(Ruth Carr) *prom: pushed along 1/2-way: wknd ins fnl f (jockey said gelding was never travelling)* **7/2**[2]

05-0 **7** *2 ½* **King Crimson**[22] 1817 7-8-12 **65**.................... KieranO'Neill 1 33
(John Butler) *led: plld hrd: hdd wl over 1f out: wknd ins fnl f* **25/1**

1m 1.01s (-0.89) **Going Correction** +0.10s/f (Slow) 7 Ran SP% **113.4**
Speed ratings (Par 103): **111,108,108,107,99 96,92**
CSF £47.69 CT £141.59 TOTE £4.10: £2.40, £4.00; EX 47.80 Trifecta £199.70.
Owner Jim Biggane **Bred** Miss H Botterill & Mr D R Botterill **Trained** Ardleigh, Essex

FOCUS
Competitive enough for the grade and they went a strong gallop, which suited the winner who loves to swoop late.

2516 HELLERMANNTYTON/STARRETT H'CAP 1m 1f 104y (Tp)
7:30 (7:30) (Class 4) (0-80,82) 4-Y-0+

£5,530 (£1,645; £822; £411; £300; £300) **Stalls** Low

Form RPR

120- **1** **Livvys Dream (IRE)**[159] 9313 4-9-4 **77**....................(h) JimCrowley 5 83
(Charles Hills) *hld up: hdwy over 1f out: r.o u.p to ld nr fin* **11/4**[2]

046- **2** *½* **Redgrave (IRE)**[159] 9309 5-9-4 **77**.................... OisinMurphy 8 82
(Joseph Tuite) *chsd ldrs: shkn up and swtchd lft over 1f out: rdn to ld wl ins fnl f: hdd nr fin* **10/3**[3]

6-2 **3** *nse* **Paco's Prince**[10] 2124 4-8-7 **73**.................... AledBeech(7) 6 78
(Nick Littmoden) *chsd ldr tl led over 1f out: rdn and hdd wl ins fnl f* **15/2**

5-00 **4** *1* **Uther Pendragon (IRE)**[18] 1912 4-8-13 **72**............(p) CallumShepherd 7 75
(J S Moore) *hld up: hdwy over 1f out: sn rdn: r.o* **12/1**

0411 **5** *¾* **Badenscoth**[32] 1566 5-9-7 **80**.................... FrannyNorton 3 81+
(Dean Ivory) *s.i.s: hld up: shkn up over 2f out: r.o ins fnl f: nt clr run towards fin: nt rch ldrs (jockey said slowly away and was denied a clear run on the run to the line)* **9/4**[1]

050- **6** *2* **The Throstles**[143] 9563 4-9-9 **82**.................... ShaneKelly 2 79
(Kevin Frost) *led at stdy pce: qcknd over 2f out: rdn and hdd over 1f out: no ex wl ins fnl f* **10/1**

56-0 **7** *6* **Acker Bilk (IRE)**[10] 2124 5-9-0 **73**....................(p) RaulDaSilva 1 57
(Ronald Harris) *chsd ldrs: rdn over 2f out: wknd over 1f out* **50/1**

00-0 **8** *6* **Sir Hamilton (IRE)**[53] 1213 4-9-9 **82**.................... RobertHavlin 4 61
(Luke McJannet) *prom: hung lft fr over 2f out: wkng whn nt clr run over 1f out (jockey said gelding hung badly left)* **28/1**

2m 2.55s (1.75) **Going Correction** +0.10s/f (Slow) 8 Ran SP% **114.5**
Speed ratings (Par 105): **96,95,95,94,93 92,86,81**
CSF £12.42 CT £59.90 TOTE £3.20: £1.20, £1.40, £2.20; EX 13.40 Trifecta £52.50.
Owner International Plywood (Importers) Ltd **Bred** Barronstown Stud **Trained** Lambourn, Berks

FOCUS
A competitive race for the grade and this looks useful form despite the fact that the gallop looked steady enough and there wasn't much separating a few of these at the line. Muddling form and it's been rated a bit cautiously.

2517 GRAND THEATRE WOLVERHAMPTON H'CAP 1m 1f 104y (Tp)
8:00 (8:00) (Class 6) (0-65,67) 3-Y-O

£3,105 (£924; £461; £300; £300; £300) **Stalls** Low

Form RPR

-344 **1** **Lieutenant Conde**[90] 614 3-9-4 **62**........................ CharlieBennett 4 68
(Hughie Morrison) *prom: nt clr run and lost pl over 8f out: hld up: hdwy on outer over 2f out: rdn over 1f out: r.o to ld wl ins fnl f* **17/2**

4005 **2** *nk* **Archdeacon**[25] 1725 3-8-3 **47**........................(p[1]) KieranO'Neill 11 54
(Dean Ivory) *hld up: nt clr run over 2f out: swtchd rt and hdwy over 1f out: rdn and hung lft ins fnl f: r.o to go 2nd nr fin (jockey said gelding was denied a clear run on the final bend)* **6/1**[2]

6404 **3** *½* **Margaret J**[25] 1726 3-8-2 **46** oh1........................(p) LukeMorris 7 50
(Phil McEntee) *chsd ldrs: rdn and ev ch over 1f out: styd on u.p* **20/1**

000- **4** *½* **Sadlers Beach (IRE)**[139] 9604 3-8-5 **49**........................(h[1]) HayleyTurner 6 53
(Marcus Tregoning) *plld hrd early: led: hdd over 7f out: chsd ldr tl led again over 2f out: rdn over 1f out: hdd wl ins fnl f* **22/1**

66-1 **5** *½* **Sea Of Marengo (IRE)**[62] 1041 3-9-7 **65**........................ JFEgan 3 68
(Paul George) *s.i.s: hld up: swtchd rt over 2f out: sn hung rt: hdwy u.p on outer over 1f out: nt rch ldrs* **12/1**

040- **6** *½* **Craneur**[167] 9170 3-9-8 **66**........................ HectorCrouch 5 68
(Harry Dunlop) *prom: rdn over 1f out: styd on same pce wl ins fnl f* **9/1**

5502 **7** *1 ½* **Robeam (IRE)**[10] 2125 3-8-8 **52**........................ PaddyMathers 10 51
(Richard Fahey) *hld up: hmpd and carried wd over 2f out: r.o u.p ins fnl f: nvr nrr* **7/2**[1]

1305 **8** *nk* **Precision Prince (IRE)**[17] 1957 3-9-3 **61**........................ ShaneKelly 2 59
(Mark Loughnane) *chsd ldrs: rdn and ev ch over 1f out: no ex ins fnl f* **8/1**[3]

60-4 **9** *1 ¼* **Spiritual Boy (IRE)**[15] 1979 3-9-0 **58**........................ CamHardie 9 54
(David O'Meara) *s.i.s: hld up: hdwy over 1f out: rdn and swtchd lft ins fnl f: no ex* **14/1**

03-0 **10** *8* **Dark Glory (IRE)**[29] 1656 3-9-9 **67**........................(p[1]) OisinMurphy 1 48
(Brian Meehan) *w ldr: led over 7f out: hdd over 2f out: wknd fnl f* **6/1**[2]

40-4 **11** *10* **Chance Of Glory (FR)**[16] 1970 3-9-1 **59**........................ FrannyNorton 8 21
(Mark Johnston) *chsd ldrs: rdn over 3f out: wkng whn hung lft over 1f out* **12/1**

2m 2.74s (1.94) **Going Correction** +0.10s/f (Slow) **11 Ran SP% 113.6**
Speed ratings (Par 97): **95,94,94,93,93 92,91,91,90,83 74**
CSF £56.72 CT £986.22 TOTE £6.30: £2.10, £3.10, £3.10; EX 67.30 Trifecta £1676.60.
Owner MNC Racing **Bred** Melksham Craic **Trained** East Ilsley, Berks

FOCUS
A wide-open handicap in which plenty had chances entering the final furlong. The pace looked to steady mid race which wouldn't have helped some of the hold-up horses. A minor pb from the third.

2518 HELLERMANNTYTON/EDMUNDSON ELECTRICAL MAIDEN STKS 1m 142y (Tp)
8:30 (8:31) (Class 5) 3-Y-O+ **£3,752** (£1,116; £557; £278) **Stalls** Low

Form RPR

2- **1** **Tempus**[209] 8109 3-9-0 0........................ JasonWatson 1 82+
(Roger Charlton) *mde all: set stdy pce tl qcknd over 2f out: pushed clr fnl f* **4/6**[1]

2 *2 ¾* **Bardo Contiguo (IRE)** 3-9-0 0........................ JackMitchell 6 74+
(Roger Varian) *chsd ldrs: rdn to chse wnr and hung lft over 1f out: styd on same pce fnl f* **5/1**[2]

3 *2 ¼* **Abr Al Hudood (JPN)** 3-8-9 0........................ BenCurtis 13 64+
(Hugo Palmer) *wnt rt s: rcvrd to chse wnr over 7f out: rdn over 2f out: lost 2nd over 1f out: no ex fnl f* **16/1**

4 *½* **Nonchalance** 3-8-9 0........................ RobertHavlin 2 63+
(John Gosden) *s.i.s: hld up: hdwy and nt clr run over 1f out: nt clr run ins fnl f: r.o to go 4th nr fin: nvr nr to chal* **5/1**[2]

50- **5** *½* **Starczewski (USA)**[167] 9172 3-8-9 0........................ DylanHogan(5) 7 67
(David Simcock) *hld up in tch: arced keenly: rdn over 2f out: edgd lft over 1f out: styd on same pce fnl f* **66/1**

6 *shd* **Dawaaween (IRE)** 3-8-9 0........................ JimCrowley 10 62
(Owen Burrows) *chsd ldrs: rdn and hung lft over 1f out: no ex fnl f (jockey said filly ran green and hung left in the home straight)* **12/1**[3]

7 *1* **Arcadienne** 3-8-9 0........................ HarryBentley 5 59
(Ralph Beckett) *prom: rdn over 2f out: styd on same pce fr over 1f out* **25/1**

5 **8** *5* **Le Musee (FR)**[15] 1989 6-10-0 0........................(p) RossaRyan 9 55+
(Nigel Hawke) *hld up: rdn over 2f out: edgd lft over 1f out: n.d* **33/1**

9 *2 ¼* **Tronador (IRE)** 3-9-0 0........................ ShaneKelly 3 48
(David Lanigan) *s.i.s: hld up: nvr nrr* **40/1**

0-0 **10** *3* **Harry The Norseman**[122] 90 3-9-0 0........................(w) LiamKeniry 11 41
(Jonjo O'Neill) *s.i.s: hld up: n.d* **100/1**

6-6 **11** *7* **Fancy Dress (IRE)**[13] 2034 3-8-9 0........................ RobHornby 12 20
(Ralph Beckett) *in rr: pushed along over 5f out: n.d* **66/1**

1m 50.85s (0.75) **Going Correction** +0.10s/f (Slow)
WFA 3 from 6yo 14lb **11 Ran SP% 120.1**
Speed ratings (Par 103): **100,97,95,95,94 94,93,89,87,84 78**
CSF £4.22 TOTE £1.30: £1.10, £2.10, £3.00; EX 4.30 Trifecta £35.60.
Owner K Abdullah **Bred** Juddmonte Farms Ltd **Trained** Beckhampton, Wilts

FOCUS
This looked quite a useful maiden on paper but the steady tempo, dictated by the red-hot market leader, meant that they posted a slower time than the opening Class 6 handicap over this trip. The fifth may limit the level.
T/Plt: £299.40 to a £1 stake. Pool: £74,420.06 - 181.40 winning units. T/Qpdt: £20.10 to a £1 stake. Pool: £10,345.07 - 379.49 winning units. **Colin Roberts**

2311 SAINT-CLOUD (L-H)
Tuesday, May 7

OFFICIAL GOING: Turf: good to soft

2519a PRIX YOUTH (MAIDEN) (3YO COLTS & GELDINGS) (TURF) 1m 2f 110y
3:10 3-Y-O

£13,513 (£5,135; £3,783; £2,162; £1,081; £810)

RPR

1 **San Huberto (IRE)**[24] 3-9-2 0........................ TonyPiccone 8 78
(F Chappet, France) **41/10**[2]

2 *1 ¾* **Son Of Normandy**[33] 3-9-2 0........................ AurelienLemaitre 2 75
(F Head, France) **9/2**[3]

3 *1 ¼* **Monty Saga (FR)**[52] 3-9-2 0........................ AlexisBadel 5 73
(D Chenu, France) **19/1**

4 *nk* **Savoir Aimer (FR)**[15] 3-9-2 0........................ GregoryBenoist 1 72
(T Castanheira, France) **15/2**

5 *1* **Poet's Quest (FR)**[26] 3-9-2 0........................ TheoBachelot 11 70
(S Wattel, France) **47/10**

6 *¾* **Star Talent (IRE)**[143] 9556 3-9-2 0........................ ClementLecoeuvre 4 69
(Gay Kelleway) *disp ld early: tk a t.k.h: settled to trck ldrs: urged along over 2f out: rdn over 1f out: kpt on same pce fnl f* **59/1**

7 *shd* **Aquilino (FR)**[173] 3-9-2 0........................ Pierre-CharlesBoudot 6 68
(A Fabre, France) **37/10**[1]

8 *10* **Istorius (FR)**[50] 3-9-2 0........................ VincentCheminaud 10 49
(H-A Pantall, France) **5/1**

9 *1 ¼* **King And Queen (FR)**[26] 3-9-2 0........................ EddyHardouin 7 47
(A Schutz, France) *racd towards rr of mid-div: prog on outer to r promly over 3f out: sn pushed along: unable qck and rdn over 2f out: wknd ins fnl f* **28/1**

10 *10* **Bookieboy (FR)** 3-8-8 0........................ MlleMickaelleMichel(3) 9 23
(Yannick Fouin, France) **25/1**

2m 14.87s (-4.73) **10 Ran SP% 119.0**
PARI-MUTUEL (all including 1 euro stake): WIN 5.10; PLACE 1.90, 2.00, 3.70; DF 14.60.
Owner Maurice Lagasse **Bred** Gestut Zur Kuste Ag **Trained** France

CHESTER (L-H)
Wednesday, May 8

OFFICIAL GOING: Good to soft (7.2)
Wind: Moderate, half behind in straight of over 1f Weather: Rain

2520 STELLAR GROUP LILY AGNES CONDITIONS STKS (PLUS 10 RACE) 5f 15y
1:50 (1:52) (Class 2) 2-Y-O

£14,940 (£4,473; £2,236; £1,118; £559; £280) **Stalls** Low

Form RPR

01 **1** **Great Dame (IRE)**[20] 1893 2-8-11 0........................ DanielTudhope 3 78
(David O'Meara) *mde all: rdn over 1f out: kpt on gamely ins fnl f: a doing enough cl home* **7/2**[2]

1 **2** *½* **Iva Reflection (IRE)**[11] 2093 2-9-2 0........................ RichardKingscote 5 81
(Tom Dascombe) *w wnr tl rdn and unable qck over 1f out: rallied and styd on ins fnl f: ev ch but a hld* **8/1**

2 **3** *¾* **Top Buck (IRE)**[9] 2205 2-9-2 0........................ OisinMurphy 4 79
(Brian Meehan) *chsd ldrs: pushed along and lost pl after 1f: towards rr: rdn over 1f out: edgd rt whn proging ins fnl f: styd on and gaining towards fin* **5/1**[3]

14 **4** *nk* **Chasanda**[19] 1923 2-8-11 0........................ JFEgan 7 72
(David Evans) *missed break: racd keenly: towards rr: hdwy to chse ldrs after 1f: rdn over 1f out: kpt on same pce ins fnl f* **16/1**

1 **5** *nk* **Show Me Show Me**[39] 1416 2-9-5 0........................ FrankieDettori 8 79+
(Richard Fahey) *hld up: rdn and hdwy wl over 1f out: chsd ldrs ins fnl f: no ex fnl 100yds* **15/8**[1]

11 **6** *3* **Electric Ladyland (IRE)**[18] 1937 2-8-11 0........................ LukeMorris 10 61+
(Archie Watson) *awkward leaving stalls: chsd ldrs: rdn 2f out: lost pl over 1f out: wknd ins fnl f (trainer said filly was unsuited by the good to soft ground and would prefer a quicker surface)* **5/1**[3]

6 **7** *hd* **Lexi The One (IRE)**[20] 1879 2-8-11 0........................ BarryMcHugh 6 60
(Richard Fahey) *missed break: bhd: rdn over 3f out: nvr a threat* **25/1**

1m 4.7s (2.60) **Going Correction** +0.525s/f (Yiel) **7 Ran SP% 111.2**
Speed ratings (Par 99): **100,99,98,97,97 92,91**
CSF £29.04 TOTE £3.80: £1.70, £4.70; EX 35.10 Trifecta £119.30.
Owner Nick Bradley Racing 7 And Partner 2 **Bred** Mark Salmon **Trained** Upper Helmsley, N Yorks

FOCUS
The rail between the 6f and 1f points was moved out by 8yds, adding 20yds to the advertised distance of this race. After riding in the opener Frankie Dettori and Barry McHugh said the ground was on the slow side of good, Luke Morris and Oisin Murphy called it soft and Richard Kingscote said: "It's good to soft but in a couple of races it will be soft." The time for this decent conditions event was just over 5sec slower than the standard. There was a bunch finish, the first five separated by about a length and a half, and the race went to a filly for the seventh time in nine seasons. The first three came from the three lowest stalls. It's been rated in line with recent renewals.

2521 ARKLE FINANCE CHESHIRE OAKS (FOR THE ROBERT SANGSTER MEMORIAL CUP) (LISTED RACE) (FILLIES) 1m 3f 75y
2:25 (2:26) (Class 1) 3-Y-O

£42,532 (£16,125; £8,070; £4,020; £2,017; £1,012) **Stalls** Low

Form RPR

21-1 **1** **Mehdaayih**[20] 1885 3-9-0 **97**........................ RobertHavlin 6 108+
(John Gosden) *n.m.r s: midfield: nt clr run over 2f out: sn swtchd to outer and hdwy: led over 1f out: qcknd clr ins fnl f and edgd lft: readily: impressive* **3/1**[1]

11- **2** *4 ½* **Manuela De Vega (IRE)**[198] 8477 3-9-3 **99**........................ HarryBentley 3 98+
(Ralph Beckett) *in tch: nt clr run on inner over 2f out: effrt and swtchd lft over 1f out: styd on ins fnl f to take 2nd fnl 100yds: no ch w wnr* **7/2**[3]

2-1 **3** *1* **Fanny Logan (IRE)**[10] 2148 3-9-0 0........................ FrankieDettori 1 93
(John Gosden) *racd keenly: sn dropped in bhd to trck ldrs: rdn and unable qck over 1f out: styd on same pce ins fnl f* **10/3**[2]

1- **4** 1 1/4 **Grace And Danger (IRE)**[203] 8329 3-9-0 0........................ OisinMurphy 7 91
(Andrew Balding) *n.m.r s: racd keenly: hld up: swtchd rt and hdwy over 1f out: styd on ins fnl f: one pce and no further imp fnl 100yds* **8/1**

41- **5** 1 3/4 **Red Hot (FR)**[144] 9556 3-9-0 0........................ DanielTudhope 9 88
(Richard Fahey) *hld up in rr: hdwy on outer over 3f out: chsd ldrs over 2f out: chalng over 1f out: sn outpcd by wnr: no ex fnl 150yds* **28/1**

61 **6** 5 **La Voix Magique**[11] 2103 3-9-0 0........................ RichardKingscote 11 79
(Steph Hollinshead) *hld up in rr: pushed along over 2f out: rdn over 1f out: kpt on ins fnl f: nvr able to trble ldrs* **33/1**

3-11 **7** 1/2 **Love So Deep (JPN)**[15] 2021 3-9-0 74........................ JFEgan 10 78
(Jane Chapple-Hyam) *prom: racd keenly: trckd ldr: led wl over 2f out: rdn and hdd over 1f out: wknd ins fnl f* **25/1**

512- **8** 6 **Vivid Diamond (IRE)**[186] 8836 3-9-0 92........................ FrannyNorton 4 67
(Mark Johnston) *racd keenly: chsd ldrs: ev ch 3f out: rdn and wknd over 1f out* **10/1**

2534 **9** 3 1/2 **Wanaasah**[11] 2110 3-9-0 71........................(p) TrevorWhelan 5 61
(David Loughnane) *led: hdd wl over 2f out: sn rdn: wknd over 1f out (jockey said filly hung right)* **100/1**

3-5 **10** 13 **Secret Thoughts (USA)**[32] 1601 3-9-0 98........................ RyanMoore 8 37
(A P O'Brien, Ire) *hld up: pushed along 3 out: lft bhd over 1f out: eased whn wl btn fnl f* **6/1**

0-3 **11** 39 **Starlight Red (IRE)**[32] 1592 3-9-0 0........................ SilvestreDeSousa 12
(Charles Hills) *racd keenly: in tch on outer: midfield after 3f: niggled along 4f out: wknd 3f out: eased whn wl bhd wl over 1f out: t.o (jockey said filly stopped quickly)* **66/1**

2m 31.51s (4.11) **Going Correction** +0.525s/f (Yiel) **11 Ran SP% 117.5**
Speed ratings (Par 104): **106,102,102,101,99 96,95,91,88,79 51**
CSF £13.09 TOTE £4.20: £1.90, £1.70, £1.40; EX 15.20 Trifecta £47.80.
Owner Emirates Park Pty Ltd **Bred** Rabbah Bloodstock Limited **Trained** Newmarket, Suffolk

FOCUS
Add 36yds. A fillies' Listed race that has seen a huge boost in recent years, with brilliant Enable following up in the 2017 Oaks, while last year's runner-up Forever Together also triumphed at Epsom next time out. It was a typical edition on paper this season and one run at a decent enough tempo on the rain-softened ground. Solid form. The winner has been rated up with the better winners of this race, only bettered by Enable (111) this century.

2522 BOODLES DIAMOND H'CAP — 5f 15y
3:00 (3:02) (Class 2) (0-105,98) 3-Y-O
£21,165 (£6,337; £3,168; £1,584; £792; £397) **Stalls Low**

Form RPR

1-11 **1** **Leodis Dream (IRE)**[12] 2086 3-9-3 **94**........................ DanielTudhope 6 104+
(David O'Meara) *broke wl: chsd ldrs: rdn to ld over 1f out: r.o ins fnl f: pushed out whn in control towards fin* **9/2**[3]

02-4 **2** 1/2 **Recon Mission (IRE)**[12] 2086 3-9-4 **95**........................(h) TomMarquand 8 101
(Tony Carroll) *broke wl: sn dropped to midfield: pushed along over 2f out: rdn over 1f out: styd on to take 2nd towards fin and clsd on wnr but nvr able to mount serious chal* **10/1**

114- **3** 1 **She Can Boogie (IRE)**[151] 9461 3-8-11 **88**........................ RichardKingscote 5 90
(Tom Dascombe) *led early: chsd ldr: rdn and ev ch over 1f out: unable qck ent fnl f: lost 2nd towards fin and styd on same pce (jockey said filly hung left under pressure)* **9/1**

101- **4** 1 **Society Queen (IRE)**[284] 5504 3-8-0 **82**........................ SeanDavis(5) 4 81
(Richard Fahey) *missed break: in rr: rdn 2f out: hdwy ins fnl f: styd on: edgd lft and gaining towards fin: nt quite rch ldrs* **15/2**

2-11 **5** 1/2 **Top Breeze (IRE)**[21] 1851 3-9-1 **92**........................ ShaneKelly 1 89
(Richard Hughes) *chsd ldrs: effrt on inner over 1f out: one pce ins fnl f* **5/2**[1]

1540 **6** 1 **Yolo Again (IRE)**[6] 2319 3-8-8 **85**........................ SilvestreDeSousa 3 78
(Roger Fell) *sn in midfield: pushed along over 1f out and swtchd lft: sn checked: swtchd rt wl ins fnl f: kpt on but nt trble ldrs* **9/1**

120- **7** 1 **Dave Dexter**[193] 8629 3-9-7 **98**........................ HarryBentley 9 88
(Ralph Beckett) *in rr: rdn 2f out: edgd rt ins fnl f: kpt on but nvr a threat* **16/1**

222- **8** shd **Angel Alexander (IRE)**[188] 8783 3-8-1 **81**........................ JaneElliott(3) 2 70
(Tom Dascombe) *sn led: rdn and hdd over 1f out: sn nt pce of wnr: wknd fnl 100yds* **7/2**[2]

-110 **9** 4 **Liberation Day**[39] 1424 3-8-2 **79**........................(p) DavidEgan 7 54
(Tom Dascombe) *towards rr: pushed along over 2f out: rdn and outpcd over 1f out: nvr a threat* **33/1**

243- **10** 1 3/4 **No More Regrets (IRE)**[236] 7251 3-8-3 **80**........................ FrannyNorton 10 49
(Patrick Morris) *hld up: rdn over 1f out: nvr a threat* **50/1**

1m 3.81s (1.71) **Going Correction** +0.525s/f (Yiel) **10 Ran SP% 120.6**
Speed ratings (Par 105): **107,106,104,103,102 100,99,98,92,89**
CSF £50.81 CT £396.97 TOTE £4.40: £1.70, £2.50, £2.20; EX 56.50 Trifecta £329.80.
Owner Andrew Kendall-Jones I **Bred** R & M Bloodstock **Trained** Upper Helmsley, N Yorks

FOCUS
Add 20yds. A classy sprint handicap, run 0.9sec quicker than the Lily Agnes, and like that race the sire Dandy Man was responsible for the winner and the third.

2523 MBNA CHESTER VASE STKS (GROUP 3) (C&G) — 1m 4f 63y
3:35 (3:37) (Class 1) 3-Y-O
£56,710 (£21,500; £10,760; £5,360; £2,690; £1,350) **Stalls Low**

Form RPR

1 **Sir Dragonet (IRE)**[13] 2073 3-9-0 0........................ DonnachaO'Brien 8 117
(A P O'Brien, Ire) *hld up in last pl: hdwy over 2f out: led over 1f out: pushed out and r.o wl to draw clr ins fnl f: impressive* **13/2**

14- **2** 8 **Norway (IRE)**[193] 8663 3-9-0 104........................(p1) RyanMoore 6 104
(A P O'Brien, Ire) *hld up: nt clr run over 2f out: drvn and hdwy over 1f out: kpt on to take 2nd wl ins fnl f: no ch w wnr* **9/2**[2]

20-2 **3** 3/4 **Dashing Willoughby**[26] 1737 3-9-0 102........................ OisinMurphy 4 103
(Andrew Balding) *led: rdn 2f out: hdd over 1f out: sn no ch w wnr: lost 2nd wl ins fnl f* **11/2**[3]

10-1 **4** 4 1/2 **King Ottokar (FR)**[26] 1737 3-9-0 106........................ BenCurtis 5 96
(Charlie Fellowes) *chsd ldrs: effrt on outer to take 2nd over 2f out and ev ch: lost 2nd over 1f out: no ex and wl btn ins fnl f* **11/4**[1]

3-12 **5** 1 1/4 **Technician (IRE)**[12] 2084 3-9-0 105........................ FrankieDettori 3 94
(Martyn Meade) *chsd ldrs: pushed along briefly 7f out: rdn 3f out: wknd 2f out (trainer's rep said the colt was unsuited by the sharp left handed track)* **11/4**[1]

54-5 **6** 1 **Arthur Kitt**[14] 2031 3-9-0 109........................ RichardKingscote 7 92
(Tom Dascombe) *chsd ldr: drvn over 3f out: lost 2nd over 2f out: wknd over 1f out* **20/1**

1-3 **7** 11 **Kaloor**[26] 1737 3-9-0 0........................ JimCrowley 1 74
(Brian Meehan) *hld up in midfield: rdn and lost pl over 3f out: wknd over 2f out* **11/1**

2m 42.91s (0.71) **Going Correction** +0.525s/f (Yiel) **7 Ran SP% 113.3**
Speed ratings (Par 109): **118,112,112,109,108 107,100**
CSF £34.81 TOTE £6.90: £3.10, £3.00; EX 27.40 Trifecta £210.10.
Owner Mrs John Magnier & Michael Tabor & Derrick Smith **Bred** Orpendale, Wynatt & Chelston **Trained** Cashel, Co Tipperary

FOCUS
Add 38yds. Although not since Ruler In The World in 2013 has the winner of this gone on to Derby success, it's still rightly considered an important trial for the Blue Riband next month. This looked a fair edition and there was a solid early pace on. It saw a 1-2 for Aidan O'Brien, who made it eight wins in the race since 2009. The race has been rated at something like face value, with the second and third rated close to form, and Sir Dragonet as the best winner of this race since Toulon (120) in 1991.

2524 SPORTPESA MAIDEN STKS (PLUS 10 RACE) — 1m 2f 70y
4:05 (4:09) (Class 3) 3-Y-O
£11,826 (£3,541; £1,770; £885; £442; £222) **Stalls High**

Form RPR

3 **1** **Future Investment**[23] 1824 3-9-5 0........................ HarryBentley 3 88
(Ralph Beckett) *midfield: pushed along 3f out: hdwy over 1f out: styd on to ld wl ins fnl f: in command towards fin* **11/2**[3]

4-33 **2** 1 1/2 **Bo Samraan (IRE)**[19] 1928 3-9-5 79........................ FrannyNorton 9 85
(Mark Johnston) *led: rdn abt 2 l clr over 1f out: worn down and hdd wl ins fnl f: kpt on same pce towards fin* **14/1**

4-6 **3** 3 3/4 **Vindolanda**[21] 1856 3-9-0 0........................ JamieSpencer 6 73
(Charles Hills) *in rr: rdn over 2f out: hdwy over 1f out: styd on ins fnl f to take 3rd towards fin: nt trble front two* **33/1**

65- **4** 1/2 **Faylaq**[196] 8552 3-9-5 0........................ JimCrowley 7 77
(William Haggas) *hld up: hdwy on outer over 2f out: rdn over 1f out: unable to chal ins fnl f: no ex fnl 100yds* **4/1**[2]

4 **5** 2 3/4 **Mons Star (IRE)**[21] 1856 3-9-5 0........................ PatCosgrave 8 71
(Saeed bin Suroor) *racd keenly: chsd ldrs: effrt to take 2nd 2f out tl over 1f out: wknd fnl 150yds* **11/4**[1]

52-2 **6** 7 **Damon Runyon**[32] 1592 3-9-5 83........................(b1) FrankieDettori 10 57
(John Gosden) *chsd ldr tl rdn 2f out: wknd over 1f out* **8/1**

2 **7** 1 1/4 **Sneaky Peek**[26] 1739 3-9-0 0........................ OisinMurphy 1 50
(Andrew Balding) *chsd ldrs: rdn over 3f out: wknd 2f out (jockey said filly stopped quickly)* **11/4**[1]

6-3 **8** 10 **Artistic Streak**[22] 1828 3-9-0 0........................ RichardKingscote 2 30
(Tom Dascombe) *midfield: drvn over 3f out: sn wknd* **16/1**

9 1/2 **Lady Muk** 3-8-7 0........................ TobyEley(7) 5 29
(Steph Hollinshead) *hld up: rdn 4f out: lft bhd over 2f out (jockey said filly ran green and was never travelling)* **100/1**

2m 17.52s (3.22) **Going Correction** +0.525s/f (Yiel) **9 Ran SP% 116.3**
Speed ratings (Par 103): **108,106,103,103,101 95,94,86,86**
CSF £78.86 TOTE £6.20: £1.90, £2.90, £6.90; EX 63.80 Trifecta £1085.90.
Owner R N J Partnership **Bred** Theakston Stud **Trained** Kimpton, Hants
■ Stewards' Enquiry : Franny Norton two-day ban: careless riding (May 22,23)

FOCUS
Add 26yds. Fairly useful maiden form. Harbinger won this event back in 2009. The level revolves around the second.

2525 HOMESERVE H'CAP — 6f 17y
4:35 (4:39) (Class 3) (0-95,95) 3-Y-O
£11,827 (£3,541; £1,770; £885; £442; £222) **Stalls Low**

Form RPR

00-0 **1** **Lihou**[26] 1736 3-8-5 **79**........................ JFEgan 4 85
(David Evans) *trckd ldrs: rdn to ld over 1f out: hld on wl towards fin* **8/1**

435- **2** 1/2 **Cosmic Law (IRE)**[197] 8504 3-9-6 **94**........................ PJMcDonald 1 98
(Richard Fahey) *chsd ldrs: pushed along over 2f out: effrt over 1f out: wnt 2nd ins fnl f: r.o u.p to press wnr towards fin* **9/2**[3]

0-20 **3** 1/2 **Princess Power (IRE)**[12] 2078 3-8-9 **83**........................ AndrewMullen 6 85
(Nigel Tinkler) *midfield: pushed along 2f out: hdwy u.p over 1f out: r.o towards fin* **16/1**

40-3 **4** 3/4 **Pass The Gin**[12] 2086 3-8-8 **82**........................ OisinMurphy 9 82+
(Andrew Balding) *midfield: hdwy on outer 2f out: rdn to chse ldrs over 1f out: sn hung lft sltly: styd on same pce towards fin* **7/1**

650- **5** 3/4 **Revich (IRE)**[215] 7957 3-8-9 **83**........................ JamieSpencer 8 81+
(Richard Spencer) *hld up in rr: angled out over 1f out: hdwy ins fnl f: styd on: nrst fin* **33/1**

0-04 **6** 1 **Kinks**[12] 2078 3-9-0 **88**........................ SilvestreDeSousa 11 82+
(Mick Channon) *midfield: effrt over 1f out: kpt on same pce ins fnl f* **12/1**

5460 **7** nk **Quiet Endeavour (IRE)**[19] 1920 3-9-5 **93**........................(p) HollieDoyle 7 86
(Archie Watson) *midfield: sn pushed along: nt clr run over 1f out: one pce ins fnl f* **28/1**

600- **8** 1 **Gabrial The Wire**[221] 7751 3-8-0 **79**........................ SeanDavis(5) 5 69
(Richard Fahey) *midfield: pushed along on inner 2f out: kpt on ins fnl f: nvr able to trble ldrs* **20/1**

513- **9** nk **Finoah (IRE)**[167] 9210 3-8-13 **87**........................(v) RichardKingscote 12 76
(Tom Dascombe) *in rr: rdn over 1f out: kpt on ins fnl f: nvr able to trble ldrs* **10/1**

10-4 **10** nk **Wild Edric**[29] 1662 3-8-6 **83**........................ JaneElliott(3) 3 71
(Tom Dascombe) *w ldr: rdn and led briefly over 1f out: wknd fnl 150yds* **7/2**[1]

5230 **11** 6 **Uncle Jerry**[26] 1729 3-8-10 **84**........................(b) ShaneKelly 13 53
(Richard Hughes) *in rr: edgd lft ins fnl f: nvr on terms* **50/1**

-232 **12** 2 1/4 **Chapelli**[6] 2319 3-9-7 **95**........................ FrannyNorton 2 57
(Mark Johnston) *led: rdn and hdd over 1f out: sn wknd (trainer could offer no explanation for the filly's performance)* **4/1**[2]

0-00 **13** 1 3/4 **Swissterious**[39] 1434 3-9-2 **90**........................ DavidEgan 10 46
(Damian Joseph English, Ire) *chsd ldrs tl rdn and wknd over 1f out* **33/1**

1m 19.26s (3.76) **Going Correction** +0.525s/f (Yiel) **13 Ran SP% 122.7**
Speed ratings (Par 103): **95,94,93,92,91 90,89,88,88,87 79,76,74**
CSF £42.80 CT £581.18 TOTE £8.70: £2.70, £1.70, £5.20; EX 46.70 Trifecta £578.40.
Owner Trevor Gallienne **Bred** David Botterill & John Guest **Trained** Pandy, Monmouths
■ Stewards' Enquiry : J F Egan two-day ban: misuse of the whip (May 22,23)

FOCUS
Add 24yds. A decent 3yo sprint handicap. Again the draw played a huge part, but it should prove okay form. The second has been rated in line with his smart early 2yo form, and the third to form.

2526 HR OWEN MASERATI H'CAP — 7f 1y
5:05 (5:08) (Class 4) (0-85,85) 4-Y-O+
£7,698 (£2,290; £1,144; £572; £300; £300) **Stalls Low**

Form — RPR
0-01 **1** **Gossiping**[42] 1355 7-9-5 **83** ShaneKelly 8 — 92
(Gary Moore) *midfield: rdn over 2f out: hdwy over 1f out: sn wnt 2nd: r.o ins fnl f to chal strly: led fnl strides* **8/1**
14-2 **2** *nk* **Elerfaan (IRE)**[15] 2015 5-9-7 **85** DanielTudhope 2 — 93
(Rebecca Bastiman) *in tch: rdn to ld wl over 1f out: pressed ins fnl f: hdd fnl strides (jockey said gelding hung right)* **9/2**[2]
0-53 **3** *1 1/4* **Tadaawol**[16] 1977 6-8-11 **80** (p) BenSanderson[(5)] 11 — 85
(Roger Fell) *trckd ldrs: drvn over 1f out: edgd rt ins fnl f: r.o: nt quite pce of front pair* **33/1**
250- **4** *1/2* **Imperial State**[315] 4245 6-9-4 **82** (v) PaulMulrennan 14 — 85
(Michael Easterby) *hld up: rdn and hdwy over 1f out: r.o towards fin: unable to chal front two* **50/1**
0-00 **5** *1 1/2* **Penwortham (IRE)**[20] 1881 6-9-6 **84** PaulHanagan 10 — 84
(Richard Fahey) *dwlt: hld up: hdwy over 1f out: kpt on u.p towards fin: nvr able to chal* **16/1**
50-5 **6** *nk* **Humble Gratitude**[15] 2015 4-9-4 **82** DavidEgan 7 — 81
(Ian Williams) *racd keenly in midfield: hdwy over 5f out: w ldr over 4f out: rdn over 2f out: ev ch over 1f out: kpt on same pce fnl 100yds* **16/1**
000- **7** *1 1/4* **Air Raid**[159] 9324 4-9-6 **84** (w) JackGarritty 6 — 80
(Jedd O'Keeffe) *racd keenly: prom: trckd ldrs 5f out: rdn over 1f out: one pce ins fnl f* **6/1**
3- **8** *nse* **Frankelio (FR)**[180] 4-9-6 **84** PJMcDonald 9 — 79
(Micky Hammond) *hld up: rdn over 1f out: kpt on u.p fnl 150yds: no imp on ldrs* **25/1**
060- **9** *1 3/4* **My Amigo**[208] 8162 6-9-6 **84** (t w) BarryMcHugh 13 — 75
(Marjorie Fife) *midfield: pushed along 3f out: rdn on outer 2f out: no imp ins fnl f: no ex fnl 100yds* **40/1**
22-3 **10** *nk* **Queen's Sargent (FR)**[38] 1457 4-9-4 **82** ShaneGray 1 — 72
(Kevin Ryan) *midfield: lost pl over 2f out: u.p over 1f out: trying to keep on whn nt clr run and hmpd sltly fnl 150yds: n.d* **4/1**[1]
12-5 **11** *1* **Gin In The Inn (IRE)**[11] 2117 6-9-2 **85** SeanDavis[(5)] 3 — 72
(Richard Fahey) *trckd ldrs: dropped to midfield 5f out: one pce and no imp ins fnl f* **5/1**[3]
540- **12** *1 1/2* **Calder Prince (IRE)**[221] 7767 6-9-7 **85** (w) RichardKingscote 12 — 69
(Tom Dascombe) *led: rdn 2f out: hdd wl over 1f out: wknd ins fnl f: eased whn btn fnl 100yds* **16/1**
5454 **13** *nk* **Robero**[15] 2015 7-9-2 **80** (v) DavidProbert 4 — 63
(Gay Kelleway) *in tch: midfield over 4f out: rdn over 1f out: hung rt ins fnl f: wknd fnl 100yds* **16/1**
100- **14** *2 3/4* **Dark Intention (IRE)**[186] 8839 6-9-5 **83** SilvestreDeSousa 5 — 59
(Lawrence Mullaney) *sltly hmpd s: in rr: pushed along over 4f out: rdn over 2f out: nvr a threat* **15/2**

1m 32.71s (5.21) **Going Correction** +0.525s/f (Yiel) **14 Ran SP% 126.7**
Speed ratings (Par 105): **91,90,89,88,86 86,85,85,83,82 81,79,79,76**
CSF £45.07 CT £1202.32 TOTE £10.10: £2.80, £2.10, £11.50; EX 68.30 Trifecta £2933.20.
Owner The Buckwell Partnership **Bred** Darley **Trained** Lower Beeding, W Sussex

FOCUS
Add 24yds. A competitive handicap, in which three of the first four raced wide in the home straight where the ground appeared faster. The third helps set the level, rated close to his recent form.
T/Jkpt: Not won. T/Plt: £580.90 to a £1 stake. Pool: £160,919.26 - 202.20 winning units T/Qpdt: £124.30 to a £1 stake. Pool: £13,656.69 - 81.29 winning units **Darren Owen**

2345 SOUTHWELL (L-H)
Wednesday, May 8

OFFICIAL GOING: Fibresand: standard
Wind: Light behind Weather: Rain clearing

2527 SOUTHWELL GOLF CLUB H'CAP — 4f 214y(F)
6:05 (6:05) (Class 6) (0-60,65) 4-Y-O+
£3,105 (£924; £461; £300; £300; £300) **Stalls Centre**

Form — RPR
2165 **1** **Red Stripes (USA)**[3] 2433 7-8-12 **56** (b) SeamusCronin[(5)] 7 — 66
(Lisa Williamson) *w ldr: led 4f out: rdn clr and hung lft over 1f out: styd on* **4/1**[2]
400 **2** *2 1/2* **Skyva**[9] 2189 4-8-12 **54** BenRobinson[(3)] 10 — 55
(Brian Ellison) *prom: pushed along over 3f out: sn outpcd: rallied and hung lft over 1f out: wnt 2nd ins fnl f: nt trble wnr* **9/1**
630 **3** *1/2* **Le Manege Enchante (IRE)**[13] 2066 6-8-7 **46** (v) PaddyMathers 5 — 45
(Derek Shaw) *s.i.s and n.m.r s: outpcd: hrd rdn over 1f out: r.o ins fnl f: nrst fin* **12/1**
0-50 **4** *2 1/4* **Flying Foxy**[18] 1952 5-9-0 **60** (p) JessicaCooley[(7)] 1 — 51
(George Scott) *prom: chsd wnr 1/2-way: rdn over 1f out: lost 2nd and wknd no ex ins fnl f* **12/1**
0-00 **5** *hd* **Racquet**[9] 2189 6-8-13 **52** (p[1]) JamesSullivan 2 — 42
(Ruth Carr) *led 1f: chsd ldrs: rdn over 1f out: no ex fnl f* **16/1**
6136 **6** *1/2* **Kath's Boy (IRE)**[42] 1364 5-8-6 **52** (p) ElishaWhittington[(7)] 8 — 41
(Tony Carroll) *prom: pushed along over 3f out: styd on same pce fr over 1f out (vet said gelding was lame left hind)* **8/1**
00-5 **7** *shd* **Optimickstickhill**[7] 2295 4-8-2 **46** oh1 (b) TheodoreLadd[(5)] 6 — 34
(Scott Dixon) *in tch: outpcd over 3f out: styd on ins fnl f* **25/1**
0011 **8** *1 1/4* **Red Invader (IRE)**[7] 2295 9-9-12 **65** 4ex (b) StevieDonohoe 3 — 49
(John Butler) *s.i.s: sn pushed along in rr: hdwy over 1f out: wknd ins fnl f (jockey said gelding ran flat; post-race examination failed to reveal any abnormalities)* **3/1**[1]
-610 **9** *2 3/4* **Furni Factors**[42] 1364 4-8-11 **57** (b) RPWalsh[(7)] 9 — 31
(Ronald Thompson) *sn pushed along and prom: rdn 1/2-way: wknd over 1f out* **16/1**
10 *6* **Ar Saoirse**[21] 1866 4-8-13 **52** (b) LukeMorris 4 — 4
(Clare Hobson) *chsd ldrs: pushed along over 3f out: rdn and wknd 1/2-way: eased fnl f (trainer said gelding was unsuited by Fibresand surface)* **7/1**[3]
0000 **11** *8* **Independence Day (IRE)**[20] 1883 6-9-4 **57** (h) JoeyHaynes 11
(Paul Howling) *sn outpcd: eased fnl f* **40/1**

58.19s (-1.51) **Going Correction** -0.325s/f (Stan) **11 Ran SP% 112.0**
Speed ratings (Par 101): **99,95,94,90,90 89,89,87,82,73 60**
CSF £37.88 CT £397.64 TOTE £4.50: £1.60, £2.60, £3.10; EX 37.30 Trifecta £452.10.
Owner E H Jones (paints) Ltd **Bred** Tim Ahearn **Trained** Taporley, Wrexham

FOCUS
A moderate sprint handicap and there was only one horse in it from halfway.

2528 VISITSOUTHWELL.COM H'CAP — 2m 102y(F)
6:35 (6:38) (Class 6) (0-65,66) 4-Y-O+
£3,105 (£924; £461; £300; £300; £300) **Stalls Low**

Form — RPR
030- **1** **Chetwynd Abbey**[170] 9152 4-9-3 **61** GeorgeWood 7 — 69
(James Fanshawe) *hld up: hdwy over 4f out: rdn over 1f out: styd on to ld wl ins fnl f* **14/1**
30-1 **2** *1/2* **Aphaea**[6] 2351 4-9-5 **63** NathanEvans 4 — 70
(Michael Easterby) *chsd ldr: led over 1f out: rdn: hung rt and hdd wl ins fnl f* **8/13**[1]
0546 **3** *1/2* **Katie Gale**[6] 2351 9-9-5 **62** KieranO'Neill 1 — 67
(Robyn Brisland) *sn led: rdn over 3f out: hdd over 1f out: styd on u.p* **14/1**
-334 **4** *1 1/4* **Colwood**[67] 991 5-9-4 **66** DarraghKeenan[(5)] 3 — 69
(Robert Eddery) *s.i.s: hld up: hdwy over 6f out: lost pl 5f out: nt clr run and outpcd over 3f out: hdwy over 1f out: styd on* **5/1**[2]
6422 **5** *1* **High Command (IRE)**[6] 2351 6-9-1 **65** (v) GraceMcEntee[(7)] 8 — 67
(Michael Appleby) *sn pushed along to chse ldrs: rdn over 2f out: styd on same pce fnl f* **9/1**[3]
5 **6** *8* **Dharma Rain (IRE)**[9] 2196 4-8-11 **55** (tp) LukeMorris 6 — 50
(Clare Hobson) *s.i.s: drvn along early in rr: hdwy u.p 4f out: hung lft and wknd over 1f out* **33/1**
-4 **7** *27* **Brandy James (GER)**[23] 1815 4-9-7 **65** LiamKeniry 2 — 27
(Harry Whittington) *chsd ldrs: rdn over 6f out: wknd over 3f out* **18/1**

3m 38.92s (-6.58) **Going Correction** -0.325s/f (Stan)
WFA 4 from 5yo+ 1lb **7 Ran SP% 110.1**
Speed ratings (Par 101): **103,102,102,101,101 97,83**
CSF £21.63 CT £122.37 TOTE £13.40: £4.50, £1.10; EX 25.80 Trifecta £127.20.
Owner G S Shropshire **Bred** West Dereham Abbey Stud **Trained** Newmarket, Suffolk

FOCUS
Not much pace on for this modest staying handicap in which three of the seven runners had met over 1m6f here six days earlier. The 1-2-6 there finished 2-5-3 here and there was something of a turn up.

2529 ADVERTISER LADIES DAY H'CAP — 7f 14y(F)
7:05 (7:07) (Class 5) (0-75,77) 3-Y-O
£3,752 (£1,116; £557; £300; £300; £300) **Stalls Low**

Form — RPR
-432 **1** **Ollivander (IRE)**[7] 2299 3-9-1 **65** (v[1]) ConorMcGovern[(3)] 2 — 71
(David O'Meara) *s.i.s: rcvrd to chse ldr after 1f: shkn up to ld 2f out: rdn and hdd over 1f out: rallied to ld wl ins fnl f* **2/1**[1]
5136 **2** *hd* **Sylviacliffs (FR)**[7] 2299 3-9-2 **63** (p) CliffordLee 6 — 68
(K R Burke) *s.i.s: sn pushed along to go prom: shkn up over 3f out: rdn to ld over 1f out: edgd rt and hdd wl ins fnl f* **8/1**
56-2 **3** *1 1/2* **Moveonup (IRE)**[41] 1385 3-9-6 **67** LukeMorris 1 — 68
(Gay Kelleway) *sn led: rdn and hdd 2f out: styd on same pce ins fnl f* **9/2**[2]
1150 **4** *3 3/4* **Bay Of Naples (IRE)**[14] 2035 3-9-11 **77** AndrewBreslin[(5)] 4 — 68+
(Mark Johnston) *sn outpcd: rdn over 1f out: r.o strly ins fnl f: nt rch ldrs (jockey said colt didn't face the kickback on this occasion)* **13/2**[3]
060- **5** *1 3/4* **No Thanks**[184] 8880 3-9-7 **68** (h) GeorgeWood 8 — 54
(William Jarvis) *hld up: shkn up over 3f out: styd on fnl f: nvr trbld ldrs* **15/2**
02-5 **6** *3 1/4* **Usain Boat (IRE)**[42] 1360 3-9-9 **77** (h) JessicaCooley[(7)] 5 — 54
(George Scott) *hld up: pushed along over 3f out: n.d* **9/1**
06-0 **7** *3 1/2* **Straitouttacompton**[23] 1819 3-9-3 **67** GabrieleMalune[(3)] 7 — 35
(Ivan Furtado) *chsd ldrs: rdn over 2f out: sn wknd* **15/2**
1600 **8** *2* **Axel Jacklin**[15] 2024 3-9-4 **65** JoeyHaynes 3 — 27
(Paul Howling) *led early: lost pl after 1f: pushed along over 4f out: lost grnd fnl 3f* **50/1**

1m 27.92s (-2.38) **Going Correction** -0.325s/f (Stan) **8 Ran SP% 111.4**
Speed ratings (Par 99): **100,99,98,93,91 88,84,81**
CSF £17.76 CT £62.07 TOTE £3.00: £1.30, £2.10, £1.80; EX 18.50 Trifecta £52.50.
Owner York Thoroughbred Racing **Bred** Canice Farrell **Trained** Upper Helmsley, N Yorks

FOCUS
An ordinary 3yo handicap. Only two of these had raced on Fibresand before and they filled the first two places. The front three were the only ones ever in it.

2530 SKY SPORTS RACING VIRGIN 535 H'CAP — 1m 3f 23y(F)
7:35 (7:35) (Class 6) (0-60,60) 3-Y-O
£3,105 (£924; £461; £300; £300; £300) **Stalls Low**

Form — RPR
-134 **1** **Glutnforpunishment**[9] 2213 3-9-7 **60** EoinWalsh 7 — 68
(Nick Littmoden) *pushed along to chse ldr: led over 4f out: rdn clr fnl 3f: styd on wl* **9/2**[3]
000- **2** *2 1/2* **Spargrove**[165] 9254 3-9-5 **58** CharlieBennett 4 — 62+
(Hughie Morrison) *s.i.s: hld up: rdn over 3f out: hdwy to go 2nd over 1f out: nt rch wnr* **5/2**[2]
0222 **3** *5* **Bonneville (IRE)**[6] 2343 3-8-8 **52** (b) TheodoreLadd[(5)] 8 — 48
(Rod Millman) *s.i.s: hdwy over 9f out: chsd wnr over 3f out: sn outpcd: rdn and no imp whn lost 2nd over 1f out* **1/1**[1]
0-06 **4** *1 3/4* **Juals Spirit (IRE)**[9] 2190 3-8-7 **46** oh1 (p) CamHardie 1 — 39
(Brian Ellison) *chsd ldrs: rdn and outpcd over 3f out: no ch whn hung lft fnl f* **33/1**
0650 **5** *19* **Enyama (GER)**[25] 1770 3-9-0 **53** LukeMorris 6 — 16
(Michael Attwater) *sn pushed along in rr: rdn over 8f out: wknd over 4f out* **22/1**
00-6 **6** *18* **Northern Footsteps**[16] 1980 3-8-4 **46** oh1 JamieGormley[(3)] 2
(Ollie Pears) *led: hdd over 4f out: sn rdn: wknd and eased over 2f out (jockey said filly lost its action round fnl bnd; post-race examination failed to reveal any abnormalities)* **50/1**
640 **7** *16* **Golden Grenade (FR)**[57] 1165 3-8-11 **50** StevieDonohoe 3
(Ian Williams) *prom: rdn over 5f out: wknd over 3f out* **25/1**
404- **8** *44* **Jean Merci (FR)**[186] 8826 3-9-2 **55** TomEaves 5
(Keith Dalgleish) *s.i.s: hdwy 6f out: rdn and wknd 4f out* **14/1**

2m 24.15s (-3.85) **Going Correction** -0.325s/f (Stan) **8 Ran SP% 116.5**
Speed ratings (Par 97): **101,99,95,94,80 67,55,23**
CSF £15.94 CT £19.45 TOTE £6.00: £1.50, £1.10, £1.10; EX 16.70 Trifecta £33.50.
Owner A A Goodman **Bred** Rabbah Bloodstock Limited **Trained** Newmarket, Suffolk

FOCUS
A moderate 3yo middle-distance handicap containing just one previous winner, and that was in a match. They finished well spread out.

2531 ATTHERACES.COM H'CAP 1m 13y(F)
8:05 (8:06) (Class 6) (0-55,56) 3-Y-O

£3,105 (£924; £461; £300; £300; £300) Stalls Low

Form RPR

3304 1 **Crazy Spin**[6] 2350 3-9-1 **46**....................(p) JasonHart 4 53
(Ivan Furtado) *mde all: rdn and edgd rt over 2f out: edgd lft over 2f out: styd on wl* **4/1**[2]

0-53 2 2 ¼ **Antico Lady (IRE)**[15] 2016 3-9-8 **56**.................... BenRobinson(3) 7 58
(Brian Ellison) *sn chsng wnr: rdn over 2f out: styd on (jockey said filly hung right)* **15/8**[1]

5-00 3 1 **Lethal Laura**[9] 2197 3-8-10 **46**.................... DarraghKeenan(5) 5 46
(James Given) *broke wl: sn stdd to trck ldrs: racd keenly: rdn over 2f out: styd on same pce ins fnl f* **25/1**

0-03 4 ¾ **Treasured Company (IRE)**[9] 2190 3-9-1 **46**..............(e) NathanEvans 2 44
(Richard Guest) *hld up: hdwy u.p over 2f out: hung rt over 1f out: rdr dropped whip 1f out: no ex wl ins fnl f* **7/1**

00-0 5 2 ½ **Preservation**[38] 1458 3-9-7 **52**.................... CliffordLee 1 44
(Jedd O'Keeffe) *chsd ldrs: rdn over 3f out: wknd wl ins fnl f* **12/1**

-006 6 4 ½ **Jagerbond**[6] 2350 3-9-5 **50**....................(p) CamHardie 8 32
(Andrew Crook) *sn pushed along and prom: rdn over 2f out: wknd over 1f out* **14/1**

-200 7 7 **Piccolita**[44] 1332 3-9-3 **48**.................... CharlieBennett 6 14
(Hughie Morrison) *s.i.s: sn pushed along in rr: reminder 7f out: hdwy on outer over 5f out: rdn and wknd over 2f out* **9/1**

5-00 8 6 **Mi Laddo (IRE)**[15] 2016 3-9-6 **51**....................(p) DavidNolan 10 3
(Oliver Greenall) *s.i.s: pushed along and hdwy to go prom 7f out: rdn over 3f out: wknd over 2f out* **6/1**[3]

06-0 9 1 ¼ **Milistorm**[26] 1726 3-9-6 **51**.................... LukeMorris 3
(Michael Blanshard) *sn pushed along in rr: rdn and wknd over 3f out* **50/1**

500- 10 ¾ **Leebellinsummerbee (IRE)**[245] 6950 3-8-11 **49**........... EllaMcCain(7) 9
(Donald McCain) *s.i.s: in rr: rdn: hung rt and wknd over 3f out* **33/1**

1m 41.82s (-1.88) **Going Correction** -0.325s/f (Stan) 10 Ran SP% **114.7**
Speed ratings (Par 97): **96,93,92,92,89 85,78,72,70,70**
CSF £11.45 CT £161.09 TOTE £4.50: £1.50, £1.60, £4.10; EX 14.90 Trifecta £258.60.

Owner The Giggle Factor Partnership **Bred** Mrs A Shone **Trained** Wiseton, Nottinghamshire

FOCUS
A poor affair contested by ten maidens and few got into it.

2532 SKY SPORTS RACING SKY 415 H'CAP 6f 16y(F)
8:35 (8:39) (Class 6) (0-60,58) 4-Y-O+

£3,105 (£924; £461; £300; £300; £300) Stalls Low

Form RPR

0-35 1 **Space War**[17] 1967 12-8-9 **46**....................(t) NathanEvans 2 59
(Michael Easterby) *hld up: hdwy over 2f out: led over 1f out: rdn clr ins fnl f: comf* **11/2**[3]

-400 2 3 ½ **Queen Of Kalahari**[60] 1093 4-8-5 **47**.................... FayeMcManoman(5) 6 47
(Les Eyre) *chsd ldrs: shkn up and nt clr run over 1f out: swtchd lft ins fnl f: styd on to go 2nd nr fin (jockey said filly denied a clear run from 1 1/2f out)* **12/1**

0-40 3 ½ **Loulin**[15] 2013 4-9-3 **54**.................... JamesSullivan 4 52
(Ruth Carr) *sn led: hdd 5f out: chsd ldr: rdn and ev ch over 1f out: no ex ins fnl f* **11/1**

0016 4 1 **Falcao (IRE)**[9] 2194 7-9-7 **58**....................(t) KieranO'Neill 14 53
(John Butler) *restless in stalls: prom on outer: rdn over 1f out: styd on same pce fnl f* **13/2**

650- 5 nk **The Gingerbreadman**[201] 8381 4-8-3 **45**.................... PaulaMuir(5) 7 39
(Chris Fairhurst) *s.s: outpcd: hung lft over 2f out: r.o ins fnl f: nvr nrr (jockey said blindfold had become stuck on bridle and took a second attempt to move)* **14/1**

0-34 6 1 **Fortinbrass (IRE)**[42] 1368 9-8-2 **46**.................... IzzyClifton(7) 5 37
(John Balding) *prom: lost pl after 1f: pushed along over 3f out: styd on ins fnl f* **16/1**

-211 7 nse **Jazz Legend (USA)**[34] 1553 6-9-4 **55**.................... LiamKeniry 12 46
(Mandy Rowland) *led 5f out: rdn and hdd over 1f out: wknd ins fnl f* **7/2**[1]

3003 8 hd **Haader (FR)**[32] 1595 4-9-6 **57**....................(t) PaddyMathers 1 47
(Derek Shaw) *s.i.s: outpcd: styd on u.p ins fnl f: nvr trbld ldrs* **12/1**

5000 9 shd **Coiste Bodhar (IRE)**[34] 1554 8-8-5 **45**................(h) JamieGormley(3) 10 35
(Scott Dixon) *hld up: hung rt over 4f out: styd on ins fnl f: nvr on terms (jockey said gelding hung right throughout)* **40/1**

06 10 nk **Dream Ally (IRE)**[9] 2189 9-8-12 **49**.................... PhilDennis 9 38
(John Weymes) *chsd ldrs: rdn over 2f out: wknd fnl f* **16/1**

3250 11 3 **Essential**[17] 1967 5-8-13 **50**.................... RachelRichardson 3 30
(Olly Williams) *led early: remained handy: rdn over 1f out: sn wknd (jockey said gelding lost left fore shoe)* **5/1**[2]

0640 12 10 **Blistering Dancer (IRE)**[42] 1368 9-8-8 **45**................(p) LukeMorris 8
(Tony Carroll) *s.i.s: sn prom: rdn over 3f out: wknd 2f out* **33/1**

10-0 13 15 **Danish Duke (IRE)**[17] 1973 8-8-13 **50**.................... JackGarritty 11
(Ruth Carr) *racd towards outer and sn pushed along in rr: sme hdwy 4f out: wknd over 3f out* **25/1**

1m 14.85s (-1.65) **Going Correction** -0.325s/f (Stan) 13 Ran SP% **119.0**
Speed ratings (Par 101): **98,93,92,91,90 89,89,89,89,88 84,71,51**
CSF £68.46 CT £709.44 TOTE £6.00: £2.10, £3.30, £3.70; EX 72.80 Trifecta £851.80.

Owner The Laura Mason Syndicate **Bred** Shutford Stud And O F Waller **Trained** Sheriff Hutton, N Yorks

FOCUS
A moderate handicap full of the usual suspects, but the veteran showed them the way home.

T/Plt: £45.50 to a £1 stake. Pool: £69,616.22 - 1,15.53 winning units T/Qpdt: £12.40 to a £1 stake. Pool: £8,482.87 - 504.24 winning units **Colin Roberts**

2533 - 2549a (Foreign Racing) - See Raceform Interactive

2316
CHELMSFORD (A.W) (L-H)
Thursday, May 9

OFFICIAL GOING: Polytrack: standard
Wind: light, half against Weather: showers

2550 SRI LANKA THE WONDER OF ASIA NOVICE STKS 7f (P)
5:30 (5:31) (Class 5) 3-Y-O+ £4,948 (£1,472; £735; £367) Stalls Low

Form RPR

4- 1 **Daring Venture (IRE)**[278] 5749 3-8-11 0.................... AndreaAtzeni 11 75+
(Roger Varian) *chsd ldr tl led after 1f: mde rest: clr w rival 2f out: rdn and asserted over 1f out: in command and r.o wl ins fnl f: comf* **5/4**[1]

03- 2 3 **Molvaliente (USA)**[166] 9246 3-9-2 0.................... KierenFox 6 72+
(John Best) *hld up off the pce in midfield: nt clrest of runs 2f out: nt clr run and swtchd rt over 1f out: hdwy to chse ldng pair ins fnl f: r.o wl to go 2nd fnl 50yds: no threat to wnr (jockey said colt was never travelling in the early stages of the race and was denied a clear run around the bend and in the home straight)* **5/2**[2]

56 3 1 ¼ **Seraphim**[16] 2018 3-8-8 0....................(t) GabrieleMalune(3) 8 64
(Marco Botti) *chsd ldrs tl clsd to press wnr 4f out: clr w wnr 2f out: outpcd and hung lft 1f out: plugged on same pce and lost 2nd fnl 50yds* **10/1**

4 1 ¾ **Desert War (USA)** 3-9-2 0....................(h[1]) PatCosgrave 4 64
(Hugo Palmer) *rrd as stalls opened and slowly away: in rr: prog into midfield but stl off the pce 4f out: swtchd rt and hdwy over 1f out: styd on wl ins fnl f: nvr trbld ldrs* **7/1**[3]

65 5 ¾ **Bawaader (IRE)**[61] 1102 4-10-0 0.................... DaneO'Neill 13 66
(Ed Dunlop) *midfield: clsd and chsd ldrs 4f out: 4th and struggling to qckn over 2f out: kpt on same pce after and nvr getting on terms w ldrs* **16/1**

5- 6 2 ¼ **Favre (USA)**[208] 8178 3-9-2 0.................... TomMarquand 2 56
(Robert Cowell) *dwlt and pushed along leaving stalls: rcvrd and chsd ldrs after: 6th and unable qck over 2f out: btn over 1f out: wknd ins fnl f* **14/1**

66 7 hd **Luna Princess**[22] 1862 3-8-11 0.................... NicolaCurrie 1 51
(Michael Appleby) *led for 1f: chsd wnr tl 4f out: 3rd and unable qck over 1f out: btn over 1f out: wknd ins fnl f* **50/1**

0 8 hd **For Richard**[29] 1677 3-9-2 0.................... KieranO'Neill 14 55
(John Best) *midfield: nt clrest of runs jst over 2f out: unable qck and no prog whn jostled over 1f out: wl hld fnl f* **33/1**

00 9 1 **Reformed Character (IRE)**[29] 1690 3-9-2 0.................... BrettDoyle 10 52
(Lydia Pearce) *chsd ldrs early: wl in tch in midfield: rdn and unable qck over 2f out: outpcd over 1f out: wknd ins fnl f (jockey said colt hung both way up the home straight)* **100/1**

10 shd **Fountain Of Life** 3-8-11 0.................... DylanHogan(5) 3 52
(Philip McBride) *s.i.s: a towards rr: rdn 3f out: kpt on fnl f but nvr involved* **25/1**

5 11 9 **Katie O'Hara (IRE)**[17] 1984 3-8-11 0.................... EoinWalsh 9 23
(Samuel Farrell, Ire) *midfield: swtchd rt over 4f out: shkn up over 3f out: rdn and unable qck over 2f out: wl hld over 1f out: wknd fnl f* **100/1**

40 12 5 **Kiowa**[66] 1019 3-9-2 0.................... DannyBrock 5 14
(Philip McBride) *a towards rr: nvr on terms (jockey said gelding was never travelling)* **50/1**

13 6 **Red Moon Lady** 3-8-11 0.................... MartinDwyer 7
(Dean Ivory) *wd and sn towards rr: bhd fnl 2f* **20/1**

14 1 ¼ **Shawwaslucky** 3-8-11 0.................... PaddyMathers 15
(Derek Shaw) *s.i.s: a outpcd in rr* **33/1**

1m 25.82s (-1.38) **Going Correction** -0.125s/f (Stan) 14 Ran SP% **127.5**
WFA 3 from 4yo 12lb
Speed ratings (Par 103): **102,98,97,95,94 91,91,91,90,90 79,74,67,65**
CSF £4.20 TOTE £1.90: £1.10, £1.20, £2.40; EX 5.50 Trifecta £29.00.

Owner Sheikh Juma Dalmook Al Maktoum **Bred** Ecurie Normandie Pur Sang **Trained** Newmarket, Suffolk

FOCUS
Just a fair novice. The opening level is set around the third and fifth.

2551 SRI LANKA PARADISE ISLAND H'CAP 7f (P)
6:00 (6:02) (Class 2) (0-100,100) 4-Y-O+ £12,938 (£3,850; £1,924; £962) Stalls Low

Form RPR

6005 1 **Victory Wave (USA)**[19] 1942 5-9-3 **96**....................(h) PatCosgrave 2 106
(Saeed bin Suroor) *t.k.h: chsd ldrs early: in tch in last pair after 1f: effrt over 1f out: nt clr run and swtchd lft ins fnl f: rdn to ld 100yds out: sn rdn clr and r.o strly* **11/4**[2]

3622 2 2 ¼ **Raucous**[20] 1916 6-9-0 **100**....................(tp) CierenFallon(7) 4 104
(Robert Cowell) *wl in tch in midfield: effrt ent fnl 2f: clsd u.p and ev ch 1f out: led ins fnl f: sn hdd: edgd lft and nt match pce of wnr towards fin* **8/1**

43-0 3 nk **Al Barg (IRE)**[12] 2116 4-8-7 **86** oh1....................(b) HollieDoyle 1 89
(Richard Hannon) *nodded leaving stalls: pushed along and led early: sn hdd and trckd ldrs: effrt and nt clrest of runs over 1f out: swtchd lft and pressed ldrs 1f out: kpt on same pce ins fnl f (jockey said gelding hung left-handed)* **14/1**

6-50 4 1 **Breathless Times**[20] 1916 4-9-4 **97**....................(t) JasonWatson 5 97
(Roger Charlton) *in rr early: hdwy to press ldr over 4f out: rdn over 1f out: no ex ins fnl f: one pce and hld whn short of room and impeded wl ins fnl f* **8/1**

02-1 5 shd **Margub**[16] 2015 4-9-2 **95**.................... DaneO'Neill 6 95+
(Marcus Tregoning) *sn led: rdn wl over 1f out: edgd rt ent fnl f: hdd ins fnl f: no ex and one pce wl ins fnl f* **9/4**[1]

0002 6 1 **Masham Star (IRE)**[3] 2487 5-9-0 **93**.................... PJMcDonald 3 91
(Mark Johnston) *sn dropped to last pair: swtchd rt and effrt over 1f out: no imp and kpt on same pce ins fnl f* **3/1**[3]

1m 24.81s (-2.39) **Going Correction** -0.125s/f (Stan) 6 Ran SP% **111.3**
Speed ratings (Par 109): **108,105,105,103,103 102**
CSF £23.42 TOTE £3.40: £1.90, £3.40; EX 23.80 Trifecta £131.80.

Owner Godolphin **Bred** Darley **Trained** Newmarket, Suffolk

The Form Book Flat 2019, Raceform Ltd, Newbury, RG14 5SJ

FOCUS
The leaders did a bit too much in front and this set up for a closer. The winner has been rated back to the level of last year's C&D win, with the third close to his mark.

2552 AMAZING SRI LANKA FILLIES' H'CAP — 1m (P)
6:30 (6:31) (Class 3) (0-90,86) 3-Y-O — £9,703 (£2,887; £1,443; £721) Stalls Low

Form — RPR

01-3 **1** **Vivionn**[23] 1838 3-9-4 83 ... JasonWatson 7 — 88
(Sir Michael Stoute) *mde all and dictated stdy gallop: pushed along and qcknd over 2f out: rdn over 1f out: kpt on ins fnl f: a lasting home nr fin* **2/1**[1]

163- **2** *nk* **Pennywhistle (IRE)**[199] 8468 3-9-1 80 ... FrankieDettori 1 — 86+
(John Gosden) *awkward and stmbld leaving stalls: hld up in tch in rr: effrt and swtchd rt over 1f out: hdwy ins fnl f and chsd wnr wl ins fnl f: r.o strly but nvr quite getting to wnr (jockey said filly stumbled at the start)* **9/2**[3]

40-4 **3** *1* **Prairie Spy (IRE)**[16] 2008 3-9-2 81 ... JoeFanning 2 — 83
(Mark Johnston) *t.k.h: chsd wnr for over 1f: trckd ldrs after: effrt u.p over 1f out: chsd wnr ins fnl f: kpt on but no imp: lost 2nd wl ins fnl f* **9/1**

5-12 **4** *1 1/4* **Star Of War (USA)**[11] 2144 3-9-3 82 ... SeanLevey 8 — 81
(Richard Hannon) *t.k.h: hdwy to press wnr over 6f out: rdn over 1f out: unable qck and lost 2nd ins fnl f: wknd wl ins fnl f* **4/1**[2]

41-5 **5** *nk* **Sonja Henie (IRE)**[23] 1838 3-8-11 76 ... (h[1]) AndreaAtzeni 5 — 74
(Marco Botti) *dwlt and awkward leaving stalls: in tch in midfield: effrt over 2f out: swtchd rt wl over 1f out: sn drvn and chsd ldrs 1f out: no ex and outpcd ins fnl f* **20/1**

41-2 **6** *1 1/2* **Sunset Flash (IRE)**[17] 1984 3-9-7 86 ... StevieDonohoe 6 — 81
(David Lanigan) *hld up in tch in last pair: c wd and effrt wl over 1f out: no hdwy u.p: wknd ins fnl f* **9/2**[3]

22-1 **7** *nse* **Coastline (IRE)**[48] 1272 3-8-13 78 ... PJMcDonald 4 — 73
(James Tate) *t.k.h: hld up in midfield: sltly impeded over 6f out: effrt and sltly impeded over 1f out: edgd lft and wl hld ins fnl f* **8/1**

1m 39.2s (-0.70) **Going Correction** -0.125s/f (Stan) — **7** Ran SP% **115.6**
Speed ratings (Par 100): **98,97,96,95,95 93,93**
CSF £11.56 CT £65.06 TOTE £2.60: £1.50, £2.30; EX 13.60 Trifecta £61.50.
Owner Cheveley Park Stud **Bred** Newsells Park Stud **Trained** Newmarket, Suffolk

FOCUS
This was steadily run early on and it was an advantage to be handy.

2553 SRI LANKA STAYING STRONG H'CAP — 1m 2f (P)
7:00 (7:03) (Class 2) (0-105,98) 3-Y-O — £12,938 (£3,850; £1,924; £962) Stalls Low

Form — RPR

526- **1** **Fox Premier (IRE)**[245] 6995 3-8-2 79 oh2 ... SilvestreDeSousa 1 — 88+
(Andrew Balding) *hld up in tch in rr: swtchd rt over 4f out: rdn over 3f out: hdwy on inner over 1f out: led ins fnl f: a doing enough towards fin* **7/2**[2]

140- **2** *1/2* **The Trader (IRE)**[236] 7294 3-8-12 89 ... PJMcDonald 2 — 96
(Mark Johnston) *led: gng best ent fnl 2f: rdn and wnt rt over 1f out: hung lft 1f out and hdd ins fnl f: kpt on but a hld towards fin* **10/1**

5-32 **3** *2 1/2* **Ritchie Valens (IRE)**[13] 2075 3-8-2 79 oh1 ... KieranO'Neill 3 — 81
(Richard Hannon) *chsd ldrs: effrt to go 2nd ent fnl 2f: hung rt and outpcd over 1f out: kpt on same pce and hung lft ins fnl f* **9/2**

35-3 **4** *2 1/4* **Boerhan**[23] 1831 3-9-7 98 ... JamesDoyle 4 — 96
(William Haggas) *chsd ldr tl 5f out: styd handy: rdn and hung rt over 2f out: outpcd and hung lft 1f out: wl hld ins fnl f (trainers' rep could offer no explanation for the poor performance. Vet said colt lost a right fore shoe)* **6/4**[1]

2-14 **5** *11* **Travel On**[13] 2084 3-9-6 97 ... FrankieDettori 5 — 73
(John Gosden) *in tch in last pair: swtchd rt and hdwy to join ldr 5f out tl unable qck and lost 2nd over 2f out: lost pl and bhd whn swtchd rt 1f out* **4/1**[3]

2m 4.24s (-4.36) **Going Correction** -0.125s/f (Stan) — **5** Ran SP% **109.5**
Speed ratings (Par 105): **112,111,109,107,99**
CSF £32.22 TOTE £3.90: £1.80, £3.80; EX 25.70 Trifecta £61.30.
Owner King Power Racing Co Ltd **Bred** Rabbah Bloodstock Limited **Trained** Kingsclere, Hants

FOCUS
An interesting handicap, if a bit messy. The second is perhaps the key to the form and has been rated in line with his Chester win.

2554 RESOLUTE AND BEAUTIFUL SRI LANKA CONDITIONS STKS — 1m 6f (P)
7:30 (7:30) (Class 2) 4-Y-O+ — £12,938 (£3,850; £1,924; £962) Stalls Low

Form — RPR

30-6 **1** **Weekender**[8] 2269 5-9-3 114 ... FrankieDettori 3 — 115
(John Gosden) *swtchd rt sn after s: led after 2f: mde rest: pushed along ent fnl 2f: rdn over 1f out: styd on wl and in command ins fnl f* **8/13**[1]

22-5 **2** *1 1/4* **Danehill Kodiac (IRE)**[8] 2269 6-9-3 112 ... SeanLevey 5 — 112
(Richard Hannon) *chsd ldr for 1f: trckd ldrs after: swtchd rt and effrt to chse wnr over 1f out: kpt on same pce ins fnl f* **11/4**[2]

-434 **3** *5* **Higher Power**[20] 1917 7-9-3 102 ... GeorgeWood 4 — 105
(James Fanshawe) *led for over 2f: chsd ldr: rdn over 2f out: drvn: unable qck and lost 2nd over 1f out: wknd ins fnl f* **5/1**[3]

420/ **4** *4 1/2* **Cohesion**[509] 9259 6-9-3 99 ... JimmyQuinn 2 — 99?
(David Bridgwater) *stdd s: hld up in tch in rr: effrt over 3f out: outpcd and btn over 1f out* **33/1**

2m 58.15s (-5.05) **Going Correction** -0.125s/f (Stan) — **4** Ran SP% **108.2**
Speed ratings (Par 109): **109,108,105,102**
CSF £2.58 TOTE £1.40; EX 2.00 Trifecta £3.40.
Owner K Abdullah **Bred** Juddmonte Farms Ltd **Trained** Newmarket, Suffolk

FOCUS
A good opportunity for the winner to return to form over a C&D that suits him well. He's been rated to his best.

2555 SUPPORT SRI LANKA NOVICE STKS — 1m 2f (P)
8:00 (8:05) (Class 5) 4-Y-O+ — £4,948 (£1,472; £735; £367) Stalls Low

Form — RPR

1 **Freerolling** 4-9-2 0 ... SilvestreDeSousa 8 — 86+
(Charlie Fellowes) *hld up in midfield: dropped in and plld hrd after 2f: dropped to rr of main gp: effrt over 2f out: chsd ldr 1f out: led ins fnl f: r.o strly: readily* **10/3**[2]

21 **2** *1 3/4* **Kodiac Harbour (IRE)**[83] 732 4-9-9 0 ... LukeMorris 5 — 89
(Paul George) *bmpd leaving stalls: hld up in tch: effrt and swtchd rt 2f out: rdn to ld over 1f out: hung lft and hdd ins fnl f: btn and eased wl ins fnl f* **4/1**[3]

2 **3** *7* **Trailboss (IRE)**[8] 2301 4-9-2 0 ... TomMarquand 1 — 68
(Ed Vaughan) *n.m.r on inner sn after s: led after 1f: rdn ent fnl 2f: hdd over 1f out: 3rd and btn 1f out: wknd ins fnl f* **10/3**[2]

1-0 **4** *5* **Daddy's Daughter (CAN)**[19] 1941 4-9-4 0 ... RobertWinston 2 — 60
(Dean Ivory) *t.k.h: led for 1f: chsd ldr tl 7f out: styd chsng ldrs: rdn to chse ldr 2f out tl over 1f out: sn btn: wknd fnl f* **11/4**[1]

0 **5** *4 1/2* **Treble Clef**[43] 1352 4-9-2 0 ... RossaRyan 4 — 49
(Lee Carter) *in tch in midfield: rdn 3f out: outpcd and btn whn swtchd rt over 1f out: wknd fnl f* **50/1**

6 *1* **Marquisette** 4-8-11 0 ... MartinDwyer 9 — 42
(Marcus Tregoning) *wnt rt leaving stalls: in rr: hdwy on outer to press ldr over 7f out tl 2f out: hung lft and wknd over 1f out* **16/1**

7 *7* **Desert Son** 4-8-9 0 ... TristanPrice(7) 7 — 33
(Sir Michael Stoute) *wd: w ldrs early: dropped to midfield 7f out: rdn 3f out: sn btn* **6/1**

00- **8** *5* **Ginger Lacey**[248] 6885 4-9-2 0 ... (w) NicolaCurrie 6 — 23
(Harry Dunlop) *hmpd leaving stalls: a bhd* **33/1**

2m 6.07s (-2.53) **Going Correction** -0.125s/f (Stan) — **8** Ran SP% **117.9**
Speed ratings (Par 103): **105,103,98,94,90 89,84,80**
CSF £17.76 TOTE £4.00: £1.60, £1.50, £1.40; EX 16.80 Trifecta £64.90.
Owner Three Of A Kind **Bred** Whatton Manor Stud **Trained** Newmarket, Suffolk

FOCUS
An ordinary novice, but there was a gamble landed. The second has been rated in line with the better view of his maiden/novice form.

2556 SRI LANKA UNBOWED H'CAP — 5f (P)
8:30 (8:32) (Class 4) (0-85,85) 4-Y-O+ — £5,692 (£1,694; £846; £423; £300; £300) Stalls Low

Form — RPR

-610 **1** **Poyle Vinnie**[24] 1814 9-9-7 85 ... JamesSullivan 6 — 94
(Ruth Carr) *chsd ldrs: clsd and upsides over 1f out: led 1f out: rdn and kpt on: edgd rt towards fin* **7/1**[3]

0205 **2** *1* **Something Lucky (IRE)**[8] 2272 7-9-1 79 ... (v) HollieDoyle 9 — 84
(Michael Appleby) *dwlt: bhd: hdwy on outer over 1f out: styd on wl to go 2nd wl ins fnl f: nvr getting to wnr* **8/1**

6646 **3** *1 1/4* **Zac Brown (IRE)**[35] 1547 8-8-13 80 ... (t) JoshuaBryan(3) 5 — 81
(Charlie Wallis) *chsd ldr: rdn to ld over 1f out: hdd 1f out: no ex and outpcd fnl 100yds* **16/1**

10-6 **4** *1* **Our Oystercatcher**[8] 2272 5-8-8 75 ... FinleyMarsh(3) 8 — 72
(Mark Pattinson) *chsd ldrs: rdn over 1f out: struggling to qckn whn swtchd lft 1f out: kpt on same pce ins fnl f* **12/1**

-030 **5** *1/2* **Equimou**[21] 1892 5-9-1 79 ... PJMcDonald 3 — 75
(Robert Eddery) *in tch in last trio: effrt over 1f out: swtchd lft and kpt on ins fnl f: nvr threatened ldrs* **7/1**[3]

40-2 **6** *nk* **Zamjar**[13] 2079 5-9-6 84 ... SilvestreDeSousa 1 — 78
(Robert Cowell) *hld up in tch in midfield: effrt on inner over 1f out: hrd drvn 1f out: no ex and wknd ins fnl f* **9/4**[1]

0110 **7** *1 1/4* **Miracle Works**[24] 1822 4-9-1 79 ... TomMarquand 2 — 69
(Robert Cowell) *hld up in tch in midfield: effrt over 1f out: no imp u.p 1f out: wknd ins fnl f* **4/1**[2]

2000 **8** *nk* **Dynamo Walt (IRE)**[20] 1929 8-9-0 78 ... (v) PaddyMathers 7 — 67
(Derek Shaw) *dwlt: in tch in last pair: effrt towards inner over 1f out: no imp and wknd ins fnl f* **25/1**

-433 **9** *nk* **Global Academy (IRE)**[19] 1938 4-9-5 83 ... GeraldMosse 4 — 71
(Gay Kelleway) *taken down early: led: rdn and hdd over 1f out: struggling whn nt clr run and hmpd 1f out: wknd ins fnl f* **4/1**[2]

58.64s (-1.56) **Going Correction** -0.125s/f (Stan) — **9** Ran SP% **124.3**
Speed ratings (Par 105): **107,105,103,101,101 100,98,98,97**
CSF £66.40 CT £892.53 TOTE £7.40: £2.00, £2.40, £6.50; EX 78.90 Trifecta £1478.70.
Owner Formulated Polymer Products Ltd **Bred** Cecil And Miss Alison Wiggins **Trained** Huby, N Yorks

FOCUS
An open sprint handicap. The winner has been rated back to last spring's C&D form.
T/Plt: £95.10 to a £1 stake. Pool: £48,285.85 - 370.36 winning units T/Qpdt: £53.00 to a £1 stake. Pool: £5,878.63 - 82.02 winning units **Steve Payne**

2520 CHESTER (L-H)
Thursday, May 9

OFFICIAL GOING: Good to soft (soft in places) changing to soft after race 2 (2.25)
Wind: Almost nil Weather: Rain

2557 GATELEY PLC H'CAP — 5f 15y
1:50 (1:51) (Class 2) (0-105,100) 4-Y-O+ — £21,165 (£6,337; £3,168; £1,584; £792; £397) Stalls Low

Form — RPR

2203 **1** **Merhoob (IRE)**[20] 1919 7-9-5 98 ... LiamKeniry 4 — 107
(John Ryan) *hld up in midfield: hdwy over 1f out: r.o to ld ins fnl 150yds: asserted towards fin* **22/1**

41-4 **2** *1* **Copper Knight (IRE)**[19] 1946 5-9-7 100 ... (t) DavidAllan 1 — 105
(Tim Easterby) *led: rdn over 1f out: hdd ins fnl 150yds: styd on same pce nr fin* **11/8**[1]

301- **3** *1* **Confessional**[202] 8370 12-8-8 90 ... (e) JamieGormley(3) 5 — 91
(Tim Easterby) *w ldr: pushed along 2f out: rdn over 1f out: stl chalng ins fnl f: no ex towards fin (vet reported the gelding lost its right fore shoe)* **16/1**

6513 **4** *shd* **Mokaatil**[19] 1946 4-8-9 88 ... DavidEgan 2 — 89
(Ian Williams) *trckd ldrs: rdn and nt clr run over 1f out: carried hd awkwardly: styd on towards fin: nvr able to chal* **7/1**[3]

125- **5** *1 3/4* **Camacho Chief (IRE)**[194] 8632 4-8-11 95 ... PaulaMuir(5) 6 — 90
(Michael Dods) *s.i.s: in rr: rdn over 1f out: kpt on ins fnl f: nvr able to trble ldrs* **9/1**

213- **6** *1/2* **Fool For You (IRE)**[229] 7527 4-8-6 90 ... SeanDavis(5) 3 — 83
(Richard Fahey) *trckd ldrs: rdn and unable qck over 1f out: kpt on same pce ins fnl f (starter reported that the filly was the subject of a third criteria failure; trainer was informed that the filly could not run until the day after passing a stalls test)* **8/1**

503- **7** *1 1/4* **Lord Riddiford (IRE)**[194] 8632 4-8-13 92 ... JasonHart 11 — 80
(John Quinn) *midfield: pushed along 2f out: outpcd over 1f out: no imp after* **16/1**

00-0 **8** *1 1/4* **Growl**[12] 2100 7-9-2 95 ... PaulHanagan 9 — 79
(Richard Fahey) *in rr: rdn over 1f out: nvr a threat* **11/1**

4014 **9** *4* **Reflektor (IRE)**[23] 1839 6-8-13 **92**........................ RichardKingscote 8 62
(Tom Dascombe) *hld up: outpcd 2f out: rdn over 1f out: eased whn wl btn fnl 75yds* **11/2**[2]

1m 3.2s (1.10) **Going Correction** +0.675s/f (Yiel) **9** Ran SP% **115.5**
Speed ratings (Par 109): **118,116,114,114,111 111,109,107,100**
CSF £52.92 CT £535.69 TOTE £24.20: £5.40, £1.10, £4.20; EX 70.20 Trifecta £571.90.
Owner Gerry McGladery **Bred** Airlie Stud **Trained** Newmarket, Suffolk

FOCUS
The rail between the 6f and 1f had been moved in by 4yds after racing on Wednesday. The general consensus of riders after the first was that the ground rode more like proper soft. This decent sprint handicap was hit by four non-runners. Add 10yds. The second helps sets the level.

2558 HOMESERVE DEE STKS (LISTED RACE) (C&G) 1m 2f 70y
2:25 (2:26) (Class 1) 3-Y-O

£42,532 (£16,125; £8,070; £4,020; £2,017; £1,012) **Stalls** High

Form RPR
34- **1** **Circus Maximus (IRE)**[194] 8633 3-9-0 110........................ RyanMoore 5 108
(A P O'Brien, Ire) *prom: niggled along over 5f out: w ldr over 4f out: led jst over 2f out: edgd lft over 1f out: drvn out and styd on ins fnl f* **5/4**[1]

410- **2** *1 ¼* **Mohawk (IRE)**[208] 8187 3-9-5 112........................ DonnachaO'Brien 6 110
(A P O'Brien, Ire) *hld up: rdn and hdwy over 2f out: chsd wnr jst over 1f out: styd on to try and chal ins fnl f: run flattened out nr fin* **7/1**[3]

1 **3** *2* **Fox Chairman (IRE)**[26] 1754 3-9-0 0........................ SilvestreDeSousa 3 104+
(Andrew Balding) *in tch: pushed along and dropped to last over 2f out: nt clr run wl over 1f out: trapped on ins appr fnl f: swtchd rt ins fnl f: styd on fnl 100yds: tk 3rd towards fin: nt trble front two (jockey said colt hung left)* **2/1**[2]

1-11 **4** *1 ¼* **Living Legend (IRE)**[20] 1911 3-9-0 91........................ FrannyNorton 1 99
(Mark Johnston) *racd keenly: prom: rdn over 1f out: one pce ins fnl f* **8/1**

26-0 **5** *4 ½* **Dark Jedi (IRE)**[20] 1926 3-9-0 97........................ RichardKingscote 7 90
(Charles Hills) *in rr: hdwy 4f out: chsd ldrs 3f out: rdn 2f out: lost pl over 1f out: wl btn after* **33/1**

231- **6** *½* **Allmankind**[217] 7933 3-9-0 89........................ DanielTudhope 4 89
(Michael Bell) *racd keenly: led: rdn and hdd jst over 2f out: lost 2nd over 1f out: wknd ins fnl f (vet reported the colt lost its right hind shoe)* **12/1**

2m 16.51s (2.21) **Going Correction** +0.675s/f (Yiel) **6** Ran SP% **112.0**
Speed ratings (Par 107): **118,117,115,114,110 110**
CSF £10.72 TOTE £1.90: £1.40, £2.30; EX 7.50 Trifecta £10.80.
Owner Flaxman Stables, Mrs Magnier, M Tabor, D Smith **Bred** Flaxman Stables Ireland Ltd **Trained** Cashel, Co Tipperary

FOCUS
Add 14yds. No great gallop on here and, as had been the case in the Vase a day earlier, the O'Brien runners dominated. The third might have had a say, though, with a clear run and it's doubtful this result will have any bearing on the Derby in a few weeks time. It's been rated as an up-to-standard renewal, with the fourth and fifth rated to form.

2559 DEEPBRIDGE CAPITAL H'CAP 7f 127y
3:00 (3:01) (Class 2) (0-100,91) 3-Y-O

£21,165 (£6,337; £3,168; £1,584; £792; £397) **Stalls** Low

Form RPR
5-04 **1** **Lincoln Park**[19] 1945 3-9-1 **85**........................ SilvestreDeSousa 3 94
(Michael Appleby) *mde all: rdn over 1f out: kpt on wl fnl f* **7/2**[1]

1142 **2** *1* **Spirit Warning**[15] 2035 3-8-12 **82**........................ OisinMurphy 10 88
(Andrew Balding) *midfield: angled out and hdwy over 2f out: wnt 2nd wl over 1f out: edgd rt for most of fnl f and ev ch: hld towards fin* **8/1**

416- **3** *1 ¼* **Barristan The Bold**[208] 8189 3-9-6 **90**........................ AlistairRawlinson 11 93+
(Tom Dascombe) *towards rr: hdwy over 2f out: rdn over 1f out: chsd ldrs and styd on ins fnl f: nt quite pce of front two* **8/1**

23-2 **4** *1* **King Of Tonga (IRE)**[14] 2054 3-9-5 **89**........................ PaulHanagan 8 90+
(Richard Fahey) *handy on outer early: lost pl and dropped to midfield after 1f: hdwy wl over 1f out: sn chsd ldrs: kpt on u.p ins fnl f: one pce nr fin* **13/2**[3]

210- **5** *1 ½* **Lola's Theme**[187] 8836 3-8-7 **80**........................ JaneElliott(3) 2 77
(Tom Dascombe) *bhd: rdn over 2f out: hdwy for press 1f out: styd on: unable to trble ldrs* **10/1**

51-5 **6** *¾* **Sparklealot (IRE)**[27] 1736 3-9-2 **86**........................ TrevorWhelan 9 81
(Ivan Furtado) *chsd ldrs: rdn over 2f out: unable qck over 1f out: no ex fnl 150yds (jockey said gelding hung right throughout)* **11/2**[2]

6-21 **7** *6* **Pacino**[22] 1846 3-8-7 **82**........................ SeanDavis(5) 7 62
(Richard Fahey) *nt bttr than midfield: lost pl over 4f out: struggling over 2f out: plugged on ins fnl f: nvr a threat* **14/1**

13-3 **8** *nk* **Woodside Wonder**[121] 126 3-9-2 **86**........................(p) PaulMulrennan 1 65
(Keith Dalgleish) *chsd ldrs: rdn over 2f out: wknd over 1f out* **20/1**

04-1 **9** *2 ¼* **Forseti**[110] 312 3-8-10 **80**........................(h) DavidProbert 6 54
(Andrew Balding) *racd keenly: hld up: hdwy whn nt clr run over 2f out: n.m.r and hmpd wl over 1f out: no imp after* **11/1**

3-40 **10** *1* **Metatron (IRE)**[21] 1897 3-8-12 **82**........................ RichardKingscote 5 53
(Tom Dascombe) *w wnr: rdn over 3f out: lost pl 2f out: wknd over 1f out* **12/1**

202- **11** *11* **Drogon (IRE)**[204] 8322 3-9-7 **91**........................ JimCrowley 4 35
(Tom Dascombe) *in tch: rdn over 3f out: wknd over 2f out (trainer's rep said the colt was unsuited by the soft going and would prefer a sounder surface)* **12/1**

1m 40.11s (4.41) **Going Correction** +0.675s/f (Yiel) **11** Ran SP% **117.4**
Speed ratings (Par 105): **104,103,101,100,99 98,92,92,89,88 77**
CSF £31.37 CT £214.64 TOTE £4.50: £2.60, £2.60, £3.00; EX 31.70 Trifecta £288.50.
Owner Craig Buckingham & Gary Dewhurst **Bred** Plantation Stud **Trained** Oakham, Rutland

FOCUS
After the second race predictably the going was changed to soft all over. This good-quality 3yo handicap looked wide open and it was run at a frantic pace. Add 13yds. The winner has been rated in line with his Haydock win.

2560 BOODLES DIAMOND ORMONDE STKS (GROUP 3) 1m 5f 84y
3:35 (3:35) (Class 1) 4-Y-O+

£56,710 (£21,500; £10,760; £5,360; £2,690; £1,350) **Stalls** Low

Form RPR
521- **1** **Morando (FR)**[194] 8645 6-9-3 113........................ SilvestreDeSousa 1 119
(Andrew Balding) *chsd ldrs: wnt 2nd wl over 4f out: led 3f out: kicked on wl over 1f out: styd on wl to draw clr ins fnl f: pushed out towards fin: gd ride* **3/1**[2]

310- **2** *8* **Kew Gardens (IRE)**[214] 8026 4-9-7 120........................ RyanMoore 4 111
(A P O'Brien, Ire) *hld up in rr: effrt and hdwy 2f out: kpt on to take 2nd wl ins fnl f: nt trble wnr* **4/5**[1]

110- **3** *½* **Magic Circle (IRE)**[184] 8911 7-9-0 116........................ JimCrowley 6 103
(Ian Williams) *hld up: hdwy over 4f out: wnt 2nd over 2f out: no imp and unable to go w wnr over 1f out: styng on same pce and no ch whn lost 2nd wl ins fnl f (vet reported the gelding had lost its left hind shoe)* **6/1**[3]

4/4 **4** *11* **Dalgarno (FR)**[29] 1681 6-9-0 94........................ JFEgan 3 87
(Jane Chapple-Hyam) *racd keenly: in tch: swtchd rt and hdwy wl over 4f out: sn trckd ldrs: nt clr run 3f out: rdn over 2f out: wknd over 1f out* **50/1**

616- **5** *8* **Cypress Creek (IRE)**[201] 8404 4-9-3 109........................ DonnachaO'Brien 2 78
(A P O'Brien, Ire) *bustled along s: racd in cl 2nd pl: w ldr after 5f: led 6f out: rdn and hdd 3f out: wknd over 2f out* **11/1**

0-43 **6** *69* **Warnaq (IRE)**[32] 1620 5-8-11 94........................ ColinKeane 5
(Matthew J Smith, Ire) *led: hdd 6f out: wknd over 4f out: t.o* **20/1**

3m 0.66s (4.06) **Going Correction** +0.675s/f (Yiel) **6** Ran SP% **109.9**
Speed ratings (Par 113): **114,109,108,102,97 54**
CSF £5.51 TOTE £3.20: £1.80, £1.10; EX 6.10 Trifecta £15.60.
Owner King Power Racing Co Ltd **Bred** Guy Pariente Holding Sprl **Trained** Kingsclere, Hants

FOCUS
Add 23yds. Run at a good gallop courtesy of Warnaq and then Cypress Creek, it produced a clear-cut winner, but the form is questionable with excuses for those beaten. It's hard to gauge the level of the form, with the second and third not at their best.

2561 BRITISH STALLION STUDS EBF MAIDEN STKS (PLUS 10 RACE) 5f 15y
4:05 (4:08) (Class 2) 2-Y-O

£11,827 (£3,541; £1,770; £885; £442; £222) **Stalls** Low

Form RPR
1 **Full Authority (IRE)** 2-9-5 0........................ DanielTudhope 3 94+
(David O'Meara) *mde all: rdn ins fnl f: r.o wl to draw clr: pushed out towards fin: nice type* **11/4**[1]

4 **2** *6* **It's Been Noted**[12] 2115 2-9-5 0........................ RichardKingscote 6 72
(Tom Dascombe) *w wnr tl rdn over 1f out: sn outpcd: lost 2nd narrowly ins fnl f: kpt on to regain 2nd post: no ch* **8/1**[3]

3 **3** *shd* **Stars In The Night (IRE)**[20] 1923 2-9-0 0........................ KevinStott 1 67+
(Kevin Ryan) *chsd ldrs: rdn over 2f out: rn wd ent st wl over 1f out: outpcd by wnr and no ch but wnt 2nd narrowly ins fnl f: lost 2nd post (jockey said filly ran green)* **3/1**[2]

2 **4** *1 ¾* **Rose Of Kildare (IRE)**[9] 2228 2-9-0 0........................ FrannyNorton 10 60
(Mark Johnston) *missed break: midfield: rdn over 2f out: styd on ins fnl f: nt pce to get involved* **10/1**

5 *1 ½* **Utopian Lad (IRE)** 2-9-5 0........................ BenCurtis 8 60
(Tom Dascombe) *chsd ldrs: rdn over 2f out: outpcd over 1f out: wl btn ins fnl f* **33/1**

6 *1 ¼* **The New Marwan** 2-9-5 0........................ PaulHanagan 2 61+
(Richard Fahey) *missed break and hmpd s: bhd: kpt on ins fnl f: nt pce to get involved* **3/1**[2]

7 *½* **Shevchenko Park (IRE)** 2-9-5 0........................ JaneElliott 5 54
(Tom Dascombe) *dwlt: in tch: rdn over 2f out and outpcd: wknd fnl f* **16/1**

8 *hd* **Shani** 2-9-0 0........................ JFEgan 4 48
(David Evans) *dwlt: midfield: outpcd over 2f out: nvr on terms* **20/1**

9 *6* **G For Gabrial (IRE)** 2-9-5 0........................ TonyHamilton 13 31+
(Richard Fahey) *dwlt: bhd: checked after 1f: sn pushed along: nvr on terms* **33/1**

10 *4 ½* **Olivers Pursuit** 2-9-5 0........................ DavidProbert 7 15
(Gay Kelleway) *dwlt: pushed along towards rr: wl outpcd and bhd fnl 2f: nvr on terms* **25/1**

1m 5.18s (3.08) **Going Correction** +0.675s/f (Yiel) **10** Ran SP% **117.2**
Speed ratings (Par 99): **102,92,92,89,87 85,84,83,74,67**
CSF £24.28 TOTE £3.20: £1.40, £2.10, £1.30; EX 16.70 Trifecta £55.00.
Owner Sheikh Abdullah Almalek Alsabah **Bred** Epona Bloodstock Ltd **Trained** Upper Helmsley, N Yorks

■ Javea Magic was withdrawn, price at time of withdrawal 50/1. Rule 4 does not apply.

FOCUS
They were soon strung out in this juvenile maiden, rated around the third. Add 10yds.

2562 TMT GROUP H'CAP 1m 4f 63y
4:35 (4:37) (Class 3) (0-90,92) 3-Y-O

£11,827 (£3,541; £1,770; £885; £442; £222) **Stalls** Low

Form RPR
221- **1** **Sam Cooke (IRE)**[209] 8166 3-9-3 **85**........................ HarryBentley 6 95+
(Ralph Beckett) *racd keenly in midfield: lost pl 6f out: hdwy 3f out: big move 2f out: sn led: styd on and in command ins fnl f: eased cl home* **9/4**[1]

13-2 **2** *2 ½* **Lariat**[13] 2088 3-9-4 **86**........................ OisinMurphy 9 90
(Andrew Balding) *chsd ldrs: nt clr run ent fnl 3f: n.m.r briefly bef ev ch 2f out: sn in 2nd: unable to go w wnr over 1f out: no imp ins fnl f* **9/2**[3]

-414 **3** *1 ¼* **Seeusoon (IRE)**[21] 1884 3-8-4 **72**........................ DuranFentiman 5 74
(Andrew Balding) *chsd ldrs: rdn 2f out and unable qck: styd on same pce ins fnl f* **25/1**

10-6 **4** *nk* **Just Hubert (IRE)**[20] 1911 3-8-12 **80**........................ BenCurtis 2 82+
(William Muir) *hld up: rdn and nt clr run over 2f out: hdwy sn after: styd on ins fnl f: clsng towards fin: nvr able to chal* **16/1**

31-3 **5** *10* **Gabrial The One (IRE)**[22] 1845 3-8-6 **79**........................ SeanDavis(5) 8 65
(Richard Fahey) *rrd s and missed break: hld up: hdwy over 5f out: drvn to chse ldrs over 3f out: ev ch 2f out: wknd ins fnl f (jockey said gelding hung left under pressure)* **14/1**

155- **6** *hd* **Divine Gift (IRE)**[180] 9007 3-9-0 **89**........................ AledBeech(7) 4 74
(Charlie Fellowes) *hld up in rr: pushed along 6f out: plugged on fnl f: nvr a threat (jockey said gelding was never travelling)* **22/1**

41-4 **7** *2 ¼* **Mister Chiang**[39] 1462 3-8-10 **78**........................ DavidProbert 1 60
(Mark Johnston) *midfield: rdn 2f out: no imp over 1f out: wknd ins fnl f* **15/2**

11-4 **8** *4 ½* **West End Charmer (IRE)**[20] 1911 3-9-10 **92**........................ FrannyNorton 10 66
(Mark Johnston) *prom: led 3f out: rdn and pressed 2f out: sn hdd & wknd (starter reported that colt was the subject of a third criteria failure; trainer was informed that the colt could not run until the day after passing a stalls test)* **6/1**

0245 **9** *31* **Smoki Smoka (IRE)**[29] 1696 3-8-2 **70** oh2........................(v[1]) DavidEgan 7
(Tom Dascombe) *led: rdn and hdd 3f out: wknd over 2f out* **50/1**

4-11 **10** *5* **Katiesheidinlisa**[5] 2399 3-9-4 **86** 6ex........................ RichardKingscote 11 3
(Tom Dascombe) *in tch: rdn and wknd over 2f out: eased whn wl btn over 1f out (jockey said filly ran flat)* **4/1**[2]

2m 54.16s (11.96) **Going Correction** +0.675s/f (Yiel) **10** Ran SP% **117.7**
Speed ratings (Par 103): **87,85,84,84,77 77,76,73,52,49**
CSF £12.17 CT £200.38 TOTE £3.70: £1.80, £1.80, £6.10; EX 15.30 Trifecta £249.40.
Owner Chelsea Thoroughbreds - Wonderful World **Bred** R J C Wilmot-Smith **Trained** Kimpton, Hants

FOCUS
Add 20yds. A useful 3yo handicap, but several struggled on the ground and the race set up for the closers. The second has been rated to his latest.

2563 PARTNER TECH H'CAP — 1m 2f 70y
5:05 (5:09) (Class 3) (0-90,90) 4-Y-O+
£11,827 (£3,541; £1,770; £885; £442; £222) Stalls High

Form — RPR

3255 **1** **Mr Top Hat**[20] 1912 4-9-3 86 .... HarryBentley 13 — 94
(David Evans) *midfield: hdwy over 3f out: wnt 2nd over 2f out: led jst over 1f out: edgd lft ins fnl f: styd on: eased cl home* **16/1**

0-P0 **2** *1 3/4* **Ayutthaya (IRE)**[21] 1896 4-9-5 88 .... TomEaves 6 — 93
(Kevin Ryan) *chsd ldrs: wnt 2nd over 5f out: led wl over 2f out: rdn and hdd jst over 1f out: swtchd rt ins fnl f: styd on but no imp on wnr after* **8/1**

444- **3** *1 3/4* **Dance King**[191] 8716 9-9-2 85 ....(tp) DavidAllan 11 — 86
(Tim Easterby) *pushed along early: in rr: rdn and hdwy over 2f out: styd on ins fnl f: nt rch ldrs* **25/1**

40-5 **4** *nk* **Mulligatawny (IRE)**[19] 1948 6-8-13 82 ....(p) BenCurtis 9 — 82+
(Roger Fell) *hld up: rdn and hdwy over 2f out: styd on ins fnl f: nvr able to chal* **16/1**

-541 **5** *2* **Crownthorpe**[3] 2480 4-9-1 89 5ex .... SeanDavis(5) 3 — 85
(Richard Fahey) *midfield: rdn and hdwy over 2f out: kpt on u.p over 1f out: no imp on ldrs: one pce fnl 100yds (jockey said gelding ran flat)* **2/1**[1]

05-0 **6** *2 1/4* **Gossip Column (IRE)**[12] 2095 4-9-7 90 .... DavidEgan 1 — 82
(Ian Williams) *chsd ldrs: rdn over 2f out: one pce fr over 1f out* **14/1**

3533 **7** *2* **Al Jellaby**[12] 2095 4-9-6 89 ....(h) AdamKirby 2 — 77
(Clive Cox) *led: drvn 3f out: sn hdd: unable to go w ldrs over 1f out: wknd ins fnl f* **6/1**[2]

1-40 **8** *24* **Showroom (FR)**[20] 1927 4-9-5 88 .... FrannyNorton 10 — 28
(Mark Johnston) *hld up: rdn over 3f out: lft bhd fnl 2f* **12/1**

-066 **9** *6* **Mutamaded (IRE)**[12] 2119 6-9-4 87 .... JackGarritty 12 — 15
(Ruth Carr) *midfield: rdn over 3f out: wknd 2f out* **25/1**

00- **10** *4 1/2* **Empress Ali (IRE)**[180] 9002 8-9-4 87 .... AndrewMullen 4 — 6
(Tom Tate) *chsd ldrs: rdn over 3f out: wknd over 1f out: eased whn wl btn ins fnl f (jockey said mare lost its action and had no more to give)* **10/1**

640- **11** *3 3/4* **Capton**[42] 8649 6-9-7 90 .... CamHardie 7 — 1
(Michael Easterby) *in tch: rdn 4f out: drvn over 3f out: wknd over 2f out* **40/1**

016- **12** *12* **Kasbaan**[188] 8806 4-9-5 88 .... JimCrowley 14
(Owen Burrows) *hld up: lost tch 3f out: t.o: eased* **14/1**

21-4 **P** **Bobby K (IRE)**[10] 2187 4-9-7 90 ....(b[1]) JackMitchell 8
(Simon Crisford) *midfield: hdwy to chse ldrs over 7f out: rdn and wknd 3f out: t.o whn p.u wl over 1f out (jockey said gelding lost its action approximately 3 1/2 furlongs out)* **15/2**[3]

2m 22.0s (7.70) **Going Correction** +0.675s/f (Yiel) — **13** Ran SP% **122.5**
Speed ratings (Par 107): **96,94,93,92,91 89,87,68,63,60 57,47,**
CSF £139.62 CT £3208.49 TOTE £20.90: £4.50, £2.40, £6.20; EX 197.50 Trifecta £3683.90.
Owner B McCabe & Mrs E Evans **Bred** Mrs S Field, R Field & A Turbitt **Trained** Pandy, Monmouths

FOCUS
Competitive stuff. Add 14yds. The second has been rated close to his 3yo form, and the third to his late 2018 form.
T/Jkpt: Not Won. T/Plt: £11.00 to a £1 stake. Pool: £99,861.24 - 6,584.87 winning units T/Qpdt: £5.50 to a £1 stake. Pool: £13,959.95 - 1,869.08 winning units **Darren Owen**

2390 MAISONS-LAFFITTE (R-H)
Thursday, May 9

OFFICIAL GOING: Turf: heavy

2564a PRIX TEXANITA (GROUP 3) (3YO) (TURF) — 6f
2:00 3-Y-O
£36,036 (£14,414; £10,810; £7,207; £3,603)

RPR

1 **Ilanga (FR)**[26] 1780 3-8-10 0 .... AlexandreGavilan 8 — 104
(D Guillemin, France) *wl into stride: led: mde all: urged along 2f out: rdn to hold advantage over 1f out: kpt on strly ins fnl f* **36/1**

2 *3/4* **Milord's Song (FR)**[29] 3-9-0 0 .... TheoBachelot 3 — 105
(S Wattel, France) *hld up towards rr: hdwy 1 1/2f out: rdn to chse ldr over 1f out: drvn and kpt on ins fnl f: nrest at fin* **11/1**

3 *3* **Cigalera (FR)**[56] 1200 3-8-10 0 .... TonyPiccone 4 — 92
(M Delcher Sanchez, France) *led nrside gp: pushed along 2f out: rdn and ev ch over 1f out: kpt on same pce fnl f* **13/1**

4 *hd* **Sexy Metro (FR)**[26] 3-9-0 0 .... CristianDemuro 6 — 95
(D Guillemin, France) *chsd ldr down centre of crse: rowed along 2f out: rdn and hdwy over 1f out: no ex ins fnl f* **9/5**[1]

5 *1 1/4* **We Go (FR)**[37] 3-9-0 0 .... Pierre-CharlesBoudot 1 — 91
(H-A Pantall, France) *settled to trck ldr in nrside gp: urged along over 2f out: rdn w limited rspnse over 1f out: no imp fnl f* **66/10**

6 *1/2* **Happy Odyssey (IRE)**[26] 1780 3-8-10 0 ....(p) StephanePasquier 5 — 85
(N Clement, France) *settled in rr of gp down centre: rdn 2f out: sn drvn and fnd little: kpt on one pce* **51/10**[2]

7 *1 3/4* **Sicilia**[11] 2166 3-8-11 0 ow1 .... OlivierPeslier 2 — 81
(C Laffon-Parias, France) *hld up towards rr: pushed along over 2f out: rdn but no imp over 1f out: styd on same pce* **73/10**

8 *1 1/2* **Kenbaio (FR)**[26] 1780 3-9-0 0 .... GregoryBenoist 9 — 79
(P Bary, France) *hld in fnl duo: short-lived effrt over 2f out: rdn and fnd little: no ex ins fnl f* **15/1**

9 *nk* **Poetry**[209] 8145 3-8-10 0 .... MaximeGuyon 7 — 74
(Michael Bell) *trckd ldrs down centre of crse: pushed along 2f out: rdn w limited rspnse over 1f out: eased ins fnl f* **59/10**[3]

10 *6* **El Guanche (FR)**[56] 1199 3-9-0 0 .... VincentCheminaud 10 — 59
(M Delcher Sanchez, France) *settled in rr of gp nrside: rdn along 2f out: nvr a factor and eased ins fnl f* **26/1**

1m 13.11s (-0.29) — **10** Ran SP% **119.9**
PARI-MUTUEL (all including 1 euro stake): WIN 36.90; PLACE 7.80, 3.50, 3.90; DF 84.30.
Owner Zied Ben M'Rad **Bred** Zied Ben M'Rad **Trained** France

2267 ASCOT (R-H)
Friday, May 10

OFFICIAL GOING: Soft (str 6.8, rnd 6.0)
Wind: Light, across Weather: Fine but cloudy

2565 BRITISH STALLION STUDS EBF MAIDEN FILLIES' STKS (PLUS 10 RACE) — 5f
2:00 (2:01) (Class 4) 2-Y-O
£6,727 (£2,002; £1,000; £500) Stalls High

Form — RPR

1 **Final Song (IRE)** 2-9-0 0 .... OisinMurphy 10 — 93+
(Saeed bin Suroor) *mde all: briefly pressed over 1f out: pushed along and sn drew rt away* **5/2**[2]

2 *5* **Mrs Flanders (IRE)** 2-9-0 0 .... DavidProbert 3 — 75+
(Charles Hills) *green to post: s.i.s: hld up in last pair: smooth prog to take 2nd wl over 1f out and briefly pressed wnr: sn outpcd: wknd ins fnl f but hld on for 2nd* **5/1**[3]

3 *hd* **Star Alexander** 2-9-0 0 .... AdamKirby 5 — 74
(Clive Cox) *chsd ldrs: pushed along 1/2-way: outpcd over 1f out: kpt on last 100yds to press for modest 2nd nr fin* **6/4**[1]

4 *1/2* **Inyamazane (IRE)** 2-9-0 0 .... CharlesBishop 7 — 72
(Mick Channon) *chsd ldrs: pushed along and outpcd wl over 1f out: kpt on ins fnl f* **6/1**

5 *2 3/4* **Wafrah** 2-9-0 0 .... JimCrowley 11 — 62+
(Richard Hughes) *rn v green in last pair: nvr on terms* **10/1**

0 **6** *nk* **Birkie Queen (IRE)**[12] 2138 2-9-0 0 .... JoeyHaynes 2 — 61?
(J S Moore) *uns rdr bef gng in stalls: chsd wnr to wl over 1f out: wknd qckly* **66/1**

1m 3.06s (2.36) **Going Correction** +0.475s/f (Yiel) — **6** Ran SP% **110.1**
Speed ratings (Par 92): **100,92,91,90,86 86**
CSF £14.55 TOTE £2.80: £1.40, £2.70; EX 15.10 Trifecta £34.10.
Owner Godolphin **Bred** Godolphin **Trained** Newmarket, Suffolk

FOCUS
There had been 8mm of rain in the previous 24 hours and a total of 25mm since Tuesday. As a result the ground was now soft all over (GoingStick: Straight Course 6.8, Round Course 6.0). There were a total of 24 non-runners throughout the afternoon, all bar one due to the ground (declared on good ground). With the course at its widest configuration, all distances were as advertised. This opening maiden has been won by some high-class fillies in recent years, like Rizeena and Besharah, and this year's winner was particularly impressive. She's sure to rate 100+ in time. Conditions would have been tough for these youngsters and the winning time was over four seconds outside standard. Joey Haynes and Oisin Murphy said: "It's soft", Jim Crowley said: "It's soft, but not too testing", while David Probert said: "It's very holding".

2566 KAREN MILLEN MAIDEN STKS (PLUS 10 RACE) — 1m 3f 211y
2:35 (2:36) (Class 3) 3-Y-O
£9,703 (£2,887; £1,443; £721) Stalls Low

Form — RPR

1 **Kesia (IRE)** 3-9-0 0 .... RobertHavlin 7 — 87+
(John Gosden) *cl up: trckd ldr 7f out: swept into the ld 2f out and sn 2 l ahd: mostly pushed out fnl f: v readily* **7/1**[3]

2 **2** *1 1/2* **Cape Cavalli (IRE)**[23] 1856 3-9-5 0 .... OisinMurphy 6 — 88
(Simon Crisford) *led: rdn and hdd 2f out: styd on but nvr able to threaten wnr after* **10/11**[1]

3 *1 1/4* **Swift Wing** 3-9-5 0 .... FrankieDettori 5 — 86+
(John Gosden) *dwlt: rn green: in tch: pushed along at times fr 1/2-way: shkn up to take 3rd over 2f out: styd on but unable to threaten* **7/4**[2]

4 *7* **Imperium (IRE)** 3-9-5 0 .... AdamMcNamara 4 — 75
(Roger Charlton) *hld up in last pair: sme prog to take 4th over 2f out but nt on terms: shkn up and lost further grnd after* **25/1**

0-40 **5** *7* **Cherry Cola**[112] 296 3-9-0 50 .... TrevorWhelan 3 — 59
(Sheena West) *dwlt: restrained into last: nvr a factor: tk modest 5th over 1f out but already wl adrift of ldrs* **150/1**

6 *8* **Manucci (IRE)** 3-9-5 0 .... JimCrowley 1 — 51
(Amanda Perrett) *dwlt: sn chsd ldr: lost 2nd 7f out but styd prom: wknd rapidly over 2f out* **16/1**

0 **7** *33* **Aleatoric (IRE)**[27] 1754 3-9-5 0 .... GeraldMosse 2
(Martin Smith) *t.k.h: chsd ldrs to 1/2-way: wknd rapidly over 4f out: t.o* **150/1**

2m 42.28s (9.68) **Going Correction** +0.475s/f (Yiel) — **7** Ran SP% **112.3**
Speed ratings (Par 103): **86,85,84,79,74 69,47**
CSF £13.46 TOTE £7.60: £2.60, £1.30; EX 15.60 Trifecta £23.60.
Owner George Strawbridge **Bred** Philip & Carolyn Cort **Trained** Newmarket, Suffolk

FOCUS
A promising type against some beautifully bred newcomers from big yards in this interesting middle-distance maiden. The first three pulled well clear of the others and a combination of the soft ground and an ordinary pace contributed to a time nearly 14sec outside standard. The runner-up is rated close to his debut run, but the fifth casts doubts.

2567 CARERS TRUST H'CAP — 6f
3:10 (3:13) (Class 4) (0-85,82) 3-Y-O
£6,727 (£2,002; £1,000; £500; £300; £300) Stalls Centre

Form — RPR

461- **1** **Whelans Way (IRE)**[170] 9169 3-8-10 71 .... DavidProbert 17 — 79
(Roger Teal) *racd towards nr side of gp: mde all: rdn 2f out and decisive advantage: styd on wl* **20/1**

51-4 **2** *1* **Aplomb (IRE)**[21] 1924 3-9-4 79 .... ColmO'Donoghue 6 — 84+
(William Haggas) *t.k.h: hld up in rr: trckd ldrs 2f out: swtchd to outer and prog over 1f out: chsd wnr ins fnl f: hung lft but r.o: too late to chal* **10/3**[2]

6-22 **3** *2* **Tinto**[9] 2274 3-9-5 80 .... RobertHavlin 2 — 78
(Amanda Perrett) *hld up in rr: smooth prog over 2f out: chsd wnr jst over 1f out: rdn and nt qckn: lost 2nd ins fnl f and one pce after* **7/1**

20-5 **4** *2 1/4* **Sir Busker (IRE)**[7] 2364 3-9-4 79 .... WilliamBuick 12 — 70
(William Knight) *fractious to post: chsd ldrs: rdn to dispute 2nd briefly over 1f out: sn hung lft and outpcd* **9/2**[3]

10-3 **5** *1 3/4* **Motagally**[17] 2008 3-9-6 81 .... JimCrowley 4 — 67
(Charles Hills) *pressed ldrs: rdn to dispute 2nd briefly over 1f out: sn wknd* **9/1**

25-1 **6** *nk* **Shorter Skirt**[39] 1475 3-9-3 78 .... CharlesBishop 11 — 63
(Eve Johnson Houghton) *rrd s: plld hrd early and hld up in last pair: brief effrt over 2f out: sn rdn and no real prog* **9/1**

2-53 **7** *hd* **Champion Brogie (IRE)**[9] 2274 3-9-0 75 .... JoeyHaynes 13 — 59
(J S Moore) *wl in tch: rdn and no prog 2f out: wknd over 1f out* **25/1**

The Form Book Flat 2019, Raceform Ltd, Newbury, RG14 5SJ

31-5 **8** *shd* **Welcoming (FR)**[41] 1424 3-9-6 **81** .... AdamKirby 16 65
(Clive Cox) *chsd wnr to over 1f out: wknd (jockey said filly jumped right-handed leaving the stalls)* **3/1**[1]

00-0 **9** *3 ½* **Fly The Nest (IRE)**[41] 1424 3-9-5 **80** .... SeanLevey 14 52
(Tony Carroll) *chsd ldrs tl wknd wl over 1f out* **33/1**

052- **10** *nk* **Journey Of Life**[167] 9246 3-9-5 **80** .... PatDobbs 8 52
(Gary Moore) *dwlt: plld hrd early and hld up in last pair: shkn up and no prog 2f out* **25/1**

1m 16.55s (2.85) **Going Correction** +0.475s/f (Yiel) **10** Ran SP% **114.2**
Speed ratings (Par 101): **100,98,96,93,90 90,90,89,85,84**
CSF £81.12 CT £539.63 TOTE £22.50: £5.20, £1.70, £1.90; EX 109.20 Trifecta £836.50.
Owner Austin Whelan **Bred** G W Robinson **Trained** Lambourn, Berks

FOCUS
A fair 3yo sprint handicap, but the winner was never headed like the other two sprint winners on the card.

2568 MONTFORT H'CAP — 6f
3:45 (3:48) (Class 3) (0-95,95) 4-Y-O+ **£7,762** (£2,310; £1,154; £577) **Stalls** Centre

Form RPR

20-5 **1** **Louie De Palma**[40] 1459 7-9-1 **89** .... AdamKirby 12 97
(Clive Cox) *racd on nr side of gp: mde all: drvn over 1f out: hld on wl nr fin* **6/1**[2]

30-5 **2** *½* **Vegas Boy (IRE)**[15] 2061 4-8-11 **85** .... (t) PatDobbs 14 91
(Jamie Osborne) *racd towards nr side of gp: trckd ldrs gng wl: chsd wnr over 1f out: chal ins fnl f: jst hld* **14/1**

20-6 **3** *1 ¼* **Royal Residence**[6] 2396 4-8-10 **84** .... WilliamBuick 16 86
(James Tate) *hld up towards nr side of gp: pushed along wl over 2f out and no prog: rdn and hdwy over 1f out: tried to cl on ldrs fnl f: one pce last 100yds* **7/4**[1]

010- **4** *nk* **Youkan (IRE)**[223] 7767 4-8-9 **83** .... MartinDwyer 5 84+
(Stuart Kittow) *dwlt: hld up: prog on far side of gp over 2f out: tried to chal over 1f out: kpt on same pce* **20/1**

0-12 **5** *½* **Diamond Dougal (IRE)**[13] 2117 4-8-11 **92** .... ScottMcCullagh(7) 4 92
(Mick Channon) *hld up in rr: rdn 2f out: styd on towards nr side of gp over 1f out: nvr nrr* **13/2**[3]

0-40 **6** *nse* **Lightning Charlie**[32] 1654 7-8-9 **83** .... KevinStott 8 83
(Amanda Perrett) *chsd ldrs: rdn 2f out: nt quite on terms 1f out: one pce* **20/1**

000- **7** *¾* **Squats (IRE)**[195] 8634 7-9-2 **90** .... CharlesBishop 15 87
(Ian Williams) *awkward s: hld up in last pair: rdn 2f out: kpt on one pce over 1f out: n.d* **25/1**

3622 **8** *½* **Equitation**[32] 1654 5-8-9 **83** .... (t) BrettDoyle 2 79
(Stuart Williams) *t.k.h: in tch towards outer of gp: rdn 2f out: one pce and nt on terms jst over 1f out* **17/2**

16-2 **9** *½* **Dream Catching (IRE)**[20] 1932 4-8-7 **81** oh3 .... DavidProbert 11 75
(Andrew Balding) *pressed wnr: nrly upsides 2f out: lost 2nd and wknd over 1f out* **12/1**

0-00 **10** *4 ½* **Pettochside**[6] 2403 10-8-10 **84** .... JoeyHaynes 7 64
(John Bridger) *t.k.h: cl up on outer of gp tl wknd 2f out* **33/1**

353- **11** *hd* **Tawny Port**[203] 8370 5-8-10 **84** .... (t[1]) AdamMcNamara 6 63
(Stuart Williams) *t.k.h: hld up in tch towards far side: lost pl 2f out: wknd over 1f out (jockey said gelding ran too free)* **7/1**

1m 15.87s (2.17) **Going Correction** +0.475s/f (Yiel) **11** Ran SP% **117.7**
Speed ratings (Par 107): **104,103,101,101,100 100,99,98,98,92 91**
CSF £80.79 CT £203.25 TOTE £6.10: £1.60, £3.40, £1.50; EX 35.00 Trifecta £324.90.
Owner Peter Ridgers **Bred** Pantile Stud **Trained** Lambourn, Berks

FOCUS
A useful sprint handicap and another all-the-way winner. They came up the centre, but those who raced on the nearside of the field seemed to hold the advantage. The winner is rated to last year's best.

2569 WOMEN IN RACING H'CAP — 1m (S)
4:20 (4:21) (Class 4) (0-85,87) 3-Y-O **£6,727** (£2,002; £1,000; £500; £300) **Stalls** Centre

Form RPR

36-1 **1** **Aweedram (IRE)**[23] 1857 3-9-6 **84** .... WilliamBuick 2 95+
(Alan King) *plld hrd: hld up in last: pushed along to cl 3f out: chsd ldr 2f out: rdn to chal over 1f out: sustained effrt to ld last 100yds* **3/1**[2]

2151 **2** *½* **I'm Available (IRE)**[10] 2251 3-9-2 **80** 6ex .... DavidProbert 8 90
(Andrew Balding) *led: gng best over 2f out: shkn up and pressed over 1f out: styd on but hdd and hld last 100yds* **7/4**[1]

42-3 **3** *3 ¾* **Just The Man (FR)**[27] 1754 3-9-2 **80** .... AdamKirby 3 81
(Clive Cox) *in tch: pushed along 3f out: disp 2nd briefly 2f out: one pce u.p after* **5/1**[3]

23-6 **4** *4 ½* **Greek Kodiac (IRE)**[22] 1886 3-9-2 **80** .... CharlesBishop 5 71
(Mick Quinn) *in tch: shkn up 3f out: disp 2nd briefly 2f out: wknd over 1f out (vet said colt had lost its left-fore shoe)* **14/1**

16-0 **5** *2 ¼* **Flying Dragon (FR)**[40] 1462 3-9-3 **81** .... SeanLevey 1 67
(Richard Hannon) *t.k.h: chsd ldr to 2f out: wknd (vet said gelding had lost its left-hind shoe)* **11/1**

231- **P** **Fightwithme (IRE)**[135] 9708 3-9-9 **87** .... (b) FrankieDettori 7
(John Gosden) *prom tl wknd rapidly 1/2-way: t.o and p.u 2f out: dismntd (vet said colt had bled from the nose)* **5/1**[3]

1m 44.65s (3.25) **Going Correction** +0.475s/f (Yiel) **6** Ran SP% **109.7**
Speed ratings (Par 101): **102,101,97,93,91**
CSF £8.25 CT £21.10 TOTE £3.30: £1.80, £1.60; EX 9.40 Trifecta £31.40.
Owner McNeill Family & Niall Farrell **Bred** Petra Bloodstock Agency Ltd **Trained** Barbury Castle, Wilts

FOCUS
A fair 3yo handicap. The first two finished clear and look above-average types. The winner built on his Newmarket win.

2570 AGV H'CAP — 7f
4:55 (4:57) (Class 2) (0-105,97) 3-Y-O
£18,675 (£5,592; £2,796; £1,398; £699; £351) **Stalls** Centre

Form RPR

23-1 **1** **Motafaawit (IRE)**[15] 2054 3-9-7 **97** .... JimCrowley 1 108
(Richard Hannon) *trckd ldrs: clsd smoothly over 2f out: rdn to ld wl over 1f out: hung lft fnl f: kpt on wl (jockey said gelding hung left-handed)* **11/4**[1]

012- **2** *½* **Awe**[204] 8345 3-8-8 **84** .... MartinDwyer 6 94
(William Haggas) *t.k.h: hld up in tch: effrt over 2f out: chsd wnr over 1f out: edgd lft then carried lft fnl f: kpt on wl but a jst hld* **3/1**[2]

140- **3** *4 ½* **Celebrity Dancer (IRE)**[239] 7201 3-9-0 **90** .... KevinStott 8 88
(Kevin Ryan) *trckd ldr: rdn to chal and upsides 2f out: fdd over 1f out* **5/1**

1120 **4** *1 ¼* **Deep Intrigue**[21] 1920 3-9-7 **97** .... FrankieDettori 2 92
(Mark Johnston) *led: rdn jst over 2f out: hdd & wknd wl over 1f out (jockey said colt hung left-handed.)* **8/1**

15-6 **5** *nse* **Dirty Rascal (IRE)**[22] 1888 3-9-3 **93** .... PatDobbs 5 88
(Richard Hannon) *hld up in last pair: pushed along over 2f out: lft bhd over 1f out* **8/1**

214- **6** *1 ½* **Indomitable (IRE)**[225] 7700 3-8-6 **82** .... DavidProbert 4 73
(Andrew Balding) *hld up in last: prog over 2f out and cl up: wknd wl over 1f out* **4/1**[3]

1m 29.29s (1.79) **Going Correction** +0.475s/f (Yiel) **6** Ran SP% **110.6**
Speed ratings (Par 105): **108,107,102,100,100 99**
CSF £10.90 CT £34.98 TOTE £3.40: £1.90, £2.00; EX 11.50 Trifecta £69.90.
Owner Hamdan Al Maktoum **Bred** Shadwell Estate Company Limited **Trained** East Everleigh, Wilts

FOCUS
A warm 3yo handicap, but the first two were far superior to the rest. They've been rated in line with the usual standard of this race.

2571 WOOD & WOOD SIGNS APPRENTICE H'CAP — 1m 7f 209y
5:30 (5:33) (Class 3) (0-90,91) 4-Y-O+ **£7,762** (£2,310; £1,154; £577) **Stalls** Low

Form RPR

210/ **1** **Agrapart (FR)**[34] 1202 8-8-13 **77** .... MeganNicholls(3) 10 84
(Nick Williams) *pressed ldr after 4f: rdn to ld over 2f out: hdd over 1f out: rallied to ld jst ins fnl f: kpt on wl* **7/4**[1]

22-1 **2** *1* **Orin Swift (IRE)**[10] 2254 5-9-3 **83** 5ex .... TylerSaunders(5) 8 89
(Jonathan Portman) *awkward and stdd s: hld up in rr: prog to trck ldrs 1/2-way: wnt 2nd over 2f out: rdn to ld over 1f out: hdd and one pce jst ins fnl f* **4/1**[3]

0-46 **3** *3 ½* **Flintrock (GER)**[12] 2143 4-9-6 **82** .... JoshuaBryan 1 84
(Andrew Balding) *s.v.s: hld up in last and in tch: plenty to do whn prog over 6f out: rdn to chse ldrs over 2f out: hung lft over 1f out: kpt on to take 3rd nr fin (jockey said colt was slowly away)* **16/1**

411- **4** *hd* **Graceful Lady**[189] 8807 6-9-1 **79** .... DarraghKeenan(3) 5 81
(Robert Eddery) *trckd ldrs: pushed along over 3f out: rdn to chse ldng pair jst over 2f out: no imp over 1f out: lost 3rd nr fin* **5/1**

0-00 **5** *9* **Gavlar**[20] 1943 8-8-9 **77** .... (v) GeorgiaDobie(7) 9 68
(William Knight) *hld up in tch: t.k.h downhill after 6f: outpcd over 4f out: rdn and no prog over 3f out: wl btn after* **20/1**

513- **6** *3 ½* **Billy Ray**[170] 9174 4-9-10 **91** .... ScottMcCullagh(5) 6 78
(Mick Channon) *led to over 2f out: wknd* **11/4**[2]

04-6 **7** *9* **Medburn Cutler**[28] 1735 9-9-6 **81** .... (p) GaryMahon 3 57
(Peter Hedger) *t.k.h: trckd ldrs: lost pl 1/2-way: struggling in rr over 4f out: sn no ch* **33/1**

-036 **8** *nk* **Gang Warfare**[19] 1971 8-9-1 **79** .... (tp) SebastianWoods(3) 7 55
(Alexandra Dunn) *chsd ldrs: wknd 6f out: last 5f out: sn t.o* **25/1**

3m 38.31s (5.01) **Going Correction** +0.475s/f (Yiel) **8** Ran SP% **117.1**
WFA 4 from 5yo+ 1lb
Speed ratings (Par 107): **106,105,103,103,99 97,92,92**
CSF £9.16 CT £83.60 TOTE £2.50: £1.20, £1.50, £3.30; EX 8.40 Trifecta £71.90.
Owner Gascoigne, Brookes & Barker **Bred** Jean-Marc Lucas **Trained** George Nympton, Devon

FOCUS
A decent staying handicap for apprentice riders and a particularly game winner best known for his exploits over hurdles. He has the potential do better on the Flat.
T/Plt: £27.10 to a £1 stake. Pool: £72,361.84 - 1,942.76 winning units T/Qpdt: £8.40 to a £1 stake. Pool: £6,683.47 - 582.85 winning units **Jonathan Neesom**

2557 CHESTER (L-H)
Friday, May 10

OFFICIAL GOING: Soft changing to heavy after race 4 (3.35)
Wind: Almost nil Weather: Heavy Showers

2572 LIVERPOOL GIN EARL GROSVENOR H'CAP — 7f 127y
1:50 (1:51) (Class 2) (0-105,103) 4-Y-O+
£21,165 (£6,337; £3,168; £1,584; £792; £397) **Stalls** Low

Form RPR

2120 **1** **Sha La La La Lee**[21] 1916 4-8-5 **90** .... JaneElliott(3) 1 99
(Tom Dascombe) *mde all: rdn over 1f out: edgd rt whn pressed ins fnl f: kpt on wl* **12/1**

0-00 **2** *1 ¼* **Gabrial The Saint (IRE)**[20] 1946 4-8-6 **88** .... PaulHanagan 7 94
(Richard Fahey) *in tch: effrt 2f out: chsd wnr jst over 1f out: ev ch whn carried rt ins fnl f: hld towards fin* **10/1**

00-0 **3** *nk* **Baraweez (IRE)**[6] 2419 9-8-6 **91** .... BenRobinson(3) 3 96
(Brian Ellison) *hld up: rdn and hdwy 2f out: styd on chsng ldrs ins fnl f: gng on at fin* **7/1**[2]

000- **4** *hd* **Aces (IRE)**[216] 7977 7-8-13 **95** .... PJMcDonald 4 99
(Ian Williams) *in tch: pushed along over 3f out: chsd ldrs: tried to chal on inner 1f out: kpt on: one pce nr fin* **16/1**

306- **5** *¾* **Al Erayg (IRE)**[185] 8898 6-8-3 **85** .... RachelRichardson 14 87
(Tim Easterby) *in rr: rdn over 2f out: hdwy over 1f out: styd on ins fnl f: nvr able to chal* **20/1**

023- **6** *1* **Mazyoun**[228] 7610 5-8-4 **86** .... (v) LukeMorris 8 86
(Hugo Palmer) *midfield: drvn over 2f out: kpt on for press ins fnl f: nvr able to trble ldrs* **25/1**

23-0 **7** *2 ½* **Shady McCoy (USA)**[13] 2100 9-9-2 **98** .... JasonWatson 5 91
(Ian Williams) *dwlt: in rr: rdn whn nt clr run and swtchd lft over 2f out: hdwy over 1f out: no imp on ldrs: one pce fnl 150yds (jockey said gelding was slowly away)* **20/1**

12-2 **8** *1* **Ptarmigan Ridge**[13] 2100 5-8-9 **91** .... ShaneKelly 2 82
(Richard Hughes) *chsd wnr tl rdn and lost 2nd over 1f out: wknd fnl 100yds* **15/8**[1]

400- **9** *22* **Dragons Tail (IRE)**[181] 9004 4-8-7 **89** .... (p w) SilvestreDeSousa 11 25
(Tom Dascombe) *midfield: rdn over 3f out: wknd over 2f out: eased whn wl btn over 1f out (jockey said gelding had no more to give)* **11/1**

02-0 **10** *12* **Cold Stare (IRE)**[13] 2100 4-8-12 **94** ow1 .... DanielTudhope 9
(David O'Meara) *prom tl rdn and wknd over 2f out: eased whn wl btn over 1f out* **9/1**

4-06 **11** *16* **Brian The Snail (IRE)**[20] 1944 5-8-3 **90** .... SeanDavis(5) 15
(Richard Fahey) *hld up: dropped away over 2f out: sn eased whn wl btn (jockey said gelding hung right throughout)* **20/1**

4560 **12** *1 ¼* **Another Batt (IRE)**[27] 1753 4-9-7 **103** .... JamesDoyle 13
(Richard Hughes) *racd on wd outside: chsd ldrs tl rdn and wknd over 3f out: eased whn wl btn fnl 2f (jockey said gelding was never travelling from a wide draw)* **15/2**[3]

1m 36.44s (0.74) **Going Correction** +1.175s/f (Soft) **12** Ran SP% **118.2**
Speed ratings (Par 109): **109,107,107,107,106 105,103,102,80,68 52,50**
CSF £118.28 CT £924.58 TOTE £13.00: £3.70, £3.90, £2.10; EX 151.10 Trifecta £984.70.

The Form Book Flat 2019, Raceform Ltd, Newbury, RG14 5SJ

Owner Nigel And Sharon Mather & Charles Ledigo **Bred** Lady Juliet Tadgell **Trained** Malpas, Cheshire

■ Stewards' Enquiry : Jane Elliott three-day ban: careless riding (May 24-25,27)

FOCUS

The rail between the 6f and 1f points was moved back to the inside after Thursday's card, so there was no change to advertised race distances. After the first Silvestre De Sousa called the ground "soft and tacky", Ben Robinson said it was "tacky, better ground down the middle" and Jason Watson described it as "like glue." The winner came out of the inside stall and the third and fourth were drawn low too. Those three all raced against the rail until they were into the home straight. The winner picked up on his AW progress.

2573 HOMESERVE HUXLEY STKS (GROUP 2) — 1m 2f 70y

2:25 (2:25) (Class 1) 4-Y-O+

£70,887 (£26,875; £13,450; £6,700; £3,362; £1,687) **Stalls High**

Form — RPR

2-02 **1** **Forest Ranger (IRE)**[22] 1890 5-9-1 112 .... TonyHamilton 3 — 113
(Richard Fahey) *led for 1f: remained prom: chsd ldr over 7f out: rdn 2f out: led ins fnl f: drvn out (vet said gelding lost its right fore shoe)* — **9/2**[3]

1101 **2** ¾ **Matterhorn (IRE)**[21] 1921 4-9-1 115 .... JoeFanning 1 — 111
(Mark Johnston) *racd keenly: a.p: rdn and swtchd rt over 1f out: wnt 2nd fnl 110yds: styd on towards fin* — **15/8**[2]

05-0 **3** 1 ¼ **Success Days (IRE)**[27] 1777 7-9-1 104 .... (t) RyanMoore 4 — 108
(K J Condon, Ire) *led after 1f: rdn 2f out: hdd ins fnl f: styd on same pce fnl 100yds* — **7/1**

03- **4** ¾ **Addeybb (IRE)**[174] 9126 5-9-1 117 .... JamesDoyle 5 — 107
(William Haggas) *hld up: rdn over 2f out: no imp over 1f out: hdwy and edgd rt ins fnl f: styd on towards fin: nvr able to trble ldrs* — **7/4**[1]

0-30 **5** 7 **Gabrial (IRE)**[13] 2105 10-9-1 100 .... PaulHanagan 6 — 93
(Richard Fahey) *hld up in rr: rdn 2f out: nvr on terms w ldrs* — **33/1**

330- **6** 8 **Chief Ironside**[215] 8019 4-9-1 104 .... JasonWatson 2 — 77
(William Jarvis) *in tch: rdn over 2f out: wknd over 1f out (trainer was asked why he was running colt here on going described as soft, having reported that the colt did not handle the soft ground following its previous run at Tipperary on 7 October 2018; the trainer's explanation that, in his opinion, the going* — **16/1**

2m 16.26s (1.96) **Going Correction** +1.175s/f (Soft) — **6** Ran SP% **110.7**
Speed ratings (Par 115): **114,113,112,111,106 99**
CSF £13.00 TOTE £3.40: £1.60, £1.70; EX 13.90 Trifecta £47.90.
Owner Mrs H Steel **Bred** Yeguada De Milagro Sa **Trained** Musley Bank, N Yorks

FOCUS

The winner probably ran to a similar level as when taking this the previous year, with the remainder below their peak form. Pace held out, and the form's rated around the third.

2574 BOODLES DIAMOND H'CAP — 1m 2f 70y

3:00 (3:01) (Class 2) (0-105,101) 4-Y-O+

£21,165 (£6,337; £3,168; £1,584; £792; £397) **Stalls High**

Form — RPR

0220 **1** **Aquarium**[6] 2408 4-9-7 101 .... FrannyNorton 1 — 109
(Mark Johnston) *midfield: hdwy 3f out: drvn and styd on ins fnl f: led towards fin* — **13/2**[3]

12-1 **2** ½ **Epaulement (IRE)**[22] 1896 4-9-3 97 .... RichardKingscote 5 — 104
(Tom Dascombe) *led: rdn 2f out: hdd narrowly ins fnl f: regained ld briefly towards fin: nt pce of wnr fnl strides* — **11/2**[2]

0-13 **3** nk **Aasheq (IRE)**[16] 2033 6-9-2 96 .... DavidAllan 10 — 102
(Tim Easterby) *chsd ldr: rdn over 1f out: sn upsides: led narrowly ins fnl f: hdd towards fin: no ex fnl strides* — **5/1**[1]

042- **4** 2 **Restorer**[153] 9463 7-9-7 101 .... RyanMoore 3 — 103
(Ian Williams) *midfield: hdwy over 4f out: rdn and chsd front two over 2f out: abt 2 l down over 1f out: kpt on for press: lost 3rd ins fnl f: one pce fnl 100yds: nvr able to chal* — **7/1**

105- **5** 11 **Genetics (FR)**[231] 7486 5-9-0 94 .... GrahamLee 4 — 74
(Andrew Balding) *hld up: rdn over 3f out: plugged on for press fnl f: no imp* — **10/1**

40-2 **6** 5 **Frankuus (IRE)**[13] 2119 5-9-6 100 .... (b) DanielTudhope 2 — 70
(David O'Meara) *chsd ldrs: rdn over 3f out: wknd over 2f out* — **5/1**[1]

06-6 **7** 9 **Finniston Farm**[13] 2095 4-9-2 96 .... (p) AlistairRawlinson 9 — 48
(Tom Dascombe) *racd keenly: chsd ldrs tl rdn and wknd over 3f out (jockey said gelding stopped quickly)* — **14/1**

/11- **8** 2 **Sputnik Planum (USA)**[377] 2126 5-8-5 85 .... (t) SilvestreDeSousa 7 — 33
(Michael Appleby) *hld up: pushed along over 4f out: drvn in midfield 3f out: no imp: wknd 2f out* — **5/1**[1]

304- **9** 1 ½ **Banksea**[333] 3681 6-9-6 100 .... (h) TomMarquand 12 — 45
(Marjorie Fife) *dwlt: in rr: rdn over 3f out: bhd and struggling over 2f out* — **33/1**

31-6 **10** 109 **Dukhan**[31] 1664 4-9-0 94 .... JamesDoyle 11
(Hugo Palmer) *midfield: rdn 4f out: sn wknd: eased whn bhd over 2f out: t.o (jockey said gelding was never travelling)* — **10/1**

2m 16.83s (2.53) **Going Correction** +1.175s/f (Soft) — **10** Ran SP% **119.0**
Speed ratings (Par 109): **107,106,106,104,95 91,84,83,81,**
CSF £43.09 CT £196.91 TOTE £7.50: £2.70, £1.50, £1.70; EX 37.20 Trifecta £188.10.
Owner Kingsley Park Owners Club **Bred** Miss K Rausing **Trained** Middleham Moor, N Yorks

FOCUS

Solid, straightforward form amongst the front four, who finished clear of the others.

2575 SPORTPESA CHESTER CUP H'CAP — 2m 2f 140y

3:35 (3:38) (Class 2) 4-Y-O+

£92,385 (£27,810; £13,905; £6,930; £3,480; £1,755) **Stalls High**

Form — RPR

3-51 **1** **Making Miracles**[13] 2118 4-9-0 101 3ex .... FrannyNorton 16 — 113
(Mark Johnston) *led after over 1f: mde rest: rdn over 2f out: drew clr over 1f out: styd on strly and in command after* — **16/1**

/3-3 **2** 6 **Who Dares Wins (IRE)**[28] 1735 7-9-0 100 .... (p) TomMarquand 12 — 102
(Alan King) *in tch: effrt 3f out: carried rt 1f out: styd on chalng for pls ins fnl f: edgd lft clsoing stages: tk 2nd nr fin: no ch w wnr* — **6/1**

600- **3** nk **Whiskey Sour (IRE)**[19] 8860 6-9-2 102 .... AndreaAtzeni 7 — 104+
(W P Mullins, Ire) *hld up: hdwy over 3f out: carried rt 1f out: rdn and chalng for pls and tk 2nd ins fnl f: no ch w wnr: kpt on: intimidated by rival clsng stages: lost 2nd nr fin* — **9/2**[2]

1- **4** 2 **Low Sun**[209] 8188 6-9-6 106 .... (p) RyanMoore 17 — 106
(W P Mullins, Ire) *sn chsd ldr: rdn and ev ch 3f out: unable to go w wnr over 1f out: lost 2nd ins fnl f: styd on same pce* — **8/1**

400- **5** ½ **Fun Mac (GER)**[181] 9005 8-8-7 93 .... (t) CharlieBennett 4 — 92
(Hughie Morrison) *chsd ldrs: rdn over 3f out: edgd rt 1f out: one pce fnl 100yds* — **12/1**

13-3 **6** 8 **Cleonte (IRE)**[9] 2269 6-9-1 101 .... SilvestreDeSousa 1 — 92
(Andrew Balding) *hld up: rdn and hdwy over 3f out: no imp on ldrs: one pce fr over 1f out* — **5/1**[3]

6-66 **7** 4 ½ **Speedo Boy (FR)**[92] 635 5-8-12 98 .... JamesDoyle 6 — 85
(Ian Williams) *midfield: lost pl 6f out: u.p over 3f out: plugged on fnl f: nvr a threat* — **25/1**

00-0 **8** ½ **Time To Study (FR)**[97] 565 5-8-11 97 .... RichardKingscote 13 — 83
(Ian Williams) *led early and briefly: chsd ldrs after: rdn over 3f out: wknd 2f out* — **25/1**

23-1 **9** 20 **Austrian School (IRE)**[20] 1947 4-9-4 105 3ex .... JoeFanning 5 — 75
(Mark Johnston) *hld up in midfield: hdwy 7f out: on outer chsng ldrs 6f out: rdn over 3f out: wknd 2f out* — **3/1**[1]

0-5 **10** 20 **Cliffs Of Dooneen (IRE)**[20] 1943 4-9-0 101 .... HarryBentley 2 — 51
(Ralph Beckett) *chsd ldrs: rdn 4f out: wknd 3f out: t.o* — **16/1**

0-05 **11** 13 **Mirsaale**[13] 2118 9-8-6 92 .... (p) JamesSullivan 3 — 25
(Keith Dalgleish) *bhd: nvr travelled after 1/2-way: t.o* — **50/1**

1442 **12** 15 **Lucky Deal**[13] 2118 4-8-9 96 .... JFEgan 14 — 18
(Mark Johnston) *a towards rr: rdn 4f out: t.o* — **33/1**

500- **13** 26 **Montaly**[216] 8013 8-9-3 103 .... GrahamLee 11
(Andrew Balding) *led early: sn dropped to midfield: rdn and wknd 4f out: t.o* — **25/1**

541- **P** **Shabeeb (USA)**[357] 2820 6-8-12 98 .... PaulHanagan 9
(Ian Williams) *in tch on outer: rdn and wknd 7f out: t.o whn p.u 6f out (jockey said gelding stopped quickly)* — **28/1**

-321 **P** **Watersmeet**[21] 1917 8-8-10 96 3ex .... PJMcDonald 10
(Mark Johnston) *hld up: dropped away 4f out: sn p.u* — **40/1**

4m 33.09s (28.49) **Going Correction** +1.175s/f (Soft)
WFA 4 from 5yo+ 1lb — **15** Ran SP% **127.0**
Speed ratings (Par 109): **87,84,84,83,83 79,78,77,69,60 55,49,38,,**
CSF £107.23 CT £523.87 TOTE £21.60: £5.80, £2.50, £2.20; EX 175.30 Trifecta £857.80.
Owner Acorn, Brown, Parker & Scott **Bred** Cheveley Park Stud Ltd **Trained** Middleham Moor, N Yorks

FOCUS

Last year's winner Magic Circle, set to carry top weight, was a significant absentee. This was a gruelling edition of this historic handicap which was run around 33sec slower than standard, an indication both of the testing ground - officially changed to heavy after the race - and the slow pace set by Making Miracles. Drawn 16, he bucked the recent trend of low-drawn winners in this race, and Low Sun, the only other horse to get seriously involved, came out of 17. The form is rated around the second and fourth, but it's uncertain how literal it will prove.

2576 WHITE OAK UK CONDITIONS STKS — 5f 15y

4:10 (4:12) (Class 3) 3-Y-O+

£11,826 (£3,541; £1,770; £885; £442; £222) **Stalls Low**

Form — RPR

14-3 **1** **She Can Boogie (IRE)**[2] 2522 3-8-4 88 .... JaneElliott(3) 6 — 94
(Tom Dascombe) *mde all: kicked on over 1f out: tail flashed whn rdn ins fnl f: kpt on wl and in command fnl 100yds* — **5/2**[2]

0-55 **2** 3 ½ **Duke Of Firenze**[7] 2368 10-9-4 82 .... DavidAllan 4 — 87
(David C Griffiths) *hld up in rr: hdwy 2f out: kpt on and chsd wnr over 1f out: ch ins fnl f: no ex and no imp fnl 100yds* — **11/2**[3]

10-0 **3** 1 ½ **A Momentofmadness**[20] 1946 6-9-7 103 .... (h) SilvestreDeSousa 2 — 85+
(Charles Hills) *prom: squeezed out and lost pl after 1f: racd off the pce after: effrt on wd outer wl over 2f out: hdwy 1f out: styd on u.p ins fnl f: nvr able to trble ldrs* — **8/11**[1]

41-0 **4** 4 ½ **Brandy Station (IRE)**[111] 317 4-8-11 66 .... (h) ElishaWhittington(7) 1 — 66
(Lisa Williamson) *trckd ldrs: rdn over 1f out: wknd ins fnl f* — **33/1**

000- **5** 15 **I'll Be Good**[192] 8715 10-8-13 51 .... ConnorMurtagh(5) 7 — 12
(Alan Berry) *trckd ldrs tl rdn and wknd over 2f out: lft bhd over 1f out* — **100/1**

10-0 **6** hd **Angel Force (IRE)**[14] 2079 4-8-13 73 .... (b) PhilDennis 5
(David C Griffiths) *w wnr tl rdn 2f out: wknd over 1f out* — **16/1**

1m 7.58s (5.48) **Going Correction** +1.175s/f (Soft)
WFA 3 from 4yo+ 9lb — **6** Ran SP% **111.7**
Speed ratings (Par 107): **103,97,95,87,63 63**
CSF £16.14 TOTE £3.10: £1.50, £1.80; EX 12.50 Trifecta £17.50.
Owner Mike Nolan & Partner **Bred** Cooneen Stud **Trained** Malpas, Cheshire

■ Stewards' Enquiry : Jane Elliott five-day ban (reduced from 6 on appeal): careless riding (May 28- Jun 1)

FOCUS

The previous year's winner Kachy was odds-on before being withdrawn, so in his absence, and with the new favourite well below form, this was just an ordinary race of its type. The winner built on her C&D run two days earlier.

2577 ENGLISH FINE COTTONS APPRENTICE H'CAP — 1m 4f 63y

4:40 (4:43) (Class 4) (0-85,82) 4-Y-O+

£7,698 (£2,290; £1,144; £572; £300; £300) **Stalls Low**

Form — RPR

323 **1** **Heart Of Soul (IRE)**[18] 1989 4-9-6 78 .... (v[1]) CameronNoble 2 — 89
(Ian Williams) *mde all: drew clr ent fnl 3f: edgd rt ins fnl f: pushed out* — **7/2**[1]

3-35 **2** 4 **Saryshagann (FR)**[13] 2104 6-9-9 81 .... ConorMcGovern 5 — 85+
(David O'Meara) *hmpd s and sn lost pl: hld up after: hdwy 3f out: proged on wd outer after: chsd wnr wl over 1f out: styd on but no imp* — **6/1**[3]

00-3 **3** 10 **Archippos**[11] 2185 6-9-3 75 .... (b) PhilDennis 6 — 63
(Philip Kirby) *racd on and off the bridle: towards rr: hrd at work and no imp 3f out: hdwy on outer over 1f out: styd on to take 3rd towards fin: nvr able to trble front two (jockey said gelding was never travelling)* — **6/1**[3]

1153 **4** 1 ¼ **Azari**[79] 799 7-9-4 81 .... (b) ThoreHammerHansen(5) 4 — 67
(Alexandra Dunn) *hld up in midfield: rdn over 2f out: kpt on u.p ins fnl f: nvr a threat* — **8/1**

2-60 **5** ¾ **Indomeneo**[13] 2095 4-9-3 82 .... RussellHarris(7) 10 — 67
(Richard Fahey) *racd keenly: prom: rdn and outpcd over 2f out: kpt on at same pce u.p fr over 1f out* — **12/1**

6/0- **6** 1 ¾ **Beach Break**[20] 2230 5-8-8 73 .... (b) EllaMcCain(7) 9 — 55
(Donald McCain) *chsd ldrs early: dropped to midfield after 4f: rdn and wknd over 3f out* — **33/1**

616/ **7** nk **Bahama Moon (IRE)**[61] 7595 7-9-2 77 .... ConnorMurtagh(3) 12 — 59
(Jonjo O'Neill) *midfield: hdwy to chse ldrs over 4f out: one pce and n.d fnl 2f* — **8/1**

/04- **8** 5 **Marengo**[185] 8901 8-9-3 75 .... (p) WilliamCox 11 — 49
(Bernard Llewellyn) *prom: chsd wnr after 4f: drvn over 3f out: unable to go w wnr wl over 2f out: lost 2nd wl over 1f out: sn wknd* — **25/1**

03-0 **9** *12* **Midnight Wilde**[10] 2254 4-9-3 **80**.......................... CierenFallon(5) 8 34
(John Ryan) *a bhd: niggled along 6f out: nvr a threat (trainer's rep said gelding was unsuited by the Heavy going, and would prefer a faster surface)* **11/2**[2]

3520 **10** *36* **This Girl**[13] 2104 4-9-5 **77**..........................(v[1]) JaneElliott 1
(Tom Dascombe) *racd keenly: chsd ldrs: rdn over 4f out: wknd 3f out: eased whn wl btn over 1f out: t.o (jockey said filly ran too freely)* **11/2**[2]

3m 2.0s (19.80) **Going Correction** +1.175s/f (Soft) **10** Ran SP% **118.3**
Speed ratings (Par 105): **81,78,71,70,70 69,68,65,57,33**
CSF £24.79 CT £123.74 TOTE £4.30: £1.60, £2.00, £1.80; EX 23.20 Trifecta £116.30.
Owner Dr Marwan Koukash **Bred** Ecurie La Vallee Martigny **Trained** Portway, Worcs

FOCUS
Probably not form to buy into, with the winner getting his own way in front.

2578 SPORTPESA CHESTER PLATE H'CAP — 2m 2f 140y
5:15 (5:17) (Class 2) 4-Y-O+
£31,125 (£9,320; £4,660; £2,330; £1,165; £585) **Stalls** High

Form RPR

50-2 **1** **Coeur De Lion**[28] 1735 6-9-3 **88**..................(p) ThoreHammerHansen(5) 9 99
(Alan King) *hld up in midfield on outer: hdwy after 5f: chsd ldrs: wnt 2nd 6f out: rdn over 3f out: led over 2f out: asserted over 1f out: styd on wl fnl f* **13/8**[1]

665- **2** *5* **Suegioo (FR)**[209] 8197 10-9-5 **85**..................(p) PaulHanagan 12 90
(Ian Williams) *bhd: hdwy over 4f out: styd on for press to take 2nd ins fnl f: nt trble wnr* **16/1**

340- **3** *3 ½* **Always Resolute**[34] 7755 8-8-5 **74**..................(p) JamieGormley(3) 2 76
(Ian Williams) *midfield: rdn over 5f out: hdwy over 4f out: cl up chsng ldrs over 3f out: styd on u.p: one pce fnl 100yds* **9/1**

3/-0 **4** *12* **Michael's Mount**[35] 1559 6-8-11 **80**.................. CameronNoble(3) 8 70+
(Ian Williams) *led early: chsd ldrs: led after 7f: sn rdn clr whn rdr rode fin a circut too early: sn given breather: rdn 3f out: hdd over 2f out: wknd ins fnl f (vet said gelding was suffering from post-race ataxia)* **14/1**

313- **5** *8* **Faithful Mount**[20] 8197 10-9-2 **82**..................(p) AlistairRawlinson 4 64
(Ian Williams) *chsd ldrs: dropped to midfield after 7f: rdn and hdwy over 5f out: cl up over 3f out: wknd over 1f out (jockey said gelding was never travelling)* **20/1**

0600 **6** *29* **Baydar**[13] 2092 6-8-7 **78**..................(p) SeanDavis(5) 13 31
(Ian Williams) *chsd ldrs: cl up 4f out: rdn over 3f out: wknd wl over 2f out: eased whn wl btn over 1f out* **14/1**

7 *51* **Drakensberg (IRE)**[65] 1051 5-8-9 **75**..................(t) JFEgan 3
(A J Martin, Ire) *midfield: rdn over 4f out: wknd over 3f out: t.o (jockey said gelding had no more to give)* **7/1**[3]

255- **8** *2 ¾* **Arty Campbell (IRE)**[194] 7337 9-8-3 **76**.................. WilliamCarver(7) 6
(Bernard Llewellyn) *in rr: pushed along over 5f out: t.o fnl 4f* **40/1**

6-46 **9** *1 ¼* **Diocletian (IRE)**[97] 558 4-8-10 **80**.................. WilliamCox(3) 15
(Andrew Balding) *racd keenly: sn led: hdd after 7f: chsd ldr tl 6f out: rdn and wknd over 4f out: t.o (jockey said gelding stopped quickly)* **8/1**

62-0 **10** *10* **Never Surrender (IRE)**[20] 1943 5-9-5 **85**.................. SilvestreDeSousa 7
(Charles Hills) *handy: rdn over 6f out: sn wknd: eased 5f out: sn t.o* **10/1**

11 *dist* **Constancio (IRE)**[14] 3379 6-9-5 **85**.................. GrahamLee 10
(Donald McCain) *prom: lost pl after 7f: rdn and wknd 6f out: t.o* **16/1**

0320 **12** *85* **Addicted To You (IRE)**[14] 2080 5-9-5 **85**..................(v) FrannyNorton 5
(Mark Johnston) *s.i.s: a bhd: drvn over 5f out: t.o (jockey said gelding lost its left fore shoe)* **13/2**[2]

233- **P** **Paddy A (IRE)**[71] 9731 5-8-8 **79**.................. ConnorMurtagh(5) 11
(Ian Williams) *hld up: struggling after 6f: t.o whn p.u over 5f out (trainer said gelding was unsuited by the heavy going and would prefer a sounder surface)* **33/1**

4m 42.76s (38.16) **Going Correction** +1.175s/f (Soft) **13** Ran SP% **129.4**
WFA 4 from 5yo+ 1lb
Speed ratings (Par 109): **66,63,62,57,54 41,20,19,18,14 , ,**
CSF £34.89 CT £207.66 TOTE £2.40: £1.40, £3.90, £2.90; EX 40.00 Trifecta £282.10.
Owner The Barbury Boys **Bred** Mr & Mrs R Kelvin-Hughes **Trained** Barbury Castle, Wilts
■ Stewards' Enquiry : Cameron Noble ten-day ban: riding a finish a circuit too early (May 24-25,27-31, June 1-3)

FOCUS
The second running of this consolation event. It took place on the worst of the ground and was reminiscent of a Midlands National in the latter stages, the field coming home at wide margins. The time was 42.76sec outside the standard, and over 9sec slower than the Chester Cup. Coeur de Lion improved on last year's second in this race.
T/Jkpt: Not Won. T/Plt: £245.90 to a £1 stake. Pool: £149,375.66 - 443.31 winning units T/Qpdt: £27.30 to a £1 stake. Pool: £15,754.82 - 426.04 winning units **Darren Owen**

2248 NOTTINGHAM (L-H)
Friday, May 10

OFFICIAL GOING: Soft
Wind: Light across Weather: Heavy rain

2579 CASTLE ROCK ELSIE MO FILLIES' NOVICE MEDIAN AUCTION STKS (PLUS 10 RACE) — 5f 8y
5:20 (5:22) (Class 5) 2-Y-O
£3,881 (£1,155; £577; £288) **Stalls** High

Form RPR

02 **1** **Daddies Diva**[10] 2248 2-9-0 0.................. HectorCrouch 10 75
(Rod Millman) *trckd ldrs on stands' rail: hdwy over 1f out: rdn to chal ent fnl f: led last 110yds: styd on wl* **8/1**[3]

2 *2* **Go Well Spicy (IRE)** 2-9-0 0.................. GeorgeDowning 8 68
(Mick Channon) *in tch nr stands' rail: pushed along 2f out: rdn over 1f out: styd on wl fnl f* **14/1**

3 *½* **Know No Limits (IRE)** 2-9-0 0.................. LiamJones 5 66
(Tom Dascombe) *slt ld: rdn wl over 1f out: edgd lft and drvn ent fnl f: hdd and no ex last 110yds* **12/1**

4 *2 ½* **Microscopic (IRE)** 2-9-0 0.................. StevieDonohoe 6 57
(David Simcock) *wnt rt s: in tch: hdwy to chse ldrs 2f out: rdn over 1f out: kpt on fnl f* **25/1**

4 **5** *nse* **Callipygian**[15] 2052 2-9-0 0.................. BarryMcHugh 9 57
(James Given) *trckd ldrs nr stands' rail: pushed along 2f out: rdn to chse ldng pair ent fnl f: kpt on same pce* **9/1**

6 *2 ¾* **Queenoftheclyde (IRE)** 2-9-0 0.................. CliffordLee 2 47
(K R Burke) *in tch: pushed along 2f out: rdn over 1f out: sn no imp* **10/1**

7 *2 ¾* **Quiet Word (FR)** 2-9-0 0.................. HollieDoyle 4 37+
(Archie Watson) *cl up: chal 2f out: sn rdn and wknd over 1f out (trainer's rep said that the filly was unsuited by the ground which was officially described as Soft on this occasion and would prefer a faster surface)* **5/6**[1]

0 **8** *2 ¼* **Flashy Flyer**[10] 2248 2-9-0 0.................. KieranO'Neill 3 29
(Dean Ivory) *cl up on outer: rdn along over 2f out: sn wknd* **66/1**

9 *shd* **Seraphinite (IRE)** 2-9-0 0.................. NicolaCurrie 7 29
(Jamie Osborne) *bmpd and hmpd s: a bhd* **13/2**[2]

1m 2.88s (2.68) **Going Correction** +0.35s/f (Good) **9** Ran SP% **117.8**
Speed ratings (Par 90): **92,88,88,84,83 79,75,71,71**
CSF £114.02 TOTE £5.10: £1.50, £4.10, £2.60; EX 43.80 Trifecta £247.90.
Owner Daddies Girl Partnership **Bred** Porlock Vale Stud **Trained** Kentisbeare, Devon

FOCUS
Outer track in use. All distances as advertised. The going had eased to soft, and the action developed towards the stands' rail in this fillies' novice.

2580 CASTLE ROCK SCREECH OWL H'CAP — 6f 18y
5:50 (5:53) (Class 6) (0-65,65) 4-Y-O+
£3,234 (£962; £481; £400; £400; £400) **Stalls** High

Form RPR

-354 **1** **Rasheeq (IRE)**[11] 2194 6-9-2 **65**..................(p) SeamusCronin(5) 2 74
(Mohamed Moubarak) *racd centre: trckd ldrs: hdwy on wd outside to chal wl over 1f out: rdn ent fnl f: kpt on wl to ld last 75yds* **14/1**

4434 **2** *hd* **Global Melody**[9] 2296 4-9-6 **64**..................(p) JosephineGordon 5 72
(Phil McEntee) *racd centre: cl up 1/2-way: led wl over 2f out: rdn over 1f out: edgd rt ins fnl f: hdd and no ex last 75yds (jockey said gelding hung right-handed)* **20/1**

41-0 **3** *3 ¼* **Cosmic Chatter**[13] 2122 9-9-5 **63**..................(p) DavidNolan 1 61
(Ruth Carr) *racd centre: trckd ldrs: smooth hdwy wl over 1f out: ev ch appr fnl f: sn rdn and kpt on one pce* **33/1**

465- **4** *2* **Glaceon (IRE)**[292] 5244 4-8-8 **59**.................. HarryRussell(7) 6 51
(Tina Jackson) *wnt rt s: racd towards centre: chsd ldrs: rdn along wl over 1f out: drvn and kpt on fnl f* **40/1**

0-00 **5** *1* **Boundsy (IRE)**[13] 2122 5-9-4 **62**.................. BarryMcHugh 3 51
(Richard Fahey) *racd centre: chsd ldrs: rdn along 2f out: kpt on same pce appr fnl f* **13/2**[3]

1300 **6** *nse* **The Golden Cue**[11] 2194 4-8-12 **63**.................. TobyEley(7) 10 52
(Steph Hollinshead) *in tch centre: rdn along 2f out: drvn over 1f out: sn no imp* **25/1**

-463 **7** *½* **Winklemann (IRE)**[12] 2145 7-9-1 **59**..................(p) DanielMuscutt 7 47
(John Flint) *dwlt and in rr centre: swtchd rt to stands' rail wl over 1f out and sn rdn along: styd on strly fnl f: nrst fin (jockey said gelding was slowly into stride)* **6/1**[2]

131- **8** *1* **Papa Delta**[156] 9401 5-9-0 **58**.................. GeorgeDowning 9 43
(Tony Carroll) *in tch centre: rdn along and lost pl bef 1/2-way: styd on fr wl over 1f out* **20/1**

0-05 **9** *1 ½* **Penny Pot Lane**[14] 2081 6-9-7 **65**.................. LewisEdmunds 15 45+
(Richard Whitaker) *racd nr stands' side: chsd ldrs: rdn along and lost pl bef 1/2-way: kpt on again u.p fnl 2f* **11/1**

-421 **10** *½* **Poet's Pride**[79] 811 4-9-5 **63**.................. RobbieDowney 17 42+
(David Barron) *nvr bttr than midfield nr stands' rail* **8/1**

-631 **11** *4 ½* **Tricky Dicky**[64] 1072 6-8-12 **61**.................. BenSanderson(5) 16 26+
(Roger Fell) *racd nr stands' rail: led: pushed along 1/2-way: sn hdd and rdn: wknd fnl 2f* **11/4**[1]

-015 **12** *3* **Decision Maker (IRE)**[25] 1817 5-8-13 **57**.................. DaneO'Neill 14 13+
(Roy Bowring) *cl up nr stands' rail: rdn along over 2f out: sn wknd* **22/1**

60-4 **13** *4 ½* **Praxedis**[14] 2081 4-8-12 **56**.................. GeorgeWood 12 +
(James Fanshawe) *a in rr* **12/1**

4230 **14** *2* **Mount Wellington (IRE)**[30] 1682 4-9-7 **65**..................(v) HollieDoyle 13 2
(Henry Spiller) *a bhd (jockey said gelding was never travelling)* **25/1**

1m 15.3s (1.50) **Going Correction** +0.35s/f (Good) **14** Ran SP% **115.0**
Speed ratings (Par 101): **104,103,99,96,95 95,94,93,91,90 84,80,74,72**
CSF £261.63 CT £4803.77 TOTE £14.80: £3.70, £4.10, £11.80; EX 187.80 Trifecta £2928.40.
Owner David Fremel **Bred** Rabbah Bloodstock Limited **Trained** Newmarket, Suffolk
■ Stewards' Enquiry : Seamus Cronin two-day ban: misuse of whip (May 24-25)

FOCUS
In contrast to the opening 2yo race the principals in this older horse sprint turned out to be drawn low and raced up the centre of the track. The form is rated around the runner-up to his mark.

2581 CASTLE ROCK SESSION NOVICE STKS — 1m 2f 50y
6:20 (6:22) (Class 5) 3-Y-O
£3,881 (£1,155; £577; £288) **Stalls** Low

Form RPR

4 **1** **Pondus**[30] 1690 3-9-2 0.................. DanielMuscutt 8 90+
(James Fanshawe) *trckd ldrs: hdwy and cl up 4f out: slt ld 3f out: jnd and rdn wl over 1f out: drvn ins fnl f: kpt on wl* **11/4**[1]

2 *¾* **Dubai Falcon (IRE)** 3-9-2 0.................. HectorCrouch 7 88+
(Saeed bin Suroor) *in tch: hdwy 3f out: rdn along wl over 1f out: kpt on strly fnl f* **15/2**

2- **3** *1 ½* **Qarasu (IRE)**[196] 8607 3-9-2 0.................. JasonWatson 10 85
(Roger Charlton) *trckd ldrs: hdwy on outer over 3f out: sn cl up: chal 2f out: rdn to dispute ld over 1f out: ev ch ins fnl f tl no ex last 100yds* **9/2**[3]

3 **4** *¾* **Aktau**[20] 1956 3-9-2 0..................(h[1]) DavidEgan 12 83+
(Roger Varian) *towards rr: hdwy over 4f out: chsd ldrs over 2f out: sn rdn: kpt on fnl f* **7/2**[2]

51- **5** *2 ¾* **Dalaalaat (IRE)**[191] 8738 3-9-9 0.................. DaneO'Neill 5 85
(William Haggas) *trckd ldrs: hdwy on inner to dispute ld 3f out: rdn along 2f out: sn drvn and wknd* **9/2**[3]

- **6** *5* **Nette Rousse (GER)** 3-8-11 0.................. JosephineGordon 15 63
(Ralph Beckett) *towards rr: gd hdwy 3f out: rdn along 2f out: kpt on: nvr rchd ldrs* **14/1**

7 *nk* **Earth And Sky (USA)** 3-8-11 0..................(h[1]) EoinWalsh 6 62
(George Scott) *dwlt and towards rr tl styd on fnl 2f* **50/1**

02 **8** *5* **Frequency Code (FR)**[10] 2245 3-9-2 0.................. CliffordLee 2 57
(Jedd O'Keeffe) *t.k.h: sn led: pushed along 4f out: rdn over 3f out: sn hdd & wknd* **33/1**

9 *11* **Postie** 3-8-11 0..................(h[1]) RyanTate 13 30
(James Eustace) *a towards rr* **100/1**

10 *7* **Resurrected (IRE)** 3-8-11 0.................. DannyBrock 1 16
(Philip McBride) *prom: rdn along over 3f out: sn wknd* **150/1**

6 **11** *11* **Wareeda (IRE)**[36] 1543 3-8-11 0..................(t) RossaRyan 14
(Richard Hannon) *a towards rr* **50/1**

12 *½* **Pipoca** 3-8-11 0.................. BarryMcHugh 3
(James Given) *a towards rr* **66/1**

00 **13** *2 ¼* **Lexington Warlord**[20] 1956 3-8-9 0.................. EmmaTaff(7) 9
(Richard Hannon) *dwlt: a in rr* **200/1**

14 39 **Medal Winner (FR)** 3-9-2 0.. HollieDoyle 16
(Archie Watson) *dwlt: rapid hdwy to chse ldrs after 1f: sn cl up: rdn along 4f out: sn wknd* **16/1**

2m 16.46s (3.06) **Going Correction** +0.35s/f (Good) **14 Ran SP% 120.1**
Speed ratings (Par 99): **101,100,99,98,96 92,92,88,79,73 64,64,62,31**
CSF £23.95 TOTE £4.30: £2.20, £2.00, £1.90; EX 27.10 Trifecta £111.50.
Owner Hubert John Strecker **Bred** Miss K Rausing **Trained** Newmarket, Suffolk

FOCUS
A good looking novice and it should throw up a number of winners. The form as rated makes sense but could prove better.

2582 CASTLE ROCK HARVEST PALE H'CAP — 1m 2f 50y
6:50 (6:55) (Class 5) (0-75,76) 3-Y-O

£3,881 (£1,155; £577; £400; £400; £400) **Stalls** Low

Form				RPR
1-60	**1**		**Jackamundo (FR)**[23] 1846 3-9-2 **70**........ DavidNolan 3 (Declan Carroll) *in tch: hdwy 3f out: chsd ldrs 2f out: sn rdn and chal over 1f out: drvn to ld ins fnl f: kpt on wl* **10/1**	80
040-	**2**	1 1/4	**Group Stage (GER)**[196] 8608 3-9-0 **68**........ JasonWatson 10 (Alan King) *trckd ldr: cl up over 3f out: led wl over 2f out: jnd and rdn over 1f out: drvn and hdd ins fnl f: kpt on* **7/1[3]**	76
34-0	**3**	2	**Knowing**[17] 2023 3-9-4 **72**........ GeorgeWood 5 (James Fanshawe) *hld up: hdwy and in tch 1/2-way: chsd ldrs wl over 2f out: rdn wl over 1f out: kpt on fnl f* **5/1[1]**	76
-500	**4**	2 1/4	**Thinque Tank**[25] 1824 3-8-12 **66**........ StevieDonohoe 7 (Charlie Longsdon) *towards rr: hdwy on inner 4f out: swtchd rt and rdn along 2f out: swtchd lft over 1f out: sn drvn to chse ldrs: kpt on same pce* **16/1**	65
05-4	**5**	3 1/2	**El Picador (IRE)**[34] 1594 3-9-4 **72**........(b[1]) OisinMurphy 4 (Sir Michael Stoute) *trckd ldrs: hdwy 3f out: rdn along over 2f out: sn drvn and kpt on one pce* **14/1**	64
5-63	**6**	1 1/2	**Patchouli**[10] 2253 3-9-7 **75**........ DavidEgan 12 (Mick Channon) *trckd ldrs on wd outside: hdwy 4f out: rdn along wl over 2f out: drvn wl over 1f out: grad wknd* **6/1[2]**	64
42-4	**7**	1 1/2	**Silkstone (IRE)**[30] 1697 3-9-4 **72**........ KieranO'Neill 9 (Pam Sly) *prom: hdwy to ld over 4f out: rdn along over 3f out: hdd wl over 2f out: sn drvn and grad wknd* **8/1**	58
540	**8**	3 1/4	**Ardimento (IRE)**[65] 1033 3-8-13 **67**........ CharlieBennett 13 (Rod Millman) *midfield: hdwy 3f out: rdn along over 2f out: sn drvn and n.d* **25/1**	47
00-4	**9**	6	**Amorously (IRE)**[10] 2253 3-9-1 **69**........ RossaRyan 6 (Richard Hannon) *in tch: hdwy over 3f out: rdn along wl to chse ldrs wl over 2f out: sn drvn and btn* **8/1**	37
0000	**10**	1 1/4	**Showshutai**[11] 2190 3-8-2 **56** oh9........ JimmyQuinn 1 (Christopher Kellett) *a towards rr* **100/1**	21
0-62	**11**	1 1/2	**Fly Lightly**[70] 967 3-9-7 **75**........ PJMcDonald 14 (Robert Cowell) *chsd ldrs: rdn along over 4f out: sn wknd* **12/1**	37
62-1	**12**	29	**Dark Miracle (IRE)**[45] 1344 3-9-6 **74**........ DanielMuscutt 8 (Marco Botti) *chsd ldrs: rdn along over 3f out: wknd over 2f out (trainer said colt was unsuited by the Soft ground and would prefer a faster surface)* **9/1**	
2620	**13**	11	**Whenapoet**[14] 2075 3-8-5 **64**........(p) TheodoreLadd[(5)] 2 (Michael Appleby) *led: rdn along and hdd over 4f out: sn wknd (trainer said colt was unsuited by the ground which was officially described as Soft on this occasion and would prefer a faster surface)* **12/1**	

2m 17.98s (4.58) **Going Correction** +0.35s/f (Good) **13 Ran SP% 117.5**
Speed ratings (Par 99): **95,94,92,90,87 86,85,82,78,77 75,52,43**
CSF £77.07 CT £397.05 TOTE £12.40: £3.60, £3.20, £2.60; EX 135.00 Trifecta £660.90.
Owner Danny Fantom **Bred** John Kilpatrick **Trained** Malton, N Yorks

FOCUS
A competitive affair which has been rated in line with the race standard.

2583 CASTLE ROCK SONGBIRD MAIDEN FILLIES' STKS (PLUS 10 RACE) — 1m 75y
7:20 (7:22) (Class 5) 3-Y-O **£3,881** (£1,155; £577; £288) **Stalls** Centre

Form				RPR
3-2	**1**		**Twist 'N' Shake**[24] 1828 3-9-0 0........ RobertHavlin 17 (John Gosden) *mde all: qcknd clr over 2f out: unchal* **1/2[1]**	99+
2-	**2**	7	**Audarya (FR)**[177] 9048 3-9-0 0........ GeorgeWood 8 (James Fanshawe) *trckd ldrs: hdwy 3f out: rdn along to chse wnr fr over 1f out: sn drvn and kpt on: no ch w wnr* **5/1[2]**	81
	3	1/2	**Qamka** 3-9-0 0........ DavidEgan 9 (Roger Varian) *in tch: hdwy over 3f out: sn chsng ldrs: rdn along 2f out: kpt on same pce* **12/1**	80
02-	**4**	3	**Regal Banner**[151] 9485 3-9-0 0........ OisinMurphy 12 (Roger Varian) *chsd ldrs: hdwy on outer over 4f out: pushed along 3f out: rdn over 2f out: kpt on same pce* **10/1[3]**	73
	5	6	**Narina (IRE)** 3-9-0 0........ LiamJones 11 (William Haggas) *towards rr: sme hdwy 3f out: sn rdn along and n.d* **20/1**	59+
4	**6**	1/2	**Venusta (IRE)**[24] 1828 3-9-0 0........ GeorgeDowning 5 (Mick Channon) *dwlt: a towards rr* **33/1**	58+
5	**7**	3/4	**Plissken**[24] 1834 3-9-0 0........(h) PJMcDonald 14 (Tom Clover) *prom: chse wnr 1/2-way: rdn along wl over 3f out: sn drvn and wknd (vet said filly lost its right hind shoe)* **66/1**	56
00	**8**	1 3/4	**Tereshkova**[8] 2340 3-8-7 0........(h) SaraDelFabbro[(7)] 3 (Michael Bell) *trckd ldrs: hdwy on inner 4f out: rdn along 3f out: sn wknd* **80/1**	52
02-	**9**	6	**Perfect Showdance**[163] 9291 3-9-0 0........ HectorCrouch 1 (Clive Cox) *chsd ldrs: rdn along over 4f out: sn wknd* **16/1**	39
0-	**10**	1 1/2	**Tamok (IRE)**[195] 8647 3-9-0 0........ LouisSteward 6 (Michael Bell) *a towards rr* **100/1**	35
0-	**11**	3/4	**Dolly McQueen**[188] 8833 3-9-0 0........ RyanTate 10 (Anthony Carson) *a towards rr* **100/1**	33
0	**12**	3 3/4	**Inspirational (IRE)**[23] 1852 3-9-0 0........ DanielMuscutt 13 (Ed Dunlop) *a towards rr* **66/1**	25
	13	3	**Marmarr** 3-8-11 0........ GeorgiaCox[(3)] 4 (William Haggas) *dwlt: green: a outpcd and bhd* **10/1[3]**	18

1m 48.66s (1.96) **Going Correction** +0.35s/f (Good) **13 Ran SP% 129.0**
Speed ratings (Par 96): **104,97,96,93,87 87,86,84,78,77 76,72,69**
CSF £3.65 TOTE £1.50: £1.10, £2.60, £2.80; EX 5.10 Trifecta £27.40.
Owner Helena Springfield Ltd **Bred** Meon Valley Stud **Trained** Newmarket, Suffolk

FOCUS
This went as the market suggested, the odds-on winner bolting up in fine style. The form has been rated slightly above the race average.

2584 CASTLE ROCK WILLOWBROOK H'CAP — 1m 75y
7:50 (7:52) (Class 4) (0-85,87) 4-Y-O+

£6,469 (£1,925; £962; £481; £400; £400) **Stalls** Centre

Form				RPR
030-	**1**		**Nightingale Valley**[222] 7803 6-8-10 **73**........ JasonWatson 7 (Stuart Kittow) *in tch: hdwy over 3f out: cl up over 2f out: rdn to ld 1 1/2f out: kpt on wl* **16/1**	82+
0363	**2**	1/2	**Confrontational (IRE)**[20] 1955 5-9-2 **79**........ DavidEgan 5 (Jennie Candlish) *trckd ldr: hdwy 3f out: led jst over 2f out: rdn and hdd 1 1/2f out: drvn and kpt on wl fnl f* **6/1**	85
0-06	**3**	5	**Highlight Reel (IRE)**[13] 2116 4-9-1 **78**........ LewisEdmunds 8 (Rebecca Bastiman) *t.k.h: in tch: hdwy 4f out and sn trcking ldrs: effrt over 2f out: rdn wl over 1f out: kpt on same pce fnl f* **9/1**	73
210-	**4**	2	**Secret Return (IRE)**[188] 8835 6-9-3 **80**........ OisinMurphy 2 (Paul George) *trckd ldng pair: hdwy over 4f out: cl up 3f out: chal over 2f out: sn rdn and ev ch tl drvn and wknd ent fnl f* **3/1[1]**	70
5663	**5**	1/2	**Me Too Nagasaki (IRE)**[11] 2193 5-8-12 **75**........(t) PJMcDonald 10 (Stuart Williams) *hld up in rr: hdwy over 3f out: rdn along over 2f out: kpt on u.p: n.d* **5/1[2]**	64
51-1	**6**	nk	**Give It Some Teddy**[32] 1644 5-9-6 **83**........ DuranFentiman 1 (Tim Easterby) *trckd ldrs: effrt 3f out: rdn along over 2f out: drvn wl over 1f out: sn no imp* **11/2[3]**	71
000-	**7**	2	**Swift Emperor (IRE)**[213] 8095 7-9-1 **78**........ RobbieDowney 6 (David Barron) *dwlt and in rr tl sme late hdwy* **9/1**	61
14-0	**8**	4 1/2	**Big Storm Coming**[13] 2116 9-9-10 **87**........ BarryMcHugh 9 (John Quinn) *trckd ldng pair: pushed along over 3f out: rdn wl over 2f out: sn wknd* **50/1**	60
-666	**9**	1	**Noble Peace**[34] 1588 6-9-0 **77**........ RobertHavlin 11 (Lydia Pearce) *racd wd early: a towards rr* **16/1**	48
330-	**10**	2 3/4	**Plunger**[162] 9313 4-9-7 **84**........ RaulDaSilva 3 (Paul Cole) *t.k.h: led: rdn along over 3f out: hdd over 2f out: sn drvn and wknd* **9/1**	48

1m 49.14s (2.44) **Going Correction** +0.35s/f (Good) **10 Ran SP% 115.1**
Speed ratings (Par 105): **101,100,95,93,93 92,90,86,85,82**
CSF £107.56 CT £927.58 TOTE £19.90: £4.90, £2.30, £4.30; EX 107.60 Trifecta £1358.60.
Owner M E Harris **Bred** M Harris **Trained** Blackborough, Devon

FOCUS
A fair handicap and the first two finished nicely clear. The form is rated around the runner-up, with the winner value for a bit extra.

2585 CASTLE ROCK FOX & GRAPES FILLIES' H'CAP — 1m 75y
8:20 (8:21) (Class 5) (0-70,70) 4-Y-O+

£3,881 (£1,155; £577; £400; £400; £400) **Stalls** Centre

Form				RPR
2030	**1**		**Classic Charm**[55] 1231 4-8-9 **58**........ PJMcDonald 4 (Dean Ivory) *trckd ldrs on inner: hdwy over 3f out: sn cl up: led over 1f out: sn rdn: kpt on wl towards fin (trainer's rep said, regarding the apparent improvement in form, that mare appeared to appreciate the rain softened ground on this occasion)* **7/2[1]**	69
511-	**2**	1	**Vixen (IRE)**[289] 5357 5-9-7 **70**........(h) OisinMurphy 1 (Emma Lavelle) *t.k.h: trckd ldng pair: hdwy and cl up 5f out: led 4f out: pushed along 2f out and sn jnd: rdn and hdd over 1f out: drvn and rallied ins fnl f: kpt on same pce towards fin* **6/1**	78
2065	**3**	4	**Accomplice**[9] 2277 5-8-12 **61**........ StevieDonohoe 8 (Michael Blanshard) *hld up in rr: stdy hdwy 4f out: trckd ldrs over 2f out: effrt wl over 1f out: sn rdn: kpt on same pce fnl f* **7/1**	62
3-35	**4**	3	**Shazzab (IRE)**[13] 2106 4-8-11 **60**........(p) BarryMcHugh 12 (Richard Fahey) *cl up on outer: chal over 3f out: sn rdn and ev ch over 2f out: sn drvn and grad wknd appr fnl f* **4/1[2]**	52
50/0	**5**	2	**Angelical Eve (IRE)**[28] 1731 5-7-13 **51** oh6........ NoelGarbutt[(3)] 2 (Dai Williams) *in rr: hdwy on inner over 3f out: rdn along 2f out: kpt on u.p: n.d* **100/1**	38
-456	**6**	shd	**Brockagh Cailin**[9] 2277 4-8-10 **59**........ KieranO'Neill 5 (J S Moore) *trckd ldrs: hdwy 4f out: rdn along wl over 2f out: sn drvn and one pce* **16/1**	46
0-66	**7**	1/2	**Acadian Angel (IRE)**[23] 1850 5-8-9 **58**........ PaddyMathers 7 (Steph Hollinshead) *towards rr tl sme late hdwy* **12/1**	44
455-	**8**	10	**Rosy Ryan (IRE)**[227] 7643 9-8-5 **54**........ JimmyQuinn 10 (Tina Jackson) *t.k.h: chsd ldrs: pushed along over 3f out: sn rdn and wknd* **25/1**	17
50-2	**9**	1 1/4	**Sussex Girl**[17] 2019 5-8-4 **53**........ JosephineGordon 11 (John Berry) *in tch on outer: pushed along over 4f out: sn lost pl and bhd* **8/1**	13
0-30	**10**	8	**Queens Royale**[117] 233 5-8-6 **60**........(v) TheodoreLadd[(5)] 6 (Michael Appleby) *led: rdn along over 4f out: sn hdd & wknd* **9/2[3]**	2

1m 49.61s (2.91) **Going Correction** +0.35s/f (Good) **10 Ran SP% 116.7**
Speed ratings (Par 100): **99,98,94,91,89 88,88,78,77,69**
CSF £24.79 CT £143.41 TOTE £4.10: £1.60, £1.90, £2.20; EX 31.20 Trifecta £236.10.
Owner Gracelands Stud Partnership **Bred** Gracelands Stud **Trained** Radlett, Herts

FOCUS
A modest fillies' handicap but livened up by a successful gamble on the winner. The second transferred her AW improvement to turf.
T/Plt: £4,777.10 to a £1 stake. Pool: £36,515.51 - 5.58 winning units T/Qpdt: £35.90 to a £1 stake. Pool: £5,926.71 - 121.88 winning units **Joe Rowntree**

2115 RIPON (R-H)
Friday, May 10

OFFICIAL GOING: Good to soft (soft in places; 7.2)
Wind: light behind Weather: fine

2586 WETHERBY RACECOURSE LADIES' DAY 30TH MAY EBF NOVICE AUCTION STKS — 5f
6:00 (6:03) (Class 5) 2-Y-O **£3,881** (£1,155; £577; £288) **Stalls** High

Form				RPR
	1		**Three Coins** 2-8-13........ TonyHamilton 4 (Richard Fahey) *prom: rdn to ld narrowly 1f out: idled: kpt on* **10/1**	71+
6213	**2**	3/4	**Birkenhead**[13] 2115 2-9-5........(v[1]) CallumShepherd 3 (Mick Channon) *prom on outer: rdn 2f out: drvn over 1f out: kpt on* **2/1[2]**	74

2 **3** *shd* **Paper Star**[9] [2282] 2-8-8 .... LukeMorris 5 63
(Archie Watson) *led: rdn along 2f out: edgd rt over 1f out: hdd 1f out: kpt on same pce* **3/1**[3]

4 *3 ½* **Queens Blade** 2-8-9 .... RachelRichardson 7 51+
(Tim Easterby) *dwlt: hld up: bit short of room 3f out and swtchd rt: pushed along 2f out: kpt on ins fnl f: nvr threatened (jockey said filly hung left in the early stages)* **20/1**

42 **5** *4 ½* **Gin Gembre (FR)**[23] [1844] 2-9-3 .... BenCurtis 8 43
(K R Burke) *dwlt sltly: hld up: sn pushed along: drvn 2f out: sn btn (jockey said colt was never travelling)* **7/4**[1]

0 **6** *6* **Nostalgic Air**[23] [1844] 2-8-8 .... AndrewMullen 2 13
(Ruth Carr) *chsd ldrs: sn pushed along: wknd 2f out* **40/1**

1m 0.84s (1.44) **Going Correction** +0.15s/f (Good) **6 Ran SP% 111.0**
Speed ratings (Par 93): **94,92,92,87,79 70**
CSF £29.76 TOTE £8.60: £2.80, £1.60; EX 28.60 Trifecta £81.40.
Owner Bearstone Stud Limited **Bred** Bearstone Stud **Trained** Musley Bank, N Yorks

FOCUS
Conditions remained unaltered from the previous evening's good to soft, soft in places following 1.4mm of rain on Friday morning. Rail movements added 12yds to races 2 and 6. The stalls were on the stands' side for this opening juvenile novice auction event, run at a solid gallop. Ordinary form, the runner-up and third helping with the level.

2587 REDCAR LADIES' DAY SATURDAY 22ND JUNE (S) STKS 1m 1f 170y
6:30 (6:33) (Class 5) 3-4-Y-O **£3,881** (£1,155; £577; £288) **Stalls** Low

Form RPR

04-0 **1** **Izvestia (IRE)**[17] [2029] 3-8-4 85 ....(p) LukeMorris 8 54
(Archie Watson) *trckd ldrs: rdn over 2f out: led over 1f out: drvn and kpt on* **4/7**[1]

5500 **2** *3* **Amity Island**[20] [1958] 4-9-7 47 ....(b[1]) BenRobinson(3) 3 53
(Ollie Pears) *trckd ldrs on inner: hmpd over 4f out and sn dropped to rr: styd on wl fr over 1f out: wnt 2nd fnl 110yds* **6/1**[2]

6060 **3** *1 ½* **Prince Consort (IRE)**[18] [1981] 4-9-10 36 ....(p) TomEaves 1 50
(John Wainwright) *led: hdd over 6f out: rdn to ld again 3f out: hdd over 1f out: no ex and lost 2nd 110yds out* **80/1**

-000 **4** *hd* **Half Full**[11] [2213] 3-8-9 50 .... RachelRichardson 4 49
(Michael Easterby) *slowly away: hld up in rr: rdn over 3f out: sme hdwy 2f out: kpt on ins fnl f* **8/1**[3]

505- **5** *1 ½* **Mandarin Princess**[374] [2267] 4-8-12 50 .... RPWalsh(7) 2 42
(Kenny Johnson) *dwlt: hld up: racd keenly: hld up: rdn and sme hdwy 2f out: plugged on fnl f* **33/1**

0000 **6** *11* **Zoom Out**[8] [2337] 3-8-6 52 ....(t) RowanScott(3) 10 25
(Nigel Tinkler) *hld up: rdn over 2f out: sn btn* **6/1**[2]

00-0 **7** *15* **Our Boy Zeus (IRE)**[12] [2150] 3-8-9 18 ....(p[1]) AndrewMullen 5
(Micky Hammond) *midfield: rdn over 3f out: sn wknd* **50/1**

5-00 **8** *1* **Lone Voice (IRE)**[37] [1527] 4-9-10 43 .... BenCurtis 6
(Tony Carroll) *in tch: racd keenly: led over 6f out: rdn and hdd 3f out: wknd (jockey said gelding had ran too free)* **12/1**

-000 **U** **Al Mortajaz (FR)**[11] [2200] 3-8-2 67 .... LauraCoughlan(7) 9
(Adrian Nicholls) *prom on inner: stmbld and uns rdr over 4f out* **9/1**

2m 9.37s (4.77) **Going Correction** +0.15s/f (Good)
WFA 3 from 4yo 15lb **9 Ran SP% 127.2**
Speed ratings (Par 103): **88,85,84,84,83 74,62,61,**
CSF £5.55 TOTE £1.50: £1.10, £1.90, £12.00; EX 6.30 Trifecta £112.70.The winner was bought in for £13,000.
Owner Saxon Thoroughbreds **Bred** Corrin Stud **Trained** Upper Lambourn, W Berks

FOCUS
Actual race distance 1m1f182yds, stalls on inner. A weak and very one-sided seller on paper, and perhaps harder work than it ought to have been for the favourite.

2588 NEW LOOK CATTERICK OPENS 17TH JUNE H'CAP 6f
7:00 (7:05) (Class 4) (0-85,83) 4-Y-O+ **£6,301** (£1,886; £943; £472; £235) **Stalls** High

Form RPR

10-5 **1** **Dark Defender**[11] [2201] 6-9-7 **83** ....(b) DanielTudhope 9 91
(Rebecca Bastiman) *mde all: rdn over 1f out: kpt on wl to draw clr fnl f: comf* **9/2**[2]

410- **2** *3* **Final Go**[253] [6709] 4-9-0 **76** .... SamJames 8 74
(Grant Tuer) *prom: rdn along 2f out: kpt on but no ch w wnr fnl f* **12/1**

00-0 **3** *¾* **Music Society (IRE)**[22] [1895] 4-8-9 **71** ....(h[1]) RachelRichardson 1 67
(Tim Easterby) *hld up on outside: rdn and hdwy 2f out: kpt on fnl f (jockey said gelding hung left-handed)* **20/1**

4-04 **4** *nk* **Magical Effect (IRE)**[18] [1978] 7-9-1 **77** .... JamesSullivan 2 72
(Ruth Carr) *hld up: rdn along and swtchd rt appr fnl f: kpt on* **9/2**[2]

5-05 **5** *½* **Explain**[18] [1977] 7-8-9 **71** ....(b) AndrewMullen 3 64
(Ruth Carr) *dwlt: hld up: rdn over 2f out: kpt on ins fnl f: nvr trbld ldrs* **11/2**[3]

0-53 **6** *hd* **Sheepscar Lad (IRE)**[11] [2201] 5-8-11 **78** .... FayeMcManoman(5) 6 70
(Nigel Tinkler) *prom: racd quite keenly: rdn 2f out: no ex ins fnl f* **7/2**[1]

00-6 **7** *2* **Charming Guest (IRE)**[64] [1061] 4-8-11 **73** .... CallumShepherd 4 59
(Mick Channon) *midfield: rdn and outpcd over 1f out: no threat after* **8/1**

320- **8** *½* **Queens Gift (IRE)**[225] [7713] 4-9-5 **81** .... PaulMulrennan 5 65
(Michael Dods) *cl up towards outer: rdn 2f out: wknd ins fnl f* **15/2**

-100 **9** *1 ¾* **Doc Sportello (IRE)**[32] [1654] 7-9-4 **80** .... BenCurtis 7 59
(Tony Carroll) *midfield: rdn 2f out: wknd fnl f* **14/1**

1m 12.7s (0.20) **Going Correction** +0.15s/f (Good) **9 Ran SP% 116.0**
Speed ratings (Par 105): **104,100,99,98,97 97,95,94,92**
CSF £56.99 CT £986.01 TOTE £4.60: £1.70, £2.90, £4.50; EX 62.70 Trifecta £691.90.
Owner Rebecca Bastiman Racing **Bred** Mrs C J Walker **Trained** Cowthorpe, N Yorks

FOCUS
Stalls on stands' side. A reasonable handicap for the grade, but the front-running winner took it apart. It rates a pb and the form could be worth more at face value.

2589 LETS ALL "GO RACING IN YORKSHIRE" H'CAP 5f
7:30 (7:34) (Class 3) (0-90,88) 4-Y-O+
£9,337 (£2,796; £1,398; £699; £349; £175) **Stalls** High

Form RPR

3315 **1** **Canford Bay (IRE)**[14] [2079] 5-8-3 **77** .... KieranSchofield(7) 6 88
(Antony Brittain) *cl up: rdn to chal over 1f out: led ins fnl f: kpt on wl to draw clr fnl 110yds (jockey said gelding hung left-handed)* **2/1**[1]

-212 **2** *2 ¼* **Acclaim The Nation (IRE)**[21] [1915] 6-9-6 **87** ....(p) TomEaves 5 90
(Eric Alston) *rrd s but led: rdn and pressed over 1f out: hdd ins fnl f: no ex fnl 110yds* **5/2**[2]

4-35 **3** *3 ¼* **Seen The Lyte (IRE)**[9] [2292] 4-8-12 **82** ....(h) RowanScott(3) 2 73
(Nigel Tinkler) *v.s.a: hld up in rr: rdn and hdwy on outside over 1f out: no ex ins fnl f (jockey said filly missed the break)* **10/1**

0-00 **4** *2 ¾* **Henley**[6] [2421] 7-9-5 **86** .... BenCurtis 4 67
(Tracy Waggott) *pressed ldrs: rdn 2f out: wknd fnl f* **11/4**[3]

3160 **5** *2 ¼* **Boom The Groom (IRE)**[16] [2030] 8-9-7 **88** .... LukeMorris 3 61
(Tony Carroll) *chsd ldrs: sn pushed along: wknd fnl f* **10/1**

0000 **6** *hd* **Classic Pursuit**[20] [1946] 8-8-10 **77** ....(v) JamesSullivan 7 49
(Marjorie Fife) *chsd ldrs: rdn over 2f out: wknd over 1f out* **25/1**

59.09s (-0.31) **Going Correction** +0.15s/f (Good) **6 Ran SP% 110.6**
Speed ratings (Par 107): **108,104,99,94,91 90**
CSF £7.04 TOTE £2.30: £1.10, £2.90; EX 6.30 Trifecta £32.90.
Owner Northgate Racing **Bred** R McCulloch **Trained** Warthill, N Yorks

FOCUS
Stalls on stands' side. A fair feature sprint handicap. The winner is rated in line with his C&D win on his penultimate run.

2590 BILLY OCEAN AT PONTEFRACT 24TH MAY MAIDEN STKS 6f
8:00 (8:02) (Class 5) 3-Y-O **£3,881** (£1,155; £577; £288) **Stalls** High

Form RPR

54- **1** **Victory Day (IRE)**[185] [8895] 3-9-5 .... DanielTudhope 2 92+
(William Haggas) *trckd ldrs on outer: led over 1f out: cruised clr: v easily* **1/2**[1]

0-4 **2** *3 ¾* **Abate**[31] [1665] 3-9-5 .... AndrewMullen 4 74
(Adrian Nicholls) *led narrowly: rdn 2f out: hdd over 1f out: one pce: sn no ch w wnr* **6/1**[3]

00 **3** *3* **Bedtime Bella (IRE)**[8] [2332] 3-9-0 .... BenCurtis 3 59
(K R Burke) *chsd ldrs: rdn over 2f out: wknd ins fnl f* **16/1**

6-0 **4** *nk* **Saltie Girl**[8] [2332] 3-9-0 .... TomEaves 8 58
(David Barron) *dwlt: sn pressed ldr: rdn 2f out: wknd fnl f* **50/1**

5 **5** *2* **Gunnison**[10] [2243] 3-9-5 .... TonyHamilton 10 57+
(Richard Fahey) *hld up: pushed along 2f out: kpt on ins fnl f: nvr threatened* **20/1**

2 **6** *½* **In Trutina**[11] [2199] 3-9-0 .... LukeMorris 1 50+
(Archie Watson) *dwlt: hld up on outer: sn rdn along: no imp and btn over 1f out* **5/1**[2]

0 **7** *1 ½* **Torque Of The Town (IRE)**[11] [2199] 3-9-5 .... ConnorBeasley 9 51
(Noel Wilson) *chsd ldrs: rdn over 2f out: sn wknd* **66/1**

54 **8** *2 ¾* **Grey Berry (IRE)**[12] [2147] 3-9-0 .... DavidAllan 6 37
(Tim Easterby) *chsd ldrs: pushed along over 2f out: outpcd over 1f out: wknd ins fnl f* **17/2**

9 *1 ½* **Ideal Option (IRE)** 3-9-5 .... RachelRichardson 5 37
(Tim Easterby) *dwlt: sn pushed along and outpcd in rr: sme hdwy and in tch w main gp 2f out: wknd fnl f* **28/1**

0 **10** *nk* **Brutalab**[13] [2094] 3-9-1 ow1 .... DannyRedmond(5) 7 37
(Tim Easterby) *hld up: rdn over 2f out: wknd fnl f* **50/1**

1m 12.72s (0.22) **Going Correction** +0.15s/f (Good) **10 Ran SP% 127.7**
Speed ratings (Par 99): **104,99,95,94,91 91,89,85,83,83**
CSF £4.65 TOTE £1.40: £1.10, £2.40, £4.00; EX 4.80 Trifecta £39.60.
Owner Clipper Logistics **Bred** J Hanly **Trained** Newmarket, Suffolk

FOCUS
Stalls on stands' side. With Texting a non-runner and In Trutina underperforming, this took little winning, but Victory Day did it well in a fast time.

2591 EVERYBODY GET UP...TO BEVERLEY RACECOURSE H'CAP 2m
8:30 (8:34) (Class 5) (0-75,76) 4-Y-O+ **£4,528** (£1,347; £673; £336) **Stalls** High

Form RPR

1-11 **1** **Grey Mist**[11] [2217] 5-9-2 **67** 5ex ....(h) JasonHart 11 75
(Karen McLintock) *in tch: trckd ldrs over 7f out: rdn along over 3f out: led 2f out: in command 1f out: styd on pushed out fnl 110yds* **10/3**[2]

16-2 **2** *2 ¾* **Divin Bere (FR)**[18] [1981] 6-9-3 **68** ....(tp) DavidAllan 2 72
(Iain Jardine) *prom: led over 3f out: sn rdn: hdd 2f out: one pce fnl f* **9/2**[3]

20-2 **3** *¾* **So Near So Farhh**[31] [1663] 4-9-1 **67** .... CallumShepherd 10 70
(Mick Channon) *in tch: rdn to chse ldrs over 3f out: styd on* **8/1**

4U-0 **4** *nk* **Searching (IRE)**[11] [2185] 7-9-5 **70** .... ConnorBeasley 3 73
(Karen Tutty) *trckd ldrs: rdn over 3f out: styd on same pce* **33/1**

034- **5** *2 ½* **Wishing Well**[52] [8480] 7-9-0 **65** .... PaulMulrennan 9 65
(Micky Hammond) *hld up in rr: pushed along over 3f out: lot to do whn bit short of room 2f out: rdn and styd on wl fnl f: nrst fin* **18/1**

00-5 **6** *¾* **Ingleby Hollow**[13] [2092] 7-9-10 **75** ....(t) DanielTudhope 7 74
(David O'Meara) *hld up: gd hdwy 3f out: rdn 2f out: no ex ins fnl f* **6/1**

/50- **7** *2* **Prairie Town (IRE)**[34] [9128] 8-8-6 **57** ....(p) LukeMorris 1 54
(Tony Carroll) *hld up: rdn along over 3f out: sn outpcd and btn* **25/1**

4603 **8** *1 ¼* **Highway Robber**[18] [1981] 6-8-0 **56** oh11 ....(t) PaulaMuir(5) 6 51?
(Wilf Storey) *midfield: rdn over 3f out: sn outpcd and btn* **33/1**

0-12 **9** *shd* **Aphaea**[2] [2528] 4-8-11 **63** .... JamesSullivan 13 58
(Michael Easterby) *midfield: hdwy and trckd ldrs 4f out: rdn 3f out: wknd over 1f out (jockey said filly ran flat)* **11/4**[1]

102/ **10** *15* **Attention Seaker**[541] [8487] 9-9-0 **70** ....(t) DannyRedmond(5) 12 47
(Tim Easterby) *hld up in midfield: wknd 3f out* **33/1**

00-0 **11** *15* **Stormin Tom (IRE)**[14] [2080] 7-9-11 **76** .... RachelRichardson 5 35
(Tim Easterby) *led: rdn and hdd over 3f out: sn wknd* **20/1**

/00- **12** *23* **Only Orsenfoolsies**[55] [8901] 10-8-11 **62** .... TomEaves 8
(Micky Hammond) *hld up in midfield: wknd and bhd 5f out: sn t.o* **28/1**

15-0 **13** *1 ¼* **Leodis (IRE)**[31] [1663] 7-8-5 **56** oh1 .... AndrewMullen 4
(Micky Hammond) *trckd ldrs: rdn and lost pl over 7f out: wknd over 4f out: t.o fnl 3f* **50/1**

3m 33.31s (0.91) **Going Correction** +0.15s/f (Good)
WFA 4 from 5yo+ 1lb **13 Ran SP% 121.4**
Speed ratings (Par 103): **103,101,101,101,99 99,98,97,97,90 82,71,70**
CSF £17.53 CT £114.66 TOTE £4.20: £2.50, £1.90, £2.70; EX 21.40 Trifecta £64.30.
Owner Brian Chicken & Equiname Ltd **Bred** David Jamison Bloodstock And G Roddick **Trained** Ingoe, Northumberland

FOCUS
Actual race distance 2m12yds, and stalls on stands' side. Just a medium sort of gallop to this concluding stayers' handicap. The winner continues to progress and perhaps the fourth is the key.

T/Plt: £46.60 to a £1 stake. Pool: £51,117.36 - 799.59 winning units T/Qpdt: £11.90 to a £1 stake. Pool: £6,287.42 - 389.98 winning units **Andrew Sheret**

2513 WOLVERHAMPTON (A.W) (L-H)

Friday, May 10

OFFICIAL GOING: Tapeta: standard

Wind: light breeze Weather: overcast, quite mild

2592 MYRACING.COM FOR WOLVERHAMPTON TIPS H'CAP 5f 21y (Tp)

5:40 (5:40) (Class 6) (0-65,62) 3-Y-O

£3,105 (£924; £461; £400; £400; £400) Stalls Low

Form RPR

5005 1 **Superseded (IRE)**[11] [2211] 3-9-4 **59**.................. RobertWinston 4 66
(John Butler) *disp ld tl led 2f out: drvn in 1 l ld 1f out: rdn fnl f: r.o wl* **13/2**[3]

031 2 3/4 **Miss Enigma (IRE)**[11] [2211] 3-9-3 **61** 6ex..................(b) FinleyMarsh(3) 5 65
(Richard Hughes) *trckd ldrs: drvn to chse wnr over 1f out: 1 l 2nd 1f out: rdn fnl f: kpt on but a hld* **3/1**[1]

0024 3 1 1/2 **Sharrabang**[11] [2211] 3-9-5 **60**.................. CamHardie 9 59
(Stella Barclay) *hld up: drvn in 6th 2f out: hdwy on outer over 1f out: rdn and kpt on into 3rd fnl f* **8/1**

0233 4 1 3/4 **Sing Bertie (IRE)**[11] [2211] 3-8-5 **46**.................. PaddyMathers 3 39
(Derek Shaw) *mid-div: drvn over 2f out: rdn over 1f out: one pce fnl f* **4/1**[2]

3200 5 1/2 **Temple Of Wonder (IRE)**[4] [2474] 3-9-7 **62**..................(p) JackMitchell 11 53
(Charlie Wallis) *hld up in rr: rdn in last 1 1/2f out: r.o fnl f but nvr a threat* **15/2**

4402 6 3/4 **Wye Bother (IRE)**[11] [2211] 3-7-13 **47** ow2..................(t) AledBeech(7) 6 35
(Milton Bradley) *hld up: drvn 2f out: rdn over 1f out: no imp (jockey said filly hung left-handed)* **14/1**

633- 7 3 1/2 **Awarded**[198] [8533] 3-9-0 **55**.................. ShaneKelly 2 31
(Robert Cowell) *disp ld tl hdd 2f out: sn drvn: reminder and wknd over 1f out: eased fnl f* **8/1**

6-30 8 shd **Spiritually**[60] [1139] 3-9-1 **61**.................. DylanHogan(5) 8 36
(Chris Wall) *hld up: drvn over 2f out: rdn over 1f out: no imp: bled fr nose (vet said filly bled from the nose)* **20/1**

-235 9 1 1/2 **Empty Promises**[55] [1236] 3-9-7 **62**.................. LiamKeniry 1 32
(Frank Bishop) *hld up: pushed along over 1f out: reminders fnl f: no rspnse* **8/1**

4160 10 1/2 **Sister Of The Sign (IRE)**[11] [2211] 3-9-0 **60**.......... HarrisonShaw(5) 10 28
(James Given) *chsd ldrs on outer: drvn in 5th 2f out: rdn and wknd over 1f out (jockey said filly jumped right-handed leaving the stalls)* **28/1**

1m 1.34s (-0.56) **Going Correction** -0.10s/f (Stan) **10** Ran SP% **118.3**

Speed ratings (Par 97): **100,98,96,93,92 91,86,85,83,82**

CSF £26.72 CT £161.86 TOTE £7.40: £1.90, £1.60, £2.60; EX 30.30 Trifecta £182.30.

Owner Northumbria Leisure Ltd **Bred** Eimear Mulhern **Trained** Newmarket, Suffolk

FOCUS

A truly run handicap. The winner can at least match his previous best for this yard.

2593 EBC GROUP 30TH ANNIVERSARY H'CAP 1m 5f 219y (Tp)

6:10 (6:12) (Class 6) (0-60,60) 4-Y-O+

£3,105 (£924; £461; £400; £400; £400) Stalls Low

Form RPR

4-06 1 **Sacred Sprite**[46] [1331] 4-8-10 **54**.................. DylanHogan(5) 6 64+
(John Berry) *mid-div: drvn and hdwy on outer 3f out: wnt 3rd 2f out: rdn to ld over 1f out: 2 l clr 1f out: c further clr fnl f: comf* **16/1**

001 2 4 **Heron (USA)**[36] [1548] 5-9-7 **60**.................. TomQueally 3 64+
(Brett Johnson) *hld up: drvn and hdwy 2f out: rdn on outer and plenty to do 1 1/2f out: r.o wl into 2nd fnl f: nvr nr wnr* **5/2**[1]

-600 3 3 1/2 **The Wire Flyer**[20] [1958] 4-8-7 **46** oh1..................(p) KierenFox 8 46
(John Flint) *t.k.h: chsd ldrs on outer: hdwy to dispute ld 3f out: drvn into narrow ld 2f out: rdn 1 1/2f out: sn hdd: no ex fnl f but jst hld on for 3rd (jockey said gelding hung badly right-handed)* **40/1**

/5-0 4 shd **King Christophe (IRE)**[117] [232] 7-9-5 **58**.................. LiamKeniry 5 57
(Peter Fahey, Ire) *hld up: drvn and hdwy into 4th 2f out: rdn 1 1/2f out: one pce ex fnl f* **11/4**[2]

3300 5 3 **Hussar Ballad (USA)**[17] [2014] 10-8-11 **50**.................. CamHardie 1 45
(Antony Brittain) *mid-div on inner: drvn 3f out: rdn over 2f out: wnt 5th over 1f out: no ex fnl f (jockey said gelding was denied a clear run on the final bend)* **16/1**

0-40 6 1 3/4 **Incredible Dream (IRE)**[96] [589] 6-9-6 **59**..................(t[1]) TomMarquand 4 52
(Conrad Allen) *dwlt: bhd: drvn and effrt on outer 3f out: sn rdn: no ex* **20/1**

502- 7 1 3/4 **Champs Inblue**[162] [9318] 4-8-9 **48**.................. HarryBentley 11 40
(Chris Gordon) *led after 2f: drvn and jnd 3f out: hdd 2f out: sn rdn and wknd* **4/1**[3]

0/06 8 14 **Beau Knight**[17] [2014] 7-8-11 **50**.................. JackMitchell 9 23
(Alexandra Dunn) *hld up: pushed along over 2f out: nvr a factor* **20/1**

5601 9 hd **Oborne Lady (IRE)**[8] [2344] 6-9-0 **53** 5ex.................. RobHornby 2 25
(Seamus Mullins) *led 2f: trckd ldrs whn hdd: rdn and lost pl over 2f out: wknd and eased fr over 1f out* **11/2**

0320 10 2 1/4 **Shovel It On (IRE)**[13] [2111] 4-8-1 **47**..................(bt) SophieRalston(7) 10 17
(Steve Flook) *hld up on outer: drvn 3f out: sn rdn: no imp* **33/1**

060- 11 5 **Remember Nerja (IRE)**[55] [846] 5-8-7 **46** oh1..................(b) PhilipPrince 7 9
(Barry Leavy) *bhd: drvn in last 4f out: rdn 3f out: no rspnse* **125/1**

/00- 12 4 1/2 **Infiniti (IRE)**[30] [508] 6-8-7 **46** oh1..................(t) HayleyTurner 13 3
(Barry Leavy) *prom: pushed along 4f out: sn lost pl: dropped away over 2f out* **50/1**

00-0 13 27 **Kerrera**[17] [2014] 6-8-12 **51**..................(b[1]) ShaneKelly 12
(Paul Webber) *mid-div: rdn to take clsr order 5f out: wknd 4f out: heavily eased fr over 2f out (jockey said mare stopped quickly)* **25/1**

3m 1.82s (0.82) **Going Correction** -0.10s/f (Stan) **13** Ran SP% **123.9**

Speed ratings (Par 101): **93,90,88,88,86 85,84,76,76,75 72,70,54**

CSF £54.85 CT £1665.32 TOTE £12.40: £3.10, £1.70, £10.90; EX 71.80 Trifecta £2755.10.

Owner Kyan Yap **Bred** Raffles Dancers (NZ) Pty Ltd **Trained** Newmarket, Suffolk

FOCUS

A moderate handicap but the winner and third weren't exposed and the second arrived in good form.

2594 MYRACING.COM FREE TIPS EVERY DAY NOVICE STKS (PLUS 10 RACE) 6f 20y (Tp)

6:40 (6:44) (Class 4) 2-Y-O £4,787 (£1,424; £711; £355) Stalls Low

Form RPR

1 **Pinatubo (IRE)** 2-9-5 0.................. JamesDoyle 9 87+
(Charlie Appleby) *mid-div: pushed along 2f out: gd hdwy on outer over 1f out: reminder ent fnl f: qckml to ld 1/2f out: sn pushed clr: easily* **3/1**[2]

2 3 1/4 **Platinum Star (IRE)** 2-9-5 0.................. HarryBentley 5 77+
(Saeed bin Suroor) *slowly away: bhd: drvn and effrt on outer 2f out: hdwy over 1f out: rdn and drifted to inner ins fnl f: r.o wl: tk 2nd last two strides* **8/1**

3 hd **War Storm** 2-9-5 0.................. JackMitchell 2 77
(Archie Watson) *broke qckly to ld: pushed along in 1 1/2 l ld 2f out: drvn and lugged rt over 1f out: reminders ent fnl f: hdd 1/2f out: one pce: lost 2nd last two strides* **9/2**[3]

5 4 nk **Gobi Sunset**[13] [2108] 2-9-5 0.................. JoeFanning 3 76
(Mark Johnston) *prom: drvn in 1 1/2 l 2nd 2f out: no ex and lost two pls fnl f* **15/2**

4 5 1/2 **Dark Of Night (IRE)**[20] [1937] 2-9-5 0.................. PatCosgrave 8 74
(Saeed bin Suroor) *mid-div: pushed along in 6th 2f out: drvn to chse ldrs over 1f out: sn rdn: no ex fnl f* **9/4**[1]

4 6 1/2 **Ocasio Cortez (IRE)**[13] [2093] 2-9-0 0.................. TomMarquand 6 68
(Richard Hannon) *trckd ldrs: drvn 2f out: sn rdn and lost pl: no ex fnl f* **10/1**

7 4 **Genever Dragon (IRE)** 2-9-5 0.................. RichardKingscote 4 61
(Tom Dascombe) *chsd ldrs: drvn 2f out: lost pl 1 1/2f out: wknd fnl f* **16/1**

0 8 3 3/4 **Miss Chilli**[27] [1759] 2-9-0 0.................. CamHardie 13 45
(Michael Easterby) *hld up: drvn over 2f out: no imp* **125/1**

9 1 1/2 **Return To Senders (IRE)** 2-9-5 0.................. ShaneKelly 7 45
(Jamie Osborne) *hld up: reminders 1 1/2f out: no rspnse: eased fnl f (jockey said colt hung left-handed throughout)* **28/1**

0 10 1 **Percy Green (IRE)**[22] [1887] 2-9-0 0.................. HarrisonShaw(5) 12 42
(K R Burke) *prom on outer: drvn and lost pl 2f out: sn wknd* **33/1**

11 8 **Sea The Spirit** 2-9-5 0.................. TomQueally 1 18
(Mike Murphy) *slowly away: a bhd* **50/1**

1m 14.18s (-0.32) **Going Correction** -0.10s/f (Stan) **11** Ran SP% **120.9**

Speed ratings (Par 95): **98,93,93,92 91,86,81,79,78 67**

CSF £27.69 TOTE £3.50: £1.50, £2.30, £2.20; EX 27.40 Trifecta £122.40.

Owner Godolphin **Bred** Godolphin **Trained** Newmarket, Suffolk

FOCUS

One of the first juvenile 6f races of the year, and an interesting novice run at a fair pace. The winner can go forward from this.

2595 FOLLOW@MYRACINGTIPS ON TWITTER H'CAP 1m 4f 51y (Tp)

7:10 (7:11) (Class 6) (0-60,60) 4-Y-O+

£3,105 (£924; £461; £400; £400; £400) Stalls Low

Form RPR

3520 1 **Rail Dancer**[55] [1235] 7-8-13 **59**..................(v) GavinAshton(7) 4 75
(Shaun Keightley) *hld up: hdwy into 3rd gng wl 3f out: disp ld 2f out: sn led: pushed into 3 l ld over 1f out: reminder and readily c further clr fnl f: easily (trainer said regarding apparent improvement in form compared that the gelding was better suited by the slower pace on this occasion which helped the gelding get the one mile four furlong trip)* **10/1**

05-2 2 7 **Givepeaceachance**[46] [1334] 4-9-3 **56**.................. PatCosgrave 12 62+
(Denis Coakley) *bhd: hdwy 4f out: drvn 3f out: wnt 4th 2f out: chsd wnr and rdn over 1f out: one pce and position accepted fnl f* **10/3**[1]

000 3 7 **Sunshineandbubbles**[8] [2345] 6-9-7 **60**..................(v) JoeFanning 2 54
(Jennie Candlish) *hld up: drvn and effrt on outer over 2f out: rdn over 1f out: styd on fnl f: tk 3rd last stride* **14/1**

4340 4 nse **Foxrush Take Time (FR)**[10] [2234] 4-8-7 **46** oh1..........(e) PhilipPrince 5 40
(Richard Guest) *hld up: drvn over 2f out: hdwy 1 1/2f out: kpt on fnl f: denied for 3rd last stride* **12/1**

1051 5 1 1/4 **Tigerfish (IRE)**[9] [2283] 5-9-4 **57** 5ex..................(p) ShaneKelly 3 49
(William Stone) *trckd ldrs: rdn in 3rd 2f out: wknd over 1f out* **15/2**

143- 6 1 **Howardian Hills (IRE)**[206] [8300] 6-9-4 **57**..................(p) RobertWinston 9 47
(Victor Dartnall) *mid-div: hdwy to go prom after 5f: led over 5f out: drvn and jnd by wnr 2f out: sn hdd and rdn: wknd fnl f* **5/1**[2]

460 7 3/4 **Raashdy (IRE)**[18] [1988] 6-9-3 **56**..................(b) LiamKeniry 1 45
(Peter Hiatt) *hld up: pushed along and hdwy on outer 3f out: rdn in 5th 2f out: wknd over 1f out* **12/1**

0-50 8 10 **Zenith One (IRE)**[25] [1826] 4-9-6 **59**..................(t) TomQueally 8 32
(Seamus Durack) *t.k.h: in rr: effrt over 2f out: sn rdn: no imp* **11/2**[3]

00-0 9 3 3/4 **Billiebrookedit (IRE)**[17] [2012] 4-8-8 **47**.................. RoystonFfrench 6 14
(Steph Hollinshead) *hld up: last 3f out: sn rdn: no rspnse* **50/1**

500- 10 3 1/4 **Genuine Approval (IRE)**[206] [8300] 6-9-5 **58**..................(t w) JackMitchell 7 20
(John Butler) *led: hdd after 3f: sn trckd ldrs: lost pl 3f out: wknd* **16/1**

-400 11 5 **Foxy's Spirit**[10] [2234] 4-8-7 **46** oh1.................. JoeyHaynes 11
(Clare Hobson) *prom: drvn and lost pl 3f out: sn rdn and dropped away (jockey said filly hung left-handed)* **50/1**

1335 12 1 **Tesorina (IRE)**[38] [1498] 4-9-3 **56**..................(v) HarryBentley 10 8
(William Knight) *prom: led after 3f: hdd over 5f out: drvn and lost pl over 3f out: wknd* **13/2**

2m 37.05s (-3.75) **Going Correction** -0.10s/f (Stan) **12** Ran SP% **121.2**

Speed ratings (Par 101): **108,103,98,98,97 97,96,89,87,85 81,81**

CSF £44.24 CT £481.32 TOTE £10.40: £2.90, £1.50, £3.40; EX 71.00 Trifecta £821.10.

Owner Simon Lockyer **Bred** Scuderia Blueberry SRL **Trained** Newmarket, Suffolk

FOCUS

An open handicap run at a steady pace. The winner bounced back to his old form and there were big gaps between the first three.

2596 MYRACING.COM FOR DAILY TIPS H'CAP 1m 142y (Tp)

7:40 (7:41) (Class 5) (0-70,73) 4-Y-O+

£3,752 (£1,116; £557; £400; £400; £400) Stalls Low

Form RPR

0400 1 **Nezar (IRE)**[32] [1655] 8-9-0 **69**.................. SophieRalston(7) 8 81
(Dean Ivory) *hld up: pushed along and hdwy on outer 2f out: qckml to ld over 1f out: sn clr: 3 l ld 1f out: reminders but nvr in danger fnl f (jockey said gelding hung left-handed)* **12/1**

0531 2 1 3/4 **Fire Diamond**[11] [2193] 6-9-11 **73** 5ex..................(p) RichardKingscote 7 80
(Tom Dascombe) *hld up: drvn and hdwy on outer 1 1/2f out: sn rdn: wnt 2nd ent fnl f: r.o but nvr nr wnr* **4/1**[2]

-513 3 1 1/2 **Lothario**[44] [1355] 5-9-5 **67**.................. RobertWinston 4 71
(Dean Ivory) *mid-div on inner: n.m.r 2f out: drvn and squeezed through into 3rd on inner over 1f out: one pce fnl f* **15/8**[1]

5055 4 nk **Arlecchino's Leap**[13] [2124] 7-9-4 **66**..................(p) FergusSweeney 9 70
(Mark Usher) *mid-div: nt clr run fr over 1 1/2f out: in clr: drvn and r.o wl fnl f: clsng nr fin (jockey said gelding was denied a clear run)* **22/1**

-101 5 3 **International Law**[38] [1511] 5-9-10 **72**.................. CamHardie 2 68
(Antony Brittain) *chsd ldrs: pushed along on inner 2f out: trckd ldrs 1 1/2f out: drvn and nt clr run 1f out and ins fnl f: reminder and kpt on nr fin (jockey said gelding was denied a clear run)* **11/2**[3]

0-00 6 shd **Deadly Accurate**[45] 1343 4-9-1 63 .... LiamKeniry 6 59
(Roy Brotherton) prom: pushed into ld 2f out: drvn and hdd over 1f out: sn rdn: wknd fnl f **100/1**

62-1 7 1/2 **Toriano**[65] 1042 6-8-13 68 .... AledBeech(7) 5 63
(Nick Littmoden) chsd ldrs: gng wl enough 2f out: drvn and lost pl 1 1/2f out: sn rdn and wknd **9/1**

2460 8 3/4 **Zorawar (FR)**[15] 2056 5-9-5 67 ....(p) ShaneGray 10 71+
(David O'Meara) hld up: looking for room over 1f out: no ch whn hmpd ins fnl f (jockey said that the gelding had been denied a clear run; jockey said regarding running and riding that the gelding needs cover in his races he had attempted to make a run towards the inside of the field, where he was repeatedly denied a clear run, and **12/1**

0006 9 4 **Rosarno (IRE)**[17] 2019 5-8-11 59 .... JoeyHaynes 3 43
(Paul Howling) in rr: drvn 1 1/2f out: no rspnse **40/1**

0023 10 nk **Adventureman**[17] 2012 7-8-6 57 ....(b) JaneElliott(3) 1 40
(Ruth Carr) broke wl: led: drvn 3f out: rdn and hdd 2f out: wkng whn hmpd over 1f out (jockey said gelding suffered interference in running) **10/1**

5033 11 1 1/4 **Street Poet (IRE)**[18] 1983 6-8-13 61 ....(p) PhilDennis 12 41
(Michael Herrington) prom: drvn on outer over 2f out: lost pl 1 1/2f out: sn rdn and wknd **17/2**

1m 48.16s (-1.94) **Going Correction** -0.10s/f (Stan) 11 Ran SP% **122.9**
Speed ratings (Par 103): **104,102,101,100,98 98,97,96,93,93 92**
CSF £61.74 CT £135.67 TOTE £14.40: £3.50, £1.70, £1.30; EX 84.00 Trifecta £431.30.
Owner Mrs Doreen Carter **Bred** Edgeridge Ltd And Glenvale Stud **Trained** Radlett, Herts

FOCUS
A fair handicap and decent form for the grade, the 1-2 coming from the rear.

2597 MYRACING.COM FREE BETS AND TIPS H'CAP 1m 142y (Tp)
8:10 (8:10) (Class 6) (0-65,71) 3-Y-O
£3,105 (£924; £461; £400; £400; £400) **Stalls Low**

Form RPR

1211 1 **Capofaro**[8] 2350 3-9-8 66 6ex .... NicolaCurrie 4 72
(Jamie Osborne) prom: pushed along to dispute ld 2f out: drvn into narrow ld ent fnl f: sn rdn and shifted rt: qckly stened and r.o wl: asserted nr fin **7/2**[2]

60-3 2 nk **In The Cove (IRE)**[10] 2238 3-9-7 65 .... TomMarquand 7 70
(Richard Hannon) led: pushed along and jnd by wnr 2f out: rdn 1 1/2f out: hdd ent fnl f: handed ch as wnr shifted rt: r.o u.p: no ex as wnr asserted nr fin **9/1**

50-1 3 1 1/2 **Filles De Fleur**[10] 2238 3-9-13 71 6ex .... HarryBentley 1 73
(George Scott) trckd ldrs: pushed along in 3rd 2f out: sn drvn: rdn over 1f out: kpt on fnl f **9/1**

4436 4 nk **Kingdom Of Dubai (FR)**[17] 2021 3-9-7 65 ....(b[1]) JackMitchell 8 66
(Roger Varian) in rr: hdwy on outer over 2f out: sn drvn: rdn in 4th over 1f out: kpt on fnl f: jst denied for 3rd nr fin **3/1**[1]

50-4 5 1 1/4 **Swiss Peak**[17] 2021 3-9-3 61 .... HayleyTurner 6 60
(Michael Bell) hld up: drvn on inner 1 1/2f out: rdn in 5th over 1f out: one pce fnl f **6/1**

-031 6 1 1/2 **Medoras Childe**[28] 1725 3-9-0 58 ....(h) CharlesBishop 9 53
(Heather Main) trckd ldrs: drvn and lost pl 1 1/2f out: no ex **20/1**

5040 7 1 1/4 **Trouble Shooter (IRE)**[17] 2007 3-8-3 47 ....(v) CamHardie 2 40
(Shaun Keightley) hld up: drvn 1 1/2f out: rdn over 1f out: no imp **12/1**

46-1 8 nk **Anna Bunina (FR)**[18] 1980 3-9-7 65 .... JackGarritty 3 57
(Jedd O'Keeffe) prom and t.k.h early: sn hld up: pushed along in last 2f out: drvn 1 1/2f out: no imp **4/1**[3]

00-0 9 10 **Swiss Miss**[14] 2077 3-8-6 50 .... RoystonFfrench 5 21
(John Gallagher) hld up: sltly hmpd 2f out: sn wknd (jockey said filly hung right-handed) **100/1**

1m 50.72s (0.62) **Going Correction** -0.10s/f (Stan) 9 Ran SP% **115.0**
Speed ratings (Par 97): **93,92,91,91,90 88,87,87,78**
CSF £34.77 CT £262.51 TOTE £4.90: £1.80, £2.10, £3.10; EX 36.00 Trifecta £193.60.
Owner Michael Buckley **Bred** Cheveley Park Stud Ltd **Trained** Upper Lambourn, Berks

FOCUS
A fair race for the grade with four last-time-out winners in the field of nine. The first two home were always in front and the winner continues to thrive.

2598 SKY SPORTS RACING VIRGIN 535 NOVICE STKS 7f 36y (Tp)
8:40 (8:41) (Class 5) 3-Y-O+ **£3,752** (£1,116; £557; £278) **Stalls High**

Form RPR

5-3 1 **Jilbaab**[12] 2140 3-9-2 0 .... JoeFanning 4 77
(Brian Meehan) trckd ldrs: pushed along 2f out: reminder over 1f out: hdwy to chal between horses 1f out: pushed into ld wl ins fnl f: sn clr: readily **12/1**

2-1 2 1 **Jalaad (IRE)**[13] 2094 4-10-2 0 .... ThomasGreatrex(5) 2 86+
(Saeed bin Suroor) led: jnd 4f out: pushed along 2f out: drvn into ld over 1f out: rdn and hdd wl ins fnl f: no ex **5/6**[1]

656- 3 1 **Jojo (IRE)**[223] 7749 3-8-4 70 .... GeorgiaDobie(7) 8 67
(Jo Hughes, France) hld up: drvn in 5th 1 1/2f out: sn rdn: hdwy fnl f: r.o into 3rd last 25yds **80/1**

55 4 1/2 **Huddle**[30] 1676 3-8-11 0 .... HarryBentley 5 66
(William Knight) mid-div: rdn in 4th over 1f out: kpt on fnl f **66/1**

5 3 1/4 **Baraajeel** 3-9-2 0 .... TomMarquand 6 62+
(Owen Burrows) t.k.h: prom disp ld 4f out: pushed along 2f out: drvn 1 1/2f out: reminder and hdd over 1f out: wknd fnl f **9/4**[2]

30 6 7 **Lady Schannell (IRE)**[24] 1838 3-8-11 0 .... NicolaCurrie 7 38
(Marco Botti) hld up: drvn 2f out: sn lost tch (jockey said filly was outpaced throughout) **66/1**

1- P **Youthful**[170] 9183 3-9-9 0 .... HayleyTurner 3
(Michael Bell) trckd ldrs tl lost action and dropped to rr after 1f: sn p.u: lame (vet said gelding was lame right hind) **9/2**[3]

1m 28.17s (-0.63) **Going Correction** -0.10s/f (Stan) 7 Ran SP% **115.4**
WFA 3 from 4yo 12lb
Speed ratings (Par 103): **99,97,96,96,92 84,**
CSF £23.33 TOTE £12.60: £4.10, £1.10; EX 27.70 Trifecta £326.70.
Owner Hamdan Al Maktoum **Bred** Sand Dancer Partnership **Trained** Manton, Wilts

FOCUS
A fair contest. It seems a much improved effort from the winner, but the form is a bit shaky.
T/Plt: £149.50 to a £1 stake. Pool: £54,812.02 - 267.61 winning units T/Qpdt: £27.00 to a £1 stake. Pool: £7,078.37 - 193.58 winning units **Keith McHugh**

2599 - 2604a (Foreign Racing) - See Raceform Interactive

1959
CORK (R-H)
Friday, May 10

OFFICIAL GOING: Good

2605a GOFFS IRISH EBF POLONIA STKS (LISTED RACE) (FILLIES) 5f 110y
8:35 (8:38) 3-Y-O
£31,891 (£10,270; £4,864; £2,162; £1,081; £540) **Stalls Centre**

RPR

1 **Lethal Promise (IRE)**[228] 7632 3-9-0 100 ....(h) WJLee 11 102+
(W McCreery, Ire) in tch nr side: hdwy travelling wl after 1/2-way to chal 1 1/2f out: rdn to ld fr 1f out and kpt on wl clsng stages **6/1**[3]

2 1 1/4 **Servalan (IRE)**[222] 7813 3-9-0 96 .... ShaneFoley 7 97
(Mrs John Harrington, Ire) in tch far side: prog to chal on terms briefly 1 1/2f out: sn rdn in 2nd and no imp on wnr wl ins fnl f: kpt on wl **14/1**

3 1 **Nitro Boost (IRE)**[11] 2221 3-9-0 84 .... OisinOrr 12 94
(W McCreery, Ire) chsd ldrs nr side: rdn 2f out and no imp on ldrs ins fnl f: kpt on wl into 3rd nr fin **33/1**

4 nk **Rainbow Moonstone (IRE)**[12] 2156 3-9-0 93 ...... DeclanMcDonogh 14 93
(Joseph Patrick O'Brien, Ire) hld up towards rr nr side: hdwy nr side 1 1/2f out where swtchd lft and rdn: r.o u.p into 4th wl ins fnl f: nvr on terms **12/1**

5 3/4 **Forever In Dreams (IRE)**[324] 3995 3-9-0 98 .... RonanWhelan 9 91
(Aidan F Fogarty, Ire) on toes befhand: hooded to load: chsd ldrs: rdn 1 1/2f out and no imp on wnr ins fnl f where swtchd rt: kpt on same pce **16/1**

6 1/2 **Gossamer Wings (USA)**[223] 7771 3-9-0 106 .... SeamieHeffernan 1 89
(A P O'Brien, Ire) dwlt: towards rr: gng wl after 1/2-way and sme hdwy far side 1 1/2f out where swtchd rt: no imp on ldrs under hands and heels ins fnl f: one pce nr fin **7/2**[2]

7 3 **Chestnut Express (IRE)**[12] 2156 3-9-0 78 ....(t) ChrisHayes 4 79
(D J Bunyan, Ire) towards rr: tk clsr order far side after 1/2-way: no imp on ldrs under hands and heels in 7th ins fnl f: one pce clsng stages **50/1**

8 3 1/4 **Cava (IRE)**[12] 2156 3-9-0 100 .... DonnachaO'Brien 2 68
(Joseph Patrick O'Brien, Ire) chsd ldrs early tl sn settled towards rr: rdn far side after 1/2-way where tk clsr order and no ex over 1f out: one pce in 8th ins fnl f **9/4**[1]

9 1 1/4 **Fantasy (IRE)**[41] 1434 3-9-0 89 .... WayneLordan 6 64
(A P O'Brien, Ire) disp ld early tl sn led narrowly: drvn far side under 2f out and sn jnd: hdd 1f out and wknd qckly **25/1**

10 1 1/4 **Angelic Light (IRE)**[41] 1434 3-9-0 96 ....(p) LeighRoche 3 60
(M D O'Callaghan, Ire) led and disp far side early: pushed along in 2nd at 1/2-way and wknd 1 1/2f out: sn eased (jockey said that his mount didn't handle the ground) **12/1**

11 shd **Bailly**[244] 7090 3-9-0 89 .... ColinKeane 5 60
(G M Lyons, Ire) in rr of mid-div far side early: tk clsr order briefly after 1/2-way: pushed along and wknd over 1f out: sn eased **16/1**

12 shd **Chicago May (IRE)**[12] 2156 3-9-0 90 .... DonaghO'Connor 13 59
(G M Lyons, Ire) dwlt and sltly awkward s: in rr nr side: drvn and no imp after 1/2-way: kpt on one pce ins fnl f: nvr a factor **16/1**

13 nk **Shumookhi (IRE)**[21] 1913 3-9-0 0 ....(p) GaryCarroll 10 58
(Archie Watson) chsd ldrs nr side: rdn after 1/2-way and sn wknd **12/1**

14 2 3/4 **Zodiacus (IRE)**[11] 2219 3-9-0 0 .... ConorMaxwell 8 49
(T G McCourt, Ire) dwlt sltly: pushed along briefly and sn chsd ldrs down centre: drvn and wknd 2f out: eased ins fnl f **50/1**

1m 5.66s 14 Ran SP% **125.4**
Pick Six: Not won. Pool of 4,062.68 carried forward. Tote Aggregate: 2019: 80,981 - 2018: N/A
CSF £88.69 TOTE £6.90: £1.70, £3.90, £8.80; DF 82.20 Trifecta £722.50.
Owner I N S Racing **Bred** Irish National Stud **Trained** Rathbride, Co Kildare

FOCUS
A result to savour for Willie McCreery, as his smart juvenile filly \bLethal Promise\p stepped forward as a three-year-old to land this Listed sprint. His other representative \bNitro Boost\p ran a cracker in third. The first five home were drawn 11, 7, 12, 14 and 9.
T/Jkpt: Not won. T/Plt: @1,345.00. Pool: @20,136.81 **Brian Fleming**

2565
ASCOT (R-H)
Saturday, May 11

OFFICIAL GOING: Good to soft (soft in places on round course; str 7.2, rnd 6.3)
Wind: Moderate, across Weather: Fine but cloudy

2606 LES AMBASSADEURS CASINO H'CAP 1m 3f 211y
2:15 (2:16) (Class 3) (0-95,97) 4-Y-O+ **£16,172** (£4,812; £2,405; £1,202) **Stalls Low**

Form RPR

212- 1 **Sextant**[246] 7010 4-9-4 89 .... LouisSteward 8 101+
(Sir Michael Stoute) patiently rdn: hld up in last: prog on outer over 2f out: swept into the ld over 1f out: rdn out and styd on wl **7/1**[3]

220- 2 3 1/4 **Blue Laureate**[259] 6548 4-9-4 89 .... BenCurtis 3 94
(Ian Williams) hld up in tch: rdn 3f out: prog u.p over 1f out: tk 2nd last 100yds: no threat to wnr **10/1**

4612 3 nk **Eddystone Rock (IRE)**[17] 2032 7-9-4 89 .... KierenFox 5 93
(John Best) rousted to get gng: chsd ldrs: rdn whn n.m.r briefly over 2f out: sn outpcd: kpt on u.p to take 3rd last 100yds (jockey said gelding was denied a clear run) **9/1**

21/1 4 1 1/4 **Setting Sail**[19] 1989 4-9-11 96 .... WilliamBuick 4 98
(Charlie Appleby) t.k.h: pressed ldr: led over 6f out: stl looked to be gng strly over 2f out: rdn and hdd over 1f out: wknd ins fnl f **6/4**[1]

14-4 5 1/2 **Autumn War (IRE)**[14] 2095 4-9-2 87 .... TomMarquand 2 89
(Charles Hills) t.k.h: prom: trckd ldr 1/2-way: rdn over 3f out: lost 2nd over 1f out: racd awkwardly and wknd fnl f **7/1**[3]

210- 6 6 **Now Children (IRE)**[182] 9005 5-9-12 97 .... AdamKirby 6 89
(Clive Cox) wl in tch: chsd ldng pair 5f out: rdn and hanging over 2f out: dropped away tamely (jockey said gelding hung right-handed in the straight) **11/4**[2]

105/ 7 83 **Boite (IRE)**[64] 8892 9-9-3 88 .... RobertWinston 1
(Warren Greatrex) led to over 6f out: sn wknd: t.o **50/1**

2m 37.12s (4.52) **Going Correction** +0.40s/f (Good) 7 Ran SP% **112.7**
Speed ratings (Par 107): **100,97,97,96,96 92,37**
CSF £69.23 CT £630.92 TOTE £6.20: £2.70, £4.30; EX 71.10 Trifecta £253.30.
Owner The Queen **Bred** The Queen **Trained** Newmarket, Suffolk

FOCUS
The track was set up at its widest configuration and race distances were as advertised. Stalls: 5F: stands' side. Remainder of Straight Course races: Centre. Round Course: Inside. The going was good to soft in the straight (GoingStick 7.2) and good to soft, soft in places on the Round course (GoingStick 6.3). A good handicap and a nice performance from the winner, who looks set to return for the Royal meeting. The form's best rated around the second and third.

2607 CAREY GROUP BUCKHOUNDS STKS (LISTED RACE) 1m 3f 211y
2:50 (2:50) (Class 1) 4-Y-O+ £25,519 (£9,675; £4,842; £2,412) Stalls Low

Form RPR
360- 1 **Salouen (IRE)**^{153} [9473] 5-9-0 117 ... OisinMurphy 2 114
(Sylvester Kirk) *mde all: set mod pce tl kicked on 4f out: pushed clr over 2f out: rdn and drew further ahd over 1f out* **4/6**^{1}
000- 2 7 **What About Carlo (FR)**^{157} [9399] 8-9-0 100 ... CharlesBishop 3 103
(Eve Johnson Houghton) *hld up in last: wnt 3rd over 3f out: sn shkn up: no ch w wnr but kpt on to take modest 2nd nr fin* **14/1**^{3}
542- 3 nk **Barsanti (IRE)**^{225} [7737] 7-9-0 111 ... WilliamBuick 4 102
(Roger Varian) *trckd wnr: cl enough and pushed along 3f out: readily lft bhd over 2f out: lost modest 2nd nr fin* **13/8**^{2}
30/U 4 45 **Pilansberg**^{28} [1750] 7-9-0 108 ... (b) MeganNicholls 1 30
(Mark Gillard) *chsd ldng pair to over 3f out: wknd rapidly and eased: t.o* **66/1**

2m 38.0s (5.40) **Going Correction** +0.40s/f (Good) **4** Ran SP% **106.2**
Speed ratings (Par 111): **98,93,93,63**
CSF £9.43 TOTE £1.60; EX 9.10 Trifecta £7.50.
Owner H Balasuriya **Bred** Silvercon Edgerodge Ltd **Trained** Upper Lambourn, Berks

FOCUS
This proved fairly straightforward for the favourite, who dominated throughout. He reversed last year's form in this with the third.

2608 ST. JAMES'S PLACE WEALTH MANAGEMENT BRITISH EBF PREMIER FILLIES' H'CAP 1m (S)
3:25 (3:26) (Class 2) 3-Y-O+
£28,012 (£8,388; £4,194; £2,097; £1,048; £526) Stalls Centre

Form RPR
0-03 1 **Bubble And Squeak**^{11} [2230] 4-8-10 87 ... JasonWatson 4 96
(Sylvester Kirk) *hld up but wl in tch: pushed along to cl on ldrs over 2f out: brought between rivals to chal fnl f: rdn to ld last 80yds: hld on* **14/1**
11-0 2 shd **Contrive (IRE)**^{21} [1941] 4-9-0 91 ... WilliamBuick 1 99
(Roger Varian) *trckd ldr: led over 3f out: rdn 2f out: hdd last 80yds: kpt on wl: jst denied* **11/1**
2-26 3 1 ½ **Red Starlight**^{28} [1753] 4-9-9 100 ... TomMarquand 2 105
(Richard Hannon) *wl in tch: prog to press ldr 3f out: rdn to chal 2f out: nt qckn and lost 2nd fnl f: kpt on* **4/1**^{2}
24-5 4 1 ¾ **Model Guest**^{10} [2268] 3-8-3 93 ... DavidEgan 6 91
(George Margarson) *wl in tch: on terms w ldrs and rdn over 2f out: nt qckn over 1f out: grad fdd* **20/1**
101- 5 hd **Bella Ragazza**^{217} [7984] 4-9-5 96 ... AdamKirby 5 97
(Hughie Morrison) *t.k.h: hld up in last but wl in tch: pushed along 3f out: no imp on ldrs 2f out: kpt on same pce after* **11/4**^{1}
50-1 6 1 ¼ **Daddies Girl (IRE)**^{11} [2252] 4-8-5 87 ... TheodoreLadd$^{(5)}$ 10 85
(Rod Millman) *wl in tch on nr side of gp: hanging whn rdn over 2f out: no prog and btn wl over 1f out* **4/1**^{2}
06-0 7 2 ½ **Existential (IRE)**^{11} [2252] 4-8-6 83 ... JoeFanning 7 75
(Clive Cox) *t.k.h: cl up tl lost pl steadily fr 3f out* **12/1**
300- 8 4 **Adorable (IRE)**^{231} [7566] 4-9-10 101 ... OisinMurphy 3 84
(William Haggas) *taken down early: led to over 3f out: steadily fdd* **6/1**^{3}
40-3 9 18 **Labrega**^{16} [2064] 4-8-9 86 ... BenCurtis 9 27
(Hugo Palmer) *t.k.h: cl up tl wknd over 3f out: t.o (trainer's rep said that the filly was unsuited by the going, which was officially described as Good to Soft on this occasion, which in their opinion was holding)* **12/1**

1m 42.72s (1.32) **Going Correction** +0.40s/f (Good)
WFA 3 from 4yo 13lb **9** Ran SP% **116.1**
Speed ratings (Par 96): **109,108,107,105,105 104,101,97,79**
CSF £157.16 CT £736.51 TOTE £13.60: £2.90, £3.10, £1.60; EX 170.60 Trifecta £785.90.
Owner Chris Wright,Holly Wright,Chloe Forsyth **Bred** Stratford Place Stud **Trained** Upper Lambourn, Berks

FOCUS
This had the look of a good-quality fillies' handicap beforehand, but with three of the four market leaders disappointing it raises a question. The pace was a fair one. The third helps with the standard.

2609 TOTE VICTORIA CUP (HERITAGE H'CAP) 7f
4:00 (4:02) (Class 2) 4-Y-O+
£65,362 (£19,572; £9,786; £4,893; £2,446; £1,228) Stalls Centre

Form RPR
220- 1 **Cape Byron**^{217} [7977] 5-9-3 103 ... AndreaAtzeni 10 113
(Roger Varian) *hld up bhd ldrs: gng strly over 2f out: prog wl over 1f out: rdn to ld jst ins fnl f: styd on wl and a holding on* **8/1**^{2}
65-2 2 nk **Kynren (IRE)**^{42} [1415] 5-8-12 98 ... RobertWinston 22 107
(David Barron) *hld up wl in tch: shkn up and prog 2f out: rdn to chal ins fnl f: styd on to take 2nd last strides* **7/1**^{1}
6-02 3 hd **Kaeso**^{14} [2116] 5-8-1 87 ... HollieDoyle 4 95
(Nigel Tinkler) *racd on outer early: pressed ldr: chal over 1f out: upsides jst ins fnl f: styd on but a jst hld by wnr after: lost 2nd last strides* **14/1**
016- 4 1 ¼ **Raising Sand**^{203} [8409] 7-9-3 103 ... NicolaCurrie 26 108+
(Jamie Osborne) *hld up wl in rr: rdn over 2f out: prog jst over 1f out on nr side of gp: r.o wl to take 4th nr fin: too late* **16/1**
0-50 5 1 **Ripp Orf (IRE)**^{28} [1753] 5-8-9 95 ... HayleyTurner 16 97
(David Elsworth) *hld up towards rr: shkn up over 2f out: prog and angled rt wl over 1f out: chsd ldrs ins fnl f: one pce last 100yds* **10/1**
214- 6 hd **Blue Mist**^{207} [8299] 4-8-11 97 ... JasonWatson 23 99
(Roger Charlton) *hld up towards rr: shkn up and prog on nr side of gp wl over 1f out: styd on fnl f but nt pce to chal* **8/1**^{2}
0-01 7 1 **Kimifive (IRE)**^{7} [2402] 4-8-7 93 ... ShaneKelly 14 92
(Joseph Tuite) *in tch in midfield: rdn over 2f out: styd on fnl f but unable to threaten* **18/1**
410- 8 ½ **Glorious Journey**^{217} [8012] 4-9-9 109 ... WilliamBuick 18 107
(Charlie Appleby) *cl up bhd ldrs: rdn 2f out: and nt qckn wl over 1f out: fdd last 100yds (jockey said gelding ran too free)* **9/1**^{3}
0-54 9 nk **Hajjam**^{8} [2378] 5-8-7 93 ... CamHardie 8 90
(David O'Meara) *towards rr: rdn over 2f out: no prog tl styd on fnl f: nvr nrr* **25/1**
0-41 10 nse **Lake Volta (IRE)**^{11} [2260] 4-8-12 98 ... JoeFanning 19 95
(Mark Johnston) *led: rdn 2f out: hdd and fdd jst ins fnl f* **16/1**
00-0 11 shd **Qaysar (FR)**^{31} [1694] 4-8-7 93 ... TomMarquand 9 90
(Richard Hannon) *towards rr: rdn 2f out: carried rt over 1f out: kpt on fnl f but n.d* **20/1**
2245 12 1 ½ **Gallipoli (IRE)**^{8} [2378] 6-8-5 91 ... (b) PaddyMathers 11 84
(Richard Fahey) *taken down early: cl up bhd ldrs: rdn 2f out: wknd jst over 1f out* **66/1**
30-0 13 nk **George Of Hearts (FR)**^{28} [1753] 4-8-4 90 ... (p^{1}) DavidEgan 27 82
(Richard Hughes) *t.k.h early: prom: lost pl 1/2-way: tried to make prog again over 1f out: one pce* **14/1**
16-0 14 1 ¼ **Zap**^{23} [1891] 4-8-5 96 ... ConnorMurtagh$^{(5)}$ 17 84
(Richard Fahey) *cl up bhd ldrs tl wknd over 1f out* **33/1**
-341 15 1 ¼ **Sanaadh**^{63} [1097] 6-8-9 95 ... (t) ConnorBeasley 20 80
(Michael Wigham) *dwlt: hld up in last: rdn and prog into midfield over 1f out: no hdwy after* **20/1**
01-0 16 nk **Alemaratalyoum (IRE)**^{25} [1829] 5-8-10 96 ... (t) OisinMurphy 24 80
(Stuart Williams) *t.k.h: cl up bhd ldrs tl wknd over 1f out* **25/1**
13-3 17 ½ **Presidential (IRE)**^{23} [1891] 5-8-4 90 ... BenCurtis 25 73
(Roger Fell) *awkward s: wl in rr: sme prog wl over 1f out: no hdwy fnl f* **10/1**
-220 18 1 ¾ **Straight Right (FR)**^{22} [1922] 5-9-5 105 ... (h) SilvestreDeSousa 2 83
(Andrew Balding) *racd on outer of gp: nvr beyond midfield: struggling over 2f out* **20/1**
15-0 19 shd **Taurean Star (IRE)**^{63} [1097] 6-8-3 89 ... JosephineGordon 21 67
(Ralph Beckett) *wl in rr: rdn and no prog over 2f out: styd on last 150yds* **33/1**
0-53 20 hd **Nicholas T**^{7} [2419] 7-7-11 86 oh1 ... JaneElliott$^{(3)}$ 3 63
(Jim Goldie) *awkward to post: stdd s: hld up in rr and racd on outer of gp: wl btn 2f out* **40/1**
1303 21 shd **Cardsharp**^{14} [2109] 4-9-8 108 ... JFEgan 15 85
(Mark Johnston) *anticipated s and slowly away: nvr able to make significant prog (gelding anticipated the start and hit the gates and was slow to stride)* **33/1**
0-43 22 6 **Green Power**^{25} [1829] 4-8-11 97 ... TomQueally 1 58
(John Gallagher) *chsd ldrs: u.p over 2f out: sn wknd* **33/1**
0-00 23 1 ¼ **Comin' Through (AUS)**^{79} [846] 5-9-10 110 ... (b) HarryBentley 12 67
(George Scott) *racd on outer of gp: nvr on terms w ldrs: wknd 2f out* **66/1**
4010 24 3 ½ **Above The Rest (IRE)**^{22} [1922] 8-9-2 105 ... (h) JoshuaBryan$^{(3)}$ 5 53
(David Barron) *chsd ldrs on outer of gp tl wknd qckly 2f out* **50/1**
410- 25 6 **Via Serendipity**^{224} [7773] 5-8-12 98 ... (t) CharlesBishop 6 30
(Stuart Williams) *t.k.h: pressed ldrs on outer of gp tl wknd rapidly 2f out* **40/1**
01/4 P **Remarkable**^{42} [1414] 6-9-7 107 ... (b) AdamKirby 13
(David O'Meara) *hld up in rr: rdn and wknd over 2f out: t.o whn p.u 1f out (jockey said gelding moved poorly; vet said gelding was lame behind)* **20/1**

1m 27.35s (-0.15) **Going Correction** +0.40s/f (Good) **26** Ran SP% **141.6**
Speed ratings (Par 109): **116,115,115,114,112 112,111,110,110,110 110,108,108,106,105 105,104,102,102,102 102,95,93,89,8**
CSF £57.13 CT £829.53 TOTE £8.60: £2.80, £2.60, £4.90, £6.20; EX 64.10 Trifecta £1857.10.
Owner Sheikh Mohammed Obaid Al Maktoum **Bred** Darley **Trained** Newmarket, Suffolk

FOCUS
A typically competitive Victoria Cup, and they all came up the centre of the track. A smart effort from the winner, with the level set around the third.

2610 BARBADOS NOVICE STKS (PLUS 10 RACE) 5f
4:35 (4:38) (Class 3) 2-Y-O £7,762 (£2,310; £1,154; £577) Stalls High

Form RPR
1 **Expressionist (IRE)** 2-9-5 0 ... WilliamBuick 4 89+
(Charlie Appleby) *trckd ldng pair: clsd 2f out: led jst over 1f out: pushed out: readily* **5/2**^{1}
2 ¾ **Clan Royale** 2-9-5 0 ... AndreaAtzeni 1 86
(Roger Varian) *trckd ldr: chal 2f out: upsides as wnr wnt past jst over 1f out: styd on fnl f but readily hld* **4/1**
2 3 2 ¾ **Praxeology (IRE)**^{9} [2316] 2-9-5 0 ... JoeFanning 5 76
(Mark Johnston) *led and racd against nr side rail: edgd rt over 1f out: sn hdd: fdd ins fnl f* **10/3**^{3}
4 hd **Amarillo Star (IRE)** 2-9-5 0 ... NicolaCurrie 6 75+
(Charlie Fellowes) *dwlt: hld up in last pair: shkn up over 1f out: nt pce to threaten but kpt on to press for 3rd nr fin* **16/1**
5 ½ **Endowed** 2-9-5 0 ... SilvestreDeSousa 7 73
(Richard Hannon) *trckd ldrs: pushed along and no imp 2f out: shkn up over 1f out: one pce after* **11/4**^{2}
6 2 **Flash To Bang** 2-9-5 0 ... TrevorWhelan 2 66
(Ivan Furtado) *racd on outer: in tch: shkn up and rn green 2f out: fdd* **33/1**
7 87 **Brunel's Boy** 2-9-5 0 ... CharlesBishop 3
(Mick Channon) *struggling after 2f: t.o whn virtually p.u over 1f out (jockey said colt lost its action; vet said colt was lame behind)* **12/1**

1m 2.67s (1.97) **Going Correction** +0.40s/f (Good) **7** Ran SP% **114.8**
Speed ratings (Par 97): **100,98,94,94,93 90,**
CSF £13.05 TOTE £3.40: £1.70, £2.10; EX 12.40 Trifecta £37.50.
Owner Godolphin **Bred** Clarecastle Stud Ltd **Trained** Newmarket, Suffolk

FOCUS
Racing stands' side in what looked a decent novice, two appealing newcomers pulled clear of one with useful debut form.

2611 STELLA ARTOIS H'CAP 6f
5:10 (5:12) (Class 4) (0-80,81) 4-Y-O+
£6,727 (£2,002; £1,000; £500; £300; £300) Stalls Centre

Form RPR
34-2 1 **Molls Memory**^{28} [1760] 4-9-2 75 ... LiamKeniry 16 87
(Ed Walker) *trckd ldrs on nr side of gp: shkn up and clsd to take 2nd 1f out: rdn to ld last 120yds: styd on wl* **4/1**^{1}
1316 2 1 ¼ **Ballyquin (IRE)**^{60} [1160] 4-9-2 78 ... JoshuaBryan$^{(3)}$ 2 86
(Andrew Balding) *led: rdn over 1f out: styd on but hdd and outpcd last 120yds* **10/1**
0111 3 1 **Martineo**^{40} [1487] 4-9-8 81 ... AdamKirby 7 86+
(John Butler) *hld up in last pair: rdn 2f out: prog over 1f out: styd on fnl f to take 3rd last strides* **13/2**^{2}
5330 4 nk **Suzi's Connoisseur**^{22} [1916] 8-9-0 73 ... (b) DavidEgan 12 77
(Jane Chapple-Hyam) *trckd ldrs: shkn up to dispute 2nd over 1f out: one pce fnl f* **8/1**^{3}
2542 5 1 ¾ **Followthesteps (IRE)**^{35} [1597] 4-9-4 77 ... (p) TrevorWhelan 8 75
(Ivan Furtado) *taken down early: prom: drvn 2f out towards outer of gp: nt on terms w ldrs after but kpt on* **11/1**

-001 **6** ¾ **Oriental Lilly**[22] 1929 5-9-6 **79** WilliamBuick 9 75
(Jim Goldie) *stdd s: hld up in last pair: shkn up and no prog over 2f out: hdwy over 1f out: kpt on but n.d* **12/1**

10- **7** ½ **Fantasy Keeper**[280] 5712 5-9-7 **80** OisinMurphy 14 74
(Michael Appleby) *pressed ldr to 1f out: wknd fnl f (jockey said gelding hung both ways under pressure)* **8/1**[3]

05U- **8** 1 **Blaine**[220] 7911 9-9-3 **79** (b) MeganNicholls(3) 11 70
(Brian Barr) *dwlt: towards rr: shkn up and no real prog 2f out: one pce after* **33/1**

-310 **9** 1 **The Right Choice (IRE)**[113] 307 4-9-2 **75** (b) PaddyMathers 15 63
(Richard Fahey) *racd alone towards nr side: nt on terms w main gp 1/2-way: one pce u.p fnl 2f* **14/1**

0500 **10** *nk* **Mont Kiara (FR)**[45] 1357 6-8-10 **69** HarryBentley 5 56
(Simon Dow) *stdd s: hld up in rr: prog on wd outside of gp over 2f out: no hdwy over 1f out: sn wknd* **25/1**

5-23 **11** ¾ **Quick Breath**[16] 2065 4-9-2 **75** NicolaCurrie 1 59
(Jonathan Portman) *racd on outer of gp: nvr on terms w ldrs: no prog over 1f out* **14/1**

1120 **12** ¾ **Treacherous**[21] 1942 5-9-3 **76** CallumShepherd 6 58
(Ed de Giles) *stdd s: hld up towards rr: pushed along and sme prog into midfield over 1f out: no hdwy after: fdd and eased fnl f* **16/1**

-430 **13** 1 ½ **Red Alert**[39] 1496 5-9-6 **79** (p) TomMarquand 3 56
(Tony Carroll) *hld up in rr on outer of gp: rdn and no prog 2f out* **25/1**

-040 **14** 2 **George Dryden (IRE)**[10] 2272 7-8-10 **76** (t) ScottMcCullagh(7) 10 47
(Charlie Wallis) *prom tl wknd 2f out* **20/1**

0401 **15** *nse* **Full Intention**[23] 1880 5-8-13 **72** (p) JoeFanning 4 43
(Lydia Pearce) *chsd ldrs: lost pl 2f out: wknd over 1f out* **10/1**

1m 15.32s (1.62) **Going Correction** +0.40s/f (Good) **15** Ran SP% **124.4**
Speed ratings (Par 105): **105,103,102,101,99 98,97,96,94,94 93,92,90,87,87**
CSF £42.64 CT £270.24 TOTE £4.20: £2.00, £2.90, £2.50; EX 37.00 Trifecta £184.00.
Owner Andrew Buxton **Bred** Andrew Buxton **Trained** Upper Lambourn, Berks

FOCUS
Of the six 4yos in the line-up, the least exposed four all finished in the first five places. The form is rated slightly positively.

2612 STELLA ARTOIS SILK SERIES LADY RIDERS' FILLIES' H'CAP 1m 1f 212y
5:45 (5:47) (Class 4) (0-85,82) 3-Y-O+
£6,727 (£2,002; £1,000; £500; £300; £300) **Stalls** Low

Form RPR

0-41 **1** **She Believes (IRE)**[8] 2360 4-9-8 **74** PoppyBridgwater(5) 8 81
(Sylvester Kirk) *hld up off the pce: prog 4f out: chsd ldr over 1f out: drifted lft but rdn to ld 1f out: jst hld on* **8/1**

04-5 **2** *nk* **Inclyne**[25] 1828 3-8-11 **73** HayleyTurner 2 79
(Andrew Balding) *hld up in rr: rdn and prog 2f out: chsd clr ldng pair jst over 1f out: drvn and styd on wl: tk 2nd last 75yds: jst too late* **5/1**[3]

02-2 **3** ¾ **Infanta Isabella**[28] 1757 5-10-6 **81** (t) NicolaCurrie 9 86
(George Baker) *trckd ldrs: prog to ld 5f out: rdn 2f out: edgd lft and hdd 1f out: one pce and lost 2nd last 75yds* **7/2**[1]

532 **4** 6 **Lady Alavesa**[31] 1688 4-8-13 **67** (p) GraceMcEntee(7) 3 60
(Gay Kelleway) *hld up in rr: stl gng wl 3f out: pushed along and no rspnse 2f out: wl btn after* **14/1**

40-1 **5** 3 ½ **Ashazuri**[11] 2230 5-9-1 **69** (h) GeorgiaDobie(7) 5 55
(Jonathan Portman) *t.k.h: cl up: wnt 2nd over 4f out: w ldr over 3f out to 2f out: wknd over 1f out* **6/1**

-300 **6** *nk* **Villette (IRE)**[11] 2252 5-10-0 **82** SophieRalston(7) 6 67
(Dean Ivory) *t.k.h: hld up in rr: pushed along 3f out: no prog and wl btn 2f out* **10/1**

3-20 **7** 3 ½ **Air Force Amy**[13] 2141 3-8-11 **73** HollieDoyle 4 50
(Mick Channon) *sn hld up in midfield: effrt over 3f out: rdn over 2f out: sn wknd* **9/2**[2]

0-02 **8** 35 **Double Reflection**[11] 2230 4-10-4 **82** MsLO'Neill(3) 7
(K R Burke) *led 1f: chsd ldr to 5f out: dropped out qckly and t.o 3f out* **14/1**

4-33 **P** **Cabarita**[60] 1166 3-9-0 **76** JosephineGordon 1
(Ralph Beckett) *plld way into ld after 1f: hdd 5f out: immediately dropped to last and t.o: p.u 2f out (jockey said filly hung badly left-handed)* **8/1**

2m 10.33s (2.63) **Going Correction** +0.40s/f (Good)
WFA 3 from 4yo+ 15lb **9** Ran SP% **116.0**
Speed ratings (Par 102): **105,104,104,99,96 96,93,65,**
CSF £47.91 CT £167.02 TOTE £8.20: £2.20, £2.10, £1.70; EX 73.50 Trifecta £409.10.
Owner Miss A Jones **Bred** Ringfort Stud **Trained** Upper Lambourn, Berks
■ Stewards' Enquiry : Sophie Ralston caution: entered the wrong stall
Hayley Turner two-day ban: excessive use of whip (May 25,27)

FOCUS
With Cabarita pulling for her head in front, the gallop soon picked up, and it eventually played into the hands of the closers. The form's rated around the favourite.
T/Jkpt: Not Won. T/Plt: £276.90 to a £1 stake. Pool: £146,295.28 - 385.66 winning units T/Qpdt: £24.50 to a £1 stake. Pool: £16,580.90 - 498.98 winning units **Jonathan Neesom**

2099 **HAYDOCK** (L-H)
Saturday, May 11

OFFICIAL GOING: Flat course - good to soft (6.4); jumps course - good (6.4)
Wind: Light, against in straight of about 4f Weather: Fine

2613 PERTEMPS NETWORK STAYERS' H'CAP 1m 6f
2:35 (2:35) (Class 4) (0-85,86) 4-Y-O+ £7,115 (£2,117; £1,058; £529; £300) **Stalls** Low

Form RPR

156- **1** **Jedhi**[182] 8995 4-9-6 **79** GrahamLee 4 90+
(Hughie Morrison) *hld up: swtchd rt and hdwy gng wl over 2f out: led narrowly over 1f out: a in control: asserted towards fin* **9/4**[2]

2-00 **2** 1 ¾ **Royal Flag**[15] 2080 9-8-3 **65** JamieGormley(3) 3 70
(Brian Ellison) *hld up: impr to chse ldrs 6f out: drvn over 3f out: ev ch u.p fr over 1f out: outpcd by wnr towards fin* **10/1**

14/3 **3** 8 **Fibonacci**[21] 1943 5-9-7 **80** PaulHanagan 6 74
(Alan King) *led: jinked rt on bnd after 2f: rdn over 2f out: hdd over 1f out: no ex ins fnl f whn unable to go w front two* **6/1**[3]

32-2 **4** 4 **Sharja Silk**[21] 1943 4-9-13 **86** (p[1]) JimCrowley 1 75
(Roger Varian) *chsd ldr: pushed along over 4f out: lost 2nd u.p 2f out: wknd over 1f out* **6/5**[1]

1534 **5** 30 **Azari**[1] 2577 7-9-7 **80** (b) RossaRyan 2 26
(Alexandra Dunn) *t.k.h: chsd ldrs: lost pl over 5f out: rdn over 4f out: wknd over 3f out: lft bhd over 2f out* **8/1**

3m 9.09s (4.49) **Going Correction** -0.825s/f (Hard) **5** Ran SP% **110.7**
Speed ratings (Par 105): **71,70,65,63,46**
CSF £22.05 TOTE £3.10: £1.70, £3.10; EX 23.00 Trifecta £89.80.
Owner Tony Pickford & Partners **Bred** Selwood Bloodstock & Mrs S Read **Trained** East Ilsley, Berks

FOCUS
Distance increased by 58yds. All races on inner home straight. The ground was good to soft on the Flat course, a description Graham Lee said was 'spot on'. Two came clear in a staying handicap that didn't take a great deal of the winning with the favourite flopping. The form's rated around the runner-up.

2614 PERTEMPS NETWORK CONDITIONS STKS 6f
3:45 (3:46) (Class 2) 3-Y-O+ **£14,006** (£4,194; £2,097; £1,048; £524) **Stalls** Centre

Form RPR

340- **1** **Shabaaby**[301] 4933 4-9-5 100 JimCrowley 4 112
(Owen Burrows) *hld up in rr: swtchd lft and hdwy over 1f out: sn rdn: big effrt ins fnl f: r.o to ld towards fin* **4/1**[3]

133- **2** ½ **Emblazoned (IRE)**[323] 4061 4-9-5 109 KieranO'Neill 1 110
(John Gosden) *chsd ldrs: rdn over 2f out: carried hd high: chalng over 1f out: led fnl 110yds: hdd and hld towards fin* **2/1**[2]

24-4 **3** 1 ½ **Laugh A Minute**[14] 2109 4-9-5 107 RichardKingscote 5 105
(Roger Varian) *handy: rdn to chal over 1f out: ev ch ins fnl f: unable qck ins fnl 110yds: styd on same pce towards fin* **6/4**[1]

01-0 **4** *hd* **Vintage Brut**[28] 1780 3-9-2 108 (p) PaulHanagan 3 109
(Tim Easterby) *led: rdn over 1f out: hdd fnl 110yds: kpt on same pce towards fin* **9/1**

450- **5** 6 **Mythmaker**[175] 9127 7-9-9 100 GrahamLee 2 89
(Bryan Smart) *prom on outer: lost pl over 3f out: pushed along over 2f out: outpcd over 1f out* **14/1**

1m 13.92s (0.02) **Going Correction** -0.825s/f (Hard)
WFA 3 from 4yo+ 10lb **5** Ran SP% **110.0**
Speed ratings (Par 109): **83,82,80,80,72**
CSF £12.38 TOTE £4.50: £1.90, £1.80; EX 15.70 Trifecta £34.10.
Owner Hamdan Al Maktoum **Bred** Bearstone Stud Ltd **Trained** Lambourn, Berks

FOCUS
This classy conditions sprint was run at a solid pace and the main action developed down the centre. A pb from the winner with the second to form.

2615 PERTEMPS NETWORK SPRING TROPHY STKS (LISTED RACE) 6f 212y
4:20 (4:21) (Class 1) 3-Y-O+
£20,982 (£7,955; £3,981; £1,983; £995; £499) **Stalls** Low

Form RPR

10-1 **1** **Safe Voyage (IRE)**[14] 2100 6-9-8 109 JasonHart 6 116
(John Quinn) *hld up: rdn over 2f out: sn nt clr run: swtchd lft and hdwy over 1f out: r.o to ld wl ins fnl f: in command towards fin* **6/1**

164- **2** 1 ¼ **Mankib**[196] 8662 5-9-11 109 JimCrowley 4 116
(William Haggas) *hld up in rr: rdn and hdwy over 1f out: led briefly ins fnl f: r.o u.p: nt pce of wnr towards fin* **13/2**

31-1 **3** *nk* **Happy Power (IRE)**[29] 1736 3-8-10 105 RobHornby 1 108
(Andrew Balding) *hld up: rdn over 1f out: hdwy over 1f out: chalng ins fnl f: kpt on u.p: nt pce of wnr towards fin* **7/4**[1]

24-4 **4** 2 **Suedois (FR)**[15] 2085 8-9-8 115 DavidNolan 5 107
(David O'Meara) *trckd ldrs: rdn over 2f out: chalng over 1f out: ev ch ins fnl f: styd on same pce fnl 100yds* **4/1**[2]

40-1 **5** 1 ½ **Vanbrugh (USA)**[28] 1763 4-9-8 108 GrahamLee 2 103
(Charles Hills) *trckd ldrs: rdn to ld over 1f out: hdd ins fnl f: no ex fnl 100yds* **11/2**[3]

23-5 **6** 6 **Arbalet (IRE)**[42] 1412 4-9-8 106 (t) PatCosgrave 8 87
(Hugo Palmer) *w ldr: rdn and ev ch 2f out: lost pl over 1f out: wknd ins fnl f* **20/1**

10-2 **7** 5 **Larchmont Lad (IRE)**[14] 2109 5-9-8 109 (p) PaulHanagan 3 73
(Joseph Tuite) *led: rdn over 2f out: hdd over 1f out: wknd ins fnl f (jockey said horse became upset in the stalls)* **9/1**

1m 27.76s (-1.54) **Going Correction** -0.825s/f (Hard)
WFA 3 from 4yo+ 12lb **7** Ran SP% **114.1**
Speed ratings (Par 111): **92,90,90,87,86 79,73**
CSF £43.50 TOTE £7.80: £2.90, £3.50; EX 54.60 Trifecta £147.30.
Owner Ross Harmon **Bred** Schneider Adolf **Trained** Settrington, N Yorks

FOCUS
This was set up for the closers. Good form for the grade off a sound pace. Add 6yds.

2616 PERTEMPS NETWORK H'CAP 7f 212y
4:55 (4:56) (Class 3) (0-95,89) 3-Y-O **£9,703** (£2,887; £1,443; £721) **Stalls** Low

Form RPR

511 **1** **Oasis Prince**[16] 2058 3-9-6 **88** FrannyNorton 7 96+
(Mark Johnston) *a.p: rdn 2f out: led over 1f out: kpt on gamely and fnd more fnl 100yds* **7/1**

0-33 **2** *hd* **Loch Ness Monster (IRE)**[15] 2082 3-9-4 **86** AlistairRawlinson 6 93
(Michael Appleby) *hld up: rdn on outer over 2f out: hdwy over 1f out: chalng ins fnl f: kpt on: hld towards fin* **9/2**[3]

12-3 **3** 1 ½ **Politicise (IRE)**[21] 1945 3-9-3 **85** JimCrowley 2 89
(William Haggas) *in tch: rdn over 2f out: cl up chsng ldrs over 1f out: unable qck ins fnl f: styd on same pce fnl 100yds (vet said gelding lost its right fore shoe)* **15/8**[1]

4120 **4** *shd* **Harvey Dent**[33] 1645 3-8-11 **79** PaulHanagan 5 82
(Archie Watson) *led: rdn over 2f out: hdd over 1f out: stl there u.p ins fnl f: no ex fnl 75yds* **16/1**

21-5 **5** 10 **Big Baby Bull (IRE)**[15] 2088 3-9-7 **89** RossaRyan 1 69
(Richard Hannon) *chsd ldrs: rdn over 2f out: wknd over 1f out* **11/2**

321- **6** ½ **House Of Kings (IRE)**[229] 7612 3-9-4 **86** (b[1]) RobHornby 4 65
(Clive Cox) *hld up: rdn on inner wl over 1f out: no rspnse: sn dropped away* **3/1**[2]

1m 42.67s (-0.03) **Going Correction** -0.825s/f (Hard) **6** Ran SP% **111.7**
Speed ratings (Par 103): **84,83,82,82,72 71**
CSF £37.15 TOTE £6.40: £2.60, £2.50; EX 38.90 Trifecta £97.50.
Owner J David Abell **Bred** Highclere Stud And Floors Farming **Trained** Middleham Moor, N Yorks

FOCUS
This fair 3yo handicap was run at an average pace and the first pair came clear late on. Sound form, the winner progressing again. Add 6yds.

[2360]LINGFIELD (L-H)

Saturday, May 11

OFFICIAL GOING: Soft (good to soft in places; 6.6)

Wind: slight head wind Weather: overcast with sunny spells and showers

2617 VISIT ATTHERACES.COM H'CAP — 1m 2f

1:25 (1:26) (Class 6) (0-65,65) 4-Y-0+

£3,105 (£924; £461; £300; £300; £300) **Stalls** Low

Form				RPR
0	1		**Neff (GER)**[59] 1183 4-9-2 **60** .... DavidProbert 13	68+
			(Gary Moore) *settled towards rr: hdwy onto heels of ldrs 3f out: swtchd lft 2f out: rdn and gd hdwy to ld 1f out: styd on wl* **7/1**
3324	2	1 1/4	**Dashing Poet**[36] 1563 5-9-7 **65** .... DavidEgan 6	71
			(Heather Main) *led: effrt to extend ld off home bnd 3f out and hdd towards stands' side: rdn and hdd by wnr 1f out: kpt on but no ex* **11/2**[2]
0325	3	nk	**Pendo**[11] 2259 8-9-7 **65** .... JoeyHaynes 2	70
			(John Best) *settled in midfield: hdwy u.p over 2f out: rdn and ev ch 1f out: kpt on fnl f* **12/1**
-402	4	3/4	**The Lords Walk**[14] 2111 6-9-1 **64** .... (p) RyanWhile(5) 9	68
			(Bill Turner) *hld up in rr: hdwy under hands and heels over 2f out: rdn and kpt on fr 1f out* **11/2**[2]
1031	5	1/2	**Mullarkey**[14] 2111 5-9-2 **60** .... (t) RobertHavlin 4	63
			(John Best) *racd promly in 4th: cl up and travelling wl 2f out: sn rdn and no immediate rspnse: one pce fnl f* **5/1**[1]
225-	6	nse	**King Athelstan (IRE)**[221] 7878 4-9-4 **62** .... (w) HollieDoyle 11	65
			(Gary Moore) *settled in midfield: effrt to cl on ldrs 3f out: sn rdn and minor hdwy over 1f out: kpt on fnl f* **14/1**
4-00	7	3 3/4	**Tebay (IRE)**[59] 1183 4-9-2 **60** .... EoinWalsh 1	56+
			(Luke McJannet) *trckd ldr: rdn and outpcd by wnr over 2f out: drvn over 1f out: one pce fnl f (jockey said gelding became unbalanced coming down the hill; trainer's rep said gelding was unsuited by the going (soft, good to soft in places) and would prefer a quicker surface)* **33/1**
2214	8	1/2	**Affluence (IRE)**[14] 2111 4-8-9 **60** .... (p) JacobClark(7) 10	55+
			(Martin Smith) *hld up: rdn and outpcd 3f out: nvr on terms (trainer said gelding was unsuited by the going (soft, good to soft in places ground and would prefer a quicker surface)* **11/1**
6644	9	2 1/2	**Grange Walk (IRE)**[33] 1653 4-9-4 **65** .... PaddyBradley(3) 12	56
			(Pat Phelan) *racd in midfield: rdn along 3f out: drvn and struggling 2f out: no ex fnl f* **13/2**[3]
-620	10	1	**Chikoko Trail**[35] 1591 4-9-4 **62** .... (t) LiamKeniry 5	51
			(Gary Moore) *settled wl in tch: rdn along and ev ch over 1f out: wknd fnl f* **16/1**
F6-0	11	1 1/2	**Iballisticvin**[21] 1936 6-8-10 **61** .... LouisGaroghan(7) 3	47
			(Gary Moore) *hld up: rdn and detached 3f out: nvr on terms* **22/1**
-300	12	6	**Mrs Benson (IRE)**[57] 1216 4-9-6 **64** .... (h) DaneO'Neill 14	40
			(Michael Blanshard) *broke wl fr wd draw and settled in tch: rdn and outpcd 3f out: lost pl and wknd fr over 1f out* **28/1**
500-	13	36	**Ishallak**[233] 7453 4-9-7 **65** .... JosephineGordon 8
			(Mark Usher) *hld up: detached 3f out: t.o* **25/1**
01-0	14	10	**Overtrumped**[40] 1482 4-9-3 **61** .... HayleyTurner 7
			(Mike Murphy) *trckd ldr early: rdn along and lost pl over 4f out: sn detached (jockey said she felt go amiss to attempt to pull the filly up)* **10/1**

2m 11.03s (-1.17) **Going Correction** +0.075s/f (Good) **14 Ran SP% 125.5**

Speed ratings (Par 101): **107,106,105,105,104 104,101,101,99,98 97,92,63,55**

CSF £45.34 CT £472.45 TOTE £8.10: £2.60, £2.40, £3.60; EX 56.40 Trifecta £602.10.

Owner Past The Post Racing **Bred** Gestut Ebbesloh **Trained** Lower Beeding, W Sussex

FOCUS

The rail was out 4yds at the 4f on the round course, and there was a cutaway at the 3f marker on the home straight. Add 4yds to this trip. There had been 24.5mm of rain since the previous Saturday before another downpour just prior to racing. A modest handicap to start, and they raced middle to stands' side in the straight, rather forced there by the cutaway. The runner-up helps guide the bare form.

2618 RACEBETS MONEY BACK ALL LOSERS OAKS TRIAL FILLIES' STKS (LISTED RACE) — 1m 3f 133y

1:55 (1:58) (Class 1) 3-Y-O

£22,684 (£8,600; £4,304; £2,144; £1,076; £540) **Stalls** High

Form				RPR
0-1	1		**Anapurna**[101] 474 3-9-0 0 .... FrankieDettori 2	103+
			(John Gosden) *trckd ldr: niggled along for a few strides 7f out: pushed along to ld over 2f out: easily drew 4 l clr over 1f out: pushed out fnl f: comf* **7/4**[1]
31-	2	6	**Tauteke**[163] 9308 3-9-0 0 .... DavidEgan 7	91
			(Roger Varian) *racd in 3rd on outer: rdn along to chse wnr 2f out: drvn and unable to match wnr 1f out: kpt on fnl f* **11/4**[2]
5-2	3	4 1/2	**King Power**[15] 2087 3-9-0 0 .... SilvestreDeSousa 5	84
			(Andrew Balding) *racd in midfield: rdn along and outpcd over 2f out: drvn over 1f out: kpt on one pce fnl f* **7/2**[3]
51	4	3/4	**Elisheba (IRE)**[81] 794 3-9-0 0 .... RobertHavlin 4	83
			(John Gosden) *dwlt but sn rcvrd to r in midfield: drvn along over 2f out: kpt on one pce fnl f* **10/1**
0-1	5	1	**Kvetuschka**[43] 1397 3-9-0 0 .... AndreaAtzeni 8	81
			(Peter Chapple-Hyam) *hld up: pushed along 5f out: drvn over 2f out: kpt on one pce fnl f but n.d* **33/1**
21-3	6	8	**Cape Islay (FR)**[14] 2110 3-9-0 85 .... PJMcDonald 1	68+
			(Mark Johnston) *led: rdn along and hdd by wnr over 2f out: wknd fnl f* **8/1**
4-32	7	2 3/4	**Lady Cosette (FR)**[77] 884 3-9-0 77 .... (p[1]) ColmO'Donoghue 6	63
			(Harry Dunlop) *hld up: rdn and outpcd over 2f out: nvr on terms* **33/1**

2m 31.77s (-2.23) **Going Correction** +0.075s/f (Good) **7 Ran SP% 111.3**

Speed ratings (Par 104): **110,106,103,102,101 96,94**

CSF £6.33 TOTE £2.40: £1.50, £2.00; EX 7.00 Trifecta £16.90.

Owner Helena Springfield Ltd **Bred** Meon Valley Stud **Trained** Newmarket, Suffolk

FOCUS

Add 4yds. There was another heavy shower before this race. Ramruma won this ahead of her Oaks victory in 1999, Look Here was second before winning the Oaks in 2008 and Seventh Heaven won it before winning the Irish Oaks in 2016. Five of this year's runners came in with Oaks entries including the 1-2-3. They raced up the middle in the straight. The winner looks a cut above recent winning performances in this event.

2619 RACEBETS DERBY TRIAL STKS (LISTED RACE) (C&G) — 1m 3f 133y

2:30 (2:31) (Class 1) 3-Y-O

£34,026 (£12,900; £6,456; £3,216; £1,614; £810) **Stalls** High

Form				RPR
230-	1		**Anthony Van Dyck (IRE)**[190] 8821 3-9-0 118 .... RyanMoore 4	108+
			(A P O'Brien, Ire) *settled wl in midfield: effrt to chse ldr 2f out: pushed along to take narrow ld over 1f out: drifted rt u.p fnl f but sn in command* **2/1**[1]
21-2	2	2 1/4	**Pablo Escobarr (IRE)**[22] 1911 3-9-0 97 .... (t) JamesDoyle 2	104
			(William Haggas) *led for 1f then trckd new ldr tl led again gng wl 3f out: rdn and hdd by wnr over 1f out: kpt on fnl f but nt pce of wnr* **6/1**[3]
513-	3	1 3/4	**Nate The Great**[210] 8185 3-9-0 101 .... HollieDoyle 3	101
			(Archie Watson) *racd in tch in 4th: rdn along and outpcd over 2f out: kpt on wl for press fnl f* **16/1**
11-2	4	1 1/4	**Cap Francais**[17] 2031 3-9-0 103 .... GeraldMosse 5	99
			(Ed Walker) *hld up: clsd gng wl 3f out: sn rdn and no imp 2f out: kpt on one pce fnl f (vet said colt had lost its right hind shoe)* **9/4**[2]
11	5	2 1/2	**Ranch Hand**[12] 2195 3-9-0 85 .... DavidProbert 6	95
			(Andrew Balding) *hld up in rr: rdn off the pce 3f out: kpt on fr over 1f out: n.d* **20/1**
2-21	6	nk	**Eagles By Day (IRE)**[13] 2142 3-9-0 93 .... DanielTudhope 7	94
			(Michael Bell) *hld up in rr of midfield: clsd gng wl 3f out: rdn and fnd little 2f out: one pce fnl f* **7/1**
31	7	1/2	**Severance**[14] 2099 3-9-0 .... (h) GeorgeDowning 1	93
			(Mick Channon) *pushed up to ld after 1f: rdn along and hdd 3f out: sn lost pl: wknd fnl f* **20/1**
0-1	8	1 3/4	**Hiroshima**[10] 2301 3-9-0 .... BrettDoyle 8	91
			(John Ryan) *hld up: rdn along and no imp over 2f out: a in rr* **50/1**
1-12	9	3 1/2	**Themaxwecan (IRE)**[36] 1558 3-9-0 92 .... PJMcDonald 10	85
			(Mark Johnston) *racd in midfield: pushed along 5f out: rdn 3f out: nvr a factor* **16/1**
122-	10	2 1/4	**Three Comets (GER)**[201] 8477 3-9-0 95 .... AndreaAtzeni 9	81
			(Roger Varian) *trckd ldr early: drvn along and no imp 3f out: wknd fnl f (trainer's rep could offer no explanation for the colt's performance)* **14/1**

2m 31.27s (-2.73) **Going Correction** +0.075s/f (Good) **10 Ran SP% 120.8**

Speed ratings (Par 107): **112,110,109,108,106 106,106,105,102,101**

CSF £14.93 TOTE £2.30: £1.20, £2.00, £4.70; EX 9.60 Trifecta £225.60.

Owner Mrs John Magnier & Michael Tabor & Derrick Smith **Bred** Orpendale, Chelston & Wynatt **Trained** Cashel, Co Tipperary

FOCUS

Add 4yds. Not since High-Rise in 1988 has a horse won this race and the Derby, but Kew Gardens, a stablemate of this year's winner, was second before taking the St Leger last year. The main action was towards the stands' side in the straight. Anthony Van Dyck did not need to match his 2yo form in a renewal that was better contested than recent editions.

2620 MILLGATE H'CAP — 1m 5f

3:05 (3:07) (Class 4) (0-85,87) 4-Y-0+

£5,530 (£1,645; £822; £411; £300; £300) **Stalls** Low

Form				RPR
006-	1		**Dance Legend**[157] 9399 4-9-7 **85** .... DavidProbert 3	95
			(Rae Guest) *restrained into last early: quick hdwy arnd outer of field to go 3rd 5f out: c wd to grab stands' rail off home bnd 3f out: rdn to ld over 1f out: styd on wl* **4/1**[2]
4-22	2	2 1/2	**Charles Kingsley**[6] 2435 4-9-9 **87** .... PJMcDonald 1	93
			(Mark Johnston) *trckd ldr: moved stands' side off home bnd and rdn to ld briefly 2f out: sn hdd by wnr over 1f out: kpt on fnl f but no match for wnr* **1/1**[1]
013-	3	2	**Oi The Clubb Oi's**[59] 6445 4-8-4 **68** .... JoeyHaynes 4	71
			(Ian Williams) *settled in midfield: rdn along and outpcd 3f out: drvn and kpt on one pce fr over 1f out* **8/1**
25-5	4	3/4	**Noble Gift**[31] 1681 9-9-8 **86** .... CallumShepherd 2	88
			(William Knight) *led: rdn along and hdd 2f out: kpt on fnl f but unable to match pce of wnr (vet said gelding lost his left-fore shoe)* **18/1**
0-23	5	11	**Hollywood Road (IRE)**[22] 1914 6-9-4 **82** .... ColmO'Donoghue 7	67
			(Gary Moore) *hld up: rdn and no imp 3f out: eased ins fnl f whn ch had gone* **9/2**[3]
5300	6	3/4	**Battle Of Marathon (USA)**[14] 2126 7-9-4 **82** .... BrettDoyle 5	66
			(John Ryan) *hld up: rdn and outpcd 3f out: sn bhd (jockey said gelding hung right-handed throughout)* **18/1**
1140	7	1 1/4	**Temur Khan**[42] 1425 4-9-2 **80** .... GeorgeDowning 6	62
			(Tony Carroll) *trckd ldr: rdn and lost pl over 2f out: wknd fnl f* **33/1**

2m 55.58s **7 Ran SP% 112.8**

CSF £8.14 TOTE £5.20: £2.10, £1.40; EX 10.00 Trifecta £45.30.

Owner T J Cooper **Bred** T J Cooper **Trained** Newmarket, Suffolk

FOCUS

Add 4yds. Some more rain before and during this race, which was a useful handicap. They raced middle to stands' side in the straight. It's rated as straightforward form.

2621 RACEBETS MILLION CHARTWELL FILLIES' STKS (GROUP 3) — 7f

3:40 (3:41) (Class 1) 3-Y-O+

£34,026 (£12,900; £6,456; £3,216; £1,614; £810) **Stalls** Centre

Form				RPR
121-	1		**Pretty Baby (IRE)**[281] 5672 4-9-4 106 .... JamesDoyle 1	105
			(William Haggas) *mde most: steadily trckd over towards stands' rail: rdn and strly pressed by rival 2f out: hdd briefly by rival ins fnl f: rallied wl to ld again fnl 50yds* **15/8**[1]
121-	2	hd	**Perfection**[210] 8190 4-9-4 100 .... (p) DanielTudhope 5	104
			(David O'Meara) *trckd wnr: clsd gng wl 2f out: rdn along and led briefly ins fnl f: drvn and hdd by wnr fnl 50yds* **10/1**
61-4	3	1 1/4	**Devant (FR)**[31] 1706 3-8-10 100 ow1 .... GeraldMosse 7	101
			(H-A Pantall, France) *racd in midfield: stl gng wl whn briefly short of room over 1f out: swtchd rt and kpt on once in clr fnl f* **11/4**[2]
61-0	4	1/2	**Shepherd Market (IRE)**[21] 1941 4-9-4 96 .... PJMcDonald 6	99
			(Clive Cox) *trckd wnr: rdn along and ev ch 2f out: kpt on one pce fnl f* **16/1**
60-	5	1/2	**Cherry Lady (GER)**[19] 4-9-4 96 .... RyanMoore 2	98
			(P Schiergen, Germany) *hld up: hdwy to chse wnr 2f out: rdn and ev ch on outer 1f out: wknd fnl f* **10/1**

03-6 **6** *1* **Betty F**[23] [1891] 4-9-4 98....................(b) FrankieDettori 4 95
(Jeremy Noseda) *hld up: rdn and no imp over 2f out: one pce fnl f* **9/1**

3-03 **7** *1 1/2* **Eirene**[16] [2062] 4-9-4 100.................... DaneO'Neill 8 91
(Dean Ivory) *hld up: rdn along and outpcd 3f out: a towards rr* **8/1**[3]

215- **8** *13* **Dancing Star**[211] [8147] 6-9-7 105.................... DavidProbert 3 59
(Andrew Balding) *anticipated s and hit hd on stalls: v slow to s as a result: qckly t.o* **10/1**

1m 24.36s (0.06) **Going Correction** +0.075s/f (Good)
WFA 3 from 4yo+ 12lb **8 Ran SP% 115.7**
Speed ratings (Par 110): **102,101,100,99,99 98,96,81**
CSF £22.19 TOTE £2.40: £1.40, £2.20, £1.60; EX 17.00 Trifecta £77.10.

Owner Sheikh Rashid Dalmook Al Maktoum **Bred** Dayton Investments Ltd **Trained** Newmarket, Suffolk

FOCUS
This looked a good little Group 3, and it unfolded towards the stands' side. The form makes sense with the first five all close to their marks.

2622 99 (NO FLAKE) FAREWELL H'CAP 7f 135y
4:15 (4:17) (Class 3) (0-90,90) 4-Y-O+ **£7,246** (£2,168; £1,084; £542; £270) **Stalls** Centre

Form RPR

0466 **1** **War Glory (IRE)**[14] [2105] 6-9-7 **90**.................... RyanMoore 6 99+
(Richard Hannon) *settled in midfield: clsd gng wl whn briefly short of room 2f out: swtchd lft off heels and rdn to ld 1f out: styd on wl* **7/2**[2]

0-44 **2** *1 1/2* **Salt Whistle Bay (IRE)**[11] [2237] 5-8-11 **80**.................... DaneO'Neill 1 84
(Rae Guest) *hld up: hdwy u.p to ld briefly on outer over 1f out: sn hdd by wnr 1f out: kpt on fnl f* **5/1**

40-1 **3** *1/2* **Here's Two**[18] [2005] 6-8-7 **76** oh2.................... DavidProbert 4 79
(Ron Hodges) *hld up: hdwy u.p on outer over 2f out: sn rdn and ev ch 1f out: sn outpcd by wnr: no ex* **13/2**

40-5 **4** *1/2* **Regimented (IRE)**[16] [2065] 4-8-2 **76**.......... ThoreHammerHansen(5) 5 77
(Richard Hannon) *hld up in rr: rdn 2f out: swtchd lft over 1f out: kpt on wl fnl f (jockey said colt hung right-handed throughout)* **10/3**[1]

3606 **5** *hd* **Swift Approval (IRE)**[63] [1097] 7-8-10 **79**.................... PJMcDonald 2 80
(Stuart Williams) *trckd ldr on rail: rdn along whn sltly short of room 2f out: ev ch whn gap appeared over 1f out: one pce fnl f* **5/1**

00-6 **6** *2* **Lamloom (IRE)**[18] [2015] 5-9-5 **88**.................... DanielTudhope 7 84
(David O'Meara) *wnt to post early: led against stands' rail: rdn along and hdd over 1f out: wknd fnl f* **9/2**[3]

036- **7** *8* **Sir Titan**[223] [7801] 5-9-6 **89**.................... GeraldMosse 3 64
(Tony Carroll) *chsd ldr early: rdn and outpcd over 2f out: wknd fnl f* **16/1**

1m 33.39s (1.69) **Going Correction** +0.075s/f (Good) **7 Ran SP% 116.0**
Speed ratings (Par 107): **94,92,92,91,91 89,81**
CSF £21.86 TOTE £3.00: £1.80, £3.50; EX 16.60 Trifecta £92.00.

Owner Mohamed Saeed Al Shahi **Bred** Pier House Stud **Trained** East Everleigh, Wilts

FOCUS
The leaders looked to overdo it. The field raced stands' side and it's ordinary form.

2623 SKY SPORTS RACING ON VIRGIN 535 FILLIES' NOVICE STKS 6f
4:50 (4:53) (Class 5) 3-Y-O+ **£3,752** (£1,116; £557; £278) **Stalls** Centre

Form RPR

22-2 **1** **Alhakmah (IRE)**[9] [2340] 3-8-11 85.................... RyanMoore 12 81
(Richard Hannon) *wnt lft s: sn corrected and mde all on stands' rail: rdn and responded wl to press over 1f out: styd on wl* **7/4**[2]

2 **2** *3/4* **Tapisserie**[15] [2077] 3-8-11 0.................... JamesDoyle 10 78+
(William Haggas) *hld up: pushed along to chse wnr 2f out: swtchd lft and rdn 1f out: kpt on wl fnl f: nt rch wnr* **10/11**[1]

3 *3 1/4* **Hassaad** 3-8-11 0.................... DaneO'Neill 8 68
(Owen Burrows) *trckd wnr on stands' rail: rdn and outpcd over 1f out: kpt on one pce fnl f* **8/1**[3]

46- **4** *nk* **Raincall**[199] [8545] 4-9-7 0.................... DavidProbert 1 70
(Henry Candy) *chsd wnr fr wd draw: rdn along and ev ch over 1f out: one pce fnl f* **14/1**

4- **5** *nk* **Quirky Gertie (IRE)**[348] [3172] 3-8-11 0.................... GeorgeDowning 3 66
(Mick Channon) *hld up: pushed along and green 3f out: rdn and mde gd late hdwy ins fnl f: should do bttr* **14/1**

6 **6** *1 3/4* **Victory Rose**[56] [1236] 3-8-11 0.................... BrettDoyle 6 60
(Lydia Pearce) *racd in midfield: hdwy u.p 2f out: rdn over 1f out: wknd fnl f (trainer said filly was unsuited by the going (soft, good to soft in places) and would prefer a quicker surface)* **50/1**

33- **7** *3 1/4* **Rose Hip**[334] [3686] 4-9-7 0.................... GeraldMosse 9 53
(Tony Carroll) *settled in midfield: rdn and little rspnse over 2f out: kpt on one pce fnl f* **20/1**

6- **8** *1 1/4* **Fanny Chenal**[236] [7366] 3-8-4 0.................... IsobelFrancis(7) 4 46
(Jim Boyle) *hld up: rdn and outpcd 3f out: a in rr* **40/1**

9 *hd* **Twilighting** 3-8-8 0.................... GeorgiaCox(3) 5 45
(Henry Candy) *racd in midfield: rdn along 3f out: sn drvn and no imp 2f out: no ex* **20/1**

0-0 **10** *1 1/4* **Secret Treaties**[24] [1855] 3-8-11 0.................... EoinWalsh 2 41
(Christine Dunnett) *racd in tch: rdn and outpcd over 2f out: wknd fnl f (jockey said filly ran green)* **80/1**

0- **11** *28* **Vereta (IRE)**[178] [9050] 3-8-11 0.................... JoeyHaynes 11
(Emma Owen) *chsd ldr: rdn and lost pl qckly over 3f out: sn t.o (jockey said filly stumbled approximately 2 1/2 furlongs out)* **100/1**

1m 12.09s (0.59) **Going Correction** +0.075s/f (Good) **11 Ran SP% 129.3**
WFA 3 from 4yo 10lb
Speed ratings (Par 100): **99,98,93,93,92 90,86,84,84,82 45**
CSF £3.92 TOTE £2.50: £1.10, £1.40, £3.10; EX 4.60 Trifecta £18.70.

Owner Al Shaqab Racing **Bred** Ice Wine Stables **Trained** East Everleigh, Wilts

FOCUS
A useful, interesting fillies' novice and the action was stands' side. The level of the ratings will prove fluid.

T/Plt: £23.50 to a £1 stake. Pool: £83,656.37 - 2,598.28 winning units. T/Qpdt: £7.90 to a £1 stake. Pool: £6,746.24 - 626.29 winning units. **Mark Grantham**

2579 NOTTINGHAM (L-H)
Saturday, May 11

OFFICIAL GOING: Soft (good to soft in places) changing to soft after race 6 (4.40)
Wind: Light across Weather: Sunnythen cloudy with showers

2624 GENTING NIGHTS NOVICE STKS 6f 18y
1:45 (1:47) (Class 5) 3-Y-O+ **£3,881** (£1,155; £577; £288) **Stalls** Centre

Form RPR

00- **1** **Lady Monica**[197] [8593] 3-8-9 0.................... RoystonFfrench 4 66
(John Holt) *midfield: hdwy 2f out: chsd ldrs and n.m.r over 1f: sn rdn and str run ins fnl f to ld on line* **125/1**

-51 **2** *hd* **Obee Jo (IRE)**[12] [2199] 3-9-5 0.................... DavidAllan 11 75
(Tim Easterby) *trckd ldrs: hdwy 1/2-way: cl up 2f out: rdn to ld over 1f out: clr ins fnl f: sn edgd lft: hdd on line* **4/1**[2]

4 **3** *3* **Senorita Grande (IRE)**[11] [2243] 3-8-4 0.................... SeanDavis(5) 7 55
(John Quinn) *prom: led wl over 2f out and sn pushed along: rdn wl over 1f out: hdd: drvn ent fnl f and kpt on same pce* **12/1**

56 **4** *1 1/4* **Kodi King (IRE)**[22] [1924] 3-9-0 0.................... CliffordLee 1 56
(K R Burke) *trckd ldrs: hdwy on outer over 2f out: sn rdn and ev ch: drvn and kpt on same pce fnl f* **3/1**[1]

02 **5** *2 3/4* **Gonzaga**[18] [2009] 4-9-5 0.................... RachealKneller(5) 6 51
(James Bennett) *in tch: hdwy over 2f out: rdn wl over 1f out: no imp (jockey said gelding hung left-handed throughout)* **20/1**

3-1 **6** *4 1/2* **Benny And The Jets (IRE)**[129] [27] 3-9-0 0....(t w) CierenFallon(7) 10 40
(Sylvester Kirk) *prom: cl up 1/2-way: rdn along over 2f out: sn drvn and btn* **3/1**[1]

7 *1 1/2* **Bold Show** 3-9-0 0.................... TonyHamilton 13 28
(Richard Fahey) *green sn rdn along and a towards rr* **9/2**[3]

0- **8** *nk* **Fox Morgan**[136] [9709] 3-9-0 0.................... MartinDwyer 5 27
(Andrew Balding) *a towards rr (jockey said gelding his lost action in the early stages)* **14/1**

050- **9** *2 3/4* **Tilsworth Prisca**[200] [8494] 4-9-5 35....................(h) RaulDaSilva 8 17
(J R Jenkins) *qckly away and swtchd rt towards stands' rail: led: rdn along 1/2-way: sn hdd & wknd* **250/1**

03- **10** *2* **Vigorito**[262] [6411] 3-8-9 0.................... AndrewMullen 9 7
(David Barron) *t.k.h: chsd ldrs: rdn along wl over 2f out: sn wknd* **14/1**

60 **11** *5* **Wadah**[15] [2077] 4-8-12 0.................... GinaMangan(7) 14
(J R Jenkins) *a towards rr* **66/1**

0 **12** *9* **Piccupaprosecco**[22] [1924] 3-8-9 0.................... AndrewElliott 3
(Derek Shaw) *a towards rr* **100/1**

1m 14.47s (0.67) **Going Correction** +0.275s/f (Good)
WFA 3 from 4yo 10lb **12 Ran SP% 117.6**
Speed ratings (Par 103): **106,105,101,100,96 90,88,88,84,81 75,63**
CSF £577.30 TOTE £56.00: £15.50, £1.70, £3.00; EX 497.10 Trifecta £2294.80.

Owner Michael Hollier **Bred** Plantation Stud **Trained** Peckleton, Leics

FOCUS
The going was soft, good to soft in places. GoingStick: 6.2. Outer track rail was sent out 2yds on the home bend, adding 6 yards to the 2.55, 4.05, 4.40. 5.15 and 5.50. Stalls - 5f, 6f and 1m - centre; Remainder - inside. A shock result in this novice contest, but the winner flew late on and clearly has ability.

2625 SOPHIES CHOICE H'CAP (JOCKEY CLUB GRASSROOTS SPRINT SERIES QUALIFIER) 5f 8y
2:20 (2:20) (Class 4) (0-80,80) 4-Y-O+
£6,469 (£1,925; £962; £481; £300; £300) **Stalls** Centre

Form RPR

-061 **1** **Peggie Sue**[10] [2294] 4-8-10 **76**.................... TobyEley(7) 2 87
(Adam West) *trckd ldrs: cl up 1/2-way: rdn to ld ent fnl f: drvn and kpt on wl towards fin* **4/1**[1]

631- **2** *1* **Maygold**[220] [7903] 4-9-2 **75**....................(h) LukeMorris 10 82
(Ed Walker) *trckd ldrs: hdwy 2f out: rdn to chal jst over 1f out: drvn and ev ch jst ins fnl f: kpt on same pce* **9/1**

10-0 **3** *1 1/4* **Hawaam (IRE)**[15] [2079] 4-9-1 **79**....................(p[1]) BenSanderson(5) 3 82
(Roger Fell) *slt ld: rdn along 1/2-way: hdd wl over 1f out: kpt on same pce* **10/1**

1460 **4** *1/2* **Zapper Cass (FR)**[10] [2294] 6-9-1 **74**....................(v) AlistairRawlinson 4 75
(Michael Appleby) *chsd ldrs: rdn along and sltly outpcd wl over 1f out: kpt on fnl f* **8/1**

0-66 **5** *3/4* **Bengali Boys (IRE)**[50] [1274] 4-9-7 **80**....................(h) PaulMulrennan 11 78
(Tony Carroll) *towards rr: hdwy wl over 1f out: sn rdn and kpt on fnl f* **10/1**

0-02 **6** *nk* **Rickyroadboy**[10] [2294] 4-8-8 **67**.................... AndrewMullen 5 64
(Mark Walford) *cl up: rdn to take slt advantage 1 1/2f out: sn drvn: hdd appr fnl f and sn wknd* **11/2**

00-5 **7** *1 3/4* **Major Pusey**[33] [1654] 7-9-5 **78**.................... FergusSweeney 1 69
(John Gallagher) *prom on outer: rdn along bef 1/2-way: sn wknd* **5/1**[3]

6-03 **8** *shd* **Gnaad (IRE)**[10] [2272] 5-8-11 **75**.................... DarraghKeenan(5) 7 65
(Alan Bailey) *awkward and wnt rt s: stalls rug ct under sddle tl loose after 1 1/2f: a in rr* **9/2**[2]

115- **9** *6* **Dr Doro (IRE)**[192] [8742] 6-8-11 **73**.................... CameronNoble(3) 8 42
(Ian Williams) *dwlt and awkward s: a in rr* **11/1**

1m 0.28s (0.08) **Going Correction** +0.275s/f (Good) **9 Ran SP% 117.9**
Speed ratings (Par 105): **110,108,106,105,104 103,101,100,91**
CSF £41.17 CT £342.13 TOTE £4.40: £1.50, £3.20, £3.20; EX 27.30 Trifecta £544.20.

Owner West Racing Partnership **Bred** Sean Gollogly **Trained** Epsom, Surrey

FOCUS
A fair sprint handicap won in good style by an improving filly.

2626 DS DERBY SALON H'CAP (JOCKEY CLUB GRASSROOTS FLAT STAYERS SERIES QUALIFIER) 1m 6f
2:55 (2:56) (Class 5) (0-75,76) 4-Y-O+
£3,881 (£1,155; £577; £300; £300; £300) **Stalls** Low

Form RPR

15-0 **1** **Nuits St Georges (IRE)**[14] [2092] 4-9-6 **72**.................... SeanLevey 11 80
(David Menuisier) *cl up: led after 2f: rdn along over 2f out: drvn over 1f out: kpt on gamely ins fnl f (jockey said gelding hung right-handed)* **7/2**[1]

1221 **2** *1 1/2* **Singing The Blues (IRE)**[10] [2279] 4-9-4 **70**.................... DanielMuscutt 7 76
(Rod Millman) *led 2f: cl up: rdn to chal 3f out: drvn over 1f out: edgd lft and ev ch ins fnl f: no ex last 100yds* **9/2**[2]

41-5 **3** *nk* **Sassie (IRE)**[7] [2400] 4-9-7 **73**.................... LukeMorris 10 78
(Sylvester Kirk) *trckd ldng pair: effrt and cl up over 3f out: rdn along 2f out: ch and drvn over 1f out: kpt on same pce fnl f* **11/2**[3]

The Form Book Flat 2019, Raceform Ltd, Newbury, RG14 5SJ

11-5 **4** *7* **Bodacious Name (IRE)**[20] 1971 5-9-4 **70**.................... DougieCostello 5 66
(John Quinn) *hld up towards rr: hdwy 1/2-way: in tch 5f out: pushed along to chse ldrs 3f out: rdn over 2f out: sn drvn and kpt on one pce* **14/1**

630- **5** *2 ¼* **Manor Park**[214] 8081 4-9-3 **72**..........................(w) FinleyMarsh(3) 12 65
(Alan King) *hld up in rr: sme hdwy over 4f out: rdn along 3f out: sn drvn and n.d* **8/1**

21/0 **6** *nse* **Remember The Man (IRE)**[11] 2254 6-9-1 **70**.......... CameronNoble(3) 3 62
(Michael Bell) *a towards rr: nvr a factor* **18/1**

600- **7** *1 ½* **Pumblechook**[209] 8230 6-9-3 **76**.......................... CierenFallon(7) 2 66
(Amy Murphy) *hld up towards rr: sme hdwy on inner and in tch over 3f out: sn rdn and wknd (jockey said gelding hung right-handed)* **11/2**[3]

13-5 **8** *2 ¾* **Looking For Carl**[39] 1497 4-9-0 **66**.................................. AndrewMullen 9 53
(Mark Loughnane) *trckd ldrs: pushed along over 4f out: rdn over 3f out: sn drvn and wknd* **16/1**

0-55 **9** *3 ½* **Torch**[8] 2373 6-8-0 **57** oh6 ow3................................... DarraghKeenan(5) 1 39
(Laura Morgan) *chsd ldrs: rdn along over 5f out: sn outpcd* **18/1**

426- **10** *4 ½* **Principia**[151] 9492 4-9-1 **67**.. LewisEdmunds 6 42
(Michael Appleby) *hld up: hdwy 1/2-way: chsd ldrs 5f out: rdn along 4f out: wknd 3f out* **20/1**

20-0 **11** *nk* **Swordbill**[14] 2092 4-8-12 **69**..(p) SeanDavis(5) 8 44
(Ian Williams) *in tch: rdn along over 4f out: sn wknd* **16/1**

00-0 **12** *32* **Tuscan Pearl**[26] 1826 4-8-3 **55**.. MartinDwyer 4
(William Knight) *chsd ldng trio: pushed along over 5f out: rdn over 4f out: sn drvn and wknd* **33/1**

3m 8.04s (1.64) **Going Correction** +0.275s/f (Good) **12** Ran SP% **118.9**
Speed ratings (Par 103): **106,105,104,100,99 99,98,97,95,92 92,74**
CSF £18.63 CT £86.36 TOTE £4.30: £1.80, £2.00, £2.10; EX 19.50 Trifecta £53.40.
Owner Boy George Partnership **Bred** Pollards Stables **Trained** Pulborough, W Sussex

FOCUS
Add 6yds. A thorough test of stamina on this energy-sapping ground and three of the market principals dominated. The winner was very game.

2627 EBF WEATHERBYS GENERAL STUD BOOK KILVINGTON STKS (LISTED RACE) (F&M) 6f 18y

3:30 (3:30) (Class 1) 3-Y-O+

£22,684 (£8,600; £4,304; £2,144; £1,076; £540) **Stalls** Centre

Form RPR

34-5 **1** **Queen Jo Jo**[28] 1751 3-8-7 **98**.................................. SamJames 3 96
(Kevin Ryan) *racd centre: trckd ldrs: hdwy 2f out: rdn ent fnl f: drvn and styd on wl to ld nr line* **5/2**[1]

2320 **2** *hd* **Treasure Me**[22] 1918 4-9-3 **80**......................................(v) StevieDonohoe 5 98
(Charlie Fellowes) *racd centre: led: rdn along 2f out: drvn ent fnl f: hdd and no ex nr line* **16/1**

40-4 **3** *2* **Iiex Excelsa (IRE)**[16] 2069 4-9-3 **93**............................. PaulMulrennan 2 92
(J A Stack, Ire) *racd centre: cl up on outer: pushed along and sltly outpcd 1/2-way: rdn wl over 1f out: kpt on fnl f* **9/2**[2]

22-5 **4** *½* **Chynna**[70] 989 3-8-7 **94**... BarryMcHugh 1 87
(Mick Channon) *towards rr centre: pushed along over 2f out: rdn and hdwy over 1f out: styng on whn hmpd ins fnl f: kpt on wl towards fin* **5/1**[3]

1-00 **5** *1* **Come On Leicester (IRE)**[22] 1913 3-8-7 **91**................ AndrewMullen 7 84
(Richard Hannon) *chsd ldrs: rdn along wl over 1f out: drvn and edgd lft jst ins fnl f: kpt on same pce* **10/1**

2-0 **6** *nk* **One Last Night (IRE)**[22] 1913 4-9-3 **94**..........................(h[1]) SeanLevey 6 86
(Robert Cowell) *cl up centre: rdn along 2f out: ev ch ent fnl f: sn drvn and wknd* **16/1**

10-0 **7** *½* **Yourtimeisnow**[28] 1751 3-8-12 **97**................................(h) JackMitchell 12 86
(Roger Varian) *racd nr stands' rail: prom: rdn along 2f out: sn drvn and wknd* **8/1**

1-34 **8** *shd* **Indian Tygress**[21] 1942 4-9-3 **85**...................................... GeorgeWood 8 84
(James Fanshawe) *racd nr stands' rail: chsd ldrs: pushed along and grad swtchd lft towards centre 2f out: sn drvn and wknd* **9/1**

630- **9** *5* **Richenza (FR)**[177] 9091 4-9-3 **93**....................................... PatDobbs 11 68
(Ralph Beckett) *racd nr stands' rail: a towards rr* **15/2**

40-0 **10** *2 ¾* **Rock On Baileys**[16] 2062 4-9-3 **97**..........................(p) LewisEdmunds 10 59
(Amy Murphy) *swtchd lft s to r centre: chsd ldrs: rdn along 2f out: sn drvn and wknd* **20/1**

1m 13.63s (-0.17) **Going Correction** +0.275s/f (Good)
WFA 3 from 4yo 10lb **10** Ran SP% **121.9**
Speed ratings (Par 111): **112,111,109,108,107 106,106,105,99,95**
CSF £49.27 TOTE £3.30: £1.50, £4.60, £2.30; EX 51.70 Trifecta £285.30.
Owner Roger Peel & Clipper Logistics **Bred** Bearstone Stud Ltd **Trained** Hambleton, N Yorks

FOCUS
A competitive fillies' and mares' Listed contest. They split into two groups, with three of the fancied contenders keeping to the stands' rail and the rest running up the centre of the course where it ultimately paid to be. The runner-up seems the key to the form.

2628 GENTINGS LUCKY LADIES H'CAP (A JOCKEY CLUB GRASSROOTS MIDDLE DISTANCE QUALIFIER) (DIV I) 1m 2f 50y

4:05 (4:05) (Class 5) (0-75,76) 4-Y-O+

£3,881 (£1,155; £577; £300; £300; £300) **Stalls** Low

Form RPR

1001 **1** **Regular Income (IRE)**[10] 2290 4-9-0 **74**..........................(p) TobyEley(7) 9 83
(Adam West) *dwlt and bhd: hdwy 3f out: chsd ldrs over 1f out: rdn to ld jst ins fnl f: kpt on strly* **15/8**[1]

631- **2** *2 ¼* **Cornborough**[24] 7289 8-9-9 **76**....................................(v) DougieCostello 4 80
(Mark Walford) *trckd ldrs: hdwy over 3f out: rdn along and sltly outpcd 2f out: drvn and kpt on wl fnl f* **10/1**

2004 **3** *¾* **Kadrizzi (FR)**[14] 2124 6-9-3 **70**..(b[1]) PatDobbs 2 73
(Dean Ivory) *trckd ldrs: hdwy over 3f out: sn cl up: rdn to ld 2f out: sn edgd lft and drvn: hdd jst ins fnl f: kpt on same pce* **8/1**[3]

314- **4** *shd* **Snookered (IRE)**[16] 7520 5-9-6 **73**...........................(p) StevieDonohoe 8 75
(Brian Ellison) *trckd ldrs: pushed along on outer 3f out: rdn 2f out and ev ch: drvn and kpt on same pce fnl f* **8/1**[3]

2-31 **5** *1* **Glacier Fox**[16] 2056 4-9-1 **68**.. AndrewMullen 5 68
(Tom Tate) *trckd ldr: effrt 3f out: sn rdn along: drvn wl over 1f out: kpt on same pce ins fnl f* **4/1**[2]

00-0 **6** *2 ¾* **Fake News**[42] 1413 4-9-6 **73**...(b[1]) SeanLevey 7 68
(David Barron) *led: rdn along 3f out: hdd 2f out: sn drvn and wknd* **20/1**

1/60 **7** *nk* **Miss Ranger (IRE)**[11] 2244 7-8-6 **64**............................ BenSanderson(5) 1 58
(Roger Fell) *hld up in rr tl sme late hdwy (starter reported the mare kicked out in the stalls; vet said the mare finished with a slight abrasion to its right hock)* **9/1**

445- **8** *1* **Orange Suit (IRE)**[238] 7274 4-9-7 **74**.............................. BarryMcHugh 6 66
(Ed de Giles) *in tch: effrt on outer over 4f out: rdn along wl over 3f out: sn drvn and outpcd* **12/1**

00-0 **9** *6* **Yorbelucky**[13] 2151 4-9-3 **70**... MartinDwyer 3 50
(Ian Williams) *in tch: effrt 4f out: rdn along 3f out: sn btn* **14/1**

2m 16.01s (2.61) **Going Correction** +0.275s/f (Good) **9** Ran SP% **115.2**
Speed ratings (Par 103): **100,98,97,97,96 94,94,93,88**
CSF £21.93 CT £122.99 TOTE £2.90: £1.30, £2.00, £2.40; EX 15.90 Trifecta £129.00.
Owner Ian & Amanda Maybrey And Partners **Bred** Garrett O'Neill **Trained** Epsom, Surrey

FOCUS
Add 6yds. An ordinary handicap which saw trainer Adam West and jockey Toby Eley complete doubles following the earlier success of Peggie Sue.

2629 GENTINGS LUCKY LADIES H'CAP (A JOCKEY CLUB GRASSROOTS MIDDLE DISTANCE QUALIFIER) (DIV II) 1m 2f 50y

4:40 (4:41) (Class 5) (0-75,75) 4-Y-O+

£3,881 (£1,155; £577; £300; £300; £300) **Stalls** Low

Form RPR

-003 **1** **Music Seeker (IRE)**[14] 2104 5-8-12 **73**...............(t) CianMacRedmond(7) 9 83
(Declan Carroll) *trckd ldrs on outer: hdwy 3f out: cl up 2f out: led appr fnl f: sn rdn clr: comf* **4/1**[2]

64-3 **2** *3 ¼* **Highfaluting (IRE)**[33] 1653 5-9-0 **68**................................. LukeMorris 8 72
(James Eustace) *prom: rdn along and ev ch 2f out: drvn over 1f out: kpt on wl u.p fnl f* **9/2**[3]

6020 **3** *hd* **Mr Carbonator**[24] 1859 4-8-4 **61**................................... WilliamCox(3) 6 64
(Philip Kirby) *prom: led over 3f out: rdn along over 2f out: hdd and drvn appr fnl f: kpt on same pce* **5/1**

20-2 **4** *1* **Chingachgook**[14] 2104 4-9-6 **74**..................................... StevieDonohoe 5 76
(Tristan Davidson) *trckd ldrs on inner: cl up 4f out: effrt and ev ch 3f out: rdn along 2f: drvn over 1f out: grad wknd* **7/4**[1]

216/ **5** *¾* **Deinonychus**[634] 6038 8-8-12 **66**................................(h) LewisEdmunds 2 66
(Michael Appleby) *led to 1/2-way: cl up: rdn along 3f out: grad wknd fnl 2f* **12/1**

0-00 **6** *shd* **Dark Devil (IRE)**[26] 1813 6-9-2 **70**................................(p) TonyHamilton 4 70
(Richard Fahey) *t.k.h: hld up in tch: hdwy over 2f out: rdn wl over 1f out: kpt on fnl f* **11/1**

445- **7** *17* **Bhodi (IRE)**[260] 6489 4-9-7 **75**.. JackMitchell 1 43
(Kevin Frost) *t.k.h: hld up in rr: hdwy to ld 1/2-way: rdn along and hdd over 3f out: sn wknd* **50/1**

150- **8** *13* **Bollin Joan**[217] 7993 4-9-2 **70**.....................................(p) DuranFentiman 3 13
(Tim Easterby) *t.k.h: in tch: rdn along over 3f out: sn wknd* **25/1**

2m 16.99s (3.59) **Going Correction** +0.275s/f (Good) **8** Ran SP% **113.0**
Speed ratings (Par 103): **96,93,93,92,91 91,78,67**
CSF £21.79 CT £89.91 TOTE £5.30: £1.70, £1.50, £1.80; EX 22.00 Trifecta £92.00.
Owner Mrs Sarah Bryan **Bred** P J Connolly **Trained** Malton, N Yorks

FOCUS
Add 6yds. Plenty in with a chance 2f out, but the winner quickly put his seal on the second division of this handicap.

2630 GENTING CASINOS AT THE CORNERHOUSE H'CAP 1m 75y

5:15 (5:16) (Class 5) (0-75,75) 3-Y-O

£3,881 (£1,155; £577; £300; £300; £300) **Stalls** Centre

Form RPR

4403 **1** **Cardano (USA)**[14] 2101 3-8-11 **65**..................................... MartinDwyer 9 74
(Ian Williams) *in rr: stdy hdwy over 3f out: trckd ldrs 2f out: rdn to chal over 1f out: led ins fnl f: kpt on strly* **5/1**[3]

5-16 **2** *1 ½* **Prince Of Harts**[15] 2088 3-9-7 **75**.............................. DanielMuscutt 2 79
(Rod Millman) *in tch: hdwy 5f out: sn trcking ldrs: effrt to chal over 2f out: rdn and ev ch 1f out: sn drvn and kpt on same pce* **4/1**[1]

3-20 **3** *½* **Lightning Attack**[24] 1846 3-9-7 **75**...............................(p) TonyHamilton 4 78
(Richard Fahey) *led: pushed along 3f out: rdn 2f out: drvn over 1f out: hdd ins fnl f: kpt on same pce* **8/1**

44-4 **4** *1 ¾* **Gleeful**[19] 1985 3-9-3 **71**.. JackMitchell 13 70
(Roger Varian) *trckd ldrs on outer: hdwy and cl up 3f out: rdn 2f out: ev ch tl drvn and wknd appr fnl f* **9/2**[2]

0-44 **5** *3* **Glory**[14] 2114 3-9-6 **74**.. PatDobbs 11 66
(Richard Hannon) *trckd ldrs: hdwy 4f out: rdn along 3f out: drvn wl over 1f out: kpt on one pce* **13/2**

363- **6** *3 ¼* **Castle Quarter (IRE)**[214] 8066 3-9-2 **70**........................ GeorgeWood 12 55
(Seb Spencer) *hld up: hdwy over 4f out: sn trcking ldrs: rdn along and edgd lft over 2f out: drvn wl over 1f out: grad wknd* **20/1**

20-5 **7** *2 ¾* **Ellheidi (IRE)**[13] 2146 3-9-5 **73**.......................................(p[1]) CliffordLee 3 51
(K R Burke) *a midfield* **22/1**

500- **8** *½* **Brawny**[175] 9123 3-9-0 **75**...(h[1]) CierenFallon(7) 7 52
(Charles Hills) *chsd ldr: rdn along 4f out: sn wknd (jockey said gelding ran too freely)* **14/1**

25-0 **9** *¾* **Barbarosa (IRE)**[17] 2035 3-9-0 **73**......................(p[1]) ThomasGreatrex(5) 1 48
(Brian Meehan) *hld up: hdwy on inner to chse ldrs wl over 3f out: sn rdn and wknd wl over 2f out* **9/1**

1-44 **10** *1 ¼* **Jack Berry House**[31] 1677 3-9-7 **75**..........................(t) StevieDonohoe 10 48
(Charlie Fellowes) *chsd ldrs: rdn along 3f out: sn drvn and wknd* **11/1**

0-20 **11** *5* **Soul Searching**[46] 1346 3-9-0 **68**....................................... LukeMorris 8 29
(James Tate) *hld up: a towards rr* **33/1**

05-0 **12** *36* **Here's Rocco (IRE)**[33] 1646 3-8-13 **67**............................ DougieCostello 6
(John Quinn) *plld hrd: chsd ldrs: lost pl 1/2-way: sn in rr (jockey said gelding ran too freely)* **33/1**

1m 49.3s (2.60) **Going Correction** +0.275s/f (Good) **12** Ran SP% **119.3**
Speed ratings (Par 99): **98,96,96,94,91 88,85,84,84,82 77,41**
CSF £24.24 CT £160.19 TOTE £5.40: £1.80, £2.00, £3.00; EX 25.40 Trifecta £207.40.
Owner Sohi & Sohi **Bred** Mt Brilliant Broodmares II Llc **Trained** Portway, Worcs

FOCUS
Add 6yds. An ordinary handicap won by a progressive type who should be able to defy a higher mark.

2631 GENTING CASINO ROULETTE APPRENTICE H'CAP (RE APPRENTICE TRAINING SERIES) 1m 75y

5:50 (5:51) (Class 6) (0-60,60) 4-Y-O+

£3,234 (£962; £481; £300; £300; £300) **Stalls** Centre

Form RPR

0/0 **1** **Camile (IRE)**[82] 782 6-9-6 **59**.. HarryRussell(3) 2 66+
(Iain Jardine) *trckd ldrs: hdwy over 4f out: led 2f out: rdn over 1f out: drvn ins fnl f: kpt on wl towards fin* **11/4**[1]

5-66 **2** *1 ¼* **Snooker Jim**[28] 1769 4-9-1 **54**...(t) TobyEley(3) 5 58
(Steph Hollinshead) *hld up in tch: hdwy on inner 3f out: chsd ldrs wl over 1f out: sn rdn: styd on wl fnl f* **9/1**

0433 **3** ½ **Break The Silence**[60] 1163 5-8-6 **52**..................(b) ErikaParkinson(10) 15 55
(Scott Dixon) *racd wd: cl up: led over 4f out: rdn and hdd 2f out: kpt on u.p fnl f* **7/1[2]**

3334 **4** shd **Sea Shack**[18] 2012 5-9-0 **53**..............................(t) SeanKirrane(3) 10 56
(Julia Feilden) *sn led: hdd over 4f out: cl up: rdn and ev ch wl over 1f out: drvn appr fnl f: kpt on same pce* **9/1**

-230 **5** ½ **Bee Machine (IRE)**[79] 829 4-8-6 **52**......................(t) ZakWheatley(10) 7 54
(Declan Carroll) *trckd ldrs: effrt on outer 3f out and sn ev ch: rdn 2f out: drvn over 1f out: kpt on same pce* **8/1[3]**

3244 **6** 2 **Lukoutoldmakezebak**[25] 1836 6-8-5 **46**..............(p) StefanoCherchi(5) 6 43
(David Thompson) *dwlt and in rr: hdwy 3f out: rdn along over 2f out: kpt on appr fnl f: nrst fin* **12/1**

-010 **7** nk **Medici Moon**[14] 2111 5-9-2 **52**..............................(p) RobertDodsworth 14 49
(Richard Price) *in tch: rdn along over 3f out: sn wknd* **20/1**

0006 **8** ½ **Highwayman**[9] 2335 6-8-8 **47**.................................. RussellHarris(3) 16 43
(David Thompson) *a towards rr* **12/1**

500- **9** 8 **Couldn't Could She**[177] 9082 4-9-10 **60**......................... CierenFallon 9 38
(Adam West) *a in rr (trainer said filly was unsuited by the soft ground on this occasion and would prefer a faster surface)* **16/1**

3342 **10** 1½ **Baron Run**[10] 2297 9-8-13 **57**..................................... RhonaPindar(8) 11 32
(K R Burke) *cl up: led after 2f: hdd over 4f out: cl up: rdn along 3f out: wknd over 2f out* **7/1[2]**

3000 **11** 7 **Aljunood (IRE)**[96] 599 5-8-12 **51**.................................. EllaMcCain(3) 3 10
(John Norton) *a in rr* **16/1**

0020 **12** 3 **Sir Jamie**[31] 1683 6-8-6 **50**.................................. ElishaWhittington(8) 8 3
(Tony Carroll) *a towards rr* **16/1**

1m 49.7s (3.00) **Going Correction** +0.275s/f (Good) **12 Ran SP% 120.6**
Speed ratings (Par 101): **96,94,94,94,93 91,91,90,82,81 74,71**
CSF £28.11 CT £164.47 TOTE £3.90: £2.10, £2.80, £2.50; EX 27.50 Trifecta £210.80.
Owner Patsy Byrne **Bred** D Shine **Trained** Carrutherstown, D'fries & G'way
■ Stewards' Enquiry : Zak Wheatley seven-day ban: used whip above the permitted level (May 25,27-31, Jun 1)

FOCUS
Add 6yds. A run-of-the-mill apprentice handicap won by a versatile mare.
T/Plt: £45.40 to a £1 stake. Pool: £44,451.43 - 713.55 winning units T/Qpdt: £11.00 to a £1 stake. Pool: £4,110.66 - 276.22 winning units **Joe Rowntree**

2415 THIRSK (L-H)
Saturday, May 11

OFFICIAL GOING: Good to soft (good in places)
Wind: Virtually Nil Weather: Fine

2632 SCOUTING FOR GIRLS - LIVE @THIRSKRACES FRIDAY 16TH AUGUST H'CAP — 5f
5:40 (5:45) (Class 6) (0-65,65) 4-Y-O+
£3,126 (£930; £464; £400; £400; £400) **Stalls Centre**

Form RPR

-000 **1** **Indian Pursuit (IRE)**[8] 2379 6-9-4 **62**.........................(v) RobbieDowney 16 71
(John Quinn) *prom stands' side: rdn to ld appr fnl f: kpt on (trainer's rep could offer no explanation for the gelding's improved form, other than it may have been suited by a return to turf)* **33/1**

-043 **2** 1¼ **Pearl Noir**[21] 1952 9-8-5 **54**.....................................(b) AndrewBreslin(5) 14 59
(Scott Dixon) *led stands' side and overall ldr: rdn and hdd appr fnl f: kpt on same pce: 2nd of 10 in gp* **12/1**

000- **3** hd **Point Of Woods**[164] 9288 6-8-13 **60**.............................. JamieGormley(3) 15 64
(Tina Jackson) *hld up towards stands' side: hdwy 2f out: rdn to chse ldrs appr fnl f: kpt on: 3rd of 10 in gp* **12/1**

000- **4** 1 **Ambitious Icarus**[317] 4295 10-8-6 **52**.........................(h) PhilipPrince 18 52
(Richard Guest) *dwlt: hld up towards stands' side: pushed along 2f out: r.o wl fnl f: 4th of 10 in gp* **50/1**

0-54 **5** ¾ **Kinloch Pride**[9] 2324 7-9-3 **61**..................................(p) PhilDennis 17 58
(Noel Wilson) *in tch stands' side: rdn to chse ldrs appr fnl f: kpt on same pce: 5th of 10 in gp* **7/1[2]**

0-24 **6** nk **Burmese Blazer (IRE)**[8] 2368 4-9-4 **65**................(h) BenRobinson(3) 6 61+
(Jim Goldie) *hld up centre: rdn 2f out: r.o wl fr appr fnl f to ld in gp 75yds out: 1st of 9 in gp (vet said gelding lost its right hind shoe)* **9/2[1]**

4000 **7** 1 **Jacob's Pillow**[16] 2053 8-9-1 **62**..............................(p) RowanScott(3) 4 55+
(Rebecca Bastiman) *chsd ldrs centre: rdn along 3f out: kpt on fnl f: 2nd of 9 in gp* **33/1**

6000 **8** nk **Dubai Elegance**[23] 1883 5-8-5 **52**..........................(p) GabrieleMalune(3) 11 44
(Derek Shaw) *in tch stands' side: rdn 2f out: edgd lft towards centre appr fnl f: no ex: 6th of 10 in gp* **33/1**

-520 **9** ½ **Lexington Place**[9] 2324 9-9-1 **59**.................................. JackGarritty 2 49
(Ruth Carr) *dwlt: hld up centre: hdwy 2f out: rdn to ld gp 1f out: hdd in gp 75yds out: wknd: 3rd of 9 in gp* **14/1**

6-60 **10** ¾ **Teepee Time**[17] 1952 6-8-3 **52**...........................(b) FayeMcManoman(5) 12 39
(Michael Mullineaux) *chsd ldrs stands' side: rdn 2f out: wknd fnl f: 7th of 10 in gp* **33/1**

6-00 **11** nk **Stoneyford Lane (IRE)**[20] 1973 5-9-1 **59**...............(p) RoystonFfrench 9 45
(Steph Hollinshead) *hld up centre: rdn over 2f out: kpt on fnl f: nvr threatened: 4th of 9 in gp* **9/1**

0-20 **12** ½ **Kibaar**[13] 2153 7-9-2 **60**...(h) JamesSullivan 10 44
(Ruth Carr) *stdd s: hld up centre: sme late hdwy: nvr involved: 5th of 9 in gp* **14/1**

42-6 **13** ½ **Paco Escostar**[21] 1952 4-8-11 **60** ow1.......................(p) DannyRedmond(5) 19 43
(Julie Camacho) *chsd ldrs stands' side: rdn 2f out: wknd fnl f: 8th of 10 in gp (trainer found filly to be in season)* **8/1[3]**

2160 **14** nk **Spirit Power**[26] 1817 4-9-7 **65**.. TomEaves 8 46
(Eric Alston) *chsd ldrs centre: rdn 2f out: wknd fnl f: 6th of 9 in gp* **22/1**

500- **15** nse **Mitchum**[220] 7893 10-7-13 **48**..................................(p) PaulaMuir(5) 1 29
(Ron Barr) *chsd ldrs on outer of centre gp: rdn over 2f out: wknd over 1f out: 7th of 9 in gp* **33/1**

3033 **16** ½ **Atyaaf**[19] 1987 4-8-10 **54**.. AndrewElliott 3 33+
(Derek Shaw) *rrd s and v.s.a: swtchd rt to r stands' side: a in rr: 9th of 10 in gp (jockey said gelding reared as the stalls opened and missed the break)* **10/1**

2-40 **17** 2½ **One Boy (IRE)**[10] 2294 8-9-2 **60**.................................(b) KevinStott 7 30
(Paul Midgley) *led centre gp: chsd ldrs overall: rdn over 2f out: hdd in gp 1f out: wknd: 8th of 9 in gp* **16/1**

-000 **18** ½ **Oriental Relation (IRE)**[13] 2153 8-8-9 **53**..................(bt) NathanEvans 5 22
(John Balding) *chsd ldrs centre: wknd over 1f out: last of 9 in gp* **66/1**

0520 **19** 8 **Come On Dave (IRE)**[18] 2010 10-9-1 **64**........................(b) SeanDavis(5) 13 4
(John Butler) *midfield stands' side: rdn 1/2-way: wknd over 1f out: eased* **20/1**

59.83s (0.43) **Going Correction** +0.025s/f (Good) **19 Ran SP% 122.8**
Speed ratings (Par 101): **97,95,94,93,91 91,89,89,88,87 86,86,85,84,84 83,79,79,66**
CSF £358.43 CT £2785.16 TOTE £34.40: £7.60, £2.30, £3.00, £12.00; EX 496.10 Trifecta £1166.10.
Owner Malcolm Walker **Bred** Sean Gorman **Trained** Settrington, N Yorks

FOCUS
A big field for this moderate sprint handicap. Those drawn high appeared to have a clear advantage and dominated. Straightforward form.

2633 ABF THE SOLDIERS' CHARITY (S) STKS — 6f
6:15 (6:17) (Class 6) 3-5-Y-O
£3,126 (£930; £464; £400; £400; £400) **Stalls Centre**

Form RPR

0-04 **1** **Murqaab**[8] 2380 3-8-9 **64**..(b[1]) ShaneGray 12 68
(David O'Meara) *trckd ldrs: pushed into ld over 1f out: kpt on wl to draw clr fnl f* **5/1[2]**

6-15 **2** 3¾ **Dandy Highwayman (IRE)**[82] 788 5-9-8 **65**........(tp) BenRobinson(3) 1 66
(Ollie Pears) *chsd ldrs: rdn 3f out: kpt on fnl f: wnt 2nd fnl 50yds: no ch w wnr* **5/1[2]**

0000 **3** ½ **Cuppacoco**[12] 2183 4-9-0 **55**.. PaulMulrennan 9 53
(Ann Duffield) *led: rdn and hdd over 1f out: no ex and lost 2nd fnl 50yds* **13/2**

0-00 **4** 1½ **Gift In Time (IRE)**[8] 2379 4-9-8 **65**.................................(bt) DavidAllan 7 57
(Paul Collins) *hld up: rdn over 2f out: hdwy over 1f out: kpt on fnl f* **7/2[1]**

-604 **5** 1¼ **You Little Beauty**[12] 2197 3-8-4 **45**......................... RachelRichardson 10 42
(Ann Duffield) *hld up: rdn over 2f out: kpt on fnl f: nvr threatened* **6/1[3]**

3065 **6** 3½ **Sir Walter (IRE)**[100] 503 4-9-5 **43**.................................... TomEaves 11 40
(Eric Alston) *prom: rdn over 2f out: wknd fnl f* **33/1**

0-04 **7** ¾ **Slieve Donard**[9] 2327 3-8-9 **48**.......................................(b) PhilDennis 3 34
(Noel Wilson) *prom: rdn over 2f out: wknd fnl f* **28/1**

06-0 **8** 1½ **Ingleby Molly (IRE)**[18] 2013 4-8-12 **49**..............(h[1]) SebastianWoods(5) 4 31
(Jason Ward) *chsd ldrs: rdn over 2f out: wknd over 1f out* **8/1**

00/0 **9** 1½ **Circuit**[64] 1083 5-8-9 **37**..(t) PaulaMuir(5) 8 23
(Wilf Storey) *dwlt: a towards rr* **100/1**

00-4 **10** 5 **Rock Hill (IRE)**[43] 1402 4-9-5 **47**.................................... KevinStott 2 13
(Paul Midgley) *chsd ldrs: rdn 3f out: wknd over 1f out* **17/2**

0- **11** 1 **Neigh Dramas**[228] 7636 3-8-9 **0**.................................... RoystonFfrench 6 7
(Bryan Smart) *a outpcd in rr* **33/1**

0050 **12** 1¼ **Henrietta's Dream**[58] 1192 5-9-0 **42**...............................(b) NathanEvans 13 2
(John Wainwright) *chsd ldrs: rdn over 2f out: wknd over 1f out* **40/1**

060- **13** 20 **Zizum**[214] 8080 4-9-2 **38**.. JamieGormley(3) 5
(Alan Berry) *hld up: wknd and bhd fr 1/2-way* **66/1**

1m 12.98s (0.18) **Going Correction** +0.025s/f (Good) **13 Ran SP% 119.1**
WFA 3 from 4yo+ 10lb
Speed ratings (Par 101): **99,94,93,91,89 85,84,82,80,73 72,70,43**
CSF £28.72 TOTE £4.40: £2.30, £2.70, £2.10; EX 21.30 Trifecta £163.40.The winner was sold for £12,000.
Owner Sheikh Abdullah Almalek Alsabah **Bred** Whitsbury Manor Stud **Trained** Upper Helmsley, N Yorks

FOCUS
The usual mix of abilities in this seller, and three stood out on the ratings. They all made the frame, but again the draw played its part. The winner did not need to match even the balance of last year's form.

2634 DAVID LEVER MEMORIAL NOVICE STKS — 7f 218y
6:45 (6:51) (Class 5) 3-Y-O+
£5,563 (£1,655; £827; £413) **Stalls Low**

Form RPR

32-2 **1** **Emirates Knight (IRE)**[14] 2128 3-9-1 **89**.............................. DanielTudhope 7 79+
(Roger Varian) *in tch: pushed along to chse ldrs 2f out: hung lft and sn drvn: led ins fnl f: edgd lft: kpt on* **5/4[1]**

0 **2** 2 **Military Tactic (IRE)**[18] 2023 3-9-1 **0**.............................. PatCosgrave 10 74
(Saeed bin Suroor) *trckd ldrs: rdn to ld narrowly wl over 1f out: sn drvn: hdd ins fnl f: kpt on same pce* **9/1[3]**

1 **3** hd **Alexander James (IRE)**[12] 2192 3-9-5 **0**..................... JamieGormley(3) 8 81
(Iain Jardine) *led narrowly: rdn and hdd narrowly wl over 1f out: kpt on same pce ins fnl f* **7/4[2]**

0 **4** nk **Mohareb**[23] 1886 3-9-1 **0**.. KevinStott 4 73
(Saeed bin Suroor) *dwlt: sn trckd ldrs: rdn to chal strly 2f out: one pce ins fnl f* **25/1**

0 **5** 1¼ **Secretarial (IRE)**[14] 2094 3-8-10 **0**.................................. DavidAllan 12 65
(Tim Easterby) *hld up: rdn along and hdwy 2f out: kpt on ins fnl f* **28/1**

1 **6** 2¾ **Trinity Lake**[13] 2147 3-9-8 **0**.. DavidNolan 3 71
(Declan Carroll) *in tch: rdn over 2f out: no ex fnl f* **12/1**

4-0 **7** 1 **Menin Gate (IRE)**[71] 971 3-9-1 **0**.................................. JackGarritty 1 62+
(Richard Fahey) *hld up in rr: pushed along over 2f out: kpt on ins fnl f: nvr involved* **40/1**

6 **8** 3 **Kung Fu**[24] 1852 3-9-1 **0**... PaulMulrennan 5 55
(Simon Crisford) *hld up in midfield: pushed along 5f out: nvr involved* **10/1**

0-0 **9** ¾ **The Mekon**[13] 2146 4-9-7 **0**.................................... OliverStammers(7) 2 56
(Noel Wilson) *midfield: pushed along 3f out: sn outpcd and btn* **125/1**

0 **10** 1½ **Power Player**[13] 2147 3-9-1 **0**...................................... MichaelStainton 9 50
(K R Burke) *pressed ldr racing keenly: rdn over 3f out: wknd over 2f out* **66/1**

6 **11** 9 **Shamitsar**[11] 2245 5-10-0 **0**.. JamesSullivan 6 32
(Ray Craggs) *hld up: stmbld sltly coming off bnd over 3f out: sn bhd* **125/1**

1m 40.41s (-1.29) **Going Correction** +0.025s/f (Good) **11 Ran SP% 120.4**
WFA 3 from 4yo+ 13lb
Speed ratings (Par 103): **107,105,104,104,103 100,99,96,95,94 85**
CSF £13.81 TOTE £2.20: £1.10, £2.20, £1.20; EX 15.40 Trifecta £32.10.
Owner Ziad A Galadari **Bred** Gerard & Anne Corry **Trained** Newmarket, Suffolk
■ Heart In Havana was withdrawn. Price at time of withdrawal 100/1. Rule 4 does not apply

FOCUS
Rail movements added 7yds to the race distance. A modest looking contest apart from the favourite, who set a high standard based on his AW form.

2635 HAPPY RETIREMENT TIM FAITHFULL H'CAP 6f

7:15 (7:21) (Class 5) (0-75,77) 3-Y-O

£6,469 (£1,925; £962; £481; £400; £400) Stalls Centre

Form RPR
6-63 1 **Look Out Louis**[13] 2149 3-9-6 74 DavidAllan 15 84
(Tim Easterby) *racd against stands' rail: mde all: rdn 2f out: drvn over 1f out: kpt on wl* 9/2[1]
100- 2 1 3/4 **Northernpowerhouse**[182] 9006 3-9-4 72 GrahamLee 18 76
(Bryan Smart) *chsd ldr stands' side: rdn over 2f out: kpt on: 2nd of 7 in gp* 6/1[2]
660- 3 nk **Fairy Stories**[193] 8714 3-7-11 56 oh2 AndrewBreslin(5) 1 59+
(Richard Fahey) *dwlt: hld up in tch centre: hdwy over 2f out: rdn to ld in gp over 1f out: edgd rt: kpt on: 1st of 13 in gp* 33/1
025- 4 1 **Across The Sea**[189] 8827 3-9-8 76 NathanEvans 2 76
(James Tate) *trckd ldrs centre: rdn 2f out: kpt on fnl f: 2nd of 13 in gp* 14/1
1204 5 3/4 **Fair Alibi**[13] 2149 3-9-2 70 AndrewMullen 14 68
(Tom Tate) *wnt lft s: chsd ldrs centre: rdn 2f out: kpt on: 3rd of 13 in gp* 16/1
-365 6 3/4 **Serengeti Song (IRE)**[14] 2098 3-8-12 71 (h) HarrisonShaw(5) 6 66
(K R Burke) *trckd ldrs centre: rdn 2f out: hung lft 1f out: kpt on same pce: 4th of 13 in gp* 12/1[3]
4-00 7 nk **Gylo (IRE)**[14] 2094 3-9-4 72 DavidNolan 7 66
(David O'Meara) *hld up centre: pushed along 3f out: swtchd lft and hdwy appr fnl f: kpt on: 5th of 13 in gp* 25/1
41-0 8 1/2 **House Deposit**[14] 2098 3-9-1 69 (t) KevinStott 17 62
(Declan Carroll) *chsd ldrs stands' side: rdn over 2f out: one pce: 3rd of 7 in gp* 12/1[3]
42-0 9 nk **Dancing Rave**[14] 2098 3-8-13 67 DanielTudhope 10 59
(David O'Meara) *prom centre: rdn over 2f out: no ex fnl f: 6th of 13 in gp* 12/1[3]
40-0 10 1 1/4 **Goldino Bello (FR)**[42] 1424 3-9-7 75 (p[1]) PatCosgrave 12 63
(Harry Dunlop) *hld up centre: rdn 2f out: kpt on: nvr threatened: 7th of 13 in gp (vet said colt had a small wound to its right fore heel)* 25/1
0-01 11 3/4 **Mark's Choice (IRE)**[14] 2121 3-9-9 77 JamesSullivan 4 62
(Ruth Carr) *pressed ldr centre: rdn 2f out: wknd ins fnl f: 8th of 13 in gp* 16/1
600- 12 nse **Arogo**[232] 7476 3-8-12 66 (w) TomEaves 5 51
(Kevin Ryan) *led narrowly centre: rdn over 2f out: hdd in gp over 1f out: wknd ins fnl f: 9th of 13 in gp* 14/1
220- 13 2 1/2 **Kermouster**[206] 8323 3-8-8 62 (w) SamJames 20 39
(Grant Tuer) *slowly away: a towards rr stands' side: 4th of 7 in gp* 20/1
2-54 14 3/4 **Five Helmets (IRE)**[16] 2054 3-8-12 69 JamieGormley(3) 16 44
(Iain Jardine) *dwlt: a towards rr stands' side: 5th of 7 in gp (jockey said gelding was never travelling)* 20/1
100- 15 2 1/4 **The Last Party**[277] 5833 3-9-5 73 BarryMcHugh 19 41
(James Given) *chsd ldrs stands' side: rdn over 2f out: wknd over 1f out: 6th of 7 in gp* 25/1
2253 16 2 3/4 **Klopp**[8] 2380 3-8-6 67 (h) KieranSchofield(7) 8 26
(Antony Brittain) *chsd ldrs: rdn over 2f out: wknd fnl f: 10th of 13 in gp* 16/1
10-0 17 2 1/2 **Carey Street (IRE)**[32] 1662 3-9-6 74 JasonHart 11 25
(John Quinn) *hld up centre: rdn over 2f out: wknd over 1f out: 11th of 13 in gp* 33/1
-066 18 2 **Kapono**[45] 1360 3-9-0 71 (p[1]) GabrieleMalune(3) 3 15
(Amy Murphy) *prom centre rdn 2f out: wknd ins fnl f and eased: 12th of 13 in gp (jockey said gelding stopped quickly)* 20/1
341- 19 3/4 **My Boy Lewis (IRE)**[182] 9006 3-9-0 73 SeanDavis(5) 13 15
(Roger Fell) *carried lft s: sn chsd ldrs stands': wknd and bhd over 1f out: last of 7 in gp* 16/1
420- 20 1/2 **Musical Sky**[215] 8049 3-9-2 70 PaulMulrennan 9 10
(Michael Dods) *hld up centre: rdn over 2f out: wknd over 1f out* 40/1

1m 12.9s (0.10) **Going Correction** +0.025s/f (Good) **20 Ran SP% 126.6**
Speed ratings (Par 99): **100,97,97,95,94 93,93,92,92,90 89,89,86,85,82 78,75,72,71,71**
CSF £24.67 CT £844.89 TOTE £5.40: £2.20, £1.70, £7.30, £4.60; EX 36.20 Trifecta £1189.60.
Owner Habton Farms **Bred** Mildmay Bloodstock Ltd **Trained** Great Habton, N Yorks

FOCUS
This competitive 3yo handicap was run fractionally faster than the earlier seller over the trip. Those drawn high again prevailed.

2636 REBECCA MENZIES 30TH BIRTHDAY CELEBRATION H'CAP 1m 4f 8y

7:45 (7:46) (Class 4) (0-80,78) 4-Y-O+

£8,021 (£2,387; £1,192; £596; £400; £400) Stalls High

Form RPR
/621 1 **Apterix (FR)**[9] 2326 9-9-3 77 BenRobinson(3) 6 83
(Brian Ellison) *prom: rdn over 2f out: led over 1f out: drvn and styd on* 5/1[1]
2630 2 2 **Glan Y Gors (IRE)**[14] 2092 7-9-7 78 (b) CliffordLee 5 81
(David Thompson) *midfield: rdn and hdwy over 2f out: chsd ldrs over 1f out: styd on fnl f* 22/1
0-60 3 1 **Super Kid**[12] 2186 7-9-6 77 (t) DavidNolan 3 78
(Tim Easterby) *midfield: rdn over 2f out: hdwy and chsd ldr over 1f out: styd on* 12/1
644- 4 3/4 **Remember The Days (IRE)**[133] 7782 5-9-6 77 JackGarritty 10 77
(Jedd O'Keeffe) *hld up: rdn over 2f out: hdwy on outside over 1f out: styd on fnl f* 5/1[1]
0030 5 2 3/4 **Be Perfect (USA)**[12] 2185 10-8-10 67 (b) JamesSullivan 2 63
(Ruth Carr) *led: rdn over 2f out: hdd over 1f out: wknd ins fnl f* 20/1
1452 6 2 1/4 **Lopes Dancer (IRE)**[12] 2185 7-8-12 74 SeanDavis(5) 1 66
(Harriet Bethell) *trckd ldrs: rdn over 2f out: wknd fnl f* 13/2[3]
540- 7 1 1/4 **Ad Libitum**[206] 8320 4-9-5 76 DanielTudhope 8 66
(Roger Fell) *hld up in rr: pushed along over 2f out: nvr threatened* 7/1
626- 8 6 **Bill Cody (IRE)**[194] 8702 4-8-13 70 PaulMulrennan 7 51
(Julie Camacho) *chsd ldrs: rdn along over 3f out: wknd over 1f out* 8/1
13-0 9 42 **Regal Mirage (IRE)**[32] 1666 5-9-3 74 DavidAllan 9
(Tim Easterby) *hld up: hmpd by faller 7f out: rdn along over 3f out: wknd 2f out and eased (jockey said gelding was eased in the final furlong, hampered by a faller approximately 1 mile out and the gelding ran flat)* 7/1
4504 F **Native Fighter (IRE)**[7] 2398 5-8-12 74 (v[1]) DylanHogan(5) 4
(Jedd O'Keeffe) *midfield: stmbld and fell 7f out* 11/2[2]

2m 38.33s (-1.67) **Going Correction** +0.025s/f (Good) **10 Ran SP% 115.0**
Speed ratings (Par 105): **106,104,104,103,101 100,99,95,67,**
CSF £111.01 CT £1246.79 TOTE £5.60: £2.30, £6.30, £3.90; EX 112.80 Trifecta £617.00.
Owner Brian Ellison Racing Club **Bred** Joel Chaignon **Trained** Norton, N Yorks

FOCUS
Rail movements added 14yds to the race distance. The feature contest and another competitive looking handicap. It paid to race close to the pace.

2637 ELWICK STUD FILLIES' H'CAP 5f

8:15 (8:15) (Class 5) (0-75,77) 4-Y-O+

£6,469 (£1,925; £962; £481; £400; £400) Stalls Centre

Form RPR
5-40 1 **Dandy's Beano (IRE)**[10] 2294 4-8-13 67 (h[1]) KevinStott 10 76
(Kevin Ryan) *prom against stands' rail: rdn 2f out: drvn to ld appr fnl f: kpt on (trainer said, as to the apparent improvement in form, the filly settled better with the first time application of a hood)* 4/1[1]
-122 2 3/4 **Honey Gg**[10] 2296 4-8-5 66 CianMacRedmond(7) 5 72
(Declan Carroll) *racd isolated centre: chsd ldrs overall: edgd rt and jnd main gp 2f out: rdn to chal 1f out: kpt on* 11/2[2]
0430 3 3/4 **Gold Stone**[7] 2416 4-9-2 70 TomEaves 1 73
(Kevin Ryan) *midfield: rdn along over 1f out: forced way through gap to chse ldrs 1f out: kpt on* 7/1
-000 4 nse **Economic Crisis (IRE)**[6] 2433 10-8-4 58 JamesSullivan 9 61
(Alan Berry) *hld up: swtchd lft to outside appr fnl f: rdn and kpt on wl* 25/1
3130 5 1/2 **Miningggold**[16] 2053 6-8-13 72 (p) PaulaMuir(5) 11 73
(Michael Dods) *chsd ldrs: rdn 2f out: kpt on same pce* 16/1
2-66 6 1 1/2 **Justice Lady (IRE)**[8] 2358 6-9-7 75 (h) DanielTudhope 13 71
(Robert Cowell) *midfield: pushed along and chsd ldrs over 1f out: kpt on same pce* 6/1[3]
221- 7 shd **Mythical Spirit (IRE)**[309] 4612 5-9-4 72 PaulMulrennan 12 68+
(Julie Camacho) *hld up in rr: gng wl but short of room on rail over 1f out tl wl ins fnl f: no ch after: kpt on towards fin (jockey said mare was denied a clear run continuously in the final 2 furlongs)* 4/1[1]
410- 8 3/4 **Our Little Pony**[228] 7639 4-9-1 74 FayeMcManoman(5) 3 67
(Lawrence Mullaney) *hld up: pushed along 2f out: nvr threatened* 12/1
54-0 9 3/4 **Lydiate Lady**[10] 2296 7-8-8 65 JamieGormley(3) 8 55
(Eric Alston) *led narrowly: rdn 2f out: hdd appr fnl f: wknd ins fnl f* 12/1
5002 10 1 **Peggy's Angel**[15] 2081 4-8-10 69 (h) SeanDavis(5) 6 56
(Stef Keniry) *prom: rdn 2f out: wknd ins fnl f* 20/1
3425 11 3 3/4 **Eternal Sun**[37] 1551 4-9-6 77 GabrieleMalune(3) 7 50
(Ivan Furtado) *fly leapt s and slowly away: hdwy and pressed ldr over 3f out: rdn 2f out: wknd fnl f* 14/1

59.64s (0.24) **Going Correction** +0.025s/f (Good) **11 Ran SP% 118.7**
Speed ratings (Par 100): **99,97,96,96,95 93,93,91,90,89 83**
CSF £25.76 CT £153.77 TOTE £5.40: £2.10, £2.20, £2.90; EX 28.50 Trifecta £233.40.
Owner Hambleton Racing Ltd XLVII **Bred** Ruskerne Ltd **Trained** Hambleton, N Yorks
■ Kodiac Express was withdrawn. Price at time of withdrawal 33/1. Rule 4 does not apply

FOCUS
This fair fillies' handicap was run 0.19secs faster than the opening race and again it paid to race close to the stands' rail. There were several hard-luck stories.

2638 "IRISH DAY" @THIRSKRACES NEXT SATURDAY 18TH MAY H'CAP 6f

8:45 (8:46) (Class 6) (0-60,60) 4-Y-O+

£3,126 (£930; £464; £400; £400; £400) Stalls Centre

Form RPR
1434 1 **Ginger Jam**[13] 2153 4-9-3 59 RowanScott(3) 10 66+
(Nigel Tinkler) *hld up in midfield: n.m.r 2f out: pushed along and hdwy over 1f out: swtchd lft appr fnl f: sn chsd ldr: rdn to ld 110yds out: kpt on wl* 5/1[2]
00-2 2 1 1/2 **Someone Exciting**[12] 2189 6-8-9 53 HarrisonShaw(5) 7 56
(David Thompson) *dwlt: sn trckd ldrs: rdn along 2f out: drvn to chal strly 1f out: kpt on* 16/1
0-50 3 1 1/4 **Danehill Desert (IRE)**[28] 1765 4-9-0 58 SeanDavis(5) 8 57
(Richard Fahey) *prom: drvn into narrow ld over 1f out: hdd 110yds out: no ex* 25/1
400 4 1/2 **Picture Your Dream**[30] 1723 4-9-7 60 NathanEvans 14 57
(Seb Spencer) *dwlt: hld up: angled lft and hdwy and hdwy over 1f out: rdn appr fnl f: kpt on* 40/1
30-0 5 1/2 **Cliff (IRE)**[28] 1765 9-8-9 55 IzzyClifton(7) 2 51
(Nigel Tinkler) *hld up towards outer: rdn and kpt on fnl f: nvr involved* 33/1
1102 6 shd **Crosse Fire**[9] 2348 7-9-7 60 (p) TomEaves 11 55
(Scott Dixon) *led narrowly: rdn and hdd over 1f out: no ex fnl f* 14/1
6523 7 hd **Lucky Lodge**[11] 2247 9-8-11 57 (v) KieranSchofield(7) 12 52
(Antony Brittain) *chsd ldrs: rdn over 2f out: outpcd over 1f out: plugged on ins fnl f* 7/2[1]
0352 8 3/4 **Milton Road**[9] 2329 4-9-3 56 DanielTudhope 9 51
(Rebecca Bastiman) *chsd ldrs: rdn 2f out: carried lft appr fnl f: no ex ins fnl f* 11/2[3]
5- 9 1/2 **Canford Art (IRE)**[301] 4968 4-9-7 60 RobbieDowney 1 51
(Peter Fahey, Ire) *chsd ldrs on outside: rdn over 2f out: outpcd over 1f out and no threat after* 14/1
0-00 10 2 **Searanger (USA)**[28] 1766 6-9-2 60 BenSanderson(5) 13 45
(Rebecca Menzies) *s.i.s: hld up: nvr threatened* 10/1
2124 11 2 1/4 **Spirit Of Zebedee (IRE)**[21] 1930 6-9-6 59 (v) JasonHart 4 37
(John Quinn) *swtchd rt after s to r against stands' rail: pressed ldr: rdn over 2f out: wknd ins fnl f* 7/1
010- 12 1/2 **Gilmer (IRE)**[186] 8902 8-9-0 58 (v) DylanHogan(5) 15 35
(Stef Keniry) *a towards rr* 20/1
2-05 13 1 1/4 **Coastal Drive**[19] 1976 4-9-7 60 (p) KevinStott 6 33
(Paul Midgley) *prom: rdn over 2f out: wknd over 1f out* 14/1
-000 14 2 1/4 **My Name Is Rio (IRE)**[28] 1765 9-9-4 57 SamJames 5 23
(John Davies) *prom on outer: rdn over 2f out: wknd over 1f out* 22/1
066- 15 20 **Hop Maddocks (IRE)**[189] 8831 4-9-7 60 GrahamLee 3
(Fred Watson) *midfield: pushed along over 3f out: sn wknd: bhd fnl 2f* 50/1

1m 12.36s (-0.44) **Going Correction** +0.025s/f (Good) **15 Ran SP% 122.0**
Speed ratings (Par 101): **103,101,99,98,98 97,97,96,95,93 90,89,87,84,58**
CSF £75.71 CT £1850.24 TOTE £5.30: £2.60, £5.60, £7.60; EX 119.10 Trifecta £1447.90.
Owner Walter Veti **Bred** Bearstone Stud Ltd **Trained** Langton, N Yorks

FOCUS
A low-grade handicap but the time was the fastest of the three races over the trip on the night.
T/Plt: £199.60 to a £1 stake. Pool: £53,129.65 - 194.31 winning units T/Qpdt: £18.10 to a £1 stake. Pool: £8,654.39 - 352.55 winning units **Andrew Sheret**

The Form Book Flat 2019, Raceform Ltd, Newbury, RG14 5SJ

2639 - 2641a (Foreign Racing) - See Raceform Interactive

2218

NAAS (L-H)

Saturday, May 11

OFFICIAL GOING: Good (good to yielding in places)

2642a IRISH NATIONAL STUD RACING IRISH EBF BLUE WIND STKS (GROUP 3) (F&M) 1m 2f

3:20 (3:20) 3-Y-O+

£42,567 (£13,738; £6,531; £2,927; £1,486; £765)

RPR

1 **Tarnawa (IRE)**[13] 2157 3-8-9 98 .... ChrisHayes 3 104
(D K Weld, Ire) *cl up tl sn settled bhd ldrs: 4th 1/2-way: hdwy nr side 2f out: rdn in 2nd 1 1/2f out and kpt on wl u.p ins fnl f to ld cl home* **4/1**[3]

2 nk **Who's Steph (IRE)**[6] 2451 4-9-9 108 .... ColinKeane 1 103
(G M Lyons, Ire) *led: jnd bef 1/2-way and disp ld: narrow advantage after 1/2-way: stl gng wl into st and extended ld over 2f out: rdn 1 1/2f out and strly pressed wl ins fnl f: hdd cl home* **8/11**[1]

3 3/4 **Delphinia (IRE)**[48] 1307 3-8-9 91 .... ShaneCrosse 4 102+
(A P O'Brien, Ire) *sn trckd ldr: disp ld fr bef 1/2-way: cl 2nd after 1/2-way: rdn in 2nd over 2f out and u.p in 3rd ins fnl f where n.m.r briefly: kpt on same pce nr fin* **14/1**

4 shd **Peach Tree (IRE)**[209] 8241 3-8-9 104 .... SeamieHeffernan 2 101
(A P O'Brien, Ire) *chsd ldrs: 3rd 1/2-way: rdn bhd ldrs over 2f out: u.p in 4th ins fnl f where n.m.r on inner briefly: kpt on same pce nr fin* **7/2**[2]

5 1 1/2 **Chablis (IRE)**[13] 2157 3-8-9 0 .... GaryHalpin 5 98
(A P O'Brien, Ire) *hld up towards rr: 5th 1/2-way: drvn under 3f out and no imp on ldrs u.p disputing 5th ins fnl f: kpt on nr fin* **20/1**

6 3/4 **Magnolia Springs (IRE)**[34] 1627 4-9-9 92 .... WJLee 7 97
(Eve Johnson Houghton) *w.w in rr: last at 1/2-way: tk clsr order between horses after 1/2-way: 5th into st: rdn over 2f out and no imp on ldrs u.p 1 1/2f out: one pce in 6th wl ins fnl f* **20/1**

7 3/4 **Credenza (IRE)**[6] 2451 3-8-9 95 .... KillianHennessy 6 95
(A P O'Brien, Ire) *w.w in 6th: last after 1/2-way: wd into st: rdn nr side over 2f out and no imp on ldrs: one pce fnl f* **25/1**

2m 14.7s (-0.90)
WFA 3 from 4yo 15lb **7 Ran SP% 120.2**
CSF £7.66 TOTE £3.30: £2.10, £1.02; DF 8.00 Trifecta £69.20.
Owner H H Aga Khan **Bred** His Highness The Aga Khan's Studs S C **Trained** Curragh, Co Kildare
■ Stewards' Enquiry : Seamie Heffernan caution: use of whip

FOCUS
A fine finish to this contest, and the improving winner could well have earned herself a place in the field for the Investec Oaks.

2643 - 2645a (Foreign Racing) - See Raceform Interactive

BELMONT PARK (L-H)

Saturday, May 11

OFFICIAL GOING: Dirt: fast; turf: firm

2646a MAN O' WAR STKS (GRADE 1) (4YO+) (MAIN TURF) (TURF) 1m 3f (T)

11:24 4-Y-O+

£295,275 (£102,362; £55,118; £36,220; £23,622; £15,748)

RPR

1 **Channel Maker (CAN)**[70] 5-8-12 0 ....(b) JoelRosario 8 117
(William Mott, U.S.A) *racd in 3rd: rdn to chse clr ldr under 2f out: drvn ins fnl f: styd on wl to ld 100yds out: hld on clsng stages* **68/10**

2 nk **Arklow (USA)**[36] 5-8-7 0 .... FlorentGeroux 4 111
(Brad H Cox, U.S.A) *hld up in rr: rdn and hdwy fr 2f out: styd on strly fnl f: nrst fin* **31/5**

3 1/2 **Magic Wand (IRE)**[42] 1446 4-8-4 .... WayneLordan 5 108
(A P O'Brien, Ire) *hld up towards rr of midfield: rdn and hdwy fr over 2f out: drvn and styd on wl fr over 1f out: nrst fin* **61/20**[2]

4 nk **Hunting Horn (IRE)**[42] 1446 4-8-7 0 .... MichaelHussey 1 110
(A P O'Brien, Ire) *led at gd pce: sn clr: rdn 2f out: stl clr ent st: drvn and wknd fnl f: hdd 100yds out: lost two more pls cl home* **121/10**

5 3 1/2 **Epical (USA)**[43] 4-8-9 0 .... TylerBaze 7 106
(James M Cassidy, U.S.A) *chsd clr ldr: rdn 2 1/2f out: dropped to 3rd 2f out: wknd fnl f* **79/10**

6 1/2 **Focus Group (USA)**[42] 5-8-9 0 ....(b) IradOrtizJr 6 105
(Chad C Brown, U.S.A) *hld up towards rr of midfield: rdn and no imp fr over 2f out* **11/4**[1]

7 1/2 **Zulu Alpha (USA)**[21] 6-8-9 0 .... JavierCastellano 2 104
(Michael J Maker, U.S.A) *midfield: rdn and no imp fr 2 1/2f out: wknd steadily fnl f* **47/10**[3]

8 2 1/4 **Village King (ARG)**[42] 4-8-4 0 .... JohnRVelazquez 3 95
(Todd Pletcher, U.S.A) *midfield: rdn and lost pl appr 2f out: sn btn* **25/1**

9 2 1/4 **Kulin Rock (USA)**[16] 5-8-6 0 ow2........................(b) KendrickCarmouche 9 91
(Michael J Maker, U.S.A) *a towards rr* **59/1**

2m 12.43s (-2.62) **9 Ran SP% 120.0**
PARI-MUTUEL (all including 2 unit stake): WIN 15.60; PLACE (1-2) 7.20, 7.00; SHOW (1-2-3) 4.90, 4.30, 3.60; SF 103.50.
Owner Wachtel Stable, Gary Barber Et Al **Bred** Tall Oaks Farm **Trained** USA

FOCUS
A bunch finish for this Grade 1.

2498

CHANTILLY (R-H)

Saturday, May 11

OFFICIAL GOING: Turf: very soft

2647a PRIX DE VERNEUIL-EN-HALATTE (H'CAP) (4YO) (TURF) 1m 2f

11:45 4-Y-O

£8,558 (£3,423; £2,567; £1,711; £855)

RPR

1 **Peaceful City (FR)**[31] 4-9-3 0 .... MlleCoraliePacaut(3) 14 73
(M Boutin, France) **192/10**

2 2 1/2 **Raster (FR)**[31] 4-9-0 0 .... ChristopheSoumillon 1 62
(M Boutin, France) **43/10**[2]

3 3/4 **Seeking Revenge (FR)**[31] 4-8-8 0 .... MlleLauraGrosso(3) 13 58
(Mme E Siavy-Julien, France) **25/1**

4 3/4 **Formi (IRE)**[182] 4-9-3 0 ....(b) StephanePasquier 16 62
(L Gadbin, France) **14/1**

5 1 1/2 **Blocking Bet (FR)**[91] 4-9-6 0 .... CyrilleStefan 3 62
(M Boutin, France) **29/1**

6 nse **Tigresse Tianjin**[31] 4-9-1 0 ....(p) SebastienMaillot 12 57
(C Plisson, France) **42/1**

7 2 1/2 **Minnehaha (FR)**[13] 2170 4-8-7 0 .... MlleLeaBails(7) 5 51
(A Schouteet, Belgium) **77/10**[3]

8 4 1/2 **Onesarnieshort (FR)**[31] 4-8-10 0 .... MrGuilainBertrand 6 38
(G Bertrand, France) **26/1**

9 3 **Miss Alpha (FR)**[225] 4-8-13 0 .... MaximeGuyon 9 35
(F Vermeulen, France) **11/5**[1]

10 1 1/2 **Vingtcoeurs (FR)**[31] 4-9-4 0 .... AurelienLemaitre 2 37
(C Plisson, France) **16/1**

11 1 1/2 **Espoir Parfait (FR)**[29] 4-8-7 0 ....(b) MlleEleniTsouchnika(7) 10 30
(C Theodorakis, Greece) **37/1**

12 6 **Koosto (FR)**[31] 4-8-13 0 .... DelphineSantiago(3) 7 20
(A Junk, France) **84/10**

13 1/2 **Amiral Chop (FR)**[6] 4-8-9 0 .... AdrienMoreau 4 12
(C Boutin, France) **46/1**

14 nse **Dimanche A Bamako (FR)**[6] 4-9-4 0 .... AlexisBadel 15 21
(C Boutin, France) **38/1**

15 2 **Captain Kissinger**[13] 2170 4-9-2 0 ....(b) MickaelBarzalona 8 15
(Jo Hughes, France) *racd keenly: hld up in midfield on outer: clsd to be prom 1/2-way: 4th and drvn over 2f out: wknd qckly appr fnl f* **10/1**

2m 12.41s (7.61) **15 Ran SP% 119.4**
PARI-MUTUEL (all including 1 euro stake): WIN 20.20; PLACE 5.10, 2.30, 6.50; DF 53.40.
Owner Ecurie Rogier **Bred** J-C Seroul **Trained** France

2648a PRIX DU CHAUDRON (CONDITIONS) (4YO+) (TURF) 6f

12:15 4-Y-O+

£12,612 (£4,792; £3,531; £2,018; £1,009; £756)

RPR

1 **Alba Power (IRE)**[195] 4-9-0 0 ....(b[1]) StephanePasquier 5 106
(F Chappet, France) **57/10**

2 2 1/2 **Euryale (IRE)**[13] 5-9-3 0 .... AurelienLemaitre 6 101
(J-V Toux, France) **17/10**[1]

3 3 1/2 **Stormbringer**[224] 7759 4-9-0 0 .... Pierre-CharlesBoudot 1 87
(Gavin Hernon, France) **21/10**[2]

4 3/4 **Art Collection (FR)**[19] 6-9-3 0 .... EddyHardouin 3 87
(Andrew Hollinshead, France) **13/1**

5 nk **Orangefield (FR)**[19] 8-9-3 0 .... SebastienMaillot 8 86
(M Boutin, France) **54/10**[3]

6 10 **Mayleaf Shine (IRE)**[43] 1411 5-8-10 0 ....(b[1]) CristianDemuro 7 47
(Mme Doris Schoenherr, France) **9/1**

7 3 1/2 **White Feather**[334] 3690 4-9-0 0 ....(b) Louis-PhilippeBeuzelin 2 40
(Jo Hughes, France) *a towards rr: lost tch fr 1/2-way* **28/1**

1m 14.34s (2.94) **7 Ran SP% 120.4**
PARI-MUTUEL (all including 1 euro stake): WIN 6.70; PLACE 1.40, 1.10, 1.30; DF 5.30.
Owner Ms Fiona Carmichael **Bred** Shehila Partnership **Trained** France

2649 - 2659a (Foreign Racing) - See Raceform Interactive

1599

LEOPARDSTOWN (L-H)

Sunday, May 12

OFFICIAL GOING: Good to yielding

2660a COMER GROUP INTERNATIONAL AMETHYST STKS (GROUP 3) 1m

2:15 (2:15) 3-Y-O+

£33,513 (£10,810; £5,135; £2,297; £1,162; £594)

RPR

1 **Hazapour (IRE)**[29] 1777 4-9-9 110 .... OisinOrr 6 111+
(D K Weld, Ire) *chsd ldrs early tl impr to dispute 2nd after 1f: 2nd bef 1/2-way: led gng best under 2f out: sn rdn and extended advantage 1f out: pressed briefly ins fnl f tl kpt on wl to assert clsng stages: comf* **2/1**[1]

2 2 1/2 **Verbal Dexterity (IRE)**[39] 1531 4-9-9 106 .... KevinManning 4 105
(J S Bolger, Ire) *chsd ldrs: 4th 1/2-way: hdwy into 2nd 1 1/2f out: sn rdn and pressed wnr briefly ins fnl f tl no imp clsng stages* **7/2**[3]

3 1/2 **Zihba (IRE)**[39] 1531 4-9-9 104 .... ChrisHayes 1 104+
(J A Stack, Ire) *hld up bhd ldrs: pushed along briefly after 1f: 5th 1/2-way: pushed along in 5th into st and sme hdwy into 3rd ent fnl f where no imp on wnr: kpt on same pce* **9/4**[2]

4 1/2 **Dunkirk Harbour (USA)**[18] 2038 3-8-10 89 ....(b) SeamieHeffernan 2 100+
(A P O'Brien, Ire) *led briefly tl sn hdd and settled bhd ldr: jnd for 2nd after 1f: 3rd bef 1/2-way: pushed along bhd ldrs over 3f out and no imp u.p in 5th over 1f out: kpt on same pce ins fnl f into 4th cl home* **8/1**

5 1/2 **Zuenoon (IRE)**[13] 2222 3-8-10 95 ....(p[1]) ConorHoban 5 99
(D K Weld, Ire) *pushed along fr s and sn led: 1 l clr at 1/2-way: drvn and hdd under 2f out: sn no ex u.p in 3rd: wknd* **16/1**

6 26 **Psychedelic Funk**[17] 2069 5-9-9 106 .... ColinKeane 3 42
(G M Lyons, Ire) *in rr thrght: pushed along on outer 3f out and no ex under 2f out: wknd and eased fr over 1f out (jockey reported the gelding to have cut his tongue but was otherwise post race normal.)* **9/1**

1m 42.12s (-1.68) **Going Correction** +0.20s/f (Good)
WFA 3 from 4yo+ 13lb **6 Ran SP% 113.3**
Speed ratings: **116,113,113,112,112 86**
CSF £9.57 TOTE £2.90: £1.70, £2.00; DF 9.40 Trifecta £21.10.
Owner H H Aga Khan **Bred** His Highness The Aga Khan's Studs S C **Trained** Curragh, Co Kildare

FOCUS
Each one of these had a question of one sort or another to answer. In respect of the winner, last season's Derrinstown Stud Derby Trial winner and Derby fifth, it was how effectively he could cope with the 1m trip. With the help of intelligent tactics, he proved more than equal to the task. The third helps the standard in line with his C&D latest, with the winner close to his mark.

2661a DERRINSTOWN STUD 1,000 GUINEAS TRIAL (GROUP 3) (FILLIES) 1m
2:50 (2:51) 3-Y-O

£31,891 (£10,270; £4,864; £2,162; £1,081; £540)

RPR

1 **Hamariyna (IRE)**[17] 2070 3-9-0 0........................ RonanWhelan 9 99+
(M Halford, Ire) *trckd ldr: 2nd 1/2-way: led gng wl over 2f out: sn strly pressed and rdn w narrow advantage 1 1/2f out: styd on wl u.p to assert far side ins fnl f: reduced ld cl home* **5/1**

2 1 1/4 **Dean Street Doll (IRE)**[15] 2131 3-9-0 0........................ ColinKeane 5 95
(Richard John O'Brien, Ire) *hld up towards rr: disp 8th at 1/2-way: hdwy far side 2f out: rdn into 3rd ins fnl f and kpt on wl u.p into 2nd wl ins fnl f where no imp on wnr: a hld* **11/2**

3 hd **Trethias**[14] 2157 3-9-0 97........................ ShaneFoley 1 95
(Mrs John Harrington, Ire) *chsd ldrs: 4th 1/2-way: rdn into 3rd under 2f out and no imp on wnr over 1f out: u.p in 4th ins fnl f: kpt on wl into 3rd nr fin: jst hld for 2nd* **7/2**[1]

4 1 1/4 **Titanium Sky (IRE)**[6] 2493 3-9-0 0........................ OisinOrr 8 92
(D K Weld, Ire) *hld up towards rr: disp 8th at 1/2-way: stl gng wl into st: rdn and hdwy nr side 1 1/2f out to chse ldrs: no imp on wnr in 5th wl ins fnl f: kpt on same pce in 4th cl home* **4/1**[2]

5 1/2 **Fire Fly (IRE)**[36] 1601 3-9-0 89........................ DonnachaO'Brien 7 91
(A P O'Brien, Ire) *chsd ldrs: 3rd 1/2-way: tk clsr order in 2nd over 2f out gng wl: rdn in cl 2nd over 1f out and sn no imp on wnr: wknd wl ins fnl f into 5th* **9/2**[3]

6 1 **Madam Seamstress (IRE)**[39] 1533 3-9-0 77........................ KevinManning 4 88
(J S Bolger, Ire) *settled in rr: last at 1/2-way: gng wl into st: prog nr side 1f out and rdn: wnt 6th ins fnl f where edgd sltly lft and no imp on ldrs: kpt on* **25/1**

7 2 **Mia Mento (IRE)**[230] 7632 3-9-0 91........................ NGMcCullagh 6 84
(Thomas Mullins, Ire) *prom tl sn settled in mid-div: 5th 1/2-way: tk clsr order 2f out: sn rdn and no ex over 1f out: one pce fnl f* **20/1**

8 1 1/4 **Lady Wannabe (IRE)**[35] 1617 3-9-0 0........................ ChrisHayes 3 81
(J A Stack, Ire) *settled in mid-div: 6th 1/2-way: drvn over 2f out and no imp over 1f out: wknd and eased ins fnl f* **12/1**

9 1 3/4 **Beau Warrior (IRE)**[10] 2319 3-9-0 92........................ RoryCleary 2 77
(Adrian McGuinness, Ire) *dwlt and in rr early: 7th 1/2-way: rdn 2f out and no imp on ldrs: one pce after* **14/1**

10 35 **Mona Lisa's Smile (USA)**[7] 2445 3-9-0 0........................ SeamieHeffernan 10
(A P O'Brien, Ire) *sn led: extended advantage after 2f: reduced ld at 1/2-way: rdn and hdd over 2f out: sn wknd: eased in rr ins fnl f* **25/1**

1m 42.99s (-0.81) **Going Correction** +0.20s/f (Good) **10** Ran SP% **119.3**
Speed ratings: **112,110,110,109,108 107,105,104,102,67**
CSF £32.56 TOTE £5.30: £1.70, £1.90, £1.50; DF 36.60 Trifecta £205.80.

Owner H H Aga Khan **Bred** His Highness The Aga Khan's Studs S C **Trained** Doneany, Co Kildare

FOCUS
Not a particularly strong Group 3 race on paper (a 97-rated filly started favourite and finished third), but the winner and second both stepped up promisingly from a maiden win and look capable of further progress.

2662a DERRINSTOWN STUD DERBY TRIAL STKS (GROUP 3) 1m 2f
3:25 (3:26) 3-Y-O

£53,153 (£17,117; £8,108; £3,603; £1,801; £900)

RPR

1 **Broome (IRE)**[36] 1603 3-9-3 115........................ DonnachaO'Brien 3 113+
(A P O'Brien, Ire) *dwlt sltly: w.w: 6th 1/2-way: pushed along 3f out and hdwy to dispute 3rd far side 1 1/2f out: sn swtchd rt and impr to chal ins fnl f where rdn briefly to ld: drvn clr and styd on wl: comf* **2/5**[1]

2 2 1/2 **Blenheim Palace (IRE)**[14] 2159 3-9-3 86........................ EmmetMcNamara 4 105
(A P O'Brien, Ire) *sn led: over 1 l clr at 1/2-way: pushed along 3f out: rdn and strly pressed over 2f out: hdd ins fnl f and sn no ch w wnr in 2nd: kpt on wl* **33/1**

3 1/2 **Sovereign (IRE)**[36] 1603 3-9-3 103........................ SeamieHeffernan 1 104
(A P O'Brien, Ire) *sn settled bhd ldr: 2nd 1/2-way: tk clsr order almost on terms under 2f out: rdn in cl 2nd ent fnl f and sn no ch w wnr u.p in 3rd: kpt on wl* **7/1**[2]

4 1 3/4 **Rakan**[204] 8426 3-9-3 95........................ ChrisHayes 7 101
(D K Weld, Ire) *hld up in 5th: pushed along into st and impr into 3rd under 2f out: sn rdn disputing 3rd and no imp on wnr u.p in 4th ins fnl f: kpt on same pce* **7/1**[2]

5 3/4 **Buckhurst (IRE)**[36] 1599 3-9-3 0........................ WayneLordan 6 99
(Joseph Patrick O'Brien, Ire) *w.w in rr: last at 1/2-way: pushed along 3f out sme hdwy u.p into 5th 1 1/2f out: kpt on same pce ins fnl f: nvr trbld ldrs* **16/1**[3]

6 1 1/4 **Guaranteed (IRE)**[36] 1603 3-9-3 106........................(t) KevinManning 5 97
(J S Bolger, Ire) *chsd ldrs: 4th 1/2-way: pushed along 3f out and lost pl over 2f out: rdn in rr 1 1/2f out and kpt on one pce ins fnl f into 6th* **20/1**

7 1 1/4 **Pythion (FR)**[36] 1603 3-9-3 100........................ ColinKeane 2 94
(G M Lyons, Ire) *chsd ldrs: 3rd 1/2-way: drvn 3f out and no ex u.p bhd ldrs over 2f out: wknd into 6th over 1f out: no imp whn n.m.r briefly on inner ins fnl f: eased nr fin* **20/1**

2m 9.18s (-2.52) **Going Correction** +0.20s/f (Good) **7** Ran SP% **114.8**
Speed ratings: **118,116,115,114,113 112,111**
CSF £23.16 TOTE £1.30: £1.02, £6.30; DF 13.00 Trifecta £33.00.

Owner Michael Tabor & Derrick Smith & Mrs John Magnier **Bred** Epona Bloodstock Ltd **Trained** Cashel, Co Tipperary

FOCUS
A one-two-three for Aidan O'Brien, a perfect end to a week in which the stable has put itself in a strong position to mount a potent Derby challenge. The form is rated around the improving Broome and the third.

2663 - 2665a (Foreign Racing) - See Raceform Interactive

HOPPEGARTEN (R-H)
Sunday, May 12

OFFICIAL GOING: Turf: good

2666a COMER GROUP INTERNATIONAL 48TH OLEANDER-RENNEN (GROUP 2) (4YO+) (TURF) 2m
3:45 4-Y-O+ £54,054 (£18,918; £9,909; £4,954; £2,252)

RPR

1 **Raa Atoll**[304] 4871 4-9-0 0........................ JozefBojko 8 110+
(Luke Comer, Ire) *a cl up: drvn to ld wl over 2f out: styd on strly* **32/1**

2 1 1/2 **Thomas Hobson**[204] 8404 9-9-2 0........................ OisinMurphy 5 107
(W P Mullins, Ire) *w.w in fnl trio: tk clsr order after 1/2-way: 6th and drvn appr 2 1/2f out: styd on to chse wnr fr 1 1/2f out: styd on but a hld* **1/2**[1]

3 1 3/4 **Moonshiner (GER)**[21] 6-9-0 0........................(p) FilipMinarik 4 103
(Jean-Pierre Carvalho, Germany) *w.w adrift in rr: began to make grnd fr 5f out: styd on fnl 2f: wnt 3rd ins fnl f: no further imp* **122/10**[3]

4 1 3/4 **Adler (GER)**[217] 8022 5-9-0 0........................ MartinSeidl 9 101+
(Markus Klug, Germany) *settled towards rr: tk clsr order 3 1/2f out: styd on u.p: nt rch ldrs* **34/1**

5 2 **Nikkei (GER)**[217] 8022 4-9-0 0........................ AndraschStarke 11 102
(P Schiergen, Germany) *settled in midfield on outer: clsd steadily to chse ldrs after 1/2-way: rdn and nt qckn 2f out: kpt on at one pce u.p* **7/1**[2]

6 2 3/4 **Abadan**[28] 5-8-10 0........................(p) MichaelCadeddu 2 92
(Henk Grewe, Germany) *trckd ldr on inner: rdn and no imp 2 1/2f out: steadily dropped away* **64/1**

7 nse **Berghain (IRE)**[21] 6-9-0 0........................ JackMitchell 12 96
(J Hirschberger, Germany) *settled towards rr: rdn along 3f out: began to cl on outer 2f out: jinked lft as nred rival 1 1/2f out: kpt on u.p: nvr in contention* **41/1**

8 nk **Ernesto (GER)**[21] 4-9-0 0........................ AdriedeVries 6 98
(Markus Klug, Germany) *prom: dropped into midfield after 1/2-way: kpt on u.p fr 2f out: nt pce to get involved* **7/1**[2]

9 8 **Zabriskie (IRE)**[224] 7814 4-9-0 0........................ SibylleVogt 7 90
(Luke Comer, Ire) *midfield on inner: lost pl 3 1/2f out: wl hld fr 2f out* **34/1**

10 11 **Klungel (GER)**[21] 4-9-0 0........................ MaximPecheur 3 78
(Markus Klug, Germany) *w.w in fnl trio: rdn and btn 2f fr home: eased ins fnl f* **71/1**

11 2 1/2 **Quintarelli (GER)**[20] 4-9-0 0........................ RenePiechulek 1 75
(Dr A Bolte, Germany) *racd keenly: led: drvn over 3f out: hdd wl over 2f out: sn wknd* **37/1**

12 22 **Wisperwind (GER)**[21] 7-9-0 0........................(p) BauyrzhanMurzabayev 10 48
(Henk Grewe, Germany) *prom on outer: rn in snatches and tried to hang lft: drvn and began to lose pl after 1/2-way: wl bhd fnl 2f and eased* **232/10**

3m 23.1s
WFA 4 from 5yo+ 1lb **12** Ran SP% **120.1**
PARI-MUTUEL (all including 1 euro stake): WIN 33.20 PLACE 4.00, 1.50, 2.30 SF 50.20.
Owner Luke Comer **Bred** Mr & Mrs J Davis & P Mitchell B'Stock **Trained** Dunboyne, Co Meath

2426 LONGCHAMP (R-H)
Sunday, May 12

OFFICIAL GOING: Turf: heavy

2667a PRIX DE SAINT-GEORGES (GROUP 3) (3YO+) (TURF) 5f (S)
1:35 3-Y-O+ £36,036 (£14,414; £10,810; £7,207; £3,603)

RPR

1 **Sestilio Jet (FR)**[16] 2089 4-9-2 0........................ FrankieDettori 7 111
(Andrea Marcialis, France) *cl up: pushed along to chal ldr jst under 2f out: rdn 1 1/2f out: led jst ins fnl f: hung sltly lft clsng stages: r.o strly* **29/10**[1]

2 3/4 **Batwan (FR)**[44] 1411 4-9-2 0........................ Pierre-CharlesBoudot 4 108
(P Sogorb, France) *prom: pushed along and effrt 2f out: swtchd to far side rail and drvn over 1f out: prog into 2nd ins fnl f: nt quite pce to chal wnr* **9/1**

3 1 1/2 **Ken Colt (IRE)**[26] 4-9-2 0........................ StephanePasquier 8 103
(F Chappet, France) *qckly into stride: led: asked to qckn whn pressed jst under 2f out: rdn 1 1/2f out: hdd jst ins fnl f: kpt on same pce fnl 110yds* **19/1**

4 1 1/4 **Gold Vibe (IRE)**[193] 8755 6-9-2 0........................(b) CristianDemuro 9 98
(P Bary, France) *racd towards rr: prog fr over 2 1/2f out: pushed along 2f out: rdn over 1f out: kpt on clsng stages but nvr threatened* **37/10**[3]

5 3/4 **Forza Capitano (FR)**[23] 1919 4-9-2 0........................ VincentCheminaud 1 96
(H-A Pantall, France) *midfield: pushed along between rivals jst under 2f out: rdn ent fnl f: unable qck: kpt on same pce fnl 110yds* **37/10**[3]

6 1 1/2 **The Broghie Man**[183] 9003 4-9-2 0........................(b) GeraldMosse 5 90
(Adrian Paul Keatley, Ire) *towards rr: sltly outpcd and pushed along 2 1/2f out: rdn 1 1/2f out: no imp and btn ent fnl f* **22/1**

7 hd **Bakoel Koffie (IRE)**[44] 1411 5-9-2 0........................ TonyPiccone 3 90
(M Delcher Sanchez, France) *prom: asked for effrt over 2f out: no imp and sn drvn: grad wknd fr 1 1/2f out* **7/2**[2]

8 1 **Coco City (FR)**[16] 2089 5-9-2 0........................ OlivierPeslier 6 86
(M Delcher Sanchez, France) *midfield: struggling to go pce and pushed along 2f out: sn drvn: no imp and wl hld ent fnl f* **19/1**

9 2 **Sosume (FR)**[32] 3-8-7 0........................(b[1]) AntoineHamelin 2 75
(Gavin Hernon, France) *a in rr: outpcd over 1/2-way: no rspnse whn pushed along over 2f out: wl btn over 1f out* **21/1**

59.02s (2.72)
WFA 3 from 4yo+ 9lb **9** Ran SP% **119.3**
PARI-MUTUEL (all including 1 euro stake): WIN 3.90 PLACE 2.10, 2.80, 4.40 DF 11.90.
Owner Akhal Teke Properties **Bred** M Monfort **Trained** France

FOCUS
The winner is rated in line with a best view of his previous form.

2668a THE EMIRATES POULE D'ESSAI DES POULAINS (GROUP 1) (3YO COLTS) (TURF) 1m

2:55 3-Y-0 **£308,864** (£123,567; £61,783; £30,864; £15,459)

RPR

1 **Persian King (IRE)**[28] 1794 3-9-2 0 .... Pierre-CharlesBoudot 2 115
(A Fabre, France) *racd keenly: in tch in midfield on inner: stuck to rail at cutaway over 2f out: shkn up and lened to ld wl over 1f out: r.o u.p* **1/2**[1]

2 *1* **Shaman (IRE)**[35] 1625 3-9-2 0 .... MaximeGuyon 11 112
(C Laffon-Parias, France) *racd keenly: a cl up on outer: drvn to ld narrowly 2f out: hdd wl over 1f out: rallied u.p: clsng again cl home: hld on for 2nd* **32/5**[2]

3 *hd* **San Donato (IRE)**[197] 8629 3-9-2 0 .... AndreaAtzeni 8 112
(Roger Varian) *in rr of midfield on outer: 6th and n.m.r over 2f out: angled out and drvn 2f out: hdwy over 1f out: styd on u.p fnl f: chal for 2nd but no ex cl home* **28/1**

4 *1 3/4* **Graignes (FR)**[32] 1707 3-9-2 .... CristianDemuro 3 108
(Y Barberot, France) *hld up in last pair: clsd over 2f out: styd on u.p ent fnl f: tk 4th cl home: nvr trbld ldrs* **11/1**

5 *1 1/4* **Duke Of Hazzard (FR)**[28] 1794 3-9-2 0 .... OlivierPeslier 6 105
(Paul Cole) *trckd ldr on inner: rowed along to chal 2f out: ev ch over 1f out: grad lft bhd ins fnl f* **30/1**

6 *3/4* **Van Beethoven (CAN)**[43] 1443 3-9-2 0 .... RyanMoore 5 103
(A P O'Brien, Ire) *in rr of midfield on inner: drvn in pursuit of ldng gp over 1f out: no further imp ent fnl f where effrt flattened out* **40/1**

7 *1/2* **Anodor (FR)**[217] 8025 3-9-2 0 .... AurelienLemaitre 12 102
(F Head, France) *settled in fnl trio: rdn over 2f out: in last and u.p ent fnl f: styd on late: nvr in contention* **13/2**[3]

8 *nse* **Senza Limiti (IRE)**[22] 1940 3-9-2 0 .... JamesDoyle 10 102
(William Haggas) *led: drvn whn pressed over 2f out: dropped away fr over 1f out* **36/1**

9 *1 1/2* **Munitions (USA)**[32] 1707 3-9-2 0 .... MickaelBarzalona 7 99
(A Fabre, France) *in tch in midfield on outer: swtchd out and drvn w 1 1/2f to run but no imp: dropped away fnl f* **18/1**

10 *7* **Simply Striking (FR)**[14] 2166 3-9-2 0 .... TonyPiccone 1 88
(M Delcher Sanchez, France) *adrift in rr: pushed along 3f out: rdn and short-lived effrt 1 1/2f out: wknd over 1f out* **46/1**

1m 38.98s (0.58) **10 Ran SP% 121.1**
PARI-MUTUEL (all including 1 euro stake): WIN 1.40 PLACE 1.10, 1.30, 2.50 DF 2.90.
Owner Godolphin SNC & Ballymore Thoroughbred Ltd **Bred** Dayton Investments (Breeding) Limited **Trained** Chantilly, France

FOCUS
Not the most competitive French 2,000 Guineas, with just four of the 11 runners boasting a pre-race RPR above 110. Unsurprisingly it paid to be in the first half of the field. Persian King gave the fifth a slightly lesser beating than in the Prix de Fontainebleau.

2669a THE EMIRATES POULE D'ESSAI DES POULICHES (GROUP 1) (3YO FILLIES) (TURF) 1m

3:30 3-Y-0 **£257,387** (£102,972; £51,486; £25,720; £12,882)

RPR

1 **Castle Lady (IRE)**[28] 1795 3-9-0 0 .... MickaelBarzalona 6 112
(H-A Pantall, France) *racd a little keenly: prom: pushed along and effrt on outer jst under 2f out: prog to ld over 1f out: pressed ins fnl f: kpt on strly u.p: jst prevailed* **5/2**[1]

2 *nse* **Commes (FR)**[20] 3-9-0 0 .... CristianDemuro 1 112+
(J-C Rouget, France) *mid-div on inner: pushed along 2f out: rdn 1 1/2f out: picked up wl to press ldr ins fnl f: r.o wl: jst denied* **10/1**

3 *1 1/2* **East**[191] 8819 3-9-0 0 .... JamieSpencer 10 108+
(Kevin Ryan) *hld up towards rr: pushed along 2f out: rdn and prog outside rivals fr over 1f out: r.o: nt match pce of front pair* **41/10**[3]

4 *1/2* **Imperial Charm**[28] 1795 3-9-0 0 .... AndreaAtzeni 2 107
(Simon Crisford) *led early: jnd after 2f: regained narrow advantage after 3f: asked to qckn over 2f out: sn rdn: hdd over 1f out: no ex ins fnl f* **12/1**

5 *snk* **Matematica (GER)**[34] 3-9-0 0 .... MaximeGuyon 3 107
(C Laffon-Parias, France) *racd keenly: prom on inner: pushed along to chal 2f out: rdn 1 1/2f out: unable qck w ldr ins fnl f: kpt on same pce* **33/10**[2]

6 *1/2* **Watch Me (FR)**[32] 1706 3-9-0 0 .... OlivierPeslier 5 106+
(F-H Graffard, France) *mid-div: sltly outpcd and nudged along over 3f out: rdn jst under 2f out: sltly hmpd whn responding for press ins fnl f: kpt on* **9/1**

7 *1 1/4* **Rocques (FR)**[28] 1795 3-9-0 0 .... StephanePasquier 9 103
(F Chappet, France) *hld up in fnl trio: dropped to rr over 1/2-way: pushed along 2f out: sn rdn: modest prog ins fnl f but nvr in contention* **30/1**

8 *shd* **Coral Beach (IRE)**[204] 8428 3-9-0 0 .... RyanMoore 7 103
(A P O'Brien, Ire) *hld up in fnl pair: pushed along over 2f out: limited rspnse: kpt on under hands and heels riding ins fnl f: nvr a factor* **31/1**

9 *1/2* **Suphala (FR)**[32] 1706 3-9-0 0 .... Pierre-CharlesBoudot 4 102
(A Fabre, France) *cl up: jnd ldr after 2f: sn chsd ldr again: pushed along to chal 2f out: sltly hmpd whn nt qckn over 1f out: nt rcvr and grad wknd* **32/5**

10 *5 1/2* **Silva (IRE)**[80] 845 3-9-0 0 .... GregoryBenoist 8 89
(Mme Pia Brandt, France) *a towards rr: pushed along over 2f out: no imp and sn btn* **51/1**

1m 40.91s (2.51) **10 Ran SP% 120.0**
PARI-MUTUEL (all including 1 euro stake): WIN 3.50 PLACE 1.70, 2.10, 2.00 DF 16.80.
Owner Godolphin SNC **Bred** Godolphin **Trained** France

FOCUS
This year's French 1,000 Guineas was more competitive than the colts equivalent. They went just a routine pace and the first pair came clear.

2670a PRIX MAURICE ZILBER - FONDS EUROPEEN DE L'ELEVAGE (LISTED RACE) (4YO+ FILLIES & MARES) (TURF) 7f

4:05 4-Y-0+ **£21,621** (£8,648; £6,486; £4,324; £2,162)

RPR

1 **Spinning Memories (IRE)**[219] 7970 4-9-1 0 ..... Pierre-CharlesBoudot 6 104
(P Bary, France) **4/1**[2]

2 *1 1/2* **Comedia Eria (FR)**[40] 7-8-11 0 .... MaximeGuyon 4 96
(P Monfort, France) *racd keenly early: hld up in midfield: 4th and travelling wl 2f out: drvn to cl ins fnl f: disp ld 100yds out: nt match wnr fr there* **44/5**

3 *1 1/2* **Qualisaga (FR)**[14] 2167 5-8-11 0 .... EddyHardouin 8 92
(Carina Fey, France) **26/5**

4 *snk* **Style Presa (FR)**[26] 4-8-11 0 .... CristianDemuro 7 92
(Rod Collet, France) **23/5**[3]

5 *1 1/4* **River Cannes (FR)**[45] 4-8-11 0 .... GregoryBenoist 3 88
(T Castanheira, France) **62/1**

6 *3/4* **Lucie Manette**[203] 8448 4-9-1 0 .... MickaelBarzalona 5 90
(A Fabre, France) *hld up in rr: pushed along over 2f out: angled out and drvn 1 1/2f out: kpt on ins fnl f but n.d* **29/10**[1]

7 *2* **Silvery Mist (FR)**[23] 1918 4-8-11 0 .... StephanePasquier 2 81
(F Chappet, France) **47/10**

8 *shd* **Beauty Filly**[233] 7480 4-8-11 0 .... JamesDoyle 9 81
(William Haggas) *settled in 3rd: pushed along to chal over 2f out: led narrowly 1 1/2f out: hdd ent fnl f: sn wknd: no ex* **14/1**

9 *1 3/4* **Isole Canarie (IRE)**[11] 4-9-1 0 ....(b) AntoineHamelin 1 80
(Gavin Hernon, France) **27/1**

1m 22.5s (1.80) **9 Ran SP% 119.2**
PARI-MUTUEL (all including 1 euro stake): WIN 5.00 PLACE 2.40, 2.90, 2.30 DF 25.30.
Owner Sutong Pan Racing Bloodstock **Bred** Mubarak Al Naemi **Trained** Chantilly, France

2003 LES LANDES

Sunday, May 12

OFFICIAL GOING: Turf: good (good to firm in places)

2671a ARCADIA H'CAP SPRINT (TURF) 5f 100y

3:05 (3:18) 3-Y-0+ **£1,780** (£640; £380)

RPR

1 **Man Of The Sea (IRE)**[11] 2276 3-9-11 0 ....(tp) BrianHughes 61
(Neil Mulholland) *trckd ldrs in 3rd : hdwy to chal over 2f out: led 1f out: rdn out* **4/7**[1]

2 *4* **Country Blue (FR)**[258] 6645 10-10-5 0 ....(p) MattieBatchelor 51
(Mrs A Malzard, Jersey) *led: no ex whn hdd 1f out* **6/1**

3 *1 1/2* **Fruit Salad**[258] 6645 6-10-11 0 .... DaveCrosse 52
(K Kukk, Jersey) *hld up in 5 th : drvn and styd on one pce fr 2f out* **4/1**[3]

4 *3* **Doctor Parkes**[6] 2503 13-10-8 0 .... MrFrederickTett 39
(Natalie Lloyd-Beavis) *trckd ldrs in 4th: one pce fr 2f out* **9/4**[2]

5 *hd* **Honcho (IRE)**[20] 2004 7-10-2 0 .... VictoriaMalzard 32
(Mrs A Malzard, Jersey) *outpcd in last: nvr able to chal* **10/1**

6 *6* **Limelite (IRE)**[258] 6645 5-10-10 0 .... RyanWhile 20
(K Kukk, Jersey) *trckd ldr in cl 2nd: rdn and wknd fr 2f out* **11/2**

Owner Dajam Ltd **Bred** Stephanie Hanly **Trained** Limpley Stoke, Wilts

2672a JT REWARDS H'CAP (TURF) 1m 4f

4:15 (4:25) 3-Y-0+ **£1,780** (£640; £380)

RPR

1 **Island Song (IRE)**[19] 2026 5-10-3 0 .... MrFrederickTett 71
(Mrs A Malzard, Jersey) *t.k.h trcking ldr: wnt on after 3f: mde rest: qcknd clr 2f out: impressive* **6/1**

2 *10* **Moayadd (USA)**[18] 5871 7-10-9 0 .... BrianHughes 61
(Neil Mulholland) *hld up: 8 l 4th 4f out: rdn over 2f out: kpt on one pce to go 2nd 1f out: no ch w wnr* **11/8**[2]

3 *9* **White Valiant (FR)**[20] 6-10-12 0 .... DaveCrosse 50
(T Le Brocq, Jersey) *hld up: tk clsr order over 4f out: outpcd by wnr 2f out: wknd* **4/5**[1]

4 *9* **Benoordenhout (IRE)**[20] 8-10-4 0 .... GeorgeRooke 27
(T Le Brocq, Jersey) *led and t.k.h tl hdd after 3f: rdn 4f out: btn and wknd 2f out* **4/1**[3]

5 *1/2* **Hawaiian Freeze**[258] 10-9-0 0 ow7 .... MrDamienArtu 8
(J Moon, Jersey) *rel to r: a detached in last* **8/1**

Owner P G Somers **Bred** Highfort Stud **Trained** St Ouen, Jersey

2673a VICE PRESIDENT'S H'CAP (TURF) 1m 1f

4:50 (4:50) (0-55,0) 3-Y-0+ **£1,780** (£640; £380)

RPR

1 **Molliana**[35] 6080 4-9-7 0 .... BrianHughes 33
(Neil Mulholland) *trckd ldrs: hdwy fr 3f out: chal on rail and bdly hmpd 1 1/2f out: rallied to ld cl home: gamely* **11/8**[1]

2 *1* **Captain James (FR)**[20] 9-10-11 0 .... CharlieTodd 49
(Mrs C Gilbert, Jersey) *mid-div: hdwy fr 3f out: rdn to ld over 1f out: no ex whn hdd cl home* **11/4**[2]

3 *10* **William Booth (IRE)**[20] 2004 5-10-9 0 ....(v) MrWillPettis 26
(Mrs C Gilbert, Jersey) *trckd ldr: effrt to dispute ld 3f out to over 1f out: wknd* **14/1**

4 *2* **Frivolous Prince (IRE)**[258] 6-9-13 0 .... LeviWilliams 12
(Mrs C Gilbert, Jersey) *hld up: last 1/2-way: styd on fr over 2f out: nvr nrr* **16/1**

5 *1 1/2* **Brown Velvet**[20] 2004 7-10-10 0 .... MrFrederickTett 20
(Mrs C Gilbert, Jersey) *trckd ldrs: outpcd fr 3f out: kpt on one pce* **9/2**

6 *2 1/2* **Kalani Rose**[20] 2004 5-9-3 0 ....(v) MorganRaine
(Mrs A Corson, Jersey) *led: jnd 3f out: bmpd rival and unbalanced 1 1/2f out: immediately hdd & wknd* **28/1**

7 *1/2* **Ocean Crystal**[294] 7-10-5 0 .... DarraghKeogh 8
(Mrs A Malzard, Jersey) *hld up: nvr able to chal* **4/1**[3]

8 *1 1/2* **Snejinska (FR)**[20] 5-10-12 0 ....(h) MattieBatchelor 12
(Mrs C Gilbert, Jersey) *mid-div: nvr able to chal* **11/1**

9 *14* **Koshi**[20] 2004 4-10-2 0 .... DaveCrosse
(K Kukk, Jersey) *mid-div: brief effrt over 3f out: sn wknd and t.o* **4/1**[3]

10 *3/4* **Drummer Jack (IRE)**[20] 2004 3-9-11 0 .... RyanWhile
(K Kukk, Jersey) *bolted bef s: trckd ldrs: wknd fr over 3f out: t.o* **12/1**

11 *3/4* **Mendacious Harpy (IRE)**[6] 2504 8-9-8 0 .... VictoriaMalzard
(Mrs A Malzard, Jersey) *sn bhd: t.o* **6/1**

Owner Dajam Ltd **Bred** Norman Court Stud **Trained** Limpley Stoke, Wilts

2674 - (Foreign Racing) - See Raceform Interactive

2182 LYON PARILLY (R-H)

Wednesday, May 8

OFFICIAL GOING: Turf: soft

2675a PRIX DE MONPLAISIR (H'CAP) (4YO+) (TURF) — 1m

4:00 4-Y-O+ **£8,108** (£3,243; £2,432; £1,621; £810)

RPR

1 **Mascalino (GER)**[123] 5-9-5 0 ClementLecoeuvre 1 88
(H Blume, Germany) **28/1**

2 *hd* **Line Drummer (FR)**[266] 9-9-0 0 MaximeGuyon 8 82
(J Reynier, France) **17/10**[1]

3 *6 ½* **L'Optimiste (FR)**[11] 2182 6-9-8 0 FabriceVeron 3 75
(J Parize, France) **18/1**

4 *2 ½* **Agua De Valencia (FR)**[145] 5-9-1 0 AlexisLarue 12 63
(J-P Gauvin, France) **21/1**

5 *¾* **Enjoy The Silence (FR)**[8] 6-8-0 0 (p) BenjaminMarie(6) 5 52
(C Boutin, France) **13/2**

6 *3 ½* **Embajadores (IRE)**[34] 5-9-11 0 MlleMarylineEon(3) 4 66
(M Maillard, France) **71/10**

7 *nk* **Namasjar (FR)**[95] 5-9-8 0 (p) ChristopheSoumillon 6 59
(F Vermeulen, France) **47/10**[2]

8 *1 ¾* **Lefortovo (FR)**[31] 1631 6-9-11 0 MickaelBarzalona 9 58
(Jo Hughes, France) *settled towards rr of midfield: urged along over 2f out: rdn w limited rspnse over 1f out: no ex ins fnl f* **17/1**

9 *nk* **Wow (GER)**[34] 5-9-5 0 MlleCoraliePacaut(3) 2 55
(Andreas Suborics, Germany) **32/5**[3]

10 *9 ½* **Sir Bibi (FR)**[263] 7-9-10 0 TonyPiccone 10 35
(Lennart Hammer-Hansen, Germany) **23/1**

11 *½* **Alegia (FR)** 4-9-0 0 (p) LudovicProietti 7 24
(S Eveno, France) **87/1**

12 *18* **Floravise (FR)**[262] 4-9-5 0 CyrilleStefan 11
(E Caroux, France) **55/1**

1m 47.56s **12** Ran SP% **119.7**
PARI-MUTUEL (all including 1 euro stake): WIN 28.60; PLACE 6.50, 1.50, 4.00; DF 43.20.
Owner Stall Lahn-Sieg **Bred** Gestut Etzean **Trained** Germany

2676a (Foreign Racing) - See Raceform Interactive

2367 MUSSELBURGH (R-H)

Monday, May 13

OFFICIAL GOING: Good to firm (good in places; 9.1)

Wind: Light, half behind in sprints and in approximately 4f of home straight in races on the round course Weather: Cloudy, bright

2677 MUSSELBURGH RACECOURSE IS SUPPORTING #MENTALHEALTHAWARENESSWEEK MAIDEN AUCTION STKS — 1m 208y

2:00 (2:01) (Class 5) 3-Y-O **£3,234** (£962; £481; £240) **Stalls** Low

Form RPR

2-2 1 **Cape Victory (IRE)**[22] 1970 3-9-5 0 PJMcDonald 5 82+
(James Tate) *t.k.h early: mde all: rdn and pressed over 1f out: hung lft ins fnl f: kpt on strly* **10/11**[1]

3-50 2 *2* **Spirit Of Lund (IRE)**[16] 2101 3-9-2 74 JamieGormley(3) 2 75
(Iain Jardine) *trckd ldrs: pushed along and chsd wnr over 1f out: effrt and ev ch briefly over 1f out: edgd rt: one pce fnl f* **5/2**[2]

6-0 3 *5* **Catch My Breath**[26] 1856 3-9-5 0 PaulMulrennan 3 64
(John Ryan) *s.i.s: hld up in tch: pushed along over 2f out: hdwy over 1f out: no imp fnl f* **33/1**

55 4 *4 ½* **Smeaton (IRE)**[13] 2245 3-9-5 0 PaulHanagan 6 54
(Roger Fell) *s.i.s: hld up in tch: outpcd 1/2-way: shkn up and rallied 2f out: hung rt: no imp fnl f* **25/1**

0-62 5 *2 ½* **Simon's Smile (FR)**[11] 2336 3-9-5 67 (p) CliffordLee 1 49
(K R Burke) *pressed wnr tl rdn and outpcd over 2f out: btn over 1f out* **5/1**[3]

20 6 *30* **Farrdhana**[52] 1272 3-9-0 0 GrahamLee 4
(Bryan Smart) *plld hrd: chsd ldrs: drvn along 3f out: wknd 2f out: sn lost tch: b.b.v (vet said filly bled from the nose)* **40/1**

1m 54.12s (1.02) **Going Correction** +0.075s/f (Good) **6** Ran SP% **106.8**
Speed ratings (Par 99): **98,96,91,87,85 58**
CSF £2.92 TOTE £1.60: £1.10, £1.30; EX 2.90 Trifecta £24.50.
Owner Saeed Manana **Bred** Rabbah Bloodstock Limited **Trained** Newmarket, Suffolk

FOCUS
The bottom bend was out 2yds adding 7yds to all races 7f and up. There was 7mm of rain the previous week, but this was a dry, sunny, mild day. This was an ordinary maiden. The winner looks a likely improver and the runner-up is rated to form.

2678 RACING WELFARE MENTAL HEALTH FIRST AID TRAINING H'CAP — 5f 1y

2:30 (2:30) (Class 6) (0-55,56) 4-Y-O+ **£3,105** (£924; £461; £300; £300; £300) **Stalls** High

Form RPR

1-04 1 **Boudica Bay (IRE)**[12] 2295 4-9-6 54 RachelRichardson 6 61
(Eric Alston) *hld up in tch: hdwy 2f out: rdn to ld ins fnl f: edgd lft: kpt on strly* **10/1**[3]

00-0 2 *½* **Arnoul Of Metz**[28] 1820 4-9-2 55 DylanHogan(5) 10 60
(Henry Spiller) *hld up in midfield: effrt whn nt clr run over 1f out: rdn and kpt on wl fnl f to take 2nd nr fin: nt rch wnr* **25/1**

20-3 3 *nk* **Mr Shelby (IRE)**[11] 2324 5-9-6 54 (p) ShaneGray 4 58
(S Donohoe, Ire) *t.k.h: cl up: led over 1f out to ins fnl f: kpt on same pce and lost 2nd nr fin* **13/2**[2]

6-1 4 *1 ¼* **Bahlwan**[11] 2324 4-9-1 52 (t) KillianLeonard(3) 9 58+
(Denis Gerard Hogan, Ire) *dwlt and blkd s: sn pushed along in rr: angled rt and hdwy over 1f out: kpt on fnl f: nrst fin* **15/8**[1]

5-03 5 *nk* **Groundworker (IRE)**[14] 2189 8-9-0 48 (t) PaulMulrennan 5 47
(Paul Midgley) *cl up: effrt and ev ch briefly over 1f out: no ex ins fnl f* **18/1**

0-22 6 *nk* **Someone Exciting**[2] 2638 6-9-0 53 HarrisonShaw(5) 2 50
(David Thompson) *hld up: hdwy on outside 2f out: sn rdn: no further imp ins fnl f* **13/2**[2]

04-6 7 *1* **Thornaby Princess**[11] 2324 8-8-12 46 oh1 (v[1]) JasonHart 7 40
(Jason Ward) *led to over 1f out: rdn and wknd ins fnl f: lost front shoe (vet said mare lost it's right-fore shoe)* **14/1**

4000 8 *hd* **Foxy Boy**[11] 2324 5-8-13 47 DavidAllan 3 40
(Rebecca Bastiman) *cl up: effrt and ev ch briefly over 1f out: wknd ins fnl f* **18/1**

5500 9 *1* **Lord Of The Glen**[11] 2324 4-9-8 56 (b) AlistairRawlinson 8 46
(Jim Goldie) *hld up: rdn along 2f out: sme late hdwy: nvr rchd ldrs (jockey said gelding was never travelling)* **10/1**[3]

4463 10 *¾* **Roaring Rory**[15] 2153 6-9-3 54 (p) JamieGormley(3) 1 41
(Ollie Pears) *dwlt: bhd on outside: drvn along 1/2-way: nvr a factor (jockey said gelding was never travelling)* **11/1**

05-5 11 *½* **Corton Lass**[11] 2324 4-8-7 46 oh1 SeanDavis(5) 11 32
(Keith Dalgleish) *dwlt: sn midfield: rdn whn nt clr run briefly over 1f out: sn wknd* **20/1**

000- 12 *¾* **Lady Joanna Vassa (IRE)**[195] 8715 6-8-12 46 oh1 (p) PhilipPrince 13 28
(Richard Guest) *prom: rdn over 2f out: wknd over 1f out* **50/1**

000- 13 *7* **Princess Apollo**[187] 8926 5-8-9 46 oh1 (t) RowanScott(3) 12 3
(Donald Whillans) *chsd ldrs to over 2f out: wknd wl over 1f out* **100/1**

59.85s (0.15) **Going Correction** +0.075s/f (Good) **13** Ran SP% **116.7**
Speed ratings (Par 101): **101,100,99,97,97 96,95,94,93,92 91,90,78**
CSF £240.65 CT £1800.26 TOTE £12.70: £2.90, £8.60, £2.10; EX 353.90 Trifecta £2007.50.
Owner The Grumpy Old Geezers **Bred** Abbey Farm Stud **Trained** Longton, Lancs

FOCUS
A moderate handicap and routine form. The winner has the scope to do better.

2679 ALZHEIMER SCOTLAND H'CAP — 7f 33y

3:05 (3:06) (Class 3) (0-90,84) 4-Y-O+ **£8,092** (£2,423; £1,211; £605; £302; £152) **Stalls** Low

Form RPR

5-36 1 **Jacob Black**[10] 2372 8-8-9 72 (v) ShaneGray 1 80
(Keith Dalgleish) *hld up: smooth hdwy over 2f out: rdn and led over 1f out: edgd both ways ins fnl f: drvn out* **8/1**[3]

43-1 2 *1 ¾* **Right Action**[43] 1457 5-9-7 84 PaulHanagan 2 88
(Richard Fahey) *prom: rdn and outpcd over 2f out: rallied and chsd wnr ins fnl f: kpt on: nt pce to chal* **11/4**[2]

1031 3 *shd* **Kupa River (IRE)**[10] 2372 5-9-3 80 (h) PJMcDonald 7 83
(Roger Fell) *wnt lft s: t.k.h and sn chsng clr ldng pair: effrt and rdn over 2f out: disp 2nd pl over 1f out to ins fnl f: no ex* **9/4**[1]

1460 4 *1 ¼* **Gabrial The Tiger (IRE)**[30] 1768 7-8-0 68 SeanDavis(5) 6 68
(Richard Fahey) *t.k.h: led at decent gallop: rdn over 2f out: hdd over 1f out: no ex ins fnl f* **8/1**[3]

1-03 5 *2 ½* **How Bizarre**[10] 2372 4-8-10 73 (p[1]) PhilDennis 3 66
(Liam Bailey) *dwlt: t.k.h and sn pressing ldr: ev ch whn rn wd bnd over 3f out: rdn over 2f out: wknd over 1f out* **10/1**

0063 6 *1 ¾* **Logi (IRE)**[8] 2437 5-8-8 74 (b) JamieGormley(3) 4 62
(Rebecca Bastiman) *hld up: stdy hdwy over 2f out: rdn and wknd over 1f out* **9/1**

-313 7 *3 ½* **Sureyoutoldme (IRE)**[20] 2015 5-9-1 78 JamesSullivan 5 57
(Ruth Carr) *dwlt: bhd and sn outpcd: short-lived effrt over 2f out: sn btn* **9/1**

1m 28.66s (-0.34) **Going Correction** +0.075s/f (Good) **7** Ran SP% **108.7**
Speed ratings (Par 107): **104,102,102,101,98 96,92**
CSF £27.31 CT £58.83 TOTE £7.80: £3.40, £1.80; EX 28.90 Trifecta £112.70.
Owner Ken McGarrity **Bred** Miss Emma Foley **Trained** Carluke, S Lanarks

FOCUS
Add 7yds. A weak-looking race of its type, with the top weight rated 8lb below the ceiling, and the pace seemed fast. The winner was back to his 2018 form.

2680 RACING WELFARE #MENTALHEALTHAWARENESSWEEK GOLIATH CUP H'CAP — 1m 5f 216y

3:35 (3:35) (Class 3) (0-90,90) 4-Y-O+ **£9,337** (£2,796; £1,398; £699; £349) **Stalls** Low

Form RPR

3-21 1 **Bayshore Freeway (IRE)**[12] 2278 4-9-10 90 PJMcDonald 6 100
(Mark Johnston) *pressed ldr: led and rdn over 2f out: sn hrd pressed: styd on gamely ins fnl f* **11/10**[1]

56-3 2 *1* **Theglasgowwarrior**[10] 2370 5-9-9 89 AlistairRawlinson 7 97
(Jim Goldie) *hld up in last pl: hdwy over 3f out: effrt and disp ld over 2f out to ins fnl f: one pce fnl 100yds* **3/1**[2]

/ 3 *4 ½* **Desert Point (FR)**[838] 7-9-5 85 ShaneGray 3 87
(Keith Dalgleish) *t.k.h: prom: effrt and shkn up over 2f out: no imp fr over 1f out (jockey said gelding hung right-handed)* **40/1**

-613 4 *5* **Maybe Today**[19] 2032 4-9-9 89 (v) PaulMulrennan 4 84
(Simon Crisford) *t.k.h: prom: outpcd over 4f out: rallied 3f out: wknd wl over 1f out* **10/3**[3]

05-0 5 *4* **Stone The Crows**[17] 2080 5-9-3 83 (p) TomEaves 2 72
(Iain Jardine) *led to over 2f out: rdn and wknd wl over 1f out* **8/1**

3m 2.27s (-1.63) **Going Correction** +0.075s/f (Good) **5** Ran SP% **109.2**
Speed ratings (Par 107): **107,106,103,101,98**
CSF £4.59 TOTE £1.70: £1.10, £2.40; EX 4.40 Trifecta £39.30.
Owner Kingsley Park Owners Club **Bred** Lynch Bages Ltd **Trained** Middleham Moor, N Yorks

FOCUS
Add 7yds. This lacked depth, but useful form from the first two. The winner's progressive.

2681 #BEBODYKIND H'CAP (DIV I) — 7f 33y

4:10 (4:11) (Class 6) (0-60,60) 4-Y-O+ **£3,105** (£924; £461; £300; £300; £300) **Stalls** Low

Form RPR

45-1 1 **Colour Contrast (IRE)**[11] 2328 6-8-11 53 (b) JamieGormley(3) 1 63+
(Iain Jardine) *t.k.h early: hld up in midfield: smooth hdwy to ld over 2f out: rdn over 1f out: r.o wl fnl f* **9/2**[2]

2-05 2 *3 ½* **Donnelly's Rainbow (IRE)**[14] 2203 6-9-4 57 DavidAllan 8 58
(Rebecca Bastiman) *midfield on outside: effrt and c wd bnd wl over 3f out: rdn and angled rt over 2f out: sn chsng wnr: kpt on same pce fnl f* **5/1**[3]

0116 3 *2* **Mr Potter**[15] 2153 6-9-0 53 (v) ConnorBeasley 2 49
(Richard Guest) *t.k.h: in tch: effrt over 2f out: chsng ldrs whn n.m.r briefly over 1f out: outpcd fnl f* **20/1**

-355 4 *1 ¼* **Twiggy**[13] 2241 5-8-8 47 PJMcDonald 5 40
(Karen McLintock) *dwlt: hld up towards rr: hdwy over 2f out: sn rdn: kpt on fnl f: nvr able to chal* **15/2**

-063 5 *nk* **Christmas Night**[14] 2203 4-9-4 60 BenRobinson(3) 4 52
(Ollie Pears) *cl up: drvn and ev ch briefly over 1f out: rdn and outpcd fr over 1f out (jockey said gelding ran flat)* **7/2**[1]

0145 6 *3 ¼* **Tellovoi (IRE)**[12] 2298 11-8-10 49 (p) PhilipPrince 10 33
(Richard Guest) *led: rn wd bnd wl over 3f out: hdd over 2f out: sn outpcd: n.d after* **25/1**

0- **7** 1/2 **Morley Gunner (IRE)**[159] 9410 4-8-7 46 oh1..........(p[1]) AndrewMullen 6 28
(S Donohoe, Ire) *dwlt: bhd: rdn over 3f out: sme late hdwy: nvr able to chal* **50/1**

0-33 **8** hd **Chaplin Bay (IRE)**[13] 2242 7-9-5 58.......................... JamesSullivan 9 40
(Ruth Carr) *dwlt: hld up: drvn and effrt over 2f out: no imp fr over 1f out* **6/1**

000- **9** nse **Strategic (IRE)**[223] 7868 4-8-11 50.......................... JasonHart 3 33
(Eric Alston) *cl up: rdn and outpcd whn n.m.r 2f out: sn btn* **10/1**

5300 **10** 1 3/4 **Shamlan (IRE)**[14] 2215 7-8-10 54..........................(p) HarrisonShaw(5) 7 31
(Marjorie Fife) *hld up: rdn along over 2f out: nvr on terms* **33/1**

60-3 **11** 2 1/2 **Crazy Tornado (IRE)**[11] 2328 6-9-5 58..........................(h) ShaneGray 12 29
(Keith Dalgleish) *cl up on outside: c wd bnd ent st: rdn and outpcd over 2f out: hung rt and btn over 1f out* **22/1**

-404 **12** 9 **Black Hambleton**[73] 969 6-8-9 48.......................... GrahamLee 11
(Bryan Smart) *bhd: struggling over 3f out: nvr on terms* **25/1**

1m 29.07s (0.07) **Going Correction** +0.075s/f (Good) **12 Ran SP% 113.9**
Speed ratings (Par 101): **102,98,95,94,93 90,89,89,87 84,74**
CSF £23.35 CT £409.00 TOTE £4.90: £2.10, £1.60, £5.10; EX 26.20 Trifecta £433.50.
Owner Kildonan Gold Racing **Bred** J P Keappock **Trained** Carruthertown, D'fries & G'way

FOCUS
Add 7yds. The first leg of a moderate handicap. The winner was back to his best at least.

2682 #BEBODYKIND H'CAP (DIV II) — 7f 33y
4:40 (4:41) (Class 6) (0-60,58) 4-Y-O+
£2,014; £461; £300; £300; £300 **Stalls** Low

Form RPR

0-01 **1** **Mi Capricho (IRE)**[11] 2329 4-9-2 58.......................... SeanDavis(5) 5 64
(Keith Dalgleish) *trckd ldrs: led gng wl over 2f out: rdn over 1f out: kpt on fnl f: jnd on post* **4/1**[2]

-004 **1** dht **Robben Rainbow**[11] 2328 5-9-2 53.......................... JasonHart 6 59
(Katie Scott) *t.k.h in midfield: pushed along over 2f out: hdwy over 1f out: kpt on wl fnl f to dead-heat on post* **11/2**

2446 **3** 1 3/4 **Lukoutoldmakezebak**[2] 2631 6-8-6 46..........................(p) JamieGormley(3) 8 48
(David Thompson) *cl up: rdn along over 2f out: kpt on ins fnl f* **3/1**[1]

504- **4** nk **Erastus**[283] 5690 4-8-11 48..........................(w) AndrewMullen 2 50
(Ruth Carr) *dwlt: hld up: effrt whn nt clr run and swtchd rt 2f out: effrt over 1f out: kpt on fnl f: nvr able to chal* **12/1**

6/- **5** 1 1/2 **Althib**[8] 2454 5-8-9 49.......................... KillianLeonard(3) 4 46
(Denis Gerard Hogan, Ire) *t.k.h: hld up: effrt and drvn along over 2f out: kpt on fnl f: no imp* **5/1**[3]

0465 **6** 1 1/4 **Be Bold**[11] 2328 7-8-13 50..........................(b) DavidAllan 3 46
(Rebecca Bastiman) *hld up in tch: nt clr run fr over 2f out to fnl 150yds: kpt on: nvr able to chal (jockey said gelding was continually denied a clear run in the final two furlongs)* **9/1**

23-0 **7** nk **Haymarket**[11] 2330 10-9-3 54..........................(t) PJMcDonald 10 47
(R Mike Smith) *disp ld to over 2f out: drvn and no ex fr over 1f out* **20/1**

0-00 **8** 3/4 **Poyle George Two**[14] 2183 4-9-1 55.......................... RowanScott(3) 11 46
(John Hodge) *hld up on outside: drvn along over 2f out: sn outpcd: n.d after* **33/1**

0000 **9** nk **Hippeia (IRE)**[11] 2329 4-9-4 55..........................(t) TomEaves 7 45
(Grant Tuer) *slt ld to over 2f out: drvn and outpcd over 1f out* **20/1**

0406 **10** 1 3/4 **Thorntoun Lady (USA)**[11] 2329 9-8-11 48.......................... PhilDennis 1 34
(Jim Goldie) *hld up on ins: effrt and rdn over 2f out: wknd over 1f out* **10/1**

1m 29.35s (0.35) **Going Correction** +0.075s/f (Good) **10 Ran SP% 116.3**
Speed ratings (Par 101): **101,101,99,98,96 95,95,94,93,91**
WIN: 2.30 Mi Capricho, 3.30 Robben Rainbow; PL: 2.10 MC, 1.60 RR, 1.30 L; EX: MC/RR 14.50, RR/MC 15.30; CSF: MC/RR 12.74, RR/MC 13.47; TC: MC/RR/L 37.44, RR/MC/L 39.23; TF: MC/RR/L 49.60, RR/MC/L 64.30;.
Owner Charles Jones **Bred** Leslie Laverty **Trained** Carluke, S Lanarks
Owner Edward Cassie & Katie Scott **Bred** Miss A J Rawding & Mr D Macham **Trained** Galashiels, Scottish Borders

FOCUS
Add 7yds. Division two of a moderate handicap saw a dead-heat. Not many positives on show.

2683 RACING WELFARE SUPPORTING RACING'S WORKFORCE H'CAP — 5f 1y
5:10 (5:13) (Class 6) (0-65,66) 3-Y-O
£3,105 (£924; £461; £300; £300; £300) **Stalls** High

Form RPR

362- **1** **Northern Society (IRE)**[210] 8261 3-9-6 61.......................... ShaneGray 9 67+
(Keith Dalgleish) *hld up: hdwy whn n.m.r over 1f out: cl up and effrt whn checked ins fnl f: sn rcvrd and led: pushed out: comf* **6/1**[3]

50 **2** 1 **Dancing Mountain (IRE)**[25] 1894 3-8-10 56.......... BenSanderson(5) 6 58
(Roger Fell) *cl up: led over 1f out: drvn: edgd lft and hdd ins fnl f: kpt on same pce* **6/1**[3]

6303 **3** 1 **Popping Corks (IRE)**[11] 2327 3-8-11 55.......................... BenRobinson(3) 4 54
(Linda Perratt) *hld up: rdn and hdwy over 1f out: kpt on ins fnl f: nt pce to chal* **12/1**

3 **4** 1/2 **Fairy Fast (IRE)**[16] 2123 3-9-3 58.......................... DavidNolan 7 55
(David O'Meara) *cl up: rdn along 2f out: kpt on ins fnl f* **4/1**[2]

010- **5** 1/2 **Jordan Electrics**[210] 8261 3-9-11 66..........................(h) ConnorBeasley 5 61
(Linda Perratt) *led to over 1f out: checked and outpcd ins fnl f* **9/1**

006- **6** 3 1/4 **Milabella**[214] 8129 3-8-4 45..........................(t[1]) AndrewMullen 2 29+
(R Mike Smith) *slowly away: bhd and detached: sme late hdwy: nvr on terms* **50/1**

5-02 **7** 2 1/4 **Brahma Kamal**[11] 2327 3-8-0 46.......................... SeanDavis(5) 3 21
(Keith Dalgleish) *in tch: rdn over 2f out: wknd over 1f out: btn whn hung lft ins fnl f (jockey said gelding hung left-handed under pressure)* **15/8**[1]

0141 **8** nse **Gunnabedun (IRE)**[12] 2300 3-9-0 58..........................(b) JamieGormley(3) 1 33
(Iain Jardine) *in tch on outside tl rdn and wknd over 1f out (trainer said gelding was unsuited by the ground and would prefer a slower surface)* **17/2**

59.92s (0.22) **Going Correction** +0.075s/f (Good) **8 Ran SP% 113.5**
Speed ratings (Par 97): **101,99,97,97,96 91,87,87**
CSF £40.92 CT £418.20 TOTE £6.10: £1.50, £2.30, £3.00; EX 34.90 Trifecta £238.80.
Owner John Kelly, John McNeill & Alan Johnston **Bred** La Estatua Partnership **Trained** Carluke, S Lanarks

FOCUS
A moderate handicap run at a strong pace. The winner looks improved.

2684 START A CONVERSATION ON MENTAL HEALTH H'CAP — 1m 7f
5:45 (5:46) (Class 6) (0-60,62) 4-Y-O+
£3,105 (£924; £461; £300; £300; £300) **Stalls** Low

Form RPR

-404 **1** **Rock N'Stones (IRE)**[32] 1718 8-8-8 46.......................... PJMcDonald 1 53
(Gillian Boanas) *mde virtually all: rdn over 2f out: edgd lft ins fnl f: kpt on wl cl home* **25/1**

-323 **2** nk **Siyahamba (IRE)**[14] 2196 5-8-7 45.......................... RoystonFfrench 4 52
(Bryan Smart) *disp ld thrght: rdn over 2f out: edgd rt over 1f out: no ex ins fnl f* **7/1**

0031 **3** 6 **Elite Icon**[10] 2373 5-9-0 52.......................... PhilDennis 3 52
(Jim Goldie) *hld up on ins: pushed along over 3f out: hdwy to chse clr ldng pair over 2f out: no imp fr over 1f out* **9/2**[2]

51-0 **4** hd **St Andrews (IRE)**[14] 2217 6-9-0 59..........................(b) OliverStammers(7) 2 58+
(Gillian Boanas) *s.v.s: sn rcvrd to join gp: hld up: outpcd over 4f out: rallied over 1f out: kpt on: no imp (jockey said gelding was slowly away)* **7/1**

00-2 **5** 3 1/4 **Frame Rate**[10] 2373 4-9-1 56..........................(b[1]) JamieGormley(3) 7 53
(Iain Jardine) *hld up: pushed along briefly 1/2-way: outpcd and hung rt over 3f out: no imp fnl 2f* **7/4**[1]

0-06 **6** 2 **Palermo (IRE)**[10] 2373 5-8-11 49..........................(t) ConnorBeasley 6 42
(Michael Wigham) *prom: drvn along 3f out: wknd over 1f out* **6/1**[3]

41-0 **7** 8 **Richard Strauss (IRE)**[14] 2202 5-9-3 55.......................... KevinStott 8 38
(Philip Kirby) *prom: rdn along 3f out: wknd fr 2f out* **8/1**

44-4 **8** 5 **Eyreborn (IRE)**[10] 2373 5-8-2 45..........................(p) SeanDavis(5) 9 21
(Keith Dalgleish) *hld up: hdwy and prom sn after 1/2-way: rdn and wknd fr over 2f out* **18/1**

3m 16.41s **8 Ran SP% 114.1**
CSF £186.58 CT £943.44 TOTE £26.30: £6.80, £2.40, £1.70; EX 191.10 Trifecta £1575.40.
Owner Miss G Boanas **Bred** Patrick Boyle **Trained** Lingdale, Redcar & Cleveland

FOCUS
Add 7yds. A moderate handicap and the first two had the race to themselves up front. Not for to place great faith in.
T/Plt: £62.60 to a £1 stake. Pool: £46,165.58 - 537.96 winning units T/Qpdt: £10.30 to a £1 stake. Pool: £5,820.30 - 415.38 winning units **Richard Young**

2483 WINDSOR (R-H)
Monday, May 13

OFFICIAL GOING: Good (good to soft in places; 6.8)
Wind: Moderate, against Weather: Fine

2685 VISIT ATTHERACES.COM FILLIES' H'CAP — 1m 3f 99y
5:20 (5:20) (Class 5) (0-75,75) 3-Y-O+
£3,752 (£1,116; £557; £300; £300; £300) **Stalls** Low

Form RPR

6-40 **1** **Tiar Na Nog (IRE)**[14] 2209 7-9-11 70.......................... OisinMurphy 1 77
(Denis Coakley) *hld up and last to 1/2-way: prog 3f out: rdn over 2f out: tk 2nd jst over 1f out: edgd rt but drvn ahd fnl 100yds: jst hld on (trainer said, reg app imp in form, mare benefitted from the faster pace on this occasion)* **9/1**

4-23 **2** shd **Sapa Inca (IRE)**[16] 2096 3-8-13 75.......................... FrannyNorton 4 81
(Mark Johnston) *hld up: t.k.h: led after 4f: rdn 2 out: hdd 100yds out: rallied nr fin: jst failed* **10/11**[1]

626- **3** 2 **Lightening Dance**[157] 9447 5-10-0 73.......................... RobertHavlin 7 76
(Amanda Perrett) *prom: rdn over 2f out: chsd ldr briefly over 1f out: hld whn short of room ins fnl f: one pce* **8/1**

401- **4** 2 3/4 **Love And Be Loved**[217] 8059 5-9-6 68.......................... FinleyMarsh(3) 6 67
(John Flint) *sn in midfield: rdn 3f out: stl chsng ldrs over 1f out: fdd fnl f* **16/1**

40-3 **5** 2 1/4 **Gamesters Icon**[16] 2106 4-9-4 63.......................... RichardKingscote 9 58
(Oliver Greenall) *led 4f: chsd ldr: rdn wl over 1f out: lost 2nd and wknd over 1f out* **7/1**[3]

41-6 **6** nse **Shagalla**[8] 2445 3-8-13 75.......................... DavidEgan 3 69
(Roger Varian) *hld up towards rr: rdn and sme prog on outer over 2f out: no hdwy over 1f out: wknd* **6/1**[2]

20-4 **7** 14 **Last Enchantment (IRE)**[23] 1934 4-9-13 72.......................... ShaneKelly 5 43
(Neil Mulholland) *chsd ldrs: rdn 3f out: wknd rapidly 2f out: t.o* **33/1**

330- **8** 9 **Born To Please**[61] 7723 5-8-10 55.......................... JasonWatson 8 11
(Mark Usher) *dropped to last 1/2-way and sn detached: pushed along and brief effrt 3f out: no ch over 1f out and sn heavily eased (jockey said mare hung left-handed and moved poorly)* **50/1**

5006 **9** 14 **Chantresse (IRE)**[32] 1710 4-9-1 60..........................(p) JosephineGordon 2
(Mark Usher) *in tch: rdn wl over 3f out: sn wknd: t.o* **33/1**

2m 28.11s (-1.59) **Going Correction** +0.15s/f (Good) **9 Ran SP% 114.0**
WFA 3 from 4yo+ 17lb
Speed ratings (Par 100): **111,110,109,107,105 105,95,89,78**
CSF £17.22 CT £70.97 TOTE £9.20: £2.20, £1.10, £2.10; EX 21.90 Trifecta £166.20.
Owner Mrs U M Loughrey **Bred** Edmund Power **Trained** West Ilsley, Berks

FOCUS
Distance increased by 32yds. An average handicap run at a steady enough gallop. Straightforward form, rated around the winner.

2686 EBF MAIDEN STKS (PLUS 10 RACE) — 5f 21y
5:50 (5:59) (Class 3) 2-Y-O
£6,931 (£2,074; £1,037; £519; £258) **Stalls** Centre

Form RPR

3 **1** **Kemble (IRE)**[27] 1833 2-9-0 0.......................... SeanLevey 7 88+
(Richard Hannon) *pressed ldrs: led wl over 1f out: shkn up and drew clr: comf* **7/2**[3]

2 **2** 5 **Illusionist (GER)**[10] 2362 2-9-5 0.......................... OisinMurphy 2 75
(Archie Watson) *disp ld and racd against nr side rail: hdd wl over 1f out: one pce and no ch w wnr* **8/11**[1]

3 3 1/2 **Carmague (IRE)** 2-9-5 0.......................... JosephineGordon 6 62
(J S Moore) *sn outpcd and wl bhd: sed to pick up 1/2-way: styd on over 1f out to take 3rd fnl 100yds* **100/1**

4 1 3/4 **Tilly Tamworth** 2-9-0 0.......................... CharlieBennett 1 51
(Rod Millman) *outpcd and rdn after 2f: swvd lft over 2f out: brief effrt over 1f out: no prog after* **50/1**

4 **5** 1 3/4 **Making History (IRE)**[23] 1953 2-9-5 0.......................... PatCosgrave 4 49
(Saeed bin Suroor) *disp ld to 2f out: wknd qckly over 1f out* **10/3**[2]

3 **6** *1* **Constitutional (IRE)**[22] 1968 2-9-5 0 BenCurtis 3 46
(K R Burke) *w ldrs to 2f out: wknd qckly* **16/1**

P **Castle Force** 2-9-5 0 ShaneKelly 5
(John O'Shea) *s.s: bhd whn lost action and p.u after 100yds (jockey said gelding took a false step and lost it's action)* **125/1**

1m 1.66s (1.56) **Going Correction** +0.15s/f (Good) 7 Ran SP% **112.8**
Speed ratings (Par 97): **93,85,79,76,73 72,**
CSF £6.27 TOTE £4.60: £2.10, £1.10; EX 7.10 Trifecta £395.40.
Owner Mr & Mrs R Kelvin-Hughes **Bred** Richard Kelvin-Hughes **Trained** East Everleigh, Wilts

FOCUS
Little depth to this maiden, but an impressive winner of a race which fell apart.

2687 WEATHERBYS RACING BANK FILLIES' H'CAP (QUALIFIER FOR THE WINDSOR SPRINT SERIES FINAL) 6f 12y
6:20 (6:24) (Class 3) (0-90,89) 3-Y-O+ **£7,246** (£2,168; £1,084; £542; £270) **Stalls** Centre

Form RPR

2112 **1** **Second Collection**[14] 2212 3-8-5 73 (h) DavidEgan 8 81
(Tony Carroll) *hld up in tch: prog on outer to ld wl over 1f out: sn in command: shkn up and styd on fnl f* **6/1**

24-3 **2** *1 ¾* **Heritage**[15] 2144 3-9-1 83 HectorCrouch 1 86
(Clive Cox) *chsd ldrs: rdn over 1f out: chsd wnr fnl f: no imp* **2/1**[1]

121- **3** *hd* **Belated Breath**[222] 7900 4-9-13 85 OisinMurphy 2 90
(Hughie Morrison) *pressed ldr tl n.m.r against rail over 4f out: styd chsng: rdn 2f out: kpt on same pce over 1f out* **7/2**[2]

235- **4** *1 ¼* **Restless Rose**[261] 6517 4-9-9 81 SilvestreDeSousa 6 82
(Stuart Williams) *hld up in last pair: rdn and sme prog on outer over 1f out: no hdwy ins fnl f* **12/1**

03-0 **5** *2 ¾* **Pink Iceburg (IRE)**[33] 1691 3-8-8 76 KierenFox 4 65
(Peter Crate) *snatched up sn after s: hld up in detached last: sme prog on wd outside 2f out: nvr in it (stewards enquired into running and riding; jockey stated that his instructions were to settle the filly early on as she can be very keen and had bled last time out; he added that filly did not face the kick back from the loose turf and did not travel in* **33/1**

604- **6** *3 ¾* **Elizabeth Bennet (IRE)**[264] 6423 4-9-11 83 TomMarquand 5 63
(Robert Cowell) *pressed ldrs: rdn 2f out: wknd over 1f out* **16/1**

1461 **7** *¾* **Bellevarde (IRE)**[28] 1822 5-9-5 77 DaneO'Neill 7 55
(Richard Price) *led and crossed to nr side rail: hdd & wknd wl over 1f out* **11/1**

160- **8** *1 ¾* **Scintilating**[249] 6998 3-9-7 89 HarryBentley 3 58
(Ralph Beckett) *chsd ldr after 2f to 2f out: wknd qckly* **4/1**[3]

1m 12.26s (0.16) **Going Correction** +0.15s/f (Good)
WFA 3 from 4yo+ 10lb 8 Ran SP% **114.7**
Speed ratings (Par 104): **104,101,101,99,96 91,90,87**
CSF £18.50 CT £48.68 TOTE £6.50: £2.20, £1.40, £1.70; EX 21.80 Trifecta £75.40.
Owner A A Byrne **Bred** Anthony Byrne **Trained** Cropthorne, Worcs

FOCUS
A fair sprint and no surprise to see one of the 3yos triumph. The winner carried over her AW progress with a clear pb.

2688 TORI GLOBAL SUPPORTS THE SAMARITANS STKS (REG AS ROYAL WINDSOR STAKES) (LISTED RACE) (C&G) 1m 31y
6:50 (6:50) (Class 1) 3-Y-O+ **£20,982** (£7,955; £3,981; £1,983) **Stalls** Low

Form RPR

52-1 **1** **Bye Bye Hong Kong (USA)**[32] 1713 3-8-6 107 SilvestreDeSousa 1 111
(Andrew Balding) *mde virtually all: jnd and drvn wl over 1f out: kpt on u.p to assert fnl 100yds* **8/11**[1]

1016 **2** *½* **Oh This Is Us (IRE)**[17] 2085 6-9-5 113 TomMarquand 2 113
(Richard Hannon) *hld up in 3rd: shkn up to chse wnr 2f out and sn upsides: drvn fnl f: nt qckn fnl 100yds* **7/2**[2]

400- **3** *2* **Breton Rock (IRE)**[213] 8147 9-9-5 110 JamieSpencer 4 108
(David Simcock) *hld up in last: effrt over 2f out: reminders over 1f out: tk 3rd ins fnl f: nvr cl enough to threaten* **14/1**[3]

12-5 **4** *1* **Mitchum Swagger**[17] 2085 7-9-8 109 HarryBentley 3 109
(Ralph Beckett) *chsd wnr: rdn over 2f out: sn lost 2nd: fdd ins fnl f* **7/2**[2]

1m 44.72s (0.22) **Going Correction** +0.15s/f (Good)
WFA 3 from 6yo+ 13lb 4 Ran SP% **109.0**
Speed ratings (Par 111): **104,103,101,100**
CSF £3.62 TOTE £1.40; EX 3.30 Trifecta £10.90.
Owner King Power Racing Co Ltd **Bred** WinStar Farm LLC **Trained** Kingsclere, Hants

FOCUS
Distance increased by 32yds. The favourite's 3yo weight allowance made all the difference in this Listed event. The runner-up is rated similar to his mark in this race last year.

2689 ROYAL WINDSOR SPRING TO THE SKY H'CAP 1m 31y
7:20 (7:26) (Class 5) (0-70,70) 3-Y-O
£3,752 (£1,116; £557; £300; £300; £300) **Stalls** Low

Form RPR

063 **1** **Mandocello (FR)**[13] 2250 3-9-3 67 CharlieBennett 1 73
(Rod Millman) *uns rdr and cantered off bef s: trckd ldng pair: led wl over 1f out: rdn and kpt on wl fnl f* **9/2**[1]

05-0 **2** *½* **Pempie (IRE)**[26] 1855 3-9-5 69 OisinMurphy 9 74
(Andrew Balding) *trckd ldrs: prog over 2f out: chsd wnr over 1f out: styd on but a hld ins fnl f* **8/1**

33-5 **3** *hd* **Arctic Spirit**[38] 1567 3-9-4 68 RobertHavlin 7 72
(Ed Dunlop) *hld up in rr: gng wl whn waiting for room over 2f out: prog against nr side rail over 1f out: disp 2nd ins fnl f: a jst hld* **25/1**

002- **4** *2 ¾* **Clem A**[224] 7837 3-9-3 67 JoeyHaynes 8 65
(Alan Bailey) *reluctant to enter stalls: hld up wl in rr: prog 2f out: rdn to chse ldrs jst over 1f out: no imp after* **20/1**

-305 **5** *1 ½* **Four Mile Bridge (IRE)**[10] 2355 3-9-2 66 JasonWatson 6 60
(Mark Usher) *hld up wl in rr: rdn and stl there 2f out: styd on against nr side rail fnl f: nvr nrr* **20/1**

56-0 **6** *2 ½* **Parisean Artiste (IRE)**[25] 1894 3-9-3 67 CharlesBishop 4 55
(Eve Johnson Houghton) *in tch in midfield: rdn and nt qckn 2f out: wknd fnl f* **16/1**

2420 **7** *¾* **Dancing Jo**[16] 2125 3-8-13 70 GeorgeBass(7) 11 57
(Mick Channon) *hld up in rr: effrt on outer over 2f out: hanging lft and no real prog* **7/1**[3]

430- **8** *½* **Renardeau**[219] 7983 3-9-6 70 TomMarquand 13 56
(Ali Stronge) *trckd ldr to over 2f out: wknd over 1f out* **20/1**

40-5 **9** *hd* **Chains Of Love (IRE)**[14] 2200 3-9-6 70 (p) BenCurtis 10 55
(K R Burke) *taken down early: slowly away: hld up wl in rr: rdn and no prog over 2f out* **6/1**[2]

4-65 **10** *nk* **Shamkha (IRE)**[16] 2103 3-9-5 69 FergusSweeney 2 53
(Richard Hannon) *chsd ldrs: shkn up over 2f out: wknd over 1f out* **10/1**

023 **11** *2 ¾* **Gabriela Laura**[47] 1359 3-9-6 70 AdamKirby 12 48
(Clive Cox) *racd keenly: led to wl over 1f out: wknd qckly (vet said filly was treated for post-race ataxia)* **14/1**

-110 **12** *½* **Red Phoenix (IRE)**[40] 1516 3-9-6 70 FrannyNorton 14 47
(Mark Johnston) *trckd ldrs: stl cl up and waiting for room 2f out: wknd over 1f out (jockey said gelding stopped quickly)* **9/1**

1m 44.61s (0.11) **Going Correction** +0.15s/f (Good) 12 Ran SP% **105.9**
Speed ratings (Par 99): **105,104,104,101,100 97,96,96,96,95 93,92**
CSF £26.89 CT £435.99 TOTE £4.70: £2.30, £2.30, £5.10; EX 37.80 Trifecta £491.80.
Owner D J Deer **Bred** Oakgrove Stud **Trained** Kentisbeare, Devon

■ Reconnaissance was withdrawn, price at time of withdrawal 4/1f. Rule 4 applies to all bets. Deduction of 20p in the pound.

FOCUS
Distance increased by 32yds. Modest form, but at least a pair of unexposed handicap debutants came to the fore. The form is rated around the third and fourth.

2690 GASTRO STEAKHOUSE NOVICE MEDIAN AUCTION STKS 1m 2f
7:50 (7:56) (Class 5) 3-5-Y-O **£3,752** (£1,116; £557; £278) **Stalls** Low

Form RPR

4- **1** **Geizy Teizy (IRE)**[202] 8510 3-8-8 0 SilvestreDeSousa 13 77
(Marco Botti) *trckd ldr after 3f: led 2f out: shkn up and clr fnl f: readily* **3/1**[2]

0- **2** *2 ½* **Mojave**[156] 9459 3-8-13 0 JasonWatson 14 77
(Roger Charlton) *trckd ldr 3f: styd cl up: rdn over 2f out: chsd wnr over 1f out: styd on but no imp* **5/2**[1]

5 **3** *3 ¼* **Tadasana**[14] 2195 3-8-8 0 BenCurtis 16 65
(Archie Watson) *led to 2f out: rdn and one pce after* **33/1**

5 **4** *¾* **Skerryvore**[13] 2250 3-8-13 0 DanielMuscutt 4 69
(James Fanshawe) *in tch in midfield: shkn up and prog over 2f out: kpt on one pce over 1f out* **10/1**

0 **5** *¾* **Eddie Cochran (IRE)**[14] 2216 3-8-13 0 SeanLevey 11 67
(Richard Hannon) *chsd ldrs: shkn up over 2f out: fdd over 1f out* **14/1**

0 **6** *2 ¼* **Ideal Grace**[33] 1677 3-8-8 0 EdwardGreatrex 3 58
(Eve Johnson Houghton) *wl in tch: rdn and no prog over 2f out: wknd over 1f out* **33/1**

0-0 **7** *nse* **Mystical Jadeite**[35] 1652 3-8-13 0 LiamJones 12 62
(Grace Harris) *wl in rr: rdn and sme prog over 2f out: kpt on but nvr a threat* **100/1**

8 *1* **Pecorino** 3-8-13 0 ShaneKelly 6 60+
(Richard Hughes) *fractious bef ent stalls: wl in rr: swift move into midfield after 3f: rn green and pushed along 1/2-way: struggling in rr over 2f out: kpt on fnl f* **9/1**

9 *nk* **Lord Halifax (IRE)** 3-8-13 0 StevieDonohoe 15 60+
(Charlie Fellowes) *dwlt: mostly in last pair: pushed along over 2f out: styd on fnl f* **14/1**

4 **10** *1* **Kalaya (IRE)**[14] 2195 3-8-5 0 JaneElliott(3) 9 53
(Archie Watson) *a towards rr: shkn up and no real prog 3f out* **33/1**

0 **11** *1* **Peripherique**[48] 1344 3-8-8 0 LukeMorris 8 51
(James Eustace) *dwlt: mostly in last pair: nvr a factor* **40/1**

53- **12** *1* **Nordic Flight**[425] 1198 4-10-0 0 RyanTate 10 55
(James Eustace) *prog fr rr to trck ldrs after 3f: rdn 3f out: no prog 2f out: wknd qckly over 1f out (trainer's rep said gelding lost it's left fore shoe)* **20/1**

0 **13** *2 ¾* **Emojie**[11] 2321 5-9-11 0 PaddyBradley(3) 5 49
(Jane Chapple-Hyam) *chsd ldrs: lost grnd 1/2-way: wknd over 2f out* **100/1**

14 *22* **Frosty Tern** 3-8-8 0 NickyMackay 2
(Geoffrey Deacon) *difficult to load into stalls: rn green and a wl in rr: t.o (vet said filly was lame on it's left fore)* **66/1**

6-4 **15** *30* **Song Without End (IRE)**[21] 1984 3-8-13 0 DavidEgan 1
(Sir Michael Stoute) *chsd ldrs: wknd rapidly 3f out: t.o (trainers' rep could offer no explanation for the poor performance. Vet said gelding had an irregular heartbeat)* **4/1**[3]

2m 10.65s (1.65) **Going Correction** +0.15s/f (Good)
WFA 3 from 4yo+ 15lb 15 Ran SP% **125.5**
Speed ratings (Par 103): **99,97,94,93,93 91,91,90,90,89 88,87,85,68,44**
CSF £10.64 TOTE £4.40: £1.30, £1.30, £9.70; EX 13.60 Trifecta £433.00.
Owner Nick Bradley Racing 30 & Sohi & Partner **Bred** Anne Hallinan & John O' Connor **Trained** Newmarket, Suffolk

FOCUS
Distance increased by 32yds. Just a fair novice, won in good style by a potentially useful filly. The field finished a little compressed.

2691 WATCH SKY SPORTS RACING IN HD H'CAP 1m 2f
8:20 (8:24) (Class 4) (0-80,80) 4-Y-O+
£5,530 (£1,645; £822; £411; £300; £300) **Stalls** Low

Form RPR

35-1 **1** **Simoon (IRE)**[42] 1479 5-9-6 79 OisinMurphy 6 88+
(Andrew Balding) *t.k.h: led 3f: trckd ldr: led again over 2f out: pressed and drvn fnl f: kpt on wl* **1/1**[1]

2-00 **2** *¾* **Petrastar**[24] 1914 4-9-4 77 AdamKirby 3 85+
(Clive Cox) *trckd ldrs: wnt 2nd 2f out: rdn to chal 1f out: styd on but hld fnl 100yds* **6/1**[3]

/03- **3** *2 ¼* **Balmoral Castle**[266] 6358 10-8-9 75 TylerSaunders(7) 9 78
(Jonathan Portman) *hld up in last trio: prog on outer over 2f out: chsd ldng pair over 1f out and looked a threat: effrt flattened out fnl f* **33/1**

1004 **4** *1* **Unit Of Assessment (IRE)**[16] 2092 5-8-12 78(vt) Pierre-LouisJamin(7) 8 79
(William Knight) *trckd ldng pair: effrt and rdn jst over 2f out: one pce over 1f out* **12/1**

25-0 **5** *1 ½* **Moxy Mares**[30] 1757 4-9-6 79 LiamJones 1 77
(Mark Loughnane) *hld up in last trio: pushed along over 2f out: hanging lft over 1f out: rdn and kpt on fnl f: nvr in it* **10/1**

605- **6** *1 ½* **Escape The City**[199] 8609 4-9-0 80 (t) CierenFallon(7) 2 75
(Hughie Morrison) *hld up in midfield: shkn up over 2f out: nt qckn and no prog over 1f out (jockey said filly was slowly away)* **5/1**[2]

0-4 **7** *nk* **Kenstone (FR)**[23] 1955 6-9-6 79 (p) TomMarquand 7 73
(Adrian Wintle) *hld up in last trio: effrt on outer 2f out: rdn and one pce over 1f out (jockey said gelding ran too free)* **25/1**

2132 **8** *1 ¾* **Narjes**[10] 2360 5-8-12 71 (h) LukeMorris 5 62
(Laura Mongan) *hld up in midfield: rdn over 2f out and no prog: wknd over 1f out* **10/1**

The Form Book Flat 2019, Raceform Ltd, Newbury, RG14 5SJ

6-00 **9** *5* **Sir Plato (IRE)**[12] 2273 5-9-2 **75**.............................. CharlieBennett 4 56
(Rod Millman) *rousted fr s: led after 3f: hdd over 2f out: sn wknd qckly*
20/1

2m 8.68s (-0.32) **Going Correction** +0.15s/f (Good) **9** Ran SP% **118.4**
Speed ratings (Par 105): **107,106,104,103,102 101,101,99,95**
CSF £7.41 CT £125.59 TOTE £1.80: £1.10, £2.00, £5.10; EX 9.30 Trifecta £277.00.
Owner Lord Blyth **Bred** Lemington Grange Stud **Trained** Kingsclere, Hants

FOCUS
Distance increased by 32yds. No great gallop on here and those racing prominently were favoured. There's potential for the front two to do better.
T/Plt: £7.10 to a £1 stake. Pool: £75,069.58 - 7,683.14 winning units T/Qpdt: £5.60 to a £1 stake. Pool: £7,819.98 - 1,021.22 winning units **Jonathan Neesom**

2592 WOLVERHAMPTON (A.W) (L-H)
Monday, May 13

OFFICIAL GOING: Tapeta: standard
Wind: Light across Weather: Fine

2692 WOLVERHAMPTON HOLIDAY INN H'CAP 1m 142y (Tp)
1:50 (1:52) (Class 6) (0-65,65) 4-Y-O+
£3,105 (£924; £461; £300; £300; £300) **Stalls** Low

Form RPR
-603 **1** **Celtic Artisan (IRE)**[34] 1659 8-9-3 **61**.....................(bt) StevieDonohoe 2 67
(Rebecca Menzies) *prom: lost pl over 5f out: hdwy over 1f out: edgd rt and r.o to ld wl ins fnl f* **10/1**

0330 **2** *3/4* **Street Poet (IRE)**[3] 2596 6-9-3 **61**.............................. JackGarritty 4 65
(Michael Herrington) *led: qcknd over 2f out: rdn and edgd rt fr over 1f out: hdd wl ins fnl f* **3/1**[1]

6062 **3** *1 1/4* **Ghazan (IRE)**[21] 1983 4-9-2 **65**.....................(t) ThoreHammerHansen(5) 9 67
(Kevin Frost) *chsd ldrs: rdn over 2f out: styng on same pce whn carried rt wl ins fnl f* **6/1**[2]

0150 **4** *nk* **Grey Destiny**[14] 2183 9-9-5 **63**..............................(p) CamHardie 5 64
(Antony Brittain) *hld up: racd keenly: r.o ins fnl f: nt rch ldrs* **14/1**

6362 **5** *2 1/4* **Helfire**[33] 1683 6-9-0 **58**.............................. CharlieBennett 1 54
(Martin Bosley) *chsd ldrs: rdn over 1f out: no ex wl ins fnl f* **14/1**

0-05 **6** *nk* **Topology**[21] 1983 6-9-0 **58**..............................(p[1]) LukeMorris 10 54
(Joseph Tuite) *prom: chsd ldr over 6f out: rdn over 2f out: hung lft fr over 1f out: no ex fnl f* **22/1**

3404 **7** *nk* **The King's Steed**[32] 1715 6-9-0 **58**.....................(bt) NicolaCurrie 7 53
(Shaun Lycett) *hld up: hdwy on outer over 2f out: rdn over 1f out: styd on same pce fnl f* **13/2**[3]

4065 **8** *1/2* **Destinys Rock**[41] 1506 4-9-2 **60**.............................. LiamJones 8 54
(Mark Loughnane) *s.i.s: hdwy to go prom over 7f out: rdn over 1f out: no ex fnl f* **12/1**

5212 **9** *nk* **Creative Talent (IRE)**[47] 1362 7-9-0 **58**.............................. GeorgeDowning 12 52
(Tony Carroll) *s.i.s: hld up: sme hdwy on outer over 1f out: hung lft: nt trble ldrs (jockey said gelding hung left-handed under pressure)* **9/1**

4046 **10** *1* **Laqab (IRE)**[26] 1859 6-9-5 **63**.............................. RobertWinston 6 56
(Derek Shaw) *s.i.s: hdwy over 5f out: rdn over 1f out: wknd ins fnl f (jockey said gelding was denied a clear run on the run to the line)* **8/1**

6400 **11** *1 1/4* **Gabrial's Kaka (IRE)**[16] 2106 9-9-0 **58**.............................. FrannyNorton 11 47
(Patrick Morris) *s.i.s: hld up: rdn over 1f out: n.d* **33/1**

000/ **12** *2 3/4* **Dubai Mission (IRE)**[930] 7594 6-9-4 **62**..............................(h[1]) HollieDoyle 3 45
(Adrian Wintle) *hld up: racd keenly: rdn over 2f out: n.d* **50/1**

1m 50.4s (0.30) **Going Correction** +0.075s/f (Slow) **12** Ran SP% **113.1**
Speed ratings (Par 101): **101,100,99,98,96 96,96,95,95,94 93,91**
CSF £37.44 CT £200.58 TOTE £8.50: £2.80, £1.20, £2.30; EX 46.20 Trifecta £294.30.
Owner Premier Racing Partnerships **Bred** Fortbarrington Stud **Trained** Mordon, Durham

FOCUS
A modest affair. Straightforward form in behind the winner.

2693 HOTEL & CONFERENCING AT WOLVERHAMPTON RACECOURSE H'CAP 7f 36y (Tp)
2:20 (2:22) (Class 6) (0-55,54) 4-Y-O+
£3,105 (£924; £461; £300; £300; £300) **Stalls** High

Form RPR
3001 **1** **Magical Molly Joe**[27] 1837 5-9-2 **54**.............................. JaneElliott(3) 12 60
(David Barron) *s.i.s: hld up: swtchd rt and hdwy on outer over 1f out: rdn and r.o to ld nr fin* **5/1**[2]

0050 **2** *1/2* **Just An Idea (IRE)**[13] 2235 5-9-3 **52**.....................(b) KieranO'Neill 5 57+
(Roger Ingram) *plld hrd and prom: rdn over 2f out: hung rt and led wl ins fnl f: hdd nr fin* **25/1**

0012 **3** *2 1/2* **Tha'ir (IRE)**[20] 2012 9-9-4 **53**.............................. DannyBrock 7 52
(Philip McBride) *hld up: hdwy and nt clr run over 1f out: hung rt and r.o to go 3rd wl ins fnl f* **7/2**[1]

1605 **4** *1/2* **Seaforth (IRE)**[20] 2013 7-9-0 **52**.............................. FinleyMarsh(3) 10 49
(Adrian Wintle) *hld up: shkn up over 1f out: r.o ins fnl f: nvr nrr* **10/1**

401- **5** *3/4* **Langley Vale**[188] 8906 10-9-2 **51**.............................. JackMitchell 3 47+
(Roger Teal) *led to 1/2-way: rdn and hung rt over 1f out: no ex wl ins fnl f* **10/1**

2420 **6** *1 1/4* **Little Miss Kodi (IRE)**[79] 887 6-8-9 **51**.....................(t) MolliePhillips(7) 2 44
(Mark Loughnane) *s.i.s: sn prom: nt clr run and lost pl 1/2-way: hdwy over 1f out: styd on same pce wl ins fnl f* **16/1**

6205 **7** *nk* **Energia Flavio (BRZ)**[21] 1986 8-9-2 **54**..............(b[1]) CameronNoble(3) 4 46
(Patrick Morris) *s.i.s: hdwy over 4f out: led 1/2-way: rdn over 1f out: hdd wl ins fnl f: wknd towards fin (jockey said gelding ran too freely)* **5/1**[2]

600- **8** *1 1/4* **Hilight**[252] 6884 4-9-4 **53**.............................. GeorgeWood 6 42
(Martin Bosley) *s.i.s: pushed along 1/2-way: sme hdwy over 1f out: wknd fnl f* **20/1**

10-0 **9** *6* **Ace Master**[39] 1553 11-9-2 **51**..............................(b) RobertWinston 11 25
(Roy Bowring) *sn chsng ldrs: rdn over 2f out: wknd over 1f out* **16/1**

0-40 **10** *2 1/2* **Muraadef**[14] 2215 4-9-2 **51**.............................. JackGarritty 1 19
(Ruth Carr) *chsd ldr tl over 5f out: rdn 1/2-way: wknd over 1f out* **17/2**[3]

4-00 **11** *7* **Gold Club**[98] 595 8-9-2 **51**..............................(p) RossaRyan 9 2
(Lee Carter) *prom: lost pl over 4f out: wknd over 2f out* **14/1**

1m 28.88s (0.08) **Going Correction** +0.075s/f (Slow) **11** Ran SP% **111.3**
Speed ratings (Par 101): **102,101,98,98,97 95,95,93,87,84 76**
CSF £114.36 CT £485.86 TOTE £5.60: £1.80, £5.80, £1.60; EX 102.20 Trifecta £1084.00.
Owner Lee Woolams & Partner **Bred** Bambi Bloodstock **Trained** Maunby, N Yorks

FOCUS
The pace picked up leaving the back straight and that set things up for those ridden patiently. The winner is edging towards her best.

2694 WOLVERHAMPTON HOLIDAY INN NOVICE AUCTION STKS 5f 21y (Tp)
2:55 (2:57) (Class 5) 2-Y-O
£3,752 (£1,116; £557; £278) **Stalls** Low

Form RPR
1 **Probable Cause** 2-8-11.............................. HollieDoyle 5 71
(Archie Watson) *s.i.s: sn prom: chsd ldr wl ins fnl f: rdn and r.o to ld post* **4/1**[3]

12 **2** *nse* **Rodnee Tee**[16] 2115 2-9-9.............................. DanielTudhope 4 83
(David O'Meara) *led: rdn and hung rt ins fnl f: hdd post* **9/4**[2]

4 **3** *2 1/4* **Miss Matterhorn**[13] 2228 2-8-11.............................. CharlesBishop 6 63
(Eve Johnson Houghton) *chsd ldr: rdn over 1f out: no ex ins fnl f* **2/1**[1]

4 *2 3/4* **Call Me Cheers** 2-9-2.............................. JFEgan 1 58
(David Evans) *s.i.s: sn pushed along in rr: hdwy over 1f out: nt rch ldrs* **10/1**

5 *2 1/4* **Chromium** 2-8-11.............................. NicolaCurrie 10 45+
(Mark Usher) *s.i.s: shkn up over 1f out: styd on ins fnl f: nvr nrr (jockey said filly was carried wide on the bend)* **40/1**

50 **6** *1* **Mumsbirthdaygirl (IRE)**[9] 2415 2-8-11.............................. EoinWalsh 8 41
(Mark Loughnane) *prom: rdn 1/2-way: wknd over 1f out* **150/1**

0 **7** *hd* **Sassy Lassy (IRE)**[26] 1843 2-8-11.............................. TrevorWhelan 2 41
(David Loughnane) *chsd ldrs: rdn over 1f out: wknd ins fnl f* **20/1**

8 *1* **Cenario** 2-9-2.............................. TonyHamilton 9 42
(Richard Fahey) *chsd ldrs: pushed along 1/2-way: wknd fnl f* **10/1**

00 **9** *6* **Little Devil**[28] 1821 2-8-6..............................(p) ThoreHammerHansen(5) 7 15
(Bill Turner) *s.i.s: sn pushed along in rr: nt clr run and swtchd rt over 3f out: wknd 1/2-way (jockey said filly hung right-handed)* **40/1**

1m 2.57s (0.67) **Going Correction** +0.075s/f (Slow) **9** Ran SP% **112.6**
Speed ratings (Par 93): **97,96,93,88,85 83,83,81,72**
CSF £12.72 TOTE £4.10: £1.40, £1.30, £1.10; EX 13.10 Trifecta £34.50.
Owner Blackbriar Racing **Bred** Whatton Manor Stud **Trained** Upper Lambourn, W Berks

FOCUS
There was a tight finish to this interesting novice event. The winner didn't need a great effort at the weights.

2695 BOOK TICKETS ONLINE AT WOLVERHAMPTON-RACECOURSE.CO.UK H'CAP 1m 5f 219y (Tp)
3:25 (3:27) (Class 6) (0-60,60) 4-Y-O+
£3,105 (£924; £461; £300; £300; £300) **Stalls** Low

Form RPR
3005 **1** **Hussar Ballad (USA)**[3] 2593 10-8-11 **50**.............................. CamHardie 6 61
(Antony Brittain) *hld up: hdwy on outer over 2f out: led ins fnl f: styd on wl* **10/1**

4006 **2** *3 3/4* **Angel Gabrial (IRE)**[14] 2217 10-9-3 **56**..............................(p) LukeMorris 12 56
(Patrick Morris) *chsd ldr: led over 2f out: drvn along over 1f out: hdd ins fnl f: styd on same pce* **40/1**

0403 **3** *2 1/2* **Yasir (USA)**[20] 2014 11-9-1 **54**.............................. DavidProbert 5 46
(Sophie Leech) *s.i.s: hld up: swtchd rt 3f out: hdwy on outer over 2f out: styd on to go 3rd ins fnl f: nt rch ldrs* **5/1**[2]

360- **4** *1/2* **Muftakker**[272] 6131 5-9-7 **60**.............................. JackGarritty 2 51
(John Norton) *hld up: nt clr run over 2f out: hdwy over 1f out: hung lft ins fnl f: nt rch ldrs* **12/1**

000 **5** *1* **Guaracha**[20] 2014 8-8-11 **50**..............................(v) GeorgeWood 13 38
(Alexandra Dunn) *s.i.s: hld up: hdwy over 1f out: nt rch ldrs* **100/1**

0-02 **6** *1* **Urban Spirit (IRE)**[32] 1718 5-9-2 **55**.............................. DanielTudhope 8 40
(Lawrence Mullaney) *led: rdn and hdd over 2f out: wknd ins fnl f* **2/1**[1]

52-6 **7** *2 3/4* **Alacritas**[96] 616 4-9-4 **57**..............................(h) JoeFanning 4 35
(David Simcock) *hld up: hmpd over 2f out: nvr on terms (jockey said filly was denied a clear run when turning for home)* **17/2**

/00- **8** *1/2* **Paddy's Rock (IRE)**[342] 3444 8-9-2 **55**.............................. TonyHamilton 7 30
(Lynn Siddall) *chsd ldrs: rdn over 3f out: wknd over 2f out* **33/1**

3/00 **9** *shd* **Fern Owl**[26] 1861 7-9-5 **58**.............................. LiamKeniry 3 33
(John Butler) *s.i.s: hld up: nt clr run over 2f out: n.d* **9/1**

54 **10** *1* **Wally's Wisdom**[103] 482 7-9-1 **54**.............................. LiamJones 10 26
(Mark Loughnane) *hld up: hdwy 3f out: rdn over 2f out: wknd over 1f out* **10/1**

4360 **11** *1* **Mood For Mischief**[28] 1826 4-9-0 **58**.............................. RachealKneller(5) 9 28
(James Bennett) *prom: racd keenly: rdn over 2f out: wknd over 1f out* **8/1**[3]

40-0 **12** *10* **Everlasting Sea**[41] 1497 5-8-4 **46** oh1..............................(t[1]) WilliamCox(3) 1
(Stuart Kittow) *chsd ldrs tl rdn and wknd over 2f out: b.b.v (jockey said mare stopped quickly. Vet said mare bled from the nose)* **100/1**

600- **13** *1/2* **Fool To Cry (IRE)**[237] 7388 6-8-13 **52**.............................. KieranO'Neill 11
(Johnny Farrelly) *s.i.s: sn pushed along in rr: hung lft fr 1/2-way: wknd over 2f out* **28/1**

3m 3.73s (2.73) **Going Correction** +0.075s/f (Slow) **13** Ran SP% **116.4**
Speed ratings (Par 101): **95,92,91,91,90 90,88,88,88,87 86,81,80**
CSF £361.36 CT £2218.45 TOTE £10.30: £2.60, £10.20, £2.20; EX 311.10 Trifecta £989.10.
Owner Antony Brittain **Bred** Darley **Trained** Warthill, N Yorks

FOCUS
A routine moderate handicap. The winner is rated near the best of this winter's form.

2696 GRAND THEATRE WOLVERHAMPTON H'CAP 1m 4f 51y (Tp)
4:00 (4:00) (Class 5) (0-70,71) 4-Y-O+
£3,752 (£1,116; £557; £300; £300; £300) **Stalls** Low

Form RPR
0065 **1** **Star Ascending (IRE)**[14] 2202 7-9-7 **70**..............................(p) JoeFanning 12 77
(Jennie Candlish) *racd keenly: wnt 2nd over 10f out: led 2f out: rdn over 1f out: r.o* **8/1**

2400 **2** *1* **Enmeshing**[21] 1988 6-8-13 **62**.............................. GeorgeWood 4 67
(Alexandra Dunn) *hld up: swtchd rt over 2f out: hdwy on outer over 1f out: sn rdn and hung lft: r.o to go 2nd nr fin* **7/1**[3]

/53- **3** *hd* **Joyceick (FR)**[271] 5555 5-9-2 **65**.............................. EoinWalsh 8 70
(Nick Littmoden) *led: hdd 2f out: rdn and ev ch ins fnl f: styd on same pce towards fin* **50/1**

21-0 **4** *hd* **Taurean Dancer (IRE)**[118] 246 4-9-0 **63**.............................. RossaRyan 11 67
(Roger Teal) *hld up in tch: racd keenly: rdn and hung lft fr over 1f out: r.o (jockey said gelding hung left-handed)* **9/1**

5154 **5** *1 1/2* **Sir Gnet (IRE)**[21] 1983 5-9-1 **64**..............................(h) DanielTudhope 5 66
(Ed Dunlop) *hld up: hung lft and r.o ins fnl f: nt rch ldrs* **8/1**

2415 **6** *1* **Dream Magic (IRE)**[21] 1988 5-8-13 **69**..............................(b) CierenFallon(7) 2 69
(Mark Loughnane) *chsd ldrs: rdn over 2f out: hung lft and no ex ins fnl f* **3/1**[1]

0-30 **7** *1* **Punkawallah**[43] 1463 5-9-1 **67**....(t[1]) WilliamCox(3) 10 66
(Alexandra Dunn) *chsd ldrs: pushed along over 3f out: hung lft and nt clr run over 1f out: no ex ins fnl f* **40/1**

2 **8** *3/4* **Lost History (IRE)**[21] 1988 6-9-5 **71**.... JaneElliott(3) 7 71
(John Spearing) *prom: rdn and swtchd lft over 1f out: styng on same pce whn hmpd ins fnl f* **11/2**[2]

6036 **9** *6* **Thawry**[14] 2185 4-9-8 **71**.... CamHardie 9 59
(Antony Brittain) *pushed along early in rr: rdn over 2f out: n.d* **8/1**

00 **10** *9* **Black Noah**[27] 1840 4-9-1 **64**.... KieranO'Neill 3 38
(Johnny Farrelly) *hld up: rdn over 3f out: wknd over 2f out* **40/1**

1446 **11** *5* **Tetradrachm**[69] 1024 6-8-12 **61**.... StevieDonohoe 1 27
(Shaun Harris) *hld up: rdn over 2f out: sn wknd and eased (jockey said gelding hung left-handed)* **16/1**

1200 **12** *7* **Ice Canyon**[65] 1095 5-9-5 **68**....(h) LiamJones 6 22
(Mark Brisbourne) *hld up: nt clr run and wknd over 2f out* **11/1**

2m 41.95s (1.15) **Going Correction** +0.075s/f (Slow) 12 Ran SP% **117.3**
Speed ratings (Par 103): **99,98,98,98,97 96,95,95,91,85 81,77**
CSF £61.73 CT £2622.91 TOTE £8.10: £2.60, £3.60, £11.30; EX 88.50 Trifecta £3598.20.
Owner Paul Wright-Bevans **Bred** Philip Gilligan & Anne Gilligan **Trained** Basford Green, Staffs
■ Stewards' Enquiry : Cieren Fallon two-day ban; careless riding (May 27-28)

FOCUS
They didn't go a great gallop early and the pace held up well. The winner is rated to his winter best.

2697 FOLLOWUS @WOLVESRACES ON TWITTER H'CAP — 1m 4f 51y (Tp)
4:30 (4:34) (Class 5) (0-75,77) 3-Y-O
£3,752 (£1,116; £557; £300; £300; £300) **Stalls** Low

Form RPR

2-10 **1** **Dark Miracle (IRE)**[3] 2582 3-9-0 **74**.... CierenFallon(7) 6 83
(Marco Botti) *hld up: hdwy over 2f out: shkn up to ld over 1f out: rdn and hung lft ins fnl f: styd on* **6/1**[3]

622- **2** *2 3/4* **Gravistas**[217] 8048 3-9-10 **77**.... JoeFanning 5 82+
(Mark Johnston) *s.i.s: sn pushed along in rr: hdwy over 8f out: rdn and ev ch over 1f out: nt clr run ins fnl f: styd on same pce* **6/5**[1]

0503 **3** *2 1/4* **Hen (IRE)**[14] 2213 3-8-6 **59**.... NicolaCurrie 7 60
(Jamie Osborne) *hld up: hdwy u.p on outer over 2f out: rdn over 1f out: hung lft and styd on same pce ins fnl f* **25/1**

60-0 **4** *3/4* **Robert Fitzroy (IRE)**[33] 1697 3-9-0 **67**....(p[1]) DavidProbert 1 67
(Michael Bell) *hld up: hdwy over 2f out: nt clr run and swtchd rt over 1f out: styd on same pce* **14/1**

0-56 **5** *1* **Awesomedude**[35] 1643 3-8-12 **65**.... AntonioFresu 8 63
(Mrs Ilka Gansera-Leveque) *chsd ldrs: rdn to ld over 2f out: hdd over 1f out: wknd ins fnl f* **12/1**

5-53 **6** *3/4* **Gino Wotimean (USA)**[112] 343 3-9-2 **69**.... RossaRyan 2 66
(Noel Williams) *hld up: hdwy 3f out: rdn and ev ch over 1f out: wknd ins fnl f* **22/1**

2-32 **7** *13* **Nabbeyl (IRE)**[13] 2229 3-9-9 **76**....(b[1]) AndreaAtzeni 9 60
(Roger Varian) *chsd ldrs: wnt 2nd over 10f out: led over 5f out: rdn and hdd over 2f out: wknd and eased fnl f (jockey said colt stopped quickly)* **3/1**[2]

45-0 **8** *28* **Garrison Commander (IRE)**[25] 1897 3-9-5 **72**....(p[1]) DanielTudhope 10 3
(Eve Johnson Houghton) *prom: rdn over 3f out: wknd and eased over 2f out* **33/1**

36-0 **9** *5* **Tasman Sea**[13] 2253 3-9-3 **70**.... HollieDoyle 3
(Archie Watson) *led: hdd over 5f out: sn rdn: wknd over 3f out (jockey said filly was never travelling)* **40/1**

0446 **10** *30* **Gabrial The Giant (IRE)**[14] 2213 3-8-3 **56**....(v[1]) LukeMorris 4
(Patrick Morris) *prom: rdn and lost pl over 6f out: wknd over 4f out (jockey said gelding stopped quickly)* **40/1**

2m 37.76s (-3.04) **Going Correction** +0.075s/f (Slow) 10 Ran SP% **115.1**
Speed ratings (Par 99): **113,111,109,109,108 108,99,80,77,57**
CSF £12.75 CT £164.19 TOTE £7.20: £2.00, £1.10, £3.00; EX 16.70 Trifecta £221.50.
Owner H Szabo **Bred** Selwood Bloodstock Ltd & R S Hoskins **Trained** Newmarket, Suffolk

FOCUS
They went off at a good pace and the closers came through at the finish. Improvement from the winner, the third a fair guide.

2698 BLACK COUNTRY H'CAP — 1m 4f 51y (Tp)
5:00 (5:01) (Class 6) (0-55,55) 3-Y-O+
£3,105 (£924; £461; £300; £300; £300) **Stalls** Low

Form RPR

0302 **1** **Lady Of Authority**[16] 2127 4-9-2 **52**.... GeorgiaDobie(7) 3 59
(Richard Phillips) *hld up: swtchd rt and hdwy on outer over 1f out: rdn to ld and hung lft wl ins fnl f: r.o* **2/1**[1]

5004 **2** *1 3/4* **Qayed (CAN)**[20] 2014 4-9-8 **51**....(p) LiamJones 1 56
(Mark Brisbourne) *s.i.s: hld up: hdwy over 2f out: nt clr run and swtchd rt over 1f out: r.o to go 2nd nr fin (jockey said gelding was denied a clear run)* **9/1**

0101 **3** *nk* **Muraaqeb**[13] 2234 5-9-6 **49**....(p) LukeMorris 12 53
(Milton Bradley) *chsd ldrs: rdn to ld 1f out: edgd lft and hdd wl ins fnl f: styd on same pce* **12/1**

6503 **4** *1* **Ember's Glow**[16] 2127 5-9-10 **53**.... EoinWalsh 7 55
(Mark Loughnane) *hld up in tch: lost pl over 5f out: hdwy on outer over 2f out: rdn over 1f out: styd on same pce wl ins fnl f (trainer said gelding was unsuited by the Tapeta surface which, in his opinion, was riding slower than Standard on this occasion)* **9/2**[2]

0500 **5** *1 1/2* **Sellingallthetime (IRE)**[11] 2344 8-9-3 **53**....(p) EllieMacKenzie(7) 6 53
(Mark Usher) *hld up: hdwy over 5f out: led over 2f out: rdn and hdd 1f out: no ex ins fnl f* **16/1**

5446 **6** *4 1/2* **Pike Corner Cross (IRE)**[16] 2111 7-9-12 **55**.... TomQueally 5 48
(Alastair Ralph) *trckd ldrs: rdn and edgd lft over 1f out: wknd ins fnl f* **5/1**[3]

-000 **7** *5* **Cat Royale (IRE)**[11] 2350 6-9-7 **50**....(b) DannyBrock 10 35
(John Butler) *led: rdn and hdd over 2f out: carried lft over 1f out: wknd fnl f* **12/1**

-000 **8** *2* **Jack Of Diamonds (IRE)**[23] 1958 10-9-11 **54**....(p) RossaRyan 2 35
(Roger Teal) *hld up: hdwy over 2f out: rdn: hung lft and wknd over 1f out* **40/1**

3200 **9** *10* **Attain**[13] 2233 10-9-4 **54**....(b) KateLeahy(7) 9 19
(Archie Watson) *s.i.s: hdwy over 8f out: rdn and wknd over 2f out (jockey said gelding was slowly away)* **20/1**

106- **10** *8* **Kay Sera**[165] 9318 11-9-5 **48**.... KieranO'Neill 4 1
(Tony Newcombe) *hld up: racd wd leaving bk st: wknd over 2f out* **40/1**

-000 **11** *5* **Faraway Fields (USA)**[16] 2112 4-9-9 **52**.... DavidProbert 11
(Peter Hiatt) *s.i.s: hdwy to chse ldr over 10f out tl rdn and wknd over 2f out* **28/1**

000- **12** *1/2* **Just Another Idea (IRE)**[194] 8737 4-9-8 **54**....(w) WilliamCox(3) 8
(Mandy Rowland) *prom: lost plkace over 5f out: sn rdn: nt clr run and wknd 3f out (jockey said gelding stopped quickly)* **66/1**

2m 41.99s (1.19) **Going Correction** +0.075s/f (Slow) 12 Ran SP% **114.0**
Speed ratings (Par 101): **99,97,97,96,95 92,89,88,81,76 72,72**
CSF £18.72 CT £171.02 TOTE £3.00: £1.20, £2.50, £2.40; EX 21.20 Trifecta £128.20.
Owner Richard Phillips **Bred** R A G Robinson **Trained** Adlestrop, Gloucs

FOCUS
Ordinary handicap form. The winner looks back to her best.
T/Jkpt: Not Won. T/Plt: £75.70 to a £1 stake. Pool: £72,357.14 - 697.18 winning units T/Qpdt: £25.30 to a £1 stake. Pool: £7,874.86 - 229.88 winning units **Colin Roberts**

2699 - 2705a (Foreign Racing) - See Raceform Interactive

2475 BEVERLEY (R-H)
Tuesday, May 14

OFFICIAL GOING: Good to soft (good in places; 6.6)
Wind: Moderate across Weather: Warm & sunny

2706 JIM HIBBS "WE DON'T SHIP" NOVICE STKS (DIV I) — 5f
1:50 (1:50) (Class 5) 2-Y-O
£4,032 (£1,207; £603; £302; £150) **Stalls** Low

Form RPR

1 **Auchterarder (IRE)** 2-9-0 0.... PJMcDonald 1 80+
(Mark Johnston) *qckly away: mde all: rdn clr over 1f out: kpt on strly* **5/1**[2]

2 **2** *2 1/2* **Quiet Place (IRE)**[21] 2020 2-9-0 0.... PatCosgrave 3 71
(Saeed bin Suroor) *trckd ldng pair on inner: swtchd lft and effrt 2f out: sn rdn: kpt on to chse wnr ins fnl f: sn no imp* **8/13**[1]

02 **3** *3* **Bezzas Lad (IRE)**[15] 2184 2-9-5 0.... SamJames 2 65
(Phillip Makin) *cl up: pushed along 2f out: rdn over 1f out: kpt on same pce* **12/1**[3]

0 **4** *2 1/2* **Geepower (IRE)**[8] 2475 2-9-2 0.... BenRobinson(3) 5 56
(Brian Ellison) *chsd ldrs: rdn along 2f out: kpt on fnl f* **33/1**

5 *1* **Out Of Here (IRE)** 2-9-5 0.... SeanLevey 4 53
(Kevin Ryan) *in tch on inner: effrt wl over 1f out: n.m.r and rdn swtchd lft jst over 1f out: kpt on* **5/1**[2]

30 **6** *nse* **War Of Clans (IRE)**[31] 1758 2-9-5 0.... BenCurtis 10 52
(K R Burke) *chsd ldrs: rdn along 2f out: sn drvn and grad wknd (jockey said colt had no more to give)* **28/1**

03 **7** *5* **Richard R H B (IRE)**[17] 2108 2-9-5 0.... TrevorWhelan 6 34
(David Loughnane) *nvr bttr than midfield (jockey said colt missed the break)* **14/1**

5 **8** *3 1/4* **Corndavon Lad (IRE)**[13] 2288 2-9-5 0.... TonyHamilton 8 23
(Richard Fahey) *dwlt: a in rr* **20/1**

9 *nk* **Youthfilly** 2-8-11 0.... JamieGormley(3) 9 17
(Ollie Pears) *sn outpcd: a in rr* **100/1**

10 *1 1/4* **Bosun's Chair** 2-9-5 0.... DavidAllan 7 17
(Tim Easterby) *green a in rr (jockey said colt ran green)* **80/1**

1m 3.69s (0.79) **Going Correction** +0.25s/f (Good) 10 Ran SP% **123.0**
Speed ratings (Par 93): **103,99,94,90,88 88,80,75,74,72**
CSF £8.68 TOTE £7.60: £1.70, £1.10, £2.60; EX 11.10 Trifecta £59.20.
Owner Kingsley Park 11 **Bred** Newstead Breeding **Trained** Middleham Moor, N Yorks

FOCUS
The going was given as good to soft, good in places (Going Stick 5.9). An impressive debut from the winner, who clocked a time 2.14sec faster than the winner of the second division. She looks Queen Mary material. The third is rated near his Newcastle form.

2707 JIM HIBBS "WE DON'T SHIP" NOVICE STKS (DIV II) — 5f
2:20 (2:21) (Class 5) 2-Y-O
£4,032 (£1,207; £603; £302; £150) **Stalls** Low

Form RPR

1 **Execlusive (IRE)** 2-9-0 0.... DanielTudhope 7 65
(Archie Watson) *mde most: rdn and qcknd clr wl over 1f out: kpt on strly* **13/8**[1]

2 *2 3/4* **Kilig** 2-9-5 0.... DavidAllan 1 60
(Tim Easterby) *trckd ldrs on inner: hdwy 2f out: rdn to chse wnr 1f out: kpt on: no imp* **14/1**

3 *1 1/4* **Dancinginthesand (IRE)** 2-9-5 0.... GrahamLee 4 56
(Bryan Smart) *trckd ldrs: pushed along 2f out: sn rdn: kpt on fnl f* **5/1**[3]

4 *nk* **Spanish Time** 2-9-5 0.... JoeFanning 5 55+
(Keith Dalgleish) *trckd ldrs: effrt 2f out: sn rdn along and kpt on fnl f* **7/2**[2]

0 **5** *1/2* **Champagne Victory (IRE)**[8] 2476 2-8-11 0.... BenRobinson(3) 8 48
(Brian Ellison) *cl up: disp ld 1/2-way: rdn along 2f out: drvn and wknd over 1f out* **50/1**

6 **6** *1/2* **Cmon Cmon (IRE)**[31] 1758 2-9-2 0.... RowanScott(3) 3 51
(Nigel Tinkler) *chsd ldrs on inner: rdn along 2f out: sn no imp* **7/2**[2]

7 *3 3/4* **Rusalka (IRE)** 2-9-0 0.... RachelRichardson 9 32
(Tim Easterby) *rrd s: green and bhd: hdwy and in tch on outer 2f out: sn rdn and wknd (jockey said filly reared as the stalls opened and missed the break)* **16/1**

8 *3 1/2* **Castashadow** 2-9-5 0.... CamHardie 2 25
(Alan Brown) *a in rr* **33/1**

0 **9** *4 1/2* **Scotch Corner (IRE)**[8] 2475 2-9-5 0.... PhilDennis 6 9
(David C Griffiths) *green a in rr* **50/1**

1m 5.83s (2.93) **Going Correction** +0.25s/f (Good) 9 Ran SP% **118.6**
Speed ratings (Par 93): **86,81,79,79,78 77,71,65,58**
CSF £28.65 TOTE £2.00: £1.20, £2.60, £1.80; EX 23.40 Trifecta £129.10.
Owner Rabbah Racing **Bred** Azienda Agricola Gennaro Stimola **Trained** Upper Lambourn, W Berks

FOCUS
This looked the weaker of the two divisions, and the time was much slower (2.14sec). The jury's out on the form's true worth.

2708 JIM HIBBS "A DEAL IS A DEAL" (S) STKS — 5f
2:50 (2:50) (Class 6) 3-Y-O
£3,137 (£933; £466; £300; £300; £300) **Stalls** Low

Form RPR

0-00 **1** **Maid From The Mist**[36] 1650 3-8-11 50.... PJMcDonald 3 55
(John Gallagher) *trckd ldr on inner: swtchd lft and hdwy wl over 1f out: sn rdn: drvn ent fnl f: kpt on wl to ld last 50yds: and edgd lft: hld on wl* **9/1**

-000 **2** *nse* **Pearl Of Qatar**[8] 2477 3-8-13 61.... BenRobinson(3) 5 60
(Brian Ellison) *chsd ldrs: rdn along 2f out: drvn and hdwy ent fnl f: styd on to chal last 100yds and edgd rt: ev ch whn bmpd sltly last 50yds: kpt on* **4/1**[2]

6056 **3** *1 3/4* **She'Zanarab**[12] 2327 3-8-8 51.... JamieGormley(3) 4 49+
(Iain Jardine) *towards rr: hdwy 1/2-way: chsd ldrs and rdn over 1f out: styd on wl towards fin* **12/1**

The Form Book Flat 2019, Raceform Ltd, Newbury, RG14 5SJ

01-2 **4** *hd* **Scale Force**[103] 506 3-9-4 68..............................(b[1]) WilliamCox(3) 7 58
(Gay Kelleway) *sn led: rdn clr over 1f out: drvn ins fnl f: wknd and hdd last 50yds* 5/1[3]

-036 **5** *2* **Kickham Street**[24] 1954 3-9-2 60..............................(p[1]) JasonHart 6 46
(John Quinn) *prom: chsd ldr 1/2-way: rdn along wl over 1f out: wknd appr fnl f* 6/1

3540 **6** *hd* **Alicia Darcy (IRE)**[17] 2098 3-8-11 66.............................. BarryMcHugh 2 40
(James Given) *in rr and sn pushed along: rdn 2f out: hdwy and n.m.r over 1f out: n.d* 7/2[1]

04-0 **7** *hd* **Caramel Curves**[43] 1486 3-8-11 53.............................. TomEaves 1 39
(David Barron) *chsd ldrs on inner: rdn along 2f out: sn drvn and wknd* 8/1

2-50 **8** *shd* **Parion**[12] 2332 3-8-6 70.............................. SeanDavis(5) 8 39
(Richard Fahey) *a towards rr (jockey said filly was never travelling)* 7/1

-465 **9** *5* **Atwaar**[27] 1863 3-8-6 48.............................. FayeMcManoman(5) 9 21
(Charles Smith) *chsd ldrs: rdn along wl 2f out: sn drvn and wknd* 33/1

60-0 **10** *8* **Frank's Law**[12] 2327 3-9-2 55..............................(p) JoeFanning 10
(Keith Dalgleish) *a in rr* 25/1

1m 4.71s (1.81) **Going Correction** +0.25s/f (Good) **10** Ran SP% **121.3**
Speed ratings (Par 97): **95,94,92,91,88 88,87,87,79,67**
CSF £46.83 TOTE £8.40: £2.00, £1.70, £4.20; EX 51.00 Trifecta £626.40.There was no bid for the winner.
Owner M C S D Racing Partnership **Bred** Trickledown Stud Limited **Trained** Chastleton, Oxon

FOCUS
An ordinary seller and there was a tight finish.

2709 ANNIE OXTOBY MEMORIAL H'CAP 5f
3:20 (3:21) (Class 5) (0-75,75) 4-Y-O+

£4,284 (£1,282; £641; £320; £300; £300) **Stalls** Low

Form RPR

0-00 **1** **East Street Revue**[11] 2368 6-9-5 73.............................. DuranFentiman 10 82
(Tim Easterby) *cl up: led 1 1/2f out: sn rdn: hdd ent fnl f: drvn and rallied gamely to ld again towards fin (trainer could offer no explanation for the gelding's improved form other than the gelding may have benefitted from the removal of blinkers on this occasion)* 25/1

-204 **2** *nk* **Qaaraat**[7] 2515 4-9-1 69.............................. CamHardie 4 77
(Antony Brittain) *cl up: rdn to take slt ld ent fnl f: sn drvn: hdd and no ex towards fin* 6/1[1]

3-40 **3** *2 1/4* **Show Palace**[7] 2508 6-9-6 74.............................. ConnorBeasley 7 74
(Jennie Candlish) *t.k.h: chsd ldrs: effrt over 1f out: sn rdn: kpt on u.p fnl f* 17/2

5012 **4** *nk* **Johnny Cavagin**[19] 2053 10-9-5 73.............................. GrahamLee 17 72+
(Paul Midgley) *dwlt and swtchd rt to inner s: towards rr: hdwy on inner wl over 1f out: sn rdn: kpt on wl fnl f: nrst fin* 11/1

-243 **5** *hd* **Foxtrot Knight**[13] 2294 7-8-9 63.............................. AndrewMullen 5 61
(Ruth Carr) *chsd ldrs: rdn along wl over 1f out: kpt on u.p fnl f* 8/1[3]

000- **6** *1/2* **Luzum (IRE)**[147] 9596 4-9-0 68.............................. NathanEvans 3 64
(Michael Easterby) *led: rdn along 2f out: sn hdd and grad wknd* 7/1[2]

00-0 **7** *1 1/2* **Ladweb**[15] 2206 9-8-13 67.............................. PJMcDonald 2 58
(John Gallagher) *chsd ldrs: rdn along 2f out: wknd over 1f out* 12/1

0335 **8** *nk* **Deeds Not Words (IRE)**[13] 2294 8-8-12 66.............................. RoystonFfrench 1 56
(Tracy Waggott) *in tch: rdn along and hdwy wl over 1f out: sn drvn and no imp fnl f* 12/1

0-54 **9** *1* **Round The Island**[13] 2292 6-8-12 66.............................. PhilDennis 14 52
(Richard Whitaker) *chsd ldrs towards outer: rdn 2f out: wknd over 1f out* 25/1

0005 **10** *1 1/4* **Tan**[14] 2227 5-9-2 70..............................(p) AlistairRawlinson 8 52
(Michael Appleby) *a towards rr* 11/1

3206 **11** *nse* **Jan Van Hoof (IRE)**[11] 2379 8-9-1 69.............................. BarryMcHugh 6 51
(Michael Herrington) *a toward rr* 7/1[2]

5-54 **12** *1 1/2* **Afandem (IRE)**[22] 1976 5-8-12 66..............................(b) DavidAllan 9 42
(Tim Easterby) *dwlt: a in rr (jockey said gelding reared as the stalls opened and missed the break)* 6/1[1]

610- **13** *nk* **Rolladice**[229] 7710 4-9-0 75.............................. JoshQuinn(7) 11 50
(Michael Easterby) *chsd ldrs: rdn along 2f out: sn wknd* 20/1

6022 **14** *1* **Gamesome (FR)**[24] 1952 8-8-12 66.............................. PaulMulrennan 15 37
(Paul Midgley) *hld up towards outer: a in rr* 12/1

00/0 **15** *1 1/4* **Adiator**[131] 45 11-8-2 61 oh16.............................. FayeMcManoman(5) 13 28
(Seb Spencer) *in rr and swtchd rt to outer after 1f: a bhd* 66/1

1m 3.46s (0.56) **Going Correction** +0.25s/f (Good) **15** Ran SP% **128.9**
Speed ratings (Par 103): **105,104,100,100,100 99,96,96,94,92 92,90,89,88,86**
CSF £173.90 CT £1461.13 TOTE £50.10: £15.20, £2.70, £3.10; EX 448.10 Trifecta £2750.70.
Owner S A Heley & Partner **Bred** Habton Farms & Mr A Heley **Trained** Great Habton, N Yorks

FOCUS
A competitive sprint but it paid to be handy, the first three and sixth racing in the first four positions throughout. The runner-up is rated to his best.

2710 JIM HIBBS "WHERE'S YOUR BE-BACK" H'CAP 1m 100y
3:50 (3:51) (Class 4) (0-85,85) 4-Y-O+

£6,553 (£1,961; £980; £490; £300; £300) **Stalls** Low

Form RPR

6-11 **1** **Kylie Rules**[19] 2057 4-8-7 71.............................. AndrewMullen 6 81+
(Ruth Carr) *t.k.h: in tch: hdwy on outer 3f out: led over 2f out: and sn rdn clr: drvn ins fnl f: jst hld on* 9/4[1]

00-0 **2** *nk* **Swift Emperor (IRE)**[4] 2584 7-9-0 78.............................. RobbieDowney 9 85
(David Barron) *hld up towards rr: hdwy 3f out: chsd ldrs wl over 1f out: sn rdn: styd on wl fnl f* 20/1

000- **3** *nk* **Leader Writer (FR)**[106] 8806 7-9-5 83.............................. SeanLevey 12 89
(David Elsworth) *stdd and swtchd rt s: hld up in rr: swtchd lft and hdwy 2f out: rdn and nt clr run over 1f out: str run ins fnl f: kpt on* 10/1

000- **4** *2* **Rousayan (IRE)**[196] 8717 8-9-7 85..............................(h) BenCurtis 2 87+
(Roger Fell) *prom: pushed along over 2f out: rdn wl over 1f out: kpt on same pce (jockey said gelding was denied a clear run 2f out)* 20/1

1120 **5** *3/4* **Weld Al Emarat**[17] 2095 7-9-2 80.............................. CamHardie 1 80
(Michael Easterby) *hld up in rr: hdwy over 2f out: rdn over 1f out: kpt on fnl f* 8/1[3]

00 **6** *2 3/4* **Intense Style (IRE)**[14] 2246 7-8-7 76.............................. FayeMcManoman(5) 4 70+
(Les Eyre) *in tch: hdwy over 2f out: rdn wl over 1f out: sn drvn and kpt on same pce (jockey said gelding was denied a clear run 2f out)* 25/1

60-0 **7** *3/4* **Magic City (IRE)**[44] 1457 10-8-8 72.............................. NathanEvans 13 64
(Michael Easterby) *towards rr: hdwy over 2f out: sn rdn and kpt on same pce (jockey said gelding was denied a clear run 2 1/2f out)* 20/1

030- **8** *1 1/4* **Mikmak**[189] 8899 6-9-2 85.............................. DannyRedmond(5) 5 74
(Tim Easterby) *chsd ldrs: rdn along on outer over 2f out: drvn and hung bdly rt 1f out: sn wknd* 16/1

51-2 **9** *1/2* **Placebo Effect (IRE)**[19] 2057 4-8-4 71.............................. JamieGormley(3) 11 59
(Ollie Pears) *in tch: hdwy on outer 3f out: rdn along over 2f out: sn btn* 9/1

6635 **10** *1/2* **Me Too Nagasaki (IRE)**[4] 2584 5-8-9 73..............................(t) PJMcDonald 10 60
(Stuart Williams) *hld up a towards rr* 11/1

03-2 **11** *5* **Storm Ahead (IRE)**[8] 2480 6-8-11 75..............................(b) DavidAllan 8 50
(Tim Easterby) *cl up: chal over 3f out: sn rdn and ev ch: drvn 2f out and sn wknd* 6/1[2]

0-55 **12** *1 1/4* **Kharbetation (IRE)**[8] 2479 6-8-13 77..............................(b[1]) DanielTudhope 3 49
(David O'Meara) *led: rdn along over 3f out: drvn and hdd over 2f out: sn wknd* 11/1

3-30 **13** *7* **International Man**[19] 2057 4-8-12 76.............................. TonyHamilton 7 32
(Richard Fahey) *chsd ldrs: rdn along over 3f out: sn wknd* 12/1

16-0 **14** *7* **Detachment**[45] 1413 6-9-3 81.............................. JoeFanning 15 21
(Les Eyre) *a in rr* 16/1

1m 46.58s (0.18) **Going Correction** +0.25s/f (Good) **14** Ran SP% **129.5**
Speed ratings (Par 105): **109,108,108,106,105 102,102,100,100,99 94,93,86,79**
CSF £61.39 CT £426.45 TOTE £3.70: £2.40, £6.40, £3.20; EX 56.40 Trifecta £917.90.
Owner J A Knox and Mrs M A Knox **Bred** J A Knox **Trained** Huby, N Yorks

FOCUS
Add 7yds. Things got a bit messy in the straight but the winner, who avoided the trouble, quickened up well.

2711 HAPPY BIRTHDAY GRAHAM ROBERTS H'CAP 1m 1f 207y
4:20 (4:23) (Class 5) (0-70,72) 3-Y-O

£4,284 (£1,282; £641; £320; £300; £300) **Stalls** Low

Form RPR

5-40 **1** **Valence**[17] 2096 3-9-3 66..............................(p[1]) RobertHavlin 6 75
(Ed Dunlop) *hld up in tch: hdwy on outer over 2f out: rdn over 1f out: led and edgd rt jst ins fnl f: drvn and hung rt to inner 75yds out: styd on (regarding the apparent improvement in form, trainer's rep said colt benefitted from the application of cheekpieces and the drop in class)* 13/2

0-02 **2** *2* **Highwaygrey**[15] 2200 3-9-1 64.............................. DavidAllan 11 70
(Tim Easterby) *dwlt and in rr: hdwy 3f out: chsd ldrs and swtchd rt wl over 1f out: drvn and styng on whn n.m.r and sltly hmpd jst ins fnl f: kpt on wl towards fin* 8/1

060- **3** *3/4* **Euro Implosion (IRE)**[234] 7508 3-8-13 62.............................. JoeFanning 12 66
(Keith Dalgleish) *trckd ldr: cl up over 4f out: rdn to ld wl over 2f out: drvn and hdd ins fnl f: n.m.r and sltly hmpd on inner last 75yds: lost 2nd towards fin* 12/1

3 **4** *5* **Osmosis**[19] 2058 3-9-9 72.............................. BenCurtis 2 66
(Jason Ward) *trckd ldng pair: effrt over 2f out and sn pushed along: rdn wl over 1f out: kpt on same pce appr fnl f* 13/2

033- **5** *shd* **Beaufort (IRE)**[189] 8896 3-9-5 68.............................. PaulMulrennan 5 61
(Michael Dods) *trckd ldrs: hdwy over 3f out: chsd ldr over 2f out: sn rdn and ev ch: drvn and wknd appr fnl f* 9/2[1]

6453 **6** *3 1/2* **Curfewed (IRE)**[29] 1819 3-9-3 66.............................. CamHardie 10 52
(Tracy Waggott) *hld up in tch: effrt and sme hdwy over 2f out: sn rdn and n.d* 8/1

04-0 **7** *1 3/4* **Ritchie Star (IRE)**[31] 1764 3-8-11 60.............................. AndrewMullen 9 43
(Ben Haslam) *stdd s and hld up: a in rr* 33/1

10-4 **8** *5* **Firewater**[17] 2125 3-9-1 64..............................(p) TonyHamilton 3 37
(Richard Fahey) *hld up: a towards rr* 5/1[2]

52-5 **9** *1/2* **Archies Lad**[23] 1972 3-8-9 63.............................. SeanDavis(5) 7 35
(Richard Fahey) *trckd ldrs: hdwy on outer 3f out: rdn along over 2f out: sn drvn and btn* 6/1[3]

2-31 **10** *4 1/2* **Fenjal (IRE)**[106] 461 3-9-7 70..............................(b) JasonHart 8 33
(Gay Kelleway) *led: rdn along 3f out: sn hdd & wknd* 14/1

44-0 **U** **Northern Lyte**[15] 2200 3-8-13 65.............................. RowanScott(3) 4
(Nigel Tinkler) *trckd ldrs: effrt 2f out: n.m.r whn clipped heels and uns rdr 1 1/2f out* 14/1

2m 7.42s (1.72) **Going Correction** +0.25s/f (Good) **11** Ran SP% **122.0**
Speed ratings (Par 99): **103,101,100,96,96 93,92,88,88,84**
CSF £60.03 CT £623.22 TOTE £8.00: £3.50, £2.40, £4.60; EX 62.20 Trifecta £1915.10.
Owner MHS Racing **Bred** Cliveden Stud Ltd **Trained** Newmarket, Suffolk

FOCUS
Add 7yds. A competitive heat, and it was a bit messy in the straight. The first three finished clear and the form is rated in line with the race standard.

2712 JIM HIBBS "TO BE FAIR" H'CAP 1m 4f 23y
4:50 (4:50) (Class 6) (0-65,65) 3-Y-O

£3,169 (£943; £471; £300; £300; £300) **Stalls** Low

Form RPR

46-3 **1** **Lincoln Tale (IRE)**[16] 2152 3-9-2 60.............................. DanielTudhope 1 66
(David O'Meara) *trckd ldrs: effrt and n.m.r wl over 1f out: swtchd rt and rdn to chal ent fnl f: sn drvn to ld: kpt on* 5/2[1]

3-56 **2** *3/4* **Fantastic Ms Fox**[17] 2096 3-8-13 57.............................. TonyHamilton 7 62
(Richard Fahey) *trckd ldrs: hdwy and cl up wl over 2f out: rdn to ld wl over 1f out: drvn ent fnl f: sn hdd: kpt on* 13/2

00-5 **3** *2 1/2* **Homesick Boy (IRE)**[21] 2021 3-9-5 63.............................. RobertHavlin 8 64
(Ed Dunlop) *trckd ldr: cl up 4f out: rdn along to ld briefly over 2f out: sn hdd and drvn: wknd appr fnl f* 7/1

3-05 **4** *3/4* **One To Go**[16] 2150 3-9-7 65.............................. DavidAllan 9 65+
(Tim Easterby) *hld up towards rr: hdwy wl over 2f out: rdn over 1f out: kpt on fnl f: nrst fin* 6/1[3]

400- **5** *1/2* **Flo Jo's Girl**[248] 7073 3-8-6 50.............................. RachelRichardson 6 49
(Tim Easterby) *hld up in rr: hdwy on outer over 2f out: rdn along wl over 1f out: sn hung bdly lft to stands' rail: kpt on (jockey said filly hung left-handed)* 25/1

000- **6** *3/4* **Land Of Winter (FR)**[166] 9308 3-8-10 54.............................. BenCurtis 5 52
(Rae Guest) *hld up in midfield: hdwy on inner and n.m.r over 1f out: rdn and no imp fnl f* 7/1

00-5 **7** *1 3/4* **Mukha Magic**[38] 1593 3-9-1 59..............................(b[1]) DanielMuscutt 3 54
(Gay Kelleway) *trckd ldrs: pushed along 3f out: rdn over 2f out: sn btn* 11/1

3-01 **8** *1 1/4* **Jazz Hands (IRE)**[12] 2325 3-8-3 52.............................. SeanDavis(5) 10 46
(Richard Fahey) *hld up towards rr: hdwy 4f out: cl up on outer 3f out: rdn along over 2f out: sn drvn and wknd* 8/1

00-0 **9** *2 1/4* **Agravain**[12] 2336 3-8-11 55.............................. DuranFentiman 2 45
(Tim Easterby) *stmbld s: t.k.h: in tch: pushed along over 2f out: sn rdn and n.d* 20/1

04-0 **10** *11* **Jean Merci (FR)**[6] 2530 3-8-11 55..............................(p[1]) TomEaves 4 31
(Keith Dalgleish) *set stdy pce: pushed along over 3f out: rdn and hdd jst over 2f out: sn wknd* 40/1

-302 **11** *7* **Nordano (GER)**[7] 2511 3-9-7 **65**.......... PJMcDonald 12 28
(Mark Johnston) *a in rr: u.p 5f out: detached after (jockey said colt was never travelling)* **4/1**[2]
2m 44.38s (5.58) **Going Correction** +0.25s/f (Good) **11** Ran SP% **131.7**
Speed ratings (Par 97): **91,90,88,88,88 87,86,85,84,76 72**
CSF £21.64 CT £112.06 TOTE £3.80: £1.80, £2.40, £2.20; EX 28.40 Trifecta £157.80.
Owner G P S Heart of Racing (Bloodstock) Ltd **Bred** W Maxwell Ervine **Trained** Upper Helmsley, N Yorks
■ Stewards' Enquiry : Daniel Tudhope two-day ban: interference & careless riding (May 28-29)
FOCUS
Add 7yds. A modest handicap but the first two pulled clear. The pace held up.

2713 JIM HIBBS "WE ARE WHERE WE ARE" MAIDEN STKS 7f 96y
5:25 (5:25) (Class 5) 3-Y-O+ **£4,284** (£1,282; £641; £320; £159) **Stalls** Low

Form RPR
0-23 **1** **Astrologer**[14] 2236 3-8-11 77.......... DanielTudhope 2 81
(David O'Meara) *mde all: rdn clr over 1f out: kpt on strly* **5/1**[3]
2-4 **2** *2 ¾* **Jabalaly (IRE)**[17] 2094 3-9-2 0.......... DaneO'Neill 6 79
(Ed Dunlop) *trckd ldrs: hdwy 3f out: rdn along over 2f out: drvn to chse wnr 1f out: edgd rt and kpt on* **9/2**[2]
3- **3** *¾* **Pamper**[202] 8546 3-8-11 0.......... PJMcDonald 4 72
(James Fanshawe) *trckd ldrs: hdwy on inner 3f out: rdn along 2f out: swtchd lft over 1f out: kpt on fnl f* **9/1**
5 **4** *½* **Moll Davis (IRE)**[17] 2102 3-8-11 0.......... EoinWalsh 11 71
(George Scott) *trckd ldrs: hdwy over 3f out: rdn along over 2f out: drvn over 1f out: kpt on same pce* **12/1**
4-2 **5** *½* **Casanova**[20] 2034 3-9-2 0.......... RobertHavlin 10 74
(John Gosden) *trckd ldrs: hdwy to chse wnr 3f out: rdn along 2f out: sn drvn and btn* **4/5**[1]
6 *3* **Grab And Run (IRE)** 3-9-2 0.......... TonyHamilton 7 67
(Richard Fahey) *towards rr: hdwy 3f out: rdn along 2f out: kpt on u.p fr over 1f out* **16/1**
0- **7** *1 ½* **Lyrical Ballad (IRE)**[181] 9050 3-8-11 0.......... BenCurtis 12 58
(Charles Hills) *in tch: hdwy 3f out: rdn along to chse ldrs on outer 2f out: grad wknd* **33/1**
-00 **8** *5* **Martha McEwan (IRE)**[16] 2146 3-8-11 0.......... RobbieDowney 1 45
(David Barron) *midfield: effrt and in tch 3f out: rdn along over 2f out: sn wknd* **100/1**
0- **9** *9* **Hard Knock Life**[341] 3494 3-9-2 0.......... DavidAllan 3 26
(Tim Easterby) *a towards rr* **50/1**
02 **10** *1* **Basildon**[12] 2347 4-9-11 0.......... BenRobinson(3) 9 28
(Brian Ellison) *a in rr* **33/1**
6- **11** *shd* **Ateescomponent (IRE)**[320] 4296 3-9-2 0.......... TomEaves 5 23
(David Barron) *a in rr* **100/1**
60- **12** *18* **Alisia R (IRE)**[178] 9133 3-8-11 0.......... JoeFanning 8
(Les Eyre) *t.k.h: cl up: rdn along over 3f out: sn wknd (jockey said filly hung left on the bottom bend)* **100/1**
1m 34.13s (1.53) **Going Correction** +0.25s/f (Good)
WFA 3 from 4yo 12lb **12** Ran SP% **124.8**
Speed ratings (Par 103): **101,97,97,96,95 92,90,85,74,73 73,52**
CSF £28.83 TOTE £4.90: £1.20, £1.80, £2.20; EX 26.70 Trifecta £183.30.
Owner Cheveley Park Stud **Bred** Cheveley Park Stud Ltd **Trained** Upper Helmsley, N Yorks
FOCUS
Add 7yds. The favourite didn't run to his best but this is still fair maiden form. The winner showed that her Beverley form doesn't flatter her.
T/Plt: £3,744.97 to a £1 stake. Pool: £59,362.71 - 83.80 winning units T/Qpdt: £314.20 to a £1 stake. Pool: £3,894.05 - 9.17 winning units **Joe Rowntree**

2353 CHEPSTOW (L-H)
Tuesday, May 14
OFFICIAL GOING: Good (good to firm in places) changing to good to firm after race 1 (2.00)
Wind: Slight breeze, mainly across Weather: Fine

2714 BJ LLEWELLYN SUPPORTS TENOVUS CANCER CARE H'CAP 1m 14y
2:00 (2:02) (Class 5) (0-70,72) 4-Y-O+
£3,752 (£1,116; £557; £300; £300; £300) **Stalls** Centre

Form RPR
0-34 **1** **Sir Roderic (IRE)**[12] 2339 6-9-6 **69**.......... OisinMurphy 14 78
(Rod Millman) *a.p: trckd ldr 1/2-way: rdn 2f out: led appr fnl f: r.o* **3/1**[2]
3242 **2** *1 ¾* **Dashing Poet**[3] 2617 5-9-2 **65**.......... DavidEgan 8 70
(Heather Main) *led: crossed over to stands' rail after 1f: rdn over 2f out: hdd appr fnl f: kpt on same pce* **2/1**[1]
1641 **3** *½* **Waqt (IRE)**[14] 2231 5-9-0 **63**.......... RichardKingscote 5 67
(Alexandra Dunn) *s.i.s: sn midfield: hdwy 3f out: rdn to chse ldng pair over 2f out: no imp tl styd on fnl f* **11/2**[3]
0610 **4** *1 ¾* **Takeonefortheteam**[17] 2106 4-9-0 **63**.......... EdwardGreatrex 11 63
(Mark Loughnane) *t.k.h in midfield: rdn: swtchd lft and hdwy over 2f out: kpt on same pce fnl f* **25/1**
21-0 **5** *¾* **Edge (IRE)**[16] 2145 8-8-13 **62**..........(b) DavidProbert 12 60
(Bernard Llewellyn) *hld up: hdwy 3f out: rdn over 1f out: unable qck (jockey said gelding was denied a clear run)* **33/1**
066- **6** *1 ½* **Tally's Son**[210] 8297 5-8-4 **56** oh7..........(p) JaneElliott(3) 9 51
(Grace Harris) *wnt to post early: chsd ldrs: rdn over 3f out: kpt on same pce fnl 2f* **33/1**
1-05 **7** *5* **Less Of That (IRE)**[11] 2353 5-8-12 **66**.......... RachealKneller(5) 6 49
(Matthew Salaman) *chsd ldrs: rdn over 2f out: wknd over 1f out* **25/1**
600- **8** *2 ¼* **Fortune And Glory (USA)**[190] 8885 6-9-7 **70**.......... RossaRyan 4 48
(Joseph Tuite) *t.k.h towards rr: rdn over 2f out: no imp on ldrs* **10/1**
00-0 **9** *3* **Connaught Ranger (IRE)**[21] 2005 4-9-6 **69**.......... ShaneKelly 10 40
(Denis Coakley) *t.k.h: hld up: pushed along over 3f out: rdn and btn over 2f out* **25/1**
00-0 **10** *1 ¾* **Kyllachys Tale (IRE)**[103] 507 5-9-3 **66**.......... JackMitchell 3 33
(Roger Teal) *wnt to post early: prom: rdn over 3f out: wknd 2f out* **12/1**
00-4 **11** *2 ½* **Bob's Girl**[8] 2481 4-8-7 **56** oh11..........(h) JimmyQuinn 13 17
(Michael Mullineaux) *wnt to post early: cl up to 1/2-way: sn rdn: wknd over 2f out* **66/1**
506- **12** *hd* **Geranium**[200] 8599 4-9-4 **67**.......... CharlieBennett 2 28
(Hughie Morrison) *chsd ldrs 3f: sn rdn along: lost tch wl over 2f out* **14/1**
30-4 **13** *10* **Zapateado**[67] 1074 4-9-2 **65**..........(t) JFEgan 1 3
(Paul George) *midfield on outer: stmbld over 6f out: rdn over 3f out: wknd over 2f out (jockey said filly stumbled after a furlong)* **12/1**

000- **14** *23* **De Bruyne Horse**[138] 9313 4-9-9 **72**..........(tp) StevieDonohoe 15
(Bernard Llewellyn) *sn wl bhd: t.o: bled fr the nose (vet said gelding bled from nose)* **20/1**
1m 32.5s (-3.50) **Going Correction** -0.45s/f (Firm) **14** Ran SP% **128.5**
Speed ratings (Par 103): **99,97,96,95,94 92,87,85,82,80 78,78,68,45**
CSF £9.28 CT £35.19 TOTE £3.60: £1.40, £1.20, £1.50; EX 12.20 Trifecta £31.90.
Owner David Little The Links Partnership **Bred** Thomas G Cooke **Trained** Kentisbeare, Devon
FOCUS
The ground was drying all the time and changed to good to firm after this opener. A modest handicap but the right horses came to the fore. They raced stands' side. Straightforward form.

2715 BJ LLEWELLYN SUPPORTS TENOVUS NOVICE AUCTION STKS 1m 14y
2:30 (2:35) (Class 5) 3-Y-O **£3,752** (£1,116; £557; £278) **Stalls** Centre

Form RPR
0-6 **1** **Light Up Our Stars (IRE)**[31] 1755 3-9-5 0.......... PatDobbs 1 80+
(Richard Hughes) *hld up in midfield: shkn up and clsd over 1f out: led early ins fnl f: comf* **10/1**
2 *2 ½* **Zephyrina (IRE)** 3-9-0 0.......... DavidEgan 9 69
(Daniel Kubler) *midfield: rdn over 2f out: r.o u.p fnl f: wnt 2nd last strides* **33/1**
034- **3** *shd* **Itizzit**[208] 8344 3-9-0 77.......... OisinMurphy 5 68
(Hughie Morrison) *led: rdn over 1f out: hdd early ins fnl f: no ex: lost 2nd last strides* **11/10**[1]
3 **4** *1* **Noble Fox**[15] 2210 3-9-5 0.......... HectorCrouch 7 71
(Clive Cox) *chsd ldrs: rdn 3f out: sn sltly outpcd: styd on fnl f* **11/4**[2]
20 **5** *nk* **Doughan Alb**[27] 1856 3-9-5 0.......... RossaRyan 6 70
(Richard Hannon) *trckd ldr: rdn over 2f out: lost 2nd over 1f out: kpt on same pce* **7/2**[3]
0-3 **6** *9* **Flying Moon (GER)**[13] 2284 3-9-5 0.......... RobHornby 10 50
(Jonathan Portman) *trckd ldrs: rdn over 2f out: wknd over 1f out* **14/1**
0 **7** *1* **Bayaanaat**[15] 2210 3-9-5 0.......... LiamKeniry 8 47
(Peter Hiatt) *awkward s: hld up: pushed along over 3f out: sn outpcd and no ch* **66/1**
00- **8** *12* **Don Diego Vega**[223] 7907 3-9-5 0.......... GeorgeDowning 4 20
(Daniel Kubler) *towards rr: rdn 1/2-way: sn lost tch (trainer's rep said gelding was unsuited by the undulations of the track)* **100/1**
1m 33.62s (-2.38) **Going Correction** -0.45s/f (Firm) **8** Ran SP% **117.7**
Speed ratings (Par 99): **93,90,90,89,89 80,79,67**
CSF £240.19 TOTE £9.60: £1.70, £5.10, £1.10; EX 248.90 Trifecta £567.10.
Owner D Boocock **Bred** D Boocock **Trained** Upper Lambourn, Berks
FOCUS
Not a strong novice, with the 77-rated third not running to that mark. They raced down the centre this time. The winner was a big improver.

2716 MAKING WAVES WITH GULF NOVICE AUCTION STKS 5f 16y
3:00 (3:03) (Class 5) 2-Y-O **£3,752** (£1,116; £557; £278) **Stalls** Centre

Form RPR
3 **1** **Flippa The Strippa (IRE)**[14] 2248 2-9-0 0.......... RichardKingscote 5 79
(Charles Hills) *cl up: led wl over 1f out: sn rdn: hld on wl fnl f* **2/1**[1]
2 *½* **Ivatheengine (IRE)** 2-9-5 0.......... OisinMurphy 8 82+
(David Evans) *s.s: bhd: hdwy over 3f out: pushed along 2f out: rdn and chsd wnr ins fnl f: r.o* **12/1**
33 **3** *1 ¾* **Audio**[14] 2228 2-9-5 0.......... TomMarquand 3 76
(Richard Hannon) *led 100yds: chsd ldrs: pushed along 3f out: rdn and hung lft fr over 1f out: nt qckn (jockey said colt hung left-handed)* **5/2**[2]
630 **4** *1 ¼* **Lili Wen Fach (IRE)**[15] 2191 2-9-0 0.......... JFEgan 4 67
(David Evans) *led after 100yds: jnd 3f out: rdn 2f out: sn hdd: lost 2nd and no ex ins fnl f (vet said filly lost left fore shoe)* **8/1**[3]
1 **5** *5* **Gold Venture (IRE)**[12] 2331 2-9-0 0.......... HollieDoyle 7 49
(Archie Watson) *w ldrs: rdn 2f out: wknd fnl f* **5/2**[2]
0 **6** *1 ¼* **Es Que Pearl (IRE)**[39] 1556 2-9-0 0.......... CharlieBennett 6 44
(Rod Millman) *chsd ldrs: stmbld sltly after 150yds and lost grnd: rdn and outpcd after 2f: no ch after* **20/1**
7 *1 ¾* **Charabanc** 2-9-0 0.......... ShaneKelly 1 38
(Richard Hughes) *wnt sltly lft s and s.i.s: sn chsd along: rdn and outpcd 2f out* **33/1**
0 **8** *4* **Twentyonered**[12] 2338 2-9-2 0.......... FinleyMarsh(3) 2 28
(Grace Harris) *in rr: last and struggling over 3f out* **100/1**
58.69s (-0.71) **Going Correction** -0.45s/f (Firm) **8** Ran SP% **118.0**
Speed ratings (Par 93): **87,86,83,81,73 71,68,62**
CSF £27.72 TOTE £2.70: £1.30, £3.00, £1.10; EX 25.60 Trifecta £70.10.
Owner Christopher Wright **Bred** Linacre House Limited **Trained** Lambourn, Berks
FOCUS
They raced stands' side in what looked an ordinary juvenile novice. The front four were clear.

2717 COUNTY MARQUEES H'CAP 6f 16y
3:30 (3:32) (Class 5) (0-70,70) 4-Y-O+
£3,752 (£1,116; £557; £300; £300; £300) **Stalls** Centre

Form RPR
0-13 **1** **Major Valentine**[11] 2358 7-8-11 **67**.......... KateLeahy(7) 1 78
(John O'Shea) *mde virtually all: pushed along 2f out: kpt on wl* **14/1**
000 **2** *2* **The Establishment**[31] 1767 4-9-7 **70**..........(h) OisinMurphy 5 75
(David Evans) *trckd wnr over 2f: remained prom: rdn over 2f out: wnt 2nd again early ins fnl f: kpt on but a being hld* **17/2**
3263 **3** *nk* **Secondo (FR)**[24] 1930 9-8-5 **59**..........(v) PoppyBridgwater(5) 14 63+
(Robert Stephens) *s.i.s: hld up: hdwy 1/2-way: rdn 2f out: nt clr run over 1f out: swtchd lft ins fnl f: r.o* **8/1**
130- **4** *½* **Swanton Blue (IRE)**[208] 8350 6-9-7 **70**.......... CallumShepherd 13 72
(Ed de Giles) *a.p: chsd wnr over 3f out: rdn 2f out: lost 2nd early ins fnl f: no ex* **11/1**
5310 **5** *¾* **Secret Potion**[17] 2122 5-9-1 **64**.......... DavidProbert 11 64
(Ronald Harris) *chsd ldrs: rdn 2f out: unable qck fnl f* **10/1**
0-01 **6** *1 ¼* **Who Told Jo Jo (IRE)**[13] 2287 5-8-9 **58**.......... JasonWatson 9 54
(Joseph Tuite) *midfield: rdn over 2f out: edgd lft over 1f out: unable to chal* **12/1**
5302 **7** *1 ¼* **The Groove**[12] 2339 6-9-0 **70**.......... GinaMangan(7) 10 62+
(David Evans) *hld up: rdn and hdwy over 1f out: no further imp fnl f (trainer said gelding was unsuited by the ground (good to firm) and would prefer an easier surface)* **11/4**[1]
30-0 **8** *¾* **Alfie's Angel (IRE)**[17] 2122 5-8-11 **60**..........(p) DavidEgan 15 49
(Milton Bradley) *midfield: hdwy 1/2-way: rdn 2f out: hung lft and wknd fnl f* **33/1**
34-4 **9** *nse* **Champagne Bob**[16] 2145 7-8-12 **61**.......... HollieDoyle 3 50
(Richard Price) *towards rr: rdn over 3f out: no imp on ldrs* **10/1**
155- **10** *2 ¾* **Mabo**[386] 2033 4-8-11 **60** ow1..........(p[1]) RossaRyan 7 40
(Grace Harris) *bmpd leaving stalls: rdn over 2f out: a towards rr* **33/1**

02-2 **11** 1/2 **Trotter**[29] 1820 5-8-10 **59** LiamKeniry 12 38
(Stuart Kittow) *s.i.s: towards rr: rdn over 2f out: no imp* **15/2[3]**
432- **12** 1 3/4 **Compton Poppy**[196] 8725 5-8-12 **61** GeorgeDowning 6 34
(Tony Carroll) *s.i.s and bmpd leaving stalls: a towards rr* **33/1**
60-0 **13** 1 1/2 **Field Of Vision (IRE)**[12] 2339 6-9-4 **70** (p) FinleyMarsh(3) 2 38
(John Flint) *prom: rdn over 2f out: grad wknd (jockey said gelding was never travelling)* **5/1[2]**
0-00 **14** 3 3/4 **Jacksonfire**[123] 180 7-8-7 **56** oh10 (p) JimmyQuinn 8 12
(Michael Mullineaux) *midfield: rdn and lost pl 1/2-way: no ch after* **66/1**
1m 9.45s (-2.05) **Going Correction** -0.45s/f (Firm) **14** Ran SP% **127.9**
Speed ratings (Par 103): **95,92,91,91,90 88,86,85,85,82 81,79,77,72**
CSF £133.33 CT £1072.64 TOTE £15.00: £3.50, £3.30, £2.90; EX 164.70 Trifecta £1843.40.
Owner Pete Smith **Bred** J R Salter **Trained** Elton, Gloucs
FOCUS
Racing down the centre, little got involved in this moderate sprint, with the winner making all. The winner was surprisingly back to something like his best.

2718 BJ LLEWELLYN SUPPORTS TENOVUSCANCERCARE.ORG.UK H'CAP 2m
4:00 (4:01) (Class 6) (0-65,65) 4-Y-0+
£3,105 (£924; £461; £300; £300; £300) **Stalls** Low

Form RPR
0-05 **1** **Master Grey (IRE)**[12] 2344 4-9-4 **60** OisinMurphy 6 74+
(Rod Millman) *chsd ldrs: clsd over 3f out: rdn to go 2nd 2f out: led over 1f out: styd on strly and drew clr fnl f* **11/4[1]**
041 **2** 6 **Panatos (FR)**[11] 2359 4-9-4 **60** RossaRyan 12 66
(Alexandra Dunn) *chsd along early: sn trcking ldr: led 3f out: sn rdn: hdd over 1f out: outpcd by wnr fnl f* **7/2[2]**
000/ **3** 5 **Daghash**[648] 5590 10-9-5 **60** RichardKingscote 10 58
(Stuart Kittow) *hld up: shkn up and hdwy 3f out: rdn 2f out: styd on to go modest 3rd towards fin: no threat to ldrs* **20/1**
0052 **4** 1 **Agent Gibbs**[8] 2468 7-9-8 **63** (p) ShaneKelly 3 60
(John O'Shea) *led tl rdn and hdd 3f out: lost 2nd 2f out: wknd fnl f: ct for modest 3rd towards fin* **9/1**
4-30 **5** 1 1/2 **Love To Breeze**[10] 2400 4-9-9 **65** (t) RobHornby 4 62
(Jonathan Portman) *trckd ldrs: rdn wl over 3f out: flashed tail and one pce fnl 3f* **6/1[3]**
/ **6** 1 1/2 **Mountain Rock (IRE)**[37] 3131 7-9-10 **65** MartinDwyer 1 58
(Ian Williams) *chsd ldrs: stmbld sltly and lost grnd after 2f: rdn 4f out: sn outpcd by ldrs and no ch* **6/1[3]**
56/6 **7** 5 **Norab (GER)**[11] 2359 8-9-7 **62** (b) StevieDonohoe 9 49
(Bernard Llewellyn) *hld up: rdn 4f out: no imp on ldrs* **25/1**
00-5 **8** 1 1/4 **Mustaaqeem (USA)**[11] 2359 7-9-2 **57** (b) LiamKeniry 5 43
(Bernard Llewellyn) *chsd along early: midfield: lost pl and reminder after 4f: rdn over 5f out: lost tch over 3f out: styd on fnl f* **16/1**
5020 **9** 2 1/2 **Tilsworth Sammy**[12] 2344 4-8-9 **51** DavidProbert 13 36
(J R Jenkins) *hld up towards rr: hdwy 6f out: rdn over 3f out: wknd 2f out* **20/1**
0433 **10** 1 1/4 **Seasearch**[12] 2351 4-9-2 **61** (b[1]) JoshuaBryan(3) 8 44
(Andrew Balding) *hld up: rdn over 5f out: wknd 3f out* **7/1**
/20- **11** 23 **Aristocracy**[19] 6444 8-8-9 **50** (b) LiamJones 11 3
(John O'Shea) *chsd ldrs: rdn 1/2-way: wknd 3f out: t.o* **50/1**
3m 28.9s (-13.20) **Going Correction** -0.45s/f (Firm)
WFA 4 from 7yo+ 1lb **11** Ran SP% **121.2**
Speed ratings (Par 101): **115,112,109,109,108 107,105,104,103,102 91**
CSF £12.00 CT £164.78 TOTE £3.10: £1.20, £1.20, £7.20; EX 14.20 Trifecta £320.30.
Owner David Little The Links Partnership **Bred** Summerhill & J Osborne **Trained** Kentisbeare, Devon
FOCUS
They got racing a long way out in this moderate staying handicap and the market leaders pulled clear. The winner confirmed that he was unlucky last time.

2719 BJ LLEWELLYN SUPPORTS TENOVUS CANCER CARE FILLIES' H'CAP 1m 2f
4:30 (4:34) (Class 5) (0-70,72) 3-Y-O
£3,752 (£1,116; £557; £300; £300; £300) **Stalls** Low

Form RPR
60-1 **1** **Lady Reset**[11] 2355 3-9-10 **72** RossaRyan 6 79+
(David Evans) *hld up early: hdwy to chse ldrs after 2f: rdn 2f out: led appr fnl f: sn edgd rt: r.o* **3/1[1]**
0-55 **2** 2 1/4 **Mystiquestar (IRE)**[18] 2087 3-9-3 **65** JasonWatson 5 68+
(Roger Charlton) *t.k.h: trckd ldrs: rdn to ld jst over 2f out: hdd appr fnl f: kpt on same pce* **3/1[1]**
-032 **3** 2 1/4 **Mongolia**[24] 1935 3-8-7 **55** HollieDoyle 7 53
(Richard Hannon) *prom early: lost pl and in rr after 2f: rdn 4f out: hdwy 3f out: wnt 3rd 1f out: styd on but hld by ldrs* **5/1[2]**
20-5 **4** hd **Ballet Red (FR)**[48] 1351 3-9-2 **67** MitchGodwin(3) 1 65
(Harry Dunlop) *led over 1f: trckd ldr: led again narrowly 3f out to jst over 2f out: sn outpcd by ldrs: disp hld 3rd fnl f* **18/1**
6-35 **5** 1 **Canford Dancer**[17] 2125 3-9-4 **69** (p[1]) FinleyMarsh(3) 8 65
(Richard Hughes) *t.k.h: hld up: hdwy after 4f: rdn and nt clr run on ins over 2f out: styd on same pce after* **7/1[3]**
04-5 **6** 6 **Tartlette**[14] 2251 3-9-0 **62** (b[1]) OisinMurphy 3 46
(Hughie Morrison) *chsd ldrs tl led over 8f out: hdd 3f out: sn pushed along: wknd 2f out* **3/1[1]**
26-5 **7** 5 **Embrace The Moment (IRE)**[44] 1462 3-9-10 **72** TomMarquand 10 46
(Richard Hannon) *in tch towards rr: rdn 1/2-way: wknd 2f out* **11/1**
04-0 **8** 28 **Island Reel (IRE)**[32] 1739 3-9-3 **65** DavidEgan 4
(Heather Main) *chsd ldrs 3f: dropped to rr 6f out: rdn over 4f out: lost tch over 3f out: t.o* **33/1**
2m 4.98s (-7.82) **Going Correction** -0.45s/f (Firm) **8** Ran SP% **120.7**
Speed ratings (Par 96): **113,111,109,109,108 103,99,77**
CSF £12.74 CT £44.58 TOTE £4.30: £1.50, £1.70, £1.30; EX 13.60 Trifecta £46.40.
Owner R S Brookhouse **Bred** R S Brookhouse **Trained** Pandy, Monmouths
FOCUS
Modest enough fillies' handicap form but the right pair came to the fore. The winner is on the upgrade.

2720 BJ LLEWELLYN SUPPORTS TENOVUS H'CAP 1m 4f
5:00 (5:02) (Class 6) (0-65,65) 4-Y-O+
£3,105 (£924; £461; £300; £300; £300) **Stalls** Low

Form RPR
-053 **1** **Ascot Day (FR)**[11] 2353 5-9-3 **61** (p) StevieDonohoe 15 69
(Bernard Llewellyn) *mde virtually all: rdn 2f out: hld on wl u.p* **3/1[2]**
3455 **2** 3/4 **Iconic Girl**[27] 1848 4-9-7 **65** DavidProbert 3 72+
(Andrew Balding) *t.k.h in midfield: rdn and hdwy over 2f out: wnt 2nd 1f out: r.o: nt rch wnr* **2/1[1]**
3 3 3/4 **Born To Frolic (IRE)**[197] 8710 4-8-9 **58** RachealKneller(5) 10 59
(Matthew Salaman) *midfield: hdwy to chse ldrs over 2f out: sn rdn: one pce fnl f* **16/1**
60-0 **4** nk **General Brook (IRE)**[8] 2468 9-9-7 **65** (h) ShaneKelly 8 65
(John O'Shea) *wnt to post early: prom: trckd wnr after 4f: rdn over 2f out: lost 2nd 1f out: kpt on same pce* **14/1**
050 **5** hd **Lafilia (GER)**[15] 2217 4-9-4 **62** HollieDoyle 2 62
(Archie Watson) *trckd wnr 4f: 3rd whn stmbld over 5f out: rdn 4f out: kpt on same pce fnl 2f (jockey said filly changed legs and stumbled in the back straight)* **8/1**
20-4 **6** 1/2 **Earthly (USA)**[12] 2344 5-8-7 **51** (tp) JimmyQuinn 4 52
(Bernard Llewellyn) *midfield: rdn over 3f out: styd on fnl f: nt clr run nr fin (jockey said gelding was denied a clear run in closing stages)* **10/1**
35-0 **7** 3/4 **Bleu Et Noir**[17] 2124 8-9-6 **64** (h) LiamKeniry 5 62
(Tim Vaughan) *towards rr: hdwy 5f out: rdn over 2f out: edgd lft and no imp fnl f* **33/1**
650- **8** 3 3/4 **Lzaaz (IRE)**[225] 7831 4-9-4 **62** CallumShepherd 7 54
(Alan King) *chsd ldrs: rdn and outpcd over 3f out: wknd over 1f out* **7/1[3]**
306- **9** 2 **Powerful Society (IRE)**[20] 6163 4-9-0 **58** RobHornby 14 47
(Mark Gillard) *chsd ldrs: rdn over 3f out: wknd over 1f out (trainer said filly was unsuited by the ground (good to firm) and would prefer an easier surface)* **12/1**
30-0 **10** 1 1/2 **Tilsworth Lukey**[15] 2196 6-8-8 **52** EdwardGreatrex 6 38
(J R Jenkins) *hld up: rdn 3f out: wknd over 1f out* **14/1**
460- **11** 7 **Windsorlot (IRE)**[208] 8338 6-8-8 **57** PoppyBridgwater(5) 1 32
(Tony Carroll) *dwlt sltly: in rr: rdn and sme prog over 3f out: wknd over 2f out* **25/1**
455- **12** 11 **Rahmah (IRE)**[38] 9409 7-9-0 **58** JosephineGordon 13 16
(Geoffrey Deacon) *a wl bhd* **18/1**
00-0 **13** 9 **Kenmare River**[17] 2127 4-8-4 **51** (p[1]) JaneElliott(3) 12
(Tim Vaughan) *awkward s: t.k.h: a wl bhd (jockey said gelding jumped awkwardly from the stalls and ran too free)* **33/1**
2m 33.86s (-6.44) **Going Correction** -0.45s/f (Firm) **13** Ran SP% **132.9**
Speed ratings (Par 101): **103,102,100,99,99 99,98,96,95,94 89,82,76**
CSF £10.45 CT £90.80 TOTE £4.30: £1.60, £1.20, £4.70; EX 13.80 Trifecta £89.60.
Owner Michael Edwards & Partner **Bred** Christophe Jouandou **Trained** Fochriw, Caerphilly
FOCUS
A modest handicap. The winner is rated to the balance of his form.
T/Jkpt: Not won. T/Plt: £35.00 to a £1 stake. Pool: £71,748.15 - 1494.07 winning units T/Qpdt: £10.80 to a 31 stake. Pool: £6,088.88 - 415.31 winning units **Richard Lowther**

2721 - 2727a (Foreign Racing) - See Raceform Interactive

2468 BATH (L-H)
Wednesday, May 15

OFFICIAL GOING: Firm (8.9)
Wind: Light across Weather: Fine

2728 VALUE RATER RACING CLUB IS FREE H'CAP 5f 160y
5:25 (5:26) (Class 6) (0-55,55) 4-Y-O+
£3,105 (£924; £461; £300; £300; £300) **Stalls** Centre

Form RPR
00-0 **1** **Jaganory (IRE)**[16] 2206 7-8-13 **52** (v) PoppyBridgwater(5) 3 61
(Christopher Mason) *sn led: shkn up whn rdr dropped whip over 1f out: styd on wl* **33/1**
0502 **2** 2 3/4 **Dalness Express**[9] 2483 6-8-12 **46** (bt) ShaneKelly 4 46
(John O'Shea) *s.i.s: sn rcvrd to be hld up in tch: rdn to chse wnr over 1f out: styd on same pce ins fnl f* **4/1[1]**
360- **3** hd **Amberine**[257] 6766 5-9-0 **48** FrannyNorton 6 47
(Malcolm Saunders) *chsd ldrs: rdn over 1f out: styd on same pce ins fnl f* **9/2[2]**
-000 **4** shd **Waneen (IRE)**[34] 1716 6-9-2 **50** (b[1]) LiamKeniry 10 50
(John Butler) *hld up: hdwy and nt clr run over 1f out: r.o: nt rch ldrs* **25/1**
0004 **5** hd **Toolatetodelegate**[9] 2503 5-8-10 **47** (tp) FinleyMarsh(3) 14 45+
(Brian Barr) *stmbld s: hld up: hdwy over 1f out: r.o: nrst fin (jockey said mare stumbled leaving the stalls)* **8/1[3]**
30-5 **6** 1 3/4 **Lily Of Year (FR)**[30] 1820 4-9-0 **55** ScottMcCullagh(7) 7 48
(Denis Coakley) *s.i.s: hld up: rdn and hdwy over 1f out: nt rch ldrs* **4/1[1]**
0536 **7** 1/2 **Kellington Kitty (USA)**[20] 2066 4-8-12 **46** HectorCrouch 12 37
(Mike Murphy) *broke wl: sn lost pl: styd on ins fnl f: nt trble ldrs* **11/1**
00-5 **8** 1 3/4 **Aquadabra (IRE)**[9] 2473 4-9-3 **51** (h[1]) NicolaCurrie 1 36
(Christopher Mason) *awkward s: jnd wnr 5f out tl pushed along 1/2-way: wknd ins fnl f (jockey said filly reared and jumped awkwardly from the stalls)* **14/1**
-040 **9** nse **Sugar Plum Fairy**[100] 596 4-8-13 **47** TomMarquand 5 32
(Tony Carroll) *s.i.s: swtchd rt 1/2-way: rdn over 1f out: nvr on terms (jockey said filly jumped awkwardly from the stalls)* **8/1[3]**
4305 **10** 3 1/4 **Captain Ryan**[23] 1987 8-9-6 **54** (p) TrevorWhelan 9 28
(Geoffrey Deacon) *chsd ldrs: wnt 2nd 1/2-way tl rdn over 1f out: sn wknd* **20/1**
5363 **11** 4 1/2 **Storm Lightning**[67] 1093 10-8-12 **46** oh1 KieranO'Neill 2 5
(Mark Brisbourne) *chsd ldrs: sn pushed along: wknd wl over 1f out* **20/1**
1200 **12** 11 **New Rich**[61] 1210 9-9-0 **48** (b) EdwardGreatrex 15
(Eve Johnson Houghton) *s.i.s: outpcd (jockey said gelding was slowly away and never travelling)* **28/1**
1m 9.48s (-1.62) **Going Correction** -0.20s/f (Firm) **12** Ran SP% **115.2**
Speed ratings (Par 101): **102,98,98,97,97 95,94,92,92,87 81,67**
CSF £148.50 CT £727.66 TOTE £37.50: £9.30, £1.60, £1.80; EX 177.30 Trifecta £1415.00.
Owner Brian Hicks **Bred** Canice Farrell Jnr **Trained** Caewent, Monmouthshire
FOCUS
The ground was riding as per the official description. A surprise winner of this very modest sprint handicap.

2729 "AROUND THE PADDOCK" AT VALUERATER.CO.UK FILLIES' H'CAP 5f 160y
5:55 (6:00) (Class 5) (0-70,69) 4-Y-O+
£3,752 (£1,116; £557; £300; £300; £300) **Stalls** Centre

Form RPR
660- **1** **Roys Dream**[207] 8418 5-9-7 **69** (p) FrannyNorton 4 75
(Paul Collins) *mde virtually all: rdn over 1f out: edgd rt wl ins fnl f: styd on* **5/1[2]**

00-5 2 ½ **Ghepardo**[22] 2010 4-9-1 **63**..........(t) TomMarquand 9 67
(Patrick Chamings) *trckd ldrs: rdn and swtchd rt over 1f out: r.o* **14/1**

-652 3 1½ **Powerful Dream (IRE)**[9] 2473 6-9-3 **65**..........(p) DavidProbert 6 64+
(Ronald Harris) *hmpd sn after s: hld up: hdwy 2f out: edgd lft and bmpd over 1f out: styd on same pce ins fnl f (jockey said mare suffered interference shortly after the start)* **9/4**[1]

426- 4 hd **Kath's Lustre**[162] 9393 4-9-6 **68**.......... ShaneKelly 10 67
(Richard Hughes) *chsd ldr: rdn and ev ch over 1f out: styd on same pce ins fnl f* **12/1**

656- 5 1¾ **Edged Out**[254] 6865 9-8-10 **61**.......... MitchGodwin(3) 2 54
(Christopher Mason) *chsd ldrs: nt clr run over 1f out: no ex ins fnl f* **33/1**

0-06 6 nk **Tundra**[19] 2081 5-9-5 **67**..........(b¹) KieranO'Neill 5 59
(Anthony Carson) *hld up: nt clr run 5f out: swtchd rt and hdwy 2f out: sn rdn: edgd lft ins fnl f: nt trble ldrs* **11/2**[3]

-004 7 1¼ **Tally's Song**[9] 2473 6-8-2 **50** oh5..........(p) JimmyQuinn 1 38
(Grace Harris) *s.i.s: sn pushed along in rr: no ch whn hmpd over 1f out* **66/1**

260- 8 21 **Babyfact**[197] 8724 8-8-11 **59**.......... MartinDwyer 3
(Malcolm Saunders) *trckd ldrs: rdn 1/2-way: wknd wl over 1f out: eased* **20/1**

0635 U **Mooroverthebridge**[9] 2483 5-8-10 **58**.......... LiamJones 7
(Grace Harris) *sn pushed along to chse ldrs: rdn and ev ch whn hmpd: clipped heels and uns rdr over 1f out* **6/1**

1m 9.36s (-1.74) **Going Correction** -0.20s/f (Firm) **9** Ran SP% **100.7**
Speed ratings (Par 100): **103,102,100,100,97 97,95,67,**
CSF £53.10 CT £137.37 TOTE £5.10: £1.90, £3.90, £1.10; EX 48.20 Trifecta £202.70.
Owner Mrs A Pickering **Bred** Dr A Gillespie **Trained** Saltburn, Cleveland
■ Exceedingly Diva was withdrawn. Price at time of withdrawal 8/1. Rule 4 applies to all bets - deduction 10p in the £.

FOCUS
Another quick time, inside the standard and 0.12sec faster than the preceding Class 6 handicap. The form's rated a bit cautiously.

2730 LET'S PLAY "FOUR FROM THE TOP" H'CAP 5f 10y
6:25 (6:28) (Class 5) (0-75,77) 3-Y-O
£3,752 (£1,116; £557; £300; £300; £300) **Stalls** Centre

Form RPR

23-3 1 **Shining**[43] 1492 3-9-7 **75**.......... TomMarquand 7 79
(Jim Boyle) *mde all: edgd lft over 4f out: rdn 1/2-way: edgd rt ins fnl f: styd on u.p* **12/1**

6136 2 1 **Major Blue**[18] 2098 3-9-3 **71**.......... RyanTate 1 72
(James Eustace) *chsd ldrs: nt clr run fr over 1f out: unbalanced wl ins fnl f: sn swtchd lft: r.o* **11/2**[3]

4-64 3 1¾ **Enchanted Linda**[18] 2121 3-9-9 **77**.......... PatDobbs 8 71
(Richard Hannon) *chsd ldrs: rdn and ev ch over 1f out: styd on same pce ins fnl f* **9/2**[2]

3433 4 2¼ **Key To Power**[15] 2255 3-9-7 **75**.......... FrannyNorton 6 63+
(Mark Johnston) *prom: hmpd and lost pl over 4f out: hdwy on outer 1/2-way: ev ch over 1f out: no ex ins fnl f: eased nr fin (jockey said filly lost its action on the run to the line)* **11/4**[1]

60-3 5 nse **Mykindofsunshine (IRE)**[22] 2024 3-9-6 **74**.......... HectorCrouch 2 60
(Clive Cox) *chsd ldrs: rdn 1/2-way: styd on same pce fnl f* **11/2**[3]

0-00 6 ½ **Knockabout Queen**[18] 2114 3-8-7 **61** oh1.......... CharlieBennett 3 45
(Dai Burchell) *s.s: outpcd: r.o ins fnl f: nvr nrr (jockey said filly was slowly away)* **40/1**

6-12 7 nse **Swiss Pride (IRE)**[43] 1492 3-9-9 **77**..........(b) ShaneKelly 5 61+
(Richard Hughes) *prom: hmpd and lost pl over 4f out: hdwy u.p on outer over 1f out: no ex ins fnl f (jockey said gelding suffered interference)* **9/2**[2]

40-3 8 1¼ **Abanica**[16] 2212 3-8-13 **67**..........(p) RobertHavlin 4 46
(Amanda Perrett) *prom: rdn over 1f out: wknd fnl f* **10/1**

1m 0.96s (-1.04) **Going Correction** -0.20s/f (Firm) **8** Ran SP% **113.0**
Speed ratings (Par 99): **100,98,95,92,91 91,91,89**
CSF £74.29 CT £346.79 TOTE £12.00: £2.60, £2.50, £1.60; EX 76.70 Trifecta £435.30.
Owner The Clean Sweep Partnership **Bred** Paddock Space **Trained** Epsom, Surrey

FOCUS
Just a modest event, and quite a messy race. There are a few doubts over the form.

2731 BRAKES GROUP/EBF NOVICE STKS 1m 3f 137y
6:55 (7:02) (Class 4) 3-Y-O+ **£5,530** (£1,645; £822; £411) **Stalls** Low

Form RPR

1-4 1 **Great Bear**[18] 2099 3-9-2 .... AdamMcNamara 11 84+
(Roger Charlton) *a.p: shkn up to ld over 2f out: rdn over 1f out: clr fnl f: easily* **10/11**[1]

0 2 3¾ **Moghram (IRE)**[17] 2142 3-8-9 .... DaneO'Neill 12 69
(Marcus Tregoning) *chsd ldrs: rdn over 2f out: styd on to go 2nd wl ins fnl f: no ch w wnr* **16/1**

0 3 ¾ **Desert Mission (IRE)**[18] 2128 3-8-4 .... KieranO'Neill 9 63
(Simon Crisford) *led: hdd 7f out: chsd ldr: rdn and ev ch over 2f out: styd on same pce fr over 1f out* **33/1**

5 4 2½ **Johnny Kidd**[17] 2142 3-8-9 .... DavidProbert 3 63
(Andrew Balding) *hld up in tch: rdn: hung lft and outpcd over 2f out: styd on ins fnl f* **7/2**[2]

-04 5 1½ **Test Valley (IRE)**[14] 2280 4-9-9 .... KatherineBegley(5) 6 63
(Tracey Barfoot-Saunt) *s.s: hld up: rdn over 2f out: styd on u.p fr over 1f out: nt trble ldrs* **50/1**

6 shd **Ekayburg (FR)**[65] 5-9-11 .... FinleyMarsh(3) 1 63
(David Pipe) *hld up: nt clr run over 4f out: hdwy and n.m.r over 2f out: swtchd rt over 1f out: nt rch ldrs* **12/1**

0 7 1 **Lucy Lou (IRE)**[33] 1738 3-8-4 .... MartinDwyer 2 54
(Charles Hills) *s.i.s: sn chsng ldrs: led 7f out: rdn and hdd over 2f out: hung lft fr over 1f out: wknd ins fnl f (jockey said filly hung badly left-handed)* **20/1**

54 8 2½ **Stone Cougar (USA)**[14] 2289 3-8-4 .... FrannyNorton 5 50
(Mark Johnston) *hld up: shkn up over 2f out: nvr on terms* **8/1**[3]

6 9 7 **Constraint**[14] 2301 3-8-4 .... JimmyQuinn 10 38
(Andrew Balding) *s.i.s: rn green in rr: nvr on terms* **50/1**

-31 10 1¾ **Pacificadora (USA)**[111] 380 3-8-11 .... TomMarquand 8 43
(Simon Dow) *hld up in tch: rdn over 2f out: wknd over 1f out* **9/1**

0 11 ½ **Dancing Lilly**[12] 2354 4-9-4 .... RachealKneller(5) 4 37
(Matthew Salaman) *s.i.s: hld up: n.d (jockey said filly hung right-handed)* **100/1**

00- 12 37 **Longville Lilly**[179] 9134 4-9-9 .... TrevorWhelan 7
(Trevor Wall) *chsd ldrs: rdn over 3f out: sn edgd lft: wknd over 2f out (jockey said filly hung left-handed 2 furlongs out)* **150/1**

2m 29.16s (-1.64) **Going Correction** -0.20s/f (Firm)
WFA 3 from 4yo+ 19lb **12** Ran SP% **122.6**
Speed ratings (Par 105): **97,94,94,92,91 91,90,88,84,83 82,58**
CSF £19.43 TOTE £2.00: £1.10, £4.60, £7.60; EX 17.30 Trifecta £230.60.
Owner Exors Of The Late Lady Rothschild **Bred** Kincorth Investments Inc **Trained** Beckhampton, Wilts

FOCUS
A high draw was a plus in what was no more than a fair novice event. There wasn't much depth to this.

2732 READ "GROUP ONE GRIFF" AT VALUERATER.CO.UK H'CAP 1m 2f 37y
7:25 (7:28) (Class 5) (0-70,75) 4-Y-O+
£3,752 (£1,116; £557; £300; £300; £300) **Stalls** Low

Form RPR

-004 1 **Uther Pendragon (IRE)**[8] 2516 4-9-9 **72**..........(p) LiamKeniry 4 80
(J S Moore) *broke wl: sn stdd and lost pl: hdwy over 2f out: rdn to chse ldr over 1f out: styd on u.p to ld wl ins fnl f* **12/1**

6-10 2 ½ **Amaretto**[30] 1826 4-8-7 **56** oh1..........(v) CharlieBennett 1 63
(Jim Boyle) *sn led: racd keenly: rdn over 2f out: hdd wl ins fnl f* **8/1**

350- 3 1½ **Il Sicario (IRE)**[171] 9033 5-8-12 **66**.......... RyanWhile(5) 6 70
(Bill Turner) *chsd ldrs: rdn over 1f out: styd on* **25/1**

00-2 4 ½ **Champs De Reves**[9] 2471 4-9-6 **69**.......... DavidProbert 9 72
(Michael Blake) *led early: chsd ldrs: rdn over 2f out: styd on same pce ins fnl f* **10/3**[2]

3402 5 ½ **Francophilia**[14] 2279 4-9-4 **67**.......... FrannyNorton 3 69
(Mark Johnston) *s.i.s: pushed along early in rr: hld up: shkn up over 2f out: nt clr run and swtchd rt over 1f out: styd on: nt pce to chal* **7/4**[1]

603 6 1½ **Zephyros (GER)**[9] 2471 8-8-7 **61**.......... PoppyBridgwater(5) 7 60
(David Bridgwater) *s.i.s: hld up: hdwy u.p on outer 2f out: no ex ins fnl f* **14/1**

3-21 7 1 **Simbirsk**[9] 2471 4-9-12 **75** 5ex.......... ShaneKelly 8 72
(John O'Shea) *led early: chsd ldrs: rdn over 2f out: wknd wl ins fnl f* **7/2**[3]

050- 8 9 **Highway Bess**[252] 6945 4-8-7 **56**.......... KieranO'Neill 5 35
(Patrick Chamings) *s.i.s: hdwy 8f out: pushed along on outer over 4f out: wknd over 1f out (jockey said filly hung right-handed)* **66/1**

2m 7.9s (-3.20) **Going Correction** -0.20s/f (Firm) **8** Ran SP% **112.5**
Speed ratings (Par 103): **104,103,102,102,101 100,99,92**
CSF £99.28 CT £2335.40 TOTE £13.40: £2.10, £2.20, £5.50; EX 118.70 Trifecta £1314.10.
Owner Mrs Wendy Jarrett & J S Moore **Bred** Jill Finegan & Noel Cogan **Trained** Upper Lambourn, Berks

FOCUS
A modest handicap, run at a solid initial pace. The winner's performance is hard to assess.

2733 FREE TIPS FROM "SANDSTORM" AT VALUERATER.CO.UK H'CAP 1m 5f 11y
7:55 (7:55) (Class 6) (0-65,69) 4-Y-O+
£3,024 (£905; £452; £300; £300; £300) **Stalls** High

Form RPR

6222 1 **Top Rock Talula (IRE)**[41] 1548 4-9-1 **58**.......... EdwardGreatrex 11 65
(Warren Greatrex) *chsd ldr tl over 9f out: wnt 2nd again 7f out: shkn up to ld over 2f out: rdn over 1f out: edgd lft ins fnl f: styd on wl* **3/1**[2]

0031 2 1¾ **Gendarme (IRE)**[9] 2468 4-9-12 **69** 5ex..........(b) FrannyNorton 7 73
(Alexandra Dunn) *a.p: rdn and hung lft over 1f out: chsd wnr ins fnl f: styd on* **11/4**[1]

3-40 3 ¾ **Filament Of Gold (USA)**[18] 2127 8-8-7 **50**..........(b) JFEgan 13 53
(Roy Brotherton) *hld up: hdwy 2f out: nt clr run over 1f out: r.o to go 3rd wl ins fnl f: nvr able to chal* **14/1**

1-00 4 ¾ **Affair**[112] 363 5-8-11 **54**.......... CharlieBennett 10 56
(Hughie Morrison) *hld up in tch: rdn over 2f out: styd on same pce ins fnl f* **8/1**

2130 5 ¾ **Double Legend (IRE)**[11] 2400 4-9-6 **63**..........(b) RobertHavlin 2 64
(Amanda Perrett) *hld up in tch: shkn up and nt clr run over 1f out: styd on same pce ins fnl f* **13/2**[3]

030- 6 1¼ **Just Right**[280] 5851 4-8-6 **49**.......... LiamJones 6 48
(John Flint) *led: rdn and hdd over 2f out: wknd wl ins fnl f* **25/1**

00/6 7 1¼ **Cougar Kid (IRE)**[9] 2468 8-8-2 **45**..........(p) KieranO'Neill 1 42
(John O'Shea) *prom: chsd ldr over 9f out tl 7f out: shkn up over 4f out: rdn and nt clr run over 1f out: no ex fnl f* **8/1**

-044 8 nse **Millie May**[9] 2468 5-8-0 **48** ow1.......... ThoreHammerHansen(5) 3 45
(Jimmy Fox) *hld up: hdwy u.p on outer 2f out: no ex fnl f (jockey said mare was never travelling)* **13/2**[3]

00-5 9 2¼ **Buxlow Belle (FR)**[14] 2283 4-8-2 **45**..........(h) JimmyQuinn 12 39
(David Menuisier) *s.s: hld up: rdn over 2f out: n.d* **14/1**

500- 10 47 **De Beau Tant**[179] 9134 4-8-3 **46** ow1..........(p) MartinDwyer 4
(John Flint) *s.i.s: sn pushed along in rr: rdn over 3f out: sn wknd* **33/1**

2m 51.53s (-1.27) **Going Correction** -0.20s/f (Firm) **10** Ran SP% **120.7**
Speed ratings (Par 101): **95,93,93,93,92 91,91,90,89,60**
CSF £12.20 CT £101.98 TOTE £3.60: £1.50, £1.90, £2.60; EX 12.30 Trifecta £78.50.
Owner Fitorfat Racing **Bred** Maurice Regan **Trained** Upper Lambourn, Berks
■ Stewards' Enquiry : Liam Jones caution: careless riding

FOCUS
Low-grade form.

2734 BRAKES GROUP H'CAP 1m
8:25 (8:29) (Class 6) (0-60,60) 3-Y-O
£3,105 (£924; £461; £300; £300; £300) **Stalls** Low

Form RPR

00-4 1 **Poetic Motion**[33] 1731 3-8-9 **48**.......... CharlieBennett 10 53
(Jim Boyle) *led: hdd over 5f out: chsd ldr tl led again over 2f out: rdn over 1f out: jst hld on* **14/1**

-543 2 hd **Lippy Lady (IRE)**[22] 2007 3-9-0 **53**..........(h) JFEgan 8 58
(Paul George) *s.s: hld up: hdwy on outer over 2f out: rdn to chse wnr ins fnl f: r.o wl (jockey said filly was slowly away)* **9/2**[2]

2216 3 ½ **Greyzee (IRE)**[44] 1481 3-9-6 **59**.......... RobHornby 2 62
(Rod Millman) *hld up: hdwy on outer over 2f out: rdn over 1f out: edgd lft ins fnl f: r.o wl (jockey said gelding was never travelling)* **9/2**[2]

5021 4 1½ **Act Of Magic (IRE)**[15] 2262 3-9-1 **54**.......... KieranO'Neill 14 54
(Mohamed Moubarak) *hld up: shkn up over 2f out: hdwy and nt clr run over 1f out: r.o ins fnl f: nt rch ldrs (jockey said gelding was denied a clear run)* **7/2**[1]

4643 **5** *shd* **Truckingby**[13] 2325 3-9-5 **58** .... FrannyNorton 13 58
(Mark Johnston) *prom: sn pushed along: lost pl over 6f out: hdwy over 3f out: rdn to chse wnr over 1f out: sn edgd rt: styd on same pce ins fnl f (jockey said gelding had no more to give)* **11/2**[3]

40-0 **6** *4* **Smith (IRE)**[37] 1652 3-9-7 **60** .... (p[1]) CharlesBishop 7 51
(Eve Johnson Houghton) *hld up: hdwy over 2f out: rdn over 1f out: no ex ins fnl f* **10/1**

40-0 **7** *2 1/2* **Legend Island (FR)**[15] 2238 3-9-7 **60** .... LiamKeniry 12 45
(Ed Walker) *prom: pushed along and awkward bnd over 4f out: rdn over 2f out: wknd over 1f out* **14/1**

00-0 **8** *1 1/4* **Sari Mareis**[14] 2280 3-8-13 **52** .... ShaneKelly 16 34
(Denis Coakley) *s.s: racd keenly: hdwy over 5f out: rdn over 2f out: wknd over 1f out (jockey said filly was slowly away)* **40/1**

000- **9** *hd* **Harbour Times (IRE)**[240] 7366 3-8-12 **51** .... DavidProbert 9 32
(Patrick Chamings) *hld up: swtchd rt over 2f out: n.d* **25/1**

0606 **10** *1 1/4* **Sacred Warner (IRE)**[22] 2007 3-8-13 **52** .... (p[1]) HectorCrouch 6 31
(Clive Cox) *chsd ldrs: rdn over 3f out: wknd fnl f* **9/1**

-000 **11** *2 1/2* **Magnetic (IRE)**[12] 2357 3-8-8 **47** .... JohnFahy 5 20
(J S Moore) *s.i.s: hld up: nvr on terms* **100/1**

-000 **12** *3* **Quarto Cavallo**[16] 2190 3-8-4 **48** .... ThoreHammerHansen(5) 15 14
(Adam West) *prom: rdn over 2f out: wknd over 1f out* **20/1**

60-0 **13** *13* **Power Seeker (IRE)**[20] 2066 3-8-7 **46** .... (b[1]) EdwardGreatrex 4
(Rod Millman) *w ldr tl led over 5f out: rdn and hdd over 2f out: wknd fnl f* **40/1**

1m 39.71s (-1.99) **Going Correction** -0.20s/f (Firm) **13** Ran SP% **120.9**
Speed ratings (Par 97): **101,100,100,98,98 94,92,90,90,89 87,84,71**
CSF £73.72 CT £350.91 TOTE £13.90: £4.00, £2.10, £1.40; EX 80.60 Trifecta £599.40.
Owner The 'In Recovery' Partnership **Bred** The 'In Recovery' Partnership **Trained** Epsom, Surrey

FOCUS
This very modest event was run at a frenetic early gallop. The winner was always prominent but the next three came from off the pace.
T/Plt: £271.90 to a £1 stake. Pool: £57,980.12 - 155.62 winning units. T/Qpdt: £110.40 to a £1 stake. Pool: £7,806.65 - 52.31 winning units. **Colin Roberts**

2256 YARMOUTH (L-H)
Wednesday, May 15

OFFICIAL GOING: Good (ovr 6.7, str 6.8, bk str 6.7)
Wind: light, across Weather: fine and sunny

2735 AKS SKIPS OF NORWICH H'CAP — 6f 3y
2:00 (2:00) (Class 6) (0-60,60) 3-Y-O
£3,105 (£924; £461; £300; £300; £300) **Stalls** Centre

Form — RPR

3-02 **1** **Lincoln Red**[23] 1982 3-8-9 **48** .... JackMitchell 14 55+
(Olly Williams) *broke wl: sn stdd and chsd ldrs: effrt and rdn to ld 2f out: styd on wl ins fnl f: rdn out* **3/1**[1]

0402 **2** *1 1/2* **Valley Belle (IRE)**[15] 2238 3-9-3 **56** .... JosephineGordon 6 58
(Phil McEntee) *taken down early: chsd ldr early: sn settled in tch in midfield: effrt 2f out: chsd ldrs and swtchd lft over 1f out: chsd wnr ins fnl f: kpt on but nvr getting on terms* **9/1**

44-4 **3** *1/2* **Liam's Lass (IRE)**[22] 2016 3-9-2 **55** .... CallumShepherd 8 55
(Pam Sly) *midfield: effrt ent fnl 2f: hdwy u.p over 1f out: wnt 3rd ins fnl f: styd on but nvr getting on terms w wnr* **7/2**[2]

3-00 **4** *1/2* **Budaiya Fort (IRE)**[46] 1430 3-8-9 **55** .... (p[1]) GraceMcEntee(7) 12 54
(Phil McEntee) *awkward leaving stalls: sn rcvrd and chsd ldr tl jst over 2f out: rdn and chsd wnr over 1f out: kpt on same pce and lost 2 pls ins fnl f* **25/1**

0 **5** *hd* **Sweet Forgetme Not (IRE)**[20] 2063 3-8-9 **48** .... HayleyTurner 3 46
(Samuel Farrell, Ire) *hld up towards rr: effrt over 2f out: hdwy and edging rt over 1f out: styd on steadily ins fnl f: nvr threatened ldrs* **8/1**

4200 **6** *1 1/2* **Sussudio**[16] 2199 3-9-4 **60** .... (b[1]) GeorgeBuckell(3) 5 53
(Richard Spencer) *sn led: hdd 2f out: unable qck u.p over 1f out: wknd ins fnl f* **9/1**

50-0 **7** *3 1/2* **Pageant Master (IRE)**[44] 1486 3-9-5 **58** .... (t[1]) DanielMuscutt 10 41
(Mark H Tompkins) *dwlt: towards rr: effrt jst over 2f out: no imp u.p 1f out: wknd ins fnl f* **16/1**

00-5 **8** *3/4* **Dance To Freedom**[132] 32 3-8-11 **57** .... (t) MarcoGhiani(7) 1 38
(Stuart Williams) *stdd s: hld up in rr: effrt ent fnl 2f: no real imp: nvr involved* **8/1**

00-0 **9** *nk* **Yes Can Do (USA)**[12] 2356 3-9-4 **57** .... GeorgeWood 4 37
(Ed Dunlop) *midfield: effrt ent fnl 2f: no hdwy u.p and btn over 1f out: wknd ins fnl f* **33/1**

34-0 **10** *7* **Such Promise**[42] 1516 3-9-7 **60** .... RossaRyan 16 19+
(Mike Murphy) *racd against stands' rail: chsd ldrs: rdn over 2f out: lost pl u.p over 1f out: wknd fnl f* **5/1**[3]

5506 **11** *13* **Spirit Of Lucerne (IRE)**[14] 2281 3-9-3 **56** ow1 .... (be) LukeMorris 13 +
(Phil McEntee) *racd against stands' rail: a bhd* **50/1**

1m 11.6s (-1.00) **Going Correction** -0.175s/f (Firm) **11** Ran SP% **120.7**
Speed ratings (Par 97): **99,97,96,95,95 93,88,87,87,78 60**
CSF £31.31 CT £103.14 TOTE £4.30: £2.30, £2.00, £1.60; EX 30.00 Trifecta £86.90.
Owner Top Of The Wolds Racing **Bred** Genesis Green Stud Ltd **Trained** Market Rasen, Lincs

FOCUS
Clerk of the course Richard Aldous reported prior to racing "We've had 31mm of rain since the last meeting which put us soft but it's now dried back to good. There is a good covering and it may be a touch slower on the stands rail." Five non-runners in the opener but it still remained a competitive moderate event.

2736 HAVEN CAISTER HOLIDAY PARK NOVICE STKS — 6f 3y
2:35 (2:36) (Class 5) 3-Y-O+ **£3,752** (£1,116; £557; £278) **Stalls** Centre

Form — RPR

1 **1** **Archer's Dream (IRE)**[19] 2077 3-9-4 0 .... GeorgeWood 2 99+
(James Fanshawe) *travelled strly thrght: chsd ldrs tl clsd to ld on bridle over 1f out: sn shkn up and qcknd clr 1f out: v easily* **4/5**[1]

2 *4 1/2* **Philipine Cobra**[16] 2219 3-8-11 0 .... JosephineGordon 3 77
(Phil McEntee) *racd keenly: led tl rdn and hdd over 1f out: sn brushed aside by wnr: clr 2nd and kpt on same pce ins fnl f* **20/1**

-222 **3** *2 3/4* **You Little Ripper (IRE)**[15] 2243 3-9-2 79 .... LukeMorris 1 73
(Peter Chapple-Hyam) *wl in tch in midfield: effrt over 2f out: outpcd and wl hld over 1f out: no ch w wnr but plugged on to go 3rd towards fin* **3/1**[2]

0 **4** *1* **Aperitif**[33] 1740 3-8-11 0 .... HayleyTurner 9 65
(Michael Bell) *stdd s: off the pce in last quartet: pushed along over 3f out: hdwy whn rn green and shifted lft 2f out: hung rt over 1f out: no ch w wnr but plugged on to go 4th on post* **9/1**[3]

-0 **5** *nse* **Lost In Alaska (USA)**[27] 1886 3-9-2 0 .... DanielMuscutt 4 70
(Jeremy Noseda) *chsd ldrs: rdn ent fnl 2f: 3rd and outpcd over 1f out: wknd and lost 2 pls towards fin* **16/1**

4 **6** *4 1/2* **Raspberry**[13] 2332 3-8-11 0 .... JackMitchell 8 50
(Olly Williams) *racd in last quartet: effrt and sme prog whn pushed lft 2f out: no prog over 1f out: wknd ins fnl f (jockey said filly ran green)* **33/1**

242- **7** *5* **Tilghman (IRE)**[393] 1871 4-9-12 80 .... CallumShepherd 6 42
(William Jarvis) *chsd ldrs: lost pl u.p and edgd lft over 1f out: wknd and eased wl ins fnl f* **10/1**

6 **8** *5* **Trust Me (IRE)**[16] 2210 3-9-2 0 .... RobertWinston 5 23
(Dean Ivory) *dwlt: a in rr: wl bhd and eased ins fnl f* **16/1**

00 **9** *21* **Piccupaprosecco**[4] 2624 3-8-11 0 .... PaddyMathers 7
(Derek Shaw) *sn outpcd in rr: lost tch 1/2-way: t.o and eased ins fnl f* **100/1**

1m 10.34s (-2.26) **Going Correction** -0.175s/f (Firm)
WFA 3 from 4yo 10lb **9** Ran SP% **120.1**
Speed ratings (Par 103): **108,102,98,97,96 90,84,77,49**
CSF £24.58 TOTE £1.70: £1.10, £4.50, £1.20; EX 15.90 Trifecta £40.50.
Owner Fred Archer Racing - Wheel Of Fortune **Bred** Ms Anne Coughlan **Trained** Newmarket, Suffolk

FOCUS
This looked nothing more than a fair novice event for sprinters before the offer, but the winner proved to be different class to her rivals and might end up being up to pattern company. It's hard to pin down the ratings with her form rivals not at their best.

2737 GOLD & SILVER EXCHANGE FILLIES' H'CAP — 1m 2f 23y
3:10 (3:11) (Class 5) (0-70,72) 4-Y-O+
£3,752 (£1,116; £557; £300; £300; £300) **Stalls** Low

Form — RPR

1502 **1** **Voi**[11] 2399 5-9-2 **72** .... (t) WilliamCarver(7) 9 79
(Conrad Allen) *stdd s: hld up in last pair: nt clr run 3f out: clsd to chse ldrs and swtchd rt 2f out: chalng and hung lft 1f out: rdn to ld ins fnl f: kpt on and a doing enough fnl 100yds* **4/1**[3]

1-33 **2** *nk* **Birch Grove (IRE)**[16] 2214 4-9-4 **72** .... DylanHogan(5) 4 78
(David Simcock) *hld up in tch: clsd to press ldr and travelling wl ent fnl 2f: rdn to ld 2f out: sn hrd pressed: drvn and hdd 1f out: kpt on u.p but a jst hld fnl 100yds (two-day ban: used whip above the permitted level (May 29-30))* **9/4**[1]

0-33 **3** *3 1/4* **Velvet Vision**[20] 2056 4-9-7 **70** .... DanielMuscutt 8 70
(Mark H Tompkins) *sn led: rdn over 2f out: hdd 2f out: 3rd and no ex 1f out: outpcd fnl 100yds* **13/2**

200- **4** *2 1/4* **Kismat**[233] 7611 4-8-9 **65** .... (w) TobyEley(7) 5 60
(Alan King) *in tch in midfield: effrt over 2f out: unable qck and outpcd over 1f out: wl hld: hung lft and plugged on same pce ins fnl f (jockey said filly hung left-handed in the final furlong)* **12/1**

4000 **5** *3/4* **Lulu Star (IRE)**[41] 1546 4-7-9 **51** .... SophieRalston(7) 1 45
(Julia Feilden) *chsd ldrs: effrt over 2f out: sn struggling and outpcd over 1f out: wl hld fnl f* **25/1**

335- **6** *hd* **Lilypad (IRE)**[212] 8260 4-9-1 **64** .... GeorgeWood 10 58
(James Fanshawe) *wnt rt leaving stalls: in tch in midfield on outer: effrt over 2f out: no imp u.p over 1f out: wl hld and plugged on same pce ins fnl f* **7/2**[2]

50 **7** *6* **Warning Light**[16] 2215 4-8-4 **53** .... JosephineGordon 6 35
(Shaun Keightley) *chsd ldrs tl lost pl and pushed along 5f out: unable qck 2f out and sn outpcd: wknd fnl f* **25/1**

4343 **8** *1 3/4* **Going Native**[13] 2345 4-8-1 **53** .... JaneElliott(3) 7 31
(Olly Williams) *hld up in rr: effrt 4f out: no imp u.p 2f out: wknd fnl f* **10/1**

050- **9** *11* **Roser Moter (IRE)**[72] 5027 4-8-7 **56** .... LukeMorris 3 12
(Michael Appleby) *mostly chsd ldr tl over 2f out: sn u.p and lost pl: bhd and eased ins fnl f* **20/1**

2m 6.39s (-2.41) **Going Correction** -0.175s/f (Firm) **9** Ran SP% **115.6**
Speed ratings (Par 100): **102,101,99,97,96 96,91,90,81**
CSF £13.05 CT £54.72 TOTE £4.40: £1.80, £1.30, £2.10; EX 14.10 Trifecta £52.00.
Owner B Homewood & Partners **Bred** Al Asayl Bloodstock Ltd **Trained** Newmarket, Suffolk

FOCUS
The first race on the round track on the card, and two came slightly away from the remainder. Modest form, with doubts over plenty.

2738 INJURED JOCKEY'S FUND H'CAP — 1m 2f 23y
3:45 (3:45) (Class 6) (0-60,60) 4-Y-O+
£3,105 (£924; £461; £300; £300; £300) **Stalls** Low

Form — RPR

5201 **1** **Rail Dancer**[5] 2595 7-9-0 **60** 4ex .... (v) GavinAshton(7) 2 71+
(Shaun Keightley) *hld up in tch: clsd to press ldr and travelling strly jst over 2f out: led over 1f out: sn pushed along to assert but hung rt: stl hanging but in command ins fnl f: eased cl home* **10/3**[1]

1-20 **2** *2* **Hard Toffee (IRE)**[90] 724 8-9-6 **59** .... CallumShepherd 4 63
(Louise Allan) *t.k.h: effrt 3f out: clsd u.p to chse ldrs 2f out: kpt on ins fnl f to go 2nd towards fin: nvr enough pce to threaten wnr* **25/1**

6543 **3** *1* **Hidden Dream (IRE)**[18] 2112 4-8-7 **46** .... (p) EoinWalsh 6 48
(Christine Dunnett) *t.k.h: hld up in tch in midfield: effrt 3f out: hdwy and rdn to ld over 2f out: hdd and swtchd lft over 1f out: unable to match pce of wnr and one pce ins fnl f: lost 2nd towards fin (jockey said filly ran too freely)* **20/1**

3-03 **4** *1* **Telekinetic**[25] 1958 4-8-9 **48** .... RoystonFfrench 13 48
(Julia Feilden) *rousted along leaving stalls: in tch in midfield: effrt over 2f out: kpt on ins fnl f: no threat to wnr* **20/1**

0056 **5** *2 1/4* **Star Of Valour (IRE)**[20] 2056 4-9-6 **59** .... (p[1]) StevieDonohoe 14 55
(David C Griffiths) *wd early: hdwy to chse ldr after 2f tl 6f out: lost pl u.p over 2f out: wl hld and plugged on same pce fnl f (vet said gelding lost its right fore shoe)* **14/1**

50-0 **6** *2* **Grasmere (IRE)**[29] 1841 4-8-6 **50** .... (t) DarraghKeenan(5) 5 43
(Alan Bailey) *t.k.h: pressed ldr for 2f: styd chsng ldrs tl unable qck ent fnl 2f: wl hld and plugged on same pce fnl f* **50/1**

222 **7** *3 3/4* **Loose Chippings (IRE)**[13] 2345 5-8-12 **54** .... JaneElliott(3) 1 40
(Ivan Furtado) *t.k.h: chsd ldrs: wnt 2nd 6f out tl unable qck ent fnl 2f: wknd fnl f (jockey said gelding ran too freely)* **4/1**[2]

00-0 **8** *2 1/4* **Oceanus (IRE)**[111] 387 5-8-11 **57** .... TobyEley(7) 10 39
(Julia Feilden) *s.i.s: hld up in last quintet: effrt on inner over 2f out: nvr threatened to get on terms: wl hld over 1f out (jockey said gelding slowly away)* **14/1**

64-3 **9** *1/2* **Bigshotte**[16] 2215 4-9-7 **60** .... (t) LukeMorris 7 41
(George Scott) *awkward leaving stalls: in tch in last quintet: effrt u.p over 2f out: sn no imp and wl hld over 1f out: wknd* **12/1**

0012 **10** ½ **Cosmic Ray**[13] 2330 7-9-3 **56**.....................(h) JackMitchell 3 36
(Les Eyre) *led: hung rt bnd 5f out: rdn wl over 2f out: sn hdd and struggling: lost pl and wl btn over 1f out: wknd (jockey said gelding hung right-handed; vet said gelding had lost its left fore shoe)* **10/3**[1]

060- **11** 1 **Battle Of Issus (IRE)**[225] 7876 4-9-1 **59**..........(b) ThomasGreatrex(5) 16 37
(David Menuisier) *sltly impeded leaving stalls: a towards rr: no hdwy u.p 3f out: wl hld fnl 2f (jockey said gelding was never travelling)* **28/1**

000- **12** 6 **Ness Of Brodgar**[161] 9408 4-9-2 **55**.....................(t w) DanielMuscutt 8 23
(Mark H Tompkins) *swtchd lft after s: midfield: effrt over 2f out: sn btn* **66/1**

000 **13** ½ **Farhhmoreexciting**[16] 2192 4-9-2 **55**..................... HayleyTurner 11 22
(David Elsworth) *a towards rr: rdn 4f out: sn struggling and bhd fnl 2f (vet said gelding lost its left fore shoe)* **8/1**[3]

00-0 **14** 2 **Tyrsal (IRE)**[112] 363 8-8-9 **48**..................... JosephineGordon 12 11
(Shaun Keightley) *v.s.a: a in rr (jockey said gelding slowly away)* **16/1**

2m 6.36s (-2.44) **Going Correction** -0.175s/f (Firm) **14** Ran SP% **124.4**
Speed ratings (Par 101): **102,100,99,98,97 95,92,90,90,89 89,84,83,82**
CSF £100.86 CT £1499.79 TOTE £4.00: £1.50, £6.80, £4.10; EX 99.50 Trifecta £2648.70.
Owner Simon Lockyer **Bred** Scuderia Blueberry SRL **Trained** Newmarket, Suffolk

FOCUS
A moderate contest, which seemed to run at an overly strong gallop.

2739 MOMENTS RESTAURANT OF SCRATBY H'CAP 1m 3y
4:15 (4:17) (Class 4) (0-80,82) 4-Y-0+

£5,530 (£1,645; £822; £411; £300; £300) **Stalls** Centre

Form RPR

242- **1** **Balgair**[238] 7433 5-9-9 **82**.....................(h) LukeMorris 8 89
(Tom Clover) *t.k.h: hld up in tch in last trio: swtchd rt and clsd over 1f out: ev ch and rdn 1f out: sustained effrt ins fnl f: led on post* **13/2**

6420 **2** nse **Glory Awaits (IRE)**[28] 1859 9-8-11 **75**.....................(b) DylanHogan(5) 7 81
(David Simcock) *t.k.h: wl in tch in midfield: effrt ent fnl 2f: drvn to chal over 1f out: led 1f out: hung lft ins fnl f: kpt on: hdd on post* **15/2**

2255 **3** 2 **Majestic Moon (IRE)**[14] 2297 9-8-9 **68**.....................(p) RoystonFfrench 6 69
(Julia Feilden) *led and set stdy gallop: rdn wl over 1f out: hrd pressed and nudged lft over 1f out: hdd 1f out: carried lft jst ins fnl f: no ex and outpcd fnl 100yds* **9/1**

1251 **4** ½ **Harbour Vision**[20] 2065 4-9-3 **76**..................... PaddyMathers 2 76
(Derek Shaw) *in tch in rr: swtchd lft and clsd over 2f out: pressed ldrs u.p 1f out: no ex and outpcd fnl 100yds* **8/1**

/6-0 **5** ¾ **Mandarin (GER)**[14] 2273 5-9-4 **80**..................... CameronNoble(3) 5 79
(Ian Williams) *dwlt and sltly short of room leaving stalls: t.k.h: hld up in tch: clsd over 2f out: ev ch u.p over 1f out: carried lft jst ins fnl f: no ex and sn outpcd* **5/2**[1]

0210 **6** 3 ¾ **Juanito Chico (IRE)**[14] 2273 5-9-6 **79**.....................(t) DanielMuscutt 4 69
(Stuart Williams) *wnt rt and jostled leaving stalls: sn chsng ldr: rdn and ev ch ent fnl 2f tl outpcd ent fnl f: sn wknd* **9/2**[2]

50-1 **7** 3 ¾ **Itsakindamagic**[20] 2064 5-9-9 **82**..................... StevieDonohoe 3 63
(Ismail Mohammed) *wnt rt leaving stalls: chsd ldrs tl lost pl ent fnl 2f: wl hld whn hung lft and wknd ins fnl f* **6/1**[3]

0V0- **8** ½ **Colonel Frank**[167] 9309 5-9-8 **81**..................... TomQueally 1 61
(Mick Quinn) *t.k.h: wl in tch: clsd and effrtr over 2f out: sn outpcd and lost pl over 1f out: sn btn and wknd ins fnl f* **10/1**

1m 36.54s (-1.66) **Going Correction** -0.175s/f (Firm) **8** Ran SP% **116.3**
Speed ratings (Par 105): **101,100,98,98,97 93,90,89**
CSF £54.78 CT £347.25 TOTE £5.60: £1.90, £1.80, £3.20; EX 53.80 Trifecta £518.10.
Owner Exors The Late J T Habershon-Butcher **Bred** G Doyle & Lord Margadale **Trained** Newmarket, Suffolk

■ Stewards' Enquiry : Dylan Hogan caution: careless riding

FOCUS
The early pace for this fair handicap was pretty slow, with a lot of the field racing keenly. Modest form for the grade.

2740 SKY SPORTS RACING ON SKY 415 H'CAP 1m 3y
4:45 (4:52) (Class 6) (0-60,60) 4-Y-0+

£3,105 (£924; £461; £300; £300; £300) **Stalls** Centre

Form RPR

034- **1** **Scoffsman**[197] 8729 4-9-1 **57**..................... JoshuaBryan(3) 9 68+
(Kevin Frost) *chsd ldr tl led 2f out: edgd lft u.p over 1f out: kpt on wl ins fnl f* **7/2**[1]

00-5 **2** 1 ½ **Hi Ho Silver**[22] 2019 5-8-13 **52**..................... GeorgeWood 3 58
(Chris Wall) *chsd ldrs: effrt u.p ent fnl 2f: drvn and chsd wnr 1f out: kpt on same pce ins fnl f* **6/1**[2]

06-0 **3** 1 ¾ **Navarra Princess (IRE)**[20] 2066 4-8-8 **47**..................... HayleyTurner 8 49
(Don Cantillon) *hld up in tch in last quintet: hdwy u.p over 1f out: chsd ldrs and kpt on same pce ins fnl f* **16/1**

34-0 **4** 1 ¼ **Show The Money**[88] 759 4-9-4 **60**..................... GabrieleMalune(3) 13 59
(Ivan Furtado) *in tch in midfield: clsd to chse ldrs 1/2-way: effrt to chse wnr 2f out tl no ex 1f out: outpcd ins fnl f* **14/1**

-503 **5** 2 ¼ **Tommycole**[13] 2347 4-9-4 **57**..................... JackMitchell 12 50
(Olly Williams) *in rr: reminders over 4f out: shkn up 2f out: hdwy and styd on to pass btn horses ins fnl f: nvr trbld ldrs* **18/1**

-000 **6** nk **Brigand**[19] 2076 4-8-9 **53**..................... DarraghKeenan(5) 11 46
(John Butler) *hld up in tch in midfield: shkn up ent fnl 2f: unable qck over 1f out: wknd ins fnl f (trainer said gelding had a breathing problem)* **40/1**

4420 **7** ½ **Red Cossack (CAN)**[34] 1717 8-8-7 **46**.....................(b) JoeyHaynes 5 38
(Dean Ivory) *racd keenly: led tl 2f out: no ex u.p over 1f out: wknd ins fnl f* **12/1**

0-02 **8** shd **Cape Cyclone (IRE)**[88] 753 4-8-12 **51**..................... CallumShepherd 14 42
(Stuart Williams) *stdd s: hld up in tch towards rr: effrt over 2f out: no imp and swtchd lft over 1f out: no threat to ldrs and plugged on same pce fnl f* **9/1**

2114 **9** 1 ¾ **Irish Times**[61] 1214 4-8-12 **56**..................... DylanHogan(5) 1 43
(Henry Spiller) *stdd s: hld up in tch: effrt over 2f out: no hdwy u.p over 1f out: wknd ins fnl f* **10/1**

105 **10** hd **Ubla (IRE)**[32] 1769 6-8-12 **54**.....................(p) WilliamCox(3) 6 41
(Gay Kelleway) *chsd ldrs: u.p and struggling to qckn ent fnl 2f: lost pl and btn over 1f out: wknd ins fnl f* **10/1**

0-60 **11** nse **Mississippi Miss**[32] 1769 5-8-12 **51**..................... KierenFox 4 38
(Dr Jon Scargill) *in tch in midfield: u.p and struggling to qckn over 2f out: lost pl and btn over 1f out: wknd ins fnl f* **12/1**

030- **12** 1 ½ **Dor's Law**[189] 8917 6-9-0 **53** ow1.....................(p) RobertWinston 7 36
(Dean Ivory) *sn dropped towards rr: effrt in centre over 2f out: no imp and btn over 1f out: wknd ins fnl f* **15/2**[3]

5500 **13** nk **I'm British**[12] 2376 6-9-4 **57**..................... RossaRyan 10 40
(Don Cantillon) *in tch in midfield: lost pl over 2f out: bhd whn wnt lft over 1f out: wknd ins fnl f* **14/1**

050- **14** 19 **Eternal Destiny**[181] 9077 4-8-5 **47**..................... CameronNoble(3) 16
(Ian Williams) *dwlt: hld up in rr: effrt over 2f out: sn struggling and btn over 1f out: bhd and eased ins fnl f* **15/2**[3]

1m 37.18s (-1.02) **Going Correction** -0.175s/f (Firm) **14** Ran SP% **130.5**
Speed ratings (Par 101): **98,96,94,93,91 90,90,90,88,88 88,86,86,67**
CSF £25.22 CT £327.85 TOTE £4.80: £2.20, £2.30, £7.90; EX 31.20 Trifecta £543.30.
Owner David & Jan Mead **Bred** Juddmonte Farms Ltd **Trained** Newcastle-under-Lyme, Staffs

FOCUS
A moderate even won by a horse well backed in the market.

2741 READE CATERING HOGG ROASTS AT YARMOUTH RACECOURSE H'CAP 7f 3y
5:15 (5:19) (Class 6) (0-60,60) 3-Y-0+

£3,105 (£924; £461; £300; £300; £300) **Stalls** Centre

Form RPR

U5-4 **1** **Diva Star**[13] 2318 4-10-0 **60**.....................(t) LukeMorris 15 69+
(Rae Guest) *stdd s: hld up in tch in rr: impeded over 5f out: swtchd rt over 2f out: gd hdwy to chal over 1f out: sn hung lft but rdn to ld 1f out: in command and r.o wl ins fnl f* **6/1**[2]

0002 **2** 2 **Holy Tiber (IRE)**[34] 1715 4-9-13 **59**.....................(b) JoeyHaynes 6 62
(Paul Howling) *stdd s: hld up in tch in rr: hdwy jst over 2f out: rdn to chse ldrs over 1f out: wnt 2nd ins fnl f: no imp on wnr towards fin* **12/1**

1244 **3** 1 **Catapult**[62] 1192 4-9-2 **55** ow2..................... GavinAshton(7) 8 55
(Shaun Keightley) *t.k.h: led: rdn over 1f out: hdd 1f out: no ex: lost 2nd and one pce ins fnl f* **13/2**[3]

3465 **4** ½ **Rivas Rob Roy**[14] 2286 4-9-2 **53**..................... TheodoreLadd(5) 2 52
(John Gallagher) *chsd ldrs: effrt to chse ldr jst over 2f out tl jst over 1f out: kpt on same pce ins fnl f* **11/4**[1]

-351 **5** ½ **Space War**[7] 2532 12-8-11 **50** 4ex.....................(t) TobyEley(7) 12 48
(Michael Easterby) *taken down early: hld up in tch in midfield: clsd over 2f out: unable qck over 1f out: kpt on again ins fnl f* **13/2**[3]

0030 **6** shd **Haader (FR)**[7] 2532 4-9-11 **57**..................... PaddyMathers 3 54
(Derek Shaw) *stdd after s: hld up in tch in midfield: effrt jst over 2f out: rdn over 1f out: kpt on same pce ins fnl f* **16/1**

-004 **7** hd **Showdance Kid**[16] 2215 5-9-9 **58**.....................(p) JoshuaBryan(3) 7 55
(Kevin Frost) *hld up in tch in midfield: effrt and swtchd lft over 1f out: unable qck and kpt on same pce ins fnl f* **10/1**

-006 **8** nk **Meshardal (GER)**[16] 2183 9-9-6 **52**.....................(p) SamJames 9 48
(Ruth Carr) *hld up in tch: clsd to trck ldrs ent fnl 2f: effrt jst over 1f out: unable qck and wknd ins fnl f* **11/1**

00-0 **9** nk **Stand Firm (IRE)**[15] 2235 4-9-0 **51**..................... DylanHogan(5) 1 46
(Robert Cowell) *in tch in midfield: unable qck u.p over 1f out: wknd ins fnl f* **14/1**

22-0 **10** ¾ **My Society (IRE)**[40] 1565 4-9-12 **58**.....................(tp) StevieDonohoe 11 51
(David Dennis) *chsd ldrs: rdn over 2f out: unable qck over 1f out: wknd ins fnl f* **20/1**

3-00 **11** 25 **Rock On Bertie (IRE)**[18] 2112 4-9-2 **48**.....................(p) RobertWinston 4
(Derek Shaw) *chsd ldr tl jst over 2f out: sn lost pl: wl bhd ins fnl f* **20/1**

1500 **12** 6 **Mochalov**[22] 2019 4-9-10 **59**..................... PaddyBradley(3) 13 +
(Jane Chapple-Hyam) *chsd ldrs tl j. path and dropped to midfield over 5f out: lost pl and u.p in rr 2f: no rspnse and wl bhd ins fnl f (jockey said gelding jumped the path approximately 5 1/2f out)* **16/1**

1m 24.03s (-1.07) **Going Correction** -0.175s/f (Firm) **12** Ran SP% **120.7**
Speed ratings (Par 101): **99,96,95,95,94 94,94,93,93,92 63,57**
CSF £77.57 CT £490.32 TOTE £6.80: £2.30, £4.00, £1.70; EX 53.90 Trifecta £283.90.
Owner FTP Equine Holdings Ltd **Bred** Berend Van Dalfsen **Trained** Newmarket, Suffolk

FOCUS
Nothing more than a modest contest at best, but the winner can hold her own in slightly better company.

T/Plt: £57.50 to a £1 stake. Pool: £52,376.33 - 664.49 winning units. T/Qpdt: £32.60 to a £1 stake. Pool: £4,346.22 - 98.48 winning units. **Steve Payne**

YORK (L-H)
Wednesday, May 15

OFFICIAL GOING: Good to firm (good in places; watered; ovr 7.3, stands' 7.3, ctr 7.3, far 7.3)
Wind: light across Weather: Sunny and warm

2742 SKY BET RACE TO THE EBOR JORVIK H'CAP 1m 3f 188y
1:50 (1:54) (Class 2) 4-Y-0+

£31,125 (£9,320; £4,660; £2,330; £1,165; £585) **Stalls** Centre

Form RPR

513- **1** **First Eleven**[221] 7975 4-9-9 **104**.....................(t) FrankieDettori 5 116
(John Gosden) *trckd ldrs: pushed along over 3f out: hdwy over 2f out: rdn to chal jst over 1f out: drvn ins fnl f: led last 100yds: kpt on wl* **5/1**[2]

11-1 **2** nk **Fujaira Prince (IRE)**[18] 2095 5-9-0 **95**..................... AndreaAtzeni 2 106
(Roger Varian) *trckd ldrs: hdwy over 3f out: led 2f out: rdn over 1f out: drvn ins fnl f: hdd last 100yds: kpt on wl u.p towards fin* **7/2**[1]

226- **3** 2 ¼ **Corgi**[263] 6548 4-9-3 **98**.....................(w) JimCrowley 7 105
(Hughie Morrison) *hld up: hdwy on outer 3f out: rdn along 2f out: sn chsng ldrs: drvn and kpt on same pce fnl f* **8/1**[3]

10-1 **4** nse **Collide**[35] 1681 4-9-3 **98**.....................(t) JamesDoyle 1 105
(Hugo Palmer) *trckd ldrs on inner: smooth hdwy over 3f out: sn cl up: rdn along 2f out: ev ch tl drvn appr fnl f: kpt on same pce* **12/1**

630- **5** 1 **Te Akau Caliburn (IRE)**[264] 6501 4-8-11 **92**..................... SilvestreDeSousa 3 97
(Andrew Balding) *hld up in tch on inner: hdwy 3f out: rdn along to chse ldrs 2f out: drvn over 1f out and kpt on same pce* **12/1**

0-2 **6** ½ **Indianapolis (IRE)**[45] 1460 4-9-1 **96**..................... BarryMcHugh 13 101
(James Given) *hld up towards rr: pushed along over 3f out: rdn and hdwy 2f out: kpt on u.p fnl f* **33/1**

2220 **7** hd **Red Galileo**[46] 1441 8-9-10 **105**..................... OisinMurphy 18 109
(Saeed bin Suroor) *cl up: rdn along wl over 2f out: sn drvn and grad wknd* **20/1**

02-6 **8** 1 ¼ **Proschema (IRE)**[32] 1750 4-9-10 **105**..................... RichardKingscote 8 107
(Tom Dascombe) *trckd ldng pair: cl up over 3f out: rdn along wl over 2f out: grad wknd* **8/1**[3]

0-32 **9** ½ **Everything For You (IRE)**[12] 2370 5-8-12 **93**.....................(v[1]) KevinStott 16 94
(Kevin Ryan) *in tch: effrt over 3f out: sn rdn along: kpt on same pce fnl 2f* **25/1**

0-31 **10** 1 1/4 **Rare Groove (IRE)**[10] 2435 4-8-12 **93** 5ex........................ PJMcDonald 4 92
(Jedd O'Keeffe) *towards rr: effrt over 3f out and sn rdn along: no imp fnl 2f* **12/1**

01-1 **11** *hd* **Crystal King**[18] 2126 4-8-10 **91**.............................. RyanMoore 11 90
(Sir Michael Stoute) *hld up in tch: effrt on outer over 3f out: rdn along to chse ldrs 2f out: sn edgd lft and wknd* **17/2**

5-41 **12** 1 1/2 **Stealth Fighter (IRE)**[22] 2022 4-8-9 **90**.......................... PatCosgrave 6 87
(Saeed bin Suroor) *trckd ldrs: hdwy 4f out: rdn along wl over 2f out: sn drvn and wknd wl over 1f out* **10/1**

111- **13** 1/2 **Byron Flyer**[199] 8084 8-9-9 **104**.............................. BenCurtis 10 100
(Ian Williams) *hld up towards rr: effrt and sme hdwy towards outer over 3f out: sn rdn along and n.d* **33/1**

14 1 3/4 **Perfect City (IRE)**[143] 4-8-10 **91**.............................. JamieSpencer 14 84
(Jonjo O'Neill) *stdd s: hld up: a in rr (starter said the gelding was reluctant to load; trainer was informed that the gelding could not run until the day after passing a stalls test)* **66/1**

15-0 **15** 1/2 **Blakeney Point**[32] 1750 6-9-9 **104**.....................(bt) JasonWatson 17 96
(Roger Charlton) *towards rr: sme hdwy over 3f out: rdn along wl over 2f out: n.d* **40/1**

00-0 **16** 1 **My Reward**[25] 1947 7-9-2 **97**.............................. DavidAllan 12 88
(Tim Easterby) *led: rdn along 3f out: hdd 2f out: sn wknd* **50/1**

521- **17** 2 3/4 **Twin Star (IRE)**[137] 7237 5-9-0 **95**.......................(t w) AdamKirby 9 81
(Noel Williams) *a in rr* **66/1**

6-60 **18** 1 3/4 **Sir Chauvelin**[25] 1947 7-9-8 **103**.............................. DanielTudhope 15 87
(Jim Goldie) *a in rr* **33/1**

2m 31.2s (-2.00) **Going Correction** +0.05s/f (Good) **18 Ran SP% 128.6**
Speed ratings (Par 109): **108,107,106,106,105 105,105,104,103,103 103,102,101,100,100 99,97,96**
CSF £21.65 CT £146.47 TOTE £5.50: £1.80, £1.50, £2.30, £3.10; EX 23.80 Trifecta £140.60.
Owner K Abdullah **Bred** Juddmonte Farms Ltd **Trained** Newmarket, Suffolk
■ Stewards' Enquiry : Andrea Atzeni two-day ban: used whip in the incorrect place (May 29-30)

FOCUS
The going was given as good to firm, good In places (Going Stick 7.3. Home straight; Stands' side 7.3; Centre 7.3; Far side 7.2). The rail on the home bend from 9f to the entrance to the home straight was out 10yds from its innermost position, adding 32yds to races of 1m2f plus. They were spread across the track in this competitive handicap which was run at an even pace, although the first five home were all drawn in stall 7 or lower. The front two pulled clear in the closing stages after a protracted battle. A strong handicap. The form looks solid and it is a race that should produce plenty of winners. The time of the first race was 3.80sec slower than RP Standard with the jockeys describing the ground as "beautiful", "nice", "gorgeous" and "perfect".

2743 INFINITY TYRES H'CAP — 6f

2:25 (2:28) (Class 2) (0-105,104) 4-Y-O+

£18,675 (£5,592; £2,796; £1,398; £699; £351) **Stalls Centre**

Form RPR

-150 **1** **Soldier's Minute**[25] 1946 4-8-9 **92**.............................. JoeFanning 3 105
(Keith Dalgleish) *prom: led over 1f out: r.o strly and sn sn clr (trainer's rep said, as to the apparent improvement in form, the gelding was suited by a better draw on this occasion)* **20/1**

3-52 **2** 3 **Wentworth Falls**[11] 2396 7-8-12 **95**.....................(p) ConnorBeasley 15 98
(Geoffrey Harker) *hld up: stl plenty to do whn n.m.r over 1f out: rdn and hdwy appr fnl f: kpt on wl to go 2nd 110yds out: wnr beyond recall* **12/1**

162- **3** 3/4 **Aljady (FR)**[222] 7950 4-8-12 **95**.............................. TonyHamilton 22 96
(Richard Fahey) *hld up towards stands' side: swtchd lft over 1f out: sn pushed along and hdwy: rdn and kpt on wl fnl f: nrst fin* **8/1**[2]

03-0 **4** *nk* **Savalas (IRE)**[25] 1946 4-8-12 **95**.............................. TomEaves 18 96
(Kevin Ryan) *prom towards stands' side: rdn 2f out: kpt on same pce* **20/1**

0004 **5** 1/2 **Intisaab**[18] 2117 8-9-7 **104**.....................(p) DavidNolan 20 102
(David O'Meara) *dwlt: hld up towards stands' side: rdn and sme hdwy over 1f out: kpt on ins fnl f* **20/1**

0-00 **6** 1/2 **Roundhay Park**[11] 2396 4-8-2 **90**.............................. FayeMcManoman(5) 1 87
(Nigel Tinkler) *hld up towards far side: rdn and hdwy over 1f out: kpt on ins fnl f* **20/1**

00-4 **7** *hd* **Spoof**[33] 1734 4-9-0 **97**.....................(h) AndreaAtzeni 4 93
(Charles Hills) *midfield: rdn and hdwy appr fnl f: one pce ins fnl f* **16/1**

50-1 **8** *nse* **Reputation (IRE)**[18] 2117 6-9-1 **98**.............................. JamesSullivan 16 94
(Ruth Carr) *dwlt sltly: sn midfield: rdn and hdwy to chse ldr 1f out: wknd fnl 110yds* **14/1**

30-0 **9** 1 1/4 **Citron Major**[12] 2378 4-8-5 **88**.............................. AndrewMullen 14 80+
(Nigel Tinkler) *hld up in rr: short of room 3f out and sn pushed along: rdn over 1f out: kpt on fnl f: nvr threatened* **33/1**

00-0 **10** 1 1/4 **Golden Apollo**[18] 2100 5-8-12 **95**.............................. JasonHart 7 83+
(Tim Easterby) *hld up: stl on bit 2f out: pushed along and sme hdwy whn sltly short of room ins fnl f: nvr involved (jockey said gelding was denied a clear run inside 2 furlongs out)* **8/1**[2]

3430 **11** 1 **Gulliver**[79] 909 5-9-1 **98**.....................(tp) AdamKirby 2 83
(David O'Meara) *midfield towards far side: rdn over 2f out: wknd ins fnl f* **33/1**

5-60 **12** 1/2 **Flying Pursuit**[18] 2117 6-9-3 **100**.....................(p) RachelRichardson 21 83
(Tim Easterby) *midfield: rdn over 2f out: wknd ins fnl f* **50/1**

26-3 **13** 1 1/2 **Staxton**[18] 2117 4-9-3 **100**.............................. DavidAllan 11 78
(Tim Easterby) *pressed ldr: rdn 2f out: wknd fnl f (trainer could offer no explanation for the gelding's performance)* **6/1**[1]

200- **14** *hd* **Holmeswood**[200] 8632 5-8-6 **89**.............................. PJMcDonald 5 67
(Julie Camacho) *led narrowly: rdn and hdd over 1f out: sn wknd* **10/1**[3]

26-2 **15** 3/4 **Whinmoor**[15] 2260 4-8-5 **91**.............................. RowanScott(3) 6 66
(Nigel Tinkler) *dwlt: sn trckd ldrs: rdn 2f out: wknd appr fnl f* **14/1**

00-0 **16** 2 1/4 **Arecibo (FR)**[18] 2117 4-9-0 **97**.....................(p[1]) DanielTudhope 19 65
(David O'Meara) *in tch towards stands' side: rdn over 2f out: wknd over 1f out* **20/1**

5130 **17** *hd* **Desert Doctor (IRE)**[29] 1829 4-8-12 **95**.............................. GeraldMosse 10 63
(Ed Walker) *midfield: rdn over 2f out: hmpd over 1f out: eased (trainer's rep said gelding was unsuited by the going (good to firm, good in places) and is better suited to an all-weather surface)* **14/1**

-600 **18** 3 1/4 **Captain Colby (USA)**[11] 2396 7-8-7 **93**.............................. BenRobinson(3) 12 50
(Paul Midgley) *midfield: rdn over 3f out: lost pl over 2f out: sn wknd* **66/1**

-000 **19** *nk* **Double Up**[18] 2100 8-8-6 **89**.....................(vt) BenCurtis 8 45
(Ian Williams) *pressed ldr: rdn over 2f out: wknd appr fnl f* **33/1**

00-2 **20** 1 **Vibrant Chords**[25] 1942 6-9-2 **99**.............................. RyanMoore 13 52
(Henry Candy) *midfield: rdn over 2f out: wknd over 1f out* **14/1**

2-40 **21** 12 **Sandra's Secret (IRE)**[18] 2117 6-8-11 **94**.............................. SilvestreDeSousa 17 9
(Les Eyre) *prom: rdn over 2f out: wknd over 1f out: eased (jockey said mare stopped quickly; vet said mare had a small wound to the inside of its left fore)* **16/1**

1m 10.06s (-1.54) **Going Correction** +0.05s/f (Good) **21 Ran SP% 127.8**
Speed ratings (Par 109): **112,108,107,106,105 105,105,104,103,101 100,99,97,97,96 93,93,88,88,87 71**
CSF £223.67 CT £2147.08 TOTE £33.00: £6.40, £3.10, £2.10, £8.30; EX 570.60 Trifecta £4540.80.
Owner Weldspec Glasgow Limited **Bred** Rabbah Bloodstock Limited **Trained** Carluke, S Lanarks

FOCUS
A competitive sprint handicap on paper, but, just like last year, one came out of the pack to win easily. There appeared to be no track bias. A wide margin win for a race of this nature and the form could rate a bit higher.

2744 DUKE OF YORK CLIPPER LOGISTICS STKS (GROUP 2) — 6f

3:00 (3:01) (Class 1) 3-Y-O+

£70,887 (£26,875; £13,450; £6,700; £3,362; £1,687) **Stalls Centre**

Form RPR

00-1 **1** **Invincible Army (IRE)**[46] 1412 4-9-8 112.............................. PJMcDonald 8 118+
(James Tate) *hld up in tch: hdwy nr stands' rail 2f out: rdn over 1f out: qcknd to ld ent fnl f: sn edgd lft and clr* **7/2**[1]

1-23 **2** 2 1/4 **Major Jumbo**[11] 2409 5-9-8 107.............................. JamieSpencer 5 110
(Kevin Ryan) *trckd ldrs: hdwy over 2f out: chal wl over 1f out: rdn and ev ch ent fnl f: sn drvn and kpt on same pce* **8/1**

10-2 **3** 3/4 **Yafta**[28] 1853 4-9-8 109.............................. JimCrowley 1 108
(Richard Hannon) *dwlt: sn trcking ldrs in centre pushed along and sltly outpcd 2f out: rdn wl over 1f out: styd on fnl f* **7/2**[1]

110- **4** 1/2 **Limato (IRE)**[207] 8405 7-9-11 113.............................. HarryBentley 9 109
(Henry Candy) *hld up in rr: hdwy towards stands' rail wl over 1f out: sn rdn: kpt on fnl f* **4/1**[2]

32-2 **5** 1/2 **Hey Jonesy (IRE)**[20] 2062 4-9-8 107.....................(p) KevinStott 4 104
(Kevin Ryan) *trckd ldrs centre: hdwy and cl up over 2f out: rdn wl over 1f out: grad wknd* **14/1**

1-26 **6** *hd* **El Astronaute (IRE)**[11] 2409 6-9-8 106.............................. JasonHart 3 104
(John Quinn) *racd towards stands' side: led: rdn along 1 1/2f out: drvn and hdd ent fnl f: grad wknd* **20/1**

24-3 **7** 1 1/2 **Brando**[28] 1853 7-9-8 114.............................. TomEaves 6 99
(Kevin Ryan) *stmbld s: sn trcking ldrs centre: hdwy 1/2-way: pushed along 2f out: sn rdn and wknd over 1f out* **7/1**[3]

3012 **8** 3/4 **George Bowen (IRE)**[26] 1919 7-9-8 106.....................(v) PaulHanagan 7 97
(Richard Fahey) *hld up: a towards rr* **16/1**

515 **9** 1 **Ornate**[11] 2409 6-9-8 99.............................. PhilDennis 2 93
(David C Griffiths) *racd centre: cl up: disp ld 4f out: rdn along 2f out: sn wknd* **66/1**

316- **10** 1 1/4 **Projection**[207] 8405 6-9-8 111.............................. JasonWatson 10 89
(Roger Charlton) *hld up: a in rr* **12/1**

1m 9.9s (-1.70) **Going Correction** +0.05s/f (Good) **10 Ran SP% 114.6**
Speed ratings (Par 115): **113,110,109,108,107 107,105,104,103,101**
CSF £31.40 CT £106.54 TOTE £4.50: £1.80, £2.60, £1.30; EX 28.60 Trifecta £124.20.
Owner Saeed Manana **Bred** Rabbah Bloodstock Limited **Trained** Newmarket, Suffolk

FOCUS
The Cammidge Trophy form had already received a boost when the second and third switched places in the Palace House, and this time the first two from Doncaster replicated their form virtually to the pound. The form is best rated through the runner-up.

2745 TATTERSALLS MUSIDORA STKS (GROUP 3) (FILLIES) — 1m 2f 56y

3:35 (3:35) (Class 1) 3-Y-O

£56,710 (£16,130; £5,360; £2,690; £1,350) **Stalls Low**

Form RPR

1-4 **1** **Nausha**[25] 1939 3-9-0 0.............................. AndreaAtzeni 2 102+
(Roger Varian) *hld up towards rr: swtchd rt and hdwy 3f out: rdn to chal over 1f out: led ent fnl f: sn drvn: edgd lft and hld on gamely* **14/1**

61- **2** *nk* **Entitle**[147] 9607 3-9-0 0.............................. FrankieDettori 5 101+
(John Gosden) *hld up towards rr: hdwy 3f out: cl up wl over 1f out: sn rdn to chal: ev ch ent fnl f: sn drvn: kpt on wl* **12/1**

1- **2** *dht* **Frankellina**[204] 8510 3-9-0 0.............................. JamesDoyle 8 101+
(William Haggas) *dwlt and lost 3 l s: in rr: gd hdwy on outer 3f out: chsd ldrs 2f out: rdn jst over 1f out: ev ch ent fnl f: sn drvn: kpt on wl (jockey said filly missed the break)* **11/4**[2]

54 **4** 1 1/2 **Fresnel**[17] 2157 3-9-0 98.............................. GaryHalpin 3 98
(Jack W Davison, Ire) *trckd ldrs: pushed along 3f out: rdn and cl up 2f out: drvn whn carried sltly rt 1 1/2f out: edgd lft and kpt on same pce ins fnl f* **16/1**

521- **5** 1 1/4 **Blue Gardenia (IRE)**[193] 8836 3-9-0 93.............................. ShaneGray 1 96
(David O'Meara) *hld up in rr: hdwy 3f out: rdn along to chse ldrs and n.m.r wl over 1f out: sn swtchd lft and drvn: kpt on fnl f* **40/1**

3-63 **6** 3/4 **I'll Have Another (IRE)**[10] 2445 3-9-0 97.............................. SilvestreDeSousa 9 94
(Mark Johnston) *cl up: led after 1f: pushed along 3f out: rdn 2f out: edgd rt 1 1/2f out: sn drvn: hdd ent fnl f: wknd* **28/1**

51-1 **7** 1 3/4 **Sparkle Roll (FR)**[19] 2087 3-9-0 92.............................. OisinMurphy 6 91
(John Gosden) *hld up in tch: hdwy 3f out: rdn along to chse ldrs 2f out: hld whn n.m.r and sltly hmpd 1 1/2f out: wknd* **7/4**[1]

134- **8** 1 1/4 **Sand Share**[203] 8562 3-9-0 101.............................. HarryBentley 4 88
(Ralph Beckett) *trckd ldrs on inner: pushed along 3f out: rdn over 2f out: sn drvn and wknd* **8/1**[3]

5025 **9** *shd* **Swift Rose (IRE)**[46] 1443 3-9-0 99.............................. JasonWatson 10 88
(Saeed bin Suroor) *qckly away and crossed to inner rail: led and t.k.h: hdd after 1f: trckd ldr: pushed along 3f out: rdn over 2f out: sn btn* **25/1**

01- **10** 21 **Dubai Blue (USA)**[242] 7298 3-9-0 0.............................. AdamKirby 7 46
(Saeed bin Suroor) *prom: pushed along and lost pl 3f out: sn rdn: wknd and bhd whn eased fr wl over 1f out* **10/1**

2m 10.5s (0.20) **Going Correction** +0.05s/f (Good) **10 Ran SP% 113.2**
Speed ratings (Par 106): **101,100,100,99,98 97,96,95,95,78**
WIN: 14.30 Nausha; PL: 3.10 Entitle, 3.70 Nausha, 1.40 Frankellina; EX: N/E 87.30, N/F 29.40; CSF: N/E 80.41, N/F 25.08; TF: N/E/F 280.20, N/F/E 203.20;.
Owner Nurlan Bizakov **Bred** Hesmonds Stud Ltd **Trained** Newmarket, Suffolk

FOCUS
Add 32yds. It's a decade since the last winner of the Musidora went on to win at Epsom, and the feeling beforehand was that this might prove more of a Ribblesdale trial than one for the Oaks. A bunched finish didn't do a great deal to change that view, but there were one or two notable performances nevertheless. The first three turned into the straight in the last three positions. The bare form looks just ordinary.

2746 CONUNDRUM ROWING FOR CHRISTIAN HOBBS GYM H'CAP 7f
4:05 (4:08) (Class 3) (0-95,93) 3-Y-O

£12,450 (£3,728; £1,864; £932; £466; £234) **Stalls** Low

Form RPR
1-42 **1** **Space Blues (IRE)**[15] 2249 3-9-7 **93**............................ JamesDoyle 10 107+
(Charlie Appleby) hld up: hdwy over 2f out: sn nt clr run: swtchd rt and effrt whn nt clr run over 1f out: sn swtchd markedly rt to outer and str run fnl f to ld last 100yds: sn clr **5/2**[1]
1-25 **2** *2* **Reeves**[19] 2082 3-8-13 **85**..(p[1]) RaulDaSilva 15 91
(Robert Cowell) hld up in tch: hdwy over 2f out: rdn to chse ldrs over 1f out: drvn to ld ent fnl f: hdd last 100yds: kpt on **20/1**
4-04 **3** *nk* **Fastman (IRE)**[8] 2510 3-9-0 **86**.............................. DanielTudhope 14 91
(David O'Meara) prom: hdwy and cl up over 2f out: rdn to ld 1 1/2f out: hdd ent fnl f: sn drvn and kpt on **14/1**
46-0 **4** *1 1/2* **I Am A Dreamer**[20] 2054 3-8-7 **79**.............................. PJMcDonald 4 80
(Mark Johnston) led: rdn along over 2f out: hdd 1 1/2f out: sn drvn and kpt on same pce fnl f **33/1**
41-6 **5** *1/2* **Karnavaal (IRE)**[28] 1857 3-8-9 **81**.............................. JimCrowley 6 81+
(Sir Michael Stoute) in tch: hdwy over 2f out: rdn wl over 1f out: drvn and kpt on fnl f **5/1**[2]
2-21 **6** *1 1/4* **Magical Wish (IRE)**[35] 1685 3-9-5 **91**.............................. SeanLevey 9 87
(Richard Hannon) t.k.h: in tch: hdwy over 2f out: rdn to chse ldrs over 1f out: kpt on same pce fnl f **20/1**
4-15 **7** *3/4* **Nefarious (IRE)**[20] 2054 3-8-11 **83**.............................. HarryBentley 2 77
(Henry Candy) trckd ldrs on inner: hdwy over 2f out: rdn and n.m.r over 1f out: kpt on fnl f **25/1**
152 **8** *3/4* **Songkran (IRE)**[17] 2140 3-8-7 **79**.............................. SilvestreDeSousa 17 71
(David Elsworth) towards rr: hdwy wl over 2f out: sn rdn: kpt on fnl f: nrst fin **14/1**
20-5 **9** *hd* **Irv (IRE)**[27] 1897 3-8-2 **74**.............................. JamesSullivan 12 66
(Micky Hammond) in rr: hdwy 3f out: rdn wl over 1f out: kpt on fnl f: nrst fin **50/1**
23-1 **10** *nk* **Zip**[127] 126 3-8-5 **77**.............................. CamHardie 5 68
(Richard Fahey) towards rr: hdwy over 2f out: rdn and kpt on fnl f: nrst fin (jockey said gelding reared as the stalls opened and missed the break) **20/1**
12-6 **11** *hd* **Shallow Hal**[33] 1736 3-9-2 **88**.............................. BenCurtis 1 78
(K R Burke) trckd ldrs on inner: hdwy over 2f out: cl up and rdn over 1f out: drvn and wknd fnl f **16/1**
0-20 **12** *1/2* **Black Magic Woman (IRE)**[16] 2222 3-8-11 **83**..........(b) GeraldMosse 7 72
(Jack W Davison, Ire) prom: cl up 3f out: rdn along over 2f out: drvn and wknd over 1f out **33/1**
201 **13** *1/2* **Conaglen**[34] 1723 3-8-6 **78**.............................. DavidEgan 18 66
(James Bethell) a towards rr **33/1**
51-2 **14** *2 1/4* **The Night Watch**[17] 2139 3-8-4 **83**.............................. CierenFallon[(7)] 3 65
(William Haggas) prom: cl up 3f out: rdn along over 2f out: sn drvn and wknd (jockey said gelding ran too freely) **11/2**[3]
13-5 **15** *2 1/2* **Breath Of Air**[28] 1851 3-9-7 **93**.............................. RyanMoore 19 68
(Charles Hills) chsd ldrs on outer: cl up 1/2-way: rdn along 2f out: wkng whn sltly hmpd appr fnl f (jockey said colt ran flat) **12/1**
051- **16** *1* **The Great Heir (FR)**[244] 7201 3-9-4 **90**.............................. AndrewMullen 13 62
(Kevin Ryan) a towards rr **33/1**
-406 **17** *6* **Chairmanoftheboard (IRE)**[25] 1940 3-9-4 **90**.........(v[1]) AndreaAtzeni 11 46
(Mick Channon) a towards rr (vet said colt finished lame on its left hind) **33/1**
022- **18** *5* **Watchmyeverymove (IRE)**[214] 8189 3-8-8 **80**..........(t) JasonWatson 16 22
(Stuart Williams) a towards rr (jockey said gelding hung right) **25/1**
2253 **19** *5* **James Street (IRE)**[26] 1920 3-9-3 **89**.............................. (t[1]) OisinMurphy 8 18
(Hugo Palmer) t.k.h: chsd ldrs: rdn along over 2f out: sn wknd **25/1**

1m 23.35s (-1.25) **Going Correction** +0.05s/f (Good) **19** Ran **SP% 130.0**
Speed ratings (Par 103): **109,106,106,104,104 102,101,100,100,100 100,99,99,96,93 92,85,79,74**
CSF £61.48 CT £637.86 TOTE £3.40: £1.70, £4.00, £2.80, £8.30; EX 52.10 Trifecta £549.10.
Owner Godolphin **Bred** Godolphin **Trained** Newmarket, Suffolk

FOCUS
A race run at a decent clip which ideally suited the winner, who needed to be extracted from a pocket late on. The main action unfolded towards the stands' side with the winner coming widest of all. He was the seventh winning favourite of this race in the last ten years, which is somewhat surprising given that it usually attracts big fields full of largely unexposed runners.

2747 BRITISH STALLION STUDS EBF NOVICE STKS (PLUS 10 RACE) 5f
4:35 (4:36) (Class 3) 2-Y-O

£12,450 (£3,728; £1,864; £932; £466; £234) **Stalls** High

Form RPR
1 **Bomb Proof (IRE)** 2-9-2 0.............................. FrankieDettori 1 95+
(Jeremy Noseda) trckd ldrs: pushed into ld over 1f out: sn rdn: kpt on wl: pushed out towards fin **7/1**
2 *1 1/4* **Monoski (USA)** 2-9-2 0.............................. JamesDoyle 4 90+
(Mark Johnston) w ldr: led 2f out: hdd over 1f out: sn rdn: wandered: kpt on **7/1**
3 *2 1/2* **Summer Sands** 2-9-2 0.............................. BarryMcHugh 9 81+
(Richard Fahey) hld up in tch: pushed along over 2f out: rdn over 1f out: kpt on wl: wnt 3rd fnl 110yds **11/2**[3]
5 **4** *2 1/4* **Dazzling Des (IRE)**[32] 1759 2-9-2 0.............................. DanielTudhope 2 73
(David O'Meara) trckd ldrs: chal over 1f out: sn rdn: wknd ins fnl f **5/1**[2]
5 *3/4* **Sun Power (FR)** 2-9-2 0.............................. SilvestreDeSousa 6 70
(Richard Hannon) s.i.s: sn in tch: pushed along over 2f out: rdn over 2f out: wknd ins fnl f **5/2**[1]
51 **6** *nse* **Kidda**[14] 2288 2-9-8 0.............................. TonyHamilton 10 76+
(Richard Fahey) chsd ldrs: pushed along over 2f out: rdn over 2f out: wknd ins fnl f **10/1**
7 *3/4* **Barbarella (IRE)** 2-8-11 0.............................. TomEaves 11 62
(Kevin Ryan) dwlt: hld up: rdn along over 2f out: minor late hdwy: nvr threatened **25/1**
01 **8** *1/2* **Harswell (IRE)**[12] 2367 2-9-8 0.............................. DavidNolan 8 72
(Liam Bailey) led narrowly: rdn and hdd 2f out: wknd fnl f **25/1**
5 **9** *1 1/4* **Holloa**[18] 2115 2-8-11 0.............................. DavidAllan 3 56
(Tim Easterby) hld up: pushed along over 2f out: nvr threatened **8/1**
6 **10** *2 1/4* **Irish Eileen**[18] 2093 2-8-11 0.............................. NathanEvans 7 48
(Michael Easterby) prom: rdn over 2f out: wknd over 1f out **50/1**
0 **11** *6* **Bankawi**[37] 1642 2-8-11 0.............................. JamesSullivan 12 26
(Michael Easterby) hld up: racd keenly: rdn over 2f out: wknd over 1f out (jockey said filly hung left) **66/1**

58.63s (0.43) **Going Correction** +0.05s/f (Good) **11** Ran **SP% 117.0**
Speed ratings (Par 97): **98,96,92,88,87 87,85,85,83,79 69**
CSF £53.23 TOTE £5.90: £2.00, £2.50, £2.40; EX 33.20 Trifecta £271.60.
Owner C Fox & Shalfleet Partnership **Bred** Michael O'Mahony **Trained** Newmarket, Suffolk

FOCUS
Usually a good novice, with three of the last four winners going on to be placed in Group company at two. They finished quite well strung out and the winner did it nicely.

2748 LINDUM CONSTRUCTION GROUP H'CAP 1m 3f 188y
5:05 (5:06) (Class 4) (0-85,85) 4-Y-O+

£12,699 (£3,802; £1,901; £950; £475; £300) **Stalls** Centre

Form RPR
30-2 **1** **Starcaster**[32] 1761 4-9-4 **82**.............................. JamieSpencer 7 96+
(Jedd O'Keeffe) hld up towards rr: smooth hdwy towards inner 3f out: cl up 2f out: shkn up to ld ent fnl f: sn rdn clr: kpt on strly **7/2**[1]
0-00 **2** *4* **Armandihan (IRE)**[32] 1761 5-9-2 **80**..............................(p w) KevinStott 17 86
(Kevin Ryan) hld up in rr: smooth hdwy 3f out: swtchd rt to outer and chsd ldrs wl over 1f out: rdn to ld briefly appr fnl f: sn hdd and drvn: kpt on same pce last 150yds **33/1**
5566 **3** *1/2* **Winged Spur (IRE)**[15] 2230 4-8-13 **77**.............................. PJMcDonald 11 82
(Mark Johnston) towards rr: hdwy on wd outside 3f out: rdn along 2f out: styd on wl fnl f **20/1**
12-1 **4** *1/2* **Get Back Get Back (IRE)**[18] 2092 4-9-6 **84**.............................. AdamKirby 12 90+
(Clive Cox) hld up in rr: hdwy on outer wl over 2f out: rdn and nt clr run over 1f out: sn swtchd rt: styd on wl fnl f **5/1**[3]
-032 **5** *1 1/2* **Delph Crescent (IRE)**[12] 2374 4-9-3 **81**....................(p) PaulHanagan 15 83
(Richard Fahey) trckd ldrs: hdwy 3f out: cl up 2f out: sn rdn and ev ch: drvn ent fnl f: one pce **12/1**
6302 **6** *1* **Glan Y Gors (IRE)**[4] 2636 7-9-0 **78**..............................(b) CliffordLee 19 78
(David Thompson) trckd ldrs: hdwy and cl up 3f out: rdn along 2f out: sn drvn and grad wknd **20/1**
3-54 **7** *1/2* **Framley Garth (IRE)**[10] 2435 7-8-8 **77**.............................. PaulaMuir[(5)] 8 76
(Liam Bailey) trckd ldrs: pushed along 3f out: rdn 2f out: kpt on one pce fnl f **14/1**
3153 **8** *1/2* **Desert Ruler**[32] 1761 6-9-6 **84**.............................. JackGarritty 18 83
(Jedd O'Keeffe) hld up towards rr tl styd on fnl 2f **20/1**
000- **9** *5* **Thomas Cranmer (USA)**[190] 8899 5-9-5 **83**.............. JamesSullivan 20 74
(Tina Jackson) hld up: hdwy 3f out: chsd ldrs 2f out: sn rdn and n.m.r over 1f out: no imp fnl f **25/1**
10/- **10** *1* **Aldreth**[779] 1405 8-9-2 **80**.............................. PhilDennis 13 69
(Michael Easterby) hld up in rr: hdwy wl over 2f out: styd on fnl f **66/1**
212- **11** *1* **Past Master**[200] 8642 6-9-4 **82**.............................. RyanMoore 10 69
(Henry Candy) sn led: pushed along 3f out: rdn over 2f out: drvn and hdd wl over 1f out: sn wknd **9/2**[2]
0-32 **12** *shd* **Addis Ababa (IRE)**[16] 2186 4-9-7 **85**.............................. DanielTudhope 16 72
(David O'Meara) trckd ldr: cl up over 3f out: rdn along over 2f out: sn drvn and wknd (jockey said gelding failed to stay the 1 mile 3 furlong 188 yard trip, which the gelding was trying for the first time at York) **11/2**
10-0 **13** *nse* **Tapis Libre**[11] 2398 11-8-7 **78**.............................. JoshQuinn[(7)] 6 65
(Jacqueline Coward) hld up: a towards rr **66/1**
6244 **14** *6* **Technological**[39] 1596 4-9-0 **78**.............................. OisinMurphy 2 56
(George Margarson) mdifield: effrt on inner and in tch over 3f out: sn rdn and wknd **16/1**
24-4 **15** *2* **Benadalid**[32] 1761 4-9-7 **85**.............................. MichaelStainton 1 59
(Chris Fairhurst) in tch on inner: rdn along over 3f out: sn wknd **12/1**
420- **16** *2 1/4* **Qawamees (IRE)**[91] 7729 4-9-2 **80**..............................(w) NathanEvans 3 51
(Michael Easterby) trckd ldrs on inner: rdn along 4f out: sn wknd **50/1**
310- **17** *18* **Moving Forward (IRE)**[219] 8045 4-9-2 **80**.............................. DougieCostello 5 22
(Tony Coyle) chsd ldrs: rdn along 3f out: sn wknd **66/1**

2m 31.97s (-1.23) **Going Correction** +0.05s/f (Good) **17** Ran **SP% 127.9**
Speed ratings (Par 105): **106,103,103,102,101 101,100,100,97,96 95,95,95,91,90 88,76**
CSF £140.10 CT £2088.40 TOTE £4.50: £1.80, £7.20, £4.30, £1.80; EX 168.90 Trifecta £4932.90.
Owner Quantum **Bred** Meon Valley Stud **Trained** Middleham Moor, N Yorks

FOCUS
Add 32yds. The first four were in the last seven positions turning into the straight. Improvement from the winner.
T/Jkpt: Not Won. T/Plt: £161.80 to a £1 stake. Pool: £209,939.56 - 946.93 winning units. T/Qpdt: £33.90 to a £1 stake. Pool: £15,533.57 - 338.26 winning units. **Joe Rowntree & Andrew Sheret**

2749 - 2756a (Foreign Racing) - See Raceform Interactive

2564
MAISONS-LAFFITTE (R-H)
Wednesday, May 15

OFFICIAL GOING: Turf: good to soft

2757a PRIX ILLINOIS II (MAIDEN) (2YO) (TURF) 5f 110y
11:25 2-Y-O **£12,162** (£4,864; £3,648; £2,432; £1,216)

RPR
1 **Alkaid (FR)**[19] 2-9-2 0.............................. StephanePasquier 8 81
(Gianluca Bietolini, France) **69/10**
2 *3/4* **Ammobaby (FR)**[37] 1657 2-9-0 0 ow1.............. ChristopheSoumillon 7 77
(H De Nicolay, France) **12/5**[1]
3 *1/2* **Yomogi (FR)**[13] 2-8-13 0.............................. FabriceVeron 2 74
(Hiroo Shimizu, France) **11/1**
4 *nse* **Sayidah Kodiac**[13] 2-8-13 0.............................. CristianDemuro 1 74
(E J O'Neill, France) **79/10**
5 *3/4* **Miss Tiche (IRE)**[19] 2-8-13 0.............................. TheoBachelot 6 71
(S Wattel, France) **3/1**[3]
6 *9* **Panthera Tigris**[15] 2263 2-8-9.............................. GeorgiaDobie[(4)] 3 42
(Jo Hughes, France) urged along early: settled towards rr: pushed along over 2f out: rdn w little rspnse over 1f out: wknd fnl f **58/1**
7 *13* **Mayana Chope (FR)** 2-8-13 0..............................(p) HugoJourniac 5
(A Chopard, France) **31/1**
P **It's A Heartache (IRE)**[21] 2-8-13 0.............................. AlexisBadel 4
(H-F Devin, France) **5/2**[2]

1m 6.77s (-0.53) **8** Ran **SP% 120.0**
PARI-MUTUEL (all including 1 euro stake): WIN 7.90; PLACE 2.10, 1.50, 2.70; DF 11.40.
Owner Scuderia Allevamento Il Quadrifoglio **Bred** Thousand Dreams & T Grandsir **Trained** France

2758a PRIX EMPERY (MAIDEN) (3YO COLTS & GELDINGS) (TURF) 1m 2f 110y
1:07 3-Y-O £11,261 (£4,504; £3,378; £2,252; £1,126)

RPR

1 **Aramhes (FR)**[23] 3-9-2 0 .... FabienLefebvre 1 79
(Carla O'Halloran, France) **4/1**[3]

2 2 1/2 **Reliable Son (FR)**[22] 3-9-2 0 .... StephanePasquier 8 74
(N Clement, France) **12/5**[2]

3 3/4 **Segarelli (IRE)**[23] 3-8-8 0 .... AugustinMadamet(8) 5 73
(A Fabre, France) **21/10**[1]

4 1 1/4 **Kolsche Jung (GER)** 3-9-2 0 .... CristianDemuro 10 70
(Dr A Bolte, Germany) **44/1**

5 4 1/2 **Sharp Rock (GER)**[25] 3-9-2 0 .... RenePiechulek 3 62
(Frau S Steinberg, Germany) **37/1**

6 2 **Yaazaain**[202] 3-9-2 0 .... RonanThomas 2 58
(J E Hammond, France) *settled towards rr: shkn up over 2f out: rdn to chse ldr over 1f out: kpt on same pce fnl f* **24/1**

7 hd **Fort Templier (FR)**[32] 3-9-2 0 .... TheoBachelot 4 58
(Vaclav Luka Jr, Czech Republic) **31/5**

8 snk **Mojano (FR)** 3-9-2 0 .... MickaelBarzalona 7 57
(S Richter, Germany) **9/1**

9 7 **San Pablo (FR)**[44] 3-9-2 0 .... OlivierPeslier 6 44
(H-A Pantall, France) **20/1**

10 nk **Hawk Cliff (FR)**[33] 1741 3-8-13 .... GeorgiaDobie(3) 9 44
(Jo Hughes, France) *midfield early: pushed along over 2f out: rdn and outpcd over 1f out: wknd ins fnl f* **94/1**

2m 13.43s (133.43) **10 Ran SP% 120.2**
PARI-MUTUEL (all including 1 euro stake): WIN 5.00; PLACE 1.50, 1.30, 1.30; DF 7.50.
Owner Ecurie Dimongo, C German Et Al **Bred** Haras De La Perelle **Trained** France

2759a PRIX NOBILIARY (MAIDEN) (3YO FILLIES) (TURF) 1m 2f 110y
1:42 3-Y-O £11,261 (£4,504; £3,378; £2,252; £1,126)

RPR

1 **Edisa (USA)**[31] 3-9-2 0 .... ChristopheSoumillon 2 77
(A De Royer-Dupre, France) **49/10**[3]

2 3/4 **Hawkamah (IRE)**[23] 3-9-2 .... MickaelBarzalona 11 76
(A Fabre, France) *trckd ldr: urged along and sltly outpcd over 2f out: rdn to chse ldr over 1f out: kpt on wl ins fnl f but a being hld* **9/5**[1]

3 1 1/2 **Villa Marina**[41] 3-9-2 0 .... OlivierPeslier 9 73
(C Laffon-Parias, France) **23/5**[2]

4 shd **Olympic Light (FR)**[276] 3-9-2 0 .... StephanePasquier 3 73
(F Chappet, France) **10/1**

5 8 **A Fine Romance (FR)**[167] 3-9-2 0 .... MaximeGuyon 4 58
(Mme Pia Brandt, France) **12/1**

6 1 **Nefyn Beach (IRE)**[42] 1515 3-8-13 0 .... GeorgiaDobie(3) 10 56
(Jo Hughes, France) *wl into stride: led: rowed along over 2f out: rdn and hdd over 1f out: no ex ins fnl f* **86/1**

7 nk **Koubalibre (IRE)**[255] 3-9-2 0 .... AurelienLemaitre 7 55
(F Head, France) **23/1**

8 1 1/4 **Suquitho (FR)**[22] 2029 3-9-2 0 .... VincentCheminaud 6 53
(H-A Pantall, France) **71/10**

9 2 **Lake Alexandrina (IRE)**[30] 3-9-2 0 ....(b) Pierre-CharlesBoudot 8 49
(A Fabre, France) *settled midfield: pushed along over 2f out: rdn but fnd little over 1f out: styd on one pce fnl f* **31/5**

10 9 **Cinquain**[15] 2265 3-9-2 0 .... Louis-PhilippeBeuzelin 5 32
(Jo Hughes, France) *hld up in fnl duo: rdn along 2f out: sn lost tch and nvr a factor* **127/1**

2m 12.19s (132.19) **10 Ran SP% 119.6**
PARI-MUTUEL (all including 1 euro stake): WIN 5.90; PLACE 1.60, 1.30, 1.50; DF 10.50.
Owner H H Aga Khan **Bred** H H The Aga Khan Studs Sc **Trained** Chantilly, France

2440 NEWMARKET (R-H)

Thursday, May 16

OFFICIAL GOING: Good to firm (good in places; watered; 7.3)
Wind: light, against Weather: light cloud, dry

2760 HEATH COURT HOTEL FILLIES' H'CAP (A JOCKEY CLUB GRASSROOTS MIDDLE DISTANCE SERIES QUALIFIER) 1m
5:10 (5:11) (Class 5) (0-75,77) 3-Y-O
£4,528 (£1,347; £673; £336; £300; £300) **Stalls Low**

Form RPR

34-2 1 **I Am Magical**[19] 2103 3-9-8 76 .... HayleyTurner 6 85+
(Charlie Fellowes) *hld up in tch in midfield: nt clr run ent fnl 2f: swtchd lft over 1f out: str run u.p ins fnl f to ld towards fin* **6/1**[3]

22-4 2 1 **Al Messila**[16] 2251 3-9-2 70 .... TomMarquand 8 73
(Richard Hannon) *sn prom: chsd ldr over 6f out: rdn and ev ch whn bmpd jst over 2f out: stl chsng ldr and swtchd lft wl over 1f out: kpt on u.p ins fnl f: nt match wnr towards fin* **8/1**

61-6 3 1/2 **Dashed**[19] 2102 3-9-3 71 .... DavidEgan 9 73+
(Roger Varian) *stdd s: t.k.h: hld up wl in tch in midfield: effrt and clsd to ld but edgd rt jst over 2f out: wnt rt to r against far rail wl over 1f out: drvn ins fnl f: hdd and lost 2 pls towards fin* **3/1**[1]

5-50 4 1/2 **Ventura Glory**[19] 2101 3-9-1 69 .... HollieDoyle 13 70
(Richard Hannon) *in tch in last trio: effrt 3f out: edgd rt and hdwy over 1f out: styd on wl ins fnl f* **12/1**

35-2 5 1 1/4 **New Jazz (USA)**[23] 2018 3-9-9 77 .... NickyMackay 1 75+
(John Gosden) *chsd ldr for over 1f out: styd chsng ldrs tl pushed along and lost pl over 2f out: swtchd rt over 1f out: kpt on ins fnl f wout threatening ldrs* **7/2**[2]

0-41 6 2 **Material Girl**[12] 2420 3-9-0 75 ....(p) SeanKirrane(7) 12 69
(Richard Spencer) *chsd ldrs: ev ch and rdn whn pushed rt over 2f out: rallied over 1f out: no imp and one pce ins fnl f* **10/1**

0031 7 3/4 **Molly Mai**[10] 2482 3-8-7 61 .... JasonHart 11 53
(Philip McBride) *stdd s: hld up towards rr: effrt over 2f out: keeping on whn impeded and swtchd lft over 1f out: kpt on but no threat to ldrs ins fnl f* **6/1**[3]

64-0 8 2 1/2 **Elsie Violet (IRE)**[19] 2114 3-8-1 60 .... DarraghKeenan(5) 4 46
(Robert Eddery) *stdd s: hld up in last pair: effrt wl over 2f out: modest hdwy and swtchd lft over 1f out: nvr threatened ldrs* **50/1**

5-12 9 3/4 **Yimkin (IRE)**[42] 1543 3-9-8 76 .... HarryBentley 3 60
(Roger Charlton) *wl in tch: effrt to chal whn pushed rt jst over 2f out: lost pl u.p over 1f out: wknd ins fnl f* **6/1**[3]

23-0 10 7 **Canavese**[16] 2253 3-8-12 66 .... MartinDwyer 5 34
(Eve Johnson Houghton) *led tl jst over 2f out: sn struggling and lost pl: wknd fnl f* **40/1**

255- 11 2 1/4 **Loving Pearl**[231] 7709 3-9-0 68 .... NicolaCurrie 14 31
(John Berry) *a bhd* **66/1**

1m 42.56s (4.16) **Going Correction** +0.425s/f (Yiel) **11 Ran SP% 123.9**
Speed ratings (Par 96): **96,95,94,94,92 90,90,87,86,79 77**
CSF £56.03 CT £177.11 TOTE £7.50: £2.30, £3.20, £1.80; EX 58.40 Trifecta £209.70.
Owner Pearson, Magnier & Shanahan **Bred** Saleh Al Homaizi & Imad Al Sagar **Trained** Newmarket, Suffolk
■ Stewards' Enquiry : Hayley Turner two-day ban: used whip without giving time to respond (19 May & 2 Jun)
David Egan two-day ban: careless riding (30 May - 2 Jun)

FOCUS
The going was good, to firm in places with a stick reading of 7.3. Stands'-side course used. Stalls far side except 1m4f: centre. An interesting 3yo fillies handicap which will probably be worth following, even though the bare form is ordinary.

2761 HEATH COURT HOTEL EMPLOYEE AWARD NOVICE AUCTION STKS (PLUS 10 RACE) 6f
5:45 (5:47) (Class 4) 2-Y-O £5,175 (£1,540; £769; £384) **Stalls Low**

Form RPR

1 **Dancinginthewoods** 2-9-1 0 .... JoeyHaynes 9 77
(Dean Ivory) *hld up towards rr: effrt and hdwy whn shifted rt wl over 1f out: styd on wl to chse ldr wl ins fnl f: str run to ld last stride* **50/1**

1 2 shd **Apollinaire**[12] 2394 2-9-5 0 .... HarryBentley 7 81
(Ralph Beckett) *led: rdn over 2f out: kpt on u.p ins fnl f: hdd last stride* **11/2**[2]

3 1 1/4 **Gallaside (FR)** 2-9-3 0 .... HollieDoyle 14 75
(Archie Watson) *chsd ldr: rdn and unable qck over 1f out: kpt on same pce and lost 2nd wl ins fnl f* **7/2**[1]

4 1/2 **Broughtons Gold** 2-8-13 0 .... HayleyTurner 8 70
(Tom Clover) *trckd ldrs: effrt u.p over 1f out: kpt on same pce ins fnl f* **50/1**

5 3/4 **Hamish Macbeth** 2-9-5 0 .... AdamKirby 12 74
(Hugo Palmer) *dwlt: hld up in tch: effrt jst over 2f out: hdwy and rdn over 1f out: chse ldr jst ins fnl f: no imp: lost 2nd and wknd wl ins fnl f* **7/2**[1]

6 1 1/2 **Little Bird (IRE)** 2-8-10 0 .... TomMarquand 18 60
(Richard Hannon) *towards rr: rdn 3f out: hdwy and swtchd lft over 1f out: styd on ins fnl f: nvr threatened ldrs* **20/1**

7 1 1/4 **London Calling (IRE)** 2-9-3 0 .... DanielMuscutt 3 63
(Richard Spencer) *in tch in midfield: effrt and rn green ent fnl 2f: unable qck and wnt rt over 1f out: kpt on same pce ins fnl f* **33/1**

8 3/4 **Grove Ferry (IRE)** 2-9-5 0 .... MartinDwyer 17 63
(Andrew Balding) *s.i.s: towards rr: effrt over 2f out: sme prog over 1f out: swtchd lft and kpt on ins fnl f: nvr trbld ldrs* **16/1**

9 3/4 **Goddess Of Fire** 2-8-8 0 .... JasonHart 16 50
(Ed Dunlop) *in tch in midfield: effrt: rn green and unable qck over 1f out: kpt on same pce ins fnl f* **50/1**

10 hd **Jungle Book (GER)** 2-8-13 0 .... LukeMorris 11 54
(Jonathan Portman) *in tch in midfield: rn green unable qck and hung rt over 1f out: wl hld and kpt on same pce ins fnl f* **20/1**

11 3 **Pitchcombe** 2-9-1 0 .... HectorCrouch 6 47+
(Clive Cox) *midfield: shkn up and outpcd jst over 2f out: nt clr run and swtchd lft wl over 1f out: no threat to ldrs but kpt on ins fnl f* **14/1**

12 hd **Hot Date** 2-8-8 0 .... PaddyMathers 13 40
(George Margarson) *in rr: rdn over 2f out: sme hdwy to pass btn ins fnl f: nvr involved* **50/1**

13 1 1/2 **Fair Warning** 2-8-13 0 .... BrettDoyle 10 40
(Henry Spiller) *wnt rt leaving stalls and s.i.s: towards rr and rdn 3f out: sn struggling and wl btn whn swtchd lft wl over 1f out* **50/1**

2 14 1/2 **What A Business (IRE)**[28] 1879 2-9-1 0 .... NicolaCurrie 5 41
(Jamie Osborne) *trckd ldrs unable qck u.p and btn over 1f out: wknd fnl f* **7/1**

0 15 2 1/2 **Amber Road (IRE)**[31] 1821 2-8-5 0 .... ThoreHammerHansen(5) 1 28
(Richard Hannon) *chsd ldrs tl over 2f out: sn struggling u.p and lost pl: wknd fnl f* **6/1**[3]

16 2 3/4 **Sparkling Diamond** 2-8-8 0 .... DannyBrock 19 18
(Philip McBride) *in tch midfield: effrt ent fnl 2f: sn unable qck and struggling: wknd fnl f* **50/1**

0 17 4 1/2 **Dover Light**[38] 1651 2-9-3 0 .... RyanTate 4 19+
(Dean Ivory) *in tch in midfield: rdn 3f out: struggling and lost pl whn hmpd ent fnl 2f: no ch after* **66/1**

4 18 5 **Red Maharani**[28] 1879 2-8-10 0 .... DavidEgan 2
(James Given) *chsd ldrs tl lost pl qckly over 2f out: edgd rt wl over 1f out: bhd and eased ins fnl f (trainer said filly was unsuited by the good, good to firm in places ground)* **16/1**

19 19 **Lily Bonnette** 2-8-8 0 .... CharlieBennett 20
(Julia Feilden) *s.i.s: a bhd: t.o over 1f out (jockey said filly ran green)* **50/1**

1m 15.13s (3.23) **Going Correction** +0.425s/f (Yiel) **19 Ran SP% 132.7**
Speed ratings (Par 95): **95,94,93,92,91 89,87,86,85,85 81,81,79,78,75 71,65,59,33**
CSF £312.54 TOTE £55.50: £20.00, £2.30, £2.00; EX 835.30 Trifecta £2420.20.
Owner Solario Racing (Ashridge) **Bred** M E Broughton **Trained** Radlett, Herts

FOCUS
A big-field novice auction with another winner coming from the clouds. The race averages help with rating the form.

2762 NEWMARKET JOURNAL RACING AHEAD MAIDEN FILLIES' STKS (PLUS 10 RACE) 7f
6:20 (6:20) (Class 4) 3-Y-O £5,822 (£1,732; £865; £432) **Stalls Low**

Form RPR

0-6 1 **Manana Chica (IRE)**[14] 2340 3-9-0 0 .... HectorCrouch 4 72
(Clive Cox) *w ldr: drvn to ld jst over 1f out: hld on wl ins fnl f* **16/1**

0- 2 1/2 **Red Romance**[218] 8099 3-9-0 0 .... HollieDoyle 10 71
(Clive Cox) *sn led: rdn over 1f out: sn hdd but stl ev ch thrght fnl f: kpt on wl but a jst hld* **16/1**

3 shd **Powerful Star (IRE)** 3-9-0 0 .... DanielMuscutt 2 70
(David Lanigan) *hld up in tch towards rr: hdwy on far rail over 2f out: pressed ldrs and drvn 1f out: kpt on but a jst hld ins fnl f* **33/1**

4 3/4 **Clarion** 3-9-0 0 .... JasonWatson 5 68
(Sir Michael Stoute) *wl in tch in midfield: effrt over 1f out: kpt on ins fnl f: nvr quite enough pce to rch ldrs* **8/1**[3]

5- **5** 1 1/4 **Molly's Game**[205] 8525 3-9-0 77 HayleyTurner 19 65
(David Elsworth) *broke wl: sn stdd and hld up wl in tch in midfield: effrt over 1f out: kpt on same pce u.p ins fnl f* **16/1**

0 **6** shd **Raha**[23] 2023 3-9-0 0 CharlieBennett 15 65
(Julia Feilden) *chsd ldrs: unable qck u.p over 1f out: no imp and one pce ins fnl f* **100/1**

7 3/4 **Elena** 3-9-0 0 LukeMorris 11 63
(Charles Hills) *in tch in midfield: rdn wl over 1f out: keeping on but no threat to ldrs whn swtchd rt ins fnl f* **25/1**

2 **8** nk **Gentlewoman (IRE)**[29] 1855 3-9-0 0 RobertHavlin 9 62
(John Gosden) *t.k.h: chsd ldrs: effrt 2f out: drvn and unable qck ent fnl 2f: wknd fnl 100yds* **8/13**[1]

9 1 1/4 **Daryana** 3-9-0 0 CharlesBishop 3 59
(Eve Johnson Houghton) *in tch in midfield: effrt and unable qck over 1f out: no imp whn nudged rt ins fnl f* **25/1**

10 1 1/4 **Colonelle (USA)** 3-9-0 0 HarryBentley 1 55
(Ed Vaughan) *s.i.s: hld up in rr: effrt over 2f out: hung rt and swtchd lft over 1f out: kpt on but no threat to ldrs ins fnl f* **50/1**

6-0 **11** 1 3/4 **Sweet Jemima (USA)**[14] 2340 3-9-0 0 MartinDwyer 16 50
(William Muir) *in tch in midfield: effrt ent fnl 2f: rn green and unable qck over 1f out: wl hld but kpt on ins fnl f* **50/1**

12 2 1/2 **Break Of Day** 3-9-0 0 TomMarquand 14 44
(William Haggas) *a towards rr: effrt over 2f out: no imp: swtchd rt and kpt on same pce fr over 1f out* **5/1**[2]

6-0 **13** nk **Masai Spirit**[23] 2018 3-9-0 0 DannyBrock 13 43
(Philip McBride) *in tch in midfield: rdn over 2f out: sn struggling and lost pl over 1f out: wknd ins fnl f* **66/1**

0 **14** 3/4 **Ximena**[30] 1834 3-9-0 0 NicolaCurrie 8 41
(Samuel Farrell, Ire) *t.k.h: hld up in tch in midfield: pushed along 2f out: sn struggling and lost pl over 1f out: wknd fnl f (jockey said filly ran too free)* **66/1**

00 **P** **Gonbutnotforgotten (FR)**[30] 1838 3-9-0 0 JasonHart 18
(Philip McBride) *t.k.h: hld up in tch in rr: effrt ent fnl 2f: sn eased: p.u and dismntd 1f out* **50/1**

1m 28.45s (3.05) **Going Correction** +0.425s/f (Yiel) **15 Ran SP% 127.8**
Speed ratings (Par 98): **99,98,98,97,96 95,95,94,93,91 89,87,86,85,**
CSF £242.73 TOTE £21.00: £4.60, £3.70, £6.70; EX 248.40 Trifecta £3332.40.
Owner Martin McHale & Partners **Bred** Breeding Capital Plc **Trained** Lambourn, Berks

FOCUS
A maiden for fillies with the weak favourite turned over.

2763 BESTWESTERN.CO.UK H'CAP 1m 4f
6:55 (6:56) (Class 4) (0-85,85) 4-Y-O+

£7,762 (£2,310; £1,154; £577; £300; £300) **Stalls** Centre

Form RPR

211- **1** **Hameem**[236] 7544 4-9-7 85 JimCrowley 4 95+
(John Gosden) *chsd ldr tl clsd to ld travelling strly over 2f out: rdn and kicked clr over 1f out: r.o wl: comf* **9/4**[1]

40-2 **2** 3 1/2 **C'Est No Mour (GER)**[17] 2209 6-9-1 79 TomMarquand 3 82
(Peter Hedger) *stdd s: hld up in tch in last pair: hdwy to chse ldrs 4f out: effrt to chse wnr 2f out: no imp and kpt on same pce ins fnl f* **7/2**[2]

55- **3** 3/4 **Needs To Be Seen (FR)**[67] 6937 4-8-11 75 BrettDoyle 6 77
(John Ryan) *wnt rt leaving stalls: hld up in tch in last pair: hdwy 5f out: effrt in 5th over 2f out: nt clr run and swtchd lft 2f out: racd awkwardly but wnt 3rd over 1f out: kpt on same pce ins fnl f* **33/1**

65-0 **4** 3 1/2 **Blazing Saddles**[19] 2092 4-8-13 77 (b[1]) HarryBentley 9 73
(Ralph Beckett) *in tch in last trio: dropped to rr and rdn over 2f out: no ch w wnr but plugged on u.p ins fnl f* **5/1**

1444 **5** 1 **The Night King**[16] 2259 4-8-2 71 DarraghKeenan(5) 8 66
(Mick Quinn) *in tch in midfield tl dropped to rr 4f out: sme prog u.p but no threat to wnr: plugged on same pce ins fnl f* **12/1**

65-5 **6** 6 **Medalla De Oro**[22] 2032 5-9-2 80 LukeMorris 1 65
(Tom Clover) *led tl over 2f out: sn u.p and struggling to qckn: lost pl and wknd over 1f out* **9/2**[3]

11-3 **7** 14 **The Pinto Kid (FR)**[21] 2059 4-8-13 77 (t) GeorgeWood 2 40
(James Fanshawe) *chsd ldrs: drvn and unable qck over 2f out: lost pl and wknd fnl f (jockey said gelding was never travelling)* **5/1**

2m 37.89s (5.39) **Going Correction** +0.425s/f (Yiel) **7 Ran SP% 115.1**
Speed ratings (Par 105): **99,96,96,93,93 89,79**
CSF £10.49 CT £196.56 TOTE £2.60: £2.00, £2.10; EX 11.20 Trifecta £121.80.
Owner Ms Hissa Hamdan Al Maktoum **Bred** Haras De Chevotel **Trained** Newmarket, Suffolk
■ Amourice was withdrawn. Price at time of withdrawal 9-1. Rule 4 applies to all bets struck prior to withdrawal, but not to SP bets. Deduction - 10p in the pound. New market formed.

FOCUS
Race distance increased by 12yds. A competitive-looking handicap but the favourite racked up a hat-trick without any fuss. There's a bit of doubt over the depth to this.

2764 HEATH COURT HOTEL BRITISH EBF MAIDEN STKS (PLUS 10 RACE) 1m 2f
7:30 (7:37) (Class 4) 3-Y-O **£5,822** (£1,732; £865; £432) **Stalls** Low

Form RPR

2-5 **1** **Apparate**[19] 2099 3-9-5 0 DavidEgan 11 81+
(Roger Varian) *mde all and sn crossed to far rail: gng best ent fnl 2f: 3 l clr and rdn over 1f out: much reduced ld towards fin but a holding on: rdn out* **7/4**[1]

2 1/2 **Harrovian** 3-9-5 0 RobertHavlin 3 80+
(John Gosden) *s.i.s: t.k.h: hld up in rr and rn green: pushed along 3f out: wnt rt over 1f out and nt clr run over 1f out: hdwy 1f out: str run to go 2nd and swtchd lft wl ins fnl f: nt quite rch wnr (jockey said colt was denied a clear run)* **10/1**

3 1 3/4 **Dilmun Dynasty (IRE)** 3-9-5 0 JasonWatson 8 76+
(Sir Michael Stoute) *in tch in midfield: rdn 3f out: sn struggling to qckn and outpcd: wnt 3rd over 1f out: kpt on to chse wnr 100yds out: 3rd and kpt on steadily fnl 75yds* **7/1**

- **4** 4 **Albadr (USA)** 3-9-5 0 JimCrowley 2 68
(John Gosden) *s.i.s: hld up in last trio: effrt over 2f out: sn outpcd: kpt on u.p and modest 4th 1f out: plugged on same pce and no imp ins fnl f* **5/1**[3]

5 1 **Mr Carpenter (IRE)** 3-9-5 0 DanielMuscutt 1 66
(David Lanigan) *wnt lft leaving stalls: chsd ldrs tl wnt 2nd ent fnl 2f: hung rt and unable qck over 1f out: lost wl hld 2nd 100yds out and wknd towards fin* **11/2**

6 3/4 **Noble Account** 3-9-5 0 CharlieBennett 10 65
(Julia Feilden) *restless in stalls: dwlt: t.k.h: hld up in tch in last trio: effrt wl over 2f out: sn outpcd: no ch w wnr but plugged on ins fnl f* **50/1**

00 **7** 1 3/4 **Crystal Tribe (IRE)**[23] 2023 3-8-12 0 GianlucaSanna(7) 4 61
(William Haggas) *chsd ldrs tl wnt 2nd over 2f out: sn hung lft and outpcd: lost pl over 1f out: wknd fnl f* **25/1**

00 **8** 1 1/4 **Best Haaf**[23] 2023 3-9-5 0 AlistairRawlinson 7 59
(Michael Appleby) *chsd wnr tl over 2f out: sn struggling and bhd over 1f out: wknd fnl f* **100/1**

0- **9** nk **Youarestar**[202] 8607 3-9-5 0 TomMarquand 6 58
(William Haggas) *t.k.h: hld up in tch in midfield: rdn over 2f out: sn struggling and lost pl over 1f out: wknd fnl f* **9/2**[2]

10 32 **Carleen** 3-9-0 0 GeorgeWood 9
(Chris Wall) *in tch in midfield on outer tl dropped to rr 4f out: lost tch over 2f out: t.o (jockey said filly ran green)* **33/1**

2m 10.45s (5.05) **Going Correction** +0.425s/f (Yiel) **10 Ran SP% 117.9**
Speed ratings (Par 101): **96,95,94,91,90 89,88,87,86,61**
CSF £21.11 TOTE £2.50: £1.10, £3.10, £2.70; EX 23.00 Trifecta £109.80.
Owner Sheikh Mohammed Obaid Al Maktoum **Bred** Sheikh Mohammed Obaid Al Maktoum **Trained** Newmarket, Suffolk

FOCUS
Some interesting sorts in this maiden and an eye-catching runner-up. The level of the form is set around the sixth.

2765 HEATH COURT HOTEL DINING CLUB H'CAP 1m 2f
8:05 (8:07) (Class 4) (0-80,78) 3-Y-O

£7,762 (£2,310; £1,154; £577; £300; £300) **Stalls** Low

Form RPR

36-6 **1** **Arctic Fox**[16] 2251 3-9-0 71 PaddyMathers 3 85+
(Richard Fahey) *stdd after s: t.k.h: hld up in tch in rr: hdwy and swtchd rt jst over 2f out: rdn to ld over 1f out: in command and r.o wl ins fnl f* **16/1**

5-62 **2** 2 **Holy Kingdom (IRE)**[110] 442 3-9-5 76 LukeMorris 6 85
(Tom Clover) *hld up wl in tch: effrt and swtchd lft over 2f out: styd on to chse wnr wl ins fnl f: nvr getting on terms but kpt on for clr 2nd* **13/2**

022- **3** 3 3/4 **Sezim**[168] 9314 3-9-6 77 DavidEgan 1 79
(Roger Varian) *pressed ldrs: rdn and ev ch 3f out tl chsd wnr but unable to match her pce 1f out: lost 2nd and wknd wl ins fnl f* **11/4**[1]

541- **4** hd **Battle Of Wills (IRE)**[148] 9611 3-9-7 78 AdamKirby 5 79
(James Tate) *led early: sn busted but styd pressing ldr: rdn to ld over 2f out: hdd and unable qck over 1f out: wknd ins fnl f* **7/1**

02-0 **5** 1/2 **Mary Somerville**[16] 2251 3-9-5 76 RobertHavlin 7 76
(John Gosden) *hld up in tch: clsd to chal 3f out: unable qck and wandered over 1f out: wknd ins fnl f* **5/1**[3]

642- **6** 4 1/2 **Copal**[181] 9105 3-9-7 78 HarryBentley 2 69
(Ralph Beckett) *t.k.h: hld up in tch: outpcd and hung rt 2f out: wl btn over 1f out: wknd fnl f* **7/2**[2]

641- **7** 6 **Minnelli**[253] 6950 3-8-12 69 JasonHart 4 48
(Philip McBride) *sn led: rdn and hdd over 2f out: sn lost pl and bhd over 1f out: wknd fnl f* **33/1**

333- **8** nk **Amjaady (USA)**[180] 9131 3-9-5 76 (b) JimCrowley 8 55
(Owen Burrows) *t.k.h: hld up in tch: clsd to chse ldrs 3f out: pushed along and fnd little over 2f out: wl btn over 1f out: wknd fnl f (jockey said gelding ran too free)* **6/1**

2m 8.9s (3.50) **Going Correction** +0.425s/f (Yiel) **8 Ran SP% 114.5**
Speed ratings (Par 101): **103,101,98,98,97 94,89,89**
CSF £115.02 CT £376.95 TOTE £15.10: £3.40, £2.30, £1.60; EX 85.40 Trifecta £703.20.
Owner Sir Robert Ogden **Bred** Sir Robert Ogden **Trained** Musley Bank, N Yorks

FOCUS
A decent Class 4 with a surprise runaway winner. The 1-2 came from the rear.

2766 PARK REGIS KRIS KIN HOTEL DUBAI H'CAP 1m
8:35 (8:36) (Class 4) (0-85,86) 3-Y-O

£7,762 (£2,310; £1,154; £577; £300; £300) **Stalls** Low

Form RPR

5-22 **1** **Migration (IRE)**[20] 2082 3-10-0 86 JasonWatson 1 94+
(David Menuisier) *s.i.s: hld up wl in tch in last trio: clsd and nt clr run ent fnl 2f: hdwy over 1f out: str run u.p to ld wl ins fnl f: sn in command and eased cl home* **6/4**[1]

2-40 **2** 1 **Ginger Fox**[20] 2078 3-9-3 75 DavidEgan 8 78
(Ian Williams) *in tch in midfield: effrt over 2f out: drvn and ev ch over 1f out: kpt on ins fnl f: nt match pce of wnr fnl 75yds: wnt 2nd last strides* **16/1**

0-13 **3** nk **Balladeer**[22] 2035 3-9-7 79 HayleyTurner 9 81
(Michael Bell) *chsd ldrs tl wnt 2nd 6f out: led 4f out: rdn jst over 2f out: drvn over 1f out: hdd and no ex wl ins fnl f: lost 2nd last strides* **9/2**[2]

40-1 **4** 1 **Smile A Mile (IRE)**[13] 2371 3-9-7 79 SilvestreDeSousa 4 79
(Mark Johnston) *wnt lft leaving stalls: sn rcvrd and chsd ldr: led over 6f out: hdd but styd upsides ldr 4f out: hrd drvn over 1f out: no ex and outpcd wl ins fnl f* **9/2**[2]

30-0 **5** nk **Production**[12] 2395 3-9-7 79 TomMarquand 3 78
(Richard Hannon) *led tl over 6f out: styd chsng ldrs: unable qck u.p 1f out: kpt on same pce ins fnl f* **20/1**

050- **6** hd **Bullington Boy (FR)**[229] 7765 3-9-4 76 CharlieBennett 2 75
(Jane Chapple-Hyam) *hld up in tch in last trio: nt clr run 2f out and swtchd lft over 1f out: kpt on on u.p ins fnl f* **33/1**

052- **7** 1 1/2 **Crimewave (IRE)**[159] 9459 3-9-7 79 LukeMorris 5 74
(Tom Clover) *nudged leaving stalls: wl in tch in midfield: n.m.r 2f out: unable qck over 1f out: wl hld and kpt on same pce ins fnl f* **12/1**

4-64 **8** hd **Bataar (IRE)**[13] 2371 3-8-11 69 PaddyMathers 11 64
(Richard Fahey) *stdd s: hld up in tch in last trio: clsd ent fnl 2f: no imp u.p 1f out: wl hld and plugged on same pce ins fnl f* **16/1**

5-60 **9** 6 **Venedegar (IRE)**[20] 2075 3-9-5 77 RobertHavlin 7 58
(Ed Dunlop) *wl in tch in midfield: rdn: outpcd and btn over 1f out: wknd ins fnl f* **12/1**

0 **10** 7 **The Corporal (IRE)**[29] 1857 3-9-4 76 GeorgeWood 6 41
(Chris Wall) *in tch in midfield tl lost pl and bhd 2f out: wknd over 1f out* **10/1**[3]

1m 40.26s (1.86) **Going Correction** +0.425s/f (Yiel) **10 Ran SP% 120.3**
Speed ratings (Par 101): **107,106,105,104,104 104,102,102,96,89**
CSF £31.27 CT £98.38 TOTE £2.50: £1.20, £3.60, £1.90; EX 28.80 Trifecta £110.90.
Owner Gail Brown Racing (IX) **Bred** Ms C Peddie **Trained** Pulborough, W Sussex

FOCUS
A decent 3yo handicap with an improving winner who could rank much higher. The form's rated around the second and third.
T/Plt: £2,502.10 to a £1 stake. Pool: £55,629.25 - 16.23 winning units T/Qpdt: £434.50 to a £1 stake. Pool: £7,957.11 - 13.55 winning units **Steve Payne**

2338 **SALISBURY** (R-H)
Thursday, May 16

OFFICIAL GOING: Good to firm (good in places; watered; 8.5)
Wind: virtually nil Weather: sunny with some cloud

2767 SIMON & NERYS DUTFIELD MEMORIAL NOVICE STKS (PLUS 10 RACE) 5f
1:40 (1:41) (Class 4) 2-Y-O £5,110 (£1,520; £759; £379) Stalls Low

Form RPR
1 **Symbolize (IRE)** 2-9-5 0 .... DavidProbert 3 88+
(Andrew Balding) *led early: trckd ldrs: led ent fnl f: r.o wl: readily* **7/2[2]**
4 2 1 ¾ **Aroha (IRE)**[18] 2138 2-9-0 0 .... CallumShepherd 6 75
(Brian Meehan) *sn led: rdn and hdd ent fnl f: kpt on but nt pce of wnr* **10/1**
3 ¾ **Shammah (IRE)** 2-9-0 0 .... SeanLevey 7 72
(Richard Hannon) *trckd ldr: rdn and ev ch 2f out: hld ent fnl f: kpt on same pce* **6/1[3]**
4 ¾ **Born To Destroy** 2-9-5 0 .... CharlesBishop 9 74
(Richard Spencer) *carried lft s: sn trcking ldrs: rdn over 1f out: kpt on same pce fnl f* **7/2[2]**
5 2 **Dark Kris (IRE)** 2-9-5 0 .... ShaneKelly 8 67
(Richard Hughes) *wnt lft s: trckd ldrs: rdn 2f out: kpt on but nt pce to get on terms* **7/1**
6 6 **Welcome Surprise (IRE)** 2-9-5 0 .... JasonWatson 5 46+
(Saeed bin Suroor) *edgd rt 1st f cl to rails: in tch: rdn over 2f out: nt pce to get involved: fdd ins fnl f* **11/4[1]**
7 2 ¾ **Magical Force** 2-9-0 0 .... RobHornby 2 31
(Rod Millman) *sn pushed along: a towards rr* **40/1**
8 2 ½ **Summers Way** 2-8-9 0 .... ThoreHammerHansen(5) 10 22
(Bill Turner) *mid-div: rdn over 2f out: nvr any imp: wknd ent fnl f* **50/1**
9 nk **Newton Jack** 2-9-5 0 .... GeorgeDowning 11 26
(Stuart Kittow) *s.i.s: a towards rr* **50/1**
10 4 **Mungo's Quest (IRE)** 2-9-5 0 .... KierenFox 4 11
(Simon Dow) *sn pushed along: a towards rr* **50/1**
11 ½ **Sir Chancealot (IRE)** 2-9-5 0 .... RobertHavlin 1 9
(Amanda Perrett) *sn outpcd: a towards rr* **25/1**

1m 0.26s (-0.24) **Going Correction** -0.275s/f (Firm) 11 Ran SP% **119.2**
Speed ratings (Par 95): **90,87,86,84,81 72,67,63,63,56 55**
CSF £37.05 TOTE £4.10: £1.70, £2.10, £2.00; EX 31.50 Trifecta £141.40.
Owner Sheikh Juma Dalmook Al Maktoum **Bred** Dc Investments Ltd **Trained** Kingsclere, Hants

FOCUS
Not many got into what was probably a decent novice event. On quickish ground, the time was only 0.56sec outside standard. The winner looks useful.

2768 BYERLEY STUD BRITISH EBF FILLIES' H'CAP 1m 1f 201y
2:10 (2:12) (Class 3) (0-90,83) 3-Y-O £12,450 (£3,728; £1,864; £932; £466; £234) Stalls Low

Form RPR
26-1 1 **Bella Vita**[13] 2361 3-9-1 77 .... CharlesBishop 3 85
(Eve Johnson Houghton) *trckd ldrs: pushed along briefly 6f out: shkn up over 3f out: rdn and hdwy over 1f out: r.o wl ins fnl f: led fnl 100yds: won gng away* **11/4[2]**
41-0 2 1 ¾ **Baba Ghanouj (IRE)**[15] 2268 3-9-6 82 .... DavidProbert 2 86
(Ed Walker) *led early: trckd ldrs: nt clrest of runs tl 2f out: rdn to ld ent fnl f: kpt on but nt pce of wnr whn hdd fnl 100yds* **4/1[3]**
130- 3 ¾ **Quintada**[212] 8302 3-9-2 78 .... FrannyNorton 5 80
(Mark Johnston) *trckd ldr: rdn and ev ch 2f out: kpt on same pce fnl f* **6/1**
13-0 4 1 ¼ **Ideological (IRE)**[28] 1897 3-9-7 83 .... JackMitchell 1 83
(Roger Varian) *hld up in last pair: rdn over 2f out: hdwy over 1f out: kpt on ins fnl f* **9/1**
23-1 5 nse **Frisella**[70] 1064 3-9-4 80 ....(h) RobertHavlin 4 79
(John Gosden) *sn led: rdn jst over 2f out: sn hung lft: hdd ent fnl f: no ex fnl 120yds (jockey said filly hung left handed)* **2/1[1]**
16-4 6 5 **Sufficient**[18] 2144 3-9-2 78 .... RobHornby 6 67
(Rod Millman) *racd keenly: hld up: hdwy over 3f out: rdn w ch over 2f out: wknd over 1f out* **12/1**

2m 6.92s (-3.58) **Going Correction** -0.275s/f (Firm) 6 Ran SP% **112.0**
Speed ratings (Par 100): **103,101,101,100,99 95**
CSF £13.97 TOTE £3.40: £3.20, £1.80; EX 13.10 Trifecta £59.20.
Owner Mrs Heather Raw **Bred** Shoreham Stud **Trained** Blewbury, Oxon

FOCUS
A competitive fillies' handicap. The form is rated around the race average.

2769 PENANG TURF CLUB MALAYSIA NOVICE STKS (C&G) 1m 1f 201y
2:45 (2:46) (Class 5) 3-Y-O+ £4,787 (£1,424; £711; £355) Stalls Low

Form RPR
21- 1 **Humanitarian (USA)**[180] 9123 3-9-5 0 .... RobertHavlin 4 98
(John Gosden) *mde all: rdn ent fnl f: kpt on wl* **1/3[1]**
0- 2 ¾ **Alignak**[204] 8552 3-8-12 0 .... RichardKingscote 3 89
(Sir Michael Stoute) *hmpd 1st f: trckd ldrs: rdn 2f out: chsd wnr ent fnl f: kpt on wl but a being hld* **14/1**
52 3 3 **Storting**[19] 2120 3-8-12 0 .... FrannyNorton 6 83
(Mick Channon) *trckd wnr: chal 3f out tl rdn over 2f out: hld in 3rd whn drifted lft to stands' side rails ent fnl f: sn no ex* **5/1[2]**
60 4 7 **Corncrake**[17] 2208 3-8-12 0 .... SeanLevey 1 69
(Richard Hannon) *hmpd 1st f: hld up bhd ldrs: rdn into 4th over 2f out: nt pce to get on terms: fdd ins fnl f* **50/1**
0-3 5 ¾ **Sawasdee (IRE)**[47] 1419 3-8-12 0 .... DavidProbert 7 68
(Andrew Balding) *last pair: hdwy over 3f out: effrt over 2f out: nt pce to threaten: fdd ins fnl f* **9/1**
0-4 6 10 **Platform Nineteen (IRE)**[19] 2120 3-8-9 0 .... CameronNoble(3) 2 48
(Michael Bell) *s.i.s: in rr: nvr threatened to get involved* **66/1**
7 15 **Paseo** 3-8-12 0 .... JasonWatson 8 18
(Amanda Perrett) *trckd ldrs: rdn over 3f out: wknd over 2f out* **20/1**
2- 8 10 **Galileo Silver (IRE)**[346] 3434 4-9-12 0 .... LouisSteward 5
(Alan King) *hmpd 1st f: trckd ldrs: rdn over 3f out: wknd over 2f out* **7/1[3]**

2m 6.24s (-4.26) **Going Correction** -0.275s/f (Firm) 8 Ran SP% **129.1**
WFA 3 from 4yo 14lb
Speed ratings (Par 103): **106,105,103,97,96 88,76,68**
CSF £9.44 TOTE £1.20: £1.02, £2.90, £1.40; EX 8.10 Trifecta £28.40.
Owner HH Sheikh Zayed bin Mohammed Racing **Bred** W S Farish **Trained** Newmarket, Suffolk

FOCUS
The first three finished clear in this novice event. The time was 0.68sec quicker than the preceding Class 3 fillies' handicap and the winner is potentially smart.

2770 SMITH & WILLIAMSON FILLIES' NOVICE STKS (DIV I) 1m 1f 201y
3:20 (3:23) (Class 5) 3-Y-O+ £4,787 (£1,424; £711; £355) Stalls Low

Form RPR
0 1 **Motivate Me (FR)**[20] 2087 3-8-12 0 .... JackMitchell 2 81+
(Roger Varian) *trckd ldrs: rdn over 2f out: styd on ins fnl f: led fnl 120yds: rdn out* **10/1**
5 2 ¾ **Norma**[17] 2208 3-8-12 0 .... GeorgeWood 12 79
(James Fanshawe) *in tch: shkn up and hdwy over 2f out: styd on to hold ev ch fnl 120yds: hld towards fin* **7/1[2]**
4-0 3 1 ¼ **Promise Of Success**[91] 727 3-8-12 0 .... PatCosgrave 14 76
(Saeed bin Suroor) *trckd ldrs: chal 3f out: sn rdn: ev ch ins fnl f: no ex fnl 75yds* **15/2[3]**
2 4 nk **Inference**[18] 2148 3-8-12 0 .... RobertHavlin 3 75
(John Gosden) *led: rdn wl over 2f out: hdd fnl 120yds: no ex towards fin* **11/10[1]**
5 1 ¾ **Hazaranda** 3-8-12 0 .... RichardKingscote 9 72
(Sir Michael Stoute) *trckd ldr: rdn 3f out: one pce fnl 2f* **15/2[3]**
6 1 ¾ **Hereby (IRE)** 3-8-12 0 .... JosephineGordon 8 68+
(Ralph Beckett) *s.i.s: towards rr: hmpd over 5f out: stdy prog over 1f out: styd on nicely fnl f wout ever threatening to get on terms* **16/1**
4 7 ½ **Libbretta**[13] 2361 4-9-5 0 .... EllieMacKenzie(7) 7 68
(John E Long) *mid-div: rdn over 2f out: kpt on but nt pce to get on terms fnl f* **50/1**
0 8 nk **Mousebird (IRE)**[13] 2361 3-8-12 0 .... SeanLevey 6 66
(Hughie Morrison) *mid-div: rdn over 2f out: kpt on but nt pce to get involved* **66/1**
9 1 ¼ **Monica Sheriff** 3-8-12 0 .... LiamJones 10 64+
(William Haggas) *swtchd rt 1st f: towards rr: jinked lft over 5f out: styd on fnl f wout ever threatening* **25/1**
3- 10 3 ¾ **Oydis**[194] 8833 3-8-12 0 ....(h[1]) PatDobbs 13 56
(Ralph Beckett) *s.i.s: towards rr: sme late prog but nvr any threat* **12/1**
11 nk **Canoodling** 3-8-12 0 .... JasonWatson 5 56
(Ian Williams) *mid-div: rdn over 2f out: wknd ent fnl f* **50/1**
0-6 12 3 ¾ **Dear Miriam (IRE)**[48] 1397 3-8-12 0 .... CallumShepherd 11 48
(Mick Channon) *hmpd s: a towards rr* **66/1**
0-0 13 15 **Vakilita (IRE)**[13] 2354 3-8-12 0 .... DavidProbert 4 18
(Andrew Balding) *mid-div: rdn over 3f out: wknd over 2f out* **80/1**
14 9 **Ord River** 4-9-12 0 .... DaneO'Neill 1 1
(Henry Candy) *mid-div: rdn over 3f out: wknd over 2f out* **50/1**

2m 7.81s (-2.69) **Going Correction** -0.275s/f (Firm) 14 Ran SP% **120.3**
WFA 3 from 4yo 14lb
Speed ratings (Par 100): **99,98,97,97,95 94,93,93,92,89 89,86,74,67**
CSF £76.07 TOTE £11.20: £1.90, £2.30, £2.40; EX 102.30 Trifecta £568.90.
Owner Saif Ali **Bred** Dermot Cantillon **Trained** Newmarket, Suffolk

FOCUS
There were some well-bred fillies on parade, and it's a race that should produce winners. It was the slower division by 1.25sec and the slowest of four 1m2f races on the day. The first two were improvers.

2771 SMITH & WILLIAMSON FILLIES' NOVICE STKS (DIV II) 1m 1f 201y
3:55 (3:56) (Class 5) 3-Y-O+ £4,787 (£1,424; £711; £355) Stalls Low

Form RPR
6 1 **La Lune**[20] 2087 3-8-12 0 .... CharlesBishop 14 87
(Henry Candy) *trckd ldrs: rdn to chal over 2f out: led ent fnl f: styd on wl: readily* **12/1**
2 2 ½ **The Very Moon** 3-8-12 0 .... RichardKingscote 9 82
(Sir Michael Stoute) *mid-div: hdwy fr 3f out: rdn to chse ldng pair over 1f out: styd on wl to go 2nd fnl 130yds: no threat to wnr* **14/1**
2- 3 3 **Stratification (USA)**[154] 9522 3-8-12 0 .... RobertHavlin 7 76
(John Gosden) *trckd ldrs led over 2f out: sn rdn: hdd ent fnl f: no ex fnl 130yds* **1/1[1]**
4 8 **Monaafasah (IRE)** 3-8-12 0 .... DaneO'Neill 11 60
(Marcus Tregoning) *s.i.s: towards rr: rdn and hdwy fr 2f out: styd on into 4th fnl f wout ever threatening to get on terms* **25/1**
0-4 5 1 ¾ **Tamachan**[34] 1739 3-8-12 0 ....(h) JasonWatson 12 57
(Roger Charlton) *mid-div: pushed along over 3f out: wnt hld 5th over 2f out: styd on same pce fnl f* **20/1**
6 7 **Ela Katrina** 3-8-12 0 .... PatDobbs 6 43
(Roger Varian) *hld up towards rr: stdy prog fr 2f out: styd on wout ever threatening fnl f* **16/1**
7 2 **Quiet Shy (FR)** 4-9-12 0 .... JohnFahy 2 40
(Michael Scudamore) *s.i.s: towards rr: struggling 3f out: styd on fnl f: n.d* **100/1**
0 8 1 ¼ **Nespola**[19] 2103 3-8-12 0 .... JackMitchell 1 36
(Roger Varian) *led: rdn and hdd over 2f out: wknd ent fnl f* **33/1**
9 2 **Eagle Queen** 3-8-12 0 .... DavidProbert 4 32
(Andrew Balding) *mid-div: rdn 3f out: nvr any imp: wknd over 1f out* **7/1[2]**
5- 10 ¾ **Isabella Brant (FR)**[211] 8329 3-8-12 0 .... RobHornby 8 31
(Ralph Beckett) *a towards rr* **9/1**
0 11 1 ¼ **All Right**[38] 1652 3-8-12 0 .... PatCosgrave 10 28
(Henry Candy) *mid-div: pushed along over 4f out: rdn over 3f out: little imp: wknd fnl f* **66/1**
0- 12 nk **Wannie Mae (IRE)**[201] 8643 3-8-9 0 .... GeorgiaCox(3) 5 27
(William Haggas) *s.i.s: a in rr (jockey said filly was never travelling)* **15/2[3]**
13 1 ¾ **Lady Elysia** 3-8-9 0 .... MitchGodwin(3) 13 24
(Harry Dunlop) *in tch: rdn over 3f out: wknd over 2f out* **100/1**
14 ¾ **Avorisk Et Perils (FR)**[34] 4-9-5 0 .... RhysClutterbuck(7) 3 23
(Gary Moore) *trckd ldr tl rdn 3f out: sn wknd* **200/1**

2m 6.56s (-3.94) **Going Correction** -0.275s/f (Firm) 14 Ran SP% **120.0**
WFA 3 from 4yo 14lb
Speed ratings (Par 100): **104,102,99,93,91 86,84,83,82,81 80,80,78,78**
CSF £161.22 TOTE £12.10: £2.90, £2.90, £1.10; EX 170.70 Trifecta £650.90.
Owner Alizeti Partners, Clive & Pamela Brandon **Bred** Haddenham Stud Farm Ltd **Trained** Kingston Warren, Oxon

FOCUS
The quickest of the three ten-furlong races on the card, this was 1.25sec faster than the first division. They finished well spread out and the form could rate a little higher.

2772 PENANG TURF CLUB MALAYSIA H'CAP 6f
4:25 (4:27) (Class 5) (0-70,72) 3-Y-O

£4,075 (£1,212; £606; £303; £300; £300) **Stalls** Low

Form RPR

215- **1** **Chitra**[189] 8955 3-9-5 **68**.................................... RichardKingscote 7 76
(Daniel Kubler) *trckd ldr: rdn to ld over 1f out: hld on wl fnl 120yds* **5/1**[3]

03-1 **2** *nk* **Spirit Of May**[21] 2063 3-9-7 **70**.................................... PatDobbs 11 77
(Roger Teal) *trckd ldrs: rdn over 1f out: pressed wnr ins fnl f: kpt on but a being hld* **9/2**[2]

-505 **3** *2* **Under Curfew**[19] 2114 3-9-0 **63**.................................... JosephineGordon 8 64
(Tony Carroll) *mid-div: rdn over 2f out: hdwy over 1f out: r.o fnl f* **15/2**

30-0 **4** *1 ½* **Cracking Speed (IRE)**[17] 2204 3-9-4 **67**..........................(t) SeanLevey 5 63
(Richard Hannon) *mid-div: swtchd lft 2f out: hdwy over 1f out: kpt on ins fnl f* **6/1**

300- **5** *¾* **Boorowa**[199] 8692 3-8-13 **62**.................................... RobHornby 6 56
(Ali Stronge) *s.i.s: towards rr: rdn and hdwy over 1f out: r.o fnl f* **40/1**

2-16 **6** *1 ¾* **Warning Fire**[18] 2149 3-9-9 **72**.................................... FrannyNorton 4 60
(Mark Johnston) *chsd ldrs: rdn 2f out: fdd ins fnl f* **3/1**[1]

060- **7** *nk* **Song Of The Isles (IRE)**[247] 7151 3-8-5 **61**........... EllieMacKenzie(7) 1 48
(Heather Main) *trckd ldrs: rdn over 2f out: sn one pce* **33/1**

040- **8** *hd* **Drumnadrochit**[212] 8296 3-9-2 **65**..........................(b[1]) CallumShepherd 3 51
(Charles Hills) *led: rdn and hdd 2f out: kpt on tl no ex fnl 140yds (jockey said gelding lost its action in final 110yds)* **12/1**

10-0 **9** *1 ¼* **Penarth Pier (IRE)**[62] 1219 3-9-6 **69**.................................... DaneO'Neill 9 51
(Richard Hannon) *dwlt bdly: in rr: nvr rcvrd* **25/1**

300- **10** *1 ¾* **Cavalry Park**[162] 9396 3-9-3 **66**.................................... DavidProbert 2 43
(Charlie Fellowes) *chsd ldrs: rdn over 2f out: wknd jst over 1f out* **10/1**

0-00 **11** *2 ¼* **Clubora (USA)**[23] 2007 3-8-2 **51**.................................... JimmyQuinn 13 21
(Richard Hannon) *hmpd s: a towards rr* **40/1**

003- **12** *6* **Atty's Edge**[199] 8690 3-9-1 **64**.................................... ShaneKelly 12 14
(Christopher Mason) *awkwardly away: mid-div: hung lft and wknd 2f out (jockey said colt hung left-handed)* **18/1**

1m 13.17s (-1.33) **Going Correction** -0.275s/f (Firm) **12** Ran SP% **119.6**
Speed ratings (Par 99): **97,96,93,91,90 88,88,87,86,83 80,72**
CSF £27.15 CT £168.94 TOTE £6.70: £2.20, £1.80, £2.70; EX 35.60 Trifecta £188.90.
Owner Mr & Mrs G Middlebrook **Bred** Mr & Mrs G Middlebrook **Trained** Lambourn, Berks

FOCUS
Just an ordinary sprint handicap. The winner built on her progressive 2yo form.

2773 PETER SYMONDS CATERING CLAIMING STKS 6f 213y
4:55 (4:56) (Class 5) 3-Y-O

£4,075 (£1,212; £606; £303; £300; £300) **Stalls** Low

Form RPR

60-0 **1** **Oofy Prosser (IRE)**[17] 2190 3-8-8 50..........................(p[1]) MitchGodwin(3) 1 63
(Harry Dunlop) *trckd ldrs: swtchd to centre and rdn 2f out: led ins fnl f: r.o wl* **20/1**

0-66 **2** *1* **Jungle Inthebungle (IRE)**[23] 2008 3-9-7 79.................... FrannyNorton 2 71
(Mick Channon) *led early: prom: rdn for str chal over 2f out: led briefly ent fnl f: kpt on but hld fnl 120yds* **1/1**[1]

4-00 **3** *2 ½* **Superstition**[13] 2357 3-8-3 52..........................(b[1]) JosephineGordon 5 46
(Eve Johnson Houghton) *trckd ldr: led over 2f out: sn rdn: hdd ent fnl f: sn no ex* **10/1**[3]

0 **4** *4* **Heldtoransom**[10] 2488 3-7-7 0.................................... IsobelFrancis(7) 4 33
(Joseph Tuite) *sn rousted along in last pair: wnt 4th over 1f out: nvr gng pce to get on terms w ldrs (jockey said filly was slowly away)* **80/1**

00-0 **5** *17* **Dark Impulse (IRE)**[18] 2140 3-8-7 34.................................... LiamJones 6
(John Bridger) *stmbld leaving stalls: racd keenly and sn led: rdn and hdd over 2f out: sn wknd (jockey said gelding stumbled leaving the stalls)* **80/1**

336 **6** *14* **Altar Boy**[36] 1677 3-8-11 68.................................... RobHornby 3
(Sylvester Kirk) *nvr really travelling in last pair: btn 2f out (jockey said colt moved poorly throughout)* **5/4**[2]

1m 27.72s (-0.98) **Going Correction** -0.275s/f (Firm) **6** Ran SP% **110.8**
Speed ratings (Par 99): **94,92,90,85,66 50**
CSF £40.13 TOTE £20.70: £5.80, £1.30; EX 57.40 Trifecta £238.40.
Owner The Megsons **Bred** Michael Staunton **Trained** Lambourn, Berks

FOCUS
A weak claimer, particularly with the second favourite not running a race. Improvement from the winner.

2774 SHADWELL RACING EXCELLENCE APPRENTICE H'CAP (WHIPS SHALL BE CARRIED BUT NOT USED) 6f 213y
5:25 (5:26) (Class 5) (0-70,70) 4-Y-0+

£4,722 (£1,405; £702; £351; £300; £300) **Stalls** Low

Form RPR

0-23 **1** **Marshal Dan (IRE)**[33] 1768 4-9-5 **70**.................................... StefanoCherchi(5) 4 79
(Heather Main) *chsd ldrs: led fnl 120yds: kpt on wl* **7/2**[2]

5-03 **2** *¾* **Crystal Casque**[14] 2339 4-9-0 **67**.................................... OliverSearle(7) 10 73
(Rod Millman) *chsd ldr: led 2f out: hdd fnl 120yds: kpt on but no ex* **7/1**

540 **3** *3* **Creek Harbour (IRE)**[26] 1933 4-8-11 **64**.................................... AngusVilliers(7) 8 62
(Richard Hughes) *t.k.h to post: racd freely: led tl 2f out: kpt on tl no ex ins fnl f* **16/1**

00-1 **4** *hd* **Fieldsman (USA)**[18] 2145 7-9-4 **67**.................................... ElishaWhittington(3) 3 64
(Tony Carroll) *cl up: effrt 2f out: kpt on same pce fnl f* **9/4**[1]

500 **5** *4 ½* **Magical Ride**[21] 2060 4-8-13 **62**..........................(h) GraceMcEntee(3) 7 47
(Richard Spencer) *in tch: effrt in cl 3rd 2f out: fdd fnl f* **16/1**

55-0 **6** *1 ¾* **Hedging (IRE)**[18] 2145 5-8-12 **58**..........................(b) GeorgiaDobie 2 38
(Eve Johnson Houghton) *rousted along leaving stalls: in tch: swtchd lft 2f out: wknd fnl f (jockey said gelding was slowly away)* **7/1**

1-23 **7** *nk* **Tamerlane (IRE)**[77] 942 4-9-10 **70**..........................(b w) AmeliaGlass 1 50
(Clive Cox) *a towards rr* **6/1**[3]

00-0 **8** *nk* **Good Luck Charm**[13] 2365 10-9-0 **65**..........................(b) RhysClutterbuck(5) 9 44
(Gary Moore) *hld up: hdwy over 1f out: nvr quite on terms: wknd fnl f* **66/1**

00-3 **9** *¾* **N Over J**[26] 1933 4-8-6 **57**..........................(v) JackDinsmore(5) 5 34
(William Knight) *in tch: effrt 3f out: wknd 2f out* **8/1**

/03- **U** **Angel Islington (IRE)**[162] 9404 4-9-5 **70**.................................... LukeCatton(5) 11
(Andrew Balding) *jinked bdly rt and uns rdr leaving stalls* **22/1**

1m 26.39s (-2.31) **Going Correction** -0.275s/f (Firm) **10** Ran SP% **121.0**
Speed ratings (Par 103): **102,101,97,97,92 90,90,89,88,**
CSF £29.64 CT £362.95 TOTE £5.00: £1.60, £1.80, £5.00; EX 33.90 Trifecta £397.10.
Owner Coxwell Partnership **Bred** Deerpark Stud **Trained** Kingston Lisle, Oxon

FOCUS
Modest form, and a race not many got into. It's rated around the runner-up.
T/Plt: £169.00 to a £1 stake. Pool: £38,357.80 - 165.63 winning units T/Qpdt: £24.90 to a £1 stake. Pool: £4,262.33 - 126.64 winning units **Tim Mitchell**

[2742]YORK (L-H)
Thursday, May 16

OFFICIAL GOING: Good to firm (good in places; watered; ovr 7.4, stands' 7.4, ctr 7.4, far 7.3)
Wind: Moderate across Weather: Fine & dry

2775 MATCHBOOK BETTING EXCHANGE H'CAP 5f
1:50 (1:57) (Class 2) (0-105,104) 4-Y-0+

£18,675 (£5,592; £2,796; £1,398; £699; £351) **Stalls** Centre

Form RPR

1-42 **1** **Copper Knight (IRE)**[7] 2557 5-9-3 **100**..........................(t) DavidAllan 11 109
(Tim Easterby) *cl up centre: led 2f out: sn rdn: kpt on strly* **8/1**[3]

0130 **2** *1* **Foolaad**[12] 2396 8-9-1 **98**..........................(t) RobertWinston 17 103
(Roy Bowring) *racd towards stands' side: chsd ldrs: hdwy 2f out: rdn over 1f out: drvn and kpt on fnl f* **16/1**

-600 **3** *shd* **Marnie James**[26] 1946 4-9-7 **104**..........................(t) PaulMulrennan 9 108
(Iain Jardine) *trckd ldrs: hdwy 2f out: rdn over 1f out: drvn and kpt on fnl f* **50/1**

10-0 **4** *¾* **Eeh Bah Gum (IRE)**[26] 1946 4-8-5 **88**.................................... RachelRichardson 20 90
(Tim Easterby) *racd towards stands' side: hld up in tch: hdwy 2f out: rdn over 1f out: sn chsng ldrs: kpt on fnl f* **14/1**

00-2 **5** *hd* **Dark Shot**[22] 2030 6-8-3 **86**..........................(p) PaddyMathers 14 87
(Scott Dixon) *chsd ldrs towards centre: hdwy 2f out: rdn over 1f out: kpt on fnl f* **20/1**

20-1 **6** *1 ½* **Cowboy Soldier (IRE)**[26] 1938 4-8-10 **93**.................................... LukeMorris 8 89
(Robert Cowell) *trckd ldrs centre: hdwy 2f out: cl up and rdn over 1f out: drvn and edgd lft ent fnl f: kpt on same pce* **8/1**[3]

0-35 **7** *¾* **Open Wide (USA)**[12] 2403 5-8-10 **93**..........................(b) JimCrowley 13 86
(Amanda Perrett) *midfield: pushed along 2f out: rdn over 1f out: kpt on fnl f* **12/1**

0-12 **8** *shd* **Fendale**[77] 953 7-8-4 **87**.................................... PhilDennis 6 80
(Bryan Smart) *chsd ldrs towards far side: rdn along and sltly outpcd wl over 1f out: kpt on fnl f* **25/1**

6101 **9** *hd* **Poyle Vinnie**[7] 2556 9-8-5 **88** 4ex.................................... JamesSullivan 16 80
(Ruth Carr) *racd towards stands' side: prom: effrt and cl up 2f out: sn rdn: drvn and wknd appr fnl f* **28/1**

60-0 **10** *hd* **Harome (IRE)**[26] 1946 5-8-5 **88**.................................... PJMcDonald 10 79
(Roger Fell) *cl up centre: rdn along 2f out: drvn over 1f out: grad wknd* **20/1**

0-00 **11** *nse* **Quick Look**[17] 2201 6-8-2 **85** oh1.................................... NathanEvans 4 76
(Michael Easterby) *bhd towards far side: hdwy 2f out: sn rdn: kpt on wl fnl f* **40/1**

1421 **12** *¾* **Saaheq**[26] 1946 5-8-9 **92**.................................... SilvestreDeSousa 1 80
(Michael Appleby) *racd towards far side: chsd ldrs: rdn along 2f out: wknd over 1f out* **6/1**[1]

240- **13** *hd* **Justanotherbottle (IRE)**[236] 7512 5-9-4 **101**.................... DanielTudhope 5 89
(Declan Carroll) *racd centre: slt ld: rdn along and hdd 2f out: sn drvn and wknd* **9/1**

0-41 **14** *hd* **Abel Handy (IRE)**[13] 2368 4-8-9 **92**.................................... KevinStott 3 79
(Declan Carroll) *chsd ldrs towards far side: rdn along 2f out: sn wknd* **13/2**[2]

4400 **15** *1 ¼* **Orvar (IRE)**[34] 1734 6-8-12 **95**.................................... JoeFanning 12 77
(Paul Midgley) *dwlt: a towards rr* **28/1**

1505 **16** *hd* **Royal Birth**[26] 1938 8-8-7 **90**..........................(t) ShaneGray 22 72
(Stuart Williams) *a towards rr* **33/1**

0-25 **17** *shd* **Line Of Reason (IRE)**[26] 1946 9-8-9 **92**.................................... OisinMurphy 18 73
(Paul Midgley) *hmpd s and towards rr: hdwy and in tch 1/2-way: rdn along over 2f out: sn wknd* **20/1**

-603 **18** *hd* **Tommy Taylor (USA)**[12] 2396 5-8-8 **91**..........................(v) TomEaves 2 71
(Kevin Ryan) *towards rr far side: hdwy over 2f out: rdn along wl over 1f out: n.d* **9/1**

1440 **19** *1 ¼* **Outrage**[26] 1938 7-8-9 **92**..........................(b) KieranO'Neill 21 68
(Daniel Kubler) *racd towards stands' side: a in rr* **50/1**

00-5 **20** *¾* **Powerallied (IRE)**[31] 1814 6-7-12 **86**.................................... SeanDavis(5) 19 59
(Richard Fahey) *wnt lft and hmpd s: a in rr* **28/1**

-004 **21** *2 ¼* **Henley**[6] 2589 7-8-5 **88** oh2 ow3.................................... RoystonFfrench 7 53
(Tracy Waggott) *towards rr: rdn along 1/2-way: sn outpcd and bhd* **80/1**

57.54s (-0.66) **Going Correction** +0.20s/f (Good) **21** Ran SP% **129.1**
Speed ratings (Par 109): **113,111,111,110,109 107,106,105,105,105 105,104,103,103,101 101,100,100,98,97 93**
CSF £113.11 CT £6082.30 TOTE £8.50: £2.40, £4.90, £9.80, £3.10; EX 161.70 Trifecta £3415.50.
Owner Ventura Racing (copper) & Partner **Bred** Wardstown Stud Ltd **Trained** Great Habton, N Yorks

FOCUS
Jockeys in the main felt the ground was similar to the previous day. Luke Morris said it was 'good to firm', while Oisin Murphy felt it was "beautiful" and "good and fast". A typically competitive edition of this sprint, they raced as one big group, but the pace was down the middle of the track. Those racing on the wings, therefore, may have been at a touch of a disadvantage. The level of the form is sound, rated around the runner-up.

2776 AL BASTI EQUIWORLD DUBAI MIDDLETON FILLIES' STKS (GROUP 2) 1m 2f 56y
2:25 (2:27) (Class 1) 4-Y-0+

£70,887 (£26,875; £13,450; £6,700; £3,362; £1,687) **Stalls** Low

Form RPR

123- **1** **Lah Ti Dar**[208] 8406 4-9-0 114.................................... FrankieDettori 2 116
(John Gosden) *t.k.h: trckd ldng pair: hdwy on inner to ld 3f out and sn pushed along rdn 2f out: kpt on wl u.p fnl f* **1/3**[1]

21-3 **2** *nk* **Rawdaa**[26] 1941 4-9-0 97.................................... RyanMoore 5 115
(Sir Michael Stoute) *t.k.h: trckd ldrs: hdwy over 3f out: cl up 2f out: sn rdn to chal: drvn and ev ch ins fnl f: no ex towards fin* **6/1**[2]

436- **3** *4 ½* **Sun Maiden**[230] 7733 4-9-0 100.................................... JimCrowley 3 106
(Sir Michael Stoute) *trckd ldrs: hdwy on outer over 3f out: sn cl up: pushed along over 2f out: rdn wl over 1f out: kpt on same pce ins fnl f* **16/1**

32-2 **4** 4 ½ **Nyaleti (IRE)**[11] 2441 4-9-0 109 JoeFanning 6 97
(Mark Johnston) *trckd ldr: pushed along 3f out: sn rdn and one pce* **10/1**[3]

0-05 **5** 4 ½ **Queen Of Time**[12] 2404 5-9-0 94 (p) JamesDoyle 1 88
(Henry Candy) *led: jnd over 3f out: sn hdd and rdn: grad wknd fnl 2f* **66/1**

412- **6** 10 **Mrs Sippy (USA)**[230] 7733 4-9-0 103 JamieSpencer 4 68
(David Simcock) *hld up: a in rr* **16/1**

2m 10.38s (0.08) **Going Correction** +0.20s/f (Good) **6 Ran SP% 111.7**
Speed ratings (Par 112): **107,106,103,99,95 87**
CSF £2.82 TOTE £1.20: £1.10, £1.90; EX 2.70 Trifecta £9.40.
Owner Lord Lloyd-Webber **Bred** Watership Down Stud **Trained** Newmarket, Suffolk

FOCUS
Distance increased by 43yds. Solid Group 2 form with the winner a proven class-act and the runner-up is a fast-improving filly. Lah Ti Dar is rated a bit below his best. They didn't go a great gallop but the pace quickened early in the straight.

2777 AL BASTI EQUIWORLD DUBAI DANTE STKS (GROUP 2) 1m 2f 56y
3:00 (3:00) (Class 1) 3-Y-O

£93,571 (£35,475; £17,754; £8,844; £4,438; £2,227) **Stalls Low**

Form RPR

21 **1** **Telecaster**[31] 1824 3-9-0 0 OisinMurphy 5 117
(Hughie Morrison) *trckd ldr: effrt and cl up over 2f out: rdn to ld wl over 1f out: drvn and edgd rt ins fnl f: hld on wl u.p towards fin* **7/1**

111- **2** 1 **Too Darn Hot**[215] 8187 3-9-0 126 FrankieDettori 8 116
(John Gosden) *hld up: gd hdwy over 3f out and sn chsng ldng pair: chal on inner wl over 1f out: sn rdn: drvn and ev ch ins fnl f: no ex and eased nr fin* **1/1**[1]

31-1 **3** 4 **Surfman**[16] 2245 3-9-0 101 AndreaAtzeni 2 108
(Roger Varian) *t.k.h: hld up towards rr: hdwy over 3f out: rdn along to chse ldrs 2f out: sn drvn and kpt on same pce* **5/1**[2]

1- **4** ¾ **Japan**[228] 7818 3-9-0 111 RyanMoore 3 106
(A P O'Brien, Ire) *hld up towards rr: hdwy over 3f out: rdn along wl over 2f out: kpt on fnl f* **8/1**

0-03 **5** ½ **Turgenev**[22] 2031 3-9-0 102 KieranO'Neill 6 105
(John Gosden) *led: rdn along 3f out: drvn and hdd 2f out: grad wknd* **40/1**

03-1 **6** 1 **Nayef Road (IRE)**[11] 2446 3-9-0 96 SilvestreDeSousa 4 103
(Mark Johnston) *chsd ldng pair: hdwy over 3f out: rdn along wl over 2f out: sn outpcd* **25/1**

111- **7** 3 ¾ **Line of Duty (IRE)**[195] 8821 3-9-0 114 JamesDoyle 7 96
(Charlie Appleby) *hld up: effrt over 3f out: sn rdn along and btn* **13/2**[3]

41- **8** hd **Almania (IRE)**[258] 6753 3-9-0 0 JimCrowley 1 96+
(Sir Michael Stoute) *dwlt: a bhd (jockey said colt was slowly away)* **20/1**

2m 10.24s (-0.06) **Going Correction** +0.20s/f (Good) **8 Ran SP% 114.7**
Speed ratings (Par 111): **108,107,104,103,103 102,99,99**
CSF £14.25 CT £38.91 TOTE £8.00: £2.10, £1.10, £1.60; EX 16.20 Trifecta £61.10.
Owner Castle Down Racing **Bred** Meon Valley Stud **Trained** East Ilsley, Berks

FOCUS
A mouth-watering Dante Stakes featuring last year's champion 2yo Too Darn Hot, Breeders' Cup Juvenile Turf winner Line Of Duty and Group 2 Beresford winner Japan, up against a host of promising 3yos.\n\x\x Add 43yds. The strong early pace ensured no hiding place, although the closers still struggled to have a say, and once again it went the way of a colt with fitness on his side. Telecaster's rating is up there with the best Derby trial figures. Too Darn Hot was 10lb off his 2yo form.

2778 MATCHBOOK BETTING PODCAST HAMBLETON H'CAP 7f 192y
3:35 (3:37) (Class 2) 4-Y-O+

£31,125 (£9,320; £4,660; £2,330; £1,165; £585) **Stalls Low**

Form RPR

00-3 **1** **What's The Story**[13] 2378 5-9-5 **96** (p) JoeFanning 16 106
(Keith Dalgleish) *in tch: hdwy 3f out: chal on outer over 1f out: rdn to ld ent fnl f: kpt on strly* **9/1**

34-0 **2** 1 ½ **Firmament**[12] 2419 7-9-2 **93** (p) ShaneGray 5 100
(David O'Meara) *in tch: hdwy 3f out: rdn along to chse ldrs wl over 1f out: drvn and kpt on fnl f* **20/1**

-321 **3** nk **Hayadh**[12] 2419 6-9-0 **91** LewisEdmunds 4 97
(Rebecca Bastiman) *trckd ldrs: hdwy 3f out: chsd ldr wl over 1f out: sn rdn: drvn ent fnl f: kpt on same pce* **14/1**

022 **4** ½ **Love Dreams (IRE)**[12] 2402 5-9-4 **95** (b) PJMcDonald 11 100
(Mark Johnston) *led: rdn along 2f out: drvn over 1f out: hdd ent fnl f: kpt on wl u.p* **8/1**

0-31 **5** ¾ **Beringer**[28] 1889 4-9-8 **99** AndreaAtzeni 7 102
(Alan King) *hld up towards rr: hdwy over 3f out: rdn along to chse ldrs 2f out: drvn over 1f out: kpt on same pce* **9/2**[1]

3-11 **6** nk **Hortzadar**[24] 1977 4-9-5 **96** DanielTudhope 18 98+
(David O'Meara) *hld up towards rr: hdwy 3f out: rdn along and in tch 2f out: drvn over 1f out: kpt on fnl f* **7/1**[3]

030- **7** 1 **Bless Him (IRE)**[278] 5991 5-9-4 **95** (h) JamieSpencer 2 95+
(David Simcock) *dwlt and hld up in rr: hdwy wl over 2f out: rdn wl over 1f out: plugged on: nt rch ldrs* **12/1**

043- **8** nk **Ulshaw Bridge (IRE)**[223] 7949 4-8-12 **89** (p) OisinMurphy 13 88
(James Bethell) *hld up: a in rr* **16/1**

-006 **9** 3 ½ **Waarif (IRE)**[12] 2419 6-9-1 **95** (p) ConorMcGovern(3) 17 86
(David O'Meara) *midfield: hdwy and in tch over 3f out: rdn along wl over 2f out: sn wknd* **20/1**

2-00 **10** 1 **Escobar (IRE)**[19] 2105 5-9-9 **100** (t) DavidNolan 6 89
(David O'Meara) *hld up: a in rr* **12/1**

311- **11** 1 ¼ **Mutafani**[338] 3718 4-9-0 **91** SilvestreDeSousa 10 77
(Simon Crisford) *t.k.h: prom: pushed along 3f out: rdn over 2f out: sn drvn and wknd* **5/1**[2]

00-0 **12** nk **Tricorn (IRE)**[27] 1912 5-9-6 **97** JamesSullivan 14 83
(Ruth Carr) *chsd ldrs: rdn along 3f out: wknd over 2f out (jockey said gelding was denied a clear run approaching the line)* **66/1**

2-32 **13** 1 **Commander Han (FR)**[12] 2419 4-8-13 **90** (p) TomEaves 9 73
(Kevin Ryan) *chsd ldr: rdn along over 2f out: sn drvn and wknd over 1f out* **20/1**

26-5 **14** 22 **Plutonian (IRE)**[33] 1753 5-9-10 **101** JamesDoyle 8 34
(Charles Hills) *midfield: pushed along 4f out: rdn 3f out: sn wknd: bhd and eased fr wl over 1f out (jockey said gelding stopped quickly)* **10/1**

1m 38.15s (0.65) **Going Correction** +0.20s/f (Good) **14 Ran SP% 121.3**
Speed ratings (Par 109): **104,102,102,101,100 100,99,99,95,94 93,93,92,70**
CSF £183.57 CT £2573.83 TOTE £11.00: £3.20, £6.10, £4.20; EX 244.40 Trifecta £4149.30.
Owner Weldspec Glasgow Limited **Bred** Mrs Liz Nelson Mbe **Trained** Carluke, S Lanarks
■ Stewards' Enquiry : David Nolan caution: careless riding

FOCUS
Add 36yds. This high-quality handicap was run at a strong pace and the main action again came down the middle of the home straight. Decent form.

2779 BRITISH STALLION STUDS EBF WESTOW STKS (LISTED RACE) 5f
4:05 (4:07) (Class 1) 3-Y-O

£28,355 (£10,750; £5,380; £2,680; £1,345; £675) **Stalls Centre**

Form RPR

44-1 **1** **Garrus (IRE)**[36] 1692 3-9-2 103 RyanMoore 8 108
(Jeremy Noseda) *trckd ldrs: pushed along and hdwy 2f out: rdn to chal jst over 1f out: drvn ins fnl f: kpt on wl to ld nr fin* **3/1**[2]

13-3 **2** shd **Shades Of Blue (IRE)**[20] 2077 3-8-11 96 OisinMurphy 9 102
(Clive Cox) *dwlt: sn prom: cl up 1/2-way: rdn to chal over 1f out: drvn ins fnl f: kpt to ld last 40yds: hdd and no ex nr fin* **8/1**[3]

136- **3** nk **Soldier's Call**[195] 8818 3-9-7 114 DanielTudhope 5 111
(Archie Watson) *led: pushed along over 1f out: sn rdn: drvn ins fnl f: hdd last 40yds: no ex nr fin* **11/4**[1]

200- **4** 6 **Deia Glory**[216] 8145 3-8-11 97 PaulMulrennan 1 79
(Michael Dods) *chsd ldng pair: rdn along wl over 1f out: sn drvn and wknd appr fnl f* **33/1**

-162 **5** 2 ½ **No Nonsense**[15] 2270 3-9-2 102 GeraldMosse 7 75
(David Elsworth) *awkward s: sn outpcd and a bhd* **11/1**

-316 **6** 2 ¼ **Charming Kid**[27] 1920 3-9-2 97 BarryMcHugh 6 67
(Richard Fahey) *chsd ldrs: rdn along 2f out: sn wknd* **25/1**

57.61s (-0.59) **Going Correction** +0.20s/f (Good) **6 Ran SP% 77.9**
Speed ratings (Par 107): **112,111,111,101,97 94**
CSF £11.46 TOTE £2.40: £1.60, £1.90; EX 10.30 Trifecta £19.50.
Owner Mrs Susan Roy **Bred** Mrs Max Morris **Trained** Newmarket, Suffolk
■ Semoum and Well Done Fox were both withdrawn. Prices at time of withdrawal were 4/1 and 5/1. Rule 4 applies to all bets. Deduction - 35p in the pound

FOCUS
Drama at the start with Well Done Fox and Semoum having to be withdrawn, but still a good Listed race with the third used as a benchmark. The form is rated around the winner and third.

2780 STRATFORD PLACE STUD BREEDS GROUP WINNERS EBFSTALLIONS.COM MAIDEN STKS (PLUS 10 RACE) 6f
4:35 (4:37) (Class 2) 2-Y-O

£12,450 (£3,728; £1,864; £932; £466; £234) **Stalls High**

Form RPR

1 **Repartee (IRE)** 2-9-5 0 AndreaAtzeni 9 96+
(Kevin Ryan) *mde most: rdn wl over 1f out: clr ins fnl f: kpt on strly* **9/2**[3]

2 5 **Forbidden Land (IRE)** 2-9-5 0 RossaRyan 8 81
(Richard Hannon) *cl up: chal over 2f out: rdn and ev ch wl over 1f out: drvn ent fnl f: kpt on same pce* **25/1**

3 ¾ **Boma Green** 2-9-5 0 FrankieDettori 14 79+
(Jeremy Noseda) *dwlt and in rr: stdy hdwy 1/2-way: chsd ldrs 2f out: sn rdn: kpt on wl fnl f* **10/1**

2 **4** nk **When Comes Here (IRE)**[14] 2338 2-9-5 0 OisinMurphy 2 78
(Andrew Balding) *cl up: disp ld 1/2-way: rdn along wl over 1f out: sn drvn and kpt on one pce* **3/1**[2]

5 ¾ **Story Of Light (IRE)** 2-9-5 0 JamesDoyle 4 76
(Charlie Appleby) *t.k.h: chsd ldrs: rdn along 2f out: sn no imp* **11/8**[1]

5 **6** 3 **Vardon Flyer**[31] 1812 2-9-5 0 JamesSullivan 12 67
(Michael Easterby) *towards rr: hdwy 1/2-way: in tch whn n.m.r and stmbld 2f out: kpt on fnl f* **100/1**

7 2 ¾ **My Kinda Day (IRE)** 2-9-5 0 PaulHanagan 3 59
(Richard Fahey) *trckd ldrs: hdwy 1/2-way: rdn along over 2f out: wknd wl over 1f out* **8/1**

3 **8** 2 ½ **River Of Kings (IRE)**[15] 2288 2-9-5 0 JoeFanning 6 51
(Keith Dalgleish) *in tch: rdn along wl over 2f out: n.d* **20/1**

9 1 **Herbert Pocket** 2-9-5 0 DavidAllan 5 48
(Tim Easterby) *a towards rr* **33/1**

0 **10** 4 ½ **Must Dream**[33] 1759 2-9-5 0 CamHardie 7 35
(Seb Spencer) *midfield: rdn along 1/2-way: wknd over 2f out* **50/1**

0 **11** 8 **Stittenham**[38] 1642 2-9-0 0 NathanEvans 15 6
(Michael Easterby) *dwlt: a in rr* **100/1**

12 35 **Dorcha Knight (IRE)** 2-9-5 0 PhilDennis 11
(David C Griffiths) *dwlt: a in rr* **100/1**

1m 11.68s (0.08) **Going Correction** +0.20s/f (Good) **12 Ran SP% 122.0**
Speed ratings (Par 99): **107,100,99,98,97 93,90,86,85,79 68,22**
CSF £114.54 TOTE £5.60: £1.80, £5.60, £2.30; EX 123.60 Trifecta £878.20.
Owner Sheikh Mohammed Obaid Al Maktoum **Bred** Wansdyke Farms Ltd & J M Burke **Trained** Hambleton, N Yorks

FOCUS
The first 6f 2yo race of the campaign. Tricky form to assess, although the winner looks smart. He's rated in line with the previous best winner of this event.

2781 INVESTEC WEALTH H'CAP 2m 56y
5:05 (5:05) (Class 3) (0-90,92) 4-Y-O+

£12,450 (£3,728; £1,864; £932; £466; £234) **Stalls Low**

Form RPR

12-2 **1** **Carnwennan (IRE)**[20] 2080 4-8-12 **79** StevieDonohoe 2 89+
(Charlie Fellowes) *hld up: stdy hdwy over 3f out: chsd ldrs 2f out: led jst over 1f out: rdn and edgd lft ins fnl f: kpt on wl* **7/1**[3]

00-4 **2** 1 ½ **Mancini**[18] 2143 5-9-10 **90** JamesDoyle 1 97
(Jonathan Portman) *trckd ldr: effrt and cl up 3f out: led over 2f out: sn rdn: drvn and hdd jst over 1f out: drvn and kpt on same pce fnl f* **9/2**[2]

134- **3** ¾ **Bal De Rio (FR)**[259] 4808 6-8-9 **78** BenRobinson(3) 16 84
(Brian Ellison) *hld up in rr: hdwy on inner over 2f out: rdn to chse ldrs whn n.m.r over 1f out: styd on strly fnl f (vet said gelding to be lame on its left fore)* **33/1**

5111 **4** shd **Champarisi**[25] 1971 4-8-9 **76** SamJames 11 82
(Grant Tuer) *trckd ldrs: hdwy over 4f out: rdn and ev ch 2f out: drvn appr fnl f: kpt on same pce* **11/1**

4-33 **5** 2 ¼ **Running Cloud (IRE)**[17] 2209 4-8-12 **79** (v) RyanMoore 15 82
(Alan King) *hld up towards rr: smooth hdwy 3f out: rdn to chse ldrs over 1f out: sn drvn and kpt on one pce* **8/1**

00-0 **6** 1 ¼ **Guns Of Leros (USA)**[22] 2032 6-9-5 **85** (v) DanielTudhope 10 87
(Gary Moore) *hld up towards rr: hdwy on outer over 3f out: rdn to chse ldrs and hung rt to stands' side 2f out: styd on u.p appr fnl f* **25/1**

42-3 **7** 1 ¼ **River Glades**[81] 124 4-8-7 **74** AndrewMullen 12 74
(Tom Tate) *sn led and set str pce: rdn along over 3f out: drvn and hdd over 2f out: sn wknd* **28/1**

2355 **8** *1* **Loud And Clear**[11] 2435 8-9-0 **80** PhilDennis 4 79
(Jim Goldie) *trckd ldrs: pushed along on inner: over 3f out: rdn along over 2f out: sn drvn and no imp* **50/1**

03/4 **9** *shd* **The Cashel Man (IRE)**[34] 1735 7-9-12 **92** (b) OisinMurphy 5 91
(Nicky Henderson) *hld up in rr: sme hdwy over 2f out: n.d* **4/1**[1]

45-1 **10** *1 1/4* **Handiwork**[20] 2080 9-9-4 **84** (p) PJMcDonald 8 81
(Steve Gollings) *midfield: effrt and sme hdwy over 3f out: rdn along over 2f out: sn wknd* **16/1**

4-06 **11** *1* **Manjaam (IRE)**[22] 2032 6-9-2 **87** SeanDavis(5) 7 83
(Ian Williams) *hld up: a in rr* **11/1**

-423 **12** *1 1/4* **Pipes Of Peace (IRE)**[26] 1947 5-9-12 **92** (t) TomQueally 14 87
(Seamus Durack) *hld up towards rr: hdwy 5f out: rdn along over 3f out: sn drvn and wknd* **7/1**[3]

0/04 **13** *3/4* **Red Tornado (FR)**[26] 737 7-8-13 **79** JoeFanning 6 73
(Chris Fairhurst) *chsd ldrs: rdn along 4f out: sn wknd* **40/1**

60-4 **14** *1/2* **Northwest Frontier (IRE)**[19] 2118 5-9-8 **88** (b) DougieCostello 9 81
(Micky Hammond) *s.i.s and in rr: hdwy to chse ldrs after 2f: rdn along over 3f out: sn wknd (jockey said gelding missed the break)* **20/1**

3/1- **15** *14* **Waiting For Richie**[364] 2800 6-8-9 **75** JamesSullivan 13 51
(Tom Tate) *chsd ldng pair: rdn along 3f out: sn drvn and wknd* **9/1**

3m 35.14s (1.24) **Going Correction** +0.20s/f (Good)
WFA 4 from 5yo+ 1lb **15** Ran SP% **126.2**
Speed ratings (Par 107): **104,103,102,102,101 101,100,99,99,99 98,98,97,97,90**
CSF £37.32 CT £1015.48 TOTE £7.80: £2.60, £2.20, £9.10; EX 42.20 Trifecta £769.40.
Owner Dr Vincent K F Kong **Bred** Brian Williamson **Trained** Newmarket, Suffolk
■ Stewards' Enquiry : Sam James four-day ban: used whip above permitted level (30 May, 2-4 Jun)

FOCUS
Distance increased by 43yds. Run at a good gallop, this is useful staying form. The form makes sense.
T/Jkpt: £35,420.30 to a £1 stake. Pool: £53,130.56 - 1.50 winning units T/Plt: £678.00 to a £1 stake. Pool: £208,715.50 - 224.71 winning units T/Qpdt: £76.60 to a £1 stake. Pool: £16,424.67 - 158.55 winning units **Joe Rowntree/Andrew Sheret**

2667 LONGCHAMP (R-H)
Thursday, May 16

OFFICIAL GOING: Turf: good

2782a PRIX DE L'ATHENEE (CONDITIONS) (4YO) (NEW COURSE: 2ND POST) (TURF) 7f
3:40 4-Y-O
£12,612 (£4,792; £3,531; £2,018; £1,009; £756)

RPR

1 **Salt Lake City (FR)**[72] 1029 4-9-0 **0** TonyPiccone 9 76
(B Audouin, France) **27/1**

2 *1/2* **Pretreville (FR)**[30] 4-9-7 **0** CristianDemuro 2 82
(J-C Rouget, France) **16/5**[2]

3 *nk* **Zavrinka (FR)**[49] 4-9-4 **0** StephanePasquier 10 78
(V Sartori, France) **9/1**[3]

4 *snk* **Naif (FR)**[24] 4-9-3 **0** OlivierPeslier 14 77
(Y Durepaire, France) **12/1**

5 *snk* **Deemster (IRE)**[18] 4-9-0 **0** MickaelBarzalona 4 73
(A Fabre, France) *midfield early: pushed along over 2f out: rdn and gd hdwy over 1f out: kpt on wl ins fnl f* **1/1**[1]

6 *1/2* **Pedro The First (FR)**[18] 4-9-0 **0** (p) MaximeGuyon 3 72
(F Rossi, France) **15/1**

7 *nse* **Leonio (FR)**[20] 2089 4-9-6 **0** (b) ChristopheSoumillon 1 78
(Andrea Marcialis, France) **15/1**

8 *1/2* **La Canche (FR)**[31] 1827 4-8-10 **0** EddyHardouin 11 67
(Carina Fey, France) **20/1**

9 *1 1/4* **French Pegasus (FR)**[18] 4-9-0 **0** TheoBachelot 7 67
(Y Barberot, France) **25/1**

10 *1 1/4* **Alonso Cano (IRE)**[16] 2266 4-9-0 **0** (b) Louis-PhilippeBeuzelin 6 64
(Jo Hughes, France) *hld up in midfield: rowed along over 2f out: rdn over 1f out: kpt on same pce fnl f* **146/1**

11 *3* **Global Hope (IRE)**[24] 2002 4-9-0 **0** FranckBlondel 8 56
(Gay Kelleway) *wl into stride: led: urged along 2f out: rdn and hdd over 1f out: wknd ins fnl f* **117/1**

12 *4 1/2* **Warren (FR)**[357] 4-9-0 **0** JeffersonSmith 5 44
(Y Barberot, France) **125/1**

13 *6* **Rue De Paradis (FR)**[30] 4-8-7 **0** DelphineSantiago(3) 13 23
(Mlle C Neveux, France) **88/1**

1m 21.09s (0.39) **Going Correction** +0.675s/f (Yiel) **13** Ran SP% **119.6**
Speed ratings: **112,111,111,110,110 110,110,109,108,106 103,98,91**
PARI-MUTUEL (all including 1 euro stake): WIN 28.00; PLACE 5.90, 1.80, 3.10; DF 42.20.
Owner Anthony Couane **Bred** Haras Du Mezeray S.A. **Trained** France

2433 HAMILTON (R-H)
Friday, May 17

OFFICIAL GOING: Good to firm (8.8)
Wind: Breezy, half against in sprints and in over 4f of home straight in races on the round course Weather: Overcast, dry

2783 BB FOODSERVICE EBF NOVICE STKS (PLUS 10 RACE) (A £20,000 BB FOODSERVICE 2YO SERIES QUALIFIER) 5f 7y
5:55 (5:56) (Class 4) 2-Y-O **£5,757** (£1,713; £856; £428) **Stalls** High

Form RPR

2 **1** **Glasvegas (IRE)**[14] 2367 2-9-0 **0** SeanDavis(5) 1 84
(Keith Dalgleish) *sn pushed along towards rr on outside: hdwy 1/2-way: effrt and disp ld over 1f out: led ins fnl f: kpt on wl* **9/4**[1]

2 **2** *nk* **Taxiwala (IRE)**[20] 2093 2-9-5 **0** LukeMorris 7 83
(Archie Watson) *led: rdn: hung rt and jnd over 1f out: hdd ins fnl f: rallied: hld nr fin (jockey said colt hung right throughout)* **11/4**[2]

3 *2 1/2* **No Mercy** 2-9-2 **0** BenCurtis 6 71+
(K R Burke) *dwlt: hld up in tch: pushed along and effrt 2f out: chsd clr ldng pair ins fnl f: r.o* **11/2**[3]

4 *2 1/4* **Bella Brazil (IRE)** 2-8-11 **0** TomEaves 4 58+
(David Barron) *missed break: bhd: shkn up and stdy hdwy whn checked over 1f out: kpt on steadily fnl f: improve* **25/1**

0 **5** *3/4* **Penmellyn (IRE)**[28] 1923 2-9-0 **0** (h) SamJames 3 58
(Phillip Makin) *hld up: rdn along and effrt over 1f out: no imp fnl f* **8/1**

3 **6** *2 3/4* **Perregrin**[11] 2469 2-9-5 **0** JoeFanning 5 53
(Mark Johnston) *cl up: rdn over 2f out: edgd lft over 1f out: wknd ins fnl f* **9/1**

44 **7** *4 1/2* **Il Maestro (IRE)**[16] 2288 2-9-5 **0** JasonHart 2 37
(John Quinn) *prom: rdn along over 2f out: wknd over 1f out* **8/1**

8 *9* **Laughing Crusader** 2-9-2 **0** DavidNolan 8
(David O'Meara) *cl up: rdn along over 2f out: wknd over 1f out* **14/1**

59.38s (-1.02) **Going Correction** -0.30s/f (Firm) **8** Ran SP% **115.6**
Speed ratings (Par 95): **96,95,91,87,86 82,75,60**
CSF £8.67 TOTE £2.70: £1.20, £1.30, £1.90; EX 10.40 Trifecta £34.40.
Owner Weldspec Glasgow Limited **Bred** Gigginstown House Stud **Trained** Carluke, S Lanarks

FOCUS
A fair juvenile novice contest won in 2017 by Karl Burke's subsequent Group 1 Prix Morny victor Unfortunately. The winning time just over a second outside standard. It's's been rated as straightforward form.

2784 CONTRAFLOW TRAFFIC MANAGEMENT LTD H'CAP 1m 68y
6:25 (6:26) (Class 4) (0-85,86) 4-Y-O+
£6,727 (£2,002; £1,000; £500; £400; £400) **Stalls** Low

Form RPR

236- **1** **Universal Gleam**[259] 6771 4-9-4 **80** (w) JoeFanning 8 91
(Keith Dalgleish) *plld hrd: mde all: shkn up over 1f out: r.o wl fnl f: unchal* **7/2**[2]

6-00 **2** *1 3/4* **Markazi (FR)**[20] 2116 5-9-10 **86** DavidNolan 4 93
(David O'Meara) *trckd ldrs: effrt and wnt 2nd 2f out: sn rdn: kpt on ins fnl f: nt pce of wnr* **7/4**[1]

-406 **3** *2 1/2* **Windsor Cross (IRE)**[22] 2057 4-9-1 **77** TonyHamilton 6 78
(Richard Fahey) *chsd wnr to 2f out: drvn and outpcd fnl f* **5/1**[3]

6230 **4** *7* **Scots Sonnet**[17] 2247 5-8-5 **70** (h) JamieGormley(3) 2 55
(Jim Goldie) *hld up: outpcd 1/2-way: sme hdwy over 1f out: kpt on steadily fnl f: nvr nrr (trainer said gelding was unsuited by the ground (good to firm) on this occasion and would prefer a slower surface)* **7/2**[2]

5-05 **5** *nk* **Set In Stone (IRE)**[14] 2369 5-9-0 **79** RowanScott(3) 7 63
(Andrew Hughes, Ire) *s.i.s: sn in tch: effrt and rdn over 2f out: wknd over 1f out* **14/1**

60-6 **6** *1* **Carbon Dating (IRE)**[12] 2435 7-9-5 **81** TomEaves 5 63
(Andrew Hughes, Ire) *hld up: hdwy and in tch over 2f out: rdn and wknd over 1f out* **10/1**

1m 44.19s (-4.21) **Going Correction** -0.30s/f (Firm) **6** Ran SP% **113.2**
Speed ratings (Par 105): **109,107,104,97,97 96**
CSF £10.26 CT £28.80 TOTE £3.90: £1.50, £1.90; EX 10.80 Trifecta £37.10.
Owner Weldspec Glasgow Limited **Bred** Mrs D O'Brien **Trained** Carluke, S Lanarks

FOCUS
A decent handicap. The ready winner made all in under standard time despite failing to settle for much of the journey.

2785 PDM MAINS TO DRAINS H'CAP 1m 68y
7:00 (7:02) (Class 5) (0-70,72) 4-Y-O+
£4,140 (£1,232; £615; £400; £400; £400) **Stalls** Low

Form RPR

35-0 **1** **Never Be Enough**[22] 2056 4-9-7 **70** TomEaves 3 79
(Keith Dalgleish) *t.k.h in midfield: stdy hdwy whn n.m.r over 2f out: effrt and led over 1f out: rdn and r.o wl fnl f* **12/1**

0-56 **2** *1/2* **Four Kingdoms (IRE)**[15] 2326 5-9-3 **66** JamesSullivan 9 74
(R Mike Smith) *hld up: hdwy on outside 2f out: rdn and chsd wnr ins fnl f: kpt on: hld nr fin* **20/1**

0-00 **3** *2 1/4* **Anchises**[20] 2104 4-9-4 **67** GrahamLee 4 70
(Rebecca Menzies) *dwlt: sn in tch: effrt and ev ch briefly over 1f out: no ex ins fnl f* **16/1**

3456 **4** *shd* **Restive (IRE)**[15] 2330 6-8-12 **61** (t) PhilDennis 2 65
(Jim Goldie) *hld up in midfield on ins: effrt over 2f out: hdwy and prom whn n.m.r briefly over 1f out: kpt on ins fnl f: no imp (jockey said gelding was denied a clear run 1f out)* **14/1**

20-3 **5** *1 3/4* **Granite City Doc**[12] 2436 6-8-10 **62** JamieGormley(3) 11 61
(Lucy Normile) *hld up: rdn along 2f out: kpt on fnl f: nvr able to chal* **3/1**[2]

0-61 **6** *nk* **Thornaby Nash**[18] 2203 8-8-11 **65** (b) SebastianWoods(5) 7 63
(Jason Ward) *hld up in tch on outside: effrt whn hung rt wl over 1f out: sn no ex* **7/1**[3]

6401 **7** *3/4* **Captain Pugwash (IRE)**[10] 2512 5-9-0 **68** 5ex (v) SeanDavis(5) 5 64
(Stef Keniry) *led to over 3f out: rallied and ev ch to over 1f out: rdn and wknd ins fnl f* **10/1**

22-5 **8** *1 3/4* **Kingdom Brunel**[17] 2246 4-9-9 **72** DavidNolan 1 64+
(David O'Meara) *prom: rdn along 3f out: wknd over 1f out (jockey said gelding was denied a clear run inside final 1 1/2f)* **11/4**[1]

030- **9** *3/4* **Al Ozzdi**[268] 6416 4-9-0 **63** BenCurtis 6 53
(Roger Fell) *t.k.h: pressed ldr: led over 3f out to over 1f out: wknd fnl f* **12/1**

56-0 **10** *1 1/2* **Forever A Lady (IRE)**[18] 2203 6-8-13 **62** ShaneGray 8 49
(Keith Dalgleish) *s.i.s: hld up: rdn over 2f out: nvr rchd ldrs* **25/1**

51-0 **11** *3* **Gabrials Centurion (IRE)**[56] 1271 4-9-4 **67** TonyHamilton 10 47
(Richard Fahey) *trckd ldrs tl rdn and wknd fr 2f out* **10/1**

55-6 **12** *14* **Chinese Spirit (IRE)**[12] 2439 5-8-12 **64** BenRobinson(3) 12 12
(Linda Perratt) *bhd: struggling 4f out: btn and eased fnl 2f* **33/1**

1m 44.35s (-4.05) **Going Correction** -0.30s/f (Firm) **12** Ran SP% **121.8**
Speed ratings (Par 103): **108,107,105,105,103 103,102,100,99,98 95,81**
CSF £236.31 CT £3872.00 TOTE £8.60: £2.00, £6.60, £4.40; EX 346.50 Trifecta £3546.30.
Owner Straightline Bloodstock **Bred** J L Skinner **Trained** Carluke, S Lanarks

FOCUS
An ordinary handicap. A 4yo filly could be seen travelling all over this field 3f out and she made no mistake in a promising time for the grade. It was in-form trainer Keith Dalgleish's third win in the first three races on the card.

2786 PALMARIS SERVICES BRAVEHEART H'CAP 1m 4f 15y
7:30 (7:30) (Class 3) (0-95,94) 4-Y-O+
£15,562 (£4,660; £2,330; £1,165; £582; £292) **Stalls** Low

Form RPR

6-32 **1** **Theglasgowwarrior**[4] 2680 5-8-13 **89** BenRobinson(3) 3 95
(Jim Goldie) *hld up: effrt and rdn 2f out: kpt on wl fnl f to ld towards fin* **5/2**[2]

0504 **2** *shd* **Fire Fighting (IRE)**[12] 2440 8-9-7 **94** LukeMorris 1 99
(Mark Johnston) *dwlt: sn in tch: rdn over 3f out: effrt and angled lft 2f out: led ins fnl f: kpt on u.p: hdd nr fin* **8/1**

-246 **3** 1 3/4 **Employer (IRE)**[18] 2186 4-8-10 **83** PhilDennis 5 85
(Jim Goldie) *stdd s: hld up: hdwy over 2f out: effrt and cl up appr fnl f: rdn and one pce ins fnl f* **14/1**

-222 **4** hd **Charles Kingsley**[6] 2620 4-9-0 **87** JoeFanning 2 89
(Mark Johnston) *cl up: led over 2f out: rdn and hdd ins fnl f: kpt on same pce* **6/4**[1]

2-0 **5** 1 1/2 **Ashington**[28] 1927 4-9-3 **90** (v[1]) JasonHart 8 89
(John Quinn) *t.k.h: pressed ldr: rdn over 2f out: outpcd over 1f out: n.d after* **28/1**

-552 **6** 1 **Seafarer (IRE)**[16] 2278 5-9-4 **91** (b) LouisSteward 6 89
(Marcus Tregoning) *hld up in tch: rdn over 2f out: outpcd over 1f out* **15/2**[3]

615- **7** 3 1/4 **Morning Wonder (IRE)**[168] 9333 4-9-5 **92** TomEaves 7 85
(Kevin Ryan) *led to over 2f out: rdn and wknd fnl f* **10/1**

-400 **8** 6 **Tor**[20] 2118 5-8-9 **85** JamieGormley(3) 4 68
(Iain Jardine) *hld up: struggling over 3f out: sn btn* **18/1**

2m 33.81s (-4.79) **Going Correction** -0.30s/f (Firm) **8 Ran SP% 115.9**
Speed ratings (Par 107): **103,102,101,101,100 99,97,93**
CSF £23.23 CT £233.96 TOTE £3.60: £1.30, £1.90, £3.40; EX 20.90 Trifecta £172.40.
Owner Mrs Lucille Bone **Bred** Mrs Lucille Bone **Trained** Uplawmoor, E Renfrews

FOCUS
The feature contest was a fairly good middle-distance handicap. The second-favourite got up in the final stride out wider from off the pace.

2787 PALMARIS INTEGRATED FACILITIES SERVICES WILLIAM WALLACE H'CAP 6f 6y
8:05 (8:05) (Class 4) (0-80,81) 3-Y-O £6,727 (£2,002; £1,000; £500) Stalls Centre

Form RPR

45-1 **1** **Shimmering Dawn (IRE)**[46] 1476 3-9-6 **79** TomEaves 5 86+
(James Tate) *trckd ldrs: nt clr run over 2f out to over 1f out: shkn up to ld ins fnl f: pushed out: comf* **9/2**

15-3 **2** 1 **Hafeet Alain (IRE)**[21] 2078 3-9-7 **80** AndrewMullen 2 83
(Adrian Nicholls) *t.k.h: sn cl up: rdn and led over 1f out: hdd ins fnl f: kpt on same pce* **7/4**[1]

11 **3** 1 1/2 **Sandret (IRE)**[39] 1649 3-9-7 **80** GrahamLee 3 78
(Ben Haslam) *prom: effrt and drvn along over 1f out: kpt on same pce fnl f* **85/40**[2]

16-3 **4** 2 3/4 **Epona**[20] 2098 3-8-5 **69** SeanDavis(5) 6 58
(Keith Dalgleish) *led: rdn and hdd over 1f out: wknd ins fnl f* **7/2**[3]

1m 11.01s (-1.69) **Going Correction** -0.30s/f (Firm) **4 Ran SP% 108.8**
Speed ratings (Par 101): **99,97,95,92**
CSF £12.64 TOTE £4.50; EX 13.60 Trifecta £23.20.
Owner Sheikh Juma Dalmook Al Maktoum **Bred** Cloneymore Farm Ltd **Trained** Newmarket, Suffolk

FOCUS
A fair 3yo handicap. The favourite edged right under pressure allowing the winner clear passage up the near rail to neatly prevail in a modest comparative time.

2788 PATERSONS OF GREENOAKHILL H'CAP 6f 6y
8:35 (8:36) (Class 5) (0-75,76) 3-Y-O+ £4,140 (£1,232; £615; £400; £400; £400) Stalls Centre

Form RPR

10-6 **1** **Cool Spirit**[124] 230 4-10-0 **75** BarryMcHugh 7 84
(Richard Fahey) *racd in centre: mde all: shkn up over 1f out: hld on wl fnl f* **10/1**

324- **2** nk **Global Spirit**[235] 7611 4-9-3 **64** GrahamLee 5 72
(Roger Fell) *prom in centre: effrt and pushed along 2f out: chsd wnr ins fnl f: kpt on: hld nr fin* **16/1**

3502 **3** 3/4 **Black Salt**[34] 1760 5-9-7 **68** BenCurtis 3 74
(David Barron) *hld up in centre: hdwy to chse wnr over 1f out to ins fnl f: kpt on same pce towards fin* **2/1**[1]

5060 **4** 2 3/4 **Chookie Dunedin**[14] 2368 4-9-11 **72** ShaneGray 8 69
(Keith Dalgleish) *hld up in centre: rdn and hdwy over 1f out: kpt on fnl f: nvr able to chal* **8/1**

3022 **5** 1 1/2 **Tommy G**[12] 2437 6-9-8 **76** CoreyMadden(7) 2 68
(Jim Goldie) *prom in centre: rdn along 2f out: outpcd fnl f* **5/1**[2]

6-00 **6** 3/4 **Mr Wagyu (IRE)**[18] 2201 4-9-11 **72** (v) JasonHart 9 62
(John Quinn) *prom nr side: rdn and outpcd over 1f out: no imp fnl f* **11/1**

446 **7** hd **Mujassam**[16] 2297 7-9-10 **71** (v) DavidNolan 11 60
(David O'Meara) *cl up nr side: drvn along over 2f out: outpcd fr over 1f out* **11/2**[3]

4560 **8** 3 1/4 **Vallarta (IRE)**[15] 2328 9-8-10 **57** JamesSullivan 6 36
(Ruth Carr) *prom centre: rdn over 2f out: wknd over 1f out* **28/1**

035- **9** 1 3/4 **Carlovian**[148] 9648 6-8-9 **56** oh1 (v) LukeMorris 1 29
(Mark Walford) *midfield on outer of centre bunch: effrt over 2f out: wknd over 1f out* **33/1**

035- **10** 2 **Miss Sabina**[176] 9205 3-8-4 **60** JoeFanning 12 25
(Ann Duffield) *dwlt: sn in tch nr side: drvn and outpcd over 2f out: btn over 1f out* **28/1**

05-0 **11** 6 **Naples Bay**[18] 2203 5-9-0 **61** PhilDennis 4 9
(Katie Scott) *bhd in centre: struggling over 2f out: sn btn (jockey said gelding was never travelling)* **12/1**

406- **12** 18 **Taexali (IRE)**[194] 8856 6-9-11 **75** (b) RowanScott(3) 10
(Andrew Hughes, Ire) *sn bhd and outpcd nr side: struggling whn hung rt over 3f out: t.o* **28/1**

1m 10.55s (-2.15) **Going Correction** -0.30s/f (Firm)
WFA 3 from 4yo+ 9lb **12 Ran SP% 120.8**
Speed ratings (Par 103): **102,101,100,96,94 93,93,89,87,84 76,52**
CSF £154.50 CT £453.71 TOTE £10.90: £3.00, £4.10, £1.40; EX 152.90 Trifecta £470.90.
Owner The Cool Silk Partnership **Bred** John Hanson **Trained** Musley Bank, N Yorks

FOCUS
A fair sprint handicap. The winner bravely made all towards the centre by a diminishing margin.

2789 HAMILTON PARK SUPPORTING MENTAL HEALTH AWARENESS WEEK H'CAP 5f 7y
9:05 (9:05) (Class 6) (0-65,66) 4-Y-O+ £3,493 (£1,039; £519; £400; £400; £400) Stalls Centre

Form RPR

061- **1** **Highly Focussed (IRE)**[197] 8778 5-9-7 **64** JoeFanning 6 70
(Ann Duffield) *hld up: nt clr run over 2f out: effrt over 1f out: led wl ins fnl f: r.o* **4/1**[2]

04-0 **2** nk **Bronze Beau**[12] 2433 12-9-5 **62** (tp) ShaneGray 2 67
(Linda Stubbs) *led and sn crossed to stands' rail: rdn over 1f out: hdd wl ins fnl f: r.o* **14/1**

30-0 **3** 1 1/2 **Funkadelic**[135] 25 4-8-8 **51** AndrewMullen 7 51
(Ben Haslam) *trckd ldrs: effrt and drvn along 2f out: kpt on ins fnl f* **11/2**

00-0 **4** 5 **Kodimoor (IRE)**[15] 2324 6-8-2 **45** (p) LukeMorris 5 27
(Mark Walford) *missed break: hld up on outside: effrt and drvn along over 2f out: wknd ins fnl f* **5/1**

0-04 **5** 1/2 **Super Florence (IRE)**[12] 2433 4-9-6 **66** (h) JamieGormley(3) 4 46
(Iain Jardine) *cl up: drvn and ev ch over 1f out: wknd ins fnl f* **5/2**[1]

06-5 **6** 3/4 **Oriental Splendour (IRE)**[18] 2189 7-8-3 **46** (p) JamesSullivan 1 23
(Ruth Carr) *slowly away: hld up: effrt and rdn over 1f out: sn no imp: btn fnl f* **9/2**[3]

520- **7** 1/2 **Duba Plains**[66] 6416 4-8-5 **51** RowanScott(3) 3 26
(Kenny Johnson) *prom: rdn over 2f out: wknd over 1f out* **40/1**

5-50 **8** 1 **Corton Lass**[4] 2678 4-7-13 **47** ow2 (p) SeanDavis(5) 8 19
(Keith Dalgleish) *in tch: rdn along and hung rt fr 1/2-way: wknd over 1f out* **10/1**

59.1s (-1.30) **Going Correction** -0.30s/f (Firm) **8 Ran SP% 117.0**
Speed ratings (Par 101): **98,97,95,87,86 85,84,82**
CSF £58.20 CT £314.92 TOTE £3.90: £1.50, £3.40, £2.00; EX 36.30 Trifecta £482.30.
Owner Evelyn Duchess Of Sutherland **Bred** Ballylinch Stud **Trained** Constable Burton, N Yorks
■ Stewards' Enquiry : Shane Gray one-day ban: failure to ride to the draw (Jun 2)

FOCUS
A pretty modest sprint handicap. The second-favourite came through to win well in a fair comparative time on the straight track for the grade. The first three finished clear.
T/Plt: £274.80 to a £1 stake. Pool: £55,915.50 - 148.53 winning units T/Qpdt: £430.50 to a £1 stake. Pool: £5,993.19 - 10.30 winning units **Richard Young**

1750 NEWBURY (L-H)
Friday, May 17

OFFICIAL GOING: Good (good to firm in places; 8.0)
Wind: moderate across Weather: overcast

2790 STARLIGHT WISHES NOVICE STKS (PLUS 10 RACE) (DIV I) 7f (S)
1:35 (1:36) (Class 4) 3-Y-O £6,727 (£2,002; £1,000; £500) Stalls Centre

Form RPR

1 **1** **Biometric**[19] 2140 3-9-8 0 RobHornby 12 97
(Ralph Beckett) *mde all: rdn whn strly chal fr 2f out: kpt on gamely fnl f: hld on wl towards fin* **8/1**

423- **2** hd **Red Armada (IRE)**[213] 8305 3-9-2 86 AdamKirby 5 90
(Clive Cox) *trckd ldrs: rdn in cl 3rd over 1f out: kpt on to press wnr fnl 120yds: hld nring fin* **15/8**[1]

3 nk **Reynolds** 3-9-2 0 CharlesBishop 10 89
(Eve Johnson Houghton) *in tch: rdn in 5th 2f out: kpt on into 3rd ins fnl f: clsng qckly on front pair at fin* **50/1**

206- **4** 3 1/2 **Posted**[238] 7490 3-8-11 88 (h) SeanLevey 13 75
(Richard Hannon) *s.i.s: sn trcking ldrs: chal 2f out: sn rdn: ev ch ent fnl f: no ex fnl 150yds (jockey said filly was slowly away)* **5/1**[3]

5 1 1/2 **Majaalis (FR)** 3-9-2 0 JimCrowley 4 76+
(William Haggas) *mid-div: kpt on nicely under hands and heels fr over 1f out but nvr gng pce to get on terms* **7/2**[2]

03 **6** 4 **City Wanderer (IRE)**[13] 2405 3-9-2 0 CallumShepherd 2 65+
(Mick Channon) *hld up towards rr: styd on fnl 2f but nvr gng pce to get involved* **20/1**

7 3/4 **Excellent Magic** 3-8-11 0 JasonWatson 11 58
(Roger Charlton) *mid-div: outpcd wl over 2f out: kpt on fnl f but no threat to ldrs* **8/1**

8 3 3/4 **Levanter (FR)** 3-8-8 0 MitchGodwin(3) 3 48
(Harry Dunlop) *pressed ldr tl rdn over 2f out: wknd over 1f out* **66/1**

9 1 1/2 **Strict (IRE)** 3-9-2 0 DavidProbert 7 49
(Andrew Balding) *hld up towards rr: rdn and sme prog over 2f out: wknd over 1f out* **16/1**

10 2 3/4 **Four Feet (IRE)** 3-8-9 0 AmeliaGlass(7) 1 41
(Henry Candy) *s.i.s: a towards rr* **66/1**

0-0 **11** 6 **Aiguillette**[19] 2140 3-9-2 0 HectorCrouch 6 25
(Gary Moore) *t.k.h early: a towards rr* **100/1**

12 4 **Cool Possibility (IRE)** 3-9-2 0 (w) RobertWinston 8 14
(Charles Hills) *racd green: sn pushed along towards rr: midfield 3f out: wknd 2f out* **33/1**

1m 24.0s (-3.00) **Going Correction** -0.20s/f (Firm) **12 Ran SP% 115.4**
Speed ratings (Par 101): **109,108,108,104,102 98,97,93,91,88 81,76**
CSF £21.91 TOTE £7.80: £2.10, £1.40, £8.60; EX 25.50 Trifecta £974.30.
Owner K Abdullah **Bred** Juddmonte Farms Ltd **Trained** Kimpton, Hants

FOCUS
Watered ground, on the quick side of good. A fair novice to start, and the penalised Biometric put up a time 17lb faster than the winner of division two. The form's rated around the second.

2791 COOLMORE STUD H'CAP 6f
2:10 (2:12) (Class 2) (0-100,100) 4-Y-O+ £19,407 (£5,775; £2,886; £1,443) Stalls Centre

Form RPR

-613 **1** **Embour (IRE)**[13] 2393 4-8-10 **89** SeanLevey 5 97
(Richard Hannon) *mid-div: hdwy over 2f out: rdn into 3rd over 1f out: led fnl 120yds: r.o wl* **11/2**[2]

630- **2** 1 1/4 **Miracle Of Medinah**[266] 6477 8-8-12 **91** FergusSweeney 4 95
(Mark Usher) *mid-div: hdwy over 2f out: rdn to chse ldr over 1f out: ev ch briefly fnl 120yds: kpt on* **16/1**

2-11 **3** hd **Walk On Walter (IRE)**[22] 2061 4-9-2 **95** (h) RobHornby 2 98
(Jonathan Portman) *led tl 2f out: sn rdn: looked hld in 4th ent fnl f: kpt on wl fnl 120yds: snatched 3rd fnl stride* **6/1**[3]

4116 **4** hd **Global Tango (IRE)**[27] 1942 4-8-1 **87** (b) CierenFallon(7) 8 90
(Charles Hills) *trckd ldrs: led 2f out: sn drifted bdly lft to far rails: rdr dropped rein ins fnl f: hdd fnl 120yds: lost 3rd fnl stride (jockey said gelding hung left-handed)* **17/2**

0-00 **5** 3 **Normandy Barriere (IRE)**[20] 2117 7-8-10 **94** FayeMcManoman(5) 6 87
(Nigel Tinkler) *mid-div: outpcd in last trio over 2f out: kpt on again ent fnl f* **11/1**

503- **6** 2 1/4 **Fighting Irish (IRE)**[244] 7299 4-9-7 **100** AdamKirby 7 86
(Harry Dunlop) *broke wl: sn stdd to trck ldrs: effrt 2f out: wknd ins fnl f* **12/1**

1-1 **7** 1 1/4 **Habub (USA)**[24] 2009 4-9-0 **93** JimCrowley 11 75
(Owen Burrows) *awkwardly away: racd freely: sn trcking ldrs: rdn over 2f out: sn hld: wknd over 1f out (jockey said colt ran too freely)* **7/2**[1]

110- **8** 10 **Fille De Reve**[223] 7980 4-9-1 **94** JamieSpencer 10 44
(Ed Walker) *s.i.s: a towards rr* **7/1**

0-56 **9** *6* **Ice Age (IRE)**[20] 2117 6-9-6 **99**.................................. CharlesBishop 9 30
(Eve Johnson Houghton) *disp ld most of way tl over 2f out: sn hung lft: eased whn appearing to lose action over 1f out (jockey said gelding hung left-handed and lost its action)* **11/2**[2]

1m 11.38s (-1.82) **Going Correction** -0.20s/f (Firm) **9** Ran SP% **112.2**
Speed ratings (Par 109): **104,102,102,101,97 94,93,79,71**
CSF £84.52 CT £423.69 TOTE £5.80: £1.90, £5.80, £2.70; EX 84.30 Trifecta £494.20.
Owner Sullivanb'Stock,Ruxleyholdings,Mrs Doyle **Bred** Carpet Lady Partnership **Trained** East Everleigh, Wilts

FOCUS
This fell apart somewhat, with the fourth horse blowing a winning chance, and the seventh, eighth and ninth all running well short of pre-race expectations. The winner maintained his progressive profile.

2792 STARLIGHT RACEDAY MAIDEN STKS (PLUS 10 RACE) 6f
2:45 (2:49) (Class 4) 2-Y-O **£6,663** (£1,982; £990; £495) **Stalls** Centre

Form RPR

2 **1** **Light Angel**[13] 2394 2-9-5 0.................................. RobertHavlin 12 80+
(John Gosden) *mid-div: rdn and hdwy over 1f out: sn hanging lft: led ins fnl f: r.o wl: readily* **9/2**[3]

2 *1 ½* **Heaven Forfend** 2-9-5 0.................................. ColmO'Donoghue 5 76+
(Sir Michael Stoute) *hld up towards rr: hdwy over 2f out but looking to hang lft: chal ent fnl f: sn carried lft: kpt on but nt pce of wnr fnl 120yds: dead-heated for 2nd: awrdd 2nd outrt* **7/2**[1]

0 **3** *dht* **Jim 'N' Tomic (IRE)**[18] 2205 2-9-5 .... KieranO'Neill 8 76
(Dominic Ffrench Davis) *prom: rdn 2f out: sn hung lft: led over 1f out: drifting lft whn hdd ins fnl f: kpt on: dead-heated for 2nd: disqualified and plcd 3rd* **33/1**

4 *1 ¾* **Golden Horde (IRE)** 2-9-5 0.................................. AdamKirby 9 70+
(Clive Cox) *mid-div: hdwy 2f out: wnt 4th and hmpd jst ins fnl f: kpt on nicely wout threatening: improve* **6/1**

6 **5** *1 ¾* **Swiss Bond**[44] 1513 2-9-0 0.................................. DavidProbert 6 60
(J S Moore) *s.i.s: towards rr: swtchd lft 2f out: hdwy over 1f out: kpt on same pce fnl f* **100/1**

6 *nse* **Sir Oliver (IRE)** 2-9-5 0.................................. JamieSpencer 1 65
(Richard Hughes) *in tch: rdn 2f out: edgd rt over 1f out: kpt on but nt quite pce to chal: no ex fnl 120yds* **10/1**

7 *nse* **Baadirr** 2-9-5 0.................................. JimCrowley 10 65+
(William Haggas) *s.i.s: towards rr: hdwy over 1f out: kpt on ins fnl f but nvr any threat* **13/2**

8 *2 ½* **Indian Creak (IRE)** 2-9-5 0.................................. CharlesBishop 2 57
(Mick Channon) *mid-div: rdn whn carried rt over 1f out: fdd fnl f* **14/1**

0 **9** *¾* **Walton Thorns (IRE)**[48] 1416 2-8-12 0.................................. OwenLewis(7) 3 55
(Charles Hills) *led: rdn and hdd over 1f out: wknd fnl f* **66/1**

10 *shd* **Ziggle Pops** 2-9-5 0.................................. SeanLevey 7 55+
(Richard Hannon) *trckd ldrs: rdn over 2f out: wkng whn bdly hmpd over 1f out* **4/1**[2]

11 *6* **Gypsy Rocker (IRE)** 2-9-5 0.................................. CallumShepherd 11 37
(Brian Meehan) *s.i.s: towards rr: effrt over 2f out: wknd over 1f out* **25/1**

12 *4 ½* **Pilsdon Pen** 2-9-5 0.................................. RobHornby 4 23
(Joseph Tuite) *prom: rdn over 2f out: wkng whn bdly hmpd over 1f out* **66/1**

1m 13.98s (0.78) **Going Correction** -0.20s/f (Firm) **12** Ran SP% **114.5**
Speed ratings (Par 95): **86,84,84,81,79 79,79,75,74,74 66,60**
CSF £19.25 TOTE £3.90: £1.30, £2.00, £3.80; EX 17.10 Trifecta £216.20.
Owner Gestut Ammerland **Bred** Ammerland Verwaltung Gmbh & Co Kg **Trained** Newmarket, Suffolk
■ Stewards' Enquiry : Kieran O'Neill caution: careless riding

FOCUS
This can be a good race - subsequent Group 1 winner Advertise won a division of it last year - and this also looked a useful enough edition.

2793 SIPP WINE H'CAP 1m 4f
3:20 (3:21) (Class 5) (0-75,77) 4-Y-O+
£4,787 (£1,424; £711; £355; £300; £300) **Stalls** Low

Form RPR

56-5 **1** **Follow Intello (IRE)**[18] 2207 4-9-4 **71**.................................. JimCrowley 2 79+
(Chris Wall) *s.i.s: towards rr: stdy hdwy fr 3f out: str run ent fnl f: led fnl 100yds: styd on wl: rdn out* **4/1**[1]

206- **2** *½* **Sufi**[198] 8735 5-9-3 **70**.................................. ColmO'Donoghue 5 77
(Ken Cunningham-Brown) *trckd ldrs: swtchd rt 2f out: sn rdn: styd on to ld ent fnl f: kpt on but no ex whn hdd fnl 100yds* **16/1**

/4-6 **3** *1 ¼* **Harmonise**[13] 2400 5-8-13 **66**.................................. HectorCrouch 3 71
(Sheena West) *mid-div: hdwy fr over 3f out: rdn over 2f out: wnt 4th ent fnl f: styd on* **12/1**

52-0 **4** *nk* **Give Him Time**[13] 2400 8-9-5 **72**..........................(p) RobertWinston 1 76
(Nick Gifford) *trckd ldrs: rdn to ld over 2f out: hdd ent fnl f: kpt on* **33/1**

4-01 **5** *1 ¼* **Carp Kid (IRE)**[14] 2353 4-9-4 **74**..........................(p) FinleyMarsh(3) 4 76
(John Flint) *led for 7f: prom: rdn over 2f out: kpt on same pce fr over 1f out* **6/1**

64-0 **6** *¾* **Rake's Progress**[20] 2104 5-9-10 **77**.................................. RobertHavlin 16 78
(Heather Main) *trckd ldrs: chal gng wl enough 3f out: rdn and ev ch over 1f out: no ex ins fnl f* **14/1**

00/- **7** *1 ½* **Navajo War Dance**[41] 4413 6-9-6 **73**.................................. CharlesBishop 8 72
(Ali Stronge) *mid-div: pushed along over 5f out: rdn and styd on fnl 2f but nt pce to get involved* **66/1**

-000 **8** *hd* **Outofthequestion**[17] 2254 5-9-0 **67**..........................(p[1]) JasonWatson 11 65
(Alan King) *mid-div: hdwy 3f out: sn rdn: 7th ent fnl f: styd on same pce* **25/1**

20-1 **9** *¾* **Buckland Boy (IRE)**[18] 2202 4-9-1 **68**..........................(p) StevieDonohoe 15 65
(Charlie Fellowes) *dwlt bdly: latched onto main gp after 4f: rdn and stdy prog fr over 2f out but nvr any threat to ldrs (jockey said gelding was slowly away)* **9/2**[2]

04-0 **10** *4* **The Secrets Out**[32] 1826 5-8-7 **60**.................................. NickyMackay 14 53
(Luke Dace) *prom: led 7f out: rdn over 3f out: hdd over 2f out: short of room over 1f out: sn wknd* **33/1**

212- **11** *1 ½* **Encryption (IRE)**[183] 9076 4-9-5 **72**.................................. JamieSpencer 13 60
(David Simcock) *s.i.s: bhd: sme minor prog u.p 2f out: nvr any threat (vet said gelding lost its right fore shoe)* **10/1**

0/0- **12** *4* **Winter Lion (IRE)**[250] 7100 9-9-7 **74**.................................. LiamJones 9 56
(John O'Shea) *s.i.s: a towards rr* **100/1**

-500 **13** *½* **Gawdawpalin (IRE)**[55] 1291 6-9-4 **74**..........................(t) GaryMahon(3) 10 55
(Sylvester Kirk) *mid-div: rdn over 3f out: little imp: wknd 2f out* **20/1**

6-30 **14** *26* **Consultant**[14] 2353 4-9-3 **70**.................................. DavidProbert 7 9
(Andrew Balding) *mid-div: rdn over 3f out: wknd over 2f out (jockey said gelding hung right-handed)* **14/1**

011- **15** *76* **Brancaster (IRE)**[231] 7717 5-9-1 **68**.................................. DavidEgan 6
(David Elsworth) *mid-div tl wknd over 3f out (jockey said gelding stopped quickly; vet said the gelding to have a fibrillating heart)* **11/2**[3]

2m 34.29s (-3.71) **Going Correction** -0.20s/f (Firm) **15** Ran SP% **120.8**
Speed ratings (Par 103): **104,103,102,102,101 101,100,100,99,97 96,93,93,75,25**
CSF £64.54 CT £722.28 TOTE £5.10: £2.30, £4.90, £3.60; EX 70.80 Trifecta £1065.40.
Owner Ms Aida Fustoq **Bred** Deerfield Farm **Trained** Newmarket, Suffolk
■ Stewards' Enquiry : Nicky Mackay one-day ban: weighed in 2lb overweight (Jun 2)

FOCUS
Add 10yds. A fair handicap, which has been rated around the runner-up.

2794 STARLIGHT WISHES NOVICE STKS (PLUS 10 RACE) (DIV II) 7f (S)
3:55 (3:58) (Class 4) 3-Y-O **£6,727** (£2,002; £1,000; £500) **Stalls** Centre

Form RPR

-1 **1** **Jubiloso**[22] 2060 3-9-3 0.................................. ColmO'Donoghue 6 102+
(Sir Michael Stoute) *travelled strly: mde all: pushed clr over 1f out: impressive* **4/5**[1]

3 **2** *7* **After John**[19] 2139 3-9-2 0.................................. CallumShepherd 10 79
(Mick Channon) *trckd ldrs: rdn 2f out: kpt on to chse wnr ent fnl f but nvr any ch* **6/1**[2]

3- **3** *2 ¼* **Penrhos**[237] 7531 3-9-2 0.................................. RobertWinston 3 73
(Charles Hills) *pressed wnr tl rdn over 2f out: outpcd by wnr over 1f out: lost 2nd ent fnl f: kpt on* **8/1**

4 *1 ¾* **Puerto Banus** 3-9-2 0.................................. DavidProbert 2 68
(Andrew Balding) *s.i.s: sn chsng ldrs: rdn over 2f out: kpt on same pce fr over 1f out* **20/1**

01- **5** *2 ¾* **Island Glen (USA)**[189] 8975 3-9-5 0.................................. JasonWatson 1 64
(Heather Main) *in tch: rdn over 2f out: sn one pce* **33/1**

6 *hd* **Falsehood (IRE)** 3-9-2 0..........................(t[1]) RobertHavlin 5 60+
(John Gosden) *awkward leaving stalls: towards rr: kpt on fnl f: n.d* **7/1**[3]

P **7** *½* **River Dawn**[52] 1346 3-9-2 0.................................. RaulDaSilva 7 59
(Paul Cole) *racd keenly trcking ldrs: rdn over 2f out: wknd fnl f (jockey said gelding ran too freely)* **25/1**

00- **8** *shd* **Kaafy (IRE)**[205] 8548 3-9-2 0.................................. JimCrowley 4 59
(Brian Meehan) *s.i.s: racd keenly and sn in tch: rdn over 2f out: sn one pce* **25/1**

6-0 **9** *1* **Illywhacker (IRE)**[18] 2210 3-9-2 0.................................. HectorCrouch 8 56
(Gary Moore) *a towards rr* **80/1**

10 *nk* **Soldier's Son** 3-8-13 0.................................. GeorgiaCox(3) 12 55
(Henry Candy) *mid-div: rdn over 2f out: nvr any imp* **66/1**

0 **11** *½* **A Hundred Echoes**[42] 1570 3-9-2 0.................................. DavidEgan 9 54
(Roger Varian) *a towards rr* **50/1**

0 **12** *21* **Immoral (IRE)**[19] 2139 3-9-2 0.................................. JamieSpencer 11
(Ed Walker) *a towards rr: wknd 3f out: t.o* **20/1**

1m 24.8s (-2.20) **Going Correction** -0.20s/f (Firm) **12** Ran SP% **118.3**
Speed ratings (Par 101): **104,96,93,91,88 88,87,87,86,85 85,61**
CSF £4.89 TOTE £1.60: £1.10, £2.00, £1.90; EX 6.90 Trifecta £24.40.
Owner K Abdullah **Bred** Juddmonte Farms Ltd **Trained** Newmarket, Suffolk

FOCUS
They didn't look to go that quick early and the final time was 0.80sec slower than the first division, but it was some going from the winner to pull so far clear. This was a smart performance.

2795 ROSSDALES LAMBOURN VETERINARY SURGEONS BRITISH EBF MAIDEN STKS (PLUS 10 RACE) 1m 2f
4:25 (4:30) (Class 4) 3-Y-O **£6,727** (£2,002; £1,000; £500) **Stalls** Low

Form RPR

1 **Logician** 3-9-5 0.................................. KieranO'Neill 2 91+
(John Gosden) *s.i.s: sn in tch: hdwy over 2f out: swtchd rt wl over 1f out: sn led: qcknd clr: quite impressive* **3/1**[1]

6- **2** *2* **High Commissioner (IRE)**[203] 8607 3-9-5 0..............(w) RaulDaSilva 1 87
(Paul Cole) *led: rdn and hdd over 1f out: kpt on for clr 2nd but nt pce of wnr* **4/1**[2]

3 *3 ¼* **Dubai Tradition (USA)** 3-9-5 0.................................. AdamKirby 8 80
(Saeed bin Suroor) *in tch: hdwy 3f out: rdn to chse ldng pair over 1f out: hung lft: kpt on same pce fnl f* **6/1**[3]

0 **4** *4 ½* **Geomatrician (FR)**[30] 1852 3-9-5 0.................................. DavidProbert 14 71
(Andrew Balding) *trckd ldr: rdn over 2f out: lost 2nd sn after: kpt on same pce fnl f* **16/1**

5 *4* **Arabist** 3-9-5 0.................................. RobertHavlin 17 63+
(John Gosden) *mid-div: rdn and hdwy 2f out: styd on wl to go 5th ins fnl f: improve* **15/2**

0- **6** *1* **Military Move**[226] 7905 3-9-5 0.................................. DavidEgan 10 61
(Roger Varian) *hld up towards rr: rdn and stdy prog fr over 3f out but hanging lft: wnt hld 5th ent fnl f: styd on same pce (jockey said colt hung left-handed in the final 3f)* **8/1**

00- **7** *½* **Cambric**[237] 7539 3-9-0 0.................................. JasonWatson 13 55+
(Roger Charlton) *towards rr of midfield: rdn over 2f out: no imp tl styd on fnl f* **33/1**

0 **8** *½* **Verify**[34] 1755 3-9-5 0..........................(h[1]) JamieSpencer 9 59+
(Ed Walker) *s.i.s: in last pair: nt best of runs but styd on fnl 2f: n.d (jockey said colt ran too freely)* **28/1**

9 *nk* **Raining Fire (IRE)** 3-9-5 0.................................. DanielMuscutt 6 58
(James Fanshawe) *nvr bttr than mid-div* **16/1**

0-6 **10** *2* **Najib (IRE)**[18] 2208 3-9-2 0.................................. GabrieleMalune(3) 12 54
(Saeed bin Suroor) *trckd ldrs: disputing 3rd u.p 2f out: wknd ent fnl f* **12/1**

00 **11** *1 ¼* **Born Leader (FR)**[21] 2087 3-9-0 0.................................. SeanLevey 16 47
(Hughie Morrison) *trckd ldrs: rdn 3f out: wknd over 1f out* **66/1**

05 **12** *2 ½* **Air Hair Lair (IRE)**[18] 2210 3-9-5 0.................................. FergusSweeney 11 47
(Sheena West) *awkwardly away: sn mid-div: rdn and sme prog over 2f out: wknd fnl f* **50/1**

4-0 **13** *¾* **Almokhtaar (USA)**[15] 2321 3-9-5 0.................................. JimCrowley 20 45
(Owen Burrows) *trckd ldrs: rdn 2f out: sn wknd* **25/1**

0-0 **14** *1* **Admirals Bay (GER)**[14] 2354 3-9-5 0.................................. RobHornby 19 43
(Andrew Balding) *a towards rr* **50/1**

15 *1* **Mr Nice Guy (IRE)** 3-9-2 0.................................. GaryMahon(3) 3 41
(Sylvester Kirk) *mid-div: rdn over 2f out: sn wknd* **40/1**

16 *8* **Master Milliner (IRE)** 3-9-5 0.................................. EdwardGreatrex 5 25
(Eve Johnson Houghton) *mid-div: rdn over 3f out: wknd 2f out (jockey said colt ran green)* **40/1**

17 *½* **Capricorn Prince** 3-9-5 0.................................. HectorCrouch 7 24
(Gary Moore) *a towards rr* **50/1**

30 **18** *14* **William McKinley**[18] 2210 3-9-5 0..........................(h[1]) CharlesBishop 4
(Ali Stronge) *towards rr of midfield: rdn over 3f out: sn wknd* **100/1**

0 **19** *15* **Prime Approach (IRE)**[11] 2488 3-9-5 0 TomQueally 18
(Brett Johnson) *a towards rr* **100/1**
2m 7.01s (-2.69) **Going Correction** -0.20s/f (Firm) **19** Ran SP% **126.1**
Speed ratings (Par 101): **102,100,97,94,91 90,89,89,89,87 86,84,83,83,82 75,75,64,52**
CSF £13.28 TOTE £4.10: £2.20, £1.70, £2.30; EX 16.70 Trifecta £58.70.
Owner K Abdullah **Bred** Juddmonte Farms Ltd **Trained** Newmarket, Suffolk

FOCUS
Add 10yds. This looked a useful enough maiden and the winner, who had his rivals strung out, is likely to prove a 100+ horse. The form is rated in line with the race standard.

2796 JOHN SUNLEY MEMORIAL H'CAP 1m 3f
4:55 (4:57) (Class 4) (0-85,85) 3-Y-O

£6,727 (£2,002; £1,000; £500; £300; £300) **Stalls** Low

Form RPR
0-62 **1** **Kiefer**[19] 2142 3-8-11 **75** CharlesBishop 8 83+
(Eve Johnson Houghton) *hld up: hdwy over 2f out: r.o wl to ld fnl 100yds: pushed out* **8/1**
34-4 **2** *3/4* **Alhaazm**[27] 1956 3-8-13 **77** JimCrowley 11 83
(Sir Michael Stoute) *hld up: hdwy over 2f out: rdn to ld jst over 1f out: hdd fnl 100yds: kpt on* **5/1**[3]
1231 **3** *1/2* **Gantier**[28] 1928 3-9-7 **85** (b) RobertHavlin 9 90
(John Gosden) *s.i.s: in last pair: rdn and hdd over 1f out: ev ch fnl 120yds: no ex towards fin* **9/1**
513- **4** *2* **Prejudice**[203] 8590 3-9-7 **85** JamieSpencer 10 87
(David Simcock) *stdd s: hld up: hdwy over 2f out: drvn to chal ent fnl f: no ex fnl 120yds* **10/3**[2]
34-2 **5** *4* **Ballylemon (IRE)**[42] 1568 3-9-3 **81** AdamKirby 5 76
(Richard Hughes) *s.i.s: last: rdn over 2f out: hdwy jst over 1f out: kpt on fnl f: snatched 4th cl home (trainer could offer no explanation for the colt's performance)* **3/1**[1]
6-15 **6** *hd* **Sash**[19] 2141 3-9-4 **82** ColmO'Donoghue 7 76
(Amanda Perrett) *trckd ldr: rdn to ld over 1f out: sn hdd: wknd ins fnl f: lost 4th cl home* **33/1**
1-53 **7** *3 1/2* **The Pink'n**[19] 2141 3-8-13 **77** SeanLevey 3 66
(Seamus Mullins) *trckd ldrs: rdn 3f out: wknd over 1f out* **9/1**
41-0 **8** *hd* **War Eagle (IRE)**[21] 2075 3-8-11 **75** (p) StevieDonohoe 1 63
(Ian Williams) *led: rdn over 2f out: hdd over 1f out: wknd fnl f* **100/1**
5215 **9** *4 1/2* **Blood Eagle (IRE)**[28] 1911 3-8-13 **77** DavidProbert 6 58
(Andrew Balding) *mid-div: hdwy over 2f out: sn rdn: wknd over 1f out* **14/1**
4-34 **10** *20* **Guildhall**[19] 2141 3-9-0 **78** RobHornby 2 25
(Ralph Beckett) *trckd ldrs: rdn over 3f out: wknd over 2f out (jockey said gelding stopped quickly)* **12/1**
2m 19.78s (-3.42) **Going Correction** -0.20s/f (Firm) **10** Ran SP% **114.1**
Speed ratings (Par 101): **104,103,103,101,98 98,96,95,92,78**
CSF £46.71 CT £368.30 TOTE £9.10: £3.00, £1.80, £2.40; EX 49.00 Trifecta £564.90.
Owner Aston House Stud **Bred** Aston House Stud **Trained** Blewbury, Oxon

FOCUS
Add 10yds. This has been rated around the race average, and is likely to prove strong form.

2797 STARLIGHT HAPPY MEMORIES APPRENTICE H'CAP 1m (S)
5:30 (5:36) (Class 5) (0-75,77) 4-Y-O+

£4,787 (£1,424; £711; £355; £300; £300) **Stalls** Centre

Form RPR
530- **1** **Wind In My Sails**[322] 4331 7-9-7 **75** TobyEley 15 84
(Ed de Giles) *mid-div: hdwy 2f out: sn rdn: str chal ins fnl f: won on nod* **33/1**
0-54 **2** *nse* **Regimented (IRE)**[6] 2622 4-9-3 **76** LukeCatton(5) 11 85
(Richard Hannon) *trckd ldrs: led over 2f out: rdn and strly chal fnl f: kpt on: lost on nod* **12/1**
160- **3** *6* **Keeper's Choice (IRE)**[203] 8611 5-9-6 **74** ScottMcCullagh 4 69
(Denis Coakley) *mid-div: hdwy over 2f out: sn rdn: chsd ldng pair ent fnl f: kpt on same pce* **8/1**[3]
0264 **4** *nk* **High Acclaim (USA)**[18] 2207 5-9-5 **73** (p) CierenFallon 1 68
(Roger Teal) *s.i.s: towards rr: hdwy 2f out: sn rdn: kpt on ins fnl f: wnt 4th fnl 120yds (jockey said gelding was slowly away)* **5/1**[1]
0-00 **5** *2* **Biotic**[16] 2273 8-8-11 **72** OliverSearle(7) 6 62
(Rod Millman) *s.i.s: towards rr: hdwy over 2f out: disp 3rd ent fnl f: fdd* **16/1**
1630 **6** *nse* **Magic Mirror**[20] 2106 6-8-7 **61** oh1 ThoreHammerHansen 8 51
(Mark Rimell) *mid-div: rdn over 2f out: little imp tl kpt on ins fnl f* **9/1**
1-05 **7** *1* **Chetan**[83] 876 7-8-12 **66** KatherineBegley 10 53
(Tony Carroll) *led: rdn and hdd over 2f out: sn one pce* **40/1**
0552 **8** *nse* **Lacan (IRE)**[24] 2006 8-8-9 **70** JoeBradnam(7) 12 57
(Michael Bell) *s.i.s: towards rr: styd on fnl f: n.d* **16/1**
26-4 **9** *2 1/4* **Kingston Kurrajong**[16] 2273 6-9-7 **75** Pierre-LouisJamin 2 57
(William Knight) *mid-div: hdwy 2f out: sn rdn: wknd fnl f* **7/1**[2]
0120 **10** *hd* **Misu Pete**[48] 1418 7-8-2 **61** (p) IsobelFrancis(5) 7 43
(Mark Usher) *prom tl rdn over 2f out: wknd ent fnl f* **25/1**
-325 **11** *1 1/2* **Arctic Sea**[24] 2005 5-8-11 **72** CaitlinTaylor(7) 9 50
(Paul Cole) *s.i.s: towards rr: midfield 2f out: no further imp fnl f* **14/1**
00-2 **12** *5* **Dreaming Of Paris**[24] 2005 5-9-5 **73** WilliamCarver 17 40
(Patrick Chamings) *racd keenly: trckd ldrs tl wknd over 2f out* **20/1**
2-34 **13** *1/2* **Indiscretion (IRE)**[50] 1387 4-9-5 **73** TylerSaunders 3 39
(Jonathan Portman) *trckd ldrs: rdn over 2f out: wknd over 1f out* **14/1**
0-23 **14** *3/4* **Grapevine (IRE)**[11] 2486 6-9-2 **77** (b[1]) OwenLewis(7) 13 41
(Charles Hills) *mid-div: pulling hrd whn swtchd rt over 2f out: sn wknd* **16/1**
46-2 **15** *1/2* **Redgrave (IRE)**[10] 2516 5-9-9 **77** AledBeech 14 40
(Joseph Tuite) *a towards rr* **14/1**
2300 **16** *5* **Margie's Choice (GER)**[14] 2365 4-8-10 **67** AmeliaGlass(3) 16 18
(Michael Madgwick) *in tch tl wknd over 2f out* **66/1**
00-1 **17** *8* **Bristol Missile (USA)**[20] 2106 5-9-0 **68** KieranSchofield 5 1
(Richard Price) *trckd ldrs: rdn over 2f out: wknd over 1f out* **7/1**[2]
1m 38.81s (-1.09) **Going Correction** -0.20s/f (Firm) **17** Ran SP% **123.6**
Speed ratings (Par 103): **97,96,90,90,88 88,87,87,85,85 83,78,78,77,76 71,63**
CSF £379.93 CT £3593.94 TOTE £22.30: £4.70, £3.90, £2.60, £1.60; EX 194.70 Trifecta £775.50.
Owner John Manser **Bred** Meon Valley Stud **Trained** Ledbury, H'fords

FOCUS
Two horses finished clear in this fair, big-field handicap for apprentice riders. The winner is rated close to last year's C&D form.
T/Plt: £139.50 to a £1 stake. Pool: £59,970.66 - 313.70 winning units T/Qpdt: £11.80 to a £1 stake. Pool: £6,181.84 - 385.18 winning units **Tim Mitchell**

2760 NEWMARKET (R-H)
Friday, May 17

OFFICIAL GOING: Good to firm (watered; 7.6)
Wind: light, across Weather: overcast

2798 RACING TV H'CAP 7f
2:00 (2:01) (Class 5) (0-70,71) 3-Y-O

£4,528 (£1,347; £673; £336; £300; £300) **Stalls** Low

Form RPR
0-00 **1** **Broughtons Flare (IRE)**[44] 1516 3-8-11 **60** MartinDwyer 7 73
(Philip McBride) *racd in centre: led gp and midfield overall: clsd to ld over 2f out: rdn and wnt clr over 1f out: r.o strly: v readily: 1st of 8 in gp* **11/1**
2542 **2** *4* **Redemptive**[32] 1825 3-8-13 **65** JoshuaBryan(3) 8 67
(David Elsworth) *racd in centre: chsd gp ldrs and midfield overall: clsd and pressing wnr over 2f out: outpcd over 1f out: no ch w wnr and kpt on same pce ins fnl f: 2nd of 8 in gp* **11/2**[1]
3-33 **3** *nse* **Saikung (IRE)**[14] 2356 3-9-6 **69** NicolaCurrie 14 71
(Charles Hills) *racd in centre: hld up in last quartet: effrt and hdwy over 2f out: wnt 3rd but stl plenty to do over 1f out: styd on to press for 2nd towards fin: no ch w wnr: 3rd of 8 in gp* **11/2**[1]
605- **4** *6* **Salmon Fishing (IRE)**[200] 8692 3-9-2 **65** (w) RossaRyan 9 51
(Mohamed Moubarak) *racd in centre: midfield overall: effrt over 2f out: drifting rt and no imp over 1f out: no ch and plugged on same pce ins fnl f: 4th of 8 in gp* **16/1**
046- **5** *3/4* **Old Red Eyes (USA)**[233] 7675 3-9-3 **66** OisinMurphy 11 50
(Joseph Tuite) *racd in centre: s.i.s: hld up in last quartet: effrt over 2f out: nvr any ch w ldrs but plugged on to pass btn horses ins fnl f: 5th of 8 in gp* **8/1**[2]
006- **6** *1 1/2* **Orliko (IRE)**[177] 9171 3-8-13 **62** TomMarquand 3 42
(Richard Hannon) *racd in far side quintet: midfield overall: niggled along 1/2-way: no imp whn hung lft and nt clrest of runs ent fnl 2f: plugged on same pce and wl hld fnl f: 1st of 5 in gp (jockey said colt hung left-handed throughout)* **11/1**
230- **7** *1/2* **Rosamour (IRE)**[227] 7875 3-9-8 **71** ShaneKelly 13 49
(Richard Hughes) *racd in centre: chsd gp ldr (wnr) and midfield overall: clsd and pressing ldrs over 2f out: 4th and btn over 1f out: wknd ins fnl f: 6th of 8 in gp* **12/1**
32-0 **8** *1 1/2* **Winter Gleam (IRE)**[23] 2035 3-9-7 **70** (v[1]) PatCosgrave 4 44
(William Knight) *racd in far side quintet: broke wl and led early: sn hdd and chsd overall ldr for over 1f out: styd chsng ldrs tl btn u.p 2f out: wknd over 1f out: 2nd of 5 in gp* **16/1**
060- **9** *shd* **City Master**[177] 9170 3-9-1 **64** PatDobbs 12 38
(Ralph Beckett) *racd in centre: restless in stalls: in last pair: lost tch over 2f out: no ch after: plugged on to pass btn horses ins fnl f: 7th of 8 in gp* **8/1**[2]
0-36 **10** *1* **Chop Chop (IRE)**[90] 761 3-8-11 **60** AdamMcNamara 5 31
(Roger Charlton) *racd in far side quintet: in rr: effrt whn nt clr run 2f out: nvr any ch w wnr after: hung lft and nt clr run again ins fnl f: eased fnl 100yds: 3rd of 5 in gp* **12/1**
5-44 **11** *shd* **Toro Dorado**[25] 1980 3-9-0 **63** (v[1]) LiamKeniry 2 34
(Ed Dunlop) *racd in far side quintet: chsd ldr over 5f out tl over 2f out: sn u.p and lost pl: wknd over 1f out: 4th of 5 in gp* **12/1**
6000 **12** *23* **Axel Jacklin**[9] 2529 3-9-2 **65** JoeyHaynes 10
(Paul Howling) *racd in centre: restless in stalls: stmbld leaving stalls: a in rr: lost tch over 2f out: t.o: 8th of 8 in gp* **100/1**
54-0 **13** *3/4* **Mohogany**[17] 2238 3-8-12 **61** (b) JackMitchell 1
(Tom Clover) *racd in far side quintet: sn led: hdd over 2f out: dropped out over 1f out: eased ins fnl f: t.o: 5th of 5 in gp* **10/1**[3]
1m 26.5s (1.10) **Going Correction** +0.325s/f (Good) **13** Ran SP% **114.6**
Speed ratings (Par 99): **106,101,101,94,93 91,91,89,89,88 88,62,61**
CSF £67.42 CT £384.87 TOTE £12.00: £4.30, £1.70, £2.40; EX 77.20 Trifecta £403.60.
Owner Broughton Thermal Insulation **Bred** W Maxwell Ervine **Trained** Newmarket, Suffolk

FOCUS
Stands-side track used. Stalls far side except 1m6f: centre. The ground continued to dry out and was now good to firm all over. Repositioning of the bend into the home straight increased the distance of race 4 by 12yds. An ordinary 3yo handicap to start featuring just two previous winners. The field split into two early with the group against the far rail looking in control to halfway, but then the complexion completely changed with the those racing up the centre eventually dominating. The first three came clear and the form is rated around the second and third.

2799 CHEMTEST ENVIRONMENTAL LABORATORIES H'CAP 7f
2:35 (2:36) (Class 4) (0-80,85) 4-Y-O+

£6,469 (£1,925; £962; £481; £300; £300) **Stalls** Low

Form RPR
3111 **1** **Glenn Coco**[29] 1881 5-9-9 **82** (t) OisinMurphy 9 90
(Stuart Williams) *racd in centre: hld up in last pair: clsd over 2f out: effrt and rdn 2f out: drvn to chal ent fnl f: styd on to ld ins fnl f: rdn out: 1st of 5 in gp* **7/2**[1]
5021 **2** *1/2* **Rock Of Estonia (IRE)**[15] 2348 4-9-3 **76** NicolaCurrie 4 82
(Charles Hills) *mounted in chute and taken down early: racd in far side trio: in tch in midfield overall: effrt and clsd to chse ldrs over 2f out: chal over 1f out: kpt on wl ins fnl f but hld cl home: 1st of 3 in gp* **7/2**[1]
4143 **3** *1 1/4* **Call Out Loud**[51] 1356 7-9-2 **75** (vt) AlistairRawlinson 8 78
(Michael Appleby) *racd in centre: overall ldr: rdn over 2f out: drvn and edgd rt over 1f out: hdd ins fnl f: no ex and outpcd towards fin: 2nd of 5 in gp* **17/2**
5-26 **4** *3* **Young John (IRE)**[17] 2237 6-9-5 **78** RossaRyan 6 73
(Mike Murphy) *racd in centre: midfield overall: clsd and rdn to chse ldr 2f out tl over 1f out: outpcd whn swtchd rt 1f out: wknd ins fnl f: 3rd of 5 in gp* **15/2**[3]
-161 **5** *2* **Mr Tyrrell (IRE)**[11] 2472 5-9-12 **85** 5ex PatDobbs 7 75
(Richard Hannon) *racd in centre: chsd gp ldrs and chsd ldrs overall: clsd to chse overall ldr and rdn 2f out: lost 2nd 2f out and sn outpcd: wknd fnl f: 4th of 5 in gp* **9/2**[2]
5600 **6** *1 1/4* **Sea Fox (IRE)**[16] 2273 5-9-5 **78** (vt[1]) JFEgan 5 64
(David Evans) *racd in centre: midfield overall: unable qck u.p over 2f out: btn over 1f out: wknd ins fnl f: 5th of 5 in gp* **9/2**[2]
454- **7** *12* **Trulee Scrumptious**[266] 6493 10-8-7 **66** (v) JimmyQuinn 1 20
(Peter Charalambous) *racd in far side trio: a in rr: lost tch over 2f out: 2nd of 3 in gp* **25/1**

60-0 **8** *22* **Dance Teacher (IRE)**[20] 2097 5-8-13 **79**................(p1) GavinAshton(7) 2
(Shaun Keightley) *racd in far side trio: led gp and chsd overall ldr tl over 2f out: sn dropped out: bhd and eased over 1f out: t.o: 3rd of 3 in gp* **20/1**

1m 27.32s (1.92) **Going Correction** +0.325s/f (Good) **8** Ran SP% **111.7**
Speed ratings (Par 105): **102,101,100,96,94 92,79,54**
CSF £14.91 CT £92.80 TOTE £3.60: £1.70, £1.70, £2.40; EX 14.60 Trifecta £98.50.

Owner Miss Emily Stevens Partnership **Bred** Old Mill Stud And S C Williams **Trained** Newmarket, Suffolk

FOCUS
An interesting handicap with a few of these coming into the race in form, albeit mainly on the AW. Again they split into two groups and again those who came up the middle were at a big advantage. The winning time was 0.82sec slower than the 3yos in the opener, and the winner was close to his AW level.

2800 MOYES INVESTMENTS H'CAP 1m 2f
3:10 (3:10) (Class 3) (0-90,91) 4-Y-0+ **£9,056** (£2,695; £1,346; £673) **Stalls** Low

Form RPR
3-15 **1** **Lunar Jet**[20] 2095 5-9-9 **91**................ JimmyQuinn 5 98
(John Mackie) *stdd after s: hld up in tch in rr: clsd over 2f out: rdn to chse ldrs over 1f out: led jst ins fnl f: r.o wl* **9/2[1]**

4-54 **2** *2* **Lawmaking**[34] 1757 6-9-2 **84**................(b) LiamKeniry 8 87
(Michael Scudamore) *mounted in chute and taken down early: stdd after s: hld up in tch in rr: clsd over 2f out: effrt in 4th and hung rt 1f out: kpt on to chse wnr wl ins fnl f: no threat to wnr* **9/1**

320- **3** *½* **You're Hired**[237] 7537 6-9-5 **87**................ PatDobbs 3 89
(Amanda Perrett) *dwlt: sn in tch in midfield: clsd to chse ldr 2f out: rdn to chal over 1f out: no ex and outpcd by wnr ins fnl f: kpt on same pce and lost 2nd wl ins fnl f* **5/1[2]**

1220 **4** *2* **Star Of Southwold (FR)**[48] 1422 4-9-5 **87**................ AlistairRawlinson 4 85
(Michael Appleby) *chsd ldr tl led over 2f out: wandered lft and hrd pressed over 1f out: hdd jst ins fnl f: sn outpcd* **6/1[3]**

-440 **5** *11* **C Note (IRE)**[34] 1757 6-9-0 **85**................ JaneElliott(3) 6 61
(Heather Main) *led: rdn and hdd over 2f out: outpcd u.p and btn over 1f out: wknd fnl f* **9/2[1]**

5-00 **6** *6* **Nayel (IRE)**[20] 2095 7-9-5 **87**................(p) TomMarquand 11 51
(Richard Hannon) *chsd ldrs: effrt over 2f out: outpcd and btn whn edgd lft over 1f out: wknd fnl f* **12/1**

54-4 **7** *1 ¼* **Perfect Illusion**[18] 2209 4-8-12 **80**................ MartinDwyer 9 42
(Andrew Balding) *taken down early: stdd s: hld up in tch in rr: rdn over 3f out: nvr threatened to get on terms w ldrs: btn 2f out: sn wknd (trainer's rep could offer no explanation for the gelding's performance)* **9/2[1]**

5-50 **8** *1* **Secret Art (IRE)**[15] 2320 9-9-7 **89**................ ShaneKelly 2 49
(Gary Moore) *chsd ldrs: rdn over 2f out: sn lost pl and wknd over 1f out* **66/1**

643- **9** *nse* **Rotherwick (IRE)**[196] 8806 7-9-2 **87**................ CameronNoble(3) 7 46
(Paul Cole) *in tch in rr: rdn over 3f out: sn struggling and wl btn 2f out: wknd* **14/1**

2m 7.46s (2.06) **Going Correction** +0.325s/f (Good) **9** Ran SP% **111.3**
Speed ratings (Par 107): **104,102,102,100,91 86,85,85,84**
CSF £42.70 CT £202.52 TOTE £3.80: £1.70, £2.80, £2.30; EX 44.60 Trifecta £201.90.

Owner Ladas **Bred** Ladas **Trained** Church Broughton, Derbys

FOCUS
A fair handicap, though not with much recent winning form. The jockeys had clearly learned from the earlier races and made straight for the centre of the track. They finished well spread out. The form's rated around the runner-up.

2801 EDMONDSON HALL SOLICITORS & SPORTS LAWYERS H'CAP 1m 6f
3:45 (3:48) (Class 3) (0-95,95) 4-Y-0+
£18,675 (£5,592; £2,796; £1,398; £699; £351) **Stalls** Centre

Form RPR
20-4 **1** **Lissitzky (IRE)**[15] 2342 4-8-7 **81**................ MartinDwyer 9 91+
(Andrew Balding) *stdd and dropped in bhd after s: hld up in rr: effrt and hdwy 3f out: chsd ldrs and drvn over 1f out: led and wnt lft ins fnl f: r.o wl* **16/1**

30/4 **2** *1 ¾* **All Set To Go (IRE)**[20] 2126 8-8-11 **88**................(t) JoshuaBryan(3) 4 94
(Kevin Frost) *hld up in tch in midfield: clsd to chse ldr 4f out tl led over 2f out: rdn and hung lft over 1f out: wandered rt 1f out: hdd and one pce ins fnl f* **33/1**

20-0 **3** *2 ¼* **Fire Jet (IRE)**[27] 1947 6-8-11 **85**................ JimmyQuinn 5 88
(John Mackie) *hld up in tch in last trio: hdwy 4f out: rdn to chse ldrs over 2f out: drvn: unable qck and edgd rt over 1f out: kpt on same pce ins fnl f* **10/1**

111 **4** *4 ½* **Gumball (FR)**[19] 2143 5-9-2 **90**................ OisinMurphy 2 87
(Philip Hobbs) *t.k.h: led tl hdd over 2f out: stl ev ch but struggling qckn whn nudged lft over 1f out: wknd ins fnl f* **6/5[1]**

3213 **5** *5* **Busy Street**[46] 1483 7-9-6 **94**................ AlistairRawlinson 3 84
(Michael Appleby) *hld up in tch in midfield: clsd to chse ldrs 4f out: unable qck u.p over 2f out: wl btn over 1f out: wknd* **16/1**

32-1 **6** *9* **Hareeq**[28] 1914 4-9-0 **88**................(p) ShaneKelly 10 65
(Richard Hughes) *chsd ldrs: rdn 3f out: sn drvn and outpcd: wknd over 1f out (trainer's rep said colt was unsuited by the ground (good to firm) which in his opinion, was riding loose on this occasion)* **7/1[3]**

2130 **7** *3 ¼* **Stamford Raffles**[28] 1917 6-9-4 **92**................ JFEgan 8 65
(Jane Chapple-Hyam) *t.k.h: hld up in tch in midfield: struggling u.p over 3f out: wl btn fnl 2f* **66/1**

410- **8** *3 ½* **Master Archer (IRE)**[216] 8197 5-9-2 **90**................(v) GeorgeWood 6 58
(James Fanshawe) *hld up in tch in last trio: effrt: rdn and hdwy 3f out: sn no imp and btn u.p 2f out: wknd* **25/1**

30-3 **9** *30* **Reshoun (FR)**[19] 2143 5-9-7 **95**................(p) PatDobbs 1 21
(Ian Williams) *chsd ldrs tl rdn and lost pl over 3f out: wl btn and eased over 2f out: t.o (trainer said gelding had a breathing problem)* **4/1[2]**

10-0 **10** *33* **Artarmon (IRE)**[27] 1947 4-9-0 **88**................(p) JackMitchell 7
(Michael Bell) *chsd ldr tl 4f out: sn dropped to rr: wl bhd and eased over 1f out: t.o (jockey said gelding stopped quickly)* **33/1**

3m 2.16s (5.06) **Going Correction** +0.325s/f (Good) **10** Ran SP% **110.0**
Speed ratings (Par 107): **98,97,95,93,90 85,83,81,64,45**
CSF £430.29 CT £5124.79 TOTE £18.60: £3.70, £7.60, £2.50; EX 681.00 Trifecta £2779.30.

Owner Nigel Morris **Bred** Frank Hutchinson **Trained** Kingsclere, Hants

FOCUS
Add 12yds. A useful staying handicap with a few in here who normally like to force it. However, on this occasion they allowed the favourite an uncontested lead, not that it did him any good. They made straight for the centre of the track on straightening for home. Improvement from the winner.

2802 PLANCHE PROPERTY INVESTMENT & RENTALS NOVICE STKS (PLUS 10 RACE) 1m
4:15 (4:19) (Class 4) 3-Y-O **£5,563** (£1,655; £827; £413) **Stalls** Low

Form RPR
2- **1** **Velorum (IRE)**[231] 7736 3-9-2 0................ BrettDoyle 3 94+
(Charlie Appleby) *chsd ldrs: effrt over 2f out: rdn to ld over 1f out: clr ins fnl f: styd on* **2/1[2]**

05- **2** *1 ¼* **Moqtarreb**[212] 8327 3-9-2 0................ MartinDwyer 12 90
(Roger Varian) *rn green and impeded sn after s: in tch towards rr: nt clr run and swtchd lft over 2f out: hdwy over 1f out: chsd clr wnr jst ins fnl f: nvr getting to wnr but r.o wl* **50/1**

41 **3** *4 ½* **Desert Icon (FR)**[16] 2289 3-9-9 0................ OisinMurphy 7 86
(William Haggas) *dwlt: sn rcvrd to chse ldrs: wnt 2nd 5f out: rdn and ev ch 3f out: chsd wnr but outpcd over 1f out: lost 2nd jst ins fnl f: wknd fnl 100yds* **6/1[3]**

4 *½* **Meqdam (IRE)** 3-9-2 0................ JosephineGordon 4 78
(Saeed bin Suroor) *hld up in tch in midfield: effrt jst over 1f out: rn green: hung rt and rn green over 1f out: hdwy ins fnl f: no threat to ldrs but kpt on wl ins fnl f* **20/1**

2 **5** *½* **Land Of Legends (IRE)**[24] 2023 3-9-2 0................ PatCosgrave 9 77
(Saeed bin Suroor) *chsd ldrs: effrt and clsd jst over 2f out: pressing ldrs but unable qck u.p over 1f out: wknd ins fnl f* **11/8[1]**

6 **6** *1 ¾* **Recondite (IRE)**[19] 2139 3-9-2 0................ PatDobbs 5 73
(Ralph Beckett) *restless in stalls: pressed ldrs: rdn and struggling to qckn whn sltly short of room 2f out: outpcd over 1f out: wknd ins fnl f* **33/1**

2-5 **7** *hd* **Real Smooth (IRE)**[19] 2139 3-9-2 0................ TomMarquand 6 73
(Richard Hannon) *led: drvn and hdd over 1f out: sn outpcd and wknd ins fnl f* **14/1**

3 **8** *1 ½* **Edaraat**[24] 2023 3-9-2 0................ JackMitchell 10 69
(Roger Varian) *in tch in midfield: rdn wl over 2f out: outpcd whn rn green and wandered over 1f out: wl hld fnl f* **8/1**

66-5 **9** *4* **Leo Davinci (USA)**[17] 2236 3-9-2 0................ EoinWalsh 2 60
(George Scott) *stdd s: t.k.h: hld up in tch in last quartet: clsd over 2f out: rdn 2f out: sn btn and wknd over 1f out* **100/1**

10 *1 ¼* **Smoke On The Water** 3-9-2 0................(t1) GeorgeWood 1 57
(Charlie Fellowes) *hld up in midfield: rn green and edgd rt over 3f out: outpcd whn sltly impeded over 1f out: sn wknd* **50/1**

0 **11** *22* **Aide Memoire (IRE)**[35] 1740 3-8-11 0................ LiamKeniry 11
(David Elsworth) *plld hrd: hld up in rr: struggling 1/2-way: wl bhd fnl 2f: t.o* **100/1**

0 **12** *¾* **Kostantina**[19] 2148 3-8-11 0................ RachelRichardson 13
(Olly Williams) *a in rr: struggling 1/2-way: wl bhd fnl 2f: t.o* **200/1**

00 **13** *18* **Samba Saravah (USA)**[18] 2208 3-9-2 0................ ShaneKelly 8
(Jeremy Noseda) *chsd ldr for 3f: rdn and lost pl wl over 2f out: wl bhd and eased ins fnl f: t.o (jockey said colt stopped quickly)* **100/1**

1m 39.65s (1.25) **Going Correction** +0.325s/f (Good) **13** Ran SP% **122.6**
Speed ratings (Par 101): **106,104,100,99,99 97,97,95,91,90 68,67,49**
CSF £115.21 TOTE £2.90: £1.10, £14.10, £1.90; EX 139.50 Trifecta £875.80.

Owner Godolphin **Bred** Phillistown House Ltd **Trained** Newmarket, Suffolk

FOCUS
An interesting novice event, though not that competitive. Two of the three Godolphin horses dominated the market and one of them won impressively. The first two are rated up to the race standard (it was a maiden in previous years).

2803 FEDERATION OF BLOODSTOCK AGENTS H'CAP 1m
4:45 (4:48) (Class 3) (0-90,90) 4-Y-0+ **£9,056** (£2,695; £1,346; £673) **Stalls** Low

Form RPR
2-30 **1** **Laieth**[106] 513 4-9-5 **88**................ OisinMurphy 4 101
(Saeed bin Suroor) *sn led and mde rest: pushed along and kicked clr 2f out: in command and styd on strly ins fnl f: comf* **11/2**

-450 **2** *3 ¼* **Dawaaleeb (USA)**[13] 2419 5-9-7 **90**................(v) JackMitchell 3 96
(Les Eyre) *chsd wnr thrght: rdn 3f out: unable to match pce of wnr 2f out: clr 2nd and kpt on same pce ins fnl f* **4/1[3]**

5-53 **3** *2* **Medieval (IRE)**[16] 2273 5-8-11 **83**................(t1) CameronNoble(3) 1 84
(Paul Cole) *hld up in tch in last pair: effrt over 2f out: hdwy to chse ldrs over 1f out: no imp and wl hld ins fnl f* **3/1[2]**

60-1 **4** *½* **Enigmatic (IRE)**[16] 2273 5-9-2 **90**................ DarraghKeenan(5) 5 90
(Alan Bailey) *in tch in midfield: no hdwy over 1f out: wl hld and kpt on same pce ins fnl f* **11/4[1]**

/12- **5** *1* **Caradoc (IRE)**[338] 3740 4-9-4 **87**................ LiamKeniry 6 85
(Ed Walker) *stdd s: hld up in tch in last pair: swtchd lft and effrt over 1f out: no prog and wl hld ins fnl f* **5/1**

130- **6** *hd* **Arigato**[195] 8839 4-9-0 **83**................(p) JosephineGordon 7 80
(William Jarvis) *t.k.h: chsd ldrs: rdn over 2f out: lost pl and wl hld fnl f* **14/1**

1m 39.22s (0.82) **Going Correction** +0.325s/f (Good) **6** Ran SP% **110.4**
Speed ratings (Par 107): **108,104,102,102,101 101**
CSF £26.32 TOTE £6.10: £3.10, £2.40; EX 24.60 Trifecta £67.90.

Owner Godolphin **Bred** Rabbah Bloodstock Ltd **Trained** Newmarket, Suffolk

FOCUS
A fair handicap, but the winner dictated and the order didn't change much. The runner-up is rated to his Spring Mile level.

2804 PORSCHE CENTRE CAMBRIDGE APPRENTICE H'CAP (HANDS AND HEELS) (PART OF RACING EXCELLENCE) 6f
5:15 (5:16) (Class 5) (0-75,77) 4-Y-0+
£4,528 (£1,347; £673; £336; £300; £300) **Stalls** Low

Form RPR
6436 **1** **Emily Goldfinch**[27] 1932 6-9-6 **77**................(p) GraceMcEntee(6) 5 86
(Phil McEntee) *chsd ldr tl led wl over 1f out: styd on wl and a doing enough ins fnl f (trainer said, regarding the apparent improvement in form, that mare benefitted from a short break following several quick runs)* **12/1**

40-3 **2** *¾* **Lethal Angel**[21] 2081 4-8-10 **67**................(b1) MarcoGhiani(6) 7 74
(Stuart Williams) *chsd ldrs: effrt to chse wnr over 1f out: kpt on but a hld ins fnl f* **12/1**

006- **3** *2 ¾* **Seprani**[137] 9772 5-9-4 **72**................ StefanoCherchi(3) 4 70
(Amy Murphy) *chsd ldrs: effrt but outpcd by ldng pair over 1f out: 3rd and kpt on same pce ins fnl f* **25/1**

-000 **4** *hd* **Valley Of Fire**[21] 2076 7-9-3 68......................................(b) HarryRussell 1 66
(Les Eyre) *wnt rt sn after s: in tch in midfield: effrt over 2f out: hdwy over 1f out: kpt on but no threat to ldng pair ins fnl f* **16/1**

5400 **5** *1 1/4* **Human Nature (IRE)**[16] 2272 6-9-7 75......................(t) GavinAshton(3) 8 69
(Stuart Williams) *midfield: effrt and swtchd lft over 1f out: no threat to ldrs but kpt on ins fnl f* **12/1**

0230 **6** *1/2* **Madrinho (IRE)**[20] 2107 6-9-5 76.......................... ElishaWhittington(6) 3 68
(Tony Carroll) *awkward leaving stalls and slowly away: in rr: effrt 2f out: hdwy 1f out: kpt on ins fnl f: nvr trbld ldrs* **9/1**

6053 **7** *1 1/2* **National Glory (IRE)**[11] 2483 4-9-1 66......................(b) GeorgiaDobie 6 53
(Archie Watson) *led tl wl over 1f out: sn pushed along and no ex: wknd ins fnl f* **10/1**

-131 **8** *1/2* **Major Valentine**[3] 2717 7-9-0 71 4ex.............................. KateLeahy(6) 11 57
(John O'Shea) *in tch in midfield: unable qck over 1f out: wl hld and plugged on same pce fnl f* **5/2[1]**

-604 **9** *1* **Big Lachie**[20] 2107 5-9-8 73.............................. JessicaCooley 9 55
(Mark Loughnane) *stdd s: hld up in tch in rr: effrt and swtchd rt over 1f out: sn no imp: wknd ins fnl f* **7/1[3]**

3304 **10** *4 1/2* **Suzi's Connoisseur**[6] 2611 8-9-8 73......................(b) TristanPrice 10 41
(Jane Chapple-Hyam) *in tch towards rr: effrt over 2f out: sn struggling and hung rt over 1f out: wknd fnl f (jockey said gelding hung right-handed under pressure)* **7/2[2]**

-000 **11** *1* **Rockies Spirit**[34] 1767 4-9-0 68............................(t w) LauraPearson(3) 2 33
(Denis Quinn) *midfield: rdn and lost pl 2f out: bhd ins fnl f* **40/1**

1m 13.07s (1.17) **Going Correction** +0.325s/f (Good) **11 Ran SP% 117.6**
Speed ratings (Par 103): **105,104,100,100,98 97,95,95,93,87 86**
CSF £147.58 CT £3507.94 TOTE £15.30: £3.60, £2.60, £7.70; EX 183.60 Trifecta £2987.60.
Owner Miss R McEntee & J Paxton **Bred** J M Paxton & Mrs S J Wrigley **Trained** Newmarket, Suffolk

FOCUS
Quite a few of these appeared to have become well handicapped, including the winner. He's was close to the form of last year's C&D win off this mark.
T/Plt: £725.80 to a £1 stake. Pool: £55,762.78 - 56.08 winning units T/Qpdt: £116.20 to a £1 stake. Pool: £4,871.05 - 31.00 winning units **Steve Payne**

2775 YORK (L-H)

Friday, May 17

OFFICIAL GOING: Good to firm (good in places; watered; ovr 7.3, stands' 7.3, ctr 7.2, far 7.3)
Wind: Moderate against Weather: Cloudy

2805 LANGLEYS SOLICITORS BRITISH EBF MARYGATE FILLIES' STKS (LISTED RACE) 5f

1:50 (1:52) (Class 1) 2-Y-O

£28,355 (£10,750; £5,380; £2,680; £1,345; £675) **Stalls** High

Form RPR

21 **1** **Good Vibes**[19] 2138 2-8-12 0.............................. HarryBentley 8 100
(David Evans) *slt bump s and towards rr: gd hdwy in centre over 2f out: chsd ldrs and rdn over 1f out: str run fnl f to ld fnl 75yds* **10/1**

2 **2** *1 1/2* **Mighty Spirit (IRE)**[28] 1923 2-8-12 0.............................. PJMcDonald 2 95+
(Richard Fahey) *racd towards far side: trckd ldrs: hdwy 2f out and sn chal: rdn over 1f out: ev ch ins fnl f: kpt on same pce towards fin* **13/2[2]**

11 **3** *1* **Lady Kermit (IRE)**[28] 1923 2-8-12 0.............................. HollieDoyle 16 91+
(Archie Watson) *qckly away and racd towards stands' side: led: rdn along over 1f out: drvn ins fnl f: hdd last 75yds: kpt on same pce* **11/4[1]**

4 *3* **Galadriel** 2-8-12 0.............................. AndreaAtzeni 21 80+
(Kevin Ryan) *green: outpcd and detached nr stands' rail after 1f: swtchd lft to centre and rdn along 1/2-way: gd hdwy wl over 1f out: fin strly* **16/1**

6 **5** *1 1/4* **Macho Touch (IRE)**[28] 1923 2-8-12 0.............................. BenCurtis 19 76+
(K R Burke) *racd towards stands' side: in rr and rdn along bef 1/2-way: hdwy 2f out: styd on wl fnl f* **50/1**

2 **6** *1/2* **Separate**[35] 1733 2-8-12 0.............................. FrankieDettori 11 74
(Richard Hannon) *towards rr: pushed along 1/2-way: rdn and hdwy 2f out: styng on whn n.m.r over 1f out: kpt on wl fnl f* **11/1**

21 **7** *1/2* **Iva Go (IRE)**[22] 2051 2-8-12 0.............................. DavidAllan 15 72+
(Tim Easterby) *racd centre: cl up: rdn along 2f out: grad wknd (jockey said filly ran too freely)* **16/1**

1 **8** *1/2* **Baileys In Bloom (FR)**[22] 2052 2-8-12 0.............................. PaulHanagan 13 70
(Richard Fahey) *chsd ldrs centre: rdn along 2f out: wknd over 1f out* **20/1**

1 **9** *1/2* **Companion**[24] 2020 2-8-12 0.............................. SilvestreDeSousa 18 69
(Mark Johnston) *wnt rt s and bhd: rdn along 1/2-way: hdwy nr stands' wl over 1f out: kpt on fnl f* **11/1**

1 **10** *1/2* **Silver Start**[16] 2275 2-8-12 0.............................. RichardKingscote 5 67+
(Charles Hills) *cl up centre: chal 2f out: rdn over 1f out: wknd ent fnl f* **20/1**

1 **11** *1* **Lady Fanditha (IRE)**[17] 2248 2-8-12 0.............................. GeraldMosse 7 63
(Clive Cox) *sltly hmpd s: t.k.h and chsd ldrs: rdn along 2f out: grad wknd* **9/1**

2 **12** *hd* **Taste The Nectar (USA)**[17] 2257 2-8-12 0.............................. LukeMorris 1 62
(Robert Cowell) *racd towards far side: towards rr: sme hdwy 2f out: sn rdn and n.d* **20/1**

1 **13** *3/4* **Fleeting Princess**[17] 2257 2-8-12 0.............................. RyanMoore 12 60
(Jeremy Noseda) *chsd ldrs centre: rdn along 2f out: drvn: edgd rt and wknd appr fnl f* **8/1[3]**

011 **14** *hd* **Great Dame (IRE)**[9] 2520 2-8-12 0.............................. DanielTudhope 4 59
(David O'Meara) *racd towards far side: cl up: rdn along 2f out: sn wknd (jockey said filly hung left from halfway)* **20/1**

1 **15** *1 3/4* **Lady Quickstep (IRE)**[16] 2282 2-8-12 0.............................. WilliamCox 20 53
(Gay Kelleway) *racd nr stands' rail: towards rr: pushed along 1/2-way: rdn and hdwy 2f out: sn in tch: wknd appr fnl f* **50/1**

21 **16** *1 1/4* **Infinite Grace**[11] 2476 2-8-12 0.............................. CamHardie 6 48
(David O'Meara) *wnt rt s: chsd ldrs centre: rdn along 2f out: sn wknd* **40/1**

144 **17** *1/2* **Chasanda**[9] 2520 2-8-12 0.............................. PaddyMathers 17 46
(David Evans) *racd towards stands' side: chsd ldrs: rdn along 2f out: grad wknd* **100/1**

22 **18** *shd* **Ruby Wonder**[11] 2475 2-8-12 0.............................. RobbieDowney 9 46
(David O'Meara) *prom: rdn along 1/2-way: sn wknd* **100/1**

59.75s (1.55) **Going Correction** +0.30s/f (Good) **18 Ran SP% 126.0**
Speed ratings (Par 98): **99,96,95,90,88 87,86,85,85,84 82,82,81,80,77 75,75,75**
CSF £67.70 TOTE £11.50: £3.10, £2.60, £1.70; EX 86.30 Trifecta £383.80.
Owner Paul & Clare Rooney **Bred** Whitsbury Manor Stud **Trained** Pandy, Monmouths

FOCUS
Ground conditions looked pretty similar to the first two days as PJ McDonald said: "It's nice, quick ground," Paul Hanagan said: "It's safe, good to firm ground" and Ben Curtis and Cam Hardie both called it 'pretty similar to yesterday'. The principal race for juvenile fillies before Royal Ascot, the first three finishing clear, and it's been rated the best ever renewal. They went a strong gallop and the time was 2.45sec outside standard, racing into a headwind. Three previous winners of this event have gone to win the Queen Mary Stakes: Gilded in 2006, Ceiling Kitty in 2012 and Signora Cabello last year.

2806 OAKS FARM STABLES FILLIES' STKS (REG AS THE MICHAEL SEELEY MEMORIAL FILLIES' STAKES) (LISTED RACE) 7f 192y

2:25 (2:30) (Class 1) 3-Y-O

£28,355 (£10,750; £5,380; £2,680; £1,345; £675) **Stalls** Low

Form RPR

164- **1** **Magnetic Charm**[246] 7199 3-9-0 100.............................. JamesDoyle 5 105
(William Haggas) *hld up in rr: gd hdwy on outer wl over 2f out: chal over 1f out: sn rdn: drvn to ld ins fnl f: edgd lft and kpt on wl* **7/1[3]**

3-21 **2** *nk* **Twist 'N' Shake**[7] 2583 3-9-0 0.............................. FrankieDettori 9 104
(John Gosden) *trckd ldrs: hdwy on outer 3f out: led 2f out and sn edgd lft: jnd and rdn over 1f out: drvn: edgd lft and hdd ins fnl f: kpt on* **11/8[1]**

142- **3** *3* **Glance**[202] 8648 3-9-0 94.............................. HarryBentley 7 97
(Ralph Beckett) *hld up: hdwy 3f out: rdn to chse ldrs wl over 1f out: drvn and kpt on same pce appr fnl f* **20/1**

13-0 **4** *1/2* **Sunday Star**[31] 1832 3-9-0 100.............................. GeraldMosse 12 96
(Ed Walker) *hld up in rr: gd hdwy 3f out: chsd ldrs and rdn wl over 1f out: drvn and kpt on same pce fnl f* **25/1**

1-63 **5** *3* **Modern Millie**[16] 2268 3-9-0 95.............................. BenCurtis 1 89
(Mick Channon) *chsd ldrs: hdwy on inner 3f out: sn cl up: rdn 2f out: grad wknd* **25/1**

5-1 **6** *1 3/4* **Flighty Almighty**[41] 1594 3-9-0 0.............................. RichardKingscote 2 85
(Tom Dascombe) *chsd ldrs: rdn along 3f out: sn btn* **25/1**

54-0 **7** *1/2* **Impulsion (IRE)**[19] 2144 3-9-0 87.............................. DanielTudhope 10 84
(Roger Varian) *trckd ldng pair: pushed along over 3f out: sn rdn and wknd over 2f out* **40/1**

3-1 **8** *1* **Clerisy**[30] 1855 3-9-0 0.............................. RyanMoore 6 81
(Sir Michael Stoute) *hld up towards rr: effrt over 3f out: sn rdn along and n.d* **9/1**

101- **9** *3 1/2* **Natalie's Joy**[301] 5172 3-9-0 100.............................. FrannyNorton 3 73
(Mark Johnston) *led: rdn along and hdd 3f out: sn wknd* **13/2[2]**

32-1 **10** *1* **El Gumryah (IRE)**[27] 1939 3-9-0 93.............................. SilvestreDeSousa 8 71
(Simon Crisford) *cl up: led 3f out: sn rdn: hdd 2f out and sn wknd* **14/1**

03-1 **11** *3/4* **Divinity**[29] 1897 3-9-0 90.............................. CliffordLee 4 69
(K R Burke) *s.i.s: a in rr* **20/1**

1m 38.8s (1.30) **Going Correction** +0.30s/f (Good) **11 Ran SP% 108.1**
Speed ratings (Par 104): **105,104,101,101,98 96,95,94,91,90 89**
CSF £13.34 TOTE £5.70: £1.60, £1.10, £5.40; EX 17.80 Trifecta £207.20.
Owner The Queen **Bred** Godolphin **Trained** Newmarket, Suffolk
■ Invitational was withdrawn. Price at time of withdrawal 12/1. Rule 4 applies to all bets - deduction 5p in the pound

FOCUS
Add 36 yards. Four of the last ten winners of this went on to win at Group level, while Threading finished second in the Group 1 Coronation Stakes at Royal Ascot after taking this last year. This running featured seven last-time-out winners and looked well up to scratch, although a couple of these appeared unsuited by the fast conditions. The winner progressed again and the second also improved on her novice form.

2807 MATCHBOOK YORKSHIRE CUP STKS (GROUP 2) (BRITISH CHAMPIONS SERIES) 1m 5f 188y

3:00 (3:02) (Class 1) 4-Y-O+

£93,571 (£35,475; £17,754; £8,844; £4,438; £2,227) **Stalls** Low

Form RPR

111- **1** **Stradivarius (IRE)**[209] 8404 5-9-4 120.............................. FrankieDettori 4 120+
(John Gosden) *hld up in tch: hdwy on outer over 3f out: cl up and rdn 2f out: sn edgd rt to stands' rail: slt ld ent fnl f: sn drvn and kpt on wl towards fin* **4/5[1]**

30-3 **2** *3/4* **Southern France (IRE)**[19] 2158 4-9-1 111.............................. RyanMoore 5 115
(A P O'Brien, Ire) *trckd ldng pair: hdwy 3f out: sn cl up: rdn to ld briefly jst over 1f out: drvn ins fnl f: ev ch tl kpt on same pce fnl 75yds* **11/2[3]**

2-03 **3** *5* **Mildenberger**[13] 2410 4-9-1 109.............................. SilvestreDeSousa 7 108
(Mark Johnston) *trckd ldr: hdwy 3f out: led over 2f out: sn rdn: drvn and hdd appr fnl f: kpt on one pce (vet said colt lost its left fore shoe)* **7/1**

2112 **4** *1* **Ispolini**[48] 1441 4-9-1 116..(t) JamesDoyle 8 107
(Charlie Appleby) *trckd ldrs: hdwy over 3f out: rdn along over 2f out: sn drvn and one pce* **7/2[2]**

450- **5** *5* **Desert Skyline (IRE)**[202] 8645 5-9-1 109......................(p) GeraldMosse 1 100
(David Elsworth) *hld up in rr: hdwy over 4f out: pushed along 3f out: rdn over 2f out: sn no imp* **20/1**

1-11 **6** *6* **Mootasadir**[48] 1420 4-9-1 104.............................. BenCurtis 2 91
(Hugo Palmer) *hld up effrt and sme hdwy 4f out: rdn along over 3f out: sn wknd* **16/1**

000- **7** *3/4* **Sevenna Star (IRE)**[224] 7951 4-9-1 105......................(t w) AndreaAtzeni 6 90
(John Ryan) *led: rdn along over 3f out: hdd over 2f out: grad wknd* **50/1**

-146 **8** *34* **Aircraft Carrier (IRE)**[28] 1917 4-9-1 100..............(p) RichardKingscote 3 43
(John Ryan) *a in rr* **50/1**

3m 1.21s (1.01) **Going Correction** +0.30s/f (Good) **8 Ran SP% 120.2**
Speed ratings (Par 115): **109,108,105,105,102 98,98,79**
CSF £6.22 CT £19.86 TOTE £1.60: £1.02, £1.70, £2.20; EX 6.00 Trifecta £20.90.
Owner B E Nielsen **Bred** Bjorn Nielsen **Trained** Newmarket, Suffolk

FOCUS
Race run over an additional 43yds. This up-to-par edition of the Yorkshire Cup wasn't run at a true pace for the first half of the race, before winding up in the straight. Stradivarius was close to form, with Southern France rated as having improved.

2808 MATCHBOOK "BEST VALUE" EXCHANGE H'CAP 1m 2f 56y

3:35 (3:36) (Class 2) (0-100,100) 4-Y-O+

£18,675 (£4,194; £1,398; £699; £351) **Stalls** Low

Form RPR

254- **1** **UAE Prince (IRE)**[217] 8162 6-9-6 99.............................. AndreaAtzeni 8 109+
(Roger Varian) *trckd ldrs: hdwy over 3f out: cl up 2f out: rdn to ld jst over 1f out: edgd lft ins fnl f kpt on* **15/8[1]**

4-45 **2** *nk* **Lucius Tiberius (IRE)**[23] 2033 4-9-7 100.............................. JamesDoyle 7 107
(Charlie Appleby) *trckd ldng pair: smooth hdwy over 3f out: led 2f out: sn jnd and rdn: hdd jst over 1f out: drvn fnl f: kpt on* **6/1[2]**

-025 **2** *dht* **Society Red**[29] 1896 5-8-11 **90**........ PaulHanagan 6 97
(Richard Fahey) *hld up in tch: hdwy 3f out: chsd ldrs and rdn along 2f out: drvn and styd on wl fnl f* **12/1**

6-41 **4** *2* **Grandee (IRE)**[36] 1719 5-8-6 **90**........ BenSanderson(5) 12 93+
(Roger Fell) *hld up in rr: hdwy on outer 3f out: rdn along to chse ldrs over 1f out: drvn and kpt on fnl f* **13/2**[3]

5241 **5** *6* **Mythical Madness**[15] 2320 8-9-3 **96**........(v) DanielTudhope 11 87
(David O'Meara) *hld up in rr: hdwy 3f out: rdn along 2f out: sn no imp* **16/1**

3-20 **6** *1 1/2* **The Emperor Within (FR)**[13] 2429 4-9-2 **95**........ GeraldMosse 5 83
(Martin Smith) *trckd ldr: hdwy and cl up over 3f out: rdn along over 2f out: sn drvn and grad wknd* **9/1**

00-2 **7** *1 1/2* **Mistiroc**[20] 2095 8-8-13 **92**........(v) SilvestreDeSousa 9 77
(John Quinn) *sn led: rdn along 3f out: hdd 2f out: sn drvn and wknd* **8/1**

2402 **8** *nk* **Tough Remedy (IRE)**[18] 2187 4-8-7 **86**........ PJMcDonald 2 70
(Keith Dalgleish) *hld up: a in rr* **11/1**

205- **9** *1/2* **Scottish Summit (IRE)**[226] 7901 6-8-8 **87** ow1........ ConnorBeasley 4 70
(Geoffrey Harker) *chsd ldrs: rdn along 3f out: wknd over 2f out* **25/1**

0-65 **10** *12* **Abe Lincoln (USA)**[104] 565 6-9-5 **98**........(bt) RyanMoore 10 57
(Jeremy Noseda) *hld up: a in rr* **20/1**

2-00 **11** *shd* **Kyllachy Gala**[72] 1031 6-8-13 **92**........(p) HollieDoyle 1 51
(Warren Greatrex) *midfield: pushed along over 3f out: rdn wl over 2f out: sn wknd* **50/1**

2m 11.05s (0.75) **Going Correction** +0.30s/f (Good) **11 Ran SP% 116.0**
Speed ratings (Par 109): **109,108,108,107,102 101,99,99,99,89 89**
WIN: 2.70 Uae Prince; Place: 1.10 UP, 3.20 SR, 2.30 LT; Exacta: UP/LT 6.40, UP/SR 13.80; CSF: UP/LT 6.09, UP/SR 12.63; Tricast: UP/LT/SR 52.82, UP/SR/LT 58.03; Trifecta: UP/LT/SR 45.40, UP/SR/LT 71.10;.
Owner Sheikh Mohammed Obaid Al Maktoum **Bred** John Connaughton **Trained** Newmarket, Suffolk

FOCUS
Add 43 yards. The market got this spot on, the short-priced favourite coming home in front, despite pulling fiercely. The dead-heating runner-ups have been rated as running to form.

2809 BRITISH EBF FRANK WHITTLE PARTNERSHIP FILLIES' H'CAP 7f
4:05 (4:08) (Class 3) (0-90,92) 3-Y-0+
£12,450 (£3,728; £1,864; £932; £466; £234) **Stalls** Low

Form RPR

01-2 **1** **Agincourt (IRE)**[20] 2097 4-9-9 **82**........ DanielTudhope 11 92
(David O'Meara) *prom on outer: effrt and cl up 2f out: rdn to chal ent fnl f: sn drvn: kpt on gamely to ld on line* **6/1**[2]

5030 **2** *nse* **Starlight Romance (IRE)**[28] 1916 5-9-12 **85**........ PaulHanagan 3 95
(Richard Fahey) *trckd ldrs on inner: hdwy and cl up 2f out: rdn to take slt ld over 1f out: drvn ins fnl f: kpt on gamely: hdd on line* **11/1**

151- **3** *nk* **Breathtaking Look**[170] 9287 4-9-6 **79**........ PJMcDonald 6 88
(Stuart Williams) *trckd ldrs: hdwy and cl up 2f out: rdn to chal over 1f out: drvn and ev ch ins fnl f: no ex nr line* **16/1**

260- **4** *1 1/2* **New Day Dawn (IRE)**[197] 8769 4-10-5 **92**........ RichardKingscote 17 97+
(Tom Dascombe) *stdd and swtchd lft s: hld up in rr: hdwy over 2f out: rdn over 1f out: styd on strly fnl f* **20/1**

5611 **5** *2* **Dream World (IRE)**[17] 2261 4-8-13 **72**........ SilvestreDeSousa 4 72
(Michael Appleby) *t.k.h: cl up: rdn to ld 1 1/2f out: sn drvn and hdd: wknd ins fnl f (jockey said filly ran too freely)* **6/1**[2]

10-6 **6** *nk* **Silca Mistress**[20] 2097 4-9-9 **82**........(b[1]) JamesDoyle 7 81
(Clive Cox) *t.k.h: sn led: rdn along 2f out: hdd 1 1/2f out: sn drvn: wknd ins fnl f* **25/1**

010- **7** *1 1/2* **Ladies First**[238] 7496 5-9-6 **79**........ NathanEvans 9 74
(Michael Easterby) *towards rr: hdwy wl over 2f out: rdn wl over 1f out: kpt on fnl f* **11/1**

41-0 **8** *3/4* **Lady Dancealot (IRE)**[12] 2442 4-10-0 **87**........ GeraldMosse 8 80
(David Elsworth) *towards rr: hdwy over 2f out: rdn to chse ldrs over 1f out: sn drvn and kpt on same pce* **12/1**

00-2 **9** *1 3/4* **Electric Landlady (IRE)**[42] 1561 4-9-9 **82**........ DaneO'Neill 1 70
(Denis Coakley) *hld up towards rr: hdwy on inner 3f out: chsd ldrs 2f out: sn rdn: wknd ent fnl f* **7/1**[3]

00-0 **10** *1 1/4* **Rose Marmara**[19] 2151 6-9-0 **73**........(tp) CamHardie 10 58
(Brian Rothwell) *chsd ldrs: rdn along wl over 2f out: sn wknd* **100/1**

0-26 **11** *1 3/4* **Zofelle (IRE)**[19] 2144 3-9-1 **85**........ DavidAllan 12 61
(Hugo Palmer) *chsd ldrs on outer: rdn along wl over 2f out: sn wknd* **16/1**

20-0 **12** *nse* **Daffy Jane**[29] 1895 4-9-9 **82**........ AndreaAtzeni 2 62
(Nigel Tinkler) *dwlt: a towards rr* **33/1**

0-51 **13** *1 3/4* **Florenza**[20] 2097 6-9-13 **86**........ MichaelStainton 15 61
(Chris Fairhurst) *midfield: hdwy to chse ldrs on outer 1/2-way: rdn along over 2f out: sn wknd* **20/1**

600- **14** *3/4* **Maggies Angel (IRE)**[223] 7980 4-9-9 **87**........ ConnorMurtagh(5) 13 60
(Richard Fahey) *a towards rr* **20/1**

441- **15** *shd* **Accommodate (IRE)**[225] 7932 3-8-13 **83**........(w) RyanMoore 5 52
(Sir Michael Stoute) *prom: effrt and cl up 3f out: led briefly 2f out: sn hdd & wknd: eased fnl f* **7/2**[1]

1m 26.21s (1.61) **Going Correction** +0.30s/f (Good)
WFA 3 from 4yo+ 11lb **15 Ran SP% 121.5**
Speed ratings (Par 104): **102,101,101,99,97 97,95,94,92,91 89,89,87,86,86**
CSF £63.84 CT £1039.27 TOTE £6.50: £2.10, £2.90, £4.70; EX 68.60 Trifecta £3875.90.
Owner Sir Robert Ogden **Bred** Sir Robert Ogden **Trained** Upper Helmsley, N Yorks

FOCUS
They went what looked a decent pace and this is solid fillies' form. Improvement from the winner and third.

2810 YORKSHIRE EQUINE PRACTICE H'CAP 5f
4:35 (4:38) (Class 3) (0-90,88) 3-Y-0
£12,450 (£3,728; £1,864; £932; £466; £234) **Stalls** Centre

Form RPR

-425 **1** **Wedding Date**[20] 2121 3-8-13 **80**........ CliffordLee 7 88
(Richard Hannon) *trckd ldrs: pushed along and sltly outpcd over 2f out: rdn and hdwy to chse ldrs over 1f out: str run ins fnl f: led last 50yds* **20/1**

0-22 **2** *3/4* **Moss Gill (IRE)**[14] 2377 3-8-7 **74**........ PJMcDonald 12 79
(James Bethell) *wnt rt s: cl up: led 3f out: rdn clr jst over 1f out: drvn ins fnl f: hdd and no ex last 50yds* **12/1**

25-1 **3** *1 1/4* **Roulston Scar (IRE)**[19] 2149 3-9-1 **82**........ KevinStott 6 83
(Kevin Ryan) *chsd ldrs: hdwy 2f out: rdn over 1f out: drvn to chse ldr ent fnl f: kpt on same pce towards fin* **9/2**[1]

40-0 **4** *1/2* **Alfie Solomons (IRE)**[30] 1851 3-9-5 **86**........ HarryBentley 5 85
(Richard Spencer) *towards rr: hdwy over 2f out: rdn to chse ldrs over 1f out: drvn and kpt on same pce fnl f* **9/1**

-32 **5** *1 1/2* **Tenax (IRE)**[17] 2255 3-9-0 **81**........ RyanMoore 1 74
(Nigel Tinkler) *trckd ldrs on inner: hdwy and cl up 2f out: sn rdn: drvn over 1f out: kpt on same pce* **5/1**[2]

10-0 **6** *2 1/4* **Good Luck Fox (IRE)**[21] 2086 3-9-6 **87**........ SilvestreDeSousa 14 72
(Richard Hannon) *sltly hmpd s and towards rr: hdwy over 2f out: sn rdn: kpt on fnl f* **14/1**

614- **7** *3* **Vee Man Ten**[151] 9589 3-8-7 **74**........(h) PaulHanagan 13 48
(Ivan Furtado) *hmpd s and towards rr: hdwy 2f out: sn rdn and kpt on fnl f* **25/1**

-643 **8** *hd* **Enchanted Linda**[2] 2730 3-8-10 **77**........ HollieDoyle 2 51
(Richard Hannon) *cl up: disp ld 2f out: sn rdn and wknd over 1f out* **8/1**

2-11 **9** *shd* **Free Love**[17] 2255 3-9-2 **88**........ TheodoreLadd(5) 4 61
(Michael Appleby) *cl up: disp ld over 2f out: sn rdn: drvn and wknd over 1f out* **13/2**

10-6 **10** *2 3/4* **Three Card Trick**[34] 1762 3-9-0 **81**........ DougieCostello 15 44
(Kevin Ryan) *prom: rdn along over 2f out: sn wknd* **18/1**

6-50 **11** *3/4* **Mawde (IRE)**[21] 2086 3-8-9 **76**........ CharlieBennett 8 37
(Rod Millman) *a towards rr* **33/1**

1600 **12** *3/4* **Sandridge Lad (IRE)**[28] 1920 3-8-12 **79**........ RichardKingscote 3 37
(John Ryan) *a towards rr* **66/1**

020- **13** *3 1/2* **Daphinia**[219] 8107 3-8-12 **79**........ GeraldMosse 11 24
(Peter Charalambous) *chsd ldrs: rdn along wl over 2f out: sn wknd* **40/1**

6-21 **14** *2* **Ustath**[20] 2123 3-9-0 **81**........ DaneO'Neill 9 19
(Owen Burrows) *cl up: rdn along and lost pl 1/2-way: sn in rr (jockey said colt ran flat)* **6/1**[3]

59.28s (1.08) **Going Correction** +0.30s/f (Good) **14 Ran SP% 118.7**
Speed ratings (Par 103): **103,101,99,99,96 93,88,87,87,83 82,80,75,72**
CSF £230.08 CT £1282.73 TOTE £20.40: £5.50, £4.30, £2.30; EX 305.80 Trifecta £2578.30.
Owner Middleham Park Racing CXIV **Bred** Llety Farms **Trained** East Everleigh, Wilts
■ True Hero was withdrawn. Price at time of withdrawal 16/1. Rule 4 does not apply

FOCUS
This 3yo sprint handicap invariably takes plenty of winning and this edition looked no exception. It was strongly run and the first four pulled clear. The winner is rated back to her early best.

2811 LONGINES IRISH CHAMPIONS WEEKEND H'CAP 1m 3f 188y
5:05 (5:06) (Class 4) (0-85,85) 3-Y-0
£12,699 (£3,802; £1,901; £950; £475; £300) **Stalls** Centre

Form RPR

36-1 **1** **Summer Moon**[11] 2485 3-9-5 **83** 6ex........ PJMcDonald 9 97
(Mark Johnston) *mde all: rdn over 2f out: drvn and clr ent fnl f: kpt on strly* **3/1**[2]

52-1 **2** *4* **Laafy (USA)**[20] 2113 3-9-5 **83**........ RyanMoore 7 90
(Sir Michael Stoute) *trckd ldrs: hdwy wl over 2f out: rdn wl over 1f out: drvn and kpt on to take 2nd ins fnl f* **2/1**[1]

213 **3** *nk* **Rochester House (IRE)**[17] 2258 3-9-4 **82**........ FrannyNorton 6 88
(Mark Johnston) *trckd ldng pair: hdwy on outer over 3f out: sn swtchd rt to stands' rail: rdn to chse wnr 2f out: drvn wl over 1f out: kpt on same pce fnl f* **12/1**

61-0 **4** *6* **Dark Lochnagar (USA)**[28] 1926 3-9-4 **82**........ DanielTudhope 1 78
(Keith Dalgleish) *trckd ldrs: hdwy 3f out: rdn along 2f out: drvn over 1f out: sn no imp* **12/1**

321- **5** *nk* **Skymax (GER)**[205] 8550 3-9-7 **85**........ HarryBentley 5 81
(Ralph Beckett) *hld up: effrt over 3f out and sn pushed along: rdn over 2f out: plugged on u.p fnl f* **5/1**[3]

3-43 **6** *1/2* **Tucson**[15] 2336 3-8-9 **73**........ AndreaAtzeni 10 68
(James Bethell) *hld up in rr: hdwy on inner wl over 2f out: rdn wl over 1f out: styd on fnl f* **25/1**

3-12 **7** *nk* **Fraser Island (IRE)**[12] 2446 3-9-5 **83**........ SilvestreDeSousa 2 78
(Mark Johnston) *chsd wnr: rdn along 3f out: drvn over 2f out: grad wknd* **6/1**

1-60 **8** *9* **Amadeus Grey (IRE)**[27] 1945 3-9-2 **80**........(t) DavidAllan 8 60
(Tim Easterby) *hld up: a towards rr* **40/1**

04-2 **9** *3 1/2* **Beechwood Jude (FR)**[20] 2096 3-8-10 **74**........ GeraldMosse 3 49
(Keith Dalgleish) *a in rr* **12/1**

2m 34.46s (1.26) **Going Correction** +0.30s/f (Good) **9 Ran SP% 118.6**
Speed ratings (Par 101): **107,104,104,100,99 99,99,93,91**
CSF £9.72 CT £62.58 TOTE £3.90: £1.40, £1.40, £3.00; EX 9.70 Trifecta £88.30.
Owner The Originals **Bred** Miss K Rausing **Trained** Middleham Moor, N Yorks

FOCUS
Race run over an additional 43yds. An easy winner of this decent 3yo handicap, in which they came towards the stands' side in the home straight. The form is rated in line with the race standard.
T/Jkpt: Not Won. T/Plt: £58.40 to a £1 stake. Pool: £201,244.42 - 2,512.67 winning units T/Qpdt: £23.50 to a £1 stake. Pool: £15,020.86 - 472.23 winning units **Joe Rowntree**

2812 - 2818a (Foreign Racing) - See Raceform Interactive

2393
DONCASTER (L-H)
Saturday, May 18

OFFICIAL GOING: Good to firm (good in places; watered; 8.1)
Wind: Virtually nil Weather: Cloudy

2819 OWLERTON GREYHOUND STADIUM SHEFFIELD APPRENTICE H'CAP 1m 3f 197y
5:30 (5:32) (Class 5) (0-70,72) 4-Y-0+
£3,752 (£1,116; £557; £400; £400; £400) **Stalls** Low

Form RPR

2-40 **1** **Just Wait (IRE)**[31] 1848 4-9-13 **72**........ AndrewBreslin 5 84+
(Mark Johnston) *in rr whn sltly hmpd and rn wd after 2f: pushed along over 4f out: hdwy wl over 3f out: in tch and swtchd lft wl over 2f out: sn rdn: chal wl over 1f out: led appr fnl f: sn clr: kpt on strly* **8/1**

230- **2** *4 1/2* **Albert Boy (IRE)**[221] 8079 6-8-11 **59**........ WilliamCarver(3) 14 64
(Scott Dixon) *prom: cl up 4f out: rdn along to ld 2 1/2f out: jnd and drvn wl over 1f out: hdd appr fnl f: kpt on* **10/1**

6631 **3** *3 1/2* **Cold Harbour**[16] 2345 4-8-7 **57**........(t) SeanKirrane(5) 6 56
(Robyn Brisland) *trckd ldng pair: effrt 3f out: rdn along over 2f out: drvn wl over 1f out: kpt on same pce* **9/2**[2]

5-06 **4** *1/2* **Motahassen (IRE)**[19] 2202 5-8-6 **56**........(t[1]) CianMacRedmond(5) 4 55+
(Declan Carroll) *hld up towards rr: hdwy on outer over 3f out: pushed along over 2f out: sn rdn: kpt on fnl f* **7/1**[3]

U-04 **5** *2* **Searching (IRE)**[8] 2591 7-9-10 **69**........(p) HarrisonShaw 11 64
(Karen Tutty) *cl up: chal over 3f out and sn pushed along: rdn over 2f out: drvn wl over 1f out: kpt on one pce* **10/1**

545- **6** 3 1/4 **Contrebasse**[211] 8386 4-9-7 **66** DannyRedmond 13 56
(Tim Easterby) *in tch: hdwy over 4f out: rdn along to chse ldrs over 2f out: sn drvn and no imp* **8/1**

623- **7** 4 **War Brigade (FR)**[77] 8808 5-9-5 **69** LukeCatton(5) 2 53
(Ian Williams) *in rr whn n.m.r and sltly hmpd after 2f: pushed along 4f out: rdn over 3f out: nvr nr ldrs (trainer could offer no explanation for the gelding performance)* **7/2**[1]

2-00 **8** 1/2 **Enemy Of The State (IRE)**[15] 2373 5-8-6 **56** oh10 ow1(p) HarryRussell(5) 15 39
(Jason Ward) *in tch: hdwy to chse ldrs 5f out: rdn along over 3f out: sn wknd (jockey said gelding hung left under pressure)* **25/1**

5P04 **9** 6 **Omotesando**[15] 2359 9-9-2 **61** (b) BenSanderson 1 34
(Oliver Greenall) *in rr whn n.m.r and sltly hmpd after 2f: nvr a factor after* **20/1**

524- **10** shd **Jawshan (USA)**[139] 9768 4-9-10 **69** DarraghKeenan 10 42
(Ian Williams) *hld up towards rr: sme hdwy 4f out: rdn along 3f out: sn drvn and wknd* **12/1**

3460 **11** 2 3/4 **Ezanak (IRE)**[14] 2400 6-9-8 **67** (v) TheodoreLadd 9 36
(Michael Appleby) *sn led: rdn along 4f out: hdd 2 1/2f out: sn wknd* **8/1**

33/0 **12** nk **Aislabie (FR)**[19] 2185 6-8-13 **58** SebastianWoods 7 26
(Jason Ward) *trckd ldrs: hdwy on inner 4f out: chsd ldrs 3f out: sn rdn and wknd* **33/1**

2m 34.4s (-2.20) **Going Correction** -0.075s/f (Good) 12 Ran SP% **123.7**
Speed ratings (Par 103): **104,101,98,98,97 94,92,91,87,87 85,85**
CSF £87.24 CT £413.88 TOTE £8.00: £2.50, £3.20, £2.00; EX 113.50 Trifecta £488.10.
Owner Abdulla Al Mansoori **Bred** Grangecon Stud **Trained** Middleham Moor, N Yorks

FOCUS
An overcast evening and a drying breeze meant quick ground. Add 6yds to the official distance to this modest handicap for apprentice riders, which was run at an even gallop.

2820 HOWCROFT GROUP NOVICE AUCTION STKS 5f 3y
6:00 (6:02) (Class 5) 2-Y-O £3,752 (£1,116; £557; £278) Stalls High

Form RPR

1 **Romero (IRE)** 2-9-3 0 JamieSpencer 8 83+
(Kevin Ryan) *dwlt: hld up in tch: n.m.r and swtchd rt wl over 1f out: shkn up and str run ent fnl f: led last 110yds: readily* **6/5**[1]

4 **2** 1 1/2 **Mecca's Hot Steps**[23] 2051 2-8-12 0 GrahamLee 4 70
(Michael Dods) *prom: effrt on outer to chal over 1f out and sn edgd lft: rdn to take slt ld ent fnl f: hdd last 110yds: kpt on* **9/1**

3 1 **She Looks Like Fun** 2-9-0 0 CliffordLee 10 68
(K R Burke) *in tch: hdwy to chse ldrs over 2f out: rdn to chal over 1f out: ev ch ent fnl f: sn drvn and kpt on same pce* **8/1**

2 **4** 3/4 **Dandizette (IRE)**[14] 2415 2-8-12 0 AndrewMullen 6 63
(Adrian Nicholls) *prom: cl up 1/2-way: rdn to take slt ld wl over 1f out: hdd ent fnl f: kpt on same pce* **13/2**[2]

4 **5** 1 1/4 **Queens Blade**[8] 2586 2-8-10 0 NathanEvans 5 57
(Tim Easterby) *led: rdn along over 2f out: hdd wl over 1f out: wknd appr fnl f* **20/1**

60 **6** 1 3/4 **The Ginger Bullet**[14] 2415 2-9-0 0 SebastianWoods(5) 3 60
(Richard Fahey) *towards rr tl styd on fnl 2f* **12/1**

45 **7** 1/2 **Ambyfaeirvine (IRE)**[19] 2191 2-9-1 0 LiamKeniry 11 54
(Ivan Furtado) *in tch: rdn along over 2f out: sn wknd* **66/1**

8 1/2 **Puffthemagicdragon** 2-9-5 0 EoinWalsh 7 56
(George Scott) *dwlt: a in rr (jockey said gelding missed the break)* **12/1**

9 1 1/4 **Mr Gus (IRE)** 2-9-5 0 PaulHanagan 2 51
(Richard Fahey) *dwlt: a in rr* **7/1**[3]

06 **10** 1/2 **Comeatchoo (IRE)**[14] 2415 2-9-1 0 DuranFentiman 9 46
(Tim Easterby) *chsd ldrs: rdn along 2f out: grad wknd* **66/1**

2 **11** hd **Doncaster Rosa**[12] 2476 2-8-7 0 GabrieleMalune(3) 1 40
(Ivan Furtado) *chsd ldrs: rdn along 1/2-way: sn wknd (jockey said filly was never travelling)* **11/1**

1m 0.17s (0.57) **Going Correction** -0.075s/f (Good) 11 Ran SP% **123.9**
Speed ratings (Par 93): **92,89,88,86,84 82,81,80,78,77 77**
CSF £13.86 TOTE £2.00: £1.10, £3.00, £2.70; EX 14.40 Trifecta £96.50.
Owner Romero Partners **Bred** Deveron Ltd **Trained** Hambleton, N Yorks

FOCUS
A decent novice auction sprint for the grade and the winner, who came from off the pace, was visually impressive. The form has been rated with reference to the five-year race average.

2821 ALAN WOOD 70TH BIRTHDAY CELEBRATION H'CAP 7f 213y(R)
6:35 (6:35) (Class 3) (0-95,93) 3-Y-O £7,762 (£2,310; £1,154; £577) Stalls High

Form RPR

51-3 **1** **Artistic Rifles (IRE)**[11] 2510 3-8-5 **77** LukeMorris 3 88
(Charles Hills) *trckd ldng pair: hdwy 3f out: chal wl over 1f out and sn rdn: drvn ent fnl f: kpt on gamely to ld last 40yds* **11/2**

1-54 **2** hd **Brian Epstein (IRE)**[14] 2414 3-8-10 **82** HollieDoyle 6 92
(Richard Hannon) *trckd ldrs: cl up 1/2-way: led 2f out: sn jnd and rdn: drvn ent fnl f: hdd and no ex last 40yds* **7/4**[1]

5-65 **3** 5 **Dirty Rascal (IRE)**[8] 2570 3-8-11 **90** LukeCatton(7) 1 89
(Richard Hannon) *trckd ldng pair: effrt on inner 3f out: rdn along 2f out: drvn over 1f out: kpt on same pce* **8/1**

41-3 **4** shd **Gallic**[31] 1857 3-8-13 **85** LiamKeniry 7 83
(Ed Walker) *hld up in rr: effrt and sme hdwy on outer 3f out: rdn along 2f out: sn drvn and no imp* **5/1**[3]

6-13 **5** 6 **Hesslewood (IRE)**[30] 1897 3-8-12 **84** (h[1]) JamieSpencer 4 68
(James Bethell) *hld up in rr: effrt 3f out and sn pushed along: rdn over 2f out: swtchd rt and drvn wl over 1f out: sn btn* **7/2**[2]

02-6 **6** 7 **Massam**[24] 2031 3-9-7 **93** JoeFanning 5 61
(Mark Johnston) *led: rdn along wl over 2f out: sn hdd & wknd* **7/1**

1m 37.24s (-3.56) **Going Correction** -0.075s/f (Good) 6 Ran SP% **114.2**
Speed ratings (Par 103): **109,108,103,103,97 90**
CSF £16.04 TOTE £6.40: £2.70, £1.60; EX 16.10 Trifecta £87.10.
Owner Mrs Fitri Hay **Bred** Lynn Lodge Stud **Trained** Lambourn, Berks

FOCUS
A decent handicap, run at a fair pace and the first two drew a little way clear after a protracted battle.

2822 BRITISH EBF PREMIER FILLIES' H'CAP 1m 2f 43y
7:05 (7:06) (Class 3) (0-90,90) 3-Y-O+
£12,450 (£3,728; £1,864; £932; £466; £234) Stalls High

Form RPR

22-3 **1** **Black Lotus**[18] 2252 4-9-1 **77** DavidAllan 6 87
(Chris Wall) *hld up: hdwy on outer wl over 2f out: rdn to ld over 1f out: edgd lft ins fnl f: kpt on strly* **9/4**[1]

055- **2** 2 1/4 **Lady Of Shalott**[224] 7985 4-9-11 **87** (h) JamieSpencer 3 92
(David Simcock) *hld up: hdwy wl over 2f out: chsd ldrs and swtchd lft to inner wl over 1f out: sn rdn to chal and ev ch: drvn ins fnl f and kpt on same pce* **5/1**[3]

10-0 **3** 2 **Lady Bergamot (FR)**[29] 1927 5-10-0 **90** GeorgeWood 4 91
(James Fanshawe) *trckd ldrs: hdwy over 3f out: cl up wl over 2f out: rdn wl over 1f out: ev ch: drvn and kpt on same pce fnl f* **3/1**[2]

31-0 **4** 1 **Time Change**[35] 1757 4-9-7 **83** HarryBentley 8 82
(Ralph Beckett) *sn trcking ldr: hdwy and cl up over 3f out: led over 2f out and sn rdn: heed wl over 1f out: sn drvn and kpt on same pce* **11/2**

063- **5** nse **First Dance (IRE)**[152] 9585 5-8-9 **71** oh3 AndrewMullen 1 70
(Tom Tate) *hld up in rr: hdwy over 2f out: rdn over 1f out: styd on fnl f* **10/1**

260- **6** 1 **Railport Dolly**[252] 7074 4-8-12 **74** (h) LiamKeniry 5 71
(David Barron) *sn led: hdd over 7f out: prom: pushed along over 3f out: rdn wl over 2f out: sn wknd* **20/1**

00-0 **7** 19 **Rayna's World (IRE)**[35] 1757 4-9-1 **77** JimmyQuinn 7 36
(Philip Kirby) *dwlt: hdwy to ld over 7f out: pushed along 4f out: rdn 3f out: sn hdd & wknd* **16/1**

2m 10.95s (-1.35) **Going Correction** -0.075s/f (Good) 7 Ran SP% **107.6**
Speed ratings (Par 104): **102,100,98,97,97 96,81**
CSF £12.11 CT £27.83 TOTE £2.60: £1.70, £2.60; EX 11.90 Trifecta £36.30.
Owner Ms Aida Fustoq **Bred** Deerfield Farm **Trained** Newmarket, Suffolk
■ Hunni was withdrawn. Price at time of withdrawal 10/1. Rule 4 applies to all bets - deduction 5p in the pound

FOCUS
Add 6yds to the official distance. A fair fillies' handicap and the pace was steady early on. They gradually wound it up from 3.5f out and the winner did it comfortably. Decent form.

2823 LEXUS SHEFFIELD NOVICE STKS 6f 2y
7:35 (7:38) (Class 5) 3-Y-O+ £3,752 (£1,116; £557; £278) Stalls High

Form RPR

1- **1** **Bielsa (IRE)**[211] 8390 4-10-0 0 KevinStott 7 89
(Kevin Ryan) *trckd ldr: pushed along and sltly outpcd wl over 1f out: hdwy to chal appr fnl f: sn rdn: styd on wl to ld last 100yds* **7/1**

62- **2** 1/2 **Dreaming Away (IRE)**[171] 9283 3-8-7 0 DavidEgan 3 73
(Simon Crisford) *trckd ldrs: hdwy over 2f out: rdn to ld 1 1/2f out: drvn ins fnl f: sn edgd rt: hdd last 100yds: no ex towards fin* **11/4**[1]

2- **3** 1 3/4 **Johnny Reb**[207] 8496 3-8-12 0 DanielMuscutt 13 72
(Jeremy Noseda) *chsd ldng pair: effrt over 2f out: rdn wl over 1f out: drvn and kpt on same pce fnl f* **7/2**[2]

31 **4** 1 **Stoney Lane**[11] 2507 4-10-0 0 PhilDennis 5 78
(Richard Whitaker) *led: rdn along 2f out: hdd 1 1/2f out: sn drvn: edgd rt and one pce fnl f* **5/1**[3]

-230 **5** 1 **Harry's Bar**[12] 2484 4-9-7 76 JamieSpencer 2 68
(James Fanshawe) *hld up towards rr: hdwy 2f out: rdn to chse ldrs over 1f out: sn drvn and no imp fnl f* **11/4**[1]

50 **6** 3 3/4 **Jet Set Go**[14] 2397 4-9-2 0 NathanEvans 8 51
(Seb Spencer) *in tch: pushed along 2 1/2f out: sn rdn and plugged on one pce* **16/1**

00 **7** 2 1/4 **Brutalab**[8] 2590 3-8-12 0 DavidAllan 4 47
(Tim Easterby) *chsd ldrs: rdn along over 2f out: sn wknd* **50/1**

0-0 **8** 1 3/4 **Shall We Begin (IRE)**[29] 1924 3-8-7 0 CamHardie 10 36
(Michael Easterby) *plld hrd: chsd ldrs: rdn along over 2f out: sn wknd* **40/1**

9 nk **Cheam Avenue (IRE)** 3-8-7 0 LukeMorris 6 35
(James Bethell) *green and sn pushed along: a towards rr* **25/1**

05 **10** 1/2 **The Thorny Rose**[16] 2332 3-8-2 0 PaulaMuir(5) 12 34
(Michael Dods) *dwlt: a in rr* **40/1**

11 8 **Guarded Secret** 3-8-7 0 AndrewMullen 11 8
(Michael Dods) *dwlt: a in rr* **25/1**

0 **12** 14 **Doncaster Star**[21] 2094 4-9-2 0 CliffordLee 1
(Ivan Furtado) *a in rr* **66/1**

1m 12.17s (-0.53) **Going Correction** -0.075s/f (Good) 12 Ran SP% **126.6**
WFA 3 from 4yo 9lb
Speed ratings (Par 103): **100,99,97,95,94 89,86,84,83,82 72,53**
CSF £27.26 TOTE £7.90: £2.30, £1.50, £1.80; EX 33.30 Trifecta £176.40.
Owner Highbank Stud **Bred** Highbank Stud **Trained** Hambleton, N Yorks

FOCUS
A well-contested, ordinary novices' sprint and they wound it up from 3f out. It paid to be up with the pace.

2824 YATES DRYWALL LTD H'CAP 6f 2y
8:05 (8:08) (Class 4) (0-80,82) 4-Y-O+
£5,530 (£1,645; £822; £411; £400; £400) Stalls High

Form RPR

2212 **1** **Equiano Springs**[14] 2416 5-9-2 **75** AndrewMullen 8 85
(Tom Tate) *hld up and bhd: gd hdwy 2f out: rdn and str run jst over 1f out: led ins fnl f: kpt on strly* **4/1**[1]

0-03 **2** 2 **Prestbury Park (USA)**[23] 2053 4-8-11 **70** KevinStott 15 74
(Paul Midgley) *hld up in tch: hdwy over 2f out: sn chsng ldrs: rdn to chal over 1f out: led briefly ent fnl f: sn hdd and drvn: kpt on same pce towards fin* **16/1**

660- **3** 3/4 **Normal Equilibrium**[140] 9748 9-8-4 **66** oh2 GabrieleMalune(3) 7 68
(Ivan Furtado) *trckd ldr centre: led 1/2-way: rdn wl over 1f out: drvn and hdd ent fnl f: kpt on wl u.p towards fin* **50/1**

3343 **4** hd **Athollblair Boy (IRE)**[14] 2416 6-9-2 **80** FayeMcManoman(5) 1 81
(Nigel Tinkler) *in rr and swtchd rt to centre bef 1/2-way: rdn along 2f out: hdwy and swtchd rt towards stands' side wl over 1f out: styd on strly fnl f* **14/1**

00-1 **5** hd **Lucky Beggar (IRE)**[35] 1765 9-8-10 **69** DavidAllan 10 69
(David C Griffiths) *in tch: hdwy 2f out: rdn to chse ldrs over 1f out: kpt on fnl f* **12/1**

352- **6** 3/4 **Zeyzoun (FR)**[210] 8415 5-9-4 **77** (h) GeorgeWood 2 75
(Chris Wall) *racd towards far side: hld up: hdwy over 2f out: rdn to chse ldrs over 1f out: kpt on fnl f* **10/1**

0-14 **7** nk **Galloway Hills**[14] 2416 4-9-7 **80** SamJames 14 77
(Phillip Makin) *chsd ldrs centre: rdn along over 2f out: sn drvn and kpt on same pce* **6/1**[2]

0000 **8** 3/4 **Kodiline (IRE)**[19] 2201 5-8-2 **68** GinaMangan(7) 4 63
(David Evans) *bhd centre: rdn along and hdwy 2f out: kpt on fnl f* **33/1**

1226 **9** 1/2 **Socialites Red**[17] 2292 6-8-4 **68** (p) TheodoreLadd(5) 18 61
(Scott Dixon) *racd wd towards stands' side: towards rr: pushed along 1/2-way: rdn and hdwy 2f out: chsd ldrs over 1f out: sn drvn and no imp* **33/1**

20-0 **10** *hd* **Iconic Knight (IRE)**[17] 2272 4-9-7 **80** LiamKeniry 9 72
(Ed Walker) *towards rr centre: hdwy 2f out: sn rdn and kpt on fnl f (vet said gelding lost both of its front shoes)* **14/1**

0-00 **11** *1 ¼* **Kenny The Captain (IRE)**[19] 2201 8-8-10 **69** RachelRichardson 13 57
(Tim Easterby) *chsd ldng pair centre: rdn along over 2f out: sn drvn and wknd* **25/1**

0-00 **12** *2 ¼* **Mostahel**[19] 2201 5-9-1 **74** GrahamLee 11 55
(Paul Midgley) *in tch centre: rdn along and wkng whn n.m.r wl over 1f out* **33/1**

-006 **13** *nk* **Bahamian Sunrise**[12] 2484 7-8-12 **71** (p) BenCurtis 16 51
(John Gallagher) *nvr bttr than midfield* **50/1**

-604 **14** *2* **Blazed (IRE)**[15] 2365 5-8-11 **70** (bt[1]) HarryBentley 3 44
(Ed Vaughan) *chsd ldrs centre: rdn along 2f out: sn wknd* **10/1**

1-32 **15** *4* **Wrenthorpe**[19] 2201 4-8-12 **78** (p) HarryRussell(7) 5 39
(Bryan Smart) *racd centre: led to 1/2-way: cl up and rdn over 2f out: sn wknd* **10/1**

20-0 **16** *16* **Black Isle Boy (IRE)**[19] 2201 5-9-7 **80** (t[1]) DanielTudhope 6
(David O'Meara) *chsd ldrs towards centre: rdn along wl over 2f out: sn wknd* **7/1**[3]

02-3 **17** *10* **Airshow**[31] 1847 4-9-9 **82** LukeMorris 17
(Michael Appleby) *swtchd rt s to r nr stands' rail: prom: rdn along wl over 2f out: sn outpcd (jockey said gelding hung right)* **9/1**

1m 11.42s (-1.28) **Going Correction** -0.075s/f (Good) **17 Ran SP% 127.6**
Speed ratings (Par 105): **105,102,101,101,100 99,99,98,97,97 95,92,92,89,84 63,49**
CSF £69.87 CT £2944.20 TOTE £5.20: £1.50, £3.30, £17.10, £3.60; EX 76.80 Trifecta £2424.40.

Owner T T Racing **Bred** Paddock Space **Trained** Tadcaster, N Yorks
■ Stewards' Enquiry : Faye McManoman two-day ban: interference & careless riding (Jun 2-3)

FOCUS
Fairly competitive for the grade. Bar \bAirshow\p, who ploughed a lone furrow up the stands' side, they came up the centre to far side and they went a strong early pace. The first two came from off the pace.

2825 INCOGNITO "ALWAYS ON TREND" FASHION H'CAP 7f 6y
8:35 (8:38) (Class 4) (0-85,87) 3-Y-O **£5,530** (£1,645; £822; £411; £400) **Stalls High**

Form RPR

3-41 **1** **Gentle Look**[16] 2333 3-9-7 **83** PatCosgrave 10 94
(Saeed bin Suroor) *mde most: rdn wl over 1f out: drvn and kpt on strly fnl f* **5/6**[1]

00-0 **2** *2 ¼* **Gabrial The Wire**[10] 2525 3-8-10 **77** ConnorMurtagh(5) 2 81
(Richard Fahey) *hld up: hdwy wl over 1f out: rdn to chse wnr ins fnl f: sn drvn: edgd lft and no imp towards fin* **12/1**

21-0 **3** *3* **Triple Distilled**[14] 2395 3-9-1 **80** RowanScott(3) 3 76
(Nigel Tinkler) *trckd ldng pair: pushed along 2f out: rdn wl over 1f out and sltly outpcd: styd on u.p fnl f* **11/1**

0-51 **4** *1 ¼* **Buckingham (IRE)**[15] 2364 3-9-7 **83** CharlesBishop 8 76
(Eve Johnson Houghton) *trckd ldrs: hdwy over 2f out: rdn wl over 1f out: drvn and wknd appr fnl f: hung lft towards fin* **11/4**[2]

5-40 **5** *nk* **Self Assessment (IRE)**[31] 1857 3-9-1 **77** BenCurtis 5 69
(K R Burke) *cl up: rdn along 2f out: drvn wl over 1f out: wknd ent fnl f: wl hld whn bmpd nr fin* **7/1**[3]

1m 24.92s (-1.48) **Going Correction** -0.075s/f (Good) **5 Ran SP% 109.7**
Speed ratings (Par 101): **105,102,99,97,97**
CSF £11.60 TOTE £1.70: £1.10, £3.40; EX 11.50 Trifecta £44.80.
Owner Godolphin **Bred** Godolphin **Trained** Newmarket, Suffolk

FOCUS
With six non-runners, this fair handicap lost a little lustre, but the pace was honest, the front two drew clear and the winner looks progressive. Decent form.
T/Plt: £87.00 to a £1 stake. Pool: £77,957.77 - 653.44 winning units T/Qpdt: £11.00 to a £1 stake. Pool: £10,388.40 - 693.55 winning units **Joe Rowntree**

2790 NEWBURY (L-H)
Saturday, May 18

OFFICIAL GOING: Good (good to firm in places; 7.9)
Wind: virtually nil Weather: overcast but warm (showers from 4.30)

2826 SHALAA CARNARVON STKS (LISTED RACE) 6f
1:50 (1:52) (Class 1) 3-Y-O
£39,697 (£15,050; £7,532; £3,752; £1,883; £945) **Stalls Centre**

Form RPR

311- **1** **Khaadem (IRE)**[248] 7168 3-9-0 105 JamesDoyle 7 108
(Charles Hills) *trckd ldrs: tight for room 1st f: rdn to chal jst ins fnl f: led fnl 100yds: asserting at fin* **11/2**

5-1 **2** *½* **Oxted**[20] 2139 3-9-0 0 PJMcDonald 4 106
(Roger Teal) *prom: led jst over 2f out: sn rdn: hdd fnl 100yds: kpt on* **20/1**

00-2 **3** *2* **Space Traveller**[32] 1830 3-9-0 103 DanielTudhope 3 100
(Richard Fahey) *in tch: rdn over 2f out: hdwy over 1f out: kpt on into 3rd fnl 120yds: nt pce of front pair* **4/1**[2]

1-46 **4** *1 ¾* **Barbill (IRE)**[35] 1780 3-9-3 102 GeraldMosse 6 97
(Mick Channon) *hld up: hdwy over 2f out: rdn over 1f out: r.o fnl f: wnt 4th towards fin* **16/1**

11-3 **5** *½* **Red Impression**[16] 2319 3-8-9 96 JasonWatson 1 87
(Roger Charlton) *trckd ldrs: rdn 2f out: sn edgd lft in cl 3rd: no ex fnl 140yds* **7/2**[1]

13- **6** *2 ½* **Sunsprite (IRE)**[264] 6628 3-9-0 99 RyanMoore 2 84
(Richard Hughes) *hld up: struggling 3f out: r.o wl ent fnl f but nvr any threat to ldrs* **14/1**

264- **7** *2 ¾* **Dunkerron**[233] 7702 3-9-0 104 OisinMurphy 12 76
(Alan King) *trckd ldrs: rdn over 2f out: sn one pce* **25/1**

200- **8** *shd* **Junius Brutus (FR)**[217] 8214 3-9-0 100 SilvestreDeSousa 9 75
(Ralph Beckett) *led: rdn and hdd jst over 2f out: kpt on tl no ex ent fnl f* **33/1**

4-16 **9** *2 ¼* **The Cruising Lord**[17] 2270 3-9-0 98 JFEgan 8 68
(Michael Attwater) *racd keenly early: trckd ldrs: tight for room 1st f: rdn over 2f out: nt pce to threaten: wknd fnl f* **25/1**

2-01 **10** *½* **Moyassar**[14] 2412 3-9-0 107 JimCrowley 10 66
(Richard Hannon) *hld up: rdn 2f out: nvr any imp (jockey said colt ran flat)* **9/2**[3]

46-3 **11** *¾* **Konchek**[17] 2270 3-9-0 104 AdamKirby 11 64
(Clive Cox) *mid-div: struggling and lost pl over 2f out: wknd fnl f* **16/1**

04-2 **12** *1* **Kurious**[22] 2086 3-8-9 95 AndreaAtzeni 5 56
(Henry Candy) *mid-div: outpcd over 2f out: wknd fnl f* **8/1**

1m 11.23s (-1.97) **Going Correction** -0.05s/f (Good) **12 Ran SP% 120.7**
Speed ratings (Par 107): **111,110,107,105,104 101,97,97,94,93 92,91**
CSF £116.52 TOTE £6.90: £2.20, £4.70, £1.90; EX 113.40 Trifecta £542.30.

Owner Hamdan Al Maktoum **Bred** Yeomanstown Stud **Trained** Lambourn, Berks

FOCUS
The 7f and 5f bends were moved out overnight, adding 19yds to race distances starting in the back straight. There was some light rain after racing the previous day but nothing measurable, so good/fast ground again. The form is rated around the race standard.

2827 AL RAYYAN STKS (REGISTERED AS THE ASTON PARK STAKES) (GROUP 3) 1m 4f
2:25 (2:25) (Class 1) 4-Y-O+
£56,710 (£21,500; £10,760; £5,360; £2,690; £1,350) **Stalls Low**

Form RPR

22-1 **1** **Crystal Ocean**[22] 2083 5-9-3 125 RyanMoore 2 119+
(Sir Michael Stoute) *trckd ldr: chal over 3f out: sn pushed along: led 2f out: styd on wl: rdn out* **2/9**[1]

61-3 **2** *2* **Laraaib (IRE)**[35] 1750 5-9-3 112 JimCrowley 5 116
(Owen Burrows) *trckd ldrs: rdn over 2f out: swtchd rt whn chsng wnr over 1f out: styd on but a being hld* **6/1**[2]

1-62 **3** *3* **Raymond Tusk (IRE)**[17] 2269 4-9-5 111 JamieSpencer 7 113
(Richard Hannon) *trckd ldrs: qcknd to ld jst over 3f out: sn rdn: hdd 2f out: kpt on same pce fnl f* **10/1**[3]

0-66 **4** *1* **Pivoine (IRE)**[22] 2083 5-9-0 104 (b) SilvestreDeSousa 1 107
(Andrew Balding) *hld up bhd ldrs: outpcd 3f out: disp hld 4th 2f out: kpt on fnl f* **33/1**

630- **5** *shd* **Top Tug (IRE)**[217] 8188 8-9-0 101 AndreaAtzeni 6 106
(Alan King) *hld up last: outpcd 3f out: styd on fnl f: wnt 5th nring fin* **40/1**

0-15 **6** *1* **Red Verdon (USA)**[14] 2410 6-9-0 108 (b) OisinMurphy 4 105
(Ed Dunlop) *hld up bhd ldrs: outpcd 3f out: disp hld 4th 2f out: no ex fnl 120yds* **16/1**

-516 **7** *15* **Count Calabash (IRE)**[49] 1422 5-9-0 102 CharlesBishop 3 81
(Eve Johnson Houghton) *s.i.s: sn led: hdd over 3f out: wknd over 1f out* **50/1**

2m 33.78s (-4.22) **Going Correction** -0.05s/f (Good) **7 Ran SP% 118.4**
Speed ratings (Par 113): **112,110,108,108,107 107,97**
CSF £2.42 TOTE £1.20: £1.10, £2.40; EX 2.30 Trifecta £5.20.
Owner Sir Evelyn De Rothschild **Bred** Southcourt Stud **Trained** Newmarket, Suffolk

FOCUS
Add 19 yards. Upwards of 13lb clear of his six rivals, this proved relatively straightforward for the odds-on favourite, who became the first dual winner of this contest in its 31-year history. The race was being run as a Group 3 for only the fourth year, having been upgraded from Listed status in 2016. It was steadily run and turned into a bit of dash in the final 3f. Crystal Ocean didn't need to be at his best, and the form's rated around the second and third.

2828 AL ZUBARAH LONDON GOLD CUP H'CAP 1m 2f
3:00 (3:01) (Class 2) 3-Y-O
£43,575 (£13,048; £6,524; £3,262; £1,631; £819) **Stalls Low**

Form RPR

12-6 **1** **Headman**[36] 1737 3-9-7 **95** JasonWatson 14 108
(Roger Charlton) *mid-div: gd hdwy in centre to ld over 2f out: styd on wl whn strly chal thrght fnl f: drifted lft fnl 100yds: hld on* **12/1**

5-21 **2** *shd* **Sinjaari (IRE)**[19] 2208 3-9-1 **89** OisinMurphy 6 102
(William Haggas) *mid-div: hdwy over 3f out: rdn in cl 3rd over 1f out: str chal ins fnl f: kpt on wl: jst hld (vet said colt lost right fore shoe)* **3/1**[1]

21-1 **3** *1* **Good Birthday (IRE)**[48] 1462 3-9-2 **90** SilvestreDeSousa 16 101
(Andrew Balding) *stdd s and sn swtchd lft: bhd: gd hdwy of far rails 3f out: rdn for str chal wl over 1f out: ev ch ins fnl f: no ex fnl 100yds* **6/1**

-121 **4** *2 ¾* **Forest Of Dean**[22] 2075 3-9-5 **93** FrankieDettori 3 99
(John Gosden) *mid-div: hdwy 3f out: rdn w ev ch 2f out: kpt on same pce fnl f* **7/2**[2]

40-2 **5** *¾* **The Trader (IRE)**[9] 2553 3-9-4 **92** JamesDoyle 9 96
(Mark Johnston) *hld up towards rr: hdwy 3f out: rdn w ev ch 2f out: kpt on same pce fnl f* **33/1**

-323 **6** *¾* **Ritchie Valens (IRE)**[9] 2553 3-7-13 **78** ThoreHammerHansen(5) 13 81
(Richard Hannon) *mid-div on outer: hdwy 5f out: led briefly over 2f out: sn rdn: edgd lft: kpt on but no ex ins fnl f* **33/1**

-221 **7** *¾* **Majestic Dawn (IRE)**[35] 1756 3-9-2 **90** DanielTudhope 11 91
(Paul Cole) *stmbld leaving stalls: towards rr: rdn and stdy prog fr 2f out: styd on fnl f but nvr gng pce to get on terms (jockey said colt stumbled leaving stalls)* **14/1**

14-1 **8** *1* **Korcho**[33] 1823 3-8-8 **82** CharlieBennett 7 81
(Hughie Morrison) *mid-div: hdwy 3f out: sn rdn to chse ldrs: wknd ent fnl f* **20/1**

21-1 **9** *¾* **Solid Stone (IRE)**[32] 1835 3-9-3 **91** RyanMoore 5 89
(Sir Michael Stoute) *in tch: rdn to chse ldrs 3f out: ev ch briefly jst over 2f out: wknd ent fnl f* **5/1**[3]

1-14 **10** *8* **Mackaar (IRE)**[24] 2031 3-9-4 **92** AndreaAtzeni 10 74
(Roger Varian) *hld up towards rr of midfield: outpcd wl over 2f out: no threat after* **16/1**

4322 **11** *nk* **Htilominlo**[14] 2407 3-8-2 **76** (t) KieranO'Neill 4 57
(Sylvester Kirk) *hld up towards rr of midfield: rdn over 2f out: wknd over 1f out* **20/1**

3112 **12** *shd* **War Tiger (USA)**[32] 1835 3-9-3 **91** TonyHamilton 1 72
(Richard Fahey) *set decent pce: rdn and hdd 3f out: sn wknd* **10/1**

11-3 **13** *1* **Riviera Nights**[28] 1940 3-9-3 **91** JimCrowley 8 70
(Richard Hannon) *in tch: rdn to chse ldrs 3f out: wknd 2f out* **25/1**

6-41 **14** *3* **Dubai Instinct**[28] 1956 3-8-12 **86** CallumShepherd 15 59
(Brian Meehan) *prom: led 4f out: sn rdn: hdd jst over 2f out: sn wknd (jockey said colt hung left-handed throughout)* **25/1**

03-1 **15** *14* **Sky Defender**[12] 2470 3-8-12 **86** PJMcDonald 12 31
(Mark Johnston) *trckd ldrs: rdn to chal 3f out: wknd 2f out* **20/1**

2m 5.33s (-4.37) **Going Correction** -0.05s/f (Good) **15 Ran SP% 135.4**
Speed ratings (Par 105): **115,114,114,111,111 110,110,109,108,102 102,102,101,98,87**
CSF £49.15 CT £257.93 TOTE £13.80: £4.20, £2.00, £2.10; EX 69.20 Trifecta £1089.90.

Owner K Abdullah **Bred** Juddmonte Farms (east) Ltd **Trained** Beckhampton, Wilts

FOCUS
Add 19 yards. This valuable 3yo handicap has a rich roll of honour, Green Moon, Al Kazeem and Cannock Chase all having won it enroute to Group 1 success. Three of the past four winners have since scored in Group 2s. This looked a typically competitive renewal and the first three pulled clear. Strong form.

2829 AL SHAQAB LOCKINGE STKS (GROUP 1) (BRITISH CHAMPIONS SERIES) 1m (S)
3:40 (3:40) (Class 1) 4-Y-O+
£198,485 (£75,250; £37,660; £18,760; £9,415; £4,725) **Stalls** Centre

Form RPR

10-3 **1** **Mustashry**[30] 1890 6-9-0 115 JimCrowley 5 122
(Sir Michael Stoute) *trckd ldrs: rdn to chal ent fnl f: sn qcknd clr: drifted lft: r.o wl* **9/1**

110- **2** 2 ½ **Laurens (FR)**[210] 8407 4-8-11 117 PJMcDonald 12 113
(K R Burke) *travelled strly: prom: led 2f out: rdn and hdd jst ins fnl f: kpt on but nt pce of wnr* **5/1**[1]

105- **3** ½ **Accidental Agent**[232] 7735 5-9-0 116 CharlesBishop 3 115
(Eve Johnson Houghton) *hld up: hdwy 2f out: rdn into 3rd ins fnl f: kpt on but nt quite pce to get on terms (vet said horse lost is right fore shoe)* **33/1**

50-5 **4** ¾ **Romanised (IRE)**[35] 1776 4-9-0 117 (t) WJLee 9 113
(K J Condon, Ire) *racd keenly: mid-div: rdn and hdwy over 1f out: kpt on to go 4th fnl 100yds* **16/1**

/6-3 **5** hd **Le Brivido (FR)**[35] 1776 5-9-0 116 RyanMoore 14 113+
(A P O'Brien, Ire) *s.i.s: towards rr: nt clr run 2f out and swtchd rt: hdwy over 1f out: r.o ins fnl f but nvr any ch: nrly snatched 4th fnl stride* **8/1**

20-0 **6** ½ **I Can Fly**[49] 1445 4-8-11 115 WayneLordan 8 109
(A P O'Brien, Ire) *s.i.s: towards rr: hdwy 2f out: sn rdn: chal for hld 4th ent fnl f: no ex nring fin* **14/1**

550- **7** 1 ¾ **Sir Dancealot (IRE)**[160] 9474 5-9-0 116 GeraldMosse 6 108
(David Elsworth) *hld up in last pair: hdwy 2f out: sn swtchd lft and rdn to dispute 3rd: wknd fnl 120yds* **33/1**

11-0 **8** 4 ½ **Ostilio**[17] 2313 4-9-0 115 (t) OisinMurphy 10 97
(Simon Crisford) *led: rdn and hdd 2f out: wknd ent fnl f* **25/1**

45-3 **9** ¾ **Billesdon Brook**[13] 2441 4-8-11 110 SeanLevey 2 93
(Richard Hannon) *mid-div: hdwy over 3f out: effrt over 2f out: wknd fnl f* **33/1**

1-12 **10** 2 **Sharja Bridge**[22] 2085 5-9-0 115 AndreaAtzeni 7 91
(Roger Varian) *hld up: pushed along and sme prog over 2f out: rdn over 1f out: wknd ins fnl f* **8/1**

00-1 **11** hd **Beat The Bank**[22] 2085 5-9-0 116 SilvestreDeSousa 1 91
(Andrew Balding) *mid-div: pushed along 4f out: hdwy 3f out: sn rdn and hung lft: wknd over 1f out (jockey said gelding hung left-handed throughout)* **5/1**[1]

2-21 **12** 6 **Mythical Magic (IRE)**[86] 846 4-9-0 115 JamesDoyle 4 77
(Charlie Appleby) *trckd ldrs: rdn over 2f out: wknd over 1f out (jockey said gelding stopped quickly)* **11/1**

66-3 **13** 1 **Lord Glitters (FR)**[49] 1445 6-9-0 116 DanielTudhope 11 75
(David O'Meara) *in tch: outpcd whn briefly short of room jst over 2f out: wknd over 1f out (jockey said gelding ran too free)* **13/2**[2]

66-5 **14** 31 **Without Parole**[49] 1445 4-9-0 116 (b[1]) FrankieDettori 13 3
(John Gosden) *mid-div: u.p whn appearing to lose action and eased wl over 1f out (jockey said colt lost its action)* **7/1**[3]

1m 35.8s (-4.10) **Going Correction** -0.05s/f (Good) **14 Ran SP% 124.9**
Speed ratings (Par 117): **118,115,115,114,114 113,111,107,106,104 104,98,97,66**
CSF £53.82 CT £1473.39 TOTE £13.30: £3.60, £2.20, £10.60; EX 101.20 Trifecta £3837.40.

Owner Hamdan Al Maktoum **Bred** Shadwell Estate Company Limited **Trained** Newmarket, Suffolk

FOCUS
There was just 6lb between the entire field on RPRs beforehand and, although there was a clear, improved winner, he's a 6yo gelding who doesn't look a star, plus a couple in behind shaped better than the result. So, this division still seems wide open. They raced up the middle, with those towards the near side dominating. Laurens is rated similar to her reappearance last year.

2830 OLYMPIC GLORY CONDITIONS STKS (PLUS 10 RACE) 6f
4:15 (4:16) (Class 2) 2-Y-O **£32,345** (£9,625; £4,810; £2,405) **Stalls** Centre

Form RPR

1 **1** **Temple Of Heaven**[28] 1953 2-9-5 0 SeanLevey 2 98
(Richard Hannon) *trckd ldr: chalng whn hmpd over 1f out: led jst ins fnl f: r.o: all out (vet said colt lost left hind shoe)* **3/1**[2]

2 shd **Fort Myers (USA)**[24] 2036 2-9-5 0 RyanMoore 6 98
(A P O'Brien, Ire) *trckd ldr: chalng whn hmpd over 1f out: rdn to ld ent fnl f: sn hdd: kpt on w ev ch: jst hld* **7/2**[3]

1 **3** nse **Well Of Wisdom**[30] 1887 2-9-5 0 JamesDoyle 7 98
(Charlie Appleby) *trckd ldrs: chalng whn hmpd over 1f out: kpt on w ev ch ins fnl f: jst hld* **11/4**[1]

4 2 ½ **United Front (USA)** 2-9-2 0 WayneLordan 3 88+
(A P O'Brien, Ire) *in tch: hdwy 2f out: sn rdn: nt pce to chal but kpt on to go 4th fnl 100yds (vet said colt lost right hind shoe)* **12/1**

5 nk **Toro Strike (USA)** 2-9-2 0 TonyHamilton 8 87+
(Richard Fahey) *s.i.s: last but in tch: rdn and hdwy 2f out: kpt on same pce fnl f* **33/1**

1 **6** hd **Firepower (FR)**[16] 2338 2-9-5 0 AdamKirby 5 89
(Clive Cox) *in tch: trckd ldrs 2f out: sn swtchd rt for effrt: kpt on fnl f but nt pce to chal* **7/1**

7 1 ¼ **Joker On Jack (USA)**[30] 2-9-7 0 (b) FrankieDettori 1 87
(Wesley A Ward, U.S.A) *led: drifted rt and bmpd whn chal over 1f out: hdd ent fnl f: sn no ex* **4/1**

043 **8** 2 ¼ **Dark Optimist (IRE)**[16] 2338 2-9-5 0 JFEgan 4 79
(David Evans) *hld up: hdwy over 2f out: sn rdn: wknd ins fnl f* **33/1**

1m 13.23s (0.03) **Going Correction** -0.05s/f (Good) **8 Ran SP% 120.0**
Speed ratings (Par 99): **97,96,96,93,93 92,91,88**
CSF £14.83 TOTE £5.40: £1.70, £1.60, £1.10; EX 18.70 Trifecta £68.10.

Owner Rockcliffe Stud **Bred** Highclere Stud & Jake Warren Ltd **Trained** East Everleigh, Wilts

FOCUS
Five of these had won their only start, including the first three finishers. They all gradually drifted over to the far rail. Probably Listed-class form, but they finished compressed and it's hard to rate the race much higher.

2831 HARAS DE BOUQUETOT FILLIES' TRIAL STKS (LISTED RACE) 1m 2f
4:50 (4:50) (Class 1) 3-Y-O
£39,697 (£15,050; £7,532; £3,752; £1,883; £945) **Stalls** Low

Form RPR

1-2 **1** **Queen Power (IRE)**[17] 2268 3-9-0 0 SilvestreDeSousa 6 101
(Sir Michael Stoute) *wnt lft s: in last pair: swtchd to centre over 2f out: rdn and hdwy over 1f out: kpt on wl fnl f: led nring fin* **13/8**[1]

1 **2** nk **Lavender's Blue (IRE)**[32] 1834 3-9-0 0 JimCrowley 4 100
(Amanda Perrett) *trckd ldrs: tk narrow advantage over 1f out: sn rdn: kpt on but no ex whn hdd nring fin* **5/1**[3]

6-1 **3** nk **Star Catcher**[36] 1738 3-9-0 0 FrankieDettori 8 99
(John Gosden) *led: rdn and narrowly hdd over 1f out: kpt on w ev ch ins fnl f: hld cl home* **6/1**

3-40 **4** 2 **Star Terms**[13] 2443 3-9-0 104 RyanMoore 1 95
(Richard Hannon) *trckd ldr: rdn 2f out: ch over 1f out: kpt on same pce fnl 120yds* **9/1**

4 **5** ½ **Sea Of Faith (IRE)**[22] 2087 3-9-0 0 JamesDoyle 5 94
(William Haggas) *s.i.s and hmpd s: in last pair: hdwy 2 out: sn rdn: kpt on same pce fnl f (jockey said filly was slowly away)* **5/2**[2]

51- **6** 1 ½ **Sh Boom**[238] 7539 3-9-0 0 TomQueally 2 91
(Peter Chapple-Hyam) *trckd ldrs: rdn whn tight for room over 1f out: swtchd rt: kpt on but nt pce to get bk on terms* **33/1**

1- **7** 1 ½ **Lastochka**[203] 8639 3-9-0 0 AndreaAtzeni 9 88
(Roger Varian) *hld up: rdn over 2f out: nt pce to threaten* **20/1**

1-2 **8** 1 ½ **Kimblewick (IRE)**[37] 1711 3-9-0 0 OisinMurphy 7 85
(John Gosden) *trckd ldr tl rdn over 2f out: wknd over 1f out* **40/1**

2m 9.47s (-0.23) **Going Correction** -0.05s/f (Good) **8 Ran SP% 117.8**
Speed ratings (Par 104): **98,97,97,95,95 94,93,91**
CSF £10.49 TOTE £2.80: £1.40, £1.60, £1.70; EX 15.70 Trifecta £60.70.

Owner King Power Racing Co Ltd **Bred** Roundhill Stud **Trained** Newmarket, Suffolk

FOCUS
Add 19 yards. This fillies' Listed event was won last year by subsequent Irish Oaks and Yorkshire Oaks heroine Sea Of Class. They went no pace early on and it looked more of a test of speed than stamina. There was rain around but it didn't change the ground. The form is rated at the bottom end of the race averages, with the winner not needing to improve.

2832 TORONADO H'CAP 1m (S)
5:25 (5:27) (Class 2) (0-105,105) 4-Y-O+
£24,900 (£7,456; £3,728; £1,864; £932; £468) **Stalls** Centre

Form RPR

4235 **1** **Breden (IRE)**[30] 1889 9-9-0 98 RobertWinston 1 106
(Linda Jewell) *mid-div: hdwy over 2f out: tk narrow advantage jst onside fnl f: kpt on wl: hld on* **10/1**

45-4 **2** hd **Thrave**[30] 1889 4-8-7 91 JasonWatson 2 98
(Henry Candy) *trckd ldrs: shkn up to ld over 2f out: drvn over 1f out: narrowly hdd jst ins fnl f: kpt on w ev ch: jst hld* **4/1**[2]

0026 **3** ½ **Masham Star (IRE)**[9] 2551 5-8-9 93 PJMcDonald 11 98
(Mark Johnston) *trckd ldrs: rdn for str chal over 1f out: ev ch fnl f: no ex cl home* **20/1**

0-11 **4** ¾ **Petrus (IRE)**[29] 1912 4-9-2 100 (p) MartinDwyer 14 104+
(Brian Meehan) *hld up: hdwy over 2f out: sn drifted lft: rdn in 4th over 1f out: kpt on ins fnl f* **9/1**

-000 **5** ¾ **Hors De Combat**[86] 847 8-8-13 97 (p[1]) OisinMurphy 10 99+
(Denis Coakley) *s.i.s: in last pair: swtchd rt 2f out: sn rdn: kpt on wl fnl f but no ch w ldrs* **16/1**

0035 **6** 3 **Wahash (IRE)**[21] 2100 5-8-12 96 TonyHamilton 7 91
(Richard Hannon) *trckd ldr: rdn over 2f out: sn one pce (vet said gelding lost left hind shoe)* **16/1**

-003 **7** nk **Robin Of Navan (FR)**[17] 2271 6-9-7 105 RyanMoore 9 106+
(Harry Dunlop) *mid-div: lost pl whn nt clr run wl over 1f out: no ch after but kpt on fnl f (jockey said horse was denied a clear run)* **9/2**[3]

000- **8** nse **Medahim (IRE)**[231] 7777 5-9-0 98 SeanLevey 6 92
(Ivan Furtado) *hld up: hdwy over 1f out: sn rdn: kpt on same pce fnl f* **12/1**

20-3 **9** 2 **Graphite Storm**[15] 2363 5-8-3 87 KieranO'Neill 3 77
(Clive Cox) *mid-div: rdn over 2f out: kpt on but nt pce to get involved* **16/1**

110- **10** 2 **Jackpot Royale**[211] 8371 4-8-5 89 ow2 SilvestreDeSousa 12 74
(Michael Appleby) *mid-div: rdn whn tight for room wl over 1f out: wknd ins fnl f* **20/1**

43/0 **11** hd **Max Zorin (IRE)**[14] 2408 5-8-13 97 RobHornby 13 82
(Andrew Balding) *mid-div: rdn whn hmpd wl over 1f out: wknd ins fnl f* **50/1**

540 **12** 8 **Arcanada (IRE)**[29] 1922 6-8-5 92 (p) JaneElliott(3) 5 58
(Tom Dascombe) *led: rdn and hdd over 2f out: wknd over 1f out (jockey said gelding stopped quickly)* **16/1**

2-12 **13** 2 ¾ **Salute The Soldier (GER)**[29] 1912 4-8-13 97 (p[1]) JamesDoyle 4 57
(Clive Cox) *trckd ldrs: rdn over 2f out: sn wknd (jockey said gelding ran too free and stopped quickly)* **7/2**[1]

2300 **14** 3 ¾ **Cosmeapolitan**[21] 2105 6-8-11 95 AndreaAtzeni 8 46
(Alan King) *s.i.s: a towards rr* **33/1**

1m 38.02s (-1.88) **Going Correction** -0.05s/f (Good) **14 Ran SP% 125.1**
Speed ratings (Par 109): **107,106,106,105,104 101,101,101,99,97 97,89,86,82**
CSF £49.67 CT £839.02 TOTE £12.10: £3.20, £2.30, £5.10; EX 53.30 Trifecta £721.50.

Owner The Breden Racing Partnership **Bred** Mrs C L Weld **Trained** Sutton Valence, Kent

FOCUS
A useful, competitive handicap but it proved hard to make up ground, with the first three always handy enough.

T/Jkpt: Not Won. T/Plt: £61.10 to a £1 stake. Pool: £177,701.48 - 2,122.33 winning units T/Qpdt: £14.50 to a £1 stake. Pool: £10,250.72 - 521.63 winning units **Tim Mitchell**

The Form Book Flat 2019, Raceform Ltd, Newbury, RG14 5SJ

2798 NEWMARKET (R-H)

Saturday, May 18

OFFICIAL GOING: Good (good to firm in places; watered; 7.3)
Wind: virtually nil Weather: overcast, bright spells later

2833 BETWAY FAIRWAY STKS (LISTED RACE) 1m 2f
2:05 (2:06) (Class 1) 3-Y-O

£22,684 (£8,600; £4,304; £2,144; £1,076; £540) **Stalls High**

Form RPR

2-1 **1** **Raise You (IRE)**[35] 1755 3-9-3 0 DavidProbert 4 108
(Andrew Balding) *led trio racing away fr stands' rail: and chsd overall ldr: led 4f out: pushed clr over 1f out: in command and r.o wl fnl f: comf* **1/1**[1]

1-31 **2** *3¾* **Eightsome Reel**[21] 2120 3-9-3 92 ColmO'Donoghue 1 100
(Michael Bell) *racd in trio away fr stands' rail: hld up in last pair overall: effrt ent fnl 2f: rdn over 1f out: sn swtchd rt: styd on to chse clr ins fnl f: nvr a threat* **8/1**

11-0 **3** *1½* **Al Hilalee**[14] 2411 3-9-3 105 BrettDoyle 3 97
(Charlie Appleby) *racd in trio away fr stands' rail: t.k.h: midfield overall: effrt to chse wnr over 2f out: outpcd u.p and edgd lft over 1f out: lost 2nd ins fnl f* **3/1**[2]

2135 **4** *10* **Target Zone**[28] 1940 3-9-3 92 HayleyTurner 2 77
(David Elsworth) *swtchd lft sn after s: t.k.h: hld up in rr of stands' rail trio: effrt over 2f out: sn outpcd and wl hld whn hung rt 2f out: plugged on into modest 4th fnl f* **33/1**

21- **5** *7* **Khuzaam (USA)**[157] 9500 3-9-3 0 DaneO'Neill 6 63
(Roger Varian) *racd in trio against stands' rail: stdd s: t.k.h: wl in tch in midfield: clsd over 2f out: sn rdn and btn over 1f out: wknd and eased wl ins fnl f* **9/2**[3]

1-0 **6** *12* **Stormwave (IRE)**[36] 1737 3-9-3 0 HarryBentley 5 39
(Ralph Beckett) *racd against stands' rail: overall ldr tl 4f out: rdn 3f out: sn lost pl: wl bhd and eased ins fnl f* **25/1**

2m 5.21s (-0.19) **Going Correction** +0.20s/f (Good) **6** Ran SP% **111.1**
Speed ratings (Par 107): **108,105,103,95,90 80**
CSF £9.81 TOTE £1.80: £1.20, £2.60; EX 7.80 Trifecta £22.60.
Owner J Palmer-Brown **Bred** Brucetown Farms Ltd **Trained** Kingsclere, Hants

FOCUS
Stands'-side course used. Stalls on stands' side except 1m4f: centre. The race times tallied with the official ground description. They split into two groups of three, with the trio positioned a little way off the stands' rail finishing well ahead of the three that raced on the fence. The form is rated to the top end of the race standard.

2834 BETWAY KING CHARLES II STKS (LISTED RACE) 7f
2:40 (2:40) (Class 1) 3-Y-O **£22,684** (£8,600; £4,304; £2,144; £1,076) **Stalls High**

Form RPR

112- **1** **Jash (IRE)**[231] 7772 3-9-0 118 DaneO'Neill 4 107
(Simon Crisford) *broke wl: sn restrained: t.k.h and trckd ldrs: effrt over 1f out: chal u.p 1f out: led ins fnl f: styd on wl: rdn out* **10/11**[1]

2-30 **2** *nk* **Azano**[14] 2411 3-9-0 104 (t) RobertHavlin 1 106
(John Gosden) *taken down early: sn led: rdn and hdd over 1f out: sltly outpcd 1f out: rallied u.p ins fnl f: kpt on wl towards fin: snatched 2nd on post* **6/1**[3]

51-6 **3** *nse* **Watan**[31] 1854 3-9-0 103 TomMarquand 2 106
(Richard Hannon) *sn chsng ldr: effrt ent fnl 2f: drvn to ld over 1f out: hdd ins fnl f: kpt on wl but a jst hld towards fin: lost 2nd on post* **9/1**

1 **4** *2¾* **Far Above (IRE)**[30] 1886 3-9-0 0 HarryBentley 5 98
(James Tate) *stdd s: t.k.h: hld up in tch in last pair: effrt and swtchd lft over 1f out: chsd ldrs u.p 1f out: sn no imp: wknd towards fin* **3/1**[2]

12-2 **5** *1* **Glorious Lover (IRE)**[15] 2378 3-9-0 98 LiamKeniry 3 96
(Ed Walker) *hld up in last pair: effrt over 1f out: sn no imp: wl hld and kpt on same pce ins fnl f* **16/1**

1m 24.79s (-0.61) **Going Correction** +0.20s/f (Good) **5** Ran SP% **107.6**
Speed ratings (Par 107): **111,110,110,107,106**
CSF £6.45 TOTE £1.60: £1.20, £2.30; EX 5.10 Trifecta £15.20.
Owner Hamdan Al Maktoum **Bred** William Pilkington **Trained** Newmarket, Suffolk

FOCUS
A slightly muddling Listed contest. Jash set a high standard on his 2yo form and was below his best.

2835 BETWAY H'CAP 6f
3:15 (3:16) (Class 2) (0-105,95) 3-Y-O

£31,125 (£9,320; £4,660; £2,330; £1,165; £585) **Stalls High**

Form RPR

21-2 **1** **Dazzling Dan (IRE)**[22] 2078 3-9-7 95 DavidProbert 7 102
(Pam Sly) *a.p: rdn and ev ch over 1f out: led ins fnl f: styd on wl u.p* **5/1**[2]

-221 **2** *nk* **Dominus (IRE)**[14] 2405 3-8-6 80 (h) DavidEgan 15 86
(Brian Meehan) *wnt keenly to post and sltly overshot the s: chsd ldrs: clsd to ld over 2f out: drvn and hrd pressed over 1f out: hdd ins fnl f: kpt on wl but hld cl home* **10/1**

-046 **3** *shd* **Kinks**[10] 2525 3-8-13 87 NicolaCurrie 11 93
(Mick Channon) *wl in tch in midfield: clsd to chse ldrs and drvn ent fnl f: swtchd rt and styd on strly u.p ins fnl f: nt quite rch wnr (starter reported that the gelding was the subject of a third criteria failure; trainer was informed that the gelding could not run until the day after passing a stalls test)* **14/1**

2-21 **4** *2¼* **Moraawed**[22] 2078 3-9-0 88 DaneO'Neill 2 86+
(Roger Varian) *hld up in tch in rr: nt clr run over 2f out: rdn and hdwy over 1f out: styd on wl ins fnl f: nt rch ldrs* **3/1**[1]

-223 **5** *½* **Tinto**[8] 2567 3-8-8 82 RobertHavlin 1 79
(Amanda Perrett) *chsd ldrs: effrt jst over 1f out: rdn and no ex ins fnl f: wknd towards fin* **25/1**

10-4 **6** *4* **Naughty Rascal (IRE)**[31] 1851 3-9-2 90 TomMarquand 9 74
(Richard Hannon) *pressed ldrs: rdn and no ex over 1f out: wknd ins fnl f* **12/1**

4-33 **7** *½* **James Watt (IRE)**[14] 2412 3-8-11 85 (b[1]) HayleyTurner 4 67
(Michael Bell) *led tl over 2f out: hung lft and no ex over 1f out: wknd ins fnl f* **12/1**

3600 **8** *1¾* **Don Armado (IRE)**[14] 2412 3-9-1 89 (vt[1]) RichardKingscote 5 66
(Stuart Williams) *in tch in midfield: no hdwy u.p and btn over 1f out: wknd ins fnl f* **16/1**

106- **9** *nk* **Octave (IRE)**[231] 7776 3-9-2 90 FrannyNorton 10 66
(Mark Johnston) *wnt lft leaving stalls: bhd: effrt and swtchd lft jst over 2f out: no imp: plugged on to pass btn horses ins fnl f: nvr involved* **25/1**

21-0 **10** *nse* **Kamikaze Lord (USA)**[31] 1857 3-8-6 80 JimmyQuinn 16 56
(Jeremy Noseda) *wnt lft s: hld up in tch towards rr: clsd over 2f out: hung rt and no imp over 1f out: swtchd rt and kpt on ins fnl f: nvr trbld ldrs* **33/1**

1-23 **11** *nk* **Rocket Action**[13] 2434 3-9-0 88 HarryBentley 13 63
(Robert Cowell) *hld up in tch towards rr: rdn and no hdwy over 1f out: wl hld fnl f* **11/1**

26-2 **12** *nk* **Yousini**[31] 1851 3-9-6 94 TomEaves 14 68
(Kevin Ryan) *hld up in tch towards rr: clsd and flashed tail over 2f out: rdn over 1f out: sn btn and wknd ins fnl f (trainer could offer no explanation for the gelding's performance)* **13/2**[3]

0-00 **13** *1¼* **He'Zanarab (IRE)**[14] 2412 3-9-2 90 (h) RossaRyan 8 60
(Richard Hannon) *stdd s: hld up in tch towards rr: effrt over 1f out: no hdwy and wknd ins fnl f* **25/1**

131- **14** *½* **Luxor**[203] 8644 3-9-4 92 LiamJones 6 60
(William Haggas) *t.k.h: hld up in tch in midfield: rdn and no hdwy over 1f out: wknd ins fnl f* **7/1**

1m 12.1s (0.20) **Going Correction** +0.20s/f (Good) **14** Ran SP% **127.3**
Speed ratings (Par 105): **106,105,105,102,101 96,95,93,93,93 92,92,90,89**
CSF £55.44 CT £700.11 TOTE £5.50: £2.10, £4.30, £6.40; EX 58.90 Trifecta £1033.80.
Owner Thorney Racing Partners **Bred** Peter & Hugh McCutcheon **Trained** Thorney, Cambs

FOCUS
A good-quality sprint handicap, and a tight finish with the first three drawing clear. Pace held up.

2836 BETWAY BRITISH EBF FILLIES' NOVICE STKS (PLUS 10 RACE) 6f
3:50 (3:51) (Class 4) 2-Y-O **£5,175** (£1,540; £769; £384) **Stalls High**

Form RPR

1 **Daahyeh** 2-9-0 0 DavidEgan 5 89+
(Roger Varian) *hld up in tch in midfield: clsd to chse ldrs 2f out: rdn to chal over 1f out: led jst ins fnl f: r.o wl* **3/1**[1]

2 *1¾* **Raffle Prize (IRE)** 2-9-0 0 FrannyNorton 1 84+
(Mark Johnston) *sn led: clr over 2f out: rdn and hrd pressed over 1f out: hdd jst ins fnl f: kpt on but unable to match pce of wnr* **9/2**[2]

3 *½* **Declaring Love** 2-9-0 0 BrettDoyle 4 82+
(Charlie Appleby) *chsd ldrs tl wnt 2nd over 2f out: 3rd and unable qck jst over 1f out: kpt on but nvr enough pce to threaten wnr ins fnl f* **3/1**[1]

4 *¾* **Picture Frame** 2-9-0 0 HarryBentley 8 80+
(Saeed bin Suroor) *hmpd leaving stalls: in tch in rr: hdwy into midfield 1/2-way: chsd ldrs and rdn over 1f out: kpt on wl ins fnl f: no threat to wnr* **9/2**[2]

5 *7* **Blausee (IRE)** 2-9-0 0 DannyBrock 7 59
(Philip McBride) *hmpd leaving stalls and rousted along: sn rcvrd and in tch in rr: outpcd 2f out: wl hld after but plugged on ins fnl f* **50/1**

4 **6** *¾* **Falconidae (IRE)**[16] 2338 2-9-0 0 TomMarquand 10 57
(Richard Hannon) *hld up in tch in midfield: effrt to chse ldrs over 2f out: outpcd 2f out: wknd and no ch whn hung rt ins fnl f* **6/1**[3]

7 *½* **Too Shy Shy (IRE)** 2-9-0 0 NicolaCurrie 9 55
(Richard Spencer) *wnt rt leaving stalls: t.k.h: chsd ldr tl over 2f out: outpcd and btn over 1f out: wknd fnl f (jockey said filly jumped right leaving stalls)* **20/1**

8 *½* **Willa** 2-9-0 0 PatDobbs 6 54
(Richard Hannon) *wnt lft leaving stalls: in tch in rr: rdn over 2f out: sn outpcd and wl hld over 1f out* **20/1**

5 **9** *12* **Luna Wish**[25] 2020 2-9-0 0 DavidProbert 2 18
(George Margarson) *chsd ldrs tl over 2f out: lost pl and bhd over 1f out: wknd fnl f* **25/1**

1m 13.18s (1.28) **Going Correction** +0.20s/f (Good) **9** Ran SP% **116.0**
Speed ratings (Par 92): **99,96,96,95,85 84,84,83,67**
CSF £15.94 TOTE £4.90: £1.60, £1.90, £1.30; EX 20.60 Trifecta £96.00.
Owner Fawzi Abdulla Nass **Bred** D J And Mrs Deer **Trained** Newmarket, Suffolk

FOCUS
Four finished clear, and they should all pay to follow. Last year's second and third, Beyond Reason and Angel's Hideaway, have both made up into Group fillies. The form has been rated towards the top end of the race average.

2837 BETWAY HEED YOUR HUNCH H'CAP 7f
4:25 (4:30) (Class 3) (0-95,94) 4-Y-O+ **£9,703** (£2,887; £1,443; £721) **Stalls High**

Form RPR

4-62 **1** **Pettifogger (IRE)**[15] 2363 4-8-12 85 (h) ShaneKelly 6 93
(Marco Botti) *mounted in the chute: led: hung rt: rdn and hung lft 2f out: drvn and hanging rt again 1f out: hdd ins fnl f: battled bk u.p to ld again last strides* **3/1**[2]

646- **2** *nk* **Spanish City**[231] 7777 6-9-7 94 DavidEgan 4 101
(Roger Varian) *stdd after s: hld up in tch in last pair: clsd gng wl over 2f out: pushed along to chal ent fnl f: rdn to ld ins fnl f: hdd and no ex last strides* **7/4**[1]

-000 **3** *1½* **Rufus King**[14] 2402 4-9-6 93 FrannyNorton 2 96
(Mark Johnston) *dwlt: t.k.h and sn chsng ldrs: effrt to chse wnr over 2f out tl 2f out: kpt on same pce u.p ins fnl f* **10/1**

-050 **4** *hd* **Buridan (FR)**[21] 2117 4-8-13 86 TomMarquand 5 88
(Richard Hannon) *wl in tch in midfield: effrt and clsd over 2f out: chsd wnr 2f out tl ent fnl f: kpt on same pce ins fnl f* **9/2**[3]

50-0 **5** *2¾* **Perfect Hustler (USA)**[37] 1714 4-8-10 83 RobertHavlin 3 78
(Jeremy Noseda) *stdd s: hld up in tch in last pair: effrt over 1f out: rdn and no imp 1f out: wknd ins fnl f* **11/1**

1-60 **6** *2¾* **Ghayadh**[29] 1912 4-8-13 86 (t) RichardKingscote 1 74
(Stuart Williams) *chsd wnr tl over 2f out: sn rdn: lost pl and bhd 1f out: wknd ins fnl f* **20/1**

1m 25.76s (0.36) **Going Correction** +0.20s/f (Good) **6** Ran SP% **101.7**
Speed ratings (Par 107): **105,104,102,102,99 96**
CSF £7.06 TOTE £4.00: £2.10, £1.10; EX 8.50 Trifecta £56.80.
Owner Scuderia Effevi SRL **Bred** Effevi Srl **Trained** Newmarket, Suffolk
■ Last Page was withdrawn. Price at time of withdrawal 9/1. Rule 4 applies to all bets - deduction 10p in the pound

FOCUS
A decent small-field handicap.

2838 BETWAY FILLIES' NOVICE STKS (PLUS 10 RACE) 1m 4f
5:00 (5:00) (Class 3) 3-Y-O **£9,703** (£2,887; £1,443; £721) **Stalls Centre**

Form RPR

43 **1** **Happy Hiker (IRE)**[20] 2148 3-9-0 0 HayleyTurner 5 83
(Michael Bell) *chsd ldrs tl wnt 2nd 4f out: effrt 3f out: swtchd lft 2f out: clsd u.p to ld 1f out: styd on and sn clr* **9/2**[3]

2 *3½* **High Above** 3-9-0 0 RichardKingscote 3 77
(Charlie Fellowes) *in tch in last pair: effrt and hdwy over 3f out: chsd clr ldng pair 2f out: nvr getting on terms w wnr but kpt on ins fnl f to go 2nd fnl 50yds* **7/1**

423- **3** 2 **Ambling (IRE)**[204] 8591 3-9-0 **78**...............(h) RobertHavlin 1 74
(John Gosden) *led: clr 3f out: pushed along over 1f out: sn rdn and hdd 1f out: sn btn and wknd ins fnl f* **7/4**[1]

0 **4** 13 **Jaidaa**[25] 2018 3-9-0 0............... JackMitchell 6 53
(Simon Crisford) *in tch in midfield: effrt to go 3rd but getting outpcd 3f out: wl btn 4th 2f out: wknd* **7/1**

1 **5** 11 **Moment Of Hope (IRE)**[52] 1351 3-9-1 0............... DylanHogan(5) 4 42
(David Simcock) *stdd s: hld up in rr: rdn over 3f out: sn struggling: wl bhd fnl 2f* **7/2**[2]

6 6 **Salve Etoiles (IRE)** 3-9-0 0............... DavidProbert 2 26
(Henry Candy) *chsd ldr tl 4f out: rdn and lost pl 3f out: wl btn 2f out: eased ins fnl f* **14/1**

2m 37.14s (4.64) **Going Correction** +0.20s/f (Good) **6** Ran SP% **108.4**
Speed ratings (Par 100): **92,89,88,79,72 68**
CSF £31.83 TOTE £4.40: £2.20, £4.50; EX 33.80 Trifecta £124.70.
Owner Sir Edmund Loder **Bred** Sir E J Loder **Trained** Newmarket, Suffolk

FOCUS
Add 12yds. This was run in a time 10sec slower than standard, and it doesn't look strong form. The first three came a long way clear. The form is rated close to the race average.

2839 BETWAY SPRINT H'CAP 5f
5:35 (5:36) (Class 4) (0-85,84) 4-Y-O+

£6,469 (£1,925; £962; £481; £300; £300) **Stalls** High

Form RPR

05-2 **1** **Daschas**[17] 2272 5-9-5 **82**...............(t) RichardKingscote 1 88
(Stuart Williams) *chsd ldrs: rdn and edgd rt over 1f out: str chal 1f out: stl wanting to edgd rt but kpt on wl to ld last strides* **11/4**[1]

4623 **2** nk **Harry Hurricane**[14] 2403 7-9-6 **83**...............(p) JosephineGordon 6 88
(George Baker) *led: rdn and hrd pressed over 1f out: kpt on wl u.p tl hdd no ex last strides* **13/2**[3]

06-0 **3** nse **Rio Ronaldo (IRE)**[17] 2272 7-9-4 **81**............... RossaRyan 2 85
(Mike Murphy) *hld up in tch: clsd 1/2-way: rdn to chse ldrs 1f out: hdwy and ev ch ins fnl f: kpt on wl* **16/1**

20-1 **4** shd **Boundary Lane**[22] 2079 4-9-2 **79**............... TomEaves 7 83
(Julie Camacho) *chsd ldrs: effrt over 1f out: kpt on wl u.p fnl 100yds: nt quite rch ldrs* **4/1**[2]

6042 **5** 3/4 **Foxy Forever (IRE)**[15] 2368 9-9-4 **81**...............(bt) FrannyNorton 10 82
(Michael Wigham) *stdd and dropped in bhd after s: hld up in tch in rr: hdwy over 1f out: chsd ldrs and kpt on u.p ins fnl f* **8/1**

30-0 **6** 1/2 **Move In Time**[30] 1892 11-9-7 **84**............... DavidProbert 8 84
(Paul Midgley) *wl in tch in midfield: effrt over 1f out: kpt on same pce ins fnl f* **8/1**

0-00 **7** 2 1/2 **Leo Minor (USA)**[17] 2272 5-9-5 **82**............... NicolaCurrie 9 73
(Robert Cowell) *in tch in midfield: wandered lft and unable qck over 1f out: wl hld and kpt on same pce ins fnl f* **9/1**

0-26 **8** nse **Zamjar**[9] 2556 5-9-7 **84**............... TomMarquand 3 74
(Robert Cowell) *restless in stalls: in tch towards rr: rdn and struggling 3f out: wl hld and kpt on same pce ins fnl f* **12/1**

0305 **9** 1 **Equimou**[9] 2556 5-9-5 **82**............... DaneO'Neill 4 69
(Robert Eddery) *short of room leaving stalls: t.k.h: hld up in tch: hdwy 1/2-way: effrt ent fnl 2f: outpcd over 1f out: bhd ins fnl f* **8/1**

59.61s (0.51) **Going Correction** +0.20s/f (Good) **9** Ran SP% **116.9**
Speed ratings (Par 105): **103,102,102,102,101 100,96,96,94**
CSF £21.23 CT £244.14 TOTE £2.70: £1.20, £2.10, £4.80; EX 18.20 Trifecta £234.30.
Owner T W Morley **Bred** Juddmonte Farms Ltd **Trained** Newmarket, Suffolk

FOCUS
Fairly useful form, but something of a blanket finish, and probably only the winner an to his best. The main action took place out towards the centre.
T/Plt: £65.00 to a £1 stake. Pool: £92,161.63 - 1,033.48 winning units T/Qpdt: £18.20 to a £1 stake. Pool: £4,793.25 - 194.49 winning units **Steve Payne**

2632 THIRSK (L-H)
Saturday, May 18

OFFICIAL GOING: Good to firm (good in places; watered)
Wind: light across Weather: fine

2840 IRISH STALLION FARMS EBF MAIDEN FILLIES' STKS (PLUS 10 RACE) 5f
2:10 (2:10) (Class 4) 2-Y-O £6,727 (£2,002; £1,000; £500) **Stalls** Centre

Form RPR

1 **Althiqa** 2-9-0 0............... JoeFanning 11 83+
(Charlie Appleby) *dwlt: sn midfield: hdwy 2f out: pushed into ld appr fnl f: rdn out fnl 110yds: kpt on wl* **3/1**[2]

2 3/4 **Nasaiym (USA)** 2-9-0 0............... DavidAllan 14 80+
(James Tate) *s.i.s: hld up: hdwy 2f out: pushed along to chse ldr appr fnl f: rdn and kpt on wl* **9/2**[3]

5 **3** 4 1/2 **Blitzle**[12] 2476 2-8-11 0............... BenRobinson(3) 13 64
(Ollie Pears) *pressed ldr: rdn to ld over 1f out: hdd appr fnl f: no ex* **40/1**

3 **4** nk **Endless Joy**[25] 2020 2-9-0 0............... HollieDoyle 9 63
(Archie Watson) *chsd ldrs: rdn 2f out: sn one pce* **9/4**[1]

5 nse **She Can Dance** 2-9-0 0............... KevinStott 2 63
(Kevin Ryan) *chsd ldrs: rdn 2f out: sn one pce* **16/1**

53 **6** 2 3/4 **Lara Silvia**[15] 2367 2-8-11 0............... JamieGormley(3) 5 53
(Iain Jardine) *led narrowly: rdn 2f out: hdd over 1f out: wknd fnl f* **20/1**

7 1 **Vintage Times** 2-9-0 0............... RachelRichardson 3 49
(Tim Easterby) *in tch: rdn and hung lft over 1f out: wknd ins fnl f* **40/1**

8 1/2 **Jaunty** 2-9-0 0............... PaulHanagan 6 47
(Richard Fahey) *s.i.s: hld up: pushed along over 2f out: sme late hdwy: nvr involved* **8/1**

9 1/2 **Beautrix** 2-9-0 0............... ConnorBeasley 7 46
(Michael Dods) *hld up: rdn and sme hdwy 2f out: drvn over 1f out: no imp* **25/1**

34 **10** 1/2 **Bare All (IRE)**[30] 1893 2-9-0 0............... BenCurtis 4 44
(K R Burke) *chsd ldrs: rdn along over 2f out: wknd fnl f* **14/1**

11 2 3/4 **Navajo Dawn (IRE)** 2-9-0 0............... AndrewMullen 1 34
(Robyn Brisland) *wnt lft s and slowly away: rcvrd to sn chsd ldrs: rdn 2f out: wknd fnl f* **66/1**

12 3 1/2 **Shepherds Way (IRE)** 2-9-0 0............... PaulMulrennan 8 21
(Michael Dods) *chsd ldrs: rdn over 2f out: wknd over 1f out* **28/1**

13 4 1/2 **Banmi (IRE)** 2-8-7 0............... CierenFallon(7) 12 5
(Mohamed Moubarak) *a towards rr* **66/1**

14 2 1/4 **Krabi** 2-9-0 0............... CamHardie 10
(Tim Easterby) *dwlt: hld up: sn pushed along: a towards rr* **33/1**

58.95s (-0.45) **Going Correction** -0.125s/f (Firm) **14** Ran SP% **120.5**
Speed ratings (Par 92): **98,96,89,89,89 84,83,82,81,80 76,70,63,59**
CSF £15.45 TOTE £3.20: £1.40, £1.80, £15.00; EX 19.80 Trifecta £499.10.
Owner Godolphin **Bred** Godolphin **Trained** Newmarket, Suffolk

FOCUS
Light rain on watered ground saw the ground change to good, good to firm in places in late morning and the winning rider reported the ground to be just on the easy side of good (though the times suggested the ground was as the official). A wide range of ability on show but a decent gallop and useful form from the first two, who pulled clear in the closing stages. The field raced in the centre of the course (winner and second came more towards the near side of the bunch) and this form should prove reliable.

2841 CELEBRATING THE LIFE OF SANDRA ROWCROFT H'CAP 5f
2:45 (2:47) (Class 4) (0-80,82) 4-Y-O+

£5,692 (£1,694; £846; £423; £300; £300) **Stalls** Centre

Form RPR

-552 **1** **Duke Of Firenze**[8] 2576 10-9-10 **82**............... DavidAllan 5 91
(David C Griffiths) *racd centre: hld up in midfield: rdn and hdwy over 1f out: r.o wl: led towards fin* **8/1**[3]

0/62 **2** nk **Lathom**[13] 2433 6-8-12 **70**............... GrahamLee 4 78
(Paul Midgley) *in tch in centre: pushed along to chse ldrs over 1f out: n.m.r ins fnl f: r.o wl fnl 75yds: wnt 2nd nr fin* **8/1**[3]

3-23 **3** nk **Jabbarockie**[14] 2421 6-9-7 **79**............... JasonHart 6 86
(Eric Alston) *prom centre: rdn to ld over 1f out: strly pressed fnl f: kpt on but hdd towards fin* **4/1**[1]

60-6 **4** 3/4 **Excessable**[14] 2421 6-9-7 **79**............... RachelRichardson 1 83
(Tim Easterby) *prom on far side of centre gp: rdn over 1f out: edgd rt and chal 1f out: no ex towards fin* **14/1**

-015 **5** 2 1/4 **Secretinthepark**[14] 2416 9-9-5 **77**...............(b) PaulMulrenan 8 73
(Michael Mullineaux) *chsd ldrs centre: rdn over 2f out: no ex fnl f* **22/1**

2401 **6** nse **Samovar**[17] 2296 4-8-13 **71**...............(b) PaddyMathers 16 67
(Scott Dixon) *1 of 2 to r stands' side: chsd ldrs: rdn over 2f out: no ex fnl f* **12/1**

04-2 **7** 3/4 **Suwaan (IRE)**[28] 1950 5-8-13 **71**............... JackGarritty 13 64
(Ruth Carr) *chsd ldrs towards stands' side of centre gp: rdn over 2f out: wknd ins fnl f* **10/1**

-246 **8** 1 **Burmese Blazer (IRE)**[7] 2632 4-8-4 **65** oh1........(h) JamieGormley(3) 17 55
(Jim Goldie) *1 of 2 to r stands' side: hld up: rdn over 2f out: sme late hdwy: nvr involved* **5/1**[2]

155 **9** shd **Tabaahy**[11] 2508 4-9-1 **73**............... DavidNolan 12 62
(David O'Meara) *hld up centre: pushed along 2f out: nvr threatened* **10/1**

00-0 **10** nk **Longroom**[46] 1501 7-9-4 **81**...............(w) DannyRedmond(5) 3 69
(Noel Wilson) *led towards far side of centre gp: rdn and hdd over 1f out: wknd fnl f* **80/1**

5203 **11** nk **Landing Night (IRE)**[11] 2508 7-9-0 **72**...............(tp) CamHardie 15 59
(Rebecca Menzies) *in tch towards stands' side of centre gp: rdn over 2f out: wknd over 1f out* **12/1**

3-45 **12** 1 **Alqaab**[15] 2377 4-8-12 **70**............... JamesSullivan 7 53
(Ruth Carr) *dwlt: hld up on far side of centre gp: nvr threatened* **40/1**

-005 **13** 3/4 **Bashiba (IRE)**[14] 2421 8-8-11 **72**...............(t) RowanScott(3) 9 53
(Nigel Tinkler) *midfield: rdn over 2f out: wknd over 1f out* **12/1**

4003 **14** 1/2 **Smokey Lane (IRE)**[21] 2107 5-8-8 **73**............... GinaMangan(7) 10 52
(David Evans) *racd towards far side of centre gp: a towards rr* **10/1**

00-0 **15** 4 1/2 **Mutafarrid (IRE)**[48] 1457 4-9-6 **78**............... KevinStott 2 41
(Paul Midgley) *chsd ldrs towards far side of centre gp: rdn over 2f out: wknd over 1f out* **33/1**

0006 **16** 2 **Classic Pursuit**[8] 2589 8-9-2 **74**...............(b) BarryMcHugh 14 30
(Marjorie Fife) *midfield centre: rdn over 2f out: wknd over 1f out* **66/1**

58.36s (-1.04) **Going Correction** -0.125s/f (Firm) **16** Ran SP% **128.4**
Speed ratings (Par 105): **103,102,102,100,97 97,95,94,94,93 93,91,90,89,82 79**
CSF £72.07 CT £250.10 TOTE £11.10: £2.50, £2.40, £1.90, £4.50; EX 77.10 Trifecta £274.60.
Owner Adlam,Damary-Thompson,Wilson,Griffiths **Bred** Cheveley Park Stud Ltd **Trained** Bawtry, S Yorks

FOCUS
Mainly exposed performers in a reasonable handicap. The gallop was sound and, although the field fanned across the course, the first four home (a few lengths clear of the rest) - drawn 5, 4, 6 and 1 respectively - raced centre to the far side of the group. Sound form.

2842 MARION GIBSON BROWN MEMORIAL H'CAP 7f 218y
3:20 (3:22) (Class 4) (0-80,80) 4-Y-O+

£5,692 (£1,694; £846; £423; £300; £300) **Stalls** Low

Form RPR

1/-4 **1** **Furzig**[16] 2348 4-8-9 **73**............... SeanDavis(5) 4 83+
(Richard Fahey) *trckd ldrs: pushed along over 2f out: drvn to chal ins fnl f: led 75yds out: kpt on wl* **12/1**

3311 **2** 1 1/2 **Saisons D'Or (IRE)**[20] 2151 4-9-6 **79**............... JackGarritty 8 85
(Jedd O'Keeffe) *racd keenly and led after 1f: rdn along over 2f out: edgd rt 1f out: sn pressed: hdd 75yds out: one pce (jockey said gelding hung right-handed in the straight)* **3/1**[1]

221- **3** 3/4 **Make Me**[201] 8703 4-8-13 **72**...............(p) JasonHart 11 76
(Tim Easterby) *chsd ldrs towards outer: rdn over 2f out: kpt on same pce* **7/1**

-505 **4** 1 1/4 **Dubai Acclaim (IRE)**[11] 2509 4-8-12 **71**............... PaulHanagan 9 72
(Richard Fahey) *midfield on inner: pushed along over 2f out: hung lft over 1f out: bit short of room appr fnl f: drvn ins fnl f: r.o fnl 110yds* **11/2**[3]

56-4 **5** 1 **Autretot (FR)**[23] 2057 4-9-7 **80**............... DavidNolan 3 79
(David O'Meara) *prom: rdn over 2f out: no ex ins fnl f* **17/2**

0-25 **6** 1 3/4 **Mutarakez (IRE)**[17] 2291 7-9-0 **73**............... JamesSullivan 6 68
(Ruth Carr) *midfield: rdn and sme hdwy towards outer over 1f out: wknd ifnl 110yds* **12/1**

-121 **7** 2 1/2 **Paparazzi**[126] 209 4-9-4 **77**............... CamHardie 1 66
(Tracy Waggott) *slowly away: hld up: rdn and hdwy on outer 2f out: wknd ins fnl f* **7/1**

-533 **8** 1 3/4 **Tadaawol**[10] 2526 6-9-7 **80**...............(p) BenCurtis 5 65
(Roger Fell) *led for 1f: prom: rdn over 2f out: wknd over 1f out (jockey said gelding ran flat)* **4/1**[2]

0-00 **9** 1 1/2 **Intense Pleasure (IRE)**[18] 2246 4-8-9 **68**...............(h[1]) AndrewMullen 7 50
(Ruth Carr) *dwlt: hld up: pushed along 2f out: nvr threatened* **12/1**

0126 **10** hd **Mont Kinabalu (IRE)**[12] 2480 4-9-2 **75**............... ShaneGray 2 56
(Kevin Ryan) *dwlt: hld up: rdn along over 2f out: nvr threatened* **12/1**

0000 11 *11* **Starplex**[11] 2509 9-8-2 **66** oh2 .... TheodoreLadd(5) 10 22
(Kenny Johnson) *a in rr* **40/1**
1m 39.33s (-2.37) **Going Correction** -0.125s/f (Firm) **11** Ran SP% **129.1**
Speed ratings (Par 105): **106,104,103,102,101 99,97,95,94,93 82**
CSF £52.79 CT £296.29 TOTE £16.60: £5.90, £1.40, £2.70; EX 101.00 Trifecta £754.90.
Owner Mr & Mrs P Ashton **Bred** Mr & Mrs P Ashton **Trained** Musley Bank, N Yorks

FOCUS
A fair handicap but one in which an ordinary gallop saw those held up at a disadvantage. The form's rated around the runner-up.

2843 JW 4X4 NORTHALLERTON H'CAP 6f
3:55 (3:56) (Class 3) (0-95,94) 4-Y-O+ **£9,703** (£2,887; £1,443; £721) **Stalls** Centre

Form RPR
3-66 1 **Muscika**[14] 2393 5-9-0 **87** ....(v) CamHardie 2 96
(David O'Meara) *prom far side: rdn into overall ld over 1f out: drvn and kpt on* **18/1**
02-6 2 *hd* **Hyperfocus (IRE)**[15] 2378 5-9-1 **88** .... DavidAllan 4 96
(Tim Easterby) *trckd ldrs: drvn to chal strly appr fnl f: kpt on: 2nd of 7 in gp* **16/1**
64-0 3 *1 1/4* **Dalton**[19] 2201 5-8-10 **83** .... GrahamLee 1 87
(Julie Camacho) *hld up far side: rdn and sme hdwy over 1f out: drvn and kpt on fnl f: 3rd of 7 in gp* **12/1**
-051 4 *2* **Paddy Power (IRE)**[14] 2416 6-8-6 **79** .... PaulHanagan 14 77
(Richard Fahey) *hld up stands' side: pushed along and hdwy over 1f out: rdn to ld gp 110yds out: kpt on: 1st of 7 in gp* **9/2**[2]
-060 5 *1/2* **Brian The Snail (IRE)**[8] 2572 5-8-9 **87** .... ConnorMurtagh(5) 10 83
(Richard Fahey) *trckd ldrs stands' side: led gp 2f out: sn rdn: hdd in gp 110yds out: one pce: 2nd of 7 in gp* **8/1**
1464 6 *1 3/4* **Primo's Comet**[14] 2421 4-8-4 **80** .... JamieGormley(3) 7 70
(Jim Goldie) *hld up far side: rdn over 2f out: nvr threatened: 4th of 7 in gp* **22/1**
54-1 7 *3/4* **The Armed Man**[26] 1978 6-8-8 **86** .... PaulaMuir(5) 11 74
(Chris Fairhurst) *pressed ldr stands' side: rdn 2f out: edgd lft and no ex fnl f: 3rd of 7 in gp* **8/1**
0-40 8 *nk* **Royal Brave (IRE)**[28] 1946 8-9-2 **89** .... RoystonFfrench 16 76
(Rebecca Bastiman) *hld up stands' side: nvr threatened: 4th of 7 in gp* **20/1**
01-3 9 *1/2* **Confessional**[9] 2557 12-9-3 **90** ....(e) JackGarritty 6 75
(Tim Easterby) *prom far side: rdn over 2f out: wknd fnl f: 5th of 7 in gp* **12/1**
-111 10 *3/4* **Pennsylvania Dutch**[19] 2201 5-8-7 **85** ....(e) SeanDavis(5) 12 68
(Kevin Ryan) *dwlt: sn chsd ldrs stands' side: rdn over 2f out: wknd ins fnl f: 5th of 7 in gp* **5/1**[3]
-020 11 *1/2* **Pipers Note**[21] 2117 9-9-7 **94** .... JamesSullivan 5 75
(Ruth Carr) *racd far side: overall ldr: rdn and hdd over 1f out: wknd ins fnl f: 6th of 7 in gp* **25/1**
56-5 12 *1/2* **Get Knotted (IRE)**[14] 2396 7-9-7 **94** ....(p) RobbieDowney 8 74
(Michael Dods) *swtchd lft to far side gp after 1f: hld up: nvr threatened: last of 7 in gp (vet said gelding had lost its left-fore shoe)* **12/1**
20-4 13 *3/4* **Orion's Bow**[19] 2201 8-8-7 **80** .... RachelRichardson 13 57
(Tim Easterby) *led narrowly in stands' side gp: rdn along and hdd 2f out: wknd fnl f: 6th of 7 in gp* **16/1**
3-32 14 *nk* **Jawwaal**[14] 2393 4-9-2 **89** .... PaulMulrennan 15 65
(Michael Dods) *dwlt: sn trckd ldrs: pushed along over 2f out: rdn over 1f out: wknd (vet said gelding had bled from the nose)* **7/2**[1]
1m 10.65s (-2.15) **Going Correction** -0.125s/f (Firm) **14** Ran SP% **132.4**
Speed ratings (Par 107): **109,108,107,104,103 101,100,100,99,98 97,97,96,95**
CSF £298.56 CT £2157.75 TOTE £28.90: £7.50, £7.90, £4.00; EX 322.90 Trifecta £1909.80.
Owner Gallop Racing & Dynast Racing **Bred** Dukes Stud & Overbury Stallions Ltd **Trained** Upper Helmsley, N Yorks

FOCUS
A decent sprint handicap in which the field split into two equal groups but, as earlier on the card, it was dominated by three low-drawn runners (in stalls 2, 4 and 1 respectively). The gallop was sound and the performances of the fourth and fifth, who raced in the stands' side septet, can be upgraded.

2844 CONSTANT SECURITY SERVICES H'CAP 7f
4:30 (4:33) (Class 2) (0-105,103) 4-Y-O+ **£12,938** (£3,850; £1,924; £962) **Stalls** Low

Form RPR
15- 1 **Admirality**[197] 8816 5-8-8 **90** .... BenCurtis 10 98
(Roger Fell) *prom: racd keenly: pushed along over 2f out: led over 1f out: sn rdn: edgd lft ins fnl f: drvn out* **12/1**
0-20 2 *3/4* **Danielsflyer (IRE)**[14] 2396 5-8-9 **91** .... AndrewMullen 7 97
(Michael Dods) *chsd ldrs towards outer: rdn over 2f out: drvn to chal appr fnl f: kpt on* **7/1**
-410 3 *1* **Lake Volta (IRE)**[7] 2609 4-9-2 **98** .... JoeFanning 9 102+
(Mark Johnston) *led: rdn over 2f out: hdd over 1f out: keeping on same pce whn hmpd on rail 50yds out* **11/4**[1]
-410 4 *1/2* **Three Saints Bay (IRE)**[14] 2402 4-9-5 **101** .... DavidNolan 4 103
(David O'Meara) *trckd ldrs towards inner: rdn along 2f out: kpt on* **9/1**
06-5 5 *nk* **Al Erayg (IRE)**[8] 2572 6-8-2 **84** .... RachelRichardson 6 85+
(Tim Easterby) *hld up: pushed along over 2f out: rdn and r.o wl fnl f: nrst fin* **4/1**[2]
-040 6 *nk* **Aeolus**[14] 2396 8-8-11 **93** .... SamJames 8 93
(Ruth Carr) *dwlt: hld up in midfield: pushed along over 2f out: kpt on fnl f: nvr threatened* **20/1**
0100 7 *3/4* **Above The Rest (IRE)**[7] 2609 8-9-7 **103** ....(h) RobbieDowney 5 108
(David Barron) *trckd ldrs: persistently short of room fr appr fnl f: eased towards fin (vet said gelding had lost its right fore shoe)* **8/1**
20-0 8 *3/4* **Gabrial The Devil (IRE)**[48] 1459 4-8-1 **88** .... SeanDavis(5) 2 84
(Richard Fahey) *in tch on inner: rdn over 2f out: hung lft over 1f out and no imp: sltly hmpd towards fin* **11/1**
050- 9 *3/4* **Breanski**[203] 8634 5-8-4 **86** .... CamHardie 3 80
(Jedd O'Keeffe) *hld up in rr: rdn over 2f out: nvr threatened* **13/2**[3]
111- 10 *2 1/4* **Byron's Choice**[309] 4923 4-8-11 **93** .... PaulMulrennan 1 81
(Michael Dods) *hld up in midfield: pushed along over 2f out: sn btn* **7/1**
1m 26.03s (-1.57) **Going Correction** -0.125s/f (Firm) **10** Ran SP% **126.9**
Speed ratings (Par 109): **103,102,101,100,100 99,98,98,97,94**
CSF £101.59 CT £271.29 TOTE £13.20: £4.50, £2.70, £1.60; EX 172.90 Trifecta £1092.40.
Owner Ventura Racing & Partners **Bred** Newsells Park Stud **Trained** Nawton, N Yorks
■ Stewards' Enquiry : Andrew Mullen three-day ban: interference & careless riding (Jun 2-4)
Ben Curtis three-day ban: interference & careless riding (Jun 2-4)

FOCUS
The feature event on the card but a muddling gallop suited those up with the pace and a couple (notably \bAbove The Rest\p) met trouble late on. This form isn't reliable.

2845 RICHARD FOSTER TRIBUTE NOVICE STKS (PLUS 10 RACE) 1m 4f 8y
5:05 (5:06) (Class 4) 3-Y-O **£6,727** (£2,002; £1,000; £500) **Stalls** High

Form RPR
12 1 **Almost Midnight**[79] 949 3-9-9 0 .... SamJames 5 92+
(David Simcock) *midfield: pushed along and hdwy on outer over 2f out: rdn to ld appr fnl f: edgd lft: styd on* **6/1**
2 2 *1 1/4* **Selino**[17] 2289 3-9-2 .... DanielMuscutt 2 82
(James Fanshawe) *trckd ldrs: rdn over 2f out: drvn over 1f out: styd on same pce: wnt 2nd towards fin (jockey said gelding had stumbled on the bend entering the back straight)* **11/4**[2]
-332 3 *1/2* **Bo Samraan (IRE)**[10] 2524 3-9-2 **79** .... JoeFanning 9 82
(Mark Johnston) *sn led: rdn along over 2f out: hdd appr fnl f: no ex and lost 2nd towards fin* **3/1**[3]
63 4 *2 1/4* **Just You Wait**[21] 2113 3-8-9 0 .... CierenFallon(7) 7 78
(Charlie Appleby) *prom: rdn along 3f out: no ex fnl f (jockey said colt hung left-handed in the home straight)* **5/2**[1]
1 5 *2 1/2* **Kashagan**[15] 2375 3-9-9 0 .... PaulMulrennan 1 81
(Archie Watson) *trckd ldrs: rdn along over 2f out: sn outpcd and btn* **6/1**
0 6 *21* **Ozark**[21] 2099 3-8-11 0 .... ConnorBeasley 6 35
(Jennie Candlish) *a towards rr* **66/1**
7 *1* **Greek Hero** 3-9-2 0 .... DavidNolan 4 39
(Declan Carroll) *dwlt: sn midfield: rdn along 3f out: sn wknd* **25/1**
00 8 *17* **Yasmin From York**[20] 2148 3-8-11 0 .... CamHardie 8 7
(Brian Rothwell) *a in rr* **125/1**
6-0 9 *2 1/4* **Bagatino**[21] 2094 3-9-2 ....(t[1]) KevinStott 3 8
(Declan Carroll) *hld up in midfield: wknd and bhd over 2f out* **66/1**
2m 38.23s (-1.77) **Going Correction** -0.125s/f (Firm) **9** Ran SP% **116.4**
Speed ratings (Par 101): **100,99,98,97,95 81,81,69,68**
CSF £22.89 TOTE £7.60: £1.90, £1.10, £1.40; EX 32.40 Trifecta £91.60.
Owner R A Pegum, Ken & Maree Lowe **Bred** Card Bloodstock **Trained** Newmarket, Suffolk

FOCUS
Rail movements added 7yds to the official distance. A useful event in which the five at the head of the market pulled clear when the (ordinary) gallop increased early in the straight. The third is the best guide to the worth of this form.

2846 SCOUTING FOR GIRLS - LIVE @THIRSKRACES FRIDAY 16TH AUGUST H'CAP (DIV I) 6f
5:40 (5:41) (Class 6) (0-65,69) 4-Y-O+
£3,398 (£1,011; £505; £300; £300; £300) **Stalls** Centre

Form RPR
6310 1 **Tricky Dicky**[8] 2580 6-9-1 **59** .... BenCurtis 9 67
(Roger Fell) *mde all: rdn and edgd rt over 1f out: kpt on* **7/2**[2]
/30- 2 *1/2* **Debawtry (IRE)**[211] 8383 4-9-5 **63** .... ShaneGray 4 70
(Phillip Makin) *hld up in midfield: pushed along and hdwy over 1f out: rdn and kpt on wl* **16/1**
4341 3 *1* **Ginger Jam**[7] 2638 4-9-3 **64** .... RowanScott(3) 6 68
(Nigel Tinkler) *hld up in midfield: rdn and hdwy to chse ldr over 1f out: kpt on same pce ins fnl f* **7/4**[1]
4210 4 *1 3/4* **Poet's Pride**[8] 2580 4-9-4 **62** .... RobbieDowney 8 60
(David Barron) *prom: rdn along over 1f out: no ex ins fnl f* **8/1**
10-4 5 *3/4* **Sfumato**[19] 2203 5-9-6 **64** .... ConnorBeasley 11 60
(Adrian Nicholls) *chsd ldr: drvn over 1f out: no ex ins fnl f* **6/1**[3]
5-00 6 *3 1/2* **Etikaal**[14] 2418 5-9-6 **64** .... SamJames 10 50
(Grant Tuer) *in tch: rdn over 2f out: wknd fnl f* **16/1**
25-0 7 *1* **Shortbackandsides (IRE)**[14] 2416 4-9-0 **65** .... RobertDodsworth(7) 5 48
(Tim Easterby) *trckd ldr: rdn over 2f out: wknd over 1f out* **25/1**
000- 8 *3/4* **Sherzy Boy**[325] 4239 4-8-9 **60** ....(t[1] w) JoshQuinn(7) 3 40
(Jacqueline Coward) *midfield: rdn over 2f out: sn outpcd and btn* **25/1**
3541 9 *1* **Rasheeq (IRE)**[8] 2580 6-9-4 **69** ....(p) CierenFallon(7) 1 46
(Mohamed Moubarak) *slowly away: hld up: nvr threatened (jockey said gelding was slowly away)* **8/1**
-000 10 *1 1/4* **Royal Connoisseur (IRE)**[22] 2076 8-8-10 **61** ....(v[1]) RussellHarris(7) 2 35
(Richard Fahey) *prom: rdn over 2f out: wknd over 1f out* **25/1**
06 11 *1/2* **At Your Service**[42] 1590 5-9-3 **61** ....(h) JoeyHaynes 12 33
(Paul Howling) *a towards rr* **25/1**
1m 11.68s (-1.12) **Going Correction** -0.125s/f (Firm) **11** Ran SP% **122.2**
Speed ratings (Par 101): **102,101,100,97,96 92,90,89,88,86 86**
CSF £56.93 CT £126.28 TOTE £4.60: £1.60, £5.50, £1.40; EX 67.10 Trifecta £210.60.
Owner Eight Gents and a Lady **Bred** Onslow, Stratton & Parry **Trained** Nawton, N Yorks

FOCUS
Division one of a modest handicap in which the field raced as one group in the centre of the track. The gallop was sound and the first five pulled a few lengths clear. The winner was well treated on old AW form.

2847 SCOUTING FOR GIRLS - LIVE @THIRSKRACES FRIDAY 16TH AUGUST H'CAP (DIV II) 6f
6:10 (6:10) (Class 6) (0-65,65) 4-Y-O+
£3,398 (£1,011; £505; £300; £300; £300) **Stalls** Centre

Form RPR
-422 1 **Sczueme**[19] 2183 5-9-6 **64** ....(h) SamJames 10 74
(Phillip Makin) *racd stands' side: mde all: stl on bit over 1f out: kpt on pushed out fnl f: comf* **11/4**[1]
0652 2 *2 1/2* **Holdenhurst**[17] 2287 4-8-7 **58** .... CierenFallon(7) 1 61
(Bill Turner) *chsd ldr centre: rdn to ld gp ins fnl f and 2nd overall: kpt on but no ch w wnr: 1st of 7 in gp* **7/1**
0602 3 *hd* **Atletico (IRE)**[19] 2203 7-9-0 **65** ....(v) GinaMangan(7) 12 67
(David Evans) *chsd ldr stands' side: rdn over 1f out: kpt on fnl f: 2nd of 4 in gp* **7/2**[2]
30-0 4 *3 1/2* **Kodicat (IRE)**[19] 2203 5-9-3 **61** .... DougieCostello 6 52
(Kevin Ryan) *chsd ldr centre: rdn to ld in gp over 1f out and chsd overall ldr: hdd in gp ins fnl 1f: wknd fnl 110yds: 2nd of 7 in gp* **11/1**
5-06 5 *1 1/4* **Patrick (IRE)**[33] 1817 7-9-1 **59** .... PaulMulrennan 2 47
(Paul Midgley) *hld up in tch: rdn over 1f out: no imp: 3rd of 7 in gp* **11/1**
000- 6 *2* **Fard**[232] 7726 4-9-6 **64** .... BenCurtis 3 46
(Roger Fell) *in tch: rdn over 1f out: wknd ins fnl f: 4th of 7 in gp (jockey said gelding hung right-handed)* **10/1**
0-06 7 *1 1/2* **Chickenfortea (IRE)**[19] 2203 5-9-4 **62** .... JasonHart 5 39
(Eric Alston) *led centre gp and chsd overall ldr: rdn and hdd in gp over 1f out: wknd fnl f: 5th of 7 in gp* **6/1**[3]

1-03 **8** *3/4* **Cosmic Chatter**[8] 2580 9-9-4 **62**..............................(p) DavidNolan 11 37
(Ruth Carr) *chsd ldr stands' side: rdn 2f out: wknd fnl f: 3rd of 4 in gp* **18/1**

045- **9** *1 3/4* **Extrasolar**[210] 8412 9-9-7 **65**..............................(t) ConnorBeasley 9 35
(Geoffrey Harker) *racd centre: a towards rr: 6th of 7 in gp* **20/1**

4-35 **10** *3 1/4* **Orient Express**[107] 500 4-9-0 **63**.............................. SeanDavis(5) 4 23
(Richard Fahey) *midfield centre: rdn over 2f out: hung lft over 1f out: wknd: last of 7 in gp* **14/1**

4300 **11** *2 1/2* **Global Exceed**[16] 2318 4-9-6 **64**..............................(p) ShaneGray 7 16
(Karen Tutty) *dwlt: a towards rr stands' side* **25/1**

1m 11.69s (-1.11) **Going Correction** -0.125s/f (Firm) **11 Ran SP% 122.0**
Speed ratings (Par 101): **102,98,98,93,92 89,87,86,84,79 76**
CSF £23.40 CT £72.67 TOTE £3.00: £1.10, £2.70, £2.00; EX 28.50 Trifecta £127.00.
Owner P J Makin **Bred** R S Hoskins & Hermes Services **Trained** Easingwold, N Yorks

FOCUS
Division two of a race featuring mainly exposed sorts. The gallop was a good one and the field split into two groups before merging in the centre of the track soon after halfway. The winner is rated back towards his best.
T/Plt: £513.60 to a £1 stake. Pool: £68,539.85 - 97.40 winning units T/Qpdt: £169.00 to a £1 stake. Pool: £3,563.30 - 15.60 winning units **Andrew Sheret**

2848 - 2852a (Foreign Racing) - See Raceform Interactive

2154

NAVAN (L-H)

Saturday, May 18

OFFICIAL GOING: Good to firm (watered)

2853a IRISH STALLION FARMS EBF YEATS STKS (LISTED RACE) 1m 5f

4:05 (4:07) 3-Y-O £39,864 (£12,837; £6,081; £2,702; £1,351)

RPR

1 **Western Australia (IRE)**[32] 1831 3-9-3 **107**.............. DonnachaO'Brien 3 102+
(A P O'Brien, Ire) *trckd ldr in 2nd: pushed along to dispute 2f out: led narrowly ent fnl f: rdn clr clsng stages* **2/1**[2]

2 *1 1/2* **Pythion (FR)**[6] 2662 3-9-3 **97**.............................. ColinKeane 1 100
(G M Lyons, Ire) *led: strly pressed and jnd 2f out: hdd ent fnl f: kpt on wl tl no ex w wnr clsng stages* **6/1**

3 *2 3/4* **Masaff (IRE)**[203] 8656 3-9-3 **106**.............................. ChrisHayes 2 96+
(D K Weld, Ire) *awkward leaving stalls: settled off ldng pair in 3rd: rdn 2f out: no imp appr fnl f: kpt on same pce* **5/4**[1]

4 *7 1/2* **Chablis (IRE)**[7] 2642 3-8-12 **95**.............................. SeamieHeffernan 4 83
(A P O'Brien, Ire) *hld up in 4th: pushed along over 2f out: no imp over 1f out: sn one pce* **9/2**[3]

5 *60* **Johnyfortycoats (IRE)** 3-9-3 **0**.............................. GaryCarroll 5
(Michael Mulvany, Ire) *slowly away and a detached in rr: nvr a factor: t.o* **100/1**

2m 49.97s (-10.03) **5 Ran SP% 111.2**
CSF £13.83 TOTE £2.50: £2.00, £3.50; DF 11.30 Trifecta £23.50.
Owner Derrick Smith & Mrs John Magnier & Michael Tabor **Bred** Pier House Stud **Trained** Cashel, Co Tipperary

FOCUS
Comfortable and classy from \bWestern Australia\p, a horse who could come into his own over these staying trips. The favourite \bMasaff\p probably underperformed but take nothing away from the winner who was very good.

2854 - 2855a (Foreign Racing) - See Raceform Interactive

PIMLICO (L-H)

Saturday, May 18

OFFICIAL GOING: Dirt: fast; turf: firm

2856a PREAKNESS STKS (GRADE 1) (3YO) (MAIN TRACK) (DIRT) 1m 1f 110y(D)

11:48 3-Y-O £779,527 (£259,842; £142,913; £77,952; £38,976)

RPR

1 **War Of Will (USA)**[14] 2425 3-9-0 **0**.............................. TylerGaffalione 1 114
(Mark Casse, Canada) *racd keenly: in tch: rdn 2f out: squeezed through gap on inner to ld over 1f out: sn drvn: edgd rt ins fnl f: kpt on wl* **61/10**[3]

2 *1 1/4* **Everfast (USA)**[14] 3-9-0 **0**.............................. JoelRosario 10 111
(Dale Romans, U.S.A) *in rr pair wl bhd main gp: latched on to main gp 3f out: rdn and gd hdwy fr 2f out: drvn fnl f: styd on wl to snatch 2nd cl home: nt rch wnr* **29/1**

3 *nse* **Owendale (USA)**[35] 3-9-0 **0**..............................(b) FlorentGeroux 5 111+
(Brad H Cox, U.S.A) *hld up towards rr of midfield: rdn 3f out: wd into st: gd hdwy fr under 2f out: drvn and styd on fr over 1f out: nrst fin* **79/10**

4 *1 1/4* **Warrior's Charge (USA)**[36] 3-9-0 **0**.............................. JavierCastellano 3 108
(Brad H Cox, U.S.A) *led: rdn 2f out: hdd over 1f out: edgd rt ins fnl f: no ex fnl 100yds* **126/10**

5 *1 1/4* **Laughing Fox (USA)**[14] 3-9-0 **0**.............................. RicardoSantanaJr 11 106
(Steven Asmussen, U.S.A) *in rr pair wl bhd main gp: latched on to main gp 3f out: rdn over 2f out: drvn and styd on fr 1 1/2f out: nrst fin* **216/10**

6 *nse* **Improbable (USA)**[14] 2425 3-9-0 **0**.............................. MikeESmith 4 106
(Bob Baffert, U.S.A) *in tch in midfield: rdn and stdy hdwy fr 3f out: briefly wnt 3rd over 1f out: no ex ins fnl f* **5/2**[1]

7 *1 3/4* **Win Win Win (USA)**[14] 2425 3-9-0 **0**..............................(b) JulianPimentel 13 102
(Michael Trombetta, U.S.A) *midfield on outside: rdn 3f out: wd into st: drvn and rallied briefly appr fnl f: wknd ins fnl f* **138/10**

8 *4* **Bourbon War (USA)**[49] 1452 3-9-0 **0**..............................(b[1]) IradOrtizJr 2 94
(Mark Hennig, U.S.A) *hld up towards rr of midfield: rdn and outpcd under 3f out: sn no imp* **56/10**[2]

9 *1* **Signalman (USA)**[42] 1615 3-9-0 **0**.............................. BrianJosephHernandezJr 8 91
(Kenneth McPeek, U.S.A) *hld up towards rr of main gp: hdwy into midfield on inner 3f out: rdn 2 1/2f out: wknd steadily fr 2f out* **207/10**

10 *nk* **Anothertwistafate (USA)**[35] 3-9-0 **0**.............................. JoselOrtiz 12 91
(Blaine D Wright, U.S.A) *trckd ldrs on outer: chsd ldr 1/2-way: rdn 3f out: wknd fr 1 1/2f out* **145/10**

11 *2 3/4* **Alwaysmining (USA)**[28] 3-9-0 **0**.............................. DanielCenteno 7 85
(Kelly Rubley, U.S.A) *in tch on outside: trckd ldrs over 3f out: rdn 2 1/2f out: wknd qckly under 2f out: eased fnl f* **66/10**

12 *10 1/4* **Market King (USA)**[42] 1615 3-9-0 **0**.............................. JonKentonCourt 6 64
(D Wayne Lukas, U.S.A) *w ldr: dropped to 3rd 1/2-way: dropped to midfield 3f out: rdn and struggling fr 2f out* **32/1**

U **Bodexpress (USA)**[14] 2425 3-9-0 **0**.............................. JohnRVelazquez 9
(Gustavo Delgado, U.S.A) *rrd and uns rdr leaving stalls* **201/10**

1m 54.34s (-1.25) **13 Ran SP% 122.9**
PARI-MUTUEL (all including 2 unit stake): WIN 14.20; PLACE (1-2) 7.40, 32.00; SHOW (1-2-3) 5.40, 14.40, 6.00; SF 947.00.
Owner Gary Barber **Bred** Flaxman Holdings Limited **Trained** Canada

FOCUS
Leg two of the Triple Crown. The first four across the line in the Kentucky Derby were absent this time, with only the 5th, 8th, 10th and 14th past the post at Churchill Downs making it, but today's winner was one of them. There was a fast, contested pace: 22.50 (2f), 23.66 (4f), 24.40 (6f), 24.92 (1m), 18.86 (line).

2857 - 2868a (Foreign Racing) - See Raceform Interactive

2586

RIPON (R-H)

Sunday, May 19

OFFICIAL GOING: Good (watered; 8.1)
Wind: Light, across in straight of nearly 5f Weather: Overcast

2869 CASTLEHOUSE CONSTRUCTION SUPPORTING WOODEN SPOON CHARITY NOVICE STKS (PLUS 10 RACE) 6f

2:00 (2:01) (Class 4) 2-Y-O £5,175 (£1,540; £769; £384) Stalls High

Form RPR

3 **1** **Misty Grey (IRE)**[16] 2362 2-9-5 **0**.............................. JasonHart 7 89
(Mark Johnston) *wnt rt s: qckly c across to nrside rail: mde all: qcknd clr over 1f out: r.o wl: eased cl home* **17/2**

2 *7* **Oso Rapido (IRE)** 2-9-5 **0**.............................. DanielTudhope 6 70+
(David O'Meara) *wnt rt and bmpd s: in tch: wnt 2nd over 1f out: kpt on: no imp on wnr: eased fnl 100yds* **3/1**[2]

3 *1 1/4* **Lexington Warfare (IRE)** 2-9-5 **0**.............................. PaulHanagan 5 66+
(Richard Fahey) *dwlt: squeezed out s: bhd and outpcd: hdwy over 1f out: styd on ins fnl f: nvr gng pce to chal* **8/1**

64 **4** *1* **King Lenox**[13] 2475 2-9-2 **0**.............................. RowanScott(3) 4 61
(Nigel Tinkler) *bmpd s: prom: rdn over 2f out: outpcd by wnr and lost 2nd over 1f out: styd on same pce ins fnl f* **20/1**

5 *3* **Rich Belief** 2-9-5 **0**.............................. PatCosgrave 8 52
(James Bethell) *missed break: outpcd and bhd: kpt on ins fnl f: nvr gng pce to get involved* **25/1**

33 **6** *1 1/2* **Don't Joke**[19] 2257 2-9-5 **0**.............................. FrannyNorton 3 48
(Mark Johnston) *chsd ldrs: rdn over 3f out: no ex over 1f out: wl btn ins fnl f* **11/4**[1]

56 **7** *1 3/4* **Mystic Knight (IRE)**[28] 1968 2-9-5 **0**.............................. DavidAllan 2 42
(Tim Easterby) *in tch: rdn over 3f out: wknd 1f out* **33/1**

5 **8** *8* **Cock Robin**[32] 1843 2-9-5 **0**.............................. KevinStott 1 18
(Kevin Ryan) *in tch: rdn and lost pl over 3f out: bhd fnl f* **7/1**

9 *5* **Abadie** 2-9-5 **0**..............................(t[1]) PaulMulrennan 9 3
(Archie Watson) *green to post: chsd ldrs: rdn over 3f out: wknd over 2f out (jockey said colt ran green)* **9/2**[3]

1m 12.2s (-0.30) **Going Correction** -0.075s/f (Good) **9 Ran SP% 115.5**
Speed ratings (Par 95): **99,89,88,86,82 80,78,67,61**
CSF £33.49 TOTE £10.20: £2.60, £1.20, £3.00; EX 41.60 Trifecta £290.30.
Owner Barbara & Alick Richmond **Bred** Skymarc Farm **Trained** Middleham Moor, N Yorks

FOCUS
Rail movements added 12yds to races 4, 5 and 7. The stalls were on the stands' side for this opening juvenile novice sprint in which the winner made all up the rail. He's obviously useful.

2870 VW VAN CENTRE (LEEDS) STIRRING SPOON SMILES CHARITY H'CAP (DIV I) 6f

2:35 (2:37) (Class 6) (0-60,62) 3-Y-O
£3,816 (£1,135; £567; £400; £400; £400) Stalls High

Form RPR

20-0 **1** **Kermouster**[8] 2635 3-9-7 **60**.............................. SamJames 6 67+
(Grant Tuer) *rrd s and missed break: bhd: stl last 2f out: hdwy over 1f out: sn swtchd rt: r.o strly fnl 100yds to ld nr fin (trainer said, as to the apparent improvement in form, the filly may have benefited from the drop in class)* **7/1**

3214 **2** *nk* **Ascot Dreamer**[18] 2293 3-9-4 **57**..............................(t) LewisEdmunds 1 63
(David Brown) *chsd ldrs: led over 2f out: kpt on for press ins fnl f: hdd nr fin* **9/2**[1]

03-0 **3** *1* **Highjacked**[17] 2337 3-8-11 **50**.............................. ConnorBeasley 9 53
(John Davies) *wnt rt s: midfield: rdn over 3f out: hdwy over 1f out: chsd ldrs ins fnl f: kpt on: sltly short of room whn hld nr fin* **9/1**

4-52 **4** *1/2* **Tizwotitiz**[16] 2357 3-9-0 **60**.............................. TobyEley(7) 3 62
(Steph Hollinshead) *midfield: rdn and hdwy ins fnl f: r.o fnl 100yds: nt pce to mount serious chal (jockey said gelding became unbalanced on the undulations)* **13/2**

0-02 **5** *shd* **Ey Up Its Mick**[20] 2197 3-9-5 **58**..............................(b) DougieCostello 8 59
(Tony Coyle) *carried rt s: chsd ldrs: rdn over 2f out: edgd lft wl over 1f out: sn wnt 2nd tl ins fnl 100yds: styd on same pce* **6/1**[3]

60-0 **6** *1/2* **Separable**[27] 1980 3-9-1 **54**..............................(p[1]) RachelRichardson 11 54
(Tim Easterby) *prom: rdn over 2f out: unable qck over 1f out: styd on same pce ins fnl f* **20/1**

2230 **7** *2* **Amor Kethley**[33] 1842 3-9-4 **62**..............................(t[1]) DylanHogan(5) 4 56
(Amy Murphy) *s.i.s: midfield: rdn and hdwy 2f out: chsd ldrs over 1f out: no ex fnl 100yds* **14/1**

5530 **8** *1 1/4* **One One Seven (IRE)**[13] 2477 3-9-2 **55**.............................. CamHardie 10 45
(Antony Brittain) *prom: rdn over 2f out: unable qck over 1f out: wknd fnl 100yds* **5/1**[2]

4-00 **9** *2 1/2* **Caramel Curves**[5] 2708 3-8-11 **53**.............................. JaneElliott(3) 2 36+
(David Barron) *swtchd lft qckly early on: towards rr: effrt but no imp over 1f out: nvr gng pce to get involved (jockey said filly jumped awkwardly leaving the stalls)* **11/1**

0-50 **10** *11* **Early Edition (IRE)**[13] 2482 3-9-1 **54**..............................(p) DanielTudhope 12 4
(Roger Fell) *led: rdn and hdd over 2f out: sn wknd* **33/1**

-004 **11** *3/4* **Budaiya Fort (IRE)**[4] 2735 3-8-9 **55**..............................(v[1]) GraceMcEntee(7) 5 2
(Phil McEntee) *a outpcd: nvr on terms* **10/1**

00-0 **12** *3 1/2* **Justice Shallow (FR)**[20] 2197 3-8-7 **46** oh1.............................. NathanEvans 7
(Alan Berry) *carried rt s: chsd ldrs tl rdn and wknd over 2f out (jockey said gelding became restless in stalls)* **100/1**

1m 12.91s (0.41) **Going Correction** -0.075s/f (Good) **12 Ran SP% 117.8**
Speed ratings (Par 97): **94,93,92,91,91 90,88,86,83,68 67,62**
CSF £37.64 CT £294.35 TOTE £9.70: £2.80, £1.50, £3.40; EX 47.90 Trifecta £377.00.
Owner D R Tucker **Bred** D R Tucker **Trained** Birkby, N Yorks

FOCUS
The first division of a modest sprint and the winner (matched at 1,000-1 in-running) produced a remarkable effort to come from last. This was a pb from her.

2871 VW VAN CENTRE (LEEDS) STIRRING SPOON SMILES CHARITY H'CAP (DIV II) 6f

3:10 (3:10) (Class 6) (0-60,61) 3-Y-O

£3,816 (£1,135; £567; £400; £400; £400) **Stalls** High

Form RPR

34 **1** **Fairy Fast (IRE)**[6] 2683 3-9-5 **58**....(p[1]) DanielTudhope 6 64
(David O'Meara) *racd keenly disputing ld: rdn and def ld over 1f out: sn hung rt: kpt on for press ins fnl f: all out nr fin: jst hld on* **5/1**[3]

5-03 **2** *shd* **Seanjohnsilver (IRE)**[20] 2197 3-9-5 **58**....(t) DavidNolan 2 64
(Declan Carroll) *midfield: rdn 1/2-way: hdwy for press 2f out: chse ldrs over 1f out: edgd lft ent fnl f: r.o towards fin: jst failed* **10/3**[2]

0-03 **3** *1 1/2* **Timetodock**[13] 2477 3-9-8 **61**....(b) DavidAllan 3 62
(Tim Easterby) *disp ld: rdn over 2f out: hdd over 1f out and hung rt: stl ev ch ins fnl f: no ex fnl 50yds* **15/8**[1]

560- **4** *nse* **Perfect Swiss**[202] 8698 3-9-1 **54**.... RachelRichardson 7 55+
(Tim Easterby) *towards rr: swtchd rt u.p whn hdwy over 1f out: styd on fnl 100yds: gng on at fin (jockey said gelding was restless in stalls)* **14/1**

0530 **5** *3/4* **Deconso**[32] 1863 3-9-1 **54**.... ShaneKelly 8 53
(Christopher Kellett) *racd off the pce: rdn 1/2-way: hdwy over 1f out: styd on ins fnl f: one pce towards fin* **28/1**

-050 **6** *1* **Zalmi Angel**[13] 2482 3-8-8 **52**.... PaulaMuir(5) 11 48
(Adrian Nicholls) *chsd ldrs: rdn over 2f out: unable qck over 1f out: styd on same pce ins fnl f* **10/1**

00-5 **7** *nse* **Josiebond**[20] 2197 3-8-13 **55**.... RowanScott(3) 9 51
(Rebecca Bastiman) *midfield: rdn 1/2-way: nt clr run over 1f out: kpt on fnl 100yds: nvr able to chal (jockey said filly was denied a clear run approaching the final furlong)* **12/1**

60-0 **8** *3/4* **Good Looker (IRE)**[13] 2482 3-9-0 **53**.... DougieCostello 4 46
(Tony Coyle) *in tch: hdwy u.p over 1f out: one pce ins fnl f* **33/1**

000- **9** *1 1/4* **Just A Rumour (IRE)**[222] 8091 3-8-8 **47**.... PhilDennis 12 37
(Noel Wilson) *chsd ldrs: rdn 2f out: wknd over 1f out* **50/1**

0000 **10** *3 1/2* **Isabella Red (IRE)**[19] 2238 3-8-0 **46** oh1....(b[1]) ElishaWhittington(7) 1 25
(Lisa Williamson) *bhd: outpcd 1/2-way: nvr a threat (jockey said filly was slowly away)* **100/1**

00-0 **11** *26* **Rock N Roll Queen**[26] 2016 3-9-3 **56**.... FrannyNorton 5
(John Mackie) *chsd ldrs tl rdn and wknd 1/2-way* **25/1**

-360 **12** *11* **Madame Vitesse (FR)**[88] 813 3-9-2 **60**.... SeanDavis(5) 10
(Richard Fahey) *midfield: rdn over 3f out: wknd over 2f out: eased when wl btn over 1f out (jockey said filly became unbalanced on the undulations from half way; vet said filly was found to have a small wound right hind)* **14/1**

1m 12.83s (0.33) **Going Correction** -0.075s/f (Good) **12** Ran SP% **117.8**
Speed ratings (Par 97): **94,93,91,91,90 89,89,88,86,82 47,32**
CSF £20.97 CT £42.53 TOTE £5.40: £2.10, £1.70, £1.20; EX 23.40 Trifecta £45.30.
Owner Blessingndisguise Partnership **Bred** Tom Mahon **Trained** Upper Helmsley, N Yorks

FOCUS
The second division was run in a 0.08secs faster time, and they raced more towards the stands' side. The second seems the best guide.

2872 TRADITIONAL FAMILY FUN DAY H'CAP 1m 1f 170y

3:45 (3:45) (Class 4) (0-85,87) 3-Y-O

£7,051 (£2,098; £1,048; £524; £400; £400) **Stalls** Low

Form RPR

23-2 **1** **Global Heat (IRE)**[20] 2208 3-9-7 **83**.... HectorCrouch 2 94+
(Saeed bin Suroor) *prom on inner: rdn over 2f out: swtchd lft over 1f out: str chal wl ins fnl f: r.o to ld nr fin* **6/4**[1]

30-1 **2** *nk* **Takumi (IRE)**[15] 2407 3-9-3 **79**.... JackMitchell 5 89
(Roger Varian) *chsd ldr: rdn to ld over 2f out: strly pressed ins fnl f: hdd nr fin* **5/2**[2]

1-10 **3** *hd* **Sameem (IRE)**[25] 2031 3-9-11 **87**.... DavidAllan 6 96
(James Tate) *led: rdn and hdd over 2f out: stl ev ch and rallying ins fnl f: hld nr fin* **3/1**[3]

4-65 **4** *9* **Sir Victor (IRE)**[25] 2035 3-9-1 **80**.... JaneElliott(3) 3 71
(Tom Dascombe) *in rr: rdn over 5f out: outpcd over 3f out: edgd lft u.p over 3f out: kpt on whn no ch ins fnl f* **16/1**

434- **5** *1/2* **Sootability (IRE)**[218] 8195 3-8-10 **77**.... SeanDavis(5) 1 67
(Richard Fahey) *in tch: rdn over 4f out: effrt over 3f out: no imp and one pce fnl 2f* **14/1**

250- **6** *1 1/2* **Bullion Boss (IRE)**[235] 7667 3-8-13 **75**.... PaulMulrennan 7 61
(Michael Dods) *hld up: pushed along over 5f out: outpcd over 4f out: plugged on and no ch ins fnl f* **25/1**

05-0 **7** *51* **Off Piste**[31] 1897 3-9-0 **76**....(t) JasonHart 4
(Tim Easterby) *racd keenly: chsd ldrs: rdn and lost pl over 4f out: wknd 3f out: eased whn wl btn over 1f out* **33/1**

2m 2.21s (-2.39) **Going Correction** -0.075s/f (Good) **7** Ran SP% **112.9**
Speed ratings (Par 101): **108,107,107,100,100 98,58**
CSF £5.29 TOTE £2.20: £1.20, £2.00; EX 5.80 Trifecta £13.60.
Owner Godolphin **Bred** Wellsummers Farm **Trained** Newmarket, Suffolk
■ Stewards' Enquiry : Jack Mitchell two-day ban: used whip above permitted level (2-3 Jun)

FOCUS
Race distance increased by 12yds. Several improvers on show for this small handicap, and the three most fancied runners came clear in fighting out a tight finish.

2873 WILMOT-SMITH MEMORIAL H'CAP 1m 1f

4:20 (4:23) (Class 2) (0-105,102) 4-Y-O+

£17,118 (£5,126; £2,563; £1,281; £640; £321) **Stalls** Low

Form RPR

4103 **1** **Fayez (IRE)**[22] 2116 5-8-6 **87**.... ShaneGray 10 96
(David O'Meara) *wnt lft s: hld up in rr: hdwy over 2f out: rdn over 1f out: r.o to ld ins fnl f: drew clr towards fin* **14/1**

0-55 **2** *3* **Fennaan (IRE)**[15] 2419 4-8-7 **88**....(h) SamJames 7 91
(Phillip Makin) *racd keenly: chsd ldrs: lft in 2nd pl under 5f out: rdn upsides chalng fr 2f out tl unable qck ins fnl f: nt pce of wnr towards fin* **10/1**

144- **3** *1/2* **Red Mist**[219] 8176 4-9-7 **102**.... JackMitchell 3 104
(Simon Crisford) *led: rdn whn jnd 2f out: hdd ins fnl f: unable to go w wnr fnl 100yds: styd on same pce* **3/1**[1]

0-40 **4** *1 3/4* **Anythingtoday (IRE)**[15] 2419 5-8-7 **88**....(p) CamHardie 2 86
(David O'Meara) *hld up in midfield: hdwy over 4f out: rdn whn cl up 2f out: styd on same pce ins fnl f* **12/1**

6-41 **5** *1 3/4* **Kripke (IRE)**[18] 2291 4-7-13 **83** oh1.... JaneElliott(3) 1 78
(David Barron) *trckd ldrs: rdn and outpcd over 3f out: kpt on ins fnl f: no real imp* **11/2**[3]

13-3 **6** *1/2* **Just Hiss**[22] 2105 6-8-9 **90**....(p) RachelRichardson 6 84
(Tim Easterby) *hld up: hdwy over 3f out: rdn to chse ldrs over 2f out: one pce fr over 1f out* **8/1**

00-6 **7** *7* **Carry On Deryck**[132] 121 7-9-4 **102**.... BenRobinson(3) 9 81
(Ollie Pears) *midfield: lost pl over 4f out: wknd over 3f out* **66/1**

1-16 **8** *1 1/2* **Give It Some Teddy**[9] 2584 5-8-2 **83**.... DuranFentiman 8 59
(Tim Easterby) *midfield: hdwy 4f out: rdn to chse ldrs over 2f out: wknd over 1f out* **9/1**

0-64 **9** *142* **Knighted (IRE)**[22] 2105 4-8-9 **90**.... KevinStott 4
(Kevin Ryan) *chsd ldr tl stmbld on bnd under 5f out: lost pl qckly: eased whn bhd fnl 3f: t.o (jockey said gelding slipped on the bend turning into the home straight)* **5/1**[2]

-030 **R** **Gurkha Friend**[20] 2187 7-8-13 **94**.... JasonHart 5
(Karen McLintock) *ref to r: tk no part* **11/2**[3]

1m 52.42s (-2.28) **Going Correction** -0.075s/f (Good) **10** Ran SP% **118.5**
Speed ratings (Par 109): **107,104,103,102,100 100,94,92, ,**
CSF £148.17 CT £551.27 TOTE £16.90: £4.60, £2.90, £1.60; EX 150.30 Trifecta £974.60.
Owner Northern Lads & Nawton Racing **Bred** Miss Siobhan Ryan **Trained** Upper Helmsley, N Yorks

FOCUS
Race distance increased by 12yds. A competitive handicap and they went a good gallop.

2874 BRITISH EBF PREMIER FILLIES' H'CAP 6f

4:55 (4:55) (Class 3) (0-95,96) 3-Y-O+

£14,006 (£4,194; £2,097; £1,048; £524; £263) **Stalls** High

Form RPR

0-12 **1** **Gold Filigree (IRE)**[30] 1913 4-10-0 **95**.... ShaneKelly 1 102
(Richard Hughes) *racd keenly: chsd ldr: rdn over 2f out: led wl over 1f out: kpt on wl towards fin* **4/1**[3]

5-31 **2** *1/2* **Isaan Queen (IRE)**[17] 2319 3-9-6 **96**.... DanielTudhope 2 99
(Archie Watson) *chsd ldrs: rdn and ev ch over 1f out: continued to chal ins fnl f: hld nr fin* **9/2**

12-5 **3** *3/4* **Excellent Times**[22] 2097 4-9-5 **86**.... DavidAllan 4 89
(Tim Easterby) *chsd ldrs: rdn over 2f out: styd on ins fnl f: unable to trble front two* **7/2**[2]

114- **4** *3/4* **Dizzy G (IRE)**[303] 5181 4-8-13 **80**.... CliffordLee 3 80
(K R Burke) *led: rdn over 2f out: hdd wl over 1f out: sn sltly outpcd: styd on same pce ins fnl f* **11/2**

10-0 **5** *1 3/4* **Our Little Pony**[8] 2637 4-8-4 **76** oh4.... FayeMcManoman(5) 6 71
(Lawrence Mullaney) *hld up: effrt over 1f out: nvr able to chal: one pce fnl 100yds* **12/1**

23-1 **6** *1 1/4* **Kareena Kapoor (USA)**[127] 211 3-8-6 **82**.... DavidEgan 5 71
(Simon Crisford) *hld up: hdwy on outer over 1f out: sn cl up and rdn: fdd fnl 100yds* **2/1**[1]

1m 11.3s (-1.20) **Going Correction** -0.075s/f (Good)
WFA 3 from 4yo 9lb **6** Ran SP% **116.8**
Speed ratings (Par 104): **105,104,103,102,100 98**
CSF £23.02 TOTE £3.90: £1.80, £1.90; EX 19.00 Trifecta £53.10.
Owner Galloway,Lawrence,Merritt & Mrs Blake **Bred** Grangecon Holdings Ltd **Trained** Upper Lambourn, Berks

FOCUS
It was a case of quality rather than quantity for this fillies sprint handicap. Most held a chance a furlong out.

2875 CHRIS WESTERMAN HAPPY 60TH BIRTHDAY NOVICE STKS 1m 1f 170y

5:30 (5:36) (Class 5) 3-Y-O **£4,916** (£1,463; £731; £365) **Stalls** Low

Form RPR

63 **1** **Great Example**[17] 2321 3-9-2 0.... PatCosgrave 12 88+
(Saeed bin Suroor) *chsd ldr: led over 2f out: rdn clr over 1f out: r.o wl: eased towards fin* **11/4**[1]

61- **2** *8* **Millions Memories**[242] 7431 3-9-9 0.... DanielMuscutt 11 79
(David Lanigan) *led: rdn and hdd over 2f out: no ch w wnr fnl f* **11/2**[3]

45 **3** *4* **Itchingham Lofte (IRE)**[18] 2301 3-9-2 0.... RobbieDowney 6 63+
(David Barron) *hld up: hdwy over 3f out: chsd ldrs over 2f out: no imp* **33/1**

03 **4** *2 1/4* **Theatro (IRE)**[19] 2245 3-8-11 0.... GrahamLee 4 54
(Jedd O'Keeffe) *in tch: rdn 4f out: sn lost pl and outpcd: kpt on one pce fnl 2f and n.d* **28/1**

02 **5** *1 1/4* **Australis (IRE)**[12] 2505 3-9-2 0.... DavidEgan 8 56
(Roger Varian) *missed break: sn in midfield: effrt 3f out: nvr able to trble ldrs: rdn and outpcd over 2f out: sn hung rt: nvr a real threat (jockey said colt became unbalanced on the undulations)* **3/1**[2]

0- **6** *2* **Funny Man**[193] 8930 3-9-2 0....(p[1]) DanielTudhope 2 52
(William Haggas) *trckd ldrs: rdn over 3f out: wknd 2f out* **11/4**[1]

5 **7** *1 1/2* **Kenica (IRE)**[12] 2505 3-8-11 0.... CliffordLee 9 44
(K R Burke) *trckd ldrs: drvn over 3f out: wknd over 2f out* **16/1**

8 *16* **Nataleena (IRE)** 3-8-11 0.... AndrewMullen 7 11
(Ben Haslam) *s.i.s: a bhd: pushed along and outpcd over 4f out: nvr a threat* **66/1**

2m 4.52s (-0.08) **Going Correction** -0.075s/f (Good) **8** Ran SP% **107.5**
Speed ratings (Par 99): **98,91,88,86,85 84,82,70**
CSF £15.85 TOTE £3.00: £1.10, £2.10, £4.10; EX 14.50 Trifecta £180.10.
Owner Godolphin **Bred** Usk Valley Stud **Trained** Newmarket, Suffolk
■ International Guy and Can Can Nights were withdrawn. Prices at time of withdrawal 12/1 and 200/1. Rule 4 applies to all bets - deduction 5p in the £.

FOCUS
Race distance increased by 12yds. An average novice, but an impressive winner.

2876 LADIES DAY 20TH JUNE APPRENTICE H'CAP 5f

6:00 (6:01) (Class 5) (0-70,72) 4-Y-O+

£4,204 (£1,251; £625; £400; £400; £400) **Stalls** High

Form RPR

4446 **1** **Musharrif**[12] 2508 7-9-7 **71**.... ZakWheatley(7) 12 83
(Declan Carroll) *mde all: rdn and edgd rt over 1f out: r.o wl to draw clr fnl 100yds* **9/1**

2042 **2** *3 1/4* **Qaaraat**[5] 2709 4-9-5 **67**.... KieranSchofield(5) 3 67
(Antony Brittain) *chsd ldrs: rdn and ev ch over 1f out: unable qck ins fnl f: styd on same pce and no ch w wnr fnl 100yds* **7/4**[1]

2121 **3** *shd* **Ticks The Boxes (IRE)**[17] 2349 7-8-13 **56**.... BenRobinson 11 56
(Brian Ellison) *rdn 1/2-way: hdwy over 1f out: r.o and gng on towards fin: nt trble wnr* **4/1**[2]

0360 **4** 1 **Dapper Man (IRE)**[16] 2368 5-9-12 72......................(b) BenSanderson(3) 1 68
(Roger Fell) *chsd ldrs: rdn and ev ch over 1f out: unable qck ins fnl f: kpt on same pce* **11/2**[3]

0-00 **5** 3/4 **B Fifty Two (IRE)**[18] 2294 10-9-4 64......................(vt) HarrisonShaw(3) 9 58
(Marjorie Fife) *in tch: rdn 1/2-way: kpt on u.p ins fnl f: nt pce to trble ldrs: no imp* **33/1**

213- **6** 3/4 **Pavers Pride**[200] 8742 5-9-10 67......................(b) PhilDennis 4 58
(Noel Wilson) *hld up: hdwy 1/2-way: rdn whn chsd ldrs over 1f out: one pce ins fnl f* **20/1**

1-03 **7** 1 3/4 **Astrophysics**[122] 277 7-9-2 59...................... ConorMcGovern 2 44
(Lynn Siddall) *in tch: rdn and outpcd over 1f out: no imp after* **25/1**

1651 **8** shd **Red Stripes (USA)**[11] 2527 7-8-10 56......................(b) DylanHogan(3) 5 40
(Lisa Williamson) *hld up: hdwy 1/2-way: sn rdn: nvr able to trble ldrs: no imp fnl f* **12/1**

0000 **9** 3/4 **Celerity (IRE)**[86] 848 5-8-3 53 oh8......................(p) ElishaWhittington(7) 10 35
(Lisa Williamson) *chsd wnr tl rdn 2f out: wknd ins fnl f* **100/1**

00-0 **10** 3/4 **Haveoneyerself (IRE)**[58] 1266 4-9-0 60...................... DarraghKeenan(3) 8 39
(John Butler) *chsd ldrs: rdn 2f out: wknd over 1f out* **50/1**

0001 **11** 2 1/4 **Indian Pursuit (IRE)**[8] 2632 6-9-6 66......................(v) SeanDavis(3) 6 37
(John Quinn) *midfield: pushed along 1/2-way: lost pl over 1f out: eased whn btn fnl 100yds (trainer's rep could offer no explanation for the run)* **12/1**

-540 **12** 1 **Afandem (IRE)**[5] 2709 5-9-4 66......................(p) RobertDodsworth(5) 7 33
(Tim Easterby) *in rr: rdn and outpcd whn edgd rt 1/2-way: nvr a threat (jockey said gelding was never travelling)* **10/1**

58.85s (-0.55) **Going Correction** -0.075s/f (Good) **12** Ran SP% **120.7**
Speed ratings (Par 103): **101,95,95,94,92 91,88,88,87,86 82,81**
CSF £24.51 CT £78.52 TOTE £11.30: £3.10, £1.10, £1.90; EX 32.10 Trifecta £157.90.
Owner Ray Flegg & John Bousfield **Bred** Mr & Mrs J Davis & P Mitchell B'Stock **Trained** Malton, N Yorks

FOCUS
This sprint was won by the highest drawn runner, who raced nearest to the stands' rail and came clear.
T/Jkpt: Not Won. T/Plt: £99.80 to a £1 stake. Pool: £99,655.88 - 728.62 winning units. T/Qpdt: £8.30 to a £1 stake. Pool: £11,152.58 - 985.83 winning units. **Darren Owen**

2877 - 2878a (Foreign Racing) - See Raceform Interactive

2639
NAAS (L-H)
Sunday, May 19

OFFICIAL GOING: Good to firm (watered)

2879a OWENSTOWN STUD STKS (LISTED RACE) 7f
2:40 (2:40) 3-Y-O+

£25,247 (£8,130; £3,851; £1,711; £855; £427)

RPR

1 **Surrounding (IRE)**[46] 1531 6-9-9 97......................(t) RonanWhelan 3 103+
(M Halford, Ire) *chsd ldrs: stmbld sltly after 1f: 4th 1/2-way: hdwy gng wl over 2f out: disp ld briefly under 2f out: rdn over 1f out and sn hdd briefly tl regained narrow advantage wl ins fnl f: kpt on wl* **5/1**[3]

2 nk **Chessman (IRE)**[50] 1434 5-9-11 101...................... OisinOrr 2 104
(Richard John O'Brien, Ire) *hld up in 6th: swtchd lft in 5th under 2f out and gd hdwy to chal on terms over 1f out where rdn: sn led narrowly briefly tl hdd wl ins fnl f: kpt on wl wout matching wnr* **7/2**[2]

3 3 **King's Field (IRE)**[129] 173 4-9-11 104...................... DonnachaO'Brien 1 96
(Joseph Patrick O'Brien, Ire) *w.w in rr: rdn 2f out: hdwy 1/2-way and u.p 2f out: prog over 1f out and impr into 3rd ins fnl f where no imp on ldrs: kpt on same pce* **3/1**[1]

4 nk **Texas Rock (IRE)**[13] 2497 8-9-11 94......................(p) RobbieColgan 5 95
(M C Grassick, Ire) *trckd ldr: cl 2nd at 1/2-way: rdn 2f out and disp ld briefly tl sn hdd: no ex in 3rd ent fnl f: one pce after and dropped to 4th ins fnl f* **20/1**

5 1 1/2 **Wisdom Mind (IRE)**[14] 2449 4-9-6 85......................(t) GaryHalpin 7 86
(Joseph Patrick O'Brien, Ire) *w.w towards rr: 8th 1/2-way: drvn over 2f out and no imp u.p in rr 1 1/2f out: kpt on into nvr threatening 5th wl ins fnl f* **25/1**

6 1/2 **Annie Fior (IRE)**[14] 2449 5-9-6 87...................... ColinKeane 8 85
(B A Murphy, Ire) *broke wl to ld: narrow advantage at 1/2-way: rdn over 2f out and sn hdd: wknd over 1f out* **20/1**

7 1/2 **Rionach**[13] 2493 4-9-6 101...................... LeighRoche 4 83
(M D O'Callaghan, Ire) *chsd ldrs: 3rd 1/2-way: effrt nr side 2f out: rdn almost on terms 1 1/2f out and sn wknd* **3/1**[1]

8 3 **Settle For Bay (FR)**[122] 285 5-9-11 106...................... WJLee 6 80
(David Marnane, Ire) *w.w in 5th and racd keenly early: pushed along 2f out and no imp on ldrs 1f out where dropped to rr: eased cl home (jockey said gelding travelled well but found nothing in the closing stages)* **7/1**

1m 28.02s (0.52) **8** Ran SP% **114.8**
CSF £22.21 TOTE £6.00: £2.20, £1.40, £1.30; DF 19.10 Trifecta £68.20.
Owner P E I Newell **Bred** P E I Newell **Trained** Doneany, Co Kildare

FOCUS
Another good display from the thoroughly likeable \bSurrounding\p, who is proving to be the gift that keeps on giving.

2880a SOLE POWER SPRINT STKS (LISTED RACE) 5f
3:15 (3:15) 3-Y-O+

£26,576 (£8,558; £4,054; £1,801; £900; £450)

RPR

1 **Soffia**[20] 2221 4-9-4 96...................... DeclanMcDonogh 4 107+
(Edward Lynam, Ire) *chsd ldrs: 3rd 1/2-way: gng wl bhd ldrs after 1/2-way and impr to chal over 1f out: rdn to ld jst ins fnl f and kpt on wl to assert clsng stages* **3/1**[1]

2 1 1/2 **Final Venture**[29] 1946 7-9-9 106...................... LeighRoche 2 106
(Paul Midgley) *dismntd bef s: sn led: narrow advantage at 1/2-way: drvn far side under 2f out and hdd u.p jst ins fnl f: no imp on wnr clsng stages* **3/1**[1]

3 1 3/4 **Julia's Magic (IRE)**[40] 1668 4-9-4 92...................... GaryCarroll 1 95+
(Mrs Denise Foster, Ire) *prom tl sn settled bhd ldrs: pushed along far side disputing 4th fr 1/2-way: u.p in 4th ent fnl f: kpt on into nvr threatening 3rd nr fin* **20/1**

4 1/2 **Fantasy (IRE)**[9] 2605 3-8-10 86...................... WayneLordan 5 90
(A P O'Brien, Ire) *trckd ldr: cl 2nd at 1/2-way: sn drvn and dropped to 3rd u.p over 1f out: no imp on ldrs ins fnl f and dropped to 4th nr fin* **25/1**

5 1 1/2 **Rapid Reaction (IRE)**[217] 8239 4-9-4 81...................... AndrewSlattery 3 88
(J F Grogan, Ire) *dwlt sltly: mid-div early: tk clsr order and disp 4th at 1/2-way: rdn over 1f out and no imp on ldrs disputing 5th ins fnl f: kpt on one pce* **50/1**

6 nse **Gossamer Wings (USA)**[9] 2605 3-8-11 105 ow1...................... RyanMoore 8 85
(A P O'Brien, Ire) *dwlt sltly: settled in rr: tk clsr order fr bef 1/2-way: rdn in 6th 1 1/2f out and no imp on ldrs u.p disputing 5th ins fnl f: kpt on one pce* **3/1**[1]

7 2 1/4 **Beckford**[386] 4-9-9 110...................... ColinKeane 9 85
(Gordon Elliott, Ire) *w.w towards rr nr side early: pushed along in 7th and no imp over 1f out: one pce after: nt hrd-rdn* **5/1**[2]

8 1/2 **All The King's Men (IRE)**[50] 1434 3-9-4 97...................... SeamieHeffernan 6 83
(A P O'Brien, Ire) *wnt down to s early: hld up in 5th early: pushed along bef 1/2-way where dropped towards rr and no imp after: rdn briefly in 8th over 1f out and kpt on one pce* **14/1**[3]

9 9 **Show Must Go On (FR)**[352] 3338 3-9-1 96......................(p[1]) WJLee 7 47
(Aidan F Fogarty, Ire) *hld up: dropped to rr bef 1/2-way and sn lost tch: wknd: eased ins fnl f* **16/1**

58.17s (-3.83) **9** Ran SP% **114.8**
WFA 3 from 4yo+ 8lb
CSF £11.46 TOTE £3.10: £1.30, £1.40, £5.50; DF 9.60 Trifecta £105.80.
Owner Lady O'Reilly **Bred** Newsells Park Stud **Trained** Dunshaughlin, Co Meath
■ Stewards' Enquiry : Ryan Moore caution: weighed in 1.1lbs over

FOCUS
Not the strongest of Listed sprints but the winner seems to be improving. She'll go down as a fitting winner representing Eddie Lynam, trainer of Sole Power, for whom the race was named after.

2881a COOLMORE STUD IRISH EBF FILLIES' SPRINT STKS (GROUP 3) 6f
3:50 (3:52) 2-Y-O

£42,522 (£13,693; £6,486; £2,882; £1,441; £720)

RPR

1 **Etoile (USA)** 2-9-0 0...................... SeamieHeffernan 3 100+
(A P O'Brien, Ire) *chsd ldrs: 5th 1/2-way: hdwy 1 1/2f out: rdn in 2nd ent fnl f and r.o wl to ld ins fnl 100yds* **12/1**

2 1/2 **Peace Charter**[20] 2218 2-9-0 0...................... ColinKeane 8 99
(G M Lyons, Ire) *chsd ldrs: 4th 1/2-way: rdn nr side 1 1/2f out and r.o between horses wl ins fnl f into 2nd: a hld by wnr* **2/1**[2]

3 1/2 **Celtic Beauty (IRE)**[20] 2218 2-9-1 0 ow1...................... WJLee 5 98
(K J Condon, Ire) *dwlt: hld up in rr: last at 1/2-way: hdwy nr side after 1/2-way: rdn into 3rd ins fnl f where edgd sltly lft briefly: kpt on wl nr fin: nt trble wnr* **25/1**

4 1 1/2 **American Lady (IRE)**[13] 2491 2-9-0 0...................... LeighRoche 1 93
(J A Stack, Ire) *wnt rt s and bmpd rival: led narrowly tl jnd after 1f and sn hdd: disp cl 2nd at 1/2-way: regained ld after 1/2-way: rdn and extended advantage over 1f out: hdd far side ins fnl 100yds and wknd cl home* **25/1**

5 3/4 **So Wonderful (USA)**[20] 2218 2-9-0 0...................... RyanMoore 7 90
(A P O'Brien, Ire) *w.w: pushed along and swtchd rt in rr under 2f out: rdn briefly into 7th ins fnl f and kpt on under hands and heels into nvr threatening 5th nr fin* **5/6**[1]

6 3/4 **In The Present (USA)**[13] 2491 2-9-0 0...................... ShaneFoley 2 88
(Mrs John Harrington, Ire) *bmpd s: cl up tl disp ld after 1f and sn led narrowly: hdd narrowly after 1/2-way: drvn in 2nd under 2f out and no ex u.p in 3rd ent fnl f: sn wknd* **9/1**[3]

7 1 1/4 **Yesterdayoncemore (IRE)**[32] 1864 2-9-0 0...................... WayneLordan 4 85
(J A Stack, Ire) *on toes befhand and rrd at times bef s: towards rr: pushed along and sme hdwy over 1f out where swtchd lft: rdn in 6th ins fnl f where n.m.r briefly and wknd nr fin where eased* **25/1**

8 7 **Feminista (IRE)**[21] 2154 2-9-0 0...................... KevinManning 6 63
(J S Bolger, Ire) *chsd ldrs early: tk clsr order and disp 2nd after 2f: drvn bhd ldrs over 2f out and sn wknd: dropped to rr over 1f out: eased ins fnl f* **16/1**

1m 12.0s (-1.20) **8** Ran SP% **123.0**
CSF £38.61 TOTE £13.60: £2.70, £1.02, £6.20; DF 57.60 Trifecta £617.60.
Owner Mrs John Magnier & Michael Tabor & Derrick Smith **Bred** Orpendale, Chelston & Wynatt **Trained** Cashel, Co Tipperary

FOCUS
It's been well documented that the Ballydoyle juveniles are plenty forward in comparison to normal years but even so, for a newcomer to account for a field of fillies with experience like this, it has to go down as a classy performance. She was introduced at 5-1 for the Albany on the strength of this.

2882a GOFFS LACKEN STKS (GROUP 3) 6f
4:25 (4:25) 3-Y-O

£34,549 (£11,126; £5,270; £2,342; £1,171; £585)

RPR

1 **So Perfect (USA)**[36] 1751 3-9-0 110...................... RyanMoore 6 107+
(A P O'Brien, Ire) *chsd ldrs: swtchd rt under 2f out and bmpd rival: pushed along and prog into 3rd over 1f out: rdn to ld ins fnl f and kpt on wl to assert nr fin* **9/10**[1]

2 2 1/4 **Gustavus Weston (IRE)**[21] 2156 3-9-3 92...................... GaryCarroll 9 103
(Joseph G Murphy, Ire) *hld up bhd ldrs in 6th early: gng wl at 1/2-way: tk clsr order and bmpd under 2f out: sn rdn in 5th and clsd u.p into 2nd ins fnl f where no imp on wnr: kpt on wl* **50/1**

3 1 3/4 **Flash Gordon (IRE)**[13] 2492 3-9-3 0...................... ShaneFoley 7 97+
(Mrs John Harrington, Ire) *dwlt: towards rr: pushed along after 1/2-way: rdn into 7th over 1f out and r.o wl into nvr threatening 3rd cl home* **12/1**

4 1/2 **Western Frontier (USA)**[29] 1962 3-9-3 96...................... SeamieHeffernan 2 95
(A P O'Brien, Ire) *bmpd s: sn trckd ldr in cl 2nd: rdn on terms 1 1/2f out and sn led tl hdd u.p ins fnl f: wknd far side nr fin* **12/1**

5 1 **Gee Rex (IRE)**[211] 8428 3-9-3 86...................... WJLee 1 92
(J C Hayden, Ire) *wnt rt s and bmpd rival: sn settled in mid-div: pushed along after 1/2-way: rdn 2f out and no imp on ldrs in 6th ent fnl f: dropped to 7th ins fnl f tl kpt on again nr fin* **50/1**

6 1/2 **Mia Mento (IRE)**[7] 2661 3-9-0 91...................... RonanWhelan 8 88
(Thomas Mullins, Ire) *chsd ldrs: drvn in 3rd 2f out and no imp on ldrs over 1f out where dropped to 5th: one pce u.p ins fnl f* **50/1**

7 1/2 **Empire Line (IRE)**[8] 2644 3-9-3 96......................(p) LeighRoche 3 89
(J A Stack, Ire) *bmpd sltly s and sn led narrowly: rdn on terms 1 1/2f out and sn hdd: wknd u.p ins fnl f* **6/1**[3]

8 1 3/4 **Inverleigh (IRE)**[21] 2156 3-9-3 104...................... ColinKeane 5 83
(G M Lyons, Ire) *hld up in rr: pushed along after 1/2-way and no imp over 1f out where rdn briefly: one pce under hands and heels into fnl f: eased* **5/1**[2]

9 ½ **The Irish Rover (IRE)**[21] 2156 3-9-3 103 DonnachaO'Brien 4 82
(A P O'Brien, Ire) *hld up in 8th early: drvn far side 2f out and no imp over 1f out where hmpd: rdn briefly in 8th ins fnl f and no ex: eased nr fin* **7/1**

10 hd **On A Session (USA)**[330] 4103 3-9-3 90 WayneLordan 10 81
(Aidan F Fogarty, Ire) *chsd ldrs: pushed along nr side over 2f out and sn sltly impeded: no ex towards rr 1 1/2f out: one pce after: eased nr fin* **50/1**

1m 10.46s (-2.74) **10** Ran SP% **119.3**
CSF £73.52 TOTE £1.60: £1.02, £15.60, £2.70; DF 58.50 Trifecta £706.00.
Owner Derrick Smith & Mrs John Magnier & Michael Tabor **Bred** Machmer Hall **Trained** Cashel, Co Tipperary

FOCUS
This race has proved a good pointer towards Royal Ascot in the past and \bSo Perfect\p will go there with a live chance.

2883 - 2884a (Foreign Racing) - See Raceform Interactive

2161 CAPANNELLE (R-H)
Sunday, May 19

OFFICIAL GOING: Turf: heavy

2885a PREMIO CARLO D'ALESSIO (GROUP 3) (4YO+) (GRANDE COURSE) (TURF) 1m 4f
12:55 4-Y-0+ **£29,279** (£12,882; £7,027; £3,513)

RPR

1 **Assiro**[27] 2001 4-8-9 0 (bt) AndreaMezzatesta 5 104
(R Biondi, Italy) *hld up in tch: hdwy on outside 3f out: led 1f out: sn hrd pressed: kpt on wl towards fin* **13/2**

2 hd **Azzurro Cobalto (ITY)**[27] 2001 4-8-9 0 FabioBranca 2 103
(Nicolo Simondi, Italy) *hld up in tch: rdn and hdwy on outside over 2f out: pressed wnr ins fnl f: kpt on: hld nr fin* **89/20**

3 2 ½ **O'Juke (FR)**[42] 4-8-11 0 (b) SergioUrru 3 101
(Nicolo Simondi, Italy) *chsd ldr: rdn over 3f out: lost 2nd 2f out: sn edgd lft: kpt on same pce ins fnl f* **5/4**[1]

4 ½ **Presley (ITY)**[27] 2001 6-8-9 0 DarioVargiu 4 98
(A Botti, Italy) *t.k.h: led at modest gallop: qcknd against ins rail over 3f out: rdn and hdd 1f out: sn no ex* **23/10**[2]

5 dist **Henry Mouth (IRE)**[344] 4-8-9 0 (b) CristianDemuro 1
(A Botti, Italy) *s.i.s: sn chsng ldrs: drvn and outpcd 3f out: lost tch and eased over 1f out* **16/5**[3]

2m 33.5s (6.30) **5** Ran SP% **130.2**
PARI-MUTUEL (all including 1 euro stake): WIN 7.47 PLACE 4.58, 3.87 DF 42.33.
Owner Luigi Roveda **Bred** Gestut Zur Kuste Ag **Trained** Italy

2886a PREMIO PRESIDENTE DELLA REPUBBLICA (GROUP 2) (4YO+) (GRANDE COURSE) (TURF) 1m 1f
3:25 4-Y-0+ **£82,882** (£36,468; £19,891; £9,945)

RPR

1 **Stormy Antarctic**[35] 1793 6-9-2 0 FrankieDettori 3 116+
(Ed Walker) *mde all at modest gallop: shkn up and qcknd clr wl over 2f out: v easily* **4/9**[1]

2 4 **Anda Muchacho (IRE)**[196] 8865 5-9-2 0 FabioBranca 2 106
(Nicolo Simondi, Italy) *t.k.h: chsd ldrs: effrt and chsd (clr) wnr over 1f out: no imp fnl f* **242/100**[2]

3 1 **Wait Forever (IRE)**[56] 4-9-2 0 DarioVargiu 4 104
(A Botti, Italy) *chsd wnr: rdn along over 2f out: lost 2nd over 1f out: sn no ex* **103/20**[3]

4 4 **Dirk (IRE)**[27] 2001 5-9-2 0 CristianDemuro 1 101
(A Botti, Italy) *s.v.s: last and detached: hdwy and in tch bef 1/2-way: effrt and drvn over 2f out: sn no imp: btn fnl f* **11/2**

1m 53.2s (-1.50) **4** Ran SP% **130.1**
PARI-MUTUEL (all including 1 euro stake): WIN 1.44 PLACE 1.13, 1.33 DF 2.70.
Owner P K Siu **Bred** East Bloodstock Ltd **Trained** Upper Lambourn, Berks

2887a 136TH DERBY ITALIANO (GROUP 2) (3YO COLTS & FILLIES) (GRANDE COURSE) (TURF) 1m 3f
4:40 3-Y-0 **£288,288** (£126,846; £69,189; £34,594)

RPR

1 **Keep On Fly (IRE)** 3-9-2 0 (b) CristianDemuro 11 107+
(A Botti, Italy) *s.i.s: hld up: drvn along over 3f out: sn outpcd: hdwy over 1f out: sustained run fnl f to ld cl home* **25/4**

2 snk **Mission Boy**[21] 2162 3-9-2 0 CarloFiocchi 8 107
(A Botti, Italy) *hld up in midfield: smooth hdwy to ld over 2f out: rdn fnl f: kpt on: hdd cl home* **77/20**[2]

3 2 ¼ **Call Me Love**[210] 3-8-13 0 DarioVargiu 9 100
(A Botti, Italy) *hld up in tch: hdwy and cl up over 2f out: sn rdn along: pressed ldr over 1f out to ins fnl f: one pce towards fin* **6/4**[1]

4 1 ¾ **Frozen Juke (IRE)**[21] 3-9-2 0 FrankieDettori 2 100
(Fabio Marchi, Italy) *hld up in tch: stdy hdwy over 3f out: effrt and rdn over 2f out: kpt on same pce ins fnl f* **5/1**

5 1 **Agente Segreto (IRE)**[27] 3-9-2 0 FabioBranca 3 98
(Nicolo Simondi, Italy) *prom: rdn along over 3f out: no ex fr over 1f out* **4/1**[3]

6 hd **Trita Sass (IRE)** 3-9-2 0 SalvatoreSulas 12 98
(A Botti, Italy) *chsd ldr: led over 4f out to over 2f out: drvn and outpcd fr over 1f out* **96/10**

7 3 ½ **Jighen (IRE)**[21] 3-9-2 0 (b) AndreaAtzeni 1 91
(A Botti, Italy) *chsd ldrs: drvn and outpcd over 3f out: n.d after* **6/4**[1]

8 snk **Passion Return (IRE)** 3-9-2 0 (t) PasqualeEmmanuele 10 91
(Gianluca Verricelli, Italy) *s.v.s: bhd: drvn over 4f out: sme hdwy over 1f out: nvr rchd ldrs* **197/10**

9 1 ½ **Garden Of Eden (ITY)** 3-9-2 0 GermanoMarcelli 7 88
(F Saggiomo, Italy) *hld up: drvn along and outpcd over 3f out: sn btn* **89/10**

10 6 **Zoman (ITY)**[21] 2162 3-9-2 0 (t) SilvanoMulas 4 78
(Grizzetti Galoppo SRL, Italy) *t.k.h: hld up on ins: drvn and outpcd 3f out: btn fnl 2f* **46/1**

11 1 ¼ **Atom Hearth Mother (IRE)**[196] 8864 3-9-2 0 (b) MickaelBarzalona 6 75
(A Botti, Italy) *hld up: drvn along over 3f out: sn struggling: nvr on terms* **89/10**

12 dist **Irish Girl** 3-8-13 0 DPerovic 5
(Georgi Zhekov, Bulgaria) *t.k.h: led to over 4f out: wknd over 3f out: eased whn no ch fnl 2f* **26/1**

2m 22.5s **12** Ran SP% **191.4**
PARI-MUTUEL (all including 1 euro stake): WIN 7.25 PLACE 1.94, 1.93, 1.45 DF 46.12.
Owner Dioscuri Srl **Bred** Dioscuri Srl **Trained** Italy

FOCUS
A 1-2-3 for trainer Alduino Botti.

2888a PREMIO TUDINI (GROUP 3) (3YO+) (DRITTA COURSE) (TURF) 6f
5:20 3-Y-0+ **£29,279** (£12,882; £7,027; £3,513)

RPR

1 **Buonasera (IRE)**[27] 4-8-10 0 (t) MarioSanna 11 100
(P L Giannotti, Italy) *cl up: led over 1f out: rdn and r.o wl fnl f* **269/10**

2 ¾ **Charline Royale (IRE)**[196] 8868 4-8-13 0 SalvatoreBasile 5 101
(Silvia Amendola, Italy) *led against stands' rail: rdn over 1f out: edgd rt and hdd ins fnl f: kpt on same pce nr fin* **29/20**[1]

3 nse **Foot Of King (IRE)**[21] 2162 3-8-5 0 (t) AndreaAtzeni 9 100
(Endo Botti, Italy) *hld up in tch: effrt and angled lft over 2f out: rdn and r.o ins fnl f: nrst fin* **758/100**

4 hd **Trust You**[196] 8868 7-9-0 0 (p) CarloFiocchi 8 101
(Endo Botti, Italy) *hld up: effrt and hdwy over 2f out: rdn and r.o ins fnl f* **162/10**

5 1 ¼ **The Conqueror (IRE)**[196] 8868 4-9-0 0 DarioVargiu 2 97
(A Botti, Italy) *trckd ldrs: rdn along 2f out: edgd rt and one pce ins fnl f* **91/20**[3]

6 ½ **Bloody Love (IRE)** 3-8-5 0 (t) AntonioFresu 4 93
(Endo Botti, Italy) *hld up bhd ldng gp: rdn and effrt wl over 1f out: no imp ins fnl f* **231/10**

7 ¾ **Zapel**[190] 9009 6-9-0 0 CristianDemuro 1 93
(A Botti, Italy) *hld up: rdn along 1/2-way: hdwy fnl f: kpt on: nt pce to chal* **41/10**[2]

8 2 ½ **Pensierieparole**[27] 7-9-0 0 (t) SilvanoMulas 7 85
(Grizzetti Galoppo SRL, Italy) *hld up in midfield: drvn and outpcd over 2f out: n.d after* **41/5**

9 1 ¾ **Noriac (ITY)** 6-9-0 0 (t) MickaelBarzalona 13 79
(Roberto Di Paolo, Italy) *in tch: hdwy on outside and cl up over 2f out: sn rdn and hung rt: wknd fnl f* **101/10**

10 1 ¼ **Zan O'Bowney (ITY)**[27] 7-9-0 0 FabioBranca 15 75
(Nicolo Simondi, Italy) *prom on outside: rdn over 2f out: hung rt over 1f out: wknd and eased ins fnl f* **127/10**

11 1 **Robranov (ITY)**[364] 2896 6-9-0 0 (bt) GianpasqualeFois 12 72
(Roberto Di Paolo, Italy) *s.i.s: bhd and outpcd: sme hdwy over 1f out: nvr rchd ldrs* **101/10**

12 hd **Gold Tail (IRE)**[309] 4977 4-9-0 0 (tp) FrankieDettori 6 72
(Paola Maria Gaetano, Italy) *cl up: rdn over 2f out: edgd rt and wknd over 1f out* **221/10**

13 shd **Macho Wind (IRE)**[232] 3-8-5 0 (t) DPerovic 3 69
(M M Peraino, Italy) *bhd: struggling 1/2-way: nvr on terms* **41/1**

14 7 **Harlem Shake (IRE)**[196] 8868 8-9-0 0 DarioDiTocco 10 49
(Marco Gasparini, Italy) *bhd and sn struggling: no ch fr 1/2-way* **269/10**

15 6 **Robiano (IRE)**[196] 8866 6-9-0 0 (t) SalvatoreSulas 14 30
(Ottavio Di Paolo, Italy) *bhd: struggling 1/2-way: btn fnl 2f* **101/10**

1m 10.7s (0.40)
WFA 3 from 4yo+ 9lb **15** Ran SP% **159.1**
PARI-MUTUEL (all including 1 euro stake): WIN 27.53 PLACE 6.04, 1.61, 2.70 DF 135.09.
Owner Scuderia Cavalli Da Corsa Giannotti **Bred** Scuderia Cavalli Da Corsa Giannotti Pier **Trained** Italy

2455 COLOGNE (R-H)
Sunday, May 19

OFFICIAL GOING: Turf: good

2889a MEHL-MULHENS-RENNEN - GERMAN 2000 GUINEAS (GROUP 2) (3YO COLTS & FILLIES) (TURF) 1m
3:40 3-Y-0 **£90,090** (£27,027; £11,711; £6,306; £2,702)

RPR

1 **Fox Champion (IRE)**[31] 1888 3-9-2 0 OisinMurphy 3 110+
(Richard Hannon) *mde all: rdn over 2f out: edgd lft and hrd pressed ins fnl f: kpt on gamely towards fin* **22/5**[2]

2 nk **Arctic Sound**[33] 1830 3-9-2 0 JoeFanning 7 109+
(Mark Johnston) *prom: rdn over 2f out: chsd wnr over 1f out: kpt on u.p fnl f: hld nr fin* **9/1**

3 nk **Great Scot**[15] 2411 3-9-2 0 RichardKingscote 8 108+
(Tom Dascombe) *hld up in midfield: drvn and outpcd over 2f out: rallied fnl f: kpt on wl cl home* **17/10**[1]

4 2 ¼ **Marie's Diamond (IRE)**[30] 1926 3-9-2 0 PJMcDonald 10 103
(Mark Johnston) *chsd wnr to over 1f out: drvn and one pce ins fnl f* **171/10**

5 nk **Golden Spectrum**[32] 1854 3-9-2 0 (p) GeraldMosse 9 102
(Gay Kelleway) *dwlt: t.k.h in rr: rdn over 2f out: rallied over 1f out: kpt on ins fnl f: nt pce to chal* **235/10**

6 nk **Wargrave (IRE)**[43] 1600 3-9-2 0 JamieSpencer 2 102
(J A Stack, Ire) *prom: effrt and drvn along 2f out: no ex ins fnl f* **174/10**

7 1 ¾ **Pogo (IRE)**[15] 2414 3-9-2 0 FranckBlondel 11 98
(Charles Hills) *hld up: rdn over 2f out: no imp fr over 1f out* **33/1**

8 ½ **Sibelius (GER)**[21] 2163 3-9-2 0 AdriedeVries 4 97
(Markus Klug, Germany) *hld up: shortlived effrt 2f out: outpcd fnl f* **195/10**

9 nse **Revelstoke**[13] 3-9-2 0 (p) BauyrzhanMurzabayev 1 96
(A Wohler, Germany) *hld up: drvn and outpcd over 2f out: sme late hdwy: nvr on terms* **73/10**

10 ½ **Noble Moon (GER)**[21] 2163 3-9-2 0 AndraschStarke 5 95
(P Schiergen, Germany) *midfield: stdy hdwy over 2f out: rdn over 1f out: wknd fnl f* **6/1**[3]

11 10 **Lady Te (GER)**[42] 1626 3-8-13 0 AlexisBadel 6 69
(Carina Fey, France) *hld up on outside: drvn and struggling over 2f out: btn and eased over 1f out* **213/10**

1m 37.87s (-0.52) **11** Ran SP% **119.2**
PARI-MUTUEL (all including 1 euro stake): WIN 5.40 PLACE 2.30, 3.20, 1.50 SF 16.60.
Owner King Power Racing Co Ltd **Bred** Con Marnane **Trained** East Everleigh, Wilts

FOCUS
A triumph for British stables.

SAINT-MALO (L-H)
Sunday, May 19

OFFICIAL GOING: Turf: good to soft

2890a PRIX DE SAINT-YDEUC (MAIDEN) (2YO) (TURF) 5f 110y
1:30 2-Y-O £6,756 (£2,702; £2,027; £1,351; £675)

RPR
1 **Agilmente (FR)** 2-8-13 0......................................(p) MathieuAndrouin 6 70
(L Gadbin, France) 148/10[1]
2 *hd* **Musetta**[12] 2-8-7 0.. ThomasTrullier(6) 2 69
(H-F Devin, France)
3 *1 1/2* **Belle Impression (FR)** 2-8-3 0........................ QuentinPerrette(5) 5 59
(Mlle L Kneip, France)
4 *1* **Fact Or Fable (IRE)**[18] 2315 2-9-2 0...............................(p) TheoBachelot 7 64
(J S Moore) *led early: hdd after 3f: trckd ldr: pushed along 2f out: rdn ent fnl f: unable qck and kpt on same pce clsng stages*
5 *1 3/4* **Danzig Issue (FR)**[12] 2-9-2 0.................................(p) AdrienFouassier 3 58
(Matthieu Palussiere, France)
6 *8* **Cassata** 2-8-5 0.. MlleMickaelleMichel(3) 1 24
(R Rohne, Germany)
D *15* **Swapan (FR)** 2-8-3 0...................................... MllePerrineCheyer(8) 4 27
(Mlle L Kneip, France)
1m 3.5s 7 Ran SP% 6.3

Owner Bernd Raber **Bred** E Dibatista & Mlle C Dibatista **Trained** France

2891 - (Foreign Racing) - See Raceform Interactive

CARLISLE (R-H)
Monday, May 20

OFFICIAL GOING: Good to firm (watered; 8.0)
Wind: Breezy, half against in over 2f of home straight Weather: Cloudy, bright

2892 BRITISH STALLION STUDS EBF NOVICE STKS (PLUS 10 RACE) 5f
2:10 (2:11) (Class 4) 2-Y-O £6,469 (£1,925; £962; £481) Stalls Low

Form RPR
1 **Rayong** 2-9-5 0.. BenCurtis 10 78+
(K R Burke) *prom on outside: rdn along 2f out: hdwy to ld ins fnl f: kpt on wl* 7/2[2]
5 2 *3/4* **Dragon Command**[23] 2093 2-9-5 0............................ ConnorBeasley 3 76+
(George Scott) *led: rdn along over 1f out: hdd ins fnl f: kpt on: hld towards fin* 11/4[1]
3 *nse* **Leapers Wood** 2-9-5 0.. PaulMulrennan 6 74+
(Michael Dods) *s.s: hld up: hdwy and edgd lft over 1f out: kpt on wl fnl f: improve* 11/1
4 *3/4* **Spartan Fighter** 2-9-5 0.. DanielTudhope 2 71+
(Declan Carroll) *prom: pushed along and hdwy whn checked appr fnl f: rdn and hung lft last 150yds: kpt on: nrst fin (jockey said colt hung left throughout)* 11/4[1]
5 *1 1/4* **Silver Mission (IRE)** 2-9-5 0.. JackGarritty 4 67
(Richard Fahey) *t.k.h: pressed ldr to over 1f out: drvn and no ex ins fnl f* 9/1[3]
6 *3* **Star Of St James (GER)** 2-9-0 0................................ SeanDavis(5) 8 56
(Richard Fahey) *cl up on outside: drvn along 2f out: wknd fnl f* 16/1
0 7 *1/2* **Ice Skate**[23] 2115 2-9-0 0.. RachelRichardson 7 49
(Tim Easterby) *hld up on outside: rdn and hung lft wl over 1f out: sn outpcd: n.d after* 40/1
8 *1* **Pearl Stream** 2-9-0 0.. LewisEdmunds 1 45
(Michael Dods) *hld up on ins: pushed along and outpcd 2f out: n.d after: lost hind shoe (vet said filly lost right hind shoe)* 40/1
9 *4 1/2* **Breguet Man (IRE)** 2-9-5 0.. JoeFanning 5 34
(Keith Dalgleish) *plld hrd: hld up: checked over 3f out: rdn and wknd fr 2f out* 12/1
10 *5* **Stormy Bay** 2-9-5 0.. ShaneGray 9 16
(Keith Dalgleish) *t.k.h: hld up: rdn and struggling over 2f out: sn btn* 28/1
U6 U **Tonquin Valley**[19] 2288 2-8-12 0.................................(h[1]) KieranSchofield(7) 11
(Brian Ellison) *swvd bdly lft and uns rdr leaving stalls* 125/1
1m 2.15s (0.05) **Going Correction** -0.175s/f (Firm) 11 Ran SP% 116.6
Speed ratings (Par 95): **92,90,90,89,87 82,81,80,73,65**
CSF £13.12 TOTE £4.50: £1.50, £1.30, £2.80; EX 15.40 Trifecta £116.30.
Owner King Power Racing Co Ltd **Bred** Houghton Bloodstock Uk Ltd **Trained** Middleham Moor, N Yorks

FOCUS
A fair juvenile novice sprint won last year by subsequent Epsom Woodcote Stakes victor Cosmic Law. The third-favourite won a shade cosily on debut from a modest draw. The winning jockey described the ground as good to firm with a good covering of grass. The level is fluid.

2893 PENRITH H'CAP (A JOCKEY CLUB GRASSROOTS SPRINT SERIES QUALIFIER) 5f 193y
2:45 (2:46) (Class 4) (0-80,80) 4-Y-O+
£7,439 (£2,213; £1,106; £553; £300; £300) Stalls Low

Form RPR
-002 1 **Firmdecisions (IRE)**[23] 2107 9-9-4 80.............................. RowanScott(3) 11 88
(Nigel Tinkler) *hld up: hdwy on wd outside over 1f out: led ins fnl f: pushed out towards fin* 18/1
0-65 2 *3/4* **Proud Archi (IRE)**[25] 2057 5-9-5 78.............................. ConnorBeasley 9 84
(Michael Dods) *sn pushed along in rr: hdwy on outside over 1f out: kpt on to take 2nd towards fin: nt rch wnr* 7/1[2]
0-40 3 *nk* **Redrosezorro**[16] 2418 5-8-1 67.............................(h) RobertDodsworth(7) 7 72
(Eric Alston) *cl up on outside: effrt and led over 1f out: hdd ins fnl f: no ex and lost 2nd towards fin* 16/1
06-6 4 *1 1/4* **Uncle Charlie (IRE)**[16] 2418 5-8-7 66.............................. JoeFanning 12 67
(Ann Duffield) *hld up: rdn over 2f out: hdwy on outside appr fnl f: kpt on to take 4th cl home* 11/2[1]
0045 5 *hd* **Luis Vaz De Torres (IRE)**[20] 2242 7-9-0 78.............(h) SeanDavis(5) 10 78
(Richard Fahey) *in tch on outside: effrt and drvn along wl over 1f out: kpt on same pce ins fnl f* 12/1
0-63 6 *nse* **Mr Orange (IRE)**[19] 2292 6-9-3 76..................................(p) KevinStott 8 76
(Paul Midgley) *in tch: drvn along over 2f out: rallied: kpt on same pce ins fnl f* 10/1
0/36 7 *nk* **Cartmell Cleave**[16] 2416 7-9-7 80.............................. JackGarritty 5 79+
(Ruth Carr) *dwlt: hld up: hdwy over 1f out: sn edgd lft: kpt on same pce ins fnl f* 7/1[2]
526- 8 *hd* **Rux Ruxx (IRE)**[214] 8340 4-8-13 72.............................. RachelRichardson 13 70
(Tim Easterby) *s.i.s: bhd: pushed along 2f out: kpt on fnl f: nvr rchd ldrs* 50/1
1312 9 *3/4* **Gowanbuster**[17] 2379 4-8-10 74.............................(t) TheodoreLadd(5) 14 70
(Susan Corbett) *led to over 1f out: rdn and wknd ins fnl f* 7/1[2]
5031 10 *1* **Highly Sprung (IRE)**[19] 2292 6-8-10 74.............................. FayeMcManoman(5) 1 67
(Les Eyre) *midfield on ins: drvn along and hdwy 2f out: wknd ins fnl f* 9/1[3]
00-3 11 *1/2* **Signore Piccolo**[24] 2079 8-9-3 76..................................(p) TrevorWhelan 2 67+
(David Loughnane) *s.s: hdwy to join main gp over 4f out: rdn over 2f out: no further imp fr over 1f out (jockey said gelding was slowly away)* 16/1
10-2 12 *2* **Final Go**[10] 2588 4-9-3 76.............................. SamJames 6 61
(Grant Tuer) *chsd ldrs tl rdn and wknd over 1f out* 11/1
60-2 13 *2 1/4* **Cale Lane**[19] 2292 4-9-1 74.............................. PaulMulrennan 3 51
(Julie Camacho) *in tch: effrt whn n.m.r over 2f out to over 1f out: sn rdn: wknd fnl f (jockey said filly weakened quickly)* 11/2[1]
0060 14 *8* **Classic Pursuit**[2] 2841 8-9-1 74..................................(v) BenCurtis 4 26
(Marjorie Fife) *s.i.s: sn pushed along in rr: struggling over 2f out: sn btn (jockey said gelding was slowly away)* 66/1
1m 12.18s (-2.42) **Going Correction** -0.175s/f (Firm) 14 Ran SP% 123.9
Speed ratings (Par 105): **109,108,107,105,105 105,105,104,103,102 101,99,96,85**
CSF £143.09 CT £2097.12 TOTE £20.80: £6.00, £2.70, £7.00; EX 158.30 Trifecta £3260.10.
Owner White Bear Racing **Bred** Thomas O'Meara **Trained** Langton, N Yorks

FOCUS
A fair sprint handicap. A strong gallop set it up for the finishers and, in terms of surface, the first two horses home weren't inconvenienced by challenging late and wide. This has been rated around the winner.

2894 THURSBY H'CAP 7f 173y
3:15 (3:18) (Class 4) (0-85,85) 4-Y-O+
£7,439 (£2,213; £1,106; £553; £300; £300) Stalls Low

Form RPR
5330 1 **Tadaawol**[2] 2842 6-8-11 80.................................(p) BenSanderson(5) 3 86
(Roger Fell) *chsd ldng pair: hdwy to ld over 1f out: sn hung rt: hld on wl u.p ins fnl f* 3/1[2]
060- 2 *3/4* **The Navigator**[85] 5758 4-8-10 77.............................. JamieGormley(3) 8 81
(Dianne Sayer) *slowly away: bhd: rdn over 2f out: hdwy on outside over 1f out: kpt on wl fnl f to take 2nd cl home* 50/1
0-66 3 *hd* **Ghayyar (IRE)**[17] 2369 5-8-7 71..................................(t) RachelRichardson 7 74
(Tim Easterby) *hld up in tch: effrt and drvn over 2f out: chsd wnr over 1f out: kpt on fnl f: lost 2nd cl home* 7/1
0-66 4 *2 1/4* **Lamloom (IRE)**[9] 2622 5-9-7 85.................................(h[1]) DanielTudhope 6 83
(David O'Meara) *t.k.h: trckd ldr: led after 1f: rdn and hdd over 1f out: outpcd fnl f* 7/2[3]
0043 5 *2 1/2* **Zeshov (IRE)**[17] 2369 8-8-8 72.................................(p) LewisEdmunds 2 64
(Rebecca Bastiman) *hld up: rdn over 2f out: hdwy over 1f out: no further imp fnl f* 10/1
5-05 6 *3 1/4* **Moxy Mares**[7] 2691 4-9-1 79.............................. BenCurtis 1 64
(Mark Loughnane) *hld up in tch: drvn and outpcd over 2f out: n.d after* 11/4[1]
0-06 7 *nk* **Royal Shaheen (FR)**[19] 2291 6-9-0 78.............................(v) PaulMulrennan 5 62
(Alistair Whillans) *t.k.h: hld up: rdn along and outpcd over 2f out: sn btn* 20/1
0-00 8 *3/4* **Lualiwa**[23] 2116 5-9-0 83.................................(v[1]) SeanDavis(5) 4 65
(Kevin Ryan) *t.k.h to post and in r: led 1f: chsd ldr: drvn and outpcd over 2f out: wknd over 1f out* 8/1
1m 38.61s (-1.39) **Going Correction** -0.175s/f (Firm) 8 Ran SP% 113.3
Speed ratings (Par 105): **99,98,98,95,93 90,89,89**
CSF £117.32 CT £970.69 TOTE £4.50: £1.40, £7.90, £2.30; EX 143.00 Trifecta £1661.70.
Owner Fell, Hamilton & Smeaton **Bred** Christopher & Annabelle Mason **Trained** Nawton, N Yorks

FOCUS
14 yards added. The feature contest was a decent handicap. The second-favourite won well in a good comparative time.

2895 DURDAR NOVICE STKS 6f 195y
3:45 (3:48) (Class 5) 3-5-Y-O £4,204 (£1,251; £625; £312) Stalls Low

Form RPR
1- 1 **I Could Do Better (IRE)**[195] 8895 3-9-9 0.............................. JoeFanning 1 88+
(Keith Dalgleish) *plld hrd: prom: hdwy to ld over 2f out: shkn up: edgd to stands' rail and qcknd clr over 1f out: eased towards fin: promising* 5/6[1]
32-3 2 *7* **Brandy Spirit**[22] 2147 3-9-2 80.............................. BenCurtis 10 62
(Michael Easterby) *chsd ldrs: drvn and outpcd over 2f out: rallied and chsd (clr) wnr over 1f out: kpt on fnl f: no imp* 11/4[2]
22- 3 *1 1/4* **So Macho (IRE)**[198] 8831 4-9-13 0.............................. SamJames 7 63
(Grant Tuer) *led to over 2f out: rdn whn edgd lft and lost 2nd over 1f out: kpt on same pce fnl f* 6/1[3]
0 4 *1 3/4* **Bold Show**[9] 2624 3-9-2 0.............................. JackGarritty 6 54
(Richard Fahey) *hld up bhd ldng gp: rdn and outpcd over 2f out: rallied whn short of room briefly over 1f out: sn no imp (jockey said colt hung left home straight)* 16/1
0 5 *3 3/4* **The Retriever (IRE)**[13] 2505 4-9-13 0.............................. DougieCostello 2 48
(Micky Hammond) *hld up: rdn and outpcd over 2f out: shortlived effrt wl over 1f out: wknd fnl f* 150/1
06 6 *4 1/2* **Ghathanfar (IRE)**[28] 1975 3-9-2 0.............................. RoystonFfrench 8 32
(Tracy Waggott) *cl up: rdn and ev ch over 2f out: outpcd whn short of room over 1f out: sn btn* 80/1
10- 7 *11* **Ride The Monkey (IRE)**[213] 8387 3-9-9 0.............................. PaulMulrennan 9 9
(Michael Dods) *dwlt and wnt lft s: bhd and detached: rdn along 1/2-way: nvr on terms* 12/1
1m 26.29s (-1.71) **Going Correction** -0.175s/f (Firm)
WFA 3 from 4yo 11lb 7 Ran SP% 111.0
Speed ratings (Par 103): **102,94,92,90,86 81,68**
CSF £3.04 TOTE £1.80: £1.20, £1.40; EX 4.00 Trifecta £7.70.
Owner Paul & Clare Rooney **Bred** Minch Bloodstock **Trained** Carluke, S Lanarks

FOCUS
14 yards added. A fair novice contest won last year by the subsequently Group 3-placed Arbalet. The odds-on favourite is clearly still learning but won this race pretty much as he liked in a good comparative time.

2896 WREAY H'CAP (DIV I) — 6f 195y

4:15 (4:17) (Class 5) (0-75,77) 3-Y-O

£4,204 (£1,251; £625; £312; £300; £300) **Stalls** Low

Form | | | | RPR
2363 **1** **Howzer Black (IRE)**[17] 2371 3-9-9 **77**....(p) ShaneGray 4 — 84
(Keith Dalgleish) *hld up towards rr: angled lft and hdwy over 1f out: sustained run against stands' rail to ld cl home* **5/1**[2]
3-45 **2** *nk* **Arletta Star**[17] 2371 3-8-3 **60**.... JamieGormley(3) 5 — 66
(Tim Easterby) *t.k.h: led: rdn and asserted over 1f out: kpt fnl f: hdd cl home* **7/1**[3]
32-1 **3** *2 ¼* **Ramesses**[23] 2114 3-9-1 **74**.... SeanDavis(5) 3 — 74+
(Richard Fahey) *prom: effrt on wd outside of gp 2f out: kpt on same pce ins fnl f* **6/5**[1]
050- **4** *¾* **Ifton**[159] 9498 3-8-12 **66**.... BenCurtis 1 — 64
(Ruth Carr) *t.k.h: hld up: rdn and effrt 2f out: kpt on ins fnl f: nt pce to chal* **12/1**
0-35 **5** *hd* **Port Of Leith (IRE)**[25] 2055 3-9-3 **71**.... JoeFanning 9 — 68
(Mark Johnston) *dwlt and blkd s: t.k.h and disp ld after 1f to over 1f out: no ex ins fnl f* **28/1**
24-0 **6** *2 ¼* **Dancing Speed (IRE)**[21] 2200 3-9-0 **68**.... DanielTudhope 8 — 59
(Marjorie Fife) *blkd s: hld up: rdn over 2f out: effrt against stands' rail over 1f out: sn no imp* **33/1**
40-0 **7** *1 ½* **Evie Speed (IRE)**[13] 2510 3-9-7 **75**.... JackGarritty 10 — 62
(Jedd O'Keeffe) *hld up bhd ldng gp: drvn and outpcd over 2f out: edgd lft wl over 1f out: sn no imp* **9/1**
-300 **8** *1 ¾* **Dream Chick (IRE)**[18] 2337 3-8-8 **62**.... SamJames 7 — 45
(Kevin Ryan) *blkd s: sn prom: rdn along over 2f out: wknd over 1f out* **28/1**
60-6 **9** *10* **Kolossus**[13] 2510 3-9-4 **72**.... ConnorBeasley 2 — 28
(Michael Dods) *t.k.h: hld up in tch: effrt and rdn over 2f out: wknd over 1f out: eased whn no ch ins fnl f (jockey said gelding ran too free)* **8/1**
604- **10** *2 ¼* **She's Awake**[186] 9083 3-7-9 **56**.... RobertDodsworth(7) 6 — 5
(Michael Easterby) *hld up on outside: drvn and struggling over 2f out: sn lost tch: eased whn no ch ins fnl f* **40/1**

1m 26.55s (-1.45) **Going Correction** -0.175s/f (Firm) 10 Ran SP% **115.7**
Speed ratings (Par 99): **101,100,98,97,97 94,92,90,79,76**
CSF £37.83 CT £67.59 TOTE £5.30: £1.80, £2.10, £1.20; EX 32.20 Trifecta £97.20.
Owner Middleham Park Racing LXXVI **Bred** Kildaragh Stud **Trained** Carluke, S Lanarks

FOCUS
14 yards added. The first division of a fair 3yo handicap. The second-favourite used the seemingly favoured near-rail strip of ground to ultimate effect in the final furlong. This has been rated around the runner-up.

2897 WREAY H'CAP (DIV II) — 6f 195y

4:45 (4:48) (Class 5) (0-75,76) 3-Y-O

£4,204 (£1,251; £625; £312; £300; £300) **Stalls** Low

Form | | | | RPR
30-3 **1** **Wild Hope**[23] 2114 3-9-4 **72**.... KevinStott 8 — 83
(Kevin Ryan) *cl up on outside: led nr stands' rail over 2f out: drew clr fnl f: eased cl home* **5/2**[1]
-001 **2** *4* **Barasti Dancer (IRE)**[19] 2285 3-9-3 **71**.... BenCurtis 5 — 71
(K R Burke) *hld up on outside: effrt against stands' rail and disp ld over 1f out to ins fnl f: kpt on same pce last 100yds* **7/1**[3]
05-1 **3** *hd* **Gale Force Maya**[19] 2293 3-9-0 **68**.... PaulMulrennan 1 — 68+
(Michael Dods) *hld up in tch: hdwy in centre of trck to chse wnr over 1f out: kpt on ins fnl f: nt pce to chal* **6/1**[2]
4-15 **4** *3 ¼* **City Tour**[33] 1846 3-9-8 **76**.... JoeFanning 6 — 67+
(Mark Johnston) *dwlt: bhd and pushed along: drvn over 2f out: kpt on fnl f: nvr able to chal* **5/2**[1]
2511 **5** *½* **Plumette**[17] 2356 3-9-7 **75**.... TrevorWhelan 9 — 65+
(David Loughnane) *hld up on ins: effrt in centre of trck 2f out: rdn and no further imp appr fnl f* **9/1**
-540 **6** *2 ½* **Five Helmets (IRE)**[9] 2635 3-8-9 **66**....(p) JamieGormley(3) 4 — 49
(Iain Jardine) *dwlt: bhd: outpcd over 4f out: rallied fnl f: kpt on: n.d* **20/1**
0305 **7** *1* **Alfred The Grey (IRE)**[22] 2152 3-8-4 **57** ow1.... RoystonFfrench 10 — 38
(Tracy Waggott) *hld up in tch: effrt over 2f out: edgd rt over 1f out: wknd fnl f* **40/1**
620- **8** *hd* **Flint Said No**[224] 8049 3-8-12 **73**.... HarryRussell(7) 2 — 53
(Bryan Smart) *t.k.h: pressed ldr on ins: rdn on outside of gp and edgd rt wl over 1f out: btn fnl f* **20/1**
56-6 **9** *4* **Euro No More (IRE)**[23] 2101 3-8-10 **64**.... ShaneGray 3 — 33
(Keith Dalgleish) *prom: drvn and outpcd over 2f out: btn over 1f out* **11/1**
504- **10** *13* **Lady Kinsale**[261] 6796 3-7-9 **56** oh4.... RobertDodsworth(7) 7 —
(Eric Alston) *t.k.h: led to over 2f out: sn rdn and struggling: lost tch over 1f out* **80/1**

1m 26.46s (-1.54) **Going Correction** -0.175s/f (Firm) 10 Ran SP% **115.5**
Speed ratings (Par 99): **101,96,96,92,91 89,87,87,83,68**
CSF £19.95 CT £97.75 TOTE £3.30: £1.10, £1.70, £2.10; EX 21.40 Trifecta £129.30.
Owner Hambleton Racing Ltd XLIV **Bred** Watership Down Stud **Trained** Hambleton, N Yorks

FOCUS
14 yards added. The second division of a fair 3yo handicap. One of the joint-favourites won readily up the favoured near rail once again in a marginally quicker time. This has been rated around the first two.

2898 BLACKWELL H'CAP (DIV I) — 6f 195y

5:15 (5:18) (Class 5) (0-75,76) 4-Y-O+

£4,204 (£1,251; £625; £312; £300; £300) **Stalls** Low

Form | | | | RPR
1-00 **1** **Redarna**[13] 2509 5-9-0 **68**....(p[1]) PaulMulrennan 12 — 82
(Dianne Sayer) *cl up on outside: led and edgd (lft) to stands' rail over 2f out: hrd pressed fr over 1f out: hld on wl fnl f* **14/1**
0-20 **2** *½* **Stringybark Creek**[25] 2057 5-9-4 **72**.... BenCurtis 4 — 84
(David Loughnane) *trckd ldrs: effrt and disp ld wl over 1f out to ins fnl f: kpt on: hld towards fin* **8/1**
-361 **3** *5* **Jacob Black**[7] 2679 8-9-8 **76** 4ex....(v) ShaneGray 11 — 75
(Keith Dalgleish) *hld up in midfield on outside: stdy hdwy whn n.m.r and bmpd over 2f out: effrt and edgd rt over 1f out: no ex fnl f* **10/1**
0046 **4** *¾* **Zylan (IRE)**[21] 2201 7-9-1 **74**....(p) BenSanderson(5) 8 — 70
(Roger Fell) *prom: effrt and rdn over 2f out: kpt on same pce fr over 1f out* **14/1**
3-04 **5** *½* **Star Shield**[17] 2372 4-9-7 **75**.... DanielTudhope 9 — 70
(David O'Meara) *midfield: effrt whn hmpd over 2f out: effrt over 1f out: no imp fnl f (jockey said gelding was hampered approaching final 2f)* **11/4**[1]
0-02 **6** *hd* **Cameo Star (IRE)**[14] 2478 4-8-10 **69**.... SeanDavis(5) 7 — 64
(Richard Fahey) *hld up on outside: effrt against stands' rail whn n.m.r and bmpd over 2f out: drvn and no imp fr over 1f out (jockey said gelding hung left throughout)* **8/1**
-401 **7** *nk* **Kentuckyconnection (USA)**[21] 2183 6-8-7 **68**.... HarryRussell(7) 5 — 62
(Bryan Smart) *hld up: drvn and outpcd over 2f out: rallied in centre of trck fnl f: kpt on: no imp* **7/1**[3]
5-11 **8** *¾* **Colour Contrast (IRE)**[7] 2681 6-8-4 **61** 5ex....(b) JamieGormley(3) 3 — 53
(Iain Jardine) *dwlt and swvd lft s: bhd and detached: hdwy over 1f out: kpt on fnl f: nvr able to chal (jockey said gelding missed the break)* **5/1**[2]
3-05 **9** *2* **Our Charlie Brown**[17] 2372 5-8-11 **65**.... RachelRichardson 6 — 51
(Tim Easterby) *t.k.h: hld up in midfield: stdy hdwy over 2f out: rdn over 1f out: sn wknd* **15/2**
0-05 **10** *9* **Dasheen**[14] 2478 6-8-9 **63**....(v) JoeFanning 10 — 25
(Karen Tutty) *prom: rdn whn hmpd over 2f out: sn lost pl and struggling* **40/1**
6/0 **11** *1* **Eldelbar (SPA)**[28] 1976 5-8-12 **66**....(h) ConnorBeasley 1 — 25
(Geoffrey Harker) *t.k.h: led to over 2f out: wknd over 1f out* **66/1**
-002 **12** *2* **Roaring Forties (IRE)**[17] 2372 6-8-8 **62**....(p) LewisEdmunds 2 — 16
(Rebecca Bastiman) *hld up on ins: drvn and struggling over 2f out: sn wknd* **25/1**

1m 25.87s (-2.13) **Going Correction** -0.175s/f (Firm) 12 Ran SP% **120.0**
Speed ratings (Par 103): **105,104,98,97,97 97,96,95,93,83 82,79**
CSF £121.70 CT £1204.52 TOTE £17.20: £4.70, £2.40, £2.90; EX 187.80 Trifecta £926.50.
Owner Graham Lund And Dianne Sayer **Bred** A H Bennett **Trained** Hackthorpe, Cumbria
■ Stewards' Enquiry : Paul Mulrennan four-day ban: interference & careless riding (May 23, Jun 3-5)

FOCUS
14 yards added. The first division of a fair handicap. The winner toughed it out up the near stands' rail once again in a quick comparative winning time. A length pb for the winner, with the runner-up to form.

2899 BLACKWELL H'CAP (DIV II) — 6f 195y

5:45 (5:47) (Class 5) (0-75,76) 4-Y-O+

£4,204 (£1,251; £625; £312; £300; £300) **Stalls** Low

Form | | | | RPR
-450 **1** **Smugglers Creek (IRE)**[17] 2372 5-8-8 **64**....(p) JamieGormley(3) 11 — 71
(Iain Jardine) *led: rdn and hdd 2f out: rallied fnl f: regained ld towards fin* **20/1**
460- **2** *nk* **Zoravan (USA)**[217] 8264 6-8-9 **62**....(v) JoeFanning 6 — 68
(Keith Dalgleish) *t.k.h: pressed wnr: led nr stands' rail 2f out: edgd rt ins fnl f: no ex and hdd towards fin* **14/1**
0-01 **3** *1 ½* **Supaulette (IRE)**[16] 2418 4-8-13 **66**....(bt) JackGarritty 7 — 68+
(Tim Easterby) *hld up: rdn over 2f out: hdwy on outside and chsd ldng pair over 1f out: kpt on: nt enough pce to chal* **17/2**
3-50 **4** *1 ¾* **John Kirkup**[16] 2416 4-9-9 **76**....(p) ConnorBeasley 8 — 73
(Michael Dods) *hld up in midfield on outside: effrt against stands' rail over 1f out: kpt on fnl f: nvr able to chal* **17/2**
-055 **5** *hd* **Explain**[10] 2588 7-9-2 **69**....(b) SamJames 5 — 66
(Ruth Carr) *hld up: rdn over 2f out: angled lft and hdwy against stands' rail fnl f: kpt on: no imp* **8/1**[3]
25-0 **6** *1 ¼* **Bibbidibobbidiboo (IRE)**[17] 2379 4-9-1 **68**.... PaulMulrennan 1 — 61
(Ann Duffield) *wnt lft s: bhd: outpcd after 2f: hdwy on outside fnl f: nvr rchd ldrs* **16/1**
04-2 **7** *2 ¾* **Knowing Glance (IRE)**[16] 2418 4-9-0 **72**.... SeanDavis(5) 4 — 58
(Richard Fahey) *plld hrd early: prom: rdn in centre of crse over 2f out: wknd fnl f* **9/4**[1]
6403 **8** *1 ½* **Dirchill (IRE)**[17] 2379 5-8-9 **67**....(b) HarrisonShaw(5) 9 — 49
(David Thompson) *chsd ldrs on outside: rdn over 2f out: wknd over 1f out* **10/1**
5-30 **9** *shd* **Proceeding**[21] 2203 4-8-7 **60**.... RoystonFfrench 2 — 42
(Tracy Waggott) *trckd ldrs: rdn over 2f out: edgd lft and wknd over 1f out* **33/1**
0-44 **10** *3* **Twin Appeal (IRE)**[22] 2151 8-9-7 **74**....(p[1]) ShaneGray 10 — 59
(Karen Tutty) *hld up: rdn and outpcd over 2f out: rallied whn nt clr run over 1f out: sn wknd (jockey said gelding was denied a clear run 1½f out causing the gelding to become unbalanced, resulting in him easing the gelding as he thought something was amiss)* **5/1**[2]
000- **11** *7* **Desert Dream**[152] 9614 5-8-8 **68**.... JoshQuinn(7) 3 — 23
(Michael Easterby) *slowly away: bhd and sn detached: nvr on terms* **12/1**

1m 26.5s (-1.50) **Going Correction** -0.175s/f (Firm) 11 Ran SP% **116.6**
Speed ratings (Par 103): **101,100,98,96,96 95,92,90,90,86 78**
CSF £271.17 CT £2600.24 TOTE £22.90: £5.30, £4.40, £2.40; EX 284.40 Trifecta £1121.20.
Owner Allan McLuckie **Bred** Ballygallon Stud Limited **Trained** Carruthertown, D'fries & G'way

FOCUS
14 yards added. The second division of a fair handicap. One of the outsiders rallied bravely to victory and the winning time was over half-a-second slower. This has been rated around the first two.
T/Plt: £83.60 to a £1 stake. Pool: £55,104.67 - 480.75 winning units T/Qpdt: £4.90 to a £1 stake. Pool: £5,544.10 - 829.44 winning units **Richard Young**

2107 LEICESTER (R-H)

Monday, May 20

OFFICIAL GOING: Good to firm (good in places; watered; 7.5)
Wind: Nil Weather: Cloudy with sunny spells

2900 BRITISH STALLION STUDS EBF MAIDEN STKS — 7f

6:15 (6:16) (Class 4) 3-Y-O+ £5,854 (£1,742; £870; £435) **Stalls** High

Form | | | | RPR
3-22 **1** **Regular**[22] 2146 3-9-3 78....(p[1]) JasonWatson 3 — 80
(Michael Bell) *mde all: edgd rt 2f out: rdn and hung lft fr over 1f out: styd on* **5/2**[1]
04- **2** *¾* **Shawaaheq (IRE)**[163] 9460 3-9-3 0.... DaneO'Neill 2 — 77
(Ed Dunlop) *trckd ldrs: racd keenly: chsd wnr over 1f out: sn carried lft: styd on* **10/1**
00- **3** *nk* **Eligible (IRE)**[208] 8548 3-9-3 0.... HectorCrouch 7 — 76
(Clive Cox) *s.i.s: hld up: hdwy over 1f out: r.o* **8/1**
3- **4** *4* **Dubai Ice (USA)**[178] 9225 3-8-12 0.... HayleyTurner 6 — 60
(Saeed bin Suroor) *s.i.s: hld up: racd keenly: nt clr run 2f out: hdwy over 1f out: edgd lft ins fnl f: nt rch ldrs* **7/2**[2]

5 4 ½ **Attorney General** 3-9-3 0........................ SeanLevey 11 53
(Ed Vaughan) *s.i.s: hld up: rdn over 2f out: styd on fr over 1f out: nvr on terms* **16/1**

20 6 *nk* **King Shamardal**[22] 2147 3-9-3 0........................ FrannyNorton 4 52
(Mark Johnston) *chsd ldr tl rdn over 1f out: wknd fnl f* **6/1**

6 7 5 **Haadef**[19] 2280 3-9-3 0........................ JosephineGordon 9 39
(Brian Meehan) *dwlt: rn green in rr: sme hdwy over 1f out: wknd ins fnl f* **33/1**

4- 8 5 **Corrida De Toros (IRE)**[170] 9355 3-9-3 0........................ CallumShepherd 5 25
(Ed de Giles) *chsd ldrs: rdn over 2f out: wkng whn wandered over 1f out (jockey said colt lost its action approximately 1½f out)* **5/1**[3]

40- 9 1 ¼ **Come On Bear (IRE)**[234] 7731 4-9-9 0........................(v[1]) JoeyHaynes 1 21
(Alan Bailey) *hld up: hdwy over 2f out: sn rdn and wknd* **100/1**

10 1 ¾ **Stepaside Boy** 3-9-3 0........................ JFEgan 12 17
(David Evans) *hld up: sme hdwy 1/2-way: rdn and wknd over 2f out* **50/1**

0 11 1 ½ **Juan De Valdes**[30] 1940 3-9-3 0........................ FergusSweeney 10 13
(Shaun Keightley) *chsd ldrs: rdn over 2f out: sn wknd* **50/1**

1m 26.05s (0.35) **Going Correction** +0.025s/f (Good) **11 Ran SP% 115.7**
WFA 3 from 4yo 11lb
Speed ratings (Par 105): **99,98,97,93,88 87,82,76,74,72 71**
CSF £27.99 TOTE £3.10: £1.30, £3.80, £1.60; EX 26.60 Trifecta £202.00.
Owner The Queen **Bred** The Queen **Trained** Newmarket, Suffolk
■ Sharqeyya was withdrawn. Price at time of withdrawal 33/1. \n\x\x Rule 4 does not appl
■ Stewards' Enquiry : Callum Shepherd two-day ban: violent or improper conduct towards stewards or officials (3-4 Jun)

FOCUS
Not the strongest of maidens and the most experienced runner got off the mark despite hanging all over the track in the closing stages. The winner set the standard and the race has been rated around him.

2901 JAMES WARD (S) STKS — 1m 3f 179y
6:45 (6:47) (Class 5) 3-Y-O+
£4,334 (£1,289; £644; £322; £300; £300) **Stalls Low**

Form / RPR

-060 1 **Eye Of The Storm (IRE)**[15] 2435 9-9-10 77........................ SeanLevey 5 80+
(Keith Dalgleish) *s.i.s: pushed along to go prom over 10f out: led over 2f out: shkn up to go clr over 1f out: comf* **5/2**[2]

06-6 2 6 **Nabhan**[24] 1463 7-9-10 70........................(tp) FrannyNorton 11 70
(Bernard Llewellyn) *hld up: hdwy over 3f out: rdn to chse wnr over 1f out: no imp fnl f* **8/1**[3]

-025 3 6 **Brinkleys Katie**[18] 2343 3-8-3 51 ow1........................(v[1]) JFEgan 12 54
(Paul George) *hld up: plld hrd: hdwy 8f out: rdn over 2f out: wknd fnl f* **9/1**

-600 4 8 **Far Cry**[40] 1679 6-8-12 46........................ JosephLyons(7) 2 41
(Hughie Morrison) *uns rdr leaving paddock: hld up: swtchd lft over 2f out: styd on to go 4th wl ins fnl f: nvr nrr* **25/1**

04-0 5 ¾ **Tingo In The Tale (IRE)**[116] 387 10-9-3 40........................(p) TobyEley(7) 8 45
(Tony Forbes) *in rr and pushed along early: rdn over 3f out: sn outpcd (jockey said gelding was never travelling)* **66/1**

4/11 6 7 **Clayton**[18] 2335 10-10-0 87........................(t) HollieDoyle 7 38
(Archie Watson) *led: hung lft and hdd over 2f out: wknd over 1f out (jockey said gelding hung left-handed)* **8/13**[1]

00-0 7 1 ½ **Ishallak**[9] 2617 4-9-10 60........................(v[1]) FergusSweeney 9 31
(Mark Usher) *chsd ldrs: ev ch 3f out: sn rdn: wknd 2f out* **50/1**

6205 8 4 ½ **Ejabah (IRE)**[14] 2481 5-9-5 34........................ JoeyHaynes 10 19
(Charles Smith) *chsd ldrs: pushed along 5f out: wknd over 2f out* **100/1**

0-00 9 10 **Pontecarlo Boy**[33] 1849 5-9-10 39........................ PhilDennis 6 8
(Richard Whitaker) *w ldr tl rdn over 3f out: wknd over 2f out* **100/1**

6 10 6 **Queen Emily**[16] 2417 3-7-9 0........................(h[1]) RPWalsh(7) 1
(Conor Dore) *led to post: s.s: a in rr: bhd fr 1/2-way (jockey said filly was slowly away)* **100/1**

2m 33.66s (-1.34) **Going Correction** +0.025s/f (Good) **10 Ran SP% 121.9**
WFA 3 from 4yo+ 17lb
Speed ratings (Par 103): **105,101,97,91,91 86,85,82,75,71**
CSF £22.77 TOTE £4.10: £1.50, £1.10, £3.00; EX 20.00 Trifecta £100.40.The winner was sold to Conor Dore for £8,200.
Owner J S Morrison **Bred** Kevin J Molloy **Trained** Carluke, S Lanarks

FOCUS
Add 15 yards. Not a bad seller and the winner, who has been Group class in his time, relished the drop in grade.

2902 J.F. HERRING H'CAP — 1m 2f
7:15 (7:15) (Class 4) (0-80,79) 4-Y-O+
£5,530 (£1,645; £822; £411) **Stalls Low**

Form / RPR

21-5 1 **Geetanjali (IRE)**[20] 2230 4-9-4 76........................(p) HayleyTurner 2 83+
(Michael Bell) *s.i.s: hld up in tch: swtchd lft over 2f out: rdn to chse ldr over 1f out: styd on u.p to ld nr fin* **9/4**[2]

0-20 2 *nk* **Billy Roberts (IRE)**[41] 1659 6-8-8 66........................ PhilDennis 1 72
(Richard Whitaker) *led at stdy pce: qcknd over 3f out: rdn over 1f out: hdd nr fin* **6/1**

-102 3 10 **Casement (IRE)**[19] 2291 5-9-6 78........................ AlistairRawlinson 3 64
(Michael Appleby) *chsd ldr: shkn up over 3f out: rdn and lost 2nd over 1f out: wknd ins fnl f* **7/4**[1]

6 4 1 ½ **Meagher's Flag (IRE)**[31] 1914 4-9-4 79........................(t) MeganNicholls(3) 4 62
(Paul Nicholls) *s.i.s: hld up: rdn over 3f out: outpcd fr over 2f out* **5/2**[3]

2m 10.1s (0.90) **Going Correction** +0.025s/f (Good) **4 Ran SP% 110.0**
Speed ratings (Par 105): **97,96,88,87**
CSF £13.94 TOTE £2.40; EX 8.10 Trifecta £24.10.
Owner Hugo Merry **Bred** G S K International **Trained** Newmarket, Suffolk
■ Stewards' Enquiry : Phil Dennis two-day ban: used whip above permitted level (23 May & 3 Jun)
Hayley Turner two-day ban: used whip above permitted level (3-4 Jun)

FOCUS
Add 15 yards. A disappointing turnout for this 0-80 handicap but the winner has been rated to form.

2903 SARTORIUS NOVICE AUCTION STKS — 5f
7:45 (7:45) (Class 5) 2-Y-O
£4,075 (£1,212; £606; £303) **Stalls High**

Form / RPR

3 1 **Bushtucker Trial (IRE)**[19] 2282 2-9-2 0........................ HayleyTurner 1 76
(Michael Bell) *wnt rt s: hung rt almost thrght: chsd ldrs: led wl over 1f out: sn rdn: r.o: comf (jockey said gelding hung right-handed throughout)* **4/1**[2]

2 1 ¼ **Spring Bloom** 2-9-2 0........................ SeanLevey 2 72
(K R Burke) *racd keenly: w ldrs: ev ch wl over 1f out: sn rdn: styd on* **5/1**

3 *shd* **My Motivate Girl (IRE)** 2-8-11 0........................(v[1]) HollieDoyle 5 66
(Archie Watson) *s.i.s: outpcd: hdwy over 1f out: r.o* **7/1**

4 4 6 **Royal Ambition (IRE)**[19] 2275 2-9-2 0........................ HectorCrouch 8 50+
(Clive Cox) *chsd ldrs: rdn over 1f out: wknd ins fnl f* **9/2**[3]

4 5 2 ½ **Royal Lightning**[16] 2415 2-8-11 0........................ BarryMcHugh 6 36
(James Given) *chsd ldrs: pushed along 1/2-way: wknd ins fnl f* **7/1**

4 6 1 **Call Me Cheers**[7] 2694 2-9-2 0........................ JFEgan 7 37
(David Evans) *w ldrs tl pushed along 1/2-way: sn rdn and wknd over 1f out* **10/1**

013 7 *hd* **Manolith**[16] 2415 2-9-5 0........................ ConorMcGovern(3) 4 42
(David O'Meara) *plld hrd: sn led: hdd wl over 1f out: wknd fnl f* **7/2**[1]

8 7 **Ossco** 2-9-2 0........................ JasonWatson 3 11+
(Mohamed Moubarak) *s.i.s: outpcd* **20/1**

1m 1.21s (-0.59) **Going Correction** +0.025s/f (Good) **8 Ran SP% 115.9**
Speed ratings (Par 93): **105,103,102,93,89 87,87,76**
CSF £24.67 TOTE £3.20: £1.90, £3.00, £2.40; EX 29.70 Trifecta £186.20.
Owner Christopher Wright & David Kilburn **Bred** Ambrose Madden **Trained** Newmarket, Suffolk

FOCUS
This looked a decent event of its type and the front three are all of interest with the future in mind. The level is fluid.

2904 JOHN FERNELEY FILLIES' H'CAP — 7f
8:15 (8:16) (Class 5) (0-70,72) 3-Y-O
£3,816 (£1,135; £567; £300; £300; £300) **Stalls High**

Form / RPR

0-25 1 **Kwela**[21] 2204 3-9-2 72........................ GeorgiaDobie(7) 11 80
(Eve Johnson Houghton) *chsd ldrs: shkn up to ld over 1f out: rdn out* **7/1**[2]

2335 2 1 **Beryl The Petal (IRE)**[89] 798 3-9-2 68........................ ConorMcGovern(3) 1 73
(David O'Meara) *hld up: nt clr run and swtchd lft over 2f out: hdwy sn after: chsd wnr fnl f: sn rdn and ev ch: unable qck towards fin* **9/2**[1]

04-5 3 4 **Lady Lavinia**[28] 1980 3-8-10 59........................ PhilDennis 4 53
(Michael Easterby) *chsd ldrs: rdn over 1f out: styd on same pce fnl f (jockey said filly was denied a clear run)* **16/1**

-204 4 2 ½ **Moneta**[17] 2356 3-9-2 65........................ JasonWatson 2 52
(Jonathan Portman) *hld up: hdwy to ld over 2f out: rdn and hdd over 1f out: wknd ins fnl f* **9/2**[1]

-305 5 1 ¼ **Tie A Yellowribbon**[21] 2212 3-9-3 66........................(b[1]) JosephineGordon 13 50
(James Bethell) *hld up: hdwy 1/2-way: rdn over 1f out: wknd ins fnl f* **10/1**

1362 6 2 ¼ **Sylviacliffs (FR)**[12] 2529 3-8-10 66........................(p) JonathanFisher(7) 7 44
(K R Burke) *mid-div: pushed along 1/2-way: swtchd lft sn after: nt trble ldrs (jockey said filly suffered interference in running)* **12/1**

305- 7 4 ½ **Winterkoenigin**[174] 9275 3-9-7 70........................ PatDobbs 3 36
(David Lanigan) *s.i.s: hld up: rdn over 2f out: n.d* **8/1**[3]

00-5 8 5 **Double Coffee**[19] 2280 3-8-6 55........................ CharlieBennett 6 7
(Peter Hiatt) *led: hdd over 4f out: remained handy tl rdn and wknd over 1f out* **50/1**

06-0 9 ¾ **Cookupastorm (IRE)**[48] 1492 3-9-0 70........................ SeanKirrane(7) 10 20
(Richard Spencer) *hld up: hmpd over 4f out: n.d* **14/1**

-450 10 2 ½ **Diva D (IRE)**[21] 2212 3-9-3 66........................ FrannyNorton 8 10
(Mark Johnston) *plld hrd: w ldrs tl led over 4f out: hdd over 2f out: wknd over 1f out* **7/1**[2]

0-14 11 *nk* **Gregorian Girl**[20] 2238 3-9-0 63........................ JoeyHaynes 12 6
(Dean Ivory) *hld up in tch: rdn over 2f out: sn wknd* **10/1**

005- 12 *nk* **Aquarius (IRE)**[216] 8306 3-9-8 71........................(h) AlistairRawlinson 9 13
(Michael Appleby) *w ldrs: rdn and ev ch over 2f out: wknd over 1f out* **16/1**

1m 26.23s (0.53) **Going Correction** +0.025s/f (Good) **12 Ran SP% 118.7**
Speed ratings (Par 96): **98,96,92,89,88 85,80,74,73,70 70,70**
CSF £38.55 CT £501.08 TOTE £11.30: £2.60, £1.50, £7.30; EX 45.30 Trifecta £438.30.
Owner Mr & Mrs James Blyth Currie **Bred** Exors Of The Late Sir Eric Parker **Trained** Blewbury, Oxon

FOCUS
The biggest field of the evening and a good finish with the front two pulling nicely clear. This has been rated around the runner-up to a better view of her form.

2905 HENRY ALKEN H'CAP — 1m 3f 179y
8:45 (8:45) (Class 4) (0-85,85) 3-Y-O
£5,530 (£1,645; £822; £411) **Stalls Low**

Form / RPR

4-21 1 **Babbo's Boy (IRE)**[20] 2258 3-9-7 85........................ JasonWatson 2 93
(Michael Bell) *mde all: shkn up over 1f out: r.o wl: comf* **5/4**[1]

-232 2 2 ¼ **Sapa Inca (IRE)**[7] 2685 3-8-11 75........................ FrannyNorton 1 79
(Mark Johnston) *prom: rdn and swtchd lft over 2f out: chsd wnr over 1f out: hung rt ins fnl f: styd on same pce* **15/8**[2]

12-3 3 6 **Fearless Warrior (FR)**[31] 1911 3-9-6 84........................ PatDobbs 4 78
(Ralph Beckett) *s.i.s: rcvrd to join wnr after 1f: rdn and ev ch over 2f out: lost 2nd over 1f out: wknd ins fnl f* **3/1**[3]

212 4 ½ **Tigray (USA)**[18] 2317 3-8-10 74........................ AlistairRawlinson 3 68
(Michael Appleby) *w wnr 1f: remained handy: rdn over 2f out: wknd over 1f out* **16/1**

2m 33.83s (-1.17) **Going Correction** +0.025s/f (Good) **4 Ran SP% 110.1**
Speed ratings (Par 101): **104,102,98,98**
CSF £3.99 TOTE £2.20; EX 3.80 Trifecta £5.10.
Owner Amo Racing Limited **Bred** Lynch Bages & Camas Park Stud **Trained** Newmarket, Suffolk

FOCUS
Add 15 yards. Another disappointing turnout for a useful handicap but the progressive winner rounded off a fine evening for Michael Bell.
T/Plt: £204.80 to a £1 stake. Pool: £60,699.50 - 216.30 winning units T/Qpdt: £31.50 to a £1 stake. Pool: £5,843.00 - 136.93 winning units **Colin Roberts**

2331
REDCAR (L-H)
Monday, May 20

OFFICIAL GOING: Good to firm (good in places; watered; 8.2)
Wind: virtually nil Weather: fine

2906 RACINGTV.COM EBF NOVICE AUCTION STKS (PLUS 10 RACE) (DIV I) — 5f 217y
2:00 (2:05) (Class 4) 2-Y-O
£5,822 (£1,732; £865; £432) **Stalls Centre**

Form / RPR

0 1 **Troubador (IRE)**[33] 1844 2-9-3 0........................ AndrewMullen 9 76
(Michael Dods) *chsd ldrs: rdn 2f out: led jst ins fnl f: drvn and edgd lft: kpt on* **28/1**

51 2 *nk* **Insania**[16] 2415 2-9-5 0........................ CliffordLee 4 77
(K R Burke) *trckd ldrs: drvn to chal ins fnl f: edgd lft: kpt on* **11/8**[1]

0 3 3 ¼ **Bob's Oss (IRE)**[16] 2415 2-9-3 0........................ JasonHart 2 65
(John Quinn) *trckd ldrs: rdn 2f out: no ex fnl 110yds* **40/1**

4 nk **Don Ramiro (IRE)** 2-9-3 0 TomEaves 3 64+
(Kevin Ryan) led narrowly: rdn and hdd over 1f out: sn outpcd: kpt on fnl 110yds 4/1[2]

35 5 ½ **Knightcap**[25] 2052 2-8-12 0 DavidAllan 8 57
(Tim Easterby) prom: rdn to ld narrowly over 1f out: hdd jst ins fnl f: wknd fnl 110yds (jockey said filly hung left) 7/1

6 2 **Pearlwood (IRE)** 2-8-12 0 TonyHamilton 1 51
(Richard Fahey) dwlt: hld up: sn pushed along: nvr threatened 15/2

7 6 **Great Aspirations** 2-8-12 0 PJMcDonald 7 31
(Mark Johnston) trckd ldrs: rdn over 2f out: wknd over 1f out 13/2[3]

1m 12.56s (0.76) **Going Correction** 0.0s/f (Good) 7 Ran SP% 105.6
Speed ratings (Par 95): **98,97,93,92,92 89,81**
CSF £57.42 TOTE £25.40: £8.20, £1.40; EX 72.00 Trifecta £1362.70.
Owner J Sagar And S Lowthian **Bred** Worksop Manor Stud **Trained** Denton, Co Durham
■ Harry Love and Loolabelle were withdrawn. Prices at time of withdrawal 14/1 and 40/1 respectively. Rule 4 applies to all bets - deduction 5p in the pound

FOCUS
The first leg of an ordinary novice and one of the outsiders turned over the favourite.

2907 RACINGTV.COM EBF NOVICE AUCTION STKS (PLUS 10 RACE) (DIV II) 5f 217y
2:35 (2:38) (Class 4) 2-Y-O £5,822 (£1,732; £865; £432) Stalls Centre

Form RPR

24 1 **Rose Of Kildare (IRE)**[11] 2561 2-9-0 0 PJMcDonald 1 73
(Mark Johnston) mde all: narrow ld tl appr fnl f: drvn and hung lft ins fnl f: kpt on 6/5[1]

2 1¼ **Huraa** 2-9-0 0 GrahamLee 5 69+
(Bryan Smart) dwlt: hld up: pushed along and hdwy over 1f out: chsd ldr ins fnl f: rdn and kpt on 4/1[2]

3 2¼ **Calippo (IRE)** 2-9-0 0 HollieDoyle 3 63
(Archie Watson) s.i.s: rcvrd to trck ldrs 4f out: rdn to chal over 1f out: no ex fnl 110yds 9/2[3]

6 4 1¾ **Classy Lady**[25] 2051 2-8-11 0 BenRobinson(3) 2 57
(Ollie Pears) sn pressed ldr: rdn 2f out: no ex ins fnl f 33/1

06 5 1¾ **Sparkling Breeze**[23] 2115 2-9-5 0 AndrewMullen 6 57
(Michael Dods) chsd ldrs: rdn and bit outpcd whn hung lft over 1f out: kpt on same pce ins fnl f 66/1

6 2¼ **The Trendy Man (IRE)** 2-9-5 0 DavidNolan 4 50
(David O'Meara) trckd ldrs: rdn over 2f out: wknd over 1f out 17/2

0 7 ¾ **Bosun's Chair**[6] 2706 2-9-5 0 DavidAllan 8 48
(Tim Easterby) pressed ldr: rdn over 2f out: wknd appr fnl f 80/1

44 8 2 **Leave Em Alone (IRE)**[33] 1843 2-9-0 0 JimCrowley 9 37
(David Evans) chsd ldrs: rdn over 2f out: wknd over 1f out 8/1

9 23 **Clay Motion (IRE)** 2-9-5 0 RobbieDowney 7
(David Barron) slowly away: early reminders and a bhd 25/1

1m 12.3s (0.50) **Going Correction** 0.0s/f (Good) 9 Ran SP% 114.8
Speed ratings (Par 95): **100,98,95,93,90 87,86,84,53**
CSF £5.91 TOTE £2.20: £1.30, £1.20, £1.20; EX 7.10 Trifecta £25.00.
Owner Kingsley Park 14 **Bred** Wansdyke Farms Ltd **Trained** Middleham Moor, N Yorks

FOCUS
The time was 0.26secs quicker than the first leg, with the favourite winning well, but again ordinary form.

2908 JOIN RACING TV NOW H'CAP 5f
3:05 (3:07) (Class 6) (0-60,61) 3-Y-O
£3,823 (£1,137; £568; £300; £300; £300) Stalls Centre

Form RPR

05-3 1 **Frosted Lass**[28] 1982 3-9-1 54 RobbieDowney 3 61
(David Barron) prom: rdn 2f out: drvn to ld 75yds out: kpt on 9/2[2]

-441 2 ½ **Tomahawk Ridge (IRE)**[14] 2489 3-9-8 61 PJMcDonald 4 66
(John Gallagher) led narrowly: rdn 2f out: hdd over 1f out but remained chalng: drvn and kpt on fnl f 15/8[1]

0-06 3 1½ **Raquelle (IRE)**[19] 2300 3-8-8 47 DuranFentiman 7 47
(Tim Easterby) pressed ldr: rdn to ld narrowly over 1f out: drvn fnl f: hdd 75yds out: no ex 100/1

0-65 4 ½ **Newgate Angel**[19] 2300 3-8-9 48 AndrewMullen 5 46
(Tony Coyle) chsd ldrs: rdn 2f out: kpt on same pce 16/1

4005 5 1¾ **Ghost Buy (FR)**[19] 2296 3-9-7 60 (t) JasonHart 9 52
(Ivan Furtado) dwlt: hld up in rr: pushed along over 2f out: rdn and kpt on fnl f: nrst fin (jockey said colt hung right early stages) 8/1

502 6 nk **Dancing Mountain (IRE)**[7] 2683 3-9-3 56 GrahamLee 8 47
(Roger Fell) hld up: rdn over 2f out: kpt on ins fnl f: nvr threatened 5/1[3]

03-0 7 1¼ **The Grey Zebedee**[21] 2197 3-9-3 56 (p) DavidAllan 2 42
(Tim Easterby) stmbld sltly s: sn chsd ldrs: rdn over 2f out: wknd ins fnl f (jockey said gelding stumbled leaving stalls) 5/1[3]

6006 8 ½ **North Korea (IRE)**[14] 2474 3-9-0 53 CamHardie 10 37
(Brian Baugh) hld up: nvr threatened 50/1

04-0 9 1 **Show The World**[75] 1034 3-8-3 49 VictorSantos(7) 1 30
(Lucinda Egerton) bmpd sltly s: sn chsd ldrs: rdn over 2f out: wknd fnl f 50/1

006- 10 4 **Miss President**[185] 9093 3-9-6 59 JimCrowley 6 25
(Robert Cowell) hld up: rdn over 2f out: sn btn 20/1

59.0s (0.50) **Going Correction** 0.0s/f (Good) 10 Ran SP% 113.0
Speed ratings (Par 97): **96,95,92,92,89 88,86,85,84,77**
CSF £12.57 CT £710.25 TOTE £4.40: £1.50, £1.20, £17.00; EX 14.50 Trifecta £914.90.
Owner Mrs Anne Atkinson & Partner **Bred** Harrowgate Bloodstock Ltd **Trained** Maunby, N Yorks

FOCUS
Ordinary sprinting form.

2909 PAT AND LES HOLMES CELEBRATION FILLIES' NOVICE STKS 7f
3:35 (3:39) (Class 5) 3-Y-O+ £4,528 (£1,347; £673; £336) Stalls Centre

Form RPR

324- 1 **Make A Wish (IRE)**[235] 7708 3-8-11 76 GrahamLee 8 81
(Simon Crisford) prom: led over 4f out: pushed along 2f out: rdn and kpt on wl fnl f 11/2

6 2 1 **Royal Welcome**[18] 2332 3-8-11 0 DavidAllan 4 78
(James Tate) pressed ldr: rdn over 2f out: drvn appr fnl f: kpt on same pce ins fnl f 3/1[2]

3 8 **Corinthian Girl (IRE)** 3-8-11 0 StevieDonohoe 9 57
(David Lanigan) slowly away: hld up: pushed along and hdwy over 1f out: kpt on to go remote 3rd fnl 50yds 25/1

4 3 **Soft Cover** 3-8-11 0 PaulHanagan 1 49
(William Haggas) in tch: trckd ldrs over 4f out: rdn 2f out: edgd lft and wknd ins fnl f 11/4[1]

53-4 5 ½ **Take Fright**[17] 2366 3-8-11 76 RossaRyan 14 47
(Hugo Palmer) chsd ldrs: rdn over 2f out: wknd fnl f 20/1

6 hd **Summer Bride (IRE)** 3-8-11 0 JasonHart 2 47
(Tim Easterby) slowly away: hld up: sn pushed along: sme late hdwy: nvr involved 20/1

00 7 1 **Al Anaab (FR)**[46] 1543 3-8-4 0 VictorSantos(7) 5 44
(Lucinda Egerton) trckd ldrs: rdn over 2f out: wknd fnl f (vet said filly was slightly lame left hind) 250/1

4- 8 1¼ **Bea Ryan (IRE)**[377] 2527 4-9-8 0 TomEaves 6 45
(Declan Carroll) led narrowly: hdd over 4f out: trckd ldrs: rdn over 2f out: wknd over 1f out 20/1

9 ½ **Dilly Dilly (IRE)** 3-8-11 0 (h[1]) CamHardie 7 39
(John Wainwright) trckd ldrs: racd quite keenly: rdn over 2f out: wknd appr fnl f 250/1

6 10 2½ **Sharp Breath**[21] 2199 3-8-11 0 TonyHamilton 15 33
(Richard Fahey) hld up: pushed along 3f out: nvr involved 50/1

11 1¼ **Pearl Jam** 3-8-11 0 DanielMuscutt 11 29
(James Fanshawe) dwlt: hld up: sn pushed along: a towards rr 11/1

32- 12 2¼ **Falathaat (USA)**[236] 7675 3-8-11 0 JimCrowley 10 23
(Saeed bin Suroor) trckd ldrs: rdn 3f out: wknd wl over 1f out (jockey said filly was never travelling; vet said she was lame left fore) 5/1[3]

04 13 1¾ **Followme Followyou (IRE)**[13] 2506 3-8-11 0 PJMcDonald 12 18
(Mark Johnston) chsd ldrs: pushed along and lost pl 2f out: sn wknd 18/1

1m 24.36s (-1.04) **Going Correction** 0.0s/f (Good)
WFA 3 from 4yo 11lb 13 Ran SP% 118.2
Speed ratings (Par 100): **105,103,94,91,90 90,89,87,87,84 83,80,78**
CSF £20.54 TOTE £5.40: £1.60, £1.50, £7.60; EX 23.60 Trifecta £377.90.
Owner Michael Tabor **Bred** Chelston Ireland **Trained** Newmarket, Suffolk

FOCUS
The front two pulled right away and have been rated as improving, although it's hard to pin down the exact level.

2910 WATCH RACING TV IN STUNNING HD H'CAP 5f
4:05 (4:10) (Class 3) (0-90,91) 3-Y-O+ £9,703 (£2,887; £1,443; £721) Stalls Centre

Form RPR

6-21 1 **Venturous (IRE)**[44] 1597 6-9-5 80 RobbieDowney 9 91
(David Barron) hld up in tch: hdwy and briefly short of room appr fnl f: rdn and kpt on wl to ld towards fin 9/1

65-1 2 ¾ **Makanah**[16] 2421 4-9-11 86 PaulHanagan 8 94
(Julie Camacho) trckd ldrs: hung repeatedly lft fr over 1f out: rdn to ld ins fnl f: kpt on but hdd towards fin (jockey said gelding hung left throughout) 7/2[1]

5520 3 1¼ **Nibras Again**[19] 2294 5-9-0 75 GrahamLee 3 79
(Paul Midgley) hld up in tch: pushed along 2f out: rdn and kpt on fnl f: wnt 3rd towards fin 6/1[2]

24-1 4 ½ **Bossipop**[32] 1895 6-9-8 83 (b) DavidAllan 5 85
(Tim Easterby) prom: rdn 2f out: one pce fnl f 10/1

-204 5 nk **Blue De Vega (GER)**[16] 2403 6-10-2 91 JimCrowley 1 92
(Robert Cowell) hld up in tch: pushed along over 2f out: rdn and kpt on fnl f: nvr threatened ldrs 7/2[1]

1-53 6 ¾ **Merry Banter**[26] 2030 5-9-6 84 BenRobinson(3) 10 82
(Paul Midgley) led: rdn 2f out: hdd ins fnl f: wknd 13/2[3]

2-00 7 nse **Requinto Dawn (IRE)**[16] 2416 4-9-0 75 (p) PaddyMathers 2 73
(Richard Fahey) dwlt: hld up: pushed along over 2f out: kpt on ins fnl f: nvr threatened 16/1

00-0 8 ¾ **Soie D'Leau**[32] 1892 7-10-2 91 TonyHamilton 4 86
(Linda Stubbs) chsd ldrs: rdn over 1f out: wknd ins fnl f 25/1

-050 9 ½ **Haddaf (IRE)**[15] 2442 4-9-12 87 (v[1]) CamHardie 7 80
(Robert Cowell) in tch: pushed along and lost pl 3f out: sn struggling (jockey said saddle slipped) 22/1

-242 10 shd **Bowson Fred**[16] 2421 7-9-4 79 (p[1]) NathanEvans 11 72
(Michael Easterby) trckd ldrs: rdn over 2f out: wknd fnl f 10/1

58.05s (-0.45) **Going Correction** 0.0s/f (Good) 10 Ran SP% 114.3
Speed ratings (Par 107): **103,101,99,99,98 97,97,96,95,95**
CSF £39.74 CT £210.40 TOTE £11.50: £2.60, £1.40, £2.70; EX 50.30 Trifecta £272.10.
Owner Laurence O'Kane/Harrowgate BloodstockLtd **Bred** John Doyle **Trained** Maunby, N Yorks

FOCUS
A fair sprint and the form looks sound.

2911 RACING TV STRAIGHT MILE FILLIES' H'CAP (RACING UK STRAIGHT MILE SERIES QUALIFIER) 7f 219y
4:35 (4:37) (Class 5) (0-70,68) 4-Y-O+
£4,075 (£1,212; £606; £303; £300; £300) Stalls Centre

Form RPR

0431 1 **La Sioux (IRE)**[18] 2330 5-8-12 64 SebastianWoods(5) 4 71
(Richard Fahey) trckd ldrs: rdn to ld over 1f out: hung lft: kpt on 9/4[1]

50-0 2 1 **Verdigris (IRE)**[19] 2290 4-9-0 61 TomEaves 12 66
(Ruth Carr) hld up: racd keenly: hdwy and trckd ldrs 3f out: rdn to chal 1f out: kpt on 33/1

0410 3 1 **Midnight Vixen**[20] 2241 5-8-9 56 (p) AndrewMullen 10 59
(Ben Haslam) hld up: pushed along over 1f out: rdn and hung lft 1f out: kpt on: wnt 3rd fnl 50yds 14/1

200- 4 1½ **Elysee Star**[198] 8830 4-7-13 50 ow1 PaulaMuir(5) 7 50
(Ben Haslam) hld up: pushed along over 2f out: hdwy over 1f out: kpt on same pce fnl f 8/1

00-5 5 1 **Dominannie (IRE)**[33] 1850 6-7-13 49 oh3 JaneElliott(3) 9 46
(Ron Barr) midfield: rdn 2f out: kpt on same pce fnl f 18/1

0000 6 ½ **Dutch Melody**[20] 2244 5-7-11 49 oh4 ow2 VictorSantos(7) 5 47
(Lucinda Egerton) prom: rdn over 2f out: outpcd over 1f out and no threat after 100/1

55-0 7 hd **Rosy Ryan (IRE)**[10] 2585 9-8-5 52 CamHardie 1 47
(Tina Jackson) trckd ldrs: rdn over 2f out: no ex fnl f 16/1

6-02 8 ¾ **Kwanza**[20] 2244 4-8-13 60 PJMcDonald 3 54
(Mark Johnston) led: rdn over 2f out: hdd over 1f out: wknd ins fnl f 9/2[2]

2203 9 1¾ **Elixsoft (IRE)**[20] 2246 4-9-7 68 (p) GrahamLee 6 58
(Roger Fell) trckd ldrs: rdn 2f out: wknd fnl f 5/1[3]

4004 10 3½ **Alexandrakollontai (IRE)**[33] 1850 9-9-1 67 (b) ConnorMurtagh(5) 11 49
(Alistair Whillans) hld up: rdn over 2f out: wknd over 1f out (trainer's rep said mare had a breathing problem) 8/1

0005 11 2¼ **Tarnhelm**[17] 2376 4-8-6 53 (h) NathanEvans 8 29
(Wilf Storey) hld up: rdn over 2f out: wknd over 1f out (trainer said filly may not have faced the use of a different bridle) 14/1

1m 38.13s (1.53) **Going Correction** 0.0s/f (Good) 11 Ran SP% 116.3
Speed ratings (Par 100): **92,91,90,88,87 87,86,86,84,80 78**
CSF £90.13 CT £878.17 TOTE £3.50: £1.40, £9.30, £3.60; EX 89.20 Trifecta £556.30.
Owner Mrs Una Towell **Bred** P J Towell **Trained** Musley Bank, N Yorks

The Form Book Flat 2019, Raceform Ltd, Newbury, RG14 5SJ

FOCUS
Moderate form but a pb from the winner.

2912 RACING TV PROFITS RETURNED TO RACING MEDIAN AUCTION MAIDEN STKS — 7f 219y

5:05 (5:10) (Class 6) 3-5-Y-O — **£3,881** (£1,155; £577; £288) **Stalls** Centre

Form — RPR

1 **Kirstenbosch** 3-8-11 0 .... DanielMuscutt 3 78+
(James Fanshawe) *midfield: smooth hdwy 2f out: pushed along to ld ins fnl f: rdn and kpt on wl to draw clr* **7/1[3]**

0 **2** 3 ½ **Universal Effect**[23] 2103 3-8-11 0 ....(h) StevieDonohoe 12 66
(David Lanigan) *midfield: hdwy and trckd ldrs over 2f out: rdn appr fnl f: kpt on: wnt 2nd post* **33/1**

3 shd **Don't Jump George (IRE)** 4-10-0 0 ....(t[1]) RossaRyan 8 74
(Shaun Lycett) *led narrowly: rdn 2f out: hung lft appr fnl f: hdd ins fnl f: one pce: lost 2nd post* **11/2[2]**

632 **4** 2 **Puzzle**[18] 2334 3-9-2 74 .... PJMcDonald 4 66
(Richard Hughes) *trckd ldrs: pushed along 2f out: n.m.r appr fnl f: rdn and one pce ins fnl f (vet said gelding had wound outside of right cannon)* **15/8[1]**

00-6 **5** 1 **The Rutland Rebel (IRE)**[22] 2147 3-9-2 68 .... GrahamLee 11 64
(Micky Hammond) *trckd ldrs: rdn over 2f out: no ex ins fnl f* **12/1**

0500 **6** 7 **Henrietta's Dream**[9] 2633 5-9-9 42 .... TomEaves 2 46
(John Wainwright) *hld up: sme late hdwy: nvr threatened* **200/1**

60- **7** 1 ½ **Calevade (IRE)**[194] 8922 3-9-2 0 .... AndrewMullen 7 45
(Ben Haslam) *hld up: nvr threatened* **33/1**

0- **8** ½ **Coco Motion (IRE)**[342] 3714 3-9-2 0 .... RobbieDowney 5 43
(Michael Dods) *trckd ldrs: rdn and losing pl whn bit short of room over 1f out: sn wknd* **18/1**

9 1 **Fasterkhani** 3-9-2 0 .... AndrewElliott 9 41
(Philip Kirby) *hld up: sn pushed along: nvr threatened* **66/1**

6- **10** nk **Gordalan**[226] 7987 3-9-2 0 .... CliffordLee 13 40
(Philip Kirby) *stmbld s: sn midfield: rdn over 3f out: sn btn* **40/1**

6 **11** ¾ **Freshfield Ferris**[18] 2334 3-8-11 0 .... CamHardie 6 34
(Brian Rothwell) *a towards rr (vet said filly lost left fore shoe)* **300/1**

06 **12** 4 ½ **Pandora's Minder**[20] 2243 3-8-4 0 .... VictorSantos(7) 1 23
(Lucinda Egerton) *pressed ldr: racd keenly: rdn over 2f out: wknd over 1f out* **300/1**

1m 39.25s (2.65) **Going Correction** 0.0s/f (Good) — **12 Ran SP% 86.6**
WFA 3 from 4yo+ 12lb
Speed ratings (Par 101): **86,82,82,80,79 72,70,70,69,69 68,63**
CSF £120.94 TOTE £7.00: £1.90, £5.80, £1.40; EX 141.90 Trifecta £693.00.
Owner Fittocks Stud **Bred** Fittocks Stud **Trained** Newmarket, Suffolk
■ Risaala was withdrawn. Price at time of withdrawal 5/2. Rule 4 applies to all bets - deduction 25p in the pound

FOCUS
A maiden that didn't take a great deal of winning with the favourite disappointing and Risaala having to be withdrawn at the start.

2913 INTRODUCING RACING TV H'CAP — 1m 5f 218y

5:35 (5:36) (Class 6) (0-60,60) 3-Y-O — **£3,823** (£1,137; £568; £300; £300; £300) **Stalls** Low

Form — RPR

0-00 **1** **Agravain**[6] 2712 3-9-2 55 .... DavidAllan 7 61+
(Tim Easterby) *hld up: smooth hdwy over 2f out: trckd ldr gng wl over 1f out: pushed into ld 1f out: drvn and sustained duel w 2nd ins fnl f: hld on wl* **14/1**

006 **2** hd **Thomas Cubitt (FR)**[20] 2249 3-9-7 60 .... LouisSteward 4 65+
(Michael Bell) *in tch: hdwy and trckd ldrs over 2f out: led over 1f out: rdn and hdd narrowly 1f out: drvn and edgd lft: styd on wl* **3/1[1]**

5-53 **3** nk **Well Funded (IRE)**[22] 2150 3-9-0 53 .... PaulHanagan 11 58
(James Bethell) *hld up: pushed along and hdwy on outer 2f out: drvn and styd on wl fnl f* **13/2[3]**

60-4 **4** 2 ½ **Victoriano (IRE)**[46] 1555 3-9-2 60 ....(b) ThomasGreatrex(5) 9 62
(Archie Watson) *hld up in rr: sn pushed along: hrd drvn 4f out: bhd tl styd on fr over 1f out* **12/1**

04-0 **5** 4 ½ **Blowing Dixie**[18] 2343 3-9-7 60 .... AdamMcNamara 6 56
(Roger Charlton) *midfield: rdn along 3f out: no imp* **7/2[2]**

-234 **6** 1 ¾ **Tabou Beach Boy**[22] 2150 3-9-3 56 ....(p[1]) NathanEvans 8 50+
(Michael Easterby) *prom: rdn to chal strly over 2f out: wknd appr fnl f* **8/1**

04-4 **7** 1 **Swerved (IRE)**[29] 1972 3-9-4 60 .... BenRobinson(3) 3 52
(Ollie Pears) *trckd ldrs: rdn over 2f out: wknd appr fnl f* **15/2**

00-0 **8** 2 **Langholm (IRE)**[18] 2337 3-8-7 53 ....(t[1]) CianMacRedmond(7) 5 43+
(Declan Carroll) *led: rdn 3f out: hdd over 1f out: wknd* **28/1**

00-0 **9** 4 ½ **Lucky Circle**[18] 2341 3-8-13 52 .... CliffordLee 1 36
(David Evans) *trckd ldrs: rdn over 3f out: wknd 2f out* **28/1**

0-40 **10** 2 ½ **Spiritual Boy (IRE)**[13] 2517 3-9-3 56 .... DavidNolan 12 37
(David O'Meara) *hld up in rr: rdn and hdwy over 3f out: wknd over 1f out* **12/1**

0-50 **11** 2 ½ **Surrey Breeze (IRE)**[66] 1221 3-9-4 57 ....(b[1]) AndrewMullen 2 34+
(Archie Watson) *trckd ldrs: rdn along over 3f out: wknd over 2f out* **16/1**

3m 2.74s (-4.26) **Going Correction** 0.0s/f (Good) — **11 Ran SP% 118.3**
Speed ratings (Par 97): **108,107,107,106,103 102,102,101,98,97 95**
CSF £56.16 CT £306.63 TOTE £17.50: £4.70, £1.80, £2.30; EX 79.50 Trifecta £465.40.
Owner Geoff & Sandra Turnbull **Bred** Elwick Stud **Trained** Great Habton, N Yorks

FOCUS
Moderate 3yo staying form, but a few of these can progress throughout the year.
T/Jkpt: Not Won T/Plt: £71.80 to a £1 stake. Pool: £63,543.83 - 645.47 winning units T/Qpdt: £41.60 to a £1 stake. Pool: £5,220.83 - 92.76 winning units **Andrew Sheret**

2685 WINDSOR (R-H)

Monday, May 20

OFFICIAL GOING: Good (good to firm in places; 7.5)
Wind: Light, behind Weather: Fine but cloudy

2914 FOLLOW AT THE RACES ON TWITTER H'CAP — 1m 3f 99y

5:30 (5:31) (Class 5) (0-75,75) 3-Y-O — **£3,752** (£1,116; £557; £300; £300; £300) **Stalls** Low

Form — RPR

6-5 **1** **Earl Of Harrow**[13] 2511 3-8-11 65 .... OisinMurphy 10 74
(Mick Channon) *dwlt: hld up in 7th: prog 3f out towards outer: drvn to ld over 1f out: edgd rt fnl f: hld on (trainer's rep said, regarding the apparent improvement in form, that gelding has strengthened up over the winter and he felt that he was suited by the trip)* **11/1**

6-00 **2** nk **Monsieur Lambrays**[16] 2406 3-9-3 71 ....(p[1]) JackMitchell 6 79
(Tom Clover) *tended to run in snatches: in tch in midfield: rdn and clsd towards outer over 2f out: chal over 1f out: nt qckn and carried sltly rt ins fnl f: jst hld* **15/2**

6-52 **3** 3 ¾ **Gold Fleece**[103] 615 3-9-0 68 .... JamesDoyle 5 70
(Hugo Palmer) *hld up in last trio: prog 3f out: rdn to chal towards outer over 1f out: one pce fnl f* **8/1**

03-4 **4** 1 ¼ **Vexed**[20] 2258 3-9-5 73 .... JamieSpencer 8 73
(David Simcock) *stdd s: hld up in last: gng easily but lot to do over 2f out: taken to wd outside over 1f out and drvn: tk 4th fnl f but nvr any ch* **5/2[1]**

-352 **5** nk **Mr Zoom Zoom**[14] 2485 3-9-2 70 ....(b[1]) RobertHavlin 9 69
(Luke McJannet) *trckd ldng pair: led over 2f out gng strly but racd against nr side rail: hdd & wknd over 1f out* **7/2[2]**

44-5 **6** 4 ½ **Natty Night**[19] 2299 3-9-7 75 .... MartinDwyer 7 66
(William Muir) *pressed ldrs: rdn to chal wl over 2f out tl wknd over 1f out* **9/1**

-365 **7** 2 ¼ **Cromwell**[16] 2407 3-8-5 59 .... RaulDaSilva 1 47
(Luke Dace) *dwlt: rcvrd to chse ldrs after 4f: rdn wl over 2f out: styd against rail and wknd wl over 1f out* **16/1**

03-0 **8** 10 **Ring Cycle**[130] 156 3-9-1 72 .... GaryMahon(3) 3 43
(Sylvester Kirk) *hld up in last trio: urged along 4f out: sn struggling: no ch fnl 2f* **25/1**

-333 **9** 2 **Bolt N Brown**[54] 1351 3-8-13 67 .... ShaneKelly 2 34
(Gay Kelleway) *t.k.h: pressed ldr: led 1/2-way: hdd & wknd qckly over 2f out* **25/1**

01-5 **10** 34 **Sky Cross (IRE)**[23] 2120 3-9-1 69 .... SilvestreDeSousa 4
(Mark Johnston) *led to 1/2-way: w ldr to 3f out: wknd rapidly: t.o (trainer's rep had no explanation for the performance)* **7/1[3]**

2m 27.25s (-2.45) **Going Correction** -0.15s/f (Firm) — **10 Ran SP% 118.1**
Speed ratings (Par 99): **102,101,99,98,97 94,93,85,84,59**
CSF £92.00 CT £699.26 TOTE £10.80: £3.60, £2.30, £2.90; EX 79.20 Trifecta £1193.90.
Owner Peter Taplin & Partner **Bred** Norman Court Stud **Trained** West Ilsley, Berks

FOCUS
After a dry weekend, the ground for this overcast evening meeting was on the fast side. Rail realignment added 32yds to official distance of this run-of-the-mill handicap, which was run at a fair gallop. The first two came from off the pace and have been rated as improving.

2915 BRITISH STALLION STUDS EBF FILLIES' NOVICE STKS (PLUS 10 RACE) — 6f 12y

6:00 (6:04) (Class 4) 2-Y-O — **£6,301** (£1,886; £943; £472; £235) **Stalls** Centre

Form — RPR

1 **Theory Of Time (IRE)** 2-9-0 0 .... JamesDoyle 3 86+
(Charlie Appleby) *trckd ldr: led over 1f out: nudged out fnl f: promising debut* **1/1[1]**

2 1 ¼ **Star In The Making** 2-9-0 0 .... AdamKirby 5 80+
(Clive Cox) *chsd ldrs: pushed along sn after 1/2-way: styd on to take 2nd fnl f: no threat to wnr: shaped wl* **12/1**

5 **3** 2 **Love Love**[22] 2138 2-9-0 0 .... SilvestreDeSousa 1 74
(Richard Hannon) *led to over 1f out: one pce but clr of rest* **7/2[2]**

4 2 ½ **Rosadora (IRE)** 2-9-0 0 .... HarryBentley 11 67+
(Ralph Beckett) *in tch: prog to chse ldrs 1/2-way: tk 4th over 1f out but nt on terms* **8/1[3]**

5 5 **Santorini Sal** 2-9-0 0 .... KieranO'Neill 10 52
(John Bridger) *s.i.s: t.k.h and rn green in last quartet: prog 1/2-way: pushed along and kpt on to take modest 5th fnl f* **100/1**

6 ½ **Where Next Jo** 2-8-7 0 .... GinaMangan(7) 7 50
(David Evans) *in tch in midfield: pushed along and no prog over 2f out: fdd* **50/1**

7 ½ **Fashion Free** 2-9-0 0 .... EdwardGreatrex 13 49
(Archie Watson) *spd to press ldrs 4f: wknd* **12/1**

0 **8** 2 ½ **Shani**[11] 2561 2-9-0 0 .... OisinMurphy 6 41
(David Evans) *prom to 1/2-way: sn rdn and lost pl* **18/1**

9 ¾ **Ebony Adams** 2-9-0 0 .... MartinDwyer 9 39
(Brian Meehan) *sn pushed along towards rr: nvr any prog* **33/1**

10 ¾ **Lethal Talent** 2-9-0 0 .... RobHornby 2 37
(Jonathan Portman) *dwlt: a in last quartet: nvr any prog* **14/1**

11 ¾ **Xquisite (IRE)** 2-9-0 0 .... ShaneKelly 8 35
(J S Moore) *dwlt: rn green in last quartet: no prog* **100/1**

12 5 **Resplendent Rose** 2-9-0 0 .... LiamKeniry 4 20
(Michael Madgwick) *dwlt: a in last quartet and bhd* **100/1**

1m 11.98s (-0.12) **Going Correction** -0.15s/f (Firm) — **12 Ran SP% 118.5**
Speed ratings (Par 92): **94,92,89,86,79 79,78,75,74,73 72,65**
CSF £15.19 TOTE £2.00: £1.10, £3.00, £1.30; EX 13.80 Trifecta £39.00.
Owner Godolphin **Bred** Godolphin **Trained** Newmarket, Suffolk

FOCUS
An interesting fillies' novice and a truly run affair, which should produce a few future winners.

2916 WEATHERBYS HAMILTON STKS (REGISTERED AS THE LEISURE STAKES) (LISTED RACE) — 6f 12y

6:30 (6:34) (Class 1) 3-Y-O+ — **£20,982** (£7,955; £3,981; £1,983; £995; £499) **Stalls** Centre

Form — RPR

20-1 **1** **Dream Of Dreams (IRE)**[25] 2062 5-9-5 109 .... RyanMoore 3 115
(Sir Michael Stoute) *trckd ldng pair: waiting for a gap 2f out tl eased out jst over 1f out: urged along and r.o to ld last 100yds: quite decisive* **11/4[2]**

10-0 **2** 1 **Glorious Journey**[9] 2609 4-9-5 108 .... JamesDoyle 4 112
(Charlie Appleby) *pressed ldr: led over 1f out: hrd rdn fnl f: hdd and outpcd last 100yds* **7/2[3]**

The Form Book Flat 2019, Raceform Ltd, Newbury, RG14 5SJ

310- **3** *1* **The Tin Man**[212] 8405 7-9-12 117........................ OisinMurphy 2 116
(James Fanshawe) *hld up in last pair: trapped on rail over 2f out tl swtchd lft wl over 1f out: rdn to cl on ldrs fnl f: one pce last 100yds* **11/10**[1]

21-6 **4** *½* **Foxtrot Lady**[25] 2062 4-9-0 100........................ DavidProbert 6 102
(Andrew Balding) *led: sn racd against rail: hdd and nt qckn over 1f out: one pce after* **20/1**

053- **5** *3¾* **Spring Loaded (IRE)**[226] 7974 7-9-5 106........................ AdamKirby 7 95
(Paul D'Arcy) *trckd ldrs: shkn up briefly 2f out: wknd jst over 1f out* **16/1**

11-5 **6** *½* **Baron Bolt**[25] 2062 6-9-5 108........................ HarryBentley 5 94
(Paul Cole) *dwlt: hld up in last pair: rdn on outer 2f out: no prog over 1f out: wknd* **33/1**

1m 10.75s (-1.35) **Going Correction** -0.15s/f (Firm) **6** Ran SP% **110.1**
Speed ratings (Par 111): **103,101,100,99,94 94**
CSF £12.20 TOTE £3.50: £1.50, £2.20; EX 12.00 Trifecta £22.00.
Owner Saeed Suhail **Bred** Prostock Ltd **Trained** Newmarket, Suffolk

FOCUS
A decent renewal of this Listed sprint, although they did not go a great gallop. A small pb from the winner, with the runner-up to form.

2917 WINDSOR'S 1866 RESTAURANT H'CAP 6f 12y

7:00 (7:02) (Class 3) (0-95,95) 4-Y-O+ **£7,246** (£2,168; £1,084; £542; £270) **Stalls Centre**

Form RPR

6220 **1** **Equitation**[10] 2568 5-8-8 82........................(t) OisinMurphy 2 91
(Stuart Williams) *nt that wl away: settled in last pair: effrt and waiting for room 2f out: urged along and prog over 1f out: led last 75yds: styd on wl* **5/2**[1]

-460 **2** *¾* **Danzan (IRE)**[91] 786 4-9-5 93........................ DavidProbert 6 99
(Andrew Balding) *led to over 4f out: chsd ldr: rdn to ld jst over 2f out: drvn fnl f: hdd and one pce last 75yds* **8/1**

23-2 **3** *hd* **Goodnight Girl (IRE)**[39] 1712 4-9-4 92........................ RobHornby 4 97
(Jonathan Portman) *trckd ldrs: swtchd rt and effrt 2f out: clsd on ldrs fnl f: styd on u.p but jst outpcd nr fin* **9/2**[2]

466- **4** *¾* **Show Stealer**[242] 7474 6-8-13 87........................(p) DavidEgan 5 90
(Rae Guest) *hld up on outer: rdn and prog over 1f out: styd on same pce fnl f: nvr able to chal* **12/1**

05-0 **5** *2* **Helvetian**[16] 2403 4-9-1 89........................ CharlesBishop 9 86
(Mick Channon) *t.k.h: hld up towards outer: rdn 2f out: no prog fnl f* **25/1**

000- **6** *1* **Oeil De Tigre (FR)**[240] 7510 8-8-3 84........................ ElishaWhittington(7) 10 77
(Tony Carroll) *tk fierce hold: plld way into ld over 4f out: hdd jst over 2f out: wknd fnl f (jockey said gelding ran too free)* **50/1**

0-24 **7** *¾* **Storm Over (IRE)**[25] 2061 5-9-4 92........................ HarryBentley 8 83
(George Scott) *in tch: drvn wl over 1f out and chsng ldrs: wknd fnl f* **10/1**

0334 **8** *½* **Tropics (USA)**[25] 2062 11-9-7 95........................(h) RobertWinston 7 86
(Dean Ivory) *prom: rdn to chal wl over 1f out: wknd qckly fnl f and eased (jockey said gelding stopped quickly)* **16/1**

0-52 **9** *1¾* **Vegas Boy (IRE)**[10] 2568 4-8-13 87........................(t) NicolaCurrie 3 71
(Jamie Osborne) *t.k.h: hld up and racd against rail: rdn and no prog 2f out: wknd over 1f out (jockey said gelding ran too free)* **11/2**[3]

00-4 **10** *1* **Victory Angel (IRE)**[15] 2442 5-9-4 92........................ JamesDoyle 1 73
(Robert Cowell) *sn hld up in last: checked 2f out: shuffled along and no prog: nvr in it* **6/1**

1m 10.75s (-1.35) **Going Correction** -0.15s/f (Firm) **10** Ran SP% **116.0**
Speed ratings (Par 107): **103,102,101,100,98 96,95,95,92,91**
CSF £23.11 CT £85.89 TOTE £3.30: £1.20, £2.40, £1.70; EX 26.80 Trifecta £178.10.
Owner A Lyons & T W Morley **Bred** Newsells Park Stud **Trained** Newmarket, Suffolk

FOCUS
A decent sprint handicap; straightforward form.

2918 SKY SPORTS RACING ON SKY 415 FILLIES' NOVICE STKS (PLUS 10 RACE) 5f 21y

7:30 (7:33) (Class 4) 2-Y-O **£4,787** (£1,424; £711; £355) **Stalls Centre**

Form RPR

1 **Divine Spirit** 2-9-0........................ JamesDoyle 2 88+
(Charlie Appleby) *free to post: trckd ldrs: swtchd to rail to cl over 1f out: led ins fnl f: sn clr: easily* **4/5**[1]

2 *1¾* **Pink Sands (IRE)** 2-9-0........................ OisinMurphy 3 79
(William Haggas) *led: shkn up over 1f out: rn green and hdd ins fnl f: outpcd* **11/4**[2]

46 **3** *2¼* **Ocasio Cortez (IRE)**[10] 2594 2-9-0........................ TomMarquand 7 71
(Richard Hannon) *pressed ldr: rdn over 1f out: lost 2nd and one pce fnl f* **10/1**[3]

4 *½* **Dynamighty** 2-9-0........................ HarryBentley 5 69
(Richard Spencer) *cl up: shkn up over 1f out: outpcd sn after: kpt on* **25/1**

543 **5** *2¼* **Bainne Dubh**[22] 2138 2-8-9........................ ThoreHammerHansen(5) 10 61
(Bill Turner) *chsd ldrs: shkn up wl over 1f out: wknd fnl f* **14/1**

6 *¾* **Jungle Boogaloo (IRE)** 2-9-0........................ CharlesBishop 4 58
(Ali Stronge) *slowly away: t.k.h and sn in tch: cl enough 2f out: shkn up and wknd jst over 1f out* **50/1**

06 **7** *2* **Birkie Queen (IRE)**[10] 2565 2-9-0........................ LiamKeniry 1 51
(J S Moore) *hld up in midfield: gng bttr than many 1/2-way: reminders over 1f out and racd against rail: no prog* **100/1**

8 *hd* **Candid (IRE)** 2-9-0........................ RobHornby 8 50
(Jonathan Portman) *in tch: pushed along and no prog wl over 1f out: fdd* **50/1**

9 *6* **Company Minx (IRE)** 2-9-0........................ DavidProbert 6 29
(Clive Cox) *rn green and sn wl off the pce in rr* **10/1**[3]

10 *1¾* **Red Cinderella** 2-9-0........................ NicolaCurrie 9 23
(David Evans) *slowly away: a wl bhd* **20/1**

11 *6* **Casi Casi** 2-9-0........................ LiamJones 11
(Charlie Wallis) *spd on outer: green and wknd qckly sn after 1/2-way* **50/1**

5 **12** *4½* **Ask Siri (IRE)**[17] 2362 2-9-0........................ KieranO'Neill 12
(John Bridger) *racd v awkwardly and hanging bdly lft: sn wl bhd* **100/1**

59.56s (-0.54) **Going Correction** -0.15s/f (Firm) **12** Ran SP% **123.5**
Speed ratings (Par 92): **98,95,91,90,87 86,82,82,72,70 60,53**
CSF £2.97 TOTE £1.90: £1.10, £1.20, £2.70; EX 3.50 Trifecta £14.40.
Owner Godolphin **Bred** Saleh Al Homaizi & Imad Al Sagar **Trained** Newmarket, Suffolk

FOCUS
Possibly a deep fillies' novice and the winner impressed. This has been rated positively.

2919 MPM FLOORING LTD. MAIDEN FILLIES' STKS 1m 31y

8:00 (8:02) (Class 5) 3-Y-O+ **£3,752** (£1,116; £557; £278) **Stalls Low**

Form RPR

34 **1** **Bighearted**[20] 2236 3-8-11........................ CameronNoble(3) 11 77
(Michael Bell) *pressed ldr: narrow ld 3f out: drvn over 1f out: hld on wl* **20/1**

4-2 **2** *nk* **Birdcage Walk**[14] 2488 3-9-0........................(h) JamesDoyle 10 76
(Hugo Palmer) *mde most to 3f out: pressed wnr after: drvn over 1f out: kpt on but nt qckn ins fnl f* **3/1**[2]

2 **3** *shd* **Ocean Paradise**[37] 1755 3-9-0........................(h) RyanMoore 3 76
(Charles Hills) *trckd ldng pair: shkn up over 2f out: swtchd rt over 1f out: drvn fnl f: kpt on but nvr quite got there* **15/8**[1]

64 **4** *¾* **Specialise**[14] 2488 3-9-0........................ DavidEgan 2 74
(Roger Varian) *hld up in 8th: swtchd lft to outer wl over 1f out and prog: shkn up and styd on fnl f: nrst fin* **8/1**

5 *½* **Society Guest (IRE)** 3-9-0........................ CharlesBishop 6 73
(Mick Channon) *hld up in 9th: pushed along over 2f out: prog over 1f out: styd on fnl f: nrst fin* **66/1**

6 *shd* **Magical Rhythms (USA)** 3-9-0........................ RobertHavlin 4 72+
(John Gosden) *s.i.s: wl off the pce in last trio: stl same pl 2f out and pushed along: styd on takingly fnl f (jockey said filly was denied a clear run)* **12/1**

7 *½* **Quiet Note** 3-9-0........................ OisinMurphy 13 71
(Saeed bin Suroor) *dwlt but sn trckd ldng pair: shkn up 2f out: nt qckn over 1f out: one pce and lost pls fnl f (jockey said filly ran too free)* **9/2**[3]

0 **8** *¾* **Forbidden Dance**[14] 2488 3-9-0........................ DavidProbert 5 69
(Hughie Morrison) *trckd ldrs disputing 5th: pushed along over 2f out: no prog over 1f out: lost pls but stl kpt on fnl f* **50/1**

9 *3* **Bated Beauty (IRE)**[360] 3073 4-9-12........................ TomQueally 7 65
(John Butler) *hld up in 10th: rdn over 2f out: no prog over 1f out: kpt on nr fin* **100/1**

6-4 **10** *2* **Rachel Zane (IRE)**[21] 2210 3-9-0........................(h) PatCosgrave 12 57
(Hugo Palmer) *hld up in 7th: pushed along over 2f out: no prog and wknd over 1f out* **40/1**

11 *1¼* **Rewrite The Stars (IRE)** 3-9-0........................ TomMarquand 1 54
(James Tate) *slowly away: a in last trio and nvr a factor* **25/1**

12 *4½* **Dandy Lass (IRE)** 3-9-0........................ LiamKeniry 9 43
(Richard Phillips) *dwlt: a in last trio and bhd* **100/1**

13 *1¾* **Distant Image (IRE)** 3-9-0........................ HarryBentley 8 39
(Saeed bin Suroor) *chsd ldrs but racd awkwardly: wknd 2f out: heavily eased whn btn (jockey said filly lost its action)* **12/1**

1m 43.73s (-0.77) **Going Correction** -0.15s/f (Firm)
WFA 3 from 4yo 12lb **13** Ran SP% **120.9**
Speed ratings (Par 100): **97,96,96,95,95 95,94,94,91,89 87,83,81**
CSF £78.43 TOTE £18.90: £4.80, £1.40, £1.30; EX 70.90 Trifecta £180.80.
Owner M E Perlman **Bred** R Frisby **Trained** Newmarket, Suffolk

FOCUS
Rail realignment added 32yds to the distance. This is usually a good fillies' maiden but the field finished too compressed to rate the winner up to the usual standard.
T/Plt: £20.80 to a £1 stake. Pool: £93,833.50 - 3,291.62 winning units T/Qpdt: £4.40 to a £1 stake. Pool: £12,041.55 - 1,981.99 winning units **Jonathan Neesom**

2920- 2923a (VOID NUMBERS)

2281 **BRIGHTON** (L-H)

Tuesday, May 21

OFFICIAL GOING: Good to firm (good in places; watered) changing to good to firm after race 1 (2.00)
Wind: light, half behind Weather: sunny

2924 CLODHOPPERS (LEE) & THE DONOVAN NEWLYWEDS CLASSIFIED STKS 5f 60y

2:00 (2:02) (Class 6) 3-Y-O+

£3,105 (£924; £461; £300; £300; £300) **Stalls Centre**

Form RPR

0-00 **1** **Pocket Warrior**[50] 1477 8-9-7 45........................(t) TomMarquand 8 53
(Paul D'Arcy) *off the pce in rr of main gp: rdn over 2f out: sme prog and swtchd rt ent fnl f: styd on strly to ld towards fin (trainer said, regarding improved form shown, the gelding benefited from a drop down in trip)* **16/1**

0004 **2** *1¼* **Waneen (IRE)**[6] 2728 6-9-7 50........................(b) LiamKeniry 11 49
(John Butler) *broke fast: led for 1f: trckd ldrs after: effrt to chse ldr over 1f out: kpt on ins fnl f: nt match pce of wnr cl home but snatched 2nd last stride* **5/2**[2]

66-0 **3** *shd* **Glyder**[29] 1987 5-9-7 47........................(p[1]) RoystonFfrench 1 48
(John Holt) *t.k.h: chsd ldrs tl led 2f out: sn rdn: kpt on u.p ins fnl f: hdd and lost 2 pls towards fin (jockey said mare ran too free)* **8/1**

0000 **4** *1½* **Tina Teaspoon**[20] 2295 5-9-7 35........................(h) JoeyHaynes 5 43
(Derek Shaw) *stdd s: hld up in midfield: hdwy u.p to chse ldrs and edging lft 1f out: no ex and one pce fnl 100yds* **66/1**

6-60 **5** *½* **Ask The Guru**[80] 986 9-9-7 46........................(p w) KierenFox 12 41
(Michael Attwater) *chsd ldrs: effrt ent fnl 2f: edgd lft u.p over 1f out: kpt on same pce and no imp ins fnl f (jockey said gelding hung right handed in the first half of the race)* **10/1**

0-30 **6** *1* **Poppy Jag (IRE)**[20] 2295 4-9-2 45........................(b) ThoreHammerHansen(5) 9 38
(Kevin Frost) *midfield: effrt over 2f out: edgd lft u.p over 1f out: kpt on ins fnl f: nvr threatened ldrs* **13/2**[3]

0000 **7** *1½* **Milldean Panther**[21] 2240 3-8-13 48........................(b[1]) TomQueally 6 30
(Suzi Best) *off the pce in rr of main gp: effrt 2f out: kpt on ins fnl f: nvr trbld ldrs* **16/1**

0-00 **8** *1* **Hornby**[80] 986 4-9-7 38........................ CharlieBennett 7 29
(Michael Attwater) *midfield: effrt but no imp u.p over 1f out: wl hld and plugged on same pce ins fnl f* **50/1**

16-3 **9** *1¾* **Cool Strutter (IRE)**[20] 2287 7-9-7 50........................(p) AdamKirby 10 23+
(John Spearing) *anticipated s: hit gate and dwlt: rousted along and hdwy to ld after 1f: hdd 2f out and lost pl u.p over 1f out: wknd ins fnl f* **2/1**[1]

0-60 **10** *2¼* **Two Faced**[26] 2063 3-8-6 43........................ MorganCole(7) 3 12
(Lydia Pearce) *midfield: pushed along and no hdwy over 1f out: wknd ins fnl f* **40/1**

3630 **11** *7* **Storm Lightning**[6] 2728 10-9-0 45........................ CierenFallon(7) 4
(Mark Brisbourne) *a outpcd in rr (trainer said the gelding was unsuited by the good to firm, good in places ground. he added that as the gelding is getting older he is preferring artificial surfaces)* **9/1**

1m 2.73s (-0.27) **Going Correction** -0.225s/f (Firm)
WFA 3 from 4yo+ 8lb **11** Ran SP% **123.1**
Speed ratings (Par 101): **93,91,90,88,87 86,83,82,79,75 64**
CSF £58.47 TOTE £27.00: £5.70, £1.20, £2.30; EX 97.10 Trifecta £531.90.
Owner Mrs Bernice Cuthbert **Bred** Dr Philip J Brown **Trained** Newmarket, Suffolk
■ Hurricane Alert was withdrawn. Price at time of withdrawal 4/1. Rule 4 applies to all bets struck prior to withdrawal, but not to SP bets. Deduction - 20p in the £. New market formed.

The Form Book Flat 2019, Raceform Ltd, Newbury, RG14 5SJ

FOCUS
Not a race to dwell on. The second has been rated near his recent form.

2925 DOVES PLAYING LIVE HERE 26TH JULY NOVICE MEDIAN AUCTION STKS — 7f 211y
2:35 (2:37) (Class 5) 3-Y-O — **£3,752** (£1,116; £557; £278) **Stalls** Centre

Form — RPR

2- **1** **Dudley's Boy**[287] 5831 3-9-0 **0** ... JoshuaBryan(3) 7 — 85+
(Andrew Balding) *chsd ldr and travelled strly: effrt and rdn to ld over 1f out: sn clr and r.o strly ins fnl f: v readily* **1/1[1]**

63-4 **2** 7 **Voltaic**[23] 2139 3-9-3 **76** ... HarryBentley 6 — 69
(Paul Cole) *t.k.h: hld up in tch in midfield: effrt ent fnl 2f: chsd clr wnr and hung lft 1f out: plugged on but no imp fnl f* **6/4[2]**

51 **3** 3 ½ **Liliofthelamplight (IRE)**[29] 1984 3-9-5 **0** ... JoeFanning 1 — 63
(Mark Johnston) *led: hdd and rdn over 1f out: sn outpcd and btn 3rd 1f out: wknd ins fnl f* **6/1[3]**

54 **4** nk **Clap Your Hands**[56] 1344 3-8-12 **0** ... DylanHogan(5) 5 — 60
(David Simcock) *v.s.a: sn rcvrd and in tch in last pair: effrt wl over 2f out: 4th and no imp whn hung lft over 1f out: wl hld and plugged on ins fnl f* **20/1**

0 **5** 5 **Zappiness (USA)**[39] 1740 3-8-12 **0** ... JackMitchell 3 — 44
(Peter Chapple-Hyam) *stmbld leaving stalls: midfield: rdn 3f out: sn struggling and outpcd: wl btn 1f out (jockey said filly stumbled leaving the stalls)* **33/1**

0-0 **6** ½ **Je M'En Fiche**[41] 1676 3-8-12 **0** ... LiamKeniry 4 — 43
(Patrick Chamings) *chsd ldrs: rdn 3f out: sn lost pl and bhd 2f out* **66/1**

00 **7** 2 ¾ **I'm Brian**[28] 2023 3-9-3 **0** ... CharlieBennett 2 — 41
(Julia Feilden) *dwlt: hld up in last pair: rdn 3f out: sn btn and bhd* **100/1**

1m 34.33s (-2.57) **Going Correction** -0.225s/f (Firm) — **7 Ran SP% 114.5**
Speed ratings (Par 99): **103,96,92,92,87 86,83**
CSF £2.72 TOTE £1.80: £1.30, £1.10; EX 3.10 Trifecta £6.90.
Owner Ms Karen Gough **Bred** Ms Karen Gough **Trained** Kingsclere, Hants

FOCUS
They went just an ordinary pace in this modest 3yo novice event. The second has been rated close to his reappearance run.

2926 SKY SPORTS RACING ON SKY 415 H'CAP — 6f 210y
3:05 (3:06) (Class 6) (0-60,62) 3-Y-O — **£3,428** (£1,020; £509; £300; £300; £300) **Stalls** Centre

Form — RPR

00-0 **1** **Sonnetina**[39] 1726 3-9-1 **53** ... TomQueally 3 — 61
(Denis Coakley) *hld up in midfield: effrt to chse ldrs ent fnl 2f: rdn to ld and edgd rt over 1f out: clr and styd on wl ins fnl f* **9/1**

-063 **2** 2 ½ **Tarrzan (IRE)**[20] 2281 3-8-7 **52** ... CierenFallon(7) 7 — 54
(John Gallagher) *hld up in midfield: shuffled bk and nt clr run over 2f out: swtchd lft 2f out: hdwy over 1f out: chsd clr wnr ins fnl f: kpt on but nvr getting on terms (jockey said gelding hung right-handed throughout)* **8/1[3]**

0-05 **3** ¾ **Dark Poet**[18] 2357 3-9-4 **56** ... (p[1]) AdamKirby 10 — 56
(Clive Cox) *chsd ldr tl 2f out: hrd drvn and unable qck over 1f out: kpt on same pce ins fnl f* **11/4[1]**

-600 **4** 1 ½ **Melo Pearl**[54] 1383 3-8-7 **45** ... (v[1]) RoystonFfrench 4 — 41
(Mrs Ilka Gansera-Leveque) *hld up in midfield: effrt over 2f out: kpt on ins fnl f: nvr enough pce to threaten wnr* **25/1**

00-6 **5** 1 **Beg For Mercy**[115] 438 3-9-0 **52** ... CharlieBennett 5 — 45
(Michael Attwater) *chsd ldrs: effrt ent fnl 2f: unable qck u.p over 1f out: wknd ins fnl f* **40/1**

0-40 **6** nk **Rum Lad**[24] 2098 3-9-7 **62** ... GabrieleMalune(3) 1 — 54
(Ivan Furtado) *sn led: rdn and hdd over 1f out: sn outpcd by wnr and wknd ins fnl f* **9/1**

0006 **7** 1 **Frea**[18] 2357 3-8-10 **48** ... JoeFanning 12 — 39
(Harry Dunlop) *wnt rt s: in tch in midfield: no imp u.p over 1f out: kpt on same pce ins fnl f: eased towards fin* **7/1[2]**

2460 **8** ½ **Shug**[29] 1982 3-9-7 **59** ... (b[1]) LiamKeniry 6 — 47
(Ed Walker) *t.k.h: hld up towards rr: effrt and hung lft over 1f out: kpt on u.p ins fnl f: nvr trbld ldrs (vet reported gelding lost its right fore shoe)* **8/1[3]**

0-00 **9** ½ **Deerfoot**[18] 2366 3-8-4 **45** ... (b[1]) WilliamCox(3) 2 — 32
(Anthony Carson) *s.i.s: detached in last: rdn over 2f out: styd on under ins fnl f: nvr trbld ldrs (jockey said gelding was very unbalanced throughout)* **33/1**

0-00 **10** 2 ¾ **We Are All Dottie**[48] 1514 3-8-7 **45** ... JFEgan 13 — 27
(Pat Phelan) *short of room leaving stalls: hld up in rr: effrt on inner jst over 2f out: no imp and btn over 1f out: wknd ins fnl f* **66/1**

50-0 **11** 1 **Savoy Brown**[41] 1678 3-9-7 **59** ... KierenFox 8 — 40
(Michael Attwater) *broke wl: sn dropped to midfield: rdn over 2f out: sn struggling and wl btn over 1f out (trainer said the gelding was unsuited by the undulating track)* **10/1**

000- **12** 2 ½ **Lady Morpheus**[206] 8647 3-8-13 **51** ... HectorCrouch 11 — 22
(Gary Moore) *t.k.h: chsd ldrs: wnt 2nd 2f out: sn rdn and btn: wknd fnl f* **9/1**

00- **13** 4 **On The Bob**[167] 9403 3-8-8 **51** ... ThoreHammerHansen(5) 9 — 11
(Paddy Butler) *in tch in midfield: rdn over 2f out: sn struggling: bhd ins fnl f* **50/1**

4-02 **14** 14 **Global Goddess (IRE)**[111] 476 3-9-7 **59** ... (p) GeraldMosse 14
(Gay Kelleway) *wnt lft s: hld up towards rr: clsd on outer 3f out: rdn 2f out: sn btn: bhd and eased ins fnl f (jockey said filly lost its action from the road crossing)* **8/1[3]**

1m 23.44s (-0.36) **Going Correction** -0.225s/f (Firm) — **14 Ran SP% 124.3**
Speed ratings (Par 97): **95,92,91,89,88 88,86,86,85,82 81,78,74,58**
CSF £79.05 CT £263.62 TOTE £8.90: £2.50, £3.60, £1.90; EX.114.20 Trifecta £349.30.
Owner The Good Mixers **Bred** Minster Stud **Trained** West Ilsley, Berks

■ Stewards' Enquiry : Adam Kirby two-day ban: misuse of the whip (Jun 4-5)

FOCUS
A moderate 3yo handicap, run at a generous pace. The winner has been rated back to last year's form.

2927 SKY SPORTS RACING ON VIRGIN 535 H'CAP — 7f 211y
3:35 (3:35) (Class 4) (0-80,81) 3-Y-O+ — **£5,530** (£1,645; £822; £411; £300; £300) **Stalls** Centre

Form — RPR

32-6 **1** **Gin Palace**[27] 2035 3-8-9 **72** ... MartinDwyer 1 — 80
(Eve Johnson Houghton) *sn led and mde rest: pushed along 2f out: rdn and asserted over 1f out: in command and styd on strly ins fnl f* **6/1**

45-4 **2** 2 ¼ **Majestic Mac**[27] 2035 3-8-13 **76** ... CharlieBennett 4 — 79
(Hughie Morrison) *hld up in tch in last pair: effrt on inner 2f out: drvn to chse clr wnr 2f out: kpt on but no imp ins fnl f* **7/2[1]**

2223 **3** ¾ **Strawberry Jack**[22] 2200 3-8-10 **73** ... (vt[1]) HarryBentley 3 — 74
(George Scott) *chsd ldrs tl chsd wnr 6f out: hrd drvn and unable qck over 1f out: 3rd and kpt on same pce ins fnl f* **9/2[2]**

2106 **4** 1 ½ **Juanito Chico (IRE)**[6] 2739 5-10-0 **79** ... (v[1]) AdamKirby 9 — 80
(Stuart Williams) *dwlt: hld up in tch in last pair: effrt on outer over 2f out: wl hld 4th and plugged on same pce ins fnl f* **13/2**

40-1 **5** 2 ¼ **He's Our Star (IRE)**[21] 2232 4-9-8 **73** ... TomMarquand 2 — 68
(Ali Stronge) *s.i.s: sn rcvrd and in tch in midfield: chsd ldrs over 2f out: no ex u.p and wandered lft ent fnl f* **11/1**

4140 **6** hd **First Link (USA)**[20] 2273 4-9-4 **69** ... RichardKingscote 5 — 64
(Jean-Rene Auvray) *stdd s: t.k.h: hld up in tch in midfield: effrt over 2f out: unable qck and no hdwy over 1f out: wl hld fnl f* **11/2[3]**

0-43 **7** nk **Prairie Spy (IRE)**[12] 2552 3-9-4 **81** ... JoeFanning 6 — 72
(Mark Johnston) *chsd ldr for 2f: styd chsng ldrs: rdn ent fnl 2f: sn outpcd and lost pl over 1f out: bhd ins fnl f (trainer's rep had no explanation for the poor form shown)* **7/2[1]**

1m 34.51s (-2.39) **Going Correction** -0.225s/f (Firm)
WFA 3 from 4yo+ 12lb — **7 Ran SP% 114.0**
Speed ratings (Par 105): **102,99,99,97,95 95,94**
CSF £26.99 CT £102.96 TOTE £7.70: £4.90, £2.00; EX 32.00 Trifecta £109.40.
Owner Mrs Zara Campbell-Harris **Bred** Mrs Z C Campbell-Harris **Trained** Blewbury, Oxon

FOCUS
It paid to be handy in this feature handicap. It's been rated around the third.

2928 RAG'N'BONE MAN HERE LIVE 27TH JULY H'CAP — 1m 3f 198y
4:10 (4:10) (Class 5) (0-70,70) 4-Y-O+ — **£3,752** (£1,116; £557; £300; £300; £300) **Stalls** Centre

Form — RPR

0-35 **1** **King Of The Sand (IRE)**[18] 2360 4-9-7 **70** ... AdamKirby 6 — 83
(Gary Moore) *mde all and sn wl clr w runner-up: rdn ent fnl 2f: wnt clr and in command whn hung lft ins fnl f: r.o strly: heavily eased wl ins fnl f* **6/4[1]**

0312 **2** 13 **Gendarme (IRE)**[6] 2733 4-9-6 **69** ... (b) RichardKingscote 9 — 61
(Alexandra Dunn) *pressed wnr and sn wl clr: upsides ent fnl 2f: sn u.p and easily brushed aside over 1f out: wl btn but plugged on for clr 2nd ins fnl f* **7/2[2]**

530- **3** 4 **Star Of Athena**[223] 8113 4-8-13 **62** ... (h[1] w) TomMarquand 8 — 48
(Ali Stronge) *s.i.s: sn rcvrd to chse clr ldng pair: pushed along 4f out: no imp and plugged on same pce fnl 2f* **33/1**

40-0 **4** ½ **Hatsaway (IRE)**[17] 2400 8-9-1 **67** ... PaddyBradley(3) 7 — 52
(Pat Phelan) *hld up wl off the pce in last trio: effrt 3f out: drvn over 1f out: nvr getting on terms w ldrs: plugged on fnl f* **7/1**

6463 **5** 6 **Makambe (IRE)**[51] 1463 4-9-5 **68** ... JoeyHaynes 4 — 43
(Paul Howling) *restless in stalls and v.s.a: a wl off the pce in last trio: effrt over 3f out: no prog and hung lft over 1f out: nvr involved (jockey said gelding was restless in the stalls and slowly away)* **9/1**

-054 **6** 1 ¾ **Roy Rocket (FR)**[21] 2233 9-9-1 **64** ... JFEgan 1 — 37
(John Berry) *broke wl: sn restrained and racd wl off the pce in 4th: effrt u.p wl over 2f out: no prog: wknd over 1f out* **10/1**

6-00 **7** 15 **Iballisticvin**[10] 2617 6-8-9 **58** ... LiamKeniry 2 — 7
(Gary Moore) *wl off the pce in last trio: effrt 3f out: no prog and nvr involved: t.o ins fnl f* **16/1**

134- **8** 4 ½ **Highland Sky (IRE)**[251] 7179 4-9-0 **68** ... (h) DylanHogan(5) 5 — 9
(David Simcock) *racd off the pce in 5th: rdn over 2f out: no prog: lost pl and bhd over 1f out: t.o ins fnl f* **5/1[3]**

2m 30.6s (-5.40) **Going Correction** -0.225s/f (Firm) — **8 Ran SP% 119.3**
Speed ratings (Par 103): **109,100,97,97,93 92,82,79**
CSF £7.20 CT £121.61 TOTE £2.50: £1.20, £1.50, £7.30; EX 7.70 Trifecta £118.30.
Owner Jacobs Construction & J Harley **Bred** R Coffey **Trained** Lower Beeding, W Sussex

FOCUS
The closers struggled in this moderate handicap and it proved one-way traffic. The winner has been rated close to his best.

2929 GREAT BRITISH GIN FESTIVAL 20TH JULY H'CAP — 6f 210y
4:45 (4:46) (Class 6) (0-65,67) 4-Y-O+ — **£3,105** (£924; £461; £300; £300; £300) **Stalls** Centre

Form — RPR

-560 **1** **Swissal (IRE)**[23] 2145 4-9-4 **62** ... (p) AdamKirby 2 — 68
(David Dennis) *hld up in tch: n.m.r 2f out: rdn and hdwy to chse ldrs 1f out: ev ch ins fnl f: r.o wl to ld on post* **5/1[3]**

0201 **2** shd **De Little Engine (IRE)**[31] 1933 5-9-8 **66** ... (p) JoeFanning 8 — 72
(Alexandra Dunn) *led for over 1f out: styd chsng ldr tl led again 2f out: sn drvn: battled on gamely ins fnl f: hdd on post* **5/1[3]**

0-26 **3** ¾ **Barritus**[17] 2397 4-9-0 **65** ... (t[1]) CierenFallon(7) 1 — 69
(George Baker) *dwlt: t.k.h: sn in midfield: clsd to chse ldrs over 4f out: edgd lft jst over 2f out: drvn to chse ldr jst over 1f out: ev ch ins fnl f: no ex towards fin (jockey said gelding ran too free)* **4/1[2]**

0364 **4** ½ **Storm Melody**[36] 1820 6-9-1 **59** ... (p) TomMarquand 7 — 61
(Ali Stronge) *hld up in tch towards rr: nt clrest of runs ent fnl 2f: hdwy and hung lft 1f out: stl hanging but kpt on wl ins fnl f* **7/1**

-045 **5** 2 ¾ **Perfect Symphony (IRE)**[23] 2145 5-9-0 **61** ... PaddyBradley(3) 9 — 57
(Mark Pattinson) *in tch in midfield: unable qck u.p over 1f out: kpt on same pce ins fnl f (jockey said gelding hung left-handed in the straight)* **12/1**

-505 **6** 3 **Wilson (IRE)**[21] 2232 4-9-6 **64** ... (p) CharlieBennett 5 — 56
(Julia Feilden) *dwlt: hld up in tch in rr: hdwy on inner whn nt clr run ent fnl 2f: sme hdwy whn nt clr run again ent fnl f: wknd ins fnl f (jockey said gelding was denied a clear run)* **25/1**

6021 **7** 1 **Blessed To Empress (IRE)**[20] 2286 4-9-3 **61** ... RichardKingscote 4 — 46
(Amy Murphy) *midfield: hdwy to ld over 5f out: edgd rt and hdd 2f out: sn drvn and no ex ent fnl f: wknd ins fnl f* **3/1[1]**

/0-0 **8** nse **Mahna Mahna (IRE)**[126] 243 5-8-2 **53** oh6 ow2... EllieMacKenzie(7) 10 — 38
(David W Drinkwater) *chsd ldr early but sn dropped to midfield: struggling u.p 2f out: wl hld over 1f out* **66/1**

00-6 **9** 10 **Andalusite**[135] 104 6-9-2 **60** ... (v) RoystonFfrench 6 — 19
(John Gallagher) *stmbld leaving stalls: in tch in last trio: effrt on outer over 2f out: no prog and wl hld over 1f out: wknd fnl f (jockey said mare stumbled leaving the stalls)* **12/1**

The Form Book Flat 2019, Raceform Ltd, Newbury, RG14 5SJ

2123 **10** 3 ½ **Sir Ottoman (FR)**[22] 2194 6-9-6 **67**......................(tp) GabrieleMalune(3) 3 43+
(Ivan Furtado) *hld up in tch towards rr: clsd and squeezed through on inner jst over 2f out: chsng ldrs whn nt clr run and hmpd ent fnl f: nt rcvr and eased fnl f (jockey said gelding suffered interference in running)* **9/1**

1m 21.1s (-2.70) **Going Correction** -0.225s/f (Firm) **10** Ran SP% **121.6**
Speed ratings (Par 101): **103,102,102,101,98 94,93,93,82,78**
CSF £31.69 CT £114.61 TOTE £5.70: £2.10, £2.10, £1.50; EX 40.50 Trifecta £233.30.
Owner Scott Wilson & Partner **Bred** Deal Gharrafa Syndicate **Trained** Hanley Swan, Worcestershire

FOCUS
There was a tight four-way finish in this ordinary handicap. The second has been rated to his best, and the third to his pre-race mark.

2930 RUM & REGGAE FESTIVAL 20 JULY CLASSIFIED STKS 7f 211y
5:15 (5:16) (Class 6) 3-Y-O+
£3,105 (£924; £461; £300; £300; £300) **Stalls** Centre

Form RPR

05-5 **1** **Kahina (IRE)**[21] 2262 3-8-9 55.............................(p) JackMitchell 1 58
(Hugo Palmer) *chsd ldrs: effrt and rdn to ld jst over 2f out: styd on wl and in command ins fnl f* **7/2**[3]

-400 **2** 1 ¼ **Don't Cry About It (IRE)**[57] 1333 4-9-7 52..............(bt) TomMarquand 9 58
(Ali Stronge) *short of room leaving stalls: in tch in midfield: effrt over 2f out: hdwy u.p 1f out: clsng and bmpd ins fnl f: wnt 2nd wl ins fnl f: kpt on but nvr getting to wnr* **12/1**

06P4 **3** nk **Confrerie (IRE)**[21] 2231 4-9-0 53.......................... CierenFallon(7) 2 57
(George Baker) *t.k.h: w ldrs for 1f: chsd ldrs after: effrt 2f out: keeping on whn hung rt ins fnl f: wnt 3rd wl ins fnl f: nvr getting to wnr* **9/4**[2]

5021 **4** 1 **Imperial Act**[21] 2240 4-9-0 51........................ WilliamCarver(7) 11 56
(Andrew Balding) *dwlt: steadily rcvrd and midfield after 2f: clsd to press wnr and rdn ent fnl 2f: no ex ins fnl f: lost 2 pls and wknd wl ins fnl f* **2/1**[1]

-500 **5** 3 ½ **Sea Tea Dea**[21] 2234 5-9-4 42.................................... FinleyMarsh(3) 12 47
(Adrian Wintle) *hld up in tch in rr: clsd over 2f out: chsd ldrs but no ex u.p 1f out: wknd ins fnl f* **50/1**

-000 **6** 1 ¼ **Jupiter**[14] 2513 4-9-7 52.. RichardKingscote 6 44
(Alexandra Dunn) *led for 1f: chsd ldr tl over 2f out: unable qck and lost pl over 1f out: wknd ins fnl f* **8/1**

0-40 **7** 10 **Chance Of Glory (FR)**[14] 2517 3-8-9 55.......................... JoeFanning 5 18
(Mark Johnston) *w ldrs for 1f: dropped to rr 6f out: c towards centre and rdn 3f out: sn struggling and wl btn over 1f out* **12/1**

0-60 **8** 6 **Song Of Summer**[110] 501 4-9-0 43......................... GraceMcEntee(7) 10 7+
(Phil McEntee) *in tch in midfield: rdn over 2f out: sn struggling and lost pl: bhd over 1f out* **33/1**

-000 **9** ½ **Following Breeze (IRE)**[21] 2231 4-9-0 39.............(b[1]) IsobelFrancis(7) 7 6
(Jim Boyle) *dashed up to ld after 1f and sn clr: hdd jst over 2f out: sn struggling and lost pl over 1f out: fdd fnl f* **66/1**

1m 35.41s (-1.49) **Going Correction** -0.225s/f (Firm)
WFA 3 from 4yo+ 12lb **9** Ran SP% **119.2**
Speed ratings (Par 101): **98,96,96,95,91 90,80,74,74**
CSF £45.29 TOTE £5.00: £1.20, £3.00, £1.10; EX 55.30 Trifecta £162.10.
Owner Mph Close Regards **Bred** Pat & Eoghan Grogan **Trained** Newmarket, Suffolk

FOCUS
Thanks to Following Breeze this moderate affair was run at a solid pace. The winner has been rated to her best.
T/Plt: £61.70 to a £1 stake. Pool: £57,723.40 - 682.61 winning units T/Qpdt: £21.00 to a £1 stake. Pool: £6,453.02 - 226.99 winning units **Steve Payne**

2624 NOTTINGHAM (L-H)
Tuesday, May 21

OFFICIAL GOING: Good to firm (good in places; watered; 7.9)
Wind: Light across Weather: Cloudy with sunny spells

2931 EBF NOVICE STKS 6f 18y
2:10 (2:11) (Class 5) 2-Y-O **£3,881** (£1,155; £577; £288) **Stalls** High

Form RPR

1 **Oh Purple Reign (IRE)** 2-9-5 0.................................... SeanLevey 1 85+
(Richard Hannon) *w ldrs: rdn to ld over 1f out: r.o* **12/1**[3]

2 ¾ **Dubai Station** 2-9-5 0.. JamieSpencer 3 83+
(K R Burke) *s.i.s: hld up: swtchd lft and hdwy over 1f out: shkn up to chse wnr ins fnl f: r.o* **16/1**

3 ¾ **Be Prepared** 2-9-5 0.. AndreaAtzeni 6 80+
(Simon Crisford) *w ldrs: rdn and ev ch over 1f out: styd on* **14/1**

4 1 ¼ **Homespin (USA)** 2-9-5 0.. FrannyNorton 2 77+
(Mark Johnston) *led: rdn and hdd over 1f out: no ex ins fnl f* **7/1**[2]

5 3 **Ottoman Court** 2-9-5 0.. JamesDoyle 4 68+
(Charlie Appleby) *s.i.s: in rr and pushed along over 4f out: reminder over 3f out: nrr trbld ldrs* **4/9**[1]

3 **6** hd **Port Winston (IRE)**[22] 2205 2-9-5 0........................... OisinMurphy 7 67
(Alan King) *prom: rdn and edgd lft over 1f out: wknd ins fnl f* **14/1**

7 5 **Ropey Guest** 2-9-2 0... JaneElliott(3) 5 52
(George Margarson) *s.i.s: outpcd (jockey said colt ran green)* **66/1**

1m 14.45s (0.65) **Going Correction** -0.15s/f (Firm) **7** Ran SP% **110.2**
Speed ratings (Par 93): **89,88,87,85,81 81,74**
CSF £159.36 TOTE £14.80: £4.50, £5.60; EX 160.80 Trifecta £1601.00.
Owner Team Wallop **Bred** Tally-Ho Stud **Trained** East Everleigh, Wilts

FOCUS
This had the look of a fair novice, even with the red-hot favourite disappointing. It's been rated positively.

2932 PETER HUDSON (L'ESPION) BIRTHDAY NOVICE MEDIAN AUCTION STKS 1m 75y
2:45 (2:45) (Class 5) 3-Y-O **£3,881** (£1,155; £577; £288) **Stalls** Centre

Form RPR

3 **1** **Tabassor (IRE)**[24] 2102 3-9-0 0.............................. DaneO'Neill 5 77+
(Charles Hills) *chsd ldr tl led over 3f out: rdn over 1f out: r.o: comf* **9/4**[2]

55 **2** 1 ½ **Sweet Celebration (IRE)**[22] 2216 3-9-0 0............ AndreaAtzeni 10 72
(Marco Botti) *prom: pushed along over 3f out: rdn to chse wnr over 1f out: r.o* **10/1**

2 **3** 5 **Aegeus (USA)**[20] 2280 3-9-5 0................................ RobertHavlin 4 65
(Amanda Perrett) *prom: chsd wnr over 2f out tl rdn over 1f out: no ex ins fnl f* **2/1**[1]

4 1 ¼ **Aldente** 3-9-0 0.. RobHornby 7 57
(Andrew Balding) *sn pushed along towards rr: styd on fnl 2f: nt trble ldrs* **14/1**

5 6 **Sleepdancer (IRE)** 3-9-5 0.. JamesDoyle 11 48
(William Haggas) *s.i.s: sn pushed along and prom: racd wd 3f: rdn over 2f out: hung lft and wknd over 1f out* **11/4**[3]

0-6 **6** hd **Keith**[23] 2140 3-9-5 0.. AdamMcNamara 8 48
(Rod Millman) *hld up: pushed along over 3f out: nvr on terms* **50/1**

7 ¾ **Mirabelle Plum (IRE)** 3-9-0 0.................................. TomEaves 6 41
(Robyn Brisland) *s.i.s: a in rr* **50/1**

8 2 **Interrogator (IRE)** 3-9-5 0.................................... CharlesBishop 2 42
(Alan Bailey) *s.i.s: a in rr* **50/1**

0- **9** 2 ½ **Pourmorechampagne**[304] 5209 3-9-5 0..................... DougieCostello 3 36
(Paul Webber) *hld up: rdn over 3f out: wknd over 2f out* **100/1**

0- **10** ½ **Mallons Spirit (IRE)**[216] 8329 3-8-9 0..................... TheodoreLadd(5) 9 30
(Michael Appleby) *led: hdd over 3f out: wknd over 2f out* **100/1**

11 46 **Gregory The Great** 3-9-5 0.. FrannyNorton 1
(Steph Hollinshead) *hld up in tch: racd keenly: hung lft and wknd 3f out (jockey said gelding lost its action in the final half furlong)* **50/1**

1m 46.51s (-0.19) **Going Correction** -0.15s/f (Firm) **11** Ran SP% **116.4**
Speed ratings (Par 99): **94,92,87,86,80 80,79,77,74,74 28**
CSF £23.80 TOTE £2.60: £1.10, £2.20, £1.30; EX 21.50 Trifecta £60.10.
Owner Hamdan Al Maktoum **Bred** Shadwell Estate Company Limited **Trained** Lambourn, Berks

FOCUS
Distance increased by 12yds. Little got into this novice and the front pair pulled clear. The level is a bit fluid. The third has been rated similar to his debut.

2933 BET AT RACINGTV.COM CLASSIFIED STKS 1m 75y
3:15 (3:20) (Class 5) 3-Y-O
£3,881 (£1,155; £577; £300; £300; £300) **Stalls** Centre

Form RPR

1-44 **1** **Rambaldi (IRE)**[40] 1720 3-9-0 70..........................(t[1]) AndreaAtzeni 8 73
(Marco Botti) *hld up: hdwy over 1f out: rdn and r.o to ld post* **7/1**

505- **2** nse **Kings Royal Hussar (FR)**[196] 8889 3-9-0 68.................. JamesDoyle 3 72
(Alan King) *s.i.s: hdwy over 6f out: rdn to ld ins fnl f: hdd post* **9/2**[2]

0544 **3** 1 ¼ **Fiction Writer (USA)**[20] 2299 3-9-0 70........................ FrannyNorton 4 69
(Mark Johnston) *chsd ldrs: shkn up over 3f out: rdn to ld over 1f out: edgd rt and hdd ins fnl f: styd on same pce* **15/2**

-645 **4** nk **Lady Mascara**[28] 2018 3-9-0 69.................................. GeorgeWood 6 68
(James Fanshawe) *hld up: hdwy over 3f out: led over 2f out: rdn: edgd rt and hdd over 1f out: styd on same pce ins fnl f* **6/1**[3]

4-00 **5** nk **God Has Given**[24] 2114 3-9-0 70................................ DavidEgan 2 68
(Ian Williams) *led early: chsd ldr: led again over 3f out: rdn and hdd over 2f out: no ex wl ins fnl f* **13/2**

-000 **6** 2 ½ **Gylo (IRE)**[10] 2635 3-9-0 70...................................... ShaneGray 9 62
(David O'Meara) *s.i.s: hld up: shkn up and hung lft over 4f out: rdn and hung lft fr over 1f out: nt trble ldrs* **14/1**

-504 **7** 7 **Ventura Glory**[5] 2760 3-9-0 69................................. OisinMurphy 7 46
(Richard Hannon) *broke wl: sn lost pl: hdwy 3f out: rdn and edgd lft over 1f out: wknd fnl f (trainer's rep said the filly ran flat having raced 5 days previously. vet reported filly was lame on its right fore)* **5/2**[1]

250- **8** 3 **Abie's Hollow**[251] 7162 3-9-0 67............................. DougieCostello 1 39
(Tony Coyle) *sn led: hdd over 3f out: rdn and wknd over 1f out* **50/1**

015- **9** 9 **Sesame (IRE)**[201] 8782 3-8-9 64............................ TheodoreLadd(5) 5 18
(Michael Appleby) *restless in stalls: s.i.s: hld up: rdn and wknd over 2f out* **33/1**

1m 45.52s (-1.18) **Going Correction** -0.15s/f (Firm) **9** Ran SP% **110.2**
Speed ratings (Par 99): **99,98,97,97,97 94,87,84,75**
CSF £35.73 TOTE £6.70: £2.40, £1.80, £2.30; EX 32.80 Trifecta £135.70.
Owner Abbas Alalawi & Partner **Bred** Camas Park, Lynch Bages & Summerhill **Trained** Newmarket, Suffolk

FOCUS
Distance increased by 12yds. Plenty held their chance in this modest but competitive classified event. The third and fifth have been rated close to form.

2934 INTRODUCING RACING TV FILLIES' H'CAP 1m 75y
3:45 (3:46) (Class 3) (0-95,93) 3-Y-O **£9,703** (£2,887; £1,443; £721) **Stalls** Centre

Form RPR

56-0 **1** **Layaleena (IRE)**[25] 2088 3-8-11 **83**.............................. DaneO'Neill 6 93
(Sir Michael Stoute) *mde all: qcknd over 2f out: pushed clr over 1f out: comf* **9/1**

1-1 **2** 3 **Nearooz**[28] 2018 3-8-13 **85**.. AndreaAtzeni 3 88
(Roger Varian) *sn chsng wnr: rdn over 2f out: styd on same pce fnl f* **5/4**[1]

21-4 **3** nse **Duneflower (IRE)**[14] 2507 3-8-12 **84**.......................... RobertHavlin 2 87+
(John Gosden) *s.i.s: hld up: outpcd over 2f out: r.o ins fnl f* **8/1**

66- **4** 2 ¼ **Aim Power (IRE)**[206] 8648 3-9-7 **93**............................ OisinMurphy 1 91
(Richard Hannon) *racd keenly: trckd ldrs: rdn over 2f out: styd on same pce fr over 1f out* **15/2**[3]

4-21 **5** 2 ½ **I Am Magical**[5] 2760 3-8-10 **82** 6ex............................ JamieSpencer 5 74+
(Charlie Fellowes) *s.i.s: hld up: plld hrd: hdwy over 2f out: rdn over 1f out: wknd fnl f* **11/4**[2]

616 **6** 10 **La Voix Magique**[13] 2521 3-8-11 **83**.......................... FrannyNorton 4 52
(Steph Hollinshead) *stdd s: plld hrd and sn prom: shkn up 3f out: wknd wl over 1f out* **16/1**

1m 44.93s (-1.77) **Going Correction** -0.15s/f (Firm) **6** Ran SP% **109.9**
Speed ratings (Par 100): **102,99,98,96,94 84**
CSF £20.02 TOTE £8.40: £3.20, £1.20; EX 23.70 Trifecta £109.50.
Owner Hamdan Al Maktoum **Bred** Sunderland Holdings Inc **Trained** Newmarket, Suffolk

FOCUS
Distance increased by 12yds. A decent fillies' handicap, albeit little got into it from off the pace with the winner making all. The fourth has been rated close to her 2yo form.

2935 BRITISH STALLION STUDS EBF FILLIES' H'CAP 1m 2f 50y
4:20 (4:21) (Class 4) (0-80,78) 3-Y-O
£6,469 (£1,925; £962; £481; £300; £300) **Stalls** Low

Form RPR

41-0 **1** **Manorah (IRE)**[18] 2354 3-9-5 **76**............................ AndreaAtzeni 6 85
(Roger Varian) *sn prom: shkn up over 3f out: rdn to ld wl ins fnl f: r.o (trainer's rep said, regarding the improved form shown, the filly was more settled in the preliminaries for wearing a hood in the parade ring, and was better suited to a flatter track)* **16/1**

55-2 **2** ¾ **Thanks Be**[24] 2102 3-9-7 **78**................................ StevieDonohoe 7 85
(Charlie Fellowes) *hld up: racd keenly: hdwy on outer over 2f out: led 1f out: rdn: edgd rt and hdd wl ins fnl f: styd on same pce* **7/2**[2]

4-52 **3** nse **Inclyne**[10] 2612 3-9-4 **75**.. RobHornby 2 84+
(Andrew Balding) *sn chsng ldrs: nt clr run over 2f out: swtchd rt over 1f out: rdn and r.o wl ins fnl f* **15/8**[1]

-636 **4** *4* **Patchouli**[11] 2582 3-9-2 **73**........................ FrannyNorton 4 72
(Mick Channon) *hld up: nt clr run over 2f out: sn swtchd rt: nt trble ldrs (jockey said filly was denied a clear run approaching the final 2 furlongs)* **15/2**

222- **5** *4* **Lady Lizzy**[155] 9590 3-9-6 **77**........................ BenCurtis 5 68
(K R Burke) *chsd ldr: shkn up and ev ch over 1f out: hung lft and wknd fnl f (jockey said filly hung left in the final furlong)* **9/2**[3]

5-21 **6** *hd* **Cuban Sun**[21] 2253 3-9-4 **75**........................ BarryMcHugh 3 66
(James Given) *led: rdn and hdd 1f out: sn wknd* **9/2**[3]

2m 11.65s (-1.75) **Going Correction** -0.15s/f (Firm) **6 Ran SP% 111.0**
Speed ratings (Par 98): **101,100,100,97,93 93**
CSF £68.62 CT £151.43 TOTE £10.90: £5.10, £2.10; EX 58.60 Trifecta £319.40.
Owner Abdullatif M Al-Abdulrazzaq **Bred** Ms Ashling Burke **Trained** Newmarket, Suffolk

FOCUS
Distance increased by 12yds. Bit of a turn up here, the complete outsider triumphing.

2936 JOIN RACING TV NOW H'CAP (A JOCKEY CLUB GRASSROOTS STAYERS SERIES QUALIFIER) 2m
4:55 (4:56) (Class 5) (0-75,76) 4-Y-O+

£3,881 (£1,155; £577; £300; £300; £300) **Stalls Low**

Form RPR

-312 **1** **True Destiny**[21] 2239 4-9-3 **69**........................ AdamMcNamara 3 84+
(Roger Charlton) *chsd ldr: led over 3f out: rdn clr fnl 2f: eased ins fnl f* **6/1**[3]

1-34 **2** *3 1/4* **Bailarico (IRE)**[25] 2080 6-9-8 **73**........................(v[1]) EdwardGreatrex 5 80
(Warren Greatrex) *hld up: hdwy over 2f out: rdn to chse wnr and hung rt over 1f out: no imp* **7/2**[2]

/30- **3** *7* **Fields Of Fortune**[150] 6500 5-9-6 **71**........................ JamesDoyle 1 70
(Alan King) *hld up: hdwy over 3f out: rdn to chse wnr and hung rt over 2f out: lost 2nd over 1f out: wknd fnl f* **9/1**

0-60 **4** *4* **Dagueneau (IRE)**[25] 2080 4-9-9 **75**........................ BenCurtis 9 69
(Ed Dunlop) *hld up: racd wd: hdwy over 2f out: rdn: hung lft and wknd over 1f out* **16/1**

-051 **5** *1 1/2* **Master Grey (IRE)**[7] 2718 4-8-13 **65** 5ex........................ OisinMurphy 8 57
(Rod Millman) *chsd ldr tl rdn over 3f out: wknd wl over 1f out (trainer's rep said the race may have come too soon having raced 7 days previously)* **11/8**[1]

4342 **6** *nk* **Knight Commander**[9] 1840 6-8-9 **60**........................(t) RaulDaSilva 7 52
(Steve Flook) *hld up: rdn over 2f out: sn wknd* **20/1**

0245 **7** *8* **Navajo Star (IRE)**[17] 2398 5-9-11 **76**........................(v) SeanLevey 4 58
(Robyn Brisland) *prom: racd keenly: rdn over 2f out: wknd wl over 1f out* **18/1**

-560 **8** *6* **Akavit (IRE)**[42] 1663 7-9-2 **67**........................ CallumShepherd 2 42
(Ed de Giles) *led: rdn and hdd over 3f out: wknd wl over 1f out* **14/1**

3m 30.33s (-4.17) **Going Correction** -0.15s/f (Firm) **8 Ran SP% 111.2**
WFA 4 from 5yo+ 1lb
Speed ratings (Par 103): **104,102,98,96,96 95,91,88**
CSF £25.73 CT £180.30 TOTE £4.80: £1.80, £1.10, £2.60; EX 28.60 Trifecta £145.50.
Owner H R H Sultan Ahmad Shah **Bred** M J & L A Taylor Llp **Trained** Beckhampton, Wilts

FOCUS
Distance increased by 24yds. Modest staying form but a clear-cut winner. The second has been rated in line with the better view of his form.

2937 RACING TV PROFITS RETURNED TO RACING H'CAP (A JOCKEY CLUB GRASSROOTS SPRINT SERIES QUALIFIER) 6f 18y
5:25 (5:25) (Class 5) (0-75,77) 3-Y-O

£3,881 (£1,155; £577; £300; £300; £300) **Stalls High**

Form RPR

3-16 **1** **Benny And The Jets (IRE)**[10] 2624 3-9-7 **75**........................(t) DavidEgan 4 87
(Sylvester Kirk) *chsd ldr tl led over 1f out: rdn and edgd rt ins fnl f: r.o (trainer said, regarding the improved form shown, the gelding was better suited to the faster ground)* **10/1**

-322 **2** *3* **Staycation (IRE)**[20] 2293 3-9-6 **74**........................(p) DavidAllan 1 76
(Rebecca Bastiman) *led over 4f: edgd rt and no ex ins fnl f* **5/2**[1]

40-1 **3** *3 1/4* **Aghast**[22] 2197 3-8-9 **63**........................ KevinStott 9 55
(Kevin Ryan) *hmpd s: hld up: hdwy over 2f out: rdn over 1f out: wknd wl ins fnl f* **9/2**[3]

44-1 **4** *4* **Socru (IRE)**[24] 2098 3-9-5 **73**........................ NathanEvans 7 52
(Michael Easterby) *stmbld s: hdwy over 2f out: wknd over 1f out (jockey said gelding stumbled badly leaving the stalls)* **7/2**[2]

22-6 **5** *3/4* **Time For Bed (IRE)**[25] 2077 3-9-5 **73**........................ SeanLevey 6 49
(Richard Hannon) *hmpd s: hld up: hdwy over 2f out: rdn over 1f out: wknd fnl f (jockey said filly hung right under pressure)* **13/2**

110- **6** *nse* **Lively Lydia**[259] 6900 3-9-7 **75**........................ CharlesBishop 10 51
(Eve Johnson Houghton) *chsd ldrs: rdn over 2f out: wknd over 1f out* **6/1**

44-5 **7** *11* **Hello Bangkok (IRE)**[20] 2285 3-9-5 **73**........................ RobHornby 5 14
(Andrew Balding) *chsd ldrs: lost pl over 3f out: wknd over 2f out* **16/1**

1m 13.02s (-0.78) **Going Correction** -0.15s/f (Firm) **7 Ran SP% 111.6**
Speed ratings (Par 99): **99,95,90,85,84 84,69**
CSF £33.57 CT £127.31 TOTE £11.80: £4.10, £1.60; EX 43.50 Trifecta £199.00.
Owner Deauville Daze Partnership **Bred** Pier House Stud **Trained** Upper Lambourn, Berks

FOCUS
Ordinary sprint form but the winner did it tidily. The second has been rated in line with the better view of his form.
T/Plt: £488.70 to a £1 stake. Pool: £45,739.42 - 68.32 winning units T/Qpdt: £20.60 to a £1 stake. Pool: £6,187.17 - 149.36 winning units **Colin Roberts**

2692 WOLVERHAMPTON (A.W) (L-H)
Tuesday, May 21

OFFICIAL GOING: Tapeta: standard
Wind: Moderate cross wind Weather: Sunny

2938 JPR ROOFING AND FLOORING LTD NOVICE STKS 6f 20y (Tp)
1:50 (1:52) (Class 5) 3-Y-O **£3,752** (£1,116; £557; £278) **Stalls Low**

Form RPR

3 **1** **Alkaraama (USA)**[24] 2094 3-9-5 0........................ JimCrowley 7 87+
(Sir Michael Stoute) *t.k.h: prom: sn led: qcknd 2f out: sn clr: pushed out: readily* **1/4**[1]

52-0 **2** *4* **Journey Of Life**[11] 2567 3-9-5 76........................(h) JasonWatson 5 74
(Gary Moore) *t.k.h: a.p: rdn 2f out: unable qck w wnr: kpt on wl fnl f: no ch w wnr (jockey said gelding moved poorly in the home straight)* **16/1**

66 **3** *3* **Victory Rose**[10] 2623 3-9-0 0........................ PatCosgrave 4 59
(Lydia Pearce) *trckd ldrs: rdn 2f out: kpt on same pce under hands and heels ride* **66/1**

- **4** *1 3/4* **Chil Chil** 3-9-0 0........................ DavidProbert 6 54
(Andrew Balding) *slowly away: chsd ldrs: hdwy on outer over 2f out: kpt on same pce fnl 1f* **5/1**[2]

5 *hd* **Alliseeisnibras (IRE)** 3-9-0 0........................ StevieDonohoe 8 53
(Ismail Mohammed) *hld up: hdwy arnd outer over 2f out: styd on past btn horses fnl 1f* **25/1**

54- **6** *1/2* **Alabama Dreaming**[327] 4310 3-9-0 0........................ EoinWalsh 12 52
(George Scott) *hld up: rdn and one pce fnl 2f* **20/1**

7 *1/2* **Sterling Price** 3-9-5 0........................ RyanTate 9 55
(James Eustace) *rdn sn after s: chsd ldrs: rdn 3f out: one pce fnl 2f (vet reported gelding was lame on its left fore)* **80/1**

00 **8** *6* **Jumeirah (IRE)**[19] 2340 3-8-7 0........................ GeorgiaDobie(7) 3 31
(Eve Johnson Houghton) *mid-div: rdn 2f out: sn wknd (vet reported filly had bled from the nose)* **80/1**

6 **9** *1 1/4* **Ice Cave (IRE)**[26] 2060 3-9-5 0........................ JosephineGordon 2 32
(Saeed bin Suroor) *t.k.h: led: hdd 4f: sn rdn and grad wknd* **6/1**[3]

0- **10** *3 1/2* **Broadhaven Dream (IRE)**[396] 1945 3-9-5 0........................ RaulDaSilva 10 21
(Ronald Harris) *chsd ldrs on outer: outpcd over 2f out: swtchd to inner 1f out: eased whn btn (jockey said gelding hung badly left-handed throughout and was virtually unsteerable, which caused the saddle to slip)* **200/1**

0 **11** *9* **Shawwaslucky**[12] 2550 3-9-0 0........................ PaddyMathers 1
(Derek Shaw) *dwlt: a in rr* **200/1**

1m 13.64s (-0.86) **Going Correction** -0.05s/f (Stan) **11 Ran SP% 130.4**
Speed ratings (Par 99): **103,97,93,91,91 90,89,81,80,75 63**
CSF £8.89 TOTE £1.10: £1.10, £3.30, £11.40; EX 7.70 Trifecta £104.40.
Owner Hamdan Al Maktoum **Bred** Frank Hutchinson **Trained** Newmarket, Suffolk

FOCUS
This proved very straightforward for the heavy odds-on favourite. The second has been rated in line with the better view of his form, with the third confirming her latest form.

2939 NFRC MIDLANDS H'CAP 6f 20y (Tp)
2:20 (2:22) (Class 6) (0-65,65) 3-Y-O

£3,105 (£924; £461; £300; £300; £300) **Stalls Low**

Form RPR

2530 **1** **Klopp**[10] 2635 3-9-7 **65**........................(h) CamHardie 4 71
(Antony Brittain) *chsd ldrs: rdn 2f out: drvn fnl f: kpt on wl to ld fnl 75yds* **9/2**[2]

1320 **2** *hd* **Eye Of The Water (IRE)**[18] 2357 3-9-2 **60**........................ DavidProbert 6 65
(Ronald Harris) *trckd ldrs: brought wd off home turn: rdn and hdwy fr 2f: r.o: jst hld* **9/2**[2]

-500 **3** *3/4* **Freedom And Wheat (IRE)**[22] 2204 3-9-7 **65**........(v) FergusSweeney 10 68+
(Mark Usher) *hld up: hdwy fnl 2f: kpt on wl: nrst fin* **12/1**

20-0 **4** *nk* **Jill Rose**[33] 1894 3-9-6 **64**........................ PhilDennis 2 66
(Richard Whitaker) *trckd ldrs: rdn 2f out: kpt on same pce fnl 1f* **12/1**

0-65 **5** *hd* **Hard Solution**[20] 2293 3-9-6 **64**........................(b[1]) DavidNolan 1 66
(David O'Meara) *sn led: kicked on ins fnl 2f: sn drvn: hdd fnl 100yds: no ex* **3/1**[1]

1000 **6** *1/2* **Greybychoice (IRE)**[22] 2204 3-9-7 **65**........................(b) EoinWalsh 5 65
(Nick Littmoden) *mid-div: rdn 2f out: sme late hdwy whn sltly hmpd 100yds out: nrst fin (jockey said gelding hung left-handed throughout)* **16/1**

55-0 **7** *1* **Miss Liberty Belle (AUS)**[19] 2340 2-9-4 **62**........................ JasonWatson 3 59
(William Jarvis) *dwlt: sn pushed along: rdn 2f out: sme late hdwy tl n.m.r fnl 100yds (jockey said filly was denied a clear run in the closing stages)* **11/1**[3]

4-24 **8** *1* **Bluebell Time (IRE)**[20] 2276 3-9-6 **64**........................ PatCosgrave 8 58
(Malcolm Saunders) *trckd ldrs: rdn and unable qck over 2f out: styd on same pce fnl 1f* **14/1**

-064 **9** *3/4* **Te Amo Te Amo**[15] 2489 3-9-1 **59**........................ NickyMackay 9 51
(Simon Dow) *hld up: rdn over 2f out: no imp* **11/1**[3]

3206 **10** *1/2* **Maisie Moo**[34] 1863 3-9-1 **59**........................ ShaneKelly 12 49
(Shaun Keightley) *hld up: rdn and one pce fnl 2f* **22/1**

0243 **11** *shd* **Sharrabang**[11] 2592 3-8-10 **59**........................ SeanDavis(5) 7 49
(Stella Barclay) *mid-div: rdn 2f out: sn wknd (jockey said gelding was never travelling)* **14/1**

-440 **12** *7* **Griggy (IRE)**[26] 2063 3-9-5 **63**........................ KieranO'Neill 13 32
(John Butler) *t.k.h: hld up: rdn and wknd fr over 2f out* **16/1**

1m 14.56s (0.06) **Going Correction** -0.05s/f (Stan) **12 Ran SP% 122.9**
Speed ratings (Par 97): **97,96,95,95,95 94,93,91,90,90 89,80**
CSF £26.11 CT £238.62 TOTE £5.90: £1.90, £1.70, £3.90; EX 26.60 Trifecta £277.40.
Owner Antony Brittain **Bred** Northgate Lodge Stud Ltd **Trained** Warthill, N Yorks

FOCUS
The favourite set a good gallop and the closers had their day. Straightforward form.

2940 ROOFCARE (NORTH STAFFS) LTD CLAIMING STKS 5f 21y (Tp)
2:55 (2:55) (Class 6) 3-Y-O+

£3,105 (£924; £461; £300; £300; £300) **Stalls Low**

Form RPR

3112 **1** **Steelriver (IRE)**[23] 2153 9-9-7 77........................ PhilDennis 8 83
(Michael Herrington) *hld up in tch: travelled wl: brought wd to chal off home turn: rdn and hung lft over 1f out: kpt on to ld nr fin* **4/1**[3]

0-60 **2** *hd* **Green Door (IRE)**[67] 1211 8-9-5 82........................(v) PJMcDonald 6 80
(Robert Cowell) *trckd ldr: led wl over 1f out: sn drvn: kpt on wl but no ex cl home* **13/2**

0-00 **3** *3 1/4* **Tomily (IRE)**[20] 2272 5-10-0 91........................ RossaRyan 11 78
(Richard Hannon) *hld up: rdn 2f out: styd on u.p fnl f* **9/4**[1]

0400 **4** *nk* **George Dryden (IRE)**[10] 2611 7-8-11 73........................ SeanDavis(5) 5 65
(Charlie Wallis) *hld up: rdn 2f out: styd on fnl f* **11/2**

0-60 **5** *1/2* **Billy Dylan (IRE)**[17] 2421 4-9-9 84........................(p) ConorMcGovern(3) 7 73
(David O'Meara) *prom: sn led: rdn 2f out: one pce fnl f* **20/1**

2052 **6** *1 1/4* **Something Lucky (IRE)**[12] 2556 7-9-9 79........................(v) AlistairRawlinson 9 65
(Michael Appleby) *hld up: brought wd to chal whn rdn 2f out: one pce* **7/2**[2]

0002 **7** *nk* **Pearl Of Qatar**[7] 2708 3-7-12 57........................ KieranSchofield(7) 10 51
(Brian Ellison) *hld up: rdn 2f out: sn one pce* **16/1**

-005 **8** *4 1/2* **Kyllachy Princess**[17] 2420 3-8-3 49 ow1........................(p[1]) JosephineGordon 4 33
(David Loughnane) *hld up in rr: rdn and one pce fr 2f* **100/1**

401/ **9** *3* **Lucky Clover**[581] 8128 8-8-11 59........................ PatCosgrave 1 25
(Malcolm Saunders) *trckd ldrs: rdn 2f out: grad wknd fnl f* **50/1**

41-5 **10** 1 3/4 **Gifted Zebedee (IRE)**[24] 2123 3-8-12 75....................(p) NickyMackay 2 25
(Luke McJannet) *trckd ldrs: rdn and wknd fr 2f out* **33/1**

1m 1.49s (-0.41) **Going Correction** -0.05s/f (Stan)
WFA 3 from 4yo+ 8lb **10 Ran SP% 118.2**
Speed ratings (Par 101): **101,100,95,95,94 92,91,84,79,76**
CSF £29.69 TOTE £6.00: £2.10, £2.40, £1.40; EX 31.90 Trifecta £148.30.There were no Claims from this race
Owner Mrs H Lloyd-Herrington **Bred** Kildaragh Stud **Trained** Cold Kirby, N Yorks

FOCUS
The first two finished nicely clear in this claimer.

2941 MIDLAND ROOF TRAINING GROUP H'CAP 1m 4f 51y (Tp)
3:25 (3:28) (Class 6) (0-60,59) 3-Y-O

£3,105 (£924; £461; £300; £300; £300) **Stalls** Low

Form RPR
3032 **1** **Willkommen**[22] 2213 3-8-11 **56**....................(b) StefanoCherchi(7) 12 71
(Marco Botti) *trckd ldrs: hdwy over 3f out: led wl over 1f out: r.o wl: comf* **5/1**[3]

05-0 **2** 3 1/4 **Junior Rip (IRE)**[24] 2101 3-9-6 **58**.................... JasonWatson 9 69+
(Roger Charlton) *trckd ldrs: rdn 2f out: kpt on: no ch w wnr* **6/4**[1]

6-04 **3** 4 1/2 **Highway Robbery**[28] 2011 3-8-0 **45**....................(p) SophieRalston(7) 11 48
(Julia Feilden) *led: rdn 2f out: hdd wl over 1f out: one pce fnl f* **16/1**

000 **4** 5 **Lock Seventeen (USA)**[19] 2343 3-8-12 **57**.................... AledBeech(7) 1 52
(Charlie Fellowes) *hld up: rdn 3f out: styd on fr 2f out* **12/1**

0-00 **5** nse **Global Freedom**[24] 2128 3-9-3 **55**.................... PJMcDonald 5 50
(Ed Dunlop) *hld up in rr: hdwy 4f out: rdn 2f out: one pce (jockey said colt hung left-handed)* **11/4**[2]

006 **6** 1 1/4 **Watch And Learn**[59] 1288 3-9-6 **58**.................... DavidProbert 4 51
(Andrew Balding) *hld up: hdwy over 2f out: rdn and wknd over 1f out* **11/1**

-064 **7** 14 **Juals Spirit (IRE)**[13] 2530 3-8-7 **45**....................(p) CamHardie 2 16
(Brian Ellison) *hld up: rdn 6f out and again 4f out: one pce fnl 2f* **25/1**

-604 **8** nk **Frenchmans Creek (IRE)**[22] 2216 3-9-1 **58**..... ThomasGreatrex(5) 10 28
(Seamus Durack) *prom: rdn 3f out: grad wknd* **16/1**

040- **9** 40 **Belle Bayeux**[179] 9225 3-8-11 **49**.................... ShaneKelly 3
(Mark H Tompkins) *trckd ldrs: rdn 4f out: eased whn btn fnl 2f (jockey said the filly stopped quickly)* **40/1**

00-0 **10** nk **Moor Top**[24] 2099 3-8-7 **45**....................(p[1]) AndrewMullen 8
(Jennie Candlish) *trckd ldrs: rdn 4f out: grad wknd (jockey said gelding stopped quickly)* **33/1**

2m 40.92s (0.12) **Going Correction** -0.05s/f (Stan) **10 Ran SP% 120.4**
Speed ratings (Par 97): **97,94,91,88,88 87,78,78,51,51**
CSF £13.12 CT £116.21 TOTE £4.20: £1.50, £1.20, £5.60; EX 15.50 Trifecta £156.70.
Owner Mrs Lucie Botti **Bred** Peter Harper **Trained** Newmarket, Suffolk
■ Hen was withdrawn. Price at time of withdrawal 5/1. Rule 4 applies to all bets struck prior to withdrawal, but not to SP bets. Deduction - 15p in the £. New market formed.
■ Stewards' Enquiry : Thomas Greatrex one-day ban: failed to ride to draw (Jun 4)

FOCUS
There was a lack of depth to this race. It was run at a good gallop and they finished well strung out.

2942 WRIGHT'S ROOFING H'CAP 1m 142y (Tp)
4:00 (4:03) (Class 4) (0-80,82) 3-Y-O

£5,530 (£1,645; £822; £411; £300; £300) **Stalls** Low

Form RPR
3-26 **1** **Fields Of Athenry (USA)**[36] 1823 3-9-10 **82**.................... PJMcDonald 7 90+
(James Tate) *t.k.h: hld up: hdwy on outer over 3f out: rdn to ld wl over 1f out: sn clr: hung lft fnl f: kpt on wl* **7/2**[2]

34-6 **2** 1 1/4 **Fares Poet (IRE)**[41] 1696 3-9-1 **73**....................(h[1]) JasonWatson 1 77
(Marco Botti) *led: rdn over 2f out: wnt clr 2nd 1f out: kpt on: no ch w wnr (jockey said colt hung right-handed in the home straight)* **16/1**

535- **3** 2 **Chicago Doll**[239] 7612 3-9-1 **73**.................... DavidProbert 4 72
(Alan King) *trckd ldrs: rdn 2f out: styd on fr wl over 1f out* **16/1**

53-5 **4** 1 1/4 **Snow Storm (IRE)**[24] 2101 3-9-2 **74**.................... PatCosgrave 11 71
(Saeed bin Suroor) *trckd ldrs: effrt 2f out whn swtchd wd: styd on fnl f* **6/1**[3]

1-04 **5** hd **Shir Khan**[16] 2446 3-9-10 **82**....................(p[1]) RossaRyan 6 78
(Paul Cole) *hld up: rdn 2f out: drifted rt fr 1f out: styd on same pce (jockey said colt was denied a clear run)* **11/1**

2-10 **6** nse **Pytilia (USA)**[23] 2141 3-9-4 **76**.................... ShaneKelly 12 72
(Richard Hughes) *led briefly: remained prom: rdn over 2f out: one pce fnl f* **25/1**

0161 **7** 1 **Havana Ooh Na Na**[28] 2016 3-8-9 **67**....................(p) CliffordLee 10 61
(K R Burke) *trckd ldr: rdn over 3f out: sn drvn: wknd fnl f* **12/1**

-100 **8** 1 3/4 **Rock Up In Style**[19] 2336 3-8-13 **71**.................... PaddyMathers 8 61
(Clare Ellam) *hld up in rr: rdn 3f out: styd on one pce fnl 2f* **100/1**

-316 **9** hd **Balata Bay**[18] 2364 3-9-1 **78**.................... KatherineBegley(5) 9 67
(Richard Hannon) *hld up: rdn 3f out: swtchd wd off home turn: sn one pce (jockey said colt hung left handed)* **20/1**

-133 **10** 1 1/2 **Balladeer**[5] 2766 3-9-7 **79**.................... HayleyTurner 2 65
(Michael Bell) *hld up: rdn 4f out: n.d (trainer's rep said gelding had missed the break)* **5/2**[1]

456- **11** 19 **Wave Walker**[208] 8576 3-8-13 **74**.................... GaryMahon(3) 5 16
(Sylvester Kirk) *hld up: rdn and wknd fr 3f out: eased fnl f* **25/1**

50-1 **12** 10 **Joe The Beau**[22] 2200 3-9-3 **75**.................... PaulMulrennan 3
(Michael Easterby) *uns rdr bef ent stalls: trckd ldrs: hdwy 3f out: rdn 2f out and grad wknd* **6/1**[3]

1m 49.4s (-0.70) **Going Correction** -0.05s/f (Stan) **12 Ran SP% 120.6**
Speed ratings (Par 101): **101,99,98,97,96 96,95,94,94,92 75,67**
CSF £56.72 CT £820.96 TOTE £4.20: £1.50, £4.90, £3.00; EX 58.80 Trifecta £862.30.
Owner Saeed Manana **Bred** Highland Yard LLC **Trained** Newmarket, Suffolk

FOCUS
The winner's task was made easier as a result of his two main market rivals failing to run their races. Sound form, with the second rated to the better view of his form, and the third to form.

2943 CAPITAL ROOFING CENTRE H'CAP 1m 142y (Tp)
4:35 (4:38) (Class 6) (0-55,55) 3-Y-O

£3,105 (£924; £461; £300; £300; £300) **Stalls** Low

Form RPR
-532 **1** **Antico Lady (IRE)**[13] 2531 3-9-4 **55**.................... BenRobinson(3) 6 69
(Brian Ellison) *a.p: rdn 2f out: sn clr: pushed out: readily* **2/1**[1]

50-6 **2** 5 **Juniors Fantasy (IRE)**[29] 1979 3-9-5 **53**.................... DuranFentiman 8 56
(Tim Easterby) *trckd ldrs: rdn 3f out: drvn fnl 1f: kpt on: no ch w wnr* **11/1**

000- **3** 3 3/4 **Kybosh (IRE)**[145] 9725 3-9-7 **55**....................(t[1]) AlistairRawlinson 13 50+
(Ed Walker) *slowly away: sn rdn towards rr: rdn 4f out: styd on fnl 2f: nrst fin (jockey said gelding was never travelling)* **15/2**

-064 **4** 3 3/4 **Symphony (IRE)**[46] 1567 3-9-3 **51**.................... DavidProbert 12 38
(James Unett) *prom: rdn 2f out: one pce fnl f* **14/1**

0026 **5** 1 1/2 **Power Of Life (USA)**[21] 2262 3-9-4 **52**....................(v[1]) HayleyTurner 10 36
(Michael Bell) *hld up: rdn and n.m.r 3f out: swtchd ins 2f out: styd on one pce* **11/2**[2]

6540 **6** 4 **Geography Teacher (IRE)**[19] 2337 3-9-4 **52**.................... JasonHart 4 28
(Roger Fell) *hld up: rdn 3f out: one pce fr wl over 1f out* **11/1**

0-05 **7** nse **Jailbreak (IRE)**[21] 2238 3-9-5 **53**....................(b) ShaneKelly 11 29
(Richard Hughes) *hld up: rdn 4f out: drvn and one pce fnl 2f* **7/1**[3]

00-0 **8** 3 1/4 **Laura Louise (IRE)**[21] 2262 3-9-1 **52**....................(v[1]) RowanScott(3) 7 21
(Nigel Tinkler) *hld up: sltly hmpd over 3f out: rdn and one pce fr 2f out* **20/1**

4000 **9** nk **Tsarmina (IRE)**[45] 1593 3-9-3 **51**....................(v[1]) PJMcDonald 9 19
(David Evans) *hld up: rdn 4f out: one pce fnl 2f* **20/1**

0-00 **10** 8 **Sherella**[21] 2238 3-9-5 **53**.................... FergusSweeney 1 4
(J R Jenkins) *hld up: swtchd rt and rdn over 3f out: sn wknd* **100/1**

000- **11** 9 **Corinthian Star**[210] 8493 3-9-6 **54**....................(h[1]) JasonWatson 2
(George Scott) *prom: rdn 3f out: grad wknd* **20/1**

50-0 **12** 1 **Maktay**[18] 2357 3-9-1 **49**....................(h[1]) JimmyQuinn 3
(David Bridgwater) *in rr: rdn 3f out: sn wknd: nvr involved* **25/1**

0-00 **13** 68 **Vena D'Amore (IRE)**[26] 2063 3-9-5 **53**.................... RobertWinston 5
(Dean Ivory) *trckd ldrs: rdn 4f out: eased whn btn fr wl over 1f out (jockey said filly lost its action)* **20/1**

1m 50.61s (0.51) **Going Correction** -0.05s/f (Stan) **13 Ran SP% 120.2**
Speed ratings (Par 97): **95,90,87,83,82 79,78,76,75,68 60,59,**
CSF £22.51 CT £149.77 TOTE £2.70: £1.30, £3.80, £2.30; EX 24.90 Trifecta £247.30.
Owner Julie & Keith Hanson **Bred** Ms Agathe Lebailly **Trained** Norton, N Yorks
■ Stewards' Enquiry : Ben Robinson two-day ban: careless riding (Jun 4-5)

FOCUS
Another race in which they finished well strung out. The second has been rated pretty much to last year's mark.

2944 BLACK COUNTRY BUSINESS FESTIVAL H'CAP 7f 36y (Tp)
5:05 (5:08) (Class 6) (0-60,60) 4-Y-O+

£3,105 (£924; £461; £300; £300; £300) **Stalls** High

Form RPR
6001 **1** **Little Miss Daisy**[22] 2215 5-9-5 **58**.................... NicolaCurrie 3 65
(William Muir) *t.k.h: trckd ldrs: swtchd rt and pushed into ld wl over 1f out: r.o* **6/1**[3]

3302 **2** 1 1/2 **Street Poet (IRE)**[8] 2692 6-9-7 **60**.................... PhilDennis 5 65
(Michael Herrington) *trckd ldrs: travelled wl: rdn to chal and no room over 1f out: r.o fnl f: nt rch wnr* **7/2**[1]

002 **3** 1/2 **Skyva**[13] 2527 4-8-10 **52**.................... BenRobinson(3) 8 54
(Brian Ellison) *hld up: rdn 2f out: styd on wl fnl f on ins rail: nrst fin* **8/1**

0-62 **4** 1 3/4 **Rockesbury**[22] 2215 4-9-7 **60**....................(p) TrevorWhelan 7 58
(David Loughnane) *prom: trckd ldrs: rdn over 2f out: hung lft whn chalng ldr over 1f out: kpt on same pce (jockey said gelding jumped right-handed leaving the stalls)* **11/2**[2]

6263 **5** 3/4 **Sooqaan**[19] 2349 8-9-7 **60**....................(p) CamHardie 9 56
(Antony Brittain) *trckd ldrs: rdn 2f out: drvn and on ex fnl f (jockey said gelding hung right-handed from 3 furlongs out)* **12/1**

340- **6** 1 1/4 **Burren View Lady (IRE)**[27] 2042 9-9-5 **58**....................(bt) JimmyQuinn 2 51
(Denis Gerard Hogan, Ire) *hld up: rdn and one pce fr 2f out (jockey said mare was denied a clear run inside the final furlong)* **13/2**

1200 **7** 1 **Viola Park**[29] 1986 5-9-5 **58**....................(p) DavidProbert 6 48
(Ronald Harris) *hld up: rdn and one pce fr 2f out* **6/1**[3]

-010 **8** 3/4 **Caledonia Laird**[83] 925 8-8-12 **58**....................(v) GeorgiaDobie(7) 11 47
(Jo Hughes, France) *hld up: rdn and hdwy on outside over 2f out: one pce fnl f (jockey said gelding was slowly away)* **20/1**

0-00 **9** 2 1/4 **Conqueress (IRE)**[28] 2019 5-8-12 **51**....................(p) EoinWalsh 12 34
(Lydia Pearce) *hld up: rdn 2f out: grad wknd* **80/1**

0230 **10** 1 3/4 **Adventureman**[11] 2596 7-9-4 **57**....................(b) JackGarritty 10 36+
(Ruth Carr) *led: rdn over 2f out: sltly impeded whn hdd over 1f out: sn wknd* **7/1**

1m 29.77s (0.97) **Going Correction** -0.05s/f (Stan) **10 Ran SP% 116.8**
Speed ratings (Par 101): **92,90,89,87,86 85,84,83,80,78**
CSF £27.35 CT £170.96 TOTE £7.40: £2.40, £2.20, £3.00; EX 23.30 Trifecta £175.30.
Owner Mrs J M Muir **Bred** Hungerford Park Stud **Trained** Lambourn, Berks
■ Stewards' Enquiry : Phil Dennis three-day ban: careless riding (Jun 4-6)

FOCUS
Just an ordinary handicap. The third has been rated near his recent form.
T/Jkpt: £6,728.00 to a £1 stake. Pool: £23,690.26 - 2.5 winning units T/Plt: £18.50 to a £1 stake. Pool: £64,513.75 - 2,536.42 winning units T/Qpdt: £12.40 to a £1 stake. Pool: £6,110.49 - 362.90 winning units **Jonathan Doidge**

2945- 2952a (Foreign Racing) - See Raceform Interactive

2757 MAISONS-LAFFITTE (R-H)
Tuesday, May 21

OFFICIAL GOING: Turf: very soft

2953a PRIX BIRUM (CONDITIONS) (3YO COLTS & GELDINGS) (TURF) 1m
2:00 3-Y-O

£12,612 (£4,792; £3,531; £2,018; £1,009; £756)

RPR
1 **Melicertes**[29] 3-9-3 0.................... MickaelBarzalona 1 100
(A Fabre, France) *trckd ldrs in 3rd: hdwy between rivals to ld 2f out: rdn clr over 1f out: kpt on strly ins fnl f* **4/5**[1]

2 3 **Fun Legend**[68] 1198 3-9-0 0.................... Pierre-CharlesBoudot 5 90
(P Bary, France) **51/10**[3]

3 2 **Kiloecho (FR)**[12] 3-9-3 0.................... AurelienLemaitre 4 88
(J-V Toux, France) **14/1**

4 1 1/2 **Isidro (FR)**[62] 3-9-0 0.................... AlexisBadel 6 82
(H-F Devin, France) **10/1**

5 1/2 **Boitron (FR)**[23] 2162 3-9-5 0.................... CristianDemuro 2 85
(Richard Hannon) *wl into stride: led: rowed along 2f out: rdn and outpcd over 1f out: kpt on same pce fnl f* **37/10**[2]

6 1 **Santi Del Mare (FR)**[21] 3-9-0 0.................... MlleCoraliePacaut(3) 7 81
(J-C Rouget, France) **15/1**

7 1/2 **Dassom (IRE)**[21] 2265 3-9-0 0.................... GregoryBenoist 9 77
(Mlle A Wattel, France) **23/1**

8 3/4 **Gaur D'Emra (FR)**[189] 9044 3-8-5 0.................... MlleAudeDuporte(9) 3 75
(Brian Beaunez, France) **85/1**

9 ¾ **Antigua Biwi (IRE)**[17] 3-8-8 0.................................... ThomasTrullier(6) 8 74
(M Rolland, France) **66/1**
1m 44.21s (1.91) **9** Ran SP% **122.1**
PARI-MUTUEL (all including 1 euro stake): WIN 1.80; PLACE 1.10, 1.40, 1.90; DF 4.80.
Owner Godolphin SNC **Bred** Godolphin **Trained** Chantilly, France

2954a PRIX NUBIENNE (CONDITIONS) (3YO FILLIES) (TURF) 1m
3:10 3-Y-O
£12,612 (£4,792; £3,531; £2,018; £1,009; £756)

RPR
1 **Simona (FR)**[43] 3-9-0 0.............................(b) Pierre-CharlesBoudot 3 96
(F-H Graffard, France) **7/1**[3]
2 4 **Hermiona (USA)**[33] 3-9-3 0................................ StephanePasquier 1 90
(F Chappet, France) **17/2**
3 2 **Rose Flower (GER)**[215] 3-9-3 0........................ ChristopheSoumillon 6 86
(G Botti, France) **9/1**
4 2 **Fonthill Abbey (IRE)**[27] 3-9-0 0........................ MickaelBarzalona 10 78
(A Fabre, France) *hld up towards rr of gp down centre: swtchd lft and hdwy 2f out: rdn to chse ldr over 1f out: kpt on one pce fnl f* **9/10**[1]
5 5 **Hold True**[29] 3-9-3 0.. CristianDemuro 7 70
(D Smaga, France) **11/2**[2]
6 ¾ **Danseur D'Argent (FR)**[25] 2091 3-8-10 0..................... AntoineHamelin 2 61
(Jo Hughes, France) *trckd ldr against rail: urged along 2f out: rdn and no imp over 1f out: wknd fnl f* **60/1**
7 2 ½ **Red Curry (FR)**[43] 3-9-0 0................................ VincentCheminaud 4 59
(H-A Pantall, France) **10/1**
8 1 ¼ **La Mariniere (FR)**[38] 3-9-3 0............................ AnthonyCrastus 5 59
(D De Watrigant, France) **21/1**
9 dist **Philippine Cobra (FR)**[10] 3-9-3 0............................ PierreBazire 9
(G Botti, France) **97/1**
10 2 **Angelica (FR)**[16] 3-8-7 0.............................. MlleMickaelleMichel(3) 8
(Laura Lemiere, France) **49/1**
1m 41.81s (-0.49) **10** Ran SP% **119.3**
PARI-MUTUEL (all including 1 euro stake): WIN 8.00; PLACE 2.60, 2.70, 3.00; DF 20.50.
Owner Nigel & Carolyn Elwes **Bred** N Elwes **Trained** France

2955a PRIX DE ROLLEBOISE (CLAIMER) (4YO+) (TURF) 7f
3:45 4-Y-O+
£8,558 (£3,423; £2,567; £1,711; £855)

RPR
1 **Brian Ryan**[14] 4-8-11 0.. MaximeGuyon 10 78
(Andrea Marcialis, France) **11/5**[1]
2 nk **Alfieri (FR)**[10] 6-9-4 0.................................(b) ThomasTrullier(6) 16 90
(F Rossi, France) **47/10**[3]
3 1 ¼ **Yuman (FR)**[74] 5-9-1 0..............................(b[1]) Pierre-CharlesBoudot 12 78
(H-A Pantall, France) **37/10**[2]
4 hd **Dylan Dancing (IRE)**[226] 6-9-1 0........................ DelphineSantiago(3) 13 80
(C Le Veel, France) **13/1**
5 4 ½ **Skydiving**[106] 600 4-8-11 0.. GlenBraem 4 61
(Mlle S Houben, France) **67/1**
6 7 **Red Kitten (FR)**[5] 6-9-2 0................................ MlleCoraliePacaut(3) 2 50
(D De Waele, France) **15/1**
7 2 ½ **Torna A Surriento (ITY)**[198] 8866 6-9-1 0..................... CristianDemuro 3 39
(Gianluca Bietolini, France) **11/1**
8 hd **Ali Spirit (IRE)**[19] 6-9-1 0.................................(p) AurelienLemaitre 7 39
(Elias Mikhalides, France) **17/1**
9 ¾ **Mr Slicker (FR)**[10] 5-9-1 0.. EddyHardouin 14 37
(Andrew Hollinshead, France) **45/1**
10 1 ½ **Flor De Seda (FR)**[18] 2391 4-8-11 0......................... IoritzMendizabal 11 29
(Jo Hughes, France) *chsd ldrs on outer: shkn up over 2f out: rdn and limited rspnse over 1f out: wknd ins fnl f* **54/1**
11 ¾ **Monteverdi (FR)**[35] 6-8-10 0........................ AnnaelleDidon-Yahlali(5) 5 35
(G Botti, France) **22/1**
12 ½ **Ancient City (FR)**[171] 4-9-4 0.................................(p) RonanThomas 6 32
(C Theodorakis, Greece) **40/1**
13 1 ¾ **Favori Royal (FR)**[56] 1349 4-8-3 0........................ MlleAudeDuporte(8) 17 21
(E Lyon, France) **79/1**
14 15 **Mapocho (FR)**[21] 2264 4-8-13 0.................................. JimmyTastayre(5) 1
(Frederic Lamotte D'Argy, France) **163/1**
15 2 ½ **Laucitu (FR)** 6-8-3 0.. MohammedLyesTabti(5) 9
(Mlle M-L Mortier, France) **219/1**
16 3 **Daring Match (GER)**[36] 8-9-4 0................................... AntoineHamelin 8
(J Hirschberger, Germany) **10/1**
1m 31.69s (3.69) **16** Ran SP% **121.0**
PARI-MUTUEL (all including 1 euro stake): WIN 3.20; PLACE 1.50, 1.90, 1.70; DF 6.60.
Owner Torsten Raber **Bred** D Curran **Trained** France

2956a PRIX DE LAMBOURN (H'CAP) (4YO+) (TURF) 6f
4:20 4-Y-O+
£11,711 (£4,450; £3,279; £1,873; £936; £702)

RPR
1 **Slickteg (FR)**[29] 4-9-1 0... VincentCheminaud 8 79
(H-A Pantall, France) **189/10**
2 hd **Canouville (FR)**[24] 2182 4-9-1 0.............................(b) GregoryBenoist 1 79
(Mlle Y Vollmer, France) **12/1**
3 3 **Tallinski (IRE)**[35] 5-9-5 0.. AurelienLemaitre 16 73
(Sofie Lanslots, France) **68/10**[3]
4 hd **Be A Wave**[230] 7919 4-8-11 0.................................... AntoineHamelin 7 64
(Gerald Geisler, Germany) **41/1**
5 2 ½ **O Dee**[29] 7-9-2 0... StephaneBreux 2 61
(Patrick Dejaeger, Belgium) **12/1**
6 1 ¾ **Koutsounakos**[138] 4-9-2 0..................................(p) MickaelBarzalona 18 56
(Mario Hofer, Germany) **17/1**
7 ½ **Blue Tango (GER)**[35] 4-9-6 0.. TonyPiccone 10 58
(M Munch, Germany) **13/1**
8 snk **Smart Move (FR)**[19] 4-8-11 0.................................. MlleAlisonMassin(4) 3 53
(D & P Prod'Homme, France) **60/1**
9 1 **Royal Diplomat (IRE)**[29] 4-8-11 0...............................(b) AlexisBadel 12 45
(P Monfort, France) **11/1**
10 1 **Marvellous Night (FR)**[128] 4-9-4 0................................ HugoJourniac 4 49
(H De Nicolay, France) **46/1**
11 ¾ **Lightoller (IRE)**[29] 5-9-3 0.....................................(b) MaximeGuyon 5 46
(P Monfort, France) **32/5**[2]
12 hd **Xenophanes (IRE)**[29] 9-8-7 0................................ MlleCoraliePacaut(3) 14 38
(M Boutin, France) **16/1**
13 1 ¾ **Cloud Eight (IRE)**[36] 4-9-5 0...........................(p) Pierre-CharlesBoudot 17 42
(P Monfort, France) **11/1**
14 1 ½ **Bohemien (IRE)**[19] 6-8-13 0................................ MlleLauraGrosso(3) 15 34
(Joeri Goossens, Belgium) **38/1**
15 ¾ **Shamdor**[19] 4-9-5 0.. ChristopheSoumillon 9 34
(A De Royer-Dupre, France) **17/5**[1]
16 dist **Get Even**[24] 2182 4-9-1 0... IoritzMendizabal 13
(Jo Hughes, France) *settled towards rr of gp down centre: rdn over 2f out: sn btn and heavily eased* **25/1**
17 15 **Castle Dream (FR)**[36] 5-9-1 0...................................... ClementLecoeuvre 11
(Matthieu Palussiere, France) **35/1**
1m 14.86s (1.46) **17** Ran SP% **120.1**
PARI-MUTUEL (all including 1 euro stake): WIN 19.90; PLACE 5.50, 4.10, 3.30; DF 132.20.
Owner Derek Clee **Bred** D Clee **Trained** France

AYR (L-H)
Wednesday, May 22

OFFICIAL GOING: Good to firm (watered; 8.6)
Wind: Breezy, half against in sprints and in over 3f of home straight in races on the round course Weather: Cloudy, bright

2957 EBF STALLIONS MENABREA MAIDEN STKS (PLUS 10 RACE) 6f
2:00 (2:01) (Class 4) 2-Y-O **£4,787** (£1,424; £711; £355) **Stalls High**

Form RPR
1 **Lord Of The Lodge (IRE)** 2-9-5 0.. BenCurtis 4 84+
(K R Burke) *dwlt: hld up: gd hdwy against stands' rail to ld over 1f out: rdn and edgd lft ins fnl f: r.o strly* **4/1**[3]
2 1 ¾ **Clay Regazzoni** 2-9-5 0.. DanielTudhope 6 79+
(Keith Dalgleish) *in tch: effrt and chsd wnr over 1f out: rdn and hung lft ins fnl f: kpt on same pce last 100yds* **9/1**
55 3 8 **Puerto Sol (IRE)**[23] 2184 2-9-2 0.............................. BenRobinson(3) 5 53
(Brian Ellison) *dwlt: bhd: rdn along and outpcd over 2f out: rallied to chse clr ldng pair ins fnl f: r.o: no imp* **50/1**
4 nk **Mellad** 2-9-5 0.. PaulHanagan 3 52
(Richard Fahey) *dwlt: sn pushed along bhd ldng gp: rdn and green over 2f out: angled rt over 1f out: kpt on fnl f: no imp* **3/1**[2]
33 5 ½ **Danny Ocean (IRE)**[37] 1812 2-9-5 0................................ CliffordLee 1 51+
(K R Burke) *prom on outside: pushed along over 2f out: wknd over 1f out* **4/1**[3]
6 5 **Streaker** 2-9-5 0.. TomEaves 8 36
(Kevin Ryan) *pressed ldrs: shkn up and green over 2f out: wknd over 1f out* **9/1**
7 1 **Capelli Rossi (IRE)**[24] 2154 2-9-0 0............................ RobbieColgan 9 28
(Miss Clare Louise Cannon, Ire) *led tl rdn and hdd over 1f out: sn wknd* **66/1**
8 2 ½ **Fred** 2-9-5 0... JoeFanning 2 25
(Mark Johnston) *noisy and green in preliminaries: cl up: rdn over 2f out: edgd lft and wknd over 1f out* **11/4**[1]
1m 13.29s (0.19) **Going Correction** -0.15s/f (Firm) **8** Ran SP% **115.1**
Speed ratings (Par 95): **92,89,79,78,77 71,69,66**
CSF £39.57 TOTE £5.80: £1.80, £3.00, £8.80; EX 45.60 Trifecta £894.10.
Owner Mrs Elaine M Burke **Bred** Mountarmstrong Stud **Trained** Middleham Moor, N Yorks

FOCUS
The watered ground was given as good to firm (Going Stick 8.6). Distances as advertised. The first two drew right away in this juvenile maiden.

2958 HEVERLEE H'CAP 6f
2:30 (2:36) (Class 6) (0-60,60) 3-Y-O+
£3,105 (£924; £461; £300; £300; £300) **Stalls High**

Form RPR
604- 1 **Tai Sing Yeh (IRE)**[75] 1120 5-9-1 **52**........................ DonaghO'Connor(3) 3 61
(J F Levins, Ire) *prom centre: rdn to ld over 1f out: clr ins fnl f: kpt on strly* **7/1**[3]
3320 2 1 ½ **Firsteen**[20] 2337 3-8-11 **54**... GrahamLee 16 58+
(Alistair Whillans) *hld up stands' side: nt clr run over 2f out: effrt and hdwy over 1f out: chsd wnr ins fnl f: kpt on: nt pce to chal* **14/1**
0250 3 1 ¼ **Joey Boy (IRE)**[30] 1982 3-9-0 **57**...................................(p[1]) ShaneGray 4 56
(Kevin Ryan) *dwlt: hld up centre: rdn and hdwy over 1f out: kpt on ins fnl* **33/1**
31-0 4 1 ½ **Tadaany (IRE)**[23] 2183 7-9-5 **53**...............................(p) BarryMcHugh 13 49
(Ruth Carr) *cl up towards stands' side: effrt and ev ch over 1f out: kpt on same pce ins fnl f* **14/1**
60-4 5 hd **Cupid's Arrow (IRE)**[29] 2013 5-9-5 **53**................................ JackGarritty 17 49
(Ruth Carr) *racd against stands' rail: w ldrs: rdn over 2f out: kpt on same pce ins fnl f* **12/1**
2301 6 hd **Star Cracker (IRE)**[23] 2189 7-9-1 **49**...................................(p) PhilDennis 7 44
(Jim Goldie) *led in centre to over 1f out: no ex ins fnl f* **25/1**
00-4 7 ½ **Raffle King (IRE)**[30] 1987 5-9-6 **54**.. TomEaves 2 48
(Ruth Carr) *hld up in tch in centre: effrt and rdn over 1f out: no imp ins fnl f* **25/1**
-500 8 ¾ **Ninjago**[23] 2203 9-9-12 **60**...(v) DanielTudhope 14 51
(Paul Midgley) *hld up bhd ldrs stands' side: effrt and rdn over 1f out: no further imp ins fnl f* **6/1**[2]
0-00 9 nse **Havana Go**[17] 2433 4-9-7 **55**...(b[1]) JoeFanning 8 46
(Keith Dalgleish) *dwlt: sn cl up in centre: rdn over 2f out: wknd ins fnl f (jockey said gelding was denied a clear run approaching the winning line)* **9/1**
0-33 10 ½ **Mr Shelby (IRE)**[9] 2678 5-9-6 **54**..(p) BenCurtis 15 44
(S Donohoe, Ire) *cl up nr stands' rail: rdn over 2f out: wknd fnl f* **9/2**[1]
05-4 11 4 ½ **Brendan (IRE)**[23] 2189 6-8-12 **49**............................ JamieGormley(3) 1 25
(Jim Goldie) *reluctant to go to post and walked to s: hld up in tch in centre: rdn over 2f out: wknd over 1f out (starter reported that the gelding had been reluctant to load into the stalls; trainer was informed that the gelding could not run until the day after passing a stalls test)* **12/1**
-030 12 1 ½ **Jessie Allan (IRE)**[39] 1765 8-9-0 **55**............................ CoreyMadden(7) 12 27
(Jim Goldie) *s.i.s: bhd towards stands' side: rdn along 1/2-way: nvr able to chal* **20/1**
4060 13 ¾ **Thorntoun Lady (USA)**[9] 2682 9-8-11 **48**........................ BenRobinson(3) 9 17
(Jim Goldie) *bhd in centre: rdn along over 2f out: nvr on terms* **20/1**

-005 **14** *1 ¼* **Racquet**[14] [2527] 6-9-1 **49**.......................(p) NathanEvans 11 15
(Ruth Carr) *cl up towards stands' side: rdn and ev ch over 2f out: wknd over 1f out* **25/1**

-006 **15** *2 ¼* **Red Cymbal**[25] [2122] 4-9-9 **57**.......................(vt[1]) RobbieColgan 6 16
(Anthony McCann, Ire) *hld up in centre: drvn and outpcd over 2f out: sn wknd* **12/1**

-403 **16** *1 ¼* **Loulin**[14] [2532] 4-9-4 **52**....................... PaulHanagan 10 7
(Ruth Carr) *prom in centre tl rdn and wknd wl over 1f out* **12/1**

1m 12.94s (-0.16) **Going Correction** -0.15s/f (Firm)
WFA 3 from 4yo+ 9lb **16** Ran SP% **123.1**
Speed ratings (Par 101): **95,93,91,89,89 88,88,87,87,86 80,78,77,75,72 71**
CSF £91.44 CT £3161.29 TOTE £7.70: £2.10, £3.00, £11.20, £3.60; EX 218.30 Trifecta £1620.00.
Owner Hugh P Ward **Bred** Rabbah Bloodstock Limited **Trained** The Curragh, Co Kildare

FOCUS
A moderate but competitive handicap. They came centre to stands' side and there looked to be no track bias. The third has been rated to the balance of his form.

2959 ORCHARD PIG H'CAP — 1m

3:05 (3:10) (Class 4) (0-80,85) 4-Y-O+

£5,530 (£1,645; £822; £411; £300; £300) **Stalls** Low

Form RPR

36-1 **1** **Universal Gleam**[5] [2784] 4-9-12 **85** 5ex....................... DanielTudhope 3 94+
(Keith Dalgleish) *prom: shkn up and hdwy to ld over 1f out: rdn out fnl f* **11/10**[1]

0-64 **2** *1 ½* **Strong Steps**[17] [2439] 7-8-7 **69**....................... JamieGormley[(3)] 4 73
(Jim Goldie) *hld up in tch: effrt and hdwy wl over 1f out: chsd wnr ins fnl f: kpt on* **13/2**

54-5 **3** *½* **Outside Inside (IRE)**[61] [1273] 4-9-4 **77**....................... JoeFanning 5 80
(Mark Johnston) *cl up: effrt and chsd wnr over 1f out to ins fnl f: kpt on same pce* **15/2**

403- **4** *3 ¾* **Najashee (IRE)**[221] [8181] 5-9-1 **74**....................... JasonHart 2 68
(Roger Fell) *s.i.s: hld up: rdn and edgd lft 2f out: kpt on fnl f: nvr able to chal* **5/1**[3]

0010 **5** *½* **Orobas (IRE)**[51] [1482] 7-8-0 **66** oh4.......................(v) VictorSantos[(7)] 6 59
(Lucinda Egerton) *led and sn clr: rdn and hdd over 1f out: wknd ins fnl f* **40/1**

1223 **6** *11* **Trevithick**[23] [2187] 4-9-2 **75**....................... GrahamLee 1 43
(Bryan Smart) *replated bef s: chsd clr ldr to over 2f out: rdn and wknd over 1f out* **9/2**[2]

1m 39.19s (-3.61) **Going Correction** -0.15s/f (Firm) **6** Ran SP% **110.0**
Speed ratings (Par 105): **112,110,110,106,105 94**
CSF £8.45 TOTE £2.10: £1.20, £3.10; EX 7.60 Trifecta £27.50.
Owner Weldspec Glasgow Limited **Bred** Mrs D O'Brien **Trained** Carluke, S Lanarks

FOCUS
This was soundly run and the favourite won with a degree of ease. It's been rated around the second and third.

2960 MAGNERS H'CAP — 5f

3:35 (3:37) (Class 4) (0-85,84) 3-Y-O

£5,530 (£1,645; £822; £411; £300; £300) **Stalls** High

Form RPR

-010 **1** **Mark's Choice (IRE)**[11] [2635] 3-8-13 **76**....................... JackGarritty 1 82
(Ruth Carr) *hld up on far side of gp: hdwy to ld over 1f out: drvn and hld on wl fnl f* **5/1**[3]

5406 **2** *nk* **Yolo Again (IRE)**[14] [2522] 3-9-6 **83**....................... BenCurtis 8 88
(Roger Fell) *led on nr side of gp: rdn and hdd over 1f out: rallied fnl f: hld cl home* **3/1**[2]

3-51 **3** *1 ¼* **Friendly Advice (IRE)**[16] [2477] 3-8-11 **74**....................... JoeFanning 2 74+
(Keith Dalgleish) *hld up in tch in centre of gp: effrt whn nt clr run briefly over 1f out: sn edgd lft: rdn and one pce ins fnl f* **11/8**[1]

10-5 **4** *nse* **Jordan Electrics**[9] [2683] 3-8-0 **66**.......................(h) JamieGormley[(3)] 4 66
(Linda Perratt) *cl up in centre of gp: effrt and ev ch over 1f out: kpt on same pce ins fnl f* **16/1**

16-0 **5** *1 ¾* **On The Stage**[25] [2121] 3-9-3 **80**....................... CliffordLee 7 74
(K R Burke) *chsd ldrs towards nr side of gp: drvn along 2f out: kpt on same pce fnl f* **16/1**

24-0 **6** *3 ¾* **Beechwood Izzy (IRE)**[50] [1504] 3-8-9 **72**....................... ShaneGray 3 52
(Keith Dalgleish) *w ldr on far side of gp: rdn over 2f out: wknd over 1f out* **12/1**

1-60 **7** *2 ¼* **Primeiro Boy (IRE)**[21] [2293] 3-8-4 **67**....................... AndrewMullen 6 39
(Richard Fahey) *dwlt: bhd on nr side of gp: struggling 2f out: sn btn* **16/1**

Going Correction -0.15s/f (Firm) **7** Ran SP% **109.1**
Speed ratings (Par 101): **94,93,91,91,88 82,79**
CSF £18.44 CT £27.60 TOTE £5.70: £2.70, £1.50; EX 20.40 Trifecta £48.50.
Owner Cragg Wood Racing **Bred** Northern Bloodstock Agency Ltd **Trained** Huby, N Yorks

FOCUS
A fair sprint. The second has been rated close to her best.

2961 TENNENT'S LAGER BRITISH STALLION STUDS EBF ROTHESAY STKS (LISTED RACE) (F&M) — 1m 2f

4:05 (4:05) (Class 1) 4-Y-O+

£28,355 (£10,750; £5,380; £2,680; £1,345; £675) **Stalls** Low

Form RPR

52-4 **1** **Shenanigans (IRE)**[32] [1941] 5-9-0 96....................... AndreaAtzeni 1 103
(Roger Varian) *trckd ldr: led gng wl over 2f out: rdn over 1f out: kpt on wl fnl f* **11/10**[1]

56-0 **2** *1 ¾* **Exhort**[34] [1889] 4-9-0 93....................... PaulHanagan 2 99
(Richard Fahey) *t.k.h: hld up: stdy hdwy over 2f out: rdn and chsd wnr over 1f out: kpt on fnl f: nt pce to chal* **13/2**[3]

2/5 **3** *8* **Coeur D'amour (IRE)**[17] [2451] 4-9-0 0....................... RobbieColgan 3 83
(Madeleine Tylicki, Ire) *s.i.s: hld up in rr: effrt on outside over 2f out: rdn: edgd lft and no imp on first two fr over 1f out* **20/1**

21- **4** *3 ¼* **Skill Set (IRE)**[270] [6516] 4-9-0 0....................... BenCurtis 6 77
(Henry Candy) *dwlt: sn chsng ldrs: effrt and rdn over 2f out: edgd lft and outpcd over 1f out: sn btn* **9/2**[2]

-106 **5** *5* **Plait**[18] [2401] 4-9-0 90....................... DavidAllan 5 67
(Michael Bell) *prom: drvn and outpcd over 2f out: sn wknd* **8/1**

4-03 **6** *7* **Vivianite (IRE)**[18] [2404] 4-9-0 94....................... DanielTudhope 7 53
(Archie Watson) *led to over 2f out: sn rdn: wknd over 1f out (trainer said the filly failed to stay the 1 mile 2 furlongs)* **9/2**[2]

2m 6.33s (-6.07) **Going Correction** -0.15s/f (Firm) **6** Ran SP% **113.2**
Speed ratings (Par 111): **116,114,108,105,101 96**
CSF £9.10 TOTE £1.70: £1.20, £2.40; EX 8.20 Trifecta £45.30.
Owner Ann Black,M Al Qatami & K M Al Mudhaf **Bred** Ringfort Stud **Trained** Newmarket, Suffolk

FOCUS
Not a strong Listed race. The winner has been rated to form.

2962 TENNENT'S STORY H'CAP — 1m 2f

4:35 (4:35) (Class 5) (0-75,76) 4-Y-O+

£3,752 (£1,116; £557; £300; £300; £300) **Stalls** Low

Form RPR

2-64 **1** **Maulesden May (IRE)**[20] [2326] 6-9-2 **69**....................... GrahamLee 3 77
(Keith Dalgleish) *sn niggled along in rr: hdwy over 2f out: led over 1f out: pushed clr ins fnl f: comf* **3/1**[1]

32-0 **2** *3* **Corton Lad**[17] [2436] 9-9-4 **71**.......................(vt) ShaneGray 7 73
(Keith Dalgleish) *dwlt: hdwy to ld after 1f: rdn and hrd pressed over 2f out: hdd over 1f out: kpt on same pce fnl f* **17/2**

0-05 **3** *nk* **Dragon Mountain**[19] [2370] 4-9-9 **76**....................... JoeFanning 5 77
(Keith Dalgleish) *cl up: wnt 2nd after 3f: effrt and ev ch over 2f out to over 1f out: one pce ins fnl f* **7/2**[2]

-433 **4** *10* **Guvenor's Choice (IRE)**[20] [2335] 4-9-7 **74**.......................(t) DanielTudhope 1 55
(Marjorie Fife) *prom: effrt over 2f out: outpcd over 1f out: btn fnl f* **5/1**[3]

613- **5** *1 ¾* **Can Can Sixty Two**[163] [7581] 4-8-13 **66**....................... AndrewMullen 2 44
(R Mike Smith) *led 1f: chsd ldr 2f: cl up: drvn: edgd lft and outpcd over 2f out: btn over 1f out* **22/1**

3000 **6** *¾* **Remmy D (IRE)**[22] [2244] 4-8-8 **64**....................... JamieGormley[(3)] 6 40
(Jim Goldie) *s.i.s: hld up: rdn over 3f out: outpcd 2f out: sn btn* **3/1**[1]

304- **7** *22* **X Rated (IRE)**[219] [8267] 5-8-6 **66**....................... AidanRedpath[(7)] 4
(Mark Johnston) *hld up in tch: rdn and struggling over 2f out: sn wknd: t.o* **8/1**

2m 9.09s (-3.31) **Going Correction** -0.15s/f (Firm) **7** Ran SP% **114.9**
Speed ratings (Par 103): **107,104,104,96,94 94,76**
CSF £28.98 TOTE £5.70: £3.10, £3.90; EX 24.90 Trifecta £99.80.
Owner The County Set (Two) **Bred** Yeomanstown Stud **Trained** Carluke, S Lanarks

FOCUS
A fair handicap. The winner has been rated back to her best, the second in line with his late 2018 form and the third close to his recent/turf best.

2963 TSINGTAO APPRENTICE H'CAP (DIV I) — 1m

5:05 (5:06) (Class 6) (0-65,65) 4-Y-O+

£3,105 (£924; £461; £300; £300; £300) **Stalls** Low

Form RPR

24-3 **1** **Jackhammer (IRE)**[20] [2330] 5-8-4 **51**.......................(bt) EllaMcCain[(3)] 13 62
(Dianne Sayer) *t.k.h in midfield: smooth hdwy to ld over 2f out: edgd lft and pushed clr fnl f: readily* **5/1**[2]

5-04 **2** *3* **Rebel State (IRE)**[22] [2241] 6-8-6 **57**.......................(p) OwenPayton[(7)] 11 60
(Jedd O'Keeffe) *hld up: hdwy on outside over 2f out: chsd (clr) wnr ins fnl f: kpt on: nt pce to chal* **5/1**[2]

4-06 **3** *2 ¼* **Lucky Violet (IRE)**[110] [525] 7-9-1 **64**.......................(h) CianMacRedmond[(5)] 2 62
(Linda Perratt) *prom: effrt and ev ch over 2f out: chsd wnr to ins fnl f: one pce* **16/1**

000- **4** *¾* **Foxy Rebel**[240] [7625] 5-7-13 **46** oh1....................... GavinAshton[(3)] 3 42
(Ruth Carr) *led: jnd after 2f and sn increased pce: rdn and hdd over 2f out: rallied: one pce fr over 1f out* **33/1**

5 *½* **War Advocate (IRE)**[19] [2387] 4-8-11 **62**....................... MikeyMelia[(7)] 6 57
(Adrian Paul Keatley, Ire) *prom: drvn and hung lft fr over 2f out: one pce fr over 1f out* **9/2**[1]

00-5 **6** *nk* **Pudding Chare (IRE)**[17] [2439] 5-8-10 **54**.......................(t) TobyEley 8 48
(R Mike Smith) *t.k.h early: prom: effrt over 2f out: no ex fr over 1f out* **10/1**[3]

0/00 **7** *hd* **Circuit**[11] [2633] 5-8-0 **49** oh1 ow3....................... RhonaPindar[(5)] 12 43
(Wilf Storey) *hld up: hdwy on outside over 2f out: shkn up and no further imp over 1f out* **50/1**

8 *nk* **Elzaa**[14] [2540] 5-7-9 **46** oh1.......................(b) IzzyClifton[(7)] 10 39
(Anthony McCann, Ire) *s.i.s: bhd: pushed along 3f out: kpt on fr over 1f out: nvr rchd ldrs* **25/1**

0-00 **9** *nse* **Quiet Moment (IRE)**[20] [2328] 5-7-11 **46** oh1.......................(t) IsobelFrancis[(5)] 4 39
(Maurice Barnes) *missed break: plld hrd in rr: rdn over 2f out: hdwy over 1f out: nvr rchd ldrs (jockey said mare was slowly away)* **50/1**

0356 **10** *1* **Testa Rossa (IRE)**[22] [2246] 9-9-2 **65**.......................(b) CoreyMadden[(5)] 7 56
(Jim Goldie) *hld up: pushed along over 2f out: nvr able to chal* **5/1**[2]

0-20 **11** *nk* **Captain Peaky**[29] [2012] 6-7-11 **46**....................... ElishaWhittington[(5)] 14 36
(Liam Bailey) *hld up in midfield: hdwy over 2f out: rdn and wknd fr over 1f out* **11/1**

6-00 **12** *1 ¼* **Let Right Be Done**[20] [2329] 7-8-2 **46** oh1.......................(v) RobertDodsworth 9 33
(Linda Perratt) *missed break: bhd: effrt and swtchd rt over 2f out: nvr on terms* **66/1**

2220 **13** *2* **Thecornishbarron (IRE)**[23] [2196] 7-8-4 **48**....................... KieranSchofield 1 31
(Brian Ellison) *hld up in midfield on ins: drvn and struggling over 2f out: sn btn* **5/1**[2]

0-0 **14** *shd* **Morley Gunner (IRE)**[9] [2681] 4-7-11 **46** oh1.......................(p) SaraDelFabbro[(5)] 5 28
(S Donohoe, Ire) *cl up: jnd ldr after 2f: rdn over 2f out: sn wknd* **33/1**

1m 41.12s (-1.68) **Going Correction** -0.15s/f (Firm) **14** Ran SP% **123.3**
Speed ratings (Par 101): **102,99,96,96,95 95,95,94,94,93 93,92,90,90**
CSF £29.51 CT £396.05 TOTE £6.20: £2.40, £1.50, £4.60; EX 30.50 Trifecta £342.60.
Owner Mrs Dianne Sayer **Bred** F Dunne **Trained** Hackthorpe, Cumbria
■ Stewards' Enquiry : Toby Eley one-day ban: failing to ride out (Jun 5)

FOCUS
Ordinary form, but the quicker of the two divisions by 0.46sec. The second has been rated close to his recent form.

2964 TSINGTAO APPRENTICE H'CAP (DIV II) — 1m

5:40 (5:42) (Class 6) (0-65,65) 4-Y-O+

£3,105 (£924; £461; £300; £300; £300) **Stalls** Low

Form RPR

4-12 **1** **Betty Grable (IRE)**[22] [2241] 5-8-0 **49** ow1....................... RhonaPindar[(5)] 7 55
(Wilf Storey) *hld up in midfield: smooth hdwy to ld wl over 1f out: pushed along and edgd lft ins fnl f: kpt on wl* **10/3**[1]

40-0 **2** *1 ¼* **Mywayistheonlyway (IRE)**[23] [2203] 6-9-1 **62**....................... HarryRussell[(3)] 12 65
(Grant Tuer) *midfield: effrt on outside over 2f out: chsd wnr ins fnl f: kpt on: nt pce to chal* **9/2**[3]

0-00 **3** *hd* **Clary (IRE)**[22] [2241] 9-8-2 **46** oh1....................... RobertDodsworth 11 49
(Alistair Whillans) *plld hrd early: hld up: effrt and swtchd rt 2f out: kpt on wl fnl f: nrst fin* **33/1**

34-0 **4** *1* **Retirement Beckons**[20] [2329] 4-7-11 **46** oh1.......................(h) IsobelFrancis[(5)] 1 46
(Linda Perratt) *dwlt: plld hrd early and sn in tch: effrt and ev ch over 1f out: kpt on same pce ins fnl f (jockey said gelding hung right throughout)* **25/1**

46-0 **5** ¾ **Bareed (USA)**[20] 2328 4-7-11 **46** oh1 ....(h) SaraDelFabbro(5) 8 45
(Linda Perratt) *prom: effrt and ev ch briefly over 1f out: rdn and no ex ins fnl f* **40/1**

230- **6** 1 **Rosemay (FR)**[163] 9481 5-8-9 **53** ....(p) TobyEley 14 49
(R Mike Smith) *hld up in tch: effrt 2f out: no imp fnl f (jockey said mare was slowly away)* **9/1**

0-03 **7** 1¼ **My Valentino (IRE)**[20] 2329 6-8-1 **48** ....(bt) EllaMcCain(3) 6 41
(Dianne Sayer) *s.i.s: bhd: pushed along and hdwy 2f out: no imp fnl f (jockey said gelding missed the break and was never travelling)* **4/1**[2]

0550 **8** 3¾ **Rioja Day (IRE)**[6] 2436 9-8-0 **49** oh1 ow3 ....(v) CoreyMadden(5) 13 34
(Jim Goldie) *bhd: pushed along over 2f out: nvr rchd ldrs* **40/1**

00-0 **9** ½ **Lagenda**[25] 2106 6-9-7 **65** ....(p) JonathanFisher 2 49
(Liam Bailey) *led or disp ld to wl over 1f out: sn wknd* **9/1**

4-40 **10** 1½ **Eyreborn (IRE)**[9] 2684 5-7-13 **46** oh1 .... GavinAshton(3) 4 26
(Keith Dalgleish) *t.k.h: w ldrs: lost pl over 2f out: btn over 1f out* **16/1**

000- **11** nk **Skito Soldier**[168] 9412 4-7-11 **46** oh1 .... ElishaWhittington(5) 10 26
(Ruth Carr) *hld up towards rr: pushed along over 2f out: edgd lft and wknd over 1f out* **22/1**

056- **12** 2¼ **Blue Whisper**[68] 1227 4-8-6 **55** ....(t[1]) CianMacRedmond(5) 3 29
(S Donohoe, Ire) *t.k.h: led or disp ld to 2f out: sn lost pl and struggling* **12/1**

1m 41.58s (-1.22) **Going Correction** -0.15s/f (Firm) **12** Ran SP% **110.8**
Speed ratings (Par 101): **100,98,98,97,96 95,94,90,90,88 88,86**
CSF £14.36 CT £304.01 TOTE £3.40: £1.40, £1.40, £11.50; EX 16.20 Trifecta £233.50.
Owner W Storey **Bred** Tally-Ho Stud **Trained** Muggleswick, Co Durham
■ Footstepsintime was withdrawn. Price at time of withdrawal 17-2. Rule 4 applies to all bets - 10p in the pound
■ Stewards' Enquiry : Jonathan Fisher one-day ban: failing to ride out (Jun 5)

FOCUS
The slower of the two divisions by 0.46sec. The fourth and fifth offer perspective on the level of the form.
T/Plt: £281.80 to a £1 stake. Pool: £56,488.07 - 146.31 winning units T/Qpdt: £16.80 to a £1 stake. Pool: £4,987.76 - 218.98 winning units **Richard Young**

1937 **KEMPTON (A.W)** (R-H)
Wednesday, May 22

OFFICIAL GOING: Polytrack: standard to slow (watered)
Wind: Nil Weather: Fine

2965 100% PROFIT BOOST AT 32REDSPORT.COM APPRENTICE H'CAP 1m (P)
5:55 (5:55) (Class 5) (0-70,70) 3-Y-O
£3,752 (£1,116; £557; £300; £300; £300) **Stalls** Low

Form RPR

2111 **1** **Capofaro**[12] 2597 3-9-7 **70** .... ThomasGreatrex 2 78
(Jamie Osborne) *pushed along leaving stalls to sn ld: rdn over 2f out: pressed fr 1f out: kpt on wl at fin* **11/4**[1]

4364 **2** 1¼ **Kingdom Of Dubai (FR)**[12] 2597 3-9-2 **65** ....(b) SeanDavis 1 70
(Roger Varian) *racd in mid-div on inner and t.k.h for 4f: rdn over 2f out and chal wnr fr 1f out: kpt on wl but no ex last 55yds* **10/3**[2]

0-64 **3** 3½ **Reasoned (IRE)**[23] 2199 3-8-10 **64** .... LukeCatton(5) 4 61
(James Eustace) *trckd wnr: swtchd off rail wl over 2f out and sn rdn in 2nd: lost 2nd over 1f out: plugged on to hold 3rd (vet said filly lost right fore shoe)* **20/1**

560- **4** 1½ **Trelinney (IRE)**[211] 8493 3-8-8 **62** .... GeorgiaDobie(5) 10 56+
(Marcus Tregoning) *ct wd in mid-div and bmpd at times: sltly hmpd on heels 2f out w plenty to do: swtchd out and shuffled along on outer sn after: mde pleasing hdwy fr over 1f out to take 4th wl ins fnl f: can do bttr (jockey said filly hung right-handed)* **16/1**

113- **5** ¾ **Padura Brave**[180] 9227 3-8-12 **66** ....(p) AmeliaGlass(5) 5 58
(Mark Usher) *bhd ldrs: rdn over 2f out: kpt on one pce fr over 1f out: lost 4th wl ins fnl f* **12/1**

4200 **6** nk **Dancing Jo**[9] 2689 3-9-4 **70** .... ScottMcCullagh(3) 9 61+
(Mick Channon) *hld up in last trio: rdn over 2f out in last: no immediate imp tl kpt on wl on outer fr over 1f out (jockey said colt was never travelling)* **7/1**[3]

20-6 **7** 1¼ **Diviner (IRE)**[37] 1819 3-9-7 **70** .... AndrewBreslin 8 58
(Mark Johnston) *in last trio: shkn up 4f out w plenty to do: rdn over 2f out: slt hmpd 2f out: kpt on fr over 1f out* **33/1**

4250 **8** nk **Rakastava (IRE)**[25] 2101 3-8-10 **66** .... GeorgeBass(7) 7 54
(Mick Channon) *in rr: rdn over 2f out: plugged on fr over 1f out* **9/1**

006 **9** 1 **Circle Of Stars (IRE)**[24] 2146 3-9-0 **66** .... AledBeech(3) 3 51
(Charlie Fellowes) *hld up in rr-div on inner: rdn over 2f out and wnt to inner: plenty to do whn shuffled along fr over 1f out* **15/2**

046- **10** 2½ **London Pride**[219] 8257 3-9-1 **67** .... TylerSaunders(3) 13 46
(Jonathan Portman) *t.k.h in mid-div: rdn over 2f out: no imp fr over 1f out* **50/1**

600- **11** 1¾ **Sephton**[226] 8057 3-8-13 **65** .... ThoreHammerHansen(3) 14 40
(Alan King) *w ldr: nudged along to go pce 3f out: lost pl over 2f out: no ex sn after* **10/1**

050 **12** nk **San Diaco (IRE)**[39] 1754 3-8-10 **64** .... MarcoGhiani(5) 12 39
(Ed Dunlop) *racd in mid-div but cl up: effrt over 2f out: wknd over 1f out* **66/1**

1m 40.28s (0.48) **Going Correction** +0.05s/f (Slow) **12** Ran SP% **117.8**
Speed ratings (Par 99): **99,97,94,92,92 91,90,90,89,86 84,84**
CSF £11.15 CT £144.61 TOTE £2.50: £1.30, £1.50, £6.20; EX 12.00 Trifecta £144.10.
Owner Michael Buckley **Bred** Cheveley Park Stud Ltd **Trained** Upper Lambourn, Berks
■ Stewards' Enquiry : Marco Ghiani four-day ban: careless riding (5-8 Jun)

FOCUS
The track had been ameliorated to a depth of 100mm before being compressed back to 'standard to slow'. 50mm of water had been applied over two days immediately before the meeting to help consolidate the Polytrack and reduce kickback. A modest apprentice handicap in which it paid to be prominent. The third has been rated to her maiden form.

2966 32RED ON THE APP STORE H'CAP (LONDON MILE SERIES QUALIFIER) 1m (P)
6:25 (6:26) (Class 4) (0-85,84) 4-Y-O+
£6,469 (£1,925; £962; £481; £300; £300) **Stalls** Low

Form RPR

0-05 **1** **Bacacarat (IRE)**[27] 2064 4-9-4 **81** .... SilvestreDeSousa 6 89+
(Andrew Balding) *bhd ldrs between horses: shkn up over 2f out and ct on heels tl wl over 1f out: decisively rdn through small gap over 1f out and qcknd up wl to ld ent fnl f: kpt on wl whn chal cl home* **5/1**[2]

43-0 **2** ½ **Manton Grange**[18] 2402 6-9-6 **83** ....(p) NicolaCurrie 12 90
(George Baker) *racd in mid-div and ct sltly wd: effrt on outer 2f: stuck on wl fr over 1f out take 2nd cl home* **11/1**

1130 **3** hd **Merchant Of Venice**[21] 2273 4-9-7 **84** .... OisinMurphy 11 90
(James Fanshawe) *bhd ldrs on outer: rdn 2f out and ev ch over 1f out: tk 2nd jst ins fnl f: kpt on wl but lost 2nd cl home* **3/1**[1]

1-30 **4** 1¼ **Astonished (IRE)**[32] 1941 4-9-4 **81** ....(h[1]) PJMcDonald 3 84
(James Tate) *racd in mid-div between horses: shkn up on heels wl over 2f out: rdn wl over 1f out and unable to instantly qckn: swtchd to inner ent fnl f and styd on wl: gng on at fin* **8/1**[3]

1000 **5** 1½ **Rampant Lion (IRE)**[16] 2480 4-9-7 **84** ....(p) DavidProbert 13 84+
(William Jarvis) *in rr: shuffled along on heels over 2f out waiting for cutaway: rdn 2f out and darted to inner: kpt on wl fr over 1f out: ch ent fnl f but one pce last 150yds* **16/1**

6312 **6** 1¼ **Divine Messenger**[40] 1727 5-9-5 **82** ....(p) CharlesBishop 8 79
(Emma Owen) *early spd: sn trckd ldr: rdn over 2f out: kpt on wl tl began to weaken fr 1f out* **10/1**

11 **7** ¾ **Nahham (IRE)**[21] 2280 4-9-4 **81** .... SeanLevey 14 76
(Richard Hannon) *pushed along fr wdst draw to ld after 2f: rdn 2f out: pressed all rnd over 1f out: hdd ent fnl f and sn wknd* **9/1**

45-0 **8** 1½ **Orange Suit (IRE)**[11] 2628 4-8-10 **73** .... CallumShepherd 7 65
(Ed de Giles) *s.s and in rr: effrt 2f out w plenty to do: no imp over 1f out: sn shuffled along and styd on w wl past btn horses (jockey said gelding was slowly away)* **40/1**

21-0 **9** ½ **Merweb (IRE)**[23] 2186 4-8-12 **75** .... DavidEgan 2 68
(Heather Main) *mid-div on inner: effrt over 2f out: kpt on one pce fr over 1f out (vet said colt lost right fore shoe)* **11/1**

1-01 **10** 1¼ **Directory**[21] 2297 4-9-1 **78** .... RyanTate 10 65
(James Eustace) *early pce: sn bhd ldr: rdn 2f out: ch over 1f out: wknd ent fnl f and eased fnl 150yds* **11/1**

52-0 **11** ¾ **Madeleine Bond**[22] 2252 5-8-13 **79** .... GeorgiaCox(3) 1 65
(Henry Candy) *in rr-div: niggled along at 1/2-way: effrt wl over 2f out: no imp over 1f out* **25/1**

12-6 **12** 2 **One Cool Daddy (USA)**[25] 2128 4-9-6 **83** .... RobertWinston 4 64
(Dean Ivory) *bhd ldrs on inner: rdn 2f out and ev ch over 1f out: no ex fr 1f out* **12/1**

1200 **13** 2½ **Inaam (IRE)**[34] 1880 6-8-11 **74** .... KieranO'Neill 9 49
(John Butler) *hld up in rr-div: sltly lost pl at 1/2-way: rdn wl over 2f out: no imp* **66/1**

1m 39.09s (-0.71) **Going Correction** +0.05s/f (Slow) **13** Ran SP% **118.2**
Speed ratings (Par 105): **105,104,104,103,101 100,99,98,97,96 95,93,91**
CSF £57.71 CT £200.38 TOTE £5.70: £1.90, £4.60, £1.60; EX 69.20 Trifecta £113.70.
Owner King Power Racing Co Ltd **Bred** Patrick Cosgrove **Trained** Kingsclere, Hants

FOCUS
A competitive handicap and the form looks up to scratch. A decent race for the grade.

2967 32RED CASINO NOVICE MEDIAN AUCTION STKS 7f (P)
6:55 (6:56) (Class 6) 3-4-Y-O
£3,105 (£924; £461; £230) **Stalls** Low

Form RPR

31 **1** **Hotsy Totsy (IRE)**[20] 2340 3-9-4 0 .... LiamKeniry 2 89+
(Ed Walker) *mde all: shkn up 2f out: qcknd clr over 1f out: pushed out fnl f: easily* **30/100**[1]

245- **2** 6 **Gaslight**[187] 9095 3-8-11 72 ....(t) OisinMurphy 4 65
(James Fanshawe) *w wnr: rdn 2f out: lft bhd by wnr over 1f out: no ch 1f out and pushed out: rdn again cl home to jst hold 2nd* **9/2**[2]

46 **3** ½ **Venusta (IRE)**[12] 2583 3-8-11 0 .... DavidEgan 7 64+
(Mick Channon) *hld up in rr-div: effrt in 6th over 2f out: rdn 2f out and wnt to inner over 1f out: styd on wl fnl f take 3rd cl home* **11/1**

4 1 **Undercolours (IRE)** 3-9-2 0 .... DanielMuscutt 3 67
(Marco Botti) *trckd wnr: rdn 2f out: styd on tl lost 3rd cl home and jst hld 4th* **7/1**[3]

5 **5** nse **Foxes Flyer (IRE)**[42] 1677 3-8-13 0 ow2 .... JamieJones(5) 5 68
(Luke McJannet) *bhd ldrs: rdn 2f out: sltly green fr over 1f out and jockey unbalanced: shuffled along fnl f and kpt on (jockey said gelding hung right-handed)* **20/1**

00 **6** 6 **For Richard**[13] 2550 3-9-2 0 .... KierenFox 9 51
(John Best) *in last pair: niggled along to go pce at times: rdn wl over 2f out: no imp* **66/1**

7 3¼ **Dee Dee Dottie** 3-8-11 0 .... TrevorWhelan 8 37
(Geoffrey Deacon) *s.s: in rr and sltly detached: reminders to cl over 3f out: effrt over 2f out: plugged on (jockey said filly was slowly away and ran green)* **66/1**

03- **8** 2¾ **Midoura**[205] 8696 3-8-11 0 .... LiamJones 6 32
(Laura Mongan) *in rr-div and tk fierce hold for 4f: pushed along 3f out: lft bhd 2f out* **40/1**

9 shd **Tilsworth Diamond** 4-9-8 0 .... RossaRyan 1 34
(Mike Murphy) *in rr-div on inner: rdn wl over 2f out in 5th: no ex over 1f out and wknd* **40/1**

1m 26.73s (0.73) **Going Correction** +0.05s/f (Slow) **9** Ran SP% **128.6**
WFA 3 from 4yo 11lb
Speed ratings (Par 101): **97,90,89,88,88 81,77,74,74**
CSF £2.62 TOTE £1.20: £1.10, £1.30, £2.60; EX 2.70 Trifecta £7.00.
Owner Mrs T Walker **Bred** Ringfort Stud **Trained** Upper Lambourn, Berks

FOCUS
A lop-sided look to this novice auction, with a penalised filly justifying strong favouritism. The winner has been rated to her Salisbury mark.

2968 32RED.COM / BRITISH STALLION STUDS EBF FILLIES' NOVICE STKS (PLUS 10 RACE) 6f (P)
7:25 (7:25) (Class 4) 2-Y-O
£5,822 (£1,732; £865; £432) **Stalls** Low

Form RPR

0 **1** **Seraphinite (IRE)**[12] 2579 2-9-0 0 .... NicolaCurrie 3 74
(Jamie Osborne) *bhd ldr: shkn up 2f out and cruised upsides ldr on inner: hld together tl rdn 1f out to ld: green in front fnl f and cajoled along to win snugly at fin: nice ride* **33/1**

2 ½ **Rubia Bella** 2-9-0 0 .... SeanLevey 6 73
(David Simcock) *bhd ldrs on outer: rdn 2f out on outer: kpt on wl fr over 1f out to take 2nd last 110yds* **13/2**

51 **3** nk **Brazen Safa**[22] 2228 2-9-3 0 .... HayleyTurner 4 75
(Michael Bell) *sn led: rdn 2f out: styd on tl hdd 1f out: lost 2nd 110yds out: kpt on* **7/1**

4 7 **Dream Kart (IRE)** 2-9-0 0 .... PJMcDonald 7 51
(Mark Johnston) *w ldr: rdn 2f out: outpcd over 1f out: no ex and pushed out fnl f* **14/1**

The Form Book Flat 2019, Raceform Ltd, Newbury, RG14 5SJ

5 nk **Sneaky** 2-9-0 0 .... OisinMurphy 2 50
(Archie Watson) *rrd s: in rr-div on outer: effrt over 2f out and wnt to inner: briefly hld pl ch ent 1f out: emptied fnl f (jockey said filly reared leaving the stalls and was subsequently slow into stride)* **2/1**[1]

6 4 **Dubai Romance (IRE)** 2-9-0 0 .... HectorCrouch 1 38
(Saeed bin Suroor) *racd in rr-div on inner and sltly keen: effrt 2f out: no ex over 1f out* **10/3**[2]

7 8 **Sri Sene Power (IRE)** 2-9-0 0 .... SilvestreDeSousa 5 14
(Richard Hannon) *a in rr and v green thrght (vet said filly was coughing post-race)* **4/1**[3]

1m 13.73s (0.63) **Going Correction** +0.05s/f (Slow) **7 Ran SP% 111.9**
Speed ratings (Par 92): **97,96,95,86,86 80,70**
CSF £217.77 TOTE £24.00: £6.10, £4.00; EX 145.50 Trifecta £1089.20.
Owner The 10 For 10 Partnership **Bred** Yeomanstown Stud **Trained** Upper Lambourn, Berks

FOCUS
Little to go on in this fillies' juvenile and it did not go the way the market expected. The level is fluid.

2969 32RED H'CAP (LONDON MIDDLE DISTANCE SERIES QUALIFIER) 2f 219y(P)
7:55 (7:56) (Class 3) (0-95,93) 4-Y-O+

£9,337 (£2,796; £1,398; £699; £349; £175) **Stalls** Low

Form RPR

-301 1 **Harbour Breeze (IRE)**[23] 2186 4-8-11 **83** .... JasonWatson 9 92
(Lucy Wadham) *led after 1f and mde rest: tk a keen grip in bk st: shkn up 3f out: rdn 2f out and stole two l advantage: styd on wl fnl f and jst hld on* **7/1**

14-3 2 shd **Koeman**[17] 2440 5-9-6 **92** .... DavidEgan 7 100
(Mick Channon) *bhd ldrs: squeezed along at times to go pce: briefly pushed along wl over 3f out: rdn to chse wnr wl over 1f out: inching clsr w ev stride fr 110yds out: jst failed* **7/1**

34-2 3 3 **Sleeping Lion (USA)**[25] 2126 4-9-5 **91** .... JamieSpencer 5 94
(James Fanshawe) *hld up in rr-div: rdn over 2f out: kpt on and tk 3rd 1f out: stuck on but no ch w ldng pair* **3/1**[1]

-363 4 3 1/2 **Wimpole Hall**[90] 825 6-8-8 **80** ....(p) SilvestreDeSousa 3 77
(William Jarvis) *hld up in last: rdn at cutaway 2f out and swtchd to inner: kpt on fr over 1f out (jockey said gelding was slowly away)* **20/1**

302- 5 nk **Western Duke (IRE)**[94] 9487 5-8-13 **85** .... RichardKingscote 1 82
(Ian Williams) *racd in mid-div: rdn 2f out: plugged on fr over 1f out* **16/1**

025- 6 3/4 **Landue**[153] 9639 4-9-3 **89** .... HayleyTurner 10 85+
(Marcus Tregoning) *in rr: shuffled along fr over 2f out and styd on past wkng horses fnl f: nvr involved* **16/1**

31-1 7 1 3/4 **Lexington Empire**[34] 1882 4-9-3 **89** .... DanielMuscutt 4 82
(David Lanigan) *early pce: sn bhd wnr: rdn over 2f out: no ex in 3rd over 1f out and wknd* **9/2**[2]

204- 8 2 3/4 **Rock Force (IRE)**[208] 8596 4-8-10 **82** .... DavidProbert 2 71
(Alan King) *mid-div on inner: drvn over 2f out: no ex ent fnl f* **5/1**[3]

1150 9 11 **Ilhabela Fact**[23] 2209 5-8-8 **80** .... KieranO'Neill 6 51
(Tony Carroll) *trckd wnr: rdn 3f out to hold pl: swamped 2f out and sn wknd* **14/1**

-006 10 1 3/4 **North Face (IRE)**[20] 2320 4-9-6 **92** ....(tp) GeraldMosse 8 60
(Marco Botti) *racd in rr-div on outer: rdn over 3f out: wknd over 2f out* **20/1**

2m 18.61s (-2.39) **Going Correction** +0.05s/f (Slow) **10 Ran SP% 112.8**
Speed ratings (Par 107): **113,112,110,108,107 107,106,104,96,94**
CSF £53.38 CT £176.57 TOTE £8.10: £2.60, £2.10, £1.50; EX 39.40 Trifecta £151.30.
Owner B J Painter **Bred** Gestut Zur Kuste Ag **Trained** Newmarket, Suffolk

FOCUS
Competitive stuff, decent form and a good ride aboard the all-the-way winner. The third has been rated a bit below form.

2970 MAKING WAVES WITH GULF H'CAP 1m 3f 219y(P)
8:25 (8:29) (Class 6) (0-55,57) 4-Y-O+

£3,105 (£924; £461; £300; £300; £300) **Stalls** Low

Form RPR

-311 1 **Croeso Cymraeg**[97] 721 5-9-5 **54** .... RaulDaSilva 3 61+
(James Evans) *hld up in rr-div on inner: shkn up 3f out and smooth prog to take clsr order over 1f out: sn pushed along and chal ldr fr 1f out: rdn to ld wl ins fnl f: snugly at fin* **7/2**[1]

-064 2 nk **Barca (USA)**[21] 2279 5-8-13 **55** .... TylerSaunders(7) 14 62
(Marcus Tregoning) *trckd ldrs on outer: tk clsr order over 3f out: rdn wl over 2f out: led over 1f out: pressed fr 1f out: hdd wl ins fnl f: no ex fin* **8/1**

004 3 2 3/4 **Lauberhorn Rocket (GER)**[25] 2127 4-9-2 **51** .... KieranO'Neill 7 53
(Tim Vaughan) *bhd ldr on inner: effrt wl over 2f out: plugged on to take 3rd 1f out: kpt on but no ch w ldng pair* **11/2**[2]

00 4 4 1/2 **Barrier Reef (IRE)**[25] 2128 4-9-4 **53** .... DavidProbert 9 48
(Tim Vaughan) *in rr-div and niggled along thrght: lost pl wl over 4f out: effrt 3f out: styd on fr wl over 1f out* **33/1**

-103 5 nk **Kingfast (IRE)**[25] 2111 4-9-2 **51** .... OisinMurphy 11 45
(David Dennis) *racd in rr-div on outer: rdn 3f out: styd on out wd fr 2f out: nvr nrr* **8/1**

060- 6 shd **Aria Rose**[186] 9128 4-9-5 **54** .... HayleyTurner 10 48
(David Arbuthnot) *bhd ldr: upsides wl over 4f out: rdn to ld 3f out: hdd 2f out lost 4th 1f out: wknd fnl f* **10/1**

5005 7 3/4 **Sellingallthetime (IRE)**[9] 2698 8-8-11 **53** ....(p) EllieMacKenzie(7) 2 46
(Mark Usher) *mid-div on inner: rdn wl over 2f out: styd on fr over 1f out* **14/1**

3021 8 hd **Lady Of Authority**[9] 2698 4-9-1 **57** 5ex .... GeorgiaDobie(7) 12 50
(Richard Phillips) *in rr: rdn wl over 2f out: plugged on fr over 1f out* **6/1**[3]

44/ 9 1 1/2 **Asknotwhat (IRE)**[39] 3487 8-9-6 **55** ....(bt) RobHornby 8 45
(Tom Gretton) *in rr: rdn wl over 2f out: sme hdwy fr 2f out* **66/1**

0042 10 4 1/2 **Qayed (CAN)**[9] 2698 4-9-2 **51** ....(p) LiamJones 6 34
(Mark Brisbourne) *racd in mid-div: gng okay whn rdn 2f out: nt qckn and sn hld* **10/1**

0305 11 1 3/4 **Apex Predator (IRE)**[25] 2127 4-9-5 **54** ....(bt w) TomQueally 5 34
(Seamus Durack) *cl up in mid-div: rdn wl over 2f out: wandered sn after: no ex over 1f out* **8/1**

-000 12 19 **Officer Drivel (IRE)**[15] 2513 8-9-2 **51** .... CallumShepherd 1 1
(Paddy Butler) *led: rdn over 3f out: hdd wl over 2f out: wknd sn after* **66/1**

0042 13 2 1/2 **Diamond Reflection (IRE)**[42] 1680 7-9-2 **51** ....(bt) CamHardie 13
(Alexandra Dunn) *hld up in rr-div: effrt 3f out: no imp* **16/1**

500/ 14 53 **Casado (IRE)**[639] 6257 5-9-5 **54** .... RobertWinston 4
(Linda Jewell) *bhd ldr: rdn wl over 2f out: lost pl and eased wl over 1f out: t.o (jockey said gelding stopped quickly)* **66/1**

2m 35.13s (0.63) **Going Correction** +0.05s/f (Slow) **14 Ran SP% 123.4**
Speed ratings (Par 101): **99,98,96,93,93 93,93,93,92,89 87,75,73,38**
CSF £31.98 CT £155.14 TOTE £4.10: £1.40, £4.10, £2.10; EX 43.40 Trifecta £279.30.
Owner Richard Evans Bloodstock **Bred** Richard Evans **Trained** Broadwas, Worcs

FOCUS
The full 14 went to post for this modest handicap and it was a bit messy to the first bend as jockey's hustled for position. The right horses came to the fore. The second has been rated as running his best race so far for his current yard.

2971 TONY SHEEDY IS GETTING MARRIED H'CAP 7f (P)
8:55 (8:55) (Class 5) (0-70,72) 4-Y-O+

£3,752 (£1,116; £557; £300; £300; £300) **Stalls** Low

Form RPR

-024 1 **Coverham (IRE)**[18] 2418 5-9-7 **70** .... RyanTate 1 78
(James Eustace) *cl up in mid-div: niggled along to hold pl at 1/2-way: cajoled along 2f out: prog and ct on heels ent fnl f: drvn between horses to ld 110yds out: wl on top at fin* **5/2**[2]

4656 2 1 **Little Palaver**[20] 2339 7-9-2 **72** ....(p) AmeliaGlass(7) 8 77
(Clive Cox) *trckd ldr on outer: clsr and upsides 2f out: rdn wl over 1f out: ev ch ent fnl f: tk 2nd nr fin: no ex cl home and tk false step last strides* **8/1**

-124 3 hd **Chloellie**[34] 1880 4-9-8 **71** .... SilvestreDeSousa 4 75
(J R Jenkins) *bhd ldrs on outer: rdn 2f out: kpt on fr over 1f out: styd on on outer fnl f to take 3rd nr fin* **2/1**[1]

0160 4 1/2 **Miracle Garden**[39] 1765 7-9-5 **68** ....(v) RichardKingscote 3 71
(Ian Williams) *bhd ldr on inner: rdn 2f out: led narrowly 1f out: hdd 110yds out and lost two pls nr fin* **13/2**[3]

03-0 5 1 **Bounty Pursuit**[20] 2339 7-9-2 **68** .... MitchGodwin(3) 11 68+
(Michael Blake) *hld up in rr: rdn 2f out w a bit to do: styd on wl fr over 1f out and tk 5th nr fin: nvr nrr* **33/1**

4010 6 1 1/4 **My Town Chicago (USA)**[20] 2349 4-8-9 **63**.. ThoreHammerHansen(5) 2 60
(Kevin Frost) *uns rdr bhd stalls: sn led: rdn 2f out: hdd 1f out: rallied briefly tl no ex wl ins fnl f* **9/1**

1-42 7 1/2 **Soar Above**[83] 944 4-9-5 **68** .... TomQueally 10 64+
(John Butler) *in rr-div on outer: niggled along 4f out: rdn on outer over 2f out: nt qckn over 1f out: kpt on being shuffled along fnl f* **12/1**

0-00 8 hd **Reshaan (IRE)**[23] 2193 4-8-9 **58** .... CamHardie 5 53
(Alexandra Dunn) *racd in mid-div: hrd rdn wl over 2f out: styng on over 1f out: no ex ent fnl f* **66/1**

1-30 9 3 1/4 **Garth Rockett**[42] 1684 5-9-1 **64** .... RossaRyan 6 50
(Mike Murphy) *mid-div: effrt over 2f out: sme prog over 1f out: emptied fnl f* **10/1**

03-U 10 7 **Angel Islington (IRE)**[6] 2774 4-9-7 **70** .... DavidProbert 7 37
(Andrew Balding) *sltly hmpd s and a in rr* **12/1**

360- 11 1 3/4 **Dutiful Son (IRE)**[156] 9587 9-9-7 **70** .... PJMcDonald 9 33
(Emma Owen) *a in rr (jockey said gelding hung left-handed)* **66/1**

1m 26.04s (0.04) **Going Correction** +0.05s/f (Slow) **11 Ran SP% 126.8**
Speed ratings (Par 103): **101,99,99,99,97 96,95,95,91,83 81**
CSF £25.24 CT £50.53 TOTE £3.20: £1.40, £2.50, £1.20; EX 22.60 Trifecta £82.50.
Owner Blue Peter Racing 15 **Bred** Peter & James Jones **Trained** Newmarket, Suffolk

FOCUS
Plenty of previous course form on offer in this modest handicap. A small pb from the winner, with the second rated to his recent 7f form.
T/Plt: £72.60 to a £1 stake. Pool: £67,805.37 - 681.58 winning units T/Qpdt: £24.10 to a £1 stake. Pool: £7,407.95 - 227.24 winning units **Cathal Gahan**

2735 YARMOUTH (L-H)
Wednesday, May 22

OFFICIAL GOING: Good to firm (watered; 7.3)
Wind: medium, against Weather: light cloud

2972 HAVEN HOPTON PARK H'CAP 1m 3y
2:10 (2:12) (Class 6) (0-55,56) 4-Y-O+

£3,105 (£924; £461; £300; £300; £300) **Stalls** Centre

Form RPR

0200 1 **Sir Jamie**[11] 2631 6-9-1 **48** ....(b) TomMarquand 15 57
(Tony Carroll) *swtchd lft after s: hld up in rr: clsd and n.m.r ent fnl 2f: hdwy to chse ldr over 1f out: sn drvn: r.o wl ins fnl f to ld towards fin (trainer's rep said, regarding the improved form shown, the gelding benefitted from the re-application of blinkers)* **18/1**

6301 2 1/2 **King Oswald (USA)**[50] 1506 6-9-6 **53** ....(tp) LiamJones 2 61
(James Unett) *hld up in tch towards rr: clsd and nt clr run 2f out: rdn to hdwy to ld over 1f out: wandered ins fnl f: edging lft after but kpt on: hdd and no ex towards fin (jockey said gelding hung left-handed)* **7/2**[2]

06-0 3 2 3/4 **Khaan**[25] 2094 4-8-9 **45** .... GeorgeBuckell(3) 4 47+
(Michael Appleby) *stdd s: hld up in detached last: clsd and swtchd lft over 2f out: effrt to chse ldng pair jst over 1f out: kpt on but no imp ins fnl f* **20/1**

0040 4 6 **Percy Toplis**[22] 2256 5-8-12 **45** ....(b) EoinWalsh 7 34
(Christine Dunnett) *dwlt: in tch towards rr: rdn over 3f out: sme prog and nt clr run ent fnl 2f: swtchd lft and hdwy over 1f out: kpt on to go 4th ins fnl f: no threat to ldrs (jockey said gelding was denied a clear run from approximately 2 and a half furlongs out)* **28/1**

0450 5 2 1/2 **Dukes Meadow**[41] 1717 8-8-12 **45** .... JackMitchell 3 27
(Roger Ingram) *in tch in midfield: effrt and hdwy to press ldrs ent fnl 2f: unable qck u.p and btn 1f out: wknd ins fnl f* **20/1**

-000 6 nk **Cloud Nine (FR)**[56] 1362 6-8-12 **45** ....(b) EdwardGreatrex 11 26
(Tony Carroll) *in tch in midfield: effrt over 2f out: unable qck over 1f out: wknd ins fnl f* **20/1**

0/05 7 1 3/4 **Angelical Eve (IRE)**[12] 2585 5-8-9 **45** .... NoelGarbutt(3) 13 22
(Dai Williams) *in tch in midfield: no ex u.p over 1f out: wknd fnl f (vet reported mare lost its left fore shoe)* **40/1**

0236 8 3 **Molten Lava (IRE)**[25] 2112 7-9-6 **53** ....(p) RobertHavlin 6 23
(Steve Gollings) *t.k.h: chsd ldrs: chsd ldr and bmpd jst over 2f out: lost pl u.p and btn over 1f out: wknd fnl f* **3/1**[1]

-055 9 1 3/4 **Mezmaar**[41] 1715 10-9-6 **56** .... GaryMahon(3) 5 22
(Mark Usher) *taken down early: chsd ldrs: rdn over 2f out: unable qck and btn over 1f out: wknd fnl f* **12/1**

2205 10 1/2 **Voice Of A Leader (IRE)**[22] 2240 8-9-1 **48** ....(p) JoeyHaynes 10 13
(Paul Howling) *taken down early: led tl over 1f out: sn btn and eased ins fnl f* **10/1**

-355 11 1 1/2 **Boxatricks (IRE)**[22] 2256 4-9-5 **52** .... RoystonFfrench 12 14
(Julia Feilden) *t.k.h: wl in tch in midfield: effrt and pushed along ent fnl 2f: reminder and lost pl over 1f out: wknd fnl f (jockey said gelding hung right-handed)* **6/1**[3]

0-3F 12 2 1/4 **Spanish Mane (IRE)**[22] 2261 4-9-4 **56**.......... DylanHogan[(5)] 1 13
(Julia Feilden) *stdd after s: hld up in tch towards rr: effrt over 2f out: sn struggling and hung rt over 1f out: wknd fnl f* **15/2**

3000 13 2 1/2 **Shamlan (IRE)**[9] 2681 7-9-2 **54**..........(p) HarrisonShaw[(5)] 14 5
(Marjorie Fife) *chsd ldr tl over 2f out: sn losing pl and jostled: bhd over 1f out: wknd* **33/1**

50-0 14 10 **Harvest Ranger**[22] 2256 5-8-7 **45**..........(p) TheodoreLadd[(5)] 16
(Michael Appleby) *in tch in midfield: rdn over 3f out: steadily lost pl and bhd over 1f out: wknd* **11/1**

1m 38.69s (0.49) **Going Correction** +0.25s/f (Good) **14** Ran SP% **126.8**
Speed ratings (Par 101): **107,106,103,97,95 94,93,90,88,87 86,84,81,71**
CSF £77.51 CT £1373.75 TOTE £16.80: £5.50, £1.40, £8.00; EX 124.40.
Owner Mayden Stud **Bred** Mayden Stud, J A And D S Dewhurst **Trained** Cropthorne, Worcs

FOCUS
Drying ground and it was changed to good to firm all over before racing. Lowly form, the race very much set up for the closers with the pace not holding up. The second has been rated near his best 2018 turf form.

2973 BRITISH STALLION STUDS EBF NOVICE STKS (PLUS 10 RACE) 6f 3y
2:45 (2:45) (Class 3) 2-Y-O £9,703 (£2,887; £1,443; £721) **Stalls** Centre

Form RPR

1 **Maxi Boy** 2-9-5.......... RyanMoore 6 79+
(Michael Bell) *dwlt: in tch: shkn up and effrt to press ldrs over 1f out: reminder and led ins fnl f: r.o wl* **11/4**[2]

3 2 nk **Path Of Thunder (IRE)**[17] 2444 2-9-5.......... JamesDoyle 8 78
(Charlie Appleby) *chsd ldr for 2f: styd prom: rdn to ld over 1f out: hdd ins fnl f: kpt on wl but hld towards fin* **5/4**[1]

3 1 **Rusper's Lad** 2-9-5.......... JackMitchell 4 75
(Tom Clover) *hld up in tch: j. path sn after s: nt clrest of runs over 1f out: swtchd rt 1f out: rdn and kpt on wl ins fnl f: snatched 3rd last strides* **66/1**

4 hd **Historic (IRE)** 2-9-5.......... HarryBentley 1 74+
(Saeed bin Suroor) *broke okay but rn green and j. path sn after s: in tch towards rr after: shkn up and clsd to chse ldrs ent fnl f: kpt on same pce fnl 150yds* **6/1**

5 1 1/2 **St Ives** 2-9-5.......... TomMarquand 3 70+
(William Haggas) *chsd ldrs: nt clrest of runs 2f out: pushed along and unable qck over 1f out: kpt on same pce ins fnl f* **14/1**

6 1 1/2 **Deverell** 2-9-5.......... RobertHavlin 2 65+
(John Gosden) *chsd ldrs tl wnt 2nd 4f out: rdn and ev ch over 1f out tl no ex 1f: outpcd ins fnl f* **5/1**[3]

7 shd **Arthur's Court (IRE)** 2-9-5.......... PatCosgrave 5 67+
(Hugo Palmer) *dwlt: hld up in tch: nt clrest of runs wl over 1f out: swtchd lft and effrt 1f out: no imp and sn outpcd* **25/1**

4 8 6 **Dark Side Division**[22] 2257 2-9-5.......... BrettDoyle 7 47
(John Ryan) *got loose in the paddock: led tl rdn and hdd over 1f out: sn lost pl: bhd and wknd ins fnl f* **50/1**

1m 14.64s (2.04) **Going Correction** +0.25s/f (Good) **8** Ran SP% **116.0**
Speed ratings (Par 97): **96,95,94,94,92 90,89,81**
CSF £6.61 TOTE £3.00: £1.20, £1.10, £11.00; EX 8.30 Trifecta £150.90.
Owner Amo Racing Limited **Bred** Al-Baha Bloodstock **Trained** Newmarket, Suffolk

FOCUS
Debatable how strong a juvenile race this was, with the field finishing bunched. Still, it should throw up winners. The second has been rated up a bit on his debut effort.

2974 GROSVENOR CASINO OF GREAT YARMOUTH H'CAP 1m 6f 17y
3:15 (3:19) (Class 6) (0-65,63) 4-Y-O+
£3,105 (£924; £461; £300; £300; £300) **Stalls** High

Form RPR

-644 1 **The Resdev Way**[30] 1981 6-9-0 **61**.......... PaulaMuir[(5)] 6 67
(Philip Kirby) *stdd s and t.k.h early: hld up in rr: gd hdwy 4f out: led over 1f out: hung lft but sn asserted: pushed along and r.o wl ins fnl f: quite comf* **9/2**[2]

6066 2 1 **Strictly Art (IRE)**[37] 1815 6-8-12 **61**.......... JessicaCooley[(7)] 7 66
(Alan Bailey) *chsd ldrs: pushed along and clsd to press ldrs 4f out: rdn and unable to match pce of wnr over 1f out: chsd wnr 1f out: kpt on but a hld* **8/1**[3]

4603 3 1 1/4 **Butterfield (IRE)**[16] 2468 6-8-10 **52**..........(p) EoinWalsh 9 55
(Tony Carroll) *hld in tch in midfield: rdn over 3f out: unable qck and outpcd over 2f out: rallied u.p 1f out: kpt on wl to go 3rd wl ins fnl f: no threat to wnr* **12/1**

-406 4 hd **Princess Harley (IRE)**[51] 1482 4-9-7 **63**.......... TomQueally 4 66
(Mick Quinn) *t.k.h: chsd ldrs: nt clr run and swtchd rt over 2f out: effrt 2f out: kpt on u.p ins fnl f: wnt 4th towards fin* **9/1**

2221 5 1 **Top Rock Talula (IRE)**[7] 2733 4-9-7 **63** 5ex.......... EdwardGreatrex 3 65
(Warren Greatrex) *t.k.h: hld up in tch in midfield: effrt to press ldrs ent fnl 2f: unable to match pce of wnr over 1f out: kpt on same pce and lost 2 pls wl ins fnl f* **5/4**[1]

00-0 6 1 1/4 **Cue's Folly**[48] 1548 4-8-3 **45**.......... JosephineGordon 2 45
(Ed Dunlop) *hld up in last pair: outpcd u.p over 2f out: rallied and styd on ins fnl f: nvr trbld ldrs* **16/1**

306- 7 1/2 **Sir Fred (IRE)**[219] 8281 4-7-13 **48**.......... SophieRalston[(7)] 5 47
(Julia Feilden) *chsd ldr: ev ch over 3f out tl unable to match pce of wnr over 1f out: wknd ins fnl f* **8/1**[3]

05-0 8 1/2 **Approaching Menace**[21] 2283 4-8-0 **45**.......... JaneElliott[(3)] 1 44
(Amy Murphy) *taken down early: led: rdn and hdd over 1f out: wknd ins fnl f* **20/1**

0060 9 10 **Chantresse (IRE)**[9] 2685 4-9-1 **60**..........(p) GaryMahon[(3)] 8 46
(Mark Usher) *hld up in midfield: clsd on inner to chse ldrs over 2f out: no ex u.p and btn over 1f out: wknd ins fnl f* **33/1**

3m 9.57s (4.87) **Going Correction** +0.25s/f (Good) **9** Ran SP% **116.1**
Speed ratings (Par 101): **96,95,94,94,94 93,93,92,87**
CSF £40.45 CT £405.19 TOTE £5.20: £1.50, £2.40, £2.40; EX 41.40 Trifecta £350.70.
Owner Resdev **Bred** Mickley Stud **Trained** East Appleton, N Yorks

FOCUS
Moderate staying form, with there being no great pace on and several racing keenly.

2975 LAVISH HAIR BEAUTY AESTHETICS H'CAP 1m 3f 104y
3:45 (3:48) (Class 6) (0-60,62) 4-Y-O+
£3,105 (£924; £461; £300; £300; £300) **Stalls** Low

Form RPR

05-2 1 **Nasee**[22] 2259 4-9-9 **62**..........(p) StevieDonohoe 10 70+
(Ed Vaughan) *hld up in tch: rdn 3f out: swtchd rt and effrt over 1f out: hdwy and rdn to chse ldr jst ins fnl f: kpt on to ld cl home (gelding ran without its right fore shoe)* **7/4**[1]

6-30 2 nk **Mistress Nellie**[126] 257 4-8-4 **46** oh1.......... GabrieleMalune[(3)] 11 54
(William Stone) *chsd ldr tl led 2f out: rdn over 1f out: drvn ins fnl f: kpt on but hdd and no ex cl home* **20/1**

000- 3 2 1/2 **Maroon Bells (IRE)**[224] 8100 4-9-6 **59**.......... TomMarquand 2 63
(David Menuisier) *hld up in midfield: clsd to chse ldrs over 2f out: chsd ldr but unable qck u.p over 1f out: lost 2nd and kpt on same pce ins fnl f* **10/1**

000- 4 2 1/2 **Misty Breese (IRE)**[240] 7614 4-8-4 **46** oh1.......... NoelGarbutt[(3)] 7 46
(Sarah Hollinshead) *hld up in rr: hdwy on inner to chse ldrs over 2f out: no ex u.p over 1f out: wknd ins fnl f* **50/1**

6000 5 hd **Seventii**[25] 2111 5-8-4 **46** oh1.......... JaneElliott[(3)] 8 45
(Robert Eddery) *hld up in tch towards rr: clsd 4f out: chsd ldrs and swtchd lft over 1f out: no ex 1f out: wknd ins fnl f* **20/1**

23-3 6 2 1/4 **Johni Boxit**[21] 2277 4-9-5 **61**.......... MeganNicholls[(3)] 3 57
(Brian Barr) *chsd ldrs: squeezed for room 2f out: unable qck over 1f out: wknd ins fnl f* **10/1**

-034 7 3 1/2 **Telekinetic**[7] 2738 4-8-9 **48**.......... RoystonFfrench 6 38
(Julia Feilden) *chsd ldr: rdn 2f out: sn outpcd and btn over 1f out: wknd ins fnl f* **4/1**[2]

30-0 8 2 1/2 **Viento De Condor (IRE)**[123] 309 4-9-7 **60**..........(v) JackMitchell 4 46
(Tom Clover) *led tl 2f out: sn rdn and lost pl: wknd ins fnl f* **25/1**

-000 9 1/2 **Tebay (IRE)**[11] 2617 4-9-5 **58**.......... EoinWalsh 9 43
(Luke McJannet) *hld up in tch in midfield: rdn over 2f out: sn edging lft and outpcd: wl hld over 1f out: wknd fnl f (jockey said gelding ran flat)* **20/1**

5040 10 3 3/4 **Roc Astrale (IRE)**[16] 2468 5-9-6 **59**..........(t) JosephineGordon 5 38
(Phil McEntee) *hld up in tch in last trio: rdn over 3f out: bhd and hung lft 2f out: no ch after* **18/1**

50-0 11 19 **Widnes**[60] 1297 5-8-12 **56**..........(vt) DarraghKeenan[(5)] 12 5
(Alan Bailey) *in tch in midfield: rdn 4f out: sn struggling and bhd 2f out: sn wknd (trainer's rep said gelding had a breathing problem)* **10/1**

5034 12 22 **Ember's Glow**[9] 2698 5-9-0 **53**.......... EdwardGreatrex 1
(Mark Loughnane) *in tch in midfield: lost pl u.p and bhd 2f out: t.o and eased ins fnl f (jockey said gelding stopped quickly)* **6/1**[3]

2m 26.95s (-0.85) **Going Correction** +0.25s/f (Good) **12** Ran SP% **123.3**
Speed ratings (Par 101): **110,109,107,106,106 104,101,100,99,96 83,67**
CSF £48.72 CT £298.13 TOTE £2.50: £1.80, £6.10, £2.50; EX 45.80 Trifecta £529.60.
Owner Saeed Suhail **Bred** Highclere Stud **Trained** Newmarket, Suffolk

FOCUS
Run at a fair gallop, the favourite came from last. The second has been rated to her best.

2976 PALM COURT HOTEL OF GREAT YARMOUTH MEDIAN AUCTION MAIDEN STKS 6f 3y
4:15 (4:18) (Class 5) 3-5-Y-O £3,752 (£1,116; £557; £278) **Stalls** Centre

Form RPR

53- 1 **Local History**[184] 9151 3-9-0.......... RyanMoore 1 71
(James Tate) *t.k.h: sn led and mde virtually all: rdn wl over 1f out: hrd pressed 1f out: kpt on wl u.p ins fnl f: drvn out* **6/4**[1]

0-3 2 hd **Delachance (FR)**[22] 2243 3-9-0..........(h[1]) DylanHogan[(5)] 2 75
(David Simcock) *stdd s: hld up in tch: clsd ent fnl 2f: rdn to press wnr over 1f out: ev ch and hung lft fr 1f out: kpt on u.p: hld towards fin* **13/2**[3]

3 3 **Fashionesque (IRE)** 3-9-0.......... ShaneKelly 6 61
(Rae Guest) *dwlt: t.k.h: hld up in tch: effrt over 1f out: rn green and edgd lft ent fnl f: swtchd rt and r.o wl fnl 100yds: no threat to ldng pair* **14/1**

2 4 hd **Casarubina (IRE)**[25] 2123 3-8-9..........(t) DarraghKeenan[(5)] 3 60
(Nick Littmoden) *t.k.h: pressed wnr for 2f: styd prom: unable qck u.p 1f out: hung rt and outpcd ins fnl f: lost 3rd last strides (jockey said filly hung right-handed)* **14/1**

62-2 5 hd **Sirius Slew**[29] 2024 3-9-5 **76**..........(b) TomMarquand 5 64
(Alan Bailey) *broke wl: sn in tch in midfield and t.k.h: effrt over 1f out: unable to match pce of ldrs and wandered lft 1f out: kpt on same pce ins fnl f* **7/4**[2]

0-20 6 1 1/4 **Miaella**[58] 1336 4-9-9.......... JoeyHaynes 4 57
(Paul Howling) *hld up in tch: effrt wl over 1f out: no imp over 1f out: kpt on ins fnl f but no threat to ldrs* **20/1**

7 nk **George Thomas** 3-9-5.......... TomQueally 9 60
(Mick Quinn) *chsd ldrs: wnt 2nd 4f out tl unable qck u.p over 1f out: wknd ins fnl f* **20/1**

8 5 **Exning Queen (IRE)** 3-9-0.......... RoystonFfrench 7 39
(Julia Feilden) *s.i.s: hld up in tch: effrt 2f out: sn hung lft: wknd ins fnl f* **33/1**

50 9 4 1/2 **Manzoni**[23] 2199 3-9-5.......... JackMitchell 8 29
(Mohamed Moubarak) *stdd s: t.k.h: effrt 2f out: sn struggling and outpcd: bhd ins fnl f (jockey said gelding ran too freely)* **66/1**

1m 13.97s (1.37) **Going Correction** +0.25s/f (Good)
WFA 3 from 4yo 9lb **9** Ran SP% **117.0**
Speed ratings (Par 103): **100,99,95,95,95 93,93,86,80**
CSF £11.60 TOTE £2.60: £1.20, £2.20, £1.50; EX 10.60 Trifecta £86.00.
Owner Saeed Manana **Bred** West Dereham Abbey Stud **Trained** Newmarket, Suffolk

FOCUS
Ordinary maiden form, they went steady and the favourite made all. It's been rated around the winner to last year's debut form.

2977 NORWICH OFFICE FURNITURE H'CAP 7f 3y
4:45 (4:48) (Class 4) (0-80,81) 4-Y-O+
£5,530 (£1,645; £822; £411; £300; £300) **Stalls** Centre

Form RPR

012- 1 **Mubhij (IRE)**[302] 5325 4-9-8 **81**.......... DaneO'Neill 10 96+
(Roger Varian) *awkward leaving stalls: hld up in tch in last trio: clsd ent fnl 2f: rdn and qcknd to ld over 1f out: clr and r.o strly ins fnl f: readily* **3/1**[2]

504- 2 2 1/2 **Envisaging (IRE)**[209] 8578 5-9-1 **74**..........(t) GeorgeWood 8 80+
(James Fanshawe) *t.k.h: hld up wl in tch in midfield: nt clr run wl over 1f out: swtchd rt and hdwy 1f out: r.o to snatch 2nd last strides: no ch w wnr* **8/1**

510- 3 nk **Choco Box**[237] 7701 4-9-7 **80**.......... StevieDonohoe 9 85
(Ed Vaughan) *stdd s: t.k.h: hld up in tch in last trio: swtchd lft and effrt over 1f out: chsd wnr ins fnl f: no imp and lost 2nd last strides* **10/1**

6065 4 3 1/4 **Swift Approval (IRE)**[11] 2622 7-9-4 **77**..........(p) HarryBentley 2 73
(Stuart Williams) *w ldrs: dropped in bhd ldrs but t.k.h after 1f: rdn over 1f out: chsd clr wnr 1f out: no imp and lost 2 pls ins fnl f* **11/4**[1]

400- 5 1 **Bint Dandy (IRE)**[179] 9242 8-9-5 **78**..........(b) LewisEdmunds 6 72
(Charlie Wallis) *hld up wl in tch in midfield: nt clrest of runs wl over 1f out: effrt u.p jst over 1f out: sn no imp and wknd ins fnl f* **25/1**

24-2 6 3/4 **Bbob Alula**[22] 2232 4-8-11 **75**..........(t) RyanWhile[(5)] 4 67
(Bill Turner) *led: rdn and nt match pce of wnr over 1f out: lost 2nd 1f out and wknd ins fnl f* **20/1**

4202 **7** *1 ¼* **Glory Awaits (IRE)**[7] 2739 9-8-11 **75**..........................(b) DylanHogan(5) 3 63
(David Simcock) *t.k.h: hld up in tch in midfield: effrt to press ldrs u.p over 1f out: sn outpcd and wknd ins fnl f* **4/1**[3]

400- **8** *1* **Marilyn**[198] 8884 5-9-2 **80**.......................... SebastianWoods(5) 5 65
(Shaun Keightley) *w ldr: rdn and unable qck over 1f out: sn outpcd and wknd ins fnl f* **20/1**

214- **9** *4 ½* **Counter Spirit (IRE)**[215] 8379 5-9-2 **75**.......................... TomMarquand 7 48
(Ismail Mohammed) *wl in tch: effrt 2f out: unable qck over 1f out: wknd ins fnl f* **8/1**

1/P- **10** *9* **Kestrel Dot Com**[288] 5832 7-9-4 **80**..........................(p[1]) JoshuaBryan(3) 1 29
(Charlie Wallis) *s.i.s: hld up in rr: pushed along 2f out: sn btn* **33/1**

1m 26.21s (1.11) **Going Correction** +0.25s/f (Good) **10** Ran SP% **119.3**
Speed ratings (Par 105): **103,100,99,96,94 94,92,91,86,76**
CSF £26.27 CT £189.04 TOTE £3.50: £1.70, £2.80, £3.30; EX 32.20 Trifecta £211.40.
Owner Hamdan Al Maktoum **Bred** S V Schilcher **Trained** Newmarket, Suffolk

FOCUS
A fair handicap won in good style by what looks a potentially really useful sort. It's been rated around the second.

2978 FAT LARRY'S BURGERS AT GREAT YARMOUTH H'CAP — 1m 3y
5:15 (5:17) (Class 5) (0-70,70) 4-Y-O+
£3,752 (£1,116; £557; £300; £300; £300) **Stalls** Centre

Form RPR

-026 **1** **Casina Di Notte (IRE)**[25] 2124 5-9-4 **70**..........................(b) AaronJones(3) 7 76
(Marco Botti) *t.k.h: trckd ldrs: pushed along over 1f out: ev ch and rdn ins fnl f: r.o to ld last strides* **6/1**[3]

0-51 **2** *hd* **Oud Metha Bridge (IRE)**[22] 2256 5-8-13 **69**.......................... SeanKirrane(7) 4 74
(Julia Feilden) *t.k.h: pressed ldr tl rdn to ld over 1f out: kpt on u.p ins fnl f: hdd and no ex last strides* **2/1**[2]

5-41 **3** *½* **Diva Star**[7] 2741 4-9-2 **65** 5ex..........................(t) ShaneKelly 2 68
(Rae Guest) *wl in tch in midfield: effrt over 1f out: ev ch 1f out: drvn and kpt on same pce fnl 100yds* **13/8**[1]

6104 **4** *1* **Takeonefortheteam**[8] 2714 4-9-0 **63**.......................... EdwardGreatrex 1 64
(Mark Loughnane) *t.k.h: hld up in tch in last pair: effrt over 1f out: nt clr run and swtchd lft ins fnl f: kpt on same pce fnl 100yds (jockey said gelding ran too freely)* **9/1**

1040 **5** *1* **Blame Culture (USA)**[21] 2273 4-9-4 **70**.......................... JaneElliott(3) 6 69
(George Margarson) *t.k.h: hld up in tch in last pair: effrt 2f out: drvn over 1f out: kpt on ins fnl f: nt enough pce to threaten ldrs* **8/1**

0-00 **6** *¾* **Pumaflor (IRE)**[20] 2335 7-8-3 **57**..........................(p) PaulaMuir(5) 5 54
(Philip Kirby) *sn led: pushed along 2f out: hdd over 1f out: no ex and wknd ins fnl f* **22/1**

1m 39.63s (1.43) **Going Correction** +0.25s/f (Good) **6** Ran SP% **111.2**
Speed ratings (Par 103): **102,101,101,100,99 98**
CSF £18.10 TOTE £6.30: £2.50, £1.10; EX 17.60 Trifecta £35.70.
Owner Mrs Lucie Botti **Bred** John T Heffernan & Grainne Dooley **Trained** Newmarket, Suffolk

FOCUS
They raced tightly bunched down the centre, going slowly, and it developed into a dash. Most of them raced keenly. The winner has been rated to his recent AW form, and the second to his turf best.
T/Jkpt: Not won. T/Plt: £88.10 to a £1 stake. Pool: £67,254.25 - 556.91 winning units T/Qpdt: £33.20 to a £1 stake. Pool: £6,080.45 - 135.24 winning units **Steve Payne**

2979 - 2993a (Foreign Racing) - See Raceform Interactive

2714
CHEPSTOW (L-H)
Thursday, May 23

OFFICIAL GOING: Good to firm (good in places; 6.2)
Wind: Moderate breeze, partly against in the home straight Weather: Fine

2994 STEEL HORSE MAD DASH H'CAP — 1m 14y
1:50 (1:50) (Class 5) (0-75,75) 4-Y-O+
£3,752 (£1,116; £557; £300; £300; £300) **Stalls** Centre

Form RPR

2-46 **1** **Ocala**[16] 2509 4-9-7 **75**.......................... DavidProbert 4 84
(Andrew Balding) *hld up: hdwy over 3f out: led wl over 1f out: sn rdn: r.o* **5/6**[1]

0-02 **2** *2* **Ragstone View (IRE)**[20] 2365 4-9-3 **71**..........................(h) TrevorWhelan 7 75
(Rod Millman) *s.s: in rr: hdwy over 2f out: swtchd rt and chsd wnr over 1f out: kpt on (jockey said gelding was slowly away)* **13/2**[3]

141 **3** *5* **Anif (IRE)**[58] 1343 5-8-8 **69**.......................... GinaMangan(7) 5 62
(David Evans) *trckd ldr: rdn to ld narrowly over 2f out: hdd wl over 1f out: kpt on same pce* **11/4**[2]

400- **4** *10* **Outer Space**[209] 8611 8-9-1 **69**..........................(p) LiamJones 6 39
(John Flint) *led: rdn 3f out: hdd over 2f out: sn hung lft: wknd over 1f out* **14/1**

0-43 **5** *27* **Be Thankful**[128] 248 4-8-9 **63**.......................... EdwardGreatrex 2
(Martin Keighley) *t.k.h: prom: rdn over 3f out: sn wknd: eased over 1f out: t.o (jockey said filly stopped quickly)* **20/1**

66-6 **6** *18* **Tally's Son**[9] 2714 5-8-7 **61** oh12..........................(p) JimmyQuinn 1
(Grace Harris) *wnt to post early: chsd ldrs on outer but hanging rt: lost pl 1/2-way: sn t.o (jockey said gelding hung right-handed throughout)* **20/1**

1m 34.85s (-1.15) **Going Correction** -0.10s/f (Good) **6** Ran SP% **110.7**
Speed ratings (Par 103): **101,99,94,84,57 39**
CSF £6.76 TOTE £1.70: £1.30, £2.30; EX 7.00 Trifecta £18.00.
Owner George Strawbridge **Bred** George Strawbridge **Trained** Kingsclere, Hants

FOCUS
The ground had been watered to maintain it at good to firm, good in places, although on a warm sunny day it was only going to be drying further. A modest handicap won in fair style by the favourite. The second has been rated to his latest.

2995 POLO AT THE MANOR H'CAP — 7f 16y
2:25 (2:25) (Class 6) (0-65,66) 3-Y-O
£3,105 (£924; £461; £300; £300; £300) **Stalls** Centre

Form RPR

56-2 **1** **Chance**[24] 2192 3-9-8 **66**.......................... JackMitchell 13 77+
(Simon Crisford) *racd alone on stands' rail: chsd ldrs overall: rdn 3f out: led over 1f out: sn edgd lft: r.o: pushed out towards fin* **5/6**[1]

65-3 **2** *¾* **Glamorous Crescent**[17] 2474 3-8-7 **51** oh2.......................... JimmyQuinn 5 58
(Grace Harris) *wnt to post early: led: rdn over 2f out: hdd over 1f out: kpt on* **20/1**

3-00 **3** *4 ½* **Dark Glory (IRE)**[16] 2517 3-9-6 **64**..........................(p) RichardKingscote 10 59
(Brian Meehan) *prom: rdn over 2f out: outpcd by ldng pair fnl f: got bttr of duel for 3rd last strides* **13/2**[3]

3-04 **4** *nse* **Jungle Juice (IRE)**[24] 2212 3-9-0 **65**.......................... ScottMcCullagh(7) 9 60
(Mick Channon) *chsd ldrs: rdn and hung lft 2f out: outpcd by ldng pair fnl f: lost duel for 3rd last strides* **6/1**[2]

6-00 **5** *4 ½* **Little Anxious**[22] 2276 3-8-7 **51** oh6..........................(h[1]) LiamJones 12 34
(Grace Harris) *s.i.s: in rr: hdwy 1/2-way: rdn over 2f out: one pce* **100/1**

00-0 **6** *2 ¼* **Anonymous Blonde**[22] 2277 3-8-11 **55**..........................(t) RossaRyan 4 32
(David Evans) *chsd ldrs tl rdn and sltly outpcd over 2f out: wknd fnl f* **50/1**

6-65 **7** *2* **Miss Gargar**[22] 2276 3-9-2 **60**.......................... ShaneKelly 7 32
(Harry Dunlop) *midfield: rdn 3f out: n.m.r over 2f out: wknd over 1f out* **20/1**

8 *hd* **Dandy Belle (IRE)**[36] 1865 3-8-11 **55**.......................... RobHornby 6 27
(Richenda Ford) *prom: rdn over 2f out: wknd over 1f out* **28/1**

405- **9** *5* **Pegasus Bridge**[226] 8067 3-9-5 **63**.......................... EdwardGreatrex 1 22
(Eve Johnson Houghton) *s.i.s: sn chsng ldrs on outer: rdn 3f out: hung lft and wknd 2f out (jockey said gelding hung right-handed throughout)* **8/1**

4015 **10** *3 ¼* **Brother Bentley**[17] 2474 3-8-12 **56**..........................(b) DavidProbert 3 6
(Ronald Harris) *midfield on outer: rdn and lost pl over 3f out: wknd 2f out (jockey said gelding hung lerft-handed; trainer's rep said gelding was unsuited by the good to firm, good in places going, and would prefer a slower surface)* **14/1**

000- **11** *3 ½* **Barb's Prince (IRE)**[218] 8327 3-9-0 **58**.......................... GeorgeDowning 8
(Ian Williams) *hld up: rdn over 3f out: sn wknd (trainer's rep said, regarding the performance, gelding was unsuited by the good to firm, good in places going, and would prefer a slower surface)* **16/1**

6265 **12** *7* **Dandy Lad (IRE)**[48] 1557 3-9-1 **59**.......................... PhilipPrince 11
(Natalie Lloyd-Beavis) *wnt to post early: hld up and plld hrd: rdn over 3f out: sn wknd* **50/1**

1m 23.44s (-0.46) **Going Correction** -0.10s/f (Good) **12** Ran SP% **123.7**
Speed ratings (Par 97): **98,97,92,91,86 84,81,81,76,72 68,60**
CSF £28.58 CT £85.02 TOTE £1.60: £1.10, £4.40, £2.60; EX 22.80 Trifecta £119.40.
Owner Khalifa Saeed Sulaiman **Bred** Haras D'Etreham & Eric De Chambure **Trained** Newmarket, Suffolk

FOCUS
Moderate handicap form, although the front pair came clear. The form has been rated at face value for now.

2996 CHEPSTOW PLANT INTERNATIONAL FILLIES' NOVICE STKS (PLUS 10 RACE) — 6f 16y
3:00 (3:02) (Class 5) 2-Y-O
£3,752 (£1,116; £557; £278) **Stalls** Centre

Form RPR

222 **1** **Bettys Hope**[24] 2191 2-9-0 0.......................... RobHornby 5 72
(Rod Millman) *trckd ldr: led over 2f out: rdn over 1f out: pushed out ins fnl f* **3/1**[1]

6304 **2** *1* **Lili Wen Fach (IRE)**[9] 2716 2-9-0 0.......................... RichardKingscote 1 69
(David Evans) *trckd ldng pair: rdn over 2f out: chsd wnr over 1f out: kpt on* **11/2**[2]

3 *shd* **Faldetta** 2-9-0 0.......................... EdwardGreatrex 7 69
(Eve Johnson Houghton) *s.s: in rr: pushed along over 2f out: rdn and hdwy over 1f out: r.o fnl f to press for 2nd* **12/1**

0 **4** *2* **Bacchalot (IRE)**[23] 2248 2-9-0 0.......................... RossaRyan 9 63
(Richard Hannon) *chsd ldrs: rdn 1/2-way: sn sltly outpcd by ldrs: rallied over 1f out: kpt on same pce fnl f* **3/1**[1]

65 **5** *1* **Swiss Bond**[6] 2792 2-8-9 0.......................... ThoreHammerHansen(5) 8 60
(J S Moore) *midfield: rdn over 2f out: swtchd lft over 1f out: styd on fnl f* **8/1**

42 **6** *2 ¾* **Forced**[17] 2469 2-9-0 0.......................... ShaneKelly 2 51
(Richard Hughes) *led tl hdd over 2f out: sn rdn: lost 2nd and wknd over 1f out* **13/2**[3]

7 *1 ½* **Strawberry Hind (IRE)** 2-9-0 0.......................... DavidProbert 3 47
(Mick Channon) *midfield: rdn over 2f out: wknd fnl f* **10/1**

04 **8** *3 ½* **Show Me Heaven**[17] 2469 2-8-9 0.......................... RyanWhile(5) 6 36
(Bill Turner) *s.i.s and hung lft in early stages: reminders over 2f out: a in rr* **80/1**

5 **9** *2 ¾* **Maisie Ellie (IRE)**[23] 2248 2-8-11 0.......................... MeganNicholls(3) 4 28
(Paul George) *trckd ldrs tl clipped heels: stmbld and lost pl over 4f out: rdn over 2f out: wknd over 1f out* **8/1**

1m 12.34s (0.84) **Going Correction** -0.10s/f (Good) **9** Ran SP% **119.0**
Speed ratings (Par 90): **90,88,88,85,84 80,78,74,70**
CSF £20.46 TOTE £3.70: £1.30, £2.20, £4.80; EX 16.20 Trifecta £161.10.
Owner Mrs Louise Millman **Bred** Llety Farms **Trained** Kentisbeare, Devon

FOCUS
Ordinary juvenile form, the field raced stands' side. The winner has been credited with slight improvement.

2997 ALLIANCE LEISURE H'CAP — 6f 16y
3:35 (3:38) (Class 4) (0-85,84) 3-Y-O+
£5,530 (£1,645; £822; £411; £300; £300) **Stalls** Centre

Form RPR

0040 **1** **Bungee Jump (IRE)**[26] 2107 4-9-8 **76**.......................... RossaRyan 8 85
(Grace Harris) *mde all: rdn over 2f out: r.o wl fnl f* **17/2**[3]

224- **2** *2* **Great Midge**[247] 7374 4-9-7 **75**.......................... DavidProbert 9 78+
(Henry Candy) *awkward s: sn in midfield: rdn and hdwy 2f out: kpt on fnl f: wnt 2nd towards fin* **8/1**[2]

-133 **3** *nk* **Nubough (IRE)**[20] 2364 3-9-7 **84**.......................... RichardKingscote 7 84
(Charles Hills) *wnt to post early: chsd ldrs: rdn to go 2nd over 2f out: outpcd by wnr fnl f: lost 2nd towards fin* **11/10**[1]

3020 **4** *1* **The Groove**[9] 2717 6-8-9 **70**.......................... GinaMangan(7) 5 69
(David Evans) *hld up in rr: swtchd rt after 1f: hdwy 2f out: sn rdn: kpt on same pce fnl f* **9/1**

15-0 **5** *4 ½* **Dr Doro (IRE)**[12] 2625 6-9-4 **72**..........................(p) GeorgeDowning 2 56
(Ian Williams) *midfield: rdn over 2f out: kpt on fnl f but nvr a threat* **50/1**

21-0 **6** *nse* **Cool Reflection (IRE)**[19] 2412 3-9-4 **81**.......................... RaulDaSilva 10 63
(Paul Cole) *jinked rt leaving stalls: trckd wnr: rdn and lost 2nd over 2f out: wknd fnl f* **9/1**

106- **7** *2* **More Than Likely**[182] 9210 3-9-6 **83**..........................(h) ShaneKelly 4 59
(Richard Hughes) *awkward s: chsd ldrs: rdn over 2f out: wknd appr fnl f* **12/1**

00-0 **8** *¾* **Indian Sounds (IRE)**[20] 2364 3-9-2 **84**.......................... AndrewBreslin(5) 6 57
(Mark Johnston) *towards rr: rdn and outpcd wl over 3f out: edgd lft 2f out* **14/1**

60-0 **9** *½* **Bahuta Acha**[35] 1899 4-9-9 **77**..........................(p) TrevorWhelan 3 51
(David Loughnane) *s.i.s: a in rr (jockey said gelding hung left-handed throughout)* **33/1**

The Form Book Flat 2019, Raceform Ltd, Newbury, RG14 5SJ

6-06 **10** ½ **Tin Hat (IRE)**[22] [2274] 3-9-5 **82**........................ EdwardGreatrex 1 52
(Eve Johnson Houghton) *towards rr: rdn over 3f out: wknd fnl f* **10/1**

1m 10.74s (-0.76) **Going Correction** -0.10s/f (Good)
WFA 3 from 4yo+ 9lb **10** Ran SP% **117.6**
Speed ratings (Par 105): **101,98,97,96,90 90,87,86,86,85**
CSF £75.32 CT £133.36 TOTE £9.10: £2.50, £2.20, £1.10; EX 68.90 Trifecta £125.30.
Owner Ronald Davies & Mrs Candida Davies **Bred** Roundhill Stud **Trained** Shirenewton, Monmouthshire

FOCUS
They again raced stands' side in this fair handicap and the winner made all. The third has been rated a bit below his latest form, but in line with his 6f form.

2998 WILLMOTT DIXON - BUILDING ON BETTER H'CAP — 1m 2f
4:10 (4:12) (Class 6) (0-65,66) 4-Y-O+
£3,752 (£1,116; £557; £300; £300; £300) **Stalls** Low

Form RPR

440- **1** **Banksy's Art**[170] [7122] 4-8-9 **59**........................ ScottMcCullagh(7) 14 68
(Mick Channon) *chsd ldrs: shkn up and wnt 2nd 2f out: rdn to ld 1f out: r.o* **14/1**

000- **2** 3 ¼ **Cwynar**[249] [7336] 4-9-0 **60**........................ JoshuaBryan(3) 6 63
(Rebecca Curtis) *chsd ldrs tl led over 2f out: sn rdn: hdd 1f out: outpcd by wnr* **25/1**

00-0 **3** 2 **Couldn't Could She**[12] [2631] 4-9-1 **58**........................ EdwardGreatrex 5 58
(Adam West) *bmpd s: chsd ldrs: rdn over 2f out and briefly in 2nd: one pce fnl f* **14/1**

1-05 **4** 3 ½ **Edge (IRE)**[9] [2714] 8-9-5 **62**........................(b) DavidProbert 13 55
(Bernard Llewellyn) *midfield: rdn and hdwy over 2f out: styd on same pce fnl f* **12/1**

5312 **5** ½ **Fire Diamond**[13] [2596] 6-9-3 **60**........................(p) RichardKingscote 15 52
(Tom Dascombe) *hld up towards rr: rdn and hdwy over 2f out: styd on fnl f: nvr able to chal* **9/4**[1]

30-6 **6** 4 **Just Right**[8] [2733] 4-8-1 **49**........................ AndrewBreslin(5) 16 34+
(John Flint) *racd keenly: sn w ldr: clr of rest after 3f to 4f out: led 3f out: sn hdd and rdn: one pce (jockey said filly hung right-handed)* **14/1**

4024 **7** 2 **The Lords Walk**[12] [2617] 6-9-2 **64**........................(p) RyanWhile(5) 3 46
(Bill Turner) *midfield: hdwy over 3f out: sn rdn: wknd over 1f out (vet said gelding lost left fore shoe)* **3/1**[2]

5605 **8** 3 ½ **Dimmesdale**[17] [2468] 4-8-13 **56**........................ LiamJones 10 31
(John O'Shea) *s.s: in rr: rdn over 4f out: no imp tl styd on fnl f* **20/1**

-446 **9** nk **Gates Pass**[77] [1065] 4-9-9 **66**........................ TrevorWhelan 2 41
(Brian Barr) *led 100yds: chsd ldrs: rdn over 2f out: wknd over 1f out (jockey said gelding ran too freely and hung left-handed)* **10/1**

240- **10** 1 ½ **Guardiola (USA)**[169] [9407] 4-8-8 **51**........................(t w) JimmyQuinn 4 23
(Bernard Llewellyn) *wnt to post early: hmpd leaving stalls: rdn 4f out: a in rr* **16/1**

000- **11** 2 ½ **Mamnoon (IRE)**[177] [9271] 6-7-9 **45**........................(b) SaraDelFabbro(7) 8 13
(Roy Brotherton) *midfield: rdn over 2f out: wknd wl over 1f out* **33/1**

360- **12** 1 ¾ **Innstigator**[211] [8537] 5-8-2 **45**........................ RaulDaSilva 9 9+
(Sue Gardner) *wnt to post early: racd keenly: led after 100yds and set str gallop: clr w one other after 3f to 4f out: hdd 3f out: wknd qckly (jockey said gelding hung right-handed)* **20/1**

4002 **13** ½ **Enmeshing**[10] [2696] 6-9-0 **62**........................ ThoreHammerHansen(5) 7 25
(Alexandra Dunn) *a towards rr (jockey said gelding was never travelling)* **8/1**[3]

0460 **14** 1 ¾ **Folies Bergeres**[21] [2344] 4-8-8 **51**........................(b) RobHornby 11 11
(Grace Harris) *s.s: a in rr* **33/1**

2m 6.96s (-5.84) **Going Correction** -0.10s/f (Good) **14** Ran SP% **128.8**
Speed ratings (Par 101): **116,113,111,109,108 105,103,101,100,99 97,96,95,94**
CSF £343.69 CT £4941.04 TOTE £17.30: £4.40, £8.20, £4.30; EX 493.40 Trifecta £1401.10.
Owner Mrs Janet Evans & Partners **Bred** Mike Channon Bloodstock Ltd **Trained** West Ilsley, Berks
■ Unzipped was withdrawn. Price at time of withdrawal 50-1. Rule 4 does not apply.

FOCUS
No hanging about here and they were strung out from an early stage.

2999 ACORN, LEADING RECRUITMENT SPECIALISTS NOVICE STKS — 1m 4f
4:45 (4:48) (Class 5) 3-Y-O+ **£3,752** (£1,116; £557; £278) **Stalls** Low

Form RPR

21- **1** **Brasca**[196] [8956] 3-9-4........................ RobHornby 4 86
(Ralph Beckett) *hld up in tch: rdn and sltly outpcd over 3f out: chsd ldng pair 2f out: styd on to ld ent fnl f: sn in command: readily* **9/4**[2]

0-3 **2** 2 ½ **Goscote**[30] [2017] 4-9-9........................ DavidProbert 1 71
(Henry Candy) *led: rdn over 3f out: styd on u.p: hdd ent fnl f: one pce* **9/2**[3]

0-4 **3** 2 ¼ **Motaraabet**[31] [1989] 4-10-0........................ RichardKingscote 2 72
(Owen Burrows) *trckd ldr: rdn over 3f out: lost 2nd 1f out: no ex* **5/6**[1]

00 **4** 5 **And The New (IRE)**[24] [2192] 8-10-0........................ GeorgeDowning 5 64
(Johnny Farrelly) *dwlt: hld up and sn wl bhd: shkn up and sme prog 4f out: reminder over 1f out: sn styd on to go modest 4th: gng on fin (jockey said gelding was slowly into stride)* **25/1**

00 **5** 6 **Doune Castle**[25] [2142] 3-8-11........................ ShaneKelly 3 54
(Andrew Balding) *chsd ldrs: rdn 4f out: wknd 3f out (vet said colt lost right fore shoe)* **8/1**

0 **6** 12 **Miss Harriett**[20] [2354] 3-8-6........................ JimmyQuinn 8 30
(Stuart Kittow) *t.k.h early: chsd ldrs: rdn over 3f out: wknd 2f out* **66/1**

7 1 ¾ **Voice Of Salsabil** 3-8-6........................ LiamJones 6 27
(David Evans) *s.s: in rr: hdwy over 5f out: rdn 4f out: wknd over 2f out* **16/1**

0-0 **8** 91 **Evadala (FR)**[128] [242] 4-9-9........................ TrevorWhelan 7
(Michael Blanshard) *a towards rr: lost tch 6f out: t.o (jockey said filly lost its action)* **125/1**

2m 37.5s (-2.80) **Going Correction** -0.10s/f (Good)
WFA 3 from 4yo+ 17lb **8** Ran SP% **126.6**
Speed ratings (Par 103): **105,103,101,98,94 86,85,24**
CSF £14.57 TOTE £3.10: £1.20, £1.70, £1.10; EX 17.30 Trifecta £35.10.
Owner Frank Brady & Brian Scanlon **Bred** Mrs C R Philipson & Lofts Hall Stud **Trained** Kimpton, Hants

FOCUS
An ordinary novice, they went a decent enough gallop and it proved a thorough test at the trip. The second and third have been rated close to their latest form for now.

3000 CHEPSTOW MENCAP H'CAP — 1m 4f
5:20 (5:20) (Class 5) (0-75,77) 4-Y-O+
£3,752 (£1,116; £557; £300; £300; £300) **Stalls** Low

Form RPR

136- **1** **Charlie D (USA)**[164] [9487] 4-9-7 **73**........................(tp) RichardKingscote 1 79
(Tom Dascombe) *trckd ldr: rdn over 3f out: led 2f out: styd on wl* **9/4**[2]

6-30 **2** 1 ¾ **The Detainee**[44] [947] 6-9-2 **68**........................(p w) ShaneKelly 2 71
(Neil Mulholland) *chsd ldng pair: rdn and unable qck 3f out: styd on to go 2nd ins fnl f: hld by wnr* **8/1**

0-04 **3** 2 ¾ **General Brook (IRE)**[9] [2720] 9-8-11 **63**........................(p) LiamJones 3 62
(John O'Shea) *wnt to post early: led tl rdn and hdd 2f out: kpt on same pce: lost 2nd ins fnl f (jockey said gelding hung left-handed)* **9/2**[3]

5663 **4** 2 ½ **Winged Spur (IRE)**[8] [2748] 4-9-6 **77**........................ AndrewBreslin(5) 6 78
(Mark Johnston) *s.i.s: in rr: hdwy into 4th 6f out: rdn and unable qck 4f out: stl 4th but styng on whn hmpd ins fnl f* **11/10**[1]

5 10 **True Thoughts (IRE)**[64] 4-8-4 **59**........................(b) NoelGarbutt(3) 5 38
(Laura Young) *slowly in stride: hld up in 4th: lost pl 6f out: rdn and no ch fnl 4f* **66/1**

-000 **6** 41 **Mouchee (IRE)**[72] [1159] 4-9-2 **68**........................(p[1]) RobHornby 7
(Michael Blake) *a in last pair: lost tch over 4f out: t.o* **25/1**

2m 38.19s (-2.11) **Going Correction** -0.10s/f (Good) **6** Ran SP% **113.0**
Speed ratings (Par 103): **103,101,100,98,91 64**
CSF £20.12 TOTE £3.00: £1.40, £3.10; EX 16.80 Trifecta £53.20.
Owner D R Passant & T Dascombe **Bred** Rabbah Bloodstock Ltd **Trained** Malpas, Cheshire

FOCUS
Another race run at a fair gallop, but it's ordinary form. The winner has been rated close to his AW level off his lower turf mark, and the second in line with the better view of last year's form.
T/Plt: £39.40 to a £1 stake. Pool: £49,623.42. 917.93 winning units. T/Qpdt: £25.90 to a £1 stake. Pool: £5,024.97. 143.20 winning units. **Richard Lowther**

2550 CHELMSFORD (A.W) (L-H)
Thursday, May 23

OFFICIAL GOING: Polytrack: standard
Wind: Light behind Weather: Fine

3001 £20 FREE BETS AT TOTESPORT.COM H'CAP — 5f (P)
5:50 (5:52) (Class 6) (0-60,59) 4-Y-O+
£3,428 (£1,020; £509; £300; £300; £300) **Stalls** Low

Form RPR

0015 **1** **Precious Plum**[35] [1883] 5-9-7 **59**........................(p) BenCurtis 5 65
(Charlie Wallis) *mde all: rdn ins fnl f: styd on u.p* **5/1**[1]

0532 **2** nk **Always Amazing**[35] [1883] 5-9-3 **55**........................ TomQueally 8 60
(Derek Shaw) *chsd ldrs: rdn over 1f out: chsd wnr ins fnl f: r.o* **7/1**[3]

303 **3** ½ **Le Manege Enchante (IRE)**[15] [2527] 6-8-8 **46**........(v) PaddyMathers 7 49
(Derek Shaw) *mid-div: hdwy u.p over 1f out: r.o* **6/1**[2]

0000 **4** ¾ **Dubai Elegance**[12] [2632] 5-8-11 **49**........................(p) LewisEdmunds 6 49+
(Derek Shaw) *hld up: rdn over 1f out: r.o ins fnl f: nt rch ldrs* **12/1**

-504 **5** ½ **Flying Foxy**[15] [2527] 5-9-6 **58**........................(p) HayleyTurner 4 57
(George Scott) *chsd wnr: rdn over 1f out: no ex ins fnl f* **8/1**

0-00 **6** 1 **Tiger Lyon (USA)**[30] [2013] 4-9-2 **54**........................(t) JoeyHaynes 12 49
(John Butler) *chsd ldrs: rdn over 2f out: no ex ins fnl f* **14/1**

6202 **7** nk **Kyllukey**[28] [2066] 6-8-10 **48**........................ DavidEgan 11 42
(Charlie Wallis) *s.i.s: hld up: edgd rt and styd on u.p ins fnl f: nvr nrr (jockey said gelding jumped awkwardly from the stalls and was slowly away as a result)* **6/1**[2]

-260 **8** nk **Alaskan Bay (IRE)**[35] [1883] 4-8-11 **54**........................ TheodoreLadd(5) 3 47
(Rae Guest) *s.i.s: hld up: rdn over 1f out: n.d (jockey said filly reared as stalls opened and was slowly away as a result)* **6/1**[2]

404 **9** ¾ **Royal Mezyan (IRE)**[35] [1883] 8-8-12 **55**........................ DylanHogan(5) 9 45
(Henry Spiller) *hld up: rdn over 1f out: n.d* **8/1**

10-0 **10** 3 ¾ **Good Business (IRE)**[35] [1883] 5-9-5 **57**........................(b) KieranO'Neill 1 34
(Henry Spiller) *hld up: rdn over 1f out: n.d* **16/1**

06-0 **11** 2 **John Joiner**[31] [1987] 7-8-11 **49**........................(v) JosephineGordon 2 18
(Shaun Keightley) *chsd ldrs: rdn over 1f out: wknd fnl f* **16/1**

1m 0.53s (0.33) **Going Correction** -0.10s/f (Stan) **11** Ran SP% **120.4**
Speed ratings (Par 101): **93,92,91,90,89 88,87,87,85,79 76**
CSF £40.61 CT £219.15 TOTE £5.10: £2.00, £2.00, £2.70; EX 20.50 Trifecta £183.70.
Owner Mrs Julia Hughes **Bred** Mrs J V Hughes **Trained** Ardleigh, Essex

FOCUS
An ordinary sprint controlled from the front by the winner. The winner has been rated similar to her C&D win in March.

3002 TOTEPOOL CASHBACK CLUB AT TOTESPORT.COM H'CAP — 1m (P)
6:20 (6:23) (Class 5) (0-70,70) 4-Y-O+
£5,433 (£1,617; £808; £404; £300; £300) **Stalls** Low

Form RPR

5133 **1** **Lothario**[13] [2596] 5-9-4 **67**........................ RobertWinston 6 76
(Dean Ivory) *chsd ldrs: rdn to ld ins fnl f: edgd rt: styd on* **5/2**[1]

5321 **2** ¾ **Zodiakos (IRE)**[16] [2509] 6-9-5 **68**........................(p) BenCurtis 11 75
(Roger Fell) *pushed along and prom: chse ldr over 6f out: rdn over 1f out: ev ch ins fnl f: styd on (vet said gelding lost left fore shoe)* **9/2**[2]

6662 **3** 1 ¼ **Pearl Spectre (USA)**[23] [2237] 8-9-2 **65**........................(v) CallumShepherd 5 69
(Phil McEntee) *sn led: rdn over 1f out: hdd ins fnl f: no ex towards fin* **9/1**

-063 **4** 1 ¾ **Militry Decoration (IRE)**[43] [1675] 4-9-2 **65**........................ KierenFox 4 65
(Dr Jon Scargill) *hld up in tch: rdn over 2f out: styd on: nt rch ldrs* **8/1**

0554 **5** nk **Arlecchino's Leap**[13] [2596] 7-9-3 **66**........................(p) FergusSweeney 3 65
(Mark Usher) *chsd ldrs: rdn over 2f out: styd on same pce ins fnl f* **6/1**[3]

15-0 **6** 1 ¼ **Roof Garden**[52] [1479] 4-9-3 **66**........................ DavidEgan 1 63
(Mark H Tompkins) *hld up: hdwy over 1f out: no ex wl ins fnl f (vet said gelding lost left hind shoe)* **16/1**

6546 **7** ½ **The Warrior (IRE)**[30] [2005] 7-9-3 **69**........................ PaddyBradley(3) 2 64
(Lee Carter) *hld up: hdwy over 1f out: nt clr run sn after: nt trble ldrs (jockey said gelding was unsuited by the polytrack surface, which in his opinion was riding deep on this occasion)* **8/1**

150- **8** 4 ½ **Sayesse**[168] [9428] 5-9-3 **66**........................(h) HectorCrouch 9 51
(Lisa Williamson) *sn pushed along in rr: bhd 6f out: r.o u.p ins fnl f* **50/1**

1211 **9** ½ **Amor Fati (IRE)**[17] [2504] 4-8-13 **62**........................ HayleyTurner 8 46
(David Evans) *hld up: rdn over 1f out: edgd lft and wknd fnl f (trainer said gelding was never travelling)* **7/1**

2-10 **10** *11* **Weloof (FR)**[30] 2005 5-9-3 **66**.......... KieranO'Neill 7 25
(John Butler) *chsd ldrs: rdn over 3f out: wknd over 1f out (trainer said gelding ran flat)* **25/1**

1-00 **11** *38* **Folie Douze**[35] 1880 4-8-13 **67**..........(p[1]) DylanHogan(5) 12
(Henry Spiller) *hld up: rdn: hung and lost pl over 4f out: wknd over 3f out: eased (jockey said gelding hung right from 5f out; vet said gelding to be lame on its right hind)* **50/1**

1m 38.87s (-1.03) **Going Correction** -0.10s/f (Stan) **11** Ran SP% **119.4**
Speed ratings (Par 103): **101,100,99,97,96 95,95,90,90,79 41**
CSF £13.38 CT £89.35 TOTE £2.90: £1.40, £1.80, £2.60; EX 15.60 Trifecta £71.30.
Owner Michael & Heather Yarrow **Bred** J Troy, Mrs R Philipps & Highbury Stud **Trained** Radlett, Herts

FOCUS
Few got into this, the first three being up there throughout. It's been rated around the second and third.

3003 EXTRA PLACES AT TOTESPORT.COM NOVICE STKS 1m (P)
6:55 (6:59) (Class 4) 3-Y-O+ **£6,145** (£1,828; £913; £456) **Stalls** Low

Form RPR

53 **1** **Piper Arrow**[24] 2192 3-9-2 0.......... JosephineGordon 10 86
(Andrew Balding) *a.p: chsd ldr over 5f out: rdn and hung rt ins fnl f: styd on to ld nr fin* **25/1**

1-4 **2** *nk* **Almashriq (USA)**[35] 1888 3-9-8 0.......... AdamKirby 7 91
(John Gosden) *s.i.s: hdwy over 6f out: rdn over 2f out: r.o to go 2nd nr fin* **11/4**[2]

3-1 **3** *hd* **Muraad (IRE)**[26] 2128 3-9-8 0.......... DaneO'Neill 2 91
(Owen Burrows) *sn led: rdn over 1f out: hdd nr fin* **6/4**[1]

1 **4** *2* **Search For Light (IRE)**[26] 2102 3-9-3 0.......... HectorCrouch 5 81
(Saeed bin Suroor) *sn chsng ldr: lost 2nd over 5f out: remained handy: rdn and hung lft over 1f out: styd on same pce ins fnl f* **5/1**[3]

4- **5** *1* **Madeeh**[188] 9105 3-9-2 0..........(w) LouisSteward 6 78
(Sir Michael Stoute) *chsd ldrs: lost pl over 6f out: hdwy over 1f out: r.o* **7/1**

0 **6** *3* **Thunder And Light**[57] 1352 3-8-13 0..........(t[1]) AaronJones(3) 9 71
(Marco Botti) *hld up: hdwy over 2f out: rdn and hung lft fr over 1f out: styd on same pce fnl f* **50/1**

4- **7** *hd* **Mutasaamy (IRE)**[203] 8774 3-9-2 0..........(w) DavidEgan 11 71
(Roger Varian) *mid-div: hdwy u.p on outer over 1f out: sn hung lft: no ex ins fnl f* **14/1**

0 **8** *2* **Unplugged (IRE)**[24] 2192 3-9-2 0.......... TomQueally 3 66
(Andrew Balding) *s.i.s: hld up: shkn up over 2f out: edgd lft and styd on ins fnl f: nvr nrr* **100/1**

9 *1 ½* **Petite Malle (USA)** 3-8-11 0.......... HayleyTurner 8 58
(James Fanshawe) *s.i.s: sme hdwy over 2f out: rdn over 1f out: wknd ins fnl f* **50/1**

10 *1 ¾* **Global Command (IRE)** 3-9-2 0.......... GeraldMosse 16 59
(Ed Dunlop) *hld up: pushed along 1/2-way: sme hdwy u.p over 1f out: n.d* **50/1**

11 *shd* **Helian (IRE)** 3-9-2 0.......... BenCurtis 4 58
(Ed Dunlop) *chsd ldrs: rdn over 1f out: wknd fnl f* **40/1**

- **12** *3 ¼* **Ghaly** 3-9-2 0.......... GeorgeWood 13 51
(Saeed bin Suroor) *s.i.s: pushed along in rr: hung lft ins fnl f: nvr on terms* **12/1**

4 **13** *3 ¼* **Second Sight**[20] 2375 3-8-9 0.......... AledBeech(7) 15 43
(Charlie Fellowes) *hld up: a in rr* **50/1**

14 *½* **Bricklebrit** 3-8-11 0.......... KieranO'Neill 12 37
(Rae Guest) *s.i.s: pushed along and a in rr* **100/1**

15 *3 ½* **Dutch Story** 3-9-2 0.......... RobertWinston 14 34
(Amanda Perrett) *prom: rdn over 3f out: wknd over 1f out* **80/1**

0 **16** *2 ¾* **Hurricane Heidi**[93] 795 3-8-11 0.......... PaddyMathers 1 23
(Derek Shaw) *hld up: rdn over 3f out: wknd over 2f out* **100/1**

1m 37.85s (-2.05) **Going Correction** -0.10s/f (Stan) **16** Ran SP% **128.5**
Speed ratings (Par 105): **106,105,105,103,102 99,99,97,95,94 93,90,87,86,83 80**
CSF £96.55 TOTE £41.10: £4.60, £1.30, £1.10; EX 149.60 Trifecta £549.00.
Owner David Brownlow **Bred** Mrs J E Laws **Trained** Kingsclere, Hants

FOCUS
This looked a good novice and, although there was a surprise winner, the form looks sound. It's been rated slightly positively.

3004 IRISH LOTTO AT TOTESPORT.COM H'CAP 1m 2f (P)
7:25 (7:30) (Class 4) (0-85,87) 4-Y-O+ **£6,016** (£1,790; £894; £447; £300; £300) **Stalls** Low

Form RPR

4115 **1** **Badenscoth**[16] 2516 5-9-5 **80**.......... RobertWinston 7 89+
(Dean Ivory) *led at stdy pce after 1f: hdd over 4f out: chsd ldr: rdn: carried rt and led over 1f out: edgd lft ins fnl f: r.o (vet said gelding lost right hind shoe)* **9/2**[3]

2551 **2** *1 ¾* **Global Art**[26] 2124 4-9-6 **81**.......... GeraldMosse 5 86
(Ed Dunlop) *prom: qcknd to ld over 4f out: rdn: hung rt and hdd over 1f out: styd on same pce ins fnl f* **11/4**[1]

-23 **3** *1 ½* **Paco's Prince**[16] 2516 4-8-5 **73**.......... AledBeech(7) 6 75
(Nick Littmoden) *chsd wnr after 1f tl over 4f out: rdn over 2f out: styd on* **7/1**

20-0 **4** *1* **Oh It's Saucepot**[28] 2064 5-9-3 **78**.......... GeorgeWood 3 78
(Chris Wall) *led at stdy pce 1f: chsd ldrs: outpcd over 3f out: styd on ins fnl f* **8/1**

1230 **5** *1* **Dommersen (IRE)**[54] 1422 6-9-7 **82**.......... BenCurtis 1 80
(Roger Fell) *s.i.s: hld up: outpcd 4f out: styd on ins fnl f: nvr on terms (jockey said gelding reared as the stalls opened and hung right)* **7/2**[2]

3630 **6** *8* **Philamundo (IRE)**[40] 1757 4-9-5 **80**..........(b) DavidEgan 2 62
(Richard Spencer) *hld up: plld hrd: outpcd over 4f out: n.d after (jockey said gelding ran too free)* **7/2**[2]

2m 10.64s (2.04) **Going Correction** -0.10s/f (Stan) **6** Ran SP% **112.9**
Speed ratings (Par 105): **87,85,84,83,82 76**
CSF £17.43 CT £83.42 TOTE £5.20: £2.70, £1.80; EX 15.00 Trifecta £54.40.
Owner Peter J Skinner **Bred** Peter J Skinner **Trained** Radlett, Herts

FOCUS
The early gallop was slow before picking up significantly leaving the back straight. Muddling form, but the second has been rated to form for now.

3005 BET IN PLAY AT TOTESPORT.COM H'CAP 1m 2f (P)
7:55 (7:56) (Class 2) (0-105,101) 4-Y-O+**£16,172** (£4,812; £2,405; £1,202) **Stalls** Low

Form RPR

031- **1** **Star Of Bengal**[187] 9134 4-9-7 **101**.......... NickyMackay 1 110+
(John Gosden) *led early: chsd ldr: shkn up to ld 1f out: rdn out* **1/1**[1]

-204 **2** *½* **Exec Chef (IRE)**[19] 2408 4-9-1 **95**.......... PatCosgrave 7 103
(Jim Boyle) *prom: shkn up over 2f out: rdn and ev ch ins fnl f: styd on* **9/2**[2]

0605 **3** *2 ¾* **Dark Red (IRE)**[78] 1031 7-8-13 **93**.......... BenCurtis 5 96
(Ed Dunlop) *hld up: nt clr run over 1f out: rdn and r.o to go 3rd wl ins fnl f: nt rch ldrs* **10/1**

030- **4** *1 ½* **Highbrow**[222] 8192 4-9-3 **97**.......... HayleyTurner 2 97
(David Simcock) *hld up in tch: rdn over 1f out: styd on same pce ins fnl f (vet said gelding lost its right hind shoe)* **7/1**

2-25 **5** *1 ¼* **Al Hamdany (IRE)**[34] 1927 5-9-3 **97**.......... GeraldMosse 3 94
(Marco Botti) *prom: chsd ldr 8f out: shkn up to ld over 2f out: rdn: edgd rt and hdd 1f out: wknd wl ins fnl f* **6/1**[3]

4124 **6** *1* **Nonios (IRE)**[21] 2320 7-8-9 **94**..........(h) DylanHogan(5) 4 89
(David Simcock) *s.i.s: hld up: hdwy on outer over 1f out: wknd ins fnl f* **12/1**

6/4- **7** *7* **Domagnano (IRE)**[263] 4-8-11 **98**.......... StefanoCherchi(7) 6 79
(Marco Botti) *s.i.s: hld up: hdwy and nt clr run over 1f out: wknd fnl f* **40/1**

6-00 **8** *19* **Mount Tahan (IRE)**[29] 2032 7-9-6 **100**.......... ShaneGray 8 43
(Kevin Ryan) *sn led: rdn and hdd over 2f out: wknd over 1f out (jockey said gelding stopped quickly)* **40/1**

2m 3.61s (-4.99) **Going Correction** -0.10s/f (Stan) **8** Ran SP% **116.6**
Speed ratings (Par 109): **115,114,112,111,110 109,103,88**
CSF £5.92 CT £27.40 TOTE £1.50: £1.10, £1.50, £2.60; EX 5.50 Trifecta £36.80.
Owner Lady Bamford **Bred** Lady Bamford **Trained** Newmarket, Suffolk

FOCUS
A good race won by a horse bred to be better than a handicapper. The second has been rated in line with the better view of his Spring Mile form.

3006 DOUBLE DELIGHT HAT-TRICK HEAVEN AT TOTESPORT.COM H'CAP 1m 2f (P)
8:30 (8:31) (Class 6) (0-55,57) 4-Y-O+
£3,428 (£1,020; £509; £300; £300; £300) **Stalls** Low

Form RPR

1013 **1** **Muraaqeb**[10] 2698 5-9-2 **49**..........(p) AdamMcNamara 4 55
(Milton Bradley) *hld up: hdwy over 2f out: rdn and r.o to ld nr fin* **6/1**[3]

30-0 **2** *hd* **Dor's Law**[8] 2740 6-8-12 **52**..........(p) SophieRalston(7) 6 58
(Dean Ivory) *sn pushed along in rr: gd hdwy fnl f: fin wl (an inquiry was held into the running and riding of the mare which was held up towards the rear throughout before being asked for an effort approaching 2f out and staying on strongly under a hands and heels ride to finish 2nd of 15 beaten a head; the rid* **25/1**

22-0 **3** *nk* **Luxford**[138] 80 5-9-3 **50**.......... HectorCrouch 13 55
(Gary Moore) *prom: rdn to ld over 1f out: hdd nr fin* **12/1**

0000 **4** *¾* **Cat Royale (IRE)**[10] 2698 6-9-3 **50**..........(b) DannyBrock 1 54+
(John Butler) *sn led: hdd over 6f out: led again 4f out: rdn and hdd over 1f out: edgd rt ins fnl f: styd on same pce towards fin* **20/1**

0045 **5** *½* **Carvelas (IRE)**[42] 1710 10-9-10 **57**.......... NickyMackay 3 60
(J R Jenkins) *hld up: rdn: hdwy over 1f out: edgd lft ins fnl f: r.o* **10/1**

0311 **6** *1* **Arlecchino's Arc (IRE)**[49] 1546 4-9-10 **57**..........(v) FergusSweeney 7 58
(Mark Usher) *trckd ldrs: rdn and ev ch over 1f out: styd on same pce wl ins fnl f* **7/2**[1]

3031 **7** *½* **Mans Not Trot (IRE)**[30] 2012 4-9-7 **57**..........(p) MeganNicholls(3) 10 57
(Brian Barr) *awkward s: sn prom: chsd ldr over 8f out: led over 6f out tl 4f out: rdn and ev ch over 1f out: no ex wl ins fnl f (jockey said gelding fly-leapt leaving the stalls, jumped left and she lost an iron as a result.)* **20/1**

3404 **8** *1* **Foxrush Take Time (FR)**[13] 2595 4-8-12 **45**..........(e) PhilipPrince 15 43
(Richard Guest) *hld up: nt clr run and swtchd rt ins fnl f: nt trble ldrs* **12/1**

3005 **9** *½* **Tobacco Road (IRE)**[26] 2112 9-9-7 **57**..........(t) PaddyBradley(3) 5 54
(Mark Pattinson) *s.i.s: hld up: wd on home turn: rdn and r.o ins fnl f: nvr nrr (jockey said gelding was slowly away)* **12/1**

0-06 **10** *½* **Island Flame (IRE)**[23] 2244 6-9-7 **54**..........(p) RobertWinston 8 51
(Les Eyre) *hmpd s: sn prom: rdn and nt clr run over 1f out: no ex ins fnl f* **33/1**

0002 **11** *¾* **Ronni Layne**[23] 2234 5-8-13 **46**..........(b) DavidEgan 9 41
(Louise Allan) *hmpd s: hld up: rdn over 2f out: nt trble ldrs* **12/1**

3344 **12** *hd* **Sea Shack**[12] 2631 5-9-5 **52**..........(t) GeraldMosse 2 47
(Julia Feilden) *chsd ldrs: rdn and ev ch over 1f out: eased whn btn ins fnl f* **5/1**[2]

5022 **13** *1 ¾* **Sharp Operator**[23] 2231 6-9-10 **57**..........(h) BenCurtis 14 49
(Charlie Wallis) *plld hrd and prom: hmpd and lost pl after 1f: hdwy over 1f out: wknd ins fnl f* **6/1**[3]

00-0 **14** *5* **Wynfaul The Wizard (USA)**[90] 859 4-8-12 **45**..(t[1]) CallumShepherd 11 28
(Laura Morgan) *hld up: a in rr* **50/1**

00-0 **15** *¾* **Argent Bleu**[50] 1519 4-8-12 **45**.......... KieranO'Neill 12 26
(Roger Ingram) *hld up: a in rr* **50/1**

2m 6.82s (-1.78) **Going Correction** -0.10s/f (Stan) **15** Ran SP% **127.6**
Speed ratings (Par 101): **103,102,102,102,101 100,100,99,99,98 98,98,96,92,92**
CSF £162.62 CT £1778.23 TOTE £6.90: £2.50, £6.90, £4.40; EX 199.80 Trifecta £1952.20.
Owner E A Hayward **Bred** Peter Winkworth **Trained** Sedbury, Gloucs

FOCUS
An ordinary affair but it was run at a good gallop. The winner has been rated as finding a bit on his recent form.

3007 FAMILY FUNDAY MONDAY 27TH H'CAP 7f (P)
9:00 (9:02) (Class 6) (0-55,56) 4-Y-O+
£3,428 (£1,020; £509; £300; £300; £300) **Stalls** Low

Form RPR

0423 **1** **Rock In Society (IRE)**[28] 2066 4-8-9 **47**..........(b) DarraghKeenan(5) 14 59+
(John Butler) *led 6f out: rdn clr and hung lft ins fnl f* **8/1**[3]

4002 **2** *3 ¼* **Queen Of Kalahari**[15] 2532 4-8-9 **47**.......... FayeMcManoman(5) 13 51
(Les Eyre) *prom: chsd wnr over 5f out: rdn over 1f out: no ex ins fnl f* **12/1**

U305 **3** *¾* **Cristal Pallas Cat (IRE)**[41] 1731 4-9-0 **47**.......... FergusSweeney 4 49+
(Roger Ingram) *restless in stalls: s.i.s hld up: hdwy over 1f out: rdn and r.o to go 3rd wl ins fnl f (jockey said gelding became upset in stalls)* **7/1**[2]

6013 **4** *¾* **Tarseekh**[79] 1026 6-9-4 **51**..........(b) DavidEgan 10 51
(Charlie Wallis) *sn led: hdd 6f out: chsd ldrs: rdn over 1f out: no ex ins fnl f* **8/1**[3]

1163 **5** *½* **Mr Potter**[10] 2681 6-9-9 **56**..........(v) PhilipPrince 3 55
(Richard Guest) *led early: chsd ldrs: rdn over 1f out: no ex ins fnl f* **6/1**[1]

0563 **6** *nse* **Caledonian Gold**[23] 2235 6-8-12 **45**.......... HectorCrouch 7 44
(Lisa Williamson) *trckd ldrs: rdn over 1f out: no ex ins fnl f* **20/1**

0-00 **7** *1 ¼* **Stand Firm (IRE)**[8] 2741 4-8-13 **51**..........(v) DylanHogan(5) 2 46
(Robert Cowell) *sn pushed along in rr: rdn over 1f out: styd on ins fnl f: nt trble ldrs* **6/1**[1]

1060 **8** 1 1/2 **Black Truffle (FR)**[41] 1731 9-8-5 **45**......................(p) EllieMacKenzie(7) 1 37
(Mark Usher) *hld up in tch: rdn over 1f out: wknd ins fnl f* **14/1**

6524 **9** 1 3/4 **Slipalongtrevaskis**[28] 2066 6-8-13 **46**......................(b) JoeyHaynes 12 33
(Paul Howling) *hld up: swtchd rt over 1f out: sn rdn: n.d* **7/1**[2]

4206 **10** 2 **Little Miss Kodi (IRE)**[10] 2693 6-9-4 **51**......................(t) LiamJones 5 33
(Mark Loughnane) *sn pushed along into mid-div: rdn over 2f out: wknd ins fnl f* **9/1**

4450 **11** 2 1/4 **Malaysian Boleh**[33] 1933 9-8-12 **45**......................(be) CallumShepherd 16 21
(Phil McEntee) *s.i.s: sn pushed along in rr: n.d* **12/1**

-064 **12** 1 **Footstepsintherain (IRE)**[78] 1042 9-9-7 **54**...................... RobertWinston 6 27
(J R Jenkins) *s.i.s: hld up: plld hrd: racd wd: n.d (jockey said gelding was slowly away)* **16/1**

0060 **13** 20 **Rosarno (IRE)**[13] 2596 5-9-9 **56**...................... ShaneGray 11
(Paul Howling) *s.i.s: outpcd (vet said gelding was lame right fore)* **16/1**

1m 25.22s (-1.98) **Going Correction** -0.10s/f (Stan) **13** Ran SP% **124.4**
Speed ratings (Par 101): **107,103,102,101,101 100,99,97,95,93 90,89,66**
CSF £104.76 CT £741.72 TOTE £10.80: £3.60, £4.20, £2.70; EX 119.40 Trifecta £1224.30.
Owner Dave James **Bred** Mrs Eithne Hamilton **Trained** Newmarket, Suffolk

FOCUS
An ordinary handicap, but the winner did it well from the front.
T/Jkpt: Not won. T/Plt: £34.40 to a £1 stake. Pool: £41,276.68. 1,197.66 winning units. T/Qpdt: £10.50 to a £1 stake. Pool: £5,138.24. 487.24 winning units. **Colin Roberts**

2400 **GOODWOOD** (R-H)
Thursday, May 23

OFFICIAL GOING: Good (good to firm in places; 7.9)
Wind: light, across Weather: sunny

3008 EUROPEAN BREEDERS FUND EBF NOVICE STKS (PLUS 10 RACE) 6f
2:00 (2:00) (Class 4) 2-Y-O **£6,792** (£2,021; £1,010; £505) **Stalls** High

Form RPR

1 **Wild Thunder (IRE)** 2-9-5 0...................... SeanLevey 2 85
(Richard Hannon) *str; bmpd sn after leaving stalls: in tch in midfield: hdwy to chse ldr over 4f out: clsd to press ldr and reminders 2f out: rdn to ld ins fnl f: r.o wl* **10/1**[3]

2 3/4 **Buhturi (IRE)** 2-9-5 0...................... JimCrowley 4 83+
(Charles Hills) *athletic; looked wl; broke okay but bmpd sn after leaving stalls: dropped to rr and t.k.h: hdwy jst over 2f out: chsd ldng pair ent fnl f: rdn to press wnr ins fnl f: r.o but hld* **11/2**[2]

2 **3** 1 1/2 **Clan Royale**[12] 2610 2-9-5 0...................... AndreaAtzeni 1 78
(Roger Varian) *str; broke fast to ld and crossed to stands' rail: rdn over 1f out: hdd ins fnl f: sn btn and wknd wl ins fnl f* **1/3**[1]

4 3 **Swinley (IRE)** 2-9-2 0...................... FinleyMarsh(3) 8 69
(Richard Hughes) *leggy; chsd ldr for over 1f: chsd ldrs after: swtchd rt and effrt over 1f out: unable qck and wknd ins fnl f* **50/1**

5 3 3/4 **Subutai (IRE)** 2-9-5 0...................... AdamKirby 3 58
(Clive Cox) *compact; bit bkwrd; bmpd and squeezed for room sn after s: in tch in last pair: effrt and shifted lft over 1f out: no imp and wknd ins fnl f* **14/1**

6 3/4 **Activius (IRE)** 2-9-5 0...................... OisinMurphy 5 56
(Brian Meehan) *leggy; wnt rt leaving stalls: chsd ldrs for 2f: rdn and struggling over 2f out: wknd fnl f* **25/1**

7 6 **Rain Cap** 2-9-5 0...................... CharlesBishop 6 38
(Mick Channon) *leggy; pressing ldrs whn squeezed for room sn after s: midfield: rn green and sn pushed along: dropped to rr 3f out: wknd over 1f out* **50/1**

1m 13.07s (0.97) **Going Correction** -0.075s/f (Good) **7** Ran SP% **113.9**
Speed ratings (Par 95): **90,89,87,83,78 77,69**
CSF £61.01 TOTE £9.30: £2.70, £2.30; EX 69.00 Trifecta £120.30.
Owner Saeed Manana **Bred** Anthony Kirwan **Trained** East Everleigh, Wilts

FOCUS
Top and bottom bends and the straight to the 2f mark dolled out 6yds. Add 10yds. The betting suggested this would be one-sided but it certainly wasn't. The winner looks useful. Andrea Atzeni described the going as "good to firm, pretty fast", while Charles Bishop called it "fast". The level is fluid.

3009 THREE FRIDAY NIGHTS H'CAP 7f
2:35 (2:35) (Class 2) (0-105,105) 4-Y-O+ **£15,562** (£4,660; £2,330; £1,165; £582; £292) **Stalls** Low

Form RPR

6304 **1** **Apex King (IRE)**[19] 2402 5-8-2 **86** oh1...................... HollieDoyle 4 94
(David Loughnane) *chsd ldr for over 1f: styd chsng ldrs: effrt and hdwy to chse ldr again over 1f out: clsd u.p to ld ins fnl f: sn in command and r.o wl* **10/1**

2-41 **2** 1 1/4 **Game Player (IRE)**[20] 2363 4-8-10 **94**...................... AndreaAtzeni 5 99+
(Roger Varian) *wnt lft leaving stalls: in tch in midfield: effrt over 2f out: hdwy u.p over 1f out: chsd wnr ins fnl f: kpt on but nvr getting on terms w wnr* **9/4**[2]

000- **3** 1 1/4 **Zhui Feng (IRE)**[246] 7424 6-9-7 **105**......................(w) JimCrowley 8 106
(Amanda Perrett) *chsd ldrs and t.k.h: sn restrained and hld up in tch in midfield: effrt ent fnl 2f: hdwy u.p over 1f out: kpt on same pce to go 3rd ins fnl f: nvr getting on terms w wnr* **16/1**

224 **4** 1 1/4 **Love Dreams (IRE)**[7] 2778 5-8-11 **95**......................(b) PJMcDonald 3 93
(Mark Johnston) *looked wl; sn led: rdn 1f out: drvn over 1f out: hdd ins fnl f: sn btn and wknd towards fin* **7/4**[1]

050- **5** hd **Makzeem**[299] 5457 6-9-4 **102**......................(t) JasonWatson 2 99+
(Roger Charlton) *hld up in tch in last trio: swtchd rt and effrt inner over 1f out: kpt on same pce ins fnl f* **10/1**

6222 **6** 1 1/2 **Raucous**[14] 2551 6-8-9 **100**......................(tp) CierenFallon(7) 6 93
(Robert Cowell) *squeezed for room sn after leaving stalls: hld up in last pair: swtchd lft and effrt over 2f out: nvr threatened to get on terms w ldrs: hung rt 1f out and one pce fnl f* **16/1**

12-4 **7** 4 1/2 **Intransigent**[132] 176 10-7-13 **86** oh1......................(b) WilliamCox(3) 7 67
(Andrew Balding) *wnt rt leaving stalls: hld up in rr: reminders 3f out: sn rdn and no prog: wl btn over 1f out* **66/1**

0-00 **8** 3/4 **George Of Hearts (FR)**[12] 2609 4-8-4 **88**..........(b[1]) SilvestreDeSousa 9 67
(Richard Hughes) *dropped into midfield sn after s: t.k.h and hdwy to chse ldr over 5f out tl 4f out: effrt 2f out: 3rd and no ex over 1f out: sn wknd* **6/1**[3]

046- **9** 8 **Rum Runner**[185] 9153 4-8-2 **86**...................... JoeFanning 1 44
(Richard Hannon) *t.k.h: chsd ldrs after 2f: rdn over 2f out: lost 2nd over 1f out: sn dropped out and bhd wh eased wl ins fnl f* **20/1**

1m 26.21s (-0.49) **Going Correction** -0.075s/f (Good) **9** Ran SP% **117.6**
Speed ratings (Par 109): **99,97,96,94,94 92,87,86,77**
CSF £33.48 CT £372.65 TOTE £10.40: £2.70, £1.30, £3.80; EX 36.50 Trifecta £392.20.
Owner G B & G H Firmager **Bred** Dr W O'Brien **Trained** Tern Hill, Shropshire

FOCUS
Add 10yds. An open-looking and very useful handicap, won in good style. The winner has been rated to his best since his 2yo days.

3010 BRITISH EBF PREMIER FILLIES' H'CAP 1m 3f 218y
3:10 (3:10) (Class 3) (0-90,90) 3-Y-O+ **£12,450** (£3,728; £1,864; £932; £466; £234) **Stalls** High

Form RPR

100- **1** **Spirit Of Appin**[209] 8610 4-10-0 **90**...................... OisinMurphy 3 101
(Brian Meehan) *trckd ldr: clsd and travelling best over 2f out: pushed into ld over 1f out: in command and styd on wl ins fnl f: rdn out* **16/1**

2212 **2** 2 3/4 **Dono Di Dio**[21] 2342 4-8-11 **80**...................... CierenFallon(7) 7 86+
(Michael Madgwick) *hld up wl off the pce in last quartet: effrt in 6th but stl plenty to do over 2f out: hdwy and hung rt over 1f out: styd on to go 2nd ins fnl f: no threat to wnr* **9/1**

2-61 **3** 1 1/2 **Hyanna**[21] 2342 4-9-13 **89**...................... CharlesBishop 8 93
(Eve Johnson Houghton) *hld up in tch in 4th: effrt over 2f out: chsd clr wnr and hung rt over 1f out: nvr getting on terms: kpt on same pce and lost 2nd ins fnl f* **9/2**[2]

306- **4** 3 1/2 **White Chocolate (IRE)**[208] 8649 5-9-13 **89**...................... JamieSpencer 1 87
(David Simcock) *hld up off the pce in last quartet: 7th and stl plenty to do over 2f out: shkn up over 1f out: kpt on but no real imp after: nvr trbld ldrs* **8/1**

26-3 **5** shd **Lightening Dance**[10] 2685 5-8-11 **73**......................(b) JimCrowley 5 71
(Amanda Perrett) *edgy; chsd ldng pair and in tch: effrt over 2f out: drvn and no imp over 1f out: wknd ins fnl f* **6/1**

-333 **6** 4 1/2 **Velvet Vision**[8] 2737 4-8-9 **71** oh1...................... SilvestreDeSousa 4 62
(Mark H Tompkins) *sweating; stdd s: t.k.h: hld up wl off the pce in last quartet: effrt in 5th but stl plenty to do over 2f out: nvr getting on terms w ldrs: wknd ins fnl f* **7/1**

31-3 **7** 3 1/4 **Hulcote**[53] 1461 4-9-7 **83**...................... AdamKirby 6 69
(Clive Cox) *restless in stalls: stdd s: hld up wl off the pce in last pair: effrt u.p but stl plenty to do over 3f out: no prog and nvr involved (jockey said filly hung left-handed in home straight)* **3/1**[1]

100- **8** 1/2 **Mystic Meg**[199] 8883 4-9-5 **81**......................(h) PJMcDonald 2 66
(Hughie Morrison) *mounted in chute: led: clr 5f out: rdn and pressed ent fnl 2f: hdd over 1f out: sn btn and fdd fnl f* **11/2**[3]

2m 37.37s (-2.23) **Going Correction** -0.075s/f (Good) **8** Ran SP% **112.3**
Speed ratings (Par 104): **104,102,101,98,98 95,93,93**
CSF £143.85 CT £758.52 TOTE £16.20: £4.10, £2.40, £1.70; EX 133.00 Trifecta £1060.70.
Owner James Stewart **Bred** Wellsummers Farm **Trained** Manton, Wilts

FOCUS
Add 10yds. A surprise winner but a clear-cut one. The pace looked sound and they were well strung out from an early stage. A clear pb from the second.

3011 JIM BARRY H'CAP 1m 1f 11y
3:45 (3:45) (Class 4) (0-85,87) 3-Y-O **£6,986** (£2,079; £1,038; £519; £300; £300) **Stalls** Low

Form RPR

02-3 **1** **Wedding Blue**[20] 2354 3-9-2 **79**...................... OisinMurphy 2 92
(Andrew Balding) *str; dwlt: steadily rcvrd to trck ldrs after 3f and travelled strly: swtchd lft jst over 2f out: rdn to ld over 1f out: styd on strly and drew clr fnl f: readily* **4/1**[3]

52-2 **2** 3 3/4 **Al Mureib (IRE)**[20] 2364 3-9-7 **84**...................... PatCosgrave 8 89
(Saeed bin Suroor) *hld up in tch in midfield: effrt jst over 2f out: hdwy to go 2nd and pressed wnr over 1f out: readily outpcd jst ins fnl f: kpt on same pce after* **4/1**[3]

1-22 **3** 1 1/2 **Sucellus**[26] 2113 3-9-10 **87**...................... FrankieDettori 6 89
(John Gosden) *athletic; looked wl; stdd s: hld up in tch in last pair: effrt jst over 2f out: hdwy u.p to chse ldng pair: kpt on same pce and no ch w wnr ins fnl f* **7/2**[2]

1204 **4** 4 **Harvey Dent**[12] 2616 3-9-2 **79**...................... HollieDoyle 3 73
(Archie Watson) *t.k.h: hld up in tch in midfield: effrt jst over 2f out: 4th and no ex ent fnl f: wknd ins fnl f* **14/1**

115- **5** 1 1/4 **Sophosc (IRE)**[225] 8110 3-9-3 **80**...................... CharlesBishop 4 71
(Joseph Tuite) *stdd after s: t.k.h: hld up in tch in last quartet: nt clr run over 2f out: effrt u.p over 1f out: no imp and nvr threatened ldrs* **40/1**

432- **6** 1 3/4 **Baryshnikov**[187] 9122 3-9-2 **79**...................... AndreaAtzeni 5 66
(Ed Walker) *looked wl; s.i.s: in tch in rr but sn pushed along and nvr travelling wl: swtchd ins 2f out: no real imp and wknd fnl f (jockey said gelding was slowly away and was never travelling)* **3/1**[1]

6-05 **7** 1/2 **Flying Dragon (FR)**[13] 2569 3-9-0 **77**...................... TomMarquand 7 63
(Richard Hannon) *t.k.h: hld up in tch in last quartet: effrt over 2f out: no prog and btn over 1f out: wknd fnl f* **25/1**

03-5 **8** 5 **Culture (FR)**[20] 2354 3-8-11 **74**...................... JasonWatson 10 50
(George Baker) *sn led: hdd over 7f out but styd upsides ldrs: rdn over 2f out: led 2f out: sn hdd and outpcd: wknd fnl f* **25/1**

2362 **9** 6 **Mustadun**[20] 2369 3-9-0 **77**...................... JoeFanning 1 40
(Mark Johnston) *chsd ldrs tl led over 7f out: rdn over 2f out: sn hdd and lost pl over 1f out: wknd fnl f* **12/1**

5-40 **10** 14 **Two Blondes (IRE)**[16] 2510 3-9-6 **83**...................... SilvestreDeSousa 9 17
(Mick Channon) *led: sn hdd and chsd ldrs: rdn: lost pl and bhd 2f out: sn wknd: t.o* **16/1**

1m 54.91s (-2.49) **Going Correction** -0.075s/f (Good) **10** Ran SP% **117.6**
Speed ratings (Par 101): **108,104,103,99,98 97,96,92,86,74**
CSF £20.19 CT £61.60 TOTE £4.30: £1.60, £1.60, £1.70; EX 17.30 Trifecta £71.40.
Owner George Strawbridge **Bred** George Strawbridge **Trained** Kingsclere, Hants

FOCUS
Add 10yds. A competitive handicap but won easily by an improving winner. The third has been rated to form.

3012 HEIGHT OF FASHION STKS (LISTED RACE) (FILLIES) 1m 1f 197y
4:20 (4:20) (Class 1) 3-Y-O

£25,519 (£9,675; £4,842; £2,412; £1,210; £607) **Stalls** Low

Form RPR

1 **1** **Aloe Vera**[20] 2354 3-9-0 0 HarryBentley 6 96+
(Ralph Beckett) *str; dwlt: hld up in tch towards rr: clsd and nt clr run jst over 2f out: swtchd rt and hdwy to chse ldrs whn swtchd rt over 1f out: rdn to ld 1f out: styd on strly and drew clr ins fnl f: readily* **11/4**[2]

40-2 **2** *3* **Shambolic (IRE)**[18] 2445 3-9-0 100 FrankieDettori 1 90
(John Gosden) *dwlt: sn rcvrd and led over 7f out: rdn ent fnl 2f: drvn over 1f out: wandered and hdd 1f out: nt match pce of wnr ins fnl f and btn ins fnl f (jockey said filly was slowly away)* **7/4**[1]

-110 **3** *nk* **Love So Deep (JPN)**[15] 2521 3-9-0 82 JFEgan 9 89
(Jane Chapple-Hyam) *sn stdd and hld up in tch: in rr: clsd and nt clr run 2f out: hdwy and swtchd lft 1f out: styd on u.p ins fnl f and pressing for 2nd cl home: no threat to wnr* **20/1**

1-01 **4** *1 ¾* **Muchly**[22] 2268 3-9-0 102 RobertHavlin 4 86+
(John Gosden) *looked wl; t.k.h: hld up wl in tch in midfield: clsd to chse ldrs over 3f out: swtchd lft and effrt over 2f out: ev ch but unable qck u.p over 1f out: wknd ins fnl f* **5/1**

61-0 **5** *nk* **Garrel Glen**[18] 2443 3-9-0 92 DanielMuscutt 8 85
(Mark H Tompkins) *led tl over 7f out: chsd ldr: effrt ent fnl 2f: ev ch but unable qck u.p over 1f out: wknd ins fnl f* **20/1**

-112 **6** *2 ¼* **Cafe Espresso**[35] 1885 3-9-0 78 (b) HollieDoyle 3 80?
(Archie Watson) *hld up in tch towards rr: effrt 2f out: sn u.p: unable qck and hung rt over 1f out: wknd fnl f (jockey said filly hung right-handed)* **80/1**

5 **7** *2* **Love Explodes**[91] 827 3-9-0 0 StevieDonohoe 2 76
(Ed Vaughan) *str; trckd ldrs on inner: effrt and swtchd rt wl over 1f out: no ex u.p ent fnl f: sn wknd* **50/1**

1-4 **8** *1* **Grace And Danger (IRE)**[15] 2521 3-9-0 0 OisinMurphy 7 74
(Andrew Balding) *leggy; stdd after s: hld up in tch towards rr: effrt over 2f out: sn struggling and wl hld over 1f out* **7/2**[3]

-320 **9** *18* **Lady Cosette (FR)**[12] 2618 3-9-0 76 TomMarquand 5 38
(Harry Dunlop) *chsd ldrs on outer: rdn over 2f out: sn lost pl: bhd and eased ins fnl f* **100/1**

2m 7.5s (-1.40) **Going Correction** -0.075s/f (Good) **9** Ran SP% **115.6**
Speed ratings (Par 104): **102,99,99,97,97 95,94,93,79**
CSF £7.65 TOTE £3.70: £1.30, £1.10, £4.00; EX 9.30 Trifecta £79.40.

Owner Miss K Rausing **Bred** Miss K Rausing **Trained** Kimpton, Hants

FOCUS
Add 10yds. A good quality Listed event, and while it won't have any bearing on Epsom this year, the winner looks distinctly useful. Ordinary form, with the third and sixth likely limiting the level.

3013 BRITISH EUROPEAN BREEDERS FUND EBF MAIDEN FILLIES' STKS (PLUS 10 RACE) 1m 1f 197y
4:55 (4:55) (Class 4) 3-Y-O

£6,792 (£2,021; £1,010; £505) **Stalls** Low

Form RPR

1 **Terebellum (IRE)** 3-9-0 0 FrankieDettori 10 97+
(John Gosden) *ly; looked wl; styd wd early: prom: chsd ldr after 2f: wnt clr w runner-up and led 2f out: rdn and kicked clr over 1f out: r.o strly: readily* **2/1**[1]

0-22 **2** *4 ½* **Maamora (IRE)**[21] 2321 3-9-0 80 AndreaAtzeni 1 88
(Simon Crisford) *led: hdd 2f out: sn u.p and brushed aside by wnr 1f out: wl hld but kpt on for clr 2nd ins fnl f* **9/4**[2]

3 *4 ½* **Promissory (IRE)** 3-9-0 0 RobertHavlin 11 79+
(John Gosden) *leggy; athletic; stdd s and dropped in: hld up in last trio: clsd and nt clr run over 2f out: swtchd 2f out: hdwy and swtchd rt over 1f out: chsd clr ldng pair 1f out: styd on but nvr getting on terms: eased cl home* **9/1**

02- **4** *5* **Chartered**[236] 7763 3-9-0 0 HarryBentley 7 69
(Ralph Beckett) *str; stmbld leaving stalls: hld up in tch in midfield: lost pl and pushed along over 4f out: modest prog to pass btn horses and hung rt 1f out: no ch and plugged on same pce ins fnl f (jockey said filly stumbled leaving stalls)* **5/1**[3]

6 **5** *1 ¼* **Dawaaween (IRE)**[16] 2518 3-9-0 0 JimCrowley 2 67
(Owen Burrows) *str; looked wl; t.k.h: hld up in tch in midfield: effrt to go 3rd but ldrs gng clr over 2f out: lost wl hld 3rd 1f out: wknd ins fnl f* **10/1**

6 *1 ¾* **Wild Cat** 3-9-0 0 JasonWatson 6 63
(Roger Charlton) *leggy; hld up in tch in midfield: rdn over 2f out: sn struggling and outpcd: wknd over 1f out* **20/1**

7 *1* **Uncertain Smile (IRE)** 3-9-0 0 HollieDoyle 4 61
(Clive Cox) *workmanlike; t.k.h: w ldrs early: sn restrained and in tch in midfield: rdn and outpcd whn edgd lft over 2f out: sn wl btn and wknd over 1f out* **50/1**

0 **8** *2 ¾* **Sibylline**[26] 2102 3-9-0 0 StevieDonohoe 9 56
(David Simcock) *leggy; stdd after s: t.k.h: hld up in rr: swtchd rt and short-lived effrt over 2f out: wl btn over 1f out: wknd* **100/1**

9 *1 ¼* **Hawafez (IRE)** 3-9-0 0 TomMarquand 3 53
(Saeed bin Suroor) *ly; dwlt: rcvrd to chse ldrs after 2f: drvn and unable qck over 2f out: sn outpcd and wl btn over 1f out: fdd fnl f* **12/1**

6-0 **10** *13* **Seeing Red (IRE)**[27] 2087 3-8-11 0 CameronNoble(3) 8 27
(Amanda Perrett) *str; chsd ldng trio: rdn and losing pl whn sltly impeded over 2f out: wl bhd and eased ins fnl f* **50/1**

11 *35* **If At Sea** 3-8-9 0 (h[1]) ThomasGreatrex(5) 5
(Amanda Perrett) *athletic; stdd after s: hld up in rr: struggling u.p over 3f out: sn lost tch: t.o and eased fnl f (jockey said filly ran green and was never travelling)* **50/1**

2m 7.47s (-1.43) **Going Correction** -0.075s/f (Good) **11** Ran SP% **119.2**
Speed ratings (Par 98): **102,98,94,90,89 88,87,85,84,74 46**
CSF £6.51 TOTE £2.90: £1.40, £1.20, £2.30; EX 7.40 Trifecta £39.30.

Owner HRH Princess Haya Of Jordan **Bred** Alan O'Flynn **Trained** Newmarket, Suffolk

FOCUS
Add 10yds. An intriguing maiden that should produce plenty of good types. The winner looks smart and they came home at decent intervals. The time was marginally quicker than the preceding Listed race over the same trip.

3014 FARMER BUTCHER CHEF APPRENTICE H'CAP 6f
5:30 (5:30) (Class 5) (0-70,72) 4-Y-O+

£5,692 (£1,694; £846; £423; £300; £300) **Stalls** High

Form RPR

3-46 **1** *nk* **Atalanta's Boy**[27] 2076 4-9-6 66 (h) ThomasGreatrex 1 79
(David Menuisier) *t.k.h: hld up in tch in midfield: effrt to chse ldrs over 1f out: ev ch and edgd lft 1f out: sustained chal and carried rt ins fnl f: hld towards fin: fin 2nd: awrdd the r* **7/2**[1]

00-1 **2** **Spanish Star (IRE)**[17] 2473 4-9-2 65 WilliamCarver(3) 5 79
(Patrick Chamings) *stdd leaving stalls: t.k.h: hld up in midfield: cl to chse ldrs over 1f out: rdn and hung rt 1f out: sn led: kpt edging rt u.p ins fnl f: hld on wl: fin 1st: disqualified and plcd 2nd* **6/1**

0530 **3** *3 ½* **National Glory (IRE)**[6] 2804 4-9-3 66 (b) Pierre-LouisJamin(3) 9 68
(Archie Watson) *led after 1f: rdn over 1f out: hdd jst ins fnl f: sn outpcd and wknd towards fin* **10/1**

-264 **4** *3 ¾* **The Lamplighter (FR)**[16] 2514 4-9-7 72 (tp) GeorgiaDobie(5) 8 62
(George Baker) *chsd ldrs: effrt to chse ldr ent fnl 2f: 4th and no ex 1f out: sn wknd* **12/1**

1621 **5** *½* **Real Estate (IRE)**[17] 2483 4-9-9 72 (p) CierenFallon(3) 4 60
(Michael Attwater) *looked wl; hld up in tch in midfield: effrt ent fnl 2f: no imp and btn 1f out: hung rt and wknd ins fnl f: fin lame (vet said colt was lame left fore)* **4/1**[2]

30-4 **6** *nk* **Born To Finish (IRE)**[17] 2483 6-9-10 70 (p) WilliamCox 6 57
(Ed de Giles) *wnt lft s and stdd: hld up in rr: sme hdwy u.p over 1f out: keeping on but no ch whn bdly hmpd and swtchd rt ins fnl f (jockey said gelding was never travelling)* **10/1**

3011 **7** *¾* **Hic Bibi**[25] 2153 4-9-6 66 CameronNoble 11 51
(David Loughnane) *sweating; w ldrs for 1f: chsd ldrs after tl wnt 2nd 3f out: rdn and lost 2nd ent fnl 2f: sn btn and wknd fnl f* **5/1**[3]

0-60 **8** *½* **Charming Guest (IRE)**[13] 2588 4-9-4 71 GeorgeBass(7) 2 54
(Mick Channon) *a towards rr: effrt 2f out: no imp u.p over 1f out: wknd fnl f* **12/1**

03/0 **9** *1 ½* **Bullseye Bullet**[23] 2235 4-8-3 56 oh10 (p) IsobelFrancis(7) 7 34
(Mark Usher) *squeezed for room leaving stalls: sn swtchd lft and outpcd in rr: nvr on terms (jockey said gelding moved poorly)* **100/1**

0005 **10** *9* **Deer Song**[69] 1210 6-8-7 56 oh11 KatherineBegley(5) 10 6
(John Bridger) *led for 1f: chsd ldr tl 1/2-way: lost pl and bhd whn hung bdly rt over 1f out (jockey said gelding hung right-handed)* **100/1**

5-30 **11** *9* **Red Tycoon (IRE)**[21] 2339 7-8-11 62 TristanPrice(5) 3
(Ken Cunningham-Brown) *stdd: awkward leaving stalls and slowly away: bhd and racd in centre: sme prog after 2f out: wknd over 1f out* **12/1**

1m 10.7s (-1.40) **Going Correction** -0.075s/f (Good) **11** Ran SP% **116.4**
Speed ratings (Par 103): **105,106,100,95,95 94,93,93,91,79 67**
CSF £24.33 CT £194.18 TOTE £4.20: £1.50, £2.30, £3.30; EX 24.50 Trifecta £253.40.
Owner Mrs Monica Josefina Borton & Partner **Bred** Monica Martinez-Trumm **Trained** Pulborough, W Sussex

■ Stewards' Enquiry : Katherine Begley two-day ban: weighed-in more than 2lb over (Jun 6)
William Carver four-day ban: careless riding (6-9 Jun)

FOCUS
A dramatic end to this modest handicap with the first past the post being demoted to second following interference. The level is a bit fluid, but the winner's Bath form could possibly be this good taking into account his jockey's claim.
T/Plt: £107.60 to a £1 stake. Pool: £70,540.38. 478.21 winning units. T/Qpdt: £7.30 to a £1 stake. Pool: £9,254.26. 933.15 winning units. **Steve Payne**

2617 LINGFIELD (L-H)
Thursday, May 23

OFFICIAL GOING: Good to firm (good in places) changing to good to firm after race 3 (2.50)
Wind: gentle breeze Weather: sunny with light cloud, warm

3015 VISIT ATTHERACES.COM H'CAP 1m 3f 133y
1:40 (1:41) (Class 6) (0-65,67) 4-Y-O+

£3,105 (£924; £461; £300; £300; £300) **Stalls** High

Form RPR

4025 **1** **Francophilia**[8] 2732 4-9-10 67 FrannyNorton 6 75
(Mark Johnston) *trckd ldr: led 3f out: drifted to far rail and drvn in 2 l ld 2f out: kpt up to work and in command ins fnl f: comf* **11/4**[2]

0/-1 **2** *2 ½* **Seaborn (IRE)**[23] 2233 5-8-11 61 WilliamCarver(7) 5 65+
(Patrick Chamings) *hld up in rr: pushed along and plenty to do on outer 3f out: rdn 2f out: hdwy ins fnl f: r.o strly nr fin: tk 2nd last three strides: nvr nr wnr* **6/4**[1]

424- **3** *nk* **Miss M (IRE)**[189] 9075 5-9-1 58 MartinDwyer 4 62
(William Muir) *chsd ldrs: drvn 3f out: rdn in 3rd over 1f out: kpt on fnl f* **9/1**

3316 **4** *½* **Iley Boy**[33] 1935 5-8-10 53 (p) CharlieBennett 8 56
(John Gallagher) *hld up: slt stumble over 3f out: drvn and hdwy over 2f out: sn rdn into 4th: no ex fnl f (jockey said gelding stumbled rounding the home bend)* **20/1**

6440 **5** *shd* **Grange Walk (IRE)**[12] 2617 4-9-4 64 PaddyBradley(3) 9 67
(Pat Phelan) *mid-div: hdwy on outer over 2f out: drvn into 2nd 2f out: rdn over 1f out: wknd fnl f* **12/1**

5-22 **6** *4 ½* **Givepeaceachance**[13] 2595 4-8-13 56 PatDobbs 7 51
(Denis Coakley) *led: drvn and hdd 3f out: sn wknd* **7/2**[3]

3600 **7** *7* **Mood For Mischief**[10] 2695 4-8-10 58 (p) RachealKneller(5) 2 42
(James Bennett) *hld up: pushed along in 6th whn stmbld over 3f out: sn bk on even keel and drvn: dropped to last over 2f out (jockey said gelding stumbled rounding home bend)* **40/1**

2m 29.67s (-4.33) **Going Correction** -0.425s/f (Firm) **7** Ran SP% **113.8**
Speed ratings (Par 101): **97,95,95,94,94 91,87**
CSF £7.20 CT £29.72 TOTE £3.20: £1.60, £1.60; EX 8.00 Trifecta £41.10.
Owner Miss K Rausing **Bred** Miss K Rausing **Trained** Middleham Moor, N Yorks

The Form Book Flat 2019, Raceform Ltd, Newbury, RG14 5SJ

FOCUS
The rail was moved out 4 yards at the 4f point on the round course. There was a cut away added at the 3f marker on the home straight. The official distance had an extra 4yds, making it to 1m3f 137yds. After the third race, the going was changed to good to firm from good to firm, good in places.

3016 PARKER ANDREWS H'CAP — 1m 3f 133y
2:15 (2:19) (Class 4) (0-85,86) 4-Y-O+ £5,530 (£1,645; £822; £411; £300) Stalls High

Form — RPR

1-45 **1** **Oasis Fantasy (IRE)**[62] 1267 8-9-4 86 .... DylanHogan(5) 5 — 93
(David Simcock) *mde all: shkn up in 2 l ld 2f out: drvn 1f out: in command and r.o wl ins fnl f: eased nr fin* — 6/1

3321 **2** ½ **Lawn Ranger**[17] 2486 4-9-5 82 .... KierenFox 6 — 87
(Michael Attwater) *a chsng wnr: pushed along 3f out: rdn in 2 l 2nd 2f out and ent fnl f: kpt on but a hld* — 7/4[1]

6-00 **3** 2¼ **El Borracho (IRE)**[61] 1291 4-8-11 74 .... (h) NickyMackay 3 — 75
(Simon Dow) *sweating: reluctant to load: slowly away and in rr: drvn and rn wd on home turn over 3f out: rdn over 2f out: wnt 3rd over 1f out: one pce fnl f* — 10/1

4-05 **4** 1 **Amourice (IRE)**[19] 2399 4-9-4 84 .... (h) PaddyBradley(3) 1 — 84
(Jane Chapple-Hyam) *reluctant to load: racd in 3rd: pushed along 3f out: rdn and dropped to 4th over 1f out: no ex fnl f* — 11/4[2]

-235 **5** 7 **Hollywood Road (IRE)**[12] 2620 6-9-5 82 .... HectorCrouch 2 — 70
(Gary Moore) *racd in 4th: drvn and dropped to last over 3f out where rn v wd on home turn: bhd and no ch fr over 2f out: eased fnl f* — 3/1[3]

2m 27.43s (-6.57) **Going Correction** -0.425s/f (Firm) — 5 Ran SP% **111.4**
Speed ratings (Par 105): **104,103,102,101,96**
CSF £17.19 TOTE £4.50: £2.10, £1.50; EX 13.20 Trifecta £52.60.
Owner Abdulla Al Mansoori **Bred** Windflower Overseas **Trained** Newmarket, Suffolk

FOCUS
This race distance had an extra 4yds, making it to 1m3f 137yds. The first two home were pretty much the first two throughout. It's been rated around the first two.

3017 WITHEFORD EQUINE BARRIER TRIALS 13TH JUNE H'CAP — 1m 6f
2:50 (2:55) (Class 6) (0-60,62) 4-Y-O+
£3,105 (£924; £461; £300; £300; £300) Stalls Low

Form — RPR

2246 **1** **Banta Bay**[49] 1548 5-8-8 47 .... JosephineGordon 4 — 56
(John Best) *chsd ldrs: pushed into ld over 2f out: reminders and wnt 3 l clr 2f out: 4 l ld 1f out: pushed out fnl f: eased nr fin* — 13/2

0410 **2** 2 **Sea's Aria (IRE)**[46] 1361 8-8-1 47 .... AledBeech(7) 10 — 51
(Mark Hoad) *mid-div: hdwy 4f out: pushed along 3f out: rdn in 3rd over 2f out: wnt 2nd over 1f out: kpt on fnl f: no ch w wnr* — 28/1

00-0 **3** 3½ **Essgee Nics (IRE)**[132] 185 6-8-7 46 oh1 .... (p) KierenFox 7 — 46
(Paul George) *hld up: pushed along 3f out: rdn over 2f out: r.o ins fnl f: tk 3rd last 25yds* — 20/1

0-00 **4** nk **Becky Sharp**[22] 2283 4-8-10 49 .... (b[1]) CharlieBennett 5 — 48
(Jim Boyle) *chsd ldrs: pushed along 3f out: rdn and kpt on fr 2f out: lost 3rd last 25yds* — 16/1

0310 **5** ¾ **Thresholdofadream (IRE)**[21] 2344 4-9-2 55 .... PatDobbs 6 — 53
(Amanda Perrett) *hld up: hdwy on inner and slipped over 3f out: drvn over 2f out: rdn ent fnl f: one pce (jockey said filly slipped on bend turning in)* — 6/1[3]

50 **6** 1 **Le Musee (FR)**[16] 2518 6-9-9 62 .... (p) TomQueally 1 — 59
(Nigel Hawke) *hld up: drvn 3f out: sn rdn: styd on fnl f: nvr a threat* — 2/1[1]

0-46 **7** 1 **Earthly (USA)**[9] 2720 5-8-5 51 .... (tp) WilliamCarver(7) 11 — 47
(Bernard Llewellyn) *hld up on outer: drvn over 2f out: sn rdn: no imp* — 3/1[2]

0060 **8** 2½ **Galitello**[20] 2373 4-9-9 62 .... (v[1]) FrannyNorton 12 — 55
(Mark Johnston) *dwlt losing several l: bhd: last over 3f out: sn rdn: mod hdwy fnl 2f (jockey said gelding was slowly away)* — 11/1

6003 **9** 2¼ **Zahraani**[19] 2417 4-8-13 52 .... LiamKeniry 14 — 42
(J R Jenkins) *chsd ldr: drvn and dropped to 3rd over 3f out: sn rdn and wknd (trainer's rep said colt was unsuited by the going (good to firm, good in places) and would prefer an easier surface)* — 20/1

546- **10** 4½ **Bay Dude**[289] 5839 4-9-2 58 .... PaddyBradley(3) 13 — 42
(Brett Johnson) *led: pushed along and hdd over 2f out: sn rdn and wknd* — 20/1

3200 **11** ½ **Shovel It On (IRE)**[13] 2593 4-8-7 46 .... (bp) NickyMackay 8 — 29
(Steve Flook) *bhd: drvn 3f out: rdn 2f out: no rspnse* — 25/1

00-0 **12** 9 **Ginger Lacey**[14] 2555 4-8-8 47 .... NicolaCurrie 2 — 19
(Harry Dunlop) *mid-div: lost pl 4 out: sn drvn and wknd* — 33/1

3m 3.22s (-7.98) **Going Correction** -0.425s/f (Firm) — 12 Ran SP% **124.7**
Speed ratings (Par 101): **105,103,101,101,101 100,100,98,97,94 94,89**
CSF £186.31 CT £3466.97 TOTE £7.10: £2.40, £12.50, £7.60; EX 165.10 Trifecta £2908.30.
Owner Jones, Fuller & Paine **Bred** R, J D & M R Bromley Gardner **Trained** Oad Street, Kent

FOCUS
This race distance had an extra 4yds, making it to 1m6f 4yds. A moderate staying event, won by a long-standing maiden.

3018 SKY SPORTS RACING ON SKY 415 CLAIMING STKS — 7f 135y
3:25 (3:27) (Class 6) 3-Y-O+
£3,105 (£924; £461; £300; £300) Stalls Centre

Form — RPR

2030 **1** **Motajaasid (IRE)**[22] 2273 4-9-7 74 .... (t[1]) AngusVilliers(7) 4 — 81
(Richard Hughes) *mde all: 2 l ld 2f out: sn drifted to lft: rdn over 1f out: wnt further lft and drvn out in diminishing ld fnl f: hld on* — 9/2[2]

4540 **2** ¾ **Robero**[15] 2526 7-9-7 78 .... (p) TobyEley(7) 2 — 79
(Gay Kelleway) *prom: rdn over 2f out: wnt 2nd over 1f out: kpt on u.p fnl f* — 6/1

6566 **3** nk **Scofflaw**[17] 2472 5-9-4 74 .... (v) SeanDavis(5) 6 — 73
(David Evans) *hld up: drvn 3f out: rdn and effrt 2f out: hdwy into 3rd 1f out: kpt on fnl f* — 5/1[3]

5203 **4** 2¾ **Facethepuckout (IRE)**[43] 1685 3-9-2 75 .... (v) FrannyNorton 8 — 69
(John Ryan) *prom: rdn and lost pl over 2f out: 5th 1f out: kpt on into 4th nr fin* — 3/1[1]

5-00 **5** hd **Barbarosa (IRE)**[12] 2630 3-8-6 71 .... MartinDwyer 5 — 58
(Brian Meehan) *hld up: pushed along and hdwy to go prom over 2f out: drvn and lost pl over 1f out: sn rdn and wknd: lost 4th nr fin* — 3/1[1]

2-10 **6** 3¾ **Toriano**[13] 2596 6-8-12 63 .... AledBeech(7) 10 — 53
(Nick Littmoden) *chsd ldr: drvn and lost pl over 2f out: sn rdn and wknd* — 8/1

0-01 **7** 21 **Oofy Prosser (IRE)**[7] 2773 3-8-6 50 .... (p) MitchGodwin(3) 1 — 1
(Harry Dunlop) *wnt lft s: hld up: lost tch over 2f out (trainer said gelding lost his action and hung left-handed)* — 16/1

0-00 **8** 16 **Time To Rock**[50] 1517 4-10-0 30 .... KierenFox 9
(John Bridger) *a bhd: lost tch bef 1/2-way* — 100/1

1m 28.09s (-3.61) **Going Correction** -0.425s/f (Firm)
WFA 3 from 4yo+ 12lb — 8 Ran SP% **117.1**
Speed ratings (Par 101): **101,100,99,97,97 93,72,56**
CSF £32.33 TOTE £4.60: £1.50, £2.30, £1.70; EX 30.90 Trifecta £138.30.Barbarosa was claimed by Mr M. Herrington for £5,000.
Owner Graham Doyle & Hazel Lawrence **Bred** Powerstown Stud Ltd **Trained** Upper Lambourn, Berks

FOCUS
The first race of the day on the straight track saw the field come more towards the stands' rail than the middle.

3019 SKY SPORTS RACING ON VIRGIN 535 NOVICE STKS — 7f
4:00 (4:07) (Class 5) 3-Y-O
£3,752 (£1,116; £557; £278) Stalls Centre

Form — RPR

31 **1** **Mutaraffa (IRE)**[20] 2366 3-9-9 .... (h) DaneO'Neill 5 — 80+
(Charles Hills) *disp ld tl tk over after 3f: pushed along 2f out: drvn in 1 l ld 1f out: c clr ins fnl f: easily* — 1/5[1]

0- **2** 2¾ **Baalbek (USA)**[175] 9314 3-9-2 .... PatDobbs 2 — 66
(Owen Burrows) *hld up: drvn and hdwy over 1f out: 3rd 1f out: r.o wl to take 2nd ins fnl f* — 14/1[3]

00- **3** 1 **So Claire**[155] 9603 3-8-11 .... MartinDwyer 3 — 58
(William Muir) *disp ld tl hdd after 3f: drvn in 1 l 2nd 1f out: no ex and lost 2nd ins fnl f* — 50/1

4 1¼ **Aljari** 3-8-13 .... GabrieleMalune(3) 1 — 60
(Marco Botti) *hld up: shkn up over 2f out: rdn over 1f out: one pce fnl f (jockey said colt ran green)* — 8/1[2]

0-0 **5** 1¾ **Basilisk (USA)**[26] 2128 3-9-2 .... (t[1]) AdamMcNamara 4 — 55
(Roger Charlton) *t.k.h: chsd ldr: rdn and effrt on outer over 2f out: wknd over 1f out* — 8/1[2]

6 4 **Ecstasea (IRE)** 3-8-11 .... NickyMackay 8 — 39
(Rae Guest) *bhd: pushed along and tk sltly clsr order 3f out: lost tch 2f out* — 33/1

4 **7** ½ **Confab (USA)**[19] 2405 3-9-2 .... NicolaCurrie 7 — 43
(George Baker) *dismntd to enter stalls: chsd ldrs: lost pl 1/2-way: drvn 3f out: sn lost tch (trainer's rep said gelding would prefer an easier surface)* — 14/1[3]

1m 21.16s (-3.14) **Going Correction** -0.425s/f (Firm) — 7 Ran SP% **123.8**
Speed ratings (Par 99): **100,96,95,94,92 87,87**
CSF £6.44 TOTE £1.10: £1.10, £4.50; EX 4.70 Trifecta £80.50.
Owner Hamdan Al Maktoum **Bred** Messrs Mark Hanly & James Hanly **Trained** Lambourn, Berks

FOCUS
The betting suggested this was pretty much a non-event and those that backed the market leader had few worries. The level is fluid.

3020 DAILY QUESTIONS, DAILY ANSWERS, DAILY MAIL FILLIES' H'CAP — 6f
4:35 (4:35) (Class 6) (0-65,67) 4-Y-O+
£3,105 (£924; £461; £300; £300; £300) Stalls Centre

Form — RPR

-066 **1** **Tundra**[8] 2729 5-9-8 67 .... (b) DarraghKeenan(5) 8 — 73
(Anthony Carson) *mde all: 2 l ld 3f out: 1 1/2 l ld 1f out: sn rdn: kpt on in diminishing ld fnl f: hld on wl* — 13/2

13-3 **2** ½ **Princess Keira (IRE)**[30] 2025 4-9-6 60 .... FrannyNorton 6 — 65
(Mick Quinn) *mid-div: hdwy over 2f out: drvn into 2nd over 1f out: rdn fnl f: r.o wl to cl on ldr but nvr getting there* — 9/2[2]

-141 **3** ¾ **Javelin**[23] 2237 4-9-13 67 .... MartinDwyer 3 — 69
(William Muir) *bhd and sltly outpcd early: drvn over 2f out: rdn over 1f out: hdwy ins fnl f: r.o nr fin: nvr nrr* — 11/4[1]

0560 **4** ½ **Alba Del Sole (IRE)**[27] 2081 4-9-3 57 .... (p) LiamKeniry 1 — 58
(Ivan Furtado) *bhd: pushed along and plenty to do 2f out: sn rdn: r.o into 4th fnl f: nrst fin* — 5/1[3]

5-50 **5** 1¼ **Quick Recovery**[38] 1820 4-9-5 59 .... CharlieBennett 7 — 56
(Jim Boyle) *prom: pushed along 3f out: rdn over 2f out: one pce fr over 1f out* — 11/2

400- **6** ½ **Exceedingly Diva**[168] 9432 4-9-13 67 .... NicolaCurrie 5 — 63
(George Baker) *chsd ldrs: drvn 2f out: sn rdn: 3rd 1f out: wknd fnl f* — 9/1

6-60 **7** 17 **Porto Ferro (IRE)**[17] 2483 5-9-9 66 .... MitchGodwin(3) 2 — 11
(John Bridger) *in rr: drvn and lost tch over 3f out: wl bhd and eased fnl f* — 6/1

1m 8.78s (-2.72) **Going Correction** -0.425s/f (Firm) — 7 Ran SP% **114.5**
Speed ratings (Par 98): **101,100,99,98,97 96,73**
CSF £35.56 CT £99.04 TOTE £7.20: £3.40, £2.30; EX 41.40 Trifecta £87.60.
Owner W H Carson **Bred** Nawara Stud Co Ltd **Trained** Newmarket, Suffolk

FOCUS
Being drawn high here was no minus in what was a modest sprint.

3021 FOLLOW AT THE RACES ON TWITTER H'CAP — 4f 217y
5:10 (5:10) (Class 5) (0-75,76) 4-Y-O+
£3,752 (£1,116; £557; £300; £300; £300) Stalls Centre

Form — RPR

0-00 **1** **Harrogate (IRE)**[17] 2484 4-9-7 75 .... (b) CharlieBennett 3 — 83
(Jim Boyle) *mde all: sn trckd across to stands' rail: pushed along 2f out: rdn in narrow ld 1f out: r.o wl to repel chalrs ins fnl f* — 14/1

2240 **2** ¾ **Enthaar**[26] 2107 4-8-11 72 .... (t) MarcoGhiani(7) 8 — 77
(Stuart Williams) *bhd: pushed along 2f out: sn drvn: 3 l to find ent fnl f: r.o wl: tk 2nd last 25yds: nt rch wnr* — 5/1[3]

14-3 **3** 1 **Maid Of Spirit (IRE)**[30] 2009 4-9-5 73 .... LiamKeniry 9 — 75
(Clive Cox) *mid-div: pushed along and hdwy 2f out: rdn to chal over 1f out: ev ch ins fnl f: no ex last 100yds* — 4/1[2]

34-4 **4** shd **Jack Taylor (IRE)**[23] 2227 4-9-4 75 .... (e[1]) FinleyMarsh(3) 5 — 76
(Richard Hughes) *hld up: pushed along 2f out: drvn and hdwy over 1f out: rdn and ev ch ins fnl f: no ex last 100yds* — 3/1[1]

40-1 **5** ¾ **Grandfather Tom**[30] 2025 4-9-0 73 .... SeanDavis(5) 4 — 72
(Robert Cowell) *chsd ldr: pushed along 2f out: rdn over 1f out: wknd fnl f* — 9/1

1100 **6** 1½ **Miracle Works**[14] 2556 4-9-8 76 .... (p[1]) NicolaCurrie 7 — 69
(Robert Cowell) *hld up: drvn over 1f out: no imp (jockey said gelding was denied a clear run)* — 9/1

1-04 **7** 1½ **Brandy Station (IRE)**[13] 2576 4-8-5 66 .... (h) ElishaWhittington(7) 6 — 54
(Lisa Williamson) *chsd ldr: lost pl 2f out: reminder and wknd over 1f out* — 33/1

4522 **8** 2 **Wiff Waff**[30] 2025 4-9-3 71 MartinDwyer 2 52
(Chris Gordon) *awkward leaving stalls: bhd: pushed along and effrt 1/2-way: rdn over 1f out: wknd and eased fnl f* **9/1**

5030 **9** 4 1/2 **Verne Castle**[61] 1295 6-9-8 76 (h) ConnorBeasley 1 40
(Michael Wigham) *prom: sn settled in mid-div: drvn and lost pl over 2f out: sn dropped to last and wl bhd (trainer said gelding was unsuited by undulating track)* **5/1**[3]

56.49s (-2.21) **Going Correction** -0.425s/f (Firm) **9** Ran SP% **117.9**
Speed ratings (Par 103): **100,98,97,97,95 93,91,87,80**
CSF £84.18 CT £341.98 TOTE £19.80: £4.60, £2.10, £1.60; EX 124.00 Trifecta £654.80.
Owner Goff, Walsh & Zerdin **Bred** P O'Rourke **Trained** Epsom, Surrey

FOCUS
Probably just a modest sprint. The winner came up the stands' rail. The winner has been rated back to his 3yo form.
T/Plt: £192.60 to a £1 stake. Pool: £46,728.73. 177.09 winning units. T/Qpdt: £48.40 to a £1 stake. Pool: £4,904.84. 74.87 winning units. **Keith McHugh**

2082 SANDOWN (R-H)

Thursday, May 23

OFFICIAL GOING: Good to firm (good in places on round course; rnd 7.6, spr 7.7)
Wind: Light, across Weather: Fine, warm

3022 MATCHBOOK BETTING EXCHANGE H'CAP (A JOCKEY CLUB GRASSROOTS MIDDLE DISTANCE SERIES QUALIFIER) 1m 1f 209y
6:00 (6:06) (Class 5) (0-75,76) 4-Y-O+
£4,528 (£1,347; £673; £336; £300; £300) **Stalls** Low

Form RPR

61-4 **1** **My Boy Sepoy**[20] 2360 4-9-7 **75** DanielTudhope 6 84
(Stuart Williams) *trckd ldrs disputing 5th: nt clr run briefly over 2f out: prog after: drvn to ld jst over 1f out and edgd rt: kpt on u.p (jockey said gelding hung both ways)* **5/1**[3]

0000 **2** 3/4 **Tangramm**[58] 1343 7-8-12 **66** (p) RyanTate 12 73
(Dean Ivory) *hld up in 9th on outer: prog 2f out: gd hdwy to chal fnl f and looked likely to win: fnd nil last 150yds and hld after (jockey said gelding hung right-handed final furlong)* **50/1**

0041 **3** 1 1/4 **Uther Pendragon (IRE)**[8] 2732 4-9-8 **76** 5ex (p) JamieSpencer 5 83+
(J S Moore) *hld up disputing 7th: clsd to trck ldrs 3f out: nt clr run after: swtchd rt 2f out but stl nowhere to go: gap fnlly appeared fnl f and r.o to take 3rd last strides* **10/1**

2110 **4** hd **Singing Sheriff**[26] 2092 4-9-0 **68** SilvestreDeSousa 8 73
(Ed Walker) *hld up in 10th: nt clr run briefly over 2f out: prog wl over 1f out gng easily: rdn to chse ldng pair fnl f: carried rt and fnd little: lost 3rd last strides* **9/2**[2]

41-3 **5** 3/4 **Sudona**[20] 2360 4-9-6 **74** JackMitchell 3 77
(Hugo Palmer) *trckd ldng pair: rdn to take narrow ld on inner 2f out: hdd and one pce jst over 1f out* **7/1**

300/ **6** 1/2 **Tulane (IRE)**[570] 8467 4-8-4 **61** oh1 JaneElliott(3) 14 63
(Richard Phillips) *t.k.h: hld up in last trio: rdn on outer over 2f out: no prog tl styd on jst over 1f out: nvr nrr* **40/1**

243- **7** nse **Jumping Jack (IRE)**[168] 9431 5-9-4 **72** CharlesBishop 7 74
(Chris Gordon) *sltly awkward s: hld up in last trio: shkn up 3f out: prog over 1f out: styd on but nvr able to threaten* **9/1**

03-3 **8** 1/2 **Cogital**[17] 2472 4-9-1 **69** (h) PatDobbs 13 70
(Amanda Perrett) *hld up in last quartet: trying to cl on ldrs whn impeded on inner 2f out: nt clr run after tl fnl f: r.o but no ch* **14/1**

3-56 **9** 2 1/2 **Sea Tide**[20] 2353 5-9-0 **68** GrahamLee 9 64
(Laura Mongan) *s.s and lost 6 l: mostly in last: rdn over 2f out: passed wkng rivals over 1f out* **25/1**

4031 **10** 3/4 **Bayston Hill**[52] 1482 5-9-0 **71** GaryMahon(3) 2 65
(Mark Usher) *trckd ldng pair: rdn to chal on outer 2f out: wknd u.p jst over 1f out* **16/1**

3-63 **11** 1 1/4 **Nawar**[30] 2005 4-9-2 **70** (t) SeanLevey 4 62
(Martin Bosley) *trckd ldrs disputing 5th: rdn to chal 2f out: wknd over 1f out* **14/1**

2-66 **12** 1/2 **Ruby Gates (IRE)**[93] 793 6-9-4 **72** EoinWalsh 1 63
(John Butler) *drvn to rcvr fr modest s and sn led: hdd 2f out: sn wknd* **50/1**

211- **13** 1 1/4 **Matewan (IRE)**[246] 7416 4-9-4 **72** (p) RyanMoore 10 60
(Ian Williams) *trckd ldrs disputing 5th: clsd to chal u.p 2f out: btn over 1f out: wkng whn impeded ins fnl f and eased* **4/1**[1]

321- **14** 7 **Lyrica's Lion (IRE)**[232] 7901 5-8-12 **71** RobJFitzpatrick(5) 11 45
(Camilla Poulton) *w ldr: stl upsides 3f out: wknd rapidly 2f out (vet said gelding lost right fore and left hind shoe)* **10/1**

2m 8.41s (-1.79) **Going Correction** -0.05s/f (Good) **14** Ran SP% **125.0**
Speed ratings (Par 103): **105,104,103,103,102 102,102,101,99,99 98,97,96,91**
CSF £255.77 CT £2440.46 TOTE £5.40: £1.60, £24.60, £3.70; EX 423.60 Trifecta £3009.70.
Owner Mr & Mrs George Bhatti **Bred** Old Mill Stud Ltd **Trained** Newmarket, Suffolk

FOCUS
The rail was out 2yds from 1m to home straight, adding 7yds to all races on the round course. This was a decent handicap for the class. There was an uneven pace and it got rough in the home straight. The fifth has been rated a bit below her latest effort.

3023 MATCHBOOK BETTING PODCAST NATIONAL STKS (LISTED RACE) 5f 10y
6:35 (6:37) (Class 1) 2-Y-O
£17,013 (£6,450; £3,228; £1,608; £807; £405) **Stalls** High

Form RPR

31 **1** **Flippa The Strippa (IRE)**[9] 2716 2-8-12 0 SilvestreDeSousa 4 95
(Charles Hills) *hld up in tch: clsd smoothly on outer to ld over 1f out and sn at least 2 l clr: hanging and racd awkwardly fnl f: a holding on* **16/1**

2 **2** 1 1/4 **Jm Jackson (IRE)**[40] 1759 2-8-12 0 RyanMoore 7 91
(Mark Johnston) *sn in last and pushed along: styd on over 1f out: rdn to take 2nd last 100yds: styd on but nt quite able to chal* **10/1**[3]

1 **3** hd **Strive For Glory (USA)**[24] 2184 2-9-3 0 JoeFanning 3 95
(Robert Cowell) *dwlt but sn trckd ldng trio: trapped on inner fr 2f out tl swtchd lft jst over 1f out: styd on fnl f but no ch to chal* **33/1**

116 **4** 3/4 **Electric Ladyland (IRE)**[15] 2520 2-8-12 0 OisinMurphy 6 87
(Archie Watson) *disp ld: narrow advantage jst over 2f out to over 1f out: outpcd after: one pce fnl f (jockey said filly changed leads on numerous occasions)* **12/1**

1 **5** 2 1/4 **Full Authority (IRE)**[14] 2561 2-9-3 0 DanielTudhope 1 84
(David O'Meara) *racd against rail: disp ld to jst over 2f out: outpcd over 1f out: stl ch of 2nd ins fnl f: wknd last 100yds* **8/15**[1]

1 **6** 6 **Proper Beau**[51] 1499 2-9-3 0 GrahamLee 2 62
(Bryan Smart) *w ldng pair to 1/2-way: rdn and fdd over 1f out: wl btn whn sltly impeded sn after* **7/2**[2]

1m 0.85s (-0.45) **Going Correction** -0.05s/f (Good) **6** Ran SP% **113.1**
Speed ratings (Par 101): **101,99,98,97,93 84**
CSF £151.36 TOTE £13.50: £5.00, £3.20; EX 73.10 Trifecta £444.90.
Owner Christopher Wright **Bred** Linacre House Limited **Trained** Lambourn, Berks

FOCUS
Another interesting edition of this 2yo Listed sprint. A suicidal early pace teed it up for the closers. It's been rated in line with the lesser renewals of this race.

3024 MATCHBOOK VIP HENRY II STKS (GROUP 3) 2m 50y
7:05 (7:06) (Class 1) 4-Y-O+ **£39,697** (£15,050; £7,532; £3,752; £1,883) **Stalls** Centre

Form RPR

43-1 **1** **Dee Ex Bee**[22] 2269 4-9-4 112 SilvestreDeSousa 3 119
(Mark Johnston) *mde all: urged along 3f out: asserted wl over 1f out: galloped on relentlessly* **4/7**[1]

412- **2** 1 3/4 **Mekong**[230] 7951 4-9-1 104 RyanMoore 1 113
(Sir Michael Stoute) *t.k.h: trckd ldng pair: pushed along over 2f out: drvn to take 2nd fnl f: styd on but nvr able to threaten wnr* **7/2**[2]

3-10 **3** hd **Austrian School (IRE)**[13] 2575 4-9-1 110 JoeFanning 6 113
(Mark Johnston) *trckd wnr: rdn over 2f out: nt qckn over 1f out: styd on but lost 2nd fnl f* **6/1**[3]

-511 **4** 5 **Making Miracles**[13] 2575 4-9-1 108 FrannyNorton 5 107
(Mark Johnston) *dwlt sltly: racd in 4th and nvr gng that wl: rdn over 3f out: tried to raise an effrt 2f out but hanging rt: wknd fnl f* **10/1**

5345 **5** 6 **Fearsome**[34] 1917 5-9-2 100 EoinWalsh 2 99
(Nick Littmoden) *a in last: rdn over 3f out: wknd 2f out* **66/1**

3m 34.0s (-3.90) **Going Correction** -0.05s/f (Good)
WFA 4 from 5yo+ 1lb **5** Ran SP% **110.7**
Speed ratings (Par 113): **107,106,106,103,100**
CSF £2.93 TOTE £1.40: £1.10, £1.60; EX 2.60 Trifecta £5.20.
Owner Sheikh Hamdan bin Mohammed Al Maktoum **Bred** Godolphin **Trained** Middleham Moor, N Yorks

FOCUS
Add 7yds. A single-figure field for the fifth year running and, with Mark Johnston running three, it was unsurprisingly tactical. The third has been rated close to form.

3025 MATCHBOOK BRIGADIER GERARD STKS (GROUP 3) 1m 1f 209y
7:35 (7:40) (Class 1) 4-Y-O+
£39,697 (£15,050; £7,532; £3,752; £1,883; £945) **Stalls** Low

Form RPR

33-3 **1** **Regal Reality**[27] 2085 4-9-0 113 RyanMoore 6 119+
(Sir Michael Stoute) *fractious preliminaries: failed to appear in paddock and arrived at s 5 minutes after the rest: hld up in 4th: prog to trck ldr over 2f out: pushed into ld wl over 1f out: rdn and r.o wl: quite impressive* **9/4**[2]

1012 **2** 3 3/4 **Matterhorn (IRE)**[13] 2573 4-9-0 112 JoeFanning 3 111
(Mark Johnston) *trckd ldr: led 3f out and sent for home: hdd wl over 1f out: styd on but readily outpcd* **11/8**[1]

04-1 **3** 3 **Danceteria (FR)**[43] 1708 4-9-0 105 JamieSpencer 4 105+
(David Menuisier) *s.i.s: hld up in 5th: shkn up over 2f out: kpt on to take 3rd fnl f but no ch w ldng pair* **7/1**

010- **4** 1/2 **Here Comes When (IRE)**[214] 8464 9-9-3 110 (h) OisinMurphy 5 107
(Andrew Balding) *hld up in last: shkn up over 2f out: sn outpcd: tk 4th fnl f but nvr any ch* **33/1**

133- **5** 1 1/2 **Bombyx**[247] 7399 4-9-0 98 DanielMuscutt 2 101
(James Fanshawe) *trckd ldng pair: shkn up over 2f out: lost pl u.p over 1f out: fdd* **16/1**

115- **6** nk **Elwazir**[285] 6011 4-9-0 105 JimCrowley 1 100
(Owen Burrows) *led to 3f out: lost 2nd over 2f out and no ch w ldng pair after: hanging and wknd fnl f* **9/2**[3]

2m 5.84s (-4.36) **Going Correction** -0.05s/f (Good) **6** Ran SP% **112.4**
Speed ratings (Par 113): **115,112,109,109,108 107**
CSF £5.75 TOTE £2.50: £1.50, £1.40; EX 6.30 Trifecta £24.10.
Owner Cheveley Park Stud **Bred** Cheveley Park Stud Ltd **Trained** Newmarket, Suffolk

FOCUS
Add 7yds. This year's Brigadier Gerard Stakes was run at an uneven pace and those held up were disadvantaged, although the second is a useful guide. The second has been rated to his turf latest, with the fifth close to form.

3026 MATCHBOOK LOW COMMISSION EXCHANGE HERON STKS (LISTED RACE) 1m
8:10 (8:14) (Class 1) 3-Y-O
£22,684 (£8,600; £4,304; £2,144; £1,076; £540) **Stalls** Low

Form RPR

12-1 **1** **King Of Comedy (IRE)**[30] 2023 3-9-0 100 FrankieDettori 2 113+
(John Gosden) *ref to go to post tl dismntd and led: hld up in 5th: stdy prog over 2f out: shkn up to ld over 1f out: carried hd high but sn clr: comf* **9/4**[1]

31 **2** 2 1/2 **Roseman (IRE)**[23] 2250 3-9-0 0 AndreaAtzeni 7 106
(Roger Varian) *disp ld: rdn and def advantage briefly wl over 1f out: sn hdd and outpcd fnl f* **8/1**

114- **3** 1 1/4 **Sangarius**[222] 8187 3-9-3 106 (t[1]) RyanMoore 6 106
(Sir Michael Stoute) *trckd ldng pair: effrt 2f out but hanging bdly rt and nt qckn: kpt on same pce in 3rd fnl f* **11/2**[3]

6-30 **4** 1/2 **Dark Vision (IRE)**[19] 2411 3-9-0 106 SilvestreDeSousa 4 102
(Mark Johnston) *hld up in 6th: shkn up and no prog over 2f out: kpt on one pce fnl f* **10/1**

1-22 **5** 3/4 **Walkinthesand (IRE)**[19] 2413 3-9-0 106 SeanLevey 8 100
(Richard Hannon) *disp ld to wl over 1f out: fdd u.p* **7/2**[2]

1- **6** 1/2 **Bell Rock**[211] 8548 3-9-0 0 OisinMurphy 5 102+
(Andrew Balding) *t.k.h: trckd ldng pair: shkn up and nt qckn 2f out: one pce and no ch whn nt clr run briefly ins fnl f* **11/2**[3]

10- **7** hd **Raakib Alhawa (IRE)**[208] 8633 3-9-0 0 JamieSpencer 3 99
(David Simcock) *s.i.s: hld up in last pair: rdn and no prog over 2f out: nvr a factor* **25/1**

1-1 **8** 1 3/4 **Lord North (IRE)**[24] 2188 3-9-0 0........................ RobertHavlin 1 99+
(John Gosden) *reluctant to enter stalls: hld up in last pair: pushed along over 2f out: no prog whn appeared short of room over 1f out: eased but lost little grnd after (jockey said colt was denied a clear run)* **10/1**

1m 40.29s (-3.01) **Going Correction** -0.05s/f (Good) **8** Ran SP% **116.9**
Speed ratings (Par 107): **113,110,109,108,108 107,107,105**
CSF £21.75 TOTE £2.60: £1.50, £2.50, £1.70; EX 19.50 Trifecta £139.90.
Owner Lady Bamford **Bred** Lady Bamford **Trained** Newmarket, Suffolk

FOCUS
Add 7yds. A decent bunch on paddock inspection and, run at a strong pace, this year's Heron Stakes looks form to be positive about. The winner has been rated up with the better winners of this race. The second has been rated in line with the race average and the third to form.

3027 MATCHBOOK CASINO WHITSUN CUP H'CAP 1m
8:40 (8:42) (Class 3) (0-95,94) 4-Y-O+
£9,337 (£2,796; £1,398; £699; £349; £175) **Stalls** Low

Form RPR
10-3 **1** **Lush Life (IRE)**[17] 2487 4-9-4 **91**........................ JamieSpencer 9 99+
(Jamie Osborne) *hld up in last pair off str pce: stl there over 1f out: cajoled along on outer and gd prog after: r.o to ld fnl strides (vet said filly lost left hind shoe)* **11/4**[2]

4661 **2** *nk* **War Glory (IRE)**[12] 2622 6-9-6 **93**........................ RyanMoore 4 99
(Richard Hannon) *trckd ldrs: weaved through fr 2f out to ld 1f out: styd on but hdd last strides* **11/2**

04-0 **3** *hd* **History Writer (IRE)**[40] 1753 4-9-4 **91**........................(t) JasonWatson 7 97
(David Menuisier) *hld up in last pair off str pce: shkn up over 2f out: prog on outer over 1f out: drvn to chse ldr ins fnl f: styd on but nvr qckning and lost 2nd nr fin* **9/4**[1]

11/0 **4** 2 **I'vegotthepower (IRE)**[17] 2487 5-9-0 **87**........................(v) OisinMurphy 2 88
(Brian Meehan) *led at gd pce: drvn whn jnd 2f out: kpt on but hdd and no ex 1f out* **16/1**

030- **5** 1 3/4 **Data Protection**[202] 8809 4-8-7 **80**........................(t) NicolaCurrie 10 77
(William Muir) *t.k.h: trckd ldng pair and racd on outer: rdn to chal and upsides 2f out: lost pl over 1f out: fdd* **20/1**

121 **6** 3/4 **Masked Identity**[21] 2347 4-8-5 **85**........................ GavinAshton(7) 1 80
(Kevin Frost) *cl up on inner: rdn 2f out: fdd over 1f out* **12/1**

252- **7** 2 **Kitaabaat**[230] 7949 4-9-1 **88**........................ JimCrowley 5 79
(Owen Burrows) *hld up in last trio off str pce: clsd on ldrs on outer 2f out: rdn and wknd over 1f out* **4/1**[3]

42-2 **8** 8 **Azzeccagarbugli (IRE)**[131] 212 6-9-7 **94**........................ RossaRyan 8 66
(Mike Murphy) *chsd ldr to jst over 2f out: wknd rapidly over 1f out* **25/1**

1m 42.21s (-1.09) **Going Correction** -0.05s/f (Good) **8** Ran SP% **115.0**
Speed ratings (Par 107): **103,102,102,100,98 98,96,88**
CSF £18.47 CT £39.06 TOTE £3.40: £1.40, £1.60, £1.20; EX 19.70 Trifecta £58.50.
Owner Michael Buckley And Mrs Paul Shanahan **Bred** Lynch Bages **Trained** Upper Lambourn, Berks

FOCUS
Add 7yds. This decent handicap saw a thrilling finish. The second has been rated to his turf latest.
T/Plt: £133.30 to a £1 stake. Pool: £94,005.69. 514.79 winning units. T/Qpdt: £2.00 to a £1 stake. Pool: £10,803.11. 3,882.54 winning units. **Jonathan Neesom**

AMIENS (R-H)
Thursday, May 23

OFFICIAL GOING: Turf: good to firm

3028a PRIX DES HORTILLONNAGES (CLAIMER) (3YO FILLIES) (TURF) 1m 55y
6:17 3-Y-O
£6,306 (£2,522; £1,891; £1,261; £630)

RPR
1 **Sandy Dream (FR)**[45] 1658 3-9-0 0........................(b) MlleLauraGrosso(6) 5 69
(Mme R Philippon, France) **104/10**

2 *hd* **Storm Katy (FR)**[27] 2090 3-8-3 0........................ MlleEugenieLaffargue(8) 2 60
(M Boutin, France) **47/1**

3 *shd* **Crop Over Queen (FR)**[14] 3-8-6 0........................ QuentinPerrette(5) 3 60
(Andrea Marcialis, France) **9/1**

4 *nse* **Covefe (FR)**[140] 3-8-10 0........................ JeremieMonteiro(6) 1 65
(Frau Hella Sauer, Germany) **6/1**[3]

5 1 1/2 **Queen Morny (FR)**[20] 2390 3-8-10 0........................ TristanBaron(6) 14 61
(H-A Pantall, France) **12/1**

6 1/2 **La Regle Du Jeu (FR)**[45] 3-8-10 0........................ PierreGraux(6) 9 60
(J-C Rouget, France) **23/10**[1]

7 1 **Grandee Daisy**[20] 2390 3-8-10 0........................(p) AlexisPouchin(6) 10 58
(Jo Hughes, France) *hld up towards rr: in fnl trio and drvn along after 2 1/2f: clsd over 2f out: drvn in midfield ent fnl f: nt pce to get in contention* **23/1**

8 1 1/2 **Got Will (FR)**[12] 3-8-8 0........................(p) ClementGuitraud(6) 12 54
(Y Barberot, France) **39/1**

9 1 1/4 **Royale Theyss (FR)**[59] 3-8-6 0........................ TomLefranc(5) 6 46
(C Boutin, France) **60/1**

10 1/2 **Million Dreams (FR)**[23] 3-9-1 0........................(b) HugoBesnier(5) 4 54
(Laurent Loisel, France) **16/1**

11 1 1/4 **Profit (IRE)**[44] 3-9-7 0........................(p) AlexandreChesneau(4) 8 56
(Henk Grewe, Germany) **29/10**[2]

12 10 **Rapsody (FR)** 3-8-6 0........................ JackyNicoleau(5) 11 19
(E Libaud, France) **30/1**

13 3 **Echelle Du Levant (IRE)**[41] 3-8-3 0........................(b) MlleCrystalMiette(8) 13 13
(F Chappet, France) **22/1**

1m 39.8s **13** Ran SP% **120.5**
PARI-MUTUEL (all including 1 euro stake): WIN 11.40; PLACE 4.10, 9.70, 3.10; DF 182.40.
Owner Jean-Christophe Daoudal & Nicolas Tournier **Bred** Haras D'Haspel **Trained** France

2782 LONGCHAMP (R-H)
Thursday, May 23

OFFICIAL GOING: Turf: good to soft

3029a PRIX DE PONTARME (LISTED RACE) (3YO) (TURF) 1m
4:50 3-Y-O
£24,774 (£9,909; £7,432; £4,954; £2,477)

RPR
1 **Noor Sahara (IRE)**[31] 3-8-10 0........................ StephanePasquier 6 102+
(F Chappet, France) **102/10**

2 1 1/2 **Dave (FR)**[21] 2352 3-9-0 0........................ MaximeGuyon 1 102
(Mme Pia Brandt, France) **10/1**

3 1 **Savvy Nine (FR)**[17] 2499 3-9-0 0........................ JamesDoyle 3 100
(William Haggas) *wl into stride: led: urged along 2f out: rdn to hold advantage over 1f out: drvn and hdd ins fnl f: no ex fnl 75yds* **27/10**[2]

4 1/2 **Eagle Hunter**[31] 3-9-0 0........................ Pierre-CharlesBoudot 4 99
(F-H Graffard, France) **11/10**[1]

5 3 **Price Range (USA)**[39] 1794 3-9-0 0........................ VincentCheminaud 7 92
(P Bary, France) **68/10**[3]

6 3/4 **Quindio (FR)**[30] 2027 3-9-0 0........................ MickaelBarzalona 2 90
(X Thomas-Demeaulte, France) **13/1**

7 1 1/4 **Isalys (FR)**[102] 683 3-8-10 0........................ AlexandreGavilan 8 84
(D Guillemin, France) **28/1**

8 3 1/2 **Muraikh (FR)**[45] 3-9-0 0........................ AlexisBadel 5 79
(H-F Devin, France) **20/1**

1m 41.59s (3.19) **8** Ran SP% **120.8**
PARI-MUTUEL (all including 1 euro stake): WIN 11.20; PLACE 2.30, 2.50, 1.60; DF 22.00.
Owner Ecurie Jean-Louis Bouchard **Bred** Southacre Bloodstock **Trained** France

3030a PRIX DE MONTRETOUT (LISTED RACE) (4YO+) (TURF) 1m
6:00 4-Y-O+
£23,423 (£9,369; £7,027; £4,684; £2,342)

RPR
1 **Barney Roy**[22] 2271 5-9-0 0........................ JamesDoyle 3 109+
(Charlie Appleby) *bmpd w rival sn after s: racd keenly: restrained in 3rd on inner: nt clr run fr 2f out: drvn and qcknd through gap 50yds out: led cl home and jinked lft rching line* **4/5**[1]

2 1/2 **Bayoun (FR)**[27] 2089 6-9-0 0........................ OlivierPeslier 4 106+
(T Lemer, France) **53/10**[3]

3 *snk* **Stunning Spirit**[214] 8446 5-9-4 0........................ AurelienLemaitre 6 110
(F Head, France) **78/10**

4 1/2 **Orbaan**[31] 4-9-0 0........................ MaximeGuyon 5 105
(A Fabre, France) **49/10**[2]

5 2 **Rayon Vert (FR)**[25] 5-9-0 0........................ FabriceVeron 7 100
(Laurent Loisel, France) **49/1**

6 1 3/4 **Dhevanafushi**[21] 6-9-0 0........................ MickaelBarzalona 1 96
(H-A Pantall, France) **43/5**

7 3/4 **Indyco (FR)**[34] 1922 4-9-0 0........................ VincentCheminaud 2 94
(H-A Pantall, France) **11/1**

1m 43.46s (5.06) **7** Ran SP% **120.5**
PARI-MUTUEL (all including 1 euro stake): WIN 1.80; PLACE 1.30, 2.30; SF 4.30.
Owner Godolphin **Bred** Eliza Park International Pty Ltd **Trained** Newmarket, Suffolk

2541 LYON PARILLY (R-H)
Thursday, May 23

OFFICIAL GOING: Turf: good

3031a COUPE DES TROIS ANS (LISTED RACE) (3YO) (TURF) 1m 4f
12:10 3-Y-O
£24,774 (£9,909; £7,432; £4,954; £2,477)

RPR
1 **San Huberto (IRE)**[16] 2519 3-9-0 0........................ TonyPiccone 7 101+
(F Chappet, France) **17/2**

2 1 1/4 **Chouain (FR)**[22] 3-9-0 0........................ CyrilleStefan 2 99
(M Rulec, Germany) **31/1**

3 *snk* **Milestone (FR)**[21] 3-9-0 0........................ VincentCheminaud 4 99+
(A Fabre, France) **59/10**[3]

4 1 1/4 **Alabaa**[27] 3-9-0 0........................ TheoBachelot 6 97+
(L Gadbin, France) **11/1**

5 *snk* **Himola (FR)**[31] 3-9-0 0........................ OlivierPeslier 1 97
(C Laffon-Parias, France) **17/5**[2]

6 1/2 **Court Poet**[256] 7106 3-9-0 0........................ JamesDoyle 3 96
(Charlie Appleby) *led: pushed along over 2f out: rdn and hdd over 1f out: wknd ins fnl f* **9/10**[1]

7 4 1/2 **Seduction (FR)**[26] 3-8-10 0........................ FranckBlondel 5 85
(C Escuder, France) **9/1**

2m 35.42s (1.91) **7** Ran SP% **121.8**
PARI-MUTUEL (all including 1 euro stake): WIN 9.50; PLACE 5.90, 10.50; SF 163.60.
Owner Maurice Lagasse **Bred** Gestut Zur Kuste Ag **Trained** France

2728 BATH (L-H)
Friday, May 24

OFFICIAL GOING: Firm (9.2)
Wind: Light half-against Weather: Cloudy

3032 OCTAGON CONSULTANCY H'CAP 5f 160y
2:00 (2:01) (Class 5) (0-75,76) 4-Y-O+ **£3,752** (£1,116; £557; £300; £300) **Stalls** Centre

Form RPR
4300 **1** **Red Alert**[13] 2611 5-9-9 **76**........................(p) TomMarquand 1 85
(Tony Carroll) *prom: shkn up over 3f out: sn outpcd: hdwy over 1f out: rdn to ld ins fnl f: r.o* **2/1**[1]

3-10 **2** 1 1/2 **Coronation Cottage**[18] 2473 5-9-2 **69**........................ CharlieBennett 5 73
(Malcolm Saunders) *led: rdn: hung lft and hdd ins fnl f: styd on same pce* **8/1**

0302 **3** 3 1/4 **Union Rose**[21] 2358 7-9-6 **73**........................(p) DavidProbert 2 65
(Ronald Harris) *chsd ldr: rdn over 1f out: no ex wl ins fnl f* **3/1**[3]

The Form Book Flat 2019, Raceform Ltd, Newbury, RG14 5SJ

335- **4** 3/4 **Three Little Birds**[188] 9135 4-9-3 **73**.............................. GaryMahon(3) 3 62
(Sylvester Kirk) *chsd ldrs: rdn over 1f out: no ex ins fnl f* **7/1**

-125 **5** 7 **Field Gun (USA)**[24] 2237 4-9-9 **76**..............................(vt[1]) CallumShepherd 4 40
(Stuart Williams) *dwlt: hdwy 1/2-way: rdn over 1f out: wknd and eased ins fnl f (jockey said gelding slipped leaving the stalls and as a result was slowly away)* **5/2[2]**

1m 10.24s (-0.86) **Going Correction** -0.075s/f (Good) **5** Ran SP% **110.5**
Speed ratings (Par 103): **102,100,95,94,85**
CSF £17.36 TOTE £2.10: £1.20, £3.50; EX 13.50 Trifecta £35.20.
Owner A A Byrne **Bred** Miss Jacqueline Goodearl **Trained** Cropthorne, Worcs

FOCUS
A fair sprint handicap, with the winner rated close to his best.

3033 MJ CHURCH CONTRACTING EBF STALLIONS FILLIES' NOVICE STKS (PLUS 10 RACE) 5f 10y
2:30 (2:30) (Class 4) 2-Y-O £4,787 (£1,424; £711; £355) **Stalls** Centre

Form RPR

1 **Applecross (IRE)** 2-9-0 0.............................. HayleyTurner 1 76+
(Michael Bell) *wnt rt s: chsd ldr tl over 3f out: nt clr run and swtchd rt over 1f out: sn rdn to chse ldr again: r.o to ld nr fin* **5/2[3]**

4 **2** hd **Inyamazane (IRE)**[14] 2565 2-9-0 0.............................. CharlesBishop 6 75
(Mick Channon) *led: rdn over 1f out: edgd rt and hdd nr fin* **9/4[2]**

3 5 **Gert Lush (IRE)** 2-9-0 0.............................. DavidProbert 4 57
(Roger Teal) *s.i.s and hmpd s: outpcd: hdwy over 1f out: styd on to go 3rd wl ins fnl f: nt trble ldrs (jockey said filly was slowly away)* **8/1**

42 **4** 1/2 **Aroha (IRE)**[8] 2767 2-9-0 0.............................. CallumShepherd 5 55
(Brian Meehan) *s.i.s and hmpd s: sn prom: chsd ldr over 3f out tl rdn over 1f out: wknd ins fnl f* **6/4[1]**

4 **5** 24 **Star's Daughter**[22] 2316 2-8-7 0.............................. VictorSantos(7) 3
(Lucinda Egerton) *hmpd s: in tch: sn pushed along: edgd rt and wknd 1/2-way* **100/1**

1m 2.34s (0.34) **Going Correction** -0.075s/f (Good) **5** Ran SP% **111.4**
Speed ratings (Par 92): **94,93,85,84,46**
CSF £8.65 TOTE £3.30: £1.90, £1.40; EX 7.80 Trifecta £22.60.
Owner The In-N-Out Partnership **Bred** Thomas Cahalan & Sophie Hayley **Trained** Newmarket, Suffolk

FOCUS
A fair juvenile fillies' novice contest.

3034 EMPIRE FIGHTING CHANCE H'CAP 1m 2f 37y
3:05 (3:05) (Class 6) (0-65,67) 3-Y-O
£3,105 (£924; £461; £300; £300; £300) **Stalls** Low

Form RPR

00-4 **1** **Sadlers Beach (IRE)**[17] 2517 3-8-8 **49**..............................(h) HayleyTurner 4 55
(Marcus Tregoning) *trckd ldrs: plld hrd early: lost grnd 7f out: hdwy on outer over 2f out: led over 1f out: sn rdn and hung lft: styd on* **11/2**

6201 **2** 2 1/4 **Vin D'Honneur (IRE)**[60] 1332 3-9-5 **60**..............................(p) DavidProbert 7 62
(Stuart Williams) *chsd ldrs: lost pl over 8f out: hung rt over 4f out: hdwy over 3f out: rdn and ev ch over 1f out: styd on same pce ins fnl f* **10/1**

0-54 **3** 1/2 **Ballet Red (FR)**[10] 2719 3-9-9 **67**.............................. MitchGodwin(3) 5 68
(Harry Dunlop) *led 1f: chsd ldrs: wnt 2nd over 4f out: led over 3f out: rdn over 2f out: hdd over 1f out: no ex wl ins fnl f* **5/1**

044- **4** 2 **Irish Art (IRE)**[190] 9073 3-9-11 **66**.............................. StevieDonohoe 6 63+
(David Lanigan) *s.i.s: sn pushed along and outpcd: rdn over 2f out: styd on fr over 1f out: nt trble ldrs (jockey said gelding was never travelling)* **11/4[1]**

00-2 **5** 4 1/2 **Catch The Cuban**[22] 2341 3-9-4 **59**..............................(tp) CharlieBennett 2 47
(Colin Tizzard) *s.i.s: pushed along and hdwy to chse ldr over 8f out: lost 2nd over 4f out: rdn over 3f out: wknd fnl f* **4/1[3]**

3604 **6** 4 **Azets**[20] 2406 3-9-6 **61**..............................(b) PatDobbs 1 42
(Amanda Perrett) *led at gd pce after 1f: hdd over 3f out: rdn over 2f out: wknd fnl f* **3/1[2]**

2m 10.07s (-1.03) **Going Correction** -0.075s/f (Good) **6** Ran SP% **112.8**
Speed ratings (Par 97): **101,99,98,97,93 90**
CSF £54.58 TOTE £5.60: £2.50, £3.10; EX 51.30 Trifecta £214.50.
Owner R Kingston **Bred** Ken Carroll **Trained** Whitsbury, Hants

FOCUS
A modest 3yo handicap. The pace collapsed up front and it paid to be delivered later.

3035 CMD RECRUITMENT NOVICE STKS 1m 2f 37y
3:40 (3:40) (Class 5) 3-Y-O £3,752 (£1,116; £557; £278) **Stalls** Low

Form RPR

12- **1** **Universal Order**[205] 8731 3-9-7 0.............................. StevieDonohoe 3 86+
(David Simcock) *hld up: hdwy over 3f out: led over 2f out: rdn clr fnl f* **4/6[1]**

5 **2** 4 1/2 **Narina (IRE)**[14] 2583 3-8-11 0.............................. FrannyNorton 4 67
(William Haggas) *trckd ldrs: lft 2nd over 3f out: rdn and ev ch over 2f out: styd on same pce fnl f* **6/5[2]**

0 **3** 5 **Lady Elysia**[8] 2771 3-8-8 0.............................. MitchGodwin(3) 2 57?
(Harry Dunlop) *chsd ldr who wnt clr over 7f out: tk clsr order over 4f out: lft in ld over 3f out: hdd over 2f out: nt clr run wl over 1f out: sn outpcd* **33/1[3]**

060 **4** 60 **Pandora's Minder**[4] 2912 3-8-4 0.............................. VictorSantos(7) 5
(Lucinda Egerton) *led: racd freely: hung rt almost thrght: clr over 7f out tl hung bdly rt 5f out: hdd over 3f out: wknd over 2f out (jockey said filly hung badly right-handed throughout)* **100/1**

2m 10.76s (-0.34) **Going Correction** -0.075s/f (Good) **4** Ran SP% **109.4**
Speed ratings (Par 99): **98,94,90,42**
CSF £1.75 TOTE £1.50; EX 1.80 Trifecta £2.00.
Owner Abdulla Al Mansoori **Bred** Rabbah Bloodstock Limited **Trained** Newmarket, Suffolk

FOCUS
A fair novice contest, rated around the winner.

3036 MJ CHURCH PLANT AND TRANSPORT H'CAP 5f 160y
4:15 (4:16) (Class 6) (0-55,57) 4-Y-O+
£3,105 (£924; £461; £300; £300; £300) **Stalls** Centre

Form RPR

-001 **1** **Pocket Warrior**[3] 2924 8-9-4 **49** 4ex..............................(t) TomMarquand 4 57
(Paul D'Arcy) *s.i.s: in rr: hdwy on outer 2f out: rdn to ld over 1f out: edgd lft: r.o* **5/2[2]**

64-0 **2** 2 1/4 **Spirit Of Ishy**[42] 1732 4-9-0 **45**..............................(b[1]) HayleyTurner 1 46
(Stuart Kittow) *hld up: swtchd rt over 1f out: r.o wl ins fnl f: wnt 2nd post: nt rch wnr* **18/1**

000- **3** shd **Bayards Cove**[289] 5856 4-9-0 **45**.............................. KieranO'Neill 3 45
(Stuart Kittow) *s.i.s: sn pushed along in rr: swtchd rt over 2f out: rdn and r.o ins fnl f: wnt 3rd post* **20/1**

60-3 **4** shd **Amberine**[9] 2728 5-9-3 **48**.............................. FrannyNorton 6 48+
(Malcolm Saunders) *w ldrs tl n.m.r over 4f out: remained handy: rdn and ev ch over 1f out: no ex wl ins fnl f* **9/4[1]**

0000 **5** 3/4 **Burauq**[23] 2287 7-8-7 **45**..............................(p) TobyEley(7) 8 42
(Milton Bradley) *mid-div: hdwy 1/2-way: rdn and nt clr run over 1f out: styd on same pce ins fnl f* **33/1**

53-0 **6** 2 3/4 **Spot Lite**[18] 2483 4-9-12 **57**.............................. CharlieBennett 14 45
(Rod Millman) *prom: ct out wd: stdd and lost pl over 4f out: hdwy over 1f out: sn rdn: styd on same pce fnl f* **10/1**

0-01 **7** hd **Jaganory (IRE)**[9] 2728 7-9-6 **56** 4ex..............................(v) FayeMcManoman(5) 7 44
(Christopher Mason) *w ldr tl led 1/2-way: hdd over 1f out: wknd wl ins fnl f* **4/1[3]**

0040 **8** 3/4 **Tally's Song**[9] 2729 6-9-0 **45**..............................(p) JimmyQuinn 13 30
(Grace Harris) *hld up: nt clr run over 1f out: nt trble ldrs (jockey said mare was denied a clear run)* **40/1**

0-50 **9** 1 1/2 **Aquadabra (IRE)**[9] 2728 4-9-4 **49**.............................. CallumShepherd 9 29
(Christopher Mason) *s.i.s: hdwy over 3f out: rdn and ev ch over 1f out: wknd ins fnl f* **14/1**

4004 **10** 1 **Compton Prince**[86] 925 10-9-0 **45**..............................(v) HollieDoyle 11 22
(Milton Bradley) *chsd ldrs: rdn over 1f out: wknd ins fnl f* **33/1**

-340 **11** 3 **Pranceabootthetoon (IRE)**[86] 919 4-9-0 **45**..............................(tp) DavidProbert 5 12
(Milton Bradley) *s.i.s: sn prom: rdn over 2f out: wknd over 1f out (jockey said colt stopped quickly)* **50/1**

-503 **12** 1 **Brogans Bay (IRE)**[112] 520 4-9-7 **52**.............................. CharlesBishop 2 16
(Simon Dow) *racd keenly: sn led: edgd rt over 4f out: hdd 1/2-way: wknd over 1f out (jockey said filly became unbalanced on the undulations of the track)* **22/1**

1m 11.31s (0.21) **Going Correction** -0.075s/f (Good) **12** Ran SP% **119.8**
Speed ratings (Par 101): **95,92,91,91,90 87,86,85,83,82 78,77**
CSF £42.06 CT £607.52 TOTE £3.30: £1.30, £4.60, £8.30; EX 43.80 Trifecta £625.10.
Owner Mrs Bernice Cuthbert **Bred** Dr Philip J Brown **Trained** Newmarket, Suffolk

FOCUS
A moderate sprint handicap. The first three horses home came through from towards the rear off an overly-strong pace.

3037 REXEL H'CAP 5f 10y
4:50 (4:50) (Class 4) (0-85,83) 4-Y-O+ £5,530 (£1,645; £822; £411) **Stalls** Centre

Form RPR

56-0 **1** **Waseem Faris (IRE)**[35] 1915 10-9-3 **79**.............................. PatDobbs 5 85
(Ken Cunningham-Brown) *mde all: shkn up ins fnl f: r.o* **6/1[3]**

156- **2** shd **Peace Dreamer (IRE)**[345] 3749 5-8-8 **75**.............................. DylanHogan(5) 3 80
(Robert Cowell) *n.m.r sn after s: hld up: hdwy on outer over 1f out: rdn and ev ch wl ins fnl f: r.o* **3/1[2]**

2633 **3** 1 3/4 **Little Boy Blue**[24] 2227 4-9-2 **83**..............................(h) RyanWhile(5) 1 82
(Bill Turner) *stmbld s: chsd wnr tl over 3f out: remained handy: nt clr run over 1f out: sn rdn: styd on same pce ins fnl f* **8/11[1]**

10-0 **4** 3 3/4 **Glamorous Rocket (IRE)**[23] 2272 4-9-1 **77**.............................. TomMarquand 4 62
(Christopher Mason) *prom: chsd wnr over 3f out: shkn up and ev ch over 1f out: edgd rt and no ex ins fnl f* **8/1**

1m 1.5s (-0.50) **Going Correction** -0.075s/f (Good) **4** Ran SP% **108.3**
Speed ratings (Par 105): **101,100,98,92**
CSF £22.37 TOTE £4.80; EX 19.70 Trifecta £33.50.
Owner Danebury Racing Stables **Bred** Rabbah Bloodstock Limited **Trained** Danebury, Hants

FOCUS
The feature contest was a fair little sprint handicap. The winner had dropped to a good mark.

3038 BEST FREE TIPS AT VALUERATER.CO.UK H'CAP 1m
5:20 (5:21) (Class 6) (0-65,63) 4-Y-O+
£3,105 (£924; £461; £300; £300; £300) **Stalls** Low

Form RPR

4566 **1** **Brockagh Cailin**[14] 2585 4-8-13 **55**.............................. JosephineGordon 6 62
(J S Moore) *pushed along early in rr: swtchd rt and hdwy over 2f out: rdn to ld over 1f out: edgd lft: r.o* **16/1**

6413 **2** 1 **Waqt (IRE)**[10] 2714 5-9-7 **63**.............................. FrannyNorton 11 68
(Alexandra Dunn) *s.i.s: sn prom: rdn and ev ch over 1f out: styd on same pce towards fin* **15/8[1]**

0-05 **3** 3/4 **Mister Musicmaster**[18] 2472 10-9-7 **63**.............................. DavidProbert 2 66
(Ron Hodges) *broke wl: sn lost pl: hdwy on outer over 2f out: rdn to ld over 1f out: sn hdd: edgd lft ins fnl f: styd on same pce* **20/1**

45-1 **4** 1/2 **Junoesque**[34] 1936 5-9-1 **57**..............................(p) CharlieBennett 5 59
(John Gallagher) *chsd ldr 1f: remained handy: shkn up over 3f out: rdn and nt clr run over 1f out: nt clr run again ins fnl f: styd on to go 4th nr fin* **13/2[3]**

3504 **5** nk **Screaming Gemini (IRE)**[24] 2256 5-9-5 **61**.............................. PatDobbs 3 62
(Tony Carroll) *prom: lost pl over 5f out: hdwy over 1f out: sn rdn: styd on same pce wl ins fnl f* **9/1**

0105 **6** 2 1/4 **Orobas (IRE)**[2] 2959 7-8-13 **62**..............................(v) VictorSantos(7) 13 58
(Lucinda Egerton) *pushed along to ld: clr 5f out tl over 2f out: rdn and hdd over 1f out: no ex ins fnl f* **7/1**

0600 **7** 1/2 **Ramblow**[33] 1967 6-8-3 **45**..............................(vt) HollieDoyle 4 40
(Alexandra Dunn) *hld up: rdn on outer over 2f out: styd on ins fnl f: nvr nrr* **50/1**

0653 **8** 3 1/2 **Accomplice**[14] 2585 5-9-4 **60**.............................. StevieDonohoe 8 47
(Michael Blanshard) *hld up: hdwy and nt clr run over 1f out: sn rdn: wknd ins fnl f* **17/2**

16-0 **9** hd **Coachella (IRE)**[17] 2513 5-8-12 **54**..............................(b) CallumShepherd 12 40
(Ed de Giles) *prom: chsd ldr over 2f out: rdn over 1f out: wknd ins fnl f* **14/1**

63-4 **10** 1 **Aye Aye Skipper (IRE)**[23] 2277 9-8-7 **49**..............................(b) KieranO'Neill 9 33
(Ken Cunningham-Brown) *chsd ldr 7f out: rdn and lost 2nd over 2f out: nt clr run over 1f out: sn wknd* **20/1**

2020 **11** 1/2 **Aqua Libre**[24] 2231 6-9-5 **61**.............................. TomMarquand 10 44
(Tony Carroll) *s.i.s: hld up: racd keenly: hdwy over 5f out: rdn over 2f out: wknd over 1f out* **6/1[2]**

00/0 **12** 20 **Machiavelian Storm (IRE)**[26] 2145 7-8-0 **45**..............................(t) WilliamCox(3) 1
(Richard Mitchell) *a in rr* **100/1**

1m 39.8s (-1.90) **Going Correction** -0.075s/f (Good) **12** Ran SP% **120.5**
Speed ratings (Par 101): **106,105,104,103,103 101,100,97,97,96 95,75**
CSF £45.59 CT £653.18 TOTE £22.20: £4.00, £2.20, £5.30; EX 78.40 Trifecta £1441.00.
Owner Gridline Racing **Bred** W G H Barrons **Trained** Upper Lambourn, Berks

FOCUS
A modest handicap. A 4yo filly got off the mark at the tenth attempt from off a strong gallop in a good comparative time for the grade.

GOODWOOD, May 24, 2019

T/Plt: £992.70 to a £1 stake. Pool: £51,471.64 - 37.85 winning units. T/Qpdt: £133.20 to a £1 stake. Pool: £4,936.78 - 27.42 winning units. **Colin Roberts**

3008 **GOODWOOD** (R-H)

Friday, May 24

OFFICIAL GOING: Good to firm (good in places; 8.0)

Wind: light, half against Weather: light cloud, warm

3039 THAMES MATERIALS MUCK AWAY EBF NOVICE AUCTION STKS (PLUS 10 RACE) 5f

1:50 (1:50) (Class 4) 2-Y-O **£6,792** (£2,021; £1,010; £505) **Stalls High**

Form RPR

1 **Dream Shot (IRE)** 2-9-2 0 JamieSpencer 5 78+
(James Tate) *athletic; sweating; edgy; coltish; stdd s: sn chsng ldrs: drifting rt and effrt to chse ldng pair wl over 1f out: rdn and chsd ldr ins fnl f: r.o wl to ld 50yds out: pushed out towards fin* **7/2**[2]

4 2 *nk* **Spanish Angel (IRE)**[19] 2444 2-9-2 0 OisinMurphy 6 76
(Andrew Balding) *looked wl; led: rdn and forged ahd over 1f out: hdd 50yds out: one pce towards fin* **9/2**[3]

0 3 *2 1/4* **Twice As Likely**[39] 1821 2-8-11 0 ShaneKelly 4 63+
(Richard Hughes) *compact; pushed along early: in tch in last trio: effrt 2f out: rn green and no imp tl styd on u.p ins fnl f: wnt 3rd 50yds out: nvr getting to ldrs but gng on at fin* **80/1**

333 4 *1* **Audio**[10] 2716 2-9-2 0 (b[1]) SeanLevey 1 64
(Richard Hannon) *tall; w ldr: rdn over 1f out: sn outpcd and flashed tail u.p ent fnl f: lost 2nd and wknd ins fnl f* **5/4**[1]

5 *hd* **Flash Henry** 2-9-2 0 HarryBentley 3 64
(George Scott) *workmanlike; in tch in last trio: effrt 2f out: kpt on same pce and no imp u.p ins fnl f* **13/2**

6 *3/4* **Treaty Of Dingle** 2-8-12 0 ow1 GeraldMosse 2 57
(Hughie Morrison) *workmanlike; in tch in midfield: effrt and hung rt 2f out: kpt on same pce and no imp fnl f* **7/1**

515 7 *2 1/4* **Copacabana Dancer (IRE)**[24] 2228 2-9-3 0 ThomasGreatrex[(5)] 7 59
(Joseph Tuite) *workmanlike; chsd ldrs tl lost pl and rdn jst over 2f out: wknd over 1f out and bhd ins fnl f* **20/1**

6 8 *3/4* **Secret Cecil (FR)**[22] 2338 2-9-2 0 RobHornby 8 50
(Joseph Tuite) *leggy; in rr: effrt 2f out: unable qck and outpcd over 1f out: bhd ins fnl f* **40/1**

58.92s (0.82) **Going Correction** +0.075s/f (Good) **8 Ran SP% 119.1**
Speed ratings (Par 95): **96,95,91,90,90 88,85,84**
CSF £20.23 TOTE £4.60: £1.40, £1.80, £11.40; EX 23.20 Trifecta £421.50.
Owner Saeed Manana **Bred** Gerard & Anne Corry **Trained** Newmarket, Suffolk

FOCUS
Top and bottom bends, and the straight to the 2f marker, were out 6yds. The ground was watered the previous evening but it was a dry, warmish day, so conditions on the fast side. This looked an ordinary 2yo novice but it should produce winners. They raced near side.

3040 THAMES MATERIALS RECYCLED/PRIMARY AGGREGATES H'CAP 7f

2:20 (2:20) (Class 4) (0-85,84) 4-Y-O+ **£6,986** (£2,079; £1,038; £519; £300; £300) **Stalls Low**

Form RPR

0-10 1 **La Maquina**[42] 1727 4-9-2 79 (t) NicolaCurrie 8 85+
(George Baker) *stdd s: t.k.h: hld up in last trio: effrt over 2f out: hdwy u.p over 1f out: edgd rt but r.o wl ins fnl f and str chal towards fin: led on post* **6/1**

510- 2 *nse* **Wufud**[248] 7377 4-9-4 81 (t[1] w) JimCrowley 9 87
(Charles Hills) *looked wl; chsd ldng pair: effrt jst over 2f out: chsd ldr ins fnl f: styd on u.p and grad clsd to ld towards fin: hdd on post* **13/2**

-302 3 *3/4* **Handytalk (IRE)**[18] 2472 6-8-12 75 (b) OisinMurphy 7 79
(Rod Millman) *led and sn clr: rdn and drifted rt over 1f out: kpt on u.p tl hdd: no ex and lost 2 pls towards fin* **8/1**

66-4 4 *1/2* **Charles Molson**[21] 2363 8-9-7 84 JoeFanning 2 87
(Patrick Chamings) *in tch in midfield: effrt over 1f out: drvn and chsd ldrs 1f out: kpt on ins fnl f wout quite getting to ldrs* **10/3**[2]

-506 5 *1 1/2* **Jellmood**[18] 2487 4-9-3 80 (t) ShaneKelly 5 79
(Chris Gordon) *in tch in midfield: effrt over 1f out: swtchd lft ent fnl f: kpt on ins fnl f: nvr quite enough pce to get on terms* **14/1**

134- 6 *1 1/4* **Department Of War (IRE)**[359] 3245 4-9-7 84 (t[1]) AdamKirby 3 79
(Stuart Williams) *looked wl; hld up in last trio: effrt and swtchd rt over 1f out: no imp and kpt on same pce ins fnl f* **5/1**[3]

6-20 7 *1 1/2* **Dream Catching (IRE)**[14] 2568 4-8-12 78 JoshuaBryan[(3)] 1 69
(Andrew Balding) *chsd ldr: effrt ent fnl 2f: no imp u.p over 1f out: lost 2nd and wknd ins fnl f* **3/1**[1]

40-0 8 *1 1/2* **Pour La Victoire (IRE)**[23] 2273 9-9-2 79 GeorgeDowning 6 66
(Tony Carroll) *racd in tch in last trio: effrt over 2f out: no imp and swtchd lft over 1f out: wl fnl f (jockey said gelding hung left-handed)* **33/1**

402- 9 *1 1/2* **Baltic Prince (IRE)**[160] 9564 9-8-9 79 ElishaWhittington[(7)] 4 62
(Tony Carroll) *hld up in rr: effrt over 2f out: no imp and wl hld fnl f (jockey said gelding anticipated the start)* **33/1**

1m 26.13s (-0.57) **Going Correction** +0.075s/f (Good) **9 Ran SP% 116.0**
Speed ratings (Par 105): **106,105,105,104,102 101,99,97,96**
CSF £44.83 CT £253.29 TOTE £6.20: £2.20, £2.50, £2.00; EX 50.10 Trifecta £385.30.
Owner George Baker And Partners - Super Six **Bred** Equine Breeding Limited **Trained** Chiddingfold, Surrey

FOCUS
Add 10yds. A fair handicap, rated around the third to this year's form.

3041 THAMES MATERIALS LAND RESTORATION FILLIES' H'CAP 1m

2:55 (2:55) (Class 4) (0-80,82) 3-Y-O **£6,986** (£2,079; £1,038; £519; £300; £300) **Stalls Low**

Form RPR

221- 1 **Desirous**[214] 8468 3-9-9 82 HarryBentley 5 90
(Ralph Beckett) *looked wl; in tch in midfield: effrt over 2f out: clsd u.p to chal over 1f out: led and hung rt 1f out: r.o wl ins fnl f: rdn out* **9/4**[1]

155- 2 *1 1/4* **Clara Peeters**[190] 9068 3-9-7 80 JimCrowley 2 85
(Gary Moore) *stdd s: hld up in tch in midfield: effrt over 1f out: hdwy ins fnl f: styd on strly fnl 100yds to go 2nd last strides: nvr getting to wnr* **8/1**

63-2 3 *nk* **Pennywhistle (IRE)**[15] 2552 3-9-9 82 FrankieDettori 1 86
(John Gosden) *looked wl; sltly awkward leaving stalls: in tch in midfield: swtchd rt and effrt on inner over 1f out: drvn to press ldrs 1f out: wnt 2nd ins fnl f: kpt on but no imp: lost 2nd last strides* **3/1**[2]

2-42 4 *3/4* **Al Messila**[8] 2760 3-8-11 70 RossaRyan 6 73
(Richard Hannon) *t.k.h: chsd ldr: effrt and chal u.p over 1f out: no ex ins fnl f and one pce fnl 100yds* **10/3**[3]

232- 5 *3/4* **Tronada**[212] 8547 3-9-3 76 OisinMurphy 8 77
(Alan King) *led: drvn and hrd pressed over 1f out: hdd 1f out: no ex ins fnl f: wknd towards fin* **7/1**

0-03 6 *4 1/2* **Sweet Poem**[31] 2018 3-8-5 71 AmeliaGlass[(7)] 7 62
(Clive Cox) *chsd ldrs: unable qck u.p and lost pl over 1f out: wknd ins fnl f* **50/1**

0-00 7 *4 1/2* **Desert Lantern (USA)**[24] 2251 3-9-0 73 JoeFanning 3 53
(Mark Johnston) *hld up in tch in last trio: clsd over outer over 2f out: unable qck u.p and btn over 1f out: wknd fnl f* **16/1**

554 8 *2* **Huddle**[14] 2598 3-8-6 65 NicolaCurrie 4 41
(William Knight) *str; stdd after s: hld up in tch in rr: effrt over 2f out: sn struggling and outpcd over 1f out: bhd fnl f (jockey said filly ran green)* **25/1**

1m 40.46s (1.26) **Going Correction** +0.075s/f (Good) **8 Ran SP% 114.1**
Speed ratings (Par 98): **96,94,94,93,92 88,83,81**
CSF £21.16 CT £54.57 TOTE £3.10: £1.30, £2.40, £1.20; EX 20.40 Trifecta £74.90.
Owner K Abdullah **Bred** Juddmonte Farms Ltd **Trained** Kimpton, Hants

FOCUS
Add 10yds. A useful handicap, rated positively, with the fourth helping to set the standard. In 2016 it was won by Persuasive, who later won the Sandringham at Royal Ascot and the Group 1 Queen Elizabeth II Stakes.

3042 BRITISH STALLION STUDS EBF COCKED HAT STKS (LISTED RACE) (C&G) 1m 3f 44y

3:30 (3:31) (Class 1) 3-Y-O **£25,519** (£9,675; £4,842; £2,412; £1,210; £607) **Stalls High**

Form RPR

2-11 1 **Private Secretary**[28] 2088 3-9-0 92 FrankieDettori 7 106+
(John Gosden) *compact; hld up in rr: effrt over 2f out: hdwy u.p over 1f out: chsd ldr ins fnl f: r.o under hands and heels riding fnl 100yds to ld towards fin: eased last strides* **11/10**[1]

31-5 2 *nk* **Spanish Mission (USA)**[79] 1035 3-9-0 95 JamieSpencer 4 105
(David Simcock) *str; hld up in tch in last trio: effrt on inner over 2f out: hdwy u.p to chal 1f out: drvn to ld ins fnl f: hdd and no ex towards fin* **20/1**

41 3 *2 1/4* **Fifth Position (IRE)**[24] 2249 3-9-0 0 AndreaAtzeni 1 101
(Roger Varian) *ly; looked wl; chsd ldr for over 1f: swtchd lft and effrt to chal over 2f out: drvn over 1f out: no ex and outpcd fnl 100yds* **7/1**[3]

1-33 4 *1/2* **Persian Moon (IRE)**[20] 2413 3-9-0 101 JoeFanning 2 100
(Mark Johnston) *led: rdn and hrd pressed ent fnl 2f: drvn over 1f out: hdd ins fnl f: no ex and outpcd fnl 100yds* **4/1**[2]

6-1 5 *5* **Duckett's Grove (USA)**[22] 2321 3-9-0 92 GeraldMosse 5 92
(Ed Walker) *in tch in midfield: effrt and clsd to chal ent fnl 2f: unable qck u.p and outpcd over 1f out wknd* **9/1**

1-30 6 *3 1/2* **Kaloor**[16] 2523 3-9-0 96 (p[1]) OisinMurphy 6 86
(Brian Meehan) *chsd ldr after over 1f tl over 2f out: sn u.p and outpcd whn hung rt over 1f out: wknd fnl f* **14/1**

1-5 7 *7* **Alfaatik**[28] 2084 3-9-0 0 JimCrowley 3 74
(John Gosden) *str; ly; looked wl; reluctant to go to post and led down by rdr fnl 5f: racd lazily: in tch in last trio: rdn over 4f out: dropped to rr 3f out: sn wl btn* **7/1**[3]

2m 24.11s (-4.19) **Going Correction** +0.075s/f (Good) **7 Ran SP% 114.0**
Speed ratings (Par 107): **118,117,116,115,112 109,104**
CSF £26.30 TOTE £1.90: £1.20, £6.40; EX 26.30 Trifecta £160.30.
Owner Denford Stud **Bred** Denford Stud Ltd **Trained** Newmarket, Suffolk

FOCUS
Add 10yds. Often a good race, the most notable recent winners being Rewilding (later won two Group 1s), Masked Marvel (won St Leger) and Storm The Stars (placed in the Derby and Irish Derby). The first three in this latest edition rate as improving.

3043 THAMES MATERIALS BULK EXCAVATIONS H'CAP 6f

4:05 (4:05) (Class 2) (0-105,103) 3-Y-O+ **£15,562** (£4,660; £2,330; £1,165; £582; £292) **Stalls High**

Form RPR

4103 1 **Lake Volta (IRE)**[6] 2844 4-9-9 98 JoeFanning 4 109
(Mark Johnston) *mde all: rdn over 1f out: clr and styd on strly ins fnl f: rdn out* **3/1**[1]

1321 2 *2 1/4* **Puds**[20] 2403 4-9-1 90 ShaneKelly 6 94+
(Richard Hughes) *stdd after s: hld up in tch in last pair: clsd and nt clr run wl over 1f out: swtchd lft and effrt ent fnl f: hdwy u.p to chse clr wnr 100yds out: nvr a threat* **11/2**

1113 3 *3/4* **Martineo**[13] 2611 4-8-9 84 oh3 OisinMurphy 9 85
(John Butler) *t.k.h: chsd ldrs early: sn restrained and hld up in tch in midfield: effrt over 1f out: kpt on ins fnl f to go 3rd towards fin: no threat to wnr* **13/2**

0-40 4 *1* **Tis Marvellous**[34] 1942 5-10-0 103 (t) AdamKirby 5 101
(Clive Cox) *squeezed for room leaving stalls: chse ldrs tl chsd wnr 1/2-way: rdn and unable qck over 1f out: hung rt and lost 2nd 100yds out: wknd towards fin* **5/1**[3]

050- 5 *1* **Enjazaat**[300] 5499 4-9-13 102 JimCrowley 8 97
(Owen Burrows) *looked wl; dwlt and short room leaving stalls: outpcd in rr early: swtchd rt towards centre and hdwy 4f out: clsd u.p to chse ldrs over 1f out: no ex 1f out: wknd ins fnl f* **15/2**

2252 6 *1 1/4* **Areen Heart (FR)**[29] 2061 5-9-4 93 DavidNolan 3 84
(David O'Meara) *mounted in chute and taken down early: hld up in tch in midfield: no imp u.p over 1f out: wknd ins fnl f* **11/1**

-430 7 *2 3/4* **Green Power**[13] 2609 4-9-8 97 AndreaAtzeni 2 79
(John Gallagher) *racd away fr rivals towards centre: in tch in midfield: no ex u.p over 1f out: wknd ins fnl f* **7/2**[2]

05-4 8 *7* **Jashma (IRE)**[143] 3 5-8-2 84 oh3 GeorgeRooke[(7)] 7 44
(Richard Hughes) *taken down early: chsd ldr tl 1/2-way: sn rdn and struggling: bhd fnl f* **25/1**

1m 10.45s (-1.65) **Going Correction** +0.075s/f (Good) **8 Ran SP% 116.6**
Speed ratings (Par 109): **114,111,110,108,107 105,102,92**
CSF £20.31 CT £100.83 TOTE £4.20: £1.60, £2.00, £1.80; EX 14.20 Trifecta £71.40.
Owner Sheikh Hamdan bin Mohammed Al Maktoum **Bred** Godolphin **Trained** Middleham Moor, N Yorks

FOCUS
The winner was allowed to dominate and is rated back to last year's Listed win. The main action was near side.

3044 THAMESMATERIALS.COM H'CAP 2m
4:40 (4:40) (Class 4) (0-85,82) 4-Y-O+

£6,986 (£2,079; £1,038; £519; £300; £300) **Stalls** Low

Form				RPR
44-2	1		**Age Of Wisdom (IRE)**[33] 1144 6-8-8 **67**.....(p) HarryBentley 6	76+
			(Gary Moore) *hld up wl in tch in midfield: n.m.r and edgd rt over 2f out: chsd ldrs and drvn over 1f out: wnt 2nd 1f out: styd on to ld ins fnl f: rdn out* **10/1**	
4312	2	1	**Knight Crusader**[24] 2254 7-9-6 **79**..... AdamKirby 11	86
			(John O'Shea) *looked wl; hld up in tch in midfield: hdwy u.p to ld 2f out: drvn over 1f out: hdd and kpt on same pce ins fnl f* **15/2[3]**	
0-16	3	2 ¼	**Seinesational**[20] 2398 4-9-3 **77**.....(v) JimCrowley 4	82
			(William Knight) *hld up in tch in midfield: nt clr run and shuffled bk over 2f out: swtchd rt and rallied jst over 1f out: styd on to go 3rd towards fin: no threat to ldrs (jockey said gelding was denied a clear run)* **10/1**	
12-1	4	shd	**Rydan (IRE)**[20] 2400 8-9-5 **78**.....(v) TomQueally 13	83
			(Gary Moore) *hld up in tch in last trio: rdn and effrt over 2f out: hdwy u.p to chse ldrs 1f out: kpt on same pce and one pce ins fnl f* **8/1**	
4-06	5	½	**Archimento**[34] 1943 6-9-9 **82**..... OisinMurphy 10	86
			(William Knight) *chsd ldrs: shkn up 2f out: drvn over 1f out: kpt on same pce ins fnl f: lost 2 pls towards fin* **25/1**	
65-3	6	¾	**October Storm**[28] 2080 6-8-11 **77**..... ScottMcCullagh(7) 8	80
			(Mick Channon) *hld up in tch in midfield: nt clrest of runs over 2f out: swtchd lft 2f out and effrt over 1f out: keeping on whn squeezed for room 1f out: kpt on same pce ins fnl f* **7/1[2]**	
1225	7	1 ¼	**Atomic Jack**[60] 1330 4-8-8 **68**..... NicolaCurrie 7	70
			(George Baker) *w ldr tl led over 2f out: sn drvn and hdd: no ex and lost 2nd 1f out: wknd ins fnl f* **14/1**	
34-3	8	2 ¼	**Elysees (IRE)**[62] 916 4-9-3 **77**..... AndreaAtzeni 9	76
			(Alan King) *looked wl; t.k.h to post: hld up in tch in last quartet: effrt over 2f out: nvr threatened to get on terms: kpt on ins fnl f* **5/2[1]**	
5324	9	2 ¼	**Emenem**[30] 2032 5-9-8 **81**..... JamieSpencer 2	77
			(Simon Dow) *stdd s: t.k.h: hld up in last pair: nt clr run on inner over 2f out: nvr threatened to get involved and wl hld fnl f* **8/1**	
-463	10	2 ¾	**Flintrock (GER)**[14] 2571 4-9-4 **81**..... JoshuaBryan(3) 12	74
			(Andrew Balding) *v.s.a: grad clsd on to rr of field 13f out: rdn 3f out: sn struggling and wl btn over 1f out (jockey said colt was very slowly away)* **8/1**	
00-2	11	3 ¾	**Blue Rambler**[20] 2398 9-9-9 **82**..... GeorgeDowning 3	70
			(Tony Carroll) *led tl over 2f out: sn u.p and lost pl over 1f out: wknd fnl f* **33/1**	
4-60	12	2 ¾	**Medburn Cutler**[14] 2571 9-9-7 **80**.....(p) ShaneKelly 1	65
			(Peter Hedger) *chsd ldrs: effrt on inner over 3f out: unable qck: lost pl and wl hld over 1f out: wknd fnl f* **66/1**	
5-30	R		**Jacob Cats**[20] 2400 10-8-12 **71**.....(v) KierenFox 5	
			(William Knight) *ref to r: tk no part* **25/1**	

3m 32.83s (1.93) **Going Correction** +0.075s/f (Good)
WFA 4 from 5yo+ 1lb **13 Ran SP% 123.1**
Speed ratings (Par 105): **98,97,96,96,96 95,95,93,92,91 89,88,**
CSF £83.02 CT £788.34 TOTE £12.00: £3.00, £2.50, £3.80; EX 112.30 Trifecta £843.90.
Owner The 1901 Partnership **Bred** Darley **Trained** Lower Beeding, W Sussex

FOCUS
Add 15yds. Ordinary form.

3045 THAMES MATERIALS CHARITY GOLF DAY H'CAP 5f
5:10 (5:11) (Class 5) (0-70,72) 3-Y-O

£5,692 (£1,694; £846; £423; £300; £300) **Stalls** High

Form				RPR
06-2	1		**All Back To Mine**[23] 2281 3-9-2 **63**..... OisinMurphy 4	69
			(Joseph Tuite) *hld up in tch in midfield: effrt over 1f out: chsd ldrs and drvn ins fnl f: styd on strly to ld last stride* **6/1**	
0051	2	shd	**Superseded (IRE)**[14] 2592 3-9-3 **64**..... RobertWinston 3	70
			(John Butler) *chsd ldrs: clsd and upsides ldrs 2f out: rdn to ld jst over 1f out: drvn ins fnl f: kpt on but hdd last stride* **8/1**	
0-41	3	nk	**Devils Roc**[23] 2276 3-9-7 **68**..... RobHornby 6	73
			(Jonathan Portman) *looked wl; in tch in midfield: effrt over 1f out: clsd and drvn 1f out: ev ch towards fin: kpt on wl* **5/2[1]**	
-251	4	¾	**Show Me The Bubbly**[18] 2474 3-9-10 **71**..... LiamJones 7	73
			(John O'Shea) *sn pushed along: squeezed for room and dropped towards rr after 1f: rdn and hdwy over 1f out: chsd ldr ins fnl f: kpt on but no imp: lost 2 pls towards fin* **9/1**	
0525	5	1	**Hanakotoba (USA)**[23] 2281 3-8-13 **67**.....(t) MarcoGhiani(7) 1	66
			(Stuart Williams) *racd away fr stands' rail towards centre: in tch in midfield: effrt over 1f out: rdn and kpt on same pce ins fnl f* **12/1**	
-363	6	nk	**Valentino Sunrise**[18] 2489 3-9-0 **61**..... GeraldMosse 9	59
			(Mick Channon) *chsd ldrs: nt clr run and hmpd ent fnl f: swtchd lft ins fnl f: styd on towards fin: no threat to ldrs* **5/1[2]**	
312	7	hd	**Miss Enigma (IRE)**[14] 2592 3-8-13 **63**.....(b) FinleyMarsh(3) 2	60
			(Richard Hughes) *led tl over 3f out: chsd ldr: ev ch and rdn over 1f out: no ex ent fnl f: wknd ins fnl f* **17/2**	
5004	8	2	**Starchant**[23] 2281 3-8-12 **59**..... NicolaCurrie 5	49
			(John Bridger) *sn in rr: rdn over 1f out: kpt on ins fnl f: nvr trbld ldrs* **33/1**	
4-25	9	2 ¾	**Khafooq**[24] 2255 3-9-11 **72**.....(p[1]) JimCrowley 8	52
			(Robert Cowell) *jostled leaving stalls: sn rcvrd and prom: led over 3f out: rdn and hdd jst over 1f out: sn btn and wknd ins fnl f* **11/2[3]**	
0-05	10	5	**Dark Impulse (IRE)**[8] 2773 3-8-0 **54** oh9..... AledBeech(7) 10	16
			(John Bridger) *prom early: sn struggling and bhd 1/2-way* **100/1**	

59.07s (0.97) **Going Correction** +0.075s/f (Good) **10 Ran SP% 118.2**
Speed ratings (Par 99): **95,94,94,93,91 91,90,87,83,75**
CSF £54.07 CT £152.11 TOTE £5.70: £1.80, £2.80, £1.30; EX 53.00 Trifecta £168.90.
Owner LECH Racing Limited **Bred** Eminent Kind Ltd **Trained** Lambourn, Berks

FOCUS
A modest but competitive handicap. This rates a small pb from the winner, with the runner-up to his best.
T/Plt: £158.30 to a £1 stake. Pool: £91,519.84 - 421.96 winning units. T/Qpdt: £16.60 to a £1 stake. Pool: £9,850.09 - 436.73 winning units. **Steve Payne**

[2613] HAYDOCK (L-H)
Friday, May 24

OFFICIAL GOING: Good to firm (watered; 7.9)
Wind: Moderate, half against in straight of over 4f Weather: Fine

3046 ALBERT BROWN MEMORIAL H'CAP 1m 2f 42y
2:10 (2:11) (Class 5) (0-70,68) 4-Y-O+

£4,851 (£1,443; £721; £360; £300; £300) **Stalls** Centre

Form				RPR
000-	1		**Briardale (IRE)**[193] 9029 7-9-6 **67**..... PaulHanagan 5	77
			(James Bethell) *racd keenly in midfield: hdwy 2f out: led ent fnl f: sn edgd lft: rdn out* **7/1[3]**	
-110	2	½	**Mr Coco Bean (USA)**[17] 2512 5-9-0 **61**..... BenCurtis 12	71+
			(David Barron) *hld up: nt clr run bef swtchd rt and hdwy over 1f out: r.o strly towards fin* **7/1[3]**	
-110	3	1 ½	**Citta D'Oro**[27] 2106 4-9-1 **62**..... RichardKingscote 6	68
			(James Unett) *a.p: led over 2f out: rdn and hdd ent fnl f: styd on same pce fnl 75yds* **7/1[3]**	
-363	4	5	**Bit Of A Quirke**[23] 2290 6-9-6 **67**..... DougieCostello 8	63
			(Mark Walford) *midfield: pushed along over 3f out: drvn and hdwy over 1f out whn hung lft: kpt on ins fnl f: nt pce to chal (jockey said gelding hung left in the closing stages)* **11/1**	
100	5	1	**Manfadh (IRE)**[73] 1169 4-9-6 **67**..... PaulMulrennan 17	61
			(Mark Brisbourne) *racd keenly in midfield: rdn and swtchd lft 2f out and nt clr run: styd on ins fnl f: gng on at fin* **50/1**	
-562	6	¾	**Four Kingdoms (IRE)**[7] 2785 5-9-5 **66**..... PJMcDonald 14	59
			(R Mike Smith) *in tch: effrt over 2f out: styd on same pce fnl f (trainer could offer no explanation for the gelding's performance)* **3/1[1]**	
5116	7	½	**False Id**[24] 2231 6-9-0 **66**.....(b) DarraghKeenan(5) 16	58
			(David Loughnane) *hld up: racd keenly and hdwy after 2f to press ldr: rdn and wknd over 1f out* **14/1**	
0354	8	1 ¼	**Seaborough (IRE)**[17] 2512 4-9-0 **61**.....(p) ConnorBeasley 13	50
			(David Thompson) *midfield: drvn and outpcd over 3f out: kpt on ins fnl f* **16/1**	
400-	9	nk	**Blue Medici**[210] 8597 5-9-3 **64**..... EdwardGreatrex 1	52
			(Mark Loughnane) *hld up: outpcd 3f out: kpt on ins fnl f: nvr a threat (jockey said gelding was denied a clear run on two occasions in the back straight)* **25/1**	
0040	10	1 ¾	**Staplegrove (IRE)**[27] 2106 4-9-7 **68**..... SamJames 2	53
			(Philip Kirby) *racd keenly: in tch: rdn over 2f out: one pce fr over 1f out* **20/1**	
40-0	11	¾	**Rebel Cause (IRE)**[17] 2512 6-9-1 **62**..... RoystonFfrench 9	45
			(John Holt) *chsd ldrs: rdn over 2f out: wknd over 1f out* **25/1**	
34-0	12	5	**Bogardus (IRE)**[19] 2436 8-9-2 **63**..... DanielTudhope 10	36
			(Liam Bailey) *missed break: hld up: struggling over 4f out: nvr a threat* **33/1**	
0060	13	¾	**Rock Warbler (IRE)**[69] 1231 6-8-8 **55** ow1.....(h) TomEaves 4	27
			(Michael Mullineaux) *hld up: rdn over 2f out: nvr a threat* **50/1**	
23-3	14	½	**Tomorrow's Angel**[22] 2326 4-9-1 **65**..... JamieGormley(3) 3	36
			(Iain Jardine) *struggling over 4f out: a bhd* **13/2[2]**	
0-30	15	9	**Maghfoor**[27] 2092 5-9-6 **67**..... JasonHart 7	20
			(Eric Alston) *sn led: rdn and hdd over 2f out: wknd over 1f out* **8/1**	

2m 9.75s (-1.05) **Going Correction** -0.20s/f (Firm) **15 Ran SP% 127.1**
Speed ratings (Par 103): **96,95,94,90,89 89,88,87,87,85 85,81,80,80,73**
CSF £54.16 CT £368.24 TOTE £9.00: £3.10, £2.70, £2.00; EX 66.60 Trifecta £389.70.
Owner J Carrick&Clarendon Thoroughbred Racing **Bred** Rabbah Bloodstock Limited **Trained** Middleham Moor, N Yorks

FOCUS
Inner home straight used. Add 33yds. The watered ground (12mm over the previous two days) was given as good to firm (Going Stick 7.9). A modest handicap run at a good pace. The winner has been rated in line with last year's best.

3047 BRITISH STALLION STUDS EBF NOVICE STKS (PLUS 10 RACE) 6f
2:45 (2:45) (Class 4) 2-Y-O £6,469 (£1,925; £962; £481) **Stalls** Centre

Form				RPR
	1		**Pierre Lapin (IRE)** 2-9-5 0..... DavidEgan 7	88+
			(Roger Varian) *hld up: j. road after nrly 1f: rdn and hdwy over 1f out: led ins fnl f: r.o wl: won gng away: nice prospect* **1/1[1]**	
	2	3 ½	**Visible Charm (IRE)** 2-9-5 0..... JamesDoyle 4	76
			(Charlie Appleby) *hld up in rr: angled out jst bef 1/2-way: hdwy to ld 2f out: rdn over 1f out: hdd ins fnl f: outpcd by wnr fnl 100yds* **9/4[2]**	
6	3	1 ¼	**Bravo Faisal (IRE)**[27] 2108 2-9-5 0..... PaulHanagan 5	72+
			(Richard Fahey) *hld up: rdn 2f out: hdwy ins fnl f: styd on fnl 150yds: gng on at fin: nt pce to chal* **25/1**	
	4	shd	**Clog Maker (IRE)** 2-9-5 0..... PJMcDonald 6	71
			(Mark Johnston) *a.p: rdn and ev ch over 1f out: unable qck ins fnl f: styd on same pce fnl 100yds* **16/1**	
23	5	3	**Top Buck (IRE)**[16] 2520 2-9-5 0..... JasonWatson 3	62
			(Brian Meehan) *led: rdn and hdd 2f out: unable qck u.p over 1f out: fdd ins fnl f* **5/1[3]**	
4	6	4 ½	**Mr Kodi (IRE)**[27] 2108 2-9-5 0..... CliffordLee 2	49
			(David Evans) *prom: rdn over 2f out: wknd fnl f* **33/1**	
	7	2 ½	**Bad Rabbit (IRE)** 2-9-5 0..... TrevorWhelan 1	41
			(David Loughnane) *chsd ldrs: rdn over 2f out: wknd over 1f out* **80/1**	

1m 14.1s (0.20) **Going Correction** -0.20s/f (Firm) **7 Ran SP% 111.3**
Speed ratings (Par 95): **90,85,83,83,79 73,70**
CSF £3.18 TOTE £1.80: £1.40, £1.40; EX 4.00 Trifecta £29.80.
Owner Sheikh Mohammed Obaid Al Maktoum **Bred** Cbs Bloodstock **Trained** Newmarket, Suffolk

FOCUS
Last year's winner took the Chesham Stakes on his next start, and it's possible this year's winner could also follow up at Royal Ascot. He certainly marked himself as a Pattern performer in the making.

3048 JOANNE KELLY 50TH BIRTHDAY H'CAP 6f
3:20 (3:21) (Class 4) (0-85,87) 3-Y-O

£7,115 (£2,117; £1,058; £529; £300; £300) **Stalls** Centre

Form				RPR
-631	1		**Look Out Louis**[13] 2635 3-9-4 **80**..... DavidAllan 3	87
			(Tim Easterby) *chsd ldrs: led over 2f out: rdn over 1f out: kpt on wl fnl f: a doing enough towards fin* **4/1[2]**	

50-5 **2** *nk* **Revich (IRE)**[16] 2525 3-9-6 82 .... DavidEgan 2 88
(Richard Spencer) *midfield: rdn and hdwy 2f out: chalng ins fnl f: kpt on wl towards fin* **7/1**

112 **3** *1 ¼* **With Caution (IRE)**[73] 1168 3-9-7 83 .... PJMcDonald 7 85
(James Tate) *in tch: rdn over 1f out: chsd ldrs ins fnl f: nvr able to chal front two* **4/1**[2]

13-0 **4** *½* **Finoah (IRE)**[16] 2525 3-9-10 86 ....(v) RichardKingscote 8 86
(Tom Dascombe) *prom: rdn over 2f out: unable qck over 1f out: styd on same pce fnl 100yds* **7/2**[1]

014- **5** *¾* **Glorious Charmer**[191] 9051 3-9-5 81 .... LiamKeniry 9 79
(Ed Walker) *hld up: rdn and hdwy over 1f out: hung lft: kpt on ins fnl f: nvr able to chal* **10/1**

221- **6** *1 ¼* **Golden Force**[263] 6880 3-9-3 79 .... HectorCrouch 5 73
(Clive Cox) *missed break: hld up: effrt over 1f out: one pce fnl 100yds* **8/1**

-640 **7** *1 ¾* **Fares Kodiac (IRE)**[35] 1920 3-9-11 87 ....(t) SilvestreDeSousa 6 75
(Marco Botti) *trckd ldrs: rdn and outpcd over 2f out: no imp after* **13/2**[3]

34-0 **8** *2 ¼* **Excelled (IRE)**[28] 2078 3-9-4 80 .... DanielMuscutt 4 61
(James Fanshawe) *hld up: rdn over 1f out: nvr a threat (jockey said filly stopped quickly)* **12/1**

1100 **9** *10* **Liberation Day**[16] 2522 3-9-2 78 ....(p) BenCurtis 1 27
(Tom Dascombe) *led: rdn and hdd over 2f out: sn wknd* **25/1**

1m 13.07s (-0.83) **Going Correction** -0.20s/f (Firm) 9 Ran SP% **119.8**
Speed ratings (Par 101): **97,96,94,94,93 91,89,86,72**
CSF £33.48 CT £121.89 TOTE £5.10: £2.10, £2.00, £1.50; EX 37.00 Trifecta £205.00.
Owner Habton Farms **Bred** Mildmay Bloodstock Ltd **Trained** Great Habton, N Yorks

FOCUS
A competitive sprint for 3yos. Sound form, with the winner progressing.

3049 GEORGE FORMBY BIRTHDAY FILLIES' NOVICE STKS (PLUS 10 RACE) 6f 212y
3:55 (3:56) (Class 4) 2-Y-O
£4,851 (£1,443; £721; £360) **Stalls** Low

Form RPR

1 **Rhea** 2-9-0 0 .... DavidEgan 4 80+
(Kevin Ryan) *chsd ldrs: effrt to take 2nd over 2f out: led ins fnl f: rdn out and kpt on wl* **8/1**[3]

3 **2** *¾* **Perfect Rose**[51] 1513 2-9-0 0 .... PJMcDonald 1 78
(Mark Johnston) *led: rdn over 1f out: hdd ins fnl f: kpt on but hld after* **8/1**[3]

3 *hd* **Sacred Dance** 2-9-0 0 .... JamesDoyle 2 78+
(Charlie Appleby) *fly-jmpd s: hld up: effrt and hdwy over 2f out: tried to chal over 1f out: stl cl up whn changed legs fnl 75yds: kpt on: nt quite pce of wnr (jockey said filly jumped awkwardly from the stalls)* **10/11**[1]

4 *½* **Zmile** 2-9-0 0 .... DanielTudhope 9 76+
(Michael Bell) *midfield: effrt 2f out: rn green and lugged lft whn hdwy over 1f out: kpt on towards fin* **12/1**

5 *¾* **Byzantia** 2-9-0 0 .... RobertHavlin 8 75
(John Gosden) *midfield: hdwy 3f out: cl up 2f out: rdn and unable qck chsng ldrs over 1f out: kpt on: eased fnl 50yds (jockey said filly was denied a clear run in the closing stages)* **3/1**[2]

6 *3 ¾* **Golden Lips (IRE)** 2-9-0 0 .... SilvestreDeSousa 3 65
(Harry Dunlop) *towards rr: rdn over 2f out: sme hdwy over 1f out: no imp on ldrs* **33/1**

7 *3* **Roman's Empress (IRE)** 2-9-0 0 .... TrevorWhelan 6 57
(David Loughnane) *chsd ldrs: rdn 3f out: wknd over 2f out* **100/1**

8 *¾* **Prestigious (IRE)** 2-9-0 0 .... EdwardGreatrex 7 55
(Archie Watson) *chsd ldr tl rdn over 2f out: sn wknd* **20/1**

9 *4* **Laughter Lounge (IRE)** 2-9-0 0 .... CliffordLee 5 45
(David Evans) *rdn along thrght: a bhd: outpcd over 4f out: nvr a threat* **100/1**

1m 28.05s (-1.25) **Going Correction** -0.20s/f (Firm) 9 Ran SP% **117.0**
Speed ratings (Par 92): **99,98,97,97,96 92,88,87,83**
CSF £67.75 TOTE £10.40: £2.40, £1.70, £1.30; EX 54.30 Trifecta £173.00.
Owner Sheikh Mohammed Obaid Al Maktoum **Bred** Blue Blood Breeding 2 Ltd **Trained** Hambleton, N Yorks

FOCUS
Add 11yds. A test of stamina for these 2yo fillies and there was something of a bunched finish.

3050 GERRY LOWE MEMORIAL FILLIES' NOVICE STKS (PLUS 10 RACE) 7f 212y
4:30 (4:31) (Class 5) 3-Y-O
£4,851 (£1,443; £721; £360) **Stalls** Low

Form RPR

4 **1** **Nonchalance**[17] 2518 3-9-0 0 .... RobertHavlin 1 83+
(John Gosden) *trckd ldrs: rdn to ld over 1f out: r.o wl to draw clr fnl 100yds* **6/4**[1]

0-3 **2** *3* **Infuse (IRE)**[27] 2103 3-9-0 0 .... JasonWatson 3 74
(Roger Charlton) *in tch: rdn over 2f out: styd on to chse wnr fnl 130yds: no imp* **4/1**[2]

0- **3** *hd* **Whimbrel (IRE)**[177] 9291 3-9-0 0 .... NickyMackay 7 73+
(John Gosden) *hld up: rdn and hdwy over 2f out: nt clr run over 1f out: styd on fnl 100yds: gng on at fin* **5/1**[3]

4 *2* **Regal Lilly (IRE)** 3-9-0 0 .... SilvestreDeSousa 5 69+
(Mark Johnston) *s.i.s: bhd: green over 4f out: angled out and rdn ent fnl 3f: styd on wl fnl 150yds: nrst fin* **20/1**

1-4 **5** *nse* **Conga**[27] 2103 3-9-7 0 .... KevinStott 6 76
(Kevin Ryan) *led: rdn over 2f out: hdd over 1f out: styd on same pce fnl 100yds* **8/1**

6 *nk* **Casting Spells** 3-9-0 0 .... PJMcDonald 9 68
(Tom Dascombe) *chsd ldr after 1f: rdn and ev ch over 2f out: unable qck and lost 2nd over 1f out: no ex fnl 150yds* **12/1**

00 **7** *shd* **Soloist (IRE)**[26] 2148 3-9-0 0 .... JamesDoyle 8 68
(William Haggas) *midfield: rdn over 2f out: hdwy over 1f out: one pce ins fnl f* **40/1**

4-6 **8** *2 ¾* **Lilligram**[136] 128 3-9-0 0 .... DavidEgan 4 61
(Roger Varian) *hld up: effrt on outer over 2f out: no imp over 1f out* **16/1**

44- **9** *2 ½* **Lucky Turn (IRE)**[191] 9050 3-9-0 0 .... DanielTudhope 2 64
(Michael Bell) *trckd ldrs: rdn over 3f out: wknd over 1f out: eased fnl 100yds* **10/1**

10 *13* **Caster Semenya** 3-9-0 0 .... RoystonFfrench 10 26
(Steph Hollinshead) *a bhd: green and intimidated by rival over 4f out: nvr a threat* **100/1**

1m 40.39s (-2.31) **Going Correction** -0.20s/f (Firm) 10 Ran SP% **118.6**
Speed ratings (Par 96): **103,100,99,97,97 97,97,94,92,79**
CSF £7.37 TOTE £2.20: £1.30, £1.80, £2.10; EX 8.40 Trifecta £35.40.
Owner HH Sheikha Al Jalila Racing **Bred** Godolphin **Trained** Newmarket, Suffolk

FOCUS
Add 11yds. A fair novice, and the winner won it with a nice turn of foot, progressing from her debut.

3051 EVERY RACE LIVE ON RACING TV H'CAP 7f 212y
5:00 (5:01) (Class 4) (0-80,81) 3-Y-O
£7,115 (£2,117; £1,058; £529; £300; £300) **Stalls** Low

Form RPR

0-14 **1** **Smile A Mile (IRE)**[8] 2766 3-9-7 79 .... JamesDoyle 1 86
(Mark Johnston) *chsd ldr tl over 3f out: effrt 2f out: rdn to ld over 1f out: r.o wl and asserted fnl 75yds* **7/2**[2]

44-3 **2** *2* **Jaleel**[21] 2366 3-9-6 78 .... DavidEgan 4 80
(Roger Varian) *chsd ldrs: wnt 2nd over 3f out: led wl over 1f out: sn hdd: edgd lft ent fnl f: nt pce of wnr fnl 75yds* **7/2**[2]

6-60 **3** *1* **Kuwait Station (IRE)**[17] 2510 3-9-9 81 .... DanielTudhope 2 83+
(David O'Meara) *chsd ldrs: rdn 2f out: effrt whn n.m.r and checked ent fnl f: kpt on after but hld* **14/1**

22 **4** *hd* **Assimilation (IRE)**[59] 1345 3-9-4 76 .... LiamKeniry 5 75
(Ed Walker) *hld up: rdn over 3f out: kpt on u.p ins fnl f: nvr able to chal* **8/1**

260- **5** *3* **Golden Parade**[214] 8474 3-8-12 70 .... DavidAllan 3 62
(Tim Easterby) *hld up: rdn over 3f out: nvr able to trble ldrs (jockey said gelding was denied a clear run approximately half furlong out)* **18/1**

335- **6** *1 ¼* **Zoffee**[258] 7068 3-9-5 77 .... RichardKingscote 6 66
(Tom Dascombe) *led: clr over 4f out: rdn and reduced advantage over 2f out: hdd wl over 1f out: btn whn n.m.r ent fnl f* **4/1**[3]

1520 **7** *17* **Songkran (IRE)**[9] 2746 3-9-7 79 .... SilvestreDeSousa 8 29
(David Elsworth) *in rr: pushed along 4f out: nvr a threat: eased wl over 1f out (jockey said colt was never travelling)* **11/4**[1]

1m 39.97s (-2.73) **Going Correction** -0.20s/f (Firm) 7 Ran SP% **114.2**
Speed ratings (Par 101): **105,103,102,101,98 97,80**
CSF £16.10 CT £149.31 TOTE £3.60: £2.10, £1.90; EX 14.10 Trifecta £125.40.
Owner Sheikh Hamdan bin Mohammed Al Maktoum **Bred** Godolphin **Trained** Middleham Moor, N Yorks

FOCUS
Add 11yds. This was run at a good gallop, the leader going off too quick, and the winner progressed again.

3052 JOIN RACING TV NOW H'CAP (A JOCKEY CLUB GRASSROOTS MIDDLE DISTANCE SERIES QUALIFIER) 1m 2f 42y
5:35 (5:35) (Class 5) (0-70,68) 3-Y-O
£4,851 (£1,443; £721; £360; £300; £300) **Stalls** Centre

Form RPR

-022 **1** **Highwaygrey**[10] 2711 3-9-3 64 .... DavidAllan 7 73
(Tim Easterby) *completely missed break: in rr: hdwy over 3f out: led over 1f out: r.o* **5/1**[2]

060- **2** *1 ¼* **Edmond Dantes (IRE)**[207] 8700 3-9-4 65 .... DavidEgan 9 71
(David Menuisier) *hld up: hdwy over 3f out: wnt 2nd over 2f out: rdn and ev ch fr over 1f out: styd on same pce fnl 75yds* **20/1**

00-0 **3** *1 ¼* **Frankadore (IRE)**[27] 2101 3-9-7 68 ....(p[1]) RichardKingscote 4 72
(Tom Dascombe) *led: rdn over 2f out: hdd over 1f out: stl cl up u.p ins fnl f: no ex fnl 75yds* **10/1**[3]

002- **4** *1 ¾* **Swansdown**[183] 9208 3-9-4 65 .... JamesDoyle 6 65
(William Haggas) *hld up: rdn over 3f out: hdwy u.p over 1f out: nt trble ldrs (vet said filly lost its right fore shoe)* **4/6**[1]

0-34 **5** *2 ½* **Kensington Art**[18] 2482 3-9-4 65 .... TonyHamilton 3 60
(Richard Fahey) *midfield: rdn over 2f out: one pce fnl f* **12/1**

0-46 **6** *¾* **George Mallory**[25] 2200 3-9-7 68 .... TomEaves 2 62
(Kevin Ryan) *trckd ldrs: rdn and outpcd 2f out: n.d after* **10/1**[3]

00-0 **7** *1 ½* **Ransomed Dreams (USA)**[32] 1979 3-9-2 63 .... LiamKeniry 8 54
(Ed Walker) *prom: rdn over 2f out: wknd over 1f out* **28/1**

5-30 **8** *9* **She's Apples (IRE)**[44] 1696 3-9-5 66 .... JasonWatson 10 39
(Roger Charlton) *trckd ldrs: rdn over 2f out: wknd over 1f out* **14/1**

2m 9.33s (-1.47) **Going Correction** -0.20s/f (Firm) 8 Ran SP% **117.4**
Speed ratings (Par 99): **97,96,95,93,91 91,89,82**
CSF £96.27 CT £968.14 TOTE £4.60: £1.40, £3.80, £2.30; EX 59.20 Trifecta £349.40.
Owner Reality Partnerships VII **Bred** Habton Farms **Trained** Great Habton, N Yorks

FOCUS
Add 33yds. They went a good gallop and this was run to suit those coming from off the pace. This has been rated in line with the race standard for now.
T/Jkpt: Part won. £10,000.00 to a £1 stake - 0.50 winning units. T/Plt: £23.60 to a £1 stake. Pool: £67,183.10 - 2,077.82 winning units. T/Qpdt: £4.40 to a £1 stake. Pool: £7,423.69 - 1,240.38 winning units. **Darren Owen**

2288 PONTEFRACT (L-H)
Friday, May 24

OFFICIAL GOING: Good to firm (good in places; 8.0)
Wind: Moderate behind Weather: Fine & dry

3053 ALAMO BUSINESS SYSTEMS H'CAP 1m 6y
6:30 (6:30) (Class 5) (0-75,74) 4-Y-O+
£3,881 (£1,155; £577; £400; £400; £400) **Stalls** Low

Form RPR

00-0 **1** **Miss Sheridan (IRE)**[20] 2418 5-9-2 69 .... NathanEvans 2 76
(Michael Easterby) *led 1f: chsd ldr: rdn to chal wl over 1f out and sn led: jnd and drvn ent fnl f: hdd narrowly ins fnl 75yds: led again nr line* **8/1**

0-03 **2** *hd* **Straight Ash (IRE)**[18] 2478 4-8-8 64 .... BenRobinson(3) 3 70
(Ollie Pears) *trckd ldrs on inner: hdwy over 2f out: rdn to chal ent fnl f: drvn and slt ld ins fnl 75yds: hdd and no ex nr line* **5/1**[3]

0-04 **3** *3 ¼* **Quoteline Direct**[23] 2291 6-9-2 69 ....(h) GrahamLee 4 68
(Micky Hammond) *hld up in rr: hdwy 3f out: chsd ldrs appr fnl f: n.m.r and swtchd rt jst ins fnl f: sn rdn and kpt on same pce* **8/1**

60-0 **4** *nk* **Final Frontier (IRE)**[26] 2151 6-9-2 69 ....(b[1]) JackGarritty 5 67
(Ruth Carr) *reminders s and rdn along: rapid hdwy to ld after 1f: pushed along 2f out: rdn and hdd over 1f out: drvn and wknd fnl f* **12/1**

55-4 **5** *1* **Frankster (FR)**[23] 2290 6-8-6 64 ow3 ....(tp) RobJFitzpatrick(5) 1 60
(Micky Hammond) *t.k.h: trckd ldrs: pushed along over 2f out: rdn on outer wl over 1f out: sn drvn and no imp (jockey said ran too free)* **3/1**[1]

1015 **6** *shd* **International Law**[14] 2596 5-9-4 71 .... CamHardie 6 66
(Antony Brittain) *hld up in tch: hdwy 3f out: rdn along over 2f out: sn drvn and btn* **8/1**

The Form Book Flat 2019, Raceform Ltd, Newbury, RG14 5SJ

22-0 **7** 1 1/2 **Trinity Star (IRE)**[56] 1401 8-9-7 **74**............................(v) ConnorBeasley 9 66
(Karen McLintock) *hld up in tch: sme hdwy 3f out: sn rdn along and n.d* **9/2**[2]

6330 **8** 40 **Channel Packet**[46] 1647 5-8-8 **66**............................ TheodoreLadd(5) 7
(Michael Appleby) *chsd ldrs on outer: pushed along 3f out: rdn over 2f out: sn wknd and bhd whn eased fnl f (jockey said horse stopped quickly)* **6/1**

1m 45.48s (-0.42) **Going Correction** -0.05s/f (Good) **8 Ran SP% 115.2**
Speed ratings (Par 103): **100,99,96,96,95 95,93,53**
CSF £47.87 CT £332.77 TOTE £9.00: £2.30, £1.70, £1.90; EX 50.70 Trifecta £289.10.
Owner J Blackburn & A Turton **Bred** Drumlin Bloodstock **Trained** Sheriff Hutton, N Yorks

FOCUS
A dry run up to a meeting staged on watered ground. Rail movements added 8yds to all races. This looks modest, with the one-two rated to form.

3054 CONSTANT SECURITY SERVING YORKSHIRE RACECOURSES H'CAP 1m 4f 5y

7:00 (7:00) (Class 5) (0-70,72) 4-Y-O+
£3,881 (£1,155; £577; £400; £400; £400) **Stalls** Low

Form RPR

2326 **1** **Champagne Rules**[32] 1988 8-9-4 **67**............................ PhilDennis 1 74+
(Sharon Watt) *in tch: smooth hdwy 4f out: trckd ldrs over 2f out: hdwy on outer to chal over 1f out: rdn to ld ent fnl f: kpt on strly* **12/1**

6-06 **2** 1 1/4 **Low Profile**[18] 2479 4-9-5 **68**............................(p) DanielTudhope 4 72
(Rebecca Bastiman) *trckd ldrs: hdwy over 2f out: rdn to ld briefly jst over 1f out: hdd ent fnl f: sn drvn and kpt on* **25/1**

4-00 **3** 3/4 **Airplane (IRE)**[25] 2202 4-8-13 **62**............................ RachelRichardson 6 65
(Tim Easterby) *led: pushed along over 2f out: rdn and hdd wl over 1f out: sn drvn: kpt on u.p fnl f* **22/1**

3242 **4** nse **Duke Of Alba (IRE)**[25] 2202 4-8-12 **61**............................ GrahamLee 12 64
(John Mackie) *trckd ldr: cl up over 3f out: rdn along to ld briefly wl over 1f out: sn hdd and drvn: kpt on same pce fnl f* **5/1**[2]

-401 **5** 1/2 **Just Wait (IRE)**[6] 2819 4-9-4 **72**............................ AndrewBreslin(5) 3 74+
(Mark Johnston) *in rr: pushed along 1/2-way: rdn along 4f out: hdwy 3f out: styd on to chse ldrs fr over 1f out: nrst fin* **1/1**[1]

0-40 **6** 1 1/4 **Zihaam**[19] 2436 5-9-1 **64**............................(p) BenCurtis 2 64
(Roger Fell) *trckd ldrs on inner: pushed along 3f out: rdn 2f out: swtchd rt and drvn ent fnl f: kpt on one pce* **9/1**

306- **7** 1/2 **Correggio**[239] 7714 9-8-2 **51**............................ AndrewMullen 5 50+
(Micky Hammond) *towards rr: hdwy on inner 4f out: chsd ldrs wl over 1f out: sn rdn and no imp fnl f (jockey said gelding was denied a clear run on several occasions in the home straight)* **40/1**

1-20 **8** 8 **Sempre Presto (IRE)**[20] 2399 4-9-2 **70**............................ SeanDavis(5) 9 56
(Richard Fahey) *hld up towards rr: hdwy and in tch 1/2-way: chsd ldrs over 3f out: sn rdn and wknd wl over 2f out* **8/1**[3]

4-20 **9** 6 **Flower Power**[24] 2254 8-9-6 **69**............................(p) DougieCostello 7 46
(Tony Coyle) *hld up: a towards rr* **25/1**

/0-4 **10** 12 **Spark Of War (IRE)**[22] 2330 4-9-0 **63**............................ ShaneGray 10 21
(Keith Dalgleish) *chsd ldrs: rdn along over 3f out: sn wknd* **12/1**

033- **11** 2 3/4 **Jan De Heem**[216] 8416 9-8-6 **55**............................ NathanEvans 8 8
(Tina Jackson) *a towards rr* **50/1**

2514 **12** 19 **Love Rat**[22] 2345 4-8-6 **55**............................(p) PaddyMathers 11
(Scott Dixon) *chsd ldrs on outer: hung rt bnd after 4f: rdn along 5f out: sn lost pl and bhd fnl 3f* **25/1**

2m 39.71s (-1.39) **Going Correction** -0.05s/f (Good) **12 Ran SP% 123.4**
Speed ratings (Par 103): **102,101,100,100,100 99,99,93,89,81 79,67**
CSF £286.80 CT £6381.45 TOTE £12.20: £2.80, £5.80, £5.00; EX 455.20 Trifecta £2182.00.
Owner Rosey Hill Partnership **Bred** Heather Raw **Trained** Brompton-on-Swale, N Yorks

FOCUS
Add 8yds. With short-priced market leader failing to live up to expectations, this didn't take as much winning as seemed likely. This has been rated around the second/third/fourth but with some doubts over the form.

3055 EBF STALLIONS VW VAN CENTRE (LEEDS) LTD YOUNGSTERS CONDITIONS STKS (PLUS 10 RACE) 6f

7:30 (7:31) (Class 2) 2-Y-O **£15,397** (£4,635; £2,317; £1,155) **Stalls** Low

Form RPR

2 **1** **Monoski (USA)**[9] 2747 2-9-2 0............................ PJMcDonald 2 95+
(Mark Johnston) *mde all: rdn and qcknd clr over 1f out: readily* **4/7**[1]

15 **2** 6 **Show Me Show Me**[16] 2520 2-9-5 0............................ PaulHanagan 1 80
(Richard Fahey) *chsd ldng pair: pushed along 1/2-way: rdn 2f out: styd on to chse wnr fnl f: no imp* **9/4**[2]

021 **3** 2 **Daddies Diva**[14] 2579 2-9-0 0............................ DanielTudhope 3 69
(Rod Millman) *trckd wnr: effrt over 2f out: sn rdn: drvn over 1f out: kpt on same pce* **8/1**[3]

00 **4** 5 **Grace Plunkett**[27] 2108 2-8-11 0............................ GrahamLee 4 51
(Richard Spencer) *a in rr: rdn along over 2f out: sn outpcd* **40/1**

1m 16.55s (-0.55) **Going Correction** -0.05s/f (Good) **4 Ran SP% 108.0**
Speed ratings (Par 99): **101,93,90,83**
CSF £2.09 TOTE £1.30; EX 1.90 Trifecta £2.90.
Owner Sheikh Hamdan bin Mohammed Al Maktoum **Bred** Godolphin **Trained** Middleham Moor, N Yorks

FOCUS
Add 8yds. Only four runners and no more than a fair gallop but a smart performance by the winner, who was giving his trainer his third win in the last four renewals of this contest, and who is the sort to improve further.

3056 CONSTANT SECURITY SERVICES H'CAP 5f 3y

8:00 (8:00) (Class 4) (0-80,81) 4-Y-O+
£6,469 (£1,925; £962; £481; £400; £400) **Stalls** Low

Form RPR

3604 **1** **Dapper Man (IRE)**[5] 2876 5-9-2 **72**............................(b) BenCurtis 7 80
(Roger Fell) *mde all: rdn clr over 1f out: drvn ins fnl f: hld on wl towards fin* **13/2**

2260 **2** 1/2 **Socialites Red**[6] 2824 6-8-5 **68**............................(p) WilliamCarver(7) 8 74
(Scott Dixon) *chsd ldng pair: rdn along 2f out: drvn over 1f out: kpt on wl towards fin* **14/1**

4064 **3** nk **Van Gerwen**[17] 2508 6-9-0 **70**............................(p[1]) DavidAllan 1 75
(Les Eyre) *chsd wnr: rdn along wl over 1f out: drvn ins fnl f: kpt on* **5/1**[2]

4461 **4** 1/2 **Musharrif**[5] 2876 7-8-8 **71**............................ ZakWheatley(7) 6 74+
(Declan Carroll) *in tch: hdwy 2f out: rdn to chse ldrs over 1f out: drvn and kpt on fnl f* **9/2**[1]

1030 **5** nk **Another Angel (IRE)**[20] 2421 5-9-7 **77**............................ CamHardie 2 79
(Antony Brittain) *in tch on inner: hdwy 2f out: rdn over 1f out: kpt on fnl f* **12/1**

2430 **6** 1/2 **Amazing Grazing (IRE)**[17] 2508 5-9-0 **73**............................ BenRobinson(3) 4 73
(Rebecca Bastiman) *hld up: hdwy on inner 2f out: rdn over 1f out: kpt on fnl f (jockey said gelding was briefly denied a clear run approaching the final furlong)* **11/2**[3]

-536 **7** 1/2 **Sheepscar Lad (IRE)**[14] 2588 5-9-6 **76**............................ LewisEdmunds 9 75+
(Nigel Tinkler) *towards rr: effrt on outer 2f out: sn rdn: kpt on fnl f* **9/1**

25-0 **8** 1/2 **Case Key**[17] 2508 6-8-9 **70**............................(p) TheodoreLadd(5) 3 67
(Michael Appleby) *chsd ldrs: rdn along 2f out: drvn over 1f out: grad wknd* **12/1**

0425 **9** 1 1/2 **Foxy Forever (IRE)**[6] 2839 9-9-11 **81**............................(bt) ConnorBeasley 5 72
(Michael Wigham) *t.k.h towards rr: hdwy 2f out: n.m.r over 1f out: n.d* **6/1**

40-0 **10** 1/2 **Suitcase 'N' Taxi**[39] 1817 5-8-12 **68**............................ JasonHart 11 58
(Tim Easterby) *in tch: rdn along 2f out: sn wknd* **33/1**

4303 **11** 1 3/4 **Gold Stone**[13] 2637 4-9-0 **70**............................ TomEaves 10 53
(Kevin Ryan) *a in rr* **14/1**

024- **12** 9 **Computable**[230] 7994 5-9-1 **71**............................(e) NathanEvans 12 22
(Tim Easterby) *stdd and swtchd lft s: t.k.h and hld up on outer: a in rr* **28/1**

1m 3.03s (-0.87) **Going Correction** -0.05s/f (Good) **12 Ran SP% 123.0**
Speed ratings (Par 105): **104,103,102,101,101 100,99,99,96,95 93,78**
CSF £97.74 CT £510.38 TOTE £8.60: £2.50, £4.10, £2.20; EX 102.30 Trifecta £495.00.
Owner Colne Valley Racing & Partner **Bred** William Joseph Martin **Trained** Nawton, N Yorks

FOCUS
Add 8yds. Mainly exposed performers in an open handicap. The gallop was sound throughout but only those right up with the pace figured.

3057 NAPOLEONS CASINO BRADFORD FILLIES' H'CAP 1m 2f 5y

8:30 (8:31) (Class 5) (0-70,75) 3-Y-O+
£3,881 (£1,155; £577; £400; £400; £400) **Stalls** Low

Form RPR

0-46 **1** **Navigate By Stars (IRE)**[24] 2253 3-8-12 **68**............................(p[1]) RichardKingscote 6 79+
(Tom Dascombe) *trckd ldrs: hdwy 3f out: chsd ldr wl over 1f out: sn rdn: led ent fnl f: sn jnd and drvn: kpt on wl towards fin* **6/4**[1]

5-01 **2** 1 3/4 **Never Be Enough**[7] 2785 4-10-5 **75** 5ex............................ TomEaves 10 83
(Keith Dalgleish) *hld up in rr: hdwy 3f out: chsd ldrs wl over 1f out: rdn to chal ins fnl f and ev ch: kpt on same pce last 100yds* **4/1**[2]

305 **3** 3 1/2 **Samstar**[31] 2017 3-8-4 **60**............................ JoeFanning 2 60
(Mark Johnston) *trckd ldrs: cl up over 3f out: led wl over 2f out: rdn wl over 1f out: hdd and drvn ent fnl f: kpt on same pce* **5/1**[3]

2341 **4** 4 1/2 **Kilbaha Lady (IRE)**[46] 1647 5-9-9 **68**............................ RowanScott(3) 8 60
(Nigel Tinkler) *hld up: hdwy over 4f out: chsd ldrs 2f out: sn rdn and no imp fnl f* **6/1**

50-0 **5** 6 **Bollin Joan**[13] 2629 4-9-12 **68**............................(p) DavidAllan 7 48
(Tim Easterby) *hmpd s and hld up in rr: sme hdwy over 2f out: plugged on: nvr nr ldrs* **16/1**

5005 **6** 3 1/4 **Beatbybeatbybeat**[44] 1688 6-9-10 **66**............................(v) CamHardie 9 40
(Antony Brittain) *hld up: hdwy on outer over 2f out: sn rdn and nvr a factor* **20/1**

00-6 **7** 1 **Moretti (IRE)**[84] 969 4-8-9 **51** oh3............................ NathanEvans 5 23
(Les Eyre) *sn led: pushed along over 3f out: rdn and hdd wl over 2f out: sn wknd (jockey said filly ran too free)* **12/1**

640 **8** 17 **Hikayah**[31] 2018 3-8-6 **62**............................(p) ShaneGray 3
(David O'Meara) *chsd ldrs on inner: rdn along 3f out: sn wknd* **16/1**

6000 **9** 8 **Bravantina**[25] 2202 4-8-9 **51** oh1............................ JasonHart 1
(Mark Walford) *chsd ldng pair: rdn along over 3f out: sn wknd (jockey said filly hung right-handed throughout)* **33/1**

-000 **10** 10 **Lots Ov (IRE)**[45] 1663 5-8-9 **51** oh6............................(p) RachelRichardson 4
(John Wainwright) *chsd ldrs: rdn along 4f out: sn wknd* **66/1**

2m 13.38s (-1.62) **Going Correction** -0.05s/f (Good)
WFA 3 from 4yo+ 14lb **10 Ran SP% 119.6**
Speed ratings (Par 100): **104,102,99,96,91 88,88,74,68,60**
CSF £7.46 CT £24.87 TOTE £2.40: £1.30, £1.60, £2.00; EX 9.10 Trifecta £53.60.
Owner The Wilmshurst Partnership **Bred** Sunderland Holdings Inc **Trained** Malpas, Cheshire

FOCUS
Add 8yds. A couple of unexposed types and a race in which the gallop was reasonable. It's worth viewing the form of the first two in a positive light. This could prove better than rated, with the third unexposed.

3058 VIRGINIA BEARDSLEY 50TH BIRTHDAY NOVICE STKS 6f

9:00 (9:00) (Class 5) 3-Y-O+ **£3,881** (£1,155; £577; £288) **Stalls** Low

Form RPR

32 **1** **After John**[7] 2794 3-9-2 0............................ BenCurtis 5 85
(Mick Channon) *trckd ldr: hdwy and cl up over 2f out: rdn to ld 1 1/2f out: drvn ins fnl f: kpt on strly* **7/4**[2]

3-32 **2** 2 1/4 **Qutob (IRE)**[20] 2405 3-9-2 80............................ PJMcDonald 4 78
(Charles Hills) *dwlt: hld up in rr: hdwy 3f out: chsd ldng pair 2f out: rdn to chse wnr and edgd lft ins fnl f: sn drvn and one pce* **1/1**[1]

20-5 **3** 2 3/4 **Dream Of Honour (IRE)**[17] 2506 3-9-2 77............................(p) DavidAllan 2 69
(Tim Easterby) *led: rdn along over 2f out: hdd 1 1/2f out: sn drvn: kpt on same pce fnl f* **6/1**[3]

3-2 **4** 2 3/4 **Texting**[39] 1816 3-8-11 0............................ JasonHart 3 55
(Mohamed Moubarak) *chsd ldrs: rdn along 2f out: drvn and no imp appr fnl f* **12/1**

50-5 **5** 10 **The Gingerbreadman**[16] 2532 4-9-6 41............................ PaulaMuir(5) 1 30
(Chris Fairhurst) *chsd ldrs: rdn along 3f out: outpcd fnl 2f* **50/1**

1m 16.26s (-0.84) **Going Correction** -0.05s/f (Good)
WFA 3 from 4yo 9lb **5 Ran SP% 110.3**
Speed ratings (Par 103): **103,100,96,92,79**
CSF £3.87 TOTE £2.70: £1.40, £1.10; EX 3.80 Trifecta £8.10.
Owner Mrs John Lee, Alf Heaney, Alec Tuckerman **Bred** Southcourt Stud **Trained** West Ilsley, Berks

FOCUS
Not much in the way of a gallop but a useful effort from the winner. The race distance increased by 8yds due to rail movements. The winner progressed again but the runner-up has been rated a bit below form.

T/Plt: £1,546.80 to a £1 stake. Pool: £68,761.62 - 32.45 winning units. T/Qpdt: £6.70 to a £1 stake. Pool: £7,856.36 - 864.58 winning units. **Joe Rowntree**

3059 - 3061a (Foreign Racing) - See Raceform Interactive

2490 CURRAGH (R-H)
Friday, May 24

OFFICIAL GOING: Good to firm (good in places on straight course; watered)

3062a TRM EXCELLENCE IN EQUINE NUTRITION H'CAP (PREMIER HANDICAP) 7f
6:35 (6:37) 4-Y-0+

£53,153 (£17,117; £8,108; £3,603; £1,801; £900)

RPR

1 **Jassaar**[27] 2133 4-7-13 **85**............................ AndrewSlattery(7) 6 90
(D K Weld, Ire) *cl up bhd ldr early: 4th 1/2-way: impr to dispute ld under 2f out and led narrowly gng best over 1f out: sn rdn and kpt on wl u.p ins fnl f: reduced ld cl home where pressed* **9/2**[1]

2 ½ **Flight Risk (IRE)**[209] 8654 8-9-13 **106**............................ KevinManning 1 110
(J S Bolger, Ire) *hld up in tch: disp 6th at 1/2-way: tk clsr order in 4th over 1f out: n.m.r ins fnl f and swtchd lft: rdn into 2nd and r.o to press wnr cl home: nrst fin* **16/1**

3 1¾ **Texas Rock (IRE)**[5] 2879 8-9-1 **94**............................(p) RobbieColgan 13 93+
(M C Grassick, Ire) *chsd ldrs early: 2nd 1/2-way: disp ld nr side fr 2f out tl rdn and hdd over 1f out: no imp on wnr ins fnl f where sltly impeded and dropped to 3rd: kpt on same pce* **14/1**

4 hd **Verhoyen**[13] 2640 4-8-4 **83** oh2............................(b) WayneLordan 2 82
(M C Grassick, Ire) *trckd ldrs in 3rd early tl impr to sn ld: rdn and jnd 2f out: hdd u.p over 1f out and no imp on wnr in 4th far side wl ins fnl f: kpt on same pce* **20/1**

5 ½ **Annie Fior (IRE)**[5] 2879 5-8-3 **87**............................ DannySheehy(5) 15 84+
(B A Murphy, Ire) *dwlt sltly: sn settled in mid-div early: clsr in 5th bef 1/2-way: rdn over 2f out and no imp on ldrs u.p in 6th ins fnl f: swtchd rt wl ins fnl f and kpt on again into 5th cl home* **16/1**

6 hd **St Brelades Bay (IRE)**[14] 2604 7-8-13 **92**............................(t[1]) ShaneFoley 11 89+
(Mrs John Harrington, Ire) *in rr of mid-div: 9th 1/2-way: prog u.p over 1f out: no imp on wnr in 5th wl ins fnl f: no ex nr fin where dropped to 6th* **8/1**[3]

7 ¾ **Kimifive (IRE)**[13] 2609 4-9-2 **95**............................ RyanMoore 5 90
(Joseph Tuite) *hld up in rr of mid-div: 10th 1/2-way: tk clsr order and pushed along 2f out: rdn in 7th over 1f out and no imp on ldrs: kpt on one pce* **9/2**[1]

8 nk **Freescape**[85] 960 4-9-0 **96**............................(b) OisinOrr(3) 3 90
(David Marnane, Ire) *dwlt: towards rr: 11th 1/2-way: sme hdwy far side under 2f out: rdn in 8th over 1f out and sn no ex* **20/1**

9 hd **Ahlan Bil Zain (FR)**[18] 2497 5-8-4 **83** oh1............................(b) ConorHoban 10 76
(M Halford, Ire) *dwlt: in rr: 13th 1/2-way: rdn 2f out: no imp over 1f out: no ex* **33/1**

10 nse **Saltonstall**[18] 2497 5-9-1 **94**............................(t[1]) RonanWhelan 4 87
(Adrian McGuinness, Ire) *hld up: pushed along in rr fr 1/2-way and no imp u.p 1 1/2f out: r.o ins fnl f: nvr on terms* **10/1**

11 ¾ **Downforce (IRE)**[29] 2069 7-9-10 **103**............................(v) WJLee 8 94
(W McCreery, Ire) *hld up in tch: 8th 1/2-way: gng wl bhd horses 2f out where nt clr run: pushed along over 1f out and sn no imp u.p in 10th ins fnl f: one pce nr fin* **16/1**

12 ¾ **Equitant**[113] 513 4-9-2 **95**............................ DonnachaO'Brien 7 84
(Joseph Patrick O'Brien, Ire) *broke wl to ld briefly tl sn settled bhd ldrs: disp 6th at 1/2-way: pushed along after 1/2-way and n.m.r under 2f out: swtchd rt over 1f out and no ex towards rr: one pce after* **14/1**

13 1 **Turbine (IRE)**[14] 2604 6-8-5 **84**............................(tp) RoryCleary 12 71
(Denis Gerard Hogan, Ire) *chsd ldrs: pushed along in 3rd fr 1/2-way and sn no ex bhd ldrs u.p over 2f out: wknd* **9/1**

14 2 **Sanaadh**[13] 2609 6-9-3 **96**............................(t) ColinKeane 14 77
(Michael Wigham) *dwlt: towards rr: 12th 1/2-way: drvn nr side 2f out and no ex u.p 1 1/2f out: wknd and eased ins fnl f* **13/2**[2]

1m 23.68s (-1.32) **Going Correction** -0.025s/f (Good) **14 Ran SP% 123.3**
Speed ratings: **106,105,103,103,102 102,101,101,100,100 100,99,98,95**
CSF £80.11 CT £981.75 TOTE £4.50: £1.80, £4.00, £4.20; DF 61.90 Trifecta £454.30.
Owner Hamdan Al Maktoum **Bred** Shadwell Estate Company Limited **Trained** Curragh, Co Kildare

FOCUS
A pb from the winner, with the second and third helping to set the standard.

3063a KERRYGOLD GALLINULE STKS (GROUP 3) 1m 2f
7:05 (7:09) 3-Y-0

£34,549 (£11,126; £5,270; £2,342; £1,171; £585)

RPR

1 **Constantinople (IRE)**[47] 1621 3-9-3 99............................ RyanMoore 3 108+
(A P O'Brien, Ire) *hld up towards rr: 6th 1/2-way: tk clsr order bhd ldrs fr 3f out: 3rd over 2f out: rdn into 2nd ins fnl f and r.o wl cl home: readily* **10/11**[1]

2 ½ **Buckhurst (IRE)**[12] 2662 3-9-3 0............................ DonnachaO'Brien 4 107
(Joseph Patrick O'Brien, Ire) *cl up bhd ldr early: dropped to 3rd after 1f: tk clsr order in 2nd after 1/2-way and led gng wl over 2f out: rdn ent fnl f and strly pressed wl ins fnl f: hdd cl home* **6/1**[3]

3 4¼ **U S S Michigan (USA)**[18] 2492 3-9-3 98............................ SeamieHeffernan 6 98+
(A P O'Brien, Ire) *led tl jnd briefly bef 1/2-way: drvn w narrow advantage 3f out and hdd over 2f out: no ex u.p ins fnl f where dropped to 3rd: one pce nr fin where pressed for 3rd* **7/1**

4 ½ **Antilles (USA)**[18] 2492 3-9-3 103............................ WayneLordan 2 97
(A P O'Brien, Ire) *s.i.s: in rr: last at 1/2-way: pushed along bef st and sme hdwy fr over 2f out between horses into 4th over 1f out where rdn briefly: r.o under hands and heels ins fnl f: nvr nrr* **12/1**

5 7 **Wee Jim (IRE)**[265] 6833 3-9-3 92............................ DeclanMcDonogh 7 83
(Luke Comer, Ire) *reluctant and hooded to load: trckd ldrs early tl impr into 2nd after 1f: disp ld briefly bef 1/2-way: hung sltly after 1/2-way where dropped to 3rd: rdn over 2f out and sn wknd* **50/1**

6 shd **Bold Approach (IRE)**[302] 5408 3-9-3 96............................ KevinManning 1 83
(J S Bolger, Ire) *dwlt and pushed along towards rr briefly after s: disp 4th at 1/2-way: rdn bhd ldrs over 2f out and sn no ex: wknd over 1f out* **14/1**

7 8 **Tinandali (IRE)**[51] 1529 3-9-3 91............................ ChrisHayes 5 67
(D K Weld, Ire) *trckd ldrs in 3rd and t.k.h early 4th after 1f: disp 4th at 1/2-way: disp 3rd briefly on outer over 3f out: eased to rr over 2f (jockey said regarding running that his instructions were to sit in second or third position, and to get his mount to stay on as best he could. The jockey stated that his mount got worked up on the way to the start and also down at the stalls. In running* **7/2**[2]

2m 10.23s (-1.27) **Going Correction** -0.025s/f (Good) **7 Ran SP% 117.7**
Speed ratings: **104,103,100,99,94 94,87**
CSF £7.54 TOTE £1.60: £1.20, £2.70; DF 7.00 Trifecta £27.30.
Owner Derrick Smith & Mrs John Magnier & Michael Tabor **Bred** One Moment In Time Syndicate **Trained** Cashel, Co Tipperary

FOCUS
A 16th win in this race for Aidan O'Brien. The first two posted personal bests.

3064 - 3065a (Foreign Racing) - See Raceform Interactive

DIEPPE (R-H)
Friday, May 24

OFFICIAL GOING: Turf: soft

3066a PRIX MARIE AMELIE (CLAIMER) (3YO) (TURF) 5f 110y
6:50 3-Y-0 £6,756 (£2,702; £2,027; £1,351; £675)

RPR

1 **Spanish Miss (IRE)**[13] 3-9-1 0............................ TonyPiccone 8 78
(M Delcher Sanchez, France) **5/2**[1]

2 5 **Hit The Track Jack**[21] 2392 3-8-5 0 ow1............................ JeremieMonteiro(7) 2 59
(N Caullery, France) **24/1**

3 1¾ **Imotep (FR)**[13] 3-8-8 0............................ MlleCoraliePacaut(3) 9 52
(M Boutin, France) **12/1**

4 1¼ **Velvet Vixen (IRE)**[21] 2392 3-9-1 0............................(h) MickaelBarzalona 13 52
(Jo Hughes, France) *away wl fr wd draw: sn cl up towards ins rail: drvn ins fnl 2f but no imp: kpt on at same pce fnl f* **8/1**

5 1¾ **Will Ness (IRE)**[205] 8753 3-9-1 0............................ JeromeMoutard 4 46
(D Allard, France) **31/1**

6 ½ **Blury (ITY)**[21] 2392 3-9-4 0............................ CristianDemuro 15 48
(Andrea Marcialis, France) **22/5**[3]

7 1¼ **Elieden (IRE)**[21] 2390 3-8-8 0............................(b) AlexisBadel 1 33
(Gay Kelleway) *broke wl: chsd ldr on rail: drvn and nt match ldrs fnl 1 1/2f* **4/1**[2]

8 3 **Charlene Du Champ (FR)**[217] 8400 3-8-3 0............................ AlexisPouchin(5) 10 24
(Tamara Richter, Austria) **93/1**

9 nk **Oui Madame (IRE)**[13] 3-8-6 0............................(p) MlleChloeHue(9) 16 30
(Hue & Lamotte D'Argy, France) **50/1**

10 nk **Fabled (FR)**[15] 3-9-1 0............................(b) EddyHardouin 3 29
(Matthieu Palussiere, France) **42/1**

11 1 **Hello Is You (FR)**[23] 3-8-4 0............................(b[1]) BenjaminMarie(7) 7 21
(F Head, France) **41/5**

12 1¼ **Hamper (FR)**[13] 3-8-8 0............................(p) FrancoisRenaut(8) 5 22
(P Adda, France) **45/1**

13 1¾ **Sign O'The Time (FR)**[57] 3-8-8 0............................ MickaelBerto 6 8
(J Parize, France) **58/1**

14 hd **Wakily (FR)**[285] 3-8-5 0............................ MlleAlisonMassin(3) 12 8
(H Fortineau, France) **129/1**

15 4 **Adirondack (IRE)**[28] 2090 3-8-6 0............................(b) ThomasTrullier(5) 14
(F Chappet, France) **47/1**

16 8 **Oh Say Can You See (FR)**[21] 2392 3-8-11 0............................(b[1]) AntoineHamelin 11
(Matthieu Palussiere, France) **31/1**

1m 2.92s **16 Ran SP% 119.1**
PARI-MUTUEL (all including 1 euro stake): WIN 3.50; PLACE 1.60, 5.00, 2.70; DF 32.00.
Owner J Maldonado Trinchant **Bred** Mrs Diane Williams **Trained** France

2572 CHESTER (L-H)
Saturday, May 25

OFFICIAL GOING: Good (good to firm in places; watered; 7.9)
Wind: Moderate, half against in straight of over 1f Weather: Cloudy

3067 CONTROLLED SOLUTIONS GROUP NOVICE STKS 7f 127y
1:45 (1:47) (Class 4) 3-Y-0+

£6,162 (£1,845; £922; £461; £230; £115) **Stalls Low**

Form RPR

2-3 1 **Hero Hero (IRE)**[30] 2060 3-9-2 0............................ SilvestreDeSousa 4 95+
(Andrew Balding) *mde all: a in control: wnt clr ins fnl f: easily* **4/7**[1]

5 2 8 **Guandi (USA)**[42] 1754 3-8-13 0............................ JaneElliott(3) 8 71
(Tom Dascombe) *chsd wnr to 5f out: remained prom: rdn to take 2nd ent fnl 2f: no ch w wnr fnl f* **6/1**[3]

0 3 1¼ **Torochica**[25] 2236 3-8-11 0............................ KierenFox 5 63
(John Best) *dwlt: towards rr: hdwy 4f out: styd on u.p ins fnl f: tk 3rd towards fin: nvr able to chal* **25/1**

2 4 1½ **Bardo Contiguo (IRE)**[18] 2518 3-9-2 0............................ JackMitchell 6 65
(Roger Varian) *chsd ldrs: rdn over 2f out: one pce over 1f out: no ex ins fnl f* **5/2**[2]

5636 5 9 **Caledonian Gold**[2] 3007 6-9-9 44............................ RossaRyan 9 40
(Lisa Williamson) *midfield: hdwy over 3f out: rdn to chse ldrs over 2f out: wknd ins fnl f* **66/1**

6 4 **Mogsy (IRE)** 3-9-2 0............................ DavidProbert 12 32
(Tom Dascombe) *prom: chsd wnr 5f out: rdn over 2f out: lost 2nd ent fnl 2f: sn wknd* **14/1**

0500 7 4 **Lambrini Lullaby**[23] 2318 4-9-4 43............................ ConnorMurtagh(5) 2 20
(Lisa Williamson) *dwlt: midfield: rdn over 2f out: wknd over 1f out* **100/1**

0600 8 7 **Just Heather (IRE)**[33] 1983 5-9-9 39............................(p) JackGarritty 11 3
(John Wainwright) *bhd: hdwy u.p over 2f out: nvr able to get involved* **100/1**

0-0 9 11 **Dolly McQueen**[15] 2583 3-8-11 0............................ CallumShepherd 7
(Anthony Carson) *dwlt: towards rr: rdn over 4f out: nvr on terms* **66/1**

0000 10 2¾ **Isabella Red (IRE)**[6] 2871 3-8-4 42............................(b) GavinAshton(7) 3
(Lisa Williamson) *wnt lft s: chsd ldrs tl rdn and wknd 3f out* **100/1**

0000 11 nk **Mr Wing (IRE)**[23] 2350 4-9-7 17............................ VictorSantos(7) 10
(John Wainwright) *sn pushed along: midfield on outer: wknd over 3f out* **100/1**

The Form Book Flat 2019, Raceform Ltd, Newbury, RG14 5SJ

12 12 **Piccolo Ramoscello**[157] 6-9-2 0......................(b[1]) ElishaWhittington(7) 1
(Lisa Williamson) *dwlt: rdn over 4f out: a bhd: nvr on terms (jockey said mare was never travelling)* **100/1**

1m 35.04s (-0.66) **Going Correction** +0.15s/f (Good)
WFA 3 from 4yo+ 12lb **12** Ran SP% **125.0**
Speed ratings (Par 105): **105,97,95,94,85 81,77,70,59,56 56,44**
CSF £5.45 TOTE £1.30: £1.10, £1.20, £7.50; EX 6.40 Trifecta £58.00.
Owner King Power Racing Co Ltd **Bred** Fancy Syndicate **Trained** Kingsclere, Hants

FOCUS
The rail was moved out after the May Festival to provide fresher ground. Add 37 yards. There weren't too many in here with serious winning claims, as the market highlighted.

3068 CHESTER HERITAGE FESTIVAL FILLIES' H'CAP 6f 17y
2:20 (2:21) (Class 4) (0-85,87) 3-Y-O
£8,021 (£2,387; £1,192; £596; £500; £500) **Stalls** Low

Form RPR
1115 1 **Probability (IRE)**[32] 2008 3-9-7 **85**.................................. HollieDoyle 5 91
(Archie Watson) *in tch: effrt over 2f out: led over 1f out: narrowly hdd briefly ins fnl f: kpt on wl towards fin* **8/1**
3-02 2 *nk* **Be Like Me (IRE)**[32] 2008 3-9-2 **83**......................... GabrieleMalune(3) 9 88
(Marco Botti) *midfield: hdwy 2f out: nosed ahd briefly ins fnl f: hld towards fin* **12/1**
0-34 3 *1* **Pass The Gin**[17] 2525 3-9-4 **82**.. DavidProbert 3 84
(Andrew Balding) *racd keenly: in tch: rdn over 1f out: styd on to chse ldrs ins fnl f: styd on same pce fnl 100yds* **9/4**[1]
01-4 4 *1 ¾* **Society Queen (IRE)**[17] 2522 3-9-4 **82**............................ DavidNolan 10 78
(Richard Fahey) *missed break: hld up in rr: rdn over 1f out: hdwy sn after: styd on u.p ins fnl f: no imp on front trio fnl 75yds* **8/1**
-203 5 *¾* **Princess Power (IRE)**[17] 2525 3-9-6 **84**...................... AndrewMullen 2 78
(Nigel Tinkler) *hld up towards rr: rdn and hdwy 1f out: kpt on u.p ins fnl f: nvr able to chal* **7/2**[2]
4251 6 *¾* **Wedding Date**[8] 2810 3-9-6 **87**................................... JamieGormley(3) 7 79
(Richard Hannon) *hld up towards rr: pushed along 2f out: swtchd rt ins fnl f: kpt on: nvr able to get involved* **4/1**[3]
43-0 7 *2 ¼* **No More Regrets (IRE)**[17] 2522 3-8-13 **77**................. StevieDonohoe 4 61
(Patrick Morris) *prom: chsd ldr 3f out tl rdn wl over 1f out: wknd wl ins fnl f* **33/1**
4334 8 *2* **Key To Power**[10] 2730 3-8-9 **73**............................... SilvestreDeSousa 6 51
(Mark Johnston) *led: rdn 2f out: hdd over 1f out: wknd ins fnl f (jockey said filly hung right from 2f out)* **8/1**
15-0 9 *6* **Sylvia's Mother**[27] 2149 3-8-8 **72**............................... CallumShepherd 1 31
(Joseph Tuite) *broke wl: chsd ldr to 3f out: sn rdn: wknd over 1f out* **20/1**

1m 16.4s (0.90) **Going Correction** +0.15s/f (Good) **9** Ran SP% **121.7**
Speed ratings (Par 98): **100,99,98,95,94 93,90,88,80**
CSF £103.55 CT £292.78 TOTE £9.50: £2.30, £3.70, £1.30; EX 106.30 Trifecta £493.40.
Owner Mrs C Cashman **Bred** Marie & Mossy Fahy **Trained** Upper Lambourn, W Berks

FOCUS
Add 37 yards. This was well contested and was won in admirable fashion by prolific AW scorer Probability on her belated turf debut. The third has been rated close to her C&D latest.

3069 MBNA H'CAP 7f 127y
2:55 (2:56) (Class 2) (0-105,104) 4-Y-O+
£28,012 (£8,388; £4,194; £2,097; £1,048; £526) **Stalls** Low

Form RPR
-023 1 **Kaeso**[14] 2609 5-8-7 **90**... HollieDoyle 6 97
(Nigel Tinkler) *racd keenly: effrt over 1f out: r.o to ld wl ins fnl f: pushed out cl home* **3/1**[2]
0263 2 *½* **Masham Star (IRE)**[7] 2832 5-8-10 **93**..................... SilvestreDeSousa 11 99
(Mark Johnston) *chsd ldr: rdn to ld over 1f out: hdd wl ins fnl f: hld cl home* **12/1**
-305 3 *½* **Gabrial (IRE)**[15] 2573 10-9-3 **100**...................................... DavidNolan 2 105
(Richard Fahey) *midfield: rdn and hdwy over 1f out whn plld off rail: styd on ins fnl f: gng on at fin* **20/1**
-002 4 *nk* **Gabrial The Saint (IRE)**[15] 2572 4-8-5 **88**.................... AndrewMullen 8 92
(Richard Fahey) *racd keenly: in tch: rdn 2f out: nt clr run and swtchd rt over 1f out: styd on ins fnl f: nvr able to chal wnr* **7/1**[3]
1201 5 *1 ¼* **Sha La La La Lee**[15] 2572 4-8-7 **93**........................... JaneElliott(3) 9 94+
(Tom Dascombe) *missed break: towards rr: pushed along 5f out: hdwy u.p ins fnl f: styd on towards fin: nvr able to trble ldrs (jockey said gelding was slowly away)* **8/1**
0-03 6 *nk* **Baraweez (IRE)**[15] 2572 9-8-5 **91**............................... BenRobinson(3) 5 91
(Brian Ellison) *midfield: pushed along 2f out: rdn over 1f out: styd on ins fnl f: no further imp nr fin and nt rch ldrs* **8/1**
00-4 7 *1 ¼* **Aces (IRE)**[15] 2572 7-8-12 **95**.. StevieDonohoe 3 92
(Ian Williams) *chsd ldrs: rdn over 2f out: unable qck over 1f out: one pce fnl 150yds* **8/1**
-015 8 *1 ¼* **Crossing The Line**[36] 1918 4-9-3 **100**............................. DavidProbert 1 94
(Andrew Balding) *towards rr: rdn 2f out: nvr able to get involved* **5/2**[1]
400 9 *¾* **Arcanada (IRE)**[7] 2832 6-8-0 **88**............................(v[1]) TheodoreLadd(5) 7 80
(Tom Dascombe) *led: rdn and hdd over 1f out: sn edgd rt: wknd fnl 150yds* **20/1**
051- 10 *4* **Di Fede (IRE)**[231] 7978 4-9-7 **104**............................ JosephineGordon 4 86
(Ralph Beckett) *missed break: in rr: pushed along over 3f out: rdn on wd outer over 1f out: no imp* **14/1**

1m 34.17s (-1.53) **Going Correction** +0.15s/f (Good) **10** Ran SP% **123.3**
Speed ratings (Par 109): **109,108,108,107,106 106,104,103,102,98**
CSF £41.73 CT £637.72 TOTE £4.40: £2.00, £2.10, £5.50; EX 39.60 Trifecta £744.20.
Owner M Webb **Bred** Sir Eric Parker **Trained** Langton, N Yorks

FOCUS
Add 37 yards. A competitive feature with some consistent sorts fighting out the finish. It's been rated around the second to his best form in Britain since his 3yo days.

3070 CANTER CARPET H'CAP 1m 5f 84y
3:30 (3:30) (Class 3) (0-90,89) 4-Y-O+
£13,383 (£4,007; £2,003; £1,001; £500; £500) **Stalls** Low

Form RPR
6123 1 **Eddystone Rock (IRE)**[14] 2606 7-9-7 **89**............................ KierenFox 5 96
(John Best) *s.i.s: hld up: hdwy ent fnl 2f: edgd lft over 1f out: r.o to ld wl ins fnl f: in command nr fin* **4/1**[3]
0-54 2 *1* **Ravenous**[12] 1693 8-8-2 **75**...................................... TheodoreLadd(5) 4 80
(Luke Dace) *led after 1f: rdn over 2f out: hdd wl ins fnl f: no ex fnl strides* **12/1**
1231 3 *1* **Claire Underwood (IRE)**[22] 2370 4-8-13 **86**.......... ConnorMurtagh(5) 6 89
(Richard Fahey) *chsd ldrs: wnt 2nd over 2f out: drvn and unable qck ins fnl f: sn lost 2nd: styd on same pce fnl 100yds* **5/2**[1]
-603 4 *3 ¼* **Super Kid**[14] 2636 7-8-8 **76**...................................(t[1]) SilvestreDeSousa 8 74
(Tim Easterby) *in tch: drvn over 1f out: kpt on ins fnl f: no imp on ldrs* **4/1**[3]
2-53 5 *1 ¼* **Jabbaar**[20] 2435 6-9-2 **87**... JamieGormley(3) 7 83
(Iain Jardine) *missed break: hld up: rdn 4f out: drvn over 2f out: nvr able to trble ldrs (jockey said gelding ran flat; post-race examination failed to reveal any abnormalities)* **3/1**[2]
6 *2 ¼* **Dawn Trouper (IRE)**[169] 9454 4-9-2 **84**.........................(t) RossaRyan 1 77
(Nigel Hawke) *led for 1f: chsd ldr tl rdn over 2f out: wknd over 1f out* **12/1**
04-4 7 *7* **Machine Learner**[24] 2278 6-9-5 **87**................................... DavidProbert 3 68
(Joseph Tuite) *in tch: rdn 3f out: drvn and wknd over 1f out* **12/1**

2m 59.11s (2.51) **Going Correction** +0.15s/f (Good) **7** Ran SP% **116.6**
Speed ratings (Par 107): **98,97,96,94,94 92,88**
CSF £50.14 CT £143.68 TOTE £4.50: £1.90, £4.90; EX 37.50 Trifecta £153.80.
Owner Curtis, Malt & Williams **Bred** Ballygallon Stud Limited **Trained** Oad Street, Kent

FOCUS
Add 67 yards. A decent staying handicap and a good performance from top weight Eddystone Rock on his first visit to Chester. The second sets the level.

3071 BRITISH STALLION STUDS EBF MAIDEN STKS (PLUS 10 RACE) 6f 17y
4:05 (4:06) (Class 2) 2-Y-O
£11,827 (£3,541; £1,770; £885; £500; £500) **Stalls** Low

Form RPR
2 1 **Raffle Prize (IRE)**[7] 2836 2-9-0 0............................ SilvestreDeSousa 1 90+
(Mark Johnston) *chsd ldr: led over 4f out: rdn over 1f out: r.o wl to draw clr ins fnl f* **8/13**[1]
6 2 *5* **The New Marwan**[16] 2561 2-9-5 0.. JackGarritty 4 80+
(Richard Fahey) *racd off the pce: sn pushed along: outpcd over 4f out: clsd on front trio 2f out: styd on to take 2nd ins fnl f: no ch w wnr* **10/1**
5 3 *2 ¼* **Endowed**[14] 2610 2-9-5 0... RossaRyan 5 73
(Richard Hannon) *chsd ldrs: wnt 2nd 2f out: rdn and hung lft over 1f out: no imp on wnr: lost 2nd ins fnl f: no ex* **3/1**[2]
4 *7* **We Owen A Dragon** 2-9-5 0.. DavidProbert 3 52
(Tom Dascombe) *squeezed out jst after s and shuffled bk to last pl: outpcd: plugged on to chse front three ins fnl f: nvr any ch* **14/1**
42 5 *10* **It's Been Noted**[16] 2561 2-9-5 0.. JaneElliott 6 22
(Tom Dascombe) *displayed gd pce and led: hdd over 4f out: rdn over 2f out: sn lost 2nd: wknd over 1f out* **8/1**[3]
0 6 *22* **G For Gabrial (IRE)**[16] 2561 2-9-5 0........................... ConnorMurtagh 2
(Richard Fahey) *sn rdn along: a outpcd and bhd* **25/1**

1m 16.66s (1.16) **Going Correction** +0.15s/f (Good) **6** Ran SP% **117.6**
Speed ratings (Par 99): **98,91,88,79,65 36**
CSF £8.98 TOTE £1.40: £1.30, £2.90; EX 7.50 Trifecta £24.10.
Owner Sheikh Hamdan bin Mohammed Al Maktoum **Bred** Godolphin **Trained** Middleham Moor, N Yorks

FOCUS
Add 37 yards. This was strongly run and was won emphatically by the heavily punted favourite.

3072 1539 H'CAP 1m 2f 70y
4:40 (4:40) (Class 4) (0-85,83) 4-Y-O+
£6,404 (£1,905; £952; £476; £300; £300) **Stalls** High

Form RPR
341- 1 **Hats Off To Larry**[182] 6358 5-9-0 **76**............................ CallumShepherd 6 85
(Mick Channon) *hld up: hdwy over 2f out: rdn to ld 1f out: r.o ins fnl f: in command fnl 100yds* **9/1**
0-56 2 *1 ¾* **Humble Gratitude**[17] 2526 4-9-4 **80**............................ StevieDonohoe 2 85
(Ian Williams) *chsd ldrs: rdn over 2f out: led briefly over 1f out: styd on same pce and hld fnl 100yds* **9/1**
0342 3 *½* **Sands Chorus**[19] 2479 7-8-10 **77**..........................(p) TheodoreLadd(5) 8 81
(Scott Dixon) *led: rdn over 2f out: hdd over 1f out: styd on same pce ins fnl f* **13/2**[3]
30-0 4 *1 ½* **Mikmak**[11] 2710 6-9-7 **83**..(p) NathanEvans 9 84
(Tim Easterby) *missed break: in rr: effrt 2f out: styd on to chse front three ins fnl f: nvr able to chal (jockey said gelding anticipated the start, hit the gates and stumbled as a result)* **14/1**
5-11 5 *3* **Simoon (IRE)**[12] 2691 5-9-7 **83**.. DavidProbert 5 78
(Andrew Balding) *midfield: hdwy 3f out: rdn and ev ch ent fnl 2f: unable qck over 1f out: no ex ins fnl f* **1/1**[1]
6450 6 *3 ½* **Mickey (IRE)**[45] 1694 6-9-0 **79**.................................(v) JaneElliott(3) 7 67
(Tom Dascombe) *racd keenly: w ldr for nrly 3f: remained prom: rdn over 2f out: wknd over 1f out* **20/1**
050- 7 *4 ½* **Chai Chai (IRE)**[247] 7447 4-9-3 **79**.....................(t[1] w) SilvestreDeSousa 4 58
(Tom Dascombe) *chsd ldrs: lost pl over 2f out: sn pushed along: wknd over 1f out* **6/1**[2]
-605 8 *¾* **Indomeneo**[15] 2577 4-8-13 **80**................................... ConnorMurtagh(5) 3 58
(Richard Fahey) *hld up: rdn and outpcd over 1f out: nvr a threat* **9/1**

2m 14.36s (0.06) **Going Correction** +0.15s/f (Good) **8** Ran SP% **119.0**
Speed ratings (Par 105): **105,103,103,102,99 96,93,92**
CSF £88.94 CT £570.19 TOTE £10.70: £2.80, £2.60, £2.00; EX 110.40 Trifecta £794.00.
Owner T Radford & Partner **Bred** W A Harrison-Allan **Trained** West Ilsley, Berks

FOCUS
Add 41 yards. A fair handicap but it was run at a stop/starting pace and proved a bit messy. The fourth has been rated close to his recent form.

3073 THYME PEOPLE H'CAP 1m 4f 63y
5:15 (5:17) (Class 4) (0-85,85) 3-Y-O+
£6,404 (£1,905; £952; £476; £300; £300) **Stalls** Low

Form RPR
1-35 1 **Gabrial The One (IRE)**[16] 2562 3-7-12 **77**......................... SeanDavis(5) 5 85
(Richard Fahey) *hld up: rdn and hdwy over 3f out: chsd ldrs 2f out: chalng and hung lft over 1f out: hung lft and led ins fnl f: r.o: cosily* **4/1**[3]
1-33 2 *¾* **Never Do Nothing (IRE)**[20] 2446 3-8-8 **82**..................... DavidProbert 4 88
(Andrew Balding) *s.i.s: hld up: hdwy after 2f: chse ldr after 4f: chalng fr 3f out: rdn over 2f out: stl ev ch ins fnl f: nt pce of wnr fnl 100yds but kpt on (jockey said gelding hung right when in front)* **3/1**[1]
1452 3 *1* **Berrahri (IRE)**[21] 2400 8-9-4 **75**.. KierenFox 2 80
(John Best) *led: rdn over 2f out: hrd pressed over 1f out: hdd ins fnl f: styd on same pce fnl 100yds* **7/1**
-011 4 *½* **Sioux Frontier (IRE)**[20] 2436 4-9-1 **72**......................... LewisEdmunds 7 76
(Iain Jardine) *hld up in rr: rdn over 3f out: hdwy on outer over 2f out: styd on ins fnl f: gng on at fin: nvr able to threaten front three* **11/1**
3231 5 *3 ½* **Heart Of Soul (IRE)**[15] 2577 4-9-13 **84**.....................(v) StevieDonohoe 1 83
(Ian Williams) *chsd ldrs: rdn over 2f out: outpcd over 1f out: no imp after* **7/2**[2]

6211 **6** *2* **Apterix (FR)**[14] 2636 9-9-7 **81** .... BenRobinson(3) 8 76
(Brian Ellison) *chsd ldr after 1f tl after 4f: remained handy: rdn over 2f out: one pce over 1f out* **8/1**

36-1 **7** *3 ½* **Charlie D (USA)**[2] 3000 4-9-4 **78** 5ex.......... (tp) JaneElliott(3) 3 68
(Tom Dascombe) *hld up: rdn over 4f out: outpcd 3f out: nvr a threat* **10/1**

44-3 **8** *¾* **Dance King**[16] 2563 9-10-0 **85**.......... (tp) NathanEvans 6 74
(Tim Easterby) *racd keenly: chsd ldrs: rdn 3f out: wknd over 1f out (jockey said gelding had no more to give)* **14/1**

1530 **9** *1 ¼* **Desert Ruler**[10] 2748 6-9-12 **83**.......... JackGarritty 9 70
(Jedd O'Keeffe) *s.i.s: hld up in rr: rdn 3f out: outpcd after and no imp (jockey said gelding ran flat)* **12/1**

2m 43.25s (1.05) **Going Correction** +0.15s/f (Good)
WFA 3 from 4yo+ 17lb **9** Ran **SP%** **122.6**
Speed ratings (Par 105): **102,101,100,100,98 96,94,94,93**
CSF £17.62 CT £84.74 TOTE £4.00: £1.10, £2.00, £2.40; EX 18.70 Trifecta £149.50.
Owner Dr Marwan Koukash **Bred** Donoughmore Bloodstock **Trained** Musley Bank, N Yorks

FOCUS
Add 60 yards. This was truly run and represents solid form for the level. The finish was dominated by the two 3yos in the race. It's been rated around the third, with the fourth close to form.
T/Plt: £269.80 to a £1 stake. Pool: £71,770.86 - 194.19 winning units T/Qpdt: £62.60 to a £1 stake. Pool: £5,009.68 - 59.21 winning units **Darren Owen**

3039 GOODWOOD (R-H)
Saturday, May 25

OFFICIAL GOING: Good to firm (good in places; watered; 7.9)
Wind: light, across Weather: fine

3074 BETFAIR BEST ODDS ON ITV RACES FESTIVAL STKS (LISTED RACE) 1m 1f 197y
1:55 (1:55) (Class 1) 4-Y-O+
£28,355 (£10,750; £5,380; £2,680; £1,345; £675) **Stalls** Low

Form RPR

34-4 **1** **Elarqam**[37] 1890 4-9-1 109.......... DaneO'Neill 3 116
(Mark Johnston) *chsd ldrs: clsd and upsides ldr travelling strly over 2f out: led and rdn ent fnl 2f: kicked clr and drifted rt over 1f out: styd on strly and in command fnl f* **11/4**[1]

10-4 **2** *2 ½* **Willie John**[55] 1460 4-9-1 98.......... DavidEgan 6 111
(Roger Varian) *looked wl; broke wl: sn restrained and hld up in last pair: nt clr of runs over 2f out: hdwy u.p to chse clr wnr 1f out: styd on for clr 2nd but nvr getting on terms w wnr* **7/1**

20-0 **3** *3 ½* **Thundering Blue (USA)**[29] 2083 6-9-6 116.......... SeanLevey 8 109
(David Menuisier) *stdd after s: hld up in rr: effrt on outer over 2f out: styd on ins fnl f to go 3rd fnl 75yds: no threat to ldng pair* **9/1**

-003 **4** *1 ¾* **Vintager**[21] 2408 4-9-1 110.......... OisinMurphy 5 101
(Charlie Appleby) *chsd ldrs for 2f: wl in tch in midfield after: clsd to join ldrs over 2f out: rdn ent fnl 2f: chsd wnr but unable to match his pce over 1f out: lost 2nd 1f out: wknd fnl 100yds* **3/1**[2]

0-23 **5** *½* **Extra Elusive**[29] 2083 4-9-1 107.......... (b[1]) JasonWatson 4 100
(Roger Charlton) *taken down early: stmbld leaving stalls and in rr: t.k.h: hdwy to chse ldrs after 2f: rdn and unable qck wl over 1f out: wl hld and kpt on same pce fnl f* **11/2**[3]

3-44 **6** *½* **Fabricate**[29] 2083 7-9-1 107.......... (p) PJMcDonald 1 99
(Michael Bell) *in tch in midfield: nt clrest of runs over 2f out: effrt and through 2f out: sn outpcd: kpt on same pce and wl hld ins fnl f* **11/2**[3]

111- **7** *2 ¾* **Francis Xavier (IRE)**[240] 7711 5-9-1 97.......... HarryBentley 7 93
(Kevin Frost) *hld up in tch in last trio: effrt over 2f out: sn struggling and outpcd over 1f out: wl btn fnl f* **16/1**

0-23 **8** *4* **Glendevon (USA)**[36] 1922 4-9-1 102.......... PatDobbs 2 85
(Richard Hughes) *taken down early: led tl rdn and hdd ent fnl 2f: lost pl over 1f out: bhd ins fnl f* **25/1**

2m 5.68s (-3.22) **Going Correction** +0.25s/f (Good) **8** Ran **SP%** **114.7**
Speed ratings (Par 111): **117,115,112,110,110 110,107,104**
CSF £22.56 TOTE £3.20: £1.40, £2.20, £2.40; EX 23.90 Trifecta £177.90.
Owner Hamdan Al Maktoum **Bred** Floors Farming **Trained** Middleham Moor, N Yorks

FOCUS
Top and bottom bends, and the straight to the 2f mark, were out 6yds. Add 10yds to this race distance. The ground was watered some more after the previous afternoon's racing but it was another dry, warm day, so conditions on the fast side again. This race looked to fall apart somewhat, with the likes of the third, fourth, fifth and sixth below form, but the winner did it well. The winner has been rated back to his best.

3075 BETFAIR EACH WAY EDGE H'CAP 7f
2:30 (2:32) (Class 2) 3-Y-O
£62,250 (£18,640; £9,320; £4,660; £2,330; £1,170) **Stalls** Low

Form RPR

-104 **1** **Beat Le Bon (FR)**[21] 2412 3-8-12 **94**.......... PatDobbs 4 104
(Richard Hannon) *hld up in tch in midfield: nt clrest of runs over 2f out: hdwy u.p to chse ldr 1f out: led 100yds out: r.o strly* **11/2**[3]

35-0 **2** *2* **Jack's Point**[38] 1851 3-8-11 **93**.......... CharlesBishop 5 98
(William Muir) *led for 2f: styd pressing ldr tl led again ent fnl 2f: drvn over 1f out: hdd 100yds out: no ex* **33/1**

01-1 **3** *¾* **Dubai Legacy (USA)**[22] 2378 3-9-2 **98**.......... PatCosgrave 12 101
(Saeed bin Suroor) *hld up in tch in midfield: swtchd lft and effrt over 2f out: hdwy to chse ldr 2f out: sn drvn: 3rd and no ex 1f out: kpt on same pce ins fnl f* **5/1**[2]

4-10 **4** *1* **Fanaar (IRE)**[44] 1713 3-9-2 **98**.......... (p[1]) DaneO'Neill 11 100+
(William Haggas) *looked wl; t.k.h: hld up in tch in midfield: swtchd rt over 5f out: bmpd over 2f out: nt clr run ent fnl 2f: squeezed through jst over 1f out: styd on u.p ins fnl f: no threat to ldrs* **11/1**

14-1 **5** *1 ¼* **Mr Diamond (IRE)**[18] 2510 3-7-11 **82** oh3.......... NoelGarbutt(3) 2 79
(Richard Fahey) *t.k.h: chsd ldrs: swtchd rt and effrt u.p wl over 1f out: unable qck 1f out: outpcd ins fnl f* **14/1**

112- **6** *1 ¼* **Flashcard (IRE)**[251] 7346 3-8-11 **93**.......... OisinMurphy 6 87
(Andrew Balding) *looked wl; chsd ldrs: squeezed for room and jostled ent fnl 2f: swtchd rt and effrt u.p over 1f out: unable qck u.p and wknd ins fnl f* **5/2**[1]

64-0 **7** *¾* **Dunkerron**[7] 2826 3-8-13 **102**.......... TobyEley(7) 3 94
(Alan King) *in tch in midfield: nt clr run ent fnl 2f: swtchd lft and effrt u.p over 1f out: sn pushed rt and no imp ent fnl f: wknd ins fnl f* **16/1**

150- **8** *1 ¼* **Indian Viceroy**[224] 8189 3-7-7 **82**.......... IsobelFrancis(7) 8 70
(Hughie Morrison) *nudged leaving stalls: hld up towards rr: sltly impeded over 5f out: nt clrest of runs and swtchd lft over 2f out: effrt u.p and swtchd rt over 1f out: wnt rt again 1f out: one pce fnl f* **40/1**

1204 **9** *¾* **Deep Intrigue**[15] 2570 3-8-13 **95**.......... PJMcDonald 13 81
(Mark Johnston) *in tch in midfield: unable qck u.p and no imp over 1f out: wknd ins fnl f* **20/1**

2-54 **10** *9* **Chynna**[14] 2627 3-8-10 **92**.......... JasonWatson 10 54
(Mick Channon) *hld up towards rr: squeezed for room and hmpd over 2f out: no hdwy u.p over 1f out: wknd fnl f* **25/1**

3410 **11** *2* **Sporting Chance**[21] 2411 3-9-7 **103**.......... HarryBentley 14 59
(Simon Crisford) *hld up in rr: sme hdwy on outer and edgd lft over 2f out: drvn 2f out: no imp and btn over 1f out: wknd fnl f* **18/1**

2-21 **12** *2 ¾* **Alhakmah (IRE)**[14] 2623 3-8-3 **85**.......... JFEgan 7 34
(Richard Hannon) *t.k.h: chsd ldrs: rdn ent fnl 2f: sn edging rt and bmpd wl over 1f out: btn ent fnl f: sn eased* **12/1**

2320 **13** *7* **Chapelli**[17] 2525 3-8-13 **95**.......... JoeFanning 1 25
(Mark Johnston) *wnt lft leaving stalls: sn rcvrd to press ldrs: led 5f out tl over 2f out: sn u.p and struggling: lost pl and wl hld whn sltly impeded 1f out: eased fnl f* **8/1**

10-0 **14** *1* **Prince Of Rome (IRE)**[29] 2086 3-8-2 **84**.......... (t) DavidEgan 9 11
(Richard Hughes) *stdd and edgd lft leaving stalls: hld up in rr: hmpd over 5f out: squeezed for room and hmpd again over 2f out: no hdwy u.p and wl btn over 1f out: eased ins fnl f* **33/1**

1m 26.84s (0.14) **Going Correction** +0.25s/f (Good) **14** Ran **SP%** **122.5**
Speed ratings (Par 105): **109,106,105,104,103 101,101,99,98,88 86,83,75,73**
CSF £189.64 CT £1007.83 TOTE £6.10: £1.80, £11.70, £2.10; EX 206.90 Trifecta £1077.50.
Owner Sullivan B'Stock/ Merriebelle Irish Farm **Bred** Gestut Zur Kuste Ag **Trained** East Everleigh, Wilts

FOCUS
Add 10yds. Most of the runners stayed up the middle of the track in the straight after the false rail ended, with only a few dropping down towards the fixed rail, so the main action was centre-field. This usually proves a good handicap and it's been rated in line with that.

3076 READ RYAN MOORE EXCLUSIVELY AT BETTING.BETFAIR EBF MAIDEN FILLIES' STKS (PLUS 10 RACE) 6f
3:10 (3:10) (Class 4) 2-Y-O
£6,792 (£2,021; £1,010; £505) **Stalls** High

Form RPR

1 **Silent Wave** 2-9-0 0.......... OisinMurphy 5 84+
(Charlie Appleby) *athletic; sltly awkward leaving stalls: mde all: rn green and edgd rt ent fnl 3f: pushed along and asserted over 1f out: r.o wl and gng away at fin* **10/11**[1]

2 *2 ¾* **Miss Villanelle** 2-9-0 0.......... DaneO'Neill 4 76
(Charles Hills) *leggy; stdd s: t.k.h: chsd ldrs: effrt to chse ldng pair and nt clrest of runs over 1f out: swtchd rt ins fnl f: kpt on to go 2nd wl ins fnl f: no threat to wnr* **4/1**[3]

3 *nk* **Atmospheric** 2-9-0 0.......... HectorCrouch 1 75
(Clive Cox) *athletic; chsd ldr: shkn up 2f out: rdn and unable to match pce of wnr over 1f out: kpt on same pce after and lost 2nd wl ins fnl f* **5/2**[2]

4 *10* **Penny Diamond** 2-9-0 0.......... HarryBentley 2 45
(Amanda Perrett) *ly; dwlt: rn green: in tch in rr: shkn up 2f out: sn outpcd and wknd over 1f out* **12/1**

5 *7* **Kahpehlo** 2-8-11 0.......... MitchGodwin(3) 6 24
(John Bridger) *tall; t.k.h: chsd ldrs tl 1/2-way: rdn and outpcd jst over 2f out: wl bhd fnl f* **40/1**

1m 14.64s (2.54) **Going Correction** +0.25s/f (Good) **5** Ran **SP%** **111.1**
Speed ratings (Par 92): **93,89,88,75,66**
CSF £5.07 TOTE £1.80: £1.30, £1.70; EX 4.50 Trifecta £5.90.
Owner Godolphin **Bred** Godolphin **Trained** Newmarket, Suffolk

FOCUS
Five newcomers, and the winner had the run of the race in front. Three of them finished clear.

3077 BET YOUR WAY ON THE BETFAIR EXCHANGE TAPSTER STKS (LISTED RACE) 1m 3f 218y
3:40 (3:43) (Class 1) 4-Y-O+
£28,355 (£10,750; £5,380; £2,680) **Stalls** High

Form RPR

120- **1** **Mirage Dancer**[167] 9473 5-9-1 116.......... PatDobbs 2 117+
(Sir Michael Stoute) *looked wl; stdd s: t.k.h: hld up in tch in rr: wnt 3rd 1/2-way: jnd ldrs travelling strly 3f out: pushed along and qcknd to ld over 1f out: in command and styd on wl fnl f: pushed out* **4/6**[1]

2-52 **2** *1 ½* **Danehill Kodiac (IRE)**[16] 2554 6-9-1 110.......... SeanLevey 4 114
(Richard Hannon) *led: jnd 3f out: sn drvn: hdd and unable to match pce of wnr over 1f out: battled on wl u.p to hold 2nd ins fnl f: no threat to wnr* **9/1**

42-3 **3** *nk* **Barsanti (IRE)**[14] 2607 7-9-1 111.......... DavidEgan 5 113
(Roger Varian) *looked wl; t.k.h: hld up in 3rd tl dropped to rr 1/2-way: clsd on outer to join ldrs 3f out: rdn ent fnl 2f: unable to match pce of wnr over 1f out: battling for 2nd and kpt on ins fnl f* **9/2**[3]

141- **4** *1 ½* **Rock Eagle**[225] 8149 4-9-1 97.......... HarryBentley 1 111
(Ralph Beckett) *chsd ldr tl dropped to last and outpcd u.p over 2f out: wl hld 1f out: kpt on again fnl 100yds: no threat to wnr* **7/2**[2]

2m 39.43s (-0.17) **Going Correction** +0.25s/f (Good) **4** Ran **SP%** **110.4**
Speed ratings (Par 111): **110,109,108,107**
CSF £7.19 TOTE £1.40; EX 8.20 Trifecta £10.70.
Owner K Abdullah **Bred** Juddmonte Farms Ltd **Trained** Newmarket, Suffolk

FOCUS
Add 10yds. A poor turnout numerically and the pace was slow. The second has been rated to his best, and the third close to form.

3078 BET IN PLAY ON THE BETFAIR EXCHANGE H'CAP 1m 6f
4:20 (4:20) (Class 2) (0-105,102) 4-Y-O+ **£15,762** (£4,715; £2,357; £1,180; £587) **Stalls** Low

Form RPR

1111 **1** **King's Advice**[28] 2119 5-9-3 **98**.......... JoeFanning 5 104+
(Mark Johnston) *looked wl; mde all: hrd pressed over 2f out: shkn up 2f out: rdn over 1f out: kpt finding ex and hld on gamely fnl f* **10/11**[1]

11-0 **2** *nse* **What A Welcome**[35] 1943 5-9-3 **98**.......... JoeyHaynes 4 103+
(Patrick Chamings) *chsd ldrs: clsd on inner and rdn over 2f out: sn chalng: sustained effrt and hrd drvn ins fnl f: kpt on wl: jst hld* **6/1**[3]

4320 **3** *1* **Amazing Red (IRE)**[24] 2269 6-9-0 **102**.......... CierenFallon(7) 3 106
(Ed Dunlop) *stdd s: hld up in tch in last: swtchd lft and effrt over 2f out: drifted rt over 1f out: clsd to chse ldrs and nt clr run ins fnl f: swtchd lft and kpt on fnl 100yds* **12/1**

150- **4** *½* **Sovereign Duke (GER)**[339] 3996 4-8-9 **90**.......... OisinMurphy 8 93
(Henry Candy) *in tch in last pair: effrt on inner over 2f out: drvn and clsd to chse ldrs 1f out: no ex and one pce ins fnl f* **11/1**

20-2 **5** *1 ½* **Blue Laureate**[14] 2606 4-8-8 **89**.......... PJMcDonald 7 90
(Ian Williams) *looked wl; chsd wnr tl jst over 2f out: unable qck u.p and lost pl over 1f out: hld and kpt on same pce ins fnl f* **7/2**[2]

050- 6 1 1/2 **Platitude**[246] 7486 6-9-5 **100**........(w) PatDobbs 6 99
(Amanda Perrett) *hld up in tch in midfield: effrt 2f out: unable qck u.p and btn 1f out: wknd ins fnl f* **16/1**
3m 5.26s (1.56) **Going Correction** +0.25s/f (Good) 6 Ran SP% **110.8**
Speed ratings (Par 109): **105,104,104,104,103 102**
CSF £6.70 CT £35.32 TOTE £1.60: £1.30, £2.30; EX 7.40 Trifecta £27.80.
Owner Saeed Jaber **Bred** Rabbah Bloodstock Limited **Trained** Middleham Moor, N Yorks
FOCUS
Add 10yds. A useful staying handicap.

3079 BETFAIR 3/1 FREE BET OFFER VETERANS' H'CAP 6f
4:55 (5:05) (Class 4) (0-80,81) 6-Y-O+
£6,986 (£2,079; £1,038; £519; £300; £300) Stalls High

Form RPR
0514 1 **Paddy Power (IRE)**[7] 2843 6-9-7 **79**........ DaneO'Neill 6 88
(Richard Fahey) *stdd s: hld up in tch: clsd and nt clr run over 2f out: effrt and hdwy to chal ent fnl f: led jst ins fnl f: sn in command and eased cl home: burst blood vessel (vet said gelding bled from nse)* **5/2**[1]
-000 2 1 3/4 **Boy In The Bar**[21] 2393 8-9-7 **79**........(v) PJMcDonald 7 82+
(Ian Williams) *chsd ldrs: nt clr run ent fnl 2f: swtchd rt over 1f out: stl nowhere to go and swtchd rt again ins fnl f: r.o to chse wnr wl ins fnl f: no ch of getting to wnr: eased cl home (jockey said gelding was persistently denied a clear run in fnl 2f)* **9/2**[3]
5641 3 1 1/2 **Shamshon (IRE)**[25] 2227 8-9-9 **81**........ OisinMurphy 3 80
(Stuart Williams) *trckd ldrs: clsd and upsides ldr travelling strly 2f out: rdn to ld over 1f out: hdd jst ins fnl f: sn outpcd and lost 2nd wl ins fnl f (vet said gelding had post-race ataxia)* **3/1**[2]
650- 4 1 3/4 **Toofi (FR)**[194] 9030 8-8-12 **70**........(t[1]) JoeyHaynes 4 63
(John Butler) *wl in tch: n.m.r 2f out: effrt over 1f out: sn no imp and wl hld ins fnl f* **8/1**
0-00 5 5 **Englishman**[19] 2484 9-9-0 **72**........ PatCosgrave 1 49
(Milton Bradley) *led and grad crossed to r against stands' rail: rdn ent fnl 2f: hdd over 1f out: sn btn and wknd ins fnl f (vet said gelding had post-race ataxia)* **9/1**
220 6 11 **Upavon**[35] 1930 9-8-7 **72**........ CierenFallon(7) 2 14
(Tony Carroll) *wl in tch: clsd 1/2-way: sn rdn: struggling and btn over 1f out: sn btn and wknd fnl f (vet said gelding had post-race ataxia)* **20/1**
1m 14.32s (2.22) **Going Correction** +0.25s/f (Good) 6 Ran SP% **97.6**
Speed ratings: **95,92,90,88,81 67**
CSF £10.07 TOTE £2.50: £1.70, £2.40; EX 10.90 Trifecta £26.00.
Owner M Scaife & R A Fahey **Bred** Yeguada De Milagro Sa **Trained** Musley Bank, N Yorks
■ Zac Brown was withdrawn. Price at time of withdrawal 4/1. Rule 4 applies to all bets - deduction 20p in the pound
■ Stewards' Enquiry : Pat Cosgrave caution: careless riding
FOCUS
This was unsatisfactory. A race for 6yos+, there was a false start after Zac Brown (subsequently withdrawn) had forced his gate open fractionally sooner than the others and got a jump on his rivals. They all covered a few furlongs before being asked to go again and, sprinters who'd been revved up twice, four of them finished with reported issues. All runners had reportedly been checked by the vet at the start and deemed fit to race. The winner has been rated back to something like his best.

3080 BETFAIR CASH OUT EBF FILLIES' NOVICE STKS 7f
5:30 (5:36) (Class 4) 3-Y-O+ £6,792 (£2,021; £1,010; £505) Stalls Low

Form RPR
2-5 1 **Neon Sea (FR)**[23] 2340 3-8-12 0........ OisinMurphy 7 88
(Sir Michael Stoute) *compact; sweating; wnt lft leaving stalls: mde all and travelled strly: rdn and kicked clr over 1f out: in n.d and r.o strly ins fnl f: readily* **1/1**[1]
30-2 2 3 3/4 **Rhossili Down**[50] 1570 3-8-12 79........ DaneO'Neill 5 77
(Charles Hills) *leggy; squeezed for room leaving stalls: hld up in tch in midfield: effrt 2f out: drvn and nt match pce of wnr over 1f out: chsd clr wnr 1f out: no imp* **7/2**[2]
055- 3 1 3/4 **Just My Type**[211] 8591 3-8-12 73........ DavidEgan 6 73
(Roger Varian) *neat; looked wl; hld up in tch in midfield: effrt 2f out: wnt 2nd but wnr gng clr over 1f out: lost 2nd 1f out and plugged on same pce ins fnl f* **4/1**[3]
3- 4 1 **Parish Poet (IRE)**[243] 7608 3-8-12 0........ PJMcDonald 4 70
(Paul Cole) *str; chsd ldrs: effrt ent fnl 2f: unable to match pce of wnr and btn over 1f out: wknd ins fnl f (trainer was informed filly could run until the day after passing a stalls test)* **6/1**
0 5 4 1/2 **Avorisk Et Perils (FR)**[9] 2771 4-9-9 0........ FergusSweeney 2 62
(Gary Moore) *str; hld up in tch in midfield: edging lft over 2f out: swtchd rt: rdn and outpcd over 1f out: sn wl btn and wknd ins fnl f* **100/1**
6 2 1/4 **Rebecke (IRE)** 3-8-12 0........ HectorCrouch 8 52
(Clive Cox) *tall; t.k.h: chsd wnr tl 2f out: sn u.p and outpcd: wknd fnl f* **20/1**
0 7 3/4 **Break Of Day**[9] 2762 3-8-12 0........ PatDobbs 3 50
(William Haggas) *compact; in tch in last pair: effrt whn tk a false step over 2f out: outpcd and btn over 1f out: wknd fnl f* **16/1**
00 8 hd **Inspirational (IRE)**[15] 2583 3-8-5 0........ CierenFallon(7) 1 49
(Ed Dunlop) *s.i.s: a last: rdn jst over 2f out: sn outpcd and wl btn over 1f out* **40/1**
1m 28.28s (1.58) **Going Correction** +0.25s/f (Good)
WFA 3 from 4yo 11lb 8 Ran SP% **120.6**
Speed ratings (Par 102): **101,96,94,93,88 85,85,84**
CSF £5.09 TOTE £1.80: £1.10, £1.40, £1.60; EX 5.30 Trifecta £15.10.
Owner Qatar Racing Limited **Bred** E A R L Qatar Bloodstock Ltd **Trained** Newmarket, Suffolk
FOCUS
Add 10yds. An ordinary looking fillies' novice. It's been rated around the third and fourth.
T/Plt: £25.20 to a £1 stake. Pool: £82,336.98 - 2,380.44 winning units T/Qpdt: £5.70 to a £1 stake. Pool: £4,594.07 - 594.07 winning units **Steve Payne**

3046 HAYDOCK (L-H)
Saturday, May 25

OFFICIAL GOING: Good to firm (watered; 7.9)
Wind: light breeze, across Weather: overcast, quite mild

3081 AMIX READY MIXED CONCRETE H'CAP 2m 45y
2:15 (2:15) (Class 2) (0-100,100) 4-Y-O+ **£16,172** (£4,812; £2,405; £1,202) Stalls Low

Form RPR
4420 1 **Lucky Deal**[15] 2575 4-9-7 **98**........ FrannyNorton 6 108
(Mark Johnston) *hld up in rr: pushed along 4f out: swtchd to outer and hdwy over 2f out: drvn to ld over 1f out: shifted lft 1f out: rdn clr fnl f: pushed out nr fin: comf (trainer rep said, regarding improvement in form, colt was better suited by the Good to Firm ground at Haydock)* **4/1**[2]
2-11 2 5 **Eden Rose**[35] 1943 4-8-13 **90**........ BenCurtis 4 94
(Mick Channon) *prom: led 3f out: rdn in narrow ld over 2f out: hdd over 1f out: kpt on fnl f: no match for wnr* **7/2**[1]
/3 3 1 **Desert Point (FR)**[12] 2680 7-8-9 **85**........ TomEaves 7 88
(Keith Dalgleish) *hld up: pushed along 3f out: rdn 2f out: styd on u.p fnl f: tk 3rd last two strides* **22/1**
46-3 4 hd **Pirate King**[21] 2398 4-8-8 **85**........ ShaneKelly 5 88
(Harry Dunlop) *hld up: gd hdwy on outer 3f out: cl up and rdn 2f out: no ex fr over 1f out* **15/2**
321P 5 hd **Watersmeet**[15] 2575 8-9-3 **93**........ RichardKingscote 2 95
(Mark Johnston) *trckd ldrs: drvn and reminder over 2f out: sn rdn: wknd fr over 1f out* **9/2**[3]
2135 6 2 1/4 **Busy Street**[8] 2801 7-9-0 **90**........ AlistairRawlinson 3 90
(Michael Appleby) *mid-div: rdn over 2f out: one pce fnl f* **9/1**
00-0 7 6 **Nakeeta**[27] 2158 8-9-10 **100**........(t) JimCrowley 8 92
(Iain Jardine) *hld up: pushed along and effrt on outer over 2f out: sn drvn: nt clr run over 1f out: reminders over 1f out and ins fnl f: no ex* **9/2**[3]
0-00 8 3 3/4 **My Reward**[10] 2742 7-9-5 **95**........ GeraldMosse 1 83
(Tim Easterby) *led: pushed along and hdd 3f out: sn rdn and wknd: eased ins fnl f* **14/1**
460- 9 1 3/4 **Magellan**[18] 9155 5-9-0 **90**........ RobertHavlin 10 76
(Philip Kirby) *mid-div: drvn and lost pl 3f out: dropped to last 2f out: wl bhd and eased fnl f* **22/1**
3m 33.62s (-3.08) **Going Correction** -0.15s/f (Firm)
WFA 4 from 5yo+ 1lb 9 Ran SP% **115.7**
Speed ratings (Par 109): **101,98,98,97,97 96,93,91,90**
CSF £18.47 CT £264.61 TOTE £3.80: £1.30, £1.60, £5.40; EX 18.30 Trifecta £336.30.
Owner Kai Fai Leung **Bred** Fittocks Stud **Trained** Middleham Moor, N Yorks
FOCUS
This decent staying handicap was run at a routine pace. Add 29yds. The third and fourth help set the standard.

3082 AMIX SILVER BOWL H'CAP 1m 37y
2:50 (2:52) (Class 2) 3-Y-O
£49,800 (£14,912; £7,456; £3,728; £1,864; £936) Stalls Low

Form RPR
10-4 1 **Beatboxer (USA)**[21] 2413 3-8-11 **95**........(t[1]) RobertHavlin 7 104
(John Gosden) *in rr: plenty to do 3f out: swtchd to outer over 2f out: rdn and hdwy over 1f out: str run u.p fnl f: led last few strides (trainer's rep said, regarding the apparent improvement in form, colt benefitted from first-time applications of both a hood and a tongue-tie)* **20/1**
121 2 nk **Munhamek**[26] 2198 3-8-0 **84** oh1........ DuranFentiman 1 92
(Ivan Furtado) *led: shkn up in 2 l ld 2f out: rdn over 1f out: 3 l ld ent fnl f: r.o: ct last few strides* **9/1**
0040 3 2 **Victory Command (IRE)**[21] 2414 3-8-8 **92**........ ConnorBeasley 6 95
(Mark Johnston) *hld up: pushed along and hdwy on outer over 2f out: rdn over 1f out: kpt on into 3rd wl ins fnl f* **25/1**
6-56 4 1 **Certain Lad**[21] 2414 3-9-0 **98**........ BenCurtis 8 99
(Mick Channon) *sweating: chsd ldrs: n.m.r 3f out: sn swtchd to outer: rdn ent fnl 2f: 4th 1f out: one pce fnl f* **16/1**
16-3 5 shd **Barristan The Bold**[16] 2559 3-8-6 **90**........ LiamJones 15 91+
(Tom Dascombe) *mid-div on outer: hdwy to go prom over 4f out: cl 2nd 3f out: sn drvn: rdn over 1f out: no ex fnl f* **10/1**
6-11 6 1 1/2 **Aweedram (IRE)**[15] 2569 3-8-8 **92**........ RichardKingscote 13 89
(Alan King) *hld up: drvn over 2f out: sn rdn: kpt on fnl f* **9/2**[2]
1-35 7 hd **Duke Of Hazzard (FR)**[13] 2668 3-9-7 **105**........ RaulDaSilva 10 102
(Paul Cole) *trckd ldr: pushed along 3f out: drvn and ev ch over 2f out: sn rdn: wknd fnl f: lost shoe* **14/1**
12-2 8 nse **Awe**[15] 2570 3-8-4 **88**........ MartinDwyer 4 88+
(William Haggas) *involved in scrimmaging first 2f: t.k.h: mid-div: drvn over 2f out: btn whn nt clr run ins fnl f* **4/1**[1]
2126 9 1 1/2 **Reggae Runner (FR)**[29] 2082 3-7-10 **85**........ AndrewBreslin(5) 9 78
(Mark Johnston) *mid-div: drvn over 2f out: wknd fnl f* **16/1**
5111 10 3 1/2 **Oasis Prince**[14] 2616 3-8-8 **92**........ FrannyNorton 5 77+
(Mark Johnston) *involved in scrimmaging first 2f: mid-div: pushed along 3f out: drvn and lost pl 2f out: wknd and eased fnl f* **5/1**[3]
-332 11 2 3/4 **Loch Ness Monster (IRE)**[14] 2616 3-8-0 **89**........ SeanDavis(5) 2 68+
(Michael Appleby) *hmpd ins first f: bhd: drvn over 3f out: no imp* **12/1**
0-11 12 1 1/4 **Masaru**[29] 2082 3-9-0 **98**........ JimCrowley 16 74
(Richard Hannon) *hld up on outer: drvn and effrt on outer over 2f out: sn rdn and wknd* **5/1**[3]
06-0 13 1 1/4 **Octave (IRE)**[7] 2835 3-8-4 **88**........ RoystonFfrench 3 61+
(Mark Johnston) *bdly hmpd first 2f and shuffled bk to last: pushed along 4f out: reminders over 2f and 1f out: no imp* **33/1**
02-0 14 23 **Drogon (IRE)**[16] 2559 3-8-8 **89** ow3........ ShaneKelly 14 12
(Tom Dascombe) *prom: drvn and lost pl 3f out where buffeted arnd: wknd qckly and heavily eased* **50/1**
1m 39.77s (-5.13) **Going Correction** -0.15s/f (Firm) 14 Ran SP% **130.2**
Speed ratings (Par 105): **119,118,116,115,115 114,113,113,112,108 106,104,103,80**
CSF £199.16 CT £4637.05 TOTE £23.60: £5.50, £3.70, £7.70; EX 284.40 Trifecta £4879.50.
Owner HRH Princess Haya Of Jordan **Bred** Ramspring Farm **Trained** Newmarket, Suffolk

FOCUS
Always a strong 3yo handicap. It was run at a searching pace and proved a rough race. Add 6yds. The fourth help set the standard.

3083 ARMSTRONG AGGREGATES SANDY LANE STKS (GROUP 2) 6f
3:25 (3:26) (Class 1) 3-Y-O £51,039 (£19,350; £9,684; £4,824) Stalls Centre

Form RPR
21-4 1 **Hello Youmzain (FR)**[42] 1752 3-9-0 113 KevinStott 3 118
(Kevin Ryan) *prom: drvn and led 1 1/2f out: 2 l ld 1f out: rdn further clr fnl f: pushed out nr fin* **5/1**[2]
11-1 2 3 1/4 **Calyx**[24] 2270 3-9-0 115 RobertHavlin 1 108
(John Gosden) *sltly hmpd as rival wnt lft s: racd in 3rd: gng wl over 2f out: shkn up and hung lft 1 1/2f out: rdn fnl f: no rspnse* **2/13**[1]
12-4 3 nk **Royal Intervention (IRE)**[23] 2319 3-8-11 99 GeraldMosse 2 104
(Ed Walker) *broke qckly and wnt lft first two strides: led: drvn 2f out: hdd 1 1/2f out: sn rdn: one pce fnl f* **33/1**
20-4 4 2 3/4 **True Mason**[42] 1780 3-9-0 104 (v[1]) BenCurtis 4 98
(K R Burke) *hld up in rr: drvn 1 1/2f out: sn rdn: no imp (jockey said colt hung left in fnl furlong)* **20/1**[3]
1m 12.13s (-1.77) **Going Correction** -0.05s/f (Good) 4 Ran SP% **111.0**
Speed ratings (Par 111): **109,104,104,100**
CSF £6.65 TOTE £7.40; EX 8.70 Trifecta £15.80.
Owner Jaber Abdullah **Bred** Rabbah Bloodstock Limited **Trained** Hambleton, N Yorks

FOCUS
With just the four runners not surprisingly this Group 2 proved tactical. The winner and third have been rated to form.

3084 ARMSTRONG AGGREGATES TEMPLE STKS (GROUP 2) 5f
4:00 (4:00) (Class 1) 3-Y-O+
£56,710 (£21,500; £10,760; £5,360; £2,690; £1,350) Stalls Centre

Form RPR
144- 1 **Battaash (IRE)**[230] 8028 5-9-4 123 (w) JimCrowley 6 125+
(Charles Hills) *chsd ldrs: eased into ld gng wl 2f out: pushed 3 l clr 1f out: rdn and in command fnl f: pushed out nr fin: impressive* **5/6**[1]
210- 2 2 1/2 **Alpha Delphini**[230] 8028 8-9-4 115 GrahamLee 5 114
(Bryan Smart) *prom: pushed along and cl up 2f out: rdn in pursuit of wnr 1f out: r.o fnl f: nvr nr wnr* **20/1**
21-1 3 3/4 **Mabs Cross**[21] 2409 5-9-6 115 PaulMulrennan 2 113
(Michael Dods) *pushed along and sltly outpcd early: racd in 5th: reminder and effrt over 2f out: wnt 3rd and reminders over 1f out: one pce fnl f: lost shoe (jockey said mare lost left hind shoe)* **7/2**[3]
0-24 4 4 1/2 **Pocket Dynamo (USA)**[24] 2270 3-8-10 104 BenCurtis 4 92
(Robert Cowell) *slowly away: bhd: pushed along over 2f out: sn drifted lft: rdn 1 1/2f out: hung lft but kpt on into 4th fnl f* **33/1**
1-11 5 3/4 **Kachy**[36] 1919 6-9-4 115 RichardKingscote 3 92
(Tom Dascombe) *disp ld: drvn and hdd 2f out: rdn and wknd over 1f out* **3/1**[2]
220- 6 16 **Caspian Prince (IRE)**[274] 6504 10-9-4 114 (t) AlistairRawlinson 1 35
(Michael Appleby) *disp ld: hdd 2f out: sn drvn and wknd qckly: dropped to last over 1f out* **40/1**
57.7s (-2.70) **Going Correction** -0.05s/f (Good)
WFA 3 from 5yo+ 8lb 6 Ran SP% **111.9**
Speed ratings (Par 115): **119,115,113,106,105 79**
CSF £19.74 TOTE £1.70: £1.30, £4.70; EX 14.20 Trifecta £35.90.
Owner Hamdan Al Maktoum **Bred** Ballyphilip Stud **Trained** Lambourn, Berks

FOCUS
Despite a poor numerical turn out this was Group 2 sprint to savour. It was predictably run at a fierce pace and the form is outstanding. The winner has been rated close to his best, the second to the balance of his form and third close to her latest.

3085 EBF BRITISH STALLION STUDS CECIL FRAIL (SPONSORED BY ARMSTRONG AGGREGATES) (LISTED RACE) 6f
4:35 (4:36) (Class 1) 3-Y-O+
£26,653 (£10,105; £5,057; £2,519; £1,264; £634) Stalls Centre

Form RPR
0-5 1 **Forever In Dreams (IRE)**[15] 2605 3-8-8 98 MartinDwyer 6 101
(Aidan F Fogarty, Ire) *prom: drvn to ld 1 1/2f out: rdn and r.o wl fnl f: pushed out nr fin* **16/1**
413- 2 3/4 **Solar Gold (IRE)**[231] 7978 4-9-3 94 MarcMonaghan 7 100
(William Haggas) *dismntd to enter stalls: hld up: hdwy 2f out: rdn to chal over 1f out: r.o fnl f: a hld by wnr* **7/1**
15-1 3 1 **Heavenly Holly (IRE)**[36] 1918 4-9-3 97 JimCrowley 8 97
(Hugo Palmer) *trckd ldrs: pushed along and hdwy 1 1/2f out: sn rdn into 3rd: kpt on fnl f* **9/2**[2]
10-0 4 nk **Ocelot**[36] 1913 5-9-3 83 KevinStott 10 96
(Robert Cowell) *hld up: plenty to do 2f out: drvn and hdwy over 1f out: rdn and kpt on into 4th ins fnl f* **40/1**
16-0 5 hd **Glass Slippers**[42] 1751 3-8-8 92 TomEaves 11 93
(Kevin Ryan) *hld up: pushed along and hdwy on stands' side 2f out: rdn 1f out: one pce fnl f* **20/1**
-122 6 2 1/4 **Island Of Life (USA)**[36] 1918 5-9-3 101 (tp) RichardKingscote 4 88
(William Haggas) *hld up: pushed along 1 1/2f out: sn drvn: reminder fnl f: no imp* **3/1**[1]
20-4 7 1 1/4 **Signora Cabello (IRE)**[24] 2270 3-8-8 112 BenCurtis 3 82
(John Quinn) *chsd ldrs: cl up and pushed along 2f out: rdn over 1f out: wknd fnl f* **5/1**[3]
0-0 8 nk **Zain Hana**[39] 1829 4-9-3 88 GeraldMosse 1 83
(John Butler) *hld up: drvn 2f out: rdn over 1f out: no imp* **50/1**
-121 9 1 **Gold Filigree (IRE)**[6] 2874 4-9-3 95 ShaneKelly 5 80
(Richard Hughes) *led: pushed along 2f out: drvn and hdd 1 1/2f out: sn rdn and wknd* **11/1**
21-2 10 1/2 **Perfection**[14] 2621 4-9-6 101 (p) DavidNolan 2 81
(David O'Meara) *mid-div: drvn 2f out: rdn 1f out: wknd fnl f* **5/1**[3]
0-00 11 1 3/4 **Yourtimeisnow**[14] 2627 3-8-13 95 JackMitchell 9 76
(Roger Varian) *chsd ldrs: drvn and lost pl 2f out: reminder and dropped to last over 1f out* **8/1**
1m 12.29s (-1.61) **Going Correction** -0.05s/f (Good)
WFA 3 from 4yo+ 9lb 11 Ran SP% **123.5**
Speed ratings (Par 111): **108,107,105,105,105 102,100,99,98,97 95**
CSF £127.88 TOTE £15.40: £3.50, £3.10, £2.30; EX 129.80 Trifecta £852.50.
Owner Mrs Theresa Marnane **Bred** Con Marnane **Trained** Kilfeacle, Tipperary, Co Tipperary

FOCUS
An open-looking fillies' Listed sprint, run at an average pace down the centre. The second, third and fifth help set the standard.

3086 AMIX H'CAP 1m 3f 175y
5:10 (5:10) (Class 3) (0-95,88) 3-Y-O £10,582 (£3,168; £1,584; £792) Stalls Centre

Form RPR
24-1 1 **Sir Ron Priestley**[37] 1898 3-9-5 86 FrannyNorton 4 101+
(Mark Johnston) *slowly away: rcvrd to ld after 1f: jnd 3f out: pushed into 1 l ld 2f out: sn drvn and readily wnt 4 l clr 1f out: pushed out fnl f: eased nr fin: easily* **1/2**[1]
3-22 2 3 3/4 **Lariat**[16] 2562 3-9-7 88 MartinDwyer 2 93
(Andrew Balding) *led 1f: trckd ldr whn hdd: disp ld 3f out: drvn and hdd over 2f out: rdn 1 1/2f out: kpt on fnl f: no ch w wnr* **7/2**[2]
-120 3 3 1/2 **Fraser Island (IRE)**[8] 2811 3-9-2 83 RichardKingscote 3 82
(Mark Johnston) *prom: sn settled in 3rd: dropped to 4th bef 1/2-way: pushed along over 2f out: reminder 2f out: wnt 3rd over 1f out: no ex fnl f* **7/1**[3]
101- 4 12 **Felix The Poet**[190] 9106 3-9-6 87 HollieDoyle 1 67
(Archie Watson) *hld up in last: wnt 3rd bef 1/2-way: hdwy to chal between horses over 2f out: sn drvn and lost pl: rdn and dropped to 4th over 1f out: wl bhd fnl f* **12/1**
2m 31.4s (-1.90) **Going Correction** -0.15s/f (Firm) 4 Ran SP% **109.1**
Speed ratings (Par 103): **100,97,95,87**
CSF £2.59 TOTE £1.30; EX 2.10 Trifecta £4.50.
Owner Paul Dean **Bred** Mascalls Stud **Trained** Middleham Moor, N Yorks

FOCUS
Another small-field, tactical affair but it's solid 3yo form. Add 16yds.

3087 ARMSTRONG FAMILY H'CAP 1m 2f 100y
5:45 (5:45) (Class 3) (0-95,93) 4-Y-O+ £10,997 (£3,272; £1,635; £817) Stalls Centre

Form RPR
6-60 1 **Finniston Farm**[15] 2574 4-9-7 93 (p) RichardKingscote 3 100
(Tom Dascombe) *led: rdn and hdd 3f out: dropped to 3rd and looked btn 2f out: rallied over 1f out: styd on ins fnl f: led last two strides* **11/10**[1]
10-2 2 hd **Red Force One**[75] 617 4-9-0 89 (p) MeganNicholls[(3)] 1 95
(Paul Nicholls) *chsd ldr: pushed along to share ld 3f out: sn hdd: rdn in 1 l 2nd 2f out: fought bk to ld 1f out: 1/2 l ld ins fnl f: kpt on: hdd last two strides* **4/1**[3]
05-0 3 7 **Scottish Summit (IRE)**[8] 2808 6-8-13 85 ConnorBeasley 2 78
(Geoffrey Harker) *racd in 3rd: hdwy into share of ld 3f out: sn led: drvn in 1 l ld 2f out: rdn and hdd 1f out: wknd fnl f: jst hld on for 3rd* **7/1**
-010 4 nse **New Show (IRE)**[20] 2440 4-9-2 88 (b) HayleyTurner 4 81
(Michael Bell) *hld up in last: rdn 3f out: plugged on fr 2f out: jst hld for 3rd* **9/4**[2]
2m 12.44s (-4.16) **Going Correction** -0.15s/f (Firm) 4 Ran SP% **110.9**
Speed ratings (Par 107): **110,109,104,104**
CSF £5.93 TOTE £1.90; EX 5.20 Trifecta £16.80.
Owner Godel Technologies Europe Limited **Bred** Stetchworth & Middle Park Studs Ltd **Trained** Malpas, Cheshire

FOCUS
A fair little handicap and it saw a dramatic finish. Add 6yds. The winner has been rated close to his best, and the second to form.
T/Plt: £4,534.10 to a £1 stake. Pool: £106,397.47 - 17.13 winning units T/Qpdt: £191.20 to a £1 stake. Pool: £5,568.10 - 21.55 winning units **Keith McHugh**

2767 SALISBURY (R-H)
Saturday, May 25

OFFICIAL GOING: Good to firm (watered; 8.5)
Wind: Light half across Weather: Sunny periods

3088 GEORGE SMITH HORSEBOXES BRITISH EBF MAIDEN STKS (PLUS 10 RACE) 5f
5:50 (5:54) (Class 4) 2-Y-O £5,498 (£1,636; £817; £408) Stalls Low

Form RPR
0430 1 **Dark Optimist (IRE)**[7] 2830 2-9-5 0 (t[1]) JFEgan 6 80
(David Evans) *led for over 1f: prom: led over 2f out: sn rdn: hdd ent fnl f: rallied wl: led cl home (trainer said, regarding improvement in form, colt benefited from the fitting of a tongue-tie and a drop in class)* **7/1**
2 nse **Partridge (IRE)** 2-9-0 0 SeanLevey 3 75
(Richard Hannon) *prom tl squeezed out 1st f: in tch: hdwy over 2f out: chal over 1f out: led ent fnl f: kpt on but no ex whn hdd cl home* **11/8**[1]
4 3 2 1/4 **Born To Destroy**[9] 2767 2-9-5 0 CharlesBishop 4 72
(Richard Spencer) *hung rt thrght: prom: rdn and ev ch 2f out tl jst ins fnl f: no ex fnl 120yds (jockey said colt hung right-handed in closing stages)* **9/4**[2]
5 4 7 **Goodwood Rebel (IRE)**[23] 2338 2-9-5 0 HarryBentley 1 47
(Ralph Beckett) *led for 1f: prom: rdn jst over 2f out: wknd fnl f* **9/2**[3]
05 5 1 **Good Times Too**[35] 1931 2-8-12 0 ScottMcCullagh[(7)] 5 43
(Mick Channon) *chsd ldrs: rdn over 2f out: wknd jst over 1f out* **25/1**
6 1 1/4 **Shaun's Delight (IRE)** 2-9-5 0 JasonWatson 7 38
(Ronald Harris) *wnt bdly lft s: a bhd* **33/1**
7 2 1/4 **Royal Optimist (IRE)** 2-9-5 0 LiamKeniry 2 30
(David Evans) *chsd ldrs: outpcd and hanging rt over 3f out: wknd over 1f out* **25/1**
1m 2.87s (2.37) **Going Correction** +0.175s/f (Good) 7 Ran SP% **114.2**
Speed ratings (Par 95): **88,87,84,73,71 69,65**
CSF £17.09 TOTE £6.90: £2.70, £1.50; EX 18.80 Trifecta £49.40.
Owner The United Optimists **Bred** Ciara Eglington **Trained** Pandy, Monmouths

FOCUS
Not a particularly deep maiden and experience won the day for Dark Optimist who looks to be going the right way.

3089 SHARP'S DOOM BAR H'CAP 6f
6:20 (6:20) (Class 6) (0-65,65) 4-Y-O+
£3,493 (£1,039; £519; £400; £400; £400) Stalls Low

Form RPR
46-4 1 **Raincall**[14] 2623 4-9-7 65 HarryBentley 4 74+
(Henry Candy) *travelled wl: trckd ldrs: led over 1f out: kpt on wl: rdn out* **2/1**[1]
-016 2 1 **Who Told Jo Jo (IRE)**[11] 2717 5-9-0 58 JasonWatson 2 63
(Joseph Tuite) *mid-div: rdn over 2f out: hdwy over 1f out: kpt on to press wnr ins fnl f but a being hld* **7/1**

-001 **3** 3/4 **Air Of York (IRE)**[23] 2339 7-9-0 **65**......................(p) ScottMcCullagh(7) 13 68
(John Flint) *hld up: hdwy over 3f out: sn rdn: kpt on to go 3rd ins fnl f but nt pce to get on terms (vet said lost right hind shoe)* **6/1**[3]

635U **4** 3/4 **Mooroverthebridge**[10] 2729 5-8-10 **57**...................... FinleyMarsh(3) 6 58
(Grace Harris) *s.i.s: towards rr: rdn over 2f out: no imp tl hdwy over 1f out: kpt on ins fnl f* **7/1**

6-00 **5** *shd* **Harry Beau**[23] 2339 5-9-7 **65**...................................(v) JFEgan 9 65
(David Evans) *led: rdn over 2f out: hdd over 1f out: no ex ins fnl f* **6/1**[3]

10-5 **6** *shd* **Cent Flying**[23] 2339 4-9-7 **65**...............................(t) SeanLevey 11 65
(William Muir) *trckd ldrs: rdn over 2f out: kpt on same pce fnl f* **5/1**[2]

0R00 **7** 2 **Gold Hunter (IRE)**[28] 2107 9-9-6 **64**.....................(t[1] w) CharlesBishop 10 58
(Steve Flook) *prom: led over 2f out: hdd over 1f out: no ex clsng stages* **14/1**

4-00 **8** *nk* **Vincenzo Coccotti (USA)**[19] 2483 7-8-8 **57**.....(p) ThomasGreatrex(5) 1 50
(Ken Cunningham-Brown) *struggling over 1/2-way: a towards rr* **14/1**

20-0 **9** 1 1/2 **Picket Line**[136] 144 7-9-4 **62**...(b) TrevorWhelan 7 51
(Geoffrey Deacon) *in tch: rdn over 2f out: wknd ent fnl f* **33/1**

1m 15.05s (0.55) **Going Correction** +0.175s/f (Good) **9** Ran SP% **119.8**
Speed ratings (Par 101): **103,101,100,99,99 99,96,96,94**
CSF £17.44 CT £75.18 TOTE £2.40: £1.10, £2.50, £2.20; EX 15.00 Trifecta £90.10.

Owner Rockcliffe Stud **Bred** Rockcliffe Stud **Trained** Kingston Warren, Oxon

FOCUS
Very few in-form contenders in what was no more than an ordinary handicap. It was, however, won by the least-exposed runner in the field and the most interesting one from a handicapping perspective.

3090 SAUNTON SANDS HOTEL NORTH DEVON MAIDEN STKS 6f
6:50 (6:51) (Class 5) 3-Y-O+ £4,787 (£1,424; £711; £355) Stalls Low

Form RPR

3625 **1** **Amplify (IRE)**[29] 2078 3-9-5 81.. JasonWatson 5 84
(Brian Meehan) *a.p: led over 3f out: rdn clr over 1f out: in command after* **7/2**[2]

2-50 **2** 1 **Real Smooth (IRE)**[8] 2802 3-9-5 77.................................. SeanLevey 9 81
(Richard Hannon) *in tch: hdwy over 2f out: rdn to chse wnr ent fnl f: kpt on but a being hld* **7/1**

64 **3** 3 1/4 **Somethingaboutjack (IRE)**[21] 2397 3-9-5 0.............. CharlesBishop 4 70
(Eve Johnson Houghton) *mid-div: rdn over 2f out: hdwy over 1f out: wnt 3rd ent fnl f: kpt on but nt pce to rch ldrs* **5/1**[3]

422- **4** 1 3/4 **Monsieur Noir**[211] 8606 3-9-5 86.................................. CharlieBennett 6 65
(Roger Varian) *wnt lft s: chsd ldrs: rdn to chse wnr 2f out tl 1f out: nvr threatened: one pce fnl f* **10/11**[1]

5 1 **Annexation (FR)** 3-9-5 0... LiamKeniry 10 62+
(Ed Dunlop) *s.i.s: towards rr: hdwy over 1f out: kpt on fnl f: improve* **40/1**

25 **6** 2 1/4 **Hey Ho Let's Go**[43] 1728 3-9-5 0.................................. TrevorWhelan 1 54
(Clive Cox) *trckd ldrs: rdn over 2f out: wknd ent fnl f* **20/1**

63- **7** 3 3/4 **Foxy Femme**[263] 6912 3-9-0 0...............................(h[1]) JoeyHaynes 3 37
(John Gallagher) *mid-div: rdn over 2f out: sn one pce* **50/1**

0 **8** 3 **Twilighting**[14] 2623 3-9-0 0.. HarryBentley 8 28
(Henry Candy) *s.i.s and hmpd s: mid-div: sme prog 2f out: kpt on fnl f but nvr gng pce to get involved* **16/1**

0- **9** *shd* **Bonny Blue**[234] 7907 3-9-0 0.. JFEgan 2 27
(Rod Millman) *mid-div: rdn 3f out: sn hung lft: wknd over 1f out (jockey said filly ran very green)* **66/1**

00- **10** 3 1/2 **Just Martha**[184] 9209 4-9-6 0................................ WilliamCox(3) 11 18
(John Flint) *s.i.s: mid-div: veered bdly lft u.p 2f out: sn wknd (jockey said filly ran green)* **100/1**

11 2 1/4 **Chizzi** 3-9-0 0.. GeorgeDowning 7 9
(Rod Millman) *a towards rr* **100/1**

0 **12** 5 **Scarlet Red**[45] 1676 4-9-6 0...................................... AaronJones(3) 12
(Malcolm Saunders) *racd freely: sn led: rdn and hdd over 2f out: hung lft fr over 2f out: sn wknd (jockey said filly ran too freely)* **100/1**

13 8 **Yet Another (IRE)** 4-9-11 0..................................... FinleyMarsh(3) 13
(Grace Harris) *hmpd s: hung lft thrght: a bhd (jockey said gelding hung left-handed throughout)* **100/1**

1m 14.5s **Going Correction** +0.175s/f (Good)
WFA 3 from 4yo 9lb **13** Ran SP% **124.3**
Speed ratings (Par 103): **107,105,101,99,97 94,89,85,85,80 77,71,60**
CSF £28.59 TOTE £3.70: £1.40, £1.90, £1.70; EX 28.40 Trifecta £111.60.

Owner Manton Thoroughbreds III **Bred** Drumlin Bloodstock **Trained** Manton, Wilts

FOCUS
Quite an interesting maiden but they didn't go a great gallop for a sprint and it proved hard for the hold-up horses to land a blow. The form makes sense rated around the first three.

3091 COMEC VOICE & DATA H'CAP 1m 6f 44y
7:20 (7:21) (Class 4) (0-80,82) 4-Y-O+
£5,757 (£1,713; £856; £428; £400; £400) Stalls Far side

Form RPR

303- **1** **Ship Of The Fen**[261] 7000 4-9-9 **82**................................. JasonWatson 91+
(Ian Williams) *trckd ldrs: rdn whn swtchd lft 2f out: led fnl 120yds: styd on strly* **2/1**[1]

221- **2** 4 1/2 **General Zoff**[242] 7654 4-8-9 **68**... JFEgan 71
(William Muir) *trckd ldr: led 2f out: sn rdn: hdd fnl 120yds: no ex* **4/1**[3]

0026 **3** 1 1/4 **Thaqaffa (IRE)**[28] 2092 6-9-7 **80**................................(h) CharlesBishop 81
(Amy Murphy) *hld up last but in tch: hdwy to ld over 4f out: rdn and hdd 2f out: kpt on tl no ex ins fnl f* **11/2**

00-2 **4** *nse* **Moayadd (USA)**[13] 2672 7-9-5 **78**............................(p[1]) OisinMurphy 79
(Neil Mulholland) *led tl over 4f out: rdn 3f out: kpt on same pce fnl 2f* **12/1**

030- **5** 3 1/2 **Airton**[10] 8538 6-9-0 **76**..(t[1]) FinleyMarsh(3) 72
(David Pipe) *hld up bhd ldrs: rdn whn outpcd 3f out: no threat after but styd on fnl f* **5/2**[2]

34-0 **6** 3 1/4 **Sunblazer (IRE)**[127] 291 9-9-3 **76**..................................(t w) SeanLevey 68
(Kim Bailey) *hld up bhd ldng trio: rdn over 2f out: wknd over 1f out* **10/1**

3m 13.44s (6.84) **Going Correction** +0.175s/f (Good) **6** Ran SP% **114.1**
Speed ratings (Par 105): **87,84,83,83,81 79**
CSF £10.66 TOTE £2.50: £1.10, £2.50; EX 12.20 Trifecta £32.50.

Owner Michael Watt & Roy David **Bred** Pantile Stud **Trained** Portway, Worcs

FOCUS
One or two tackling the trip for the first time, not least the winner, but the early pace was very steady until Thaqaffa made a swift move half a mile from home. Muddling form, but the second has been rated to form.

3092 DEREK BURRIDGE GOLF & RACING TROPHIES H'CAP 1m 4f 5y
7:50 (7:50) (Class 6) (0-65,71) 3-Y-O
£3,493 (£1,039; £519; £400; £400; £400) Stalls Low

Form RPR

05-0 **1** **Twenty Years On**[21] 2407 3-9-3 **64**........................... FinleyMarsh(3) 10 70
(Richard Hughes) *prom: led 2f out: sn rdn: styd on wl (trainer rep said, regarding improvement in form, gelding benefited from the better ground on this occasion, which in his opinion was a bit sticky at Goodwood last time out following rain and a step up in trip)* **15/2**

4-24 **2** 1 **Hummdinger (FR)**[19] 2485 3-9-6 **64**................................ HarryBentley 6 68
(Alan King) *mid-div: hdwy fr 2f out: sn rdn: str chal ent fnl f: styd on tl no ex cl home* **7/2**[1]

006 **3** *shd* **Yellow Label (USA)**[28] 2113 3-9-4 **62**.............................. OisinMurphy 2 66
(Andrew Balding) *trckd ldrs: rdn whn nt clrest of runs 2f out: chal ent fnl f: styd on but no ex nring fin* **7/1**[3]

-406 **4** 2 1/2 **Oliver Hardy**[42] 1770 3-9-2 **60**...............................(p[1] w) CharlesBishop 9 60
(Paul Cole) *mid-div: hdwy 3f out: rdn to chse ldrs 2f out: styd on same pce fnl f* **12/1**

6-60 **5** 1 3/4 **Spring Run**[22] 2361 3-9-4 **62**... RobHornby 3 59+
(Jonathan Portman) *s.i.s: in last pair: struggling 3f out: styd on fr over 1f out: fin wl* **11/1**

3250 **6** *hd* **Debbonair (IRE)**[28] 2096 3-9-1 **66**...............................(b[1]) CierenFallon(7) 5 63
(Hugo Palmer) *trckd ldrs: rdn over 2f out: one pce fnl f* **8/1**

005- **7** 3/4 **Midport (IRE)**[156] 9635 3-9-1 **59**.................................. JasonWatson 1 55+
(Roger Charlton) *mid-div: pushed along over 3f out: rdn over 2f out: no imp tl hdwy over 1f out: styd on same pce fnl f* **11/2**[2]

0-00 **8** 3/4 **Universal Song**[27] 2142 3-8-2 **46** oh1 ow3.................. AaronJones(3) 14 44
(Seamus Mullins) *squeezed up and lost pl 1st f: towards rr: rdn over 2f out: sme late prog: n.d* **33/1**

0-03 **9** *hd* **Miss Havana**[35] 1935 3-8-2 **53**....................................... GeorgiaDobie(7) 11 47
(Eve Johnson Houghton) *hld up: hdwy over 3f out: rdn over 2f out: fdd fnl f* **7/1**[3]

0-53 **10** 1/2 **Homesick Boy (IRE)**[11] 2712 3-9-4 **62**.......................(p[1]) LiamKeniry 7 56
(Ed Dunlop) *hld up: hdwy 3f out: sn rdn: nt pce to get involved* **7/1**[3]

0-00 **11** 4 **Purbeck Hills (IRE)**[27] 2141 3-9-5 **63**............................ SeanLevey 4 50
(Richard Hannon) *sn led: rdn and hdd 2f out: wknd fnl f* **18/1**

2m 40.57s (2.97) **Going Correction** +0.175s/f (Good) **11** Ran SP% **122.2**
Speed ratings (Par 97): **97,96,96,94,93 93,92,92,92,91 89**
CSF £35.32 CT £199.49 TOTE £7.90: £2.70, £1.80, £2.60; EX 35.90 Trifecta £320.70.

Owner HP Racing Twenty Years On **Bred** Mr & Mrs G Middlebrook **Trained** Upper Lambourn, Berks

FOCUS
They didn't go a great gallop here with those held up not able to get into it.

3093 GRAHAM FITCH BIRTHDAY CELEBRATION CLASSIFIED STKS 1m 1f 201y
8:20 (8:20) (Class 5) 3-Y-O £4,091 (£1,217; £608; £400) Stalls Low

Form RPR

5-02 **1** **Pempie (IRE)**[12] 2689 3-9-3 71.. OisinMurphy 4 78+
(Andrew Balding) *trckd ldr: led 2f out: styd on wl: rdn out* **5/4**[1]

50-5 **2** 1 1/2 **Starczewski (USA)**[18] 2518 3-9-2 69........................... CharlesBishop 2 73
(David Simcock) *trckd ldrs: rdn 2f out: sn edging lft: styd on to chse wnr jst ins fnl f but a being hld* **13/2**

54-3 **3** 4 **Akwaan (IRE)**[22] 2355 3-9-2 70.. DaneO'Neill 1 65
(Simon Crisford) *little slowly away: sn led: rdn and hdd 2f out: kpt on same pce fnl f* **2/1**[2]

324 **4** 14 **Ifreet (QA)**[51] 1550 3-9-2 70... SeanLevey 3 37
(Richard Hannon) *trckd ldrs: rdn over 2f out: wknd jst over 1f out* **9/2**[3]

2m 9.56s (-0.94) **Going Correction** +0.175s/f (Good) **4** Ran SP% **109.3**
Speed ratings (Par 99): **110,108,105,94**
CSF £9.10 TOTE £1.70; EX 8.90 Trifecta £18.40.

Owner Thurloe Thoroughbreds Xlv **Bred** Richard Ahern **Trained** Kingsclere, Hants

FOCUS
A tight little classified event on paper but the market got it right and in fairly straightforward fashion. They didn't go a great gallop and the winner was always close enough.
T/Plt: £72.00 to a £1 stake. Pool: £55,584.57 - 536.50 winning units T/Qpdt: £27.10 to a £1 stake. Pool: £6,319.38 - 172.16 winning units **Tim Mitchell**

2805 YORK (L-H)
Saturday, May 25

OFFICIAL GOING: Good to firm (watered; ovr 7.3, far 7.3, ctr 7.2, stands' 7.3)
Wind: Light across Weather: Cloudy with sunny periods

3094 WILLIAM HILL EXTRA PLACE RACES EVERYDAY H'CAP 7f
2:00 (2:00) (Class 2) (0-110,107) 3-Y-O+
£15,562 (£4,660; £2,330; £1,165; £582; £292) Stalls Low

Form RPR

3030 **1** **Cardsharp**[14] 2609 4-9-13 **107**... JasonHart 6 116
(Mark Johnston) *cl up: led 5f out: rdn clr over 1f out: kpt on strly* **4/1**[2]

4-34 **2** 2 1/4 **So Beloved**[28] 2100 9-9-11 **105**...............................(p[1]) DanielTudhope 3 108
(David O'Meara) *hld up towards rr: swtchd towards stands' rail 1/2-way: hdwy over 2f out: rdn to chse wnr ent fnl f: sn drvn and no imp towards fin* **11/4**[1]

6-00 **3** 1 **Zap**[14] 2609 4-9-2 **96**.. TonyHamilton 8 96
(Richard Fahey) *hld up in rr: racd nr stands' rail fr 1/2-way: hdwy 2f out: rdn over 1f out: drvn and kpt on fnl f* **7/1**

1054 **4** 3/4 **Salateen**[36] 1922 7-9-8 **102**...(p) AdamKirby 7 100
(David O'Meara) *slt ld 2f: chsd wnr: rdn along over 2f out: drvn over 1f out: grad wknd* **13/2**

-005 **5** 1 3/4 **Normandy Barriere (IRE)**[8] 2791 7-8-11 **96**..(p[1]) FayeMcManoman(5) 1 89
(Nigel Tinkler) *prom on inner: chsd ldng pair 1/2-way: rdn along over 2f out: wknd over 1f out* **16/1**

145- **6** *nk* **Polybius**[161] 9557 8-9-2 **96**..(h[1]) TomMarquand 2 89
(David Simcock) *hld up: hdwy to chse ldrs 3f out: rdn along over 2f out: drvn and wknd over 1f out* **18/1**

15-0 **7** 3 1/2 **Dancing Star**[14] 2621 6-9-11 **105**..................................... RobHornby 5 88
(Andrew Balding) *trckd ldrs: effrt 3f out: sn rdn along: wknd wl over 1f out* **11/2**[3]

10-0 **8** ½ **Via Serendipity**[14] 2609 5-9-3 **97**..................(t) DanielMuscutt 4 79
(Stuart Williams) *chsd ldrs: rdn along wl over 2f out: sn wknd* **6/1**

1m 23.98s (-0.62) **Going Correction** +0.125s/f (Good) **8** Ran SP% **113.3**
Speed ratings (Par 109): **108,105,104,103,101 101,97,96**
CSF £15.14 CT £73.21 TOTE £4.10: £1.40, £1.50, £2.50; EX 16.70 Trifecta £122.30.

Owner Sheikh Hamdan bin Mohammed Al Maktoum **Bred** Godolphin **Trained** Middleham Moor, N Yorks

FOCUS
The ground was officially good to firm and clerk of the course William Derby said: "We've had no rain since the Dante meeting and we've been putting on around 2mm of water each night to replace the moisture that's been lost." Smart handicap form, they raced down the centre in the straight and the winner was not for passing. The winner has been rated to his AW win in March.

3095 JIGSAW SPORTS BRANDING H'CAP 1m 3f 188y

2:35 (2:35) (Class 4) (0-80,79) 4-Y-O+
£10,285 (£3,060; £1,529; £764; £300; £300) **Stalls** Centre

Form RPR

31-2 **1** **Makawee (IRE)**[20] 2436 4-9-2 **74**.................. DanielTudhope 6 90+
(David O'Meara) *trckd ldrs: cl up over 2f out: led wl over 1f out: kpt on strly fnl f* **3/1**[1]

-305 **2** 1½ **Tamreer**[26] 2186 4-8-12 **75**..................(h) BenSanderson(5) 9 87
(Roger Fell) *trckd ldng pair: hdwy over 3f out: led briefly jst over 2f out: sn rdn and hdd wl over 1f out: kpt on u.p fnl f* **25/1**

4-40 **3** 5 **Perfect Illusion**[8] 2800 4-9-7 **79**..................(p[1]) RobHornby 13 83
(Andrew Balding) *dwlt and hld up towards rr: stdy hdwy 4f out: chsd ldrs 2f out: sn rdn: styd on fnl f* **10/1**

5-00 **4** 3½ **Appointed**[28] 2104 5-9-4 **76**..................(t) DavidAllan 3 74
(Tim Easterby) *hld up: hdwy 4f out: rdn along to chse ldrs 2f out: drvn over 1f out: kpt on same pce* **8/1**

-540 **5** *hd* **Framley Garth (IRE)**[10] 2748 7-8-12 **75**.................. PaulaMuir(5) 11 73
(Liam Bailey) *trckd ldrs: hdwy 4f out: pushed along on outer and outpcd wl over 2f out: sn rdn: styd on appr fnl f* **9/1**

0-56 **6** 1¼ **Ingleby Hollow**[15] 2591 7-9-2 **74**..................(t) RobbieDowney 4 70
(David O'Meara) *hld up towards rr: hdwy over 3f out: rdn along 2f out: kpt on fr over 1f out: nt rch ldrs* **14/1**

5-00 **7** ½ **Mapped (USA)**[28] 2116 4-9-3 **75**..................(p[1]) RobertWinston 12 70
(Iain Jardine) *trckd ldr: cl up 4f out: rdn along and ev ch over 2f out: drvn wl over 1f out: grad wknd* **13/2**[2]

40-6 **8** 1¾ **Armed (IRE)**[42] 1771 4-9-4 **76**..................(h[1]) SamJames 7 68
(Phillip Makin) *hld up in rr: effrt and sme hdwy 3f out: sn rdn along and n.d* **15/2**

0-22 **9** ½ **Ideal Candy (IRE)**[24] 2290 4-8-13 **74**..................(h) RowanScott(3) 5 66
(Karen Tutty) *led: pushed along over 3f out: rdn and hdd over 2f out: sn wknd* **7/1**[3]

44-4 **10** 2½ **Breathable**[19] 2479 4-8-11 **69**.................. RachelRichardson 1 57
(Tim Easterby) *a towards rr* **25/1**

4111 **11** 6 **Archive (FR)**[26] 2185 9-9-1 **73**.................. AdamKirby 8 51
(Brian Ellison) *midfield: hdwy over 4f out: rdn along over 3f out: sn btn (trainer could offer no explanation for gelding's performance; post-race examination failed to reveal any abnormalities)* **13/2**[2]

/60- **12** 1¼ **Near Kettering**[14] 9610 5-9-1 **73**..................(t) CamHardie 2 49
(Sam England) *a in rr* **50/1**

40-0 **13** *nse* **Ad Libitum**[14] 2636 4-9-2 **74**.................. JasonHart 10 50
(Roger Fell) *trckd ldrs: pushed along over 4f out: rdn over 3f out: sn wknd* **18/1**

2m 28.56s (-4.64) **Going Correction** +0.125s/f (Good) **13** Ran SP% **127.7**
Speed ratings (Par 105): **114,113,109,107,107 106,106,104,104,102 98,98,98**
CSF £99.27 CT £709.99 TOTE £3.50: £1.70, £10.30, £4.20; EX 127.20 Trifecta £1274.60.

Owner Geoff & Sandra Turnbull **Bred** Geoff & Sandra Turnbull **Trained** Upper Helmsley, N Yorks

FOCUS
Two of the fillies came clear in a fair handicap. The level is a bit fluid.

3096 WILLIAM HILL BRONTE CUP FILLIES' STKS (GROUP 3) (F&M) 1m 5f 188y

3:05 (3:08) (Class 1) 4-Y-O+
£51,039 (£19,350; £9,684; £4,824; £2,421; £1,215) **Stalls** Low

Form RPR

11-0 **1** **Dramatic Queen (USA)**[27] 2167 4-9-0 99.................. DanielTudhope 5 110
(William Haggas) *trckd ldrs: hdwy 3f out: sn chsng ldr: rdn to chal wl over 1f out: drvn ent fnl f: kpt on wl to ld fnl 75yds* **7/1**

14-1 **2** ½ **Enbihaar (IRE)**[21] 2401 4-9-0 105.................. AdamKirby 3 109
(John Gosden) *sn led: pushed along and edgd rt 3f out: rdn 2f out: drvn and edgd rt ent fnl f: hdd and no ex fnl 75yds* **6/4**[1]

-211 **3** 3 **Bayshore Freeway (IRE)**[12] 2680 4-9-0 94.................. JasonHart 8 105
(Mark Johnston) *trckd ldrs: effrt on outer over 4f out: rdn along wl over 2f out: drvn over 1f out: kpt on u.p fnl f* **6/1**[3]

30-3 **4** 1 **Pilaster**[45] 1693 4-9-0 106.................. ColmO'Donoghue 2 104
(Roger Varian) *in tch on inner: hdwy 3f out: chsd ldrs 2f out: sn rdn: drvn and kpt on same pce fnl f (jockey said his saddle slipped on filly when leaving stalls)* **3/1**[2]

10-0 **5** 9 **Maid Up**[21] 2410 4-9-0 105.................. RobHornby 7 91
(Andrew Balding) *hld up: stdy hdwy whn nt clr run and hmpd 2f out: nt rcvr* **8/1**

121- **6** ½ **Alexana**[260] 7010 4-9-0 86.................. TomMarquand 4 90
(William Haggas) *trckd ldng pair: pushed along 4f out: rdn on inner whn edgd rt over 2f out: sn drvn and wknd* **14/1**

5021 **7** 10 **Voi**[10] 2737 5-9-0 75..................(t) NickyMackay 6 76
(Conrad Allen) *a in rr* **66/1**

155- **8** 1 **Altra Vita**[205] 8770 4-9-0 92.................. RyanTate 9 75
(Sir Mark Prescott Bt) *chsd ldr: pushed along 4f out: rdn 3f out: drvn and edgd lft 2f out: sn wknd* **25/1**

50-6 **R** **Jet Streaming (IRE)**[21] 2404 5-9-0 88.................. TomQueally 1
(Samuel Farrell, Ire) *ref to r* **50/1**

2m 55.35s (-4.85) **Going Correction** +0.125s/f (Good) **9** Ran SP% **116.9**
Speed ratings (Par 110): **118,117,116,115,110 110,104,103,**
CSF £18.01 TOTE £8.00: £2.00, £1.20, £1.80; EX 23.80 Trifecta £132.50.

Owner Sheikh Juma Dalmook Al Maktoum **Bred** Gary Chervenell **Trained** Newmarket, Suffolk

■ Stewards' Enquiry : Daniel Tudhope two-day ban: used whip above permitted level (Jun 8,9)

FOCUS
Perhaps not the strongest of Group 3s, they headed centre-field in the straight and the favourite was worn down late. The second has been rated as finding a bit on her Goodwood win.

3097 WILLIAM HILL LEADING ON COURSE BOOKMAKER SPRINT H'CAP 5f

3:45 (3:48) (Class 2) (0-105,105) 3-Y-O+
£31,125 (£9,320; £4,660; £2,330; £1,165; £585) **Stalls** Centre

Form RPR

5521 **1** **Duke Of Firenze**[7] 2841 10-8-4 **85**.................. PhilDennis 19 94
(David C Griffiths) *hld up towards rr: smooth hdwy over 2f out: chsd ldrs over 1f out: rdn to chal ins fnl f: edgd lft and kpt on to ld fnl 75yds* **16/1**

0-25 **2** *nk* **Dark Shot**[9] 2775 6-8-5 **86**..................(p) PaddyMathers 16 94
(Scott Dixon) *in tch: hdwy to chse ldrs over 2f out: rdn over 1f out: drvn to take slt briefly ins fnl f: hdd and no ex fnl 75yds* **25/1**

-421 **3** 1¼ **Copper Knight (IRE)**[9] 2775 5-9-10 **105**..................(t) DavidAllan 15 109
(Tim Easterby) *cl up centre: led 2f out: rdn over 1f out: drvn and hdd ins fnl f: kpt on* **6/1**[3]

10-5 **4** *nk* **Gunmetal (IRE)**[20] 2442 6-9-8 **103**.................. RobbieDowney 14 105+
(David Barron) *hld up in rr: swtchd rt to stands' rail and hdwy 2f out: rdn over 1f out: kpt on strly fnl f* **20/1**

000- **5** *hd* **Koditime (IRE)**[276] 6425 4-8-13 **94**.................. CliffordLee 18 96
(Clive Cox) *trckd ldrs centre: hdwy and cl up 2f out: rdn and ev ch over 1f out: drvn ent fnl f: kpt on same pce* **25/1**

0-00 **6** ½ **Harome (IRE)**[9] 2775 5-8-4 **85**.................. NicolaCurrie 1 85
(Roger Fell) *racd towards far side: cl up: disp ld 1/2-way: rdn along and ev ch over 1f out: grad wknd fnl f* **25/1**

4000 **7** ½ **Orvar (IRE)**[9] 2775 6-8-11 **92**.................. BarryMcHugh 12 90
(Paul Midgley) *towards rr: hdwy 2f out: rdn to chse ldrs over 1f out: kpt on u.p fnl f* **66/1**

0-04 **8** 1 **Eeh Bah Gum (IRE)**[9] 2775 4-8-7 **88**.................. RachelRichardson 13 83+
(Tim Easterby) *t.k.h: hld up towards rr: hdwy 2f out: rdn and styng on whn n.m.r and sltly hmpd over 1f out: kpt on fnl f (jockey said gelding was denied a clear run appr 1 1/2f out)* **8/1**

-266 **9** ½ **El Astronaute (IRE)**[10] 2744 6-9-5 **105**.................. DylanHogan(5) 8 98
(John Quinn) *dwlt: racd towards far side: in tch: pushed along and hdwy to chse ldrs 2f out: sn rdn: drvn and wknd appr fnl f* **9/2**[2]

3151 **10** ½ **Canford Bay (IRE)**[15] 2589 5-8-2 **83**.................. CamHardie 11 74
(Antony Brittain) *chsd ldrs centre: rdn along 2f out: grad wknd* **33/1**

03-0 **11** ¾ **Lord Riddiford (IRE)**[16] 2557 4-8-10 **91**.................. JasonHart 2 79
(John Quinn) *racd towards far side: cl up: disp ld 1/2-way: rdn along wl over 1f out: grad wknd* **14/1**

-661 **12** ¾ **Muscika**[7] 2843 5-8-6 **90**..................(v) ConorMcGovern(3) 17 76
(David O'Meara) *chsd ldrs centre: rdn along 2f out: sn drvn and wknd* **25/1**

00-0 **13** ½ **Holmeswood**[10] 2743 5-8-6 **87**.................. KieranO'Neill 9 71
(Julie Camacho) *trckd ldrs centre: rdn along 2f out: sn wknd* **20/1**

6003 **14** 1¼ **Marnie James**[9] 2775 4-9-10 **105**..................(t) RobertWinston 4 84
(Iain Jardine) *chsd ldrs towards far side: rdn along 2f out: sn wknd* **16/1**

6- **15** 1 **Acqume (AUS)**[112] 4-9-1 **96**..................(b) AdamKirby 3 72
(Toby Edmonds, Australia) *cl up centre: slt ld 3f out: rdn and hdd 2f out: sn wknd* **20/1**

0-03 **16** 1¾ **A Momentofmadness**[15] 2576 6-9-7 **102**.................. ColmO'Donoghue 7 71
(Charles Hills) *towards rr: hdwy towards far side 2f out: sn rdn and n.d (jockey said gelding was slowly away having anticipated the start)* **14/1**

-410 **17** 2¼ **Abel Handy (IRE)**[9] 2775 4-8-11 **92**..................(b[1]) TonyHamilton 6 53
(Declan Carroll) *cl up centre: rdn along 2f out: sn wknd* **20/1**

2122 **18** ½ **Acclaim The Nation (IRE)**[15] 2589 6-8-6 **87**..................(p) PaulHanagan 5 46
(Eric Alston) *towards rr: effrt and sme hdwy towards far side 1/2-way: rdn along 2f out: n.d (jockey said gelding was restless in stalls)* **16/1**

-111 **19** 31 **Leodis Dream (IRE)**[17] 2522 3-8-11 **100**.................. DanielTudhope 10
(David O'Meara) *dwlt and awkward s: sn swtchd markedly rt and bhd: hdwy towards stands' rail 1/2-way and in touich: rdn 2f out: sn wknd and eased (jockey said gelding missed the break having anticipated the start and hit its head in the stalls. vet said gelding bled from nose)* **7/2**[1]

58.33s (0.13) **Going Correction** +0.125s/f (Good) **19** Ran SP% **135.6**
WFA 3 from 4yo+ 8lb
Speed ratings (Par 109): **104,103,101,101,100 99,99,97,96,95 94,93,92,90,89 86,82,81,32**
CSF £385.44 CT £1673.83 TOTE £21.60: £4.00, £5.40, £2.00, £5.10; EX 312.70 Trifecta £6134.60.

Owner Adam,Damary-Thompson,Wilson,Griffiths **Bred** Cheveley Park Stud Ltd **Trained** Bawtry, S Yorks

FOCUS
A typically competitive 5f burn up and the veteran of the field triumphed. The second has been rated to last year's best, and the third to his latest effort.

3098 YORKSHIRE REGIMENT BRITISH EBF NOVICE MEDIAN AUCTION STKS (PLUS 10 RACE) 6f

4:15 (4:16) (Class 3) 2-Y-O
£9,703 (£2,887; £1,443; £721) **Stalls** High

Form RPR

3 **1** **War Storm**[15] 2594 2-9-5 0.................. DanielTudhope 1 83
(Archie Watson) *trckd ldr: hdwy 2f out: rdn to chal jst over 1f out: drvn to ld ins fnl f: kpt on wl towards fin* **5/2**[1]

2 2 **Makyon (IRE)** 2-9-5 0.................. JasonHart 7 77
(Mark Johnston) *led: pushed along over 2f out: rdn over 1f out and sn jnd: drvn and hdd ins fnl f: kpt on same pce towards fin* **7/2**[2]

3 2 **Jump The Gun (IRE)** 2-9-5 0.................. NicolaCurrie 5 71
(Jamie Osborne) *dwlt and wnt lft s: in rr: hdwy on outer to trck ldrs 1/2-way: rdn along wl over 1f out: kpt on same pce (jockey said colt was slowly away)* **5/1**[3]

4 **4** 1½ **Dutch Decoy**[26] 2184 2-9-5 0.................. TonyHamilton 4 66
(Richard Fahey) *in tch: pushed along and hdwy over 2f out: rdn wl over 1f out: sn no imp* **7/2**[2]

5 ¾ **International Lion** 2-9-5 0.................. PaulHanagan 6 64+
(Richard Fahey) *towards rr: green: outpcd and detached 1/2-way: hdwy wl over 1f out: styd on wl fnl f: nrst fin* **13/2**

6 **6** 1¼ **Van Dijk**[19] 2476 2-9-5 0.................. CamHardie 2 60
(Antony Brittain) *a towards rr* **20/1**

04 **7** 3¾ **Geepower (IRE)**[11] 2706 2-9-5 0.................. AdamKirby 8 49
(Brian Ellison) *chsd ldng pair on inner: rdn along over 2f out: sn wknd* **16/1**

8 2¾ **Break Cover** 2-9-5 0.................. DanielMuscutt 3 41
(Mark H Tompkins) *chsd ldrs: rdn along wl over 2f out: sn wknd* **33/1**

1m 13.29s (1.69) **Going Correction** +0.125s/f (Good) **8** Ran SP% **116.6**
Speed ratings (Par 97): **93,90,87,85,84 83,78,74**
CSF £11.68 TOTE £3.20: £1.30, £1.50, £2.00; EX 13.30 Trifecta £58.90.

Owner Saeed Bin Mohammed Al Qassimi **Bred** Gary Hodson & Peter Moule **Trained** Upper Lambourn, W Berks

FOCUS

They raced stands' side in this juvenile novice and the right pair came clear.

3099 INFINITY TYRES IRISH CHAMPIONS WEEKEND EBF FILLIES' H'CAP — 1m 2f 56y

4:50 (4:50) (Class 3) (0-90,89) 3-Y-O — £9,703 (£2,887; £1,443; £721) Stalls Low

Form — RPR

6-61 **1** **Arctic Fox**[9] 2765 3-8-11 **79** .... PaddyMathers 2 — 87
(Richard Fahey) *dwlt: hld up in rr: hdwy on inner 3f out: rdn to ld over 1f out: drvn ins fnl f: kpt on wl towards fin* **15/8**[1]

12-0 **2** *nk* **Vivid Diamond (IRE)**[17] 2521 3-9-7 **89** .... JasonHart 5 — 96
(Mark Johnston) *trckd ldr: effrt and cl up over 2f out: rdn to dispute ld over 1f out: drvn and ev ch ins fnl f: kpt on same pce towards fin* **9/2**

30-3 **3** *3* **Quintada**[9] 2768 3-8-9 **77** .... TomMarquand 4 — 78
(Mark Johnston) *led: pushed along 3f out: rdn 2f out: hdd over 1f out: kpt on same pce* **7/2**[3]

34 **4** *3/4* **Osmosis**[11] 2711 3-8-2 **70** .... CamHardie 3 — 70?
(Jason Ward) *chsd ldrs: rdn along over 2f out: drvn and wknd over 1f out* **11/1**

514 **5** *1/2* **Elisheba (IRE)**[14] 2618 3-9-1 **83** .... KieranO'Neill 1 — 82
(John Gosden) *trckd ldng pair: effrt and cl up 3f out: rdn along over 2f out: drvn wl over 1f out: sn wknd* **11/4**[2]

2m 10.42s (0.12) **Going Correction** +0.125s/f (Good) — **5** Ran SP% **110.2**
Speed ratings (Par 100): **104,103,101,100,100**
CSF £10.54 TOTE £2.60: £1.50, £1.90; EX 9.50 Trifecta £23.00.
Owner Sir Robert Ogden **Bred** Sir Robert Ogden **Trained** Musley Bank, N Yorks

FOCUS

A decent fillies' handicap, but the pace was only steady and it didn't suit them all. The third and fourth have been rated close to form.

3100 JOHN WRIGHT ELECTRICAL H'CAP (FOR GENTLEMAN AMATEUR RIDERS) — 7f

5:25 (5:25) (Class 3) (0-90,90) 4-Y-O+ — £9,358 (£2,902; £1,450; £726) Stalls Low

Form — RPR

0-00 **1** **Citron Major**[10] 2743 4-11-3 **86** .... MrTHamilton 1 — 95
(Nigel Tinkler) *stdd s and hld up in rr: smooth hdwy on inner over 2f out: rdn to chal over 1f out: led ins fnl f: kpt on* **9/2**[2]

00-0 **2** *1* **Dark Intention (IRE)**[17] 2526 6-10-13 **82** .... MrWilliamEasterby 2 — 88
(Lawrence Mullaney) *cl up on inner: led wl over 1f out: sn rdn: drvn and hdd ins fnl f: kpt on same pce towards fin* **14/1**

0-00 **3** *1/2* **Magic City (IRE)**[11] 2710 10-9-11 **71** oh1 .... MrJTeal(5) 8 — 76
(Michael Easterby) *hld up: hdwy on outer 2f out: chal over 1f out: rdn ent fnl f and ev ch: kpt on same pce* **5/1**[3]

-341 **4** *2 1/2* **Sir Roderic (IRE)**[11] 2714 6-10-4 **73** .... MrPatrickMillman 10 — 71
(Rod Millman) *trckd ldrs: hdwy over 2f out: rdn over 1f out: drvn and one pce fnl f* **9/2**[2]

3-12 **5** *1* **Right Action**[12] 2679 5-10-10 **84** .... MrMatthewEnnis(5) 7 — 79
(Richard Fahey) *led: pushed along 3f out: rdn and hdd over 2f out: grad wknd* **5/1**[3]

2450 **6** *3 3/4* **Gallipoli (IRE)**[14] 2609 6-11-0 **90** ....(b) MrEireannCagney(7) 6 — 75
(Richard Fahey) *trckd ldrs: cl up 1/2-way: led over 2f out: rdn and hdd wl over 1f out: sn drvn and wknd* **8/1**

4-22 **7** *6* **Saluti (IRE)**[33] 1978 5-10-13 **82** .... MrSimonWalker 3 — 51
(Paul Midgley) *t.k.h: trckd ldrs: pushed along over 2f out: sn rdn and btn (jockey said gelding stopped quickly; post-race examination failed to reveal any abnormalities)* **7/2**[1]

632- **8** *2 1/2* **Muraahin**[254] 7216 4-10-5 **74** .... MrAlexFerguson 5 — 36
(Jamie Osborne) *chsd ldrs: rdn along wl over 2f out: sn wknd (vet said gelding was lame left hind)* **12/1**

1m 25.61s (1.01) **Going Correction** +0.125s/f (Good) — **8** Ran SP% **117.4**
Speed ratings (Par 107): **99,97,97,94,93 89,82,79**
CSF £65.21 CT £330.89 TOTE £4.80: £1.80, £2.80, £1.70; EX 62.20 Trifecta £364.80.
Owner Walter Veti & Sara Hattersley **Bred** Bearstone Stud Ltd **Trained** Langton, N Yorks

FOCUS

This was run at a steady pace and developed into a bit of a dash. The second has been rated to form.

T/Jkpt: Not Won. T/Plt: £102.20 to a £1 stake. Pool: £130,240.50 - 929.88 winning units T/Qpdt: £18.20 to a £1 stake. Pool: £10,365.88 - 419.99 winning units **Joe Rowntree**

3101 - 3102a (Foreign Racing) - See Raceform Interactive

3059 CURRAGH (R-H)

Saturday, May 25

OFFICIAL GOING: Good to firm (good in places on straight course; watered)

3103a WEATHERBYS IRELAND GREENLANDS STKS (GROUP 2) — 6f

3:00 (3:00) 4-Y-O+ — £63,783 (£20,540; £9,729; £4,324; £2,162; £1,081) Stalls Centre

RPR

1 **Mr Lupton (IRE)**[231] 7974 6-9-3 110 .... JamieSpencer 2 — 115+
(Richard Fahey) *hld up in rr tl 2f out: prog stands' side to chse ldrs ent fnl f: qckdn wl to ld ins fnl 100yds: comf* **5/1**[3]

2 *3/4* **Speak In Colours**[217] 8405 4-9-3 111 ....(t) DonnachaO'Brien 4 — 113
(Joseph Patrick O'Brien, Ire) *trckd ldr in 2nd: rdn to ld ent fnl f: sn strly pressed and hdd ins fnl 100yds: no ex cl home w wnr* **4/1**[1]

3 *1 3/4* **Gordon Lord Byron (IRE)**[15] 2604 11-9-3 104 .... ChrisHayes 6 — 107
(T Hogan, Ire) *trckd ldrs in 3rd: rdn over 2f out: briefly squeezed for room appr fnl f in 5th: rallied wl into 3rd cl home* **20/1**

4 *1/2* **Ardhoomey (IRE)**[26] 2221 7-9-3 106 ....(t) ColinKeane 5 — 105
(G M Lyons, Ire) *led tl hdd 1f out: kpt on same pce: dropped to 4th cl home* **10/1**

5 *3/4* **Chessman (IRE)**[6] 2879 5-9-3 102 .... OisinOrr 7 — 103
(Richard John O'Brien, Ire) *chsd ldrs: 6th at 1/2-way: travelled wl under 2f out: sltly hmpd 1f out: kpt on same pce fnl f* **5/1**[3]

6 *1 1/2* **Smash Williams (IRE)**[42] 1776 6-9-3 105 ....(t) KevinManning 9 — 98
(J S Bolger, Ire) *bit slowly away: racd in mid-div: 5th at 1/2-way: rdn and nt qckn over 1f out: styd on again clsng stages* **9/2**[2]

7 *1/2* **Urban Beat (IRE)**[26] 2221 4-9-3 102 .... ShaneFoley 1 — 97
(J P Murtagh, Ire) *hld up: pushed along 2f out: no imp ent fnl f: sn one pce* **8/1**

8 *4 1/2* **Gobi Desert**[594] 7855 4-9-3 97 .... WJLee 3 — 82
(P Twomey, Ire) *chsd ldrs on outer in 4th: pushed along under 2f out: nt qckn ent fnl f: wknd* **8/1**

9 *5* **St Patrick's Day (USA)**[223] 8239 4-9-3 100 ....(t) RyanMoore 8 — 66
(A P O'Brien, Ire) *racd in rr of mid-div: rdn and nt qckn in rr under 2f out: sn no ex* **8/1**

1m 11.51s (-2.69) **Going Correction** -0.05s/f (Good) — **9** Ran SP% **118.7**
Speed ratings: **115,114,111,111,110 108,107,101,94**
CSF £26.12 TOTE £4.20: £1.80, £1.90, £5.50; DF 13.60 Trifecta £189.80.
Owner N D Kershaw & Partner **Bred** Ms E O'Neill **Trained** Musley Bank, N Yorks

FOCUS

Last year's winner, Merchant Navy, was rated 117, while Tasleet was in there with a mark of 114 at the time. The highest-rated runner in this field was 111 so it was certainly not a vintage renewal. There was a brisk tempo from the outset.

3104a TATTERSALLS IRISH 2,000 GUINEAS (GROUP 1) (ENTIRE COLTS & FILLIES) — 1m

3:35 (3:40) 3-Y-O — £209,009 (£68,468; £32,432; £10,810; £7,207; £3,603)

RPR

1 **Phoenix Of Spain (IRE)**[210] 8633 3-9-0 112 .... JamieSpencer 1 — 120+
(Charles Hills) *mde all: strly pressed to 3f out: shkn up to extend advantage over 1f out: clr ent fnl f: kpt on strly* **16/1**[3]

2 *3* **Too Darn Hot**[9] 2777 3-9-0 126 .... FrankieDettori 11 — 113
(John Gosden) *racd in mid-div: clsr to chse ldrs 1/2-way: rdn to chse ldr in 2nd over 2f out: no imp on ldr 1f out: kpt on same pce* **6/4**[1]

3 *1/2* **Decrypt**[35] 1962 3-9-0 105 .... WJLee 8 — 112
(P Twomey, Ire) *racd in rr of mid-div: pushed along to chse ldrs under 2f out: wnt 4th ent fnl f: kpt on wl into 3rd cl home: nvr nrr* **20/1**

4 *nk* **Skardu**[21] 2411 3-9-0 111 .... JamesDoyle 2 — 111
(William Haggas) *chsd ldrs far side: 5th at 1/2-way: rdn into 3rd over 1f out: nt qckn ins fnl f: kpt on same pce and ct for 3rd cl home* **13/2**[2]

5 *2* **Magna Grecia (IRE)**[21] 2411 3-9-0 118 .... RyanMoore 9 — 106
(A P O'Brien, Ire) *chsd ldrs in 4th: 3rd at 1/2-way: rdn and nt qckn under 2f out: no imp in 5th ent fnl f: kpt on same pce (vet said colt was post-race normal)* **6/4**[1]

6 *nk* **I Am Superman (IRE)**[19] 2492 3-9-0 101 .... LeighRoche 4 — 106
(M D O'Callaghan, Ire) *racd towards rr: prog over 2f out into mid-div: no imp in 7th appr fnl f: kpt on wl clsng stages* **66/1**

7 *shd* **Van Beethoven (CAN)**[13] 2668 3-9-0 106 .... SeamieHeffernan 14 — 105
(A P O'Brien, Ire) *racd towards rr: prog in centre of trck under 2f out: kpt on wl ins fnl f: nvr nrr* **66/1**

8 *1 1/2* **Mohawk (IRE)**[16] 2558 3-9-0 112 .... DonnachaO'Brien 13 — 102
(A P O'Brien, Ire) *racd in mid-div: clsr on outer to briefly chse ldrs 1/2-way: sn rdn and nt qckn over 2f out: kpt on same pce fr over 1f out* **16/1**[3]

9 *2* **Old Glory (IRE)**[217] 8428 3-9-0 103 .... WayneLordan 3 — 97
(A P O'Brien, Ire) *racd in rr of mid-div: pushed along 3f out: no imp over 1f out in 7th: wknd* **25/1**

10 *1 3/4* **Guaranteed (IRE)**[13] 2662 3-9-0 103 ....(t) KevinManning 6 — 93
(J S Bolger, Ire) *trckd ldrs in 3rd: 4th at 1/2-way: sn pushed along and wknd qckly under 3f out* **100/1**

11 *3/4* **Shelir (IRE)**[19] 2492 3-9-0 101 .... ChrisHayes 5 — 92
(D K Weld, Ire) *racd in mid-div: pushed along 3f out: nt qckn under 2f out: sn one pce* **25/1**

12 *4 3/4* **Emaraaty Ana**[21] 2411 3-9-0 109 .... AndreaAtzeni 10 — 81
(Kevin Ryan) *sn pressed ldr in 2nd: pushed along 3f out: wknd fr 2f out* **66/1**

13 *11* **Globe Theatre (USA)**[62] 1310 3-9-0 81 .... PBBeggy 7 — 55
(A P O'Brien, Ire) *a towards rr: rdn 1/2-way: detached under 3f out* **150/1**

14 *30* **Hillwalker**[335] 4163 3-9-0 90 ....(t[1]) RoryCleary 12
(Thomas Cleary, Ire) *racd in rr of mid-div: pushed along 1/2-way and sn dropped to rr: detached under 3f out: eased* **100/1**

1m 36.52s (-4.08) **Going Correction** -0.05s/f (Good) — **14** Ran SP% **124.7**
Speed ratings: **118,115,114,114,112 111,111,110,108,106 105,101,90,60**
CSF £40.40 CT £550.90 TOTE £16.40: £2.70, £1.10, £4.40; DF 59.10 Trifecta £665.70.
Owner Tony Wechsler & Ann Plummer **Bred** Mrs Cherry Faeste **Trained** Lambourn, Berks

FOCUS

This was billed as a match between champion juvenile Too Darn Hot and the 2,000 Guineas winner Magna Grecia but neither colt could live with Phoenix Of Spain who put in a very good performance from the front. This looked an above average renewal and while the gallop was sedate early the winner looked all class. The standard fits rated around the fourth, sixth and seventh.

3105a LANWADES STUD STKS (GROUP 2) (F&M) — 1m

4:10 (4:12) 4-Y-O+ — £63,783 (£20,540; £9,729; £4,324; £2,162; £1,081)

RPR

1 **Beshaayir**[239] 7732 4-9-0 101 ....(t) FrankieDettori 3 — 112
(William Haggas) *mde all: extended advantage under 3f out: styd on wl fnl f: nvr in danger* **8/1**

2 *1 1/2* **I Can Fly**[7] 2829 4-9-0 113 .... RyanMoore 7 — 109+
(A P O'Brien, Ire) *bit slowly away and racd in rr: pushed along over 2f out: gd hdwy into 3rd ent fnl f: kpt on same pce into 2nd clsng stages: nvr nrr* **11/8**[1]

3 *hd* **Red Tea**[19] 2497 6-9-1 107 ow1 .... DonnachaO'Brien 4 — 109+
(Joseph Patrick O'Brien, Ire) *chsd ldrs in mod 4th: pushed along over 3f out: nt qckn 2f out: swtchd rt ent fnl f: styd on wl far side into 3rd cl home: nvr nrr* **9/2**[3]

4 *1/2* **One Master**[167] 9476 5-9-3 113 .... JamesDoyle 6 — 110+
(William Haggas) *hld up in 6th: pushed along and clsr under 2f out to chse ldrs in 3rd: wnt 2nd over 1f out: kpt on same pce: dropped to 4th cl home* **3/1**[2]

5 *2 1/2* **Normandel (FR)**[62] 1307 5-9-0 99 .... KevinManning 2 — 102+
(J S Bolger, Ire) *chsd ldng pair in 3rd: rdn and nt qckn 2f out: hmpd and checked 1f out where dropped to rr: kpt on again into 5th cl home* **20/1**

6 *3/4* **Yulong Gold Fairy**[62] 1307 4-9-0 105 .... ShaneFoley 1 — 100+
(D K Weld, Ire) *hld up in 5th: rdn along over 2f out on far rails: no imp appr fnl f: kpt on one pce* **9/1**

7 *nse* **Shekiba (IRE)**[20] 2451 4-9-0 91 ....(b[1]) GaryCarroll 5 — 100
(Joseph G Murphy, Ire) *trckd ldr in clr 2nd tl 2f out: wknd fnl f* **66/1**

1m 37.06s (-3.54) **Going Correction** -0.05s/f (Good) — **7** Ran SP% **112.7**
Speed ratings: **115,113,113,112,110 109,109**
CSF £18.94 TOTE £8.60: £2.80, £1.50; DF 22.00 Trifecta £94.30.
Owner Sheikh Rashid Dalmook Al Maktoum **Bred** Exors Of The Late Sir Eric Parker **Trained** Newmarket, Suffolk

■ Stewards' Enquiry : Donnacha O'Brien caution; weighed in 1.1lbs overweight

FOCUS
A career best from Beshaayir who did it the hard way from the front. The second and fifth have been rated close to their marks.

3106 - 3107a (Foreign Racing) - See Raceform Interactive

2226 **BORDEAUX LE BOUSCAT** (R-H)
Saturday, May 25

OFFICIAL GOING: Turf: good to soft

3108a **163RD DERBY DU MIDI (LISTED RACE) (3YO) (TURF)** **1m 1f 110y**
12:45 3-Y-O **£24,774** (£9,909; £7,432; £4,954; £2,477)

RPR
1 **Taos (FR)**[32] 3-8-13 0 Jean-BernardEyquem 5 100+
(J-C Rouget, France) **4/1**[3]
2 3/4 **Corando**[23] 2352 3-8-13 0 OlivierPeslier 6 98
(C Laffon-Parias, France) **9/1**
3 3/4 **Fairmont (FR)**[23] 2352 3-8-13 0 JulienAuge 3 96
(C Ferland, France) **66/10**
4 snk **Wookie (FR)**[70] 3-8-13 0 CristianDemuro 4 96
(J-C Rouget, France) **3/1**[2]
5 snk **Sagauteur (FR)**[32] 2027 3-9-3 0 Francois-XavierBertras 7 99
(D Guillemin, France) **5/1**
6 1 **Fureur De Vivre (FR)**[26] 3-8-13 0 MaximeGuyon 2 93
(B De Montzey, France) **5/2**[1]
7 nse **Barys**[27] 2163 3-9-3 0 (b) EdwardGreatrex 1 97
(Archie Watson) *pushed along to secure ld on rail: kicked for home ins fnl 2f: rdn 1 1/2f out: hdd w 1f to run: kpt on at same pce: hld whn short of room cl home* **15/1**

2m 2.96s 7 Ran SP% **119.6**
PARI-MUTUEL (all including 1 euro stake): WIN 5.00; PLACE 2.20, 4.20; SF 27.60.
Owner Martin S Schwartz Racing **Bred** B Jeffroy & T Jeffroy **Trained** Pau, France

3109 - 3113a (Foreign Racing) - See Raceform Interactive

3101 **CURRAGH** (R-H)
Sunday, May 26

OFFICIAL GOING: Good to firm (good in places on straight course; watered)

3114 **TATTERSALLS GOLD CUP (GROUP 1)** **1m 2f 110y**
3:50 (3:50) 4-Y-O+ **£212,612** (£68,468; £32,432; £14,414; £7,207)

Form RPR
2-11 1 **Magical (IRE)**[20] 2494 4-9-0 122 RyanMoore 1 121+
(A P O'Brien, Ire) *settled bhd ldr in 2nd: over 2 l bhd and clr of remainder at 1/2-way: impr travelling wl to dispute ld 2f out and sn led: pushed clr over 1f out and in command: easily* **2/7**[1]
5-22 2 7 **Flag Of Honour (IRE)**[20] 2494 4-9-3 117 DonnachaO'Brien 4 110
(A P O'Brien, Ire) *led: over 2 l clr of nrest rival at 1/2-way and clr of remainder: rdn over 2f out and sn jnd: hdd under 2f out and sn no ch w easy wnr: kpt on same pce ins fnl f* **4/1**[2]
1-02 3 4 3/4 **Mustajeer**[28] 2158 6-9-3 108 (h) ColinKeane 3 101
(G M Lyons, Ire) *sn settled in rr: last at 1/2-way: sme hdwy on outer under 2f out into mod 3rd ins fnl f where no imp on ldrs: kpt on* **16/1**[3]
0-23 4 3/4 **Zihba (IRE)**[14] 2660 4-9-3 104 (t[1]) ChrisHayes 2 100
(J A Stack, Ire) *chsd ldrs and disp 3rd early: 3rd at 1/2-way: drvn in mod 3rd and no imp on ldrs over 3f out: u.p disputing mod 3rd 1 1/2f out: kpt on one pce in 4th ins fnl f* **33/1**
6-52 5 1 3/4 **Verbal Dexterity (IRE)**[14] 2660 4-9-3 105 KevinManning 5 97
(J S Bolger, Ire) *chsd ldrs and disp 3rd early: 4th 1/2-way: drvn in mod 4th and no imp on ldrs over 3f out: u.p disputing mod 3rd 1 1/2f out: no ex and dropped to rr ins fnl f* **18/1**

2m 13.85s (-4.25) **Going Correction** -0.075s/f (Good) 5 Ran SP% **111.8**
Speed ratings: **112,106,103,102,101**
CSF £1.88 TOTE £1.10: £1.02, £1.50; DF 1.70 Trifecta £3.50.
Owner Derrick Smith & Mrs John Magnier & Michael Tabor **Bred** Orpendale, Chelston & Wynatt **Trained** Cashel, Co Tipperary

FOCUS
Very easy for the odds-on favourite, toying with a stablemate who wants further. The other three had their own private battle for a share of the generous prize-fund. The winner has been rated to her best.

3115 **TATTERSALLS IRISH 1,000 GUINEAS (GROUP 1) (FILLIES)** **1m**
4:25 (4:28) 3-Y-O
£209,009 (£68,468; £32,432; £10,810; £7,207; £3,603)

Form RPR
22-1 1 **Hermosa (IRE)**[21] 2443 3-9-0 112 RyanMoore 2 115+
(A P O'Brien, Ire) *mde all: narrow advantage at 1/2-way: rdn clr 1f out and styd on strly to assert ins fnl f: comf* **5/2**[1]
143- 2 4 **Pretty Pollyanna**[226] 8148 3-9-0 116 FrankieDettori 10 106
(Michael Bell) *chsd ldrs: disp 3rd at 1/2-way: effrt nr side 2f out and sn pressed wnr briefly: no imp on wnr u.p in 2nd ins fnl f: kpt on same pce* **9/1**
22-5 3 1 1/2 **Foxtrot Liv**[12] 2722 3-9-0 102 WJLee 8 102
(P Twomey, Ire) *cl up bhd ldr: edgd sltly rt after 1f: cl 2nd at 1/2-way: drvn fr over 2f out and no imp on wnr u.p in 3rd over 1f out: kpt on same pce ins fnl f* **25/1**
1-30 4 3/4 **Iridessa (IRE)**[21] 2443 3-9-0 110 WayneLordan 3 101
(Joseph Patrick O'Brien, Ire) *chsd ldrs: pushed along in 5th 3f out and clsd u.p into 4th ins fnl f where no imp on ldrs: kpt on same pce* **9/1**
2 5 1 **Dean Street Doll (IRE)**[14] 2661 3-9-0 98 ColinKeane 9 98
(Richard John O'Brien, Ire) *hld up towards rr early: last at 1/2-way: drvn and prog 1 1/2f out: rdn into 6th ins fnl f and wnt nvr threatening 5th nr fin: nvr trbld ldrs* **50/1**
11-5 6 1 **Fairyland (IRE)**[21] 2443 3-9-0 112 SeamieHeffernan 5 96
(A P O'Brien, Ire) *chsd ldrs and short of room early where bmpd sltly: disp 6th at 1/2-way: rdn nr side over 2f out and no imp on ldrs u.p disputing 6th over 1f out: kpt on one pce* **12/1**
14-6 7 nk **Just Wonderful (USA)**[21] 2443 3-9-0 111 DonnachaO'Brien 1 95
(A P O'Brien, Ire) *settled bhd ldrs: disp 3rd at 1/2-way: pushed along in 4th 2f out and no ex over 1f out: wknd ins fnl f* **9/2**[3]
51-0 8 1/2 **Coral Beach (IRE)**[14] 2669 3-9-0 102 MichaelHussey 4 94
(A P O'Brien, Ire) *short of room briefly early and sn settled in rr: tk clsr order in 7th after 2f: disp 6th at 1/2-way: rdn and no imp on ldrs over 2f out: no ex disputing 6th ins fnl f and wknd nr fin* **66/1**
1-13 9 3 1/4 **Qabala (USA)**[21] 2443 3-9-0 109 DavidEgan 6 87
(Roger Varian) *w.w: 8th after 2f: drvn 3f out: sn swtchd lft and rdn over 2f out where short of room briefly and bmpd sltly: swtchd rt after and no imp towards rr 1 1/2f out: eased nr fin: scoped abnormally post r (vet reported filly scoped abnormally post race)* **3/1**[2]
12-3 10 6 1/2 **East**[14] 2669 3-9-0 107 JamieSpencer 7 72
(Kevin Ryan) *w.w: 9th after 2f: 9th at 1/2-way: pushed along over 2f out where bmpd sltly and sn no ex u.p 1 1/2f out: wknd and eased ins fnl f* **7/1**

1m 35.07s (-5.53) **Going Correction** -0.075s/f (Good) 10 Ran SP% **119.2**
Speed ratings: **124,120,118,117,116 115,115,114,111,105**
CSF £26.49 CT £478.88 TOTE £2.80: £1.50, £2.90, £4.30; DF 26.70 Trifecta £506.50.
Owner Michael Tabor & Derrick Smith & Mrs John Magnier **Bred** Beauty Is Truth Syndicate **Trained** Cashel, Co Tipperary

FOCUS
The Newmarket winner is a straightforward type. She gave a polished follow-up display to win readily from a filly making her seasonal debut, and consolidating smart juvenile form. Career-best efforts from third and fifth, the pair split by a former Group 1-winning juvenile. The third and fifth help set the standard, with the second rated to her 1m form.

3116 - 3118a (Foreign Racing) - See Raceform Interactive

1793 **DUSSELDORF** (R-H)
Sunday, May 26

OFFICIAL GOING: Turf: good

3119a **WEMPE 99TH GERMAN 1000 GUINEAS (GROUP 2) (3YO FILLIES) (TURF)** **1m**
3:55 3-Y-O **£63,063** (£25,225; £13,513; £7,207; £3,603)

RPR
1 **Main Edition (IRE)**[40] 1832 3-9-2 0 JoeFanning 10 103+
(Mark Johnston) *cl up on outer: pushed along to chal ldr 2f out: no immediate rspnse and rdn over 1f out: responded for press ins fnl f: led fnl 50yds: drvn out* **48/10**[3]
2 nk **Axana (GER)**[34] 1990 3-9-2 0 EduardoPedroza 7 102
(A Wohler, Germany) *led: asked to qckn 2f out: rdn over 1f out: hrd pressed ins fnl f: hdd fnl 50yds: drvn out* **11/5**[2]
3 nk **Shalona (FR)**[29] 2137 3-9-2 0 BayarsaikhanGanbat 1 101
(Henk Grewe, Germany) *prom on inner: pushed along and effrt 2f out: rdn over 1f out: kpt on wl ins fnl f: nt quite pce to chal* **36/5**
4 2 1/2 **Best On Stage (GER)**[29] 2137 3-9-2 0 AndraschStarke 3 95+
(P Schiergen, Germany) *mid-div on inner: swtchd off rail and asked for effrt between rivals 2f out: rdn over 1f out: kpt on ins fnl f: nvr gng pce of front trio* **244/10**
5 1/2 **Sharoka (IRE)**[29] 2137 3-9-2 0 AdriedeVries 9 94+
(Markus Klug, Germany) *mid-div on outer: pushed along over 2f out: limited rspnse and sn drvn: sme modest prog ins fnl f: n.d* **155/10**
6 shd **Satomi (GER)**[34] 1990 3-9-2 0 MartinSeidl 8 94+
(Markus Klug, Germany) *mid-div: sltly hmpd after 2f: angled out and pushed along over 2f out: rdn over 1f out: kpt on but nvr in contention* **229/10**
7 1/2 **Iconic Choice**[21] 2443 3-9-2 0 RichardKingscote 5 93+
(Tom Dascombe) *rrd sltly s: racd in fnl pair: outpcd and nudged along 4f out: rdn over 2f out: prog fr over 1f out: kpt on but n.d* **21/10**[1]
8 1/2 **Diajaka (GER)**[29] 2137 3-9-2 0 RenePiechulek 4 92+
(Markus Klug, Germany) *in tch: pushed along over 2f out: no imp: rdn over 1f out: kpt on same pce ins fnl f* **46/1**
9 1 1/4 **Gold (GER)**[20] 3-9-2 0 MaximPecheur 11 89+
(Markus Klug, Germany) *hld up in rr: outpcd over 3f out: rdn 2f out: passed btn rivals ins fnl f: nvr a factor* **221/10**
10 nk **Linaria (GER)**[34] 1990 3-9-2 0 FilipMinarik 2 88+
(J Hirschberger, Germany) *towards rr: pushed along over 2f out: rdn over 1f out: sn no ex and wknd ins fnl f* **40/1**
11 1 3/4 **Ivanka (GER)**[29] 2137 3-9-2 0 BauyrzhanMurzabayev 6 84+
(A Wohler, Germany) *a towards rr* **28/1**

1m 36.46s (-4.70) 11 Ran SP% **119.5**
PARI-MUTUEL (all including 1 euro stake): WIN 5.80 PLACE 2.10, 1.40, 2.00 SF 20.30.
Owner Saif Ali **Bred** Minch Bloodstock **Trained** Middleham Moor, N Yorks

3029 **LONGCHAMP** (R-H)
Sunday, May 26

OFFICIAL GOING: Turf: good to soft

3120a **PRIX DU LYS (GROUP 3) (3YO) (TURF)** **1m 4f**
2:10 3-Y-O **£36,036** (£14,414; £10,810; £7,207; £3,603)

RPR
1 **Quest The Moon (GER)**[25] 2310 3-9-2 0 CristianDemuro 1 110+
(Frau S Steinberg, Germany) *hld up in fnl pair: pushed along and effrt outside rivals over 2f out: sn rdn: picked up wl to chal over 1f out: led jst ins fnl f: gng away at fin* **13/2**[3]
2 2 1/2 **Khagan (IRE)**[22] 2426 3-9-2 0 MickaelBarzalona 5 105
(A Fabre, France) *led: shkn up and asked to qckn 2f out: rdn 1 1/2f out: chal ent fnl f: sn hdd: kpt on clsng stages* **11/1**
3 1 1/4 **Moonlight Spirit (IRE)**[29] 2110 3-9-2 0 JamesDoyle 2 103+
(Charlie Appleby) *settled in 3rd: pushed along 2 1/2f out: unable qck and rdn 1 1/2f out: kpt on ins fnl f: nvr gng pce to chal* **1/1**[1]
4 1 1/4 **Talk Or Listen (IRE)**[61] 1347 3-9-2 0 StephanePasquier 3 101
(F Rossi, France) *trckd ldr: asked for effrt 2f out: sn drvn: nt qckn and kpt on same pce ins fnl f* **76/10**
5 2 **Ballet Russe (IRE)**[33] 3-9-2 0 Pierre-CharlesBoudot 4 98
(A Fabre, France) *a in rr: pushed along 2 1/2f out: limited rspnse and sn rdn: kpt on same pce fr over 1f out* **17/10**[2]

2m 31.27s (0.87) 5 Ran SP% **120.3**
PARI-MUTUEL (all including 1 euro stake): WIN 7.50 PLACE 3.50, 3.00 DF 40.80.
Owner Stall Salzburg **Bred** Gestut Gorlsdorf **Trained** Germany

3121a SAXON WARRIOR COOLMORE PRIX SAINT ALARY (GROUP 1) (3YO FILLIES) (TURF) 1m 2f

3:28 3-Y-0 £128,693 (£51,486; £25,743; £12,860; £6,441)

RPR

1 **Siyarafina (FR)**34 3-9-0 0 ChristopheSoumillon 4 110+
(A De Royer-Dupre, France) *midfield: clsd smoothly fr 2f out: drvn to chse ldr wl over 1f out: sustained run to last 100yds: drvn out* **7/10**[1]

2 1 **Olendon (FR)**28 [2165] 3-9-0 0 StephanePasquier 7 107
(P Bary, France) *t.k.h: hld up towards rr: drvn fr 2f out: styd on u.p ins fnl 1 1/2f: wnt 2nd cl home: nvr trbld wnr* **49/1**

3 ½ **Imperial Charm**14 [2669] 3-9-0 0 AndreaAtzeni 11 106
(Simon Crisford) *moved up steadily fr wdst draw to ld after 2f: drvn for home ins fnl 2 1/2f: 2 l ld and styng on w less than 1 1/2f to run: kpt on for press: hdd fnl 150yds: lost 2nd cl home* **10/1**

4 1 ¾ **Cala Tarida**42 [1795] 3-9-0 0 GregoryBenoist 2 102+
(F Rossi, France) *w.w towards rr: hemmed in towards ins rail 2f out: angled out w less that 1 1/2f to run: styd on u.p fnl f: nt pce to get on terms* **31/1**

5 1 ½ **Merimbula (USA)**22 [2430] 3-9-0 0 AurelienLemaitre 6 99
(F Head, France) *sn led: hdd after 2f and settled in 3rd on rail: rdn and nt qckn over 1 1/2f out: kpt on at same pce* **37/1**

6 ¾ **Fount**13 3-9-0 0 Pierre-CharlesBoudot 3 98
(A Fabre, France) *racd keenly: trckd ldr: shkn up to chal 2f out: sn outpcd by ldr: grad dropped away fr over 1f out* **63/10**[3]

7 1 ¼ **Montviette (FR)**42 [1795] 3-9-0 0 CristianDemuro 10 95
(J-C Rouget, France) *impeded leaving stalls: w.w in last: swtchd to outer and began to cl 2f out: kpt on wout ever threatening to be involved* **28/1**

8 1 ¼ **Phoceene (FR)**25 [2312] 3-9-0 0 MickaelBarzalona 8 93
(F Rossi, France) *chsd ldrs: 4th and scrubbed along to hold pl w 4f to run: outpcd and rdn 2f fr home: wl hld fnl f* **15/1**

9 nk **Morning Dew (FR)**28 [2165] 3-9-0 0 EddyHardouin 5 92
(N Caullery, France) *settled in fnl trio: no imp u.p fr 2 1/2f out: sme mod late prog: nvr in contention* **118/1**

10 2 ½ **Platane**49 [1626] 3-9-0 0 MaximeGuyon 9 87
(C Laffon-Parias, France) *stmbld leaving stalls and bmpd rival: racd keenly: hld up in fnl trio: pushed along more than 2f out: nvr involved* **49/10**[2]

11 1 ¼ **Idiosa (GER)**23 3-9-0 0 OlivierPeslier 1 84
(Mlle L Kneip, France) *racd keenly: prom early but sn dropped into midfield: no imp whn asked 2f out: wknd fnl f* **27/1**

2m 6.48s (2.48) **11 Ran SP% 120.4**
PARI-MUTUEL (all including 1 euro stake): WIN 1.70 PLACE 1.10, 4.70, 2.10 DF 32.50.
Owner H H Aga Khan **Bred** Haras De S.A. Aga Khan Scea **Trained** Chantilly, France

FOCUS
This has a mixed history with regards to producing really top-class horses out of this contest. Last year's winner Laurens is among the better recent ones, and she went on to land three more events at the highest level that season.

3122a PRIX D'ISPAHAN (GROUP 1) (4YO+) (TURF) 1m 1f 55y

4:03 4-Y-0+ £128,693 (£51,486; £25,743; £12,860; £6,441)

RPR

1 **Zabeel Prince (IRE)**38 [1890] 6-9-2 0 AndreaAtzeni 2 116+
(Roger Varian) *in tch: racd a little keenly: pushed along and effrt on outer 2f out: rdn to chal over 1f out: led jst ins fnl f: kpt on strly: a doing enough cl home* **3/1**[2]

2 ¾ **Study Of Man (IRE)**28 [2168] 4-9-2 0 StephanePasquier 8 115
(P Bary, France) *hld up in fnl trio: shkn up 2f out: drvn and prog fr 2f out: kpt on strly on outer ins fnl f: nt quite pce to chal wnr* **4/1**[3]

3 ¾ **Trais Fluors**30 [2083] 5-9-2 0 Pierre-CharlesBoudot 1 113
(A Fabre, France) *racd keenly towards rr of mid-div on inner: asked for effrt 2f out: rdn bhd ldrs over 1f out: responded for press ins fnl f: snatched 3rd fnl strides* **41/5**

4 snk **Intellogent (IRE)**28 [2168] 4-9-2 0 (p) CristianDemuro 7 113+
(F Chappet, France) *hld up in fnl pair: dropped to rr after 3f: pushed along over 2f out: sn rdn: prog fr over 1f out: picked up wl ins fnl f: nrst fin* **46/1**

5 shd **Dream Castle**57 [1445] 5-9-2 0 ChristopheSoumillon 5 112
(Saeed bin Suroor) *in tch on inner: pushed along to chse ldrs over 2f out: drvn and ev ch over 1f out: unable to match eventual wnr ins fnl f: kpt on same pce* **89/10**

6 ¾ **Wild Illusion**204 [8844] 4-8-13 0 (p) JamesDoyle 4 108
(Charlie Appleby) *trckd ldr after 1f: pushed along to dispute ld over 2f out: led narrowly over 1f out: hdd jst ins fnl f: grad wknd clsng stages* **2/1**[1]

7 1 ¼ **Knight To Behold (IRE)**30 [2083] 4-9-2 0 (p) OisinMurphy 6 108
(Harry Dunlop) *led after 1f: asked to qckn over 2f out: jnd and sn hdd over 1f out: wknd ins fnl f: no ex* **10/1**

8 2 **With You**231 [8027] 4-8-13 0 AurelienLemaitre 3 101
(F Head, France) *mid-div: outpcd and pushed along 2 1/2f out: sn rdn: no imp and btn ent fnl f: kpt on same pce* **12/1**

9 7 **Subway Dancer (IRE)**218 [8408] 7-9-2 0 RadekKoplik 9 89
(Z Koplik, Czech Republic) *a towards rr: pushed along over 2f out: no rspnse and wl btn over 1f out* **92/1**

1m 53.07s (-2.23) **9 Ran SP% 119.3**
PARI-MUTUEL (all including 1 euro stake): WIN 4.00 PLACE 1.50, 1.60, 2.10 DF 12.90.
Owner Sheikh Mohammed Obaid Al Maktoum **Bred** Roundhill Stud **Trained** Newmarket, Suffolk

FOCUS
This looked really competitive and it was run at a sound gallop. The first few were close up but it should be reliable form. It's been rated around the balance of the second, third and fourth.

3123a PRIX VICOMTESSE VIGIER (GROUP 2) (4YO+) (TURF) 1m 7f

4:38 4-Y-0+ £66,756 (£25,765; £12,297; £8,198; £4,099)

RPR

1 **Called To The Bar (IRE)**28 [2169] 5-9-0 0 TheoBachelot 2 112
(Mme Pia Brandt, France) *settled in midfield: dropped into fnl trio after 5f: hdwy on outer ins fnl 3f: sustained run to ld 1 1/2f out: styd on strly: drvn out* **53/10**[3]

2 3 **Way To Paris**28 [2169] 6-9-0 0 CristianDemuro 1 108
(Andrea Marcialis, France) *a cl up: towards inner: angled out in share of 4th 2 1/2f out: drvn to chal appr fnl 1 1/2f: styd on but nt pce of wnr* **9/1**

3 1 ½ **Call The Wind**57 [1441] 5-9-4 0 AurelienLemaitre 5 111
(F Head, France) *chsd ldrs: dropped into midfield after 5f: 7th and shkn up 3f out: sn rdn but no imp: styd on fnl f but wl hld by front two* **21/10**[1]

4 1 **Malkoboy (FR)**42 [1796] 5-9-0 0 FabriceVeron 3 105
(Claudia Erni, Switzerland) *prom: dropped towards rr of midfield wl bef 1/2-way: outpcd towards rr 3f out: styd on u.p fr 1 1/2f out: effrt flattened out last 75yds: nvr trbld ldrs* **25/1**

5 1 ½ **Holdthasigreen (FR)**28 [2169] 7-9-4 0 TonyPiccone 11 108
(B Audouin, France) *put into r steadily fr wdst stall to ld after 2 1/2f: hdd after 5f and chsd ldrs on outer: 2nd and pushed along over 2 1/2f out: jst shading ldr u.p whn eventual wnr tk over 1 1/2f out: plugged on at one pce* **16/5**[2]

6 snk **Bartaba (FR)**22 [2427] 4-8-10 0 StephanePasquier 8 100
(A Fabre, France) *w.w in fnl pair on outer: drvn more than 2 1/2f out: hrd rdn 2f out: styd on fr over 1f out: nvr trbld ldrs* **24/1**

7 4 **Boulevard (IRE)**38 4-9-0 0 ChristopheSoumillon 7 100
(Charley Rossi, France) *settled in midfield: take wd (w Funny Kid) at crse intersection to ld after 5f but qckly rejnd main gp towards inner: kicked for home wl over 2f out: hdd 1 1/2f out: wknd fnl f* **79/10**

8 8 **Funny Kid (USA)**42 [1796] 6-9-0 0 MaximeGuyon 10 89
(C Ferland, France) *w.w in fnl trio: followed Boulevard out wd at crse intersection to r cl up after 5f but qckly rejnd main gp towards inner: lost pl and shkn up wl over 2 1/2f out: sn wknd: eased ins fnl f* **11/1**

9 snk **Magical Touch**22 [2427] 4-8-10 0 MickaelBarzalona 9 86
(H-A Pantall, France) *settled in midfield on inner: drvn and short-lived effrt over 2f out: sn btn* **12/1**

10 7 **My Swashbuckler (IRE)**41 4-9-0 0 IoritzMendizabal 6 81
(Alain Couetil, France) *racd keenly: sn led: hdd after 2 1/2f: racd promly under restraint: chsd ldrs 2 1/2f out: sn no imp: rdn and wknd 1 1/2f out* **55/1**

11 12 **Impertinente (IRE)**22 [2427] 4-8-10 0 VincentCheminaud 4 63
(A Fabre, France) *w.w in fnl pair on inner: pushed along w 5f to run: no imp u.p over 2f out: ins whn bhd fnl f* **61/1**

3m 12.23s (-3.77) **11 Ran SP% 120.4**
PARI-MUTUEL (all including 1 euro stake): WIN 6.30 PLACE 2.00, 2.40, 1.60 DF 18.70.
Owner Fair Salinia Ltd & Pia Brandt **Bred** Fair Salinia Ltd **Trained** France

3124 - 3135a (Foreign Racing) - See Raceform Interactive

2519 SAINT-CLOUD (L-H)

Monday, May 20

OFFICIAL GOING: Turf: very soft

3136a PRIX TEDDY (H'CAP) (4YO) (TURF) 1m

12:50 4-Y-0 £23,423 (£8,900; £6,558; £3,747; £1,873; £1,405)

RPR

1 **Infirmier (USA)**34 4-9-4 0 GregoryBenoist 2 91
(Mlle A Wattel, France) **128/10**

2 shd **Ziveri (FR)**18 4-9-0 0 (b) ChristopheSoumillon 6 87
(F Rossi, France) **17/2**

3 hd **Babar (FR)**34 4-9-2 0 (p) JeromeClaudic 11 89
(E Lyon, France) **23/1**

4 1 ¼ **Sandyssime (FR)**51 4-8-10 0 EddyHardouin 1 80
(G Botti, France) **8/1**[3]

5 hd **Ego Dancer (FR)**16 [2429] 4-8-11 0 StephanePasquier 4 80
(M Delzangles, France) **73/10**[2]

6 ½ **Teston (FR)**73 4-9-7 0 AurelienLemaitre 3 89
(P Bary, France) **17/1**

7 nk **Nosdargent (FR)**18 4-8-8 0 FabriceVeron 16 75
(D & P Prod'Homme, France) **25/1**

8 hd **Gloria**18 4-8-13 0 ClementLecoeuvre 14 80
(Mme M Bollack-Badel, France) **61/1**

9 nk **Qatar Bolt**21 [2226] 4-8-10 0 OlivierPeslier 7 76
(H-A Pantall, France) **3/1**[1]

10 1 ½ **Falco Delavilliere (FR)**21 [2226] 4-8-13 0 AntoineHamelin 12 76
(R Avial Lopez, Spain) **25/1**

11 ¾ **For Ever Fun (FR)**51 [1449] 4-8-11 0 TheoBachelot 18 72
(L Gadbin, France) **13/1**

12 1 ¾ **Gold Lake (FR)**18 4-8-6 0 CristianDemuro 15 63
(Frau Hella Sauer, Germany) **23/1**

13 1 ¼ **Iserman (FR)**158 4-8-8 0 MickaelBarzalona 5 62
(Vaclav Luka Jr, Czech Republic) **23/1**

14 16 **Beyond My Dreams (IRE)**21 [2226] 4-8-11 0(b) Pierre-CharlesBoudot 17 28
(H-A Pantall, France) **23/1**

15 1 ½ **El Indio (FR)**21 [2226] 4-8-8 0 VincentCheminaud 10 22
(H-A Pantall, France) **33/1**

16 hd **All This Time (GER)**34 4-8-7 0 MaximeGuyon 13 20
(F Rossi, France) **12/1**

17 4 **Fairy Tale (IRE)**21 [2226] 4-9-2 0 AlexisBadel 8 20
(Gay Kelleway) *trckd ldrs: rowed along over 2f out: qckly dropped away over 1f out: heavily eased fnl f* **23/1**

1m 45.03s (-2.47) **17 Ran SP% 119.4**
PARI-MUTUEL (all including 1 euro stake): WIN 13.80; PLACE 4.50, 3.50, 7.60; DF 45.70.
Owner Capt A Pratt & Lord Clinton **Bred** Wertheimer & Frere **Trained** France

3137a PRIX CLEOPATRE (GROUP 3) (3YO FILLIES) (TURF) 1m 2f 110y

2:00 3-Y-0 £36,036 (£14,414; £10,810; £7,207; £3,603)

RPR

1 **Etoile (FR)**43 [1626] 3-8-11 0 CristianDemuro 1 102+
(J-C Rouget, France) *settled in 3rd on inner: prog to dispute ld 2f out: sn led: kpt on strly ins fnl f: readily* **2/1**[2]

2 1 ¾ **Villa D'Amore (IRE)**16 [2430] 3-8-11 0 Pierre-CharlesBoudot 4 99
(A Fabre, France) *led: asked to qckn over 2 1/2f out: rdn whn jnd 2f out: sn hdd and lost position: kpt on gamely u.p: regained 2nd clsng stages* **57/10**

3 shd **Volskha (FR)**27 [2029] 3-8-11 0 MaximeGuyon 3 99
(Simone Brogi, France) *racd a little keenly in 4th: pushed along and effrt on nr side rail over 2f out: drvn over 1f out: kpt on wl: jst denied 2nd* **49/10**[3]

4 1 **Paramount (FR)**27 [2029] 3-8-11 0 JulienAuge 6 97
(C Ferland, France) *hld up in rr: asked to improve over 2f out: swtchd lft and drvn 1 1/2f out: unable qck and kpt on same pce ins fnl f* **83/10**

5 1 **Shamiyla (FR)**[19] 3-8-13 0 ow2 ChristopheSoumillon 2 97
(A De Royer-Dupre, France) *hld up in fnl pair: pushed along 2f out: prog to dispute 2nd 1 1/2f out: nt qckn: kpt on same pce under hands and heels riding ins fnl f* **9/5**[1]

6 6 **Got Wind**[27] 2027 3-8-11 0 MickaelBarzalona 5 84
(C Ferland, France) *trckd ldr on outer: pushed along 2 1/2f out: unable qck and sn dropped to rr: no ex and allowed to fin in own time ins fnl f* **12/1**

2m 23.07s (3.47) 6 Ran SP% 119.4
PARI-MUTUEL (all including 1 euro stake): WIN 3.00; PLACE 1.90, 2.90; SF 15.60.
Owner Ecurie Philippe Segalot & Martin S Schwartz Racing **Bred** Mme P Ades-Hazan, Mme G Henochsberg & P Fellous **Trained** Pau, France

3138a PRIX CORRIDA (GROUP 2) (4YO+ FILLIES & MARES) (TURF) 1m 2f 110y
3:10 4-Y-0+ £66,756 (£25,765; £12,297; £8,198; £4,099)

RPR

1 **Morgan Le Faye**[22] 2167 5-9-0 0 MickaelBarzalona 2 111+
(A Fabre, France) *hld up in 4th: clsd gng wl fr 2f out: pushed along to chse ldr 1 1/2f out: led ent fnl f: r.o strly clsng stages* **2/5**[1]

2 2 **Listen In (IRE)**[211] 8450 5-9-2 0 AurelienLemaitre 5 109+
(F Head, France) *hld up in fnl pair: pushed along over 2f out: sn rdn: responded for press ins fnl f: kpt on wl: snatched 2nd fnl strides* **15/1**

3 snk **Shahnaza (FR)**[22] 2167 4-8-13 0 ow2 (p) ChristopheSoumillon 1 106
(A De Royer-Dupre, France) *settled in 3rd on inner: pushed along to chse ldr under 2f out: rdn to chse eventual wnr jst ins fnl f: nt qckn and lost 2nd fnl strides* **19/5**[2]

4 2 1/2 **Golden Legend (FR)**[219] 8229 5-9-0 0 AlexisBadel 3 102
(H-F Devin, France) *led: asked to qckn 2f out: hdd ent fnl f: wknd clsng stages: no ex towards fin* **15/2**[3]

5 nk **Musikaline (FR)**[32] 4-8-11 0 CristianDemuro 6 99
(Y Barberot, France) *hld up in rr: asked for effrt over 2f out: rdn ent fnl f: kpt on same pce: nvr involved* **17/1**

6 hd **Tosen Gift (IRE)**[22] 2167 4-8-11 0 FabriceVeron 4 98
(S Kobayashi, France) *trckd ldr on outer: pushed along 2 1/2f out: sn struggling to go pce: grad wknd fr over 1f out* **16/1**

2m 19.5s (-0.10) 6 Ran SP% 121.7
PARI-MUTUEL (all including 1 euro stake): WIN 1.40; PLACE 1.10, 2.60; SF 9.70.
Owner Godolphin SNC **Bred** Dieter Burkle **Trained** Chantilly, France

FOCUS
The first two posted pbs, with the third helping to set the standard.

3139a PRIX DU PRIEURE DE JARDY (CLAIMER) (3YO) (TURF) 1m 4f 110y
3:45 3-Y-0 £10,360 (£4,144; £3,108; £2,072; £1,036)

RPR

1 **Hasturies (FR)**[94] 3-8-8 0 (p) MaximeGuyon 7 60
(Mme Pia Brandt, France) **77/10**

2 1/2 **Hapt (FR)**[38] 3-8-10 0 QuentinPerrette(6) 1 67
(M Nigge, France) **56/10**[3]

3 shd **Chipiron (FR)**[13] 3-8-11 0 (b) TheoBachelot 3 62
(Y Barberot, France) **68/10**

4 2 1/2 **Rue Dauphine (FR)**[19] 2311 3-8-5 0 DelphineSantiago(3) 9 55
(Artus Adeline De Boisbrunet, France) **20/1**

5 snk **Bygeorgemygeorge (FR)**[13] 3-9-1 0 (p) Pierre-CharlesBoudot 8 62
(P Adda, France) **78/10**

6 1 1/2 **Serendipite (FR)**[19] 3-8-13 0 AurelienLemaitre 10 57
(F Head, France) **53/10**[2]

7 snk **Montilien (FR)** 3-8-4 0 (b) GuillaumeGuedj-Gay(7) 2 55
(X Thomas-Demeaulte, France) **46/1**

8 1/2 **Ondin (IRE)**[27] 3-8-9 0 ThomasTrullier(6) 4 58
(C Ferland, France) **67/10**

9 1 1/4 **Break Down (FR)** 3-7-13 0 MlleRomaneViolet(9) 11 49
(P Chevillard, France) **38/1**

10 20 **Hurricane Hero (FR)**[18] 2323 3-8-11 0 (p) TonyPiccone 5 20
(K R Burke) *wl into stride: led: pushed along over 2f out: rdn and hdd over 1f out: wknd ins fnl f* **5/2**[1]

11 5 **Giving Wings (FR)**[20] 2265 3-9-1 0 AntoineHamelin 6 16
(Matthieu Palussiere, France) **90/1**

2m 51.17s 11 Ran SP% 118.8
PARI-MUTUEL (all including 1 euro stake): WIN 8.70; PLACE 2.50, 2.20, 2.30; DF 17.90.
Owner Haras D'Etreham **Bred** Haras D'Etreham **Trained** France

3140a PRIX DE BLANQUEFORT (CLAIMER) (4YO) (TURF) 1m 2f
4:20 4-Y-0 £8,558 (£3,423; £2,567; £1,711; £855)

RPR

1 **Breath Of Fire (FR)**[32] 4-9-1 0 MaximeGuyon 9 88
(Mme Pia Brandt, France) **4/1**[2]

2 4 **Midgrey (IRE)**[97] 4-8-11 0 (p) MickaelBarzalona 1 76
(X Thomas-Demeaulte, France) **5/1**[3]

3 3/4 **Ultra Petita**[55] 4-9-1 0 TheoBachelot 8 79
(K Borgel, France) **18/1**

4 2 **Billabong Cat (FR)**[51] 1449 4-9-10 0 TonyPiccone 10 84
(F Vermeulen, France) **9/10**[1]

5 1 3/4 **Story Begins (FR)**[128] 4-8-5 0 MlleMickaelleMichel(3) 7 64
(A Spanu, France) **45/1**

6 1/2 **Karsador**[11] 4-8-9 0 (p) ThomasTrullier(6) 6 70
(M Rolland, France) **19/1**

7 shd **Debatable (IRE)**[32] 1908 4-9-1 0 ClementLecoeuvre 2 70
(Gay Kelleway) *qckly into stride: led: jnd and hdd after 1f: remained cl up: pushed into ld over 2f out: rdn and hdd over 1f out: kpt on same pce fnl f* **11/1**

8 nse **Action Pauliene (FR)**[55] 4-8-13 0 MlleElauraCieslik(6) 3 74
(K Borgel, France) **14/1**

9 15 **Salaasel** 4-9-4 0 FabriceVeron 4 43
(Georgios Alimpinisis, France) **28/1**

2m 13.99s (-2.01) 9 Ran SP% 120.2
PARI-MUTUEL (all including 1 euro stake): WIN 5.00; PLACE 1.90, 1.80, 3.60; DF 9.10.
Owner Ecurie Des Charmes **Bred** Haras D'Etreham **Trained** France

3001

CHELMSFORD (A.W) (L-H)
Monday, May 27

OFFICIAL GOING: Polytrack: standard
Wind: strong, across Weather: light cloud, bright spells, breezy

3141 BET TOTEPLACEPOT AT TOTESPORT.COM NOVICE MEDIAN AUCTION STKS 6f (P)
1:25 (1:25) (Class 5) 2-Y-O £4,527 (£1,347; £673; £336) Stalls Centre

Form RPR

1 **Malotru** 2-9-5 0 HarryBentley 6 81+
(Marco Botti) *hld up in tch in last pair: clsd ent fnl 2f: rdn and hdwy to ld 1f out: edgd lft but r.o wl ins fnl f: comf* **1/1**[1]

2 3 **Nat Love (IRE)** 2-8-12 0 ScottMcCullagh(7) 3 68
(Mick Channon) *dwlt: hld up in tch in rr: effrt and hdwy over 1f out: no ch w wnr but kpt on ins fnl f to go 2nd towards fin* **11/4**[2]

0 3 3/4 **Zain Storm (FR)**[37] 1953 2-9-5 0 PaddyMathers 2 66
(John Butler) *chsd ldr tl led ent fnl 2f: drvn and hdd 1f out: sn outpcd and lost 2nd wl ins fnl f* **7/1**[3]

4 1 3/4 **Fumbleintheforest** 2-9-0 0 KieranO'Neill 4 56
(Robyn Brisland) *hung rt thrght: led tl hdd ent fnl 2f: unable qck u.p over 1f out: wknd ins fnl f (jockey said the bit slipped through the mouth of the filly and she also hung right-handed)* **25/1**

5 nse **Billy Button (IRE)** 2-9-5 0 JoeyHaynes 8 60
(Dean Ivory) *chsd ldrs: effrt to press ldrs and rdn over 1f out: unable qck and wknd ins fnl f* **8/1**

00 6 3 **Dover Light**[11] 2761 2-9-5 0 (h[1]) RyanTate 5 51
(Dean Ivory) *stdd s: t.k.h: hld up in tch in midfield: unable qck u.p and lost pl over 1f out: wknd fnl f* **16/1**

1m 14.81s (1.11) **Going Correction** -0.175s/f (Stan) 6 Ran SP% 110.0
Speed ratings (Par 93): **85,81,80,77,77 73**
CSF £3.70 TOTE £1.70: £1.10, £1.80; EX 4.50 Trifecta £14.50.
Owner Les Boyer Partnership 1 **Bred** Wattlefield Stud Ltd & Partner **Trained** Newmarket, Suffolk

FOCUS
An ordinary juvenile novice auction contest, lacking in depth. The clear favourite won easily from off a modest gallop.

3142 BET TOTEEXACTA AT TOTESPORT.COM H'CAP 1m (P)
2:00 (2:04) (Class 7) (0-50,50) 4-Y-O+ £2,911 (£866; £432; £216) Stalls Low

Form RPR

0334 1 **Casey Banter**[27] 2240 4-8-11 47 SeanKirrane(7) 8 57
(Julia Feilden) *hld up in tch: swtchd rt and effrt jst over 2f out: rdn to ld over 1f out: sn clr and r.o strly: readily* **7/1**[3]

0404 2 4 **Percy Toplis**[5] 2972 5-9-2 45 (b) EoinWalsh 11 46
(Christine Dunnett) *dwlt: swtchd lft after s: hld up towards rr: effrt over 2f out: hdwy u.p over 1f out: styd on u.p to go 2nd last strides: no ch w wnr* **20/1**

6-03 3 1/2 **Navarra Princess (IRE)**[12] 2740 4-9-1 47 MeganNicholls(3) 13 47
(Don Cantillon) *midfield: effrt over 2f out: clsd whn nt clr run and swtchd lft over 1f out: styd on ins fnl f to snatch 3rd last stride: no ch w wnr* **12/1**

0025 4 shd **Seaquinn**[46] 1717 4-9-2 45 KierenFox 2 44
(John Best) *chsd ldrs: effrt ent fnl 2f: edgd rt over 1f out: 3rd and no threat to wnr 1f out: kpt on same pce and chsd clr wnr wl ins fnl f: lost 2 pls last strides (jockey said filly hung right-handed)* **8/1**

0612 5 3/4 **Nicky Baby (IRE)**[27] 2240 5-8-13 49 (b) SophieRalston(7) 9 47
(Dean Ivory) *t.k.h: sn pressing ldr: ev ch and rdn ent fnl 2f: nt match pce of wnr over 1f out: stl 2nd but no imp 1f out: wknd towards fin and lost 3 pls cl home* **5/1**[1]

0066 6 2 1/4 **Cool Echo**[27] 2235 5-9-5 48 (p) DavidProbert 3 41
(J R Jenkins) *wnt lft leaving stalls: sn rcvrd and wl in tch in midfield: effrt whn pushed lft over 1f out: unable qck: wl hld and plugged on same pce ins fnl f* **14/1**

5454 7 2 **Blyton Lass**[27] 2234 4-9-6 49 BarryMcHugh 5 37
(James Given) *niggled along early: towards rr: effrt and sme prog 2f out: nvr getting to ldrs (trainer said filly was in season)* **5/1**[1]

1456 8 5 **Tellovoi (IRE)**[14] 2681 11-9-5 48 (p) BrettDoyle 14 24
(Richard Guest) *taken down early: hld up in midfield: rdn over 3f out: lost pl over 2f out: no treat to ldrs fnl 2f* **14/1**

0652 9 3/4 **Luath**[25] 2350 6-9-3 46 NickyMackay 10 21
(Suzzanne France) *towards rr: drvn 2f out: sme hdwy to pass btn horses 1f out but nvr on terms w ldrs: eased wl ins fnl f* **6/1**[2]

460- 10 1 **Gulland Rock**[165] 9523 8-9-4 47 RyanTate 4 19
(Anthony Carson) *led: rdn ent fnl 2f: edgd rt: hdd and bmpd over 1f out: sn outpcd: wknd ins fnl f (jockey said gelding hung right-handed and stopped quickly)* **22/1**

100 11 hd **Ainne**[27] 2240 4-9-7 50 (tp) RobHornby 7 22
(Sylvester Kirk) *hld up in midfield: effrt on inner over 1f out: no prog: wknd ins fnl f* **33/1**

6- 12 1 **Could Be Gold (IRE)**[430] 1326 5-9-2 45 (h[1]) DannyBrock 1 15
(John Butler) *stdd s: hld up in rr: n.d* **20/1**

5643 13 6 **Merdon Castle (IRE)**[27] 2234 7-9-2 45 RobertWinston 12
(Frank Bishop) *a towards rr: effrt ent fnl 2f: no prog: nvr involved (jockey said gelding was never travelling)* **7/1**[3]

50-0 14 5 **Eternal Destiny**[12] 2740 4-9-2 45 MartinDwyer 15
(Ian Williams) *a towards rr: nvr involved* **33/1**

0-03 15 6 **Freddy With A Y (IRE)**[45] 1732 9-9-4 47 AlistairRawlinson 6
(J R Jenkins) *chsd ldrs tl over 2f out: sn losing pl: eased over 1f out (jockey said the gelding lost its action)* **33/1**

1m 39.57s (-0.33) **Going Correction** -0.175s/f (Stan) 15 Ran SP% 127.5
Speed ratings (Par 97): **94,90,89,89,88 86,84,79,78,77 77,76,70,65,59**
CSF £151.32 CT £1667.67 TOTE £7.10: £2.80, £6.80, £3.50; EX 226.80 Trifecta £1343.90.
Owner Newmarket Equine Tours Racing Club **Bred** Lady Jennifer Green **Trained** Exning, Suffolk

FOCUS
A moderate handicap. In a wide open betting market, one of the shorter-priced contenders routed her opposition from just off the pace. The winner found improvement from somewhere and the form is rated cautiously.

3143 BET TOTEQUADPOT AT TOTESPORT.COM H'CAP (DIV I) 6f (P)

2:35 (2:36) (Class 6) (0-60,61) 4-Y-O+

£3,428 (£1,020; £509; £300; £300; £300) **Stalls** Centre

Form / RPR

0455 **1** **Perfect Symphony (IRE)**[6] 2929 5-9-6 **61**..............(p) JoshuaBryan(3) 3 68
(Mark Pattinson) *sn chsng ldr: pushed along and clsd over 1f out: led 1f out: rdn and asserted ins fnl f: pushed out and a gng to hold on towards fin* **7/2**[1]

0322 **2** *nk* **Daring Guest (IRE)**[25] 2318 5-9-4 **56**..........................(bt) HarryBentley 10 62
(Tom Clover) *swtchd lft sn after s: hld up towards rr: effrt jst over 2f out: hdwy u.p over 1f out: styd on to chse clr wnr wl ins fnl f: clsng towards fin but nvr quite getting to wnr* **7/2**[1]

3100 **3** *1 ¼* **Elliot The Dragon (IRE)**[61] 1368 4-8-7 **45**.................. PaddyMathers 2 47
(Derek Shaw) *taken down early: t.k.h: hld up in tch in midfield: effrt and swtchd rt ent fnl 2f: kpt on u.p to go 3rd wl ins fnl f: nvr getting to wnr* **16/1**

6605 **4** *1* **Hello Girl**[28] 2206 4-9-5 **57**...(p[1]) MartinDwyer 5 56
(Dean Ivory) *t.k.h: effrt over 1f out: kpt on same pce u.p ins fnl f* **6/1**

0 **5** *½* **Ar Saoirse**[19] 2527 4-8-13 **51**.................................(b) CallumShepherd 6 49
(Clare Hobson) *sn led and clr after 2f: rdn and hdd 1f out: no ex: lost 2nd and wknd wl ins fnl f (vet reported gelding lost its right fore shoe)* **20/1**

0512 **6** *1 ½* **Poppy May (IRE)**[34] 2013 5-9-1 **53**.................................. BarryMcHugh 1 46
(James Given) *chsd ldrs: rdn over 2f out: unable qck u.p and btn whn hung rt 1f out: wknd ins fnl f* **4/1**[2]

0022 **7** *1 ¼* **Holy Tiber (IRE)**[12] 2741 4-9-7 **59**..............................(b) JoeyHaynes 4 49
(Paul Howling) *t.k.h: hld up in last trio: effrt u.p over 1f out: nvr threatened to get on terms w ldrs: wknd ins fnl f* **5/1**[3]

2020 **8** *1 ¾* **Kyllukey**[4] 3001 6-8-5 **48**... SeanDavis(5) 8 32
(Charlie Wallis) *stdd and swtchd lft after s: hld up in last pair: effrt ent fnl 2f: swtchd rt and no hdwy u.p over 1f out: wknd ins fnl f* **11/1**

420 **9** *½* **Fantasy Justifier (IRE)**[42] 1820 8-9-3 **55**..................(p) DavidProbert 11 38
(Ronald Harris) *in tch in midfield: effrt over 2f out: sn struggling and lost pl over 1f out: wknd fnl f* **14/1**

-600 **10** *5* **Song Of Summer**[6] 2930 4-8-1 **46** ow1..................... GraceMcEntee(7) 7 14
(Phil McEntee) *v.s.a: clsd on to rr of field after 2f: struggling over 2f out: hung lft and wl btn over 1f out* **50/1**

1m 11.95s (-1.75) **Going Correction** -0.175s/f (Stan) **10 Ran SP% 123.0**
Speed ratings (Par 101): **104,103,101,100,99 97,96,93,93,86**
CSF £16.74 CT £183.43 TOTE £4.10: £1.50, £1.40, £6.30; EX 19.50 Trifecta £266.80.
Owner Lynne Stanbrook & Julian Power **Bred** Ballyhane Stud **Trained** Epsom, Surrey

FOCUS
The first division of a modest sprint handicap. One of the joint-favourites narrowly held off his main market rival in a good comparative time. Routine form.

3144 BET TOTEQUADPOT AT TOTESPORT.COM H'CAP (DIV II) 6f (P)

3:10 (3:10) (Class 6) (0-60,60) 4-Y-O+

£3,428 (£1,020; £509; £300; £300; £300) **Stalls** Centre

Form / RPR

0043 **1** **Billyoakes (IRE)**[34] 2013 7-9-0 **53**..............................(p) JackMitchell 2 60
(Charlie Wallis) *led: rdn ent fnl 2f: hdd over 1f out: drvn and sustained duel w runner-up fnl f: battled on and led again cl home* **7/2**[1]

30-1 **2** *nse* **Olaudah**[34] 2013 5-9-4 **57**.. DavidProbert 8 64
(Henry Candy) *taken down early: sn w wnr: pushed along and led narrowly over 1f out: kpt on and sustained duel w wnr fnl f: hdd cl home* **7/2**[1]

0-02 **3** *2 ¾* **Arnoul Of Metz**[14] 2678 4-8-12 **56**.............................. DylanHogan(5) 3 55
(Henry Spiller) *chsd ldrs: effrt over 1f out: unable qck and kpt on same pce ins fnl f* **5/1**[2]

0230 **4** *shd* **Spenny's Lass**[25] 2318 4-9-4 **57**.................................(p) BrettDoyle 1 55
(John Ryan) *chsd ldrs: effrt over 1f out: unable qck and kpt on same pce ins fnl f* **7/2**[1]

5056 **5** *1* **Mother Of Dragons (IRE)**[26] 2287 4-8-6 **52**.........(v) GraceMcEntee(7) 6 47+
(Phil McEntee) *swtchd rt and racd wd after 1f: midfield: v wd and outpcd 2f out: kpt on again ins fnl f: nvr trbld ldrs* **14/1**

4616 **6** *shd* **Bond Street Beau**[52] 1565 4-9-2 **60**................................ SeanDavis(5) 9 55
(Philip McBride) *swtchd lft after 1f: midfield: u.p over 1f out: kpt on ins fnl f: no threat to ldrs* **8/1**[3]

060- **7** *1* **Prince Rock (IRE)**[221] 8342 4-8-7 **46** oh1.....................(h) NickyMackay 5 38
(Simon Dow) *rrd as stalls opened and v.s.a: bhd: effrt over 1f out: styd on ins fnl f: nvr trbld ldrs (jockey said gelding was slowly away)* **11/1**

5660 **8** *shd* **Indian Affair**[28] 2215 9-8-11 **50**......................................(vt) RobHornby 7 42
(Milton Bradley) *in tch in midfield: lost pl u.p and outpcd over 2f out: no threat to ldrs but kpt on ins fnl f* **14/1**

2200 **9** *3* **Baby Gal**[26] 2287 5-8-4 **46** oh1...................................(b) NoelGarbutt(3) 10 29
(Roger Ingram) *in tch on midfield: unable qck and outpcd u.p over 1f out: wknd ins fnl f* **40/1**

-500 **10** *8* **Mountain Of Stars**[28] 2189 4-8-7 **46** oh1..................(t[1]) PaddyMathers 4 5
(Suzzanne France) *wnt rt leaving stalls: sn rdn and outpcd: a in last pair: wl bhd fnl f* **40/1**

1m 12.03s (-1.67) **Going Correction** -0.175s/f (Stan) **10 Ran SP% 121.0**
Speed ratings (Par 101): **104,103,100,100,98 98,97,97,93,82**
CSF £16.08 CT £62.83 TOTE £5.10: £1.60, £1.40, £2.10; EX 12.60 Trifecta £68.50.
Owner Roalco Limited **Bred** Mrs M Cusack **Trained** Ardleigh, Essex

FOCUS
The second division of a modest sprint handicap, and the pace held up. Two of the three co-favourites fought this out in the straight and the winning time was only marginally slower in a photo-finish.

3145 BET TOTETRIFECTA AT TOTESPORT.COM H'CAP 2m (P)

3:45 (3:48) (Class 4) (0-85,87) 4-Y-O+

£6,016 (£1,790; £894; £447; £300; £300) **Stalls** Low

Form / RPR

2-21 **1** **Carnwennan (IRE)**[11] 2781 4-9-10 **83**........................ StevieDonohoe 8 93+
(Charlie Fellowes) *hld up wl in tch in midfield: effrt over 2f out: hdwy u.p over 1f out: chsd ldr 1f out: sn chalng: edging lft but styd on wl to ld wl ins fnl f* **11/8**[1]

5214 **2** *1 ½* **Vampish**[28] 2214 4-8-7 **71**... SeanDavis(5) 4 78
(Philip McBride) *chsd ldr for 1f: wl in tch in midfield after: hdwy u.p to press ldr 2f out: led over 1f out: drvn and hrd pressed ins fnl f: hdd and no ex wl ins fnl f* **20/1**

5233 **3** *4 ½* **Alabaster**[27] 2239 5-9-5 **77**...(b) RyanTate 9 79
(Sir Mark Prescott Bt) *led: rdn over 2f out: hdd and unable qck u.p over 1f out: 3rd and outpcd ins fnl f* **5/1**[2]

2440 **4** *2* **Technological**[12] 2748 4-10-0 **87**.................................... DavidProbert 2 86
(George Margarson) *in tch in midfield: effrt over 2f out: unable qck u.p jst over 1f out: edgd rt and wknd ins fnl f* **12/1**

/0-5 **5** *4 ½* **Steaming (IRE)**[27] 2254 5-9-0 **72**.................................... HarryBentley 5 66
(Ralph Beckett) *chsd ldr after 1f: rdn and lost 2nd jst over 2f out: unable qck and btn 1f out: wknd ins fnl f* **7/1**[3]

11-4 **6** *7* **Graceful Lady**[17] 2571 6-9-1 **78**................................ AndrewBreslin(5) 6 63
(Robert Eddery) *t.k.h: hld up wl in tch in rr: rdn over 3f out: sn struggling and outpcd over 2f out: wl btn over 1f out* **12/1**

13-5 **7** *27* **Faithful Mount**[17] 2578 10-9-10 **82**..............................(p) KieranO'Neill 1 35
(Ian Williams) *rousted along early: chsd ldrs: reminder 4f out: sn rdn and lost pl: bhd fnl 2f: t.o* **25/1**

3m 27.52s (-2.48) **Going Correction** -0.175s/f (Stan)
WFA 4 from 5yo+ 1lb **7 Ran SP% 95.3**
Speed ratings (Par 105): **99,98,96,95,92 89,75**
CSF £20.40 CT £53.81 TOTE £2.10: £1.30, £5.80; EX 13.40 Trifecta £51.30.
Owner Dr Vincent K F Kong **Bred** Brian Williamson **Trained** Newmarket, Suffolk

FOCUS
The feature contest was a decent staying handicap. The strong favourite got well on top by the line from off a tactical gallop, and is progressing.

3146 BET TOTESWINGER AT TOTESPORT.COM FILLIES' H'CAP 7f (P)

4:20 (4:20) (Class 5) (0-70,72) 3-Y-O+

£5,433 (£1,617; £808; £404; £300; £300) **Stalls** Low

Form / RPR

1531 **1** **Chica De La Noche**[24] 2365 5-10-0 **70**........................(p) HarryBentley 4 79
(Simon Dow) *led for 1f: styd chsng ldrs: swtchd rt and effrt over 1f out: rdn to chal 1f out: led ins fnl f: styd on* **5/1**[3]

563 **2** *1* **Seraphim**[18] 2550 3-8-12 **65**......................................(t) DanielMuscutt 10 67
(Marco Botti) *chsd ldrs tl led after 1f: hdd over 4f out: chsd ldr: ev ch u.p over 1f out: led 1f out: hdd and one pce ins fnl f* **10/1**

4-44 **3** *¾* **Gleeful**[16] 2630 3-9-3 **70**.. AndreaAtzeni 9 70+
(Roger Varian) *awkward as stalls opened and s.i.s: steadily rcvrd and hdwy to ld over 4f out: rdn and hrd pressed over 1f out: hdd 1f out: no ex and one pce ins fnl f* **6/4**[1]

0-11 **4** *1 ½* **Fantastic Flyer**[27] 2235 4-9-5 **61**.................................... MartinDwyer 5 61
(Dean Ivory) *t.k.h: chsd ldr for 1f: styd wl in tch: effrt in 4th over 1f out: unable qck and kpt on same pce ins fnl f* **9/2**[2]

1460 **5** *hd* **Black Medick**[25] 2339 3-9-5 **72**..................................... LiamJones 1 68
(Laura Mongan) *s.i.s: pushed in rr: swtchd rt and styd on ins fnl f: nvr trbld ldrs* **33/1**

2-04 **6** *¾* **Agent Of Fortune**[27] 2261 4-9-6 **62**................................ EoinWalsh 6 60
(Christine Dunnett) *in tch in midfield: effrt u.p over 1f out: unable qck and kpt on same pce ins fnl f* **14/1**

5242 **7** *2* **Sweet And Dandy (IRE)**[32] 2065 4-10-0 **70**...................... KieranO'Neill 8 62
(Luke McJannet) *hld up in tch in last trio: effrt u.p over 1f out: swtchd lft and no real imp ins fnl f: eased towards fin* **5/1**[3]

1-60 **8** *1 ½* **The Meter**[42] 1819 3-8-11 **69**....................................... JamieJones(5) 3 53
(Mohamed Moubarak) *hld up in last trio: effrt 1f out: sme prog ins fnl f but nvr involved* **66/1**

-300 **9** *1 ½* **Queens Royale**[17] 2585 5-9-2 **58**................................ RobertWinston 7 42
(Michael Appleby) *sn prom: chsd ldr 6f out tl over 4f out: sn swtchd rt: unable qck over 1f out: wknd ins fnl f* **28/1**

2-30 **10** *2 ½* **Sophia Maria**[23] 2418 3-9-1 **68**..................................... DavidProbert 2 41
(James Bethell) *in tch in midfield: effrt over 1f out: unable qck and btn 1f out: eased ins fnl f (jockey said filly stopped quickly)* **14/1**

1m 25.95s (-1.25) **Going Correction** -0.175s/f (Stan)
WFA 3 from 4yo+ 11lb **10 Ran SP% 121.8**
Speed ratings (Par 100): **100,98,98,96,96 95,92,91,89,86**
CSF £55.68 CT £114.74 TOTE £5.50: £1.90, £2.40, £1.20; EX 60.20 Trifecta £227.30.
Owner Robert Moss **Bred** Horizon Bloodstock Limited **Trained** Epsom, Surrey

FOCUS
An ordinary fillies' handicap. The winner is rated better than ever.

3147 CELEBRATE MAY'S HERO NIGEL SEAMAN H'CAP 7f (P)

4:55 (4:56) (Class 5) (0-75,77) 4-Y-O+

£5,433 (£1,617; £808; £404; £300; £300) **Stalls** Low

Form / RPR

0-05 **1** **Sword Exceed (GER)**[25] 2348 5-9-5 **72**.......................... KieranO'Neill 5 82
(Ivan Furtado) *taken down early: chsd ldr tl rdn and qcknd to ld over 1f out: clr and in command ins fnl f: comf (trainer's rep said, regarding the improved form shown, the gelding may have benefited from the drop in class on this occasion)* **28/1**

4604 **2** *2 ½* **Zapper Cass (FR)**[16] 2625 6-9-6 **73**....................... AlistairRawlinson 4 76
(Michael Appleby) *taken down early: chsd ldrs: effrt but unable to match pce of wnr over 1f out: chsd clr wnr ins fnl f: kpt on but no imp* **20/1**

000- **3** *hd* **Papa Stour (USA)**[163] 9564 4-9-9 **76**............................. DavidProbert 2 79+
(Andrew Balding) *s.i.s: hld up in tch in midfield: swtchd rt and effrt over 1f out: hdwy and swtchd rt again 1f out: styd on wl to snatch 3rd last strides: no threat to wnr (jockey said gelding was slowly away)* **6/1**[3]

0253 **4** *hd* **Murdanova (IRE)**[20] 2514 6-9-5 **72**........................(p) StevieDonohoe 13 74
(Rebecca Menzies) *chsd ldrs: effrt 2f out: drvn and chsd clr wnr over 1f out: no imp and kpt on same pce ins fnl f: lost 2 pls ins fnl f* **25/1**

2514 **5** *½* **Harbour Vision**[12] 2739 4-9-9 **76**................................... PaddyMathers 3 77+
(Derek Shaw) *midfield: sn rdn: swtchd rt and drvn over 1f out: styd on wl ins fnl f: no threat to wnr* **4/1**[2]

-230 **6** *½* **Quick Breath**[16] 2611 4-9-7 **74**.. RobHornby 12 73
(Jonathan Portman) *hld up towards rr: effrt and c wd wl over 1f out: styd on ins fnl f: no threat to wnr* **8/1**

1413 **7** *1* **Javelin**[4] 3020 4-9-2 **72**.. JoshuaBryan(3) 1 69
(William Muir) *wl in tch in midfield: effrt 2f out: unable qck u.p and kpt on same pce ins fnl f* **5/2**[1]

00-1 **8** *1 ¾* **Desert Fox**[25] 2318 5-9-0 **67**.. HarryBentley 8 59
(Mike Murphy) *s.i.s: swtchd lft and hld up in rr: rdn over 1f out: hdwy and swtchd lft ins fnl f: styd on: nvr trbld ldrs (jockey said gelding was slowly away)* **8/1**

6623 **9** *2 ¼* **Pearl Spectre (USA)**[4] 3002 8-8-12 **65**....................(v) CallumShepherd 7 51
(Phil McEntee) *midfield on outer: effrt wl over 1f out: no imp: edgd lft and rdr dropped whip ins fnl f* **8/1**

421/ **10** *½* **Gustavo Fring (IRE)**[522] 9344 5-9-7 **74**........................ DanielMuscutt 10 58
(Richard Spencer) *led: rdn and hdd over 1f out: sn outpcd and wknd ins fnl f* **25/1**

0030 **11** 1/2 **Able Jack**[32] 2064 6-9-10 **77** .... MartinDwyer 6 60
(Stuart Williams) *in tch in midfield: unable qck u.p and lost pl over 1f out: wknd ins fnl f* **14/1**

6240 **12** 2 1/4 **Aguerooo (IRE)**[51] 1597 6-8-11 **69** .... (tp) SeanDavis(5) 9 46
(Charlie Wallis) *stdd and swtchd lft after s: hld up in rr: effrt over 1f out: no prog and nvr involved* **50/1**

655 **13** 1 3/4 **Bawaader (IRE)**[18] 2550 4-8-12 **65** .... (b[1]) DaneO'Neill 14 37
(Ed Dunlop) *wnt rt s: t.k.h: hld up in tch in rr: no prog over 1f out: wl hld and eased ins fnl f* **25/1**

0065 **14** *nk* **Top Boy**[20] 2515 9-8-12 **65** .... (p) BrettDoyle 11 36
(Derek Shaw) *s.i.s: t.k.h: hld up in rr: nvr involved (jockey said gelding was slowly away)* **33/1**

1m 24.79s (-2.41) **Going Correction** -0.175s/f (Stan) **14** Ran SP% **127.5**
Speed ratings (Par 103): **106,103,102,102,102 101,100,98,95,95 94,92,90,89**
CSF £498.33 CT £2405.34 TOTE £27.60: £7.80, £4.90, £2.20; EX 805.20 Trifecta £3399.30.
Owner 21st Century Racing & Nigel Sennett **Bred** Gestut Wittekindshof **Trained** Wiseton, Nottinghamshire

FOCUS
A fair handicap. One of the outsiders burst back to form in a good comparative time. The form's rated around the runner-up.

3148 CCR SUPPORTING HELP FOR HEROES H'CAP 5f (P)
5:30 (5:30) (Class 6) (0-55,62) 3-Y-O
£3,428 (£1,020; £509; £300; £300; £300) Stalls Low

Form RPR

4002 **1** **Thegreyvtrain**[21] 2474 3-9-4 **52** .... KieranO'Neill 8 57
(Ronald Harris) *wnt sltly lft leaving stalls: sn led: rdn and edgd rt 1f out: hdd ins fnl f: sn led again: kpt on* **14/1**

341 **2** 1/2 **Fairy Fast (IRE)**[8] 2871 3-10-0 **62** 6ex .... (b[1]) DavidNolan 7 65
(David O'Meara) *squeezed for room leaving stalls: hdwy to join wnr over 3f out: rdn over 1f out: led ins fnl f: wandered rt and sn hdd: no ex towards fin* **9/2**[3]

33-0 **3** *1* **Awarded**[17] 2592 3-9-1 **54** .... (p[1]) DylanHogan(5) 5 54
(Robert Cowell) *chsd wnr for over 1f: chsd ldrs after: effrt over 1f out: kpt on ins fnl f: nt enough pce to threaten ldrs* **14/1**

0-00 **4** 3/4 **Sarsaparilla Kit**[60] 1381 3-9-7 **55** .... MartinDwyer 1 52+
(Stuart Williams) *in tch in midfield: effrt over 1f out: chsd ldrs and kpt on same pce ins fnl f* **5/2**[1]

4022 **5** 1/2 **Valley Belle (IRE)**[12] 2735 3-9-8 **56** .... JosephineGordon 12 51+
(Phil McEntee) *taken down early: wd: in tch towards rr: effrt over 1f out: styd on ins fnl f: nvr trbld ldrs* **5/1**

-654 **6** 1 1/4 **Laura's Legacy**[26] 2300 3-8-12 **46** oh1 .... DavidProbert 9 37
(Andrew Balding) *swtchd lft after s: hld up in tch towards rr: effrt over 1f out: kpt on ins fnl f: nvr trbld ldrs* **10/1**

0402 **7** *hd* **Lysander Belle (IRE)**[26] 2300 3-9-7 **55** .... NickyMackay 6 45
(Sophie Leech) *wnt rt leaving stalls: in tch towards rr: effrt over 1f out: kpt on ins fnl f: nvr trbld ldrs* **7/2**[2]

4026 **8** 3/4 **Wye Bother (IRE)**[17] 2592 3-8-12 **46** .... (t) RobHornby 2 33
(Milton Bradley) *chsd ldrs: unable qck u.p over 1f out: wknd ins fnl f* **25/1**

06-0 **9** 1 1/2 **Little Tipple**[27] 2238 3-8-5 **46** .... (p[1]) LauraPearson(7) 3 28
(John Ryan) *pushed early: in tch in midfield: rdn and unable qck over 1f out: wknd ins fnl f* **33/1**

5-60 **10** *4* **Nervous Nerys (IRE)**[77] 1140 3-8-12 **46** .... CallumShepherd 10 13
(Alex Hales) *hld up in rr: effrt over 1f out: no prog and wknd ins fnl f* **14/1**

59.93s (-0.27) **Going Correction** -0.175s/f (Stan) **10** Ran SP% **121.5**
Speed ratings (Par 97): **95,94,92,91,90 88,88,87,84,78**
CSF £79.24 CT £926.57 TOTE £11.10: £2.70, £2.00, £3.30; EX 39.60 Trifecta £909.30.
Owner Ridge House Stables Ltd **Bred** David C Mead **Trained** Earlswood, Monmouths

FOCUS
A moderate 3yo sprint, effectively a fillies' handicap. The first three all arrived in good form and the pace held up.
T/Plt: £47.50 to a £1 stake. Pool: £47,416.03 - 727.48 winning units T/Qpdt: £5.30 to a £1 stake. Pool: £5,518.42 - 768.17 winning units **Steve Payne**

2900 LEICESTER (R-H)
Monday, May 27

OFFICIAL GOING: Good to firm (good on the bends; 8.0)
Wind: Fresh across Weather: Overcast

3149 FOXTON H'CAP 1m 53y
1:45 (1:45) (Class 4) (0-85,85) 4-Y-O+
£5,530 (£1,645; £822; £411; £300; £300) Stalls Low

Form RPR

212 **1** **Kodiac Harbour (IRE)**[18] 2555 4-9-5 **83** .... JFEgan 9 93
(Paul George) *hld up: pushed along and hdwy over 2f out: rdn to ld wl ins fnl f: r.o* **5/1**[3]

42-3 **2** 1 1/4 **Dourado (IRE)**[27] 2237 5-9-3 **81** .... LiamKeniry 6 88
(Patrick Chamings) *trckd ldrs: racd keenly: led over 1f out: rdn and hdd wl ins fnl f: styd on same pce* **13/2**

0-16 **3** 1 1/2 **Candelisa (IRE)**[26] 2273 6-9-0 **78** .... (t[1]) TrevorWhelan 4 82
(David Loughnane) *hld up: hdwy over 2f out: rdn over 1f out: styd on u.p to go 3rd nr fin* **10/3**[2]

13-0 **4** *hd* **Sod's Law**[58] 1413 4-9-5 **83** .... PJMcDonald 2 86
(Hughie Morrison) *hld up: pushed along over 3f out: rdn over 1f out: r.o ins fnl f: nt rch ldrs* **5/2**[1]

5-00 **5** *hd* **Prevent**[29] 2151 4-8-12 **76** .... DavidEgan 7 79
(Ian Williams) *chsd ldr tl led 6f out: hdd over 4f out: led again over 2f out: rdn and hdd over 1f out: no ex ins fnl f* **14/1**

3-03 **6** *7* **Al Barg (IRE)**[18] 2551 4-9-7 **85** .... (b) RossaRyan 8 72
(Richard Hannon) *led: hung lft thrght: hdd 6f out: led again over 4f out: rdn and hdd over 2f out: wknd ins fnl f (jockey said gelding hung left-handed throughout)* **8/1**

30-0 **7** 3 1/4 **Plunger**[17] 2584 4-9-5 **83** .... RaulDaSilva 10 62
(Paul Cole) *stdd s: hld up: rdn over 2f out: n.d* **12/1**

/0-0 **8** 3 1/4 **Quixote (GER)**[34] 2015 9-9-7 **85** .... (t) TomEaves 1 57
(James Unett) *s.i.s: hld up: hdwy over 1f out: wknd ins fnl f* **50/1**

-004 **9** 1 1/2 **Burguillos**[27] 2260 6-9-4 **82** .... (bt[1]) PatCosgrave 5 50
(Stuart Williams) *s.i.s: plld hrd: hdwy over 6f out: wknd 2f out* **12/1**

1m 43.89s (-2.41) **Going Correction** -0.075s/f (Good) **9** Ran SP% **116.8**
Speed ratings (Par 105): **109,107,106,106,105 98,95,92,90**
CSF £37.87 CT £124.69 TOTE £4.50: £2.10, £1.90, £1.20; EX 34.70 Trifecta £89.40.
Owner Cross Channel Racing **Bred** Tally-Ho Stud **Trained** Crediton, Devon

FOCUS
Good to firm was the ground view of Rossa Ryan and PJ McDonald, while John Egan said it was "real good ground." A fair handicap won by a progressive sort. It's rated around the runner-up.

3150 ENDERBY (S) STKS 1m 2f
2:20 (2:20) (Class 5) 3-5-Y-O
£3,816 (£1,135; £567; £300; £300) Stalls Low

Form RPR

4-01 **1** **Izvestia (IRE)**[17] 2587 3-8-11 **80** .... (b[1]) EdwardGreatrex 6 75
(Archie Watson) *w ldrs tl settled into 4th pl 8f out: shkn up over 2f out: rdn to ld over 1f out: sn edgd lft: edgd rt wl ins fnl f: styd on* **2/1**[1]

50-3 **2** 2 3/4 **Il Sicario (IRE)**[12] 2732 5-9-2 **65** .... RyanWhile(5) 3 67
(Bill Turner) *chsd ldrs: rdn and ev ch over 1f out: styd on same pce ins fnl f* **9/4**[2]

4156 **3** *1* **Dream Magic (IRE)**[14] 2696 5-9-3 **68** .... (be) CierenFallon(7) 4 68
(Mark Loughnane) *a.p: chsd ldr over 7f out: led over 3f out: rdn and hdd over 1f out: no ex wl ins fnl f* **3/1**[3]

2356 **4** 1 1/4 **Harbour Quay**[40] 1861 5-9-7 **61** .... (p[1]) PJMcDonald 2 63
(Robyn Brisland) *sn led: rdn and hdd over 3f out: no ex ins fnl f* **7/2**

-010 **5** *6* **Oofy Prosser (IRE)**[4] 3018 3-8-7 **60** .... (b[1]) MitchGodwin(3) 7 54
(Harry Dunlop) *hld up: swtchd lft over 2f out: hrd rdn over 1f out: no rspnse* **20/1**

2m 9.05s (-0.15) **Going Correction** -0.075s/f (Good)
WFA 3 from 4yo+ 14lb **5** Ran SP% **116.1**
Speed ratings (Par 103): **97,94,94,93,88**
CSF £7.34 TOTE £2.50: £1.50, £1.60; EX 9.60 Trifecta £13.30.The winner was bought in for £11,500.
Owner Saxon Thoroughbreds **Bred** Corrin Stud **Trained** Upper Lambourn, W Berks

FOCUS
A lowly seller, with the winner not worth his rating, and four of the five runners were wearing first-time headgear. It's rated as straightforward form.

3151 VICTORIA PARK H'CAP 6f
2:55 (2:56) (Class 3) (0-95,96) 3-Y-O
£9,703 (£2,887; £1,443; £721) Stalls High

Form RPR

00-1 **1** **Rathbone**[48] 1665 3-9-7 **88** .... TomEaves 5 96
(Kevin Ryan) *trckd ldrs: shkn up and swtchd rt over 2f out: hrd rdn over 1f out: led and edgd rt ins fnl f: jst hld on* **3/1**[3]

010- **2** *hd* **Blown By Wind**[317] 4945 3-10-1 **96** .... FrannyNorton 1 103
(Mark Johnston) *s.i.s: sn prom: jnd ldr 5f out: shkn up to ld over 1f out: edgd rt and hdd ins fnl f: r.o* **13/2**

1-16 **3** *4* **Intuitive (IRE)**[23] 2412 3-9-4 **85** .... PJMcDonald 3 80
(James Tate) *s.i.s: sn pushed along in rr: hdwy over 1f out: styd on same pce ins fnl f* **11/4**[2]

4-32 **4** *2* **Heritage**[14] 2687 3-9-2 **83** .... DavidEgan 2 71
(Clive Cox) *w ldrs: shkn up over 2f out: wknd fnl f* **5/2**[1]

0-06 **5** *1* **Good Luck Fox (IRE)**[10] 2810 3-9-3 **84** .... SilvestreDeSousa 4 69
(Richard Hannon) *led: pushed along 1/2-way: hdd over 1f out: wknd ins fnl f* **9/2**

1m 11.62s (-0.48) **Going Correction** -0.075s/f (Good) **5** Ran SP% **111.8**
Speed ratings (Par 103): **100,99,94,91,90**
CSF £21.29 TOTE £3.60: £1.80, £3.20; EX 21.50 Trifecta £52.90.
Owner Mrs Angie Bailey **Bred** Whitsbury Manor Stud **Trained** Hambleton, N Yorks

FOCUS
A useful 3yo sprint with two - the improving favourite and the class act of the race - drawing clear. They raced stands' side. The winner built on his Pontefract run.

3152 BRITISH STALLION STUDS EBF NOVICE STKS (PLUS 10 RACE) 1m 3f 179y
3:30 (3:32) (Class 3) 3-Y-O
£9,703 (£2,887; £1,443; £721) Stalls Low

Form RPR

2 **1** **Dubai Falcon (IRE)**[17] 2581 3-9-2 0 .... PatCosgrave 3 93
(Saeed bin Suroor) *mde all: set stdy pce: plld hrd: qcknd over 3f out: rdn over 1f out: hung lft ins fnl f: all out* **15/8**[2]

12 **2** *hd* **Questionare**[27] 2258 3-9-8 0 .... (t) RobertHavlin 4 98
(John Gosden) *s.i.s: in rr: pushed along over 3f out: hdwy on outer over 2f out: rdn to chse wnr over 1f out: nt clr run ins fnl f: r.o* **11/2**

22 **3** *5* **Cape Cavalli (IRE)**[17] 2566 3-9-2 0 .... SilvestreDeSousa 2 84
(Simon Crisford) *chsd ldrs: rdn to chse wnr over 2f out tl over 1f out: no ex ins fnl f* **13/8**[1]

3-0 **4** *4* **Oydis**[11] 2770 3-8-11 0 .... DavidEgan 5 73
(Ralph Beckett) *chsd wnr tl rdn over 2f out: wknd over 1f out* **66/1**

6-2 **5** *6* **High Commissioner (IRE)**[10] 2795 3-9-2 0 .... RaulDaSilva 1 68
(Paul Cole) *hld up: hdwy over 9f out: rdn over 2f out: wknd wl over 1f out* **7/2**[3]

2m 30.25s (-4.75) **Going Correction** -0.075s/f (Good) **5** Ran SP% **112.0**
Speed ratings (Par 103): **112,111,108,105,101**
CSF £12.35 TOTE £2.40: £1.10, £2.10; EX 10.90 Trifecta £15.50.
Owner Godolphin **Bred** Godolphin **Trained** Newmarket, Suffolk

FOCUS
A good-quality novice and the front two, both of whom look capable of mixing it at a higher level, pulled clear.

3153 VIS-A-VIS SYMPOSIUMS FILLIES' H'CAP 1m 3f 179y
4:05 (4:05) (Class 4) (0-85,79) 3-Y-O £5,530 (£1,645; £822; £411; £300) Stalls Low

Form RPR

22-4 **1** **Dorah**[29] 2148 3-9-6 **78** .... EdwardGreatrex 2 84
(Archie Watson) *chsd ldrs: rdn over 1f out: led and edgd rt ins fnl f: r.o: comf* **7/2**[2]

-443 **2** *2* **Luck Of Clover**[25] 2343 3-8-7 **65** .... PJMcDonald 5 68
(Andrew Balding) *sn led: hdd over 2f out: rallied to ld over 1f out: hdd ins fnl f: styd on same pce* **9/4**[1]

20-0 **3** *nse* **Arctic Ocean (IRE)**[27] 2253 3-8-9 **67** .... DavidEgan 3 70
(Sir Michael Stoute) *led early: chsd ldr tl led over 2f out: rdn and hdd over 1f out: styd on same pce ins fnl f* **9/2**[3]

0-11 **4** *5* **Lady Reset**[13] 2719 3-9-7 **79** .... RossaRyan 4 74
(David Evans) *hld up: hdwy over 2f out: rdn and hung rt over 1f out: no ex fnl f* **9/4**[1]

5-66 **5** *3* **Suakin (IRE)**[34] 2017 3-8-13 **71** .... (b[1]) RobertHavlin 1 61
(John Gosden) *s.i.s: plld hrd early: shkn up over 2f out: rdn and hung rt over 1f out: sn btn* **15/2**

2m 33.92s (-1.08) **Going Correction** -0.075s/f (Good) **5** Ran SP% **113.7**
Speed ratings (Par 98): **100,98,98,95,93**
CSF £12.18 TOTE £5.20: £2.60, £1.50; EX 12.30 Trifecta £39.00.
Owner Ms Sharon Kinsella **Bred** Seasons Holidays Plc **Trained** Upper Lambourn, W Berks

FOCUS
No great gallop on here in what was an ordinary fillies' handicap. The second and third are rated close to form.

3154 ANSTY FILLIES' H'CAP — 1m 53y
4:40 (4:41) (Class 5) (0-70,70) 3-Y-O
£3,816 (£1,135; £567; £300; £300; £300) **Stalls** Low

Form — RPR

0-40 **1** **Amorously (IRE)**[17] 2582 3-9-4 **67**.................................. RossaRyan 10 75
(Richard Hannon) *hld up: hdwy on outer over 2f out: rdn to ld and edgd rt wl ins fnl f: styd on (trainer's rep said, regarding the apparent improvement in form, that filly had been more settled in the preliminaries on this occasion)* **5/1**[2]

03-0 **2** *1* **Beguiling Charm (IRE)**[41] 1828 3-9-2 **65**......................... LiamKeniry 9 71
(Ed Walker) *s.i.s: sn rcvrd to chse ldr: led 2f out: rdn and edgd rt over 1f out: hdd wl ins fnl f* **17/2**

52-0 **3** *5* **Solfeggio (IRE)**[30] 2114 3-9-7 **70**............................(h) GeorgeWood 4 64
(Chris Wall) *hld up: plld hrd: shkn up and nt clr run over 2f out: rdn over 1f out: r.o to go 3rd wl ins fnl f* **6/1**[3]

4-00 **4** *1 1/4* **Sukalia**[27] 2253 3-8-4 **60**.. CierenFallon(7) 6 51
(Alan King) *s.i.s: hdwy over 5f out: rdn over 2f out: styd on same pce fr over 1f out* **12/1**

-546 **5** *nk* **Lethal Lover**[24] 2356 3-9-1 **64**........................... EdwardGreatrex 8 55
(Clive Cox) *sn led: shkn up over 3f out: hdd 2f out: hmpd over 1f out: wknd ins fnl f* **14/1**

5422 **6** *nk* **Redemptive**[10] 2798 3-9-2 **65**................................ PJMcDonald 7 55
(David Elsworth) *chsd ldrs: ev ch 2f out: sn rdn: wknd ins fnl f* **6/4**[1]

430 **7** *1* **Any Smile (IRE)**[25] 2340 3-9-4 **67**................................ DavidEgan 3 55
(Michael Bell) *hld up: racd keenly: rdn over 2f out: nvr on terms* **16/1**

30-6 **8** *3/4* **Schnapps**[60] 1385 3-8-12 **61**.................................... GrahamLee 1 47
(Jedd O'Keeffe) *chsd ldrs: rdn over 2f out: wknd fnl f* **16/1**

0030 **9** *1 1/2* **Dusty Damsel**[25] 2322 3-9-0 **63**............................ FergusSweeney 2 45
(Mike Murphy) *s.i.s: hld up: pushed along over 3f out: n.d* **33/1**

6-06 **10** *1/2* **Parisean Artiste (IRE)**[14] 2689 3-9-1 **64**..................... LouisSteward 5 45
(Eve Johnson Houghton) *prom: rdn over 2f out: wknd over 1f out* **14/1**

1m 45.6s (-0.70) **Going Correction** -0.075s/f (Good) **10 Ran SP% 117.2**
Speed ratings (Par 96): **100,99,94,92,92 92,91,90,88,88**
CSF £47.35 CT £267.97 TOTE £6.30: £1.90, £2.60, £1.70; EX 49.90 Trifecta £274.60.
Owner Ali Bahbahani **Bred** Haras Don Alberto **Trained** East Everleigh, Wilts

FOCUS
Modest fillies' form, but the first two did put some distance between themselves and the rest. The winner is rated back to her 2yo best.

3155 TIGERS APPRENTICE H'CAP — 1m 3f 179y
5:15 (5:15) (Class 5) (0-70,70) 4-Y-O+
£3,816 (£1,135; £567; £300; £300; £300) **Stalls** Low

Form — RPR

24-2 **1** **Broad Appeal**[42] 1826 5-8-13 **60**.......................... TylerSaunders(3) 5 68+
(Jonathan Portman) *chsd ldrs: shkn up to ld over 1f out: pushed out* **11/10**[1]

30-2 **2** *1 1/2* **Albert Boy (IRE)**[9] 2819 6-9-2 **60**......................... KieranSchofield 2 64
(Scott Dixon) *led: hdd over 10f out: chsd ldr: rdn and ev ch over 1f out: styd on* **7/2**[3]

0531 **3** *nk* **Ascot Day (FR)**[13] 2720 5-9-7 **65**.....................(p) ScottMcCullagh 6 69
(Bernard Llewellyn) *s.i.s: rcvrd to ld over 10f out: rdn and hdd over 1f out: no ex nr fin* **9/4**[2]

410- **4** *1/2* **Life Knowledge (IRE)**[140] 9054 7-8-10 **54**..............(p) JonathanFisher 1 57
(Liam Bailey) *s.i.s: hld up: hdwy over 5f out: rdn over 2f out: styd on* **11/1**

6024 **5** *11* **Smiley Bagel (IRE)**[61] 1363 6-8-10 **64**..................... MolliePhillips(10) 3 49
(Mark Loughnane) *hld up: shkn up over 3f out: sn outpcd* **25/1**

60-0 **6** *3 1/2* **Remember Nerja (IRE)**[17] 2593 5-8-4 **51** oh6..........(p) AmeliaGlass(3) 7 31
(Barry Leavy) *chsd ldrs: lost pl over 5f out: shkn up on outer over 4f out: sn outpcd* **66/1**

2m 36.84s (1.84) **Going Correction** -0.075s/f (Good) **6 Ran SP% 114.3**
Speed ratings (Par 103): **90,89,88,88,81 78**
CSF £5.59 TOTE £1.80: £1.10, £3.20; EX 5.30 Trifecta £9.90.
Owner J G B Portman **Bred** S Dibb & J Repard **Trained** Upper Lambourn, Berks

FOCUS
Not much pace on in this moderate handicap and they finished in a bit of a heap. This may not be solid form.
T/Plt: £131.10 to a £1 stake. Pool: £39,959.16 - 222.40 winning units T/Qpdt: £73.10 to a £1 stake. Pool: £2,987.96 - 30.21 winning units **Colin Roberts**

2906 REDCAR (L-H)
Monday, May 27

OFFICIAL GOING: Good to firm (watered)
Wind: Light largely against Weather: Overcast, sunny after 4th

3156 RACINGTV.COM NOVICE AUCTION STKS — 5f
1:50 (1:50) (Class 5) 2-Y-O
£4,528 (£1,347; £673; £336) **Stalls** Centre

Form — RPR

1 **Liberty Beach** 2-8-12 0.. JasonHart 4 79
(John Quinn) *restrained sn after s and hld up in tch: pushed along and hdwy to chse ldr 1f out: led narrowly 110yds out: rdn and kpt on* **16/1**

10 **2** *1/2* **Lady Quickstep (IRE)**[10] 2805 2-8-9 0............................ TobyEley(7) 6 81
(Gay Kelleway) *sltly awkward s: hld up: hdwy and in tch over 2f out: rdn to chse ldr 1f out: chal strly 110yds out: one pce towards fin* **11/2**[3]

42 **3** *3* **Mecca's Hot Steps**[9] 2820 2-8-12 0........................ PaulMulrennan 5 66
(Michael Dods) *chsd ldr: rdn 2f out: sn one pce* **5/2**[2]

210 **4** *nse* **Iva Go (IRE)**[10] 2805 2-9-2 0...................................... DavidAllan 1 70
(Tim Easterby) *led: pushed along and edgd rt 1f out: rdn and hdd 110yds out: wknd* **6/5**[1]

5 *1 1/2* **Havana Dawn** 2-9-0 0... SamJames 3 63
(Phillip Makin) *dwlt: sn in tch: hung lft and outpcd over 2f out: rdn over 1f out: kpt on ins fnl f but no threat* **25/1**

0 **6** *7* **Baileys Prayer (FR)**[30] 2115 2-9-2 0........................ PaulHanagan 2 39
(Richard Fahey) *chsd ldrs: outpcd and dropped to rr over 3f out: wknd and bhd over 1f out* **16/1**

7 *2 3/4* **Samsar (IRE)** 2-9-5 0.. AndrewMullen 7 33
(Adrian Nicholls) *dwlt and wnt rt s: hld up: wknd and bhd over 1f out* **18/1**

59.41s (0.91) **Going Correction** -0.15s/f (Firm) **7 Ran SP% 110.3**
Speed ratings (Par 93): **91,90,85,85,82 71,67**
CSF £92.56 TOTE £13.00: £4.80, £2.00; EX 98.20 Trifecta £622.50.
Owner Philip Wilkins **Bred** Phillip Wilkins **Trained** Settrington, N Yorks

FOCUS
There was 4mm of water applied the previous Monday, Wednesday and Friday, plus 2mm of rain overnight into Sunday and 3mm on Sunday morning. It was dry after until race day. This looked an ordinary juvenile novice, rated around the runner-up.

3157 RACING TV PROFITS RETURNED TO RACING MEDIAN AUCTION MAIDEN STKS — 5f 217y
2:25 (2:27) (Class 5) 3-Y-O
£4,528 (£1,347; £673; £336) **Stalls** Centre

Form — RPR

26 **1** **In Trutina**[17] 2590 3-9-0 0.. HollieDoyle 4 68
(Archie Watson) *mde all: rdn over 1f out: edgd lft: kpt on* **3/1**[2]

-05 **2** *1* **Lost In Alaska (USA)**[12] 2736 3-9-5 0...........................(t[1]) BenCurtis 2 70
(Jeremy Noseda) *pressed ldr: rdn over 1f out: edgd lft: one pce fnl 50yds* **4/1**

3 *2* **Diamond Shower (IRE)** 3-9-0 0.................................. PaulHanagan 3 59+
(Richard Fahey) *chsd ldrs: pushed along over 2f out: rdn over 1f out: kpt on ins fnl f* **13/2**

4 *2 1/4* **Raksha (IRE)** 3-9-0 0.. DanielTudhope 5 51
(David O'Meara) *chsd ldrs towards nr side: pushed along over 2f out: outpcd over 1f out: kpt on same pce ins fnl f* **11/4**[1]

00 **5** *nk* **Torque Of The Town (IRE)**[17] 2590 3-9-5 0.............. ConnorBeasley 8 55
(Noel Wilson) *hld up: rdn over 2f out: drvn over 1f out: kpt on ins fnl f* **66/1**

05 **6** *nk* **Mea Culpa (IRE)**[28] 2199 3-9-5 0..........................(h[1]) PaulMulrennan 9 54+
(Julie Camacho) *slowly away: hld up: pushed along 2f out: kpt on ins fnl f* **20/1**

7 *shd* **Fortamour (IRE)** 3-9-5 0.. AndrewMullen 7 54
(Ben Haslam) *dwlt: sn chsd ldrs: pushed along over 2f out: rdn over 1f out: no ex ins fnl f* **7/2**[3]

0-0 **8** *4 1/2* **Hard Knock Life**[13] 2713 3-9-5 0................................ DavidAllan 1 40
(Tim Easterby) *chsd ldrs: rdn along over 2f out: wknd over 1f out* **33/1**

00 **9** *13* **Corralejo (IRE)**[20] 2506 3-9-5 0..............................(p[1]) JackGarritty 6
(John Wainwright) *hld up: wknd and bhd over 1f out* **100/1**

1m 12.49s (0.69) **Going Correction** -0.15s/f (Firm) **9 Ran SP% 117.4**
Speed ratings (Par 99): **98,96,94,91,90 90,90,84,66**
CSF £15.34 TOTE £4.10: £1.50, £1.70, £2.00; EX 16.40 Trifecta £94.90.
Owner Mrs S E A Sloan **Bred** Bearstone Stud Ltd **Trained** Upper Lambourn, W Berks

FOCUS
An ordinary maiden, rated around the bottom end of the race averages.

3158 CONGRATULATIONS COMPETITION WINNER MARIA FERGUSON (S) STKS — 7f
3:00 (3:07) (Class 5) 3-5-Y-O
£4,075 (£1,212; £606; £303; £300; £300) **Stalls** Centre

Form — RPR

0-00 **1** **Magwadiri (IRE)**[27] 2256 5-9-10 56........................ RichardKingscote 8 60
(Mark Loughnane) *trckd ldrs: led over 1f out: rdn and kpt on (vet reported gelding lost its left fore shoe)* **7/1**[3]

2 *1 3/4* **Kind Review** 3-8-10 0.. JasonHart 7 48
(Tracy Waggott) *slowly away and outpcd in rr: hdwy whn n.m.r over 1f out: rdn 1f out: r.o wl: wnt 2nd post* **28/1**

-524 **3** *nk* **Tizwotitiz**[8] 2870 3-8-3 60.. TobyEley(7) 1 48
(Steph Hollinshead) *midfield: racd keenly: hdwy over 2f out: pushed along to chse ldr over 1f out: rdn and one pce fnl f: lost 2nd post (jockey said the gelding ran too freely)* **15/8**[1]

-000 **4** *1/2* **Quiet Moment (IRE)**[5] 2963 5-8-9 42.........................(t) IsobelFrancis(7) 5 45
(Maurice Barnes) *hld up: hdwy towards far side over 2f out: rdn to chse ldr over 1f out: kpt on same pce* **25/1**

000- **5** *2* **Radjash**[205] 8828 5-9-7 54....................................... JackGarritty 10 45
(Ruth Carr) *hld up: smooth hdwy and trckd ldrs over 2f out: rdn over 1f out: edgd lft and no ex* **8/1**

6045 **6** *nk* **You Little Beauty**[16] 2633 3-8-5 45.............................. HollieDoyle 16 35
(Ann Duffield) *hld up towards nr side: rdn over 2f out: kpt on fnl f: nvr threatened ldrs* **10/1**

0-00 **7** *hd* **Smashing Lass (IRE)**[28] 2190 3-8-5 52..................... JamieGormley(3) 14 38
(Ollie Pears) *hld up: rdn over 2f out: kpt on fnl f: nvr threatened ldrs* **14/1**

34-0 **8** *3 3/4* **Itsupforgrabsnow (IRE)**[24] 2376 4-8-9 43...............(h) RussellHarris(7) 11 29
(Susan Corbett) *dwlt: hld up: nvr threatened* **50/1**

000U **9** *nse* **Al Mortajaz (FR)**[17] 2587 3-8-10 64.......................... AndrewMullen 2 30
(Adrian Nicholls) *chsd ldrs: rdn over 2f out: wknd fnl f* **9/1**

0000 **10** *1 1/2* **Scenery**[27] 2235 4-9-2 52.................................(t[1]) FayeMcManoman(5) 4 30
(Marjorie Fife) *prom: rdn over 2f out: wknd over 1f out* **11/2**[2]

604- **11** *2 3/4* **Jungle Room (USA)**[325] 4608 4-9-10 0.......................(p[1]) AndrewElliott 13 26
(Denis Quinn) *prom: led after 1f: rdn over 2f out: hdd over 1f out: wknd* **12/1**

-040 **12** *nk* **Slieve Donard**[16] 2633 3-8-5 47.................................. PaulaMuir(5) 12 18
(Noel Wilson) *led for 1f: remained cl up tl wknd over 1f out* **40/1**

0000 **13** *6* **Mr Wing (IRE)**[2] 3067 4-9-0 17.................................. VictorSantos(7) 15 7
(John Wainwright) *chsd ldrs: wknd over 1f out* **100/1**

4-00 **14** *10* **Royal Rattle**[29] 2147 4-9-7 44.................................. PaulMulrennan 6
(John Norton) *w ldr: wknd 2f out* **50/1**

0/50 **15** *5* **Cryogenics (IRE)**[13] 1550 5-9-2 48...................... ThomasGreatrex(5) 3
(Kenny Johnson) *dwlt: sn chsd ldrs towards far side: rdn over 2f out: wknd (jockey said gelding stopped quickly)* **100/1**

1m 25.76s (0.36) **Going Correction** -0.15s/f (Firm)
WFA 3 from 4yo+ 11lb **15 Ran SP% 122.9**
Speed ratings (Par 103): **96,94,93,93,90 90,90,85,85,84 81,80,73,62,56**
CSF £198.48 TOTE £9.30: £2.70, £9.40, £1.20; EX 216.60 Trifecta £1745.00.There was no bid for the winner. Radjash was claimed by Mrs Sarah Bryan for £6,000
Owner Shropshire Wolves **Bred** Peter & Hugh McCutcheon **Trained** Rock, Worcs

■ Last Glance and Our Secret were withdrawn. Prices at time of withdrawal 100-1 and 20-1 respectively. Rule 4 does not apply

■ Stewards' Enquiry : Toby Eley two-day ban: careless riding (Jun 10-11)

FOCUS
A moderate seller, the likes of the fourth highlighting obvious limitations.

3159 NORTH EAST AUTISM SOCIETY GOING4GOLD H'CAP — 5f
3:35 (3:41) (Class 5) (0-75,75) 3-Y-O
£4,075 (£1,212; £606; £303; £300; £300) **Stalls** Centre

Form — RPR

2431 **1** **Wise Words**[24] 2380 3-9-7 **75**...................................... DavidAllan 13 88+
(James Tate) *trckd ldrs: pushed into ld over 1f out: rdn ins fnl f: kpt on wl* **11/2**[3]

6430 **2** *1 1/2* **Enchanted Linda**[10] 2810 3-9-6 **74**.............................. HollieDoyle 6 81
(Richard Hannon) *hld up: racd keenly: swtchd rt over 2f out: sn hdwy: rdn to chse ldr appr fnl f: kpt on but a hld* **15/2**

0-42 **3** 1 ¾ **Abate**[17] 2590 3-9-7 **75** .... AndrewMullen 7 75
(Adrian Nicholls) *dwlt: hld up: pushed along over 2f out: rdn over 1f out: kpt on ins fnl f* **9/2**[2]

62-1 **4** ¾ **Northern Society (IRE)**[14] 2683 3-9-0 **68** .... ShaneGray 1 66
(Keith Dalgleish) *s.i.s: hld up: rdn 2f out: kpt on ins fnl f (jockey said filly missed the break)* **9/1**

5300 **5** *nk* **One One Seven (IRE)**[8] 2870 3-8-2 **56** oh1 .... CamHardie 5 53
(Antony Brittain) *hld up: rdn over 2f out: kpt on ins fnl f: nvr threatened ldrs* **14/1**

0112 **6** ½ **Arishka (IRE)**[21] 2489 3-9-5 **73** .... RichardKingscote 12 68
(Daniel Kubler) *prom: rdn 2f out: wknd ins fnl f* **13/2**

00 **7** ¾ **Montalvan (IRE)**[21] 2477 3-7-13 **58** .... PaulaMuir(5) 10 50
(Roger Fell) *prom: rdn over 2f out: wknd ins fnl f* **20/1**

23-0 **8** ¾ **Collect Call (IRE)**[42] 1816 3-9-2 **75** .... HarrisonShaw(5) 11 64
(K R Burke) *led narrowly: rdn over 2f out: hdd over 1f out: wknd ins fnl f* **33/1**

30-6 **9** 1 ¾ **Autumn Flight (IRE)**[30] 2121 3-9-4 **72** .... PaulMulrennan 2 55
(Tim Easterby) *in tch: rdn over 2f out: wknd ins fnl f* **12/1**

-050 **10** 5 **Raypeteafterme**[21] 2477 3-8-11 **65** ....(t¹) TonyHamilton 3 30
(Declan Carroll) *prom: rdn over 2f out: wknd over 1f out* **28/1**

-252 **11** 27 **Kyllachy Warrior (IRE)**[21] 2477 3-9-5 **73** .... DanielTudhope 8 +
(Lawrence Mullaney) *rrd s and v.s.a: t.o thrght (jockey said gelding was slowly away)* **7/2**[1]

58.64s (0.14) **Going Correction** -0.15s/f (Firm) **11 Ran SP% 116.4**
Speed ratings (Par 99): **97,94,91,90,90 89,88,86,84,76 32**
CSF £44.78 CT £206.54 TOTE £4.90: £2.40, £2.60, £1.90; EX 49.90 Trifecta £203.70.
Owner Sheikh Rashid Dalmook Al Maktoum **Bred** Ropsley Bloodstock Llp **Trained** Newmarket, Suffolk

FOCUS
A fair handicap, although the favourite took no worthwhile part. The form's rated around the runner-up.

3160 RACING TV ZETLAND GOLD CUP H'CAP — 1m 2f 1y
4:10 (4:11) (Class 2) (0-105,103) 3-Y-O+

£28,012 (£8,388; £4,194; £2,097; £1,048; £526) **Stalls** Low

Form — RPR

14-5 **1** **Al Muffrih (IRE)**[23] 2408 4-8-12 **91** ....(h¹) DanielTudhope 4 100
(William Haggas) *in tch on inner: trckd ldrs 3f out: drvn to chal 2f out: led narrowly 1f out: hld on wl* **6/4**[1]

6-45 **2** *hd* **Leroy Leroy**[23] 2414 3-8-0 **93** oh1 .... HollieDoyle 9 101
(Richard Hannon) *trckd ldrs: rdn to chal strly 2f out: drvn over 1f out: kpt on wl but a jst hld* **16/1**

0000 **3** 3 **Ventura Knight (IRE)**[58] 1415 4-9-2 **95** .... JoeFanning 6 98
(Mark Johnston) *hld up in midfield: gd hdwy on outer over 3f out: rdn to ld narrowly over 2f out: hdd 1f out: no ex ins fnl f* **25/1**

-530 **4** 2 ¼ **Nicholas T**[16] 2609 7-8-2 **84** .... JamieGormley(3) 5 83
(Jim Goldie) *hld up in midfield: pushed along and hdwy to chse ldrs over 2f out: rdn and kpt on same pce* **9/1**[3]

00-0 **5** 3 **Thomas Cranmer (USA)**[12] 2748 5-8-2 **81** .... NathanEvans 2 74
(Tina Jackson) *midfield on inner: rdn along 3f out: no imp* **18/1**

-552 **6** 1 ¼ **Fennaan (IRE)**[8] 2873 4-8-9 **88** ....(h) SamJames 13 78
(Phillip Makin) *hld up in rr: stl lot to do whn swtchd rt to wd outside over 1f out: kpt on ins fnl f* **25/1**

-320 **7** 1 ¼ **Commander Han (FR)**[11] 2778 4-8-10 **89** ....(p) KevinStott 3 77
(Kevin Ryan) *prom: rdn 3f out: wknd fnl f* **20/1**

0252 **8** 2 ¼ **Society Red**[10] 2808 5-8-13 **92** .... PaulHanagan 8 75
(Richard Fahey) *midfield: pushed along and n.m.r wl over 2f out: rdn and no imp* **10/1**

2-12 **9** ½ **Epaulement (IRE)**[17] 2574 4-9-5 **98** .... RichardKingscote 14 80
(Tom Dascombe) *prom: rdn over 3f out: wknd 2f out* **4/1**[2]

0-00 **10** 1 ¼ **Tricorn (IRE)**[11] 2778 5-9-0 **93** .... JackGarritty 12 73
(Ruth Carr) *hld up: pushed along and sme hdwy on outer over 2f out: wknd over 1f out* **66/1**

-151 **11** 1 ¼ **Lunar Jet**[10] 2800 5-9-2 **95** .... JimmyQuinn 11 72
(John Mackie) *hld up: nvr threatened (jockey said gelding was never travelling)* **16/1**

2463 **12** 2 ½ **Employer (IRE)**[10] 2786 4-8-3 **82** .... PhilDennis 10 54
(Jim Goldie) *dwlt: hld up: nvr threatened (vet reported gelding lost its right hind shoe)* **25/1**

3423 **13** *nk* **Sands Chorus**[2] 3072 7-7-13 **81** oh2 ow2 ....(p) GabrieleMalune(3) 1 52
(Scott Dixon) *led: rdn over 3f out: hdd over 2f out: wknd over 1f out (vet reported gelding had a small wound to its left fore cannon bone)* **25/1**

44-0 **14** 7 **First Sitting**[23] 2408 8-9-10 **103** .... DavidAllan 7 60
(Chris Wall) *in tch: rdn over 2f out: wknd over 1f out and eased* **25/1**

2m 2.28s (-4.62) **Going Correction** -0.15s/f (Firm)
WFA 3 from 4yo+ 14lb **14 Ran SP% 121.6**
Speed ratings (Par 109): **112,111,109,107,105 104,103,101,101,100 99,97,96,91**
CSF £26.45 CT £460.98 TOTE £2.20: £1.10, £5.60, £6.20; EX 36.60 Trifecta £670.70.
Owner Sheikh Juma Dalmook Al Maktoum **Bred** Sunderland Holdings Inc **Trained** Newmarket, Suffolk

FOCUS
A competitive running of this good handicap. The winner progressed again.

3161 MARKET CROSS JEWELLERS H'CAP — 1m 2f 1y
4:45 (4:48) (Class 4) (0-80,80) 4-Y-O+

£6,663 (£1,982; £990; £495; £300; £300) **Stalls** Low

Form — RPR

42-4 **1** **Archie Perkins (IRE)**[24] 2374 4-8-8 **70** .... RowanScott(3) 5 78
(Nigel Tinkler) *trckd ldrs: pushed into ld 2f out: rdn appr fnl f: pressed ins fnl f: drvn and styd on* **11/2**

33-4 **2** *nk* **Aiya (IRE)**[24] 2370 4-9-7 **80** ....(h) DavidAllan 7 87
(Tim Easterby) *led: rdn 3f out: hdd 2f out: sn drvn: rallied to chal again ins fnl f: styd on* **8/1**

6-45 **3** 1 ¾ **Autretot (FR)**[9] 2842 4-9-5 **78** .... DanielTudhope 1 82
(David O'Meara) *trckd ldrs: rdn along over 2f out: styd on same pce* **2/1**[1]

0-50 **4** 5 **Juneau (IRE)**[39] 1882 4-9-4 **77** .... JoeFanning 2 71
(Mark Johnston) *prom: rdn over 2f out: wknd ins fnl f* **5/1**[3]

0360 **5** 2 ¼ **Thawry**[14] 2696 4-8-11 **70** .... CamHardie 3 59
(Antony Brittain) *midfield: rdn over 2f out: wknd over 1f out* **16/1**

0031 **6** 1 ¾ **Music Seeker (IRE)**[16] 2629 5-8-12 **78** ....(t) CianMacRedmond(7) 6 64+
(Declan Carroll) *hld up in rr: rdn along over 4f out: drvn 3f out: sn btn (trainer said the gelding was unsuited by the good to firm going and would prefer some cut in the ground)* **9/2**[2]

-006 **7** *nk* **Dark Devil (IRE)**[16] 2629 6-8-9 **68** ....(p) PaulHanagan 8 53
(Richard Fahey) *midfield: rdn 3f out: wknd 2f out* **10/1**

/64- **8** 12 **Watheer**[303] 5495 4-9-4 **77** .... BenCurtis 4 52
(Roger Fell) *hld up: wknd over 2f out and eased* **14/1**

2m 3.84s (-3.06) **Going Correction** -0.15s/f (Firm) **8 Ran SP% 116.3**
Speed ratings (Par 105): **106,105,104,100,98 97,96,87**
CSF £49.18 CT £117.56 TOTE £5.90: £1.60, £2.40, £1.30; EX 41.80 Trifecta £157.20.
Owner J Raybould & S Perkins **Bred** Helen Lyons **Trained** Langton, N Yorks

FOCUS
A fair handicap in which the pace held out. The winner found a bit of improvement.

3162 COME RACING AGAIN TOMORROW H'CAP (DIV I) — 1m 2f 1y
5:20 (5:21) (Class 6) (0-60,62) 4-Y-O+

£3,823 (£1,137; £568; £300; £300; £300) **Stalls** Low

Form — RPR

1102 **1** **Mr Coco Bean (USA)**[3] 3046 5-9-8 **61** .... BenCurtis 14 68
(David Barron) *midfield: pushed along and hdwy on outer 2f out: rdn to ld narrowly ins fnl f: drvn out* **6/5**[1]

300- **2** ½ **Red Seeker**[196] 9032 4-9-2 **55** ....(t¹) DavidAllan 8 61
(Tim Easterby) *prom: rdn along to ld wl over 1f out: drvn and hdd ins fnl f: one pce* **6/1**[3]

5022 **3** *hd* **Splash Of Verve (IRE)**[24] 2376 7-8-3 **49** .... TobyEley(7) 9 55
(David Thompson) *hld up in midfield: hdwy and trckd ldrs over 2f out: rdn over 1f out: styd on wl fnl 110yds (jockey said gelding hung right throughout)* **16/1**

0203 **4** 1 ¼ **Mr Carbonator**[16] 2629 4-9-7 **60** .... KevinStott 12 63
(Philip Kirby) *hld up: rdn 2f out: styd on wl ins fnl f* **11/2**[2]

3301 **5** *hd* **King Of Naples**[91] 911 6-9-9 **62** ....(h) JackGarritty 5 65
(Ruth Carr) *in tch: trckd ldrs gng wl 2f out: drvn 1f out: sn no ex* **12/1**

36-0 **6** *nk* **Odds On Oli**[27] 2241 4-9-5 **58** .... TonyHamilton 13 61
(Richard Fahey) *hld up on inner: pushed along over 1f out: rdn and styd on ins fnl f* **22/1**

0-04 **7** 5 **Sulafaat (IRE)**[24] 2376 4-8-12 **51** ....(p) CamHardie 7 45
(Rebecca Menzies) *trckd ldrs: outpcd over 2f out and sn btn* **33/1**

000- **8** 3 ¼ **Kissesforeveryone**[268] 6787 4-8-7 **46** oh1 .... AndrewElliott 11 34
(Andrew Crook) *hld up: nvr threatened* **100/1**

-606 **9** 1 ¾ **Shakiah (IRE)**[24] 2376 4-8-7 **46** oh1 .... PhilDennis 3 31
(Sharon Watt) *trckd ldrs: rdn 3f out: wknd over 1f out* **20/1**

00-0 **10** *nk* **Geneva Trumpet**[140] 117 8-8-7 **46** oh1 .... NathanEvans 2 30
(Seb Spencer) *led: rdn and hdd over 2f out: wknd over 1f out* **100/1**

202- **11** *nse* **Midnight Warrior**[251] 7396 9-8-12 **56** ....(t) RachealKneller(5) 4 40
(Ron Barr) *trckd ldrs: rdn over 2f out: wknd over 1f out* **33/1**

6-00 **12** 2 **Mont Royal (FR)**[32] 2056 5-9-3 **56** ....(b¹) HollieDoyle 10 36
(Ollie Pears) *hld up: racd keenly and hdwy on wd outside 5f out: wknd over 2f out (jockey said gelding hung both ways)* **11/1**

/000 **P** **Rock Island Line**[26] 2290 5-8-9 **48** ....(b) JasonHart 6
(Mark Walford) *racd keenly in midfield: eased over 3f out: p.u over 2f out and dismntd (jockey said gelding lost its action. vet reported gelding was showing signs of atrial fibrillation)* **20/1**

2m 7.96s (1.06) **Going Correction** -0.15s/f (Firm) **13 Ran SP% 118.8**
Speed ratings (Par 101): **89,88,88,87,87 87,83,80,79,78 78,77,**
CSF £7.35 CT £79.20 TOTE £3.30: £1.60, £1.60, £3.40; EX 11.80 Trifecta £160.70.
Owner S Raines **Bred** Stewart Larkin Armstrong **Trained** Maunby, N Yorks

FOCUS
The early pace looked steady. The winner did not need to quite replicate his latest form.

3163 COME RACING AGAIN TOMORROW H'CAP (DIV II) — 1m 2f 1y
5:55 (5:56) (Class 6) (0-60,62) 4-Y-O+

£3,823 (£1,137; £568; £300; £300; £300) **Stalls** Low

Form — RPR

5340 **1** **Sosian**[24] 2376 4-8-7 **45** ....(b) PaulHanagan 8 51
(Richard Fahey) *hld up in midfield: pushed along and hdwy over 2f out: swtchd rt over 1f out: rdn and styd on wl: led 50yds out* **10/1**

3540 **2** ½ **Seaborough (IRE)**[3] 3046 4-9-9 **61** ....(p) ConnorBeasley 1 66
(David Thompson) *hld up: hdwy 3f out: sn trckd ldrs: drvn to chal over 1f out: led narrowly ins fnl f: hdd 50yds out: one pce* **4/1**[2]

3 ½ **Machiavelli**[9] 2854 4-9-10 **62** ....(p) BenCurtis 9 66
(Denis Gerard Hogan, Ire) *midfield: pushed along and hdwy 3f out: sn chsd ldrs: drvn into narrow ld over 1f out: hdd ins fnl f: one pce* **3/1**[1]

0-61 **4** *shd* **Allux Boy (IRE)**[20] 2513 5-8-13 **56** ....(p) FayeMcManoman(5) 2 60
(Nigel Tinkler) *trckd ldrs: led over 2f out: sn rdn: hdd over 1f out: styd on same pce* **13/2**

50-4 **5** 4 ½ **Hayward Field (IRE)**[37] 1949 6-8-9 **47** ....(e¹) PhilDennis 7 43
(Noel Wilson) *hld up: rdn over 2f out: styd on fr over 1f out: nvr threatened ldrs* **28/1**

200- **6** 5 **Ninepin Bowler**[178] 9322 5-9-7 **59** ....(h) JoeFanning 14 46
(Ann Duffield) *prom: rdn 3f out: wknd over 1f out* **14/1**

0565 **7** 2 ¼ **Star Of Valour (IRE)**[12] 2738 4-9-5 **57** ....(p) DougieCostello 3 40
(David C Griffiths) *trckd ldrs: rdn along 3f out: wknd over 1f out* **8/1**

050- **8** *hd* **Royal Liberty**[245] 7626 4-8-12 **50** .... DavidAllan 4 33
(Geoffrey Harker) *led: rdn along and hdd over 2f out: wknd over 1f out* **33/1**

3343 **9** 5 **Muqarred (USA)**[25] 2346 7-8-12 **55** ....(b) BenSanderson(5) 11 29
(Roger Fell) *trckd ldrs: rdn over 3f out: wknd 2 out* **12/1**

0050 **10** 4 ½ **Tarnhelm**[7] 2911 4-8-8 **53** .... RhonaPindar(7) 5 18
(Wilf Storey) *hld up: hdwy on outside 5f out: rdn over 3f out: wknd over 2f out* **33/1**

-064 **11** 1 ¾ **Motahassen (IRE)**[9] 2819 5-8-10 **55** ....(t) CianMacRedmond(7) 10 17
(Declan Carroll) *midfield: lost pl over 3f out: sn wknd* **5/1**[3]

0603 **12** 1 **Prince Consort (IRE)**[17] 2587 4-8-10 **48** ....(p) KevinStott 6 8
(John Wainwright) *in tch: rdn over 3f out: wknd over 1f out* **50/1**

0000 **13** 8 **Lord Rob**[27] 2241 8-8-4 **45** ....(b) JamieGormley(3) 12
(David Thompson) *slowly away: a in rr (jockey said the blindfold was caught on the blinkers and took two attempts to remove it, resulting in the gelding being slow away)* **50/1**

250- **14** 21 **Graceful Act**[244] 7643 11-8-7 **45** ....(p) AndrewMullen 13
(Ron Barr) *trckd ldrs on outer: rdn along over 3f out: wknd and eased (jockey said mare stopped quickly)* **50/1**

2m 5.51s (-1.39) **Going Correction** -0.15s/f (Firm) **14 Ran SP% 124.8**
Speed ratings (Par 101): **99,98,98,98,94 90,88,88,84,80 79,78,72,55**
CSF £49.46 CT £154.40 TOTE £12.90: £5.20, £1.90, £1.30; EX 62.10 Trifecta £254.50.
Owner H J P Farr **Bred** Worksop Manor Stud **Trained** Musley Bank, N Yorks

FOCUS
The second division of a moderate handicap. The first three cam from off the pace.
T/Jkpt: Not won. T/Plt: £412.40 to a £1 stake. Pool: £63,398.18 - 112.20 winning units T/Qpdt: £14.70 to a £1 stake. Pool: £7,599.84 - 381.95 winning units **Andrew Sheret**

2914 WINDSOR (R-H)

Monday, May 27

OFFICIAL GOING: Good to firm (good in places; 7.7)

Wind: strong tail wind Weather: Overcast with bright spells

3164 GEMS H'CAP 6f 12y

1:55 (1:56) (Class 4) (0-85,86) 4-Y-0+

£5,563 (£1,655; £827; £413; £300; £300) Stalls Centre

Form RPR

21-3 1 **Belated Breath**[14] 2687 4-9-7 85 OisinMurphy 3 93
(Hughie Morrison) *broke smartly and led on rail: rdn along and hdd by runner-up 1f out: rallied wl u.p to ld again fnl 50yds* 13/8[1]

0504 2 *nk* **Buridan (FR)**[9] 2837 4-9-7 85 SeanLevey 4 92
(Richard Hannon) *trckd wnr: clsd gng wl 2f out: rdn to ld briefly 1f out: drvn and hdd by wnr fnl 50yds* 11/4[2]

1-00 3 *3/4* **Lady Dancealot (IRE)**[10] 2809 4-9-7 85 GeraldMosse 5 90
(David Elsworth) *hld up in last pair: niggled along 1/2-way: hdwy u.p on outer in 3rd over 1f out: sn rdn and kpt on fnl f* 5/1[3]

/00- 4 *3 1/2* **Clear Spring (IRE)**[307] 5299 11-9-1 79 ShaneKelly 6 72
(John Spearing) *racd in midfield: effrt to chse wnr 2f out: rdn and ev ch over 1f out: wknd fnl f* 66/1

30-5 5 *1/2* **Delagate This Lord**[38] 1915 5-8-10 74 CharlieBennett 2 66
(Michael Attwater) *trckd wnr on rail: rdn and no imp over 1f out: one pce fnl f: lost a shoe (vet reported gelding lost its left fore shoe)* 10/1

40-0 6 *3 3/4* **Hart Stopper**[22] 2442 5-9-8 86 (t) JasonWatson 1 66
(Stuart Williams) *hld up in last: rdn and unable qck 2f out: one pce fnl f* 8/1

3001 7 *1* **Red Alert**[3] 3032 5-9-3 81 5ex (p) TomMarquand 7 58
(Tony Carroll) *settled in midfield: rdn and no imp 2f out: nvr on terms* 12/1

1m 10.36s (-1.74) **Going Correction** -0.125s/f (Firm) 7 Ran SP% 110.8
Speed ratings (Par 105): **106,105,104,99,99 94,92**
CSF £5.77 TOTE £2.40: £1.20, £1.80; EX 6.90 Trifecta £19.20.
Owner Lady Blyth **Bred** Lemington Grange Stud **Trained** East Ilsley, Berks

FOCUS
The bend from the winning post into the back straight was realigned to fit in with the reduced width of the back straight. Rail moved back to inside as per first meeting of season. The principals came clear in this fair sprint handicap with the winner rated similar to her C&D run last time.

3165 VISIT MARATHONBET.CO.UK NOVICE AUCTION STKS 6f 12y

2:30 (2:32) (Class 5) 2-Y-0 £3,752 (£1,116; £557; £278) Stalls Centre

Form RPR

2 1 **Ivatheengine (IRE)**[13] 2716 2-9-1 0 OisinMurphy 7 79
(David Evans) *trckd ldr: rdn to ld over 1f out: drvn out fnl f: a jst doing enough* 5/6[1]

2 *1* **Alabama Whitman** 2-8-12 0 JasonWatson 10 73+
(Richard Spencer) *hld up: hdwy u.p on outer over 2f out: rdn and styd on wl fnl f: nt rch wnr* 28/1

3 *shd* **Romsey** 2-8-10 0 CharlieBennett 4 71
(Hughie Morrison) *racd in tch in 5th: prog to chse wnr over 1f out: kpt on fnl f: nt rch wnr* 20/1

5 4 *2 1/4* **I'm Digby (IRE)**[28] 2205 2-9-5 0 ShaneKelly 3 73
(Richard Hughes) *trckd ldr: rdn along and ev ch over 1f out: one pce fnl f* 6/1[3]

5 *1 3/4* **Able Kane** 2-9-2 0 GeorgeDowning 1 65
(Rod Millman) *racd in midfield: rdn and unable qck 2f out: kpt on one pce fnl f* 50/1

4 6 *hd* **Champagne Highlife (GER)**[26] 2282 2-9-2 0 CharlesBishop 2 64
(Eve Johnson Houghton) *led on stands' rail: rdn along and hdd over 1f out: wknd fnl f* 9/2[2]

0 7 *4* **Pitchcombe**[11] 2761 2-9-2 0 HectorCrouch 5 52
(Clive Cox) *chsd ldr early: pushed along and lost pl over 2f out: one pce fnl f* 7/1

0 8 *3/4* **Red Cinderella**[7] 2918 2-8-10 0 JohnFahy 13 44
(David Evans) *hld up: rdn and outpcd 1/2-way: nvr on terms* 66/1

9 *1 3/4* **Depeche Toi (IRE)** 2-8-8 0 WilliamCox(3) 9 40
(Jonathan Portman) *t.k.h to post: racd in rr of midfield: rdn and no imp over 1f out: one pce fnl f* 50/1

10 *1/2* **Rajan** 2-9-4 0 TomMarquand 6 45
(Tom Clover) *racd in midfield: rdn along and outpcd 2f out: one pce fnl f* 33/1

11 *6* **Love My Life (IRE)** 2-9-0 0 NicolaCurrie 12 23
(Jamie Osborne) *slowly away and racd in rr: a bhd* 20/1

12 *6* **Mac McCarthy (IRE)** 2-9-0 0 FinleyMarsh(3) 8 8
(Richard Hughes) *dwlt and racd in rr: a bhd* 50/1

13 *3 3/4* **Son Of Prancealot (IRE)** 2-8-11 0 TheodoreLadd(5) 11
(David Evans) *hld up: rdn and no imp 2f out: eased cl home* 40/1

1m 11.87s (-0.23) **Going Correction** -0.125s/f (Firm) 13 Ran SP% 125.3
Speed ratings (Par 93): **96,94,94,91,89 88,83,82,80,79 71,63,58**
CSF £40.95 TOTE £1.70: £1.10, £8.60, £3.70; EX 43.00 Trifecta £495.70.
Owner E R Griffiths **Bred** D Byrne **Trained** Pandy, Monmouths

FOCUS
This modest 2yo contest was run at a strong pace. The form has a fluid look to it.

3166 DOWNLOAD THE MARATHONBET APP H'CAP (WINDSOR SPRINT SERIES QUALIFIER) 5f 21y

3:05 (3:05) (Class 2) (0-105,100) 3-Y£02,450 (£3,728; £1,864; £932; £466) Stalls Centre

Form RPR

106- 1 **Street Parade**[275] 6551 3-9-2 95 (t[1]) JasonWatson 4 103
(Stuart Williams) *led after 100yds and mde rest: effrt to qckn tempo w 1 l ld 2f out: drvn out fnl f: a doing enough* 7/1

-115 2 *1 1/4* **Top Breeze (IRE)**[19] 2522 3-8-12 91 ShaneKelly 2 94
(Richard Hughes) *broke wl and sn restrained to trck wnr: clsd gng wl over 1f out: rdn and ev ch 1f out: kpt on fnl f but nvr quite getting to wnr* 11/8[1]

440- 3 *2 1/4* **Firelight (FR)**[247] 7511 3-9-4 97 OisinMurphy 3 92
(Andrew Balding) *wnt to post early: hld up: effrt on outer to go 3rd 2f out: rdn over 1f out: no ex fnl f* 5/2[2]

1-24 4 *5* **Deputise**[22] 2434 3-9-7 100 RyanMoore 1 77
(William Haggas) *hld up in last: rdn and no imp 2f out: nvr on terms (trainer's rep could offer no explanation for the performance shown other than the colt may benefit from a break)* 3/1[3]

-400 5 *6* **Oberyn Martell**[31] 2086 3-8-2 88 (p[1] w) GeorgiaDobie(7) 5 43
(Eve Johnson Houghton) *dwlt but sn rcvrd to chse wnr: rdn and lost pl 2f out: wknd fnl f (jockey said gelding stumbled leaving the stalls)* 20/1

58.45s (-1.65) **Going Correction** -0.125s/f (Firm) 5 Ran SP% 112.9
Speed ratings (Par 105): **108,106,102,94,84**
CSF £17.72 TOTE £7.40: £3.00, £1.10; EX 16.90 Trifecta £37.60.
Owner T W Morley **Bred** Julian Pittam **Trained** Newmarket, Suffolk

FOCUS
A decent 3yo sprint handicap. There was no hanging around and the form's been taken at face value.

3167 MARATHONBET SUPPORTS RESPONSIBLE GAMBLING NOVICE STKS 5f 21y

3:40 (3:41) (Class 5) 3-Y-0+ £3,752 (£1,116; £557; £278) Stalls Centre

Form RPR

32- 1 **Celtic Manor (IRE)**[202] 8903 3-9-3 0 TomMarquand 5 77
(William Haggas) *chsd ldr: pushed along and upsides ldr 2f out: rdn to ld jst over 1f out: kpt on wl fnl f* 1/1[1]

1-0 2 *nk* **Mercenary Rose (IRE)**[41] 1832 3-9-5 0 (w) SeanLevey 2 78
(Paul Cole) *trckd ldr: swtchd lft over 1f out: drvn and styd on wl fnl f: nt rch wnr* 11/4[2]

2-02 3 *1 3/4* **Journey Of Life**[6] 2938 3-9-3 76 (h) RyanMoore 4 71
(Gary Moore) *led: rdn along and hdd by wnr over 1f out: no ex fnl f (jockey said the gelding hung badly left-handed, making it difficult to ride the gelding out in the closing stages)* 11/4[2]

040- 4 *3 1/4* **Deptford Mick (IRE)**[198] 9001 3-9-3 69 ShaneKelly 3 60
(Rae Guest) *hld up: rdn along and outpcd 2f out: nvr on terms* 14/1[3]

59.21s (-0.89) **Going Correction** -0.125s/f (Firm) 4 Ran SP% 110.0
Speed ratings (Par 103): **102,101,98,93**
CSF £4.13 TOTE £1.60; EX 3.10 Trifecta £5.60.
Owner Sheikh Rashid Dalmook Al Maktoum **Bred** Patrick M Ryan **Trained** Newmarket, Suffolk

FOCUS
This fair little novice sprint for 3yos was run at a decent pace. The first two both progressed.

3168 MARATHONBET OFFICIAL BETTING PARTNER OF MANCHESTER CITY H'CAP 1m 2f

4:15 (4:15) (Class 3) (0-95,95) 4-Y-0+ £7,313 (£2,236; £1,152; £610) Stalls Low

Form RPR

0060 1 **Waarif (IRE)**[11] 2778 6-9-4 92 AdamKirby 5 100
(David O'Meara) *racd in last but wl in tch: hdwy on outer into 3rd over 2f out: sn rdn and clsd on ldng pair over 1f out: drvn to ld ins fnl f: kpt on wl* 5/1[3]

2-01 2 *1/2* **Shareef Star**[24] 2374 4-8-11 85 RyanMoore 4 92
(Sir Michael Stoute) *led: effrt to qckn tempo over 1f out: sn rdn and strly pressed by rivals over 1f out: kpt on but hdd hdd by wnr ins fnl f* 1/1[1]

4-00 3 *1 3/4* **Banditry (IRE)**[33] 2033 7-9-7 95 (h) JasonWatson 2 99
(Ian Williams) *trckd ldr: rdn along to chse ldr 2f out: hld whn squeezed for room 1f out: no ex* 25/1

00-0 4 *15* **Borderforce (FR)**[30] 2105 6-9-2 90 NicolaCurrie 3 64
(George Baker) *racd in midfield: rdn along and outpcd over 2f out: wknd fnl f (trainer's rep said the gelding was unsuited by the good to firm, good in places ground on this occasion and would prefer a slower surface)* 33/1

60-1 P **He's Amazing (IRE)**[28] 2207 4-8-11 85 OisinMurphy 1
(Ed Walker) *trckd ldr: pushed along and lost grnd qckly over 2f out: sn p.u and dismntd on crse (jockey said gelding stopped quickly. vet reported the gelding had an irregular heartbeat)* 7/4[2]

2m 7.06s (-1.94) **Going Correction** -0.125s/f (Firm) 5 Ran SP% 109.8
Speed ratings (Par 107): **102,101,100,88,**
CSF £10.53 TOTE £5.70: £2.30, £1.10; EX 9.70 Trifecta £60.20.
Owner Middleham Park Racing XLIX **Bred** Joseph Stewart Investments **Trained** Upper Helmsley, N Yorks

■ Stewards' Enquiry : Ryan Moore caution: careless riding

FOCUS
Despite just five runners this good-quality handicap was run at a fair pace. The winner's rated close to last year's best.

3169 MARATHONBET SPORTSBOOK FILLIES' H'CAP 1m 3f 99y

4:50 (4:50) (Class 4) (0-85,84) 3-Y-0+ £5,563 (£1,655; £827; £413) Stalls Low

Form RPR

-332 1 **Birch Grove (IRE)**[12] 2737 4-9-12 74 OisinMurphy 1 79
(David Simcock) *mde all: pushed along to maintain short ld 2f out: rdn out fnl f and a doing enough* 9/4[2]

14-1 2 *3/4* **Mannaal (IRE)**[21] 2481 3-9-7 84 RyanMoore 4 88
(Simon Crisford) *trckd wnr: effrt to chse wnr 2f out: sn rdn over 1f out: kpt on but a hld by wnr fnl f* 8/11[1]

30-1 3 *3/4* **Eesha My Flower (USA)**[34] 2017 3-8-10 73 NicolaCurrie 5 75
(Marco Botti) *a in 3rd: rdn to chse wnr over 2f out: kpt on fnl f but a hld (jockey said filly ran green)* 7/1[3]

602- 4 *5* **Miss Mumtaz (IRE)**[39] 9096 4-9-13 75 JasonWatson 2 67
(Ian Williams) *hld up in last: rdn and outpcd by rivals over 2f out: nvr able to land a blow* 9/1

2m 29.52s (-0.18) **Going Correction** -0.125s/f (Firm)
WFA 3 from 4yo 15lb 4 Ran SP% 111.2
Speed ratings (Par 102): **95,94,93,90**
CSF £4.47 TOTE £2.60; EX 4.30 Trifecta £11.00.
Owner Rathordan Partnership **Bred** Glenvale Stud **Trained** Newmarket, Suffolk

FOCUS
This tight-looking fillies' handicap developed into a dash for home, and the order didn't change. The winner's rated similar to her recent form.

3170 ZUPERMAN AUTOMOTIVE UK H'CAP 1m 31y

5:25 (5:26) (Class 5) (0-75,75) 3-Y-0

£3,752 (£1,116; £557; £300; £300) Stalls Low

Form RPR

0-21 1 **Lethal Missile (IRE)**[49] 1656 3-9-5 73 AdamKirby 3 82+
(Clive Cox) *racd in midfield: swtchd lft to outer and gd hdwy over 2f out: rdn to ld 1f out: styd on strly ins fnl f* 11/4[1]

060- 2 *2 1/2* **Rock The Cradle (IRE)**[198] 9001 3-9-1 69 ShaneKelly 1 72+
(Ed Vaughan) *hld up: hdwy between rivals over 2f out: swtchd rt to stands' rail over 1f out: styd on wl fnl f: no ch w wnr* 28/1

2-03 3 *nk* **Sassoon**[26] 2280 3-9-4 72 (p[1]) SeanLevey 13 74
(Paul Cole) *trckd ldr: rdn along and ev ch 2f out: led briefly over 1f out: one pce fnl f* 10/1

03-3 **4** *1 ¼* **Canal Rocks**[54] 1516 3-8-13 **74**.................... GeorgiaDobie(7) 4 73+
(Henry Candy) *racd in midfield: rdn and no immediate imp 2f out: kpt on one pce ins fnl f* **4/1**[2]

1111 **5** *¾* **Capofaro**[5] 2965 3-9-2 **70**.................... NicolaCurrie 14 68
(Jamie Osborne) *pushed up to ld after 2f: rdn and strly pressed by rivals 2f out: hdd over 1f out: no ex fnl f* **4/1**[2]

63 **6** *nk* **Onebaba (IRE)**[52] 1570 3-9-7 **75**....................(v[1]) JasonWatson 7 72+
(Michael Bell) *squeezed for room out of stalls and restrained in last as a result: rdn over 2f out: mde sme late hdwy passed btn horses* **9/2**[3]

1-00 **7** *¾* **Toybox**[23] 2407 3-9-4 **72**.................... CharlieBennett 11 67
(Jonathan Portman) *settled in midfield: rdn and unable qck 2f out: kpt on one pce ins fnl f* **50/1**

050 **8** *hd* **Air Hair Lair (IRE)**[10] 2795 3-9-0 **68**.................... CharlesBishop 10 63
(Sheena West) *racd in midfield on outer: drvn along over 1f out: one pce fnl f: n.d* **40/1**

26-6 **9** *1* **Startego**[47] 1697 3-9-4 **72**.................... OisinMurphy 9 65
(Archie Watson) *racd promly in 4th: rdn along and ev ch 2f out: wknd fnl f* **12/1**

-000 **10** *2 ¼* **My Lady Claire**[25] 2340 3-8-11 **65**.................... GeraldMosse 12 52
(Ed Walker) *racd in rr of midfield: rdn and no imp over 1f out: one pce fnl f* **20/1**

004- **11** *hd* **No Trouble (IRE)**[198] 8993 3-8-5 **62**.................... WilliamCox(3) 5 49
(Stuart Williams) *racd in rr: rdn and no imp over 2f out: nvr on terms* **33/1**

142- **12** *1* **Max Guevara (IRE)**[231] 8056 3-8-12 **69**.................... FinleyMarsh(3) 2 54
(William Muir) *hld up: rdn and little rspnse over 2f out: n.d* **20/1**

436- **13** *¾* **Denis The Diva**[192] 9095 3-9-3 **71**.................... RoystonFfrench 8 54
(Marcus Tregoning) *settled in midfield: rdn and outpcd over 2f out: wknd whn btn ins fnl f* **20/1**

520- **14** *12* **Sunvisor (IRE)**[170] 9459 3-9-7 **75**.................... TomMarquand 6 30
(William Muir) *hld up: rdn along and sn detached over 2f out: a bhd* **50/1**

1m 41.57s (-2.93) **Going Correction** -0.125s/f (Firm) **14 Ran SP% 128.7**
Speed ratings (Par 99): **109,106,106,104,104 103,103,102,101,99 99,98,97,85**
CSF £98.19 CT £734.36 TOTE £3.60: £1.50, £7.70, £4.00; EX 136.30 Trifecta £2198.10.
Owner B Allen, G Hill & N Wagland **Bred** J McGlynn & C Lyons **Trained** Lambourn, Berks

FOCUS
A modest handicap which was sound run. The winner built on his previous C&D win to give Clive Cox his third win in the last four runnings of this race.
T/Plt: £39.30 to a £1 stake. Pool: £64,370.90 - 1193.37 winning units T/Qpdt: £24.10 to a £1 stake. Pool: £3,083.03 - 127.91 winning units **Mark Grantham**

3136 **SAINT-CLOUD** (L-H)
Monday, May 27

OFFICIAL GOING: Turf: good to soft

3171a **PRIX DE VAUREAL (CLAIMER) (2YO) (TURF)** **6f**
3:45 2-Y-O **£12,162** (£4,864; £3,648; £2,432; £1,216)

RPR

1 **Has D'Emra (FR)**[21] 2-8-11 0....................(b) MaximeGuyon 3 77
(F Rossi, France) **7/5**[1]

2 *3 ½* **Goldmembers (FR)**[58] 1448 2-9-4 0.................... IoritzMendizabal 4 74
(D Guillemin, France) **12/5**[2]

3 *1 ¼* **Pink Princess** 2-9-1 0.................... MickaelBarzalona 6 67
(P Monfort, France) **17/2**

4 *4 ½* **Carmague (IRE)**[14] 2686 2-9-1 0.................... TonyPiccone 5 53
(J S Moore) *chsd ldrs: pushed along over 2f out: rdn w little rspnse over 1f out: kpt on same pce fnl f* **37/10**[3]

5 *¾* **Golden Warrior (FR)** 2-8-9 0.................... AlexandreChesneau(6) 2 51
(G Botti, France) **14/1**

6 *8* **Morgenstern (FR)**[20] 2-8-6 0.................... ThomasTrullier(5) 8 23
(A Giorgi, Italy) **25/1**

7 *4 ½* **On The Nod** 2-8-11 0.................... PierreBazire 7 10
(E J O'Neill, France) **16/1**

1m 15.92s (-0.88) **7 Ran SP% 119.3**
PARI-MUTUEL (all including 1 euro stake): WIN 2.40; PLACE 1.20, 1.20, 1.30; DF 2.60.
Owner L Haegel **Bred** J Boitteau & C Plisson **Trained** France

3172 - (Foreign Racing) - See Raceform Interactive

2671 **LES LANDES**
Monday, May 27

OFFICIAL GOING: Good to firm changing to good to firm (good in places) after race 2 (3.05)

3173a **YKTR H'CAP** **5f 100y**
3:05 (3:05) 3-Y-O+ **£1,780** (£640; £380)

RPR

1 **Man Of The Sea (IRE)**[15] 2671 3-10-4 0....................(tp) PhilipPrince 62
(Neil Mulholland) *trckd ldrs: 3 rd into st: led wl ins fnl f: drvn out* **8/11**[1]

2 *¾* **Country Blue (FR)**[15] 2671 10-10-5 0....................(p) MattieBatchelor 56
(Mrs A Malzard, Jersey) *led: no ex whn hdd wl ins fnl f* **6/1**

3 *3 ½* **Fruit Salad**[15] 2671 6-10-10 0.................... MarkQuinlan 49
(K Kukk, Jersey) *trckd ldr: 2nd into st: ev ch fnl f: wknd cl home* **4/1**[3]

4 *2 ½* **Chapeau Bleu (IRE)**[35] 7-10-2 0.................... MissSerenaBrotherton 33
(Mrs C Gilbert, Jersey) *outpcd: 7th 1f out: kpt on: nvr* **14/1**

5 *nse* **Sing Something**[35] 6-10-12 0....................(v) MrWillPettis 43
(Mrs C Gilbert, Jersey) *outpcd: nvr able to chal* **10/3**[2]

6 *1 ½* **Limelite (IRE)**[15] 2671 5-10-8 0.................... GaryMahon 34
(K Kukk, Jersey) *s.s: brief effrt fr over 2f out: wknd* **12/1**

7 *2 ½* **Doctor Parkes**[15] 2671 13-10-7 0.................... MrFrederickTett 25
(Natalie Lloyd-Beavis) *chsd ldrs to 2f out: wknd* **9/2**

8 *½* **Spanish Bounty**[351] 14-9-6 0.................... VictoriaMalzard 8
(Mrs A Malzard, Jersey) *s.s: a bhd* **20/1**

1m 8.8s **8 Ran SP% 152.6**
WFA 3 from 5yo+ 8lb

Owner Dajam Ltd **Bred** Stephanie Hanly **Trained** Limpley Stoke, Wilts

3174a **WINDSOR HOUSE H'CAP** **1m 100y**
4:15 (4:15) 3-Y-O+ **£1,780** (£640; £380)

RPR

1 **Honcho (IRE)**[15] 2671 7-10-12 0.................... VictoriaMalzard 49
(Mrs A Malzard, Jersey) *led: narrowly hdd 6f out: wnt on again 3f out: sn clr: rdn out* **7/2**[2]

2 *5* **Koshi**[15] 2673 4-9-9 0....................(p) GaryMahon 21
(K Kukk, Jersey) *trckd ldrs tl hmpd turn after 1f: drvn along and 5th in st: kpt on one pce* **10/1**

3 *½* **William Booth (IRE)**[15] 2673 5-10-4 0....................(v) MrWillPettis 29
(Mrs C Gilbert, Jersey) *trckd ldrs: 3rd into st but sn 2nd: tired late: lost 2nd cl home* **7/1**

4 *4* **Kalani Rose**[15] 2673 5-8-10 0....................(v) MissSerenaBrotherton
(Mrs A Corson, Jersey) *trckd ldrs: 4th into st: one pce* **18/1**

5 *4* **Brown Velvet**[15] 2673 7-10-4 0.................... MrFrederickTett 11
(Mrs C Gilbert, Jersey) *hld up: nvr able to chal* **6/1**[3]

6 *½* **Drummer Jack (IRE)**[15] 2673 3-9-6 0.................... PhilipPrince 7
(K Kukk, Jersey) *hld up whn bdly hmpd turn after 1f: nt rcvr* **14/1**

7 *½* **Mendacious Harpy (IRE)**[15] 2673 8-9-2 0....................(p) DarraghKeogh
(Mrs A Malzard, Jersey) *hld up: brief effrt fr over 3f out: wknd* **18/1**

8 *15* **Coastguard Watch (FR)**[21] 2504 3-9-8 0....................(p) MattieBatchelor
(Natalie Lloyd-Beavis) *pressed ldr: wnt on 6f out: hdd 3f out: sn wknd* **12/1**

S **Molliana**[15] 2673 4-9-9 0.................... GeorgeRooke
(Neil Mulholland) *trcking ldrs whn slipped up turn after 1f* **1/2**[1]

1m 51.7s **9 Ran SP% 149.7**
WFA 3 from 4yo+ 12lb

Owner Sheik A Leg Racing **Bred** Paul Hancock **Trained** St Ouen, Jersey

2957 **AYR** (L-H)
Tuesday, May 28

OFFICIAL GOING: Good to firm (good in places; 8.5)
Wind: Fresh, half against in sprint and in over 3f of home straight in races on the round course Weather: Sunny

3175 **BOOK FOR THE JUNE TENNENT'S RACENIGHT H'CAP (FOR LADY AMATEUR RIDERS)** **1m 5f 26y**
5:45 (5:49) (Class 6) (0-65,65) 4-Y-O+
£2,994 (£928; £464; £300; £300; £300) **Stalls Low**

Form RPR

104- **1** **Perla Blanca (USA)**[213] 8650 5-10-2 **65**.................... SophieSmith(5) 5 71
(Ed Dunlop) *t.k.h: hld up in tch: effrt over 2f out: led wl ins fnl f: r.o* **5/1**[2]

1-22 **2** *nk* **Shine Baby Shine**[34] 1429 5-10-6 **64**.................... MissAmieWaugh 10 70
(Philip Kirby) *hld up in midfield: hdwy on outside to ld over 2f out: hdd wl ins fnl f: r.o* **12/1**

33-5 **3** *2 ¾* **Donnachies Girl (IRE)**[23] 2436 6-10-3 **61**.................... MissBeckySmith 8 63
(Alistair Whillans) *w ldr: led over 3f out to over 2f out: sn pushed along: one pce fnl f* **4/1**[1]

005/ **4** *2* **Poitin**[25] 2382 9-9-4 **51**.................... MsHMooney(3) 4 50
(Keith Henry Clarke, Ire) *missed break: hld up: hdwy on outside and prom over 3f out: effrt and ev ch over 2f out: no ex fr over 1f out* **16/1**

0-55 **5** *3* **Thorntoun Care**[21] 2512 8-10-0 **63**....................(p) MissAmyCollier(5) 1 57
(Karen Tutty) *t.k.h: trckd ldrs: pushed along over 2f out: wknd over 1f out* **6/1**

0303 **6** *¾* **Gravity Wave (IRE)**[29] 2217 5-9-12 **63**....................(p) MissImogenMathias(7) 6 56
(John Flint) *t.k.h: hld up on ins: shkn up over 2f out: no imp fr over 1f out* **11/2**[3]

0662 **7** *1 ½* **Strictly Art (IRE)**[6] 2974 6-9-10 **61**.................... MissEmmaJack(7) 2 52
(Alan Bailey) *led to over 3f out: sn pushed along: wknd over 1f out* **7/1**

-526 **8** *4* **Pammi**[23] 2436 4-9-5 **56**.................... MissShannonWatts(7) 9 41
(Jim Goldie) *dwlt: hld up: shortlived effrt on outside over 2f out: sn btn* **11/1**

0313 **9** *¾* **Elite Icon**[15] 2684 5-9-7 **51**.................... MissSerenaBrotherton 11 35
(Jim Goldie) *prom: rdn and outpcd 2f out: sn btn* **7/1**

0 **10** *15* **Go Guarantor**[23] 2436 5-9-2 **46** oh1....................(t) MrsCarolBartley 7 7
(R Mike Smith) *dwlt: bhd: outpcd whn hung lft 2f out: sn btn: t.o* **66/1**

2m 53.05s (-1.35) **Going Correction** -0.325s/f (Firm) **10 Ran SP% 114.7**
Speed ratings (Par 101): **103,102,101,99,98 97,96,94,93,84**
CSF £62.25 CT £262.34 TOTE £5.50: £2.20, £3.70, £1.50; EX 69.40 Trifecta £430.60.
Owner Mrs C L Smith **Bred** Ted Folkerth Et Al **Trained** Newmarket, Suffolk

FOCUS
The going was given as good to firm, good in places (Going Stick 8.5). The home straight stands' rail was in 3yds and far rail in 3yds but that didn't affect the race distances. A modest affair, but there was a bit of a gamble landed. A minor pb for the winner.

3176 **WEDDINGS AT WESTERN HOUSE HOTEL MAIDEN FILLIES' STKS** **6f**
6:20 (6:21) (Class 5) 3-Y-O+ **£4,463** (£1,328; £663; £331) **Stalls High**

Form RPR

46 **1** **Raspberry**[13] 2736 3-8-9 0.................... ConnorMurtagh(5) 8 70
(Olly Williams) *prom: shkn up to ld over 1f out: qcknd clr ins fnl f: comf* **14/1**

20 **2** *5* **Sound Of Iona**[39] 1924 3-9-0 0.................... PhilDennis 7 54
(Jim Goldie) *t.k.h: led to over 1f out: no ch w wnr* **7/2**[3]

0-50 **3** *6* **Ellheidi (IRE)**[17] 2630 3-9-0 **70**.................... CliffordLee 4 35
(K R Burke) *blkd s: cl up: drvn along over 2f out: outpcd fr over 1f out* **11/10**[1]

6-60 **4** *nk* **Euro No More (IRE)**[8] 2897 3-9-0 **64**....................(b[1]) PaulMulrennan 2 34
(Keith Dalgleish) *wnt rt and blkd s: cl up: rdn over 2f out: outpcd fr over 1f out* **9/4**[2]

06-6 **5** *8* **Milabella**[15] 2683 3-9-0 **38**....................(t) AndrewMullen 6 8
(R Mike Smith) *prom: drvn along 1/2-way: wknd fr 2f out* **50/1**

4-6 **6** *3 ½* **Lady Steps**[25] 2377 3-8-7 0.................... CoreyMadden(7) 1
(Jim Goldie) *wnt lft s: bhd: struggling over 3f out: nvr on terms* **80/1**

1m 12.86s (-0.24) **Going Correction** -0.325s/f (Firm) **6 Ran SP% 110.5**
Speed ratings (Par 100): **88,81,73,72,62 57**
CSF £59.63 TOTE £10.80: £3.30, £1.60; EX 52.20 Trifecta £130.80.
Owner Olly Williams Rhys Williams James Hanna **Bred** D J And Mrs Deer **Trained** Market Rasen, Lincs

The Form Book Flat 2019, Raceform Ltd, Newbury, RG14 5SJ

FOCUS
A modest maiden, and they finished well strung out. Tricky form to assess with the market leaders below par, and it's been rated cautiously.

3177 BOOK DIRECT AT WESTERN HOUSE HOTEL H'CAP 1m
6:50 (6:50) (Class 6) (0-65,64) 4-Y-O+
£3,105 (£924; £346; £300; £300) **Stalls** Low

Form RPR
0-56 **1** **Pudding Chare (IRE)**[6] 2963 5-8-8 **54**....................(t) JamieGormley(3) 9 61
(R Mike Smith) *chsd ldr: led over 2f out: hrd pressed and edgd lft over 1f out: kpt on gamely ins fnl f* **16/1**
440 **2** *nk* **Ascot Week (USA)**[21] 2512 5-9-6 **63**................................(v) JasonHart 14 69
(John Quinn) *hld up in tch: hdwy and ev ch over 1f out to ins fnl f: kpt on: hld nr fin* **14/1**
5-60 **3** *1 ½* **Chinese Spirit (IRE)**[11] 2785 5-9-3 **60**............................. DavidNolan 4 64
(Linda Perratt) *prom: effrt over 2f out: ch whn carried lft over 1f out: short of room briefly ins fnl f: kpt on (jockey said gelding suffered interference in the final furlong)* **33/1**
4-31 **3** *dht* **Jackhammer (IRE)**[6] 2963 5-8-1 **51**..........................(bt) EllaMcCain(7) 10 54+
(Dianne Sayer) *dwlt: t.k.h in rr: hdwy on ins and prom over 1f out: rdn and r.o ins fnl f* **1/1**[1]
6-05 **5** *1* **Edgar Allan Poe (IRE)**[26] 2330 5-9-6 **63**..................... LewisEdmunds 6 64
(Rebecca Bastiman) *hld up towards rr: pushed along over 2f out: hdwy on outside over 1f out: edgd lft: kpt on ins fnl f: no imp* **25/1**
6 *¾* **Rosin Box (IRE)**[279] 6436 6-8-9 **59**........................... HarryRussell(7) 1 58
(Tristan Davidson) *led to over 2f out: rallied: no ex ins fnl f* **3/1**[2]
0-30 **7** *1 ¼* **Crazy Tornado (IRE)**[15] 2681 6-9-0 **57**..........................(h) ShaneGray 11 53
(Keith Dalgleish) *hld up in midfield: effrt and pushed along over 2f out: no imp over 1f out* **22/1**
4564 **8** *1* **Restive (IRE)**[11] 2785 6-9-4 **61**....................................... PhilDennis 8 55
(Jim Goldie) *s.i.s: hld up: effrt whn n.m.r briefly 2f out: rdn and no imp fnl f* **11/1**[3]
-000 **9** *1 ¾* **Poyle George Two**[15] 2682 4-8-1 **51**........................... CoreyMadden(7) 5 41
(John Hodge) *t.k.h: hld up: effrt on outside over 2f out: no imp fr over 1f out* **66/1**
0-60 **10** *½* **Ventura Secret (IRE)**[24] 2418 5-9-2 **59**....................(t) PaulMulrennan 12 47
(Michael Dods) *hld up in midfield: hdwy and prom 2f out: wknd fnl f* **25/1**
0-05 **11** *1 ¾* **Joyful Star**[26] 2329 9-8-9 **52**... PaulHanagan 3 36
(Fred Watson) *hld up: rdn over 2f out: sn no imp: btn fnl f* **28/1**
016- **12** *10* **Majdool (IRE)**[193] 9101 6-9-5 **62**..(e) CliffordLee 2 23
(Noel Wilson) *t.k.h: prom tl rdn and wknd 2f out* **50/1**
-000 **13** *1 ¾* **Intense Pleasure (IRE)**[10] 2842 4-9-7 **64**.....................(h) AndrewMullen 7 21
(Ruth Carr) *missed break: bhd: struggling over 2f out: nvr on terms* **25/1**

1m 39.7s (-3.10) **Going Correction** -0.325s/f (Firm) **13** Ran SP% **121.6**
Speed ratings (Par 101): **102,101,100,100,99 98,97,96,94,93 92,82,80**
PL: 1.80 Ascot Week, 0.50 Jackhammer, 3.40 Chinese Spirit, 4.90 Pudding Chare; EX: 424.70; CSF: 199.58; TC: PC/AW/CS 3659.39, PC/AW/J 217.35; TF: PC/AW/CS 894.30, PC/AW/J 648.00; TOTE £26.50.
Owner Ayr Racecourse Club **Bred** Mrs Eleanor Kent **Trained** Galston, E Ayrshire
■ Stewards' Enquiry : Jamie Gormley three-day ban: interference & careless riding (Jun 11-13)

FOCUS
It didn't pay to be too far off the pace here. The runner-up's amongst those to help set the level.

3178 BOOK THE SUMMER SATURDAY RACEDAY H'CAP 7f 50y
7:20 (7:23) (Class 6) (0-65,65) 4-Y-O+
£3,105 (£924; £461; £300; £300; £300) **Stalls** High

Form RPR
412- **1** **Polyphony (IRE)**[221] 8388 4-9-6 **64**..(h) JasonHart 8 71+
(John Mackie) *t.k.h and sn trcking ldrs: effrt and rdn over 1f out: led ins fnl f: kpt on wl cl home* **9/2**[2]
-063 **2** *nk* **Lucky Violet (IRE)**[6] 2963 7-9-6 **64**...................................(h) DavidNolan 6 70
(Linda Perratt) *t.k.h: prom: rdn to ld over 1f out: hdd ins fnl f: rallied: hld nr fin* **13/2**
-052 **3** *nse* **Donnelly's Rainbow (IRE)**[15] 2681 6-8-13 **57**........... LewisEdmunds 9 63
(Rebecca Bastiman) *dwlt and sn swtchd lft: hld up on ins: effrt 2f out: ev ch and rdn fnl f: kpt on: hld nr fin* **4/1**[1]
-110 **4** *½* **Colour Contrast (IRE)**[8] 2898 6-9-0 **61**................(b) JamieGormley(3) 7 66
(Iain Jardine) *t.k.h: hld up in tch: n.m.r over 2f out: angled rt and hdwy over 1f out: kpt on fnl f: hld nr fin* **11/2**[3]
-616 **5** *1 ¾* **Thornaby Nash**[11] 2785 8-9-2 **65**........................(b) AndrewBreslin(5) 13 66
(Jason Ward) *dwlt: hld up: rdn over 2f out: gd hdwy fnl f: nrst fin* **8/1**
264- **6** *1 ¼* **Royal Duchess**[229] 8135 9-9-0 **63**........................ ConnorMurtagh(5) 5 60
(Lucy Normile) *t.k.h: in tch: rdn along over 2f out: no ex over 1f out* **16/1**
2100 **7** *nk* **Insurplus (IRE)**[28] 2246 6-9-6 **64**... PhilDennis 10 61
(Jim Goldie) *t.k.h: hld up towards rr: rdn and outpcd over 2f out: sme late hdwy: nvr rchd ldrs* **14/1**
R560 **8** *1* **Desai**[30] 2147 5-9-6 **64**... CliffordLee 3 58
(Noel Wilson) *pressed ldr: rdn and ev ch over 2f out to over 1f out: wknd ins fnl f* **28/1**
0041 **9** *½* **Robben Rainbow**[15] 2682 5-8-12 **56**............................. PaulHanagan 11 49
(Katie Scott) *hld up: rdn and outpcd over 2f out: nvr on terms* **10/1**
-330 **10** *1 ½* **Chaplin Bay (IRE)**[15] 2681 7-8-12 **56**.........................(p) AndrewMullen 1 45
(Ruth Carr) *led: rdn over 2f out: hdd over 1f out: wknd ins fnl f* **15/2**

1m 30.46s (-2.04) **Going Correction** -0.325s/f (Firm) **10** Ran SP% **114.9**
Speed ratings (Par 101): **98,97,97,97,95 93,93,92,91,89**
CSF £33.34 CT £125.92 TOTE £3.60: £1.80, £2.20, £1.70; EX 33.80 Trifecta £143.70.
Owner D Ward **Bred** Mrs Natasha Drennan **Trained** Church Broughton, Derbys

FOCUS
There was a bunched finish to this modest handicap, and the form's ordinary.

3179 CELEBRATE AT AWARD WINNING WESTERN HOUSE HOTEL H'CAP 7f 50y
7:50 (7:50) (Class 4) (0-85,86) 4-Y-O+
£5,530 (£1,645; £822; £411; £300; £300) **Stalls** High

Form RPR
0225 **1** **Tommy G**[11] 2788 6-8-5 **76**.. CoreyMadden(7) 10 84
(Jim Goldie) *stdd fr outside draw: hld up: effrt and hdwy on outside over 1f out: hung lft and qcknd to ld ins fnl f: kpt on strly* **7/1**
-044 **2** *1* **Magical Effect (IRE)**[18] 2588 7-8-11 **75**..................... AndrewMullen 9 80
(Ruth Carr) *hld up in tch: effrt and rdn over 1f out: ev ch briefly ins fnl f: sn pressing wnr: kpt on: hld nr fin* **12/1**
0313 **3** *1 ¼* **Kupa River (IRE)**[15] 2679 5-9-2 **80**..................................(h) CliffordLee 8 82
(Roger Fell) *t.k.h: led: rdn along 2f out: hdd ins fnl f: kpt on same pce* **11/4**[1]
-063 **4** *1 ¼* **Highlight Reel (IRE)**[18] 2584 4-8-12 **76**........................ LewisEdmunds 7 77+
(Rebecca Bastiman) *dwlt: hld up on ins: stdy hdwy 2f out: cl 5th and styng on whn hmpd ins fnl f: r.o* **4/1**[2]
01-2 **5** *nse* **Glengarry**[28] 2242 6-9-7 **85**... ShaneGray 3 87+
(Keith Dalgleish) *dwlt: sn trcking ldrs: rdn and ev ch over 1f out tl hmpd and snatched up ins fnl f: nt rcvr* **6/1**
-005 **6** *1 ½* **Penwortham (IRE)**[20] 2526 6-9-4 **82**............................... PaulHanagan 1 77
(Richard Fahey) *plld hrd: sn pressing ldr: rdn and outpcd over 1f out: btn fnl f* **13/2**
233- **7** *hd* **Bertog**[231] 8085 4-8-10 **74**...(w) JasonHart 6 68
(John Mackie) *trckd ldrs: rdn and outpcd 2f out: no imp whn checked ent fnl f* **9/2**[3]

1m 29.18s (-3.32) **Going Correction** -0.325s/f (Firm) **7** Ran SP% **112.7**
Speed ratings (Par 105): **105,103,102,101,100 99,99**
CSF £79.86 CT £284.32 TOTE £3.50: £4.20, £5.00; EX 74.90 Trifecta £203.70.
Owner Johnnie Delta Racing **Bred** Jim Goldie **Trained** Uplawmoor, E Renfrews
■ Stewards' Enquiry : Corey Madden two-day ban: interference & careless riding (Jun 11-12)

FOCUS
The early pace was good and the closers came to the fore at the finish. The winner added to a good C&D record.

3180 CONFERENCES AT AYR RACECOURSE H'CAP 1m 2f
8:20 (8:21) (Class 4) (0-85,86) 4-Y-O+ **£5,530** (£1,645; £822; £411; £300) **Stalls** Low

Form RPR
0-54 **1** **Mulligatawny (IRE)**[19] 2563 6-9-3 **81**...........................(p) CliffordLee 7 88
(Roger Fell) *cl up: rdn to ld over 2f out: clr whn edgd lft over 1f out: hld on wl fnl f* **7/2**[2]
-320 **2** *nk* **Addis Ababa (IRE)**[13] 2748 4-9-7 **85**..........................(p[1]) DavidNolan 4 91
(David O'Meara) *s.i.s: rcvrd and led after 1f: hdd over 2f out: drvn and hd high over 1f out: rallied ins fnl f: kpt on: hld nr fin* **5/4**[1]
0660 **3** *2 ¾* **Mutamaded (IRE)**[19] 2563 6-9-7 **85**.............................. AndrewMullen 2 86
(Ruth Carr) *prom: rdn over 2f out: hdwy and edgd lft over 1f out: one pce ins fnl f* **8/1**
000- **4** *2 ¾* **Gworn**[238] 7870 9-8-7 **71** oh5.. PhilDennis 1 66
(R Mike Smith) *hld up in tch: stdy hdwy on ins over 2f out: rdn over 1f out: wknd ins fnl f* **20/1**
06-4 **5** *1 ½* **Royal Regent**[25] 2369 7-8-7 **76**................................. ConnorMurtagh(5) 3 68
(Lucy Normile) *led 1f: cl up: drvn along over 2f out: wknd over 1f out* **10/1**
0-0R **R** **Mooltazem (IRE)**[25] 2370 5-9-8 **86**............................... PaulMulrennan 5
(Michael Dods) *ref to r (starter reported that the gelding had refused to race after the start had been effected; trainer's rep was informed that any future similar behaviour from the gelding may result in being reported to the Head Office of the BHA)* **4/1**[3]

2m 7.82s (-4.58) **Going Correction** -0.325s/f (Firm) **6** Ran SP% **111.6**
Speed ratings (Par 105): **105,104,102,100,99**
CSF £8.22 TOTE £3.40: £1.60, £1.60; EX 7.50 Trifecta £33.90.
Owner Middleham Park Racing Li & Partner **Bred** Pat O'Rourke **Trained** Nawton, N Yorks

FOCUS
They went fairly steady early and the first two dominated throughout. The winner is rated close to last year's best.

3181 SUMMER PROSECCO MINI BREAK @ WESTERN HOUSE H'CAP 1m 2f
8:50 (8:50) (Class 6) (0-60,62) 4-Y-O+
£3,557 (£1,058; £529; £300; £300; £300) **Stalls** Low

Form RPR
00-0 **1** **Hillgrove Angel (IRE)**[28] 2244 7-8-8 **54**........................ CoreyMadden(7) 11 65
(Jim Goldie) *s.i.s: hld up: smooth hdwy over 2f out: shkn up to ld over 1f out: rdn and r.o wl fnl f* **17/2**[3]
/0-6 **2** *nk* **Ishebayorgrey (IRE)**[28] 2241 7-9-3 **59**..............(h) JamieGormley(3) 9 69
(Iain Jardine) *dwlt: sn prom: smooth hdwy to ld over 2f out: rdn and hdd over 1f out: rallied fnl f: hld nr fin* **6/4**[1]
4664 **3** *7* **Home Before Dusk**[23] 2436 4-9-9 **62**.................................. ShaneGray 8 60
(Keith Dalgleish) *hld up on ins: stdy hdwy over 2f out: sn rdn: outpcd by first two fr fnl f* **13/8**[2]
02-0 **4** *4* **Remember Rocky**[26] 2330 10-9-2 **60**....................(b) ConnorMurtagh(5) 1 51
(Lucy Normile) *trckd ldrs: effrt and rdn over 2f out: wknd over 1f out* **14/1**
3-00 **5** *3* **Haymarket**[15] 2682 10-8-13 **52**..(t) AndrewMullen 10 37
(R Mike Smith) *cl up: led over 4f out to over 2f out: rdn and wknd over 1f out (jockey said gelding weakened quickly in the final 2f)* **12/1**
6 *5* **Hard Times (IRE)**[160] 9620 8-8-0 **46** oh1.......................... EllaMcCain(7) 4 22
(Philip Kirby) *slowly away: hld up: rdn over 2f out: sn wknd* **33/1**
34/0 **7** *8* **About Glory**[25] 2373 5-9-2 **55**...(w) LewisEdmunds 6 17
(Iain Jardine) *led to over 4f out: rdn and wknd over 2f out* **14/1**

2m 7.73s (-4.67) **Going Correction** -0.325s/f (Firm) **7** Ran SP% **112.6**
Speed ratings (Par 101): **105,104,99,95,93 89,83**
CSF £21.10 CT £31.15 TOTE £9.20: £3.50, £1.40; EX 22.40 Trifecta £58.70.
Owner Johnnie Delta Racing **Bred** Carrigbeg Stud Co Ltd **Trained** Uplawmoor, E Renfrews

FOCUS
An ordinary handicap, but the first two came well clear and look to be ahead of the handicapper.
T/Plt: £136.50 to a £1 stake. Pool: £55,050.58 - 294.25 winning units T/Qpdt: £14.70 to a £1 stake. Pool: £6,797.20 - 341.22 winning units **Richard Young**

2924 BRIGHTON (L-H)
Tuesday, May 28

OFFICIAL GOING: Good to firm (watered)
Wind: light, half against Weather: light cloud, bright spells

3182 INJURED JOCKEYS FUND H'CAP 6f 210y
2:00 (2:00) (Class 6) (0-60,60) 3-Y-O
£3,105 (£924; £461; £300; £300; £300) **Stalls** Centre

Form RPR
4402 **1** **Your Mothers' Eyes**[35] 2016 3-8-11 **55**.................(p) DarraghKeenan(5) 3 66
(Alan Bailey) *chsd ldrs: shkn up and effrt wl over 1f out: rdn to chse ldr 1f out: led ins fnl f: r.o strly: pushed out* **11/4**[2]
00-2 **2** *2* **Lonicera**[25] 2355 3-9-6 **59**.. OisinMurphy 8 65
(Henry Candy) *chsd ldrs tl clsd to join ldr over 3f out: rdn to ld over 1f out: hdd and no ex ins fnl f* **6/5**[1]
5060 **3** *4 ½* **Spirit Of Lucerne (IRE)**[13] 2735 3-8-6 **52**.................. GraceMcEntee(7) 4 45
(Phil McEntee) *hld up in tch: nt clr run over 2f out: swtchd rt wl over 1f out: kpt on to go 3rd wl ins fnl f: no threat to ldrs* **66/1**
5450 **4** *½* **Fox Happy (IRE)**[48] 1678 3-9-7 **60**................................ TomMarquand 5 52
(Richard Hannon) *broke fast: led: rdn ent fnl 2f: hdd over 1f out: 3rd and outpcd 1f out: wknd ins fnl f* **15/2**

400 **5** *shd* **Jeanette May**[28] 2236 3-8-8 **47**.............................. HollieDoyle 6 39
(William Stone) *restless in stalls: s.i.s: t.k.h: hld up in rr: effrt 3f out: styd on ins fnl f: nvr trbld ldrs (jockey said filly was slowly away)* **33/1**

5020 **6** *1 1/4* **Thedevilinneville**[54] 1549 3-8-4 **50**.............................. TobyEley(7) 2 38
(Adam West) *t.k.h: hld up in tch in last trio: effrt u.p 2f out: swtchd rt and kpt on ins fnl f: nvr trbld ldrs (jockey said gelding hung right-handed throughout)* **14/1**

0-00 **7** *3* **Princess Florence (IRE)**[29] 2190 3-8-7 **46** oh1..............(p) BrettDoyle 7 26
(John Ryan) *dwlt: t.k.h: sn rcvrd to chse ldrs: unable qck u.p over 1f out: wknd ins fnl f* **40/1**

0632 **8** *2 1/2* **Tarrzan (IRE)**[7] 2926 3-8-13 **52**.............................. TomQueally 1 26
(John Gallagher) *in tch in midfield: effrt over 2f out: no imp u.p over 1f out: wknd ins fnl f and eased towards fin* **5/1**[3]

50 **9** *hd* **Katie O'Hara (IRE)**[19] 2550 3-8-4 **46** oh1.............................. WilliamCox(3) 10 19
(Samuel Farrell, Ire) *w ldr tl over 3f out: lost pl u.p and btn over 1f out: wknd ins fnl f* **100/1**

0000 **10** *3 3/4* **Milldean Panther**[7] 2924 3-8-9 **48**..............................(b) KierenFox 9 11
(Suzi Best) *a in rr: nvr involved* **33/1**

1m 22.64s (-1.16) **Going Correction** -0.175s/f (Firm) **10** Ran SP% **118.0**
Speed ratings (Par 97): **99,96,91,91,90 89,86,83,82,78**
CSF £6.34 CT £169.53 TOTE £3.20: £1.10, £1.10, £16.80; EX 6.70 Trifecta £193.10.
Owner Capla Developments And A Bailey **Bred** Strawberry Fields Stud **Trained** Newmarket, Suffolk

FOCUS
A modest 3yo handicap. The second-favourite came clear with the market leader and won going away on the climb to the line. The winner's credited with a minor pb.

3183 WEATHERBYS STALLION BOOK H'CAP 6f 210y
2:30 (2:30) (Class 4) (0-80,81) 4-Y-0+ **£5,530** (£1,645; £822; £411) **Stalls** Centre

Form RPR
2040 **1** **Key Player**[27] 2273 4-9-3 **78**..............................(w) CharlesBishop 2 86
(Eve Johnson Houghton) *mde all: rdn over 2f out: drvn over 1f out: forged ahd ins fnl f: kpt on wl* **7/2**[3]

65-5 **2** *3/4* **Elysium Dream**[22] 2487 4-9-6 **81**.............................. RossaRyan 3 87?
(Richard Hannon) *in rr tl chsd clr ldng pair over 4f out: effrt u.p 2f out: edgd lft but kpt on to chse wnr wl ins fnl f: a hld (jockey said filly hung left-handed in the straight)* **5/2**[2]

-631 **3** *3* **Mamillius**[38] 1932 6-9-6 **81**.............................. PatCosgrave 4 79
(George Baker) *trckd ldrs tl wnt 2nd 5f out: jnd wnr and wnt clr over 4f out: effrt over 2f out: nt qckn u.p 1f out: lost 2nd and wknd wl ins fnl f* **10/11**[1]

20-0 **4** *9* **Robsdelight (IRE)**[59] 1413 4-9-2 **77**..............................(p[1]) TomQueally 5 51
(Gay Kelleway) *chsd wnr for 2f: dropped to last and rdn over 4f out: nvr bk on terms and wknd over 1f out* **20/1**

1m 21.55s (-2.25) **Going Correction** -0.175s/f (Firm) **4** Ran SP% **107.9**
Speed ratings (Par 105): **105,104,100,90**
CSF £12.05 TOTE £4.60; EX 14.40 Trifecta £22.40.
Owner Raw, Reeve & Wollaston **Bred** Heather Raw **Trained** Blewbury, Oxon

FOCUS
The feature contest was a fair little handicap. The third-favourite toughed out a second career victory and his winning time was over a second quicker than the opening C&D 3yo handicap. The winner's rated close to his best.

3184 SKY SPORTS RACING ON SKY 415 NOVICE STKS 7f 211y
3:00 (3:00) (Class 5) 3-Y-0+ **£3,752** (£1,116; £557; £278) **Stalls** Centre

Form RPR
-223 **1** **Franz Kafka (IRE)**[21] 2506 3-9-5 **86**.............................. RobertHavlin 1 87
(John Gosden) *mde all: shkn up over 1f out: kpt on u.p and a doing enough ins fnl f* **8/15**[1]

23-3 **2** *1* **Current Option (IRE)**[34] 2034 3-9-5 **84**.............................. OisinMurphy 2 84
(William Haggas) *taken down early: stdd s: t.k.h: chsd ldrs tl trckd wnr after 2f: effrt 2f out: drvn over 1f out: kpt on but a hld ins fnl f: eased cl home* **13/8**[2]

0 **3** *10* **Cool Possibility (IRE)**[11] 2790 3-9-5.............................. TomQueally 4 61
(Charles Hills) *chsd wnr for 2f: chsd ldrs after: outpcd u.p over 2f out: wl btn over 1f out* **28/1**[3]

P0 **4** *3/4* **River Dawn**[11] 2794 3-9-5.............................. RaulDaSilva 3 59
(Paul Cole) *stdd s: t.k.h: hld up in last pair: 4th and effrt over 2f out: sn outpcd and wl btn over 1f out* **33/1**

40 **5** *12* **Potters Question**[29] 2192 3-9-5.............................. TomMarquand 5 32
(Amy Murphy) *bhd and rdn over 3f out: sn struggling and wl hld whn edgd rt 2f out: sn wknd* **66/1**

1m 33.3s (-3.60) **Going Correction** -0.175s/f (Firm) **5** Ran SP% **111.2**
Speed ratings (Par 103): **111,110,100,99,87**
CSF £1.65 TOTE £1.40: £1.10, £1.10; EX 1.30 Trifecta £4.40.
Owner HH Sheikha Al Jalila Racing **Bred** Godolphin **Trained** Newmarket, Suffolk

FOCUS
A decent little, effectively 3yo novice contest. The odds-on favourite controlled the race from the front and found more than his main market rival on the uphill section. The form could prove to be worth a little higher.

3185 I.T. ELECTRICAL CONTRACTORS EXETER H'CAP 7f 211y
3:30 (3:30) (Class 5) (0-75,73) 4-Y-0+ **£3,752** (£1,116; £557; £300; £300; £300) **Stalls** Centre

Form RPR
433- **1** **De Vegas Kid (IRE)**[167] 9506 5-9-6 **72**.............................. GeorgeDowning 4 79
(Tony Carroll) *stdd s: hld up in tch in last pair: effrt 2f out: edgd lft and clsd to chal 1f out: led ins fnl f: r.o wl (jockey said gelding hung left-handed under pressure)* **9/2**

6-40 **2** *1* **Kingston Kurrajong**[11] 2797 6-9-7 **73**.............................. KierenFox 3 78
(William Knight) *pressed ldr early: sn restrained and hld up in tch: effrt over 1f out: chsng ldrs u.p whn squeezed for room and swtchd rt ins fnl f: styd on to go 2nd cl home* **5/2**[1]

0-43 **3** *nk* **Kachumba**[25] 2365 4-9-2 **68**.............................. OisinMurphy 2 72
(Rae Guest) *sn pressing ldr: rdn to ld over 2f out: drvn over 1f out: hdd and one pce ins fnl f: lost 2nd cl home* **11/4**[2]

200- **4** *hd* **Fleeting Freedom**[194] 9069 4-9-0 **73**..............................(p) JessicaCooley(7) 6 76
(Alan Bailey) *fly j. leaving stalls: sn pressing ldrs: ev ch and rdn over 2f out: unable qck ins fnl f: jst outpcd fnl 100yds* **6/1**

1320 **5** *1* **Narjes**[15] 2691 5-8-12 **71**..............................(h) SophieRalston(7) 5 75+
(Laura Mongan) *taken down early: hld up in tch in rr: effrt and clsd over 1f out: chsd ldrs 1f out: nt clr run thrght fnl f and unable to cl (jockey said mare was denied a clear run)* **7/2**[3]

54-0 **6** *5* **Trulee Scrumptious**[11] 2799 10-8-4 **63**..............................(v) GraceMcEntee(7) 1 53
(Peter Charalambous) *led: rdn and hdd over 2f out: outpcd and lost pl over 1f out: wknd ins fnl f* **25/1**

1m 35.99s (-0.91) **Going Correction** -0.175s/f (Firm) **6** Ran SP% **113.8**
Speed ratings (Par 103): **97,96,95,95,94 89**
CSF £16.50 TOTE £4.30: £2.40, £2.10; EX 19.50 Trifecta £37.00.
Owner The Rebelle Boys **Bred** Miriam O'Donnell & Kevin F O'Donnell **Trained** Cropthorne, Worcs

FOCUS
A fair handicap. The fourth-favourite's winning time was comparatively modest, and it's ordinary form.

3186 RAG'N'BONE MAN LIVE HERE 27TH JULY H'CAP 1m 1f 207y
4:00 (4:01) (Class 6) (0-60,61) 4-Y-0+ **£3,105** (£924; £461; £300; £300; £300) **Stalls** High

Form RPR
0-03 **1** **Couldn't Could She**[5] 2998 4-9-0 **58**.............................. TobyEley(7) 3 66
(Adam West) *pushed along leaving stalls: hld up in tch: effrt towards inner ent fnl 2f: hdwy to chal 1f out: led ins fnl f: r.o wl* **9/4**[2]

0-06 **2** *1* **Fair Power (IRE)**[28] 2256 5-9-5 **56**.............................. OisinMurphy 8 62
(John Butler) *stdd after s: hld up in tch: clsd over 2f out: sn ev ch: rdn to ld over 1f out: hdd and one pce ins fnl f* **2/1**[1]

25-6 **3** *nk* **King Athelstan (IRE)**[17] 2617 4-9-10 **61**.............................. HectorCrouch 5 67
(Gary Moore) *hld up in tch: effrt and swtchd rt 3f out: hdwy u.p over 1f out: chsd ldrs ins fnl f: kpt on same pce fnl 100yds* **9/2**[3]

0462 **4** *2* **Passing Clouds**[55] 1520 4-8-8 **45**.............................. KierenFox 9 47
(Michael Attwater) *chsd ldr tl led 5f out: edgd lft to rail over 4f out: drvn and hdd ent fnl 2f: no ex 1f out: wknd ins fnl f* **20/1**

6000 **5** *1* **Prerogative (IRE)**[31] 2111 5-8-11 **48**..............................(p) TomMarquand 6 48
(Tony Carroll) *chsd ldrs tl lft chsng ldr over 4f out: rdn to ld ent fnl 2f: sn drvn and hdd: no ex 1f out: wknd ins fnl f* **8/1**

0-00 **6** *1* **Mahna Mahna (IRE)**[7] 2929 5-8-1 **45**.............................. EllieMacKenzie(7) 1 43
(David W Drinkwater) *sn led: hdd 5f out: squeezed for room: hmpd and lost 2nd over 4f out: lost pl u.p over 1f out: wl hld and kpt on same pce ins fnl f* **40/1**

0-20 **7** *hd* **Sussex Girl**[18] 2585 5-9-0 **51**.............................. RobertHavlin 4 49
(John Berry) *dwlt: in tch in last trio: effrt 2f out: no imp u.p 1f out: wl hld and kpt on same pce ins fnl f* **10/1**

6451 **8** *2 1/4* **Herm (IRE)**[22] 2500 5-8-13 **50**.............................. HollieDoyle 2 43
(David Evans) *chsd ldrs: lost pl and bhd whn drvn over 1f out: wknd ins fnl f* **10/1**

2m 4.67s (-0.33) **Going Correction** -0.175s/f (Firm) **8** Ran SP% **118.8**
Speed ratings (Par 101): **94,93,92,91,90 89,89,87**
CSF £7.53 CT £18.29 TOTE £3.20: £1.30, £1.40, £1.20; EX 9.30 Trifecta £28.90.
Owner Ross Deacon & Partners **Bred** D R Botterill & E Boumans **Trained** Epsom, Surrey

FOCUS
A modest handicap, and straightforward form.

3187 RACING WELFARE H'CAP 7f 211y
4:30 (4:32) (Class 6) (0-60,60) 4-Y-0+ **£3,105** (£924; £461; £300; £300; £300) **Stalls** Centre

Form RPR
6P43 **1** **Confrerie (IRE)**[7] 2930 4-9-0 **53**.............................. PatCosgrave 13 59
(George Baker) *midfield and pushed along 5f out: reminders 3f out: clsd u.p over 1f out: hung lft but styd on to ld ins fnl f: a jst holding on cl home* **11/4**[1]

4600 **2** *nk* **Brother In Arms (IRE)**[21] 2514 5-8-7 **46** oh1.............................. BrettDoyle 12 51
(Tony Carroll) *midfield: effrt ent fnl 2f: hdwy over 1f out: styd on strly u.p ins fnl f: clsng but nvr quite getting to wnr* **66/1**

5-60 **3** *1/2* **Imbucato**[30] 2145 5-8-11 **50**.............................. TomMarquand 9 54
(Tony Carroll) *chsd ldr: drvn to ld over 1f out: sn hung lft: hdd ins fnl f: kpt on but lost 2nd towards fin (jockey said gelding ran around under pressure)* **9/1**

2552 **4** *3 1/4* **Maazel (IRE)**[27] 2286 5-9-4 **57**.............................. RobertWinston 5 54
(Lee Carter) *stdd s: t.k.h: hld up towards rr: clsd over 2f out: hdwy to chse ldrs whn pushed lft ent fnl f: rdn ins fnl f: fnd little and wknd fnl 75yds* **7/1**

0220 **5** *3/4* **Sharp Operator**[5] 3006 6-9-1 **57**..............................(h) JoshuaBryan(3) 10 52
(Charlie Wallis) *stdd s: t.k.h: hld up tch in midfield: clsd over 2f out: rdn to chse ldrs ent fnl f: no ex ins fnl f: wknd fnl 100yds* **4/1**[2]

-025 **6** *1 1/4* **Khazix (IRE)**[28] 2231 4-8-12 **54**.............................. WilliamCox(3) 14 46
(Daniele Camuffo) *chsd ldrs: keeping on same pce and jst getting outpcd whn carried lft ent fnl f: wknd ins fnl f* **11/2**[3]

0003 **7** *1* **Swiss Cross**[27] 2286 12-8-1 **47** oh1 ow1..............................(p) GraceMcEntee(7) 3 37
(Phil McEntee) *led: rdn and hdd over 1f out: struggling to qckn whn carried lft ent fnl f: wknd ins fnl f* **40/1**

5304 **8** *nk* **Sweet Nature (IRE)**[28] 2232 4-9-0 **60**.............................. SophieRalston(7) 15 49
(Laura Mongan) *chsd ldrs: lost pl u.p over 1f out: wknd ins fnl f* **33/1**

4-50 **9** *1 3/4* **Duchess Of Avon**[96] 835 4-9-7 **60**.............................. HectorCrouch 8 45
(Gary Moore) *midfield: effrt over 2f out: no imp u.p over 1f out: wknd ins fnl f* **10/1**

4654 **10** *1* **Rivas Rob Roy**[13] 2741 4-8-13 **52**.............................. TomQueally 1 35
(John Gallagher) *hld up towards rr: effrt on inner jst over 2f out: no imp u.p over 1f out: wknd ins fnl f* **10/1**

05-0 **11** *nk* **Hidden Stash**[28] 2234 5-8-8 **47**..............................(p) HollieDoyle 7 29
(William Stone) *restless in stalls: s.i.s: a in rr: effrt over 2f out: no prog and nvr involved (jockey said gelding was restless in the stalls and missed the break)* **10/1**

-000 **12** *14* **Twistsandturns (IRE)**[62] 1353 8-8-8 **47** oh1 ow1.............................. KierenFox 2
(Adrian Wintle) *midfield but sn pushed along: dropped towards rr 6f out: a struggling after and wl bhd ins fnl f* **50/1**

/00- **13** *11* **Birthday Girl (IRE)**[302] 5550 4-8-7 **46** oh1..............................(p[1]) MartinDwyer 4
(Amanda Perrett) *chsd ldrs: lost pl u.p 2f out: wl bhd ins fnl f* **40/1**

1m 35.1s (-1.80) **Going Correction** -0.175s/f (Firm) **13** Ran SP% **123.1**
Speed ratings (Par 101): **102,101,101,97,97 95,94,94,92,91 91,77,66**
CSF £233.52 CT £1508.25 TOTE £3.10: £1.10, £13.60, £3.00; EX 230.50 Trifecta £2709.80.
Owner New Confidence Partnership **Bred** Hyde Park Stud **Trained** Chiddingfold, Surrey
■ Stewards' Enquiry : Tom Marquand two-day ban; careless riding (tba)

FOCUS
A modest handicap. A line of ten horses stretched across the track over 1f out but the narrow winning favourite came clear with two others in a fair winning time for the grade. He's rated near to his best.

3188 SKY SPORTS RACING ON VIRGIN 535 H'CAP — 5f 215y
5:00 (5:01) (Class 5) (0-70,70) 4-Y-O+
£3,752 (£1,116; £557; £300; £300; £300) **Stalls** Centre

Form RPR

5-00 **1** **King Crimson**[21] 2515 7-8-13 **62** OisinMurphy 1 71
(John Butler) *mde all: rdn over 1f out: sn edgd lft but kpt on ins fnl f (trainer said, reg app imp in form, gelding was suited by the return to Brighton)* **8/1**

0-56 **2** 1 3/4 **Cent Flying**[3] 3089 4-9-2 **65** (t) MartinDwyer 6 68
(William Muir) *off the pce in midfield: effrt over 2f out: kpt on u.p ins fnl f: chsd wnr towards fin: nvr getting on terms* **7/2**[3]

5303 **3** hd **National Glory (IRE)**[5] 3014 4-8-9 **65** (b) Pierre-LouisJamin(7) 2 67
(Archie Watson) *chsd wnr: rdn ent fnl 2f: unable qck: hld and kpt on same pce ins fnl f: lost 2nd towards fin* **5/2**[1]

5000 **4** 1 3/4 **Mont Kiara (FR)**[17] 2611 6-9-4 **67** TomMarquand 5 64
(Simon Dow) *chsd clr ldng pair: effrt over 2f out: kpt on ins fnl f: nvr trbld ldrs: burst blood vessel (vet said gelding bled from the nose)* **13/2**

1110 **5** hd **Foreign Legion (IRE)**[87] 982 4-9-4 **67** (p) TomQueally 4 63
(Luke McJannet) *off the pce in midfield: effrt over 2f out: rdn over 1f out: kpt on ins fnl f: nvr trbld ldrs* **12/1**

0-46 **6** hd **Born To Finish (IRE)**[5] 3014 6-9-7 **70** PatCosgrave 3 65
(Ed de Giles) *s.i.s: off the pce in rr of main gp: effrt over 2f out: kpt on ins fnl f: nvr trbld ldrs* **3/1**[2]

6003 **7** 45 **The British Lion (IRE)**[28] 2232 4-9-1 **64** (t) RobertHavlin 7
(Alexandra Dunn) *s.i.s and awkward leaving stalls: sn outpcd: t.o and eased ins fnl f: rn wout tongue tie (jockey said gelding was slowly away and raced awkwardly in the first stages of the race)* **14/1**

1m 8.85s (-2.25) **Going Correction** -0.175s/f (Firm) **7 Ran SP% 114.6**
Speed ratings (Par 103): **108,105,105,103,102 102,42**
CSF £36.12 TOTE £9.00: £4.20, £2.00; EX 36.40 Trifecta £140.10.
Owner Power Geneva Ltd **Bred** Mickley Stud **Trained** Newmarket, Suffolk

FOCUS
An ordinary sprint handicap. It proved hard to make up ground on the leaders after a ragged start, particularly with the winner making all in the quickest comparative time on the day. The form might have been rated higher at face value, but there are doubts.
T/Plt: £34.50 to a £1 stake. Pool: £56,448.03 - 1,191.62 winning units T/Qpdt: £5.50 to a £1 stake. Pool: £4,714.25 - 631.96 winning units **Steve Payne**

3149 LEICESTER (R-H)
Tuesday, May 28

OFFICIAL GOING: Good to firm (good on the bends; watered) changing to good after race 1 (2.10)
Wind: Light across Weather: Showers

3189 SAFFRON 3-Y-O FILLIES' H'CAP — 6f
2:10 (2:10) (Class 5) (0-70,71) 3-Y-O
£3,816 (£1,135; £567; £300; £300; £300) **Stalls** High

Form RPR

60-0 **1** **Queen Of Burgundy**[41] 1855 3-9-7 **69** JoeyHaynes 11 80+
(Christine Dunnett) *hld up in tch: shkn up to ld over 1f out: pushed clr ins fnl f: comf (trainer said, regarding apparent improvement in form, that filly had strengthened up for her first run at Newmarket 41 days ago, was better suited to this track and the drop down in trip)* **40/1**

3055 **2** 3 1/4 **Tie A Yellowribbon**[8] 2904 3-9-4 **66** (p) SilvestreDeSousa 9 67
(James Bethell) *led: rdn and hdd over 1f out: styd on same pce ins fnl f* **3/1**[2]

3352 **3** 1 **Beryl The Petal (IRE)**[8] 2904 3-9-3 **68** (p[1]) ConorMcGovern(3) 3 66
(David O'Meara) *hld up: rdn over 2f out: hdwy over 1f out: hung rt and styd on to go 3rd ins fnl f: nt trble ldrs* **7/4**[1]

25-0 **4** 3/4 **Miss Elsa**[31] 2114 3-9-2 **71** GeorgiaDobie(7) 8 66
(Eve Johnson Houghton) *chsd ldr: rdn over 2f out: styd on same pce fnl f* **16/1**

003 **5** 1 1/2 **Bedtime Bella (IRE)**[18] 2590 3-9-0 **62** PJMcDonald 1 53
(K R Burke) *chsd ldrs: rdn over 2f out: no ex fnl f* **13/2**[3]

501 **6** 2 3/4 **Sepahi**[61] 1380 3-9-1 **63** (p) BenCurtis 5 45
(Henry Spiller) *prom: sn lost pl: pushed along 4f out: rdn over 1f out: nt trble ldrs (trainers' rep said, regarding the poor form shown, that filly would prefer a flatter track)* **33/1**

40-5 **7** 3/4 **Showu**[143] 83 3-9-6 **68** AdamKirby 2 47
(Tony Carroll) *hld up: plld hrd: hdwy over 1f out: sn rdn: wknd fnl f* **14/1**

2044 **8** 1 1/4 **Moneta**[8] 2904 3-9-3 **65** RobHornby 4 40
(Jonathan Portman) *chsd ldrs: rdn over 1f out: wknd fnl f* **7/1**

00-1 **9** 5 **Lady Monica**[17] 2624 3-9-6 **68** RoystonFfrench 10 27
(John Holt) *s.i.s: racd keenly in rr: hdwy over 3f out: wknd wl over 1f out* **12/1**

1m 11.76s (-0.34) **Going Correction** -0.075s/f (Good) **9 Ran SP% 112.8**
Speed ratings (Par 96): **99,94,93,92,90 86,85,84,77**
CSF £154.06 CT £334.95 TOTE £38.10: £7.20, £1.30, £1.20; EX 262.90 Trifecta £1605.30.
Owner Trevor Milner **Bred** Cheveley Park Stud Ltd **Trained** Hingham, Norfolk

FOCUS
This ordinary 3yo fillies' handicap was run at a fair pace. Big improvement from the winner, with the runner-up to form.

3190 BRITISH STALLION STUDS EBF NOVICE STKS (PLUS 10 RACE) — 5f
2:40 (2:40) (Class 4) 2-Y-O **£6,016** (£1,790; £894; £447) **Stalls** High

Form RPR

1 **Majestic Sands (IRE)** 2-9-5 0 BarryMcHugh 6 83+
(Richard Fahey) *chsd ldrs: shkn up to ld over 1f out: sn edgd lft: wandered ins fnl f: r.o* **3/1**[1]

2 3/4 **Cool Sphere (USA)** 2-9-5 0 LouisSteward 8 79+
(Robert Cowell) *led: drifted rt fr over 3f out tl rdn: hdd and edgd lft over 1f out: edgd rt wl ins fnl f: styd on* **9/2**[3]

6 **3** 3/4 **Ivor**[38] 1931 2-9-5 0 SeanLevey 5 77+
(Richard Hannon) *prom: outpcd over 3f out: hdwy over 1f out: hung lft ins fnl f: r.o* **7/1**

4 4 1/2 **Zuckerberg (IRE)** 2-9-5 0 SilvestreDeSousa 1 60+
(Ivan Furtado) *s.i.s and edgd rt s: sn pushed along in rr: hdwy and hung lft over 1f out: nt trble ldrs (jockey said colt ran greenly)* **7/2**[2]

5 1 **Wentworth Amigo (IRE)** 2-9-5 0 NicolaCurrie 2 57
(Jamie Osborne) *broke wl: sn outpcd: r.o wl ins fnl f* **11/2**

00 **6** 3/4 **Percy Green (IRE)**[18] 2594 2-9-5 0 BenCurtis 3 54+
(K R Burke) *hld up: racd keenly: hdwy 3f out: wknd over 1f out* **12/1**

7 1 3/4 **Lincoln Blue** 2-9-5 0 JFEgan 4 48
(Jane Chapple-Hyam) *s.i.s and edgd rt sn after s: hdwy over 3f out: rdn and wknd over 1f out: slipped wl ins fnl f (jockey said colt lost it's footing shortly before the line)* **11/1**

8 7 **Prissy Missy (IRE)** 2-9-0 0 DavidEgan 7 18
(David Loughnane) *chsd ldr: rdn 1/2-way: wknd over 1f out* **28/1**

1m 0.91s (-0.89) **Going Correction** -0.075s/f (Good) **8 Ran SP% 112.8**
Speed ratings (Par 95): **104,102,101,94,92 91,88,77**
CSF £16.21 TOTE £4.00: £1.60, £2.40, £2.50; EX 15.50 Trifecta £47.20.
Owner The Cool Silk Partnership **Bred** Paul Monaghan & T J Monaghan **Trained** Musley Bank, N Yorks

FOCUS
For the third successive season this juvenile affair went to a well-fancied newcomer. Sound form, the first three clear.

3191 STATHERN CLAIMING STKS — 7f
3:10 (3:11) (Class 5) 3-Y-O **£3,816** (£1,135; £567; £300; £300) **Stalls** High

Form RPR

2-50 **1** **Archies Lad**[14] 2711 3-8-5 60 PaddyMathers 2 61+
(Richard Fahey) *s.i.s: hdwy over 2f out: shkn up to ld over 1f out: rdn and edgd lft ins fnl f: styd on wl* **5/2**[2]

4-53 **2** 2 3/4 **Lady Lavinia**[8] 2904 3-8-4 59 FrannyNorton 6 53
(Michael Easterby) *chsd ldrs: pushed along over 2f out: rdn over 1f out: styd on same pce fnl f: wnt 2nd towards fin* **5/4**[1]

-662 **3** 1/2 **Jungle Inthebungle (IRE)**[12] 2773 3-9-2 77 ScottMcCullagh(7) 3 71
(Mick Channon) *chsd ldr: led 1/2-way: rdn and hdd over 1f out: nt run on* **3/1**[3]

-023 **4** 9 **Haats Off**[22] 2503 3-8-6 63 NicolaCurrie 1 30
(Brian Barr) *s.i.s: plld hrd and hdwy over 4f out: rdn and wknd over 1f out* **17/2**

60-0 **5** 1/2 **Alisia R (IRE)**[14] 2713 3-8-6 34 JFEgan 4 29
(Les Eyre) *led to 1/2-way: rdn over 2f out: wknd over 1f out* **66/1**

1m 25.12s (-0.58) **Going Correction** -0.075s/f (Good) **5 Ran SP% 110.0**
Speed ratings (Par 99): **100,96,96,86,85**
CSF £6.04 TOTE £3.40: £1.60, £1.10; EX 6.00 Trifecta £10.70.The winner was claimed by Mr R. Michael Smith £5,000
Owner Mark Barlow & Partner **Bred** J Weatherby,Myriad,Naseby & New England **Trained** Musley Bank, N Yorks

FOCUS
Typically weak 3yo plating form.

3192 LEICESTER STUDENTS RACEDAY H'CAP — 1m 2f
3:40 (3:40) (Class 4) (0-80,80) 4-Y-O+ **£4,884** (£1,453; £726; £363) **Stalls** Low

Form RPR

01-6 **1** **Victory Chime (IRE)**[29] 2209 4-9-7 **80** HarryBentley 7 89
(Ralph Beckett) *sn drvn along to ld: shkn up over 3f out: rdn over 1f out: edgd lft: all out* **11/2**[3]

6-00 **2** 1/2 **Existential (IRE)**[17] 2608 4-9-5 **78** AdamKirby 2 86
(Clive Cox) *trckd ldrs: shkn up over 3f out: chsd wnr over 2f out: sn rdn and hung rt: styd on u.p (jockey said filly hung right-handed)* **11/4**[2]

10-2 **3** 1 3/4 **Allegiant (USA)**[29] 2207 4-8-13 **72** RichardKingscote 8 77
(Stuart Williams) *sn chsng wnr: rdn and lost 2nd over 2f out: no ex wl ins fnl f* **15/8**[1]

36- **4** 1 1/2 **Dramatic Device**[203] 4-9-7 **80** GeorgeWood 9 82
(Chris Wall) *hld up: hdwy 2f out: sn hung rt: styd on: nt rch ldrs* **33/1**

-005 **5** hd **Biotic**[11] 2797 8-8-11 **70** RobHornby 3 71
(Rod Millman) *s.i.s: hld up: hdwy u.p 2f out: nt rch ldrs* **8/1**

16/0 **6** 10 **Bahama Moon (IRE)**[18] 2577 7-9-1 **74** LiamKeniry 6 55
(Jonjo O'Neill) *chsd ldrs: rdn over 3f out: wknd over 2f out* **20/1**

150- **7** 4 **Bartholomew J (IRE)**[37] 8513 5-9-1 **74** (p) RoystonFfrench 10 47
(Lydia Pearce) *hld up: rdn and wknd over 2f out* **50/1**

606- **8** 5 **Paddy The Chef (IRE)**[127] 9313 4-8-13 **72** JimCrowley 4 35
(Ian Williams) *hld up: shkn up over 3f out: wknd 2f out* **6/1**

2m 7.9s (-1.30) **Going Correction** -0.075s/f (Good) **8 Ran SP% 111.9**
Speed ratings (Par 105): **102,101,100,99,98 90,87,83**
CSF £20.01 CT £37.62 TOTE £5.70: £1.70, £1.10, £1.40; EX 18.10 Trifecta £58.90.
Owner A Nevin **Bred** M Downey & Kildaragh Stud **Trained** Kimpton, Hants

FOCUS
This looked competitive on paper but you had to be handy. The form's rated around the third.

3193 CORONATION FILLIES' H'CAP — 7f
4:10 (4:10) (Class 4) (0-85,87) 3-Y-O
£6,249 (£1,859; £929; £464; £300; £300) **Stalls** High

Form RPR

066- **1** **Mulan (IRE)**[224] 8295 3-9-2 **72** DavidEgan 6 79+
(Sir Michael Stoute) *s.i.s and edgd lft s: rcvrd to ld 6f out: rdn and hung rt fr over 1f out: styd on* **3/1**[1]

50-0 **2** 1 1/4 **No Way Jose (IRE)**[30] 2144 3-10-3 **87** JasonWatson 5 90
(Brian Meehan) *chsd ldrs: rdn over 2f out: chsd wnr and flashed tail ins fnl f: no imp towards fin* **8/1**

33-0 **3** 2 **Knightshayes**[25] 2356 3-9-3 **76** MeganNicholls(3) 4 74
(Paul George) *s.i.s: hld up: hdwy 1/2-way: rdn over 1f out: styd on same pce ins fnl f* **6/1**

-002 **4** 1 1/2 **Cotubanama**[25] 2356 3-9-7 **77** SilvestreDeSousa 1 71
(Mick Channon) *stmbld s: hld up: hdwy to join wnr 4f out: rdn and ev ch over 1f out: wknd wl ins fnl f (jockey said filly stumbled leaving the stalls)* **5/1**

20-6 **5** 3/4 **Ajrar**[27] 2268 3-10-3 **87** SeanLevey 2 79
(Richard Hannon) *chsd ldrs: rdn over 2f out: no ex ins fnl f* **10/3**[2]

3-10 **6** 1/2 **Isango**[28] 2251 3-9-5 **75** StevieDonohoe 3 65
(Charlie Fellowes) *led 1f: remained handy: racd keenly: rdn over 2f out: styd on same pce fr over 1f out* **7/2**[3]

1m 25.8s (0.10) **Going Correction** -0.075s/f (Good) **6 Ran SP% 112.4**
Speed ratings (Par 98): **96,94,92,90,89 89**
CSF £26.35 TOTE £3.00: £1.40, £3.70; EX 23.40 Trifecta £111.20.
Owner Kin Hung Kei & Qatar Racing Ltd **Bred** Skymarc Farm Inc And Ecurie Des Monceaux **Trained** Newmarket, Suffolk

FOCUS
Not a bad fillies' handicap for 3yos, with the level of the form a bit solid.

3194 BRITISH STALLION STUDS EBF MAIDEN STKS (PLUS 10 RACE) 6f
4:40 (4:42) (Class 4) 2-Y-O £5,110 (£1,520; £759; £379) **Stalls High**

Form RPR

2 **1** **Platinum Star (IRE)**[18] 2594 2-9-5 0 HarryBentley 9 83
(Saeed bin Suroor) *dwlt: sn prom: led over 1f out: pushed out* **5/6**[1]

2 2 **Zim Baby** 2-8-11 0 MeganNicholls(3) 4 72
(Paul George) *chsd ldrs: ev ch over 1f out: styd on same pce wl ins fnl f* **100/1**

0 **3** 1 1/2 **Return To Senders (IRE)**[18] 2594 2-9-5 0 NicolaCurrie 5 73
(Jamie Osborne) *hld up in tch: lost pl 4f out: swtchd rt and hdwy over 1f out: sn rdn and edgd lft: styd on same pce ins fnl f (jockey said colt hung left-handed in the closing stages)* **50/1**

4 4 **Asfurasagira (IRE)** 2-9-0 0 JimCrowley 7 56+
(Owen Burrows) *s.i.s: hld up: pushed along over 2f out: hdwy over 1f out: nt trble ldrs* **9/1**

5 3/4 **Otago** 2-9-5 0 HayleyTurner 11 58+
(Michael Bell) *hld up: pushed along 1/2-way: r.o ins fnl f: nvr nrr* **14/1**

6 1 **Capp It All (IRE)** 2-9-0 0 DavidEgan 1 50
(David Loughnane) *w ldr tl led 2f out: rdn and hdd over 1f out: wknd ins fnl f* **80/1**

7 1/2 **Javea Magic (IRE)** 2-9-5 0 RichardKingscote 8 54
(Tom Dascombe) *sn led: hdd 2f out: wknd ins fnl f* **20/1**

8 1 1/2 **Sky Commander (IRE)** 2-9-5 0 PJMcDonald 3 49
(James Tate) *s.s: sn pushed along in rr: hdwy over 1f out: wknd ins fnl f* **6/1**[3]

0 **9** 4 1/2 **Port Noir**[43] 1821 2-9-0 0 JFEgan 13 31
(Paul George) *sn pushed along in rr: hdwy 1/2-way: rdn and wknd 2f out* **100/1**

10 1 3/4 **Handsome Yank (USA)** 2-9-5 0 TrevorWhelan 10 31
(Ivan Furtado) *chsd ldrs: rdn over 2f out: wknd over 1f out* **50/1**

11 nk **Big City** 2-9-5 0 AndreaAtzeni 12 30
(Saeed bin Suroor) *hld up: hdwy 1/2-way: wknd 2f out* **11/2**[2]

12 2 1/2 **Haafel (IRE)** 2-9-5 0 DaneO'Neill 6 22
(Charles Hills) *dwlt: rn green and a in rr* **14/1**

1m 12.13s (0.03) **Going Correction** -0.075s/f (Good) **12 Ran SP% 119.5**
Speed ratings (Par 95): **96,93,91,86,85 83,83,81,75,72 72,68**
CSF £175.87 TOTE £1.60: £1.10, £24.90, £11.10; EX 169.90 Trifecta £3450.60.
Owner Godolphin **Bred** Corduff Stud & Farmleigh Bloodstock Ltd **Trained** Newmarket, Suffolk

FOCUS
This had been won by top-notchers such as Thunder Snow and Toormore in the past decade. Juvenile form to be positive about.

3195 OADBY H'CAP 1m 2f
5:10 (5:10) (Class 5) (0-75,75) 3-Y-O
£3,816 (£1,135; £567; £300; £300; £300) **Stalls Low**

Form RPR

3-13 **1** **Conundrum**[26] 2333 3-9-5 **73** JackGarritty 12 79
(Jedd O'Keeffe) *mde all: grad crossed over fr wd draw: rdn over 1f out: edgd lft ins fnl f (jockey said gelding hung right-handed in the home straight)* **7/2**[1]

2-40 **2** nk **Silkstone (IRE)**[18] 2582 3-9-3 **71** RobHornby 1 76
(Pam Sly) *prom: shkn up over 2f out: chsd wnr ins fnl f: r.o* **17/2**

32-0 **3** 2 **Starfighter**[32] 2082 3-9-6 **74** RichardKingscote 8 75
(Ed Walker) *hld up: hdwy 3f out: rdn over 1f out: styd on same pce ins fnl f* **11/2**[2]

33-3 **4** 1/2 **Fragrant Dawn**[36] 1975 3-9-7 **75** (h[1]) DaneO'Neill 4 75
(Charles Hills) *prom: ev ch 2f out: sn rdn: edgd rt ins fnl f: no ex towards fin* **16/1**

5-00 **5** 3/4 **Garrison Commander (IRE)**[15] 2697 3-9-0 **68** (b[1]) SilvestreDeSousa 13 67
(Eve Johnson Houghton) *dwlt: hld up: rdn over 2f out: nt clr run and swtchd lft over 1f out: styd on: nt rch ldrs* **16/1**

04-0 **6** nse **Baasem (USA)**[25] 2354 3-9-6 **74** JimCrowley 5 72
(Owen Burrows) *hld up: rdn over 2f out: r.o ins fnl f: nvr nrr* **7/2**[1]

00-0 **7** 2 **Jimmy Greenhough (IRE)**[36] 1975 3-8-4 **58** PaddyMathers 2 52
(Richard Fahey) *sn chsng ldrs: rdn over 2f out: styng on same pce whn nt clr run ins fnl f* **28/1**

3055 **8** hd **Four Mile Bridge (IRE)**[15] 2689 3-8-10 **64** FergusSweeney 3 58
(Mark Usher) *hld up: racd keenly: rdn over 2f out: nt rch ldrs* **33/1**

5004 **9** 2 3/4 **Thinque Tank**[18] 2582 3-8-11 **65** LiamKeniry 6 54
(Charlie Longsdon) *chsd wnr over 8f out: rdn and ev ch over 1f out: wknd ins fnl f* **9/1**

4-42 **10** 1 3/4 **Dancingwithwolves (IRE)**[36] 1975 3-9-7 **75** (h) DanielMuscutt 11 60
(Ed Dunlop) *hld up: racd keenly: hdwy 3f out: rdn and hung rt over 1f out: sn wknd (jockey said gelding ran too freely and also ran greenly)* **14/1**

006- **11** 14 **Road To Paris (IRE)**[208] 8767 3-8-4 **58** JosephineGordon 7 15
(Sir Mark Prescott Bt) *s.i.s: sn pushed along and a in rr* **7/1**[3]

2m 8.9s (-0.30) **Going Correction** -0.075s/f (Good) **11 Ran SP% 117.7**
Speed ratings (Par 99): **98,97,96,95,95 95,93,93,91,89 78**
CSF £34.02 CT £162.58 TOTE £4.40: £1.70, £3.00, £1.90; EX 34.00 Trifecta £235.90.
Owner Highbeck Racing 2 **Bred** Mr & Mrs A E Pakenham **Trained** Middleham Moor, N Yorks

FOCUS
There was a stop-start pace on in this modest 3yo handicap. The second and third are rated in line with a better view of their form.
T/Plt: £9.10 to a £1 stake. Pool: £46,994.57 - 3,754.90 winning units T/Qpdt: £5.90 to a £1 stake. Pool: £3,373.51 - 421.97 winning units **Colin Roberts**

3156 REDCAR (L-H)
Tuesday, May 28

OFFICIAL GOING: Good to firm (watered; 8.6)
Wind: fresh largely against Weather: cool and overcast

3196 LONGINES IRISH CHAMPION WEEKEND EBF FILLIES' NOVICE MEDIAN AUCTION STKS (PLUS 10 RACE) 5f 217y
2:20 (2:26) (Class 5) 2-Y-O £5,175 (£1,540; £769; £384) **Stalls Centre**

Form RPR

4 **1** **Bella Brazil (IRE)**[11] 2783 2-9-0 0 TomEaves 5 69
(David Barron) *trckd ldrs: pushed along 2f out: chal ent fnl f: sn rdn: led 75yds out: kpt on* **7/1**[3]

512 **2** 3/4 **Insania**[8] 2906 2-9-2 0 HarrisonShaw(5) 13 74
(K R Burke) *led narrowly: rdn 2f out: hung lft and strly pressed ent fnl f: hdd 75yds out: one pce (jockey said filly hung left)* **4/1**[1]

3 2 1/2 **Fashion Advice** 2-9-0 0 JoeFanning 12 60
(Keith Dalgleish) *trckd ldrs: rdn 2f out: one pce fnl f* **11/1**

0 **4** 3/4 **Rusalka (IRE)**[14] 2707 2-9-0 0 DavidAllan 9 57
(Tim Easterby) *midfield: pushed along 2f out: kpt on wl fnl 110yds* **33/1**

4 **5** nk **Microscopic (IRE)**[18] 2579 2-9-0 0 DavidProbert 4 56
(David Simcock) *trckd ldrs: rdn 2f out: no ex fnl 110yds* **4/1**[1]

6 1 3/4 **Secret Identity** 2-9-0 0 GrahamLee 10 51
(Jedd O'Keeffe) *trckd ldrs: pushed along over 2f out: outpcd fr over 1f out* **33/1**

43 **7** 4 **Amnaa**[33] 2051 2-9-0 0 ConnorBeasley 8 39
(Adrian Nicholls) *pressed ldr: rdn over 2f out: hung lft over 1f out and wknd* **5/1**[2]

0 **8** 1 **Mist In The Valley**[29] 2191 2-9-0 0 TonyHamilton 3 36
(David Brown) *hld up: nvr threatened* **100/1**

6 **9** 8 **South Light (IRE)**[22] 2475 2-9-0 0 CamHardie 1 12
(Antony Brittain) *s.i.s: a in rr* **66/1**

10 nk **Fulbeck Rose** 2-8-11 0 RowanScott(3) 7 11
(Nigel Tinkler) *slowly away: a outpcd in rr* **33/1**

11 1/2 **Moonlighting** 2-9-0 0 KevinStott 11 10
(Kevin Ryan) *s.i.s: a towards rr* **12/1**

1m 14.32s (2.52) **Going Correction** +0.025s/f (Good) **11 Ran SP% 96.5**
Speed ratings (Par 90): **88,87,83,82,82 79,74,73,62,62 61**
CSF £21.42 TOTE £6.00: £2.00, £2.30, £2.60; EX 21.60 Trifecta £205.10.
Owner P Savill & T Savill **Bred** Cottage Lodge Stud **Trained** Maunby, N Yorks
■ Three Coins & Quiet Word were withdrawn. Prices at time of withdrawal both 5/2. Rule 4 applies to board prices prior to withdrawal - deduction 45p in the pound. New market formed. Rule 4 applies to all bets - deduction 25p in the pound

FOCUS
A fillies' novice that was significantly weakened late on with both Three Coins and Quiet Words, the market leaders, having to be withdrawn. Improvement from the winner.

3197 FOLLOW REDCARRACING ON FACEBOOK & TWITTER MAIDEN H'CAP (DIV I) 1m 5f 218y
2:50 (2:51) (Class 6) (0-65,65) 3-Y-O
£3,823 (£1,137; £568; £300; £300; £300) **Stalls Low**

Form RPR

-562 **1** **Fantastic Ms Fox**[14] 2712 3-9-1 **59** TonyHamilton 2 65
(Richard Fahey) *in tch: pushed along over 3f out: rdn to chse ldrs over 1f out: led 150yds out: styd on* **11/4**[1]

0006 **2** nk **Champagne Marengo (IRE)**[21] 2511 3-8-10 **54** (p) GrahamLee 10 60
(Ian Williams) *pressed ldr: rdn to ld over 2f out: hdd over 1f out but remained chalng: styd on (vet reported gelding bled from the nose)* **33/1**

000- **3** 1/2 **Anyonecanhaveitall**[216] 8549 3-9-7 **65** JoeFanning 5 70
(Mark Johnston) *midfield: hdwy and trckd ldrs 9f out: pushed along over 2f out: rdn into narrow ld over 1f out: sn rdn: hdd 150yds out: no ex and short of room nr fin* **3/1**[2]

600- **4** 1 1/2 **Land Of Oz**[220] 8420 3-9-2 **60** RyanTate 4 63+
(Sir Mark Prescott Bt) *trckd ldrs: pushed along over 4f out: rdn over 2f out: lugged lft and n.m.r bhd horses: swtchd rt ins fnl f: styd on* **11/4**[1]

6-04 **5** 6 **Sea Art**[26] 2343 3-9-6 **64** (v) DavidProbert 7 58
(William Knight) *led narrowly: rdn and hdd over 2f out: wknd fnl f* **13/2**[3]

00-5 **6** 1 1/4 **Flo Jo's Girl**[14] 2712 3-8-5 **49** RachelRichardson 8 42
(Tim Easterby) *hld up in rr: pushed along and sme hdwy 3f out: rdn 2f out: wknd ins fnl f* **14/1**

6050 **7** 1/2 **Munstead Moonshine**[45] 1770 3-8-2 **46** (b[1]) DuranFentiman 1 38
(Andrew Balding) *hld up: rdn along over 3f out: nvr threatened* **14/1**

6-00 **8** hd **Feebi**[30] 2148 3-7-12 **47** oh1 ow1 PaulaMuir(5) 3 39
(Chris Fairhurst) *hld up: rdn along over 3f out: nvr threatened* **33/1**

9 16 **Bendzonic (IRE)**[16] 2664 3-9-3 **61** (p[1]) RobbieDowney 6 30
(Denis Gerard Hogan, Ire) *midfield on outer: hung lft and wknd over 2f out* **22/1**

000 **10** 7 **Lexington Warlord**[18] 2581 3-7-13 **48** oh1 ow2 (b[1]) SeanDavis(5) 9 7
(Richard Hannon) *trckd ldrs: lost pl and dropped to midfield 9f out: rdn along over 4f out: hung lft and wknd over 2f out (vet reported gelding finished lame on its right fore)* **50/1**

3m 4.7s (-2.30) **Going Correction** +0.025s/f (Good) **10 Ran SP% 117.2**
Speed ratings (Par 97): **107,106,106,105,102 101,101,101,92,88**
CSF £101.31 CT £294.15 TOTE £3.50: £1.50, £8.10, £1.10; EX 89.70 Trifecta £247.70.
Owner Mel Roberts & Ms Nicola Meese 1 **Bred** Mel Roberts & R A Fahey **Trained** Musley Bank, N Yorks

FOCUS
The first leg of a moderate 3yo staying handicap, it was run at a fair gallop and provided a good test at the distance. The winner can perhaps be rated a shade better than the bare facts.

3198 FOLLOW REDCARRACING ON FACEBOOK & TWITTER MAIDEN H'CAP (DIV II) 1m 5f 218y
3:20 (3:20) (Class 6) (0-65,64) 3-Y-O
£3,823 (£1,137; £568; £300; £300; £300) **Stalls Low**

Form RPR

0-44 **1** **Victoriano (IRE)**[8] 2913 3-9-3 **60** (b) EdwardGreatrex 2 66
(Archie Watson) *midfield: wnt a little in snatches: bit outpcd and hmpd over 3f out: rdn and hdwy to 2f out: styd on wl to ld 50yds out* **10/3**[2]

2220 **2** 1 1/4 **Rich Cummins**[30] 2150 3-9-4 **61** JoeFanning 3 65
(Mark Johnston) *led: rdn and pressed over 1f out: hdd 50yds out: one pce* **2/1**[1]

5020 **3** nk **Robeam (IRE)**[21] 2517 3-8-9 **52** TonyHamilton 9 56
(Richard Fahey) *midfield: rdn and hdwy to chse ldrs 2f out: styd on* **8/1**

0-40 **4** 2 **Battle Of Pembroke (USA)**[77] 1165 3-9-5 **62** DavidProbert 7 63
(David Simcock) *hld up: hdwy and trckd ldrs on inner 3f out: rdn along 2f out: n.m.r fr over 1f out til swtchd lft 110yds: drvn and one pce* **9/2**[3]

50-6 **5** nk **Geyser**[23] 2438 3-8-2 **45** DuranFentiman 4 45
(Barry Murtagh) *prom: rdn to chal strly over 1f out: no ex fnl 110yds* **66/1**

2346 **6** nk **Tabou Beach Boy**[8] 2913 3-8-13 **56** (p) GrahamLee 1 56
(Michael Easterby) *trckd ldrs: rdn over 2f out: no ex fnl 110yds* **5/1**

05-0 **7** 1/2 **Play It By Ear (IRE)**[29] 2200 3-9-7 **64** DanielTudhope 8 63
(David O'Meara) *hld up in rr: bit clsr 3f out: rdn 2f out: kpt on ins fnl f* **10/1**

0-00 **8** 28 **Ventura Island (FR)**[29] 2213 3-7-13 **47** (b[1]) SeanDavis(5) 6 7
(Richard Hannon) *trckd ldrs: rdn over 3f out: sn wknd* **20/1**

000 **9** 9 **Yasmin From York**[10] 2845 3-8-2 **45** NathanEvans 5
(Brian Rothwell) *hld up: rdn over 3f out: sn wknd* **66/1**

3m 5.14s (-1.86) **Going Correction** +0.025s/f (Good) **9 Ran SP% 119.2**
Speed ratings (Par 97): **106,105,105,103,103 103,103,87,82**
CSF £10.70 CT £48.98 TOTE £3.60: £1.20, £1.30, £2.50; EX 11.70 Trifecta £55.00.

Owner Ebury Racing 3 **Bred** Godolphin **Trained** Upper Lambourn, W Berks
FOCUS
They went more steadily in this than the first leg and the time was 0.44secs slower. Ordinary form.

3199 JOIN RACING TV NOW H'CAP 7f 219y
3:50 (3:55) (Class 5) (0-70,72) 4-Y-0+
£4,075 (£1,212; £606; £303; £300; £300) **Stalls** Centre

Form RPR
0-02 1 **Verdigris (IRE)**[8] 2911 4-8-12 **61** .... TomEaves 4 71+
(Ruth Carr) *stdd s: hld up in rr: smooth hdwy 2f out: led 1f out: kpt on pushed out: cosily* **8/1**
00 2 1 1/4 **First Response**[39] 1925 4-9-9 **72** ....(p[1]) TonyHamilton 3 79
(Linda Stubbs) *midfield: rdn over 2f out: hdwy and chsd ldrs over 1f out: kpt on: wnt 2nd fnl 50yds* **4/1**[1]
60-2 3 3/4 **Tukhoom (IRE)**[32] 2076 6-9-7 **70** .... DuranFentiman 1 75
(Michael Herrington) *trckd ldrs: rdn over 2f out: chal strly 1f out: one pce ins fnl f: lost 2nd fnl 50yds* **11/2**[3]
1-20 4 1/2 **Placebo Effect (IRE)**[14] 2710 4-9-5 **71** .... BenRobinson(3) 7 75
(Ollie Pears) *midfield: rdn over 2f out: kpt on ins fnl f* **4/1**[1]
50-0 5 2 1/2 **Coviglia (IRE)**[21] 2509 5-9-2 **65** .... NathanEvans 6 63
(Jacqueline Coward) *trckd ldrs: rdn over 2f out: outpcd over 1f out* **33/1**
0-06 6 2 **Fake News**[17] 2628 4-9-7 **70** ....(b) RobbieDowney 2 64
(David Barron) *led narrowly: rdn over 2f out: drvn and hdd 1f out: sn wknd* **10/1**
010- 7 1 **Shamaheart (IRE)**[225] 8262 9-9-0 **63** ....(p) DavidAllan 10 54
(Geoffrey Harker) *hld up: pushed along over 1f out: nvr threatened* **50/1**
3212 8 3/4 **Zodiakos (IRE)**[5] 3002 6-9-0 **68** ....(p) BenSanderson(5) 12 58
(Roger Fell) *prom: rdn over 2f out: drvn to chal strly over 1f out: wknd ins fnl f* **9/2**[2]
0-00 9 nk **Jennies Gem**[28] 2241 6-8-2 **56** oh11 .... FayeMcManoman(5) 5 45
(Ollie Pears) *prom: rdn and lost pl 3f out: no threat after* **66/1**
-000 10 1 **Stoneyford Lane (IRE)**[17] 2632 5-8-8 **57** .... DavidProbert 8 44
(Steph Hollinshead) *chsd ldrs: rdn over 2f out: wknd over 1f out* **33/1**
5054 11 1/2 **Dubai Acclaim (IRE)**[10] 2842 4-9-2 **70** .... SeanDavis(5) 15 56
(Richard Fahey) *trckd ldrs: rdn over 2f out: wknd over 1f out (vet reported gelding lost both of its front shoes)* **9/1**
-006 12 2 **Etikaal**[10] 2846 5-8-13 **62** ....(p) KevinStott 13 43
(Grant Tuer) *hld up: nvr threatened* **33/1**
-600 13 4 1/2 **Jo's Girl (IRE)**[21] 2509 4-9-2 **65** ....(t) DougieCostello 11 36
(Micky Hammond) *a towards rr* **50/1**
-035 14 2 **How Bizarre**[15] 2679 4-9-8 **71** .... GrahamLee 14 37
(Liam Bailey) *prom: rdn 3f out: sn wknd* **25/1**
1m 39.15s (2.55) **Going Correction** +0.025s/f (Good) **14** Ran SP% **121.9**
Speed ratings (Par 103): **88,86,86,85,83 81,80,79,78,77 77,75,70,68**
CSF £38.55 CT £171.63 TOTE £8.40: £2.50, £2.00, £1.70; EX 58.90 Trifecta £317.10.
Owner Ms Gillian Khosla **Bred** Vimal And Gillian Khosla **Trained** Huby, N Yorks
■ Hitman was withdrawn. Price at time of withdrawal 25/1. Rule 4 does not apply
FOCUS
Modest form, but a progressive winner. The form seems sound.

3200 WATCH IRISH RACING ON RACINGTV MEDIAN AUCTION MAIDEN STKS 1m 2f 1y
4:20 (4:28) (Class 5) 3-5-Y-O **£4,528** (£1,347; £673; £336) **Stalls** Low

Form RPR
20 1 **Sneaky Peek**[20] 2524 3-8-9 0 .... DavidProbert 14 76+
(Andrew Balding) *prom: pushed along to ld over 2f out: rdn over 1f out: pressed briefly appr fnl f: styd on to draw clr ins fnl f* **5/1**[1]
04- 2 3 1/2 **No Dress Rehearsal**[187] 9203 3-8-9 0 .... NathanEvans 4 69
(Michael Easterby) *trckd ldrs: rdn along 3f out: chal appr fnl f: one pce ins fnl f* **15/2**[2]
3-2 3 2 1/2 **Sweet Marmalade (IRE)**[24] 2417 4-9-4 0 .... FayeMcManoman(5) 5 65
(Lawrence Mullaney) *in tch: rdn over 3f out: styd on fr over 1f out to go 3rd fnl 50yds* **40/1**
53 4 3 1/2 **Tadasana**[15] 2690 3-8-9 0 .... EdwardGreatrex 8 57
(Archie Watson) *led: rdn and hdd over 2f out: wknd fnl f: lost 3rd fnl 50yds* **20/1**
5 2 1/2 **Vintage Rose** 3-8-9 0 .... KevinStott 3 52
(Mark Walford) *dwlt: hld up: styd on fnl 2f: nvr involved* **80/1**
6-0 6 hd **Ateescomponent (IRE)**[14] 2713 3-9-0 0 .... TonyHamilton 12 57
(David Barron) *in tch: rdn over 3f out: wknd over 1f out* **125/1**
0 7 6 **Stormin Norman**[21] 2505 4-10-0 0 .... GrahamLee 2 46
(Micky Hammond) *nvr bttr than midfield* **50/1**
0 8 3 1/4 **Fasterkhani**[8] 2912 3-9-0 0 .... AndrewElliott 10 38
(Philip Kirby) *hld up: sme hdwy over 1f out: nvr involved* **100/1**
6-0 9 9 **Gordalan**[8] 2912 3-9-0 0 .... DougieCostello 9 20
(Philip Kirby) *a towards rr* **125/1**
05 10 2 1/2 **Gloryella**[25] 2375 3-8-9 0 .... TomEaves 6 10
(Ruth Carr) *hld up: wknd over 2f out* **150/1**
11 6 **Gracie** 3-8-9 0 .... JoeFanning 11
(James Fanshawe) *trckd ldrs: rdn over 4f out: sn wknd* **8/1**[3]
60 12 8 **Freshfield Ferris**[8] 2912 3-8-8 0 ow2 .... BenRobinson(3) 13
(Brian Rothwell) *midfield: wknd over 2f out* **150/1**
6 13 37 **Melwood**[36] 1984 3-9-0 0 .... DavidAllan 7
(Antony Brittain) *hld up in midfield: wknd over 3f out: eased and t.o* **125/1**
14 11 **Thinking Cutely** 3-8-9 0 .... DuranFentiman 15
(Antony Brittain) *slowly away: a in rr* **100/1**
2m 7.23s (0.33) **Going Correction** +0.025s/f (Good)
WFA 3 from 4yo 14lb **14** Ran SP% **55.6**
Speed ratings (Par 103): **99,96,94,91,89 89,84,81,74,72 67,61,31,23**
CSF £5.47 TOTE £3.00: £1.10, £1.60, £3.80; EX 13.80 Trifecta £80.60.
Owner Kingsclere Racing Club **Bred** Kingsclere Stud **Trained** Kingsclere, Hants
■ Hamish was withdrawn. Price at time of withdrawal 1/3F. Rule 4 applies to all bets - deduction 70p in the pound
FOCUS
With the late withdrawal of red-hot favourite Hamish, who refused to go in the stalls, this was left looking a modest maiden, in terms of depth anyway. They were strung out a long way from the finish and the winner built on his debut promise.

3201 WATCH RACING TV IN STUNNING HD FILLIES' H'CAP 5f
4:50 (4:55) (Class 4) (0-85,87) 4-Y-0+
£6,663 (£1,982; £990; £495; £300; £300) **Stalls** Centre

Form RPR
51-0 1 **Machree (IRE)**[40] 1899 4-9-0 **80** .... CianMacRedmond(7) 5 88
(Declan Carroll) *mde all: drvn and edgd rt 2f out: rdr dropped whip over 1f out: kpt on (trainer's rep said, regarding the improved form shown, the filly stripped fitter for its seasonal reappearance)* **14/1**
20-0 2 3/4 **Queens Gift (IRE)**[18] 2588 4-9-7 **80** .... TomEaves 2 85
(Michael Dods) *hld up: swtchd rt over 1f out: pushed along and sn over 1f out: rdn and kpt on wl fnl f* **10/1**
-353 3 nk **Seen The Lyte (IRE)**[18] 2589 4-9-3 **79** ....(h) RowanScott(3) 4 83
(Nigel Tinkler) *dwlt: sn chsd ldr: rdn 2f out: kpt on fnl f* **11/1**
0-14 4 shd **Boundary Lane**[10] 2839 4-9-6 **79** .... GrahamLee 1 83+
(Julie Camacho) *stmbld bdly s and slowly away: hld up in rr: pushed along and hdwy over 1f out: kpt on fnl f (jockey said filly stumbled leaving the stalls)* **2/1**[1]
040- 5 2 1/2 **Stewardess (IRE)**[187] 9212 4-9-0 **73** .... TonyHamilton 6 68
(Richard Fahey) *chsd ldrs: rdn over 2f out: outpcd over 1f out: plugged on fnl f* **50/1**
1010 6 hd **Midnight Malibu (IRE)**[34] 2030 6-10-0 **87** .... RachelRichardson 3 81
(Tim Easterby) *chsd ldr: rdn and outpcd over 2f out: plugged on fnl f* **11/1**
4610 7 1 3/4 **Bellevarde (IRE)**[15] 2687 5-9-4 **77** .... EdwardGreatrex 10 65
(Richard Price) *chsd ldrs: rdn over 2f out: wknd over 1f out* **33/1**
-401 8 1/2 **Dandy's Beano (IRE)**[17] 2637 4-8-12 **71** ....(h) KevinStott 9 57
(Kevin Ryan) *dwlt: hld up: rdn 2f out: wknd over 1f out* **9/1**
0/ 9 1/2 **Betsey Trotter (IRE)**[29] 2220 4-9-4 **77** .... DanielTudhope 8 61
(David O'Meara) *hld up: rdn over 2f out: wknd over 1f out* **13/2**[3]
/401 10 nk **Fair Cop**[25] 2358 5-9-5 **78** ....(p) DavidProbert 7 61
(Andrew Balding) *chsd ldr: rdn over 2f out: edgd lft over 1f out and wknd (vet reported mare had bled from the nose)* **7/2**[2]
59.06s (0.56) **Going Correction** +0.025s/f (Good) **10** Ran SP% **116.2**
Speed ratings (Par 102): **96,94,94,94,90 89,87,86,85,84**
CSF £145.42 CT £1601.45 TOTE £15.70: £3.80, £2.90, £2.90; EX 146.00 Trifecta £1126.10.
Owner B Cooney **Bred** Camogue Stud Ltd **Trained** Malton, N Yorks
FOCUS
No hanging around here with the winner blasting them from the word go. With the jockey's claim, this rated a pb from her.

3202 RACING TV PROFITS RETURNED TO RACING H'CAP 5f 217y
5:20 (5:24) (Class 5) (0-75,75) 3-Y-O
£4,075 (£1,212; £606; £303; £300; £300) **Stalls** Centre

Form RPR
112 1 **Inspired Thought (IRE)**[25] 2380 3-9-7 **75** .... DanielTudhope 1 87+
(Archie Watson) *trckd ldrs: pushed into narrow ld appr fnl f: rdn ins fnl f: hld on wl* **7/4**[1]
31-2 2 1/2 **Magical Spirit (IRE)**[57] 1488 3-9-3 **71** .... KevinStott 6 81
(Kevin Ryan) *prom: led over 2f out: rdn and edgd lft over 1f out: hdd appr fnl f: kpt on but a hld* **8/1**
00-2 3 2 **Northernpowerhouse**[17] 2635 3-9-5 **73** .... GrahamLee 3 77
(Bryan Smart) *midfield: rdn over 2f out: kpt on ins fnl f: wnt 3rd fnl 50yds* **4/1**[2]
2142 4 1 1/2 **Ascot Dreamer**[9] 2870 3-8-3 **57** ....(t) DuranFentiman 2 56
(David Brown) *trckd ldrs: rdn 2f out: no ex ins fnl f: lost 3rd fnl 50yds* **15/2**
5340 5 1 1/2 **Muhallab (IRE)**[29] 2197 3-8-2 **56** ....(w) JoeFanning 5 50
(Adrian Nicholls) *led: rdn and hdd over 2f out: no ex fnl f* **33/1**
46-3 6 2 1/4 **Defence Treaty (IRE)**[33] 2055 3-8-10 **69** .... SeanDavis(5) 10 56
(Richard Fahey) *hld up: sn pushed along: kpt on fnl f: nvr threatened* **20/1**
-452 7 2 **Arletta Star**[8] 2896 3-8-6 **60** .... RachelRichardson 7 41
(Tim Easterby) *trckd ldrs: rdn 2f out: wknd fnl f* **6/1**[3]
-041 8 nk **Murqaab**[17] 2633 3-9-1 **69** ....(b) DavidAllan 4 49
(John Balding) *hld up in midfield: rdn over 2f out: sn btn* **33/1**
636- 9 1 1/4 **Olivia R (IRE)**[251] 7414 3-9-1 **69** .... TonyHamilton 11 45
(David Barron) *dwlt: hld up: rdn 2f out: nvr threatened* **40/1**
2045 10 1/2 **Fair Alibi**[17] 2635 3-9-0 **68** .... TomEaves 12 42
(Tom Tate) *dwlt: hld up: rdn over 2f out: sn btn* **20/1**
-330 11 1 **Fume (IRE)**[27] 2293 3-9-3 **71** .... DavidProbert 8 42
(James Bethell) *midfield: rdn along 3f out: wknd over 1f out* **25/1**
-032 12 3/4 **Seanjohnsilver (IRE)**[9] 2871 3-8-4 **58** ....(t) JimmyQuinn 9 27
(Declan Carroll) *trckd ldrs: rdn over 2f out: wknd over 1f out (jockey said gelding stopped quickly)* **16/1**
1m 11.8s **Going Correction** +0.025s/f (Good) **12** Ran SP% **121.1**
Speed ratings (Par 99): **105,104,101,99,97 94,92,91,89,89 87,86**
CSF £15.22 CT £53.29 TOTE £2.30: £1.10, £2.80, £1.70; EX 17.20 Trifecta £51.30.
Owner Clipper Logistics **Bred** L Wright **Trained** Upper Lambourn, W Berks
FOCUS
Modest enough sprint form, but an unexposed and progressive winner. The form's rated around the race average.

3203 WATCH RACE REPLAYS AT RACINGTV.COM AMATEUR RIDERS' H'CAP 5f 217y
5:55 (5:57) (Class 6) (0-65,66) 4-Y-0+
£3,770 (£1,169; £584; £300; £300; £300) **Stalls** Centre

Form RPR
0335 1 **Mansfield**[31] 2122 6-10-5 **55** .... MissJoannaMason 10 62
(Stella Barclay) *trckd ldrs: rdn to ld appr fnl f: kpt on* **7/1**
-013 2 3/4 **Supaulette (IRE)**[8] 2899 4-11-2 **66** ....(bt) MissEmilyEasterby 1 71
(Tim Easterby) *dwlt: sn in tch: hdwy and chal ent fnl f: kpt on pushed out: sddle slipped shortly after s (jockey said her saddle slipped shortly after the start)* **4/1**[3]
1121 3 3/4 **Steelriver (IRE)**[7] 2940 9-10-11 **61** 4ex .... MrPatrickMillman 11 64
(Michael Herrington) *hld up: rdn along and hdwy over 1f out: kpt on fnl f* **6/1**
600- 4 3/4 **Pearl's Calling (IRE)**[223] 8326 4-9-7 **50** oh5 .... AidanMacdonald(7) 6 51
(Ron Barr) *outpcd in rr tl kpt on fr over 1f out: nrst fin* **125/1**
0552 5 nse **Shepherd's Purse**[21] 2514 7-10-9 **64** .... MissEmilyBullock(5) 5 64
(Ruth Carr) *led narrowly: rdn 2f out: edgd rt ahd hdd appr fnl f: no ex* **3/1**[2]
0000 6 2 **Royal Connoisseur (IRE)**[10] 2846 8-10-1 **58** ..(v) MrEireannCagney(7) 8 52
(Richard Fahey) *pressed ldr: rdn over 2f out: wknd fnl f* **40/1**

0002 **7** ½ **Letmestopyouthere (IRE)**[30] 2145 5-10-7 **57**(p) MissBrodieHampson 9 50
(Archie Watson) *s.i.s: hld up: sn pushed along and sn hung lft: hdwy into midfield over 2f out: no further imp (jockey said gelding hung left throughout)* **5/2**[1]

200- **8** ½ **Sunstorm**[211] 8704 4-10-1 **56**.................. MissKellyAdams(5) 12 47
(Stef Keniry) *dwlt: hld up: nvr involved* **50/1**

00-0 **9** ¾ **Mitchum**[17] 2632 10-9-9 **50** oh3..........................(p) MissSarahBowen(5) 3 39
(Ron Barr) *chsd ldrs: rdn over 2f out: wknd fnl f* **40/1**

0162 **10** 1½ **Who Told Jo Jo (IRE)**[3] 3089 5-10-1 **58**......... MissMatildaBlundell(7) 13 43
(Joseph Tuite) *a towards rr* **20/1**

-005 **11** ¾ **B Fifty Two (IRE)**[9] 2876 10-11-0 **64**..........................(vt) MrJohnDawson 2 46
(Marjorie Fife) *chsd ldrs: rdn over 2f out: wknd over 1f out* **20/1**

00-0 **12** 5 **Khitaamy (IRE)**[21] 2509 5-10-7 **57**..........................(t[1]) MissEmmaTodd 4 24
(Tina Jackson) *midfield: rdn over 2f out: wknd over 1f out* **33/1**

1m 12.92s (1.12) **Going Correction** +0.025s/f (Good) **12** Ran SP% **120.5**
Speed ratings (Par 101): **97,96,95,94,93 91,90,89,88,86 85,79**
CSF £33.61 CT £186.07 TOTE £9.70: £2.80, £1.50, £1.90; EX 39.40 Trifecta £249.10.
Owner The Style Council **Bred** Newsells Park Stud **Trained** Garstang, Lancs
■ Moonshine Dancer was withdrawn. Price at time of withdrawal 66/1. Rule 4 does not apply

FOCUS
Moderate form and the runner-up would surely have won but for a slipped saddle. The fourth limits the form.
T/Jkpt: Partly Won. £10,000.00 to a £1 stake. Pool: £14,084.51 - 0.5 winning unit. T/Plt: £84.60 to a £1 stake. Pool: £62,071.28 - 535.0 winning units T/Qpdt: £26.50 to a £1 stake. Pool: £5,210.70 - 145.04 winning units **Andrew Sheret**

2527 SOUTHWELL (L-H)
Tuesday, May 28

OFFICIAL GOING: Fibresand: standard (watered)
Wind: Moderate half behind Weather: Cloudy with heavy showers

3204 DOWNLOAD THE MANSIONBET APP H'CAP — 1m 13y(F)
6:10 (6:10) (Class 6) (0-65,65) 3-Y-O

£3,105 (£924; £461; £300; £300; £300) **Stalls** Low

Form RPR

5406 **1** **Geography Teacher (IRE)**[7] 2943 3-8-8 **52**..................(p) BenCurtis 1 60
(Roger Fell) *in tch: hdwy over 3f out: chal 2f out and sn rdn: drvn to ld appr fnl f: kpt on strly (trainer's rep said, regarding the improved form shown, the gelding jumped better from the stalls on this occasion)* **16/1**

3041 **2** 2½ **Crazy Spin**[20] 2531 3-8-2 **49**..........................(p) GabrieleMalune(3) 12 51
(Ivan Furtado) *qckly away: sn led and swtchd lft to inner: pushed along 3f out: jnd and rdn 2f out: hdd and drvn appr fnl f: kpt on same pce towards fin* **5/1**[3]

6012 **3** 4½ **Termonator**[22] 2482 3-9-7 **65**.......................... SamJames 10 57
(Grant Tuer) *dwlt and sn pushed along in rr: hdwy on outer over 3f out: wd st: sn chsng ldrs: rdn and edgd lft over 1f out: kpt on fnl f* **5/2**[1]

6046 **4** 1 **Monsieur Piquer (FR)**[30] 2152 3-8-9 **60**..............(v) JonathanFisher(7) 5 50
(K R Burke) *midfield: hdwy and in tch 3f out: rdn to chse ldrs over 2f out: drvn over 1f out: kpt on one pce* **11/1**

-605 **5** 4 **Biscuit Queen**[29] 2190 3-8-4 **48**..........................(b) CamHardie 11 28
(Brian Ellison) *prom: pushed along over 3f out: rdn wl over 2f out: grad wknd* **22/1**

6301 **6** 2¾ **Peruvian Summer (IRE)**[29] 2190 3-9-6 **64**.................. JackMitchell 3 38
(Kevin Frost) *trckd ldrs on inner: pushed along 3f out: rdn over 2f out: sn drvn and wknd (trainer could offer no explanation for the gelding's performance)* **4/1**[2]

660 **7** 1 **Luna Princess**[19] 2550 3-8-5 **54**.......................... TheodoreLadd(5) 2 26
(Michael Appleby) *prom: rdn along 3f out: sn wknd* **40/1**

-003 **8** 2¼ **Dark Glory (IRE)**[5] 2995 3-9-1 **64**..........................(v[1]) ThomasGreatrex(5) 8 31
(Brian Meehan) *in rr: sme hdwy on inner 3f out: rdn along over 2f out: nvr nr ldrs* **12/1**

-031 **9** 3 **Spirit Of Angel (IRE)**[26] 2322 3-9-7 **65**.................. RoystonFfrench 13 25
(Marcus Tregoning) *in tch on outer: rdn along to chse ldrs over 3f out: drvn wl over 2f out: sn wknd* **8/1**

000- **10** 2¼ **Ramatuelle**[246] 7607 3-8-10 **54**.......................... RyanTate 9 9
(Sir Mark Prescott Bt) *a towards rr* **20/1**

500- **11** ¾ **Big Ian**[215] 8575 3-8-13 **57**.......................... ShaneKelly 7 10
(Alan Jones) *a towards rr* **33/1**

000- **12** 24 **Ocean Reach**[187] 9208 3-8-2 **46** oh1.................. KieranO'Neill 4
(Richard Price) *chsd ldrs: rdn along wl over 3f out: sn wknd* **40/1**

006- **13** 1¼ **Amelia R (IRE)**[223] 8323 3-9-0 **58**.......................... ConnorBeasley 6
(Ray Craggs) *in tch: chsd ldrs wl over 3f out: sn rdn along and wknd* **20/1**

1m 43.84s (0.14) **Going Correction** -0.05s/f (Stan) **13** Ran SP% **119.9**
Speed ratings (Par 97): **97,94,90,89,85 82,81,79,76,73 73,49,47**
CSF £86.80 CT £281.48 TOTE £10.70: £2.00, £1.80, £1.60; EX 183.30 Trifecta £1599.10.
Owner Northern Marking Ltd & Partners **Bred** E Higgins **Trained** Nawton, N Yorks

FOCUS
The kickback was bad through the card. An open handicap run at a sound pace with the front two pulling clear. The form's rated cautiously.

3205 MANSIONBET YOUR FAVOURITE PLACE TO BET H'CAP — 1m 6f 21y(F)
6:40 (6:44) (Class 6) (0-60,62) 4-Y-O+

£3,105 (£924; £461; £300; £300; £300) **Stalls** Low

Form RPR

012 **1** **Heron (USA)**[18] 2593 5-9-7 **60**..........................(p) DanielMuscutt 7 70
(Brett Johnson) *trckd ldrs: hdwy over 3f out: chal over 2f out: sn led: drvn ent fnl f: styd on strly* **5/1**[3]

6-31 **2** 3½ **Thahab Ifraj (IRE)**[9] 2196 6-8-10 **49**.......................... BenCurtis 1 54
(Alexandra Dunn) *trckd ldrs on inner: hdwy over 3f out: cl up 2f out: sn rdn and ev ch: drvn ent fnl f: kpt on same pce* **9/2**[2]

3232 **3** 3½ **Siyahamba (IRE)**[15] 2684 5-8-8 **47**.......................... CamHardie 6 48
(Bryan Smart) *trckd ldrs: hdwy over 3f out: chse ldr wl over 2f out: sn led: rdn and hdd 2f out: drvn over 1f out: wknd fnl f* **11/2**

1-30 **4** 10 **Constituent**[14] 185 4-8-3 **47**..........................(b[1]) TheodoreLadd(5) 13 35
(Michael Appleby) *sn chsng ldr: hdwy over 4f out and sn cl up: rdn along 3f out: drvn over 2f out: sn one pce* **25/1**

50-0 **5** nk **Prairie Town (IRE)**[18] 2591 8-9-1 **54**..........................(p) FrannyNorton 4 42
(Tony Carroll) *bhd and sn rdn along: detached 7f out: hdwy 4f out: chsd ldrs 3f out: sn drvn and kpt on one pce* **12/1**

0630 **6** 1½ **Lady Makfi (IRE)**[29] 2196 7-9-1 **54**.......................... ShaneKelly 2 40
(Johnny Farrelly) *trckd ldrs: hdwy 4f out: rdn along 3f out: drvn over 2f out: sn outpcd* **50/1**

560- **7** 3¾ **Kaylen's Mischief**[371] 2943 6-8-7 **46** oh1..........................(h) JFEgan 12 27
(D J Jeffreys) *bhd: sme hdwy 1/2-way: rdn along wl over 3f out: nvr a factor* **33/1**

5140 **8** 4½ **Love Rat**[4] 3054 4-9-9 **62**..........................(be[1]) KieranO'Neill 11 37
(Scott Dixon) *led: clr after 4f: pushed along and jnd 4f out: rdn over 3f out: sn drvn and hdd: sn wknd* **8/1**

6266 **9** 99 **Demophon**[28] 2239 5-8-9 **48**.......................... NicolaCurrie 3
(Steve Flook) *a bhd: t.o fr over 3f out (jockey said gelding was never travelling)* **20/1**

30-1 **10** shd **Chetwynd Abbey**[20] 2528 4-9-9 **62**.......................... GeorgeWood 8
(James Fanshawe) *hld up towards rr: pushed along after 4f: swtchd rt and rdn along 7f out: sn drvn: outpcd and bhd: over 4f out: eased and t.o fr over 3f out (jockey said filly didn't face the kickback; starter reported that the filly was reluctant to load; trainer was informed that the filly could not run until the day after passing a stalls test)* **11/4**[1]

44/0 **P** **Asknotwhat (IRE)**[6] 2970 8-8-13 **55**..........................(bt) FinleyMarsh(3) 10
(Tom Gretton) *chsd ldrs: rdn along and lost pl 1/2-way: sn bhd: t.o whn p.u 2f out (jockey said gelding hung badly left and lost its action approximately 1f out when tailed off)* **66/1**

R **Yo Tambien**[20] 2536 4-9-3 **56**..........................(tp) RobbieDowney 5
(John C McConnell, Ire) *ref to r (starter reported that the filly was reluctant to load; trainer was informed that the filly could not run until the day after passing a stalls test)* **14/1**

3m 7.35s (-0.95) **Going Correction** -0.05s/f (Stan) **12** Ran SP% **117.4**
Speed ratings (Par 101): **100,98,96,90,90 89,87,84,27,27** ,
CSF £26.01 CT £129.34 TOTE £6.20: £1.60, £2.20, £1.80; EX 32.00 Trifecta £120.90.
Owner 01 Racing Partnership **Bred** Juddmonte Farms Inc **Trained** Epsom, Surrey

FOCUS
A moderate handicap in which only three mattered.

3206 MANSIONBET H'CAP — 4f 214y(F)
7:10 (7:14) (Class 5) (0-75,76) 4-Y-O+

£3,752 (£1,116; £557; £300; £300; £300) **Stalls** Centre

Form RPR

3102 **1** **Big Time Maybe (IRE)**[21] 2515 4-8-10 **69**..........(p) ScottMcCullagh(7) 2 78
(Michael Attwater) *racd towards far side: cl up: rdn to ld and edgd lft over 1f out: sn drvn and kpt on wl towards fin* **18/1**

3101 **2** ½ **Tricky Dicky**[10] 2846 6-9-7 **73**.......................... BenCurtis 10 80
(Roger Fell) *racd centre: narrow ld: rdn along wl over 1f out: sn hdd: drvn and ev ch ins fnl f: kpt on wl u.p towards fin* **5/2**[1]

4016 **3** 1¼ **Samovar**[10] 2841 4-9-5 **71**..........................(b) PaddyMathers 8 74
(Scott Dixon) *cl up centre: rdn 2f out and ev ch: drvn ent fnl f: kpt on same pce towards fin* **12/1**

1026 **4** 1¼ **Crosse Fire**[17] 2638 7-9-10 **76**..........................(p) KieranO'Neill 5 74
(Scott Dixon) *in tch centre: rdn along 1/2-way: hdwy 2f out: styd on u.p fnl f* **17/2**

0422 **5** shd **Qaaraat**[9] 2876 4-9-7 **73**.......................... CamHardie 11 71
(Antony Brittain) *swtchd lft towards centre s: prom: rdn along 2f out: drvn over 1f out: kpt on same pce fnl f* **16/1**

1305 **6** 3 **Miningold**[17] 2637 6-9-0 **71**..........................(p) PaulaMuir(5) 13 58+
(Michael Dods) *racd nr stands' rail: prom: rdn along over 2f out: drvn wl over 1f out: grad wknd* **14/1**

00-0 **7** 2 **Han Solo Berger (IRE)**[43] 1822 4-9-5 **71**.................. GeorgeWood 3 51
(Chris Wall) *racd towards far side: in tch: rdn along over 2f out: sn no imp* **12/1**

1222 **8** ¾ **Honey Gg**[17] 2637 4-9-1 **67**.......................... CallumShepherd 9 44
(Declan Carroll) *racd centre: towards rr: pushed along 1/2-way: rdn wl over 1f out: hdwy and swtchd rt appr fnl f: sn no imp (jockey said filly didn't face the kickback)* **6/1**[2]

4-20 **9** ¾ **Suwaan (IRE)**[10] 2841 5-9-4 **70**.......................... JackGarritty 4 44
(Ruth Carr) *racd towards centre: cl up: rdn along 2f out: grad wknd* **10/1**

-403 **10** 1½ **Show Palace**[14] 2709 6-9-6 **72**.......................... ConnorBeasley 1 41
(Jennie Candlish) *racd centre: towards rr: rdn along bef 1/2-way: sn bhd* **8/1**[3]

0/0- **11** ¾ **Sahreej (IRE)**[17] 2645 6-8-8 **60**..........................(t) JFEgan 12 26
(Paul W Flynn, Ire) *racd towards stands' side: chsd ldrs: rdn along over 2f out: sn wknd* **33/1**

4250 **12** 3¼ **Eternal Sun**[17] 2637 4-9-7 **76**.......................... GabrieleMalune(3) 7 31
(Ivan Furtado) *sn rdn along and bhd centre: swtchd rt to stands' rail over 3f out: nvr a factor* **20/1**

0220 **13** 6 **Archimedes (IRE)**[88] 970 6-9-0 **66**..........................(tp) JosephineGordon 6
(David C Griffiths) *sn outpcd and bhd in centre: detached fr 1/2-way* **33/1**

59.03s (-0.67) **Going Correction** -0.05s/f (Stan) **13** Ran SP% **117.4**
Speed ratings (Par 103): **103,102,100,98,98 93,90,88,87,85 84,78,69**
CSF £60.46 CT £596.47 TOTE £19.50: £5.80, £1.20, £4.00; EX 79.90 Trifecta £828.40.
Owner Dare To Dream Racing **Bred** Joe Fogarty **Trained** Epsom, Surrey

FOCUS
Plenty of course specialists lined up for this sprint handicap which was run at a decent pace. The first three raced towards the far side and the winner is rated to his best.

3207 MANSIONBET AT SOUTHWELL H'CAP — 6f 16y(F)
7:40 (7:46) (Class 5) (0-70,71) 4-Y-O+

£3,752 (£1,116; £557; £300; £300; £300) **Stalls** Low

Form RPR

2322 **1** **Liamba**[26] 2349 4-9-0 **63**..........................(v[1]) ConorMcGovern(3) 3 77
(David O'Meara) *cl up: led after 2f: rdn clr over 1f out: readily* **7/2**[1]

00-6 **2** 6 **Luzum (IRE)**[14] 2709 4-9-6 **66**.......................... NathanEvans 5 61
(Michael Easterby) *chsd ldrs: hdwy 1/2-way: rdn along 2f out: drvn over 1f out: kpt on ins fnl f: no ch w wnr* **12/1**

2120 **3** 1 **Kraka (IRE)**[31] 2107 4-9-11 **71**..........................(v) KieranO'Neill 11 63
(Christine Dunnett) *cl up: n.m.r and swtchd lft and over 2f out: rdn wl over 1f out: sn drvn and kpt on same pce* **8/1**

2602 **4** shd **Socialites Red**[4] 3056 6-8-9 **62**..........................(p) WilliamCarver(7) 10 53
(Scott Dixon) *towards rr: rdn along and wd st: hdwy nr stands' rail 2f out: kpt on u.p fnl f: nrst fin* **6/1**[3]

450 **5** ½ **Poeta Brasileiro (IRE)**[31] 2122 4-9-0 **65**..........(p[1]) ThomasGreatrex(5) 12 55
(Seamus Durack) *dwlt and towards rr on outer: swtchd markedly lft to inner over 2f out and sn rdn: kpt on: n.d* **16/1**

4342 **6** nk **Global Melody**[18] 2580 4-9-7 **67**..........................(p) JosephineGordon 8 56
(Phil McEntee) *slt ld 2f: cl up: wd st: rdn and edgd rt over 2f out: drvn wl over 1f out: grad wknd* **8/1**

0-20 **7** ½ **Inexes**[26] 2348 7-9-11 **71**..........................(p) LiamKeniry 2 58
(Ivan Furtado) *in tch: hdwy to chse ldrs 1/2-way: rdn wl over 2f out: sn drvn and wknd* **14/1**

0- **8** *11* **Vinnie's Wish (IRE)**[17] 2640 4-9-6 **66**..........................(t) RobbieDowney 6 18
(John C McConnell, Ire) *a in rr* **25/1**

350- **9** *7* **Bobby's Charm (USA)**[260] 7130 4-9-2 **67**..............(p) TheodoreLadd(5) 1
(Scott Dixon) *chsd ldrs on inner: rdn along and lost pl over 3f out: sn in rr* **25/1**

-332 **10** *5* **Gunmaker (IRE)**[28] 2247 5-9-7 **67**.................................. JackGarritty 4
(Ruth Carr) *chsd ldrs on inner: rdn along wl over 2f out: sn drvn and wknd (jockey said gelding didn't face the kickback)* **5/1**[2]

-200 **11** *2 1/4* **Granny Roz**[45] 1760 5-9-11 **71**.................................. ConnorBeasley 9
(Ray Craggs) *a in rr* **20/1**

0-30 **12** *7* **Crystal Deauville (FR)**[28] 2227 4-9-11 **71**........................ ShaneKelly 7
(Gay Kelleway) *dwlt: a in rr (jockey said gelding stumbled leaving the stalls)* **10/1**

1m 15.65s (-0.85) **Going Correction** -0.05s/f (Stan) **12** Ran SP% **117.2**
Speed ratings (Par 103): **103,95,93,93,92 92,91,77,67,61 58,48**
CSF £44.94 CT £315.09 TOTE £3.70: £1.10, £4.00, £2.30; EX 36.00 Trifecta £310.50.
Owner Diamond Racing Ltd **Bred** Thoroughbreds For The Future Ltd **Trained** Upper Helmsley, N Yorks
■ Hollander was withdrawn. Price at time of withdrawal 50/1. Rule 4 does not apply

FOCUS
This looked a competitive race for the grade, but produced a clear winner. The form's hard to pin down.

3208 MANSIONBET BEATEN BY A HEAD H'CAP 7f 14y(F)
8:10 (8:16) (Class 6) (0-60,61) 3-Y-0+
£3,105 (£924; £461; £300; £300; £300) **Stalls** Low

Form RPR

6-03 **1** **Khaan**[6] 2972 4-8-11 **46** oh1.................................. GeorgeBuckell(3) 7 57+
(Michael Appleby) *dwlt and bhd: detached 1/2-way: hdwy and wd st: str run nr stands' rail to chse ldrs over 1f out: sn rdn: led jst ins fnl f: kpt on strly* **13/2**[3]

011 **2** *3 1/4* **Atalanta Queen**[27] 2298 4-9-6 **52**..................................(v) NicolaCurrie 14 55
(Robyn Brisland) *chsd ldrs on outer: hdwy 3f out: chal wl over 1f out: sn rdn and slt ld appr fnl f: sn drvn and hdd jst ins fnl f: kpt on same pce (jockey said filly hung right in the home straight)* **8/1**

2443 **3** *1/2* **Catapult**[13] 2741 4-8-13 **52**..(p) GavinAshton(7) 10 54
(Shaun Keightley) *cl up: led 1/2-way: rdn along over 2f out: drvn over 1f out: hdd appr fnl f: kpt on same pce u.p* **5/1**[2]

600- **4** *2 1/4* **The Game Is On**[248] 7524 3-9-4 **61**.................................. RyanTate 13 53
(Sir Mark Prescott Bt) *in tch on outer: rdn along 3f out: hdwy over 2f out: drvn: edgd lft and kpt on fnl f* **11/1**

2305 **5** *3 1/4* **Bee Machine (IRE)**[17] 2631 4-9-7 **53**........................(t) CallumShepherd 5 40
(Declan Carroll) *trckd ldrs: hdwy over 3f out: chsd ldr wl over 2f out: sn rdn and ev ch: drvn wl over 1f out: grad wknd* **9/2**[1]

-000 **6** *5* **Kimberley Girl**[29] 2197 3-8-12 **55**.................................. NathanEvans 6 25
(Michael Easterby) *in tch: rdn along and outpcd 1/2-way: plugged on fnl 2f* **25/1**

0-00 **7** *1 1/4* **Tigerinmytank**[29] 2197 3-8-6 **49**.................................. RoystonFfrench 8 16
(John Holt) *a towards rr* **50/1**

-560 **8** *2 1/2* **Just Once**[36] 1979 3-9-2 **59**..(v[1]) PaddyMathers 12 20
(Mrs Ilka Gansera-Leveque) *a towards rr* **33/1**

5005 **9** *5* **Magical Ride**[12] 2774 4-9-13 **59**.................................. DanielMuscutt 4 11
(Richard Spencer) *chsd ldrs: rdn along 3f out: sn drvn and wknd* **10/1**

50-0 **10** *nse* **Chez Vegas**[119] 467 6-9-4 **55**.................................. TheodoreLadd(5) 11 7
(Scott Dixon) *chsd ldrs: rdn along wl over 3f out: sn wknd* **16/1**

6-50 **11** *30* **High Contrast**[21] 2510 3-8-12 **60**.............................(p[1]) HarrisonShaw(5) 2
(K R Burke) *led: hdd 1/2-way and sn rdn along on inner: wknd wl over 2f out* **8/1**

1m 30.22s (-0.08) **Going Correction** -0.05s/f (Stan)
WFA 3 from 4yo+ 11lb **11** Ran SP% **102.5**
Speed ratings (Par 101): **98,94,93,91,87 81,80,77,71,71 37**
CSF £42.19 CT £180.16 TOTE £5.70: £2.60, £2.80, £1.10; EX 36.00 Trifecta £150.10.
Owner I R Hatton **Bred** Howdale Bloodstock Ltd **Trained** Oakham, Rutland
■ Fly True and Vicky Cristina were withdrawn. Prices at time of withdrawal 11/2 & 33/1 respectively. Rule 4 applies to all bets - deduct 15p in the pound

FOCUS
A modest contest but the unexposed winner came from a long way back. The form's rated as straightforward.

3209 MANSIONBET PROUD TO SUPPORT BRITISH RACING H'CAP 1m 4f 14y(F)
8:40 (8:41) (Class 6) (0-65,65) 4-Y-0+
£3,105 (£924; £461; £300; £300; £300) **Stalls** Low

Form RPR

6313 **1** **Cold Harbour**[10] 2819 4-8-12 **56**..................................(t) NicolaCurrie 8 64+
(Robyn Brisland) *sn led: rdn along over 2f out: drvn over 1f out: kpt on strly* **11/8**[1]

5-04 **2** *2 1/2* **King Christophe (IRE)**[18] 2593 7-8-13 **57**....................(b) LiamKeniry 2 61
(Peter Fahey, Ire) *trckd ldrs on inner: swtchd rt and smooth hdwy 3f out: chal over 2f out: sn rdn and ev ch tl drvn ent fnl f and kpt on same pce* **9/2**[2]

0-46 **3** *7* **Foresee (GER)**[115] 560 6-9-0 **58**...............................(h[1] w) FrannyNorton 3 51
(Tony Carroll) *trckd ldrs: hdwy 3f out: sn chsng ldng pair and rdn: drvn wl over 1f out: sn no imp* **6/1**

3/5- **4** *4* **Phebes Dream (IRE)**[130] 301 6-8-2 **46** oh1....................(h) CamHardie 4 32
(John C McConnell, Ire) *hld up: hdwy 4f out: effrt 3f out: sn chsng ldrs: rdn over 2f out and sn one pce* **12/1**

020 **5** *3 1/4* **Basildon**[14] 2713 4-8-11 **58**.................................. BenRobinson(3) 1 39
(Brian Ellison) *prom early: pushed along and lost pl after 3f: towards rr: hdwy 5f out: chsd ldrs over 3f out: sn rdn: wknd over 2f out (jockey said gelding was never travelling)* **11/2**[3]

50-0 **6** *7* **Lzaaz (IRE)**[14] 2720 4-8-13 **60**.................................. FinleyMarsh(3) 9 30
(Alan King) *trckd wnr: pushed along 4f out: rdn over 3f out: sn drvn and wknd* **15/2**

/00- **7** *27* **So You Thought (USA)**[242] 7729 5-9-7 **65**..................(bt w) AndrewElliott 6
(Simon West) *sltly hmpd s: a in rr: bhd fnl 3f* **33/1**

/20- **8** *35* **Ceyhan**[65] 2101 7-9-3 **61**..(p[1]) AlistairRawlinson 5
(Barry Brennan) *chsd ldrs: rdn along over 5f out: lost pl and bhd over 4f out: sn t.o (vet said gelding bled from the nose)* **40/1**

2m 39.97s (-1.03) **Going Correction** -0.05s/f (Stan) **8** Ran SP% **114.8**
Speed ratings (Par 101): **101,99,94,92,89 85,67,43**
CSF £7.76 CT £27.49 TOTE £2.00: £1.30, £1.20, £1.80; EX 9.80 Trifecta £34.80.
Owner Mrs Jackie Cornwell And Mrs Jo Brisland **Bred** Exors Of The Late Mrs Liz Nelson **Trained** Danethorpe, Notts

FOCUS
Not a strong handicap but the winner looks progressive. The form could be rated 3lb higher.

T/Plt: £50.10 to a £1 stake. Pool: £71,905.32 - 1,047.53 winning units T/Qpdt: £12.70 to a £1 stake. Pool: £8,542.59 - 496.57 winning units **Joe Rowntree**

3210 - 3211a (Foreign Racing) - See Raceform Interactive

2706 BEVERLEY (R-H)
Wednesday, May 29

OFFICIAL GOING: Good to soft (soft in places; 6.0)
Wind: Moderate across Weather: Cloudy with sunny periods

3212 ETTON CLAIMING STKS 5f
1:40 (1:44) (Class 6) 2-Y-O
£3,492 (£1,039; £519; £300; £300; £300) **Stalls** Low

Form RPR

1 **Allhallowtide (IRE)**[31] 2154 2-8-8 0.................................. FrannyNorton 5 63
(Kevin Thomas Coleman, Ire) *trckd ldrs: pushed along 2f out: hdwy over 1f out: to chse ldr ins fnl f: styd on strly to ld nr line* **10/1**

2132 **2** *nk* **Birkenhead**[19] 2586 2-9-5 0..................................(v) CallumShepherd 4 73
(Mick Channon) *led: rdn clr wl over 1f out: drvn ins fnl f: hdd nr line* **4/6**[1]

20 **3** *hd* **What A Business (IRE)**[13] 2761 2-8-11 0.......................... NicolaCurrie 1 64
(Jamie Osborne) *towards rr: swtchd to inner and hdwy over 2f out: nt clr run and hmpd wl over 1f out: sn swtchd lft and rdn to chse ldrs: styd on wl fnl f (jockey said colt was denied a clear run approx 1 1/2f out)* **4/1**[3]

0 **4** *6* **Not Another Word**[25] 2415 2-8-1 0.......................... FayeMcManoman(5) 3 38
(Nigel Tinkler) *towards rr: hdwy on outer 2f out: sn rdn and edgd rt over 1f out: kpt on fnl f (jockey said saddle slipped)* **40/1**

03 **5** *3 1/4* **Frida Kahlo (IRE)**[27] 2331 2-8-0 0..............................(v[1]) HollieDoyle 6 20
(Archie Watson) *awkward s: in tch: rdn along over 2f out: sn one pce* **7/2**[2]

66 **6** *3 1/2* **Vodka Dawn (IRE)**[27] 2331 2-8-1 0.......................... AndrewBreslin(5) 8 13
(Phillip Makin) *prom: rdn along 1/2-way: sn wknd* **40/1**

06 **7** *2 1/4* **Spiritulist**[28] 2275 2-8-5 0.................................. KieranO'Neill 7 4
(David Evans) *cl up: rdn along over 2f out: sn drvn and wknd* **25/1**

00 **8** *1* **Stittenham**[13] 2780 2-8-0 0.................................. NathanEvans 2
(Michael Easterby) *sn outpcd and a bhd* **50/1**

1m 5.79s (2.89) **Going Correction** +0.60s/f (Yiel) **8** Ran SP% **122.0**
Speed ratings (Par 91): **100,99,99,89,84 78,75,73**
CSF £18.34 TOTE £16.80: £2.40, £1.10, £1.50; EX 32.10 Trifecta £112.90.The winner was claimed by Mr Claes Bjorling for £9,000. What A Business was claimed by Mr R. G. Fell for £8,000.
Owner Mrs Eileen Coleman **Bred** Kevin Coleman **Trained** Kildare, Co Kildare
■ Scotch Corner was withdrawn, price at time of withdrawal 100/1. Rule 4 does not apply.

FOCUS
There had been 26mm of rain over the last two days and the going had eased to good to soft, soft in places (GoingStick 6.0). The inside rail around the bottom bend was out, adding 7yds to races using the bend. The complexion of this claimer changed dramatically in the closing stages. The form's been rated with feet on the ground.

3213 RACING TV NOW IN HD H'CAP 5f
2:10 (2:12) (Class 6) (0-60,60) 3-Y-0+
£3,493 (£1,039; £519; £300; £300; £300) **Stalls** Low

Form RPR

6-56 **1** **Oriental Splendour (IRE)**[12] 2789 7-8-10 **46** oh1.........(p) SamJames 3 53
(Ruth Carr) *in tch: hdwy 2f out: rdn over 1f out: drvn ins fnl f: kpt on strly to ld nr line (trainer said, regarding the apparent improvement in form, she could offer no explanation other than the yard appears to be in better form)* **10/1**

0003 **2** *hd* **Cuppacoco**[18] 2633 4-9-4 **54**.................................. PaulHanagan 6 60
(Ann Duffield) *prom on inner: effrt and n.m.r over 1f out: sn rdn and chal ins fnl f: led briefly towards fin: hdd nr line* **10/1**

-035 **3** *shd* **Groundworker (IRE)**[16] 2678 8-8-8 **47**.......................... BenRobinson(3) 7 53
(Paul Midgley) *cl up: rdn wl over 1f out: led appr fnl f and sn drvn: hdd and no ex towards fin* **12/1**

0-50 **4** *nk* **Optimickstickhill**[21] 2527 4-8-10 **46** oh1....................(b) KieranO'Neill 11 52+
(Scott Dixon) *towards rr: hdwy 1/2-way: rdn and edgd rt wl over 1f out: sn swtchd lft and hdwy to chse ldrs ent fnl f: drvn and styd on wl towards fin (jockey said filly was was denied a clear run approximately 1 1/2 f out)* **25/1**

6-03 **5** *2 1/4* **Glyder**[8] 2924 5-8-11 **47**..(p) RoystonFfrench 4 44
(John Holt) *prom: effrt and cl up wl over 1f out: sn rdn and ev ch: drvn ent fnl f and kpt on same pce* **13/2**

-400 **6** *1/2* **One Boy (IRE)**[18] 2632 8-9-7 **57**.................................. DavidNolan 1 52
(Paul Midgley) *trckd ldrs: effrt and n.m.r over 1f out: rdn ent fnl f: sn drvn and kpt on same pce* **4/1**[1]

0432 **7** *1 3/4* **Pearl Noir**[18] 2632 9-8-13 **54**..................................(b) TheodoreLadd(5) 15 43
(Scott Dixon) *led: rdn along wl over 1f out: drvn and hdd appr fnl f: grad wknd* **14/1**

600- **8** *nk* **Young Tiger**[161] 9617 6-8-12 **48**..................................(h) TomEaves 14 36+
(Tom Tate) *towards rr: hdwy on outer 2f out: sn rdn and no imp* **33/1**

00-3 **9** *1 3/4* **Point Of Woods**[18] 2632 6-9-3 **60**..........................(p) SophieRalston(7) 8 41
(Tina Jackson) *a towards rr* **6/1**[3]

-041 **10** *1/2* **Boudica Bay (IRE)**[16] 2678 4-9-7 **57**.......................... RachelRichardson 10 36+
(Eric Alston) *midfield: rdn along over 2f out: sn drvn and n.d* **5/1**[2]

0-50 **11** *1 1/2* **Quduraat**[124] 409 3-9-1 **59**.................................. AlistairRawlinson 2 30
(Michael Appleby) *a towards rr* **20/1**

00-4 **12** *2* **Ambitious Icarus**[18] 2632 10-9-2 **52**..........................(h) PhilipPrince 12 19
(Richard Guest) *in tch on outer: rdn along 1/2-way: sn wknd* **25/1**

0000 **13** *nk* **Foxy Boy**[16] 2678 5-8-10 **46**.................................. DavidAllan 17 12
(Rebecca Bastiman) *in tch on outer: rdn along over 2f out: sn wknd* **20/1**

1240 **14** *hd* **Spirit Of Zebedee (IRE)**[18] 2638 6-9-7 **57**.......................... DougieCostello 9 22
(John Quinn) *a in rr* **14/1**

6100 **15** *1 3/4* **Furni Factors**[21] 2527 4-9-5 **55**..................................(b) AndrewElliott 16 14
(Ronald Thompson) *chsd ldrs on outer: rdn along over 2f out: sn wknd* **40/1**

1m 5.16s (2.26) **Going Correction** +0.60s/f (Yiel)
WFA 3 from 4yo+ 8lb **15** Ran SP% **126.1**
Speed ratings (Par 101): **105,104,104,104,100 99,96,96,93,92 90,87,86,86,83**
CSF £100.81 CT £1241.35 TOTE £10.70: £3.20, £2.90, £4.20; EX 107.00 Trifecta £1492.70.
Owner J A Swinburne & Mrs Ruth A Carr **Bred** H R H Sultan Ahmad Shah **Trained** Huby, N Yorks

FOCUS
There was a bunched finish to this ordinary sprint handicap, which was dominated by those drawn low.

3214 VERY HAPPY RETIREMENT BILL GRAY H'CAP (DIV I) 7f 96y
2:40 (2:41) (Class 5) (0-70,71) 4-Y-O+

£4,599 (£1,376; £688; £344; £300; £300) Stalls Low

Form RPR
4604 1 **Gabrial The Tiger (IRE)**[16] 2679 7-9-4 **67** PaulHanagan 8 75
(Richard Fahey) *mde all: rdn along 2f out: drvn ent fnl f: kpt on wl towards fin* **11/2**[2]
4031 2 *nk* **Abushamah (IRE)**[23] 2478 8-8-12 **61** TomEaves 1 68
(Ruth Carr) *trckd ldrs: hdwy over 2f out: chsd wnr over 1f out: rdn ent fnl f: kpt on* **11/2**[2]
6023 3 ½ **Atletico (IRE)**[11] 2847 7-9-2 **65** (v) HollieDoyle 12 71
(David Evans) *hld up in rr: hdwy on inner over 2f out: chsd ldrs and swtchd lft over 1f out: rdn to chse ldng pair ent fnl f: sn drvn and kpt on* **6/1**[3]
-152 4 3 ¼ **Dandy Highwayman (IRE)**[18] 2633 5-8-13 **65** (tp) BenRobinson(3) 5 62
(Ollie Pears) *hld up towards rr: effrt and n.m.r over 2f out: sn swtchd lft and rdn: styd on wl fnl f* **14/1**
00-0 5 2 **Make On Madam (IRE)**[29] 2256 7-8-9 **58** NicolaCurrie 3 50
(Les Eyre) *trckd ldrs: hdwy over 2f out: rdn wl over 1f out: kpt on same pce* **16/1**
460 6 4 **Mujassam**[12] 2788 7-9-5 **68** (b) DavidNolan 6 50
(David O'Meara) *trckd ldng pair: hdwy over 3f out: rdn along 2f out: drvn and wknd over 1f out (vet said gelding lost right hind shoe)* **5/1**[1]
0-02 7 2 ½ **Mywayistheonlyway (IRE)**[7] 2964 6-8-13 **62** SamJames 7 37
(Grant Tuer) *chsd ldrs: rdn along over 2f out: drvn wl over 1f out: sn wknd* **5/1**[1]
-540 8 ½ **Round The Island**[15] 2709 6-9-0 **63** FrannyNorton 10 37
(Richard Whitaker) *stdd and swtchd rt s: hld up in rr: hdwy towards outer whn n.m.r over 2f out: sn rdn along and n.d* **12/1**
-400 9 3 ¼ **Kroy**[30] 2183 5-8-7 **56** oh4 (p) RachelRichardson 4 21
(Ollie Pears) *midfield: pushed along over 3f out: sn rdn and wknd* **33/1**
-510 10 ¾ **Tiercel**[40] 1925 6-9-7 **70** DavidAllan 2 33
(Rebecca Bastiman) *hld up in midfield: effrt and sme hdwy 3f out: rdn over 2f out: sn wknd* **10/1**
30-0 11 12 **Al Ozzdi**[12] 2785 4-8-11 **60** CliffordLee 9
(Roger Fell) *chsd wnr: rdn along 3f out: sn drvn and wknd* **10/1**
1m 35.46s (2.86) **Going Correction** +0.60s/f (Yiel) 11 Ran SP% **119.8**
Speed ratings (Par 103): **107,106,106,102,100 95,92,92,88,87 73**
CSF £36.58 CT £194.95 TOTE £6.00: £2.50, £1.90, £1.90; EX 24.60 Trifecta £99.00.
Owner Dr Marwan Koukash **Bred** Kenneth Heelan **Trained** Musley Bank, N Yorks

FOCUS
Add 7yds. The pace held up here.

3215 VERY HAPPY RETIREMENT BILL GRAY H'CAP (DIV II) 7f 96y
3:10 (3:10) (Class 5) (0-70,70) 4-Y-O+

£4,599 (£1,376; £688; £344; £300; £300) Stalls Low

Form RPR
504- 1 **Keepup Kevin**[198] 9029 5-9-5 **68** CallumShepherd 2 78
(Pam Sly) *mde most: rdn along wl over 1f out: drvn ins fnl f: kpt on wl towards fin* **5/2**[1]
0020 2 1 ¼ **Roaring Forties (IRE)**[9] 2898 6-8-13 **62** (p) ConnorBeasley 10 69
(Rebecca Bastiman) *hld up towards rr: hdwy on inner wl over 2f out: rdn over 1f out: styd on to chse wnr ins fnl f: sn drvn and kpt on* **12/1**
-040 3 2 ½ **Somewhere Secret**[25] 2418 5-8-8 **57** (p) CliffordLee 1 58
(Michael Mullineaux) *trckd ldrs on inner: hdwy over 2f out: rdn wl over 1f out: drvn and kpt on same pce fnl f* **11/2**[3]
-256 4 *nk* **Mutarakez (IRE)**[11] 2842 7-9-7 **70** (p) TomEaves 9 70
(Ruth Carr) *hld up in rr: hdwy 3f out: rdn along wl over 1f out: kpt on fnl f* **10/1**
10-0 5 3 ¾ **Silk Mill Blue**[36] 2012 5-8-7 **56** oh6 CamHardie 5 46
(Richard Whitaker) *trckd ldrs: hdwy wl over 2f out: sn rdn along: no imp fnl f* **50/1**
0635 6 ¾ **Christmas Night**[16] 2681 4-8-6 **58** BenRobinson(3) 3 46
(Ollie Pears) *trckd ldng pair: hdwy to chse wnr over 2f out: rdn wl over 1f out: drvn appr fnl f: grad wknd* **7/2**[2]
0000 7 ¾ **Kodiline (IRE)**[11] 2824 5-9-3 **66** HollieDoyle 8 52
(David Evans) *cl up: disp ld 5f out: rdn along 3f out: wknd over 2f out* **10/1**
00-6 8 *hd* **Fard**[11] 2847 4-8-12 **61** NicolaCurrie 4 47
(Roger Fell) *hld up: a towards rr* **11/1**
-050 9 ½ **Dasheen**[9] 2898 6-9-0 **63** (v) NathanEvans 6 47
(Karen Tutty) *a in rr* **11/1**
10-0 10 *nk* **Relight My Fire**[23] 2478 9-8-11 **60** (p) DavidAllan 12 43
(Tim Easterby) *chsd ldrs: rdn along over 2f out: drvn and wknd wl over 1f out* **25/1**
-340 11 1 ¼ **Mudawwan (IRE)**[68] 1273 5-9-6 **69** (p w) PaulHanagan 11 49
(James Bethell) *a towards rr* **14/1**
1m 36.56s (3.96) **Going Correction** +0.60s/f (Yiel) 11 Ran SP% **121.2**
Speed ratings (Par 103): **101,99,96,96,92 91,90,90,89,89 87**
CSF £35.79 CT £160.52 TOTE £3.30: £1.50, £3.20, £2.20; EX 35.90 Trifecta £164.30.
Owner Mrs P M Sly **Bred** Mrs P M Sly **Trained** Thorney, Cambs

FOCUS
Add 7yds. The slower of the two divisions by 1.10sec. The winner's three runs last term all worked out well.

3216 DR EDDIE MOLL H'CAP 1m 100y
3:40 (3:41) (Class 4) (0-80,80) 4-Y-O+

£6,868 (£2,055; £1,027; £514; £300; £300) Stalls Low

Form RPR
-111 1 **Kylie Rules**[15] 2710 4-9-1 **74** TomEaves 6 87
(Ruth Carr) *hld up in tch: smooth hdwy over 3f out: sn trcking ldng pair: chal 2f out: led over 1f out: sn rdn: styd on strly and clr ins fnl f* **5/4**[1]
-663 2 3 ¾ **Ghayyar (IRE)**[9] 2894 5-8-12 **71** (t[1]) RachelRichardson 7 76
(Tim Easterby) *hld up: hdwy 3f out: chsd ldrs 2f out: sn rdn: styd on to chse wnr ins fnl f: sn drvn and no imp* **8/1**
00-5 3 ¾ **Poet's Dawn**[23] 2480 4-9-6 **79** DavidAllan 3 82
(Tim Easterby) *led: rdn along over 2f out: drvn and hdd over 1f out: kpt on same pce* **3/1**[2]
-500 4 2 ½ **Beverley Bullet**[50] 1660 6-8-7 **66** (p) PaulHanagan 5 64
(Lawrence Mullaney) *bhd and rdn along 5f out: hdwy 3f out: rdn to chse ldrs 2f out: sn drvn and n.d* **12/1**
30-4 5 9 **Club Wexford (IRE)**[23] 2480 8-9-6 **79** CliffordLee 4 57
(Roger Fell) *cl up: chal 3f out: rdn 2f out and ev ch: drvn wl over 1f out: sn wknd* **6/1**[3]
050- 6 11 **Barton Mills**[287] 6157 4-9-7 **80** (h w) NathanEvans 1 34
(Michael Easterby) *chsd ldng pair: rdn along over 3f out: sn wknd* **50/1**
2-50 7 38 **Kingdom Brunel**[12] 2785 4-8-11 **70** (b[1]) CamHardie 2
(David O'Meara) *chsd ldng pair: hung lft bnd over 4f out: rdn along over 3f out: sn wknd (jockey said gelding didn't handle the bend)* **8/1**
1m 50.52s (4.12) **Going Correction** +0.60s/f (Yiel) 7 Ran SP% **115.6**
Speed ratings (Par 105): **103,99,98,96,87 76,38**
CSF £12.75 TOTE £2.00: £1.50, £3.10; EX 8.20 Trifecta £23.20.
Owner J A Knox and Mrs M A Knox **Bred** J A Knox **Trained** Huby, N Yorks

FOCUS
Add 7yds. They went a good gallop here and the race set up for the closers. The form's rated at face value.

3217 HULL FC H'CAP 1m 1f 207y
4:10 (4:11) (Class 5) (0-70,68) 4-Y-O+

£4,599 (£1,376; £688; £344; £300; £300) Stalls Low

Form RPR
3414 1 **Kilbaha Lady (IRE)**[5] 3057 5-9-2 **68** FayeMcManoman(5) 5 72
(Nigel Tinkler) *dwlt: sn trcking ldrs: effrt 2f out: rdn to ld appr fnl f: kpt on wl* **4/1**[3]
0060 2 ½ **Dark Devil (IRE)**[2] 3161 6-9-7 **68** (p) PaulHanagan 7 71
(Richard Fahey) *hld up in rr: hdwy wl over 2f out: rdn over 1f out: chsd wnr and edgd rt ins fnl f: kpt on* **9/2**
100- 3 1 ¾ **Bollin Ted**[222] 8391 5-9-1 **62** DavidAllan 2 62
(Tim Easterby) *trckd ldng pair on inner: hdwy 2f out: rdn over 1f out: chsd wnr ent fnl f: sn drvn and kpt on same pce* **6/1**
0-40 4 2 **Bob's Girl**[15] 2714 4-8-7 **54** oh9 (b) CliffordLee 3 50?
(Michael Mullineaux) *hld up in rr: hdwy on inner over 2f out: rdn wl over 1f out: chsd ldrs: kpt on same pce fnl f* **50/1**
-315 5 3 **Glacier Fox**[18] 2628 4-9-6 **67** TomEaves 6 57
(Tom Tate) *led: pushed along over 2f out: rdn and hdd over 1f out: sn wknd* **7/2**[2]
10-4 6 ¾ **Whatwouldyouknow (IRE)**[34] 2056 4-9-5 **66** PhilipPrince 4 54
(Richard Guest) *t.k.h: trckd ldrs: hdwy and cl up over 2f out: led briefly over 1f out: sn rdn: hdd appr fnl f and sn wknd* **5/2**[1]
1056 7 3 ¾ **Orobas (IRE)**[5] 3038 7-8-8 **62** (v) VictorSantos(7) 8 43
(Lucinda Egerton) *trckd ldrs on outer: cl up 3f out: rdn along over 2f out: sn drvn and wknd* **12/1**
2m 12.06s (6.36) **Going Correction** +0.60s/f (Yiel) 7 Ran SP% **112.9**
Speed ratings (Par 103): **98,97,96,94,92 91,88**
CSF £21.61 CT £104.81 TOTE £4.20: £1.50, £2.80; EX 20.00 Trifecta £121.80.
Owner The Dapper Partnership **Bred** Helen Lyons **Trained** Langton, N Yorks

FOCUS
Add 7yds. The early pace was steady but they got racing soon enough and the hold-up horses came through at the finish. The form might not prove too reliable.

3218 SKIDBY NOVICE STKS 7f 96y
4:40 (4:41) (Class 5) 3-Y-O+ £4,599 (£1,376; £688; £344; £171) Stalls Low

Form RPR
25- 1 **Kodiac Pride**[179] 9355 3-9-5 0 TomMarquand 7 86
(William Haggas) *mde all: rdn and qcknd 2f out: drvn ins fnl f: kpt on wl* **9/4**[2]
2 1 **Maydanny (IRE)** 3-9-5 0 JimCrowley 8 83
(Mark Johnston) *trckd wnr: pushed along over 2f out: rdn wl over 1f out: drvn and kpt on fnl f* **5/2**[3]
43 3 2 **Noble Prospector (IRE)**[30] 2198 3-9-5 0 PaulHanagan 4 78+
(Richard Fahey) *trckd ldrs: hdwy on outer over 2f out: rdn to chse ldng pair over 1f out: drvn and no imp fnl f* **6/4**[1]
05 4 4 ½ **Canasta**[79] 1142 3-9-0 0 GeorgeWood 3 61
(James Fanshawe) *trckd ldng pair on inner: effrt 2 1/2f out: rdn wl over 1f out: grad wknd* **7/1**
00- 5 8 **Rodney After Dave (IRE)**[212] 8700 3-9-5 0 NathanEvans 6 44
(Marjorie Fife) *in tch: rdn along wl over 2f out: sn outpcd* **80/1**
00 6 13 **Fabulous View (FR)**[36] 2018 3-9-0 0 TomEaves 10 4
(Ruth Carr) *a in rr* **100/1**
7 3 ½ **Lady Sebastian** 3-9-0 0 CamHardie 9
(Jason Ward) *in tch: rdn along 3f out: sn outpcd* **50/1**
0 8 4 **Olivia On Green**[60] 1417 3-9-0 0 AndrewElliott 5
(Ronald Thompson) *a in rr* **100/1**
9 55 **Nouvelli Solo (FR)** 3-8-7 0 VictorSantos(7) 1
(Lucinda Egerton) *v.s.a: green and sn t.o (jockey said filly was slowly away)* **100/1**
1m 37.35s (4.75) **Going Correction** +0.60s/f (Yiel) 9 Ran SP% **118.0**
Speed ratings (Par 103): **96,94,92,87,78 63,59,54,**
CSF £8.62 TOTE £3.10: £1.20, £1.30, £1.10; EX 9.70 Trifecta £17.70.
Owner Sheikh Rashid Dalmook Al Maktoum **Bred** New England Stud & Sir Peter Vela **Trained** Newmarket, Suffolk

FOCUS
Add 7yds. One-way traffic as the winner dictated things in front and wasn't for catching. The level of the form makes sense.

3219 COTTINGHAM H'CAP 1m 4f 23y
5:10 (5:12) (Class 6) (0-60,60) 3-Y-O

£3,493 (£1,039; £519; £300; £300; £300) Stalls Low

Form RPR
-001 1 **Agravain**[9] 2913 3-9-3 **56** 6ex DavidAllan 7 63
(Tim Easterby) *mde all: rdn along over 2f out: drvn and kpt on wl fnl f* **3/1**[2]
0-60 2 ¾ **Dear Miriam (IRE)**[13] 2770 3-9-6 **59** CallumShepherd 5 65
(Mick Channon) *trckd ldng pair on inner: pushed along 3f out: rdn and n.m.r wl over 1f out: swtchd lft to outer and drvn ent fnl f: kpt on wl towards fin* **12/1**
540 3 1 ½ **Stone Cougar (USA)**[14] 2731 3-9-4 **57** FrannyNorton 1 61
(Mark Johnston) *trckd ldrs: hdwy 3f out: rdn along 2f out: drvn over 1f out: kpt on same pce fnl f* **6/1**[3]
0062 4 1 **Thomas Cubitt (FR)**[9] 2913 3-9-7 **60** (v[1]) HayleyTurner 2 62
(Michael Bell) *sn trcking wnr: hdwy over 3f out: rdn to chal 2f out: drvn over 1f out: wknd ent fnl f* **4/6**[1]
0000 5 7 **Showshutai**[19] 2582 3-8-7 **46** oh1 HollieDoyle 6 38
(Christopher Kellett) *a in rr* **66/1**
64-0 6 ½ **Burnage Boy (IRE)**[31] 2152 3-9-2 **55** GrahamLee 4 46
(Micky Hammond) *in tch: pushed along over 3f out: sn rdn and outpcd* **20/1**

500 7 64 **Parker's Pride**[50] 1665 3-8-9 **48**........................ NathanEvans 8
(Brian Rothwell) *a in rr: outpcd and bhd fnl 3f* **66/1**
2m 46.21s (7.41) **Going Correction** +0.60s/f (Yiel) 7 Ran SP% **114.7**
Speed ratings (Par 97): **99,98,97,96,92 91,49**
CSF £35.51 CT £201.61 TOTE £3.40: £1.40, £3.50; EX 31.30 Trifecta £102.00.
Owner Geoff & Sandra Turnbull **Bred** Elwick Stud **Trained** Great Habton, N Yorks
FOCUS
Add 7yds. An ordinary handicap dominated from the front. The form looks a little fluid.
T/Jkpt: Not Won. T/Plt: £166.40 to a £1 stake. Pool: £58,501.41 - 256.58 winning units T/Qpdt: £18.60 to a £1 stake. Pool: £6,034.10 - 239.98 winning units **Joe Rowntree**

[2783] HAMILTON (R-H)

Wednesday, May 29

OFFICIAL GOING: Good to soft changing to soft after race 4 (3.25)
Wind: Light, half behind in sprints and in over 4f of home straight in races on the round course Weather: Cloudy, showers

3220 BB FOODSERVICE NOVICE AUCTION STKS (PLUS 10 RACE) (A £20,000 BB FOODSERVICE 2YO SERIES QUALIFIER) 5f 7y

1:50 (1:52) (Class 4) 2-Y-O **£5,433** (£1,617; £808; £404) **Stalls** High

Form RPR
241 1 **Rose Of Kildare (IRE)**[9] 2907 2-9-0 0........................ PJMcDonald 6 74+
(Mark Johnston) *prom: effrt whn nt clr run and swtchd lft over 1f out: squeezed through to chse ldr ent fnl f: sustained run to ld cl home* **1/1**[1]
23 2 1 1/4 **Paper Star**[19] 2586 2-8-9 0........................ EdwardGreatrex 5 65
(Archie Watson) *led: rdn over 1f out: kpt on fnl f: hdd and no ex cl home* **7/2**[2]
3 2 1/2 **Castlehill Retreat** 2-9-3 0........................ AndrewMullen 4 64+
(Ben Haslam) *s.i.s: rn green in rr: hdwy and swtchd rt over 1f out: kpt on fnl f: nt rch first two* **14/1**
23 4 2 **Mr Fudge**[23] 2476 2-9-0 0........................ SeanDavis(5) 8 58
(Richard Fahey) *trckd ldrs: effrt and rdn over 1f out: outpcd ins fnl f* **5/1**[3]
0 5 1 3/4 **Stormy Bay**[9] 2892 2-9-2 0........................ PaulMulrennan 3 49
(Keith Dalgleish) *dwlt: bhd and detached: stdy hdwy over 1f out: kpt on fnl f: nvr nrr* **40/1**
03 6 2 **Bob's Oss (IRE)**[9] 2906 2-8-13 0........................ JasonHart 1 39
(John Quinn) *t.k.h: pressed ldr: rdn over 1f out: wknd ent fnl f* **18/1**
50 7 nse **Holloa**[14] 2747 2-8-13 0........................ DuranFentiman 2 39
(Tim Easterby) *t.k.h: prom on outside: rdn along 2f out: wknd fnl f* **10/1**
1m 0.49s (0.09) **Going Correction** -0.05s/f (Good) 7 Ran SP% **112.3**
Speed ratings (Par 95): **97,95,91,87,85 81,81**
CSF £4.46 TOTE £1.80: £1.10, £1.50; EX 5.40 Trifecta £38.00.
Owner Kingsley Park 14 **Bred** Wansdyke Farms Ltd **Trained** Middleham Moor, N Yorks
FOCUS
The ground had predictably eased following a fair bit of rain. Ordinary juvenile form, but a fair effort from the winner to defy a penalty. The winner's credited with a minor step forward.

3221 LOCKTON COMPANIES H'CAP 6f 6y

2:20 (2:22) (Class 5) (0-75,73) 3-Y-O+ **£5,433** (£1,617; £808; £404; £300; £300) **Stalls** Centre

Form RPR
24-2 1 **Global Spirit**[12] 2788 4-9-8 **67**........................ BenCurtis 1 77
(Roger Fell) *in tch on far side of centre gp: rdn and hdwy to ld over 1f out: edgd lft ins fnl f: r.o wl* **3/1**[1]
3145 2 1 1/4 **Avenue Of Stars**[29] 2247 6-9-6 **65**........................(v) JasonHart 6 71
(Karen McLintock) *prom in centre gp: effrt and chsd wnr over 1f out: kpt on fnl f: nt pce to chal* **18/1**
-000 3 1 **Kenny The Captain (IRE)**[11] 2824 8-9-7 **66**........................ DuranFentiman 8 69
(Tim Easterby) *early to post: led stands' side gp: overall ldr over 2f out to over 1f out: drvn and kpt on ins fnl f* **10/1**
0-03 4 3/4 **Music Society (IRE)**[19] 2588 4-9-11 **70**........................(h) PhilDennis 9 70
(Tim Easterby) *dwlt: hld up on outside of stands' side gp: hdwy over 2f out: kpt on same pce ins fnl f* **11/1**
0636 5 1 1/2 **Logi (IRE)**[16] 2679 5-9-9 **71**........................(b) JamieGormley(3) 4 67
(Rebecca Bastiman) *early to post: chsd centre ldrs: effrt and rdn 2f out: kpt on same pce ins fnl f* **17/2**[3]
-036 6 1/2 **Captain Dion**[38] 1973 6-8-12 **57**........................(p) TonyHamilton 10 51
(Ivan Furtado) *hung rt thrght: prom on outside of stands' side gp: rdn over 2f out: one pce over 1f out* **11/1**
4030 7 nk **Dirchill (IRE)**[9] 2899 5-9-8 **67**........................(b) JoeFanning 3 60
(David Thompson) *dwlt: hld up in centre gp: effrt and pushed along over 1f out: kpt on fnl f: nvr able to chal* **8/1**[2]
0-04 8 3/4 **Mighty Mac (IRE)**[54] 1560 4-9-5 **64**........................(p) PJMcDonald 5 55
(Karen McLintock) *disp ld in centre to over 1f out: rdn and wknd ins fnl f* **16/1**
0604 9 1/2 **Chookie Dunedin**[12] 2788 4-9-11 **70**........................ ShaneGray 12 59
(Keith Dalgleish) *hld up in tch in stands' side gp: rdn along over 2f out: no imp over 1f out* **8/1**[2]
5021 10 1/2 **Epeius (IRE)**[26] 2379 6-10-0 **73**........................(v) AndrewMullen 11 60
(Ben Haslam) *dwlt: bhd stands' side gp: rdn over 2f out: nvr able to chal (jockey said gelding lost left hind shoe)* **8/1**[2]
30-4 11 1 1/4 **Swanton Blue (IRE)**[15] 2717 6-9-10 **69**........................ BarryMcHugh 2 52
(Ed de Giles) *overall ldr in centre to over 2f out: rdn and wknd over 1f out* **12/1**
-030 12 1/2 **Cosmic Chatter**[11] 2847 9-9-1 **60**........................(p) JackGarritty 13 42
(Ruth Carr) *towards rr stands' side: drvn along 1/2-way: nvr on terms* **28/1**
0000 13 7 **Jacob's Pillow**[18] 2632 8-9-1 **60**........................(p) LewisEdmunds 14 19
(Rebecca Bastiman) *early to post: chsd stands' side ldrs: rdn over 2f out: wknd over 1f out* **40/1**
10-0 14 16 **Rolladice**[15] 2709 4-10-0 **73**........................ PaulMulrennan 7
(Michael Easterby) *bhd centre: struggling 1/2-way: sn btn: eased whn no ch fnl f* **25/1**
1m 11.83s (-0.87) **Going Correction** -0.05s/f (Good) 14 Ran SP% **123.2**
Speed ratings (Par 103): **103,101,100,99,97 96,95,94,94,93 91,91,81,60**
CSF £64.37 CT £513.13 TOTE £2.80: £1.10, £7.80, £3.70; EX 61.80 Trifecta £618.00.
Owner Arthington Barn Racing **Bred** Car Colston Hall Stud **Trained** Nawton, N Yorks
FOCUS
A modest sprint and there was little between the two groups.

3222 CADZOW CASTLE H'CAP 1m 3f 15y

2:50 (2:51) (Class 4) (0-85,87) 4-Y-O+ **£8,021** (£2,387; £1,192; £596; £300; £300) **Stalls** Low

Form RPR
2224 1 **Charles Kingsley**[12] 2786 4-9-9 **87**........................ JoeFanning 6 95+
(Mark Johnston) *prom: smooth hdwy on outside to ld over 2f out: shkn up and clr whn drifted rt over 1f out: eased towards fin: readily* **2/1**[1]
1324 2 4 1/2 **Royal Cosmic**[30] 2185 5-8-2 **71**........................ SeanDavis(5) 3 72
(Richard Fahey) *hld up in tch: rdn and outpcd 3f out: rallied over 1f out: chsd (clr) wnr ins fnl f: kpt on: nt pce to chal* **13/2**[3]
-053 3 nk **Dragon Mountain**[7] 2962 4-8-12 **76**........................ PaulMulrennan 7 76
(Keith Dalgleish) *cl up: wnt 2nd after 2f: led over 3f out to over 2f out: chsd (clr) wnr to ins fnl f: no ex* **12/1**
4000 4 1 1/2 **Tor**[12] 2786 5-9-1 **82**........................ JamieGormley(3) 1 79
(Iain Jardine) *hld up: shkn up over 2f out: stdy hdwy whn nt clr run briefly over 1f out: kpt on fnl f: nvr nrr (jockey said gelding was denied a clear run approaching final furlong)* **14/1**
664- 5 1/2 **Done Deal (IRE)**[236] 7958 4-9-0 **78**........................ RyanTate 2 75
(Sir Mark Prescott Bt) *t.k.h early: pressed ldr 2f: prom: drvn and outpcd over 2f out: rallied ins fnl f: kpt on: no imp* **11/2**[2]
002- 6 3/4 **Overhaugh Street**[391] 2345 6-8-2 **66** oh2........................ AndrewMullen 5 61
(Ed de Giles) *led to over 3f out: rallied and ev ch over 2f out: drvn and outpcd fnl f* **33/1**
131- 7 3/4 **Alabanza**[258] 7223 4-8-8 **72**........................ ShaneGray 4 66
(Keith Dalgleish) *dwlt: t.k.h: hld up: effrt on outside over 2f out: no further imp fr over 1f out* **7/1**
-002 8 1 3/4 **Armandihan (IRE)**[14] 2748 5-9-5 **83**........................(p) KevinStott 9 74
(Kevin Ryan) *s.s: hld up: pushed along over 2f out: sn n.d: btn over 1f out* **11/2**[2]
00-0 9 1 1/2 **Multellie**[46] 1761 7-9-7 **85**........................ JasonHart 10 74
(Tim Easterby) *prom on outside: effrt and ev ch over 3f out: wknd over 2f out* **18/1**
60-0 10 3 3/4 **Diodorus (IRE)**[30] 2186 5-9-2 **80**........................(v[1]) PJMcDonald 8 62
(Karen McLintock) *hld up on outside: struggling over 3f out: btn fnl 2f* **18/1**
2m 22.89s (-2.61) **Going Correction** -0.05s/f (Good) 10 Ran SP% **117.8**
Speed ratings (Par 105): **107,103,103,102,102 101,100,99,98,95**
CSF £15.31 CT £126.55 TOTE £2.80: £1.50, £1.90, £3.80; EX 15.30 Trifecta £65.80.
Owner Sheikh Hamdan bin Mohammed Al Maktoum **Bred** Godolphin **Trained** Middleham Moor, N Yorks
FOCUS
A fair handicap won in good style by the favourite.

3223 HAMILTON PARK SUPPORTING RACING TO SCHOOL FILLIES' H'CAP 1m 68y

3:25 (3:26) (Class 5) (0-70,72) 3-Y-O+ **£5,433** (£1,617; £808; £404; £300; £300) **Stalls** Low

Form RPR
4662 1 **Ivory Charm**[27] 2337 3-8-9 **60**........................ PJMcDonald 10 69
(Richard Fahey) *cl up: wnt 2nd after 1f: rdn to ld appr fnl f: drew clr fnl 100yds* **2/1**[2]
6-00 2 3 1/2 **Forever A Lady (IRE)**[12] 2785 6-9-6 **59**........................ JoeFanning 9 63
(Keith Dalgleish) *led: rdn and hdd appr fnl f: outpcd fnl 100yds* **10/1**
6/0- 3 hd **Bobby Jean (IRE)**[21] 2536 8-9-3 **56**........................(t) BenCurtis 1 59
(Miss Tara Lee Cogan, Ire) *trckd ldr 1f: cl up: nt clr run over 2f out: rdn and angled lft over 1f out: kpt on wl fnl 100yds: no imp* **9/5**[1]
5010 4 1 1/2 **Wall Of Sapphire (IRE)**[30] 2200 3-9-2 **67**........................ EdwardGreatrex 5 64
(Mark Loughnane) *s.i.s: hld up in tch: rdn and outpcd 2f out: n.d after* **7/1**
4103 5 2 **Midnight Vixen**[9] 2911 5-9-3 **56**........................(p) AndrewMullen 3 51
(Ben Haslam) *slowly away: hld up in last pl: drvn and outpcd over 2f out: rchd ldrs* **5/1**[3]
0040 6 nk **Alexandrakollontai (IRE)**[9] 2911 9-9-9 **67**..........(b) ConnorMurtagh(5) 8 62
(Alistair Whillans) *hld up in tch on ins: effrt and rdn 2f out: sn no imp: btn fnl f* **20/1**
1m 48.42s (0.02) **Going Correction** -0.05s/f (Good)
WFA 3 from 5yo+ 12lb 6 Ran SP% **112.1**
Speed ratings (Par 100): **97,93,93,91,89 89**
CSF £21.14 CT £40.34 TOTE £2.90: £2.00, £3.90; EX 18.80 Trifecta £53.70.
Owner John Dance **Bred** Mr & Mrs J Dance **Trained** Musley Bank, N Yorks
FOCUS
The first leg of a moderate handicap, it was depleted somewhat with four non-runners and it was no surprise to see one of the unexposed 3yos come to the fore. Little got into it from off the pace.

3224 RACINGTV.COM H'CAP (DIV I) 1m 1f 35y

3:55 (3:57) (Class 6) (0-55,57) 4-Y-O+ **£3,493** (£1,039; £519; £300; £300; £300) **Stalls** Low

Form RPR
-121 1 **Betty Grable (IRE)**[7] 2964 5-8-7 **48**........................ RhonaPindar(7) 7 55
(Wilf Storey) *w ldr: led over 2f out: shkn up over 1f out: edgd lft and hld on wl fnl f* **3/1**[1]
-040 2 3/4 **Spirit Of Sarwan (IRE)**[24] 2439 5-9-8 **56**........................(p) JoeFanning 5 62
(Stef Keniry) *hld up: hdwy and prom over 3f out: rdn and outpcd 2f out: rallied and chsd wnr ins fnl f: r.o* **6/1**
0223 3 1/2 **Splash Of Verve (IRE)**[2] 3162 7-8-8 **49**........................ TobyEley(7) 12 54
(David Thompson) *s.i.s: t.k.h in rr: hdwy and prom on outside over 2f out: effrt and ev ch over 1f out: one pce ins fnl f* **5/1**[2]
02-6 4 1 1/4 **Broctune Red**[32] 2127 4-9-2 **50**........................ PhilDennis 3 52
(Gillian Boanas) *led to over 2f out: rallied: kpt on same pce fnl f* **12/1**
0060 5 shd **Highwayman**[18] 2631 6-8-9 **46** oh1........................ JamieGormley(3) 9 48
(David Thompson) *hld up: pushed along over 2f out: kpt on fnl f: nvr able to chal* **7/1**
30-6 6 1 3/4 **Rosemay (FR)**[7] 2964 5-9-5 **53**........................(p) PJMcDonald 6 51
(R Mike Smith) *hld up in midfield: rdn and outpcd 3f out: rallied over 1f out: no imp fnl f* **11/2**[3]
-000 7 2 1/2 **Prancing Oscar (IRE)**[26] 2376 5-9-9 **57**........................(v[1]) AndrewMullen 10 50
(Ben Haslam) *cl up on outside: rdn over 2f out: edgd rt and wknd over 1f out* **7/1**
5500 8 3/4 **Rioja Day (IRE)**[7] 2964 9-8-5 **46** oh1........................(b) CoreyMadden(7) 2 38
(Jim Goldie) *hld up on ins: rdn along 3f out: no further imp fr 2f out* **25/1**
-060 9 2 **John Caesar (IRE)**[32] 2112 8-8-12 **46** oh1............(p) LewisEdmunds 11 34
(Rebecca Bastiman) *hld up: drvn along over 2f out: nvr able to chal* **25/1**

000- **10** *hd* **The Brora Pobbles**[180] 9327 4-9-4 **55**.......................... RowanScott(3) 1 42
(Alistair Whillans) *t.k.h: prom: rdn over 2f out: wknd over 1f out* **33/1**

600- **11** *3 ½* **Jazz Magic (IRE)**[235] 8001 4-8-9 **46**.......................... ConorMcGovern(3) 4 26
(Lynn Siddall) *in tch: lost pl over 3f out: sn struggling* **18/1**

000- **12** *13* **Newspeak (IRE)**[258] 7222 7-8-12 **46** oh1..........................(w) JasonHart 8
(Fred Watson) *hld up in midfield on outside: struggling 3f out: sn btn* **66/1**

1m 58.84s (-0.16) **Going Correction** -0.05s/f (Good) **12** Ran SP% **121.4**
Speed ratings (Par 101): **98,97,96,95,95 94,91,91,89,89 86,74**
CSF £20.70 CT £90.22 TOTE £2.90: £1.10, £1.90, £1.80; EX 23.00 Trifecta £107.00.
Owner W Storey **Bred** Tally-Ho Stud **Trained** Muggleswick, Co Durham
■ Irish Times and Shamlan were withdrawn, prices at time of withdrawal 16/1 and 50/1. Rule 4 does not apply.

FOCUS
Lowly form, but the right horses at least came to the fore.

3225 RACINGTV.COM H'CAP (DIV II) 1m 1f 35y
4:25 (4:27) (Class 6) (0-55,57) 4-Y-0+
£3,493 (£1,039; £519; £300; £300; £300) **Stalls** Low

Form RPR

0-63 **1** **Majeste**[24] 2439 5-9-9 **57**.......................... LewisEdmunds 9 63
(Rebecca Bastiman) *hld up on ins: hdwy and prom over 1f out: sn rdn: angled lft ins fnl f: kpt on wl to ld cl home* **8/1**[3]

4463 **2** *shd* **Lukoutoldmakezebak**[16] 2682 6-8-9 **46** oh1.......(p) JamieGormley(3) 12 52
(David Thompson) *pressed ldr: led over 2f out: rdn over 1f out: edgd lft and kpt on fnl f: hdd cl home* **9/1**

4630 **3** *½* **I Am Dandy (IRE)**[27] 2329 4-9-2 **50**..........................(t) AndrewMullen 5 55
(James Ewart) *prom: rdn along 3f out: hdwy wl over 1f out: kpt on fnl f: hld cl home* **12/1**

0-6 **4** *¾* **Milan Reef (IRE)**[32] 2106 4-9-7 **55**.......................... BenCurtis 3 58
(David Loughnane) *led to over 2f out: rallied and ev ch over 1f out: kpt on same pce ins fnl f* **9/4**[1]

3554 **5** *½* **Twiggy**[16] 2681 5-8-12 **46** oh1.......................... JasonHart 10 48
(Karen McLintock) *s.i.s: t.k.h: hld up: hdwy and prom over 1f out: drvn and one pce ins fnl f* **5/1**[2]

-256 **6** *4* **Optima Petamus**[39] 1958 7-9-0 **48**..........................(b) PhilDennis 2 42
(Liam Bailey) *hld up in midfield: effrt whn nt clr run over 2f out: rdn and wknd over 1f out* **8/1**[3]

0-00 **7** *5* **Dutch Coed**[32] 2112 7-9-2 **53**.......................... RowanScott(3) 11 37
(Nigel Tinkler) *hld up: short-lived effrt on outside over 2f out: wknd wl over 1f out* **11/1**

8 *1 ¼* **War Ensign (IRE)**[266] 6958 4-9-1 **49**.......................... DuranFentiman 6 31
(Tim Easterby) *midfield: rdn along 3f out: wknd fr 2f out* **12/1**

0-60 **9** *1 ¼* **Sebastiano Ricci (IRE)**[27] 2349 4-9-6 **54**.......................... EdwardGreatrex 8 33
(Mark Loughnane) *s.i.s: hld up: rdn and outpcd 3f out: btn fnl 2f (jockey said gelding was never travelling)* **12/1**

642- **10** *hd* **Sunhill Lad (IRE)**[212] 8701 4-9-2 **50**.......................... PaulMulrennan 1 29
(Ann Duffield) *chsd ldrs: rdn along over 3f out: wknd over 2f out* **8/1**[3]

40P- **11** *21* **Indie Groove (IRE)**[273] 6692 4-9-0 **55**.......................... HarryRussell(7) 13
(Linda Perratt) *s.i.s: hld up: struggling over 3f out: sn lost tch: t.o* **66/1**

1m 58.47s (-0.53) **Going Correction** -0.05s/f (Good) **11** Ran SP% **123.7**
Speed ratings (Par 101): **100,99,99,98,98 94,90,89,88,87 69**
CSF £82.21 CT £879.42 TOTE £7.20: £2.40, £2.90, £3.70; EX 47.30 Trifecta £743.70.
Owner Let's Be Lucky Racing 17 & Partner **Bred** Marston Stud **Trained** Cowthorpe, N Yorks
■ Stewards' Enquiry : Andrew Mullen two-day ban: used whip above permitted level (Jun 12-13)

FOCUS
Similarly competitive to the first leg, it produced a tight finish. The winner can have his effort upgraded as he came from much further back than the placed runners.

3226 DUNCAN AND KATHLEEN DIAMOND WEDDING ANNIVERSARY H'CAP 1m 1f 35y
4:55 (4:56) (Class 6) (0-65,67) 3-Y-0
£3,493 (£1,039; £519; £300; £300; £300) **Stalls** Low

Form RPR

3530 **1** **Creek Island (IRE)**[30] 2200 3-9-9 **67**.......................... JoeFanning 4 74
(Mark Johnston) *cl up: led over 3f out: clr whn veered lft 1f out: kpt on wl towards fin* **9/2**[2]

554 **2** *¾* **Smeaton (IRE)**[16] 2677 3-9-6 **64**.......................... BenCurtis 2 70
(Roger Fell) *hld up on ins: hdwy over 2f out: effrt and chsd wnr over 1f out: hung lft ins fnl f: r.o* **13/2**[3]

00-6 **3** *2 ¼* **Royal Countess**[27] 2325 3-7-12 **47**.......................... PaulaMuir(5) 7 48
(Lucy Normile) *s.i.s: hld up: pushed along over 3f out: hdwy on outside 2f out: kpt on fnl f: nvr rchd ldrs* **33/1**

-054 **4** *2 ¾* **One To Go**[15] 2712 3-9-5 **63**..........................(p[1]) DuranFentiman 11 59
(Tim Easterby) *in tch: hdwy and cl up over 2f out: rdn: edgd rt and one pce appr fnl f* **10/1**

60-3 **5** *2* **Euro Implosion (IRE)**[15] 2711 3-9-5 **63**.......................... PaulMulrennan 1 55
(Keith Dalgleish) *taken early to post: hld up in midfield: effrt over 2f out: no imp fr over 1f out* **3/1**[1]

05-4 **6** *2* **God Of Dreams**[24] 2438 3-9-3 **64**.......................... JamieGormley(3) 12 52
(Iain Jardine) *midfield on outside: drvn over 2f out: no imp fr over 1f out* **25/1**

4-0U **7** *nse* **Northern Lyte**[15] 2711 3-9-4 **65**.......................... RowanScott(3) 13 52
(Nigel Tinkler) *hld up: rdn and outpcd over 3f out: rallied wl over 1f out: sn no imp* **16/1**

0-05 **8** *2 ¼* **Preservation**[21] 2531 3-8-0 **49**.......................... SeanDavis(5) 8 32
(Jedd O'Keeffe) *hld up: drvn and outpcd over 4f out: sme late hdwy: nvr on terms* **20/1**

4-00 **9** *shd* **Menin Gate (IRE)**[18] 2634 3-9-7 **65**.......................... TonyHamilton 3 48
(Richard Fahey) *hld up: drvn and outpcd over 3f out: btn fnl 2f* **13/2**[3]

050- **10** *hd* **Hydroplane (IRE)**[193] 9122 3-9-6 **64**.......................... RyanTate 10 46
(Sir Mark Prescott Bt) *led 1f: chsd ldrs: drvn over 2f out: wknd over 1f out* **15/2**

00-0 **11** *5* **Magrevio (IRE)**[31] 2150 3-9-2 **60**.......................... PhilDennis 5 32
(Liam Bailey) *sn pressing ldr: drvn along 3f out: wknd 2f out* **40/1**

44-5 **12** *10* **Hoffa**[42] 1845 3-9-9 **67**..........................(b) AndrewMullen 9 19
(Michael Dods) *t.k.h: hdwy to ld after 1f: hdd over 3f out: sn wknd: eased whn btn over 1f out* **9/1**

1m 57.9s (-1.10) **Going Correction** -0.05s/f (Good) **12** Ran SP% **120.6**
Speed ratings (Par 97): **102,101,99,96,95 93,93,91,91,91 86,77**
CSF £33.04 CT £876.39 TOTE £4.30: £1.60, £2.50, £7.60; EX 40.40 Trifecta £522.70.
Owner Hamad Rashed Bin Ghedayer **Bred** Rabbah Bloodstock Limited **Trained** Middleham Moor, N Yorks

FOCUS
Modest 3yo form, it was another race where little got involved.

3227 WATCH RACING TV IN HD APPRENTICE H'CAP 5f 7y
5:25 (5:27) (Class 6) (0-65,64) 4-Y-0+
£3,493 (£1,039; £519; £300; £300; £300) **Stalls** High

Form RPR

-114 **1** **Everkyllachy (IRE)**[26] 2379 5-9-7 **62**..........................(v) SebastianWoods(3) 5 68
(Karen McLintock) *hld up bhd ldng gp: hdwy over 1f out: led ins fnl f: edgd lft: hld on wl cl home* **9/2**[1]

-005 **2** *hd* **Boundsy (IRE)**[19] 2580 5-9-5 **60**..........................(p[1]) SeanDavis(3) 4 65
(Richard Fahey) *early to post: chsd ldrs: drvn and effrt over 1f out: chsd wnr ins fnl f: kpt on: hld cl home* **6/1**[2]

1-66 **3** *1* **The Bull (IRE)**[36] 2013 4-8-12 **53**..........................(p) HarrisonShaw(3) 3 55
(Ben Haslam) *hld up: effrt on outside over 1f out: chsd ldrs ins fnl f: kpt on* **17/2**

-030 **4** *2 ¼* **Astrophysics**[10] 2876 7-9-4 **59**.......................... BenSanderson(3) 7 53
(Lynn Siddall) *prom: rdn and edgd rt over 1f out: outpcd ins fnl f* **20/1**

1-54 **5** *½* **Seamster**[26] 2358 12-9-8 **63**..........................(t) PaulaMuir(3) 2 55
(David Loughnane) *led: rdn over 1f out: edgd lft and hdd ins fnl f: sn btn* **10/1**

4-02 **6** *¾* **Bronze Beau**[12] 2789 12-9-9 **64**..........................(tp) ConnorMurtagh(3) 11 53
(Linda Stubbs) *early to post: cl up against stands' rail: drvn along over 2f out: no ex fnl f* **12/1**

-000 **7** *shd* **Havana Go**[7] 2958 4-8-10 **55**..........................(b) HarryRussell(7) 10 44
(Keith Dalgleish) *dwlt: bhd and outpcd: hdwy fnl f: nvr rchd ldrs* **12/1**

3016 **8** *½* **Star Cracker (IRE)**[7] 2958 7-8-11 **49**..........................(p) PhilDennis 12 36
(Jim Goldie) *in tch against stands' rail: drvn 1/2-way: sn no imp: btn over 1f out* **10/1**

5003 **9** *1* **Leeshaan (IRE)**[24] 2433 4-8-12 **50**.......................... RowanScott 9 33
(Rebecca Bastiman) *bhd and sn outpcd: nvr on terms* **8/1**[3]

1005 **10** *4 ½* **Rockley Point**[30] 2183 6-8-13 **56**..........................(b) TobyEley(5) 8 23
(Katie Scott) *fly-jmpd and lost several l s: a outpcd and bhd (jockey said gelding missed the break)* **6/1**[2]

00-0 **11** *nk* **Argon**[141] 129 4-8-2 **45**..........................(p) RobertDodsworth(5) 6 11
(Noel Wilson) *t.k.h: cl up tl rdn and wknd over 1f out* **80/1**

1m 0.09s (-0.31) **Going Correction** -0.05s/f (Good) **11** Ran SP% **108.0**
Speed ratings (Par 101): **100,99,98,94,93 92,92,91,89,82 82**
CSF £24.44 CT £127.52 TOTE £5.20: £1.90, £2.80, £3.00; EX 27.20 Trifecta £166.00.
Owner Ever Equine & Self Preservation Society **Bred** Mrs T Mahon **Trained** Ingoe, Northumberland
■ Foxtrot Knight was withdrawn, price at time of withdrawal 11/2. Rule 4 applies to all bets. Deduction of 15p in the pound.

FOCUS
A wide-open sprint.
T/Plt: £19.80 to a £1 stake. Pool: £48,939.08 - 1,800.86 winning units T/Qpdt: £10.10 to a £1 stake. Pool: £5,151.57 - 376.73 winning units **Richard Young**

3228 - 3243a (Foreign Racing) - See Raceform Interactive

2892 CARLISLE (R-H)
Thursday, May 30

OFFICIAL GOING: Soft changing to soft (heavy in places) after race 5 (7.15)
Wind: Breezy, half against in over 2f of home straight Weather: Overcast, raining

3244 CARLETON EBF MAIDEN FILLIES' STKS (PLUS 10 RACE) 5f
5:05 (5:06) (Class 5) 2-Y-0 **£4,204** (£1,251; £625; £312) **Stalls** Low

Form RPR

1 **Exceptional** 2-9-0 0.......................... TonyHamilton 9 75
(Richard Fahey) *dwlt: bhd and green: shkn up and hdwy over 1f out: squeezed through to ld ins fnl f: kpt on wl: improve* **7/1**

4 **2** *¾* **Yarrow Gate**[24] 2476 2-9-0 0.......................... PaulMulrennan 6 72
(Michael Dods) *dwlt: t.k.h and sn prom: effrt and rdn over 1f out: squeezed through ins fnl f: wnt 2nd cl home: nt rch wnr* **3/1**[2]

4 **3** *nk* **Dream Kart (IRE)**[8] 2968 2-9-0 0.......................... JoeFanning 1 71
(Mark Johnston) *led: crossed to stands' rail over 2f out: hrd pressed and rdn over 1f out: hdd ins fnl f: one pce and lost 2nd cl home* **7/1**

4 *nk* **Miss Lucy (IRE)** 2-9-0 0.......................... BenCurtis 3 70
(K R Burke) *dwlt: chsd ldrs: effrt and rdn 2f out: kpt on same pce ins fnl f* **9/2**[3]

33 **5** *2 ¾* **Stars In The Night (IRE)**[21] 2561 2-9-0 0.......................... KevinStott 7 60
(Kevin Ryan) *cl up: effrt and ev ch over 1f out: wknd ins fnl f* **6/4**[1]

6 *½* **Roseina's Voice** 2-9-0 0.......................... TrevorWhelan 8 58
(David Loughnane) *dwlt: t.k.h in rr: hdwy and prom whn edgd lft over 3f out: lost pl over 2f out: n.d after (jockey said filly ran too free)* **66/1**

7 *nk* **Angels Faces (IRE)** 2-9-0 0.......................... TomEaves 10 57
(Grant Tuer) *in tch: hmpd and lost pl over 3f out: n.d after* **33/1**

8 *2 ¾* **Orlaith (IRE)** 2-8-11 0.......................... JamieGormley(3) 4 47+
(Iain Jardine) *dwlt: hld up: effrt on outside over 1f out: no further imp fnl f* **16/1**

0 **9** *5* **Beautrix**[12] 2840 2-9-0 0.......................... ConnorBeasley 5 29
(Michael Dods) *bhd: rdn and shortlived effrt 2f out: sn wknd* **12/1**

05 **U** **Champagne Victory (IRE)**[16] 2707 2-9-0 0.......................... PhilDennis 11
(Brian Ellison) *prom on outside: lost grnd whn hmpd: faltered: hit rail and uns rdr over 3f out* **50/1**

1m 4.43s (2.33) **Going Correction** +0.55s/f (Yiel) **10** Ran SP% **128.2**
Speed ratings (Par 90): **103,101,101,100,96 95,95,90,82,**
CSF £31.17 TOTE £8.60: £2.40, £1.70, £2.00; EX 48.10 Trifecta £190.80.
Owner Cheveley Park Stud **Bred** Cheveley Park Stud Ltd **Trained** Musley Bank, N Yorks

FOCUS
A fair juvenile fillies' maiden. The field came over to the stands' side rail and the neat winner's time was nearly five seconds outside standard in deteriorating conditions. They went a decent pace, perhaps overly fast.

3245 RACING TV IN HD NOVICE AUCTION STKS 5f 193y
5:40 (5:40) (Class 5) 2-Y-0 **£4,204** (£1,251; £625; £312) **Stalls** Low

Form RPR

1 **Coase** 2-9-5 0.......................... BenCurtis 7 89+
(Hugo Palmer) *trckd ldrs: rdn to ld over 1f out: drew clr ins fnl f: readily* **9/2**[2]

56 **2** *4* **Vardon Flyer**[14] 2780 2-9-5 0.......................... NathanEvans 10 77
(Michael Easterby) *led or disp ld to over 1f out: kpt on fnl f: nt rch wnr* **16/1**

3 **3** *nse* **Gallaside (FR)**[14] 2761 2-9-5 0.......................... HollieDoyle 15 77
(Archie Watson) *led or disp ld to over 1f out: kpt on same pce ins fnl f* **4/5**[1]

	4 5	**Frasard** 2-9-5 0 .... GrahamLee 6	62+

(Bryan Smart) *bhd and v green: shkn up and veered rt over 1f out: kpt on wl fnl f to take 4th cl home: bttr for r* **25/1**

4 **5** *nk* **Coast Ofalfujairah (IRE)**[58] 1499 2-9-5 0 .... JamieSpencer 2 61+
(Kevin Ryan) *trckd ldrs: effrt on outside over 1f out: wknd ins fnl f* **6/1**[3]

0 **6** *6* **Congratulate**[47] 1758 2-9-0 0 .... DavidAllan 8 38
(Tim Easterby) *in tch: rdn along 1/2-way: wknd over 1f out* **20/1**

06 **7** *3/4* **Never Said Nothing (IRE)**[31] 2191 2-9-5 0 .... PhilDennis 3 41
(Brian Ellison) *midfield: drvn along 1/2-way: no further imp fr over 1f out* **40/1**

8 *3* **One Bite (IRE)** 2-9-5 0 .... TomEaves 1 32
(Keith Dalgleish) *s.i.s: bhd and sn pushed along: nvr able to chal* **20/1**

9 *1 3/4* **Milltown Star** 2-8-12 0 .... ScottMcCullagh(7) 9 26
(Mick Channon) *colty in paddock: dwlt and checked s: bhd and green: nvr able to chal* **14/1**

10 *1/2* **Teasel's Rock (IRE)** 2-9-0 0 .... DuranFentiman 14 20
(Tim Easterby) *blkd sn after s: midfield: outpcd 1/2-way: btn fnl 2f* **66/1**

11 *2 1/4* **Indra Dawn (FR)** 2-9-5 0 .... AdamMcNamara 13 18
(Archie Watson) *blkd s: bhd and outpcd: nvr on terms (jockey said colt ran green)* **12/1**

12 *nk* **Inductive** 2-9-5 0 .... PaulMulrennan 12 17
(Michael Dods) *bmpd s: bhd and green: nvr on terms* **25/1**

0 **13** *4 1/2* **Mr Gus (IRE)**[12] 2820 2-9-5 0 .... TonyHamilton 5
(Richard Fahey) *bhd: rdn along 1/2-way: sn struggling* **25/1**

0 **14** *nk* **Castashadow**[16] 2707 2-9-5 0 .... KevinStott 11
(Alan Brown) *dwlt and bmpd s: sn midfield: rdn over 2f out: sn wknd* **66/1**

0 **15** *2* **Moneyball**[41] 1923 2-9-0 0 .... ShaneGray 4
(Keith Dalgleish) *midfield: drvn along after 2f: wknd over 2f out* **40/1**

1m 16.25s (1.65) **Going Correction** +0.55s/f (Yiel) **15 Ran SP% 137.2**
Speed ratings (Par 93): **111,105,105,98,98 90,89,85,83,82 79,79,73,72,70**
CSF £74.92 TOTE £6.00: £1.90, £4.70, £1.10; EX 101.70 Trifecta £433.80.
Owner Lit Lung Lee **Bred** St Albans Bloodstock Llp **Trained** Newmarket, Suffolk

FOCUS
The stalls were moved forward 10yds owing to a false patch of ground. An ordinary juvenile novice auction contest. The second-favourite come home far too strongly for his opponents up the stands' rail. The runner-up is probably the key to the race.

3246 WATCH RACING TV IN HD H'CAP — 1m 1f
6:10 (6:11) (Class 6) (0-60,60) 3-Y-O
£3,493 (£1,039; £519; £300; £300; £300) **Stalls Low**

Form RPR

1 **Champagne Terri (IRE)**[22] 2539 3-8-12 **51** .... (p[1]) GrahamLee 7 61
(Adrian Paul Keatley, Ire) *hld up in tch: smooth hdwy to ld over 2f out: shkn up and kpt on wl fnl 150yds: comf (trainer said, regarding improvement in form, that the filly may have benefited from the first time cheek-pieces and appreciated the softer ground on this occasion)* **11/2**[3]

4-00 **2** *2* **Ritchie Star (IRE)**[16] 2711 3-9-3 **56** .... PaulMulrennan 12 59
(Ben Haslam) *trckd ldrs: effrt and ev ch over 2f out: sn rdn: kpt on same pce last 150* **14/1**

0066 **3** *hd* **Jagerbond**[22] 2531 3-8-4 **46** .... (p) JamieGormley(3) 9 49
(Andrew Crook) *hld up: shkn up and hdwy over 2f out: kpt on fnl f: nvr able to chal* **9/1**

5300 **4** *1/2* **Tails I Win (CAN)**[47] 1770 3-9-4 **57** .... (h) BenCurtis 4 59
(Roger Fell) *s.i.s: hld up: smooth hdwy and prom over 2f out: effrt and rdn over 1f out: one pce ins fnl f* **7/1**

3050 **5** *1 1/4* **Precision Prince (IRE)**[23] 2517 3-9-7 **60** .... ShaneGray 2 59
(Mark Loughnane) *hld up: hdwy on outside over 2f out: drvn along over 1f out: no further imp fnl f* **7/1**

00-0 **6** *4* **Myklachi (FR)**[38] 1980 3-9-7 **60** .... (h[1]) RobbieDowney 3 51
(David O'Meara) *t.k.h early: chsd ldrs: rdn along 3f out: wknd over 1f out* **14/1**

0-04 **7** *5* **Potenza (IRE)**[27] 2355 3-8-10 **54** .... SeanDavis(5) 6 35
(Stef Keniry) *midfield: drvn and outpcd 3f out: n.d after (jockey said gelding was never travelling)* **7/2**[2]

00-6 **8** *3 1/4* **Keska**[26] 2420 3-8-9 **48** .... TonyHamilton 5 23
(Richard Fahey) *midfield: rdn along over 3f out: wknd fnl 2f* **12/1**

-600 **9** *3/4* **Amourie**[49] 1721 3-9-0 **53** .... ConnorBeasley 11 26
(Ray Craggs) *hld up on outside: rdn and outpcd over 3f out: btn fnl 2f* **28/1**

0-04 **10** *6* **Jack Randall**[32] 2152 3-9-3 **56** .... DavidAllan 10 17
(Tim Easterby) *led to 1/2-way: cl up: regained ld over 3f out to over 2f out: wknd over 1f out* **5/2**[1]

0640 **11** *1 3/4* **Juals Spirit (IRE)**[9] 2941 3-8-7 **46** oh1 .... (p) PhilDennis 1 4
(Brian Ellison) *awkward s: hld up: struggling 4f out: nvr on terms* **20/1**

0-00 **12** *37* **Sittin Handy (IRE)**[57] 1514 3-8-10 **49** .... AdamMcNamara 14
(Mark Loughnane) *dwlt: bhd: lost tch fr 1/2-way: t.o* **66/1**

4-00 **13** *12* **Jean Merci (FR)**[16] 2712 3-8-12 **51** .... (b[1]) TomEaves 15
(Keith Dalgleish) *w ldr: led 1/2-way to over 3f out: wknd fnl 2f: t.o* **25/1**

2m 4.09s (5.09) **Going Correction** +0.55s/f (Yiel) **13 Ran SP% 135.8**
Speed ratings (Par 97): **99,97,97,96,95 91,87,84,83,78 77,44,33**
CSF £88.38 CT £721.37 TOTE £10.30: £3.70, £5.10, £3.70; EX 173.10 Trifecta £1625.70.
Owner Mrs B Keatley **Bred** John R Jeffers **Trained** Rossmore Cottage, Co Kildare

FOCUS
10 yards added. A modest 3yo handicap. The third-favourite's winning time was nearly ten seconds outside of the standard. Improvement from the winner, the form rated through the runner-up.

3247 CUMWHINTON MAIDEN STKS (DIV I) — 1m 1f
6:45 (6:46) (Class 5) 3-Y-O+ £4,204 (£1,251; £625; £312) **Stalls Low**

Form RPR

05 **1** **Secretarial (IRE)**[19] 2634 3-8-10 0 .... DanielTudhope 6 78
(Tim Easterby) *mde all: rdn 2f out: hld on wl fnl f* **9/2**

2 *nk* **Caravan Of Hope (IRE)** 3-9-1 0 .... BenCurtis 2 82+
(Hugo Palmer) *midfield: effrt and hdwy on outside 2f out: chsd wnr ins fnl f: clsng at fin* **9/4**[2]

26-0 **3** *2* **James Park Woods (IRE)**[34] 2088 3-9-1 81 .... KevinStott 9 78
(Ralph Beckett) *trckd ldrs: wnt 2nd over 2f out to ins fnl f: one pce last 100yds* **6/4**[1]

4-6 **4** *10* **Tarbeyah (IRE)**[32] 2148 4-9-9 0 .... TomEaves 8 55
(Kevin Frost) *w wnr to over 2f out: rdn and wknd over 1f out* **33/1**

55- **5** *1 3/4* **Skyman**[195] 9104 3-9-1 0 .... AdamMcNamara 5 55+
(Roger Charlton) *trckd ldrs: effrt and disp 2nd pl over 2f out to over 1f out: sn wknd* **4/1**[3]

6 *hd* **At Peace (IRE)** 3-8-10 0 .... RobbieDowney 1 49+
(John Quinn) *dwlt: bhd: pushed along over 3f out: hdwy over 1f out: nvr rchd ldrs* **20/1**

0 **7** *1* **Kaizer**[90] 968 4-10-0 0 .... GrahamLee 10 54
(Alistair Whillans) *prom on outside tl rdn and wknd over 2f out* **100/1**

0- **8** *1/2* **General Mischief (IRE)**[278] 6534 3-9-1 0 .... ConnorBeasley 12 51
(Michael Dods) *hld up in midfield: drvn and outpcd 3f out: btn fnl 2f* **33/1**

0 **9** *5* **Storm Approaching**[24] 2488 3-8-10 0 .... JoeFanning 4 36
(James Fanshawe) *hld up on outside: pushed along over 2f out: sn wknd* **28/1**

10 *9* **Thornton Le Clay** 3-8-8 0 .... JoshQuinn(7) 13 23
(Michael Easterby) *bhd: struggling over 4f out: nvr on terms* **50/1**

0 **11** *5* **Global Rock (FR)**[47] 1755 3-9-1 0 .... PaulMulrennan 11 13
(Ed Dunlop) *hld up: rdn and struggling 4f out: sn btn* **20/1**

0/ **12** *3 3/4* **Howbaar (USA)**[583] 8316 4-10-0 0 .... TonyHamilton 3 8
(James Bethell) *dwlt: hld up: shkn up over 3f out: sn wknd* **66/1**

13 *37* **Ayr Poet** 4-10-0 0 .... (h[1]) PhilDennis 7
(Jim Goldie) *s.s: sn wl bhd: t.o (jockey said gelding was slowly away and never travelling)* **50/1**

2m 4.28s (5.28) **Going Correction** +0.55s/f (Yiel)
WFA 3 from 4yo 13lb **13 Ran SP% 134.2**
Speed ratings (Par 103): **98,97,95,87,85 85,84,84,79,71 67,63,30**
CSF £15.91 TOTE £6.40: £1.90, £1.20, £1.30; EX 25.30 Trifecta £70.30.
Owner Clipper Logistics **Bred** Rabbah Bloodstock Limited **Trained** Great Habton, N Yorks

FOCUS
10 yards added. The first division of a fair maiden. The fourth-favourite's winning time was marginally slower than the previous C&D 3yo handicap. The first three were clear and the form's rated at face value.

3248 CUMWHINTON MAIDEN STKS (DIV II) — 1m 1f
7:15 (7:18) (Class 5) 3-Y-O+ £4,204 (£1,251; £625; £312) **Stalls Low**

Form RPR

5- **1** **Proton (IRE)**[205] 8895 3-9-1 0 .... PaulMulrennan 6 81+
(Jedd O'Keeffe) *prom: rdn and outpcd over 3f out: rallied and swtchd rt 2f out: effrt whn hmpd over 1f out: rcvrd and led ins fnl f: kpt on strly* **16/1**

523 **2** *1 1/2* **Storting**[14] 2769 3-9-1 81 .... BenCurtis 11 78+
(Mick Channon) *prom: led gng wl 3f out: rdn and veered rt 2f out: sn stened: hdd ins fnl f: kpt on same pce (jockey said colt hung left throughout until ducking sharply right)* **1/1**[1]

5 **3** *4 1/2* **Sincerity**[30] 2249 3-8-10 0 .... TonyHamilton 12 64
(James Fanshawe) *dwlt: hld up: pushed along 3f out: effrt and swtchd rt over 1f out: chsd clr ldng pair ins fnl f: r.o* **5/2**[2]

0 **4** *2 1/2* **Greek Hero**[12] 2845 3-9-1 0 .... DanielTudhope 1 64
(Declan Carroll) *trckd ldrs: rdn over 2f out: edgd lft over 1f out: wknd ins fnl f* **25/1**

4-5 **5** *2 1/4* **Tajdeed (IRE)**[26] 2417 4-10-0 0 .... DougieCostello 10 62
(Michael Appleby) *w ldr to 3f out: cl up tl rdn and wknd over 1f out* **25/1**

3 **6** *1 1/4* **Stone Mason (IRE)**[23] 2505 3-9-1 0 .... (t[1]) AdamMcNamara 9 57
(Roger Charlton) *hld up in midfield: stdy hdwy and cl up over 1f out: rdn and wknd ins fnl f* **7/2**[3]

7 *nk* **Villiersdorp**[149] 4-9-2 0 .... (h) CoreyMadden(7) 8 53
(John Hodge) *missed break: bhd: pushed along over 4f out: kpt on fr 2f out: nvr rchd ldrs* **80/1**

3 **8** *3 1/2* **Clovenstone**[25] 2438 3-9-1 0 .... GrahamLee 7 49
(Alistair Whillans) *dwlt: bhd: rdn and outpcd wl over 3f out: n.d after* **25/1**

0- **9** *10* **Philyaboots**[314] 5163 3-9-1 0 .... TomEaves 3 29
(Donald McCain) *dwlt: hld up: outpcd 4f out: sn btn* **66/1**

10 *18* **Philip's Wish** 3-8-10 0 .... SeanDavis(5) 5
(Keith Dalgleish) *mde most to 3f out: sn rdn and wknd: t.o* **16/1**

0-0 **11** *7* **Mullion Dreams**[23] 2505 5-9-11 0 .... JamieGormley(3) 4
(James Ewart) *hld up: drvn and outpcd 4f out: sn btn: t.o (jockey said gelding hung right throughout)* **100/1**

6 **12** *8* **Tanaawol**[33] 2120 3-9-1 0 .... JoeFanning 2
(Mark Johnston) *in tch: struggling wl over 3f out: sn wknd: t.o* **20/1**

2m 5.65s (6.65) **Going Correction** +0.55s/f (Yiel)
WFA 3 from 4yo+ 13lb **12 Ran SP% 132.6**
Speed ratings (Par 103): **92,90,86,84,82 81,81,77,69,53 46,39**
CSF £35.09 TOTE £26.10: £3.70, £1.10, £1.10; EX 59.50 Trifecta £150.90.
Owner Geoff & Sandra Turnbull **Bred** Elwick Stud **Trained** Middleham Moor, N Yorks

FOCUS
10 yards added. The second division of a fair maiden. The going was officially changed to soft, heavy in places after this race. One of the lesser-fancied runners outstayed the hanging favourite close home in a slower time.

3249 RACING TV DAY PASS JUST £10 H'CAP — 7f 173y
7:50 (7:50) (Class 5) (0-75,78) 3-Y-O
£4,204 (£1,251; £625; £312; £300; £300) **Stalls Low**

Form RPR

402 **1** **Global Gift (FR)**[32] 2147 3-9-7 **75** .... (h) TomEaves 5 83
(Ed Dunlop) *hld up: hdwy on outside to ld over 1f out: rdn and drifted lft ins fnl f: kpt on strly* **14/1**

-203 **2** *2 1/4* **Lightning Attack**[19] 2630 3-9-7 **75** .... (p) TonyHamilton 7 78
(Richard Fahey) *prom: effrt and rdn 2f out: chsd wnr ins fnl f: kpt on: nt pce to chal* **4/1**[2]

41-0 **3** *nk* **My Boy Lewis (IRE)**[19] 2635 3-9-1 **72** .... JamieGormley(3) 2 74
(Roger Fell) *hld up: hdwy on outside over 2f out: chsd wnr over 1f out to ins fnl f: one pce towards fin* **16/1**

0012 **4** *hd* **Barasti Dancer (IRE)**[10] 2897 3-9-3 **71** .... BenCurtis 9 73+
(K R Burke) *hld up in tch: stdy hdwy and prom over 3f out: effrt whn nt clr run over 2f out tl angled rt ins fnl f: kpt on fin (jockey said gelding was denied a clear run 1f out)* **5/1**[3]

33-5 **5** *2 1/4* **Beaufort (IRE)**[16] 2711 3-8-12 **66** .... (p[1]) PaulMulrennan 4 63
(Michael Dods) *s.i.s: hld up: pushed along whn checked over 3f out: effrt and swtchd rt over 1f out: kpt on fnl f: nt pce to chal* **15/2**

4321 **6** *1/2* **Ollivander (IRE)**[22] 2529 3-9-1 **69** .... (v) DanielTudhope 8 65
(David O'Meara) *led to over 3f out: rallied and ev ch over 1f out: wknd ins fnl f* **9/1**

0-62 **7** *shd* **Stronsay (IRE)**[27] 2371 3-9-4 **72** .... GrahamLee 11 67
(Bryan Smart) *pressed ldr: led over 3f out to over 1f out: wknd fnl f* **6/1**

20-0 **8** *nk* **Al Suil Eile (FR)**[60] 1462 3-9-7 **75** .... (t) JasonHart 6 70
(John Quinn) *plld hrd in midfield: rdn over 2f out: wknd over 1f out* **9/1**

0-31 **9** *1 1/2* **Wild Hope**[10] 2897 3-9-5 **78** 6ex .... SeanDavis(5) 10 69+
(Kevin Ryan) *trckd ldrs: effrt and hanging lft whn no room fr over 2f out to ins fnl f: nt rcvr and eased (jockey said gelding hung left)* **9/4**[1]

3000 **10** *1* **Harperelle**[31] 2197 3-8-2 **56** oh1 .... NathanEvans 3 45
(Alistair Whillans) *hld up: drvn and outpcd over 3f out: btn fnl 2f* **50/1**

1m 46.46s (6.46) **Going Correction** +0.55s/f (Yiel) **10 Ran SP% 128.0**
Speed ratings (Par 99): **89,86,86,86,84 83,83,83,81,80**
CSF £76.20 CT £972.56 TOTE £19.40: £4.40, £1.80, £5.80; EX 109.70 Trifecta £1243.80.

The Form Book Flat 2019, Raceform Ltd, Newbury, RG14 5SJ

Owner Dr Johnny Hon **Bred** Ecurie Des Monceaux, Lordship Stud Et Al **Trained** Newmarket, Suffolk

FOCUS

9 yards added. A fair 3yo handicap. Those in the frame help with the standard.

3250 RACING TV H'CAP — 1m 3f 39y

8:20 (8:21) (Class 4) (0-80,81) 4-Y-O+

£7,698 (£2,290; £1,144; £572; £300; £300) Stalls High

Form				RPR
-642	1		**Roar (IRE)**[33] 2092 5-8-13 **72** BarryMcHugh 5	81

(Ed de Giles) *trckd ldrs: smooth hdwy to ld 3f out: rdn over 1f out: kpt on wl fnl f* **11/4**[2]

41-1 2 ½ **Hats Off To Larry**[5] 3072 5-9-1 **81** 5ex ScottMcCullagh(7) 6 — 89

(Mick Channon) *hld up in tch: n.m.r over 2f out: hdwy to press wnr over 1f out: kpt on fnl f: hld nr fin: lost front shoe (vet said gelding lost left fore shoe)* **15/8**[1]

0114 3 3¼ **Sioux Frontier (IRE)**[5] 3073 4-8-13 **72** LewisEdmunds 8 — 74

(Iain Jardine) *s.i.s: hld up: hdwy on outside and prom over 1f out: rdn and outpcd ins fnl f* **3/1**[3]

2-02 4 ½ **Corton Lad**[8] 2962 9-8-12 **71** (vt) ShaneGray 4 — 73

(Keith Dalgleish) *pressed ldr: led briefly over 3f out: outpcd 2f out: rallied ins fnl f: no imp* **14/1**

212/ 5 2¼ **Kilowatt**[689] 4691 5-9-7 **80** PaulMulrennan 2 — 78

(Tim Easterby) *chsd ldrs: ev ch over 3f out to over 2f out: rdn and wknd over 1f out* **11/1**

60-2 6 7 **The Navigator**[10] 2894 4-9-1 **77** JamieGormley(3) 7 — 63

(Dianne Sayer) *s.i.s: hld up: drvn along over 3f out: wknd fr 2f out* **8/1**

3-00 7 7 **Regal Mirage (IRE)**[19] 2636 5-9-0 **73** DavidAllan 1 — 47

(Tim Easterby) *hld up in tch: effrt whn nt clr run over 2f out: rdn and wknd over 1f out* **12/1**

13-5 8 14 **Can Can Sixty Two**[8] 2962 4-8-7 **66** AndrewMullen 3 — 16

(R Mike Smith) *t.k.h: led to over 3f out: sn rdn and wknd (jockey said filly ran too free)* **28/1**

2m 34.29s (4.59) **Going Correction** +0.55s/f (Yiel) **8 Ran SP% 123.7**

Speed ratings (Par 105): **105,104,102,101,100 95,90,79**

CSF £9.18 CT £17.02 TOTE £4.40: £1.50, £1.10, £1.90; EX 9.70 Trifecta £22.80.

Owner P Inglett, J Basquill And E Frost **Bred** Wollemie Park Stud **Trained** Ledbury, H'fords

FOCUS

10 yards added. The feature contest was a fair middle-distance handicap. They went a sensible gallop on the testing ground and, with the benefit of the stands' rail, the second-favourite saw off his main market rival close home. Sound form.

3251 WREAY H'CAP — 1m 3f 39y

8:50 (8:51) (Class 6) (0-60,64) 4-Y-O+

£3,493 (£1,039; £519; £300; £300; £300) Stalls High

Form — RPR

23-3 1 **Majestic Stone (IRE)**[30] 2244 5-8-3 **49** VictorSantos(7) 2 — 55

(Julie Camacho) *dwlt: t.k.h and sn prom: wnt 2nd 1/2-way: effrt on outside and led over 2f out: sn edgd lft: hrd pressed fr over 1f out: hld on wl cl home* **6/1**

-400 2 nse **Onda District (IRE)**[80] 1145 7-8-7 **46** oh1 (p[1]) ShaneGray 8 — 52

(Stella Barclay) *led: hdd over 1f out: styd w wnr: kpt on u.p: jst hld* **33/1**

3 4 **Law Equity (FR)**[414] 1748 8-8-7 **46** oh1 (t[1]) NathanEvans 11 — 46

(Rebecca Menzies) *chsd ldr to 1/2-way: cl up: outpcd over 3f out: rallied over 2f out: kpt on same pce fr over 1f out* **33/1**

40-1 4 8 **Banksy's Art**[7] 2998 4-9-4 **64** 5ex ScottMcCullagh(7) 3 — 51

(Mick Channon) *prom: outpcd over 3f out: no imp fr 2f out* **6/4**[1]

425- 5 ½ **Kitty's Cove**[272] 6743 4-8-10 **49** DavidAllan 1 — 35

(Tim Easterby) *hld up towards rr: drvn and outpcd over 3f out: n.d after* **9/1**

60-0 6 7 **Pinchpoint (IRE)**[23] 2512 4-9-7 **60** (h) AndrewMullen 12 — 35

(John Butler) *hld up: rdn over 3f out: no imp fr over 2f out: sn btn* **12/1**

/600 7 3¼ **Miss Ranger (IRE)**[19] 2628 7-9-9 **62** (p) BenCurtis 4 — 32

(Roger Fell) *prom: drvn and outpcd over 3f out: btn fnl 2f* **11/2**[3]

00-0 8 3 **Jock Talk (IRE)**[58] 1506 5-8-4 **46** oh1 (h) JamieGormley(3) 9 — 11

(Patrick Morris) *t.k.h towards rr: struggling over 3f out: sn btn (jockey said gelding ran too free)* **33/1**

- 9 ½ **Greengage (IRE)**[264] 7093 4-9-3 **56** JasonHart 6 — 20

(Tristan Davidson) *t.k.h: hld up towards rr: shortlived effrt over 2f out: sn btn* **11/4**[2]

2m 35.29s (5.59) **Going Correction** +0.55s/f (Yiel) **9 Ran SP% 122.9**

Speed ratings (Par 101): **101,100,98,92,91 86,84,82,81**

CSF £185.88 CT £5923.61 TOTE £9.90: £2.70, £8.60, £9.80; EX 356.20 Trifecta £895.60.

Owner Majestic Stone Partnership **Bred** Rabbah Bloodstock Limited **Trained** Norton, N Yorks

FOCUS

10 yards added. A modest middle-distance handicap. The winner's credited with a minor step forward.

T/Plt: £76.90 to a £1 stake. Pool: £43,680.01. 414.17 winning units. T/Qpdt: £33.30 to a £1 stake. Pool: £6,201.90. 137.48 winning units. **Richard Young**

3015 LINGFIELD (L-H)

Thursday, May 30

OFFICIAL GOING: Good to firm (good down the hill; 9.4)

Wind: light, across Weather: light cloud

3252 BET365.COM H'CAP — 1m 3f 133y

2:00 (2:01) (Class 6) (0-55,53) 4-Y-O+

£3,105 (£924; £461; £300; £300; £300) Stalls High

Form — RPR

02-0 1 **Champs Inblue**[20] 2593 4-9-2 **48** CharlesBishop 11 — 54

(Chris Gordon) *chsd ldrs tl hdwy to chse ldr over 10f out: effrt over 2f out: styd on ins fnl f to ld towards fin* **7/1**

-302 2 shd **Mistress Nellie**[8] 2975 4-8-10 **45** GabrieleMalune(3) 4 — 51

(William Stone) *broke wl: sn restrained and chsd ldrs: effrt over 2f out: drvn over 1f out: styd on ins fnl f: ev ch towards fin: jst hld* **15/8**[1]

0005 3 ½ **Seventii**[8] 2975 5-8-8 **45** DarraghKeenan(5) 6 — 50

(Robert Eddery) *hld up in tch in midfield: clsd and shkn up 2f out: styd on u.p ins fnl f: pressing ldrs and snatched 3rd last strides* **10/1**

/0-5 4 nk **Templier (IRE)**[39] 185 6-9-7 **53** (b) HectorCrouch 12 — 58

(Gary Moore) *sn led: rdn 2f out: drvn jst ins fnl f: grad worn down: hdd and lost 3 pls towards fin* **14/1**

0332 5 1 **Sigrid Nansen**[29] 2283 4-8-13 **45** (tp) OisinMurphy 1 — 48

(Alexandra Dunn) *walked rdrless to s: dwlt: hld up in last trio: effrt and hdwy over 1f out: drvn and chsd ldrs over 1f out: kpt on ins fnl f: nvr quite enough pce to get on terms* **5/1**[3]

23- 6 shd **Royal Hall (FR)**[18] 7302 7-9-2 **48** (v) SilvestreDeSousa 2 — 51

(Gary Moore) *in tch in midfield: effrt over 2f out: sn drvn: kpt on ins fnl f: nvr enough pce to get on terms* **7/2**[2]

4102 7 shd **Sea's Aria (IRE)**[7] 3017 8-8-8 **47** AledBeech(7) 10 — 50

(Mark Hoad) *s.i.s: hld up in last trio: effrt over 2f out: hdwy and nt clrest of runs 1f out: swtchd rt and styd on ins fnl f: nvr getting to ldrs* **15/2**

0-00 8 6 **Kerrera**[20] 2593 6-9-5 **51** RobertWinston 8 — 44+

(Paul Webber) *led briefly sn after s: chsd ldrs fr over 10f out: unable qck and btn over 1f out: wknd ins fnl f (jockey said mare hung right-handed)* **25/1**

-000 9 19 **Phobos**[30] 2231 4-9-1 **47** (h[1]) DavidProbert 9 — 10

(Michael Blanshard) *stdd s: hld up in rr: effrt over 2f out: sn struggling and bhd* **50/1**

2m 31.32s (-2.68) **Going Correction** -0.45s/f (Firm) **9 Ran SP% 119.5**

Speed ratings (Par 101): **90,89,89,89,88 88,88,84,71**

CSF £21.29 CT £136.84 TOTE £8.10: £1.90, £1.20, £3.70; EX 23.50 Trifecta £151.30.

Owner Paul Cox **Bred** West Dereham Abbey Stud **Trained** Morestead, Hampshire

■ Lady Of York was withdrawn. Price at time of withdrawal 16-1. Rule 4 does not apply.

FOCUS

All distances as advertised, though a cut away was in place on the downhill section of the round course until the 3f marker. Robert Winston and Oisin Murphy were full of praise for the ground after riding in the opener, describing it as lovey and beautiful respectively. \nLow grade stuff with the first seven finishing in a bit of a heap.

3253 BET365 (S) STKS — 1m 3f 133y

2:30 (2:30) (Class 6) 3-Y-O

£3,105 (£924; £461; £300) Stalls High

Form — RPR

1126 1 **Cafe Espresso**[7] 3012 3-9-3 **78** (b) OisinMurphy 1 — 66+

(Archie Watson) *t.k.h: trckd ldr for 2f: swtchd rt and effrt to chal over 2f out: led u.p 2f out: forged ahd 1f out: styd on strly* **2/9**[1]

6505 2 5 **Enyama (GER)**[22] 2530 3-8-9 **50** DavidProbert 3 — 50

(Michael Attwater) *trckd ldr after 2f: shkn up and ev ch 3f out: drvn 2f out: no ex and btn 1f out: wknd ins fnl f* **33/1**[3]

5230 3 3¾ **Hurricane Hero (FR)**[10] 3139 3-9-0 **74** (v[1]) CliffordLee 2 — 49

(K R Burke) *t.k.h: led: rdn 3f out: hdd 2f out: sn btn and wknd fnl f* **7/2**[2]

00-0 4 11 **On The Bob**[9] 2926 3-9-0 **51** (h[1]) JoeyHaynes 4 — 31

(Paddy Butler) *mounted in the chute: stdd s: t.k.h: hld up in tch in rr: effrt over 2f out: sn outpcd: wl hld and eased ins fnl f* **100/1**

2m 29.39s (-4.61) **Going Correction** -0.45s/f (Firm) **4 Ran SP% 108.0**

Speed ratings (Par 97): **93,89,87,79**

CSF £9.62 TOTE £1.10; EX 7.40 Trifecta £7.00.The winner was sold to Chelsea Banham Pre Training Ltd for £20,000. Hurricane Hero was claimed by Oliver Jack Murphy for £6,400.

Owner Boadicea Bloodstock **Bred** Churchill Bloodstock Investments Ltd **Trained** Upper Lambourn, W Berks

FOCUS

This seller lacked depth and the long odds-on favourite gradually stamped her authority on proceedings.

3254 BET365 MAIDEN AUCTION STKS (PLUS 10 RACE) — 1m 3f 133y

3:00 (3:01) (Class 5) 3-Y-O

£3,752 (£1,116; £557; £278) Stalls High

Form — RPR

243- 1 **Mind The Crack (IRE)**[218] 8549 3-9-5 **82** SilvestreDeSousa 1 — 83+

(Mark Johnston) *trckd ldr tl 7f out: styd handy: swtchd ins and clsd to ld ent fnl 2f: nudged along and asserted over 1f out: eased towards fin: v easily* **1/3**[1]

2340 2 5 **Ydra**[23] 2511 3-8-12 **70** (b) OisinMurphy 5 — 64

(Archie Watson) *led: rdn wl over 2f out: hdd ent fnl 2f: nt match pce of wnr and wknd ins fnl f* **12/1**[3]

40 3 1¼ **Kalaya (IRE)**[17] 2690 3-8-7 **0** DavidProbert 4 — 57

(Archie Watson) *chsd ldrs tl wnt 2nd 7f out: shkn up and ev ch wl over 2f out: unable to match pce of wnr over 1f out: one pce fnl f* **40/1**

3-3 4 1¼ **Dubai Philosopher (FR)**[33] 2128 3-9-2 **0** CliffordLee 3 — 64

(Michael Bell) *restless in stalls: dwlt: t.k.h: hld up in tch in rr: effrt wl over 2f out: unable qck and kpt on same pce fr over 1f out (jockey said colt was restless in stalls)* **7/2**[2]

2m 28.62s (-5.38) **Going Correction** -0.45s/f (Firm) **4 Ran SP% 107.4**

Speed ratings (Par 99): **99,95,94,94**

CSF £5.12 TOTE £1.10; EX 4.30 Trifecta £10.10.

Owner Paul & Clare Rooney **Bred** H & M Biebel **Trained** Middleham Moor, N Yorks

FOCUS

Another uncompetitive contest but the winner impressed. There are doubts over the form.

3255 BET365 H'CAP — 1m 1f

3:30 (3:30) (Class 4) (0-80,82) 4-Y-O+

£5,530 (£1,645; £822; £411) Stalls Low

Form — RPR

5343 1 **Enzemble (IRE)**[24] 2480 4-9-3 **76** SilvestreDeSousa 2 — 88

(James Fanshawe) *taken down early: mde all: pushed along and readily asserted wl over 1f out: in n.d fnl f: v easily* **11/8**[1]

-542 2 8 **Regimented (IRE)**[13] 2797 4-9-7 **80** PatDobbs 4 — 74

(Richard Hannon) *hld up in tch in 3rd: effrt to chse wnr 2f out: sn brushed aside and wl hld whn flashing tail ins fnl f* **11/8**[1]

0043 3 3 **Kadrizzi (FR)**[19] 2628 6-8-11 **70** (b) JasonWatson 5 — 58

(Dean Ivory) *hld up in tch in rr: effrt over 2f out: unable qck and wl hld over 1f out: wnt modest 3rd ins fnl f* **11/2**[2]

-020 4 1¼ **Double Reflection**[19] 2612 4-9-9 **82** CliffordLee 1 — 67

(K R Burke) *chsd wnr: rdn over 3f out: lost 2nd and btn ent fnl 2f: wknd fnl f* **8/1**[3]

1m 50.45s (-6.45) **Going Correction** -0.45s/f (Firm) course record **4 Ran SP% 110.7**

Speed ratings (Par 105): **106,98,96,95**

CSF £3.59 TOTE £2.20; EX 3.80 Trifecta £5.90.

Owner Ben CM Wong **Bred** Minch Bloodstock **Trained** Newmarket, Suffolk

FOCUS
Punters couldn't find a favourite but there was no doubting the winner. It might not have taken much winning.

3256 BEST ODDS GUARANTEED AT BET365 H'CAP 1m 1f
4:00 (4:01) (Class 6) (0-60,61) 3-Y-O
£3,105 (£924; £461; £300; £300; £300) **Stalls** Low

Form RPR

0214 **1** **Act Of Magic (IRE)**[15] 2734 3-9-2 **54** KieranO'Neill 8 65+
(Mohamed Moubarak) *hld up in tch in midfield: effrt to chse ldrs over 2f out: clsd u.p over 1f out: led jst ins fnl f: r.o strly: readily* **7/2**[2]

03-5 **2** *3* **Temujin (IRE)**[37] 2007 3-9-7 **59** RobertWinston 3 63
(Charles Hills) *chsd ldr: effrt over 2f out: kpt on u.p and ev ch ent fnl f: chsd wnr but easily outpcd ins fnl f* **10/1**

0-50 **3** *½* **Mukha Magic**[16] 2712 3-9-3 **58** (b) WilliamCox(3) 11 61
(Gay Kelleway) *in tch in midfield: effrt over 2f out: drvn over 1f out: hdwy ins fnl f: styd on wl towards fin: no threat to wnr* **20/1**

0-45 **4** *¾* **Swiss Peak**[20] 2597 3-9-7 **59** DavidProbert 13 61
(Michael Bell) *stdd and wnt rt s: sn swtchd lft and t.k.h in rr: effrt over 2f out: swtchd lft and hdwy 2f out: chsd ldrs and swtchd rt ins fnl f: kpt on but no threat to wnr (jockey said gelding was slowly away)* **7/1**

3650 **5** *nk* **Cromwell**[10] 2914 3-9-2 **59** TheodoreLadd(5) 2 60
(Luke Dace) *led and sn clr: rdn jst over 2f out: drvn and hrd pressed ent fnl f: hdd jst ins fnl f: no ex and wknd towards fin* **8/1**

4043 **6** *3* **Margaret J**[23] 2517 3-8-8 **46** (p) NicolaCurrie 1 41
(Phil McEntee) *chsd ldrs: effrt 3f out: unable qck and outpcd 2f out: wl hld and plugged on same pce fnl f* **20/1**

-440 **7** *3 ¼* **Toro Dorado**[13] 2798 3-9-9 **61** (b) DanielMuscutt 5 49
(Ed Dunlop) *wnt rt and bmpd leaving stalls: hld up in tch in midfield: effrt jst over 2f out: no imp u.p over 1f out: wknd fnl f* **16/1**

4-00 **8** *½* **Elsie Violet (IRE)**[14] 2760 3-9-0 **57** DarraghKeenan(5) 6 44
(Robert Eddery) *wnt rt and bmpd leaving stalls: hld up in rr: effrt on inner 3f out: nvr trbld ldrs* **33/1**

600- **9** *5* **Queen Of Bradgate**[230] 8163 3-8-4 **45** GabrieleMalune(3) 4 22
(Ivan Furtado) *short of room leaving stalls: hld up in tch in midfield: effrt over 2f out: sn struggling and wl btn over 1f out* **40/1**

5432 **10** *hd* **Lippy Lady (IRE)**[15] 2734 3-9-3 **55** (h) OisinMurphy 14 32
(Paul George) *taken down early: unruly coming onto crse and led rdrless to s: pushed rt leaving stalls: sn rcvrd and in tch in midfield: clsd to chse ldrs 5f out: shkn up over 2f out: sn btn: wknd over 1f out (jockey said filly found little under pressure; trainer could offer no further explanation for the filly's performance)* **3/1**[1]

0-41 **11** *1 ¼* **Poetic Motion**[15] 2734 3-8-13 **51** PatCosgrave 9 26
(Jim Boyle) *t.k.h: chsd ldrs: unable qck u.p over 2f out: sn lost pl: wknd over 1f out (jockey said filly became unbalanced coming down the hill)* **9/2**[3]

00-0 **12** *3 ½* **Bader**[45] 1824 3-9-5 **57** PatDobbs 10 25
(Richard Hannon) *in tch in midfield tl lost pl over 2f out: sn bhd* **16/1**

460 **13** *1 ¾* **Jazzy Card (IRE)**[31] 2210 3-9-3 **55** GeorgeDowning 7 19
(Linda Jewell) *wnt lft and bmpd s: in tch: lost pl u.p over 2f out: bhd over 1f out* **66/1**

06-0 **14** *24* **Florence Rose**[54] 1593 3-9-1 **53** RobHornby 12
(Jonathan Portman) *a towards rr: bhd 3f out: sn lost pl: t.o* **50/1**

1m 52.52s (-4.38) **Going Correction** -0.45s/f (Firm) **14 Ran SP% 128.2**
Speed ratings (Par 97): **97,94,93,93,92 90,87,86,82,82 81,78,76,55**
CSF £38.57 CT £664.38 TOTE £4.90: £1.80, £3.10, £8.70; EX 50.50 Trifecta £921.40.
Owner The Mojito Partnership **Bred** Mr & Mrs W Evans **Trained** Newmarket, Suffolk

FOCUS
A competitive if only moderate 3yo handicap.

3257 BET365 NOVICE MEDIAN AUCTION STKS 6f
4:30 (4:33) (Class 5) 2-Y-O
£3,752 (£1,116; £557; £278) **Stalls** Centre

Form RPR

3 **1** **Calippo (IRE)**[10] 2907 2-9-0 0 OisinMurphy 7 72
(Archie Watson) *mde all: rdn and hung rt over 1f out: hrd pressed ins fnl f: hld on u.p cl home* **2/1**[1]

43 **2** *hd* **Miss Matterhorn**[17] 2694 2-9-0 0 CharlesBishop 9 71
(Eve Johnson Houghton) *chsd ldrs tl wnt 2nd over 2f out: drvn and swtchd lft over 1f out: kpt on wl u.p and str chal ins fnl f: jst hld cl home* **5/1**[3]

3 *1 ¾* **Dorset Blue (IRE)** 2-9-5 0 RossaRyan 4 71
(Richard Hannon) *midfield: effrt over 2f out: hdwy u.p to chse ldrs ent fnl f: kpt on but nvr quite getting on terms* **5/1**[3]

4 *1 ¼* **Decora (IRE)** 2-9-0 0 DavidProbert 8 62
(Mick Channon) *chsd ldrs: rdn over 2f out: unable qck over 1f out: hld and kpt on same pce ins fnl f* **20/1**

0 **5** *3* **London Calling (IRE)**[14] 2761 2-9-5 0 DanielMuscutt 6 58
(Richard Spencer) *chsd wnr tl over 2f out: unable qck over 1f out: btn whn sltly impeded jst ins fnl f: wknd* **7/2**[2]

6 *nk* **Full Spectrum (IRE)** 2-9-0 0 JFEgan 2 52
(Paul George) *pushed lft s: towards rr of main gp: wnt lft and effrt over 2f out: hdwy 2f out: sn no imp and kpt on same pce ins fnl f* **25/1**

7 *1 ¼* **Overpriced Mixer** 2-9-5 0 NicolaCurrie 14 53
(Jamie Osborne) *wnt lft s: racd in midfield: effrt over 2f out: no imp whn rn green and edgd lft over 1f out: wl hld and plugged on same pce ins fnl f* **12/1**

0 **8** *1* **Rain Cap**[7] 3008 2-9-5 0 GeorgeDowning 3 50
(Mick Channon) *rn green in rr of main gp: effrt ent fnl 2f: kpt on steadily fnl f: nvr involved* **50/1**

9 *3 ½* **Rodney Le Roc** 2-9-5 0 KierenFox 12 40
(John Best) *wnt rt s: in rr of main gp: effrt and swtchd rt ent fnl 2f: no prog and wknd fnl f (jockey said colt ran green)* **33/1**

0 **10** *1* **Sir Chancealot (IRE)**[14] 2767 2-9-5 0 PatDobbs 10 37+
(Amanda Perrett) *chsd ldrs tl pl over 2f out: sn edging lft and btn: wknd over 1f out* **33/1**

11 *1* **Boasty (IRE)** 2-9-5 0 StevieDonohoe 11 34
(Charlie Fellowes) *a towards rr of main gp: struggling 1/2-way: bhd fnl 2f* **10/1**

12 *½* **Lafontaine (FR)** 2-8-11 0 GaryMahon(3) 13 27+
(Sylvester Kirk) *squeezed for room leaving stalls: towards rr of main gp: prog into midfield over 3f out: pushed along and lost pl 2f out: sn wknd and hung lft over 1f out* **50/1**

13 *64* **Broughtons Compass** 2-9-5 0 JackMitchell 1
(Mark Hoad) *s.i.s: swtchd rt: sn t.o (jockey said colt ran green)* **66/1**

1m 10.32s (-1.18) **Going Correction** -0.45s/f (Firm) **13 Ran SP% 125.6**
Speed ratings (Par 93): **90,89,87,85,81 81,79,78,73,72 71,70,**
CSF £12.09 TOTE £2.70: £1.30, £1.70, £1.90; EX 13.40 Trifecta £56.90.
Owner Marco Polo **Bred** Padraig Williams **Trained** Upper Lambourn, W Berks

FOCUS
An informative, though likely only ordinary affair.

3258 BET365 FILLIES' H'CAP 7f
5:00 (5:06) (Class 5) (0-70,72) 3-Y-O
£3,752 (£1,116; £557; £300; £300; £300) **Stalls** Centre

Form RPR

50-2 **1** **King's Girl**[30] 2251 3-9-7 **69** OisinMurphy 7 76
(Sir Michael Stoute) *t.k.h: trckd ldrs: effrt to ld 2f out: drvn over 1f out: styd on wl ins fnl f* **11/10**[2]

1-63 **2** *1 ¼* **Dashed**[14] 2760 3-9-10 **72** JackMitchell 4 76
(Roger Varian) *t.k.h: trckd ldr for over 1f out: styd trcking ldrs: effrt 2f out: drvn to press ldrs over 1f out: nt match pce of wnr and btn fnl 100yds* **1/1**[1]

03-0 **3** *2 ¼* **Mrs Worthington (IRE)**[28] 2340 3-9-3 **65** RobHornby 5 63
(Jonathan Portman) *t.k.h: hld up in tch: clsd to join ldrs jst over 2f out: ev ch and edgd lft over 1f out: no ex and wknd ins fnl f* **20/1**

00-5 **4** *½* **Boorowa**[14] 2772 3-8-11 **59** RossaRyan 3 56
(Ali Stronge) *wnt lft s: t.k.h: hld up in tch in last pair: effrt ent fnl 2f: swtchd lft and kpt on same pce ins fnl f* **14/1**[3]

306 **5** *1 ¼* **Lady Schannell (IRE)**[20] 2598 3-9-4 **66** (t[1]) DanielMuscutt 1 59
(Marco Botti) *t.k.h: jnd ldr after over 1f: led 4f out: hdd 2f out: sn rdn and unable qck over 1f out: wknd ins fnl f (jockey said filly hung right-handed under pressure)* **40/1**

-300 **6** *3 ¼* **Hanbury Dreams**[30] 2251 3-8-11 **59** StevieDonohoe 2 43
(Tom Clover) *bmpd leaving stalls: t.k.h: hld up in tch: effrt ent fnl 2f: wnt lft and no imp wl over 1f out: wknd ins fnl f* **40/1**

0-00 **7** *12* **Aegean Mist**[24] 2489 3-9-5 **67** KieranO'Neill 8 19
(John Bridger) *led tl 4f out: styd prom tl ent fnl 2f: lost pl and towards rr and wnt lft wl over 1f out: wknd* **33/1**

1m 22.61s (-1.69) **Going Correction** -0.45s/f (Firm) **7 Ran SP% 116.9**
Speed ratings (Par 96): **92,90,88,87,86 82,68**
CSF £2.52 CT £7.56 TOTE £2.00: £1.80, £1.10; EX 2.60 Trifecta £10.10.
Owner Mohamed Obaida **Bred** Rabbah Bloodstock Limited **Trained** Newmarket, Suffolk
■ Bequest was withdrawn. Price at time of withdrawal 8-1. Rule 4 only applies to board prices prior to withdrawal - deduction 10p in the pound. New market formed.

FOCUS
This was considered a match in the betting and that played out in the race itself. The winner's rated back to her 2yo best.
T/Plt: £56.90 to a £1 stake. Pool: £50,944.21. 653.56 winning units. T/Qpdt: £15.70 to a £1 stake. Pool: £4,264.81. 200.92 winning units. **Steve Payne**

3022 SANDOWN (R-H)
Thursday, May 30

OFFICIAL GOING: Good to firm (good in places bottom bend)
Wind: Moderate, against Weather: Fine but cloudy, warm

3259 DOWNLOAD THE STAR SPORTS APP NOW! EBF FILLIES' NOVICE STKS (PLUS 10 RACE) 5f 10y
5:55 (5:56) (Class 4) 2-Y-O
£4,851 (£1,443; £721; £360) **Stalls** Low

Form RPR

1 **Graceful Magic** 2-9-0 0 CharlesBishop 2 76
(Eve Johnson Houghton) *racd against rail: trckd ldng pair: wnt 2nd over 1f out: clsd fnl f: pushed into ld last 75yds: styd on wl* **33/1**

5 **2** *1* **Sneaky**[8] 2968 2-9-0 0 OisinMurphy 1 72
(Archie Watson) *led and racd against rail: pushed along over 1f out: hdd and outpcd last 75yds* **7/2**[2]

3 *hd* **Multiply By Eight (FR)** 2-9-0 0 SilvestreDeSousa 6 72+
(Tom Dascombe) *sn in last: pushed along on outer 2f out: rn green but prog over 1f out: r.o fnl f to take 3rd last 100yds and nrly snatched 2nd* **10/1**

4 *3* **Cece Ceylon** 2-9-0 0 HarryBentley 3 61
(Ralph Beckett) *dwlt sltly: sn in tch in 5th: pushed along 2f out: sltly checked jst over 1f out: kpt on fnl f: nt pce to threaten* **8/1**

0 **5** *hd* **Crime Of Passion (IRE)**[45] 1821 2-9-0 0 NicolaCurrie 7 60
(Jamie Osborne) *chsd ldrs on outer: pushed along 2f out: no prog over 1f out: fdd fnl f* **11/2**[3]

6 *1* **Divine Covey** 2-9-0 0 TomMarquand 4 57
(Richard Hannon) *pressed ldr: pushed along 2f out: lost 2nd over 1f out and sn wknd* **10/11**[1]

7 *2 ¼* **Dragon Flight (IRE)** 2-9-0 0 EoinWalsh 5 48
(George Scott) *sn pushed along in last pair: no prog over 1f out: nvr a factor* **25/1**

1m 3.66s (2.36) **Going Correction** +0.075s/f (Good) **7 Ran SP% 117.0**
Speed ratings (Par 92): **84,82,82,77,76 75,71**
CSF £149.23 TOTE £33.20: £7.20, £1.70; EX 138.00 Trifecta £1803.80.
Owner The Kimber Family **Bred** Dr Scott Kimber **Trained** Blewbury, Oxon

FOCUS
All distances as advertised and Sprint track at full width. A surprise outcome to this fair event, which was run around 4sec outside the standard. Stall 2 beat stall 1. The form's fluid initially.

3260 STARSPORTS.BET H'CAP 1m 6f
6:30 (6:31) (Class 4) (0-85,85) 3-Y-O
£9,586 (£2,870; £1,435; £717; £358; £300) **Stalls** Low

Form RPR

1215 **1** **Lord Lamington**[28] 2317 3-9-2 **80** SilvestreDeSousa 3 85
(Mark Johnston) *mde all: stretched on 3f out: rdn over 1f out: hrd pressed ins fnl f: a holding on* **7/1**

216- **2** *nk* **Prefontaine (IRE)**[218] 8550 3-9-7 **85** AndreaAtzeni 1 89
(Roger Varian) *dwlt and pushed along early: sn wl in tch: pushed along 3f out: chsd wnr over 2f out: edgd lft u.p over 1f out: grad clsd ins fnl f: a jst hld* **4/1**[3]

653 **3** *1 ¾* **Tidal Point (IRE)**[33] 2099 3-8-8 **72** NicolaCurrie 6 73
(Steph Hollinshead) *wl in tch: pushed along 3f out: effrt u.p on outer 2f out: kpt on same pce fnl f* **33/1**

4-21 **4** *¾* **Rowland Ward**[33] 2096 3-9-3 **81** HarryBentley 2 81
(Ralph Beckett) *hld up in tch: effrt to dispute 2nd over 2f out: u.p and hld whn nudged by rival jst over 1f out: one pce after* **5/4**[1]

4143 **5** *2 ½* **Seeusoon (IRE)**[21] 2562 3-8-8 **72** OisinMurphy 4 69
(Andrew Balding) *trckd wnr: pushed along 3f out: lost 2nd over 2f out and btn wl over 1f out* **5/2**[2]

21-2 **6** *2* **Queen Constantine (GER)**[30] 2253 3-8-10 **74**..........(h) DavidProbert 5 68
(William Jarvis) *hld up in last: effrt on wd outside over 2f out: nt qckn over 1f out: wknd fnl f* **16/1**

3m 11.02s (5.02) **Going Correction** +0.075s/f (Good) **6** Ran SP% **114.3**
Speed ratings (Par 101): **88,87,86,86,84 83**
CSF £35.30 TOTE £7.00: £2.50, £2.20; EX 37.50 Trifecta £200.40.
Owner Netherfield House Stud **Bred** Newsells Park Stud **Trained** Middleham Moor, N Yorks
■ Stewards' Enquiry : Andrea Atzeni caution: careless riding

FOCUS
This decent little handicap was run at a modest initial gallop. This is perhaps not the most solid piece of form.

3261 READ SILVESTRE DE SOUSA'S BLOG STARSPORTSBET.CO.UK H'CAP — 1m

7:05 (7:06) (Class 4) (0-85,83) 3-Y-O
£6,469 (£1,925; £962; £481; £300; £300) **Stalls** Low

Form — RPR

-143 **1** **Fox Leicester (IRE)**[26] 2414 3-9-6 **82**.................... SilvestreDeSousa 7 93+
(Andrew Balding) *led after 1f: mde rest: at least 2 l clr fr 3f out: shkn up and wl in command over 1f out: won decisively* **5/6**[1]

541- **2** *2 ½* **Hold Still (IRE)**[197] 9051 3-9-3 **79**.................... JasonWatson 5 83
(William Muir) *hld up off the pce in last trio: shkn up and gd prog on outer over 2f out: chsd wnr over 1f out: styd on but nvr able to land a blow* **10/1**[3]

630- **3** *1 ½* **Conspiritor**[216] 8602 3-8-11 **73**.................... RichardKingscote 3 74
(Charles Hills) *led 1f: chsd wnr to over 5f out: wnt 2nd again 2f out to over 1f out: kpt on same pce u.p* **25/1**

213 **4** *1* **Sparkle In His Eye**[24] 2488 3-9-6 **82**.................... OisinMurphy 1 80
(William Haggas) *dwlt: hld up in midfield: prog on inner jst over 2f out: rdn to dispute 2nd jst over 1f out: one pce fnl f* **7/2**[2]

155 **5** *1 ½* **Eardley Road (IRE)**[32] 2147 3-9-0 **76**..............(p[1]) HectorCrouch 2 71
(Clive Cox) *chsd clr ldrs: rdn to try to cl over 2f out: ch of a pl over 1f out: fdd fnl f* **20/1**

3160 **6** *½* **Balata Bay**[9] 2942 3-8-9 **78**.................... LukeCatton(7) 9 72
(Richard Hannon) *hld up in rr: shkn up over 2f out and briefly nt clr run: styd on same pce fr over 1f out: nvr nrr* **33/1**

332- **7** *9* **Steeve**[218] 8553 3-9-2 **78**.................... RobHornby 8 51
(Rod Millman) *stdd s: hld up in detached last: pushed along 3f out: passed wkng rivals fnl 2f: nvr in it* **20/1**

420- **8** *4* **Dawn Treader (IRE)**[239] 7904 3-9-3 **79**.................... TomMarquand 6 43
(Richard Hannon) *nvr beyond midfield: rdn and no prog over 2f out: sn wknd* **16/1**

4-03 **9** *2 ¼* **Promise Of Success**[14] 2770 3-9-0 **76**.................... PatCosgrave 10 35
(Saeed bin Suroor) *dwlt: rcvrd on outer to chse wnr over 5f out to 2f out: wknd rapidly* **10/1**[3]

2-11 **10** *36* **Renegade Master**[134] 258 3-9-7 **83**.................... NicolaCurrie 4
(George Baker) *t.k.h: prom to 1/2-way: wknd rapidly over 3f out: eased 2f out: t.o (jockey said gelding took a false step and she eased the gelding in the last 1 1/2f)* **25/1**

1m 42.95s (-0.35) **Going Correction** +0.075s/f (Good) **10** Ran SP% **121.0**
Speed ratings (Par 101): **104,101,100,99,97 97,88,84,81,45**
CSF £9.92 CT £136.45 TOTE £1.60: £1.10, £2.70, £8.20; EX 11.90 Trifecta £188.30.
Owner King Power Racing Co Ltd **Bred** Marston Stud **Trained** Kingsclere, Hants

FOCUS
Fairly useful handicap form. The winner was another to boost the form of Pogo's Newmarket race.

3262 CALL STAR SPORTS ON 08000 521 321 H'CAP — 1m 1f 209y

7:35 (7:36) (Class 3) (0-90,89) 3-Y-O
£9,337 (£2,796; £1,398; £699; £349; £175) **Stalls** Low

Form — RPR

26-1 **1** **Fox Premier (IRE)**[21] 2553 3-9-3 **85**.................... SilvestreDeSousa 5 102
(Andrew Balding) *t.k.h: trckd ldng pair: pushed along to take 2nd 2f out: led over 1f out: shkn up and drew clr fnl f: v readily* **9/4**[1]

-103 **2** *3 ½* **Sameem (IRE)**[11] 2872 3-9-5 **87**.................... OisinMurphy 4 97
(James Tate) *led at gd pce: rdn and hdd over 1f out: kpt on same pce and no ch w wnr fnl f* **4/1**[3]

3312 **3** *3 ¼* **Albert Finney**[45] 1823 3-9-2 **84**.................... FrankieDettori 3 88
(John Gosden) *trckd ldr: briefly tried to chal over 2f out: sn dropped to 3rd and wl hld after* **6/1**

211- **4** *2* **Jersey Wonder (IRE)**[230] 8157 3-9-3 **85**.................... NicolaCurrie 1 85
(Jamie Osborne) *dwlt: hld up in last: shkn up over 3f out: tk 4th 2f out but nt on terms: no real imp after* **20/1**

3-41 **5** *1 ¾* **Pour Me A Drink**[33] 2101 3-8-11 **79**.................... HectorCrouch 6 75
(Clive Cox) *hld up in 5th: shkn up and no rspnse over 2f out: sn wl btn* **7/2**[2]

2-21 **6** *1 ¾* **Emirates Knight (IRE)**[19] 2634 3-9-7 **89**.................... AndreaAtzeni 2 82
(Roger Varian) *chsd ldng trio: urged along wl over 3f out: sn struggling* **7/2**[2]

2m 7.89s (-2.31) **Going Correction** +0.075s/f (Good) **6** Ran SP% **114.3**
Speed ratings (Par 103): **112,109,106,105,103 102**
CSF £11.90 TOTE £2.90: £2.00, £2.40; EX 12.70 Trifecta £47.40.
Owner King Power Racing Co Ltd **Bred** Rabbah Bloodstock Limited **Trained** Kingsclere, Hants

FOCUS
Last year's winner, Corgi, went on to finish second in the King George V at Royal Ascot. This edition was run at a solid gallop and the form is taken at face value.

3263 WATCH THE #BETTINGPEOPLE VIDEOS STARSPORTSBET.CO.UK EBF NOVICE STKS — 1m 1f 209y

8:10 (8:10) (Class 5) 3-Y-O+
£4,851 (£1,443; £721; £360) **Stalls** Low

Form — RPR

41 **1** **Pondus**[20] 2581 3-9-7 0.................... OisinMurphy 2 107+
(James Fanshawe) *mde virtually all: drew clr 2f out: in n.d after: rdn out tl last 50yds* **7/4**[1]

34 **2** *5* **Aktau**[20] 2581 3-9-0 0.................... AndreaAtzeni 11 87+
(Roger Varian) *t.k.h early: hld up in 6th: pushed along over 2f out: prog over 1f out: tk 2nd ins fnl f: no ch w wnr but styd on (jockey said gelding hung right-handed under pressure)* **3/1**[2]

-6 **3** *1* **Nette Rousse (GER)**[20] 2581 3-8-9 0.................... HarryBentley 8 80
(Ralph Beckett) *mostly in 5th tl chsd clr ldng trio over 2f out: sn shkn up: styd on over 1f out to take 3rd last 100yds* **20/1**

51 **4** *1 ¼* **Gold Stick (IRE)**[23] 2505 3-9-7 0.................... FrankieDettori 3 90
(John Gosden) *sn trckd ldng pair: shkn up over 2f out: pressed for 2nd 1f out: one pce fnl f* **9/2**[3]

4-2 **5** *¾* **Maiden Castle**[27] 2354 3-9-0 0.................... DavidProbert 7 81
(Henry Candy) *sn chsd wnr: outpcd 2f out: tending to hang over 1f out: lost 2nd and wknd ins fnl f* **3/1**[2]

6 **6** *3 ½* **Tribal Craft** 3-8-9 0.................... RobHornby 14 69+
(Andrew Balding) *hld up towards rr: nt clr run wl over 2f out and in last trio: prog wl over 1f out: pushed along and styd on w promise fnl f* **50/1**

7 *1 ¼* **Mizuki (IRE)** 4-9-6 0.................... JoshuaBryan(3) 9 68
(Andrew Balding) *mostly in 8th: pushed along and effrt over 2f out: no real prog over 1f out* **50/1**

23 **8** *3 ¼* **Trailboss (IRE)**[21] 2555 4-10-0 0.................... StevieDonohoe 6 66
(Ed Vaughan) *dwlt: hld up in 10th: shkn up and no prog over 2f out: wknd over 1f out* **50/1**

5/4 **9** *nk* **Flying Tiger (IRE)**[19] 2354 6-10-0 0.................... TomMarquand 12 65
(Nick Williams) *hld up in last pair: pushed along over 2f out: modest prog over 1f out: nvr in it* **20/1**

6 **10** *1 ½* **Ekayburg (FR)**[15] 2731 5-9-11 0..............(t[1]) FinleyMarsh(3) 5 62
(David Pipe) *racd in 7th: shkn up and no prog over 2f out: wknd over 1f out* **66/1**

11 *2 ¼* **Indignation (FR)** 3-9-0 0.................... PatDobbs 10 57
(Sir Michael Stoute) *dwlt: hld up in last pair: pushed along and no prog over 2f out: passed a few fnl f* **20/1**

06 **12** *1 ½* **Ideal Grace**[17] 2690 3-8-9 0.................... NicolaCurrie 4 49
(Eve Johnson Houghton) *briefly chsd wnr but sn in 4th: wknd over 2f out* **66/1**

13 *1 ¾* **The Cruix (IRE)**[21] 4-10-0 0.................... JoeyHaynes 1 51
(Dean Ivory) *dwlt: pushed up into midfield: wknd 2f out* **50/1**

0 **14** *1* **Postie**[20] 2581 3-8-9 0..........(h) RyanTate 13 43
(James Eustace) *a in rr: shkn up and no prog over 2f out* **100/1**

2m 7.45s (-2.75) **Going Correction** +0.075s/f (Good)
WFA 3 from 4yo+ 14lb **14** Ran SP% **130.6**
Speed ratings (Par 103): **114,110,109,108,107 104,103,101,100,99 97,96,95,94**
CSF £7.25 TOTE £2.50: £1.10, £1.70, £5.60; EX 9.40 Trifecta £87.70.
Owner Hubert John Strecker **Bred** Miss K Rausing **Trained** Newmarket, Suffolk

FOCUS
Winners ought to come out of this novice event, which was 0.44sec quicker than the preceding class 3 handicap. The first three all came from the same race at Nottingham. The form's rated around the runner-up.

3264 FIRST FOR INDUSTRY JOBS VISIT STARRECRUITMENT.BET FILLIES' H'CAP — 1m 1f

8:40 (8:42) (Class 5) (0-75,76) 3-Y-O+
£4,528 (£1,347; £673; £336; £300; £300) **Stalls** Low

Form — RPR

0-15 **1** **Ashazuri**[19] 2612 5-9-8 **69**..........(h) NicolaCurrie 1 78
(Jonathan Portman) *mde all and set str pce: clr w one rival over 3f out: rdn 2f out and looked vulnerable over 1f out: kpt on wl fnl f* **9/1**

6001 **2** *1* **Emma Point (USA)**[33] 2125 3-8-12 **72**..........(h) JasonWatson 2 77
(Marco Botti) *chsd ldng trio: outpcd over 4f out: shkn up to cl over 2f out: rdn to chse wnr jst ins fnl f: kpt on but no imp last 100yds* **8/1**[3]

011- **3** *nk* **Hallalulu**[279] 6497 3-8-8 **75**.................... CierenFallon(7) 5 79+
(William Haggas) *hld up in 8th: plenty to do over 3f out: shkn up and no great prog over 2f out: sed to run on over 1f out: fin wl but too late to chal* **9/4**[1]

5012 **4** *4* **Comeonfeeltheforce (IRE)**[37] 2007 3-7-11 **60** oh4...(t) NoelGarbutt(3) 6 55
(Lee Carter) *s.i.s: hld up in last pair: plenty to do whn shkn up 3f out: gd prog on outer to take 2nd wl over 1f out and looked a threat: fdd fnl f* **25/1**

35-3 **5** *4 ½* **Chicago Doll**[9] 2942 3-8-13 **73**.................... DavidProbert 3 58
(Alan King) *mostly in same pl: outpcd over 4f out: drvn and no imp on ldrs 2f out: fdd* **9/1**

6-30 **6** *2* **Artistic Streak**[22] 2524 3-9-0 **74**.................... RichardKingscote 8 55
(Tom Dascombe) *pressed ldng pair tl outpcd over 4f out: sn urged along: wknd over 2f out* **12/1**

0-34 **7** *1* **Sweet Charity**[30] 2230 4-10-0 **75**.................... OisinMurphy 11 56
(Denis Coakley) *hld up in 7th: tried to cl over 2f out and gng bttr than sme: rdn and wknd over 1f out* **4/1**[2]

3000 **8** *2 ¾* **Margie's Choice (GER)**[13] 2797 4-9-1 **62**..........(v) HectorCrouch 9 37
(Michael Madgwick) *a towards rr: rdn and no prog over 2f out: wknd over 1f out* **50/1**

505- **9** *3 ½* **Dependable (GER)**[267] 6954 4-9-4 **65**.................... TomMarquand 4 32
(Charles Hills) *t.k.h: pressed wnr: clr of rest over 4f out: lost 2nd and wknd wl over 1f out* **20/1**

022- **10** *61* **Dubrava**[204] 8915 3-8-13 **73**.................... AndreaAtzeni 7
(Roger Varian) *chsd ldrs: lost pl 3f out and sltly impeded sn after: wknd rapidly: t.o (jockey said filly stopped quickly)* **4/1**[2]

02-0 **11** *2 ½* **Perfect Showdance**[20] 2583 3-9-2 **76**.................... RobHornby 12
(Clive Cox) *s.s: nvr gng wl and sn t.o* **16/1**

1m 57.62s (1.32) **Going Correction** +0.075s/f (Good)
WFA 3 from 4yo+ 13lb **11** Ran SP% **126.0**
Speed ratings (Par 100): **97,96,95,92,88 86,85,83,80,25 23**
CSF £83.16 CT £223.99 TOTE £12.00: £3.20, £2.70, £2.00; EX 91.40 Trifecta £359.20.
Owner RWH Partnership **Bred** G Wickens And J Homan **Trained** Upper Lambourn, Berks
■ Stewards' Enquiry : Jason Watson caution: careless riding

FOCUS
An ordinary fillies' race. The winner is rated in line with a better view of her form.
T/Jkpt: Not won. T/Plt: £166.60 to a £1 stake. Pool: £75,817.22. 332.02 winning units. T/Qpdt: £10.70 to a £1 stake. Pool: £11,240.38. 772.02 winning units. **Jonathan Neesom**

[2505]WETHERBY (L-H)
Thursday, May 30

OFFICIAL GOING: Good to firm (8.7)
Wind: Fresh and blustery behind Weather: Cloudy and blustery with showers

3265 BRITISH STALLION STUDS EBF MEDIAN AUCTION MAIDEN STKS (PLUS 10 RACE) — 5f 110y

2:10 (2:12) (Class 4) 2-Y-O
£5,498 (£1,636; £817; £408) **Stalls** High

Form — RPR

1 **Coastal Mist (IRE)** 2-9-5 0.................... JasonHart 8 73+
(John Quinn) *cl up on outer: chal over 1f out: rdn: green and edgd lft ins fnl f: kpt on wl to ld towards fin* **2/1**[1]

6 **2** *shd* **Star Of St James (GER)**[10] 2892 2-9-0 0.................... SeanDavis(5) 6 73
(Richard Fahey) *cl up: led wl over 1f out: sn rdn: jnd and drvn ent fnl f: sn edgd lft: kpt on: hdd towards fin* **6/1**

The Form Book Flat 2019, Raceform Ltd, Newbury, RG14 5SJ

3 3 **Cruising** 2-9-5 0 PaulMulrennan 5 63
(David Brown) *trckd ldrs: hdwy over 2f out: rdn and ch over 1f out: kpt on same pce fnl f* **25/1**

36 4 2 ¼ **Perregrin**[13] [2783] 2-9-5 0 JoeFanning 1 55
(Mark Johnston) *led: pushed along over 2f out: sn rdn and hdd wl over 1f out: grad wknd* **10/1**

5 hd **Wots The Wifi Code** 2-9-5 0 DougieCostello 7 55
(Tony Coyle) *chsd ldrs on inner: rdn along over 2f out: wknd over 1f out* **66/1**

5 6 nk **Out Of Here (IRE)**[16] [2706] 2-9-5 0 KevinStott 4 54
(Kevin Ryan) *trckd ldrs: hdwy and cl up 2f out: sn rdn and wknd over 1f out* **5/2**[2]

7 ½ **Asstech (IRE)** 2-9-5 0 TonyHamilton 9 52
(Richard Fahey) *dwlt: green and in rr tl styd on appr fnl f: n.d* **14/1**

8 1 ¼ **Ellenor Gray (IRE)** 2-9-0 0 PaulHanagan 2 43
(Richard Fahey) *dwlt: green and in rr: sme late hdwy* **5/1**[3]

9 3 **Pacific Coast** 2-9-5 0 CamHardie 3 38
(Antony Brittain) *a towards rr* **100/1**

1m 6.14s (0.34) **Going Correction** -0.125s/f (Firm) 2y crse rec **9 Ran SP% 114.9**
Speed ratings (Par 95): **92,91,87,84,84 84,83,81,77**
CSF £14.46 TOTE £2.70: £1.30, £1.90, £4.80; EX 15.90 Trifecta £205.00.
Owner Hart Inn 1 & Partner **Bred** R & R Bloodstock **Trained** Settrington, N Yorks

FOCUS
Hard to know what to make of this form yet, but two pulled away.

3266 FOLLOW @RACINGTV ON TWITTER NOVICE MEDIAN AUCTION STKS 1m
2:40 (2:41) (Class 6) 3-4-Y-O **£4,204** (£1,251; £625; £312) **Stalls** Low

Form RPR

2-3 1 **Mokammal**[31] [2216] 3-9-5 DaneO'Neill 5 81
(Sir Michael Stoute) *trckd ldr: hdwy on inner over 2f out: sn chal: rdn to ld jst over 1f out: edgd lft and kpt on* **2/5**[1]

34-3 2 1 ¼ **Itizzit**[16] [2715] 3-9-0 74 GrahamLee 2 73
(Hughie Morrison) *set stdy pce: pushed along and qcknd over 2f out: sn jnd and rdn: hdd over 1f out: drvn and kpt on fnl f* **3/1**[2]

4-6 3 3 ¾ **Poetic Era**[31] [2216] 3-9-0 PaulHanagan 1 65
(David Simcock) *trckd ldng pair: hdwy on outer over 2f out: rdn along wl over 1f out: sn one pce* **8/1**[3]

- 4 2 ¼ **Sweet Dreamer** 3-8-9 HarrisonShaw(5) 3 60
(K R Burke) *hld up: a in rr* **66/1**

1m 43.34s (1.74) **Going Correction** -0.125s/f (Firm) **4 Ran SP% 109.0**
Speed ratings (Par 101): **86,84,81,78**
CSF £1.93 TOTE £1.20; EX 1.80 Trifecta £2.30.
Owner Hamdan Al Maktoum **Bred** G R Bailey Ltd **Trained** Newmarket, Suffolk

FOCUS
Hard to rate this as anything more than fair form for now considering the pre-race profiles of the two leading contenders.

3267 AMT VEHICLE RENTAL LEEDS FILLIES' H'CAP 1m 2f
3:10 (3:12) (Class 5) (0-70,74) 4-Y-O+ **£4,722** (£1,405; £702; £351; £300; £300) **Stalls** Centre

Form RPR

60-6 1 **Railport Dolly**[12] [2822] 4-9-9 71 (h) LiamKeniry 1 79
(David Barron) *trckd ldng pair on inner: hdwy and cl up 3f out: led over 2f out: rdn over 1f out: kpt on wl fnl f* **6/1**[3]

0056 2 1 **Beatbybeatbybeat**[6] [3057] 6-8-11 66 (v) KieranSchofield(7) 3 72
(Antony Brittain) *t.k.h: trckd ldrs: hdwy 3f out: rdn 2f out: chsd wnr ent fnl f: sn drvn and ch: sn edgd rt and kpt on same pce towards fin* **25/1**

0414 3 1 **Perceived**[23] [2513] 7-8-6 54 (p) CamHardie 6 58
(Antony Brittain) *led: pushed along and jnd 3f out: rdn and hdd 2f out: sn drvn and kpt on same pce fnl f* **10/1**

63-5 4 hd **First Dance (IRE)**[12] [2822] 5-9-5 67 AndrewMullen 2 71
(Tom Tate) *hld up in rr: hdwy 3f out: rdn along to chse ldrs wl over 1f out: sn drvn and kpt on same pce fnl f* **4/1**[1]

043- 5 1 ¾ **Reassurance**[219] [8507] 4-9-6 68 DavidAllan 9 68
(Tim Easterby) *hld up in rr: hdwy on inner wl over 2f out: sn rdn: kpt on fnl f: nrst fin* **9/2**[2]

-641 6 nk **Maulesden May (IRE)**[8] [2962] 6-9-12 74 5ex GrahamLee 4 74
(Keith Dalgleish) *trckd ldrs: hdwy wl over 2f out: sn rdn along: drvn and no imp fnl f* **9/2**[2]

500- 7 ¾ **Delirium (IRE)**[194] [9128] 5-8-7 55 (p) BarryMcHugh 8 53
(Ed de Giles) *trckd ldng pair on outer: rdn along wl over 2f out: sn drvn and one pce* **16/1**

00-4 8 ¾ **Kismat**[15] [2737] 4-8-8 63 TobyEley(7) 7 60
(Alan King) *hld up: a towards rr* **10/1**

0-35 9 2 ½ **Gamesters Icon**[17] [2685] 4-8-13 61 PaulHanagan 5 53
(Oliver Greenall) *trckd ldr: effrt and cl up over 3f out: rdn along wl over 2f out: drvn wl over 1f out and sn wknd* **9/2**[2]

2m 10.0s (0.70) **Going Correction** -0.125s/f (Firm) **9 Ran SP% 116.7**
Speed ratings (Par 100): **92,91,90,90,88 88,88,87,85**
CSF £139.32 CT £1474.33 TOTE £6.80: £2.50, £6.60, £3.00; EX 134.00 Trifecta £886.30.
Owner A C Cook **Bred** A C Cook **Trained** Maunby, N Yorks

FOCUS
The early pace for this fillies handicap didn't look overly strong, suggesting the latter stages were a bit of a burn up.

3268 KENDALL'S JEWELLERS WETHERBY BEST DRESSED LADY H'CAP 1m
3:40 (3:40) (Class 4) (0-85,86) 4-Y-O+ **£6,016** (£1,790; £894; £447; £300; £300) **Stalls** Low

Form RPR

0-45 1 **Club Wexford (IRE)**[1] [3216] 8-8-10 79 BenSanderson(5) 2 86
(Roger Fell) *dwlt: sn trcking ldrs: hdwy on inner over 2f out: rdn along over 1f out: styd on wl u.p fnl f to ld nr fin (trainer said, regarding the improved form shown, the gelding was suited by a change of tactics to be ridden more patiently)* **13/2**

-002 2 nk **Markazi (FR)**[13] [2784] 5-9-8 86 (p) DanielTudhope 4 92
(David O'Meara) *trckd ldrs: hdwy on outer over 2f out: chal over 1f out: sn rdn: drvn to take slt ld last 60yds: hdd and no ex nr fin* **11/4**[1]

40-0 3 ¾ **Calder Prince (IRE)**[22] [2526] 6-9-4 82 LiamKeniry 6 86
(Tom Dascombe) *led: pushed clr 3f out: rdn wl over 1f out: drvn ins fnl f: hdd last 6 yds: kpt on same pce towards fin* **12/1**

3-0 4 1 ¾ **Frankelio (FR)**[22] [2526] 4-9-4 82 PaulHanagan 5 82
(Micky Hammond) *t.k.h: sn chsng ldr: pushed along 3f out: rdn 2f out: sn drvn and kpt on same pce* **8/1**

21-3 5 hd **Make Me**[12] [2842] 4-8-8 72 (p) JasonHart 1 72
(Tim Easterby) *trckd ldng pair: hdwy over 2f out: rdn wl over 1f out: drvn and kpt on same pce fnl f* **4/1**[2]

362- 6 2 ½ **Cheer The Title (IRE)**[305] [5522] 4-9-2 80 DaneO'Neill 9 74
(Tom Clover) *hld up: hdwy wl over 2f out: sn rdn along: nvr rchd ldrs* **7/1**

23-6 7 nk **Mazyoun**[20] [2572] 5-9-2 85 (v) DylanHogan(5) 7 78
(Hugo Palmer) *hld up towards rr: sme hdwy over 3f out: rdn along wl over 2f out: n.d* **5/1**[3]

4-00 8 2 ¾ **Big Storm Coming**[20] [2584] 9-9-7 85 DougieCostello 8 72
(John Quinn) *hld up: rdn along 3f out: a in rr* **50/1**

3130 9 nk **Sureyoutoldme (IRE)**[17] [2679] 5-8-13 77 JackGarritty 3 63
(Ruth Carr) *hld up towards rr: effrt 3f out: sn rdn along and nvr a factor* **22/1**

1m 39.72s (-1.88) **Going Correction** -0.125s/f (Firm) **9 Ran SP% 114.3**
Speed ratings (Par 105): **104,103,102,101,101 98,98,95,95**
CSF £24.45 CT £211.23 TOTE £6.60: £2.10, £1.20, £3.20; EX 28.10 Trifecta £225.40.
Owner C Varley **Bred** J S Bolger **Trained** Nawton, N Yorks

FOCUS
A decent contest and the form should prove to be reliable.

3269 THANKS & GOOD LUCK JOE TUFFIN FILLIES' H'CAP 1m 6f
4:10 (4:10) (Class 4) (0-80,82) 4-Y-O+ **£6,016** (£1,790; £894; £447; £300; £300) **Stalls** Low

Form RPR

1-21 1 **Makawee (IRE)**[5] [3095] 4-9-11 79 5ex DanielTudhope 7 93+
(David O'Meara) *trckd ldrs: smooth hdwy on outer 3f out: led on bit wl over 1f out: v easily* **4/11**[1]

06-0 2 2 **Iconic Belle**[15] [803] 5-9-2 75 ConnorMurtagh(5) 3 80
(Philip Kirby) *trckd ldng pair: hdwy over 3f out: sn chsng ldr: rdn to chal 2f out: drvn over 1f out: kpt on: no ch w wnr* **33/1**

01-6 3 2 ¼ **Miss Latin (IRE)**[26] [2399] 4-9-2 75 DylanHogan(5) 6 77
(David Simcock) *hld up in rr: hdwy on inner 3f out: chsd ldrs 2f out and sn rdn: drvn and no imp fnl f* **25/1**

14-3 4 2 ¾ **Quicksand (IRE)**[26] [2399] 4-10-0 82 DaneO'Neill 1 80
(Hughie Morrison) *led: pushed along 3f out: sn jnd and rdn: drvn and hdd wl over 1f out: sn one pce* **5/1**[2]

-200 5 2 ¾ **Flower Power**[6] [3054] 8-9-1 69 DougieCostello 5 63
(Tony Coyle) *hld up: effrt and sme hdwy over 3f out: rdn along wl over 2f out: sn outpcd* **50/1**

225- 6 2 ¾ **Potters Lady Jane**[169] [9503] 7-9-3 71 (p) PaulHanagan 4 61
(Lucy Wadham) *trckd ldr: hdwy and cl up over 3f out: rdn along wl over 2f out: sn drvn and wknd* **8/1**[3]

3m 2.96s (-4.04) **Going Correction** -0.125s/f (Firm) **6 Ran SP% 109.8**
Speed ratings (Par 102): **106,104,103,102,100 98**
CSF £18.12 TOTE £1.30: £1.10, £6.00; EX 12.60 Trifecta £55.30.
Owner Geoff & Sandra Turnbull **Bred** Geoff & Sandra Turnbull **Trained** Upper Helmsley, N Yorks

FOCUS
The two fillies at the head of the market looked to be improving types, albeit one was more heavily backed than the other.

3270 RACINGTV.COM H'CAP (DIV I) 1m
4:40 (4:41) (Class 6) (0-60,62) 3-Y-O **£4,075** (£1,212; £606; £303; £300; £300) **Stalls** Low

Form RPR

-020 1 **Fitzy**[30] [2262] 3-8-11 50 (p) CamHardie 14 56
(David Brown) *stdd and swtchd lft s: hld up in rr: gd hdwy on inner over 2f out: chsd ldrs over 1f out: sn rdn to chal: styd on wl to ld last 100yds* **11/1**[3]

00-0 2 1 ½ **Bumblekite**[40] [1957] 3-8-2 48 TobyEley(7) 11 51
(Steph Hollinshead) *hld up in rr: gd hdwy on inner over 2f out: led wl over 1f out: sn rdn: jnd and drvn ins fnl f: hdd and kpt on same pce last 100yds* **33/1**

000 3 1 ¼ **Brutalab**[12] [2823] 3-8-13 52 RachelRichardson 3 52
(Tim Easterby) *hld up towards rr: hdwy on inner wl over 2f out: rdn over 1f out: styd on u.p fnl f* **14/1**

0-42 4 hd **Hector's Here**[32] [2152] 3-9-6 59 JasonHart 7 59+
(Ivan Furtado) *prom: trckd ldr after 2f: effrt over 2f out and sn pushed along: cl up and rdn wl over 1f out: sn drvn and kpt on same pce* **7/4**[1]

1253 5 1 **Macs Blessings (IRE)**[28] [2337] 3-9-2 55 (p) LiamKeniry 6 52
(Stef Keniry) *hld up: hdwy wl over 2f out: rdn along wl over 1f out: kpt on fnl f* **9/2**[2]

40-0 6 ¾ **Dragons Will Rise (IRE)**[32] [2152] 3-9-1 54 MichaelStainton 10 50
(Micky Hammond) *hld up towards rr: hdwy on outer 3f out: rdn along to chse ldrs over 1f out: drvn and wknd fnl f* **40/1**

43-0 7 5 **Bumbledom**[52] [1649] 3-9-9 62 DavidNolan 1 47
(Michael Dods) *led: pushed along 3f out: rdn over 2f out: sn hdd and drvn: grad wknd* **14/1**

06-0 8 2 **Secret Magic (IRE)**[57] [1515] 3-8-6 48 ConorMcGovern(3) 8 28
(Mark Loughnane) *a towards rr* **50/1**

0-66 9 6 **Northern Footsteps**[22] [2530] 3-8-2 46 oh1 PaulaMuir(5) 2 13
(Ollie Pears) *chsd ldng pair on inner: pushed along 3f out: rdn over 2f out: sn wknd* **66/1**

3-40 10 1 ½ **Call Him Al (IRE)**[33] [2101] 3-9-8 61 PaulHanagan 12 25
(Richard Fahey) *trckd ldrs on outer: pushed along over 3f out: sn rdn and btn* **9/2**[2]

500- 11 2 ¼ **George's Law**[254] [7390] 3-9-3 56 JackGarritty 5 15
(Tim Easterby) *chsd ldrs: hdwy 3f out: rdn along over 2f out: sn wknd* **14/1**

050 12 2 ½ **Opera Kiss (IRE)**[45] [1816] 3-8-4 46 oh1 RowanScott(3) 9
(Lawrence Mullaney) *a towards rr* **100/1**

456- 13 ½ **Delectable**[217] [8575] 3-9-7 60 AndrewMullen 4 12
(Adrian Nicholls) *trckd ldrs: rdn along over 3f out: sn wknd* **16/1**

1m 40.35s (-1.25) **Going Correction** -0.125s/f (Firm) **13 Ran SP% 116.8**
Speed ratings (Par 97): **101,99,98,98,97 96,91,89,83,81 79,77,76**
CSF £333.70 CT £5213.08 TOTE £11.20: £2.80, £8.10, £3.40; EX 390.00 Trifecta £5057.60.
Owner Ron Hull **Bred** A C Cook **Trained** Averham Park, Notts

FOCUS
The first division of a modest handicap, and plenty held chances around 2f out.

3271 RACINGTV.COM H'CAP (DIV II) 1m
5:10 (5:15) (Class 6) (0-60,62) 3-Y-O

£4,075 (£1,212; £606; £303; £300; £300) Stalls Low

Form RPR

5321 **1** **Antico Lady (IRE)**[9] 2943 3-9-6 61 6ex........ BenRobinson(3) 4 71+
(Brian Ellison) *trckd ldr: hdwy to ld 2f out: rdn over 1f out: drvn and kpt on wl fnl f* 5/6[1]

5-00 **2** 2 1/2 **The Big House (IRE)**[31] 2197 3-8-10 48........ AndrewMullen 10 52
(Adrian Nicholls) *toot.k.h: trckd ldrs whn n.m.r: jinked lft and hmpd after 2f: in tch: hdwy over 3f out: chsd ldrs 2f out: rdn to chal jst over 1f out: drvn and ev ch ent fnl f: kpt on same pce last 150yds* 12/1

00-5 **3** 1 **Neileta**[24] 2482 3-9-2 54........ JackGarritty 1 56
(Tim Easterby) *t.k.h: trckd ldrs on inner: hdwy 3f out: rdn along 2f out: drvn and kpt on u.p fnl f* 8/1[3]

311- **4** 4 1/2 **Melgate Majeure**[181] 9325 3-9-0 59........ TobyEley(7) 8 51+
(Michael Easterby) *dwlt: sn in tch: hdwy over 3f out: rdn along 2f out: drvn over 1f out: kpt on one pce* 7/1[2]

-400 **5** 1 **Spiritual Boy (IRE)**[10] 2913 3-9-4 56........(p[1]) DavidNolan 9 46
(David O'Meara) *hld up towards rr: hdwy 3f out: rdn along 2f out: kpt on fnl f* 20/1

00-0 **6** 1/2 **Supreme Dream**[24] 2482 3-9-0 52........ RachelRichardson 14 41
(Ollie Pears) *led: pushed along and jnd 3f out: rdn and hdd 2f out: grad wknd fr over 1f out* 50/1

2000 **7** 2 1/4 **Piccolita**[22] 2531 3-8-7 45........ BarryMcHugh 12 29
(Hughie Morrison) *towards rr: sme hdwy wl over 2f out: sn rdn along and n.d* 20/1

0-60 **8** hd **Seafaring Girl (IRE)**[28] 2350 3-8-5 48........ ConnorMurtagh(5) 7 31
(Mark Loughnane) *t.k.h: trcking ldrs whn edgd lft after 2f: rdn along 1/2-way: rdn over 3f out: n.d* 40/1

03-0 **9** 1 3/4 **Dothraki (IRE)**[137] 228 3-9-1 53........ AndrewElliott 3 32
(Ronald Thompson) *a towards rr* 80/1

0555 **10** 3 1/4 **Klipperty Klopp**[37] 2016 3-9-5 57........ CamHardie 11 29
(Antony Brittain) *chsd ldrs: rdn along 3f out: sn wknd* 18/1

4-60 **11** 2 **Lethal Guest**[28] 2325 3-9-7 62........ ConorMcGovern(3) 13 30
(Ollie Pears) *hld up: a in rr (jockey said gelding had reared in the stalls)* 25/1

60-0 **12** 3/4 **Angel Sarah (IRE)**[28] 2337 3-8-11 49........ PaulHanagan 6 15
(Richard Fahey) *dwlt: a in rr (jockey said filly was restless in the stalls and missed the break)* 18/1

0-00 **13** nse **Laura Louise (IRE)**[9] 2943 3-8-11 52........(p[1]) RowanScott(3) 2 18
(Nigel Tinkler) *t.k.h: in tch on inner: whn bdly hmpd after 2f: towards rr after* 40/1

000 **14** 16 **Two For Three (IRE)**[29] 2289 3-8-2 45........(p[1]) PaulaMuir(5) 5
(Roger Fell) *chsd ldrs: rdn along over 3f out: sn wknd* 50/1

1m 39.85s (-1.75) **Going Correction** -0.125s/f (Firm) **14 Ran SP% 119.8**
Speed ratings (Par 97): **103,100,99,95,94 93,91,91,89,86 84,83,83,67**
CSF £10.31 CT £57.47 TOTE £1.80: £1.40, £3.00, £2.20; EX 13.20 Trifecta £79.10.
Owner Julie & Keith Hanson **Bred** Ms Agathe Lebailly **Trained** Norton, N Yorks

FOCUS
The second and slightly quicker division of a modest handicap. Not many got into it.

3272 WATCH IRISH RACING ON RACINGTV APPRENTICE H'CAP (YORKSHIRE FUTURE STARS APPRENTICE RIDER SERIES) 2m
5:50 (5:51) (Class 6) (0-60,60) 4-Y-O+

£4,075 (£1,212; £606; £303; £300; £300) Stalls Low

Form RPR

/ **1** **Maid In Manhattan (IRE)**[16] 414 5-8-7 46........(h) HarrisonShaw 7 53
(Rebecca Menzies) *hld up: hdwy over 3f out: rdn along to chse ldrs over 1f out: led ins fnl f: sn drvn and kpt on wl* 25/1

360- **2** 1/2 **General Allenby**[23] 5605 5-8-9 51........(p) WilliamCarver(3) 1 57
(Peter Bowen) *trckd ldrs: hdwy over 3f out: chsd ldrs 2f out: rdn and n.m.r jst over 1f out: sn swtchd lft and ev ch: drvn ins fnl f: kpt on* 5/1[2]

50-0 **3** 1 1/4 **The Fiddler**[31] 2202 4-8-11 51........ DylanHogan 5 57
(Chris Wall) *in tch: hdwy on outer 3f out: rdn along 2f out: drvn and ev ch whn edgd lft jst over 1f out: edgd lft ins fnl f: kpt on same pce* 11/1

254/ **4** 2 1/4 **Another Lincolnday**[934] 7846 8-9-2 55........ ConnorMurtagh 12 58
(Rebecca Menzies) *dwlt: sn chsng ldrs: led after 2f: pushed along 3f out: rdn over 2f out: drvn over 1f out: hdd jst ins fnl f: hld whn nt much after* 12/1

00-3 **5** 3 1/4 **Misscarlett (IRE)**[49] 1718 5-8-9 48........(p[1]) PaulaMuir 11 46
(Philip Kirby) *trckd ldrs: hdwy 3f out: rdn along 2f out: drvn wl over 1f out: sn one pce* 6/1[3]

125 **6** 1 **Geordielad**[65] 1341 5-8-13 52........ ThomasGreatrex 3 49
(Oliver Sherwood) *led 2f: prom: effrt on inner 3f out: rdn along 2f out: drvn over 1f out: grad wknd* 12/1

-061 **7** shd **Sacred Sprite**[20] 2593 4-9-1 60........ GeorgiaDobie(5) 4 58
(John Berry) *hld up in rr: hdwy 3f out: sn rdn: kpt on fnl f: n.d* 9/4[1]

0-53 **8** shd **Dew Pond**[27] 2373 7-9-1 54........(bt) DannyRedmond 15 51
(Tim Easterby) *hld up in rr: hdwy 3f out: rdn along 2f out: kpt on: n.d* 8/1

1-04 **9** 1 3/4 **St Andrews (IRE)**[17] 2684 6-9-3 59........(b) KieranSchofield(3) 2 54
(Gillian Boanas) *chsd ldrs: rdn along over 3f out: sn wknd* 14/1

0-06 **10** 3 1/2 **Cue's Folly**[8] 2974 4-8-6 46 oh1........ BenSanderson 10 38
(Ed Dunlop) *a towards rr* 16/1

4-50 **11** 1 1/2 **Dizoard**[49] 1718 9-8-2 46 oh1........ EllaMcCain(5) 13 35
(Iain Jardine) *a towards rr* 50/1

1000 **12** 5 **Sweetest Smile (IRE)**[43] 1861 4-8-6 49........ TobyEley(3) 14 33
(Ed de Giles) *a towards rr (jockey said filly was never travelling)* 28/1

0000 **13** 1 3/4 **Lots Ov (IRE)**[6] 3057 5-8-4 46 oh1........ RobertDodsworth(3) 6 27
(John Wainwright) *t.k.h: prom: rdn along over 4f out: wknd over 3f out* 150/1

5-00 **14** 12 **Leodis (IRE)**[20] 2591 7-8-8 52........(p[1]) HarryRussell(5) 8 18
(Micky Hammond) *chsd ldrs on outer: rdn along 5f out: wknd over 3f out (vet said gelding lost its right fore shoe)* 50/1

3m 29.64s (-4.06) **Going Correction** -0.125s/f (Firm) **14 Ran SP% 121.0**
WFA 4 from 5yo+ 1lb
Speed ratings (Par 101): **105,104,104,103,101 100,100,100,99,98 97,94,94,88**
CSF £143.85 CT £1494.80 TOTE £24.00: £5.70, £1.80, £2.80; EX 203.50 Trifecta £1245.20.
Owner Stoneleigh Racing **Bred** John Breslin **Trained** Mordon, Durham
■ Stewards' Enquiry : William Carver caution: careless riding

FOCUS
A moderate staying contest for apprentice riders. It appeared to be run at an even tempo.
T/Plt: £587.10 to a £1 stake. Pool: £45,154.84. 56.14 winning units. T/Qpdt: £160.40 to a £1 stake. Pool: £5,308.85. 24.48 winning units. **Joe Rowntree**

2972 YARMOUTH (L-H)
Thursday, May 30

OFFICIAL GOING: Good to firm (7.3)
Wind: breezy Weather: hot and sunny; 24 degrees

3273 HAVEN WILD DUCK HOLIDAY PARK H'CAP 7f 3y
2:20 (2:20) (Class 5) (0-75,75) 3-Y-O

£3,752 (£1,116; £557; £300; £300; £300) Stalls Centre

Form RPR

2233 **1** **Strawberry Jack**[9] 2927 3-9-5 73........(vt) JamesDoyle 6 80
(George Scott) *prom: rdn to ld wl over 1f out: edgd lft whn forging clr fnl 100yds* 7/2[2]

1610 **2** 2 1/2 **Havana Ooh Na Na**[9] 2942 3-8-13 67........(p) DavidEgan 1 67
(K R Burke) *prom: drvn and w wnr wl over 1f out tl outpcd fnl 100yds* 7/1

01-2 **3** 3 **John Clare (IRE)**[33] 2114 3-9-6 74........ ShaneKelly 2 66
(Pam Sly) *led: rdn and hdd wl over 1f out: kpt on same pce whn hld fnl f* 6/4[1]

2-10 **4** 1 1/4 **Coastline (IRE)**[21] 2552 3-9-7 75........ FrannyNorton 8 64
(James Tate) *t.k.h in midfield: rdn and outpcd over 2f out: n.d after* 6/1[3]

60-5 **5** 1 1/4 **No Thanks**[22] 2529 3-8-12 66........(h) GeorgeWood 3 51
(William Jarvis) *towards rr: rdn 1/2-way: sme prog to midfield wl over 1f out: sn no ch w ldrs* 33/1

2034 **6** 2 **Facethepuckout (IRE)**[7] 3018 3-9-7 75........(p) GeraldMosse 7 55
(John Ryan) *midfield: rdn 1/2-way: nt looking keen and wl btn fnl 2f* 13/2

5-5 **7** 2 3/4 **Molly's Game**[14] 2762 3-9-6 74........ HayleyTurner 4 47
(David Elsworth) *missed break: a bhd: rdn and btn over 2f out* 14/1

1m 25.56s (0.46) **Going Correction** 0.0s/f (Good) **7 Ran SP% 111.9**
Speed ratings (Par 99): **97,94,90,89,87 85,82**
CSF £26.46 CT £49.69 TOTE £5.70: £1.90, £3.00; EX 21.00 Trifecta £79.20.
Owner Jack Stephenson **Bred** Whitsbury Manor Stud **Trained** Newmarket, Suffolk

FOCUS
Modest 3yo form, they raced nearer to the stands' side and the winner scored with a bit in hand.

3274 BRITISH STALLION STUDS EBF NOVICE STKS 7f 3y
2:50 (2:51) (Class 5) 2-Y-O

£3,752 (£1,116; £557; £278) Stalls Centre

Form RPR

1 **Boccaccio (IRE)** 2-9-5 0........ JamesDoyle 4 81+
(Charlie Appleby) *w ldrs: led 3f out: rdn 2f out: hld on wl thrght fnl f* 5/4[1]

2 1 1/2 **Dramatic Sands (IRE)** 2-9-5 0........ EdwardGreatrex 3 77+
(Archie Watson) *rn loose in paddock: dwlt: sn chsng ldrs: drvn 2f out: effrt and chsd wnr fnl f: kpt on but a hld* 14/1

3 1/2 **Al Namir (IRE)** 2-9-5 0........ JimCrowley 9 76+
(Richard Hannon) *pressed ldrs: rdn 2f out: wnt 3rd ins fnl f: kpt on steadily wout threatening wnr* 6/1[3]

0 **4** 3/4 **Ropey Guest**[9] 2931 2-9-5 0........ TomQueally 6 74
(George Margarson) *prom: rdn over 2f out: nt qckn ins fnl f* 66/1

5 1 3/4 **Mass Media** 2-9-5 0........ NickyMackay 1 69+
(John Gosden) *chsd ldrs on outer: rn green and outpcd over 1f out but styd on nicely ins fnl f: will improve* 14/1

6 3/4 **Herman Hesse** 2-9-5 0........ RobertHavlin 7 67+
(John Gosden) *missed break: sn in midfield: nvr looked like chalng fnl f but kpt on v pleasingly: sure to do bttr* 3/1[2]

45 **7** nk **Dark Of Night (IRE)**[20] 2594 2-9-5 0........ GeorgeWood 10 66
(Saeed bin Suroor) *cl up: drvn over 2f out: lost pl wl over 1f out* 9/1

8 1 3/4 **Order Of St John** 2-9-5 0........ GeraldMosse 12 61
(John Ryan) *bhd: rdn and wl hld over 2f out* 50/1

9 1/2 **Pitcher** 2-9-5 0........ SeanLevey 8 60
(Richard Hannon) *midfield early: rdn and btn over 2f out* 25/1

10 nse **Progressive Rating** 2-9-5 0........ DavidEgan 5 60
(William Knight) *led narrowly 4f: rdn and wknd wl over 1f out* 50/1

11 5 **Selsey Sizzler** 2-9-5 0........ CallumShepherd 11 46
(William Knight) *towards rr and sn rdn: t.o fnl 2f* 33/1

P **Austin Taetious** 2-9-5 0........ RoystonFfrench 2
(Adam West) *awkward s: sn t.o: p.u and dismntd after 2f (jockey said he pulled up the gelding shortly after the start as he felt something was amiss)* 66/1

1m 25.9s (0.80) **Going Correction** 0.0s/f (Good) **12 Ran SP% 120.8**
Speed ratings (Par 93): **95,93,92,91,89 89,88,86,86,86 80,**
CSF £21.69 TOTE £2.00: £1.10, £3.80, £2.30; EX 21.00 Trifecta £127.00.
Owner Godolphin **Bred** Andrew Rosen **Trained** Newmarket, Suffolk

FOCUS
A potentially useful juvenile novice and the market spoke favourably of the winner.

3275 SEADELL SHOPS & HOLIDAY CHALETS HEMSBY H'CAP 1m 3f 104y
3:20 (3:23) (Class 6) (0-55,57) 3-Y-O

£3,105 (£924; £461; £300; £300; £300) Stalls Low

Form RPR

0-00 **1** **Admirals Bay (GER)**[13] 2795 3-9-9 57........ FrannyNorton 5 63+
(Andrew Balding) *dropped out in last pl tl home turn: plenty to do tl stdy prog on far rails 3f out: styd on dourly to ld 100yds out: sn clr (trainer said, regarding the improved form shown, the gelding appreciated the step up in trip from 1m2f to 1m3f½f)* 3/1[2]

305 **2** 1 1/2 **Miss Green Dream**[47] 1770 3-8-6 47........ SeanKirrane(7) 1 51
(Julia Feilden) *cl up: led over 2f out: sn rdn and edgd rt: 2 l clr 1f out: hdd 100yds out: no ex* 11/1

00-0 **3** 3/4 **New Expo (IRE)**[32] 2150 3-8-12 46 oh1........ RoystonFfrench 11 48
(Julia Feilden) *prom: rdn 2f out: kpt on same pce fnl f* 100/1

-005 **4** 1/2 **Global Freedom**[9] 2941 3-9-7 55........(t) GeraldMosse 7 57
(Ed Dunlop) *towards rr: effrt 1/2-way: rdn over 2f out: kpt on ins fnl f: nt get in a blow* 12/1

00-0 **5** 1 **Cheng Gong**[50] 1690 3-9-2 50........(p[1]) DavidEgan 8 50
(Tom Clover) *prom: rdn on outer over 2f out: no imp fnl f* 18/1

5615 **6** 3 1/4 **Ignatius (IRE)**[26] 2406 3-9-7 55........ JimCrowley 2 50
(John Best) *cl up: lost pl over 3f out: sme prog fnl f but n.d* 5/2[1]

0-60 **7** nk **Dinah Washington (IRE)**[33] 2102 3-9-6 54........ HayleyTurner 3 48
(Michael Bell) *nvr bttr than midfield: rdn 4f out: n.d after* 7/1

-000 **8** 5 **Deerfoot**[9] 2926 3-8-12 46 oh1........(b) NickyMackay 6 32
(Anthony Carson) *hdwy towards rails on far side 4f out: rdn and n.m.r 2f out: sn btn: eased* 66/1

1006 **9** 3 1/2 **Ginge N Tonic**[37] 2011 3-9-0 48........ CharlieBennett 10 29
(Adam West) *sn led tl rdn and hdd over 2f out: lost pl wl over 1f out* 25/1

The Form Book Flat 2019, Raceform Ltd, Newbury, RG14 5SJ

0-54 **10** *3 3/4* **Parknacilla (IRE)**[30] 2262 3-9-4 **52**................................ RobertHavlin 9 27
(Henry Spiller) *bhd: short-lived effrt 3f out: stopped qckly: t.o and eased (jockey said filly stopped quickly)* **6/1**[3]
00-3 **11** *13* **Kybosh (IRE)**[9] 2943 3-9-7 **55**................................ AlistairRawlinson 4 9
(Michael Appleby) *towards rr: rdn 4f out: racd awkwardly and sn struggling: t.o and eased (jockey said gelding hung left-handed in the home straight)* **9/1**

2m 26.87s (-0.93) **Going Correction** 0.0s/f (Good) **11** Ran SP% **118.0**
Speed ratings (Par 97): **103,101,101,101,100 97,97,94,91,88 79**
CSF £35.98 CT £2710.08 TOTE £3.90: £1.60, £2.90, £34.10; EX 41.20 Trifecta £2332.90.
Owner Lord Blyth **Bred** Lemington Grange Stud **Trained** Kingsclere, Hants

FOCUS
Moderate 3yo form, but an unexposed winner who did well to come from so far back.

3276 LEN BURGESS MEMORIAL H'CAP 1m 2f 23y
3:50 (3:51) (Class 6) (0-65,65) 4-Y-0+
£3,105 (£924; £461; £300; £300; £300) **Stalls** Low

Form RPR
12-0 **1** **Lucky's Dream**[33] 2111 4-9-2 **60**................................ JimCrowley 6 67+
(Ian Williams) *towards rr: rdn and taken to outside 3f out: chal strly 1f out: led fnl 100yds: styd on wl* **8/1**
000- **2** *1/2* **Le Maharajah (FR)**[225] 8316 4-9-7 **65**................................(w) DavidEgan 5 71
(Tom Clover) *sn led: rdn 2f out: hrd pressed 1f out: hdd 100yds out: nt qckn* **5/1**[3]
20 **3** *1 3/4* **Movie Star (GER)**[38] 1988 4-9-5 **63**................................ GeorgeWood 4 66
(Amy Murphy) *t.k.h: prom: drvn over 1f out: no imp ins fnl f* **20/1**
00-5 **4** *3/4* **Peace Prevails**[138] 202 4-8-13 **57**................................ CharlieBennett 9 59
(Jim Boyle) *pressed ldr: rdn 2f out: one pce and hld fnl f* **7/2**[1]
324 **5** *2 3/4* **Lady Alavesa**[19] 2612 4-9-0 **65**................................(p) GraceMcEntee[(7)] 2 62
(Gay Kelleway) *t.k.h towards rr: rdn and brief effrt over 2f out: sn btn* **7/2**[1]
-000 **6** *1/2* **Conqueress (IRE)**[9] 2944 5-8-7 **51**................................ RoystonFfrench 1 47
(Lydia Pearce) *midfield: rdn 3f out: nvr making any imp after* **100/1**
-202 **7** *3 1/4* **Hard Toffee (IRE)**[15] 2738 8-9-1 **59**................................ CallumShepherd 7 49
(Louise Allan) *cl up: drvn 3f out: sn wandering: btn 2f out* **11/2**
-031 **8** *2 1/2* **Couldn't Could She**[2] 3186 4-9-5 **63** 5ex................................ EdwardGreatrex 3 48
(Adam West) *t.k.h towards rr: drvn over 2f out: no ch after (jockey said filly ran too freely)* **4/1**[2]
0-00 **9** *1 1/4* **Oceanus (IRE)**[15] 2738 5-8-4 **55**................................ SeanKirrane[(7)] 8 38
(Julia Feilden) *lost 6 l and rdn s: a bhd* **20/1**

2m 9.28s (0.48) **Going Correction** 0.0s/f (Good) **9** Ran SP% **118.1**
Speed ratings (Par 101): **98,97,96,95,93 93,90,88,87**
CSF £47.73 CT £783.11 TOTE £9.80: £2.70, £1.90, £5.20; EX 64.60 Trifecta £1151.50.
Owner R S Brookhouse **Bred** R S Brookhouse **Trained** Portway, Worcs

FOCUS
Modest form and it was similar to the previous race in that the winner did well to come from off the pace and run down the prominent racers.

3277 EASTERN POWER SYSTEMS OF NORWICH NOVICE STKS 1m 3y
4:20 (4:21) (Class 5) 3-Y-0+ **£3,752** (£1,116; £557; £278) **Stalls** Centre

Form RPR
2-1 **1** **Velorum (IRE)**[13] 2802 3-9-9 0................................ JamesDoyle 8 98+
(Charlie Appleby) *cl up: rdn to ld over 2f out: clr w one chalr 1f out: drvn to repel her fnl 100yds* **1/6**[1]
2-2 **2** *1* **Audarya (FR)**[20] 2583 3-8-11 0................................ GeorgeWood 9 83
(James Fanshawe) *t.k.h chsng ldrs: rdn to chse wnr over 1f out and sn clr of rest: sustained effrt tl jst hld fnl 100yds: game effrt* **3/1**[2]
3 *2* **Informed Front (USA)** 3-9-2 0................................(t[1]) RobertHavlin 5 83+
(John Gosden) *racd in midfield: outpcd and rn green wl over 1f out: rallied ins fnl f: kpt on strly cl home* **6/1**[3]
6 **4** *7* **Noble Account**[14] 2764 3-9-2 0................................ CharlieBennett 14 66
(Julia Feilden) *prom tl drvn and racing awkwardly 2f out: sn wknd: eased cl home* **33/1**
0 **5** *6* **Strict (IRE)**[13] 2790 3-9-2 0................................ FrannyNorton 12 52
(Andrew Balding) *prom tl rdn 2f out: sn fdd* **16/1**
0 **6** *3/4* **Tronador (IRE)**[23] 2518 3-9-2 0................................ ShaneKelly 11 50
(David Lanigan) *lost 12 l s: rchd midfield by 1/2-way but nvr in sight of ldrs* **66/1**
0-0 **7** *1 1/2* **Tamok (IRE)**[20] 2583 3-8-11 0................................ HayleyTurner 1 42
(Michael Bell) *awkward s: chsd ldrs: outpcd over 2f out* **50/1**
00 **8** *1/2* **Emojie**[17] 2690 5-9-7 0................................ SeanKirrane[(7)] 13 48
(Jane Chapple-Hyam) *midfield: drvn over 2f out: sn btn* **100/1**
0 **9** *4 1/2* **Fountain Of Life**[21] 2550 3-9-2 0................................ TomQueally 3 35
(Philip McBride) *dwlt: rn green in rr: t.o* **66/1**
5-6 **10** *1* **Favre (USA)**[21] 2550 3-9-2 0................................ SeanLevey 7 32
(Robert Cowell) *prom: drvn and wknd rapidly 2f out: t.o (vet said colt lost its left fore shoe)* **40/1**
0-0 **11** *4 1/2* **Tattenhams**[78] 1182 3-8-11 0................................ RoystonFfrench 2 16
(Adam West) *led tl rdn and hdd over 2f out: dropped out rapidly (jockey said filly jumped the path approximately 5 1/2f out)* **100/1**
00P **12** *45* **Gonbutnotforgotten (FR)**[14] 2762 3-8-11 0.......... JosephineGordon 10
(Philip McBride) *nvr on terms: t.o over 2f out: heavily eased* **100/1**

1m 37.46s (-0.74) **Going Correction** 0.0s/f (Good)
WFA 3 from 5yo 12lb **12** Ran SP% **144.2**
Speed ratings (Par 103): **103,102,100,93,87 86,84,84,79,78 74,29**
CSF £1.85 TOTE £1.10: £1.10, £1.10, £2.10; EX 1.80 Trifecta £4.80.
Owner Godolphin **Bred** Phillistown House Ltd **Trained** Newmarket, Suffolk

FOCUS
Only three mattered in the market and they pulled 7l clear of the remainder.

3278 NICHOLSONS STALHAM ENGINEERING H'CAP 1m 3y
4:50 (4:52) (Class 4) (0-80,78) 3-Y-0
£5,530 (£1,645; £822; £411; £300; £300) **Stalls** Centre

Form RPR
21-6 **1** **Listen To The Wind (IRE)**[33] 2103 3-9-7 **78**................................ JamesDoyle 3 84
(William Haggas) *chsd ldrs: effrt 2f out: led over 1f out and sn drew clr wout recrse to whip* **3/1**[2]
3-64 **2** *2* **Greek Kodiac (IRE)**[20] 2569 3-9-6 **77**................................ FrannyNorton 8 78
(Mick Quinn) *prom: drvn and ev ch over 1f out: outpcd by wnr ins fnl f* **6/1**[3]
6-03 **3** *nk* **Catch My Breath**[17] 2677 3-8-0 **64**................................ LauraPearson[(7)] 6 64
(John Ryan) *lost 6 l s: bhd: urged along and hdwy over 1f out: styd on wl ins fnl f: too much to do* **33/1**
0-11 **4** *1 3/4* **Dragon Sun**[35] 2055 3-9-5 **76**................................ SeanLevey 1 72
(Richard Hannon) *prom: rdn and ev ch 2f out: no ex over 1f out* **7/4**[1]
41-2 **5** *1/2* **Carnival Rose**[30] 2236 3-9-6 **77**................................ GeorgeWood 7 72
(James Fanshawe) *prom tl rdn and outpcd over 1f out* **7/1**
13-0 **6** *1* **Spencers Son (IRE)**[34] 2075 3-9-5 **76**................................(p[1]) JimCrowley 4 68
(Richard Spencer) *nvr bttr than midfield: rdn and btn 2f out* **16/1**
1-55 **7** *nk* **Sonja Henie (IRE)**[21] 2552 3-9-3 **74**................................ GeraldMosse 2 65
(Marco Botti) *racd freely in ld: rdn 2f out: hdd over 1f out: fdd ins fnl f* **10/1**
-101 **8** *3/4* **Love Your Work (IRE)**[29] 2299 3-9-6 **77**................................ RoystonFfrench 5 67
(Adam West) *nvr bttr than midfield: rdn over 2f out: sn wl hld* **14/1**

1m 37.65s (-0.55) **Going Correction** 0.0s/f (Good) **8** Ran SP% **112.7**
Speed ratings (Par 101): **102,100,99,97,97 96,96,95**
CSF £20.70 CT £485.00 TOTE £3.10: £1.40, £1.40, £4.70; EX 19.50 Trifecta £189.90.
Owner Sheikh Rashid Dalmook Al Maktoum **Bred** Macha Bloodstock & Ptn **Trained** Newmarket, Suffolk

FOCUS
A fair handicap won in good style by the top weight.

3279 FOLLOW AT THE RACES ON TWITTER H'CAP 1m 3y
5:20 (5:21) (Class 6) (0-65,65) 4-Y-0+
£3,105 (£924; £461; £300; £300; £300) **Stalls** Centre

Form RPR
06-0 **1** **Club Tropicana**[84] 1065 4-9-6 **64**................................(t) SeanLevey 8 71
(Richard Spencer) *towards rr: hdwy 2f out: led 1f out: rdn and hld on wl after* **5/1**[3]
0146 **2** *1/2* **Lunar Deity**[30] 2233 10-8-9 **60**................................ MarcoGhiani[(7)] 1 66
(Stuart Williams) *towards rr: rdn and effrt over 2f out: chsd wnr ins fnl f: no imp cl home* **6/1**
6-53 **3** *1* **Angel's Whisper (IRE)**[30] 2261 4-9-3 **61**................................(h) DavidEgan 5 65
(Amy Murphy) *chsd ldrs: rdn to ld narrowly 2f out tl 1f out: nt qckn fnl 100yds* **3/1**[1]
0-52 **4** *shd* **Hi Ho Silver**[15] 2740 5-8-10 **54**................................ GeorgeWood 7 57
(Chris Wall) *tk keen and prom: led briefly over 2f out: sn rdn: one pce fnl 100yds* **3/1**[1]
00-4 **5** *4 1/2* **Spinart**[28] 2349 6-9-7 **65**................................ ShaneKelly 10 58
(Pam Sly) *midfield: cajoled on to heels of ldrs 2f out: racd awkwardly and fnd nthing after* **7/2**[2]
-000 **6** *11* **Stay In The Light**[64] 1353 4-8-2 **46** oh1................................ JimmyQuinn 4 14
(Roger Ingram) *t.k.h: chsd ldrs tl rdn and fdd wl over 1f out: t.o* **28/1**
6000 **7** *2* **Song Of Summer**[3] 3143 4-8-2 **46** oh1................................(p) JosephineGordon 9 9
(Phil McEntee) *nvr on terms: t.o* **40/1**
/5-0 **8** *2 3/4* **Ocean Spray**[56] 1546 4-8-3 **46** oh1 ow1................................ RoystonFfrench 2 4
(Eugene Stanford) *led tl hdd and rdn over 2f out: fdd rapidly: t.o* **100/1**
041/ **9** *47* **Tom Dooley (IRE)**[97] 863 8-7-11 **46** oh1................................(p) AndrewBreslin[(5)] 3
(Philip Kirby) *stood in stalls tl rest had covered 150yds: virtually p.u over 1f out* **12/1**
000- **10** *1 1/4* **Fata Morgana**[303] 5589 4-8-2 **49** oh1 ow3................................(h) AaronJones[(3)] 12
(Christine Dunnett) *wore a nosenet: spd to 1/2-way: reluctant and sn t.o: virtually p.u over 1f out* **66/1**

1m 38.31s (0.11) **Going Correction** 0.0s/f (Good) **10** Ran SP% **119.2**
Speed ratings (Par 101): **99,98,97,97,92 81,79,77,30,28**
CSF £35.22 CT £110.24 TOTE £6.00: £1.70, £2.10, £1.30; EX 41.60 Trifecta £118.60.
Owner Rebel Racing **Bred** Redgate Bloodstock Ltd **Trained** Newmarket, Suffolk

FOCUS
Moderate handicap form and it set up for the closers.
T/Plt: £336.20 to a £1 stake. Pool: £67,079.31. 145.61 winning units. T/Qpdt: £60.70 to a £1 stake. Pool: £6,856.32. 83.54 winning units. **Iain Mackenzie**

3280 - 3286a (Foreign Racing) - See Raceform Interactive

BADEN-BADEN (L-H)
Thursday, May 30

OFFICIAL GOING: Turf: good

3287a 41ST BADENER MEILE POWERED BY GELDERMANN PRIVATSEKTKELLEREI (GROUP 2) (3YO+) (TURF) 1m
4:10 3-Y-0+ **£36,036** (£13,963; £7,207; £3,603; £2,252)

RPR
1 **The Revenant**[61] 1451 4-9-2 0................................(h) RonanThomas 8 108+
(F-H Graffard, France) *hld up in fnl trio: asked to improve 2 1/2f out: prog fr 2f out: rdn to chse ldr ent fnl f: picked up wl clsng stages: led fnl 100yds* **11/5**[2]
2 *1/2* **Imaging**[47] 1776 4-9-2 0................................ OisinOrr 7 107
(D K Weld, Ire) *bmpd s: mid-div on outer: prog fr 3f out: pushed along to chal under 2f out: led ent fnl f: hrd pressed clsng stages: hdd fnl 100yds* **13/10**[1]
3 *1 3/4* **Go To Hollywood (FR)**[51] 3-8-4 0................................ FabriceVeron 4 100
(Y Barberot, France) *mid-div: pushed along between rivals 2f out: rdn to chse ldng pair over 1f out: kpt on: nt quite pce to chal eventual wnr* **94/10**[3]
4 *nse* **Volfango (IRE)**[53] 1628 5-9-2 0................................ FranckBlondel 5 103
(F Vermeulen, France) *awkward s: in rr: asked to improve 2f out: swtchd rt and prog fr 1 1/2f out: kpt on strly u.p: nrst fin* **143/10**
5 *2* **Palace Prince (GER)**[46] 1793 7-9-2 0................................(p) FilipMinarik 3 98
(Jean-Pierre Carvalho, Germany) *qckly into stride: led: asked to qckn over 2f out: rdn whn chal 1 1/2f out: hdd ent fnl f: grad wknd and no ex clsng stages* **144/10**
6 *1/2* **Kronprinz (GER)**[76] 1230 4-9-2 0................................ AndraschStarke 1 97
(P Schiergen, Germany) *hld up in last pair: effrt 2f out: sltly short of racing room whn making hdwy on inner 1 1/2f out: kpt on ins fnl f but nvr threatened* **161/10**
7 *1* **Aviateur (FR)**[50] 1708 4-9-2 0................................ BauyrzhanMurzabayev 6 95
(A Kleinkorres, Germany) *sltly bmpd s: mid-div: swtchd off rail over 3f out: pushed along and effrt on outer over 2f out: unable qck and sn rdn: kpt on same pce ins fnl f* **149/10**
8 *5 1/2* **Melodino (GER)**[39] 4-9-2 0................................(p) MaximPecheur 9 82
(K Demme, Germany) *prom: pushed along to chse ldr over 2f out: sn rdn: no rspnse and sn struggling: wl btn ent fnl f* **35/1**
9 *1/2* **Degas (GER)**[46] 1793 6-9-2 0................................ AdriedeVries 2 81
(Markus Klug, Germany) *cl up: pushed along to chse ldr over 2f out: limited rspnse and rdn 1 1/2f out: no imp and wknd ins fnl f: eased clsng stages* **149/10**

1m 38.77s (-0.34)
WFA 3 from 4yo+ 12lb **9** Ran SP% **118.6**
PARI-MUTUEL (all including 1 euro stake): WIN 3.20 PLACE: 1.40, 1.30, 1.70; SF: 4.60.
Owner Al Asayl Bloodstock Ltd **Bred** Al Asayl Bloodstock Ltd **Trained** France

DORTMUND (R-H)
Thursday, May 30

OFFICIAL GOING: Turf: good

3288a GROSSER PREIS DER SPARKASSE DORTMUND (LISTED RACE) (4YO+ FILLIES & MARES) (TURF) 1m
4:25 4-Y-O+ £12,612 (£5,855; £2,702; £1,351)

RPR
1 **Nica (GER)**[29] 4-8-13 0 CarlosHenrique 9 105
(Dr A Bolte, Germany) **31/5**
2 2 1/4 **Madita (GER)**[46] 1793 4-9-2 0 EduardoPedroza 7 102
(S Smrczek, Germany) **31/10**[2]
3 1/2 **Akua'rella (GER)**[29] 4-8-13 0 JozefBojko 6 98
(D Moser, Germany) **188/10**
4 3/4 **Emerita (GER)**[29] 4-8-13 0 MichaelCadeddu 3 97
(H-J Groschel, Germany) **36/5**
5 nse **Folie De Louise (FR)**[29] 5-9-5 0 TonyPiccone 8 102
(Carmen Bocskai, Germany) **33/10**[3]
6 1 **Dathanna (IRE)**[342] 4063 4-8-13 0 BrettDoyle 10 94
(Charlie Appleby) *t.k.h early and wd: trckd ldr: pushed along to chal 2f out: rdn and outpcd over 1f out: kpt on same pce fnl f* **29/10**[1]
7 1/2 **Viva Gloria (GER)**[29] 4-8-13 0 MiguelLopez 4 93
(J Hirschberger, Germany) **178/10**
8 1 1/4 **Lovelett (IRE)**[256] 5-8-13 0 StephenHellyn 2 90
(M Figge, Germany) **50/1**
9 1 1/4 **Afsane (FR)**[56] 6-8-13 0 BayarsaikhanGanbat 5 87
(S Smrczek, Germany) **28/1**
10 8 1/2 **Dina (GER)**[29] 4-8-13 0 MartinSeidl 1 68
(Markus Klug, Germany) **28/1**

1m 35.98s **10** Ran SP% **118.6**
PARI-MUTUEL (all including 1 euro stake): WIN 7.20 PLACE: 2.20, 2.10, 3.40; SF: 23.80.
Owner R Nicolay **Bred** Frau Christel & Achim Stahn **Trained** Germany

3120 LONGCHAMP (R-H)
Thursday, May 30

OFFICIAL GOING: Turf: good

3289a PRIX DU PALAIS-ROYAL (GROUP 3) (3YO+) (TURF) 7f
4:55 3-Y-O+ £36,036 (£14,414; £10,810; £7,207; £3,603)

RPR
1 **Hey Gaman**[33] 2109 4-9-4 0 PJMcDonald 4 111+
(James Tate) *chsd ldr outside rival: drvn to ld over 1 1/2f out: styd on wl fnl f: a holding pursuers* **19/5**[3]
2 1 **King Malpic (FR)**[22] 6-9-4 0 OlivierPeslier 5 108
(T Lemer, France) *midfield on outer: drvn and clsd appr fnl f: styd on to go 2nd cl home: no threat to wnr* **31/1**
3 snk **Polydream (IRE)**[29] 2313 4-9-7 0 MaximeGuyon 1 111
(F Head, France) *chsd ldr on inner: n.m.r 1 1/2f out: sn in clr and rallied to chse ldr ins fnl f: nvr able to chal: lost 2nd cl home* **31/10**[2]
4 hd **Spinning Memories (IRE)**[18] 2670 4-9-1 0 ChristopheSoumillon 2 104
(P Bary, France) *midfield on inner: shkn up to chse ldng pair 1 1/2f out: styd on fnl f: nt pce to chal* **9/1**
5 nk **Marianafoot (FR)**[97] 869 4-9-4 0 Pierre-CharlesBoudot 6 106
(J Reynier, France) *prom: nt clr run 2f out: angled out w 1 1/2f to run: styd on ins fnl f: nvr on terms* **10/1**
6 3/4 **Urwald**[32] 2166 3-8-7 0 MickaelBarzalona 3 100
(A Fabre, France) *towards rr: clsd ins fnl 1 1/2f: styd on u.p fnl f: nvr trbld ldrs* **9/1**
7 3/4 **Tornibush (IRE)**[29] 2313 5-9-6 0 StephanePasquier 8 104
(P Decouz, France) *towards rr: drvn but no imp 2f out: kpt on ins fnl f: nvr in contention* **10/1**
8 2 **Tour To Paris (FR)**[38] 4-9-4 0 GregoryBenoist 7 97
(Mme Pia Brandt, France) *broke wl fr wd draw: led: hdd over 1 1/2f out: wknd fnl f* **19/10**[1]
9 1/2 **Fas (IRE)**[98] 843 5-9-4 0 (b) AurelienLemaitre 9 95
(Mme Pia Brandt, France) *a in rr: scrubbed along 2 1/2f out: kpt on ins fnl f: nvr involved* **112/1**

1m 18.6s (-2.10) **9** Ran SP% **121.9**
WFA 3 from 4yo+ 11lb
PARI-MUTUEL (all including 1 euro stake): WIN 4.80; PLACE 2.00, 4.10, 1.80; DF 62.20.
Owner Sultan Ali **Bred** Rabbah Bloodstock Limited **Trained** Newmarket, Suffolk

3244 CARLISLE (R-H)
Friday, May 31

OFFICIAL GOING: Heavy (soft in places; 6.2)
Wind: Breezy, half against in over 2f of home straight Weather: Overcast, raining to race 2 (1.40)

3290 RACING TV IN HD EBF NOVICE STKS (PLUS 10 RACE) 5f
1:10 (1:12) (Class 4) 2-Y-O £6,469 (£1,925; £962; £481) Stalls Low

Form RPR
1 **Iffraaz (IRE)** 2-9-5 0 JoeFanning 9 82+
(Mark Johnston) *sn cl up: shkn up to ld against stands' rail 1f out: kpt on strly to draw clr last 100yds: comf* **4/1**[3]
3 2 2 1/4 **Hurstwood**[43] 1893 2-9-5 0 DavidAllan 6 74+
(Tim Easterby) *t.k.h early: cl up: rdn and outpcd 2f out: rallied to chse wnr ins fnl f: r.o* **13/8**[1]
3 3 **Kilham** 2-9-5 0 DavidNolan 8 63
(Declan Carroll) *led: drvn and hdd 1f out: lost 2nd ins fnl f: sn wknd* **3/1**[2]
4 1 **Stone Soldier** 2-9-5 0 BarryMcHugh 3 60
(James Given) *dwlt: sn in tch: effrt on outside 2f out: wknd ins fnl f* **14/1**
4 5 2 **Spanish Time**[17] 2707 2-9-0 0 SeanDavis(5) 5 52
(Keith Dalgleish) *in tch: drvn and outpcd over 2f out: n.d after* **6/1**
6 1/2 **Unifier** 2-9-5 0 PaulMulrennan 4 51
(Michael Dods) *missed break: bhd: hdwy to join gp after 2f: shkn up 2f out: wknd appr fnl f (jockey said colt was slowly away)* **11/1**

1m 6.51s (4.41) **Going Correction** +0.425s/f (Yiel) **6** Ran SP% **112.4**
Speed ratings (Par 95): **81,77,72,71,67 67**
CSF £11.00 TOTE £4.20: £2.00, £1.40; EX 10.40 Trifecta £26.30.

Owner Sheikh Hamdan bin Mohammed Al Maktoum **Bred** Godolphin **Trained** Middleham Moor, N Yorks

FOCUS
There were a large number of non-runners due to the ground, including three in this opener. The time was respectable however, 6.71sec outside standard, so perhaps conditions weren't as testing as they might have been. As they'd been doing here on Thursday evening, the runners came over to the stands' side. It's been rated at face value.

3291 THURSBY H'CAP 5f
1:40 (1:42) (Class 5) (0-70,67) 3-Y-O+ £4,204 (£1,251; £625; £312; £300; £300) Stalls Low

Form RPR
5400 1 **Afandem (IRE)**[12] 2876 5-9-10 63 (p) DuranFentiman 2 74
(Tim Easterby) *hld up: smooth hdwy over 2f out: effrt and chsd ldr over 1f out: led ins fnl f: pushed clr: readily* **11/1**
1165 2 5 **Santafiora**[33] 2153 5-8-10 56 VictorSantos(7) 7 49
(Julie Camacho) *dwlt: hld up: hdwy and rdn over 1f out: kpt on wl fnl f to take 2nd last stride: no ch w easy wnr* **3/1**[1]
-545 3 hd **Seamster**[2] 3227 12-9-3 63 (t) LauraCoughlan(7) 4 55+
(David Loughnane) *dwlt: hld up: hdwy on outside to ld 2f out: rdn and over 2 l clr over 1f out: hdd ins fnl f: sn outpcd: lost 2nd cl home* **5/1**[3]
0030 4 4 **Leeshaan (IRE)**[2] 3227 4-8-11 50 DavidProbert 1 28
(Rebecca Bastiman) *w ldrs to 2f out: sn rdn and outpcd: btn fnl f* **7/2**[2]
0-33 5 4 **Sapphire Jubilee**[28] 2377 3-8-12 62 BenRobinson(3) 5 22
(Ollie Pears) *prom: effrt and ev ch briefly 2f out: sn rdn and wknd* **7/1**
-600 6 hd **Teepee Time**[20] 2632 6-8-11 50 (b) PhilDennis 9 13
(Michael Mullineaux) *mde most to 2f out: sn rdn and wknd* **16/1**
13-6 7 hd **Pavers Pride**[12] 2876 5-9-9 67 (b) DannyRedmond(5) 8 29
(Noel Wilson) *hld up on ins: effrt and shkn up over 2f out: wknd over 1f out (jockey said he felt something was amiss in the final furlong on the gelding; vet said the gelding to be lame left fore)* **11/2**
00-0 8 2 1/4 **Minty Jones**[144] 118 10-8-4 48 oh3 (v) FayeMcManoman(5) 6 2
(Michael Mullineaux) *w ldrs to over 2f out: sn lost pl and struggling* **66/1**
-450 9 4 1/2 **Alqaab**[13] 2841 4-9-13 66 JackGarritty 10 4
(Ruth Carr) *missed break: bhd and outpcd: struggling fr 1/2-way* **8/1**

1m 5.49s (3.39) **Going Correction** +0.425s/f (Yiel)
WFA 3 from 4yo+ 8lb **9** Ran SP% **118.6**
Speed ratings (Par 103): **89,81,80,74,67 67,67,63,56**
CSF £45.35 CT £193.43 TOTE £10.00: £3.20, £1.80, £2.00; EX 52.00 Trifecta £240.00.

Owner Reality Partnerships Xi **Bred** Rabbah Bloodstock Limited **Trained** Great Habton, N Yorks

FOCUS
A low-grade sprint handicap in testing ground. It's hard to pin down the level.

3292 LONGTOWN H'CAP 5f 193y
2:15 (2:19) (Class 6) (0-65,65) 3-Y-O £3,234 (£962; £481; £300; £300; £300) Stalls Low

Form RPR
-033 1 **Timetodock**[12] 2871 3-9-3 61 (b) DavidAllan 2 68
(Tim Easterby) *racd in far side gp: mde all: rdn over 1f out: hld on wl fnl f: first of five in gp* **7/2**[1]
33-4 2 nk **Sarasota Bay**[64] 1389 3-9-7 65 JasonHart 5 71
(John Quinn) *trckd wnr far side: effrt and rdn over 1f out: edgd lft ins fnl f: r.o: hld nr fin: 2nd of five in gp* **8/1**
03-0 3 1 **Vigorito**[20] 2624 3-9-2 60 RobbieDowney 4 63
(David Barron) *hld up in tch on far side gp: effrt and hdwy over 1f out: kpt on fnl f: nrst fin: 3rd of five in gp* **20/1**
2-00 4 6 **Dancing Rave**[20] 2635 3-9-7 65 DavidNolan 13 50+
(David O'Meara) *hld up in tch on nr side: smooth hdwy to ld that gp over 2f out: plld clr of that gp over 1f out: no ch w far side ldrs: first of five in gp* **9/2**[2]
5-00 5 5 **Here's Rocco (IRE)**[20] 2630 3-9-5 63 BarryMcHugh 3 33
(John Quinn) *t.k.h: hld up far side: pushed along and no imp whn checked over 1f out: nvr able to chal: 4th of five in gp (jockey said gelding was hampered by the faller 2f out)* **40/1**
000- 6 1 1/4 **Allsfineandandy (IRE)**[202] 9000 3-8-2 51 SeanDavis(5) 1 17
(Lynn Siddall) *dwlt: hld up in tch on far side: rdn along over 2f out: sn n.d: btn over 1f out: last of five in gp* **12/1**
3-03 7 3 1/2 **Highjacked**[12] 2870 3-8-6 50 PhilDennis 15 6+
(John Davies) *cl up in nr side gp: disp ld that gp over 2f out to over 1f out: sn wknd: 2nd of five in gp* **5/1**[3]
6-23 8 1 1/4 **Pinarella (FR)**[32] 2199 3-9-3 61 AndrewMullen 14 13+
(Ben Haslam) *cl up in nr side gp tl lost pl 2f out: sn struggling: 3rd of five in gp* **6/1**
050 9 3 1/4 **The Thorny Rose**[13] 2823 3-8-10 59 PaulaMuir(5) 10 +
(Michael Dods) *prom nr side gp: effrt over 2f out: wknd over 1f out: 4th of five in gp* **25/1**
0213 10 25 **Lexikon**[25] 2482 3-8-7 54 JamieGormley(3) 12 +
(Ollie Pears) *led nr side gp to over 2f out: sn struggling: t.o: last of five in gp (trainer said filly was unsuited by the ground (heavy, soft in places) on this occasion and would prefer a sounder surface)* **5/1**[3]
3033 U **Popping Corks (IRE)**[18] 2683 3-8-7 54 BenRobinson(3) 7
(Linda Perratt) *trckd ldrs in far side gp: effrt and cl 3rd whn faltered bdly and uns rdr over 1f out* **20/1**

1m 16.46s (1.86) **Going Correction** +0.425s/f (Yiel) **11** Ran SP% **122.6**
Speed ratings (Par 97): **104,103,102,94,87 85,81,79,75,41**
CSF £32.02 CT £506.02 TOTE £3.70: £2.20, £2.20, £4.10; EX 28.70 Trifecta £326.30.

Owner E A Brook & Partner **Bred** Crossfields Bloodstock Ltd **Trained** Great Habton, N Yorks

■ Darwina was withdrawn. Price at time of withdrawal 50-1. Rule 4 does not apply

FOCUS
The stalls were moved forward 10yds to avoid a patch of false ground. Modest form. This time there was a split opinion, with five runners tacking over to the stands' side and six staying on the far side, which hadn't been used over the two days. It was the far side that came out on top, the five who finished comprising the first three plus the fifth and sixth home. The second has been rated to her pre-race mark.

3293 BRITISH EBF PREMIER FILLIES' H'CAP 5f 193y
2:50 (2:50) (Class 3) (0-90,92) 3-Y-0

£15,562 (£4,660; £2,330; £1,165; £582; £292) Stalls Low

Form RPR

0-13 **1** **Lady Calcaria**[30] 2293 3-8-7 **71**.................................. DuranFentiman 11 79
(Tim Easterby) *trckd ldr: led gng wl 2f out: sn hrd pressed and rdn: kpt on wl last 100yds* **9/2**[3]

1-02 **2** *1½* **Lorton**[24] 2510 3-9-2 **85**.................................. DannyRedmond(5) 5 89
(Julie Camacho) *hld up in tch on outside: hdwy and ev ch over 1f out to ins fnl f: rdn and one pce last 100yds* **4/1**[2]

411- **3** *2* **Gold Arrow**[249] 7617 3-9-5 **83**.................................. KevinStott 3 81
(Ralph Beckett) *hld up: angled lft and hdwy over 1f out: kpt on fnl f: nt rch first two* **14/1**

154- **4** *1½* **Praxidice**[224] 8369 3-9-0 **78**.................................. BenCurtis 4 71
(K R Burke) *in tch: effrt and rdn 2f out: outpcd ins fnl f* **6/1**

26-5 **5** *2¼* **Strict Tempo**[33] 2144 3-9-4 **82**.................................. DavidProbert 1 68
(Andrew Balding) *hld up in tch on ins: rdn over 2f out: n.m.r briefly over 1f out: sn btn (trainer said filly was unsuited by the ground (heavy, soft in places) on this occasion and would prefer a sounder surface)* **5/1**

-540 **6** *7* **Chynna**[6] 3075 3-9-7 **92**.................................. ScottMcCullagh(7) 8 57
(Mick Channon) *dwlt: hld up: rdn and hung lft 2f out: sn wknd* **10/1**

25-4 **7** *1½* **Across The Sea**[20] 2635 3-8-11 **75**.................................. DavidAllan 10 36
(James Tate) *trckd ldrs: rdn over 2f out: wknd over 1f out* **3/1**[1]

4-00 **8** *½* **Little Legs**[42] 1929 3-9-3 **84**.................................. BenRobinson(3) 2 43
(Brian Ellison) *led to 2f out: sn rdn and wknd* **33/1**

4062 **9** *11* **Yolo Again (IRE)**[9] 2960 3-9-0 **83**.................................. BenSanderson(5) 7 9
(Roger Fell) *awkward s: hld up on outside: rdn and outpcd over 2f out: sn btn (jockey said filly missed the break and hung left)* **14/1**

1m 15.49s (0.89) **Going Correction** +0.425s/f (Yiel) **9** Ran SP% **119.5**
Speed ratings (Par 100): **111,109,106,104,101 92,90,89,74**
CSF £23.78 CT £239.12 TOTE £5.30: £1.60, £1.90, £3.00; EX 31.80 Trifecta £386.30.
Owner Ontoawinner 10 & Partner **Bred** Lady Juliet Tadgell **Trained** Great Habton, N Yorks

FOCUS
The stalls were moved forward 10yds to avoid a patch of false ground. Quite a valuable fillies' handicap. This time the whole field remained on the far side. The time was around a second quicker than the preceding class 6 handicap. The second has been rated to her Wetherby latest.

3294 RACING TV DAY PASS JUST £10 H'CAP 2m 1f 47y
3:25 (3:25) (Class 4) (0-80,78) 4-Y-0+

£7,439 (£2,213; £1,106; £553; £300; £300) Stalls Low

Form RPR

00-0 **1** **Only Orsenfoolsies**[21] 2591 10-8-7 **59**......................(p[1]) AndrewElliott 3 65
(Micky Hammond) *trckd ldr: rdn 3f out: led and hrd pressed fr over 1f out: hld on wl towards fin (trainer said, regarding the apparent improvement in form, that gelding may have appreciated the ground (heavy, soft in places) on this occasion and benefitted from the first-time application of cheekpieces)* **33/1**

3/5- **2** *nk* **Cornerstone Lad**[55] 8901 5-8-13 **65**..............................(p) GrahamLee 8 71+
(Micky Hammond) *plld hrd: in tch: stdy hdwy whn nt clr run and plld out over 1f out: rdn and cl 2nd ins fnl f: kpt on: hld cl home (jockey said gelding ran too free)* **6/4**[1]

02/0 **3** *nk* **Attention Seaker**[21] 2591 9-9-2 **68**..............................(t) DavidAllan 9 73
(Tim Easterby) *cl up: ev ch 3f out to over 1f out: kpt on fnl f: hld towards fin* **16/1**

1-54 **4** *2* **Bodacious Name (IRE)**[20] 2626 5-9-3 **69**.................................. JasonHart 11 72
(John Quinn) *hld up: rdn and hdwy over 3f out: kpt on same pce fnl f* **4/1**[3]

-002 **5** *4* **Royal Flag**[20] 2613 9-8-11 **66**.................................. BenRobinson(3) 10 65
(Brian Ellison) *hld up in tch: rdn and outpcd over 2f out: no imp fnl f (jockey said gelding was never travelling)* **12/1**

0-23 **6** *nk* **So Near So Farhh**[21] 2591 4-9-0 **67**.................................. BenCurtis 6 67
(Mick Channon) *led: rdn and hdd over 1f out: wknd ins fnl f* **7/4**[2]

345/ **7** *10* **Wynford (IRE)**[21] 1092 6-8-13 **72**..............................(bt) VictorSantos(7) 12 59
(Lucinda Egerton) *hld up: outpcd whn hung lft bnd over 2f out: sn wknd* **100/1**

04-0 **8** *3¾* **Question Of Faith**[32] 2185 8-9-3 **74**.................................. HarrisonShaw(5) 5 57
(Martin Todhunter) *missed break: hld up: drvn and outpcd over 2f out: edgd lft and wknd over 2f out* **20/1**

4m 1.71s (7.41) **Going Correction** +0.425s/f (Yiel)
WFA 4 from 5yo+ 1lb **8** Ran SP% **118.6**
Speed ratings (Par 105): **99,98,98,97,95 95,91,89**
CSF £85.51 CT £896.28 TOTE £47.30: £6.60, £1.10, £3.60; EX 112.80 Trifecta £2411.40.
Owner M H O G **Bred** Redmyre Bloodstock & Newhall Farm Estate **Trained** Middleham, N Yorks

FOCUS
A tight finish to this modest staying handicap, which saw a 1-2 for the Micky Hammond stable. It was Hammond's first winner of the season. The third has been rated close to her old best.

3295 RACING TV IN HD H'CAP 1m 3f 39y
4:00 (4:01) (Class 4) (0-80,80) 3-Y-0

£7,439 (£2,213; £1,106; £553; £300; £300) Stalls High

Form RPR

35-2 **1** **Buriram (IRE)**[51] 1696 3-9-5 **78**.................................. KevinStott 1 87
(Ralph Beckett) *trckd ldrs: led over 2f out: sn edgd lft: rdn and edgd rt over 1f out: drew clr fnl f: comf* **9/4**[2]

4-60 **2** *3¼* **Artistic Language**[34] 2096 3-9-0 **73**..............................(v[1]) BenCurtis 2 76
(Brian Meehan) *hld up in tch: rdn and effrt over 2f out: chsd wnr over 1f out: hung rt and no ex ins fnl f* **6/1**

0-62 **3** *1* **London Eye (USA)**[27] 2406 3-9-1 **74**.................................. DavidAllan 5 75
(Sir Michael Stoute) *t.k.h early: hld up bhd ldng gp: effrt and rdn 2f out: kpt on same pce fnl f* **15/8**[1]

50-6 **4** *1* **Bullion Boss (IRE)**[12] 2872 3-9-2 **75**..............................(p) PaulMulrennan 4 74
(Michael Dods) *pressed ldr tl rdn and outpcd over 2f out: swtchd lft over 1f out: hung rt and sn outpcd* **16/1**

1-56 **5** *1¼* **Landa Beach (IRE)**[29] 2321 3-9-7 **80**.................................. DavidProbert 6 78
(Andrew Balding) *s.i.s: hld up: pushed along over 4f out: effrt 3f out: no imp fr 2f out* **4/1**[3]

532- **6** *10* **Ticklish (FR)**[190] 9205 3-9-5 **78**.................................. JoeFanning 3 58
(Mark Johnston) *t.k.h: led to over 2f out: rdn and wknd over 1f out* **12/1**

2m 30.07s (0.37) **Going Correction** +0.425s/f (Yiel) **6** Ran SP% **113.4**
Speed ratings (Par 101): **112,109,108,108,107 100**
CSF £16.15 TOTE £3.50: £2.60, £2.60; EX 16.90 Trifecta £41.60.
Owner King Power Racing Co Ltd **Bred** Irish National Stud **Trained** Kimpton, Hants

FOCUS
Fairly useful handicap form. The winner has been rated to his 2yo form, with the third close to his latest.

3296 RACING TV IN GLORIOUS HD H'CAP (DIV I) 1m 1f
4:45 (4:45) (Class 6) (0-60,64) 4-Y-0+

£3,234 (£962; £481; £300; £300; £300) Stalls Low

Form RPR

-631 **1** **Majeste**[2] 3225 5-9-10 **62** 5ex.................................. DavidProbert 8 69
(Rebecca Bastiman) *prom: effrt and rdn 2f out: led ent fnl f: rdn out* **5/2**[2]

00-0 **2** *1¼* **Tom's Anna (IRE)**[29] 2328 9-8-7 **45**.................................. AndrewElliott 9 48
(Sean Regan) *pressed ldr: rdn and led over 1f out: hdd ent fnl f: rallied: one pce towards fin* **50/1**

0-64 **3** *1* **Milan Reef (IRE)**[2] 3225 4-9-3 **55**.................................. JasonHart 2 56
(David Loughnane) *t.k.h early: led: rdn and hdd over 1f out: rallied: one pce ins fnl f* **11/10**[1]

0-00 **4** *2¾* **Im Dapper Too**[32] 2203 8-9-6 **58**.................................. SamJames 12 54
(John Davies) *hld up in tch: drvn and outpcd 3f out: rallied over 1f out: kpt on fnl f: no imp* **7/2**[3]

0-55 **5** *2* **Dominannie (IRE)**[11] 2911 6-8-8 **46**.................................. PhilDennis 3 38
(Ron Barr) *trckd ldrs: drvn along 3f out: wknd over 1f out* **8/1**

6000 **6** *8* **Just Heather (IRE)**[6] 3067 5-8-9 **47** ow2.................................. BarryMcHugh 1 23
(John Wainwright) *hld up towards rr: drvn and outpcd over 3f out: n.d after* **28/1**

20-0 **7** *7* **Duba Plains**[14] 2789 4-8-10 **48**.................................. GrahamLee 5 10
(Kenny Johnson) *slowly away: hld up: rdn and struggling over 3f out: nvr on terms* **40/1**

000- **8** *8* **Symbolic Star (IRE)**[41] 8829 7-8-10 **53**................(p) ConnorMurtagh(5) 6
(Barry Murtagh) *hld up: rdn and struggling over 3f out: sn btn* **40/1**

0006 **9** *3* **Dutch Melody**[11] 2911 5-8-0 **45**.................................. VictorSantos(7) 7
(Lucinda Egerton) *dwlt: bhd: struggling 4f out: sn btn (trainer said mare was unsuited by the ground (heavy, soft in places) on this occasion and would prefer a sounder surface)* **25/1**

2m 2.38s (3.38) **Going Correction** +0.425s/f (Yiel) **9** Ran SP% **123.7**
Speed ratings (Par 101): **102,100,100,97,95 88,82,75,72**
CSF £128.03 CT £217.18 TOTE £3.70: £1.60, £7.10, £1.10; EX 61.50 Trifecta £276.40.
Owner Let's Be Lucky Racing 17 & Partner **Bred** Marston Stud **Trained** Cowthorpe, N Yorks

FOCUS
Division one of a weak handicap. Only a few became involved. It's been rated negatively.

3297 RACING TV IN GLORIOUS HD H'CAP (DIV II) 1m 1f
5:20 (5:21) (Class 6) (0-60,62) 4-Y-0+

£3,234 (£962; £481; £300; £300; £300) Stalls Low

Form RPR

-313 **1** **Jackhammer (IRE)**[3] 3177 5-8-13 **51**..............................(bt) PaulMulrennan 5 63+
(Dianne Sayer) *hld up: smooth hdwy to trck ldrs over 3f out: shkn up to ld over 1f out: sn clr: readily* **15/8**[1]

0605 **2** *3½* **Highwayman**[2] 3224 6-8-2 **45**.................................. PaulaMuir(5) 8 49
(David Thompson) *dwlt: hld up: rdn along 3f out: hdwy on outside to chse (clr) wnr over 1f out: edgd rt: no imp fnl f* **4/1**[2]

06-0 **3** *2¼* **Metronomic (IRE)**[30] 2290 5-8-10 **48**.................................. JasonHart 1 48
(Peter Niven) *fly-jmpd s: plld hrd early: hld up on ins: hdwy and prom 1/2-way: outpcd 3f out: rallied to chse ldrs over 1f out: one pce* **8/1**

3430 **4** *3½* **Muqarred (USA)**[4] 3163 7-8-12 **55**..............................(b) BenSanderson(5) 11 48
(Roger Fell) *mde most tl hdd over 1f out: sn wknd* **6/1**[3]

000- **5** *2¾* **Mr Cool Cash**[249] 7599 7-8-8 **46**..............................(t) SamJames 7 33
(John Davies) *trckd ldrs: effrt and ch over 2f out: wknd over 1f out* **12/1**

0560 **6** *½* **Orobas (IRE)**[2] 3217 7-9-3 **62**..............................(v) VictorSantos(7) 3 48
(Lucinda Egerton) *pressed ldr: chal over 4f out to over 2f out: rdn and wknd over 1f out* **16/1**

65-4 **7** *4½* **Glaceon (IRE)**[21] 2580 4-9-0 **57**.................................. ConnorMurtagh(5) 4 34
(Tina Jackson) *hld up in tch: outpcd over 4f out: n.d after* **8/1**

3-00 **8** *2¾* **Zealous (IRE)**[31] 2244 6-9-10 **62**.................................. GrahamLee 9 34
(Alistair Whillans) *hld up on outside: drvn and outpcd over 4f out: sn btn* **15/2**

2m 2.78s (3.78) **Going Correction** +0.425s/f (Yiel) **8** Ran SP% **116.6**
Speed ratings (Par 101): **100,96,94,91,89 88,84,82**
CSF £9.56 CT £48.61 TOTE £2.30: £1.30, £1.20, £3.20; EX 9.60 Trifecta £51.30.
Owner Mrs Dianne Sayer **Bred** F Dunne **Trained** Hackthorpe, Cumbria

FOCUS
This was 0.4sec slower than the first division. Low-grade form.
T/Plt: £78.40 to a £1 stake. Pool: £41,867.28 - 389.34 winning units. T/Qpdt: £27.90 to a £1 stake. Pool: £4,313.33 - 114.24 winning units. **Richard Young**

3141 CHELMSFORD (A.W) (L-H)
Friday, May 31

OFFICIAL GOING: Polytrack: standard
Wind: virtually nil Weather: dry and warm

3298 £20 FREE BETS AT TOTESPORT.COM H'CAP 1m 2f (P)
6:10 (6:12) (Class 7) (0-50,54) 4-Y-0+ £2,911 (£866; £432; £216) Stalls Low

Form RPR

0163 **1** **Murhib (IRE)**[51] 1679 7-9-7 **50**..............................(h) JFEgan 3 58
(Lydia Richards) *t.k.h: trckd ldrs: rdn to ld over 1f out: clr 1f out: r.o wl* **5/1**[2]

4040 **2** *3* **Foxrush Take Time (FR)**[8] 3006 4-9-2 **45**......................(e) PhilipPrince 5 48
(Richard Guest) *taken down early: effrt over 1f out: chsd clr wnr ins fnl f: kpt on but no imp* **8/1**

030- **3** *nk* **It's How We Roll (IRE)**[81] 9643 5-9-2 **45**......................(p) RyanTate 15 47
(John Spearing) *swtchd lft after s: hld up towards rr: sme hdwy 3f out: nt clrest of runs 2f out: drvn and styd on on wl ins fnl f: no threat to wnr* **33/1**

0131 **4** *½* **Muraaqeb**[8] 3006 5-9-11 **54** 5ex..............................(p) AdamMcNamara 6 55
(Milton Bradley) *bustled along early: racd in last trio: effrt over 1f out: styng on whn nt clr run and swtchd lft ins fnl f: kpt on but no threat to wnr* **7/2**[1]

0-00 **5** *1 ¼* **Tilsworth Lukey**[17] 2720 6-9-7 **50** .... RaulDaSilva 4 49
(J R Jenkins) *in tch in midfield: effrt and hdwy on inner over 1f out: drvn and kpt on same pce fnl f (vet said gelding lost its right fore shoe)* **12/1**

0005 **6** *1 ¼* **Lulu Star (IRE)**[16] 2737 4-9-3 **49** .... JoshuaBryan(3) 10 46
(Julia Feilden) *chsd ldrs: effrt to chal 2f out: unable qck and outpcd over 1f out: wknd ins fnl f* **12/1**

0004 **7** *nk* **Cat Royale (IRE)**[8] 3006 6-9-1 **49** .... (b) DarraghKeenan(5) 1 45
(John Butler) *sn led: drvn ent fnl 2f: hdd over 1f out: no ex and wknd ins fnl f* **5/1**[2]

0-06 **8** *shd* **Grasmere (IRE)**[16] 2738 4-8-12 **48** .... (t[1]) CierenFallon(7) 2 44
(Alan Bailey) *in tch in midfield: effrt 2f out: keeping on same pce and no threat to wnr whn hmpd ins fnl f* **12/1**

0430 **9** *¾* **Woggle (IRE)**[41] 1958 4-8-13 **45** .... (b) GeorgiaCox(3) 14 40
(Geoffrey Deacon) *bdly hmpd s: in rr: effrt over 1f out: swtchd lft and kpt on ins fnl f: nvr trbld ldrs (jockey said filly suffered interference shortly after the start)* **33/1**

0000 **10** *1* **Officer Drivel (IRE)**[9] 2970 8-9-8 **51** .... (v) JoeyHaynes 11 44
(Paddy Butler) *hld up in tch in midfield: effrt over 1f out: unable qck u.p: wl hld and plugged on same pce ins fnl f* **50/1**

0020 **11** *nk* **Ronni Layne**[8] 3006 5-9-3 **46** .... (b) MartinDwyer 9 38
(Louise Allan) *s.i.s: pushed early: hdwy to chse ldrs over 7f out: unable qck and lost pl u.p over 1f out: wknd ins fnl f* **25/1**

0500 **12** *5* **Herringswell (FR)**[31] 2234 4-8-10 **46** .... LauraPearson(7) 8 29
(Henry Spiller) *hld up in tch in midfield: unable qck u.p and btn over 1f out: wknd fnl f* **50/1**

5433 **13** *7* **Hidden Dream (IRE)**[16] 2738 4-9-3 **46** .... (p) LewisEdmunds 16 17
(Christine Dunnett) *in tch in midfield: hung rt and reminder over 4f out: lost pl u.p over 1f out: wknd fnl f (jockey said filly hung right-handed)* **7/1**[3]

00-5 **14** *11* **Master Poet**[24] 2513 4-9-8 **51** .... DougieCostello 12 2
(Gary Moore) *led for 2f: w ldr: drvn and unable qck ent fnl 2f: lost pl and bhd 1f out: eased ins fnl f: burst blood vessel (jockey said gelding hung left-handed; vet said gelding had bled from the nose)* **7/1**[3]

-000 **P** **More Harry**[81] 1146 4-9-2 **45** .... (w) RobertWinston 13
(Clare Ellam) *wnt rt leaving stalls: wd thrght and a bhd: eased and p.u over 1f out (jockey said gelding was never travelling and stopped quickly)* **50/1**

2m 6.89s (-1.71) **Going Correction** -0.25s/f (Stan) **15 Ran SP% 130.4**
Speed ratings (Par 97): **96,93,93,92,91 90,90,90,90,89 89,85,79,70,**
CSF £46.20 CT £1236.41 TOTE £5.10: £2.10, £2.80, £35.20; EX 50.50 Trifecta £960.10.
Owner The Murhib Partnership **Bred** A Stroud And J Hanly **Trained** Funtington, W Sussex

FOCUS
A moderate handicap.

3299 TOTEPOOL CASHBACK CLUB AT TOTESPORT.COM H'CAP 1m 2f (P)
6:40 (6:44) (Class 6) (0-60,60) 3-Y-O
£3,428 (£1,020; £509; £400; £400; £400) **Stalls Low**

Form RPR

0052 **1** **Archdeacon**[24] 2517 3-8-9 **48** .... (p) KieranO'Neill 5 59
(Dean Ivory) *chsd ldrs: travelling best 3f out: swtchd rt and clsd jst over 2f out: rdn to ld over 1f out: sn in command but drifting rt fnl f: easily* **3/1**[1]

4254 **2** *5* **Picture Poet (IRE)**[29] 2322 3-9-0 **60** .... CierenFallon(7) 2 61
(Henry Spiller) *hld up in midfield: swtchd rt and effrt jst over 2f out: hdwy and drvn to chse clr wnr 1f out: kpt on but no imp* **5/1**[3]

0400 **3** *shd* **Trouble Shooter (IRE)**[21] 2597 3-8-7 **46** oh1 .... (v) RaulDaSilva 13 47
(Shaun Keightley) *hld up in rr: effrt and swtchd rt ent fnl 2f: drvn and hdwy over 1f out: styd on ins fnl f: no threat to wnr (vet said gelding lost its left fore shoe)* **5/1**[3]

000- **4** *1 ¼* **Percy's Prince**[220] 8502 3-9-2 **55** .... RyanTate 7 54
(Sir Mark Prescott Bt) *midfield: rdn over 4f out: drvn over 2f out: no ch w wnr and plugged on same pce ins fnl f* **8/1**

0040 **5** *1 ¾* **Tunky**[31] 2262 3-8-12 **51** .... JFEgan 4 46
(James Given) *stdd s: hld up towards rr: effrt and hdwy u.p over 1f out: no ch w wnr and plugged on same pce ins fnl f* **14/1**

-003 **6** *4* **Lethal Laura**[23] 2531 3-8-7 **46** oh1 .... JosephineGordon 9 34
(James Given) *sn chsng ldr: rdn to ld jst over 2f out: hdd and nt match pce of wnr over 1f out: wknd ins fnl f* **14/1**

000- **7** *2 ½* **Drumshanbo Destiny (FR)**[162] 9637 3-8-12 **51** .... DougieCostello 3 35
(Gary Moore) *in tch in midfield: effrt over 2f out: sn struggling and outpcd over 1f out: wknd ins fnl f* **9/2**[2]

0-0 **8** *2 ¼* **Cala Sveva (IRE)**[119] 532 3-8-7 **46** oh1 .... DavidEgan 8 26
(Mark Usher) *led: rdn and hdd jst over 2f out: outpcd and lost pl over 1f out: wknd fnl f* **33/1**

660 **9** *4* **Matilda Bay (IRE)**[46] 1824 3-8-11 **50** .... NicolaCurrie 10 22
(Jamie Osborne) *hld up in rr: nvr involved (jockey said filly was outpaced throughout)* **25/1**

0004 **10** *¾* **Half Full**[21] 2587 3-8-9 **48** .... NathanEvans 12 19
(Michael Easterby) *chsd ldrs: rdn over 4f out: lost pl and wl btn fnl 2f* **20/1**

0-00 **11** *1 ¾* **Supreme Chance**[38] 2007 3-8-7 **46** oh1 .... EoinWalsh 6 14
(Michael Blanshard) *rrd as stalls opened and s.i.s: a in rr (jockey said gelding reared as the stalls opened)* **66/1**

000- **12** *2* **Catalogue**[154] 9730 3-9-3 **56** .... (p[1]) JoeyHaynes 1 20
(Christine Dunnett) *t.k.h: chsd ldrs: rdn and struggling to qckn jst over 2f out: lost pl and btn over 1f out: wknd fnl f (jockey said filly ran too freely)* **66/1**

000- **13** *9* **Mister Fawkes**[183] 9308 3-9-7 **60** .... MartinDwyer 11 8
(Andrew Balding) *racd awkwardly towards rr: bhd fnl 2f* **8/1**

2m 7.03s (-1.57) **Going Correction** -0.25s/f (Stan) **13 Ran SP% 126.6**
Speed ratings (Par 97): **96,92,91,90,89 86,84,82,79,78 77,75,68**
CSF £18.08 CT £76.83 TOTE £3.20: £1.40, £1.50, £2.30; EX 17.70 Trifecta £90.90.
Owner K T Ivory & Michael Yarrow **Bred** Miss K Rausing **Trained** Radlett, Herts

FOCUS
A modest 3yo handicap.

3300 EXTRA PLACES AT TOTESPORT.COM H'CAP 1m 2f (P)
7:10 (7:14) (Class 4) (0-85,86) 4-Y-O+
£6,727 (£2,002; £1,000; £500; £400; £400) **Stalls Low**

Form RPR

50-5 **1** **Grand Inquisitor**[41] 1949 7-9-7 **82** .... (v) DavidEgan 1 90
(Ian Williams) *led sn after s: hdd over 8f out and chsd ldr tl 6f out: styd chsng ldrs: effrt to ld on inner over 1f out: styd on wl ins fnl f (trainers rep said regarding apparent improvement in form that the gelding benefitted from the re-application of a visor)* **10/1**

20-1 **2** *1 ¼* **Livvys Dream (IRE)**[24] 2516 4-9-4 **79** .... (h) JFEgan 4 84+
(Charles Hills) *stdd after s: t.k.h: hld up in tch in rr: effrt on inner over 1f out: hdwy to chse wnr and swtchd rt jst ins fnl f: kpt on wl ins fnl f: a hld (jockey said filly ran too freely)* **3/1**[2]

-500 **3** *4* **Secret Art (IRE)**[14] 2800 9-9-11 **86** .... (v[1]) JoshuaBryan 6 83
(Gary Moore) *hld up in tch: effrt on outer over 2f out: drvn over 1f out: outpcd by ldng pair jst ins fnl f: wnt 3rd and wl hld fnl 100yds* **6/1**

3006 **4** *2 ¼* **Villette (IRE)**[20] 2612 5-9-5 **80** .... JoeyHaynes 5 73
(Dean Ivory) *led: sn hdd: chsd ldrs tl wnt 2nd 6f out: effrt over 2f out: ev ch u.p over 1f out tl no ex 1f out: wknd ins fnl f* **5/1**[3]

112- **5** *1* **Grey Spirit (IRE)**[301] 5699 4-9-2 **77** .... RyanTate 3 68
(Sir Mark Prescott Bt) *s.i.s: swtchd rt and hdwy to ld over 8f out: rdn ent fnl 2f: hdd over 1f out: sn outpcd and wknd ins fnl f* **6/4**[1]

3U4/ **6** *2 ¾* **First Voyage (IRE)**[680] 5060 6-9-3 **78** .... AlistairRawlinson 2 63
(Michael Appleby) *awkward leaving stalls: hld up in tch: rdn 3f out: unable qck over 1f out: wknd ins fnl f* **14/1**

2m 4.31s (-4.29) **Going Correction** -0.25s/f (Stan) **6 Ran SP% 111.7**
Speed ratings (Par 105): **107,106,102,101,100 98**
CSF £39.37 TOTE £12.40: £4.50, £1.50; EX 33.00 Trifecta £271.50.
Owner Macable Partnership & S Hassiakos **Bred** Floors Farming And Dominic Burke **Trained** Portway, Worcs

FOCUS
A decent handicap and the winning time was notably quicker than the previous two 1m2f contests. However, there are some doubts over the form.

3301 IRISH LOTTO AT TOTESPORT.COM H'CAP 6f (P)
7:40 (7:41) (Class 3) (0-90,92) 4-Y-O+ **£9,703** (£2,887; £1,443; £721) **Stalls Centre**

Form RPR

1016 **1** **Katheefa (USA)**[24] 2515 5-8-11 **80** .... NathanEvans 5 88
(Ruth Carr) *sn in tch in midfield: clsd to chse ldrs over 2f out: rdn and chal on inner over 1f out: led 1f out: styd on: rdn out (vet said gelding lost its right fore shoe and the gelding was subsequently lame on its right fore)* **25/1**

4003 **2** *1* **Ultimate Avenue (IRE)**[50] 1714 5-9-3 **86** .... (h) DougieCostello 2 91
(David Simcock) *sn outpcd in rr: pushed along and clsd over 1f out: swtchd rt jst ins fnl f: r.o wl to chse wnr towards fin: nvr getting on terms* **7/1**

-240 **3** *¾* **Storm Over (IRE)**[11] 2917 5-9-9 **92** .... (p[1]) HarryBentley 3 94
(George Scott) *mostly chsd ldr: drvn and clsd over 1f out: no ex jst ins fnl f: kpt on same pce and lost 2nd towards fin* **4/1**[3]

-660 **4** *2 ½* **Moon Trouble (IRE)**[27] 2402 6-9-2 **85** .... AlistairRawlinson 1 79
(Michael Appleby) *taken down early: led: rdn and hrd pressed over 1f out: hdd 1f out: no ex and wknd ins fnl f* **11/4**[1]

0436 **5** *¾* **Giogiobbo**[26] 2442 6-9-7 **90** .... (p) EoinWalsh 8 82
(Nick Littmoden) *mounted on the crse: hmpd leaving stalls: midfield: effrt over 2f out: keeping on same pce and hld whn impeded jst ins fnl f* **10/1**

33-1 **6** *shd* **Busby (IRE)**[136] 247 4-8-10 **79** .... (p) MartinDwyer 4 71
(Conrad Allen) *chsd ldrs: rdn and struggling to qckn jst over 1f out: btn over 1f out: wknd ins fnl f* **7/2**[2]

-003 **7** *4 ½* **Tomily (IRE)**[10] 2940 5-9-3 **91** .... ThoreHammerHansen(5) 7 68
(Richard Hannon) *awkward leaving stalls and impeded sn after leaving stalls: a outpcd in rr (jockey said gelding was never travelling)* **16/1**

6631 **8** *¾* **Erissimus Maximus (FR)**[25] 2484 5-8-12 **88** .... (b) CierenFallon(7) 9 63
(Amy Murphy) *pushed lft leaving stalls: sn rousted along to chse ldrs: struggling and losing pl over 2f out: bhd 1f out* **8/1**

6-03 **9** *1 ¾* **Rio Ronaldo (IRE)**[13] 2839 7-8-12 **81** .... RobertWinston 6 50
(Mike Murphy) *hmpd leaving stalls: hld up off the pce in last trio: effrt 2f out: nvr threatened to get involved: swtchd rt 1f out and kpt on same pce ins fnl f (jockey said gelding suffered interference shortly after the start)* **20/1**

6463 **U** **Zac Brown (IRE)**[22] 2556 8-8-9 **78** .... (t) DavidEgan 10
(Charlie Wallis) *wnt sharply lft and uns rdr leaving stalls* **12/1**

1m 11.05s (-2.65) **Going Correction** -0.25s/f (Stan) **10 Ran SP% 123.8**
Speed ratings (Par 107): **107,105,104,101,100 100,94,93,90,**
CSF £201.52 CT £871.27 TOTE £36.00: £4.90, £2.60, £1.80; EX 361.90 Trifecta £1306.10.
Owner Grange Park Racing XIV & Ruth Carr **Bred** Shadwell Farm LLC **Trained** Huby, N Yorks

FOCUS
The feature contest was a decent sprint handicap. An outsider came through to win well up the far rail in the final furlong in a good comparative time. Zac Brown lost his rider leaving the stalls in an eventful start to proceedings. The winner has been rated in line with the better view of his Southwell win, with the third to his C&D latest.

3302 BET IN PLAY AT TOTESPORT.COM NOVICE STKS 6f (P)
8:10 (8:13) (Class 5) 3-Y-O **£5,271** (£1,568; £783; £391) **Stalls Centre**

Form RPR

1-0 **1** **Heath Charnock**[27] 2397 3-9-9 0 .... KieranO'Neill 3 86
(Michael Dods) *t.k.h: chsd ldrs: drvn to chal over 1f out: led 1f out: styd on* **14/1**

2-3 **2** *½* **Johnny Reb**[13] 2823 3-9-2 0 .... HarryBentley 5 79+
(Jeremy Noseda) *in tch in midfield: clsd and nt clr run over 1f out: hmpd and tried to switch rt 1f out: swtchd lft and drvn 100yds: r.o to go 2nd last strides: nvr quite getting to wnr (jockey said colt was denied a clear run)* **1/1**[1]

2254 **3** *hd* **White Coat**[33] 2146 3-9-2 76 .... (tp) RobertHavlin 1 77
(John Gosden) *chsd ldrs: clsd to trck ldrs and nt clr run over 1f out: edgd out rt and effrt ent fnl f: chsd wnr ins fnl f: kpt on but a hld: lost 2nd last strides* **7/4**[2]

4 *2 ¾* **Kodiak Attack (IRE)** 3-9-2 0 .... DavidEgan 4 68
(Sylvester Kirk) *led: sn restrained and in tch in midfield: clsd to chse ldrs over 1f out: rn green: sn hanging lft and nudged rt: stl hanging and outpcd ins fnl f (jockey said colt hung left-handed)* **33/1**

20 **5** *hd* **Derry Boy**[34] 2114 3-9-2 72 .... (v[1]) RobertWinston 2 67
(David Evans) *taken down early and led to s: nt that wl away: sn rcvrd to ld: drvn and hrd pressed over 1f out: hdd 1f out: no ex and wknd ins fnl f* **7/1**[3]

6-6 **6** *1 ¾* **Stormbomber (CAN)**[34] 2094 3-9-2 0 .... LiamKeniry 8 62
(Ed Walker) *wnt rt leaving stalls: hld up in last pair: pushed along over 1f out: swtchd rt and reminder ins fnl f: kpt on no threat to ldrs* **25/1**

345- **7** *hd* **Mendoza (IRE)**[235] 8049 3-9-2 76 .... (h[1]) RyanTate 7 61
(James Eustace) *taken down early and led to s: in tch in midfield on outer: effrt jst over 2f out: sn struggling and outpcd over 1f out: wl hld and kpt on same pce ins fnl f* **14/1**

The Form Book Flat 2019, Raceform Ltd, Newbury, RG14 5SJ

04 **8** *39* **Aperitif**[16] 2736 3-8-11 0.. JosephineGordon 6
(Michael Bell) *t.k.h: hld up in rr: lost tch and eased 3f out: t.o (jockey said filly hung badly right-handed throughout)* **16/1**

1m 11.67s (-2.03) **Going Correction** -0.25s/f (Stan) **8** Ran SP% **124.9**
Speed ratings (Par 99): **103,102,102,98,98 95,95,43**
CSF £31.36 TOTE £20.30: £3.10, £1.10, £1.10; EX 44.80 Trifecta £129.70.
Owner David W Armstrong **Bred** Highfield Farm Llp **Trained** Denton, Co Durham

FOCUS
A fair 3yo novice contest. The winner gamely defied a penalty with trouble in behind. The third has been rated a bit below form.

3303 DOUBLE DELIGHT HAT-TRICK HEAVEN AT TOTESPORT.COM H'CAP 5f (P)
8:40 (8:46) (Class 4) (0-80,79) 4-Y-0+
£6,727 (£2,002; £1,000; £500; £400; £400) **Stalls** Low

Form RPR

5625 **1** **You're Cool**[41] 1952 7-9-7 **79**..(t) LewisEdmunds 2 86
(John Balding) *chsd ldng trio: effrt and clsd over 1f out: drvn and ev ch 1f out: led ins fnl f: drvn out* **6/1**

6141 **2** *1* **Cappananty Con**[24] 2515 5-9-1 **76**................................ JoshuaBryan(3) 7 79
(Charlie Wallis) *stdd s: hld up in midfield: effrt over 1f out: clsd to chse ldrs and swtchd lft ins fnl f: r.o to go 2nd towards fin* **3/1**[2]

30-0 **3** *½* **Kodiac Express (IRE)**[46] 1814 4-9-0 **75**.......................... GabrieleMalune(3) 1 77
(Mike Murphy) *led: rdn and hrd pressed over 1f out: hdd ins fnl f: kpt on same pce after: lost 2nd towards fin* **14/1**

31-2 **4** *1* **Maygold**[20] 2625 4-9-5 **77**..(h) LiamKeniry 3 75
(Ed Walker) *w ldrs: rdn and unable qck over 1f out: kpt on same pce ins fnl f* **9/4**[1]

0526 **5** *2* **Something Lucky (IRE)**[10] 2940 7-9-7 **79**..........(v) AlistairRawlinson 4 70
(Michael Appleby) *dwlt: pushed along in rr: swtchd rt and rdn over 1f out: kpt on ins fnl f: nvr trbld ldrs* **5/1**[3]

00-5 **6** *1¾* **La Fortuna**[50] 1712 6-9-2 **74**..(t) DavidEgan 9 59
(Charlie Wallis) *stdd and dropped in bhd after s: hld up in rr: c centre and effrt over 1f out: nvr trbld ldrs* **33/1**

0000 **7** *½* **Dynamo Walt (IRE)**[22] 2556 8-9-3 **75**..........................(v) PaddyMathers 8 58
(Derek Shaw) *dwlt and pushed along: rdn and sme hdwy into midfield 1/2-way: no hdwy over 1f out: wknd ins fnl f* **16/1**

3050 **8** *nk* **Equimou**[13] 2839 5-9-0 **77**.. DarraghKeenan(5) 5 59
(Robert Eddery) *sn pressing ldrs: unable qck u.p over 1f out: wknd ins fnl f* **8/1**

58.75s (-1.45) **Going Correction** -0.25s/f (Stan) **8** Ran SP% **113.3**
Speed ratings (Par 105): **101,99,98,97,93 91,90,89**
CSF £22.15 CT £184.79 TOTE £6.40: £1.70, £1.20, £4.00; EX 24.20 Trifecta £193.80.
Owner D Bichan & F Connor **Bred** Tirnaskea Stud **Trained** Scrooby, S Yorks

FOCUS
A fair sprint handicap. The fourth-favourite came through to win well in the final furlong. The winner has been rated to his best and the second in line with his recent form.

3304 LADIES DAY 20TH JUNE H'CAP 7f (P)
9:10 (9:14) (Class 6) (0-55,55) 4-Y-0+
£3,428 (£1,020; £509; £400; £400; £400) **Stalls** Low

Form RPR

000- **1** **Quick Monet (IRE)**[162] 9644 6-8-12 **46** oh1.......................... MartinDwyer 4 52
(Shaun Harris) *dwlt: hld up in rr: nt clr run 2f out: clsd and nt clr run again over 1f out: str run u.p ins fnl f to ld towards fin* **33/1**

4200 **2** *½* **Red Cossack (CAN)**[16] 2740 8-8-12 **46** oh1..................(b) JoeyHaynes 9 51
(Dean Ivory) *restless in stalls: t.k.h: hld up towards rr: nt clr run 2f out: hdwy over 1f out: styd on wl u.p ins fnl f: wnt 2nd towards fin* **8/1**

U122 **3** *¾* **Magicinthemaking (USA)**[93] 919 5-9-6 **54**.................... RobertHavlin 6 57
(John E Long) *chsd ldrs: effrt over 1f out: chsd ldr ins fnl f: kpt on but lost 2nd towards fin* **9/2**[2]

0134 **4** *shd* **Tarseekh**[8] 3007 6-9-3 **51**..(b) DavidEgan 12 53+
(Charlie Wallis) *wnt lft sn after s: chsd ldr: rdn to ld over 1f out: drvn ins fnl f: hdd and no ex towards fin* **8/1**

0-30 **5** *3¾* **N Over J**[15] 2774 4-9-0 **55**..(v) JackDinsmore(7) 13 48
(William Knight) *midfield but sn rdn: hung lft u.p over 1f out: no threat to ldrs and kpt on same pce ins fnl f* **12/1**

5-00 **6** *nk* **Sunbright (IRE)**[29] 2350 4-8-12 **46** oh1.......................... AlistairRawlinson 5 38
(Michael Appleby) *chsd ldng trio: unable qck over 1f out: wknd ins fnl f* **25/1**

000 **7** *1½* **Breathoffreshair**[38] 2013 5-9-4 **52**..............................(tp) PhilipPrince 3 40
(Richard Guest) *taken down early: midfield: rdn over 3f out: kpt on ins fnl f: no threat to ldrs* **20/1**

4231 **8** *¾* **Rock In Society (IRE)**[8] 3007 4-8-13 **52** 5ex......(b) DarraghKeenan(5) 11 38+
(John Butler) *led: rdn and hdd over 1f out: wknd ins fnl f* **7/4**[1]

0640 **9** *nk* **Footstepsintherain (IRE)**[8] 3007 9-9-6 **54**.................... RobertWinston 1 39+
(J R Jenkins) *chsd ldrs: drvn and unable qck over 1f out: wknd ins fnl f* **20/1**

0306 **10** *1½* **Haader (FR)**[16] 2741 4-9-7 **55**.. PaddyMathers 7 36
(Derek Shaw) *restless in stalls: midfield: no hdwy u.p and shifted lft over 1f out: wknd ins fnl f* **7/1**[3]

0236 **11** *nk* **My Girl Maisie (IRE)**[49] 1731 5-8-9 **46** oh1..................(e) WilliamCox(3) 2 27
(Richard Guest) *taken down early: in tch in midfield: rdn over 2f out: sme prog on inner over 1f out: nt clr run and no prog ins fnl f* **16/1**

04-4 **12** *5* **Erastus**[18] 2682 4-9-0 **48**.. NathanEvans 15 16
(Ruth Carr) *taken down early: s.i.s: steadily rcvrd to chse ldrs on outer after 3f: rdn and unable qck over 1f out: sn btn and wknd fnl f* **14/1**

0/5- **13** *5* **Lady Gwhinnyvere (IRE)**[372] 3025 5-8-12 **46** oh1............ RyanTate 10
(John Spearing) *pushed lft sn after s: a towards rr: bhd and eased ins fnl f (vet said mare was struck into on its left fore)* **40/1**

50-0 **14** *½* **Tilsworth Prisca**[20] 2624 4-8-12 **46** oh1.......................(h) RaulDaSilva 8
(J R Jenkins) *taken down early: hood off late: stdd after s: a in rr: lost tch over 1f out (jockey said that the blindfold was tucked too tightly into the bridle resulting in the slow removal)* **50/1**

1m 25.6s (-1.60) **Going Correction** -0.25s/f (Stan) **14** Ran SP% **130.2**
Speed ratings (Par 101): **99,98,97,97,93 92,91,90,89,88 87,82,76,75**
CSF £282.96 CT £1457.00 TOTE £72.60: £17.90, £2.70, £1.70; EX 901.90 Trifecta £1809.20.
Owner J Morris **Bred** Ms Nadja Humphreys **Trained** Carburton, Notts

FOCUS
A moderate handicap. It paid to be delivered late off a strong gallop and an outsider won going away from well out of the weights.
T/Plt: £97.60 to a £1 stake. Pool: £35,147.60 - 359.90 winning units. T/Qpdt: £20.60 to a £1 stake. Pool: £4,385.63 - 212.25 winning units. **Steve Payne**

2819

DONCASTER (L-H)
Friday, May 31

OFFICIAL GOING: Good to firm (watered; 8.2)
Wind: Moderate against Weather: Cloudy with sunny periods and breezy

3305 XPO LOGISTICS FIGHTING CANCER WITH WPCC H'CAP 1m (S)
6:00 (6:00) (Class 5) (0-75,76) 4-Y-0+
£3,752 (£1,116; £557; £400; £400; £400) **Stalls** High

Form RPR

1501 **1** **Hammer Gun (USA)**[35] 2076 6-8-11 **65**..................(v) RichardKingscote 3 73
(Derek Shaw) *hld up towards rr: smooth hdwy over 2f out: chsd ldrs over 1f out: rdn ent fnl f: kpt on wl to ld last 75yds* **6/1**[2]

512- **2** *½* **Lucky Louie**[309] 5390 6-9-4 **72**..............................(p) JackMitchell 11 79
(Roger Teal) *hld up towards rr: hdwy 2f out: rdn and kpt on wl fnl f (jockey said gelding was denied a clear run)* **14/1**

-032 **3** *1* **Straight Ash (IRE)**[7] 3053 4-8-7 **64**.................... ConorMcGovern(3) 10 69
(Ollie Pears) *trckd ldrs: pushed along and sltly outpcd over 2f out: rdn to chal over 1f out: slt ld ins fnl f: sn drvn: hdd last 75yds: kpt on same pce (jockey said gelding suffered interference in running)* **11/1**

-230 **4** *hd* **Tamerlane (IRE)**[15] 2774 4-9-0 **68**..........................(vt[1]) HectorCrouch 12 72
(Clive Cox) *hld up in midfield: hdwy nr stands' rail over 2f out: rdn to ld 1 1/2f out: drvn and hdd ent fnl f: kpt on same pce* **20/1**

0-03 **5** *1* **Kannapolis (IRE)**[36] 2057 4-8-10 **71**.......................... JoshQuinn(7) 13 74
(Michael Easterby) *hld up in tch: effrt over 2f out and sn pushed along: rdn wl over 1f out: kpt on fnl f* **6/1**[2]

0-06 **6** *½* **Brother McGonagall**[39] 1977 5-9-7 **75**.......................... JackGarritty 9 76
(Tim Easterby) *trckd ldrs: hdwy wl over 2f out: chsd ldrs and rdn whn n.m.r and swtchd lft over 1f out: sn drvn and kpt on same pce* **11/1**

1210 **7** *1¾* **Paparazzi**[13] 2842 4-9-6 **74**.. CamHardie 6 71
(Tracy Waggott) *hld up towards rr: hdwy over 3f out: chsd ldrs 2f out: sn rdn and ev ch on outer: wknd fnl f* **14/1**

-000 **8** *1½* **Fingal's Cave (IRE)**[27] 2418 7-8-9 **63**..........................(p) PaulHanagan 7 56
(Philip Kirby) *stmbld bdly s: a in rr (jockey said gelding stumbled badly leaving the stalls and was slowly away)* **25/1**

000- **9** *¾* **Bombastic (IRE)**[189] 9228 4-9-6 **74**.......................... CallumShepherd 5 66
(Ed de Giles) *led: rdn along 3f out: drvn 2f out: sn hdd & wknd* **9/1**

3232 **10** *3* **Ambient (IRE)**[30] 2273 4-9-8 **76**.......................... RossaRyan 2 61
(Mohamed Moubarak) *chsd ldng pair: rdn along 3f out: drvn and wkng whn n.m.r over 1f out (trainer said that too much use was made of the gelding in the first half of the race)* **5/1**[1]

-005 **11** *1¼* **Prevent**[4] 3149 4-9-8 **76**..(p[1]) PJMcDonald 8 58
(Ian Williams) *trckd ldr: pushed along over 2f out: sn rdn and wknd* **7/1**[3]

3125 **12** *¾* **Fire Diamond**[8] 2998 6-8-7 **61** oh1..........................(p) NickyMackay 4 41
(Tom Dascombe) *awkward and wnt lft s: in tch on outer: rdn along 3f out: sn wknd (jockey said gelding jumped very awkwardly from the stalls and was slowly away)* **16/1**

1000 **13** *½* **Insurplus (IRE)**[3] 3178 6-8-3 **64**.......................... CoreyMadden(7) 1 43
(Jim Goldie) *racd wd: chsd ldrs: rdn along 3f out: wknd over 2f out* **14/1**

1m 39.62s (-0.58) **Going Correction** -0.075s/f (Good) **13** Ran SP% **118.9**
Speed ratings (Par 103): **99,98,97,97,96 95,94,92,91,88 87,86,86**
CSF £86.94 CT £937.35 TOTE £5.70: £2.30, £3.00, £3.00; EX 72.20.
Owner A Flint **Bred** Her Majesty The Queen **Trained** Sproxton, Leics

FOCUS
The going was good to firm on a watered track and there was quite a strong headwind. They went a decent pace in this handicap and it set up for the closers. The winner has been rated back to his old turf form, the second as running a pb, and the third close to his Pontefract latest.

3306 WELDRICKS PHARMACY SUPPORTING WPCC NOVICE STKS 1m (S)
6:30 (6:33) (Class 5) 3-Y-0 **£3,752** (£1,116; £557; £278) **Stalls** High

Form RPR

1- **1** **Motakhayyel**[211] 8767 3-9-9 0.. DaneO'Neill 3 85+
(Richard Hannon) *dwlt: sn trcking ldrs: hdwy over 2f out: led 1 1/2f out: rdn: green and edgd sharply rt ins fnl f: pushed out* **3/1**[2]

4 **2** *nk* **Double Honour**[61] 1458 3-9-2 0.. PJMcDonald 6 75
(James Bethell) *trckd ldng pair: hdwy over 2f out: cl up and ev ch over 1f out: sn rdn: chsd wnr and swtchd lft ins fnl f: drvn and kpt on wl towards fin* **9/4**[1]

4 **3** *2¼* **Better Than Ever (IRE)**[34] 2128 3-8-13 0.......................... AaronJones(3) 7 70
(Marco Botti) *hld up in tch: hdwy over 2f out: rdn to chse ldrs over 1f out: kpt on fnl f* **20/1**

3 **4** *¾* **Assembled**[24] 2507 3-9-2 0.. PatCosgrave 1 68
(Hugo Palmer) *hld up: hdwy 3f out: chsd ldrs over 2f out: rdn along wl over 1f out: kpt on same pce fnl f* **4/1**

40- **5** *2¼* **Heavenly Bliss**[324] 4815 3-8-11 0.. PatDobbs 2 58
(Sir Michael Stoute) *hld up: a in rr* **12/1**

0-0 **6** *5* **Lyrical Ballad (IRE)**[17] 2713 3-8-11 0.......................... RichardKingscote 4 46
(Charles Hills) *cl up: rdn along 3f out: wknd over 2f out* **20/1**

4-0 **7** *2¾* **Mutasaamy (IRE)**[8] 3003 3-9-2 0.. JackMitchell 5 45
(Roger Varian) *led: rdn along over 2f out: hdd wl over 1f out: sn wknd* **7/2**[3]

1m 39.5s (-0.70) **Going Correction** -0.075s/f (Good) **7** Ran SP% **115.2**
Speed ratings (Par 99): **100,99,97,96,94 89,86**
CSF £10.38 TOTE £3.20: £1.90, £2.20; EX 10.30 Trifecta £69.50.
Owner Hamdan Al Maktoum **Bred** Crossfields Bloodstock Ltd **Trained** East Everleigh, Wilts

FOCUS
The two market leaders pulled clear in this novice event. The second has been rated in line with his debut run.

3307 ALAN WOOD PLUMBING & HEATING SUPPORTING WPCC H'CAP 7f 6y
7:00 (7:03) (Class 4) (0-80,79) 3-Y-0
£5,530 (£1,645; £822; £411; £400; £400) **Stalls** High

Form RPR

0-02 **1** **Gabrial The Wire**[13] 2825 3-9-5 **77**.......................... PaulHanagan 10 86
(Richard Fahey) *hld up towards rr: hdwy over 2f out: chsd ldrs over 1f out: rdn ent fnl f: kpt on wl to ld last 100yds* **7/1**[3]

61-1 **2** *1¾* **Whelans Way (IRE)**[21] 2567 3-9-6 **78**.......................... JackMitchell 8 82+
(Roger Teal) *trckd ldrs: hdwy and cl up over 2f out: sn led: rdn wl over 1f out: drvn and edgd lft ins fnl f: hdd last 100yds* **5/1**[2]

2-50 **3** *nk* **Punjab Mail**[52] 1662 3-9-1 **73**.. PJMcDonald 9 76
(Ian Williams) *hld up towards rr: hdwy over 2f out: rdn to chse ldrs over 1f out: styng on whn n.m.r and swtchd rt ins fnl f: kpt on towards fin* **40/1**

1-03 **4** 2 ½ **Triple Distilled**[13] 2825 3-9-3 78..............................(t[1]) RowanScott(3) 2 74
(Nigel Tinkler) *racd wd: prom: hdwy over 2f out: rdn to dispute ld 1 1/2f out: ev ch tl drvn and kpt on same pce ins fnl f* **20/1**

0-05 **5** ½ **Production**[15] 2766 3-9-6 78.............................. PatDobbs 12 73
(Richard Hannon) *hld up in rr: hdwy over 2f out: rdn wl over 1f out: kpt on fnl f* **8/1**

-005 **6** 1 ½ **Jem Scuttle (USA)**[24] 2510 3-8-9 67..............................(t) TomEaves 4 58
(Declan Carroll) *t.k.h: in tch: hdwy on outer 2f out: rdn over 1f out: no imp* **11/1**

2-42 **7** ¾ **Jabalaly (IRE)**[17] 2713 3-9-7 79.............................. DaneO'Neill 6 68
(Ed Dunlop) *dwlt: sn in tch: trckd ldrs 1/2-way: hdwy and prom over 2f out: sn rdn along: wknd over 1f out* **11/4[1]**

15-0 **8** 1 **Axe Axelrod (USA)**[44] 1846 3-9-3 75..............................(p[1]) RobbieDowney 5 61
(Michael Dods) *led: pushed along 3f out: rdn and hdd 2f out: sn drvn and grad wknd* **25/1**

4-52 **9** 2 ¼ **Entertaining (IRE)**[25] 2470 3-9-4 76.............................. RossaRyan 11 56
(Richard Hannon) *trckd ldrs: effrt over 2f out: sn rdn and btn* **7/1[3]**

-020 **10** 1 **Azor Ahai**[34] 2114 3-9-7 79.............................. CallumShepherd 7 57
(Mick Channon) *chsd ldrs: rdn along 3f out: sn wknd* **20/1**

0-61 **11** nk **Manana Chica (IRE)**[15] 2762 3-9-6 78.............................. HectorCrouch 3 55
(Clive Cox) *chsd ldrs: rdn along wl over 2f out: wknd wl over 1f out* **16/1**

5-05 **12** 2 ¼ **Baby Steps**[33] 2149 3-9-3 75.............................. RichardKingscote 1 46
(David Loughnane) *racd wd: cl up: rdn along over 2f out: sn wknd* **12/1**

1m 26.34s (-0.06) **Going Correction** -0.075s/f (Good) **12 Ran SP% 117.2**
Speed ratings (Par 101): **97,95,94,91,91 89,88,87,84,83 83,80**
CSF £39.25 CT £1312.96 TOTE £7.80: £2.00, £2.30, £13.60; EX 37.10 Trifecta £3344.20.
Owner Dr Marwan Koukash **Bred** S Emmet And Miss R Emmet **Trained** Musley Bank, N Yorks

FOCUS
They went a fair pace and the winner scored from some way back. The main action unfolded near the stands' rail. The third has been rated to his novice form.

3308 BLUE LINE TAXIS BARNSLEY SUPPORTING WPCC H'CAP 7f 6y
7:30 (7:33) (Class 3) (0-95,95) 4-Y-O+ **£7,762** (£2,310; £1,154; £577) **Stalls** High

Form RPR

12-5 **1** **Diocles Of Rome (IRE)**[28] 2363 4-8-6 80.............................. BenCurtis 5 91
(Ralph Beckett) *trckd ldrs: hdwy over 2f out: rdn to chal over 1f out: led ent fnl f: sn drvn and edgd lft: kpt on wl towards fin (trainer said regarding apparent improvement in form that the gelding had benefited from returning to a flatter track on this occasion)* **10/1**

6030 **2** 2 **Tommy Taylor (USA)**[15] 2775 5-9-1 89.............................. KevinStott 4 94
(Kevin Ryan) *hld up in rr: hdwy over 2f out: chsd ldrs over 1f out: rdn and squeezed through ent fnl f: kpt on wl towards fin* **7/1[2]**

-250 **3** hd **Raselasad (IRE)**[27] 2419 5-8-13 87.............................. RoystonFfrench 8 91
(Tracy Waggott) *led: rdn along and jnd over 2f out: drvn over 1f out: hdd ent fnl f: sn edgd lft and rt: kpt on same pce* **12/1**

-301 **4** 1 ¾ **Laieth**[14] 2803 4-9-7 95.............................. PatCosgrave 10 94
(Saeed bin Suroor) *cl up: chal over 2f out: rdn and ev ch over 1f out: drvn and wknd fnl f* **11/8[1]**

6-20 **5** hd **Whinmoor**[16] 2743 4-8-12 89.............................. RowanScott(3) 12 88
(Nigel Tinkler) *dwlt and towards rr: hdwy on outer over 2f out: rdn to chse ldrs and hung lft over 1f out: kpt on fnl f* **8/1**

6-0 **6** 2 ¼ **New Look (FR)**[34] 2105 4-8-11 85.............................. CamHardie 9 78
(Tim Easterby) *a towards rr* **50/1**

00-0 **7** ¾ **Dragons Tail (IRE)**[21] 2572 4-8-13 87..............................(p) RichardKingscote 7 78
(Tom Dascombe) *chsd ldng pair: rdn along 3f out: drvn and wknd 2f out* **14/1**

-621 **8** 5 **Pettifogger (IRE)**[13] 2837 4-8-13 87..............................(h) DaneO'Neill 1 64
(Marco Botti) *trckd ldrs on outer: pushed along and cl up 3f out: rdn along over 2f out: sn drvn and wknd* **15/2[3]**

3632 **9** ½ **Confrontational (IRE)**[21] 2584 5-8-7 81..............................(p) AndrewMullen 11 57
(Jennie Candlish) *in tch: rdn along 3f out: sn wknd (jockey said gelding finished lame left-fore)* **14/1**

0302 **10** 2 ¼ **Starlight Romance (IRE)**[14] 2809 5-9-0 88.............................. PaulHanagan 2 58
(Richard Fahey) *trckd ldrs: pushed along and lost pl over 3f out: sn rdn and btn (trainers rep said that the mare had ran flat)* **8/1**

1m 24.61s (-1.79) **Going Correction** -0.075s/f (Good) **10 Ran SP% 120.7**
Speed ratings (Par 107): **107,104,104,102,102 99,98,93,92,89**
CSF £80.97 CT £865.11 TOTE £10.80: £3.30, £2.30, £4.90; EX 70.30.
Owner Mrs Philip Snow & Partners **Bred** Petra Bloodstock Agency Ltd **Trained** Kimpton, Hants

FOCUS
The pace was strong and the winner forged clear under a hold-up ride. The winner has been rated in line with the better view of his AW form, and the second close to this year's 6f form.

3309 NAPOLEONS CASINO & RESTAURANT SHEFFIELD SUPPORTING WPCC H'CAP 6f 2y
8:00 (8:02) (Class 4) (0-85,86) 4-Y-O+ **£5,530** (£1,645; £822; £411; £400; £400) **Stalls** High

Form RPR

0605 **1** **Brian The Snail (IRE)**[13] 2843 5-9-9 86.............................. PaulHanagan 3 95
(Richard Fahey) *trckd ldrs: smooth hdwy to ld 1 1/2f out: rdn and kpt on wl fnl f* **6/5[1]**

-505 **2** 1 ¼ **Buccaneers Vault (IRE)**[26] 2437 7-9-1 78.............................. KevinStott 9 83
(Paul Midgley) *hld up: hdwy over 2f out: chsd ldrs over 1f out: sn rdn: chsd wnr ins fnl f: kpt on* **10/1**

0-00 **3** 2 ¼ **Lucky Lucky Man (IRE)**[27] 2393 4-9-7 84.............................. JackGarritty 7 82
(Richard Fahey) *hld up: rdn along 2f out: hdd 1 1/2f out: drvn and kpt on same pce fnl f (jockey said gelding hung right-handed)* **14/1**

15-0 **4** nse **Consequences (IRE)**[43] 1892 4-9-5 82..............................(t) PJMcDonald 2 80
(Ian Williams) *hld up: hdwy over 2f out: chsd ldrs over 1f out: rdn and kpt on same pce fnl f* **14/1**

0016 **5** 1 ¼ **Oriental Lilly**[20] 2611 5-8-8 78.............................. CoreyMadden(7) 5 72
(Jim Goldie) *hld up: hdwy 2f out: rdn over 1f out: kpt on fnl f* **8/1[3]**

1145 **6** 1 ¼ **Highland Acclaim (IRE)**[91] 964 8-9-5 82..............................(h) DavidNolan 6 72
(David O'Meara) *chsd ldr: rdn along over 2f out: wknd wl over 1f out* **16/1**

14-4 **7** nk **Dizzy G (IRE)**[12] 2874 4-9-3 80.............................. CliffordLee 11 69
(K R Burke) *chsd ldrs: rdn along 2f out: sn drvn and wknd (trainer's rep said that the filly would now appreciate a step up in trip)* **6/1[2]**

0-30 **8** nk **Signore Piccolo**[11] 2893 8-8-13 76..............................(p) TrevorWhelan 4 64
(David Loughnane) *a towards rr* **11/1**

000- **9** 1 ¼ **Choosey (IRE)**[220] 8498 4-8-8 78..............................(t w) JoshQuinn(7) 8 62
(Michael Easterby) *chsd ldr: rdn along wl over 2f out: sn wknd* **33/1**

0-00 **10** 2 ¼ **Daffy Jane**[14] 2809 4-8-12 80.............................. FayeMcManoman(5) 10 57
(Nigel Tinkler) *a towards rr (jockey said filly was restless in the stalls and jumped away awkwardly)* **18/1**

1m 12.35s (-0.35) **Going Correction** -0.075s/f (Good) **10 Ran SP% 115.7**
Speed ratings (Par 105): **99,97,94,94,92 90,90,90,88,85**
CSF £14.05 CT £118.79 TOTE £1.90: £1.10, £2.70, £3.00; EX 14.30 Trifecta £125.60.
Owner Dr Marwan Koukash **Bred** A Kirwan **Trained** Musley Bank, N Yorks

FOCUS
The hot favourite scored with authority in this sprint handicap. The second has been rated to this year's form.

3310 ANT MARKETING SUPPORTING WESTON PARK CANCER CHARITY FILLIES' H'CAP 1m 2f 43y
8:30 (8:31) (Class 5) (0-70,74) 3-Y-O **£3,752** (£1,116; £557; £400; £400; £400) **Stalls** High

Form RPR

1250 **1** **Colony Queen**[34] 2125 3-9-4 65.............................. PJMcDonald 9 71
(Steve Gollings) *trckd ldrs: hdwy 3f out: rdn along 2f out: drvn to chse clr ldr ent fnl f: styd on wl to ld last 50yds* **16/1**

6-34 **2** ½ **Perfecimperfection (IRE)**[32] 2200 3-9-7 68.............................. DaneO'Neill 5 73
(Marco Botti) *hld up towards rr: hdwy 3f out: rdn over 2f out: chsd ldng pair ent fnl f: sn drvn and ev ch: kpt on* **6/1[3]**

0-43 **3** hd **Little India (FR)**[31] 2229 3-9-11 72.............................. CliffordLee 4 76
(K R Burke) *led: rdn along and clr wl over 2f out: drvn ent fnl f: hdd and no ex last 50yds* **14/1**

-461 **4** 3 ½ **Navigate By Stars (IRE)**[7] 3057 3-9-13 74 6ex...(p) RichardKingscote 6 71
(Tom Dascombe) *trckd ldrs: hdwy 4f out: pushed along 3f out: rdn 2f out: sn drvn and one pce* **6/5[1]**

-552 **5** 6 **Mystiquestar (IRE)**[17] 2719 3-9-6 67.............................. JasonWatson 2 52
(Roger Charlton) *trckd ldrs: hdwy on inner over 3f out: rdn over 2f out: drvn wl over 1f out: sn outpcd* **5/2[2]**

-650 **6** 2 ¼ **Shamkha (IRE)**[18] 2689 3-9-6 67.............................. FergusSweeney 7 48
(Richard Hannon) *hld up: a in rr* **18/1**

0-40 **7** 6 **Grape Shot**[32] 2210 3-9-2 63.............................. RossaRyan 3 32
(Richard Hannon) *hld up: a in rr* **18/1**

6-00 **8** ¾ **Tasman Sea**[18] 2697 3-9-5 66..............................(p[1]) AndrewMullen 1 33
(Archie Watson) *t.k.h: trckd ldr: pushed along 4f out: rdn 3f out: sn wknd* **40/1**

2m 11.1s (-1.20) **Going Correction** -0.075s/f (Good) **8 Ran SP% 113.8**
Speed ratings (Par 96): **101,100,100,97,92 91,86,85**
CSF £106.83 CT £1384.44 TOTE £18.90: £2.90, £1.80, £3.00; EX 125.40 Trifecta £702.70.
Owner David & Ros Chapman **Bred** Mrs J A Cornwell **Trained** Scamblesby, Lincs

FOCUS
Race distance increased by 6 yards. The favourite didn't fire but there was an exciting three-way finish in this middle-distance handicap. It's been rated around the third, with the winner back to her best.

3311 PINDERS SUPPORTING WESTON PARK CANCER CHARITY H'CAP 1m 3f 197y
9:00 (9:00) (Class 5) (0-70,71) 3-Y-O **£3,752** (£1,116; £557; £400; £400; £400) **Stalls** Low

Form RPR

-004 **1** **West Newton**[24] 2511 3-9-0 63..............................(p) JasonWatson 12 69
(Roger Charlton) *trckd ldr: pushed along to ld 3f out: rdn 2f out: drvn and edgd rt ins fnl f: kpt on wl towards fin* **12/1**

045 **2** nk **Message**[48] 1771 3-9-3 66.............................. PJMcDonald 2 71
(Mark Johnston) *trckd ldrs: pushed along over 2f out: rdn wl over 1f out: styd on wl fnl f* **9/1**

0-04 **3** ½ **Enhanced**[34] 2113 3-9-8 71.............................. CharlieBennett 3 75+
(Hughie Morrison) *hld up: pushed along over 3f out: swtchd on outer and hdwy 2f out: sn rdn and styd on wl fnl f* **6/1[3]**

0-04 **4** shd **Robert Fitzroy (IRE)**[18] 2697 3-9-2 65..............................(p) RichardKingscote 8 69
(Michael Bell) *trckd ldrs: hdwy 3f out: sn chsng wnr: cl up 2f out: rdn and ev ch over 1f out: drvn and kpt on same pce fnl f* **3/1[1]**

40-6 **5** 1 ½ **Craneur**[24] 2517 3-9-1 64.............................. HectorCrouch 4 65
(Harry Dunlop) *chsd ldrs: rdn along over 2f out: drvn over 1f out: kpt on same pce* **16/1**

-433 **6** 1 ¾ **What Will Be (IRE)**[50] 1721 3-8-7 61.............................. SeanDavis(5) 9 59
(Olly Murphy) *in tch: hdwy to chse ldrs 3f out: rdn along over 2f out: sn drvn and one pce* **6/1[3]**

06-0 **7** hd **Manton Warrior (IRE)**[38] 2021 3-9-3 66.............................. StevieDonohoe 11 64
(Charlie Fellowes) *hld up in rr: hdwy 3f out: rdn along 2f out: kpt on fnl f* **9/1**

053 **8** 4 ½ **Nathanielhawthorne**[48] 1771 3-9-4 70..............................(h) AaronJones(3) 6 61
(Marco Botti) *a in rr* **16/1**

6-31 **9** 2 ¼ **Lincoln Tale (IRE)**[17] 2712 3-9-2 65.............................. DanielTudhope 10 52
(David O'Meara) *hld up in midfield: hdwy over 3f out: rdn along wl over 2f out: sn btn (trainers rep said that the one mile four furlong trip on a flatter track, appeared an insufficient test of stamina)* **7/2[2]**

0-66 **10** 1 **Darwin Dream**[30] 2289 3-9-0 63..............................(p[1]) PatCosgrave 7 49
(Sophie Leech) *a towards rr* **25/1**

0-30 **11** 2 **Starlight Red (IRE)**[23] 2521 3-9-6 69.............................. PaulHanagan 1 51
(Charles Hills) *led: pushed along 4f out: rdn and hdd 3f out: sn drvn and wknd* **33/1**

4-06 **12** 34 **Achaeus (GER)**[59] 1510 3-8-12 61.............................. BenCurtis 5
(Ed Dunlop) *midfield: rdn along 4f out: sn outpcd* **33/1**

2m 34.22s (-2.38) **Going Correction** -0.075s/f (Good) **12 Ran SP% 125.0**
Speed ratings (Par 99): **104,103,103,103,102 101,101,98,96,95 94,71**
CSF £119.88 CT £726.64 TOTE £12.20: £3.50, £3.10, £2.50; EX 129.70 Trifecta £1188.30.
Owner The Queen **Bred** The Queen **Trained** Beckhampton, Wilts

FOCUS
Race distance increased by 6 yards. The winner was always prominent and toughed it out to hold off some closers in this handicap. The fourth has been rated to his 2yo form.
T/Plt: £1,768.60 to a £1 stake. Pool: £67,473.85 - 27.85 winning units. T/Qpdt: £152.40 to a £1 stake. Pool: £8,206.13 - 39.82 winning units. **Joe Rowntree**

[2030] **EPSOM** (L-H)
Friday, May 31

OFFICIAL GOING: Good (good to firm in places; watered; 7.1)
Wind: Fairly strong, across in straight of over 3f Weather: Overcast

3312 INVESTEC WOODCOTE EBF STKS (CONDITIONS RACE) (PLUS 10 RACE) 6f 3y
2:00 (2:01) (Class 2) 2-Y-O

£37,350 (£11,184; £5,592; £2,796; £1,398; £702) **Stalls** High

Form RPR
1 **1** **Pinatubo (IRE)**[21] 2594 2-9-5 0 JamesDoyle 5 97
(Charlie Appleby) *str; dwlt: sn chsd ldrs: wnt 2nd over 2f out: rdn and hung lft over 1f out: led 1f out: r.o: pushed out towards fin (jockey said colt stumbled coming out of the stalls)* **1/1**[1]

1 **2** 1 ½ **Oh Purple Reign (IRE)**[10] 2931 2-9-5 0 SeanLevey 6 93
(Richard Hannon) *leggy; athletic; chsd ldr: outpcd by ldr over 3f out: rdn and hung lft whn lost 2nd over 2f out: outpcd by front two over 1f out: sn edgd rt: rallied wl ins fnl f: r.o to take 2nd towards fin: nt rch wnr* **4/1**[3]

31 **3** ¾ **Misty Grey (IRE)**[12] 2869 2-9-5 0 FrannyNorton 7 90
(Mark Johnston) *str; led and displayed plenty of pce: clr over 3f out: reduced advantage ent fnl 2f: hdd 1f out: no ex and lost 2nd towards fin* **11/4**[2]

1 **4** 6 **Dancinginthewoods**[15] 2761 2-9-5 0 JoeyHaynes 1 72
(Dean Ivory) *unfurnished; in tch: rdn and outpcd over 2f out: edgd rt wl over 1f out: no imp* **14/1**

52 **5** 6 **Dragon Command**[11] 2892 2-9-0 0 HarryBentley 3 49
(George Scott) *tall; towards rr: pushed along over 3f out: tried to cl over 2f out: no imp: wknd over 1f out* **20/1**

00 **6** 19 **Barry Magoo**[30] 2288 2-9-0 0 PaddyMathers 4
(Adam West) *sn outpcd and bhd: lost tch over 3f out* **80/1**

1m 9.22s (-0.68) **Going Correction** -0.10s/f (Good) **6** Ran SP% **109.3**
Speed ratings (Par 99): **100,98,97,89,81 55**
CSF £5.06 TOTE £1.70: £1.10, £1.60; EX 4.60 Trifecta £8.60.
Owner Godolphin **Bred** Godolphin **Trained** Newmarket, Suffolk

FOCUS
It was dry overnight and the going was given as good, good to firm in places (Going Stick 7.1). The rail was out up to 5yds from 1m to the winning post. Add 9yds. Fast and furious stuff. The form is possibly a bit better than rated.

3313 INVESTEC MILE H'CAP 1m 113y
2:35 (2:37) (Class 2) (0-105,101) 4-Y-O+

£31,125 (£9,320; £4,660; £2,330; £1,165; £585) **Stalls** Low

Form RPR
-011 **1** **Gossiping**[23] 2526 7-8-7 **87** AndreaAtzeni 9 100
(Gary Moore) *chsd ldr: rdn to ld over 2f out: wnt clr 1f out: r.o wl and in command fnl f (starter reported the gelding was the subject of a third criteria failure; trainer was informed that the gelding could not run until the day after passing a stalls test)* **10/1**

0-40 **2** 5 **Seniority**[120] 515 5-9-7 **101** RyanMoore 1 103
(William Haggas) *trckd ldrs: rdn over 2f out: wnt 2nd over 1f out: unable to go w wnr and no imp fnl f: jst hld on for 2nd* **11/2**[1]

4-41 **3** nse **Greenside**[25] 2487 8-9-0 **94** HarryBentley 13 96+
(Henry Candy) *looked wl; midfield: pushed along over 3f out: rdn over 2f out: hdwy 1f out: r.o fnl 75yds: nt trble wnr* **6/1**[2]

2632 **4** 2 ¼ **Masham Star (IRE)**[6] 3069 5-8-13 **93** SilvestreDeSousa 14 90
(Mark Johnston) *chsd ldrs: rdn 3f out: unable qck over 1f out: styd on same pce fnl 100yds* **6/1**[2]

-116 **5** ¾ **Hortzadar**[15] 2778 4-9-2 **96** DanielTudhope 15 91+
(David O'Meara) *sweating; midfield: rdn over 2f out: hdwy ins fnl f: styd on towards fin: nvr able to chal* **17/2**[3]

0356 **6** 1 ½ **Wahash (IRE)**[13] 2832 5-9-0 **94** SeanLevey 6 86
(Richard Hannon) *hld up: rdn over 2f out: kpt on ins fnl f: nvr able to get competitive* **11/1**

30-6 **7** shd **Arigato**[14] 2803 4-8-2 **82** (p) JosephineGordon 10 74
(William Jarvis) *looked wl; towards rr: u.p whn lugged lft over 2f out and bmpd rival: kpt on ins fnl f: nt pce to trble ldrs* **20/1**

301- **8** hd **Nicklaus**[254] 7434 4-8-13 **93** JamesDoyle 3 84
(William Haggas) *led: rdn and hdd over 2f out: kpt on u.p: wknd fnl 150yds* **14/1**

0003 **9** ½ **Rufus King**[13] 2837 4-8-12 **92** FrannyNorton 7 82
(Mark Johnston) *chsd ldrs: drvn over 2f out: unable qck over 1f out: no ex fnl 100yds* **20/1**

50-0 **10** ½ **Breanski**[13] 2844 5-8-4 **84** DavidEgan 11 73
(Jedd O'Keeffe) *towards rr: pushed along over 3f out: u.p whn bmpd over 2f out: nvr a threat* **25/1**

0005 **11** hd **Hors De Combat**[13] 2832 8-9-3 **97** OisinMurphy 5 86
(Denis Coakley) *s.i.s: bustled along early: in rr: rdn over 3f out: no imp* **14/1**

4-02 **12** ½ **Firmament**[15] 2778 7-9-0 **94** (p) ShaneGray 4 82
(David O'Meara) *midfield: n.m.r and hmpd early: rdn over 2f out: outpcd over 1f out: no imp after* **16/1**

4-03 **13** hd **History Writer (IRE)**[8] 3027 4-8-11 **91** (t) JasonWatson 8 78
(David Menuisier) *bhd: u.p over 3f out: nvr able to get on terms* **6/1**[2]

-606 **14** ½ **Ghayadh**[13] 2837 4-8-4 **84** (t[1]) KieranO'Neill 2 70
(Stuart Williams) *midfield: n.m.r on inner after 1f: rdn over 2f out: outpcd and no imp over 1f out: eased whn nt clr run towards fin* **50/1**

1m 42.76s (-3.64) **Going Correction** -0.10s/f (Good) **14** Ran SP% **120.7**
Speed ratings (Par 109): **112,107,107,105,104 103,103,103,102,102 102,101,101,101**
CSF £61.35 CT £377.94 TOTE £12.60: £3.80, £2.20, £2.60; EX 84.00 Trifecta £411.90.
Owner The Buckwell Partnership **Bred** Darley **Trained** Lower Beeding, W Sussex

FOCUS
Add 14yds. This race was light on unexposed improvers and the pace wasn't that fast, so it was hard to make ground. The winner has been rated back to his 2017 best.

3314 INVESTEC CORONATION CUP (GROUP 1) 1m 4f 6y
3:10 (3:13) (Class 1) 4-Y-O+

£252,359 (£95,675; £47,882; £23,852; £11,970; £6,007) **Stalls** Centre

Form RPR
2-42 **1** **Defoe (IRE)**[27] 2410 5-9-0 115 AndreaAtzeni 2 122
(Roger Varian) *s.i.s: hld up: hdwy on inner turning in over 3f out: c through gap between horses jst over 1f out: led fnl 110yds: r.o* **11/1**

10-2 **2** ½ **Kew Gardens (IRE)**[22] 2560 4-9-0 120 RyanMoore 8 121
(A P O'Brien, Ire) *looked wl; hld up: rdn and hdwy on outer over 2f out: led over 1f out: hdd fnl 110yds: kpt on but nt pce of wnr towards fin* **10/3**[2]

60-1 **3** 5 **Salouen (IRE)**[20] 2607 5-9-0 117 OisinMurphy 7 113
(Sylvester Kirk) *looked wl; w ldr: rdn to ld 3f out: hdd over 1f out: styd on same pce ins fnl f* **10/1**

5-01 **4** 2 **Communique (IRE)**[27] 2410 4-9-0 114 FrannyNorton 5 110
(Mark Johnston) *led: rdn and hdd narrowly 3f out: stl ev ch 2f out: kpt on same pce ins fnl f* **25/1**

22-1 **5** 1 ½ **Marmelo**[48] 1750 6-9-0 117 GeraldMosse 10 107
(Hughie Morrison) *hld up in midfield on outer: effrt and hdwy to chse ldrs whn hung lft over 2f out: wanted to lug lft and bmpd rival wl over 1f out: one pce ins fnl f* **12/1**

23-1 **6** 5 **Lah Ti Dar**[15] 2776 4-8-11 114 FrankieDettori 6 96
(John Gosden) *hld up no bttr than midfield: lost pl 5f out: last 4f out: plugged on fnl f: nvr a threat (trainer said gelding was unsuited by the downhill section of the track and the camber at Epsom)* **11/4**[1]

5-11 **7** ½ **Old Persian**[62] 1446 4-9-0 122 JamesDoyle 1 99
(Charlie Appleby) *sweating; in tch: chsd ldrs 5f out: rdn and unable qck whn bmpd wl over 1f out: wknd ins fnl f* **10/3**[2]

21-1 **8** 1 **Morando (FR)**[22] 2560 6-9-0 117 SilvestreDeSousa 4 97
(Andrew Balding) *trckd ldrs: pushed along and lost pl 4f out: struggling and n.d after (vet said the gelding was struck into on its right-hind leg)* **8/1**[3]

16-5 **9** 14 **Cypress Creek (IRE)**[22] 2560 4-9-0 109 (p) DonnachaO'Brien 9 75
(A P O'Brien, Ire) *prom: pushed along 5f out: wkng whn n.m.r and hmpd wl over 2f out: eased whn bhd over 1f out* **100/1**

2m 33.94s (-6.86) **Going Correction** -0.10s/f (Good) **9** Ran SP% **113.9**
Speed ratings (Par 117): **118,117,114,113,112 108,108,107,98**
CSF £46.99 CT £383.39 TOTE £11.40: £2.70, £1.70, £2.40; EX 56.10 Trifecta £433.30.
Owner Sheikh Mohammed Obaid Al Maktoum **Bred** Darley **Trained** Newmarket, Suffolk

FOCUS
Add 14yds. A competitive Coronation Cup but one that was short of a star. The first two came from the last two positions early on. The runner-up has been rated to form.

3315 INVESTEC WEALTH & INVESTMENT H'CAP 1m 2f 17y
3:45 (3:49) (Class 2) 4-Y-O+

£37,350 (£11,184; £5,592; £2,796; £1,398; £702) **Stalls** Low

Form RPR
20-1 **1** **Mountain Angel (IRE)**[37] 2033 5-9-4 **101** AndreaAtzeni 6 111+
(Roger Varian) *looked wl; midfield: hdwy over 2f out: led over 1f out: drvn out and r.o ins fnl f* **11/4**[1]

41-2 **2** 1 **Jazeel (IRE)**[27] 2408 4-8-8 **91** JamieSpencer 8 98
(Jedd O'Keeffe) *midfield: rdn and hdwy over 2f out: big effrt and styd on to take 2nd fnl 110yds: nt quite able to chal wnr* **7/1**

6502 **3** ¾ **Mr Scaramanga**[25] 2486 5-8-0 **83** DavidEgan 5 89
(Simon Dow) *led: rdn over 2f out: hdd over 1f out: kpt on u.p ins fnl f: no ex nr fin* **33/1**

1/14 **4** ½ **Setting Sail**[20] 2606 4-8-12 **95** JamesDoyle 4 100
(Charlie Appleby) *prom: rdn over 2f out: unable qck and edgd rt over 1f out: kpt on ins fnl f* **4/1**[3]

00-4 **5** 1 ¾ **Lorelina**[27] 2401 6-8-12 **95** OisinMurphy 2 96
(Andrew Balding) *hld up in midfield: rdn over 3f out: hdwy on inner 1f out: kpt on ins fnl f: nvr able to chal* **16/1**

0011 **6** ½ **Regular Income (IRE)**[20] 2628 4-8-0 **83** oh4 (p) JimmyQuinn 10 83
(Adam West) *dwlt: towards rr: rdn over 3f out: hdwy over 1f out: styd on towards fin: nvr able to threaten ldrs* **40/1**

3-34 **7** ½ **Borodin (IRE)**[27] 2419 4-8-8 **91** (p[1]) PaddyMathers 7 90
(Richard Fahey) *prom: rdn over 2f out and unable to go w ldr: outpcd whn bmpd over 1f out: kpt on same pce ins fnl f* **9/1**

33-1 **8** hd **Elector**[27] 2408 4-8-12 **95** RyanMoore 3 94
(Sir Michael Stoute) *trckd ldrs: rdn over 2f out: sn outpcd: no imp after* **3/1**[2]

00-2 **9** 2 ½ **What About Carlo (FR)**[20] 2607 8-9-3 **100** CharlesBishop 1 94
(Eve Johnson Houghton) *s.i.s: hld up in midfield: rdn over 3f out: sn outpcd: nvr a threat* **16/1**

-542 **10** 1 ¾ **Lawmaking**[14] 2800 6-8-1 **84** (b) KieranO'Neill 9 74
(Michael Scudamore) *in rr: rdn over 3f out: sme prog on outer to midfield over 2f out: no imp on ldrs: wknd fnl 150ds* **25/1**

-000 **11** ¾ **Comin' Through (AUS)**[20] 2609 5-9-10 **107** (t) HarryBentley 11 96
(George Scott) *hld up: rdn over 3f out: nvr a threat* **66/1**

2m 6.08s (-3.92) **Going Correction** -0.10s/f (Good) **11** Ran SP% **116.7**
Speed ratings (Par 109): **111,110,109,109,107 107,107,106,104,103 102**
CSF £21.67 CT £521.62 TOTE £3.60: £1.60, £2.00, £5.30; EX 22.60 Trifecta £482.20.
Owner Ziad A Galadari **Bred** Yeomanstown Stud **Trained** Newmarket, Suffolk

FOCUS
Add 14yds. A useful handicap. It's been rated around the third.

3316 INVESTEC OAKS (GROUP 1) (FILLIES) 1m 4f 6y
4:30 (4:33) (Class 1) 3-Y-O

£297,727 (£112,875; £56,490; £28,140; £14,122; £7,087) **Stalls** Centre

Form RPR
0-11 **1** **Anapurna**[20] 2618 3-9-0 103 FrankieDettori 3 113
(John Gosden) *athletic; on toes; sweating; trckd ldrs: 3rd st: rdn and swtchd lft to ld briefly over 2f out: unable qck w ldr over 1f out: edgd rt and rallied ins fnl f: led fnl 110yds: r.o: pushed out nr fin* **8/1**

5-1 **2** nk **Pink Dogwood (IRE)**[33] 2157 3-9-0 104 RyanMoore 12 112+
(A P O'Brien, Ire) *str; looked wl; hld up in midfield: 9th st: rdn and hdwy over 2f out: sn led: hdd fnl 110yds: r.o u.p: hld towards fin* **3/1**[2]

31-0 **3** 1 ¼ **Fleeting (IRE)**[26] 2443 3-9-0 105 WayneLordan 10 111+
(A P O'Brien, Ire) *hld up in rr: 13th st: pushed along over 2f out: rdn and hdwy whn nt clr run over 1f out: swtchd lft ent fnl f: r.o to take 3rd fnl 150yds: fin wl: nt rch front pair* **25/1**

11-2 **4** 1 **Manuela De Vega (IRE)**[23] 2521 3-9-0 99 HarryBentley 1 108
(Ralph Beckett) *ly; sweating; midfield: 10th st: rdn 3f out: hdwy over 2f out: edgd rt and bmpd whn chsng ldrs over 1f out: sn n.m.r: styd on ins fnl f: nt pce to chal* **16/1**

63 **5** 1 ½ **Delphinia (IRE)**[20] 2642 3-9-0 98 SeamieHeffernan 13 106
(A P O'Brien, Ire) *str; in tch: 6th st: effrt over 3f out: lost pl over 2f out: bmpd 1f out: rallied ins fnl f: kpt on: nvr able to chal* **66/1**

1-2 **6** ¾ **Frankellina**[16] 2745 3-9-0 0 JamesDoyle 14 105
(William Haggas) *str; hld up: 11th st: rdn on outer over 2f out: hdwy over 1f out: kpt on ins fnl f: one pce towards fin* **12/1**

1-11 **7** *1 1/2* **Mehdaayih**[23] 2521 3-9-0 105 .... RobertHavlin 6 102
(John Gosden) *leggy; athletic; racd keenly: midfield: n.m.r and hmpd after 3f: 7th st: rdn and nt clr run towards outer over 2f out: n.m.r and hmpd jst over 1f out: one pce fnl 100yds* **11/4**[1]

3-11 **8** *3 3/4* **Maqsad (FR)**[26] 2445 3-9-0 109 .... JimCrowley 5 96+
(William Haggas) *looked wl; in tch: 5th st: gng wl 3f out: rdn and ev ch 2f out: edgd rt whn unable to go w front two over 1f out: wknd fnl 150yds* **4/1**[3]

21-5 **9** *1* **Blue Gardenia (IRE)**[16] 2745 3-9-0 96 .... JamieSpencer 11 95
(David O'Meara) *rdr adjsted iron leaving stalls: in rr: struggling over 3f out and 14th st: kpt on fnl f: nvr a threat* **100/1**

01-4 **10** *2 1/4* **Peach Tree (IRE)**[20] 2642 3-9-0 103 .... DonnachaO'Brien 9 91
(A P O'Brien, Ire) *w ldr: 2nd st: rdn to ld 3f out: hdd over 2f out: wknd over 1f out* **33/1**

2-31 **11** *shd* **Tarnawa (IRE)**[20] 2642 3-9-0 101 .... ChrisHayes 7 91
(D K Weld, Ire) *compact; midfield: 8th st: rdn 3f out whn bmpd sltly: wknd over 2f out* **20/1**

31-2 **12** *1 1/2* **Tauteke**[20] 2618 3-9-0 90 .... AndreaAtzeni 8 89
(Roger Varian) *str; looked wl; trckd ldrs: pushed along 4f out: 4th st: effrt 3f out: rdn and ev ch over 2f out: wknd over 1f out* **25/1**

51-6 **13** *5* **Sh Boom**[13] 2831 3-9-0 90 .... TomQueally 2 81
(Peter Chapple-Hyam) *s.i.s: in rr: struggling over 3f out and 12th st: nvr a threat* **100/1**

12 **14** *21* **Lavender's Blue (IRE)**[13] 2831 3-9-0 0 .... SilvestreDeSousa 4 47
(Amanda Perrett) *led: rdn and hdd 3f out: wknd over 2f out (jockey said filly lost its action approximately 1f out; vet said the filly was suffering from thumps)* **16/1**

2m 36.09s (-4.71) **Going Correction** -0.10s/f (Good) **14 Ran SP% 121.1**
Speed ratings (Par 110): **111,110,109,109,108 107,106,104,103,102 102,101,97,83**
CSF £30.66 CT £592.63 TOTE £6.70: £2.40, £1.60, £6.70; EX 38.60 Trifecta £680.00.
Owner Helena Springfield Ltd **Bred** Meon Valley Stud **Trained** Newmarket, Suffolk
■ Stewards' Enquiry : Frankie Dettori two-day ban: used whip above the permitted level (Jun 14-15)

FOCUS
Add 14yds. This looked a pretty open Oaks beforehand, and it's hard to rate highly. The first two had it between them inside the last, but the time was 2.15sec slower than the Coronation Cup. It's been rated at the bottom end of the race averages, with the winner matching the historic low for an Oaks winner.

3317 INVESTEC SURREY STKS (LISTED RACE) 7f 3y
5:15 (5:18) (Class 1) 3-Y-O

£28,355 (£10,750; £5,380; £2,680; £1,345; £675) **Stalls Low**

Form RPR

-421 **1** **Space Blues (IRE)**[16] 2746 3-9-0 103 .... JamesDoyle 4 110+
(Charlie Appleby) *looked wl; hld up: hdwy over 2f out: rdn to ld over 1f out: kpt on wl and a doing enough towards fin* **6/5**[1]

1-30 **2** *nk* **Urban Icon**[27] 2411 3-9-0 107 .... TomMarquand 6 109
(Richard Hannon) *looked wl; chsd ldrs: str chal and upsides over 1f out: kpt on to press wnr ins fnl f: hld towards fin* **7/2**[3]

-544 **3** *1 1/2* **Marie's Diamond (IRE)**[12] 2889 3-9-0 104 .... FrannyNorton 5 105
(Mark Johnston) *chsd ldr: led over 2f out: rdn and hdd over 1f out: kpt on ins fnl f: swtchd rt whn nt pce of front two towards fin* **14/1**

2-34 **4** *4* **Angel's Hideaway (IRE)**[26] 2443 3-8-9 109 .... RobertHavlin 2 89
(John Gosden) *slowly away: hld up: rdn over 2f out: no imp and one pce fnl f* **11/4**[2]

1-04 **5** *3* **Vintage Brut**[20] 2614 3-9-3 108 ....(p) SilvestreDeSousa 3 89
(Tim Easterby) *led: rdn over 3f out: hdd over 2f out: wknd 1f out (trainer's rep said colt was unsuited by the undulations at Epsom causing him to become unbalanced)* **33/1**

3-04 **6** *1 3/4* **Sunday Star**[14] 2806 3-8-9 98 .... GeraldMosse 8 76
(Ed Walker) *racd keenly: hld up: rdn over 2f out: no imp* **20/1**

410- **7** *12* **Miss Celestial (IRE)**[260] 7199 3-8-9 90 ....(b) AndreaAtzeni 1 44
(Sir Mark Prescott Bt) *on toes; chsd ldrs: rdn and hung lft over 2f out: sn wknd: eased whn wl btn over 1f out (jockey said filly ran freely to post and hung left-handed in the race)* **33/1**

1m 22.74s (-0.66) **Going Correction** -0.10s/f (Good) **7 Ran SP% 111.7**
Speed ratings (Par 107): **99,98,96,92,88 86,73**
CSF £5.33 TOTE £2.00: £1.30, £1.90; EX 5.60 Trifecta £25.90.
Owner Godolphin **Bred** Godolphin **Trained** Newmarket, Suffolk

FOCUS
Add 13yds. A good Listed race. It's been rated around the second and third.

3318 INVESTEC ZEBRA H'CAP 7f 3y
5:50 (5:53) (Class 2) (0-100,97) 3-Y-O+

£31,125 (£9,320; £4,660; £2,330; £1,165; £585) **Stalls Low**

Form RPR

-564 **1** **Corazon Espinado (IRE)**[25] 2487 4-8-13 82 .... TomMarquand 2 89
(Simon Dow) *mde all: rdn over 2f out: hrd pressed after: all out towards fin: jst hld on* **7/1**[3]

5-32 **2** *shd* **Hateya (IRE)**[31] 2252 4-9-11 94 .... AndreaAtzeni 1 100
(Jim Boyle) *chsd ldrs: pushed along over 3f out: rdn and no imp over 2f out: swtchd rt over 1f out: r.o strly fnl 75yds: fin wl: jst failed* **9/2**[2]

244 **3** *1/2* **Love Dreams (IRE)**[8] 3009 5-9-12 95 ....(b) FrannyNorton 10 100
(Mark Johnston) *looked wl; w wnr: rdn over 2f out: continued to chal strly ins fnl f: hld fnl strides* **7/1**[3]

1-00 **4** *shd* **Alemaratalyoum (IRE)**[20] 2609 5-9-11 94 ....(t) OisinMurphy 5 99
(Stuart Williams) *chsd ldrs: rdn and ev ch over 1f out: continued to chal for press ins fnl f: hld towards fin* **14/1**

6612 **5** *3/4* **War Glory (IRE)**[8] 3027 6-9-10 93 .... SeanLevey 8 98+
(Richard Hannon) *midfield: rdn over 2f out: hdwy u.p whn edgd lft over 1f out: swtchd rt fnl 75yds: running on whn nt clr run and checked towards fin (jockey said gelding was denied a clear run)* **8/1**

3-00 **6** *1 3/4* **Shady McCoy (USA)**[21] 2572 9-10-0 97 .... JimCrowley 4 95
(Ian Williams) *midfield: rdn and outpcd over 2f out: styd on ins fnl f: nt rch ldrs* **25/1**

2-62 **7** *1 1/2* **Blackheath**[25] 2484 4-9-2 85 .... LiamKeniry 9 79
(Ed Walker) *midfield: rdn over 3f out: kpt on ins fnl f: nt trble ldrs* **16/1**

60-0 **8** *nk* **Start Time (IRE)**[61] 1457 6-8-9 78 oh1 .... GeraldMosse 11 71
(Paul Midgley) *in tch: rdn over 2f out: hung lft u.p whn bmpd over 1f out: kpt on same ins fnl f* **25/1**

0-00 **9** *3/4* **Gabrial The Devil (IRE)**[13] 2844 4-9-3 86 .... PaddyMathers 12 77
(Richard Fahey) *awkward s and slowly away: towards rr: pushed along over 3f out: kpt on towards fin: nvr able to get involved* **33/1**

-505 **10** *2 3/4* **Ripp Orf (IRE)**[20] 2609 5-9-11 94 .... HayleyTurner 6 78
(David Elsworth) *hld up: rdn over 3f out: nvr a threat* **7/2**[1]

00-0 **11** *4 1/2* **Adorable (IRE)**[20] 2608 4-10-0 97 .... JamesDoyle 3 69
(William Haggas) *hld up: rdn over 3f out: sn outpcd: nvr a threat* **8/1**

551- **12** *11* **Nobleman's Nest**[253] 7475 4-9-11 94 ....(t[1]) SilvestreDeSousa 7 36
(Simon Crisford) *in rr: rdn over 3f out: nvr on terms: eased whn wl btn over 1f out* **10/1**

1m 22.14s (-1.26) **Going Correction** -0.10s/f (Good) **12 Ran SP% 119.9**
Speed ratings (Par 109): **103,102,102,102,101 99,97,97,96,93 88,75**
CSF £38.17 CT £237.92 TOTE £7.80: £2.40, £2.00, £2.40; EX 33.70 Trifecta £205.10.
Owner Robert Moss **Bred** M P & R J Coleman **Trained** Epsom, Surrey
■ Stewards' Enquiry : Andrea Atzeni two-day ban: interference & careless riding (Jun 14-15)

FOCUS
Add 13yds. This unfolded in unusual fashion; half the runners were detached from the other six by the time they reached the straight and, on fast, drying ground, it was those in the 'breakaway group', led by the winner and third who flew out of the traps and took each other on, who had the edge. It's been rated around the third to his recent form.
T/Jkpt: Not Won. T/Plt: £70.20 to a £1 stake. Pool: £259,082.23 - 2,690.73 winning units. T/Qpdt: £26.00 to a £1 stake. Pool: £21,978.80 - 623.22 winning units. **Darren Owen**

2938 WOLVERHAMPTON (A.W) (L-H)
Friday, May 31

OFFICIAL GOING: Tapeta: standard
Wind: light breeze Weather: overcast, mild

3319 SMARTVETMEDS.COM H'CAP 6f 20y (Tp)
1:50 (1:51) (Class 6) (0-55,55) 3-Y-O

£3,105 (£924; £461; £300; £300; £300) **Stalls Low**

Form RPR

4020 **1** **Lysander Belle (IRE)**[4] 3148 3-9-7 55 .... ShaneKelly 2 61
(Sophie Leech) *trckd ldrs: pushed along in 3rd 2f out: drvn to chal over 1f out: reminder and led ent fnl f: sn rdn clr* **4/1**[2]

60-4 **2** *1 1/2* **Perfect Swiss**[12] 2871 3-9-6 54 .... RachelRichardson 3 56
(Tim Easterby) *quite slowly away: sn rcvrd to r in mid-div: drvn over 2f out: hdwy over 1f out: rdn fnl f: r.o wl to take 2nd last 75yds: nvr a threat to wnr* **6/4**[1]

0-50 **3** *nk* **Josiebond**[12] 2871 3-9-4 55 .... RowanScott[(3)] 7 56
(Rebecca Bastiman) *hld up: pushed along and plenty to do 2f out: drvn and hdwy ent fnl f: sn rdn: kpt on into 3rd last 75yds* **9/1**[3]

4 *nk* **Betty's Heart (IRE)**[161] 9672 3-8-13 47 .... KierenFox 8 47+
(John Best) *t.k.h: hld up in rr: pushed along in last 2f out: hdwy on outer 1f out: rdn and rn wl fnl f: nvr nrr (jockey said filly jumped awkwardly from the stalls and ran too freely)* **10/1**

0050 **5** *3/4* **Kyllachy Princess**[10] 2940 3-8-13 47 ....(b[1]) TrevorWhelan 12 44
(David Loughnane) *disp ld tl led on own over 2f out: pushed along in 2 l ld 2f out: sn rdn: hdd ent fnl f: no ex* **40/1**

4650 **6** *1 1/4* **Atwaar**[17] 2708 3-8-5 46 .... WilliamCarver[(7)] 6 41
(Charles Smith) *hld up: pushed along and nt clr run 1 1/2f out: sn swtchd to outer: r.o fnl f* **12/1**

00-0 **7** *nk* **Andies Armies**[28] 2357 3-9-0 48 ....(b[1]) CamHardie 4 41
(Lisa Williamson) *hld up on outer: pushed along 2f out: sn drvn: rdn fnl f: no imp* **33/1**

0120 **8** *nk* **Champagne Mondays**[44] 1863 3-9-3 51 ....(p) NicolaCurrie 11 43
(Scott Dixon) *disp ld tl hdd over 2f out: rdn and wknd fnl f* **9/1**[3]

0260 **9** *nse* **Wye Bother (IRE)**[4] 3148 3-8-5 46 ....(t) TobyEley[(7)] 1 38
(Milton Bradley) *mid-div on inner: pushed along 2f out: rdn 1f out: wknd fnl f (jockey said filly was never travelling)* **16/1**

000- **10** *1 1/4* **Grey Hare**[184] 9289 3-9-3 51 .... GeorgeDowning 10 39
(Tony Carroll) *trckd ldrs: drvn in 4th 2f out: sn rdn and wknd (jockey said gelding jumped left leaving the stalls)* **50/1**

0040 **11** *1/2* **Budaiya Fort (IRE)**[12] 2870 3-8-13 54 ....(p) GraceMcEntee[(7)] 13 41
(Phil McEntee) *prom on outer: drvn and lost pl over 2f out: sn rdn and wknd* **25/1**

0-00 **12** *11* **Solesmes**[30] 2276 3-9-7 55 .... EoinWalsh 5 9
(Tony Newcombe) *hld up on inner: drvn and reminder 1 1/2f out: dropped to last 1f out* **33/1**

1m 15.07s (0.57) **Going Correction** +0.025s/f (Slow) **12 Ran SP% 116.8**
Speed ratings (Par 97): **97,95,94,94,93 91,91,90,90,89 88,73**
CSF £9.65 CT £51.01 TOTE £4.00: £1.60, £1.20, £2.10; EX 13.70 Trifecta £73.80.
Owner Mike Harris Racing Club **Bred** Mattock Stud **Trained** Elton, Gloucs

FOCUS
This was run at a steady pace, which came from two of the widest draws, with the winner tracking the leaders and getting the perfect trip.

3320 SMARTVETMEDS.COM ONLINE PHARMACY H'CAP 5f 21y (Tp)
2:25 (2:25) (Class 6) (0-55,55) 3-Y-O+

£3,105 (£924; £461; £300; £300; £300) **Stalls Low**

Form RPR

-04 **1** **Awsaaf**[32] 2206 4-9-6 54 ....(t[1]) TonyHamilton 4 63
(Michael Wigham) *chsd ldrs: pushed along in 4th 2f out: rdn 1 1/2f out: hdwy u.p ins fnl f: r.o wl to ld last 50yds: sn in command and gng away at fin* **9/2**[3]

-006 **2** *1 1/4* **Tiger Lyon (USA)**[8] 3001 4-9-1 54 ....(t) DarraghKeenan[(5)] 8 59
(John Butler) *disp ld tl led on own 2f out: 2 l ld ent fnl f: rdn 1/2f out: no ex and hdd last 50yds* **9/1**

0526 **3** *1/2* **Bahango (IRE)**[30] 2295 7-9-3 51 ....(p) ShaneKelly 2 54
(Patrick Morris) *restless in stalls: mid-div on inner: pushed along 1 1/2f out: hdwy ent fnl f: sn rdn: kpt on into 3rd fr 1/2f out* **14/1**

5322 **4** *1 1/4* **Always Amazing**[8] 3001 5-9-7 55 .... KierenFox 1 54
(Derek Shaw) *chsd ldrs: pushed along in 3rd 2f out: rdn 1 1/2f out: one pce and lost 3rd fnl f* **5/2**[1]

05 **5** *1 1/4* **Ar Saoirse**[4] 3143 4-9-3 51 ....(b) CallumShepherd 5 45
(Clare Hobson) *disp ld tl hdd 2f out: rdn over 1f out: wknd fnl f* **6/1**

0011 **6** *nse* **Pocket Warrior**[7] 3036 8-9-5 53 8ex ....(t) AdamKirby 6 47
(Paul D'Arcy) *in rr: drvn and swtchd to outer 1 1/2f out: rdn and r.o fnl f: nvr nrr (jockey said gelding was never travelling; vet said gelding lost both of its front shoes)* **7/2**[2]

35-0 **7** *nk* **Carlovian**[14] 2788 6-9-6 54 ....(v) DougieCostello 7 47
(Mark Walford) *mid-div: drvn in 6th 2f out: sn rdn and wknd* **20/1**

2400 **8** *shd* **Dandilion (IRE)**[33] 2153 6-9-4 52 ....(t) NicolaCurrie 3 44
(Alex Hales) *hld up: pushed along on inner 2f out: rdn over 1f out: no imp* **11/1**

003- **9** *shd* **Marcella**[223] 8417 4-8-12 46 oh1 .... CamHardie 10 38
(Ruth Carr) *bhd: pushed along 2f out: sn drvn: reminder 1f out: no imp (jockey said filly hung left in the final furlong)* **50/1**

6-00 **10** *4 1/2* **John Joiner**[8] 3001 7-8-8 **49**........................(v) GavinAshton(7) 9 25
(Shaun Keightley) *bhd: pushed along 1 1/2f out: reminder over 1f out: no rspnse: wknd fnl f* **66/1**

1m 1.29s (-0.61) **Going Correction** +0.025s/f (Slow) **10** Ran SP% **116.5**
Speed ratings (Par 101): **105,103,102,100,98 98,97,97,97,90**
CSF £43.74 CT £540.86 TOTE £6.50: £1.60, £3.10, £3.50; EX 39.80 Trifecta £429.40.

Owner Tugay Akman & Ms I D Heerowa **Bred** Lordship Stud **Trained** Newmarket, Suffolk

FOCUS
A moderate handicap run at a good pace thanks to two duelling pacesetters, Tiger Lyon and Ar Saoirse, who were clear at halfway.

3321 VISIT SMARTVETMEDS.COM ONLINE PHARMACY H'CAP 1m 4f 51y (Tp)
3:00 (3:00) (Class 5) (0-70,75) 4-Y-0+
£3,752 (£1,116; £557; £300; £300; £300) **Stalls** Low

Form RPR

20 **1** **Lost History (IRE)**[18] 2696 6-9-8 **71**........................ JackMitchell 8 78
(John Spearing) *mid-div: tk clsr order 3f out: gng wl in 4th 2f out: shkn up and hdwy to chal over 1f out: sn led: rdn in 2 l ld ins fnl f: pushed out nr fin* **8/1**[3]

-135 **2** *1 1/4* **Ebqaa (IRE)**[32] 2214 5-9-3 **66**........................(p[1]) RobHornby 2 71
(James Unett) *trckd ldrs: 3rd 2f out: pushed along to chal over 1f out: rdn in 2nd 2f out: kpt on fnl f* **9/1**

560/ **3** *3/4* **California Lad**[18] 2702 6-9-3 **66**........................(vt) StevieDonohoe 4 70
(Fergal Birrane, Ire) *hld up: drvn into 5th 2f out: rdn on outer over 1f out: wnt 3rd 1/2f out: gng on at fin* **16/1**

-351 **4** *3 3/4* **King Of The Sand (IRE)**[10] 2928 4-9-12 **75** 5ex........................ AdamKirby 1 73
(Gary Moore) *led: drvn 3f out: reminder over 2f out: narrow ld 2f out: hdd over 1f out: wknd fnl f: lost 3rd 1/2f out* **1/2**[1]

0651 **5** *2 3/4* **Star Ascending (IRE)**[18] 2696 7-9-9 **72**........................(p) RossaRyan 6 65
(Jennie Candlish) *prom: rdn in cl 2nd 2f out: wknd over 1f out* **5/1**[2]

0420 **6** *3/4* **Qayed (CAN)**[9] 2970 4-8-0 **52**........................(p) WilliamCox(3) 3 44
(Mark Brisbourne) *hld up: rdn in 6th 2f out: no imp* **20/1**

60-0 **7** *8* **Accessor (IRE)**[44] 1848 4-9-7 **70**........................ TonyHamilton 9 49
(Michael Wigham) *hld up in rr: drvn over 2f out: no imp and sn lost tch* **25/1**

2000 **8** *3 1/4* **Ice Canyon**[18] 2696 5-9-5 **68**........................(h) EoinWalsh 5 42
(Mark Brisbourne) *hld up: drvn 3f out: no rspnse: sn lost tch (jockey said gelding ran flat)* **33/1**

2m 38.5s (-2.30) **Going Correction** +0.025s/f (Slow) **8** Ran SP% **121.9**
Speed ratings (Par 103): **108,107,106,104,102 101,96,94**
CSF £77.92 CT £1143.42 TOTE £8.40: £1.40, £2.40, £2.20; EX 80.90 Trifecta £676.60.

Owner John J Reilly **Bred** J Mangan **Trained** Kinnersley, Worcs

FOCUS
This was all about the favourite, who was red-hot in the betting, but in the end it did not go to plan. It's been rated around the first two.

3322 SMARTVETMEDS.COM CLAIMING STKS 1m 1f 104y (Tp)
3:35 (3:36) (Class 6) 4-Y-0+ **£3,105** (£924; £461; £300; £300) **Stalls** Low

Form RPR

5663 **1** **Scofflaw**[8] 3018 5-9-8 **74**........................(v) AdamKirby 4 71+
(David Evans) *hld up: pushed along in 4th 2f out: nt clr run over 1f out: swtchd to inner ent fnl f: sn rdn and r.o wl: drvn to ld last stride* **11/8**[2]

5605 **2** *nse* **Calling Out (FR)**[29] 2320 8-9-7 **91**........................(h[1]) DylanHogan(5) 2 75+
(David Simcock) *trckd ldrs: pushed into ld on inner 2f out: rdn in narrow ld 1f out: r.o u.p fnl f: hdd last stride* **8/11**[1]

4466 **3** *1 3/4* **Pike Corner Cross (IRE)**[18] 2698 7-8-10 **54**........................ RobHornby 5 56
(Alastair Ralph) *prom: drvn in cl 2nd 2f out: rdn and ev ch 1f out: no ex and dropped to 3rd fnl f* **14/1**[3]

0/0- **4** *2 1/4* **Cash In Mind (FR)**[24] 2071 8-9-8 **61**........................(p) ShaneKelly 1 63
(Des Donovan, Ire) *hld up in rr: pushed along and hdwy on outer 3f out: sn drvn: reminder and dropped to last 2f out: rdn on outer over 1f out: one pce fnl f* **28/1**

5 *1 1/2* **Taylor Velvet (IRE)**[8] 9232 4-9-3 **44**........................(h) StevieDonohoe 3 55
(Fergal Birrane, Ire) *led: drvn 3f out: hdd 2f out: reminders over 1f out and ins fnl f: sn wknd into last* **100/1**

2m 4.57s (3.77) **Going Correction** +0.025s/f (Slow) **5** Ran SP% **111.1**
Speed ratings (Par 101): **84,83,82,80,79**
CSF £2.71 TOTE £2.30: £1.10, £1.10; EX 2.70.Pike Corner Cross was claimed by Mr J. E. Abbey for £4,000

Owner John Abbey & Emma Evans **Bred** Mrs M E Slade **Trained** Pandy, Monmouths

FOCUS
The market was focused on the top two on official ratings, who fought out a tight finish off a steady pace.

3323 SMARTVETMEDS.COM FILLIES' H'CAP 7f 36y (Tp)
4:10 (4:10) (Class 4) (0-85,85) 3-Y-0+
£5,530 (£1,645; £822; £411; £300; £300) **Stalls** High

Form RPR

2-04 **1** **Maid For Life**[36] 2060 3-8-9 **73**........................(h) GeorgeWood 6 78+
(Charlie Fellowes) *t.k.h: mid-div: hdwy to chse ldrs 1 1/2f out: rdn over 1f out: led 1/2f out: sn clr: pushed out nr fin* **8/1**

-102 **2** *2* **Turanga Leela**[24] 2508 5-9-3 **70**........................(b) StevieDonohoe 8 74
(John Mackie) *led: pushed along in narrow ld 2f out: sn drvn: rdn in 1 l ld 1f out: hdd 1/2f out: no ex* **14/1**

6-45 **3** *3/4* **Queen Penn**[31] 2252 4-9-8 **75**........................(p) TonyHamilton 5 77+
(Richard Fahey) *t.k.h: prom: cl 2nd 2f out: drvn over 1f out: rdn and dropped to 3rd ent fnl f: one pce (starter reported that the filly was the subject of a third criteria failure; trainer was informed that the filly could not run until the day after passing a stalls test)* **4/1**[1]

41-0 **4** *hd* **Winter Light**[51] 1685 3-9-7 **85**........................ ShaneKelly 2 82
(Richard Hughes) *chsd ldrs: pushed along 2f out: rdn 1f out: one pce fnl f* **7/1**[3]

021- **5** *1/2* **Mums Hope**[210] 8796 3-9-2 **80**........................ CharlieBennett 4 76
(Hughie Morrison) *hld up: pushed along on outer over 2f out: drvn 1 1/2f out: sn rdn: no imp* **4/1**[1]

26-0 **6** *hd* **Rux Ruxx (IRE)**[11] 2893 4-9-5 **72**........................ RachelRichardson 7 72
(Tim Easterby) *chsd ldrs: pushed along 2f out: lost pl 1 1/2f out: rdn over 1f out: one pce* **18/1**

0-10 **7** *3/4* **Kodiac Lass (IRE)**[29] 2340 3-8-5 **72**........................ GabrieleMalune(3) 3 66
(Marco Botti) *hld up: drvn 2f out: reminder ent fnl f: no ch whn hmpd 1/2f out: kpt on nr fin* **9/2**[2]

1-00 **8** *nse* **Deira Surprise**[33] 2144 3-8-11 **80**........................ DylanHogan(5) 1 73
(Hugo Palmer) *in rr: drvn 1 1/2f out: rdn and effrt over 1f out: trying to run on but hld whn nt clr run ins fnl f* **4/1**[1]

1m 29.54s (0.74) **Going Correction** +0.025s/f (Slow)
WFA 3 from 4yo+ 11lb **8** Ran SP% **113.7**
Speed ratings (Par 102): **96,93,92,92,92 91,90,90**
CSF £108.26 CT £512.84 TOTE £7.40: £2.80, £4.50, £1.10; EX 94.30 Trifecta £335.60.

Owner Normandie Stud Ltd **Bred** Normandie Stud Ltd **Trained** Newmarket, Suffolk

FOCUS
A competitive handicap won by an improving filly. Muddling form.

3324 SMARTVETMEDS.COM NOVICE MEDIAN AUCTION STKS 1m 142y (Tp)
4:55 (4:57) (Class 5) 3-5-Y-O **£3,752** (£1,116; £557; £278) **Stalls** Low

Form RPR

41 **1** **Cristal Breeze (IRE)**[29] 2334 3-9-8 **0**........................ AdamKirby 11 84+
(William Haggas) *trckd across fr wd draw: mde all: pushed along and kicked 3 l clr 2f out: rdn in reduced ld 1f out: r.o u.p fnl f: sn 1 l clr: pushed out nr fin (jockey said gelding hung right throughout)* **6/4**[1]

02 **2** *3/4* **Universal Effect**[11] 2912 3-8-10 **0**........................(h) StevieDonohoe 2 70
(David Lanigan) *t.k.h: mid-div: drvn in 4th 2f out: rdn into cl 2nd 1f out: r.o fnl f but a hld* **13/2**

3 *3/4* **Muhaarar's Nephew** 3-9-1 **0**........................ TonyHamilton 1 73
(Owen Burrows) *hld up: drvn in 6th 2f out: hdwy over 1f out: wnt 3rd 1/2f out: pushed along and kpt on wl* **22/1**

3-1 **4** *1/2* **Sea Sculpture**[32] 2216 3-9-5 **0**........................ WilliamCox(3) 8 79
(Andrew Balding) *trckd ldrs: wnt 2nd over 3f out: reminder in 3 l 2nd 2f out: drvn and dropped to 3rd 1f out: rdn and lost 3rd ins fnl f (jockey said gelding was briefly short of room in the closing stages)* **9/2**[3]

5 *7* **Clifton** 3-8-8 **0**........................ TobyEley(7) 6 56
(Michael Easterby) *hld up on outer: pushed along 2f out: reminders over 1f out: kpt on past btn rivals fnl f* **100/1**

6 *hd* **Rudy Lewis (IRE)** 3-8-8 **0**........................ AledBeech(7) 7 56
(Charlie Fellowes) *mid-div on outer: pushed along 2f out: reminder 1 1/2f out: one pce fr over 1f out* **40/1**

1-5 **7** *hd* **Fragrant Belle**[59] 1495 3-9-3 **0**........................ RobHornby 5 57
(Ralph Beckett) *hld up: pushed along 2f out: swtchd to inner fnl f: no imp* **4/1**[2]

4 **8** *3/4* **Undercolours (IRE)**[9] 2967 3-9-1 **0**........................ DanielMuscutt 9 53
(Marco Botti) *trckd ldr: pushed along over 2f out: drvn and lost pl 1 1/2f out: rdn 1f out: wknd fnl f* **20/1**

9 *1 1/4* **Reine Magnifique (FR)** 3-8-10 **0**........................ GeorgeWood 3 46
(James Fanshawe) *t.k.h: hld up: drvn 2f out: no imp* **20/1**

10 *1* **Social Calendar** 3-9-1 **0**........................ ShaneKelly 4 48
(James Tate) *rrd leaving stalls: bhd: reminders over 2f out: nvr involved (jockey said colt reared as the stalls opened)* **20/1**

00- **11** *2 1/2* **Miss Swift**[175] 9443 3-8-10 **0**........................ RachelRichardson 10 37
(Marcus Tregoning) *hld up: drvn and lost tch fr over 2f out* **150/1**

1m 50.55s (0.45) **Going Correction** +0.025s/f (Slow) **11** Ran SP% **114.2**
Speed ratings (Par 103): **99,98,97,97,91 90,90,89,88,87 85**
CSF £10.22 TOTE £2.10: £1.10, £1.90, £6.10; EX 11.40 Trifecta £98.20.

Owner G & M Roberts, Green, Savidge & Whittal-Williams **Bred** Mrs K Prendergast **Trained** Newmarket, Suffolk

FOCUS
Four finished clear of the field in a fair novice event. The second has been rated up a bit on her latest effort.

3325 SMARTVETMEDS.COM APPRENTICE H'CAP 1m 142y (Tp)
5:30 (5:30) (Class 6) (0-55,55) 4-Y-0+
£3,105 (£924; £461; £300; £300; £300) **Stalls** Low

Form RPR

0214 **1** **Imperial Act**[10] 2930 4-9-0 **51**........................ WilliamCarver(3) 12 65+
(Andrew Balding) *mid-div: hdwy on outer over 2f out: wnt into 2 l 2nd gng wl 2f out: shkn up to ld over 1f out: pushed clr fnl f: easily* **4/1**[2]

0123 **2** *3 1/2* **Tha'ir (IRE)**[18] 2693 9-9-5 **53**........................(t) DylanHogan 2 57
(Philip McBride) *disp ld tl led on own after 3f: pushed along in 2 l ld 2f out: rdn and hdd over 1f out: no ex fnl f* **3/1**[1]

-662 **3** *nk* **Snooker Jim**[20] 2631 4-9-3 **54**........................(t) TobyEley(3) 6 57
(Steph Hollinshead) *hld up: drvn and hdwy on outer 2f out: rdn into 3rd 1f out: kpt on fnl f (jockey said gelding received a slight bump approximately 4f out)* **4/1**[2]

-006 **4** *2 1/2* **Perfect Soldier (IRE)**[39] 1983 5-9-2 **55**........................(p) GavinAshton(5) 1 53
(Shaun Keightley) *disp ld tl hdd after 3f: pushed along and dropped to 3rd 2f out: sn rdn: no ex fnl f* **9/1**

205- **5** *nse* **Pact Of Steel**[32] 2224 4-9-2 **50**........................(t) WilliamCox 7 48
(Fergal Birrane, Ire) *chsd ldrs: pushed along 2f out: nt clr run over 1f out: reminder and kpt on fnl f (jockey said colt was denied a clear run approaching the final furlong)* **22/1**

1200 **6** *1 1/2* **Misu Pete**[14] 2797 7-9-0 **55**........................(p) MorganCole(7) 8 50
(Mark Usher) *prom: pushed along and lost pl over 2f out: wknd over 1f out* **16/1**

60-0 **7** *1/2* **Windsorlot (IRE)**[17] 2720 6-9-0 **55**........................ ElishaWhittington(7) 9 49
(Tony Carroll) *hld up: drvn over 2f out: rdn 1 1/2f out: one pce fnl f* **18/1**

5-0 **8** *3/4* **The Third Man**[85] 1060 8-9-2 **55**........................ SeanKirrane(5) 13 47
(Henry Spiller) *hld up: effrt on outer 2f out: rdn over 1f out: one pce fnl f* **40/1**

4056 **9** *3/4* **Soldier Blue (FR)**[55] 1595 5-8-10 **47**........................ KieranSchofield(3) 11 38
(Brian Ellison) *hld up: drvn over 2f out: rdn over 1f out: no imp* **14/1**

4333 **10** *3 3/4* **Break The Silence**[20] 2631 5-9-3 **51**........................(b) TheodoreLadd 4 34
(Scott Dixon) *mid-div: drvn and lost pl over 2f out: wknd* **5/1**[3]

3/00 **11** *1/2* **Bullseye Bullet**[8] 3014 4-8-5 **46**........................(p) IsobelFrancis(7) 5 28
(Mark Usher) *slowly away: a bhd* **66/1**

1m 49.07s (-1.03) **Going Correction** +0.025s/f (Slow) **11** Ran SP% **117.8**
Speed ratings (Par 101): **105,101,101,99,99 98,97,96,96,92 92**
CSF £16.18 CT £52.15 TOTE £4.30: £2.00, £1.10, £2.40; EX 15.80 Trifecta £46.60.

Owner A M Balding **Bred** The Victrix Ludorum Partnership **Trained** Kingsclere, Hants

FOCUS
A moderate handicap won in some style by a well-handicapped filly.

T/Plt: £107.40 to a £1 stake. Pool: £43,307.38 - 294.24 winning units. T/Qpdt: £43.10 to a £1 stake. Pool: £4,471.74 - 76.71 winning units. **Keith McHugh**

3326 - 3332a (Foreign Racing) - See Raceform Interactive

2953 MAISONS-LAFFITTE (R-H)

Friday, May 31

OFFICIAL GOING: Turf: good to soft changing to good after race 3 (2.30)

3333a PRIX LA FLECHE (LISTED RACE) (2YO) (TURF) 5f

3:00 2-Y-O £27,027 (£10,810; £8,108; £5,405; £2,702)

RPR

1 **Real Appeal (GER)**[12] 2-9-2 0..........(b[1]) AntoineHamelin 10 99
(Matthieu Palussiere, France) 9/1

2 hd **Jolie (FR)**[11] 2-8-13 0.......... MaximeGuyon 2 95
(Andrea Marcialis, France) 89/10

3 snk **My Love's Passion (FR)**[29] 2-8-13 0.......... ChristopheSoumillon 6 95
(Y Barberot, France) 51/10[3]

4 1 **Lady Kermit (IRE)**[14] 2805 2-8-13 0.......... EdwardGreatrex 8 91
(Archie Watson) *settled bhd ldrs: shkn up in 2nd 2f out: briefly chal bef wknd and lost position ins fnl f: rdn out* 11/5[1]

5 1 1/4 **Great Dame (IRE)**[14] 2805 2-8-13 0.......... MickaelBarzalona 7 87
(David O'Meara) *qckly into stride: trckd ldrs: rdn along 1 1/2f out: kpt on same pce* 11/1

6 2 1/2 **Show Kena (FR)** 2-8-13 0.......... Pierre-CharlesBoudot 4 78
(P Sogorb, France) 16/5[2]

7 snk **Littledidyouknow (IRE)**[32] 2191 2-8-13 0..........(b[1]) HollieDoyle 5 77
(Archie Watson) *pushed along in rr of midfield: tk clsr order and rdn along over 1f out: wknd fnl f* 32/5

8 6 **Galio Chop (FR)** 2-9-2 0.......... MickaelForest 3 58
(A Chopard, France) 40/1

9 snk **Fan Club Rules (IRE)**[27] 2-9-2..........(b[1]) ClementLecoeuvre 9 58+
(Matthieu Palussiere, France) 22/1

59.05s **9 Ran SP% 120.2**
PARI-MUTUEL (all including 1 euro stake): WIN 7.40 (winner coupled with Fan Club Rules); PLACE 2.90, 3.00, 2.20; DF 43.20.
Owner Mrs Theresa Marnane **Bred** Gestut Kussaburg **Trained** France

FOCUS
Fan Club Rules ensured this was a well-run Listed sprint.

3305 DONCASTER (L-H)

Saturday, June 1

OFFICIAL GOING: Good to firm (watered; 8.4)
Wind: Light against Weather: Cloudy

3334 1ST SECURITY SOLUTIONS H'CAP 1m 6f 115y

1:20 (1:20) (Class 5) (0-70,71) 4-Y-O+ £3,752 (£1,116; £557; £300; £300; £300) Stalls Low

Form RPR

0-00 1 **Swordbill**[21] 2626 4-9-2 65..........(p) AdamKirby 3 74
(Ian Williams) *dwlt: hld up towards rr: hdwy over 3f out: chsd ldrs 2f out: rdn to ld appr fnl f: kpt on strly (trainer's rep said, regarding the improved form shown, the gelding had appreciated the quicker going (good to Firm) on this occasion and also the slight step up in trip to 1m6f½f)* 6/1[3]

-111 2 3/4 **Echo (IRE)**[40] 1981 4-9-8 71..........(b) JackGarritty 7 78
(Jedd O'Keeffe) *hld up: hdwy on outer 3f out: chal 2f out: sn rdn and hung rt over 1f out: drvn and ev ch whn edgd lft jst ins fnl f: kpt on towards fin* 3/1[1]

0062 3 3 1/2 **Angel Gabrial (IRE)**[19] 2695 10-8-8 57..........(p) DavidEgan 4 59
(Patrick Morris) *trckd ldr: cl up over 4f out: led 3f out and sn pushed along: jnd and rdn 2f out: drvn and hdd jst over 1f out: kpt on same pce* 14/1

5/0- 4 1/2 **Big Time Dancer (IRE)**[15] 3557 6-8-12 61.......... GrahamLee 6 62
(Jennie Candlish) *hld up in rr: hdwy over 2f out: rdn wl over 1f out: kpt on fnl f* 3/1[1]

13-6 5 2 1/4 **Jumping Cats**[37] 2059 4-9-8 71.......... JackMitchell 1 69
(Chris Wall) *trckd ldrs on inner: pushed along over 3f out: rdn wl over 2f out: sn drvn and wknd* 7/1

6-22 6 2 **Divin Bere (FR)**[22] 2591 6-9-6 69..........(tp) AndrewMullen 5 65
(Iain Jardine) *trckd ldrs: pushed along 4f out: rdn 2f out: sn drvn and wknd* 4/1[2]

-003 7 4 **Airplane (IRE)**[8] 3054 4-8-13 62.......... RachelRichardson 2 52
(Tim Easterby) *led: pushed along over 4f out: rdn and hdd over 3f out: sn drvn and wknd* 8/1

3m 6.8s (-4.80) **Going Correction** -0.10s/f (Good) **7 Ran SP% 114.6**
Speed ratings (Par 103): **108,107,105,105,104 103,101**
CSF £24.41 TOTE £6.80: £3.00, £2.40; EX 19.70 Trifecta £239.10.
Owner Sohi & Sohi **Bred** Juddmonte Farms Ltd **Trained** Portway, Worcs

FOCUS
Races 1, 3, 4 & 5 increased by 6yds. It was good to firm on a watered track prior to the opener, a small staying handicap of which three of the last six winners followed up. They went an even gallop and most were travelling well entering the home straight, where speed proved crucial.

3335 EUROPEAN BREEDERS FUND EBF NOVICE STKS (PLUS 10 RACE) 6f 111y

1:55 (1:55) (Class 4) 2-Y-O £4,787 (£1,424; £711; £355) Stalls Centre

Form RPR

63 1 **Full Verse (IRE)**[31] 2267 2-9-5 0.......... AdamKirby 9 81
(Charlie Appleby) *cl up: effrt 2f out and sn rdn: drvn to ld 150yds out: sn edgd lft: kpt on wl towards fin* 4/6[1]

0 2 nse **Kuwait Direction (IRE)**[33] 2205 2-9-5 0.......... PatDobbs 7 81
(Richard Hannon) *trckd ldrs: hdwy over 1f out: n.m.r jst ins fnl f: sn swtchd lft and rdn: fin wl: jst hld (jockey said colt ran green)* 9/1

3 shd **Raahy** 2-9-5 0.......... EoinWalsh 5 81
(George Scott) *slt ld: rdn along over 1f out: drvn jst ins fnl f: hdd 150yds out: kpt on wl u.p towards fin* 22/1

4 1/2 **Saqqara King (USA)** 2-9-5 0.......... JackMitchell 6 79+
(Charlie Appleby) *t.k.h: hld up in rr: swtchd rt to outer and hdwy over 2f out: green and rdn along to chse ldrs over 1f out: kpt on wl fnl f* 5/2[2]

63 5 2 1/4 **Bravo Faisal (IRE)**[8] 3047 2-9-5 0.......... PaulHanagan 10 73
(Richard Fahey) *trckd ldrs: pushed along over 2f out: rdn wl over 1f out: sn drvn and wknd appr fnl f* 6/1[3]

6 1 1/4 **Broken Rifle** 2-9-5 0.......... DavidProbert 4 70
(Ivan Furtado) *trckd ldrs: hdwy 2f out: sn rdn and ch tl wknd fnl f* 25/1

7 5 **Moonshine Mo** 2-9-5 0.......... RossaRyan 1 56
(Kevin Frost) *trckd ldrs: hdwy and cl up 2f out: rdn wl over 1f out: wkng and hld whn n.m.r and hmpd jst ins fnl f* 40/1

8 5 **Majarra (IRE)** 2-9-0 0.......... AndrewMullen 8 37
(Adrian Nicholls) *dwlt: a towards rr* 66/1

9 hd **Little Ted** 2-9-5 0..........(t[1]) DavidNolan 3 42
(Tim Easterby) *dwlt: a towards rr (vet said colt lost its left fore shoe)* 20/1

10 12 **Dream Isle (IRE)** 2-8-12 0.......... TobyEley[(7)] 2 9
(Steph Hollinshead) *in tch: rdn along 1/2-way: sn wknd* 66/1

1m 21.7s (2.10) **Going Correction** -0.10s/f (Good) **10 Ran SP% 131.2**
Speed ratings (Par 95): **84,83,83,83,80 79,73,67,67,53**
CSF £9.37 TOTE £1.60: £1.30, £2.00, £6.50; EX 9.70 Trifecta £106.70.
Owner Godolphin **Bred** Mountarmstrong Stud **Trained** Newmarket, Suffolk

FOCUS
A fair juvenile fillies' novice contest, but there wasn't much between the first four home.

3336 50 YEARS OF INDUSTRIAL ANCILLARIES FILLIES' H'CAP 1m 2f 43y

2:30 (2:31) (Class 3) (0-90,87) 3-Y-O+ £7,561 (£2,263; £1,131; £566; £282) Stalls High

Form RPR

1-31 1 **Vivionn**[23] 2552 3-9-0 86.......... PatDobbs 6 92+
(Sir Michael Stoute) *set stdy pce: rdn and qcknd 2f out: kpt on strly fnl f* 6/5[1]

430- 2 1 1/2 **Amber Spark (IRE)**[213] 8754 3-8-6 78.......... PaulHanagan 3 81
(Richard Fahey) *trckd ldrs: hdwy wl over 2f out: sn pushed along: rdn wl over 1f out: kpt on u.p fnl f: tk 2nd nr line* 7/1

1-51 3 hd **Geetanjali (IRE)**[12] 2902 4-9-5 78..........(p) DavidProbert 5 82
(Michael Bell) *trckd wnr: pushed along 3f out: rdn wl over 1f out: drvn and kpt on fnl f* 10/1

-411 4 3/4 **She Believes (IRE)**[21] 2612 4-9-4 77.......... LiamKeniry 1 80
(Sylvester Kirk) *trckd ldrs on inner: effrt 2f out: sn n.m.r: rdn and n.m.r ent fnl f: kpt on same pce* 5/1[3]

55-2 5 hd **Lady Of Shalott**[14] 2822 4-9-9 87..........(h) DylanHogan[(5)] 4 89
(David Simcock) *hld up in rr: hdwy on outer 3f out: chsd ldrs 2f out: sn rdn: drvn and no imp fnl f* 4/1[2]

234- 6 1 3/4 **Hunni**[238] 7984 4-9-5 78.......... JackMitchell 2 77
(Tom Clover) *in tch: pushed along 3f out: rdn 2f out: sn one pce* 8/1

2m 12.81s (0.51) **Going Correction** -0.10s/f (Good)
WFA 3 from 4yo 13lb **6 Ran SP% 114.8**
Speed ratings (Par 104): **94,92,92,92,91 90**
CSF £10.75 TOTE £1.90: £1.20, £3.70; EX 9.80 Trifecta £62.80.
Owner Cheveley Park Stud **Bred** Newsells Park Stud **Trained** Newmarket, Suffolk

FOCUS
Add 6yds to the official distance. A good fillies' handicap featuring three last time out winners, and the victor was impressive.

3337 DONCASTER GROUNDWORKS H'CAP 1m 6f 115y

3:05 (3:06) (Class 2) 3-Y-O £37,350 (£11,184; £5,592; £2,796; £1,398; £702) Stalls Low

Form RPR

32-4 1 **Durston**[33] 2208 3-8-7 79.......... PaulHanagan 1 86
(David Simcock) *hld up in rr: hdwy 3f out: rdn to chse ldrs over 1f out: styd on to ld ins fnl f: hld on wl towards fin* 6/1

-120 2 hd **Themaxwecan (IRE)**[21] 2619 3-9-6 92.......... FrannyNorton 6 99
(Mark Johnston) *hld up in rr: hdwy on outer wl over 2f out: rdn wl over 1f out: styd on wl fnl f: jst failed* 9/2[3]

6-11 3 nk **Summer Moon**[15] 2811 3-9-7 93.......... PJMcDonald 3 99
(Mark Johnston) *cl up: led after 2f: pushed along 3f out: rdn 2f out: drvn over 1f out: hdd ins fnl f: kpt on wl u.p* 6/4[1]

-211 4 2 3/4 **Emirates Empire (IRE)**[30] 2317 3-9-4 90.......... DavidProbert 4 92
(Michael Bell) *t.k.h: sn trcking ldr: effrt 3f out: rdn along to chal 12f out: drvn over 1f out: kpt on same pce fnl f* 10/3[2]

21-5 5 1/2 **Skymax (GER)**[15] 2811 3-8-13 85.......... PatDobbs 2 86
(Ralph Beckett) *led 2f: trckd ldrs: pushed along over 3f out: rdn wl over 2f out: sn drvn and wknd (jockey said gelding hung right throughout)* 10/1

401- 6 2 **Buckman Tavern (FR)**[262] 7163 3-8-7 79.......... DavidEgan 5 78
(Sir Mark Prescott Bt) *trckd ldrs: pushed along 4f out: rdn 3f out: sn wknd* 12/1

3m 5.29s (-6.31) **Going Correction** -0.10s/f (Good) **6 Ran SP% 112.3**
Speed ratings (Par 105): **112,111,111,110,110 108**
CSF £32.34 TOTE £6.40: £2.70, £2.60; EX 30.70 Trifecta £78.40.
Owner Highclere Thoroughbred Racing - Durston **Bred** Miss K Rausing **Trained** Newmarket, Suffolk

FOCUS
Add 6yds to the official distance. Just six runners for this staying handicap, but strong form. They went a fair clip and the winner came from last place.

3338 29TH JUNE RITA ORA LIVE @ DONCASTER H'CAP 1m 2f 43y

3:40 (3:40) (Class 3) (0-90,90) 3-Y-O+ £7,762 (£2,310; £1,154; £577) Stalls High

Form RPR

1-40 1 **West End Charmer (IRE)**[23] 2562 3-9-2 90.......... FrannyNorton 4 106+
(Mark Johnston) *mde: rdn along and qcknd over 2f out: clr ent fnl f: styd on strly (trainer's rep could offer no explanation for the colt's improved form)* 3/1[2]

6-05 2 4 **Mandarin (GER)**[17] 2739 5-9-3 78..........(t[1]) PJMcDonald 2 86
(Ian Williams) *hld up towards rr: hdwy 3f out: chsd wnr 2f out: sn rdn: drvn and no imp fnl f* 11/2

2-31 3 7 **Black Lotus**[14] 2822 4-9-6 81.......... GeorgeWood 6 75
(Chris Wall) *hld up in rr: hdwy on wd outside 3f out: rdn along 2f out: sn drvn and no imp* 9/4[1]

0325 4 5 **Delph Crescent (IRE)**[17] 2748 4-9-6 81..........(p) PaulHanagan 3 65
(Richard Fahey) *hld up: hdwy over 3f out and sn pushed along: rdn over 2f out: plugged on: n.d* 5/1[3]

1-4P 5 6 **Bobby K (IRE)**[23] 2563 4-10-0 89..........(b) JackMitchell 1 61
(Simon Crisford) *trckd ldng pair: pushed along 3f out: rdn over 2f out: drvn and wknd wl over 1f out* 8/1

5-06 6 1 **Gossip Column (IRE)**[23] 2563 4-10-0 89.......... DavidEgan 5 59
(Ian Williams) *trckd wnr: pushed along 4f out: rdn over 3f out: wknd wl over 2f out* 7/1

40-0 7 1/2 **Capton**[23] 2563 6-9-4 86.......... JoshQuinn[(7)] 8 55
(Michael Easterby) *chsd ldrs: rdn along over 3f out: sn wknd* 33/1

2m 5.57s (-6.73) **Going Correction** -0.10s/f (Good) **7 Ran SP% 114.4**
WFA 3 from 4yo+ 13lb
Speed ratings (Par 107): **118,114,109,105,100 99,99**
CSF £19.76 CT £42.71 TOTE £3.60: £1.90, £3.10; EX 24.20.
Owner Martin McHale **Bred** Niarchos Family **Trained** Middleham Moor, N Yorks

FOCUS
Add 6yds to the official distance. A fair handicap in which the winner took them along at a good gallop, and they finished strung out.

3339 HAPPY BIRTHDAY LUCY TITCHENER NOVICE STKS 5f 3y
4:15 (4:17) (Class 5) 3-Y-O+ **£3,752** (£1,116; £557; £278) **Stalls** Centre

Form RPR
-222 **1** **Moss Gill (IRE)**[15] 2810 3-9-3 78 PJMcDonald 6 85
(James Bethell) *t.k.h: trckd ldr: smooth hdwy to ld 1 1/2f out: sn clr: readily* **1/4**[1]
53-4 **2** *6* **Ginvincible**[127] 412 3-8-12 65 DavidEgan 3 58
(James Given) *chsd ldng pair: rdn along wl over 1f out: hung rt 1f out: sn drvn and kpt on to take 2nd nr line (jockey said filly hung right under pressure)* **10/1**[3]
342 **3** *nk* **Brigadier**[56] 1598 3-9-3 69 AdamKirby 1 62
(Robert Cowell) *led: pushed along and jnd 2f out: hdd 1 1/2f out: sn drvn and one pce: lost modest 2nd nr line* **6/1**[2]
55 **4** *3 1/2* **Gunnison**[22] 2590 3-9-3 PaulHanagan 5 50
(Richard Fahey) *dwlt and bhd: sme hdwy fnl 2f: nvr a factor* **10/1**[3]
5 *3/4* **Cominginonmonday (IRE)** 4-8-12 SeanKirrane(7) 4 45
(Robyn Brisland) *sn outpcd and a in rr* **50/1**
0 **6** *3 1/4* **Dilly Dilly (IRE)**[12] 2909 3-8-12 (h) AndrewMullen 2 30
(John Wainwright) *chsd ldrs: rdn along 1/2-way: sn wknd* **50/1**

59.35s (-0.25) **Going Correction** -0.10s/f (Good)
WFA 3 from 4yo 7lb **6 Ran SP% 116.4**
Speed ratings (Par 103): **98,88,87,82,81 75**
CSF £4.42 TOTE £1.10: £1.10, £3.10; EX 3.80 Trifecta £8.70.
Owner G Van Cutsem & Partner **Bred** Camas Park & Lynch Bages **Trained** Middleham Moor, N Yorks

FOCUS
An uncompetitive novice sprint that centred on the hot favourite, who won easily.

3340 ST LEGER FESTIVAL 11-14 SEPTEMBER H'CAP 1m (S)
4:50 (4:52) (Class 4) (0-85,85) 3-Y-O **£5,530** (£1,645; £822; £411; £300) **Stalls** Centre

Form RPR
1-31 **1** **Artistic Rifles (IRE)**[14] 2821 3-9-5 83 DavidProbert 2 89+
(Charles Hills) *mde all: rdn wl over 1f out: drvn ins fnl f: hld on gamely* **11/4**[2]
2010 **2** *nse* **Conaglen**[17] 2746 3-8-11 75 PJMcDonald 3 81
(James Bethell) *in tch: pushed along and sltly outpcd over 2f out: hdwy over 1f out: sn rdn: swtchd rt jst ins fnl f: fin strly: jst failed* **16/1**
05-2 **3** *1 1/2* **Moqtarreb**[15] 2802 3-9-7 85 DaneO'Neill 1 87
(Roger Varian) *trckd ldrs: hdwy over 2f out: chal over 1f out: sn rdn and ev ch: drvn ins fnl f: kpt on same pce towards fin* **1/1**[1]
-402 **4** *1/2* **Ginger Fox**[16] 2766 3-8-13 77 DavidEgan 4 78
(Ian Williams) *trckd wnr: hdwy and cl up wl over 1f out: sn rdn and ev ch: drvn ent fnl f: kpt on same pce* **5/1**[3]
20-1 **5** *3 1/4* **Irreverent**[34] 2146 3-9-4 82 PaulHanagan 5 75
(Richard Fahey) *t.k.h: trckd wnr: pushed along 2f out: rdn over 1f out: wknd appr fnl f* **7/1**

1m 38.77s (-1.43) **Going Correction** -0.10s/f (Good) **5 Ran SP% 111.7**
Speed ratings (Par 101): **103,102,101,100,97**
CSF £36.23 TOTE £3.30: £1.50, £5.60; EX 33.00 Trifecta £63.50.
Owner Mrs Fitri Hay **Bred** Lynn Lodge Stud **Trained** Lambourn, Berks

FOCUS
A classy 3yo handicap to keep an eye on, with four of the last six winners following-up, two at Royal Ascot (Britannia/Group 3), and another in Group 3 company. It was run at only a sedate tempo down the middle, and the first four were bunched at the finish, the front two locked in a photo.
T/Plt: £46.70 to a £1 stake. Pool: £62,610.16 - 977.08 winning units T/Qpdt: £17.20 to a £1 stake. Pool: £4,245.55 - 182.09 winning units **Joe Rowntree**

3312 EPSOM (L-H)
Saturday, June 1

OFFICIAL GOING: Good (good to firm in home straight and on 5f course; watered) changing to good to firm after race 1 (2.00)
Wind: light, across Weather: sunny and warm

3341 INVESTEC PRIVATE BANKING H'CAP 1m 2f 17y
2:00 (2:03) (Class 2) (0-105,105) 3-Y-O
£31,125 (£9,320; £4,660; £2,330; £1,165; £585) **Stalls** Low

Form RPR
53-1 **1** **Le Don De Vie**[38] 2034 3-8-2 86 MartinDwyer 4 100
(Andrew Balding) *chsd ldr tl led after 1f: mde rest: rdn and kicked clr w runner-up jst over 2f out: drvn over 1f out: forged ahd 1f out and styd on strly ins fnl f: eased towards fin* **5/1**[3]
0-25 **2** *4 1/2* **The Trader (IRE)**[14] 2828 3-8-8 92 SilvestreDeSousa 9 97
(Mark Johnston) *chsd wnr over 8f out: rdn and kicked clr w wnr jst over 2f out: drvn over 1f out: jst getting outpcd whn wandered rt and btn jst ins fnl f: wknd towards fin but a holding 2nd* **7/2**[1]
1222 **3** *nk* **Alkaamel**[28] 2414 3-8-5 89 ChrisHayes 6 93+
(William Haggas) *looked wl; stdd s: hld up in last pair: effrt and swtchd rt 3f out: sn rdn: kpt on to chse clr ldng pair jst ins fnl f: styd and pressing for 2nd cl home: no threat to wnr* **6/1**
0403 **4** *1* **Victory Command (IRE)**[7] 3082 3-8-9 93 JoeFanning 7 95
(Mark Johnston) *chsd ldrs: rdn 3f out: outpcd by ldng pair jst over 2f out: no threat to ldrs after: kpt on same pce ins fnl f* **11/1**
3-16 **5** *nk* **Nayef Road (IRE)**[16] 2777 3-9-7 105 RyanMoore 2 107
(Mark Johnston) *hld up in tch in last trio: effrt over 2f out: sn outpcd by ldng pair: no threat to ldrs after and kpt on same pce ins fnl f* **4/1**[2]
13-5 **6** *2* **Kheros**[146] 103 3-8-1 85 HollieDoyle 3 83
(Archie Watson) *t.k.h: led for 1f: chsd ldrs after: rdn wl over 2f out: sn u.p and unable qck: wl hld and plugged on same pce fr over 1f out* **25/1**
2-33 **7** *hd* **Politicise (IRE)**[21] 2616 3-8-1 85 (p[1]) JFEgan 1 82
(William Haggas) *in tch in midfield: effrt wl over 2f out: sn u.p and unable qck: no threat to ldrs after and plugged on same pce fr over 1f out* **6/1**
41-5 **8** *6* **Red Hot (FR)**[24] 2521 3-8-6 90 BarryMcHugh 8 75
(Richard Fahey) *hld up in last pair: effrt wl over 2f out: sn struggling and outpcd: wl btn over 1f out* **11/1**
115 **9** *25* **Creationist (USA)**[43] 1926 3-8-10 94 JasonWatson 5 29
(Roger Charlton) *in tch in midfield: effrt over 3f out: sn struggling: bhd whn hung lft over 2f out: lost tch and wl bhd whn eased ins fnl f* **10/1**

2m 4.37s (-5.63) **Going Correction** -0.325s/f (Firm) **9 Ran SP% 117.1**
Speed ratings (Par 105): **109,105,105,104,104 102,102,97,77**
CSF £23.22 CT £108.21 TOTE £6.20: £2.20, £1.50, £2.00; EX 26.40 Trifecta £208.60.
Owner Mick and Janice Mariscotti **Bred** Miss K Rausing **Trained** Kingsclere, Hants

FOCUS
A total of 3mm of water was applied overnight to the 1m4f course, except from 6f to the home straight crossing. It was a warm day and, while the going was described as good on the Derby course (GoingStick 7.6) and good to firm in the home straight (GoingStick 7.9) to begin with, it was soon changed to good to firm all round after the first race. The rail was at its innermost configuration and all distances were as advertised. They didn't go that quick early and the pace held up. It's been rated at face value.

3342 PRINCESS ELIZABETH STKS (SPONSORED BY INVESTEC) (GROUP 3) (F&M) 1m 113y
2:35 (2:39) (Class 1) 3-Y-O+
£51,039 (£19,350; £9,684; £4,824; £2,421; £1,215) **Stalls** Low

Form RPR
6-02 **1** **Anna Nerium**[28] 2404 4-9-6 106 TomMarquand 6 110
(Richard Hannon) *looked wl; hld up in rr: effrt 3f out: hdwy u.p to chse ldrs over 1f out: styd on strly to ld wl ins fnl f: gng away at fin* **9/2**[3]
26-1 **2** *1 1/4* **Awesometank**[28] 2404 4-9-6 106 (p[1]) JamesDoyle 3 107+
(William Haggas) *led for 1f: chsd ldr tl over 5f out: styd trcking ldrs tl led on inner over 2f out: sn rdn: drvn over 1f out: kpt on tl hdd and no ex wl ins fnl f* **3/1**[2]
16-4 **3** *nk* **Veracious**[27] 2441 4-9-9 110 (t[1]) RyanMoore 5 109
(Sir Michael Stoute) *looked wl; hld up in tch in last trio: effrt 3f out: hdwy u.p to chse ldr 2f out: drvn over 1f out: kpt on but lost 2nd ins fnl f* **2/1**[1]
01-5 **4** *3* **Bella Ragazza**[21] 2608 4-9-6 96 OisinMurphy 2 100
(Hughie Morrison) *hld up in tch in last trio: effrt 3f out: nt clr run and swtchd rt over 2f out: drvn and hdwy over 1f out: no imp and one pce ins fnl f* **7/1**
-036 **5** *1 3/4* **Vivianite (IRE)**[10] 2961 4-9-6 94 HollieDoyle 1 96
(Archie Watson) *in tch in midfield: swtchd lft and effrt on inner over 2f out: chsd ldrs and drvn over 1f out: wknd ins fnl f* **40/1**
1-02 **6** *16* **Contrive (IRE)**[21] 2608 4-9-6 94 AndreaAtzeni 4 59
(Roger Varian) *chsd ldrs early: sn settled in midfield: effrt 3f out: unable qck u.p 2f out: sn outpcd and btn: wknd* **10/1**
14-0 **7** *5* **Akvavera**[28] 2404 4-9-6 94 HarryBentley 7 47
(Ralph Beckett) *rousted along leaving stalls: led after 1f: rdn over 3f out: hdd over 2f out and sn struggling: btn over 1f out: wknd and eased ins fnl f* **33/1**
2-24 **8** *12* **Nyaleti (IRE)**[16] 2776 4-9-6 109 JoeFanning 8 20
(Mark Johnston) *chsd ldrs after 1f: chsd ldr over 5f out tl lost pl over 2f out: sn bhd: wknd and eased ins fnl f: t.o: lame (jockey said filly stopped quickly; vet said filly was lame on her right-fore)* **6/1**

1m 40.82s (-5.58) **Going Correction** -0.325s/f (Firm) **8 Ran SP% 117.8**
Speed ratings (Par 113): **111,109,109,106,105 91,86,76**
CSF £19.06 TOTE £5.00: £1.40, £1.40, £1.20; EX 20.70 Trifecta £67.70.
Owner Mrs R J McCreery **Bred** Stowell Hill Ltd **Trained** East Everleigh, Wilts

FOCUS
A solid enough renewal, though the top four in the market had won just four races between them in their last 25 races combined. They went hard up front and the winner came from last. The winner has been rated back to her best.

3343 INVESTEC DIOMED STKS (GROUP 3) 1m 113y
3:10 (3:15) (Class 1) 3-Y-O+
£51,039 (£19,350; £9,684; £4,824; £2,421; £1,215) **Stalls** Low

Form RPR
30-1 **1** **Zaaki**[31] 2271 4-9-6 112 RyanMoore 2 114
(Sir Michael Stoute) *dwlt: hld up in tch in last pair: effrt over 2f out: swtchd rt over 1f out: clsd u.p 1f out: led 75yds out: r.o strly* **11/8**[1]
0162 **2** *1* **Oh This Is Us (IRE)**[19] 2688 6-9-6 111 TomMarquand 4 112
(Richard Hannon) *looked wl; stdd s: hld up in last pair: effrt wl over 1f out: drvn and clsd 1f out: kpt on to chse wnr wl ins fnl f: r.o but a hld towards fin* **8/1**
30-6 **3** *1 1/4* **Chief Ironside**[22] 2573 4-9-6 104 JasonWatson 1 109
(William Jarvis) *led tl over 5f out: chsd ldr tl rdn to ld again over 2f out: edging lft u.p 1f out: hdd 75yds out: no ex and wknd cl home* **16/1**
2-11 **4** *nk* **Bye Bye Hong Kong (USA)**[19] 2688 3-8-8 112 SilvestreDeSousa 6 107
(Andrew Balding) *dwlt: hdwy on outer to join ldr over 6f out: led over 5f out: hdd and rdn over 2f out: keeping on whn n.m.r briefly ins fnl f: kpt on same pce fnl 100yds* **13/8**[2]
22-1 **5** *1/2* **Mordin (IRE)**[35] 2105 5-9-6 106 (p) PatCosgrave 7 107
(Simon Crisford) *looked wl; chsd ldrs after over 1f out: effrt over 2f out: drvn over 1f out: kpt on same pce ins fnl f* **13/2**[3]
00-0 **6** *7* **Zabriskie (IRE)**[20] 2666 4-9-6 100 ChrisHayes 5 91
(Luke Comer, Ire) *chsd ldr for over 1f: midfield after: unbalanced on downhill run 4f out: u.p and dropped to rr 3f out: no ch after* **66/1**

1m 40.46s (-5.94) **Going Correction** -0.325s/f (Firm) course record
WFA 3 from 4yo+ 12lb **6 Ran SP% 112.0**
Speed ratings (Par 113): **113,112,111,110,110 104**
CSF £12.97 TOTE £2.10: £1.30, £2.70; EX 12.10 Trifecta £65.30.
Owner Ahmad Alotaibi **Bred** Miss K Rausing **Trained** Newmarket, Suffolk

FOCUS
The leaders appeared to get racing a little soon and the first two came through from off the pace. They finished in a bit of a heap but the track record was lowered by 0.29sec. The third is the key to the form. The winner has been rated a bit below his Ascot latest.

3344 INVESTEC "DASH" H'CAP 5f
3:45 (3:50) (Class 2) 3-Y-O+
£61,590 (£18,540; £9,270; £4,620; £2,320; £1,170) **Stalls** High

Form RPR
150 **1** **Ornate**[17] 2744 6-8-13 99 PhilDennis 2 107
(David C Griffiths) *mde all: pushed along 2f out: drvn ent fnl f: hld on gamely towards fin: all out* **33/1**
-252 **2** *nk* **Dark Shot**[7] 3097 6-8-0 86 (p) PaddyMathers 9 93
(Scott Dixon) *stmbld sltly leaving stalls: midfield: rdn 1/2-way: hdwy u.p over 1f out: hrd drvn and chsd wnr ins fnl f: kpt on wl: a jst hld* **14/1**
2045 **3** *nk* **Blue De Vega (GER)**[12] 2910 6-8-5 91 (p) MartinDwyer 7 97
(Robert Cowell) *towards rr: effrt over 1f out: clsd and nt clr run 1f out: sn swtchd lft and r.o v strly fnl 100yds: nt quite rch ldrs* **25/1**

-040 **4** *hd* **Eeh Bah Gum (IRE)**[7] 3097 4-7-13 **88**.................... JamieGormley(3) 14 93+
(Tim Easterby) *looked wl; in rr: effrt over 1f out: hdwy jst ins fnl f: swtchd lft and r.o strly wl ins fnl f: nt rch ldrs* **9/1**[3]

300- **5** *shd* **Muthmir (IRE)**[196] 9127 9-9-5 **105**..............................(p) JimCrowley 16 110
(William Haggas) *towards rr: swtchd lft: rdn and hdwy 2f out: chsd ldrs 1f out: nt clrest of runs ins fnl f: kpt towards fin* **8/1**[2]

-006 **6** *¾* **Harome (IRE)**[7] 3097 5-8-2 **88**.. NicolaCurrie 13 90+
(Roger Fell) *impeded leaving stalls: in rr: rdn wl over 2f out: swtchd lft 1f out: hdwy ins fnl f: styd on strly towards fin: nt rch ldrs (jockey said gelding anticipated the start)* **20/1**

5211 **7** *hd* **Duke Of Firenze**[7] 3097 10-8-3 **89** 7ex.......................... NathanEvans 19 90
(David C Griffiths) *midfield: effrt whn nt clr run and hmpd over 1f out: rdn and kpt on wl ins fnl f: nt rch ldrs (jockey said gelding was denied a clear run)* **8/1**[2]

1605 **8** *½* **Boom The Groom (IRE)**[22] 2589 8-7-11 **88**........... DarraghKeenan(5) 6 88
(Tony Carroll) *taken down early: wl in tch in midfield: effrt and clsd 2f out: chsd ldrs and drvn 1f out: no ex and one pce wl ins fnl f* **33/1**

20-6 **9** *hd* **Caspian Prince (IRE)**[7] 3084 10-10-0 **114**...........(t) AlistairRawlinson 10 113
(Michael Appleby) *pressed wnr: ev ch and drvn over 1f out: no ex and lost 2nd ins fnl f: wknd towards fin* **20/1**

-350 **10** *nk* **Open Wide (USA)**[16] 2775 5-8-7 **93**..........................(b) HarryBentley 11 91
(Amanda Perrett) *in rr: effrt wl over 1f out: hdwy whn nt clr run and swtchd rt ins fnl f: styd on wl towards fin: nvr trbld ldrs* **25/1**

54-2 **11** *nk* **Just Glamorous (IRE)**[28] 2403 6-8-0 **86**.................... JimmyQuinn 12 83
(Grace Harris) *broke fast and wnt sltly rt leaving stalls: chsd ldrs: edgd rt after 1f: rdn and sltly impeded over 1f out: no ex u.p ins fnl f: wknd towards fin* **25/1**

4213 **12** *hd* **Copper Knight (IRE)**[7] 3097 5-9-4 **104** 4ex.....................(t) DavidAllan 15 103+
(Tim Easterby) *looked wl; chsd ldrs: sltly impeded after 1f and lost pl: towards rr 1/2-way: effrt over 1f out: hdwy but stl plenty to do whn nt clr run and eased ins fnl f (jockey said gelding was denied a clear run and became unbalanced on the road crossings)* **8/1**[2]

-250 **13** *hd* **Line Of Reason (IRE)**[16] 2775 9-8-6 **92**...................... JoeFanning 4 87
(Paul Midgley) *midfield: shkn up over 1f out: kpt on ins fnl f: nvr threatened ldrs* **33/1**

5134 **14** *nk* **Mokaatil**[23] 2557 4-7-10 **87**.....................................(p[1]) AndrewBreslin(5) 3 81
(Ian Williams) *racd wd: midfield: effrt over 1f out: kpt on ins fnl f: nvr enough pce to threaten ldrs* **33/1**

2-42 **15** *hd* **Recon Mission (IRE)**[24] 2522 3-8-2 **95**........................ HollieDoyle 17 86
(Tony Carroll) *sltly on toes; chsd ldrs: effrt and jostled over 1f out: rdn and no ex 1f out: wknd ins fnl f (jockey said colt hung left-handed throughout)* **9/1**[3]

1651 **16** *¾* **Just That Lord**[38] 2030 6-8-1 **87**.. JFEgan 5 78
(Michael Attwater) *wl in tch in midfield: effrt over 1f out: unable qck and wknd ins fnl f* **16/1**

221/ **17** *2* **Hathiq (IRE)**[6] 3113 5-8-2 **88** 4ex..................................(t) RoryCleary 18 72
(Denis Gerard Hogan, Ire) *wl in tch in midfield: lost pl 2f out: struggling after and no hdwy over 1f out: wl hld ins fnl f (trainer could offer no explanation for the gelding's performance other than he showed his inexperience and may have been unsuited by the large field)* **7/2**[1]

13-6 **18** *nk* **Fool For You (IRE)**[23] 2557 4-8-4 **90**........................ ShaneGray 8 73
(Richard Fahey) *s.i.s: a in rr: effrt over 1f out: no prog and nvr involved* **40/1**

5-21 **19** *3 ¼* **Daschas**[14] 2839 5-8-0 **86** 4ex....................................(t) KieranO'Neill 20 57
(Stuart Williams) *chsd ldrs: rdn and jostled over 1f out: sn struggling: wknd ins fnl f* **16/1**

54.0s (-1.30) **Going Correction** -0.325s/f (Firm) course record
WFA 3 from 4yo+ 7lb **19** Ran SP% **129.3**
Speed ratings (Par 109): **97,96,96,95,95 94,94,93,92,92 91,91,91,90,90 89,86,85,80**
CSF £418.73 CT £11447.97 TOTE £47.00: £8.00, £3.30, £6.50, £2.50; EX 479.20 Trifecta £16728.70.
Owner Kings Road Racing Partnership **Bred** Cheveley Park Stud Ltd **Trained** Bawtry, S Yorks
■ Stewards' Enquiry : Jim Crowley two-day ban: used whip above the permitted level (Jun 23-24)
J F Egan one-day ban: weighing in at 2lb overweight (Jun 15)
Jimmy Quinn two-day ban: interference & careless riding (tba)

FOCUS
A typically fast and furious edition, featuring three-time winner of the race Caspian Prince and 2013 scorer, Duke Of Firenze. Much of the early pace was middle to high, though the winner showed plenty of early dash from stall two. They all congregated towards the stands' rail and there were plenty of hard luck stories. The winning time was within 0.31sec of Stone Of Folca's world record. The second has been rated similar to his latest/2017 form in this race.

3345 INVESTEC DERBY STKS (GROUP 1) (ENTIRE COLTS & FILLIES) 1m 4f 6y
4:30 (4:33) (Class 1) 3-Y-O
£921,537 (£349,375; £174,850; £87,100; £43,712; £21,937) **Stalls** Centre

Form RPR

30-1 **1** **Anthony Van Dyck (IRE)**[21] 2619 3-9-0 118........... SeamieHeffernan 7 119+
(A P O'Brien, Ire) *str; sweating; midfield and pushed along at times: 9th and pushed along st: swtchd rt jst over 2f out: hdwy u.p to chse ldrs whn nt clr run and swtchd lft 1f out: edging lft and led 100yds out: styd on* **13/2**

1-24 **2** *½* **Madhmoon (IRE)**[28] 2411 3-9-0 113................................ ChrisHayes 6 117+
(Kevin Prendergast, Ire) *stdd after s: hld up towards rr: clipped heels and stmbld 4f out: 10th st: swtchd rt and gd hdwy to chal over 2f out: battled on wl u.p: nt quite pce of wnr fnl 100yds: regained 2nd on post* **10/1**

1-4 **3** *nse* **Japan**[16] 2777 3-9-0 111.. WayneLordan 11 117
(A P O'Brien, Ire) *tall; hld up towards rr: 11th st: effrt over 2f out: rdn and hdwy over 1f out: clsng to press ldrs whn rdr dropped whip 100yds out: styd on wl to snatch 3rd last stride* **20/1**

2-11 **4** *shd* **Broome (IRE)**[20] 2662 3-9-0 114...................... DonnachaO'Brien 8 116
(A P O'Brien, Ire) *athletic; looked wl; restless in stalls: hld up towards rr: hdwy and 7th st: clsd over 2f out: drvn to chse ldrs over 1f out: kpt on u.p ins fnl f: no ex towards fin* **4/1**[2]

1 **5** *shd* **Sir Dragonet (IRE)**[24] 2523 3-9-0 115......................... RyanMoore 13 116
(A P O'Brien, Ire) *workmanlike; hld up in midfield: 6th st: effrt to chal and edgd lft over 2f out: led 2f out: drvn and sustained duel w runner-up after: hdd 100yds out: no ex and nt quite match pce of wnr after: lost 3 pls last strides* **11/4**[1]

34-1 **6** *4 ½* **Circus Maximus (IRE)**[23] 2558 3-9-0 110.................(p[1]) FrankieDettori 5 109
(A P O'Brien, Ire) *str; sweating; stmbld and wnt lft leaving stalls: rcvrd to ld: hdd after 1f: chsd ldrs: 4th st: rdn wl over 2f out: chsng ldrs but getting outpcd whn pushed lft 1f out: sn btn and eased ins fnl f* **10/1**

21-1 **7** *1 ¾* **Humanitarian (USA)**[16] 2769 3-9-0 95........................ RobertHavlin 9 106
(John Gosden) *stdd after s: hld up in last pair: 12th st: hdwy to pass btn horses and edgd lft u.p over 1f out: kpt on ins fnl f: nvr trbld ldrs* **33/1**

14-2 **8** *shd* **Norway (IRE)**[24] 2523 3-9-0 104..................................(p) JamieSpencer 10 108+
(A P O'Brien, Ire) *chsd ldr after 2f: 2nd st: rdn to ld 3f out: hdd 2f out: unable qck and getting outpcd whn nudged lft 1f out: wknd ins fnl f* **33/1**

11-0 **9** *1* **Line of Duty (IRE)**[16] 2777 3-9-0 114..........................(p[1]) JamesDoyle 1 104
(Charlie Appleby) *sweating; in tch in midfield: 5th st: effrt to chse ldrs over 2f out: unable qck u.p and btn over 1f out: wknd fnl f* **25/1**

3-23 **10** *1 ¼* **Sovereign (IRE)**[20] 2662 3-9-0 105................................ PBBeggy 4 102
(A P O'Brien, Ire) *short of room and hmpd leaving stalls: rcvrd and hdwy to ld after 1f: rdn and hdd 3f out: lost pl over 1f out: wknd fnl f (vet said colt lost its left-fore shoe)* **50/1**

0-10 **11** *2 ¼* **Hiroshima**[21] 2619 3-9-0 87... BrettDoyle 3 98
(John Ryan) *bmpd leaving stallls: t.k.h: hld up in last pair: 13th st: rdn and outpcd 3f out: n.d after: plugged on ins fnl f* **100/1**

4-11 **12** *1 ¼* **Bangkok (IRE)**[36] 2084 3-9-0 104.................. SilvestreDeSousa 12 96
(Andrew Balding) *on toes; sweating; t.k.h: hld up in midfield: 8th st: effrt and drvn wl over 2f out: sn struggling and btn over 1f out: wknd fnl f (trainer said colt was unsuited by the undulations at Epsom)* **9/1**

211 **13** *6* **Telecaster**[16] 2777 3-9-0 115.. OisinMurphy 2 87
(Hughie Morrison) *tall; on toes; sweating; t.k.h: chsd ldr for 2f: 3rd st: rdn over 2f out: sn struggling and lost pl: bhd and eased ins fnl f (trainer said colt ran flat)* **5/1**[3]

2m 33.38s (-7.42) **Going Correction** -0.325s/f (Firm) **13** Ran SP% **122.3**
Speed ratings (Par 113): **111,110,110,110,110 107,106,106,105,104 103,102,98**
CSF £66.61 CT £1253.04 TOTE £8.30: £2.70, £3.60, £5.90; EX 83.70 Trifecta £1317.50.
Owner Mrs John Magnier & Michael Tabor & Derrick Smith **Bred** Orpendale, Chelston & Wynatt **Trained** Cashel, Co Tipperary
■ Stewards' Enquiry : Seamie Heffernan two-day ban: interference & careless riding (Jun 15-16)

FOCUS
It looked an open Derby beforehand, and a bunched finish (Aidan O'Brien-trained runners filled five of the first six spots) suggests the form could be turned around in future, depending on who gets the run of the race. They went a good early gallop which suited those ridden with a bit of patience. The winner has been rated below par for the race. The fourth and fifth have been rated to their trial winning marks.

3346 INVESTEC OUT OF THE ORDINARY H'CAP 1m 4f 6y
5:15 (5:17) (Class 2) (0-105,104) 4-Y-O+
£31,125 (£9,320; £4,660; £2,330; £1,165; £585) **Stalls** Centre

Form RPR

0-51 **1** **Soto Sizzler**[38] 2032 4-8-5 **88**.. JimmyQuinn 11 96+
(William Knight) *looked wl; hld up in tch in midfield: clsd to chse ldrs and travelling strly over 3f out: rdn to ld jst over 2f out: styd on wl ins fnl f* **9/2**[2]

11-0 **2** *1 ½* **Byron Flyer**[17] 2742 8-9-7 **104**................................ JamesDoyle 6 110
(Ian Williams) *led tl 7f out: styd w ldr and rdn to ld again wl over 2f out: hdd and drvn jst over 2f out: kpt on but a hld ins fnl f* **25/1**

1231 **3** *nk* **Eddystone Rock (IRE)**[7] 3070 7-8-9 **92**...................... KierenFox 10 97
(John Best) *chsd ldrs: effrt 3f out: edging lft and unable qck over 1f out: kpt on ins fnl f: nt enough pce to threaten wnr* **14/1**

12-1 **4** *1 ½* **Sextant**[21] 2606 4-9-0 **97**.. RyanMoore 7 100+
(Sir Michael Stoute) *looked wl; t.k.h: sn stdd to rr: hld up in rr: hdwy into midfield 5f out: effrt and chsd ldng trio over 1f out: kpt on same pce ins fnl f* **2/1**[1]

-414 **5** *3 ½* **Grandee (IRE)**[15] 2808 5-8-7 **90**.............................. NicolaCurrie 3 87
(Roger Fell) *in tch in midfield: lost pl and last trio over 3f out: effrt on inner wl over 1f out: kpt on ins fnl f: no threat to ldrs* **7/1**[3]

5042 **6** *1 ¾* **Fire Fighting (IRE)**[15] 2786 8-8-12 **95**.................... SilvestreDeSousa 1 89
(Mark Johnston) *s.i.s: steadily rcvrd and chsd ldrs 9f out: rdn 3f out: unable qck and outpcd over 1f out: wknd ins fnl f* **12/1**

2-03 **7** *nk* **Mazzuri (IRE)**[28] 2401 4-8-12 **95**.............................. JasonWatson 9 89
(Amanda Perrett) *midfield: effrt over 2f out: unable qck: no threat to ldrs and kpt on same pce fr over 1f out* **33/1**

215- **8** *1 ¼* **Breath Caught**[232] 8149 4-8-11 **94**............................ JimCrowley 8 86
(Ian Williams) *looked wl; hld up in last trio: effrt 3f out: no imp and nvr threatened to get on terms: wl hld fnl f (vet said gelding received treatment for post-race ataxia)* **14/1**

05-5 **9** *nk* **Genetics (FR)**[22] 2574 5-8-11 **94**.............................. OisinMurphy 4 85
(Andrew Balding) *chsd ldr tl led 7f out: rdn wl over 2f out: lost pl 2f out: sn wknd* **8/1**

2201 **10** *nk* **Aquarium**[22] 2574 4-9-6 **103**.. JoeFanning 5 94
(Mark Johnston) *hld up in last trio: swtchd rt and effrt wl over 2f out: no imp and hung lft over 1f out: wknd fnl f* **7/1**[3]

-000 **11** *14* **Kyllachy Gala**[15] 2808 6-8-4 **87**....................................(p) KieranO'Neill 2 55
(Warren Greatrex) *pushed along leaving stalls: chsd ldrs early: midfield 5f out: rdn 3f out: sn dropped out and bhd* **66/1**

2m 34.55s (-6.25) **Going Correction** -0.325s/f (Firm) **11** Ran SP% **116.9**
Speed ratings (Par 109): **107,106,105,104,102 101,101,100,100,99 90**
CSF £112.67 CT £1460.75 TOTE £5.40: £1.90, £5.70, £3.30; EX 126.60 Trifecta £1051.70.
Owner I J Heseltine **Bred** D A Yardy **Trained** Angmering, W Sussex

FOCUS
They appeared to go steadily and nothing got into it from off the pace. It's been rated around the second and third.

3347 INVESTEC ASSET MANAGEMENT H'CAP (FOR THE TOKYO TROPHY) 6f 3y
5:50 (5:54) (Class 2) (0-105,103) 4-Y-O+
£31,125 (£9,320; £4,660; £2,330; £1,165; £585) **Stalls** High

Form RPR

3141 **1** **Watchable**[28] 2393 9-8-11 **93**...................................(p) OisinMurphy 5 104
(David O'Meara) *mde all: rdn and kicked clr over 1f out: styd on strly ins fnl f: v readily* **8/1**[3]

1031 **2** *3 ½* **Lake Volta (IRE)**[8] 3043 4-9-7 **103**.......................... JoeFanning 12 103
(Mark Johnston) *looked wl; stmbld leaving stalls: chsd wnr: effrt 2f out: sn drvn and unable to match pce of wnr over 1f out: wl hld and kpt on same pce ins fnl f* **4/1**[1]

00-0 **3** *nk* **Squats (IRE)**[22] 2568 7-8-6 **88**.................................... JasonWatson 1 87
(Ian Williams) *chsd ldrs: effrt ent fnl 2f: unable to match pce of wnr over 1f out: kpt on same pce ins fnl f* **16/1**

0-10 **4** *3 ¾* **Reputation (IRE)**[17] 2743 6-9-1 **97**............................ BarryMcHugh 3 84
(Ruth Carr) *chsd ldrs: rdn over 2f out: unable qck 2f out: sn outpcd and wl hld fnl f* **9/2**[2]

46-2 **5** *shd* **Spanish City**[14] 2837 6-8-13 **95**................................ AndreaAtzeni 14 82+
(Roger Varian) *looked wl; hld up in rr: effrt but stl plenty to do whn nt clrest of runs over 1f out: rdn and hdwy 1f out: styd on: nvr trbld ldrs* **4/1**[1]

5-05 **6** ¾ **Helvetian**[12] 2917 4-8-0 **87** .... TheodoreLadd(5) 11 71+
(Mick Channon) *stmbld leaving stalls: racd in last quartet: effrt wl over 1f out: hdwy 1f out: kpt on ins fnl f: no threat to ldrs (jockey said gelding stumbled leaving the stalls)* **16/1**

2526 **7** ¾ **Areen Heart (FR)**[8] 3043 5-8-7 **89** .... ShaneGray 7 71
(David O'Meara) *t.k.h: hld up in tch in midfield: effrt 2f out: fnd little and btn over 1f out: wknd ins fnl f* **25/1**

3200 **8** ¾ **Stone Of Destiny**[43] 1919 4-9-6 **102** .... SilvestreDeSousa 9 81+
(Andrew Balding) *looked wl; t.k.h: hld up in last quartet: effrt 2f out: drvn and no hdwy over 1f out: nvr involved* **8/1**[3]

-061 **9** 1 ¼ **Manshood (IRE)**[25] 2508 6-8-2 **84** oh4........(b) JimmyQuinn 13 59
(Paul Midgley) *in tch in midfield on outer: effrt 2 out: no imp and wknd ins fnl f (jockey said gelding ran too free)* **33/1**

1-04 **10** 1 ¼ **Beyond Equal**[28] 2393 4-8-5 **87** .... MartinDwyer 6 58
(Stuart Kittow) *chsd ldrs: rdn over 2f out: unable qck and outpcd over 1f out: wknd fnl f* **8/1**[3]

5U-0 **11** nse **Blaine**[21] 2611 9-7-13 **84** oh7........(b) JamieGormley(3) 2 55
(Brian Barr) *s.i.s: a towards rr: effrt u.p on inner over 2f out: no prog and wknd fnl f* **33/1**

-001 **12** ½ **Harrogate (IRE)**[9] 3021 4-7-13 **84** oh5........(b[1]) GabrieleMalune(3) 4 54
(Jim Boyle) *hood off late and slowly away: bhd: hdwy into midfield after 2f: rdn over 2f out: lost pl and bhd over 1f out: wknd fnl f* **20/1**

12-0 **13** shd **Mountain Peak**[28] 2403 4-8-6 **88** .... CharlieBennett 8 57
(Ed Walker) *midfield: effrt ent fnl 2f: sn struggling and btn over 1f out: wknd fnl f* **20/1**

546- **14** nk **Ashpan Sam**[261] 7217 10-7-11 **86**........(p) EllieMacKenzie(7) 10 54
(David W Drinkwater) *midfield: lost pl and bhd whn stmbld over 1f out* **40/1**

1m 6.2s (-3.70) **Going Correction** -0.325s/f (Firm) course record **14** Ran SP% **125.0**
Speed ratings (Par 109): **111,106,105,100,100 99,98,97,96,94 94,93,93,93**
CSF £38.13 CT £534.58 TOTE £9.00: £2.50, £2.40, £4.40; EX 56.40 Trifecta £707.90.
Owner Hambleton Xxxix P Bamford Roses Partners **Bred** Cheveley Park Stud Ltd **Trained** Upper Helmsley, N Yorks

FOCUS
Run around the bend, this often favours the low drawn horses. Few got involved as Watchable took the race apart from the front in a course record time. The winner has been rated as running his best race in nearly three years.
T/Jkpt: Not won. T/Plt: £378.10 to a £1 stake. Pool: £248,370.06 - 479.46 winning units T/Qpdt: £150.70 to a £1 stake. Pool: £25,030.39 - 122.84 winning units **Steve Payne**

3252 LINGFIELD (L-H)
Saturday, June 1

OFFICIAL GOING: Good to firm (good in places; watered; 8.7)
Wind: virtually nil Weather: warm and sunny

3348 VISIT ATTHERACES.COM H'CAP — 1m 2f
5:45 (5:46) (Class 6) (0-55,60) 3-Y-O+
£3,105 (£924; £461; £400; £400; £400) **Stalls** Low

Form / RPR

000 **1** **Sir Canford (IRE)**[57] 1562 3-9-3 **55**........(p[1]) CharlesBishop 6 63
(Ali Stronge) *racd in tch in 5th: effrt on inner to chse ldr 2f out: rdn and gd prog over 1f out: styd on wl to ld wl ins fnl f* **12/1**

2141 **2** hd **Act Of Magic (IRE)**[2] 3256 3-9-8 **60** 6ex........ RobbieDowney 9 68
(Mohamed Moubarak) *racd in rr of midfield: hdwy over 2f out to chse ldr: rdn along to ld briefly 1f out: kpt on but unable to match wnr fnl 100yds* **5/6**[1]

0323 **3** 2 **Mongolia**[18] 2719 3-9-3 **55**........(p[1]) HollieDoyle 4 59
(Richard Hannon) *trckd ldr: pushed along to ld 2f out: rdn and hdd 1f out: one pce fnl f* **4/1**[2]

-405 **4** 1 ¼ **Cherry Cola**[22] 2566 3-9-3 **55** .... TrevorWhelan 1 57+
(Sheena West) *in rr of midfield: effrt on inner over 2f out: rdn 1f out: kpt on wl fnl f* **28/1**

0-06 **5** 2 ¼ **Forty Four Sunsets (FR)**[30] 2341 3-9-2 **54** .... SeanLevey 14 52
(Richard Hannon) *hld up: effrt to cl on outer over 2f out: rdn over 1f out: kpt on* **12/1**

0000 **6** 2 **With Pride**[56] 1593 3-8-4 **45**........(w) AaronJones(3) 3 40
(Clare Ellam) *led: rdn along and hdd 2f out: one pce fnl f* **50/1**

0-50 **7** 1 ¼ **Rocksette**[31] 2277 5-9-12 **51**........(p) TomQueally 8 44
(Gary Moore) *racd in midfield: rdn along and no imp 2f out: kpt on one pce fnl f (jockey said mare ran too freely)* **12/1**

306- **8** hd **Allofmelovesallofu**[257] 7361 5-9-4 **48** .... ThomasGreatrex(5) 10 41
(Ken Cunningham-Brown) *hld up: hdwy on outer to go 3rd 5f out: rdn along and ev ch 2f out: wknd fnl f* **20/1**

0005 **9** nse **Altaira**[66] 1362 8-9-6 **45**........(p) TomMarquand 5 38
(Tony Carroll) *racd in midfield: effrt to chse ldr 2f out: sn rdn and no imp 1f out: one pce after* **25/1**

-010 **10** 1 ¼ **Jazz Hands (IRE)**[18] 2712 3-8-9 **52** .... ConnorMurtagh(5) 7 42
(Richard Fahey) *racd in tch: pushed along 3f out: sn rdn and no imp 2f out: one pce fnl f* **10/1**[3]

0000 **11** 8 **Chutzpah (IRE)**[32] 2240 3-8-7 **48** .... WilliamCox(3) 12 23
(Mark Hoad) *trckd ldr: drvn along and lost pl 3f out: wknd over 1f out (jockey said gelding hung right-handed throughout)* **50/1**

4253 **12** ½ **Ahfad**[52] 1683 4-9-7 **46**........(b) HectorCrouch 11 21
(Gary Moore) *dwlt and racd in last: rdn along in rr over 3f out: nvr on terms (jockey said gelding reared as the stalls opened, was slowly away and ran too freely)* **22/1**

-000 **13** 11 **Invincible Sea (IRE)**[50] 1725 3-9-2 **54** .... GeorgeDowning 13 8
(Linda Jewell) *hld up: rdn along in rr 3f out: a bhd* **40/1**

2m 7.24s (-4.96) **Going Correction** -0.30s/f (Firm)
WFA 3 from 4yo+ 13lb **13** Ran SP% **129.5**
Speed ratings (Par 101): **107,106,105,104,102 100,99,99,99,98 92,91,83**
CSF £22.88 CT £57.32 TOTE £18.40: £4.10, £1.10, £1.90; EX 39.60 Trifecta £124.90.
Owner www.Select-Racing-Club.co.uk **Bred** Thomas Maher **Trained** Eastbury, Berks

FOCUS
A weak handicap but the winner pulled clear with a bang in-form rival so it should pay to be positive about the form.

3349 KAREN MILLS HAPPY BIRTHDAY H'CAP — 1m 3f 133y
6:15 (6:16) (Class 4) (0-80,81) 4-Y-O+ **£5,530** (£1,645; £822; £411) **Stalls** High

Form / RPR

6634 **1** **Winged Spur (IRE)**[9] 3000 4-9-6 **78** .... TomMarquand 4 86
(Mark Johnston) *hld up: rdn along to chse ldng pair over 2f out: drvn and styd on strly to ld wl ins fnl f* **7/2**[3]

5-04 **2** 2 **Blazing Saddles**[16] 2763 4-9-2 **74**........(b) HarryBentley 2 79
(Ralph Beckett) *chsd ldr: rdn to ld over 2f out: hung lft u.p ins fnl f: hdd by wnr fnl 50yds: no ex* **5/4**[1]

122- **3** 1 **Final Rock**[283] 6407 4-9-9 **81**........(p) RyanTate 3 84
(Sir Mark Prescott Bt) *pushed along fr stalls to ld: rdn along and hdd over 2f out: kpt on one pce fr over 1f out: nt match wnr fnl f* **10/3**[2]

540- **4** 2 ¾ **Vision Clear (GER)**[26] 8414 4-9-6 **78** .... HectorCrouch 1 77
(Gary Moore) *hld up: rdn and no imp 2f out: nvr able to land a blow* **7/2**[3]

2m 27.17s (-6.83) **Going Correction** -0.30s/f (Firm) **4** Ran SP% **112.0**
Speed ratings (Par 105): **110,108,108,106**
CSF £8.65 TOTE £4.70; EX 9.10.
Owner Kingsley Park 12 - Ready To Run **Bred** Mrs M B Brady **Trained** Middleham Moor, N Yorks
■ Stewards' Enquiry : Harry Bentley caution: careless riding

FOCUS
A tight little handicap run at a strong pace thanks to Final Rock. The winner swooped late from off the pace.

3350 MARTIN MATTHEWS 50TH BIRTHDAY FILLIES' NOVICE MEDIAN AUCTION STKS (PLUS 10 RACE) — 4f 217y
6:45 (6:45) (Class 5) 2-Y-O **£3,752** (£1,116; £557; £278) **Stalls** Centre

Form / RPR

26 **1** **Separate**[15] 2805 2-8-12 0 .... SeanLevey 3 84+
(Richard Hannon) *in tch: clsd on ldr gng wl 2f out: effrt to ld over 1f out: pushed out fnl f: comf* **4/6**[1]

1 **2** 3 ¾ **Probable Cause**[19] 2694 2-9-5 0 .... HollieDoyle 4 77
(Archie Watson) *broke smartly and led on stands' rail: rdn along and hdd by wnr over 1f out: kpt on fnl f (jockey said filly hung right-handed throughout)* **3/1**[2]

4 **3** 5 **Dynamighty**[12] 2918 2-8-12 0 .... HarryBentley 5 52
(Richard Spencer) *chsd ldr on rail: rdn and outpcd by front pair over 2f out: kpt on one pce fnl f* **4/1**[3]

00 **4** 2 **Flashy Flyer**[22] 2579 2-8-12 0 .... JoeyHaynes 1 45
(Dean Ivory) *racd in last and rn green: sme late hdwy u.p ins fnl f* **50/1**

5 2 ½ **A Go Go** 2-8-12 0 .... JFEgan 2 36
(David Evans) *hld up: pushed along and green 2f out: wknd fnl f* **20/1**

57.13s (-1.57) **Going Correction** -0.30s/f (Firm) **5** Ran SP% **111.7**
Speed ratings (Par 90): **100,94,86,82,78**
CSF £3.06 TOTE £1.50: £1.10, £1.80; EX 3.40 Trifecta £4.30.
Owner Martin Hughes & Mark Murphy **Bred** Guy Bloodstock Ltd **Trained** East Everleigh, Wilts

FOCUS
No depth to this fillies' event and they finished quite well strung out.

3351 MID-SUSSEX TIMBER 90TH ANNIVERSARY NOVICE STKS — 6f
7:15 (7:16) (Class 5) 3-Y-O+ **£3,752** (£1,116; £557; £278) **Stalls** Centre

Form / RPR

1 **1** **Nahaarr (IRE)**[28] 2397 3-9-4 0 .... GeorgiaCox(3) 4 76+
(William Haggas) *hld up: gd hdwy to chse ldr 2f out: rdn to ld jst ins fnl f: styd on wl* **13/8**[2]

11 **2** ¾ **Biometric**[15] 2790 3-10-0 92 .... HarryBentley 5 80+
(Ralph Beckett) *in tch in midfield: clsd on ldr u.p over 1f out: rdn and kpt on wl fnl f: nt pce of wnr* **8/13**[1]

5-00 **3** 1 **Global Hope (IRE)**[16] 2782 4-9-1 61........(t[1]) TobyEley(7) 6 65
(Gay Kelleway) *trckd ldr: rdn along to ld and ev ch over 1f out: kpt on one pce once hdd jst ins fnl f by wnr* **33/1**

0-0 **4** 2 **Broadhaven Dream (IRE)**[11] 2938 3-9-0 0 .... KieranO'Neill 3 57
(Ronald Harris) *hld up: hung lft to far rail u.p over 2f out: rdn and ev ch 1f out: one pce fnl f (jockey said gelding hung left-handed)* **100/1**

5 1 **Good Answer**[245] 7785 3-9-0 0 .... PatCosgrave 2 53
(Robert Cowell) *led: rdn along and hdd over 1f out: wknd fnl f* **50/1**

6 shd **Perfect Charm** 3-8-9 0 .... EdwardGreatrex 1 48
(Archie Watson) *dwlt and racd in last: rdn over 2f out and no imp: one pce fnl f* **12/1**[3]

1m 9.61s (-1.89) **Going Correction** -0.30s/f (Firm)
WFA 3 from 4yo 8lb **6** Ran SP% **113.6**
Speed ratings (Par 103): **100,99,97,95,93 93**
CSF £2.99 TOTE £2.30: £1.30, £1.10; EX 3.10 Trifecta £8.30.
Owner Sheikh Ahmed Al Maktoum **Bred** Rossenarra Bloodstock Limited **Trained** Newmarket, Suffolk

FOCUS
Effectively a match between two very promising colts.

3352 MALCOLM BROWN'S BIRTHDAY CELEBRATION H'CAP — 7f
7:45 (7:47) (Class 6) (0-55,59) 3-Y-O+
£3,105 (£924; £461; £400; £400; £400) **Stalls** Centre

Form / RPR

4-43 **1** **Liam's Lass (IRE)**[17] 2735 3-8-13 **54**........(p[1]) RobHornby 14 60
(Pam Sly) *racd in tch: effrt to chse ldr 2f out: rdn to ld on stands' rail 1f out: kpt on strly* **11/4**[1]

31-0 **2** 1 ¾ **Papa Delta**[22] 2580 5-9-10 **55** .... GeorgeDowning 12 60
(Tony Carroll) *racd in midfield: gd hdwy to ld 2f out: sn rdn and hdd by wnr 1f out: kpt on (jockey said gelding ran too freely)* **6/1**[3]

-430 **3** 1 **Three C's (IRE)**[52] 1683 5-9-6 **51**........(p) HollieDoyle 8 54
(Adrian Wintle) *chsd ldr: rdn along 2f out: drvn and no imp 1f out: no ex fnl f* **8/1**

5005 **4** shd **Sea Tea Dea**[11] 2930 5-8-12 **46** oh1........ FinleyMarsh(3) 16 49
(Adrian Wintle) *racd in midfield: effrt to chse wnr on rail 2f out: kpt on wl fnl f: nrst fin* **14/1**

0011 **5** 1 **Little Miss Daisy**[11] 2944 5-10-0 **59** .... SeanLevey 5 59
(William Muir) *racd in rr of midfield: rdn 2f out: kpt on but no imp fnl f* **7/2**[2]

/00- **6** nk **Golden Deal (IRE)**[155] 9735 4-9-7 **52** .... TomQueally 2 51
(Richard Phillips) *racd in midfield: hdwy u.p 2f out: rdn over 1f out: plugged on one pce fnl f* **33/1**

000 **7** 3 ¾ **Reformed Character (IRE)**[23] 2550 3-9-0 **55** .... BrettDoyle 17 40
(Lydia Pearce) *racd in rr of midfield: rdn along and no imp 3f out: hung lft 1f out: one pce fnl f* **20/1**

5240 **8** 1 ¼ **Slipalongtrevaskis**[9] 3007 6-9-1 **46** oh1........(v) JoeyHaynes 9 32
(Paul Howling) *racd in tch in 5th: rdn along and outpcd over 2f out: wknd ins fnl f* **12/1**

0364 **9** ¾ **Classy Cailin (IRE)**[51] 1722 4-9-6 **51** .... EdwardGreatrex 11 35
(Mark Loughnane) *walked to post early: racd in rr: rdn along 3f out: nvr on terms* **10/1**

5006 **10** ½ **Rapid Rise (IRE)**[31] 2286 5-9-1 **46** oh1........(p) TomMarquand 6 29
(Milton Bradley) *hld up: rdn along 1/2-way: nvr a factor* **25/1**

006- **11** ½ **Illustrious Spirit**[333] 4489 4-9-1 **46** .... CharlesBishop 7 28
(Ali Stronge) *led: rdn along and hdd 2f out: wknd fr 1f out* **22/1**

600- **12** 2 1/4 **Crimson Princess**[185] 9293 4-9-1 **46** oh1 TrevorWhelan 1 22
(Nikki Evans) *chsd ldr: drvn along over 2f out: wknd fr over 1f out (jockey said filly hung left-handed throughout)* **50/1**

00-6 **13** 1/2 **Flying Sakhee**[29] 2365 6-9-3 **48** KieranO'Neill 10 23
(John Bridger) *racd in rr: rdn and unable qck over 2f out: one pce fr 1f out* **10/1**

000- **14** 14 **Sussex Spirit**[164] 9603 3-7-12 **46** SophieRalston(7) 15
(Luke Dace) *hld up: a in rr: eased fnl f* **33/1**

1m 22.83s (-1.47) **Going Correction** -0.30s/f (Firm)
WFA 3 from 4yo+ 10lb **14** Ran SP% **127.6**
Speed ratings (Par 101): **96,94,92,92,91 91,86,85,84,84 83,80,80,64**
CSF £18.89 CT £126.86 TOTE £3.90: £2.20, £2.10, £2.70; EX 22.00 Trifecta £107.60.
Owner Mrs P M Sly **Bred** L Lynch & R Sherrard **Trained** Thorney, Cambs

FOCUS
The rail so often proves the place to be in big-field events on the straight course here and that once again proved to be the case.

3353 SKY SPORTS RACING ON SKY 415 MEDIAN AUCTION MAIDEN STKS 7f
8:15 (8:17) (Class 6) 3-5-Y-O **£3,105** (£924; £461; £230) **Stalls** Centre

Form RPR

004- **1** **Heroic**[217] 8630 3-9-2 73 KieranShoemark 7 75
(Charles Hills) *mde all: rdn to maintain short ld wl over 1f out: drvn and kpt on wl for press fnl f: a doing enough* **15/8**[2]

3-42 **2** nk **Voltaic**[11] 2925 3-9-2 76 HarryBentley 1 74
(Paul Cole) *hld up: effrt to chse wnr on outer over 2f out: drvn along and kpt on wl fnl f: nvr quite doing enough* **8/11**[1]

6- **3** nk **Jack D'Or**[241] 7907 3-9-2 0 HectorCrouch 4 73
(Ed Walker) *settled wl in 3rd: rdn along to chse wnr 2f out: drvn and ev ch 1f out: kpt on* **6/1**[3]

0 **4** 14 **Stepaside Boy**[12] 2900 3-9-2 0 JFEgan 3 37
(David Evans) *hld up: rdn and outpcd over 2f out: sn bhd* **50/1**

0 **5** 1 1/2 **Mousquetaire (FR)**[57] 1562 3-9-2 0 (h[1]) JasonWatson 2 33
(David Menuisier) *chsd ldr: j. path and briefly unbalanced 4f out: sn rdn and grad wknd fr 2f out (jockey said gelding jumped the road crossing and moved poorly thereafter)* **40/1**

6 3 1/4 **Ewell Spring** 3-8-4 0 LeviWilliams(7) 6 20
(Brett Johnson) *racd in midfield: rdn and readily lft bhd 2f out* **66/1**

1m 23.22s (-1.08) **Going Correction** -0.30s/f (Firm)
WFA 3 from 4yo 10lb **6** Ran SP% **112.9**
Speed ratings (Par 101): **94,93,93,77,75 71**
CSF £3.62 TOTE £2.80: £1.60, £1.10; EX 3.60 Trifecta £6.10.
Owner Mrs J K Powell **Bred** R Kent & D Evans **Trained** Lambourn, Berks
■ Perfect Challenge was withdrawn. Price at time of withdrawal 40-1. Rule 4 does not apply.

FOCUS
Not a strong maiden by any means and the front three came a long way clear.

3354 SKY SPORTS RACING ON VIRGIN 535 H'CAP 7f 135y
8:45 (8:47) (Class 6) (0-65,67) 3-Y-O
£3,105 (£924; £461; £400; £400; £400) **Stalls** Centre

Form RPR

60-0 **1** **Song Of The Isles (IRE)**[16] 2772 3-8-7 **58** EllieMacKenzie(7) 15 66
(Heather Main) *settled wl handily: rdn to chse ldr 2f out: drvn and kpt on strly to ld fnl 50yds (trainer's rep said, regarding the improved form shown, the filly has been slow to come to hand and benefited from the step up in trip)* **14/1**

-640 **2** 1/2 **Bataar (IRE)**[16] 2766 3-9-4 **67** ConnorMurtagh(5) 17 74
(Richard Fahey) *trckd ldr: swtchd lft off rail over 1f out: rdn to ld 1f out: kpt on but hdd by wnr fnl 50yds* **7/4**[1]

-360 **3** 3 **Chop Chop (IRE)**[15] 2798 3-8-13 **57** (b[1]) JasonWatson 14 57
(Roger Charlton) *led and got to stands' rail 4f out: rdn along and hdd 1f out: one pce fnl f* **5/1**[2]

3202 **4** 2 1/2 **Eye Of The Water (IRE)**[11] 2939 3-9-4 **62** KieranO'Neill 3 56
(Ronald Harris) *hld up: effrt to chse ldr over 2f out: kpt on wl fnl f* **6/1**

0-00 **5** 6 **Mystical Jadeite**[19] 2690 3-9-4 **62** RossaRyan 16 42
(Grace Harris) *chsd ldr: rdn and outpcd over 2f out: kpt on one pce fnl f* **14/1**

5-40 **6** 1 **Global Destination (IRE)**[67] 1346 3-9-9 **67** (w) TomQueally 5 44
(Ed Dunlop) *hld up: rdn and little imp over 2f out: kpt on fnl f* **11/2**[3]

00-0 **7** 1/2 **Grandad's Legacy**[30] 2341 3-9-0 **58** (h[1]) TomMarquand 9 34
(Ali Stronge) *racd in midfield: rdn and no imp 2f out: one pce fnl f* **20/1**

50-0 **8** 3 3/4 **Ragstone Cowboy (IRE)**[33] 2204 3-9-4 **62** (h) ShaneKelly 7 29
(Murty McGrath) *racd in rr of midfield: rdn and outpcd 3f out: nvr on terms* **50/1**

5-40 **9** nk **Invincible One (IRE)**[68] 1337 3-9-2 **65** PoppyBridgwater(5) 6 32
(Sylvester Kirk) *racd in midfield: rdn along and outpcd over 2f out: one pce fnl f (jockey said gelding did not handle the undulations of the track and became unbalanced)* **8/1**

-405 **10** 2 **Paddy's Pursuit (IRE)**[80] 1178 3-9-7 **65** (p[1]) EdwardGreatrex 13 27
(Mark Loughnane) *racd keenly in midfield: rdn over 2f out: nvr on terms* **33/1**

-000 **11** 1 1/4 **Sussex Solo**[50] 1726 3-8-1 **52** IsobelFrancis(7) 12 11
(Luke Dace) *awkward leaving stalls and racd in rr: rdn 1/2-way: nvr a factor* **16/1**

0000 **12** 1 1/2 **Axel Jacklin**[15] 2798 3-9-3 **61** (p[1]) JoeyHaynes 2 17
(Paul Howling) *hld up: a in rr* **50/1**

03-0 **13** 4 1/2 **Adena Star (IRE)**[66] 1359 3-9-7 **65** RobHornby 11 10
(Jonathan Portman) *racd in midfield on stands' rail: rdn along and wknd fr 2f out (jockey said filly lost its action)* **25/1**

1m 30.1s (-1.60) **Going Correction** -0.30s/f (Firm) **13** Ran SP% **128.5**
Speed ratings (Par 97): **96,95,92,90,84 83,82,78,78,76 75,73,69**
CSF £40.04 CT £154.20 TOTE £17.50: £4.60, £1.30, £2.30; EX 59.40.
Owner Donald M Kerr **Bred** Seamus Phelan **Trained** Kingston Lisle, Oxon
■ Stewards' Enquiry : Connor Murtagh four-day ban: used whip above the permitted level (Jun 15-17, 23)

FOCUS
Very few with good recent form to their name and they finished well strung out.
T/Plt: £9.70 to a £1 stake. Pool: £46,627.46 - 3,499.84 winning units T/Qpdt: £2.00 to a £1 stake. Pool: £4,621.57 - 1,699.63 winning units **Mark Grantham**

2677 **MUSSELBURGH** (R-H)
Saturday, June 1
OFFICIAL GOING: Good to soft (soft in places)
Wind: fresh across Weather: Cloudy

3355 EBFSTALLIONS.COM EDINBURGH CASTLE STKS (A CONDITIONS RACE) (PLUS 10 RACE) 5f 1y
1:40 (1:41) (Class 2) 2-Y-O **£12,450** (£3,728; £1,864) **Stalls** High

Form RPR

1 **Bill Neigh** 2-8-11 0 CierenFallon 5 79+
(John Ryan) *stmbld sltly jst after s: trckd ldrs: pushed along to ld over 1f out: rdn and kpt on fnl f* **7/1**[3]

0 **2** 3 **My Kinda Day (IRE)**[16] 2780 2-9-0 0 TonyHamilton 2 71
(Richard Fahey) *led: rdn and hdd over 1f out: no ex ins fnl f* **10/11**[1]

3 **3** 13 **She Looks Like Fun**[14] 2820 2-8-9 0 CliffordLee 1 19
(K R Burke) *prom: rdn over 2f out: hung rt and sn wknd (jockey said filly hung right from half way)* **5/4**[2]

1m 1.55s (1.85) **Going Correction** +0.375s/f (Good) **3** Ran SP% **109.3**
Speed ratings (Par 99): **100,95,74**
CSF £13.71 TOTE £5.50; EX 11.00 Trifecta £9.60.
Owner Gerry McGladery **Bred** Selwood Bloodstock Ltd **Trained** Newmarket, Suffolk

FOCUS
The going was good to soft, soft in places. Rails on innermost position so all distances as advertised. Some nice juveniles have won this contest over the years, including the subsequent Group 2 winner Frederick Engels, but with the absence of Strive For Glory this was reduced to an uncompetitive three-runner event for the money. Still, no shortage of drama with the outsider of the trio proving much too good.

3356 PACE YOURSELF TO GO THE DISTANCE H'CAP 1m 208y
2:15 (2:16) (Class 4) (0-80,86) 4-Y-O+
£5,692 (£1,694; £846; £423; £300; £300) **Stalls** Low

Form RPR

-541 **1** **Mulligatawny (IRE)**[4] 3180 6-9-8 **86** 5ex (p) BenSanderson(5) 6 92
(Roger Fell) *in tch: hdwy and chsd ldr 2f out: rdn to ld 110yds: drvn and kpt on* **4/1**[3]

63- **2** 1/2 **Be Kool (IRE)**[290] 6147 6-9-1 **77** (v) BenRobinson(3) 5 82
(Brian Ellison) *prom: rdn to ld narrowly 2f out: drvn and hdd 110yds out: one pce* **8/1**

0-02 **3** nk **Swift Emperor (IRE)**[18] 2710 7-9-7 **80** BenCurtis 1 84
(David Barron) *trckd ldrs on inner: pushed along and n.m.r over 2f out tl over 1f out: rdn and kpt on fnl f* **15/8**[1]

1260 **4** nk **Mont Kinabalu (IRE)**[14] 2842 4-9-1 **74** TomEaves 7 78
(Kevin Ryan) *in tch: rdn along over 2f out: angled lft to outer ent fnl f: kpt on* **14/1**

/-41 **5** 1/2 **Furzig**[14] 2842 4-9-0 **78** SeanDavis(5) 3 81
(Richard Fahey) *in tch: pushed along and hdwy over 2f out: rdn to chal 2f out: no ex fnl 110yds* **11/4**[2]

410- **6** 3/4 **Rose Tinted Spirit**[191] 9204 4-9-7 **80** JasonHart 8 81
(Karen McLintock) *led: rdn and hdd 2f out: sn outpcd: kpt on ins fnl f* **7/1**

034- **7** 1/2 **First Flight (IRE)**[204] 8974 8-9-2 **75** CamHardie 4 75
(Brian Ellison) *slowly away: hld up in rr: rdn along over 2f out: one pce and nvr threatened (jockey said gelding missed the break)* **16/1**

1m 56.47s (3.37) **Going Correction** +0.375s/f (Good) **7** Ran SP% **117.6**
Speed ratings (Par 105): **100,99,99,99,98 97,97**
CSF £36.55 CT £78.95 TOTE £4.00: £2.10, £3.80; EX 44.40 Trifecta £136.10.
Owner Middleham Park Racing Li & Partner **Bred** Pat O'Rourke **Trained** Nawton, N Yorks

FOCUS
A fair handicap, but the pace was ordinary and the main protagonists finished in a heap. The winner has been rated in line with his best form over the past year.

3357 MADELEINE CUP H'CAP 7f 33y
2:50 (2:54) (Class 3) (0-90,89) 3-Y-O **£12,161** (£3,619; £1,808; £904) **Stalls** Low

Form RPR

-542 **1** **Brian Epstein (IRE)**[14] 2821 3-9-5 **87** RichardKingscote 4 98
(Richard Hannon) *trckd ldrs: pushed along to ld 2f out: sn in command: rdn and edgd rt ins fnl f: kpt on wl* **9/2**[3]

3-24 **2** 2 3/4 **King Of Tonga (IRE)**[23] 2559 3-9-1 **88** SeanDavis(5) 2 92
(Richard Fahey) *trckd ldrs: drvn to chse ldr over 1f out: kpt on but a hld* **7/2**[2]

-252 **3** 1 1/2 **Reeves**[17] 2746 3-9-5 **87** (p) RaulDaSilva 6 87
(Robert Cowell) *hld up: rdn over 2f out: kpt on fr over 1f out: wnt 3rd ins fnl f* **9/2**[3]

1-42 **4** 4 **Aplomb (IRE)**[22] 2567 3-9-1 **83** DanielTudhope 7 72+
(William Haggas) *dwlt sltly: hld up: pushed along and hdwy on outer 3f out: chsd ldr 2f out: wknd fnl f* **9/4**[1]

40-3 **5** nk **Celebrity Dancer (IRE)**[22] 2570 3-9-7 **89** KevinStott 9 77
(Kevin Ryan) *prom: rdn over 2f out: wknd over 1f out* **16/1**

6-04 **6** nse **I Am A Dreamer**[17] 2746 3-8-11 **79** JasonHart 1 67
(Mark Johnston) *midfield on inner: rdn over 2f out: wknd over 1f out* **12/1**

-004 **7** 1 **Battle Of Waterloo (IRE)**[29] 2364 3-8-4 **79** CierenFallon(7) 3 65
(John Ryan) *midfield: rdn over 2f out: wknd over 1f out* **12/1**

222- **8** 2 1/2 **Theatre Of War (IRE)**[198] 9083 3-8-12 **80** TomEaves 5 59
(Keith Dalgleish) *led: rdn and hdd 2f out: sn wknd* **20/1**

-210 **9** 10 **Pacino**[23] 2559 3-8-13 **81** TonyHamilton 8 33
(Richard Fahey) *midfield: rdn over 2f out: wknd and bhd* **25/1**

1m 30.38s (1.38) **Going Correction** +0.375s/f (Good) **9** Ran SP% **119.2**
Speed ratings (Par 103): **107,103,102,97,97 97,96,93,81**
CSF £21.42 CT £76.69 TOTE £5.60: £1.70, £1.50, £1.60; EX 22.00 Trifecta £104.40.
Owner Chelsea Thoroughbreds & Martin Hughes **Bred** Epona Bloodstock Ltd **Trained** East Everleigh, Wilts

FOCUS
A warm 3yo handicap, but they finished well spread out and this is form to view positively. The level is a bit fluid.

3358 GAYNOR WINYARD H'CAP 1m 4f 104y
3:25 (3:25) (Class 3) (0-90,85) 3-Y-O
£15,562 (£4,660; £2,330; £1,165; £582; £292) **Stalls** Low

Form RPR

021 **1** **Just Benjamin**[31] 2284 3-9-1 **79** DanielTudhope 5 90+
(William Haggas) *midfield: smooth hdwy over 3f out and sn trckd ldrs: pushed into ld over 1f out: drvn ins fnl f: styd on wl* **9/2**[3]

22-2 **2** 2 1/2 **Gravistas**[19] 2697 3-9-1 **79** JasonHart 7 86
(Mark Johnston) *hld up: sltly impeded 4f out: sn rdn along: hdwy over 2f out: chsd ldr jst ins fnl f: styd on* **10/3**[1]

13-5 **3** 3 1/4 **Aspire Tower (IRE)**[27] 2446 3-9-7 **85** RichardKingscote 8 87
(Steve Gollings) *pressed ldr: rdn 3f out: led 2f out: hdd over 1f out: wknd ins fnl f* **12/1**

2133 **4** 7 **Rochester House (IRE)**[15] 2811 3-9-6 **84** ConnorBeasley 4 75
(Mark Johnston) *hld up: rdn along 4f out: plugged on to go remote 4th ins fnl f* **4/1**[2]

1-04 **5** 1 1/4 **Dark Lochnagar (USA)**[15] 2811 3-8-12 **81** SeanDavis(5) 3 70
(Keith Dalgleish) *midfield: rdn over 3f out: no imp* **7/1**

4-20 **6** 1 **Beechwood Jude (FR)**[15] 2811 3-8-10 **74** TomEaves 6 62
(Keith Dalgleish) *led narrowly: rdn and hdd 2f out: sn wknd* **33/1**

22-1 **7** 18 **Dancin Boy**[30] 2336 3-9-5 **83** PaulMulrennan 10 43
(Michael Dods) *hld up in midfield: rdn over 3f out: wknd over 2f out* **10/1**

6-42 **8** 23 **L'Un Deux Trois (IRE)**[34] 2150 3-8-7 **71** HayleyTurner 2
(Michael Bell) *trckd ldrs: rdn along over 4f out: wknd over 3f out: eased* **4/1**[2]

112- **9** 20 **Calling The Wind (IRE)**[212] 8782 3-9-2 **80** (b) BenCurtis 9
(Sir Mark Prescott Bt) *trckd ldrs: rdn along over 5f out: wknd 4f out: sn t.o* **9/1**

2m 45.0s (0.50) **Going Correction** +0.375s/f (Good) **9** Ran SP% **123.5**
Speed ratings (Par 103): **113,111,109,104,103 103,91,75,62**
CSF £21.49 CT £175.82 TOTE £5.20: £1.90, £1.50, £3.70; EX 22.70 Trifecta £264.20.
Owner Ian and Christine Beard **Bred** Mrs J M Quy **Trained** Newmarket, Suffolk

FOCUS
Another nice 3yo handicap and another race where they finished well spread out, won by the least-exposed runner in the field. Solid form. The third has been rated close to his 2yo form.

3359 STOBO CASTLE LADIES' DAY GOLD CUP FILLIES' STKS (REGISTERED AS THE MAGGIE DICKSON STAKES) (LISTED) 7f 33y

4:00 (4:02) (Class 1) 3-Y-O+

£22,684 (£8,600; £4,304; £2,144; £1,076; £540) **Stalls** Low

Form RPR

33-0 **1** **Indian Blessing**[26] 2493 5-9-1 105 GeraldMosse 6 103+
(Ed Walker) *prom: led over 2f out: rdn clr appr fnl f: kpt on wl: eased nr fin* **6/1**

06-5 **2** 1 1/2 **Wisdom Mind (IRE)**[13] 2879 4-9-1 85 (t) JasonHart 5 98
(Joseph Patrick O'Brien, Ire) *hld up: pushed along and n.m.r over 1f out: angled lft and in clr appr fnl f: kpt on wl: wnt 2nd nr fin* **16/1**

-263 **3** hd **Red Starlight**[21] 2608 4-9-1 100 DanielTudhope 1 97
(Richard Hannon) *trckd ldrs: rdn over 2f out: chsd ldr appr fnl f: kpt on same pce: lost 2nd nr fin* **5/4**[1]

3-30 **4** 1 1/4 **Cava (IRE)**[22] 2605 3-8-5 99 HayleyTurner 2 90
(Joseph Patrick O'Brien, Ire) *hld up in tch on inner: pushed along and bit short of room over 2f out: rdn over 1f out: styd on ins fnl f* **11/2**[3]

60-4 **5** 1 1/4 **New Day Dawn (IRE)**[15] 2809 4-9-1 92 RichardKingscote 7 91
(Tom Dascombe) *trckd ldrs: rdn over 2f out: wknd ins fnl f* **16/1**

10-4 **6** 1 1/2 **Concello (IRE)**[39] 2027 3-8-5 92 (b1) BenCurtis 4 83
(Archie Watson) *led: rdn and hdd over 2f out: wknd ins fnl f* **14/1**

13-1 **7** 1 1/2 **Ice Gala**[34] 2144 3-8-5 95 JosephineGordon 8 79
(William Haggas) *wnt rt s and bmpd into rival: hld up: rdn and sme hdwy on outer over 2f out: wknd fnl f* **3/1**[2]

145- **8** 7 **Nicki's Angel (IRE)**[308] 5455 3-8-5 90 SeanDavis 3 60
(Richard Fahey) *midfield: rdn over 2f out: wknd over 1f out* **25/1**

1m 30.61s (1.61) **Going Correction** +0.375s/f (Good)
WFA 3 from 4yo+ 10lb **8** Ran SP% **121.4**
Speed ratings (Par 108): **105,103,103,101,100 98,96,88**
CSF £98.47 TOTE £7.60: £2.10, £3.70, £1.10; EX 94.40 Trifecta £313.60.
Owner P K Siu **Bred** Jocelyn Targett **Trained** Upper Lambourn, Berks

FOCUS
An interesting fillies' Listed contest won in fine style by the class act of the race. The winner has been rated close to form.

3360 MCGLADERY AND FRIENDS H'CAP 5f 1y

4:55 (4:55) (Class 3) (0-90,89) 4-Y-O+

£12,031 (£3,602; £1,801; £900; £450; £226) **Stalls** High

Form RPR

5-12 **1** **Makanah**[12] 2910 4-9-7 **89** PaulMulrennan 3 99
(Julie Camacho) *trckd ldr: pushed along to ld ins fnl f: kpt on wl: comf* **13/8**[1]

4646 **2** 2 1/4 **Primo's Comet**[14] 2843 4-8-2 **77** CoreyMadden(7) 4 79
(Jim Goldie) *hld up: pushed along over 1f out: n.m.r appr fnl f: r.o wl fnl 150yds: wnt 2nd post (jockey said gelding hung left was was denied a clear run 1f out)* **5/1**

0-03 **3** nse **Hawaam (IRE)**[21] 2625 4-8-10 **78** (p) BenCurtis 7 80
(Roger Fell) *led: rdn over 1f out: hdd ins fnl f: sn no ex: lost 2nd post* **9/2**[3]

315- **4** 1 1/2 **Fairy Falcon**[253] 7480 4-9-6 **88** DanielTudhope 6 84
(Bryan Smart) *dwlt sltly: hld up: pushed along over 2f out: rdn over 1f out: one pce fnl f and nvr threatened* **4/1**[2]

2030 **5** 3/4 **Landing Night (IRE)**[14] 2841 7-8-2 **70** (tp) CamHardie 1 64
(Rebecca Menzies) *hld up: rdn and sme hdwy on outer over 1f out: no ex fnl 75yds* **14/1**

-000 **6** shd **Requinto Dawn (IRE)**[12] 2910 4-7-13 **72** (p) SeanDavis(5) 2 65
(Richard Fahey) *in tch: rdn over 1f out: no ex whn n.m.r 75yds out* **7/1**

5-00 **7** 1 1/2 **Robot Boy (IRE)**[28] 2421 9-8-5 **78** HarrisonShaw(5) 8 66
(Marjorie Fife) *chsd ldr: rdn over 1f out: sn wknd* **16/1**

1m 0.56s (0.86) **Going Correction** +0.375s/f (Good) **7** Ran SP% **118.0**
Speed ratings (Par 107): **108,104,104,101,100 100,98**
CSF £10.78 CT £31.43 TOTE £2.40: £1.50, £3.50; EX 11.00 Trifecta £37.90.
Owner Axom Lxxi **Bred** Y E Mullin & Theobalds Stud **Trained** Norton, N Yorks

FOCUS
A useful sprint handicap and fast and furious stuff.

3361 SILK SERIES LADY RIDERS' H'CAP (PRO-AM LADY RIDERS' RACE) 1m 5f 216y

5:30 (5:30) (Class 4) (0-80,78) 4-Y-O+

£5,692 (£1,694; £846; £423; £300; £300) **Stalls** Low

Form RPR

3242 **1** **Royal Cosmic**[3] 3222 5-9-11 **71** MeganNicholls(3) 2 78
(Richard Fahey) *trckd ldrs: rdn to ld narrowly over 1f out: drvn fnl f: hld on wl* **7/4**[1]

6006 **2** hd **Baydar**[22] 2578 6-9-11 **73** (v) MissJoannaMason(5) 3 79
(Ian Williams) *trckd ldrs: rdn to chal strly over 1f out: styd on wl but a jst hld* **3/1**[2]

-045 **3** 2 1/4 **Searching (IRE)**[14] 2819 7-9-8 **68** GemmaTutty(3) 4 71
(Karen Tutty) *led: rdn and hdd 2f out: remained chalng tl no ex fnl 110yds* **10/1**

550 **4** hd **Loud And Clear**[16] 2781 8-9-13 **75** MissCatherineWalton(5) 8 78
(Jim Goldie) *hld up: rdn along over 2f out: styd on wl fnl 150yds: nrst fin* **6/1**

00-2 **5** 1/2 **Sebastian's Wish (IRE)**[30] 2326 6-10-0 **71** HayleyTurner 5 73
(Keith Dalgleish) *prom: rdn over 2f out: led narrowly 2f out: hdd over 1f out: wknd fnl 110yds* **11/2**[3]

050/ **6** 1 1/4 **Ballynanty (IRE)**[50] 1171 7-10-6 **77** (t) LucyAlexander 10 77
(N W Alexander) *midfield: rdn over 2f out: styd on fnl f: nvr trbld ldrs* **25/1**

3006 **7** 5 **Battle Of Marathon (USA)**[21] 2620 7-10-0 **78** LauraPearson(7) 1 71
(John Ryan) *s.i.s: hld up: rdn over 3f out: sn wknd* **25/1**

55-3 **8** 5 **Needs To Be Seen (FR)**[16] 2763 4-10-4 **75** (p) JosephineGordon 7 61
(John Ryan) *v.s.a and briefly detached in rr: in tch w main field 10f out: rdn over 3f out: sn btn (jockey said gelding was slowly away)* **6/1**

156- **9** 4 1/2 **An Fear Ciuin (IRE)**[16] 5737 8-10-0 **74** MrsCarolBartley(3) 6 54
(R Mike Smith) *midfield: rdn over 2f out: wknd over 1f out* **25/1**

3m 13.89s (9.99) **Going Correction** +0.375s/f (Good) **9** Ran SP% **125.9**
Speed ratings (Par 105): **86,85,84,84,84 83,80,77,75**
CSF £7.72 CT £40.31 TOTE £2.70: £1.20, £1.40, £2.60; EX 8.50 Trifecta £69.60.
Owner The Cosmic Cases **Bred** The Cosmic Cases **Trained** Musley Bank, N Yorks

FOCUS
A fair staying handicap, though the pace was steady and there were four in a line entering the last furlong. Again the winner was well backed. It's been rated a bit cautiously.
T/Plt: £495.30 to a £1 stake. Pool: £47,221.32 - 69.59 winning units T/Qpdt: £14.20 to a £1 stake. Pool: £5,354.80 - 279.01 winning units **Andrew Shert**

3362 - 3368a (Foreign Racing) - See Raceform Interactive

3287

BADEN-BADEN (L-H)

Saturday, June 1

OFFICIAL GOING: Turf: good

3369a PREIS DER ANNETTE HELLWIG STIFTUNG - SILBERNE PEITSCHE (GROUP 3) (3YO+) (TURF) 6f

4:10 3-Y-O+ **£28,828** (£10,810; £5,405; £2,702; £1,801)

RPR

1 **Namos (GER)**[15] 3-8-13 0 WladimirPanov 5 107
(D Moser, Germany) *w.w in rr: shkn up and stdy prog over 1 1/2f out: sustained run fnl f to ld fnl 75yds: readily* **152/10**

2 1/2 **The Right Man**[63] 1442 7-9-6 0 Francois-XavierBertras 3 106
(D Guillemin, France) *a cl up: drvn to ld ins fnl 1 1/2f: rdn and styd on fnl f but edgd lft: hdd fnl 75yds: no ex* **1/2**[1]

3 3 3/4 **McQueen (FR)**[21] 2676 7-9-6 0 MichaelCadeddu 4 94
(Yasmin Almenrader, Germany) *racd in fnl trio: drvn to chse ldrs 2f out: 4th and rdn wl over 1f out: kpt on at same pce* **132/10**

4 3/4 **Iron Duke (GER)**[21] 2676 3-8-13 0 AndraschStarke 7 91
(P Schiergen, Germany) *midfield: nt qckn whn asked ent fnl 2f: kpt on same pce: nvr able to mount a chal* **15/1**

5 hd **Yuman (FR)**[11] 2955 5-9-6 0 (b) BauyrzhanMurzabayev 6 91
(M Rulec, Germany) *chsd ldr: 2nd and ev ch whn rdn 1 1/2f out: nt match ldrs appr fnl f: one pce u.p* **181/10**

6 1/2 **Julio (GER)**[21] 2676 4-9-6 0 AdriedeVries 2 89
(Jean-Pierre Carvalho, Germany) *racd in fnl trio: outpcd and drvn ins fnl 2f: kpt on fnl f but nt pce to get involved* **105/10**[3]

7 1/2 **Shining Emerald**[21] 2676 8-9-6 0 EduardoPedroza 1 88
(A Wohler, Germany) *bmpd leaving stalls: racd in fnl trio: rdn and no imp 2f out: nvr able to get in contention* **105/10**[3]

8 1 1/4 **Zargun (GER)**[21] 2676 4-9-6 0 (p) AntoineHamelin 8 84
(Henk Grewe, Germany) *bmpd rival leaving stalls: led: brought field stands' side st: hdd ins fnl 1 1/2f: sn dropped away* **93/10**[2]

1m 8.32s (-1.97)
WFA 3 from 4yo+ 8lb **8** Ran SP% **118.5**
PARI-MUTUEL (all including 1 euro stake): WIN 16.20 PLACE: 2.90, 1.60, 2.50; SF: 32.90.
Owner Stall Namaskar **Bred** Gestut Brummerhof **Trained** Germany

3370 - (Foreign Racing) - See Raceform Interactive

2931

NOTTINGHAM (L-H)

Sunday, June 2

OFFICIAL GOING: Good (good to firm in places; watered) changing to good after race 3 (3.20)
Wind: Light against Weather: Raining

3371 EBF MAIDEN STKS 5f 8y

2:10 (2:13) (Class 5) 2-Y-O **£3,881** (£1,155; £577; £288) **Stalls** High

Form RPR

1 **Al Aakif (IRE)** 2-9-5 0 JimCrowley 7 84+
(William Haggas) *uns rdr to post: restless in stalls: a.p: racd keenly: shkn up to ld over 1f out: edgd lft ins fnl f: pushed out* **13/8**[1]

50 **2** 2 3/4 **Corndavon Lad (IRE)**[19] 2706 2-9-5 0 PaulHanagan 2 73
(Richard Fahey) *led over 3f: edgd lft and no ex wl ins fnl f* **16/1**

3 1/2 **Tom Tulliver** 2-9-5 0 DavidNolan 3 71
(Declan Carroll) *uns rdr to post: sn prom: rdn over 1f out: edgd lft ins fnl f: styd on* **7/1**[3]

24 **4** 3 **Beignet (IRE)**[33] 2248 2-9-0 0 SeanLevey 6 55
(Richard Hannon) *chsd ldr: led briefly over 1f out: wknd ins fnl f* **9/4**[2]

00 **5** 1 1/2 **Walton Thorns (IRE)**[16] 2792 2-9-5 0 KieranShoemark 1 55
(Charles Hills) *trckd ldrs: racd keenly: shkn up over 1f out: edgd lft and wknd fnl f* **9/1**

6 1/2 **Jazz Style (IRE)** 2-9-5 0 PaulMulrennan 4 53
(David Brown) *s.i.s: sn pushed along towards rr: rdn and wknd over 1f out* **20/1**

7 2 1/2 **Jochi Khan (USA)** 2-9-0 0 SeanDavis(5) 5 44
(Robert Cowell) *restless in stalls: dwlt: rn green in rr: bhd fr 1/2-way* **9/1**

8 7 **Apachito** 2-9-5 0 RossaRyan 8 19
(Kevin Frost) *s.i.s: pushed along and sme hdwy 3f out: wknd 1/2-way* **66/1**

1m 2.14s (1.94) **Going Correction** 0.0s/f (Good) **8** Ran SP% **113.5**
Speed ratings (Par 93): **84,79,78,74,71 70,66,55**
CSF £29.27 TOTE £2.30: £1.10, £3.00, £2.20; EX 23.00 Trifecta £171.70.

The Form Book Flat 2019, Raceform Ltd, Newbury, RG14 5SJ

Owner Hamdan Al Maktoum **Bred** Rathbarry Stud **Trained** Newmarket, Suffolk

FOCUS

Outer track in use, and the rail was out 4yds all round. There was rain in the hour before racing and the going was changed to good, good to firm in places before the first race. Jockeys returning after the opener said the ground was no faster than good, with one even saying it was good to soft. A maiden that probably lacked strength in depth.

3372 LIKE RACING TV ON FACEBOOK NOVICE STKS — 1m 75y

2:45 (2:48) (Class 5) 3-Y-O — £3,881 (£1,155; £577; £288) Stalls Centre

Form					RPR
51-	1		**Dal Horrisgle**[190] 9254 3-9-9 SilvestreDeSousa 5 (William Haggas) *mde all: shkn up over 2f out: styd on*	3/1[2]	90+
1-	2	3/4	**Loolwah (IRE)**[218] 8637 3-9-4 JimCrowley 4 (Sir Michael Stoute) *a.p: shkn up and swtchd rt over 2f out: rdn to chse wnr over 1f out: styd on*	5/1[3]	83
	3	1 3/4	**Saffran (IRE)** 3-9-2 DaneO'Neill 2 (Simon Crisford) *s.s: hld up: hdwy over 2f out: r.o to go 3rd wl ins fnl f: nt rch ldrs*	12/1	77+
5	4	nk	**San Sebastian (IRE)**[58] 1562 3-9-2 RobertHavlin 10 (Ed Dunlop) *broke wl: sn stdd and lost pl: hdwy over 2f out: r.o: nt rch ldrs*	33/1	76
-4	5	1 1/2	**My Style (IRE)**[33] 2249 3-9-2 CharlesBishop 9 (Eve Johnson Houghton) *chsd ldrs: rdn over 2f out: no ex ins fnl f*	7/1	73
4	6	hd	**Meqdam (IRE)**[16] 2802 3-9-2 PatCosgrave 8 (Saeed bin Suroor) *sn pushed along to chse wnr: rdn over 2f out: lost 2nd over 1f out: wknd wl ins fnl f*	10/11[1]	73
00	7	7	**Verify**[16] 2795 3-9-2 (h) LiamKeniry 3 (Ed Walker) *s.s: hld up: racd keenly: nvr nrr*	40/1	56
50	8	7	**Plissken**[23] 2583 3-8-11 (h) PJMcDonald 1 (Tom Clover) *broke wl: sn pushed along and lost pl: rdn over 3f out: sn wknd*	50/1	35
66	9	12	**Night Fury**[34] 2195 3-8-9 VictorSantos(7) 11 (Lucinda Egerton) *chsd ldrs on outer: rdn over 4f out: wknd 3f out*	150/1	13
0-0	10	4	**Pourmorechampagne**[12] 2932 3-9-2 DougieCostello 6 (Paul Webber) *hld up: plld hrd: wknd over 3f out*	100/1	4

1m 45.8s (-0.90) **Going Correction** 0.0s/f (Good) 10 Ran SP% **123.2**
Speed ratings (Par 99): **104,103,101,101,99 99,92,85,73,69**
CSF £19.35 TOTE £3.80: £1.10, £1.80, £2.50; EX 17.70 Trifecta £120.00.
Owner St Albans Bloodstock Limited **Bred** St Albans Bloodstock Ltd **Trained** Newmarket, Suffolk

FOCUS

Add 12yds. After this race the jockeys agreed that the ground had eased further and was riding more like good to soft. A good battling performance from the winner out in front.

3373 DS DERBY SALON H'CAP — 1m 2f 50y

3:20 (3:20) (Class 5) (0-75,76) 3-Y-O — £3,881 (£1,155; £577; £400; £400; £400) Stalls Low

Form					RPR
41-4	1		**Battle Of Wills (IRE)**[17] 2765 3-9-8 76 PJMcDonald 6 (James Tate) *chsd ldr tl led over 2f out: rdn over 1f out: styd on gamely*	9/2[2]	86
3220	2	1/2	**Htilominlo**[15] 2828 3-9-8 76 (t[1]) JimCrowley 8 (Sylvester Kirk) *hld up: hdwy u.p on outer over 2f out: chsd wnr over 1f out: ev ch ins fnl f: nt run on*	11/2	85
-311	3	3 1/2	**Mayfair Spirit (IRE)**[35] 2141 3-9-6 74 (t) StevieDonohoe 10 (Charlie Fellowes) *hld up: hdwy 6f out: rdn over 2f out: edgd lft over 1f out: styd on same pce ins fnl f*	5/1[3]	76
606-	4	1	**Salam Zayed**[244] 7830 3-8-13 67 PaulHanagan 7 (Richard Fahey) *led: hdd over 8f out: chsd ldrs: rdn over 2f out: hung lft and no ex ins fnl f*	20/1	67
205	5	2 3/4	**Doughan Alb**[19] 2715 3-9-4 72 SeanLevey 11 (Richard Hannon) *prom: lost pl 6f out: rdn over 3f out: styd on same pce fnl 2f*	20/1	67
503-	6	1/2	**Fantastic Blue**[228] 8327 3-9-5 73 SilvestreDeSousa 2 (Ismail Mohammed) *s.i.s: hdwy to ld over 8f out: rdn and hdd over 2f out: nt clr run over 1f out: wknd ins fnl f*	7/2[1]	67
403-	7	1/2	**Avenue Foch**[215] 8728 3-9-4 72 DanielMuscutt 3 (James Fanshawe) *trckd ldrs: hung lft fr over 3f out: wknd fnl f (jockey said gelding hung left in the straight)*	13/2	65
2-26	8	4 1/2	**Deebee**[26] 2507 3-9-7 75 DavidNolan 5 (Declan Carroll) *s.i.s: hld up: rdn over 2f out: wknd over 1f out*	13/2	59
00-0	9	42	**Barb's Prince (IRE)**[10] 2995 3-8-2 55 oh1 KieranO'Neill 4 (Ian Williams) *s.i.s: sn pushed along in rr: j. path arnd 8f out: wknd and eased fnl 4f*	50/1	
300-	P		**Tribal Commander**[221] 8553 3-9-5 73 JasonWatson 1 (Ian Williams) *rrd s: tk no part: p.u after leaving the stalls (starter reported that the gelding was unruly in the stalls; trainer was informed that the gelding could not run until the day after passing a stalls test; jockey said gelding reared as the start was effected, losing many lengths and in the interests of*	16/1	

2m 11.67s (-1.73) **Going Correction** 0.0s/f (Good) 10 Ran SP% **116.5**
Speed ratings (Par 99): **106,105,102,102,99 99,99,95,61,**
CSF £28.70 CT £128.80 TOTE £5.20: £1.90, £2.00, £2.30; EX 25.00 Trifecta £142.50.
Owner Saeed Manana **Bred** Fermoir Ltd **Trained** Newmarket, Suffolk

FOCUS

Add 12yds. This looked a competitive affair, but the first two drew clear of the rest.

3374 BRITISH STALLION STUDS EBF NOTTINGHAMSHIRE OAKS STKS (LISTED RACE) (F&M) — 1m 2f 50y

3:55 (3:55) (Class 1) 4-Y-O+ — £22,684 (£8,600; £4,304; £2,144; £1,076; £540) Stalls Low

Form					RPR
36-3	1		**Sun Maiden**[17] 2776 4-9-0 100 JimCrowley 7 (Sir Michael Stoute) *chsd ldr tl led over 2f out: shkn up over 1f out: pushed out: comf*	4/5[1]	106+
0-66	2	2 1/2	**Shailene (IRE)**[28] 2440 4-9-0 92 FrannyNorton 1 (Andrew Balding) *trckd ldrs: racd keenly: rdn and hung lft over 1f out: styd on to go 2nd nr fin*	7/1	100
-055	3	shd	**Queen Of Time**[17] 2776 5-9-0 94 (p) JasonWatson 6 (Henry Candy) *chsd ldrs: rdn over 2f out: styd on same pce wl ins fnl f*	20/1	100
6-02	4	1 3/4	**Exhort**[11] 2961 4-9-0 93 PaulHanagan 5 (Richard Fahey) *hld up: rdn over 1f out: styd on ins fnl f: nt rch ldrs*	6/1[2]	96
24-6	5	shd	**Savaanah (IRE)**[43] 1941 4-9-0 95 SilvestreDeSousa 2 (Roger Charlton) *sn led at stdy pce: shkn up and qcknd over 3f out: rdn and hdd over 2f out: wknd wl ins fnl f*	13/2[3]	96
1-05	6	3 3/4	**Rasima**[28] 2441 4-9-3 102 CharlesBishop 3 (Roger Varian) *s.i.s: hld up: shkn up over 1f out: sn wknd*	12/1	92
0-16	7	1 1/2	**Daddies Girl (IRE)**[22] 2608 4-9-0 87 RobHornby 4 (Rod Millman) *hld up: shkn up and outpcd fnl 3f*	33/1	86

2m 11.86s (-1.54) **Going Correction** 0.0s/f (Good) 7 Ran SP% **111.1**
Speed ratings (Par 111): **106,104,103,102,102 99,98**
CSF £6.52 TOTE £1.80: £1.10, £2.60; EX 6.80 Trifecta £45.70.
Owner K Abdullah **Bred** Juddmonte Farms Ltd **Trained** Newmarket, Suffolk

FOCUS

Add 12yds. This proved fairly straightforward for the class-dropping winner, who didn't need to improve to win.

3375 RACINGTV.COM H'CAP — 5f 8y

4:30 (4:30) (Class 3) (0-95,97) 4-Y-O+ — £9,703 (£2,887; £1,443; £721) Stalls High

Form					RPR
305-	1		**Danzeno**[313] 5299 8-9-13 97 AlistairRawlinson 8 (Michael Appleby) *s.i.s: sn chsng ldrs: led over 1f out: sn pushed clr: easily*	15/2	110+
-001	2	6	**East Street Revue**[19] 2709 6-8-8 78 DuranFentiman 6 (Tim Easterby) *s.i.s: outpcd: r.o to go 2nd ins fnl f: no ch w wnr*	7/1[3]	69
0-40	3	3 1/4	**Spoof**[18] 2743 4-9-12 96 (h) KieranShoemark 5 (Charles Hills) *half-rrd s and s.i.s: hld up: hdwy over 1f out: wknd ins fnl f (jockey said gelding reared and missed the break)*	9/2[2]	76
1-51	4	hd	**Burford Brown**[32] 2272 4-9-0 84 PJMcDonald 7 (Robert Cowell) *chsd ldrs: rdn and edgd lft over 1f out: wknd ins fnl f*	7/2[1]	63
11/4	5	2	**Indian Raj**[32] 2272 5-8-6 76 MartinDwyer 4 (Stuart Williams) *s.i.s: sn pushed along in rr: hdwy u.p on outer over 1f out: wknd ins fnl f (jockey said gelding was never travelling)*	7/2[1]	48
4100	6	4	**Abel Handy (IRE)**[8] 3097 4-9-7 91 (b) DavidNolan 9 (Declan Carroll) *w ldr tl led 2f out: rdn and hdd over 1f out: wknd fnl f*	7/2[1]	48
00-0	7	8	**Cox Bazar (FR)**[39] 2030 5-9-7 91 (t[1]) SilvestreDeSousa 10 (Ivan Furtado) *led 3f: wknd over 1f out*	16/1	20

58.92s (-1.28) **Going Correction** 0.0s/f (Good) 7 Ran SP% **115.0**
Speed ratings (Par 107): **110,100,95,94,91 85,72**
CSF £58.05 CT £264.64 TOTE £9.00: £4.80, £4.50; EX 64.50 Trifecta £382.20.
Owner A M Wragg **Bred** A M Wragg **Trained** Oakham, Rutland

FOCUS

This was strongly run, the two leaders setting off at an unsustainable gallop, and they finished well strung out behind the back-to-form winner.

3376 BET AT RACINGTV.COM H'CAP — 5f 8y

5:05 (5:05) (Class 6) (0-65,66) 3-Y-O — £3,234 (£962; £481; £400; £400; £400) Stalls High

Form					RPR
60-3	1		**Fairy Stories**[22] 2635 3-8-12 56 PaulHanagan 2 (Richard Fahey) *racd stands' side: s.i.s: hld up: hdwy 1/2-way: led overall over 1f out: shkn up and wnt readily clr ins fnl f: easily*	7/4[1]	75
3412	2	6	**Fairy Fast (IRE)**[6] 3148 3-9-4 62 (b) DavidNolan 4 (David O'Meara) *racd stands' side: chsd ldr: led that gp 1/2-way: rdn and hdd over 1f out: sn hdd: no ex ins fnl f*	9/2[3]	59
3-55	3	2	**Amazing Alba**[27] 2477 3-9-6 64 PaulMulrennan 6 (Michael Dods) *led gp on stands' side: sn hung lft: hdd 1/2-way: wknd ins fnl f*	5/1	54
0512	4	2 1/4	**Superseded (IRE)**[9] 3045 3-9-8 66 RobertWinston 5 (John Butler) *racd stands' side: prom: hmpd and lost pl over 4f out: n.d after (jockey said gelding ran flat)*	3/1[2]	48
044-	5	1 1/2	**Swell Song**[183] 9353 3-8-6 55 SeanDavis(5) 3 (Robert Cowell) *racd stands' side: chsd ldrs: lost pl 1/2-way: sn wknd*	18/1	31
-240	6	shd	**Cobweb Catcher**[27] 2474 3-9-2 60 (b[1]) RobHornby 1 (Rod Millman) *racd alone in centre: racd freely and sn led overall: hdd over 1f out: wknd fnl f (jockey said he felt the stride of the gelding shorten in the closing stages and so he held the gelding together to the line)*	8/1	36

1m 0.42s (0.22) **Going Correction** 0.0s/f (Good) 6 Ran SP% **112.6**
Speed ratings (Par 97): **98,88,85,81,79 79**
CSF £10.08 TOTE £2.40: £1.60, £2.20; EX 8.10 Trifecta £40.60.
Owner Richard Fahey Ebor Racing Club Ltd **Bred** Mrs Sheila Oakes **Trained** Musley Bank, N Yorks

FOCUS

A modest sprint, but it was run at a good gallop.

3377 INTRODUCING RACING TV H'CAP (JOCKEY CLUB GRASSROOTS FLAT STAYERS QUALIFIER) — 1m 6f

5:40 (5:40) (Class 5) (0-75,75) 4-Y-O+ £3,881 (£1,155; £577; £400; £400) Stalls Low

Form					RPR
13-3	1		**Oi The Clubb Oi's**[22] 2620 4-8-13 67 JimCrowley 2 (Ian Williams) *a.p: chsd ldr 12f out: led over 2f out: rdn over 1f out: hdd wl ins fnl f: rallied to ld nr fin*	8/13[1]	73
-604	2	hd	**Dagueneau (IRE)**[12] 2936 4-9-5 73 (p) RobertHavlin 5 (Ed Dunlop) *hld up: hdwy to chse wnr over 2f out: rdn to ld wl ins fnl f: hdd nr fin*	9/2[2]	78
-005	3	8	**Gavlar**[23] 2571 8-9-7 75 (v) CallumShepherd 4 (William Knight) *chsd ldr 2f: remained handy: rdn over 2f out: wknd fnl f*	8/1[3]	69
16/5	4	3/4	**Deinonychus**[22] 2629 8-8-6 65 (h) TheodoreLadd(5) 1 (Michael Appleby) *hld up: rdn over 3f out: hdwy over 1f out: wknd fnl f*	9/1	57
1400	5	23	**Temur Khan**[22] 2620 4-9-7 75 GeraldMosse 6 (Tony Carroll) *led at stdy pce: qcknd over 4f out: rdn and hdd over 2f out: wknd over 1f out*	12/1	35

3m 9.46s (3.06) **Going Correction** 0.0s/f (Good) 5 Ran SP% **108.9**
Speed ratings (Par 103): **91,90,86,85,72**
CSF £3.59 TOTE £1.50: £1.10, £1.50; EX 3.20 Trifecta £7.60.
Owner The Albatross Club **Bred** Marcia Gray **Trained** Portway, Worcs

FOCUS

Add 24yds. The first two pulled clear and had a good battle inside the final furlong.

T/Jkpt: £3,227.20 to a £1 stake. Pool: £50,021.64 - 15.50 winning units T/Plt: £74.90 to a £1 stake. Pool: £92,915.07 - 905.34 winning units T/Qpdt: £17.50 to a £1 stake. Pool: £9,732.01 - 411.17 winning units **Colin Roberts**

3378- 3383a (Foreign Racing) - See Raceform Interactive

LISTOWEL (L-H)

Sunday, June 2

OFFICIAL GOING: Good to yielding changing to yielding after race 1 (1.45)

3384a OVER 1000 GAMES AT BETVICTOR CASINO (Q.R.) RACE 1m 6f 170y

5:15 (5:18) 4-Y-0+ £9,434 (£2,925; £1,393; £627; £245)

RPR

1 **Newcross (IRE)**[35] 2160 6-10-9 83...(t) MrTHamilton(5) 2 90+
(A J Martin, Ire) *led and disp early tl hdd after 1f and settled bhd ldr: 3rd 1/2-way: disp 2nd over 3f out: travelling wl in 2nd over 2f out and impr to ld over 1f out: rdn clr ins fnl f: eased cl home: comf* **2/1**[1]

2 2 1/2 **Pearl Of The West (IRE)**[21] 1406 5-10-2 84......(t) MrMJMO'Sullivan(7) 4 79
(John C McConnell, Ire) *s.i.s and in rr early: 6th 1/2-way: cl 6th over 3f out: prog and disp 4th fr 2f out: rdn into 2nd ins fnl f where no imp on easy wnr: kpt on same pce* **10/3**[3]

3 1/2 **Hot Beat (IRE)**[539] 5803 7-11-0 87... MrDerekO'Connor 1 83
(T M Walsh, Ire) *chsd ldrs: 5th 1/2-way: cl 5th over 3f out: sn tk clsr order bhd ldrs: disp 4th gng wl 2f out: drvn 1f out and no imp on easy wnr u.p in 3rd wl ins fnl f: kpt on same pce* **20/1**

4 5 **Yabass (IRE)**[36] 2118 4-10-9 92...(t) MissBrodieHampson(5) 5 76
(Archie Watson) *unruly and uns rdr on way to s: led down and reluctant to load: loaded wout rdr: sn led narrowly tl jnd after 3f: narrow ld bef 1/2-way: rdn under 2f out and hdd over 1f out: no ex and wknd ins fnl f (jockey said gelding made a noise in running)* **5/2**[2]

5 3/4 **Flat To The Max (FR)**[19] 2727 4-11-0 88...(b) MsLO'Neill 7 75
(Gordon Elliott, Ire) *chsd ldrs in 3rd early: 4th 1/2-way: disp 2nd over 3f out: rdn in 3rd fr 2f out and sn no ex: wknd into 5th over 1f out* **9/1**

6 7 1/2 **Woodland Opera (IRE)**[20] 9-10-11 0...(bt) MrFinianMaguire(3) 6 48
(Mrs John Harrington, Ire) *dwlt and hld up in 5th early: disp ld after 3f: cl 2nd bef 1/2-way: pushed along over 4f out and sn reminders: wknd over 3f out: mod 6th into st and eased briefly: mod 7th over 1f out: fin 7th: plcd 6th* **4/1**

D 12 **Sweet Cassie (IRE)**[51] 8205 4-10-2 52... MissNCKelly(7) 3 53
(Leonard Paul Flynn, Ire) *a bhd: in rr and detached at 1/2-way: no imp trailing bef st: kpt on one pce in mod 6th ins fnl f: nvr a factor: disqualified: rdr weighed-in 2lb light* **100/1**

3m 27.27s **7 Ran SP% 120.7**

Pick Six: Not won. Pool of 1,723.50 carried over to Gowran Park on 16th June. Tote aggregates: 2018 - 380,048.00; 2019 - 243,347.00. CSF £9.90 TOTE £3.20: £2.00, £2.40; DF 9.80 Trifecta £120.90.

Owner Newtown Anner Stud Farm Ltd **Bred** Newtown Anner Stud **Trained** Summerhill, Co. Meath

■ Stewards' Enquiry : Miss N C Kelly caution: use of whip

FOCUS

The winner came in for good support late on to start favourite and didn't let his backers down with a smooth win. For a race of this nature, the pace looked decent. The winner produced a pb but the sixth is a doubt over the form.

T/Jkpt: Not won. T/Plt: @219.50. Pool: @32,527.88 - 103.70 winning units **Brian Fleming**

3369 BADEN-BADEN (L-H)

Sunday, June 2

OFFICIAL GOING: Turf: good

3385a DERBY TRIAL - FRUHJAHRS-PREIS (GROUP 3) (3YO) (TURF) 1m 2f

1:40 3-Y-0 £28,828 (£10,810; £5,405; £2,702; £1,801)

RPR

1 **Accon (GER)**[32] 2310 3-9-2 0... JiriPalik 1 103
(Markus Klug, Germany) *racd keenly: in tch in midfield: gd hdwy on inner of bnd appr 2f out: rdn to ld 2f out: kpt on strly f: comf* **195/10**

2 1 3/4 **Skyful Sea (FR)**[27] 3-8-13 0... AndraschStarke 8 97
(P Schiergen, Germany) *hld up in rr: rdn over 2f out: styd on fr 2f out: snatched 2nd cl home* **79/10**

3 nk **Surrey Thunder (FR)**[49] 1797 3-9-2 0... ShaneKelly 4 99
(Joseph Tuite) *racd keenly towards rr of midfield: smooth hdwy on wd outside of bnd appr 2f out: rdn to chse wnr under 2f out: kpt on same pce fnl f: lost 2nd cl home* **33/10**[2]

4 1 1/4 **Runnymede**[28] 3-9-2 0... FabriceVeron 3 97
(Frau S Steinberg, Germany) *t.k.h in midfield: nt clr run over 2f out: rdn and outpcd 2f out: kpt on fnl f* **6/1**

5 nk **Moonlight Man (GER)**[35] 2163 3-9-2 0... AdriedeVries 5 96
(Markus Klug, Germany) *hld up towards rr: hdwy appr 2f out: rdn and kpt on same pce fr 2f out* **53/10**[3]

6 hd **King (GER)**[35] 2163 3-9-2 0... RenePiechulek 2 96
(C J M Wolters, Holland) *led: rdn over 2f out: hdd 2f out: wknd steadily fnl f* **106/10**

7 3/4 **Peppone (GER)**[217] 3-9-2 0... BauyrzhanMurzabayev 7 94
(A Wohler, Germany) *racd keenly: trckd ldrs: rdn 2f out: wknd ins fnl f* **19/10**[1]

8 3 1/2 **Konig Platon (GER)**[35] 3-9-2 0... LukasDelozier 6 87
(J Hirschberger, Germany) *racd keenly: chsd ldr: rdn 2f out: wknd over 1f out* **148/10**

2m 4.64s (-0.35) **8 Ran SP% 119.0**

PARI-MUTUEL (all including 1 euro stake): WIN 20.50 PLACE: 3.90, 2.40, 2.00; SF: 131.50.

Owner Holger Renz **Bred** Gestut Hof Ittlingen **Trained** Germany

3386a GROSSER PREIS DER BADISCHEN WIRTSCHAFT (GROUP 2) (4YO+) (TURF) 1m 3f

3:30 4-Y-0+ £36,036 (£13,963; £7,207; £3,603; £2,252)

RPR

1 **Itobo (GER)**[42] 7-9-2 0... MarcoCasamento 3 114
(H-J Groschel, Germany) *in tch: rdn 2f out: led over 1f out: kpt on wl fnl f: drvn out* **8/1**

2 1/2 **Royal Youmzain (FR)**[213] 8794 4-9-2 0... EduardoPedroza 2 113
(A Wohler, Germany) *trckd ldrs: rdn over 2f out: drvn and kpt on wl fnl f: nt quite able to chal wnr* **11/5**[1]

3 1/2 **Windstoss (GER)**[28] 2455 5-9-2 0... AdriedeVries 1 112+
(Markus Klug, Germany) *midfield: pushed along and sltly outpcd 3f out: rdn 2f out: styd on fr over 1f out: nrst fin* **7/2**[2]

4 1 1/4 **Alounak (FR)**[28] 2455 4-9-2 0... AntoineHamelin 7 110
(Waldemar Hickst, Germany) *chsd ldr: rdn over 2f out: led under 2f out: hdd over 1f out: no ex fnl 100yds* **79/10**

5 2 1/4 **Walsingham (GER)**[28] 2455 5-9-2 0... AndraschStarke 8 106
(P Schiergen, Germany) *towards rr of midfield: rdn and kpt on steadily fr under 2f out* **63/10**

6 2 **Oriental Eagle (GER)**[258] 7373 5-9-2 0... FilipMinarik 4 102
(J Hirschberger, Germany) *led: wnt clr at 1/2-way: rdn over 2f out: hdd under 2f out: wknd over 1f out* **125/10**

7 nk **Wai Key Star (GER)**[28] 6-9-2 0... FabriceVeron 6 102
(Frau S Steinberg, Germany) *a towards rr* **49/10**[3]

8 4 1/4 **Matchwinner (GER)**[14] 8-9-2 0... AndreBest 5 94
(J M Snackers, Germany) *a in rr* **188/10**

2m 17.25s (-2.02) **8 Ran SP% 118.9**

PARI-MUTUEL (all including 1 euro stake): WIN 9.00 PLACE: 2.00, 1.50, 1.50; SF: 27.30.

Owner Stall Totti **Bred** Gestut Gorlsdorf **Trained** Germany

2647 CHANTILLY (R-H)

Sunday, June 2

OFFICIAL GOING: Turf: good

3387a PRIX DE SANDRINGHAM (GROUP 2) (3YO FILLIES) (TURF) 1m

1:30 3-Y-0 £66,756 (£25,765; £12,297; £8,198; £4,099)

RPR

1 **Obligate**[27] 2498 3-8-13 0 ow2... Pierre-CharlesBoudot 7 103
(P Bary, France) *mde all: rdn whn pressed 1 1/2f out: drvn and hld on wl fr over 1f out: hrd drvn fnl 50yds: jst prevailed* **9/10**[1]

2 hd **Pure Zen (FR)**[27] 2498 3-8-13 0 ow2... StephanePasquier 1 103
(Gianluca Bietolini, France) *chsd ldr: rdn over 2f out: pressed wnr fr 1 1/2f out: drvn and kpt on wl fnl f: jst hld* **14/1**

3 1 1/4 **Glance**[16] 2806 3-8-13 0 ow2... HarryBentley 3 100
(Ralph Beckett) *midfield: rdn over 3f out: styd on fr over 1f out: nt gng pce to rch front pair* **19/1**

4 nk **Hidden Message (USA)**[32] 2268 3-8-13 0 ow2... AndreaAtzeni 2 99+
(William Haggas) *hld up towards rr: rdn 3f out: kpt on wl fr 2f out: nrst fin* **18/1**

5 1 1/2 **Matematica (GER)**[21] 2669 3-8-13 0 ow2... MaximeGuyon 4 96
(C Laffon-Parias, France) *towards rr of midfield: rdn and kpt on steadily fr 2f out* **23/10**[2]

6 1/2 **Olympe (FR)**[27] 2498 3-8-13 0 ow2... ChristopheSoumillon 5 95
(J-C Rouget, France) *hld up in rr: rdn under 2f out: kpt on last 100yds: n.d* **43/5**[3]

7 1 1/4 **Rocques (FR)**[21] 2669 3-8-13 0 ow2... CristianDemuro 6 92
(F Chappet, France) *in tch: trckd ldrs: over 2f out: rdn 2f out: wknd fnl f* **10/1**

1m 34.59s (-3.41) **7 Ran SP% 119.4**

PARI-MUTUEL (all including 1 euro stake): WIN 1.90; PLACE 1.40, 3.30; SF 9.30.

Owner K Abdullah **Bred** Juddmonte Farms Ltd **Trained** Chantilly, France

FOCUS

The second, third and fourth have all been rated as running small personal bests.

3388a PRIX DU GROS-CHENE (GROUP 2) (3YO+) (TURF) 5f

2:05 3-Y-0+ £66,756 (£25,765; £12,297; £8,198; £4,099)

RPR

1 **Inns Of Court (IRE)**[37] 2089 5-9-4 0 ow1... MickaelBarzalona 1 121+
(A Fabre, France) *trckd ldrs: smooth hdwy fr 2f out: rdn to ld over 1f out: drvn clr fnl f: readily* **13/10**[1]

2 2 1/2 **Sestilio Jet (FR)**[21] 2667 4-9-4 0 ow1... FrankieDettori 5 112
(Andrea Marcialis, France) *chsd ldr: rdn under 2f out: kpt on wl fnl f: no imp on clr wnr* **31/10**[3]

3 1/2 **Major Jumbo**[18] 2744 5-9-4 0 ow1... JamieSpencer 3 110
(Kevin Ryan) *led: rdn 1 1/2f out: drvn whn hdd over 1f out: kpt on same pce fnl f* **2/1**[2]

4 1 1/4 **Gold Vibe (IRE)**[21] 2667 6-9-4 0 ow1...(b) CristianDemuro 4 106
(P Bary, France) *hld up in tch: rdn and no imp fr under 2f out* **74/10**

5 nk **Gossamer Wings (USA)**[14] 2880 3-8-8 0 ow1... WayneLordan 2 98
(A P O'Brien, Ire) *hld up: rdn and no imp fr under 2f out* **16/1**

57.64s (-0.66)

WFA 3 from 4yo+ 7lb **5 Ran SP% 119.0**

PARI-MUTUEL (all including 1 euro stake): WIN 2.30; PLACE 1.20, 1.80; SF 5.50.

Owner Godolphin SNC **Bred** Darley **Trained** Chantilly, France

3389a GRAND PRIX DE CHANTILLY (GROUP 2) (4YO+) (TURF) 1m 4f

2:40 4-Y-0+ £66,756 (£25,765; £12,297; £8,198; £4,099)

RPR

1 **Aspetar (FR)**[29] 2428 4-9-1 0 ow1... JamesDoyle 4 114+
(Roger Charlton) *racd keenly: towards rr of midfield: rdn to chse ldrs 2f out: styd on wl to ld 100yds out: rdn out* **11/1**

2 3/4 **Ziyad**[25] 2541 4-9-1 0 ow1... OlivierPeslier 1 113
(C Laffon-Parias, France) *chsd ldr: rdn and kpt on wl fr under 2f out: nt quite able to chal: short of room clsng stages* **20/1**

3 1/2 **Silverwave (FR)**[25] 2541 7-9-1 0 ow1... ChristopheSoumillon 7 112
(F Vermeulen, France) *led: rdn 1 1/2f out: hdd 100yds out: no ex clsng stages* **5/2**[1]

4 1 3/4 **Folamour**[29] 2428 4-9-1 0 ow1... MaximeGuyon 6 109+
(A Fabre, France) *hld up towards rr: rdn 2 1/2f out: kpt on wl fr 1 1/2f out* **7/2**[2]

5 3 1/2 **Gyllen (USA)**[29] 2428 4-9-1 0 ow1... MickaelBarzalona 5 104
(A Fabre, France) *hld up in rr: rdn under 3f out: kpt on fnl f: n.d* **10/1**

6 shd **Listen In (IRE)**[13] 3138 5-9-2 ow1... AurelienLemaitre 2 104
(F Head, France) *hld up towards rr of midfield: rdn and no imp fr over 2f out* **5/2**[1]

7 4 1/2 **Petit Fils (FR)**[29] 2428 4-9-1 ow1... TheoBachelot 3 96
(J-P Gauvin, France) *in tch: rdn 2f out: wknd fr 1 1/2f out: eased fnl 150yds* **9/2**[3]

2m 24.6s (-6.40) **7 Ran SP% 119.7**

PARI-MUTUEL (all including 1 euro stake): WIN 12.30; PLACE 4.90, 6.80; SF 121.10.

Owner H H Sheikh Mohammed Bin Khalifa Al Thani **Bred** Hh Sheikh Mohammed Bin Khalifa Al Thani **Trained** Beckhampton, Wilts

3390a QIPCO PRIX DU JOCKEY CLUB (GROUP 1) (3YO COLTS & FILLIES) (TURF) 1m 2f 110y

3:25 3-Y-O £772,162 (£308,918; £154,459; £77,162; £38,648)

RPR

1 **Sottsass (FR)**[31] 2352 3-9-3 0 ow1 CristianDemuro 5 121+
(J-C Rouget, France) *towards rr of midfield: gd hdwy appr 2f out: rdn 2f out: drvn to ld 1f out: kpt on strly fnl 100yds: readily* 13/1

2 2 **Persian King (IRE)**[21] 2668 3-9-3 0 ow1 Pierre-CharlesBoudot 14 117
(A Fabre, France) *midfield on outside: smooth hdwy appr 2f out: rdn to ld under 2f out: drvn and hdd 1f out: outpcd by wnr fnl 100yds: kpt on* 9/5[1]

3 2 **Motamarris (IRE)**[22] 3-9-3 0 ow1 AurelienLemaitre 4 113
(F Head, France) *led: rdn 2f out: hdd under 2f out: no ex fnl f* 44/5

4 ¾ **Cape Of Good Hope (IRE)**[39] 2031 3-9-3 0 ow1 RyanMoore 13 112
(A P O'Brien, Ire) *hld up towards rr: rdn and hdwy fr over 2f out: kpt on same pce fnl f* 24/1

5 2 ½ **Roman Candle**[32] 2314 3-9-3 0 ow1 MickaelBarzalona 3 107
(A Fabre, France) *midfield: rdn and nt clr run fr 2f out: kpt on same pce fr 1 1/2f out* 14/1

6 ¾ **Rockemperor (IRE)**[56] 1625 3-9-3 0 ow1 IoritzMendizabal 7 106
(Simone Brogi, France) *in tch: rdn 2 1/2f out: wknd fr 1 1/2f out* 23/1

7 1 **Mohawk (IRE)**[8] 3104 3-9-3 0 ow1 DonnachaO'Brien 15 104
(A P O'Brien, Ire) *hld up in rr: rdn 2 1/2f out: styd on fr 1 1/2f out: n.d* 43/1

8 2 ½ **Surfman**[17] 2777 3-9-3 0 ow1 AndreaAtzeni 6 99
(Roger Varian) *in tch in midfield: rdn 2 1/2f out: outpcd fr 2f out: wknd steadily fnl f* 13/1

9 3 ½ **Kick On**[29] 2411 3-9-3 0 ow1 OisinMurphy 12 93
(John Gosden) *trckd ldrs: rdn over 2f out: lost pl under 2f out: wknd over 1f out* 37/1

10 ½ **Raise You (IRE)**[15] 2833 3-9-3 0 ow1 DavidProbert 8 92
(Andrew Balding) *midfield: rdn and lost pl over 2f out: sn btn* 18/1

11 7 **Joe Francais (FR)**[49] 1797 3-9-3 0 ow1 Jean-BernardEyquem 1 78
(J-C Rouget, France) *in tch in midfield: nt clr run 2f out: sn lost pl and wl btn: eased fnl f* 50/1

12 *hd* **Slalom (FR)**[49] 1797 3-9-3 0 ow1 MaximeGuyon 10 78
(A Fabre, France) *s.v.s: a towards rr* 67/10[3]

13 2 ½ **Zarkallani (FR)**[7] 3-9-3 0 ow1 ChristopheSoumillon 9 73
(A De Royer-Dupre, France) *hld up towards rr: pushed along and no imp fr 2f out: eased fnl f* 11/2[2]

14 3 ½ **Blenheim Palace (IRE)**[21] 2662 3-9-3 0 ow1 SeamieHeffernan 2 66
(A P O'Brien, Ire) *chsd ldr: rdn under 3f out: wknd 2f out: eased fr 1 1/2f out* 53/1

15 10 **Starmaniac**[32] 2314 3-9-3 0 ow1 OlivierPeslier 11 47
(C Laffon-Parias, France) *towards rr of midfield: rdn under 3f out: wkng whn sltly hmpd 2f out: sn eased* 36/1

2m 2.9s (-5.90) **15 Ran SP% 120.1**
PARI-MUTUEL (all including 1 euro stake): WIN 14.60; PLACE 3.50, 1.50, 3.00; DF 16.90.
Owner White Birch Farm **Bred** Ecurie Des Monceaux **Trained** Pau, France

FOCUS
A fair renewal of the French Derby with a trio of Andre Fabre-trained runners, headed by Persian King, trying to repel an interesting bunch of rivals from the UK and Ireland. However, it was one of the home team that provided a bit of an upset in a race which was run at a good early gallop thanks to Motamarris and Blenheim Palace. The English and Irish raiders were generally disappointing.

3391a PRIX DE ROYAUMONT (GROUP 3) (3YO FILLIES) (TURF) 1m 4f

4:45 3-Y-O £36,036 (£14,414; £10,810; £7,207; £3,603)

RPR

1 **Pelligrina (IRE)**[20] 3-9-1 ow1 Pierre-CharlesBoudot 4 105+
(A Fabre, France) *Held up in rr: gd hdwy on inner fr 3f out: rdn to ld under 2f out: drvn clr over 1f out: in command fnl f: comf* 27/10[2]

2 2 ½ **Malevra (FR)**[36] 3-9-1 ow1 MaximeGuyon 8 101
(G Botti, France) *chsd ldr: led over 2f out: rdn 2f out: hdd under 2f out: kpt on wl fnl f: no imp on comfortable wnr* 12/1

3 1 ¼ **Je Ne Regretterien**[13] 3-9-1 ow1 MickaelBarzalona 7 99
(A Fabre, France) *trckd ldrs: rdn and kpt on fr over 2f out: nt able to chal* 9/1

4 2 **Eliade (FR)**[29] 2430 3-9-1 ow1 OlivierPeslier 5 96
(F Rohaut, France) *hld up towards rr of midfield: rdn over 2f out: kpt on fnl f* 63/10

5 *hd* **Psara**[29] 2426 3-9-1 ow1 AlexisBadel 1 96
(H-F Devin, France) *hld up towards rr of midfield: rdn 2 1/2f out: kpt on steadily fr 1 1/2f out* 49/10[3]

6 1 **Burning Victory (FR)**[31] 3-9-1 ow1 TheoBachelot 6 94
(S Wattel, France) *hld up towards rr: rdn and no imp fr 2f out* 17/2

7 *hd* **Dariyza (FR)**[16] 3-9-1 ow1 ChristopheSoumillon 9 94
(A De Royer-Dupre, France) *midfield: tk clsr order appr 2f out: rdn under 2f out: wknd tamely fnl f* 13/5[1]

8 15 **Sagama**[21] 3-9-1 ow1 MickaelBerto 3 70
(M Delzangles, France) *led: rdn and hdd over 2f out: sn drvn and wknd: eased fr 1 1/2f out* 16/1

2m 25.99s (-5.01) **8 Ran SP% 119.6**
PARI-MUTUEL (all including 1 euro stake): WIN 3.70; PLACE 2.00, 3.40, 3.00; DF 23.10.
Owner H H Sheikh Mohammed Bin Khalifa Al Thani **Bred** Al Shahania Stud **Trained** Chantilly, France

3392 - 3403a (Foreign Racing) - See Raceform Interactive

3182 BRIGHTON (L-H)

Monday, June 3

OFFICIAL GOING: Good to firm (watered)
Wind: virtually nil Weather: warm and sunny

3404 EAGLES SOARING HIGH H'CAP 5f 60y

2:00 (2:04) (Class 6) (0-65,66) 4-Y-O+

£3,105 (£924; £461; £300; £300) **Stalls Centre**

Form RPR

56-2 1 **Essaka (IRE)**[35] 2206 7-8-9 **59** SophieRalston(7) 1 72
(Tony Carroll) *wnt to post early: settled wl in midfield: clsd gng wl 2f out: effrt between rivals to ld 1f out: rdn out* 7/2[2]

0-52 2 4 **Ghepardo**[19] 2729 4-9-9 **66** TomMarquand 4 65
(Patrick Chamings) *racd in midfield: effrt on outer to chse ldr 2f out: sn rdn and kpt on fnl f: nt match wnr* 4/1[3]

0004 3 1 ½ **Tina Teaspoon**[13] 2924 5-8-5 **48** ow3 (h) JoeyHaynes 7 41
(Derek Shaw) *hld up: rdn to chse ldr 2f out: kpt on fnl f* 33/1

1012 4 ½ **Hurricane Alert**[41] 2010 7-7-13 **49** AledBeech(7) 5 40
(Mark Hoad) *wnt to post early: chsd ldr tl led after 2f: rdn along and hdd 1f out: wknd fnl f* 16/1

60-3 5 *shd* **Normal Equilibrium**[16] 2824 9-9-4 **64** GabrieleMalune(3) 2 55
(Ivan Furtado) *led for 2f then chsd ldr: rdn over 2f out: one pce fnl f (trainer's rep said gelding would be better suited to a flatter track and was unsuited by the going (good to Firm) and would prefer a slower surface)* 2/1[1]

00-6 6 1 **Exceedingly Diva**[11] 3020 4-9-7 **64** PatCosgrave 8 51
(George Baker) *dwlt and racd in rr: rdn along to chal over 2f out: no hdwy and wknd fnl f* 7/2[2]

-000 7 ½ **Hornby**[13] 2924 4-8-2 **45** JimmyQuinn 6 31
(Michael Attwater) *reluctant to go to post and walked to s: hld up: rdn 3f out: nvr on terms* 100/1

5200 8 3 ¼ **Come On Dave (IRE)**[23] 2632 10-9-5 **62** (b) LiamKeniry 3 36
(John Butler) *chsd ldr: rdn 2f out: wkng whn short of room over 1f out: no ex* 11/1

1m 3.2s (0.20) **Going Correction** -0.025s/f (Good) **8 Ran SP% 115.9**
Speed ratings (Par 101): **97,90,88,87,87 85,84,79**
CSF £18.23 CT £395.45 TOTE £5.00: £1.60, £1.40, £5.90; EX 17.30 Trifecta £185.70.
Owner Mrs J Carrington **Bred** Dream Vision Partnership **Trained** Cropthorne, Worcs

FOCUS
6 yards added. A weak sprint handicap, with a pb from the winner.

3405 WATCH ROYAL ASCOT ON SKY SPORTS RACING MAIDEN AUCTION STKS 5f 215y

2:30 (2:31) (Class 5) 2-Y-O £3,752 (£1,116; £557; £278) **Stalls Centre**

Form RPR

3 1 **Faldetta**[11] 2996 2-8-13 CharlesBishop 1 73+
(Eve Johnson Houghton) *mde all: rdn to maintain 1 l ld over 1f out: kpt on wl fnl f: a doing enough* 9/4[2]

3 2 1 ¼ **My Motivate Girl (IRE)**[14] 2903 2-8-13 (v) OisinMurphy 4 69
(Archie Watson) *wnt rt s and gave away a couple of l: pushed along to cl on wnr 2f out: rdn over 1f out: kpt on but a hld by wnr* 8/11[1]

04 3 3 ¼ **Bacchalot (IRE)**[11] 2996 2-8-13 RossaRyan 2 59
(Richard Hannon) *chsd wnr: rdn along and no imp over 1f out: wknd fnl f (jockey said filly hung left-handed from 3f out)* 9/2[3]

4 11 **Moontide (IRE)** 2-9-2 LiamKeniry 3 26
(J S Moore) *hld up: rdn and outpcd over 2f out: nvr on terms* 25/1

1m 12.9s (1.80) **Going Correction** -0.025s/f (Good) **4 Ran SP% 110.7**
Speed ratings (Par 93): **87,85,81,66**
CSF £4.44 TOTE £3.10; EX 5.00 Trifecta £7.00.
Owner Mrs M E Slade & Partner **Bred** Lofti Raissi **Trained** Blewbury, Oxon

FOCUS
6 yards added. An ordinary little juvenile maiden. The second-favourite dominated in game fashion and is rated a minor improver.

3406 DOVES PLAYING LIVE HERE 26 JULY H'CAP 5f 215y

3:00 (3:00) (Class 6) (0-65,65) 3-Y-O+ £3,105 (£924; £461; £300) **Stalls Centre**

Form RPR

0-04 1 **Cracking Speed (IRE)**[18] 2772 3-9-6 **65** (t) SeanLevey 5 72
(Richard Hannon) *trckd ldr: rdn to chse ldr 2f out: led gng best 1f out: pushed out* 4/1[3]

-000 2 2 ¼ **Soaring Spirits (IRE)**[28] 2483 9-9-3 **61** (b) SophieRalston(7) 2 63
(Dean Ivory) *trckd ldr: rdn and sltly outpcd 2f out: kpt on to go 2nd wl ins fnl f* 10/1

5053 3 ½ **Under Curfew**[18] 2772 3-9-3 **62** TomMarquand 3 60
(Tony Carroll) *hld up: effrt on outer to chse wnr 2f out: rdn and no imp 1f out: one pce fnl f (jockey said gelding hung left-handed in the straight)* 2/1[2]

-263 4 1 ½ **Barritus**[13] 2929 4-10-0 **65** (p[1]) PatCosgrave 1 60
(George Baker) *led: rdn along and hdd by wnr 1f out: wknd fnl f* 5/4[1]

0045 U **Noble Deed**[33] 2287 9-8-9 **46** oh1 KierenFox 4
(Michael Attwater) *j. awkwardly and uns rdr sn after s* 33/1

1m 11.53s (0.43) **Going Correction** -0.025s/f (Good)
WFA 3 from 4yo+ 8lb **5 Ran SP% 109.8**
Speed ratings (Par 101): **96,93,92,90,**
CSF £36.60 TOTE £4.60: £2.50, £4.10; EX 22.70 Trifecta £64.80.
Owner Dragon Gate **Bred** Highfort Stud & R Foley **Trained** East Everleigh, Wilts

FOCUS
6 yards added. A modest handicap. The form's been rated cautiously.

3407 PHIL O'HARA BIRTHDAY CITY H'CAP 1m 1f 207y

3:30 (3:33) (Class 6) (0-60,62) 3-Y-O

£3,105 (£924; £461; £300; £300; £300) **Stalls High**

Form RPR

4064 1 **Oliver Hardy**[9] 3092 3-9-6 **59** (t) RossaRyan 10 67
(Paul Cole) *trckd pce: pushed along and briefly outpcd over 2f out: drvn to chse ldr 1f out: styd on strly to ld post (jockey said colt hung left-handed)* 7/1

4-56 2 *nk* **Tartlette**[20] 2719 3-9-6 **59** SeanLevey 3 66
(Hughie Morrison) *in tch: rdn along to ld 2f out: drvn to maintain 1 l ld 1f out: kpt on but hdd by wnr post* 4/1[2]

-063 3 3 ¾ **Red Archangel (IRE)**[32] 2341 3-9-3 **56** NicolaCurrie 6 56
(Richard Spencer) *racd in midfield: rdn over 2f out: hung lft u.p 1f out: kpt on but no ch w front pair (jockey said filly hung left-handed in the straight)* 11/2[3]

044 4 3 ¼ **Winter Snowdrop (IRE)**[54] 1689 3-8-0 **46** oh1 SophieRalston(7) 8 40
(Julia Feilden) *racd in midfield: pushed along on outer over 2f out: rdn and no imp over 1f out: kpt on one pce fnl f (jockey said filly hung right-handed under pressure)* 66/1

0-60 5 ½ **Confils (FR)**[32] 2343 3-9-6 **59** PatCosgrave 9 52
(George Baker) *restrained in rr: hdwy u.p over 1f out: kpt on one pce fnl f* 8/1

3053 6 *shd* **Samstar**[10] 3057 3-9-7 **60** FrannyNorton 2 56
(Mark Johnston) *led: rdn along and hdd 2f out: hmpd whn wkng 1f out: no ex* 3/1[1]

125 7 2 **Mr Fox**[32] 2322 3-9-4 **62** ScottMcCullagh(5) 7 51
(Michael Attwater) *hld up: effrt on the outer over 2f out: sn rdn and no imp over 1f out: one pce fnl f* 14/1

-030 8 1 ½ **Miss Havana**[9] 3092 3-9-0 **53** (p[1]) CharlesBishop 4 39
(Eve Johnson Houghton) *chsd ldr: rdn along and ev ch 2f out: wknd fnl f* 13/2

The Form Book Flat 2019, Raceform Ltd, Newbury, RG14 5SJ

6040 **9** *7* **Frenchmans Creek (IRE)**[13] 2941 3-8-11 **53**............(t) JoshuaBryan(3) 1 25
(Seamus Durack) *racd in midfield: rdn and lost pl 2f out: sn bhd* **25/1**

2m 4.14s (-0.86) **Going Correction** -0.025s/f (Good) 9 Ran SP% **109.3**
Speed ratings (Par 97): **102,101,98,96,95 95,94,92,87**
CSF £30.31 CT £124.29 TOTE £8.00: £2.60, £1.80, £1.70; EX 44.00 Trifecta £138.60.
Owner Chelsea T'breds, Sophie Magnier, Oliver Cole **Bred** Bugley Stud & D B Clark **Trained** Whatcombe, Oxon

■ Whistler Bowl was withdrawn, price at time of withdrawal 7/1. Rule 4 applies to all bets. Deduction of 10p in the pound.

FOCUS
6 yards added. A modest 3yo handicap. The winner picked up strongly centrally to deny the second-favourite close home. A small step up from the winner.

3408 PARK LANE GROUP H'CAP — 1m 3f 198y
4:00 (4:00) (Class 4) (0-85,92) 4-Y-O+ **£5,530** (£1,645; £822; £411) **Stalls** High

Form RPR

2241 **1** **Charles Kingsley**[5] 3222 4-10-1 **92** 5ex............................ FrannyNorton 3 102+
(Mark Johnston) *settled wl in 3rd: effrt to cl on ldr 2f out: rdn along to ld wl over 1f out: sn in command and pushed out fnl f* **8/13**[1]

-403 **2** *1 ½* **Perfect Illusion**[9] 3095 4-8-11 **77**..............................(p) JoshuaBryan(3) 1 83
(Andrew Balding) *hld up: pushed along to chse wnr over 2f out: rdn and wnt 2nd 1f out: kpt on but no match for wnr* **2/1**[2]

3122 **3** *4 ½* **Gendarme (IRE)**[13] 2928 4-8-4 **70**..............................(b) WilliamCox(3) 4 69
(Alexandra Dunn) *trckd ldr: pushed along to ld 3f out: sn rdn: hdd by wnr wl over 1f out: no ex fnl f* **25/1**

120- **4** *hd* **Trouble And Strife (IRE)**[229] 8313 4-9-7 **84**........................ RyanTate 2 82
(Sir Mark Prescott Bt) *led: rdn along and hdd 3f out: kpt on one pce fr over 1f out* **8/1**[3]

2m 32.0s (-4.00) **Going Correction** -0.025s/f (Good) 4 Ran SP% **110.2**
Speed ratings (Par 105): **112,111,108,107**
CSF £2.17 TOTE £1.40; EX 2.10 Trifecta £7.30.
Owner Sheikh Hamdan bin Mohammed Al Maktoum **Bred** Godolphin **Trained** Middleham Moor, N Yorks

FOCUS
6 yards added. The feature race was a decent little middle-distance handicap. The odds-on favourite got well on top on the uphill section in the best comparative time on the card despite a tactical gallop. The winner backed up his latest Hamilton improvement.

3409 SKY SPORTS RACING ON SKY 415 H'CAP — 7f 211y
4:30 (4:30) (Class 6) (0-60,60) 3-Y-O
£3,105 (£924; £461; £300; £300; £300) **Stalls** Centre

Form RPR

06-6 **1** **Orliko (IRE)**[17] 2798 3-9-7 **60**...................................(b[1]) RossaRyan 6 64
(Richard Hannon) *mde all: rdn along to maintain short ld wl over 1f out: drvn ins fnl f: hung on gamely* **3/1**[2]

-000 **2** *nk* **Princess Florence (IRE)**[6] 3182 3-8-0 **46** oh1............ CierenFallon(7) 5 49
(John Ryan) *in tch in midfield: effrt to chse wnr over 1f out: kpt on wl fnl f nt rch wnr (jockey said filly ran too free early on)* **20/1**

600- **3** *¾* **Lady Mazie (IRE)**[224] 8470 3-9-3 **56**......................... JoeyHaynes 4 58
(Dominic Ffrench Davis) *hld up: hdwy on outer 2f out: rdn and kpt on wl fnl f: nt rch front pair* **11/2**[3]

040 **4** *3* **Followme Followyou (IRE)**[14] 2909 3-9-7 **60**.............. FrannyNorton 1 55
(Mark Johnston) *racd in midfield: rdn and no imp 2f out: drvn 1f out: one pce fnl f* **3/1**[2]

0-06 **5** *3 ¼* **Smith (IRE)**[19] 2734 3-9-4 **57**.................................... CharlesBishop 7 44
(Eve Johnson Houghton) *trckd wnr on outer: rdn and no imp 2f out: sn outpcd: plugged on fnl f* **5/2**[1]

60-3 **6** *1* **Daniel Dravot**[33] 2285 3-9-2 **60**..............................(h[1]) ScottMcCullagh(5) 2 45
(Michael Attwater) *chsd wnr: rdn along and ev ch on inner over 1f out: wknd ins fnl f* **8/1**

-000 **7** *3* **Clubora (USA)**[18] 2772 3-8-9 **48**................................ FergusSweeney 3 26
(Richard Hannon) *hld up: rdn along and outpcd over 2f out: wknd whn btn fnl f* **12/1**

1m 37.07s (0.17) **Going Correction** -0.025s/f (Good) 7 Ran SP% **117.5**
Speed ratings (Par 97): **98,97,96,93,90 89,86**
CSF £58.07 TOTE £3.80: £1.60, £5.70; EX 33.60 Trifecta £119.90.
Owner Axom Lxxv **Bred** Old Carhue Stud **Trained** East Everleigh, Wilts

FOCUS
6 yards added. A very modest 3yo handicap. One of the joint-second favourites bravely scrambled home from the front.

3410 RAG'N'BONE MAN LIVE HERE 27 JULY APPRENTICE H'CAP — 6f 210y
5:00 (5:01) (Class 6) (0-55,58) 3-Y-O+
£3,105 (£924; £461; £300; £300; £300) **Stalls** Centre

Form RPR

P431 **1** **Confrerie (IRE)**[6] 3187 4-9-10 **58** 5ex........................ CierenFallon(5) 2 65+
(George Baker) *hld up: hdwy between rivals over 2f out: swtchd lft to far rail over 1f out: drvn and styd on strly to ld cl home* **6/5**[1]

2030 **2** *½* **Joyful Dream (IRE)**[43] 1967 5-8-13 **45**..................... DarraghKeenan(3) 8 51
(John Butler) *racd in midfield: effrt to cl on outer 2f out: led gng wl over 1f out: sn rdn and hdd by wnr cl home (jockey said mare hung left-handed under pressure)* **17/2**

23-0 **3** *1* **Harlequin Rose (IRE)**[33] 2286 5-8-11 **45**..................(v) WilliamCarver(5) 5 48
(Patrick Chamings) *racd in rr of midfield: hdwy u.p 3f out: swtchd lft and rdn 2f out: kpt on wl fnl f: nt match wnr* **7/1**[2]

0604 **4** *4* **Diamond Pursuit**[33] 2298 4-9-2 **45**............................ GabrieleMalune 7 38
(Ivan Furtado) *racd in midfield: rdn on inner over 2f out: kpt on one pce fnl f* **8/1**[3]

0000 **5** *2 ¾* **Quarto Cavallo**[19] 2734 3-7-13 **45**............................ IsobelFrancis(7) 9 26
(Adam West) *racd in rr: rdn and hung lft over 1f out: kpt on one pce fnl f (jockey said filly fly-leapt from the stalls)* **25/1**

-000 **6** *¾* **Cedar**[34] 2240 3-8-6 **48**..(t[1]) PoppyBridgwater(3) 3 27
(Mohamed Moubarak) *racd in tch in 4th: rdn and unable qck over 2f out: kpt on one pce fnl f* **25/1**

-300 **7** *2 ½* **Star Attraction (FR)**[96] 924 4-8-11 **45**......................... TobyEley(5) 13 21
(Tony Carroll) *racd in midfield: rdn and no imp 2f out: kpt on one pce* **40/1**

0-65 **8** *1* **Beg For Mercy**[13] 2926 3-8-11 **50**............................... JoshuaBryan 1 20
(Michael Attwater) *racd in rr of midfield: rdn and no imp 2f out: nvr on terms* **14/1**

13-6 **9** *1 ¼* **Keep It Country Tv**[129] 400 3-8-7 **53**......................... EllaBoardman(7) 12 19
(Pat Phelan) *racd in midfield on outer: rdn along and no imp over 2f out: nvr on terms* **16/1**

5360 **10** *1 ¼* **Kellington Kitty (USA)**[19] 2728 4-8-11 **45**.........(p[1]) ScottMcCullagh(5) 6 12
(Mike Murphy) *led: rdn along and hdd over 1f out: wknd fnl f* **10/1**

0030 **11** *1 ½* **Swiss Cross**[6] 3187 12-8-9 **45**..................................(p) GraceMcEntee(7) 4 8
(Phil McEntee) *chsd ldr: rdn and little rspnse 2f out: wknd fnl f* **14/1**

/0-0 **12** *1* **Paco Dawn**[124] 476 5-8-9 **45**.................................... ElishaWhittington(7) 11 5
(Tony Carroll) *slowly away and racd in rr: a bhd (jockey said mare jumped awkwardly from the stalls)* **33/1**

-500 **13** *1* **Dragon Kuza**[34] 2240 3-8-9 **48**..................................(v[1]) MeganNicholls 10
(Hugo Palmer) *racd in tch: rdn along and outpcd over 2f out: wknd fnl f* **16/1**

1m 23.21s (-0.59) **Going Correction** -0.025s/f (Good)
WFA 3 from 4yo+ 10lb 13 Ran SP% **126.9**
Speed ratings (Par 101): **102,101,100,95,92 91,88,87,86,84 83,82,80**
CSF £12.29 CT £61.79 TOTE £2.10: £1.30, £4.00, £1.60; EX 14.40 Trifecta £81.30.
Owner New Confidence Partnership **Bred** Hyde Park Stud **Trained** Chiddingfold, Surrey

FOCUS
6 yards added. A moderate apprentice riders' handicap. The favourite came with a withering late run up the far rail to win well in a good comparative time for the grade.
T/Plt: £323.70 to a £1 stake. Pool: £57,391.65 - 129.42 winning units T/Qpdt: £55.90 to a £1 stake. Pool: £4,731.55 - 62.58 winning units **Mark Grantham**

2840 THIRSK (L-H)
Monday, June 3

OFFICIAL GOING: Good to firm (good in places; watered)
Wind: fairly strong behind Weather: fine

3411 LIKE RACING TV ON FACEBOOK MAIDEN STKS — 6f
2:15 (2:17) (Class 5) 2-Y-O **£4,347** (£1,301; £650; £325; £162) **Stalls** Centre

Form RPR

5 **1** **Toro Strike (USA)**[16] 2830 2-9-5 0.............................. TonyHamilton 9 80+
(Richard Fahey) *prom: led 4f out: pushed along 2f out: sn pressed: drvn fnl 75yds: kpt on* **6/4**[1]

2 *nk* **The Bell Conductor (IRE)** 2-9-5 0.............................. SamJames 7 79+
(Phillip Makin) *in tch: racd keenly: hdwy to chal 2f out: sn rdn along: drvn ins fnl f: kpt on* **8/1**

2 **3** *1 ¼* **Oso Rapido (IRE)**[15] 2869 2-9-5 0.............................. DanielTudhope 6 75
(David O'Meara) *trckd ldrs: rdn to chal over 1f out: hung lft and no ex fnl 75yds* **5/2**[2]

3 **4** *2* **No Mercy**[17] 2783 2-9-5 0.. CliffordLee 4 69
(K R Burke) *trckd ldrs: rdn 2f out: kpt on same pce fnl f* **7/1**

3 **5** *2 ¼* **Leapers Wood**[14] 2892 2-9-5 0.................................... TomEaves 3 62
(Michael Dods) *hld up in tch: rdn 2f out: kpt on ins fnl f* **6/1**[3]

6 *3* **Refuge** 2-9-5 0.. NathanEvans 1 53+
(Michael Easterby) *veered lft s: rcvrd to chse ldrs 4f out: rdn over 2f out: wknd ins fnl f (jockey said gelding veered left at the start and ran green)* **50/1**

00 **7** *hd* **Ice Skate**[14] 2892 2-9-0 0.. DavidAllan 10 48
(Tim Easterby) *dwlt: hld up in tch: pushed along over 2f out: wknd ins fnl f* **66/1**

8 *3 ½* **Queen Moya (IRE)** 2-8-9 0.................................... FayeMcManoman(5) 8 37
(Nigel Tinkler) *trckd ldrs: lost pl over 3f out: wknd over 1f out* **100/1**

3 **9** *2* **Dancinginthesand (IRE)**[20] 2707 2-9-5 0...................... GrahamLee 5 36
(Bryan Smart) *led: hdd 4f out: remained cl up tl wknd over 1f out* **20/1**

10 *½* **My Havana** 2-9-2 0... RowanScott(3) 2 35+
(Nigel Tinkler) *dwlt and wnt lft s: a outpcd in rr* **66/1**

1m 10.77s (-2.03) **Going Correction** -0.45s/f (Firm) 10 Ran SP% **117.2**
Speed ratings (Par 93): **95,94,92,90,87 83,83,78,75,75**
CSF £14.36 TOTE £2.50: £1.20, £2.30, £1.20; EX 18.50 Trifecta £62.30.
Owner Al Shaqab Racing **Bred** Al Shaqab Racing **Trained** Musley Bank, N Yorks

FOCUS
A fair maiden, they raced centre-track and the favourite just did enough. The winner won with a bit up his sleeve.

3412 JOIN RACING TV NOW NOVICE STKS — 7f 218y
2:45 (2:47) (Class 5) 3-Y-O+ **£5,175** (£1,540; £769; £384) **Stalls** Low

Form RPR

0-1 **1** **Davydenko**[28] 2488 3-9-9 0.. LouisSteward 7 89+
(Sir Michael Stoute) *settled in tch: hdwy over 2f out: pushed into ld over 1f out: sn in command: eased fnl 50yds* **1/6**[1]

0-50 **2** *1 ¾* **Irv (IRE)**[19] 2746 3-9-2 72.. GrahamLee 3 73
(Micky Hammond) *led: rdn and hdd over 1f out: sn outpcd: kpt on but flattered by proximity to eased wnr* **9/2**[2]

6 **3** *6* **Summer Bride (IRE)**[14] 2909 3-8-12 0 ow1.................... DanielTudhope 4 55
(Tim Easterby) *trckd ldr: rdn and outpcd 2f out: plugged on to go modest 3rd ins fnl f* **12/1**[3]

0 **4** *2* **Heart In Havana**[34] 2250 3-9-2 0................................ NathanEvans 5 54
(Michael Easterby) *trckd ldr: rdn to chal briefly over 2f out: wknd over 1f out* **100/1**

00 **5** *2* **Voiceoftheemirates**[33] 2289 3-9-2 0............................. KevinStott 1 49
(Kevin Ryan) *in tch: rdn over 2f out: wknd over 1f out* **40/1**

6 *nk* **High Fort (IRE)**[12] 4-9-13 0....................................... JasonHart 8 51
(Karen McLintock) *hld up in rr: outpcd and bhd over 2f out: minor late hdwy* **80/1**

0 **7** *shd* **Taaldara (IRE)**[41] 2018 3-8-6 0.................................. HarrisonShaw(5) 6 43
(Ben Haslam) *hld up: pushed along over 2f out: nvr threatened* **80/1**

1m 38.61s (-3.09) **Going Correction** -0.45s/f (Firm)
WFA 3 from 4yo 11lb 7 Ran SP% **117.5**
Speed ratings (Par 103): **97,95,89,87,85 84,84**
CSF £1.58 TOTE £1.10: £1.10, £1.70; EX 1.60 Trifecta £3.50.
Owner Cheveley Park Stud **Bred** Cheveley Park Stud Ltd **Trained** Newmarket, Suffolk

FOCUS
An uncompetitive novice and it played out as the market expected. The winner was value for a bit extra.

3413 FOLLOW @RACINGTV ON TWITTER (S) H'CAP — 6f
3:15 (3:16) (Class 6) (0-65,62) 3-Y-O+
£3,398 (£1,011; £505; £300; £300; £300) **Stalls** Centre

Form RPR

5000 **1** **Ninjago**[12] 2958 9-9-9 **57**..(v) DanielTudhope 10 64
(Paul Midgley) *hld up in midfield: hdwy and chsd ldrs over 1f out: led ins fnl f: kpt on* **7/1**

0135 **2** *nk* **Brockey Rise (IRE)**[28] 2503 4-9-12 **60**..........................(b) CliffordLee 5 66
(David Evans) *chsd ldrs: rdn to ld over 1f out: hdd ins fnl f: kpt on* **10/1**

0000 **3** *1 ¾* **Jacob's Pillow**[5] 3221 8-9-12 **60**................................(p) DavidAllan 16 61
(Rebecca Bastiman) *prom: rdn 2f out: kpt on same pce fnl f* **14/1**

5600 4 3/4 **Vallarta (IRE)**[17] 2788 9-9-6 **54**.......... JackGarritty 7 53
(Ruth Carr) *chsd ldrs: led over 2f out: rdn and hdd over 1f out: no ex ins fnl f* **14/1**

-050 5 nk **Coastal Drive**[23] 2638 4-9-9 **57**.......... KevinStott 6 55
(Paul Midgley) *chsd ldrs: rdn and hung lft over 1f out: no ex fnl 50yds* **11/1**

10-0 6 nk **Gilmer (IRE)**[23] 2638 8-9-9 **57**.......... JoeFanning 14 54
(Stef Keniry) *midfield: rdn and sme hdwy over 1f out: one pce fnl f* **16/1**

0-45 7 1/2 **Cupid's Arrow (IRE)**[12] 2958 5-9-1 **52**.......... JamieGormley(3) 1 47
(Ruth Carr) *racd alone on far side: chsd ldrs overall: rdn over 2f out: wknd ins fnl f* **13/2**[3]

00-0 8 1 **Billy Wedge**[35] 2203 4-9-7 **55**.......... BarryMcHugh 11 47
(Tracy Waggott) *hld up: sme late hdwy: nvr threatened* **11/1**

1600 9 3/4 **Spirit Power**[23] 2632 4-10-0 **62**.......... JasonHart 8 52
(Eric Alston) *led narrowly: hdd over 2f out: wknd over 1f out* **20/1**

-500 10 hd **Parion**[20] 2708 3-9-1 **62**.......... SeanDavis(5) 3 49
(Richard Fahey) *midfield: rdn and outpcd over 2f out: nvr threatened* **16/1**

-226 11 1/2 **Someone Exciting**[21] 2678 6-9-0 **53**.......... HarrisonShaw(5) 13 41
(David Thompson) *nvr bttr than midfield* **5/1**[1]

-000 12 nk **Searanger (USA)**[23] 2638 6-9-9 **57**..........(p) PJMcDonald 12 44
(Rebecca Menzies) *chsd ldrs: rdn over 2f out: wknd over 1f out* **11/2**[2]

4-40 13 1 1/2 **Dark Confidant (IRE)**[81] 1192 6-8-4 **45**..........(p) EllaMcCain(7) 15 28
(Donald McCain) *chsd ldrs: wknd 2f out* **28/1**

00-5 14 2 1/4 **Ad Vitam (IRE)**[150] 64 11-8-12 **46**..........(bt) TomEaves 9 22
(Suzzanne France) *a towards rr* **33/1**

000- 15 23 **Nifty Niece (IRE)**[237] 8080 5-8-11 **45**.......... ShaneGray 4
(Ann Duffield) *a towards rr: t.o fnl 2f* **50/1**

1m 9.34s (-3.46) **Going Correction** -0.45s/f (Firm)
WFA 3 from 4yo+ 8lb **15 Ran SP% 121.9**
Speed ratings (Par 101): **105,104,102,101,100 100,99,98,97,97 96,96,94,91,60**
CSF £72.86 CT £989.40 TOTE £7.70: £2.60, £2.80, £4.70; EX 69.00 Trifecta £400.00.The winner was bought in for £3,200.
Owner Taylor's Bloodstock Ltd & P T Midgley **Bred** Newsells Park Stud **Trained** Westow, N Yorks

FOCUS
Lowly sprinting form. The first two came up the middle.

3414 CHARLIE DENT 70 REASONS TO CELEBRATE FILLIES' H'CAP 7f
3:45 (3:46) (Class 5) (0-70,69) 3-Y-O+
£5,175 (£1,540; £769; £384; £300; £300) **Stalls** Low

Form RPR

505- 1 **Aliento**[275] 6787 4-9-6 **58**.......... TomEaves 13 68
(Michael Dods) *hld up: hdwy on outside to ld over 1f out: sn hrd pressed: kpt on wl towards fin* **11/1**[3]

0132 2 3/4 **Supaulette (IRE)**[6] 3203 4-10-0 **66**..........(bt) DavidAllan 12 74
(Tim Easterby) *hld up: hdwy on outside and disp ld over 1f out: drifted to far rail ins fnl f: one pce fnl 50yds* **6/4**[1]

0-60 3 1 1/4 **Moretti (IRE)**[10] 3057 4-8-9 **47** oh1.......... JasonHart 4 52
(Les Eyre) *plld hrd: chsd ldrs: rdn whn checked and outpcd over 1f out: rallied ins fnl f: tk 3rd cl home: nt rch first two (jockey said filly ran too free)* **16/1**

0-32 4 nk **Elikapeka (FR)**[66] 1400 3-9-1 **63**.......... KevinStott 11 63
(Kevin Ryan) *trckd ldr: disp ld over 2f out: rdn and carried hd high over 1f out: no ex fnl f* **11/1**[3]

000- 5 hd **Groupie**[276] 6747 5-9-11 **63**.......... GrahamLee 9 66+
(Tom Tate) *s.i.s: hld up: stdy hdwy whn nt clr run briefly over 1f out: rdn and r.o wl fnl f: nrst fin (jockey said mare did not get the clearest of runs in the home straight)* **25/1**

0-01 6 1/2 **Kermouster**[15] 2870 3-9-1 **63**.......... SamJames 10 61
(Grant Tuer) *s.i.s: t.k.h towards rr: effrt and angled rt over 1f out: kpt on fnl f: no imp* **6/1**[2]

5-00 7 4 **Rosy Ryan (IRE)**[14] 2911 9-8-12 **50**.......... CamHardie 15 41
(Tina Jackson) *hld up in midfield on outside: rdn over 2f out: outpcd fr over 1f out* **16/1**

0-00 8 1 1/4 **Seek The Moon (USA)**[66] 1399 4-9-7 **59**..........(h[1]) DanielTudhope 6 47
(Lawrence Mullaney) *t.k.h: in tch: nt clr run over 2f out: lost pl over 1f out: n.d after (jockey said filly was denied a clear run continuously between the 2f marker and the final furlong marker)* **11/1**[3]

-532 9 3/4 **Lady Lavinia**[6] 3191 3-8-9 **57**.......... RachelRichardson 1 39
(Michael Easterby) *s.i.s: hld up: rdn over 2f out: sn no imp: btn over 1f out* **12/1**

0-60 10 shd **Lexington Palm (IRE)**[35] 2212 3-8-12 **60**.......... JoeFanning 7 41
(Keith Dalgleish) *led: hrd pressed fr over 2f out: already hdd and jst outpcd whn checked 1f out: wknd* **16/1**

540 11 1 1/4 **Grey Berry (IRE)**[24] 2590 3-9-3 **65**.......... DuranFentiman 2 43
(Tim Easterby) *s.i.s: sn in tch on ins: rdn over 2f out: wknd over 1f out* **33/1**

4004 12 3 1/2 **Picture Your Dream**[23] 2638 4-9-6 **58**.......... NathanEvans 16 31
(Seb Spencer) *prom on outside: rdn along over 2f out: sn wknd (jockey said filly was unsuited by the ground (good to firm) and would prefer a slower surface)* **12/1**

000/ 13 nk **Peach Pavlova (IRE)**[696] 4559 5-8-12 **50**.......... ShaneGray 5 22
(Ann Duffield) *hld up towards rr: struggling over 2f out: sn wknd* **50/1**

1m 25.09s (-2.51) **Going Correction** -0.45s/f (Firm)
WFA 3 from 4yo+ 10lb **13 Ran SP% 121.1**
Speed ratings (Par 100): **96,95,93,93,93 92,88,86,85,85 84,80,79**
CSF £27.64 CT £293.65 TOTE £12.40: £3.80, £1.10, £5.20; EX 43.10 Trifecta £1049.10.
Owner J A Knox and Mrs M A Knox **Bred** J A And M A Knox **Trained** Denton, Co Durham

FOCUS
A moderate handicap that was run at a strong gallop and set up nicely for the closers. The form's rated around the second.

3415 RACINGTV.COM H'CAP 1m 4f 8y
4:15 (4:15) (Class 5) (0-75,76) 3-Y-O+
£5,175 (£1,540; £769; £384; £300; £300) **Stalls** High

Form RPR

-566 1 **Ingleby Hollow**[9] 3095 7-10-0 **72**..........(t) DanielTudhope 8 80+
(David O'Meara) *hld up: smooth hdwy to chal over 2f out: shkn up to ld over 1f out: pushed out fnl f: snugly* **5/2**[2]

0251 2 3/4 **Francophilia**[11] 3015 4-10-0 **72**.......... JoeFanning 2 78+
(Mark Johnston) *trckd ldrs: effrt whn nt clr run over 2f out tl swtchd rt over 1f out: chsd wnr ins fnl f: kpt on fin* **15/8**[1]

6-21 3 2 1/4 **Glorious Dane**[30] 2417 3-8-10 **69**.......... ShaneGray 10 70
(Stef Keniry) *hld up: drvn and ev ch over 2f out to over 1f out: chsd wnr tl edgd lft and lost 2nd ins fnl f: sn no ex* **9/1**

0-00 4 3 1/2 **Tapis Libre**[19] 2748 11-9-11 **76**.......... JoshQuinn(7) 4 71
(Jacqueline Coward) *hld up towards rr: rdn along and outpcd 3f out: rallied over 1f out: kpt on: nt pce of first three* **33/1**

-350 5 3/4 **Biz Markee (IRE)**[88] 1066 3-8-1 **63**..........(p) JamieGormley(3) 1 57
(Roger Fell) *wnt lft s: bhd: pushed along over 4f out: sn outpcd: rallied over 1f out: nvr rchd ldrs* **33/1**

44-4 6 1 **Remember The Days (IRE)**[23] 2636 5-10-4 **76**.......... GrahamLee 6 69
(Jedd O'Keeffe) *in tch: drvn along over 3f out: outpcd over 2f out: n.d after (jockey said gelding was unsuited by the going (good to firm) and would prefer a slower surface)* **7/2**[3]

0305 7 1 1/2 **Be Perfect (USA)**[23] 2636 10-9-7 **65**..........(b) JackGarritty 9 55
(Ruth Carr) *led: hrd pressed fr over 2f out: hdd over 1f out: sn wknd* **17/2**

25-6 8 30 **Move In Faster**[27] 2512 4-9-6 **64**.......... TomEaves 3 6
(Michael Dods) *in tch: drvn and struggling 3f out: lost tch over 1f out: eased whn no ch ins fnl f* **20/1**

2m 32.69s (-7.31) **Going Correction** -0.45s/f (Firm)
WFA 3 from 4yo+ 15lb **8 Ran SP% 116.7**
Speed ratings (Par 103): **106,105,104,101,101 100,99,79**
CSF £7.63 CT £33.41 TOTE £2.90: £1.30, £1.10, £1.70; EX 7.70 Trifecta £40.70.
Owner Dave Scott & The Fallen Angels **Bred** Dave Scott **Trained** Upper Helmsley, N Yorks

FOCUS
The right pair came to the fore in this ordinary handicap. The winner scored comfortably off a good mark.

3416 WATCH RACING TV NOW MAIDEN STKS 5f
4:45 (4:46) (Class 5) 3-Y-O+
£4,851 (£1,443; £721; £360) **Stalls** Centre

Form RPR

3 1 **Mendamay**[32] 2332 3-9-0.......... DavidAllan 10 70
(Tim Easterby) *pressed ldr: effrt and rdn over 1f out: disp ld thrght fnl f: led cl home* **7/2**[2]

-423 2 shd **Abate**[7] 3159 3-9-5 75.......... JoeFanning 8 74
(Adrian Nicholls) *t.k.h: led: rdn 2f out: hrd pressed and edgd lft ins fnl f: kpt on: hdd cl home* **8/11**[1]

4 3 3 **Raksha (IRE)**[7] 3157 3-9-0.......... DanielTudhope 2 58
(David O'Meara) *t.k.h: prom: hung lft thrght: effrt and rdn over 1f out: outpcd fnl f* **7/1**[3]

0-4 4 1 3/4 **Kodiac Dancer (IRE)**[31] 2377 3-9-0.......... GrahamLee 4 52
(Julie Camacho) *t.k.h: prom: effrt and rdn over 1f out: outpcd fnl f* **12/1**

00 5 1 3/4 **Harry's Ridge (IRE)**[27] 2506 4-9-12.......... TomEaves 3 54
(Eric Alston) *hld up: shkn up and hung lft wl over 1f out: sn no imp* **33/1**

330- 6 2 **Magical Duchess**[222] 8533 3-9-0 67..........(h) ConnorBeasley 1 38
(Michael Dods) *bhd: rdn and outpcd 1/2-way: btn over 1f out* **8/1**

0-0 7 2 1/2 **Ingenium (IRE)**[37] 2123 3-9-0.......... (h) RobbieDowney 7 29
(David O'Meara) *t.k.h: trckd ldrs: rdn 1/2-way: wknd over 1f out* **40/1**

60- 8 6 **Red Hot Fusion (IRE)**[227] 8390 5-9-7.......... ConnorMurtagh(5) 5 16
(Alan Berry) *dwlt: bhd and outpcd: struggling fnl 2f* **200/1**

57.13s (-2.27) **Going Correction** -0.45s/f (Firm)
WFA 3 from 4yo+ 7lb **8 Ran SP% 117.3**
Speed ratings (Par 103): **100,99,95,92,89 86,82,72**
CSF £6.56 TOTE £4.10: £1.60, £1.10, £1.70; EX 6.80 Trifecta £25.00.
Owner Habton Farms **Bred** P Balding **Trained** Great Habton, N Yorks

FOCUS
Little depth to this sprint maiden and the two market leaders dominated. It's rated around the runner-up.

3417 SCOUTING FOR GIRLS - LIVE @THIRSKRACES FRIDAY 16TH AUGUST H'CAP 5f
5:15 (5:16) (Class 6) (0-60,62) 3-Y-O
£3,534 (£1,051; £525; £300; £300; £300) **Stalls** Centre

Form RPR

-161 1 **The Defiant**[32] 2327 3-9-10 **62**.......... KevinStott 5 69
(Paul Midgley) *wnt rt s: mde all: rdn over 1f out: edgd lft ins fnl f: r.o wl* **3/1**[2]

4122 2 2 **Fairy Fast (IRE)**[1] 3376 3-9-10 **62**..........(b) DanielTudhope 2 62
(David O'Meara) *hld up in tch: effrt and pushed along over 1f out: sn chsng wnr: r.o same pce fnl 100yds* **11/4**[1]

0060 3 1 1/2 **North Korea (IRE)**[14] 2908 3-8-12 **50**..........(p[1]) ConnorBeasley 3 45
(Brian Baugh) *chsd wnr to over 1f out: rdn and one pce ins fnl f* **20/1**

5026 4 shd **Dancing Mountain (IRE)**[14] 2908 3-8-13 **56**.......... BenSanderson(5) 7 50
(Roger Fell) *blkd s: bhd and sn pushed along: hdwy over 1f out: kpt on fnl f: nrst fin* **6/1**

5-31 5 1/2 **Frosted Lass**[14] 2908 3-9-7 **59**.......... RobbieDowney 8 51
(David Barron) *hld up: rdn along 1/2-way: hdwy over 1f out: no imp fnl f* **4/1**[3]

-020 6 3/4 **Brahma Kamal**[21] 2683 3-8-8 **46**..........(v[1]) JoeFanning 1 36
(Keith Dalgleish) *prom: outpcd and hung lft 2f out: sn n.d* **9/1**

1410 7 nk **Gunnabedun (IRE)**[21] 2683 3-9-2 **57**..........(b) JamieGormley(3) 9 46
(Iain Jardine) *in tch: rdn and outpcd wl over 1f out: n.d after* **20/1**

06-0 8 1/2 **Se Green**[42] 1982 3-8-7 **45**..........(b[1]) RachelRichardson 10 32
(Tim Easterby) *dwlt: bhd: rdn and outpcd 2f out: sn btn* **33/1**

-063 9 1 **Raquelle (IRE)**[14] 2908 3-8-9 **47**..........(p[1]) DuranFentiman 4 30
(Tim Easterby) *prom: rdn over 2f out: wknd over 1f out* **14/1**

04-0 10 6 **Lady Kinsale**[14] 2897 3-8-12 **50**.......... TomEaves 6 12
(Eric Alston) *blkd s: bhd and sn rdn: struggling 1/2-way: sn wknd (trainer said filly was unsuited by the ground (good to firm) and would prefer a slower surface)* **50/1**

57.18s (-2.22) **Going Correction** -0.45s/f (Firm) **10 Ran SP% 117.0**
Speed ratings (Par 97): **99,95,93,93,92 91,90,89,88,78**
CSF £11.17 CT £138.31 TOTE £4.00: £1.20, £1.30, £4.80; EX 12.90 Trifecta £175.40.
Owner Joe And Frank Brady **Bred** Frank Brady **Trained** Westow, N Yorks

FOCUS
Moderate sprinting form, but a dominate winner.

T/Jkpt: Part Won. £10,000.00 to a £1 stake. Pool: £14,084.51 - 0.5 winning units. T/Plt: £9.00 to a £1 stake. Pool: £62,626.10 - 5,039.45 winning units T/Qpdt: £7.70 to a £1 stake. Pool: £6,400.89 - 612.23 winning units **Richard Young/Andrew Sheret**

[3164] WINDSOR (R-H)

Monday, June 3

OFFICIAL GOING: Good to firm (good in places; watered; 7.3)

Wind: moderate, half behind Weather: Fine but cloudy

3418 VISIT MARATHONBET.CO.UK H'CAP — 1m 3f 99y

5:30 (5:33) (Class 6) (0-60,61) 3-Y-O

£3,105 (£924; £461; £300; £300; £300) Stalls Low

Form — RPR

4054 1 **Cherry Cola**[2] 3348 3-9-2 **55** .... TrevorWhelan 15 67+
(Sheena West) *hld up in last pair: gd prog over 3f out to press ldng pair 2f out: drvn to ld ins fnl f: styd on wl* **16/1**

5-02 2 1 1/4 **Junior Rip (IRE)**[13] 2941 3-9-7 **60** .... (bt[1]) JasonWatson 9 70
(Roger Charlton) *trckd ldr: led wl over 2f out: sn rdn: edgd lft and hdd ins fnl f: styd on* **7/2[2]**

0-53 3 6 **Queen's Soldier (GER)**[30] 2407 3-9-8 **61** .... AdamKirby 10 61
(Andrew Balding) *trckd ldrs: effrt to go 2nd over 2f out to over 1f out: wknd fnl f* **9/2[3]**

00-1 4 2 1/2 **Gold Arch**[35] 2213 3-9-8 **61** .... StevieDonohoe 14 57+
(David Lanigan) *rousted along to chse ldrs: rdn 3f out: nt pce to threaten and lft bhd u.p fnl 2f* **3/1[1]**

0253 5 3/4 **Brinkleys Katie**[14] 2901 3-8-12 **51** .... (v) JFEgan 7 46
(Paul George) *chsd ldrs: rdn 3f out: wknd u.p fr 2f out* **16/1**

0-00 6 3 3/4 **Harry The Norseman**[27] 2518 3-9-7 **60** .... LiamKeniry 11 49
(Jonjo O'Neill) *hld up wl in rr: rdn over 3f out: no prog over 2f out: kpt on to pass wkng rivals over 1f out* **66/1**

5-00 7 1 3/4 **Loch Lady**[32] 2343 3-9-4 **57** .... (b[1]) HarryBentley 12 43
(Ralph Beckett) *led to wl over 2f out: sn wknd* **14/1**

-040 8 3/4 **Another Approach (FR)**[32] 2341 3-9-3 **56** .... (p[1]) JamieSpencer 8 40
(George Baker) *hld up in rr: prog on outer over 3f out: no hdwy 2f out: wknd over 1f out* **25/1**

5033 9 3 **Hen (IRE)**[21] 2697 3-9-6 **59** .... DougieCostello 2 38
(Jamie Osborne) *hld up wl in rr: shkn up 3f out: nvr clrst of runs but no real prog* **10/1**

0-25 10 shd **Catch The Cuban**[10] 3034 3-9-6 **59** .... (tp) CharlieBennett 6 38
(Colin Tizzard) *a in rr: rdn and struggling over 3f out* **16/1**

06-0 11 1 **Arbuckle**[32] 2341 3-8-13 **52** .... GeorgeWood 5 30
(Michael Madgwick) *chsd ldrs: lost pl 1/2-way: struggling in rr 3f out* **100/1**

0 12 1 **Dandy Belle (IRE)**[11] 2995 3-8-13 **52** .... RichardKingscote 4 28
(Richenda Ford) *chsd ldrs: rdn over 3f out: wknd over 2f out* **66/1**

5564 13 4 **Lucky Lou (IRE)**[32] 2341 3-9-7 **60** .... (p[1]) PatDobbs 3 29
(Ken Cunningham-Brown) *chsd ldng pair to 3f out: wknd qckly* **25/1**

00-3 14 18 **Brooklyn Boy**[41] 2011 3-9-7 **60** .... TomMarquand 1
(Harry Dunlop) *chsd ldrs but sn pushed along: lost pl 3f out: bhd and eased over 1f out: t.o* **10/1**

2m 27.71s (-1.99) **Going Correction** -0.125s/f (Firm) **14** Ran SP% **119.6**
Speed ratings (Par 97): **102,101,96,94,94 91,90,89,87,87 86,86,83,70**
CSF £68.99 CT £305.67 TOTE £17.60: £5.70, £1.50, £2.20; EX 125.90 Trifecta £630.00.
Owner Ashley Head **Bred** Norman Court Stud **Trained** Falmer, E Sussex

FOCUS
Rail movements added 15yds to the race distance. A competitive looking low-grade handicap for 3yos, but the first two came clear. The winner is progressing now.

3419 SYNERGY COMMERCIAL FINANCE FUNDING UK BUSINESSES EBF NOVICE STKS (PLUS 10 RACE) — 6f 12y

6:00 (6:01) (Class 4) 2-Y-O £5,175 (£1,540; £769; £384) Stalls Centre

Form — RPR

4 1 **Golden Horde (IRE)**[17] 2792 2-9-5 .... AdamKirby 1 90
(Clive Cox) *mde virtually all: shkn up to assert 2f out: styd on wl fnl f: readily* **6/5[1]**

0 2 4 1/2 **Indian Creak (IRE)**[17] 2792 2-9-5 .... PatDobbs 7 77
(Mick Channon) *chsd ldng quartet: pushed along 1/2-way: prog 2f out: tk 2nd ins fnl f: kpt on but no ch w wnr* **25/1**

45 3 1 **Making History (IRE)**[21] 2686 2-9-5 .... HectorCrouch 9 74
(Saeed bin Suroor) *chsd ldng pair: shkn up to chse wnr wl over 1f out: no imp: lost 2nd ins fnl f* **8/1[3]**

4 2 3/4 **Stone Circle (IRE)** 2-9-5 .... JamieSpencer 4 65+
(Michael Bell) *chsd ldng pair: pushed along over 2f out: rn green and fdd over 1f out* **7/1[2]**

5 shd **Atlantic Crossing (IRE)** 2-9-5 .... HarryBentley 5 65+
(Paul Cole) *off the pce in 7th and sn pushed along: kpt on steadily over 1f out: nvr nrr* **14/1**

6 3/4 **Hexagon (IRE)** 2-9-5 .... JasonWatson 11 63
(Roger Charlton) *towards rr and off the pce: shkn up over 2f out: kpt on steadily after: nvr nrr* **12/1**

7 1 1/4 **Eton College (IRE)** 2-9-5 .... RichardKingscote 12 59
(Mark Johnston) *gd spd fr wd draw: w wnr to jst over 2f out: wknd over 1f out* **8/1[3]**

8 2 3/4 **New Jack Swing (IRE)** 2-9-5 .... SeanLevey 8 51+
(Richard Hannon) *chsd ldrs disputing 5th: pushed along 1/2-way: wknd 2f out* **10/1**

9 5 **Apples Acre (IRE)** 2-9-0 .... JFEgan 6 31
(Paul George) *dwlt: a outpcd and bhd* **50/1**

0 10 3 1/2 **Gypsy Rocker (IRE)**[17] 2792 2-9-5 .... TomMarquand 3 25
(Brian Meehan) *awkward s and slowly away: a bhd* **20/1**

11 1 1/4 **Glamorous Anna** 2-9-0 .... LiamKeniry 10 16+
(Christopher Mason) *s.v.s: detached in last early: a bhd (jockey said filly was slowly away)* **100/1**

12 2 **Made Guy (USA)** 2-9-5 .... JosephineGordon 13 15
(J S Moore) *dwlt: sn rdn: outpcd and a bhd* **66/1**

13 8 **Power Of Love** 2-9-5 .... NicolaCurrie 2
(George Baker) *a bhd: t.o* **50/1**

1m 11.18s (-0.92) **Going Correction** -0.125s/f (Firm) **13** Ran SP% **118.6**
Speed ratings (Par 95): **101,95,93,90,89 88,87,83,76,72 70,67,57**
CSF £45.08 TOTE £2.00: £1.10, £6.10, £2.40; EX 31.50 Trifecta £141.60.
Owner AlMohamediya Racing **Bred** Cn Farm Ltd **Trained** Lambourn, Berks

FOCUS
An interesting juvenile maiden which last year was won by a colt who was subsequently placed at Group 2 level. Those with experience dominated the closing stages and the winner produced a useful performance.

3420 DOWNLOAD THE MARATHONBET APP CLASSIFIED STKS — 6f 12y

6:30 (6:31) (Class 5) 3-Y-O

£3,752 (£1,116; £557; £300; £300; £300) Stalls Centre

Form — RPR

302- 1 **Night Secret (IRE)**[205] 9000 3-9-0 75 .... (t[1]) TomMarquand 6 78
(William Haggas) *in tch: rdn to cl on ldrs on outer fr over 2f out: drvn to ld wl ins fnl f: kpt on wl* **10/11[1]**

2-33 2 nk **Mr Buttons (IRE)**[43] 1969 3-9-0 71 .... ShaneKelly 2 77
(Linda Stubbs) *trckd ldr: rdn to ld wl over 1f out: hdd wl ins fnl f: kpt on but jst hld* **12/1**

2-25 3 4 **Sirius Slew**[12] 2976 3-9-0 75 .... RaulDaSilva 4 64
(Alan Bailey) *chsd ldng pair: urged along 1/2-way: in tch jst over 1f out: fdd ins fnl f* **13/2[2]**

05-0 4 2 1/4 **Aquarius (IRE)**[14] 2904 3-9-0 67 .... (p[1]) AlistairRawlinson 5 57
(Michael Appleby) *led: rdn and hdd wl over 1f out: wknd fnl f* **11/1**

-530 5 3 3/4 **Champion Brogie (IRE)**[24] 2567 3-9-0 73 .... LiamKeniry 7 45
(J S Moore) *dwlt: outpcd in last pair: nvr a factor* **10/1**

-500 6 10 **Mawde (IRE)**[17] 2810 3-9-0 73 .... NicolaCurrie 1 13
(Rod Millman) *s.s: outpcd and a bhd (jockey said filly was slowly away and never travelling)* **10/1**

2-56 7 1 **Usain Boat (IRE)**[26] 2529 3-9-0 74 .... (v[1]) HarryBentley 3 10
(George Scott) *awkward s: in tch to over 2f out: sn wknd: eased fnl f (jockey said gelding was slowly away)* **7/1[3]**

1m 10.87s (-1.23) **Going Correction** -0.125s/f (Firm) **7** Ran SP% **112.4**
Speed ratings (Par 99): **103,102,97,94,89 75,74**
CSF £12.77 TOTE £1.80: £1.20, £4.10; EX 12.50 Trifecta £42.20.
Owner Clipper Logistics **Bred** Liam Phelan **Trained** Newmarket, Suffolk

FOCUS
Not much between the whole field on ratings in this classified sprint. The time was 0.31secs faster than the preceding 2yo novice. The form is rated through the runner-up.

3421 MARATHONBET OFFICIAL GLOBAL PARTNER OF MANCHESTER CITY NOVICE STKS — 6f 12y

7:00 (7:00) (Class 5) 3-Y-O+ £3,752 (£1,116; £557; £278) Stalls Centre

Form — RPR

1 **Drummond Warrior (IRE)** 3-9-2 .... ShaneKelly 10 77
(Pam Sly) *nt that wl away: prog fr rr by 1/2-way: jnd ldrs on outer 2f out: rdn to ld jst over 1f out: hld on wl* **20/1**

5 2 hd **Alliseeisnibras (IRE)**[13] 2938 3-8-11 .... SeanLevey 5 71
(Ismail Mohammed) *chsd ldrs: rdn 2f out: str chal towards outer fnl f: jst denied* **10/1**

30-0 3 1/2 **Gambon (GER)**[36] 2139 3-9-2 77 .... CharlesBishop 6 76+
(Eve Johnson Houghton) *chsd ldrs: nt clr run briefly wl over 1f out then nudged by rival: rdn and styd on fnl f to take 3rd last strides* **4/1[2]**

022- 4 3/4 **Ricochet (IRE)**[173] 9497 3-9-2 79 .... NicolaCurrie 7 72
(Jamie Osborne) *t.k.h: sn pressed ldr: led after 1/2-way: edgd lft over 1f out: hdd and nt qckn sn after: one pce ins fnl f* **11/10[1]**

4- 5 3 **Meghan Sparkle (IRE)**[180] 9395 3-8-11 .... HectorCrouch 2 57
(Clive Cox) *led: hdd after 1/2-way: fdd over 1f out* **9/2[3]**

06 6 4 **Caesonia**[27] 2506 3-8-11 .... RichardKingscote 1 45
(Charles Hills) *chsd ldr early: styd clsd up towards nr side rail: steadily wknd fr 2f out* **7/1**

6-0 7 1/2 **Fanny Chenal**[23] 2623 3-8-11 .... CharlieBennett 4 43
(Jim Boyle) *outpcd and nvr a factor* **40/1**

0-0 8 3/4 **Mallons Spirit (IRE)**[13] 2932 3-8-11 .... AlistairRawlinson 9 41
(Michael Appleby) *spd on wd outside and prom over 3f: wknd wl over 1f out (jockey said filly hung left-handed)* **100/1**

0 9 10 **Red Moon Lady**[25] 2550 3-8-11 .... JoeyHaynes 8 9
(Dean Ivory) *outpcd and a bhd* **80/1**

10 nk **Mottaham (FR)** 4-9-10 .... JFEgan 3 15
(Christian Williams) *mostly in last: allowed to come home in own time* **50/1**

1m 12.13s (0.03) **Going Correction** -0.125s/f (Firm)
WFA 3 from 4yo 8lb **10** Ran SP% **118.8**
Speed ratings (Par 103): **94,93,93,92,88 82,82,81,67,67**
CSF £200.72 TOTE £24.80: £5.00, £2.90, £1.60; EX 287.30 Trifecta £1108.30.
Owner G A Libson & Mrs P M Sly **Bred** Ronan Fitzpatrick **Trained** Thorney, Cambs

FOCUS
Those with ratings set a fair standard in this 3yo novice. The time compared unfavourably with the two earlier races over the trip, suggesting the form is not that strong. It seems to make sense at face value.

3422 MARATHONBET SPORTSBOOK H'CAP (WINDSOR SPRINT SERIES QUALIFIER) — 5f 21y

7:30 (7:32) (Class 3) (0-90,89) 3-Y-O £7,246 (£2,168; £1,084; £542; £270) Stalls Centre

Form — RPR

0-01 1 **Dark Shadow (IRE)**[33] 2274 3-8-13 **81** .... HectorCrouch 3 87
(Clive Cox) *hld up in last pair: prog on outer 1/2-way: clsd on ldrs over 1f out: rdn to ld ins fnl f: styd on* **5/1[3]**

0-46 2 3/4 **Naughty Rascal (IRE)**[16] 2835 3-9-7 **89** .... TomMarquand 2 92
(Richard Hannon) *pushed along in last pair and struggling to stay in tch: prog u.p 2f out: trying to cl on outer whn impeded ins fnl f: styd on to take 2nd last strides* **2/1[1]**

4-62 3 hd **Thegreatestshowman**[36] 2149 3-8-12 **80** ow1 .... (p[1]) DougieCostello 6 82+
(Amy Murphy) *prom: chsd ldr 1/2-way: led wl over 1f out: edgd lft u.p fnl f: hdd and nt qckn sn after* **9/4[2]**

2300 4 1 **Uncle Jerry**[26] 2525 3-9-0 **82** .... (b) ShaneKelly 1 81
(Richard Hughes) *in tch: effrt to chse ldrs over 1f out: nt qckn and kpt on same pce fnl f* **11/1**

3-31 5 2 1/2 **Shining**[19] 2730 3-8-11 **79** .... CharlieBennett 5 69
(Jim Boyle) *chsd ldr to 1/2-way: steadily wknd over 1f out* **6/1**

0-00 6 4 1/2 **Fly The Nest (IRE)**[24] 2567 3-8-9 **77** .... NicolaCurrie 7 50
(Tony Carroll) *chsd ldrs to 1/2-way: sn lost pl and btn* **20/1**

060- 7 nk **Country Rose (IRE)**[256] 7454 3-8-12 **80** .... (h[1]) LiamKeniry 4 52
(Ronald Harris) *led: styd against nr side rail: 2 l ahd 1/2-way: hdd & wknd qckly wl over 1f out* **20/1**

59.04s (-1.06) **Going Correction** -0.125s/f (Firm) **7** Ran SP% **112.9**
Speed ratings (Par 103): **103,101,101,99,95 88,88**
CSF £15.05 TOTE £5.70: £2.40, £1.70; EX 19.60 Trifecta £44.30.
Owner J Goddard **Bred** Redpender Stud Ltd **Trained** Lambourn, Berks
■ Stewards' Enquiry : Dougie Costello caution; careless riding

The Form Book Flat 2019, Raceform Ltd, Newbury, RG14 5SJ

FOCUS
The first of the two feature races and a pretty decent handicap over the minimum distance.\n\x\x
The pace was frantic early and the first two came from the back. The winner built on his Bath win.

3423 TIM PARKINS H'CAP — 1m 31y
8:00 (8:01) (Class 3) (0-90,89) 4-Y-O **£7,246** (£2,168; £1,084; £542; £270) **Stalls** Low

Form				RPR
0061	**1**		**Ballard Down (IRE)**[27] 2514 6-9-3 **88**...(v) FinleyMarsh(3) 7	96
(David Pipe) *rel to r and lft 8 l s: adrift in last most of way: urged along over 2f out: stl last over 1f out: sed to run on after: str burst on outer fnl f to ld post (jockey said gelding was slowly away)* **9/1**
1615 | **2** | *nse* | **Mr Tyrrell (IRE)**[17] 2799 5-9-3 **85**... SeanLevey 2 | 92
(Richard Hannon) *trckd ldng pair: led jst over 2f out: drvn over 1f out: looked in command fnl f: styd on but hdd post* **4/1**[3]
2120 | **3** | *1 ¼* | **Family Fortunes**[72] 1294 5-9-2 **89**... ScottMcCullagh(5) 3 | 93
(Michael Madgwick) *hld up disputing 5th: clsd on ldrs 2f out: waiting for a gap over 1f out: drvn to chse ldr briefly fnl f: one pce* **7/1**
30-1 | **4** | *1* | **Wind In My Sails**[17] 2797 7-8-5 **80**... TobyEley(7) 5 | 82
(Ed de Giles) *taken down early: t.k.h: hld up disputing 5th: clsd over 2f out: rdn and nt qckn over 1f out: one pce after (jockey said gelding hung right-handed)* **7/2**[2]
0-40 | **5** | *1 ¼* | **Letsbe Avenue (IRE)**[33] 2273 4-8-11 **79**... FergusSweeney 6 | 78
(Richard Hannon) *trckd ldr: led over 3f out to jst over 2f out: wknd fnl f* **12/1**
1/04 | **6** | *1 ½* | **I'vegotthepower (IRE)**[11] 3027 5-9-4 **86**...(v) JasonWatson 1 | 82
(Brian Meehan) *led: racd against rail and hdd over 3f out: styd in tch tl wknd over 1f out (vet said gelding was lame left fore)* **9/4**[1]
004- | **7** | *2 ½* | **Maratha (IRE)**[184] 9358 5-8-12 **80**...(t) RichardKingscote 8 | 70
(Stuart Williams) *chsd ldng trio: rdn over 2f out: lost pl and wknd over 1f out* **8/1**

1m 43.54s (-0.96) **Going Correction** -0.125s/f (Firm) **7 Ran SP% 114.3**
Speed ratings (Par 107): **99,98,97,96,95 93,91**
CSF £44.49 CT £268.94 TOTE £10.30: £4.70, £2.50; EX 45.50 Trifecta £228.40.
Owner W Frewen **Bred** D Harron, Ederidge Ltd & Glenvale Stud **Trained** Nicholashayne, Devon

FOCUS
Rail movements added 15yds to the race distance. The second feature contest and only 10lb covered the field in this handicap. It was a race of changing fortunes and the winner passed all his rivals in the closing stages to snatch the race. It's hard to be confident in the form.

3424 SKY SPORTS RACING VIRGIN 535 H'CAP — 1m 2f
8:30 (8:30) (Class 4) (0-85,86) 4-Y-O+ **£5,530** (£1,645; £822; £411) **Stalls** Low

Form				RPR
3212	**1**		**Lawn Ranger**[11] 3016 4-9-7 **82**... KierenFox 3	94+
(Michael Attwater) *mde all: set str pce and sn clr: stl 6 l ahd over 2f out: drvn and edgd lft over 1f out: nvr in any danger and heavily eased nr fin* **9/4**[2]
-230 | **2** | *¾* | **Grapevine (IRE)**[17] 2797 6-9-0 **75**...(p[1]) RichardKingscote 6 | 79
(Charles Hills) *hld up in 3rd and off the pce: coaxed along over 2f out: kpt on fnl f to take 2nd last strides: no ch w wnr and flattered by proximity* **11/2**
-002 | **3** | *nk* | **Petrastar**[21] 2691 4-9-4 **79**... AdamKirby 5 | 82
(Clive Cox) *chsd wnr: rdn and no imp over 2f out: one pce after and lost 2nd nr fin: flattered to fin so cl* **7/4**[1]
0116 | **4** | *1* | **Regular Income (IRE)**[3] 3315 4-8-11 **79**...(p) TobyEley(7) 2 | 80
(Adam West) *s.s: hld up in last: brief effrt 3f out: sn no prog and btn: flattered to fin so cl* **3/1**[3]

2m 6.75s (-2.25) **Going Correction** -0.125s/f (Firm) **4 Ran SP% 107.5**
Speed ratings (Par 105): **104,103,103,102**
CSF £12.92 TOTE £3.20; EX 15.00 Trifecta £30.80.
Owner Canisbay Bloodstock **Bred** Jacqueline Doyle **Trained** Epsom, Surrey

FOCUS
Rail movements added 15yds to the race distance. A small field for this fair handicap but it turned into something of a procession. The winner was value for further.
T/Plt: £308.30 to a £1 stake. Pool: £72,281.70 - 171.12 winning units T/Qpdt: £122.00 to a £1 stake. Pool: £7,376.97 - 44.72 winning units **Jonathan Neesom**

3319 WOLVERHAMPTON (A.W) (L-H)
Monday, June 3

OFFICIAL GOING: Tapeta: standard
Wind: Light behind Weather: Cloudy with sunny spells

3425 GRAND THEATRE WOLVERHAMPTON H'CAP — 5f 21y (Tp)
5:45 (5:45) (Class 6) (0-55,59) 3-Y-O+ **£3,105** (£924; £461; £300; £300; £300) **Stalls** Low

Form				RPR
041	**1**		**Awsaaf**[3] 3320 4-9-12 **59** 5ex...(t) TonyHamilton 3	69
(Michael Wigham) *trckd ldrs: plld hrd: hmpd over 3f out: shkn up and swtchd rt over 1f out: rdn: edgd lft and r.o to ld wl ins fnl f: comf* **10/11**[1]
5030 | **2** | *½* | **Brogans Bay (IRE)**[10] 3036 4-9-2 **49**... DavidProbert 11 | 57
(Simon Dow) *led 4f out: sn edgd lft: rdn over 1f out: hdd wl ins fnl f* **50/1**
3033 | **3** | *2 ½* | **Le Manege Enchante (IRE)**[11] 3001 6-8-13 **46**...(v) PaddyMathers 5 | 45
(Derek Shaw) *s.i.s: sn pushed along in rr: hdwy over 1f out: rdn and r.o to go 3rd nr fin: nt rch ldrs* **9/1**[3]
224 | **4** | *½* | **Prominna**[58] 1590 9-9-7 **54**... GeorgeDowning 9 | 51
(Tony Carroll) *s.i.s: hld up: nt clr run 1/2-way: hdwy over 1f out: sn rdn: styd on same pce wl ins fnl f* **25/1**
0004 | **5** | *1 ¾* | **Dubai Elegance**[11] 3001 5-9-1 **48**...(p) LewisEdmunds 4 | 39
(Derek Shaw) *s.i.s: sn pushed along in rr: rdn over 1f out: styd on ins fnl f: nvr nrr* **9/1**[3]
0042 | **6** | *nk* | **Waneen (IRE)**[13] 2924 6-9-1 **48**...(b) SilvestreDeSousa 8 | 38
(John Butler) *chsd ldrs: hmpd over 3f out: rdn over 1f out: wknd ins fnl f* **7/2**[2]
6365 | **7** | *½* | **Caledonian Gold**[9] 3067 6-8-5 **45**... GavinAshton(7) 6 | 33
(Lisa Williamson) *prom: nt clr run and lost pl 4f out: n.d after* **16/1**
3050 | **8** | *½* | **Captain Ryan**[19] 2728 8-9-5 **52**...(p) KieranO'Neill 2 | 38
(Geoffrey Deacon) *chsd ldrs: rdn over 1f out: wknd ins fnl f* **12/1**
630- | **9** | *½* | **Mysusy (IRE)**[231] 8258 3-8-13 **53**...(p) EdwardGreatrex 10 | 35
(Robert Cowell) *prom: lost pl over 4f out: n.d after* **16/1**
0-00 | **10** | *14* | **Ballesteros**[35] 2206 10-8-13 **46**...(p[1]) EoinWalsh 7 |
(Emma Owen) *led 1f: rdn 1/2-way: wknd over 1f out (jockey said gelding stopped quickly)* **80/1**

1m 1.31s (-0.59) **Going Correction** -0.125s/f (Stan) **10 Ran SP% 121.1**
WFA 3 from 4yo+ 7lb
Speed ratings (Par 101): **99,98,94,93,90 90,89,88,87,65**
CSF £76.22 CT £310.16 TOTE £1.80: £1.10, £12.90, £2.30; EX 77.70 Trifecta £509.40.
Owner Tugay Akman & Ms I D Heerowa **Bred** Lordship Stud **Trained** Newmarket, Suffolk
■ Stewards' Enquiry : David Probert two-day ban; careless riding (June 6,23)

FOCUS
A low-grade affair to open proceedings but the front two will remain of interest, the favourite following up Friday's C&D win in good style. The runner-up is the best guide.

3426 VISIT THE BLACK COUNTRY NOVICE STKS — 6f 20y (Tp)
6:15 (6:17) (Class 5) 2-Y-O **£3,752** (£1,116; £557; £278) **Stalls** Low

Form				RPR
5	**1**		**Sun Power (FR)**[19] 2747 2-9-5 0... SilvestreDeSousa 6	83
(Richard Hannon) *sn w ldr tl 4f out: remained handy: shkn up and hung lft fr over 1f out: styd on to ld wl ins fnl f: comf* **3/1**[1]
4 | **2** | *2* | **Homespin (USA)**[13] 2931 2-9-5 0... DavidEgan 1 | 77
(Mark Johnston) *sn led: shkn up over 2f out: rdn over 1f out: hdd wl ins fnl f: styd on same pce* **3/1**[1]
6 | **3** | *shd* | **Welcome Surprise (IRE)**[18] 2767 2-9-5 0... DavidProbert 7 | 77
(Saeed bin Suroor) *led early: remained w ldr: rdn and ev ch fr over 1f out tl styd on same pce wl ins fnl f* **6/1**
2 | **4** | *4* | **Miss Villanelle**[9] 3076 2-9-0 0... KieranShoemark 2 | 60
(Charles Hills) *chsd ldrs: shkn up over 2f out: styd on same pce fr over 1f out* **17/2**
3 | **5** | *¾* | **Royal Council (IRE)**[30] 2394 2-9-5 0... TonyHamilton 5 | 62
(James Tate) *broke wl: plld hrd: sn stdd to trck ldrs: rdn over 1f out: styd on same pce* **9/2**[3]
 | **6** | *19* | **Yalata** 2-9-5 0... BrettDoyle 3 | 5
(Charlie Appleby) *s.i.s: outpcd (jockey said colt ran green)* **4/1**[2]

1m 14.17s (-0.33) **Going Correction** -0.125s/f (Stan) **6 Ran SP% 113.0**
Speed ratings (Par 93): **97,94,94,88,87 62**
CSF £12.32 TOTE £3.80: £2.60, £1.40; EX 12.80 Trifecta £49.70.
Owner King Power Racing Co Ltd **Bred** Seven Hills Bloodstock Nh Ltd **Trained** East Everleigh, Wilts
■ Casi Casi was withdrawn, price at time of withdrawal 150/1. Rule 4 does not apply.

FOCUS
Some powerful stables represented and probably a good novice for the track. The eventual second and third helped got racing quite a long way out and shaped better than their distance beaten would suggest.

3427 SKY SPORTS RACING SKY 415 FILLIES' H'CAP — 6f 20y (Tp)
6:45 (6:46) (Class 4) (0-85,86) 3-Y-O+ **£5,530** (£1,645; £822; £411; £300; £300) **Stalls** Low

Form				RPR
516-	**1**		**Furious**[213] 8805 3-9-7 **82**... OisinMurphy 1	91
(David Simcock) *sn led at stdy pce: shkn up and qcknd 2f out: styd on wl* **9/4**[1]
06-0 | **2** | *2* | **More Than Likely**[11] 2997 3-8-12 **80**... GeorgeRooke(7) 7 | 83
(Richard Hughes) *hld up: hdwy on outer over 1f out: rdn whn rdr dropped whip wl ins fnl f: r.o to go 2nd nr fin: nt rch wnr (jockey dropped his whip on the run to the line)* **14/1**
-304 | **3** | *hd* | **Reticent Angel (IRE)**[33] 2274 3-9-4 **79**...(p) HollieDoyle 2 | 81
(Clive Cox) *chsd ldrs: rdn over 1f out: r.o* **6/1**[3]
4061 | **4** | *¾* | **Di Matteo**[35] 2212 3-8-7 **68**... DavidEgan 3 | 68
(Marco Botti) *sn prom: rdn to chse wnr over 1f out tl no ex wl ins fnl f* **5/2**[2]
-311 | **5** | *nk* | **Always A Drama (IRE)**[102] 824 4-9-10 **77**... KieranShoemark 4 | 78
(Charles Hills) *prom: chsd wnr over 4f out tl rdn over 1f out: styd on same pce ins fnl f* **7/1**
5-16 | **6** | *2* | **Shorter Skirt**[24] 2567 3-9-1 **76**... EdwardGreatrex 8 | 69
(Eve Johnson Houghton) *s.i.s: hld up: rdn over 1f out: nt trble ldrs* **9/1**
2616 | **7** | *1 ½* | **Rose Berry**[45] 1913 5-10-0 **86**...(h) SeanDavis(5) 6 | 76
(Charlie Wallis) *broke wl: sn stdd and lost pl: shkn up over 1f out: nt trble ldrs* **10/1**
04-6 | **8** | *7* | **Elizabeth Bennet (IRE)**[21] 2687 4-9-9 **81**... DylanHogan(5) 5 | 48
(Robert Cowell) *s.i.s: hld up: rdn over 2f out: wknd over 1f out* **25/1**

1m 14.29s (-0.21) **Going Correction** -0.125s/f (Stan) **8 Ran SP% 115.7**
WFA 3 from 4yo+ 8lb
Speed ratings (Par 102): **96,93,93,92,91 89,87,77**
CSF £34.92 CT £170.64 TOTE £3.40: £1.70, £3.50, £2.70; EX 36.90 Trifecta £204.30.
Owner Qatar Racing Ltd & Kin Hung Kei **Bred** Sir Nicholas & Lady Nugent **Trained** Newmarket, Suffolk

FOCUS
An interesting fillies' handicap with the impressive winner able to dictate at a steady tempo. The runner-up is rated close to her Chelmsford win.

3428 JESS GLYNNE - LIVE AT LADIES DAY CLAIMING STKS — 1m 4f 51y (Tp)
7:15 (7:15) (Class 6) 4-Y-O+ **£3,105** (£924; £461; £300; £300; £300) **Stalls** Low

Form				RPR
3140	**1**		**Noble Expression**[40] 2032 4-8-13 81...(b[1]) OisinMurphy 7	81+
(Jim Boyle) *s.i.s: pushed along early in rr: hdwy to chse ldr over 8f out: led over 3f out: rdn clr fr over 2f out* **11/8**[1]
6506 | **2** | *10* | **Lexington Law (IRE)**[37] 2126 6-9-3 87...(p) SeanDavis(5) 6 | 74
(Alan King) *chsd ldr over 3f: remained handy: rdn to chse wnr 3f out: styd on same pce fnl 2f* **7/4**[2]
1563 | **3** | *1 ½* | **Dream Magic (IRE)**[7] 3150 5-9-0 68...(p) EdwardGreatrex 2 | 64
(Mark Loughnane) *chsd ldrs: rdn over 2f out: sn outpcd* **4/1**[3]
/000 | **4** | *4* | **Fern Owl**[21] 2695 7-8-12 56... DavidEgan 8 | 55
(John Butler) *s.i.s: hld up: rdn and outpcd fr over 2f out* **16/1**
0400 | **5** | *2 ½* | **Roc Astrale (IRE)**[12] 2975 5-8-10 55... CallumShepherd 1 | 49
(Phil McEntee) *s.i.s: hld up: rdn and outpcd fr over 2f out: eased wl ins fnl f* **16/1**
-500 | **6** | *8* | **Bertie Moon**[35] 2196 9-8-7 42...(tp) JaneElliott(3) 3 | 36
(Barry Leavy) *s.i.s: bhd and pushed along 8f out: wknd over 3f out* **200/1**
2500 | **7** | *26* | **Essential**[26] 2532 5-8-12 48... JackMitchell 4 |
(Olly Williams) *led at stdy pce tl rdn and hdd over 3f out: wknd over 2f out* **50/1**

2m 36.36s (-4.44) **Going Correction** -0.125s/f (Stan) **7 Ran SP% 112.7**
Speed ratings (Par 101): **109,102,101,98,97 91,74**
CSF £3.88 TOTE £2.30: £1.50, £1.20; EX 4.40 Trifecta £8.10.Noble Expression was claimed by Mr R K Watson for £7,000
Owner Lycett Racing Ltd **Bred** Horizon Bloodstock Limited **Trained** Epsom, Surrey

FOCUS
An uncompetitive claimer with the well-backed winner coming home as he pleased.

3429 WATCH ROYAL ASCOT ON SKY SPORTS RACING H'CAP 1m 1f 104y (Tp)
7:45 (7:45) (Class 6) (0-65,67) 4-Y-O+
£3,105 (£924; £461; £300; £300; £300) Stalls Low

Form / RPR

3022 **1** **Street Poet (IRE)**[13] 2944 6-9-4 **62** .... OisinMurphy 6 68
(Michael Herrington) *led 1f: chsd ldr: shkn up to ld over 1f out: rdn and hung rt ins fnl f: styd on* **3/1**[2]

5-06 **2** *nk* **Roof Garden**[11] 3002 4-9-5 **63** .... DanielMuscutt 5 68
(Mark H Tompkins) *sn prom: rdn over 1f out: chsd wnr wl ins fnl f: r.o* **33/1**

-056 **3** *nk* **Topology**[21] 2692 6-8-13 **57** ....(v) EdwardGreatrex 1 62
(Joseph Tuite) *sn chsng ldrs: rdn over 1f out: r.o* **25/1**

1230 **4** *1 ½* **Subliminal**[35] 2202 4-9-6 **64** .... NickyMackay 4 66
(Simon Dow) *s.i.s: rcvrd to ld over 8f out: rdn and hdd over 1f out: no ex wl ins fnl f* **4/1**[3]

1005 **5** *shd* **Manfadh (IRE)**[10] 3046 4-9-9 **67** .... EoinWalsh 3 69+
(Mark Brisbourne) *hld up: shkn up over 3f out: nt clr run over 2f out: hdwy over 1f out: sn rdn: r.o: nt rch ldrs* **12/1**

0003 **6** *3 ½* **Clive Clifton (IRE)**[70] 1333 6-8-2 **46** oh1........(v) KieranO'Neill 2 41+
(Mark Brisbourne) *dwlt: hld up: shkn up and nt clr run over 2f out: hdwy over 1f out: sn rdn: no ex ins fnl f* **25/1**

026- **7** *hd* **Is It Off (IRE)**[259] 7369 4-9-6 **64** ....(p) DavidEgan 9 59+
(Sean Curran) *stdd s: hld up: shkn up over 2f out: edgd rt over 1f out: n.d* **50/1**

04-0 **8** *½* **X Rated (IRE)**[12] 2962 5-9-6 **64** .... SilvestreDeSousa 11 58+
(Mark Johnston) *hld up: rdn and rn wd wl over 1f out: nvr nrr* **7/1**

0623 **9** *5* **Ghazan (IRE)**[21] 2692 4-9-2 **65** ....(t) ThoreHammerHansen(5) 8 49
(Kevin Frost) *chsd ldrs: rdn over 2f out: wknd over 1f out* **8/1**

01 **10** *1 ¾* **Neff (GER)**[23] 2617 4-9-5 **63** .... DavidProbert 7 44+
(Gary Moore) *prom: lost pl after 1f: pushed along over 3f out: rdn and no ch whn hmpd over 1f out (trainers' rep said gelding was unsuited by the sharp track)* **9/4**[1]

1m 59.67s (-1.13) **Going Correction** -0.125s/f (Stan) **10 Ran SP% 119.7**
Speed ratings (Par 101): **100,99,99,98,98 94,94,94,89,88**
CSF £105.72 CT £2124.13 TOTE £3.40: £1.40, £5.40, £5.10; EX 121.70 Trifecta £2405.00.
Owner Mrs H Lloyd-Herrington **Bred** Mrs C Regalado-Gonzalez **Trained** Cold Kirby, N Yorks

FOCUS
Modest fare with the winner providing Oisin Murphy with a treble on the card.

3430 STAY AT THE WOLVERHAMPTON HOLIDAY INN H'CAP 7f 36y (Tp)
8:15 (8:17) (Class 6) (0-60,60) 4-Y-O+
£3,105 (£924; £461; £300; £300; £300) Stalls High

Form / RPR

0-00 **1** **Al Ozzdi**[5] 3214 4-9-7 **60** .... HollieDoyle 11 67
(Roger Fell) *prom but ct out wd: stdd and lost pl over 6f out: hdwy over 1f out: rdn and r.o to ld post (trainers' rep said, reg app imp in form, gelding appeared to benefit from the switch to a Tapeta surface)* **16/1**

303- **2** *shd* **Calin's Lad**[168] 9588 4-9-6 **59** .... SilvestreDeSousa 3 66
(Michael Appleby) *hld up: plld hrd: nt clr run 6f out: hdwy over 1f out: sn swtchd lft: rdn and r.o to ld ins fnl f: hdd post* **5/4**[1]

50-0 **3** *¾* **Masquerade Bling (IRE)**[36] 2145 5-9-5 **58** .... StevieDonohoe 10 63
(Neil Mulholland) *chsd ldrs: rdn to ld over 1f out: hdd wl ins fnl f* **16/1**

/60- **4** *¾* **Gold Flash**[486] 531 7-9-7 **60** ....(v) OisinMurphy 12 63
(Rod Millman) *hld up: hdwy on outer over 1f out: sn rdn: styd on* **14/1**

-624 **5** *1* **Rockesbury**[13] 2944 4-9-0 **60** ....(p) LauraCoughlan(7) 6 61
(David Loughnane) *chsd ldr over 6f out: led 2f out: rdn and hdd over 1f out: no ex wl ins fnl f* **6/1**[3]

-604 **6** *3 ½* **Ventriloquist**[122] 517 7-9-6 **59** .... DavidProbert 1 51
(Simon Dow) *hld up: hdwy over 1f out: sn rdn: styd on same pce ins fnl f* **22/1**

0011 **7** *¾* **Magical Molly Joe**[21] 2693 5-9-2 **58** .... JaneElliott(3) 7 48
(David Barron) *hld up: plld hrd: hdwy over 5f out: hung rt fr over 3f out: wknd over 1f out (jockey said mare hung badly right-handed)* **5/1**[2]

55-0 **8** *¾* **Mabo**[20] 2717 4-9-4 **57** ....(p) LiamJones 5 45
(Grace Harris) *chsd ldrs: nt clr run over 6f out: rdn whn hmpd over 1f out: wknd ins fnl f* **80/1**

3060 **9** *nk* **Tavener**[53] 1715 7-9-7 **60** ....(p) MartinDwyer 2 48
(David C Griffiths) *sn led: rdn and hdd 2f out: wknd ins fnl f* **22/1**

4-40 **10** *hd* **Champagne Bob**[20] 2717 7-8-12 **58** .... JonathanFisher(7) 8 45
(Richard Price) *hld up: effrt over 2f out: wknd over 1f out* **33/1**

0040 **11** *¾* **Showdance Kid**[19] 2741 5-8-11 **55** ....(b) ThoreHammerHansen(5) 4 40
(Kevin Frost) *hood removed late: s.s: hld up: nvr on terms (jockey was slow to remove the blindfold, he explained that the gelding had been attempting to put it's head in an adjoining stall as the start had been effected which had made it difficult for him to remove the blindfold on the first attempt before succ* **7/1**

05/- **12** *48* **Fitzrovia**[587] 8309 4-9-4 **57** .... CallumShepherd 9
(Ed de Giles) *chsd ldrs: hung rt fr over 3f out: wknd over 2f out (jockey said gelding hung badly right-handed)* **25/1**

1m 28.42s (-0.38) **Going Correction** -0.125s/f (Stan) **12 Ran SP% 123.0**
Speed ratings (Par 101): **97,96,96,95,94 90,89,88,87,87 86,32**
CSF £36.03 CT £369.95 TOTE £22.30: £4.60, £1.10, £4.60; EX 65.20 Trifecta £555.40.
Owner Northern Marking Ltd & Partners **Bred** Good Breeding **Trained** Nawton, N Yorks

FOCUS
A low-grade handicap but run at a good pace and a thrilling finish, the winner coming from well off the pace to defy the heavily backed favourite.

3431 COME TO ARMED SERVICES DAY - 1ST JULY FILLIES' NOVICE STKS 7f 36y (Tp)
8:45 (8:47) (Class 5) 3-Y-O+ £3,752 (£1,116; £557; £278) Stalls High

Form / RPR

233- **1** **Ascended (IRE)**[311] 5436 3-8-11 **80** .... SilvestreDeSousa 7 83
(William Haggas) *got loose on the way to post: sn trcking ldrs: wnt 2nd 1/2-way: led over 1f out: rdn and edgd lft ins fnl f: jst hld on* **10/3**[2]

1-0 **2** *hd* **Turn 'n Twirl (USA)**[151] 48 3-9-4 .... JackMitchell 3 89
(Simon Crisford) *sn led: racd keenly: hdd over 5f out: lost 2nd 1/2-way: rallied to chse wnr ins fnl f: r.o wl* **7/1**

20 **3** *2 ¼* **Gentlewoman (IRE)**[18] 2762 3-8-11 ....(h[1]) RobertHavlin 6 76
(John Gosden) *chsd ldr tl led over 5f out: rdn and hdd over 1f out: styd on same pce ins fnl f* **11/2**

62 **4** *1 ¾* **Royal Welcome**[14] 2909 3-8-11 .... OisinMurphy 1 71
(James Tate) *chsd ldrs: lost pl 1/2-way: rdn over 2f out: styd on fr over 1f out* **6/4**[1]

4- **5** *1 ½* **Alma Linda**[341] 4250 3-8-11 .... RyanTate 8 67+
(Sir Mark Prescott Bt) *hld up: shkn up over 1f out: nvr nr to chal* **50/1**

3 **6** *4 ½* **Powerful Star (IRE)**[18] 2762 3-8-11 .... StevieDonohoe 2 55
(David Lanigan) *s.i.s: hdwy 1/2-way: wknd over 1f out* **4/1**[3]

00 **7** *1 ¾* **Impressionable**[32] 2332 3-8-11 .... DavidEgan 4 50
(Marco Botti) *hld up: hdwy 1/2-way: pushed along and hung rt over 2f out: wknd over 1f out* **25/1**

00 **8** *½* **Hooriya**[72] 1288 3-8-4 .... StefanoCherchi(7) 5 49
(Marco Botti) *s.i.s: shkn up over 2f out: nvr on terms* **100/1**

1m 27.54s (-1.26) **Going Correction** -0.125s/f (Stan) **8 Ran SP% 117.8**
Speed ratings (Par 100): **102,101,99,97,95 90,88,87**
CSF £27.15 TOTE £2.50: £1.10, £1.90, £2.50; EX 24.90 Trifecta £100.80.
Owner Mike And Michelle Morris **Bred** R J Cornelius **Trained** Newmarket, Suffolk

FOCUS
A useful novice event to round off proceedings, the winner showing no ill effects of unshipping her rider on the way to post. Improvement from the 1-2.
T/Plt: £48.50 to a £1 stake. Pool: £68,515.40 - 1,029.69 winning units T/Qpdt: £14.60 to a £1 stake. Pool: £9,082.83 - 457.63 winning units **Colin Roberts**

3432 - 3439a (Foreign Racing) - See Raceform Interactive

3348 LINGFIELD (L-H)
Tuesday, June 4

OFFICIAL GOING: Polytrack: standard
Wind: light, half behind Weather: bright spells following rain before racing

3440 VISIT ATTHERACES.COM H'CAP 7f 1y(P)
5:40 (5:44) (Class 5) (0-70,72) 3-Y-O
£3,752 (£1,116; £557; £300; £300; £300) Stalls Low

Form / RPR

0-32 **1** **In The Cove (IRE)**[25] 2597 3-9-5 **68** .... SeanLevey 7 77
(Richard Hannon) *wl in tch in midfield: effrt to chse ldng pair 2f out: drvn to press ldrs 1f out: r.o to ld 50yds out* **6/1**[3]

55-4 **2** *½* **Revolutionise (IRE)**[104] 796 3-9-7 **70** .... AndreaAtzeni 3 77
(Roger Varian) *led: rdn wl over 1f out: drvn 1f out: hdd and one pce fnl 100yds* **11/8**[1]

-044 **3** *¾* **Jungle Juice (IRE)**[12] 2995 3-9-0 **63** .... DavidEgan 10 68
(Mick Channon) *chsd ldr: effrt 2f out: drvn and stl pressing ldr 1f out: 3rd and kpt on same pce ins fnl f* **16/1**

60-0 **4** *3* **City Master**[18] 2798 3-8-12 **61** .... HarryBentley 6 58+
(Ralph Beckett) *midfield: rdn over 4f out: hdwy 1f out: styd on u.p ins fnl f: nvr trbld ldrs* **12/1**

0006 **5** *1* **Greybychoice (IRE)**[14] 2939 3-8-10 **64** ....(h[1]) DylanHogan(5) 8 58
(Nick Littmoden) *uns rdr and galloped loose on the way to s: in tch in midfield: drvn ent fnl 2f: kpt on same pce: no threat to ldrs fnl f* **25/1**

-350 **6** *½* **Bug Boy (IRE)**[50] 1825 3-8-8 **60** ....(p) MeganNicholls(3) 4 53
(Paul George) *tk keel hold: hld up in tch in last quartet: effrt over 1f out: hdwy and kpt on ins fnl f: nvr trbld ldrs* **20/1**

644- **7** *¾* **Dove Divine (FR)**[167] 9603 3-9-9 **72** .... CharlieBennett 12 63
(Hughie Morrison) *in tch in midfield: effrt on outer bnd 2f out: rdn and kpt on ins fnl f: nvr trbld ldrs* **16/1**

5003 **8** *½* **Freedom And Wheat (IRE)**[14] 2939 3-9-2 **65**......(v) FergusSweeney 11 54+
(Mark Usher) *stdd s: effrt and swtchd rt over 1f out: nt clr run tl wl ins fnl f: kpt on towards fin: nvr involved (jockey said gelding hung left-handed throughout)* **20/1**

065- **9** *shd* **Fancy Flyer**[214] 8796 3-8-11 **67** .... LukeBacon(7) 5 56
(Dean Ivory) *in tch in midfield: effrt ent fnl 2f: unable qck over 1f out: wl hld and kpt on same pce ins fnl f* **20/1**

0640 **10** *½* **Te Amo Te Amo**[14] 2939 3-8-7 **56** .... NickyMackay 13 44
(Simon Dow) *chsd ldrs: rdn over 2f out: unable qck and lost pl over 1f out: wknd ins fnl f* **33/1**

6U0- **11** *1* **Sirinapha (IRE)**[201] 9065 3-9-5 **68** .... SilvestreDeSousa 2 53
(Richard Hannon) *s.i.s: hld up in last quartet: swtchd rt and shkn up over 1f out: no prog: nvr involved* **14/1**

1120 **12** *1 ½* **Pentland Lad (IRE)**[36] 2204 3-9-4 **67** ....(tp) OisinMurphy 1 48
(Charlie Fellowes) *rousted along leaving stalls: chsd ldrs: unable qck u.p over 1f out: wknd fnl f* **11/2**[2]

045- **13** *3 ½* **Reddiac (IRE)**[259] 7390 3-9-3 **66** ....(b[1] w) RobertHavlin 9 38
(Ed Dunlop) *stdd s: hld up in rr: nvr involved* **14/1**

1m 23.24s (-1.56) **Going Correction** -0.175s/f (Stan) **13 Ran SP% 125.6**
Speed ratings (Par 99): **101,100,99,96,95 94,93,93,92,92 91,89,85**
CSF £14.14 CT £142.12 TOTE £6.40: £1.70, £1.10, £3.70; EX 20.70 Trifecta £99.00.
Owner Owners Group 027 **Bred** John & Jennifer Coleman **Trained** East Everleigh, Wilts

FOCUS
A modest handicap in which few got involved. Further progress from the winner and runner-up.

3441 WATCH SKY SPORTS RACING IN HD EBF FILLIES' NOVICE STKS (PLUS 10 RACE) 6f 1y(P)
6:10 (6:11) (Class 5) 2-Y-O £3,752 (£1,116; £557; £278) Stalls Low

Form / RPR

1 **Last Surprise (IRE)** 2-9-0 0 .... JackMitchell 9 85+
(Simon Crisford) *trckd ldr: upsides and carried rt wl over 1f out: shkn up and led 1f out: r.o strly and drew clr ins fnl f: v readily* **2/1**[2]

22 **2** *3 ½* **Quiet Place (IRE)**[21] 2706 2-9-0 0 .... PatCosgrave 4 76
(Saeed bin Suroor) *wnt sharply rt leaving stalls: led: rdn drifted rt wl over 1f out: hdd 1f out: easily outpcd by wnr but stl clr 2nd ins fnl f* **8/11**[1]

0 **3** *4* **Fashion Free**[15] 2915 2-9-0 0 .... EdwardGreatrex 6 62
(Archie Watson) *sltly impeded leaving stalls: sn in tch in midfield: effrt in 4th 2f out: outpcd by ldng pair over 1f out: no ch w ldrs but kpt on to snatch 3rd cl home* **10/1**

4 *½* **Angel Of Delight (IRE)** 2-9-0 0 .... JamesDoyle 5 61
(Hugo Palmer) *sltly awkward as stalls opened and dwlt: in last trio: effrt ent fnl 2f: no threat to ldrs but kpt on steadily ins fnl f* **7/1**[3]

5 *3* **Chateau Peapod** 2-9-0 0 .... BrettDoyle 3 52
(Lydia Pearce) *in tch in midfield: rdn over 2f out: sn struggling and outpcd over 1f out: wknd fnl f* **100/1**

020 **6** *¾* **Hollaback Girl**[35] 2248 2-9-0 0 .... OisinMurphy 8 49
(Richard Spencer) *chsd ldrs: unable qck over 1f out: wknd ins fnl f* **18/1**

7 *hd* **Aust Ferry** 2-9-0 0 .... CharlesBishop 2 49
(Eve Johnson Houghton) *s.i.s: a outpcd in last pair* **16/1**

8 7 **Get The Look (IRE)** 2-9-0 0 .... JosephineGordon 7 28
(J S Moore) *s.i.s: a outpcd in rr* 66/1

1m 11.52s (-0.38) **Going Correction** -0.175s/f (Stan) 8 Ran SP% 126.5
Speed ratings (Par 90): **95,90,85,84,80 79,79,69**
CSF £4.27 TOTE £3.30: £1.10, £1.10, £2.60; EX 5.40 Trifecta £21.60.
Owner Sheikh Rashid Dalmook Al Maktoum **Bred** Mr & Mrs C Booth & Mrs S Cammidge **Trained** Newmarket, Suffolk

FOCUS
A nice performance from the winner, who looks useful. The ratings are a bit fluid.

3442 SKY SPORTS RACING ON SKY 415 H'CAP 6f 1y(P)
6:40 (6:41) (Class 6) (0-60,60) 3-Y-O
£3,105 (£924; £461; £300; £300; £300) Stalls Low

Form RPR

200- 1 **Kennocha (IRE)**[220] 8638 3-9-4 57 .... (t) SilvestreDeSousa 11 62
(Amy Murphy) *hdwy to chse ldr after 1f: effrt to press ldr 2f out: drvn and led 1f out: edgd lft and kpt on wl ins fnl f (jockey said filly hung left-handed)* 8/1

0225 2 ½ **Valley Belle (IRE)**[8] 3148 3-9-3 56 .... JosephineGordon 8 60
(Phil McEntee) *jostled leaving stalls and sn dropped to rr: effrt wl over 1f out: hdwy and swtchd rt ins fnl f: r.o strly to go 2nd nr fin: nvr quite getting to wnr* 4/1[2]

2-00 3 ¾ **Vino Rosso (IRE)**[36] 2204 3-9-4 57 .... DavidProbert 1 58
(Michael Blanshard) *in tch in midfield: effrt and swtchd rt over 1f out: chsd ldrs 1f out: wnt 2nd ins fnl f: kpt on but a hld: lost 2nd nr fin* 20/1

2006 4 ½ **Sussudio**[20] 2735 3-9-5 58 .... (v[1]) HarryBentley 2 58
(Richard Spencer) *chsd ldr for 1f: 3rd whn swtchd lft and effrt over 1f out: kpt on same pce ins fnl f* 3/1[1]

4-00 5 nk **Such Promise**[20] 2735 3-9-4 57 .... (v[1]) RossaRyan 4 56
(Mike Murphy) *led: rdn ent fnl 2f: drvn and hdd 1f out: lost 2nd ins fnl f: wknd towards fin* 9/1

0-03 6 shd **My Law**[36] 2204 3-9-0 60 .... IsobelFrancis(7) 5 59
(Jim Boyle) *hld up in last trio: pushed along over 1f out: swtchd rt ins fnl f: styd on wl fnl 100yds: nt rch ldrs (jockey said filly became unbalanced coming down the hill)* 9/2[3]

5000 7 nk **Islay Mist**[60] 1557 3-9-0 53 .... (tp) RobertWinston 6 51
(Lee Carter) *in tch in midfield: rdn over 2f out: kpt on u.p ins fnl f: nvr enough pce to threaten ldrs* 20/1

1260 8 hd **Global Acclamation**[32] 2357 3-9-5 58 .... (b) LiamKeniry 10 55
(Ed Dunlop) *stdd after s: hld up in rr: hdwy on inner 2f out: rdn and kpt on same pce ins fnl f* 10/1

5010 9 ½ **Ever Rock (IRE)**[34] 2276 3-8-10 56 .... LauraCoughlan(7) 7 52
(J S Moore) *awkward leaving stalls: sn bhd: styd on ins fnl f: nvr trbld ldrs* 11/1

00-0 10 nk **Shaffire**[32] 2356 3-9-6 59 .... (h[1]) ShaneKelly 9 54
(Joseph Tuite) *chsd ldrs: unable qck u.p over 1f out: kpt on same pce ins fnl f* 25/1

6-00 11 1¾ **Little Tipple**[8] 3148 3-8-0 46 .... LauraPearson(7) 3 35
(John Ryan) *chsd ldrs for 2f: steadily lost pl: bhd ins fnl f* 50/1

4400 12 1 **Griggy (IRE)**[14] 2939 3-9-7 60 .... KieranO'Neill 12 46
(John Butler) *midfield on outer: effrt and stl wd bnd 2f out: lost pl: bhd ins fnl f* 12/1

1m 11.83s (-0.07) **Going Correction** -0.175s/f (Stan) 12 Ran SP% 124.7
Speed ratings (Par 97): **93,92,91,90,90 90,89,89,88,88 86,84**
CSF £40.38 CT £653.64 TOTE £10.90: £2.90, £1.90, £5.20; EX 36.30 Trifecta £444.60.
Owner Dale, Knight, Darlington & Robson **Bred** R & T Bloodstock **Trained** Newmarket, Suffolk

FOCUS
An ordinary affair, with the field finishing compressed.

3443 INJURED JOCKEYS FUND H'CAP 5f 6y(P)
7:10 (7:11) (Class 4) (0-80,80) 4-Y-O+
£5,530 (£1,645; £822; £411; £300; £300) Stalls High

Form RPR

2305 1 **Harry's Bar**[17] 2823 4-9-1 74 .... OisinMurphy 2 85+
(James Fanshawe) *chsd ldrs: effrt jst over 1f out: pressing ldr 1f out: rdn to ld 75yds out: r.o wl* 5/4[1]

-602 2 1 **Green Door (IRE)**[14] 2940 8-9-7 80 .... (v) LouisSteward 7 87
(Robert Cowell) *chsd ldr tl rdn to ld over 1f out: hdd and nt match pce of wnr fnl 75yds* 16/1

1412 3 2½ **Cappananty Con**[4] 3303 5-9-0 76 .... JoshuaBryan(3) 5 74
(Charlie Wallis) *hld up in 6th: effrt and hdwy over 1f out: styd on ins fnl f: nvr trbld ldrs* 4/1[2]

-000 4 ½ **Pettochside**[25] 2568 10-9-7 80 .... HollieDoyle 1 76
(John Bridger) *chsd ldrs: effrt ent fnl 2f: unable qck over 1f out: kpt on same pce ins fnl f* 25/1

5-40 5 ½ **Jashma (IRE)**[11] 3043 5-9-7 80 .... (b) ShaneKelly 3 74
(Richard Hughes) *dwlt and sltly short of room: rcvrd and hld up in midfield after 1f: effrt over 1f out: no imp ins fnl f* 8/1

0010 6 nse **Harrogate (IRE)**[3] 3347 4-9-6 79 .... (b) CharlieBennett 6 73
(Jim Boyle) *led: rdn and hdd over 1f out: no ex and wknd ins fnl f* 6/1

5265 7 1½ **Something Lucky (IRE)**[4] 3303 7-9-5 78 .... (bt) SilvestreDeSousa 4 67
(Michael Appleby) *v.s.a: clsd onto rr of field and t.k.h 3f out: effrt wd bnd 2f out: no prog: wl hld fnl f (jockey said gelding was slowly away)* 11/2[3]

002- 8 4 **Roundabout Magic (IRE)**[243] 7946 5-8-7 66 .... NickyMackay 8 40
(Simon Dow) *hld up in last pair: effrt on inner over 1f out: no prog: wknd ins fnl f* 25/1

57.71s (-1.09) **Going Correction** -0.175s/f (Stan) 8 Ran SP% 118.8
Speed ratings (Par 105): **101,99,95,94,93 93,91,84**
CSF £26.30 CT £66.46 TOTE £2.10: £1.30, £2.90, £1.40; EX 19.40 Trifecta £68.70.
Owner Jan and Peter Hopper **Bred** Jan & Peter Hopper **Trained** Newmarket, Suffolk

FOCUS
This went the way of the least exposed runner in the line-up. The runner-up is rated to last year's form.

3444 RACING WELFARE H'CAP 1m 7f 169y(P)
7:40 (7:41) (Class 6) (0-65,66) 4-Y-O+
£3,105 (£924; £461; £300; £300; £300) Stalls Low

Form RPR

3344 1 **Colwood**[27] 2528 5-9-2 65 .... DarraghKeenan(5) 8 72
(Robert Eddery) *chsd ldr after 2f: rdn and effrt jst over 2f out: clsd and drvn to ld jst ins fnl f: hrd pressed fnl 100yds: hld on wl u.p* 3/1[1]

0265 2 hd **Nafaayes (IRE)**[28] 946 5-9-2 60 .... (p) MartinDwyer 5 67
(Jean-Rene Auvray) *hld up in rr of main gp: nt clr run over 2f out: swtchd rt jst over 2f out: hdwy and rdn to chse ldrs over 1f out: str chal 100yds out: kpt on: a jst hld* 11/2

1631 3 5 **Murhib (IRE)**[4] 3298 7-8-10 54 4ex .... (h) JFEgan 6 55
(Lydia Richards) *t.k.h: hld up in tch in rr of main gp: nt clr run over 2f out: swtchd lft and hdwy over 1f out: styd on to snatch 3rd last strides: no threat to 1st 2* 7/2[2]

53-3 4 nk **Joyceick (FR)**[22] 2696 5-9-2 65 .... (t) DylanHogan(5) 11 65
(Nick Littmoden) *t.k.h: led and set stdy gallop: rdn wl over 1f out: hdd jst ins fnl f: sn btn and wknd fnl 100yds* 4/1[3]

-003 5 2¾ **Fitzwilly**[32] 2359 9-9-1 64 .... ScottMcCullagh(5) 4 61
(Mick Channon) *in tch in midfield: effrt u.p 3f out: 5th and no imp 2f out: wl hld fnl f* 10/1

-004 6 2¼ **Affair**[20] 2733 5-8-9 53 .... CharlieBennett 1 47
(Hughie Morrison) *t.k.h: led for 1f: chsd ldr tl 14f out: styd prom: rdn over 2f out: sn struggling to qckn: wknd fnl f (jockey said mare ran too free)* 14/1

0200 7 1 **Tilsworth Sammy**[21] 2718 4-8-7 51 oh2 .... KieranO'Neill 7 45
(J R Jenkins) *in tch: rdn and struggling to qckn over 2f out: outpcd and wl hld over 1f out* 16/1

34R- 8 10 **Threediamondrings**[272] 6926 6-8-7 51 oh5 .... (t) JosephineGordon 2 32
(Mark Usher) *rel to r and v.s.a: grad rcvrd and jst abt in tch but stl rr 5f out: nt clr run ent fnl 2f: sn btn and wknd over 1f out* 28/1

6-35 9 15 **Mary Elise (IRE)**[33] 2342 4-9-5 63 .... OisinMurphy 10 27
(Michael Blake) *chsd ldrs: losing pl u.p whn squeezed for room and hmpd jst over 2f out: sn bhd (jockey said filly stopped quickly)* 10/1

3m 25.04s (-0.66) **Going Correction** -0.175s/f (Stan) 9 Ran SP% 116.8
Speed ratings (Par 101): **94,93,91,91,89 88,88,83,75**
CSF £20.11 CT £60.15 TOTE £3.60: £1.50, £2.10, £1.50; EX 22.80 Trifecta £99.30.
Owner R J Creese **Bred** Snowdrop Stud Co Ltd **Trained** Newmarket, Suffolk
■ Ardamir was withdrawn. Price at time of withdrawal 20-1. Rule 4 does not apply

FOCUS
This was steadily run. Weak form, with the front pair clear.

3445 FOLLOW AT THE RACES ON TWITTER NOVICE STKS 1m 2f (P)
8:10 (8:13) (Class 5) 3-Y-O+
£3,752 (£1,116; £557; £278) Stalls Low

Form RPR

2 1 **First In Line**[45] 1956 3-9-1 0 .... FrankieDettori 1 80+
(John Gosden) *in tch in midfield: chsd ldng trio and gng clr of field but v wd over 2f out: drvn over 1f out: clsd and chal ins fnl f: led and hung rt towards fin* 4/6[1]

2 2 ½ **Harrovian**[19] 2764 3-9-1 0 .... RobertHavlin 7 79+
(John Gosden) *chsd ldrs: effrt to chal ent fnl 2f: kpt on and drvn to ld ins fnl f: hdd and no ex towards fin* 15/8[2]

0 3 1 **Rum Baba**[47] 1886 3-9-1 0 .... RichardKingscote 13 77
(Charlie Fellowes) *chsd ldr: ev ch u.p ent fnl 2f: led jst ins fnl f: sn hdd and no ex towards fin* 20/1

620 4 ½ **Fly Lightly**[25] 2582 3-9-1 75 .... OisinMurphy 4 76
(Robert Cowell) *led: rdn ent fnl 2f: hdd jst ins fnl f: kpt on same pce after* 16/1[3]

0 5 10 **Desert Son**[26] 2555 4-10-0 0 .... LouisSteward 12 57
(Sir Michael Stoute) *midfield: outpcd over 2f out: no threat to ldrs after: plugged on ins fnl f* 25/1

00 6 ½ **Peripherique**[22] 2690 3-8-10 0 .... RyanTate 3 50
(James Eustace) *dwlt: towards rr: midfield but ldrs clr whn nt clr run over 2f out: kpt on ins fnl f: no threat to ldrs* 100/1

0 7 4½ **Arcadienne**[28] 2518 3-8-10 0 .... HarryBentley 5 41
(Ralph Beckett) *chsd ldrs: 5th and outpcd u.p over 2f out: sn wl btn and wknd over 1f out* 16/1[3]

0- 8 2 **Para Queen (IRE)**[291] 6238 3-8-3 0 .... EllieMacKenzie(7) 11 37
(Heather Main) *s.i.s: rdn along and outpcd in rr: styd on ins fnl f: n.d* 100/1

06 9 1½ **Thunder And Light**[12] 3003 3-8-12 0 .... (t) AaronJones(3) 10 39
(Marco Botti) *a towards rr: outpcd over 2f out: no ch after* 33/1

6 10 shd **Triple Genius (IRE)**[28] 2505 3-9-1 0 .... DanielMuscutt 14 39
(Ed Dunlop) *s.i.s: rn in snatches: a towards rr: no ch over 2f out* 100/1

0- 11 1¾ **Logan's Choice**[217] 8729 4-10-0 0 .... AdamMcNamara 6 36
(Roger Charlton) *midfield: outpcd u.p over 2f out: disputing wl hld 5th whn hung lft u.p over 1f out: wknd fnl f* 66/1

00 12 10 **All Right**[19] 2771 3-8-10 0 .... DavidProbert 9 10
(Henry Candy) *midfield: outpcd over 2f out: sn btn: wknd over 1f out (vet said filly lost it's right fore shoe)* 80/1

13 32 **Kimbriki** 3-9-1 0 .... LiamKeniry 8
(Ed Walker) *a in rr: lost tch 3f out: t.o* 28/1

2m 3.16s (-3.44) **Going Correction** -0.175s/f (Stan) 13 Ran SP% 127.2
WFA 3 from 4yo 13lb
Speed ratings (Par 103): **106,105,104,104,96 96,92,90,89,89 88,80,54**
CSF £2.04 TOTE £1.50: £1.10, £1.10, £2.80; EX 2.40 Trifecta £23.50.
Owner A E Oppenheimer **Bred** Hascombe And Valiant Studs **Trained** Newmarket, Suffolk

FOCUS
There was a good battle up the straight but ultimately it went they way the market had predicted. The Gosden 1-2 are likely to prove better than the bare form.

3446 TAKE THE REINS H'CAP 1m 4f (P)
8:40 (8:40) (Class 5) (0-75,74) 3-Y-O
£3,752 (£1,116; £557; £300; £300; £300) Stalls Low

Form RPR

1341 1 **Glutnforpunishment**[27] 2530 3-8-11 64 .... SilvestreDeSousa 7 70
(Nick Littmoden) *mde all: rdn 2f out: kpt on u.p ins fnl f: jst hld on: all out* 7/1

03-5 2 hd **Tammooz**[29] 2488 3-9-7 74 .... AndreaAtzeni 5 79
(Roger Varian) *dwlt: hld up in tch in midfield: effrt over 2f out: clsd u.p 1f out: wnt 2nd and press wl ins fnl f: styd on: jst hld* 9/2[2]

4-63 3 1 **Vindolanda**[27] 2524 3-9-2 69 .... KieranShoemark 8 72
(Charles Hills) *chsd ldrs and wd early: chsd wnr over 9f out: rdn ent fnl 2f: stl pressing wnr and drvn over 1f out: lost 2nd and kpt on same pce wl ins fnl f* 6/1[3]

30-0 4 ¾ **Calculation**[36] 2208 3-9-2 69 .... RyanMoore 6 71
(Sir Michael Stoute) *sltly impeded leaving stalls: chsd wnr tl over 9f out: styd chsng ldrs: effrt over 2f out: drvn over 1f out: nt clrest of runs and kpt on same pce ins fnl f* 11/8[1]

000- 5 ½ **Mon Frere (IRE)**[237] 8108 3-8-10 63 .... RyanTate 4 64
(Sir Mark Prescott Bt) *in tch in last pair: rdn over 2f out: no imp tl hdwy ins fnl f: styd on wl towards fin: nt rch ldrs* 20/1

4240 6 1½ **Thunderoad**[38] 2096 3-9-3 70 .... OisinMurphy 1 69
(Marco Botti) *hld up in tch in rr: clsd and nt clr run 2f out: swtchd rt and effrt over 1f out: no imp fnl f* 14/1

-441 **7** *1 1/4* **Torolight**[42] 2011 3-9-4 **71**.. ShaneKelly 3 68
(Richard Hughes) *hld up in tch in midfield: effrt 2f out: swtchd rt jst ins fnl f: no prog* **9/2**[2]

2m 30.45s (-2.55) **Going Correction** -0.175s/f (Stan) **7** Ran SP% **116.7**
Speed ratings (Par 99): **101,100,100,99,99 98,97**
CSF £39.43 CT £202.55 TOTE £7.80: £3.10, £2.70; EX 40.80 Trifecta £200.50.
Owner A A Goodman **Bred** Rabbah Bloodstock Limited **Trained** Newmarket, Suffolk

FOCUS
A good ride from the front saw the winner home in what was something of a tactical affair. The form could be rated a bit higher at face value.
T/Plt: £8.80 to a £1 stake. Pool: £77,153.87 - 6,361.58 winning units T/Qpdt: £5.80 to a £1 stake. Pool: £7,646.05 - 960.75 winning units **Steve Payne**

2374 NEWCASTLE (A.W) (L-H)

Tuesday, June 4

OFFICIAL GOING: Tapeta: standard
Wind: Breezy, half behind in sprints and in over 3f of home straight in races on the round course Weather: Overcast, raining

3447 WATCH ROYAL ASCOT ON SKY SPORTS RACING H'CAP 1m 4f 98y (Tp)
5:50 (5:51) (Class 6) (0-55,54) 4-Y-O+

£3,105 (£924; £461; £300; £300; £300) **Stalls** High

Form RPR

5-05 **1** **Steel Helmet (IRE)**[13] 593 5-8-12 **45**.. JoeFanning 6 51
(Harriet Bethell) *trckd ldrs: led over 1f out: hrd pressed fnl f: hld on wl cl home* **14/1**

041 **2** *shd* **Kodi Koh (IRE)**[32] 2376 4-8-11 **47**.. RowanScott(3) 7 53
(Simon West) *hld up in midfield: nt clr run over 2f out: hdwy over 1f out: sn rdn and edgd lft: kpt on wl to press wnr last 30yds: jst hld* **8/1**

025/ **3** *3/4* **My Mo (FR)**[670] 3756 7-9-3 **50**.. JasonHart 8 55
(Tristan Davidson) *led at ordinary gallop: rdn over 2f out: hdd over 1f out: rallied and ev ch ins fnl f: no ex and lost 2nd last 30yds* **9/4**[1]

33-0 **4** *1* **Jan De Heem**[11] 3054 9-9-0 **52**.. ConnorMurtagh(5) 5 55
(Tina Jackson) *hld up in midfield: stdy hdwy and prom whn nt clr run over 2f out tl angled rt over 1f out: rdn and ch ins fnl f: hld cl home* **33/1**

060- **5** *1 3/4* **Melabi (IRE)**[259] 7395 6-9-1 **48**.. JackGarritty 2 49
(Stella Barclay) *midfield on ins: effrt over 2f out: rdn over 1f out: kpt on same pce ins fnl f* **33/1**

650- **6** *nk* **Clayton Hall (IRE)**[6] 3468 6-8-12 **45**..(p) GrahamLee 12 45
(John Wainwright) *t.k.h: hld up: rdn 3f out: hdwy whn edgd lft over 1f out: no imp fnl f* **100/1**

10-4 **7** *1 1/2* **Life Knowledge (IRE)**[8] 3155 7-9-7 **54**..(p) DanielTudhope 10 52
(Liam Bailey) *hld up on outside: stdy hdwy after 4f: effrt on outside and prom over 1f out: rdn and one pce fnl f* **11/4**[2]

2-00 **8** *1/2* **Nearly There**[54] 1718 6-9-7 **54**..(t) NicolaCurrie 1 51
(Wilf Storey) *t.k.h: hld up on ins: effrt over 2f out: no imp over 1f out* **7/1**[3]

6-00 **9** *shd* **Gabriel's Oboe (IRE)**[36] 2202 4-9-5 **52**..(b[1]) DougieCostello 9 49
(Mark Walford) *trckd ldrs: rdn over 2f out: wknd over 1f out (jockey said gelding hung left in the home straight)* **33/1**

5002 **10** *3/4* **Amity Island**[25] 2587 4-9-2 **52**..(b) BenRobinson(3) 4 48
(Ollie Pears) *prom on ins: effrt and rdn over 2f out: wknd over 1f out* **16/1**

/0-0 **11** *2 3/4* **Bigbadboy (IRE)**[143] 208 6-9-0 **47**.. CamHardie 11 39
(Clive Mulhall) *in tch: drvn over 2f out: wknd over 1f out* **18/1**

-000 **12** *2 1/4* **Enemy Of The State (IRE)**[17] 2819 5-9-5 **52**..(p) TomEaves 13 40
(Jason Ward) *chsd ldr to over 3f out: rdn and wknd fr 2f out* **22/1**

520/ **13** *1/2* **Byronegetonefree**[31] 6898 8-9-0 **47**..(p) PaddyMathers 14 35
(Stuart Coltherd) *hld up: drvn and outpcd over 2f out: nvr on terms* **40/1**

/500 **14** *1* **Cryogenics (IRE)**[8] 3158 5-8-10 **48**.. ThoreHammerHansen(5) 3 34
(Kenny Johnson) *dwlt: hld up: bhd: struggling over 2f out: nvr on terms* **100/1**

2m 47.22s (6.12) **Going Correction** +0.30s/f (Slow) **14** Ran SP% **116.4**
Speed ratings (Par 101): **91,90,90,89,88 88,87,87,87,86 84,83,82,82**
CSF £111.98 CT £349.35 TOTE £11.50: £2.40, £2.00, £1.30; EX 76.40 Trifecta £1280.90.
Owner W A Bethell **Bred** Rabbah Bloodstock Limited **Trained** Arnold, E Yorks

FOCUS
A very moderate middle-distance handicap. The favourite couldn't dominate off his own modest gallop after a lengthy absence. The winner's rated back to last year's high.

3448 SKY SPORTS RACING ON VIRGIN CHANNEL 535 H'CAP 1m 2f 42y (Tp)
6:20 (6:25) (Class 6) (0-65,63) 4-Y-O+

£3,105 (£924; £461; £300; £300; £300) **Stalls** High

Form RPR

0-35 **1** **Granite City Doc**[18] 2785 6-9-1 **62**.. PaulaMuir(5) 4 68
(Lucy Normile) *prom: effrt and rdn over 1f out: led ins fnl f: sn hrd pressed and edgd lft: kpt on wl nr fin* **11/2**[3]

2566 **2** *3/4* **Optima Petamus**[6] 3225 7-8-6 **48**..(b) PhilDennis 3 53
(Liam Bailey) *reluctant to enter stalls: hld up: smooth hdwy and cl up: effrt and ev ch whn blkd ins fnl f: rdn and no ex nr fin* **20/1**

0-62 **3** *1 1/4* **Ishebayorgrey (IRE)**[7] 3181 7-9-0 **59**..(h) JamieGormley(3) 5 61
(Iain Jardine) *dwlt: t.k.h: hld up: rdn and hdwy over 1f out: chsd ldrs ins fnl f: kpt on: hld towards fin* **2/1**[1]

5503 **4** *nk* **Zarkavon**[32] 2376 5-8-3 **45**..(p) NathanEvans 1 47
(John Wainwright) *t.k.h in midfield: n.m.r briefly over 2f out: sn rdn: hdwy over 1f out: kpt on fnl f* **25/1**

-040 **5** *1 1/4* **Sulafaat (IRE)**[8] 3162 4-8-9 **51**..(p) PaulHanagan 7 51
(Rebecca Menzies) *t.k.h: led at slow pce for 1f: chsd ldr: regained ld over 2f out: rdn: edgd lft and hdd ins fnl f: sn no ex: lost hind shoe (vet said filly lost it's left hind shoe)* **12/1**

6 **6** *hd* **Rosin Box (IRE)**[7] 3177 6-9-3 **59**.. JasonHart 2 58
(Tristan Davidson) *t.k.h: prom: effrt whn nt clr run briefly 2f out: rdn and one pce fnl f* **9/2**[2]

0205 **7** *nk* **Basildon**[7] 3209 4-8-13 **58**..(b[1]) BenRobinson(3) 8 57
(Brian Ellison) *hld up: rdn over 2f out: hdwy on outside over 1f out: kpt on fnl f: nrst fin* **10/1**

4320 **8** *2 1/2* **Traveller (FR)**[43] 1983 5-9-2 **58**..(t) CamHardie 12 52
(Antony Brittain) *hld up towards rr: rdn along 3f out: kpt on fnl f: nvr rchd ldrs* **18/1**

5640 **9** *1 1/2* **Restive (IRE)**[7] 3177 6-9-2 **63**.. SeanDavis(5) 10 55
(Jim Goldie) *hld up: rdn over 2f out: no imp fr over 1f out* **9/1**

0006 **10** *1 3/4* **Remmy D (IRE)**[13] 2962 4-9-5 **61**..(p) LewisEdmunds 11 49
(Jim Goldie) *sn cl up: effrt and ev ch over 2f out to over 1f out: wknd fnl f* **22/1**

-003 **11** *1* **Clary (IRE)**[13] 2964 9-8-3 **45**..(h[1]) AndrewMullen 6 32
(Alistair Whillans) *midfield on outside: drvn along over 2f out: wknd over 1f out* **28/1**

05-5 **12** *15* **Mandarin Princess**[13] 2587 4-8-1 **48**.. ThoreHammerHansen(5) 13 8
(Kenny Johnson) *hdwy to ld after 1f and sn 3 l clr: rdn and hdd over 2f out: sn wknd* **150/1**

2m 14.02s (3.62) **Going Correction** +0.30s/f (Slow) **12** Ran SP% **116.0**
Speed ratings (Par 101): **97,96,95,95,94 94,93,91,90,89 88,76**
CSF £114.55 CT £293.24 TOTE £6.10: £1.90, £6.00, £1.20; EX 138.40 Trifecta £335.50.
Owner Corsby Racing **Bred** Corsby Racing **Trained** Duncrievie, Perth & Kinross

■ Home Before Dusk (13-2) was withdrawn. Rule 4 applies to all bets struck prior to withdrawal but not to SP bets. Deduction - 10p in the pound. New market formed

■ Stewards' Enquiry : Paula Muir two-day ban; careless riding (June 23-24)

FOCUS
A modest handicap. The favourite couldn't quite get into contention from off a muddling gallop.

3449 EQUINE PRODUCTS FILLIES' H'CAP 1m 2f 42y (Tp)
6:50 (6:52) (Class 4) (0-80,79) 4-Y-O+

£5,530 (£1,645; £822; £411; £300; £300) **Stalls** High

Form RPR

3052 **1** **Tamreer**[10] 3095 4-9-1 **78**..(h) BenSanderson(5) 3 87
(Roger Fell) *mde all: set v stdy pce: pushed along 2f out: kpt on wl fnl f* **9/4**[1]

2030 **2** *1/2* **Elixsoft (IRE)**[15] 2911 4-9-1 **73** ow1.. DanielTudhope 5 80
(Roger Fell) *hld up on ins: hdwy and shkn up over 1f out: angled rt and chsd wnr last 100yds: kpt on: hld nr fin* **6/1**[3]

122- **3** *3/4* **Snowdon**[281] 6626 4-8-12 **75**.. PaulaMuir(5) 6 80
(Michael Dods) *trckd ldrs: effrt and wnt 2nd over 2f out to last 100yds: one pce towards fin* **11/1**

0210 **4** *4 1/2* **Voi**[10] 3096 5-8-10 **75**..(t) WilliamCarver(7) 7 71
(Conrad Allen) *slowly away: t.k.h: hld up: rdn and outpcd over 2f out: hung lft: hdwy over 1f out: kpt on fnl f: nrst fin (jockey said mare hung left in the home straight)* **9/2**[2]

4202 **5** *shd* **Apache Blaze**[28] 2512 4-8-6 **64**..(p) NicolaCurrie 1 60
(Robyn Brisland) *t.k.h: chsd wnr to over 2f out: rallied: no ex whn short of room briefly ins fnl f: sn btn* **9/1**

6-03 **6** *1 1/2* **Lucy's Law (IRE)**[28] 2512 5-8-5 **63**.. AndrewMullen 4 56
(Tom Tate) *t.k.h: hld up in tch: drvn and outpcd over 2f out: n.d after* **15/2**

-012 **7** *nk* **Never Be Enough**[11] 3057 4-9-7 **79**.. TomEaves 2 71
(Keith Dalgleish) *t.k.h: in tch: smooth hdwy to dispute 2nd pl over 2f out: shkn up and wknd over 1f out* **9/2**[2]

2m 17.28s (6.88) **Going Correction** +0.30s/f (Slow) **7** Ran SP% **111.5**
Speed ratings (Par 102): **84,83,83,79,79 78,77**
CSF £15.23 TOTE £2.60: £2.00, £2.90; EX 13.40 Trifecta £123.30.
Owner Arcane Racing Partnership **Bred** Shadwell Estate Company Limited **Trained** Nawton, N Yorks

FOCUS
A fair fillies' handicap. The favourite made all off her own pedestrian gallop and backed up her York form.

3450 MEGAN O'BRIEN 30TH BIRTHDAY H'CAP 1m 5y (Tp)
7:20 (7:20) (Class 3) (0-95,94) 4-Y-O+ **£7,762** (£2,310; £1,154; £577) **Stalls** Low

Form RPR

5415 **1** **Crownthorpe**[26] 2563 4-8-10 **88**.. SeanDavis(5) 11 99
(Richard Fahey) *hld up: hdwy nr side of gp 3f out: led over 1f out: drvn out fnl f* **10/1**

4566 **2** *2* **Bedouin's Story**[47] 1889 4-9-6 **93**.. KevinStott 8 99
(Saeed bin Suroor) *hld up in centre of gp: hdwy and prom 2f out: rdn and chsd wnr ins fnl f: kpt on: nt pce to chal* **11/2**[2]

43-0 **3** *2* **Ulshaw Bridge (IRE)**[19] 2778 4-9-1 **88**..(p) PaulHanagan 2 90
(James Bethell) *dwlt: hld up: rdn and hdwy nr side of gp over 2f out: wnt 3rd ins fnl f: no ex last 50yds* **12/1**

0-06 **4** *nk* **Ibraz**[31] 2408 4-9-4 **91**.. DaneO'Neill 7 92
(Roger Varian) *prom: hdwy to ld briefly wl over 1f out: chsd wnr to ins fnl f: no ex last 75yds* **5/2**[1]

4020 **5** *3 3/4* **Tough Remedy (IRE)**[18] 2808 4-9-2 **89**.. PJMcDonald 9 81
(Keith Dalgleish) *dwlt: sn midfield: effrt and hung lft over 2f out: rdn and no imp fr over 1f out* **8/1**[3]

0-31 **6** *1 1/2* **Lush Life (IRE)**[12] 3027 4-9-7 **94**.. JamieSpencer 12 83
(Jamie Osborne) *hld up: hdwy nr side of gp and in tch over 1f out: wknd ins fnl f* **5/2**[1]

0-51 **7** *2* **Algaffaal (USA)**[35] 2242 4-8-5 **78**.. CamHardie 10 62
(Brian Ellison) *hld up in midfield in centre of gp: hdwy to chse ldrs over 2f out: wknd fnl f* **12/1**

1-00 **8** *2 1/2* **Parys Mountain (IRE)**[31] 2419 5-9-1 **88**..(h) DavidAllan 6 67
(Tim Easterby) *led at decent gallop in centre of gp: rdn and hdd wl over 1f out: sn wknd* **33/1**

-510 **9** *3/4* **Florenza**[18] 2809 6-8-13 **86**.. MichaelStainton 1 63
(Chris Fairhurst) *chsd ldr on far side of gp: struggling over 2f out: sn wknd* **100/1**

30/0 **10** *hd* **Shrewd**[30] 2435 9-8-11 **87**.. JamieGormley(3) 3 64
(Iain Jardine) *hld up in centre of gp: rdn and outpcd over 2f out: sn wknd* **100/1**

06-0 **11** *26* **London Protocol (FR)**[29] 2480 6-8-9 **82**..(p) JoeFanning 4
(John Mackie) *chsd ldrs on far side of gp: struggling over 2f out: sn btn: t.o* **80/1**

1m 38.1s (-0.50) **Going Correction** +0.30s/f (Slow) **11** Ran SP% **114.3**
Speed ratings (Par 107): **114,112,110,109,105 104,102,99,99,99 73**
CSF £61.90 CT £682.74 TOTE £11.00: £2.30, £2.00, £2.70; EX 56.50 Trifecta £396.00.
Owner Richard Fahey Ebor Racing Club Ltd **Bred** Mrs Sheila Oakes **Trained** Musley Bank, N Yorks

FOCUS
The feature contest was a good handicap. It paid to be played late from off a strong gallop. The winner continued his improved run this year.

3451 JULIET THOMPSON SUPPORTING LEGER LEGENDS EBF NOVICE STKS (PLUS 10 RACE) 5f (Tp)
7:50 (7:51) (Class 4) 2-Y-O **£7,051** (£2,098; £1,048; £524) **Stalls** Low

Form RPR

1 **Mrs Bouquet** 2-8-11.. JoeFanning 4 75
(Mark Johnston) *trckd ldr: effrt over 1f out: led ins fnl f: kpt on strly* **8/1**

2 *1 1/4* **Olcan** 2-9-2.. DanielTudhope 6 76
(David O'Meara) *hld up: effrt and hdwy over 1f out: kpt on fnl f: tk 2nd last stride* **13/2**

24 **3** *nse* **Dandizette**[17] 2820 2-8-11 .... AndrewMullen 1 71
(Adrian Nicholls) *led: faltered 1/2-way: rdn over 1f out: hdd ins fnl f: sn one pce: lost 2nd last stride (jockey said filly jumped the path 2f out)* **12/1**

31 **4** *1 1/4* **Chattanooga Boy (IRE)**[38] 2108 2-9-8 .... ConnorBeasley 8 77
(George Scott) *in tch: stdy hdwy 1/2-way: effrt and rdn over 1f out: one pce ins fnl f* **9/2**[3]

3 **5** *1* **Jump The Gun (IRE)**[10] 3098 2-9-2 .... NicolaCurrie 2 67
(Jamie Osborne) *dwlt: sn prom: rdn along 1/2-way: outpcd fnl f* **11/4**[1]

6 *3* **Balancing Act (IRE)** 2-8-11 .... PJMcDonald 7 52+
(Jedd O'Keeffe) *s.s: rn green and sn wl bhd: hdwy fnl f: nrst fin: bttr for r* **10/1**

7 *nse* **Street Life** 2-9-2 .... PaulHanagan 3 56
(Richard Fahey) *dwlt: hld up: drvn and outpcd over 2f out: btn over 1f out* **10/3**[2]

0 **8** *12* **Laughing Crusader**[18] 2783 2-9-2 .... DavidNolan 5 13
(David O'Meara) *prom: drvn along and edgd lft 2f out: sn wknd* **50/1**

1m 0.24s (0.74) **Going Correction** +0.30s/f (Slow) **8** Ran SP% **111.1**
Speed ratings (Par 95): **106,104,103,101,100 95,95,76**
CSF £55.23 TOTE £7.10: £2.60, £2.30, £2.30; EX 59.20 Trifecta £1016.90.
Owner Garrett J Freyne **Bred** Hatford Enterprises **Trained** Middleham Moor, N Yorks

FOCUS
A fair juvenile novice contest. A likeable debutante won well from just off the pace.

3452 PARKLANDS MINI GOLF H'CAP 5f (Tp)
8:20 (8:21) (Class 6) (0-65,64) 4-Y-0+

£3,105 (£924; £461; £300; £300; £300) **Stalls Low**

Form RPR

0150 **1** **Decision Maker (IRE)**[25] 2580 5-8-13 **56** .... AndrewMullen 7 63
(Roy Bowring) *w ldrs in centre: led 2f out: hrd pressed and edgd lft wl ins fnl f: hld on wl* **7/2**[1]

06-0 **2** *hd* **Arnold**[30] 2433 5-9-3 **60** ....(p) JoeFanning 5 66
(Ann Duffield) *early to post: prom in centre: rdn and hdwy over 1f out: disp ld wl ins fnl f: jst hld* **6/1**[3]

6510 **3** *1 3/4* **Red Stripes (USA)**[16] 2876 7-9-4 **61** ....(b) PJMcDonald 10 61
(Lisa Williamson) *racd centre: disp ld to 2f out: lost 2nd and one pce ins fnl f* **5/1**[2]

0050 **4** *2 1/4* **Rockley Point**[6] 3227 6-9-2 **59** ....(p) JasonHart 3 51
(Katie Scott) *prom far side: effrt and rdn 2f out: no ex ins fnl f* **13/2**

0-40 **5** *3/4* **Ambitious Icarus**[6] 3213 10-8-9 **52** ....(h) PhilipPrince 8 41
(Richard Guest) *early to post: hld up in tch centre: drvn and outpcd 1/2-way: rallied fnl f: nt pce to chal* **11/1**

626- **6** *nse* **Phantasmal**[186] 9327 5-9-7 **64** .... PaddyMathers 12 53
(Stuart Coltherd) *dwlt: bhd and outpcd centre: hdwy over 1f out: r.o fnl f: no imp* **8/1**

0620 **7** *shd* **Windforpower (IRE)**[67] 1402 9-8-2 **45** ....(p) CamHardie 4 34
(Tracy Waggott) *chsd far side ldr 2f: cl up: drvn and outpcd 2f out: n.d after* **14/1**

5000 **8** *2* **Lord Of The Glen**[22] 2678 4-8-11 **54** ....(b) PhilDennis 1 35
(Jim Goldie) *hld up far side: pushed along over 2f out: no imp whn checked appr fnl f* **5/1**[2]

0-60 **9** *2 1/4* **Jorvik Prince**[95] 970 5-9-4 **61** .... NathanEvans 2 34
(Julia Brooke) *racd far side: disp ld to 2f out: hung rt and wknd over 1f out* **20/1**

0-00 **10** *2 3/4* **Duba Plains**[4] 3296 4-8-4 **52** .... ThoreHammerHansen[(5)] 6 15
(Kenny Johnson) *s.i.s: bhd and outpcd centre: nvr on terms* **100/1**

59.89s (0.39) **Going Correction** +0.30s/f (Slow) **10** Ran SP% **115.0**
Speed ratings (Par 101): **108,107,104,101,100 100,99,96,93,88**
CSF £24.10 CT £104.06 TOTE £4.80: £2.20, £2.30, £1.40; EX 23.70 Trifecta £175.50.
Owner K Nicholls **Bred** Brian Miller **Trained** Edwinstowe, Notts

FOCUS
A modest sprint handicap.
T/Jkpt: Not Won. T/Plt: £487.10 to a £1 stake. Pool: £76,220.98 - 114.21 winning units T/Qpdt: £86.30 to a £1 stake. Pool: £8,363.24 - 71.65 winning units **Richard Young**

3453 - 3460a (Foreign Racing) - See Raceform Interactive

2965

KEMPTON (A.W) (R-H)
Wednesday, June 5

OFFICIAL GOING: Polytrack: standard to slow

3461 WISE BETTING AT RACINGTV.COM MAIDEN FILLIES' STKS (PLUS 10 RACE) 6f (P)
5:15 (5:17) (Class 5) 2-Y-O £3,881 (£1,155; £577; £288) **Stalls Low**

Form RPR

1 **Shadn (IRE)** 2-9-0 0 .... OisinMurphy 3 81+
(Andrew Balding) *cl up in mid-div: travelling wl on heels 2f out: rdn sn after and wnt to inner: qcknd wl: led ent fnl f and sn clr* **9/1**

2 *3 1/4* **Fair Pass (IRE)** 2-9-0 0 .... ShaneKelly 9 71
(Marco Botti) *racd in rr-div: rdn 2f out and swtchd to inner: kpt on wl fr over 1f out: pushed out to take 2nd nr fin: nrst fin* **16/1**

3 *1/2* **Diva Kareem (IRE)** 2-9-0 0 .... PatCosgrave 5 70
(George Baker) *sltly bttr than rr-div: t.k.h at times: rdn 2f out to chse ldrs: styd on strly ins fnl f: nrst fin* **20/1**

4 *nse* **Silent Agenda** 2-9-0 0 .... HollieDoyle 4 70
(Archie Watson) *bhd ldrs on inner: effrt over 2f out: ev ch ent fnl f: wnr sn swept by: plugged on fnl 110yds* **7/2**[1]

5 *1* **Zulu Girl** 2-9-0 0 .... CharlesBishop 7 67
(Eve Johnson Houghton) *racd in mid-div: rdn along to hold pl fr 4f out: styd on wl fr over 1f out: nvr nrr* **16/1**

0 **6** *hd* **Too Shy Shy (IRE)**[18] 2836 2-9-0 0 .... JasonWatson 8 66
(Richard Spencer) *sn led: rdn 2f out: hdd ent fnl f: stl 2nd 150yds out: wknd qckly after* **10/1**

7 *2* **Cindy Bear (IRE)** 2-9-0 0 .... AndreaAtzeni 11 60
(Roger Varian) *trckd ldrs and t.k.h most of r: effrt 2f out: outpcd over 1f out: pushed out* **5/1**[3]

3 **8** *shd* **Shammah (IRE)**[20] 2767 2-9-0 0 .... SeanLevey 12 60
(Richard Hannon) *free to post: w ldr on outer: rdn 2f out: 4th ent fnl f: emptied fnl 150yds* **4/1**[2]

0 **9** *1 3/4* **Love My Life (IRE)**[9] 3165 2-9-0 0 .... NicolaCurrie 1 54
(Jamie Osborne) *slow into stride: rn green and t.k.h for 1f: sltly detached 1/2-way: stuck on fr over 2f out* **50/1**

20 **10** *2* **Taste The Nectar (USA)**[19] 2805 2-9-0 0 .... JamesDoyle 6 48
(Robert Cowell) *racd in mid-div on outer: effrt wl over 2f out: nt qckn and wknd over 1f out* **7/1**

11 *11* **Go With Grace** 2-9-0 0 .... JosephineGordon 2 15
(J S Moore) *a towards rr* **66/1**

12 *4* **Divine Queen** 2-9-0 0 .... JamieSpencer 10 3
(James Tate) *missed break and a in rr: attempted to make hdwy 4f out: no ex and nudged out fr 2f out* **12/1**

1m 12.99s (-0.11) **Going Correction** -0.025s/f (Stan) **12** Ran SP% **118.2**
Speed ratings (Par 90): **99,94,94,93,92 92,89,87,84 69,64**
CSF £141.11 TOTE £11.10: £3.10, £5.90, £7.50; EX 190.90 Trifecta £1595.80.
Owner Alrabban Racing **Bred** Barronstown Stud **Trained** Kingsclere, Hants

FOCUS
A decent evening meeting, with the Polytrack once again given as 'standard to slow'. \n\x\x The time was nothing special, despite what looked like a good gallop, but a taking performance from the winner of this okay fillies' maiden.

3462 100% PROFITS BOOST AT 32REDSPORT.COM H'CAP 7f (P)
5:45 (5:45) (Class 5) (0-75,75) 4-Y-O+

£3,752 (£1,116; £557; £300; £300; £300) **Stalls Low**

Form RPR

2306 **1** **Quick Breath**[9] 3147 4-8-13 **74** .... TylerSaunders[(7)] 3 85
(Jonathan Portman) *cl up in mid-div on inner: clung to rail and rdn 2f out: qcknd wl and led ent fnl f: wnt clr last 110yds* **4/1**[1]

-033 **2** *2 1/4* **Choral Music**[68] 1392 4-9-5 **73** .... RobHornby 12 78
(John E Long) *rrd leaving stalls and jockey did wl to keep on: in rr: stdy prog wl over 3f out: rdn 2f out: qcknd and briefly led over 1f out: kpt on in duel for 2nd ins fnl f: jst hld 2nd* **25/1**

-410 **3** *nse* **Met By Moonlight**[34] 2339 5-9-2 **70** ....(b[1]) DavidProbert 1 75
(Ron Hodges) *bhd ldrs and t.k.h: rdn 2f out: ev ch over 1f out: kpt on wl in duel for 2nd ins fnl f: no ex last strides* **10/1**

2-04 **4** *1 1/4* **Grey Galleon (USA)**[30] 2484 5-8-13 **74** ....(p) AmeliaGlass[(7)] 9 75+
(Clive Cox) *hld up in rr: swtchd wd w plenty to do over 2f out: kpt on fr over 1f out: styd on strly ins fnl f* **16/1**

4010 **5** *2 1/2* **Full Intention**[25] 2611 5-9-3 **71** ....(p) AdamKirby 4 66
(Lydia Pearce) *in rr-div: rdn over 2f out: one pce fr over 1f out* **8/1**

0241 **6** *2 3/4* **Coverham (IRE)**[14] 2971 5-9-5 **73** .... RyanTate 13 60
(James Eustace) *in rr-div: rdn over 2f out: plugged on* **8/1**

00-0 **7** *3/4* **Fortune And Glory (USA)**[22] 2714 6-9-0 **68** .... RossaRyan 10 53
(Joseph Tuite) *bhd ldrs: rdn over 2f out: wknd over 1f out* **16/1**

24-4 **8** *nk* **Yimou (IRE)**[144] 206 4-9-4 **72** .... MartinDwyer 11 56
(Dean Ivory) *t.k.h and cl up: impr to ld after 2f: pressed either side over 2f out: hdd wl over 1f out: wknd* **11/1**

0030 **9** *nk* **Smokey Lane (IRE)**[18] 2841 5-9-4 **72** .... OisinMurphy 6 56
(David Evans) *bhd ldrs: pushed along 3f out: began to weaken fr over 2f out* **5/1**[3]

2644 **10** *1/2* **The Lamplighter (FR)**[13] 3014 4-9-7 **75** ....(tp) PatCosgrave 5 57
(George Baker) *mid-div: rdn over 2f out plugged on* **8/1**

5450 **11** *1/2* **Choice Encounter**[32] 2416 4-9-2 **75** .... ThomasGreatrex[(5)] 14 56
(Archie Watson) *in rr: rdn over 2f out: plugged on* **33/1**

0261 **12** *1* **Tum Tum**[36] 2246 4-9-7 **75** ....(h) GeorgeWood 2 53
(Michael Herrington) *racd in mid-div: rdn over 2f out: no ex fr over 1f out* **9/2**[2]

30-0 **13** *7* **Dark Side Dream**[48] 1880 7-9-7 **75** ....(p) SilvestreDeSousa 8 34
(Charlie Wallis) *led for 2f: styd w ldr: rdn over 2f out: no ex over 1f out: wknd qckly and eased fnl f* **16/1**

004- **14** *15* **Dark Crocodile (IRE)**[292] 6264 4-9-1 **69** ....(t) TomQueally 7
(Seamus Durack) *a towards rr: no ex fr 2f out: eased over 1f out* **66/1**

1m 25.05s (-0.95) **Going Correction** -0.025s/f (Stan) **14** Ran SP% **131.5**
Speed ratings (Par 103): **104,101,101,99,97 93,93,92,92,91 91,90,82,64**
CSF £118.25 CT £1009.55 TOTE £5.30: £2.30, £7.70, £3.70; EX 180.70 Trifecta £3284.20.
Owner Wood Street Syndicate **Bred** S Dibb & J Repard **Trained** Upper Lambourn, Berks

FOCUS
Another winner who made use of the cutaway in this modest handicap.

3463 32RED ON THE APP STORE NOVICE STKS (DIV I) 7f (P)
6:15 (6:16) (Class 4) 3-Y-O+ £6,469 (£1,925; £962; £481) **Stalls Low**

Form RPR

5 **1** **Tipperary Jack (USA)**[32] 2397 3-9-2 0 .... KierenFox 5 81
(John Best) *bhd ldr between horses and t.k.h thrght: cajoled along over 1f out: almost upsides whn rdn ent fnl f: fnd stride 200yds out and qcknd smartly to ld 110yds out: pushed out nr fin: promising* **6/1**[3]

-51 **2** *1 3/4* **Destination**[29] 2506 3-9-8 0 .... JamesDoyle 12 82
(William Haggas) *bhd ldr on outer: rdn 2f out: ev ch over 1f out: kpt on wl pressing ldr: tk 2nd cl home but no ch w wnr* **8/11**[1]

0- **3** *nk* **Lapidary**[168] 9604 3-8-4 0 .... EllieMacKenzie[(7)] 9 70
(Heather Main) *sn led: rdn 2f out: kpt on wl tl pressed either side fr 1f out: hdd 110yds out and lost 2nd sn after* **50/1**

4 *1/2* **Motfael (IRE)** 3-9-2 0 .... PatDobbs 1 74+
(Owen Burrows) *racd in mid-div: tk clsr over gng wl fr over 2f out: rdn in 5th 2f out: plugged on fr over 1f out* **10/1**

0- **5** *3/4* **Debonair Don Juan (IRE)**[188] 9320 3-9-2 0 ....(t[1]) StevieDonohoe 14 72
(Ed Vaughan) *cl up bhd ldrs: rdn on outer 2f out: stuck on w promise fr over 1f out wout being able to qckn: can do bttr* **40/1**

6 *nk* **Laurier (USA)** 3-8-11 0 .... JamieSpencer 7 66+
(Kevin Ryan) *in rr-div: sltly green at times: shuffled along fr 2f out: kpt on wl being pushed out ins fnl f: nvr involved* **20/1**

0 **7** *2 1/2* **Soldier's Son**[19] 2794 3-8-13 0 .... GeorgiaCox[(3)] 4 64
(Henry Candy) *w ldr on inner: rdn 2f out: no ex ent fnl f* **50/1**

8 *1 1/4* **Tuk Power** 3-8-11 0 .... SilvestreDeSousa 6 56+
(Andrew Balding) *t.k.h in mid-div: plld hrd over 3f out: green and shuffled along fr over 1f out* **9/2**[2]

34 **9** *2 3/4* **Noble Fox**[22] 2715 3-9-2 0 .... AdamKirby 13 53
(Clive Cox) *mid-div on outer: shuffled along fr over 2f out: nvr involved* **25/1**

0 **10** *1/2* **Daryana**[20] 2762 3-8-11 0 .... CharlesBishop 2 47
(Eve Johnson Houghton) *racd in mid-div: niggled along at times: rdn over 2f out: plugged on* **25/1**

0 **11** *1/2* **Pecorino**[23] 2690 3-9-2 0 .... ShaneKelly 10 51
(Richard Hughes) *in rr-div on outer: effrt over 2f out: plugged on* **50/1**

0 **12** *1* **Bated Beauty (IRE)**[16] 2919 4-9-7 0 .... TomQueally 3 47
(John Butler) *racd in rr-div and t.k.h: no ex fr 2f out* **50/1**

04 **13** *18* **Heldtoransom**[20] 2773 3-8-6 0 .... ThomasGreatrex[(5)] 11
(Joseph Tuite) *rrd leaving stalls: a in rr: eased over 1f out (jockey said filly reared as the stalls opened and was never travelling)* **100/1**

14 2 **Lambristo (IRE)** 3-9-2 0 JosephineGordon 8
(J S Moore) *a in rr: sltly detached fr 1/2-way: eased wl over 1f out* **100/1**
1m 25.73s (-0.27) **Going Correction** -0.025s/f (Stan)
WFA 3 from 4yo 10lb 14 Ran SP% **124.2**
Speed ratings (Par 105): **100,98,97,97,96 95,93,91,88,87 87,86,65,63**
CSF £10.35 TOTE £7.50: £2.40, £1.10, £10.10; EX 13.80 Trifecta £233.40.
Owner Curtis & Tomkins **Bred** Edward A Cox Jr **Trained** Oad Street, Kent

FOCUS
Some expensive sorts took their chance, the right horses came to the fore and probably the deeper of the two divisions. The inside once again looked the place to be.

3464 32RED ON THE APP STORE NOVICE STKS (DIV II) 7f (P)
6:45 (6:47) (Class 4) 3-Y-0+ £6,469 (£1,925; £962; £481) Stalls Low

Form / RPR

25 1 **Land Of Legends (IRE)**19 2802 3-9-2 0 PatCosgrave 3 85+
(Saeed bin Suroor) *mde all: shkn up and drew clr 2f out: drifted to nrside rail fr over 1f out: pushed out fnl f: v easily (jockey said colt hung left-handed under pressure)* **4/11**1

2 2 1/4 **Mutamaasik** 3-9-2 0 JimCrowley 7 78+
(Roger Varian) *bhd wnr: rdn wl over 1f out: kpt on wl in clr 2nd but no ch w wnr: pushed out fnl 150yds* **9/2**2

3 3 2 3/4 **Corinthian Girl (IRE)**16 2909 3-8-11 0 ShaneKelly 9 66
(David Lanigan) *bhd wnr on inner: rdn 2f out: stuck on to hold 3rd* **25/1**

00 4 1/2 **Royal Sands (FR)**39 2094 3-9-2 0 BarryMcHugh 1 70
(James Given) *racd in mid-div on inner: rdn 2f out: kpt on one pce fr over 1f out* **66/1**

6- 5 1 **Young Bernie**293 6193 4-9-12 0 RobHornby 13 71
(Andrew Balding) *hld up in rr-div: effrt 2f out: no imp* **33/1**

24- 6 4 1/2 **Lilbourne Star (IRE)**452 1119 4-9-12 0 (w) AdamKirby 6 59+
(Clive Cox) *bhd ldrs between horses and t.k.h: effrt wl over 1f out: green and kpt on tl shuffled along ent fnl f: nvr involved: can do bttr* **16/1**

7 shd **Elena Osorio (IRE)** 3-8-11 0 GeraldMosse 10 50
(David Elsworth) *in rr: effrt over 2f out: kpt on being shuffled along fr wl over 1f out* **16/1**

3-3 8 2 3/4 **Penrhos**19 2794 3-9-2 0 KieranShoemark 12 47
(Charles Hills) *in rr-div: effrt over 2f out: plugged on (jockey said colt ran too free early on)* **8/1**3

0 9 nk **Four Feet (IRE)**19 2790 3-8-9 0 AmeliaGlass(7) 11 46
(Henry Candy) *racd in rr-div: effrt 2f out: pushed out fr over 1f out* **16/1**

60 10 2 1/4 **Trust Me (IRE)**21 2736 3-9-2 0 RobertWinston 4 40
(Dean Ivory) *w ldr and plld hrd: effrt 2f out: emptied and pushed out ent fnl f* **50/1**

0 11 hd **Bambys Boy**33 2354 8-9-12 0 JamieSpencer 8 44
(Neil Mulholland) *s.s: a towards rr (jockey said gelding was slowly away)* **66/1**

40 12 1 **Confab (USA)**13 3019 3-9-2 0 NicolaCurrie 5 37
(George Baker) *racd in rr-div: pushed along over 2f out: no imp* **80/1**

13 shd **Set Point Charlie (IRE)** 3-9-2 0 TomQueally 2 37
(Seamus Durack) *s.i.s: a in rr (jockey said gelding was slowly away)* **50/1**

1m 26.34s (0.34) **Going Correction** -0.025s/f (Stan)
WFA 3 from 4yo+ 10lb 13 Ran SP% **130.3**
Speed ratings (Par 105): **97,94,91,90,89 84,84,81,80,78 78,76,76**
CSF £2.67 TOTE £1.30: £1.10, £1.40, £5.30; EX 3.00 Trifecta £28.00.
Owner Godolphin **Bred** Godolphin **Trained** Newmarket, Suffolk

FOCUS
Less depth than the first division and the time was the slowest of the four 7f events on the card. The winner didn't need to match his debut form.

3465 32RED.COM H'CAP 7f (P)
7:15 (7:15) (Class 4) (0-85,87) 3-Y-O
£6,469 (£1,925; £962; £481; £300; £300) Stalls Low

Form / RPR

-142 1 **Mawakib**32 2412 3-9-3 81 AndreaAtzeni 6 92+
(Roger Varian) *hld up in mid-div: swtchd to outer over 2f out: shkn up wl over 1f out: rdn and qcknd smartly ent fnl f: styd on wl to ld 100yds out: pushed out nr fin* **9/4**1

-150 2 1 1/4 **Nefarious (IRE)**21 2746 3-9-4 82 DavidProbert 7 90
(Henry Candy) *racd in mid-div: rdn 2f out: led ent fnl f: kpt on wl tl hdd 110yds out* **16/1**

1-35 3 2 1/4 **Cool Exhibit**43 2023 3-9-6 84 (p1) SilvestreDeSousa 10 86
(Simon Crisford) *in rr-div: rdn 2f out: kpt on wl to take 3rd ins fnl f* **15/2**3

-310 4 1 1/2 **Global Warning**32 2414 3-9-7 85 GeraldMosse 1 83
(Ed Dunlop) *initially entered wrong stall: bhd ldr on inner: rdn 2f out: briefly led over 1f out: plugged on fnl f* **10/1**

-653 5 nse **Dirty Rascal (IRE)**18 2821 3-9-9 87 TomMarquand 14 85+
(Richard Hannon) *w ldrs on outer: rdn 2f out: ev ch over 1f out: no ex fnl f* **25/1**

22-3 6 nk **Alfred Boucher**57 1665 3-9-4 82 DaneO'Neill 12 79
(Henry Candy) *racd in mid-div on outer: effrt over 2f out: kpt on fnl f* **11/1**

1430 7 1/2 **Dahawi**40 2078 3-9-0 78 (t) JamesDoyle 5 74
(Hugo Palmer) *racd in mid-div on inner: haken up over 2f out: effrt 2f out: kpt on wl over 1f out: no ex fnl f* **12/1**

-514 8 1/2 **Buckingham (IRE)**18 2825 3-9-5 83 CharlesBishop 13 77
(Eve Johnson Houghton) *rousted along fr wd draw to sit w ldr after 2f: rdn 2f out: ev ch and briefly led over 1f out: no ex 1f out and wknd* **40/1**

1-23 9 hd **Attainment**49 1846 3-9-5 83 PJMcDonald 9 77
(James Tate) *bhd ldrs between horses: effrt 2f out: on heels whn hmpd and eased ent fnl f: no ex sn after (jockey said colt was denied a clear run)* **11/2**2

-140 10 nk **Oloroso (IRE)**33 2364 3-8-11 78 JoshuaBryan(3) 3 71+
(Andrew Balding) *in last: rdn over 2f out: mod hdwy past btn horses over 1f out* **8/1**

01-0 11 1 **Hackle Setter (USA)**54 1736 3-9-1 79 JasonWatson 2 69
(Sylvester Kirk) *racd in rr-div on inner: rdn over 2f out: no imp sn after* **40/1**

045- 12 2 3/4 **Hawridge Storm (IRE)**245 7906 3-9-4 82 JFEgan 4 65
(Rod Millman) *in rr-div on outer: effrt over 2f out: nt qckn and plugged on* **33/1**

33-1 13 3 1/4 **Scat King (IRE)**62 1550 3-9-6 84 ShaneKelly 8 58
(Richard Hughes) *led: rdn 2f out: hdd over 1f out: emptied ent fnl f and hmpd: eased (jockey said gelding suffered interference in running)* **12/1**

1m 24.87s (-1.13) **Going Correction** -0.025s/f (Stan) 13 Ran SP% **119.4**
Speed ratings (Par 101): **105,103,101,99,99 98,98,97,97,97 96,92,89**
CSF £41.54 CT £237.41 TOTE £3.40: £1.40, £5.80, £3.20; EX 48.10 Trifecta £447.60.
Owner Sheikh Ahmed Al Maktoum **Bred** Mrs J E Laws **Trained** Newmarket, Suffolk

FOCUS
The quickest of the four 7f races and form to be positive about.

3466 32RED H'CAP 1m 3f 219y(P)
7:45 (7:46) (Class 3) (0-95,96) 4-Y-O+
£9,337 (£2,796; £1,398; £699; £349; £175) Stalls Low

Form / RPR

4-30 1 **Desert Wind (IRE)**42 2033 4-9-7 93 StevieDonohoe 11 104
(Ed Vaughan) *hld up in rr: shkn up over 3f out: prog over 2f out: rdn 2f out: qcknd sharply over 1f out and led ent fnl f: kpt on wl* **9/2**1

1-02 2 1 3/4 **Big Kitten (USA)**34 2320 4-9-7 93 JamesDoyle 9 101
(William Haggas) *hld up in rr-div: effrt on outer 2f: kpt on wl ins fnl f: styd on but nt get to wnr* **5/1**2

5624 3 2 3/4 **Cosmelli (ITY)**46 1943 6-9-10 96 (b) DanielMuscutt 6 100
(Gay Kelleway) *in rr-div on inner: clsr whn rdn 2f out: briefly chal tl no ex 1f out and plugged on* **33/1**

202- 4 1 **Volcanic Sky**219 8702 4-8-11 83 PatCosgrave 1 85
(Saeed bin Suroor) *bhd ldrs: shkn up and cruised into ld 2f out: rdn wl over 1f out: hdd ent fnl f: one pce after* **9/2**1

25-6 5 2 1/2 **Landue**14 2969 4-9-2 88 HayleyTurner 12 86
(Marcus Tregoning) *hld up in rr: rdn over 2f out: no immediate imp tl styd on wl fr over 1f out* **14/1**

5526 6 2 **Seafarer (IRE)**19 2786 5-9-5 91 MartinDwyer 10 86
(Marcus Tregoning) *hld up in last: rdn over 2f out: styd on wl fr over 1f out: nvr nrr* **20/1**

114- 7 2 1/2 **Canford Heights (IRE)**236 8164 4-9-1 90 GeorgiaCox(3) 5 81
(William Haggas) *t.k.h into first bnd: sn bhd ldr: niggled along over 3f out: rdn wl over 2f out: plugged on one pce (jockey said gelding hung left-handed)* **6/1**3

-255 8 3/4 **Al Hamdany (IRE)**13 3005 5-9-10 96 JFEgan 8 86
(Marco Botti) *in rr-div on outer: effrt over 2f out: pushed out fr over 1f out* **12/1**

20-1 9 shd **Al Kout**67 1425 5-9-1 87 CharlesBishop 3 76
(Heather Main) *sn led: 3 l clr 1/2-way: rdn over 2f out: hdd 2f out: grad wknd* **7/1**

4-24 10 4 **Exceeding Power**75 1267 8-9-6 92 GeorgeWood 7 75
(Martin Bosley) *mid-div: effrt over 2f out: no ex* **50/1**

10-0 11 hd **Envoy**151 82 5-9-2 88 RyanTate 2 71
(James Eustace) *bhd ldr: rdn over 2f out: no ex and wknd qckly 2f out* **10/1**

0/0- 12 11 **Torcello (IRE)**19 2816 5-9-2 88 RaulDaSilva 4 53
(Shaun Lycett) *mid-div: pushed along wl over 3f out: no ex 2f out* **33/1**

2m 31.38s (-3.12) **Going Correction** -0.025s/f (Stan) 12 Ran SP% **115.9**
Speed ratings (Par 107): **109,107,106,105,103 102,100,100,100,97 97,89**
CSF £24.95 CT £659.74 TOTE £5.40: £1.80, £1.80, £8.10; EX 22.60 Trifecta £556.70.
Owner Sheikh Juma Dalmook Al Maktoum **Bred** Irish National Stud **Trained** Newmarket, Suffolk

FOCUS
An above average event run at a good pace.

3467 BET AT RACINGTV.COM H'CAP (JOCKEY CLUB GRASSROOTS FLAT STAYERS' QUALIFIER) 1m 7f 218y(P)
8:15 (8:17) (Class 4) (0-80,82) 4-Y-O+
£6,469 (£1,925; £962; £481; £300; £300) Stalls Low

Form / RPR

1-53 1 **Sassie (IRE)**25 2626 4-9-1 74 OisinMurphy 8 85
(Sylvester Kirk) *kpt tabs on clr ldr w clr break to pack: shkn up over 3f out: effrt 2f out and reeled in ldr over 1f out: pushed out fnl f: easily: astute ride* **5/1**2

2 11 **Superb Story (IRE)**885 8-9-9 82 JamieSpencer 2 79+
(Harry Fry) *racd in mid-div: rdn over 3f out: stuck on wl and tk 2nd fnl 110yds: no ch w wnr: too much to do* **5/1**2

1-24 3 1 3/4 **Cristal Spirit**32 2400 4-8-11 70 (p) PatCosgrave 12 66+
(George Baker) *racd in mid-div: rdn 3f out: kpt on one pce: too much to do* **12/1**

1115 4 1 **Blazon**63 1524 6-8-11 70 (p) JasonWatson 5 64+
(Kim Bailey) *in rr-div: rdn over 3f out: plugged on fr over 1f out: too much to do* **8/1**3

33-P 5 3/4 **Paddy A (IRE)**26 2578 5-9-6 79 (p) PJMcDonald 1 72
(Ian Williams) *led pack chsng clr ldrs: effrt over 3f out: plugged on and no imp: too much to do* **14/1**

-000 6 1 3/4 **Mapped (USA)**11 3095 4-9-0 73 (b1) RobertWinston 10 65
(Iain Jardine) *clr ldr: built up big ld at 1/2-way: rdn over 3f out: hdd over 1f out: stl 2nd tl wknd qckly fnl 110yds (jockey said gelding hung right-handed)* **10/1**

3122 7 nse **Knight Crusader**12 3044 7-9-8 81 (p) AdamKirby 6 71
(John O'Shea) *racd in 5th: rdn over 3f out: plugged on: too much to do* **11/4**1

-30R 8 1 **Jacob Cats**12 3044 10-8-12 71 (v) SilvestreDeSousa 7 60
(William Knight) *s.s: in rr: effrt over 3f out: one pce (jockey said gelding was slowly away)* **25/1**

/0-0 9 2 **Winter Lion (IRE)**19 2793 9-9-2 75 LiamJones 4 62
(John O'Shea) *a in rr* **100/1**

231- 10 3 1/4 **Dance To Paris**153 9608 4-9-2 75 (p) JimCrowley 9 59
(Lucy Wadham) *racd in mid-div: effrt 3f out: plugged on (jockey said filly hung left-handed)* **10/1**

5-03 11 4 1/2 **Inn The Bull (GER)**39 2126 6-9-7 80 DavidProbert 11 58
(Alan King) *a in rr* **16/1**

-550 12 3 1/4 **Galactic Spirit**74 1291 4-9-4 77 (p) RaulDaSilva 3 52
(James Evans) *a in rr: sme effrt over 3f out: one pce* **50/1**

3m 28.66s (-1.44) **Going Correction** -0.025s/f (Stan) 12 Ran SP% **116.3**
Speed ratings (Par 105): **102,96,95,95,94 93,93,93,92,90 88,86**
CSF £29.29 CT £285.75 TOTE £6.10: £1.70, £1.90, £3.90; EX 41.30 Trifecta £309.60.
Owner Neil Simpson **Bred** Worksop Manor Stud **Trained** Upper Lambourn, Berks

The Form Book Flat 2019, Raceform Ltd, Newbury, RG14 5SJ

FOCUS
Pre-race this had all the right ingredients to think that this should rate as solid staying AW form, but it proved very unsatisfactory, with seemingly only winning jockey Oisin Murphy alive to the pace.

3468 32RED CASINO FILLIES' H'CAP (LONDON MILE SERIES QUALIFIER) 1m (P)

8:45 (8:50) (Class 4) (0-80,82) 3-Y-O+
£6,469 (£1,925; £962; £481; £300; £300) **Stalls** Low

Form	Pos	Dist	Horse / Comment	Jockey	RPR
33-	1		**Kitcarina (FR)**[182] 4-9-9 **73** (Andrew Balding) *mde all: shkn up and increased ld over 2f out: rdn wl over 1f out: kpt on wl to hold on cl home* **9/2**[3]	OisinMurphy 1	81
-106	2	1/2	**Pytilia (USA)**[15] 2942 3-8-13 **74** (Richard Hughes) *hld up in last: cruising 2f out: swtchd to outer w plenty to do over 1f out: rdn sn after: kpt on strly and jst failed: too much to do* **16/1**	ShaneKelly 12	78+
-660	3	3/4	**Ruby Gates (IRE)**[13] 3022 6-9-1 **70** (John Butler) *in rr: rdn over 2f out: gd hdwy over 1f out: kpt on wl ins fnl f* **66/1**	DarraghKeenan(5) 9	75
412-	4	shd	**Camelot Rakti (IRE)**[226] 8474 3-9-3 **78** (James Tate) *bhd ldr: rdn over 2f out: styd on wl tl* **8/1**	PJMcDonald 4	80
4605	5	3 1/4	**Black Medick**[9] 3146 3-8-11 **72** (Laura Mongan) *cl up in mid-div on inner: rdn over 2f out: one pce over 1f out* **66/1**	LiamJones 5	66
421-	6	1/2	**Spanish Aria**[202] 9068 3-9-7 **82** (John Gosden) *s.s and lost several l: in rr: rdn on inner 2f out: ct on heels fr over 1f out tl 1f out: no ch after and pushed out (jockey said filly was slowly away and denied a clear run)* **11/4**[1]	RobertHavlin 3	75+
30-1	7	2 3/4	**Nightingale Valley**[26] 2584 6-10-0 **78** (Stuart Kittow) *mid-div and niggled along at times to hold pl: effrt over 2f out: one pce* **20/1**	JasonWatson 7	68
55-2	8	1 1/4	**Clara Peeters**[12] 3041 3-9-7 **82** (Gary Moore) *bhd ldrs on inner: rdn over 2f out: kpt on tl no ex ent fnl f* **3/1**[2]	JimCrowley 2	66
0-13	9	hd	**Here's Two**[25] 2622 6-9-8 **72** (Ron Hodges) *hld up in mid-div on outer: rdn over 2f out: kpt on* **33/1**	KieranO'Neill 11	58
3-04	10	11	**Ideological (IRE)**[20] 2768 3-9-6 **81** (Roger Varian) *bhd wnr on outer: rdn over 2f out to hold pl: sn hld and wknd (jockey said filly stopped quickly)* **9/2**[3]	AndreaAtzeni 10	39

1m 38.95s (-0.85) **Going Correction** -0.025s/f (Stan) **10 Ran SP% 115.7**
WFA 3 from 4yo+ 11lb
Speed ratings (Par 102): **103,102,101,101,98 97,95,93,93,82**
CSF £68.55 CT £4157.76 TOTE £4.80: £1.90, £3.70, £10.50; EX 67.10 Trifecta £3399.20.
Owner Windmill Racing-Kitcarina **Bred** S C E A Haras De Saint Pair **Trained** Kingsclere, Hants

FOCUS
A fair fillies' handicap.
T/Plt: £229.30 to a £1 stake. Pool: £62,757.40. 199.77 winning units. T/Qpdt: £4.40 to a £1 stake. Pool: £10,555.20. 1,760.08 winning units. **Cathal Gahan**

3371 NOTTINGHAM (L-H)

Wednesday, June 5

OFFICIAL GOING: Good (good to soft in places; 7.5)
Wind: Light, against Weather: Cloudy with sunny spells

3469 EBF MAIDEN FILLIES' STKS (PLUS 10 RACE) 5f 8y

12:00 (12:02) (Class 5) 2-Y-O **£3,881** (£1,155; £577; £288) **Stalls** Centre

Form	Pos	Dist	Horse / Comment	Jockey	RPR
	1		**Flaming Princess (IRE)** 2-9-0 (Richard Fahey) *w ldrs: led 2f out: hdd over 1f out: rdn and edgd lft ins fnl f: r.o to ld nr fin* **12/1**	BarryMcHugh 12	88
	2	nk	**Al Raya** 2-9-0 (Simon Crisford) *hld up: racd keenly: hdwy 1/2-way: shkn up to ld and edgd rt over 1f out: rdn and wandered ins fnl f: hdd nr fin* **15/8**[1]	SilvestreDeSousa 4	87+
	3	2 1/4	**Poets Dance** 2-9-0 (Rae Guest) *s.i.s: sn swtchd rt: hld up: nt clr run: hdwy and swtchd lft over 1f out: r.o* **50/1**	DavidProbert 7	79
3	4	3 3/4	**Know No Limits (IRE)**[26] 2579 2-9-0 (Tom Dascombe) *led 3f: rdn over 1f out: wknd ins fnl f* **8/1**[3]	RichardKingscote 10	65
0	5	3/4	**Navajo Dawn (IRE)**[18] 2840 2-9-0 (Robyn Brisland) *w ldrs: ev ch 2f out: sn rdn: hung lft and wknd ins fnl f* **100/1**	NicolaCurrie 9	63
4	6	1/2	**Picture Frame**[18] 2836 2-9-0 (Saeed bin Suroor) *chsd ldrs: pushed along 1/2-way: nt clr run and swtchd lft over 1f out: wkng whn carried lft ins fnl f* **15/8**[1]	HarryBentley 11	61
	7	nse	**Sobriquet (IRE)** 2-9-0 (Ed de Giles) *prom on outer: rdn and hung lft over 1f out: sn wknd* **33/1**	CallumShepherd 3	61
	8	1/2	**Knock Annie (IRE)** 2-9-0 (K R Burke) *s.i.s: sme hdwy on outer 2f out: btn whn carried lft ins fnl f* **20/1**	BenCurtis 2	59
45	9	nk	**Queens Blade**[18] 2820 2-9-0 (Tim Easterby) *hld up: racd keenly: pushed along 1/2-way: n.d* **50/1**	DavidAllan 5	58
	10	1 3/4	**With Virtue** 2-9-0 (James Tate) *prom: pushed along 1/2-way: sn hung lft: wknd over 1f out* **11/2**[2]	PJMcDonald 8	51

1m 0.89s (0.69) **Going Correction** +0.05s/f (Good) **10 Ran SP% 116.4**
Speed ratings (Par 90): **96,95,91,85,84 83,83,83,82,79**
CSF £33.98 TOTE £12.80: £3.70, £1.10, £8.40; EX 44.10 Trifecta £979.00.
Owner The Cool Silk Partnership **Bred** Linacre House Limited **Trained** Musley Bank, N Yorks

FOCUS
Outer track in use. There was 6mm of rain the previous day and the going was given as good, good to soft in places (Going Stick 7.5). The rail was out 6yds on the home bend and 4yds on the stands' bend. The first two pulled nicely clear and look useful sorts.

3470 RACINGTV.COM FILLIES' H'CAP 6f 18y

12:30 (12:32) (Class 5) (0-70,72) 4-Y-O+
£3,881 (£1,155; £577; £300; £300; £300) **Stalls** Centre

Form	Pos	Dist	Horse / Comment	Jockey	RPR
33-0	1		**Rose Hip**[25] 2623 4-8-13 **62** (Tony Carroll) *s.i.s: hld up: racd keenly: hdwy on outer 4f out: shkn up to ld over 1f out: rdn and wandered ins fnl f: r.o (trainers' rep said, regarding the apparent improvement in form, that filly was hampered on her previous start and appreciated the better ground on this occasion)* **16/1**	TomMarquand 1	71+
-050	2	1	**Penny Pot Lane**[26] 2580 6-9-0 **63** (Richard Whitaker) *s.i.s: hld up: hdwy nt clr run and swtchd lft over 1f out: edgd lft and r.o to go 2nd wl ins fnl f* **8/1**	LewisEdmunds 9	68
0-10	3	nk	**Incentive**[34] 2339 5-8-13 **62** (Stuart Kittow) *chsd ldrs: rdn over 1f out: edgd lft ins fnl f: styd on* **15/2**	(p) BenCurtis 7	66
6115	4	hd	**Dream World (IRE)**[19] 2809 4-9-4 **72** (Michael Appleby) *s.i.s: hld up: hdwy and nt clr run over 1f out: rdn and hung lft ins fnl f: kpt on* **9/2**[3]	SeanDavis(5) 5	75
4-33	5	1 1/4	**Maid Of Spirit (IRE)**[13] 3021 4-9-9 **72** (Clive Cox) *sn chsng ldr: led over 2f out: rdn: carried hd high and hdd over 1f out: no ex ins fnl f* **5/1**	HectorCrouch 2	71
30-2	6	1 1/2	**Debawtry (IRE)**[18] 2846 4-9-3 **66** (Phillip Makin) *s.i.s: hld up: racd keenly: hdwy on outer over 1f out: rdn: whn carried lft ins fnl f: no ex (trainer said filly was slowly away and would have appreciated a stronger gallop)* **5/2**[1]	ShaneGray 3	61+
3221	7	1/2	**Liamba**[8] 3207 4-9-2 **68** 5ex (David O'Meara) *chsd ldrs: led over 3f: no ex fr over 1f out* **4/1**[2]	(v) ConorMcGovern(3) 8	61
000-	8	shd	**Ocean Temptress**[225] 8516 5-8-6 **55** (Louise Allan) *prom: pushed along over 2f out: sn lost pl* **40/1**	FrannyNorton 4	48

1m 14.5s (0.70) **Going Correction** +0.05s/f (Good) **8 Ran SP% 114.6**
Speed ratings (Par 100): **97,95,95,95,93 91,90,90**
CSF £135.80 CT £1051.97 TOTE £13.60: £3.20, £2.40, £2.30; EX 135.30 Trifecta £823.40.
Owner Lady Whent **Bred** Lady Whent **Trained** Cropthorne, Worcs

FOCUS
Quite a competitive little sprint, rated around the second and third.

3471 BET AT RACINGTV.COM H'CAP 1m 75y

1:00 (1:00) (Class 4) (0-85,87) 3-Y-O
£6,469 (£1,925; £962; £481; £300; £300) **Stalls** Centre

Form	Pos	Dist	Horse / Comment	Jockey	RPR
55-2	1		**Ouzo**[39] 2101 3-8-11 **74** (Richard Hannon) *chsd ldr: led over 6f out: rdn and hdd over 2f out: rallied to ld ins fnl f: styd on* **9/2**[3]	SeanLevey 2	87
42-2	2	nk	**King Ademar (USA)**[56] 1690 3-9-10 **87** (Martyn Meade) *s.i.s: hld up: hdwy 5f out: led over 2f out: rdn over 1f out: hdd ins fnl f: styd on* **7/2**[2]	OisinMurphy 10	99+
51-5	3	3 1/4	**Dalaalaat (IRE)**[26] 2581 3-9-5 **82** (William Haggas) *hld up in tch: n.m.r over 2f out: rdn over 1f out: styd on (jockey said colt was denied a clear run approx 2f out. Vet said colt lost it's right fore shoe)* **15/8**[1]	JimCrowley 4	87+
-600	4	nk	**Amadeus Grey (IRE)**[19] 2811 3-9-0 **77** (Tim Easterby) *prom: lost pl 7f out: swtchd rt over 2f out: r.o ins fnl f* **100/1**	(t) DavidAllan 1	81
5-33	5	1 1/2	**Entrusting**[37] 2208 3-9-5 **82** (James Fanshawe) *sn chsng ldrs: shkn up over 3f out: ev ch over 2f out: sn rdn: styd on same pce fnl f* **7/1**	SilvestreDeSousa 12	83
61-2	6	1 1/4	**Millions Memories**[17] 2875 3-9-4 **81** (David Lanigan) *chsd ldrs: rdn over 2f out: wknd over 1f out* **20/1**	DanielMuscutt 9	79
0504	7	shd	**Burj**[49] 1857 3-9-7 **84** (Saeed bin Suroor) *broke wl: sn lost pl: rdn 1/2-way: styd on ins fnl f* **16/1**	(h) HayleyTurner 6	81
2-61	8	1/2	**Gin Palace**[15] 2927 3-9-0 **77** (Eve Johnson Houghton) *led: hdd over 6f out: chsd ldr tl rdn over 2f out: wknd over 1f out* **16/1**	CharlesBishop 3	73
-654	9	1 3/4	**Sir Victor (IRE)**[17] 2872 3-9-2 **79** (Tom Dascombe) *s.i.s: hld up: nvr on terms (jockey said gelding jumped awkwardly from the stalls)* **33/1**	RichardKingscote 8	71
42-6	10	2 1/4	**Copal**[20] 2765 3-8-13 **76** (Ralph Beckett) *plld hrd and prom: stdd and lost pl after 1f: rdn over 3f out: wknd 2f out* **25/1**	HarryBentley 11	63
22-0	11	1 3/4	**Watchmyeverymove (IRE)**[21] 2746 3-9-2 **79** (Stuart Williams) *prom: lost pl over 6f out: rdn over 3f out: wknd over 2f out* **66/1**	(t) PJMcDonald 5	62

1m 45.44s (-1.26) **Going Correction** +0.05s/f (Good) **11 Ran SP% 113.5**
Speed ratings (Par 101): **108,107,104,104,102 101,101,100,99,96 95**
CSF £18.84 CT £38.99 TOTE £4.90: £1.70, £1.70, £1.20; EX 20.10 Trifecta £48.70.
Owner Michael Kerr-Dineen & Martin Hughes **Bred** Equine Breeding Limited **Trained** East Everleigh, Wilts

■ Stewards' Enquiry : Sean Levey two-day ban; misuse of whip (June 19,23)

FOCUS
Add 18yds. The first two pulled clear and had a good battle. It's easy to be positive about both of them, and the third.

3472 INTRODUCING RACING TV H'CAP 1m 75y

1:30 (1:31) (Class 2) (0-110,98) 3-Y-O+ **£16,172** (£4,812; £2,405; £1,202) **Stalls** Centre

Form	Pos	Dist	Horse / Comment	Jockey	RPR
6000	1		**Circus Couture (IRE)**[35] 2271 7-9-3 **97** (Jane Chapple-Hyam) *hld up: hdwy over 2f out: ev ch whn hmpd sn after: swtchd rt over 1f out: sn rdn: led ins fnl f: r.o* **7/1**[3]	(v[1]) JFEgan 6	100
4-	2	3/4	**Baltic Baron (IRE)**[230] 4-9-2 **96** (David O'Meara) *chsd ldr: shkn up and ev ch whn hmpd 2f out: rallied fnl f: r.o* **7/1**[3]	DavidNolan 3	97
6324	3	1/2	**Masham Star (IRE)**[5] 3313 5-9-2 **96** (Mark Johnston) *led: qcknd 3f out: hdd over 2f out: hmpd sn after: rdn over 1f out: r.o* **9/4**[1]	FrannyNorton 5	96
11-0	4	nk	**Mutafani**[20] 2778 4-9-2 **96** (Simon Crisford) *s.i.s: hld up: hdwy on outer to ld over 2f out: sn hung lft: rdn over 1f out: hdd ins fnl f: styd on same pce (jockey said colt hung left under pressure)* **3/1**[2]	SilvestreDeSousa 4	95+
3/00	5	3/4	**Max Zorin (IRE)**[18] 2832 5-9-2 **96** (Andrew Balding) *stmbld s: sn chsng ldrs: nt clr run over 2f out: swtchd rt and stmbld over 1f out: styd on (jockey said gelding stumbled leaving the stalls)* **9/1**	RobHornby 2	93

1m 45.48s (-1.22) **Going Correction** +0.05s/f (Good) **5 Ran SP% 90.8**
Speed ratings (Par 109): **108,107,106,106,105**
CSF £31.25 TOTE £5.40: £1.90, £2.20; EX 34.40 Trifecta £33.40.
Owner Mrs Jane Chapple-Hyam **Bred** Azienda Agricola Mariano **Trained** Dalham, Suffolk

■ Escobar was withdrawn. Price at time of withdrawal 3/1. Rule 4 applies to all bets - deduction 25p in the £.

FOCUS
Add 18yds. A good handicap, although it was a bit tactical and they finished bunched up. Only the winner raced off their correct mark and the form's rated cautiously.

3473 LIKE RACING TV ON FACEBOOK H'CAP — 1m 2f 50y
2:00 (2:02) (Class 6) (0-60,65) 4-Y-O+
£3,234 (£962; £481; £300; £300; £300) **Stalls** Low

Form — RPR

2-01 **1** **Lucky's Dream**[6] 3276 4-9-12 **65** 5ex PJMcDonald 4 — 73
(Ian Williams) *a.p: shkn up over 2f out: rdn to ld ins fnl f: r.o* — **4/1**[2]

0315 **2** 1 3/4 **Mullarkey**[25] 2617 5-9-6 **59** (t) KierenFox 6 — 64
(John Best) *led: rdn over 2f out: hdd and unable qck ins fnl f* — **11/2**

040- **3** 1 1/2 **Das Kapital**[218] 8718 4-8-11 **50** JFEgan 10 — 52
(John Berry) *hld up: rdn and hung lft fr over 3f out: hdwy over 1f out: r.o: nt rch ldrs* — **40/1**

-614 **4** nse **Allux Boy (IRE)**[9] 3163 5-8-12 **56** FayeMcManoman[(5)] 13 — 58
(Nigel Tinkler) *prom: rdn over 1f out: styd on same pce ins fnl f* — **5/1**[3]

0-60 **5** hd **Doctor Wonderful**[104] 835 4-9-5 **58** (p w) DanielMuscutt 15 — 60
(Kevin Frost) *s.i.s: hld up: hdwy over 1f out: rdn and hung lft ins fnl f: r.o* — **50/1**

00-2 **6** 1 1/2 **Red Seeker**[9] 3162 4-9-2 **55** (t) DavidAllan 7 — 54
(Tim Easterby) *prom: racd keenely: wnt 2nd 8f out: rdn over 2f out: lost 2nd over 1f out: no ex ins fnl f (jockey said gelding ran too freely)* — **7/2**[1]

0-00 **7** nk **Ebbisham (IRE)**[29] 2509 6-9-7 **60** (v) BenCurtis 3 — 58
(John Mackie) *hld up: hdwy over 2f out: rdn over 1f out: styd on same pce fnl f* — **11/1**

6036 **8** 1/2 **Zephyros (GER)**[21] 2732 8-8-13 **57** PoppyBridgwater[(5)] 2 — 55
(David Bridgwater) *hld up: shkn up over 2f out: styd on ins fnl f: nvr nrr* — **16/1**

0650 **9** 2 1/2 **Destinys Rock**[23] 2692 4-8-12 **58** (p[1]) CierenFallon[(7)] 5 — 51
(Mark Loughnane) *chsd ldrs: rdn over 2f out: wknd ins fnl f* — **14/1**

-005 **10** shd **Little Choosey**[96] 969 9-8-8 **47** (tp) JimmyQuinn 14 — 40
(Roy Bowring) *hld up in tch: rdn over 1f out: wknd ins fnl f* — **66/1**

5035 **11** 5 **Tommycole**[21] 2740 4-9-2 **55** JackMitchell 11 — 39
(Olly Williams) *chsd ldr 2f: remained handy: shkn up over 4f out: rdn and hung lft over 2f out: sn hung rt: wknd over 1f out* — **16/1**

4-05 **12** 3/4 **Castle Talbot (IRE)**[36] 2233 7-9-5 **58** (b) DavidProbert 1 — 41
(Tom Clover) *hld up: rdn over 3f out: nvr on terms* — **20/1**

0600 **13** 5 **Chantresse (IRE)**[14] 2974 4-9-2 **55** (p) FergusSweeney 9 — 29
(Mark Usher) *s.i.s: hld up: n.d* — **50/1**

06-5 **14** 1 3/4 **Turnbury**[36] 2234 8-8-7 **46** (p) EdwardGreatrex 8 — 16
(Nikki Evans) *hld up: rdn over 3f out: sn wknd (jockey said gelding was hampered shortly after leaving the stalls and was unable to obtain a prominent position)* — **33/1**

-660 **15** hd **Acadian Angel (IRE)**[26] 2585 5-9-3 **56** PaddyMathers 16 — 26
(Steph Hollinshead) *s.i.s: a in rr* — **22/1**

2m 12.73s (-0.67) **Going Correction** +0.05s/f (Good) **15 Ran SP% 120.9**
Speed ratings (Par 101): **104,102,101,101,101 100,99,99,97,97 93,92,88,87,87**
CSF £24.47 CT £784.20 TOTE £4.50: £1.70, £3.10, £17.30; EX 25.20 Trifecta £1236.10.
Owner R S Brookhouse **Bred** R S Brookhouse **Trained** Portway, Worcs

FOCUS
Add 18yds. An ordinary handicap. The winner can do better again.

3474 JOIN RACING TV NOW H'CAP — 1m 6f
2:35 (2:35) (Class 5) (0-75,75) 3-Y-O
£3,881 (£1,155; £577; £300; £300; £300) **Stalls** Low

Form — RPR

2-11 **1** **Moon King (FR)**[29] 2511 3-9-2 **70** HarryBentley 6 — 81+
(Ralph Beckett) *pushed along early in rr: hdwy over 3f out: chsd ldr over 2f out: led over 1f out: rdn clr ins fnl f* — **11/8**[1]

0-24 **2** 4 **Palladium**[39] 2096 3-9-5 **73** RobHornby 8 — 77
(Martyn Meade) *sn prom: chsd ldr and carried wd over 11f out: led over 2f out: rdn and hdd over 1f out: no ex ins fnl f* — **7/2**[2]

00-3 **3** nk **Anyonecanhaveitall**[8] 3197 3-8-11 **65** PJMcDonald 1 — 68
(Mark Johnston) *chsd ldrs: rdn over 3f out: styd on same pce fnl f* — **11/2**

2124 **4** 2 3/4 **Tigray (USA)**[16] 2905 3-9-1 **69** AlistairRawlinson 2 — 68
(Michael Appleby) *ld early: chsd ldrs: rdn over 2f out: hung lft and no ex fnl f* — **14/1**

1-40 **5** 3/4 **Mister Chiang**[27] 2562 3-9-7 **75** FrannyNorton 3 — 73
(Mark Johnston) *sn led: rdn and hdd over 2f out: wknd ins fnl f* — **5/1**[3]

3246 **6** 1/2 **Alpasu (IRE)**[70] 1365 3-8-12 **73** (tp) Pierre-LouisJamin[(7)] 5 — 70
(Archie Watson) *s.i.s: hld up: pushed along 6f out: rdn and hung lft fr over 2f out: nvr nrr* — **50/1**

2-35 **7** 9 **Fox Fearless**[47] 1928 3-9-7 **75** (p) SilvestreDeSousa 4 — 60
(K R Burke) *awkward leaving stalls: bhd: rdn and hung lft fr over 2f out: eased over 1f out* — **14/1**

25-3 **8** 8 **Surrey Warrior (USA)**[48] 1884 3-9-7 **75** (b) EdwardGreatrex 7 — 48
(Archie Watson) *chsd ldrs: lost pl over 11f out: sn pushed along: rdn over 5f out: wkng whn hmpd over 1f out* — **33/1**

3m 5.42s (-0.98) **Going Correction** +0.05s/f (Good) **8 Ran SP% 114.6**
Speed ratings (Par 99): **104,101,101,99,99 99,94,89**
CSF £6.26 CT £19.28 TOTE £2.50: £1.40, £1.30, £1.20; EX 8.00 Trifecta £25.20.
Owner What Asham Partnership **Bred** Rashit Shaykhutdinov **Trained** Kimpton, Hants

FOCUS
Add 30yds. The winner is on a roll and won comfortably. The form's rated round the second.

3475 FOLLOW @RACINGTV ON TWITTER "HANDS AND HEELS" APPRENTICE H'CAP (RE INITIATIVE) (DIV I) — 6f 18y
3:10 (3:11) (Class 6) (0-55,60) 4-Y-O+
£3,557 (£1,058; £529; £300; £300; £300) **Stalls** Centre

Form — RPR

3515 **1** **Space War**[21] 2741 12-9-1 **52** (t) ZakWheatley[(3)] 2 — 62
(Michael Easterby) *hld up: hdwy over 2f out: shkn up to ld ins fnl f: pushed out* — **14/1**

0022 **2** 2 1/4 **Queen Of Kalahari**[13] 3007 4-8-13 **47** JessicaCooley 7 — 50
(Les Eyre) *led: shkn up over 1f out: hdd ins fnl f: styd on same pce* — **8/1**

1213 **3** shd **Ticks The Boxes (IRE)**[17] 2876 7-9-8 **56** TristanPrice 1 — 59
(Brian Ellison) *chsd ldrs: shkn up and ev ch over 1f out: edgd lft and styd on same pce ins fnl f* — **3/1**[1]

-000 **4** 3/4 **Jacksonfire**[22] 2717 7-8-12 **46** (b) CianMacRedmond 10 — 46
(Michael Mullineaux) *s.i.s: hld up: swtchd lft and hdwy over 1f out: r.o: nt rch ldrs* — **66/1**

0-05 **5** 1/2 **Cliff (IRE)**[25] 2638 9-9-0 **53** IzzyClifton[(5)] 8 — 52
(Nigel Tinkler) *hld up: swtchd rt and hdwy over 1f out: r.o: nt rch ldrs* — **8/1**

0060 **6** nse **Meshardal (GER)**[21] 2741 9-9-1 **49** (p) GavinAshton 14 — 48
(Ruth Carr) *hld up: hdwy over 2f out: shkn up over 1f out: styd on* — **8/1**

3520 **7** nk **Milton Road**[25] 2638 4-9-8 **56** HarryRussell 3 — 54
(Rebecca Bastiman) *wnt rt s: sn prom: shkn up over 1f out: no ex ins fnl f* — **6/1**[3]

-306 **8** 2 1/4 **Poppy Jag (IRE)**[15] 2924 4-8-12 **45** oh1 (b) SeanKirrane 12 — 37
(Kevin Frost) *w ldrs to 1/2-way: no ex fnl f* — **33/1**

3351 **9** 1/2 **Mansfield**[8] 3203 6-9-12 **60** 5ex GeorgiaDobie 13 — 50
(Stella Barclay) *s.i.s: hdwy over 4f out: shkn up over 1f out: wknd ins fnl f* — **4/1**[2]

4500 **10** 1 1/2 **Malaysian Boleh**[13] 3007 9-8-9 **45** oh1 (p) GraceMcEntee[(3)] 11 — 31
(Phil McEntee) *mid-div: pushed along and lost pl over 3f out: n.d after* — **33/1**

40-0 **11** 3 1/4 **Give Em A Clump (IRE)**[98] 920 4-8-9 **45** oh1.(v) ElishaWhittington[(3)] 9 — 21
(Victor Dartnall) *prom: pushed along over 4f out: lost pl over 3f out* — **25/1**

0000 **12** 1 1/2 **Celerity (IRE)**[17] 2876 5-8-12 **45** oh1 (p) RussellHarris 6 — 17
(Lisa Williamson) *w ldr over 3f: wknd over 1f out* — **100/1**

005- **13** 9 **Sandkissed (IRE)**[230] 8342 4-8-13 **47** RhonaPindar 15 — +
(Amy Murphy) *chsd ldrs: pushed along 1/2-way: wknd 2f out* — **14/1**

405- **14** 8 **Raise A Little Joy**[226] 8466 4-8-9 **45** oh1 (p) KeelanBaker[(3)] 4
(J R Jenkins) *s.i.s and hmpd s: a in rr* — **100/1**

60/0 **15** 4 1/2 **Rio Glamorous**[35] 2296 6-8-11 **50** (b) JoeBradnam[(5)] 16 — +
(Roy Bowring) *prom: lost pl whn nt clr run over 3f out: sn wknd* — **80/1**

1m 15.08s (1.28) **Going Correction** +0.05s/f (Good) **15 Ran SP% 120.4**
Speed ratings (Par 101): **93,90,89,88,88 87,87,84,84,82 77,75,63,53,47**
CSF £117.38 CT £433.21 TOTE £14.40: £4.20, £2.40, £2.00; EX 138.80 Trifecta £452.90.
Owner The Laura Mason Syndicate **Bred** Shutford Stud And O F Waller **Trained** Sheriff Hutton, N Yorks

FOCUS
The quicker of the two divisions by 0.22sec. A moderate sprint, but the first three have all been in good heart of late so the form looks sound enough. Those in the middle of the track dominated.

3476 FOLLOW @RACINGTV ON TWITTER "HANDS AND HEELS" APPRENTICE H'CAP (RE INITIATIVE) (DIV II) — 6f 18y
3:45 (3:50) (Class 6) (0-55,57) 4-Y-O+
£3,557 (£1,058; £529; £300; £300; £300) **Stalls** Centre

Form — RPR

6-43 **1** **Viking Way (IRE)**[35] 2295 4-8-13 **49** (b) LukeCatton[(3)] 8 — 55
(Olly Williams) *prom: nt clr run over 1f out: shkn up ins fnl f: r.o to ld post (vet said gelding lost it's right fore shoe)* — **10/1**

1-04 **2** nse **Tadaany (IRE)**[14] 2958 7-9-5 **52** (p) GavinAshton 2 — 58
(Ruth Carr) *trckd ldrs: led over 1f out: shkn up and edgd rt ins fnl f: hdd post (jockey said gelding hung right in the closing stages)* — **9/2**[1]

0000 **3** 1/2 **Major Crispies**[35] 2298 8-8-9 **45** (b) IsobelFrancis[(3)] 13 — 49
(Ronald Thompson) *hld up: pushed along and hdwy over 2f out: r.o* — **20/1**

3650 **4** 1/2 **Caledonian Gold**[2] 3425 6-8-12 **45** RussellHarris 9 — 48
(Lisa Williamson) *chsd ldrs: shkn up over 1f out: styd on* — **20/1**

6446 **5** 1 1/2 **Coastal Cyclone**[38] 2145 5-9-1 **48** (b) SeanKirrane 15 — 46
(Harry Dunlop) *hld up: pushed along and hdwy over 2f out: styd on same pce wl ins fnl f* — **9/1**

1604 **6** 3/4 **Miracle Garden**[14] 2971 7-9-10 **57** (v) TristanPrice 3 — 60+
(Ian Williams) *edgd rt s: hld up: swtchd lft away fr loose horse over 5f out and racd alone on far side: sn wl bhd: shkn up: hung rt and r.o ins fnl f: nt rch ldrs* — **7/1**[3]

2235 **7** 1 **First Excel**[122] 586 7-9-4 **54** (v) ElishaWhittington[(3)] 1 — 47
(Roy Bowring) *sn led: shkn up: hung rt and hdd over 1f out: no ex ins fnl f (jockey said gelding hung right in the final 2f)* — **10/1**

5022 **8** 3/4 **Dalness Express**[21] 2728 6-9-4 **51** (bt) GeorgiaDobie 4 — 42
(John O'Shea) *edgd rt s: chsd ldrs: shkn up over 2f out: no ex ins fnl f* — **6/1**[2]

0660 **9** 1/2 **Tilsworth Rose**[35] 2295 5-8-9 **45** (b) KeelanBaker[(3)] 10 — 34
(J R Jenkins) *chsd ldrs: shkn up and hung rt over 1f out: wknd ins fnl f* — **66/1**

-000 **10** 1 3/4 **Lisnamoyle Lady (IRE)**[69] 1384 4-8-7 **45** (bt) JacobClark[(5)] 5 — 29+
(Martin Smith) *hmpd s: hmpd again by loose horse over 5f out: sn wl bhd: r.o ins fnl f* — **40/1**

2-00 **11** 1 1/2 **My Society (IRE)**[21] 2741 4-9-6 **56** (vt[1]) StefanoCherchi[(3)] 14 — 36
(David Dennis) *hld up: pushed along over 2f out: n.d* — **8/1**

0565 **12** hd **Mother Of Dragons (IRE)**[9] 3144 4-9-2 **52** (v) GraceMcEntee[(3)] 12 — 31
(Phil McEntee) *hld up in tch: pushed along and lost pl over 3f out: n.d after* — **12/1**

0600 **13** 1 1/2 **Black Truffle (FR)**[13] 3007 9-8-7 **45** (p) EllaBoardman[(5)] 11 — 20
(Mark Usher) *sn pushed along in rr: n.d* — **66/1**

6-00 **14** 1 1/2 **Ingleby Molly (IRE)**[25] 2633 4-9-0 **47** HarryRussell 6 — 17
(Jason Ward) *prom: edgd rt over 5f out: shkn up over 2f out: wknd over 1f out (jockey said filly hung right throughout)* — **14/1**

30-0 **U** **Red Allure**[40] 2081 4-8-13 **46** (p[1]) CianMacRedmond 7
(Michael Mullineaux) *clipped heels and uns rdr over 5f out* — **12/1**

1m 15.3s (1.50) **Going Correction** +0.05s/f (Good) **15 Ran SP% 121.3**
Speed ratings (Par 101): **92,91,91,90,88 87,86,85,84,82 80,80,78,76,**
CSF £51.94 CT £920.15 TOTE £9.60: £3.80, £1.90, £7.30; EX 61.70 Trifecta £1841.80.
Owner Folk From The Shire **Bred** Ennistown Stud **Trained** Market Rasen, Lincs

FOCUS
This leg was run in a time 0.22sec slower than the first division, and featured several hard-to-win-with types. A rather messy race, rated around the second.
T/Plt: £369.10 to a £1 stake. Pool: £47,088.22. 93.13 winning units. T/Qpdt: £17.70 to a £1 stake. Pool: £7,882.59. 329.42 winning units. **Colin Roberts**

2869 RIPON (R-H)
Wednesday, June 5

OFFICIAL GOING: Good to soft (7.5)
Wind: Light, across Weather: overcast

3477 BRITISH STALLION STUDS EBF NOVICE STKS — 5f
6:30 (6:31) (Class 5) 2-Y-O **£3,881** (£1,155; £577; £288) **Stalls** High

Form — RPR

4 **1** **Spartan Fighter**[16] 2892 2-9-5 0 DanielTudhope 7 — 93+
(Declan Carroll) *led narrowly: rdn 2f out: drvn and hdd narrowly ent fnl f: kpt on: led again nr fin* — **7/4**[2]

2 nk **A'Ali (IRE)** 2-9-5 0 JackMitchell 6 — 92+
(Simon Crisford) *trckd ldrs: swtchd rt over 2f out: smooth hdwy to chal 2f out: pushed into narrow ld ent fnl f: drvn fnl 110yds: kpt on but hdd nr fin* — **5/4**[1]

0 **3** 9 **Javea Magic (IRE)**[8] 3194 2-9-5 0 RichardKingscote 4 60
(Tom Dascombe) *pressed ldr: rdn over 2f out: wknd over 1f out* **9/1**
4 hd **Precocity (IRE)** 2-9-0 0 PaulHanagan 2 54
(Richard Fahey) *trckd ldrs: t.k.h early: rdn along over 2f out: wknd over 1f out* **6/1**[3]
5 1 **Arriba Arriba (IRE)** 2-9-5 0 GrahamLee 5 56
(Rebecca Menzies) *slowly away: hld up: nvr threatened* **40/1**
00 **6** 1 **Bankawi**[21] 2747 2-8-7 0 JoshQuinn(7) 3 47
(Michael Easterby) *prom: rdn and outpcd over 2f out: wknd over 1f out* **100/1**
7 9 **Pronghorn** 2-9-5 0 NathanEvans 1 20
(Michael Easterby) *v.s.a: a towards rr* **66/1**

58.74s (-0.66) **Going Correction** 0.0s/f (Good) **7 Ran SP% 110.0**
Speed ratings (Par 93): **105,104,90,89,88 86,72**
CSF £3.91 TOTE £2.70: £1.10, £1.50; EX 4.00 Trifecta £11.50.
Owner Clipper Logistics **Bred** Cheveley Park Stud Ltd **Trained** Malton, N Yorks
FOCUS
Over 21mm of rain since Tuesday evening had turned the ground to the softer side of good. The market told the story in this novice, with two useful types pulling clear.

3478 YORKSHIRE ACCOUNTANTS RIPON H'CAP 1m
7:00 (7:00) (Class 5) (0-70,70) 3-Y-O
£4,075 (£1,212; £606; £303; £300; £300) **Stalls** Low

Form RPR
4031 **1** **Cardano (USA)**[25] 2630 3-9-7 **70** RichardKingscote 8 88+
(Ian Williams) *trckd ldrs: rdn 2f out: drvn to ld ins fnl f: kpt on* **9/4**[1]
6-10 **2** 1 1/4 **Anna Bunina (FR)**[26] 2597 3-9-2 **65** JackGarritty 9 79
(Jedd O'Keeffe) *led: rdn and pressed 2f out: hdd ins fnl f: one pce* **10/1**
3-02 **3** 6 **Beguiling Charm (IRE)**[9] 3154 3-9-2 **65** LiamKeniry 10 65
(Ed Walker) *prom: rdn to chal 2f out: wknd ins fnl f* **7/1**[3]
6-44 **4** 3/4 **Ventura Bay (IRE)**[39] 2101 3-8-11 **65** SeanDavis(5) 4 63
(Richard Fahey) *trckd ldrs: rdn and outpcd 3f out: plugged on ins fnl f* **9/2**[2]
4-06 **5** 1 3/4 **Mecca's Gift (IRE)**[30] 2482 3-9-0 **63** ConnorBeasley 3 57
(Michael Dods) *hld up: rdn along over 3f out: no imp: plugged on fnl f* **16/1**
0006 **6** 1/2 **Gylo (IRE)**[15] 2933 3-9-4 **67** (p[1]) DanielTudhope 5 60
(David O'Meara) *midfield: rdn over 2f out: wknd over 1f out* **8/1**
60-5 **7** nse **Golden Parade**[12] 3051 3-9-5 **68** DavidAllan 2 61
(Tim Easterby) *hld up on inner: rdn along and sme hdwy 2f out: wknd ins fnl f (vet said gelding had lost its left hind shoe)* **15/2**
2500 **8** 4 **Rakastava (IRE)**[14] 2965 3-9-0 **63** DavidEgan 6 47
(Mick Channon) *midfield: hdwy and chsd ldrs 3f out: sn rdn: wknd over 1f out (jockey said gelding ran too free)* **14/1**
206 **9** 13 **King Shamardal**[16] 2900 3-9-4 **67** JoeFanning 7 21
(Mark Johnston) *s.i.s: hld up: wknd and bhd fnl 3f* **14/1**
665- **F** **Cawthorne Lad**[224] 8541 3-8-4 **53** RachelRichardson 1
(Tim Easterby) *hld up: plld hrd: stmbld and fell over 6f out* **33/1**

1m 41.02s (0.02) **Going Correction** 0.0s/f (Good) **10 Ran SP% 115.6**
Speed ratings (Par 99): **99,97,91,91,89 88,88,84,71,**
CSF £25.79 CT £127.97 TOTE £3.10: £1.70, £2.80, £2.10; EX 27.40 Trifecta £224.90.
Owner Sohi & Sohi **Bred** Mt Brilliant Broodmares II Llc **Trained** Portway, Worcs
FOCUS
Add 6yds. Two pulled clear in what was a modest handicap. A clear pb from the progressive winner.

3479 RIPON FARM SERVICES H'CAP 6f
7:30 (7:31) (Class 4) (0-85,85) 3-Y-O
£5,692 (£1,694; £846; £423; £300; £300) **Stalls** High

Form RPR
0101 **1** **Mark's Choice (IRE)**[14] 2960 3-9-2 **80** JackGarritty 5 87
(Ruth Carr) *s.i.s: hld up in tch: racd quite keenly: swtchd rt over 2f out: sn hdwy: rdn to chse ldr appr fnl f: drvn to ld 75yds out: kpt on* **16/1**
5-32 **2** 3/4 **Hafeet Alain (IRE)**[19] 2787 3-9-2 **80** AndrewMullen 3 85+
(Adrian Nicholls) *s.i.s: hld up: sn pushed along: drvn and sme hdwy over 1f out: r.o fnl f: wnt 2nd nr fin* **11/2**[3]
6311 **3** hd **Look Out Louis**[12] 3048 3-9-7 **85** DavidAllan 1 89+
(Tim Easterby) *prom: led 4f out: rdn 2f out: drvn appr fnl f: hdd 75yds out: no ex: lost 2nd nr fin* **4/1**[2]
2035 **4** 2 **Princess Power (IRE)**[11] 3068 3-9-2 **83** RowanScott(3) 2 81
(Nigel Tinkler) *in tch on outside: rdn over 2f out: kpt on same pce* **10/1**
56-0 **5** 2 1/4 **Constant**[40] 2078 3-9-3 **81** DanielTudhope 6 71
(David O'Meara) *in tch towards outer: rdn over 2f out: wknd ins fnl f* **8/1**
3040 **6** 1 1/4 **Coolagh Magic**[38] 2149 3-8-10 **79** (p) SeanDavis(5) 10 65
(Richard Fahey) *led: hdd 4f out but remained cl up: rdn over 2f out: drvn over 1f out: wknd ins fnl f* **33/1**
3-04 **7** 3/4 **Finoah (IRE)**[12] 3048 3-9-4 **85** (v) JaneElliott(3) 9 69
(Tom Dascombe) *trckd ldrs: rdn over 2f out: wknd over 1f out (trainer's rep said gelding became unbalanced on the undulations)* **12/1**
3-00 **8** 4 **No More Regrets (IRE)**[11] 3068 3-8-11 **75** PaulHanagan 7 46
(Patrick Morris) *chsd ldrs: rdn over 2f out: wknd over 1f out* **50/1**
2-44 **9** 14 **Converter (IRE)**[36] 2255 3-9-4 **82** BenCurtis 4 8
(Mick Channon) *hld up: wknd and bhd fnl 2f (vet said colt had bled from the nose)* **16/1**
2212 **U** **Dominus (IRE)**[18] 2835 3-9-5 **83** (h) DavidEgan 8
(Brian Meehan) *stmbld and uns rdr s* **7/4**[1]

1m 12.59s (0.09) **Going Correction** 0.0s/f (Good) **10 Ran SP% 116.3**
Speed ratings (Par 101): **99,98,97,95,92 90,89,84,65,**
CSF £101.35 CT £427.95 TOTE £11.60: £3.00, £2.00, £1.20; EX 67.50 Trifecta £439.90.
Owner Cragg Wood Racing **Bred** Northern Bloodstock Agency Ltd **Trained** Huby, N Yorks
FOCUS
A useful 3yo handicap, but it instantly became more winnable when short-priced favourite Dominus stumbled and unseated his rider leaving the stalls. The form seems sound, with a pb from the winner.

3480 DIRECTORS CUP H'CAP 6f
8:00 (8:01) (Class 3) (0-95,97) 4-Y-O+
£9,337 (£2,796; £1,398; £699; £349; £175) **Stalls** High

Form RPR
2-62 **1** **Hyperfocus (IRE)**[18] 2843 5-9-2 **90** DavidAllan 1 98
(Tim Easterby) *1 of 3 who racd far side: mde all: strly pressed thrght: rdn over 1f out: kpt on wl* **7/2**[1]
-560 **2** shd **Ice Age (IRE)**[19] 2791 6-9-2 **97** GeorgiaDobie(7) 8 104
(Eve Johnson Houghton) *prom stands' side: rdn to ld in gp over 1f out and pressed overall ldr: kpt on: jst failed: 1st of 8 in gp* **11/1**
4300 **3** shd **Gulliver**[21] 2743 5-9-7 **95** (tp) DanielTudhope 11 101
(David O'Meara) *chsd ldrs stands' side: rdn to chal appr fnl f: drvn and kpt on: 2nd of 8 in gp (vet said gelding was lame right hind)* **16/1**
0-00 **4** nk **Growl**[27] 2557 7-9-4 **92** PaulHanagan 4 97
(Richard Fahey) *hld up far side: pushed along and hdwy 2f out: rdn to chal ins fnl f: kpt on: 2nd of 3 in gp* **6/1**[2]
1300 **5** nk **Desert Doctor (IRE)**[21] 2743 4-9-4 **92** LiamKeniry 14 96
(Ed Walker) *trckd ldrs stands' side: rdn over 2f out: kpt on fnl f: 3rd of 8 in gp* **20/1**
-000 **6** 1/2 **Quick Look**[20] 2775 6-8-9 **83** NathanEvans 13 86
(Michael Easterby) *s.i.s: sn midfield stands' side: rdn and edgd rt to outer appr fnl f: kpt on: 4th of 8 in gp* **8/1**[3]
0-00 **7** hd **Golden Apollo**[21] 2743 5-9-5 **93** JasonHart 3 95
(Tim Easterby) *trckd ldr far side: rdn 2f out: kpt on same pce: last of 3 in gp* **7/2**[1]
4-14 **8** 1 **Bossipop**[16] 2910 6-8-9 **83** (b) CamHardie 12 82
(Tim Easterby) *led stands' side gp: pressed ldr overall: rdn and hdd in gp over 1f out: no ex ins fnl f: 5th of 8 in gp* **14/1**
-400 **9** 1/2 **Royal Brave (IRE)**[18] 2843 8-8-13 **87** RoystonFfrench 9 84
(Rebecca Bastiman) *hld up stands' side: rdn 2f out: kpt on ins fnl f: nvr threatened: 6th of 8 in gp* **28/1**
-006 **10** 2 **Roundhay Park**[21] 2743 4-8-9 **88** FayeMcManoman(5) 5 79
(Nigel Tinkler) *hld up on outside of stands' side gp: pushed along over 2f out: edgd rt and btn over 1f out: 7th of 8 in gp* **6/1**[2]
0200 **11** 1 3/4 **Pipers Note**[18] 2843 9-9-4 **92** JackGarritty 7 77
(Ruth Carr) *hld up in tch stands' side: rdn over 2f out: wknd over 1f out* **16/1**

1m 11.44s (-1.06) **Going Correction** 0.0s/f (Good) **11 Ran SP% 119.1**
Speed ratings (Par 107): **107,106,106,106,105 105,105,103,103,100 98**
CSF £44.84 CT £561.40 TOTE £3.60: £1.30, £3.50, £4.80; EX 55.30 Trifecta £590.30.
Owner Ryedale Partners No 14 **Bred** Stephanie Von Schilcher & Gavan Kinch **Trained** Great Habton, N Yorks
FOCUS
A useful and competitive sprint, they raced in two groups with the winner coming from the trio who raced far side. Ordinary form for the grade.

3481 RIPON RACES SUPPORTS RACING WELFARE H'CAP 2m
8:30 (8:30) (Class 5) (0-75,77) 4-Y-O+
£4,075 (£1,212; £606; £303; £300; £300) **Stalls** High

Form RPR
0623 **1** **Angel Gabrial (IRE)**[4] 3334 10-8-4 **57** (p) DavidEgan 2 65
(Patrick Morris) *trckd ldrs: dropped to midfield 12f out: hdwy to trck ldrs 3f out: rdn to ld over 1f out: styd on* **3/1**[2]
40-3 **2** 2 1/2 **Always Resolute**[26] 2578 8-9-7 **74** (v) PaulHanagan 3 79
(Ian Williams) *midfield: trckd ldrs 8f out: rdn to ld over 2f out: hdd over 1f out: one pce* **11/8**[1]
125- **3** 6 **Indian Vision (IRE)**[303] 5789 5-8-8 **61** AndrewMullen 8 59
(Micky Hammond) *hld up: rdn over 2f out: plugged on to go modest 3rd ins fnl f* **12/1**
0-00 **4** 3/4 **Stormin Tom (IRE)**[26] 2591 7-9-7 **74** DavidAllan 1 71
(Tim Easterby) *prom: led 4f out: sn rdn along: hdd over 2f out: wknd over 1f out* **5/1**[3]
004- **5** 3/4 **Buyer Beware (IRE)**[149] 7453 7-8-8 **61** SamJames 9 57
(Liam Bailey) *hld up in rr: rdn over 4f out: sn btn* **12/1**
0360 **6** 28 **Gang Warfare**[26] 2571 8-9-10 **77** (bt) BenCurtis 4 39
(Alexandra Dunn) *v.s.a: rcvrd to trck ldrs after 3f: rdn over 4f out: wknd qckly: t.o* **16/1**
0000 **7** nk **Tebay (IRE)**[14] 2975 4-8-3 **56** oh1 ow1 RoystonFfrench 7 19
(Luke McJannet) *led: rdn and hdd 4f out: wknd: t.o* **25/1**
0600 **S** **Galitello**[13] 3017 4-8-7 **60** (v) JoeFanning 5
(Mark Johnston) *hld up: slipped up over 6f out* **11/1**

3m 29.77s (-2.63) **Going Correction** 0.0s/f (Good) **8 Ran SP% 117.2**
Speed ratings (Par 103): **106,104,101,101,101 87,86,**
CSF £7.73 CT £41.53 TOTE £3.30: £1.10, £1.10, £2.40; EX 9.00 Trifecta £50.00.
Owner Dr Marwan Koukash **Bred** K And Mrs Cullen **Trained** Prescot, Merseyside
FOCUS
Add 6yds. The market leaders dominated this modest staying handicap. There were doubts over most of these beforehand.

3482 TOPSPORT EQUISAND NOVICE STKS 1m 2f 190y
9:00 (9:02) (Class 5) 3-Y-O+
£3,881 (£1,155; £577; £288) **Stalls** Low

Form RPR
31 **1** **Future Investment**[28] 2524 3-9-7 0 HarryBentley 9 90+
(Ralph Beckett) *trckd ldrs: rdn along to chal 3f out: drvn into narrow ld 110yds out: all out* **11/8**[1]
3 **2** shd **Dubai Tradition (USA)**[19] 2795 3-9-0 0 HectorCrouch 5 83+
(Saeed bin Suroor) *prom: led narrowly over 3f out: rdn over 2f out: drvn and hdd narrowly 110yds out: styd on* **7/4**[2]
1 **3** 1/2 **Alright Sunshine (IRE)**[34] 2323 4-10-5 0 DanielTudhope 1 87+
(Keith Dalgleish) *prom: gng wl but no much room in bhd ldrs over 2f out: angled lft and in clr over 1f out: drvn and styd on fnl f* **7/2**[3]
4 2 1/4 **Grenadier Guard (IRE)** 3-9-0 0 AndrewMullen 6 78+
(Mark Johnston) *midfield: hdwy and trckd ldrs over 3f out: rdn over 2f out: no ex fnl 110yds* **14/1**
0 **5** 2 1/4 **Canoodling**[20] 2770 3-8-9 0 BenCurtis 4 69
(Ian Williams) *midfield on inner: pushed along over 2f out: kpt on ins fnl f* **66/1**
0-0 **6** nk **Philonikia**[146] 156 3-8-9 0 KevinStott 2 68
(Ralph Beckett) **33/1**
0 **7** 17 **Thornton Le Clay**[6] 3247 3-8-7 0 JoshQuinn(7) 7 43
(Michael Easterby) *racd keenly and sn led: rdn along and hdd over 3f out: wknd over 1f out* **100/1**
00 **8** 1/2 **Stormin Norman**[8] 3200 4-10-0 0 GrahamLee 3 42
(Micky Hammond) *hld up in midfield: rdn along over 3f out: wknd 2f out* **66/1**
0 **9** 1 1/2 **Marmarr**[26] 2583 3-8-9 0 PaulHanagan 10 34
(William Haggas) *slowly away: a towards rr* **14/1**
/0-0 **10** nk **Reedway (IRE)**[37] 2192 6-9-9 0 SeanDavis(5) 11 39
(Robyn Brisland) *a towards rr* **200/1**
0 **11** 16 **Hasili Filly**[32] 2420 3-8-9 0 ConnorBeasley 8 5
(Noel Wilson) *hld up in midfield: rdn over 3f out: wknd 2f out* **80/1**

2m 22.47s (3.47) **Going Correction** 0.0s/f (Good) **11 Ran SP% 122.7**
WFA 3 from 4yo+ 14lb
Speed ratings (Par 103): **87,86,86,84,83 83,70,70,69,69 57**
CSF £4.21 TOTE £2.30: £1.10, £1.40, £1.20; EX 5.00 Trifecta £10.70.
Owner R N J Partnership **Bred** Theakston Stud **Trained** Kimpton, Hants

FOCUS
Add 6yds. A useful novice that should produce plenty of winners. The first three are rated close to form.
T/Jkpt: Not won. T/Plt: £19.40 to a £1 stake. Pool: £86,781.20. 3,253.50 winning units. T/Qpdt: £8.90 to a £1 stake. Pool: £10,472.04. 870.70 winning units. **Andrew Sheret**

3483 - 3490a (Foreign Racing) - See Raceform Interactive

3298
CHELMSFORD (A.W) (L-H)
Thursday, June 6

OFFICIAL GOING: Polytrack: standard
Wind: light, half behind Weather: sunny

3491 £20 FREE BETS AT TOTESPORT.COM NOVICE AUCTION STKS (PLUS 10 RACE) 6f (P)
5:25 (5:30) (Class 4) 2-Y-O **£6,145** (£1,828; £913; £456) **Stalls** Centre

Form RPR
1 **Above (FR)** 2-9-5 0 OisinMurphy 14 78
(Archie Watson) *chsd ldrs: effrt to chal over 1f out: rdn to ld 1f out: drew clr and styd on strly ins fnl f: readily* **4/5**[1]

2 2 3 **Nat Love (IRE)**[10] 3141 2-9-0 0 ScottMcCullagh(5) 8 69
(Mick Channon) *dwlt: sn rcvrd and in tch in midfield on outer: effrt over 2f out: unable qck and hung lft over 1f out: kpt on ins fnl f to go 2nd last strides: no ch w wnr* **10/1**[2]

3 nk **Second Love (IRE)** 2-9-5 0 CliffordLee 11 68
(K R Burke) *chsd ldr: rdn over 2f out: drvn to ld over 1f out: hdd 1f out: sn outpcd and btn: wknd towards fin and lost 2nd last strides* **12/1**[3]

4 nk **The Blue Bower (IRE)** 2-9-0 0 KierenFox 2 62+
(Suzy Smith) *s.i.s: hld up in rr of main gp: nt clr run on inner 3f out: swtchd rt ent fnl 2f: hdwy u.p 1f out: styd on strly ins fnl f: no threat to wnr (jockey said filly was slowly away)* **33/1**

0 5 ¾ **Lethal Talent**[17] 2915 2-9-0 0 RobHornby 12 60
(Jonathan Portman) *in tch in midfield: unable qck u.p over 1f out: no threat to wnr but kpt on again ins fnl f* **20/1**

0 6 2 **Constanzia**[36] 2282 2-9-0 0 RossaRyan 5 54
(Jamie Osborne) *chsd ldng trio: outpcd u.p over 1f out: wknd ins fnl f* **16/1**

0 7 1 **Sparkling Diamond**[21] 2761 2-9-0 0 TomMarquand 13 51
(Philip McBride) *in rr of main gp: effrt over 2f out: short of room briefly wl over 1f out: hdwy u.p whn rn green and edgd lft 1f out: kpt on but no threat to wnr* **33/1**

0 8 shd **Mac McCarthy (IRE)**[10] 3165 2-9-5 0 ShaneKelly 6 56
(Richard Hughes) *wl in tch in midfield: rdn 3f out: unable qck and outpcd over 1f out: wknd ins fnl f* **33/1**

9 shd **Beat The Breeze** 2-9-5 0 HarryBentley 4 55
(Simon Dow) *dwlt and rdn leaving stalls: in rr of main gp: rdn over 2f out: nt clrest of runs briefly wl over 1f out: plugged on to pass btn horses fnl f: nvr involved* **14/1**

0 10 1 **Great Aspirations**[17] 2906 2-9-0 0 DavidEgan 10 47
(Mark Johnston) *led: hdd and no ex u.p over 1f out: wknd ins fnl f* **20/1**

11 2 **Boy George** 2-9-5 0 CallumShepherd 9 46
(Dominic Ffrench Davis) *uns rdr in the paddock: v.s.a: rn green and detached in last: plugged on to pass btn horses ins fnl f: nvr involved (jockey said colt ran green)* **20/1**

5 12 1 **Chromium**[24] 2694 2-9-0 0 FergusSweeney 3 38
(Mark Usher) *in tch in midfield: lost pl over 1f out: bhd ins fnl f* **20/1**

0 13 ¾ **Village Rock (IRE)**[37] 2228 2-9-5 0 StevieDonohoe 1 41
(Richard Hughes) *in tch in midfield: rdn over 2f out: sn struggling and lost pl over 1f out: bhd ins fnl f* **12/1**[3]

0 14 ¾ **Fair Warning**[21] 2761 2-9-5 0 BrettDoyle 7 39
(Henry Spiller) *midfield: struggling u.p over 2f out: lost pl and bhd over 2f out* **14/1**

1m 13.09s (-0.61) **Going Correction** -0.15s/f (Stan) **14 Ran SP% 127.1**
Speed ratings (Par 95): **98,94,93,93,92 89,88,88,87,86 83,82,81,80**
CSF £8.59 TOTE £1.30: £1.10, £2.20, £3.00; EX 8.70 Trifecta £26.20.
Owner Qatar Racing Limited **Bred** J Kilpatrick & Mme D Ades Hazan **Trained** Upper Lambourn, W Berks

FOCUS
An ordinary juvenile novice auction contest. The odds-on favourite won well from a poor draw here on debut.

3492 TOTEPOOL CASHBACK CLUB AT TOTESPORT.COM H'CAP 6f (P)
6:00 (6:00) (Class 3) (0-90,92) 4-Y-O+ **£9,703** (£2,887; £1,443; £721) **Stalls** Centre

Form RPR
6604 1 **Moon Trouble (IRE)**[6] 3301 6-9-2 **85** OisinMurphy 1 96
(Michael Appleby) *taken down early: trckd ldr for over 1f: styd trcking ldrs and travelled strly: effrt to chal over 1f out: sn rdn to ld: r.o strly and in command ins fnl f* **5/2**[2]

3-23 2 2 **Goodnight Girl (IRE)**[17] 2917 4-9-9 **92** (p[1]) RobHornby 2 97
(Jonathan Portman) *in tch in midfield: effrt ent fnl 2f: edgd lft u.p and chsd ldrs 1f out: chsd wnr 100yds out: no imp and one pce after* **9/4**[1]

463U 3 1 **Zac Brown (IRE)**[6] 3301 8-8-9 **78** (t) DavidEgan 5 80
(Charlie Wallis) *t.k.h: led: rdn and hrd pressed over 1f out: sn hdd: no ex and lost 2nd 100yds out: kpt on same pce after* **12/1**

4365 4 1 **Giogiobbo**[6] 3301 6-9-2 **90** (b) DylanHogan(5) 4 89
(Nick Littmoden) *wnt lft leaving stalls: pushed along and hdwy to press ldr over 4f out: unable qck u.p and lost pl over 1f out: kpt on same pce ins fnl f* **7/1**

1213 5 1 **Steelriver (IRE)**[9] 3203 9-8-11 **80** JamieSpencer 7 75
(Michael Herrington) *hld up in last pair: effrt and c towards outer 2f out: edgd lft and no prog 1f out: plugged on same pce fnl f* **12/1**

5-00 6 1 ½ **Count Otto (IRE)**[33] 2402 4-9-6 **89** (b) RobertHavlin 3 80
(Amanda Perrett) *in tch in midfield: effrt jst over 2f out: no imp u.p over 1f out: wl hld and plugged on same pce ins fnl f* **9/2**[3]

1255 7 8 **Field Gun (USA)**[13] 3032 4-8-6 **75** (v) JasonWatson 6 40
(Stuart Williams) *hld up in tch in last pair: effrt jst over 2f out: swtchd lft and no hdwy u.p over 1f out: wknd ins fnl f* **10/1**

1m 11.23s (-2.47) **Going Correction** -0.15s/f (Stan) **7 Ran SP% 114.5**
Speed ratings (Par 107): **110,107,106,104,103 101,90**
CSF £8.60 TOTE £3.30: £1.60, £1.60; EX 8.70 Trifecta £52.20.
Owner Rob Oliver & The Horse Watchers **Bred** Haras Du Mezeray **Trained** Oakham, Rutland

FOCUS
A decent sprint handicap. The second-favourite tracked a good pace and strongly asserted for a decisive victory in the final furlong. The winner can do better based on his old French form.

3493 EXTRA PLACES AT TOTESPORT.COM H'CAP 1m (P)
6:30 (6:31) (Class 2) (0-100,94) 3-Y-O **£12,938** (£3,850; £1,924; £962) **Stalls** Low

Form RPR
1422 1 **Spirit Warning**[28] 2559 3-8-11 **84** RobHornby 1 90
(Andrew Balding) *broke wl: sn hdd and stdd bk into last pair: effrt on inner over 1f out: rdn to chse ldr 1f out: led ins fnl f: styd on and a doing enough towards fin* **5/1**

-261 2 ½ **Fields Of Athenry (USA)**[16] 2942 3-9-2 **89** OisinMurphy 5 94+
(James Tate) *t.k.h: sn prom: chsd ldr after 2f: effrt ent fnl 2f: rdn to ld over 1f out: hdd ins fnl f: kpt on but a hld towards fin* **4/1**[2]

51-1 3 1 ½ **San Carlos**[37] 2236 3-8-13 **86** ShaneKelly 6 88
(Shaun Keightley) *dropped in sn after s: hld up in tch in midfield: effrt ent fnl 2f: drvn and pressed ldrs 1f out: no ex and outpcd fnl 100yds* **9/2**[3]

1-20 4 1 **Woven**[126] 511 3-9-7 **94** JamieSpencer 2 93
(David Simcock) *stdd after s: hld up in tch in rr: clsd and swtchd rt over 1f out: rdn to chse ldrs 1f out: kpt on same pce ins fnl f* **7/1**

-411 5 1 ¼ **Gentle Look**[19] 2825 3-9-2 **89** PatCosgrave 4 85
(Saeed bin Suroor) *dwlt and squeezed for room leaving stalls: sn rcvrd to ld and tk keen ld: rdn ent fnl 2f: hdd over 1f out: no ex and wknd ins fnl f* **5/2**[1]

1-50 6 2 ½ **Fintas**[89] 1110 3-9-6 **93** AdamKirby 3 84
(David O'Meara) *dwlt and squeezed for room leaving stalls: sn rcvrd to chse ldr for 2f: rdn and lost pl over 1f out: bhd and wl hld ins fnl f: eased towards fin* **9/2**[3]

1m 38.18s (-1.72) **Going Correction** -0.15s/f (Stan) **6 Ran SP% 114.1**
Speed ratings (Par 105): **102,101,100,99,97 95**
CSF £25.47 TOTE £6.30: £3.10, £1.90; EX 33.80 Trifecta £133.70.
Owner Kingsclere Racing Club **Bred** Kingsclere Stud **Trained** Kingsclere, Hants

FOCUS
A fairly good 3yo handicap, which was well run. The winner continues to progress.

3494 IRISH LOTTO AT TOTESPORT.COM FILLIES' H'CAP 1m (P)
7:05 (7:06) (Class 2) (0-100,101) 3-Y-O+ **£12,938** (£3,850; £1,924; £962) **Stalls** Low

Form RPR
0051 1 **Victory Wave (USA)**[28] 2551 5-10-7 **101** (h) PatCosgrave 5 109
(Saeed bin Suroor) *stdd s: hld up wl in tch in rr: effrt and qcknd between horses to ld over 1f out: rdn and r.o wl ins fnl f* **2/1**[1]

1-21 2 ¾ **Agincourt (IRE)**[20] 2809 4-9-6 **86** AdamKirby 2 92
(David O'Meara) *wl in tch: effrt over 1f out: drvn to chse wnr 1f out: kpt on wl but a hld ins fnl f* **4/1**[2]

21-6 3 ½ **Romola**[33] 2395 3-8-4 **81** DavidEgan 1 83
(Sir Michael Stoute) *chsd ldrs: effrt on inner over 1f out: chsd ldrs and kpt on u.p ins fnl f* **2/1**[1]

5-52 4 3 **Elysium Dream**[9] 3183 4-9-1 **81** TomMarquand 4 79
(Richard Hannon) *chsd ldr: rdn over 2f out: outpcd and btn 1f out: wknd ins fnl f* **8/1**

6-00 5 1 ½ **Octave (IRE)**[12] 3082 3-8-10 **87** OisinMurphy 3 79
(Mark Johnston) *led: rdn ent fnl 2f: hdd over 1f out: no ex and btn 1f out: wknd ins fnl f* **7/1**[3]

1m 38.21s (-1.69) **Going Correction** -0.15s/f (Stan)
WFA 3 from 4yo+ 11lb **5 Ran SP% 110.3**
Speed ratings (Par 96): **102,101,100,97,96**
CSF £10.29 TOTE £2.90: £1.30, £2.10; EX 7.40 Trifecta £15.30.
Owner Godolphin **Bred** Darley **Trained** Newmarket, Suffolk

FOCUS
The feature contest was a good fillies' handicap. One of the joint-favourites did well to come from last to first under her welter burden in the straight. The winner is rated in line with last year's good win here.

3495 BET IN PLAY AT TOTESPORT.COM BRITISH EBF "CONFINED" FILLIES' NOVICE STKS (NO MORE THAN TWO RUNS) 1m 2f (P)
7:35 (7:40) (Class 3) 3-Y-O+ **£9,703** (£2,887; £1,443; £721) **Stalls** Low

Form RPR
0-3 1 **Whimbrel (IRE)**[13] 3050 3-8-11 0 RobertHavlin 15 81+
(John Gosden) *bmpd and pushed rt leaving stalls: rcvrd and hdwy to chse ldr over 7f out: rdn to ld 2f out: sn kicked clr: kpt on ins fnl f* **9/2**[2]

1- 2 2 **Dame Malliot**[171] 9590 3-9-3 0 StevieDonohoe 14 82+
(Ed Vaughan) *wnt rt and bmpd wnr leaving stalls: t.k.h: hld up in midfield: effrt on outer 3f out: edgd lft over 1f out: styd on to chse wnr wl ins fnl f: gng on fin* **11/4**[1]

54 3 1 ¼ **Moll Davis (IRE)**[23] 2713 3-8-11 0 HarryBentley 12 74
(George Scott) *in tch in midfield: effrt 2f out: unable qck and outpcd over 1f out: rallied and swtchd rt jst ins fnl f: kpt on wl fnl 100yds* **8/1**

4-1 4 nk **Geizy Teizy (IRE)**[24] 2690 3-9-3 0 OisinMurphy 9 79
(Marco Botti) *t.k.h: chsd ldrs: effrt in 3rd 2f out: unable qck over 1f out: kpt on same pce ins fnl f* **5/1**[3]

03 5 1 ½ **Desert Mission (IRE)**[22] 2731 3-8-11 0 JackMitchell 13 70
(Simon Crisford) *chsd ldrs tl led 8f out: hdd and rdn 2f out: sn outpcd: wknd ins fnl f* **20/1**

3-4 6 2 ¼ **Parish Poet (IRE)**[12] 3080 3-8-11 0 RaulDaSilva 3 65
(Paul Cole) *pressed ldrs tl settled into midfield: swtchd rt and effrt ent fnl 2f: no imp over 1f out: wl hld and kpt on same pce ins fnl f* **14/1**

35 7 2 **Scenesetter (IRE)**[55] 1739 3-8-11 0 ShaneKelly 5 61
(Marco Botti) *led for 2f: chsd ldrs: rdn ent fnl 2f: unable qck and btn over 1f out: wknd ins fnl f* **25/1**

42 8 6 **Cherries At Dawn (IRE)**[44] 2017 4-9-10 0 CallumShepherd 2 50
(Dominic Ffrench Davis) *hld up in tch in midfield: effrt ent fnl 2f: sn outpcd and btn over 1f out: wknd fnl f* **16/1**

3-0 9 nse **Dubawi Meeznah (IRE)**[44] 2017 4-9-5 0 DylanHogan(5) 11 50
(David Simcock) *s.i.s: hld up in last quartet: effrt 2f out: sn btn* **50/1**

10 shd **Hindaam (USA)** 3-8-11 0 JimCrowley 7 49
(Owen Burrows) *chsd ldrs early: dropped to midfield over 7f out: rdn 2f out: sn btn* **7/1**

11 1 ½ **Albanderi** 3-8-11 0 TomMarquand 4 46
(Sir Michael Stoute) *a last quartet: rdn wl over 2f out: sn struggling and no ch over 1f out* **10/1**

12 ¾ **Astral Girl** 3-8-8 0 MitchGodwin(3) 1 45
(Hughie Morrison) *restless in stalls: s.i.s: a towards rr: no hdwy u.p over 1f out: sn wknd* **33/1**

13 ¾ **Giving Back**15 5-9-10 0 .... AdamKirby 6 44
(Alan King) *s.i.s: a bhd* **40/1**

2m 6.24s (-2.36) **Going Correction** -0.15s/f (Stan) 13 Ran SP% **122.7**
WFA 3 from 4yo+ 13lb
Speed ratings (Par 104): **103,101,100,100,98 97,95,90,90,90 89,88,88**
CSF £16.77 TOTE £4.20: £1.70, £1.60, £2.90; EX 18.10 Trifecta £147.90.

Owner HH Sheikha Al Jalila Racing **Bred** Mrs T Mahon **Trained** Newmarket, Suffolk

FOCUS
A fair fillies' novice contest. The improving second-favourite won readily from a prominent pitch and the form's rated around the fourth.

3496 DOUBLE DELIGHT HAT-TRICK HEAVEN AT TOTESPORT.COM H'CAP 7f (P)
8:05 (8:08) (Class 3) (0-90,90) 4-Y-O+ **£9,703** (£2,887; £1,443; £721) **Stalls** Low

Form RPR

063/ **1** **That Is The Spirit**92 1047 8-8-5 **74** .... DavidEgan 2 84+
(Michael Appleby) *sn led and mde rest: 3 l clr 2f out: rdn over 1f out: kpt on ins fnl f* **8/1**3

0233 **2** 1 ¼ **Atletico (IRE)**8 3214 7-8-8 **77** ....(v) HollieDoyle 6 83
(David Evans) *midfield tl dropped to last pair over 5f out: effrt over 1f out: hdwy 1f out: edgd lft but chsd wnr ins fnl f: kpt on but nvr getting on terms* **12/1**

641- **3** 1 ½ **Tahreek**275 6913 4-9-3 **86** .... JimCrowley 3 88+
(Sir Michael Stoute) *t.k.h: wl in tch in midfield: effrt over 1f out: chsd wnr 1f out: no imp: lost 2nd and one pce ins fnl f* **9/4**2

2-12 **4** 4 **Jalaad (IRE)**27 2598 4-9-4 **87** .... AdamKirby 4 78
(Saeed bin Suroor) *chsd ldr over 5f out: effrt ent fnl 2f: unable qck and lost 2nd 1f out: sn wknd* **7/4**1

242- **5** 1 **Monaadhil (IRE)**310 5578 5-9-1 **84** .... JasonWatson 8 72
(Marcus Tregoning) *hld up in tch in last trio: effrt over 1f out: no hdwy u.p 1f out: wknd ins fnl f* **10/1**

00-3 **6** 2 ¾ **Rogue**49 1881 4-9-7 **90** .... RossaRyan 5 71
(Alexandra Dunn) *in tch in midfield: effrt to chse ldrs jst over 2f out: unable qck and btn over 1f out: wknd ins fnl f* **16/1**

0-20 **7** 2 **Top Mission**31 2487 5-9-2 **85** ....(p) OisinMurphy 7 61
(Marco Botti) *hld up in tch in trio: swtchd lft over 5f out: effrt over 1f out: sn btn and wknd ins fnl f* **8/1**3

000/ **8** 10 **Sea Of Flames**824 1023 6-9-5 **88** ....(t[1]) TomMarquand 1 37
(Richard Spencer) *led: sn hdd: chsd ldrs tl lost pl u.p over 2f out: bhd 1f out* **40/1**

1m 24.37s (-2.83) **Going Correction** -0.15s/f (Stan) 8 Ran SP% **114.5**
Speed ratings (Par 107): **110,108,106,102,101 98,95,84**
CSF £96.65 CT £289.61 TOTE £10.10: £2.40, £2.00, £1.20; EX 90.90 Trifecta £385.10.

Owner William Esdaile **Bred** Cliveden Stud Ltd **Trained** Oakham, Rutland

FOCUS
A decent handicap dominated by a well-treated previous C&D winner in a good comparative time here on stable debut. This form could be rated higher.

3497 FALCO SUPPORTING MATES IN MIND H'CAP 1m 6f (P)
8:40 (8:40) (Class 6) (0-60,62) 4-Y-O+
£3,428 (£1,020; £509; £300; £300; £300) **Stalls** Low

Form RPR

0455 **1** **Carvelas (IRE)**14 3006 10-9-3 **55** .... NickyMackay 1 61
(J R Jenkins) *t.k.h: hld up in tch in midfield: effrt to chse ldrs over 2f out: styd on u.p to chal ins fnl f: led wl ins fnl f: styd on* **6/1**3

00-0 **2** ½ **Ness Of Brodgar**22 2738 4-8-12 **50** ....(t) DanielMuscutt 2 55
(Mark H Tompkins) *t.k.h: led for over 1f: chsd ldr tl over 11f out: chsd ldrs tl wnt 2nd again 6f out: effrt and swtchd rt over 1f out: drvn to ld ins fnl f: sn hdd and one pce towards fin* **33/1**

3111 **3** 2 **Croeso Cymraeg**15 2970 5-9-7 **59** .... RaulDaSilva 6 62+
(James Evans) *taken down early: t.k.h: hdwy to ld over 12f out: bit slipped through mouth and hung rt fr 6f out: rdn over 1f out: drvn and hdd ins fnl f: sn btn and hung rt towards fin (jockey said gelding hung right-handed and that the bit slipped through the mouth; post-race examination failed to reveal any abnormalities)* **8/11**1

3050 **4** 6 **Normandy Blue**34 2359 4-8-7 **45** .... JimmyQuinn 3 39
(Louise Allan) *chsd ldr early: sn stdd and t.k.h in last trio: effrt on outer over 2f out: no imp and wl hld fr over 1f out* **7/1**

0005 **5** 1 ½ **Guaracha**24 2695 8-8-8 **46** ....(v) HollieDoyle 7 38
(Alexandra Dunn) *s.i.s: rousted along leaving stalls: hdwy to chse ldr over 11f out tl 6f out: lost pl over 3f out: wl btn over 1f out (jockey said gelding was slowly away)* **14/1**

0000 **6** *hd* **Allleedsaren'Twe**64 1520 4-8-7 **45** ....(t) GeorgeWood 10 37
(Robyn Brisland) *hld up in tch in last pair: effrt over 2f out: no imp u.p and btn over 1f out: wknd fnl f (jockey said gelding was never travelling)* **10/1**

6004 **7** 11 **Far Cry**17 2901 6-8-8 **46** .... CharlieBennett 8 22
(Hughie Morrison) *chsd ldrs tl stdd bk towards rr after 2f: hdwy to chse ldrs over 3f out: rdn and lost pl over 2f out: bhd and wknd over 1f out* **11/2**2

-304 **8** 54 **Constituent**9 3205 4-8-6 **47** ....(b) GabrieleMalune(3) 5
(Michael Appleby) *wnt rt leaving stalls: midfield: rdn over 4f out: dropped to rr 3f out: sn lost tch and eased over 1f out: t.o (jockey said gelding was never travelling)* **12/1**

3m 1.07s (-2.13) **Going Correction** -0.15s/f (Stan) 8 Ran SP% **126.5**
Speed ratings (Par 101): **100,99,98,95,94 94,87,57**
CSF £178.25 CT £314.72 TOTE £7.40: £1.50, £7.30, £1.10; EX 280.90 Trifecta £1009.20.

Owner Crofters Racing Syndicate **Bred** George Grothier **Trained** Royston, Herts

FOCUS
A modest staying handicap. The odds-on favourite had steering problems and a veteran handicapper came through to win in the slowest comparative time on the night.

T/Plt: £31.20 to a £1 stake. Pool: £49,845.40 - 1,164.25 winning units T/Qpdt: £18.60 to a £1 stake. Pool: £6,066.60 - 240.17 winning units **Steve Payne**

3220 HAMILTON (R-H)
Thursday, June 6

OFFICIAL GOING: Soft (5.9)
Wind: Breezy, half behind in sprints and in over 4f of home straight in races on the round course Weather: Cloudy, bright

3498 BB FOODSERVICE NOVICE AUCTION STKS (PLUS 10 RACE) (A £20,000 BB FOODSERVICE 2YO SERIES QUALIFIER) 6f 6y
2:00 (2:00) (Class 4) 2-Y-O **£5,433** (£1,617; £808; £404) **Stalls** High

Form RPR

2 **1** **Makyon (IRE)**12 3098 2-9-2 0 .... SilvestreDeSousa 5 91+
(Mark Johnston) *blkd s: mde all: clr and shkn up over 1f out: v easily* **4/9**1

01 **2** 6 **Troubador (IRE)**17 2906 2-9-5 0 .... GrahamLee 8 76
(Michael Dods) *chsd wnr thrght: drvn 1/2-way: no imp fr over 1f out* **11/2**2

3 3 ¼ **Glory Maker (FR)** 2-9-2 .... DanielTudhope 2 63+
(K R Burke) *hld up on outside: rdn 1/2-way: hdwy over 1f out: no imp fnl f* **12/1**

4 2 ½ **Typsy Toad** 2-8-12 0 .... BarryMcHugh 6 52
(Richard Fahey) *wnt rt s: in tch: drvn along over 2f out: no imp over 1f out* **28/1**

05 **5** 8 **Stormy Bay**8 3220 2-8-9 0 .... AndrewBreslin(5) 9 30
(Keith Dalgleish) *missed break: bhd and outpcd: nvr rchd ldrs* **40/1**

30 **6** 4 ½ **River Of Kings (IRE)**21 2780 2-9-2 0 .... TomEaves 3 18
(Keith Dalgleish) *dwlt: outpcd and sn struggling: nvr on terms* **18/1**

7 5 **Teenar** 2-8-11 0 .... SeanDavis(5) 4 3
(Richard Fahey) *chsd ldrs: drvn along over 2f out: wknd over 1f out* **10/1**3

1m 13.89s (1.19) **Going Correction** +0.20s/f (Good) 7 Ran SP% **112.6**
Speed ratings (Par 95): **100,92,87,84,73 67,61**
CSF £3.19 TOTE £1.20: £1.10, £2.30; EX 3.20 Trifecta £12.40.
Owner The Makyowners **Bred** Ballylinch Stud **Trained** Middleham Moor, N Yorks

FOCUS
There was 11.6mm of rain on the previous day and the going was given as soft, heavy in places (Going Stick 5.9). The rail was out 3yds on the loop.\n\x\x Straightforward stuff, the odds-on favourite bagging the rail and in control thereafter. There's every chance he can improve on this. Typsy Toad went right leaving the stalls, causing minor interference to a trio of rivals.

3499 MACROBERTS SOLICITORS LLP NOVICE STKS 6f 6y
2:30 (2:33) (Class 5) 3-Y-O+ **£4,787** (£1,424; £711; £355) **Stalls** Centre

Form RPR

3- **1** **Last Empire**230 8369 3-8-12 0 ow1 .... DanielTudhope 1 77
(Kevin Ryan) *cl up centre: drvn and overall ldr over 1f out: r.o wl fnl f* **4/1**3

4 **2** 2 ½ **Puerto Banus**20 2794 3-9-2 0 .... SilvestreDeSousa 2 73
(Andrew Balding) *chsd centre ldr: rdn over 2f out: kpt on fnl f: nt pce to chal* **2/1**1

13 **3** 1 **Alexander James (IRE)**26 2634 3-9-6 0 .... JamieGormley(3) 5 77
(Iain Jardine) *cl up stands' side: effrt and ev ch that gp over 2f out: kpt on same pce fnl f* **9/4**2

4 1 ¼ **Victory Ahead (IRE)** 3-9-2 0 .... SamJames 8 66
(David Simcock) *hld up stands' side: pushed along and hdwy 2f out: kpt on fnl f: no imp* **9/1**

31 **5** *nk* **Mina Velour**35 2332 3-9-4 0 ....(h) GrahamLee 11 67
(Bryan Smart) *led: rdn and hdd over 1f out: sn outpcd* **15/2**

6 ¾ **Twentysixthstreet (IRE)**29 2533 3-9-2 0 .... TadhgO'Shea 4 63
(Andrew Hughes, Ire) *dwlt: sn midfield stands' side: drvn and outpcd 1/2-way: n.d after* **50/1**

0 **7** 2 **Cheam Avenue (IRE)**19 2823 3-8-11 0 .... TomEaves 12 51
(James Bethell) *chsd stands' side ldrs tl rdn and wknd over 1f out* **40/1**

43 **8** 2 ¼ **Senorita Grande (IRE)**26 2624 3-8-6 0 .... SeanDavis(5) 6 44
(John Quinn) *in tch stands' side: rdn over 2f out: wknd over 1f out* **20/1**

9 4 ½ **Indiaro** 3-9-2 0 .... NathanEvans 9 35
(Linda Perratt) *missed break: a bhd and outpcd stands' side* **100/1**

0 **10** 18 **Gatesy (IRE)**145 211 3-9-2 0 ....(t[1]) JackGarritty 10
(John Davies) *slowly away: a struggling stands' side* **100/1**

0 **11** 1 ¼ **Gregory The Great**16 2932 3-9-2 0 ....(t[1]) PaddyMathers 13
(Steph Hollinshead) *dwlt: bhd and outpcd stands' side: hung rt 1/2-way: sn wknd* **100/1**

1m 13.46s (0.76) **Going Correction** +0.20s/f (Good) 11 Ran SP% **118.0**
Speed ratings (Par 103): **102,98,97,95,95 94,91,88,82,58 56**
CSF £12.14 TOTE £4.50: £1.40, £1.10, £1.30; EX 15.90 Trifecta £43.30.
Owner Clipper Logistics **Bred** Mrs G S Rees And Douglas McMahon **Trained** Hambleton, N Yorks

FOCUS
Those towards the head of the betting dominated so, while the front pair were the only ones to race down the middle, there was no clear-cut evidence to suggest there was a track bias. The pace was solid from the outset and the winner was a big improver.

3500 MACROBERTS SOLICITORS LLP H'CAP 1m 5f 16y
3:00 (3:00) (Class 6) (0-65,67) 4-Y-O+
£3,493 (£1,039; £519; £300; £300; £300) **Stalls** High

Form RPR

60-0 **1** **Battle Of Issus (IRE)**22 2738 4-8-11 **55** ....(b) SilvestreDeSousa 7 65
(David Menuisier) *prom: hdwy to ld over 3f out: clr over 1f out: kpt on strly (trainer's rep said, regarding the improved form shown, the gelding may have appreciated the step up in trip to 1m5f and the soft ground)* **11/1**

242- **2** 3 ¼ **Auxiliary**267 7167 6-9-9 **67** ....(p) DanielTudhope 10 72
(Liam Bailey) *hld up: hdwy on outside over 2f out: chsd (clr) wnr over 1f out: kpt on fnl f: no imp* **8/1**

3130 **3** ¾ **Elite Icon**9 3175 5-8-1 **50** .... SeanDavis(5) 4 54
(Jim Goldie) *hld up: rdn over 3f out: hdwy on outside over 1f out: kpt on fnl f: no imp (jockey said gelding was never travelling)* **11/1**

5260 **4** 1 **Pammi**9 3175 4-8-9 **56** .... JamieGormley(3) 2 58
(Jim Goldie) *hld up: drvn and outpcd over 4f out: rallied on outside over 2f out: kpt on fnl f: no imp* **13/2**2

5 2 ¼ **Give Battle (IRE)**615 1993 7-8-11 **55** .... GrahamLee 6 54
(C Byrnes, Ire) *hld up in midfield: hdwy over 3f out: rdn and wknd over 1f out* **6/5**1

00-0 **6** 1 ¾ **Wise Coco**22 2373 6-7-11 **46** oh1 ....(p) AndrewBreslin(5) 9 43
(Alistair Whillans) *dwlt: hld up: hdwy on outside and prom 1/2-way: rdn and wknd over 1f out* **100/1**

0-0 **7** 3 ¾ **Excalibur (POL)**56 1718 6-8-2 **46** oh1 ....(p) NathanEvans 5 37
(Micky Hammond) *midfield: drvn and outpcd 3f out: n.d after* **22/1**

400- **8** 6 **Qasr**234 8267 5-9-8 **66** .... TomEaves 1 49
(Keith Dalgleish) *t.k.h early: led to over 3f out: rdn and wknd 2f out* **14/1**

4002 **9** *5* **Onda District (IRE)**[7] 3251 7-8-2 **46** oh1....................(p) PaddyMathers 8 21
(Stella Barclay) *prom: rdn over 3f out: hung rt and wknd 2f out* **7/1**[3]

6/54 **10** *19* **Deinonychus**[4] 3377 8-9-4 **65**.......................(h) GeorgeBuckell(3) 3 13
(Michael Appleby) *chsd ldr to over 3f out: wknd over 2f out: t.o* **9/1**

2m 57.41s (2.71) **Going Correction** +0.20s/f (Good) **10** Ran SP% **121.1**
Speed ratings (Par 101): **99,97,96,95,94 93,91,87,84,72**
CSF £99.55 CT £1008.21 TOTE £13.70: £3.60, £2.40, £1.80; EX 95.80 Trifecta £517.90.
Owner Clive Washbourn **Bred** J Higgins **Trained** Pulborough, W Sussex

FOCUS
They were soon strung out in this moderate handicap. Add 8yds.

3501 BRITISH STALLION STUDS CLYDE EBF CONDITIONS STKS 6f 6y
3:30 (3:30) (Class 2) 3-Y-0+

£16,807 (£5,032; £2,516; £1,258; £629; £315) **Stalls** Centre

Form RPR

4-30 **1** **Brando**[22] 2744 7-9-4 112..TomEaves 6 119
(Kevin Ryan) *hld up stands' side: shkn up and hdwy 2f out: led and edgd rt ins fnl f: kpt on strly* **7/2**[3]

31-6 **2** *1 ¾* **Donjuan Triumphant (IRE)**[40] 2109 6-9-4 111....... SilvestreDeSousa 2 113
(Andrew Balding) *chsd clr centre ldr: drvn along over 2f out: rallied: wnt 2nd ins fnl f: kpt on: nt pce of wnr* **5/2**[2]

51-6 **3** *3* **Sands Of Mali (FR)**[68] 1442 4-9-4 118.......................... BarryMcHugh 4 103
(Richard Fahey) *dwlt: in tch stands' side: effrt and rdn 2f out: edgd rt 1f out: no imp* **1/1**[1]

412- **4** *4 ½* **Lomu (IRE)**[307] 5677 5-9-4 89......................................(w) DanielTudhope 1 89
(Keith Dalgleish) *led and sn clr centre: rdn over 1f out: hdd ins fnl f: sn wknd* **33/1**

03-6 **5** *nse* **Fighting Irish (IRE)**[20] 2791 4-9-4 97..............................(p[1]) GrahamLee 5 89
(Harry Dunlop) *in tch centre: drvn over 2f out: wknd over 1f out* **50/1**

66-0 **6** *3 ¼* **Lahore (USA)**[42] 2061 5-9-4 93.. SamJames 3 78
(Phillip Makin) *hld up centre: effrt over 2f out: wknd over 1f out* **50/1**

1m 12.46s (-0.24) **Going Correction** +0.20s/f (Good) **6** Ran SP% **107.7**
Speed ratings (Par 109): **109,106,102,96,96 92**
CSF £11.47 TOTE £3.30: £1.80, £1.50; EX 11.60 Trifecta £17.40.
Owner Mrs Angie Bailey **Bred** Car Colston Hall Stud **Trained** Hambleton, N Yorks

FOCUS
A high-quality sprint. There was a difference of opinion regarding the best ground, but the main action developed in the centre. Brando is rated to last year's best.

3502 WEATHERBYS PRINTING SERVICES HAMILTONIAN H'CAP 1m 1f 35y
4:00 (4:02) (Class 4) (0-85,84) 4-Y-0+

£8,021 (£2,387; £1,192; £596; £300; £300) **Stalls** Low

Form RPR

0-00 **1** **Ghalib (IRE)**[31] 2480 7-9-0 **77**.. LewisEdmunds 2 87
(Rebecca Bastiman) *chsd clr ldng pair: effrt and swtchd lft over 1f out: led ins fnl f: kpt on strly (trainer said, regarding the improved form shown, the gelding appreciated the return to soft ground)* **40/1**

11-0 **2** *2 ¼* **Sputnik Planum (USA)**[27] 2574 5-9-7 **84**...............(t) AlistairRawlinson 3 90
(Michael Appleby) *pressed ldr: led over 1f out to ins fnl f: kpt on: nt pce of wnr* **12/1**

-461 **3** *nk* **Ocala**[14] 2994 4-9-4 **81**.. SilvestreDeSousa 5 86
(Andrew Balding) *hld up in tch: effrt over 2f out: kpt on fnl f: no imp* **7/4**[1]

20-0 **4** *½* **Falmouth Light (FR)**[21] 1461 4-8-13 **79**..........(h) JamieGormley(3) 13 83
(Iain Jardine) *hld up in midfield: rdn along over 2f out: kpt on fnl f nt pce to chal* **25/1**

4230 **5** *shd* **Sands Chorus**[10] 3160 7-8-8 **76**...............................(p) TheodoreLadd(5) 10 80
(Scott Dixon) *led: rdn and hdd over 1f out: rallied and ev ch ins fnl f: no ex* **8/1**[3]

2-00 **6** *½* **Trinity Star (IRE)**[13] 3053 8-8-8 **71**............................(v) BarryMcHugh 15 74+
(Karen McLintock) *hld up: rdn over 2f out: hdwy over 1f out: nvr rchd ldrs* **33/1**

1205 **7** *½* **Weld Al Emarat**[23] 2710 7-9-1 **78**...................................... NathanEvans 12 80+
(Michael Easterby) *hld up in last pl: rdn over 3f out: hdwy over 1f out: nvr rchd ldrs* **6/1**[2]

5004 **8** *shd* **Beverley Bullet**[8] 3216 6-8-3 **66**................................(p) PaddyMathers 11 67
(Lawrence Mullaney) *hld up towards rr: drvn and outpcd over 3f out: sme late hdwy: nvr rchd ldrs* **20/1**

010- **9** *1* **Iconic Code**[203] 9087 4-7-12 **66**................................ AndrewBreslin(5) 14 65
(Keith Dalgleish) *s.i.s: hld up: hdwy over 2f out: no further imp over 1f out* **28/1**

-055 **10** *5* **Set In Stone (IRE)**[20] 2784 5-8-13 **76**............................ TadhgO'Shea 1 65
(Andrew Hughes, Ire) *dwlt: hld up: rdn and outpcd 3f out: n.d after* **14/1**

-060 **11** *1 ½* **Royal Shaheen (FR)**[17] 2894 6-8-12 **75**............................(v) GrahamLee 4 61
(Alistair Whillans) *prom: drvn along over 3f out: edgd rt and wknd 2f out* **33/1**

5162 **12** *5* **Illustrissime (USA)**[56] 1719 6-9-6 **83**..............................(p) TomEaves 6 58
(Ivan Furtado) *midfield: rdn and outpcd over 2f out: sn wknd* **14/1**

5-04 **13** *shd* **Vive La Difference (IRE)**[30] 2509 5-8-13 **76**.................. DuranFentiman 7 51
(Tim Easterby) *hld up in midfield: effrt and rdn 3f out: wknd 2f out (trainer's rep could offer no explanation for the gelding's performance)* **6/1**[2]

212/ **14** *7* **Ennjaaz (IRE)**[560] 8923 5-9-5 **82**...................................... DanielTudhope 9 42
(Marjorie Fife) *dwlt: hld up: struggling over 2f out: nvr on terms* **33/1**

-642 **15** *1 ¼* **Strong Steps**[15] 2959 7-8-1 **69**.. SeanDavis(5) 8 27
(Jim Goldie) *in tch: drvn along over 3f out: wknd over 2f out* **20/1**

2m 0.31s (1.31) **Going Correction** +0.20s/f (Good) **15** Ran SP% **125.2**
Speed ratings (Par 105): **102,100,99,99,99 98,98,98,97,92 91,87,87,80,79**
CSF £442.65 CT £1314.02 TOTE £47.60: £10.70, £3.40, £1.30; EX 598.40 Trifecta £2342.40.
Owner Ms M Austerfield **Bred** T Molan **Trained** Cowthorpe, N Yorks

FOCUS
Add 8yds. A useful handicap in which it proved difficult to make up ground despite a reasonable gallop and the form doesn't look strong. The second and fourth are the best guides.

3503 BETTRENDSSHOP.CO.UK H'CAP 6f 6y
4:30 (4:32) (Class 4) (0-80,82) 4-Y-0+

£8,021 (£2,387; £1,192; £596; £300; £300) **Stalls** Centre

Form RPR

00-0 **1** **Air Raid**[29] 2526 4-9-10 **82**.. JackGarritty 2 104
(Jedd O'Keeffe) *mde all in centre: rdn clr over 1f out: kpt on wl fnl f: eased towards fin: readily* **5/1**[2]

0-20 **2** *4* **Zumurud (IRE)**[33] 2416 4-9-5 **77**.. DanielTudhope 5 85
(Rebecca Bastiman) *chsd wnr centre: rdn over 2f out: kpt on same pce fr over 1f out* **9/1**

-140 **3** *1 ¼* **Galloway Hills**[19] 2824 4-9-2 **79**................................ SeanDavis(5) 10 83
(Phillip Makin) *hld up in midfield in centre gp: effrt and rdn 2f out: kpt on fnl f: no imp* **14/1**

0003 **4** *1 ½* **Kenny The Captain (IRE)**[8] 3221 8-8-8 **66**................. DuranFentiman 9 65
(Tim Easterby) *prom in centre gp: drvn along over 2f out: edgd rt and one pce over 1f out* **6/1**[3]

-513 **5** *1 ½* **Equidae**[30] 2509 4-8-9 **67**..(t) TomEaves 3 62
(Iain Jardine) *prom centre: drvn along over 2f out: outpcd fr over 1f out* **11/1**

1452 **6** *¾* **Avenue Of Stars**[8] 3221 6-8-7 **65**.......................(v) SilvestreDeSousa 14 57
(Karen McLintock) *racd stands' side: in tch: rdn and edgd rt 2f out: sn n.d* **4/1**[1]

60-0 **7** *nk* **My Amigo**[29] 2526 6-9-10 **82**...(t) SamJames 6 73
(Marjorie Fife) *hld up centre: drvn along over 2f out: sn no imp* **14/1**

3100 **8** *2 ½* **The Right Choice (IRE)**[26] 2611 4-8-13 **71**................. BarryMcHugh 4 54
(Richard Fahey) *hld up centre: rdn and struggling over 2f out: sn btn* **7/1**

00-1 **9** *1 ½* **Zig Zag Zyggy (IRE)**[32] 2437 4-9-9 **81**.......................... TadhgO'Shea 13 59
(Andrew Hughes, Ire) *racd stands' side: in tch tl edgd rt and wknd 2f out* **10/1**

50-4 **10** *4* **Imperial State**[29] 2526 6-9-10 **82**.................................(vt) NathanEvans 8 48
(Michael Easterby) *dwlt: bhd centre: struggling over 2f out: sn btn* **6/1**[3]

426- **11** *4 ½* **Mable Lee (IRE)**[173] 9558 4-8-2 **63**............................ JamieGormley(3) 11 14
(Iain Jardine) *bhd: struggling over 2f out: sn btn* **28/1**

1m 12.49s (-0.21) **Going Correction** +0.20s/f (Good) **11** Ran SP% **121.9**
Speed ratings (Par 105): **109,103,102,100,98 97,96,93,91,85 79**
CSF £51.62 CT £615.74 TOTE £6.20: £1.90, £2.90, £4.70; EX 68.10 Trifecta £714.10.
Owner Caron & Paul Chapman **Bred** Meon Valley Stud **Trained** Middleham Moor, N Yorks

FOCUS
The bulk of them came down the middle this time so, while it made no difference so far as the winner was concerned, the pair that raced on the stands rail could perhaps be excused. There was no obvious pace bias. The winner got back to his early form.

3504 DM HALL H'CAP 5f 7y
5:00 (5:04) (Class 5) (0-75,77) 4-Y-0+

£5,433 (£1,617; £808; £404; £300; £300) **Stalls** Centre

Form RPR

-034 **1** **Music Society (IRE)**[8] 3221 4-9-4 **70**........................(h) DanielTudhope 5 79
(Tim Easterby) *hld up: rdn and hdwy over 1f out: led ins fnl f: r.o wl* **11/2**[2]

0163 **2** *nk* **Samovar**[9] 3206 4-9-5 **71**..(b) PaddyMathers 12 79
(Scott Dixon) *led: rdn 2f out: hdd ins fnl f: kpt on: hld nr fin (c out of stall 12 but should have racd fr stall 7) (starter reported that the gelding was the subject of a third criteria failure; trainer was informed that the gelding could not run until the day after passing a stalls test)* **14/1**

5425 **3** *1* **Followthesteps (IRE)**[26] 2611 4-9-10 **76**........................(p) TomEaves 13 80
(Ivan Furtado) *upset in stalls: midfield: rdn over 2f out: hdwy over 1f out: r.o ins fnl f* **8/1**

1141 **4** *hd* **Everkyllachy (IRE)**[8] 3227 5-8-3 **62**.......................... LauraCoughlan(7) 3 66
(Karen McLintock) *in tch: effrt and rdn over 1f out: kpt on ins fnl f* **4/1**[1]

-320 **5** *½* **Wrenthorpe**[19] 2824 4-9-4 **77**......................................(p) HarryRussell(7) 2 79
(Bryan Smart) *disp ld to over 1f out: rdn and no ex ins fnl f* **6/1**[3]

0004 **6** *2 ¾* **Economic Crisis (IRE)**[26] 2637 10-8-2 **57**................ JamieGormley(3) 4 49
(Alan Berry) *chsd ldr: drvn along over 2f out: wknd fnl f* **25/1**

0643 **7** *1 ¾* **Van Gerwen**[13] 3056 6-9-5 **71**..................................(p) SilvestreDeSousa 1 57
(Les Eyre) *in tch: rdn over 2f out: wknd fnl f* **8/1**

4306 **8** *hd* **Amazing Grazing (IRE)**[13] 3056 5-9-6 **72**.................... LewisEdmunds 11 57
(Rebecca Bastiman) *hld up: drvn along over 2f out: kpt on fnl f: no imp* **11/1**

004 **9** *2 ¼* **Gift In Time (IRE)**[26] 2633 4-8-10 **62**..........................(bt) NathanEvans 7 39
(Paul Collins) *s.v.s: bhd and outpcd: sme late hdwy: nvr on terms (c out of stall 7 but should have racd fr stall 12) (jockey said gelding reared as the stalls opened)* **40/1**

0004 **10** *nk* **Camanche Grey (IRE)**[37] 2247 8-7-10 **55** oh5 ow1(w) VictorSantos(7) 6 31
(Lucinda Egerton) *blindfold slow to remove and s.s: bhd and outpcd: nvr rchd ldrs* **50/1**

0124 **11** *4* **Johnny Cavagin**[23] 2709 10-9-7 **73**.................................... GrahamLee 10 34
(Paul Midgley) *midfield: drvn along over 2f out: sn no imp: btn over 1f out* **13/2**

3006 **12** *hd* **The Golden Cue**[27] 2580 4-8-9 **61**............................... DuranFentiman 8 22
(Steph Hollinshead) *t.k.h: hld up: struggling over 2f out: sn btn* **25/1**

0052 **13** *7* **Boundsy (IRE)**[8] 3227 5-8-3 **60**..................................(p) SeanDavis(5) 9
(Richard Fahey) *midfield: drvn along 1/2-way: wknd fnl 2f (vet said gelding bled from the nose and had an irregular heartbeat)* **6/1**[3]

1m 1.09s (0.69) **Going Correction** +0.20s/f (Good) **13** Ran SP% **126.6**
Speed ratings (Par 103): **102,101,99,99,98 94,91,91,87,87 80,80,69**
CSF £82.32 CT £650.73 TOTE £6.90: £2.10, £5.20, £2.80; EX 97.90 Trifecta £918.70.
Owner Richard Taylor & Philip Hebdon **Bred** Pier House Stud **Trained** Great Habton, N Yorks
■ Stewards' Enquiry : Victor Santos four-day ban: used whip above the permitted level (Jun 23-26)
Nathan Evans one-day ban: started from wrong stall (Jun 23)
Paddy Mathers one-day ban: started from wrong stall (Jun 23)

FOCUS
The centre was again the place to be in this modest sprint handicap. Gift In Time and Samovar somehow came out of the wrong stalls, but the result was allowed to stand. (Gift In Time was orginally drawn in stall 12 and Samovar in stall 7). The runner-up was the best guide.
T/Plt: £122.00 to a £1 stake. Pool: £53,825.36 - 321.84 winning units T/Qpdt: £111.30 to a £1 stake. Pool: £4,395.64 - 29.20 winning units **Richard Young**

3081 HAYDOCK (L-H)
Thursday, June 6

OFFICIAL GOING: Good to soft (7.4), changing to soft after race 1 (2.10)
Wind: mainly negligible; very windy during shower before race 1 Weather: mainly sunny and warm, heavy shower before race 1

3505 REWARDING OWNERSHIP WITH THE ROA H'CAP 1m 3f 140y
2:10 (2:11) (Class 5) (0-70,72) 3-Y-0

£4,851 (£1,443; £721; £360; £300; £300) **Stalls** Centre

Form RPR

51 **1** **Earl Of Harrow**[17] 2914 3-9-9 **71**.. AndreaAtzeni 4 77
(Mick Channon) *chsd ldrs on outer: hdwy over 3f out: sn cl up: pushed into ld ent fnl 2f: drvn in narrow ld 1f out: rdn fnl f: r.o wl: pushed out nr fin* **10/3**[2]

25-0 **2** 1 **Say Nothing**[37] 2253 3-9-10 **72** .... ConnorBeasley 7 76
(Hughie Morrison) *hld up in rr: hdwy on outer over 2f out: rdn to chal over 1f out: r.o u.p fnl f: tk 2nd last few strides* **12/1**

0221 **3** 1/2 **Highwaygrey**[13] 3052 3-9-7 **69** .... DavidAllan 3 72
(Tim Easterby) *hld up: pushed along and hdwy 2f out: drvn over 1f out: rdn and ev ch ins fnl f: kpt on: lost 2nd last few strides* **9/4**[1]

-345 **4** 1 **Kensington Art**[13] 3052 3-9-2 **64** .... TonyHamilton 6 65
(Richard Fahey) *chsd ldrs: pushed along and nt clr run 2f out: in clr and rdn over 1f out: kpt on into 4th ins fnl f* **12/1**

-436 **5** 1 1/4 **Tucson**[20] 2811 3-9-9 **71** .... PJMcDonald 1 70
(James Bethell) *led: pushed along and jnd 3f out: sn drvn and hdd: wknd 2f out* **9/2**[3]

5542 **6** 1 **Smeaton (IRE)**[8] 3226 3-9-2 **64** .... BenCurtis 2 62
(Roger Fell) *chsd ldr: disp ld 3f out: sn drvn into ld: rdn and hdd ent fnl 2f: wknd* **10/3**[2]

2m 37.16s (3.86) **Going Correction** +0.025s/f (Good) **6** Ran SP% **110.5**
Speed ratings (Par 99): **88,87,87,86,85 84**
CSF £37.63 CT £100.31 TOTE £3.80: £1.70, £3.50; EX 42.90 Trifecta £162.40.
Owner Peter Taplin & Partner **Bred** Norman Court Stud **Trained** West Ilsley, Berks

FOCUS
All races on Inner Home Straight. Add 30yds. Plenty of rain resulted in the ground easing further (changed to soft after this race) and, despite this being run at an ordinary gallop, stamina was certainly needed. The form's rated around the third and fourth.

3506 BRITISH STALLION STUDS EBF MAIDEN FILLIES' STKS (PLUS 10 RACE) 6f
2:40 (2:43) (Class 4) 2-Y-O £4,851 (£1,443; £721; £360) **Stalls** Centre

Form RPR

1 **Aleneva (IRE)** 2-9-0 0 .... PJMcDonald 4 76
(Richard Fahey) *mde all: drvn 2f out: narrow ld 1f out: rdn fnl f: r.o wl: jst hld persistent chal of runner-up* **4/1**[1]

2 shd **Walk In Marrakesh (IRE)** 2-9-0 0 .... AndreaAtzeni 2 76
(Mark Johnston) *hmpd by rival leaving stalls: sn rcvrd to go prom: pushed along in cl 2nd 2f out: drvn over 1f out: r.o wl and persistent chal to wnr thrght fnl f: jst hld* **4/1**[1]

60 **3** 1/2 **Irish Eileen**[22] 2747 2-9-0 0 .... CamHardie 8 74
(Michael Easterby) *prom: pushed along 2f out: drvn over 1f out: rdn and r.o wl fnl f: gaining on first two nr fin* **40/1**

4 1 **Anfield Girl (IRE)** 2-9-0 0 .... RichardKingscote 1 71
(Tom Dascombe) *hld up: pushed along over 2f out: reminders 2f out and over 1f out: kpt on into 4th fnl f* **7/1**

5 hd **Masaakin** 2-9-0 0 .... DaneO'Neill 7 71
(Richard Hannon) *chsd ldrs: pushed along over 2f out: sn drvn: cl up and reminder over 1f out: rdn and no ex fnl f* **7/1**

6 2 **Guipure** 2-9-0 0 .... BenCurtis 9 65+
(K R Burke) *slowly away: bhd: pushed along over 2f out: reminder 1 1/2f out: no imp* **9/2**[2]

6 **7** 1/2 **Internationalangel (IRE)**[37] 2248 2-9-0 0 .... TonyHamilton 6 63+
(Richard Fahey) *chsd ldrs: drvn over 2f out: sn rdn and wknd* **6/1**

8 4 1/2 **Dublin Rocker (IRE)** 2-9-0 0 .... KevinStott 5 50
(Kevin Ryan) *chsd ldrs: pushed along and lost pl over 2f out: rn green and wknd over 1f out* **5/1**[3]

9 2 1/2 **Eileen's Magic** 2-8-7 0 .... GavinAshton[(7)] 3 42
(Lisa Williamson) *wnt lft leaving stalls: hld up: drvn 2f out: wnt lft 1 1/2f out: sn dropped away* **50/1**

1m 14.33s (0.43) **Going Correction** +0.025s/f (Good) **9** Ran SP% **118.5**
Speed ratings (Par 92): **98,97,97,95,95 92,92,86,82**
CSF £20.68 TOTE £4.80: £1.90, £1.60, £8.10; EX 22.60 Trifecta £356.80.
Owner John Dance **Bred** M J Rozenbroek **Trained** Musley Bank, N Yorks

FOCUS
The market got this fillies maiden right, the two market leader being separated by just a short head. Despite the presence of a 40-1 outsider in third, it looked an okay field that should produce winners. It wasn't as strong a race as it often is, however.

3507 BENEFITS FOR ROA MEMBERS AT ROA.CO.UK NOVICE STKS (PLUS 10 RACE) 5f
3:10 (3:10) (Class 4) 2-Y-O £6,469 (£1,925; £962; £481) **Stalls** Centre

Form RPR

2 **1** **Dubai Station**[16] 2931 2-9-2 0 .... JamieSpencer 2 87+
(K R Burke) *hld up: hdwy and sltly hmpd by rival over 2f out: drvn into ld over 1f out: rdn fnl f: r.o wl* **11/8**[1]

2 **2** 1 **Partridge (IRE)**[12] 3088 2-8-11 0 .... SeanLevey 3 78
(Richard Hannon) *hld up: trckd ldrs over 2f out: sn pushed along: hdwy into 3rd over 1f out: drvn and reminder fnl f: wnt 3rd 1/2f out: reminder and r.o wl: hld nr fin* **15/8**[2]

3 2 1/4 **Sermon (IRE)** 2-9-2 0 .... RichardKingscote 7 75
(Tom Dascombe) *prom: wnt lft and sltly hamepered wnr over 2f out: sn stened: led 2f out: hdd and reminder over 1f out: wknd fnl f* **9/1**

4 2 **Matera** 2-9-2 0 .... KevinStott 6 68+
(Kevin Ryan) *rn green: hld up: pushed along 1/2-way: reminder over 1f out: kpt on steadily into 4th fnl f* **9/2**[3]

2 **5** 4 1/2 **Kilig**[23] 2707 2-9-2 0 .... DavidAllan 4 52
(Tim Easterby) *chsd ldrs: pushed along and lost pl bef 1/2-way: drvn over 2f out: rdn over 1f out: one pce fnl f* **16/1**

6 2 3/4 **Saras Hope** 2-9-2 0 .... PJMcDonald 9 42
(John Gallagher) *led: pushed along and hdd 2f out: sn wknd* **40/1**

7 3/4 **Invincible Bertie (IRE)** 2-8-13 0 .... RowanScott[(3)] 5 39
(Nigel Tinkler) *chsd ldrs: cl up over 2f out: drvn and lost pl over 1f out: wknd fnl f* **66/1**

1m 0.73s (0.33) **Going Correction** +0.025s/f (Good) **7** Ran SP% **114.9**
Speed ratings (Par 95): **98,96,92,89,82 78,76**
CSF £4.22 TOTE £1.90: £1.20, £1.40; EX 4.40 Trifecta £14.60.
Owner Ahmad Alshaikh & Co **Bred** Hall Of Fame Stud **Trained** Middleham Moor, N Yorks

FOCUS
A fair juvenile novice, in which the market leaders pulled away late on. The winner came from a good race at Nottingham.

3508 ROA OWNERS JACKPOT H'CAP 5f
3:40 (3:40) (Class 5) (0-70,68) 3-Y-O £4,851 (£1,443; £721; £360; £300; £300) **Stalls** Centre

Form RPR

000- **1** **Celsius (IRE)**[168] 9636 3-8-11 **58** .... (t[1]) MartinDwyer 11 67+
(Tom Clover) *t.k.h: hld up: hdwy 1/2-way: drvn into ld over 1f out: sn hung lft: stened and rdn clr fnl f (jockey said gelding hung left-handed under pressure)* **25/1**

1-24 **2** 1 1/2 **Scale Force**[23] 2708 3-9-0 **68** .... (v[1]) TobyEley[(7)] 1 71
(Gay Kelleway) *prom: drvn in 3rd over 1f out: wnt 2nd ins fnl f: kpt on* **20/1**

0660 **3** nk **Kapono**[26] 2635 3-9-7 **68** .... BenCurtis 2 70
(Roger Fell) *mid-div: drvn and hdwy over 1f out: sn rdn: kpt on wl fnl f* **8/1**

3636 **4** 1 **Valentino Sunrise**[13] 3045 3-8-13 **60** .... AndreaAtzeni 10 58
(Mick Channon) *prom: pushed along 2f out: sn drvn: nt clr run and bmpd rival over 1f out: rdn and no ex fnl f* **7/2**[2]

000 **5** 1 **Dream House**[30] 2507 3-8-13 **60** .... DavidAllan 8 55
(Tim Easterby) *bhd: pushed along 2f out: drvn and hdwy over 1f out: rdn and r.o fnl f: nvr nrr* **12/1**

5301 **6** 3/4 **Klopp**[16] 2939 3-9-7 **68** .... (h) CamHardie 12 60
(Antony Brittain) *hld up: pushed along 1/2-way: rdn 1 1/2f out: one pce fnl f* **20/1**

0-56 **7** 1/2 **Skeetah**[31] 2477 3-9-7 **68** .... JasonHart 3 60
(John Quinn) *led: pushed along 2f out: sn drvn: hdd over 1f out: wkng whn bdly hmpd over 1f out* **14/1**

00-1 **8** 1 **Tone The Barone**[38] 2204 3-9-1 **62** .... (t) RichardKingscote 14 49
(Stuart Williams) *prom: pushed along 2f out: sn rdn and wknd* **7/4**[1]

5-00 **9** 1 **Sylvia's Mother**[12] 3068 3-9-4 **68** .... (b) FinleyMarsh[(3)] 6 51
(Joseph Tuite) *chsd ldrs: drvn and lost pl over 2f out: sn rdn and wknd (jockey said filly ran flat)* **33/1**

-600 **10** hd **Primeiro Boy (IRE)**[15] 2960 3-9-4 **65** .... TonyHamilton 9 47
(Richard Fahey) *hld up: pushed along over 2f out: sn btn* **40/1**

500- **11** 1 1/4 **No Bills**[203] 9085 3-8-10 **57** .... ConnorBeasley 4 35
(Michael Easterby) *bhd: drvn 1/2-way: rdn 2f out: no imp* **14/1**

4412 **12** 2 1/2 **Tomahawk Ridge (IRE)**[17] 2908 3-9-3 **64** .... PJMcDonald 13 33
(John Gallagher) *prom: lost pl over 2f out: sn wknd (trainer said the gelding had been uncharacteristically restless in the stalls and appeared to be unsuited by the ground, which was officially described as soft)* **13/2**[3]

3540 **13** 6 **Swiss Chime**[59] 1650 3-8-3 **55** .... FayeMcManoman[(5)] 5 2
(Alan Berry) *hld up: pushed along and dropped to rr 2f out: sn lost tch* **50/1**

59.9s (-0.50) **Going Correction** +0.025s/f (Good) **13** Ran SP% **124.8**
Speed ratings (Par 99): **105,102,102,100,98 97,96,95,93,93 91,87,77**
CSF £442.71 CT £4449.23 TOTE £62.30: £11.30, £3.30, £2.60; EX 603.90.
Owner J Collins, C Fahy & S Piper **Bred** Owenstown Stud **Trained** Newmarket, Suffolk

FOCUS
A moderate handicap that looked more open than the betting suggested and two of the outsiders came to the fore. The form's rated around the runner-up.

3509 SHAPE CONSULTING ENGINEERS H'CAP 5f
4:10 (4:11) (Class 4) (0-85,83) 4-Y-O+ £7,115 (£2,117; £1,058; £529; £300; £300) **Stalls** Centre

Form RPR

-233 **1** **Jabbarockie**[19] 2841 6-9-4 **80** .... JasonHart 4 94
(Eric Alston) *mde all: 2 l ld 2f out: drvn in 1 l ld 1f out: rdn and asserted fnl f* **6/1**[3]

-144 **2** 1 1/4 **Boundary Lane**[9] 3201 4-9-3 **79** .... PaulMulrennan 5 89
(Julie Camacho) *chsd wnr: 2 l 2nd 2f out: rdn in 1 l 2nd 1f out: kpt on fnl f: a hld* **11/2**[2]

1510 **3** 2 **Canford Bay (IRE)**[12] 3097 5-9-6 **82** .... CamHardie 10 84
(Antony Brittain) *mid-div: hdwy 1/2-way: sn drvn: rdn in 3rd over 1f out: kpt on fnl f* **10/1**

-300 **4** 2 1/2 **Signore Piccolo**[6] 3309 8-8-12 **74** .... (h) TrevorWhelan 2 67
(David Loughnane) *slowly away: bhd: pushed along over 2f out: sn rdn: kpt on into 4th fnl f (jockey said gelding missed the break)* **14/1**

0-06 **5** 2 **Move In Time**[19] 2839 11-9-6 **82** .... DougieCostello 11 68
(Paul Midgley) *mid-div: pushed along 2f out: sn drvn: one pce fnl f* **20/1**

0-50 **6** 1 3/4 **Major Pusey**[26] 2625 7-8-13 **75** .... PJMcDonald 7 55
(John Gallagher) *prom: pushed along and lost pl 1/2-way: rdn 2f out: no ex* **7/1**

4030 **7** nk **Show Palace**[9] 3206 6-8-10 **72** .... ConnorBeasley 8 51
(Jennie Candlish) *hld up: drvn 2f out: sn rdn: no imp* **15/2**

-665 **8** 3/4 **Bengali Boys (IRE)**[26] 2625 4-9-2 **78** .... GeorgeDowning 6 54
(Tony Carroll) *bhd: drvn 1/2-way: rdn over 1f out: no imp* **12/1**

10-4 **9** nse **Youkan (IRE)**[27] 2568 4-9-7 **83** .... BenCurtis 14 59
(Stuart Kittow) *mid-div: pushed along 1/2-way: sn rdn and wknd (trainer could offer no explanation for the gelding's performance other than he appeared to be outpaced over the 5f on this occasion and may appreciate a step up in trip)* **3/1**[1]

0-40 **10** 1 **Orion's Bow**[19] 2843 8-9-1 **77** .... (p) DavidAllan 13 49
(Tim Easterby) *prom: pushed along and lost pl 2f out: sn rdn and wknd* **7/1**

-040 **11** 2 3/4 **Brandy Station (IRE)**[14] 3021 4-7-10 **65** .... (h) ElishaWhittington[(7)] 15 27
(Lisa Williamson) *a bhd* **40/1**

1m 0.21s (-0.19) **Going Correction** +0.025s/f (Good) **11** Ran SP% **122.1**
Speed ratings (Par 105): **102,100,96,92,89 86,86,85,85,83 79**
CSF £40.64 CT £339.59 TOTE £5.60: £1.90, £1.30, £3.00; EX 24.30 Trifecta £179.80.
Owner M Balmer, K Sheedy, P Copple, C Dingwall **Bred** Paul Green **Trained** Longton, Lancs

FOCUS
A fair sprint handicap, little got into it with the front two in their final placings throughout. The form could be rated a bit better at face value.

3510 VOICE FOR RACEHORSE OWNERS NOVICE STKS (PLUS 10 RACE) 6f 212y
4:40 (4:41) (Class 4) 3-Y-O £6,469 (£1,925; £962; £481) **Stalls** Low

Form RPR

1 **Vitralite (IRE)** 3-9-5 0 .... BenCurtis 3 83+
(K R Burke) *mde all: pushed along in 1 l ld 2f out: rdn and qcknd 3 l clr over 1f out: kpt on wl fnl f: comf* **6/1**[3]

63- **2** 1 **Enough Already**[310] 5586 3-9-5 0 .... AndreaAtzeni 4 80+
(Roger Varian) *chsd ldrs: hdwy gng wl 2f out: drvn in 2nd as wnr qcknd over 1f out: rdn and r.o wl fnl f: nvr getting to wnr* **6/4**[1]

0 **3** 2 3/4 **Sendeed (IRE)**[44] 2023 3-9-5 0 .... KevinStott 10 73+
(Saeed bin Suroor) *bhd: last over 3f out: pushed along and hdwy on outer over 2f out: reminders over 1f out and ins fnl f: tk 3rd over 1/2f out: kpt on wl nr fin* **6/1**[3]

4 3 1/4 **Modakhar (IRE)** 3-9-5 0 .... DaneO'Neill 5 64
(Richard Hannon) *chsd ldrs: pushed along in 3rd 2f out: drvn over 1f out: rdn and wknd fnl f* **10/1**

52 **5** 3/4 **Guandi (USA)**[12] 3067 3-9-5 0 .... RichardKingscote 6 62
(Tom Dascombe) *prom: drvn 2f out: lost pl over 1f out: one pce under hands and heels fnl f* **3/1**[2]

0 **6** *nse* **Ripon Spa**[30] 2506 3-9-2 0 .... JaneElliott(3) 9 62
(Jedd O'Keeffe) *hld up: pushed along 3f out: reminder 2f out: one pce fnl f* **33/1**

7 *¾* **Hurricane Ali (IRE)** 3-9-5 0 .... CamHardie 7 60
(John Mackie) *hld up: pushed along over 2f out: drvn over 1f out: mod hdwy whn nt clr run ins fnl f* **66/1**

0 **8** *nk* **Lucky Number**[30] 2507 3-9-2 0 .... GeorgiaCox(3) 12 59
(William Haggas) *mid-div: drvn over 2f out: rdn and wknd over 1f out* **14/1**

0 **9** *½* **Vita Vivet**[108] 785 3-9-0 0 .... PaulMulrennan 1 52
(Dianne Sayer) *hld up: pushed along 2f out: wknd over 1f out* **100/1**

04 **10** *½* **Bold Show**[17] 2895 3-9-5 0 ....(p[1]) TonyHamilton 2 56
(Richard Fahey) *trckd ldrs: drvn over 2f out: sn rdn and wknd* **28/1**

11 *2½* **Key Choice** 3-9-5 0 .... JasonHart 8 49
(Eric Alston) *t.k.h: hld up: pushed along 2f out: drvn and dropped to last over 1f out* **28/1**

1m 28.97s (-0.33) **Going Correction** +0.025s/f (Good) **11** Ran SP% **121.6**
Speed ratings (Par 101): **102,100,97,94,93 93,92,91,91,90 87**
CSF £15.52 TOTE £6.80: £2.30, £1.10, £2.30; EX 16.70 Trifecta £107.20.
Owner S P C Woods **Bred** Donnchadh Higgins **Trained** Middleham Moor, N Yorks

FOCUS
Add 15yds. A decent novice and with the experienced runners not setting a particularly high bar it was no surprise one of the newcomers stepped up.

3511 ROA MEMBERS PARK IN O & T H'CAP (FOR LADY AMATEUR RIDERS) 1m 3f 140y
5:10 (5:14) (Class 5) (0-70,70) 4-Y-0+
£4,679 (£1,451; £725; £363; £300; £300) **Stalls Centre**

Form RPR

-555 **1** **Thorntoun Care**[9] 3175 8-9-9 **63** ....(p) MissAmyCollier(5) 4 71
(Karen Tutty) *hld up: pushed along and plenty to do 2f out: swtchd and hdwy over 1f out: led on rail 100yds out: pushed out nr fin* **11/2[1]**

-460 **2** *½* **Earthly (USA)**[14] 3017 5-8-9 **51** oh3 ....(tp) MissJessicaLlewellyn(7) 10 58
(Bernard Llewellyn) *hld up: hdwy 2f out: sn rdn: led 1/2f out: hdd 100yds out: no ex* **12/1**

50-0 **3** *¾* **Iolani (GER)**[41] 2080 7-10-0 **63** .... MissEmmaSayer 11 69
(Dianne Sayer) *prom: pushed into ld 2f out: rdn over 1f out: hdd 1/2f out: no ex* **12/1**

22-0 **4** *nk* **Canford Thompson**[56] 1718 6-9-2 **51** .... MissSerenaBrotherton 13 56
(Micky Hammond) *reluctant to load: hld up: hdwy 2f out: rdn over 1f out: kpt on into 4th fnl f (starter reported that the gelding was reluctant to enter the stalls; trainer was informed that the gelding could not run until the day after passing a stalls test)* **16/1**

06-0 **5** *2½* **Correggio**[13] 3054 9-9-3 **52** ow1 .... MissBeckySmith 12 53
(Micky Hammond) *hld up: hdwy on outer 3f out: drvn 2f out: rdn over 1f out: no ex fnl f* **11/1**

00-0 **6** *3* **Duke Of Yorkshire**[59] 1648 9-9-13 **62** ....(p) MissEmilyEasterby 1 59
(Tim Easterby) *led: pushed along and hdd 2f out: sn wknd* **16/1**

-302 **7** *nk* **The Detainee**[14] 3000 6-10-0 **68** ....(p) MissMillieWonnacott(5) 7 64
(Neil Mulholland) *mid-div on inner: rdn 3f out: swtchd over 2f out: bk on inner and one pce fnl f* **8/1[3]**

651- **8** *2¼* **Firby (IRE)**[268] 7145 4-9-13 **69** .... MissRachelTaylor(7) 8 61
(Michael Dods) *prom on outer: pushed along in 3rd 3f out: drifted lft and lost pl 2f out: sn wknd (jockey said gelding hung left-handed in the home straight)* **13/2[2]**

00-0 **9** *1¾* **Paddy's Rock (IRE)**[24] 2695 8-9-2 **51** oh1 .... MissJoannaMason 3 41
(Lynn Siddall) *reluctant to load: in rr: pushed along in last 3f out: rdn on outer over 2f out: no imp (starter reported that the gelding was reluctant to enter the stalls; trainer was informed that the gelding could not run until the day after passing a stalls test)* **10/1**

-300 **10** *1¼* **Punkawallah**[24] 2696 5-9-12 **64** ....(tp) MissHannahWelch(3) 5 52
(Alexandra Dunn) *mid-div: rdn over 2f out: wknd over 1f out* **16/1**

50- **11** *nk* **Zenafire**[366] 3083 10-9-9 **63** ....(p) MissAntoniaPeck(5) 14 50
(Sarah Hollinshead) *mid-div: drvn 3f out: rdn and wknd fr 2f out* **25/1**

/0-6 **12** *2¾* **Beach Break**[27] 2577 5-10-7 **70** ....(b) MissAbbieMcCain 6 53
(Donald McCain) *mid-div: lost pl 4f out: sn rdn and wknd* **9/1**

1-00 **13** *1½* **Richard Strauss (IRE)**[8] 2684 5-9-5 **54** ....(p) MissAmieWaugh 2 34
(Philip Kirby) *mid-div: trckd ldrs 4f out: rdn and wknd 3f out* **11/2[1]**

66-0 **14** *3¾* **Golden Jeffrey (SWI)**[21] 2326 6-10-1 **69** ....(p) MissSarahBowen(5) 9 43
(Iain Jardine) *mid-div on outer: lost pl over 4f out: sn drvn and wknd* **12/1**

-000 **15** *7* **Esspeegee**[110] 754 6-9-6 **62** ....(p) MissEmmaJack(7) 15 25
(Alan Bailey) *slowly away: bhd tl hdwy on outer to go prom after 3f: wknd over 4f out: dropped to last 2f out (jockey said gelding hung right-handed)* **40/1**

2m 35.1s (1.80) **Going Correction** +0.025s/f (Good) **15** Ran SP% **129.6**
Speed ratings (Par 103): **95,94,94,93,92 90,90,88,87,86 86,84,83,81,76**
CSF £76.63 CT £792.70 TOTE £6.20: £2.10, £4.30, £5.40; EX 86.40 Trifecta £1616.60.
Owner Irvine Lynch & Thoroughbred Homes Ltd **Bred** W M Johnstone **Trained** Osmotherley, N Yorks

FOCUS
Add 30yds. As in most lady riders' races there were varying degrees of ability in the saddle on show and it proved wide-open late on, with plenty still in with a chance entering the last 2f. The pace was good and the form's ordinary.
T/Jkpt: Not Won. T/Plt: £382.00 to a £1 stake. Pool: £61,975.84 - 118.43 winning units T/Qpdt: £64.00 to a £1 stake. Pool: £5,640.07 - 65.12 winning units **Keith McHugh**

3477 RIPON (R-H)
Thursday, June 6
OFFICIAL GOING: Good (good to soft in places; 7.6)
Wind: fresh half behind Weather: cloudy, heavy shower during race 6

3512 BRITISH STALLION STUDS EBF NOVICE STKS 6f
2:20 (2:20) (Class 5) 2-Y-0 **£3,881** (£1,155; £577; £288) **Stalls High**

Form RPR

23 **1** **Praxeology (IRE)**[26] 2610 2-9-5 0 .... FrannyNorton 6 81
(Mark Johnston) *mde all: rdn over 1f out: kpt on wl to draw clr ins fnl f* **5/4[1]**

2 *5* **Just Jean (IRE)** 2-9-0 0 .... AndrewMullen 4 61
(Micky Hammond) *chsd ldrs: rdn over 2f out: kpt on same pce: wnt 2nd nr fin* **66/1**

3 *½* **Istanbul (IRE)** 2-9-5 0 .... PaulHanagan 2 65+
(Richard Fahey) *wnt rt s: sn prom: rdn 2f out: wknd ins fnl f: lost 2nd nr fin* **2/1[2]**

4 *hd* **Red Hot Streak** 2-9-5 0 .... ShaneGray 5 64+
(Tim Easterby) *chsd ldrs: rdn over 2f out: one pce* **16/1**

03 **5** *12* **Return To Senders (IRE)**[9] 3194 2-9-5 0 .... NicolaCurrie 3 28+
(Jamie Osborne) *slowly away: a in rr (jockey said colt missed the break and hung left-handed throughout)* **4/1[3]**

6 *6* **Red Jasper** 2-9-5 0 .... RobertWinston 7 10
(Michael Appleby) *s.i.s: sn in tch: rdn over 2f out: sn wknd* **12/1**

1m 11.61s (-0.89) **Going Correction** -0.025s/f (Good) **6** Ran SP% **112.8**
Speed ratings (Par 93): **104,97,96,96,80 72**
CSF £61.97 TOTE £1.90: £1.40, £6.50; EX 45.60 Trifecta £113.40.
Owner Dr J Walker **Bred** Yeomanstown Stud **Trained** Middleham Moor, N Yorks

FOCUS
The going was given as good, good to soft in places (Going Stick 7.6). The rail on the bend from the back straight to the home straight was dolled out 3yds, adding about 6yds to races on the round course. The first two in the market had a good battle, but the favourite was well on top at the line. There wasn't much depth to this.

3513 CHARLIE WALLER MEMORIAL TRUST H'CAP 1m 1f 170y
2:50 (2:51) (Class 5) (0-70,71) 3-Y-O
£4,075 (£1,212; £606; £303; £300; £300) **Stalls Low**

Form RPR

6364 **1** **Patchouli**[16] 2935 3-9-8 **71** .... NicolaCurrie 11 77
(Mick Channon) *dwlt: hld up in midfield: hdwy 3f out: rdn to chal over 1f out: led 75yds out: kpt on* **5/1[2]**

0-53 **2** *nk* **Neileta**[7] 3271 3-8-5 **54** .... ShaneGray 5 59
(Tim Easterby) *prom: rdn over 2f out: drvn to ld narrowly appr fnl f: hdd 75yds out: kpt on* **9/2[1]**

0-00 **3** *1¼* **Slaithwaite (IRE)**[56] 1721 3-7-12 **52** ow1 ....(p[1]) PaulaMuir(5) 8 54
(Roger Fell) *midfield: rdn and hdwy on outer over 3f out: sn chsd ldrs: kpt on same pce fnl f* **50/1**

453 **4** *nse* **Itchingham Lofte (IRE)**[18] 2875 3-9-7 **70** .... RobbieDowney 7 72
(David Barron) *midfield on inner: n.m.r over 3f out: swtchd lft over 2f out: sn rdn along: kpt on fnl f* **7/1**

4536 **5** *nse* **Curfewed (IRE)**[23] 2711 3-9-1 **64** ....(p[1]) DavidNolan 4 66
(Tracy Waggott) *trckd ldrs: rdn over 2f out: swtchd lft over 1f out: kpt on same pce fnl f* **13/2**

0-60 **6** *nk* **Diviner (IRE)**[15] 2965 3-9-4 **67** .... FrannyNorton 1 68
(Mark Johnston) *led: rdn over 2f out: hdd appr fnl f: no ex ins fnl f* **13/2**

000 **7** *1* **Soloist (IRE)**[13] 3050 3-9-0 **70** ....(p) CierenFallon(7) 6 69
(William Haggas) *dwlt: hld up: rdn along over 4f out: minor late hdwy: nvr involved* **11/2[3]**

0-40 **8** *1½* **Firewater**[23] 2711 3-8-13 **62** ....(p) PaulHanagan 3 58
(Richard Fahey) *trckd ldrs: rdn over 3f out: outpcd and btn whn n.m.r over 1f out* **10/1**

625 **9** *3* **Simon's Smile (FR)**[24] 2677 3-8-12 **66** ....(p) HarrisonShaw(5) 9 56
(K R Burke) *trckd ldrs on outer: rdn 3f out: wknd over 1f out* **25/1**

0-65 **10** *2¾* **The Rutland Rebel (IRE)**[17] 2912 3-9-4 **67** .... AndrewMullen 2 51
(Micky Hammond) *s.i.s: hld up in midfield: rdn along 3f out: short of room over 2f out: no ch after* **10/1**

446- **11** *4½* **Palazzo**[211] 8932 3-8-3 **52** .... KieranO'Neill 10 27
(Bryan Smart) *a towards rr* **33/1**

2m 5.26s (0.66) **Going Correction** -0.025s/f (Good) **11** Ran SP% **116.3**
Speed ratings (Par 99): **98,97,96,96,96 96,95,94,92,89 86**
CSF £27.00 CT £1005.90 TOTE £4.80: £2.10, £2.10, £13.00; EX 26.90 Trifecta £427.30.
Owner M Channon **Bred** Mike Channon Bloodstock Ltd **Trained** West Ilsley, Berks
■ Stewards' Enquiry : Paul Hanagan caution: careless riding

FOCUS
Add 6yds. A modest but competitive handicap and the form makes a fair bit of sense.

3514 SKY SPORTS RACING SKY 415 H'CAP 1m 4f 10y
3:20 (3:21) (Class 4) (0-85,86) 4-Y-0+
£5,692 (£1,694; £846; £423; £300; £300) **Stalls Centre**

Form RPR

2-00 **1** **Speed Company (IRE)**[40] 2095 6-9-3 **80** .... PaulHanagan 4 90
(Ian Williams) *dwlt: hld up in rr: pushed along and gd hdwy on outer 2f out: chal appr fnl f: led 110yds out: kpt on wl pushed out (trainer said, regarding the improved form shown, the gelding was suited by the step up in trip)* **11/2[3]**

-404 **2** *1½* **Anythingtoday (IRE)**[18] 2873 5-9-9 **86** ....(p) DavidNolan 5 93
(David O'Meara) *hld up in tch: pushed along and hdwy 2f out: rdn to ld appr fnl f: sn strly pressed: hdd 110yds out: kpt on same pce* **7/2[1]**

4-40 **3** *4* **Benadalid**[22] 2748 4-9-6 **83** .... MichaelStainton 6 84
(Chris Fairhurst) *in tch: trckd ldrs over 3f out: sn rdn along: one pce fnl f* **9/2[2]**

/33 **4** *nk* **Desert Point (FR)**[12] 3081 7-9-7 **84** .... ShaneGray 3 85
(Keith Dalgleish) *in tch: rdn along over 3f out: drvn over 2f out: no imp: kpt on nr fin* **8/1**

3-42 **5** *nse* **Aiya (IRE)**[10] 3161 4-9-3 **80** ....(h) RobertWinston 7 80
(Tim Easterby) *sn led: rdn over 2f out: hdd appr fnl f: wknd ins fnl f* **7/2[1]**

106- **6** *1¾* **Doctor Cross (IRE)**[219] 8716 5-8-7 **75** .... ConnorMurtagh(5) 1 73
(Richard Fahey) *hld up in tch: pushed along and n.m.r on inner over 2f out: nvr threatened* **7/1**

2305 **7** *2¼* **Dommersen (IRE)**[14] 3004 6-8-13 **81** .... BenSanderson(5) 2 75
(Roger Fell) *trckd ldrs: rdn 3f out: wknd fnl f* **11/1**

0-00 **8** *38* **Dr Richard Kimble (IRE)**[31] 2479 4-9-1 **78** ....(v[1]) FrannyNorton 8 11
(Mark Johnston) *prom: rdn along 3f out: wknd over 1f out* **16/1**

2m 36.03s (-0.27) **Going Correction** -0.025s/f (Good) **8** Ran SP% **115.8**
Speed ratings (Par 105): **99,98,95,95,95 93,92,67**
CSF £25.44 CT £94.19 TOTE £6.10: £1.60, £1.70, £1.60; EX 31.40 Trifecta £152.10.
Owner Allan Stennett **Bred** Rathasker Stud **Trained** Portway, Worcs

FOCUS
Add 6yds. The first two were well handicapped on old form and finished clear of the rest. Ordinary form for the grade.

3515 WEATHERBYS TBA H'CAP 1m 1f 170y
3:50 (3:52) (Class 3) (0-95,97) 4-Y-O+
£9,337 (£2,796; £1,398; £699; £349; £175) **Stalls Low**

Form RPR

1031 **1** **Fayez (IRE)**[18] 2873 5-9-7 **93** .... ShaneGray 10 102+
(David O'Meara) *dwlt: hld up: gng wl but n.m.r over 2f out: sn swtchd lft and in clr over 1f out: sn gd hdwy: qcknd to ld 110yds out: kpt on wl* **13/2**

3-36 **2** *1½* **Just Hiss**[18] 2873 6-9-0 **89** ....(p) BenRobinson(3) 6 93
(Tim Easterby) *trckd ldrs: rdn 2f out: kpt on fnl f* **10/1**

2551 **3** *shd* **Mr Top Hat**[28] 2563 4-9-4 **90**........................ KieranShoemark 2 94
(David Evans) *led: rdn and strly pressed 2f out: hdd 110yds out: one pce (vet said gelding had a wound to its right fore)* **5/1**[2]

-000 **4** *nse* **King's Pavilion (IRE)**[33] 2419 6-8-11 **88**................ ConnorMurtagh(5) 3 92
(Jason Ward) *midfield on inner: hdwy and trckd ldrs 2f out: rdn to chal 1f out: one pce fnl 110yds* **16/1**

0601 **5** *1 ½* **Waarif (IRE)**[10] 3168 6-9-8 **97** 5ex.......................... ConorMcGovern(3) 1 98
(David O'Meara) *trckd ldrs: racd quite keenly: rdn along and n.m.r over 1f out: no ex ins fnl f* **4/1**[1]

20-0 **6** *½* **Qawamees (IRE)**[22] 2748 4-8-4 **76**........................ KieranO'Neill 4 76
(Michael Easterby) *hld up in rr: pushed along and hdwy on inner over 2f out: kpt on ins fnl f* **33/1**

7 *1 ¾* **Cockalorum (IRE)**[229] 8431 4-8-7 **79**........................ PaulHanagan 11 75
(Roger Fell) *hld up: pushed along over 3f out: sme hdwy on outer over 1f out: nvr threatened ldrs* **6/1**[3]

-410 **8** *2* **Stealth Fighter (IRE)**[22] 2742 4-9-1 **90**................ WilliamCox(3) 9 82
(Saeed bin Suroor) *midfield: rdn along 3f out: n.m.r over 2f out: wknd ins fnl f* **13/2**

6-11 **9** *3* **Universal Gleam**[15] 2959 4-9-3 **89**........................ RobertWinston 7 75
(Keith Dalgleish) *prom: rdn over 2f out: wknd fnl f (trainer's rep could offer no explanation for the gelding's performance)* **5/1**[2]

12-5 **10** *nk* **Garden Oasis**[40] 2116 4-8-10 **82**........................ AndrewElliott 8 67
(Tim Easterby) *trckd ldrs: rdn over 3f out: wknd over 1f out (jockey said gelding stumbled leaving the stalls)* **12/1**

2m 3.68s (-0.92) **Going Correction** -0.025s/f (Good) **10** Ran SP% **119.9**
Speed ratings (Par 107): **104,102,102,102,101 101,99,98,95,95**
CSF £71.69 CT £357.15 TOTE £6.80: £2.10, £3.30, £1.80; EX 78.50 Trifecta £359.70.
Owner Northern Lads & Nawton Racing **Bred** Miss Siobhan Ryan **Trained** Upper Helmsley, N Yorks

FOCUS
Add 6yds. A good, competitive handicap, rated around the second, third and fourth.

3516 VML JAN NORTON HAPPY BIRTHDAY H'CAP — 6f
4:20 (4:21) (Class 5) (0-70,75) 3-Y-O
£4,075 (£1,212; £606; £303; £300; £300) **Stalls High**

Form RPR

1-22 **1** **Magical Spirit (IRE)**[9] 3202 3-9-9 **71**........................ AndrewMullen 2 82+
(Kevin Ryan) *prom: led after 1f: mde rest: pushed along 2f out: kpt on wl* **2/1**[1]

0-01 **2** *1 ½* **Queen Of Burgundy**[9] 3189 3-9-8 **75** 6ex.............. DarraghKeenan(5) 1 81+
(Christine Dunnett) *chsd ldrs on outside: rdn along 2f out: chsd ldr 1f out: kpt on but a hld* **3/1**[2]

3050 **3** *1 ¼* **Alfred The Grey (IRE)**[17] 2897 3-8-6 **54**........................ PaulHanagan 6 56
(Tracy Waggott) *midfield: pushed along and sme hdwy on outer over 1f out: rdn and kpt on fnl f* **20/1**

2-14 **4** *2 ½* **Northern Society (IRE)**[10] 3159 3-9-6 **68**........................ ShaneGray 4 62
(Keith Dalgleish) *dwlt sltly: sn chsd ldrs: rdn to chal 2f out: wknd ins fnl f* **12/1**

6-04 **5** *1 ¼* **Saltie Girl**[27] 2590 3-8-13 **61**........................ RobbieDowney 10 51
(David Barron) *led for 1f: dropped to midfield: rdn over 2f out: no imp* **14/1**

-655 **6** *2* **Hard Solution**[16] 2939 3-9-1 **63**........................(b) DavidNolan 7 47
(David O'Meara) *hld up: rdn over 3f out: wknd appr fnl f* **6/1**[3]

0410 **7** *hd* **Murqaab**[9] 3202 3-9-7 **69**........................(v) KieranShoemark 8 52
(John Balding) *hld up: nvr threatened (jockey said gelding lost his action approximately 2f out)* **25/1**

1-00 **8** *10* **Gremoboy**[30] 2510 3-9-1 **63**........................(p[1]) RobertWinston 5 14
(Tim Easterby) *chsd ldrs: rdn over 2f out: wknd over 1f out (jockey said gelding hung left-handed)* **8/1**

0-04 **9** *½* **Jill Rose**[16] 2939 3-8-11 **64**........................ ConnorMurtagh(5) 9 13
(Richard Whitaker) *hld up: rdn over 2f out: sn wknd and bhd* **10/1**

1m 11.75s (-0.75) **Going Correction** -0.025s/f (Good) **9** Ran SP% **115.8**
Speed ratings (Par 99): **104,102,100,97,95 92,92,79,78**
CSF £7.92 CT £89.51 TOTE £2.50: £1.20, £1.40, £4.70; EX 9.40 Trifecta £93.90.
Owner Hambleton Racing Ltd XXXII **Bred** S E B/Stock,W J B/Stock& Norrismount **Trained** Hambleton, N Yorks

FOCUS
As the market expected, the two who were well in at the weights came home in front. The form's rated slightly positively.

3517 CWMT MENTAL WELLBEING MAIDEN STKS — 1m
4:50 (4:50) (Class 5) 3-Y-O+ £3,881 (£1,155; £577; £288) **Stalls Low**

Form RPR

-222 **1** **Maamora (IRE)**[14] 3013 3-8-12 83........................ FrannyNorton 5 85+
(Simon Crisford) *mde all: pushed clr fnl 2f: easily* **4/5**[1]

2 *6* **New Arrangement** 3-9-3 0........................ KieranShoemark 10 76+
(James Tate) *slowly away: hld up in rr: swtchd lft to outer over 2f out: hung rt but kpt on wl fr over 1f out: wnt 2nd fnl 50yds: no ch w wnr (jockey said gelding was slowly away)* **7/1**[3]

3 *1 ¼* **Morning Duel (IRE)** 3-9-3 0........................ DavidNolan 3 73
(David O'Meara) *trckd ldrs: rdn over 2f out: wnt 2nd over 1f out: one pce: lost 2nd 50yds out* **16/1**

55 **4** *4 ½* **Foxes Flyer (IRE)**[15] 2967 3-8-12 0....................(t[1]) DarraghKeenan(5) 4 63
(Luke McJannet) *midfield: racd quite keenly: pushed along 3f out: kpt on same pce* **100/1**

5 *2 ½* **Incredulous** 3-8-12 0........................ PaulHanagan 1 52+
(William Haggas) *hld up: pushed along over 2f out and rn green: kpt on ins fnl f* **4/1**[2]

2 **6** *1* **Kind Review**[10] 3158 3-9-0 0........................ BenRobinson(3) 2 55
(Tracy Waggott) *hld up: pushed along over 2f out: nvr threatened* **33/1**

05 **7** *5* **The Retriever (IRE)**[17] 2895 4-10-0 0........................ AndrewMullen 6 46
(Micky Hammond) *nvr bttr than midfield* **100/1**

33 **8** *hd* **Battle Of Yarmouk (IRE)**[63] 1550 3-9-3 0........................ ShaneGray 7 43
(Kevin Ryan) *trckd ldrs: rdn along 3f out: wknd over 1f out* **33/1**

0 **9** *1* **Quiet Note**[17] 2919 3-8-12 0........................ JosephineGordon 8 36
(Saeed bin Suroor) *dwlt: sn prom: rdn over 3f out: edgd lft and wknd fnl 2f* **7/1**[3]

0-6 **10** *1* **Funny Man**[18] 2875 3-8-10 0........................ GianlucaSanna(7) 9 38
(William Haggas) *wnt lft s: a towards rr* **25/1**

1m 39.46s (-1.54) **Going Correction** -0.025s/f (Good)
WFA 3 from 4yo 11lb **10** Ran SP% **118.1**
Speed ratings (Par 103): **106,100,98,94,91 90,85,85,84,83**
CSF £7.00 TOTE £1.70: £1.10, £2.40, £4.10; EX 7.80 Trifecta £61.80.
Owner Sheikh Ahmed Al Maktoum **Bred** Godolphin **Trained** Newmarket, Suffolk

FOCUS
Add 6yds. Run in a thunderstorm, this proved straightforward for the odds-on favourite. The winner was the clear form pick and didn't need to improve.

3518 LADIES DAY 20TH JUNE BOOK NOW H'CAP — 5f
5:20 (5:25) (Class 6) (0-60,62) 4-Y-O+
£3,428 (£1,020; £509; £300; £300; £300) **Stalls High**

Form RPR

-504 **1** **Optimickstickhill**[8] 3213 4-8-7 **46** oh1........................(b) KieranO'Neill 10 55
(Scott Dixon) *chsd ldr stands' side: rdn over 2f out: kpt on to ld 50yds out* **11/2**[1]

4320 **2** *1* **Pearl Noir**[8] 3213 9-8-8 **54**........................(b) KieranSchofield(7) 11 59
(Scott Dixon) *led stands' side gp and overall ldr: rdn over 2f out: hdd 50yds out: one pce: 2nd of 6 in gp* **7/1**[3]

0050 **3** *nse* **Racquet**[15] 2958 6-8-7 **46**........................(p) PaulHanagan 7 51
(Ruth Carr) *led far side gp: pressed ldr overall: rdn 2f out: kpt on wl: 1st of 7 in gp (jockey said gelding hung right-handed throughout)* **10/1**

4-00 **4** *3* **Lydiate Lady**[26] 2637 7-9-2 **62**........................ RobertDodsworth(7) 8 56
(Eric Alston) *dwlt: sn chsd ldr far side: rdn over 2f out: no ex ins fnl f: 2nd of 7 in gp* **7/1**[3]

0-04 **5** *1* **Kodimoor (IRE)**[20] 2789 6-8-5 **49** oh1 ow3...........(p) ConnorMurtagh(5) 6 40
(Mark Walford) *chsd ldrs far side: rdn over 2f out: no ex ins fnl f: 3rd of 7 in gp* **16/1**

0-00 **6** *1 ¼* **Mitchum**[9] 3203 10-8-3 **47**........................(v) PaulaMuir(5) 14 33
(Ron Barr) *chsd ldrs stands' side: rdn over 2f out: wknd ins fnl f: 3rd of 6 in gp* **14/1**

1360 **7** *shd* **Twentysvnthlancers**[35] 2324 6-9-5 **58**........................ DavidNolan 12 44
(Paul Midgley) *hld up stands' side: nvr threatened: 4th of 6 in gp* **11/1**

0-40 **8** *¾* **Raffle King (IRE)**[15] 2958 5-8-13 **52**........................ ShaneGray 4 35
(Ruth Carr) *hld up far side: rdn over 2f out: kpt on ins fnl f: nvr threatened: 4th of 7 in gp* **17/2**

0-30 **9** *2* **Point Of Woods**[8] 3213 6-9-0 **60**........................(p) EllieMacKenzie(7) 2 36
(Tina Jackson) *hld up far side: rdn and sme hdwy over 1f out: wknd ins fnl f: 5th of 7 in gp (jockey said gelding stopped quickly)* **6/1**[2]

4300 **10** *shd* **Bluella**[69] 1402 4-8-7 **46** oh1........................ NicolaCurrie 13 22
(Robyn Brisland) *chsd ldrs stands' side: rdn over 2f out: wkd over 1f out: 5th of 6 in gp* **28/1**

0000 **11** *hd* **Foxy Boy**[8] 3213 5-8-7 **46**........................(t[1]) AndrewElliott 9 21
(Rebecca Bastiman) *racd stands' side: a towards rr: last of 6 in gp* **20/1**

0-00 **12** *2 ¼* **Whispering Soul (IRE)**[150] 118 6-8-7 **46** oh1.....(b) JosephineGordon 3 13
(Brian Baugh) *chsd ldrs far side: rdn over 2f out: wknd over 1f out: 6th of 7 in gp* **66/1**

0-03 **13** *6* **Funkadelic**[20] 2789 4-8-11 **50**........................ AndrewMullen 5
(Ben Haslam) *chsd ldrs far side: wknd 2f out* **8/1**

326 **R** **Piazon**[64] 1521 8-9-1 **57**........................(b) BenRobinson(3) 1
(Julia Brooke) *ref to r (starter reported that the gelding was unruly in the stalls; trainer was informed that the gelding could not run until the day after passing a stalls test)* **14/1**

1m 0.57s (1.17) **Going Correction** -0.025s/f (Good) **14** Ran SP% **122.7**
Speed ratings (Par 101): **89,87,87,82,80 78,78,77,74,74 73,70,60,**
CSF £43.13 CT £385.88 TOTE £7.30: £2.50, £2.50, £2.70; EX 43.10 Trifecta £475.20.
Owner Paul J Dixon **Bred** Mrs Yvette Dixon **Trained** Babworth, Notts

FOCUS
A low-grade sprint. They raced in two groups but there was little in it at the line, the first two coming from the stands' side group and the next three from the bunch on the far side. Straightforward form for the grade.
T/Plt: £58.30 to a £1 stake. Pool: £60,050.62 - 751.70 winning units T/Qpdt: £12.30 to a £1 stake. Pool: £6,633.52 - 398.83 winning units **Andrew Sheret**

3519 - 3525a (Foreign Racing) - See Raceform Interactive

3289 LONGCHAMP (R-H)
Thursday, June 6

OFFICIAL GOING: Turf: good to soft

3526a PRIX DE L'AQUEDUC (CLAIMER) (3YO) (TURF) — 7f
6:35 3-Y-O £10,360 (£4,144; £3,108; £2,072; £1,036)

RPR

1 **Adesias (FR)**[33] 3-8-9 0........................ MlleCoraliePacaut(4) 2 75
(J-C Rouget, France) **6/5**[1]

2 *¾* **So When (FR)**[57] 3-9-1 0........................ Pierre-CharlesBoudot 5 75
(P Sogorb, France) **5/1**[3]

3 *1 ¼* **Amethyst (FR)** 3-7-13 0........................(p) MlleMarieWaldhauser(9) 3 64
(C Escuder, France) **10/1**

4 *snk* **Harbour Spirit (FR)**[50] 1857 3-9-1 0........................(p) MickaelBarzalona 7 71
(Richard Hughes) *sn led: pushed along 2f out: rdn and hdd over 1f out: no ex ins fnl f* **3/1**[2]

5 *nk* **Improvising (IRE)**[13] 3-8-11 0........................(p) MaximeGuyon 1 66
(P Monfort, France) **20/1**

6 *1* **Singing Tower (FR)**[53] 3-8-7 0........................ ThomasTrullier(8) 4 67
(N Clement, France) **5/1**[3]

7 *4* **Antigua Biwi (IRE)**[16] 2953 3-8-11 0........................ TonyPiccone 6 53
(M Rolland, France) **56/1**

1m 22.74s (2.04) **7** Ran SP% **119.4**
PARI-MUTUEL (all including 1 euro stake): WIN 2.20; PLACE 1.50, 2.30; SF 6.90.
Owner Sarl Ecurie J L Tepper **Bred** Jean-Pierre-Daniel Ancelin & Mlle S Perrier **Trained** Pau, France

3032 BATH (L-H)
Friday, June 7

OFFICIAL GOING: Good to firm (firm in places; 8.6)
Wind: moderate, across Weather: showers

3527 CHARLES SAUNDERS H'CAP — 5f 160y
5:35 (5:37) (Class 6) (0-60,63) 4-Y-O+
£3,105 (£924; £461; £400; £400; £400) **Stalls Centre**

Form RPR

3644 **1** **Storm Melody**[17] 2929 6-9-5 **58**........................(p) SilvestreDeSousa 14 77
(Ali Stronge) *mde all: pushed clr over 1f out: in command after: readily* **3/1**[1]

0045 **2** *4* **Toolatetodelegate**[23] 2728 5-8-5 **47**......................(tp) MeganNicholls(3) 4 53
(Brian Barr) *mid-div: hdwy over 2f out: sn rdn: chsd wnr jst ins fnl f: kpt on but nt pce to get on terms* **14/1**

6-21 **3** *¾* **Essaka (IRE)**[4] 3404 7-9-3 **63** 4ex................................ SophieRalston(7) 9 67+
(Tony Carroll) *towards rr: hdwy in centre fr over 2f out: rdn over 1f out: kpt on to go 3rd fnl 120yds but nt pce to threaten* **9/2**[2]

200 **4** *1½* **Fantasy Justifier (IRE)**[11] 3143 8-9-2 **55**...............(p) KieranShoemark 7 54
(Ronald Harris) *racd keenly: mid-div: hdwy over 2f out: kpt on ins fnl f: wnt 4th towards fin* **33/1**

-300 **5** *½* **Red Tycoon (IRE)**[15] 3014 7-9-6 **59**.................................... PatDobbs 13 56
(Ken Cunningham-Brown) *mid-div: hdwy 2f out: sn rdn: kpt on ins fnl f: snatched 4th cl home* **20/1**

0-12 **6** *hd* **Olaudah**[11] 3144 5-9-4 **57**.. DavidProbert 6 53
(Henry Candy) *chsd wnr: rdn 2f out: sn hld: lost 2nd jst ins fnl f: no ex and lost 3 pls fnl 120yds* **11/2**[3]

4042 **7** *½* **Filbert Street**[37] 2295 4-8-7 **51**..........................(p) PoppyBridgwater(5) 2 46
(Roy Brotherton) *s.i.s: sn mid-div: kpt on ins fnl f: nvr threatened ldrs* **25/1**

0116 **8** *hd* **Pocket Warrior**[7] 3320 8-8-11 **55**.................................(t) DylanHogan(5) 12 49
(Paul D'Arcy) *s.i.s: bhd: hdwy in centre over 1f out: kpt on wl fnl f: n.d* **10/1**

0400 **9** *shd* **Sugar Plum Fairy**[23] 2728 4-8-7 **46**................................ JoeyHaynes 17 40
(Tony Carroll) *stdd s: towards rr: hdwy over 1f out: kpt on ins fnl f: n.d* **33/1**

3-06 **10** *¾* **Spot Lite**[14] 3036 4-9-2 **55**.. CharlieBennett 8 46
(Rod Millman) *chsd ldrs: rdn over 2f out: wknd ent fnl f* **25/1**

1620 **11** *nk* **Who Told Jo Jo (IRE)**[10] 3203 5-9-4 **60**.................... FinleyMarsh(3) 10 50
(Joseph Tuite) *mid-div tl outpcd 2f out* **20/1**

6522 **12** *2½* **Holdenhurst**[20] 2847 4-9-5 **58**.. JFEgan 16 40
(Bill Turner) *wnt lft s: chsd ldrs: rdn over 2f out: wknd over 1f out (jockey said gelding jumped left-handed as the stalls opened)* **10/1**

0400 **13** *½* **Tally's Song**[14] 3036 6-8-7 **46** oh1....................................(p) JimmyQuinn 5 26
(Grace Harris) *a towards rr* **66/1**

03 **14** *½* **Mrs Todd**[107] 811 5-8-11 **50**.......................................(h¹) FergusSweeney 1 29
(Tony Carroll) *in tch: rdn over 2f out: sn hung lft: wknd over 1f out* **25/1**

4-02 **15** *nk* **Spirit Of Ishy**[14] 3036 4-8-7 **46** oh1............................(b) HayleyTurner 11 24
(Stuart Kittow) *chsd ldrs: rdn over 2f out: wknd over 1f out* **20/1**

0005 **16** *1¼* **Burauq**[14] 3036 7-8-7 **46** oh1...................................(p) JosephineGordon 15 19
(Milton Bradley) *mid-div: rdn over 2f out: wknd over 1f out* **66/1**

0-00 **U** **Pastfact**[36] 2339 5-9-6 **59**.. DaneO'Neill 3
(Malcolm Saunders) *rrd and uns rdr leaving stalls* **8/1**

1m 9.16s (-1.94) **Going Correction** -0.175s/f (Firm) **17** Ran SP% **129.2**
Speed ratings (Par 101): **105,99,98,96,96 95,95,94,94,93 93,89,89,88,88 86,**
CSF £43.89 CT £205.54 TOTE £4.20: £1.30, £3.30, £1.90, £7.70; EX 61.20 Trifecta £326.80.
Owner Shaw Racing Partnership 2 **Bred** Selwood B/S, Hoskins & Jonason **Trained** Eastbury, Berks

FOCUS
After 15mm of rain during the day the official going description was changed to good to firm, good in places (from firm). A modest handicap which was dominated by the front-running favourite. The winner has been rated in line with last year's best.

3528 BIG ALS STAG H'CAP 1m 6f
6:10 (6:10) (Class 6) (0-60,64) 3-Y-O
£3,105 (£924; £461; £400; £400; £400) **Stalls High**

Form RPR

0004 **1** **Lock Seventeen (USA)**[17] 2941 3-9-1 **54**................ StevieDonohoe 10 59
(Charlie Fellowes) *prom early: trckd ldrs: rdn to ld 2f out: hld on wl fnl f: drvn out* **8/1**

44-6 **2** *hd* **Sinndarella (IRE)**[40] 2150 3-8-5 **47**................................ NoelGarbutt(3) 4 52
(Sarah Hollinshead) *hld up: hdwy fr 3f out: rdn over 1f out: sn chsng wnr: kpt on wl for str chal ins fnl f: jst hld* **25/1**

-441 **3** *1¼* **Victoriano (IRE)**[10] 3198 3-9-11 **64** 6ex.....................(b) EdwardGreatrex 2 67
(Archie Watson) *towards rr of midfield: rdn on centre over 2f out: hdwy over 1f out: styd on strly fnl f to go 3rd towards fin but no threat to front pair* **9/2**[3]

-602 **4** *1¼* **Dear Miriam (IRE)**[9] 3219 3-9-6 **59**............................ SilvestreDeSousa 6 60
(Mick Channon) *mid-div: hdwy to press ldr 6f out: rdn to ld briefly over 2f out: sn hld by wnr: styd on but no ex fnl 120yds* **3/1**[1]

4-05 **5** *5* **Blowing Dixie**[18] 2913 3-9-2 **55**..............................(p¹) AdamMcNamara 12 50
(Roger Charlton) *s.i.s: racing keenly and sn rcvrd to trck ldrs: rdn and ev ch over 2f out tl wl over 1f out: fdd fnl f* **7/2**[2]

2223 **6** *2¾* **Bonneville (IRE)**[30] 2530 3-8-13 **52**..(b) JFEgan 7 43
(Rod Millman) *trckd ldrs tl dropped to midfield 6f out: rdn and hdwy over 2f out: nt pce to chal: wknd jst over 1f out* **11/2**

-000 **7** *1¼* **So I'm Told (IRE)**[55] 1770 3-8-2 **46** oh1.................... DarraghKeenan(5) 5 36
(Gary Moore) *s.i.s: towards rr: slipped on bnd 5f out: hdwy over 3f out: sn rdn to chse ldrs: nt pce to threaten: wknd jst over 1f out (jockey said gelding slipped on the top bend)* **17/2**

0066 **8** *2* **Watch And Learn**[17] 2941 3-9-3 **56**................................... DavidProbert 11 43
(Andrew Balding) *trckd ldrs early: in tch: hdwy to ld 6f out: rdn and hdd over 2f out: wknd over 1f out* **25/1**

60-0 **9** *7* **Rainbow Spirit**[38] 2253 3-9-5 **58**....................................... TomQueally 8 36
(Ed Dunlop) *dwlt: a towards rr: nvr on terms* **20/1**

-306 **10** *29* **Tribune**[36] 2322 3-9-5 **58**... DaneO'Neill 9
(Sylvester Kirk) *mid-div tl wknd over 4f out: virtually p.u fnl 2f* **33/1**

60-5 **11** *37* **Snow In Spring**[142] 259 3-9-7 **60**......................................(v¹) PatDobbs 1
(Ralph Beckett) *led tl 6f out: wknd qckly 4f out: virtually p.u fr over 2f out* **20/1**

3m 4.61s (-1.49) **Going Correction** -0.175s/f (Firm) **11** Ran SP% **122.6**
Speed ratings (Par 97): **97,96,96,95,92 91,90,89,85,68 47**
CSF £198.65 CT £1022.84 TOTE £11.40: £3.00, £7.50, £1.40; EX 264.60 Trifecta £2299.60.
Owner Peter O'Callaghan **Bred** J Ramsey, S Ramsey & W Ramsey **Trained** Newmarket, Suffolk

FOCUS
A modest staying handicap in which the pace increased from halfway.

3529 T C BUILDING SERVICES H'CAP 1m
6:40 (6:40) (Class 4) (0-80,79) 4-Y-O+ **£5,530** (£1,645; £822; £411; £400) **Stalls Low**

Form RPR

2150 **1** **Poetic Force (IRE)**[37] 2273 5-9-3 **75**.............................(t) JoeyHaynes 6 82
(Tony Carroll) *stdd into last sn after s: travelling strly on heels of ldrs but nt clr run fr 2f out tl jst over 1f out: sn qcknd up to ld ins fnl f: pushed out* **9/2**

-442 **2** *1¼* **Salt Whistle Bay (IRE)**[27] 2622 5-9-7 **79**........................ DaneO'Neill 3 83
(Rae Guest) *prom: rdn to ld over 1f out: hdd ins fnl f: kpt on but nt pce of wnr* **7/2**[3]

-000 **3** *3* **Sir Plato (IRE)**[25] 2691 5-9-1 **73**............................(b¹) CharlieBennett 1 70
(Rod Millman) *led: rdn and hdd over 1f out: no ex ins fnl f* **9/1**

110 **4** *1¼* **Nahham (IRE)**[16] 2966 4-9-7 **79**.. PatDobbs 5 73
(Richard Hannon) *trckd ldrs: cl up 2f out: effrt over 1f out: sn one pce* **7/4**[1]

0000 **5** *3½* **Rock Icon**[43] 2064 6-9-2 **74**.. SilvestreDeSousa 2 60
(Ali Stronge) *trcking ldrs whn slipped on bnd 5f out: rdn over 2f out: btn over 1f out (jockey said gelding slipped on the bend)* **10/3**[2]

1m 39.71s (-1.99) **Going Correction** -0.175s/f (Firm) **5** Ran SP% **109.8**
Speed ratings (Par 105): **102,100,97,96,93**
CSF £19.85 TOTE £5.00: £2.30, £1.60; EX 14.00 Trifecta £62.60.
Owner S J Barton **Bred** S J Macdonald **Trained** Cropthorne, Worcs

FOCUS
A fair handicap and competitive despite the small field. The winner has been rated to his turf best, and the second to his reappearance/late 2018 form for now.

3530 BRITISH STALLION STUDS EBF NOVICE STKS (PLUS 10 RACE) 5f 10y
7:15 (7:15) (Class 3) 2-Y-O **£6,301** (£1,886; £943; £472) **Stalls Centre**

Form RPR

22 **1** **Illusionist (GER)**[25] 2686 2-9-4 ....(b¹) EdwardGreatrex 5 90
(Archie Watson) *trckd ldr: led over 2f out: sn clr: comf* **8/11**[1]

2 *8* **Red Sun (IRE)** 2-9-4 .... KieranShoemark 1 64+
(Charles Hills) *s.i.s: sn outpcd and detached in last: hdwy over 1f out: kpt on into 2nd ins fnl f: no ch w wnr* **11/2**[3]

3 *3¾* **Claudia Jean (IRE)** 2-8-13 .... PatDobbs 2 43
(Richard Hannon) *chsd ldrs: rdn 2f out: nt pce to chal: no ex ins fnl f* **4/1**[2]

1440 **4** *5* **Chasanda**[21] 2805 2-9-5 .... JFEgan 4 31
(David Evans) *broke wl: led: hung bdly rt fr 3f out: hdd over 2f out: wknd ent fnl f (jockey said filly hung badly right-handed)* **11/2**[3]

1m 1.07s (-0.93) **Going Correction** -0.175s/f (Firm) **4** Ran SP% **108.7**
Speed ratings (Par 97): **100,87,81,73**
CSF £5.07 TOTE £1.50; EX 6.80 Trifecta £10.50.
Owner Qatar Racing Limited **Bred** Edergole Thoroughbred Ltd **Trained** Upper Lambourn, W Berks

FOCUS
No drama at all for the short-priced favourite.

3531 BRICK PEERS H'CAP 5f 10y
7:45 (7:49) (Class 4) (0-85,87) 3-Y-O+
£5,387 (£1,612; £806; £403; £400; £400) **Stalls Centre**

Form RPR

4250 **1** **Foxy Forever (IRE)**[14] 3056 9-9-8 **79**......................................(bt) JFEgan 6 87
(Michael Wigham) *squeezed up sn after s: mid-div: hdwy over 2f out: sn rdn: led jst over 1f out: kpt on wl fnl f: hld on* **10/1**

4302 **2** *nk* **Enchanted Linda**[11] 3159 3-8-5 **74**............(h¹) ThoreHammerHansen(5) 8 78
(Richard Hannon) *s.i.s: towards rr: hdwy over 2f out: swtchd rt jst over 1f out: str chal fnl f: hld cl home* **8/1**

6-01 **3** *½* **Waseem Faris (IRE)**[14] 3037 10-9-11 **82**................................ PatDobbs 9 87
(Ken Cunningham-Brown) *mid-div tl lost pl over 2f out: hdwy over 1f out: fin strly: wnt 3rd towards fin* **33/1**

6333 **4** *¾* **Little Boy Blue**[14] 3037 4-9-7 **83**..............................(h) RyanWhile(5) 2 85+
(Bill Turner) *prom: rdn and ev ch over 1f out: kpt on same pce fnl f* **8/1**

20-0 **5** *¾* **Secretfact**[49] 1915 6-9-4 **75**.. JimmyQuinn 12 75+
(Malcolm Saunders) *hld up towards rr: hdwy but nt clr run fr over 1f out: kpt on wl whn clr ins fnl f but no ch* **33/1**

13-5 **6** *½* **Whataguy**[37] 2274 3-9-1 **82**... MeganNicholls(3) 11 77
(Paul Nicholls) *mid-div tl outpcd 3f out: hdwy over 1f out: kpt on fnl f* **12/1**

6523 **7** *hd* **Powerful Dream (IRE)**[23] 2729 6-8-9 **66**......................(p) DavidProbert 4 63
(Ronald Harris) *chsd ldrs: gng wl enough whn hmpd over 1f out: kpt on ins fnl f but no ch after* **16/1**

2-06 **8** *shd* **Mutawaffer (IRE)**[42] 2086 3-9-4 **82**.................................. DaneO'Neill 13 76
(Charles Hills) *s.i.s: towards rr: hdwy over 1f out: sn rdn: kpt on but nt pce to get on terms fnl f* **9/2**[2]

-102 **9** *1* **Coronation Cottage**[14] 3032 5-8-13 **70**............................ CharlieBennett 7 63
(Malcolm Saunders) *led: rdn and hdd jst over 1f out: wknd fnl f* **14/1**

00-6 **10** *1½* **Oeil De Tigre (FR)**[18] 2917 8-9-11 **82**............................ GeorgeDowning 14 70
(Tony Carroll) *a towards rr* **25/1**

-065 **11** *¾* **Good Luck Fox (IRE)**[11] 3151 3-9-6 **84**...................... SilvestreDeSousa 1 66
(Richard Hannon) *mid-div: effrt over 2f out: little imp whn nt clr run wl over 1f out: wknd fnl f* **5/1**[3]

-001 **12** *¾* **King Crimson**[10] 3188 7-8-4 **66** 4ex......................... DarraghKeenan(5) 10 48
(John Butler) *chsd ldrs: rdn 2f out: wknd fnl f* **16/1**

-216 **13** *1½* **The Daley Express (IRE)**[34] 2403 5-10-2 **87**.................... KieranShoemark 5 64
(Ronald Harris) *chsd ldrs: rdn over 2f out: hld whn hmpd jst over 1f out: wknd fnl f* **4/1**[1]

1m 1.2s (-0.80) **Going Correction** -0.175s/f (Firm)
WFA 3 from 4yo+ 7lb **13** Ran SP% **122.0**
Speed ratings (Par 105): **99,98,97,96,95 94,94,94,92,90 88,87,85**
CSF £88.12 CT £2549.96 TOTE £10.50: £3.00, £2.80, £6.10; EX 86.30 Trifecta £1757.60.
Owner D Hassan, J Cullinan **Bred** Tally-Ho Stud **Trained** Newmarket, Suffolk
■ Stewards' Enquiry : Thore Hammer Hansen four-day ban: careless riding (June 23-26)

FOCUS
A useful, competitive sprint and the pace collapsed late on. The winner has been rated to his recent best, with the second to her latest form.

3532 STEVE VICK FILLIES' NOVICE STKS 5f 160y
8:20 (8:22) (Class 5) 3-Y-O+ **£3,752** (£1,116; £557; £278) **Stalls Centre**

Form RPR

2 **1** **Philipine Cobra**[23] 2736 3-8-11 70.............................. JosephineGordon 3 81
(Phil McEntee) *mde all: set decent pce: kpt on strly to assert fnl f: readily* **7/2**[2]

-4 **2** *6* **Chil Chil**[17] 2938 3-8-11 0.. SilvestreDeSousa 1 61+
(Andrew Balding) *wnt lft s and slowly away: showed gd early spd to rcvr: trck ldrs: wnt 2nd over 2f out: rdn over 1f out: nt pce to chal: no ex fnl 120yds* **5/4**[1]

5-04 **3** *hd* **Miss Elsa**[10] 3189 3-8-11 71.. EdwardGreatrex 5 61
(Eve Johnson Houghton) *trckd ldrs: rdn over 2f out: kpt on ins fnl furlon: clsng on runner-up at fin but nt pce to threaten* **9/2**[3]

3-5 **4** *7* **Mrs Discombe**[42] 2077 3-8-11 0.. DavidProbert 6 37
(Mick Quinn) *hld up: wnt hld 4th 2f out: nvr gng pce to get on terms* **5/1**

0 **5** *14* **Cala D'Or (IRE)**[51] 1855 3-8-11 0.. JFEgan 2
(Samuel Farrell, Ire) *in tch: rdn over 2f out: nvr threatened: wknd over 1f out (jockey said filly moved poorly throughout)* **33/1**

6 *nse* **Mother Brown** 3-8-11 0.. JimmyQuinn 8
(Bill Turner) *sn outpcd: a towards rr* **33/1**

00 **7** *2¼* **Scarlet Red**[13] 3090 4-9-5 0.. CharlieBennett 4
(Malcolm Saunders) *little slowly away: pressed wnr tl 3f out: sn wandered u.p and wknd* **40/1**

24 **8** 9 **Casarubina (IRE)**[16] 2976 3-8-6 0..........................(t) DarraghKeenan(5) 7
(Nick Littmoden) *hld up: effrt 3f out: nvr threatened: wknd over 1f out (vet said filly bled from the nose)* **12/1**

1m 10.0s (-1.10) **Going Correction** -0.175s/f (Firm)
WFA 3 from 4yo 8lb **8 Ran SP% 117.5**
Speed ratings (Par 100): **100,92,91,82,63 63,60,48**
CSF £8.44 TOTE £3.90: £1.30, £1.10, £1.60; EX 9.10 Trifecta £25.30.
Owner Trevor Johnson **Bred** Al-Baha Bloodstock **Trained** Newmarket, Suffolk

FOCUS
A novice event with little strength in depth. The winner has been rated in line with the better view of her Yarmouth form.

3533 AVON VALLEY CLEANING & RESTORATION H'CAP 1m
8:50 (8:52) (Class 6) (0-60,60) 4-Y-O+
£3,105 (£924; £461; £400; £400; £400) **Stalls Low**

Form RPR
10-2 **1** **Princess Way (IRE)**[37] 2277 5-9-6 **59**..........................(v) JFEgan 12 66
(Paul George) *mde all: 8 l clr of 2nd 3f out but nrly 18 l clr of main gp: rdn over 1f out: jst hld on* **5/1**[3]

0505 **2** shd **Red Gunner**[99] 941 5-8-12 **51**.......................... EdwardGreatrex 5 58
(Mark Loughnane) *sn midfield: rdn and stdy prog fr over 2f out: 4th ent fnl f: str run fnl 120yds: jst failed* **16/1**

6530 **3** ¾ **Accomplice**[14] 3038 5-9-5 **58**.......................... DavidProbert 13 63
(Michael Blanshard) *hld up: rdn and stdy prog fr over 2f out: kpt on ins fnl f: snatched 3rd cl home* **10/1**

01-5 **4** nk **Langley Vale**[25] 2693 10-8-11 **50**.......................... FergusSweeney 1 54
(Roger Teal) *chsd clr ldr: 10 l clr of main gp 3f out: clsd on ldr over 2f out: sn rdn: nt quite pce to get on terms: no ex whn losing 2 pls cl home* **28/1**

-052 **5** ½ **Silverturnstogold**[72] 1355 4-9-7 **60**.......................... GeorgeDowning 7 63
(Tony Carroll) *chsd ldng pair: clsd on ldrs u.p fr 2f out: kpt on same pce fnl f* **7/1**

2141 **6** 3 **Imperial Act**[7] 3325 4-8-9 **51**.......................... WilliamCox(3) 10 47
(Andrew Balding) *mid-div: hdwy over 2f out: sn rdn: chal for 4th ent fnl f: fdd fnl 120yds* **11/4**[1]

-045 **7** 4 ½ **Test Valley (IRE)**[23] 2731 4-9-7 **60**.......................... TomQueally 8 46
(Tracey Barfoot-Saunt) *racd keenly in midfield: hdwy over 2f out: sn rdn: nvr threatened: wknd ent fnl f* **16/1**

5661 **8** 1 **Brockagh Cailin**[14] 3038 4-9-6 **59**.......................... JosephineGordon 11 43
(J S Moore) *a towards rr* **6/1**

4002 **9** 4 ½ **Don't Cry About It (IRE)**[17] 2930 4-9-0 **53**..........(bt) SilvestreDeSousa 6 26
(Ali Stronge) *a towards rr* **7/2**[2]

60-0 **10** 3 ¾ **Lily Jean**[37] 2280 4-8-7 **46** oh1.......................... HayleyTurner 9 11
(Stuart Kittow) *chsd clr ldrs tl wknd over 2f out* **33/1**

6-0 **11** 8 **Could Be Gold (IRE)**[11] 3142 5-8-2 **46** oh1..........(h) DarraghKeenan(5) 2
(John Butler) *in tch: rdn 3f out: sn wknd* **50/1**

1m 40.43s (-1.27) **Going Correction** -0.175s/f (Firm) **11 Ran SP% 121.5**
Speed ratings (Par 101): **99,98,98,97,97 94,89,88,84,80 72**
CSF £83.05 CT £796.65 TOTE £6.70: £2.10, £2.80, £3.20; EX 78.40 Trifecta £1058.90.
Owner David Renfree And Paul George **Bred** Tally-Ho Stud **Trained** Crediton, Devon

FOCUS
A modest handicap, in which the winner showed a tough attitude from the front. The second has been rated in line with his better AW form.
T/Plt: £185.00 to a £1 stake. Pool: £59,403.11 - 234.29 winning units T/Qpdt: £18.40 to a £1 stake. Pool: £5,912.19 - 236.53 winning units **Tim Mitchell**

3404 BRIGHTON (L-H)
Friday, June 7

OFFICIAL GOING: Good (good to soft in places) changing to soft after race 5 (4.05)
Wind: moderate head wind Weather: overcast with showers

3534 DOWNLOAD THE STAR SPORTS APP NOW! NOVICE STKS 5f 60y
2:00 (2:00) (Class 5) 2-Y-O **£3,752** (£1,116; £557) **Stalls Low**

Form RPR
22 **1** **Taxiwala (IRE)**[21] 2783 2-9-5 0..........................(b[1]) OisinMurphy 5 81
(Archie Watson) *mde all: pushed along to extend advantage 2f out: rdn 1f out: kpt up to work ins fnl f* **4/5**[1]

42 **2** 5 **Inyamazane (IRE)**[14] 3033 2-9-0 0.......................... CharlesBishop 1 58
(Mick Channon) *chsd wnr and racd keenly: rdn along to chse wnr 2f out: kpt on but no match for wnr* **7/4**[2]

63 **3** 6 **Ivor**[10] 3190 2-9-5 0.......................... SeanLevey 2 41
(Richard Hannon) *racd keenly in last: c wd into st 3f out: rdn and no imp 2f out: one pce fnl f (jockey said gelding hung right-handed)* **9/2**[3]

1m 2.59s (-0.41) **Going Correction** -0.125s/f (Firm) **3 Ran SP% 110.1**
Speed ratings (Par 93): **98,90,80**
CSF £2.59 TOTE £1.60; EX 2.70 Trifecta £2.80.
Owner Arjun Waney **Bred** River Downs Stud **Trained** Upper Lambourn, W Berks

FOCUS
All distances as advertised. There had been at least 6mm of rain this morning resulting in a going change to good, good to soft in places. It changed again to soft after race 5. Two out in the first so just three went to post, all with similar form so far but a clear win for the favourite with the time suggesting the ground is no worse than good. It's hard to set the level.

3535 STARSPORTS.BET H'CAP 5f 215y
2:30 (2:30) (Class 5) (0-75,76) 3-Y-O **£3,752** (£1,116; £557; £300; £300) **Stalls Low**

Form RPR
3340 **1** **Key To Power**[13] 3068 3-9-2 **70**.......................... JasonWatson 1 81
(Mark Johnston) *broke smartly and mde all: effrt to extend advantage 2f out: rdn and in command 1f out: pushed out: comf* **5/2**[2]

1011 **2** 3 **Pink Flamingo**[37] 2281 3-9-7 **75**.......................... HarryBentley 4 76
(Michael Attwater) *settled wl in 4th: rdn along to chse wnr in 2nd 2f out: kpt on fnl f but no match for wnr* **4/1**[3]

55-2 **3** 4 **Leopardina (IRE)**[36] 2332 3-8-11 **65**.......................... OisinMurphy 3 53
(David Simcock) *racd in 3rd: clsd on wnr gng wl 2f out: rdn and no imp over 1f out: one pce fnl f* **7/4**[1]

-120 **4** 1 ½ **Swiss Pride (IRE)**[23] 2730 3-9-8 **76**..........................(b) ShaneKelly 5 59
(Richard Hughes) *hld up: rdn and outpcd 2f out: nvr on terms* **9/2**

0-30 **5** 13 **Vikivaki (USA)**[36] 2332 3-8-13 **67**.......................... TomMarquand 2 9
(Robert Cowell) *chsd wnr: rdn along and lost pl 2f out: eased whn btn fnl f* **10/1**

1m 10.33s (-0.77) **Going Correction** -0.125s/f (Firm) **5 Ran SP% 112.2**
Speed ratings (Par 99): **100,96,90,88,71**
CSF £12.83 TOTE £3.10: £1.90, £2.10; EX 14.90 Trifecta £34.70.
Owner Sheikh Hamdan bin Mohammed Al Maktoum **Bred** Godolphin **Trained** Middleham Moor, N Yorks

FOCUS
A second all-the-way success of the day in an ordinary 3yo sprint handicap. The level is a bit fluid, but the second has been rated to her latest.

3536 READ SILVESTRE DE SOUSA'S EXCLUSIVE BLOG STARSPORTSBET.CO.UK H'CAP 5f 215y
3:05 (3:08) (Class 4) (0-80,83) 4-Y-O+
£5,530 (£1,645; £822; £411; £300; £300) **Stalls Low**

Form RPR
-215 **1** **Diamond Lady**[32] 2484 8-9-3 **75**.......................... HectorCrouch 7 83
(William Stone) *racd in midfield: drvn along to chse ldr 2f out: gd hdwy u.p to ld jst ins fnl f: rdn out and hung lft clsng stages: a doing enough* **6/1**[3]

0401 **2** ¾ **Key Player**[10] 3183 4-9-11 **83** 5ex.......................... CharlesBishop 2 88
(Eve Johnson Houghton) *bmpd at the s and chsd ldr: rdn along to ld over 1f out: drvn and hdd by wnr jst ins fnl f: kpt on* **2/1**[1]

0-00 **3** 1 ¼ **Pour La Victoire (IRE)**[14] 3040 9-9-5 **77**..........(p) GeorgeDowning 4 78
(Tony Carroll) *hld up: rdn along and outpcd over 2f out: kpt on wl u.p ins fnl f* **10/1**

-406 **4** nk **Lightning Charlie**[28] 2568 7-9-9 **81**.......................... JasonWatson 1 81
(Amanda Perrett) *j. awkwardly and racd in rr: rdn to chse ldr on inner 2f out: gd hdwy upsides ldr and ev ch 1f out: wknd clsng stages* **11/4**[2]

4-44 **5** hd **Jack Taylor (IRE)**[15] 3021 4-9-2 **74**..........................(e) ShaneKelly 3 73
(Richard Hughes) *loose briefly on way to post: racd in midfield: rdn and no imp 2f out: one pce fnl f* **6/1**[3]

4361 **6** 1 ¾ **Emily Goldfinch**[21] 2804 6-9-2 **81**..........................(p) GraceMcEntee(7) 6 75
(Phil McEntee) *led: rdn along and hdd over 1f out: wknd fnl f* **9/1**

-000 **7** 1 ¼ **Leo Minor (USA)**[20] 2839 5-9-7 **79**.......................... TomMarquand 5 69
(Robert Cowell) *trckd ldr: rdn along and outpcd over 2f out: sn drvn and no hdwy: wknd fnl f* **11/1**

1m 9.93s (-1.17) **Going Correction** -0.125s/f (Firm) **7 Ran SP% 116.0**
Speed ratings (Par 105): **102,101,99,98,98 96,94**
CSF £19.01 TOTE £7.10: £4.10, £1.70; EX 19.90 Trifecta £129.70.
Owner Miss Caroline Scott **Bred** Mickley Stud **Trained** West Wickham, Cambs

FOCUS
A fairly open sprint handicap. The second has been rated in line with his latest.

3537 DOWNLOAD THE STAR SPORTS APP NOW! H'CAP 1m 1f 207y
3:35 (3:36) (Class 6) (0-65,65) 4-Y-O+
£3,105 (£924; £461; £300; £300; £300) **Stalls Centre**

Form RPR
0515 **1** **Tigerfish (IRE)**[28] 2595 5-9-0 **58**..........................(p) TomMarquand 6 69
(William Stone) *mde all: rdn to extend advantage to 3 l wl over 1f out: sn clr: pushed out fnl f* **4/1**[2]

0-32 **2** 2 ¾ **Il Sicario (IRE)**[11] 3150 5-9-2 **65**..........................(h) RyanWhile(5) 2 69
(Bill Turner) *trckd wnr: rdn along to chse wnr over 2f out: kpt on fnl f but no imp* **10/1**

-062 **3** 2 ¼ **Fair Power (IRE)**[10] 3186 5-8-12 **56**.......................... OisinMurphy 3 56
(John Butler) *dwlt and racd in rr: hdwy between rivals over 2f out: rdn to chse wnr over 1f out: kpt on but no ch w wnr* **13/8**[1]

0-14 **4** 3 **Banksy's Art**[8] 3251 4-9-2 **65**.......................... ScottMcCullagh(5) 5 59
(Mick Channon) *hld up: pushed along over 3f out: sn rdn 2f out: kpt on one pce fnl f* **11/2**[3]

0546 **5** 6 **Roy Rocket (FR)**[17] 2928 9-9-3 **61**.......................... RobHornby 4 43
(John Berry) *hld up in rr: rdn and no imp 2f out: sme late hdwy passed rivals fnl f* **12/1**

0-56 **6** 3 **Cherbourg (FR)**[86] 1183 7-9-4 **62**..........................(p) KierenFox 7 39
(Dr Jon Scargill) *trckd wnr: rdn along and lost pl 2f out: wknd fnl f (jockey said gelding stopped quickly; vet said the gelding to be lame on its left-hind leg)* **8/1**

6-34 **7** 5 **Barrsbrook**[86] 1183 5-9-6 **64**..........................(v) HectorCrouch 1 31
(Gary Moore) *racd in midfield: rdn and no imp 2f out: sn struggling in rr* **6/1**

2m 3.15s (-1.85) **Going Correction** -0.125s/f (Firm) **7 Ran SP% 115.7**
Speed ratings (Par 101): **102,99,98,95,90 88,84**
CSF £42.86 CT £89.36 TOTE £4.60: £2.50, £3.90; EX 30.70 Trifecta £99.60.
Owner Miss Caroline Scott **Bred** Swordlestown Little **Trained** West Wickham, Cambs

FOCUS
A double for William Stone taking his course record to 7-29 in the last five years, and a convincing fourth course victory for the winner. The second helps guide the level of the form.

3538 CALL STAR SPORTS ON 08000 521 321 H'CAP 1m 3f 198y
4:05 (4:05) (Class 5) (0-70,70) 3-Y-O
£3,752 (£1,116; £557; £300; £300; £300) **Stalls High**

Form RPR
000- **1** **Goshen (FR)**[213] 8889 3-9-1 **64**.......................... HectorCrouch 1 84
(Gary Moore) *trckd ldr for 2f then mde rest: rdn and steadily drew clr 2f out: sn wl in command 1f out: easily (trainer said, regarding the improved form shown, the gelding had matured over the winter and had appreciated the step-up in trip)* **15/2**[3]

0452 **2** 12 **Message**[7] 3311 3-9-3 **66**.......................... HarryBentley 6 66
(Mark Johnston) *led for 2f then trckd wnr: rdn along to chse wnr over 2f out: kpt on one pce fr 1f out* **8/11**[1]

0-45 **3** 1 ½ **Tamachan**[22] 2771 3-9-7 **70**..........................(h) JasonWatson 5 68
(Roger Charlton) *dwlt and racd in rr: rdn along 1/2-way: drvn and hdwy on outer into 3rd 2f out: kpt on fnl f* **11/2**[2]

00-0 **4** 13 **Crackaway (FR)**[40] 2141 3-9-5 **68**..........................(p) OisinMurphy 4 45
(Harry Dunlop) *racd in midfield: rdn and readily outpcd over 3f out: nvr able to get on terms* **25/1**

-005 **5** 3 ¾ **Garrison Commander (IRE)**[10] 3195 3-9-5 **68**..........(b) TomMarquand 2 39
(Eve Johnson Houghton) *trckd ldng pair: rdn and no imp 2f out: wknd and drifted lft fnl f* **9/1**

-310 **6** 2 ½ **Fenjal (IRE)**[24] 2711 3-8-11 **67**..........................(b) TobyEley(7) 7 34
(Gay Kelleway) *in rr: racd lazily: rdn 1/2-way: a bhd (jockey said gelding was never travelling)* **25/1**

-530 **7** 43 **Homesick Boy (IRE)**[13] 3092 3-8-12 **61**.......................... RobertHavlin 3
(Ed Dunlop) *racd in midfield: rdn along and lost pl over 3f out: sn bhd and eased fnl f* **8/1**

2m 31.82s (-4.18) **Going Correction** -0.125s/f (Firm) **7 Ran SP% 113.9**
Speed ratings (Par 99): **108,100,99,90,87 86,57**
CSF £13.33 TOTE £6.70: £3.00, £1.10; EX 16.10 Trifecta £77.00.
Owner Steven Packham **Bred** Christophe Toulorge **Trained** Lower Beeding, W Sussex

FOCUS
The rain had returned. Punters got stuck into the wrong one as a handicap debutant romped in.

3539 WATCH THE #BETTINGPEOPLE VIDEOS STARSPORTSBET.CO.UK H'CAP 7f 211y

4:40 (4:40) (Class 5) (0-70,72) 4-Y-O+ £3,752 (£1,116; £557; £300; £300) Stalls Low

Form RPR

4132 1 **Waqt (IRE)**[14] 3038 5-9-7 **64** RossaRyan 2 75
(Alexandra Dunn) *trckd ldng pair: rdn along to ld on far rail 2f out: sn in command and rdn out fnl f* **13/8**[1]

0-60 2 4 1/2 **Andalusite**[17] 2929 6-9-0 **57** (v) RoystonFfrench 1 58
(John Gallagher) *led: rdn along and hdd by wnr 2f out: kpt on wl in battle for 2nd ins fnl f: no ch w wnr (jockey said mare hung right-handed turning in)* **16/1**

6200 3 nse **Chikoko Trail**[27] 2617 4-9-4 **61** (t[1]) HectorCrouch 4 62
(Gary Moore) *trckd ldr: rdn along to chse wnr 2f out: kpt on in battle for 2nd ins fnl f* **11/2**

3205 4 2 1/2 **Narjes**[10] 3185 5-10-0 **71** (h) LiamJones 3 66
(Laura Mongan) *racd in rr: rdn along 3f out: drvn and sme minor hdwy ins fnl f: n.d* **3/1**[3]

3250 5 shd **Arctic Sea**[21] 2797 5-9-9 **71** ScottMcCullagh(5) 5 66
(Paul Cole) *dwlt and racd in rr: rdn along and no rspnse 3f out: sn btn* **5/2**[2]

1m 36.93s (0.03) **Going Correction** -0.125s/f (Firm) **5** Ran SP% **112.9**
Speed ratings (Par 103): **94,89,89,86,86**
CSF £25.19 TOTE £2.90: £1.60, £4.30; EX 17.80 Trifecta £65.00.
Owner Helium Racing Ltd **Bred** Ennistown Stud **Trained** West Buckland, Somerset

FOCUS
The going was changed to soft before this race. Modest fare won in convincing fashion by an in-form course winner. The winner has been rated back to his early level.

3540 FIRST FOR INDUSTRY JOBS VISIT STARRECRUITMENT.BET H'CAP 6f 210y

5:10 (5:10) (Class 6) (0-65,67) 4-Y-O+
£3,105 (£924; £461; £300; £300; £300) Stalls Low

Form RPR

056- 1 **Canford's Joy (IRE)**[175] 9529 4-9-5 **63** DanielMuscutt 4 69
(Amy Murphy) *mde all: rdn along and strly pressed wl over 1f out: drvn and hung on gamely ins fnl f: jst prevailed* **9/1**

5-06 2 hd **Hedging (IRE)**[22] 2774 5-8-11 **55** (b) CharlesBishop 1 60
(Eve Johnson Houghton) *racd in midfield on inner: rdn along and no immediate imp over 2f out: swtchd rt and drvn 1f out: styd on strly ins fnl f: jst failed* **7/2**[2]

5056 3 nk **Wilson (IRE)**[17] 2929 4-9-1 **62** (p) JoshuaBryan(3) 6 67
(Julia Feilden) *dwlt and racd in rr: hdwy u.p to go 2nd over 1f out: rdn and kpt on wl fnl f: lost 2nd fnl strides* **11/1**

0002 4 1 1/4 **Soaring Spirits (IRE)**[4] 3406 9-8-10 **61** (b) LukeBacon(7) 9 62
(Dean Ivory) *racd in midfield: effrt on outer to chse wnr over 2f out: sn rdn and kpt on one pce ins fnl f* **14/1**

3625 5 2 1/2 **Helfire**[25] 2692 6-8-13 **57** RobertHavlin 3 52
(Martin Bosley) *mounted on crse and wnt to post early: trckd wnr: rdn along and ev ch over 1f out: one pce fnl f* **7/1**

-413 6 hd **Diva Star**[16] 2978 4-9-7 **65** (t) SeanLevey 5 59
(Rae Guest) *hld up on inner: rdn along and no imp 2f out: kpt on one pce fnl f* **11/4**[1]

-050 7 3/4 **Chetan**[21] 2797 7-8-13 **64** TobyEley(7) 10 56
(Tony Carroll) *wnt to post early: chsd ldr: rdn along and lost pl 2f out: wknd fnl f* **8/1**

2012 8 1 1/2 **De Little Engine (IRE)**[17] 2929 5-9-9 **67** (p) RossaRyan 7 56
(Alexandra Dunn) *settled wl in midfield: clsd on outer gng wl over 2f out: sn rdn and fnd little: wknd fnl f (jockey said gelding was never travelling)* **5/1**[3]

0-00 9 shd **Good Luck Charm**[22] 2774 10-9-4 **62** (b) HectorCrouch 11 50
(Gary Moore) *trckd wnr: rdn along to chse wnr wl over 1f out: wknd and lost pl fnl f* **20/1**

1m 22.94s (-0.86) **Going Correction** -0.125s/f (Firm) **9** Ran SP% **118.9**
Speed ratings (Par 101): **99,98,98,97,94 93,93,91,91**
CSF £41.86 CT £362.65 TOTE £10.70: £3.30, £1.60, £3.20; EX 44.50 Trifecta £372.90.
Owner J R Dwyer **Bred** Dr D Harron **Trained** Newmarket, Suffolk
■ Stewards' Enquiry : Daniel Muscutt four-day ban: used whip above the permitted level (Jun 23-26)

FOCUS
The most competitive race of the day and a thrilling finish. The winner has been rated near last year's best.
T/Plt: £82.80 to a £1 stake. Pool: £53,976.68 - 475.61 winning units T/Qpdt: £20.10 to a £1 stake. Pool: £5,587.09 - 205.68 winning units **Mark Grantham**

3074 GOODWOOD (R-H)

Friday, June 7

OFFICIAL GOING: Good to soft (good in places; 7.0) changing to soft after race 1 (5.55)
Wind: light, behind Weather: heavy showers

3541 NOW TV AMATEUR RIDERS' H'CAP 1m 1f 11y

5:55 (5:55) (Class 5) (0-75,77) 4-Y-O+
£6,176 (£1,915; £957; £479; £400; £400) Stalls Low

Form RPR

0-00 1 **Gloweth**[37] 2277 4-9-6 **58** MissSarahBowen(5) 4 68
(Stuart Kittow) *midfield: effrt over 2f out: clsd to chse ldrs over 1f out: pressing ldr and sltly impeded jst ins fnl f: kpt on wl to ld last stride* **7/1**

413 2 shd **Anif (IRE)**[15] 2994 5-10-0 **68** MrPhilipThomas(7) 10 77
(David Evans) *chsd ldrs: effrt over 2f out: hdwy and rdn to ld 2f out: hrd pressed jst ins fnl f: kpt on wl: hdd last stride* **5/1**[2]

5-11 3 4 **French Mix (USA)**[130] 457 5-10-13 **77** MissHannahWelch(3) 9 77
(Alexandra Dunn) *chsd ldrs tl clsd to ld 3f out: hdd 2f out: unable qck over 1f out: outpcd ins fnl f* **14/1**

-054 4 4 1/2 **Edge (IRE)**[15] 2998 8-9-13 **60** (b) MissSerenaBrotherton 13 50
(Bernard Llewellyn) *hld up towards rr: hdwy to trck ldrs 3f out: unable qck u.p and btn over 1f out: wl hld and plugged on same pce fnl f* **10/1**

4-44 5 5 **Grandscape**[43] 2059 4-10-6 **72** SophieSmith(5) 1 51
(Ed Dunlop) *midfield: rdn 3f out: sn outpcd: wl hld and plugged on same pce fnl 2f* **7/2**[1]

4334 6 8 **Guvenor's Choice (IRE)**[16] 2962 4-10-12 **73** (t) MissBeckySmith 2 35
(Marjorie Fife) *in tch in midfield: effrt fnl 2f: no imp and struggling whn swtchd lft over 1f out: sn wknd* **12/1**

2140 7 2 **Dutch Uncle**[76] 1291 7-10-3 **71** (p) MrCharlesClover(7) 3 28
(Tom Clover) *v awkward leaving stalls and lost many l: steadily rcvrd and clsd on to bk of field 1/2-way: effrt 3f out: sn outpcd and wl hld 2f out: wknd (jockey said gelding was slowly away)* **16/1**

222- 8 hd **Ban Shoof**[177] 9510 6-10-0 **68** (b) MissKatyBrooks(7) 11 25
(Gary Moore) *midfield: c to outer over 3f out: pushed along: hung rt and no hdwy over 3f out: sn outpcd and n.d after* **14/1**

2553 9 7 **Majestic Moon (IRE)**[23] 2739 9-10-6 **67** (p) MrRossBirkett 5 8
(Julia Feilden) *led tl rdn and hdd 3f out: sn struggling u.p: wl btn over 1f out: wknd (jockey said gelding stopped quickly)* **5/1**[2]

000- 10 1 3/4 **Bakht A Rawan (IRE)**[228] 8486 7-10-5 **73** MrLiamSpencer(7) 8 11
(Roger Teal) *hld up in rr: u.p 3f out: no prog and wl btn after* **20/1**

03-3 11 2 1/4 **Balmoral Castle**[25] 2691 10-10-11 **75** MrJamesHarding(3) 12 8
(Jonathan Portman) *stdd after s: hld up in rr: effrt and c towards centre 3f out: sn u.p and no prog: no ch after: eased towards fin* **6/1**[3]

2051 12 nk **Mama Africa (IRE)**[36] 2346 5-10-2 **70** (p) MissImogenMathias(7) 6 2
(John Flint) *w ldr tl 3f out: sn dropped out: fdd over 1f out* **25/1**

2m 1.7s (4.30) **Going Correction** +0.575s/f (Yiel) **12** Ran SP% **126.9**
Speed ratings (Par 103): **103,102,99,95,90 83,82,81,75,74 72,71**
CSF £45.09 CT £498.84 TOTE £9.50: £3.20, £2.10, £3.60; EX 47.60 Trifecta £664.20.
Owner M E Harris **Bred** M Harris **Trained** Blackborough, Devon

FOCUS
The ground was officially described as good to soft, good in places at the start of racing and, with plenty of rain around, conditions were expected to continue to worsen. This looked hard work on the ground and very few figured in the finish. The 1-2 are rated close to their early form.

3542 LUCKY LEAP/EBF NOVICE STKS (PLUS 10 RACE) 6f

6:30 (6:31) (Class 4) 2-Y-O £6,469 (£1,925; £962; £481) Stalls High

Form RPR

1 **Guildsman (FR)** 2-9-5 0 OisinMurphy 3 90+
(Archie Watson) *dwlt and hmpd leaving stalls: hdwy to trck ldrs after 2f tl led ent fnl 2f: rdn and gng clr whn edgd lft over 1f out: r.o strly ins fnl f: v readily* **3/1**[2]

5 2 6 **Dark Kris (IRE)**[22] 2767 2-9-5 0 ShaneKelly 2 72
(Richard Hughes) *wnt lft leaving stalls: chsd ldrs tl wnt 2nd after 2f: effrt and ev ch ent fnl 2f: outpcd by wnr and btn over 1f out: edging lft but plugged on for clr 2nd ins fnl f* **10/3**[3]

3 5 **Good Earth (IRE)** 2-9-5 0 NicolaCurrie 1 57
(Jamie Osborne) *wnt rt and rn green leaving stalls: in rr: pushed along and effrt over 2f out: sn outpcd but ldng pair and wl hld 4th over 1f out: plugged on to go modest 3rd ins fnl f (jockey said colt hung right-handed)* **20/1**

4 nk **Owney Madden** 2-9-5 0 RobHornby 4 56
(Martyn Meade) *uns rdr ent stalls and loose briefly: wnt rt leaving stalls and rn green: in tch: effrt over 2f out: sn outpcd by ldng pair and wl btn over 1f out: plugged on and swtchd rt wl ins fnl f* **10/1**

54 5 1/2 **Gobi Sunset**[28] 2594 2-9-5 0 HarryBentley 8 55
(Mark Johnston) *led but hung rt: rdn and hdd ent fnl 2f: sn outpcd and wl hld 3rd over 1f out: wknd and lost 2 pls ins fnl f* **11/4**[1]

6 6 6 **Activius (IRE)**[15] 3008 2-9-5 0 MartinDwyer 7 37
(Brian Meehan) *chsd ldr for 2f: sn pushed along: struggling and outpcd over 2f out: wl bhd over 1f out* **16/1**

7 12 **Desert Palms** 2-9-5 0 AndreaAtzeni 9 1
(Richard Hannon) *s.i.s: in tch tl dropped to rr and rdn over 2f out: sn struggling and wl btn over 1f out: eased ins fnl f* **10/3**[3]

1m 14.33s (2.23) **Going Correction** +0.575s/f (Yiel) **7** Ran SP% **117.6**
Speed ratings (Par 95): **108,100,93,92,92 84,68**
CSF £14.10 TOTE £4.00: £2.30, £1.70; EX 15.60 Trifecta £161.90.
Owner Qatar Racing Limited **Bred** S C E A Haras De Saint Pair **Trained** Upper Lambourn, W Berks

FOCUS
The going was changed to soft following the running of the first race. The three previous runnings of this had been won by subsequent Group scorers, so this was a notable effort from Guildsman on debut. The opening level is fluid.

3543 GROGGER H'CAP 6f

7:05 (7:06) (Class 5) (0-70,71) 4-Y-O+
£6,404 (£1,905; £952; £476; £400; £400) Stalls High

Form RPR

0-11 1 **Spanish Star (IRE)**[15] 3014 4-9-6 **69** LiamKeniry 2 82
(Patrick Chamings) *stdd s: hld up towards rr: clsd and swtchd rt over 2f out: chsd ldrs and effrt 2f out: rdn to ld 1f out: edgd lft and asserted ins fnl f: r.o wl: readily* **9/4**[1]

05 2 2 1/4 **Savitar (IRE)**[35] 2365 4-8-12 **61** (h) TomMarquand 14 67
(Jim Boyle) *s.i.s: outpcd and detached in last: swtchd rt and racing in centre after 2f: rdn 3f out: hdwy 1f out: styd on strly to pass btn horses and go 2nd cl home: no ch w wnr (jockey said gelding was slowly away and never travelling)* **9/1**

50-5 3 1/2 **Mad Endeavour**[62] 1595 8-8-3 **52** (b) KieranO'Neill 8 56
(Stuart Kittow) *led: rdn over 2f out: hdd 1f out: no ex and wknd ins fnl f: lost 2nd towards fin* **16/1**

1105 4 2 **Foreign Legion (IRE)**[10] 3188 4-9-4 **67** (p) NickyMackay 3 65
(Luke McJannet) *chsd ldrs: effrt 2f out: unable qck u.p and outpcd over 1f out: kpt on same pce ins fnl f* **11/1**

-005 5 1/2 **Englishman**[13] 3079 9-9-5 **68** MartinDwyer 11 64
(Milton Bradley) *stdd s: hld up in rr: hdwy 1/2-way: effrt to chse ldrs and rdn 2f out: unable qck over 1f out: wknd ins fnl f* **16/1**

-600 6 3/4 **Charming Guest (IRE)**[15] 3014 4-9-5 **68** CharlesBishop 7 62
(Mick Channon) *prom in chsng gp: nt clrest of runs and shuffled bk over 2f out: swtchd rt and nt clr run over 1f out: swtchd bk lft and rdn 1f out: kpt on but no threat to wnr* **13/2**[3]

0-00 7 nse **Field Of Vision (IRE)**[24] 2717 6-9-4 **67** (p) NicolaCurrie 12 64
(John Flint) *towards rr: effrt 2f out: swtchd rt over 1f out: nt clr run and swtchd rt jst ins fnl f: sme prog but no threat to ldrs whn nt clr run again ins fnl f (jockey said gelding was denied a clear run)* **12/1**

0-00 8 3 3/4 **Alfie's Angel (IRE)**[24] 2717 5-8-8 **57** (p) RobHornby 15 38
(Milton Bradley) *chsd ldrs: unable qck u.p and lost pl over 1f out: wknd ins fnl f* **33/1**

025 9 1 1/4 **Gonzaga**[27] 2624 4-9-0 **68** RachealKneller(5) 1 45
(James Bennett) *midfield: effrt over 2f out: unable qck and btn over 1f out: hung lft and wknd ins fnl f (jockey said gelding hung left-handed under pressure)* **16/1**

0204 **10** 3 1/4 **The Groove**[15] 2997 6-9-6 **69**........................ HarryBentley 10 36
(David Evans) *hld up in tch in midfield: unable qck u.p and nt clr run jst over 1f out: sn btn and wknd ins fnl f: burst blood vessel (vet said that the gelding had bled from the nose)* **7/2**[2]

06-3 **11** 1 1/2 **Seprani**[21] 2804 5-9-1 **71**........................ StefanoCherchi(7) 13 33
(Amy Murphy) *in tch in midfield: rdn over 2f out: unable qck and lost pl over 1f out: wknd fnl f* **10/1**

010- **12** 1/2 **Flowing Clarets**[217] 8795 6-8-7 **56**........................ LiamJones 4 17
(John Bridger) *taken down early: chsd ldr: rdn and ev ch ent fnl 2f: no ex and btn over 1f out: fdd ins fnl f* **33/1**

1m 14.97s (2.87) **Going Correction** +0.575s/f (Yiel) **12** Ran SP% **125.0**
Speed ratings (Par 103): **103,100,99,96,96 95,94,89,88,83 81,81**
CSF £25.08 CT £278.66 TOTE £3.50: £2.60, £3.10, £4.10; EX 31.60 Trifecta £336.10.
Owner Shirley Symonds & Fred Camis **Bred** David Webb **Trained** Baughurst, Hants

FOCUS
This looked competitive beforehand but was won readily by the gambled on favourite.

3544 BRITISH EBF FILLIES' H'CAP 6f
7:35 (7:35) (Class 3) (0-90,90) 3-Y-O+ **£9,451** (£2,829; £1,414; £708; £352) **Stalls** High

Form RPR

30-0 **1** **Richenza (FR)**[27] 2627 4-10-0 **90**........................ HarryBentley 3 98
(Ralph Beckett) *mde all and dictated gallop: pushed along 2f out: drvn and styd on wl ins fnl f: forged ahd fnl 100yds (trainer said regarding apparent improvement in form that the yard is in better form)* **6/1**

3212 **2** 1 1/4 **Puds**[14] 3043 4-10-0 **90**........................ ShaneKelly 1 94+
(Richard Hughes) *t.k.h: chsd ldng pair tl wnt 2nd over 3f out: upsides wnr and pushed along over 1f out: drvn ins fnl f: no ex and outpcd fnl 100yds* **15/8**[1]

-343 **3** 2 3/4 **Pass The Gin**[13] 3068 3-8-12 **82**........................ OisinMurphy 7 75
(Andrew Balding) *bmpd sn after leaving stalls: t.k.h: hld up in tch: effrt over 1f out: sn u.p and outpcd by ldng pair: wnt 3rd but no imp ins fnl f* **11/4**[2]

3-10 **4** 3 1/4 **Lufricia**[36] 2319 3-8-13 **83**........................ AndreaAtzeni 5 66
(Roger Varian) *stdd and bmpd leaving stalls: t.k.h: chsd wnr tl over 3f out: unable qck u.p and btn over 1f out: wknd ins fnl f (jockey said filly ran too free)* **4/1**[3]

1121 **5** 1/2 **Second Collection**[25] 2687 3-8-9 **79**........................(h) TomMarquand 6 60
(Tony Carroll) *wnt rt and hmpd leaving stalls: t.k.h: hld up in tch in last pair: effrt ent fnl 2f: unable qck and btn over 1f out: wknd ins fnl f* **9/2**

1m 14.84s (2.74) **Going Correction** +0.575s/f (Yiel) **5** Ran SP% **113.9**
WFA 3 from 4yo 8lb
Speed ratings (Par 104): **104,102,98,94,93**
CSF £18.32 TOTE £8.20: £2.70, £1.40; EX 22.60 Trifecta £44.90.
Owner Mrs Lynn Turner & Guy Brook **Bred** S A Le Thenney **Trained** Kimpton, Hants

FOCUS
A couple of absentees on account of the deteriorating ground, though still a fair race for the level. The two top weights pulled clear and fought out a good finish. The winner's rated in line with a better view of his form.

3545 NOW TV H'CAP 1m 3f 218y
8:10 (8:10) (Class 5) (0-75,76) 4-Y-O+
£6,404 (£1,905; £952; £476; £400; £400) **Stalls** High

Form RPR

0044 **1** **Unit Of Assessment (IRE)**[25] 2691 5-9-8 **76**..........(vt) AndreaAtzeni 2 85
(William Knight) *chsd ldrs tl wnt 2nd 4f out: upsides ldr travelling strly over 2f out: rdn to ld over 1f out: edgd rt ins fnl f: forged ahd 100yds out: styd on* **8/1**

3-12 **2** 2 **Kirkland Forever**[35] 2353 5-8-6 **67**........................ GeorgiaDobie(7) 5 73+
(Eve Johnson Houghton) *short of room sn after s: hld up in last pair: hdwy 4f out: rdn to chse ldrs 2f out: ev ch u.p over 1f out tl no ex 100yds out: wknd towards fin* **6/1**[2]

4523 **3** 1 1/2 **Berrahri (IRE)**[13] 3073 8-9-7 **75**........................ KierenFox 1 78
(John Best) *led and brought field to stands' side over 3f out: rdn over 2f out: hdd over 1f out: kpt on same pce u.p fr over 1f out* **7/1**[3]

52-0 **4** 5 **Horatio Star**[39] 2208 4-9-6 **74**........................ MartinDwyer 8 69
(Brian Meehan) *shifted rt leaving stalls: chsd ldr for 1f: styd chsng ldrs: rdn 3f out: unable qck and outpcd 2f out: wl hld and plugged on same pce after* **8/1**

-015 **5** 1 **Carp Kid (IRE)**[21] 2793 4-9-6 **74**........................(p) OisinMurphy 11 68
(John Flint) *chsd ldr after 1f tl 4f out: sn rdn: outpcd u.p 2f out: wl hld and plugged on same pce fr over 1f out* **5/1**[1]

04-0 **6** 1 **Marengo**[28] 2577 8-9-5 **73**........................(p) DanielMuscutt 4 65
(Bernard Llewellyn) *rousted along and jostled sn after leaving stalls: in tch in midfield: drvn and nt qckn over 2f out: sn outpcd: wl hld and plugged on same pce fnl 2f* **28/1**

201 **7** 2 1/4 **Lost History (IRE)**[7] 3321 6-9-5 **76** 5ex........................ JaneElliott(3) 9 65
(John Spearing) *hld up in tch in midfield: effrt over 2f out: sn u.p and no imp: wl btn over 1f out: wknd fnl f* **9/1**

04-4 **8** 3 3/4 **Cacophonous**[35] 2353 4-9-3 **71**........................(v[1]) JasonWatson 12 54
(David Menuisier) *s.i.s: hld up in last pair: rdn 4f out: no imp and btn 2f out: no ch whn swtchd lft over 1f out (jockey said gelding was never traveling. trainer said gelding did not face the first-time visor)* **5/1**[1]

434 **9** 3 **Famous Dynasty (IRE)**[53] 1826 5-8-8 **62**........................ RobHornby 3 40
(Michael Blanshard) *hld up in last quartet: effrt and sme hdwy u.p over 2f out: sn btn and wknd over 1f out* **20/1**

54-2 **10** 10 **French Riviera (FR)**[63] 1569 4-9-5 **73**........................ HarryBentley 6 35
(Ralph Beckett) *hmpd sn after s: t.k.h: hld up in tch in midfield: effrt wl over 2f out: sn rdn and bhd fnl 2f (jockey said filly suffered interference at the start and ran too free)* **5/1**[1]

0-06 **11** 34 **Ace Combat**[12] 1826 4-8-9 **63**........................ KieranO'Neill 7
(Michael Madgwick) *a towards rr: rdn over 4f out: sn btn: bhd and eased fnl 2f: t.o* **40/1**

2m 44.77s (5.17) **Going Correction** +0.575s/f (Yiel) **11** Ran SP% **119.7**
Speed ratings (Par 103): **105,103,102,99,98 98,96,94,92,85 62**
CSF £55.27 CT £359.63 TOTE £7.70: £2.80, £2.30, £2.60; EX 52.30 Trifecta £346.70.
Owner A Hetherton **Bred** Barouche Stud (IRE) Ltd **Trained** Angmering, W Sussex

FOCUS
An ordinary handicap. The winner's rated in line with his better AW form.

3546 MK FILLIES' NOVICE STKS 1m
8:40 (8:43) (Class 4) 3-Y-O+ **£6,469** (£1,925; £962; £481) **Stalls** Low

Form RPR

4-2 **1** **Be More**[31] 2507 3-8-10 **0**........................ OisinMurphy 8 86
(Andrew Balding) *wnt lft leaving stalls: mde all and styd wd early: shkn up 2f out: rdn over 1f out: styd on strly ins fnl f* **11/8**[2]

4 **2** 1 1/2 **Clarion**[22] 2762 3-8-10 **0**........................ JasonWatson 1 82
(Sir Michael Stoute) *t.k.h early: trckd ldrs tl wnt 2nd over 3f out: effrt 2f out: drvn over 1f out: kpt on same pce ins fnl f* **11/10**[1]

5 **3** 8 **Society Guest (IRE)**[18] 2919 3-8-10 **0**........................ CallumShepherd 2 64
(Mick Channon) *t.k.h: hld up in tch in midfield: effrt to chse ldng pair 2f out: sn u.p and outpcd: wknd but hld on to 3rd ins fnl f* **7/1**[3]

0 **4** 1 1/2 **Uncertain Smile (IRE)**[15] 3013 3-8-7 **0**........................ MitchGodwin(3) 4 61
(Clive Cox) *plld hrd: chsd wnr tl over 3f out: rdn ent fnl 2f: sn outpcd and btn: wknd ins fnl f (jockey said ran too free early on)* **20/1**

00 **5** shd **Misty**[32] 2488 3-8-10 **0**........................ HarryBentley 3 60
(Ralph Beckett) *short of room sn after s: hld up in tch in last pair: effrt over 2f out: sn u.p and outpcd 2f out: wknd ins fnl f* **16/1**

6 3/4 **Chamomile** 3-8-10 **0**........................ KieranO'Neill 7 59
(Daniel Kubler) *in tch in midfield: effrt over 2f out: unable qck and wl hld whn hung rt over 1f out* **25/1**

05 **7** 2 1/4 **Avorisk Et Perils (FR)**[13] 3080 4-9-7 **0**........................ HectorCrouch 5 56
(Gary Moore) *t.k.h: stdd after s: hld up in tch in rr: effrt and swtchd rt 2f out: sn btn and wknd fnl f* **50/1**

1m 43.61s (4.41) **Going Correction** +0.575s/f (Yiel)
WFA 3 from 4yo 11lb **7** Ran SP% **118.7**
Speed ratings (Par 102): **100,98,90,89,88 88,85**
CSF £3.36 TOTE £2.20: £1.40, £1.30; EX 3.50 Trifecta £6.80.
Owner George Strawbridge **Bred** George Strawbridge **Trained** Kingsclere, Hants

FOCUS
This lacked depth and was dominated by the two at the head of the betting, though not in the order the market expected. It's hard to pin down the form with the pair clear on soft ground.
T/Plt: £110.80 to a £1 stake. Pool: £62,221.75 - 409.88 winning units T/Qpdt: £9.60 to a £1 stake. Pool: £6,993.53 - 538.45 winning units **Steve Payne**

3505
HAYDOCK (L-H)
Friday, June 7

OFFICIAL GOING: Heavy (6.4)
Wind: Moderate, half behind in straight of over 4f Weather: Rain

3547 HAYDOCK PARK TRAINING SERIES APPRENTICE H'CAP (PART OF THE RACING EXCELLENCE INITIATIVE) 1m 2f 42y
5:50 (5:52) (Class 5) (0-70,71) 4-Y-O+
£4,851 (£1,443; £721; £400; £400; £400) **Stalls** Centre

Form RPR

0640 **1** **Motahassen (IRE)**[11] 3163 5-8-8 **55**..............(t) CianMacRedmond(3) 10 64
(Declan Carroll) *in rr: hdwy over 2f out: styd on to ld fnl 110yds: won gng away (trainer said regarding apparent improvement in form that the gelding had appreciated the slower ground, which was officially described as Heavy on this occasion)* **5/1**[2]

-643 **2** 2 **Milan Reef (IRE)**[7] 3296 4-8-8 **55**........................ JessicaCooley(3) 7 60
(David Loughnane) *chsd ldr: rdn over 2f out: chalng over 1f out: stl ev ch ins fnl f: styd on same pce fnl 75yds and no match for wnr* **3/1**[1]

660- **3** 1 **Pioneering (IRE)**[210] 8974 5-9-8 **69**........................ TristanPrice(3) 1 72
(Roger Fell) *led: rdn over 2f out: edgd lft over 1f out: hdd fnl 110yds: kpt on same pce towards fin* **7/1**[3]

0562 **4** 1 **Beatbybeatbybeat**[8] 3267 6-9-5 **63**........................(v) KieranSchofield 4 64
(Antony Brittain) *midfield: hdwy over 3f out: rdn to chse ldrs over 2f out: chalng ins fnl f: eased whn no ex towards fin* **7/1**[3]

1-00 **5** 5 **Overtrumped**[27] 2617 4-8-12 **61**........................ LukeCatton(5) 5 52
(Mike Murphy) *towards rr: rdn over 4f out: hdwy over 2f out: kpt on ins fnl f: nvr able to trble ldrs* **14/1**

210- **6** 1 1/4 **Maroc**[29] 7717 6-9-12 **70**........................(p) CierenFallon 8 59
(Nikki Evans) *chsd ldrs: rdn 4f out: one pce fnl 2f (jockey said that gelding was unsuited by the ground, which was officially described as heavy on this occasion, and would prefer a faster surface)* **16/1**

50-0 **7** 3/4 **Inflexiball**[38] 2244 7-8-4 **51**........................ EllaMcCain(3) 13 38
(John Mackie) *s.i.s: midfield: rdn 3f out and outpcd: plugged on ins fnl f: nvr a threat* **33/1**

-043 **8** 1/2 **Quoteline Direct**[14] 3053 6-9-6 **67**........................(h) GavinAshton(3) 2 53
(Micky Hammond) *midfield: rdn over 2f out: no imp* **9/1**

1160 **9** 2 1/4 **False Id**[14] 3046 6-9-4 **65**........................(b) RhonaPindar(3) 6 47
(David Loughnane) *hld up: plld hrd and hdwy over 6f out: sn chsd ldrs: rdn over 2f out: wknd over 1f out* **10/1**

6632 **10** 1/2 **Ghayyar (IRE)**[9] 3216 5-9-13 **71**........................(tp) RobertDodsworth 11 52
(Tim Easterby) *hld up: plld hrd: rdn 4f out: nvr a threat (jockey said gelding ran too freely and was unable to get cover from a wide draw)* **7/1**[3]

25-0 **11** 3 3/4 **Pilot Wings (IRE)**[60] 1653 4-9-7 **68**........................ HarryRussell(3) 3 41
(David Dennis) *chsd ldrs: pushed along 5f out: rdn and wknd over 2f out* **16/1**

456 **12** 6 **Captain Scott (IRE)**[46] 1989 4-9-4 **65**........................ SeanKirrane(3) 12 26
(Heather Main) *in tch: pushed along and outpcd 5f out: wknd over 2f out* **12/1**

2m 17.65s (6.85) **Going Correction** +0.425s/f (Yiel) **12** Ran SP% **127.3**
Speed ratings (Par 103): **89,87,86,85,81 80,80,79,78,77 74,69**
CSF £21.99 CT £112.21 TOTE £5.70: £2.00, £1.80, £2.70; EX 22.50 Trifecta £169.30.
Owner Mrs Sarah Bryan **Bred** Diomed Bloodstock Ltd **Trained** Malton, N Yorks
■ Stewards' Enquiry : Tristan Price seven-day ban: Improper riding (June 21-27)

FOCUS
After plenty of rain throughout the day the going was changed from soft to heavy. All races were run on the inner home straight and the opening race distance was increased by 37 yards. They went a good pace in this apprentice handicap and the winner came from last to first. The time was just over 12 seconds slower than standard. The winner built on the promise of his penultimate run.

3548 JOIN RACING TV NOW H'CAP 1m 2f 42y
6:20 (6:21) (Class 4) (0-85,87) 3-Y-O
£7,115 (£2,117; £1,058; £529; £400; £400) **Stalls** Centre

Form RPR

-601 **1** **Jackamundo (FR)**[28] 2582 3-8-11 **75**........................ KevinStott 4 86
(Declan Carroll) *chsd ldrs: gng wl over 2f out: sn led: rdn clr over 1f out: styd on wl: eased towards fin* **11/4**[2]

560- **2** 5 **Francisco Bay**[196] 9227 3-8-5 **69**........................ AndrewMullen 3 70
(Ed de Giles) *hld up: pushed along over 4f out: nt clr run over 3f out: angled out over 2f out: hdwy sn after: drvn and ev ch briefly 2f out: unable to go w wnr over 1f out: no imp after* **50/1**

4-10 **3** 7 **Korcho**[20] 2828 3-9-4 **82**........................ PJMcDonald 1 69
(Hughie Morrison) *hld up in tch: hdwy 3f out: rdn to chse ldrs over 2f out: one pce fr over 1f out* **2/1**[1]

10-5 **4** *2 ¼* **Lola's Theme**[29] 2559 3-9-2 **80**................................ RichardKingscote 2 63
(Tom Dascombe) *prom: pushed along over 3f out: outpcd over 2f out: plugged on fnl f but no ch* **6/1**

01-4 **5** *4* **Felix The Poet**[13] 3086 3-9-9 **87**..............................(p[1]) DavidAllan 8 62
(Archie Watson) *prom: led wl over 2f out: rdn and hdd 2f out: wknd over 1f out* **20/1**

1-36 **6** *nk* **Cape Islay (FR)**[27] 2618 3-9-5 **83**.............................. FrannyNorton 6 57
(Mark Johnston) *led: hdd wl over 2f out: sn rdn: wknd over 1f out* **10/1**

43-6 **7** *2* **Over The Guns (IRE)**[36] 2333 3-8-10 **74**.................(b) ConnorBeasley 7 44
(K R Burke) *midfield: pushed along over 4f out: sn lost pl: wknd over 2f out* **25/1**

12-4 **8** *38* **Felix**[42] 2075 3-9-7 **85**..(t) DavidEgan 5
(Sir Michael Stoute) *pushed along early in rr: drvn over 3f out: sn no imp: wknd over 2f out: eased whn wl btn over 1f out (trainer's rep said colt had a breathing problem and was unsuited by the ground)* **3/1**[3]

2m 16.33s (5.53) **Going Correction** +0.425s/f (Yiel) **8** Ran SP% **118.9**
Speed ratings (Par 101): **94,90,84,82,79 79,77,47**
CSF £134.38 CT £337.66 TOTE £4.30: £1.50, £8.30, £1.20; EX 158.70 Trifecta £521.00.
Owner Danny Fantom **Bred** John Kilpatrick **Trained** Malton, N Yorks

FOCUS
Race distance increased by 37 yards. The pace was steady and they were tightly grouped for a long way but they eventually finished well strung out behind the emphatic winner. It's hard to pin down this heavy-ground form.

3549 CJM MAINTENANCE H'CAP (DIV I) 6f
6:55 (6:56) (Class 5) (0-75,75) 4-Y-0+
£4,851 (£1,443; £721; £400; £400; £400) **Stalls** Centre

Form RPR

0403 **1** **Somewhere Secret**[9] 3215 5-8-3 **57**..............................(p) NathanEvans 9 66
(Michael Mullineaux) *mde most: rdn over 1f out: all out towards fin: jst hld on* **5/1**[1]

5-00 **2** *hd* **Shortbackandsides (IRE)**[20] 2846 4-8-8 **62**............... DuranFentiman 7 70
(Tim Easterby) *midfield: rdn 2f out: hdwy over 1f out: sn in 2nd pl: r.o for press towards fin: jst hld* **7/1**[2]

2306 **3** *1 ¼* **Madrinho (IRE)**[21] 2804 6-9-6 **74**.............................. FrannyNorton 11 78
(Tony Carroll) *hld up: rdn over 2f out: hdwy whn sltly short of room and checked over 1f out: r.o u.p and gng on at fin* **8/1**[3]

5410 **4** *¾* **Rasheeq (IRE)**[20] 2846 6-8-8 **69**..............................(p) CierenFallon[(7)] 10 71
(Mohamed Moubarak) *racd keenly: chsd ldrs: drvn over 2f out: unable qck ent fnl f: styd on same pce after* **5/1**[1]

0-00 **5** *1* **Mutafarrid (IRE)**[20] 2841 4-9-7 **75**.............................. KevinStott 2 73
(Paul Midgley) *in rr: rdn over 1f out: hdwy ent fnl f: kpt on for press: one pce fnl 75yds* **33/1**

15-0 **6** *1* **Delilah Park**[32] 2484 5-9-2 **70**.............................. DavidAllan 1 65
(Chris Wall) *racd keenly in midfield: effrt over 1f out: kpt on same pce fnl 100yds* **14/1**

5230 **7** *hd* **Lucky Lodge**[27] 2638 9-8-2 **56** oh1..............................(v) CamHardie 5 51
(Antony Brittain) *chsd ldrs: rdn over 2f out: outpcd over 1f out: kpt on fnl 100yds* **7/1**[2]

-403 **8** *1* **Redrosezorro**[18] 2893 5-8-13 **67**..............................(h) RachelRichardson 3 58
(Eric Alston) *prom: ev ch 2f out: rdn over 1f out: nt pce of ldrs ins fnl f: wknd fnl 75yds* **7/1**[2]

-400 **9** *1 ½* **Champagne Bob**[4] 3430 7-8-4 **58**.............................. HollieDoyle 4 45
(Richard Price) *midfield: pushed along over 3f out: drvn and outpcd over 2f out: n.d after* **7/1**[2]

1230 **10** *nk* **Sir Ottoman (FR)**[17] 2929 6-8-12 **66**..............................(tp) JasonHart 8 52
(Ivan Furtado) *w wnr tl rdn wl over 1f out: wknd fnl 150yds* **12/1**

544- **11** *2* **Pickett's Charge**[184] 9414 6-9-2 **73**.............................. BenRobinson[(3)] 6 52
(Brian Ellison) *dwlt: in rr: pushed along and outpcd over 2f out: nvr a threat* **10/1**

1m 14.54s (0.64) **Going Correction** +0.425s/f (Yiel) **11** Ran SP% **120.8**
Speed ratings (Par 103): **105,104,103,102,100 99,99,97,95,95 92**
CSF £40.72 CT £282.20 TOTE £5.90: £2.00, £2.60, £3.10; EX 49.10 Trifecta £452.20.
Owner Mia Racing **Bred** Mia Racing **Trained** Alpraham, Cheshire

FOCUS
They raced up the centre of the track and the winner toughed it out under a positive ride. The winner's rated up a length on this year's form.

3550 CJM MAINTENANCE H'CAP (DIV II) 6f
7:25 (7:29) (Class 5) (0-75,75) 4-Y-0+
£4,851 (£1,443; £721; £400; £400; £400) **Stalls** Centre

Form RPR

-504 **1** **John Kirkup**[18] 2899 4-9-6 **74**..............................(p) ConnorBeasley 7 84
(Michael Dods) *chsd ldrs: rdn over 2f out: wnt 2nd over 1f out: nosed ahd fnl 110yds: asserted nr fin* **4/1**[2]

6000 **2** *½* **Mutabaahy (IRE)**[48] 1952 4-8-13 **67**.............................. CamHardie 8 75
(Antony Brittain) *led: rdn over 1f out: hdd narrowly fnl 110yds: outpcd by wnr nr fin* **14/1**

1012 **3** *1 ½* **Tricky Dicky**[10] 3206 6-8-6 **65**.............................. BenSanderson[(5)] 5 68
(Roger Fell) *w ldr: rdn over 2f out: lost 2nd over 1f out: stl there styng on ins fnl f: kpt on same pce fnl 75yds* **5/2**[1]

3040 **4** *nk* **Suzi's Connoisseur**[21] 2804 8-9-4 **72**..............................(b) DavidEgan 3 74
(Jane Chapple-Hyam) *hld up: rdn and hdwy over 1f out: sn edgd rt: styd on towards fin: nvr able to chal* **6/1**[3]

1306 **5** *2 ¼* **Peachey Carnehan**[32] 2478 5-8-7 **61**..............................(v) NathanEvans 9 56
(Michael Mullineaux) *hld up: rdn 1/2-way: kpt on ins fnl f: nvr able to trble ldrs* **16/1**

-503 **6** *1 ¾* **Danehill Desert (IRE)**[27] 2638 4-8-0 **59** ow2.............................. SeanDavis[(5)] 4 48
(Richard Fahey) *midfield: rdn over 2f out: nvr able to chal* **12/1**

0000 **7** *shd* **Stoneyford Lane (IRE)**[10] 3199 5-8-3 **57**.............................. PaddyMathers 1 46
(Steph Hollinshead) *no bttr than midfield: rdn and outpcd over 3f out: nvr got involved* **12/1**

4001 **8** *½* **Afandem (IRE)**[7] 3291 5-8-13 **67** 5ex..............................(p) DuranFentiman 6 55
(Tim Easterby) *dwlt: midfield: effrt over 1f out: no imp: wknd fnl 150yds* **4/1**[2]

5-00 **9** *17* **Case Key**[14] 3056 6-8-10 **69**..............................(p) TheodoreLadd[(5)] 10 2
(Michael Appleby) *chsd ldrs: drvn over 2f out: wknd over 1f out (jockey said gelding stopped quickly)* **11/1**

1m 15.02s (1.12) **Going Correction** +0.425s/f (Yiel) **9** Ran SP% **119.1**
Speed ratings (Par 103): **102,101,99,98,95 93,93,92,70**
CSF £59.90 CT £169.44 TOTE £4.60: £1.90, £4.30, £1.20; EX 60.00 Trifecta £259.90.
Owner Mrs Suzanne Kirkup & Kevin Kirkup **Bred** W M Lidsey **Trained** Denton, Co Durham

FOCUS
The first three were always prominent and the hold-up performers couldn't get involved in the second division of this sprint handicap. The winner's rated close to his 3yo form.

3551 BRITISH STALLION STUDS EBF NOVICE STKS (PLUS 10 RACE) 6f 212y
8:00 (8:00) (Class 4) 2-Y-O **£7,051** (£2,098; £1,048; £524) **Stalls** Low

Form RPR

1 **Juan Elcano** 2-9-5 0.............................. KevinStott 3 86+
(Kevin Ryan) *s.s: towards rr: pushed along 4f out: rdn and hdwy 2f out: edgd rt over 1f out: sn chsd ldr: styd on ins fnl f: led nr fin* **6/4**[1]

2 *nk* **Subjectivist** 2-9-5 0.............................. FrannyNorton 5 85+
(Mark Johnston) *chsd ldr: led wl over 1f out: sn edgd lft: styd on ins fnl f: all out and ct nr fin* **3/1**[2]

3 *8* **World Title (IRE)** 2-9-5 0.............................. HollieDoyle 2 65
(Archie Watson) *chsd ldrs: drvn 2f out: intimidated and wnt rt over 1f out: one pce and no ch w front two fnl f* **4/1**[3]

4 **4** *1 ½* **Mellad**[16] 2957 2-9-5 0.............................. PaulHanagan 4 62
(Richard Fahey) *led: rdn and hdd wl over 1f out: sn wl hld* **4/1**[3]

5 *6* **Saoirse's Gift (IRE)** 2-9-5 0.............................. DavidAllan 6 47
(Tim Easterby) *dwlt: in rr: hdwy over 3f out: rdn over 2f out: sn wknd* **12/1**

6 *nk* **Dwyfran** 2-9-0 0.............................. JasonHart 1 41
(David Loughnane) *chsd ldrs: lost pl 3f out: rdn and wknd over 2f out* **20/1**

1m 32.37s (3.07) **Going Correction** +0.425s/f (Yiel) **6** Ran SP% **117.5**
Speed ratings (Par 95): **99,98,89,87,80 80**
CSF £6.73 TOTE £2.00: £1.50, £2.00; EX 5.90 Trifecta £20.40.
Owner Sheikh Mohammed Obaid Al Maktoum **Bred** Mr & Mrs David Brown **Trained** Hambleton, N Yorks

FOCUS
Race distance increased by 15 yards. There wasn't much form to go on but the two market leaders pulled well clear in this novice event.

3552 WATCH IRISH RACING ON RACING TV FILLIES' H'CAP 6f 212y
8:30 (8:31) (Class 4) (0-85,81) 3-Y-O **£7,115** (£2,117; £1,058; £529; £400) **Stalls** Low

Form RPR

-231 **1** **Astrologer**[24] 2713 3-9-7 **81**.............................. DavidNolan 6 88
(David O'Meara) *mde all: rdn over 1f out: styd on wl fnl f* **3/1**[2]

-416 **2** *1 ¾* **Material Girl**[22] 2760 3-8-7 **74**..............................(p) SeanKirrane[(7)] 5 76
(Richard Spencer) *chsd wnr for nrly 1f: in tch: effrt 2f out: kpt on to take 2nd ins fnl f: no imp* **3/1**[2]

1111 **3** *1* **Kylie Rules**[9] 3216 4-10-1 **79** 5ex.............................. TomEaves 1 82
(Ruth Carr) *stdd s: racd keenly: hld up: hdwy over 3f out: chsd wnr over 2f out: rdn over 1f out: no imp: lost 2nd ins fnl f: styd on same pce towards fin* **13/8**[1]

5115 **4** *7* **Plumette**[18] 2897 3-9-0 **74**..............................(t[1]) HollieDoyle 4 55
(David Loughnane) *chsd ldrs: rdn and no imp over 1f out: no ch ins fnl f* **8/1**

21-5 **5** *4* **Mums Hope**[7] 3323 3-9-6 **80**.............................. PJMcDonald 2 51
(Hughie Morrison) *s.i.s: chsd wnr after nrly 1f: rdn and lost 2nd over 2f out: wknd over 1f out* **5/1**[3]

1m 32.54s (3.24) **Going Correction** +0.425s/f (Yiel)
WFA 3 from 4yo 10lb **5** Ran SP% **115.9**
Speed ratings (Par 102): **98,96,94,86,82**
CSF £12.96 TOTE £4.10: £2.00, £2.10; EX 13.80 Trifecta £26.50.
Owner Cheveley Park Stud **Bred** Cheveley Park Stud Ltd **Trained** Upper Helmsley, N Yorks

FOCUS
Race distance increased by 15 yards. The winner made all to complete a double in this handicap, improving on her Beverley form.

3553 WATCH RACING TV FILLIES' NOVICE STKS 1m 3f 140y
9:00 (9:02) (Class 3) 3-Y-O+ **£9,703** (£2,887; £1,443; £721) **Stalls** Centre

Form RPR

0 **1** **Monica Sheriff**[22] 2770 3-8-11 0.............................. PJMcDonald 3 79
(William Haggas) *midfield: hdwy 3f out: rdn over 2f out: chalng over 1f out: led ins fnl f: styd on towards fin* **7/1**

01 **2** *¾* **Motivate Me (FR)**[22] 2770 3-9-3 0.............................. JackMitchell 4 84
(Roger Varian) *chsd ldrs: rdn over 2f out: led over 1f out: hdd ins fnl f: kpt on: hld towards fin* **11/4**[1]

3 *1* **Ahorsewithnoname**[45] 4-9-9 0.............................. BenRobinson[(3)] 1 76
(Brian Ellison) *hld up: pushed along over 3f out: hdwy over 2 out: chalng ins fnl f: styd on same pce towards fin* **12/1**

0-0 **4** *4 ½* **Wannie Mae (IRE)**[22] 2771 3-8-11 0.............................. PaulHanagan 5 69
(William Haggas) *midfield: rdn over 3f out: hdwy over 1f out: kpt on ins fnl f: nt trble front three* **12/1**

0 **5** *7* **Earth And Sky (USA)**[28] 2581 3-8-11 0.............................. DavidEgan 14 58
(George Scott) *led after over 1f out: rdn over 2f out: hdd over 1f out: wknd ins fnl f* **14/1**

50 **6** *½* **Kenica (IRE)**[19] 2875 3-8-4 0.............................. RhonaPindar[(7)] 9 57
(K R Burke) *midfield: rdn and outpcd over 3f out: n.d after* **25/1**

5 **7** *1 ½* **Dubious Affair (IRE)**[35] 2361 3-8-11 0.............................. JamieSpencer 7 55
(Sir Michael Stoute) *led for over 1f: chsd ldr tl rdn and edgd lft over 2f out: wknd over 1f out* **7/2**[3]

5 **8** *½* **Vintage Rose**[10] 3200 3-8-11 0.............................. KevinStott 6 54
(Mark Walford) *hld up: rdn over 3f out: nvr able to trble ldrs* **50/1**

00 **9** *nk* **Video Diva (IRE)**[35] 2361 3-8-11 0.............................. GeorgeWood 13 54
(James Fanshawe) *chsd ldrs: rdn 3f out: wknd over 1f out* **40/1**

2 **10** *18* **High Above**[20] 2838 3-8-11 0.............................. RichardKingscote 2 25
(Charlie Fellowes) *midfield tl rdn and wknd 3f out: eased whn wl btn over 1f out (trainer's rep said that the filly was unsuited by the ground, which was officially described as Heavy on this occasion, and would prefer a faster surface)* **3/1**[2]

0 **11** *27* **Quiet Shy (FR)**[22] 2771 4-9-12 0.............................. TomEaves 11
(Michael Scudamore) *towards rr: rdn over 3f out: eased whn wl btn over 2f out* **40/1**

0 **12** *44* **Piccolo Ramoscello**[13] 3067 6-9-5 0.............................. ElishaWhittington[(7)] 10
(Lisa Williamson) *sn chsd ldrs: rdn over 4f out: sn wknd: lft bhd over 3f out: t.o* **50/1**

2m 36.91s (3.61) **Going Correction** +0.425s/f (Yiel)
WFA 3 from 4yo+ 15lb **12** Ran SP% **121.1**
Speed ratings (Par 104): **98,97,96,93,89 88,87,87,87,75 57,27**
CSF £25.19 TOTE £8.10: £2.20, £1.60, £2.80; EX 30.40 Trifecta £180.00.
Owner Duke Of Devonshire **Bred** The Duke Of Devonshire **Trained** Newmarket, Suffolk
■ Local Affair was withdrawn. Price at time of withdrawal 12-1. Rule 4 applies to all bets. Deduction - 5p in the pound.

The Form Book Flat 2019, Raceform Ltd, Newbury, RG14 5SJ

FOCUS
Race distance increased by 30 yards. They went a decent pace in this interesting fillies' novice event and the first three pulled clear. The sixth and eighth help with the level. Local Affair refused to enter the stalls and was withdrawn.
T/Jkpt: Not won. T/Plt: £47.90 to a £1 stake. Pool: £62,873.21 - 957.77 winning units T/Qpdt: £14.50 to a £1 stake. Pool: £6,602.75 - 336.56 winning units **Darren Owen**

3554 - 3556a (Foreign Racing) - See Raceform Interactive

3111 CURRAGH (R-H)
Friday, June 7

OFFICIAL GOING: Good to yielding (yielding in places on straight course)

3557a TRM - EXCELLENCE IN EQUINE NUTRITION BALLYOGAN STKS (GROUP 3) (F&M) 6f
7:10 (7:11) 3-Y-0+

£33,486 (£10,783; £5,108; £2,270; £1,135; £567) **Stalls** Centre

RPR

1 **Soffia**[19] 2880 4-9-6 102 .... DeclanMcDonogh 10 107
(Edward Lynam, Ire) *cl up nr side: gng wl in 2nd after 1/2-way and led 2f out: rdn ins fnl f and strly pressed nr fin: hld on* 11/4[2]

2 *nk* **Dan's Dream**[32] 2493 4-9-6 107 .... RonanWhelan 5 106+
(Mick Channon) *chsd ldrs nr side early: pushed along over 2f out and clsd u.p fr over 1f out: wnt 3rd wl ins fnl f and r.o far side to strly press wnr nr fin: jst hld* 3/1[3]

3 *1/2* **Queen Jo Jo**[27] 2627 3-8-12 98 .... DanielTudhope 7 102
(Kevin Ryan) *dwlt sltly: w.w towards rr nr side early: clsr in 4th fr 1/2-way: prog 2f out: sn rdn in 2nd and no imp on wnr wl ins fnl f where dropped to 3rd: kpt on wl* 4/1

4 *4 1/2* **Julia's Magic (IRE)**[19] 2880 4-9-6 92 .... GaryCarroll 4 90
(Mrs Denise Foster, Ire) *cl up nr side: pushed along in 3rd after 1/2-way and no imp on ldrs u.p in 5th over 1f out: kpt on one pce ins fnl f into 4th cl home* 16/1

5 *nk* **Lethal Promise (IRE)**[28] 2605 3-8-12 101 ....(h) WJLee 3 87
(W McCreery, Ire) *sn led far side: hdd 2f out: sn rdn and no ex bhd ldrs over 1f out: wknd in 4th ins fnl f: denied 4th cl home* 9/4[1]

6 *1 3/4* **Rapid Reaction (IRE)**[19] 2880 4-9-6 84 .... AndrewSlattery 1 83
(J F Grogan, Ire) *led narrowly far side early tl sn hdd and settled bhd ldr: 5th fr 1/2-way: rdn and no ex 2f out: one pce after* 50/1

7 *6* **Sakura (FR)**[65] 1533 3-8-12 69 .... RobbieColgan 9 62
(Ms Sheila Lavery, Ire) *chsd ldrs nr side early: disp 6th at 1/2-way: pushed along in 7th after 1/2-way and no imp under 2f out: wknd* 66/1

8 *14* **Mm Sixsevei (IRE)**[389] 2719 4-9-6 96 .... ColmO'Donoghue 11 19
(John M Oxx, Ire) *dwlt: in rr thrght: no imp detached bef 1/2-way: nvr a factor* 25/1

1m 13.86s (-0.34) **Going Correction** +0.275s/f (Good)
WFA 3 from 4yo 8lb 8 Ran SP% 115.6
Speed ratings: **113,112,111,105,105 103,95,76**
CSF £11.50 TOTE £3.50: £1.10, £1.20, £1.40; DF 10.80 Trifecta £35.30.
Owner Lady O'Reilly **Bred** Newsells Park Stud **Trained** Dunshaughlin, Co Meath
■ Stewards' Enquiry : Ronan Whelan two-day ban: excessive use of whip (tba)

FOCUS
This trip might just be at the limits of her stamina, but it was a very gutsy performance from the winner. She's rated to her mark.

3558 - 3560a (Foreign Racing) - See Raceform Interactive

2646 BELMONT PARK (L-H)
Friday, June 7

OFFICIAL GOING: Dirt: fast; turf: firm

3561a BELMONT GOLD CUP INVITATIONAL STKS (GRADE 2) (4YO+) (WIDENER TURF) (TURF) 2m (T)
10:48 4-Y-0+

£173,228 (£62,992; £37,795; £18,897; £9,448; £6,299)

RPR

1 **Amade (IRE)**[49] 1917 5-8-7 0 ....(b) FlavienPrat 3 108
(G Botti, France) 66/10

2 *nk* **Arklow (USA)**[27] 2646 5-8-11 0 .... FlorentGeroux 6 112
(Brad H Cox, U.S.A) 41/20[1]

3 *1* **Highland Sky (USA)**[69] 6-8-3 0 ....(b) ManuelFranco 5 103
(Barclay Tagg, U.S.A) 28/1

4 *1/2* **Canessar (FR)**[48] 6-8-6 0 ow3 .... JoelRosario 8 105
(Arnaud Delacour, U.S.A) 19/5[3]

5 *1 1/2* **Red Knight (USA)**[48] 5-8-3 0 .... JoseLOrtiz 4 101
(William Mott, U.S.A) 23/10[2]

6 *2 3/4* **Raa Atoll**[26] 2666 4-8-9 0 .... JozefBojko 7 105
(Luke Comer, Ire) *pressed ldr: rdn and chal strly fr 2f out: sing to drop away whn squeezed for room and stdd fnl half f* 36/5

7 *2 3/4* **Mootasadir**[21] 2807 4-8-9 0 .... BenCurtis 1 102
(Hugo Palmer) *pushed along fr stalls to ld: pressed thrght: hrd rdn 2 1/2f out: hdd ins last 1 1/2f: grad fdd* 191/10

8 *1* **Noble Thought (USA)**[22] 6-8-4 0 ow1 ....(b) IradOrtizJr 2 95
(Michael J Maker, U.S.A) 44/1

3m 19.95s 8 Ran SP% 119.9

Owner OTI Racing, Lauren Dassault & Elisa Berte **Bred** Eamonn McEvoy **Trained** France

2026 COMPIEGNE (L-H)
Friday, June 7

OFFICIAL GOING: Turf: soft

3562a PRIX DE CAISNES (CLAIMER) (2YO) (TURF) 7f
12:50 2-Y-0 £8,558 (£3,423; £2,567; £1,711; £855)

RPR

1 **Salar Island (ITY)** 2-8-11 0 .... CristianDemuro 6 78+
(Andrea Marcialis, France) 57/10[3]

2 *3* **Spencer** 2-8-9 0 .... ErwannLebreton(6) 5 74
(P De Chevigny, France) 43/1

3 *4* **Atlantica (FR)** 2-9-1 0 ....(p) MaximeGuyon 8 64
(P Monfort, France) 43/5

4 *1/2* **Can't Hold Us (FR)**[58] 1709 2-8-5 0 .... MlleAlisonMassin(3) 7 56
(D Allard, France) 29/1

5 *nk* **Brown Eyes Blue (IRE)**[39] 2205 2-8-9 0 ow1 ....(b) TonyPiccone 9 56
(J S Moore) *towards rr: no imp u.p fr 2 1/2f out: kpt on ins fnl f: nvr trbld ldrs* 16/1

6 *1 1/2* **Kikana (FR)** 2-9-4 0 .... StephanePasquier 4 61
(L Rovisse, France) 6/4[1]

7 *4 1/2* **Swiss Bond**[15] 2996 2-8-11 0 .... MickaelBarzalona 10 43
(J S Moore) *racd in fnl trio: no hdwy whn asked wl over 2f out: kpt on at same pce* 23/10[2]

8 *shd* **Saga Bee (FR)**[21] 2-8-8 0 .... AnthonyCrastus 2 40
(C Boutin, France) 42/1

9 *snk* **Proun (FR)**[58] 1709 2-8-3 0 .... ThomasTrullier(5) 3 39
(Andrea Marcialis, France) 40/1

10 *3/4* **Astrosamantha (FR)** 2-8-9 0 .... QuentinPerrette(6) 1 45
(A Giorgi, Italy) 11/1

1m 27.52s 10 Ran SP% 120.2
PARI-MUTUEL (all including 1 euro stake): WIN 6.70; PLACE 2.80, 10.00, 3.20 DF 84.00.
Owner Mme Eleonora Marcialis **Bred** Giovanni Latina **Trained** France

3212 BEVERLEY (R-H)
Saturday, June 8

OFFICIAL GOING: Good to firm (7.4) changing to good after race 2 (2.00) and good to soft after race 5 (3.45)
Wind: Light half against Weather: Cloudy and heavy showers

3563 DADIE OUGHTRED MEMORIAL H'CAP 7f 96y
1:25 (1:25) (Class 3) (0-95,95) 3-Y-0+

£9,337 (£2,796; £1,398; £699; £349; £175) **Stalls** Low

Form RPR

2443 1 **Love Dreams (IRE)**[8] 3318 5-9-12 95 ....(v) FrannyNorton 3 102
(Mark Johnston) *mde all: rdn along over 1f out: drvn ins fnl f: hld on wl towards fin* 2/1[1]

11-0 2 *1/2* **Byron's Choice**[21] 2844 4-9-8 91 .... PaulMulrennan 2 96
(Michael Dods) *t.k.h: early: trckd ldng pair: effrt on inner 2f out: nt clr run and swtchd lft over 1f out: sn rdn to chse wnr: drvn and ev ch ins fnl f: no ex towards fin* 12/1

0-00 3 *3 1/4* **Qaysar (FR)**[28] 2609 4-9-8 91 .... PatDobbs 4 89+
(Richard Hannon) *hld up in tch: hdwy 2f out: nt clr run and swtchd rt over 1f out: sn rdn and kpt on fnl f* 7/2[2]

-003 4 *1 3/4* **Zap**[14] 3094 4-9-11 94 .... TonyHamilton 6 86
(Richard Fahey) *hld up towards rr: hdwy over 2f out: rdn wl over 1f out: kpt on fnl f* 8/1

0-53 5 *nse* **Poet's Dawn**[10] 3216 4-8-12 81 oh2 .... DavidAllan 8 72
(Tim Easterby) *bmpd s: in tch: hdwy on outer over 2f out: rdn wl over 1f out: kpt on u.p fnl f (jockey said gelding slipped leaving the stalls and didn't handle the bend)* 9/1

00-4 6 *1 1/4* **Rousayan (IRE)**[25] 2710 8-8-10 84 ....(h) BenSanderson(5) 5 72
(Roger Fell) *t.k.h: trckd wnr: effrt over 2f out and sn rdn: drvn over 1f out: sn wknd* 6/1

4-22 7 *3/4* **Elerfaan (IRE)**[31] 2526 5-9-5 88 .... PhilDennis 7 74
(Rebecca Bastiman) *wnt lft s: trckd ldrs: hdwy on outer 3f out: rdn to chse ldng pair 2f out: sn drvn and wknd over 1f out (jockey said gelding hung right in the straight)* 9/2[3]

-000 8 *2* **Big Storm Coming**[9] 3268 9-8-13 82 .... DougieCostello 1 63
(John Quinn) *a towards rr: rdn along over 2f out: sn outpcd* 40/1

1m 32.28s (-0.32) **Going Correction** +0.275s/f (Good) 8 Ran SP% 119.3
Speed ratings (Par 107): **112,111,107,105,105 104,103,101**
CSF £29.60 CT £82.93 TOTE £2.70: £1.20, £3.80, £1.40; EX 28.50 Trifecta £120.40.
Owner Crone Stud Farms Ltd **Bred** John O'Connor **Trained** Middleham Moor, N Yorks
■ Stewards' Enquiry : Paul Mulrennan two-day ban: interference & careless riding (Jun 23-24)

FOCUS
An interesting handicap with plenty coming into the race in good form but it was run at an ordinary gallop and those who raced close to the pace were favoured. The first two were clear. The winner has been rated in line with his recent form.

3564 HILARY NEEDLER TROPHY FILLIES' CONDITIONS STKS (PLUS 10 RACE) 5f
2:00 (2:01) (Class 2) 2-Y-O

£24,900 (£7,456; £3,728; £1,864; £932; £468) **Stalls** Low

Form RPR

1 1 **Liberty Beach**[12] 3156 2-8-12 0 .... DavidAllan 8 88+
(John Quinn) *hld up: hdwy and n.m.r 2f out: rdn over 1f out: str run ent fnl f: led last 100yds: sn clr* 11/2[3]

2411 2 *2 1/2* **Rose Of Kildare (IRE)**[10] 3220 2-8-12 0 .... FrannyNorton 3 79
(Mark Johnston) *in rr and sn pushed along: rdn and hdwy 2f out: drvn and styng on whn hung rt ins fnl f: kpt on wl towards fin (jockey said filly stumbled leaving the stalls)* 9/4[1]

3 *1/2* **Moon Of Love (IRE)** 2-8-9 0 .... BarryMcHugh 2 83+
(Richard Fahey) *cl up on inner: chalng and ev ch whn bdly hmpd over 1f out: sn rdn and chsng ldng pair whn edgd lft and hmpd again ins fnl f: kpt on same pce after* 4/1[2]

102 4 *1* **Lady Quickstep (IRE)**[12] 3156 2-8-12 0 .... DougieCostello 4 74
(Gay Kelleway) *led: pushed along 2f out: rdn over 1f out: sn edgd rt: drvn ins fnl f: hdd & wknd last 100yds (jockey said filly hung right under pressure)* 7/1

41 5 *3 3/4* **Bella Brazil (IRE)**[11] 3196 2-8-12 0 .... LiamKeniry 1 60
(David Barron) *in tch on inner: hdwy 2f out: sn rdn: kpt on same pce fnl f* 12/1

42 6 *3 1/2* **Yarrow Gate**[9] 3244 2-8-12 0 .... PaulMulrennan 7 48
(Michael Dods) *chsd ldrs on outer: rdn along wl over 1f out: sn wknd* 12/1

1 7 *3 3/4* **Three Coins**[29] 2586 2-8-12 0 .... TonyHamilton 5 34
(Richard Fahey) *chsd ldng pair: rdn along 2f out: edgd lft and wknd over 1f out* 7/1

1 8 *2 3/4* **Exclusive (IRE)**[25] 2707 2-8-12 0 .... EdwardGreatrex 6 24
(Archie Watson) *chsd ldrs: rdn along 2f out: sn drvn and wknd* 8/1

1m 3.8s (0.90) **Going Correction** +0.275s/f (Good) 8 Ran SP% 117.6
Speed ratings (Par 96): **103,99,98,96,90 85,79,74**
CSF £18.90 TOTE £6.60: £1.90, £1.30, £1.90; EX 21.90 Trifecta £103.00.
Owner Philip Wilkins **Bred** Phillip Wilkins **Trained** Settrington, N Yorks

FOCUS
This didn't look a vintage running of this fillies' conditions event which has thrown up some top-class winners over the years. The pace was strong and the first two were the last two at halfway. The second has been rated to her pre-race mark.

3565 ALANA, AMBER, SONNY AND ZACH MEDIAN AUCTION MAIDEN STKS 7f 96y
2:35 (2:36) (Class 5) 3-5-Y-O **£4,851** (£1,443; £721; £360) **Stalls** Low

Form RPR
04-2 **1** **Shawaaheq (IRE)**[19] 2900 3-9-2 76 .... EdwardGreatrex 2 76+
(Ed Dunlop) *t.k.h early: trckd ldng pair: pushed along 2f out: rdn over 1f out: swtchd lft and drvn to chal ent fnl f: styd on to ld last 100yds* **6/5**[1]
-502 **2** *1 ¼* **Spirit Of Lund (IRE)**[26] 2677 3-8-13 74 .... JamieGormley(3) 3 72
(Iain Jardine) *chsd ldrs: rdn along over 2f out: drvn over 1f out: styd on wl fnl f* **5/2**[2]
63 **3** *nk* **Summer Bride (IRE)**[5] 3412 3-8-11 0 .... DavidAllan 6 66
(Tim Easterby) *chsd ldr: rdn along over 2f out: drvn over 1f out: kpt on same pce* **12/1**
3656 **4** *shd* **Serengeti Song (IRE)**[28] 2635 3-8-11 69 .... HarrisonShaw(5) 7 71
(K R Burke) *led: rdn along 2f out: drvn over 1f out: hdd last 100yds: kpt on same pce* **4/1**[3]
0 **5** *10* **Guarded Secret**[21] 2823 3-8-11 0 .... AndrewMullen 8 40
(Michael Dods) *chsd ldrs: rdn along over 2f out: sn drvn and wknd* **50/1**
6 *3 ¼* **Cuba Ruba** 3-9-2 0 .... DuranFentiman 5 37
(Tim Easterby) *dwlt: green and a in rr* **28/1**
00 **7** *2 ¼* **Immoral (IRE)**[22] 2794 3-9-2 0 .... LiamKeniry 4 31
(Ed Walker) *a in rr* **14/1**
000- **8** *9* **Ganton Eagle**[245] 7989 3-9-2 43 .... NathanEvans 1 7
(Michael Easterby) *a in rr* **66/1**
1m 35.07s (2.47) **Going Correction** +0.275s/f (Good) **8 Ran SP% 115.3**
Speed ratings (Par 103): **96,94,94,94,82 78,76,66**
CSF £4.34 TOTE £1.90: £1.10, £1.10, £2.20; EX 4.20 Trifecta £14.30.
Owner Hamdan Al Maktoum **Bred** Shadwell Estate Company Limited **Trained** Newmarket, Suffolk

FOCUS
After some heavy showers the ground was changed to good from good to firm prior to this maiden for three-year-olds which lacked strength in depth. The pace was fair and the first four were clear. It's been rated around the fourth to this year's form, with the winner close to his latest.

3566 TRUCKINGBY BRIAN YEARDLEY TWO YEAR OLD TROPHY CONDITIONS STKS (PLUS 10 RACE) (C&G) 5f
3:15 (3:15) (Class 2) 2-Y-O **£24,900** (£7,456; £3,728; £1,864; £932) **Stalls** Low

Form RPR
3 **1** **Summer Sands**[24] 2747 2-8-12 0 .... BarryMcHugh 5 90+
(Richard Fahey) *trckd ldrs on outer: cl up 2f out: rdn over 1f out: led jst ins fnl f: kpt on wl towards fin* **11/4**[2]
12 **2** *½* **Oh Purple Reign (IRE)**[8] 3312 2-9-2 0 .... PatDobbs 6 93
(Richard Hannon) *trckd ldrs: pushed along and hdwy over 1f out: rdn to chse wnr jst ins fnl f: sn ev ch: drvn and no ex towards fin* **5/4**[1]
1 **3** *3 ¾* **Dream Shot (IRE)**[15] 3039 2-9-0 0 .... DavidAllan 2 77
(James Tate) *cl up: rdn to take slt ld jst over 1f out: hdd jst ins fnl f: sn drvn and kpt on same pce* **7/2**[3]
12 **4** *3 ¾* **Xcelente**[38] 2288 2-9-2 0 .... FrannyNorton 3 66
(Mark Johnston) *chsd ldrs pair: rdn along wl over 2f out: wknd appr fnl f* **13/2**
122 **5** *12* **Rodnee Tee**[26] 2694 2-9-0 0 .... CamHardie 1 20
(David O'Meara) *led: rdn along 2f out: hdd over 1f out: sn wknd* **14/1**
1m 4.15s (1.25) **Going Correction** +0.275s/f (Good) **5 Ran SP% 113.3**
Speed ratings (Par 99): **101,100,94,88,69**
CSF £6.87 TOTE £3.40: £1.70, £1.10; EX 9.10 Trifecta £26.70.
Owner The Cool Silk Partnership **Bred** Koharu Partnership **Trained** Musley Bank, N Yorks

FOCUS
Four of the five runners were previous winners and the other had shown particular promise on his debut so the form should prove sound. They finished quite well strung out. The second has been rated close to his Epsom level.

3567 BIFFA H'CAP 1m 100y
3:45 (3:47) (Class 5) (0-75,75) 4-Y-0+ **£5,607** (£1,678; £839; £420; £300; £300) **Stalls** Low

Form RPR
-066 **1** **Brother McGonagall**[8] 3305 5-9-5 73 .... DavidAllan 13 87
(Tim Easterby) *prom: trckd ldr over 3f out: cl up over 2f out: led wl over 1f out: sn rdn clr: kpt on strly* **6/1**[1]
0040 **2** *5* **Beverley Bullet**[2] 3502 6-8-10 64 ....(p) PhilDennis 5 67
(Lawrence Mullaney) *chsd ldrs: hdwy wl over 2f out: rdn to chse wnr over 1f out: drvn and no imp fnl f* **10/1**[3]
0-21 **3** *1 ½* **Harvest Day**[137] 355 4-8-12 73 ....(t) JoshQuinn(7) 15 72+
(Michael Easterby) *t.k.h early: hld up in rr: hdwy over 2f out: sn swtchd markedly lft to stands' rail: styd on wl u.p fnl f* **20/1**
-440 **4** *nk* **Twin Appeal (IRE)**[19] 2899 8-9-2 73 ....(p) GemmaTutty(3) 1 71
(Karen Tutty) *in tch: hdwy over 2f out: rdn wl over 1f out: drvn and kpt on wl fnl f* **6/1**[1]
0323 **5** *½* **Straight Ash (IRE)**[8] 3305 4-8-9 66 .... BenRobinson(3) 10 63
(Ollie Pears) *trckd ldrs: hdwy over 2f out: rdn wl over 1f out: drvn appr fnl f: kpt on same pce* **12/1**
130- **6** *¾* **Mustaqbal (IRE)**[243] 8053 7-9-7 75 .... JackGarritty 7 70
(Michael Dods) *trckd ldrs: hdwy over 2f out: rdn wl over 1f out: drvn and kpt on same pce fnl f* **20/1**
-003 **7** *5* **Magic City (IRE)**[14] 3100 10-9-2 70 .... NathanEvans 17 54
(Michael Easterby) *sn led: pushed along 3f out: rdn over 2f out: hdd wl over 1f out: grad wknd* **14/1**
3-20 **8** *¾* **Storm Ahead (IRE)**[25] 2710 6-9-5 73 ....(b) DuranFentiman 11 55
(Tim Easterby) *prom: trckd ldr after 2f: pushed along 3f out: rdn over 2f out: sn drvn and wknd over 1f out* **12/1**
-003 **9** *1 ¾* **Anchises**[22] 2785 4-8-8 67 .... HarrisonShaw(5) 8 45
(Rebecca Menzies) *t.k.h early: hld up towards rr: hdwy on outer wl over 2f out: rdn along wl over 1f out: sn no imp* **14/1**
0634 **10** *2* **Highlight Reel (IRE)**[11] 3179 4-9-7 75 .... LewisEdmunds 12 49
(Rebecca Bastiman) *trckd ldrs: pushed along 3f out: rdn over 2f out: sn one pce* **10/1**[3]
0156 **11** *½* **International Law**[15] 3053 5-9-2 70 .... CamHardie 16 42
(Antony Brittain) *in tch: rdn along wl over 2f out: sn wknd* **25/1**
0460 **12** *5* **Laqab (IRE)**[26] 2692 6-8-7 61 .... PaddyMathers 4 22
(Derek Shaw) *a midfield* **25/1**
5-06 **13** *7* **Bibbidibobbidiboo (IRE)**[19] 2899 4-8-12 66 .... TonyHamilton 14 11
(Ann Duffield) *a towards rr* **25/1**
1104 **14** *2 ½* **Singing Sheriff**[16] 3022 4-9-0 68 .... LiamKeniry 2 7
(Ed Walker) *a towards rr (trainer said gelding was unsuited by the going (good) and would prefer a sounder surface)* **6/1**[1]
45-0 **15** *1 ½* **Bhodi (IRE)**[28] 2629 4-9-2 70 ....(h[1]) DougieCostello 9 6
(Kevin Frost) *a towards rr* **100/1**
2320 **16** *nse* **Blindingly (GER)**[39] 2246 4-9-5 73 .... AndrewMullen 3 9
(Ben Haslam) *dwlt: a bhd (trainer's rep said the gelding found the good ground too soft; vet said the gelding had lost its right fore shoe)* **8/1**[2]
34-0 **R** **First Flight (IRE)**[7] 3356 8-8-12 73 .... KieranSchofield(7) 6
(Brian Ellison) *ref to r* **12/1**
1m 47.5s (1.10) **Going Correction** +0.275s/f (Good) **17 Ran SP% 130.6**
Speed ratings (Par 103): **105,100,98,98,97 96,91,91,89,87 86,81,74,72,70 70,**
CSF £63.47 CT £1209.15 TOTE £7.60: £1.80, £2.50, £4.20, £2.50; EX 71.50.
Owner Reality Partnerships VI **Bred** J P Coggan **Trained** Great Habton, N Yorks

FOCUS
Mainly exposed sorts in this big-field handicap and though it looked wide open, not many featured and the winner scored in fine style. The winner has been rated right back to his best.

3568 HAPPY BIRTHDAY GRAHAM HALLETT H'CAP 1m 1f 207y
4:20 (4:22) (Class 5) (0-75,77) 4-Y-O+ **£5,607** (£1,678; £839; £420; £300; £300) **Stalls** Low

Form RPR
2-41 **1** **Archie Perkins (IRE)**[12] 3161 4-9-4 73 .... RowanScott(3) 2 85
(Nigel Tinkler) *trckd ldrs: smooth hdwy on inner 2f out: swtchd lft and effrt over 1f out: sn chal: rdn to ld ins fnl f: sn edgd rt: styd on wl* **4/1**[2]
3634 **2** *4* **Bit Of A Quirke**[15] 3046 6-8-13 65 ....(b[1]) AndrewMullen 8 69
(Mark Walford) *prom: trckd ldr after 3f: led 2f out: sn rdn: drvn and hdd ins fnl f: kpt on same pce* **15/2**
-113 **3** *4 ½* **Ventura Gold (IRE)**[33] 2479 4-9-10 76 .... JackGarritty 4 71
(Richard Fahey) *trckd ldrs: hdwy 3f out: chsd ldng pair 2f out: sn rdn: drvn and kpt on same pce fnl f* **5/1**[3]
-220 **4** *2* **Ideal Candy (IRE)**[14] 3095 4-9-3 72 .... GemmaTutty(3) 5 63
(Karen Tutty) *sn led: pushed along 3f out: rdn and hdd 2f out: sn drvn and one pce* **3/1**[1]
6050 **5** *nk* **Indomeneo**[14] 3072 4-9-11 77 .... TonyHamilton 3 67
(Richard Fahey) *hld up in rr: pushed along and hdwy over 2f out: drvn over 1f out: plugged on fnl f* **12/1**
-204 **6** *shd* **Placebo Effect (IRE)**[11] 3199 4-9-1 70 .... BenRobinson(3) 7 60
(Ollie Pears) *trckd ldrs: pushed along over 2f out: sn rdn: drvn over 1f out: sn one pce* **11/2**
0-00 **7** *2 ½* **Ad Libitum**[14] 3095 4-9-1 72 .... BenSanderson(5) 10 57
(Roger Fell) *hld up towards rr: effrt and sme hdwy over 2f out: sn rdn and n.d* **16/1**
60-0 **8** *nk* **Near Kettering**[14] 3095 5-9-0 66 ....(t) CamHardie 9 51
(Sam England) *a towards rr* **50/1**
0-05 **9** *8* **Bollin Joan**[15] 3057 4-9-0 66 ....(p) DavidAllan 1 35
(Tim Easterby) *trckd ldr 3f: prom: rdn along wl over 2f out: sn drvn and wknd* **14/1**
3015 **10** *4 ½* **King Of Naples**[12] 3162 6-8-10 62 ....(h) BarryMcHugh 6 22
(Ruth Carr) *hld up: a towards rr* **16/1**
0-40 **11** *6* **Spark Of War (IRE)**[15] 3054 4-8-9 61 ....(p[1]) FrannyNorton 11 9
(Keith Dalgleish) *chsd ldrs: rdn along wl over 2f out: sn wknd* **16/1**
2m 7.25s (1.55) **Going Correction** +0.275s/f (Good) **11 Ran SP% 122.8**
Speed ratings (Par 103): **104,100,97,95,95 95,93,93,86,83 78**
CSF £35.98 CT £158.15 TOTE £4.10: £2.00, £2.00, £1.90; EX 36.00 Trifecta £168.50.
Owner J Raybould & S Perkins **Bred** Helen Lyons **Trained** Langton, N Yorks

FOCUS
A competitive handicap run at a fair gallop in which they finished quite well strung out. The second has been rated in line with this year's form for now.

3569 MICHAEL FOSTER MEMORIAL H'CAP (DIV I) 7f 96y
4:55 (4:55) (Class 5) (0-70,80) 3-Y-O **£5,607** (£1,678; £839; £420; £300; £300) **Stalls** Low

Form RPR
3216 **1** **Ollivander (IRE)**[9] 3249 3-9-3 68 ....(v) ConorMcGovern(3) 10 74
(David O'Meara) *mde all: rdn 2f out: drvn ent fnl f: hld on gamely towards fin* **6/1**
3523 **2** *nk* **Beryl The Petal (IRE)**[11] 3189 3-9-8 70 .... CamHardie 1 75
(David O'Meara) *prom: effrt 2f out: sn chal and rdn: drvn and ev ch ins fnl f: no ex towards fin* **7/2**[1]
50-0 **3** *1 ½* **Abie's Hollow**[18] 2933 3-9-2 64 .... DougieCostello 5 65
(Tony Coyle) *in tch: pushed along over 2f out: hdwy and rdn wl over 1f out: drvn and kpt on fnl f* **18/1**
2331 **4** *nse* **Strawberry Jack**[9] 3273 3-9-11 80 ....(vt) JessicaCooley(7) 12 81
(George Scott) *chsd ldrs: rdn along over 2f out: drvn over 1f out: kpt on same pce* **5/1**
-000 **5** *1 ½* **Smashing Lass (IRE)**[12] 3158 3-8-2 50 ....(p[1]) PaddyMathers 3 47
(Ollie Pears) *sn outpcd and bhd: rdn along and hdwy over 2f out: kpt on u.p appr fnl f* **20/1**
6055 **6** *1 ½* **Biscuit Queen**[11] 3204 3-7-9 50 oh4 ....(b) KieranSchofield(7) 2 43
(Brian Ellison) *chsd ldrs: rdn along on inner over 2f out: drvn wl over 1f out: grad wknd* **14/1**
1405 **7** *2 ¼* **Rich Approach (IRE)**[35] 2418 3-9-5 67 .... DavidAllan 7 54
(James Bethell) *a towards rr* **9/2**[3]
0500 **8** *6* **Raypeteafterme**[12] 3159 3-8-12 60 ....(t) TonyHamilton 9 32
(Declan Carroll) *a towards rr* **25/1**
2130 **9** *9* **Lexikon**[8] 3292 3-8-3 54 .... JamieGormley(3) 6 2
(Ollie Pears) *cl up: rdn along over 2f out: wknd wl over 1f out (trainer said filly was unsuited by the going (good to soft) and would prefer a sounder surface)* **9/1**
50-0 **10** *2 ½* **Mo Emmad Ali (IRE)**[56] 1764 3-9-7 69 ....(h[1]) BarryMcHugh 4 11
(Kevin Ryan) *a towards rr* **4/1**[2]
1m 36.58s (3.98) **Going Correction** +0.275s/f (Good) **10 Ran SP% 121.9**
Speed ratings (Par 99): **88,87,85,85,84 82,79,73,62,59**
CSF £28.66 CT £376.22 TOTE £8.10: £1.90, £1.40, £6.40; EX 30.30 Trifecta £331.30.
Owner York Thoroughbred Racing **Bred** Canice Farrell **Trained** Upper Helmsley, N Yorks
■ Dreamseller was withdrawn. Price at time of withdrawal 20/1. Rule 4 does not apply.

FOCUS
Not the strongest of 51-70 handicaps and though it was run at a sound pace very few got into it. The third and fourth have been rated close to form.

3570 MICHAEL FOSTER MEMORIAL H'CAP (DIV II) 7f 96y
5:30 (5:34) (Class 5) (0-70,72) 3-Y-O
£5,607 (£1,678; £839; £420; £300; £300) Stalls Low

Form RPR
06-4 **1** **Hunterwali**[35] 2420 3-9-1 **64**.................................. PhilDennis 6 79
(Michael Dods) *trckd ldrs: hdwy 3f out and sn cl up: led 2f out: rdn clr appr fnl f: kpt on strly* **10/1**
603- **2** *7* **Mac Ailey**[333] 4788 3-9-0 **63**.................................. DavidAllan 8 60
(Tim Easterby) *hld up towards rr: hdwy over 2f out: rdn wl over 1f out: styd on to chse wnr ins fnl f: sn no imp* **10/1**
1-00 **3** *1* **House Deposit**[28] 2635 3-9-4 **67**..............................(t) TonyHamilton 10 61+
(Declan Carroll) *hld up towards rr: hdwy wl over 2f out: rdn wl over 1f out: sn swtchd lft and kpt on fnl f* **7/1[2]**
060- **4** *2 ½* **Donnago (IRE)**[262] 7414 3-8-0 **56**.............................. KieranSchofield(7) 3 44+
(Brian Ellison) *hld up in midfield: hdwy on inner over 2f out: nt clr run and swtchd lft over 1f out: sn rdn: kpt on fnl f* **25/1**
0-06 **5** *1 ¼* **Separable**[20] 2870 3-8-4 **53**..................................(p) DuranFentiman 4 37
(Tim Easterby) *cl up: disp ld over 2f out: rdn wl over 1f out: sn drvn and grad wknd* **12/1**
0-06 **6** *hd* **Supreme Dream**[9] 3271 3-8-2 **51** oh3.......................... PaddyMathers 1 35
(Ollie Pears) *slt ld: rdn along 3f out: drvn and hdd 2f out: grad wknd* **12/1**
5040 **7** *nk* **Ventura Glory**[18] 2933 3-9-5 **68**..............................(p[1]) PatDobbs 9 51
(Richard Hannon) *in tch: hdwy to chse ldrs 3f out: rdn over 2f out: sn drvn and no imp* **7/1[2]**
3113 **8** *1 ¼* **Blazing Dreams (IRE)**[47] 1980 3-8-12 **61**................(p) AndrewMullen 11 41
(Ben Haslam) *dwlt: a towards rr (jockey said gelding was slowly away)* **8/1[3]**
3000 **9** *1 ½* **Dream Chick (IRE)**[19] 2896 3-8-9 **58**.......................... BarryMcHugh 7 34
(Kevin Ryan) *midfield: hdwy over 3f out: rdn along over 2f out: sn wknd* **8/1[3]**
-660 **10** *9* **Northern Footsteps**[9] 3270 3-7-13 **51** oh6.........(p[1]) JamieGormley(3) 13 4
(Ollie Pears) *dwlt: a in rr* **80/1**
-000 **11** *1 ½* **Desert Lantern (USA)**[15] 3041 3-9-5 **68**..................(v[1]) FrannyNorton 2 17
(Mark Johnston) *midfield: rdn along 3f out: sn wknd* **11/4[1]**
440 **12** *30* **Dabouk (IRE)**[32] 2507 3-9-7 **70**.................................. CamHardie 12
(David O'Meara) *prom: rdn along 1/2-way: sn wknd* **9/1**

1m 35.57s (2.97) **Going Correction** +0.275s/f (Good) **12 Ran SP% 122.5**
Speed ratings (Par 99): **94,86,84,82,80 80,80,78,76,66 64,30**
CSF £109.82 CT £760.54 TOTE £13.50: £3.50, £4.90, £2.10; EX 127.40 Trifecta £1035.90.
Owner Redgate Bloodstock **Bred** Redgate Bloodstock Ltd **Trained** Denton, Co Durham

FOCUS
The second division of a 7.5f handicap for three-year-olds. It was run at a suicidal pace but produced a runaway winner. The level is a bit fluid, but the second has been rated in line with his maiden form and the third in line with his latest.
T/Plt: £17.00 to a £1 stake. Pool: £80,466.56 - 3,450.78 winning units T/Qpdt: £6.00 to a £1 stake. Pool: £5,711.36 - 702.09 winning units **Joe Rowntree**

2994 CHEPSTOW (L-H)
Saturday, June 8

OFFICIAL GOING: Good to soft (soft in places)
Wind: Slight against Weather: Fine

3571 BIDAID.COM CHARITY FUNDRAISING EVENTS H'CAP 1m 4f
6:00 (6:04) (Class 6) (0-65,67) 4-Y-O+
£3,105 (£924; £461; £400; £400; £400) Stalls Low

Form RPR
1035 **1** **Kingfast (IRE)**[17] 2970 4-8-6 **50**..............................(p[1]) CharlieBennett 16 58
(David Dennis) *trckd ldrs: rdn 2f out: led appr fnl f: drvn out* **8/1[3]**
5313 **2** *½* **Ascot Day (FR)**[12] 3155 5-9-7 **65**..............................(p) KieranShoemark 13 72
(Bernard Llewellyn) *sed fr stall 14: s.i.s: sn prom: wnt 2nd after 3f: rdn to ld over 2f out: hdd appr fnl f: kpt on (jockey said gelding reared as the stalls opened)* **9/4[1]**
004 **3** *2* **And The New (IRE)**[16] 2999 8-9-7 **65**.............................. RyanTate 7 69+
(Johnny Farrelly) *s.i.s: towards rr: pushed along over 4f out: hdwy 3f out: sn rdn: no further imp tl styd on wl and wnt 3rd ins fnl f: nvr nrr* **5/2[2]**
3325 **4** *5* **Sigrid Nansen**[9] 3252 4-7-11 **46** oh1.......................(p) AndrewBreslin(5) 5 43
(Alexandra Dunn) *led: drvn 3f out: hdd over 2f out: sn one pce: wknd and lost 3rd ins fnl f* **18/1**
01/0 **5** *2 ¼* **Khismet**[75] 1333 6-8-8 **55**..................................(p) FinleyMarsh(3) 6 48
(John Flint) *chsd ldrs: rdn over 3f out: kpt on same pce* **33/1**
060- **6** *hd* **Rosie Royale (IRE)**[97] 8743 7-9-4 **62**..............................(w) GeorgeWood 9 55
(Roger Teal) *midfield: rdn 3f out: styd on fnl 2f* **25/1**
0240 **7** *2 ¼* **The Lords Walk**[16] 2998 6-9-0 **63**..............................(p) RyanWhile(5) 11 53
(Bill Turner) *prom: rdn 3f out: wknd over 1f out* **9/1**
0020 **8** *16* **Boycie**[101] 923 6-8-2 **53** ow1..............................(p) GeorgiaDobie(7) 1 19
(Adrian Wintle) *drvn over 3f out: a in rr* **20/1**
-043 **9** *10* **General Brook (IRE)**[16] 3000 9-9-0 **61**........................(p) WilliamCox(3) 15 12
(John O'Shea) *wnt to post early: trckd ldr 3f: remained prom tl rdn and wknd 4f out* **14/1**
4300 **10** *1 ¼* **Woggle (IRE)**[8] 3298 4-7-9 **46** oh1............................(b) IsobelFrancis(7) 4
(Geoffrey Deacon) *s.i.s: hld up in rr: rdn and hung rt over 3f out: no imp* **33/1**
050- **11** *24* **Street Jester**[219] 8785 5-8-5 **49**.................................. LiamJones 8
(Robert Stephens) *midfield: pushed along 5f out: rdn and wknd over 3f out: t.o* **28/1**
0006 **12** *13* **Mouchee (IRE)**[16] 3000 4-9-6 **67**..............................(p) MeganNicholls(3) 2
(Michael Blake) *a in rr: t.o fnl 5f (jockey said gelding was never travelling)* **66/1**
12 *dht* **Atlantic King (GER)**[111] 6-8-7 **58**.............................. Pierre-LouisJamin(7) 10
(Kevin Bishop) *dwlt: a bhd: t.o fr 1/2-way* **66/1**

2m 38.95s (-1.35) **Going Correction** +0.20s/f (Good) **13 Ran SP% 113.3**
Speed ratings (Par 101): **102,101,100,97,95 95,93,83,76,75 59,51,51**
CSF £21.21 CT £45.56 TOTE £8.40: £2.60, £1.50, £2.00; EX 23.90 Trifecta £96.80.
Owner G Saville, G Brandrick & Partner **Bred** D Veitch & B Douglas **Trained** Hanley Swan, Worcestershire
■ Stewards' Enquiry : Kieran Shoemark one-day ban: started from wrong stall (Jun 23)

FOCUS
A modest middle-distance handicap. The decent pace gradually collapsed in the straight but two prominently-ridden runners held off the closing second-favourite.

3572 BETTINGSITES.LTD.UK NEW BETTING SITES H'CAP 1m 2f
6:30 (6:30) (Class 5) (0-70,70) 4-Y-O+
£3,752 (£1,116; £557; £400; £400; £400) Stalls Low

Form RPR
1223 **1** **Gendarme (IRE)**[5] 3408 4-9-7 **70**..............................(b) GeorgeWood 11 78
(Alexandra Dunn) *trckd ldrs: led 2f out: sn rdn clr: eased cl home* **7/1**
01-4 **2** *2 ½* **Love And Be Loved**[26] 2685 5-9-1 **67**.......................... FinleyMarsh(3) 12 67
(John Flint) *wnt to post early: led to 1/2-way: sn rdn and lost pl: styd on down outer fnl 2f: wnt 2nd fnl 75yds but no ch w wnr (jockey said mare hung right-handed in the home straight)* **9/4[1]**
00-6 **3** *1 ¾* **Essenaitch (IRE)**[61] 1653 6-9-1 **64**.............................. LiamJones 4 61+
(David Evans) *t.k.h: trckd ldrs tl led 1/2-way: rdn and hdd 2f out: sn outpcd by wnr: no ex and lost 2nd fnl 75yds* **7/2[3]**
2120 **4** *¾* **Creative Talent (IRE)**[26] 2692 7-8-5 **57**.......................... WilliamCox(3) 3 52
(Tony Carroll) *hld up: effrt and hdwy on outer over 2f out: kpt on same pce fnl f* **8/1**
00-2 **5** *¾* **Cwynar**[16] 2998 4-8-11 **60**.................................. HollieDoyle 8 54
(Rebecca Curtis) *hld up: rdn and hdwy to chse ldrs over 3f out: kpt on same pce fnl 2f* **3/1[2]**
0-00 **6** *8* **Yorbelucky**[28] 2628 4-9-4 **67**..............................(t[1]) KieranShoemark 7 45
(Ian Williams) *s.i.s: gd hdwy to press ldr after 1f: lost 2nd over 5f out: sn rdn: wknd over 1f out* **14/1**
320- **7** *shd* **Momentarily**[205] 9086 4-9-7 **70**..............................(h[1]) RonanWhelan 2 47
(Mick Channon) *hld up: hdwy to trck ldrs 4f out: rdn over 2f out: wknd over 1f out* **10/1**

2m 11.94s (-0.86) **Going Correction** +0.20s/f (Good) **7 Ran SP% 117.4**
Speed ratings (Par 103): **101,99,97,97,96 90,89**
CSF £24.15 CT £65.99 TOTE £8.00: £3.20, £1.90; EX 24.40 Trifecta £101.80.
Owner Helium Racing Ltd **Bred** Gillian, Lady Howard De Walden **Trained** West Buckland, Somerset

FOCUS
A modest handicap. The fourth horse in the market won easily from off a muddling gallop. The winner has been rated back to his old best, with the second in line with her latest.

3573 COMPAREBETTINGSITES.COM BEST BETTING SITE/EBF FILLIES' NOVICE AUCTION STKS (PLUS 10 RACE) 5f 16y
7:00 (7:01) (Class 5) 2-Y-O
£3,752 (£1,116; £557; £278) Stalls Centre

Form RPR
3042 **1** **Lili Wen Fach (IRE)**[16] 2996 2-8-12 0.............................. LiamJones 1 70
(David Evans) *t.k.h: trckd ldr: rdn over 2f out: drvn and r.o fnl f: led nr fin* **7/2[3]**
2 **2** *¾* **Go Well Spicy (IRE)**[29] 2579 2-9-0 0.............................. RonanWhelan 6 69
(Mick Channon) *niggled along early: chsd ldrs: drvn and sltly outpcd over 2f out: r.o wl fnl f: tk 2nd post* **6/4[1]**
10 **3** *nse* **Silver Start**[22] 2805 2-9-4 0.............................. KieranShoemark 2 73
(Charles Hills) *led: rdn over 1f out: hdd nr fin: lost 2nd post* **5/2[2]**
03 **4** *1 ¼* **Twice As Likely**[15] 3039 2-8-9 0.............................. FinleyMarsh(3) 7 63
(Richard Hughes) *s.i.s: sn in tch: rdn to chse ldrs 2f out: unable qck and lost 3rd ins fnl f (jockey said filly was slowly away)* **13/2**
0 **5** *7* **Come On Girl**[40] 2205 2-8-11 0.............................. GeorgeDowning 8 36
(Tony Carroll) *chsd ldrs: rdn 1/2-way: lost pl over 1f out: wknd fnl f* **33/1**
00 **6** *½* **Red Cinderella**[12] 3165 2-8-11 0.............................. JohnFahy 10 35
(David Evans) *in tch towards rr: rdn over 2f out: sn outpcd and no ch* **33/1**
7 *5* **Mayflower Lady (IRE)** 2-8-11 0.............................. RyanTate 3 17
(Ronald Harris) *chsd ldrs 2f: sn rdn and outpcd* **33/1**
8 *1 ¼* **Ohnotanotherone** 2-8-9 0.............................. WilliamCox(3) 9 13
(Stuart Kittow) *hld up: rdn over 2f out: sn wknd* **20/1**

1m 1.63s (2.23) **Going Correction** +0.20s/f (Good) **8 Ran SP% 117.7**
Speed ratings (Par 90): **90,88,88,86,75 74,66,64**
CSF £9.16 TOTE £3.70: £1.40, £1.10, £1.30; EX 11.40 Trifecta £26.00.
Owner Rob Emmanuelle, Lynn Cullimore & Partner **Bred** Rathasker Stud **Trained** Pandy, Monmouths

FOCUS
A fair juvenile fillies' novice sprint contest. The right horses came to the fore off a decent gallop.

3574 WESSEX GARAGES NOVICE MEDIAN AUCTION STKS 7f 16y
7:30 (7:31) (Class 5) 3-Y-O
£3,752 (£1,116; £557; £278) Stalls Centre

Form RPR
2 **1** **Zephyrina (IRE)**[25] 2715 3-9-0 0.............................. KieranShoemark 3 65+
(Daniel Kubler) *chsd ldrs: rdn over 2f out: stl 4th ent fnl f: r.o wl u.p to ld cl home* **13/2**
6-23 **2** *¾* **Moveonup (IRE)**[31] 2529 3-9-2 67.............................. WilliamCox(3) 7 68
(Gay Kelleway) *wnt to post early: racd keenly: led: rdn appr fnl f: kpt on: hdd cl home* **6/1[3]**
4-5 **3** *hd* **Quirky Gertie (IRE)**[28] 2623 3-9-0 0.............................. RonanWhelan 8 62
(Mick Channon) *trckd ldrs: wnt 2nd 3f out: rdn 2f out: ev ch fnl f: unable qck nr fin* **8/11[1]**
0-0 **4** *1 ¾* **Bonny Blue**[14] 3090 3-9-0 0.............................. CharlieBennett 4 58
(Rod Millman) *trckd ldr tl lost 2nd 3f out: drvn over 2f out: kpt on same pce* **33/1**
36-0 **5** *3* **Denis The Diva**[12] 3170 3-9-5 68.............................. HollieDoyle 1 55
(Marcus Tregoning) *t.k.h: hld up: rdn and clsd over 2f out: no further imp fr over 1f out* **9/2[2]**
0 **6** *7* **Kasuku**[40] 2210 3-9-0 0.............................. JosephineGordon 5 31
(Ralph Beckett) *in rr: rdn over 4f out: wknd over 1f out* **16/1**
0 **7** *11* **Dee Dee Dottie**[17] 2967 3-8-9 0.............................. PoppyBridgwater(5) 2 1
(Geoffrey Deacon) *s.s: in rr: rdn and sme prog 1/2-way: wknd qckly over 1f out* **50/1**

1m 25.86s (1.96) **Going Correction** +0.20s/f (Good) **7 Ran SP% 114.5**
Speed ratings (Par 99): **96,95,94,92,89 81,68**
CSF £44.40 TOTE £7.00: £2.10, £2.50; EX 23.10 Trifecta £45.20.
Owner Patrick Whitten **Bred** Colin Kennedy **Trained** Lambourn, Berks

FOCUS
An ordinary 3yo novice contest. The favourite's promising challenge faltered in the downhill section and one of her likelier rivals made the most of a dream run up the near rail. The second sets the standard, while the third has been rated a bit below her modest Lingfield form.

3575 MICHAEL MAINE MEMORIAL H'CAP 7f 16y
8:00 (8:00) (Class 4) (0-80,82) 4-Y-0+
£5,530 (£1,645; £822; £411; £400; £400) **Stalls** Centre

Form | | | | RPR
0401 **1** **Bungee Jump (IRE)**[16] 2997 4-9-11 **82** RossaRyan 2 92
(Grace Harris) *mde all: sn c over to stands' rail: 3 l clr whn rdn 2f out: r.o wl: comf* **11/2**[3]
0212 **2** 3 1/2 **Rock Of Estonia (IRE)**[22] 2799 4-9-7 **78** KieranShoemark 9 79+
(Charles Hills) *wnt to post early: upset in stalls: s.s: t.k.h in rr: rdn over 2f out: hdwy over 1f out: r.o to go 2nd 75yds out: no ch w wnr (jockey said gelding was slowly away)* **5/2**[1]
3414 **3** 1 **Sir Roderic (IRE)**[14] 3100 6-9-2 **73** CharlieBennett 4 71
(Rod Millman) *prom: chsd wnr after 2f: rdn over 2f out: sn no imp: lost 2nd fnl 75yds* **7/2**[2]
/31- **4** 1 **Eula Varner**[356] 3908 5-9-6 **77** GeorgeWood 7 72
(Henry Candy) *hld up: rdn 3f out: hdwy over 1f out: unable qck fnl f* **8/1**
0-10 **5** 3 **Bristol Missile (USA)**[22] 2797 5-8-11 **68** RyanTate 5 55
(Richard Price) *chsd wnr 2f: remained prom: drvn over 2f out: fdd fnl f* **6/1**
0-40 **6** 1 1/2 **Kenstone (FR)**[26] 2691 6-9-3 **77** (p) FinleyMarsh(3) 8 60
(Adrian Wintle) *t.k.h: chsd ldrs: drvn over 2f out: wknd over 1f out* **8/1**
00-0 **7** 8 **Another Boy**[33] 2483 6-8-7 **64** JosephineGordon 6 25
(Ralph Beckett) *midfield tl rdn and dropped last after 3f: no ch after: eased fnl f* **14/1**
0013 **8** 6 **Air Of York (IRE)**[14] 3089 7-8-8 **65** (p) LiamJones 3 10
(John Flint) *plld hrd: chsd ldrs on outer: rdn 1/2-way: wknd over 1f out* **12/1**

1m 24.55s (0.65) **Going Correction** +0.20s/f (Good) **8 Ran SP% 117.0**
Speed ratings (Par 105): **100,96,94,93,90 88,79,72**
CSF £20.19 CT £55.80 TOTE £7.10: £1.90, £1.10, £1.60; EX 21.50 Trifecta £65.40.
Owner Ronald Davies & Mrs Candida Davies **Bred** Roundhill Stud **Trained** Shirenewton, Monmouthshire

FOCUS
The feature contest was a fair handicap. The third-favourite benefited from a fine front-running ride, proving thoroughly dominant up the stands' rail in a good comparative time. The winner has been rated back to her best.

3576 COMPAREBETTINGSITES.COM ONLINE BETTING H'CAP 5f 16y
8:30 (8:30) (Class 5) (0-75,76) 4-Y-0+
£3,752 (£1,116; £557; £400; £400; £400) **Stalls** Centre

Form | | | | RPR
1053 **1** **A Sure Welcome**[32] 2515 5-9-5 **73** (b) RyanTate 2 83
(John Spearing) *wnt lft s: sn rcvrd to chse ldrs: rdn 2f out: r.o to ld appr fnl f: edgd rt towards fin* **10/3**[1]
0-00 **2** 1 1/2 **Ladweb**[25] 2709 9-8-8 **65** ow1 GeorgeBuckell(3) 1 70
(John Gallagher) *carried lft s: wl in rr and rdn along: hdwy on outer over 1f out: chsd wnr ins fnl f: no imp fnl 50 yds* **12/1**
3033 **3** 1 1/4 **National Glory (IRE)**[11] 3188 4-8-10 **64** (b) HollieDoyle 10 66
(Archie Watson) *chsd ldrs: rdn over 2f out: nt clr run over 1f out tl swtchd rt ent fnl f: r.o wl* **9/2**[2]
3023 **4** 1 **Union Rose**[15] 3032 7-9-5 **73** (p) KieranShoemark 6 70
(Ronald Harris) *midfield: rdn 1/2-way: clsd over 1f out: no imp fnl f* **5/1**[3]
20-0 **5** 3/4 **Kinglami**[33] 2483 10-8-12 **66** RossaRyan 4 60
(John O'Shea) *sn towards rr: rdn 1/2-way: hdwy over 1f out: unable qck fnl f* **8/1**
6100 **6** 1/2 **Bellevarde (IRE)**[11] 3201 5-9-3 **76** SeamusCronin(5) 8 68
(Richard Price) *trckd ldr: rdn 2f out: ev ch over 1f out: lost 2nd ins fnl f: wknd* **5/1**[3]
-300 **7** hd **Crystal Deauville (FR)**[11] 3207 4-8-11 **68** (v[1]) WilliamCox(3) 11 59
(Gay Kelleway) *wnt to post early: prom: rdn 2f out: fdd fnl f* **12/1**
0-40 **8** 2 1/2 **Swanton Blue (IRE)**[10] 3221 6-8-8 **67** PoppyBridgwater(5) 12 49
(Ed de Giles) *in rr: rdn and sme prog after 2f: wknd fnl f (jockey said gelding was outpaced)* **11/2**
0-04 **9** 3 **Glamorous Rocket (IRE)**[15] 3037 4-9-7 **75** JosephineGordon 5 46
(Christopher Mason) *led: rdn and edgd rt over 1f out: sn hdd and briefly n.m.r: wknd qckly* **28/1**

1m 0.78s (1.38) **Going Correction** +0.20s/f (Good) **9 Ran SP% 119.9**
Speed ratings (Par 103): **97,94,92,91,89 89,88,84,79**
CSF £46.88 CT £186.82 TOTE £4.10: £1.70, £4.10, £1.80; EX 43.60 Trifecta £219.20.
Owner Kinnersley Partnership 3 **Bred** Richard Evans Bloodstock **Trained** Kinnersley, Worcs

FOCUS
A fair sprint handicap. The favourite did well to assert centrally after a ragged start. The winner has been rated in line with the better view of his AW form.

3577 CASINOSITES.LTD.UK CASINO SITES H'CAP 5f 16y
9:00 (9:00) (Class 6) (0-60,59) 4-Y-0+
£3,105 (£924; £461; £400; £400; £400) **Stalls** Centre

Form | | | | RPR
00-6 **1** **Sovereign State**[149] 161 4-8-11 **49** RossaRyan 7 58
(Tony Newcombe) *s.i.s: towards rr: rdn 1/2-way: hdwy and briefly nt clr run over 1f out: wnt 2nd 100 yds out: r.o wl to ld post (jockey said gelding hung left-handed)* **11/1**
-643 **2** shd **David's Beauty (IRE)**[33] 2473 6-9-4 **56** (b) HollieDoyle 1 65
(Brian Baugh) *in tch on outer: pushed along over 3f out: hdwy to ld over 1f out: edgd rt u.p ins fnl f: hdd post* **5/2**[1]
-035 **3** 3 1/4 **Glyder**[10] 3213 5-8-8 **46** (p) RoystonFfrench 6 43
(John Holt) *prom: rdn 2f out: ev ch over 1f out: no ex ins fnl f: lost 2nd 100 yds out* **7/2**[3]
-010 **4** 1 **Jaganory (IRE)**[15] 3036 7-9-1 **58** (v) PoppyBridgwater(5) 5 51
(Christopher Mason) *s.i.s: in rr: rdn 1/2-way: r.o appr fnl f: no imp towards fin* **17/2**
0000 **5** 3/4 **Celerity (IRE)**[3] 3475 5-8-4 **45** (v) WilliamCox(3) 2 36
(Lisa Williamson) *chsd ldrs: rdn 2f out: edgd lft and sltly outpcd over 1f out: kpt on fnl f* **25/1**
56-5 **6** hd **Edged Out**[24] 2729 9-9-7 **59** JosephineGordon 4 49
(Christopher Mason) *cl up: led after 2f: rdn 2f out: hdd over 1f out: fdd fnl f* **10/1**
00-0 **7** 3 1/4 **Hellofagame**[145] 239 4-8-0 **45** EllieMacKenzie(7) 11 23
(Richard Price) *wnt rt s: pushed along and sn chsng ldrs: rdn after 2f: n.m.r 2f out: sn wknd* **25/1**
6050 **8** 2 **Fethiye Boy**[33] 2473 5-9-5 **57** KieranShoemark 9 28
(Ronald Harris) *t.k.h: led 2f: remained prom: rdn 2f out: wknd fnl f* **11/4**[2]
60-0 **9** 3 **Babyfact**[24] 2729 8-9-4 **56** (p) CharlieBennett 3 16
(Malcolm Saunders) *chsd ldrs: rdn 2f out: wknd appr fnl f* **14/1**

1m 1.37s (1.97) **Going Correction** +0.20s/f (Good) **9 Ran SP% 119.8**
Speed ratings (Par 101): **92,91,86,85,83 83,78,75,70**
CSF £40.27 CT £120.21 TOTE £14.50: £3.30, £1.40, £1.30; EX 62.30 Trifecta £204.90.
Owner SS Partnership **Bred** Whitsbury Manor Stud **Trained** Yarnscombe, Devon

FOCUS
A moderate sprint handicap.
T/Plt: £22.90 to a £1 stake. Pool: £55,345.46 - 2,412.52 winning units T/Qpdt: £7.70 to a £1 stake. Pool: £5,953.55 - 772.51 winning units **Richard Lowther**

3491 CHELMSFORD (A.W) (L-H)
Saturday, June 8

OFFICIAL GOING: Polytrack: standard
Wind: strong, across Weather: cloudy, brightening up later

3578 FEDERATION OF BLOODSTOCK AGENTS MAIDEN AUCTION FILLIES' STKS (PLUS 10 RACE) 7f (P)
1:55 (1:59) (Class 5) 2-Y-0
£4,527 (£1,347; £673; £336) **Stalls** Low

Form | | | | RPR
3 **1** **Romsey**[12] 3165 2-8-11 0 PJMcDonald 2 81+
(Hughie Morrison) *in tch: clsd to trck ldr and switching rt 2f out: pushed into ld ent fnl f: r.o wl easily* **10/11**[1]
5 **2** 4 1/2 **Blausee (IRE)**[21] 2836 2-8-11 0 DannyBrock 9 66
(Philip McBride) *midfield early: sn dropped to last trio: effrt on inner over 1f out: swtchd rt and drvn ins fnl f: r.o to go 2nd towards fin: no ch w wnr* **10/1**[3]
00 **3** 1 1/4 **The Lazy Monkey (IRE)**[44] 2052 2-8-12 0 SilvestreDeSousa 4 64
(Mark Johnston) *led for 2f: chsd ldr tl led again over 3f out: rdn ent fnl 2f: hdd ent fnl f: sn outpcd and lost 2nd towards fin* **12/1**
4 2 **Hashtagmetoo (USA)** 2-9-0 0 NicolaCurrie 6 61
(Jamie Osborne) *chsd ldr for over 1f: in tch in midfield after: effrt 2f out: no ch w wnr and kpt on same pce fnl f* **12/1**
5 1 3/4 **Pink Tulip** 2-9-0 0 StevieDonohoe 5 56
(David Simcock) *in tch in midfield: effrt over 2f out: outpcd and btn over 1f out: wknd ins fnl f* **8/1**[2]
45 **6** 2 **Callipygian**[29] 2579 2-8-5 0 CierenFallon(7) 10 49
(James Given) *chsd ldrs early: hung rt 4f out: lost pl and towards rr whn rdn over 2f out: wknd over 1f out* **20/1**
7 4 **Boston Girl (IRE)** 2-8-12 0 RobertHavlin 7 39
(Ed Dunlop) *slowly into strdrn green in rr: hung rt over 2f out: sn bhd* **33/1**
8 4 **Lightning Bug (IRE)** 2-8-11 0 KierenFox 8 27
(Suzy Smith) *s.i.s: hdwy to ld after 2f: hdd over 3f out: lost pl u.p over 1f out: fdd ins fnl f (jockey said filly was slowly away)* **33/1**

1m 26.25s (-0.95) **Going Correction** -0.325s/f (Stan) **8 Ran SP% 98.6**
Speed ratings (Par 90): **92,86,85,83,81 78,74,69**
CSF £6.97 TOTE £1.30: £1.20, £1.50, £1.80; EX 6.40 Trifecta £29.60.
Owner The End-R-Ways Partnership & Partners **Bred** The Lavington Stud **Trained** East Ilsley, Berks
■ Mrs Dukesbury was withdrawn. Price at time of withdrawal 9/2. Rule 4 applies to all bets - deduction 15p in the £.

FOCUS
Not much depth to this, especially following the late withdrawal of the paper favourite Mrs Dukesbury, and it proved easy pickings for the heavily backed Romsey.

3579 BET TOTEEXACTA AT TOTESPORT.COM NOVICE AUCTION STKS 6f (P)
2:30 (2:33) (Class 6) 2-Y-0
£3,492 (£1,039; £519; £259) **Stalls** Centre

Form | | | | RPR
06 **1** **Constanzia**[2] 3491 2-9-0 0 NicolaCurrie 1 67
(Jamie Osborne) *broke wl: sn hdd and chsd ldr for 2f: styd handy: effrt ent fnl 2f: kpt on u.p to ld and edgd rt 100yds out: styd on* **7/1**
2 1/2 **Space Ace (FR)** 2-9-0 0 OisinMurphy 6 66
(Archie Watson) *sn led: rdn over 1f out: drvn and hdd 100yds out: kpt on same pce after* **8/11**[1]
0 **3** 1 1/4 **Ossco**[19] 2903 2-9-5 0 SeanLevey 2 67
(Mohamed Moubarak) *in tch in last pair: effrt ent fnl 2f: clsd to chse ldrs whn hung lft and swtchd lft ins fnl f: kpt on to snatch 3rd last stride* **20/1**
40 **4** shd **Red Maharani**[23] 2761 2-9-0 0 SilvestreDeSousa 4 61
(James Given) *chsd ldrs tl wnt 2nd 4f out: drvn and ev ch over 2f out: hung rt and no ex ins fnl f: wknd towards fin (jockey said filly hung right-handed)* **5/1**[2]
0 **5** nk **Boasty (IRE)**[9] 3257 2-9-5 0 StevieDonohoe 5 66
(Charlie Fellowes) *in tch in midfield: effrt over 2f out: unable qck over 1f out: kpt on ins fnl f: nt enough pce to threaten ldrs* **6/1**[3]
0 **6** 3 3/4 **Mungo's Quest (IRE)**[23] 2767 2-9-5 0 KierenFox 3 54
(Simon Dow) *dwlt: in tch in rr: effrt over 1f out: no imp and hung rt 1f out: wknd ins fnl f* **14/1**

1m 12.78s (-0.92) **Going Correction** -0.325s/f (Stan) **6 Ran SP% 112.8**
Speed ratings (Par 91): **93,92,90,90,90 85**
CSF £12.80 TOTE £8.10: £2.40, £1.20; EX 17.00 Trifecta £93.60.
Owner The Judges & Partner **Bred** Saeed Nasser Al Romaithi **Trained** Upper Lambourn, Berks

FOCUS
This didn't look a strong race on paper beforehand and the result tends to support that view. The level is fluid.

3580 BET TOTEQUADPOT AT TOTESPORT.COM H'CAP 1m (P)
3:05 (3:08) (Class 5) (0-75,77) 3-Y-0
£5,498 (£1,636; £817; £408; £300; £300) **Stalls** Low

Form | | | | RPR
6315 **1** **Solar Heights (IRE)**[37] 2333 3-9-6 **74** (v[1]) PJMcDonald 8 86
(James Tate) *chsd ldr tl shkn up to ld over 1f out: r.o strly and drew clr fnl f: v readily* **6/1**[3]
-114 **2** 4 1/2 **Dragon Sun**[9] 3278 3-9-8 **76** SeanLevey 9 78+
(Richard Hannon) *t.k.h: hld up in tch in midfield: effrt over 1f out: kpt on u.p ins fnl f to snatch 2nd last strides: no ch w wnr* **5/1**[2]
5-25 **3** hd **New Jazz (USA)**[23] 2760 3-9-8 **76** RobertHavlin 10 78
(John Gosden) *led: rdn and hdd over 1f out: outpcd by wnr fnl f: lost 2nd last strides* **7/1**
5-31 **4** 1 **Jilbaab**[29] 2598 3-9-9 **77** JamesSullivan 1 76
(Brian Meehan) *t.k.h early: chsd ldrs: effrt over 2f out: no ch w wnr and kpt on same pce ins fnl f* **5/1**[2]

-162 **5** ½ **Prince Of Harts**[28] 2630 3-9-8 **76**........................ CharlesBishop 13 74+
(Rod Millman) *stdd and dropped in bhd after s: effrt and hdwy over 1f out: swtchd lft and kpt on ins fnl f: no threat to wnr* **5/1**[2]

636 **6** ¾ **Onebaba (IRE)**[12] 3170 3-9-4 **75**........................(v) CameronNoble(3) 4 71
(Michael Bell) *t.k.h: chsd ldrs: unable qck over 1f out: keeping on same pce whn hung lft ins fnl f* **9/2**[1]

1504 **7** 2½ **Bay Of Naples (IRE)**[31] 2529 3-9-7 **75**........................ SilvestreDeSousa 2 66
(Mark Johnston) *sddle slipped leaving stalls: hld up in tch in last trio: effrt on inner over 1f out: no imp (jockey said the saddle slipped)* **7/1**

6-60 **8** nk **Startego**[12] 3170 3-9-2 **70**........................ OisinMurphy 6 60
(Archie Watson) *taken down early: hld up in tch in midfield: effrt over 1f out: hung lft and nt qckn: wl hld and plugged on same pce fnl f* **25/1**

05-2 **9** 3¼ **Kings Royal Hussar (FR)**[18] 2933 3-9-4 **72**........................ TomQueally 11 54
(Alan King) *hld up in tch in midfield on outer: effrt over 2f out: unable qck and lost pl over 1f out: wknd fnl f* **14/1**

-000 **10** 6 **Mitigator**[39] 2238 3-8-7 **61** ow1........................ BrettDoyle 3 30
(Lydia Pearce) *short of room and jostled leaving stalls: a in rr (jockey said he was tightened for room shortly after the start)* **50/1**

1m 37.47s (-2.43) **Going Correction** -0.325s/f (Stan) **10 Ran SP% 119.9**
Speed ratings (Par 99): **99,94,94,93,92 92,89,89,86,80**
CSF £37.23 CT £219.41 TOTE £7.40: £2.20, £2.10, £2.50; EX 53.50 Trifecta £384.60.
Owner Saeed Manana **Bred** Norelands Bloodstock & Yarraman Park **Trained** Newmarket, Suffolk

FOCUS
Three non-runners but still plenty of potential on show in what looked a decent race for the level. Four of the runners were unusually rated in excess of the ceiling mark of 75. It's been rated at face value, with the second to the fifth all rated close to form.

3581 BET TOTETRIFECTA AT TOTESPORT.COM MOULSHAM MILE H'CAP 1m (P)
3:40 (3:48) (Class 2) (0-105,102) 3-Y-O+ **£25,876** (£7,700; £3,848; £1,924) **Stalls Low**

Form RPR

6125 **1** **War Glory (IRE)**[8] 3318 6-9-7 **94**........................ SeanLevey 1 103
(Richard Hannon) *hld up in tch in midfield: swtchd rt and effrt over 1f out: hdwy u.p to chse ldr ins fnl f: r.o strly to ld towards fin* **5/1**[3]

1-23 **2** ¾ **Qaroun**[35] 2402 4-9-1 **88**........................ OisinMurphy 10 95
(Sir Michael Stoute) *led: rdn over 1f out: drvn ins fnl f: hdd and no ex towards fin* **9/2**[2]

01-0 **3** 2 **Nicklaus**[8] 3313 4-8-13 **93**........................ CierenFallon(7) 5 95
(William Haggas) *chsd ldr tl over 4f out: styd handy tl chsd ldr again over 2f out tl ins fnl f: kpt on same pce fnl 100yds* **16/1**

30-0 **4** ¾ **Bless Him (IRE)**[23] 2778 5-9-7 **94**........................(h) RobertHavlin 11 95+
(David Simcock) *stdd and dropped in bhd after s: t.k.h: hld up in rr: stl last and nt clr run over 1f out: hdwy 1f out: r.o strly ins fnl f* **10/1**

1-10 **5** 2 **Name The Wind**[35] 2411 3-9-1 **99**........................ PJMcDonald 2 92
(James Tate) *t.k.h: hld up in tch in midfield: clsd to chse ldrs over 2f out: drvn and unable qck over 1f out: wknd ins fnl f* **2/1**[1]

3200 **6** ½ **Commander Han (FR)**[12] 3160 4-9-1 **88**........................ SamJames 3 83
(Kevin Ryan) *t.k.h: hld up in tch in midfield: effrt on inner over 1f out: sme hdwy and swtchd rt 1f out: no imp after and nvr trbld ldrs* **6/1**

3041 **7** 1¾ **Apex King (IRE)**[16] 3009 5-9-3 **90**........................ NicolaCurrie 7 81
(David Loughnane) *awkward leaving stalls: sn chsng ldrs: lost pl u.p over 1f out: wknd ins fnl f (starter reported that the gelding was the subject of a third criteria failure; trainer was informed that the gelding could not run until the day after passing a stalls test)* **25/1**

31-0 **8** 1¼ **Hot Team (IRE)**[41] 2163 3-9-4 **102**........................(v) PatCosgrave 8 87
(Hugo Palmer) *dwlt: t.k.h: hld up in tch in last pair: swtchd rt and effrt over 1f out: no imp and wl hld ins fnl f* **25/1**

5015 **9** 1¾ **Goring (GER)**[35] 2402 7-10-0 **101**........................(v) CharlesBishop 4 85
(Eve Johnson Houghton) *chsd ldrs tl rdn and lost pl over 1f out: wknd ins fnl f* **25/1**

-051 **10** 1¼ **Bacacarat (IRE)**[17] 2966 4-8-11 **84**........................ SilvestreDeSousa 9 65
(Andrew Balding) *in tch in midfield: hdwy to chse ldr over 4f out tl over 2f out: sn struggling u.p and lost pl over 1f out: wknd ins fnl f* **9/1**

-031 **11** nse **Bubble And Squeak**[28] 2608 4-9-1 **91**........................ GaryMahon(3) 6 72+
(Sylvester Kirk) *in tch in midfield: rdn and hdwy on outer over 2f out: lost pl u.p and btn over 1f out: wknd ins fnl f* **25/1**

1m 36.65s (-3.25) **Going Correction** -0.325s/f (Stan)
WFA 3 from 4yo+ 11lb **11 Ran SP% 122.8**
Speed ratings (Par 109): **103,102,100,99,97 97,95,94,92,91 90**
CSF £27.08 CT £332.66 TOTE £6.20: £1.80, £1.90, £4.10; EX 35.00 Trifecta £417.40.
Owner Mohamed Saeed Al Shahi **Bred** Pier House Stud **Trained** East Everleigh, Wilts

FOCUS
The first of three class 2 handicaps on the card and it looked a good one. The winner translated his recent turf improvement and went two places better than last year. The third has been rated close to form.

3582 BET TOTESWINGER AT TOTESPORT.COM ESSEX SPRINT H'CAP 5f (P)
4:15 (4:19) (Class 2) (0-105,104) 3-Y-O+ **£25,876** (£7,700; £3,848; £1,924) **Stalls Low**

Form RPR

3-00 **1** **Lord Riddiford (IRE)**[14] 3097 4-8-13 **89**........................ PJMcDonald 1 97
(John Quinn) *chsd ldrs: effrt over 1f out: drvn and clsd to ld ins fnl f: r.o wl* **7/2**[2]

3340 **2** ¾ **Tropics (USA)**[19] 2917 11-9-13 **103**........................(h) JoeyHaynes 8 108
(Dean Ivory) *led: rdn over 1f out: hdd and one pce ins fnl f* **20/1**

1660 **3** ¾ **Encore D'Or**[35] 2409 7-9-9 **104**........................ DylanHogan(5) 9 106
(Robert Cowell) *chsd ldr: rdn over 1f out: kpt on same pce fnl 100yds* **25/1**

0063 **4** 1 **Udontdodou**[44] 2061 6-8-13 **89**........................ PhilipPrince 7 88+
(Richard Guest) *taken down early: hld up in last pair: effrt over 1f out: styd on u.p fnl 100yds: nt rch ldrs* **20/1**

5050 **5** shd **Royal Birth**[23] 2775 8-9-10 **100**........................(t) OisinMurphy 5 98
(Stuart Williams) *in tch in last quartet: effrt over 1f out: kpt on ins fnl f: nt rch ldrs* **6/1**

1010 **6** nse **Poyle Vinnie**[23] 2775 9-8-12 **88**........................ JamesSullivan 3 86
(Ruth Carr) *hld up in tch in midfield: swtchd rt and effrt over 1f out: kpt on same pce ins fnl f* **8/1**

4210 **7** nk **Saaheq**[23] 2775 5-8-10 **91**........................ ThoreHammerHansen(5) 6 88
(Michael Appleby) *chsd ldrs: unable qck u.p over 1f out: kpt on same pce ins fnl f: burst blood vessel (vet said gelding bled from the nose)* **8/1**

-211 **8** hd **Venturous (IRE)**[19] 2910 6-8-10 **86**........................ RobbieDowney 10 82
(David Barron) *in tch in midfield: unable qck and outpcd over 1f out: kpt on same pce ins fnl f* **14/1**

0-16 **9** 2¼ **Cowboy Soldier (IRE)**[23] 2775 4-9-3 **93**........................ HayleyTurner 4 81
(Robert Cowell) *shifted lft sn after s: in tch in last quartet: effrt over 2f out: no imp and wknd ins fnl f* **11/4**[1]

-030 **10** 1¼ **A Momentofmadness**[14] 3097 6-9-3 **100**........................(h) CierenFallon(7) 2 84
(Charles Hills) *dwlt and hmpd sn after s: a bhd (jockey said he was tightened for room shortly after the start)* **5/1**[3]

57.6s (-2.60) **Going Correction** -0.325s/f (Stan) **10 Ran SP% 122.1**
Speed ratings (Par 109): **107,105,104,103,102 102,102,101,98,96**
CSF £76.64 CT £1588.73 TOTE £4.30: £1.80, £6.80, £6.90; EX 95.80 Trifecta £1186.60.
Owner The Jam Partnership **Bred** Malachy M Harney **Trained** Settrington, N Yorks

FOCUS
A competitive edition of this quality sprint handicap, in which Tropics was bidding to repeat last year's triumph. The winner has been rated to his 3yo form, and the second similar to his last 5f run here.

3583 BILL BRIGHT MEMORIAL FILLIES' H'CAP 7f (P)
4:50 (4:52) (Class 2) (0-100,87) 3-Y-O **£19,407** (£5,775; £2,886; £1,443) **Stalls Low**

Form RPR

2-51 **1** **Neon Sea (FR)**[14] 3080 3-9-5 **85**........................ OisinMurphy 5 92+
(Sir Michael Stoute) *sn led and mde rest: rdn over 1f out: drvn 1f out: kpt on u.p and a doing enough ins fnl f* **8/11**[1]

4-00 **2** ½ **Impulsion (IRE)**[22] 2806 3-9-6 **86**........................ JackMitchell 1 91
(Roger Varian) *t.k.h: trckd ldng pair: effrt on inner: drvn and clsd to press wnr ins fnl f: styd on wl but a hld* **4/1**[2]

10-0 **3** 2 **Porcelain Girl (IRE)**[41] 2144 3-8-6 **79**........................ SaraDelFabbro(7) 2 79
(Michael Bell) *rdr slow to remove hood and dwlt: t.k.h: hld up in tch in rr: clsd and swtchd rt 2f out: rdn and kpt on same pce ins fnl f: snatched 3rd on post* **33/1**

1123 **4** nse **With Caution (IRE)**[15] 3048 3-9-3 **83**........................ PJMcDonald 6 82
(James Tate) *chsd wnr: drvn over 1f out: unable qck and lost 2nd ins fnl f: outpcd towards fin and lost 3rd on post* **6/1**

-022 **5** 1½ **Lorton**[8] 3293 3-9-2 **87**........................ DannyRedmond(5) 4 82
(Julie Camacho) *taken down early: t.k.h: hld up in tch in last pair: effrt over 1f out: unable qck and kpt on same pce ins fnl f* **5/1**[3]

1m 25.23s (-1.97) **Going Correction** -0.325s/f (Stan) **5 Ran SP% 111.8**
Speed ratings (Par 102): **98,97,95,95,93**
CSF £4.12 TOTE £1.70: £1.10, £1.80; EX 4.00 Trifecta £31.40.
Owner Qatar Racing Limited **Bred** E A R L Qatar Bloodstock Ltd **Trained** Newmarket, Suffolk

FOCUS
With top weight Lorton rated just 87, this was well below the standard generally associated with a race at this level. The odds-on favourite dictated throughout. The second has been rated back to her 2yo best.

3584 COMMODORE KITCHENS MAIDEN STKS 1m 2f (P)
5:25 (5:30) (Class 5) 3-Y-O+ **£5,271** (£1,568; £783; £391) **Stalls Low**

Form RPR

32-2 **1** **Durrell**[40] 2210 3-9-1 84........................ DanielMuscutt 8 89
(James Fanshawe) *chsd ldrs: clsd and swtchd rt 2f out: rdn to ld over 1f out: styd on wl and a doing enough ins fnl f* **11/4**[2]

35 **2** ¾ **Ironclad**[70] 1417 3-9-1 0........................ PatCosgrave 9 87
(Hugo Palmer) *in tch in midfield: chsd ldrs and effrt jst over 2f out: swtchd rt and rdn over 1f out: pressed wnr 1f out: kpt on but a hld ins fnl f* **9/2**[3]

3 2½ **Dante's View (IRE)** 3-9-1 0........................ PJMcDonald 10 82
(Sir Michael Stoute) *chsd ldrs: effrt jst over 2f out: chsd ldng pair and swtchd lft ins fnl f: kpt on same pce after* **12/1**

3 **4** 1 **Dilmun Dynasty (IRE)**[23] 2764 3-9-1 0........................ OisinMurphy 1 80+
(Sir Michael Stoute) *dwlt and pushed along early: towards rr: rdn and swtchd rt over 3f out: 6th and stl plenty to do u.p over 1f out: styd on: nvr rchd ldrs* **11/8**[1]

52-0 **5** 5 **Crimewave (IRE)**[23] 2766 3-8-10 77........................ DylanHogan(5) 11 70
(Tom Clover) *chsd ldr tl rdn to ld over 2f out: edgd rt and hdd over 1f out: wknd ins fnl f* **8/1**

6 4½ **Gallatin** 3-8-10 0........................ JoeyHaynes 14 56+
(Andrew Balding) *stdd and dropped in bhd after s: hld up in rr: sme hdwy over 2f out: m green over 1f out: kpt on ins fnl f: nvr trbld ldrs* **20/1**

7 2¾ **Red Secret (CAN)** 3-9-1 0........................ BrettDoyle 13 56
(Ed Dunlop) *s.i.s: in rr: sme late hdwy to pass btn horses fnl f: nvr involved* **25/1**

0-6 **8** ½ **Star Talent (IRE)**[32] 2519 3-9-1 0........................ TomQueally 7 55
(Gay Kelleway) *midfield: struggling and outpcd over 3f out: no ch and hung rt over 1f out* **66/1**

04 **9** 1 **Jaidaa**[21] 2838 3-8-10 0........................ JackMitchell 2 48
(Simon Crisford) *led tl hdd and rdn over 1f out: sn btn and wknd fnl f* **22/1**

40 **10** ½ **Second Sight**[16] 3003 3-8-8 0........................ AledBeech(7) 6 52
(Charlie Fellowes) *a in rr: nvr involved (jockey said colt hung right-handed travelling up the home straight)* **80/1**

11 12 **Ned Pepper (IRE)** 3-8-10 0........................ ThoreHammerHansen(5) 3 28
(Alan King) *a towards rr: lost tch 3f out* **66/1**

12 10 **Thespinningwheel (IRE)** 4-10-0 0........................ RoystonFfrench 5 9
(Adam West) *s.i.s: hdwy into midfield after 2f out: dropped to rr and struggling over 3f out: t.o (jockey said gelding was slowly away)* **80/1**

13 95 **Isaac Murphy (USA)** 3-9-1 0........................ RobbieDowney 12
(Mark H Tompkins) *midfield: rdn 5f out: dropped to rr 3f out: sn lost tch and eased: t.o (jockey said gelding was never travelling)* **80/1**

2m 3.11s (-5.49) **Going Correction** -0.325s/f (Stan)
WFA 3 from 4yo 13lb **13 Ran SP% 125.4**
Speed ratings (Par 103): **108,107,105,104,100 97,94,94,93,93 83,75,**
CSF £15.55 TOTE £2.90: £1.30, £1.50, £3.30; EX 17.70 Trifecta £135.80.
Owner Silver,Steed,Gambini & Venice Consulting **Bred** Rabbah Bloodstock Limited **Trained** Newmarket, Suffolk

FOCUS
An informative maiden, though as the market suggested, only a handful of the runners could be seriously considered. It's been rated slightly positively, with the fifth to last year's 1m2f run.
T/Plt: £51.00 to a £1 stake. Pool: £31,645.66 - 619.93 winning units T/Qpdt: £38.60 to a £1 stake. Pool: £2,734.64 - 70.78 winning units **Steve Payne**

3547

HAYDOCK (L-H)

Saturday, June 8

OFFICIAL GOING: Heavy (6.0)

Wind: light breeze, against in home straight Weather: overcast, occasional rain, cool

3585 BETWAY HEED YOUR HUNCH H'CAP 1m 3f 175y

1:45 (1:45) (Class 3) (0-90,89) 3-Y-O **£10,350** (£3,080; £1,539; £769) **Stalls** Centre

Form RPR

43-1 **1** **Mind The Crack (IRE)**[9] 3254 3-9-1 **83** JasonHart 6 92+
(Mark Johnston) *mde all: pushed along in narrow ld 3f out: drvn in 1 l ld 2f out: rdn 4 l clr 1f out: in command fnl f: eased nr fin* **5/2**[2]

5-36 **2** *3* **Cormier (IRE)**[43] 2075 3-8-2 **70** oh1 DavidEgan 1 72
(Stef Keniry) *chsd wnr thrght: pushed along in cl 2nd 3f out: rdn and lost grnd on wnr 2f out: 4 l 2nd 1f out: one pce fnl f* **11/2**

4-42 **3** *4 ½* **Alhaazm**[22] 2796 3-9-0 **82** JimCrowley 3 77
(Sir Michael Stoute) *racd in 3rd: pushed along and tk clsr order 3f out: rdn 2f out: wknd over 1f out (trainer's rep said colt was unsuited by the heavy ground and would prefer a faster surface; vet said colt had sustained a minor wound to its right hind)* **13/8**[1]

1222 **4** *1 ¾* **Paradise Boy (FR)**[72] 1386 3-8-9 **77** DavidProbert 4 69
(Andrew Balding) *slowly away: a in rr: pushed along 3f out: drvn and effrt on outer over 2f out: sn rdn: no ex* **11/4**[3]

2m 44.44s (11.14) **Going Correction** +0.75s/f (Yiel) **4 Ran SP% 108.7**
Speed ratings (Par 103): **92,90,87,85**
CSF £14.33 TOTE £2.90; EX 16.30 Trifecta £31.60.

Owner Paul & Clare Rooney **Bred** H & M Biebel **Trained** Middleham Moor, N Yorks

FOCUS
All races used the stands' side home straight. Distance of the opener increased by 52yds. Further rain on the morning of racing (around 4mm) ensured the ground remained heavy. Two key non-runners and this didn't take much winning with the favourite struggling on the ground, but still a nice performance from an improving winner. It's been rated a bit cautiously, with the second in line with the better view of his form.

3586 BETWAY PINNACLE STKS (GROUP 3) (F&M) 1m 3f 175y

2:25 (2:26) (Class 1) 4-Y-O+

£35,727 (£13,545; £6,778; £3,376; £1,694; £850) **Stalls** Centre

Form RPR

12-2 **1** **Klassique**[35] 2401 4-9-0 102 DanielTudhope 4 107+
(William Haggas) *chsd ldr: pushed along to chal over 2f out: rdn to ld 1 1/2f out: 1 l ld 1f out: drvn clr fnl f: comf* **7/2**[2]

11- **2** *3* **True Self (IRE)**[31] 2535 6-9-0 112 ColinKeane 7 101
(W P Mullins, Ire) *mid-div: hdwy on outer 3f out: drvn in cl 2nd 1 1/2f out: rdn in 1 l 2nd 1f out: one pce as wnr asserted fnl f* **8/11**[1]

0-34 **3** *½* **Pilaster**[14] 3096 4-9-0 104 DavidEgan 9 100
(Roger Varian) *chsd ldr: drvn in cl 2nd 3f out: lost pl and rdn 1 1/2f out: kpt on into 3rd last 50yds* **7/1**[3]

6-66 **4** *1 ¼* **Magnolia Springs (IRE)**[28] 2642 4-9-0 92 JimCrowley 6 98
(Eve Johnson Houghton) *led: narrow ld 3f out: drvn over 2f out: sn rdn: hdd 1 1/2f out: no ex fnl f: lost 3rd last 50yds* **33/1**

06-1 **5** *2 ¾* **Dance Legend**[28] 2620 4-9-0 89 DavidProbert 2 94
(Rae Guest) *t.k.h: hld up: 5th on inner 3f out: sn drvn: reminders over 2f out and over 1f out: no imp (jockey said filly ran too freely)* **11/1**

56-1 **6** *4 ½* **Jedhi**[28] 2613 4-9-0 85 GrahamLee 5 86
(Hughie Morrison) *hld up: pushed along 3f out: reminder and wnt lft 2f out: wknd* **14/1**

12-6 **7** *1* **Mrs Sippy (USA)**[23] 2776 4-9-0 103 JamieSpencer 1 85
(David Simcock) *hld up: in rr: pushed along over 2f out: lost grnd and rdn over 1f out: no ch and eased fnl f* **8/1**

0-6R **R** **Jet Streaming (IRE)**[14] 3096 5-9-0 88 TrevorWhelan 8
(Samuel Farrell, Ire) *ref to leave stalls: tk no part (starter reported that the mare had refused to race; trainer was informed that any future similar behaviour from the mare may result in the mare being reported to the Head Office of the BHA)* **66/1**

2m 39.43s (6.13) **Going Correction** +0.75s/f (Yiel) **8 Ran SP% 123.2**
Speed ratings (Par 113): **109,107,106,105,104 101,100,**
CSF £6.95 TOTE £3.90: £1.40, £1.10, £1.70; EX 7.30 Trifecta £23.40.

Owner Miss Yvonne Jacques **Bred** R A H Evans **Trained** Newmarket, Suffolk

FOCUS
Distance increased by 52yds. Unpleasant conditions for these fillies and mares, with them racing into driving rain in the straight. Ordinary Group 3 form. The level is set around the fourth and fifth.

3587 BETWAY ACHILLES STKS (LISTED RACE) 5f

3:00 (3:01) (Class 1) 3-Y-O+

£20,982 (£7,955; £3,981; £1,983; £995; £499) **Stalls** High

Form RPR

145- **1** **Maid In India (IRE)**[210] 9003 5-8-13 92 TomEaves 8 103
(Eric Alston) *broke wl: mde all: 1 l ld 2f out: sn pushed along: rdn in 1 l ld 1f out: r.o wl fnl f: gng away at fin* **9/1**

1 **2** *1 ¾* **Lady In France**[36] 2377 3-8-6 0 BenCurtis 2 94
(K R Burke) *mid-div: carried lft by rival after 1f: pushed along to go prom 2f out: rdn in 2nd 1f out: kpt on fnl f* **20/1**

1-30 **3** *1 ½* **Tarboosh**[35] 2409 6-9-4 107 GrahamLee 9 96
(Paul Midgley) *mid-div: pushed along and hdwy into 3rd over 1f out: rdn fnl f: no ex* **7/2**[3]

00/1 **4** *½* **Stake Acclaim (IRE)**[57] 1734 7-9-4 108 RobertWinston 3 95
(Dean Ivory) *bhd: pushed along and hdwy 2f out: rdn over 1f out: kpt on fnl f: tk 4th nr fin* **10/3**[2]

20-0 **5** *nse* **Dave Dexter**[31] 2522 3-9-0 96 HarryBentley 5 94
(Ralph Beckett) *hld up: pushed along 2f out: rdn and hdwy into 4th 1f out: no ex fnl f: lost 4th nr fin* **6/1**

11-6 **6** *4 ½* **Intense Romance (IRE)**[40] 2221 5-9-2 104 GeraldMosse 7 76
(Michael Dods) *hld up: pushed along 2f out: rdn and wknd over 1f out (trainer could offer no explanation for the mare's performance other than she had missed the break)* **3/1**[1]

3202 **7** *3 ½* **Treasure Me**[28] 2627 4-8-13 90 (v) JamieSpencer 1 61
(Charlie Fellowes) *restless in stalls: trckd across fr wd draw to go prom: drvn 2f out: reminder and wknd over 1f out: eased fnl f* **15/2**

2-06 **8** *4 ½* **One Last Night (IRE)**[28] 2627 4-8-13 90 (h) JimCrowley 4 44
(Robert Cowell) *t.k.h: chsd ldrs: carried rival lft after 1f: drvn and lost pl 1 1/2f out: lost tch fnl f* **33/1**

1m 2.1s (1.70) **Going Correction** +0.75s/f (Yiel)
WFA 3 from 4yo+ 7lb **8 Ran SP% 114.1**
Speed ratings (Par 111): **116,113,110,110,109 102,97,89**
CSF £161.79 TOTE £10.10: £2.70, £4.10, £1.70; EX 149.20 Trifecta £1355.60.

Owner Con Harrington **Bred** C F Harrington **Trained** Longton, Lancs

FOCUS
Ordinary Listed form, with a couple of the key players failing to run to their best, and the winner dominated. They raced stands' side. The level is a bit fluid, but the fifth helps set the standard for now, rated close to his 2yo form.

3588 BETWAY JOHN OF GAUNT STKS (GROUP 3) 7f 37y

3:35 (3:35) (Class 1) 4-Y-O+

£35,727 (£13,545; £6,778; £3,376; £1,694; £850) **Stalls** Low

Form RPR

0-11 **1** **Safe Voyage (IRE)**[28] 2615 6-9-0 109 JasonHart 3 117
(John Quinn) *trckd ldrs: 3rd gng wl 3f out: tk clsr order 2f out: pushed into ld over 1f out: rdn and forged clr fnl f: readily* **5/4**[1]

4-44 **2** *1 ¾* **Suedois (FR)**[28] 2615 8-9-0 112 DanielTudhope 4 112
(David O'Meara) *mid-div: trckd ldrs 2f out: rdn in 3rd 1f out: r.o u.p fnl f: wnt 2nd 1/2f out: nvr a threat to wnr* **15/2**[3]

101- **3** *2 ¾* **Snazzy Jazzy (IRE)**[220] 8755 4-9-3 110 HectorCrouch 8 108
(Clive Cox) *prom: pushed along in 2 l 2nd 3f out: drvn and almost upsides ldr 2f out: rdn and ev ch 1f out: no ex fnl f: lost 2nd 1/2f out* **11/1**

1-04 **4** *nk* **Shepherd Market (IRE)**[28] 2621 4-8-11 96 PaulHanagan 2 102
(Clive Cox) *led: pushed along in 2 l ld 3f out: drvn in narrow ld 2f out: hdd and rdn over 1f out: wknd fnl f* **33/1**

2-54 **5** *shd* **Mitchum Swagger**[26] 2688 7-9-0 107 HarryBentley 12 104
(Ralph Beckett) *hld up: pushed along 2f out: rdn over 1f out: one pce fnl f* **10/1**

-115 **6** *1 ¼* **Keyser Soze (IRE)**[50] 1922 5-9-0 105 GrahamLee 9 101
(Richard Spencer) *hld up: in rr: last 2f out: rdn past btn rivals ins fnl f* **25/1**

00-3 **7** *2 ¼* **Breton Rock (IRE)**[26] 2688 9-9-0 108 JamieSpencer 10 95
(David Simcock) *hld up: pushed along over 2f out: drvn fr over 1f out: no imp* **14/1**

60-6 **8** *1* **Burnt Sugar (IRE)**[42] 2100 7-9-0 103 BenCurtis 1 93
(Roger Fell) *t.k.h: mid-div: rdn and lost pl over 1f out: dropped away fnl f* **20/1**

64-2 **9** *dist* **Mankib**[28] 2615 5-9-0 109 JimCrowley 11
(William Haggas) *rrd up and banged hd leaving stalls: situation immediately accepted: horse allowed to canter home in its own time (jockey said horse reared as the stalls opened and banged its head on the stalls and he therefore brought the colt home in its own time)* **3/1**[2]

1m 36.23s (4.83) **Going Correction** +0.75s/f (Yiel) **9 Ran SP% 116.8**
Speed ratings (Par 113): **102,100,96,96,96 94,92,91,**
CSF £11.35 TOTE £2.20: £1.10, £2.70, £2.40; EX 8.90 Trifecta £93.50.

Owner Ross Harmon **Bred** Schneider Adolf **Trained** Settrington, N Yorks

FOCUS
Distance increased by 30yds. Not the deepest of Group 3s, especially with three non-runners (one significant one) and it proved all very straightforward for the improving favourite, also helped by main market rival Mankib losing his race exiting the stalls. It's been rated around the fourth.

3589 BETWAY DASH H'CAP 6f

4:10 (4:14) (Class 3) (0-95,95) 4-Y-O+ **£10,350** (£3,080; £1,539; £769) **Stalls** High

Form RPR

2-00 **1** **Cold Stare (IRE)**[29] 2572 4-9-4 **92** (t[1]) HarryBentley 16 103
(David O'Meara) *hld up: pushed along and hdwy 2f out: rdn to ld over 1f out: forged clr fnl f (trainer's rep said, regarding the improved form shown, the gelding had benefitted from the application of the first-time tongue-strap and may have appreciated the heavy ground)* **12/1**

21-0 **2** *2 ¼* **Lord Oberon**[42] 2100 4-9-6 **94** CliffordLee 3 98
(K R Burke) *mid-div: rdn to chal over 2f out: 3rd ent fnl f: kpt on to take 2nd last 25yds* **11/2**[2]

25-5 **3** *shd* **Camacho Chief (IRE)**[30] 2557 4-9-1 **94** PaulaMuir[(5)] 8 98+
(Michael Dods) *prom: led over 2f out: hdd over 1f out: sn rdn: kpt on fnl f: lost 2nd last 25yds* **10/1**

-125 **4** *2 ½* **Diamond Dougal (IRE)**[29] 2568 4-9-3 **91** DavidEgan 11 87
(Mick Channon) *bhd: rdn 2f out: hdwy over 1f out: styd on into 4th wl ins fnl f* **7/1**[3]

-004 **5** *hd* **Growl**[3] 3480 7-9-4 **92** (p) PaulHanagan 6 88
(Richard Fahey) *prom: drvn over 2f out: rdn and cl up 1 1/2f out: one pce fnl f: lost 4th nr fin* **7/1**[3]

301- **6** *1 ¾* **Bernardo O'Reilly**[225] 8612 5-9-3 **91** GeraldMosse 4 82
(Richard Spencer) *slowly away: bhd: drvn and effrt 1/2-way: rdn in mid-div over 1f out: one pce fnl f* **14/1**

1-30 **7** *1* **Confessional**[21] 2843 12-9-0 **88** (e) JasonHart 14 76
(Tim Easterby) *reluctant to load: chsd ldrs on stands' rail: drvn 2f out: one pce fnl f* **11/1**

15-1 **8** *¾* **Admirality**[21] 2844 5-9-5 **93** BenCurtis 15 78
(Roger Fell) *chsd ldrs: rdn and wknd over 1f out* **5/1**[1]

0-51 **9** *¾* **Dark Defender**[29] 2588 6-9-1 **89** DavidProbert 13 72
(Rebecca Bastiman) *mid-div: rdn 2f out: no imp* **14/1**

0140 **10** *5* **Reflektor (IRE)**[30] 2557 6-9-1 **92** JaneElliott[(3)] 5 60
(Tom Dascombe) *prom: drvn 1/2-way: sn wknd* **20/1**

0406 **11** *½* **Aeolus**[21] 2844 8-9-3 **91** JimCrowley 1 58
(Ruth Carr) *mid-div: pushed along and lost pl over 3f out: sn bhd* **16/1**

3-04 **12** *nse* **Savalas (IRE)**[24] 2743 4-9-6 **94** TomEaves 9 60
(Kevin Ryan) *trckd across to ld on stands' rail: drvn and hdd over 2f out: sn wknd* **10/1**

6000 **13** *4 ½* **Captain Colby (USA)**[24] 2743 7-9-2 **90** GrahamLee 17 43
(Paul Midgley) *outpcd and in rr: nvr a factor: lost shoe (vet said gelding lost its left hind shoe)* **40/1**

0-00 **14** *4* **Soie D'Leau**[19] 2910 7-9-0 **88** RobertWinston 7 29
(Linda Stubbs) *prom: pushed along and wknd over 2f out* **28/1**

430- **15** *½* **Gymkhana**[169] 9675 6-9-5 **93** DanielTudhope 10 32
(David O'Meara) *mid-div: drvn and lost pl 1/2-way: bhd and eased over 1f out (jockey said gelding moved poorly and was never travelling)* **14/1**

1m 16.75s (2.85) **Going Correction** +0.75s/f (Yiel) **15 Ran SP% 127.8**
Speed ratings (Par 107): **111,108,107,104,104 101,100,99,98,91 91,91,85,79,79**
CSF £79.28 CT £727.38 TOTE £14.10: £4.20, £2.30, £3.80; EX 121.60 Trifecta £871.30.

Owner Middleham Park Racing XC **Bred** Dubois Holdings Ltd **Trained** Upper Helmsley, N Yorks

The Form Book Flat 2019, Raceform Ltd, Newbury, RG14 5SJ

FOCUS
A useful and competitive sprint, the field was spread middle-to-stands' side and 4yos filled the first four places (from five runners).

3590 BETWAY SPRINT H'CAP 6f
4:45 (4:47) (Class 4) (0-80,82) 3-Y-O

£7,115 (£2,117; £1,058; £529; £300; £300) Stalls High

Form RPR

43-0 **1** **Came From The Dark (IRE)**[57] 1728 3-9-2 **75**............ GeraldMosse 6 85
(Ed Walker) *chsd ldr in centre: pushed into ld over 1f out: rdn ent fnl f: sn 2 l clr: pushed out nr fin (trainer's rep said, regarding the improved form shown, the colt had appreciated the return to turf)* **9/1**

2-25 **2** 2¼ **Glorious Emaraty (FR)**[63] 1598 3-9-3 **76**.................... HectorCrouch 1 79
(Clive Cox) *mid-div in centre: rdn into 3rd over 1f out: tk 2nd ins fnl f: jst hld on for 2nd nr fin* **25/1**

1-12 **3** nse **Whelans Way (IRE)**[8] 3307 3-9-6 **79**.................... DavidProbert 3 82
(Roger Teal) *mid-div: drvn 2f out: hdwy and rdn in 4th over 1f out: kpt on into 3rd fnl f: jst hld for 2nd nr fin* **11/2[3]**

14-0 **4** 4½ **Vee Man Ten**[22] 2810 3-8-13 **72**.................... PaulHanagan 5 61
(Ivan Furtado) *led in centre: 1 l ld 2f out: drvn and hdd over 1f out: rdn and wknd fnl f: jst hld on for 4th* **20/1**

22-1 **5** hd **Pendleton**[39] 2243 3-9-9 **82**.................... PaulMulrennan 14 71+
(Michael Dods) *bhd: pushed along and effrt over 2f out: sn rdn: one pce fnl f (jockey said colt was slowly away)* **11/4[1]**

1-20 **6** ¾ **The Night Watch**[24] 2746 3-9-9 **82**.................... JimCrowley 12 69+
(William Haggas) *hld up: pushed along over 2f out: reminder in mid-div over 1f out: no ex fnl f* **4/1[2]**

0-60 **7** shd **Autumn Flight (IRE)**[12] 3159 3-8-10 **69**.................... AndrewElliott 8 55
(Tim Easterby) *hld up: pushed along and nt clr run over 2f out: rdn over 1f out: one pce* **33/1**

25-3 **8** 2¾ **Phosphor (IRE)**[84] 1236 3-9-7 **80**.................... (b[1]) HarryBentley 11 58
(Martyn Meade) *hld up: pushed along over 2f out: sn rdn: no imp* **8/1**

0-40 **9** 1¾ **Wild Edric**[31] 2525 3-9-5 **81**.................... JaneElliott(3) 13 54
(Tom Dascombe) *mid-div on stands' side: rdn and lost pl over 2f out: wknd* **8/1**

564 **10** 9 **Kodi King (IRE)**[28] 2624 3-8-8 **67**.................... CliffordLee 9 13
(K R Burke) *prom: drvn and wknd 2f out* **12/1**

145- **11** 7 **Requited (IRE)**[253] 7720 3-9-1 **74**.................... GrahamLee 10
(Hughie Morrison) *racd in 3rd but led gp on stands' side: drvn and wknd 2f out: sn dropped to last* **20/1**

1m 17.09s (3.19) **Going Correction** +0.75s/f (Yiel) 11 Ran SP% 118.3
Speed ratings (Par 101): **108,105,104,98,98 97,97,93,91,79 70**
CSF £217.78 CT £973.40 TOTE £10.00: £2.40, £6.30, £1.80; EX 138.50 Trifecta £1766.70.
Owner P K Siu **Bred** Yeomanstown Stud & Doc Bloodstock **Trained** Upper Lambourn, Berks

■ Stewards' Enquiry : Paul Mulrennan caution: careless riding

FOCUS
A fair 3yo sprint, the main action unfolded down the centre. It's been rated around the second and third.

3591 BETWAY H'CAP 7f 37y
5:20 (5:20) (Class 4) (0-85,87) 3-Y-O

£7,115 (£2,117; £1,058; £529; £300; £300) Stalls Low

Form RPR

-040 **1** **Finoah (IRE)**[3] 3479 3-9-4 **85**.................... (v) JaneElliott(3) 13 94
(Tom Dascombe) *chsd ldrs: pushed along in 3rd 3f out: drvn into ld 1 1/2f out: sn rdn: wandered ent fnl f: sn stened and readily plld away fr rivals* **20/1**

3-10 **2** 2¼ **Zip**[24] 2746 3-8-10 **74**.................... PaulHanagan 12 77
(Richard Fahey) *hld up: pushed along and hdwy on stands' rail over 2f out: rdn in 2nd over 1f out: almost alongside wnr ins fnl f: no ex as wnr asserted last 100yds* **7/1[3]**

431- **3** 1¾ **Wise Counsel**[253] 7719 3-9-9 **87**.................... DanielTudhope 1 85+
(Clive Cox) *hld up: pushed along and hdwy on far side over 2f out: rdn over 1f out: kpt on into 3rd fnl f* **11/8[1]**

1-56 **4** 1 **Sparklealot (IRE)**[30] 2559 3-9-7 **85**.................... TrevorWhelan 5 81
(Ivan Furtado) *led: 1/2 l ld 3f out: rdn 2f out: hdd 1 1/2f out: no ex fnl f* **9/2[2]**

50-0 **5** 1 **Red Bravo (IRE)**[43] 2082 3-9-2 **80**.................... RobertWinston 8 75
(Charles Hills) *slowly away: bhd: hdwy over 2f out: drvn to chal over 1f out: rdn and nt clr run ins fnl f: no ex* **8/1**

14-6 **6** 12 **Indomitable (IRE)**[29] 2570 3-9-2 **80**.................... DavidProbert 3 42
(Andrew Balding) *hld up: drvn 2f out: sn rdn: no imp* **9/1**

50-0 **7** 2¼ **Indian Viceroy**[14] 3075 3-9-2 **80**.................... GeraldMosse 11 36
(Hughie Morrison) *mid-div: pushed along 3f out: sn rdn and wknd* **7/1[3]**

0-55 **8** nse **Gospel**[49] 1939 3-9-3 **86**.................... ScottMcCullagh(5) 4 42
(Mick Channon) *chsd ldrs: drvn and lost pl over 3f out: sn rdn and wknd* **20/1**

-503 **9** nk **Ellheidi (IRE)**[11] 3176 3-8-2 **66** oh1.................... (v[1]) DavidEgan 10 21
(K R Burke) *prom: drvn in 1/2 l 2nd 3f out: wknd over 2f out: dropped to last over 1f out* **33/1**

1m 35.48s (4.08) **Going Correction** +0.75s/f (Yiel) 9 Ran SP% 118.9
Speed ratings (Par 101): **106,103,101,100,99 85,82,82,82**
CSF £153.51 CT £328.55 TOTE £24.80: £5.60, £2.20, £1.20; EX 227.70 Trifecta £573.00.
Owner Alan & Sue Cronshaw & Peter Birbeck **Bred** Azienda Agricola La Rovere **Trained** Malpas, Cheshire

■ Stewards' Enquiry : Jane Elliott four-day ban: interference & careless riding (Jun 25-28)

FOCUS
Distance increased by 30yds. An ordinary 3yo handicap, it looked more open than the betting suggested and it was no surprise to see the favourite turned over. The level is a bit fluid, but the second has been rated close to his AW form.

T/Jkpt: Not won. T/Plt: £233.60 to a £1 stake. Pool: £139,757.27 - 456.16 winning units T/Qpdt: £59.00 to a £1 stake. Pool: £12,050.06 - 151.12 winning units **Keith McHugh**

3440 LINGFIELD (L-H)
Saturday, June 8

OFFICIAL GOING: All-weather - polytrack: standard; turf course - good to soft
Wind: Strong, half behind Weather: Changeable; heavy shower 7.45

3592 BUY2LETCARS AMATEUR RIDERS' H'CAP 1m 1y(P)
5:40 (5:42) (Class 6) (0-55,54) 4-Y-O+

£2,994 (£928; £464; £400; £400; £400) Stalls High

Form RPR

-000 **1** **Mime Dance**[59] 1679 8-10-9 **49**.................... MrMatthewJohnson(7) 2 56
(John Butler) *trckd ldrs: rdn to chal over 1f out: led ins fnl f: kpt on wl* **16/1**

2050 **2** 1 **Voice Of A Leader (IRE)**[17] 2972 8-10-7 **47**.. MissChelseaBanham(7) 8 52
(Paul Howling) *taken down early: led after 2f: mde most after: urged along over 1f out: hdd ins fnl f: kpt on* **11/2[2]**

-033 **3** nk **Captain Marmalade (IRE)**[32] 2513 7-10-5 **45**.................... MrCharliePike(7) 6 49
(Jimmy Fox) *hld up in last: stl there over 2f out: prog on inner but only 7th 1f out: swtchd rt and r.o wl: tk 3rd last strides* **8/1**

055- **4** ½ **Arctic Flower (IRE)**[185] 9401 6-10-9 **45**.................... MrJamesHarding(3) 1 48
(John Bridger) *trckd ldrs: rdn to chse ldng pair 2f out: kpt on same pce u.p* **25/1**

-020 **5** nse **Lord Murphy (IRE)**[122] 624 6-11-2 **54**.................... (tp) MrMatthewEnnis(5) 5 57
(Mark Loughnane) *hld up in last trio: prog on inner over 2f out: styd on u.p fnl f: nvr quite pce to chal* **14/1**

06 **6** ¾ **Brecqhou Island**[59] 1683 4-10-11 **49**.................... MrWillPettis(5) 7 50
(Mark Pattinson) *in tch: rdn to chse ldng quartet over 2f out: no imp u.str.p over 1f out: kpt on same pce* **10/1**

-033 **7** ¾ **Navarra Princess (IRE)**[12] 3142 4-10-13 **46**.... MissSerenaBrotherton 4 45
(Don Cantillon) *hld up in midfield: lost pl over 2f out: nt clr run and swtchd rt over 1f out: rdn and styd on same pce fnl f: n.d* **2/1[1]**

2000 **8** shd **New Rich**[24] 2728 9-10-10 **50**.................... MissNynkeSchilder(7) 11 49
(Eve Johnson Houghton) *s.i.s: hld up in last pair: nudged along over 1f out: kpt on steadily but no ch* **33/1**

3310 **9** 1¾ **Limerick Lord (IRE)**[66] 1527 7-11-6 **53**.................... (p) MrRossBirkett 3 48
(Julia Feilden) *w ldr after 2f to over 1f out: wknd fnl f* **7/1**

0064 **10** 1¼ **Perfect Soldier (IRE)**[8] 3325 5-10-12 **52**.. (v[1]) MissJenniferPahlman(7) 9 44
(Shaun Keightley) *prom: lost pl fr 1/2-way: wl in rr 2f out: no ch after* **6/1[3]**

0003 **11** 3½ **Haraz (IRE)**[46] 2006 6-10-12 **50**.................... MissMichelleBryant(5) 12 34
(Paddy Butler) *chsd ldrs: lost pl fr 3f out: bhd fnl f* **25/1**

0040 **12** 4 **Camanche Grey (IRE)**[2] 3504 8-10-9 **49**.................... MrJoshuaScott(7) 10 24+
(Lucinda Egerton) *led to s: racd v wd: led 2f: styd prom tl wknd qckly over 2f out* **25/1**

1m 38.86s (0.66) **Going Correction** -0.10s/f (Stan) 12 Ran SP% 122.7
Speed ratings (Par 101): **92,91,90,90,90 89,88,88,86,85 82,78**
CSF £101.18 CT £790.42 TOTE £18.80: £4.40, £2.40, £2.40; EX 167.20 Trifecta £1679.40.
Owner J Butler **Bred** The Stanley Estate And Stud Company **Trained** Newmarket, Suffolk

FOCUS
18mm of rain since yesterday and the going on turf was eased to good to soft. The amateur riders went a steady pace mid-race, and those racing prominently held an advantage.

3593 F G KEEN - LIVING THE DREAM H'CAP 1m 4f (P)
6:15 (6:16) (Class 6) (0-55,57) 3-Y-O

£3,105 (£924; £461; £400; £400; £400) Stalls Low

Form RPR

-043 **1** **Highway Robbery**[18] 2941 3-8-5 **45**.................... (p) SophieRalston(7) 6 51
(Julia Feilden) *trckd ldrs: rdn over 2f out: wnt 2nd over 1f out: grad clsd fnl f: led post* **12/1**

-000 **2** nse **Elsie Violet (IRE)**[9] 3256 3-9-3 **55**.................... (p) DarraghKeenan(7) 11 61
(Robert Eddery) *led: rdn 2f out: kpt on fnl f but hdd post* **25/1**

000 **3** 1¼ **Born Leader (FR)**[22] 2795 3-9-7 **54**.................... TomMarquand 3 58
(Hughie Morrison) *free to post: wl in tch: rdn 3f out: prog over 1f out: styd on to take 3rd nr fin* **5/1[2]**

4-00 **4** 1¼ **Riverina**[37] 2343 3-9-2 **52**.................... MitchGodwin(3) 12 54
(Harry Dunlop) *chsd ldr: rdn over 2f out: nt qckn over 1f out: sn lost 2nd and one pce after* **25/1**

0203 **5** 1¾ **Robeam (IRE)**[11] 3198 3-9-0 **52**.................... SeanDavis(5) 10 51+
(Richard Fahey) *restless stalls: wl in rr: rdn over 3f out: prog u.p over 1f out: kpt on and nvr nrr* **6/1[3]**

0060 **6** ½ **Ginge N Tonic**[9] 3275 3-8-7 **47**.................... TobyEley(7) 14 45+
(Adam West) *wl in rr: rdn 3f out and no prog: styd on over 1f out: no ch but gng on at fin* **16/1**

0-00 **7** shd **Bader**[9] 3256 3-9-7 **54**.................... SeanLevey 4 52
(Richard Hannon) *rn in snatches: towards rr: prog u.p 2f out: chsd ldrs fnl f but no ch: no imp last 75yds* **14/1**

2505 **8** hd **Chakrii (IRE)**[40] 2213 3-8-12 **52**.................... CierenFallon(7) 13 50
(Henry Spiller) *a abt same pl: rdn and no prog over 2f out* **8/1**

00-6 **9** 2 **Land Of Winter (FR)**[25] 2712 3-9-4 **51**.................... ShaneKelly 5 46
(Rae Guest) *wl in rr: rdn over 3f out: no great prog fnl 2f* **5/1[2]**

0-00 **10** nse **Lucky Circle**[19] 2913 3-8-9 **47**.................... TheodoreLadd(5) 7 42
(David Evans) *s.i.s and impeded after s: wl in rr: rdn and no prog 3f out: nvr a factor* **33/1**

6-00 **11** ¾ **Padmavati**[37] 2341 3-9-10 **57**.................... NickyMackay 1 50
(Ed Walker) *trckd ldng pair: rdn over 2f out: wknd qckly on inner jst over 1f out* **20/1**

40-0 **12** 1½ **Goodwood Sonnet (IRE)**[37] 2341 3-9-9 **56**.................... CharlesBishop 8 47+
(William Knight) *slowly away: pushed along to rch midfield: prog u.p to cl on ldrs 3f out: wknd 2f out* **4/1[1]**

0-66 **13** 1 **Keith**[18] 2932 3-9-5 **52**.................... AdamMcNamara 9 41
(Rod Millman) *a in rr: u.p and no prog 4f out (jockey said gelding was never travelling and hung right-handed)* **10/1**

6-00 **14** 7 **Milistorm**[31] 2531 3-9-1 **48**.................... NicolaCurrie 2 26
(Michael Blanshard) *nvr on terms: in rr fr 1/2-way: t.o* **66/1**

2m 32.34s (-0.66) **Going Correction** -0.10s/f (Stan) 14 Ran SP% 125.0
Speed ratings (Par 97): **98,97,97,96,95 94,94,94,93,93 92,91,91,86**
CSF £296.17 CT £1713.00 TOTE £12.80: £3.10, £7.70, £2.10; EX 347.80 Trifecta £1572.20.
Owner Mrs C T Bushnell **Bred** Shortgrove Manor Stud **Trained** Exning, Suffolk

The Form Book Flat 2019, Raceform Ltd, Newbury, RG14 5SJ

FOCUS
This was run at a steady pace, and the leader looked to have just about timed it right, only to be edged out on the line.

3594 WILL BROOKE FINAL FLING H'CAP — 1m 2f (P)
6:45 (6:45) (Class 6) (0-65,65) 3-Y-O

£3,105 (£924; £461; £400; £400; £400) **Stalls** Low

Form — RPR

000 **1** **Crystal Tribe (IRE)**[23] 2764 3-9-4 **62**..........................(b[1]) TomMarquand 9 — 72+
(William Haggas) *dwlt: hld up in last: gd prog over 1f out to trck ldng pair fnl f: swtchd lft 100yds out: rdn and str burst to ld last strides (jockey said colt hung right-handed throughout; vet said colt had lost his left-fore and right-hind shoes)* **11/4**[1]

3-52 **2** *nk* **Temujin (IRE)**[9] 3256 3-9-1 **59**.......................... RichardKingscote 13 — 64
(Charles Hills) *disp ld 3f: trckd ldr: led again 3f out: sn rdn: jnd fnl f: hdd and outpcd last strides* **7/2**[2]

60-0 **3** *hd* **Bartimaeus (IRE)**[41] 2139 3-9-5 **63**.......................... CharlesBishop 5 — 68
(Denis Coakley) *wl in tch: prog over 2f out: chsd ldr over 1f out and sn chalng: upsides fnl f but wouldn't go by: dropped to 3rd last strides* **7/1**

0001 **4** *2 ¼* **Twpsyn (IRE)**[33] 2501 3-8-11 **60**..........................(b[1]) TheodoreLadd(5) 7 — 60
(David Evans) *hld up in midfield gng wl: shkn up and wd bnd 2f out: rdn and styd on fnl f to take 4th nr fin: too late (jockey said gelding ran too free)* **20/1**

406- **5** *½* **Fame N Fortune**[213] 8931 3-9-1 **59**.......................... ShaneKelly 2 — 58
(Joseph Tuite) *disp ld 3f: styd cl up: rdn 3f out: nvr gng pce to chal: kpt on u.p* **9/1**

-000 **6** *¾* **Purbeck Hills (IRE)**[14] 3092 3-9-2 **60**.......................... SeanLevey 3 — 58
(Richard Hannon) *hld up in midfield: shkn up over 2f out: kpt on same pce over 1f out and nvr a real threat* **16/1**

55-0 **7** *¾* **Seven For A Pound (USA)**[54] 1819 3-8-13 **62**.......................... SeanDavis(5) 4 — 59
(Richard Fahey) *hld up in last pair: prog on inner 2f out: briefly threatened to cl over 1f out: fdd fnl f (jockey said gelding hung right-handed in the straight)* **22/1**

6-60 **8** *nk* **Petits Fours**[39] 2253 3-9-5 **63**..........................(h) NicolaCurrie 6 — 59
(Charlie Fellowes) *hld up: a in rr: shkn up and no prog over 2f out* **10/1**

44-4 **9** *4* **Irish Art (IRE)**[15] 3034 3-9-7 **65**.......................... MartinDwyer 11 — 53
(David Lanigan) *dwlt: drvn and rapid prog arnd rivals to ld after 3f: hdd 3f out: wknd qckly over 1f out* **6/1**[3]

4-56 **10** *1* **Shifting Gold (IRE)**[36] 2355 3-8-9 **60**.......................... JackDinsmore(7) 8 — 46
(William Knight) *in tch: effrt on wd outside 3f out: v wd bnd 2f out: wknd* **33/1**

6506 **11** *shd* **Shamkha (IRE)**[8] 3310 3-9-6 **64**.......................... FergusSweeney 14 — 50
(Richard Hannon) *t.k.h: trckd ldrs: rdn whn nudged by rival over 2f out: wknd qckly* **25/1**

2m 6.14s (-0.46) **Going Correction** -0.10s/f (Stan) — 11 Ran SP% **116.5**
Speed ratings (Par 97): **97,96,96,94,94 93,93,92,89,88 88**
CSF £11.27 CT £60.43 TOTE £2.70: £1.70, £2.10, £2.30; EX 13.70 Trifecta £86.40.
Owner Lord Lloyd-Webber **Bred** Watership Down Stud **Trained** Newmarket, Suffolk
■ Stewards' Enquiry : Jack Dinsmore two-day ban: interference & careless riding (Jun 23-24)

FOCUS
Three pulled clear with the winner looking a progressive sort and the overall form looking solid.

3595 VISIT ATTHERACES.COM MAIDEN AUCTION STKS — 4f 217y
7:15 (7:17) (Class 5) 2-Y-O — **£3,752** (£1,116; £557; £278) **Stalls** Centre

Form — RPR

463 **1** **Ocasio Cortez (IRE)**[19] 2918 2-9-0.......................... TomMarquand 9 — 74
(Richard Hannon) *pressed ldng pair: shkn up to ld over 1f out: styd on wl and sn in command* **7/4**[1]

45 **2** *2 ½* **Microscopic (IRE)**[11] 3196 2-8-13.......................... NicolaCurrie 5 — 64
(David Simcock) *disp ld to over 1f out: chsd wnr after: styd on same pce* **6/1**[3]

60 **3** *2 ½* **Lexi The One (IRE)**[31] 2520 2-8-8.......................... SeanDavis(5) 2 — 55
(Richard Fahey) *dwlt: rn green in last pair and sn pushed along: prog over 1f out: kpt on to take 3rd nr fin* **18/1**

5 **4** *nk* **Santorini Sal**[19] 2915 2-8-8.......................... MitchGodwin(3) 8 — 52
(John Bridger) *dwlt: in tch towards rr: rdn and rn green over 1f out: prog to take 3rd briefly ins fnl f: one pce after (jockey said filly hung left-handed)* **16/1**

5 *¾* **Epsom Faithfull** 2-8-11.......................... FergusSweeney 1 — 49
(Pat Phelan) *hld up in rr: pushed along 2f out: n.d but kpt on steadily* **50/1**

6 *1 ¼* **Newyorkstateofmind** 2-9-5.......................... MartinDwyer 7 — 53+
(William Muir) *disp ld to over 1f out: wknd* **7/2**[2]

7 *1 ¾* **Luscifer** 2-9-2.......................... ShaneKelly 3 — 43
(Richard Hughes) *towards rr: wknd over 1f out* **20/1**

8 *5* **Knockacurra (IRE)** 2-9-3.......................... RichardKingscote 4 — 26
(Mark Loughnane) *disp ld to 1/2-way: wknd qckly* **20/1**

46 **9** *4 ½* **Champagne Highlife (GER)**[12] 3165 2-9-3.......................... CharlesBishop 6 — 10
(Eve Johnson Houghton) *trckd ldrs to 1/2-way: wknd qckly 2f out (trainer said colt was unsuited by the good to soft ground and would prefer a quicker surface)* **7/2**[2]

59.21s (0.51) **Going Correction** -0.025s/f (Good) — 9 Ran SP% **117.7**
Speed ratings (Par 93): **94,90,86,85,84 82,79,71,64**
CSF £12.89 TOTE £2.20: £1.30, £1.90, £3.30; EX 13.60 Trifecta £98.50.
Owner K Sohi **Bred** Paul McEnery **Trained** East Everleigh, Wilts

FOCUS
Experience proved key, with the winner showing superior speed.

3596 WITHEFORD EQUINE BARRIER TRIALS 13TH JUNE FILLIES' H'CAP — 4f 217y
7:45 (7:46) (Class 5) (0-75,73) 3-Y-O+

£3,752 (£1,116; £557; £400; £400; £400) **Stalls** Centre

Form — RPR

15-1 **1** **Chitra**[23] 2772 3-9-7 **73**.......................... RichardKingscote 5 — 82
(Daniel Kubler) *mde virtually all: rdn and hrd pressed fnl f: edgd rt but styd on wl* **5/2**[2]

0-31 **2** *½* **Fairy Stories**[6] 3376 3-8-5 **62** 6ex.......................... SeanDavis(5) 6 — 69
(Richard Fahey) *cl up: trckd wnr 2f out: chal 1f out: hrd rdn and styd on but nt qckn last 100yds* **4/6**[1]

35-4 **3** *3 ¼* **Three Little Birds**[15] 3032 4-9-13 **72**.......................... JasonWatson 4 — 71
(Sylvester Kirk) *trckd ldrs: rdn 2f out: chsd ldng pair over 1f out: one pce and no imp* **10/1**[3]

434- **4** *1 ¼* **Society Star**[186] 9392 3-8-13 **65**.......................... BrettDoyle 1 — 56
(Robert Cowell) *wnt lft s: racd alone in centre: on terms w wnr to 2f out: shkn up briefly and outpcd: nt disgracd* **28/1**

0-56 **5** *¾* **La Fortuna**[8] 3303 6-9-9 **71**..........................(t) JoshuaBryan(3) 3 — 62
(Charlie Wallis) *mostly in last: rdn 2f out: nvr a threat but styd on fnl f* **33/1**

-666 **6** *2* **Justice Lady (IRE)**[28] 2637 6-10-0 **73**..........................(h) ShaneKelly 2 — 57
(Robert Cowell) *hld up in last pair: pushed along 2f out: no prog and nvr in it* **16/1**

0-00 **7** *6* **Firenze Rosa (IRE)**[40] 2206 4-8-9 **54** oh4.......................... NicolaCurrie 7 — 17
(John Bridger) *prom tl wknd rapidly over 1f out* **28/1**

58.24s (-0.46) **Going Correction** -0.025s/f (Good)
WFA 3 from 4yo+ 7lb — 7 Ran SP% **113.4**
Speed ratings (Par 100): **102,101,96,94,92 89,80**
CSF £4.39 TOTE £3.30: £1.90, £1.10; EX 5.20 Trifecta £12.40.
Owner Mr & Mrs G Middlebrook **Bred** Mr & Mrs G Middlebrook **Trained** Lambourn, Berks

FOCUS
This was run in a heavy shower. The two market leaders came clear in a protracted battle.

3597 RACING WELFARE H'CAP — 6f
8:15 (8:15) (Class 4) (0-85,87) 4-Y-O+

£5,530 (£1,645; £822; £411; £400; £400) **Stalls** Centre

Form — RPR

5042 **1** **Buridan (FR)**[12] 3164 4-9-9 **87**.......................... TomMarquand 1 — 96
(Richard Hannon) *hld up in tch: rdn and prog on outer of gp to ld jst over 1f out: sn hrd pressed: r.o wl and a jst holding on* **9/4**[2]

0-63 **2** *nk* **Royal Residence**[29] 2568 4-9-6 **84**.......................... PJMcDonald 9 — 92
(James Tate) *trckd ldrs gng wl: shkn up to chal over 1f out: pressed wnr fnl f: edgd lft but r.o: jst hld* **5/4**[1]

-260 **3** *3 ¾* **Zamjar**[21] 2839 5-9-5 **83**..........................(p) CharlesBishop 3 — 79
(Robert Cowell) *t.k.h: pressed ldr: rdn 2f out: outpcd fnl f* **18/1**

-520 **4** *¾* **Vegas Boy (IRE)**[19] 2917 4-9-9 **87**..........................(t) NicolaCurrie 4 — 81
(Jamie Osborne) *led to jst over 1f out: fdd* **6/1**[3]

0030 **5** *shd* **Tomily (IRE)**[8] 3301 5-8-9 **80**.......................... LukeCatton(7) 7 — 73
(Richard Hannon) *wl in tch: urged along and nt qckn over 1f out: sn outpcd: n.d after* **9/1**

0040 **6** *10* **Burguillos**[12] 3149 6-8-13 **77**..........................(p[1]) RichardKingscote 5 — 38
(Stuart Williams) *s.i.s: mostly detached in last: pushed along 2f out: nvr in it* **12/1**

1m 12.04s (0.54) **Going Correction** -0.025s/f (Good) — 6 Ran SP% **112.5**
Speed ratings (Par 105): **95,94,89,88,88 75**
CSF £5.47 CT £33.42 TOTE £3.00: £1.80, £1.20; EX 5.90 Trifecta £31.30.
Owner Al Shaqab Racing **Bred** S C A La Perrigne **Trained** East Everleigh, Wilts
■ Stewards' Enquiry : P J McDonald two-day ban: misuse of whip (Jun 23-24)

FOCUS
The pace picked up midway when the two market leaders battled it out and came clear. The winner has been rated in line with the better view of his latest effort.

3598 WATCH SKY SPORTS RACING IN HD MAIDEN AUCTION FILLIES' STKS (PLUS 10 RACE) — 7f
8:45 (8:48) (Class 5) 3-Y-O — **£3,752** (£1,116; £557; £278) **Stalls** Centre

Form — RPR

222 **1** **Sashenka (GER)**[38] 2284 3-8-8 **78**.......................... NicolaCurrie 4 — 67
(Sylvester Kirk) *w ldrs: led 1/2-way: rdn 2f out: edgd lft over 1f out: drvn out and kpt on* **6/4**[1]

0 **2** *1* **Elena**[23] 2762 3-8-9.......................... RichardKingscote 8 — 66
(Charles Hills) *dwlt: trckd ldrs: rdn to take 2nd 2f out: sn edgd lft: nt qckn and no imp on wnr fnl f: kpt on* **5/2**[2]

0 **3** *2* **Colonelle (USA)**[23] 2762 3-8-7.......................... MartinDwyer 6 — 58
(Ed Vaughan) *sn racd against nr side rail: w ldrs: rdn over 2f out: nt qckn wl over 1f out: one pce after* **8/1**

30-0 **4** *shd* **Nostrovia (IRE)**[39] 2251 3-8-12 **73**..........................(p) JasonWatson 2 — 63
(Richard Spencer) *racd centre: hld up: rdn 3f out: kpt on u.p fnl 2f but nvr pce to pose a threat* **5/1**

-355 **5** *1 ½* **Canford Dancer**[25] 2719 3-8-13 **67**..........................(p) ShaneKelly 3 — 60
(Richard Hughes) *t.k.h: hld up in tch: rdn and no rspnse 2f out: no imp on ldrs after* **9/2**[3]

00- **6** *19* **Isla Skye (IRE)**[320] 5282 3-8-2.......................... DarraghKeenan(5) 1 — 3
(Barry Brennan) *racd centre: mde most to 1/2-way: wknd rapidly jst over 2f out: t.o* **80/1**

000 **7** *1 ½* **Al Anaab (FR)**[19] 2909 3-8-0 **53**.......................... SophieRalston(7) 5
(Lucinda Egerton) *reluctant to enter stall: in tch in rr to 3f out: wknd: t.o* **100/1**

00 **8** *16* **Hurricane Heidi**[16] 3003 3-8-11.......................... SeanDavis(5) 9
(Derek Shaw) *s.s: a in rr: bhd fnl 2f: t.o (jockey said filly lost her action)* **100/1**

1m 25.06s (0.76) **Going Correction** -0.025s/f (Good) — 8 Ran SP% **117.7**
Speed ratings (Par 96): **94,92,90,90,88 67,65,47**
CSF £5.71 TOTE £2.00: £1.10, £1.30, £2.40; EX 6.20 Trifecta £26.30.
Owner N Pickett **Bred** Stiftung Gestut Fahrhof **Trained** Upper Lambourn, Berks

FOCUS
A moderate race with the winner dropping markedly in trip. The second and third have been rated close to their Newmarket form.
T/Plt: £43.60 to a £1 stake. Pool: £48,043.00 - 1,100.95 winning units T/Qpdt: £2.30 to a £1 stake. Pool: £6,630.48 - 2,819.19 winning units **Jonathan Neesom**

2833 NEWMARKET (R-H)
Saturday, June 8

OFFICIAL GOING: Good to firm (watered; 7.5)
Wind: blustery Weather: overcast after morning rain; 15 degrees

3599 BENTLEY CAMBRIDGE H'CAP — 7f
2:10 (2:11) (Class 2) (0-105,99) 3-Y-O

£31,125 (£9,320; £4,660; £2,330; £1,165; £585) **Stalls** Low

Form — RPR

2-20 **1** **Awe**[14] 3082 3-8-10 **88**.......................... TomMarquand 5 — 96
(William Haggas) *prom and t.k.h: drvn to ld 2f out: hld on wl fnl f* **3/1**[1]

10-2 **2** *1* **Blown By Wind**[12] 3151 3-9-7 **99**.......................... JamesDoyle 8 — 104
(Mark Johnston) *prom: drvn 2f out: ev ch 1f out: chsd wnr vainly after* **6/1**[2]

4-15 **3** *½* **Mr Diamond (IRE)**[14] 3075 3-8-1 **79**.......................... RoystonFfrench 6 — 83
(Richard Fahey) *prom and racd freely: rdn 2f out: ev ch 1f out: kpt on but a hld after* **10/1**

-021 **4** *1 ¾* **Gabrial The Wire**[8] 3307 3-8-0 **83**.......................... SeanDavis(5) 4 — 82+
(Richard Fahey) *towards rr: rdn and racd awkwardly 3f out: knuckled down wl ins fnl f and kpt on stoutly* **20/1**

12-6 **5** *nse* **Flashcard (IRE)**[14] 3075 3-9-0 **92** RobHornby 3 91
(Andrew Balding) *wnt rt s: sn chsng ldrs: rdn over 2f out: no imp ins fnl f* **7/1**

5-02 **6** *shd* **Jack's Point**[14] 3075 3-9-3 **95** JasonWatson 9 94
(William Muir) *chsd ldrs: rdn over 2f out: nt qckn fnl f* **8/1**

3-6 **7** *nse* **Sunsprite (IRE)**[21] 2826 3-9-5 **97** ShaneKelly 11 96
(Richard Hughes) *midfield: rdn over 2f out: no imp fnl f* **20/1**

321 **8** *1¼* **After John**[15] 3058 3-8-8 **86** ow1 CallumShepherd 12 81
(Mick Channon) *towards rr: swtchd lft 2f out: sn btn and hung lft* **13/2**[3]

-221 **9** *shd* **Regular**[19] 2900 3-8-1 **79** (v[1]) HayleyTurner 10 74
(Michael Bell) *plld hrd: chsd ldrs: drvn over 2f out: nt keen and sn btn* **16/1**

160- **10** *2* **Athmad (IRE)**[224] 8646 3-9-2 **94** MartinDwyer 2 84
(Brian Meehan) *hmpd s: a bhd* **16/1**

1-30 **11** *6* **Riviera Nights**[21] 2828 3-8-12 **90** AndreaAtzeni 7 63
(Richard Hannon) *taken down early: led 5f: fdd rapidly: eased* **8/1**

51-0 **12** *¾* **The Great Heir (FR)**[24] 2746 3-8-10 **88** ShaneGray 1 59
(Kevin Ryan) *impeded s: a bhd: eased fnl f* **20/1**

1m 23.68s (-2.02) **Going Correction** -0.15s/f (Firm) **12** Ran SP% **122.5**
Speed ratings (Par 105): **105,103,103,101,101 101,101,99,99,97 90,89**
CSF £20.21 CT £156.34 TOTE £3.70: £1.80, £2.10, £3.20; EX 25.40 Trifecta £312.20.
Owner China Horse Club International Limited **Bred** Whatton Manor-Global Equine-L Stratton **Trained** Newmarket, Suffolk

FOCUS
The re-positioning of the bend into the home straight and the running rail between the 8f and 14f points increased the distance of the 10f, 12f and 14f races by 2yds. Stands' side course used. Despite morning rain the opening time suggested it wasn't far from good to firm going, and jockey James Doyle afterwards confirmed as much. This looked really competitive, but they went just an average pace down the centre and the first pair dominated the finish. The second and third have been rated close to form.

3600 BERNARD SUNLEY MEMORIAL H'CAP 1m 6f
2:45 (2:55) (Class 2) (0-105,104) 4-Y-O+
£31,125 (£9,320; £4,660; £2,330; £1,165; £585) **Stalls** Low

Form RPR

2200 **1** **Red Galileo**[24] 2742 8-9-10 **104** (h[1]) AdamKirby 4 114
(Saeed bin Suroor) *chsd ldrs: shown whip over 3f out: styd on to ld wl over 1f out: drvn clr ins fnl f* **8/1**

-660 **2** *2¼* **Speedo Boy (FR)**[29] 2575 5-9-2 **96** JasonWatson 8 103
(Ian Williams) *slipped and uns rdr gng to s: led 2f: sn dropped bk to midfield: swtchd lft and hdwy 2f out: chsd wnr fnl f: no imp* **11/1**

2-60 **3** *¾* **Proschema (IRE)**[24] 2742 4-9-9 **103** RichardKingscote 16 109
(Tom Dascombe) *t.k.h and prom: led 8f out: rdn and hdd wl over 1f out: one pce and no ch w wnr fnl f* **6/1**[2]

1-02 **4** *1* **What A Welcome**[14] 3078 5-9-6 **100** JoeyHaynes 10 104
(Patrick Chamings) *midfield: effrt 3f out: sn hrd drvn: no imp wl over 1f out* **8/1**

13-6 **5** *2* **Billy Ray**[29] 2571 4-8-10 **90** CallumShepherd 2 92
(Mick Channon) *bhd: hdwy 3f out: rdn and unable to cl over 1f out* **33/1**

-05 **6** *3½* **Ashington**[22] 2786 4-8-8 **88** (v) TomMarquand 9 85
(John Quinn) *tk str hold pressing ldrs: drvn wl over 1f out: no rspnse and sn btn* **33/1**

101- **7** *nk* **The Grand Visir**[134] 8595 5-9-7 **101** (t) ShaneGray 6 97
(Ian Williams) *bhd early: nvr rchd ldrs* **33/1**

-321 **8** *2* **Theglasgowwarrior**[22] 2786 5-8-6 **91** SeanDavis(5) 11 84
(Jim Goldie) *sn towards rr and pushed along: nvr gng wl: btn 3f out* **12/1**

20-0 **9** *3½* **Melting Dew**[34] 2440 5-9-6 **100** RyanMoore 13 89
(Sir Michael Stoute) *towards rr: nvr on terms* **12/1**

42-4 **10** *hd* **Restorer**[29] 2574 7-9-1 **100** DarraghKeenan(5) 14 88
(Ian Williams) *t.k.h: bhd and on outer: hdwy gng wl enough 3f out: rdn and wknd wl over 1f out* **14/1**

21-5 **11** *4½* **Spirit Ridge**[34] 2440 4-8-12 **92** AndreaAtzeni 17 74
(Amanda Perrett) *chsd ldrs: effrt on outer over 3f out: rdn and sn btn (trainer could offer no explanation for the gelding's performance)* **4/1**[1]

0-03 **12** *2* **Fire Jet (IRE)**[22] 2801 6-8-4 **84** JimmyQuinn 7 63
(John Mackie) *midfield: struggling over 3f out: t.o* **16/1**

66-5 **13** *9* **Great Hall**[146] 231 9-8-6 **86** KieranO'Neill 1 53
(Mick Quinn) *t.k.h: pressed ldrs tl rdn and wknd 4f out: t.o* **33/1**

0-41 **14** *shd* **Lissitzky (IRE)**[22] 2801 4-8-5 **85** (p[1]) MartinDwyer 5 51
(Andrew Balding) *led after 2f: hdd 8f out: lost pl over 3f out: t.o (jockey said gelding stopped quickly)* **7/1**[3]

3203 **15** *1* **Amazing Red (IRE)**[14] 3078 6-9-8 **102** JamesDoyle 15 67
(Ed Dunlop) *stdd s: last after 4f: t.o* **14/1**

2m 55.6s (-4.30) **Going Correction** -0.15s/f (Firm) **15** Ran SP% **123.7**
Speed ratings (Par 109): **106,104,104,103,102 100,100,99,97,97 94,93,88,88,87**
CSF £92.22 CT £566.00 TOTE £9.40: £3.40, £3.60, £2.00; EX 125.40 Trifecta £775.80.
Owner Godolphin **Bred** T R G Vestey **Trained** Newmarket, Suffolk

FOCUS
Add 2yds. A classy staying handicap and they finished fairly strung out on the loose surface. Again the centre of the home straight was favoured. The second helps set the standard, with the third rated close to form.

3601 MARGARET GIFFEN MEMORIAL BRITISH EBF NOVICE STKS (PLUS 10 RACE) 6f
3:20 (3:25) (Class 4) 2-Y-O **£5,175** (£1,540; £769; £384) **Stalls** Low

Form RPR

1 **Visinari (FR)** 2-9-5 0 RyanMoore 7 98+
(Mark Johnston) *mde all: clr w one rival over 1f out: rdn and wl in command after* **10/1**

5 **2** *3½* **Ottoman Court**[18] 2931 2-9-5 0 (p[1]) JamesDoyle 10 88
(Charlie Appleby) *prom: chsd wnr wl over 1f out: rdn and wl hld fnl f but a long way clr of rest* **11/8**[1]

3 *10* **Clareyblue (IRE)** 2-9-5 0 RobHornby 5 58
(Martyn Meade) *dwlt: sn rcvrd to chse ldrs: rdn 2f out: duelled for poor 3rd fnl f* **9/1**

4 *hd* **Daily Times** 2-9-0 0 NickyMackay 6 52
(John Gosden) *pressed wnr tl rdn wl over 1f out: duelled for poor 3rd fnl f* **9/2**[2]

5 *1¼* **Will To Win (GER)** 2-9-5 0 AndreaAtzeni 2 53
(Simon Crisford) *midfield: sn rdn: no ch w ldng pair fnl 2f* **7/1**

6 *1* **Little Brown Trout** 2-9-5 0 CallumShepherd 3 50
(William Stone) *chsd ldrs: rdn 1/2-way: btn 2f out* **66/1**

3 **7** *nse* **Dorset Blue (IRE)**[9] 3257 2-9-5 0 RossaRyan 4 50
(Richard Hannon) *prom: drvn 2f out: sn wknd* **5/1**[3]

8 *6* **Maysong** 2-9-5 0 TomMarquand 8 32
(Ed Dunlop) *lost 8 l s: rn green in last pl: t.o over 2f out: fin w a flourish* **40/1**

9 *nse* **Strait Of Hormuz (IRE)** 2-9-5 0 JackMitchell 9 32
(Hugo Palmer) *midfield: struggling over 2f out: t.o* **33/1**

10 *shd* **Looktothelight (USA)** 2-9-5 0 AdamKirby 1 32
(Jamie Osborne) *sn bhd and outpcd: t.o* **25/1**

1m 10.41s (-1.69) **Going Correction** -0.15s/f (Firm) **10** Ran SP% **119.3**
Speed ratings (Par 95): **105,100,87,86,85 83,83,75,75,75**
CSF £24.29 TOTE £11.10: £2.70, £1.10, £2.40; EX 30.00 Trifecta £308.50.
Owner Rob Ferguson **Bred** S A R L Ecurie Haras De Beauvoir **Trained** Middleham Moor, N Yorks

FOCUS
This time the field came stands' side and two dominated the finish. It looks 2yo form to be positive about.

3602 RWS/STRAWBERRY FIELDS STUD H'CAP 6f
3:55 (3:56) (Class 2) (0-105,102) 3-Y-O+ **£12,938** (£3,850; £1,924; £962) **Stalls** Low

Form RPR

4-13 **1** **Flavius Titus**[34] 2442 4-9-7 **95** AndreaAtzeni 9 104
(Roger Varian) *prom: rdn over 2f out: led 1f out: hld on wl cl home* **4/1**[1]

0-51 **2** *nk* **Louie De Palma**[29] 2568 7-9-5 **93** AdamKirby 11 101
(Clive Cox) *led after 1f: rdn over 2f out: hdd 1f out: kpt on wl cl home: jst hld* **9/1**

6-25 **3** *1* **Spanish City**[7] 3347 6-9-7 **95** RichardKingscote 8 100
(Roger Varian) *pressed ldrs: drvn over 2f out: wnt 3rd 100yds out and kpt on cl home* **9/2**[2]

-104 **4** *¾* **Reputation (IRE)**[7] 3347 6-9-8 **96** RobHornby 1 98+
(Ruth Carr) *stdd s: bhd: drvn 1/2-way: styd on wl despite hanging lft ins fnl f* **16/1**

6131 **5** *shd* **Embour (IRE)**[22] 2791 4-9-5 **93** RossaRyan 13 95
(Richard Hannon) *cl up: rdn 2f out: styd on same pce fnl f* **6/1**[3]

-522 **6** *nk* **Wentworth Falls**[24] 2743 7-9-7 **95** (p) ConnorBeasley 2 96
(Geoffrey Harker) *t.k.h in rr: effrt 1/2-way: rdn and no imp over 1f out* **8/1**

425- **7** *shd* **Swiss Knight**[178] 9508 4-8-12 **86** (t[1]) JasonWatson 10 87
(Stuart Williams) *towards rr: rdn over 2f out: 4th 1f out: wknd fnl 100yds* **25/1**

6-30 **8** *1¾* **Staxton**[24] 2743 4-9-10 **98** ShaneGray 4 93
(Tim Easterby) *chsd ldrs tl drvn and no ex over 1f out (jockey said gelding became unbalanced going into the dip)* **17/2**

0-40 **9** *nse* **Aces (IRE)**[14] 3069 7-9-6 **94** (t[1]) RyanMoore 5 89
(Ian Williams) *dwlt and rdn: effrt 2f out: btn over 1f out* **7/1**

0-20 **10** *hd* **Vibrant Chords**[24] 2743 6-9-11 **99** JamesDoyle 15 93
(Henry Candy) *last after 2f: effrt 1/2-way: drvn and wknd wl over 1f out* **16/1**

0610 **11** *½* **Teruntum Star (FR)**[42] 2117 7-9-10 **98** (p) KevinStott 7 91
(Kevin Ryan) *prom tl drvn and wknd over 2f out* **20/1**

2031 **12** *½* **Merhoob (IRE)**[30] 2557 7-9-9 **102** DarraghKeenan(5) 3 93
(John Ryan) *s.i.s: a bhd* **22/1**

-600 **13** *4* **Flying Pursuit**[24] 2743 6-9-10 **98** (p) RachelRichardson 14 76
(Tim Easterby) *led 1f: prom tl rdn and fdd over 1f out: eased* **25/1**

1m 10.55s (-1.55) **Going Correction** -0.15s/f (Firm) **13** Ran SP% **125.2**
Speed ratings (Par 109): **104,103,102,101,101 100,100,98,98,97 97,96,91**
CSF £40.10 CT £172.77 TOTE £4.80: £1.80, £3.10, £2.10; EX 48.10 Trifecta £266.90.
Owner Sheikh Mohammed Obaid Al Maktoum **Bred** Cheveley Park Stud Ltd **Trained** Newmarket, Suffolk

FOCUS
A highly competitive sprint handicap in which the first pair came up the middle. Solid form. The second has been rated back to his early best, with the third close to form.

3603 KEYSTONE LAW & RAE GUEST RACING FILLIES' NOVICE STKS 7f
4:30 (4:31) (Class 4) 3-Y-O+ **£5,822** (£1,732; £865; £432) **Stalls** Low

Form RPR

41 **1** **Nonchalance**[15] 3050 3-9-4 0 FrankieDettori 6 92+
(John Gosden) *pressed ldrs: led wl over 1f out: edging lft whn pushed clr ins fnl f: comf* **4/5**[1]

61- **2** *1¼* **Flarepath**[213] 8915 3-9-4 0 JamesDoyle 8 85
(William Haggas) *led at stdy pce: rdn and hdd wl over 1f out: sn racing awkwardly and hanging lft: no ch w wnr fnl f* **5/1**[3]

3 *4* **Nazeef** 3-8-11 0 NickyMackay 2 67+
(John Gosden) *stdd s: hdwy and rdn 2f out: styd on wl to go 3rd fnl 75yds: promising* **12/1**

4-1 **4** *1½* **Daring Venture (IRE)**[30] 2550 3-9-4 0 AndreaAtzeni 13 70
(Roger Varian) *prom: rdn wl over 1f out: sn carried sltly lft: one pce and n.d after: lost 3rd cl home* **9/2**[2]

5 *½* **Visionara** 3-8-11 0 KieranO'Neill 5 62+
(Simon Crisford) *midfield: effrt 2f out: modest 4th and cajoled along 1f out: no ch after* **20/1**

00- **6** *1* **Sharqeyya (IRE)**[229] 8468 3-8-11 0 RichardKingscote 11 59
(Owen Burrows) *chsd ldrs: rdn: hung lft and wl btn over 1f out (jockey said filly hung left)* **50/1**

0-2 **7** *¾* **Red Romance**[23] 2762 3-8-11 0 JasonWatson 9 57
(Clive Cox) *cl up: rdn 1/2-way: edgd lft and wknd 2f out* **9/1**

06 **8** *5* **Raha**[23] 2762 3-8-11 0 EoinWalsh 1 44
(Julia Feilden) *last early: hanging lft and a bhd (jockey said filly hung left)* **50/1**

0 **9** *nse* **Exning Queen (IRE)**[17] 2976 3-8-4 0 SeanKirrane(7) 3 43
(Julia Feilden) *dwlt and pushed along in rr: rn green and nvr on terms* **100/1**

5 **10** *4* **Lope Athena**[36] 2366 3-8-11 0 ConnorBeasley 4 33
(Stuart Williams) *bhd: drvn 1/2-way: t.o* **50/1**

46- **11** *2* **Peggy McKay**[295] 6255 4-9-7 0 RobHornby 7 31
(Andrew Balding) *towards rr: rdn 1/2-way: t.o* **40/1**

00 **12** *16* **Break Of Day**[14] 3080 3-8-8 0 GeorgiaCox(3) 14
(William Haggas) *a remote* **50/1**

1m 24.39s (-1.31) **Going Correction** -0.15s/f (Firm)
WFA 3 from 4yo 10lb **12** Ran SP% **124.1**
Speed ratings (Par 102): **101,99,95,93,92 91,90,85,84,80 78,59**
CSF £5.20 TOTE £1.70: £1.10, £1.60, £2.90; EX 5.70 Trifecta £30.90.
Owner HH Sheikha Al Jalila Racing **Bred** Godolphin **Trained** Newmarket, Suffolk

FOCUS
Few got into this good-quality 3yo fillies' event. The level is a bit fluid, but the first two have been rated as improving.

3604 JOHN HOLMES H'CAP 1m 4f
5:05 (5:09) (Class 4) (0-80,81) 3-Y-O
£6,469 (£1,925; £962; £481; £300; £300) Stalls Low

Form RPR
2-22 1 **Gravistas**[7] 3358 3-9-6 **79** RyanMoore 2 87+
(Mark Johnston) *pressed ldrs: led 2f out: sn edgd rt: pushed along and in command over 1f out* **11/8**[1]
-622 2 2 **Holy Kingdom (IRE)**[23] 2765 3-9-7 **80** JamesDoyle 7 85
(Tom Clover) *last early: drvn and effrt 3f out: last of three who were clr 2f out: chsd wnr vainly fnl f* **9/2**[3]
1-41 3 1 1/4 **Great Bear**[24] 2731 3-9-8 **81** JasonWatson 5 84
(Roger Charlton) *led 1f: led again 4f out: rdn and hdd 2f out: 3rd and wl hld fnl f* **3/1**[2]
-602 4 4 1/2 **Artistic Language**[8] 3295 3-9-1 **74** (v) CallumShepherd 3 70
(Brian Meehan) *t.k.h in rr: drvn and effrt over 2f out: no ch w ldrs fnl 2f* **18/1**
3525 5 hd **Mr Zoom Zoom**[19] 2914 3-8-10 **69** EoinWalsh 4 64
(Luke McJannet) *stdd in rr: rdn and struggling wl over 2f out* **25/1**
54-0 6 19 **Top Top (IRE)**[49] 1956 3-8-13 **72** SilvestreDeSousa 6 37
(Sir Michael Stoute) *t.k.h: led after 1f: rdn and hdd 4f out: wknd 3f out: eased and t.o* **6/1**
1-06 7 2 3/4 **Stormwave (IRE)**[21] 2833 3-9-8 **81** (b[1]) RobHornby 1 42
(Ralph Beckett) *stdd s: bhd: drvn and nt keen over 2f out: sn struggling: eased and t.o* **16/1**

2m 29.37s (-4.53) **Going Correction** -0.15s/f (Firm) 7 Ran SP% 114.6
Speed ratings (Par 101): **109,107,106,103,103 91,89**
CSF £8.03 TOTE £2.10: £1.30, £2.20; EX 6.90 Trifecta £15.90.
Owner China Horse Club International Limited **Bred** Windmill Farm Partnership Ltd **Trained** Middleham Moor, N Yorks

FOCUS
Add 2yds. A decent 3yo handicap. It once again paid to be handy. The winner backed up his latest second at Musselburgh.

3605 TUSTING H'CAP 1m 2f
5:35 (5:40) (Class 2) (0-100,99) 4-Y-O+ £12,938 (£3,850; £1,924; £962) Stalls Low

Form RPR
12-5 1 **Caradoc (IRE)**[22] 2803 4-8-8 **86** AndreaAtzeni 3 93
(Ed Walker) *racd freely in 2nd pl: rdn 3f out: chal 2f out: led 1f out: hrd pressed thrght fnl f but pushed along and hld on wl* **9/2**[3]
0003 2 1/2 **Ventura Knight (IRE)**[12] 3160 4-9-3 **95** SilvestreDeSousa 11 101
(Mark Johnston) *t.k.h and prom: wandering fnl 2f: drvn to chal over 1f out: pressed wnr hrd fnl 100yds but a jst hld* **10/3**[2]
-P02 3 1 1/2 **Ayutthaya (IRE)**[30] 2563 4-8-11 **89** ShaneGray 5 92
(Kevin Ryan) *led: rdn and hdd 1f out: styd on same pce after* **11/2**
166- 4 1/2 **Infrastructure**[260] 7486 4-8-12 **90** RobHornby 10 92
(Martyn Meade) *chsd ldrs: rdn 2f out: effrt on outer 1f out: no ex ins fnl f* **15/2**
610- 5 3 **Stylehunter**[252] 7773 4-9-7 **99** (b) KieranO'Neill 4 95+
(John Gosden) *pulling hrd in rr after 4f: drvn over 3f out: no rspnse and btn over 2f out* **3/1**[1]
066 6 1 1/4 **Gossip Column (IRE)**[7] 3338 4-8-8 **86** ConnorBeasley 8 80
(Ian Williams) *s.s: bhd: rdn and btn over 2f out* **10/1**
1510 7 7 **Lunar Jet**[12] 3160 5-9-2 **94** JimmyQuinn 6 74
(John Mackie) *nvr bttr than midfield: rdn and btn wl over 2f out* **7/1**

2m 4.98s (-2.12) **Going Correction** -0.15s/f (Firm) 7 Ran SP% 115.0
Speed ratings (Par 109): **102,101,100,100,97 96,91**
CSF £20.09 CT £83.61 TOTE £5.30: £2.60, £2.10; EX 26.80 Trifecta £101.40.
Owner P K Siu **Bred** P & B Bloodstock **Trained** Upper Lambourn, Berks

FOCUS
Add 2yds. This decent handicap was hit by non-runners and it turned into something of a dash. It's been rated around the second to this year's form.
T/Plt: £36.40 to a £1 stake. Pool: £116,117.93 - 2323.67 winning units T/Qpdt: £4.80 to a £1 stake. Pool: £8,757.98 - 1337.35 winning units **Iain Mackenzie**

3606 - 3617a (Foreign Racing) - See Raceform Interactive

3561 BELMONT PARK (L-H)
Saturday, June 8

OFFICIAL GOING: Dirt: fast; turf: firm

3618a RUNHAPPY METROPOLITAN H'CAP (GRADE 1) (3YO+) (MAIN TRACK) (DIRT) 1m (D)
9:46 3-Y-O+
£511,811 (£173,228; £94,488; £62,992; £35,433; £25,984)

RPR
1 **Mitole (USA)**[35] 2423 4-8-10 **0** RicardoSantanaJr 3 121
(Steven Asmussen, U.S.A) *chsd ldr: w ldr fr 1/2-way: led narrowly over 2f out: rdn under 2f out: drvn and kpt on wl fnl f* **7/2**[2]
2 3/4 **McKinzie (USA)**[36] 4-8-12 **0** MikeESmith 2 122+
(Bob Baffert, U.S.A) *towards rr: gd hdwy into midfield fr 2f out: nt clr run fr 1 1/2f out tl rdn and styd on strly fnl f: nt rch wnr* **33/20**[1]
3 nk **Thunder Snow (IRE)**[70] 1447 5-8-12 **0** (p) ChristopheSoumillon 4 121
(Saeed bin Suroor) *in tch: rdn 1 1/2f out: styd on fnl f: nt able to chal* **57/10**
4 3 1/4 **Promises Fulfilled (USA)**[35] 2423 4-8-8 **0** LuisSaez 6 110
(Dale Romans, U.S.A) *trckd ldrs: rdn 2f out: drvn under 2f out: no ex fnl f* **174/10**
5 1/2 **Firenze Fire (USA)**[28] 4-8-7 **0** IradOrtizJr 7 107
(Jason Servis, U.S.A) *towards rr of midfield: stdy hdwy into midfield 2 1/2f out: rdn and effrt 2f out: one pce fnl f* **42/10**[3]
6 1 1/2 **Pavel (USA)**[70] 1447 5-8-6 **0** (b) MarioGutierrez 8 103
(Doug O'Neill, U.S.A) *towards rr: rdn over 2f out: v wd into st: drvn and kpt on steadily fr 1 1/2f out: n.d* **224/10**
7 3/4 **Coal Front (USA)**[70] 1440 5-8-10 **0** JoselOrtiz 1 105
(Todd Pletcher, U.S.A) *led: rdn and hdd over 2f out: remained prom tl over 1f out: wknd fnl f* **105/10**
8 2 3/4 **Tale Of Silence (USA)**[70] 5-8-4 **0** (b) JulienRLeparoux 5 93
(Barclay Tagg, U.S.A) *a towards rr* **51/1**
9 6 **Prince Lucky (USA)**[35] 4-8-7 **0** JohnRVelazquez 9 82
(Todd Pletcher, U.S.A) *midfield on outside: awkward on turn into st and lost pl: sn struggling* **166/10**

1m 32.75s 9 Ran SP% 120.1
PARI-MUTUEL (all including 2 unit stake): WIN 9.00; PLACE (1-2) 4.40, 3.30; SHOW (1-2-3) 3.50, 2.70, 3.70; SF 23.40.
Owner L William & Corinne Heiligbrodt **Bred** Edward A Cox Jr **Trained** USA

3620a BELMONT STKS PRESENTED BY NYRA BETS (GRADE 1) (3YO) (MAIN TRACK) (DIRT) 1m 4f (D)
11:37 3-Y-O
£629,921 (£220,472; £118,110; £78,740; £47,244; £35,433)

RPR
1 **Sir Winston (USA)**[28] 3-9-0 **0** (b) JoelRosario 7 117
(Mark Casse, Canada) *hld up towards rr: hdwy on inner fr 5f out: trckd ldrs over 3f out: switch to outside and rdn under 2f out: drvn to ld 1f out: kpt on wl* **102/10**
2 1 **Tacitus (USA)**[35] 2425 3-9-0 **0** JoseLOrtiz 10 115+
(William Mott, U.S.A) *hld up towards rr of midfield: pushed along and stdy hdwy on wd outside fr 2 1/2f out: drvn 2f out: bmpd under 2f out: styd on fnl f: nt rch wnr* **39/20**[1]
3 3/4 **Joevia (USA)**[27] 3-9-0 **0** JoseLezcano 1 114
(Gregory D Sacco, U.S.A) *led: rdn whn hrd pressed 2f out: rallied 1 1/2f out: hdd 1f out: kpt on same pce* **216/10**
4 1 **Tax (USA)**[35] 2425 3-9-0 **0** IradOrtizJr 4 112
(Danny Gargan, U.S.A) *chsd ldr: rdn and ev ch 2f out: edgd rt 1 1/2f out: no ex fnl f* **117/10**
5 hd **Master Fencer (JPN)**[35] 2425 3-9-0 **0** JulienRLeparoux 3 112+
(Koichi Tsunoda, Japan) *hld up towards rr: rdn under 3f out: wd into st: styd on wl last 100yds: nrst fin* **133/10**
6 nk **Spinoff (USA)**[35] 2425 3-9-0 **0** JavierCastellano 6 111
(Todd Pletcher, U.S.A) *trckd ldrs: pushed along 3f out: nt clr run and lost pl 2f out: rdn under 2f out: kpt on fnl f* **104/10**
7 nse **Everfast (USA)**[21] 2856 3-9-0 **0** LuisSaez 2 111
(Dale Romans, U.S.A) *midfield: tk clsr order 6f out: stmbld and lost pl 2 1/2f out: sn rdn: hrd drvn and kpt on steadily fr 2f out* **165/10**
8 1 3/4 **Intrepid Heart (USA)**[28] 3-9-0 **0** (b[1]) JohnRVelazquez 8 109
(Todd Pletcher, U.S.A) *midfield: rdn and lost pl 2 1/2f out: drvn and no imp fr 2f out* **69/10**[3]
9 2 1/4 **War Of Will (USA)**[21] 2856 3-9-0 **0** TylerGaffalione 9 105
(Mark Casse, Canada) *in tch on outside: rdn and outpcd 2f out: nt clr run and bmpd rival under 2f out: wknd fnl f* **73/20**[2]
10 4 3/4 **Bourbon War (USA)**[21] 2856 3-9-0 **0** MikeESmith 5 97
(Mark Hennig, U.S.A) *a in rr* **10/1**

2m 28.3s (-0.66) 10 Ran SP% 119.9
PARI-MUTUEL (all including 2 unit stake): WIN 22.40; PLACE (1-2) 8.80, 3.90; SHOW (1-2-3) 6.10, 3.20, 8.70; SF 96.00.
Owner Tracy Farmer **Bred** Tracy Farmer **Trained** Canada

FOCUS
A competitive race but there was no Triple Crown on the line this year - only one runner had contested the first two legs - and this is relatively ordinary form. Over a track that was riding extremely fast, this was a truly run race: 23.92 (2f), 24.87 (4f), 24.75 (6f), 24.73 (1m), 24.45 (1m2f), 25.58 (line), with the winner earning a modest 95 Beyer speed figure. Justify earned 101 the previous year and American Pharoah got 105 for his 2015 triumph. It's been rated around the second, fourth, fifth, sixth and seventh.

3619 - 3620a (Foreign Racing) - See Raceform Interactive

3333 MAISONS-LAFFITTE (R-H)
Saturday, June 8

OFFICIAL GOING: Turf: very soft

3621a PRIX DE L'OFFICE DE TOURISME DE MAISONS-LAFFITTE (LISTED RACE) (3YO) (TURF) 6f 110y
4:52 3-Y-O £24,774 (£9,909; £7,432; £4,954; £2,477)

RPR
1 **Eagleway (FR)**[16] 3-8-10 **0** StephanePasquier 6 102
(Andrea Marcialis, France) **69/10**
2 3/4 **Flaming Star (FR)**[59] 3-8-7 **0** JulienGuillochon 7 97
(H-A Pantall, France) **40/1**
3 shd **Pretty Boy (IRE)**[59] 1707 3-8-10 **0** MaximeGuyon 2 100
(Mme Pia Brandt, France) **87/10**
4 nk **Milord's Song (FR)**[30] 2564 3-8-10 **0** TheoBachelot 9 99
(S Wattel, France) **33/10**[1]
5 nse **Dubai Dominion**[53] 1830 3-8-10 **0** (b[1]) AurelienLemaitre 1 99
(Ed Vaughan) *midfield on inner: outpcd and drvn 2f out: last and hrd rdn 1 1/2f out: styd on strly on stands' rail ins fnl f: nvr on terms* **42/1**
6 hd **We Go (FR)**[30] 2564 3-8-10 **0** Pierre-CharlesBoudot 3 98
(H-A Pantall, France) **16/1**
7 shd **Space Traveller**[21] 2826 3-8-10 CristianDemuro 4 98
(Richard Fahey) *w.w fnl trio: drvn but nowhere to go fr 1/2-way: effrt and gap clsd over 1 1/2f out: styd on ins fnl f but nvr able to get on terms* **18/5**[2]
7 dht **Midnight Shine (FR)**[22] 3-8-10 MickaelBarzalona 11 98
(A Fabre, France) *a cl up on outer: ev ch whn drvn 2f out: sltly outpcd 1 1/2f out: one pce fnl f* **73/10**
9 snk **Devant (FR)**[28] 2621 3-8-13 **0** VincentCheminaud 10 100
(H-A Pantall, France) **26/5**[3]
10 2 **Barbill (IRE)**[21] 2826 3-9-0 **0** JFEgan 5 95
(Mick Channon) *w.w in fnl trio on inner: taken off rails 1/2-way: drvn and beginning to stay on whn squeezed out and lost all ch appr fnl f* **13/1**
11 5 **Vintage Brut**[8] 3317 3-8-10 (p) AlexisBadel 8 77
(Tim Easterby) *led or disp ld: hdd after nrly 2f but remained virtually upsides new ldr: regained ld wl over 2f out: sn drvn and hdd 1 1/2f out: sn wknd* **20/1**

1m 18.09s 11 Ran SP% 118.7
PARI-MUTUEL (all including 1 euro stake): WIN 7.90; PLACE 2.80, 9.60, 3.20; DF 98.10.
Owner Andreina Mosca Toselli **Bred** Nikola Bockova **Trained** France

FOCUS
A bunched finish, and the second, sixth and eighth limit the level.

3541 **GOODWOOD** (R-H)

Sunday, June 9

OFFICIAL GOING: Good to soft (soft in places) changing to good to soft after race 1 (2.00)

Wind: light breeze half against Weather: sunny periods

3632 INFINITI Q30 H'CAP — 7f

2:00 (2:00) (Class 3) (0-95,90) 3-Y-O **£9,451** (£2,829; £1,414; £708; £352) **Stalls** Low

Form — RPR

10-0 **1** **Beauty Filly**[28] 2670 4-9-12 **89** .... JamesDoyle 8 — 101
(William Haggas) *fly-leapt leaving stalls: hld up last trio: nt clr run over 1f out: swtchd lft: hdwy ent fnl f: led fnl 120yds: kpt on strly: readily* **7/1**

12-1 **2** 2 1/4 **Mubhij (IRE)**[18] 2977 4-9-13 **90** .... DaneO'Neill 4 — 96
(Roger Varian) *trckd ldrs: rdn to chal over 1f out: ev ch fnl 120yds: sn hld: kpt on same pce* **7/2**[2]

46-0 **3** *hd* **Rum Runner**[17] 3009 4-9-7 **84** .... SeanLevey 5 — 89
(Richard Hannon) *hld up in last trio: hdwy 2f out: sn rdn: wnt 3rd ins fnl f: kpt on to press for 2nd towards fin* **33/1**

2-30 **4** 2 **Queen's Sargent (FR)**[32] 2526 4-9-5 **82** .... ShaneGray 6 — 82
(Kevin Ryan) *trckd ldr: rdn into narrow advantage over 1f out: hdd fnl 120yds: no ex* **9/1**

0-30 **5** *shd* **Graphite Storm**[22] 2832 5-9-7 **84** .... AdamKirby 3 — 84
(Clive Cox) *hld up in last trio: rdn and hdwy over 1f out: kpt on ins fnl f but nt pce to get on terms* **15/2**

-041 **6** 3/4 **Lincoln Park**[31] 2559 3-9-2 **89** .... SilvestreDeSousa 9 — 83
(Michael Appleby) *led: rdn and narrowly hdd over 1f out: kpt on tl wknd fnl 120yds* **3/1**[1]

5-00 **7** 11 **Taurean Star (IRE)**[29] 2609 6-9-10 **87** .... HarryBentley 7 — 55
(Ralph Beckett) *s.i.s: sn in tch: effrt over 2f out: wknd over 1f out* **9/1**

2-20 **8** 2 **Ptarmigan Ridge**[30] 2572 5-9-13 **90** .... ShaneKelly 2 — 53
(Richard Hughes) *in tch: rdn over 2f out: wknd over 1f out (jockey said gelding stopped quickly; vet said gelding broke blood vessel)* **4/1**[3]

1m 29.06s (2.36) **Going Correction** +0.35s/f (Good) — **8** Ran SP% **114.4**

WFA 3 from 4yo+ 10lb

Speed ratings (Par 107): **100,97,97,94,94 93,81,79**

CSF £31.75 CT £760.26 TOTE £7.60: £1.80, £1.30, £7.00; EX 32.20 Trifecta £380.00.

Owner Sheikh Juma Dalmook Al Maktoum **Bred** Highbank Stud **Trained** Newmarket, Suffolk

FOCUS

They went a brisk early pace in this competitive handicap. The time suggested the going was near as advertised. The second has been rated to his Yarmouth win and the third to his best.

3633 BENNINGTON FAMILY H'CAP — 1m 3f 44y

2:30 (2:33) (Class 5) (0-75,75) 4-Y-O+

£6,404 (£1,905; £952; £476; £400; £400) **Stalls** High

Form — RPR

4-06 **1** **Rake's Progress**[23] 2793 5-9-7 **75** .... DavidEgan 8 — 82
(Heather Main) *mid-div: hdwy over 2f out: rdn to take narrow advantage over 1f out: hld on wl fnl f: drvn out* **4/1**[2]

23-0 **2** *nk* **War Brigade (FR)**[22] 2819 5-9-1 **69** .... JamesDoyle 3 — 75
(Ian Williams) *mid-div: nt clrest of runs on rails whn pushed along 3f out: stdy prog fr over 2f out: sn rdn: chal ent fnl f: kpt on: hld cl home* **3/1**[1]

0-23 **3** 1/2 **Stormingin (IRE)**[28] 1934 6-9-6 **74** .... AdamKirby 10 — 79
(Gary Moore) *hld up: swtchd lft and hdwy over 2f out: sn rdn to chal: tk narrow advantage briefly over 1f out: kpt on but no ex nring fin* **12/1**

-003 **4** *shd* **El Borracho (IRE)**[17] 3016 4-9-5 **73** ....(h) TomMarquand 9 — 78
(Simon Dow) *hld up: hdwy 3f out: pushed along bhd ldrs over 1f out: rdn jst ins fnl f: kpt on wl but nt quite pce to chal: nrly snatched 3rd fnl strides* **14/1**

6350 **5** 2 **Me Too Nagasaki (IRE)**[26] 2710 5-9-2 **70** ....(h[1]) PJMcDonald 4 — 71
(Stuart Williams) *led: u.p 2f out: hdd over 1f out: no ex fnl 120yds* **9/1**

06-2 **6** 1/2 **Sufi**[23] 2793 5-9-4 **72** .... PatDobbs 6 — 73
(Ken Cunningham-Brown) *trckd ldrs: rdn 2f out: styd on same pce fnl f* **13/2**[3]

4635 **7** 6 **Makambe (IRE)**[19] 2928 4-9-0 **68** .... OisinMurphy 13 — 58
(Paul Howling) *mid-div: hdwy 3f out: sn rdn to chse ldrs: wknd ent fnl f* **20/1**

134- **8** 1/2 **Amanto (GER)**[144] 6656 9-9-1 **69** ....(tp) HollieDoyle 1 — 59
(Ali Stronge) *hld up: rdn 3f out: little imp* **25/1**

0100 **9** 23 **New Agenda**[28] 2207 7-9-6 **74** .... DavidProbert 5 — 24
(Paul Webber) *prom: rdn over 2f out: sn hung rt: wknd over 1f out: eased (jockey said gelding hung right-handed and stopped quickly)* **25/1**

3116 **10** 3/4 **Arlecchino's Arc (IRE)**[17] 3006 4-8-3 **57** ....(v) SilvestreDeSousa 2 — 6
(Mark Usher) *chsd ldr: pushed along over 5f out: wknd 2f out: eased (trainer said gelding was unsuited by the going, which was officially described as Good to Soft on this occasion, and would prefer a quicker surface or a return to the All Weather)* **9/1**

21-0 **11** 62 **Lyrica's Lion (IRE)**[17] 3022 5-8-11 **70** .... RobJFitzpatrick(5) 14
(Camilla Poulton) *in tch: rdn over 3f out: sn btn: eased (jockey said gelding was never traveling)* **25/1**

2-04 **12** 44 **Give Him Time**[23] 2793 8-9-4 **72** ....(p) RobertWinston 7
(Nick Gifford) *trckd ldrs on outer: eased up over 3f out: virtually p.u (jockey said gelding moved poorly)* **10/1**

2m 31.44s (3.14) **Going Correction** +0.35s/f (Good) — **12** Ran SP% **118.1**

Speed ratings (Par 103): **102,101,101,101,99 99,95,94,78,77 32,**

CSF £15.36 CT £127.71 TOTE £5.10: £1.80, £1.40, £3.10; EX 18.60 Trifecta £123.70.

Owner Coxwell Partnership **Bred** Mr & Mrs A E Pakenham **Trained** Kingston Lisle, Oxon

FOCUS

Another competitive handicap and it saw a cracking finish. The third has been rated close to form.

3634 INCUBEX WELLCHILD (S) STKS — 5f

3:05 (3:06) (Class 3) 2-Y-O **£9,451** (£2,829; £1,414; £708; £352) **Stalls** High

Form — RPR

00 **1** **Shani**[20] 2915 2-8-8 **0** .... PJMcDonald 7 — 60
(David Evans) *prom: rdn to take narrow advantage over 1f out: hld on wl ins fnl f: all out* **20/1**

6 **2** *nk* **Sir Gordon**[65] 1556 2-8-13 **0** .... SilvestreDeSousa 8 — 64
(Mick Channon) *outpcd and detached early: hdwy 3f out: rdn for str chal thrght fnl f: kpt on: hld cl home* **5/1**

232 **3** 2 **Paper Star**[11] 3220 2-8-8 **0** .... EdwardGreatrex 3 — 52
(Archie Watson) *led: hung rt and rdn over 2f out: hdd over 1f out: kpt on same pce fnl f* **11/10**[1]

244 **4** 5 **Beignet (IRE)**[7] 3371 2-8-8 **0** .... HollieDoyle 6 — 34
(Richard Hannon) *chsd ldrs: rdn 2f out: nt pce to chal: fdd fnl f* **4/1**[2]

0534 **5** *nk* **Fact Or Fable (IRE)**[21] 2890 2-8-13 **0** .... LiamKeniry 4 — 38
(J S Moore) *little slowly away: sn prom: rdn w ev ch over 1f out: wknd jst onside fnl f* **18/1**

536 **6** *shd* **Isobar Wind (IRE)**[41] 2205 2-8-13 **0** .... OisinMurphy 5 — 37
(David Evans) *prom: rdn w ev ch 2f out: wknd ent fnl f* **9/2**[3]

7 16 **Sooty's Return (IRE)** 2-8-13 **0** .... TrevorWhelan 1
(J S Moore) *s.i.s: sn outpcd and detached: nvr on terms* **50/1**

1m 0.82s (2.72) **Going Correction** +0.35s/f (Good) — **7** Ran SP% **114.5**

Speed ratings (Par 97): **92,91,88,80,79 79,54**

CSF £114.99 TOTE £24.20: £8.60, £2.30; EX 167.70 Trifecta £435.40.The winner was sold to J Bridger for £8,000. Paper Star was claimed by Mr George Baker for £15,000.

Owner Mark Windsor, Richard Kent **Bred** Mickley Stud & Mark Winsor **Trained** Pandy, Monmouths

FOCUS

The fillies mainly dominated this selling stakes.

3635 R L AUSTEN DIAMOND H'CAP — 2m

3:40 (3:40) (Class 3) (0-90,88) 4-Y-O+ **£12,602** (£3,772; £1,886; £944; £470) **Stalls** Low

Form — RPR

5-01 **1** **Nuits St Georges (IRE)**[29] 2626 4-8-9 **76** .... SeanLevey 9 — 82+
(David Menuisier) *led for 2f: trckd ldr: led over 3f out: styd on strly fnl 2f: rdn out* **3/1**[1]

2-12 **2** 1 **Orin Swift (IRE)**[30] 2571 5-9-4 **85** .... RobHornby 8 — 89+
(Jonathan Portman) *mid-div: hdwy 3f out: swtchd lft 2f out: sn rdn to chse wnr: styd on but nt pce to get on terms* **7/2**[2]

-342 **3** 1/2 **Bailarico (IRE)**[19] 2936 6-8-7 **74** ....(v) EdwardGreatrex 5 — 77
(Warren Greatrex) *led after 2f: rdn and hdd over 3f out: kpt chsng wnr tl over 1f out: styd on ins fnl f* **8/1**

10-0 **4** *hd* **Master Archer (IRE)**[23] 2801 5-9-7 **88** ....(v) DavidProbert 3 — 91
(James Fanshawe) *hld up: hdwy over 3f out: rdn in cl 4th over 1f out: styd on ins fnl f* **25/1**

5-36 **5** *shd* **October Storm**[16] 3044 6-8-10 **77** .... SilvestreDeSousa 7 — 80
(Mick Channon) *s.i.s: last: hdwy over 3f out: sn hung rt: rdn 2f out: chal for 3rd ins fnl f: styd on (jockey said gelding hung right-handed in the straight)* **6/1**

340- **6** 1 1/2 **Imphal**[278] 6901 5-9-3 **84** .... ShaneKelly 10 — 85
(Gary Moore) *slowly away: in last pair: struggling 3f out: sn hanging rt: styd on fnl 2f wout ever threatening to get involved* **33/1**

65-2 **7** 1/2 **Suegioo (FR)**[30] 2578 10-9-4 **85** ....(p) AdamKirby 1 — 86
(Ian Williams) *hld up: struggling over 3f out: hdwy 2f out: swtchd rt jst over 1f out: styd on ins fnl f* **8/1**

0-06 **8** 1 3/4 **Guns Of Leros (USA)**[24] 2781 6-9-2 **83** ....(v) HectorCrouch 2 — 82
(Gary Moore) *s.i.s: sn trcking ldrs: rdn and hld whn briefly tight for room jst over 2f out: wknd fnl f* **16/1**

022- **9** *hd* **Maquisard (FR)**[79] 9503 7-9-7 **88** .... CharlesBishop 11 — 86?
(Chris Gordon) *trckd ldrs: rdn 3f out: wknd fnl f* **25/1**

325- **10** 1 3/4 **Early Summer (IRE)**[230] 8471 4-8-11 **78** .... OisinMurphy 6 — 75
(Hughie Morrison) *trckd ldrs: rdn 3f out: hld over 1f out: wknd fnl f* **9/2**[3]

3m 33.7s (2.80) **Going Correction** +0.35s/f (Good) — **10** Ran SP% **118.4**

Speed ratings (Par 107): **107,106,106,106,106 105,105,104,104,103**

CSF £13.44 CT £76.82 TOTE £3.90: £1.40, £1.50, £2.60; EX 14.60 Trifecta £97.00.

Owner Boy George Partnership **Bred** Pollards Stables **Trained** Pulborough, W Sussex

FOCUS

A fair staying handicap and sound form for the class. The winner has been rated as backing up his Nottingham win.

3636 ED CHAMBERLIN CLASSIC GOLF DAY H'CAP — 6f

4:10 (4:12) (Class 4) (0-85,87) 4-Y-O+

£7,374 (£2,194; £1,096; £548; £400; £400) **Stalls** High

Form — RPR

1110 **1** **Pennsylvania Dutch**[22] 2843 5-9-1 **84** .... SeanDavis(5) 5 — 91
(Kevin Ryan) *hld up: hdwy 3f out: rdn to chal 2f out: led jst over 1f out: kpt on wl: all out (trainers rep could offer no explanation for the gelding's improved form)* **15/2**

10-0 **2** *nk* **Fantasy Keeper**[29] 2611 5-9-0 **78** .... SilvestreDeSousa 8 — 84+
(Michael Appleby) *prom: nt clrest of runs 2f out: sn rdn: ev ch fnl 120yds: kpt on but hld cl home (jockey said gelding hung right-handed throughout)* **4/1**[2]

0-00 **3** *nk* **Iconic Knight (IRE)**[22] 2824 4-9-0 **78** .... JamesDoyle 10 — 83+
(Ed Walker) *mid-div: nt clr run 2f out: swtchd rt over 1f out: sn rdn: kpt on wl fnl 120yds: snatched 3rd fnl stride (vet said gelding lost its right fore shoe)* **6/1**

U-00 **4** *nse* **Blaine**[8] 3347 9-8-13 **77** .... TrevorWhelan 6 — 82
(Brian Barr) *mid-div: hdwy over 2f out: rdn and ev ch ent fnl f: kpt on but no ex cl home* **33/1**

0-40 **5** *shd* **Youkan (IRE)**[3] 3509 4-9-5 **83** .... PJMcDonald 4 — 88
(Stuart Kittow) *dwlt: bhd: hdwy over 2f out: rdn w ch over 1f out: kpt on same pce fnl f (jockey said gelding was slowly away)* **11/2**[3]

53-0 **6** *nk* **Tawny Port**[30] 2568 5-9-5 **83** .... OisinMurphy 3 — 87
(Stuart Williams) *hld up: rdn over 1f out: r.o ins fnl f: clsng on ldrs at fin* **7/2**[1]

36-0 **7** 3 3/4 **Sir Titan**[29] 2622 5-9-9 **87** .... GeraldMosse 2 — 79
(Tony Carroll) *sn led: rdn over 2f out: hdd jst over 1f out: wknd ins fnl f* **10/1**

5-40 **8** 3 **Private Matter**[34] 2484 5-9-4 **82** .... DavidProbert 7 — 64
(Amy Murphy) *mid-div: hdwy over 2f out: rdn to chse ldrs over 1f out: wknd ent fnl f* **14/1**

000 **9** 2 3/4 **Double Up**[25] 2743 8-9-7 **85** ....(vt) AdamKirby 1 — 59
(Ian Williams) *prom: rdn and ev ch over 1f out: wknd ent fnl f* **16/1**

0-00 **10** 3 **Quench Dolly**[36] 2403 5-9-2 **83** .... GeorgeBuckell(3) 12 — 47
(John Gallagher) *trckd ldrs: rdn and ev ch over 2f out: wknd over 1f out* **9/1**

1m 12.88s (0.78) **Going Correction** +0.35s/f (Good) — **10** Ran SP% **118.2**

Speed ratings (Par 105): **108,107,107,107,107 106,101,97,93,89**

CSF £38.16 CT £195.79 TOTE £8.20: £2.00, £1.80, £1.50; EX 24.20 Trifecta £111.20.

Owner K&J Bloodstock Ltd **Bred** Lael Stables **Trained** Hambleton, N Yorks

FOCUS
There was a tight six-way finish in this fair sprint handicap. The third has been rated close to last year's C&D run.

3637 WELLCHILD FILLIES' NOVICE STKS — 1m 1f 197y
4:45 (4:45) (Class 4) 3-Y-O+ — £6,469 (£1,925; £962; £481) Stalls Low

Form — RPR

1 **Litigious** 3-9-0 0 .... RobertHavlin 7 — 91
(John Gosden) *s.i.s: in tch: hdwy 3f out: chalng whn drifted lft 2f out: sn led: r.o wl: comf* **7/1[2]**

2 6 **Merry Vale** 3-9-0 0 .... KieranO'Neill 9 — 79
(John Gosden) *hld up last but in tch: hdwy over 2f out: swtchd rt over 1f out: wnt 2nd ent fnl f: kpt on nicely but no ch w wnr* **12/1**

0-2 3 5 **Shrewdness**[37] 2361 3-9-0 0 .... JamesDoyle 2 — 69+
(William Haggas) *trckd ldr: disp ld over 2f out: sltly hmpd sn after: rdn and hdd wl over 1f out: one pce fnl f* **13/8[1]**

0-5 4 1 1/2 **Thakaa (USA)**[53] 1855 3-9-0 0 .... DaneO'Neill 5 — 66
(Charles Hills) *s.i.s: in tch: hdwy 3f out: rdn over 2f out: sn one pce: wnt wl hld 4th ins fnl 120yds* **10/1[3]**

52 5 1 **Norma**[24] 2770 3-9-0 0 .... OisinMurphy 6 — 64+
(James Fanshawe) *trckd ldrs: disp ld over 2f out: rdn and hdd wl over 1f out: fdd fnl f* **13/8[1]**

0 6 7 **Voice Of Salsabil**[17] 2999 3-9-0 0 .... RichardKingscote 3 — 50
(David Evans) *trckd ldrs: rdn over 2f out: wknd over 1f out* **50/1**

00 7 1 1/4 **Mousebird (IRE)**[24] 2770 3-9-0 0 .... PJMcDonald 1 — 48
(Hughie Morrison) *led: rdn and hdd wl over 2f out: sn wknd* **25/1**

2m 9.89s (0.99) **Going Correction** +0.35s/f (Good) — **7** Ran SP% **111.3**
Speed ratings (Par 102): **110,105,101,100,99 93,92**
CSF £77.97 TOTE £5.90: £2.00, £4.80; EX 41.30 Trifecta £167.70.
Owner Cheveley Park Stud **Bred** Cheveley Park Stud Ltd **Trained** Newmarket, Suffolk

FOCUS
This interesting 3yo fillies' contest rather fell apart. The level is fluid, but the third, fourth and fifth have all been rated below form for now.

3638 CONFIDENCE TO CARE H'CAP — 7f
5:15 (5:15) (Class 5) (0-75,77) 3-Y-O
£6,404 (£1,905; £952; £476; £400; £400) Stalls Low

Form — RPR

0-54 1 **Sir Busker (IRE)**[30] 2567 3-9-9 **77** .... (v[1]) OisinMurphy 6 — 88
(William Knight) *slowly away: in last pair: hdwy fr 3f out: mounting chal whn squeezed out 2f out: sn swtchd lft and rdn: r.o wl ent fnl f: led fnl 120yds: readily* **4/1[1]**

006- 2 3 **Bring Us Paradise**[228] 8553 3-8-5 **59** .... HollieDoyle 4 — 61
(Tony Carroll) *mid-div: hdwy 3f out: rdn for str chal fr 2f out: led briefly ins fnl f: kpt on but nt pce of wnr* **22/1**

1606 3 3/4 **Balata Bay**[10] 3261 3-9-6 **74** .... SeanLevey 1 — 74
(Richard Hannon) *trckd ldrs: chal wl over 2f out: sn rdn: led wl over 1f out: hdd ins fnl f: no ex nring fin (jockey said colt hung left-handed under pressure)* **11/2**

05-4 4 2 3/4 **Sense Of Belonging (FR)**[53] 1862 3-9-4 **72** .... ShaneGray 10 — 64
(Kevin Ryan) *hld up: rdn wl over 2f out: no imp tl over 1f out: wnt 4th ent fnl f: kpt on but nt pce to get on terms* **20/1**

036 5 2 **City Wanderer (IRE)**[23] 2790 3-9-1 **69** .... SilvestreDeSousa 5 — 56
(Mick Channon) *trckd ldrs: effrt 2f out: nt quite pce to mount chal: wknd ins fnl f (jockey said gelding ran green)* **5/1[3]**

30-3 6 3 1/2 **Conspiritor**[10] 3261 3-9-5 **73** .... RichardKingscote 7 — 51
(Charles Hills) *prom: led over 3f out tl rdn wl over 2f out: wknd ent fnl f* **11/2**

3-12 7 1 3/4 **Spirit Of May**[24] 2772 3-9-5 **73** .... PatDobbs 9 — 46
(Roger Teal) *trckd ldrs: rdn over 2f out: wknd over 1f out* **9/2[2]**

-033 8 13 **Sassoon**[13] 3170 3-9-5 **73** .... DavidProbert 3 — 11
(Paul Cole) *led tl over 3f out: led wl over 2f out: rdn and hdd wl over 1f out: appeared to lose action whn hld ent fnl f: eased (jockey said colt stopped quickly)* **9/2[2]**

01-5 9 7 **Island Glen (USA)**[23] 2794 3-9-5 **73** .... DavidEgan 8
(Heather Main) *mid-div: rdn wl over 2f out: nt pce to threaten: wknd over 1f out* **16/1**

1m 28.66s (1.96) **Going Correction** +0.35s/f (Good) — **9** Ran SP% **118.8**
Speed ratings (Par 99): **102,98,97,94,92 88,86,71,63**
CSF £93.02 CT £496.83 TOTE £3.90: £1.90, £7.00, £1.90; EX 115.30 Trifecta £901.60.
Owner Kennet Valley Thoroughbreds XI Racing **Bred** Ms Ann Foley **Trained** Angmering, W Sussex

FOCUS
A modest 3yo handicap. The second and third have been rated close to their turf form.
T/Jkpt: Not Won. T/Plt: £2,041.80 to a £1 stake. Pool: £125,447.79 - 44.85 winning units T/Qpdt: £327.80 to a £1 stake. Pool: £13,685.46 - 30.89 winning units **Tim Mitchell**

2666 HOPPEGARTEN (R-H)
Sunday, June 9

OFFICIAL GOING: Turf: good

3639a DIANA-TRIAL (GROUP 2) (3YO FILLIES) (TURF) — 1m 2f
4:40 3-Y-O — £36,036 (£13,963; £7,207; £3,603; £2,252)

RPR

1 **Akribie (GER)**[48] 1990 3-9-2 0 .... AdriedeVries 9 — 103+
(Markus Klug, Germany) *mde all: pushed along and asked to qckn over 2f out: rdn 1 1/2f out: r.o strly ins fnl f: a in command* **5/1**

2 2 **Satomi (GER)**[14] 3119 3-9-2 0 .... RenePiechulek 6 — 98+
(Markus Klug, Germany) *racd keenly in fnl trio: swtchd outside rivals and pushed along jst under 2f out: drvn ent fnl f: picked up wl to go 2nd fnl 50yds: nt rch wnr* **199/10**

3 1 1/2 **Stex (IRE)**[224] 8679 3-9-2 0 .... WladimirPanov 5 — 95
(R Dzubasz, Germany) *trckd ldr: pushed along to chal over 2f out: nt qckn and sn drvn: kpt on ins fnl f: lost 2nd fnl 50yds* **203/10**

4 1 1/4 **Anna Pivola (GER)**[48] 1990 3-9-2 0 .... MaximPecheur 4 — 93
(Markus Klug, Germany) *midfield: pushed along between rivals over 2f out: limited rspnse and sn rdn: responded for press ins fnl f: tk 4th fnl strides* **23/5[3]**

5 1 **Whispering Angel (GER)**[231] 8443 3-9-2 0 .... MartinSeidl 2 — 91
(Markus Klug, Germany) *cl up on inner: pushed along to chse ldr over 2f out: rdn 1 1/2f out: grad wknd ins fnl f: no ex* **7/2[2]**

6 1 1/4 **Shining Pass (GER)** 3-9-2 0 .... EduardoPedroza 8 — 88
(A Wohler, Germany) *midfield on outer: asked for effrt 2f out: sltly short of racing room 1 1/2f out: kpt on same pce under hands and heels riding ins fnl f: n.d* **12/5[1]**

7 2 1/2 **Global Cloud (GER)** 3-9-2 0 .... BauyrzhanMurzabayev 10 — 83
(R Dzubasz, Germany) *hld up in rr: pushed along 2f out: no imp and sn struggling: wl btn ins fnl f: passed btn rival cl home: nvr a factor* **43/5**

8 1/2 **Guardian Fay (IRE)**[33] 3-9-2 0 .... FilipMinarik 3 — 82
(Jean-Pierre Carvalho, Germany) *racd towards rr: asked for effrt 2 1/2f out: no imp and grad wknd fr over 1f out* **13/2**

2m 0.15s (-6.55) — **8** Ran SP% **119.4**
PARI-MUTUEL (all including 1 euro stake): WIN 6.00; PLACE 2.80, 4.70, 3.90; SF 115.00.
Owner Gestut Rottgen **Bred** Gestut Rottgen **Trained** Germany

3173 LES LANDES
Sunday, June 9

OFFICIAL GOING: Turf: good

3640a BRADY & GALLAGHER (1999) H'CAP — 1m 4f
3:05 (3:05) 3-Y-O+ — £1,780 (£640; £380)

RPR

1 **White Valiant (FR)**[13] 6-10-3 0 .... MarkQuinlan — 74
(T Le Brocq, Jersey) *trckd ldrs: led over 1f out: rdn out* **2/1[2]**

2 6 **Island Song (IRE)**[13] 5-10-3 0 .... MrFrederickTett — 64
(Mrs A Malzard, Jersey) *trckd ldr: effrt to dispute ld 3f out: hdd over 1f out: no ex* **3/1[3]**

3 2 **Mrs Burbidge**[21] 602 9-8-7 0 .... (tp) PhilipPrince — 37
(Neil Mulholland) *hld up: 6 th into st: kpt on one pce* **4/6[1]**

4 3/4 **Howardian Hills (IRE)**[30] 2595 6-8-5 0oh3 .... (p) ElishaWhittington — 34
(Victor Dartnall) *led: rn wd bnds over 7f out & 6f out: jnd 3f out: hdd over 1f out: wknd* **4/1**

5 5 **Winklevi (FR)**[13] 4-9-12 0 .... (h) MattieBatchelor — 47
(Mrs A Malzard, Jersey) *dwlt: trckd ldrs: rdn fr 3f out: 4 th st: wknd* **6/1**

6 5 **Safira Menina**[48] 2003 7-9-2 0 .... DarraghKeogh — 29
(Mrs A Malzard, Jersey) *hld up: rapid hdwy to press ldrs fr 5f out: 5 th st: wknd* **16/1**

7 1/2 **Frivolous Prince (IRE)**[13] 6-8-6 0 oh14 ow1 .... PoppyBridgwater — 18
(Mrs C Gilbert, Jersey) *a bhd: nvr able to chal* **25/1**

8 20 **Benoordenhout (IRE)**[13] 8-9-6 0 .... (t) GeorgeRooke
(T Le Brocq, Jersey) *trckd ldrs: outpcd and rdn over 4 out: t.o* **7/1**

9 40 **Barwick**[34] 2502 11-10-12 0 .... (p) VictoriaMalzard
(Mrs A Malzard, Jersey) *hld up: bhd fr over 4f out: t.o* **7/1**

.

Owner Maple Grove Racing **Bred** John Berry **Trained** Jersey

3641a MILLBROOK 2019 JERSEY BULLET H'CAP — 5f 100y
3:40 (3:40) 3-Y-O+ — £2,380 (£860; £510)

RPR

1 **Fruit Salad**[13] 3173 6-10-8 0 .... MarkQuinlan — 59
(K Kukk, Jersey) *hld up: last into st: styd on strly to ld wl ins fnl f: drvn out* **3/1**

2 2 3/4 **Man Of The Sea (IRE)**[13] 3173 3-10-10 0 .... (tp) SamTwiston-Davies — 56
(Neil Mulholland) *trckd ldrs: 4 th into st: ev ch 1f out: no ex cl home* **7/4[2]**

3 nk **Country Blue (FR)**[13] 3173 10-10-8 0 .... (p) MattieBatchelor — 49
(Mrs A Malzard, Jersey) *led: c stands' side st: hdd wl ins fnl f: no ex* **6/1**

4 1/2 **Sing Something**[13] 3173 6-10-10 0 .... (v) MissSerenaBrotherton — 49
(Mrs C Gilbert, Jersey) *trckd ldrs: 3rd into st: ev ch 1f out: wknd cl home* **2/1[3]**

5 nk **Limelite (IRE)**[13] 3173 5-10-6 0 .... MrFrederickTett — 44
(K Kukk, Jersey) *hld up: 5th into st: ev ch over 1f out: hung lft: one pce.* **12/1**

6 hd **Wolf Hunter (IRE)**[28] 3-10-12 0 .... (b) MrDamienArtu — 54
(J Moon, Jersey) *sn pressed ldr: 2nd into st: ev ch 1f out: wknd* **11/8[1]**

.

Owner Tim Loretto & Neil Carter **Bred** Mrs James Bethell **Trained** Jersey

3642a GREEN VALLEY H'CAP — 1m 2f
4:50 (4:50) (0-55,0) 3-Y-O+ — £1,780 (£640; £380)

RPR

1 **Molliana**[13] 3174 4-10-4 0 .... SamTwiston-Davies — 49
(Neil Mulholland) *trckd ldr: chal on bit fr over 1f out: shkn up to ld & go clr fnl 110yds: easy* **1/2[1]**

2 5 **Kenoughty (FR)**[13] 3-9-11 0 .... MrDamienArtu — 44
(J Moon, Jersey) *hld up: last 4f out: sn rdn & rapid hdwy: kpt on to take 2nd cl home* **12/1**

3 nk **Mendacious Harpy (IRE)**[13] 3174 8-9-8 0 .... (p) VictoriaMalzard — 28
(Mrs A Malzard, Jersey) *trckd ldrs: rapid hdwy to ld 5f out: no ex whn hdd fnl 110yds: lost 2nd cl home* **14/1**

4 5 **Carrera**[34] 2501 9-9-0 0 .... DarraghKeogh — 10
(Mrs A Malzard, Jersey) *hld up: mod late hdwy past btn rivals* **25/1**

5 1 1/2 **William Booth (IRE)**[13] 3174 5-10-12 0 .... (v) MissSerenaBrotherton — 33
(Mrs C Gilbert, Jersey) *trckd ldrs: n.m.r turn into st over 2f out: nt rcvr* **9/2[3]**

6 9 **Grey Panel (FR)**[48] 2003 11-10-5 0 .... GeorgeRooke — 8
(T Le Brocq, Jersey) *hld up: nvr able to chal* **4/1[2]**

7 7 **Koshi**[13] 3174 4-10-3 0 .... (p) MarkQuinlan
(K Kukk, Jersey) *trckd ldrs: wknd fr 2f out: eased* **4/1[2]**

8 14 **Little Lotte (IRE)**[34] 2500 6-9-13 0 .... (v) MorganRaine
(Mrs A Corson, Jersey) *led and t.k.h: sn clr: hdd 5f out and wknd rapidly: t.o* **14/1**

.

Owner Dajam Ltd **Bred** Norman Court Stud **Trained** Limpley Stoke, Wilts

2001 **SAN SIRO** (R-H)
Sunday, June 9

OFFICIAL GOING: Turf: good

3643a **PREMIO CARLO VITTADINI (GROUP 3) (3YO+) (GRANDE COURSE) (TURF)** **1m**
4:10 3-Y-O+ **£32,882** (£14,468; £7,891; £3,945)

RPR
1 **Anda Muchacho (IRE)**[21] [2886] 5-9-6 0........................ AntonioFresu 6 107
(Nicolo Simondi, Italy) *trckd ldr on outer: pushed along jst under 2f out: rdn to chal jst ins fnl f: kpt on strly: led fnl 75yds: drvn out* **10/11**[1]
2 *nk* **Out Of Time (ITY)**[42] [2162] 3-8-7 0........................ CristianDemuro 7 101
(A Botti, Italy) *hld up in fnl pair: pushed along over 2f out: rdn 1 1/2f out: responded for press and prog on outer fr over 1f out: r.o strly: nt quite rch wnr* **7/5**[2]
3 *snk* **Fulminix (ITY)**[22] 4-9-4 0........................(t) CarloFiocchi 5 104
(Endo Botti, Italy) *hld up in rr: pushed along and prog between rivals 2f out: rdn to chse ldrs ent fnl f: kpt on strly: nt quite pce to chal* **156/10**
4 *shd* **Time To Choose**[22] 6-9-4 0........................ FabioBranca 1 103
(A Botti, Italy) *prom on inner: pushed along to chal 2f out: rdn and ev ch over 1f out: led narrowly jst ins fnl f: sn hdd: hld towards fin* **282/100**[3]
5 *1 1/2* **Aspettatemi (ITY)**[217] [8866] 5-9-4 0........................(t) MarioSanna 3 100
(D Grilli, Italy) *led: asked to qckn over 3f out: rdn jst under 2f out: jnd over 1f out: hdd jst ins fnl f: no ex and wknd clsng stages* **84/1**
6 *2* **Wait Forever (IRE)**[21] [2886] 4-9-4 0........................ DarioVargiu 2 95
(A Botti, Italy) *midfield: asked for effrt 2 1/2f out: limited rspnse and rdn 2f out: nt qckn and kpt on same pce ins fnl f* **282/100**[3]
7 *9* **Fortissimo (GER)**[259] [7593] 5-9-4 0........................(t) IoritzMendizabal 4 75
(Nicolo Simondi, Italy) *hld up in fnl trio: outpcd and pushed along 3f out: rdn over 2f out: no imp and sn wl btn* **32/1**

1m 35.8s (-6.30) **7 Ran SP% 156.6**
WFA 3 from 4yo+ 11lb
PARI-MUTUEL (all including 1 euro stake): WIN 1.92; PLACE 1.20, 1.35; DF 2.29.
Owner Scuderia Incolinx & Diego Romeo **Bred** Thomas Hassett **Trained** Italy

3189 **LEICESTER** (R-H)
Monday, June 10

OFFICIAL GOING: Good to soft changing to soft after race 6 (5.00)
Wind: Light against Weather: Overcast turning to rain after race 2

3644 **RAGDALE MAIDEN AUCTION STKS** **6f**
2:30 (2:33) (Class 5) 2-Y-O **£4,527** (£1,347; £673; £336) **Stalls High**

Form RPR
2 1 **Zim Baby**[13] [3194] 2-8-4........................ MeganNicholls(3) 6 68+
(Paul George) *chsd ldrs: nt clr run over 1f out: rdn to ld ins fnl f: styd on (vet said filly lost it's right fore shoe)* **3/1**[1]
5 2 *hd* **Flash Henry**[17] [3039] 2-9-2 0........................ HarryBentley 2 76
(George Scott) *chsd ldrs: led and hung lft over 1f out: rdn and hdd ins fnl f: styd on* **13/2**
54 3 *2* **I'm Digby (IRE)**[14] [3165] 2-9-2 0........................ FinleyMarsh(3) 9 73
(Richard Hughes) *mid-div: pushed along and hdwy over 1f out: styd on* **12/1**
32 4 *1/2* **My Motivate Girl (IRE)**[7] [3405] 2-8-9 0........................(v) OisinMurphy 4 62
(Archie Watson) *hld up in tch: rdn over 2f out: nt clr run and swtchd rt ins fnl f: styd on* **4/1**[2]
0 5 *1/2* **Ebony Adams**[21] [2915] 2-8-7 0........................ JasonWatson 11 58
(Brian Meehan) *led 4f: sn rdn: no ex ins fnl f* **25/1**
6 *3/4* **Dubai Avenue (IRE)** 2-9-2 0........................ AdamKirby 13 65+
(Clive Cox) *chsd ldrs: rdn over 1f out: styd on same pce ins fnl f* **6/1**[3]
7 *2* **Drew Breeze (IRE)** 2-9-2 0........................ GeorgeBuckell(3) 14 62
(Richard Spencer) *hld up: pushed along over 2f out: edgd rt and styd on ins fnl f: nt trble ldrs* **22/1**
8 *shd* **Leg It Lenny (IRE)** 2-9-5 0........................ RichardKingscote 5 62+
(Robert Cowell) *s.s: sn pushed along in rr: hdwy over 1f out: styd on same pce ins fnl f* **8/1**
00 9 *1/2* **Flight Of Thunder (IRE)**[46] [2052] 2-8-9 0........................ KevinStott 3 50
(Kevin Ryan) *chsd ldr: led 2f out: rdn and hdd over 1f out: wknd ins fnl f* **25/1**
10 *1 3/4* **I Had A Dream** 2-8-7 0........................ MartinDwyer 15 43
(Tom Clover) *s.s: outpcd: nvr nrr* **33/1**
11 *3/4* **Alibaba** 2-9-5 0........................ CharlieBennett 7 53
(Julia Feilden) *s.i.s: hld up: rdn over 2f out: n.d* **33/1**
0 12 *3/4* **Dream Isle (IRE)**[9] [3335] 2-8-5 0........................ TobyEley(7) 8 44
(Steph Hollinshead) *prom: sn pushed along: rdn and lost pl after 1f: n.d after (jockey said colt ran green)* **200/1**
06 13 *1 1/4* **Baileys Prayer (FR)**[14] [3156] 2-9-0 0........................ PaulHanagan 1 42
(Richard Fahey) *stmbld s: sn prom: lost pl 4f out: n.d after* **28/1**
14 *1 3/4* **Sir Rodneyredblood** 2-8-12 0........................ KieranO'Neill 12 35
(J R Jenkins) *chsd ldrs: rdn over 2f out: wknd over 1f out* **100/1**
P 15 *22* **Austin Taetious**[11] [3274] 2-8-12 0........................ JimmyQuinn 10
(Adam West) *bhd fr 1/2-way* **150/1**

1m 14.22s (2.12) **Going Correction** +0.275s/f (Good) **15 Ran SP% 114.9**
Speed ratings (Par 93): **96,95,93,92,91 90,88,87,87,84 83,82,81,78,49**
CSF £19.00 TOTE £4.00: £1.80, £2.10, £2.90; EX 24.40 Trifecta £129.80.
Owner Fosnic Racing & Paul George **Bred** David Botterill & John Guest **Trained** Crediton, Devon

FOCUS
The first pair dominated the finish of this 2yo maiden. The winner did not need to replicate her recent debut effort.

3645 **HICKLING (S) STKS** **6f**
3:00 (3:01) (Class 5) 3-5-Y-O
£4,075 (£1,212; £606; £303; £300; £300) **Stalls High**

Form RPR
1 **Elzaam's Dream (IRE)** 3-8-5 0........................(h[1]) KieranO'Neill 1 57
(Ronald Harris) *s.i.s: rn green in rr: hdwy u.p over 1f out: sn rdn and hung lft: r.o to ld nr fin* **20/1**
6440 2 *1/2* **The Lamplighter (FR)**[5] [3462] 4-9-8 70........................(tp) PatCosgrave 5 67
(George Baker) *hld up: hdwy 1/2-way: shkn up over 2f out: led over 1f out: sn rdn: hdd nr fin* **11/4**[2]
2-20 3 *1 1/4* **Trotter**[27] [2717] 5-9-8 58........................(b) AdamKirby 9 63
(Stuart Kittow) *hld up: hdwy u.p over 1f out: styd on* **6/1**
6320 4 *4* **Tarrzan (IRE)**[13] [3182] 3-9-0 52........................ LiamJones 4 49
(John Gallagher) *chsd ldrs: led over 2f out: rdn and hdd over 1f out: nt clr run and wknd ins fnl f* **25/1**
-600 5 *1* **Nervous Nerys (IRE)**[14] [3148] 3-8-2 43........................ JaneElliott(3) 6 37
(Alex Hales) *prom: rdn over 3f out: outpcd over 2f out: rallied over 1f out: no ex ins fnl f* **50/1**
000- 6 *2 1/2* **Hellovaqueen**[198] [9257] 4-9-0 67........................(p[1]) FinleyMarsh(3) 3 36
(Richard Hughes) *chsd ldrs: rdn and ev ch wl over 1f out: wknd fnl f* **5/2**[1]
6556 7 *1* **Hard Solution**[4] [3516] 3-8-10 63........................(b) CamHardie 10 32
(David O'Meara) *prom: rdn over 2f out: wknd over 1f out* **11/2**[3]
-560 8 *shd* **Usain Boat (IRE)**[7] [3420] 3-9-0 74........................ EoinWalsh 7 35
(George Scott) *s.i.s: sn rcvrd to chse ldr: rdn and ev ch over 2f out: wknd over 1f out* **8/1**
-000 9 *3/4* **Tigerinmytank**[13] [3208] 3-8-5 45........................ RoystonFfrench 8 24
(John Holt) *led over 3f: rdn and wknd over 1f out* **50/1**
0-00 10 *9* **Maktay**[20] [2943] 3-8-5 46........................ PoppyBridgwater(5) 2 2
(David Bridgwater) *prom: rdn over 3f out: wknd 2f out* **16/1**

1m 14.45s (2.35) **Going Correction** +0.275s/f (Good)
WFA 3 from 4yo+ 8lb **10 Ran SP% 114.4**
Speed ratings (Par 103): **95,94,92,87,86 82,81,81,80,68**
CSF £71.60 TOTE £27.20: £6.30, £1.30, £1.90; EX 97.90 Trifecta £675.40.The winner was bought in for £5,500. The Lamplighter was the subject of a friendly claim. Usain Boat was claimed by Noel Kelly for £7,000.
Owner Ridge House Stables Ltd **Bred** Gerard Brady **Trained** Earlswood, Monmouths

FOCUS
The principals came clear in this moderate seller. The second and third help set the level.

3646 **SHARNFORD CONDITIONS STKS** **1m 3f 179y**
3:30 (3:30) (Class 3) 3-Y-O+ **£8,086** (£2,406; £1,202; £601) **Stalls Low**

Form RPR
0-26 1 **Getchagetchagetcha**[64] [1625] 3-8-6 95........................ JasonWatson 2 105
(Clive Cox) *prom: stdd and lost pl over 10f out: swtchd lft over 2f out: hdwy sn after: rdn to ld over 1f out: hung rt: styd on (jockey said colt lugged right under pressure)* **4/1**[3]
4-56 2 *nk* **Arthur Kitt**[33] [2523] 3-8-7 106 ow1........................ RichardKingscote 4 106+
(Tom Dascombe) *chsd ldrs: nt clr run fr over 3f out tl rdn over 1f out: chsd wnr wl ins fnl f: r.o* **6/4**[1]
33-5 3 *3* **Bombyx**[18] [3025] 4-9-7 98........................ OisinMurphy 3 100
(James Fanshawe) *prom: racd keenly: wnt 2nd over 10f out tl led over 2f out: rdn: hdd and bmpd over 1f out: no ex wl ins fnl f* **7/4**[2]
0-20 4 *1/2* **What About Carlo (FR)**[10] [3315] 8-9-7 98........................ CharlesBishop 5 99
(Eve Johnson Houghton) *hld up: hdwy over 3f out: rdn and hung rt over 1f out: no ex ins fnl f* **8/1**
20/4 5 *1 3/4* **Cohesion**[32] [2554] 6-9-7 99........................ TomQueally 1 96
(David Bridgwater) *led at stdy pce: shkn up and qcknd 3f out: hdd over 2f out: no ex fnl f: eased nr fin* **33/1**

2m 36.78s (1.78) **Going Correction** +0.275s/f (Good)
WFA 3 from 4yo+ 15lb **5 Ran SP% 110.4**
Speed ratings (Par 107): **105,104,102,102,101**
CSF £10.53 TOTE £3.80: £2.80, £1.10; EX 11.40 Trifecta £18.50.
Owner Paul & Clare Rooney **Bred** Mrs James Wigan **Trained** Lambourn, Berks

FOCUS
This feature conditions event was run at a routine gallop and the two 3yos came clear. The third has been rated close to form.

3647 **JO CADDICK 21 YEARS GOING IS GOOD H'CAP** **1m 2f**
4:00 (4:03) (Class 4) (0-80,80) 3-Y-O **£4,690** (£1,395; £697; £348) **Stalls Low**

Form RPR
33-0 1 **Amjaady (USA)**[25] [2765] 3-9-2 **75**........................ JimCrowley 9 84
(Owen Burrows) *led at stdy pce after 1f: qcknd over 3f out: rdn over 1f out: styd on u.p* **16/1**
035- 2 *1 1/2* **Asian Angel (IRE)**[222] [8738] 3-9-2 **75**........................ FrannyNorton 1 81+
(Mark Johnston) *chsd ldrs: rdn over 2f out: styd on* **5/1**[3]
2-33 3 *3/4* **Just The Man (FR)**[31] [2569] 3-9-7 **80**........................ AdamKirby 4 85
(Clive Cox) *slipped leaving stalls: hld up: hdwy over 2f out: rdn over 1f out: edgd lft ins fnl f: styd on same pce towards fin (jockey said colt slipped leaving the stalls)* **11/4**[1]
2150 4 *6* **Blood Eagle (IRE)**[24] [2796] 3-9-2 **75**........................ OisinMurphy 8 68
(Andrew Balding) *s.i.s: hld up: hdwy on outer to chse wnr over 2f out tl rdn over 1f out: wknd ins fnl f* **9/2**[2]
3-34 5 *2 3/4* **Canal Rocks**[14] [3170] 3-9-1 **74**........................ DavidProbert 7 61
(Henry Candy) *hld up: rdn and edgd lft over 2f out: nt trble ldrs* **6/1**
6-03 6 *hd* **Greeley (IRE)**[35] [2470] 3-9-0 **73**........................ RobHornby 5 60
(Rod Millman) *led 1f: chsd wnr tl rdn over 2f out: wknd wl over 1f out* **16/1**
1330 7 *12* **Balladeer**[20] [2942] 3-9-6 **79**........................ HayleyTurner 2 42
(Michael Bell) *prom: racd keenly: nt clr run over 7f out: wknd over 2f out* **5/1**[3]
041- 8 *1 1/2* **Thorn**[270] [7215] 3-9-5 **78**........................ JasonWatson 3 38
(Roger Charlton) *hld up: rdn and wknd over 2f out* **17/2**

2m 10.02s (0.82) **Going Correction** +0.275s/f (Good) **8 Ran SP% 114.8**
Speed ratings (Par 101): **107,105,105,100,98 98,88,87**
CSF £93.85 CT £291.31 TOTE £14.10: £3.10, £2.30, £1.10; EX 108.20 Trifecta £302.40.
Owner Hamdan Al Maktoum **Bred** W S Farish & Lazy F Ranch **Trained** Lambourn, Berks

FOCUS
A fair 3yo handicap, run at an a muddling pace and the winner dictated.

3648 **BRITISH STALLION STUDS EBF MAIDEN STKS** **1m 53y**
4:30 (4:36) (Class 4) 3-Y-O+ **£6,080** (£1,809; £904; £452) **Stalls Low**

Form RPR
1 **Keep Me Company (IRE)** 3-9-3 0........................ DanielMuscutt 1 93+
(James Fanshawe) *chsd ldrs: led over 1f out: rdn and edgd lft ins fnl f: r.o* **7/1**[3]
2-3 2 *1 3/4* **Vasiliev**[61] [1690] 3-9-3 0........................ AdamKirby 4 88+
(Clive Cox) *trckd ldrs: shkn up over 3f out: sn outpcd: rallied u.p over 1f out: wnt 2nd ins fnl f: r.o: nt rch wnr* **11/10**[1]
2-22 3 *3 1/2* **Al Mureib (IRE)**[18] [3011] 3-9-3 85........................ PatCosgrave 9 80
(Saeed bin Suroor) *chsd ldr: rdn over 3f out: ev ch over 1f out: no ex ins fnl f* **15/8**[2]
0-2 4 *2 1/4* **Baalbek (USA)**[18] [3019] 3-9-3 0........................ PatDobbs 8 75+
(Owen Burrows) *s.i.s: hld up: hdwy over 1f out: nt trble ldrs* **16/1**

-0 5 3 **Ghaly**[18] 3003 3-9-0 0 GabrieleMalune(3) 3 68
(Saeed bin Suroor) *sn led: qcknd over 3f out: rdn and edgd lft over 2f out: hdd over 1f out: edgd rt and wknd ins fnl f* 14/1

03 6 1 1/2 **Cool Possibility (IRE)**[13] 3184 3-9-3 0 RichardKingscote 10 64
(Charles Hills) *prom: rdn over 2f out: sn hung rt and wknd* 33/1

P0- 7 3 3/4 **Gavi Di Gavi (IRE)**[257] 7680 4-10-0 0 TomQueally 6 59
(Alan King) *plld hrd and prom: stdd and lost pl after 1f: rdn and wknd over 2f out* 100/1

0- 8 2 **Heartbreak Hotel (IRE)**[272] 7151 3-8-12 0 HayleyTurner 13 46
(Michael Bell) *s.i.s: hld up: wknd over 2f out* 50/1

9 1/2 **Cinzento (IRE)** 3-9-3 0 CallumShepherd 5 50
(Stuart Williams) *s.i.s: hld up: shkn up over 3f out: wknd over 2f out* 66/1

10 10 **Alsafa** 3-9-3 0 JimCrowley 7 27
(Brian Meehan) *s.i.s: rn green in rr: rdn and wknd 3f out* 16/1

1m 47.5s (1.20) **Going Correction** +0.275s/f (Good)
WFA 3 from 4yo 11lb **10** Ran SP% **120.7**
Speed ratings (Par 105): **105,103,99,97,94 93,89,87,86,76**
CSF £15.60 TOTE £8.90: £2.30, £1.10, £1.10; EX 23.70 Trifecta £44.70.
Owner Mrs A M Swinburn **Bred** W Maxwell Ervine **Trained** Newmarket, Suffolk

FOCUS
A fair maiden, run at a sound pace.

3649 RACING TV H'CAP 7f
5:00 (5:04) (Class 4) (0-80,80) 4-Y-O+
£5,692 (£1,694; £846; £423; £300; £300) **Stalls** High

Form RPR

1433 1 **Call Out Loud**[24] 2799 7-9-2 **75** (vt) AlistairRawlinson 5 84
(Michael Appleby) *mde all: shkn up over 1f out: rdn out* 11/2[3]

4203 2 1/2 **Esprit De Corps**[39] 2348 5-8-13 **72** RobbieDowney 7 79
(David Barron) *chsd ldrs: rdn over 1f out: chsd wnr wl ins fnl f: r.o* 8/1

-045 3 1 **Star Shield**[21] 2898 4-9-0 **73** CamHardie 9 77+
(David O'Meara) *hld up: pushed along over 2f out: hdwy and swtchd lft over 1f out: r.o: nt rch ldrs* 8/1

-264 4 1/2 **Young John (IRE)**[24] 2799 6-9-4 **77** RossaRyan 2 80
(Mike Murphy) *chsd wnr: rdn and ev ch over 1f out: no ex wl ins fnl f* 9/2[1]

V0-0 5 1 **Colonel Frank**[26] 2739 5-9-6 **79** FrannyNorton 10 79
(Mick Quinn) *hld up in tch: rdn over 1f out: no ex ins fnl f* 16/1

634 6 shd **Custard The Dragon**[41] 2242 6-9-4 **77** (v) JimmyQuinn 8 77
(John Mackie) *s.i.s: in rr: r.o ins fnl f: nt rch ldrs* 14/1

4001 7 shd **Nezar (IRE)**[31] 2596 8-8-9 **75** SophieRalston(7) 3 75
(Dean Ivory) *hld up: hdwy 2f out: styd on* 15/2

4-20 8 1/2 **Knowing Glance (IRE)**[21] 2899 4-8-13 **72** PaulHanagan 15 70
(Richard Fahey) *hld up: rdn over 1f out: r.o ins fnl f: nt trble ldrs* 15/2

0654 9 1 1/2 **Swift Approval (IRE)**[19] 2977 7-9-2 **75** OisinMurphy 12 69
(Stuart Williams) *chsd ldrs: rdn over 1f out: no ex ins fnl f* 5/1[2]

360- 10 27 **Welliesinthewater (IRE)**[279] 6913 9-9-4 **77** (v) PaddyMathers 14
(Derek Shaw) *s.s: outpcd* 50/1

0-00 11 12 **Quixote (GER)**[14] 3149 9-9-5 **78** (t) DanielMuscutt 1
(James Unett) *s.i.s: pushed along early in rr: rdn and wknd over 2f out* 40/1

5-00 12 16 **Theodorico (IRE)**[43] 2151 6-9-5 **78** TrevorWhelan 11
(David Loughnane) *plld hrd and prom: rdn and wknd 1/2-way* 16/1

1m 26.14s (0.44) **Going Correction** +0.275s/f (Good) **12** Ran SP% **118.8**
Speed ratings (Par 105): **108,107,106,105,104 104,104,103,102,71 57,39**
CSF £49.29 CT £355.61 TOTE £5.80: £2.00, £3.20, £2.80; EX 58.30 Trifecta £809.70.
Owner Kings Head Duffield Racing Partnership **Bred** Rabbah Bloodstock Limited **Trained** Oakham, Rutland

FOCUS
It paid to be handy in this modest, big-field handicap.

3650 FOLLOW @RACING TV ON TWITTER H'CAP (DIV I) 7f
5:30 (5:31) (Class 6) (0-65,67) 3-Y-O
£3,493 (£1,039; £519; £300; £300; £300) **Stalls** High

Form RPR

6-36 1 **Defence Treaty (IRE)**[13] 3202 3-9-9 **67** (p[1]) PaulMulrennan 7 77+
(Richard Fahey) *hld up in tch: pushed along over 2f out: rdn and r.o to ld wl ins fnl f* 13/2

-002 2 1 3/4 **The Big House (IRE)**[11] 3271 3-8-5 **49** PaddyMathers 11 55
(Adrian Nicholls) *s.i.s: hld up: racd keenly: hdwy 1/2-way: rdn to ld 1f out: lost number cloth sn after: hdd and unable qck wl ins fnl f* 9/2[2]

4021 3 3/4 **Your Mothers' Eyes**[13] 3182 3-8-12 **61** (p) DarraghKeenan(5) 8 65
(Alan Bailey) *hld up: hdwy 1/2-way: rdn and ev ch 1f out: styd on same pce wl ins fnl f* 9/2[2]

36-0 4 3/4 **Olivia R (IRE)**[13] 3202 3-9-8 **66** RobbieDowney 16 68
(David Barron) *hld up: rdn over 2f out: r.o ins fnl f: nt rch ldrs* 16/1

1-00 5 3/4 **Uncle Norman (FR)**[43] 2152 3-8-13 **57** (b) RachelRichardson 15 57
(Tim Easterby) *slowly into stried: hld up: hdwy 1/2-way: shkn up over 1f out: styd on same pce ins fnl f* 14/1

4-06 6 1 3/4 **Dancing Speed (IRE)**[21] 2896 3-9-7 **65** SamJames 9 61
(Marjorie Fife) *chsd ldrs: rdn and ev ch over 1f out: wknd wl ins fnl f* 28/1

46-5 7 nk **Old Red Eyes (USA)**[24] 2798 3-9-5 **63** OisinMurphy 3 58+
(Joseph Tuite) *sn led: rdn and hdd 1f out: wknd wl ins fnl f* 6/1[3]

-324 8 2 3/4 **Elikapeka (FR)**[7] 3414 3-9-5 **63** DougieCostello 13 51
(Kevin Ryan) *hld up: pushed along 3f out: nt trble ldrs* 14/1

6-00 9 nk **Sweet Jemima (USA)**[25] 2762 3-9-3 **61** MartinDwyer 4 49
(William Muir) *s.i.s: hdwy over 2f out: rdn and ev ch over 1f out: wknd ins fnl f* 20/1

50-4 10 1 **Ifton**[21] 2896 3-9-7 **65** JimCrowley 2 50
(Ruth Carr) *hld up in tch: shkn up over 1f out: wknd ins fnl f (trainer said gelding would prefer a faster surface)* 4/1[1]

-260 11 2 **Turquoise Friendly**[35] 2489 3-9-6 **64** RichardKingscote 18 44
(Robert Cowell) *chsd ldrs: rdn over 2f out: wknd over 1f out* 40/1

05 12 1 1/4 **Sweet Forgetme Not (IRE)**[26] 2735 3-8-3 **47** HayleyTurner 10 24
(Samuel Farrell, Ire) *chsd ldrs: rdn and ev ch over 1f out: wknd ins fnl f* 20/1

0150 13 3/4 **Brother Bentley**[18] 2995 3-8-11 **55** (b) RossaRyan 5 30
(Ronald Harris) *chsd ldr: rdn over 2f out: wknd over 1f out* 16/1

1m 27.88s (2.18) **Going Correction** +0.325s/f (Good) **13** Ran SP% **124.5**
Speed ratings (Par 97): **100,98,97,96,95 93,93,89,89,88 86,84,83**
CSF £35.71 CT £151.21 TOTE £3.80: £2.30, £1.90, £2.20; EX 37.20 Trifecta £170.90.
Owner Clipper Logistics **Bred** Michael Rogers **Trained** Musley Bank, N Yorks

FOCUS
They spread across the track in this moderate 3yo handicap. Fair form for the class.

3651 FOLLOW @RACING TV ON TWITTER H'CAP (DIV II) 7f
6:00 (6:02) (Class 6) (0-65,67) 3-Y-O
£3,493 (£1,039; £519; £300; £300; £300) **Stalls** High

Form RPR

0-10 1 **Run After Genesis (IRE)**[56] 1825 3-9-6 **64** DanielMuscutt 7 70
(Brett Johnson) *chsd ldrs: rdn over 2f out: hung lft and led ins fnl f: styd on u.p* 14/1

0506 2 1 1/4 **Zalmi Angel**[22] 2871 3-8-1 **50** PaulaMuir(5) 12 53
(Adrian Nicholls) *led 2f: chsd ldrs: rdn over 1f out: styd on* 14/1

256 3 1/2 **Hey Ho Let's Go**[16] 3090 3-9-6 **64** AdamKirby 14 66+
(Clive Cox) *plld hrd and prom: rdn over 1f out: styd on* 5/1[2]

06-0 4 nse **Classic Star**[152] 134 3-8-10 **61** LukeBacon(7) 6 63
(Dean Ivory) *chsd ldrs: rdn over 2f out: styd on* 7/1

650- 5 1/2 **Cambeleza (IRE)**[257] 7666 3-8-12 **56** (w) DougieCostello 3 56+
(Kevin Ryan) *hld up: swtchd lft and hdwy over 1f out: swtchd rt ins fnl f: styd on: nt rch ldrs* 25/1

54-6 6 shd **Alabama Dreaming**[20] 2938 3-9-9 **67** EoinWalsh 9 67
(George Scott) *s.i.s: hld up: hdwy over 1f out: nt rch ldrs* 16/1

0404 7 3 1/4 **Maid Millie**[48] 2007 3-8-12 **56** (v) RichardKingscote 5 48
(Robert Cowell) *led 5f out: rdn and hdd over 1f out: wknd wl ins fnl f* 10/1

200- 8 1/2 **Congress Place (IRE)**[163] 9744 3-9-4 **62** AlistairRawlinson 10 53
(Michael Appleby) *hld up in tch: hmpd 4f out: sn pushed along: rdn over 2f out: styd on same pce fr over 1f out* 25/1

05-4 9 1/2 **Salmon Fishing (IRE)**[24] 2798 3-9-5 **63** RossaRyan 2 52
(Mohamed Moubarak) *chsd ldrs: rdn to ld over 1f out: hdd & wknd ins fnl f* 11/2[3]

0-22 10 1 **Lonicera**[13] 3182 3-9-2 **60** PatCosgrave 15 47
(Henry Candy) *s.i.s: hld up: rdn over 2f out: n.d* 9/2[1]

0500 11 3/4 **Air Hair Lair (IRE)**[14] 3170 3-9-7 **65** FergusSweeney 16 50
(Sheena West) *hld up: rdn over 2f out: nvr on terms* 15/2

0-42 12 3/4 **Perfect Swiss**[10] 3319 3-8-10 **54** RachelRichardson 17 37
(Tim Easterby) *prom: racd keenly: rdn over 2f out: sn lost pl* 10/1

0206 13 hd **Thedevilinneville**[13] 3182 3-8-4 **48** JimmyQuinn 1 31
(Adam West) *hld up: hdwy over 2f out: wknd over 1f out* 25/1

006 14 6 **Fabulous View (FR)**[12] 3218 3-8-2 **46** oh1 NathanEvans 4 14
(Ruth Carr) *in rr and pushed along 5f out: rdn and bhd fr 1/2-way* 33/1

1m 29.03s (3.33) **Going Correction** +0.325s/f (Good) **14** Ran SP% **126.4**
Speed ratings (Par 97): **94,92,92,91,91 91,87,86,86,85 84,83,83,76**
CSF £197.78 CT £1137.59 TOTE £17.90: £6.90, £6.30, £1.60; EX 341.60 Trifecta £1398.60.
Owner Colin Westley **Bred** R Cantoni & G Benvenuto **Trained** Epsom, Surrey

FOCUS
This second division of the 7f 3yo handicap was 1.15secs slower than the first.
T/Plt: £29.50 to a £1 stake. Pool: £62,290.13 - 1539.33 winning units T/Qpdt: £7.20 to a £1 stake. Pool: £6,152.35 - 625.64 winning units **Colin Roberts**

3053 PONTEFRACT (L-H)
Monday, June 10

OFFICIAL GOING: Good to soft changing to soft after race 2 (6.35)
Wind: Light against Weather: Heavy cloud and rain

3652 LEEDS RHINOS EBF FILLIES' NOVICE AUCTION STKS (PLUS 10 RACE) 6f
6:05 (6:06) (Class 5) 2-Y-O
£3,881 (£1,155; £577; £288) **Stalls** Low

Form RPR

1 **Oti Ma Boati** 2-9-0 0 TonyHamilton 7 77+
(Richard Fahey) *dwlt and green in rr: hdwy over 2f out: chsd ldrs over 1f out: kpt on wl to ld last 100yds* 6/1

2 nk **Hidden Spell (IRE)** 2-8-12 0 DanielTudhope 4 72+
(K R Burke) *trckd ldr: cl up 2f out: rdn to chal over 1f out: slt ld jst ins fnl f: hdd last 100yds: kpt on same pce* 11/4[1]

31 3 2 1/4 **Calippo (IRE)**[11] 3257 2-9-5 0 (p[1]) BenCurtis 6 72
(Archie Watson) *led: pushed along 2f out: sn jnd and rdn: hdd jst ins fnl f: kpt on same pce* 3/1[2]

45 4 5 **Royal Lightning**[21] 2903 2-8-10 0 BarryMcHugh 3 48
(James Given) *trckd ldrs: hdwy on inner over 2f out: rdn along wl over 1f out: sn one pce* 11/1

5 nk **Ebony Legend** 2-9-0 0 JasonHart 1 51
(John Quinn) *dwlt: green in rr: outpcd and detached over 2f out: styd on wl fnl f* 6/1

6 1 **Hollywood Waltz** 2-8-10 0 SilvestreDeSousa 2 44
(Mick Channon) *towards rr: hdwy on outer over 2f out: sn chsng ldrs: rdn wl over 1f out: sn wknd* 7/2[3]

7 8 **Marengo Sally (IRE)** 2-8-12 0 AndrewMullen 8 22
(Ben Haslam) *chsd ldng pair: pushed along 3f out: sn rdn and wknd 2f out* 25/1

1m 20.46s (3.36) **Going Correction** +0.375s/f (Good) **7** Ran SP% **114.6**
Speed ratings (Par 90): **92,91,88,81,81 80,69**
CSF £22.98 TOTE £6.20: £2.90, £1.60; EX 21.50 Trifecta £82.00.
Owner R A Fahey **Bred** Bearstone Stud **Trained** Musley Bank, N Yorks

FOCUS
A dry night but the ground eased to "good to soft" before the opener after the course soaked up 5.5mm of rain from 1pm. A false rail added approximately 8yds to the distance of all races. Fair form from the first three, who pulled clear in the straight in a time that suggested the ground was already soft.

3653 TONY BETHELL MEMORIAL H'CAP (ROUND 3 OF THE PONTEFRACT STAYERS CHAMPIONSHIP 2019) 2m 1f 27y
6:35 (6:37) (Class 4) (0-80,80) 4-Y-O+
£6,469 (£1,925; £962; £481; £300; £300) **Stalls** Low

Form RPR

/-04 1 **Michael's Mount**[31] 2578 6-9-7 **80** SilvestreDeSousa 11 89
(Ian Williams) *mde all: rdn wl over 1f out: drvn ins fnl f: hld on gamely towards fin* 9/2[2]

3121 2 shd **True Destiny**[20] 2936 4-9-4 **77** AdamMcNamara 9 85
(Roger Charlton) *dwlt: hld up in rr: stdy hdwy 5f out: chsd ldrs 3f out: rdn wl over 1f out: kpt on to chse wnr ins fnl f: sn drvn: kpt on wl towards fin: jst hld* 13/2[3]

-531 3 5 **Sassie (IRE)**[5] 3467 4-9-3 **79** 5ex GaryMahon(3) 3 82
(Sylvester Kirk) *prom: trckd wnr 7f out: pushed along 3f out: rdn over 2f out: drvn wl over 1f out: kpt on one pce fnl f* 3/1[1]

-040 **4** *2 1/2* **St Andrews (IRE)**[11] 3272 6-8-2 **61** oh6....................(v) DuranFentiman 1 61
(Gillian Boanas) *dwlt and in rr: hdwy into midfield 1/2-way: in tch over 4f out: hdwy on inner 3f out: sn rdn along to chse ldrs: drvn and no imp fr over 1f out* **40/1**

435- **5** *5* **Wind Place And Sho**[98] 6331 7-9-1 **74**.................................. RyanTate 7 69
(James Eustace) *bhd: hdwy 4f out: rdn along 3f out: plugged on fnl 2f: nvr nr ldrs* **25/1**

-544 **6** *3* **Bodacious Name (IRE)**[10] 3294 5-8-9 **68**........................... JasonHart 5 60
(John Quinn) *in tch: hdwy on inner to chse ldrs over 3f out: rdn along over 2f out: sn drvn and grad wknd* **8/1**

1112 **7** *11* **Echo (IRE)**[9] 3334 4-9-1 **74**...(b) JackGarritty 8 55
(Jedd O'Keeffe) *hld up towards rr: sme hdwy over 5f out: rdn along over 3f out: n.d* **8/1**

6-14 **8** *15* **Valkenburg**[41] 2254 4-8-3 **67**................................... SeanDavis(5) 6 33
(Harriet Bethell) *in tch: pushed along over 6f out: rdn along over 4f out: sn drvn and wknd (jockey said gelding was never travelling)* **9/1**

3026 **9** *13* **Glan Y Gors (IRE)**[26] 2748 7-9-4 **77**..................................(b) CliffordLee 4 30
(David Thompson) *chsd ldrs: rdn along 4f out: drvn 3f out: wknd over 2f out (jockey said gelding hung left-handed under pressure)* **16/1**

60-2 **10** *3 1/2* **General Allenby**[11] 3272 5-8-2 **61** oh9...................(b) AndrewMullen 10 11
(Peter Bowen) *a towards rr: bhd fnl 4f* **14/1**

2/03 **11** *7* **Attention Seaker**[10] 3294 9-8-9 **68**....................................(t) DavidAllan 13 11
(Tim Easterby) *chsd ldrs: pushed along over 6f out: rdn wl over 4f out: sn wknd* **12/1**

/1-0 **12** *4* **Waiting For Richie**[25] 2781 6-9-2 **75**........................... JamesSullivan 12 14
(Tom Tate) *trckd wnr: pushed along over 6f out: rdn 5f out: sn wknd* **50/1**

3m 54.45s (5.25) **Going Correction** +0.375s/f (Good) **12 Ran SP% 117.2**
Speed ratings (Par 105): **102,101,99,98,96 94,89,82,76,74 71,69**
CSF £32.99 CT £101.90 TOTE £4.50: £2.20, £2.10, £1.60; EX 33.50 Trifecta £101.90.
Owner Andrew Dick And Mark Dennis **Bred** Southill Stud **Trained** Portway, Worcs
■ Stewards' Enquiry : Adam McNamara seven-day ban; misuse of whip (June 24-30)

FOCUS
A competitive handicap run at approximately 8yds further than advertised. The gallop was reasonable and the first two pulled clear in the closing stages.

3654 MR WOLF SPRINT H'CAP 6f
7:05 (7:06) (Class 3) (0-90,90) 3-Y-O
£9,238 (£2,781; £1,390; £693; £348; £175) **Stalls** Low

Form RPR

5-13 **1** **Roulston Scar (IRE)**[24] 2810 3-8-13 **82**............................ TomEaves 3 93
(Kevin Ryan) *mde all: rdn clr and drifted to stands' side over 1f out: drvn and kpt on wl towards fin* **6/1**

-034 **2** *2* **Triple Distilled**[10] 3307 3-8-4 **76**.........................(t) RowanScott(3) 1 81
(Nigel Tinkler) *trckd ldrs on inner: hdwy 1/2-way: chsd ldng pair and rdn over 1f out: sn edgd rt towards stands' side and styd on to chse wnr ins fnl f: kpt on towards fin* **9/1**

-325 **3** *2* **Tenax (IRE)**[24] 2810 3-8-7 **81**.................................. FayeMcManoman(5) 8 80+
(Nigel Tinkler) *hld up in rr: hdwy and wd st: swtchd rt and rdn wl over 1f out: kpt on fnl f* **16/1**

2-60 **4** *1* **Shallow Hal**[26] 2746 3-9-4 **87**.. BenCurtis 6 82
(K R Burke) *chsd wnr: rdn along over 2f out: drvn wl over 1f out: grad wknd* **9/2**[3]

-322 **5** *2 1/4* **Hafeet Alain (IRE)**[5] 3479 3-8-11 **80**........................... AndrewMullen 5 68
(Adrian Nicholls) *trckd ldrs whn hmpd after 1f: towards rr: hdwy over 2f out: rdn wl over 1f out: kpt on same pce fnl f* **7/2**[1]

-512 **6** *1/2* **Obee Jo (IRE)**[30] 2624 3-8-8 **77**.................................... DavidAllan 7 64
(Tim Easterby) *towards rr: rdn along over 2f out: kpt on fnl f* **9/1**

112- **7** *6* **Princes Des Sables**[230] 8504 3-9-6 **89**............................ ShaneGray 10 56
(Kevin Ryan) *chsd ldrs on outer: rdn along 2f out: sn drvn and wknd* **16/1**

0463 **8** *1 1/2* **Kinks**[23] 2835 3-9-7 **90**.. SilvestreDeSousa 4 53
(Mick Channon) *chsd ldrs: rdn along over 2f out: sn wknd (jockey said gelding ran flat)* **4/1**[2]

102- **9** *29* **Golden Circle (IRE)**[241] 8161 3-8-5 **79**............................. SeanDavis(5) 2
(Richard Fahey) *plld hrd: chsd ldng pair tl wknd qckly wl over 2f out: sn bhd (jockey said filly ran too free)* **12/1**

1m 18.18s (1.08) **Going Correction** +0.375s/f (Good) **9 Ran SP% 114.1**
Speed ratings (Par 103): **107,104,101,100,97 96,88,86,48**
CSF £57.80 CT £824.09 TOTE £7.00: £1.90, £3.20, £5.10; EX 56.40 Trifecta £573.70.
Owner K&J Bloodstock Ltd **Bred** Epona Bloodstock Ltd **Trained** Hambleton, N Yorks

FOCUS
The ground was changed to soft before this useful handicap. The gallop was only fair and the runners came centre to stands' side in the straight. Rail movements added approximately 8yds.

3655 PONTEFRACT SQUASH & LEISURE CLUB H'CAP 1m 4f 5y
7:35 (7:36) (Class 2) (0-105,102) 4-Y-O+
£12,318 (£3,708; £1,854; £924; £464; £234) **Stalls** Low

Form RPR

30-5 **1** **Te Akau Caliburn (IRE)**[26] 2742 4-8-11 **92**............ SilvestreDeSousa 3 105+
(Andrew Balding) *trckd ldrs: smooth hdwy over 2f out: sn cl up: led wl over 1f out and sn swtchd rt to stands' rail: shkn up ins fnl f: kpt on strly* **11/8**[1]

-535 **2** *2 1/2* **Jabbaar**[16] 3070 6-8-2 **86**.. JamieGormley(3) 5 93
(Iain Jardine) *dwlt and hld up in rr: hdwy over 2f out: swtchd rt towards stands' side wl over 1f out: rdn to chse wnr ins fnl f: drvn and no imp towards fin (jockey said gelding was slowly away)* **12/1**

-000 **3** *5* **My Reward**[16] 3081 7-8-11 **92**... DavidAllan 4 91
(Tim Easterby) *led: jnd and rdn over 2f out: hdd wl over 1f out: drvn and kpt on one pce fnl f* **16/1**

20-0 **4** *1 1/4* **Not So Sleepy**[47] 2032 7-9-0 **95**......................................(t) GrahamLee 6 92
(Hughie Morrison) *hld up towards rr: pushed along and outpcd over 2f out: rdn wl over 1f out: kpt on fnl f* **9/1**

-320 **5** *3/4* **Everything For You (IRE)**[26] 2742 5-8-12 **93**...........(p) KevinStott 8 89
(Kevin Ryan) *trckd ldr: cl up 3f out: rdn along and wd st towards stands' side: drvn wl over 1f out: grad wknd* **7/1**[3]

2313 **6** *1 3/4* **Claire Underwood (IRE)**[16] 3070 4-8-0 **86**.................. SeanDavis(5) 2 79
(Richard Fahey) *in tch: effrt wl over 2f out: sn rdn along: drvn and no imp fr wl over 1f out* **5/1**[2]

0-25 **7** *2* **Blue Laureate**[16] 3078 4-8-7 **88**... BenCurtis 7 78
(Ian Williams) *t.k.h: trckd ldrs: cl up over 3f out: rdn along over 2f out: sn wknd* **7/1**[3]

8 *15* **Isidor Bonheur Yes (FR)**[400] 5-9-7 **102**...................... DanielTudhope 9 68
(David O'Meara) *cl up on outer: rdn along over 2f out: sn wknd* **20/1**

2m 43.52s (2.42) **Going Correction** +0.375s/f (Good) **8 Ran SP% 112.1**
Speed ratings (Par 109): **106,104,101,100,99 98,97,87**
CSF £18.79 CT £182.07 TOTE £1.90: £1.10, £2.60, £4.40; EX 18.40 Trifecta £138.00.
Owner M M Stables **Bred** Springbank Way Stud **Trained** Kingsclere, Hants

FOCUS
Add approximately 8yds to the official distance. The feature event on the card and a performance bordering on smart from the winner, who won with a fair bit in hand. The gallop was an ordinary one and the field again raced towards the stands' side in the straight.

3656 CASTLEFORD TIGERS H'CAP (DIV I) 6f
8:05 (8:06) (Class 5) (0-70,72) 3-Y-O+
£3,881 (£1,155; £577; £300; £300; £300) **Stalls** Low

Form RPR

0366 **1** **Captain Dion**[12] 3221 6-9-0 **55**...................................(b) SilvestreDeSousa 6 69
(Ivan Furtado) *qckly away: sn clr: mde all: wd st to stands' rail: kpt on strly* **2/1**[1]

05-0 **2** *5* **Mosseyb (IRE)**[60] 1722 4-8-9 **50**...................................... GrahamLee 4 48
(Paul Midgley) *prom: hdwy towards stands' side to chse wnr over 1f out: sn rdn: drvn and no imp fnl f* **28/1**

0003 **3** *1 3/4* **Jacob's Pillow**[7] 3413 8-9-2 **57**..................................(p) DanielTudhope 3 49
(Rebecca Bastiman) *chsd wnr on inner: rdn along and swtchd rt wl over 1f out: sn drvn and kpt on same pce* **9/1**

0-04 **4** *1* **Kodicat (IRE)**[23] 2847 5-9-4 **59**... KevinStott 5 48
(Kevin Ryan) *towards rr: hdwy 2f out: sn rdn and kpt on fnl f* **6/1**[2]

3320 **5** *1/2* **Gunmaker (IRE)**[13] 3207 5-9-12 **67**.............................. JamesSullivan 1 55
(Ruth Carr) *chsd ldrs towards inner: rdn along 2f out: sn drvn and kpt on same pce* **9/1**

4000 **6** *1/2* **Mr Strutter (IRE)**[39] 2349 5-9-11 **66**.............................. AndrewElliott 7 52
(Ronald Thompson) *chsd ldrs: rdn along wl over 2f out: sn wknd* **25/1**

6-64 **7** *1 1/4* **Uncle Charlie (IRE)**[21] 2893 5-9-10 **65**...................... PaulMulrennan 12 47
(Ann Duffield) *a towards rr* **8/1**[3]

5400 **8** *nse* **Round The Island**[12] 3214 6-9-5 **60**.................................. PhilDennis 11 42
(Richard Whitaker) *chsd ldrs on outer: wd st: rdn wl over 1f out: sn btn* **6/1**[2]

0-45 **9** *5* **Sfumato**[23] 2846 5-9-8 **63**.. AndrewMullen 14 29
(Adrian Nicholls) *chsd ldrs: rdn along and wd st: wknd wl over 1f out* **10/1**

0264 **10** *1 3/4* **Crosse Fire**[13] 3206 7-9-3 **58**..(p) PaddyMathers 10 18
(Scott Dixon) *prom: rdn along 2f out: sn wknd* **12/1**

3350 **11** *1/2* **Deeds Not Words (IRE)**[27] 2709 8-9-9 **64**................. RoystonFfrench 9 23
(Tracy Waggott) *sn outpcd and a bhd* **20/1**

1m 19.27s (2.17) **Going Correction** +0.375s/f (Good) **11 Ran SP% 121.9**
Speed ratings (Par 103): **100,93,91,89,89 88,86,86,79,77 76**
CSF £77.12 CT £440.51 TOTE £2.20: £1.40, £8.70, £1.90; EX 72.10 Trifecta £607.70.
Owner Daniel Macauliffe & Anoj Don **Bred** Miss R J Dobson **Trained** Wiseton, Nottinghamshire

FOCUS
Add 8yds. A modest handicap full of exposed sorts but a race turned into a procession by the well-backed market leader, who won with plenty in hand and continued the trend of angling towards the stands' rail in the home straight.

3657 CASTLEFORD TIGERS H'CAP (DIV II) 6f
8:35 (8:37) (Class 5) (0-70,70) 3-Y-O+
£3,881 (£1,155; £577; £300; £300; £300) **Stalls** Low

Form RPR

0123 **1** **Tricky Dicky**[3] 3550 6-9-9 **65**... BenCurtis 2 74
(Roger Fell) *led main gp on inner: wd into st and led wl over 1f out: sn rdn: drvn ins fnl f: hld on wl towards fin* **5/4**[1]

2133 **2** *1/2* **Ticks The Boxes (IRE)**[5] 3475 7-8-7 **56**............... KieranSchofield(7) 13 63
(Brian Ellison) *racd v wd and overall ldr: drifted lft and jnd 2f out: sn hdd and rdn: swtchd lft and drvn ent fnl f: kpt on wl u.p towards fin* **7/1**[2]

0300 **3** *2 1/4* **Cosmic Chatter**[12] 3221 9-9-1 **57**...............................(p) JamesSullivan 12 57
(Ruth Carr) *in tch: hdwy and wd st: rdn wl over 1f out: chsd ldng pair ent fnl f: kpt on* **20/1**

6365 **4** *7* **Logi (IRE)**[12] 3221 5-9-13 **69**..(b) LewisEdmunds 11 46
(Rebecca Bastiman) *towards rr: hdwy 2f out: sn rdn: kpt on fnl f* **20/1**

50-4 **5** *1/2* **Toofi (FR)**[16] 3079 8-9-11 **67**...................................(t) SilvestreDeSousa 9 43
(John Butler) *prom: rdn along 2f out: sn drvn and kpt on same pce* **11/1**[3]

0502 **6** *1* **Penny Pot Lane**[5] 3470 6-9-7 **63**... PhilDennis 8 36
(Richard Whitaker) *cl up: rdn along and wd st: drvn wl over 1f out: sn wknd* **7/1**[2]

00-4 **7** *2 1/2* **Elysee Star**[21] 2911 4-8-9 **51** oh2.. GrahamLee 10 16
(Ben Haslam) *a towards rr* **25/1**

0040 **8** *3* **Gift In Time (IRE)**[4] 3504 4-9-6 **62**.................................(t) PaddyMathers 5 17
(Paul Collins) *a towards rr* **20/1**

0060 **9** *4* **Etikaal**[13] 3199 5-9-2 **58**.. SamJames 3
(Grant Tuer) *chsd ldrs: rdn along over 2f out: sn wknd* **12/1**

0-05 **10** *5* **Related**[90] 1160 9-10-0 **70**..(w) BarryMcHugh 6
(Paul Midgley) *a towards rr* **16/1**

03-2 **11** *5* **Calin's Lad**[7] 3430 4-9-3 **59**... AndrewMullen 7
(Michael Appleby) *prom: rdn along 2f out: sn drvn and wknd (trainer said gelding was unsuited by the Soft ground and would prefer a sounder surface)* **7/1**[2]

1m 18.63s (1.53) **Going Correction** +0.375s/f (Good) **11 Ran SP% 122.0**
Speed ratings (Par 103): **104,103,100,91,90 89,85,81,76,69 63**
CSF £9.90 CT £130.18 TOTE £2.30: £1.10, £1.80, £6.80; EX 9.90 Trifecta £174.80.
Owner Eight Gents and a Lady **Bred** Onslow, Stratton & Parry **Trained** Nawton, N Yorks
■ Stewards' Enquiry : Silvestre De Sousa caution; careless riding
Sam James caution; careless riding

FOCUS
Division two of a modest handicap and, despite the decent gallop, this was another race on the card in which very few figured. The field came stands' side in the straight and the first three pulled clear.

3658 BRADFORD BULLS H'CAP 5f 3y
9:05 (9:06) (Class 5) (0-75,75) 4-Y-O+
£3,881 (£1,155; £577; £300; £300; £300) **Stalls** Low

Form RPR

/622 **1** **Lathom**[23] 2841 6-9-4 **72**... GrahamLee 13 83+
(Paul Midgley) *trckd ldrs on outer: wd st to stands' rail: hdwy to chse ldng pair over 1f out: rdn to chal ins fnl f: drvn and kpt on wl to ld nr fin* **6/1**

5525 **2** *hd* **Shepherd's Purse**[13] 3203 7-8-8 **62**............................ JamesSullivan 14 72
(Ruth Carr) *racd wd: led: rdn along and wd to stands' rail st: drvn ins fnl f: hdd and no ex nr fin* **9/1**

-000 **3** *4* **Desert Ace (IRE)**[37] 2421 8-9-5 **73**...................................... KevinStott 5 69
(Paul Midgley) *chsd ldr: rdn along and wd st: drvn over 1f out: edgd lft ins fnl f: kpt on same pce* **14/1**

60-6 **4** *nk* **Only Spoofing (IRE)**[23] 2849 5-9-2 **75**.............................. SeanDavis(5) 11 70
(Jedd O'Keeffe) *hld up: hdwy and wd st: rdn over 1f out: styng on whn nt clr run and swtchd lft ins fnl f: kpt on towards fin* **12/1**

40-5 **5** 2 **Stewardess (IRE)**[13] 3201 4-9-3 **71** DavidNolan 16 59
(Richard Fahey) *racd wd: chsd ldng pair: rdn along and wd st: drvn over 1f out: sn one pce* **16/1**
5360 **6** 1 **Sheepscar Lad (IRE)**[17] 3056 5-9-3 **74** RowanScott(3) 8 58
(Nigel Tinkler) *in tch: hdwy to chse ldrs 2f out: rdn over 1f out: sn one pce* **11/2**[3]
6024 **7** 1 ¼ **Socialites Red**[13] 3207 6-8-9 **70** (p) WilliamCarver(7) 3 50
(Scott Dixon) *in tch: rdn along whn hmpd and lost pl 2f out: sn drvn and n.d* **9/2**[2]
4225 **8** 2 **Qaaraat**[13] 3206 4-9-3 **71** CamHardie 1 43
(Antony Brittain) *midfield: effrt on inner over 2f out: sn rdn and n.d* **4/1**[1]
5453 **9** 2 ¾ **Seamster**[10] 3291 12-8-8 **62** (t) BenCurtis 2 24
(David Loughnane) *midfield: hdwy 2f out: sn rdn and n.d* **8/1**
0-00 **10** 1 **Fumbo Jumbo (IRE)**[36] 2433 6-8-8 **62** LewisEdmunds 4 21
(Rebecca Bastiman) *dwlt: a in rr* **25/1**
0-00 **11** 2 ¾ **Suitcase 'N' Taxi**[17] 3056 5-8-11 **65** DavidAllan 10 14
(Tim Easterby) *chsd ldrs: rdn along 2f out: sn wknd* **16/1**
-000 **12** 1 ¾ **Robot Boy (IRE)**[9] 3360 9-9-0 **73** HarrisonShaw(5) 7 16
(Marjorie Fife) *a towards rr* **33/1**

1m 4.83s (0.93) **Going Correction** +0.375s/f (Good) **12 Ran SP% 121.9**
Speed ratings (Par 103): **107,106,100,99,96 95,93,89,85,83 79,76**
CSF £60.99 CT £748.29 TOTE £6.30: £1.90, £2.90, £5.30; EX 81.40 Trifecta £1053.10.
Owner David W Armstrong **Bred** T G Lane **Trained** Westow, N Yorks

FOCUS
Add approximately 8yds to the official distance. A fair handicap and a decent pace but a race in which very few figured. The field came centre to stands' side in the straight and the first two deserve credit for pulling clear.
T/Jkpt: Part won. £21,743.40 to a £1 stake - 0.5 winning units. T/Plt: £78.90 to a £1 stake. Pool: £66,017.84 - 610.43 winning units T/Qpdt: £28.00 to a £1 stake. Pool: £8,028.13 - 211.45 winning units **Joe Rowntree**

3418 WINDSOR (R-H)
Monday, June 10

OFFICIAL GOING: Good (good to soft in places) changing to soft after race 1 (5.45)
Wind: Light, behind Weather: Persistent rain most of meeting

3659 THAMES MATERIALS SUPPORTING AISLING PROJECT H'CAP 5f 21y
5:45 (5:46) (Class 4) (0-85,84) 3-Y-O
£5,530 (£1,645; £822; £411; £300; £300) **Stalls** Centre

Form RPR
22-0 **1** **Angel Alexander (IRE)**[33] 2522 3-9-0 **80** JaneElliott(3) 7 93+
(Tom Dascombe) *t.k.h: disp ld tl def advantage 2f out and racd against far rail: shkn up and clr over 1f out: styd on wl* **10/3**[3]
-330 **2** 2 ¾ **James Watt (IRE)**[23] 2835 3-9-4 **84** CameronNoble(3) 5 86
(Michael Bell) *dwlt: in tch: prog to chse wnr wl over 1f out: styd on but no imp* **11/4**[2]
3004 **3** 2 ½ **Uncle Jerry**[7] 3422 3-8-12 **82** (b) AngusVilliers(7) 1 75
(Richard Hughes) *dwlt: pushed along in last: prog in centre over 2f out: tk 3rd over 1f out: kpt on same pce* **6/1**
14-5 **4** 2 ½ **Glorious Charmer**[17] 3048 3-9-3 **80** GeraldMosse 8 64
(Ed Walker) *dwlt: chsd ldrs: rdn and no prog 1/2-way: wl btn over 1f out (vet said gelding lost it's left fore shoe)* **5/2**[1]
3-05 **5** nk **Pink Iceburg (IRE)**[28] 2687 3-8-13 **76** KierenFox 3 59
(Peter Crate) *chsd ldrs: outpcd and shkn up 2f out: no ch after* **20/1**
5-00 **6** 2 ½ **Autumn Splendour (IRE)**[40] 2274 3-9-0 **77** PJMcDonald 2 51
(Milton Bradley) *in tch: rdn and no prog over 2f out: wknd over 1f out* **22/1**
6000 **7** 4 ½ **Sandridge Lad (IRE)**[24] 2810 3-8-13 **76** StevieDonohoe 4 34
(John Ryan) *in tch to 1/2-way: sn wknd* **33/1**
0-14 **8** 2 **Lille**[69] 1492 3-8-10 **73** KieranShoemark 6 24
(Kevin Ryan) *racd freely: disp ld to 2f out: wknd rapidly* **6/1**

1m 1.46s (1.36) **Going Correction** +0.30s/f (Good) **8 Ran SP% 118.9**
Speed ratings (Par 101): **101,96,92,88,88 84,76,73**
CSF £13.23 CT £53.75 TOTE £3.90: £1.40, £1.20, £1.70; EX 13.30 Trifecta £48.10.
Owner Birbeck Mound Trowbridge & Owen **Bred** Mountarmstrong Stud **Trained** Malpas, Cheshire

FOCUS
Heavy rain throughout the day resulted in the ground easing significantly and it would only have continued to get softer as the meeting progressed. A fair 3yo sprint, but it was run in miserable conditions and not form to get carried away with. They headed centre-to-far side and the winner spearheaded the charge on the far rail.

3660 MURPHY GROUP EBF NOVICE STKS (PLUS 10 RACE) 5f 21y
6:15 (6:15) (Class 4) 2-Y-O **£4,787** (£1,424; £711; £355) **Stalls** Centre

Form RPR
1 **Diligent Deb (IRE)** 2-9-0 DavidEgan 4 71
(William Muir) *hld up in 6th: prog in centre over 1f out: rdn and styd on wl fnl f to ld last strides* **14/1**
4 **2** hd **Swinley (IRE)**[18] 3008 2-9-5 ShaneKelly 2 75
(Richard Hughes) *wnt lft s: pressed ldr: led after 2f: drvn and hrd pressed over 1f out: kpt on but hdd last strides* **11/2**[3]
0 **3** hd **Eton College (IRE)**[7] 3419 2-9-5 PJMcDonald 9 74
(Mark Johnston) *led 2f: pressed ldr and racd against far rail: n.m.r fnl f but kpt on wl: lost 2nd last strides* **2/1**[1]
4 1 **Fantom Force (IRE)** 2-9-5 TomMarquand 1 71
(Richard Hannon) *chsd ldrs in 5th: shkn up and hanging lft over 1f out: styd on ins fnl f: nrst fin* **7/1**
5 ½ **Hard Nut (IRE)** 2-9-5 SeanLevey 5 69
(Richard Hannon) *chsd ldng pair: rdn over 1f out: kpt on but lost pls ins fnl f* **8/1**
6 ½ **Tommy Cooper (IRE)** 2-9-5 KieranShoemark 3 67
(Michael Bell) *dwlt: racd in last trio: prog on outer over 1f out: kpt on steadily fnl f: nrst fin* **12/1**
7 1 ¼ **Forgetful Agent** 2-9-5 EdwardGreatrex 6 63
(Eve Johnson Houghton) *dwlt: hld up in last trio: effrt against far rail over 1f out: no real imp* **20/1**
50 **8** 4 ½ **Maisie Ellie (IRE)**[18] 2996 2-8-11 MeganNicholls(3) 8 41
(Paul George) *chsd ldrs over 3f: wknd* **18/1**
9 hd **Dark Silver (IRE)** 2-9-5 GeraldMosse 7 46
(Ed Walker) *dwlt: mostly in last: shkn up and no prog 2f out (vet said colt lost it's right fore shoe)* **7/2**[2]

1m 2.65s (2.55) **Going Correction** +0.50s/f (Yiel) **9 Ran SP% 118.9**
Speed ratings (Par 95): **99,98,98,96,95 95,93,85,85**
CSF £91.53 TOTE £13.30: £3.90, £1.90, £1.20; EX 82.40 Trifecta £379.20.
Owner Foursome Thoroughbreds **Bred** Hyde Park Stud **Trained** Lambourn, Berks

FOCUS
An average juvenile novice, the leaders again headed far side in the straight but this time the winner came more towards the centre.

3661 CAREY GROUP 50TH ANNIVERSARY NOVICE STKS 6f 12y
6:45 (6:48) (Class 5) 3-Y-O+ **£3,752** (£1,116; £557; £278) **Stalls** Centre

Form RPR
14 **1** **Far Above (IRE)**[23] 2834 3-9-9 0 PJMcDonald 5 96+
(James Tate) *a gng wl: trckd ldrs: led jst over 2f out: pushed clr over 1f out: comf* **8/13**[1]
200- **2** 5 **Crantock Bay**[270] 7201 3-9-2 **85** HarryBentley 14 69
(George Scott) *wl in tch: rdn to chse wnr wl over 1f out: kpt on but sn outpcd* **5/1**[3]
3 ½ **Hour Of The Dawn (IRE)** 3-9-2 0 ShaneKelly 11 67
(Ed Vaughan) *dwlt: wl in rr: pushed along and prog 2f out: rdn and rn green fnl f but styd on to take 3rd last strides* **66/1**
P04 **4** nk **River Dawn**[13] 3184 3-9-2 0 TomMarquand 13 66
(Paul Cole) *wl in tch: prog over 2f out: rdn to chse clr ldng pair jst over 1f out: no imp and lost 3rd last strides* **50/1**
24-2 **5** 2 ½ **Great Midge**[18] 2997 4-9-10 **75** JosephineGordon 2 60
(Henry Candy) *racd in centre: mde most to jst over 2f out: fdd over 1f out* **8/1**
6 ½ **Great Suspense** 3-9-2 0 SeanLevey 7 56
(William Jarvis) *dwlt: hld up in tch: effrt to chse ldrs over 2f out: fdd over 1f out* **25/1**
00 **7** 1 ¼ **Twilighting**[16] 3090 3-8-11 0 KieranShoemark 3 47
(Henry Candy) *dwlt: in tch: pushed along over 2f out: sn outpcd: n.d whn sltly impeded and eased last 75yds* **50/1**
06- **8** hd **Bird Of Wonder**[265] 7402 4-9-10 0 LiamKeniry 8 54
(Henry Candy) *dwlt: nvr on terms w ldrs: no great prog fnl 2f* **100/1**
2-32 **9** 1 ½ **Johnny Reb**[10] 3302 3-9-2 **78** StevieDonohoe 1 47
(Charlie Fellowes) *racd centre: w ldr to over 2f out: wknd qckly over 1f out* **4/1**[2]
0 **10** 2 ¼ **Dutch Story**[18] 3003 3-9-2 0 RobertWinston 6 40
(Amanda Perrett) *spd over 3f: wknd* **50/1**
0 **11** 8 **Vallachy**[79] 1286 4-9-10 0 CharlesBishop 10 16
(William Muir) *spd to 1/2-way: wknd rapidly over 2f out* **100/1**
12 nse **Equipped** 3-8-11 0 DavidEgan 12 9
(Mick Channon) *sn in rr: bhd over 1f out* **25/1**
13 4 **Hidden Dream (FR)**[372] 4-8-12 0 MorganCole(7) 4
(John Butler) *sn in last quartet: wknd 1/2-way* **66/1**

1m 13.93s (1.83) **Going Correction** +0.50s/f (Yiel)
WFA 3 from 4yo 8lb **13 Ran SP% 128.2**
Speed ratings (Par 103): **107,100,99,99,95 95,93,93,91,88 77,77,72**
CSF £4.44 TOTE £1.80: £1.10, £1.80, £6.20; EX 6.00 Trifecta £189.10.
Owner Sheikh Rashid Dalmook Al Maktoum **Bred** Mohamed Abdul Malik **Trained** Newmarket, Suffolk

FOCUS
No great depth to this average 3yo novice and a clear-cut win for the odds-on favourite.

3662 VISIT MARATHONBET.CO.UK H'CAP (WINDSOR SPRINT SERIES QUALIFIER) 5f 21y
7:15 (7:15) (Class 3) (0-95,97) 4-Y-O **£7,246** (£2,168; £1,084; £542; £270) **Stalls** Centre

Form RPR
3-06 **1** **Tawny Port**[1] 3636 5-8-12 **83** PJMcDonald 4 91
(Stuart Williams) *in tch: shkn up and prog 2f out: drvn to ld last 150yds: styd on wl* **7/2**[2]
4-20 **2** 1 ¼ **Just Glamorous (IRE)**[9] 3344 6-8-12 **86** CameronNoble(3) 8 90
(Grace Harris) *trckd ldr: rdn to ld 2f out: hdd and one pce u.p last 150yds* **4/1**[3]
2403 **3** ½ **Storm Over (IRE)**[10] 3301 5-9-6 **91** (p) HarryBentley 3 93
(George Scott) *pushed along in last: rdn and prog in centre over 1f out: kpt on fnl f to take 3rd last stride* **7/1**
0453 **4** shd **Blue De Vega (GER)**[9] 3344 6-9-7 **92** (p) JasonWatson 1 93
(Robert Cowell) *wl in tch: prog to chal over 1f out: nt qckn fnl f and one pce last 100yds* **9/2**
6232 **5** 2 ½ **Harry Hurricane**[23] 2839 7-8-12 **83** (p) JosephineGordon 9 75
(George Baker) *led to 2f out: rdn and wknd fnl f* **15/2**
5602 **6** 2 ½ **Ice Age (IRE)**[5] 3480 6-9-12 **97** CharlesBishop 7 80
(Eve Johnson Houghton) *awkward s: sn chsd ldng pair: shkn up briefly 2f out: sn dropped to last (jockey said gelding ran flat)* **5/2**[1]

1m 1.52s (1.42) **Going Correction** +0.50s/f (Yiel) **6 Ran SP% 113.2**
Speed ratings (Par 107): **108,106,105,105,101 97**
CSF £17.96 CT £90.71 TOTE £4.40: £2.40, £1.90; EX 17.10 Trifecta £84.40.
Owner Mrs J Morley **Bred** Mrs D O'Brien **Trained** Newmarket, Suffolk

FOCUS
An open sprint and so it played out, plenty still being in with a chance inside the final 2f. The winner has been rated to his best, with the third and fourth close to their recent efforts.

3663 GALLAGHER GROUP H'CAP 1m 3f 99y
7:45 (7:46) (Class 4) (0-85,87) 4-Y-O+
£5,530 (£1,645; £822; £411; £300; £300) **Stalls** Low

Form RPR
4-06 **1** **Dragons Voice**[35] 2486 5-9-3 **80** JasonWatson 5 91+
(David Menuisier) *hld up in last: pushed along and swift prog 3f out to ld jst over 2f out: sn clr: rdn out (trainers' rep said, regarding the improved form shown, gelding was suited by the step up in trip and the soft ground)* **16/1**
3240 **2** 2 ¼ **Emenem**[17] 3044 5-9-3 **80** HarryBentley 6 85
(Simon Dow) *trckd ldrs: rdn 3f out: outpcd 2f out: styd on u.p to take 2nd last strides* **5/1**[3]
4405 **3** nk **C Note (IRE)**[24] 2800 6-9-6 **83** CharlesBishop 4 88
(Heather Main) *hld up in last pair: nt clr run jst over 2f out and then outpcd: rdn and styd on over 1f out to take 3rd fnl stride* **10/1**
0104 **4** shd **New Show (IRE)**[16] 3087 4-9-10 **87** (b) PJMcDonald 13 91
(Michael Bell) *rousted early to chse ldng pair: led briefly over 2f out: wandered u.p and sn outpcd by wnr: lost 2 pls last strides* **5/1**[3]
12-0 **5** 3 **Past Master**[26] 2748 6-9-4 **81** DavidProbert 8 80
(Henry Candy) *trckd ldr: chal over 2f out: sn rdn and nt qckn: wknd jst over 1f out* **7/2**[2]
54-6 **6** 3 ½ **William Hunter**[44] 2104 7-8-12 **75** (t[1]) LiamKeniry 9 68
(Nigel Twiston-Davies) *t.k.h: hld up: gng wl enough 3f out: shkn up and fnd nil 2f out: wknd over 1f out* **18/1**

0000 7 3/4 **Kyllachy Gala**[9] 3346 6-9-7 **84**..........(b[1]) EdwardGreatrex 12 76
(Warren Greatrex) led to over 2f out: sltly impeded sn after and wknd **33/1**

2-14 8 1/2 **Get Back Get Back (IRE)**[26] 2748 4-9-7 **84**.......... HectorCrouch 7 75
(Clive Cox) t.k.h: hld up: rdn over 3f out: sn struggling (jockey said gelding ran too freely. Trainers' rep said gelding was unsuited by the Soft ground on this occasion and would prefer a faster surface) **11/4**[1]

04-0 9 2 **Rock Force (IRE)**[19] 2969 4-9-4 **81**.......... KieranShoemark 2 69
(Alan King) chsd ldrs: rdn whn sltly impeded over 2f out: sn wknd **11/2**

2m 34.14s (4.44) **Going Correction** +0.50s/f (Yiel) **9 Ran SP% 120.8**
Speed ratings (Par 105): **103,101,101,101,98 96,95,95,93**
CSF £98.19 CT £864.75 TOTE £15.00: £3.70, £2.00, £3.00; EX 105.30 Trifecta £1492.40.
Owner Heart Of The South Racing 106 **Bred** Parry, Stratton, Steele-Mortimer **Trained** Pulborough, W Sussex

FOCUS
Distance increased by 23yds. A couple of the key players failed to give their running in this fair handicap. They again headed centre-to-far side.

3664 CAPPAGH GIRLS GALLOP NOVICE STKS — 1m 2f
8:15 (8:28) (Class 5) 3-Y-O+ — £3,752 (£1,116; £557; £278) Stalls Low

Form | | | | RPR

2-3 1 **Qarasu (IRE)**[31] 2581 3-8-8 .... JasonWatson 5 83+
(Roger Charlton) hld up in midfield: pushed along and prog over 2f out: led over 1f out: sn drew clr **2/7**[1]

0 2 4 1/2 **Wild Animal**[54] 1852 3-8-8 .... DavidEgan 13 74
(Saeed bin Suroor) trckd ldr after 4f: led wl over 2f out to over 1f out: one pce and no ch w wnr after **4/1**[2]

3 1 1/4 **Paths Of Glory** 4-9-7 ....(t[1]) JackMitchell 8 72
(Hugo Palmer) hld up in last trio: prog over 2f out: shkn up to chse clr ldng pair over 1f out: kpt on steadily **16/1**

0 4 1/2 **Lord Halifax (IRE)**[28] 2690 3-8-8 .... EdwardGreatrex 14 70+
(Charlie Fellowes) hld up in last pair: prog over 2f out: shkn up briefly over 1f out: kpt on steadily: shaped w promise **12/1**[3]

00 5 hd **Unplugged (IRE)**[18] 3003 3-8-8 .... RobHornby 3 69
(Andrew Balding) wl in tch: effrt over 2f out: disp 3rd over 1f out: one pce after **25/1**

60 6 8 **Ekayburg (FR)**[11] 3263 5-9-4 ....(t) FinleyMarsh(3) 4 57+
(David Pipe) hld up in last: sme prog into midfield 2f out: pushed along and no hdwy after: likely to do bttr **33/1**

04- 7 3/4 **Strindberg**[243] 8108 3-8-8 .... GeorgeWood 12 52
(Marcus Tregoning) in tch: rdn 3f out: sn struggling and btn (trainer said colt was unsuited by the Soft ground and would prefer a faster surface) **14/1**

8 3/4 **Hazm (IRE)**[66] 4-9-7 .... PJMcDonald 7 51
(Tim Vaughan) chsd ldrs: rdn and wknd 2f out **25/1**

0/ 9 5 **Bird To Love**[922] 8151 5-8-9 .... EllieMacKenzie(7) 10 36
(Mark Usher) dwlt: rcvrd to chse ldrs: wknd qckly wl over 2f out **100/1**

14 10 shd **Native Silver**[42] 2192 3-9-1 .... DavidProbert 11 47
(Robert Eddery) led to wl over 2f out: wknd qckly **20/1**

00 11 1 1/2 **Marmarr**[5] 3482 3-8-3 .... LiamJones 2 32
(William Haggas) sn in rr: dropped to last and btn 4f out **40/1**

06 12 9 **Society Sweetheart (IRE)**[41] 2250 3-8-3 .... JosephineGordon 9 14
(J S Moore) t.k.h: chsd ldr 4f: wknd rapidly 3f out: t.o **66/1**

2m 14.67s (5.67) **Going Correction** +0.50s/f (Yiel) **12 Ran SP% 138.3**
WFA 3 from 4yo+ 13lb
Speed ratings (Par 103): **97,93,92,92,91 85,84,84,80,80 78,71**
CSF £2.33 TOTE £1.30: £1.10, £1.40, £3.60; EX 3.60 Trifecta £27.70.
Owner H H Sheikh Mohammed Bin Khalifa Al Thani **Bred** Al Shahania Stud **Trained** Beckhampton, Wilts

FOCUS
Distance increased by 23yds. Little depth to this novice and the heavy odds-on favourite won in decisive fashion. They headed centre-to-far side.

3665 DOWNLOAD THE MARATHONBET APP H'CAP — 1m 31y
8:45 (8:53) (Class 5) (0-70,69) 3-Y-O — £3,752 (£1,116; £557; £300; £300) Stalls Low

Form | | | | RPR

463 1 **Venusta (IRE)**[19] 2967 3-9-7 **69**.......... DavidEgan 14 74
(Mick Channon) hld up wl in rr: pushed along 3f out: prog in centre over 1f out: drvn and styd on wl fnl f to ld last stride **7/1**

0451 2 shd **Remembering You (IRE)**[43] 2152 3-9-2 **64**.......... HectorCrouch 10 69
(Clive Cox) sn trckd ldr: rdn to chal over 2f out: narrow ld over 1f out: hdd last stride **11/2**[2]

6-50 3 hd **Leo Davinci (USA)**[24] 2802 3-9-5 **67**..........(t[1]) HarryBentley 9 71
(George Scott) prom: rdn to chal 2f out: w ldr fnl f: jst hld nr fin **5/1**[1]

20-0 4 1 1/4 **Elegant Love**[38] 2355 3-9-5 **67**.......... KieranShoemark 1 68
(David Evans) hld up wl in rr: pushed along 3f out: prog in centre over 1f out: rdn and kpt on same pce fnl f **12/1**

30-0 5 hd **Renardeau**[28] 2689 3-9-5 **67**..........(p[1]) TomMarquand 13 68
(Ali Stronge) dwlt: hld up wl in rr: pushed along 3f out: prog in centre over 1f out: rdn and kpt on same pce fnl f **12/1**

6-40 5 dht **Rachel Zane (IRE)**[21] 2919 3-9-4 **66**.......... JackMitchell 4 67
(Hugo Palmer) hld up: prog over 2f out: drvn to chse ldrs over 1f out: one pce after **6/1**[3]

-000 7 2 **Toybox**[14] 3170 3-9-7 **69**.......... RobHornby 3 65
(Jonathan Portman) hld up towards rr: rdn and prog in centre over 2f out: no hdwy over 1f out: fdd **10/1**

0-30 8 nk **Poet's Magic**[38] 2355 3-9-2 **64**.......... CharlesBishop 2 60
(Jonathan Portman) prom: rdn to ld over 2f out to over 1f out: wknd fnl f **6/1**[3]

13-5 9 1 3/4 **Padura Brave**[19] 2965 3-9-3 **65**..........(p) DavidProbert 5 57
(Mark Usher) wl in tch: rdn to press ldrs 2f out: wknd jst over 1f out **20/1**

2346 10 shd **Kadiz (IRE)**[40] 2276 3-8-7 **58**.......... MeganNicholls(3) 8 49
(Paul George) hld up in midfield: rdn to chse ldrs and cl up 2f out: wknd over 1f out **20/1**

300- 11 3 **Lynchpin (IRE)**[255] 7736 3-9-4 **69**.......... FinleyMarsh(3) 12 54
(Lydia Pearce) a in rr: detached in last 3f out: no ch after **33/1**

-036 12 3 1/4 **Sweet Poem**[17] 3041 3-8-11 **66**.......... AmeliaGlass(7) 6 43
(Clive Cox) led to over 2f out: wknd qckly over 1f out **16/1**

6-00 13 10 **Illywhacker (IRE)**[24] 2794 3-9-0 **62**.......... JasonWatson 11 16
(Gary Moore) chsd ldrs: rdn over 2f out: wknd rapidly wl over 1f out **14/1**

1000 14 12 **Rock Up In Style**[20] 2942 3-9-6 **68**.......... StevieDonohoe 7
(Clare Ellam) t.k.h: hld up in midfield: wknd rapidly 3f out: t.o **40/1**

1m 50.61s (6.11) **Going Correction** +0.50s/f (Yiel) **14 Ran SP% 125.1**
Speed ratings (Par 99): **89,88,88,87,87 87,85,84,83,83 80,76,66,54**
CSF: WIN: 7.40 Venusta; PL: 2.70 Venusta 1.90 Leo Davinci 2.40 Remembering You; EX: 27.20; CSF: 45.08; TC: 218.00; TF: 73.60 CSF £45.08 CT £218.00 TOTE £7.40: £2.70, £2.40, £1.90; EX 27.20 Trifecta £73.60.
Owner N J Hitchins **Bred** Mr & Mrs Nick Hitchins **Trained** West Ilsley, Berks

FOCUS
Distance increased by 23yds. Modest enough form and plenty held a chance late, but the winner can have her effort upgraded a fair bit.
T/Plt: £144.80 to a £1 stake. Pool: £81,667.62 - 411.72 winning units T/Qpdt: £36.80 to a £1 stake. Pool: £8,627.31 - 173.19 winning units **Jonathan Neesom**

3666 - 3673a (Foreign Racing) - See Raceform Interactive

2889 COLOGNE (R-H)
Monday, June 10

OFFICIAL GOING: Turf: good

3674a SPARKASSE KOLNBONN-UNION-RENNEN (GROUP 2) (3YO) (TURF) — 1m 3f
3:40 3-Y-O — **£36,036** (£13,963; £7,207; £3,603; £2,252)

RPR

1 **Laccario (GER)**[15] 3-9-2 0.......... EduardoPedroza 3 113
(A Wohler, Germany) cl up on inner: prog to chal ldr over 2f out: sn led and a in command after: r.o strly under hands and heels riding: readily **12/5**[2]

2 2 1/2 **Django Freeman (GER)**[40] 2310 3-9-2 0.......... LukasDelozier 8 109
(Henk Grewe, Germany) hld up towards rr on outer: pushed along and prog fr over 2f out: rdn to chse ldr over 1f out: r.o strly: nvr rching wnr **21/10**[1]

3 1 3/4 **Winterfuchs (GER)**[43] 2163 3-9-2 0.......... SibylleVogt 7 106
(Carmen Bocskai, Germany) racd keenly in mid-div: asked for effrt 2 1/2f out: prog between rivals fr 2f out: kpt on strly u.p ins fnl f: nrst fin **58/10**

4 1/2 **Dschingis First (GER)**[40] 2310 3-9-2 0.......... AdriedeVries 2 105
(Markus Klug, Germany) mid-div on inner: pushed along over 2 1/2f out: rdn bhd ldr jst under 2f out: unable qck ins fnl f: kpt on same pce clsng stages **57/10**[3]

5 2 **Sibelius (GER)**[22] 2889 3-9-2 0.......... MaximPecheur 9 101
(Markus Klug, Germany) led after 1f: asked to qckn 2 1/2f out: chal over 2f out: sn hdd: grad wknd ins fnl f: no ex **269/10**

6 1 1/4 **So Chivalry (GER)**[24] 3-9-2 0.......... FilipMinarik 6 99
(Jean-Pierre Carvalho, Germany) hld up towards rr on inner: pushed along and effrt jst under 3f out: limited rspnse and sn rdn: unable qck and kpt on same pce **164/10**

7 4 1/2 **Nubius (IRE)**[22] 3-9-2 0.......... DennisSchiergen 5 91
(P Schiergen, Germany) racd keenly: mid-div on outer: outpcd and pushed along over 3f out: rdn 2 1/2f out: sn wknd and btn over 1f out **31/1**

8 1 1/2 **Man On The Moon (GER)**[43] 2163 3-9-2 0.......... FabriceVeron 1 88
(Jean-Pierre Carvalho, Germany) hld up in fnl pair: outpcd and pushed along jst under 3f out: no imp: wl btn over 1f out **206/10**

9 nk **Andoro (GER)**[30] 3-9-2 0.......... MichaelCadeddu 4 87
(R Dzubasz, Germany) cl up on outer: pushed along to chse ldr 3f out: swtchd to nrside rail and rdn 2f out: sn struggling and wknd fr over 1f out **244/10**

10 20 **Quian (GER)**[40] 2310 3-9-2 0..........(p) AndraschStarke 10 51
(P Schiergen, Germany) in rr: outpcd and detached over 3f out: sn rdn: no rspnse: t.o **153/10**

2m 14.31s (-6.49) **10 Ran SP% 118.5**
PARI-MUTUEL (all including 1 euro stake): WIN 3.40 PLACE: 1.40, 1.50, 1.60; SF: 7.10.
Owner Gestut Ittlingen **Bred** Gestut Hof Ittlingen **Trained** Germany

3526 LONGCHAMP (R-H)
Monday, June 10

OFFICIAL GOING: Turf: good

3675a PRIX DE L'OPERA COMIQUE (MAIDEN) (3YO COLTS & GELDINGS) (GRANDE COURSE) (TURF) — 1m
1:00 3-Y-O — **£13,513** (£5,135; £3,783; £2,162; £1,081; £810)

RPR

1 **Air Dance (FR)**[40] 3-9-2 0.......... CristianDemuro 1 88
(J-C Rouget, France) **6/5**[1]

2 snk **Bleu Marine (IRE)**[18] 3-9-2 0.......... Pierre-CharlesBoudot 6 88
(A Fabre, France) **2/1**[2]

3 4 **Ferid**[17] 3-9-2 0.......... VincentCheminaud 8 78
(M Delzangles, France) **5/1**[3]

4 1 3/4 **Bullington Boy (FR)**[25] 2766 3-9-2 0.......... JFEgan 2 74
(Jane Chapple-Hyam) t.k.h early: settled to trck ldrs in 3rd: pushed along over 2f out: rdn to chse ldrs over 1f out: wknd ins fnl f **19/1**

5 3/4 **Indian Pacific (FR)**[17] 3-9-2 0.......... ThibaultSpeicher 4 73
(Louis Baudron, France) **17/1**

6 shd **Visiteur Royal (FR)**[360] 3-8-8 0.......... JordanDelaunay(8) 7 72
(J-P Dubois, France) **94/1**

7 hd **Strike Bomber (FR)**[18] 3-9-2 0.......... MickaelBarzalona 9 72
(Andrea Marcialis, France) **9/1**

8 3/4 **Tactile (FR)** 3-8-11 0.......... HugoJourniac 3 65
(M Nigge, France) **81/1**

P **Uncle Colum (FR)** 3-8-11 0.......... StephanePasquier 5
(Gavin Hernon, France) **27/1**

1m 41.81s (3.41) **9 Ran SP% 121.9**
PARI-MUTUEL (all including 1 euro stake): WIN 2.20; PLACE 1.10, 1.10, 1.20; DF 2.20.
Owner Ecurie Jean-Louis Bouchard **Bred** Mme G Forien & G Forien **Trained** Pau, France

3676a PRIX MELISANDE (LISTED RACE) (3YO FILLIES) (TURF) — 1m 2f 110y
1:35 3-Y-O — **£24,774** (£9,909; £7,432; £4,954; £2,477)

RPR

1 **Edisa (USA)**[26] 2759 3-8-11 0.......... StephanePasquier 1 100
(A De Royer-Dupre, France) **18/5**[3]

2 hd **Golden Box (USA)**[20] 3-8-11 0.......... VincentCheminaud 4 100
(A De Royer-Dupre, France) **12/5**[2]

3 1 **Sand Share**[26] 2745 3-8-11 0.......... MaximeGuyon 3 98
(Ralph Beckett) settled in midfield: urged along and hdwy to chal 2f out: rdn to briefly ld over 1f out: sn hdd: kpt on ins fnl f **23/10**[1]

4 1 **Alimnia (FR)**[64] 1626 3-8-11 0.............. Pierre-CharlesBoudot 7 96
(F-H Graffard, France) **41/5**

5 snk **Shafia (FR)**[30] 3-8-11 0.............. CristianDemuro 6 96
(J-C Rouget, France) **76/10**

6 1 3/4 **Queendara (FR)**[48] 2029 3-8-11 0.............. OlivierPeslier 5 92
(D Guillemin, France) **12/1**

7 2 1/2 **Lady Te (GER)**[22] 2889 3-8-11 0.............. AlexisBadel 2 88
(Carina Fey, France) **13/1**

2m 15.46s (5.26) **7** Ran SP% **118.8**
PARI-MUTUEL (all including 1 euro stake): WIN 3.00; PLACE 2.90, 1.90; SF 14.60.
Owner H H Aga Khan **Bred** H H The Aga Khan Studs Sc **Trained** Chantilly, France

FOCUS
The sixth helps set the level.

3677a PRIX VOLTERRA (LISTED RACE) (3YO FILLIES) (TURF) 1m
3:25 3-Y-0 **£24,774** (£9,909; £7,432; £4,954; £2,477)

RPR

1 **Suphala (FR)**[29] 2669 3-8-13 0.............. Pierre-CharlesBoudot 7 100+
(A Fabre, France) **7/5**[1]

2 3/4 **Madeleine Must (FR)**[32] 3-8-13 0.............. OlivierPeslier 2 98
(H-A Pantall, France) **46/1**

3 1/2 **Waldblumchen (GER)**[28] 3-8-13 0.............. MaximeGuyon 1 97
(G Botti, France) **11/1**

4 nk **Simplicity (FR)**[35] 2498 3-8-13 0..............(b) HugoJourniac 3 96
(F Chappet, France) **11/1**

5 hd **Aviatress (IRE)**[28] 3-8-13 0.............. VincentCheminaud 4 96
(A De Royer-Dupre, France) **67/10**[3]

6 1 1/4 **Hermiona (USA)**[20] 2954 3-8-13 0.............. TonyPiccone 5 93
(F Chappet, France) **28/1**

7 nk **So Unique (FR)**[202] 9167 3-8-13 0.............. StephanePasquier 8 92
(N Clement, France) **22/1**

8 1/2 **Alzire (FR)**[33] 3-8-13 0.............. CristianDemuro 6 91
(J-C Rouget, France) **21/10**[2]

9 1 1/4 **Mistress Of Love (USA)**[55] 1832 3-8-13 0.............. AlexisBadel 9 88
(K R Burke) *sn prom: settled in 2nd: pushed along over 2f out: rdn w limited rspnse over 1f out: wknd ins fnl f* **36/1**

10 9 **Lover's Knot**[130] 510 3-8-13 0.............. MickaelBarzalona 10 68
(H-A Pantall, France) *t.k.h early: trckd ldrs on outer: urged along over 2f out: rdn and lost pl over 1f: eased ins fnl f* **23/1**

1m 42.26s (3.86) **10** Ran SP% **120.4**
PARI-MUTUEL (all including 1 euro stake): WIN 2.40; PLACE 1.50, 6.00, 2.70; DF 45.50.
Owner Lady Bamford **Bred** Haras D'Etreham & Riviera Equine S.A.R.L. **Trained** Chantilly, France

3678a LA COUPE (GROUP 3) (4YO+) (TURF) 1m 2f
4:00 4-Y-O+ **£36,036** (£14,414; £10,810; £7,207; £3,603)

RPR

1 **Danceteria (FR)**[18] 3025 4-9-0 0.............. JamieSpencer 7 112
(David Menuisier) *hld up in fnl pair: angled out and pushed along 2f out: rdn and prog fr over 1f out: picked up wl ins fnl f: r.o strly: led fnl strides* **77/10**

2 1 **Soleil Marin (IRE)**[43] 2168 5-9-2 0.............. MickaelBarzalona 2 112
(A Fabre, France) *settled in 4th on inner: gained a pl over 1/2-way: pushed along bhd ldr 2f out: rdn and ev ch over 1f out: led briefly wl ins fnl f: hdd fnl strides* **6/4**[1]

3 3/4 **Spotify (FR)**[93] 1113 5-9-2 0..............(p) JamesDoyle 1 110
(Charlie Appleby) *racd in 5th: pushed along outside rivals over 2f out: sn rdn: no immediate rspnse: prog ins fnl f: r.o to take 3rd clsng stages* **36/5**

4 nk **Royal Julius (IRE)**[37] 2428 6-9-0 0.............. CristianDemuro 5 107
(J Reynier, France) *settled in 3rd: lost a pl over 1/2-way: pushed along and effrt 2f out: rdn over 1f out: kpt on but nt pce to chal* **43/10**[2]

5 3/4 **Success Days (IRE)**[31] 2573 7-9-0 0.............. Pierre-CharlesBoudot 4 106
(K J Condon, Ire) *led: qcknd over 2f out: rdn 1 1/2f out: chal jst ins fnl f: sn hdd: no ex clsng stages* **57/10**

6 snk **Nikkei (GER)**[26] 4-9-2 0.............. TheoBachelot 6 108
(P Schiergen, Germany) *trckd ldr: pushed along wl over 2f out: nt qckn and lost position over 1f out: kpt on same pce ins fnl f* **15/1**

7 1/2 **Ligne D'Or**[226] 8665 4-8-13 0.............. VincentCheminaud 8 104
(A Fabre, France) *a in rr: pushed along over 2f out: no imp: kpt on same pce ins fnl f* **11/2**[3]

2m 9.63s (5.63) **7** Ran SP% **119.1**
PARI-MUTUEL (all including 1 euro stake): WIN 8.70; PLACE 2.20, 1.30, 2.30; DF 11.40.
Owner Australian Bloodstock & Clive Washbourn **Bred** Berend Van Dalfsen **Trained** Pulborough, W Sussex

3290 CARLISLE (R-H)
Tuesday, June 11

OFFICIAL GOING: Good to soft (soft in places; 6.2)
Wind: Breezy, half behind in over 2f of home straight Weather: Overcast, dry

3679 JOIN RACING TV NOW MAIDEN STKS 5f
5:30 (5:34) (Class 5) 2-Y-O **£4,204** (£1,251; £625; £312) **Stalls** Low

Form RPR

1 **Classy Moon (USA)** 2-9-5 0.............. CliffordLee 9 84+
(K R Burke) *dwlt: hld up: rdn over 2f out: gd hdwy on outside to ld appr fnl f: edgd rt: kpt on strly* **7/5**[1]

2 2 1/4 **Ventura Flame (IRE)** 2-9-0 0.............. ShaneGray 7 71+
(Keith Dalgleish) *prom on outside: effrt over 2f out: led briefly over 1f out: edgd rt: kpt on fnl f: nt pce of wnr* **14/1**

0 3 1/2 **Good Night Mr Tom (IRE)**[54] 1893 2-9-5 0.............. FrannyNorton 1 74+
(Mark Johnston) *noisy in paddock and reluctant to enter stalls: chsd ldrs: effrt whn n.m.r briefly over 1f out: kpt on ins fnl f* **13/2**

4 3 1/2 **Heavens Open** 2-9-0 0.............. TonyHamilton 3 57+
(Richard Fahey) *dwlt and blkd s: rn green in tch: effrt and edgd rt over 1f out: kpt on fnl f: no imp* **7/2**[2]

0 5 1 3/4 **Prissy Missy (IRE)**[14] 3190 2-9-0 0.............. DavidEgan 5 50
(David Loughnane) *led to over 1f out: rdn and wknd fnl f* **66/1**

0 6 1 1/4 **Pearl Stream**[22] 2892 2-9-0 0.............. PaulMulrennan 8 46
(Michael Dods) *wnt lft s: hld up on ins: effrt and shkn up over 2f out: wknd over 1f out* **10/1**

5 7 1 1/2 **Wafrah**[32] 2565 2-9-0 0..............(p1) BenCurtis 2 40
(David O'Meara) *prom: rdn over 2f out: wknd over 1f out* **11/2**[3]

00 8 3 **Mr Gus (IRE)**[12] 3245 2-9-0 0.............. SeanDavis(5) 6 35
(Richard Fahey) *dwlt: bhd and outpcd: nvr on terms* **33/1**

9 9 **Starfield Song (IRE)** 2-8-11 0.............. JamieGormley(3) 4
(Iain Jardine) *chsd ldr to over 2f out: rdn and wknd wl over 1f out* **25/1**

1m 1.98s (-0.12) **Going Correction** +0.175s/f (Good) **9** Ran SP% **116.6**
Speed ratings (Par 93): **107,103,102,97,94 92,89,85,70**
CSF £24.08 TOTE £2.30: £1.30, £4.20, £1.70; EX 25.20 Trifecta £136.00.
Owner C Waters **Bred** Three Chimneys Farm Llc **Trained** Middleham Moor, N Yorks

FOCUS
An ordinary juvenile maiden in terms of prior form but the strong favourite quickened up well to win in taking fashion here on debut.

3680 FOLLOW RACING TV ON TWITTER NOVICE STKS 1m 1f
6:00 (6:01) (Class 5) 3-Y-O+ **£4,204** (£1,251; £625; £312) **Stalls** Low

Form RPR

4433 1 **Mount Ararat (IRE)**[41] 2291 4-10-0 74.............. BenCurtis 2 77
(K R Burke) *t.k.h: trckd ldrs: rdn and led over 1f out: hld on wl fnl f* **7/4**[2]

4 2 nk **Regal Lilly (IRE)**[18] 3050 3-8-11 0.............. FrannyNorton 7 69+
(Mark Johnston) *cl up: effrt and pressing wnr whn edgd lft 1f out: rallied: kpt on wl cl home: jst hld* **13/8**[1]

1 3 1 1/2 **Freerolling**[33] 2555 4-10-7 0.............. StevieDonohoe 6 80+
(Charlie Fellowes) *t.k.h: stdd in tch: effrt and edgd rt 2f out: kpt on same pce ins fnl f* **5/2**[3]

0 4 7 **Lady Muk**[34] 2524 3-8-11 0..............(p1) TomEaves 5 52
(Steph Hollinshead) *led at ordinary gallop: rdn and hdd over 1f out: wknd fnl f* **66/1**

0 5 1 1/4 **Villiersdorp**[12] 3248 4-9-9 0..............(h) ShaneGray 8 51
(John Hodge) *dwlt: hld up: effrt and pushed along over 2f out: no imp fr over 1f out: fin lame on lft hind (vet said filly finished lame left hind)* **33/1**

6-6 6 1 1/2 **Transpennine Gold**[43] 2198 3-9-2 0.............. PaulMulrennan 9 51
(Michael Dods) *in tch: drvn and outpcd over 2f out: btn over 1f out* **33/1**

00 7 7 **Kaizer**[12] 3247 4-9-9 0.............. SeanDavis(5) 1 38
(Alistair Whillans) *hld up: rdn and outpcd 3f out: sn struggling* **25/1**

00 8 1 3/4 **Fasterkhani**[14] 3200 3-9-2 0.............. TonyHamilton 3 32
(Philip Kirby) *dwlt: t.k.h: hld up: outpcd 3f out: sn btn* **50/1**

0 9 6 **Ayr Poet**[12] 3247 4-10-0 0..............(h) PhilDennis 4 22
(Jim Goldie) *hld up: rdn and outpcd over 3f out: sn wknd* **50/1**

2m 1.14s (2.14) **Going Correction** +0.175s/f (Good)
WFA 3 from 4yo 12lb **9** Ran SP% **118.2**
Speed ratings (Par 103): **97,96,95,89,88 86,80,78,73**
CSF £4.89 TOTE £2.30: £1.02, £1.40, £1.10; EX 5.70 Trifecta £11.00.
Owner H Strecker & Mrs E Burke **Bred** James F Hanly **Trained** Middleham Moor, N Yorks

FOCUS
7 yards added. A fair novice contest. Only three horses had realistic winning claims and they came clear of the rest. The winner has been rated in line with his form in Britain.

3681 RACING TV H'CAP (DIV I) 1m 1f
6:30 (6:30) (Class 6) (0-60,61) 4-Y-O+
£3,234 (£962; £481; £300; £300; £300) **Stalls** Low

Form RPR

-055 1 **Edgar Allan Poe (IRE)**[14] 3177 5-9-9 **61**.............. PhilDennis 4 69
(Rebecca Bastiman) *hld up: hdwy over 2f out: effrt and pressed ldr over 1f out: led ins fnl f: drvn out* **7/1**

2034 2 nk **Mr Carbonator**[15] 3162 4-9-4 **59**.............. JamieGormley(3) 7 66
(Philip Kirby) *cl up: led after 2f: rdn over 2f out: hdd ins fnl f: kpt on: hld nr fin* **9/2**[2]

500- 3 nk **Millie The Minx (IRE)**[17] 4065 5-8-9 **47**.............. TomEaves 8 54
(Dianne Sayer) *prom: effrt and pressed ldr over 2f out to over 1f out: kpt on fnl f: hld nr fin* **16/1**

6401 4 3 1/4 **Motahassen (IRE)**[4] 3547 5-8-9 **54**..............(t) CianMacRedmond(7) 5 54+
(Declan Carroll) *hld up: hdwy on outside over 2f out: rdn over 1f out: edgd rt and kpt on fnl f: nt pce to chal* **11/10**[1]

000- 5 3/4 **Prosecute (FR)**[248] 7992 6-8-4 **45**..............(w) JaneElliott(3) 2 44
(Sean Regan) *hld up: effrt over 2f out: rdn and no further imp over 1f out* **33/1**

0006 6 2 1/4 **Just Heather (IRE)**[11] 3296 5-8-7 **45**..............(p) FrannyNorton 9 39
(John Wainwright) *led 2f: chsd ldr to over 2f out: rdn and wknd fnl f* **66/1**

00-3 7 nk **Cliff Bay (IRE)**[41] 2298 5-8-10 **48**..............(p) ShaneGray 11 42
(Keith Dalgleish) *t.k.h: hld up in tch: effrt over 2f out: wknd ins fnl f (jockey said gelding ran too free)* **5/1**[3]

0004 8 1 **Quiet Moment (IRE)**[15] 3158 5-8-2 **45**..............(t) PaulaMuir(5) 10 37
(Maurice Barnes) *dwlt: t.k.h and sn in tch: rdn over 2f out: wknd over 1f out (jockey said mare ran too free)* **40/1**

0402 9 nk **Spirit Of Sarwan (IRE)**[13] 3224 5-9-0 **57**..............(p) SeanDavis(5) 3 48
(Stef Keniry) *slowly away: hld up: effrt and rdn over 2f out: wknd over 1f out* **9/1**

000- 10 13 **Bevsboy (IRE)**[246] 8055 5-8-8 **46**.............. NathanEvans 1 11
(Lynn Siddall) *t.k.h: prom: outpcd 3f out: struggling fnl 2f* **50/1**

2m 1.43s (2.43) **Going Correction** +0.175s/f (Good) **10** Ran SP% **119.7**
Speed ratings (Par 101): **96,95,95,92,91 89,89,88,88,76**
CSF £38.92 CT £497.12 TOTE £6.60: £1.90, £2.50, £2.40; EX 32.00 Trifecta £366.40.
Owner I B Barker / P Bastiman **Bred** Paul, Ben & Charlie Cartan **Trained** Cowthorpe, N Yorks

FOCUS
7yds added. The first division of a modest handicap. The winning time was over 1.5sec slower than the second. The second and third help pin the level.

3682 RACING TV H'CAP (DIV II) 1m 1f
7:00 (7:01) (Class 6) (0-60,60) 4-Y-O+
£3,234 (£962; £481; £300; £300; £300) **Stalls** Low

Form RPR

3131 1 **Jackhammer (IRE)**[11] 3297 5-9-5 **58**..............(bt) PaulMulrennan 5 68
(Dianne Sayer) *hld up in tch: smooth hdwy to ld over 1f out: pushed clr fnl f: readily* **7/4**[2]

5444 2 1 3/4 **Born To Reason (IRE)**[40] 2346 5-8-7 **46** oh1.............. DavidEgan 10 50
(Kevin Frost) *hld up: pushed along over 3f out: hdwy and edgd rt 2f out: chsd (clr) wnr ins fnl f: r.o: no imp* **17/2**[3]

6432 3 3/4 **Milan Reef (IRE)**[4] 3547 4-9-1 **54**.............. BenCurtis 2 57
(David Loughnane) *dwlt: t.k.h and sn cl up: led over 2f out to over 1f out: no ex and lost 2nd ins fnl f* **13/8**[1]

0000 4 2 3/4 **Fingal's Cave (IRE)**[11] 3305 7-9-2 **60**..............(p) SeanDavis(5) 4 57
(Philip Kirby) *prom: effrt and rdn along over 2f out: edgd rt and one pce over 1f out* **10/1**

00-4 5 3 3/4 **Foxy Rebel**[20] 2963 5-8-7 **46** oh1.............. FrannyNorton 1 36
(Ruth Carr) *led to over 2f out: rallied: edgd lft and wknd ins fnl f* **20/1**

500- **6** *nk* **Mystical Mac (IRE)**[239] 8267 4-8-11 **53**..................(p) JamieGormley(3) 3 42
(Iain Jardine) *pressed ldr to over 2f out: drvn and wknd fnl f* **9/1**

00-0 **7** *1 1/4* **Strategic (IRE)**[29] 2681 4-8-9 **48**..................................(h[1]) PhilDennis 7 34
(Eric Alston) *dwlt: t.k.h: hld up: rdn 3f out: no imp fnl 2f* **25/1**

00-0 **8** *1 1/4* **Jazz Magic (IRE)**[13] 3224 4-8-7 **46** oh1.............................. NathanEvans 9 30
(Lynn Siddall) *dwlt: hld up: drvn and struggling over 2f out: sn btn* **40/1**

6030 **9** *20* **Prince Consort (IRE)**[15] 3163 4-8-9 **48** ow2..................(h) TomEaves 8
(John Wainwright) *hld up towards rr: drvn and struggling fr 3f out: lost tch fnl 2f: t.o* **40/1**

1m 59.72s (0.72) **Going Correction** +0.175s/f (Good) **9** Ran SP% **117.6**
Speed ratings (Par 101): **103,101,100,98,95 94,93,92,74**
CSF £16.60 CT £28.00 TOTE £2.60: £1.10, £2.50, £1.10; EX 17.10 Trifecta £54.70.

Owner Mrs Dianne Sayer **Bred** F Dunne **Trained** Hackthorpe, Cumbria

FOCUS
7yds added. The second division of a modest handicap, won in a time over 1.5sec quicker. The second and third help set a straightforward base level for the form.

3683 WATCH RACING TV NOW H'CAP 7f 173y
7:30 (7:30) (Class 4) (0-85,84) 3-Y-O
£7,439 (£2,213; £1,106; £553; £300; £300) **Stalls** Low

Form RPR

6004 **1** **Amadeus Grey (IRE)**[6] 3471 3-9-0 **77**......................(t) DuranFentiman 6 85
(Tim Easterby) *hld up in tch: hdwy against far rail to ld over 1f out: drvn and kpt on wl fnl f* **9/1**

2044 **2** *1* **Harvey Dent**[19] 3011 3-9-1 **78**.............................. PaulMulrennan 2 84
(Archie Watson) *led: rdn: edgd lft and hdd over 1f out: rallied ins fnl f: hld nr fin* **5/1**

1260 **3** *1 3/4* **Reggae Runner (FR)**[17] 3082 3-9-7 **84**.............................. FrannyNorton 1 86
(Mark Johnston) *chsd ldrs: rdn over 2f out: effrt and edgd lft over 1f out: kpt on same pce ins fnl f* **4/1**[3]

21 **4** *1 3/4* **Archaeology**[38] 2395 3-9-7 **84**.............................. JackGarritty 5 82+
(Jedd O'Keeffe) *s.i.s: hld up in last pl: smooth hdwy on outside over 2f out: rdn and edgd rt over 1f out: sn one pce* **15/8**[1]

2-13 **5** *3 1/4* **Ramesses**[22] 2896 3-8-11 **74**.............................. TonyHamilton 7 64
(Richard Fahey) *pressed ldr: drvn along 2f out: wknd fnl f* **7/2**[2]

5-35 **6** *4* **Beautiful Gesture**[43] 2198 3-7-13 **67**..........................(w) SeanDavis(5) 3 48
(K R Burke) *t.k.h: in tch: rdn over 2f out: wknd over 1f out* **11/1**

15-0 **7** *3* **Sesame (IRE)**[21] 2933 3-7-13 **65** oh3.............................. JaneElliott(3) 4 39
(Michael Appleby) *hld up: drvn and struggling over 2f out: btn over 1f out* **50/1**

1m 40.48s (0.48) **Going Correction** +0.175s/f (Good) **7** Ran SP% **114.0**
Speed ratings (Par 101): **104,103,101,99,96 92,89**
CSF £52.36 TOTE £7.40: £2.60, £3.10; EX 57.70 Trifecta £227.60.

Owner Ontoawinner 10 & Partner **Bred** Karis Bloodstock Ltd & Rathbarry Stud **Trained** Great Habton, N Yorks

FOCUS
5yds added. The feature contest was a fair 3yo handicap. The winner has been rated back to his 2yo form, while the second helps set the standard.

3684 INTRODUCING IRISH RACING ON RACING TV H'CAP 7f 173y
8:00 (8:00) (Class 6) (0-60,59) 3-Y-O
£3,234 (£962; £481; £300; £300; £300) **Stalls** Low

Form RPR

0364 **1** **Three Castles**[40] 2325 3-9-3 **55**.............................. ShaneGray 12 63+
(Keith Dalgleish) *slowly away: hld up: stdy hdwy over 2f out: effrt and rdn over 1f out: sustained run fnl f to ld towards fin* **8/1**[2]

0-62 **2** *1/2* **Juniors Fantasy (IRE)**[21] 2943 3-9-1 **53**.............................. DuranFentiman 13 60
(Tim Easterby) *trckd ldrs: effrt and rdn 2f out: led ins fnl f: hdd and no ex towards fin* **4/1**[1]

6600 **3** *2* **Luna Princess**[14] 3204 3-8-11 **52**.............................. JaneElliott(3) 16 54
(Michael Appleby) *pressed ldr: drvn to ld over 1f out: hdd ins fnl f: sn one pce* **16/1**

0456 **4** *1 1/2* **You Little Beauty**[15] 3158 3-8-2 **45**.............................. SeanDavis(5) 14 44
(Ann Duffield) *t.k.h: hld up towards rr: effrt and hdwy 2f out: kpt on fnl f: no imp* **14/1**[3]

0-63 **5** *1 1/4* **Royal Countess**[13] 3226 3-8-4 **47**.............................. PaulaMuir(5) 1 43
(Lucy Normile) *hld up: rdn along over 2f out: kpt on fnl f: nvr rchd ldrs* **4/1**

0505 **6** *1/2* **Precision Prince (IRE)**[12] 3246 3-9-7 **59**.............................. DavidEgan 8 54
(Mark Loughnane) *t.k.h: hld up on ins: effrt and c wd bnd over 2f out: rdn and no imp fr over 1f out* **4/1**[1]

6-00 **7** *3/4* **Se Green**[8] 3417 3-8-7 **45**.............................. PhilDennis 4 38
(Tim Easterby) *trckd ldrs: drvn over 2f out: outpcd over 1f out: n.d after* **25/1**

06-0 **8** *3/4* **Amelia R (IRE)**[14] 3204 3-9-2 **54**.............................. TomEaves 11 45
(Ray Craggs) *led: drvn and hdd over 1f out: wknd ins fnl f* **20/1**

6400 **9** *1* **Juals Spirit (IRE)**[12] 3246 3-8-0 **45**.............................. KieranSchofield(7) 10 34
(Brian Ellison) *hld up towards rr: rdn over 2f out: sme late hdwy: nvr able to chal* **33/1**

00-5 **10** *3/4* **Rodney After Dave (IRE)**[13] 3218 3-8-10 **53**.......... HarrisonShaw(5) 9 40
(Marjorie Fife) *hld up: rdn along over 2f out: nvr rchd ldrs* **25/1**

04-0 **11** *nk* **She's Awake**[22] 2896 3-9-0 **52**.............................. NathanEvans 2 39
(Michael Easterby) *t.k.h: in tch: drvn and outpcd wl over 2f out: sn btn* **25/1**

6-00 **12** *2 1/4* **Bagatino**[24] 2845 3-8-5 **50**..........................(t) CianMacRedmond(7) 15 32
(Declan Carroll) *hld up: effrt on outside over 2f out: wknd over 1f out* **20/1**

0-02 **13** *3* **Bumblekite**[12] 3270 3-8-13 **51**.............................. FrannyNorton 17 26
(Steph Hollinshead) *s.i.s: hld up in midfield on outside: hdwy over 2f out: rdn and wknd over 1f out* **8/1**[2]

004- **14** *6* **Oh Yes Please**[272] 7164 3-9-5 **57**.............................. PaulMulrennan 7 18
(Michael Dods) *t.k.h in midfield: drvn and struggling 3f out: sn wknd* **16/1**

5000 **15** *5* **Parker's Pride**[13] 3219 3-8-4 **45**.............................. JamieGormley(3) 6
(Brian Rothwell) *prom: drvn and struggling over 2f out: sn wknd* **66/1**

1m 42.73s (2.73) **Going Correction** +0.175s/f (Good) **15** Ran SP% **126.1**
Speed ratings (Par 97): **93,92,90,89,87 87,86,85,84,84 83,81,78,72,67**
CSF £38.13 CT £524.34 TOTE £11.00: £3.00, £2.10, £7.10; EX 50.50 Trifecta £504.40.

Owner Keith Dalgleish **Bred** W M Johnstone **Trained** Carluke, S Lanarks

■ Stewards' Enquiry : Duran Fentiman two-day ban: excessive use of whip (June 25-26)

FOCUS
5 yards added. A modest 3yo handicap. They went a decent gallop and the winning time was over two seconds slower than the previous 3yo C&D contest.

3685 RACINGTV.COM FILLIES' H'CAP 6f 195y
8:30 (8:32) (Class 5) (0-75,76) 3-Y-O+
£4,204 (£1,251; £625; £312; £300; £300) **Stalls** Low

Form RPR

6-06 **1** **Rux Ruxx (IRE)**[11] 3323 4-9-13 **70**.............................. PaulMulrennan 1 79
(Tim Easterby) *in tch: hdwy against far rail to ld over 1f out: hld on wl cl home* **11/1**

12-1 **2** *hd* **Polyphony (IRE)**[14] 3178 4-9-9 **66**.............................. TomEaves 9 74
(John Mackie) *pressed ldr: led over 2f out to over 1f out: rallied and ev ch fnl f: hld cl home* **7/2**[2]

-016 **3** *1 3/4* **Kermouster**[8] 3414 3-8-9 **62**.............................. PhilDennis 4 61
(Grant Tuer) *hld up: effrt on outside over 2f out: kpt on ins fnl f: nt rch first two* **9/1**

02-4 **4** *3/4* **Regal Banner**[32] 2583 3-9-7 **74**.............................. DavidEgan 5 71
(Roger Varian) *blkd s: sn prom: rdn over 2f out: hdwy over 1f out: no ex ins fnl f: lost front shoe (vet said filly lost its right fore shoe)* **2/1**[1]

-002 **5** *3* **Forever A Lady (IRE)**[13] 3223 6-9-1 **58**.............................. ShaneGray 2 51
(Keith Dalgleish) *hld up: effrt and pushed along over 2f out: no further imp over 1f out* **14/1**

6-34 **6** *2 1/4* **Epona**[25] 2787 3-8-10 **68**.............................. SeanDavis(5) 3 51
(Keith Dalgleish) *wnt sltly lft s: early ldr: t.k.h: cl up: rdn over 2f out: wknd over 1f out: lost hind shoe (vet said filly lost its left hind shoe)* **9/2**[3]

626 **7** *6* **Sylviacliffs (FR)**[22] 2904 3-8-10 **63**..........................(p) BenCurtis 7 30
(K R Burke) *blkd s: sn led: rdn and hdd over 2f out: wknd over 1f out* **7/1**

0 **8** *3 1/4* **Fox Hill**[54] 1894 3-7-13 **59**.............................. RobertDodsworth(7) 10 17
(Eric Alston) *hld up: drvn and struggling over 2f out: sn btn* **33/1**

1m 29.04s (1.04) **Going Correction** +0.175s/f (Good)
WFA 3 from 4yo+ 10lb **8** Ran SP% **114.2**
Speed ratings (Par 100): **101,100,98,97,94 91,85,81**
CSF £49.23 CT £370.00 TOTE £8.20: £1.90, £2.90, £2.10; EX 55.90 Trifecta £358.50.

Owner King Power Racing Co Ltd **Bred** Yeomanstown Stud **Trained** Great Habton, N Yorks

FOCUS
5 yards added. An ordinary fillies' handicap which produced an exciting photo-finish in a fair time. A pb from the winner, with the second building on her Ayr win.

3686 EVERY RACE LIVE ON RACING TV H'CAP 2m 1f 47y
9:00 (9:02) (Class 6) (0-65,66) 4-Y-O+
£3,234 (£962; £481; £300; £300; £300) **Stalls** Low

Form RPR

540/ **1** **Mr Smith**[791] 1713 8-8-0 **49**.............................. SeanDavis(5) 4 60+
(C Byrnes, Ire) *hld up in midfield: smooth hdwy 4f out: drvn to ld over 1f out: sn hrd pressed: hld on gamely fnl f* **3/1**[2]

506 **2** *nk* **Le Musee (FR)**[19] 3017 6-9-0 **58**..........................(p) FrannyNorton 5 69+
(Nigel Hawke) *prom: led briefly 2f out: w wnr: kpt on wl to pull clr of rest fnl f: hld cl home* **13/8**[1]

114/ **3** *6* **Tawseef (IRE)**[52] 8426 11-8-9 **60**.............................. EllaMcCain(7) 12 64
(Donald McCain) *in tch: rdn and outpcd over 3f out: rallied and hung rt over 1f out: chsd clr ldng pair ins fnl f: r.o* **20/1**

666- **4** *hd* **In Demand (IRE)**[235] 8386 4-9-8 **66**..........................(b[1]) StevieDonohoe 15 72
(Charlie Fellowes) *t.k.h: pressed ldr: led briefly over 2f out: rdn and outpcd fr over 1f out* **14/1**

0412 **5** *4 1/2* **Panatos (FR)**[28] 2718 4-9-3 **61**.............................. BenCurtis 6 61
(Alexandra Dunn) *hld up in tch: outpcd over 3f out: rallied over 1f out: sn no imp* **5/1**[3]

3-50 **6** *1/2* **Looking For Carl**[31] 2626 4-9-7 **65**..........................(p) DavidEgan 14 65
(Mark Loughnane) *prom: drvn and outpcd over 2f out: no ex fr over 1f out: btn fnl f* **40/1**

000/ **7** *1* **Frightened Rabbit (USA)**[15] 5701 7-7-13 **46** oh1.... JamieGormley(3) 7 42
(Dianne Sayer) *led to over 2f out: rdn and wknd fnl f* **40/1**

0-35 **8** *5* **Misscarlett (IRE)**[12] 3272 5-7-12 **47**..........................(p) PaulaMuir(5) 13 37
(Philip Kirby) *midfield: rdn over 3f out: hung rt and wknd wl over 1f out* **10/1**

000 **9** *2 3/4* **Put The Law On You (IRE)**[42] 2245 4-8-2 **46** oh1....(p[1]) NathanEvans 2 35
(Alistair Whillans) *hld up in rr: drvn and outpcd over 4f out: sme hdwy fr 2f out: nvr rchd ldrs* **50/1**

34-5 **10** *4 1/2* **Wishing Well**[32] 2591 7-9-5 **63**.............................. PaulMulrennan 9 45
(Micky Hammond) *dwlt: bhd: struggling over 4f out: nvr on terms (jockey said mare was never travelling)* **16/1**

0/ **11** *5* **Chocolat Noir (IRE)**[10] 8485 6-9-7 **65**.............................. TomEaves 1 41
(Martin Todhunter) *hld up: rdn and outpcd over 4f out: sn btn* **20/1**

0000 **12** *1/2* **Sweetest Smile (IRE)**[12] 3272 4-8-0 **47**.............................. JaneElliott(3) 11 24
(Ed de Giles) *t.k.h: hld up: rdn over 4f out: sn wknd* **40/1**

3-30 **13** *4 1/2* **Tomorrow's Angel**[18] 3046 4-8-13 **64**..........(v) CianMacRedmond(7) 8 36
(Iain Jardine) *dwlt: hld up: effrt u.p wl over 3f out: hung rt and wknd 2f out* **18/1**

0-06 **14** *1* **Wise Coco**[5] 3500 6-7-9 **46** oh1..........................(p) RobertDodsworth(7) 16 14
(Alistair Whillans) *s.v.s: rcvrd to join bk of main gp after 5f: struggling over 4f out: sn btn (jockey said mare missed the break)* **50/1**

3040 **15** *16* **Constituent**[5] 3497 4-7-9 **46**..........................(b) KieranSchofield(7) 3
(Michael Appleby) *t.k.h: prom: outpcd over 4f out: struggling fnl 3f: breathing problem (trainers rep said gelding had a breathing problem)* **50/1**

3m 54.66s (0.36) **Going Correction** +0.175s/f (Good) **15** Ran SP% **129.4**
Speed ratings (Par 101): **106,105,103,102,100 100,100,97,96,94 92,91,89,89,81**
CSF £8.17 CT £87.75 TOTE £4.10: £1.60, £1.70, £3.50; EX 12.90 Trifecta £184.50.

Owner Byrnsey Boys Syndicate **Bred** Denford Stud Ltd **Trained** Ballingarry, Co Limerick

FOCUS
12 yards added. A modest staying handicap. A gamble was narrowly landed on a long-absent Irish raider. The winner has been rated back towards his 2014 form.

T/Plt: £134.60 to a £1 stake. Pool: £54,436.94 - 295.09 winning units T/Qpdt: £69.60 to a £1 stake. Pool: £7,562.57 - 80.31 winning units **Richard Young**

^{3592}LINGFIELD (L-H)

Tuesday, June 11

OFFICIAL GOING: All-weather - polytrack: standard; turf course - heavy (soft in places) changing to soft after race 4 (3.30)

Wind: Light, across Weather: Fine but cloudy

3687 RYAN CANTER CLUB SUPPORTS LINGFIELD PARK H'CAP — 1m 1y(P)

2:00 (2:01) (Class 6) (0-55,55) 4-Y-0+

£3,105 (£924; £461; £300; £300; £300) **Stalls** High

Form RPR

00-4 **1** **Billie Beane**^{147} [243] 4-9-1 **52**............................ JoshuaBryan$^{(3)}$ 2 58
(Dr Jon Scargill) *wl in tch in midfield: rdn over 1f out: clsd on ldrs fnl f: styd on wl to ld last 75yds* **11/2^{3}**

0550 **2** ¾ **Mezmaar**^{20} [2972] 10-9-3 **54**........................(p^{1}) GaryMahon$^{(3)}$ 5 58
(Mark Usher) *taken down early: a in ldng trio: rdn to chal and upsides over 2f out: nt doing much u.p but narrow ld 100yds out: sn hdd and outpcd* **10/1**

-000 **3** ¾ **Stand Firm (IRE)**^{19} [3007] 4-9-0 **48**........................(v) SilvestreDeSousa 9 51
(Robert Cowell) *s.s: rapid prog on outer to ld over 5f out: jnd and rdn over 2f out: kpt on u.p but hdd and one pce last 100yds (jockey said gelding hung left-handed throughout)* **13/2**

-305 **4** ½ **N Over J**^{11} [3304] 4-9-5 **53**........................(v) OisinMurphy 1 55
(William Knight) *hld up towards rr: sme prog on inner 2f out: nt clr run and swtchd rt fnl f: styd on after: nrst fin (jockey said gelding was denied a clear run)* **4/1^{1}**

600- **5** nse **Classified (IRE)**^{203} [9166] 5-9-7 **55**........................ PatCosgrave 3 56
(Ed de Giles) *chsd ldrs: pushed along fr 1/2-way: wnt 3rd over 2f out: kpt on same pce u.p over 1f out* **7/1**

2530 **6** hd **Ahfad**^{10} [3348] 4-8-12 **46**........................(b) HectorCrouch 10 47
(Gary Moore) *s.i.s: hld up in last pair: rdn and prog on inner 2f out: styd on fnl f: gaining at fin but no ch* **16/1**

55-4 **7** ½ **Arctic Flower (IRE)**^{3} [3592] 6-8-12 **46** oh1........................ JosephineGordon 4 47
(John Bridger) *led to over 5f out: styd cl up: pushed along over 2f out: waiting to chal but nowhere to go over 1f out: lost pls fnl f (jockey said mare was denied a clear run)* **11/1**

00-6 **8** 1¼ **Golden Deal (IRE)**^{10} [3352] 4-9-2 **50**........................ ShaneKelly 7 47
(Richard Phillips) *prom on outer: rdn over 2f out: fdd over 1f out* **20/1**

6125 **9** 1 **Nicky Baby (IRE)**^{15} [3142] 5-8-8 **49**........................(b) SophieRalston$^{(7)}$ 6 45
(Dean Ivory) *s.i.s: hld up towards rr: pushed along over 2f out: nt clr run over 1f out: no prog (jockey said gelding ran flat)* **5/1^{2}**

00/0 **10** 3¼ **Lovely Acclamation (IRE)**^{71} [1478] 5-8-9 **48**........ RachealKneller$^{(5)}$ 8 35
(Matthew Salaman) *a in last trio: pushed along and no prog 2f out: wknd over 1f out* **50/1**

1053 **11** 1¼ **With Approval (IRE)**^{42} [2231] 7-9-6 **54**........................(p) LiamJones 12 38
(Laura Mongan) *a wl in rr: rdn and no prog over 2f out* **14/1**

-000 **12** 2 **Reshaan (IRE)**^{20} [2971] 4-9-7 **55**........................ EdwardGreatrex 11 35
(Alexandra Dunn) *racd v wd: in tch tl wknd over 2f out (jockey said gelding hung right-handed throughout)* **16/1**

1m 37.76s (-0.44) **Going Correction** -0.025s/f (Stan) **12** Ran SP% **120.5**
Speed ratings (Par 101): **101,100,99,99,98 98,98,97,96,92 91,89**
CSF £60.72 CT £376.65 TOTE £7.00: £2.40, £3.60, £1.70; EX 82.20 Trifecta £828.80.
Owner Silent Partners **Bred** Susan Scargill **Trained** Newmarket, Suffolk
■ Stewards' Enquiry : Josephine Gordon caution; entered incorrect stall

FOCUS
Although run at a fair clip little got into this moderate handicap from off the pace.

3688 WELCOME BACK HAMWAYS & GUESTS (S) STKS — 6f 1y(P)

2:30 (2:30) (Class 6) 3-Y-0+ £3,105 (£924; £461; £300) **Stalls** Low

Form RPR

403 **1** **Creek Harbour (IRE)**^{26} [2774] 4-9-6 64........................ ShaneKelly 4 70
(Richard Hughes) *taken down early: mde all: kicked on over 2f out: rdn and styd on wl fr over 1f out* **5/4^{1}**

206 **2** 1¼ **Upavon**^{17} [3079] 9-9-6 80........................ AdamKirby 2 66
(Tony Carroll) *cl up in 3rd: chsd wnr over 2f out and sn rdn: kpt on but nt qckn and no imp ins fnl f* **2/1^{2}**

0-00 **3** 1½ **Penarth Pier (IRE)**^{26} [2772] 3-8-2 66........ ThoreHammerHansen$^{(5)}$ 6 55
(Richard Hannon) *chsd wnr: rdn and lost 2nd whn pce lifted over 2f out: one pce after* **5/2^{3}**

0050 **4** 9 **Deer Song**^{19} [3014] 6-9-6 45........................ LiamJones 5 35
(John Bridger) *a last: hanging rt bnd 4f out: wl btn fnl 2f* **40/1**

00-0 **R** **Fata Morgana**^{12} [3279] 4-8-8 30........................(h) AaronJones$^{(3)}$ 3
(Christine Dunnett) *ref to r: tk no part* **100/1**

1m 12.33s (0.43) **Going Correction** -0.025s/f (Stan)
WFA 3 from 4yo+ 8lb **5** Ran SP% **109.8**
Speed ratings (Par 101): **96,94,92,80,**
CSF £4.05 TOTE £2.20: £1.30, £1.10; EX 4.10 Trifecta £4.60.There was no bid for the winner.
Owner Richard Hughes Racing Club **Bred** Keatingstown Bloodstock **Trained** Upper Lambourn, Berks

FOCUS
They finished in market order in this seller, with the winner very much enjoying the run of the race.

3689 MARK ROBERTS MOTION CONTROL FILLIES' NOVICE STKS (PLUS 10 RACE) — 6f 1y(P)

3:00 (3:00) (Class 5) 2-Y-0 £3,752 (£1,116; £557; £278) **Stalls** Low

Form RPR

4 **1** **Rosadora (IRE)**^{22} [2915] 2-9-0 0........................ OisinMurphy 6 77+
(Ralph Beckett) *chsd ldng pair: pushed along over 2f out: swtchd rt fnl f and drvn: continued to edge rt but r.o to ld last strides* **11/4^{1}**

53 **2** nk **Love Love**^{22} [2915] 2-9-0 0........................ SilvestreDeSousa 7 76
(Richard Hannon) *led: jnd over 2f out: narrowly hdd over 1f out: fought on wl and led again last 100yds: hdd fnl strides* **3/1^{2}**

10 **3** ½ **Companion**^{25} [2805] 2-9-7 0........................ AdamKirby 12 82
(Mark Johnston) *spd fr wdst draw to press ldr: rdn to take narrow ld over 1f out: hdd and one pce last 100yds* **11/2**

513 **4** 1 **Brazen Safa**^{20} [2968] 2-9-1 0........................ CameronNoble$^{(3)}$ 8 76
(Michael Bell) *racd in 5th: pushed along 1/2-way: no imp on ldrs tl styd on fnl f: nrst fin* **6/1**

5 1½ **Caspian Queen (IRE)** 2-9-0 0........................ ShaneKelly 4 67
(Richard Hughes) *s.s: rcvrd after 2f and disp 3rd pl 1/2-way: shkn up 2f out: one pce over 1f out: nt disgracd* **9/2^{3}**

6 7 **Queen Aya** 2-9-0 0........................ HectorCrouch 5 46
(Ed Walker) *jst in tch disputing 6th: no prog 2f out: wknd fnl f* **25/1**

6 **7** 4½ **Queenoftheclyde (IRE)**^{32} [2579] 2-9-0 0........................ MichaelStainton 1 33
(K R Burke) *jst in tch disputing 6th: no prog 2f out: wknd over 1f out* **33/1**

8 4½ **Little Lulu (IRE)** 2-9-0 0........................ EdwardGreatrex 11 19
(Archie Watson) *dwlt: a wl in rr* **11/1**

9 1 **Hot Poppy** 2-8-11 0........................ GeorgeBuckell$^{(3)}$ 3 16
(John Gallagher) *s.s: a wl in rr (jockey said filly ran green)* **66/1**

10 15 **Golden Slumbers** 2-9-0 0........................ LiamJones 9
(Bill Turner) *chsd ldrs: rn green and hung rt bnd after 2f: dropped to rr and sn btn: t.o (jockey said filly ran too free)* **50/1**

1m 11.68s (-0.22) **Going Correction** -0.025s/f (Stan) **10** Ran SP% **118.1**
Speed ratings (Par 90): **100,99,98,97,95 86,80,74,72,52**
CSF £11.08 TOTE £3.50: £1.40, £2.00, £1.50; EX 13.60 Trifecta £43.30.
Owner Guy Brook **Bred** Keatingstown Bloodstock Ltd **Trained** Kimpton, Hants

FOCUS
Ordinary juvenile form, but a few of these should go on to do okay in nurseries. The pace was reasonable.

3690 WITHEFORD EQUINE BARRIER TRIALS 13TH JUNE NOVICE STKS — 1m 1f

3:30 (3:30) (Class 5) 3-Y-0+ £3,752 (£1,116; £557; £278) **Stalls** Low

Form RPR

2-1 **1** **Dudley's Boy**^{21} [2925] 3-9-4........................ JoshuaBryan$^{(3)}$ 7 88+
(Andrew Balding) *led after 2f: cruised clr 2f out: unextended* **1/7^{1}**

43 **2** 7 **Better Than Ever (IRE)**^{11} [3306] 3-9-2........................ ShaneKelly 1 63
(Marco Botti) *chsd ldng pair: pushed along 1/2-way: rdn to try to press wnr 3f out: sn brushed aside* **10/3^{2}**

06/ **3** ½ **Onomatopoeia**^{1042} [5022] 5-9-4........................ RobJFitzpatrick$^{(5)}$ 4 59
(Camilla Poulton) *led 2f: w wnr to over 3f out: sn rdn: kpt on u.p to press for 2nd again fnl f* **66/1**

0 **4** 6 **Bricklebrit**^{19} [3003] 3-8-11........................ RaulDaSilva 3 45
(Rae Guest) *a in last pair: urged along and lost tch 3f out* **20/1^{3}**

00 **5** 2½ **Sibylline**^{19} [3013] 3-8-8........................ RosieJessop$^{(3)}$ 6 40
(David Simcock) *rn green in last pair: urged along and lost tch 3f out* **40/1**

1m 58.28s (1.38) **Going Correction** +0.25s/f (Good)
WFA 3 from 5yo 12lb **5** Ran SP% **119.3**
Speed ratings (Par 103): **103,96,96,91,88**
CSF £1.29 TOTE £1.10: £1.02, £1.30; EX 1.40 Trifecta £7.90.
Owner Ms Karen Gough **Bred** Ms Karen Gough **Trained** Kingsclere, Hants

FOCUS
The ground didn't look as bad as first feared and was changed to soft after this race, having initially been given as heavy. No Al Battar or Train To Georgia, so this proved little more than a racecourse canter for the 1-7 favourite. Add 4yds. The winner has been rated in line with his Brighton win, and the third close to her old 2yo debut figure.

3691 EAST PARK RDA FILLIES' H'CAP — 1m 2f

4:00 (4:00) (Class 5) (0-70,72) 4-Y-0+

£3,752 (£1,116; £557; £300; £300; £300) **Stalls** Low

Form RPR

5-14 **1** **Junoesque**^{18} [3038] 5-8-13 **57**........................(p) HectorCrouch 2 65
(John Gallagher) *led 1f: led briefly 6f out: chsd ldr: rdn to chal 2f out: led over 1f out: styd on wl and in command fnl f* **3/1^{2}**

2422 **2** 1½ **Dashing Poet**^{28} [2714] 5-9-7 **65**........................ OisinMurphy 7 70
(Heather Main) *dwlt: t.k.h: prom on outer: led over 5f out: rdn and hdd over 1f out: nt qckn and hld fnl f* **10/11^{1}**

-435 **3** ¾ **Be Thankful**^{19} [2994] 4-9-2 **60**........................(h^{1}) SilvestreDeSousa 1 63
(Martin Keighley) *hld up: rdn 3f out: chsd clr ldng pair 2f out: styd on u.p but nvr able to chal* **12/1**

0-20 **4** 9 **Dreaming Of Paris**^{25} [2797] 5-9-7 **72**........................ WilliamCarver$^{(7)}$ 3 57
(Patrick Chamings) *chsd ldrs: rdn over 2f out: sn wknd* **9/2^{3}**

0006 **5** nk **Stay In The Light**^{12} [3279] 4-8-2 **46** oh1........................ RaulDaSilva 5 30
(Roger Ingram) *slowly away: hld up in last pair: rdn and no prog 3f out: sn btn* **25/1**

014- **6** 94 **Born To Spend (IRE)**^{281} [6864] 4-9-0 **58**........................(h) ShaneKelly 4
(Samuel Farrell, Ire) *plld hrd: led on outer after 1f: hdd 6f out: sn eased: virtually p.u 3f out (jockey said filly hung badly right-handed throughout)* **16/1**

2m 11.8s (-0.40) **Going Correction** +0.25s/f (Good) **6** Ran SP% **113.0**
Speed ratings (Par 100): **108,106,106,99,98 23**
CSF £6.21 TOTE £3.20: £1.40, £1.20; EX 6.60 Trifecta £53.90.
Owner The Juniper Racing Club Ltd **Bred** Adweb Ltd **Trained** Chastleton, Oxon

FOCUS
Run at a steady gallop, the first three came clear in what was a moderate handicap. Add 4yds. The second has been rated close to her C&D form on soft.

3692 TAKE THE REINS H'CAP — 1m 3f 133y

4:30 (4:31) (Class 4) (0-85,86) 3-Y-0 £5,530 (£1,645) **Stalls** High

Form RPR

4-56 **1** **Natty Night**^{22} [2914] 3-8-13 **72**........................ SilvestreDeSousa 3 79
(William Muir) *led at decent pce: rdn and hdd over 2f out: kpt on wl to ld again over 1f out: drvn out* **5/2^{2}**

-221 **2** 4 **Agent Basterfield (IRE)**^{42} [2229] 3-9-7 **80**........................ OisinMurphy 1 80
(Andrew Balding) *trckd rival: shkn up to ld over 2f out: fnd little in front and hdd over 1f out: wl hld fnl f* **2/7^{1}**

2m 36.12s (2.12) **Going Correction** +0.25s/f (Good) **2** Ran SP% **106.3**
Speed ratings (Par 101): **102,99**
TOTE £2.80.
Owner O'Mulloy, Schwartz **Bred** Watership Down Stud **Trained** Lambourn, Berks

FOCUS
Just the two remaining runners and a bit of a turn-up. Add 4yds.

3693 INJURED JOCKEYS FUND H'CAP — 2m 68y

5:00 (5:00) (Class 5) (0-75,75) 4-Y-0+

£3,752 (£1,116; £557; £300; £300; £300) **Stalls** Centre

Form RPR

2250 **1** **Atomic Jack**^{18} [3044] 4-8-12 **66**........................ NicolaCurrie 8 72
(George Baker) *led: rdn and hdd over 2f out: rallied over 1f out: led ins fnl f: kpt on wl* **9/2**

21-2 **2** ¾ **General Zoff**^{17} [3091] 4-9-0 **68**........................ OisinMurphy 4 73
(William Muir) *trckd wnr: shkn up to ld over 2f out: lugged lft u.p after: hdd ins fnl f: outbattled* **7/2^{3}**

4-21 **3** 3½ **Age Of Wisdom (IRE)**^{18} [3044] 6-9-3 **71**........................(p) HectorCrouch 10 72
(Gary Moore) *hld up in 4th: rdn to chse ldng pair 2f out: edgd lft and no imp on them after* **11/4^{2}**

-236 **4** 1 **So Near So Farhh**^{11} [3294] 4-8-12 **66**........................ SilvestreDeSousa 3 66
(Mick Channon) *trckd ldng pair: rdn and nt qckn over 2f out: sn dropped to 4th and one pce* **2/1^{1}**

61/0 5 ½ **Mere Anarchy (IRE)**[10] 700 8-8-8 **67**..............(v) PoppyBridgwater(5) 7 66
(Robert Stephens) *hld up in last: shkn up and no rspnse over 2f out: kpt on over 1f out: n.d* **6/1**

466/ 6 9 **Be My Sea (IRE)**[733] 2021 8-9-7 **75**.......................... GeorgeDowning 1 63
(Tony Carroll) *hld up in 5th: rdn over 2f out: sn wknd* **33/1**

3m 42.53s (6.53) **Going Correction** +0.25s/f (Good) **6** Ran SP% **117.6**
Speed ratings (Par 103): **93,92,90,90,90 85**
CSF £21.61 CT £51.51 TOTE £5.90: £2.70, £2.50; EX 22.40 Trifecta £108.60.
Owner George Baker And Partners - Super Six **Bred** Newsells Park Stud **Trained** Chiddingfold, Surrey

FOCUS
A pretty uneventful staying handicap with the one-two more or less holding their positions throughout. Sound form for the level. Add 4yds. The second has been rated close to his AW form.
T/Plt: £18.50 to a £1 stake. Pool: £59,729.46 - 2,356.19 winning units T/Qpdt: £4.60 to a £1 stake. Pool: £5,461.35 - 876.20 winning units **Jonathan Neesom**

3088 SALISBURY (R-H)
Tuesday, June 11

OFFICIAL GOING: Soft (heavy in places; 6.8)
Wind: light against Weather: overcast

3694 FIRST CARLTON NOVICE AUCTION STKS (PLUS 10 RACE) (DIV I) 6f
1:45 (1:46) (Class 4) 2-Y-O **£5,110** (£1,520; £759; £379) **Stalls Low**

Form RPR

15 1 **Gold Venture (IRE)**[28] 2716 2-8-10 0.......................... HollieDoyle 2 68
(Archie Watson) *tall; a.p: led over 2f out: sn rdn and strly chal: hld on wl fnl f* **3/1**[2]

54 2 ¾ **Goodwood Rebel (IRE)**[17] 3088 2-9-5 0.......................... HarryBentley 7 75
(Ralph Beckett) *str; mid-div: pushed along over 3f out: rdn and hdwy over 1f out: kpt on wl ins fnl f: wnt 2nd towards fin* **14/1**

5 3 ¾ **Able Kane**[15] 3165 2-9-1 0.......................... RobHornby 8 69
(Rod Millman) *workmanlike; trckd ldrs: chal over 2f out: sn rdn: rdn and ev ch over 1f out: kpt on same pce fnl f* **5/2**[1]

4 2 ½ **Chairlift Chat (IRE)** 2-9-3 0.......................... CharlesBishop 3 63
(Eve Johnson Houghton) *str; green to post; trckd ldrs: rdn 2f out: kpt on but nt pce to chal* **6/1**

00 5 1 **Pitchcombe**[15] 3165 2-9-3 0.......................... LiamKeniry 5 60
(Clive Cox) *workmanlike; led tl rdn over 2f out: one pce fnl f* **10/1**

6 ½ **Souter Johnnie (IRE)** 2-9-5 0.......................... PatDobbs 4 61
(Richard Hughes) *athletic; s.i.s: bhd: styd on fr over 1f out but nvr gng pce to get on terms* **5/1**[3]

0 7 2 **Lafontaine (FR)**[12] 3257 2-8-10 0.......................... JasonWatson 6 46
(Sylvester Kirk) *leggy; trckd ldrs: rdn wl over 1f out: wknd fnl f* **20/1**

8 6 **Max's Thunder (IRE)** 2-9-5 0.......................... NicolaCurrie 1 37
(Jamie Osborne) *compact; s.i.s: a towards rr* **11/1**

00 9 3 **Sir Chancealot (IRE)**[12] 3257 2-9-3 0.......................... RobertHavlin 9 26
(Amanda Perrett) *compact; s.i.s: a towards rr* **50/1**

1m 18.88s (4.38) **Going Correction** +0.60s/f (Yiel) **9** Ran SP% **115.3**
Speed ratings (Par 95): **94,93,92,88,87 86,84,76,72**
CSF £44.13 TOTE £3.90: £1.20, £3.30, £1.30; EX 35.10 Trifecta £55.80.
Owner Saxon Thoroughbreds **Bred** Gearoid Cahill **Trained** Upper Lambourn, W Berks

FOCUS
Plenty of rain about and conditions were pretty testing, the going being described as soft, heavy in places (Going Stick 6.8). As usual when the ground is like this, they came over to the stands' rail.

3695 FIRST CARLTON NOVICE AUCTION STKS (PLUS 10 RACE) (DIV II) 6f
2:15 (2:16) (Class 4) 2-Y-O **£5,110** (£1,520; £759; £379) **Stalls Low**

Form RPR

0 1 **Grove Ferry (IRE)**[26] 2761 2-9-5 0.......................... DavidProbert 7 78+
(Andrew Balding) *athletic; looked wl; s.i.s: in last trio: hdwy over 2f out: shkn up to chal jst ins fnl f: led towards fin: cosily* **9/5**[2]

2 ¾ **Sword Beach (IRE)** 2-9-5 0.......................... TomMarquand 4 76
(Eve Johnson Houghton) *str; trckd ldrs: rdn to ld jst over 1f out: kpt on but no ex whn hdd towards fin* **10/1**

235 3 3 ½ **Top Buck (IRE)**[18] 3047 2-9-5 0.......................... RyanMoore 8 65
(Brian Meehan) *compact; edgy; hld up in last trio: rdn and hdwy over 1f out: wnt 3rd ent fnl f: nt pce of front pair* **11/8**[1]

0 4 1 ¾ **Whispering Leaves (IRE)**[57] 1821 2-8-9 0.......................... WilliamCox(3) 5 53+
(Clive Cox) *compact; bit bkward; trckd ldrs: outpcd over 2f out: kpt on again ins fnl f: snatched 4th fnl stride* **20/1**

5 hd **Al Verde** 2-9-1 0.......................... CharlesBishop 2 55
(Ali Stronge) *racd keenly: sn prom: rdn and ev ch 2f out tl ent fnl f: sn no ex* **14/1**

5 6 1 ¼ **Kahpehlo**[17] 3076 2-8-10 0.......................... KieranO'Neill 1 47
(John Bridger) *s.i.s: sn prom: rdn over 2f out: wknd ent fnl f* **100/1**

06 7 ½ **Es Que Pearl (IRE)**[28] 2716 2-8-10 0.......................... CharlieBennett 3 45
(Rod Millman) *workmanlike; led: rdn and hdd jst over 1f out: wknd ins fnl f* **25/1**

6 8 ½ **Shaun's Delight (IRE)**[17] 3088 2-9-3 0.......................... LiamKeniry 9 51
(Ronald Harris) *workmanlike; a towards rr* **50/1**

9 ½ **Summer Lake** 2-8-10 0.......................... JasonWatson 6 42
(Roger Charlton) *workmanlike; bit on the leg; slowly away: sn in tch: effrt 2f out: wknd fnl f* **8/1**[3]

1m 19.58s (5.08) **Going Correction** +0.60s/f (Yiel) **9** Ran SP% **116.2**
Speed ratings (Par 95): **90,89,84,82,81 80,79,78,78**
CSF £19.42 TOTE £2.30: £1.10, £2.50, £1.10; EX 18.50 Trifecta £45.50.
Owner Martin & Valerie Slade & Partner **Bred** Skymarc Farm **Trained** Kingsclere, Hants

FOCUS
The slower of the two divisions by 0.70sec, but the first two finished nicely clear.

3696 WILLTON HOMES NOVICE STKS 6f 213y
2:45 (2:47) (Class 5) 3-Y-O+ **£4,787** (£1,424; £711; £355) **Stalls Low**

Form RPR

22 1 **Tapisserie**[31] 2623 3-8-11 0.......................... RyanMoore 8 83+
(William Haggas) *tall; a.p: led over 2f out: sn in command: comf* **1/2**[1]

-10 2 3 ¾ **Quick**[41] 2268 3-9-4 0.......................... TomMarquand 5 79
(Richard Hannon) *in tch: hdwy 2f out: sn rdn to chse wnr kpt on but nt pce to get on terms* **8/1**[3]

4-0 3 4 ½ **Desert Land (IRE)**[36] 2488 3-9-2 0.......................... JackMitchell 7 65
(David Simcock) *compact; prom: rdn over 1f out: kpt on same pce fnl f* **3/1**[2]

4-0 4 nk **Corrida De Toros (IRE)**[22] 2900 3-9-2 0.......................... CallumShepherd 3 65
(Ed de Giles) *str; hld up towards rr: hdwy over 2f out: kpt on into 4th ent fnl f but nvr gng pce to get involved* **33/1**

0- 5 2 **Closer Than Close**[228] 8606 3-9-2 0..........(h[1]) RobHornby 15 59
(Jonathan Portman) *compact; hld up towards rr: stdy prog fr 2f out: styd on but nvr threatened to get on terms* **50/1**

05 6 1 ¼ **Strict (IRE)**[12] 3277 3-9-2 0.......................... DavidProbert 11 56
(Andrew Balding) *compact; mid-div: outpcd 3f out: sme late prog but nvr any threat* **20/1**

60- 7 ¾ **Garrison Law**[291] 6490 3-9-2 0.......................... LiamKeniry 9 54
(David Simcock) *workmanlike; s.i.s: in last pair: hdwy over 2f out: rdn in midfield over 1f out: no further imp fnl f* **33/1**

8 1 ¾ **Bear Force One** 3-9-2 0.......................... JasonWatson 2 50
(Roger Teal) *str; dwlt: bhd: hdwy into midfield 4f out: effrt in tch over 1f out: wknd ins fnl f* **25/1**

6 9 1 **Rebecke (IRE)**[17] 3080 3-8-11 0.......................... HollieDoyle 10 42
(Clive Cox) *led: rdn and hdd over 2f out: wknd ent fnl f* **25/1**

00- 10 21 **King Of The Ring**[237] 8314 3-8-13 0.......................... MeganNicholls(3) 16
(Paul Nicholls) *workmanlike; mid-div early: bhd fnl 3f: t.o (trainers' rep said gelding was unsuited by the ground and would prefer a faster surface)* **66/1**

0 11 9 **Yet Another (IRE)**[17] 3090 4-9-9 0.......................... FinleyMarsh(3) 17
(Grace Harris) *workmanlike; trckd ldrs: rdn over 2f out: sn wknd: t.o* **100/1**

1m 31.74s (3.04) **Going Correction** +0.60s/f (Yiel)
WFA 3 from 4yo 10lb **11** Ran SP% **125.6**
Speed ratings (Par 103): **106,101,96,96,93 92,91,89,88,64 54**
CSF £5.67 TOTE £1.60: £1.10, £2.00, £1.10; EX 6.00 Trifecta £16.90.
Owner Isa Salman **Bred** Newsells Park Stud **Trained** Newmarket, Suffolk

FOCUS
There was a good early gallop and they finished well strung out in this novice. The second has been rated back to her debut form.

3697 MOLSON COORS H'CAP 6f 213y
3:15 (3:17) (Class 6) (0-60,66) 3-Y-O
£3,493 (£1,039; £519; £300; £300; £300) **Stalls Low**

Form RPR

2024 1 **Eye Of The Water (IRE)**[10] 3354 3-9-7 **60**.......................... DavidProbert 14 74
(Ronald Harris) *mde virtually all: racd stands' side: styd on wl to draw clr fnl f: rdn out* **7/1**[2]

0-01 2 7 **Sonnetina**[21] 2926 3-9-6 **59**.......................... TomQueally 18 57
(Denis Coakley) *looked wl; racd stands' side: hld up: hdwy over 2f out: sn rdn: styd on to chse wnr jst ins fnl f but nvr any threat* **6/1**[1]

5-32 3 1 ¼ **Glamorous Crescent**[19] 2995 3-9-1 **54**.......................... JimmyQuinn 15 47
(Grace Harris) *racd stands' side: unsettled stalls and slowly away: sn chsng ldrs: rdn wl over 2f out: kpt on same pce* **6/1**[1]

-050 4 1 ½ **Jailbreak (IRE)**[21] 2943 3-8-11 **50**.......................... PatDobbs 11 40+
(Richard Hughes) *racd centre: in tch: rdn over 2f out: kpt on but nt pce to get involved* **8/1**[3]

2060 5 hd **Maisie Moo**[21] 2939 3-9-3 **56**.......................... RobertHavlin 17 45
(Shaun Keightley) *racd stands' side: bhd: nt clr run 2f out: hdwy over 1f out: styd on but nvr any ch* **20/1**

6-61 6 3 **Orliko (IRE)**[8] 3409 3-9-13 **66** 6ex..........(bt) RossaRyan 8 48+
(Richard Hannon) *looked wl; nvr travelling: bhd in centre: hdwy u.p over 2f out: nvr threatened ldrs: fdd ins fnl f (jockey said gelding was never travelling)* **10/1**

0030 7 shd **Dark Glory (IRE)**[14] 3204 3-9-7 **60**..........(b[1]) CallumShepherd 16 41
(Brian Meehan) *racd stands' side: chsd ldrs: rdn over 2f out: sn hld: wknd fnl f (fin lame) (vet said colt was lame left fore)* **12/1**

-053 8 2 ¼ **Dark Poet**[21] 2926 3-9-2 **55**..........(v[1]) HollieDoyle 7 31+
(Clive Cox) *racd centre: trckd ldrs: ev ch 3f out: sn rdn: hung lft and hld over 1f out: wknd fnl f (jockey said gelding hung left-handed)* **7/1**[2]

500- 9 4 ½ **Powerage (IRE)**[248] 7995 3-9-3 **56**.......................... FergusSweeney 6 21+
(Malcolm Saunders) *racd centre: nvr bttr than mid-div* **33/1**

0-00 10 shd **Swiss Miss**[32] 2597 3-8-9 **47** ow1.......................... JFEgan 5 12+
(John Gallagher) *led centre gp: pressed wnr 4f out: ev ch 3 out: sn rdn: wknd over 1f out* **40/1**

4600 11 8 **Shug**[21] 2926 3-9-4 **57**..........(v[1]) GeraldMosse 9 +
(Ed Walker) *s.i.s: towards rr in centre: hdwy 4f out: ev ch 3 out: sn rdn: wknd over 1f out* **10/1**

00-3 12 nk **So Claire**[19] 3019 3-9-6 **59**.......................... MartinDwyer 2 +
(William Muir) *prom in centre: rdn and ev ch 3f out: wknd 2f out* **17/2**

03-0 13 1 ½ **Midoura**[20] 2967 3-9-4 **57**.......................... LiamKeniry 4 +
(Laura Mongan) *trckd ldrs in centre: ev ch 3f out tl 2f out: sn wknd* **25/1**

05-0 14 3 ½ **Pegasus Bridge**[19] 2995 3-9-7 **60**..........(b[1]) TomMarquand 12
(Eve Johnson Houghton) *racd stands' side: mid-div tl dropped to rr u.p 3f out: nvr bk on terms: wknd over 1f out* **14/1**

1m 32.9s (4.20) **Going Correction** +0.60s/f (Yiel) **14** Ran SP% **121.7**
Speed ratings (Par 97): **100,92,90,88,88 85,85,82,77,77 68,67,66,62**
CSF £47.19 CT £223.22 TOTE £6.70: £2.30, £2.20, £2.40; EX 49.20 Trifecta £123.00.
Owner Malcolm E Wright **Bred** M Fahy **Trained** Earlswood, Monmouths

FOCUS
They raced in two separate groups to begin with, before they joined up approaching the half mile marker. The six who went towards the stands' rail immediately (all drawn high) included the first three, fifth and seventh.

3698 BRITISH STALLION STUDS EBF MARGADALE FILLIES' H'CAP 1m 1f 201y
3:45 (3:45) (Class 3) (0-90,81) 3-Y-O+ **£11,320** (£3,368; £1,683; £841) **Stalls Low**

Form RPR

6-11 1 **Bella Vita**[26] 2768 3-9-1 **81**.......................... CharlesBishop 2 92
(Eve Johnson Houghton) *trckd ldrs: chal 4f out: rdn over 2f out: led over 1f out: kpt on v gamely: drvn out* **7/4**[1]

00-0 2 1 ¼ **Mystic Meg**[19] 3010 4-9-12 **79**..........(h) JackMitchell 7 88
(Hughie Morrison) *trckd ldrs: pushed along whn nt clrest of runs 2f out: swtchd rt over 1f out: kpt on to press wnr ins fnl f: no ex nring fin* **11/1**

2-00 3 5 **Madeleine Bond**[20] 2966 5-9-10 **77**.......................... HarryBentley 4 76
(Henry Candy) *led: jnd 4f out: rdn over 2f out: hdd over 1f out: no ex ins fnl f* **12/1**

-021 4 1 ½ **Pempie (IRE)**[17] 3093 3-8-8 **74**.......................... DavidProbert 5 69
(Andrew Balding) *looked wl; in tch: rdn over 2f out: wnt 4th over 1f out: nt pce to threaten* **11/4**[2]

4114 5 5 **She Believes (IRE)**[10] 3336 4-9-10 **77**.......................... LiamKeniry 8 63
(Sylvester Kirk) *in tch: rdn over 2f out: nt pce to get on terms: wknd fnl f* **4/1**[3]

The Form Book Flat 2019, Raceform Ltd, Newbury, RG14 5SJ

05-6 **6** *17* **Escape The City**[29] [2691] 4-9-11 **78**..............................(t) GeraldMosse 3 30
(Hughie Morrison) *hld up in last pair: hdwy over 4f out: rdn and ev ch 3f out tl jst over 2f out: wknd over 1f out* **15/2**

332- **7** *5* **Pilgrim Soul**[13] [5682] 4-9-6 **73**..............................(t) RobertHavlin 6 15
(Kerry Lee) *hld up in last: rdn 3f out: sn btn* **40/1**

2m 13.33s (2.83) **Going Correction** +0.60s/f (Yiel)
WFA 3 from 4yo+ 13lb **7 Ran SP% 113.3**
Speed ratings (Par 104): **112,111,107,105,101 88,84**
CSF £21.83 CT £176.22 TOTE £2.60: £1.40, £4.80; EX 22.70 Trifecta £130.90.
Owner Mrs Heather Raw **Bred** Shoreham Stud **Trained** Blewbury, Oxon

FOCUS
They finished well strung out behind a very much in form and improving winner. The second has been rated to her 3yo form when with Hugo Palmer.

3699 SORVIO INSURANCE BROKERS MAIDEN STKS (PLUS 10 RACE) 1m 4f 5y

4:15 (4:16) (Class 3) 3-Y-O **£9,703** (£2,887; £1,443; £721) **Stalls** Low

Form RPR

1 **Mankayan (IRE)** 3-9-5 0.............................. KieranShoemark 4 85
(Charlie Fellowes) *tall; str; sltly on toes; s.i.s: in last pair: struggling 4f out: hdwy over 2f out: led over 1f out: styd on wl: rdn out* **25/1**

5-0 **2** *1* **Isabella Brant (FR)**[26] [2771] 3-9-0 0.............................. HarryBentley 6 78
(Ralph Beckett) *tall; trckd ldrs: rdn 3f out: edgd lft 2f out: styd on into 2nd ins fnl f: a being hld by wnr* **28/1**

60- **3** *¾* **Fox Vardy (USA)**[257] [7699] 3-9-5 0.............................. TomMarquand 8 82
(Martyn Meade) *bit bkward; trckd ldr: led after 4f: rdn 2f out: hdd over 1f out: styd on but no ex fnl 120yds* **9/1**

2 **4** *3* **Make My Day (IRE)**[45] [2099] 3-9-5 0.............................. RobertHavlin 5 77
(John Gosden) *str; edgy; s.i.s: in last trio: struggling 3f out: making prog whn sltly hmpd 2f out: swtchd rt in cl 4th jst over 1f out: fdd fnl 120yds* **13/8**[1]

-523 **5** *5* **Inclyne**[21] [2935] 3-9-0 78.............................. DavidProbert 2 64
(Andrew Balding) *trckd ldrs: rdn over 2f out: wknd ent fnl f* **9/4**[2]

33 **6** *7* **Isolate (FR)**[44] [2142] 3-9-5 0.............................. RobHornby 9 58
(Martyn Meade) *str; trckd ldrs: rdn 3f out: wknd 2f out* **8/1**[3]

43 **7** *10* **Arthur Pendragon (IRE)**[54] [1898] 3-9-5 0.............................. JasonWatson 3 42
(Brian Meehan) *str; led for 4f: trckd ldrs: rdn 4f out: drifted rt to centre over 2f out: sn wknd* **17/2**

02 **8** *14* **Moghram (IRE)**[27] [2731] 3-9-5 0.............................. JimCrowley 1 19
(Marcus Tregoning) *tall; hld up in last pair: rdn 5f out: hdwy 4f out: nvr threatened: wknd over 2f out* **16/1**

2m 41.81s (4.21) **Going Correction** +0.60s/f (Yiel) **8 Ran SP% 113.7**
Speed ratings (Par 103): **110,109,108,106,103 98,92,82**
CSF £524.58 TOTE £36.90: £6.70, £5.60, £1.80; EX 403.90 Trifecta £3034.00.
Owner Dahab Racing **Bred** B V Sangster **Trained** Newmarket, Suffolk

FOCUS
A shock result here, with the two outsiders coming home first and second. The level is a bit fluid, but the second has been rated as improving in line with last year's debut form.

3700 DEOS GROUP H'CAP 1m 4f 5y

4:45 (4:45) (Class 5) (0-70,72) 4-Y-O+
£4,075 (£1,212; £606; £303; £300; £300) **Stalls** Low

Form RPR

-000 **1** **Loving Your Work**[69] [1520] 8-8-2 **51** oh4.............................. KieranO'Neill 3 57
(Ken Cunningham-Brown) *in tch: hdwy over 2f out: led over 1f out: sn wandered u.p: hdd fnl 100yds: regained ld fnl stride* **33/1**

2212 **2** *shd* **Singing The Blues (IRE)**[31] [2626] 4-9-9 **72**.............................. RobHornby 6 78
(Rod Millman) *looked wl; prom: rdn and ev ch fr 2f out: tk narrow advantage fnl 100yds: hdd fnl stride* **15/8**[1]

6313 **3** *nk* **Murhib (IRE)**[7] [3444] 7-8-7 **56** ow1..............................(h) JFEgan 12 62+
(Lydia Richards) *looked wl; hld up towards rr: midfield 6f out: rdn over 2f out: styng on whn nt clr run ins fnl f: sn swtchd lft: fin strly: jst hld* **11/1**

0515 **4** *hd* **Master Grey (IRE)**[21] [2936] 4-9-5 **68**.............................. CharlesBishop 11 73
(Rod Millman) *pushed along leaving stalls: towards rr: hdwy over 2f out: chsd ldrs over 1f out: styd on fnl f: lost 3rd fnl strides* **15/2**[3]

3030 **5** *2 ¼* **Mobham (IRE)**[39] [2353] 4-9-1 **64**.............................. RobertHavlin 14 65
(J R Jenkins) *hld up last: hdwy fr 3f out: rdn whn swtchd rt jst over 1f out: styd on same pce fnl f* **16/1**

11-0 **6** *2 ½* **Brancaster (IRE)**[25] [2793] 5-9-5 **68**.............................. JasonWatson 8 65
(David Elsworth) *hld up towards rr: hdwy 4f out: rdn to chse ldrs over 2f out: fdd fnl 120yds* **8/1**

06-0 **7** *1 ¾* **Geranium**[28] [2714] 4-9-2 **65**.............................. GeraldMosse 2 60
(Hughie Morrison) *led for 3f: trckd ldrs: rdn over 3f out: fdd ins fnl f* **20/1**

-210 **8** *¾* **Simbirsk**[27] [2732] 4-9-9 **72**.............................. KieranShoemark 9 65
(John O'Shea) *prom: led after 3f: rdn and hdd over 1f out: sn no ex* **12/1**

4-32 **9** *9* **Highfaluting (IRE)**[31] [2629] 5-9-5 **68**.............................. RyanTate 10 47
(James Eustace) *trckd ldrs: rdn 3f out: wknd over 1f out* **5/1**[2]

1-04 **10** *8* **Taurean Dancer (IRE)**[29] [2696] 4-9-0 **63**..............................(p) RossaRyan 1 29
(Roger Teal) *mid-div: hdwy 5f out: rdn and ev ch 2f out: sn wknd* **8/1**

6-00 **11** *12* **Acker Bilk (IRE)**[35] [2516] 5-9-7 **70**..............................(p) LiamKeniry 4 17
(Ronald Harris) *rousted along s: sn mid-div: rdn over 3f out: wknd 2f out* **66/1**

430- **12** *1 ½* **Mythological (IRE)**[262] [7530] 4-8-10 **59**.............................. HollieDoyle 7 4
(Louise Allan) *chsd ldrs early: in last pair after 4f: btn 3f out* **50/1**

0-00 **R** **Camakasi (IRE)**[52] [1934] 8-9-2 **65**.............................. TomMarquand 13
(Ali Stronge) *ref to r: tk no part* **50/1**

2m 46.09s (8.49) **Going Correction** +0.60s/f (Yiel) **13 Ran SP% 120.5**
Speed ratings (Par 103): **95,94,94,94,93 91,90,89,83,78 70,69,**
CSF £93.40 CT £783.70 TOTE £44.00: £9.00, £1.20, £2.90; EX 287.00 Trifecta £3272.30.
Owner Danebury Racing Stables **Bred** Dukes Stud & Overbury Stallions Ltd **Trained** Danebury, Hants

FOCUS
In contrast to several of the races on the card, there was a bunched finish to this competitive handicap. The winner has been rated in line with last year's turf form, while the second helps with the standard.

3701 SHADWELL RACING EXCELLENCE APPRENTICE H'CAP (WHIPS SHALL BE CARRIED BUT NOT USED) 6f

5:15 (5:17) (Class 5) (0-75,77) 4-Y-O+
£4,722 (£1,405; £702; £351; £300; £300) **Stalls** Low

Form RPR

3023 **1** **Handytalk (IRE)**[18] [3040] 6-9-5 **75**..............................(b) OliverSearle(7) 9 82
(Rod Millman) *a.p: pushed along fr over 2f out: kpt on wl ins fnl f: led cl home* **13/2**

6605 **2** *½* **Princely**[69] [1522] 4-9-1 **64**.............................. JessicaCooley 4 70
(Tony Newcombe) *prom: disp ld 3f out tl edgd ahd over 1f out: no ex whn hdd cl home* **14/1**

1310 **3** *hd* **Major Valentine**[25] [2804] 7-9-5 **73**.............................. KateLeahy(5) 10 78
(John O'Shea) *chsd ldrs: swtchd lft ent fnl f: kpt on fnl 120yds (jockey said gelding hung right-handed)* **9/1**

3426 **4** *1 ½* **Global Melody**[14] [3207] 4-9-0 **66**..............................(p) GraceMcEntee(3) 7 66
(Phil McEntee) *prom: disp ld 3f out tl over 1f out: kpt on same pce ins fnl f* **7/2**[1]

4005 **5** *2 ¼* **Human Nature (IRE)**[25] [2804] 6-9-4 **72**..............................(t) MarcoGhiani(5) 6 65
(Stuart Williams) *in tch: effrt over 2f out: sn one pce* **9/2**[3]

0301 **6** *3 ¼* **Motajaasid (IRE)**[19] [3018] 4-9-9 **77**..............................(tp) AngusVilliers(5) 2 60
(Richard Hughes) *in tch: shkn up over 3f out: little imp: wknd ins fnl f* **4/1**[2]

1406 **7** *4 ½* **Elusif (IRE)**[36] [2483] 4-8-9 **58**.............................. GavinAshton 5 26
(Shaun Keightley) *s.i.s: sn pushed along in last: nvr threatened: wknd fnl f (jockey said gelding was never travelling)* **12/1**

6562 **8** *3 ¼* **Little Palaver**[20] [2971] 7-9-9 **72**..............................(p) AmeliaGlass 8 30
(Clive Cox) *led tl 3f out: wknd ent fnl f (trainer said gelding was unsuited by the Soft ground and would prefer a faster surface)* **6/1**

1m 18.66s (4.16) **Going Correction** +0.60s/f (Yiel) **8 Ran SP% 112.4**
Speed ratings (Par 103): **96,95,95,93,90 85,79,75**
CSF £86.80 CT £820.73 TOTE £7.80: £2.30, £2.90, £2.70; EX 100.60 Trifecta £841.20.
Owner Cantay Racing **Bred** Edmond Kinane & Donal Sweeney **Trained** Kentisbeare, Devon

FOCUS
An ordinary sprint handicap for apprentice riders. It's been rated around the third to his recent form.
T/Plt: £516.20 to a £1 stake. Pool: £60,058.92 - 84.93 winning units T/Qpdt: £226.50 to a £1 stake. Pool: £6,121.71 - 20.0 winning units **Tim Mitchell**

3411 THIRSK (L-H)

Tuesday, June 11

OFFICIAL GOING: Good (good to soft in places) changing to good to soft after race 1 (5.20) changing to soft after race 6 (7.50)
Wind: fresh largely across Weather: light rain, heavier after 3rd

3702 RACINGTV.COM EBF MAIDEN AUCTION STKS (DIV I) 6f

5:20 (5:21) (Class 5) 2-Y-O **£3,946** (£1,174; £586; £293) **Stalls** Centre

Form RPR

1 **Ardenlee Star (USA)** 2-9-0.............................. PaddyMathers 9 76+
(Richard Fahey) *dwlt: hld up: sn pushed along: hdwy 2f out: chal 1f out: led 110yds out: kpt on pushed out* **9/1**

2 *½* **Harry Love (IRE)** 2-8-9.............................. BenRobinson(3) 6 73
(Ollie Pears) *trckd ldrs: pushed along to ld over 1f out: rdn and pressed 1f out: hdd 110yds out: kpt on same pce* **18/1**

3 *1 ¾* **Kayewhykelly (IRE)** 2-8-9 ow1.............................. GrahamLee 5 64
(Julie Camacho) *dwlt: pushed along and outpcd in rr tl kpt on fr over 1f out: wnt 3rd 50yds out* **14/1**

5 **4** *¾* **Rich Belief**[23] [2869] 2-9-5.............................. PaulHanagan 2 72
(James Bethell) *midfield: pushed along over 2f out: rdn and kpt on fnl f* **9/2**[2]

5 *½* **Governor Of Punjab (IRE)** 2-9-3.............................. PJMcDonald 10 69
(Mark Johnston) *trckd ldrs: hdwy and pressed ldr over 2f out: rdn and hung lft appr fnl f: no ex* **6/4**[1]

6 *3 ½* **Pentewan** 2-8-13.............................. SamJames 1 54
(Phillip Makin) *led narrowly: rdn and hdd over 2f out: sn wknd* **10/1**

7 *3 ¼* **Rebel Redemption** 2-9-4.............................. JasonHart 4 49
(John Quinn) *dwlt: sn outpcd in rr: minor late hdwy* **8/1**

8 *2* **Tiltilys Rock (IRE)** 2-8-13.............................. AndrewElliott 3 38
(Andrew Crook) *prom: rdn over 2f out: sn wknd* **66/1**

3 **9** *5* **Castlehill Retreat**[13] [3220] 2-9-1.............................. AndrewMullen 8 25
(Ben Haslam) *prom tl wknd 2f out* **11/2**[3]

10 *¾* **Newsical** 2-9-0.............................. DougieCostello 7 22
(Mark Walford) *prom tl wknd 2f out* **66/1**

1m 13.92s (1.12) **Going Correction** +0.025s/f (Good) **10 Ran SP% 118.7**
Speed ratings (Par 93): **93,92,90,89,88 83,79,76,70,69**
CSF £159.61 TOTE £9.90: £2.60, £4.90, £4.80; EX 152.90 Trifecta £2371.60.
Owner Mrs L Hannity **Bred** Kirsten Rausing **Trained** Musley Bank, N Yorks

FOCUS
The first pair came away down the middle in this modest 2yo maiden. The runners kicked up the turf, although the winning time suggested the going was near advertised.

3703 RACINGTV.COM EBF MAIDEN AUCTION STKS (DIV II) 6f

5:50 (5:53) (Class 5) 2-Y-O **£3,946** (£1,174; £586; £293) **Stalls** Centre

Form RPR

1 **Commanche Falls** 2-9-0.............................. ConnorBeasley 5 74
(Michael Dods) *midfield: hdwy and chsd ldrs 2f out: swtchd lft over 1f out: sn rdn: drvn into narrow ld 110yds out: kpt on* **12/1**

2 **2** *½* **Clay Regazzoni**[20] [2957] 2-9-5.............................. KevinStott 1 77
(Keith Dalgleish) *prom: rdn along over 2f out: drvn to chal strly ins fnl f: edgd lft: kpt on but a jst hld* **6/5**[1]

3 *1 ½* **Mischief Star** 2-9-4.............................. DavidNolan 6 72
(David O'Meara) *trckd ldrs: pushed along over 1f out: rdn and kpt on fnl f* **11/1**

5 **4** *hd* **Havana Dawn**[15] [3156] 2-8-12.............................. SamJames 8 65
(Phillip Makin) *led: pushed along over 1f out: edgd rt ins fnl f: hdd 110yds out: no ex* **5/1**[3]

5 *2* **Spygate** 2-9-2.............................. DanielTudhope 9 65
(Richard Fahey) *dwlt but sn prom: rdn 2f out: bit outpcd whn n.m.r ins fnl f and swtchd lft: one pce fnl 110yds* **7/2**[2]

04 **6** *nk* **Rusalka (IRE)**[14] [3196] 2-8-10.............................. DavidAllan 7 56
(Tim Easterby) *trckd ldrs: bit short of room and lost pl over 2f out: sn pushed along: kpt on same pce ins fnl f but no threat* **16/1**

0 **7** *2 ¼* **My Havana**[8] [3411] 2-8-10.............................. RowanScott(3) 2 52
(Nigel Tinkler) *dwlt: outpcd in rr tl kpt on fnl f* **66/1**

8 *1* **Our Dave** 2-8-12.............................. JasonHart 4 48
(John Quinn) *dwlt: hld up: racd quite keenly: pushed along over 2f out: rdn appr fnl f: nvr threatened* **16/1**

9 *1 ¼* **Aiden's Reward (IRE)** 2-9-2.............................. AndrewMullen 3 49
(Ben Haslam) *s.i.s: hld up in tch: pushed along over 2f out: wknd ins fnl f* **66/1**

1m 14.08s (1.28) **Going Correction** +0.10s/f (Good) **9 Ran SP% 115.1**
Speed ratings (Par 93): **95,94,92,92,89 89,86,84,83**
CSF £26.77 TOTE £12.50: £3.30, £1.20, £1.80; EX 33.90 Trifecta £203.40.
Owner Doug Graham And Ian Davison **Bred** Redgate Bstock & Peter Bottowley Bstock **Trained** Denton, Co Durham

FOCUS
After the opener the going was downgraded to good to soft all over. This second division of the juvenile maiden was just marginally slower than the preceding event.

3704 WEATHERBYS RACING BANK H'CAP — 7f 218y

6:20 (6:22) (Class 5) (0-70,68) 4-Y-O+

£4,528 (£1,347; £673; £336; £300; £300) **Stalls** Low

Form RPR

6165 **1** **Thornaby Nash**[14] 3178 8-9-0 **64**......................(b) ConorMcGovern(3) 11 72
(Jason Ward) *midfield: pushed along and hdwy 2f out: rdn to ld 1f out: sn edgd rt: drvn and kpt on* **7/1**[2]

-500 **2** 3/4 **Kingdom Brunel**[13] 3216 4-9-7 **68**.........................(p[1]) DanielTudhope 8 74
(David O'Meara) *trckd ldrs: rdn 2f out: drvn to chal 1f out: kpt on* **7/1**[2]

3000 **3** *nse* **Global Exceed**[24] 2847 4-8-11 **61**.........................(t[1]) RowanScott(3) 7 67
(Karen Tutty) *hld up: pushed along and gd hdwy on outer 2f out: rdn to chse ldr whn hmpd ins fnl f: kpt on wl* **50/1**

0-03 **4** 1 1/2 **The Stalking Moon (IRE)**[38] 2418 5-9-2 **63**............... AndrewMullen 13 65
(Adrian Nicholls) *led narrowly: rdn over 2f out: hdd 1f out: no ex ins fnl f* **6/1**[1]

5-45 **5** 3/4 **Frankster (FR)**[18] 3053 6-9-0 **61**.........................(tp) PJMcDonald 12 62
(Micky Hammond) *prom: rdn over 2f out: no ex ins fnl f* **10/1**

2564 **6** 1 1/4 **Mutarakez (IRE)**[13] 3215 7-9-7 **68**.........................(p) JamesSullivan 4 66
(Ruth Carr) *hld up in midfield: pushed along over 2f out: rdn over 1f out: one pce and nvr threatened* **6/1**[1]

-066 **7** 2 **Fake News**[14] 3199 4-9-6 **67**................................ RobbieDowney 6 60
(David Barron) *trckd ldrs: rdn along 3f out: sn outpcd and no threat after* **9/1**[3]

0000 **8** 1/2 **Intense Pleasure (IRE)**[14] 3177 4-8-12 **59**..............(h) BarryMcHugh 14 51
(Ruth Carr) *trckd ldrs on outer: racd keenly: rdn over 2f out: wknd ins fnl f* **25/1**

00-0 **9** 1/2 **Desert Dream**[22] 2899 5-8-12 **66**................................ JoshQuinn(7) 9 57
(Michael Easterby) *midfield on outer: rdn and sme hdwy on wd outside 2f out: wknd ins fnl f* **14/1**

1524 **10** 2 1/4 **Dandy Highwayman (IRE)**[13] 3214 5-9-0 **64**........(tp) BenRobinson(3) 1 50
(Ollie Pears) *midfield on inner: rdn over 2f out: wknd over 1f out* **12/1**

-042 **11** 3/4 **Rebel State (IRE)**[20] 2963 6-8-3 **57**.........................(p) OwenPayton(7) 5 41
(Jedd O'Keeffe) *a towards rr* **9/1**[3]

-001 **12** 1 1/4 **Al Ozzdi**[8] 3430 4-9-1 **62** 5ex................................ PaulHanagan 3 43
(Roger Fell) *settled into midfield: pushed along over 2f out: rdn over 1f out: hung lft and sn btn* **10/1**

2304 **13** 3 1/4 **Scots Sonnet**[25] 2784 5-9-7 **68**.........................(h) AlistairRawlinson 2 42
(Jim Goldie) *hld up: racd keenly: rdn over 2f out: sn btn (jockey said gelding ran too free)* **20/1**

1m 42.39s (0.69) **Going Correction** +0.10s/f (Good) **13** Ran SP% **116.7**
Speed ratings (Par 103): **100,99,99,97,96 95,93,93,92,90 89,88,85**
CSF £52.81 CT £2266.62 TOTE £7.40: £2.40, £3.10, £20.70; EX 52.20 Trifecta £1696.30.
Owner Ingleby Bloodstock Limited **Bred** Dave Scott **Trained** Sessay, N Yorks
■ Stewards' Enquiry : Conor McGovern two-day ban: careless riding (June 25-26)

FOCUS
There was a rough start to this competitive handicap and they went a sound pace. The second has been rated to form, and the third as finding a bit for his new yard off a reduced mark.

3705 SCOUTING FOR GIRLS - LIVE @THIRSKRACES FRIDAY 16TH AUGUST H'CAP — 1m 4f 8y

6:50 (6:50) (C!ass 6) (0-60,60) 4-Y-O+

£3,398 (£1,011; £505; £300; £300; £300) **Stalls** High

Form RPR

-530 **1** **Dew Pond**[12] 3272 7-8-13 **52**.........................(bt) DavidAllan 2 59
(Tim Easterby) *midfield: pushed along and hdwy over 2f out: rdn to ld over 1f out: drvn and styd on* **7/2**[2]

00-3 **2** 3/4 **Maroon Bells (IRE)**[20] 2975 4-8-12 **58**..................... CierenFallon(7) 6 64
(David Menuisier) *trckd ldrs: rdn along over 2f out: drvn to chse ldr ins fnl f: styd on* **7/4**[1]

0402 **3** 2 **Foxrush Take Time (FR)**[11] 3298 4-8-7 **46** oh1...........(e) PhilipPrince 9 49
(Richard Guest) *midfield: rdn over 2f out: drvn over 1f out: edgd lft but styd on fnl f* **14/1**

50-6 **4** *nk* **Clayton Hall (IRE)**[7] 3447 6-8-9 **48** oh1 ow2...............(p) GrahamLee 10 50
(John Wainwright) *hld up: pushed along and hdwy 3f out: chsd ldrs 2f out: drvn over 1f out: one pce* **50/1**

00-0 **5** 2 **Point Of Honour (IRE)**[43] 2202 4-8-13 **52**.................. JamesSullivan 3 51
(Ruth Carr) *led: rdn over 2f out: hdd over 1f out: wknd ins fnl f* **14/1**

6643 **6** 3 **Home Before Dusk**[14] 3181 4-9-7 **60**........................ DanielTudhope 4 55
(Keith Dalgleish) *prom: rdn over 2f out: drvn and hung lft over 1f out: sn wknd* **7/2**[2]

50-0 **7** 1 1/2 **Doon Star**[39] 2376 4-8-13 **52**................................ AlistairRawlinson 12 45
(Jim Goldie) *hld up: rdn over 2f out: nvr threatened* **33/1**

0030 **8** 4 **Zahraani**[19] 3017 4-8-13 **52**................................ PaulHanagan 8 39
(J R Jenkins) *hld up in midfield: pushed along over 4f out: wknd over 2f out* **33/1**

0-25 **9** 7 **Frame Rate**[29] 2684 4-9-1 **54**.........................(b) LewisEdmunds 7 30
(Iain Jardine) *in tch: rdn over 3f out: wknd* **9/1**[3]

0600 **10** 3 1/2 **Rock Warbler (IRE)**[18] 3046 6-8-12 **51**...................(b[1]) KevinStott 11 22
(Michael Mullineaux) *hld up in midfield: rdn 3f out: sn wknd* **33/1**

4/00 **11** 4 1/2 **About Glory**[14] 3181 5-9-1 **54**................................ AndrewMullen 1 18
(Iain Jardine) *prom: rdn over 3f out: wknd* **66/1**

2m 40.28s (0.28) **Going Correction** +0.10s/f (Good) **11** Ran SP% **116.4**
Speed ratings (Par 101): **103,102,101,100,99 97,96,93,89,86 83**
CSF £9.52 CT £74.60 TOTE £4.50: £1.20, £1.50, £3.20; EX 13.40 Trifecta £76.60.
Owner Ashfield Caravan Park **Bred** Pollards Stables **Trained** Great Habton, N Yorks

FOCUS
This moderate handicap was run at a decent tempo.

3706 WEATHERBYS VAT SERVICES H'CAP — 6f

7:20 (7:22) (Class 5) (0-75,75) 4-Y-O+

£4,528 (£1,347; £673; £336; £300; £300) **Stalls** Centre

Form RPR

21-0 **1** **Gullane One (IRE)**[59] 1760 4-8-13 **67**.........................(t) JasonHart 4 75
(Tim Easterby) *prom: pushed into narrow ld over 1f out: drvn ent fnl f: kpt on wl* **33/1**

4221 **2** 3/4 **Scuzeme**[24] 2847 5-9-3 **71**.........................(h) SamJames 9 76
(Phillip Makin) *led narrowly: rdn and hdd over 1f out: remained chalng: drvn and kpt on* **5/1**[2]

0-15 **3** *nse* **Lucky Beggar (IRE)**[24] 2824 9-9-1 **69**........................ DavidAllan 15 74
(David C Griffiths) *chsd ldrs: rdn 2f out: kpt on* **8/1**[3]

0002 **4** *nk* **Mutabaahy (IRE)**[4] 3550 4-8-13 **67**........................ CamHardie 2 71
(Antony Brittain) *hld up: rdn and hdwy on outer over 1f out: sn chsd ldrs: kpt on* **8/1**[3]

4010 **5** *nse* **Dandy's Beano (IRE)**[14] 3201 4-9-2 **70**...................(h) KevinStott 14 74
(Kevin Ryan) *hld up: rdn and hdwy over 1f out: drvn to chal ins fnl f: one pce fnl 75yds* **20/1**

4-21 **6** *hd* **Global Spirit**[13] 3221 4-9-0 **73**........................ BenSanderson(5) 13 76
(Roger Fell) *midfield: rdn over 2f out: kpt on ins fnl f* **4/1**[1]

-636 **7** 3/4 **Mr Orange (IRE)**[22] 2893 6-9-6 **74**.........................(p) DougieCostello 1 75
(Paul Midgley) *hld up: rdn along 2f out: kpt on ins fnl f: nrst fin* **16/1**

-032 **7** *dht* **Prestbury Park (USA)**[24] 2824 4-9-2 **70**........................ GrahamLee 3 71
(Paul Midgley) *trckd ldrs: rdn to chal strly ent fnl f: wknd fnl 50yds* **10/1**

4031 **9** 1/2 **Somewhere Secret**[4] 3549 5-8-7 **61** 5ex...............(p) AndrewMullen 18 64+
(Michael Mullineaux) *slowly away: hld up: pushed along and hdwy whn short of room towards stands' rail fr over 1f out tl ins fnl f: no ch after: kpt on fnl 75yds (jockey said gelding was denied a clear run inside the final furlong)* **9/1**

1550 **10** *hd* **Tabaahy**[24] 2841 4-9-3 **71**................................ RobbieDowney 12 70
(David O'Meara) *hld up: racd keenly: rdn 2f out: nvr threatened* **25/1**

0/0 **11** 1 1/2 **Betsey Trotter (IRE)**[14] 3201 4-9-7 **75**..................... DanielTudhope 19 69
(David O'Meara) *chsd ldrs: rdn over 2f out: wknd fnl f* **16/1**

0161 **12** *nk* **Katheefa (USA)**[11] 3301 5-8-10 **64**........................ JamesSullivan 17 57
(Ruth Carr) *chsd ldrs: rdn over 2f out: wknd ins fnl f* **11/1**

4614 **13** 1 **Musharrif**[18] 3056 7-9-0 **75**................................ ZakWheatley(7) 5 65
(Declan Carroll) *prom: rdn over 2f out: sn lost pl: wknd ins fnl f* **25/1**

0300 **14** 1/2 **Dirchill (IRE)**[13] 3221 5-8-11 **65**.........................(b) ConnorBeasley 6 53
(David Thompson) *s.i.s: sn midfield: rdn along 3f out: sn outpcd and btn* **16/1**

0-20 **15** 7 **Red Pike (IRE)**[145] 278 8-9-0 **75**........................ HarryRussell(7) 10 41
(Bryan Smart) *chsd ldrs: rdn over 2f out: sn wknd* **22/1**

1m 12.82s (0.02) **Going Correction** +0.10s/f (Good) **15** Ran SP% **123.7**
Speed ratings (Par 103): **103,102,101,101,101 101,100,100,99,99 97,96,95,94,85**
CSF £185.14 CT £1530.84 TOTE £43.20: £12.10, £1.90, £2.30; EX 388.90 Trifecta £1313.70.
Owner Mount Pleasant Racing **Bred** E Phelan & Dream Ahead Syndicate **Trained** Great Habton, N Yorks

FOCUS
There was a blanket finish to this modest sprint handicap. The second has been rated close to his old best, and the third in line with his best since early last year.

3707 JW 4X4 NORTHALLERTON NOVICE STKS — 7f 218y

7:50 (7:57) (Class 5) 3-Y-O+

£4,357 (£1,304; £652; £326; £163; £81) **Stalls** Low

Form RPR

04 **1** **Greek Hero**[12] 3248 3-9-2 0................................ DanielTudhope 10 77
(Declan Carroll) *hld up: hdwy on outer to trck ldrs 5f out: pushed into ld over 1f out: rdn and kpt on fnl f* **10/1**[3]

6- **2** 1 3/4 **Ambersand (IRE)**[319] 5444 3-8-11 0........................ PaulHanagan 6 68
(Richard Fahey) *led: rdn and hdd over 1f out: kpt on same pce* **6/1**[2]

0 **3** 3 1/4 **Philip's Wish**[12] 3248 3-9-2 0.........................(h[1]) KevinStott 13 65
(Keith Dalgleish) *stdd s: hld up: pushed along and hdwy on outer over 2f out: styd on to go 3rd 110yds out* **50/1**

4-0 **4** 1 **Bea Ryan (IRE)**[22] 2909 4-9-8 0................................ DavidNolan 8 61
(Declan Carroll) *prom: rdn over 2f out: no ex ins fnl f* **18/1**

1-4 **5** 3/4 **Myrmidons (IRE)**[40] 2334 3-9-9 0........................ AndrewMullen 9 68
(Michael Dods) *trckd ldrs: rdn along and outpcd over 2f out: kpt on again towards fin* **10/1**[3]

3-3 **6** 3/4 **Pamper**[28] 2713 3-8-11 0................................ PJMcDonald 11 54
(James Fanshawe) *trckd ldrs: dropped bk to midfield after 1f: rdn along over 2f out: sn no imp (trainer could offer no explanation, other than the filly may benefit from being ridden more positively on a sharp track in future)* **5/6**[1]

7 3 **Spiritual Command (IRE)** 3-9-2 0........................ ConnorBeasley 2 52
(Michael Dods) *dwlt: hld up: pushed along over 3f out: nvr threatened* **20/1**

8 1 3/4 **Little Miss Muffin** 3-8-11 0................................ CamHardie 7 43
(Sam England) *midfield: pushed along 3f out: grad wknd* **100/1**

6 **9** 2 **At Peace (IRE)**[12] 3247 3-8-11 0................................ JasonHart 12 39
(John Quinn) *s.i.s: a towards rr* **14/1**

10 3 1/4 **Foxy Eloise** 4-9-3 0................................ SeamusCronin(5) 5 34
(Robyn Brisland) *dwlt: sn trckd ldrs: rdn along over 3f out: wknd 2f out* **66/1**

11 3 1/4 **Graciarose** 3-8-11 0................................ RoystonFfrench 3 24
(Tracy Waggott) *dwlt: hld up in midfield: rdn along over 3f out: sn wknd* **80/1**

1m 44.41s (2.71) **Going Correction** +0.10s/f (Good) **11** Ran SP% **109.4**
WFA 3 from 4yo+ 11lb
Speed ratings (Par 103): **90,88,85,84,83 82,79,77,75,72 69**
CSF £55.11 TOTE £8.50: £2.20, £1.70, £9.00; EX 57.20 Trifecta £462.70.
Owner Clipper Logistics **Bred** Scuderia Archi Romani **Trained** Malton, N Yorks
■ International Guy was withdrawn. Price at time of withdrawal 7-1. Rule 4 applies to all bets. Deduction - 10p in the pound.

FOCUS
The first two dominated the finish of this modest novice event, with the middle of the home straight again favoured. It's been rated a bit cautiously. Another step forward from the winner, with the fourth rated close to last year's debut run here.

3708 RACING TV CLUB EVENING @THIRSKRACES FILLIES' H'CAP — 1m 4f 8y

8:20 (8:22) (Class 5) (0-70,69) 3-Y-O+

£4,075 (£1,212; £606; £303; £300; £300) **Stalls** High

Form RPR

534- **1** **Joie De Vivre (IRE)**[256] 7724 4-9-13 **67**..................... PaulHanagan 6 74
(Martin Todhunter) *hld up: stdy hdwy on outer fr over 5f out: pushed into ld over 1f out: drvn and styd on wl fnl f* **33/1**

-523 **2** 3/4 **Gold Fleece**[22] 2914 3-8-6 **68**................................ CierenFallon(7) 8 74
(Hugo Palmer) *trckd ldrs: drvn to chal over 1f out: styd on fnl f* **7/4**[1]

-310 **3** 1 **Lincoln Tale (IRE)**[11] 3311 3-8-10 **65**........................ CamHardie 7 69
(David O'Meara) *hld up: pushed along and hdwy 3f out: rdn to chse ldrs 2f out: styd on fnl f* **10/1**

4343 **4** 1 **Fayetta**[105] 917 3-9-0 **69**.........................(v[1]) TrevorWhelan 11 71
(David Loughnane) *trckd ldrs: drvn to chal 2f out: no ex ins fnl f* **16/1**

41/3 **5** 2 1/4 **Shambra (IRE)**[38] 2400 5-9-9 **63**.........................(h) GrahamLee 10 62
(Lucy Wadham) *prom: led over 7f out: rdn over 2f out: hdd over 1f out: wknd ins fnl f* **5/1**[2]

35-6 **6** 5 **Lilypad (IRE)**[27] 2737 4-9-8 **62**.........................(v[1]) GeorgeWood 4 53
(James Fanshawe) *midfield: rdn over 2f out: no imp* **8/1**[3]

1352 **7** *nk* **Ebqaa (IRE)**[11] 3321 5-10-0 **68**..............(p) AndrewMullen 1 58
(James Unett) *midfield: rdn along 3f out: sn btn* **12/1**

344 **8** *2 1/4* **Osmosis**[17] 3099 3-8-10 **68**.............. ConorMcGovern(3) 5 55
(Jason Ward) *trckd ldrs: rdn 3f out: wknd over 1f out* **11/1**

43-5 **9** *2 3/4* **Reassurance**[12] 3267 4-9-13 **67**..............(p) DavidAllan 13 49
(Tim Easterby) *hld up: rdn over 3f out: sn btn (trainer could offer no explanation for the filly's performance)* **8/1**[3]

4-40 **10** *9* **Swerved (IRE)**[22] 2913 3-7-11 **57**.............. AndrewBreslin(5) 2 25
(Ollie Pears) *led: hdd over 7f out: remained cl up tl wknd over 2f out* **14/1**

0-50 **11** *2 1/4* **Fillydelphia (IRE)**[27] 2373 8-8-9 **49** oh4..............(p) RachelRichardson 3 13
(Liam Bailey) *a in rr* **80/1**

2m 41.99s (1.99) **Going Correction** +0.175s/f (Good)
WFA 3 from 4yo+ 15lb **11 Ran SP% 117.1**
Speed ratings (Par 100): **100,99,98,98,96 93,93,91,89,83 82**
CSF £90.66 CT £664.58 TOTE £32.90: £7.90, £1.70, £3.00; EX 209.00 Trifecta £891.30.
Owner Leeds Plywood And Doors Ltd **Bred** Sir Robert Ogden **Trained** Orton, Cumbria

FOCUS
Again the middle of the home straight was the place to be in this ordinary mares' handicap. It's been rated around the fourth to her best.

3709 LIKE RACING TV ON FACEBOOK H'CAP 6f
8:50 (8:51) (Class 6) (0-65,65) 3-Y-O

£3,398 (£1,011; £505; £300; £300; £300) **Stalls** Centre

Form RPR

-004 **1** **Dancing Rave**[11] 3292 3-9-6 **64**.............. DanielTudhope 11 71
(David O'Meara) *hld up: pushed along and hdwy 2f out: rdn and hung lft over 1f out: led ins fnl f: continued to hang lft but kpt on* **5/2**[1]

0035 **2** *3/4* **Bedtime Bella (IRE)**[14] 3189 3-9-2 **60**..............(v[1]) PJMcDonald 2 65
(K R Burke) *led: rdn 2f out: drvn and hdd ins fnl f: kpt on but a hld* **10/1**

5016 **3** *2 1/2* **Sepahi**[14] 3189 3-8-11 **62**..............(p) CierenFallon(7) 8 59
(Henry Spiller) *dwlt: hld up: sn pushed along: rdn over 3f out: kpt on fnl f: wnt 3rd fnl 75yds: no threat to ldng pair* **33/1**

-025 **4** *1 1/4* **Ey Up Its Mick**[23] 2870 3-9-0 **58**..............(v[1]) DougieCostello 1 52
(Tony Coyle) *wnt lft s: hld up: rdn along 3f out: drvn and plugged on fnl f* **10/1**

0331 **5** *nse* **Timetodock**[11] 3292 3-9-6 **64**..............(b) DavidAllan 7 57
(Tim Easterby) *prom: rdn appr fnl f: wknd ins fnl f* **5/2**[1]

0320 **6** *1 3/4* **Seanjohnsilver (IRE)**[14] 3202 3-9-3 **61**..............(t) DavidNolan 5 49
(Declan Carroll) *trckd ldrs: rdn 2f out: wknd ins fnl f* **6/1**[2]

-005 **7** *1 1/4* **Here's Rocco (IRE)**[11] 3292 3-9-2 **60**.............. BarryMcHugh 12 44
(John Quinn) *slowly away: hld up in rr: pushed along over 2f out: nvr threatened* **16/1**

-604 **8** *7* **Euro No More (IRE)**[14] 3176 3-9-1 **59**..............(p[1]) GrahamLee 6 22
(Keith Dalgleish) *prom: sn pushed along: rdn 3f out: wknd 2f out* **20/1**

0-34 **9** *3 1/2* **Tease Maid**[47] 2063 3-9-4 **62**..............(v[1]) JasonHart 10 15
(John Quinn) *trckd ldrs: rdn 2f out: wknd* **15/2**[3]

1m 14.19s (1.39) **Going Correction** +0.175s/f (Good) **9 Ran SP% 115.0**
Speed ratings (Par 97): **97,96,92,91,90 88,86,77,72**
CSF £29.84 CT £663.48 TOTE £3.30: £1.10, £2.80, £5.90; EX 29.70 Trifecta £938.70.
Owner David Lumley & Partner **Bred** Frazer Hood **Trained** Upper Helmsley, N Yorks

FOCUS
An ordinary 3yo sprint handicap and only two mattered from the furlong marker.
T/Jkpt: Not won. T/Plt: £3,200.30 to a £1 stake. Pool: £57,431.28 - 13.1 winning units T/Qpdt: £133.20 to a £1 stake. Pool: £9,803.93 - 54.45 winning units **Andrew Sheret**

3066 DIEPPE (R-H)
Tuesday, June 11

OFFICIAL GOING: Turf: heavy

3710a PRIX CLARKSON (MAIDEN) (3YO) (TURF) 1m 1f
4:25 3-Y-O **£9,009** (£3,603; £2,702; £1,801; £900)

RPR

1 **Turea**[35] 3-8-13 0.............. AurelienLemaitre 15 78
(F Head, France) **7/1**

2 *3 1/2* **Noxareno (GER)**[18] 3-9-2 0.............. Pierre-CharlesBoudot 13 74
(F Chappet, France) **63/10**[3]

3 *4* **Smart Lady (FR)**[33] 3-8-13 0.............. GregoryBenoist 11 62
(M Delzangles, France) **7/1**

4 *2* **Saint Andrews (FR)** 3-9-2 0.............. EddyHardouin 16 61
(H Blume, Germany) **42/1**

5 *3* **Kiev (FR)**[52] 3-9-2 0.............. MaximeGuyon 10 55
(Mme Pia Brandt, France) **5/2**[1]

6 *nk* **Pharoa (FR)**[18] 3-9-2 0.............. CristianDemuro 6 54
(J-P Dubois, France) **58/10**[2]

7 *8* **Pensee Spirituelle** 3-8-8 0.............. VincentCheminaud 8 29
(A Fabre, France) **44/5**

8 *1 1/4* **Noble Sky (FR)** 3-8-5 0.............. MlleCoraliePacaut(3) 12 27
(H Blume, Germany) **37/1**

9 *1 1/4* **Cinquain**[27] 2759 3-8-9 0.............. GeorgiaDobie(4) 7 29
(Jo Hughes, France) *prom: lost pl wl bef 1/2-way: rdn and wknd 2f out* **121/1**

10 *6* **Culture (FR)**[19] 3011 3-9-2 0.............. TheoBachelot 4 19
(George Baker) *broke wl: w ldrs: dropped into midfield after 3f: drvn and shortlived effrt 2 1/2f out: sn rdn and wknd* **34/1**

11 *5* **Spokesman (IRE)**[38] 3-8-10 0.............. JeremieMonteiro(6) 5 9
(Andrew Hollinshead, France) **87/1**

12 *2 1/2* **Navalmoral**[93] 3-9-2 0.............. AlexisBadel 9 4
(M Boutin, France) **13/1**

13 *3/4* **Sedrina (IRE)**[41] 3-8-9 0.............. MlleAlisonMassin(4) 3
(S Wattel, France) **18/1**

14 *1 1/2* **Hot Summer (FR)**[101] 3-9-2 0.............. FabriceVeron 2
(C Lerner, France) **24/1**

15 *10* **Wilpena (IRE)**[19] 3-8-4 0.............. MlleAudeDuporte(9) 1
(D Smaga, France) **115/1**

1m 56.12s **15 Ran SP% 119.2**
PARI-MUTUEL (all including 1 euro stake): WIN 8.00; PLACE 2.40, 2.40, 2.50; DF 26.60.
Owner George Strawbridge **Bred** G Strawbridge **Trained** France

3711a PRIX DU CLUB DES COYOTES (H'CAP) (APPRENTICE & YOUNG JOCKEYS) (4YO+) (TURF) 1m 3f
5:03 4-Y-O+ **£6,756** (£2,702; £2,027; £1,351; £675)

RPR

1 **Hexis (IRE)**[8] 5-8-9 0..............(b) MlleLeaBails(7) 12 68
(Guillaume Courbot, France) **9/2**[1]

2 *3 1/2* **Vingtcoeurs (FR)**[12] 4-8-11 0.............. QuentinPerrette(4) 3 61
(C Plisson, France) **30/1**

3 *3/4* **Snowy Sunday (FR)**[26] 5-8-3 0..............(b) ThomasTrullier(3) 6 51
(Frank Sheridan, Italy) **11/2**

4 *1 1/2* **Ma Valentine (FR)**[26] 7-8-6 0.............. JeremyMoisan 7 48
(Mme Anne-Marie Gareau, France) **49/10**[2]

5 *8* **Ayguemorte (FR)**[26] 6-8-6 0.............. TomLefranc(3) 11 37
(P-L Guerin, France) **32/5**

6 *4* **Hark**[243] 5-8-7 0.............. MaixentRemy(3) 16 30
(P Van De Poele, France) **58/1**

7 *3* **Formi (IRE)**[12] 4-9-0 0..............(p) DamienBoche(5) 13 34
(L Gadbin, France) **11/1**

8 *3* **Jazz Warrior (FR)**[231] 5-8-2 0 ow2.............. AnnaelleDidon-Yahlali(6) 8 18
(G Verheye, Belgium) **27/1**

9 *3* **Papa Winner (FR)**[26] 5-8-4 0..............(p) AdrienMoreau 4 8
(S Jesus, France) **38/1**

10 *1/2* **Thomas Crown (FR)**[29] 8-8-0 0..............(b) MohammedLyesTabti(4) 15 7
(Caroline Auvray, France) **18/1**

11 *nk* **Carbutt's Ridge (IRE)**[60] 6-8-8 0.............. JeremieMonteiro(6) 14 17
(N Caulliery, France) **11/1**

12 *6* **Never Say Never (FR)**[26] 6-8-4 0..............(p) AlexisPouchin(3) 1
(S Jesus, France) **28/1**

13 *4* **Jardin Fleuri (FR)**[8] 6-9-0 0.............. HugoLebouc(5) 5 4
(B Legros, France) **66/1**

14 *1* **Trois Roses (FR)**[631] 5-9-1 0..............(b) AlexandreChesneau 9
(J-M Lefebvre, France) **26/5**[3]

15 *12* **Tropezienne (FR)**[158] 76 4-8-13 0..............(p) MathieuPelletan 2
(R Le Dren Doleuze, France) **93/1**

16 *16* **Captain Kissinger**[31] 2647 4-8-11 0..............(b) GeorgiaDobie(4) 10
(Jo Hughes, France) *sn chsng ldng pair outside rivals: outpcd and pushed along over 3f out: sn wknd: wl bhd and eased fr 1 1/2f out* **99/1**

PARI-MUTUEL (all including 1 euro stake): WIN 5.50; PLACE 2.60, 7.50, 2.90; DF 56.60.
Owner Daniel Dumoulin **Bred** Sc Ecurie De Meautry **Trained** France

3712a PRIX NICHOLAS (MAIDEN) (3YO) (TURF) 7f
5:41 3-Y-O **£9,009** (£3,603; £2,702; £1,801; £900)

RPR

1 **Asterios (FR)**[33] 3-9-2 0..............(b) VincentCheminaud 6 77
(M Delzangles, France) **29/10**[1]

2 *nk* **Testa (IRE)**[33] 3-8-13 0.............. TheoBachelot 1 73
(S Wattel, France) **7/2**[2]

3 *1 1/2* **Jojo (IRE)**[32] 2598 3-8-9 0.............. GeorgiaDobie(4) 10 69
(Jo Hughes, France) *midfield on inner: drvn to cl and chse ldrs towards stands' side fr 2f out: styd on u.p: no ex fnl 100yds* **23/1**

4 *1 3/4* **Alvilda (USA)**[33] 3-8-13 0.............. MickaelBarzalona 8 64
(A Fabre, France) *chsd ldr in gp of four on outside rail: c stands' side st: trapped on rail and nowhere to go fr 2f out: kpt on once clr ins fnl f: nvr able to chal* **78/10**

5 *snk* **Handmaiden**[55] 1855 3-8-13 0.............. Pierre-CharlesBoudot 9 64
(H-A Pantall, France) *led gp of four on outside rail: rejnd field on inner turning out of bk st w overall ld: led field to stands' side rail st: drvn whn hrd pressed fr 2f out: hdd 1f out: grad dropped away* **22/5**[3]

6 *4* **Made To Order (FR)**[13] 3-8-13 0.............. PierreBazire 4 53
(E J O'Neill, France) **31/5**

7 *5* **Sosoft (FR)**[41] 3-9-2 0.............. MaximeGuyon 2 43
(C Laffon-Parias, France) **23/5**

8 *3 1/2* **Miss Me (GER)** 3-8-0 0.............. ThomasTrullier(8) 3 25
(N Clement, France) **29/1**

9 *5* **Sweet Smoothie (FR)** 3-8-9 0.............. MlleCoraliePacaut(4) 5 17
(H Blume, Germany) **52/1**

1m 24.87s **9 Ran SP% 118.9**
PARI-MUTUEL (all including 1 euro stake): WIN 3.90; PLACE 1.70, 1.80, 3.60; DF 6.80.
Owner John Goelet **Bred** J Goelet **Trained** France

3713a PRIX CLAUDE MONET (MAIDEN) (3YO) (TURF) 5f 110y
6:17 3-Y-O **£9,009** (£3,603; £2,702; £1,801; £900)

RPR

1 **Samskara (IRE)**[274] 3-8-7 0.............. ThomasTrullier(6) 9 75
(C Laffon-Parias, France) **53/1**

2 *1/2* **Morning Basma (FR)**[70] 1512 3-8-13 0.............. CristianDemuro 11 73
(E J O'Neill, France) **44/5**

3 *1* **Louve Dream (IRE)**[29] 3-9-2 0.............. EddyHardouin 1 73
(Carina Fey, France) **23/5**[3]

4 *1 1/2* **Alkawthar (USA)**[27] 3-8-13 0.............. MaximeGuyon 4 65
(Mme Pia Brandt, France) **27/10**[2]

5 *1 1/4* **Antonia Clara**[11] 3-8-13 0..............(b) TheoBachelot 8 61
(P Monfort, France) **39/1**

6 *1 1/4* **Lucky Bird (FR)**[18] 3-9-2 0.............. ThibaultSpeicher 2 60
(Louis Baudron, France) **36/5**

7 *1/2* **Velvet Vixen (IRE)**[18] 3066 3-8-9 0.............. GeorgiaDobie(4) 7 55
(Jo Hughes, France) *prom: 4th and drvn 1/2-way: wknd ins fnl f* **40/1**

8 *1* **Mya George (FR)**[68] 3-8-13 0..............(b[1]) AurelienLemaitre 5 52
(G Doleuze, France) **90/1**

9 *1 1/2* **Dubai Opera**[18] 3-8-13 0.............. MickaelBarzalona 3 47
(H-A Pantall, France) *towards rr on inner: rdn and n.m.r 2f out: no imp whn in clr: nvr in contention* **18/1**

10 *1 1/2* **Mubarmaj (FR)**[27] 3-9-2 0.............. RonanThomas 10 45
(J E Hammond, France) *towards rr on outer: rdn and shortlived effrt ins fnl 2f: sn btn* **8/5**[1]

1m 4.58s **10 Ran SP% 118.9**
PARI-MUTUEL (all including 1 euro stake): WIN 53.60; PLACE 7.90, 2.50, 2.10; DF 157.70.
Owner Al Shira'aa Farms **Bred** Tiger Bloodstock & Tallyho Stud **Trained** Chantilly, France

3714a PRIX A RAIMBOURG-BOURVIL (CLAIMER) (2YO) (TURF) 5f 110y
6:52 2-Y-O £7,207 (£2,882; £2,162; £1,441; £720)

RPR
1 **Diva Du Dancing (FR)**[11] 2-9-1 0 MickaelBarzalona 9 73
(T Castanheira, France) **58/10**
2 3 **Lalacelle (FR)**[36] 2-9-1 0 MaximeGuyon 4 63
(M Boutin, France) **2/1**[1]
3 2 **Ekaitzana (FR)** 2-8-11 0 MlleCoraliePacaut[(4)] 5 57
(Andrea Marcialis, France) **8/1**
4 ¾ **Vereny Ka (FR)**[48] 2-8-4 0 MlleFriedaValleSkar[(7)] 1 50
(C Lerner, France) **41/5**
5 1 **Birkie Queen (IRE)**[22] 2918 2-8-11 0 RonanThomas 2 47
(J S Moore) *chsd ldrs: lost pl 1/2-way: sn rdn and btn* **18/1**
6 snk **Carmague (IRE)**[15] 3171 2-8-13 0 (p) ThomasTrullier[(5)] 7 54
(J S Moore) *w ldrs: rdn and nt qckn 1 1/2f out: wknd fnl f* **22/5**[2]
7 2 ½ **Equinozio (IRE)**[11] 2-9-4 0 CristianDemuro 10 45
(A Giorgi, Italy) **5/1**[3]
8 1 ½ **Panthera Tigris**[27] 2757 2-8-8 0 (b) GeorgiaDobie[(3)] 6 33
(Jo Hughes, France) *towards rr: tk clsr order 1/2-way: sn rdn and btn* **15/1**
9 3 **Baie De Somme (FR)** 2-8-8 0 (p) BenjaminHubert 3 20
(P Monfort, France) **52/1**

1m 7.86s **9** Ran SP% **118.6**
PARI-MUTUEL (all including 1 euro stake): WIN 6.80; PLACE 2.20, 1.40, 2.50; DF 9.50.
Owner D Dahan, S Taieb & T Castanheira **Bred** Mlle J Castanheira & P Lamy **Trained** France

3715a PRIX VERRAZANO (CLAIMER) (4YO+) (TURF) 7f
7:27 4-Y-O+ £5,405 (£2,162; £1,621; £1,081; £540)

RPR
1 **Amadeus Wolfe Tone (IRE)**[40] 10-8-11 0 (b) JeromeClaudic 8 74
(Carina Fey, France) **77/10**
2 5 **Radja (FR)**[22] 4-9-8 0 (b) PierreBazire 6 71
(V Sartori, France) **47/10**[3]
3 1 **Surewecan**[21] 7-8-11 0 JeremieMonteiro 7 57
(Andrew Hollinshead, France) **20/1**
4 3 **Get Even**[21] 2956 4-8-11 0 GeorgiaDobie[(4)] 5 53
(Jo Hughes, France) *chsd ldr in gp of four on outside rail: returned to inner leaving bk st: chsd ldr and c stands' side st: sn rdn: dropped away ins fnl f* **29/10**[1]
5 2 ½ **Eva Glitters (FR)**[35] 4-8-13 0 JeffersonSmith 3 44
(P Demercastel, France) **16/1**
6 6 **Digicode (FR)**[35] 4-9-1 0 (p) BenjaminHubert 1 30
(P Monfort, France) **48/10**
7 2 ½ **Sant Angelo (GER)**[362] 5-8-11 0 MathieuPelletan 2 20
(S Smrczek, Germany) **16/5**[2]
8 3 **Royal Prize**[110] 9-9-2 0 GarySanchez 4 16
(Mme M Bollack-Badel, France) **68/10**

1m 23.27s **8** Ran SP% **119.2**
PARI-MUTUEL (all including 1 euro stake): WIN 8.70; PLACE 2.50, 2.10, 5.40; DF 20.30.
Owner Stall Allegra **Bred** Brian Williamson **Trained** France

3498 HAMILTON (R-H)
Wednesday, June 12

OFFICIAL GOING: Good (good to soft in places; 7.2)
Wind: Breezy, half against in sprints and in over 4f of home straight in races on the round course Weather: Overcast, dry

3716 RACINGTV.COM AMATEUR RIDERS' H'CAP 6f 6y
5:30 (5:35) (Class 6) (0-60,60) 4-Y-0+
£3,369 (£1,044; £522; £300; £300; £300) Stalls Centre

Form RPR
0222 1 **Queen Of Kalahari**[7] 3475 4-9-12 **47** (p[1]) MrJamesHarding[(3)] 8 53
(Les Eyre) *t.k.h: cl up centre: led 2f out: hrd pressed fnl f: hld on gamely nr fin* **7/1**[2]
-600 2 nk **Ventura Secret (IRE)**[15] 3177 5-10-2 **55** (t[1]) MissChloeDods[(7)] 9 60
(Michael Dods) *hld up in tch: hdwy in centre over 1f out: ev ch fnl f: kpt on but hld nr fin* **18/1**
5151 3 nk **Space War**[7] 3475 12-10-6 **52** (t) MissJoannaMason 5 56
(Michael Easterby) *chsd centre ldrs: rdn over 2f out: kpt on ins fnl f* **11/2**[1]
0050 4 nk **B Fifty Two (IRE)**[15] 3203 10-11-0 **60** (tp) MissBeckySmith 13 63
(Marjorie Fife) *bhd centre: rdn over 2f out: gd hdwy fnl f: nrst fin* **20/1**
0000 5 ½ **Havana Go**[14] 3227 4-10-6 **52** (b) MrsCarolBartley 15 54
(Keith Dalgleish) *bhd stands' side: rdn over 2f out: kpt on wl fnl f: nt rch centre ldrs* **22/1**
-030 6 ½ **My Valentino (IRE)**[21] 2964 6-10-1 **47** (p) MissEmmaSayer 4 47
(Dianne Sayer) *bhd centre: rdn over 2f out: hdwy over 1f out: hung rt ins fnl f: r.o: no imp* **16/1**
0020 7 ¾ **Letmestopyouthere (IRE)**[15] 3203 5-10-11 **57**(p) MissBrodieHampson 11 55
(Archie Watson) *cl up stands' side: drvn 2f out: edgd rt: one pce fnl f* **11/2**[1]
3300 8 nk **Chaplin Bay (IRE)**[15] 3178 7-10-3 **54** (b) MissEmilyBullock[(5)] 2 51
(Ruth Carr) *dwlt: bhd centre: hdwy on outside and cl up over 1f out: no ex ins fnl f* **7/1**[2]
3000 9 ½ **Middlescence (IRE)**[43] 2242 5-10-2 **55** (w) MrJoshuaScott[(7)] 3 51
(Lucinda Egerton) *w ldr to 2f out: drvn and outpcd fnl f* **20/1**
0600 10 nk **Thorntoun Lady (USA)**[21] 2958 9-9-7 **46** oh1. MissShannonWatts[(7)] 10 41
(Jim Goldie) *bhd towards centre: rdn over 2f out: hdwy over 1f out: nvr rchd ldrs* **50/1**
0110 11 5 **Magical Molly Joe**[9] 3430 5-10-5 **51** (h) MissCatherineWalton 12 31
(David Barron) *dwlt: bhd: effrt and swtchd rt 2f out: sn no imp: btn fnl f: bled fr nose* **9/1**
312 12 nk **La Cumparsita (IRE)**[52] 1967 5-9-13 **52** (t) MissRachelHuskisson[(7)] 6 31
(Tristan Davidson) *dwlt: t.k.h and sn chsng centre ldrs: rdn over 2f out: edgd lft and wknd over 1f out* **15/2**[3]
0006 13 1 ½ **Royal Connoisseur (IRE)**[15] 3203 8-10-2 **55**(v) MrEireannCagney[(7)] 14 29
(Richard Fahey) *cl up stands' side tl rdn and wknd over 1f out* **25/1**
0-00 14 hd **Wensley**[48] 2053 4-10-12 **58** (p) MissSerenaBrotherton 7 32
(Rebecca Bastiman) *led centre to 2f out: sn wknd* **14/1**
3320 15 3 ¼ **Dodgy Bob**[79] 1335 6-10-3 **49** (v) MissMichelleMullineaux 1 13
(Michael Mullineaux) *bhd in centre: outpcd and hung rt over 2f out: sn wknd* **28/1**

1m 13.22s (0.52) **Going Correction** 0.0s/f (Good) **15** Ran SP% **118.5**
Speed ratings (Par 101): **96,95,95,94,94 93,92,92,91,91 84,83,81,81,77**
CSF £110.04 CT £748.85 TOTE £6.70: £2.50, £6.90, £1.60; EX 168.70 Trifecta £983.50.
Owner Les Eyre Racing Partnership I **Bred** Minster Stud **Trained** Catwick, N Yorks

FOCUS
A modest amateur riders' handicap.

3717 AUDI ON DEMAND GLASGOW EBF MAIDEN AUCTION STKS (BB FOODSERVICE QUALIFIER) 5f 7y
6:00 (6:01) (Class 5) 2-Y-O £4,140 (£1,232; £615; £307) Stalls High

Form RPR
1 **Better The Devil (USA)** 2-9-5 0 BenCurtis 1 79+
(Archie Watson) *mde all: sn crossed to stands' rail: pushed along over 1f out: kpt on strly to draw clr ins fnl f* **4/1**[2]
2 2 2 ¾ **Spring Bloom**[23] 2903 2-9-5 0 AndrewMullen 4 69
(K R Burke) *dwlt: hld up in tch: hdwy on outside to press wnr over 2f out: drvn over 1f out: one pce fnl f* **6/4**[1]
3 1 ½ **Bubbly Splash (IRE)** 2-9-5 0 DanielTudhope 2 64
(David O'Meara) *dwlt: hld up: hdwy on outside and prom over 1f out: one pce ins fnl f: bttr for r* **9/2**[3]
6 4 1 ¼ **Pearlwood (IRE)**[23] 2906 2-8-9 0 SeanDavis[(5)] 3 54
(Richard Fahey) *prom: drvn and outpcd over 2f out: rallied ins fnl f: no imp* **20/1**
30 5 ¾ **Birdie Bowers (IRE)**[39] 2415 2-9-5 0 ConnorBeasley 5 56
(Michael Dods) *pressed wnr to over 2f out: hung rt and wknd over 1f out* **4/1**[2]
0 6 6 **Two Hearts**[46] 2115 2-9-5 0 SamJames 7 35
(Grant Tuer) *t.k.h: prom: rdn 2f out: sn wknd* **20/1**
00 7 7 **Moneyball**[13] 3245 2-8-7 0 HarryRussell[(7)] 8 5
(Keith Dalgleish) *s.i.s: t.k.h and sn in tch: struggling over 2f out: sn wknd* **40/1**

1m 1.11s (0.71) **Going Correction** 0.0s/f (Good) **7** Ran SP% **110.1**
Speed ratings (Par 93): **94,89,87,85,84 74,63**
CSF £9.60 TOTE £4.20: £1.90, £1.10; EX 11.20 Trifecta £34.90.
Owner Better The Devil **Bred** Two-Turn Farm Llc **Trained** Upper Lambourn, W Berks

FOCUS
A fair juvenile maiden sprint. One of the joint-second favourites broke much better than the favourite here on debut and made all in taking style after immediately tracking over to the stands' rail.

3718 WATCH RACING TV IN HD H'CAP 1m 3f 15y
6:30 (6:30) (Class 6) (0-65,65) 4-Y-0+
£3,493 (£1,039; £519; £300; £300; £300) Stalls High

Form RPR
0-01 1 **Hillgrove Angel (IRE)**[15] 3181 7-8-7 **58** CoreyMadden[(7)] 2 67+
(Jim Goldie) *hld up: smooth hdwy over 2f out: shkn up and led over 1f out: pricked ears ins fnl f: comf* **3/1**[1]
3401 2 1 ¼ **Sosian**[16] 3163 4-7-13 **48** (b) SeanDavis[(5)] 3 54
(Richard Fahey) *s.s: hld up: hdwy over 2f out: rdn and chsd wnr over 1f out: kpt on fnl f: nt pce to chal* **6/1**
6311 3 hd **Majeste**[12] 3296 5-9-7 **65** LewisEdmunds 9 71
(Rebecca Bastiman) *t.k.h early: hld up bhd ldng gp: hdwy over 2f out: rdn and outpcd over 1f out: edgd rt: kpt on ins fnl f* **11/2**[3]
00-0 4 2 **So You Thought (USA)**[15] 3209 5-9-3 **61** AndrewElliott 11 63
(Simon West) *led 1f: cl up: regained ld over 3f out: hdd over 1f out: no ex fnl f* **16/1**
00-6 5 ½ **Ninepin Bowler**[16] 3163 5-8-13 **57** JackGarritty 10 59
(Ann Duffield) *t.k.h early: chsd ldrs: rdn over 2f out: outpcd fnl f* **15/2**
3-50 6 shd **Can Can Sixty Two**[13] 3250 4-9-6 **64** BenCurtis 7 66
(R Mike Smith) *hld up: rdn over 2f out: hdwy over 1f out: nvr rchd ldrs* **25/1**
1303 7 3 ½ **Elite Icon**[6] 3500 5-8-3 **50** (v[1]) JaneElliott[(3)] 8 46
(Jim Goldie) *in tch: drvn and outpcd over 2f out: n.d after* **6/1**
5402 8 2 ½ **Seaborough (IRE)**[16] 3163 4-9-4 **62** (p) ConnorBeasley 1 54
(David Thompson) *hld up: outpcd 3f out: btn fnl 2f (regarding the performance, trainer could offer no explaantion)* **4/1**[2]
0-00 9 7 **Jock Talk (IRE)**[13] 3251 5-7-11 **46** oh1 AndrewBreslin[(5)] 4 27
(Patrick Morris) *t.k.h: led after 1f to over 3f out: rdn and wknd fnl 2f* **50/1**
0-00 10 nk **Morley Gunner (IRE)**[21] 2963 4-8-3 **47** oh1 ow1 (b[1]) AndrewMullen 6 27
(S Donohoe, Ire) *t.k.h: chsd ldrs tl rdn and wknd over 2f out* **40/1**

2m 24.57s (-0.93) **Going Correction** 0.0s/f (Good) **10** Ran SP% **114.8**
Speed ratings (Par 101): **103,102,101,100,100 100,97,95,90,90**
CSF £20.57 CT £93.65 TOTE £3.20: £1.40, £1.80, £2.00; EX 17.30 Trifecta £58.30.
Owner B Holohan **Bred** Carrigbeg Stud Co Ltd **Trained** Uplawmoor, E Renfrews
■ Stewards' Enquiry : Corey Madden caution: careless riding

FOCUS
15 yards added. A modest middle-distance handicap. The favourite won cosily from well off the pace.

3719 BOOK AN AUDI TODAY H'CAP 6f 6y
7:00 (7:03) (Class 4) (0-80,81) 3-Y-O
£8,021 (£2,387; £1,192; £596; £300; £300) Stalls Centre

Form RPR
1121 1 **Inspired Thought (IRE)**[15] 3202 3-9-9 **81** DanielTudhope 6 85+
(Archie Watson) *stdd in tch: smooth hdwy over 1f out: shkn up and qcknd to ld ins fnl f: rdn and hld on wl cl home* **7/4**[1]
0-54 2 nk **Jordan Electrics**[21] 2960 3-8-7 **68** ow3 (h) BenRobinson[(3)] 7 71
(Linda Perratt) *led: rdn along over 1f out: edgd lft and hdd ins fnl f: rallied: hld nr fin* **33/1**
5-13 3 nk **Gale Force Maya**[23] 2897 3-8-10 **68** GrahamLee 5 70
(Michael Dods) *prom: drvn and outpcd over 2f out: rallied over 1f out: kpt on fnl f: hld nr fin* **6/1**[3]
035- 4 1 ¼ **Zebzardee (IRE)**[272] 7224 3-8-7 **70** ConnorMurtagh[(5)] 4 68
(Richard Fahey) *hld up: pushed along over 2f out: hdwy over 1f out: kpt on fnl f: no imp* **20/1**
6-05 5 1 ½ **Constant**[7] 3479 3-9-9 **81** DavidNolan 1 74
(David O'Meara) *hld up: effrt over 2f out: outpcd fr over 1f out* **8/1**
3-64 6 1 ¼ **Princess Palliser (IRE)**[46] 2098 3-8-9 **67** JasonHart 8 56
(John Quinn) *t.k.h: chsd ldrs tl rdn and wknd over 1f out* **9/1**

-131 **7** *2* **Lady Calcaria**[12] [3293] 3-9-5 **77**........................ DuranFentiman 3 60
(Tim Easterby) *prom: rdn over 2f out: wknd over 1f out* **9/4**[2]

1m 12.17s (-0.53) **Going Correction** 0.0s/f (Good) 7 Ran SP% **110.2**
Speed ratings (Par 101): **103,102,102,100,98 96,94**
CSF £51.61 CT £268.85 TOTE £2.20: £1.40, £11.50; EX 42.10 Trifecta £229.60.
Owner Clipper Logistics **Bred** L Wright **Trained** Upper Lambourn, W Berks

FOCUS
A fair 3yo handicap. The winning filly, and favourite, dug deep once on the lead in the final furlong to narrowly defy top-weight in a good comparative time. The third has been rated to her Pontefract win.

3720 CAE TECHNOLOGY SERVICES HAMILTON H'CAP (DIV I) 1m 68y
7:30 (7:34) (Class 6) (0-60,62) 3-Y-O+

£3,493 (£1,039; £519; £300; £300; £300) **Stalls** Low

Form RPR
-603 **1** **Chinese Spirit (IRE)**[15] [3177] 5-9-9 **60**........................ BenRobinson(3) 2 67
(Linda Perratt) *in tch: squeezed through on ins to ld over 1f out: rdn and r.o wl fnl f* **11/1**
6-06 **2** *1/2* **Odds On Oli**[16] [3162] 4-9-3 **56**........................ ConnorMurtagh(5) 14 62
(Richard Fahey) *hld up: hdwy on outside over 2f out: sn rdn: chsd wnr ins fnl f: r.o* **12/1**
56-0 **3** *hd* **Blue Whisper**[21] [2964] 4-9-1 **49**........................(tp) PaulMulrennan 12 54
(S Donohoe, Ire) *t.k.h: hld up: effrt and swtchd lft over 1f out: rdn and kpt on wl fnl f: nrst fin* **40/1**
4632 **4** *1 1/4* **Lukoutoldmakezebak**[14] [3225] 6-8-12 **46**........................(p) BenCurtis 8 49
(David Thompson) *chsd ldrs: drvn along over 2f out: kpt on same pce ins fnl f* **13/2**[3]
0420 **5** *1* **Rebel State (IRE)**[1] [3704] 6-9-9 **57**........................(p) JackGarritty 13 58
(Jedd O'Keeffe) *hld up: outpcd over 3f out: rallied and swtchd lft over 1f out: kpt on fnl f: no imp* **7/1**
4323 **6** *3 1/4* **Milan Reef (IRE)**[1] [3682] 4-9-6 **54**........................ DanielTudhope 6 47
(David Loughnane) *led: rdn over 2f out: hdd over 1f out: wknd ins fnl f* **9/4**[1]
00-0 **7** *1/2* **Amy Blair**[70] [1527] 6-8-11 **50**........................ SeanDavis(5) 5 42
(Stef Keniry) *pressed ldr: drvn over 2f out: wknd fnl f* **16/1**
0040 **8** *5* **Quiet Moment (IRE)**[1] [3681] 5-8-7 **46** oh1........................(t) PaulaMuir(5) 1 27
(Maurice Barnes) *s.i.s: hld up: outpcd 3f out: no imp whn checked wl over 1f out* **20/1**
0-00 **9** *3 3/4* **Rebel Cause (IRE)**[19] [3046] 6-9-10 **58**........................ AndrewMullen 4 31
(John Holt) *hld up in tch: drvn and outpcd over 2f out: btn over 1f out* **11/1**
5545 **F** **Twiggy**[14] [3225] 5-8-9 **46** oh1........................(p[1]) ConorMcGovern(3) 7 48+
(Karen McLintock) *s.i.s: sn midfield: stdy hdwy to trck ldrs whn nt clr run over 2f out: cl 5th and stl looking for room whn clipped heels and fell wl over 1f out* **5/1**[2]
0000 **B** **Harperelle**[13] [3249] 3-8-5 **50**........................ JamesSullivan 3
(Alistair Whillans) *prom: drvn along 3f out: rallied: cl sixth and one pce whn bdly hmpd and b.d wl over 1f out* **28/1**

1m 48.01s (-0.39) **Going Correction** 0.0s/f (Good)
WFA 3 from 4yo+ 11lb 11 Ran SP% **114.2**
Speed ratings (Par 101): **101,100,100,99,98 94,94,89,85,**
CSF £121.99 CT £4409.48 TOTE £10.70: £3.10, £2.90, £13.20; EX 58.90 Trifecta £2614.30.
Owner Y C Luk & Miss L A Perratt **Bred** J Murphy **Trained** East Kilbride, S Lanarks
■ Kwanza was withdrawn. Price at time of withdrawal 12/1. Rule 4 applies to all bets - deduction 5p in the £.

FOCUS
15 yards added. The first division of a modest but eventful handicap.

3721 CAE TECHNOLOGY SERVICES HAMILTON H'CAP (DIV II) 1m 68y
8:00 (8:13) (Class 6) (0-60,60) 3-Y-O+

£3,493 (£1,039; £519; £300; £300; £300) **Stalls** Low

Form RPR
4020 **1** **Spirit Of Sarwan (IRE)**[1] [3681] 5-9-4 **57**........................(p) SeanDavis(5) 11 63
(Stef Keniry) *slowly away: bhd: rdn 1/2-way: hdwy on outside 2f out: sustained run fnl f to ld towards fin* **7/1**
0000 **2** *nk* **Poyle George Two**[15] [3177] 4-8-7 **46**........................ AndrewBreslin(5) 6 51
(John Hodge) *t.k.h: led 1f: chsd ldng pair: effrt over 2f out: led ins fnl f: edgd rt: hdd towards fin* **25/1**
0201 **3** *2* **Fitzy**[13] [3270] 3-8-12 **57**........................(p) CamHardie 4 55
(David Brown) *hld up: rdn 1/2-way: hdwy over 2f out: hdwy to chse ldng pair ins fnl f: r.o* **4/1**[1]
4656 **4** *2* **Be Bold**[30] [2682] 7-9-2 **50**........................(b) LewisEdmunds 8 47
(Rebecca Bastiman) *hld up: stdy hdwy 3f out: rdn 2f out: kpt on fnl f: no imp* **12/1**
0-60 **5** *3/4* **Fard**[14] [3215] 4-9-10 **58**........................ BenCurtis 3 53
(Roger Fell) *hld up on ins: hdwy over 2f out: effrt and hung lft over 1f out: sn no imp* **5/1**[2]
0464 **6** *hd* **Monsieur Piquer (FR)**[15] [3204] 3-8-8 **58**........................(v) HarrisonShaw(5) 2 49
(K R Burke) *plld hrd early: chsd ldr after 1f: effrt and led over 1f out to ins fnl f: sn wknd* **11/2**[3]
6400 **7** *1* **Restive (IRE)**[8] [3448] 6-9-5 **60**........................ CoreyMadden(7) 14 52
(Jim Goldie) *s.s: hld up: stdy hdwy on outside 2f out: kpt on fnl f: nvr nr ldrs* **10/1**
436- **8** *1 1/4* **Vicky Cristina (IRE)**[246] [8088] 4-8-12 **46** oh1........................ AndrewMullen 10 36
(John Holt) *prom: drvn along 3f out: wknd over 1f out* **16/1**
0500 **9** *2* **Dasheen**[14] [3215] 6-9-8 **59**........................(v) GemmaTutty(3) 13 45
(Karen Tutty) *in tch: drvn along 3f out: outpcd whn hmpd over 1f out: wknd* **20/1**
040 **10** *2* **Lizzie Loch**[103] [971] 3-8-9 **54**........................ GrahamLee 5 32
(Alistair Whillans) *t.k.h in midfield: struggling 3f out: btn fnl 2f* **25/1**
-300 **11** *1* **Crazy Tornado (IRE)**[15] [3177] 6-9-8 **56**........................ ShaneGray 12 35
(Keith Dalgleish) *t.k.h: led after 1f: clr bef 1/2-way: rdn and hdd over 1f out: sn wknd* **7/1**
050 **12** *4* **Gloryella**[15] [3200] 3-8-1 **46** oh1........................ JamesSullivan 9 13
(Ruth Carr) *hld up in midfield: struggling over 3f out: sn btn* **66/1**
000- **13** *23* **Dark Crystal**[244] [8133] 8-9-4 **55**........................ BenRobinson(3) 7
(Linda Perratt) *hld up: rdn and outpcd 1/2-way: sn struggling: t.o (jockey said mare hung right)* **40/1**

1m 48.27s (-0.13) **Going Correction** 0.0s/f (Good)
WFA 3 from 4yo+ 11lb 13 Ran SP% **116.1**
Speed ratings (Par 101): **100,99,97,95,94 94,93,92,90,88 87,83,60**
CSF £175.92 CT £817.16 TOTE £8.70: £2.40, £7.50, £1.40; EX 141.10 Trifecta £670.10.
Owner Mrs Stef Keniry **Bred** John Fallon **Trained** Middleham, N Yorks

FOCUS
15 yards added. The second division of a modest handicap. The winning time was marginally slower.

3722 DRIVE THE AUDI YOU BOOK H'CAP 6f 6y
8:30 (8:36) (Class 4) (0-80,87) 4-Y-O+

£8,021 (£2,387; £1,192; £596; £300; £300) **Stalls** Centre

Form RPR
0-01 **1** **Air Raid**[6] [3503] 4-10-6 **87** 5ex........................ JackGarritty 5 101+
(Jedd O'Keeffe) *mde all: shkn up over 1f out: pushed clr ins fnl f: unchal* **8/11**[1]
-200 **2** *2 3/4* **Inexes**[15] [3207] 7-9-1 **68**........................(p) JasonHart 1 71
(Ivan Furtado) *t.k.h: in tch: effrt and edgd lft over 1f out: kpt on fnl f to take 2nd towards fin: no ch w wnr* **14/1**
0-20 **3** *hd* **Cale Lane**[23] [2893] 4-9-5 **72**........................ GrahamLee 7 74
(Julie Camacho) *chsd wnr: effrt over 1f out: hung rt ins fnl f: sn no ex: lost 2nd cl home* **11/1**[3]
-216 **4** *2* **Global Spirit**[1] [3706] 4-9-6 **73**........................ BenCurtis 2 69
(Roger Fell) *chsd ldrs: rdn over 2f out: edgd rt over 1f out: sn outpcd* **5/2**[2]
0-20 **5** *2* **Final Go**[23] [2893] 4-9-7 **74**........................ SamJames 6 64
(Grant Tuer) *t.k.h: prom: rdn 2f out: wkng whn hung lft ins fnl f* **16/1**
000- **6** *6* **Yes You (IRE)**[225] [8719] 5-9-11 **81**........................ ConorMcGovern(3) 3 51
(Iain Jardine) *hld up in tch: pushed along over 2f out: wknd over 1f out* **40/1**

1m 12.22s (-0.48) **Going Correction** 0.0s/f (Good) 6 Ran SP% **109.8**
Speed ratings (Par 105): **103,99,99,96,93 85**
CSF £12.17 TOTE £1.90: £1.10, £5.50; EX 9.80 Trifecta £63.00.
Owner Caron & Paul Chapman **Bred** Meon Valley Stud **Trained** Middleham Moor, N Yorks

FOCUS
The feature contest was a fairly decent sprint handicap. The odds-on favourite proved far too good from the front. The winner has been rated similar to his recent win, and the third close to form.

3723 EVERY RACE LIVE ON RACING TV H'CAP 5f 7y
9:00 (9:00) (Class 6) (0-55,55) 4-Y-O+

£3,493 (£1,039; £519; £300; £300; £300) **Stalls** Centre

Form RPR
0353 **1** **Groundworker (IRE)**[14] [3213] 8-9-0 **48**........................ PaulMulrennan 3 56
(Paul Midgley) *prom: hdwy to ld over 1f out: edgd lft: pushed out fnl f: comf* **7/1**
-663 **2** *1 1/4* **The Bull (IRE)**[14] [3227] 4-9-5 **53**........................(v[1]) AndrewMullen 6 57+
(Ben Haslam) *dwlt: bhd: rdn and hdwy over 1f out: chsd wnr last 50yds: r.o* **3/1**[1]
0400 **3** *1 1/4* **Camanche Grey (IRE)**[4] [3592] 8-8-8 **49**........................ VictorSantos(7) 13 48
(Lucinda Egerton) *in tch: drvn along over 2f out: rallied fnl f: kpt on* **25/1**
00-5 **4** *shd* **I'll Be Good**[33] [2576] 10-8-12 **51**........................ ConnorMurtagh(5) 11 50
(Alan Berry) *w ldr: led briefly over 1f out: kpt on same pce ins fnl f* **33/1**
2260 **5** *nse* **Someone Exciting**[9] [3413] 6-9-0 **53**........................ HarrisonShaw(5) 1 51
(David Thompson) *bhd: hdwy on outside 2f out: kpt on ins fnl f: no imp* **4/1**[2]
0304 **6** *1/2* **Leeshaan (IRE)**[12] [3291] 4-9-0 **48**........................ LewisEdmunds 9 45
(Rebecca Bastiman) *hld up towards rr: rdn and hdwy over 1f out: edgd rt ins fnl f: nt pce to chal* **8/1**
-500 **7** *3 3/4* **Corton Lass**[26] [2789] 4-8-12 **46** oh1........................ ShaneGray 14 29+
(Keith Dalgleish) *racd stands' side: in tch: rdn over 2f out: wknd over 1f out* **33/1**
0503 **8** *1/2* **Racquet**[6] [3518] 6-8-12 **46**........................(p) JamesSullivan 2 27
(Ruth Carr) *prom: drvn over 2f out: effrt over 1f out: wknd ins fnl f* **5/1**[3]
-133 **9** *1 3/4* **Encoded (IRE)**[138] [411] 6-8-11 **48**........................ ConorMcGovern(3) 10 23
(Lynn Siddall) *dwlt: hld up: rdn over 2f out: wknd wl over 1f out* **28/1**
0160 **10** *1/2* **Star Cracker (IRE)**[14] [3227] 7-8-11 **48**........................(p) BenRobinson(3) 4 21
(Jim Goldie) *fly-jmpd s and sn checked: a outpcd and bhd* **14/1**
0-00 **11** *1 1/4* **Minty Jones**[12] [3291] 10-8-5 **46** oh1........................(v) IzzyClifton(7) 12 15+
(Michael Mullineaux) *dwlt: sn pushed along towards stands' side: nvr on terms* **50/1**
4006 **12** *nk* **One Boy (IRE)**[14] [3213] 8-9-7 **55**........................(b) GrahamLee 7 23
(Paul Midgley) *slt ld to over 1f out: sn wknd (jockey said gelding stopped quickly)* **6/1**

1m 0.39s (-0.01) **Going Correction** 0.0s/f (Good) 12 Ran SP% **121.4**
Speed ratings (Par 101): **100,98,96,95,95 94,88,88,85,84 82,82**
CSF £27.64 CT £522.64 TOTE £7.30: £2.50, £1.60, £6.40; EX 40.80 Trifecta £983.30.
Owner Blackburn Family **Bred** Knockainey Stud **Trained** Westow, N Yorks

FOCUS
A moderate sprint handicap.
T/Plt: £69.40 to a £1 stake. Pool: £46,402.50 - 487.90 winning units T/Qpdt: £37.70 to a £1 stake. Pool: £9,224.93 - 180.78 winning units **Richard Young**

3585 HAYDOCK (L-H)
Wednesday, June 12

OFFICIAL GOING: Heavy (6.3)
Wind: Nil Weather: Overcast

3724 RACING TO SCHOOL NOVICE STKS (PLUS 10 RACE) 1m 3f 175y
2:20 (2:24) (Class 4) 3-Y-O **£6,469** (£1,925; £962; £481) **Stalls** Low

Form RPR
4 **1** **Grenadier Guard (IRE)**[7] [3482] 3-9-5 0........................ FrannyNorton 3 79
(Mark Johnston) *led narrowly: hdd 7f out: remained w ldr: rdn to regain ld 2f out: kpt on wl fnl f* **7/2**[2]
3- **2** *1/2* **Navajo Pass**[249] [7987] 3-9-5 0........................ DavidNolan 2 78
(Donald McCain) *racd keenly in tch: rdn and nt clr run 2f out: sn swtchd rt: tried to chal ins fnl f: styd on towards fin* **25/1**
3 **3** *1 1/4* **Swift Wing**[33] [2566] 3-9-5 0........................ RobertHavlin 7 76
(John Gosden) *trckd ldrs: shkn up 3f out: chalng 2f out: hung lft over 1f out: no ex fnl 75yds* **8/15**[1]
04 **4** *7* **Geomatrician (FR)**[26] [2795] 3-9-5 0........................ DavidProbert 4 65
(Andrew Balding) *chsd ldrs: rdn 2f out: sn lost pl: hung lft and one pce ins fnl f* **6/1**[3]
50 **5** *2 1/4* **Vintage Rose**[5] [3553] 3-9-0 0........................ KevinStott 5 56
(Mark Walford) *hld up: rdn over 1f out: nvr able to trble ldrs* **66/1**
-4 **6** *1/2* **Sweet Dreamer**[13] [3266] 3-9-0 0........................ CliffordLee 1 55
(K R Burke) *w ldr: led 7f out: rdn and hdd 2f out: wknd fnl f* **50/1**

The Form Book Flat 2019, Raceform Ltd, Newbury, RG14 5SJ

7 12 **Ezzrah** 3-9-5 0 ... DougieCostello 6 41
(Mark Walford) *towards rr: niggled along over 6f out: outpcd over 4f out: lft bhd fnl 3f* 66/1

2m 41.44s (8.14) **Going Correction** +0.65s/f (Yiel) 7 Ran SP% 110.5
Speed ratings (Par 101): **98,97,96,92,90 90,82**
CSF £59.68 TOTE £3.10: £1.20, £4.20; EX 61.10 Trifecta £94.10.
Owner J Barson **Bred** Paget Bloodstock **Trained** Middleham Moor, N Yorks

FOCUS
Due to the ground, the meeting was switched at late notice to the stands' side home straight. This, plus rail movements, meant the actual distance of the opener was 1m 3f 160yds. This was a decent novice event in which three finished clear. They raced in the centre in the straight, keeping away from the inside rail. After riding in the first, Franny Norton said of the ground: "It's tough but they're getting through it." David Nolan called it heavy. The winner has been rated to his debut form.

3725 BRITISH STALLION STUDS EBF FILLIES' NOVICE STKS (PLUS 10 RACE) 6f
2:50 (2:50) (Class 4) 2-Y-0 **£4,851** (£1,443; £721) **Stalls** High

Form RPR
1 **Ursulina (IRE)** 2-9-0 0 ... RichardKingscote 2 76+
(Tom Dascombe) *chsd ldr: rdn over 2f out: sltly intimidated by rival and carried lft over 1f out: sn led: stretched clr ins fnl 100yds: r.o wl* 10/11[1]
2 4 **Woke (IRE)** 2-9-0 0 ... CliffordLee 3 64
(K R Burke) *led: rdn over 2f out: hung lft over 1f out: sn hdd: no ch w wnr fnl 100yds* 2/1[2]
3 1 1/4 **It's Not My Fault (IRE)** 2-8-11 0 ... JaneElliott[(3)] 1 60
(Tom Dascombe) *dwlt and wnt lft: in rr: pushed along 2f out: outpcd over 1f out: nvr a threat* 7/2[3]

1m 19.9s (6.00) **Going Correction** +0.65s/f (Yiel) 3 Ran SP% 107.9
Speed ratings (Par 92): **86,80,79**
CSF £2.99 TOTE £1.20; EX 2.10 Trifecta £2.90.
Owner Chasemore Farm **Bred** R O'Callaghan And D Veitch **Trained** Malpas, Cheshire

FOCUS
Only three runners, all newcomers, and two of them from the same stable. It was just under 10sec slower than standard and it's not easy to quantify the form, but the winner looks useful. A token figure has been given.

3726 PARETO FINANCIAL PLANNING H'CAP 1m 2f 100y
3:20 (3:21) (Class 3) (0-95,95) 4-Y-0+ **£10,997** (£3,272; £1,635; £817) **Stalls** Low

Form RPR
1-30 1 **Hulcote**[20] 3010 4-8-8 82 ... HollieDoyle 13 93
(Clive Cox) *midfield: hdwy over 2f out: led over 1f out: kpt on wl towards fin* 11/2[2]
413- 2 3/4 **Thistimenextyear**[32] 8649 5-8-11 85 ... HarryBentley 3 95
(Richard Spencer) *midfield: hdwy over 3f out: led over 2f out: rdn and hdd over 1f out: stl ev ch ins fnl f: hld towards fin* 4/1[1]
5100 3 2 1/2 **Lunar Jet**[4] 3605 5-9-6 94 ... JimmyQuinn 8 99
(John Mackie) *hld up: hmpd after 1f: n.m.r over 2f out: rdn and hdwy after: chsd ldrs over 1f out: styd on ins fnl f: nvr able to rch front two* 7/1[3]
0-04 4 1 1/2 **Falmouth Light (FR)**[6] 3502 4-8-5 79 ... (h) CamHardie 2 81
(Iain Jardine) *hld up: hdwy over 2f out: chsd ldrs over 1f out: styd on same pce fnl 100yds* 20/1
13-0 5 4 1/2 **Awake My Soul (IRE)**[46] 2095 10-9-6 94 ... JamesSullivan 4 88
(Tom Tate) *led: rdn and hdd over 2f out: outpcd over 1f out: kpt on ins fnl f* 11/1
40-4 6 3/4 **Zzoro (IRE)**[37] 2486 6-8-4 78 ... RoystonFfrench 12 70
(Amanda Perrett) *chsd ldr: rdn and ev ch over 2f out: no ex fnl f* 16/1
6053 7 4 **Dark Red (IRE)**[20] 3005 7-9-4 92 ... FrannyNorton 7 77
(Ed Dunlop) *midfield: lost pl 3f out: rdn over 2f out: plugged on fr over 1f out: nvr a threat* 8/1
0-45 8 3 1/4 **Lorelina**[12] 3315 6-9-6 94 ... DavidProbert 10 72
(Andrew Balding) *chsd ldrs: rdn over 2f out: sn lost pl: hung lft whn wkng over 1f out* 4/1[1]
30-0 9 9 **Daawy (IRE)**[54] 1927 5-9-0 88 ... (p) PaulHanagan 6 49
(Roger Fell) *midfield: rdn over 2f out: sn btn* 12/1
15-0 10 14 **Morning Wonder (IRE)**[26] 2786 4-9-4 92 ... KevinStott 5 27
(Kevin Ryan) *chsd ldrs tl rdn and wknd over 2f out* 10/1
162/ 11 36 **Indy (IRE)**[620] 7627 8-8-8 82 ... NathanEvans 11
(John Quinn) *shuffled bk after 1f: racd on outer: rdn and outpcd 4f out: lft bhd fnl 3f* 40/1

2m 18.58s (1.98) **Going Correction** +0.65s/f (Yiel) 11 Ran SP% 117.2
Speed ratings (Par 107): **114,113,111,110,106 106,102,100,93,81 53**
CSF £27.65 CT £157.59 TOTE £7.40: £2.70, £2.10, £1.70; EX 35.70 Trifecta £229.20.
Owner The Kathryn Stud **Bred** The Kathryn Stud **Trained** Lambourn, Berks

FOCUS
Actual race distance 1m 2f 83yds. Quite a useful standard in this handicap. Once more they came down the middle in the home straight. It's been rated around the solid third.

3727 WATCH RACING TV NOW NOVICE STKS (PLUS 10 RACE) 1m 37y
3:50 (3:50) (Class 4) 3-Y-0 **£6,469** (£1,925; £962) **Stalls** Low

Form RPR
2-1 1 **Tempus**[36] 2518 3-9-8 0 ... JasonWatson 1 83+
(Roger Charlton) *mde all: rdn over 2f out: fnd more over 1f out: styd on wl fnl f* 4/11[1]
24-2 2 1 1/4 **Lyndon B (IRE)**[46] 2094 3-9-2 82 ... HarryBentley 2 72+
(George Scott) *chsd wnr most of way: shkn up over 3f out: rdn and ev ch over 2f out: no imp over 1f out: kpt on towards fin* 5/2[2]
00 3 1 1/2 **Power Player**[32] 2634 3-9-2 0 ... CliffordLee 3 69
(K R Burke) *broke wl: sn stdd: racd keenly: mainly disp 2nd: chsd wnr over 4f out: rdn and ev ch over 2f out: unable qck over 1f out: styd on same pce ins fnl f* 33/1[3]

1m 50.48s (5.58) **Going Correction** +0.65s/f (Yiel) 3 Ran SP% 104.8
Speed ratings (Par 101): **98,96,95**
CSF £1.47 TOTE £1.80; EX 1.40 Trifecta £1.20.
Owner K Abdullah **Bred** Juddmonte Farms Ltd **Trained** Beckhampton, Wilts

FOCUS
Actual race distance 1m 20yds. They came down the centre again. An interesting little novice event, but it was steadily run and the proximity of the third could be used to hold down the form. The first two have been rated below form.

3728 RACINGTV.COM H'CAP 1m 37y
4:20 (4:20) (Class 3) (0-95,91) 3-Y-0 **£10,997** (£3,272; £1,635; £817) **Stalls** Low

Form RPR
4021 1 **Global Gift (FR)**[13] 3249 3-8-11 81 ... (h) GeraldMosse 1 87
(Ed Dunlop) *chsd ldrs: wnt 2nd over 2f out: rdn and swtchd rt over 1f out: led ins fnl f: pushed out towards fin* 3/1[3]
-102 2 1 1/2 **Zip**[4] 3591 3-8-4 74 ... RoystonFfrench 2 76
(Richard Fahey) *in rr: rdn and outpcd over 2f out: styd on ins fnl f: tk 2nd towards fin but nt trble wnr* 6/4[1]
1110 3 hd **Oasis Prince**[18] 3082 3-9-7 91 ... FrannyNorton 3 93
(Mark Johnston) *chsd ldr: pushed along 3f out: rdn and lost pl over 2f out: outpcd over 1f out: rallied fnl 110yds: styd on* 9/4[2]
3-10 4 1/2 **Divinity**[26] 2806 3-9-6 90 ... CliffordLee 5 90
(K R Burke) *led: rdn over 2f out: hdd ins fnl f: no ex fnl 75yds* 13/2

1m 48.21s (3.31) **Going Correction** +0.65s/f (Yiel) 4 Ran SP% 109.1
Speed ratings (Par 103): **109,107,107,106**
CSF £7.95 TOTE £4.20; EX 6.80 Trifecta £16.40.
Owner Dr Johnny Hon **Bred** Ecurie Des Monceaux, Lordship Stud Et Al **Trained** Newmarket, Suffolk

FOCUS
Actual race distance 1m 20yds. This fair handicap appeared to be more truly run than most races on the card and was 2.7sec quicker than the preceding novice event. This time they stayed up the inside in the straight. The second and third have been rated close to form.

3729 JOIN RACING TV NOW H'CAP 1m 6f
4:50 (4:50) (Class 4) (0-85,86) 3-Y-0
£9,703 (£2,887; £1,443; £721; £300; £300) **Stalls** Low

Form RPR
-111 1 **Moon King (FR)**[7] 3474 3-9-1 76 6ex ... HarryBentley 4 85+
(Ralph Beckett) *hld up towards rr: rdn and hdwy over 2f out: led wl over 1f out: styd on wl: eased cl home* 11/10[1]
6533 2 1/2 **Tidal Point (IRE)**[13] 3260 3-8-11 72 ... RoystonFfrench 5 77
(Steph Hollinshead) *in tch: effrt over 2f out: styd on to take 2nd wl ins fnl f: clsd on wnr towards fin (flattered) (jockey said gelding hung left-handed in the home straight)* 10/1
1334 3 2 **Rochester House (IRE)**[11] 3358 3-9-7 82 ... FrannyNorton 3 84
(Mark Johnston) *chsd ldr: rdn to ld 2f out: sn hdd: no imp on wnr ins fnl f: lost 2nd: styd on same pce* 6/1[2]
55-6 4 5 **Divine Gift (IRE)**[34] 2562 3-9-11 86 ... RichardKingscote 2 81
(Charlie Fellowes) *led: rdn over 2f out: sn hdd: btn over 1f out: wkng whn hung lft ins fnl f* 7/1[3]
1435 5 14 **Seeusoon (IRE)**[13] 3260 3-8-11 72 ... DavidProbert 6 48
(Andrew Balding) *hld up: rdn over 2f out: no imp* 7/1[3]
2-41 6 14 **Dorah**[16] 3153 3-9-7 82 ... EdwardGreatrex 1 38
(Archie Watson) *chsd ldrs: rdn and ev ch over 2f out: sn wknd (jockey said filly stopped quickly)* 8/1
04-2 7 15 **No Dress Rehearsal**[15] 3200 3-8-11 72 ... NathanEvans 7 7
(Michael Easterby) *in tch on outer: rdn and lost pl 4f out: lft bhd over 2f out (jockey said filly stopped quickly)* 25/1

3m 12.34s (7.74) **Going Correction** +0.65s/f (Yiel) 7 Ran SP% 111.0
Speed ratings (Par 101): **103,102,101,98,90 82,74**
CSF £12.33 TOTE £2.30: £1.30, £4.20; EX 10.70 Trifecta £56.50.
Owner What Asham Partnership **Bred** Rashit Shaykhutdinov **Trained** Kimpton, Hants

FOCUS
Actual race distance 1m 5f 209yds. Comfortable for the favourite in this decent staying handicap, and a 1-2 for the stallion Sea The Moon. Another step forward from the winner, with the third rated a bit below his York form.

3730 HAYDOCK PARK APPRENTICE TRAINING SERIES H'CAP (PART OF THE RACING EXCELLENCE INITIATIVE) 1m 37y
5:20 (5:23) (Class 5) (0-70,71) 4-Y-0+
£4,851 (£1,443; £721; £360; £300; £300) **Stalls** Low

Form RPR
2120 1 **Zodiakos (IRE)**[15] 3199 6-9-13 71 ... (p) TristanPrice[(3)] 4 77
(Roger Fell) *stdd s: hld up in rr: hdwy 3f out: led over 2f out: edgd lft 1f out: kpt on ins fnl f* 7/2[2]
6623 2 1/2 **Snooker Jim**[12] 3325 4-8-12 53 ... (t) TobyEley 1 57
(Steph Hollinshead) *in tch: rdn and ev ch over 2f out: unable qck over 1f out: styd on towards fin* 9/4[1]
112 3 1/2 **Atalanta Queen**[15] 3208 4-8-11 52 ... (v) AledBeech 3 55
(Robyn Brisland) *chsd ldr: led over 2f out: sn rdn and hdd: kpt on u.p ins fnl f but hld* 9/1[3]
2300 4 2 1/4 **Adventureman**[22] 2944 7-8-11 55 ... (b) EllaMcCain[(3)] 9 53
(Ruth Carr) *led: rdn and hdd over 2f out: styd on same pce ins fnl f* 20/1
00-0 5 1 **Magic Ship (IRE)**[45] 2146 4-8-4 48 oh3 ... CianMacRedmond[(5)] 2 43
(John Norton) *in tch: effrt on far rail over 2f out: one pce fnl f* 25/1
0-00 6 6 **Lagenda**[21] 2964 6-9-7 62 ... (v[1]) JonathanFisher 7 44
(Liam Bailey) *hld up: pushed along 3f out: rdn over 2f out: outpcd over 1f out* 10/1
-200 7 10 **Captain Peaky**[21] 2963 6-8-0 48 oh3 ... (p) OwenPayton[(7)] 8 7
(Liam Bailey) *plld hrd: hdwy to sn go prom: rdn and wknd over 2f out* 12/1

1m 50.21s (5.31) **Going Correction** +0.65s/f (Yiel) 7 Ran SP% 88.4
Speed ratings (Par 103): **99,98,98,95,94 88,78**
CSF £6.95 CT £22.77 TOTE £3.50: £1.60, £1.40; EX 7.70 Trifecta £19.70.
Owner C Varley & R G Fell **Bred** Brian Walsh **Trained** Nawton, N Yorks
■ Beatbybeatbybeat was withdrawn. Price at time of withdrawal 11/4. Rule 4 applies to all bets - deduction 25p in the £.

FOCUS
Actual race distance 1m 20yds. A very modest event for apprentices who, before the weekend, hadn't ridden more than ten winners under rules. This time they stayed more on the inside in the straight. The second has been rated to his Nottingham form.
T/Plt: £418.30 to a £1 stake. Pool: £46,526.82 - 81.18 winning units T/Qpdt: £21.00 to a £1 stake. Pool: £6,754.25 - 167.00 winning units **Darren Owen**

3461 KEMPTON (A.W) (R-H)
Wednesday, June 12

3731 Meeting Abandoned - burst water main

[3273]YARMOUTH (L-H)
Wednesday, June 12

OFFICIAL GOING: Soft changing to heavy after race 3 (3.00)
Wind: breezy Weather: raining; 14 degrees

3738 MANSIONBET BEATEN BY A HEAD H'CAP 6f 3y
2:00 (2:01) (Class 6) (0-55,55) 4-Y-0+
£3,105 (£924; £461; £300; £300; £300) **Stalls** Centre

Form RPR
30-5 1 **Napping**[153] 159 6-9-3 **54**........ GabrieleMalune(3) 15 62
(Amy Murphy) *prom: led 2f out: pushed along and hld on wl fnl f* **12/1**
-431 2 ¾ **Viking Way (IRE)**[7] 3476 4-9-1 **49**........(b) JackMitchell 13 55
(Olly Williams) *t.k.h: chsd ldrs: rdn 2f out: chsd wnr over 1f out: ev ch 100yds out: no imp after (vet said gelding lost its right fore shoe)* **4/1**[2]
0-00 3 3 **Good Business (IRE)**[20] 3001 5-9-2 **55**........(b) DylanHogan(5) 7 52
(Henry Spiller) *t.k.h towards rr: effrt 1/2-way: rdn and chsng ldng pair over 1f out: a hld after* **33/1**
-055 4 ¾ **Cliff (IRE)**[7] 3475 9-9-0 **53**........ FayeMcManoman(5) 2 48+
(Nigel Tinkler) *bhd: disputing last over 2f out: pushed along and kpt on wl after: snatched 4th: given too much to do* **10/3**[1]
6054 5 nse **Hello Girl**[16] 3143 4-9-1 **52**........ RowanScott(3) 8 46
(Nigel Tinkler) *t.k.h and cl up: rdn and outpcd by ldng pair 1f out: lost 4th fnl stride* **6/1**[3]
0045 6 1 **Dubai Elegance**[9] 3425 5-9-0 **48**........(p) TomEaves 14 39
(Derek Shaw) *stdd and lost 7 l s: rdn and sme prog over 1f out: nvr looked like chalng* **25/1**
4433 7 1¾ **Catapult**[15] 3208 4-8-11 **52**........(p) GavinAshton(7) 10 38
(Shaun Keightley) *led and t.k.h: drvn and hdd 2f out: wknd ins fnl f (jockey said gelding was struck into on its right hind)* **15/2**
5126 8 3¼ **Poppy May (IRE)**[16] 3143 5-9-5 **53**........ BarryMcHugh 3 29
(James Given) *a towards rr: btn 2f out* **10/1**
3060 9 2¾ **Haader (FR)**[12] 3304 4-9-5 **53**........ PaddyMathers 6 21
(Derek Shaw) *wnt to post v early and lost a shoe on the way: lost 6 l s: a bhd: drvn and struggling 1/2-way* **16/1**
0-00 10 5 **Out Of The Ashes**[43] 2235 6-8-9 **48**........(bt) SeamusCronin(5) 16
(Mohamed Moubarak) *prom: drvn 1/2-way: lost pl rapidly 2f out: t.o and eased* **33/1**
5650 11 nk **Mother Of Dragons (IRE)**[7] 3476 4-9-2 **50**........(v) RossaRyan 4 2
(Phil McEntee) *drvn and floundering 1/2-way: t.o (jockey said filly was never travelling; trainer said that the mare was unsuited by the Soft ground on this occasion and would prefer a quicker surface)* **10/1**
0-40 12 1½ **Praxedis**[33] 2580 4-9-6 **54**........ GeorgeWood 11 2
(James Fanshawe) *drvn 1/2-way: sn floundering: t.o and virtually p.u nr fin* **10/1**

1m 14.04s (1.44) **Going Correction** +0.475s/f (Yiel) **12 Ran SP% 119.7**
Speed ratings (Par 101): **109,108,104,103,102 101,99,94,91,84 84,82**
CSF £59.12 CT £1584.76 TOTE £11.10: £2.80, £1.50, £9.20; EX 76.20 Trifecta £1076.10.
Owner Eclipse Sports Racing Club **Bred** Aiden Murphy **Trained** Newmarket, Suffolk

FOCUS
The raced centre-field in what was a weak sprint.

3739 BRITISH STALLION STUDS EBF MAIDEN STKS (PLUS 10 RACE) 5f 42y
2:30 (2:31) (Class 4) 2-Y-0
£5,175 (£1,540; £769; £384) **Stalls** Centre

Form RPR
3 1 **Tom Tulliver**[10] 3371 2-9-0 0........ TomEaves 8 75
(Declan Carroll) *prom and travelled strly: led 1/2-way: drvn and hrd pressed by two rivals fnl f: hld on gamely* **9/4**[1]
0 2 nk **Lincoln Blue**[15] 3190 2-9-0 0........ JFEgan 5 74
(Jane Chapple-Hyam) *prom: drvn and sustained chal fnl f: edgd rt and hld cl home* **16/1**
5 3 shd **Otago**[15] 3194 2-9-0 0........ RyanMoore 4 74
(Michael Bell) *trckd ldrs: rdn and effrt over 1f out: ev ch fnl 100yds: jst hld* **10/3**[3]
4 2¼ **Flowing Magic (IRE)** 2-9-0 0........(t[1]) PatCosgrave 1 65
(George Scott) *bhd: effrt 2f out: rdn and outpcd by ldng trio fnl f* **7/1**
5 3 **Interrupted Dream** 2-9-0 0........ PJMcDonald 7 55
(Mark Johnston) *chsd ldrs: rdn and btn 2f out* **11/4**[2]
40 6 5 **Dark Side Division**[21] 2973 2-9-0 0........ BrettDoyle 6 37
(John Ryan) *led tl 1/2-way: rdn and lost pl rapidly* **20/1**
7 6 **Mr Bowjangles** 2-9-0 0........ TomQueally 2 15
(Gay Kelleway) *chsd ldrs: rdn and btn 2f out* **10/1**
8 11 **Dark Side Prince** 2-9-0 0........ RossaRyan 3
(Charlie Wallis) *lost 10 l s: drvn 1/2-way: t.o and eased* **28/1**

1m 4.43s (2.53) **Going Correction** +0.475s/f (Yiel) **8 Ran SP% 116.2**
Speed ratings (Par 95): **98,97,97,93,88 80,71,53**
CSF £40.30 TOTE £2.90: £1.10, £4.00, £1.50; EX 41.40 Trifecta £141.90.
Owner F Gillespie **Bred** Biddestone Stud Ltd **Trained** Malton, N Yorks

FOCUS
Ordinary juvenile form. They again raced down the centre.

3740 DOWNLOAD THE MANSIONBET APP H'CAP 1m 3f 104y
3:00 (3:01) (Class 6) (0-55,55) 4-Y-0+
£3,105 (£924; £461; £300; £300; £300) **Stalls** Low

Form RPR
60-0 1 **Kaylen's Mischief**[15] 3205 6-8-12 **46** oh1........ JFEgan 6 55
(D J Jeffreys) *mde all: rdn and edging rt fr over 2f out: hrd pressed ins fnl f: plld out ex last 100yds: gamely (trainer said that the gelding had appreciated the slower ground, which was officially described as Soft on this occasion)* **12/1**
3022 2 1½ **Mistress Nellie**[13] 3252 4-8-10 **47**........ GabrieleMalune(3) 8 54
(William Stone) *t.k.h in rr and given plenty to do: stl last home turn: pushed along and hdwy up centre fr over 2f out: wnt 2nd 1f out: threatened briefly: no ex fnl 100yds* **3/1**[1]
0053 3 2¾ **Seventii**[13] 3252 5-8-7 **46** oh1........ DarraghKeenan(5) 13 48
(Robert Eddery) *midfield: prog gng strly 4f out: rdn to chal over 1f out: wknd ins fnl f* **5/1**[2]
00-4 4 1¼ **Misty Breese (IRE)**[21] 2975 4-8-9 **46** oh1........ NoelGarbutt(3) 3 46
(Sarah Hollinshead) *dwlt and pushed along in rr: prog on far rails 3f out: chsd ldrs over 1f out: rdn and no imp after* **16/1**
06-0 5 1¾ **Sir Fred (IRE)**[21] 2974 4-8-5 **46**........ SophieRalston(7) 9 43
(Julia Feilden) *towards rr: hdwy fnl 2f: pushed along and kpt on ins fnl f: nvr threatened* **11/2**[3]
4005 6 4½ **Roc Astrale (IRE)**[9] 3428 5-9-7 **55**........(vt) RossaRyan 10 45
(Phil McEntee) *bhd: rdn and btn whn bmpd over 2f out* **16/1**
0-50 7 ½ **Buxlow Belle (FR)**[28] 2733 4-8-5 **46** oh1........(h) CierenFallon(7) 11 35
(David Menuisier) *mounted on crse: cl up on outer: rdn and wknd over 2f out* **5/1**[2]
0056 8 1¼ **Lulu Star (IRE)**[12] 3298 4-8-6 **47**........ SeanKirrane(7) 1 34
(Julia Feilden) *prom: rdn 3f out: wknd grad fnl 2f* **14/1**
00-0 9 ½ **Roue De Charrette**[56] 1850 4-8-7 **46** oh1...(p) ThoreHammerHansen(5) 7 33
(Amy Murphy) *nvr bttr than midfield: rdn and hanging rt whn struggling over 2f out* **33/1**
0-00 10 1 **Tyrsal (IRE)**[28] 2738 8-8-13 **47**........(p) JosephineGordon 14 32
(Shaun Keightley) *lost 12 l s: sme prog into midfield 4f out: rdr dropped whip 3f out: struggling after* **20/1**
0006 11 shd **Conqueress (IRE)**[13] 3276 5-8-13 **47**........ JackMitchell 15 32
(Lydia Pearce) *nvr bttr than midfield: btn 4f out* **18/1**
50-0 12 31 **Roser Moter (IRE)**[28] 2737 4-9-0 **53**........ TheodoreLadd(5) 4
(Michael Appleby) *midfield: rdn 4f out: sn btn: t.o and eased* **33/1**
0060 13 3¼ **Golconda Prince (IRE)**[46] 2111 5-9-4 **55**........(b[1]) JoshuaBryan(3) 12
(Mark Pattinson) *cl up tl fdd 4f out: t.o and eased* **16/1**
0-00 14 4½ **Interrogation (FR)**[137] 435 4-8-12 **46** oh1........ JoeyHaynes 16
(Alan Bailey) *pressed ldr tl rdn 4f out: sn lost pl: t.o and eased* **66/1**

2m 34.21s (6.41) **Going Correction** +0.60s/f (Yiel) **14 Ran SP% 123.1**
Speed ratings (Par 101): **100,98,96,96,94 91,91,90,89,89 89,66,64,60**
CSF £47.48 CT £214.67 TOTE £17.90: £6.20, £1.80, £1.50; EX 69.30 Trifecta £253.80.
Owner Mark E Smith **Bred** Trickledown Stud Limited **Trained** Stow-On-The-Wold, Gloucs

FOCUS
Weak handicap form, they headed down the centre in the straight.

3741 MANSIONBET AT YARMOUTH H'CAP 1m 2f 23y
3:30 (3:34) (Class 6) (0-65,66) 3-Y-O
£3,105 (£924; £461; £300; £300; £300) **Stalls** Low

Form RPR
4003 1 **Trouble Shooter (IRE)**[12] 3299 3-8-2 **46** oh1........(v) RaulDaSilva 15 53
(Shaun Keightley) *sn prom: led 3f out: drvn and hdd over 1f out: rallied wl to ld fnl 75yds* **11/1**
3330 2 ½ **Bolt N Brown**[23] 2914 3-9-0 **65**........(t[1]) GraceMcEntee(7) 12 71
(Gay Kelleway) *a in ldng trio: led 4f out tl rdn and hdd 3f out: stl ev ch wl ins fnl f: kpt on gamely tl no ex cl home* **20/1**
02-4 3 hd **Swansdown**[19] 3052 3-9-7 **65**........ JamesDoyle 11 71
(William Haggas) *midfield: rdn and effrt over 2f out: led over 1f out: edgd lft: hdd and rdr dropped whip 75yds out* **13/8**[1]
0633 4 10 **Red Archangel (IRE)**[9] 3407 3-8-5 **56**........(p) SeanKirrane(7) 5 44
(Richard Spencer) *plld hrd: prom tl rdn and wknd over 2f out* **7/1**[3]
003- 5 1¾ **Sea Battle (FR)**[216] 8956 3-9-7 **65**........ JFEgan 6 50
(Jane Chapple-Hyam) *bhd: last 5f out: nvr nr ldrs* **14/1**
-033 6 2 **Catch My Breath**[13] 3278 3-9-6 **64**........ BrettDoyle 13 45
(John Ryan) *chsd ldrs: effrt and hrd drvn 3f out: wandering and wl btn 2f out* **13/2**[2]
0-00 7 8 **Dolly McQueen**[18] 3067 3-8-0 **49** ow3........ DarraghKeenan(5) 9 16
(Anthony Carson) *plld hrd: prom tl rdn and fdd 3f out: t.o* **33/1**
55-0 8 7 **Loving Pearl**[27] 2760 3-9-4 **62**........ TomEaves 14 16
(John Berry) *uns bef loading and mounted in stalls: towards rr: struggling over 3f out: t.o* **33/1**
04-0 9 4 **No Trouble (IRE)**[16] 3170 3-9-0 **58**........ PJMcDonald 2 5
(Stuart Williams) *str reminders in midfield after 3f: struggling 4f out: t.o fnl 2f* **8/1**
0-55 10 ¾ **No Thanks**[13] 3273 3-8-11 **62**........(h) CierenFallon(7) 8 7
(William Jarvis) *dwlt and rdn: a bhd: t.o fnl 2f (trainer said gelding was unsuited by the going, which was officially described as Heavy on this occasion)* **7/1**[3]
0436 11 1 **Margaret J**[13] 3256 3-8-2 **46**........(p) JosephineGordon 1
(Phil McEntee) *led tl hdd and lost pl rapidly 4f out: t.o 2f out* **16/1**
-500 12 30 **Freedom's Breath**[82] 1270 3-8-0 **49** oh1 ow3 ThoreHammerHansen(5) 3
(Michael Appleby) *bhd: nvr travelling: t.o and eased 2f out (jockey said filly was never travelling)* **66/1**

2m 15.07s (6.27) **Going Correction** +0.60s/f (Yiel) **12 Ran SP% 120.6**
Speed ratings (Par 97): **98,97,97,89,88 86,80,74,71,70 69,45**
CSF £216.72 CT £547.85 TOTE £13.10: £3.50, £8.40, £1.10; EX 290.40 Trifecta £2342.40.
Owner Simon Lockyer **Bred** Kildaragh Stud & M Downey **Trained** Newmarket, Suffolk

FOCUS
Three pulled clear in what was a modest (at best) 3yo handicap. They headed centre-field in the straight and it again paid to race prominently.

3742 MANSIONBET PROUD TO SUPPORT BRITISH RACING FILLIES' H'CAP 6f 3y
4:00 (4:03) (Class 5) (0-75,77) 3-Y-O
£3,752 (£1,116; £557; £300; £300; £300) **Stalls** Centre

Form RPR
1111 1 **Camachess (IRE)**[50] 2024 3-9-5 **72**........ PhilDennis 8 80
(Philip McBride) *stdd s: racd in last trio: prog travelling strly over 1f out: led 200yds out and willingly surged clr* **3/1**[2]
3-24 2 2¼ **Texting**[19] 3058 3-9-0 **67**........ TomEaves 11 68
(Mohamed Moubarak) *stdd s: v keen in rr: effrt and swtchd lft wl over 1f out: chsd wnr ins fnl f but edgd rt and easily outpcd by her* **8/1**
5255 3 2¾ **Hanakotoba (USA)**[19] 3045 3-8-5 **65**........(t) MarcoGhiani(7) 7 57
(Stuart Williams) *t.k.h pressing ldr: led and rdn 2f out: hdd & wknd sn ins fnl f* **11/1**
6-00 4 nk **Cookupastorm (IRE)**[23] 2904 3-8-10 **66**........(v[1]) GeorgeBuckell(3) 2 57
(Richard Spencer) *cl up: jnd ldr u.p 2f out: wknd over 1f out* **7/1**
3401 5 nse **Key To Power**[5] 3535 3-9-9 **76** 6ex........ PJMcDonald 10 67
(Mark Johnston) *dwlt: chsd ldrs: rdn and racd awkwardly over 1f out: no imp after* **7/4**[1]
5-04 6 8 **Aquarius (IRE)**[9] 3420 3-9-0 **67**........(p) AlistairRawlinson 4 32
(Michael Appleby) *racd freely in ld tl rdn and hdd 2f out: fdd over 1f out* **13/2**[3]

1m 16.33s (3.73) **Going Correction** +0.475s/f (Yiel) **6 Ran SP% 106.6**
Speed ratings (Par 96): **94,91,87,86,86 76**
CSF £23.08 CT £186.19 TOTE £3.20: £1.30, £3.10; EX 20.80 Trifecta £96.70.
Owner The Narc Partnership **Bred** Yeomanstown Stud **Trained** Newmarket, Suffolk
■ Lucky Charm was withdrawn. Price at time of withdrawal 10/1. Rule 4 applies to all bets - deduction 5p in the £.

FOCUS
Modest form, with the favourite disappointing, but a clear-cut winner, who has been rated as taking another step forward.

3743 MANSIONBET YOUR FAVOURITE PLACE TO BET H'CAP — 1m 3y
4:30 (4:32) (Class 4) (0-80,80) 4-Y-0+
£5,530 (£1,645; £822; £411; £300; £300) **Stalls Centre**

Form — RPR

-512 **1** **Oud Metha Bridge (IRE)**[21] 2978 5-8-4 **70**.................. SeanKirrane(7) 6 78
(Julia Feilden) t.k.h: led 2f: pressed ldr tl led again over 2f out: pushed along and hld on gamely fnl f: readily **3/1**[1]

2320 **2** 1 1/4 **Ambient (IRE)**[12] 3305 4-8-12 **76**.................. SeamusCronin(5) 5 80
(Mohamed Moubarak) bhd: rdn and hdwy over 1f out: chsd wnr and hung lft ins fnl f: a hld **9/2**[3]

34-6 **3** 3/4 **Hunni**[11] 3336 4-9-1 **77**.................. CameronNoble(3) 7 79
(Tom Clover) cl up: drvn over 2f out: outpcd by wnr and lost 2nd ins fnl f **5/1**

2020 **4** nse **Glory Awaits (IRE)**[21] 2977 9-8-13 **77**..................(b) DylanHogan(5) 1 79
(David Simcock) plld hrd: led after 2f: hdd over 2f out: nt travelling: hung lft and btn ins fnl f **8/1**

53 **5** nk **Outside Inside (IRE)**[21] 2959 4-9-3 **76**.................. PJMcDonald 9 77
(Mark Johnston) prom: rdn 2f out: wknd over 1f out **4/1**[2]

-021 **6** 1 **Verdigris (IRE)**[15] 3199 4-8-9 **68**.................. TomEaves 3 67+
(Ruth Carr) stdd and sn detached: effrt 3f out: hung bdly lft and btn wl over 1f out **9/2**[3]

00-4 **7** 6 **Fleeting Freedom**[15] 3185 4-8-6 **72**..................(p) JessicaCooley(7) 8 57
(Alan Bailey) mounted in stalls: pressed ldrs tl rdn and wknd 2f out **12/1**

1m 41.23s (3.03) **Going Correction** +0.475s/f (Yiel) **7 Ran SP% 116.8**
Speed ratings (Par 105): **103,101,101,100,100 99,93**
CSF £17.39 CT £65.39 TOTE £4.10: £2.10, £2.70; EX 18.70 Trifecta £78.70.
Owner In It To Win Partnership **Bred** Rabbah Bloodstock Limited **Trained** Exning, Suffolk

FOCUS
Modest form. The second has been rated to his recent Ascot form.

3744 MANSIONBET APPRENTICE H'CAP — 1m 3y
5:00 (5:01) (Class 6) (0-65,67) 4-Y-0+
£3,105 (£924; £461; £300; £300; £300) **Stalls Centre**

Form — RPR

0312 **1** **Abushamah (IRE)**[14] 3214 8-9-9 **62**.................. RowanScott 8 68
(Ruth Carr) chsd ldrs: effrt over 1f out: firmly drvn to ld fnl 150yds: styd on wl **7/2**[2]

66 **2** 2 **Brecqhou Island**[4] 3592 4-8-3 **49**.................. IsobelFrancis(7) 13 51
(Mark Pattinson) lost 6 l s and urged along in rr: stl outpcd in 7th over 1f out: str late run to snatch 2nd but veered lft and no ch w wnr (jockey said gelding was outpaced early) **8/1**

3550 **3** nse **Boxatricks (IRE)**[21] 2972 4-8-3 **49**.................. SeanKirrane(7) 4 50
(Julia Feilden) lost 8 l s: swtchd to stands' rails and rcvrd after 3f: led wl over 1f out: pushed along and idling in front: hdd 150yds out and jst lost 2nd (jockey said gelding was slowly away) **5/1**

6230 **4** 1 1/2 **Pearl Spectre (USA)**[16] 3147 8-8-13 **59**..................(v) GraceMcEntee(7) 10 57
(Phil McEntee) t.k.h: led tl rdn and hdd wl over 1f out: nt qckn fnl f **12/1**

0502 **5** 1/2 **Sonnet Rose (IRE)**[43] 2261 5-9-5 **61**..................(bt) SebastianWoods(3) 11 58
(Conrad Allen) prom: rdn wl over 1f out: one pce fnl f **9/2**[3]

-031 **6** nse **Khaan**[15] 3208 4-9-1 **54**.................. GeorgeBuckell 2 51
(Michael Appleby) bhd: rdn over 2f out: nvr making any imp after: btn 1f out (trainers rep said colt was unsuited by the going, which was officially described as Heavy on this occasion) **9/4**[1]

00- **7** 2 1/4 **Thunderhooves**[177] 9585 4-8-6 **48**.................. DarraghKeenan(3) 12 40
(John Ryan) cl up tl rdn and fdd wl over 1f out **25/1**

16-0 **8** 19 **Right About Now (IRE)**[43] 2259 5-10-0 **67**..................(b) JoshuaBryan 6 17
(Charlie Wallis) prom 5f: lost pl rapidly: t.o and eased **25/1**

1m 45.25s (7.05) **Going Correction** +0.475s/f (Yiel) **8 Ran SP% 114.3**
Speed ratings (Par 101): **83,81,80,79,78 78,76,57**
CSF £31.34 CT £137.80 TOTE £3.50: £3.10, £2.20, £1.20; EX 37.10 Trifecta £189.50.
Owner Grange Park Racing VIII & Mrs R Carr **Bred** Shadwell Estate Company Limited **Trained** Huby, N Yorks

FOCUS
Lowly form.
T/Jkpt: Not Won. T/Plt: £69.80 to a £1 stake. Pool: £70,453.09 - 735.8 winning units T/Qpdt: £17.90 to a £1 stake. Pool: £6,939.23 - 285.84 winning units **Iain Mackenzie**

3745 - 3752a (Foreign Racing) - See Raceform Interactive

3724 HAYDOCK (L-H)
Thursday, June 13

3753 Meeting Abandoned - waterlogged

2826 NEWBURY (L-H)
Thursday, June 13

OFFICIAL GOING: Soft (5.8)
Wind: quite strong across Weather: light rain easing by 3pm

3760 BE WISER INSURANCE NOVICE STKS (PLUS 10 RACE) — 6f 110y
2:00 (2:02) (Class 4) 2-Y-0
£4,787 (£1,424; £711; £355) **Stalls High**

Form — RPR

1 **Mottrib (IRE)** 2-9-5 0.................. DavidEgan 6 85+
(Roger Varian) str; in tch: hdwy whn swtchd lft 3f out: led jst ins fnl f: kpt on wl **4/1**[2]

0 **2** 2 3/4 **Baadirr**[27] 2792 2-9-5 0.................. OisinMurphy 3 77
(William Haggas) looked wl; in tch: hdwy 3f out: led jst over 2f out: sn rdn: hdd jst ins fnl f: sn no ex **15/8**[1]

3 5 **Swinley Forest (IRE)** 2-9-5 0.................. MartinDwyer 9 64
(Brian Meehan) tall; str; trckd ldr: led briefly over 2f out: sn rdn: kpt on tl no ex ent fnl f **20/1**

4 2 3/4 **Bealach (IRE)** 2-9-5 0.................. CharlesBishop 4 56
(Eve Johnson Houghton) leggy; trckd ldrs: rdn wl over 2f out: sn one pce **9/1**[3]

5 8 **Rocket Dancer** 2-9-5 0.................. JimCrowley 2 34
(Sylvester Kirk) str; wnt lft s: racd in last trio: hdwy over 2f out: sn rdn: wknd over 1f out **11/1**

6 2 3/4 **Glorious Return (IRE)** 2-9-5 0.................. RobHornby 7 27
(Jonathan Portman) str; trckd ldrs: rdn over 3f out: sn wknd **20/1**

7 1/2 **Gold Souk (IRE)** 2-9-5 0.................. SilvestreDeSousa 10 25
(Mark Johnston) str; ly; led tl rdn over 2f out: sn wknd **4/1**[2]

0 **8** 5 **Made Guy (USA)**[10] 3419 2-9-5 0..................(b[1]) JFEgan 1 11
(J S Moore) workmanlike; last pair: rdn 3f out: little imp: wknd over 1f out **100/1**

9 1/2 **King's View (IRE)** 2-9-5 0.................. RyanMoore 8 10
(Richard Hannon) athletic; s.i.s: racd in last pair: struggling over 3f out: nvr on terms **12/1**

1m 23.17s (3.07) **Going Correction** +0.50s/f (Yiel) **9 Ran SP% 111.3**
Speed ratings (Par 95): **102,98,93,90,80 77,77,71,70**
CSF £11.14 TOTE £4.60: £1.70, £1.10, £4.10; EX 11.60 Trifecta £119.80.
Owner Sheikh Ahmed Al Maktoum **Bred** Mabaki Investments **Trained** Newmarket, Suffolk

FOCUS
The fifth running of this event as a novice rather than a maiden. The 2017 winner Expert Eye went on to Breeders' Cup glory and last year's scorer Confiding was placed in a couple of Group races. Barraquero, Star Terms and Anna Nerium have also debuted in this. They finished well stretched out in this year's edition, with the time 7.17sec slower than standard. After the opener the jockeys said the ground was soft and holding, but not heavy. It's been rated in line with the race average to begin with.

3761 CROSSLAND BRITISH EBF FILLIES' NOVICE STKS (PLUS 10 RACE) — 1m (S)
2:30 (2:35) (Class 4) 3-Y-0
£5,530 (£1,645; £822; £411) **Stalls High**

Form — RPR

3 **1** **Qamka**[34] 2583 3-9-0 0.................. DavidEgan 1 80+
(Roger Varian) tall; ly; s.i.s: sn cl up: chal over 2f out: rdn over 1f out: led fnl 120yds: kpt on wl: asserting towards fin **6/4**[1]

2 1 1/4 **Beauty Of Deira (IRE)** 3-9-0 0.................. OisinMurphy 5 77
(Hugo Palmer) leggy; athletic; led: rdn whn strly chal wl over 1f out: kpt on w narrow advantage tl hdd fnl 120yds: no ex **11/1**

00 **3** 1 3/4 **Forbidden Dance**[24] 2919 3-9-0 0.................. JimCrowley 2 73+
(Hughie Morrison) compact; prom tl rdn over 2f out: sn chsng ldng pair: kpt on same pce fnl f **16/1**

3-6 **4** 2 3/4 **To The Moon**[38] 2488 3-9-0 0.................. FrankieDettori 3 67
(John Gosden) workmanlike; edgy; on her toes: rrd leaving stalls: last but in tch: hdwy 3f out: rdn to chal for cl 3rd over 1f out: nt pce to threaten: no ex fnl 120yds (jockey said filly was slowly away) **9/4**[2]

6 **5** 6 **Wild Cat**[21] 3013 3-9-0 0.................. JasonWatson 7 53
(Roger Charlton) cl up: pushed along over 5f out: rdn over 2f out: wknd over 1f out **16/1**

6 26 **Kingslady** 3-9-0 0.................. CharlesBishop 11
(Eve Johnson Houghton) str; prom tl rdn over 3f out: wknd qckly **12/1**

0- **7** nk **Galileo Jade (IRE)**[322] 5386 3-9-0 0.................. SeanLevey 4
(Richard Hannon) leggy; chsd ldrs tl rdn over 3f out: sn wknd **20/1**

8 18 **Narak** 3-9-0 0.................. HarryBentley 10
(George Scott) athletic; chsd ldrs tl wknd 3f out **8/1**[3]

1m 44.96s (5.06) **Going Correction** +0.50s/f (Yiel) **8 Ran SP% 114.4**
Speed ratings (Par 98): **94,92,91,88,82 56,55,37**
CSF £19.60 TOTE £2.00: £1.10, £2.80, £4.00; EX 16.20 Trifecta £170.70.
Owner Nurlan Bizakov **Bred** Hesmonds Stud Ltd **Trained** Newmarket, Suffolk

FOCUS
A fair fillies' novice in conditions which found out several of these. The winner has been rated similar to her debut form, and the fourth similar to her reappearance.

3762 JOHNNIE LEWIS MEMORIAL BRITISH EBF STKS (REG' AS THE ABINGDON STAKES) (LISTED RACE) (FILLIES) — 1m 2f
3:00 (3:01) (Class 1) 3-Y-0
£28,355 (£10,750; £5,380; £2,680; £1,345; £675) **Stalls Low**

Form — RPR

110- **1** **Antonia De Vega (IRE)**[244] 8148 3-9-0 **99**.................. HarryBentley 1 107
(Ralph Beckett) hld up 6th: hdwy over 3f out: rdn into cl 3rd 2f out: led jst ins fnl f: styd on strly to draw clr: rdn out **4/1**[2]

-404 **2** 4 **Star Terms**[26] 2831 3-9-0 **102**.................. RyanMoore 4 99
(Richard Hannon) looked wl; led for 2f: trckd ldr: rdn wl over 2f out: led narrowly over 1f out: kpt on but no ex whn hdd jst ins fnl f **9/2**[3]

1 **3** 1 1/4 **Terebellum (IRE)**[21] 3013 3-9-0 0.................. FrankieDettori 5 97
(John Gosden) looked wl; s.i.s: led after 2f: rdn whn strly pressed over 2f out: narrowly hdd over 1f out: kpt on tl no ex ins fnl f **1/1**[1]

1-0 **4** 8 **Lastochka**[26] 2831 3-9-0 0.................. DavidEgan 3 81
(Roger Varian) tall; trckd ldrs: rdn in cl 3rd over 2f out: wknd fnl f **14/1**

3641 **5** 3 1/4 **Patchouli**[7] 3513 3-9-0 **71**.................. GeraldMosse 2 74
(Mick Channon) trckd ldrs: rdn over 3f out: nt quite pce to chal: wknd ent fnl f **40/1**

4-12 **6** 14 **Mannaal (IRE)**[17] 3169 3-9-0 **84**.................. SilvestreDeSousa 6 46
(Simon Crisford) looked wl; trckd ldrs: wnt 2nd over 4f out: rdn over 3f out: wknd 2f out **7/1**

2m 11.97s (2.27) **Going Correction** +0.50s/f (Yiel) **6 Ran SP% 109.8**
Speed ratings (Par 104): **110,106,105,99,96 85**
CSF £20.88 TOTE £4.60: £2.20, £2.40; EX 17.10 Trifecta £26.80.
Owner Waverley Racing **Bred** Fermoir Ltd **Trained** Kimpton, Hants

FOCUS
Add 19yds. This was won a year ago by Sea Of Class, who went on to finish second in the Arc, and earlier winners include Group 1 scorers Great Heavens and Speedy Boarding. They raced down the centre in the home straight and the time was 10sec outside standard. The second has been rated similar to her C&D latest, and the third similar to her debut win.

3763 COMAX H'CAP — 1m (S)
3:35 (3:36) (Class 4) (0-85,87) 4-Y-0+
£6,727 (£2,002; £1,000; £500; £300; £300) **Stalls High**

Form — RPR

2-23 **1** **Infanta Isabella**[33] 2612 5-9-5 **82**..................(t) HarryBentley 8 95
(George Baker) trckd ldrs: led over 1f out: sn rdn clr: comf **4/1**[2]

10-4 **2** 6 **Secret Return (IRE)**[34] 2584 6-9-2 **79**.................. JFEgan 3 78
(Paul George) trckd ldrs: rdn to ld over 2f out: hdd over 1f out: kpt on but nt pce of wnr fnl f **8/1**

5422 **3** 2 **Regimented (IRE)**[14] 3255 4-9-3 **80**.................. SeanLevey 4 75
(Richard Hannon) mid-div: hdwy over 2f out: sn rdn: wnt 3rd jst over 1f out: kpt on same pce fnl f **8/1**

3-04 **4** 1 **Sod's Law**[17] 3149 4-9-6 **83**.................. OisinMurphy 5 75
(Hughie Morrison) looked wl; disp ld tl edgd ahd over 3f out: rdn and hdd over 2f out: kpt on same pce fr over 1f out **4/1**[2]

00-3 **5** 4 **Leader Writer (FR)**[30] 2710 7-9-7 **84**.................. RyanMoore 1 67
(David Elsworth) little slowly away: sn in tch: hdwy 3f out: cl up whn effrt over 2f out: wknd fnl f **10/3**[1]

5065 **6** *2 ¼* **Jellmood**[20] 3040 4-9-1 **78**..............................(t) ShaneKelly 10 56
(Chris Gordon) *hmpd s: last: hdwy over 2f out: sn rdn: nvr threatened: wknd over 1f out* **50/1**

11-2 **7** *4 ½* **Vixen (IRE)**[34] 2585 5-8-10 **73**..............................(h) LiamKeniry 7 41
(Emma Lavelle) *slowly away: racd in last trio: effrt over 2f out: wknd over 1f out* **22/1**

30-5 **8** *6* **Data Protection**[21] 3027 4-9-2 **79**..............................(t) JasonWatson 11 33
(William Muir) *wnt lft s: trckd ldrs: lost pl whn nt clr run over 3f out: wknd over 2f out (jockey said gelding hung right-handed and was denied a clear run)* **20/1**

10-0 **9** *2 ¼* **Jackpot Royale**[26] 2832 4-9-10 **87**.............................. RobertWinston 2 36
(Michael Appleby) *last pair: hdwy over 4f out: effrt in cl 3rd over 2f out: sn wknd (jockey said gelding stopped quickly)* **12/1**

564 **10** *24* **Time For A Toot (IRE)**[44] 2252 4-9-4 **81**.............................. JimCrowley 9
(Charles Hills) *disp ld tl over 3f out: sn wknd (jockey said filly stopped quickly)* **6/1[3]**

1m 44.31s (4.41) **Going Correction** +0.50s/f (Yiel) **10** Ran SP% **118.3**
Speed ratings (Par 105): **97,91,89,88,84 81,77,71,69,45**
CSF £35.69 CT £247.85 TOTE £4.40: £1.70, £2.40, £2.80; EX 41.70 Trifecta £311.60.
Owner The Chriselliam Partnership **Bred** Stratford Place Stud **Trained** Chiddingfold, Surrey

FOCUS
A dominant winner of this decent handicap. The runner-up could back this form being rated higher than at face value.

3764 BE WISER INSURANCE H'CAP 7f (S)

4:10 (4:12) (Class 5) (0-70,71) 3-Y-O

£3,752 (£1,116; £557; £300; £300; £300) **Stalls** High

Form RPR

-406 **1** **Global Destination (IRE)**[12] 3354 3-9-1 **64**.............................. GeraldMosse 7 71
(Ed Dunlop) *s.i.s: towards rr: hdwy after 2f: shkn up over 2f out: led jst ins fnl f: kpt on wl: rdn out* **8/1**

0340 **2** *nk* **John Betjeman**[42] 2339 3-9-7 **70**.............................. RobHornby 5 76
(Mark Gillard) *awkwardly away: towards rr: hdwy fr 3f out: rdn to chse ldrs over 1f out: kpt on to press wnr ins fnl f: hld nring fin* **10/1**

30-0 **3** *1 ¾* **Rosamour (IRE)**[27] 2798 3-8-13 **69**.............................. GeorgeRooke(7) 1 70
(Richard Hughes) *prom: led 3f out: sn rdn: hdd jst ins fnl f: kpt on same pce* **9/1**

-140 **4** *2 ¼* **Gregorian Girl**[24] 2904 3-8-13 **62**.............................. MartinDwyer 9 57
(Dean Ivory) *prom: rdn and ev ch over 2f out: hld over 1f out: kpt on same pce fnl f* **20/1**

3652 **5** *5* **Urban Highway (IRE)**[45] 2204 3-9-0 **63**.............................. JFEgan 10 45
(Tony Carroll) *looked wl; trckd ldrs: rdn wl over 2f out: sn one pce* **6/1**

334 **6** *1* **Tulloona**[92] 1171 3-9-7 **70**.............................. JimCrowley 4 50
(Tom Clover) *trckd ldrs: rdn over 2f out: nt quite pce to chal: wknd ent fnl f* **9/2[1]**

2-65 **7** *nk* **Time For Bed (IRE)**[23] 2937 3-9-8 **71**.............................. SeanLevey 12 50
(Richard Hannon) *towards rr: sme prog and effrt over 2f out: nvr threatened to get involved: wknd ent fnl f* **10/1**

566- **8** *13* **Lordsbridge Boy**[196] 9307 3-8-13 **62**.............................. RobertWinston 6 7
(Dean Ivory) *led tl 3f out: sn wknd* **18/1**

006 **9** *3 ¼* **Storm Girl**[64] 1676 3-8-2 **54** oh2 ow3..............................(t[1]) AaronJones(3) 2
(Michael Attwater) *s.i.s: a towards rr (£650 fine: changing his breeches and boots after weighing out)* **40/1**

6-66 **10** *11* **Stormbomber (CAN)**[13] 3302 3-9-3 **66**.............................. LiamKeniry 3
(Ed Walker) *looked wl; a towards rr (jockey said he felt the colt ran poorly as it had lost its left fore shoe on the way to the start)* **5/1[2]**

6505 **11** *1* **Cromwell**[14] 3256 3-8-8 **57**..............................(t[1]) SilvestreDeSousa 13
(Luke Dace) *broke wl: prom tl rdn over 3f out: sn wknd (trainer's rep said gelding was unsuited by the soft ground and would prefer a faster surface)* **11/2[3]**

1m 30.49s (3.49) **Going Correction** +0.50s/f (Yiel) **11** Ran SP% **116.3**
Speed ratings (Par 99): **100,99,97,95,89 88,87,73,69,56 55**
CSF £84.41 CT £749.32 TOTE £9.40: £2.90, £2.50, £2.80; EX 92.10 Trifecta £618.80.
Owner Dr Johnny Hon **Bred** Norelands Bloodstock **Trained** Newmarket, Suffolk
■ Stewards' Enquiry : Aaron Jones one-day ban: weighing in at 2lb overweight (tba)

FOCUS
Just modest form. A step up on this year's form from the second, who looks back to his best.

3765 INSURE WISER H'CAP 1m 4f

4:40 (4:41) (Class 5) (0-75,78) 3-Y-O

£3,752 (£1,116; £557; £300; £300; £300) **Stalls** Low

Form RPR

2322 **1** **Sapa Inca (IRE)**[24] 2905 3-9-9 **77**.............................. SilvestreDeSousa 8 88
(Mark Johnston) *looked wl; a.p: led gng wl over 3f out: pushed clr and in command fnl 2f: comf* **5/2[2]**

40-2 **2** *5* **Group Stage (GER)**[34] 2582 3-9-3 **71**.............................. DavidEgan 5 74
(Alan King) *hld up in last pair: stdy prog fr 4f out: rdn to chse wnr over 2f out: nvr threatened to get on terms: styd on same pce* **9/4[1]**

-001 **3** *9* **Admirals Bay (GER)**[14] 3275 3-8-8 **62**.............................. RobHornby 4 51
(Andrew Balding) *prom: led briefly wl over 3f out: sn rdn: wknd fnl f* **7/2[3]**

3402 **4** *10* **Ydra**[14] 3254 3-8-9 **68**..............................(b) ThomasGreatrex(5) 1 41
(Archie Watson) *led tl wl over 3f out: sn rdn: hld over 2f out: wknd over 1f out* **20/1**

-536 **5** *1 ¼* **Gino Wotimean (USA)**[31] 2697 3-8-12 **66**.............................. ShaneKelly 3 37
(Noel Williams) *hld up in last pair: rdn over 3f out: nvr gng pce to get involved: wknd over 1f out* **14/1**

61-3 **6** *¾* **Zuba**[48] 2088 3-9-7 **75**.............................. RyanMoore 6 44
(Amanda Perrett) *trckd ldrs: rdn over 3f out: wknd over 1f out* **5/1**

2m 39.84s (1.84) **Going Correction** +0.50s/f (Yiel) **6** Ran SP% **109.7**
Speed ratings (Par 99): **111,107,101,95,94 93**
CSF £8.12 CT £16.30 TOTE £2.90: £1.30, £1.50; EX 7.70 Trifecta £23.00.
Owner China Horse Club International Limited **Bred** Desert Star Phoenix Jvc **Trained** Middleham Moor, N Yorks

FOCUS
Add 19yds. They finished well strung out in this modest handicap, in which they came down the centre in the straight. A clear step up from the winner, with the second rated to form for now.

3766 WISER ACADEMY AMATEUR RIDERS' H'CAP 1m 2f

5:15 (5:15) (Class 5) (0-70,71) 4-Y-O+

£3,618 (£1,122; £560; £300; £300; £300) **Stalls** Low

Form RPR

1400 **1** **Dutch Uncle**[6] 3541 7-10-8 **71**..............................(p) MrCharlesClover(7) 4 82
(Tom Clover) *trckd ldr: led wl over 3f out: rdn clr 2f out: styd on wl* **25/1**

-102 **2** *11* **Amaretto**[29] 2732 4-9-9 **58**..............................(v) MissSuzannahStevens(7) 1 47
(Jim Boyle) *racd keenly: trckd ldrs: chal wl over 3f out: sn rdn: hld 2f out: fdd fnl f (jockey said gelding ran too freely)* **7/2[2]**

5000 **3** *2 ½* **Gawdawpalin (IRE)**[27] 2793 6-11-0 **70**..............................(t) MissSerenaBrotherton 7 54
(Sylvester Kirk) *chsd ldrs: rdn over 3f out: sn outpcd: wnt wl hld 3rd over 1f out (vet said gelding lost its right hind shoe)* **4/1[3]**

43-0 **4** *2* **Jumping Jack (IRE)**[21] 3022 5-11-1 **71**.............................. MrSimonWalker 2 51
(Chris Gordon) *trckd ldrs: outpcd over 3f out: wnt wl hld 4th jst over 1f out* **4/1[3]**

3505 **5** *4* **Me Too Nagasaki (IRE)**[4] 3633 5-11-0 **70**..............................(h) MrPatrickMillman 6 42
(Stuart Williams) *set decent pce: hdd 3f out: sn hld: wknd over 1f out (jockey said gelding hung left-handed; vet said gelding lost its right fore and right hind)* **3/1[1]**

1204 **6** *11* **Creative Talent (IRE)**[5] 3572 7-9-10 **57**.............................. MissSarahBowen(5) 3 7
(Tony Carroll) *s.i.s: last but in tch: struggling over 3f out: wknd over 1f out* **7/2[2]**

2m 15.74s (6.04) **Going Correction** +0.50s/f (Yiel) **6** Ran SP% **113.3**
Speed ratings (Par 103): **95,86,84,82,79 70**
CSF £110.22 CT £434.46 TOTE £16.90: £4.90, £2.00; EX 124.00 Trifecta £1207.00.
Owner The Shimplingthorne Syndicate **Bred** Cheveley Park Stud Ltd **Trained** Newmarket, Suffolk

FOCUS
Add 19yds. This weak event for amateur riders fell apart in the home straight, where the action took place down the middle.
T/Plt: £337.40 to a £1 stake. Pool: £51,623.62. 111.67 winning units. T/Qpdt: £86.60 to a £1 stake. Pool: £6,635.47. 56.66 winning units. **Tim Mitchell**

3469 NOTTINGHAM (L-H)

Thursday, June 13

OFFICIAL GOING: Heavy (5.5)
Wind: Light, against Weather: Raining

3767 MANSIONBET NOVICE STKS 6f 18y

1:40 (1:40) (Class 5) 2-Y-O **£3,881** (£1,155; £577; £288) **Stalls** Centre

Form RPR

0 **1** **Big City**[16] 3194 2-9-5 0.............................. AdamKirby 5 75
(Saeed bin Suroor) *wnt rt s: sn chsng ldrs: rdn to ld and hung lft fr over 1f out: styd on* **5/1[3]**

0 **2** *¾* **Maysong**[5] 3601 2-9-5 0.............................. TomQueally 2 73
(Ed Dunlop) *chsd ldr: rdn and ev ch fr over 1f out: edgd lft ins fnl f: kpt on* **6/1**

3 *½* **Mensen Ernst (IRE)** 2-9-5 0.............................. TomMarquand 1 71+
(Richard Hannon) *s.i.s: sn chsng ldrs: shkn up over 2f out: sn outpcd: rallied ins fnl f: r.o wl* **11/4[2]**

4 *¾* **Upstate New York (IRE)** 2-9-5 0.............................. DanielTudhope 3 69
(Richard Fahey) *s.s: hld up: hdwy over 1f out: rdn and hung lft ins fnl f: no ex towards fin* **2/1[1]**

60 **5** *2* **Lexington Quest (IRE)**[56] 1887 2-9-5 0.............................. PatDobbs 4 63+
(Richard Hannon) *led over 4f: nt clr run sn after: no ex fnl f* **9/1**

6 *9* **Under Your Spell (IRE)** 2-9-5 0.............................. NicolaCurrie 6 36+
(Jamie Osborne) *s.i.s and hmpd s: hld up: shkn up over 2f out: wknd over 1f out* **9/1**

1m 20.51s (6.71) **Going Correction** +0.875s/f (Soft) **6** Ran SP% **111.0**
Speed ratings (Par 93): **90,89,88,87,84 72**
CSF £32.82 TOTE £4.10: £2.50, £2.80; EX 30.80 Trifecta £215.30.
Owner Godolphin **Bred** Newsells Park Stud **Trained** Newmarket, Suffolk

FOCUS
Outer track and standard distances. This fair little 2yo novice event was run at a fair pace considering the deep surface, which played its part. The opening level is fluid.

3768 MANSIONBET MAIDEN STKS 1m 75y

2:10 (2:12) (Class 5) 3-Y-O+ **£4,204** (£1,251; £625; £312) **Stalls** Centre

Form RPR

23 **1** **Ocean Paradise**[24] 2919 3-8-12 0..............................(h) DanielTudhope 4 82
(Charles Hills) *mde all: brought field stands' side turning for home: rdn over 1f out: styd on: eased nr fin* **1/1[1]**

2 **2** *¾* **Maydanny (IRE)**[15] 3218 3-9-3 0.............................. DaneO'Neill 7 85
(Mark Johnston) *chsd wnr over 6f out: rdn and hung lft over 1f out: styd on same pce ins fnl f* **11/10[2]**

0 **3** *6* **Helian (IRE)**[21] 3003 3-9-3 0.............................. TomQueally 6 71
(Ed Dunlop) *hld up and bhd: reminder over 2f out: wnt 3rd over 1f out: nvr nr to chal* **25/1**

0 **4** *19* **Molotov (IRE)**[45] 2210 3-9-3 0.............................. NicolaCurrie 3 28
(Jamie Osborne) *s.i.s: bhd fnl 6f (jockey said gelding was outpaced in the early stages)* **20/1[3]**

54- **5** *3 ¾* **Rock Boy Grey (IRE)**[349] 4343 4-10-0 0.............................. EdwardGreatrex 2 22
(Mark Loughnane) *racd keenly in 2nd pl tl over 6f out: remained handy: shkn up over 3f out: wknd 2f out (jockey said gelding stopped quickly)* **25/1**

1m 52.64s (5.94) **Going Correction** +0.875s/f (Soft)
WFA 3 from 4yo 11lb **5** Ran SP% **110.1**
Speed ratings (Par 103): **105,104,98,79,75**
CSF £2.30 TOTE £1.90: £1.10, £1.10; EX 2.30 Trifecta £8.30.
Owner P Winkworth **Bred** Peter Winkworth **Trained** Lambourn, Berks

FOCUS
This wasn't a bad little maiden, but it proved tactical with the stands' rail the place to be from 3f out. The winner has been rated in line with her debut form.

3769 CARLING CUSTOMER H'CAP 1m 6f

2:40 (2:42) (Class 6) (0-60,61) 4-Y-O+

£3,234 (£962; £481; £300; £300; £300) **Stalls** Low

Form RPR

/1 **1** **Maid In Manhattan (IRE)**[14] 3272 5-8-7 **49**..............................(h) HarrisonShaw(5) 2 63+
(Rebecca Menzies) *hld up: hdwy over 4f out: chsd ldr over 3f out: led over 2f out: rdn clr fr over 1f out: easily* **11/4[1]**

45-0 **2** *9* **Artic Nel**[43] 2283 5-8-8 **45**.............................. PaulHanagan 3 46
(Ian Williams) *s.i.s: hld up: racd keenly: hdwy over 3f out: chsd wnr over 2f out: outpcd fr over 1f out* **9/2**

0043 **3** *6* **Lauberhorn Rocket (GER)**[22] 2970 4-9-0 **51**.............................. DavidProbert 10 45
(Tim Vaughan) *hld up: hdwy over 3f out: rdn and wknd over 1f out* **7/2[2]**

/0-4 **4** *2 ¼* **Cash In Mind (FR)**[13] 3322 8-9-10 **61**.............................. AdamKirby 7 52
(Des Donovan, Ire) *stdd s: hld up: hdwy u.p over 2f out: hung rt and wknd over 1f out* **4/1[3]**

0006 **5** 1 **Allleedsaren'Twe**[7] 3497 4-8-8 **45**...............................(vt[1]) NicolaCurrie 9 34
(Robyn Brisland) *chsd ldrs: rdn over 2f out: wknd over 1f out* **14/1**

-000 **6** 7 **Gabriel's Oboe (IRE)**[9] 3447 4-9-1 **52**.....................(v[1]) DougieCostello 8 32
(Mark Walford) *chsd ldr tl led over 4f out: rdn and hdd over 2f out: wknd wl over 1f out* **16/1**

1400 **7** 41 **Love Rat**[16] 3205 4-9-1 **52**..(v) PJMcDonald 1
(Scott Dixon) *led: brought field towards stands' side turning for home: rdn and hdd over 4f out: wknd over 3f out* **8/1**

0051 **8** 78 **Hussar Ballad (USA)**[31] 2695 10-9-5 **56**........................... CamHardie 6
(Antony Brittain) *chsd ldrs: shkn up and lost pl over 4f out: sn wknd: virtually p.u fnl f* **28/1**

3m 18.36s (11.96) **Going Correction** +0.875s/f (Soft) **8** Ran SP% **114.2**
Speed ratings (Par 101): **100,94,91,90,89 85,62,17**
CSF £15.34 CT £43.19 TOTE £3.50: £1.50, £1.60, £1.90; EX 14.80 Trifecta £89.20.
Owner Stoneleigh Racing **Bred** John Breslin **Trained** Mordon, Durham

FOCUS
An ordinary staying handicap, run at a solid pace. Again they came stands' side after turning for home. The winner has been rated back to her best.

3770 MANSIONBET H'CAP — 6f 18y

3:15 (3:16) (Class 3) (0-90,92) 4-Y-O+

£9,337 (£2,796; £1,398; £699; £349; £175) **Stalls** Centre

Form RPR

4-03 **1** **Dalton**[26] 2843 5-9-3 **83**.. GrahamLee 8 91
(Julie Camacho) *sn pushed along in rr: swtchd lft and hdwy over 1f out: rdn to ld and hung lft ins fnl f: r.o* **9/2**[2]

010- **2** nk **Alaadel**[229] 8634 6-9-7 **87**..(t) AdamKirby 10 94
(Stuart Williams) *s.i.s: sn pushed along in rr: swtchd lft and hdwy over 1f out: rdn and ev ch whn hmpd ins fnl f: r.o* **10/1**

6-00 **3** 3 1/4 **Captain Jameson (IRE)**[49] 2061 4-9-6 **86**........................ JasonHart 5 83
(John Quinn) *chsd ldrs: shkn up over 2f out: rdn to ld briefly ins fnl f: no ex* **11/1**

4-10 **4** 3/4 **The Armed Man**[26] 2843 6-9-0 **85**............................ PaulaMuir(5) 7 79
(Chris Fairhurst) *hld up in tch: shkn up over 1f out: hung lft and no ex ins fnl f* **16/1**

-040 **5** 2 3/4 **Beyond Equal**[12] 3347 4-9-5 **85**.................................... DavidProbert 3 70
(Stuart Kittow) *led: racd freely: rdn and hung lft over 1f out: hdd & wknd ins fnl f* **10/1**

6051 **6** 2 **Brian The Snail (IRE)**[13] 3309 5-9-12 **92**...................... PaulHanagan 6 71
(Richard Fahey) *chsd ldrs: pushed along 1/2-way: wknd fnl f* **7/1**[3]

6042 **7** 1 1/2 **Zapper Cass (FR)**[17] 3147 6-8-7 **73**........................(v) NicolaCurrie 2 47
(Michael Appleby) *w ldr to 1/2-way: rdn over 1f out: wknd fnl f* **9/1**

-000 **8** 3 1/2 **Naadirr (IRE)**[40] 2393 8-9-6 **86**.................................... DougieCostello 12 49
(Kevin Ryan) *s.i.s: sn pushed along and a in rr* **40/1**

-632 **U** **Royal Residence**[5] 3597 4-9-4 **84**.................................... PJMcDonald 4
(James Tate) *s.i.s: in rr and pushed along 4f out: hdwy and edgd lft over 1f out: cl up whn nt clr run: clipped heels and uns rdr ins fnl f* **15/8**[1]

1m 17.91s (4.11) **Going Correction** +0.875s/f (Soft) **9** Ran SP% **110.3**
Speed ratings (Par 107): **107,106,102,101,97 94,92,88,**
CSF £45.06 CT £437.39 TOTE £5.60: £1.70, £2.40, £3.50; EX 43.60 Trifecta £321.10.
Owner David W Armstrong **Bred** Cheveley Park Stud Ltd **Trained** Norton, N Yorks
■ Stewards' Enquiry : Graham Lee caution: careless riding

FOCUS
Run at a strong pace, this feature sprint was set up for the closers. The winner has been rated back to his best, with a small pb from the second.

3771 DOOM BAR SUMMER H'CAP (DIV I) — 6f 18y

3:45 (3:46) (Class 6) (0-65,66) 3-Y-O+

£3,234 (£962; £481; £300; £300; £300) **Stalls** Centre

Form RPR

0-40 **1** **Stallone (IRE)**[38] 2482 3-9-6 **65**...................................(v) AdamKirby 3 70
(Richard Spencer) *hld up: pushed along over 3f out: hdwy over 2f out: rdn to ld wl ins fnl f: r.o* **5/1**

-450 **2** 3/4 **Cupid's Arrow (IRE)**[10] 3413 5-9-1 **52**........................ JackGarritty 10 57
(Ruth Carr) *led: rdn and edgd rt over 1f out: hdd and unable qck wl ins fnl f* **9/2**[3]

0-06 **3** 1 **Cardaw Lily (IRE)**[132] 533 4-8-9 **46** oh1........................... SamJames 8 48
(Ruth Carr) *chsd ldrs: rdn over 1f out: styd on same pce wl ins fnl f* **22/1**

4264 **4** shd **Global Melody**[2] 3701 4-10-1 **66**........................(p) JosephineGordon 6 67
(Phil McEntee) *chsd ldr: rdn and ev ch fr over 1f out tl no ex wl ins fnl f* **9/4**[1]

-050 **5** 11 **Our Charlie Brown**[24] 2898 5-9-11 **62**........................ PaulMulrennan 2 30
(Tim Easterby) *stall opened fractionally early: chsd ldrs: pushed along 1/2-way: wknd over 1f out* **11/4**[2]

554 **6** 1 1/4 **Gunnison**[12] 3339 3-9-2 **61**.. PaulHanagan 9 24
(Richard Fahey) *hld up: rdn over 2f out: wkng whn hung lft over 1f out* **10/1**

00-3 **7** 12 **Bayards Cove**[20] 3036 4-8-9 **46** oh1.................................... DavidProbert 4
(Stuart Kittow) *s.i.s: a in rr: wknd over 2f out* **20/1**

1m 18.03s (4.23) **Going Correction** +0.875s/f (Soft) **7** Ran SP% **110.5**
WFA 3 from 4yo+ 8lb
Speed ratings (Par 101): **106,105,103,103,88 87,71**
CSF £25.60 CT £422.92 TOTE £6.80: £2.90, £2.80; EX 34.30 Trifecta £288.50.
Owner Rebel Racing Premier **Bred** Ms Marie Higgins **Trained** Newmarket, Suffolk

FOCUS
A moderate sprint handicap, but the winning time was just 0.12sec slower than the preceding 0-95 event. A marginal pb from the winner.

3772 DOOM BAR SUMMER H'CAP (DIV II) — 6f 18y

4:20 (4:23) (Class 6) (0-65,65) 3-Y-O+

£3,234 (£962; £481; £300; £300; £300) **Stalls** Centre

Form RPR

5-00 **1** **Carlovian**[13] 3320 6-9-1 **52**..(v) DougieCostello 2 59
(Mark Walford) *sn led: shkn up over 1f out: rdn and edgd rt ins fnl f: jst hld on* **6/1**[3]

-042 **2** hd **Tadaany (IRE)**[8] 3476 7-9-1 **52**....................................(p) JackGarritty 3 58
(Ruth Carr) *broke wl: plld hrd: sn stdd to trck ldrs: rdn and edgd rt ins fnl f: r.o* **6/4**[1]

-000 **3** 3 1/4 **John Joiner**[13] 3320 7-8-9 **46** oh1........................(v) JosephineGordon 1 43
(Shaun Keightley) *a.p: racd keenly: rdn over 1f out: no ex ins fnl f* **14/1**

-562 **4** 1 1/4 **Cent Flying**[16] 3188 4-9-13 **64**....................................(t) TomMarquand 6 57
(William Muir) *hld up: hdwy over 1f out: rdn and carried rt ins fnl f: wknd towards fin* **7/2**[2]

6504 **5** 1 1/2 **Caledonian Gold**[8] 3476 6-8-2 **46** oh1........................ GavinAshton(7) 10 34
(Lisa Williamson) *racd keenly: w ldrs over 3f: rdn over 1f out: sn wknd (vet said mare lost its left hind shoe)* **9/1**

3224 **6** 1 **Always Amazing**[13] 3320 5-9-6 **57**.................................... TomQueally 9 42
(Derek Shaw) *broke wl: sn stdd and lost pl: hdwy over 1f out: sn rdn: wknd ins fnl f* **12/1**

0-55 **7** nk **The Gingerbreadman**[20] 3058 4-8-4 **46** oh1........................ PaulaMuir(5) 7 31
(Chris Fairhurst) *s.i.s: hld up: pushed along over 2f out: sn outpcd* **8/1**

1m 18.83s (5.03) **Going Correction** +0.875s/f (Soft) **7** Ran SP% **112.0**
Speed ratings (Par 101): **101,100,96,94,92 91,91**
CSF £14.81 CT £117.88 TOTE £5.30: £1.90, £1.60; EX 18.00 Trifecta £144.60.
Owner Profit Pony Racing **Bred** Bradmill Meats Ltd **Trained** Sheriff Hutton, N Yorks

FOCUS
This second division of the weak sprint handicap was 0.80sec slower than the first. The winner has been rated in line with last year's best on synthetics.

3773 MANSIONBET FILLIES' H'CAP (A JOCKEY CLUB GRASSROOTS MIDDLE DISTANCE SERIES QUALIFIER) — 1m 2f 50y

4:55 (4:55) (Class 5) (0-75,76) 3-Y-O **£3,881** (£1,155; £577; £300; £300) **Stalls** Low

Form RPR

4-22 **1** **Birdcage Walk**[24] 2919 3-9-7 **75**....................................(h) TomMarquand 1 84
(Hugo Palmer) *a.p: chsd ldr over 7f out: led over 3f out: rdn out* **5/2**[2]

564 **2** 1 3/4 **Teodora De Vega (IRE)**[66] 1652 3-8-13 **67**........................ PatDobbs 4 72
(Ralph Beckett) *chsd ldr over 2f: remained handy: chsd wnr over 3f out: ev ch over 2f out: sn rdn: styd on same pce fnl f* **11/2**

32-5 **3** 3 1/4 **Tronada**[20] 3041 3-9-7 **75**.. DavidProbert 3 73
(Alan King) *broke wl: sn stdd and lost pl: hld up: hdwy over 3f out: rdn over 1f out: no ex ins fnl f* **7/2**[3]

-342 **4** 8 **Perfecimperfection (IRE)**[13] 3310 3-9-0 **68**........................ DaneO'Neill 5 50
(Marco Botti) *prom: rdn over 2f out: wknd over 1f out* **2/1**[1]

32-6 **5** 16 **Ticklish (FR)**[13] 3295 3-9-8 **76**.. AdamKirby 6 26
(Mark Johnston) *led: rdn and hdd over 3f out: wknd sn after* **9/1**

2m 22.3s (8.90) **Going Correction** +0.875s/f (Soft) **5** Ran SP% **109.5**
Speed ratings (Par 96): **99,97,95,88,75**
CSF £15.55 TOTE £3.80: £1.40, £2.80; EX 11.10 Trifecta £55.10.
Owner G Schoeningh **Bred** G Schoeningh **Trained** Newmarket, Suffolk

FOCUS
There was a fair pace on in this modest 3yo fillies' handicap. The level is a bit fluid.

3774 DOWNLOAD THE MANSIONBET APP H'CAP — 1m 2f 50y

5:25 (5:26) (Class 6) (0-55,55) 4-Y-O+

£3,234 (£962; £481; £300; £300; £300) **Stalls** Low

Form RPR

0-02 **1** **Dor's Law**[21] 3006 6-8-13 **54**....................................(p) SophieRalston(7) 14 65
(Dean Ivory) *hld up: hdwy over 7f out: led 2f out: pushed clr ins fnl f: comf (jockey said mare stumbled after crossing the line, causing her to be unseated)* **6/1**

-005 **2** 5 **Tilsworth Lukey**[13] 3298 6-9-1 **49**.................................... TomMarquand 2 51
(J R Jenkins) *hld up: hdwy over 3f out: chsd wnr over 1f out: sn rdn: styd on same pce ins fnl f* **4/1**[2]

/00- **3** 16 **Weardiditallgorong**[47] 2135 7-8-12 **46** oh1...............(b) GeorgeDowning 8 19
(Des Donovan, Ire) *hld up: hdwy over 3f out: rdn over 2f out: wknd over 1f out* **9/2**[3]

4143 **4** 3/4 **Perceived**[14] 3267 7-9-5 **53**..(p) CamHardie 7 25
(Antony Brittain) *hld up in tch: pushed along and lost pl 6f out: hdwy u.p over 2f out: wknd over 1f out* **7/2**[1]

0200 **5** 1 **Ronni Layne**[13] 3298 5-8-12 **46** oh1................................(v[1]) RobertHavlin 10 16
(Louise Allan) *chsd ldrs: rdn over 2f out: sn wknd* **14/1**

4435 **6** 3/4 **Don't Do It (IRE)**[47] 2111 4-9-5 **53**................................(v) AlistairRawlinson 1 22
(Michael Appleby) *prom: rdn over 2f out: sn wknd* **7/1**

0-00 **7** 5 **Ishallak**[24] 2901 4-9-5 **53**..(v) FergusSweeney 15 13
(Mark Usher) *chsd ldrs: wnt 2nd over 5f out tl rdn over 2f out: wknd over 1f out* **28/1**

0-65 **8** 6 **Silvington**[132] 535 4-8-12 **46** oh1.................................... JohnFahy 6
(Mark Loughnane) *s.s: effrt over 3f out: sn wknd* **33/1**

0-00 **9** 10 **Eternal Destiny**[17] 3142 4-8-12 **46** oh1............................(p[1]) PaulHanagan 16
(Ian Williams) *led: stmbld over 4f out: rdn and hdd 2f out: sn hung lft and wknd (jockey said filly stumbled turning in)* **25/1**

0-00 **10** 20 **Viento De Condor (IRE)**[22] 2975 4-9-6 **54**...............(v) DougieCostello 12
(Tom Clover) *chsd ldrs tl rdn and wknd over 2f out* **14/1**

1140 **11** 25 **Irish Times**[29] 2740 4-9-0 **55**.. CierenFallon(7) 9
(Henry Spiller) *hld up in tch: lost pl over 5f out: sn bhd* **12/1**

2m 21.49s (8.09) **Going Correction** +0.875s/f (Soft) **11** Ran SP% **118.5**
Speed ratings (Par 101): **23,19,6,5,4 4, , , ,**
CSF £29.86 CT £120.24 TOTE £7.80: £2.80, £1.40, £2.20; EX 29.00 Trifecta £222.90.
Owner Mrs Doreen Carter **Bred** Petra Bloodstock Agency Ltd **Trained** Radlett, Herts

FOCUS
The bad ground found out all bar the first pair in this weak handicap. The winner has been rated back in line with her previous turf best.
T/Plt: £73.10 to a £1 stake. Pool: £35,029.32. 349.51 winning units. T/Qpdt: £21.40 to a £1 stake. Pool: £6,050.12. 208.40 winning units. **Colin Roberts**

3738 YARMOUTH (L-H)

Thursday, June 13

OFFICIAL GOING: Heavy changing to soft after race 1 (2.20)
Wind: strong, against Weather: bright spells, blustery, showers later

3775 RACING WELFARE H'CAP — 6f 3y

2:20 (2:21) (Class 6) (0-55,55) 3-Y-O

£3,105 (£924; £461; £300; £300; £300) **Stalls** Centre

Form RPR

-021 **1** **Lincoln Red**[29] 2735 3-9-5 **53**.. JackMitchell 4 60
(Olly Williams) *hld up in tch in last pair: swtchd lft and hdwy ent fnl 2f: effrt to chal jst over 1f out: rdn to ld ins fnl f: styd on (vet said gelding lost its right hind shoe)* **2/1**[1]

-503 **2** 1 1/4 **Josiebond**[13] 3319 3-9-3 **54**.. RowanScott(3) 3 57
(Rebecca Bastiman) *hld up in tch in midfield: effrt 2f out: rdn and hdwy to chse ldrs 1f out: squeezed for room and swtchd lft ins fnl f: kpt on to snatch 2nd last strides* **5/1**[3]

5120 **3** hd **Simba Samba**[63] 1721 3-9-0 **53**....................................(w) SeanDavis(5) 2 56
(Philip McBride) *chsd ldrs tl wnt 2nd over 2f out: rdn to ld over 1f out: hdd and one pce ins fnl f: lost 2nd last strides* **3/1**[2]

The Form Book Flat 2019, Raceform Ltd, Newbury, RG14 5SJ

5305 **4** ½ **Deconso**[25] 2871 3-9-5 **53** HollieDoyle 8 54
(Christopher Kellett) *hld up in tch in midfield: nt clr run 2f out: shuffled bk and swtchd rt over 1f out: rallied ins fnl f: styd on wl towards fin: no threat to wnr* **15/2**

0-50 **5** 3 **Chocco Star (IRE)**[77] 1380 3-9-7 **55** JoeyHaynes 9 47
(Paul Howling) *dwlt: hld up in tch in last pair: clsd to press ldrs ent fnl f: sn rdn and no ex 1f out: wknd ins fnl f* **18/1**

1200 **6** ½ **Champagne Mondays**[13] 3319 3-9-1 **49** (p) KieranO'Neill 6 40
(Scott Dixon) *led: rdn and hdd over 1f out: sn no ex and wknd ins fnl f* **8/1**

-000 **7** 1¾ **Little Tipple**[9] 3442 3-8-5 **46** oh1 (p) LauraPearson(7) 12 31
(John Ryan) *dwlt: sn rcvrd and in tch in midfield: rdn over 2f out: sn outpcd: plugged on same pce and edgd lft ins fnl f* **25/1**

0400 **8** 5 **Budaiya Fort (IRE)**[13] 3319 3-8-10 **51** (t[1]) GraceMcEntee(7) 14 21
(Phil McEntee) *chsd ldrs tl lost pl u.p over 2f out: bhd ins fnl f* **20/1**

0-00 **9** 12 **Andies Armies**[13] 3319 3-8-7 **46** (b) SeamusCronin(5) 16
(Lisa Williamson) *dwlt: t.k.h: sn rcvrd to press ldr tl rdn and lost pl qckly over 2f out: bhd and eased wl ins fnl f* **25/1**

1m 17.73s (5.13) **Going Correction** +0.725s/f (Yiel) **9 Ran SP% 115.6**
Speed ratings (Par 97): **94,92,92,91,87 86,84,77,61**
CSF £11.94 CT £27.99 TOTE £2.70: £1.20, £2.40, £1.10; EX 10.50 Trifecta £25.50.
Owner Top Of The Wolds Racing **Bred** Genesis Green Stud Ltd **Trained** Market Rasen, Lincs

FOCUS
Racing was given the go-ahead after a morning inspection, though the ground was described as heavy and there were lots of non-runners. A poor opener but a decent effort from Lincoln Red, who ran on from last to follow up last month's C&D win. The balance of the second, third and fourth suggest these ratings shouldn't be far out.

3776 BRITISH STALLION STUDS EBF MAIDEN FILLIES' STKS (PLUS 10 RACE) 6f 3y
2:50 (2:52) (Class 5) 2-Y-O £3,752 (£1,116; £557; £278) **Stalls** Centre

Form RPR

1 **Summer Romance (IRE)** 2-9-0 0 JamesDoyle 2 85+
(Charlie Appleby) *trckd ldr tl swtchd rt and effrt over 1f out: rdn and qckned to ld jst ins fnl f: r.o strly: pushed out: readily* **8/13**[1]

2 2 **Bredenbury (IRE)** 2-9-0 0 StevieDonohoe 3 76
(David Simcock) *trckd ldng pair: effrt and swtchd lft jst over 2f out: rdn and r.o ins fnl f: wnt 2nd last strides: no threat to wnr* **9/2**[3]

3 hd **Huboor (IRE)** 2-9-0 0 FrannyNorton 1 75
(Mark Johnston) *led: shkn up over 1f out: rdn and hdd jst ins fnl f: edgd lft and kpt on same pce after: lost 2nd last strides* **4/1**[2]

4 3¼ **Lady Red Moon** 2-8-11 0 GabrieleMalune(3) 4 66
(Marco Botti) *dwlt: hld up in rr: effrt 2f out: sn rdn and no imp: kpt on same pce and hung lft ins fnl f* **12/1**

1m 21.41s (8.81) **Going Correction** +0.725s/f (Yiel) **4 Ran SP% 107.8**
Speed ratings (Par 90): **70,67,67,62**
CSF £3.69 TOTE £1.30; EX 3.50 Trifecta £5.50.
Owner Godolphin **Bred** Roundhill Stud **Trained** Newmarket, Suffolk

FOCUS
This was won last year by subsequent Irish 1,000 Guineas runner-up, Pretty Pollyana. Only a small field, though a potentially smart winner. They went very steadily early on but were flat out in the final quarter-mile. A token rating has been given.

3777 GROSVENOR CASINO OF GREAT YARMOUTH H'CAP 1m 3f 104y
3:25 (3:29) (Class 6) (0-60,60) 3-Y-O £3,105 (£924; £461; £300; £300; £300) **Stalls** Low

Form RPR

0541 **1** **Cherry Cola**[10] 3418 3-9-7 **60** 6ex TrevorWhelan 16 70+
(Sheena West) *stdd and dropped in bhd after s: hld up in rr: clsd travelling strly over 3f out: led 2f out: sn rdn and ducked rt 1f out: shifted bk lft and styd on ins fnl f: rdn out* **10/3**[2]

5600 **2** 2 **Just Once**[16] 3208 3-9-3 **56** PaddyMathers 13 59
(Mrs Ilka Gansera-Leveque) *s.i.s: hld up in rr: hdwy on outer over 3f out: effrt to chse wnr and hung lft over 1f out: swtchd rt jst ins fnl f: kpt on same pce fnl 100yds (jockey said filly hung left-handed under pressure)* **50/1**

0-60 **3** ½ **Land Of Winter (FR)**[5] 3593 3-8-12 **51** RaulDaSilva 12 53
(Rae Guest) *t.k.h: chsd ldr tl led over 2f out: sn rdn and hdd 2f out: kpt on same pce ins fnl f* **9/2**[3]

5300 **4** 3¾ **Mi Manchi (IRE)**[51] 2011 3-9-0 **56** (p[1]) GabrieleMalune(3) 7 52
(Marco Botti) *s.i.s and rousted along early: racd in last quartet: rdn and hdwy over 3f out: unable qck and outpcd 2f out: wl hld and kpt on same pce fnl f* **16/1**

605- **5** 1¼ **Crystal Tiara**[240] 8307 3-9-2 **55** FrannyNorton 11 49
(Mick Channon) *t.k.h: chsd ldrs: clsd 4f out: unable qck and outpcd ent fnl 2f: wl hld and plugged on same pce fnl f* **14/1**

0-60 **6** 4 **Keska**[14] 3246 3-8-2 **46** SeanDavis(5) 6 34
(Richard Fahey) *led: rdn and hdd over 2f out: no ex and lost pl over 1f out: wknd fnl f* **28/1**

0405 **7** 5 **Tunky**[13] 3299 3-8-11 **50** KieranO'Neill 3 30
(James Given) *chsd ldrs: unable qck u.p and outpcd over 2f out: sn btn and wknd over 1f out* **20/1**

-022 **8** 12 **Junior Rip (IRE)**[10] 3418 3-9-7 **60** (bt) AdamMcNamara 1 22
(Roger Charlton) *hld up in tch in midfield: nt clr run: swtchd lft and rdn over 2f out: sn hung lft and btn: bhd and eased ins fnl f (jockey said gelding had hung badly left-handed)* **7/4**[1]

36-0 **9** 7 **Summa Force (IRE)**[59] 1825 3-9-6 **59** (p[1]) RossaRyan 10 10
(Richard Hannon) *nvr travelling: midfield: reminder 7f out: rdn 5f out: lost pl and bhd 2f out: eased ins fnl f: t.o (jockey said gelding was never travelling)* **16/1**

0-40 **10** 7 **Velvet Vista**[46] 2150 3-8-11 **50** (b[1]) LiamJones 2
(Mark H Tompkins) *t.k.h: midfield: rdn 5f out: sn struggling and dropped to rr: wl bhd fnl 2f: eased ins fnl f: t.o (jockey said filly ran too freely and stopped quickly)* **16/1**

2012 **11** 16 **Vin D'Honneur (IRE)**[20] 3034 3-9-7 **60** (p) PatCosgrave 9
(Stuart Williams) *chsd ldrs: rdn 4f out: sn lost pl: wl bhd 2f out: eased fnl f: t.o* **8/1**

2m 32.63s (4.83) **Going Correction** +0.725s/f (Yiel) **11 Ran SP% 123.2**
Speed ratings (Par 97): **108,106,106,103,102 99,96,87,82,77 65**
CSF £174.19 CT £784.65 TOTE £4.90: £1.60, £13.80, £1.70; EX 237.60 Trifecta £995.40.
Owner Ashley Head **Bred** Norman Court Stud **Trained** Falmer, E Sussex

■ Cheng Gong (5-1) and Miss Green Dream (7-1) were withdrawn. Rule 4 only applies to board prices prior to withdrawal - deduction of 25p in the pound. New market formed.

FOCUS
There was a much reduced field for this already moderate handicap. The bare form is modest.

3778 NORWICHINNS.COM H'CAP 1m 6f 17y
3:55 (3:56) (Class 5) (0-70,70) 4-Y-O+ £3,752 (£1,116; £557; £300; £300; £300) **Stalls** High

Form RPR

422- **1** **Imperial Court (IRE)**[202] 9230 4-9-5 **68** (h[1]) JamieSpencer 8 75+
(David Simcock) *stdd s: hld up in rr: clsd over 3f out: nt clr run 2f out: swtchd rt over 1f out: r.o wl u.p ins fnl f to ld cl home* **4/1**[2]

4064 **2** ½ **Princess Harley (IRE)**[22] 2974 4-8-13 **62** FrannyNorton 10 68
(Mick Quinn) *chsd ldr tl 10f out: chsd clr ldng pair after: clsd again over 3f out: led 2f out: rdn over 1f out: battled on gamely ins fnl f: hdd and no ex cl home* **12/1**

5-21 **3** shd **Nasee**[22] 2975 4-9-3 **66** (p) StevieDonohoe 4 72+
(Ed Vaughan) *t.k.h early: hld up in tch in midfield: clsd over 3f out: rdn and ev ch over 1f out: drvn 1f out: kpt on u.p: unable qck nr fin* **6/4**[1]

30-3 **4** 1¾ **Fields Of Fortune**[23] 2936 5-9-4 **67** JamesDoyle 5 71
(Alan King) *t.k.h early: chsd ldrs tl 10f out: off the pce in midfield tl clsd again over 3f out: nt clr run ent fnl 2f: swtchd lft 1f out and sn drvn: no ex and outpcd towards fin (jockey said gelding was denied a clear run)* **9/2**[3]

0-04 **5** 7 **Hatsaway (IRE)**[23] 2928 8-9-3 **66** CharlieBennett 9 60
(Pat Phelan) *broke wl and prom: sn restrained and hld up in last pair: clsd over 3f out: drvn over 2f out: sn struggling and outpcd out: wknd fnl f* **13/2**

3336 **6** ¾ **Velvet Vision**[21] 3010 4-9-4 **67** DanielMuscutt 11 60
(Mark H Tompkins) *t.k.h: hld up in midfield: hdwy to chse ldr 10f out: led 8f out and sn clr: hdd 2f out: sn u.p and no ex: wknd fnl f (jockey said filly ran too freely; vet said mare had lost its left hind shoe)* **17/2**

1155 **7** ½ **Contingency Fee**[38] 2471 4-8-9 **65** (p) GraceMcEntee(7) 3 57
(Phil McEntee) *led tl 8f out: chsd ldr tl over 2f out: sn u.p and outpcd: bhd and wknd 1f out* **25/1**

3m 13.59s (8.89) **Going Correction** +0.725s/f (Yiel) **7 Ran SP% 113.6**
Speed ratings (Par 103): **103,102,102,101,97 97,96**
CSF £47.80 CT £101.22 TOTE £3.60: £2.20, £4.20; EX 40.20 Trifecta £114.80.
Owner John Cook **Bred** Drumbaragh Stud **Trained** Newmarket, Suffolk

FOCUS
This was tactically run and the first and third came from well off the pace. The second has been rated similar to her latest.

3779 ADNAMS GHOST SHIP H'CAP 1m 3y
4:30 (4:31) (Class 4) (0-80,78) 3-Y-O £5,530 (£1,645; £822; £411; £300; £300) **Stalls** Centre

Form RPR

22-0 **1** **Wiretap (FR)**[41] 2364 3-9-7 **78** JamieSpencer 5 85
(David Simcock) *stdd s: hld up in rr: clsd and travelling strly jst over 2f out: swtchd rt and cruised up to ldrs jst over 1f out: rdn to ld ins fnl f: r.o wl* **8/1**

22-3 **2** ¾ **Sezim**[28] 2765 3-9-4 **75** JackMitchell 8 80
(Roger Varian) *in tch in midfield: clsd to chse ldrs 1/2-way: ev ch 2f out: rdn to ld over 1f out: sn shifting lft and hdd ins fnl f: kpt on same pce after and hung lft towards fin* **4/1**[2]

341- **3** 1¼ **Marronnier (IRE)**[247] 8066 3-9-6 **77** (t) DanielMuscutt 7 80+
(Stuart Williams) *hld up in tch in midfield: effrt over 1f out: swtchd lft and drvn to chse ldrs 1f out: pushed lft and short of room wl ins fnl f: hld whn pushed rt cl home* **8/1**

0310 **4** ½ **Molly Mai**[28] 2760 3-8-9 **66** DannyBrock 9 67
(Philip McBride) *hld up in tch in last pair: swtchd lft and hdwy 2f out: drvn and ev ch 1f out: no ex wl ins fnl f: wnt rt cl home* **11/1**

5-12 **5** 2½ **Camber**[42] 2333 3-8-13 **75** SeanDavis(5) 2 73+
(Richard Fahey) *dwlt and rousted along briefly leaving stalls: in tch in midfield: pushed along and clsd jst over 2f out: ev ch and pushed lft over 1f out: no ex ins fnl f: jst getting outpcd whn squeezed out wl ins fnl f* **9/2**[3]

-401 **6** 1¾ **Amorously (IRE)**[17] 3154 3-9-4 **75** RossaRyan 4 66
(Richard Hannon) *chsd ldrs: rdn over 1f out: pushed lft and then edgd lft ins fnl f: hld whn short of room wl ins fnl f* **9/1**

3-54 **7** 2 **Snow Storm (IRE)**[23] 2942 3-9-2 **73** PatCosgrave 3 60
(Saeed bin Suroor) *led: rdn: hung lft and hdd over 1f out: no ex and wknd ins fnl f* **7/2**[1]

-642 **8** 6 **Greek Kodiac (IRE)**[14] 3278 3-9-6 **77** FrannyNorton 6 50
(Mick Quinn) *t.k.h: chsd ldr tl ent fnl 2f: sn lost pl and bhd fnl f* **4/1**[2]

1m 44.01s (5.81) **Going Correction** +0.725s/f (Yiel) **8 Ran SP% 121.0**
Speed ratings (Par 101): **99,98,97,96,94 92,90,84**
CSF £42.39 CT £272.91 TOTE £10.90: £2.60, £2.40, £3.20; EX 61.60 Trifecta £388.20.
Owner Qatar Racing Limited **Bred** E A R L Qatar Bloodstock Ltd **Trained** Newmarket, Suffolk

FOCUS
The most competitive race on the card followed the trend of the day and was won by a horse coming from off the pace. The second and fifth give the form a solid look.

3780 NICHOLSONS STALHAM ENGINEERING CLASSIFIED STKS 1m 3y
5:05 (5:06) (Class 6) 3-Y-O £3,105 (£924; £461; £300; £300; £300) **Stalls** Centre

Form RPR

000- **1** **Pushmi Pullyu (IRE)**[267] 7430 3-8-11 59 RowanScott(3) 11 71+
(Jane Chapple-Hyam) *hld up in tch: clsd jst over 2f out: rdn to ld ent fnl f: pushed along and r.o v strly ins fnl f: easily* **6/1**[3]

30-6 **2** 3½ **Purgatory**[44] 2238 3-9-0 59 GeorgeWood 14 60+
(Chris Wall) *hld up in tch: nt clr run and swtchd lft over 1f out: hdwy ent fnl f: styd on to chse wnr wl ins fnl f: nvr a threat* **11/2**[2]

0-60 **3** ¾ **Tavus (IRE)**[78] 1352 3-9-0 57 AdamMcNamara 3 60+
(Roger Charlton) *stdd and dropped in after s: hld up in rr: clsd and nt clr run 2f out: pushed along: rn green but hdwy ent fnl f: kpt on to go 3rd wl ins fnl f: no ch w wnr (jockey said gelding was denied a clear run on two occasions)* **7/1**

0000 **4** 2 **Mitigator**[5] 3580 3-9-0 60 (b[1]) BrettDoyle 6 54
(Lydia Pearce) *wnt rt sn after s: prom tl chsd ldr 1/2-way: sn rdn and hdd ent fnl f: lost 2nd and wknd ins fnl f* **20/1**

0-02 **5** 3¼ **Approve The Dream (IRE)**[44] 2262 3-8-11 56 JoshuaBryan(3) 1 47
(Julia Feilden) *led tl 2f out: sn u.p and no ex jst ins fnl f: sn wknd* **11/2**[2]

-400 **6** 3¾ **Call Him Al (IRE)**[14] 3270 3-8-9 60 SeanDavis(5) 13 39
(Richard Fahey) *t.k.h: chsd ldr tl 1/2-way: styd chsng ldrs: unable qck over 1f out: fdd ins fnl f* **12/1**

-431 **7** 4½ **Liam's Lass (IRE)**[12] 3352 3-9-0 60 (p) CallumShepherd 9 29
(Pam Sly) *hld up in tch: rdn 3f out: sn drvn and struggling: wl hld fnl 2f (trainer said filly was never travelling)* **11/4**[1]

0603 **8** *1 1/4* **Spirit Of Lucerne (IRE)**[16] 3182 3-8-7 50................ GraceMcEntee(7) 8 26
(Phil McEntee) *bmpd leaving stalls: in tch in midfield: rdn 2f out: sn hung lft and btn: wknd* **50/1**

0300 **9** *9* **Zaula**[64] 1678 3-9-0 58.. FrannyNorton 10 6
(Mick Channon) *t.k.h: chsd ldrs tl over 2f out: sn lost pl: bhd ins fnl f* **10/1**

0-00 **10** *18* **Pageant Master (IRE)**[29] 2735 3-9-0 55...............(t) DanielMuscutt 5
(Mark H Tompkins) *wl in tch in midfield: rdn jst over 2f out: sn struggling and wknd over 1f out: wl bhd and eased ins fnl f: t.o (jockey said gelding stopped quickly)* **28/1**

604- **11** *11* **Rita's Folly**[252] 7931 3-8-9 58........................... DarraghKeenan(5) 4
(Anthony Carson) *wl in tch in midfield: rdn 3f out: sn struggling and lost pl: wl bhd and eased ins fnl f: t.o* **16/1**

1m 43.62s (5.42) **Going Correction** +0.725s/f (Yiel) **11** Ran SP% **117.1**
Speed ratings (Par 97): **101,97,96,94,91 87,83,82,73,55 44**
CSF £38.01 TOTE £6.00: £1.60, £2.00, £2.60; EX 48.80 Trifecta £411.80.
Owner Mrs Jane Chapple-Hyam **Bred** John O'Connor **Trained** Dalham, Suffolk

FOCUS
A weak race, though there were performances of note from both the winner and third.

3781 SKY SPORTS RACING SKY 415 H'CAP 7f 3y
5:40 (5:41) (Class 6) (0-65,65) 4-Y-O+
£3,105 (£924; £461; £300; £300; £300) **Stalls** Centre

Form RPR

5/-0 **1** **Fitzrovia**[10] 3430 4-8-13 57... PatCosgrave 10 69+
(Ed de Giles) *wl in tch in midfield: nt clr run 2f out: bdly hmpd and sddle slipped over 1f out: sn swtchd rt and hdwy to chse ldr 1f out: led ins fnl f: r.o wl: readily* **25/1**

0000 **2** *4* **Song Of Summer**[14] 3279 4-7-13 46 oh1.................(t[1]) NoelGarbutt(3) 14 45
(Phil McEntee) *s.i.s: bhd: clsd and swtchd rt 2f out: hdwy over 1f out: styd on ins fnl f to go 2nd towards fin: no threat to wnr* **33/1**

0633 **3** *1* **Evening Attire**[42] 2318 8-9-6 64.................................. HollieDoyle 12 61
(William Stone) *t.k.h: pressed ldr tl led after 2f: forged ahd u.p and hung lft over 1f out: hdd ins fnl f: sn outpcd and lost 2nd towards fin* **11/4**[1]

1054 **4** *1 1/4* **Foreign Legion (IRE)**[6] 3543 4-9-7 65..................(p) NickyMackay 3 58
(Luke McJannet) *swtchd rt after s: hld up in midfield: clsd and effrt over 2f out: drvn to chse ldrs over 1f out: no ex and wknd ins fnl f* **7/2**[2]

60-0 **5** *1* **Gulland Rock**[17] 3142 8-7-13 48 oh1 ow2............ DarraghKeenan(5) 13 39
(Anthony Carson) *led for 2f: chsd ldr tl lost pl and edgd lft 2f out: rallied and kpt on again ins fnl f: no threat to wnr* **12/1**

-206 **6** *3/4* **Miaella**[22] 2976 4-9-4 62.. JoeyHaynes 6 51
(Paul Howling) *chsd ldrs: effrt jst over 2f out: carried lft over 1f out and unable qck u.p ent fnl f: wknd ins fnl f* **16/1**

0-00 **7** *hd* **Art Echo**[48] 2076 6-9-2 60..(vt[1]) JimmyQuinn 5 49
(John Mackie) *hld up in tch in midfield: nt clr run 2f out: sn swtchd lft and drvn to chse ldrs over 1f out: no ex 1f out: wknd ins fnl f* **11/2**

0202 **8** *2 3/4* **Roaring Forties (IRE)**[15] 3215 6-9-1 62..........(p) RowanScott(3) 2 44
(Rebecca Bastiman) *towards rr: rdn and hdwy jst over 2f out: unable qck u.p over 1f out: wknd ins fnl f* **4/1**[3]

50-0 **9** *14* **Sayesse**[21] 3002 5-9-7 65... CallumShepherd 9 12
(Lisa Williamson) *s.i.s: racd in last trio: clsd and rdn to chse ldrs over 2f out: hung lft and btn wl over 1f out: bhd and eased ins fnl f* **33/1**

305- **10** *nk* **Thunderbell**[183] 9507 5-8-6 50................................. PaddyMathers 4
(Scott Dixon) *racd away fr rivals towards centre: wl in tch in midfield: rdn over 2f out: sn btn: wl bhd and eased ins fnl f* **8/1**

00-0 **11** *1 3/4* **Skito Soldier**[22] 2964 4-8-2 46 oh1............................ JamesSullivan 11
(Ruth Carr) *restless in stalls: chsd ldrs: rdn and struggling whn pushed lft and hmpd wl over 1f out: sn wknd: bhd and eased ins fnl f* **25/1**

1m 30.17s (5.07) **Going Correction** +0.725s/f (Yiel) **11** Ran SP% **122.5**
Speed ratings (Par 101): **100,95,94,92,91 90,90,87,71,71 69**
CSF £669.29 CT £2987.36 TOTE £25.00: £6.80, £9.40, £1.60; EX 817.50.
Owner Simon Treacher & Clarissa Casdagali **Bred** Mrs Fiona Denniff **Trained** Ledbury, H'fords

FOCUS
Not a strong race but an easy winner and a superb ride from Pat Cosgrave, who overcame a badly slipping saddle. Form to treat with caution.
T/Jkpt: £13,482.50 to a £1 stake. Pool: £26,965.05. 2 winning units. T/Plt: £125.40 to a £1 stake. Pool: £64,915.94. 377.67 winning units. T/Qpdt: £62.50 to a £1 stake. Pool: £7,030.04. 83.20 winning units. **Steve Payne**

3782 - 3785a (Foreign Racing) - See Raceform Interactive

3519 LEOPARDSTOWN (L-H)
Thursday, June 13

OFFICIAL GOING: Good (good to yielding in places)

3786a PLUSVITAL BALLYCORUS STKS (GROUP 3) 7f 30y
7:40 (7:41) 3-Y-O+
£33,486 (£10,783; £5,108; £2,270; £1,135; £567)

RPR

1 **Flight Risk (IRE)**[7] 3521 8-9-9 110.......................... KevinManning 2 102+
(J S Bolger, Ire) *hld up bhd ldrs in 4th: drvn nr side under 2f out and prog to chal in 2nd ent fnl f: rdn to ld ins fnl f and kpt on wl to assert nr fin* **10/11**[1]

2 *1 1/4* **Inverleigh (IRE)**[25] 2882 3-8-13 104............................ ColinKeane 4 97+
(G M Lyons, Ire) *hld up: disp 5th at 1/2-way: gng wl and swtchd lft under 2f out where pushed along: n.m.r in 4th over 1f out where swtchd rt: rdn disputing 4th ins fnl f and r.o wl to snatch 2nd on line: nt trble wnr* **4/1**[2]

3 *nse* **Gordon Lord Byron (IRE)**[19] 3103 11-9-9 104.................. WJLee 5 101
(T Hogan, Ire) *chsd ldrs in 3rd: tk clsr order bhd ldr over 2f out: rdn in 2nd 1 1/2f out and no imp on wnr u.p in 2nd wl ins fnl f: denied 2nd on line* **13/2**[3]

4 *hd* **Fire Fly (IRE)**[20] 3061 3-8-10 94.............................. WayneLordan 6 94+
(A P O'Brien, Ire) *hld up: disp 5th at 1/2-way: pushed along in 6th 2f out: sme hdwy nr side over 1f out where rdn: no imp on wnr disputing 3rd wl ins fnl f: kpt on in 4th cl home* **10/1**

5 *2 1/2* **Rionach**[25] 2879 4-9-6 101.. LeighRoche 1 95
(M D O'Callaghan, Ire) *broke wl to ld: over 1 l clr at 1/2-way: rdn over 1f out and sn strly pressed: hdd u.p ins fnl f and sn wknd* **13/2**[3]

6 *2* **I Remember You (IRE)**[20] 3061 3-8-10 80................... MichaelHussey 7 89
(A P O'Brien, Ire) *w.w in rr: last at 1/2-way: pushed along under 2f out where sltly impeded briefly: rdn in 6th over 1f out and no imp on ldrs: kpt on one pce* **33/1**

7 *5 1/2* **Ilex Excelsa (IRE)**[11] 3383 4-9-6 92........................(p) SeamieHeffernan 3 88
(J A Stack, Ire) *trckd ldr in 2nd: drvn over 2f out and sn no imp on ldr in 3rd: wknd u.p 1 1/2f out: eased in rr wl ins fnl f* **33/1**

1m 31.43s
WFA 3 from 4yo+ 10lb **7** Ran SP% **114.0**
CSF £4.78 TOTE £1.60: £1.10, £2.10; DF 4.60 Trifecta £16.20.
Owner Mrs J S Bolger **Bred** James F Hanly **Trained** Coolcullen, Co Carlow

FOCUS
It would be hard to say that the winner is improving, but he is running consistently to his mark and it proved good enough. The fourth and sixth limit the level.

3787 - 3788a (Foreign Racing) - See Raceform Interactive

3675 LONGCHAMP (R-H)
Thursday, June 13

OFFICIAL GOING: Turf: soft

3789a PRIX RIDGWAY (LISTED RACE) (3YO COLTS & GELDINGS) (TURF) 1m 2f
6:35 3-Y-O
£24,774 (£9,909; £7,432; £4,954; £2,477)

RPR

1 **Technician (IRE)**[36] 2523 3-8-11 0............................ OisinMurphy 3 99
(Martyn Meade) *wl into stride: led: shkn up over 2f out: rdn and hdd over 1f out: drvn and responded wl to regain ld ins fnl f: drvn and kpt on wl fnl 100yds* **16/5**[3]

2 *snk* **Battle Of Toro (IRE)**[17] 3-8-11 0......................... MickaelBarzalona 2 99
(A Fabre, France) *bmpd s: trckd ldr in 2nd: urged along 2f out: rdn to ld over 1f out: drvn and hdd ins fnl f: styd on wl but a being hld by wnr* **17/10**[1]

3 *1 1/4* **Diyani (FR)**[21] 3-8-11 0................................... ChristopheSoumillon 5 97
(M Delzangles, France) **47/10**

4 *1* **Veronesi (FR)**[30] 3-8-11 0.. CristianDemuro 4 95
(J-C Rouget, France) **14/5**[2]

5 *1 1/4* **Argyron (IRE)**[48] 3-8-11 0...................................... Pierre-CharlesBoudot 1 92
(A Fabre, France) **58/10**

2m 16.43s (12.43) **5** Ran SP% **119.4**
PARI-MUTUEL (all including 1 euro stake): WIN 4.20; PLACE 1.80, 1.50; SF 9.30.
Owner Team Valor 1 **Bred** Barronstown Stud **Trained** Manton, Wilts

3571 CHEPSTOW (L-H)
Friday, June 14

3790 Meeting Abandoned - waterlogged

3632 GOODWOOD (R-H)
Friday, June 14

OFFICIAL GOING: Soft (good to soft in places; 6.3)
Wind: Virtually nil Weather: Cloudy with bright sunny spells

3797 NOW TV APPRENTICE H'CAP 1m 1f 197y
6:05 (6:06) (Class 5) (0-70,76) 3-Y-O
£6,404 (£1,905; £952; £476; £400; £400) **Stalls** Low

Form RPR

60-2 **1** **Edmond Dantes (IRE)**[21] 3052 3-9-4 67............. Pierre-LouisJamin(3) 3 74
(David Menuisier) *dwlt sltly but sn rcvrd into midfield: effrt to chse clr ldr over 2f out: rdn and no immediate rspnse over 1f out: drvn and styd on strly ins fnl f to ld cl home* **9/2**[2]

0311 **2** *1* **Cardano (USA)**[9] 3478 3-10-2 76 6ex........................ DarraghKeenan 7 81
(Ian Williams) *prom on outer: pushed along to chse clr ldr over 2f out: sn rdn and clsd on ldr over 1f out: led v briefly wl ins fnl f but hdd by wnr cl home* **5/4**[1]

-533 **3** *nk* **Queen's Soldier (GER)**[11] 3418 3-8-12 61................ WilliamCarver(3) 6 65
(Andrew Balding) *trckd ldr: effrt to chse ldr over 2f out: sn rdn and ev ch 1f out: kpt on fnl f* **9/2**[2]

60-4 **4** *shd* **Trelinney (IRE)**[23] 2965 3-8-12 61......................... TylerSaunders(3) 10 65
(Marcus Tregoning) *led: slipped 6 l clr over 4f out: rdn and reduced advantage 2f out: drvn along and hdd wl ins fnl f: no ex nr fin* **16/1**

0-45 **5** *8* **Chinese Alphabet**[48] 2096 3-9-2 67.......................(h[1]) JackDinsmore(5) 2 55
(William Knight) *hld up: pushed along in rr 3f out: rdn over 2f out: nvr on terms* **6/1**[3]

0000 **6** *1* **My Lady Claire**[18] 3170 3-8-12 63................................ LukeCatton(5) 5 49
(Ed Walker) *hld up in last: rdn along in rr 3f out: sme minor late hdwy (jockey said filly was never traveling)* **33/1**

6046 **7** *4* **Azets**[21] 3034 3-9-0 60... RhiainIngram 1 38
(Amanda Perrett) *trckd ldr: rdn along 3f out: drvn and lost pl 2f out: wknd fnl f* **25/1**

40-3 **8** *shd* **Crimean Queen**[43] 2322 3-9-3 66.............................(h) AledBeech(3) 9 44
(Charlie Fellowes) *hld up: rdn and no rspnse over 2f out: nvr on terms (jockey said filly ran too free)* **12/1**

0104 **9** *nk* **Wall Of Sapphire (IRE)**[16] 3223 3-9-1 66................. GeorgiaDobie(5) 8 43
(Mark Loughnane) *racd in rr of midfield: pushed along and no imp 3f out: nvr on terms (trainer said filly was unsuited by the going (soft, good to soft in places) and would prefer a quicker surface)* **25/1**

2m 14.89s (5.99) **Going Correction** +0.55s/f (Yiel) **9** Ran SP% **119.3**
Speed ratings (Par 99): **98,97,96,96,90 89,86,86,86**
CSF £10.68 CT £27.40 TOTE £4.90: £1.40, £1.30, £1.50; EX 12.70 Trifecta £54.30.
Owner Mme C Head & Partner **Bred** Kildaragh Stud **Trained** Pulborough, W Sussex
■ Stewards' Enquiry : Tyler Saunders two-day ban: used whip above the permitted level (Jun 28-29)
Darragh Keenan four-day ban: used whip above the permitted level (Jun 28-30, Jul 1)

FOCUS
After a fairly wet week, the ground was officially soft, good to soft in places with a going stick of 6.3. A really competitive apprentice handicap to open things and a stop-start front-running ride almost pinched it. The runner-up has been rated close to his latest.

3798 SIR ERIC PARKER MEMORIAL MEDIAN AUCTION MAIDEN FILLIES' STKS (PLUS 10 RACE) 6f
6:35 (6:40) (Class 4) 2-Y-O £5,822 (£1,732; £865; £432) Stalls High

Form RPR
040 1 **Show Me Heaven**[22] 2996 2-9-0 0..............................(p[1]) KieranO'Neill 3 68
(Bill Turner) *dwlt bdly and v green early: rdn along and detached 4f out: hdwy u.p 2f out: drvn and styd on wl to ld ins fnl f (jockey said filly was slowly away)* **33/1**
3 2 ½ **Diva Kareem (IRE)**[9] 3461 2-9-0 0.................................. PatCosgrave 1 66
(George Baker) *trckd ldr: led gng best over 2f out: sn rdn over 1f out: drvn and hdd by wnr wl ins fnl f: no ex* **1/1**[1]
4 3 7 **Decora (IRE)**[15] 3257 2-9-0 0.. DavidEgan 2 45
(Mick Channon) *trckd ldr: rdn along and outpcd over 2f out: kpt on one pce fnl f* **2/1**[2]
4 ½ **Krishmaya (IRE)** 2-8-9 0............................ ThoreHammerHansen(5) 6 44
(Adam West) *hld up and rn green early: gd hdwy to chse ldr 2f out: sn rdn and fnd little over 1f out: one pce after* **14/1**
0 5 3 **Resplendent Rose**[25] 2915 2-9-0 0..................................... LiamKeniry 4 35
(Michael Madgwick) *chsd ldr: rdn along and outpcd 2f out: wknd fnl f* **66/1**
0 6 4 **Candid (IRE)**[25] 2918 2-9-0 0................................... RichardKingscote 5 23
(Jonathan Portman) *led: rdn along and hdd over 2f out: hung rt u.p over 1f out: wknd fnl f (jockey said filly hung right-handed under pressure)* **9/2**[3]

1m 16.66s (4.56) **Going Correction** +0.55s/f (Yiel) 6 Ran SP% **112.6**
Speed ratings (Par 92): **91,90,81,80,76 71**
CSF £68.20 TOTE £15.30: £3.90, £1.30; EX 45.90 Trifecta £247.90.
Owner Mrs I Eavis & Mrs L Parfitt **Bred** Mrs Isabel Eavis **Trained** Sigwells, Somerset

FOCUS
An interesting fillies' maiden, but a complete blowout as they clearly went off too fast. A step forward from the winner, with a token rating through the second's fluid debut.

3799 AD MECHANICAL H'CAP 1m 6f
7:10 (7:10) (Class 3) (0-95,96) 4-Y-O- £9,451 (£2,829; £1,414; £708; £352) Stalls Low

Form RPR
000/ 1 **Paddys Motorbike (IRE)**[766] 5879 7-8-11 85................(w) LiamKeniry 6 95
(Nigel Twiston-Davies) *led after 1f and mde rest: 8 l clr 6f out: pushed along to maintain advantage 2f out: sn rdn 1f out: kpt on and nvr chal* **16/1**
03-1 2 3 **Ship Of The Fen**[20] 3091 4-8-13 87.................................. JasonWatson 3 93
(Ian Williams) *led for 1f then sat off pce in 2nd: effrt to chse wnr 3f out: pushed along and short of room wl over 1f out: rdn and kpt on again ins fnl f* **7/4**[2]
21-0 3 3 ¼ **Twin Star (IRE)**[30] 2742 5-9-7 95........................(t) RichardKingscote 4 96
(Noel Williams) *hld up: pushed along 3f out: rdn 2f out: kpt on one pce fnl f* **16/1**
2-14 4 ¾ **Rydan (IRE)**[21] 3044 8-8-4 78.......................................(v) HollieDoyle 1 78
(Gary Moore) *settled off pce in 3rd: pushed along whn squeezed for room over 2f out: sn rdn and kpt on passed btn horses fnl f* **11/2**[3]
13-1 5 1 ½ **Mugatoo (IRE)**[41] 2398 4-9-2 90.................................. JamieSpencer 5 88+
(David Simcock) *restrained in rr: hdwy on outer to go 2nd 2f out: hung rt u.p over 1f out: wknd fnl f* **11/8**[1]
2-00 6 1 **Never Surrender (IRE)**[35] 2578 5-8-8 82..............................(p) JFEgan 8 79
(Charles Hills) *hld up: hdwy to chse wnr over 2f out: sn rdn and wknd ins fnl f* **11/1**

3m 8.55s (4.85) **Going Correction** +0.55s/f (Yiel) 6 Ran SP% **114.0**
Speed ratings (Par 107): **108,106,104,104,103 102**
CSF £45.59 CT £473.55 TOTE £12.30: £3.60, £1.50; EX 80.60 Trifecta £877.40.
Owner Walters Plant Hire Ltd Egan Waste Ltd **Bred** Peter And Jackie Grimes **Trained** Naunton, Gloucs
■ Stewards' Enquiry : Jamie Spencer two-day ban: interference & careless riding (Jun 28-29)

FOCUS
An intriguing staying contest with two progressive last-time-out winners taking on some exposed stayers but one returning from a long absence. The winner has been rated to his old form.

3800 COATES & SEELY FILLIES' H'CAP 1m 3f 218y
7:40 (7:42) (Class 3) (0-90,89) 3-Y-O- £9,451 (£2,829; £1,414; £708; £352) Stalls High

Form RPR
02-4 1 **Chartered**[22] 3013 3-8-2 78.................................... JosephineGordon 7 90
(Ralph Beckett) *trckd ldr: led gng wl 3f out: pushed along to extend advantage 2f out: sn in command: pushed out fnl f* **3/1**[2]
-613 2 4 ½ **Hyanna**[22] 3010 4-10-0 89... CharlesBishop 5 94
(Eve Johnson Houghton) *settled wl in 3rd: effrt to chse wnr 3f out: rdn and no imp 2f out: kpt on one pce fnl f* **7/2**[3]
0-15 3 3 ¼ **Kvetuschka**[34] 2618 3-8-5 81....................................... HollieDoyle 2 81
(Peter Chapple-Hyam) *racd in midfield: pushed along and dropped to last 3f out: rdn 2f out: drvn and kpt on again fnl f (jockey said filly ran in snatches)* **8/1**
06-4 4 hd **White Chocolate (IRE)**[22] 3010 5-9-13 88.................... JamieSpencer 1 87
(David Simcock) *restrained in last: effrt on outer to chse wnr 3f out: sn rdn and little imp 2f out: wknd fnl f* **7/2**[3]
-110 5 26 **Katiesheidinlisa**[36] 2562 3-8-11 87.......................... RichardKingscote 6 45
(Tom Dascombe) *led: rdn along and hdd 3f out: lost pl 2f out: eased whn btn fnl f* **9/4**[1]

2m 44.94s (5.34) **Going Correction** +0.55s/f (Yiel)
WFA 3 from 4yo+ 15lb 5 Ran SP% **111.3**
Speed ratings (Par 104): **104,101,98,98,81**
CSF £13.74 TOTE £4.00: £1.80, £2.10; EX 11.70 Trifecta £55.60.
Owner R Barnett **Bred** W & R Barnett Ltd **Trained** Kimpton, Hants

FOCUS
A tight fillies handicap with the market really struggling to find a favourite but the winner was a big improver, rated around the runner-up.

3801 BESPOKE PROPERTIES FILLIES' H'CAP 6f
8:15 (8:16) (Class 5) (0-70,70) 3-Y-O
£6,404 (£1,905; £952; £476; £400; £400) Stalls High

Form RPR
040 1 **Aperitif**[14] 3302 3-8-10 59.. JamieSpencer 7 64
(Michael Bell) *dwlt and racd in last: hdwy to chse ldrs over 1f out: rdn whn gap appeared and styd on wl to ld 75yds out: drvn out* **12/1**
-443 2 1 **Gleeful**[18] 3146 3-9-7 70.. DavidEgan 4 72
(Roger Varian) *racd in midfield: clsd gng wl on outer 2f out: rdn and ev ch 1f out: kpt on fnl f* **5/2**[2]
-001 3 nse **Maid From The Mist**[31] 2708 3-8-5 54..................... JosephineGordon 6 56
(John Gallagher) *hld up: hdwy u.p over 1f out: rdn and kpt on wl fnl f* **20/1**
3-42 4 shd **Sarasota Bay**[14] 3292 3-9-4 67.............................. RichardKingscote 2 69
(John Quinn) *trckd ldr: pushed along to chse ldr 2f out: rdn upsides and ev ch 1f out: kpt on fnl f (jockey said filly hung left-handed under pressure)* **2/1**[1]
3-03 5 shd **Mrs Worthington (IRE)**[15] 3258 3-9-0 63........................ RobHornby 1 64
(Jonathan Portman) *in tch on outer: pushed along and hdwy to ld 2f out: drvn and hdd by wnr 75yds out: no ex clsng stages (vet said filly lost its left fore shoe)* **12/1**
261 6 2 ¼ **In Trutina**[18] 3157 3-9-2 65... HollieDoyle 5 59
(Archie Watson) *trckd ldr: rdn and unable qck 2f out: wkng whn short of room ins fnl f: no ex (jockey said filly hung left-handed under pressure)* **11/2**[3]
0-5 7 ¾ **Mayfair Madame**[39] 2489 3-8-13 62............................... JasonWatson 8 54
(Stuart Kittow) *racd in midfield: rdn along and outpcd 2f out: one pce fnl f* **16/1**
-000 8 1 ¼ **Aegean Mist**[15] 3258 3-9-1 64...................................... KieranO'Neill 9 52
(John Bridger) *hld up: drvn along and outpcd 2f out: one pce fnl f* **20/1**
6-21 9 3 **All Back To Mine**[21] 3045 3-9-3 66............................... OisinMurphy 3 44
(Joseph Tuite) *led: rdn along and hdd 2f out: wknd fnl f* **7/1**

1m 15.52s (3.42) **Going Correction** +0.55s/f (Yiel) 9 Ran SP% **120.6**
Speed ratings (Par 96): **99,97,97,97,97 94,93,91,87**
CSF £44.17 CT £611.33 TOTE £13.20: £3.40, £1.40, £4.80; EX 47.10 Trifecta £1135.90.
Owner Lordship Stud **Bred** Lordship Stud **Trained** Newmarket, Suffolk

FOCUS
A tight fillies handicap and another come-from-behind victor. This has been rated a bit below the race standard with the second, third and fifth close to form.

3802 NOW TV MAIDEN STKS 1m 3f 44y
8:45 (8:46) (Class 5) 3-Y-O+ £5,239 (£1,559; £779; £389) Stalls High

Form RPR
6 1 **Hereby (IRE)**[29] 2770 3-8-9 0.. HarryBentley 5 75
(Ralph Beckett) *trckd ldr: clsd gng wl over 2f out: rdn along to ld over 1f out: styd on wl fnl f* **6/4**[1]
54 2 2 **Johnny Kidd**[30] 2731 3-9-0 0.. OisinMurphy 4 77
(Andrew Balding) *led: pushed along to maintain short ld 2f out: rdn and hdd by wnr over 1f out: kpt on wl fnl f but no match for wnr* **7/2**[2]
22 3 3 ½ **Selino**[27] 2845 3-9-0 0... DanielMuscutt 3 71
(James Fanshawe) *midfield in tch: clsd gng wl over 2f out: sn rdn and unable to match front pair over 1f out: drifted rt u.p and one pce fnl f (jockey said gelding hung right-handed under pressure)* **6/4**[1]
50 4 2 ½ **So Hi Cardi (FR)**[65] 1690 3-8-9 0................................... JasonWatson 7 62
(Roger Charlton) *hld up: pushed along 4f out: rdn and outpcd over 2f out: kpt on one pce* **16/1**[3]
0 5 5 **Lyrical Waters**[46] 2208 3-9-0 0.................................... CharlesBishop 1 59
(Eve Johnson Houghton) *settled in 3rd: rdn and no imp 3f out: wknd fnl f* **16/1**[3]

2m 34.13s (5.83) **Going Correction** +0.55s/f (Yiel)
WFA 3 from 4yo 14lb 5 Ran SP% **114.0**
Speed ratings (Par 103): **100,98,96,94,90**
CSF £7.58 TOTE £2.40: £1.20, £1.60; EX 7.30 Trifecta £9.50.
Owner J H Richmond-Watson **Bred** Lawn Stud **Trained** Kimpton, Hants

FOCUS
A hard race to assess so the level is fluid.
T/Plt: £56.40 to a £1 stake. Pool: £66,738.27 - 862.99 winning units. T/Qpdt: £22.60 to a £1 stake. Pool: £6,605.33 - 215.84 winning units. **Mark Grantham**

3259 SANDOWN (R-H)
Friday, June 14

OFFICIAL GOING: Soft (good to soft in places on round course; spr 6.4, rnd 6.7, home str - far 6.2, stands' 6.7)
Wind: Fresh, against Weather: Fine but cloudy

3803 BRITISH STALLION STUDS EBF NOVICE STKS (PLUS 10 RACE) 5f 10y
2:00 (2:06) (Class 4) 2-Y-O £4,787 (£1,424; £711) Stalls Low

Form RPR
5 1 **Wentworth Amigo (IRE)**[17] 3190 2-9-5 0........................ OisinMurphy 3 77
(Jamie Osborne) *str; pressed ldr: led 1/2-way: clr wl over 1f out: rdn out* **3/1**[2]
4 2 9 **Fumbleintheforest**[18] 3141 2-9-0 0.............................. TomMarquand 1 40
(Robyn Brisland) *leggy; dwlt: racd in last: outpcd and urged along after 2f: kpt on to take remote 2nd fnl f* **14/1**[3]
43 3 1 ¾ **Dream Kart (IRE)**[15] 3244 2-9-0 0............................ PJMcDonald 2 34
(Mark Johnston) *tall; led to 1/2-way: immediately btn: lost remote 2nd fnl f and fin tired* **4/11**[1]

1m 5.49s (4.19) **Going Correction** +0.575s/f (Yiel) 3 Ran SP% **105.0**
Speed ratings (Par 95): **89,74,71**
CSF £16.66 TOTE £3.20; EX 13.70 Trifecta £25.80.
Owner Jacobs Construction (holdings) Ltd & Ptn **Bred** Mountarmstrong Stud **Trained** Upper Lambourn, Berks

FOCUS
An uncompetitive race and, with the long odds-on favourite failing to show up, the form is difficult to weigh up.

3804 CHASEMORE FARM EBF MAIDEN STKS (PLUS 10 RACE) 7f
2:35 (2:41) (Class 4) 2-Y-O £4,787 (£1,424; £711; £355) Stalls Low

Form RPR
1 **Shared Belief (IRE)** 2-9-5 0.................................... EdwardGreatrex 2 83+
(Archie Watson) *leggy; athletic; trckd ldng pair: trapped bhd them over 2f out and dropped to last: swtchd lft over 1f out: squeezed between rivals fnl f to ld last 75yds* **17/2**[3]
2 hd **Riot (IRE)** 2-9-5 0.. OisinMurphy 3 80+
(John Gosden) *str; looked wl; s.i.s: hld up in last: prog on outer 2f out: shkn up to ld jst ins fnl f: hanging lft and green after: hdd and nt qckn last 75yds (jockey said colt hung left-handed under pressure)* **1/1**[1]
2 3 1 ½ **Visible Charm (IRE)**[21] 3047 2-9-5 0............................. JamesDoyle 5 76
(Charlie Appleby) *str; trckd ldr: shkn up to chal over 2f out: narrow ld over 1f out: hdd and one pce jst ins fnl f* **6/4**[2]

4 *hd* **King's Caper** 2-9-5 0 PJMcDonald 4 76
(Mark Johnston) *leggy; led: pressed and shkn up over 2f out: narrowly hdd over 1f out: one pce after* **12/1**

5 *3/4* **Vulcan (IRE)** 2-9-2 0 MitchGodwin(3) 6 74
(Harry Dunlop) *workmanlike; bit on the leg; in tch in 4th: effrt on outer to press ldrs 2f out: outpcd and btn over 1f out: kpt on again nr fin* **40/1**

1m 35.05s (5.75) **Going Correction** +0.575s/f (Yiel) **5** Ran SP% **110.7**
Speed ratings (Par 95): **90,89,88,87,86**
CSF £17.91 TOTE £8.00: £3.00, £1.30; EX 22.30 Trifecta £31.40.

Owner China Horse Club/Ballylinch Stud/Clipper **Bred** Ballyhane Stud **Trained** Upper Lambourn, W Berks

FOCUS
Add 15 yards. Just a small field but no shortage of potential. They finished in a bit of a heap but the first two home could be well above average. This has been rated through the third to his debut level.

3805 FOLLOW @RACINGTV H'CAP 7f
3:10 (3:15) (Class 5) (0-75,80) 3-Y-O
£4,528 (£1,347; £673; £336; £300; £300) **Stalls** Low

Form RPR

5-21 **1** **Ouzo**[9] 3471 3-9-13 **80** 6ex SeanLevey 5 86+
(Richard Hannon) *looked wl; hld up in tch: prog on wd outside to ld wl over 1f out: pressed fnl f: rdn out and a in control* **4/9**[1]

0346 **2** *1* **Facethepuckout (IRE)**[15] 3273 3-9-5 **72** (p) OisinMurphy 3 75
(John Ryan) *trckd ldng pair: clsd to chal 2f out: chsd wnr sn after: cl enough fnl f: styd on but a readily hld* **12/1**

0-00 **3** *3* **Carey Street (IRE)**[34] 2635 3-9-3 **70** PJMcDonald 6 65
(John Quinn) *mostly in last: shkn up wl over 2f out: prog over 1f out: tk 3rd ins fnl f: styd on but no ch* **33/1**

3-06 **4** *4* **Spencers Son (IRE)**[15] 3278 3-9-5 **72** (v[1]) JasonWatson 2 57
(Richard Spencer) *trckd ldr: led over 2f out to wl over 1f out: wknd fnl f* **10/1**[3]

-005 **5** *2 3/4* **God Has Given**[24] 2933 3-9-2 **69** (p[1]) JamesDoyle 1 47
(Ian Williams) *in tch: reminders and no prog 2f out: wknd and eased fnl f* **9/2**[2]

00-0 **6** *5* **Brawny**[34] 2630 3-9-6 **73** KieranShoemark 4 38
(Charles Hills) *led at gd pce to over 2f out: wknd qckly* **20/1**

1m 32.96s (3.66) **Going Correction** +0.575s/f (Yiel) **6** Ran SP% **111.9**
Speed ratings (Par 99): **102,100,97,92,89 84**
CSF £7.15 TOTE £1.20: £1.10, £2.40; EX 5.40 Trifecta £27.70.

Owner Michael Kerr-Dineen & Martin Hughes **Bred** Equine Breeding Limited **Trained** East Everleigh, Wilts

FOCUS
Add 15 yards. With the exception of the odds-on Ouzo, the majority of these were out of form. This has been rated in line with the time and race average.

3806 JOIN RACING TV NOW H'CAP 1m 1f 209y
3:45 (3:52) (Class 3) (0-90,91) 4-Y-O+
£12,450 (£3,728; £1,864; £932; £466; £234) **Stalls** Low

Form RPR

1151 **1** **Badenscoth**[22] 3004 5-9-7 **86** RobertWinston 11 97+
(Dean Ivory) *hld up in midfield: smooth prog to ld 2f out: clr over 1f out: rdn out and kpt on wl* **14/1**

-052 **2** *2 1/2* **Mandarin (GER)**[13] 3338 5-9-1 **80** (t) PJMcDonald 4 85
(Ian Williams) *s.s: wl in rr: prog over 2f out: rdn to chse clr wnr over 1f out: styd on but unable to threaten (jockey said gelding was slowly away)* **11/2**[2]

43-0 **3** *1 1/4* **Rotherwick (IRE)**[28] 2800 7-9-7 **86** (t) RaulDaSilva 8 89
(Paul Cole) *lost pl after 3f and sn in rr: urged along 3f out: prog 2f out: styd on to take 3rd ins fnl f* **33/1**

25-5 **4** *3/4* **Frontispiece**[62] 1757 5-9-5 **84** KieranShoemark 12 85
(Amanda Perrett) *hld up in midfield: lost pl 4f out and last of main gp over 3f out: rdn and prog over 2f out: tk 3rd briefly fnl f: kpt on same pce after* **14/1**

213- **5** *1 1/4* **Herculean**[231] 8596 4-9-12 **91** JasonWatson 3 90
(Roger Charlton) *looked wl; wl in tch: rdn and nt qckn over 2f out: no imp on ldrs after but plugged on* **5/4**[1]

4053 **6** *3 1/4* **C Note (IRE)**[4] 3663 6-9-4 **83** CharlesBishop 7 75
(Heather Main) *prom: overall ldr 3f out: rdn and hdd 2f out: wknd over 1f out* **11/2**[2]

0-1P **7** *5* **He's Amazing (IRE)**[18] 3168 4-9-6 **85** LiamKeniry 6 67
(Ed Walker) *wl in tch: rdn over 2f out: no prog and wknd over 1f out* **20/1**

5023 **8** *2 1/2* **Mr Scaramanga**[14] 3315 5-9-4 **83** OisinMurphy 10 60
(Simon Dow) *looked wl; cl up: rdn and stl wl there over 2f out: wknd qckly over 1f out* **12/1**[3]

5-54 **9** *1* **Noble Gift**[34] 2620 9-9-5 **84** CallumShepherd 13 59
(William Knight) *rdn to ld after 1f: set str pce but jnd: breather 1/2-way: styd alone on far side in st: sn lost ld and btn* **25/1**

253- **10** *2 3/4* **Sing Out Loud (IRE)**[197] 9313 4-9-4 **83** PatCosgrave 9 53
(Chris Gordon) *wl in tch: rdn over 2f out and wdst of main gp: wknd over 1f out and eased* **25/1**

0-31 **11** *11* **Tralee Hills**[119] 735 5-9-1 **80** (w) TomMarquand 1 28
(Peter Hedger) *sn detached in last and urged along: t.o (jockey said gelding was never travelling; trainer said gelding was unsuited by the ground (soft, good to soft in places) on this occasion and would prefer a quicker surface)* **20/1**

5003 **12** *3/4* **Secret Art (IRE)**[14] 3300 9-9-5 **84** (v) JamesDoyle 2 30
(Gary Moore) *pushed up to join ldr after 2f at str pce: led main gp towards nr side in st: hdd 3f out and wknd rapidly: eased and t.o (jockey said gelding stopped quickly)* **33/1**

0-23 **13** *14* **Allegiant (USA)**[17] 3192 4-8-7 **72** EdwardGreatrex 5
(Stuart Williams) *looked wl; led 1f: pushed along to stay prom by 1/2-way: c to nr side rail in st and sn t.o (jockey said gelding stopped quickly)* **14/1**

2m 13.5s (3.30) **Going Correction** +0.575s/f (Yiel) **13** Ran SP% **126.0**
Speed ratings (Par 107): **109,107,106,105,104 101,97,95,95,92 84,83,72**
CSF £85.98 CT £2541.52 TOTE £19.10: £3.40, £2.30, £8.10; EX 133.90 Trifecta £4302.30.

Owner Peter J Skinner **Bred** Peter J Skinner **Trained** Radlett, Herts

FOCUS
Add 15 yards. This looked competitive but the market was dominated by the lightly raced Herculean. It was strongly run and most of the runners headed to the stands' rail in the straight. The runner-up has been rated to form.

3807 BRITISH STALLIONS EBF FILLIES' H'CAP 1m
4:20 (4:25) (Class 4) (0-85,81) 3-Y-O £7,115 (£2,117; £1,058; £529) **Stalls** Low

Form RPR

6-46 **1** **Sufficient**[29] 2768 3-9-2 **76** (h) OisinMurphy 4 81
(Rod Millman) *sltly on toes; t.k.h: trckd ldr after 2f: chal and upsides 3f out: rdn to ld jst over 1f out: grad asserted* **9/2**[2]

-242 **2** *1* **Nooshin**[41] 2420 3-9-1 **75** JamesDoyle 3 78
(Charles Hills) *taken down early: led at mod pce: brought field to nr side in st: jnd 3f out: rdn and hdd jst over 1f out: nt qckn after* **6/4**[1]

-215 **3** *3/4* **I Am Magical**[24] 2934 3-9-6 **80** StevieDonohoe 5 81
(Charlie Fellowes) *stdd s: hld up in last: shkn up to chse ldng pair over 1f out: tried to cl fnl f: no imp last 100yds* **6/4**[1]

513 **4** *1 3/4* **Liliofthelamplight (IRE)**[24] 2925 3-9-5 **79** PJMcDonald 1 76
(Mark Johnston) *pressed ldr 2f: styd cl up: rdn 2f out: sn dropped to last and one pce after* **11/1**[3]

1m 48.84s (5.54) **Going Correction** +0.575s/f (Yiel) **4** Ran SP% **106.5**
Speed ratings (Par 98): **95,94,93,91**
CSF £11.35 TOTE £5.00; EX 11.70 Trifecta £20.90.

Owner Whitsbury Manor Stud And Mrs M E Slade **Bred** Whitsbury Manor Stud And Mrs M E Slade **Trained** Kentisbeare, Devon

FOCUS
Add 15 yards. This small-field fillies' handicap developed into a sprint and the form is suspect, but the winner has been rated to her best.

3808 BECK CELEBRATING 25 YEARS OF EXCELLENCE H'CAP 1m 1f 209y
4:50 (4:57) (Class 4) (0-80,78) 3-Y-O
£7,115 (£2,117; £1,058; £529; £300; £300) **Stalls** Low

Form RPR

2104 **1** **Ragnar**[39] 2470 3-9-6 **77** JasonWatson 6 87+
(Roger Charlton) *hld up in last trio: prog to trck ldrs 2f out: squeezed through to ld over 1f out: drvn and more than a l up ins fnl f: jst clung on* **10/1**

53-3 **2** *nse* **Rhythmic Intent (IRE)**[45] 2249 3-9-6 **77** PJMcDonald 8 84
(Stuart Williams) *str; looked wl; sn pressed ldr: upsides over 3f out: rdn to take narrow ld 2f out: hdd over 1f out: rallied wl last 100yds: jst failed* **9/4**[1]

-530 **3** *2 3/4* **The Pink'n**[28] 2796 3-9-5 **76** RobHornby 3 77
(Seamus Mullins) *hld up in last trio: shkn up on outer of gp over 2f out: prog jst over 1f out: styd on to take 3rd last strides* **10/1**

3236 **4** *hd* **Ritchie Valens (IRE)**[27] 2828 3-9-6 **77** TomMarquand 5 78
(Richard Hannon) *cl up: rdn jst over 2f out: nt qckn over 1f out: chsd ldng pair ins fnl f: no imp and lost 3rd last strides (jockey said colt ran too freely)* **7/2**[2]

3-14 **5** *3/4* **Sea Sculpture**[14] 3324 3-9-7 **78** OisinMurphy 4 77
(Andrew Balding) *str; led: brought field to nr side in st: jnd over 2f out: rdn and hdd 2f out: steadily fdd fnl f* **6/1**[3]

60-2 **6** *shd* **Francisco Bay**[7] 3548 3-8-12 **69** KieranShoemark 2 68
(Ed de Giles) *t.k.h: cl up: rdn 2f out: one pce over 1f out (jockey said colt ran too freely)* **10/1**

-401 **7** *3* **Valence**[31] 2711 3-9-2 **73** (p) RobertHavlin 7 66
(Ed Dunlop) *trckd ldrs: rdn and on terms jst over 2f out: wknd over 1f out* **12/1**

2202 **8** *11* **Htilominlo**[12] 3373 3-9-5 **76** (tp) JamesDoyle 1 47
(Sylvester Kirk) *a in last and nvr gng that wl: no prog over 2f out: eased over 1f out (jockey said colt was never travelling)* **6/1**[3]

2m 15.21s (5.01) **Going Correction** +0.575s/f (Yiel) **8** Ran SP% **116.5**
Speed ratings (Par 101): **103,102,100,100,100 99,97,88**
CSF £33.57 CT £238.36 TOTE £10.50: £2.80, £1.40, £2.80; EX 42.20 Trifecta £386.60.

Owner Kingwood Stud Management Co Ltd **Bred** The National Stud **Trained** Beckhampton, Wilts

FOCUS
Add 15 yards. This had a competitive look to it and was run at an honest pace. The winner has been rated as improving.

3809 CARPETRIGHT SUPPORTS THE BHF H'CAP (JOCKEY CLUB GRASSROOTS FLAT STAYERS SERIES QUALIFIER) 1m 6f
5:25 (5:26) (Class 5) (0-70,70) 3-Y-O
£4,528 (£1,347; £673; £336; £300; £300) **Stalls** Low

Form RPR

00-1 **1** **Goshen (FR)**[7] 3538 3-9-10 **70** 6ex HectorCrouch 3 88+
(Gary Moore) *mde virtually all: hung lft bnd after 2f: pushed along and drew rt away over 2f out: impressive* **10/11**[1]

4432 **2** *9* **Luck Of Clover**[18] 3153 3-9-5 **65** OisinMurphy 8 68
(Andrew Balding) *looked wl; lft chsng wnr after 2f tl 1/2-way: rdn to go 2nd again 3f out: clr of rest fnl 2f but no ch* **7/1**[3]

00-2 **3** *3* **Spargrove**[37] 2530 3-8-12 **58** CharlieBennett 9 57
(Hughie Morrison) *cl up: impeded after 2f: prog to chse wnr 1/2-way to 3f out: sn outpcd u.p: kpt on* **9/2**[2]

-605 **4** *nse* **Spring Run**[20] 3092 3-8-13 **59** RobHornby 10 58
(Jonathan Portman) *hld up: rdn and prog 3f out: disp 3rd pl fnl f but no ch w ldng pair* **16/1**

0-60 **5** *4 1/2* **Alramz**[52] 2011 3-8-12 **58** CallumShepherd 7 50
(Lee Carter) *hld up in rr: swift prog over 4f out: cl up 3f out: sn outpcd: wknd over 1f out* **40/1**

-242 **6** *3 1/2* **Hummdinger (FR)**[20] 3092 3-9-5 **65** JamesDoyle 2 53
(Alan King) *looked wl; hld up wl in rr: rdn over 3f out: passed a few wkng rivals fnl 2f* **10/1**

5-01 **7** *4 1/2* **Twenty Years On**[20] 3092 3-9-4 **67** FinleyMarsh(3) 11 48
(Richard Hughes) *in tch: rdn 3f out: wknd over 2f out (trainer said gelding was unsuited by the ground (soft, good to soft in places) on this occasion and would prefer a quicker surface)* **11/1**

5052 **8** *13* **Enyama (GER)**[15] 3253 3-8-7 **53** JohnFahy 6 16
(Michael Attwater) *w wnr whn impeded after 2f: styd cl up tl wkd qckly wl over 2f out* **40/1**

0-65 **9** *3* **Craneur**[14] 3311 3-9-3 **63** TomMarquand 4 22
(Harry Dunlop) *chsd ldrs: rdn and wknd 3f out: eased* **12/1**

0606 **P** **Ginge N Tonic**[6] 3593 3-7-13 **48** oh1 .... NoelGarbutt(3) 5
(Adam West) *sn detached in last: nvr gng wl: t.o 1/2-way: p.u and dismntd nr fin (jockey said gelding lost its action; vet said gelding was lame on its right fore)* **25/1**

3m 13.66s (7.66) **Going Correction** +0.575s/f (Yiel) **10** Ran SP% **122.8**
Speed ratings (Par 99): **101,95,94,94,91 89,86,79,77,**
CSF £8.43 CT £21.86 TOTE £1.70: £1.40, £1.60, £1.90; EX 8.30 Trifecta £33.20.
Owner Steven Packham **Bred** Christophe Toulorge **Trained** Lower Beeding, W Sussex

FOCUS
Add 15 yards. This moderate staying handicap was taken apart by an improver, and the second has been rated to form.
T/Plt: £502.40 to a £1 stake. Pool: £65,019.45 - 94.47 winning units. T/Qpdt: £65.40 to a £1 stake. Pool: £7,231.40 - 81.72 winning units. **Jonathan Neesom**

3094 YORK (L-H)
Friday, June 14

OFFICIAL GOING: Soft (5.7, home str - stands' 5.6, ctr 5.7, far 5.6)
Wind: Moderate half behind Weather: Cloudy

3810 BRITTAINS BEVERAGES BRITISH EBF NOVICE STKS (PLUS 10 RACE) 5f
1:50 (1:50) (Class 3) 2-Y-O **£9,703** (£2,887; £1,443; £721) **Stalls** High

Form RPR

32 **1** **Hurstwood**[14] 3290 2-9-5 0 .... DavidAllan 1 80
(Tim Easterby) *wnt lft s: mde all: jnd and rdn ent fnl f: sn drvn: kpt on wl towards fin* **7/2**[3]

2 ½ **Asmund (IRE)** 2-9-5 0 .... BenCurtis 8 78+
(K R Burke) *trckd ldrs: hdwy 2f out: rdn to chal ent fnl f: sn edgd lft and ev ch tl kpt on same pce towards fin* **9/1**

02 **3** 3¼ **My Kinda Day (IRE)**[13] 3355 2-9-5 0 .... TonyHamilton 2 67
(Richard Fahey) *t.k.h early: trckd ldrs: pushed along and hdwy wl over 1f out: rdn and kpt on fnl f* **5/1**

3 **4** ¾ **Kilham**[14] 3290 2-9-5 0 .... TomEaves 9 64
(Declan Carroll) *prom: cl up 2f out: rdn over 1f out: kpt on same pce fnl f* **10/1**

2 **5** 1 **Olcan**[10] 3451 2-9-5 0 .... DavidNolan 3 60
(David O'Meara) *trckd ldrs: pushed along and sltly outpcd 2f out: sn rdn and kpt on fnl f* **10/3**[2]

5 **6** ¾ **She Can Dance**[27] 2840 2-9-0 0 .... DanielTudhope 7 53
(Kevin Ryan) *cl up: rdn along 2f out: wknd over 1f out* **5/2**[1]

4 **7** 3¾ **Noddy Shuffle**[58] 1844 2-9-5 0 .... NathanEvans 6 44
(Michael Easterby) *sn outpcd and a in rr* **33/1**

0 **8** 5 **Invincible Bertie (IRE)**[8] 3507 2-9-2 0 .... RowanScott(3) 5 26
(Nigel Tinkler) *chsd ldrs: rdn along 2f out: sn drvn and wknd* **33/1**

1m 1.06s (2.86) **Going Correction** +0.45s/f (Yiel) **8** Ran SP% **115.5**
Speed ratings (Par 97): **95,94,89,87,86 85,79,71**
CSF £35.00 TOTE £4.30: £1.50, £3.00, £1.60; EX 41.20 Trifecta £239.70.
Owner David W Armstrong **Bred** Highfield Farm Llp **Trained** Great Habton, N Yorks

FOCUS
There was an additional 3mm of rain on race day morning, and the going was given as soft (Going Stick 5.7. Home straight - stands' side 5.6; centre 5.7; far side 5.6). Jockeys returning after the first concurred with the official description. There was a light (8mph) southerly tailwind. No more than a fair novice, but this rates another step forward from the winner.

3811 CONSTANT SECURITY H'CAP 1m 2f 56y
2:20 (2:20) (Class 4) (0-85,86) 4-Y-0+
£8,881 (£2,659; £1,329; £664; £332; £300) **Stalls** Low

Form RPR

0316 **1** **Music Seeker (IRE)**[18] 3161 5-8-7 **78** ....(t) CianMacRedmond(7) 9 87
(Declan Carroll) *hld up towards rr: stdy hdwy 3f out: chsd ldrs 2f out: rdn to chal jst over 1f out: slt ld ins fnl f: drvn out* **16/1**

3202 **2** 1 **Addis Ababa (IRE)**[17] 3180 4-9-8 **86** ....(v[1]) DanielTudhope 8 93
(David O'Meara) *trckd ldrs: hdwy and cl up over 3f out: rdn to ld wl over 1f out: drvn and hdd ins fnl f: ev ch tl no ex towards fin* **17/2**

-411 **3** 2 **Archie Perkins (IRE)**[6] 3568 4-8-11 **78** 5ex .... RowanScott(3) 12 81
(Nigel Tinkler) *in tch: hdwy on outer over 3f out: chsd ldrs 2f out: drvn and kpt on fnl f* **10/3**[1]

0402 **4** shd **Beverley Bullet**[6] 3567 6-7-13 **66** oh2 ....(p) JamieGormley(3) 7 69
(Lawrence Mullaney) *sn led: pushed along over 2f out: rdn and hdd wl over 1f out: sn drvn: kpt on same pce fnl f* **10/1**

0-04 **5** ½ **Mikmak**[20] 3072 6-9-4 **82** ....(p) DavidAllan 13 84
(Tim Easterby) *hld up towards rr: stdy hdwy 3f out: chsd ldrs 2f out: rdn over 1f out: drvn and kpt on wl fnl f* **8/1**[3]

60-3 **6** 4 **Pioneering (IRE)**[7] 3547 5-8-5 **69** .... BenCurtis 11 63
(Roger Fell) *hld up: hdwy over 4f out: chsd ldrs over 2f out: rdn and ev ch wl over 1f out: sn drvn: grad wknd* **8/1**[3]

000/ **7** nk **Top Notch Tonto (IRE)**[39] 2497 9-9-1 **82** .... BenRobinson(3) 16 75
(Brian Ellison) *dwlt and in rr: pushed along 4f out: rdn 3f out: styd on wl appr fnl f: nrst fin* **22/1**

3254 **8** 5 **Delph Crescent (IRE)**[13] 3338 4-9-1 **79** ....(p) PaulHanagan 10 62
(Richard Fahey) *hld up: hdwy 3f out: rdn along 2f out: sn drvn and no imp* **8/1**[3]

-001 **9** 2 **Ghalib (IRE)**[8] 3502 7-9-3 **81** 4ex .... LewisEdmunds 1 60
(Rebecca Bastiman) *trckd ldng trio: pushed along over 3f out: rdn over 2f out: grad wknd (trainer said the race may have come too soon for the gelding having ran at Hamilton 8 days ago)* **11/1**

1-02 **10** 3 **Sputnik Planum (USA)**[8] 3502 5-9-6 **84** ....(t) AlistairRawlinson 3 57
(Michael Appleby) *trckd ldrs: pushed along over 4f out: rdn 3f out: sn wknd (trainer said the race may have come too soon for the gelding having ran at Hamilton 8 days ago)* **15/2**[2]

-023 **11** 1¼ **Swift Emperor (IRE)**[13] 3356 7-9-2 **80** .... RobbieDowney 2 51
(David Barron) *hld up: effrt and sme hdwy 4f out: rdn along over 3f out: sn wknd (trainer could offer no explanation for the gelding's performance)* **16/1**

0-0 **12** 17 **Empress Ali (IRE)**[36] 2563 8-9-7 **85** .... JamesSullivan 14 22
(Tom Tate) *trckd ldng pair: pushed along on outer over 3f out: rdn wl over 2f out: sn drvn and wknd* **25/1**

5-53 **13** 1 **Zabeel Star (IRE)**[31] 2186 7-8-11 **82** .... LauraCoughlan(7) 5 17
(Karen McLintock) *s.i.s: a in rr* **25/1**

210- **14** 50 **Jamih**[231] 8596 4-9-6 **84** .... TomEaves 15
(Tina Jackson) *cl up: rdn along over 3f out: wknd qckly: bhd and eased fnl 2f* **80/1**

2m 12.11s (1.81) **Going Correction** +0.45s/f (Yiel) **14** Ran SP% **121.2**
Speed ratings (Par 105): **110,109,107,107,107 103,103,99,98,95 94,81,80,40**
CSF £141.74 CT £574.33 TOTE £17.90: £5.40, £3.20, £1.80; EX 174.30 Trifecta £763.90.
Owner Mrs Sarah Bryan **Bred** P J Connolly **Trained** Malton, N Yorks

FOCUS
A competitive affair. The winner has been rated close to his best.

3812 SKF ROUS (S) STKS 6f
2:55 (2:58) (Class 3) 2-Y-O **£12,938** (£3,850; £1,924; £962) **Stalls** High

Form RPR

430 **1** **Amnaa**[17] 3196 2-8-9 0 .... ConnorBeasley 17 70
(Adrian Nicholls) *cl up nr stands' rail: led over 2f out: rdn and edgd markedly lft to centre wl over: jnd and drvn ins fnl f: kpt on wl towards fin* **22/1**

0421 **2** ½ **Lili Wen Fach (IRE)**[6] 3573 2-8-9 0 .... AndrewMullen 6 69
(David Evans) *prom centre: rdn 2f out: chsd wnr over 1f out: drvn and ev ch ins fnl f* **11/2**[3]

5 **3** 2¼ **Speed Dating (FR)**[39] 2475 2-9-0 0 .... BenCurtis 18 67
(K R Burke) *racd nr stands' side: trckd ldrs: swtchd lft to centre after 1f: pushed along and sltly outpcd 2f out: rdn over 1f out: styd on fnl f* **9/2**[2]

065 **4** nk **Sparkling Breeze**[25] 2907 2-9-0 0 .... PaulMulrennan 3 66
(Michael Dods) *in tch centre: hdwy to chse ldrs 2f out: rdn over 1f out: kpt on u.p fnl f* **33/1**

035 **5** 1 **Return To Senders (IRE)**[8] 3512 2-8-9 0 ....(p[1]) SeanDavis(5) 8 63
(Jamie Osborne) *in tch centre: pushed along and reminder 1/2-way: rdn 2f out: sn drvn and kpt on u.p fnl f* **16/1**

313 **6** 1¼ **Calippo (IRE)**[4] 3652 2-8-9 0 ....(p) LukeMorris 20 54
(Archie Watson) *racd nr stands' rail: led: rdn along and hdd over 2f out: drvn over 1f out: grad wknd* **7/1**

314 **7** 2 **Chattanooga Boy (IRE)**[10] 3451 2-9-0 0 .... GrahamLee 9 53
(George Scott) *racd centre: prom: rdn along and ev ch wl over 1f out: sn drvn and grad wknd appr fnl f (vet said colt was lame right-fore)* **6/1**

245 **8** ½ **Out Of Breath**[44] 2275 2-9-0 0 ....(b[1]) NicolaCurrie 1 52
(Jamie Osborne) *chsd ldrs on inner: rdn along 2f out: sn drvn and grad wknd over 1f out* **16/1**

00 **9** ¾ **Beautrix**[15] 3244 2-8-9 0 .... TomEaves 5 44
(Michael Dods) *towards rr centre: hdwy to trck ldrs over 3f out: rdn along 2f out: sn drvn and grad wknd* **50/1**

62 **10** 1 **Sir Gordon**[5] 3634 2-9-0 0 .... SilvestreDeSousa 11 46
(Mick Channon) *towards rr centre: pushed along 1/2-way: hdwy over 2f out: rdn over 1f out: sn drvn and no imp* **7/2**[1]

0 **11** 2½ **Queen Moya (IRE)**[11] 3411 2-8-4 0 .... FayeMcManoman(5) 12 34
(Nigel Tinkler) *in tch centre: rdn along wl over 2f out: sn wknd* **66/1**

6 **12** 1½ **The Trendy Man (IRE)**[25] 2907 2-9-0 0 ....(p[1]) DanielTudhope 4 34
(David O'Meara) *prom centre: rdn along over 2f out: sn wknd* **16/1**

00 **13** 3½ **Rain Cap**[15] 3257 2-9-0 0 .... GeraldMosse 13 24+
(Mick Channon) *chsd ldrs centre: rdn along 2f out: sn wknd* **33/1**

0 **14** ¾ **Pronghorn**[9] 3477 2-9-0 0 .... NathanEvans 2 22
(Michael Easterby) *chsd ldrs centre: rdn along wl over 2f out: sn wknd* **66/1**

15 8 **Afterallthat (IRE)** 2-9-0 0 .... DavidNolan 14
(Richard Fahey) *chsd ldrs centre: rdn along over 2f out: sn wknd* **12/1**

64 **16** 3¼ **Classy Lady**[25] 2907 2-8-6 0 .... BenRobinson(3) 19
(Ollie Pears) *chsd ldng pair nr stands' rail: rdn along 2f out: sn wknd* **28/1**

17 3¾ **Archie Bear** 2-9-0 0 .... DougieCostello 21
(Mark H Tompkins) *dwlt: a towards rr nr stands' rail* **50/1**

18 22 **Microclimate** 2-9-0 0 .... DavidAllan 16
(Mark H Tompkins) *dwlt and towards rr stands' side whn j. path after 1f: bhd after (jockey said colt jumped the crossing shortly after the start and stumbled)* **66/1**

1m 15.35s (3.75) **Going Correction** +0.45s/f (Yiel) **18** Ran SP% **130.0**
Speed ratings (Par 97): **93,92,89,88,87 85,83,82,81,80 76,74,70,69,58 54,49,19**
CSF £139.61 TOTE £31.70: £8.80, £2.40, £2.50; EX 202.90 Trifecta £1139.10.There was no bid for the winner. Speed Dating was claimed by Mr P. W. Middleton for £18,000
Owner Ahmad Bintooq **Bred** Bearstone Stud **Trained** Sessay, N Yorks
■ My Dream Of You was withdrawn. Price at time of withdrawal 66-1. Rule 4 does not apply

FOCUS
A big field as usual, but it doesn't usually take more than running to an RPR in the low 70s to win it, and that was the case once again.

3813 IRISH THOROUGHBRED MARKETING H'CAP 7f
3:30 (3:31) (Class 4) (0-85,84) 4-Y-O+
£8,927 (£2,656; £1,327; £663; £300; £300) **Stalls** Low

Form RPR

1-22 **1** **Shawaamekh**[38] 2509 5-9-1 **78** ....(t) DavidNolan 14 88
(Declan Carroll) *trckd ldrs: hdwy 3f out: rdn to ld wl over 1f out: edgd rt over 1f out: drvn and hung rt to stands' rail ins fnl f: drvn out* **5/1**[1]

-652 **2** ¾ **Proud Archi (IRE)**[25] 2893 5-9-2 **79** .... PaulMulrennan 12 88+
(Michael Dods) *midfield: hdwy 3f out: trckd ldrs 2f out: swtchd rt and rdn over 1f out: sn chal: ev ch whn n.m.r and hmpd ins fnl f: sn swtchd lft and drvn: kpt on same pce towards fin* **14/1**

0455 **3** ½ **Luis Vaz De Torres (IRE)**[25] 2893 7-9-0 **77** ....(h) PaulHanagan 9 83
(Richard Fahey) *hld up: hdwy 2f out: rdn to chse ldrs over 1f out: drvn and kpt on fnl f* **20/1**

-125 **4** 1¼ **Right Action**[20] 3100 5-9-7 **84** .... SilvestreDeSousa 2 87
(Richard Fahey) *led: pushed along 3f out: rdn over 2f out: hdd wl over 1f out: sn drvn and kpt on same pce (vet said gelding had lost its left-fore shoe)* **13/2**[2]

0-00 **5** ¾ **Breanski**[14] 3313 5-8-11 **81** .... OwenPayton(7) 11 82+
(Jedd O'Keeffe) *hld up in rr: hdwy nr inner over 2f out: chsd ldrs and rdn over 1f out: swtchd lft and drvn ent fnl f: styd on* **20/1**

0-02 **6** nk **Dark Intention (IRE)**[20] 3100 6-9-0 **82** .... PaulaMuir(5) 13 82
(Lawrence Mullaney) *hld up towards rr: stdy hdwy wl over 2f out: rdn to chse ldrs over 1f out: kpt on fnl f* **8/1**[3]

314 **7** 2¼ **Stoney Lane**[27] 2823 4-9-0 **77** .... PhilDennis 15 71
(Richard Whitaker) *trckd ldng pair: hdwy 3f out: cl up over 2f out: sn rdn: drvn over 1f out: grad wknd* **10/1**

0442 **8** nk **Magical Effect (IRE)**[17] 3179 7-8-12 **75** .... JamesSullivan 6 68
(Ruth Carr) *hld up towards rr: hdwy over 2f out: rdn wl over 1f out: n.d* **16/1**

6-06 **9** 2 **New Look (FR)**[14] 3308 4-9-4 **81** .... DavidAllan 17 69
(Tim Easterby) *dwlt and in rr tl styd on fnl 2f* **25/1**

500- 10 nk **Dream Walker (FR)**[32] 2700 10-9-4 **84**...................(t) BenRobinson(3) 8 71
(Brian Ellison) *chsd ldrs: rdn along wl over 2f out: grad wknd* **20/1**

-163 11 1/2 **Candelisa (IRE)**[18] 3149 6-9-1 **78**...........................(tp) LukeMorris 16 64
(David Loughnane) *trckd ldrs: hdwy over 3f out: rdn along over 2f out: sn drvn and wknd over 1f out* **10/1**

5145 12 hd **Harbour Vision**[18] 3147 4-8-12 **75**........................ PaddyMathers 7 60
(Derek Shaw) *a towards rr* **33/1**

-220 13 hd **Saluti (IRE)**[20] 3100 5-9-4 **81**.................................. GrahamLee 5 66
(Paul Midgley) *trckd ldrs: hdwy to chse ldr 1/2-way: rdn along 2f out: sn drvn and ev ch: wknd appr fnl f* **25/1**

0-00 14 1 1/4 **My Amigo**[8] 3503 6-9-0 **82**...................(t) ConnorMurtagh(5) 20 63
(Marjorie Fife) *in tch on outer whn carried wd bnd after 2f: rdn along 1/2-way: wknd over 2f out* **33/1**

3133 15 1 3/4 **Kupa River (IRE)**[17] 3179 5-9-3 **80**...........................(h) BenCurtis 18 57
(Roger Fell) *midfield: hdwy to chse ldrs over 3f out: rdn along over 2f out: grad wknd (jockey said gelding ran flat)* **11/1**

3-45 16 nse **Deansgate (IRE)**[106] 952 6-8-4 **74**..................... VictorSantos(7) 1 50
(Julie Camacho) *dwlt: a towards rr (vet said gelding had lost its right hind shoe)* **25/1**

2032 17 1 1/2 **Esprit De Corps**[4] 3649 5-8-9 **72**.......................(h1) TomEaves 19 44
(David Barron) *dwlt: a towards rr* **10/1**

-000 18 10 **Lualiwa**[25] 2894 5-9-2 **79**..(p) KevinStott 10 24
(Kevin Ryan) *cl up on outer: swtchd markedly rt to stands' rail over 3f out: rdn over 2f out: sn drvn and wknd* **20/1**

360- 19 22 **Bertiewhittle**[273] 7235 11-9-5 **82**..................................... RobbieDowney 4
(David Barron) *towards rr: rdn along 3f out: sn outpcd and bhd* **40/1**

1m 26.43s (1.83) **Going Correction** +0.45s/f (Yiel) **19 Ran SP% 128.2**
Speed ratings (Par 105): **107,106,105,104,103 102,100,100,97,97 96,96,96,94,92 92,91,79,54**
CSF £65.70 CT £1335.92 TOTE £5.20: £1.60, £3.30, £4.40, £2.20; EX 108.50 Trifecta £1925.30.

Owner Highgreen Partnership **Bred** Lady Lonsdale & Richard Kent **Trained** Malton, N Yorks

■ Stewards' Enquiry : David Nolan two-day ban: interference & careless riding (Jun 28-29)

FOCUS
An open affair. The winner built on this year's form.

3814 EQUINITY TECHNOLOGY GANTON STKS (LISTED RACE) 7f 192y
4:05 (4:05) (Class 1) 3-Y-O+ **£28,355** (£10,750; £5,380; £2,680; £1,345) **Stalls** Low

Form RPR

1-13 1 **Happy Power (IRE)**[34] 2615 3-8-10 **105**.................. SilvestreDeSousa 1 113
(Andrew Balding) *trckd ldr: hdwy and cl up 3f out: led over 2f out: rdn over 1f out: kpt on wl* **6/5**[1]

11-0 2 1 1/4 **Wadilsafa**[44] 2271 4-9-10 **112**..............................(t1) DaneO'Neill 4 116
(Owen Burrows) *set stdy pce early: pushed along and qcknd 3f out: rdn and hdd over 2f out: cl up and drvn over 1f out: ev ch tl kpt on same pce ins fnl f* **11/2**[3]

1622 3 2 3/4 **Oh This Is Us (IRE)**[13] 3343 6-9-7 **111**.................. DanielTudhope 3 107
(Richard Hannon) *trckd ldng pair: hdwy 3f out: rdn along over 2f out: drvn over 1f out: no imp fnl f* **13/2**

50-0 4 3/4 **Sir Dancealot (IRE)**[27] 2829 5-9-7 **115**........................ GeraldMosse 5 105
(David Elsworth) *hld up: effrt and sme hdwy 3f out: sn pushed along: rdn 2f out and sn btn* **7/2**[2]

10-0 5 3 1/2 **Raakib Alhawa (IRE)**[22] 3026 3-8-10 **98**............................ BenCurtis 2 94
(David Simcock) *dwlt: a in rr* **13/2**

1m 39.61s (2.11) **Going Correction** +0.45s/f (Yiel)
WFA 3 from 4yo+ 11lb **5 Ran SP% 109.7**
Speed ratings (Par 111): **107,105,103,102,98**
CSF £8.10 TOTE £1.90: £1.20, £2.40; EX 7.20 Trifecta £19.50.

Owner King Power Racing Co Ltd **Bred** Yeomanstown Stud **Trained** Kingsclere, Hants

FOCUS
This proved fairly straightforward for the favourite, who progressed again, with the runner-up to last year's Sandown win.

3815 BRITISH EBF PREMIER FILLIES' H'CAP 6f
4:40 (4:41) (Class 2) (0-100,90) 3-Y-O+
£18,675 (£5,592; £2,796; £1,398; £699; £351) **Stalls** Centre

Form RPR

21 1 **Philipine Cobra**[7] 3532 3-8-6 **76** 6ex................................ LukeMorris 3 86
(Phil McEntee) *mde all: rdn clr jst over 1f out: kpt on strly* **8/1**

-000 2 1 3/4 **Daffy Jane**[14] 3309 4-8-10 **77**.......................... FayeMcManoman(5) 1 84
(Nigel Tinkler) *cl up on outer: rdn along 2f out: ev ch over 1f out: sn drvn and kpt on same pce fnl f* **25/1**

-003 3 1 3/4 **Lady Dancealot (IRE)**[18] 3164 4-9-9 **85**........................ GeraldMosse 2 86
(David Elsworth) *t.k.h early: trckd ldrs: hdwy over 2f out: chsd ldng pair and rdn over 1f out: kpt on same pce fnl f* **5/1**[2]

3433 4 3/4 **Pass The Gin**[7] 3544 3-8-12 **82**........................ SilvestreDeSousa 4 79
(Andrew Balding) *trckd ldrs: effrt 2f out: sn rdn: drvn ent fnl f: kpt on same pce* **7/2**[1]

00-5 5 1 1/4 **Hells Babe**[76] 1414 6-10-0 **90**.................................. LewisEdmunds 9 85
(Michael Appleby) *cl up: ev ch 2f out: sn rdn: drvn and wknd ent fnl f* **12/1**

00-0 6 3/4 **Maggies Angel (IRE)**[28] 2809 4-9-7 **83**........................ PaulHanagan 8 75
(Richard Fahey) *chsd ldrs: rdn along 1/2-way: drvn 2f out: n.d* **18/1**

2-53 7 nk **Excellent Times**[26] 2874 4-9-10 **86**.................................. DavidAllan 5 77
(Tim Easterby) *towards rr: effrt and sme hdwy 2f out: sn rdn and n.d (vet said filly had bled from the nose)* **7/1**

1-44 8 3 1/4 **Society Queen (IRE)**[20] 3068 3-8-6 **81**........................ SeanDavis(5) 6 60
(Richard Fahey) *a towards rr* **5/1**[2]

1-45 9 5 **Conga**[21] 3050 3-8-9 **79**... KevinStott 10 42
(Kevin Ryan) *chsd ldrs: rdn along 2f out: sn drvn and wknd* **13/2**[3]

0-02 10 1 1/4 **Queens Gift (IRE)**[17] 3201 4-9-5 **81**................................ TomEaves 7 42
(Michael Dods) *a towards rr* **11/1**

1m 13.53s (1.93) **Going Correction** +0.45s/f (Yiel)
WFA 3 from 4yo+ 8lb **10 Ran SP% 117.6**
Speed ratings (Par 96): **105,102,100,99,97 96,96,91,85,83**
CSF £186.45 CT £822.40 TOTE £10.10: £3.00, £5.90, £1.90; EX 160.80 Trifecta £1546.00.

Owner Trevor Johnson **Bred** Al-Baha Bloodstock **Trained** Newmarket, Suffolk

FOCUS
A comfortable success for the well-in winner and the runner-up has been rated close to her best.

3816 FEDERATION OF BLOODSTOCK AGENTS APPRENTICE H'CAP 1m 3f 188y
5:15 (5:15) (Class 4) (0-80,85) 4-Y-O+
£8,927 (£2,656; £1,327; £663; £300; £300) **Stalls** Centre

Form RPR

42-2 1 **Auxiliary**[8] 3500 6-8-8 **67**............................(p) JonathanFisher(5) 12 76
(Liam Bailey) *hld up: hdwy on inner over 3f out: chsd ldrs over 2f out: rdn to ld over 1f out: edgd sharply rt ent fnl f: sn drvn and kpt on wl towards fin* **25/1**

-001 2 1/2 **Speed Company (IRE)**[8] 3514 6-10-3 **85** 5ex............ CameronNoble 6 93+
(Ian Williams) *hld up towards rr: hdwy 3f out: chsd ldrs over 1f out: rdn to chal ins fnl f: kpt on same pce towards fin (jockey said gelding missed the break)* **4/1**[1]

140- 3 3 1/2 **Burn Some Dust (IRE)**[254] 7902 4-9-1 **69**.................. BenRobinson 18 72
(Brian Ellison) *hld up towards rr: hdwy 3f out: chsd ldrs on outer 2f out and sn rdn: drvn and ch ent fnl f: kpt on same pce* **12/1**[3]

-004 4 1/2 **Appointed**[20] 3095 5-9-0 **73**.............................(t) RobertDodsworth(5) 5 75
(Tim Easterby) *bhd and pushed along bef 1/2-way: hdwy on inner 3f out: rdn 2f out: styd on wl fnl f: nrst fin* **12/1**[3]

-200 5 1 **Sempre Presto (IRE)**[21] 3054 4-8-12 **69**........................ SeanDavis(3) 14 69
(Richard Fahey) *hld up in rr: hdwy 3f out: nt clr run and swtchd lft over 2f out: sn rdn: chsd ldrs appr fnl f: sn drvn and kpt on same pce* **28/1**

0-00 6 1/2 **Diodorus (IRE)**[16] 3222 5-9-2 **75**.............................. LauraCoughlan(5) 8 74
(Karen McLintock) *midfield: hdwy on outer wl over 2f out: rdn wl over 1f out: kpt on fnl f* **40/1**

2421 7 2 1/2 **Royal Cosmic**[13] 3361 5-9-3 **74**............................ ConnorMurtagh(3) 10 69
(Richard Fahey) *hld up towards rr: hdwy 3f out: rdn to chse ldrs 2f out: sn drvn and no imp* **10/1**[2]

5405 8 2 1/2 **Framley Garth (IRE)**[20] 3095 7-9-3 **74**........................ PaulaMuir(3) 13 65
(Liam Bailey) *in tch: hdwy over 4f out: chsd ldng pair 3f out: rdn along 2f out: sn drvn and btn over 1f out* **10/1**[2]

-233 9 nk **Paco's Prince**[22] 3004 4-8-13 **72**............................ ScottMcCullagh(5) 4 63
(Nick Littmoden) *midfield: effrt over 3f out: sn rdn along and n.d* **25/1**

3605 10 1 1/2 **Thawry**[18] 3161 4-8-9 **68**.. KieranSchofield(5) 9 57
(Antony Brittain) *a towards rr* **40/1**

-000 11 2 3/4 **Regal Mirage (IRE)**[15] 3250 5-8-11 **72**........................ EllaMcCain(7) 15 56
(Tim Easterby) *sn trcking ldr: hdwy and cl up over 3f out: led jst over 2f out: sn rdn: hdd 1 1/2f out and sn wknd* **33/1**

5-56 12 1 **Medalla De Oro**[29] 2763 5-9-8 **79**................................ DylanHogan(3) 19 62
(Tom Clover) *sn led: rdn along over 3f out: hdd jst over 2f out: sn wknd* **12/1**[3]

12/5 13 6 **Kilowatt**[15] 3250 5-9-7 **78**.. DannyRedmond(3) 11 51
(Tim Easterby) *trckd ldrs: effrt over 3f out and sn pushed along: rdn wl over 2f out: sn wknd* **14/1**

511- 14 5 **Itlaaq**[306] 6065 13-8-11 **70**...(t) JoshQuinn(5) 7 35
(Michael Easterby) *hld up towards rr: sme hdwy 3f out: sn rdn along and n.d* **25/1**

0/-0 15 1/2 **Aldreth**[30] 2748 8-9-12 **80**...(p) ConorMcGovern 17 44
(Michael Easterby) *chsd ldrs: rdn along 3f out: sn wknd* **40/1**

0-00 16 8 **Rayna's World (IRE)**[27] 2822 4-9-3 **74**........................ BenSanderson(5) 16 25
(Philip Kirby) *dwlt and swtchd lft s: a in rr* **14/1**

3261 17 nk **Champagne Rules**[21] 3054 8-9-5 **73**................................ PhilDennis 3 24
(Sharon Watt) *in tch on inner: pushed along 5f out: rdn 4f out: sn wknd (jockey said gelding hung left-handed throughout)* **12/1**[3]

6421 18 6 **Roar (IRE)**[15] 3250 5-9-4 **75**...................................... SeamusCronin(3) 1 16
(Ed de Giles) *trckd ldng pair: pushed along over 3f out: sn rdn and wknd over 2f out (jockey said gelding ran flat)* **4/1**[1]

26-0 19 18 **Bill Cody (IRE)**[34] 2636 4-9-0 **68**.. RowanScott 2
(Julie Camacho) *prom: rdn along over 5f out: sn wknd* **28/1**

2m 35.96s (2.76) **Going Correction** +0.45s/f (Yiel) **19 Ran SP% 131.0**
Speed ratings (Par 105): **108,107,105,105,104 104,102,100,100,99 97,96,92,89,89 83,83,79,67**
CSF £119.45 CT £1320.32 TOTE £29.40: £5.30, £1.70, £2.80, £3.20; EX 168.00 Trifecta £3173.40.

Owner Mrs C M Clarke, Foulrice Park Racing Ltd **Bred** The Pocock Family **Trained** Middleham, N Yorks

■ Stewards' Enquiry : Jonathan Fisher two-day ban: used whip above the permitted level (Jun 28-29)

FOCUS
This was run at a good gallop and suited those ridden with patience. The winner posted his best Flat figure since he was a 2yo.
T/Jkpt: Not Won. T/Plt: £224.10 to a £1 stake. Pool: £130,376.97 - 424.56 winning units. T/Qpdt: £27.10 to a £1 stake. Pool: £13,086.64 - 356.41 winning units. **Joe Rowntree**

3817 - (Foreign Racing) - See Raceform Interactive

2979
CORK (R-H)
Friday, June 14

OFFICIAL GOING: Good to yielding

3818a MATCHBOOK STRAIGHT MIDSUMMER SPRINT STKS (LISTED RACE) 5f
5:50 (5:52) 3-Y-O+
£26,576 (£8,558; £4,054; £1,801; £900; £450)

RPR

1 **El Astronaute (IRE)**[20] 3097 6-9-12 **104**............................ JasonHart 6 108+
(John Quinn) *mde all: shkn up ent fnl f: styd on wl for press fnl 150yds* **11/4**[1]

2 3/4 **Smash Williams (IRE)**[20] 3103 6-9-12 **104**.................(t) KevinManning 7 105
(J S Bolger, Ire) *chsd ldrs: 3rd at 1/2-way: rdn and no imp 1f out: kpt on wl ins fnl f into 2nd fnl 50yds: nt trble wnr* **8/1**

3 1/2 **Ardhoomey (IRE)**[20] 3103 7-9-9 **104**..........................(t) ColinKeane 1 100
(G M Lyons, Ire) *chsd ldrs towards far side: 4th at 1/2-way: wnt 3rd ent fnl f: kpt on same pce fnl 100yds* **4/1**[3]

4 3/4 **Urban Beat (IRE)**[20] 3103 4-9-12 **102**............................ ShaneFoley 12 101
(J P Murtagh, Ire) *bit slowly away and early reminders towards rr: clsr at 1/2-way and sn chsd ldrs: rdn into 2nd appr fnl f: no ex in 4th fnl 100yds* **7/2**[2]

5 1/2 **Rapid Reaction (IRE)**[7] 3557 4-9-4 **86**........................ AndrewSlattery 9 91
(J F Grogan, Ire) *racd towards rr: clsr under 2f out: rdn in 6th appr fnl f: kpt on wl into 5th fnl 100yds: nvr nrr* **33/1**

6 3 1/2 **Primo Uomo (IRE)**[46] 2221 7-9-9 104..........................(t) NGMcCullagh 3 85
(Gerard O'Leary, Ire) *bit slowly away: towards rr tl prog far side to chse ldrs after 1/2-way: no imp ent fnl f: wknd* **6/1**

7 1 1/2 **The Broghie Man**[33] 2667 4-9-9 98..........................(vt) MichaelHussey 5 78
(Adrian Paul Keatley, Ire) *racd towards rr: sn pushed along: last at 1/2-way: kpt on ins fnl f: nvr on terms* **20/1**

8 3/4 **Fantasy (IRE)**[26] 2880 3-8-11 89.......................... SeamieHeffernan 11 71
(A P O'Brien, Ire) *chsd ldrs stands' side: rdn in 5th at 1/2-way: no imp ent fnl f: wknd* **16/1**

9 shd **Optionality**[19] 3113 5-9-4 78.......................... OisinOrr 2 70
(D J Bunyan, Ire) *pressed ldr in 2nd: pushed along 1/2-way: wknd appr fnl f* **33/1**

10 3/4 **St Patrick's Day (USA)**[20] 3103 4-9-9 98..........................(t) WayneLordan 8 72
(A P O'Brien, Ire) *chsd ldrs in centre of trck: nt qckn under 2f out and sn dropped towards rr: no ex: lame (vet said colt was found to be lame on the right fore having pulled a shoe)* **14/1**

11 hd **Peshkova (IRE)**[19] 3112 4-9-4 66..........................(v[1]) WJLee 10 66
(W McCreery, Ire) *racd in mid-div to 1/2-way: pushed along and nt qckn under 2f out: one pce* **33/1**

58.7s (-0.50)
WFA 3 from 4yo+ 7lb **11** Ran SP% **120.4**
CSF £25.21 TOTE £3.60: £1.50, £2.40, £1.30; DF 30.10 Trifecta £122.20.
Owner Ross Harmon Racing **Bred** T Jones **Trained** Settrington, N Yorks

FOCUS
A dominant display from the front by the winner for his 11th career success. The first four have been rated in line with their recent form.

3820a MUNSTER OAKS STKS (GROUP 3) (F&M) 1m 4f
6:55 (6:55) 3-Y-0+

£37,207 (£11,981; £5,675; £2,522; £1,261; £630)

RPR

1 **Who's Steph (IRE)**[34] 2642 4-9-9 108.......................... ColinKeane 6 103+
(G M Lyons, Ire) *chsd ldrs in 3rd: clsr in 2nd 3f out: travelled wl to ld under 2f out: pushed clr ins fnl f under hands and heels: comf* **1/1**[1]

2 1 **Peach Tree (IRE)**[14] 3316 3-8-9 102.......................... SeamieHeffernan 5 101
(A P O'Brien, Ire) *led: strly pressed 2f out and sn hdd: kpt on wl for press tl no ex w wnr fnl 100yds* **3/1**[2]

3 1 1/2 **Moteo (IRE)**[20] 3106 4-9-9 93.......................... RonanWhelan 2 98+
(John M Oxx, Ire) *racd in mid-div: pushed along in 5th under 2f out: kpt on wl ins fnl f into 3rd cl home: nvr nrr* **16/1**

4 nse **Chablis (IRE)**[27] 2853 3-8-9 93.......................... WayneLordan 7 99
(A P O'Brien, Ire) *racd in mid-div: clsr on inner to chse ldrs in 3rd 3f out: rdn and no imp ent fnl f: kpt on same pce and ct for 3rd cl home* **10/1**

5 3/4 **Four White Socks**[279] 7054 4-9-9 97.......................... KevinManning 1 97
(Harry Fry) *hld up in rr: pushed along in 6th under 2f out: kpt on wl fnl f into 5th fnl 50yds: nvr nrr* **20/1**

6 2 1/4 **Tipitena**[32] 2701 4-9-9 86.......................... WJLee 4 93
(W McCreery, Ire) *racd towards rr tl clsr to briefly chse ldrs in 4th 2f out: no imp ent fnl f: wknd fnl 100yds* **16/1**

7 dist **Jaega (IRE)**[37] 2535 4-9-9 96..........................(v[1]) OisinOrr 3
(D K Weld, Ire) *trckd ldr in 2nd: rdn under 4f out: wknd qckly fr 3f out: eased: clinically abnormal (vet said filly was clinically abnormal post race)* **8/1**[3]

2m 38.5s (-9.40)
WFA 3 from 4yo 15lb **7** Ran SP% **111.7**
CSF £3.82 TOTE £1.70: £1.20, £1.60; DF 4.80 Trifecta £29.20.
Owner George Strawbridge **Bred** Patrick Headon **Trained** Dunsany, Co Meath

FOCUS
A convincing performance from the winner, a filly proving difficult to beat at this sort of level. The third, fourth and sixth set the standard.

3819a, 3821 - 3833a (Foreign Racing) - See Raceform Interactive

3527 BATH (L-H)
Saturday, June 15

OFFICIAL GOING: Good to soft (7.1) (race 4 (3.30) & race 7 (5.20) abandoned due to unsafe ground)
Wind: moderate against Weather: heavy showers

3834 CONGRATULATIONS CAITLIN KENNEDY H'CAP 1m 3f 137y
1:45 (1:46) (Class 6) (0-60,60) 4-Y-0+

£3,105 (£924; £461; £300; £300; £300) **Stalls** Low

Form RPR

24-3 1 **Miss M (IRE)**[23] 3015 5-9-5 **58**.......................... MartinDwyer 1 67+
(William Muir) *mid-div: smooth hdwy fr 3f out to ld 2f out: sn in command: comf* **7/2**[1]

-226 2 4 **Givepeaceachance**[23] 3015 4-9-2 **55**.......................... CharlesBishop 3 58
(Denis Coakley) *in tch: hdwy over 3f out: ev ch briefly over 2f out: sn rdn: kpt on but a being comf hld by wnr* **5/1**[2]

0000 3 3 1/2 **Happy Ending (IRE)**[46] 2234 4-8-8 **52**.......................... RhiainIngram(5) 10 49
(Seamus Mullins) *trckd ldrs tl 6f out: midfield: hdwy over 2f out: styd on into 3rd fnl f* **20/1**

0050 4 1/2 **Sellingallthetime (IRE)**[24] 2970 8-8-4 **50**..........................(v) EllieMacKenzie(7) 6 46
(Mark Usher) *trckd ldrs: rdn and ev ch briefly over 2f out: fdd ins fnl f* **11/1**

313- 5 nk **Dream Free**[37] 8745 6-8-11 **53** ow2..........................(vt[1]) FinleyMarsh(3) 9 49
(David Pipe) *hld up towards rr: rdn over 2f out: no imp tl hdwy jst over 1f out: styd on ins fnl f but nvr any threat* **6/1**[3]

30-3 6 3/4 **Star Of Athena**[25] 2928 4-9-7 **60**..........................(h) AdamKirby 4 55
(Ali Stronge) *mid-div: slipped on bnd leaving bk st: rdn 3f out: styd on same pce fnl 2f (jockey said filly slipped on the bend at the end of the back straight)* **10/1**

406 7 1 **Incredible Dream (IRE)**[36] 2593 6-8-11 **57**..........(bt[1]) WilliamCarver(7) 2 50
(Conrad Allen) *s.i.s: towards rr: midfield 3f out: sn rdn: kpt on same pce fnl 2f* **5/1**[2]

40-3 8 hd **Das Kapital**[10] 3473 4-8-10 **49**.......................... JFEgan 12 42
(John Berry) *hld up: slipped on bnd leaving bk st: hdwy into midfield over 3f out: sn rdn: no further imp fnl 2f (jockey said gelding slipped on the bend at the end of the back straight)* **6/1**[3]

0360 9 1 **Zephyros (GER)**[10] 3473 8-8-11 **55**.......................... PoppyBridgwater(5) 14 46
(David Bridgwater) *sn led: slipped on bnd leaving bk st: rdn and hdd over 2f out: wknd ent fnl f (jockey said gelding slipped on the bend at the end of the back straight)* **11/1**

00-0 10 4 1/2 **Imminent Approach**[94] 1176 4-9-6 **59**.......................... EoinWalsh 13 43
(Tony Newcombe) *mid-div tl over 6f out: towards rr: struggling 3f out: nvr bk on terms* **33/1**

03 11 1 1/2 **Sunshineandbubbles**[36] 2595 6-8-11 **55**..........................(p) DylanHogan(5) 7 36
(Jennie Candlish) *trckd ldrs: rdn and ev ch over 2f out: wknd over 1f out* **20/1**

315- 12 30 **Purple Jazz (IRE)**[56] 7122 4-9-4 **57**..........................(t) TrevorWhelan 8
(Jeremy Scott) *s.i.s: a towards rr: wknd over 1f out* **12/1**

00-R 13 37 **Duhr (IRE)**[45] 2283 5-8-12 **54**.......................... MeganNicholls(3) 11
(Ralph J Smith) *in tch: rdn 3f out: wknd qckly* **50/1**

2m 31.15s (0.35) **Going Correction** +0.25s/f (Good) **13** Ran SP% **132.0**
Speed ratings (Par 101): **108,105,103,102,102 101,101,101,100,97 96,76,51**
CSF £21.99 CT £332.14 TOTE £4.50: £1.90, £2.20, £6.60; EX 29.30 Trifecta £191.30.
Owner Brian Willis **Bred** J & J Waldron **Trained** Lambourn, Berks
■ Filament Of Gold was withdrawn. Price at time of withdrawal 14/1. Rule 4 applies to all bets struck prior to withdrawal, but not to SP bets. Deduction - 5p in the £. New market formed.

FOCUS
A weak handicap on paper, featuring mainly exposed sorts and they finished quite well string out. The winner has been rated back to her best.

3835 BRITISH EBF FILLIES' NOVICE STKS (PLUS 10 RACE) 5f 10y
2:20 (2:21) (Class 4) 2-Y-0

£4,787 (£1,424; £711; £355) **Stalls** Centre

Form RPR

3 1 **Star Alexander**[36] 2565 2-9-0 0.......................... AdamKirby 3 90
(Clive Cox) *mde all: drawing clr under hands and heels whn stmbld 1f out: easily* **6/5**[1]

0 2 6 **Sobriquet (IRE)**[10] 3469 2-9-0 0.......................... CallumShepherd 6 68
(Ed de Giles) *trckd wnr: rdn 2f out: kpt on but nt pce to chal* **14/1**

0213 3 1 1/2 **Daddies Diva**[22] 3055 2-9-3 0.......................... CharlieBennett 8 66
(Rod Millman) *mid-div: swtchd rt and hdwy over 2f out: sn rdn: kpt on but nt pce to get on terms* **4/1**[2]

4 1 1/4 **Sabaaya (IRE)** 2-9-0 0.......................... TomQueally 2 59
(Charles Hills) *trckd wnr tl rdn 2f out: sn hld: kpt on same pce* **8/1**

6 5 1/2 **Divine Covey**[16] 3259 2-9-0 0.......................... PatDobbs 4 57
(Richard Hannon) *trckd wnr tl rdn 2f out: sn hld: no ex ins fnl f* **9/2**[3]

0 6 1 1/4 **Glamorous Anna**[12] 3419 2-8-11 0.......................... MitchGodwin(3) 10 52
(Christopher Mason) *towards rr: sme prog but no threat whn nt clr run over 1f out: one pce fnl f* **66/1**

0 7 1 1/2 **Aust Ferry**[11] 3441 2-9-0 0.......................... CharlesBishop 1 47
(Eve Johnson Houghton) *s.i.s: towards rr: sme late prog but nvr gng pce to get involved* **20/1**

8 nk **Lethal Sensation** 2-9-0 0.......................... MartinDwyer 9 46
(Paul Webber) *s.i.s: towards rr: sme late prog but nvr any threat* **25/1**

6 9 2 1/2 **Jungle Boogaloo (IRE)**[26] 2918 2-8-11 0.......................... FinleyMarsh(3) 7 37
(Ali Stronge) *s.i.s: sn mid-div: effrt 2f out: wknd ent fnl f* **10/1**

0 10 10 **Summers Way**[30] 2767 2-9-0 0.......................... JFEgan 5 1
(Bill Turner) *mid-div tl wknd over 2f out* **66/1**

1m 2.82s (0.82) **Going Correction** +0.25s/f (Good) **10** Ran SP% **122.1**
Speed ratings (Par 92): **103,93,91,89,88 86,83,83,79,63**
CSF £22.02 TOTE £1.90: £1.10, £3.60, £1.50; EX 18.10 Trifecta £70.10.
Owner Noel O'Callaghan **Bred** N Bradley **Trained** Lambourn, Berks

FOCUS
One or two interesting fillies on show but the red-hot favourite dominated from the outset.

3836 CENTURY CASINO BATH / BRITISH EBF NOVICE STKS 5f 10y
2:55 (3:00) (Class 5) 3-Y-0+

£3,752 (£1,116; £557; £278) **Stalls** Centre

Form RPR

5 1 **Good Answer**[14] 3351 3-9-3 0.......................... PatDobbs 5 68
(Robert Cowell) *chsd ldrs: rdn 2f out: kpt on ins fnl f: led fnl 60yds: won gng away* **6/1**

-250 2 1 1/2 **Khafooq**[22] 3045 3-9-3 70.......................... AdamKirby 2 63
(Robert Cowell) *disp ld tl clr ldr over 2f out: rdn over 1f out: no ex whn hdd fnl 60yds* **11/10**[1]

00- 3 1 1/2 **Alyx Vance**[224] 8833 3-8-5 0.......................... MarcoGhiani(7) 4 53
(Lydia Pearce) *hld up: rdn and stdy prog over 1f out: kpt on to go 3rd fnl 100yds* **25/1**

0 4 1 **George Thomas**[24] 2976 3-9-3 0.......................... TomQueally 1 54
(Mick Quinn) *chsd ldrs: rdn to dispute 2nd 2f out: nt quite pce to chal: no ex ins fnl f* **4/1**[3]

000 5 1/2 **Scarlet Red**[8] 3532 4-9-5 10.......................... CharlieBennett 3 50?
(Malcolm Saunders) *disp ld tl rdn over 2f out: kpt on tl no ex ent fnl f* **22/1**

6 10 **Final Legacy** 3-8-12 0.......................... JoeyHaynes 6 11
(Derek Shaw) *s.i.s: sn outpcd in detached last: nvr on terms* **20/1**

0234 7 1 1/2 **Haats Off**[18] 3191 3-8-12 60.......................... TrevorWhelan 7 6
(Brian Barr) *s.i.s: outpcd towards rr: wknd over 1f out (jockey said filly was slowly away and never traveling)* **3/1**[2]

1m 4.04s (2.04) **Going Correction** +0.25s/f (Good)
WFA 3 from 4yo 7lb **7** Ran SP% **119.9**
Speed ratings (Par 103): **93,90,88,86,85 69,67**
CSF £13.69 TOTE £6.30: £3.00, £1.40; EX 15.00 Trifecta £162.70.
Owner Malih L Al Basti **Bred** Lady Fairhaven **Trained** Six Mile Bottom, Cambs

FOCUS
This didn't look a particularly strong novice on paper and it's hard to get a proper handle on the form.

3837 S.P. GREEN & CO BATH SOMERSETSHIRE H'CAP 1m
(3:30) (Class 3) (0-90,) 4-Y-0+ £

3838 BET365 SILK SERIES LADY RIDERS' H'CAP 5f 160y
4:10 (4:10) (Class 4) (0-80,79) 3-Y-0+

£5,530 (£1,645; £822; £411; £300; £300) **Stalls** Centre

Form RPR

6046 1 **Miracle Garden**[10] 3476 7-8-11 **58** oh1..........................(v) PoppyBridgwater(5) 9 68
(Ian Williams) *mid-div: hdwy in centre over 2f out: led ins fnl f: kpt on wl: readily* **14/1**

6040 2 1 3/4 **Big Lachie**[29] 2804 5-9-12 **71**.......................... GeorgiaCox(3) 10 75
(Mark Loughnane) *hld up: hdwy over 2f out: sn rdn: led ent fnl f: sn hdd: kpt on but no ex* **9/1**

-0P0 3 3/4 **Look Surprised**[47] 2206 6-9-1 **64**.......................... SophieRalston(7) 1 66
(Roger Teal) *chsd ldrs: rdn to ld briefly over 1f out: kpt on same pce fnl f* **8/1**

3-56 4 hd **Whataguy**[8] 3531 3-9-12 **79**.......................... MeganNicholls(3) 2 78
(Paul Nicholls) *prom: led over 2f out: sn rdn and hdd: kpt on same pce fnl f* **11/2**[3]

0231 5 1 1/4 **Handytalk (IRE)**[4] 3701 6-9-12 **75**..........................(b) GeorgiaDobie(7) 6 72
(Rod Millman) *prom: led over 2f out: rdn and hdd over 1f out: no ex fnl f* **13/8**[1]

6-13 **6** ½ **Gottardo (IRE)**[63] 1766 4-9-7 **70**.......... SophieSmith(7) 5 65
(Ed Dunlop) *prom: rdn and ev ch over 2f out: fdd ins fnl f* **10/1**

0-00 **7** 2 **Walkman (IRE)**[77] 1424 3-9-6 **77**..........(p) EllieMacKenzie(7) 3 63
(Mark Usher) *slipped leaving stalls: prom: rdn and ev ch over 2f out: wknd ent fnl f (jockey said colt slipped leaving the stalls)* **16/1**

-044 **8** shd **Grey Galleon (USA)**[10] 3462 5-9-10 **73**..........(p) AmeliaGlass(7) 7 61
(Clive Cox) *led tl over 2f out: sn rdn: wknd ent fnl f* **5/1**[2]

14-0 **9** 4 **The Lacemaker**[44] 2339 5-9-5 **68**..........(p) MrsDawnScott(7) 11 43
(Milton Harris) *s.i.s: bhd: hdwy 2f out: nvr threatened to get on terms: wknd fnl f* **33/1**

300- **10** 21 **Outback Traveller (IRE)**[221] 8891 8-9-10 **71**.......... KatherineBegley(5) 8
(Nikki Evans) *chsd ldrs: rdn 3f out: wknd over 1f out: eased (jockey said gelding was outpaced throughout)* **33/1**

1m 12.27s (1.17) **Going Correction** +0.25s/f (Good)
WFA 3 from 4yo+ 8lb **10** Ran SP% **118.8**
Speed ratings (Par 105): **102,99,98,98,96 96,93,93,87,59**
CSF £136.03 CT £1119.17 TOTE £12.10: £2.80, £2.40, £2.60; EX 127.90 Trifecta £715.60.
Owner M A Geobey **Bred** W And R Barnett Ltd **Trained** Portway, Worcs

FOCUS
Not many of these came here at the top of their game and but they all had their chances in the race itself, spread across the track. The winner has been rated to his best turf form.

3839 VALUE RATER RACING CLUB IS FREE H'CAP 5f 160y
4:45 (4:47) (Class 6) (0-65,65) 3-Y-O

£3,024 (£905; £452; £300; £300; £300) **Stalls** Centre

Form RPR

0100 **1** **Ever Rock (IRE)**[11] 3442 3-8-3 **54**.......... LauraCoughlan(7) 11 60
(J S Moore) *hld up towards rr: hdwy over 2f out: sn rdn: led over 1f out: kpt on* **14/1**

63-0 **2** nk **Foxy Femme**[21] 3090 3-9-1 **59**..........(h) JoeyHaynes 5 64
(John Gallagher) *hld up towards rr: hdwy 2f out: sn rdn: kpt on wl ins fnl f: wnt 2nd towards fin: jst failed* **10/1**

3603 **3** ¾ **Chop Chop (IRE)**[14] 3354 3-8-12 **56**..........(b) AdamMcNamara 8 59
(Roger Charlton) *s.i.s: towards rr: hdwy over 2f out: sn rdn: chal over 1f out: kpt on w ev ch tl no ex fnl 120yds* **7/2**[1]

6000 **4** 2 ½ **Yfenni (IRE)**[43] 2357 3-8-3 **47** oh1 ow1.......... RaulDaSilva 9 41
(Milton Bradley) *mid-div: hdwy over 2f out: sn rdn: wnt 4th ent fnl f: kpt on same pce* **50/1**

0-04 **5** 2 **Broadhaven Dream (IRE)**[14] 3351 3-8-11 **55**.......... LiamKeniry 12 43+
(Ronald Harris) *led: rdn and edgd lft over 2f out: hdd over 1f out: no ex ins fnl f (jockey said gelding hung left-handed)* **12/1**

2430 **6** 2 ½ **Sharrabang**[25] 2939 3-8-9 **58** ow1.......... DylanHogan(5) 6 37
(Stella Barclay) *prom tl rdn over 2f out: wkng whn stmbld jst ins fnl f* **10/1**

0201 **7** hd **Lysander Belle (IRE)**[15] 3319 3-9-1 **59**.......... TomQueally 2 38
(Sophie Leech) *s.i.s: towards rr: rdn and hdwy 2f out: sn chsng ldrs: wknd fnl f* **14/1**

000- **8** 1 ½ **Coutts De Ville**[187] 9484 3-7-11 **46** oh1.......... RhiainIngram(5) 1 20
(Paul George) *towards rr: sme late prog: nvr on terms* **25/1**

120 **9** hd **Miss Enigma (IRE)**[22] 3045 3-9-2 **63**..........(b) FinleyMarsh(3) 10 36
(Richard Hughes) *trckd ldrs: rdn over 2f out: wknd over 1f out (jockey said filly was restless in the stalls)* **10/1**

40-4 **10** ½ **Deptford Mick (IRE)**[19] 3167 3-9-7 **65**.......... AdamKirby 14 37
(Rae Guest) *trckd ldrs: rdn over 2f out: wknd over 1f out* **5/1**[2]

5000 **11** 1 **Rakastava (IRE)**[10] 3478 3-9-2 **60**.......... CallumShepherd 3 28
(Mick Channon) *mid-div: rdn over 2f out: nt pce to threaten: wknd ins fnl f* **8/1**

000- **12** 1 **Willa's Wish (IRE)**[236] 8470 3-8-0 **49**.......... DarraghKeenan(5) 7 14
(Tony Carroll) *mid-div: effrt over 2f out: wknd over 1f out* **16/1**

-003 **13** 8 **Vino Rosso (IRE)**[11] 3442 3-8-13 **57**.......... CharlesBishop 4
(Michael Blanshard) *trckd ldrs: rdn over 2f out: sn wknd (trainer's rep said filly was unsuited by the going (good to soft) and would prefer a firmer surface)* **6/1**[3]

-006 **14** 5 **Knockabout Queen**[31] 2730 3-8-12 **59**.......... MeganNicholls(3) 13
(Dai Burchell) *dwlt bdly: nvr rcvrd and a bhd (jockey said filly reared as the stalls opened and was subsequently slowly away)* **14/1**

1m 13.49s (2.39) **Going Correction** +0.25s/f (Good) **14** Ran SP% **130.9**
Speed ratings (Par 97): **94,93,92,89,86 83,83,81,80,80 78,77,66,60**
CSF £160.05 CT £633.01 TOTE £16.20: £4.50, £3.30, £1.80; EX 210.00 Trifecta £1266.00.
Owner Ever Equine & J S Moore **Bred** Tom Twomey **Trained** Upper Lambourn, Berks

■ Stewards' Enquiry : Laura Coughlan four-day ban: used whip above the permitted level (Jun 29-30, Jul 1-2)
Adam McNamara four-day ban: used whip above the permitted level (Jul 1-4)

FOCUS
Modest stuff and the winner is exposed, so not form to get excited about.

3840 CMD RECRUITMENT BATH H'CAP 1m 2f 37y
(5:20) (Class 6) (0-65,) 3-Y-O+

£

T/Plt: £92.50 to a £1 stake. Pool: £55,235.20 - 435.80 winning units T/Qpdt: £39.90 to a £1 stake. Pool: £4,790.21 - 88.68 winning units **Tim Mitchell**

3067 **CHESTER (L-H)**
Saturday, June 15

OFFICIAL GOING: Soft (heavy in places; 6.8)
Wind: Light, across in straight of over 1f Weather: Sunny intervals

3841 LAMB & WATT NOVICE MEDIAN AUCTION STKS (PLUS 10 RACE) 6f 17y
2:10 (2:11) (Class 4) 2-Y-O

£6,162 (£1,845; £922; £461; £230; £115) **Stalls** Low

Form RPR

34 **1** **Know No Limits (IRE)**[10] 3469 2-8-11 **0**.......... RichardKingscote 2 80
(Tom Dascombe) *led early: chsd ldr tl over 3f out and again over 2f out: rdn to ld jst over 1f out: drew clr fnl 100yds* **5/1**

12 **2** 4 **Apollinaire**[30] 2761 2-9-8 **0**.......... JosephineGordon 3 79
(Ralph Beckett) *racd keenly: sn led: rdn and hdd jst over 1f out: styd on same pce ins fnl 150yds* **5/2**[1]

0 **3** 2 ½ **Breguet Man (IRE)**[26] 2892 2-9-2 **0**.......... ShaneGray 6 65+
(Keith Dalgleish) *s.i.s: towards rr: pushed along over 4f out: hdwy u.p over 1f out: swtchd to inner ins fnl f: styd on towards fin: nvr able to trble ldrs* **33/1**

603 **4** shd **Lexi The One (IRE)**[7] 3595 2-8-11 **0**.......... PaddyMathers 1 60
(Richard Fahey) *missed break: sn in midfield: pushed along over 4f out: hdwy over 2f out: drvn to chse ldrs over 1f out: no imp: kpt on same pce ins fnl f* **10/1**

06 **5** ¾ **G For Gabrial (IRE)**[21] 3071 2-9-2 **0**.......... DavidNolan 7 62
(Richard Fahey) *bustled along towards rr: drvn over 3f out: hdwy ins fnl f: styd on: nvr able to trble ldrs* **25/1**

1 **6** 5 **Mrs Bouquet**[11] 3451 2-9-3 **0**.......... FrannyNorton 5 48
(Mark Johnston) *chsd ldrs: racd in 2nd pl fr over 3f out tl rdn over 2f out: wknd over 1f out* **11/4**[2]

4 **7** 1 ¼ **We Owen A Dragon**[21] 3071 2-8-13 **0**.......... JaneElliott(3) 8 44
(Tom Dascombe) *bhd: pushed along and outpcd 1/2-way: nvr on terms* **16/1**

4 **8** 7 **Red Hot Streak**[9] 3512 2-9-2 **0**.......... JasonHart 4
(Tim Easterby) *racd keenly: chsd ldrs: pushed along over 3f out: wknd over 1f out* **10/3**[3]

0 **9** ½ **Eileen's Magic**[9] 3506 2-8-4 **0**.......... GavinAshton(7) 9
(Lisa Williamson) *midfield: drvn 1/2-way: wknd over 1f out* **100/1**

1m 17.75s (2.25) **Going Correction** +0.45s/f (Yiel) **9** Ran SP% **117.7**
Speed ratings (Par 95): **103,97,94,94,93 86,84,75,74**
CSF £18.11 TOTE £6.70: £1.90, £1.10, £10.30; EX 20.80 Trifecta £286.90.
Owner Fdcholdings Hedges Nolan Rutherford **Bred** Ballyreddin Stud **Trained** Malpas, Cheshire

FOCUS
The going was given as soft, heavy in places (Going Stick 6.8) and all distances were as advertised. Few got into this. The winner improved, with the runner-up and fourth helping the opening level.

3842 WHITLEY NEILL HANDCRAFT GIN H'CAP 1m 4f 63y
2:40 (2:40) (Class 2) (0-100,98) 3-Y-O

£18,052 (£5,405; £2,702; £1,351; £675; £339) **Stalls** Low

Form RPR

2-41 **1** **Durston**[14] 3337 3-8-5 **82**.......... NicolaCurrie 8 93+
(David Simcock) *hld up in rr: pushed along over 2f out: wnt through gap and hdwy over 1f out: led fnl 150yds: kpt on wl towards fin* **4/1**[2]

-222 **2** 1 **Lariat**[21] 3086 3-8-11 **88**.......... RichardKingscote 5 95
(Andrew Balding) *chsd ldr: moved alongside over 4f out: led 3f out: rdn over 2f out: pressed ins fnl f: hdd fnl 150yds: styd on same pce and hld after* **5/2**[1]

16-2 **3** 1 ¾ **Prefontaine (IRE)**[16] 3260 3-8-10 **87**..........(p[1]) DavidEgan 4 91
(Roger Varian) *hld up: hdwy on outer over 2f out: rdn to chal ins fnl f: styd on same pce fnl 100yds* **11/2**

-351 **4** 2 ¼ **Gabrial The One (IRE)**[21] 3073 3-8-4 **81**.......... PaddyMathers 6 82
(Richard Fahey) *chsd ldrs: pushed along over 3f out: rdn to chse ldr over 2f out tl 1f out: no ex fnl 100yds* **11/2**

124- **5** 9 **Waldstern**[245] 8185 3-9-7 **98**.......... KieranO'Neill 3 84
(John Gosden) *trckd ldrs: nt clr run and checked 3f out: sn lost pl: tried to switch to outer over 2f out: sn briefly n.m.r: unable to get bk on terms and wknd fnl f* **9/2**[3]

2-33 **6** 6 **Fearless Warrior (FR)**[26] 2905 3-8-5 **82**.......... JosephineGordon 7 59
(Ralph Beckett) *hld up: pushed along over 3f out: no imp and outpcd over 2f out: nvr able to get involved* **9/1**

0-54 **7** 2 ¾ **Lola's Theme**[8] 3548 3-7-13 **79** oh1.......... JaneElliott(3) 1 51
(Tom Dascombe) *led: pushed along whn jnd over 4f out: hdd 3f out: n.m.r whn wkng over 1f out* **14/1**

2m 45.69s (3.49) **Going Correction** +0.45s/f (Yiel) **7** Ran SP% **114.2**
Speed ratings (Par 105): **106,105,104,102,96 92,90**
CSF £14.40 CT £53.91 TOTE £4.90: £4.30, £1.50; EX 13.20 Trifecta £58.30.
Owner Highclere Thoroughbred Racing - Durston **Bred** Miss K Rausing **Trained** Newmarket, Suffolk

FOCUS
Not a bad handicap, and the first two are on the upgrade.

3843 JJ WHITLEY FILLIES' H'CAP 7f 127y
3:10 (3:13) (Class 4) (0-80,76) 4-Y-O+

£6,404 (£1,905; £952; £476; £300; £300) **Stalls** Low

Form RPR

-604 **1** **Eponina (IRE)**[134] 525 5-7-13 **59** ow2.......... TheodoreLadd(5) 1 69
(Michael Appleby) *mde all: rdn over 1f out: edgd rt ins fnl f: kpt on wl* **9/2**[3]

-453 **2** 1 ¾ **Queen Penn**[15] 3323 4-9-5 **74**..........(p) PaddyMathers 5 80
(Richard Fahey) *chsd ldrs: rdn over 2f out to go pce of front two: styd on to cl and take 2nd ins fnl f: nvr able to trble wnr* **3/1**[1]

0612 **3** 2 ¼ **Bell Heather (IRE)**[49] 2106 6-8-12 **67**..........(p) DavidEgan 7 67
(Patrick Morris) *chsd wnr: rdn 2f out: no imp over 1f out: lost 2nd ins fnl f: styd on same pce (vet said mare lost its right hind shoe)* **4/1**[2]

535 **4** ½ **Outside Inside (IRE)**[3] 3743 4-9-7 **76**.......... FrannyNorton 2 75
(Mark Johnston) *sed awkwardly: towards rr: nt clr run wl over 2f out: hdwy sn after: chsd ldrs ins fnl f: sn one pce: nvr able to chal (jockey said filly fly-leapt leaving the stalls)* **3/1**[1]

5 1 ½ **Cracking Name (IRE)**[32] 2725 5-8-5 **60**..........(bt) NicolaCurrie 9 55
(David Marnane, Ire) *chsd ldrs: rdn to go pce over 2f out: one pce u.p fnl 150yds* **4/1**[2]

0230 **6** 7 **Corked (IRE)**[65] 1710 6-8-4 **59**.......... JosephineGordon 3 37
(Alistair Whillans) *racd off the pce: bhd 5f out: u.p over 3f out: nvr on terms* **16/1**

0040 **7** 5 **Valentine Mist (IRE)**[64] 1731 7-7-13 **57** oh12.......... NoelGarbutt(3) 8 22
(James Grassick) *midfield: pushed along over 3f out: effrt on inner over 2f out: no imp on ldrs: wknd over 1f out* **100/1**

5045 **8** 2 ¼ **Caledonian Gold**[2] 3772 6-7-9 **57** oh12.......... IsobelFrancis(7) 6 16
(Lisa Williamson) *dwlt: towards rr: pushed along and outpcd 3f out: nvr on terms: bhd over 1f out* **50/1**

1m 38.67s (2.97) **Going Correction** +0.45s/f (Yiel) **8** Ran SP% **117.0**
Speed ratings (Par 102): **103,101,99,98,97 90,85,82**
CSF £18.92 CT £58.99 TOTE £4.90: £1.70, £1.40, £1.20; EX 20.00 Trifecta £80.00.
Owner Mrs Elisabeth Cash **Bred** Rev John Naughton **Trained** Oakham, Rutland

FOCUS
This was controlled from the front by the winner, who has been rated in line with last year's form.

3844 MARYLEBONE GIN H'CAP 5f 15y
3:45 (3:47) (Class 3) (0-95,94) 3-Y-O

£11,827 (£3,541; £1,770; £885; £442; £222) **Stalls** Low

Form RPR

2-01 **1** **Angel Alexander (IRE)**[5] 3659 3-8-10 **86** 6ex.......... JaneElliott(3) 4 92+
(Tom Dascombe) *prom: chsd ldr over 3f out: rdn over 1f out: chalng ins fnl f: nosed ahd fnl 100yds: pushed out towards fin* **11/10**[1]

4-31 **2** ½ **She Can Boogie (IRE)**[36] 2576 3-9-3 **90**.......... RichardKingscote 8 94
(Tom Dascombe) *led: rdn over 1f out: pressed ins fnl f: hdd narrowly fnl 100yds: no ex fnl strides* **11/4**[2]

51-3 **3** 1 1/2 **Broken Spear**[66] 1692 3-9-7 **94**..............................(p) DougieCostello 3 93
(Tony Coyle) *prom: rdn over 2f out: edgd rt and outpcd by front two ins fnl f: no imp after* **8/1**

0406 **4** 1 3/4 **Coolagh Magic**[10] 3479 3-8-4 **77**..............................(p) PaddyMathers 6 70+
(Richard Fahey) *hld up: pushed along 3f out: hdwy fnl 175yds: styd on: nt rch ldrs* **16/1**

-000 **5** 3/4 **No More Regrets (IRE)**[10] 3479 3-8-2 **75** oh5..............(h[1]) DavidEgan 1 65
(Patrick Morris) *hld up: rdn over 1f out: nvr able to trble ldrs* **12/1**

-110 **6** 1 1/4 **Free Love**[29] 2810 3-8-9 **87**.............................. TheodoreLadd(5) 7 73
(Michael Appleby) *dwlt: hld up: effrt on outer over 1f out: no imp: no ex fnl 150yds (jockey said filly jumped awkwardly from the stalls)* **13/2**[3]

405- **7** 2 1/4 **Primeravez (IRE)**[257] 7851 3-9-5 **92**.............................. DavidNolan 5 69
(Michael Dods) *chsd ldrs: rdn over 1f out: wknd ins fnl f* **16/1**

1m 3.19s (1.09) **Going Correction** +0.45s/f (Yiel) **7 Ran SP% 118.2**
Speed ratings (Par 103): **109,108,105,103,101 99,96**
CSF £4.54 CT £15.72 TOTE £1.60: £1.70, £1.40; EX 5.40 Trifecta £25.70.
Owner Birbeck Mound Trowbridge & Owen **Bred** Mountarmstrong Stud **Trained** Malpas, Cheshire
FOCUS
A good sprint handicap and a Tom Dascombe-trained 1-2.

3845 CITY OF LONDON GIN H'CAP 1m 2f 70y
4:20 (4:23) (Class 4) (0-80,81) 4-Y-0+

£8,021 (£2,387; £1,192; £596; £300; £300) **Stalls** High

Form RPR

1164 **1** **Regular Income (IRE)**[12] 3424 4-9-5 **78**..............................(p) JimmyQuinn 1 85
(Adam West) *midfield: hdwy 2f out: led over 1f out: drvn out* **9/2**[3]

6342 **2** 1 **Bit Of A Quirke**[7] 3568 6-8-8 **67**..............................(v[1]) JosephineGordon 2 73+
(Mark Walford) *led for nrly 1f: chsd ldrs after: rdn whn n.m.r and checked over 1f out: sn lost pl: rallied ins fnl f: styd on to take 2nd fnl 100yds: nt trble wnr (jockey said gelding was denied a clear run approaching the final furlong)* **9/2**[3]

0-06 **3** 3/4 **Qawamees (IRE)**[9] 3515 4-9-1 **74**.............................. KieranO'Neill 6 77
(Michael Easterby) *in rr: rdn over 2f out: hdwy ins fnl f: styd on for press: one pce cl home* **9/1**

6320 **4** 1/2 **Confrontational (IRE)**[15] 3308 5-9-7 **80**.............................. FrannyNorton 3 82
(Jennie Candlish) *broke wl: racd keenly: in tch: rdn over 2f out: effrt whn cl up over 1f out: unable qck ins fnl f: styd on same pce fnl 100yds* **11/2**

0602 **5** nk **Dark Devil (IRE)**[17] 3217 6-8-4 **68**..............................(p) ConnorMurtagh(5) 4 69
(Richard Fahey) *hld up: hdwy whn nt clr run over 1f out: sn swtchd lft: n.m.r sn after: kpt on ins fnl f: nvr able to chal* **4/1**[2]

-562 **6** 6 **Humble Gratitude**[21] 3072 4-9-7 **80**..............................(p) DavidEgan 5 69
(Ian Williams) *chsd ldr after nrly 1f: rdn to ld over 1f out: sn hdd: wknd ins fnl f (trainer's rep said gelding is an inconsistent type)* **10/3**[1]

-425 **7** 2 1/4 **Aiya (IRE)**[9] 3514 4-9-8 **81**..............................(h) JasonHart 7 66
(Tim Easterby) *led after nrly 1f: rdn over 2f out: hdd over 1f out: wknd ins fnl f* **8/1**

2m 18.96s (4.66) **Going Correction** +0.45s/f (Yiel) **7 Ran SP% 115.9**
Speed ratings (Par 105): **99,98,97,97,96 92,90**
CSF £25.58 TOTE £5.70: £2.30, £2.70; EX 24.60 Trifecta £188.60.
Owner Ian & Amanda Maybrey And Partners **Bred** Garrett O'Neill **Trained** Epsom, Surrey
FOCUS
They finished in a bit of a heap and getting the best trip proved the difference, but this rates a length pb from the winner.

3846 LIVERPOOL GIN H'CAP 6f 17y
4:55 (4:58) (Class 4) (0-85,84) 4-Y-0+

£8,021 (£2,387; £1,192; £596; £300; £300) **Stalls** Low

Form RPR

0006 **1** **Quick Look**[10] 3480 6-9-5 **82**.............................. KieranO'Neill 1 93
(Michael Easterby) *chsd ldrs: led 2f out: drvn out and r.o ins fnl f* **5/2**[1]

1022 **2** 2 **Turanga Leela**[15] 3323 5-8-7 **70**..............................(b) FrannyNorton 6 75
(John Mackie) *n.m.r early and swtchd lft: in rr: nt clr run 2f out: hdwy on inner over 1f out: r.o ins fnl f: tk 2nd post: nt trble wnr (jockey said mare was slowly into stride)* **13/2**[3]

6041 **3** shd **Gabrial The Tiger (IRE)**[17] 3214 7-8-6 **69**.............. RoystonFfrench 12 73
(Richard Fahey) *chsd ldrs: rdn over 2f out: wnt 2nd over 1f out: no imp on wnr ins fnl f: lost 2nd post* **12/1**

0056 **4** 1/2 **Penwortham (IRE)**[18] 3179 6-9-3 **80**.............................. PaddyMathers 10 83+
(Richard Fahey) *in rr: hdwy on outer 2f out: rdn over 1f out: styd on and clsng towards fin* **14/1**

0-00 **5** shd **Dragons Tail (IRE)**[15] 3308 4-9-7 **84**..............................(p) RichardKingscote 4 86
(Tom Dascombe) *chsd ldrs: effrt over 1f out: styd on same pce ins fnl f* **6/1**[2]

-000 **6** 3/4 **Gabrial The Devil (IRE)**[15] 3318 4-9-2 **84**.............................. ConnorMurtagh(5) 13 84
(Richard Fahey) *hld up: hdwy into midfield 4f out: effrt to chse ldrs over 1f out: styd on ins fnl f: one pce fnl 50yds* **14/1**

000- **7** 3/4 **Maarek**[21] 3102 12-9-4 **81**.............................. JasonHart 8 79
(Miss Evanna McCutcheon, Ire) *towards rr: nt clr run over 2f out: rdn over 1f out: styd on ins fnl f: nt clr run towards fin: nt pce to chal* **10/1**

0-03 **8** nse **Calder Prince (IRE)**[16] 3268 6-9-2 **82**.............................. JaneElliott(3) 11 79
(Tom Dascombe) *bhd: rdn and outpcd over 4f out: hdwy and styd on ins fnl f: nvr gng pce to trble ldrs but nrst fin* **20/1**

0-50 **9** 3/4 **Powerallied (IRE)**[30] 2775 6-9-3 **83**.............................. JamieGormley(3) 5 78
(Richard Fahey) *midfield: rdn 2f out: nt clr run over 1f out: one pce ins fnl f* **7/1**

0005 **10** 1/2 **Celerity (IRE)**[7] 3577 5-7-10 **66** oh20 ow1..........(p) ElishaWhittington(7) 3 59?
(Lisa Williamson) *chsd ldrs: rdn on inner over 1f out: no imp on wnr: wknd fnl 100yds* **80/1**

1456 **11** 6 **Highland Acclaim (IRE)**[15] 3309 8-9-3 **80**..............................(h) DavidNolan 9 54
(David O'Meara) *midfield: rdn over 1f out: wknd ins fnl f* **25/1**

5000 **12** 1 3/4 **Lambrini Lullaby**[21] 3067 4-7-13 **65** oh20.............................. NoelGarbutt(3) 2 34?
(Lisa Williamson) *led: rdn and hdd 2f out: wknd over 1f out* **50/1**

-140 **13** 9 **Bossipop**[10] 3480 6-9-5 **82**..............................(b) DavidEgan 7 22
(Tim Easterby) *chsd ldr tl rdn over 2f out: wknd over 1f out (trainer could offer no explanation for the gelding's performance; vet said gelding had lost its right fore shoe)* **6/1**[2]

5103 **14** 1 1/4 **Red Stripes (USA)**[11] 3452 7-7-9 **65** oh12..........(b) IsobelFrancis(7) 14 1
(Lisa Williamson) *midfield on outer: hdwy 4f out: drvn and wknd over 2f out (trainer said gelding was unsuited by the going (soft, heavy in places) on this occasion and would prefer a quicker surface)* **50/1**

1m 17.89s (2.39) **Going Correction** +0.45s/f (Yiel) **14 Ran SP% 126.9**
Speed ratings (Par 105): **102,99,99,98,98 97,96,96,95,94 86,84,72,70**
CSF £18.59 CT £181.41 TOTE £2.90: £1.50, £2.70, £3.50; EX 24.60 Trifecta £225.10.
Owner Golden Ratio, Hull, Hollings & Winter **Bred** Susanna Ballinger **Trained** Sheriff Hutton, N Yorks
FOCUS
A big field, but the well-handicapped favourite won cosily and has been rated to his best.

3847 CRABBIE WHISKY H'CAP 1m 4f 63y
5:30 (5:32) (Class 4) (0-85,87) 4-Y-0+

£6,404 (£1,905; £952; £476; £300; £300) **Stalls** Low

Form RPR

6034 **1** **Super Kid**[21] 3070 7-8-11 **75**..............................(tp) JasonHart 5 82+
(Tim Easterby) *hld up in tch: hdwy whn nt clr run over 2f out: swtchd rt whn nt clr run over 1f out: r.o ins fnl f to ld towards fin* **7/1**

4-06 **2** 3/4 **Marengo**[8] 3545 8-8-6 **70**..............................(b[1]) FrannyNorton 7 75
(Bernard Llewellyn) *prom whn n.m.r and hmpd after 1f: chsd ldrs: w ldr 6f out: led 3f out: rdn abt 4 l clr 1f out: reduced advantage ins fnl f: hdd and no ex towards fin* **10/1**

666 **3** hd **Gossip Column (IRE)**[7] 3605 4-9-5 **83**.............................. RichardKingscote 3 87
(Ian Williams) *missed break: midfield: rdn over 2f out: hdwy over 1f out: r.o ins fnl f: nt pce of wnr fnl 50yds but styd on* **4/1**[2]

5-20 **4** 1 1/4 **Suegioo (FR)**[6] 3635 10-9-7 **85**..............................(v[1]) DavidNolan 9 87
(Ian Williams) *s.s: wl bhd: swtchd to outer and hdwy over 1f out: styd on ins fnl f: nt rch ldrs: nrst fin (jockey said gelding was slowly into stride)* **12/1**

0004 **5** 4 **Tor**[17] 3222 5-9-0 **81**.............................. JamieGormley(3) 8 77
(Iain Jardine) *prom: rdn over 2f out: chsd ldr over 1f out: no imp: lost 2nd ins fnl f: wknd fnl 100yds* **11/2**

2315 **6** 4 1/2 **Heart Of Soul (IRE)**[21] 3073 4-9-3 **84**..............................(p[1]) CameronNoble(3) 10 73
(Ian Williams) *chsd ldrs: effrt to chse ldr over 2f out tl over 1f out: wknd ins fnl f* **9/2**[3]

0-10 **7** 5 **Al Kout**[10] 3466 5-9-9 **87**.............................. DavidEgan 4 68
(Heather Main) *led: hdd over 7f out: handy tl drvn and lost pl over 3f out: wknd over 2f out* **11/2**

3132 **8** 1 1/4 **Ascot Day (FR)**[7] 3571 5-8-4 **68**..............................(p) JimmyQuinn 1 47
(Bernard Llewellyn) *hld up: angled out after 3f: hdwy after 4f: led over 7f out: drvn and hdd 3f out: wknd over 1f out* **7/2**[1]

006- **9** 23 **Lady Natasha (IRE)**[89] 7325 6-7-13 **66** oh21..............(t[1]) NoelGarbutt(3) 6 8
(James Grassick) *hld up: carried rt after 3f: drvn 7f out: lost tch 3f out* **66/1**

2m 48.87s (6.67) **Going Correction** +0.45s/f (Yiel) **9 Ran SP% 121.9**
Speed ratings (Par 105): **95,94,94,93,90 87,84,83,68**
CSF £78.43 CT £324.56 TOTE £7.70: £2.50, £3.20, £1.80; EX 60.70 Trifecta £485.10.
Owner M J Macleod **Bred** Darley **Trained** Great Habton, N Yorks
FOCUS
A messy race from a pace perspective, and it set up for the closers.
T/Plt: £38.00 to a £1 stake. Pool: £79,322.18 - 1,522.70 winning units. T/Qpdt: £13.60 to a £1 stake. Pool: £5,886.04 - 319.58 winning units. **Darren Owen**

3644 LEICESTER (R-H)
Saturday, June 15
3848 Meeting Abandoned - false patches of ground

3803 SANDOWN (R-H)
Saturday, June 15
OFFICIAL GOING: Round course - good to soft (soft in places, 6.8); straight course - soft (good to soft in places; spr 6.4, home str - far 6.3, stands' 6.8)
Wind: Moderate, against Weather: Cloudy with showers

3855 RANDOX HEALTH SCURRY STKS (LISTED RACE) 5f 10y
2:05 (2:07) (Class 1) 3-Y-O

£22,684 (£8,600; £4,304; £2,144; £1,076; £540) **Stalls** Low

Form RPR

4-20 **1** **Kurious**[28] 2826 3-8-9 95.............................. KieranShoemark 8 98
(Henry Candy) *chsd ldng pair: pushed along 2f out: clsd to ld jst over 1f out: sn hrd pressed: drvn and kpt on wl (trainer said, regarding the improved form shown, the filly appreciated being ridden more positively on this occasion)* **5/1**[2]

-160 **2** 3/4 **The Cruising Lord**[28] 2826 3-9-0 96.............................. RobertHavlin 5 100
(Michael Attwater) *hld up in midfield gng wl: prog over 1f out: rdn to chse wnr last 100yds: kpt on but no imp nr fin* **6/1**[3]

3043 **3** 1/2 **Reticent Angel (IRE)**[12] 3427 3-8-9 79..............................(p) TomMarquand 7 93?
(Clive Cox) *pushed along in last trio after 2f: rdn and prog 2f out: chal and w wnr 1f out: hanging and nt qckn after: lost 2nd fnl 100yds* **40/1**

4311 **4** 1/2 **Wise Words**[19] 3159 3-8-9 82.............................. ShaneKelly 2 91+
(James Tate) *pushed along in last trio: plld out and prog over 1f out: rdn and styd on fnl f: too late to threaten* **16/1**

20-0 **5** 1 3/4 **Well Done Fox**[45] 2270 3-9-0 106.............................. SilvestreDeSousa 6 90
(Richard Hannon) *t.k.h: sn pressed ldr: led 2f out: rdn and hdd jst over 1f out: wknd ins fnl f* **3/1**[1]

00 **6** 3 3/4 **El Guanche (FR)**[15] 3-9-0 96.............................. JimCrowley 1 77
(M Delcher Sanchez, France) *chsd ldrs: rdn 2f out: wknd over 1f out* **8/1**

06-1 **7** 1/2 **Street Parade**[19] 3166 3-9-0 101..............................(t) JasonWatson 9 75
(Stuart Williams) *racd on outer: rdn in midfield 1/2-way: no prog and wl btn over 1f out* **7/1**

1110 **8** 5 **Leodis Dream (IRE)**[21] 3097 3-9-0 100.............................. OisinMurphy 4 57
(David O'Meara) *led against far rail: hdd 2f out: sn wknd (trainer's rep could offer no explanation for the gelding's performance)* **3/1**[1]

1m 2.76s (1.46) **Going Correction** +0.45s/f (Yiel) **8 Ran SP% 112.9**
Speed ratings (Par 107): **106,104,104,103,100 94,93,85**
CSF £33.89 TOTE £5.70: £1.70, £1.80, £2.10; EX 31.10 Trifecta £539.70.
Owner Hot To Trot Racing 2 **Bred** Mrs B A Matthews **Trained** Kingston Warren, Oxon

FOCUS
A fair edition of this 3yo Listed sprint and a frantic tempo set it up for the closers. Afterwards the riders generally reported the ground to be hard work. The winner only had to run to form, with the joint-favourites below form.

3856 RANDOX.COM H'CAP (JOCKEY CLUB GRASSROOTS FLAT SPRINT SERIES QUALIFIER) 5f 10y
2:35 (2:39) (Class 4) (0-80,78) 4-Y-0+

£6,469 (£1,925; £962; £481; £300; £300) **Stalls** Low

Form RPR

0-02 **1** **Fantasy Keeper**[6] 3636 5-9-7 **78**.............................. SilvestreDeSousa 6 86+
(Michael Appleby) *chsd ldr: pushed along to cl 2f out: led 1f out: drvn and kpt on wl* **13/8**[1]

2156 **2** ½ **King Robert**[51] 2061 6-9-5 **76**.............................. OisinMurphy 5 82
(Charlie Wallis) *taken steadily to post: trckd ldrs: rdn to chse ldng pair jst over 1f out: styd on to take 2nd last 100yds: a hld* **8/1**[3]

0-64 **3** 1 **Our Oystercatcher**[37] 2556 5-9-2 **73**.............................. HectorCrouch 7 75
(Mark Pattinson) *taken steadily to post: broke wl: led: rdn and hdd 1f out: kpt on same pce and lost 2nd last 100yds* **6/1**[2]

0004 **4** ½ **Pettochside**[11] 3443 10-8-11 **75**.............................. CierenFallon(7) 9 76
(John Bridger) *racd on outer: in rr: shkn up and prog over 2f out: rdn to press ldng pair over 1f out: nt qckn and kpt on same pce fnl f* **14/1**

0-05 **5** nk **Secretfact**[8] 3531 6-9-3 **74**.............................. FergusSweeney 3 74
(Malcolm Saunders) *hld up in last trio: rdn and prog 2f out: rchd 5th jst over 1f out: styd on but nvr quite pce to chal* **20/1**

5220 **6** 2¾ **Wiff Waff**[23] 3021 4-8-13 **70**.............................. ShaneKelly 4 60
(Chris Gordon) *v awkward s and slowly away: mostly in last: shkn up 2f out: passed wkng rivals to rch 6th fnl f: no hdwy last 100yds (jockey said gelding reared as the stalls opened and was slowly away as a result)* **40/1**

36-3 **7** 1¾ **Wiley Post**[40] 2484 6-9-6 **77**..............................(b) TomMarquand 8 60
(Tony Carroll) *taken steadily to post: chsd ldrs: shkn up sn after 1/2-way: lost pl and btn over 1f out* **8/1**[3]

0060 **8** 1 **Bahamian Sunrise**[28] 2824 7-8-10 **67**..............................(b) JasonWatson 2 47
(John Gallagher) *only one to r against rail: prom: rdn 1/2-way: sn struggling* **8/1**[3]

0-03 **9** 4 **Kodiac Express (IRE)**[15] 3303 4-9-0 **74**.............................. GabrieleMalune(3) 1 39
(Mike Murphy) *taken down early: a towards rr: rdn and no prog 2f out: sn wknd* **25/1**

0-55 **10** 6 **Delagate This Lord**[19] 3164 5-9-1 **72**..............................(p) LukeMorris 10 16
(Michael Attwater) *chsd ldrs on outer: rdn 1/2-way: sn wknd: eased and t.o* **17/2**

1m 2.55s (1.25) **Going Correction** +0.45s/f (Yiel) **10** Ran SP% **114.0**
Speed ratings (Par 105): **108,107,105,104,104 99,97,95,89,79**
CSF £14.19 CT £62.54 TOTE £2.10: £1.30, £2.20, £2.20; EX 15.80 Trifecta £78.60.
Owner The Fantasy Fellowship B **Bred** Cheveley Park Stud Ltd **Trained** Oakham, Rutland

FOCUS
This modest sprint handicap was another strongly run affair.

3857 RANDOX HEALTH H'CAP 1m
3:15 (3:18) (Class 2) (0-100,95) 3-Y-0+

£24,744 (£7,416; £3,712; £1,848; £928; £468) **Stalls** Low

Form RPR

-030 **1** **History Writer (IRE)**[15] 3313 4-9-10 **91**..............................(t) JasonWatson 3 101
(David Menuisier) *t.k.h: hld up in rr: brushed rail 6f out: cajoled along and prog over 2f out: rdn to chse ldrs over 1f out and briefly hung fire: brought between rivals to ld jst ins fnl f: styd on wl (trainer said, regarding the improved form shown, the gelding appreciated the return to Sandown having won here previously)* **5/1**[3]

4-2 **2** 2 **Baltic Baron (IRE)**[10] 3472 4-10-0 **95**.............................. OisinMurphy 9 100
(David O'Meara) *trckd ldrs: prog over 2f out: rdn to ld over 1f out: hdd and one pce jst ins fnl f* **10/1**

0-00 **3** ½ **Alternative Fact**[49] 2095 4-9-8 **89**.............................. RobertHavlin 8 93
(Ed Dunlop) *w ldrs: led over 3f out and brought field to centre: rdn 2f out: hdd over 1f out: kpt on same pce fnl f* **12/1**

-413 **4** 1½ **Greenside**[15] 3313 8-10-0 **95**.............................. KieranShoemark 6 95
(Henry Candy) *hld up towards rr: shkn up over 2f out: prog u.p over 1f out: kpt on but nvr enough pce to threaten* **4/1**[1]

3320 **5** nk **Loch Ness Monster (IRE)**[21] 3082 3-8-3 **88**.............................. CierenFallon(7) 2 85
(Michael Appleby) *trckd ldrs in 5th: rdn: outpcd and lost pl over 2f out: rallied over 1f out: kpt on fnl f* **7/1**

0034 **6** 3½ **Zap**[7] 3563 4-9-12 **93**..............................(p[1]) ShaneKelly 1 85
(Richard Fahey) *mostly in midfield: rdn and no prog over 2f out: wl btn over 1f out* **25/1**

-322 **7** 1½ **Hateya (IRE)**[15] 3318 4-10-0 **95**.............................. JackMitchell 7 83
(Jim Boyle) *hld up in rr: rdn wl over 2f out and sn struggling: modest late hdwy* **10/1**

3243 **8** hd **Masham Star (IRE)**[10] 3472 5-9-13 **94**.............................. SilvestreDeSousa 10 82
(Mark Johnston) *w ldrs: chal and upsides 3f out to jst over 2f out: wknd qckly over 1f out* **14/1**

5-42 **9** ½ **Thrave**[28] 2832 4-9-11 **92**.............................. TomMarquand 5 79
(Henry Candy) *w ldrs: rdn 3f out: wknd 2f out (jockey said gelding hung right-handed travelling up the home straight)* **13/2**

3206 **10** 1½ **Pattie**[57] 1918 5-9-8 **94**.............................. ScottMcCullagh(5) 11 77
(Mick Channon) *rrd s and lost 12 l: nvr able to rcvr though passed two rivals late on (jockey said mare reared as the stalls opened and was slowly away as a result)* **33/1**

13-3 **11** 2¾ **Sawwaah**[58] 1889 4-9-12 **93**..............................(p[1]) JimCrowley 4 70
(Owen Burrows) *hld up in rr: rdn and no prog wl over 2f out: wl btn after (jockey said colt was slowly away)* **9/2**[2]

2-20 **12** 11 **Azzeccagarbugli (IRE)**[23] 3027 6-9-11 **92**..............................(p) RossaRyan 12 44
(Mike Murphy) *led to over 3f out: wknd rapidly: t.o* **80/1**

1m 45.85s (2.55) **Going Correction** +0.45s/f (Yiel) **12** Ran SP% **121.2**
WFA 3 from 4yo+ 11lb
Speed ratings (Par 109): **105,103,102,101,100 97,95,95,95,93 90,79**
CSF £54.95 CT £590.02 TOTE £6.50: £2.40, £3.20, £3.10; EX 73.80 Trifecta £1001.20.
Owner Clive Washbourn & Partner **Bred** Kildaragh Stud **Trained** Pulborough, W Sussex

FOCUS
Competitive stuff, and a pb from the winner. The centre of the home straight proved the place to be. Add 15yds.

3858 RANDOX H'CAP 7f
3:50 (3:51) (Class 3) (0-95,87) 3-Y-0

£6,066; £1,398; £699; £349; £175 **Stalls** Low

Form RPR

041- **1** **Pesto**[307] 6051 3-9-7 **87**.............................. TomMarquand 2 95+
(Richard Hannon) *hld up in tch: nt clr run briefly wl over 1f out: prog and squeezed through to chse ldr ins fnl f: r.o wl to force dead-heat post* **10/1**

31-3 **1** dht **Wise Counsel**[7] 3591 3-9-7 **87**.............................. OisinMurphy 7 94
(Clive Cox) *prom: led wl over 1f out and sent for home: nrly 2 l up fnl f w a few tail swishes: kpt on but jnd post* **3/1**[2]

1502 **3** 1¾ **Nefarious (IRE)**[10] 3465 3-9-2 **82**.............................. KieranShoemark 9 84
(Henry Candy) *racd wd: in tch: lost pl 1/2-way: rdn and prog on outer 2f out: disp 2nd 1f out and looked a threat: one pce ins fnl f (jockey said colt ran too freely and hung left-handed)* **13/2**[3]

010 **4** hd **May Sonic**[42] 2397 3-8-6 **79**.............................. CierenFallon(7) 4 80
(Charles Hills) *t.k.h: hld up bhd ldrs: rdn and prog 2f out: disp 2nd 1f out: one pce after (jockey said gelding ran too freely)* **16/1**

5-60 **5** nk **Sheila's Showcase**[43] 2364 3-8-13 **79**.............................. JasonWatson 5 79
(Denis Coakley) *led at mod pce: tk field up far side in st: tried to kick on over 2f out: hdd wl over 1f out: stl disputing 2nd fnl f: one pce after (jockey said colt hung right-handed; trainer said colt was unsuited by the ground (good to soft, soft in places) on this occasion and would prefer a quicker surface)* **16/1**

-311 **6** 3¾ **Artistic Rifles (IRE)**[14] 3340 3-9-7 **87**.............................. LukeMorris 8 77
(Charles Hills) *trckd ldr to jst over 2f out: sn lost pl and rdn: fdd* **13/2**[3]

1-65 **7** 2 **Karnavaal (IRE)**[31] 2746 3-9-1 **81**.............................. JimCrowley 6 66
(Sir Michael Stoute) *hld up in rr but wl in tch: rdn and no prog jst over 2f out: n.d after (trainer said colt was unsuited by the ground (good to soft, soft in places) on this occasion and would prefer a quicker surface)* **15/8**[1]

01-2 **8** shd **Mardle**[158] 126 3-9-0 **80**.............................. ShaneKelly 3 64
(K R Burke) *broke w ldrs but sn restrained into last: shkn up and no prog 2f out: nvr in it* **25/1**

1m 33.28s (3.98) **Going Correction** +0.45s/f (Yiel) **8** Ran SP% **111.2**
Speed ratings (Par 103): **95,95,93,92,92 88,85,85**
WIN: 1.80 Wise Counsel, 3.50 Pesto; PL: 1.20 Wise Counsel, 1.90 Pesto, 1.90 Nefarious; EX: WC/P 10.10, P/WC 15.90; CSF: WC/P 15.35, P/WC 18.96; TC: WC/P/N 87.54, P/WC/N 103.69; TF: WC/P/N 73.00, P/WC/N 102.70;.
Owner Clipper Logistics **Bred** South Acre Bloodstock **Trained** Lambourn, Berks
Owner Highclere Thoroughbred Racing - Goodwood **Bred** New England, Mount Coote & P Barrett **Trained** East Everleigh, Wilts

FOCUS
A fair 3yo handicap on paper, but it was a messy race and saw a dead-heat. The fourth and fifth have been rated close to their marks. Add 15yds.

3859 RANDOXHEALTH.COM H'CAP 1m 1f
4:25 (4:27) (Class 3) (0-95,89) 3-Y-0

£9,337 (£2,796; £1,398; £699; £349; £175) **Stalls** Low

Form RPR

1-34 **1** **New King**[50] 2088 3-9-6 **88**.............................. OisinMurphy 2 105+
(John Gosden) *w.w off the pce: clsd 4f out: prog to ld wl over 1f out: shkn up and sn clr: edgd lft fnl f but drew further away* **15/8**[1]

-415 **2** 8 **Pour Me A Drink**[16] 3262 3-8-11 **79**.............................. TomMarquand 3 79
(Clive Cox) *hld up off the pce: clsd 4f out: rdn and prog over 2f out: drvn to chse clr wnr over 1f out: kpt on but lft further bhd fnl f* **4/1**[2]

661- **3** 5 **Mubariz**[227] 8739 3-9-7 **89**.............................. JasonWatson 6 79
(Roger Charlton) *nt gng that wl in last: rdn over 2f out: kpt on to take modest 3rd ins fnl f* **5/1**[3]

1-13 **4** 2¾ **Absolutio (FR)**[42] 2395 3-9-1 **83**..............................(h) ShaneKelly 5 67
(K R Burke) *blasted off in front and sn clr: breather 1/2-way: tried to kick on over 2f out: hdd wl over 1f out: wknd* **15/2**

411 **5** 10 **Cristal Breeze (IRE)**[15] 3324 3-8-9 **84**.............................. CierenFallon(7) 1 47
(William Haggas) *briefly pressed ldr but sn restrained bhd him: lost 2nd jst over 2f out: wknd qckly (jockey said gelding hung left-handed travelling up the home straight)* **5/1**[3]

1-61 **6** 6 **Multamis (IRE)**[52] 2035 3-9-1 **83**.............................. JimCrowley 4 33
(Owen Burrows) *chsd clr ldr pair: clsd 4f out: tried to chal over 2f out: sn wknd rapidly (trainer's rep said gelding was unsuited by the ground (good to soft, soft in places) on this occasion and would prefer a quicker surface)* **8/1**

1m 58.97s (2.67) **Going Correction** +0.45s/f (Yiel) **6** Ran SP% **111.0**
Speed ratings (Par 103): **106,98,94,92,83 77**
CSF £9.29 TOTE £2.30: £1.70, £2.50; EX 8.60 Trifecta £29.80.
Owner Qatar Racing Limited **Bred** Qatar Bloodstock Ltd **Trained** Newmarket, Suffolk

FOCUS
This good-quality 3yo handicap fell apart but the winner was impressive. Add 15yds.

3860 BRITISH EBF MAIDEN STKS 1m 1f 209y
5:00 (5:02) (Class 4) 3-Y-0+ **£5,530** (£1,645; £822; £411) **Stalls** Low

Form RPR

-63 **1** **Nette Rousse (GER)**[16] 3263 3-8-10 0.............................. SilvestreDeSousa 8 84
(Ralph Beckett) *mde all: pushed along and pressed 2f out: drvn and asserted fnl f* **10/11**[1]

2-26 **2** 2¼ **Damon Runyon**[38] 2524 3-9-1 80..............................(p) RobertHavlin 9 84
(John Gosden) *prom: trckd wnr 4f out: chal 2f out: hung lft u.p over 1f out: no imp after* **9/2**[3]

3 1 **Two Bids** 3-9-1 0.............................. OisinMurphy 6 82
(William Haggas) *s.i.s: sn wl in tch: prog to trck ldng pair over 2f out and cl enough: rdn and one pce after* **3/1**[2]

2-0 **4** 3½ **Galileo Silver (IRE)**[30] 2769 4-10-0 0.............................. JimCrowley 7 76
(Alan King) *chsd wnr to 4f out: shkn up 3f out: styd cl up tl fdd fnl f* **14/1**

3 **5** 7 **Caen Na Coille (USA)**[116] 794 3-8-10 0.............................. GeorgeWood 4 56
(Ed Dunlop) *in tch in rr: outpcd over 3f out: shkn up over 2f out: fdd over 1f out but tk modest 5th fnl f* **22/1**

36 **6** 1 **Stone Mason (IRE)**[16] 3248 3-9-1 0.............................. JasonWatson 3 59
(Roger Charlton) *w ldrs to over 3f out: steadily wknd fr 2f out* **14/1**

60 **7** 22 **Triple Genius (IRE)**[11] 3445 3-9-1 0.............................. DanielMuscutt 1 15
(Ed Dunlop) *in tch 4f: sn struggling: t.o* **50/1**

8 24 **Champ Ayr** 3-9-1 0.............................. KieranShoemark 2
(David Menuisier) *s.s: a wl bhd: t.o (jockey said gelding was slowly away)* **25/1**

9 1¾ **Juniors Dream (IRE)** 3-8-12 0.............................. GabrieleMalune(3) 5
(Ivan Furtado) *dwlt: a bhd: t.o (jockey said gelding was never travelling)* **33/1**

2m 11.73s (1.53) **Going Correction** +0.45s/f (Yiel) **9** Ran SP% **122.0**
WFA 3 from 4yo 13lb
Speed ratings (Par 105): **111,109,108,105,100 99,81,62,61**
CSF £5.62 TOTE £1.80: £1.10, £1.60, £1.50; EX 6.10 Trifecta £17.40.
Owner H H Sheikh Mohammed Bin Khalifa Al Thani **Bred** Gestut Wittekindshof **Trained** Kimpton, Hants

FOCUS
A fair maiden, run at a solid tempo. The winner progressed again, with the form set by the runner-up and fourth. Add 15yds.

3861 RANDOX FOOD H'CAP 1m 6f
5:35 (5:35) (Class 4) (0-80,81) 4-Y-O+
£6,469 (£1,925; £962; £481; £300; £300) **Stalls** Low

Form RPR

-163 **1** **Seinesational**[22] [3044] 4-9-4 **77**....................(v) JasonWatson 4 86
(William Knight) *trckd ldr 3f: styd prom: rdn to ld 2f out: kpt on wl u.p after* **16/1**

-460 **2** *1 1/2* **Diocletian (IRE)**[36] [2578] 4-9-7 **80**.................... OisinMurphy 13 86
(Andrew Balding) *wl in tch in midfield: clsd over 2f out and waiting for a gap: rdn to chse wnr over 1f out: kpt on but no imp fnl f* **5/1**[2]

-012 **3** *2 1/4* **Argus (IRE)**[95] [1159] 7-9-4 **77**.................... RossaRyan 8 80
(Alexandra Dunn) *wl in tch: grad lost pl fr 1/2-way and wl in rr over 3f out: drvn and hdwy over 2f out: kpt on to take 3rd nr fin* **22/1**

03-0 **4** *nk* **Polish**[56] [1943] 4-9-8 **81**.................... HectorCrouch 14 83
(John Gallagher) *led and sn clr: hdd 3f out and sn lost pl: kpt on again over 1f out* **33/1**

0-22 **5** *nse* **C'Est No Mour (GER)**[30] [2763] 6-9-7 **80**.................... TomMarquand 3 82
(Peter Hedger) *t.k.h: hld up in rr: prog to chse ldrs over 2f out: sn rdn: kpt on to battle for 3rd ins fnl f* **12/1**

/0-3 **6** *3 1/2* **Regal Director (IRE)**[43] [2374] 4-9-2 **75**.................... JackMitchell 9 72
(Simon Crisford) *t.k.h: trckd ldrs: stl gng wl enough over 2f out: rdn and no rspnse wl over 1f out: wknd* **15/2**[3]

-065 **7** *2 3/4* **Archimento**[22] [3044] 6-9-8 **81**.................... LukeMorris 12 75
(William Knight) *chsd ldng trio: rdn over 3f out: steadily wknd u.p* **25/1**

0062 **8** *shd* **Baydar**[14] [3361] 6-9-2 **75**....................(p) DanielMuscutt 11 68
(Ivan Furtado) *slowly away: drvn to rcvr and chsd ldr after 3f: rdn to ld 3f out: hdd & wknd 2f out (jockey said gelding was slowly into stride)* **15/2**[3]

14-1 **9** *3/4* **Point In Time (IRE)**[47] [2214] 4-9-3 **76**.................... StevieDonohoe 10 68
(Mark Usher) *hld up in last pair: rdn on outer and tried to make prog over 2f out: no hdwy over 1f out: wknd* **16/1**

4-30 **10** *2 1/4* **Elysees (IRE)**[22] [3044] 4-9-3 **76**....................(p[1]) KieranShoemark 5 65
(Alan King) *a in rr: shkn up and no prog over 2f out: wknd sn after* **9/1**

3-31 **11** *7* **Oi The Clubb Oi's**[13] [3377] 4-8-12 **71**.................... JimCrowley 2 50
(Ian Williams) *hld up in midfield: prog to trck ldrs 6f out: rdn over 2f out: sn wknd* **5/1**[2]

4015 **12** *5* **Just Wait (IRE)**[22] [3054] 4-9-5 **78**.................... SilvestreDeSousa 7 50
(Mark Johnston) *c out of stall slowly: a in last pair: rdn and no prog 3f out: eased fnl f (trainer's rep could offer no explanation for the filly's performance)* **7/2**[1]

3m 11.33s (5.33) **Going Correction** +0.45s/f (Yiel) **12** Ran SP% **119.7**
Speed ratings (Par 105): **102,101,99,99,99 97,96,96,95,94 90,87**
CSF £93.15 CT £1795.32 TOTE £17.00: £3.90, £2.10, £6.80; EX 112.80 Trifecta £1456.20.
Owner One Day Rodney Partnership **Bred** Fittocks Stud **Trained** Angmering, W Sussex

FOCUS
This fair staying handicap served up a proper test. The winner progressed again, rated around the runner-up to this year's form. Add 15yds.
T/Plt: £87.30 to a £1 stake. Pool: £110,783.64 - 925.74 winning units T/Qpdt: £11.00 to a £1 stake. Pool: £10,512.27 - 701.94 winning units **Jonathan Neesom**

3810 YORK (L-H)
Saturday, June 15

OFFICIAL GOING: Good to soft (6.1, home str - stands' 6.0, ctr 6.2, far 6.2)
Wind: Moderate behind Weather: Cloudy, showery after race 4

3862 QUEEN MOTHER'S CUP H'CAP (FOR LADY AMATEUR RIDERS) 1m 3f 188y
1:50 (1:50) (Class 3) (0-95,93) 3-Y-O+
£11,992 (£3,746; £1,872; £936; £468; £236) **Stalls** Centre

Form RPR

-611 **1** **Arctic Fox**[21] [3099] 3-9-4 **84**.................... MrsCarolBartley 1 89+
(Richard Fahey) *trckd ldrs: hdwy over 4f out: led 3f out: rdn and edgd markedly rt to stands' rail over 1f out: drvn out* **5/1**[2]

6603 **2** *1/2* **Mutamaded (IRE)**[18] [3180] 6-10-1 **83**.................... MissEmilyBullock(3) 8 87
(Ruth Carr) *trckd ldrs: hdwy 4f out: chsd wnr over 2f out: rdn wl over 1f out: drvn and kpt on fnl f* **33/1**

3-41 **3** *1/2* **Where's Jeff**[40] [2479] 4-9-12 **77**.................... MissSerenaBrotherton 10 80
(Michael Easterby) *t.k.h early: hld up in tch: hdwy 3f out: rdn wl over 1f out: styd on fnl f: nrst fin* **6/1**[3]

16-5 **4** *shd* **Billy No Mates (IRE)**[50] [2075] 3-9-0 **83**.................... MissSophieDods(3) 12 86
(Michael Dods) *hld up towards rr: hdwy over 3f out: chsd ldrs 2f out: rdn and ev ch over 1f out: edgd lft and kpt on same pce fnl f (vet said gelding had lost its left fore shoe)* **5/1**[2]

-211 **5** *nse* **Makawee (IRE)**[16] [3269] 4-10-10 **89**.................... MissJoannaMason 14 92
(David O'Meara) *dwlt: hld up in rr: hdwy over 3f out: rdn to chse ldrs over 1f out: kpt on u.p fnl f* **4/1**[1]

-004 **6** *1 1/4* **Tapis Libre**[12] [3415] 11-9-9 **74** oh1.................... MissCatherineWalton 9 75
(Jacqueline Coward) *hld up towards rr: hdwy on inner 3f out: rdn along wl over 1f out: styd on fnl f* **20/1**

0-00 **7** *2 1/4* **Multellie**[17] [3222] 7-10-5 **84**.................... MissEmilyEasterby 2 81
(Tim Easterby) *trckd ldrs: hdwy over 3f out: rdn along 2f out: grad wknd* **20/1**

-113 **8** *1 3/4* **French Mix (USA)**[8] [3541] 5-9-12 **77**.................... MissHannahWelch 5 72
(Alexandra Dunn) *trckd ldrs: pushed along 3f out: rdn 2f out: sn wknd* **12/1**

013- **9** *3 1/4* **Archi's Affaire**[259] [7769] 5-10-6 **91**.................... MissChloeDods(6) 7 80
(Michael Dods) *t.k.h: trckd ldrs: pushed along wl over 2f out: rdn wl over 1f out: sn wknd* **12/1**

34-5 **10** *7* **Sootability (IRE)**[27] [2872] 3-8-9 **75**.................... MissAmieWaugh 15 53
(Richard Fahey) *dwlt: a in rr (jockey said filly was restless in the stalls and jumped awkwardly)* **8/1**

550/ **11** *3 1/2* **Promise Of Peace (JPN)**[20] 5-10-6 **85**....................(bt) MissAbbieMcCain 6 58
(Donald McCain) *cl up: led after 3f: pushed along 4f out: hdd 3f out: sn wknd* **50/1**

0/3- **12** *10* **Mister Manduro (FR)**[30] [1809] 5-10-8 **87**.................... MissBeckySmith 3 44
(Brian Ellison) *led 3f: trckd ldr: rdn along 4f out: sn wknd* **12/1**

2116 **13** *96* **Apterix (FR)**[21] [3073] 9-10-1 **80**.................... TabithaWorsley 13
(Brian Ellison) *trckd ldrs on outer: pushed along over 6f out: rdn and lost pl over 5f out: sn bhd (vet said gelding had blood in its trachea and had atrial fibrillation)* **16/1**

2m 37.31s (4.11) **Going Correction** +0.375s/f (Good)
WFA 3 from 4yo+ 15lb **13** Ran SP% **122.1**
Speed ratings (Par 107): **101,100,100,100,100 99,97,96,94,89 87,80,16**
CSF £172.12 CT £1030.40 TOTE £5.40: £2.00, £8.30, £2.40; EX 149.80 Trifecta £2409.80.
Owner Sir Robert Ogden **Bred** Sir Robert Ogden **Trained** Musley Bank, N Yorks

FOCUS
The rail around the home bend from 1m1f to the entrance to the straight was out three metres; add 11yds. There was 3.4mm of rain the previous day but dry as racing began and the ground was said to have dried to good to soft (from soft). This set up for the closers, and the second and third help the standard.

3863 JCB H'CAP 7f
2:25 (2:26) (Class 2) (0-105,102) 3-Y-O+
£24,900 (£7,456; £3,728; £1,864; £932; £468) **Stalls** Low

Form RPR

-020 **1** **Firmament**[15] [3313] 7-9-4 **93**....................(p) JamesDoyle 3 104
(David O'Meara) *trckd ldrs: rdn to chal appr fnl f: drvn to ld 110yds out: kpt on wl* **14/1**

5-10 **2** *1 3/4* **Admirality**[7] [3589] 5-9-4 **93**.................... BenCurtis 11 99+
(Roger Fell) *trckd ldrs: smooth hdwy to ld wl over 1f out: rdn and pressed appr fnl f: drvn and hdd 110yds out: one pce* **25/1**

5-03 **3** *nk* **Great Prospector (IRE)**[49] [2100] 4-9-5 **94**.................... PaulHanagan 4 99
(Richard Fahey) *dwlt: hld up: rdn and hdwy towards far side over 1f out: kpt on wl fnl f* **8/1**[3]

6000 **4** *1 1/2* **Flying Pursuit**[7] [3602] 6-9-6 **95**....................(p) RachelRichardson 12 96
(Tim Easterby) *w ldr: rdn over 2f out: no ex ins fnl f* **33/1**

-000 **5** *1/2* **Golden Apollo**[10] [3480] 5-9-3 **92**.................... PhilDennis 7 94+
(Tim Easterby) *hld up in rr: pushed along and sme hdwy whn n.m.r over 1f out: r.o wl fnl 110yds: nrst fin* **25/1**

-202 **6** *nse* **Danielsflyer (IRE)**[28] [2844] 5-9-3 **92**....................(p[1]) AndrewMullen 1 92
(Michael Dods) *midfield: drvn and hdwy to chse ldrs over 1f out: one pce ins fnl f* **20/1**

3213 **7** *3/4* **Hayadh**[30] [2778] 6-9-2 **91**.................... LewisEdmunds 15 89
(Rebecca Bastiman) *trckd ldrs: rdn over 2f out: no ex ins fnl f (vet said gelding had lost its right fore shoe)* **16/1**

-300 **8** *1/2* **Staxton**[7] [3602] 4-9-7 **96**.................... DuranFentiman 5 92
(Tim Easterby) *led narrowly: rdn and hdd wl over 1f out: wknd ins fnl f* **25/1**

0231 **9** *shd* **Kaeso**[21] [3069] 5-9-4 **93**.................... HollieDoyle 18 89+
(Nigel Tinkler) *midfield on outer: rdn over 2f out: no imp* **13/2**[1]

4431 **10** *shd* **Love Dreams (IRE)**[7] [3563] 5-9-10 **99**....................(v) PJMcDonald 6 95
(Mark Johnston) *prom: rdn along over 2f out: wknd ins fnl f* **12/1**

6-50 **11** *hd* **Get Knotted (IRE)**[28] [2843] 7-9-3 **92**....................(p) PaulMulrennan 20 87
(Michael Dods) *hld up in rr: pushed along over 2f out: sme hdwy appr fnl f: kpt on fnl 110yds: nvr involved* **9/1**

3053 **12** *nk* **Gabrial (IRE)**[21] [3069] 10-9-8 **100**.................... SeanDavis(3) 16 94
(Richard Fahey) *hld up: rdn over 2f out: nvr threatened* **33/1**

3005 **13** *1 1/2* **Desert Doctor (IRE)**[10] [3480] 4-9-2 **91**.................... GeraldMosse 9 81
(Ed Walker) *midfield: rdn and sme hdwy to chse ldrs 2f out: wknd ins fnl f* **25/1**

541- **14** *1/2* **Blizzard**[212] [9091] 4-9-10 **99**.................... HarryBentley 2 88
(Ralph Beckett) *trckd ldrs: rdn over 2f out: wknd fnl f* **33/1**

62-3 **15** *hd* **Aljady (FR)**[31] [2743] 4-9-6 **95**.................... TonyHamilton 14 83
(Richard Fahey) *midfield: pushed along over 2f out: rdn over 1f out: sn btn (trainer could offer no explanation for the gelding's performance; vet said gelding had lost its right fore shoe)* **7/1**[2]

-400 **16** *1 3/4* **Aces (IRE)**[7] [3602] 7-9-3 **92**....................(t) RyanMoore 8 76
(Ian Williams) *midfield: pushed along over 2f out: rdn along and no imp whn n.m.r appr fnl f: nt persevered w (vet said gelding had lost its left fore shoe)* **11/1**

-621 **17** *1 1/2* **Hyperfocus (IRE)**[10] [3480] 5-9-2 **91**.................... DavidAllan 10 71
(Tim Easterby) *hld up: pushed along and n.m.r over 1f out: nvr involved (jockey said gelding was denied a clear run approximately 2f out)* **14/1**

1-02 **18** *2* **Lord Oberon**[7] [3589] 4-9-6 **95**.................... CliffordLee 13 69
(K R Burke) *midfield: rdn over 2f out: wknd over 1f out (jockey said gelding ran flat)* **9/1**

1000 **19** *10* **Above The Rest (IRE)**[28] [2844] 8-9-13 **102**....................(h) RobbieDowney 19 49
(David Barron) *hld up towards outer: rdn over 2f out: wknd over 1f out: eased* **16/1**

4104 **20** *29* **Three Saints Bay (IRE)**[28] [2844] 4-9-11 **100**.................... DanielTudhope 17
(David O'Meara) *dwlt: sn prom towards outer: rdn along 3f out: wknd 2f out: eased (jockey said gelding ran too free; vet said gelding was lame right hind)* **20/1**

1m 25.14s (0.54) **Going Correction** +0.375s/f (Good) **20** Ran SP% **131.8**
Speed ratings (Par 109): **111,109,108,106,106 106,105,104,104,104 104,104,102,101,101 99,97,95,84,51**
CSF £343.50 CT £3054.94 TOTE £15.90: £3.50, £6.90, £3.00, £9.20; EX 325.00 Trifecta £4386.00.
Owner Gallop Racing **Bred** Cheveley Park Stud Ltd **Trained** Upper Helmsley, N Yorks

FOCUS
A competitive handicap in which they raced middle to near side in the straight.

3864 SKY BET RACE TO THE EBOR GRAND CUP STKS (LISTED RACE) 1m 5f 188y
3:00 (3:00) (Class 1) 4-Y-O+
£28,355 (£10,750; £5,380; £2,680; £1,345; £675) **Stalls** Low

Form RPR

36-4 **1** **Gold Mount**[77] [1441] 6-9-0 110.................... AndreaAtzeni 2 117
(Ian Williams) *hld up in rr: smooth hdwy 3f out: cl up 2f out: rdn to ld over 1f out: kpt on strly* **16/1**

444- **2** *2 1/4* **Raheen House (IRE)**[231] [8645] 5-9-0 106.................... JamesDoyle 3 113
(William Haggas) *hld up: hdwy over 4f out: cl up 3f out: led 2f out: sn rdn: hdd over 1f out: sn drvn and kpt on* **9/2**[2]

52-0 **3** *9* **Buzz (FR)**[57] [1927] 5-9-0 98.................... DanielTudhope 8 100
(Hughie Morrison) *hld up in tch: hdwy 4f out: slt ld 3f out: sn rdn and hdd 2f out: drvn and kpt on one pce fr over 1f out* **14/1**

-103 **4** *2 1/2* **Austrian School (IRE)**[23] [3024] 4-9-0 110.................... PJMcDonald 4 97
(Mark Johnston) *led 2f: trckd ldr: cl up 5f out: led 4f out: hdd and rdn 3f out: drvn over 2f out: plugged on one pce* **5/1**[3]

50-5 **5** *2* **Desert Skyline (IRE)**[29] [2807] 5-9-0 107....................(p) GeraldMosse 7 94
(David Elsworth) *trckd ldng pair: pushed along over 5f out: rdn 4f out: drvn wl over 2f out: sn outpcd* **14/1**

5114 **6** *16* **Making Miracles**[23] 3024 4-9-0 108................................ HarryBentley 1 72
(Mark Johnston) *trckd ldrs: hdwy to chse ldng pair 5f out: rdn along over 3f out: sn wknd* **8/1**

12-2 **7** *9* **Mekong**[23] 3024 4-9-0 110................................ RyanMoore 6 59
(Sir Michael Stoute) *t.k.h early: prom: led after 2f: pushed along over 4f out: sn hdd and rdn: wknd qckly (trainer's rep could offer no explanation for the gelding's performance)* **1/1**[1]

2m 59.95s (-0.25) **Going Correction** +0.375s/f (Good) **7** Ran SP% **115.2**
Speed ratings (Par 111): **115,113,108,107,106 96,91**
CSF £86.53 TOTE £13.90: £5.20, £2.60; EX 134.60 Trifecta £2813.90.
Owner Sutong Pan **Bred** Mrs L H Field **Trained** Portway, Worcs

FOCUS
Add 11yds. This looked to fall apart, with the favourite doing too much in front, pressed by the fourth-placed finisher from too far out, and the first three raced in the last three spots for most of the way. The action unfolded towards the near side in the straight. The winner has been rated to his Hong Kong best.

3865 PAVERS FOUNDATION CATHERINE MEMORIAL SPRINT H'CAP 6f
3:35 (3:41) (Class 2) (0-105,102) 3-Y-O
£62,250 (£18,640; £9,320; £4,660; £2,330; £1,170) **Stalls** Centre

Form RPR

-420 **1** **Recon Mission (IRE)**[14] 3344 3-9-2 **97**........................ RobertWinston 3 107
(Tony Carroll) *qckly away: mde all centre: rdn over 1f out: drvn ins fnl f: kpt on wl towards fin* **20/1**

54-1 **2** *hd* **Victory Day (IRE)**[36] 2590 3-8-9 **90**........................ JamieSpencer 21 100+
(William Haggas) *hld up in rr towards stands' side: hdwy over 2f out: swtchd rt wl over 1f out: rdn and chsd wnr ins fnl f: drvn and no imp towards fin* **4/1**[1]

-216 **3** *2* **Magical Wish (IRE)**[31] 2746 3-8-9 **90**........................ HollieDoyle 13 93+
(Richard Hannon) *hld up: hdwy 2f out: rdn over 1f out: styd on strly fnl f* **25/1**

35-2 **4** *nse* **Cosmic Law (IRE)**[38] 2525 3-9-1 **96**........................ PJMcDonald 12 99
(Richard Fahey) *in tch: hdwy 2f out: rdn to chse ldrs over 1f out: drvn and ch ins fnl f: kpt on same pce towards fin* **12/1**

6-20 **5** *1 1/4* **Yousini**[28] 2835 3-8-12 **93**........................ KevinStott 4 92
(Kevin Ryan) *towards rr: hdwy towards far side 2f out: rdn over 1f out: styd on fnl f* **20/1**

1-21 **6** *3/4* **Dazzling Dan (IRE)**[28] 2835 3-9-4 **99**........................ DavidProbert 7 96
(Pam Sly) *trckd ldrs centre: cl up 2f out: sn rdn: drvn and kpt on same pce ent fnl f* **6/1**[2]

-604 **7** *1/2* **Shallow Hal**[5] 3654 3-8-6 **87**........................(v[1]) BenCurtis 22 82+
(K R Burke) *racd nr stands' rail: cl up: disp ld 2f out: sn rdn and grad wknd appr fnl f* **16/1**

0-11 **8** *1 1/2* **Rathbone**[19] 3151 3-8-13 **94**........................ TomEaves 17 84
(Kevin Ryan) *wnt rt s: racd towards stands' side: trckd ldrs: hdwy 2f out: rdn over 1f out: grad wknd* **16/1**

0-22 **9** *hd* **Blown By Wind**[7] 3599 3-9-7 **102**........................ RyanMoore 1 92
(Mark Johnston) *chsd ldrs centre: hdwy 2f out: sn rdn and kpt on same pce fnl f* **11/1**[3]

-214 **10** *hd* **Moraawed**[28] 2835 3-8-7 **88**........................(b[1]) AndreaAtzeni 5 77
(Roger Varian) *in rr towards far side: hdwy 2f out: sn rdn and kpt on fnl f: n.d* **6/1**[2]

2516 **11** *nk* **Wedding Date**[21] 3068 3-8-8 **89** ow2........................ CliffordLee 19 77
(Richard Hannon) *racd towards stands' side: trckd ldrs whn n.m.r and lost pl path after 1f: hdwy over 2f out: rdn to chse ldrs wl over 1f out: drvn appr fnl f: grad wknd* **25/1**

40-3 **12** *3/4* **Firelight (FR)**[19] 3166 3-8-13 **94**........................ RobHornby 14 80
(Andrew Balding) *midfield: pushed along and sme hdwy over 2f out: sn rdn and wknd* **25/1**

4640 **13** *1 1/4* **Barbill (IRE)**[7] 3621 3-9-5 **100**........................ GeraldMosse 11 82
(Mick Channon) *racd centre: chsd ldrs: rdn along 2f out: sn drvn and wknd* **25/1**

0-05 **14** *1/2* **Dave Dexter**[7] 3587 3-9-1 **96**........................ HarryBentley 8 76
(Ralph Beckett) *midfield: rdn along centre over 2f out: n.d* **14/1**

31-0 **15** *1/2* **Luxor**[28] 2835 3-8-10 **91**........................ KerrinMcEvoy 6 69
(William Haggas) *hld up in centre: hdwy and in tch 2f out: sn rdn and wknd* **14/1**

05-1 **16** *3/4* **Ventura Ocean (IRE)**[67] 1662 3-8-11 **92**........................ PaulHanagan 16 68
(Richard Fahey) *chsd ldrs towards stands' side: rdn along over 2f out: sn drvn and wknd* **20/1**

45-0 **17** *3 1/4* **Nicki's Angel (IRE)**[14] 3359 3-8-3 **87**........................ SeanDavis(3) 15 53
(Richard Fahey) *racd towards stands' side: a towards rr* **50/1**

3-04 **18** *nse* **Triggered (IRE)**[42] 2396 3-8-7 **88**........................ AndrewMullen 9 53
(Ed Walker) *a towards rr in centre* **33/1**

4600 **19** *3 1/2* **Quiet Endeavour (IRE)**[38] 2525 3-8-3 **91**......(p) Pierre-LouisJamin(7) 20 45
(Archie Watson) *chsd ldrs towards stands' side: rdn along over 2f out: sn wknd* **33/1**

136- **20** *1/2* **Fuente**[245] 8193 3-9-1 **96**........................(w) PaulMulrennan 10 49
(Keith Dalgleish) *racd centre: a towards rr* **40/1**

03-2 **21** *4 1/2* **Secret Venture**[41] 2434 3-8-12 **93**........................ DanielTudhope 2 31
(Kevin Ryan) *in tch centre: hdwy to chse ldrs 1/2-way: rdn along 2f out: sn wknd* **14/1**

3166 **22** *2* **Charming Kid**[30] 2779 3-8-13 **94**........................ BarryMcHugh 18 26
(Richard Fahey) *dwlt and sltly hmpd s: a in rr towards stands' side* **40/1**

1m 12.48s (0.88) **Going Correction** +0.375s/f (Good) **22** Ran SP% **138.8**
Speed ratings (Par 105): **109,108,106,106,104 103,102,100,100,100 99,98,97,96,95 94,90,90,85,85 79,76**
CSF £94.61 CT £2167.52 TOTE £24.20: £4.90, £1.90, £7.00, £3.20; EX 148.30 Trifecta £5209.50.
Owner B J Millen **Bred** Tally-Ho Stud **Trained** Cropthorne, Worcs

FOCUS
There were cases to be made for so many of these in a good 3yo sprint handicap. They raced middle to near side. A pb from the winner, rated at the bottom end of the race averages.

3866 REG GRIFFIN APPRECIATION EBFSTALLIONS.COM MAIDEN STKS (PLUS 10 RACE) 6f
4:05 (4:10) (Class 3) 2-Y-O **£9,703** (£2,887; £1,443; £721) **Stalls** High

Form RPR

1 **Magical Max** 2-9-5 0........................ AndrewMullen 1 82
(Mark Walford) *in tch on outer: hdwy and cl up 2f out: rdn to chal over 1f out: kpt on wl u.p fnl f to ld last 75yds* **20/1**

562 **2** *1/2* **Vardon Flyer**[16] 3245 2-9-5 0........................ NathanEvans 5 81
(Michael Easterby) *cl up: led 2f out: rdn over 1f out: drvn ins fnl f: hdd and kpt on same pce last 75yds* **14/1**

5 **3** *1 1/2* **St Ives**[24] 2973 2-9-5 0........................ RyanMoore 13 76+
(William Haggas) *trckd ldrs: hdwy wl over 1f out: sn rdn: ev ch ent fnl f: kpt on same pce (vet said colt had wounds to both his fore legs)* **11/2**

4 **4** *3 1/4* **Historic (IRE)**[24] 2973 2-9-5 0........................ PatCosgrave 2 66
(Saeed bin Suroor) *in tch: hdwy 2f out: sn rdn and chsd ldrs over 1f out: drvn and no imp fnl f* **9/2**[3]

23 **5** *nk* **Oso Rapido (IRE)**[12] 3411 2-9-5 0........................ DanielTudhope 3 65
(David O'Meara) *prom: cl up and rdn along 2f out: drvn over 1f out: sn wknd* **4/1**[2]

6 *6* **Sun Crystal (IRE)** 2-9-0 0........................ TonyHamilton 4 42
(Richard Fahey) *wnt rt s: towards rr: hdwy 2f out: sn rdn along and n.d* **14/1**

7 *nk* **Godfather (IRE)** 2-9-5 0........................ AlistairRawlinson 8 46
(Tom Dascombe) *green in rr: pushed along and hdwy whn nt clr run wl over 1f out: sn swtchd lft: rdn and hung lft over 1f out: kpt on wl fnl f* **10/1**

5 **8** *nk* **International Lion**[21] 3098 2-9-5 0........................ PaulHanagan 9 46
(Richard Fahey) *hld up towards rr: hdwy over 2f out: n.m.r and swtchd rt wl over 1f out: sn rdn and kpt on fnl f* **12/1**

9 *1 1/2* **Singe Anglais (IRE)** 2-9-0 0........................ FayeMcManoman(5) 12 41+
(Nigel Tinkler) *chsd ldrs: rdn along wl over 2f out: sn wknd* **50/1**

6 **10** *5* **Refuge**[12] 3411 2-9-5 0........................ CamHardie 6 26
(Michael Easterby) *led: rdn along and hdd whn stmbld sltly 2f out: sn wknd* **33/1**

11 *1/2* **Idoapologise** 2-9-5 0........................ PJMcDonald 7 25
(James Bethell) *chsd ldrs: rdn along over 2f out: sn wknd (jockey said colt hung left-handed)* **25/1**

12 *4 1/2* **Black Caspian (IRE)** 2-9-5 0........................ AndreaAtzeni 14 11+
(Kevin Ryan) *dwlt and green in rr: sme hdwy over 2f out: sn rdn and eased whn btn* **11/4**[1]

66 **13** *nk* **Cmon Cmon (IRE)**[32] 2707 2-9-2 0........................ RowanScott(3) 10 10+
(Nigel Tinkler) *a towards rr* **25/1**

1m 13.76s (2.16) **Going Correction** +0.375s/f (Good) **13** Ran SP% **127.7**
Speed ratings (Par 97): **100,99,97,93,92 84,84,83,81,75 74,68,68**
CSF £278.13 TOTE £24.80: £6.90, £3.90, £3.70; EX 1179.50 Trifecta £5623.80.
Owner Mrs E Holmes, M Johnson & Mrs Walford **Bred** Poole, Trickledown & The Late Mrs Poole **Trained** Sherriff Hutton, N Yorks

FOCUS
This was run in driving rain, and they raced middle to near side. The form looks just fair.

3867 ICE CO SUPPORTING MACMILLAN H'CAP 1m 177y
4:40 (4:42) (Class 4) (0-85,87) 4-Y-O+
£8,927 (£2,656; £1,327; £663; £300; £300) **Stalls** Low

Form RPR

-535 **1** **Poet's Dawn**[7] 3563 4-9-0 **78**........................ DavidAllan 4 89
(Tim Easterby) *prom: led gng wl over 2f out: rdn out fnl f* **15/2**[2]

-415 **2** *2* **Furzig**[14] 3356 4-8-11 **78**........................ SeanDavis(3) 12 85
(Richard Fahey) *hld up in midfield: rdn 3f out: sme hdwy whn swtchd lft over 1f out: drvn and styd on wl: wnt 2nd post* **14/1**

0022 **3** *nk* **Markazi (FR)**[16] 3268 5-9-9 **87**........................(p) DanielTudhope 10 93
(David O'Meara) *in tch: pushed along and hdwy to trck ldr over 2f out: drvn appr fnl f: no ex fnl 110yds: lost 2nd post* **7/1**[1]

0 **4** *1 1/4* **Cockalorum (IRE)**[9] 3515 4-9-1 **79**........................ PaulHanagan 15 83+
(Roger Fell) *hld up in midfield on outer: pushed along and sme hdwy whn hung lft 2f out: sn rdn: styd on ins fnl f* **11/1**

10-0 **5** *1 3/4* **Ladies First**[29] 2809 5-8-13 **77**........................(t[1]) NathanEvans 16 77
(Michael Easterby) *midfield towards outer: rdn along over 2f out: plugged on fnl f* **10/1**[3]

03-4 **6** *3/4* **Najashee (IRE)**[24] 2959 5-8-8 **72**........................ BenCurtis 5 70
(Roger Fell) *trckd ldrs: rdn over 2f out: no ex fnl f* **16/1**

00-4 **7** *4 1/2* **Gworn**[18] 3180 9-8-2 **66**........................ AndrewMullen 7 55
(R Mike Smith) *s.i.s: sn rcvrd into midfield: rdn over 2f out: wknd ins fnl f* **33/1**

3-04 **8** *1 1/4* **Frankelio (FR)**[16] 3268 4-9-3 **81**........................ GrahamLee 18 67
(Micky Hammond) *dwlt: hld up: pushed along 3f out: rdn 2f out: nvr threatened* **10/1**[3]

-040 **9** *hd* **Vive La Difference (IRE)**[9] 3502 5-8-11 **75**........... RachelRichardson 8 61
(Tim Easterby) *dwlt: hld up in rr: rdn over 2f out: nvr threatened* **16/1**

4000 **10** *3/4* **Arcanada (IRE)**[21] 3069 6-9-7 **85**........................(p) AlistairRawlinson 11 69
(Tom Dascombe) *in tch: hdwy and chsd ldr over 3f out: rdn to chal over 2f out: wknd ins fnl f* **20/1**

0030 **11** *hd* **Magic City (IRE)**[7] 3567 10-8-4 **68**........................ CamHardie 9 52
(Michael Easterby) *midfield: rdn 3f out: wknd over 1f out* **14/1**

-160 **12** *1* **Give It Some Teddy**[27] 2873 5-9-4 **82**........................ DuranFentiman 13 64
(Tim Easterby) *in tch: rdn along 3f out: wknd over 1f out* **12/1**

63-2 **13** *nk* **Be Kool (IRE)**[14] 3356 6-8-11 **78**........................(v) BenRobinson(3) 6 59
(Brian Ellison) *trckd ldrs: rdn 3f out: wknd over 1f out (jockey said gelding stopped quickly)* **7/1**[1]

2305 **14** *nse* **Sands Chorus**[9] 3502 7-8-11 **75**........................(p) BarryMcHugh 17 56
(Scott Dixon) *led: rdn and hdd over 2f out: wknd over 1f out* **10/1**[3]

6-00 **15** *2* **Detachment**[32] 2710 6-9-0 **78**........................ DavidProbert 3 55
(Les Eyre) *dwlt: hld up: rdn over 2f out: sme hdwy over 1f out: hung lft and wknd ins fnl f* **20/1**

1300 **16** *2 1/4* **Sureyoutoldme (IRE)**[16] 3268 5-8-9 **73**........................ JamesSullivan 1 45
(Ruth Carr) *hld up in midfield: rdn 3f out: wknd over 1f out* **25/1**

1216 **17** *3 1/4* **Masked Identity**[23] 3027 4-9-5 **83**........................ TomEaves 14 48
(Kevin Frost) *dwlt: hld up in rr: rdn over 2f out: sn btn* **14/1**

1m 52.72s (2.32) **Going Correction** +0.375s/f (Good) **17** Ran SP% **128.1**
Speed ratings (Par 105): **104,102,101,100,99 98,94,93,93,92 92,91,91,91,89 87,84**
CSF £107.68 CT £814.68 TOTE £8.50: £2.30, £3.90, £2.20, £2.90; EX 131.10 Trifecta £1529.40.

Owner Timothy O'Gram & Partner **Bred** Mrs J K Powell & Catridge Farm Stud **Trained** Great Habton, N Yorks

FOCUS
Add 9yds. Few got into this. They raced middle to near side in the straight. The winner has been rated back to his best.

3868 PLASMOR CONCRETE PRODUCTS DIAMOND ANNIVERSARY H'CAP 6f
5:15 (5:19) (Class 4) (0-80,80) 3-Y-O+
£8,927 (£2,656; £1,327; £663; £300; £300) **Stalls** Centre

Form RPR

1403 **1** **Galloway Hills**[9] 3503 4-9-7 **78**........................(p) SeanDavis(3) 9 87
(Phillip Makin) *cl up centre: led 2f out: rdn over 1f out: drvn ins fnl f: hld on wl towards fin* **10/1**

0341 **2** 3/4 **Music Society (IRE)**[9] 3504 4-9-7 **75**....(h) DavidAllan 1 82
(Tim Easterby) *racd towards far side: prom: rdn to chse wnr over 1f out: drvn to chal ins fnl f: ev ch: no ex last 50yds* **9/2**[1]
0-05 **3** shd **Our Little Pony**[27] 2874 4-8-13 **72**.... FayeMcManoman(5) 5 78+
(Lawrence Mullaney) *racd towards far side: in tch: hdwy wl over 1f out: rdn and styd on wl fnl f* **20/1**
3533 **4** 1 1/4 **Seen The Lyte (IRE)**[18] 3201 4-9-11 **79**....(h) HollieDoyle 8 81
(Nigel Tinkler) *in tch centre: hdwy 2f out: sn chsng ldrs: rdn and ev ch jst over 1f out: drvn ins fnl f: kpt on same pce* **16/1**
-202 **5** 1 **Zumurud (IRE)**[9] 3503 4-9-9 **77**.... DanielTudhope 18 76+
(Rebecca Bastiman) *racd nr stands' rail: in tch: hdwy over 2f out: cl up and rdn: over 1f out: drvn and kpt on same pce fnl f* **8/1**[3]
0610 **6** shd **Manshood (IRE)**[14] 3347 6-9-12 **80**....(b) BarryMcHugh 11 79
(Paul Midgley) *in tch centre: hdwy 2f out: rdn to chse ldrs over 1f out: drvn and kpt on fnl f* **16/1**
5041 **7** hd **John Kirkup**[8] 3550 4-9-10 **78**....(p) ConnorBeasley 7 76
(Michael Dods) *chsd ldrs centre: effrt 2f out: sn rdn: drvn ent fnl f: kpt on same pce* **13/2**[2]
1240 **8** 1 **Johnny Cavagin**[9] 3504 10-9-4 **72**.... GrahamLee 4 67
(Paul Midgley) *racd towards far side: chsd ldrs: rdn along wl over 1f out: drvn and wknd fnl f* **16/1**
/360 **9** nk **Cartmell Cleave**[26] 2893 7-9-10 **78**.... JamesSullivan 22 72+
(Ruth Carr) *racd nr stands' rail: towards rr: hdwy over 2f out: rdn to chse ldrs over 1f out: no imp fnl f* **12/1**
5052 **10** 3 1/4 **Buccaneers Vault (IRE)**[15] 3309 7-9-12 **80**.... KevinStott 12 64
(Paul Midgley) *in tch centre: hdwy to chse ldrs 2f out: sn rdn and wknd over 1f out* **16/1**
0-00 **11** 1/2 **Start Time (IRE)**[15] 3318 6-9-7 **75**.... GeraldMosse 21 57+
(Paul Midgley) *racd nr stands' rail: hld up: hdwy over 2f out: rdn along wl over 1f out: n.d* **9/1**
0-00 **12** 2 1/4 **Upstaging**[47] 2201 7-9-4 **79**.... OakleyBrown(7) 20 54
(Noel Wilson) *racd towards stands' side: dwlt and towards rr: sme hdwy over 2f out: sn rdn and n.d* **33/1**
0310 **13** 4 1/2 **Highly Sprung (IRE)**[26] 2893 6-8-13 **72**.... HarrisonShaw(5) 19 32
(Les Eyre) *racd nr stands' rail: cl up: rdn along over 2f out: sn wknd* **40/1**
0-06 **14** 3 **Angel Force (IRE)**[36] 2576 4-9-3 **71**.... BenCurtis 6 22
(David C Griffiths) *racd towards far side: led: rdn along and hdd 2f out: sn wknd* **33/1**
000/ **15** 1 3/4 **Echo Of Lightning**[582] 8718 9-9-4 **77**....(h) BenSanderson(5) 3 22
(Roger Fell) *dwlt: a towards rr* **33/1**
0-00 **16** 1 **Black Isle Boy (IRE)**[28] 2824 5-9-9 **77**....(p) HarryBentley 16 19
(David O'Meara) *in tch centre: pushed along and outpcd over 2f out: rdn and styng on whn n.m.r and swtchd rt over 1f out: sn wknd* **25/1**
0012 **17** hd **East Street Revue**[13] 3375 6-9-9 **77**....(p1) DuranFentiman 2 18
(Tim Easterby) *racd towards far side: chsd ldrs: sme hdwy over 2f out: sn rdn and wknd over 1f out* **12/1**
1203 **18** 1/2 **Kraka (IRE)**[18] 3207 4-9-2 **70**....(v) RobertWinston 17 10
(Christine Dunnett) *racd towards stands' side: chsd ldrs: rdn along wl over 2f out: sn wknd* **20/1**
44-0 **19** hd **Pickett's Charge**[8] 3549 6-9-1 **72**.... BenRobinson(3) 13 11
(Brian Ellison) *in tch centre: pushed along and lost pl bef 1/2-way: sn bhd* **50/1**
0305 **20** nse **Another Angel (IRE)**[22] 3056 5-9-8 **76**.... CamHardie 14 15
(Antony Brittain) *chsd ldrs centre: rdn along wl over 2f out: sn wknd (jockey said gelding stopped quickly)* **33/1**
50-6 **21** nk **Barton Mills**[17] 3216 4-9-9 **77**....(h) NathanEvans 15 15
(Michael Easterby) *prom centre: rdn along wl over 2f out: sn wknd* **50/1**
055 **22** 37 **Constant**[3] 3719 3-9-3 **79**.... ShaneGray 10
(David O'Meara) *in tch centre: rdn along and lost pl 1/2-way: sn bhd and eased (jockey said gelding did not move fluently but returned sound)* **12/1**

1m 15.0s (3.40) **Going Correction** +0.375s/f (Good)
WFA 3 from 4yo+ 8lb **22** Ran SP% **139.8**
Speed ratings (Par 105): **92,91,90,89,87 87,87,86,85,81 80,77,71,67,65 64,63,63,62,62 62,13**
CSF £54.44 CT £959.62 TOTE £11.70: £3.10, £1.90, £5.10, £4.60; EX 73.10 Trifecta £1273.00.
Owner P J Makin **Bred** Rosyground Stud **Trained** Easingwold, N Yorks

FOCUS
They were spread out a fair way across the track, with near side looking the worst of the ground. The winner has been rated back to his best.
T/Jkpt: Not won. T/Plt: £3,817.80 to a £1 stake. Pool of £124,463.23 - 32.60 winning units.
T/Qpdt: £174.20 to a £1 stake. Pool of £12,620.92 - 72.43 winning units.
Joe Rowntree/Andrew Sheret

3869 - 3876a (Foreign Racing) - See Raceform Interactive

3119 DUSSELDORF (R-H)
Saturday, June 15

OFFICIAL GOING: Turf: good

3877a 30TH BMW PREIS DUSSELDORF (LISTED RACE) (3YO FILLIES) (TURF) 1m 2f 110y
4:25 3-Y-O **£12,612** (£5,855; £2,702; £1,351)

RPR
1 **Durance (GER)**[20] 3-9-2 0....(p) AndraschStarke 6 93
(P Schiergen, Germany) **9/2**[3]
2 shd **Mythica (IRE)**[42] 2430 3-9-2 0.... FilipMinarik 7 92
(Jean-Pierre Carvalho, Germany) **104/10**
3 hd **Diamanta (GER)**[62] 3-9-2 0.... AdrieDeVries 8 92
(Markus Klug, Germany) **3/1**[2]
4 1 3/4 **Ormuz (GER)** 3-9-2 0.... BauyrzhanMurzabayev 4 89
(A Wohler, Germany) **8/1**
5 1 1/4 **Vivid Diamond (IRE)**[21] 3099 3-9-2 0.... EduardoPedroza 1 86
(Mark Johnston) *racd keenly: hld up bhd ldng pair ins rival: drvn wl over 2f out but no imp: kpt on at same pce fnl f* **7/5**[1]
6 3/4 **Quantum Joy (GER)** 3-9-2 0.... MartinSeidl 5 85
(Lennart Hammer-Hansen, Germany) **139/10**
7 1/2 **La Pradera** 3-9-2 0.... LukasDelozier 3 84
(Henk Grewe, Germany) **123/10**

2m 10.16s **7** Ran SP% **119.0**
PARI-MUTUEL (all including 1 euro stake): WIN 5.50 PLACE: 1.80, 2.40, 1.50; SF: 33.70.
Owner Gestut Ebbesloh **Bred** Gestut Ebbesloh **Trained** Germany

3621 MAISONS-LAFFITTE (R-H)
Saturday, June 15

OFFICIAL GOING: Turf: good to soft

3878a PRIX DE MARCQ (CLAIMER) (3YO) (TURF) 7f
12:45 3-Y-O **£8,558** (£3,423; £2,567; £1,711; £855)

RPR
1 **Einar (IRE)**[12] 3-9-1 0.... MathieuPelletan(5) 2 77
(M Delcher Sanchez, France) **13/5**[1]
2 1/2 **Capla Gilda**[35] 3-9-5 0.... Pierre-CharlesBoudot 11 75
(Andrea Marcialis, France) **29/10**[2]
3 3 1/2 **Baylagan (FR)**[15] 3-9-1 0....(b1) TonyPiccone 8 62
(I Endaltsev, Czech Republic) **10/1**
4 snk **Fire At Midnight (FR)**[29] 3-8-10 0.... JeremieMonteiro(8) 1 64
(N Caullery, France) **23/1**
5 1 **Last Edition (FR)**[12] 3-8-8 0.... AugustinMadamet(8) 9 59
(A Fabre, France) **3/1**[3]
6 3/4 **Rum Lad**[25] 2926 3-8-11 0.... Louis-PhilippeBeuzelin 7 52
(Jo Hughes, France) *hld up in rr: rdn and kpt on fr 2f out: nrst fin* **22/1**
7 1/2 **Captain Lancelot (FR)**[50] 2090 3-8-11 0....(b) CristianDemuro 3 51
(F Chappet, France) **71/10**
8 shd **Hello Is You (FR)**[22] 3066 3-8-11 0....(b) AurelienLemaitre 4 51
(F Head, France) **18/1**
9 3 1/2 **Fabled (FR)**[22] 3066 3-9-1 0....(b) EddyHardouin 10 45
(Matthieu Palussiere, France) **43/1**
10 hd **Nonaynevernomore (IRE)**[50] 2090 3-8-6 0.... MllePerrineCheyer(9) 5 45
(A Le Duff, France) **82/1**
11 7 **Confetti (FR)**[171] 3-8-7 0.... ThomasTrullier(8) 6 26
(N Clement, France) **37/1**

1m 27.93s (-0.07) **11** Ran SP% **119.7**
PARI-MUTUEL (all including 1 euro stake): WIN 3.60; PLACE 1.50, 1.60, 2.30; DF 6.00.
Owner Cuadra Miranda S.L.U **Bred** Varstock Ltd **Trained** France

3879a PRIX CARVIN (CONDITIONS) (4YO+) (TURF) 1m
3:07 4-Y-O+ **£14,864** (£5,648; £4,162; £2,378; £1,189; £891)

RPR
1 **Impulsif**[19] 4-9-0 0.... MickaelBarzalona 15 112
(A Fabre, France) *mde all: rdn under 2f out: qcknd and wnt clr 1f out: sn in command: eased clsng stages* **17/1**
2 3 **Stunning Spirit**[23] 3030 5-9-0 0.... AurelienLemaitre 5 105
(F Head, France) **4/1**[2]
3 1 **Mer Et Nuages (FR)**[45] 2313 4-9-6 0.... Pierre-CharlesBoudot 4 109
(A Fabre, France) *hld up towards rr of midfield: stdy hdwy into midfield fr 3f out: rdn and kpt on wl fr under 2f out* **13/10**[1]
4 3 **Salt Lake City (FR)**[30] 2782 4-9-0 0.... TonyPiccone 6 96
(B Audouin, France) **19/1**
5 3/4 **Diwan Senora (FR)**[102] 1027 6-9-0 0.... JeffersonSmith 16 94
(Y Barberot, France) **35/1**
6 1/2 **Sun At Work (GER)**[19] 7-9-0 0.... MaximeGuyon 3 93
(W Haustein, Germany) **11/1**
7 shd **Rominou (FR)**[30] 6-9-0 0.... ChristopheSoumillon 10 93
(C Lerner, France) **78/10**[3]
8 1 **Ninario (GER)**[19] 4-9-0 0.... CristianDemuro 2 90
(Waldemar Hickst, Germany) **28/1**
9 1 3/4 **Indyco (FR)**[23] 3030 4-9-3 0.... VincentCheminaud 1 89
(H-A Pantall, France) **16/1**
10 hd **Perfect Pitch (GER)**[46] 2266 5-8-10 0.... CyrilleStefan 12 82
(S Smrczek, Germany) **126/1**
11 2 **Jasnin (FR)**[48] 7-9-0 0.... MlleCoraliePacaut 11 81
(Waldemar Hickst, Germany) **38/1**
12 4 **Bid Adieu (IRE)**[11] 5-9-0 0.... FabienLefebvre 9 72
(Guillaume Courbot, France) **60/1**
13 2 **Mezidon (FR)**[86] 6-9-0 0.... FabriceVeron 8 68
(D & P Prod'Homme, France) **51/1**
14 2 1/2 **Samasthiti (IRE)**[223] 8859 4-8-10 0.... EddyHardouin 13 58
(Carina Fey, France) **63/1**
15 1 1/4 **Dhevanafushi**[23] 3030 6-9-0 0.... OlivierPeslier 14 59
(H-A Pantall, France) **17/1**
16 4 **Culmination**[139] 2571 7-9-0 0.... Louis-PhilippeBeuzelin 7 50
(Jo Hughes, France) *s.i.s: a in rr* **142/1**

1m 35.19s (-7.11) **16** Ran SP% **120.6**
PARI-MUTUEL (all including 1 euro stake): WIN 2.10; PLACE 2.00, 1.60, 1.30; DF 12.80.
Owner Godolphin SNC **Bred** Godolphin **Trained** Chantilly, France

3334 DONCASTER (L-H)
Sunday, June 16

OFFICIAL GOING: Soft (good to soft in places; 6.9)
Wind: Moderate half against Weather: Cloudy with sunny periods

3880 LOTTIE CABORN LAKESIDE LUCKY WINNER H'CAP 7f 213y(R)
2:10 (2:11) (Class 4) (0-85,83) 4-Y-O+
£5,530 (£1,645; £822; £411; £400; £400) **Stalls** High

Form RPR
200 **1** **Storm Ahead (IRE)**[8] 3567 6-8-9 **71**....(b) DavidAllan 4 81
(Tim Easterby) *trckd ldrs: smooth hdwy 2f out: shkn up to ld jst over 1f out: sn rdn clr: kpt on strly (trainers rep could offer no explanation)* **3/1**[1]
0540 **2** 2 1/4 **Dubai Acclaim (IRE)**[19] 3199 4-8-3 **68**.... SeanDavis(3) 3 73
(Richard Fahey) *trckd ldrs: hdwy on inner to ld over 2f out: rdn along over 1f out: hdd appr fnl f: sn drvn and kpt on same pce* **6/1**
5011 **3** nk **Hammer Gun (USA)**[16] 3305 6-8-9 **71**....(v) PaddyMathers 1 75
(Derek Shaw) *dwlt: swtchd rt s and hld up in rr: hdwy over 2f out: rdn to chse ldng pair ent fnl f: sn drvn and kpt on same pce* **8/1**
06 **4** 3 1/4 **Intense Style (IRE)**[33] 2710 7-8-7 **74**.... FayeMcManoman(5) 2 71
(Les Eyre) *dwlt: sn trcking ldng pair: pushed along over 2f out: rdn wl over 1f out: sn one pce (vet said gelding lost its right fore shoe)* **7/2**[2]

 The Form Book Flat 2019, Raceform Ltd, Newbury, RG14 5SJ

10-2 **5** *shd* **Wufud**[23] 3040 4-9-7 **83**....................(t) DaneO'Neill 6 79
(Charles Hills) *t.k.h early: hld up towards rr: hdwy on outer wl over 2f out: rdn along and sltly outpcd wl over 1f out: kpt on fnl f* **9/2**[3]

6-00 **6** 2 1/2 **London Protocol (FR)**[12] 3450 6-9-1 **77**....................(v) CliffordLee 5 68
(John Mackie) *trckd ldr: hdwy and cl up 3f out: rdn along 2f out: sn drvn and wknd* **20/1**

64-0 **7** 1 3/4 **Watheer**[20] 3161 4-8-13 **75**....................(b[1]) BenCurtis 8 62
(Roger Fell) *set stdy pce: qcknd along 5f out: pushed along over 4f out: rdn 3f out: hdd over 2f out: sn wknd* **25/1**

-304 **8** 2 1/2 **Astonished (IRE)**[25] 2966 4-9-5 **81**....................(h) PJMcDonald 7 62
(James Tate) *t.k.h: trckd ldrs: pushed along 4f out: rdn 3f out: sn btn* **5/1**

1m 42.15s (1.35) **Going Correction** +0.425s/f (Yiel) **8** Ran SP% **116.1**
Speed ratings (Par 105): **110,107,107,104,104 101,99,97**
CSF £21.82 CT £130.75 TOTE £3.70: £1.60, £2.00, £2.00; EX 21.50 Trifecta £162.60.
Owner Ambrose Turnbull **Bred** Victor Stud And Brendan Cummins **Trained** Great Habton, N Yorks

FOCUS
A blustery day and the ground looked a bit tacky in the opening 1m handicap, which was just how winning rider David Nolan described it afterwards. The winner has been rated to a similar level as when third in this the previous year and the runner-up has been rated to this season's form.

3881 TOG24 TRUTH OVER GLORY EBF FILLIES' NOVICE STKS (PLUS 10 RACE) 7f 6y
2:45 (2:45) (Class 5) 2-Y-O **£3,752** (£1,116; £557; £278) **Stalls** Low

Form RPR

3 **1** **Sacred Dance**[23] 3049 2-9-0 0.................... KerrinMcEvoy 2 81+
(Charlie Appleby) *trckd ldng pair: smooth hdwy to ld 2f out: pushed clr ent fnl f: kpt on strly* **1/2**[1]

2 2 **Lola Paige (IRE)** 2-9-0 0.................... DanielTudhope 4 76
(William Haggas) *trckd ldr: hdwy and cl up 2f out: rdn over 1f out: drvn ins fnl f: kpt on same pce* **4/1**[2]

3 *nk* **Topkapi Star** 2-9-0 0.................... DavidEgan 1 75
(Roger Varian) *hld up in tch: hdwy over 2f out: rdn to chse ldng pair over 1f out: kpt on fnl f* **9/1**[3]

603 **4** 3 **Irish Eileen**[10] 3506 2-9-0 0.................... NathanEvans 5 68
(Michael Easterby) *dwlt: hld up in tch: pushed along and sme hdwy 2f out: sn rdn and n.d* **10/1**

5 9 **Golden Times (SWI)** 2-9-0 0.................... FrannyNorton 3 45
(Mark Johnston) *t.k.h: sn led: rdn and hdd 2f out: sn wknd* **16/1**

1m 30.38s (3.98) **Going Correction** +0.425s/f (Yiel) **5** Ran SP% **111.6**
Speed ratings (Par 90): **94,91,91,87,77**
CSF £2.92 TOTE £1.40: £1.10, £1.80; EX 2.90 Trifecta £9.80.
Owner Godolphin **Bred** Eminent Kind Ltd **Trained** Newmarket, Suffolk

FOCUS
They went a routine pace in this fair 2yo fillies' novice.

3882 THORNTONS PEARLS NEW AT LAKESIDE VILLAGE MAIDEN STKS 1m 3f 197y
3:20 (3:20) (Class 5) 3-Y-O+ **£3,752** (£1,116; £557; £278) **Stalls** Low

Form RPR

45 **1** **Sea Of Faith (IRE)**[29] 2831 3-8-9 0.................... PaulHanagan 1 93+
(William Haggas) *trckd ldr: hdwy on bit and cl up over 2f out: shkn up to ld 1 1/2f out: sn clr: unchal* **1/10**[1]

0-64 **2** 9 **Bullion Boss (IRE)**[16] 3295 3-9-0 72....................(p) PaulMulrennan 3 74
(Michael Dods) *led: pushed along 3f out: jnd and rdn over 2f out: hdd 1 1/2f out: sn drvn and kpt on: no ch w wnr* **7/2**[2]

00 **3** 13 **Kostantina**[30] 2802 3-8-9 0.................... RachelRichardson 2 48
(Olly Williams) *trckd ldng pair: effrt 4f out: pushed along over 3f out: sn rdn and one pce fnl 2f* **50/1**

00 **4** 13 **Thornton Le Clay**[11] 3482 3-9-0 0.................... NathanEvans 5 32
(Michael Easterby) *t.k.h early: chsd ldrs: lost pl after 4f: sn bhd* **25/1**[3]

4 **5** 1 1/2 **Nineteenrbo'Malley**[43] 2417 7-10-0 0.................... TomEaves 4 30
(Robyn Brisland) *hld up in rr: sme hdwy and in tch 1/2-way: rdn along wl over 3f out: sn wknd (vet said gelding lost its left hind shoe)* **25/1**[3]

2m 38.91s (2.31) **Going Correction** +0.425s/f (Yiel) **5** Ran SP% **122.8**
WFA 3 from 7yo 14lb
Speed ratings (Par 103): **109,103,94,85,84**
CSF £1.26 TOTE £1.10: £1.02, £1.30; EX 1.20 Trifecta £6.50.
Owner Sunderland Holding Inc **Bred** Sunderland Holdings Inc **Trained** Newmarket, Suffolk

FOCUS
Add 12yds. A soft opening for the 1-14 winner. The runner-up has been rated to form.

3883 LAKESIDE VILLAGE OUTLET SHOPPING DONCASTER H'CAP 5f 3y
3:55 (3:55) (Class 3) (0-95,95) 3-Y-O+ **£7,762** (£2,310; £1,154; £577) **Stalls** Low

Form RPR

5-53 **1** **Camacho Chief (IRE)**[8] 3589 4-9-12 **95**.................... PaulMulrennan 6 104
(Michael Dods) *t.k.h early: trckd ldrs: hdwy and cl up 2f out: slt ld over 1f out: rdn clr ins fnl f: kpt on wl* **9/4**[1]

2110 **2** 1 1/2 **Duke Of Firenze**[15] 3344 10-9-7 **90**.................... DavidAllan 7 94
(David C Griffiths) *hld up towards rr: hdwy wl over 1f out: rdn to chse wnr ins fnl f: drvn and no imp towards fin* **4/1**[2]

3-60 **3** 1 1/4 **Fool For You (IRE)**[15] 3344 4-9-5 **88**.................... PJMcDonald 1 88
(Richard Fahey) *t.k.h: trckd ldrs: hdwy and cl up over 2f out: rdn and ev ch over 1f out: kpt on same pce fnl f* **11/2**

-300 **4** 1 **Confessional**[8] 3589 12-9-0 **86**....................(e) JamieGormley(3) 3 82
(Tim Easterby) *cl up: slt ld over 2f out: rdn 1 1/2f out and sn hdd: drvn and wknd fnl f* **6/1**

5-04 **5** 1/2 **Consequences (IRE)**[16] 3309 4-8-9 **81**....................(t) SeanDavis(3) 2 75
(Ian Williams) *hld up in rr: sme hdwy 2f out: sn rdn and no imp* **12/1**

4033 **6** 1 1/4 **Storm Over (IRE)**[6] 3662 5-9-8 **91**....................(v[1]) HayleyTurner 8 81
(George Scott) *trckd ldrs: rdn along over 2f out: sn wknd* **9/2**[3]

310 **7** 2 1/4 **Erissimus Maximus (FR)**[16] 3301 5-8-11 **87**....................(b) CierenFallon(7) 5 69
(Amy Murphy) *slt ld: rdn along 1/2-way: sn hdd & wknd* **4/1**[2]

1m 1.88s (2.28) **Going Correction** +0.425s/f (Yiel) **7** Ran SP% **126.3**
Speed ratings (Par 107): **98,95,93,92,91 89,85**
CSF £13.26 CT £47.78 TOTE £2.80: £2.20, £2.50; EX 10.00 Trifecta £79.00.
Owner Davison & Drysdale **Bred** Doc Bloodstock **Trained** Denton, Co Durham

■ Bowson Fred was withdrawn, price at time of withdrawal 10/1. Rule 4 applies to board prices prior to withdrawal but not to SP bets. Deduction of 5p in the pound. New market formed.

■ Stewards' Enquiry : Nathan Evans ten-day ban; improper riding (June 30, July 1-9)

FOCUS
This feature sprint represents solid handicap form. The winner is progressive.

3884 SKOPES MENSWEAR LAKESIDE VILLAGE H'CAP 6f 2y
4:30 (4:31) (Class 5) (0-75,76) 3-Y-O
£3,752 (£1,116; £557; £400; £400; £400) **Stalls** Low

Form RPR

32-1 **1** **Celtic Manor (IRE)**[20] 3167 3-9-8 **76**.................... DanielTudhope 1 82+
(William Haggas) *trckd ldrs: hdwy 2f out: led 1 1/2f out: sn rdn: drvn and edgd rt ins fnl f: hld on wl towards fin* **13/8**[1]

446- **2** 1/2 **Swinging Eddie**[279] 7127 3-8-12 **66**.................... TomEaves 5 69
(Kevin Ryan) *hld up in rr: swtchd rt to stands' side and hdwy wl over 1f out: rdn and styd on strly fnl f* **25/1**

0450 **3** *shd* **Fair Alibi**[19] 3202 3-8-12 **66**.................... JamesSullivan 8 68
(Tom Tate) *trckd ldrs: hdwy 2f out: rdn over 1f out: drvn ins fnl f: kpt on wl towards fin* **14/1**

4-14 **4** *shd* **Socru (IRE)**[26] 2937 3-9-5 **73**.................... NathanEvans 7 75+
(Michael Easterby) *hld up in rr: hdwy 2f out: rdn to chse ldrs jst over 1f out: n.m.r ins fnl f: drvn and kpt on wl towards fin* **7/1**[3]

0055 **5** 1 1/4 **Ghost Buy (FR)**[27] 2908 3-8-4 **58**....................(t) FrannyNorton 9 56
(Ivan Furtado) *in tch: hdwy on outer to chse ldrs 2f out: sn rdn: drvn and kpt on fnl f (jockey said colt hung left in the closing stages and as a precautionary measure he stopped riding)* **8/1**

-332 **6** 3/4 **Mr Buttons (IRE)**[13] 3420 3-9-8 **76**.................... ShaneKelly 10 72
(Linda Stubbs) *hld up: hdwy over 2f out: chsd ldrs and nt clr run ent fnl f: sn swtchd lft and rdn: kpt on same pce* **8/1**

6102 **7** 1 1/2 **Havana Ooh Na Na**[17] 3273 3-9-0 **68**....................(p) CliffordLee 6 59
(K R Burke) *cl up: rdn along wl over 1f out: ent fnl f: grad wknd* **10/1**

0-10 **8** 1 1/2 **Lady Monica**[19] 3189 3-8-12 **66**.................... RoystonFfrench 2 52
(John Holt) *a towards rr* **20/1**

232 **9** *nse* **Moveonup (IRE)**[8] 3574 3-8-9 **70**....................(p[1]) CierenFallon(7) 3 56
(Gay Kelleway) *led: rdn along 2f out: drvn and hdd 1 1/2f out: sn wknd (jockey said gelding ran too free; vet said that the gelding lost its left hind shoe)* **6/1**[2]

-106 **10** 2 1/2 **Bugler Bob (IRE)**[46] 2293 3-9-7 **75**.................... JasonHart 4 53
(John Quinn) *chsd ldrs: rdn along over 2f out: sn wknd* **14/1**

1m 16.06s (3.36) **Going Correction** +0.425s/f (Yiel) **10** Ran SP% **118.1**
Speed ratings (Par 99): **94,93,93,93,91 90,88,86,86,83**
CSF £51.54 CT £454.93 TOTE £2.20: £1.20, £6.90, £3.20; EX 44.80 Trifecta £580.70.
Owner Sheikh Rashid Dalmook Al Maktoum **Bred** Patrick M Ryan **Trained** Newmarket, Suffolk

■ Kolossus was withdrawn, price at time of withdrawal 16/1. Rule 4 does not apply.

FOCUS
There was a bunched finish to this modest 3yo handicap, but the winner is value for further and on the upgrade.

3885 TEAM VERRICO H'CAP 7f 213y(R)
5:00 (5:00) (Class 4) (0-80,79) 3-Y-O
£5,530 (£1,645; £822; £411; £400; £400) **Stalls** High

Form RPR

-402 **1** **Silkstone (IRE)**[19] 3195 3-9-2 **74**.................... ShaneKelly 5 81
(Pam Sly) *hld up: hdwy 3f out: chsd ldrs 2f out: rdn to chal ins fnl f: led fnl 100yds: drvn out (vet said gelding lost its left fore shoe)* **10/1**

4024 **2** 1 **Ginger Fox**[15] 3340 3-9-4 **76**....................(p[1]) PJMcDonald 2 81
(Ian Williams) *trckd ldrs on inner: hdwy over 2f out: rdn to chal wl over 1f out: drvn to take slt ld ent fnl f: hdd fnl 100yds: no ex* **3/1**[2]

2032 **3** 3/4 **Lightning Attack**[17] 3249 3-9-0 **75**....................(p) SeanDavis(3) 1 78
(Richard Fahey) *cl up on inner: led after 1f: pushed along over 2f out: jnd and rdn wl over 1f out: drvn and hdd ent fnl f: kpt on same pce* **11/2**[3]

5232 **4** 2 1/4 **Storting**[17] 3248 3-9-7 **79**.................... DavidEgan 8 77+
(Mick Channon) *hld up in rr: hdwy on outer over 2f out: rdn over 1f out: kpt on fnl f (jockey said colt hung left throughout and was denied a clear run)* **11/4**[1]

-420 **5** 1 1/4 **Dancingwithwolves (IRE)**[19] 3195 3-9-1 **73**............(h) DanielMuscutt 4 68
(Ed Dunlop) *trckd ldrs: hdwy 3f out: rdn along 2f out: drvn over 1f out: sn one pce* **12/1**

2-00 **6** 2 1/2 **Watchmyeverymove (IRE)**[11] 3471 3-9-3 **75**....................(t) KevinStott 7 64
(Stuart Williams) *cl up: pushed along over 4f out: rdn wl over 3f out: sn drvn and wknd over 2f out* **22/1**

32-0 **7** 1/2 **Steeve**[17] 3261 3-9-4 **76**.................... DanielTudhope 10 64
(Rod Millman) *led 1f: trckd ldrs: pushed along over 3f out: rdn over 2f out: sn no imp* **8/1**

0-50 **8** *nk* **Golden Parade**[11] 3478 3-8-7 **65**.................... DuranFentiman 9 52
(Tim Easterby) *a towards rr* **16/1**

3620 **9** 1/2 **Mustadun**[24] 3011 3-9-3 **75**.................... FrannyNorton 3 61
(Mark Johnston) *hld up towards rr: hdwy on inner 3f out: chsd ldrs over 2f out and sn rdn: drvn wl over 1f out: sn wknd* **16/1**

0124 **10** 1 1/2 **Barasti Dancer (IRE)**[17] 3249 3-8-13 **71**.................... BenCurtis 6 54
(K R Burke) *in tch: rdn along 1/2-way: sn wknd* **6/1**

1m 43.13s (2.33) **Going Correction** +0.425s/f (Yiel) **10** Ran SP% **125.3**
Speed ratings (Par 101): **105,104,103,101,99 97,96,96,95,94**
CSF £43.28 CT £192.97 TOTE £8.70: £3.10, £1.90, £1.80; EX 58.40 Trifecta £189.70.
Owner Pam's People **Bred** Ms D Hutch **Trained** Thorney, Cambs

FOCUS
There was no hanging around in this competitive 3yo handicap. A pb from the winner, rated around the third.

3886 LAKESIDE VILLAGE SAVINGS WITH EVERY STEP FILLIES' H'CAP 1m 6f 115y
5:35 (5:36) (Class 5) (0-70,73) 3-Y-O+
£3,752 (£1,116; £557; £400; £400; £400) **Stalls** Low

Form RPR

-533 **1** **Well Funded (IRE)**[27] 2913 3-7-11 **57** oh3.................... JaneElliott(3) 6 63
(James Bethell) *trckd ldrs: hdwy and cl up 3f out: rdn 2f out: drvn to ld appr fnl f: kpt on wl* **11/2**[3]

/11 **2** 1/2 **Maid In Manhattan (IRE)**[3] 3769 5-8-9 **54** 5ex.....(h) HarrisonShaw(5) 3 58
(Rebecca Menzies) *hld up in rr: hdwy over 3f out: chsd ldrs and n.m.r wl over 2f out: sn swtchd rt and rdn: drvn and edgd rt ent fnl f: kpt on wl u.p towards fin* **6/4**[1]

5621 **3** *nk* **Fantastic Ms Fox**[19] 3197 3-8-2 **62**.................... SeanDavis(3) 10 66
(Richard Fahey) *trckd ldr: cl up over 3f out: rdn to take slt ld 2f out: drvn and hdd appr fnl f: kpt on wl u.p fnl f* **5/1**[2]

403 **4** 2 1/4 **Kalaya (IRE)**[17] 3254 3-8-3 **60**.................... HollieDoyle 9 60
(Archie Watson) *led: pushed along over 3f out: rdn over 2f out: sn hdd: drvn wl over 1f out: kpt on same pce* **16/1**

The Form Book Flat 2019, Raceform Ltd, Newbury, RG14 5SJ

/030 5 ½ **Attention Seaker**[6] 3653 9-10-0 **68**....................(t) DavidAllan 2 67
(Tim Easterby) *hld up in tch: hdwy to trck ldrs 4f out: cl up 3f out: rdn and ev ch 2f out: sn drvn and kpt on one pce* **14/1**
02-0 6 ¾ **Perfect Summer (IRE)**[12] 1172 9-10-3 **71**..............(v) DanielTudhope 5 69
(Ian Williams) *hld up in rr: hdwy 4f out: chsd ldrs over 2f out: sn rdn and no imp* **20/1**
-222 7 1 ¾ **Shine Baby Shine**[19] 3175 5-9-11 **65**.................... PhilDennis 7 60
(Philip Kirby) *hld up in tch: pushed along 4f out: rdn 3f out: sn drvn and outpcd* **9/1**
5-02 8 2 ½ **Say Nothing**[10] 3505 3-9-2 **73**.................... PJMcDonald 1 66
(Hughie Morrison) *trckd ldng pair: rdn along over 3f out: sn wknd* **5/1**[2]
6000 9 7 **Miss Ranger (IRE)**[17] 3251 7-9-5 **59**.................... BenCurtis 4 41
(Roger Fell) *hld up towards rr: effrt and sme hdwy over 3f out: sn rdn and wknd (jockey said mare hung right in the home straight)* **33/1**

3m 20.75s (9.15) **Going Correction** +0.425s/f (Yiel)
WFA 3 from 5yo+ 17lb **9** Ran SP% **119.0**
Speed ratings (Par 100): **92,91,91,90,90 89,88,87,83**
CSF £14.60 CT £45.37 TOTE £6.50: £1.80, £1.30, £1.60; EX 19.90 Trifecta £78.10.
Owner Clarendon Thoroughbred Racing **Bred** Irish National Stud **Trained** Middleham Moor, N Yorks

FOCUS
Add 12yds. Not a bad staying handicap for the class, though it turned into a dash from 3f out.
T/Plt: £18.70 to a £1 stake. Pool: £90,413.06 - 3,520.49 winning units T/Qpdt: £4.90 to a £1 stake. Pool: £8,280.12 - 1,243.44 winning units **Joe Rowntree**

3694 SALISBURY (R-H)
Sunday, June 16

OFFICIAL GOING: Soft (6.9)
Wind: Quite strong against Weather: Overcast with sunny periods

3887 SHADWELL RACING EXCELLENCE APPRENTICE H'CAP (WHIPS SHALL BE CARRIED BUT NOT USED) 6f
1:55 (1:55) (Class 6) (0-65,71) 3-Y-O
£3,832 (£1,140; £569; £400; £400; £400) **Stalls** Low

Form RPR
0443 1 **Jungle Juice (IRE)**[12] 3440 3-9-4 **64**.................... GeorgeBass(7) 6 70
(Mick Channon) *mde all: kpt on wl* **9/2**[3]
6620 2 1 **Stay Forever (FR)**[95] 1171 3-9-7 **65**.................... KayleighStephens(5) 2 68
(Andrew Balding) *dwlt: bhd: hdwy fr 3f out: chal for 2nd 2f out: kpt on ins fnl f but nt quite pce to get on terms w wnr* **6/1**
-401 3 nk **Stallone (IRE)**[3] 3771 3-10-4 **71** 6ex....................(v) SeanKirrane 1 73
(Richard Spencer) *trckd wnr: rdn 2f out: kpt on but nt pce to chal: lost 2nd fnl 120yds* **9/4**[1]
-036 4 2 ¾ **My Law**[12] 3442 3-9-0 **58**.................... IsobelFrancis(5) 5 52
(Jim Boyle) *in tch: lost pl whn clipped heels and stmbld 3f out: sn struggling: kpt on fnl f but nvr any threat: wnt 4th towards fin (jockey said filly clipped heels app 3f out)* **4/1**[2]
5406 5 nk **Alicia Darcy (IRE)**[33] 2708 3-9-4 **62**.................... KateLeahy(5) 7 55
(Archie Watson) *s.i.s: in last pair: shkn up over 2f out: kpt on fnl f but nvr any threat* **9/2**[3]
-650 6 nk **Miss Gargar**[24] 2995 3-9-1 **57**.................... LukeCatton(3) 3 49
(Harry Dunlop) *trckd ldrs: pushed along over 2f out: sn one pce* **16/1**
-004 7 1 **Anglesey Penny**[74] 1514 3-8-2 **46** oh1....................(p[1]) KeelanBaker(5) 8 35
(J R Jenkins) *in tch: hdwy 2f out: effrt over 1f out: nt pce to threaten: fdd ins fnl f* **66/1**
00-0 8 4 **Grey Hare**[16] 3319 3-8-6 **48**.................... ElishaWhittington(3) 4 25
(Tony Carroll) *racd keenly: trckd wnr: pushed along over 2f out: sn wknd (jockey said gelding ran too free)* **25/1**

1m 17.52s (3.02) **Going Correction** +0.35s/f (Good) **8** Ran SP% **112.6**
Speed ratings (Par 97): **93,91,91,87,87 86,85,80**
CSF £30.48 CT £75.17 TOTE £4.10: £1.70, £2.20, £1.10; EX 23.00 Trifecta £75.00.
Owner Insignia Racing (ribbon) **Bred** Ballybrennan Stud Ltd **Trained** West Ilsley, Berks

FOCUS
Soft ground (Going Stick 6.9), and a rail was up on the stands' side of the straight course, railing off ground used on Tuesday. Distances as advertised. A modest sprint.

3888 PAUL ELLIOTT MEMORIAL H'CAP 1m 4f 5y
2:30 (2:30) (Class 6) (0-65,66) 3-Y-O
£3,493 (£1,039; £519; £400; £400; £400) **Stalls** Low

Form RPR
00-0 1 **Cambric**[30] 2795 3-9-4 **61**.................... JasonWatson 6 74+
(Roger Charlton) *pushed along leaving stalls: towards rr: hdwy on outer 5f out: rdn to ld 2f out: styd on strly (trainers rep said regarding apparent improvement in form that that the filly benefitted from the step up in trip from 1m2f to 1m4f and the drop in grade from Class 4 to Class 6)* **4/1**[2]
-045 2 3 ½ **Sea Art**[19] 3197 3-9-6 **63**....................(v) AdamKirby 13 68
(William Knight) *led after 2f: rdn and hdd 2f out: styd on same pce fnl f (vet said gelding lost its left fore shoe)* **8/1**
-006 3 1 ½ **Harry The Norseman**[13] 3418 3-9-0 **57**.................... LiamKeniry 12 60
(Jonjo O'Neill) *pushed along towards rr early: rdn and hdwy fr 3f out: wnt 3rd ent fnl f: styd on* **40/1**
060 4 3 ½ **Ideal Grace**[17] 3263 3-9-0 **57**.................... CharlesBishop 1 55
(Eve Johnson Houghton) *led for 2f: trckd ldrs: rdn over 2f out: sn hld: styd on same pce* **16/1**
-660 5 ¾ **Keith**[8] 3593 3-8-6 **49**.................... CharlieBennett 9 45
(Rod Millman) *hld up towards rr: hdwy over 3f out: sn rdn: styd on but nt pce to get on terms* **20/1**
-044 6 3 ¾ **Robert Fitzroy (IRE)**[16] 3311 3-9-9 **66**..............(v[1]) SilvestreDeSousa 10 57
(Michael Bell) *slowly away: nvr travelling: bhd: swtchd to centre and rdn over 3f out: sme prog 2f out: nvr trbld ldrs: wknd fnl f (jockey said gelding was never travelling)* **11/4**[1]
0063 7 6 **Yellow Label (USA)**[22] 3092 3-9-6 **63**.................... RobHornby 11 45
(Andrew Balding) *trckd ldrs: rdn wl over 2f out: wknd over 1f out* **11/2**[3]
3233 8 5 **Mongolia**[15] 3348 3-8-12 **55**....................(b[1]) TomMarquand 4 29
(Richard Hannon) *mid-div: struggling over 4f out: wknd 2f out* **7/1**
0006 9 6 **Purbeck Hills (IRE)**[8] 3594 3-8-13 **56**.................... PatDobbs 3 21
(Richard Hannon) *mid-diviion: rdn over 3f out: wknd 2f out* **20/1**
-000 10 3 ½ **Universal Song**[22] 3092 3-8-2 **45**.................... RaulDaSilva 2 5
(Seamus Mullins) *in tch tl rdn over 3f out: sn btn* **20/1**
6-60 11 1 ¾ **Fancy Dress (IRE)**[40] 2518 3-9-0 **57**.................... HarryBentley 8 14
(Ralph Beckett) *in tch: rdn 5f out: wknd 2f out* **20/1**
2236 12 1 ¼ **Bonneville (IRE)**[9] 3528 3-8-8 **51**....................(b) KieranO'Neill 7 7
(Rod Millman) *nvr travelling: mid-div: rdn over 3f out: sn btn* **11/1**

2m 43.18s (5.58) **Going Correction** +0.35s/f (Good) **12** Ran SP% **121.4**
Speed ratings (Par 97): **95,92,91,89,88 86,82,79,75,72 71,70**
CSF £33.58 CT £1140.21 TOTE £4.90: £1.80, £3.10, £8.20; EX 41.60 Trifecta £1008.90.
Owner D J Deer **Bred** D J And Mrs Deer **Trained** Beckhampton, Wilts

FOCUS
They finished well strung out in this moderate handicap. This could be rated a bit higher.

3889 WATERAID MILDREN CONSTRUCTION FILLIES' NOVICE STKS 1m 1f 201y
3:05 (3:07) (Class 4) 3-Y-O+
£5,822 (£1,732; £865; £432) **Stalls** Low

Form RPR
6 1 **Tribal Craft**[17] 3263 3-8-10 0.................... DavidProbert 9 84
(Andrew Balding) *mde all: nudged clr 3f out: in command after: rdn out fnl f* **11/8**[1]
2 3 **Jomrok** 3-8-10 0.................... PatDobbs 5 78
(Owen Burrows) *mid-div: hdwy 3f out: sn rdn to chse wnr: styd on but a being hld* **9/2**[3]
4 3 9 **Tatweej**[61] 1834 3-8-10 0.................... KieranShoemark 8 60
(Owen Burrows) *trckd ldrs: rdn 3f out: styd on same pce fnl 2f* **8/1**
0- 4 1 ¼ **Mina Vagante**[179] 9604 3-8-10 0.................... SilvestreDeSousa 6 58
(Hugo Palmer) *mid-div: rdn and stdy prog fr over 2f out: styd on but nvr gng pce to get on terms (jockey said filly ran green)* **11/2**
5 ¾ **Mistral Song (FR)**[65] 5-9-5 0.................... MeganNicholls(3) 1 56
(Michael Blanshard) *mid-div tl outpcd over 3f out: n.d after but styd on again fnl f* **66/1**
0 6 1 **Eagle Queen**[31] 2771 3-8-10 0.................... HarryBentley 11 54
(Andrew Balding) *trckd wnr tl rdn wl over 2f out: grad fdd* **7/2**[2]
03 7 hd **Lady Elysia**[23] 3035 3-8-7 0.................... MitchGodwin(3) 4 54
(Harry Dunlop) *trckd ldrs: rdn wl over 2f out: wknd over 1f out (jockey said filly lost its left hind shoe)* **33/1**
8 hd **Mini Milk** 3-8-10 0.................... RobHornby 3 53
(Jonathan Portman) *hld up towards rr: stdy prog fr 2f out but nvr gng pce to get involved* **20/1**
06 9 1 ½ **Miss Harriett**[24] 2999 3-8-7 0.................... WilliamCox(3) 2 50
(Stuart Kittow) *mid-div: rdn 3f out: wknd over 1f out* **66/1**
10 17 **Sharqi (IRE)** 3-8-10 0....................(t[1]) NicolaCurrie 7 16
(Jean-Rene Auvray) *wnt lft s: a towards rr* **50/1**

2m 12.72s (2.22) **Going Correction** +0.35s/f (Good)
WFA 3 from 5yo 12lb **10** Ran SP% **121.7**
Speed ratings (Par 102): **105,102,95,94,93 93,92,92,91,77**
CSF £8.06 TOTE £2.10: £1.10, £2.00, £2.30; EX 9.00 Trifecta £34.60.
Owner J C Smith **Bred** Littleton Stud **Trained** Kingsclere, Hants

FOCUS
The early pace was steady and the winner dominated throughout.

3890 BYERLEY STUD PETER WALWYN MEMORIAL NOVICE STKS (PLUS 10 RACE) 6f
3:35 (3:35) (Class 2) 2-Y-O
£11,320 (£3,368; £1,683; £841) **Stalls** Low

Form RPR
231 1 **Praxeology (IRE)**[10] 3512 2-9-7 0.................... SilvestreDeSousa 1 87
(Mark Johnston) *mde all: rdn ent fnl f: drifted lft towards fin: r.o wl* **11/8**[1]
2 2 **Wightman (IRE)** 2-9-2 0.................... CharlesBishop 2 76
(Mick Channon) *trckd ldrs: rdn 2f out: sn swtchd lft: kpt on ins fnl f to chse wnr fnl 100yds: a being hld* **8/1**[2]
2 3 nk **Forbidden Land (IRE)**[31] 2780 2-9-2 0.................... RossaRyan 3 75
(Richard Hannon) *trckd wnr: wandered u.p fr 2f out: nt quite pce to mount chal: kpt on but no ex fnl 100yds* **11/8**[1]
0 4 2 ¾ **Pitcher**[17] 3274 2-9-2 0.................... PatDobbs 4 67
(Richard Hannon) *trckd ldrs: rdn over 2f out: sn one pce* **16/1**[3]
5 26 **Dark Moonlight (IRE)** 2-9-2 0.................... KieranShoemark 5
(Charles Hills) *dwlt bdly: a detached in last (jockey said gelding was slowly away)* **8/1**[2]

1m 16.8s (2.30) **Going Correction** +0.35s/f (Good) **5** Ran SP% **112.3**
Speed ratings (Par 99): **98,95,94,91,56**
CSF £13.49 TOTE £1.90: £1.10, £3.70; EX 8.30 Trifecta £14.00.
Owner Dr J Walker **Bred** Yeomanstown Stud **Trained** Middleham Moor, N Yorks

FOCUS
The third winner from the first four races on the card to make all the running. The level is a bit fluid.

3891 BRITISH STALLION STUDS EBF CATHEDRAL STKS (LISTED RACE) 6f
4:10 (4:10) (Class 1) 3-Y-O+
£19,552; £5,380; £2,680; £1,345; £675 **Stalls** Low

Form RPR
01-3 1 **Snazzy Jazzy (IRE)**[8] 3588 4-9-10 **110**.................... AdamKirby 4 113
(Clive Cox) *trckd ldrs: rdn over 1f out: str run ins fnl f: jnd ldr on line* **11/4**[2]
11 1 dht **Archer's Dream (IRE)**[32] 2736 3-8-7 **94**.................... GeorgeWood 1 101+
(James Fanshawe) *trckd ldrs: led jst over 1f out: sn rdn: kpt on: jnd on line* **2/1**[1]
0-01 3 ¾ **Richenza (FR)**[9] 3544 4-9-0 **93**.................... HarryBentley 2 101
(Ralph Beckett) *chsd ldrs: rdn whn sltly outpcd 2f out: r.o ins fnl f: wnt 3rd fnl 100yds: clsng on front pair cl home* **7/1**
3-56 4 2 ¼ **Arbalet (IRE)**[36] 2615 4-9-5 **105**....................(t) SilvestreDeSousa 3 98
(Hugo Palmer) *sn led: hung lft thrght: rdn 2f out: hdd jst over 1f out: no ex fnl 100yds (jockey said colt hung left-handed throughout)* **10/1**
5-00 5 ½ **Emaraaty Ana**[22] 3104 3-8-12 **107**.................... AndreaAtzeni 5 95
(Kevin Ryan) *trckd ldr: rdn and ev ch over 1f out: hld ent fnl f: no ex fnl 100yds* **3/1**[3]
0120 6 1 ½ **George Bowen (IRE)**[32] 2744 7-9-5 **105**....................(v) TonyHamilton 6 92
(Richard Fahey) *chsd ldrs: rdn 2f out: sn one pce* **5/1**

1m 14.87s (0.37) **Going Correction** +0.35s/f (Good)
WFA 3 from 4yo+ 7lb **6** Ran SP% **123.3**
Speed ratings (Par 111): **111,111,110,107,106 104**
WIN: 1.50 Snazzy Jazzy 1.40 Archer's Dream; PL: 1.50 Snazzy Jazzy 1.70 Archer's Dream; EX: SJ/AD 4.50, AD/SJ 4.00; CSF: SJ/AD/R 4.91, AD/SJ/R 4.43 CSF £4.91 TOTE £1.50: £1.50; EX 4.50 Trifecta £24.30.
Owner Fred Archer Racing - Wheel Of Fortune **Bred** Ms Anne Coughlan **Trained** Newmarket, Suffolk
Owner Mrs Olive Shaw **Bred** Bluegate Stud **Trained** Lambourn, Berks

FOCUS
An interesting edition, and the judge couldn't split the first two at the line.

3892 CARA GLASS FILLIES' H'CAP 6f 213y
4:45 (4:46) (Class 5) (0-75,76) 3-Y-O+

£4,091 (£1,217; £608; £400; £400; £400) **Stalls** Low

Form RPR

1-04 1 **Daddy's Daughter (CAN)**[38] 2555 4-9-13 **75**........(h[1]) RobertWinston 2 87
(Dean Ivory) *mde all: kpt on wl to assert fnl f: rdn out (trainers rep said regarding apparent improvement in form that the filly benefitted from the step down in trip from 1m2f to 7f and running on turf for the first time)* **7/1**

5311 2 3 1/2 **Chica De La Noche**[20] 3146 5-9-12 **74**..........(p) AdamKirby 1 77
(Simon Dow) *trckd ldrs: rdn to chse wnr 2f out: kpt on but a being readily hld fnl f* **5/1**[2]

-632 3 1/2 **Dashed**[17] 3258 3-9-2 **73**.............................. AndreaAtzeni 4 72
(Roger Varian) *s.i.s: in tch: pushed along and hdwy over 2f out: sn swtchd lft and rdn: wnt 3rd over 1f out: kpt on same pce fnl f* **7/4**[1]

4162 4 2 1/2 **Material Girl**[9] 3552 3-8-11 **75**...............(p) SeanKirrane(7) 7 67
(Richard Spencer) *in tch: hdwy over 2f out: sn rdn: one pce fnl f* **5/1**[2]

0024 5 4 1/2 **Cotubanama**[19] 3193 3-9-5 **76**.......................... CharlesBishop 5 57
(Mick Channon) *hld up in tch: swtchd lft wl over 1f out: sn rdn: nvr threatened: wknd fnl f* **17/2**

-130 6 3 1/2 **Here's Two**[11] 3468 6-9-12 **74**......................... DavidProbert 6 48
(Ron Hodges) *in tch: effrt whn nt clr run 2f out: wknd fnl f* **13/2**[3]

1406 7 1 **First Link (USA)**[26] 2927 4-9-6 **68**..................... NicolaCurrie 3 40
(Jean-Rene Auvray) *racd keenly: trckd ldr tl rdn 2f out: sn wknd* **20/1**

030- 8 3 **Wild Abandon**[265] 7622 3-9-2 **73**......................... HarryBentley 8 34
(Ralph Beckett) *hld up in tch: pushed along over 3f out: rdn over 2f out: little imp: wknd over 1f out* **8/1**

1m 30.05s (1.35) **Going Correction** +0.35s/f (Good) 8 Ran SP% 121.9
WFA 3 from 4yo+ 9lb
Speed ratings (Par 100): **106,102,101,98,93 89,88,84**
CSF £44.64 CT £90.11 TOTE £6.60: £2.80, £1.10, £1.10; EX 46.70 Trifecta £148.00.
Owner Heather & Michael Yarrow **Bred** K 5 Stables, Inc **Trained** Radlett, Herts

FOCUS
A fair handicap, but another all-the-way winner, the fourth from the first six races on the card. A pb from the winner, with the runner-up to her turf best.

3893 PAUL WILLIAMSON MEMORIAL H'CAP 5f
5:20 (5:20) (Class 4) (0-85,86) 3-Y-O+

£5,757 (£1,713; £856; £428; £400; £400) **Stalls** Low

Form RPR

1-24 1 **Maygold**[16] 3303 4-9-6 **77**.............................. LiamKeniry 3 90
(Ed Walker) *s.i.s: travelled wl: cl up: hdwy 2f out: led over 1f out: qcknd clr: readily* **4/1**[2]

-405 2 2 3/4 **Youkan (IRE)**[7] 3636 4-9-11 **82**.......................... AdamKirby 1 85
(Stuart Kittow) *trckd ldrs: rdn over 2f out: kpt on ins fnl f but nt pce of wnr: wnt 2nd towards fin* **5/2**[1]

5141 3 nk **Paddy Power (IRE)**[22] 3079 6-9-12 **83**.................... TonyHamilton 4 85
(Richard Fahey) *cl up: squeezed through gap 2f out: sn rdn to chse wnr: nt pce to chal: lost 2nd towards fin* **5/2**[1]

0044 4 3 1/4 **Pettochside**[1] 3856 10-9-1 **75**.................. MitchGodwin(3) 5 65
(John Bridger) *cl up: hdwy 2f out: sn rdn to chal for 3rd: fdd fnl 120yds* **6/1**

6050 5 2 3/4 **Boom The Groom (IRE)**[15] 3344 8-10-1 **86**............. TomMarquand 2 66
(Tony Carroll) *trckd ldr: rdn whn hmpd 2f out: wknd fnl f* **11/2**[3]

5006 6 1/2 **Mawde (IRE)**[13] 3420 3-8-7 **70**........................ CharlieBennett 7 47
(Rod Millman) *led: rdn and hdd over 1f out: wknd fnl f* **20/1**

000- 7 16 **Our Lord**[213] 9084 7-9-4 **75**.............................. LukeMorris 6
(Michael Attwater) *sn outpcd: a last (jockey said gelding was never travelling)* **14/1**

1m 1.8s (1.30) **Going Correction** +0.35s/f (Good) 7 Ran SP% 118.2
WFA 3 from 4yo+ 6lb
Speed ratings (Par 105): **103,98,98,92,88 87,62**
CSF £15.22 TOTE £4.10: £1.40, £2.40; EX 11.80 Trifecta £44.80.
Owner Farleigh Racing **Bred** Farleigh Court Racing Partnership **Trained** Upper Lambourn, Berks

FOCUS
The winner settled matters in good style.
T/Jkpt: £2,500.00 to a £1 stake. Pool: £14,084.51 - 4.0 winning units T/Plt: £26.20 to a £1 stake. Pool: £77,771.22 - 2,159.62 winning units T/Qpdt: £4.40 to a £1 stake. Pool: £6,645.49 - 1,098.49 winning units **Tim Mitchell**

3894 - 3901a (Foreign Racing) - See Raceform Interactive

BRO PARK (L-H)
Sunday, June 16

OFFICIAL GOING: Turf: good

3902a STOCKHOLMS STORA PRIS (GROUP 3) (3YO+) (TURF) 1m 165y
1:52 3-Y-0+ £62,001 (£22,143; £11,514; £7,085; £3,542)

RPR

1 **Learn By Heart**[43] 4-9-4 0.......................... RafaeldeOliveira 4 100
(Bent Olsen, Denmark) *s.i.s: chsd up to r promly on inner: swtchd off rail and pushed along to chse ldr 3f out: rdn jst under 2f out: edgd rt u.p whn led jst ins fnl f: kpt on strly* **47/1**

2 1 **King David (DEN)**[43] 4-9-4 0.......................... OliverWilson 10 98
(Marc Stott, Denmark) *hld up in rr: gained a pl jst under 1/2-way: pushed along 2 1/2f out: racd wd into st: drvn and prog fr jst under 2f out: chsd eventual wnr ent fnl f: styd on but nt quite pce to chal* **558/100**[3]

3 3/4 **Christmas (IRE)**[246] 8187 3-8-7 0...................... JacobJohansen 2 95
(Flemming Velin, Denmark) *mid-div: pushed along on inner 3f out: rdn 2f out: disp 4th ent fnl f: styd on wl: snatched 3rd last stride: nt pce to chal wnr* **79/20**[2]

4 shd **Swedish Dream (FR)**[294] 6609 5-9-4 0.................... CarlosLopez 1 96
(Annike Bye Hansen, Norway) *led: asked to qckn 2f out: rdn 1 1/2f out: sn hrd pressed: hdd jst ins fnl f: no ex clsng stages: lost 3rd last stride* **81/10**

5 1 **Duca Di Como (IRE)** 4-9-4 0.......................... ElioneChaves 7 94
(Cathrine Erichsen, Norway) *mid-div on outer: pushed along 2 1/2f out: rdn 1 1/2f out: unable qck: kpt on same pce ins fnl f* **41/5**

6 hd **Ginmann (IRE)**[309] 6049 5-9-4 0........................ NikolajStott 6 93
(Bolette Rosenlund, Denmark) *hld up in fnl pair: sltly hmpd and dropped to last jst under 1/2-way: pushed along 3f out: rdn on inner over 1 1/2f out: kpt on ins fnl f but nvr in contention* **163/10**

7 1/2 **Victor Kalejs (USA)**[28] 5-9-4 0..................... Per-AndersGraberg 9 92
(Roy Arne Kvisla, Sweden) *hld up towards rr: sltly impeded rival jst under 1/2-way: sn mde prog into mid-div: pushed along 3f out: limited rspnse: rdn 1 1/2f out: no imp and one pce ins fnl f* **116/10**

8 2 **Our Last Summer (IRE)**[266] 7590 6-9-4 0.................. RafaelSchistl 3 88
(Niels Petersen, Norway) *trckd ldr: pushed along 3f out: struggling to go pce and lost position jst under 2f out: grad wknd and btn 1f out* **23/10**[1]

9 shd **Red Hot Chili (SWE)**[28] 6-9-4 0....................(b) MartinRodriguez 8 88
(Patrick Wahl, Sweden) *mid-div: asked for effrt 2 1/2f out: rdn jst under 2f out: edgd rt u.p: wknd fr over 1f out* **604/100**

1m 48.2s 9 Ran SP% 117.6
WFA 3 from 4yo+ 11lb

Owner Lone Kaj-Nielsen **Bred** The Queen **Trained** Denmark

3387 **CHANTILLY** (R-H)
Sunday, June 16

OFFICIAL GOING: Turf: good to soft

3903a PRIX PAUL DE MOUSSAC LONGINES (GROUP 3) (3YO) (TURF) 1m
1:45 3-Y-0 £36,036 (£14,414; £10,810; £7,207; £3,603)

RPR

1 **Azano**[29] 2834 3-8-11 0.......................... RobertHavlin 7 107
(John Gosden) *cl up on outer: pushed along to chal ldr 2f out: sn led: rdn over 1f out: r.o strly ins fnl f: a jst doing enough* **69/10**

2 1 **Transcendent (ITY)**[58] 1920 3-8-11 0.............. ChristopheSoumillon 2 105
(F Chappet, France) *racd in fnl trio: angled out and prog fr jst under 2f out: drvn over 1f out: kpt on u.p ins fnl f: nt match pce of wnr* **67/10**

3 3/4 **Admiral Rous (IRE)**[34] 3-8-11 0......................... TheoBachelot 6 103
(E J O'Neill, France) *hld up in rr: pushed along outside rivals 2f out: drvn and prog fr 1f out: r.o strly ins fnl f: snatched 3rd last stride* **24/1**

4 hd **Melicertes**[26] 2953 3-8-11 0...................... MickaelBarzalona 4 103
(A Fabre, France) *hld up in fnl pair: pushed along and effrt on inner 2f out: drvn to chse ldr 1f out: unable qck: one pce clsng stages: lost 3rd last stride* **13/5**[2]

5 2 **Eagle Hunter**[24] 3029 3-8-11 0.................. Pierre-CharlesBoudot 5 98
(F-H Graffard, France) *racd keenly bhd ldrs: pushed along 2f out: rdn ent fnl f: unable to go w ldrs and sn one pce: no ex clsng stages* **67/10**

6 1/2 **Mission Boy**[28] 2887 3-9-2 0......................... CristianDemuro 1 102
(A Botti, Italy) *racd in 4th on inner: struggling to go pce and pushed along 2f out: lost position and dropped to rr 1 1/2f out: passed btn rival ins fnl f* **6/1**[3]

7 1/2 **Anodor (FR)**[35] 2668 3-9-0 0....................(b[1]) AurelienLemaitre 3 99
(F Head, France) *led: asked to qckn 2f out: sn hdd and u.p: grad wknd fr 1 1/2f out* **19/10**[1]

1m 35.96s (-2.04) 7 Ran SP% 119.2
PARI-MUTUEL (all including 1 euro stake): WIN 7.90; PLACE 4.00, 3.80; SF 70.20.
Owner M J & L A Taylor **Bred** Elysian Bloodstock Ltd **Trained** Newmarket, Suffolk

3904a PRIX HOCQUART LONGINES (GROUP 2) (3YO COLTS & FILLIES) (TURF) 1m 4f
2:20 3-Y-0 £66,756 (£25,765; £12,297; £8,198; £4,099)

RPR

1 **Al Hilalee**[29] 2833 3-9-2 0............................. JamesDoyle 5 106
(Charlie Appleby) *mde all: shkn up and wnt for home 1 1/2f out: rdn and edgd lft 1f out: wnt sltly rt whn jockey changed whip hand fnl 100yds: drvn out* **11/5**[1]

2 nk **Soft Light (FR)**[43] 2426 3-9-2 0....................... CristianDemuro 4 106
(J-C Rouget, France) *w.w in rr: drvn 2f out but no imp: hdwy over 1f out: r.o to go 2nd 100yds out: a hld by wnr fnl 50yds* **23/5**

3 nk **Khagan (IRE)**[21] 3120 3-9-2 0..................... MickaelBarzalona 1 105
(A Fabre, France) *disp 2nd on inner: drvn and chsd ldr over 1f out: sltly impeded whn wnr wnt lft 100yds out: angled out and styng on between front two whn short of room and snatched up cl home* **31/10**[2]

4 2 **Kasaman (FR)**[59] 3-9-2 0..................(p) ChristopheSoumillon 2 102
(M Delzangles, France) *settled in 4th: no imp whn asked over 1 1/2f out: sme late prog but nvr trbld ldrs* **31/10**[2]

5 2 1/2 **San Huberto (IRE)**[24] 3031 3-9-2 0..................... TonyPiccone 3 98
(F Chappet, France) *disp 2nd on outer: chsd ldr fr 3f out: sn rdn and no further imp: dropped away fr more than 1f out* **18/5**[3]

2m 29.1s (-1.90) 5 Ran SP% 119.6
PARI-MUTUEL (all including 1 euro stake): WIN 1.80 (coupled with Khagan); PLACE 2.00, 2.50; SF 11.00.
Owner Godolphin **Bred** Rabbah Bloodstock Limited **Trained** Newmarket, Suffolk

3905a PRIX DE DIANE LONGINES (GROUP 1) (3YO FILLIES) (TURF) 1m 2f 110y
3:05 3-Y-0 £514,774 (£205,945; £102,972; £51,441; £25,765)

RPR

1 **Channel (IRE)**[30] 3-9-0 0........................ Pierre-CharlesBoudot 7 109
(F-H Graffard, France) *a cl up: drvn to chal outside two rivals w 1 1/2f to run: sn rdn: led appr fnl f: styd on gamely u.p* **91/10**[3]

2 hd **Commes (FR)**[35] 2669 3-9-0 0........................ CristianDemuro 5 109
(J-C Rouget, France) *settled in midfield: drvn 2f out but nt clr run and angled out w less than 1 1/2f to run: began to cl u.p appr fnl f: r.o: jst failed* **53/10**[2]

3 1/2 **Grand Glory**[59] 3-9-0 0............................. GeraldMosse 8 108+
(Gianluca Bietolini, France) *towards rr: drvn and hdwy 1 1/2f out: styd on strly fnl f: nvr quite on terms* **28/1**

4 nk **Etoile (FR)**[27] 3137 3-9-0 0..................... MickaelBarzalona 6 107
(J-C Rouget, France) *racd keenly: hld up towards rr on inner: moved off rail but nt clr run ins fnl 2f: angled out again more than 1f out: styd on strly fnl f: nvr on terms* **12/1**

5 snk **Cala Tarida**[21] 3121 3-9-0 0......................... GregoryBenoist 9 107
(F Rossi, France) *racd keenly: hld up in midfield: dropped towards rr 4f out: drvn to cl over 1 1/2f out: styd on 1f out: run evened out late on: nvr chal ldrs* **30/1**

6 nse **Siyarafina (FR)**[21] 3121 3-9-0 0.................. ChristopheSoumillon 16 107
(A De Royer-Dupre, France) *w.w in midfield on outer: shkn up and began to cl 1 1/2f out: styd u.p fnl f: nt pce to rch ldrs* **6/4**[1]

7 1 1/2 **Wonderment (IRE)**30 3-9-0 0.............................. StephanePasquier 11 104
(N Clement, France) *racd keenly: chsd ldr: drvn to dispute ld over 2f out: led appr 1 1/2f out: hdd on run to fnl f: readily outpcd fr there* **20/1**
8 3/4 **Platane**21 3121 3-9-0 0.............................. MaximeGuyon 1 102
(C Laffon-Parias, France) *led: jnd over 2f out: hdd appr 1 1/2f out: sn rdn: dropped away ins fnl f* **17/1**
9 nk **Ebony (FR)**30 3-9-0 0.............................. Jean-BernardEyquem 3 102
(J-C Rouget, France) *racd in fnl trio: clsd into midfield bef 1/2-way: 7th and drvn 1 1/2f out: wknd ins fnl f* **30/1**
10 hd **Entitle**32 2745 3-9-0 0.............................. FrankieDettori 13 101
(John Gosden) *racd in fnl trio: sme hdwy u.p ins fnl 1 1/2f: nvr able to get in contention* **12/1**
11 snk **Noor Sahara (IRE)**24 3029 3-9-0 0.............................. OlivierPeslier 10 101
(F Chappet, France) *hld up in midfield on outer: stl travelling wl enough over 2f out: rdn and no imp fnl 1 1/2f* **25/1**
12 nk **Paramount (FR)**27 3137 3-9-0 0.............................. JulienAuge 12 101
(C Ferland, France) *hld up in fnl trio: sme late prog: nvr involved* **103/1**
13 2 **Cartiem (FR)**46 2312 3-9-0 0.............................. Christophe-PatriceLemaire 2 97
(J-C Rouget, France) *chsd ldr on inner: drvn and nt qckn 1 1/2f out: wknd fnl f* **23/1**
14 3/4 **Nausha**32 2745 3-9-0 0.............................. JamesDoyle 4 95
(Roger Varian) *midfield on inner: drvn 2 1/2f fr home: no imp fr 1 1/2f out: wl hld fnl f* **25/1**
15 3/4 **Amarena (FR)**43 2430 3-9-0 0.............................. YutakaTake 15 94
(S Kobayashi, France) *prom on outer: wkng whn sltly impeded 1 1/2f out: wl hld over 1f out* **19/1**
16 4 1/2 **Morning Dew (FR)**21 3121 3-9-0 0.............................. EddyHardouin 14 85
(N Caullery, France) *in rr: rdn and no imp over 2f out: wl hld fnl 1 1/2f* **117/1**

2m 8.7s (-0.10) **16 Ran SP% 120.0**
PARI-MUTUEL (all including 1 euro stake): WIN 10.10; PLACE 2.90, 2.40, 6.90; DF 19.30.
Owner Samuel De Barros **Bred** Kilcarn Stud **Trained** France

FOCUS
Plenty of strength in depth in this edition of the French Oaks but it was an unsatisfactory race with the lack of early pace turning it into a bunched finish, with the first six separated by just over a length. The time was the third slowest recorded this century. The two British raiders were disappointing. This rates a step up from the winner and third.

3906a PRIX BERTRAND DU BREUIL LONGINES (GROUP 3) (4YO+) (TURF) 1m
5:35 4-Y-O+ £36,036 (£14,414; £10,810; £7,207; £3,603)

RPR
1 **Vintager**22 3074 4-9-0 0.............................. JamesDoyle 5 115
(Charlie Appleby) *cl up on outer: nudged along to press ldr 2f out: qcknd and led 1 1/2f out: rdn jst ins fnl f: styd on strly: a doing enough cl home* **9/2**3
2 3/4 **Trais Fluors**21 3122 5-9-0 0.............................. Pierre-CharlesBoudot 4 113
(A Fabre, France) *w.w in rr: pushed along outside rivals to chse eventual wnr 1 1/2f out: rdn jst ins fnl f: kpt on wl: nt quite enough pce to chal* **1/2**1
3 3 1/2 **Lunch Lady**49 2167 4-8-10 0..............................(b) MaximeGuyon 3 101
(F Head, France) *racd in 4th: asked for effrt 2f out: nt qckn w ldr: drvn over 1f out: kpt on same pce ins fnl f: no match for front pair* **37/10**2
4 7 **Louis D'Or (IRE)**54 2028 4-9-0 0.............................. OlivierPeslier 2 89
(Laurent Loisel, France) *racd in 3rd: pushed along whn pce qcknd over 1 1/2f out: sltly short of racing room over 1f out: sn wl btn* **16/1**
5 snk **Geniale (JPN)**228 8755 5-9-0 0.............................. YutakaTake 1 89
(S Kobayashi, France) *led: tried to qckn 2f out: hdd 1 1/2f out and sn u.p: grad wknd fr 1f out* **13/1**

1m 36.74s (-1.26) **5 Ran SP% 119.2**
PARI-MUTUEL (all including 1 euro stake): WIN 5.50; PLACE 1.50, 1.10; SF 10.30.
Owner Godolphin **Bred** Thurso Bloodstock Ltd **Trained** Newmarket, Suffolk

FOCUS
The second and third set the standard to their latest form.

DRESDEN
Sunday, June 16

OFFICIAL GOING: Turf: good

3907a GROSSER PREIS DER LANDESHAUPTSTADT DRESDEN (GROUP 3) (3YO+) (TURF) 7f
12:25 3-Y-O+ £28,828 (£10,810; £5,405; £2,702; £1,801)

RPR
1 **Brian Ryan**14 4-9-2 0.............................. MaximPecheur 8 102
(Andrea Marcialis, France) *racd wd early: led after 2f: qcknd up 2f out: sn drvn whn pressed 1 1/2f out: hdd ent fnl f: rallied to regain ld fnl 75yds: drvn out* **127/10**
2 nk **Waldpfad (GER)**259 7822 5-9-2 0.............................. WladimirPanov 2 101
(D Moser, Germany) *in tch: pushed along to chse ldr 2f out: upsides ldr over 1f out: led narrowly ent fnl f: hdd fnl 75yds: hld nr fin* **111/10**
3 1 3/4 **Broderie**46 4-9-1 .... SoufianeSaadi 5 95
(H-A Pantall, France) *prom: edgd sltly lft whn asked to improve 2f out: rdn to chse ldng pair ent fnl f: nt qckn and kpt on same pce clsng stages* **9/10**1
4 3/4 **Coppelia (GER)**22 4-9-1 0.............................. MichaelCadeddu 4 93
(Frau C Barsig, Germany) *hld up in fnl pair: angled out and drvn jst under 2f out: prog fr 1f out: kpt on ins fnl f: nrst fin* **196/10**
5 3/4 **Cherry Lady (GER)**36 2621 4-9-1 0.............................. AndraschStarke 6 91
(P Schiergen, Germany) *mid-div: pushed along and effrt 2f out: rdn 1 1/2f out: kpt on same pce ins fnl f: n.d* **71/10**3
6 2 1/4 **Yuman (FR)**15 3369 5-9-2 0.............................. FilipMinarik 3 86
(M Rulec, Germany) *hld up in rr: outpcd and pushed along over 2f out: limited rspnse and sn rdn: passed btn rivals ins fnl f: nvr a factor* **32/1**
7 1 **Zargun (GER)**15 3369 4-9-2 0..............................(p) LukasDelozier 7 83
(Henk Grewe, Germany) *led main gp bef sn trckd ldr after 2f: asked for effrt 2f out: unable qck and sn rdn: hung rt u.p: no ex and wknd ins fnl f* **99/10**
8 1 **Revelstoke**28 2889 3-8-9 0..............................(p) BauyrzhanMurzabayev 1 80
(A Wohler, Germany) *towards rr on inner: pushed along over 2f out: sn rdn: no rspnse and grad wknd fr over 1f out* **17/5**2

1m 24.7s
WFA 3 from 4yo+ 9lb **8 Ran SP% 120.3**
PARI-MUTUEL (all including 1 euro stake): WIN 13.70 PLACE: 3.30, 3.00, 1,50; SF: 76.00.
Owner Mme Janina Burger **Bred** D Curran **Trained** France

3908 - 3918a (Foreign Racing) - See Raceform Interactive

3679 CARLISLE (R-H)
Monday, June 17

OFFICIAL GOING: Good to soft (good in places; 6.7)
Wind: Fresh, half against in over 2f of home straight Weather: Cloudy, bright

3919 JOIN RACING TV NOW NOVICE AUCTION STKS 5f 193y
2:00 (2:02) (Class 5) 2-Y-O £4,204 (£1,251; £625; £312) Stalls Low

Form RPR
012 1 **Troubador (IRE)**11 3498 2-9-9 0.............................. PaulMulrennan 7 82
(Michael Dods) *trckd ldrs: hdwy to ld 2f out: edgd lft and pushed clr fnl f: comf* **7/4**1
0 2 4 **Moonlighting**20 3196 2-8-11 0.............................. KevinStott 8 58
(Kevin Ryan) *prom: drvn along over 2f out: rallied and chsd (clr) wnr ins fnl f: kpt on: no imp* **16/1**
2 3 3/4 **Space Ace (FR)**9 3579 2-8-11 0..............................(p1) HollieDoyle 4 56
(Archie Watson) *disp ld to 2f out: chsd wnr to ins fnl f: no ex* **9/4**2
4 1 1/2 **Sir Havelock (IRE)** 2-9-2 0.............................. PaulHanagan 6 56+
(Richard Fahey) *noisy in paddock: s.i.s: rn green in rr: outpcd 1/2-way: edgd rt and rallied over 1f out: no imp* **7/1**
5 4 **Requiems Dream (IRE)** 2-8-11 0.............................. FrannyNorton 5 39
(Mark Johnston) *disp ld to 2f out: rdn and wknd appr fnl f* **4/1**3
6 31 **Swift Arion (IRE)** 2-9-2 0.............................. RobbieDowney 2
(John Quinn) *noisy and green in paddock: slowly away: bhd and green: struggling over 3f out: t.o* **14/1**

1m 16.2s (1.60) **Going Correction** +0.20s/f (Good) **6 Ran SP% 112.2**
Speed ratings (Par 93): **97,91,90,88,83 42**
CSF £28.68 TOTE £2.30: £1.10, £7.50; EX 28.50 Trifecta £81.90.
Owner J Sagar And S Lowthian **Bred** Worksop Manor Stud **Trained** Denton, Co Durham

FOCUS
After winning the opener Paul Mulrennan described it as "Quite nice ground, just on the easy side of good." Race times backed up this assessment. This looked just a modest auction event.

3920 INTRODUCING RACING TV FILLIES' NOVICE STKS 5f 193y
2:30 (2:33) (Class 5) 3-Y-O+ £4,204 (£1,251; £625; £312) Stalls Low

Form RPR
5- 1 **Gometra Ginty (IRE)**314 5815 3-9-0 0.............................. ShaneGray 2 71
(Keith Dalgleish) *prom: rdn and outpcd wl over 1f out: rallied fnl f: led last stride* **16/1**
3 2 shd **Diamond Shower (IRE)**21 3157 3-9-0 0.............................. PaulHanagan 5 70
(Richard Fahey) *bmpd s: in tch: effrt and rdn over 1f out: led ins fnl f: kpt on: hdd last stride* **5/1**3
0-22 3 3/4 **Rhossili Down**23 3080 3-9-0 77.............................. KieranShoemark 7 68
(Charles Hills) *trckd ldrs: shkn up to ld over 1f out: edgd rt: hdd ins fnl f: no ex towards fin* **5/6**1
6 4 2 1/2 **Perfect Charm**16 3351 3-9-0 0.............................. HollieDoyle 1 60
(Archie Watson) *led to over 1f out: no ex ins fnl f* **7/1**
00 5 6 **Cheam Avenue (IRE)**11 3499 3-9-0 0.............................. TomEaves 3 41
(James Bethell) *wnt lft s: sn pressing ldr: drvn over 2f out: wknd over 1f out* **25/1**
00 6 4 1/2 **Vita Vivet**11 3510 3-9-0 0.............................. JamesSullivan 6 26
(Dianne Sayer) *bmpd s: bhd and sn pushed along: struggling 1/2-way: nvr on terms* **40/1**
7 2 1/2 **Loretta (IRE)** 3-9-0 0.............................. KevinStott 8 18
(Julie Camacho) *bhd: struggling over 3f out: sn btn* **4/1**2
05 8 3 3/4 **Guarded Secret**9 3565 3-9-0 0.............................. PaulMulrennan 4 6
(Michael Dods) *dwlt: bhd: struggling over 3f out: nvr on terms* **40/1**

1m 15.36s (0.76) **Going Correction** +0.20s/f (Good) **8 Ran SP% 118.3**
Speed ratings (Par 100): **102,101,100,97,89 83,80,75**
CSF £94.67 TOTE £16.00: £4.30, £1.40, £1.10; EX 66.00 Trifecta £198.70.
Owner Keith Dalgleish **Bred** Tally-Ho Stud **Trained** Carluke, S Lanarks
■ Stewards' Enquiry : Paul Hanagan two-day ban: used whip above permitted level (1-2 Jul)

FOCUS
Just modest fillies' form. It's tricky to rate the race, with the third having not progressed from her debut.

3921 MOLSON COORS H'CAP 5f 193y
3:00 (3:02) (Class 6) (0-65,65) 3-Y-O+
£3,234 (£962; £481; £300; £300; £300) Stalls Low

Form RPR
52-2 1 **Caustic Love (IRE)**166 21 3-9-7 65.............................. ShaneGray 12 79+
(Keith Dalgleish) *towards rr: pushed along 1/2-way: gd hdwy on outside to ld over 1f out: pushed clr fnl f: eased nr fin: readily* **12/1**
6002 2 3 3/4 **Ventura Secret (IRE)**5 3716 5-9-4 55..............................(tp) PaulMulrennan 3 61
(Michael Dods) *hld up in tch: nt clr run fr 1/2-way to over 1f out: hdwy to chse (clr) wnr ins fnl f: nt pce to chal* **4/1**2
0310 3 1 1/2 **Somewhere Secret**6 3706 5-9-10 61..............................(p) AndrewMullen 10 62
(Michael Mullineaux) *midfield on outside: effrt over 2f out: hung lft and disp ld briefly over 1f out: no ex ins fnl f* **10/1**3
3000 4 1 1/4 **Dirchill (IRE)**6 3706 5-10-0 65..............................(b) LewisEdmunds 14 62
(David Thompson) *bhd: rdn along 1/2-way: hdwy over 1f out: kpt on fnl f: nvr able to chal* **22/1**
0606 5 1/2 **Meshardal (GER)**12 3475 9-8-11 48..............................(p) JamesSullivan 7 43
(Ruth Carr) *hld up: nt clr run over 2f out: effrt and rdn over 1f out: kpt on fnl f: no imp* **16/1**
0005 6 1 1/2 **Dream House**11 3508 3-9-1 59.............................. RachelRichardson 11 48
(Tim Easterby) *chsd ldrs: effrt and led briefly over 1f out: wknd ins fnl f* **12/1**
-045 7 nse **Saltie Girl**11 3516 3-9-1 59.............................. RobbieDowney 17 48
(David Barron) *bhd: rdn along 1/2-way: hdwy over 1f out: kpt on fnl f: no imp* **28/1**
3003 8 nk **Cosmic Chatter**7 3657 9-9-6 57..............................(p) JackGarritty 16 47
(Ruth Carr) *hld up on outside: drvn along and edgd lft over 2f out: sn outpcd: no imp fnl f* **10/1**3
1332 9 3/4 **Ticks The Boxes (IRE)**7 3657 7-8-12 56.............................. KieranSchofield(7) 8 43
(Brian Ellison) *midfield: drvn along over 2f out: effrt and edgd rt over 1f out: wknd ins fnl f* **5/2**1
0503 10 1 1/4 **Alfred The Grey (IRE)**11 3516 3-8-10 54.............................. PaulHanagan 2 36
(Tracy Waggott) *prom: rdn along over 1f out: wknd fnl f* **16/1**
0-0U 11 3/4 **Red Allure**12 3476 4-8-9 46..............................(p) TomEaves 6 27
(Michael Mullineaux) *dwlt: bhd: drvn along over 2f out: effrt over 1f out: no imp* **40/1**

3202 **12** *½* **Firsteen**[26] [2958] 3-8-12 **56**.............................. BarryMcHugh 15 34
(Alistair Whillans) *bhd: rdn along on wd outside over 2f out: sn no imp: btn over 1f out* **14/1**

0033 **13** *4* **Jacob's Pillow**[7] [3656] 8-9-4 **58**..............................(p) RowanScott(3) 4 26
(Rebecca Bastiman) *chsd ldrs: rdn over 2f out: wknd over 1f out* **20/1**

-060 **14** *1* **Chickenfortea (IRE)**[30] [2847] 5-9-8 **59**.............................. PhilDennis 9 24
(Eric Alston) *led at decent gallop to over 1f out: sn wknd* **20/1**

005- **15** *3½* **Dahik (IRE)**[199] [9330] 4-9-1 **59**.............................. JoshQuinn(7) 13 13
(Michael Easterby) *midfield on outside: drvn and outpcd over 2f out: sn btn* **28/1**

0040 **16** *2½* **Picture Your Dream**[14] [3414] 4-8-12 **56**.............. CianMacRedmond(7) 5 3
(Seb Spencer) *missed break: bhd: struggling over 2f out: sn btn* **40/1**

66-0 **17** *30* **Hop Maddocks (IRE)**[37] [2638] 4-9-5 **56**..............................(v1) KevinStott 1
(Fred Watson) *cl up tl rdn and wknd qckly (lost action) over 1f out: eased whn btn (jockey said gelding lost its action)* **100/1**

1m 15.12s (0.52) **Going Correction** +0.20s/f (Good) **17** Ran SP% **127.2**
WFA 3 from 4yo+ 7lb
Speed ratings (Par 101): **104,99,97,95,94 92,92,92,91,89 88,87,82,81,76 73,33**
CSF £56.03 CT £542.87 TOTE £14.80: £3.20, £1.30, £2.30, £4.70; EX 85.70 Trifecta £891.10.
Owner Weldspec Glasgow Limited **Bred** Mrs C Holohan **Trained** Carluke, S Lanarks

FOCUS
A moderate big-field sprint. They went a good gallop and it was the quickest of the three races over the trip.

3922 CELEBRATING THE LIFE OF VANESSA GRAHAM H'CAP — 7f 173y
3:30 (3:32) (Class 5) (0-70,72) 4-Y-O+
£4,204 (£1,251; £625; £312; £300; £300) **Stalls** Low

Form — RPR

-001 **1** **Redarna**[28] [2898] 5-9-10 **72**..............................(p) PaulMulrennan 6 84
(Dianne Sayer) *t.k.h: cl up: led 3f out: rdn and hung lft over 1f out: kpt on strly fnl f* **6/1**[3]

0551 **2** *2* **Edgar Allan Poe (IRE)**[6] [3681] 5-9-4 **66** 5ex.............................. PhilDennis 8 73
(Rebecca Bastiman) *midfield: effrt over 2f out: chsd wnr over 1f out: kpt on fnl f: nt pce to chal* **9/1**

-623 **3** *¾* **Ishebayorgrey (IRE)**[13] [3448] 7-8-10 **61**..............................(h) JamieGormley(3) 9 66
(Iain Jardine) *dwlt: sn in tch: effrt and rdn 2f out: kpt on ins fnl f* **8/1**

4024 **4** *shd* **Beverley Bullet**[3] [3811] 6-8-13 **64**..............................(p) RowanScott(3) 10 69
(Lawrence Mullaney) *prom on outside: effrt and drvn along over 2f out: rallied: kpt on same pce ins fnl f* **7/2**[1]

6031 **5** *½* **Chinese Spirit (IRE)**[5] [3720] 5-8-10 **65** 5ex.............. CianMacRedmond(7) 7 71+
(Linda Perratt) *hld up: effrt whn nt clr run over 2f out tl swtchd lft over 1f out: styng on whn n.m.r ins fnl f: kpt on* **12/1**

50-0 **6** *1¼* **Irish Minister (USA)**[87] [1273] 4-9-6 **68**.............................. AndrewElliott 12 69
(David Thompson) *s.i.s: bhd: pushed along over 3f out: no imp whn checked over 1f out: kpt on fnl f: nrst fin* **80/1**

1260 **7** *¾* **Showboating (IRE)**[41] [2509] 11-9-7 **69**..............................(p) LewisEdmunds 4 68
(John Balding) *towards rr: drvn along 3f out: hdwy on outside fnl f: nvr rchd ldrs* **16/1**

-004 **8** *½* **Im Dapper Too**[17] [3296] 8-8-7 **55**.............................. ShaneGray 5 53
(John Davies) *prom: effrt and rdn 2f out: wknd ins fnl f* **12/1**

1-35 **9** *½* **Make Me**[18] [3268] 4-9-9 **71**..............................(p) JackGarritty 13 68
(Tim Easterby) *midfield on outside: drvn and outpcd over 2f out: no imp over 1f out* **9/2**[2]

6420 **10** *1¼* **Strong Steps**[11] [3502] 7-9-6 **68**..............................(p) DavidNolan 14 62
(Jim Goldie) *hld up towards rr: rdn along 3f out: no imp fr 2f out* **25/1**

0660 **11** *1* **Fake News**[6] [3704] 4-9-5 **67**.............................. RobbieDowney 3 59
(David Barron) *led to 3f out: rallied: wkng whn nt clr run ins fnl f* **14/1**

0600 **12** *nk* **Royal Shaheen (FR)**[11] [3502] 6-9-10 **72**..............................(v) TomEaves 1 63
(Alistair Whillans) *dwlt: sn midfield: struggling over 2f out: sn wknd* **33/1**

0004 **13** *1¼* **Fingal's Cave (IRE)**[6] [3682] 7-8-12 **60**.............................. PaulHanagan 11 54
(Philip Kirby) *t.k.h: chsd ldrs: rdn over 2f out: wknd over 1f out* **12/1**

4-00 **14** *4½* **Gun Case**[122] [738] 7-8-9 **57**..............................(p) BarryMcHugh 2 35
(Alistair Whillans) *bhd: struggling over 3f out: nvr on terms* **66/1**

1m 42.92s (2.92) **Going Correction** +0.20s/f (Good) **14** Ran SP% **120.9**
Speed ratings (Par 103): **93,91,90,90,89 88,87,87,86,85 84,84,82,78**
CSF £58.19 CT £443.18 TOTE £6.80: £2.60, £2.60, £2.20; EX 60.60 Trifecta £435.20.
Owner Graham Lund And Dianne Sayer **Bred** A H Bennett **Trained** Hackthorpe, Cumbria

FOCUS
Add 11yds to race distance. Ordinary form. In the straight the main action took place on the stands' side. The second has been rated in line with his latest.

3923 RACINGTV.COM FILLIES' H'CAP — 6f 195y
4:00 (4:01) (Class 4) (0-80,81) 3-Y-O **£7,439** (£2,213; £1,106; £553; £300) **Stalls** Low

Form — RPR

4520 **1** **Arletta Star**[20] [3202] 3-8-7 **62**.............................. JamesSullivan 4 67
(Tim Easterby) *trckd ldr: checked and swtchd rt over 2f out: sn rdn: led ins fnl f: kpt on wl (trainer could offer no explanation for the apparent improvement in form)* **10/3**[3]

-333 **2** *¾* **Saikung (IRE)**[31] [2798] 3-9-0 **69**.............................. KieranShoemark 2 72
(Charles Hills) *trckd ldrs: effrt and drvn over 1f out: chsd wnr ins fnl f: kpt on* **3/1**[2]

54-4 **3** *2* **Praxidice**[17] [3293] 3-9-0 **76**.............................. JonathanFisher(7) 5 74
(K R Burke) *t.k.h: prom: drvn and outpcd 2f out: rallied ins fnl f: tk 3rd cl home* **2/1**[1]

-346 **4** *shd* **Epona**[6] [3685] 3-8-13 **68**.............................. ShaneGray 1 65
(Keith Dalgleish) *t.k.h: led: rdn over 2f out: hdd ins fnl f: sn outpcd* **5/1**

-430 **5** *10* **Prairie Spy (IRE)**[27] [2927] 3-9-12 **81**.............................. FrannyNorton 3 51
(Mark Johnston) *s.i.s: bhd and sn pushed along: struggling over 2f out: eased whn no ch fnl f* **7/1**

1m 30.0s (2.00) **Going Correction** +0.20s/f (Good) **5** Ran SP% **110.6**
Speed ratings (Par 98): **96,95,92,92,81**
CSF £13.57 TOTE £4.10: £1.80, £1.40; EX 14.70 Trifecta £28.10.
Owner M J Macleod **Bred** Max Weston **Trained** Great Habton, N Yorks
■ Stewards' Enquiry : James Sullivan two-day ban: careless riding (1-2 Jul)

FOCUS
Add 11yds. The feature event, this fair handicap looked to be run at a true pace. It's been rated around the first two.

3924 RACING TV H'CAP — 6f 195y
4:30 (4:32) (Class 6) (0-60,60) 3-Y-O+
£3,234 (£962; £481; £300; £300; £300) **Stalls** Low

Form — RPR

0-30 **1** **Cliff Bay (IRE)**[6] [3681] 5-9-0 **48**.............................. ShaneGray 2 53
(Keith Dalgleish) *hld up: rdn and hdwy over 1f out: led and edgd lft ins fnl f: hld on wl cl home* **10/3**[2]

0523 **2** *nk* **Donnelly's Rainbow (IRE)**[20] [3178] 6-9-9 **57**.............. LewisEdmunds 10 61
(Rebecca Bastiman) *stdd and swtchd rt s: hld up: shkn up over 2f out: effrt whn n.m.r over 1f out: swtchd rt and hdwy to chse wnr wl ins fnl f: r.o* **3/1**[1]

-400 **3** *nk* **Muraadef**[35] [2693] 4-9-2 **50**.............................. JamesSullivan 9 53
(Ruth Carr) *t.k.h: led and clr to over 2f out: hrd pressed over 1f out: hdd ins fnl f: kpt on* **25/1**

5200 **4** *hd* **Milton Road**[12] [3475] 4-9-4 **55**.............................. RowanScott(3) 1 58
(Rebecca Bastiman) *prom: effrt and ev ch on outside over 1f out to ins fnl f: one pce* **8/1**[3]

0000 **5** *½* **Searanger (USA)**[14] [3413] 6-9-6 **54**.............................. PaulMulrennan 3 56
(Rebecca Menzies) *hld up in tch: rdn over 2f out: outpcd and hung rt over 1f out: r.o ins fnl f* **10/1**

3065 **6** *shd* **Peachey Carnehan**[10] [3550] 5-9-12 **60**..............................(v) TomEaves 4 61
(Michael Mullineaux) *hld up in midfield: drvn along on wd outside over 2f out: kpt on same pce fr over 1f out* **14/1**

200- **7** *¾* **Destination Aim**[241] [8380] 12-9-2 **50**.............................. KevinStott 8 50
(Fred Watson) *midfield: drvn and outpcd over 2f out: rallied on outside fnl f: no imp* **50/1**

-300 **8** *hd* **Proceeding**[28] [2899] 4-9-8 **56**.............................. PaulHanagan 7 55
(Tracy Waggott) *chsd ldrs: drvn along over 2f out: outpcd fr over 1f out* **12/1**

2005 **9** *nk* **Temple Of Wonder (IRE)**[38] [2592] 3-9-2 **59**.............................. DavidNolan 5 57
(Liam Bailey) *hld up: pushed along over 2f out: effrt whn nt clr run over 1f out to ins fnl f: no imp (jockey said gelding was denied a clear run 1 1/2f out)* **33/1**

66 **10** *hd* **Rosin Box (IRE)**[13] [3448] 6-9-9 **57**.............................. PhilDennis 6 55
(Tristan Davidson) *chsd clr ldr: rdn over 2f out: wknd fnl f* **3/1**[1]

1m 31.1s (3.10) **Going Correction** +0.20s/f (Good) **10** Ran SP% **116.4**
WFA 3 from 4yo+ 9lb
Speed ratings (Par 101): **90,89,89,89,88 88,87,87,86,86**
CSF £13.52 CT £217.03 TOTE £3.90: £1.40, £1.40, £5.00; EX 16.00 Trifecta £366.00.
Owner K Comb **Bred** John Hutchinson **Trained** Carluke, S Lanarks

FOCUS
Add 11yds. A blanket finish to this low-grade handicap. Again, the field gravitated to the stands' side in the straight. The second has been rated near his latest effort.

3925 WATCH RACINGTV NOW H'CAP — 1m 3f 39y
5:00 (5:00) (Class 5) (0-70,72) 4-Y-O+
£4,204 (£1,251; £625; £312; £300; £300) **Stalls** High

Form — RPR

000- **1** **Bombero (IRE)**[199] [9332] 5-9-4 **67**.............................. BarryMcHugh 6 75
(Ed de Giles) *chsd ldr: led over 2f out: drifted rt ins fnl f: jst hld on* **9/1**

11-0 **2** *shd* **Matewan (IRE)**[25] [3022] 4-9-9 **72**..............................(p) PaulHanagan 7 79
(Ian Williams) *in tch: rdn and outpcd 3f out: rallied and ev ch fr over 1f out: carried rt ins fnl f: kpt on: jst hld* **9/2**[2]

1143 **3** *1½* **Sioux Frontier (IRE)**[18] [3250] 4-9-8 **71**.............................. LewisEdmunds 3 76
(Iain Jardine) *hld up: hdwy over 2f out: effrt and ev ch ins fnl f: no ex towards fin* **9/2**[2]

3-31 **4** *1½* **Majestic Stone (IRE)**[18] [3251] 5-7-9 **51** oh2.............. VictorSantos(7) 4 54
(Julie Camacho) *s.i.s: hld up: effrt and rdn on outside over 2f out: chsd ldrs over 1f out: no ex ins fnl f* **11/4**[1]

-024 **5** *¾* **Corton Lad**[18] [3250] 9-9-7 **70**..............................(vt) ShaneGray 2 71
(Keith Dalgleish) *led: rdn and hdd over 2f out: rallied: no ex fnl f* **8/1**[3]

4-40 **6** *¾* **Breathable**[23] [3095] 4-9-3 **66**.............................. RachelRichardson 1 66
(Tim Easterby) *chsd ldr: rdn over 2f out: outpcd appr fnl f* **9/2**[2]

10-0 **7** *1* **Iconic Code**[11] [3502] 4-9-2 **65**.............................. PaulMulrennan 5 64
(Keith Dalgleish) *hld up: stdy hdwy over 2f out: rdn over 1f out: sn n.d: btn fnl f* **8/1**[3]

2m 29.82s (0.12) **Going Correction** +0.20s/f (Good) **7** Ran SP% **113.4**
Speed ratings (Par 103): **107,106,105,104,104 103,102**
CSF £47.87 TOTE £9.10: £4.00, £2.20; EX 66.60 Trifecta £320.20.
Owner Woodham Walter Partnership **Bred** Nesco II **Trained** Ledbury, H'fords

FOCUS
Add 14yds. They were spread across the track approaching the final furlong in this modest handicap. The third has been rated close to form.

3926 EVERY RACE LIVE ON RACINGTV H'CAP — 1m 3f 39y
5:30 (5:31) (Class 5) (0-70,71) 3-Y-O
£4,204 (£1,251; £625; £312; £300; £300) **Stalls** High

Form — RPR

-206 **1** **Beechwood Jude (FR)**[16] [3358] 3-9-10 **71**.............................. ShaneGray 5 77
(Keith Dalgleish) *t.k.h: hld up: rdn over 3f out: hdwy on outside over 1f out: led ins fnl f: styd on wl* **5/1**[1]

0000 **2** *½* **Soloist (IRE)**[11] [3513] 3-9-7 **68**..............................(p) PaulHanagan 6 73
(William Haggas) *hld up in tch: rdn over 2f out: effrt over 1f out: chsd wnr ins fnl f: r.o* **7/1**

0003 **3** *½* **Brutalab**[18] [3270] 3-8-5 **52**.............................. RachelRichardson 10 56
(Tim Easterby) *prom: hdwy to ld over 2f out: edgd rt and hdd ins fnl f: one pce* **8/1**

0-35 **4** *nk* **Euro Implosion (IRE)**[19] [3226] 3-9-2 **63**.............................. KevinStott 1 66
(Keith Dalgleish) *trckd ldrs: effrt and ev ch over 1f out to ins fnl f: no ex* **6/1**[2]

-000 **5** *1½* **Menin Gate (IRE)**[19] [3226] 3-9-2 **63**.............................. JackGarritty 2 63
(Richard Fahey) *led to over 2f out: rallied: outpcd fnl f* **9/1**

-466 **6** *shd* **George Mallory**[24] [3052] 3-9-6 **67**.............................. TomEaves 4 67
(Kevin Ryan) *stdd s: hld up: rdn and outpcd 3f out: rallied over 1f out: kpt on: nt pce to chal* **13/2**[3]

3-55 **7** *hd* **Beaufort (IRE)**[18] [3249] 3-9-4 **65**..............................(p) PaulMulrennan 7 65
(Michael Dods) *t.k.h: cl up: ev ch over 2f out: rdn and hung rt over 1f out: sn no ex* **6/1**[2]

550- **8** *1¾* **Arms Of The Angel (GER)**[170] [9744] 3-8-10 **64**....... AidenSmithies(7) 9 61
(Mark Johnston) *hld up: rdn and outpcd 3f out: no imp fr 2f out* **20/1**

06-4 **9** *18* **Salam Zayed**[15] [3373] 3-9-5 **66**.............................. DavidNolan 8 32
(Richard Fahey) *hld up: drvn along and outpcd 3f out: struggling fr 2f out: t.o (jockey said gelding stopped quickly)* **6/1**[2]

6-06 **10** *3¾* **Ateescomponent (IRE)**[20] [3200] 3-9-1 **62**.............................. RobbieDowney 3 22
(David Barron) *plld hrd in midfield: drvn and struggling over 3f out: sn wknd: t.o* **25/1**

2m 30.19s (0.49) **Going Correction** +0.20s/f (Good) **10** Ran SP% **115.1**
Speed ratings (Par 99): **106,105,105,105,103 103,103,102,89,86**
CSF £39.18 CT £275.51 TOTE £5.30: £2.50, £1.80, £2.40; EX 44.60 Trifecta £236.60.
Owner Middleham Park Racing LXXXIV **Bred** T De La Heronniere & J Hebert **Trained** Carluke, S Lanarks

FOCUS
Add 14yds. This was marginally slower than the preceding 3yo event over the same trip. The fourth has been rated to his Beverley form two starts back.
T/Plt: £44.20 to a £1 stake. Pool: £64,946.15 - 1,070.42 winning units T/Qpdt: £16.50 to a £1 stake. Pool: £7,060.16 - 316.56 winning units **Richard Young**

CATTERICK (L-H)
Monday, June 17

OFFICIAL GOING: Soft (6.5)
Wind: fresh across Weather: cloudy

3927 EBF FILLIES' NOVICE STKS (PLUS 10 RACE) 5f
2:15 (2:16) (Class 5) 2-Y-O **£4,463** (£1,328; £663; £331) **Stalls** Low

Form RPR
3 **1** **Fashion Advice**[20] 3196 2-9-0 0 .... GrahamLee 7 78+
(Keith Dalgleish) *mde all: pushed clr appr fnl f: kpt on wl* **14/1**
3 **2** 2 1/4 **Keep Busy (IRE)**[49] 2184 2-9-0 0 .... JasonHart 4 70
(John Quinn) *chsd ldrs: pushed along over 2f out: rdn and kpt on fnl f: wnt 2nd nr fin* **8/1**
2104 **3** nk **Iva Go (IRE)**[21] 3156 2-9-4 0 .... DavidAllan 1 73
(Tim Easterby) *trckd ldrs: pushed along to chse ldr over 1f out: rdn and sn one pce: lost 2nd nr fin* **15/8**[1]
10 **4** 1/2 **Baileys In Bloom (FR)**[31] 2805 2-9-1 0 .... SeanDavis(3) 8 71
(Richard Fahey) *hld up on outer: pushed along over 2f out: rdn and sme hdwy appr fnl f: kpt on* **8/1**
5 2 1/4 **Lady Melody (IRE)** 2-9-0 0 .... DanielTudhope 2 59+
(David O'Meara) *hld up: pushed along 2f out: kpt on fnl f: nvr threatened ldrs* **8/1**
4 **6** 1 1/2 **Miss Lucy (IRE)**[18] 3244 2-9-0 0 .... BenCurtis 10 54+
(K R Burke) *dwlt and wnt rt s: chsd ldrs: rdn over 2f out: wknd ins fnl f* **5/1**[2]
53 **7** 1/2 **Blitzle**[30] 2840 2-8-11 0 .... BenRobinson(3) 5 52
(Ollie Pears) *hld up: racd quite keenly: pushed along 2f out: rdn ins fnl f: nvr threatened* **16/1**
210 **8** 1 3/4 **Infinite Grace**[31] 2805 2-9-4 0 .... CamHardie 9 50
(David O'Meara) *wnt rt s: hld up: pushed along over 2f out: rdn and wknd fnl f* **16/1**
006 **9** 1 1/2 **Bankawi**[12] 3477 2-9-0 0 .... NathanEvans 3 40
(Michael Easterby) *prom: rdn over 2f out: wknd over 1f out* **150/1**
52 **P** **Sneaky**[18] 3259 2-9-0 0 .... EdwardGreatrex 6
(Archie Watson) *hld up: rdn over 3f out: sn outpcd and bhd: eased and p.u and dismntd ins fnl f (jockey said filly lost action)* **13/2**[3]

1m 0.79s (0.29) **Going Correction** +0.075s/f (Good) **10** Ran SP% **117.2**
Speed ratings (Par 90): **100,96,95,95,91 89,88,85,83,**
CSF £121.76 TOTE £14.70: £4.50, £2.70, £1.10; EX 166.60 Trifecta £608.20.
Owner A R M Galbraith **Bred** A R M Galbraith **Trained** Carluke, S Lanarks

FOCUS
All distances as advertised. An open fillies' novice that went to one of the outsiders.

3928 MILLBRY HILL VETERANS' H'CAP 5f 212y
2:45 (2:45) (Class 5) (0-75,73) 6-Y-O+
£5,110 (£1,520; £759; £379; £300; £300) **Stalls** Low

Form RPR
606 **1** **Mujassam**[19] 3214 7-8-13 65 ....(b) DanielTudhope 4 75
(David O'Meara) *midfield: pushed along and hdwy over 1f out: drvn ins fnl f: kpt on: led towards fin* **7/2**[2]
1231 **2** 3/4 **Tricky Dicky**[7] 3657 6-9-4 70 5ex .... BenCurtis 12 78
(Roger Fell) *across fr wd stall to ld after 1f: rdn along over 1f out: drvn fnl 110yds: one pce and hdd towards fin* **13/8**[1]
-153 **3** 1 3/4 **Lucky Beggar (IRE)**[6] 3706 9-9-3 69 .... DavidAllan 1 71
(David C Griffiths) *stmbld s: sn midfield on inner: pushed along and hdwy over 1f out: sn chsd ldrs: rdn and kpt on fnl f (jockey said gelding stumbled leaving stalls)* **9/2**[3]
0010 **4** nk **Indian Pursuit (IRE)**[29] 2876 6-8-13 65 ....(v) JasonHart 5 66
(John Quinn) *led for 1f: prom: rdn over 1f out: no ex ins fnl f* **9/1**
0504 **5** 1 **B Fifty Two (IRE)**[5] 3716 10-8-5 60 ....(tp) JaneElliott(3) 8 58
(Marjorie Fife) *hld up: rdn 2f out: kpt on ins fnl f: nvr threatened* **16/1**
0240 **6** 1 1/2 **Socialites Red**[7] 3658 6-8-13 70 ....(p) TheodoreLadd(5) 9 63
(Scott Dixon) *chsd ldrs on outside: rdn and outpcd over 2f out: no threat after* **11/1**
0-00 **7** 1 1/2 **Rose Marmara**[31] 2809 6-9-5 71 ....(tp) CamHardie 7 60
(Brian Rothwell) *chsd ldrs: rdn over 2f out: wknd ins fnl f* **33/1**
45-0 **8** hd **Extrasolar**[30] 2847 9-8-11 63 ....(t) ConnorBeasley 10 51
(Geoffrey Harker) *hld up: nvr threatened* **33/1**
0000 **9** 3/4 **Robot Boy (IRE)**[7] 3658 9-9-2 73 .... HarrisonShaw(5) 3 59
(Marjorie Fife) *chsd ldrs on inner: rdn 2f out: wknd ins fnl f* **66/1**
2640 **10** 1 **Crosse Fire**[7] 3656 7-8-6 58 ....(p) PaddyMathers 11 40
(Scott Dixon) *slowly away: a towards rr* **20/1**
600 **11** 8 **Classic Pursuit**[28] 2893 8-9-3 69 ....(v) SamJames 2 26
(Marjorie Fife) *midfield on outer: racd quite keenly: rdn over 2f out: wknd over 1f out* **50/1**

1m 13.55s (-0.05) **Going Correction** +0.075s/f (Good) **11** Ran SP% **116.8**
Speed ratings: **103,102,99,99,97 95,93,93,92,91 80**
CSF £9.03 CT £25.81 TOTE £3.80: £1.10, £1.10, £1.70; EX 11.60 Trifecta £41.90.
Owner Thoroughbred British Racing **Bred** Bumble Bs, D F Powell & S Nicholls **Trained** Upper Helmsley, N Yorks

FOCUS
A weak sprint for the older boys and it was dominated by the market leaders. The second has been rated close to his old turf best.

3929 ZEEK DESIGN THANKS GERARD BROGAN CLAIMING STKS 1m 4f 13y
3:15 (3:16) (Class 6) 4-Y-O+
£3,428 (£1,020; £509; £300; £300; £300) **Stalls** Low

Form RPR
0-51 **1** **Grand Inquisitor**[17] 3300 7-10-0 86 ....(v) BenCurtis 8 75+
(Ian Williams) *prom: led gng wl over 2f out: sn clr: rdn out ins fnl f: eased nr fin* **8/11**[1]
6030 **2** 5 **Highway Robber**[38] 2591 6-8-5 44 ....(t) PaulaMuir(5) 5 49
(Wilf Storey) *midfield: rdn along 2f out: plugged on to go modest 2nd appr fnl f: no ch w wnr* **7/1**
-500 **3** 5 **Fillydelphia (IRE)**[6] 3708 8-8-9 43 ow2 ....(b1) SamJames 4 41
(Liam Bailey) *trckd ldrs: rdn over 2f out: wknd over 1f out* **16/1**
-000 **4** 3/4 **Dr Richard Kimble (IRE)**[11] 3514 4-8-7 75 .... AidanRedpath(7) 7 44
(Mark Johnston) *in tch: rdn over 2f out: wknd over 1f out* **6/1**[3]
0000 **5** 1 1/2 **Lots Ov (IRE)**[18] 3272 5-8-4 33 ....(p) RobertDodsworth(7) 6 39
(John Wainwright) *led: rdn and hdd over 2f out: sn wknd* **100/1**
5-50 **6** 1 **Mandarin Princess**[13] 3448 4-8-11 43 .... GrahamLee 1 38
(Kenny Johnson) *hld up in midfield: rdn 3f out: sn btn* **100/1**
-050 **7** 1 1/2 **Mirsaale**[38] 2575 9-9-11 88 ....(p) SeanDavis(3) 3 52
(Keith Dalgleish) *s.i.s and early reminders: hld up: rdn 4f out: sn btn (jockey said gelding was never travelling)* **3/1**[2]
8 12 **Windy Writer (IRE)**[16] 9-8-12 0 ....(tp) CamHardie 2 18
(Sam England) *slowly away: a towards rr (jockey said gelding was slowly away)* **40/1**

2m 41.73s (1.13) **Going Correction** +0.075s/f (Good) **8** Ran SP% **120.0**
Speed ratings (Par 101): **99,95,92,91,90 90,89,81**
CSF £7.51 TOTE £1.50: £1.10, £2.00, £3.00; EX 6.60 Trifecta £38.90.The winner was subject to a friendly claim of £12,000. Dr Richard Kimble was claimed by Mrs Marjorie Fife for £5,000.
Owner Macable Partnership & S Hassiakos **Bred** Floors Farming And Dominic Burke **Trained** Portway, Worcs

FOCUS
Desperately weak claiming form, with the favourite's only credible rival running a stinker. The fifth helps pin the level.

3930 EVERY RACE LIVE ON RACING TV H'CAP 7f 6y
3:45 (3:45) (Class 4) (0-80,81) 3-Y-O+
£6,727 (£2,002; £1,000; £500; £300; £300) **Stalls** Low

Form RPR
2534 **1** **Murdanova (IRE)**[21] 3147 6-9-9 71 ....(p) CamHardie 6 79
(Rebecca Menzies) *midfield: rdn and hdwy over 1f out: led 75yds out: styd on* **10/1**
0464 **2** 3/4 **Zylan (IRE)**[28] 2898 7-9-5 72 ....(p) BenSanderson(5) 8 78
(Roger Fell) *trckd ldrs: rdn to chal over 1f out: kpt on same pce* **12/1**
-620 **3** 1/2 **Stronsay (IRE)**[18] 3249 3-9-1 72 .... GrahamLee 9 74
(Bryan Smart) *trckd ldrs: rdn to ld over 1f out: hdd 75yds out: no ex* **6/1**[3]
22-0 **4** 1/2 **Theatre Of War (IRE)**[16] 3357 3-9-7 78 .... JasonHart 2 78
(Keith Dalgleish) *trckd ldrs: rdn along over 2f out: drvn and kpt on fnl f* **4/1**[2]
-603 **5** hd **Kuwait Station (IRE)**[24] 3051 3-9-10 81 .... DanielTudhope 4 81
(David O'Meara) *hld up: rdn over 2f out: sme hdwy on outside appr fnl f: kpt on: nrst fin (jockey said gelding was never travelling)* **10/3**[1]
-026 **6** 1 **Cameo Star (IRE)**[28] 2898 4-9-3 68 .... SeanDavis(3) 1 68
(Richard Fahey) *hld up: rdn over 2f out: kpt on ins fnl f: nvr involved* **8/1**
1-23 **7** hd **John Clare (IRE)**[18] 3273 3-9-0 74 .... ConorMcGovern(3) 7 71
(Pam Sly) *midfield on outside: racd quite keenly: rdn and hdwy over 1f out: wknd fnl 110yds* **10/3**[1]
-045 **8** 3 3/4 **Super Florence (IRE)**[31] 2789 4-8-12 63 ....(h) BenRobinson(3) 10 53
(Iain Jardine) *led: rdn over 2f out: hdd over 1f out: sn wknd* **33/1**
166 **9** 23 **Elenora Delight**[48] 2261 4-9-9 71 ....(t) DavidAllan 5
(Ron Barr) *dwlt: hld up: rdn 3f out: wknd and bhd* **80/1**

1m 27.58s (0.18) **Going Correction** +0.075s/f (Good)
WFA 3 from 4yo+ 9lb **9** Ran SP% **112.5**
Speed ratings (Par 105): **102,101,100,100,99 98,98,94,67**
CSF £118.18 CT £780.38 TOTE £11.30: £3.10, £3.60, £2.10; EX 144.10 Trifecta £663.80.
Owner Phil Slater **Bred** John Lyons **Trained** Mordon, Durham

FOCUS
Ordinary form. The third and fourth have been rated close to form.

3931 JOIN RACING TV NOW H'CAP 1m 7f 189y
4:15 (4:17) (Class 5) (0-70,71) 3-Y-O
£4,463 (£1,328; £663; £331; £300; £300) **Stalls** Low

Form RPR
0062 **1** **Champagne Marengo (IRE)**[20] 3197 3-8-11 55 ....(p) BenCurtis 9 66
(Ian Williams) *midfield: trckd ldrs 8f out: pushed along over 2f out: rdn to chse ldr over 1f out: drvn to ld 110yds out: styd on (vet said gelding lost left hind shoe)* **5/1**[2]
-46 **2** 1 1/4 **Platform Nineteen (IRE)**[32] 2769 3-9-3 61 ....(p1) CliffordLee 1 70+
(Michael Bell) *hld up: rdn along 3f out: hdwy on outer over 1f out: styd on wl: wnt 2nd towards fin* **17/2**
4413 **3** 1/2 **Victoriano (IRE)**[10] 3528 3-9-7 65 ....(b) EdwardGreatrex 10 73
(Archie Watson) *led after 2f: rdn 3f out: drvn over 1f out: hdd 110yds: no ex: lost 2nd towards fin* **7/1**[3]
2035 **4** 1/2 **Robeam (IRE)**[9] 3593 3-8-7 51 .... PaddyMathers 2 58
(Richard Fahey) *trckd ldrs: shuffled bk to midfield 10f out: rdn over 2f out: drvn and chse ldrs fnl f: styd on (vet said gelding lost right fore shoe)* **9/1**
0-33 **5** 1 1/2 **Anyonecanhaveitall**[12] 3474 3-9-7 65 .... PJMcDonald 5 70
(Mark Johnston) *prom: rdn along over 3f out: no ex fnl 110yds (jockey said gelding hung right-handed throughout)* **13/8**[1]
3020 **6** 1/2 **Nordano (GER)**[34] 2712 3-9-7 65 .... JasonHart 7 70
(Mark Johnston) *hld up: hdwy to trck ldrs 10f out: rdn along over 3f out: drvn and edgd lft over 1f out: no ex ins fnl f* **9/1**
-000 **7** hd **Feebi**[20] 3197 3-7-12 47 oh1 ow1 .... PaulaMuir(5) 6 51?
(Chris Fairhurst) *hld up in midfield: rdn over 2f out: no imp* **28/1**
3505 **8** 53 **Biz Markee (IRE)**[14] 3415 3-8-11 60 ....(p) BenSanderson(5) 3
(Roger Fell) *dwlt: sn midfield on inner: lost pl over 6f out: rdn 3f out: wknd* **33/1**
0-56 **9** 1 1/2 **Flo Jo's Girl**[20] 3197 3-8-3 47 .... CamHardie 4
(Tim Easterby) *led for 2f: prom: rdn over 3f out: wknd 2f out: eased* **12/1**
2466 **10** 34 **Alpasu (IRE)**[12] 3474 3-9-10 71 ....(bt1) SeanDavis(3) 8
(Archie Watson) *hld up: drvn over 4f out: sn wknd and bhd: eased* **22/1**

3m 34.67s (-1.33) **Going Correction** +0.075s/f (Good) **10** Ran SP% **116.2**
Speed ratings (Par 99): **106,105,105,104,104 103,103,77,76,59**
CSF £45.62 CT £298.87 TOTE £5.60: £1.50, £2.40, £2.20; EX 58.60 Trifecta £283.30.
Owner Champagne Charlies Club **Bred** Helen Lyons **Trained** Portway, Worcs

FOCUS
No great gallop on early in this moderate 3yo staying handicap and as a result there was a bit of a bunched finish. The winner has been rated as improving a touch on his his Redcar second.

3932 FOLLOW @RACINGTV ON TWITTER MAIDEN STKS 7f 6y
4:45 (4:45) (Class 5) 3-Y-O+ **£4,463** (£1,328; £663; £331) **Stalls** Low

Form RPR
3-00 **1** **Bumbledom**[18] 3270 3-9-5 59 ....(p1) ConnorBeasley 5 68
(Michael Dods) *led: rdn and hdd over 1f out: remained chalng: drvn to ld again 110yds out: kpt on* **6/1**[3]

6 **2** ½ **Grab And Run (IRE)**[34] 2713 3-9-2 0 SeanDavis(3) 4 67
(Richard Fahey) *trckd ldrs: rdn to chal over 2f out: edgd rt to wd outside over 1f out: drvn and edgd lft fnl f: kpt on* 7/2[2]

3 **3** ¾ **Morning Duel (IRE)**[11] 3517 3-9-5 0 DanielTudhope 1 65
(David O'Meara) *prom: rdn into narrow ld over 1f out: hdd 110yds: no ex* 10/11[1]

6 **4** 3½ **Cuba Ruba**[9] 3565 3-9-5 0 DavidAllan 10 56+
(Tim Easterby) *s.i.s: hld up in rr: swtchd rt to outside 2f out: rdn along and hdwy appr fnl f: kpt on* 14/1

00 **5** 1 **Lucky Number**[11] 3510 3-9-2 0 GeorgiaCox(3) 3 53
(William Haggas) *in tch: pushed along 3f out: rdn and outpcd fr over 1f out* 6/1[3]

6 **6** ½ **High Fort (IRE)**[14] 3412 4-10-0 0 JasonHart 8 55
(Karen McLintock) *hld up: pushed along 2f out: nvr threatened (jockey said gelding was restless in stalls)* 50/1

00-4 **7** nk **Pearl's Calling (IRE)**[20] 3203 4-9-4 46 PaulaMuir(5) 2 49
(Ron Barr) *nvr bttr than midfield* 33/1

-000 **8** nk **Duba Plains**[13] 3452 4-10-0 43 CamHardie 9 53
(Kenny Johnson) *hld up: nvr threatened* 125/1

000- **9** 12 **One For Brad (IRE)**[261] 7753 4-9-2 41 HarryRussell(7) 6 17
(Alan Berry) *midfield: rdn over 3f out: wknd 2f out* 200/1

00- **10** 12 **Mixed Up Miss (IRE)**[251] 8073 3-9-0 0 (h) GrahamLee 7
(Bryan Smart) *hld up: wknd and bhd fnl 3f* 33/1

1m 28.18s (0.78) **Going Correction** +0.075s/f (Good) **10** Ran SP% **119.0**
WFA 3 from 4yo 9lb
Speed ratings (Par 103): **98,97,96,92,91 90,90,90,76,62**
CSF £27.50 TOTE £6.20: £1.50, £1.10, £1.20; EX 30.90 Trifecta £71.20.
Owner G Thompson And M Dods **Bred** Joyce Wallsgrove **Trained** Denton, Co Durham

FOCUS
Modest maiden form. The second has been rated to his debut form.

3933 RACING AGAIN 1ST JULY APPRENTICE H'CAP 5f
5:15 (5:17) (Class 6) (0-55,54) 4-Y-O+
£3,428 (£1,020; £509; £300; £300; £300) Stalls Low

Form RPR

0046 **1** **Economic Crisis (IRE)**[11] 3504 10-9-4 54 HarryRussell(5) 6 61
(Alan Berry) *rrd s: hld up: stdy hdwy fr 3f out: chsd ldr appr fnl f: drvn to ld 110yds out: edgd rt: kpt on* 6/1[2]

3000 **2** 2½ **Bluella**[11] 3518 4-9-0 45 (v[1]) SeamusCronin 2 43
(Robyn Brisland) *led: briefly clr over 1f out: rdn and edgd lft appr fnl f: hdd 110yds out: no ex* 20/1

6600 **3** 1½ **Tilsworth Rose**[12] 3476 5-8-9 45 (b) GavinAshton(5) 9 38
(J R Jenkins) *midfield: rdn along 2f out: kpt on fnl f* 18/1

2400 **4** ¾ **Spirit Of Zebedee (IRE)**[19] 3213 6-9-9 54 (v) ThoreHammerHansen 5 44
(John Quinn) *midfield: rdn over 2f out: kpt on fnl f* 7/1

3202 **5** ½ **Pearl Noir**[11] 3518 9-9-6 54 (b) TheodoreLadd(3) 1 42
(Scott Dixon) *chsd ldrs: rdn over 2f out: outpcd and btn over 1f out* 7/2[1]

0504 **6** hd **Rockley Point**[13] 3452 6-9-8 53 BenSanderson 10 40
(Katie Scott) *slowly away: outpcd in rr tl kpt on fnl f* 13/2[3]

1000 **7** nk **Furni Factors**[19] 3213 4-9-3 53 (b) IsobelFrancis(5) 8 39
(Ronald Thompson) *hld up: sme late hdwy: nvr threatened* 14/1

5030 **8** 1¼ **Racquet**[5] 3723 6-9-1 46 (b) HarrisonShaw 11 28
(Ruth Carr) *chsd ldrs: rdn along over 2f out: edgd rt and wknd ins fnl f* 7/1

-600 **9** hd **Jorvik Prince**[13] 3452 5-9-4 54 EllaMcCain(5) 12 35
(Julia Brooke) *hld up: nvr threatened* 33/1

00-0 **10** 1 **Princess Apollo**[35] 2678 5-9-0 45 AndrewBreslin 13 22
(Donald Whillans) *a outpcd towards rr* 66/1

00-0 **11** hd **Lady Joanna Vassa (IRE)**[35] 2678 6-9-0 45 (v) DarraghKeenan 4 22
(Richard Guest) *prom: rdn over 2f out: wknd fnl f* 20/1

-006 **12** ½ **Mitchum**[11] 3518 10-9-0 45 PoppyBridgwater 7 20
(Ron Barr) *hld up: pushed along: nvr threatened* 10/1

050- **13** 1 **Mightaswellsmile**[199] 9329 5-9-0 45 PaulaMuir 3 16
(Ron Barr) *chsd ldrs: rdn over 2f out: wknd over 1f out* 12/1

1m 1.22s (0.72) **Going Correction** +0.075s/f (Good) **13** Ran SP% **117.5**
Speed ratings (Par 101): **97,93,90,89,88 88,87,85,85,83 83,82,81**
CSF £124.54 CT £2103.61 TOTE £6.80: £2.50, £7.10, £6.10; EX 146.20 Trifecta £2602.20.
Owner William Burns & Alan Berry **Bred** Philip Hore Jnr **Trained** Cockerham, Lancs

FOCUS
Lowly sprinting form, but the veteran winner did well to overcame rearing at the start. The second and third help confirm the level.
T/Plt: £35.30 to a £1 stake. Pool: £65,145.83 - 1,344.43 winning units T/Qpdt: £12.70 to a £1 stake. Pool: £7,601.43 - 441.94 winning units **Andrew Sheret**

3767 NOTTINGHAM (L-H)
Monday, June 17

OFFICIAL GOING: Soft (heavy in places; 6.1)
Wind: Fresh against Weather: Sunny spells

3934 EBF FILLIES' NOVICE AUCTION STKS (PLUS 10 RACE) 6f 18y
5:50 (5:51) (Class 5) 2-Y-O £3,881 (£1,155; £577) Stalls High

Form RPR

22 **1** **Go Well Spicy (IRE)**[9] 3573 2-9-0 0 CharlesBishop 1 70
(Mick Channon) *s.i.s: sn chsng ldr: shkn up over 2f out: led over 1f out: rdn out* 4/11[1]

2 2 **Sesame Birah (IRE)** 2-9-0 0 TomMarquand 3 64
(Richard Hannon) *led: shkn up and qcknd over 2f out: hdd over 1f out: edgd lft and styd on same pce ins fnl f* 11/4[2]

0 **3** 2¼ **Boston Girl (IRE)**[9] 3578 2-9-0 0 RobertHavlin 4 57?
(Ed Dunlop) *s.i.s: sn prom: swtchd lft over 2f out: shkn up over 1f out: no ex ins fnl f* 14/1[3]

1m 17.67s (3.87) **Going Correction** +0.375s/f (Good) **3** Ran SP% **106.6**
Speed ratings (Par 90): **89,86,83**
CSF £1.63 TOTE £1.30; EX 1.80 Trifecta £2.10.
Owner Six Or Sticks **Bred** Grangemore Stud **Trained** West Ilsley, Berks

FOCUS
Outer track in use. The course survived a 7am inspection, and a dry, breezy day improved conditions from the overnight heavy. The stands' bend rail was stepped out 8yds, adding 24yds to the concluding stayers' handicap. The stalls were on the stands' side for this fillies' auction sprint much weakened by non-runners. A token rating has been given.

3935 BET AT RACINGTV.COM H'CAP 6f 18y
6:20 (6:20) (Class 4) (0-85,87) 3-Y-O £6,469 (£1,925; £962; £481; £300) Stalls High

Form RPR

-424 **1** **Aplomb (IRE)**[16] 3357 3-9-6 83 TomMarquand 6 95+
(William Haggas) *trckd ldrs: racd keenly: swtchd lft over 2f out: nt clr run and swtchd rt over 1f out: n.m.r and r.o to ld wl ins fnl f: comf* 6/4[1]

3302 **2** 1¾ **James Watt (IRE)**[7] 3659 3-9-4 84 CameronNoble(3) 4 88
(Michael Bell) *chsd ldr tl led 2f out: rdn and edgd rt ins fnl f: sn hdd: styd on same pce towards fin* 7/2[3]

1310 **3** shd **Lady Calcaria**[5] 3719 3-9-0 77 DuranFentiman 1 80
(Tim Easterby) *chsd ldrs: rdn and ev ch ins fnl f: styd on same pce towards fin* 11/4[2]

1-50 **4** 2¼ **Welcoming (FR)**[38] 2567 3-9-2 79 SilvestreDeSousa 5 75
(Mark Johnston) *hld up: racd keenly: swtchd lft over 2f out: hdwy over 1f out: sn rdn: no ex ins fnl f* 11/2

021- **5** 6 **Essenza (IRE)**[178] 9670 3-8-7 70 RoystonFfrench 7 47
(Richard Fahey) *racd keenly: led at stdy pce: shkn up and hdd 2f out: hmpd over 1f out: wknd fnl f (jockey said filly ran too free)* 20/1

1m 16.67s (2.87) **Going Correction** +0.375s/f (Good) **5** Ran SP% **109.0**
Speed ratings (Par 101): **95,92,92,89,81**
CSF £6.89 TOTE £2.30: £1.20, £1.60; EX 7.30 Trifecta £13.30.
Owner Ms Fiona Carmichael **Bred** Anglia Bloodstock Ltd & Mr C Humber **Trained** Newmarket, Suffolk

FOCUS
Stalls on stands' side. Not hard to mark up the effort in victory of the favourite in this feature sprint handicap. The third has been rated to form.

3936 RACINGTV.COM H'CAP (FOR HORSES WHICH HAVE NOT WON IN 2019) 5f 8y
6:50 (6:51) (Class 5) (0-75,77) 4-Y-O+
£3,780 (£1,131; £565; £300; £300; £300) Stalls High

Form RPR

244 **1** **Prominna**[14] 3425 9-8-4 53 HayleyTurner 8 60
(Tony Carroll) *hld up: pushed along and hdwy 1/2-way: rdn to ld and hung lft over 1f out: styd on* 12/1

-033 **2** nk **Hawaam (IRE)**[16] 3360 4-10-0 77 (p) SilvestreDeSousa 5 83
(Roger Fell) *led: rdn and hdd over 1f out: edgd lft and rallied ins fnl f: styd on* 2/1[2]

0333 **3** ¾ **National Glory (IRE)**[9] 3576 4-9-1 64 (b) LukeMorris 2 67
(Archie Watson) *s.i.s: pushed along in rr: swtchd lft and hdwy over 1f out: sn rdn: styd on* 11/1

2644 **4** ½ **Global Melody**[4] 3771 4-8-10 66 (v) GraceMcEntee(7) 4 68
(Phil McEntee) *chsd ldrs: rdn and edgd rt over 1f out: kpt on (jockey said gelding hung right under pressure)* 15/8[1]

-026 **5** 1¾ **Rickyroadboy**[37] 2625 4-9-2 65 DougieCostello 6 60
(Mark Walford) *chsd ldr: rdn 1/2-way: lost 2nd and bmpd over 1f out: hung lft and no ex ins fnl f* 7/1[3]

2650 **6** ½ **Something Lucky (IRE)**[13] 3443 7-9-7 70 (b) AlistairRawlinson 1 63
(Michael Appleby) *s.i.s and stmbld s: outpcd: r.o ins fnl f: nvr nrr* 12/1

/450 **7** 6 **Just For The Craic (IRE)**[49] 2206 4-8-10 59 RossaRyan 3 31
(Neil Mulholland) *s.i.s: sn prom: lost pl 1/2-way: carried lft and wknd over 1f out* 14/1

1m 2.68s (2.48) **Going Correction** +0.375s/f (Good) **7** Ran SP% **111.0**
Speed ratings (Par 103): **95,94,93,92,89 88,79**
CSF £34.33 CT £267.08 TOTE £11.60: £5.40, £1.30; EX 33.90 Trifecta £147.30.
Owner Mayden Stud **Bred** Mayden Stud, J A And D S Dewhurst **Trained** Cropthorne, Worcs

FOCUS
Stalls on stands' side. A race confined to horses who had not won in 2019. The winner has been rated in line with his best over the past year.

3937 INTRODUCING RACING TV H'CAP 1m 2f 50y
7:20 (7:20) (Class 5) (0-75,73) 4-Y-O+ £3,881 (£1,155; £577; £300; £300) Stalls Low

Form RPR

0002 **1** **Tangramm**[25] 3022 7-9-2 68 (p) RyanTate 2 75+
(Dean Ivory) *led early: chsd ldr: shkn up to ld over 1f out: hung lft ins fnl f: rdn out* 5/1

-005 **2** ½ **Overtrumped**[10] 3547 4-8-8 60 HayleyTurner 7 65
(Mike Murphy) *s.i.s: sn chsng ldrs: rdn and outpcd over 3f out: rallied fnl f: r.o* 13/2

4445 **3** ½ **The Night King**[32] 2763 4-9-4 70 (p) CharlesBishop 4 74
(Mick Quinn) *hld up in tch: shkn up over 3f out: outpcd over 2f out: rallied fnl f: styd on* 3/1[2]

/540 **4** 1 **Deinonychus**[11] 3500 8-8-9 61 (p[1]) LukeMorris 5 63
(Michael Appleby) *sn led: shkn up and qcknd over 3f out: rdn and hdd over 1f out: edgd lft ins fnl f: styd on same pce* 9/2[3]

-105 **5** 14 **Bristol Missile (USA)**[9] 3575 5-9-1 67 PatCosgrave 6 41
(Richard Price) *hld up: hdwy over 3f out: rdn over 1f out: sn wknd (trainer could offer no explanation for the gelding's performance)* 13/8[1]

2m 15.95s (2.55) **Going Correction** +0.375s/f (Good) **5** Ran SP% **111.3**
Speed ratings (Par 103): **104,103,103,102,91**
CSF £34.10 TOTE £4.90: £1.30, £3.40; EX 19.30 Trifecta £87.90.
Owner Roger S Beadle **Bred** W G H Barrons **Trained** Radlett, Herts

FOCUS
Stalls on inner. Immediate compensation for one who appeared to have let slip a big-price win last time. It's been rated around the third to his recent form.

3938 LIKE RACING TV ON FACEBOOK H'CAP 1m 2f 50y
7:50 (7:50) (Class 6) (0-60,61) 3-Y-O
£3,234 (£962; £481; £300; £300; £300) Stalls Low

Form RPR

-400 **1** **Firewater**[11] 3513 3-9-7 60 (p) TonyHamilton 3 66
(Richard Fahey) *pushed along to chse ldrs: lost pl 6f out: hdwy over 2f out: chsd ldr over 1f out: rdn and r.o to ld nr fin* 6/1[3]

-503 **2** hd **Mukha Magic**[18] 3256 3-9-5 58 (v[1]) LukeMorris 5 64
(Gay Kelleway) *chsd ldrs: led over 2f out: rdn over 1f out: edgd lft ins fnl f: hdd nr fin* 9/2[1]

3004 **3** ½ **Tails I Win (CAN)**[18] 3246 3-9-1 57 (h) CameronNoble(3) 2 62
(Roger Fell) *prom: nt clr run and lost pl over 8f out: nt clr run and swtchd rt over 2f out: hdwy sn after: rdn over 1f out: r.o wl* 5/1[2]

400- **4** *3 1/2* **Pinkie Pie (IRE)**[292] 6667 3-8-7 **46** oh1 CamHardie 1 44
(Andrew Crook) *s.i.s: hld up: hdwy over 2f out: rdn over 1f out: edgd lft and styd on same pce fnl f* **66/1**

0036 **5** *6* **Lethal Laura**[17] 3299 3-8-7 **46** oh1 (p[1]) JosephineGordon 10 34
(James Given) *plld hrd and prom: ev ch over 2f out: sn rdn: wknd fnl f* **16/1**

660 **6** *2* **Blue Beirut (IRE)**[65] 1771 3-9-5 **58** CharlesBishop 4 42
(William Muir) *s.i.s: sn pushed along in rr: rdn over 3f out: nvr nrr* **5/1**[2]

0 **7** *1 1/4* **Holy Hymn (IRE)**[48] 2249 3-9-8 **61** DanielMuscutt 9 43
(Kevin Frost) *hld up: pushed along over 5f out: rdn over 3f out: wknd 2f out* **14/1**

0-00 **8** *18* **Legend Island (FR)**[33] 2734 3-9-4 **57** HectorCrouch 7 6
(Ed Walker) *sn led: hdd over 6f out: remained handy tl rdn over 2f out: sn wknd* **6/1**[3]

-400 **9** *2* **Chance Of Glory (FR)**[27] 2930 3-8-11 **50** SilvestreDeSousa 8
(Mark Johnston) *hld up in tch: chsd ldr over 5f out: led over 3f out: rdn and hdd over 2f out: wknd wl over 1f out* **8/1**

000 **10** *2* **George Formby**[68] 1676 3-9-3 **56** (h[1]) JackMitchell 11
(Hugo Palmer) *prom: led over 6f out: rdn and hdd 3f out: sn wknd* **10/1**

2m 15.88s (2.48) **Going Correction** +0.375s/f (Good) **10 Ran SP% 114.3**
Speed ratings (Par 97): **105,104,104,101,96 95,94,79,78,76**
CSF £32.47 CT £144.67 TOTE £5.30: £1.40, £1.90, £1.60; EX 36.60 Trifecta £83.10.
Owner Mrs H Steel **Bred** Mrs H Steel **Trained** Musley Bank, N Yorks

FOCUS
Stalls on inner. Competitive, and a winning time 0.07 seconds quicker than the preceding 0-75 event. The third has been rated to the best of her Irish form.

3939 JOIN RACING TV NOW H'CAP — 1m 75y
8:20 (8:21) (Class 6) (0-65,67) 4-Y-O+
£3,234 (£962; £481; £300; £300; £300) **Stalls Centre**

Form — RPR

/-01 **1** **Fitzrovia**[4] 3781 4-9-3 **59** 5ex PatCosgrave 11 71+
(Ed de Giles) *hld up: nt clr run over 2f out: sn swtchd rt: hdwy over 1f out: shkn up to ld ins fnl f: qcknd clr: easily* **9/4**[1]

0-02 **2** *2 3/4* **Tom's Anna (IRE)**[17] 3296 9-7-10 **45** SophieRalston(7) 13 48
(Sean Regan) *racd keenly: sn led: shkn up over 1f out: rdn: edgd rt and hdd ins fnl f: sn outpcd* **12/1**

2025 **3** *1 3/4* **Apache Blaze**[13] 3449 4-9-2 **63** (p) SeamusCronin(5) 14 62
(Robyn Brisland) *led early: chsd ldrs: nt clr run wl over 1f out: rdn ins fnl f: styd on same pce* **8/1**

6232 **4** *2 1/4* **Snooker Jim**[5] 3730 4-8-4 **53** (t) TobyEley(7) 4 47
(Steph Hollinshead) *prom: hung rt over 4f out: shkn up over 2f out: styd on same pce fnl f* **11/4**[2]

0-45 **5** *nk* **Foxy Rebel**[6] 3682 5-8-3 **45** CamHardie 12 38
(Ruth Carr) *s.i.s: sn prom: chsd ldr 4f out tl rdn over 1f out: wknd ins fnl f* **25/1**

0000 **6** *1 1/2* **Reshaan (IRE)**[6] 3687 4-8-13 **55** RossaRyan 2 45
(Alexandra Dunn) *prom: lost pl over 6f out: hdwy u.p over 2f out: no ex fnl f* **33/1**

3330 **7** *nse* **Break The Silence**[17] 3325 5-8-8 **50** (p) LukeMorris 5 40
(Scott Dixon) *prom: chsd ldr over 6f out tl 4f out: rdn over 2f out: no ex fnl f* **8/1**

0511 **8** *nk* **Fly True**[57] 1967 6-9-2 **58** NickyMackay 6 47
(Ivan Furtado) *s.i.s: hld up: nt clr run wl over 2f out: nvr on terms* **25/1**

-354 **9** *shd* **Shazzab (IRE)**[38] 2585 4-9-2 **58** TonyHamilton 3 47
(Richard Fahey) *chsd ldrs: rdn over 2f out: no ex fnl f* **15/2**[3]

0000 **10** *4 1/2* **Aljunood (IRE)**[37] 2631 5-8-7 **49** HayleyTurner 1 28
(John Norton) *s.i.s: hld up: hdwy u.p on outer over 2f out: wknd over 1f out* **33/1**

100- **11** *1* **Maldonado (FR)**[268] 7523 5-9-5 **61** NathanEvans 8 38
(Michael Easterby) *broke wl: sn stdd and lost pl: shkn up over 2f out: sn hung lft and wknd* **33/1**

660- **12** *6* **Kings Academy**[244] 8308 5-9-4 **60** (p) DuranFentiman 9 24
(John Mackie) *hld up: rdn over 3f out: sn rdn: wknd wl over 1f out* **20/1**

1m 47.63s (0.93) **Going Correction** +0.375s/f (Good) **12 Ran SP% 121.3**
Speed ratings (Par 101): **107,104,102,100,99 98,98,98,98,93 92,86**
CSF £28.10 CT £167.63 TOTE £3.10: £1.30, £3.60, £2.50; EX 26.10 Trifecta £171.00.
Owner Simon Treacher & Clarissa Casdagali **Bred** Mrs Fiona Denniff **Trained** Ledbury, H'fords

FOCUS
Stalls in centre. A workaday handicap taken apart by one far better than this grade. The winner has been rated as confirming his Yarmouth form.

3940 FOLLOW @RACINGTV ON TWITTER H'CAP (A JOCKEY CLUB GRASSROOTS STAYERS' SERIES QUALIFIER) — 1m 6f
8:50 (8:50) (Class 5) (0-70,70) 4-Y-O+
£3,881 (£1,155; £577; £300; £300; £300) **Stalls Low**

Form — RPR

0-01 **1** **Battle Of Issus (IRE)**[11] 3500 4-8-10 **59** (b) SilvestreDeSousa 10 68
(David Menuisier) *led after 1f: shkn up over 4f out: rdn over 2f out: all out* **11/8**[1]

-243 **2** *hd* **Cristal Spirit**[12] 3467 4-9-6 **69** (p) PatCosgrave 1 77
(George Baker) *led 1f: chsd ldrs: rdn to chse wnr over 1f out: r.o wl* **6/1**[3]

3-02 **3** *1 1/2* **War Brigade (FR)**[8] 3633 5-9-3 **69** (p[1]) CameronNoble(3) 2 75
(Ian Williams) *chsd wnr after 2f: rdn over 2f out: lost 2nd over 1f out: styd on* **11/4**[2]

0453 **4** *4 1/2* **Searching (IRE)**[16] 3361 7-9-2 **68** GemmaTutty(3) 4 68
(Karen Tutty) *hld up: bhd 10f out: hdwy over 1f out: nt trble ldrs* **12/1**

1/0- **5** *1 1/4* **Master Dancer**[23] 5872 8-9-7 **70** (p) CharlesBishop 8 68
(Tim Vaughan) *hld up: hdwy over 2f out: rdn over 1f out: no ex fnl f* **25/1**

121 **6** *3/4* **Heron (USA)**[20] 3205 5-9-3 **66** (p) DanielMuscutt 5 63
(Brett Johnson) *chsd ldrs: rdn over 3f out: no ex fnl f* **9/1**

0025 **7** *6* **Royal Flag**[17] 3349 9-9-0 **66** BenRobinson(3) 9 54
(Brian Ellison) *sn prom: pushed along over 5f out: rdn and wknd over 2f out (jockey said gelding was never travelling)* **16/1**

P040 **8** *nk* **Omotesando**[30] 2819 9-8-11 **60** (b) HayleyTurner 6 48
(Oliver Greenall) *s.i.s: hld up: hdwy over 2f out: sn rdn: wknd over 1f out* **28/1**

3m 11.5s (5.10) **Going Correction** +0.375s/f (Good) **8 Ran SP% 113.9**
Speed ratings (Par 103): **100,99,99,96,95 95,91,91**
CSF £10.16 CT £19.85 TOTE £2.50: £1.30, £1.60, £1.10; EX 8.90 Trifecta £39.10.
Owner Clive Washbourn **Bred** J Higgins **Trained** Pulborough, W Sussex

FOCUS
Actual race distance 1m6f24yds, stalls on inner. The combination of a smart ride and a runner from a yard in searing form got the job done in this stayers' event. The winner has been rated as backing up his Hamilton win, and the third to his latest.

T/Plt: £17.10 to a £1 stake. Pool: £46,474.45 - 1,974.52 winning units T/Qpdt: £9.70 to a £1 stake. Pool: £5,098.24 - 388.10 winning units **Colin Roberts**

3659 WINDSOR (R-H)
Monday, June 17

OFFICIAL GOING: Good to soft changing to good to soft (good in places) after race 2 (6.10)
Wind: Moderate, mostly behind in home straight Weather: Fine

3941 VISIT MARATHONBET.CO.UK APPRENTICE H'CAP — 1m 3f 99y
5:40 (5:43) (Class 6) (0-65,67) 4-Y-O+
£3,105 (£924; £461; £300; £300; £300) **Stalls Low**

Form — RPR

/-12 **1** **Seaborn (IRE)**[25] 3015 5-9-10 **62** WilliamCarver 13 71
(Patrick Chamings) *cl up: shkn up to ld jst over 1f out: styd on wl: readily* **3/1**[1]

203 **2** *3/4* **Movie Star (GER)**[18] 3276 4-9-10 **62** CierenFallon 3 68
(Amy Murphy) *trckd ldr after 5f: shkn up to ld 2f out: rdn and hdd jst over 1f out: styd on but readily hld* **9/1**

0-01 **3** *nk* **Kaylen's Mischief**[5] 3740 6-8-12 **50** 5ex ScottMcCullagh 9 55
(D J Jeffreys) *restrained into last pair s: rapid prog to ld after 3f: rdn and hdd 2f out: kpt on against rail fnl f (jockey said gelding jumped awkwardly leaving stalls)* **9/2**[2]

4-21 **4** *nk* **Broad Appeal**[21] 3155 5-9-12 **64** TylerSaunders 8 69+
(Jonathan Portman) *hld up in rr: prog on outer 3f out: rdn 2f out: styd on fnl f: nrst fin* **13/2**[3]

0000 **5** *1* **Esspeegee**[11] 3511 6-9-5 **60** (p) JessicaCooley(3) 12 63+
(Alan Bailey) *s.s: t.k.h: hld up in rr: prog over 2f out: urged along and kpt on over 1f out: nt pce to threaten (jockey said gelding was slowly away)* **50/1**

0533 **6** *nk* **Seventii**[5] 3740 5-8-7 **45** AledBeech 1 48
(Robert Eddery) *hld up towards rr: rdn over 2f out: kpt on against rail over 1f out: nvr able to threaten* **10/1**

4560 **7** *2* **Captain Scott (IRE)**[10] 3547 4-9-5 **62** (b[1]) LukeCatton(5) 10 62
(Heather Main) *w ldr 3f: trckd ldrs after: rdn and in tch 2f out: wknd over 1f out* **50/1**

-500 **8** *hd* **Rocksette**[16] 3348 5-8-5 **50** (p) LouisGaroghan(7) 15 49
(Gary Moore) *racd wd: prom: urged along over 2f out: wknd over 1f out (jockey said mare ran too free)* **14/1**

00/6 **9** *1 1/4* **Tulane (IRE)**[25] 3022 4-9-5 **60** GeorgiaDobie(3) 14 57
(Richard Phillips) *hld up in rr: prog over 3f out: chsd ldrs over 2f out: wknd over 1f out* **8/1**

5-63 **10** *2 1/2* **King Athelstan (IRE)**[20] 3186 4-9-3 **60** RhysClutterbuck(5) 11 53
(Gary Moore) *led 3f: lost pl rapidly 1/2-way: struggling in last pair 4f out: no ch after* **11/1**

-006 **11** *3/4* **Rainbow Jazz (IRE)**[75] 1525 4-9-6 **58** (be) Pierre-LouisJamin 6 50
(Adam West) *prom: trckd ldr after 3f tl after 5f: wknd over 2f out* **40/1**

5000 **12** *3/4* **Contrast (IRE)**[47] 2291 5-9-6 **63** MarcoGhiani(5) 4 54+
(Michael Easterby) *hld up in last pair: nvr any prog and nvr in it (jockey said gelding clipped heels 1f after start)* **20/1**

0/0- **13** *hd* **Briac (FR)**[41] 2202 8-8-4 **45** SeanKirrane(3) 2 36
(Tim Vaughan) *hld up in rr: rdn and swtchd to outer 3f out: no prog 2f out: wknd* **16/1**

2m 30.53s (0.83) **Going Correction** +0.025s/f (Good) **13 Ran SP% 118.7**
Speed ratings (Par 101): **98,97,97,97,96 96,94,94,93,91 91,90,90**
CSF £29.31 CT £121.02 TOTE £3.40: £1.50, £3.20, £2.50; EX 36.00 Trifecta £262.50.
Owner Ian Beach **Bred** Michael Fennessy **Trained** Baughurst, Hants

FOCUS
It was dry overnight and on race day. Add 23yds. A modest handicap for apprentice riders.

3942 DOWNLOAD THE MARATHONBET APP EBF NOVICE STKS — 5f 21y
6:10 (6:11) (Class 5) 2-Y-O
£3,752 (£1,116; £557; £278) **Stalls Centre**

Form — RPR

30 **1** **Shammah (IRE)**[12] 3461 2-9-0 0 SeanLevey 6 81
(Richard Hannon) *mde all: pushed along and drew clr over 1f out: v comf* **2/1**[2]

6 **2** *5* **Newyorkstateofmind**[9] 3595 2-9-5 0 JasonWatson 2 66
(William Muir) *chsd wnr: shkn up and outpcd over 1f out: kpt on same pce after* **15/2**[3]

3 *1 1/2* **Hubert (IRE)** 2-9-5 0 OisinMurphy 5 61
(Sylvester Kirk) *dwlt: sn chsd ldrs: rdn and outpcd wl over 1f out: kpt on to win battle for 3rd fnl f* **10/1**

4 *nse* **Waddat (IRE)** 2-9-5 0 ShaneKelly 4 60
(Richard Hughes) *v free to post: plld hrd: cl up: outpcd wl over 1f out: kpt on again ins fnl f* **9/1**

5 **5** *nk* **Billy Button (IRE)**[21] 3141 2-9-5 0 MartinDwyer 8 59
(Dean Ivory) *prom on outer: pushed along and outpcd wl over 1f out: stl ch of a pl ins fnl f: one pce nr fin* **16/1**

6 *5* **Passing Nod** 2-9-5 0 JamesDoyle 3 41+
(William Haggas) *nvr on terms w ldrs: pushed along and lft bhd over 1f out* **7/4**[1]

7 *4 1/2* **She Strides On** 2-9-0 0 GeorgeDowning 1 20
(Mick Channon) *scratchy to post: sn struggling in last pair: nvr a factor* **14/1**

8 *2* **Helluvasunset** 2-9-0 0 FergusSweeney 7 13
(Mark Usher) *slowly away: a in rr: wknd 2f out* **50/1**

1m 0.16s (0.06) **Going Correction** +0.025s/f (Good) **8 Ran SP% 115.1**
Speed ratings (Par 93): **100,92,89,89,89 81,73,70**
CSF £17.72 TOTE £2.80: £1.20, £1.90, £2.60; EX 17.20 Trifecta £87.30.
Owner Sheikh Abdullah Almalek Alsabah **Bred** Ammerland Verwaltung Gmbh & Co Kg **Trained** East Everleigh, Wilts

FOCUS
Following this race the going was changed to good to soft, good (from good to soft). It's hard to know the exact worth of this form but the winner looked useful.

3943 MARATHONBET LIVE CASINO NOVICE MEDIAN AUCTION STKS — 6f 12y
6:40 (6:43) (Class 6) 2-Y-O
£3,105 (£924; £461; £230) **Stalls Centre**

Form — RPR

1 **Boosala (IRE)** 2-9-5 JamesDoyle 12 86+
(William Haggas) *chsd ldrs: pushed along 1/2-way: prog to go 2nd 2f out: clsd to ld ins fnl f: sn in command: readily* **9/2**[2]

3 **2** 1 1/2 **Raahy**[16] 3335 2-9-5 .... JasonWatson 3 82+
(George Scott) *led and racd against nr side rail: sent for home 2f out: hdd and outpcd ins fnl f but stl clr of rest* **5/2[1]**

3 3 **Tomfre** 2-9-5 .... HarryBentley 9 75+
(Ralph Beckett) *dwlt: wl in rr: prog jst over 2f out: styd on wl to take 3rd ins fnl f* **12/1**

4 2 3/4 **Centurion Song (IRE)** 2-9-5 .... MartinDwyer 13 64
(Brian Meehan) *slowly away: wl in rr and rn green: prog over 2f out: shkn up and styd on same pce fnl f* **13/2**

42 **5** hd **Swinley (IRE)**[7] 3660 2-9-5 .... ShaneKelly 14 64
(Richard Hughes) *in tch in midfield: prog to chse ldrs 2f out: shkn up and outpcd over 1f out* **7/1**

6 1/2 **Ecclesiastical** 2-9-5 .... RobHornby 1 62+
(Martyn Meade) *dwlt: wl in rr: pushed along 1/2-way: prog and swtchd lft 2f out: n.d but kpt on* **14/1**

22 **7** 2 3/4 **Nat Love (IRE)**[11] 3491 2-9-5 .... OisinMurphy 4 54
(Mick Channon) *chsd ldr to 2f out: wknd* **5/1[3]**

8 1 **Winnetka (IRE)** 2-9-5 .... SeanLevey 5 52
(Richard Hannon) *dwlt: sn in midfield: pushed along 1/2-way: tried to cl 2f out: wknd over 1f out (jockey said colt hung left-handed under pressure; trainer's rep said filly Good to Soft, Good in places ground)* **14/1**

00 **9** 3 1/2 **Victochop (FR)**[76] 1493 2-9-5 .... LiamKeniry 10 40
(George Baker) *towards rr: shkn up over 2f out: sn no ch* **100/1**

0 **10** 3/4 **Sir Rodneyredblood**[7] 3644 2-9-5 .... KieranO'Neill 2 38
(J R Jenkins) *chsd ldrs but rn green: wknd wl over 1f out* **100/1**

00 **11** 2 1/2 **Love My Life (IRE)**[12] 3461 2-9-0 .... NicolaCurrie 15 26
(Jamie Osborne) *c out of stall slowly: hld up in last: nvr in it but passed a few late on: likely to do bttr (jockey said filly was outpaced throughout)* **50/1**

12 1 **Farhhmorecredit** 2-9-5 .... JFEgan 6 28
(Michael Attwater) *sn struggling in rr: nvr a factor* **66/1**

00 **13** 2 **Twentyonered**[34] 2716 2-9-5 .... LiamJones 8 22
(Grace Harris) *prom to 1/2-way: wknd qckly* **125/1**

14 5 **Hares Rocket (IRE)** 2-9-5 .... DavidProbert 7 7
(Joseph Tuite) *spd to 1/2-way: wknd qckly* **50/1**

15 2 1/4 **Meet The Parents** 2-9-5 .... KierenFox 11
(John Best) *chsd ldrs: hung lft into centre of trck 1/2-way: wknd over 2f out* **50/1**

1m 12.3s (0.20) **Going Correction** +0.025s/f (Good) **15 Ran SP% 120.4**
Speed ratings (Par 91): **99,97,93,89,89 88,84,83,78,77 74,73,70,63,60**
CSF £15.78 TOTE £5.90: £1.90, £1.30, £4.30; EX 19.50 Trifecta £213.40.
Owner Sheikh Ahmed Al Maktoum **Bred** Godolphin **Trained** Newmarket, Suffolk

FOCUS
An interesting 2yo novice. The runner-up had already shown plenty of ability and this race ought to produce a few winners.

3944 MARATHONBET OFFICIAL GLOBAL PARTNER OF MANCHESTER CITY H'CAP — 1m 31y
7:10 (7:10) (Class 4) (0-80,82) 4-Y-0+
£5,530 (£1,645; £822; £411; £300; £300) **Stalls Low**

Form RPR

2302 **1** **Grapevine (IRE)**[14] 3424 6-9-2 **75** .... (p) JamesDoyle 9 83
(Charles Hills) *racd in last pair and off the pce: nt gng that wl over 4f out: prog on outer over 2f out: hrd rdn to chse ldr jst over 1f out: styd on wl to ld fnl 100yds* **7/1[3]**

4143 **2** 1/2 **Sir Roderic (IRE)**[9] 3575 6-8-13 **72** .... OisinMurphy 7 79
(Rod Millman) *sn trckd ldr: led wl over 1f out: drvn fnl f: hdd and hld fnl 100yds* **7/4[1]**

6-20 **3** 1 1/2 **Redgrave (IRE)**[31] 2797 5-9-4 **77** .... DavidProbert 11 81
(Joseph Tuite) *hld up towards rr: stdy prog over 2f out: rdn over 1f out: tk 3rd ins fnl f: styd on but nt quite pce to chal* **9/1**

0-00 **4** 1/2 **Plunger**[21] 3149 4-9-7 **80** .... (b) RaulDaSilva 12 82
(Paul Cole) *racd freely: led: rdn and hdd wl over 1f out: sn outpcd: kpt on fnl f* **33/1**

1331 **5** shd **Lothario**[25] 3002 5-8-13 **72** .... MartinDwyer 2 74
(Dean Ivory) *awkward s and s.i.s: t.k.h towards rr: shkn up over 2f out: swtchd towards outer and prog over 1f out: kpt on but nvr able to threaten* **7/2[2]**

-405 **6** 5 **Letsbe Avenue (IRE)**[14] 3423 4-9-4 **77** .... FergusSweeney 8 68
(Richard Hannon) *trckd ldrs: shkn up to chse ldng pair 2f out: nt qckn over 1f out: wknd fnl f* **20/1**

4441 **7** nk **Chevallier**[105] 1018 7-9-9 **82** .... RobHornby 3 72
(Michael Attwater) *chsd ldrs: rdn and nt qckn 2f out: wknd over 1f out* **33/1**

346 **8** 1 **Custard The Dragon**[7] 3649 6-9-4 **77** .... (v) JimmyQuinn 10 65
(John Mackie) *sn in last and nt gng wl: nvr a factor* **14/1**

1-00 **9** hd **Merweb (IRE)**[26] 2966 4-9-0 **73** .... DavidEgan 1 60
(Heather Main) *wl in tch: rdn over 2f out: wknd over 1f out* **9/1**

6041 **10** 2 1/4 **Come On Tier (FR)**[55] 2006 4-9-0 **73** .... SeanLevey 5 55
(Lee Carter) *nt that wl away: pushed along and sn in midfield: rdn over 2f out: wknd qckly over 1f out* **20/1**

2-60 **11** 14 **One Cool Daddy (USA)**[26] 2966 4-9-6 **79** .... (b[1]) RobertWinston 4 29
(Dean Ivory) *t.k.h: prom 5f: wknd rapidly: t.o (jockey said colt had no more to give)* **12/1**

1m 43.7s (-0.80) **Going Correction** +0.025s/f (Good) **11 Ran SP% 120.9**
Speed ratings (Par 105): **105,104,103,102,102 97,97,96,95,93 79**
CSF £19.28 CT £115.13 TOTE £7.30: £2.40, £1.30, £2.20; EX 23.30 Trifecta £190.20.
Owner Mrs J K Powell **Bred** Colman O'Flynn Jnr **Trained** Lambourn, Berks

FOCUS
Add 23yds. A fair handicap. It's been rated around the second.

3945 MARATHONBET SPORTSBOOK H'CAP (WINDSOR SPRINT SERIES QUALIFIER) — 6f 12y
7:40 (7:41) (Class 3) (0-95,95) 3-Y-0+ **£7,246** (£2,168; £1,084; £542; £270) **Stalls Centre**

Form RPR

4-21 **1** **Molls Memory**[37] 2611 4-9-0 **81** .... LiamKeniry 6 88+
(Ed Walker) *trckd ldrs: stl gng strly 2f out: rdn jst over 1f out: r.o fnl f to ld nr fin* **5/2[1]**

2201 **2** nk **Equitation**[28] 2917 5-9-4 **85** .... (t) RichardKingscote 7 91
(Stuart Williams) *wl in tch: prog on outer over 2f out: rdn to chal over 1f out: hanging lft but upsides ins fnl f: led briefly fnl 75yds: outpcd fnl strides* **11/2**

4602 **3** nse **Danzan (IRE)**[28] 2917 4-9-12 **93** .... OisinMurphy 10 99
(Andrew Balding) *w ldr: sustained battle fr 2f out: stl upsides wl ins fnl f: jst outpcd* **10/3[2]**

3003 **4** 1/2 **Gulliver**[12] 3480 5-10-0 **95** .... (tp) JamesDoyle 9 99
(David O'Meara) *dropped in and hld up in last: prog on wd outside over 2f out: drvn to chal jst over 1f out: upsides fnl 100yds: jst outpcd in bunch fin* **10/1**

00-0 **5** 1/2 **Maarek**[2] 3846 12-9-0 **81** .... SeanLevey 5 84+
(Miss Evanna McCutcheon, Ire) *settled in rr: rdn and no prog wl over 1f out: stl only 8th ins fnl f: r.o wl fnl 100yds: too late* **16/1**

1000 **6** shd **Doc Sportello (IRE)**[38] 2588 7-8-2 **76** oh1 .... (p) CierenFallon(7) 4 78
(Tony Carroll) *mde most: taken to centre of crse fr 1/2-way: edgd lft 2f out whn jnd: hdd and fdd fnl 75yds (jockey said gelding hung badly left-handed)* **40/1**

1254 **7** 1/2 **Diamond Dougal (IRE)**[9] 3589 4-9-9 **90** .... DavidProbert 2 91
(Mick Channon) *in tch in rr: rdn wl over 1f out: nt pce to chal but kpt on fnl f* **8/1**

212U **8** nse **Dominus (IRE)**[12] 3479 3-8-9 **83** .... (h) JasonWatson 8 85
(Brian Meehan) *trckd ldng pair: rdn over 2f out: no rspnse and already lost pl over 1f out whn impeded: kpt on again fnl 100yds (jockey said colt suffered interference approximately 1 1/2f out)* **5/1[3]**

0055 **9** 6 **Normandy Barriere (IRE)**[23] 3094 7-9-4 **90** .... (p) FayeMcManoman(5) 1 71
(Nigel Tinkler) *in tch in rr tl wknd 2f out* **20/1**

1m 11.48s (-0.62) **Going Correction** +0.025s/f (Good)
WFA 3 from 4yo+ 7lb **9 Ran SP% 117.0**
Speed ratings (Par 107): **105,104,104,103,103 103,102,102,94**
CSF £16.90 CT £46.84 TOTE £2.80: £1.50, £1.60, £1.40; EX 14.70 Trifecta £59.70.
Owner Andrew Buxton **Bred** Andrew Buxton **Trained** Upper Lambourn, Berks
■ Stewards' Enquiry : Cieren Fallon two-day ban: careless riding (1-2 Jul)

FOCUS
They raced middle to far side in the closing stages, but it was the horse who initially challenged closest to the near side who proved strongest. It's been rated around the second and third to their C&D latest.

3946 MARATHONBET "CHECK OUR PRICES FIRST" NOVICE STKS — 1m 2f
8:10 (8:10) (Class 5) 3-Y-0+ **£3,752** (£1,116; £557; £278) **Stalls Low**

Form RPR

2 **1** **Hamish**[49] 2198 3-9-2 0 .... JamesDoyle 2 93+
(William Haggas) *led after 3f: mde most: briefly pressed and shkn up jst over 1f out: qckly drew clr fnl f* **2/5[1]**

4-03 **2** 7 **Knowing**[38] 2582 3-9-2 72 .... GeorgeWood 6 77
(James Fanshawe) *trckd ldng pair: effrt to go 2nd jst over 1f out and briefly looked a threat: sn wl outpcd* **3/1[2]**

0 **3** 4 1/2 **Mizuki (IRE)**[18] 3263 4-9-9 0 .... DavidProbert 12 63
(Andrew Balding) *trckd ldng pair: wnt 2nd wl over 2f out: outpcd and lost 2nd jst over 1f out: one pce after (jockey said saddle slipped)* **6/1[3]**

0 **4** 6 **Sherwood Forrester**[45] 2354 3-8-11 0 .... RhiainIngram(5) 5 56
(Paul George) *led 3f: w wnr to 3f out: wknd over 2f out but stl clr of rest* **28/1**

00 **5** 1 3/4 **Bambys Boy**[12] 3464 8-10-0 0 .... LiamKeniry 1 53+
(Neil Mulholland) *dwlt: hld up off the pce in rr: pushed along and prog over 2f out: tk remote 5th over 1f out: nt wout promise* **100/1**

6 2 3/4 **Eighteenhundred (IRE)** 3-8-13 0 .... MeganNicholls(3) 7 47
(Paul Nicholls) *a in midfield and off the pce: shkn up and outpcd over 2f out: no ch after* **16/1**

00 **7** 3/4 **Pecorino**[12] 3463 3-9-2 0 .... (h[1]) ShaneKelly 13 46
(Richard Hughes) *hld up off the pce in midfield: shkn up and lft bhd over 2f out* **25/1**

06 **8** 3 **Tronador (IRE)**[18] 3277 3-9-2 0 .... StevieDonohoe 3 40
(David Lanigan) *slowly away: wl off the pce in last trio: rdn and stl looked green 3f out: passed a few late on* **33/1**

0 **9** 1 **Limited Reserve (IRE)**[37] 1365 7-10-0 0 .... MartinDwyer 10 38
(Christian Williams) *wl off the pce in last trio: shkn up and no prog 3f out* **22/1**

00- **10** 3/4 **Simply Sin (IRE)**[234] 8601 4-9-7 0 .... PhilipDonovan(7) 9 36
(Neil Mulholland) *racd in midfield and nt on terms: shkn up 3f out: wknd over 2f out* **100/1**

0 **11** 1 **Thespinningwheel (IRE)**[9] 3584 4-10-0 0 .... CharlieBennett 4 34
(Adam West) *w ldrs early: mostly in 5th after tl wknd over 2f out* **100/1**

0 **12** 12 **Mottaham (FR)**[14] 3421 4-10-0 0 .... JFEgan 8 10
(Christian Williams) *a wl off the pce in last trio: t.o* **125/1**

2m 8.87s (-0.13) **Going Correction** +0.025s/f (Good)
WFA 3 from 4yo+ 12lb **12 Ran SP% 134.9**
Speed ratings (Par 103): **101,95,91,87,85 83,82,80,79,79 78,68**
CSF £2.30 TOTE £1.50: £1.10, £1.10, £2.30; EX 2.20 Trifecta £6.30.
Owner B Haggas **Bred** J B Haggas **Trained** Newmarket, Suffolk

FOCUS
Add 23yds. An uncompetitive novice - the first four raced in the first four for much of the journey - but still a good performance from the winner, who went 0.9sec quicker than the following Class 5 handicap, and the next three finishers in this had already shown reasonable ability. The second has been rated in line with his handicap latest.

3947 MARATHONBET SUPPORTS RESPONSIBLE GAMBLING H'CAP — 1m 2f
8:40 (8:42) (Class 5) (0-70,70) 3-Y-0
£3,752 (£1,116; £557; £300; £300; £300) **Stalls Low**

Form RPR

3-04 **1** **Oydis**[21] 3152 3-9-7 **70** .... HarryBentley 11 80
(Ralph Beckett) *led after 2f to 1/2-way: pushed along to ld again 3f out: rdn and hrd pressed 2f out: drifted lft fnl f but hld on wl* **7/4[1]**

3506 **2** nk **Bug Boy (IRE)**[13] 3440 3-8-5 **57** .... (p) MeganNicholls(3) 7 66
(Paul George) *racd wd: hld up: prog over 3f out: wnt 2nd jst over 2f out and sn chalng: w wnr fnl f: nt qckn fnl 100yds* **10/1**

4456 **3** 2 1/2 **Mrs Meader**[46] 2343 3-8-12 **61** .... (h[1]) SeanLevey 1 65
(Seamus Mullins) *hld up in rr: prog on outer 3f out: rdn to chse ldng pair wl over 1f out: kpt on same pce u.p* **8/1**

-0U0 **4** 3 1/4 **Northern Lyte**[19] 3226 3-8-8 **62** .... FayeMcManoman(5) 4 60
(Nigel Tinkler) *hld up in midfield: prog over 2f out: drvn to chse ldrs over 1f out: no imp after* **14/1**

2506 **5** 1 1/2 **Debbonair (IRE)**[23] 3092 3-9-2 **65** .... (b) JamesDoyle 5 60
(Hugo Palmer) *hld up in rr: taken to wd outside and prog over 2f out: no hdwy u.p over 1f out* **7/1**

0003 **6** 2 1/4 **Isle Of Wolves**[44] 2406 3-9-3 **66** .... CharlieBennett 8 56
(Jim Boyle) *wl in tch: pushed along 4f out: stl chsng ldrs over 2f out: sn wknd* **5/1[3]**

5400 **7** 6 **Ardimento (IRE)**[38] 2582 3-9-1 **64** .... OisinMurphy 9 42
(Rod Millman) *trckd wnr after 3f: led 1/2-way to 3f out: wknd tamely* **4/1[2]**

46-0 **8** 1 1/2 **London Pride**[26] 2965 3-9-0 **63** .... RobHornby 10 38
(Jonathan Portman) *prom: rdn 3f out: wknd over 2f out* **50/1**

56-0 **9** 2 ¾ **Wave Walker**[27] 2942 3-9-6 **69**.. JasonWatson 3 39
(Sylvester Kirk) *hld up in last: shkn up 3f out: no real prog and nvr in it (jockey said gelding hung left-handed under pressure)* **25/1**

4-35 **10** 12 **Lucipherus (IRE)**[42] 2485 3-9-7 **70**..............................(t[1]) ShaneKelly 6 16
(Marco Botti) *led 2f: stdy cl up tl wknd qckly over 2f out: t.o* **14/1**

00 **11** ¾ **Bayaanaat**[34] 2715 3-8-13 **62**...............................(h[1]) KieranO'Neill 2 6
(Peter Hiatt) *t.k.h: hld up: shkn up and no prog 3f out: sn wknd: t.o* **33/1**

2m 9.77s (0.77) **Going Correction** +0.025s/f (Good) **11** Ran SP% **127.8**
Speed ratings (Par 99): **97,96,94,92,90 89,84,83,80,71 70**
CSF £23.36 CT £125.46 TOTE £2.80: £1.50, £2.60, £2.30; EX 23.10 Trifecta £188.70.
Owner J C Smith **Bred** Littleton Stud **Trained** Kimpton, Hants

FOCUS
Add 23yds. A modest handicap. The second has been rated to his best, and the third to her Salisbury latest.
T/Jkpt: £5,000.00 to a £1 stake. Pool: £10,000.00 - 2.0 winning units T/Plt: £18.40 to a £1 stake. Pool: £85,679.86 - 3,388.22 winning units T/Qpdt: £4.20 to a £1 stake. Pool: £10,270.05 - 1,794.45 winning units **Jonathan Neesom**

2606
ROYAL ASCOT (R-H)
Tuesday, June 18

OFFICIAL GOING: Good (good to soft in places on round course; stands' 8.0, ctr 8.9, far 8.7, rnd 7.4) changing to good to soft after race 4 (4.20) changing to soft after race 5 (5.00)
Wind: Almost nil Weather: Rain

3948 QUEEN ANNE STKS (GROUP 1) (BRITISH CHAMPIONS SERIES) 1m (S)
2:30 (2:31) (Class 1) 4-Y-0+

£340,260 (£129,000; £64,560; £32,160; £16,140; £8,100) **Stalls** Centre

Form RPR

6-30 **1** **Lord Glitters (FR)**[31] 2829 6-9-0 116........................... DanielTudhope 1 120
(David O'Meara) *hld up in rr: hdwy 2f out: r.o to ld narrowly fnl 110yds: kpt on gamely fnl strides* **14/1**

0-10 **2** *nk* **Beat The Bank**[31] 2829 5-9-0 115........................... SilvestreDeSousa 7 119
(Andrew Balding) *midfield: hdwy over 2f out: drvn to chal over 1f out: r.o for press ins fnl f and upsides: hld fnl strides* **20/1**

50-4 **3** ¾ **One Master**[24] 3105 5-8-11 113.................... Pierre-CharlesBoudot 13 114+
(William Haggas) *hld up: hdwy ent fnl 2f: led over 1f out and drifted rt: hdd fnl 110yds: styd on same pce nr fin* **20/1**

0-54 **4** ¾ **Romanised (IRE)**[31] 2829 4-9-0 115..................................(t) WJLee 15 116+
(K J Condon, Ire) *swtchd rt s: hld up: hdwy whn nt clr run 2f out and over 1f out whn swtchd rt: clsng bhd ldrs whn nt clr run and swtchd rt fnl 100yds: styd on but unable to chal* **25/1**

6-35 **5** 1 ¼ **Le Brivido (FR)**[31] 2829 5-9-0 114.. RyanMoore 2 113
(A P O'Brien, Ire) *hld up: hdwy over 2f out: rdn over 1f out: chalng ins fnl f: no ex fnl 75yds* **11/2[2]**

10-2 **6** ½ **Laurens (FR)**[31] 2829 4-8-11 117.. PJMcDonald 6 109
(K R Burke) *chsd ldr: led ent fnl 2f: hdd over 1f out: nt pce of ldrs ins fnl f: styd on same pce fnl 150yds* **11/2[2]**

0-31 **7** *nse* **Mustashry**[31] 2829 6-9-0 121.. JimCrowley 8 111
(Sir Michael Stoute) *midfield: rdn 2f out: effrt whn bmpd ent fnl f: kpt on towards fin: nt pce to chal* **11/2[2]**

0/21 **8** 1 ½ **Barney Roy**[26] 3030 5-9-0 115.. JamesDoyle 3 108
(Charlie Appleby) *sweating; edgy; midfield: drvn over 2f out: angled lft and hdwy 1f out: styd on ins fnl f: nvr able to trble ldrs (vet said gelding had lost its left-fore shoe)* **5/1[1]**

-120 **9** ¾ **Sharja Bridge**[31] 2829 5-9-0 113.. AndreaAtzeni 11 106
(Roger Varian) *midfield: hdwy and angled out over 2f out: rdn to chse ldrs over 1f out: sn bmpd: outpcd ins fnl f* **20/1**

0122 **10** ¾ **Matterhorn (IRE)**[26] 3025 4-9-0 110.. OisinMurphy 14 105
(Mark Johnston) *looked wl; chsd ldrs: rdn over 2f out: nt qckning whn bmpd 1f out: sn lost pl and fdd* **14/1**

0-11 **11** 1 ¼ **Stormy Antarctic**[30] 2886 6-9-0 114.. GeraldMosse 9 102
(Ed Walker) *chsd ldrs: rdn over 2f out: n.m.r and bmpd whn losing pl 1f out: n.d after* **20/1**

3-51 **12** ½ **Hazapour (IRE)**[37] 2660 4-9-0 110.. FrankieDettori 4 100
(D K Weld, Ire) *chsd ldrs: rdn to chal 2f out: wknd over 1f out* **12/1[3]**

-210 **13** 1 **Mythical Magic (IRE)**[31] 2829 4-9-0 114.. KerrinMcEvoy 5 98
(Charlie Appleby) *led: rdn and hdd ent fnl 2f: wknd over 1f out* **50/1**

1105 **14** 4 ½ **Dream Castle**[23] 3122 5-9-0 114.......................... ChristopheSoumillon 12 88
(Saeed bin Suroor) *hld up in midfield: rdn over 1f out: sn btn* **20/1**

0-42 **15** *nk* **Olmedo (FR)**[48] 2313 4-9-0 115.. CristianDemuro 10 87
(J-C Rouget, France) *looked wl; midfield: rdn over 2f out: wknd and lft bhd over 1f out* **16/1**

05-3 **R** **Accidental Agent**[31] 2829 5-9-0 116.. CharlesBishop 16
(Eve Johnson Houghton) *ref to r: tk no part* **14/1**

1m 37.4s (-4.00) **Going Correction** 0.0s/f (Good) **16** Ran SP% **126.0**
Speed ratings (Par 117): **118,117,116,116,114 114,114,112,112,111 110,109,108,104,103**
CSF £275.01 CT £5733.20 TOTE £11.70: £3.05, £8.25, £9.10; EX 389.50 Trifecta £7182.00.
Owner Geoff & Sandra Turnbull **Bred** S C A Elevage De Tourgeville Et Al **Trained** Upper Helmsley, N Yorks

■ Stewards' Enquiry : Silvestre De Sousa £1,050 fine; seven-day ban: used whip above the permitted level (Jul 2-8)

FOCUS
The running rail on the round course was positioned 3yds out from approx 9f out to the home straight. Despite being forecast for midway through the card, a band of rain arrived 2hrs prior to racing. They kicked up turf in the opener, but the time was still under RP standard. Jockey Ryan Moore described the ground as 'beautiful', while Oisin Murphy thought it was on the dead side of good. Another wide-open Queen Anne, with the mile division still lacking a real star. With pace-setting Mythical Magic drawn in stall five, not surprisingly they merged down the middle, and it was teed up for closers. Interestingly, the first four are all known for liking cut underfoot. The second has been rated pretty much to his best.

3949 COVENTRY STKS (GROUP 2) 6f
3:05 (3:06) (Class 1) 2-Y-O

£85,065 (£32,250; £16,140; £8,040; £4,035; £2,025) **Stalls** Centre

Form RPR

1 **Arizona (IRE)**[23] 3111 2-9-1 0.. RyanMoore 3 108
(A P O'Brien, Ire) *str; looked wl; racd centre to far side: in tch in midfield but sn pushed along: rdn and hdwy over 1f out: chal u.p ins fnl f: styd on wl to ld towards fin: 1st of 9 in gp* **15/8[1]**

1 **2** ½ **Threat (IRE)**[44] 2444 2-9-1 0.. TomMarquand 12 107
(Richard Hannon) *sweating; racd centre to nr side: stdd and bmpd s: hld up in rr: swtchd rt and effrt wl over 1f out: hdwy and ev ch ins fnl f: edgd lft u.p but styd on to snatch 2nd last strides: 1st of 8 in gp* **4/1[2]**

1 **3** *nk* **Guildsman (FR)**[11] 3542 2-9-1 0.. OisinMurphy 7 106
(Archie Watson) *athletic; racd centre to nr side: in tch: effrt and hdwy u.p over 1f out: drvn to ld 100yds out: sn hdd and kpt on same pce towards fin: lost 2nd last strides: 2nd of 9 in gp* **6/1[3]**

2 **4** 1 **Fort Myers (USA)**[31] 2830 2-9-1 0.. DonnachaO'Brien 10 103
(A P O'Brien, Ire) *tall; racd centre to nr side: in tch in midfield: effrt ent fnl 2f: drvn over 1f out: hdwy and swtchd lft ins fnl f: styd on: nt enough pce to rch ldrs: 2nd of 8 in gp* **16/1**

41 **5** *shd* **Golden Horde (IRE)**[15] 3419 2-9-1 0.. AdamKirby 4 102
(Clive Cox) *str; racd centre to far side: chsd ldrs overall: effrt and hung lft ent fnl 2f: stl hanging and rdr dropped reins briefly ent fnl f: no ex and outpcd fnl 100yds: 3rd of 9 in gp (jockey said colt hung left-handed)* **33/1**

04 **6** ½ **Ropey Guest**[19] 3274 2-9-1 0.. TomQueally 11 101
(George Margarson) *leggy; athletic; racd centre to nr side: in tch in midfield: pushed along 1/2-way: lost pl and in rr whn drifted rt 2f out: drvn over 1f out: hdwy ins fnl f: kpt on wl nvr getting on terms w ldrs: 3rd of 8 in grou* **200/1**

7 1 ¼ **Royal Lytham (FR)**[10] 3607 2-9-1 0.. SeamieHeffernan 13 97+
(A P O'Brien, Ire) *athletic; racd centre to nr side: wnt rt leaving stalls: in tch in midfield: effrt 2f out: drvn over 1f out: keeping on whn sltly impeded ins fnl f: no imp towards fin: 4th of 8 in gp* **16/1**

1 **8** *hd* **Maxi Boy**[27] 2973 2-9-1 0.. JamieSpencer 9 96
(Michael Bell) *athletic; racd centre to far side: stdd and swtchd rt after s: pushed along early: in rr: effrt and shkn up over 1f out: rdn 1f out: kpt on but no imp fnl 100yds: 4th of 9 in gp* **14/1**

13 **9** *nk* **Well Of Wisdom**[31] 2830 2-9-1 0.. JamesDoyle 8 96
(Charlie Appleby) *racd centre to far side: in tch in midfield: effrt and carried lft over 1f out: unable qck and kpt on same pce ins fnl f: 5th of 9 in gp* **16/1**

02 **10** *shd* **Kuwait Direction (IRE)**[17] 3335 2-9-1 0.. PatDobbs 5 95
(Richard Hannon) *str; racd centre to far side: in tch in midfield: rdn ent fnl 2f: unable qck over 1f out: kpt on same pce ins fnl f: 6th of 9 in gp* **100/1**

21 **11** ½ **Makyon (IRE)**[12] 3498 2-9-1 0.. SilvestreDeSousa 16 94
(Mark Johnston) *str; racd centre to nr side: overall ldr: rdn 2f out: drvn over 1f out: hdd 100yds out: sltly impeded: no ex and wknd towards fin: 5th of 8 in gp* **25/1**

1 **12** 1 **Lord Of The Lodge (IRE)**[27] 2957 2-9-1 0.. BenCurtis 15 91
(K R Burke) *unfurnished; racd centre to nr side: t.k.h: hld up in tch: lost pl and in rr whn rdn ent fnl 2f: kpt on ins fnl f: no threat to ldrs: 6th of 8 in gp* **50/1**

13 ½ **King Of Athens (USA)**[23] 3111 2-9-1 0.. WayneLordan 6 89
(A P O'Brien, Ire) *ly; racd centre to far side: wnt rt after s: in rr and pushed along: effrt over 1f out: nvr threatened to get on terms: plugged on same pce ins fnl f: 7th of 9 in gp* **33/1**

1 **14** ½ **Majestic Sands (IRE)**[21] 3190 2-9-1 0.. BarryMcHugh 1 88
(Richard Fahey) *unfurnished; racd centre to far side: chsd ldrs: unable qck u.p over 1f out: wknd ins fnl f: 8th of 9 in gp* **66/1**

21 **15** 1 **Light Angel**[32] 2792 2-9-1 0.. FrankieDettori 14 85
(John Gosden) *leggy; sltly on toes; racd centre to nr side: t.k.h: hld up in tch in midfield: effrt ent fnl 2f: unable qck over 1f out: wknd ins fnl f: 7th of 8 in gp* **17/2**

21 **16** 1 ¼ **Monoski (USA)**[25] 3055 2-9-1 0.. PJMcDonald 2 81
(Mark Johnston) *str; racd centre to far side: led gp and chsd ldrs overall: drvn over 1f out: unable qck and btn 1f out: wknd ins fnl f: 9th of 9 in gp* **14/1**

1 **17** 2 **Coase**[19] 3245 2-9-1 0.. JamesMcDonald 17 75
(Hugo Palmer) *workmanlike; looked wl; racd centre to nr side: t.k.h: chsd ldrs tl lost pl u.p over 1f out: wknd fnl f: 8th of 8 in gp* **25/1**

1m 13.02s (-0.68) **Going Correction** 0.0s/f (Good) **17** Ran SP% **129.1**
Speed ratings (Par 105): **104,103,102,101,101 100,99,98,98,98 97,96,95,95,93 92,89**
CSF £8.56 CT £43.59 TOTE £2.20: £1.30, £1.95, £2.60; EX 13.40 Trifecta £66.70.
Owner Mrs John Magnier & Michael Tabor & Derrick Smith **Bred** Stephen Sullivan **Trained** Cashel, Co Tipperary

FOCUS
A typical field for this Group 2 prize, with no end of promising 2yos with a last-time-out win against their name, but despite the big field the market leaders came to the fore. They raced in two groups and, with neither group holding a decisive pace advantage, there were several in with a chance spread centre-to-stands' side inside the last furlong. The pace seemed a good one.

3950 KING'S STAND STKS (GROUP 1) (BRITISH CHAMPIONS SERIES) 5f
3:40 (3:40) (Class 1) 3-Y-O+

£283,550 (£107,500; £53,800; £26,800; £13,450; £6,750) **Stalls** Centre

Form RPR

-111 **1** **Blue Point (IRE)**[80] 1442 5-9-4 120.. JamesDoyle 1 127
(Charlie Appleby) *looked wl; wnt to post early: a.p: rdn to ld ins fnl 2f: pressed 1f out: r.o gamely and fnd ex fnl 75yds: in command nr fin* **5/2[2]**

44-1 **2** 1 ¼ **Battaash (IRE)**[24] 3084 5-9-4 123.. JimCrowley 12 122
(Charles Hills) *sltly on toes; hld up towards nrside: swtchd rt 1/2-way: hdwy sn after: qcknd to chal 1f out and edgd rt: no ex towards fin* **2/1[1]**

36-3 **3** 1 ½ **Soldier's Call**[33] 2779 3-8-12 113.. DanielTudhope 8 115
(Archie Watson) *looked wl; led: showed plenty of pce: rdn and hdd ins fnl 2f: stl chsng ldrs ins fnl f: rdn ot u.p but a hld* **16/1**

1-13 **4** *nse* **Mabs Cross**[24] 3084 5-9-1 115.. PaulMulrennan 4 114
(Michael Dods) *hld up: hdwy 2f out: effrt to chse ldrs over 1f out: kpt on ins fnl f: nvr able to chal* **6/1[3]**

1-56 **5** *nk* **Fairyland (IRE)**[23] 3115 3-8-9 110.. WayneLordan 10 111
(A P O'Brien, Ire) *prom: rdn and unable qck over 1f out: kpt on u.p ins fnl f: nt pce of ldrs* **16/1**

6- **6** 1 ¾ **Imprimis (USA)**[73] 5-9-4 114.. FrankieDettori 3 109
(Joseph Orseno, U.S.A) *ponied to s: midfield: rdn and bmpd 1/2-way: sme hdwy u.p over 1f out: one pce ins fnl f* **7/1**

-342 **7** 1 ½ **Equilateral**[45] 2409 4-9-4 110.. JamesMcDonald 5 104
(Charles Hills) *hld up: rdn and hdwy over 1f out: no imp on ldrs: no ex fnl 150yds* **20/1**

6- **8** 2 ¼ **Houtzen (AUS)**[157] 4-9-1 108..................................(bt) KerrinMcEvoy 11 93
(Toby Edmonds, Australia) *stmbld s: gd spd towards nrside: prom: rdn and lost pl 2f out: outpcd after (jockey said filly slipped coming out of the stalls)* **33/1**

0-40 **9** *nse* **Signora Cabello (IRE)**[24] 3085 3-8-9 109..................................(b[1]) OisinMurphy 2 91
(John Quinn) *hld up: bmpd 1/2-way: rdn and outpcd over 1f out: plugged on ins fnl f: nvr able to get involved* **66/1**

0-14 **10** 1 ¼ **Sergei Prokofiev (CAN)**[45] 2409 3-8-12 111................ RyanMoore 7 89
(A P O'Brien, Ire) *hld up: rdn 2f out: no imp* **12/1**

11 shd **Enzo's Lad (AUS)**[51] 2176 6-9-4 113...............................(b) DavidEgan 9 91
(Michael Pitman, New Zealand) *chsd ldrs: pushed along and lost pl 1/2-way: no imp after* **66/1**

05-0 **12** hd **Judicial (IRE)**[45] 2409 7-9-4 107...............................(h) PJMcDonald 6 90
(Julie Camacho) *led to post and wnt early: midfield: rdn 2f out: wknd 1f out* **66/1**

58.53s (-2.17) **Going Correction** 0.0s/f (Good)
WFA 3 from 4yo+ 6lb **12** Ran SP% **120.3**
Speed ratings (Par 117): **117,115,112,112,112 109,106,103,103,101 101,100**
CSF £7.72 CT £64.43 TOTE £3.30: £1.30, £1.30, £4.15; EX 8.40 Trifecta £98.20.
Owner Godolphin **Bred** Oak Lodge Bloodstock **Trained** Newmarket, Suffolk
■ Stewards' Enquiry : Paul Mulrennan two-day ban: used whip above the permitted level (Jun 30, Jul 2)

FOCUS
An exciting edition of the King's Stand. Run in driving rain, there was a frantic pace on down the centre and it saw a repeat of last year's 1-2. The placed horses also give the form a red-hot look. The third has been rated as running right up to his 2yo form, with the fifth close to form.

3951 ST JAMES'S PALACE STKS (GROUP 1) (BRITISH CHAMPIONS SERIES) (COLTS) 7f 213y(R)

4:20 (4:23) (Class 1) 3-Y-O

£305,525 (£115,831; £57,969; £28,877; £14,492; £7,273) **Stalls** Low

Form RPR

4-16 **1** **Circus Maximus (IRE)**[17] 3345 3-9-0 110...................(b[1]) RyanMoore 1 118
(A P O'Brien, Ire) *sweating; t.k.h: chsd ldr tl rdn to ld over 1f out: hrd pressed 1f out: edgd lft but forged ahd ins fnl f: a jst lasting home* **10/1**

2-11 **2** nk **King Of Comedy (IRE)**[26] 3026 3-9-0 111........................ AdamKirby 5 117+
(John Gosden) *athletic; sltly squeezed for room stalls: hld up in last trio: hdwy and rdn 2f out: swtchd lft and clsd to chse ldrs whn hung lft 1f out: styd on wl u.p fnl 100yds: wnt 2nd cl home: nt quite rch wnr* **4/1[3]**

1-22 **3** ¾ **Too Darn Hot**[24] 3104 3-9-0 120.. FrankieDettori 2 115
(John Gosden) *t.k.h: chsd ldng trio: swtchd lft and effrt ent fnl 2f: clsd and str chal u.p 1f out: no ex and jst outpcd wl ins fnl f: lost 2nd cl home* **2/1[1]**

-134 **4** ½ **Skardu**[24] 3104 3-9-0 111... JamesDoyle 3 114+
(William Haggas) *looked wl; hld up in tch in midfield: effrt 2f out: swtchd lft and clsd over 1f out: chsd ldrs and drvn 1f out: kpt on ins fnl f: nvr quite enough pce to chal* **7/1**

-112 **5** 2 **Shaman (IRE)**[37] 2668 3-9-0 114.. MaximeGuyon 6 109+
(C Laffon-Parias, France) *str; wnt rt leaving stalls: hld up in tch: short of room wl over 2f out: hdwy over 1f out: edging rt and kpt on wl ins fnl f: nvr trbld ldrs* **14/1**

22-1 **6** nk **Phoenix Of Spain (IRE)**[24] 3104 3-9-0 120...................... JamieSpencer 7 108
(Charles Hills) *looked wl; chsd ldrs: effrt to press ldng pair and rdn 2f out: hung rt and unable qck over 1f out: wknd ins fnl f* **5/2[2]**

-111 **7** 1 **Fox Champion (IRE)**[30] 2889 3-9-0 110.................. SilvestreDeSousa 11 106
(Richard Hannon) *looked wl; led: rdn 2f out: sn hdd and drvn: wknd ins fnl f* **25/1**

4060 **8** ½ **Van Beethoven (CAN)**[24] 3104 3-9-0 107............... DonnachaO'Brien 10 105
(A P O'Brien, Ire) *sweating; t.k.h: stdd and dropped in after s: hld up in last trio: effrt 2f out: sn drvn: hdwy 1f out: kpt on ins fnl f: nvr trbld ldrs* **66/1**

-440 **9** 2 ½ **Royal Marine (IRE)**[45] 2411 3-9-0 109................ ChristopheSoumillon 4 99
(Saeed bin Suroor) *t.k.h: hld up in tch in midfield: n.m.r and bmpd sn after s: effrt over 1f out: unable qck and sn btn: wknd ins fnl f* **33/1**

1-6 **10** 3 ½ **Bell Rock**[26] 3026 3-9-0 0.. OisinMurphy 8 91
(Andrew Balding) *in tch in midfield: hung lft bnd 3f out: sn lost pl and bhd 2f out* **33/1**

-520 **11** 5 **The Irish Rover (IRE)**[30] 2882 3-9-0 99.................. SeamieHeffernan 9 80
(A P O'Brien, Ire) *awkward leaving stalls: hld up in rr: effrt 2f out: no prog u.p: wknd fnl f* **100/1**

1m 39.9s (-0.70) **Going Correction** +0.25s/f (Good) **11** Ran SP% **122.4**
Speed ratings (Par 113): **113,112,111,111,109 109,108,107,105,101 96**
CSF £50.41 CT £116.39 TOTE £12.05: £3.25, £1.70, £1.30; EX 58.50 Trifecta £150.60.
Owner Flaxman Stables, Mrs Magnier, M Tabor, D Smith **Bred** Flaxman Stables Ireland Ltd **Trained** Cashel, Co Tipperary

FOCUS
Add 5yds. The first race on the Round course, where the ground was expected to be riding softer and the rain looked to have really got into it ground by this stage. Little gallop on early, with neither of the Ballydoyle outsiders setting the pace as expected, and it certainly didn't look the strongest edition of the race. The form is set around the fourth and fifth.

3952 ASCOT STKS (A H'CAP) 2m 3f 210y

5:00 (5:00) (Class 2) (0-100,100) 4-Y-O+

£56,025 (£16,776; £8,388; £4,194; £2,097; £1,053) **Stalls** Low

Form RPR

01-0 **1** **The Grand Visir**[10] 3600 5-9-10 **100**.....................(t) RichardKingscote 18 109
(Ian Williams) *hld up: hdwy 4f out: rdn over 2f out: led over 1f out: pressed ins fnl 100yds: styd on gamely and in command towards fin* **12/1**

450- **2** 1 ¼ **Buildmeupbuttercup**[49] 5747 5-9-1 **91**.........................(t[1]) RyanMoore 19 99
(W P Mullins, Ire) *in rr: hdwy 3f out: rdn over 2f out: styd on to take 2nd wl ins fnl f: chal briefly ins fnl 100yds: kpt on same pce and hld towards fin* **7/1[2]**

0-00 **3** 3 ½ **Time To Study (FR)**[39] 2575 5-9-6 **96**................................ JimCrowley 14 101
(Ian Williams) *midfield: hdwy 4f out: rdn and swtchd lft over 2f out: led wl over 1f out: sn hdd: stl there ins fnl f: no ex fnl 100yds* **16/1**

00-5 **4** 2 ¼ **Fun Mac (GER)**[39] 2575 8-9-1 **91**................................(t) PJMcDonald 8 94
(Hughie Morrison) *midfield: rdn over 2f out: hdwy whn edgd rt over 1f out: sn chsd ldrs: one pce fnl 100yds* **11/1**

0-21 **5** 1 **Coeur De Lion**[39] 2578 6-8-12 **93**.............(p) ThoreHammerHansen[(5)] 10 95
(Alan King) *hmpd s: chsd ldrs: rdn 3f out: cl up 2f out: outpcd over 1f out: kpt on ins fnl f* **7/1[2]**

6 1 ¼ **Arctic Fire (GER)**[35] 2727 10-9-6 **96**...........................(h) MarkGallagher 1 97
(Denis W Cullen, Ire) *hld up: drvn over 2f out: hdwy whn hung rt over 1f out: styd on ins fnl f: nt rch ldrs* **33/1**

0-42 **7** 2 **Mancini**[33] 2781 5-9-1 **91**.. SilvestreDeSousa 12 90
(Jonathan Portman) *looked wl; sn chsd ldr: rdn to ld over 2f out: hdd wl over 1f out: no ex fnl f* **13/2[1]**

4/0- **8** ½ **Batts Rock (IRE)**[25] 7313 6-9-1 **91**...........................(t) FrankieDettori 13 90
(Gordon Elliott, Ire) *hld up: hdwy bef 1/2-way: prom 8f out: rdn whn chsng ldrs over 2f out: no imp over 1f out: wknd ins fnl f* **8/1[3]**

5-34 **9** ¾ **Yabass (IRE)**[16] 3384 4-9-1 **92**....................................(t) HollieDoyle 11 91
(Archie Watson) *looked wl; wnt rt s: racd keenly: chsd ldrs: rdn to chal 2f out: unable to go w ldrs over 1f out: fdd ins fnl f* **50/1**

225/ **10** 1 **Not Never**[13] 7498 7-9-5 **95**.. HarryBentley 20 92
(Gary Moore) *in tch: rdn and lost pl 4f out: kpt on u.p 2f out: no imp: wl hld ins fnl f* **22/1**

040/ **11** ¾ **Kerosin (GER)**[10] 3609 8-9-3 **93**.................................... OisinMurphy 7 89
(Denis Gerard Hogan, Ire) *chsd ldrs: rdn over 2f out: wknd over 1f out* **16/1**

014/ **12** 10 **Mengli Khan (IRE)**[58] 7188 6-9-6 **96**............................(t) RoryCleary 2 83
(Gordon Elliott, Ire) *racd keenly: in tch: rdn and outpcd over 3f out: no imp u.p fnl 2f: wknd ins fnl f: eased fnl 150yds* **8/1[3]**

020/ **13** 7 **Snow Falcon (IRE)**[48] 8038 9-9-9 **99**.............................. ColinKeane 16 80
(Noel Meade, Ire) *hld up: pushed along 4f out: no imp: eased over 1f out* **10/1**

0/0- **14** nk **Percy Street**[12] 3965 6-9-2 **95**...............................(vt) FinleyMarsh[(3)] 15 76
(David Pipe) *hld up: rdn 3f out: nvr a threat* **66/1**

0-03 **15** 1 ¼ **Jukebox Jive (FR)**[131] 635 5-9-3 **93**................................ DougieCostello 17 73
(Jamie Osborne) *led: rdn and hdd over 2f out: wknd over 1f out* **33/1**

260/ **16** 20 **Gunnery (FR)**[14] 4059 6-9-2 **92**.................................... JamieSpencer 4 54
(Nicky Henderson) *hld up: rdn 2f out: no imp: eased whn wl btn over 1f out* **16/1**

6243 **17** 7 **Cosmelli (ITY)**[13] 3466 6-9-2 **92**.................................(b) DanielMuscutt 3 47
(Gay Kelleway) *midfield: rdn over 3f out: wknd over 2f out* **50/1**

1222 **P** **Ulster (IRE)**[59] 1947 4-9-2 **93**.. EdwardGreatrex 6
(Archie Watson) *hld up in midfield: pushed along and wknd over 4f out: t.o whn p.u 2f out: dsmntd (jockey said gelding got tired in the rain softened ground)* **20/1**

1-41 **P** **Mixboy (FR)**[76] 1524 9-9-2 **92**.. PaulMulrennan 9
(Keith Dalgleish) *prom: rdn 4f out: sn wknd: t.o whn p.u 2f out: dsmntd (jockey said gelding stopped quickly)* **28/1**

4m 28.34s (6.34) **Going Correction** +0.25s/f (Good)
WFA 4 from 5yo+ 1lb **19** Ran SP% **127.2**
Speed ratings (Par 109): **97,96,95,94,93 93,92,92,92,91 91,87,84,84,83 75,73, ,**
CSF £88.31 CT £1387.52 TOTE £14.00: £2.45, £2.55, £5.05, £2.20; EX 123.00 Trifecta £2622.70.
Owner CLXX **Bred** Qatar B'Stock, Ecurie Monceaux & Skymarc **Trained** Portway, Worcs

FOCUS
Predictably the going was officially downgraded to good to soft all over after the St James's Palace. \n\x\x Another fiercely competitive Ascot Stakes. It proved a dour test and saw a 1-3 for trainer Ian Williams. The fourth has been rated close to his Chester Cup form and the fifth similar to last year's run in this race. Add 11yds.

3953 WOLFERTON STKS (LISTED RACE) 1m 1f 212y

5:35 (5:36) (Class 1) 4-Y-O+

£56,710 (£21,500; £10,760; £5,360; £2,690; £1,350) **Stalls** Low

Form RPR

03-4 **1** **Addeybb (IRE)**[39] 2573 5-9-3 112...........................(p[1]) DanielTudhope 12 120+
(William Haggas) *looked wl; hld up in tch in midfield: pushed lft after 1f: nudged lft but clsd ent fnl 2f: sn pushed along and hdwy to ld jst ins fnl f: rdn clr and sn in command: comf* **5/1[2]**

-253 **2** 2 ½ **Magic Wand (IRE)**[38] 2646 4-8-12 108........................... RyanMoore 14 109
(A P O'Brien, Ire) *chsd ldrs: effrt ent fnl 2f: unable qck u.p over 1f out: hung rt but kpt on ins fnl f to snatch 2nd on post: no ch w wnr* **9/2[1]**

4-41 **3** nse **Elarqam**[24] 3074 4-9-6 111... JimCrowley 3 117
(Mark Johnston) *chsd ldr: effrt u.p to chal 2f out: drvn and forged ahd jst over 1f out: hdd jst ins fnl f: no match for wnr and one pce after: lost 2nd on post* **5/1[2]**

0-34 **4** shd **Latrobe (IRE)**[43] 2494 4-9-3 113............................ DonnachaO'Brien 2 114
(Joseph Patrick O'Brien, Ire) *wl in tch in midfield: short of room on inner after 1f: swtchd lft and effrt over 2f out: swtchd and hdwy u.p over 1f out: kpt on ins fnl f: no threat to wnr* **12/1**

0-11 **5** 3 ½ **Mountain Angel (IRE)**[18] 3315 5-9-3 106.......................... OisinMurphy 1 107
(Roger Varian) *looked wl; hld up in midfield: hmpd after 1f: effrt over 2f out: hdwy between rivals jst ins fnl f: kpt on: nvr trbld ldrs (jockey said gelding suffered interference approaching Swinley Bottom)* **11/1**

105- **6** shd **Riven Light (IRE)**[11] 3558 7-9-3 112............................... ColinKeane 11 107
(W P Mullins, Ire) *t.k.h: hld up towards rr: swtchd lft and effrt over 2f out: styd on ins fnl f: nvr trbld ldrs* **17/2**

5110 **7** nk **Mountain Hunter (USA)**[80] 1445 5-9-3 109...... ChristopheSoumillon 16 106
(Saeed bin Suroor) *in tch in midfield: effrt over 2f out: hung rt u.p over 1f out: kpt on but no threat to ldrs ins fnl f* **25/1**

31-1 **8** ½ **Star Of Bengal**[26] 3005 4-9-3 107..........................(p[1]) FrankieDettori 15 105
(John Gosden) *led: rdn and hrd pressed 2f out: hdd and no ex u.p jst over 1f out: wknd ins fnl f* **13/2[3]**

1-15 **9** 1 ¾ **Oasis Charm**[117] 844 5-9-3 107....................................(p) AdamKirby 4 101
(Charlie Appleby) *in tch in midfield: short of room after 1f: effrt u.p over 2f out: unable qck over 1f out: wknd ins fnl f* **20/1**

4-02 **10** ¾ **Zorion**[110] 961 5-9-3 103...(p) KerrinMcEvoy 6 100
(Charlie Appleby) *chsd ldrs: rdn over 2f out: sn struggling and outpcd over 1f out: wknd ins fnl f* **66/1**

-234 **11** 1 **Zihba (IRE)**[23] 3114 4-9-3 104.......................................(t) ChrisHayes 7 98
(J A Stack, Ire) *t.k.h: hld up in last trio: effrt jst over 2f out: nvr involved* **66/1**

-630 **12** 6 **Master The World (IRE)**[60] 1921 8-9-6 106...................(p) SeanLevey 10 89
(David Elsworth) *looked wl; hld up in tch in midfield: drvn 3f out: unable qck and btn over 1f out: wknd fnl f* **100/1**

-135 **13** ½ **First Nation**[61] 1890 5-9-3 109.. JamesDoyle 13 85
(Charlie Appleby) *awkward leaving stalls: hld up in rr: short of room: hmpd and swtchd lft after 1f: swtchd lft and effrt over 2f out: nvr involved: wknd fnl f* **12/1**

0-42 **14** 1 ¼ **Willie John**[24] 3074 4-9-3 106... AndreaAtzeni 8 82
(Roger Varian) *t.k.h: short of room: edgd rt and hmpd after 1f: effrt and nudged lft over 2f out: sn outpcd and wknd over 1f out (trainer's rep said colt was unsuited by the soft ground and would prefer a sounder surface)* **10/1**

221- **15** 1 ¼ **Global Giant**[249] 8174 4-9-6 105... GeraldMosse 5 83
(Ed Dunlop) *short of room leaving stalls: hld up in rr: short of room and hmpd after 1f: n.d* **50/1**

21-0 **16** ½ **Dolphin Vista (IRE)**[93] 1244 6-9-6 110............................ HarryBentley 9 82
(Ralph Beckett) *bustled along leaving stalls: midfield: short of room: hmpd and swtchd lft after 1f: effrt 3f out: sn drvn and struggling: wknd over 1f out (jockey said gelding suffered interference approaching Swinley Bottom)* **33/1**

2m 6.9s (-0.80) **Going Correction** +0.25s/f (Good) **16** Ran SP% **125.7**
Speed ratings (Par 111): **113,111,110,110,108 108,107,107,105,105 104,99,99,98,97 96**
CSF £27.23 CT £124.06 TOTE £6.00: £2.05, £1.95, £2.10; EX 31.60 Trifecta £165.30.
Owner Sheikh Ahmed Al Maktoum **Bred** Rabbah Bloodstock Limited **Trained** Newmarket, Suffolk

FOCUS
Add 11yds. Strong Listed form, with the first four being at least Group 2 performers. The winner has been rated close to his best, with the third backing up his Goodwood run under a penalty and running better than ever.
T/Jkpt: Not Won. T/Plt: £520.60 to a £1 stake. Pool: £572,563.35 - 802.83 winning units. T/Qpdt: £12.30 to a £1 stake. Pool: £50,726.53 - 3,028.24 winning units. **Darren Owen/Steve Payne**

3563 BEVERLEY (R-H)

Tuesday, June 18

OFFICIAL GOING: Good (good to soft in places; 5.8)
Wind: Virtually nil Weather: Cloudy with sunny periods

3954 HULL HOMELESS PROJECT NOVICE MEDIAN AUCTION STKS — 7f 96y
6:00 (6:00) (Class 5) 2-Y-O — **£4,347** (£1,301; £650; £325; £162) **Stalls** Low

Form — RPR

3 **1** **World Title (IRE)**[11] 3551 2-9-5 0 ... AdamMcNamara 3 74+
(Archie Watson) *trckd ldng pair: hdwy 2f out: rdn to ld over 1f out: drvn ins fnl f: kpt on wl towards fin* **6/4**[1]

2 *hd* **Northern Hope** 2-9-2 0 ... ConorMcGovern(3) 2 74+
(David O'Meara) *hld up towards rr: hdwy on inner wl over 2f out: chsd ldrs over 1f out: rdn to chal ent fnl f: ev ch tl no ex towards fin* **11/1**

3 *4 1/2* **Lord Of The Alps (IRE)** 2-9-5 0 ... FrannyNorton 9 62+
(Mark Johnston) *t.k.h and edging lft thrght: led 3f out: rdn and hung bdly rt to stands' rail over 1f out: sn hdd: kpt on same pce fnl f (jockey said colt hung badly left and the bit slipped through the colt's mouth)* **6/1**[3]

00 **4** *2* **Lady Erimus**[43] 2476 2-9-0 0 ... CamHardie 4 53
(Kevin Ryan) *in tch: hdwy 3f out: rdn along to chse ldrs wl over 1f out: kpt on same pce fnl f* **50/1**

0 **5** *1* **Little Ted**[17] 3335 2-9-5 0 ... DavidAllan 1 55
(Tim Easterby) *dwlt and in rr: hdwy 3f out: rdn along 2f out: kpt on fnl f* **14/1**

0 **6** *1/2* **Roman's Empress (IRE)**[25] 3049 2-9-0 0 ... TrevorWhelan 10 49
(David Loughnane) *dwlt and swtchd rt s: towards rr: hdwy and in tch 1/2-way: rdn along to chse ldrs 2f out: sn drvn and no imp* **40/1**

35 **7** *2 3/4* **Royal Council (IRE)**[15] 3426 2-9-5 0 ...(h[1]) TomEaves 6 47
(James Tate) *trckd ldrs: hdwy and cl up over 2f out: rdn along wl over 1f out: wknd ent fnl f* **4/1**[2]

0 **8** *6* **Coast Of Dubai (IRE)**[80] 1416 2-9-5 0 ... GrahamLee 7 32
(Kevin Ryan) *in tch: pushed along 2 1/2f out: sn rdn and wknd* **8/1**

9 *5* **Trickydickysimpson** 2-9-5 0 ... TonyHamilton 8 20
(Richard Fahey) *a in rr: bhd fr over 2f out* **7/1**

10 *5* **Richard Of Cambria** 2-9-5 0 ... AndrewMullen 5 8
(Adrian Nicholls) *a in rr: bhd fr over 2f out* **33/1**

00 **11** *1/2* **Bosun's Chair**[29] 2907 2-9-5 0 ... RachelRichardson 11 7
(Tim Easterby) *slt ld on outer: hdd 3f out: sn rdn and wknd* **50/1**

1m 35.08s (2.48) **Going Correction** +0.225s/f (Good) **11** Ran SP% **122.2**
Speed ratings (Par 93): **94,93,88,86,85 84,81,74,68,63 62**
CSF £21.01 TOTE £2.30: £1.10, £3.30, £1.70; EX 25.10 Trifecta £191.20.
Owner Clipper Logistics **Bred** Oghill House Stud & Joseph M Burke **Trained** Upper Lambourn, W Berks
■ Stewards' Enquiry : Adam McNamara two-day ban: misuse of whip (July 5,7)

FOCUS
A dry run up to a meeting staged on ground just on the easy side of good. Not much strength in depth but fair form from the first two, who pulled clear late on. The gallop was sound and the winning rider stated the ground was "dead". The fourth and those in behind will prove the true worth of the form.

3955 DOVE HOUSE HOSPICE FILLIES' H'CAP — 1m 4f 23y
6:30 (6:31) (Class 5) (0-70,72) 3-Y-O+
£3,969 (£1,188; £594; £300; £300; £300) **Stalls** Low

Form — RPR

0-03 **1** **Arctic Ocean (IRE)**[22] 3153 3-9-1 **67** ... JimmyQuinn 1 77
(Sir Michael Stoute) *trckd ldng pair on inner: swtchd lft and hdwy over 2f out: chal wl over 1f out: rdn to ld ent fnl f: kpt on strly* **6/1**

5232 **2** *2 1/4* **Gold Fleece**[7] 3708 3-9-2 **68** ...(p[1]) GrahamLee 2 74
(Hugo Palmer) *slt ld: rdn along 3f out: hdd 2f out: cl up and drvn over 1f out: kpt on u.p fnl f* **5/2**[1]

1-50 **3** *2 1/4* **Fragrant Belle**[18] 3324 3-9-6 **72** ... DavidAllan 3 74
(Ralph Beckett) *cl up: rdn and slt ld 2f out: sn drvn: hdd ent fnl f: kpt on same pce (vet said filly lost its left fore shoe)* **11/2**

3434 **4** *1 1/4* **Fayetta**[7] 3708 3-9-3 **69** ...(v) TrevorWhelan 6 69
(David Loughnane) *hld up in tch: hdwy 3f out: rdn along to chse ldrs 2f out: drvn over 1f out: kpt on one pce* **8/1**

-633 **5** *nk* **Vindolanda**[14] 3446 3-9-3 **69** ... KieranShoemark 4 69+
(Charles Hills) *dwlt: hld up in rr: hdwy on outer 2 1/2f out: chsd ldrs and rdn over 1f out: drvn and no imp fnl f (jockey said filly was slowly away)* **10/3**[2]

2005 **6** *1/2* **Flower Power**[19] 3269 8-10-0 **66** ...(p) DavidNolan 8 65
(Tony Coyle) *hld up in rr: hdwy over 2f out: rdn along wl over 1f out: n.d* **33/1**

3103 **7** *3/4* **Lincoln Tale (IRE)**[7] 3708 3-8-13 **65** ... CamHardie 5 63
(David O'Meara) *trckd ldrs: hdwy 3f out: rdn along 2f out: drvn and wknd over 1f out* **5/1**[3]

0005 **8** *43* **Lots Ov (IRE)**[1] 3929 5-8-9 **47** oh2 ...(p) AndrewMullen 7
(John Wainwright) *trckd ldrs: pushed along over 3f out: sn rdn and wknd* **125/1**

2m 39.39s (0.59) **Going Correction** +0.225s/f (Good)
WFA 3 from 5yo+ 14lb **8** Ran SP% **112.8**
Speed ratings (Par 100): **107,105,104,103,102 102,102,73**
CSF £20.82 CT £86.24 TOTE £7.20: £1.70, £1.10, £2.60; EX 20.90 Trifecta £93.70.
Owner Qatar Racing Limited **Bred** Martin White **Trained** Newmarket, Suffolk

FOCUS
A modest handicap in which an ordinary gallop only picked up rounding the home turn and those held up were at a disadvantage. It's been rated at face value, with the second to her latest effort.

3956 TECKNO DEVELOPMENTS EBF CONDITIONS STKS — 5f
7:00 (7:01) (Class 3) 3-Y-O+ — **£8,715** (£2,609; £1,304) **Stalls** Low

Form — RPR

1501 **1** **Ornate**[17] 3344 6-9-2 103 ... PhilDennis 1 109
(David C Griffiths) *qckly away: mde all: rdn wl over 1f out: drvn ins fnl f: hld on gamely* **6/5**[2]

3-22 **2** *1* **Final Venture**[30] 2880 7-9-2 105 ... ConnorBeasley 3 105
(Paul Midgley) *wnt lft s: sn trcking wnr: effrt 2f out and sn pushed along: rdn over 1f out: drvn to chal ent fnl f: kpt on* **10/11**[1]

15-4 **3** *1/2* **Fairy Falcon**[17] 3360 4-8-11 86 ... GrahamLee 2 99
(Bryan Smart) *wnt lft s: chsd ldng pair on inner: rdn along and sltly outpcd 1/2-way: swtchd lft and drvn jst over 1f out: kpt on wl u.p fnl f* **9/1**[3]

1m 2.19s (-0.71) **Going Correction** +0.225s/f (Good) **3** Ran SP% **107.8**
Speed ratings (Par 107): **114,112,111**
CSF £2.68 TOTE £2.00; EX 2.20 Trifecta £1.90.
Owner Kings Road Racing Partnership **Bred** Cheveley Park Stud Ltd **Trained** Bawtry, S Yorks

FOCUS
Only three runners but a decent gallop and another victory for Ornate, who is another feather in the cap of his very capable trainer. The winner has been rated to his old C&D form and not far off his old best.

3957 R-EVOLUTION H'CAP — 1m 100y
7:30 (7:31) (Class 5) (0-75,77) 3-Y-O+
£4,599 (£1,376; £688; £344; £300; £300) **Stalls** Low

Form — RPR

-202 **1** **Stringybark Creek**[29] 2898 5-9-7 **75** ... LauraCoughlan(7) 6 85
(David Loughnane) *t.k.h: chsd ldr: led after 3f: rdn wl over 1f out: drvn and kpt on wl fnl f* **13/2**

3121 **2** *1 3/4* **Abushamah (IRE)**[6] 3744 8-9-1 **62** ... JamesSullivan 9 68
(Ruth Carr) *led 3f: chsd wnr after: rdn and edgd rt over 1f out: drvn and kpt on fnl f* **5/1**[3]

0-23 **3** *1 3/4* **Tukhoom (IRE)**[21] 3199 6-9-9 **70** ... PhilDennis 1 72
(Michael Herrington) *in tch: hdwy 2f out: rdn over 1f out: drvn to chse ldng pair ins fnl f: no imp* **11/2**

4141 **4** *1/2* **Kilbaha Lady (IRE)**[20] 3217 5-9-7 **71** ... RowanScott(3) 4 72
(Nigel Tinkler) *hld up towards rr: hdwy wl over 2f out: rdn wl over 1f out: kpt on fnl f* **10/1**

6320 **5** *1 1/4* **Ghayyar (IRE)**[11] 3547 5-9-10 **71** ...(tp) RachelRichardson 2 69
(Tim Easterby) *trckd ldrs: hdwy over 2f out: rdn wl over 1f out: drvn and kpt on one pce fnl f* **9/2**[2]

5301 **6** *nk* **Creek Island (IRE)**[20] 3226 3-9-3 **74** ... FrannyNorton 3 69
(Mark Johnston) *chsd ldng pair: rdn along 3f out: drvn 2f out: sn wknd* **11/4**[1]

2604 **7** *nk* **Mont Kinabalu (IRE)**[17] 3356 4-9-13 **74** ... TomEaves 10 71
(Kevin Ryan) *hld up: a towards rr* **20/1**

304- **8** *1/2* **Sumner Beach**[242] 8381 5-8-9 **56** oh1 ... CamHardie 8 51
(Harriet Bethell) *a towards rr* **40/1**

0-00 **9** *1 1/4* **Desert Dream**[7] 3704 5-9-5 **66** ...(t) NathanEvans 7 59
(Michael Easterby) *a towards rr (jockey said mare was denied a clear run app 2f out)* **18/1**

40-3 **10** *5* **Kingson (IRE)**[54] 2058 3-9-3 **77** ... SeanDavis(3) 11 56
(Richard Fahey) *hld up: a in rr* **14/1**

0435 **11** *1 1/2* **Zeshov (IRE)**[29] 2894 8-9-9 **70** ...(p) LewisEdmunds 5 48
(Rebecca Bastiman) *chsd ldrs: rdn along wl over 2f out: drvn and wknd wl over 1f out* **25/1**

1m 46.83s (0.43) **Going Correction** +0.225s/f (Good)
WFA 3 from 4yo+ 10lb **11** Ran SP% **122.3**
Speed ratings (Par 103): **106,104,102,102,100 100,100,99,98,93 91**
CSF £39.83 CT £199.28 TOTE £8.10: £2.40, £1.50, £2.30; EX 53.50 Trifecta £309.70.
Owner Miss Sarah Hoyland **Bred** Whatton Manor Stud **Trained** Tern Hill, Shropshire

FOCUS
An ordinary handicap in which the gallop picked up turning for home and very few figured. The winner has been rated in line with the better view of his Carlisle win.

3958 CASH FOR KIDS MAIDEN STKS — 1m 1f 207y
8:00 (8:02) (Class 5) 3-Y-O+ — **£4,599** (£1,376; £688; £344; £171) **Stalls** Low

Form — RPR

352 **1** **Ironclad**[10] 3584 3-9-2 81 ... JackMitchell 1 83
(Hugo Palmer) *trckd ldr: pushed along to chal 2f out: rdn to take slt ld jst over 1f out: drvn and edgd rt ins fnl f: kpt on wl towards fin* **4/5**[1]

4-5 **2** *1* **Madeeh**[26] 3003 3-9-2 0 ... DaneO'Neill 4 81
(Sir Michael Stoute) *set stdy pce: shkn up and qcknd over 2f out: sn jnd and rdn: hdd jst over 1f out: n.m.r and drvn ins fnl f: ev ch tl no ex last 50yds* **4/1**[3]

3 *5* **Beyond The Clouds**[423] 6-10-0 0 ... TomEaves 2 71+
(Kevin Ryan) *hld up in rr: pushed along 2f out: rdn over 1f out: styd on fnl f* **7/2**[2]

53 **4** *1* **Sincerity**[19] 3248 3-8-11 0 ... GeorgeWood 5 64
(James Fanshawe) *trckd ldng pair: pushed along wl over 2f out: sn rdn: drvn over 1f out and sn one pce* **7/1**

05 **5** *1 1/2* **Canoodling**[13] 3482 3-8-11 0 ... TonyHamilton 3 61+
(Ian Williams) *plld hrd: hld up in tch: hdwy to chse ldng pair 1/2-way: rdn along over 2f out: drvn wl over 1f out: wknd* **33/1**

2m 18.2s (12.50) **Going Correction** +0.225s/f (Good)
WFA 3 from 6yo 12lb **5** Ran SP% **113.2**
Speed ratings (Par 103): **59,58,54,53,52**
CSF £4.63 TOTE £1.50: £1.10, £3.10; EX 4.50 Trifecta £12.40.
Owner K Abdullah **Bred** Juddmonte Farms Ltd **Trained** Newmarket, Suffolk

FOCUS
An interesting maiden but the dawdling gallop suited the two 3yo colts, who pulled clear as the tempo increased in the last quarter mile and this bare form isn't reliable. The winner didn't need to match his Chelmsford level to take this.

3959 DAISY APPEAL H'CAP (DIV I) — 1m 1f 207y
8:30 (8:31) (Class 6) (0-65,66) 4-Y-O+
£3,428 (£1,020; £509; £300; £300; £300) **Stalls** Low

Form — RPR

-406 **1** **Zihaam**[25] 3054 5-9-0 **62** ...(p) BenSanderson(5) 6 68
(Roger Fell) *hld up: hdwy over 2f out: rdn to chse ldrs and n.m.r ent fnl f: drvn and squeezed through to ld last 50yds* **3/1**[1]

0-00 **2** *1/2* **Bigbadboy (IRE)**[14] 3447 6-8-2 **45** ... AndrewMullen 3 50
(Clive Mulhall) *trckd ldng pair on inner: hdwy over 2f out: rdn to ld 1 1/2f out: drvn ins fnl f: hdd and no ex last 50yds* **11/2**

-000 **3** *1 1/4* **Jennies Gem**[21] 3199 6-7-13 **45** ... JamieGormley(3) 2 48
(Ollie Pears) *trckd ldrs on inner: hdwy over 2f out: rdn wl over 1f out: drvn and ev ch ins fnl f: kpt on same pce towards fin* **12/1**

0600 **4** *shd* **John Caesar (IRE)**[20] 3224 8-8-2 **45** ...(p) PaddyMathers 9 47
(Rebecca Bastiman) *hld up in tch: gd hdwy over 2f out: chsd ldrs and rdn over 1f out: drvn and ev ch jst ins fnl f: kpt on same pce towards fin* **25/1**

0-00 **5** *1 1/4* **Inflexiball**[11] 3547 7-8-6 **49**............................... JimmyQuinn 10 49
(John Mackie) *in tch: hdwy wl over 2f out: rdn wl over 1f out: drvn and kpt on same pce fnl f* **14/1**

6-03 **6** *1 3/4* **Metronomic (IRE)**[18] 3297 5-8-4 **47**..................... CamHardie 8 44
(Peter Niven) *trckd ldr: pushed along over 2f out: rdn wl over 1f out: drvn and wknd appr fnl f* **10/1**

526- **7** *2 3/4* **Dutch Artist (IRE)**[190] 9481 7-8-7 **55**.................. FayeMcManoman(5) 7 47
(Nigel Tinkler) *dwlt: a in rr (jockey said gelding was slowly away)* **12/1**

1600 **8** *8* **False Id**[11] 3547 6-9-0 **64**.......................(b) LauraCoughlan(7) 1 40+
(David Loughnane) *dwlt and towards rr: rapid hdwy on outer 6f out: sn disputing ld: rdn along 3f out: wknd over 2f out (jockey said gelding ran too freely)* **9/2**[3]

3155 **9** *1/2* **Glacier Fox**[20] 3217 4-9-9 **66**................................ JamesSullivan 4 41+
(Tom Tate) *sn led: pushed along 3f out: rdn over 2f out: drvn and hdd wl over 1f out: sn wknd (jockey said that the gelding was unsuited by being taken on for the lead)* **7/2**[2]

00-0 **10** *6* **Wedding Breakfast (IRE)**[57] 1983 5-8-10 **53**...................... DavidAllan 5 17
(Stella Barclay) *a towards rr (vet said mare lost its left fore shoe)* **33/1**

2m 8.63s (2.93) **Going Correction** +0.225s/f (Good) **10** Ran SP% **118.7**
Speed ratings (Par 101): **97,96,95,95,94 93,90,84,84,79**
CSF £20.20 CT £175.95 TOTE £4.00: £1.60, £2.20, £4.70; EX 22.60 Trifecta £169.10.
Owner Nick Bradley Racing 29 & Partner **Bred** Cheveley Park Stud Ltd **Trained** Nawton, N Yorks

FOCUS
A modest handicap in which the steady gallop picked up markedly soon after halfway and the two leaders didn't get home in the closing stages.

3960 DAISY APPEAL H'CAP (DIV II) — 1m 1f 207y
9:00 (9:00) (Class 6) (0-65,65) 4-Y-O+
£3,428 (£1,020; £509; £300; £300; £300) **Stalls Low**

Form RPR

-000 **1** **Dutch Coed**[20] 3225 7-8-5 **52** ow2.......................... RowanScott(3) 9 60
(Nigel Tinkler) *dwlt and in rr: hdwy on outer over 2f out: rdn to chse ldrs over 1f out: str run ins fnl f to ld nr fin (trainer's rep said, regarding the improved form shown, the gelding was suited by a return to Beverley)* **7/1**[3]

536- **2** *3/4* **Ventura Royal (IRE)**[330] 5269 4-9-4 **62**..............(h[1] w) RobbieDowney 8 69
(David O'Meara) *set stdy pce: pushed along and qcknd 2 1/2f out: rdn over 1f out: drvn ins fnl f: kpt on gamely: hdd and no ex towards fin* **14/1**

3113 **3** *3/4* **Majeste**[6] 3718 5-9-7 **65**.. LewisEdmunds 4 71
(Rebecca Bastiman) *trckd ldrs: hdwy 3f out: rdn along wl over 1f out: drvn and ev ch ent fnl f: kpt on same pce towards fin* **13/8**[1]

0-46 **4** *1* **Whatwouldyouknow (IRE)**[20] 3217 4-9-6 **64**.................. PhilipPrince 2 68
(Richard Guest) *hld up towards rr: stdy hdwy over 3f out: chsd ldrs wl over 1f out: rdn and ev ch ent fnl f: sn drvn and kpt on same pce* **5/2**[2]

0-66 **5** *3 1/4* **Size Matters**[30] 2349 5-8-4 **48**............................... NathanEvans 3 46
(Mike Sowersby) *trckd ldr: effrt over 2f out and sn cl up: rdn wl over 1f out: ev ch tl drvn and wknd appr fnl f* **9/1**

-000 **6** *4 1/2* **Mont Royal (FR)**[22] 3162 5-8-10 **54**............................ TomEaves 6 43
(Ollie Pears) *s.i.s: a in rr* **10/1**

0-00 **7** *2 1/2* **Late For The Sky**[99] 1146 5-8-2 **46** oh1...................... CamHardie 1 30
(Stella Barclay) *prom: rdn along over 2f out: sn wknd* **66/1**

5034 **8** *5* **Zarkavon**[14] 3448 5-8-2 **46** oh1.......................(p) JamesSullivan 5 21
(John Wainwright) *hld up towards rr: sme hdwy over 2f out: sn rdn and n.d* **10/1**

600/ **9** *3 3/4* **Aneedh**[549] 9262 9-8-2 **46** oh1...............................(b) AndrewMullen 7 14
(Clive Mulhall) *chsd ldrs: rdn along on outer wl over 2f out: sn drvn and wknd* **33/1**

2m 9.23s (3.53) **Going Correction** +0.225s/f (Good) **9** Ran SP% **118.4**
Speed ratings (Par 101): **94,93,92,92,89 85,83,79,76**
CSF £101.00 CT £235.99 TOTE £7.60: £1.90, £2.70, £1.30; EX 94.80 Trifecta £451.60.
Owner Ms Sara Hattersley **Bred** Sara Hattersley **Trained** Langton, N Yorks

FOCUS
A modest handicap in which an ordinary gallop picked up turning for home. It's been rated as straightforward form.
T/Plt: £31.90 to a £1 stake. Pool: £38,613.62 - 882.15 winning units T/Qpdt: £17.00 to a £1 stake. Pool: £4,378.95 - 189.89 winning units **Joe Rowntree**

3534 BRIGHTON (L-H)
Tuesday, June 18

OFFICIAL GOING: Good to firm (good in places; 7.9)
Wind: Virtually nil Weather: overcast with showers

3961 BRIGHTON BARBERS "CUTTER AND GRINDER" H'CAP — 5f 60y
5:50 (5:54) (Class 6) (0-65,66) 3-Y-O+
£3,105 (£924; £461; £300; £300; £300) **Stalls Low**

Form RPR

0010 **1** **King Crimson**[11] 3531 7-9-6 **66**......................... DarraghKeenan(5) 3 75
(John Butler) *mde all: rdn and sn 3 l clr over 1f out: rdn out and a doing enough ins fnl f (trainers rep said regarding apparent improvement in form that the gelding appreciated the return to Brighton, where it has won previously)* **3/1**[1]

-213 **2** *1/2* **Essaka (IRE)**[11] 3527 7-9-3 **65**............................ SophieRalston(7) 1 72
(Tony Carroll) *racd in midfield: wnt 2nd gng wl 2f: rdn to chse wnr over 1f out: kpt on wl ins fnl f but nvr quite getting to wnr (jockey said gelding hung right-handed under pressure)* **3/1**[1]

0-66 **3** *3* **Exceedingly Diva**[15] 3404 4-9-6 **61**............................ PatCosgrave 9 58
(George Baker) *dwlt and racd in rr: rdn along over 2f out: hdwy u.p over 1f out: kpt on fnl f* **7/1**

-000 **4** *3/4* **Firenze Rosa (IRE)**[10] 3596 4-8-10 **51** oh3.................. CharlieBennett 5 45
(John Bridger) *trckd wnr: pushed along over 2f out: rdn and no imp over 1f out: kpt on one pce fnl f* **40/1**

055 **5** *3/4* **Ar Saoirse**[18] 3320 4-8-3 **51** oh2............................ CierenFallon(7) 10 43
(Clare Hobson) *racd in midfield on outer: rdn and outpcd over 2f out: drvn and mde sme late hdwy fnl f* **10/1**

1021 **6** *hd* **Big Time Maybe (IRE)**[21] 3206 4-9-3 **63**..........(p) ScottMcCullagh(5) 2 54
(Michael Attwater) *midfield on inner: rdn along 2f out: wknd ins fnl f (jockey said gelding was slowly away)* **6/1**[3]

-002 **7** *1* **Ladweb**[10] 3576 9-9-7 **65**....................................... GeorgeBuckell(3) 7 52
(John Gallagher) *dwlt and racd in rr: pushed along and detached over 2f out: mde late hdwy past btn rivals fnl f (trainer said gelding had a breathing problem)* **4/1**[2]

-050 **8** *1* **True Belief (IRE)**[43] 2489 3-9-2 **63**............................(h) RossaRyan 8 45
(Brett Johnson) *racd keenly in midfield: pushed along and little rspnse 2f out: one pce after* **14/1**

10-0 **9** *1 3/4* **Flowing Clarets**[11] 3543 6-9-0 **55**............................ LiamJones 4 33
(John Bridger) *walked to post: chsd wnr: rdn along and outpcd 2f out: wknd ins fnl f* **20/1**

1m 1.45s (-1.55) **Going Correction** -0.325s/f (Firm)
WFA 3 from 4yo+ 6lb **9** Ran SP% **119.7**
Speed ratings (Par 101): **99,98,93,92,91 90,89,87,84**
CSF £12.41 CT £59.23 TOTE £3.80: £1.70, £1.30, £1.70; EX 13.10 Trifecta £101.80.
Owner Power Geneva Ltd **Bred** Mickley Stud **Trained** Newmarket, Suffolk

FOCUS
An overcast evening. Rail re-alignment added 3yds to all races on the card. A low-class handicap and the top two in the market dominated with the winner making all.

3962 EBF MAIDEN STKS — 5f 215y
6:20 (6:20) (Class 5) 2-Y-O
£3,752 (£1,116; £557; £278) **Stalls Low**

Form RPR

03 **1** **Eton College (IRE)**[8] 3660 2-9-5.................................. JFEgan 5 81
(Mark Johnston) *mde all: rdn along and strly pressed by runner-up over 1f out: kpt on really wl ins fnl f* **11/2**[3]

24 **2** *1 1/2* **When Comes Here (IRE)**[33] 2780 2-9-5 .... DavidProbert 2 76
(Andrew Balding) *trckd wnr: clsd gng wl 2f out: rdn upsides and ev ch 2f out: nt match wnr ins fnl f* **10/11**[1]

4 **3** *2 1/2* **Fantom Force (IRE)**[8] 3660 2-9-5 .... TomMarquand 6 68
(Richard Hannon) *chsd wnr: rdn and outpcd by front pair over 1f out: one pce fnl f* **5/1**[2]

4 *1 3/4* **Incinerator** 2-9-5 .... JasonWatson 3 63+
(Hugo Palmer) *hld up: pushed along and rn green over 2f out: hung rt 2f out: rdn and kpt on wl fnl f* **7/1**

4 **5** *3* **Silent Agenda**[13] 3461 2-9-0 .... HectorCrouch 4 48
(Archie Watson) *racd in rr: rdn and outpcd over 1f out: one pce fnl f* **5/1**[2]

1m 9.45s (-1.65) **Going Correction** -0.325s/f (Firm) **5** Ran SP% **113.6**
Speed ratings (Par 93): **98,96,92,90,86**
CSF £11.52 TOTE £6.60: £2.90, £1.10; EX 11.50 Trifecta £34.40.
Owner Sheikh Hamdan bin Mohammed Al Maktoum **Bred** Godolphin **Trained** Middleham Moor, N Yorks

FOCUS
Add 3yds. An ordinary maiden for juveniles and the winner made all under a well-judged ride. The third has been rated near his debut effort.

3963 MARATHONBET FESTIVAL OF RACING 7TH-9TH AUGUST H'CAP — 5f 215y
6:50 (6:51) (Class 4) (0-80,82) 4-Y-O+
£5,530 (£1,645; £822; £411; £300; £300) **Stalls Low**

Form RPR

3334 **1** **Little Boy Blue**[11] 3531 4-9-4 **82**.............................(h) RyanWhile(5) 6 95
(Bill Turner) *trckd ldr: upsides gng wl 2f out: rdn to ld over 1f out: sn clr: rdn out* **11/2**[3]

2151 **2** *4* **Diamond Lady**[11] 3536 8-9-6 **79**............................... HectorCrouch 2 79
(William Stone) *led: rdn along and hdd by wnr over 1f out: kpt on one pce fnl f* **3/1**[1]

-200 **3** *1/2* **Dream Catching (IRE)**[25] 3040 4-9-4 **77**...................(b[1]) DavidProbert 3 76
(Andrew Balding) *midfield on inner: clsng and briefly short of room 2f out: sn rdn over 1f out: kpt on one pce fnl f* **9/2**[2]

6215 **4** *1 1/4* **Real Estate (IRE)**[26] 3014 4-8-12 **71**.......................(p) CallumShepherd 9 66
(Michael Attwater) *hld up: pushed along and no imp on outer over 2f out: sn rdn and kpt on fnl f* **12/1**

-003 **5** *3/4* **Pour La Victoire (IRE)**[11] 3536 9-9-4 **77**..................(v) GeorgeDowning 7 69
(Tony Carroll) *dwlt and racd in last: rdn and bhd 2f out: kpt on passed btn horses ins fnl f* **14/1**

4064 **6** *nk* **Lightning Charlie**[11] 3536 7-9-7 **80**.......................(p[1]) JasonWatson 8 71
(Amanda Perrett) *midfield on outer: rdn along to chse wnr 2f out: wknd ins fnl f* **8/1**

6413 **7** *nse* **Shamshon (IRE)**[24] 3079 8-9-7 **80**............................ TomMarquand 1 71
(Stuart Williams) *hld up: pushed along and no imp 2f out: sn rdn over 1f out: no ex* **6/1**

6313 **8** *10* **Mamillius**[21] 3183 6-9-7 **80**...................................... PatCosgrave 5 39
(George Baker) *racd in midfield: pushed along and outpcd over 2f out: rdn and hung lft over 1f out: wknd fnl f (jockey said gelding stopped quickly)* **3/1**[1]

1m 8.06s (-3.04) **Going Correction** -0.325s/f (Firm) **8** Ran SP% **123.3**
Speed ratings (Par 105): **107,101,101,99,98 97,97,84**
CSF £24.34 CT £84.15 TOTE £5.90: £1.80, £1.50, £1.90; EX 24.80 Trifecta £161.50.
Owner Mrs Tracy Turner **Bred** Mrs P A Turner **Trained** Sigwells, Somerset

FOCUS
Add 3yds. Quite competitive for the grade and all bar one had previous course-winning form. Again it paid to be near the pace. The second has been rated 7lb off her latest C&D win.

3964 DOVES LIVE HERE 26 JULY H'CAP — 6f 210y
7:20 (7:24) (Class 6) (0-65,70) 3-Y-O
£3,105 (£924; £461; £300; £300; £300) **Stalls Low**

Form RPR

06-2 **1** **Bring Us Paradise**[9] 3638 3-9-2 **59**........................... RobertWinston 9 70+
(Tony Carroll) *midfield on outer: clsd gng wl over 2f out: pushed along to ld wl over 1f out: immediately hung lft to far rail: sn in command: rdn out* **10/3**[2]

0213 **2** *3/4* **Your Mothers' Eyes**[8] 3650 3-8-13 **61**..................(p) DarraghKeenan(5) 1 67
(Alan Bailey) *cl up on inner: effrt on inner whn short of room over 2f out: rdn once in clr over 1f out: kpt on wl (jockey said colt was denied a clear run)* **9/4**[1]

2600 **3** *1 1/4* **Global Acclamation**[14] 3442 3-8-13 **56**.....................(p[1]) TomQueally 3 59
(Ed Dunlop) *racd in rr of midfield: niggled along 3f out: rdn wl over 2f out: swtchd rt and drvn 2f out: kpt on wl fnl f* **25/1**

5-00 **4** *3* **Miss Liberty Belle (AUS)**[28] 2939 2-9-3 **60**................... JasonWatson 11 55
(William Jarvis) *dwlt and racd in rr: drvn and drifted wd on crse over 2f out: kpt on wl for press ins fnl f: nrst fin (jockey said filly was slowly away)* **10/1**

00-0 **5** *1 1/2* **Kaafy (IRE)**[32] 2794 3-9-9 **66**..................................... TomMarquand 4 56
(Brian Meehan) *prom in 5th: pushed along to chse wnr 2f out: sn rdn and no imp 1f out: one pce fnl f* **7/1**

0002 **6** *4* **Princess Florence (IRE)**[15] 3409 3-8-4 **47**.................. HayleyTurner 6 27
(John Ryan) *trckd ldr: led over 2f out: rdn and hdd wl over 1f out: wknd fnl f* **20/1**

-101 **7** *2* **Run After Genesis (IRE)**[8] 3651 3-9-6 **70** 6ex............ CierenFallon(7) 7 44
(Brett Johnson) *hld up: pushed along in rr over 3f out: rdn 2f out: nvr on terms (jockey said gelding was never travelling)* **4/1**[3]

2600 **8** *2 1/2* **Turquoise Friendly**[8] 3650 3-9-7 **64**........................ ShaneKelly 2 32
(Robert Cowell) *slowly away and racd in last: rdn in rr over 2f out: nvr on terms* **25/1**

600- **9** *4 1/2* **Loving Life (IRE)**[201] 9307 3-8-1 **47** ow2.................. GabrieleMalune(3) 5 2
(Martin Bosley) *led: pushed along and hdd over 2f out: wknd ins fnl f (jockey said filly moved poorly)* **16/1**

0440 **10** *1 1/4* **Moneta**[21] 3189 3-9-5 **62**..(b[1]) JFEgan 8 14
(Jonathan Portman) *chsd ldr: almost upsides and ev ch 2f out: sn drvn and fnd little: wknd fnl f* **16/1**

1m 21.61s (-2.19) **Going Correction** -0.325s/f (Firm) **10** Ran SP% **119.7**
Speed ratings (Par 97): **99,98,96,93,91 87,84,81,76,75**
CSF £11.27 CT £159.50 TOTE £4.00: £1.30, £1.50, £6.60; EX 12.80 Trifecta £114.60.
Owner D Boocock **Bred** Boocock Trading Ltd **Trained** Cropthorne, Worcs
■ Double Coffee was withdrawn. Price at time of withdrawal 40/1. Rule 4 does not apply.

FOCUS
Add 3yds. Modest fare and the winner was always near the pace. Sound form for the grade.

3965 RAG'N'BONE MAN LIVE HERE 27 JULY H'CAP — 1m 3f 198y
7:50 (7:51) (Class 6) (0-60,62) 3-Y-O

£3,105 (£924; £461; £300; £300; £300) **Stalls** High

Form RPR

0641 **1** **Oliver Hardy**[15] 3407 3-9-9 **62**..(t) RossaRyan 4 70+
(Paul Cole) *prom in 3rd: clsd gng wl on inner 2f out: pushed along to ld over 1f out: rdn out and in command fnl f* **5/2**[1]

0-60 **2** *3/4* **Funny Man**[12] 3517 3-9-5 **58**..(b[1]) LiamJones 8 65+
(William Haggas) *in rr of midfield: effrt to cl on outer over 2f out: rdn over 1f out and no immediate imp: kpt on strly for press wl ins fnl f (trainers rep said gelding was unsuited by the undulating track)* **8/1**

5403 **3** *1 3/4* **Stone Cougar (USA)**[20] 3219 3-9-4 **57**........................ TomMarquand 9 61
(Mark Johnston) *trckd ldr: rdn along and led briefly 2f out: sn drvn and hdd by wnr over 1f out: kpt on fnl f* **6/1**[3]

0-00 **4** *2 3/4* **Goodwood Sonnet (IRE)**[10] 3593 3-8-13 **52**.............. JasonWatson 10 52
(William Knight) *dwlt but sn rcvrd into midfield: rdn along and ev ch in 3rd over 1f out: one pce fnl f* **5/1**[2]

0431 **5** *3/4* **Highway Robbery**[10] 3593 3-8-2 **48**......................(p) SophieRalston(7) 5 46
(Julia Feilden) *racd in midfield: pushed along and outpcd 2f out: rdn and kpt on one pce fnl f* **5/1**[2]

6024 **6** *4 1/2* **Dear Miriam (IRE)**[11] 3528 3-9-7 **60**........................ CallumShepherd 7 51
(Mick Channon) *prom on outer: upsides ldr and ev ch 2f out: sn rdn and readily outpcd by wnr: wknd fnl f* **5/1**[2]

0000 **7** *1 3/4* **So I'm Told (IRE)**[11] 3528 3-8-2 **46** oh1................(v) DarraghKeenan(5) 6 34
(Gary Moore) *hld up: pushed along on outer over 2f out: rdn and one pce over 1f out: plugged on* **12/1**

0-06 **8** *36* **Je M'En Fiche**[28] 2925 3-8-13 **52**................................ JoeyHaynes 1
(Patrick Chamings) *midfield on inner: rdn and bdly outpcd over 2f out: sn bhd* **33/1**

0-50 **9** *32* **Snow In Spring**[11] 3528 3-9-4 **57**........................(p[1]) JosephineGordon 11
(Ralph Beckett) *hld up: a in rr* **33/1**

3060 **10** *nk* **Tribune**[11] 3528 3-9-2 **55**.. ShaneKelly 3
(Sylvester Kirk) *led: rdn along and hdd 2f out: wknd qckly and eased over 1f out (jockey said gelding stopped quickly)* **25/1**

2m 33.06s (-2.94) **Going Correction** -0.325s/f (Firm) **10** Ran SP% **121.4**
Speed ratings (Par 97): **96,95,94,92,92 89,87,63,42,42**
CSF £24.36 CT £111.22 TOTE £3.30: £1.10, £3.00, £1.70; EX 26.40 Trifecta £188.50.
Owner Chelsea T'breds, Sophie Magnier, Oliver Cole **Bred** Bugley Stud & D B Clark **Trained** Whatcombe, Oxon

FOCUS
Add 3yds. The early pace was adequate, but as can often be the case here, it turned into something of a sprint from the bottom of the hill. The form should hold up, however. The third helps set the opening level.

3966 RACING WELFARE H'CAP — 7f 211y
8:20 (8:33) (Class 6) (0-60,60) 4-Y-O+

£3,105 (£924; £461; £300; £300; £300) **Stalls** Low

Form RPR

-500 **1** **Duchess Of Avon**[21] 3187 4-9-5 **58**............................ HectorCrouch 16 65
(Gary Moore) *prom on outer: pushed along to cl 2f out: rdn wd on crse and styd on wl to ld wl ins fnl f: styd on wl* **10/1**

6-00 **2** *1 1/4* **Coachella (IRE)**[25] 3038 5-8-13 **52**......................(b) CallumShepherd 11 56
(Ed de Giles) *hld up: hdwy u.p on inner to ld 2f out: sn rdn over 1f out w 1 ld: kpt on wl but no match for wnr clsng stages* **16/1**

-062 **3** *nk* **Hedging (IRE)**[11] 3540 5-8-11 **57**......................(b) GeorgiaDobie(7) 10 60
(Eve Johnson Houghton) *midfield: rdn along to chse ldr 2f out: drvn and kpt on wl fnl f (vet said gelding lost its right fore shoe)* **9/2**[2]

5-00 **4** *1 1/4* **Hidden Stash**[21] 3187 5-8-7 **46** oh1..........................(p) HollieDoyle 14 46
(William Stone) *disp ld on outer: rdn and ev ch over 1f out: no ex fnl f* **12/1**

0254 **5** *1/2* **Seaquinn**[22] 3142 4-8-8 **47** oh1 ow1.................................. KierenFox 12 46
(John Best) *midfield: rdn along to chse ldr over 1f out: kpt on wl ins fnl f: no ch w wnr* **20/1**

-603 **6** *3 1/4* **Imbucato**[21] 3187 5-8-11 **50**.. TomMarquand 6 42
(Tony Carroll) *chsd ldrs: drvn and outpcd over 2f out: kpt on one pce fr over 1f out* **10/3**[1]

2205 **7** *nse* **Sharp Operator**[21] 3187 6-9-0 **56**......................(h) JoshuaBryan(3) 7 48
(Charlie Wallis) *dwlt and hld up: hdwy u.p over 2f out: rdn and short of room 1f out: kpt on once in clr* **7/1**[3]

0030 **8** *1 1/2* **Duke Of North (IRE)**[49] 2233 7-9-0 **60**..................... IsobelFrancis(7) 8 48
(Jim Boyle) *hld up in rr of midfield: rdn and little imp over 1f out: kpt on one pce fnl f* **10/1**

0530 **9** *nk* **With Approval (IRE)**[7] 3687 7-9-1 **54**........................(p) LiamJones 5 42
(Laura Mongan) *disp ld: rdn and ev ch over 1f out: wknd ins fnl f* **16/1**

0-06 **10** *1 1/4* **Pinchpoint (IRE)**[19] 3251 4-8-13 **57**......................(h) DarraghKeenan(5) 4 42
(John Butler) *disp ld tl rdn along and fnd little over 1f out: wknd fnl f* **12/1**

6002 **11** *1 1/4* **Brother In Arms (IRE)**[21] 3187 5-8-8 **47**.......................... BrettDoyle 15 29
(Tony Carroll) *hld up: pushed along in rr over 2f out: sn rdn and no imp: n.d (vet said gelding lost its right hind shoe)* **17/2**

0024 **12** *3* **Soaring Spirits (IRE)**[11] 3540 9-9-0 **60**...............(b) SophieRalston(7) 1 35
(Dean Ivory) *in tch on inner: rdn along and unable qck over 1f out: wknd qckly fnl f* **14/1**

000- **13** *1 1/2* **Sir Magnum**[257] 7941 4-9-3 **56**.................................. RobertWinston 13 27
(Tony Carroll) *midfield on outer: c wdst of all into st: rdn 2f out and fnd little: n.d* **20/1**

00-0 **14** *6* **Thunderhooves**[6] 3744 4-8-2 **48**................................(t) CierenFallon(7) 2 6
(John Ryan) *in tch on inner: rdn and lost pl 2f out: sn bhd* **14/1**

1m 34.74s (-2.16) **Going Correction** -0.325s/f (Firm) **14** Ran SP% **132.5**
Speed ratings (Par 101): **97,95,95,94,93 90,90,88,88,87 86,83,81,75**
CSF £176.43 CT £861.11 TOTE £8.50: £3.20, £6.00, £2.10; EX 172.90 Trifecta £1565.20.
Owner Caplin & Sheridan **Bred** Meon Valley Stud **Trained** Lower Beeding, W Sussex
■ Star Attraction was withdrawn. Price at time of withdrawal 50/1. Rule 4 does not apply.

FOCUS
Add 3yds. The second bank of stalls (12 to 15) failed to open, with the 11 others having to be pulled up after going 1f or so. Following the false start and a 13-minute delay, the winner came from one of the stalls that did not open at the first attempt. The form is open to question. The winner has been rated within 6lb of last year's best.

3967 SKY SPORTS RACING ON SKY 415 H'CAP — 6f 210y
8:50 (9:00) (Class 5) (0-70,71) 3-Y-O+

£3,752 (£1,116; £557; £300; £300; £300) **Stalls** Low

Form RPR

0563 **1** **Wilson (IRE)**[11] 3540 4-9-4 **63**..................................(p) JoshuaBryan(3) 11 69
(Julia Feilden) *racd in midfield: effrt to cl on outer 2f out: sn rdn and clsd on outer ent fnl f: drvn out to ld on the post* **7/1**

6-30 **2** *nse* **Seprani**[11] 3543 5-9-11 **70**.. GabrieleMalune(3) 5 76
(Amy Murphy) *midfield on inner: pushed along to chse ldr over 1f out: sn rdn and kpt on wl to ld briefly 50yds out: hd on post by wnr* **8/1**

3000 **3** *1/2* **Crystal Deauville (FR)**[10] 3576 4-9-2 **65**..................(v) CierenFallon(7) 12 70
(Gay Kelleway) *broke smartly fr a wd draw and led: rdn 5 l clr over 1f out: drvn and reduced advantage fnl f: hdd fnl 50yds* **6/1**

-166 **4** *3/4* **Warning Fire**[33] 2772 3-9-6 **71**................................ TomMarquand 8 71
(Mark Johnston) *chsd ldr: rdn to chse ldr over 1f out: kpt on fnl f* **11/2**[3]

5601 **5** *1 3/4* **Swissal (IRE)**[28] 2929 4-9-8 **64**..................................(p) DougieCostello 1 62
(David Dennis) *midfield: rdn to chse ldr over 2f out: kpt on wl for press ins fnl f* **4/1**[1]

4402 **6** *nk* **The Lamplighter (FR)**[8] 3645 4-9-13 **69**......................(tp) PatCosgrave 2 66
(George Baker) *bmpd coming out of stalls and racd in rr: hdwy on inner to chse ldr wl over 1f out: no ex ins fnl f* **9/2**[2]

0030 **7** *4 1/2* **The British Lion (IRE)**[21] 3188 4-9-8 **64**........................ RossaRyan 6 49
(Alexandra Dunn) *hld up: rdn and outpcd over 2f out: nvr on terms* **25/1**

6255 **8** *2 3/4* **Helfire**[11] 3540 6-8-13 **55**..(t) CharlieBennett 10 33
(Martin Bosley) *midfield: rdn along and lost pl over 2f out: n.d* **10/1**

-602 **9** *2* **Andalusite**[11] 3539 6-9-0 **56**......................................(v) RoystonFfrench 9 28
(John Gallagher) *midfield on outer: rdn and fnd little over 2f out: wknd fnl f* **10/1**

-300 **10** *1/2* **Golden Nectar**[61] 1880 5-9-9 **65**................................ LiamJones 3 36
(Laura Mongan) *j. awkwardly and racd in last: a in rr* **16/1**

00-0 **11** *1/2* **Ocean Temptress**[13] 3470 5-8-10 **52**...............................(p) BrettDoyle 7 22
(Louise Allan) *in tch in 3rd: rdn along to chse ldr over 2f out: sn wknd over 1f out* **33/1**

1m 21.39s (-2.41) **Going Correction** -0.325s/f (Firm)
WFA 3 from 4yo+ 9lb **11** Ran SP% **122.3**
Speed ratings (Par 103): **100,99,99,98,96 96,91,87,85,85 84**
CSF £64.65 CT £369.65 TOTE £8.10: £2.10, £2.80, £2.90; EX 67.50 Trifecta £402.40.
Owner Adrian Sparks & Partners **Bred** Castlefarm Stud **Trained** Exning, Suffolk
■ Stewards' Enquiry : Gabriele Malune two-day ban: misuse of whip (July 2-3)
Joshua Bryan two-day ban: misuse of whip (July 2-3)

FOCUS
Add 3yds. A searching pace for this ordinary handicap and the first two raced towards the centre of the track. A close finish ensued. The third has been rated to his April C&D run, and the second in line with her turf best.
T/Plt: £26.10 to a £1 stake. Pool: £61,767.49 - 1,725.97 winning units. T/Qpdt: £10.60 to a £1 stake. Pool: £7,962.93 - 552.44 winning units. **Mark Grantham**

3702 THIRSK (L-H)
Tuesday, June 18

OFFICIAL GOING: Good to soft (soft in places)
Wind: light half behind Weather: fine

3968 JOIN RACING TV NOW - EBF FILLIES' NOVICE STKS (PLUS 10 RACE) — 6f
1:40 (1:41) (Class 5) 2-Y-O

£4,204 (£1,251; £625; £312) **Stalls** Centre

Form RPR

54 **1** **Havana Dawn**[7] 3703 2-9-0 0.. SamJames 8 73
(Phillip Makin) *prom: rdn along 2f out: drvn into narrow ld 1f out: hld on wl* **5/1**[2]

2 *nk* **Hot Touch** 2-9-0 0.. JackMitchell 4 72
(Hugo Palmer) *in tch: rdn along 2f out: chsd ldrs whn searching for gap ins fnl f: swtchd lft and kpt on wl fnl 75yds* **9/1**

0 **3** *hd* **Barbarella (IRE)**[34] 2747 2-9-0 0.................................. TomEaves 7 71
(Kevin Ryan) *sn led: strly pressed thrght: drvn whn hdd narrowly 1f out: no ex towards fin* **9/2**[1]

4 *shd* **Imperial Gloriana (IRE)** 2-9-0 0.................................. DavidNolan 11 71+
(David O'Meara) *hld up in tch on outer: pushed along and hdwy over 1f out: rdn and kpt on fnl f* **9/2**[1]

6 **5** *1 1/2* **Balancing Act (IRE)**[14] 3451 2-9-0 0............................ GrahamLee 9 66
(Jedd O'Keeffe) *prom: rdn 2f out: no ex ins fnl f* **10/1**

6 **6** *1/2* **Secret Identity**[21] 3196 2-9-0 0.................................. JackGarritty 2 65
(Jedd O'Keeffe) *cl up: tk str hold: rdn 2f out: edgd lft and no ex ins fnl f* **16/1**

0 **7** *3 1/2* **Ellenor Gray (IRE)**[19] 3265 2-9-0 0............................ PaulHanagan 3 54
(Richard Fahey) *dwlt: sn cl up: rdn 2f out: wknd ins fnl f* **12/1**

4 **8** *1 3/4* **Cece Ceylon**[19] 3259 2-9-0 0.................................... RobHornby 10 49
(Ralph Beckett) *wnt rt s: sn trckd ldrs: rdn 2f out: wknd appr fnl f* **8/1**[3]

9 *nk* **Carriesmatic** 2-9-0 0.. RobbieDowney 5 48
(David Barron) *hld up in tch: pushed along over 2f out: sn outpcd and btn* **80/1**

10 *1* **The Works (IRE)** 2-9-0 0.. CamHardie 13 45
(Declan Carroll) *hld up: pushed along over 2f out: nvr threatened* **14/1**

0 **11** *9* **Knock Annie (IRE)**[13] 3469 2-9-0 0.............................. CliffordLee 12 18
(K R Burke) *dwlt: sn in tch: rdn over 2f out: wknd over 1f out* **18/1**

12 *hd* **Champagne Angel (IRE)** 2-9-0 0.................................. DavidAllan 1 17
(Tim Easterby) *hld up: rdn along over 2f out: wknd over 1f out (vet said filly lost its left fore shoe)* **16/1**

1m 14.1s (1.30) **Going Correction** +0.10s/f (Good) **12** Ran SP% **115.9**
Speed ratings (Par 90): **95,94,94,94,92 91,86,84,84,82 70,70**
CSF £48.42 TOTE £4.00: £1.80, £2.70, £2.30; EX 46.30 Trifecta £276.10.
Owner Syps (uk) Ltd **Bred** Bumble Bloodstock Ltd **Trained** Easingwold, N Yorks

FOCUS
The time for the opener was 3.6sec slower than standard, suggesting that the ground was drying out and quicker than advertised. They finished in a heap in what was probably just an ordinary novice event. The stalls were positioned in the centre for this race.

3969 REDFORD H'CAP (DIV I) 7f
2:10 (2:10) (Class 5) (0-70,71) 3-Y-O+
£4,075 (£1,212; £606; £303; £300; £300) **Stalls** Low

Form RPR

0-62 **1** **Luzum (IRE)**[21] 3207 4-9-12 **65** NathanEvans 8 74
(Michael Easterby) *prom: racd quite keenly: rdn to ld 2f out: drvn and kpt on fnl f* **3/1**[1]

0-00 **2** ½ **Billy Wedge**[15] 3413 4-8-13 **52** CamHardie 9 59
(Tracy Waggott) *trckd ldrs: rdn over 2f out: drvn appr fnl f: kpt on wl* **12/1**

3400 **3** 1 ¼ **Mudawwan (IRE)**[20] 3215 5-10-0 **67** (p) PaulHanagan 12 71
(James Bethell) *across fr wd draw to ld after 1f: rdn and hdd 2f out: sn dropped to 3rd: kpt on ins fnl f* **16/1**

0505 **4** ½ **Our Charlie Brown**[5] 3771 5-9-9 **62** (p[1]) JamesSullivan 2 64
(Tim Easterby) *led for 1f: trckd ldrs: rdn to chal strly over 1f out: wknd fnl 110yds* **7/1**

-034 **5** shd **The Stalking Moon (IRE)**[7] 3704 5-9-10 **63** AndrewMullen 7 65
(Adrian Nicholls) *dwlt: hld up: pushed along and hdwy on outer over 2f out: rdn and edgd lft appr fnl f: kpt on ins fnl f* **10/3**[2]

200- **6** 1 ¾ **Inner Circle (IRE)**[201] 9317 5-10-4 **71** (p) LewisEdmunds 10 68
(Roger Fell) *midfield: outpcd and lost pl 3f out: kpt on fnl f* **5/1**[3]

-066 **7** shd **Dancing Speed (IRE)**[8] 3650 3-9-3 **65** SamJames 3 59
(Marjorie Fife) *midfield: rdn over 2f out: one pce and nvr threatened* **14/1**

00-5 **8** 2 ¼ **Groupie**[15] 3414 5-9-10 **63** GrahamLee 6 54
(Tom Tate) *hld up in midfield: rdn over 2f out: wknd ins fnl f* **15/2**

5600 **9** 6 **Desai**[21] 3178 5-9-8 **61** (p[1]) ConnorBeasley 5 36
(Noel Wilson) *hld up: rdn over 2f out: sn btn* **33/1**

0-00 **10** 1 ½ **Khitaamy (IRE)**[21] 3203 5-8-8 **52** (t[1]) ConnorMurtagh(5) 4 23
(Tina Jackson) *midfield: rdn over 2f out: wknd over 1f out* **100/1**

0-06 **11** 2 **Benji**[152] 274 3-8-7 **58** SeanDavis(3) 1 20
(Richard Fahey) *dwlt: hld up: drvn over 2f out: sn btn (jockey said colt hung right in the home straight)* **25/1**

-000 **12** 2 **Bagatino**[7] 3684 3-7-9 **50** (t) JessicaAnderson(7) 11 7
(Declan Carroll) *dwlt: sn trckd ldrs on wd outside: rdn 3f out: sn wknd* **50/1**

1m 28.13s (0.53) **Going Correction** +0.10s/f (Good)
WFA 3 from 4yo+ 9lb **12 Ran SP% 119.0**
Speed ratings (Par 103): **101,100,99,98,98 96,96,93,86,85 82,80**
CSF £39.37 CT £505.39 TOTE £4.40: £1.90, £3.00, £4.80; EX 39.90 Trifecta £392.60.
Owner Straghalis Mason Hollings Hull & Lm Synd **Bred** Mrs Gillian McCalmont **Trained** Sheriff Hutton, N Yorks

FOCUS
Add 10yds to race distance. The principals raced prominently in this very ordinary handicap, and they all came down the centre in the straight. The third has been rated close to his recent form.

3970 REDFORD H'CAP (DIV II) 7f
2:45 (2:45) (Class 5) (0-70,72) 3-Y-O+
£4,075 (£1,212; £606; £303; £300; £300) **Stalls** Low

Form RPR

3055 **1** **Bee Machine (IRE)**[21] 3208 4-8-4 **51** (t) ZakWheatley(7) 5 59
(Declan Carroll) *trckd ldrs: racd keenly: pushed into ld wl over 1f out: drvn and kpt on* **4/1**[1]

066 **2** 1 ¼ **Ghathanfar (IRE)**[29] 2895 3-8-8 **57** CamHardie 6 59
(Tracy Waggott) *pressed ldr: led over 5f out: rdn and hdd wl over 1f out: kpt on but a hld* **22/1**

0-06 **3** 3 ¼ **I Know How (IRE)**[49] 2247 4-9-11 **65** GrahamLee 7 61
(Julie Camacho) *hld up in midfield: racd quite keenly: rdn over 2f out: kpt on fnl f: wnt modest 3rd post (vet said gelding lost its right hind shoe)* **5/1**[2]

5135 **4** shd **Equidae**[12] 3503 4-9-13 **67** (t) TomEaves 1 63
(Iain Jardine) *led: hdd over 5f out: trckd ldr: rdn and outpcd in 3rd over 1f out: one pce ins fnl f: lost 3rd post* **4/1**[1]

3-45 **5** ½ **Take Fright**[29] 2909 3-9-7 **70** JackMitchell 9 61
(Hugo Palmer) *stdd jst after s and hld up in rr: rdn and sme hdwy on outside over 2f out: kpt on same pce fnl f: nvr trbld ldrs* **7/1**

0-00 **6** nk **The Mekon**[38] 2634 4-9-2 **56** ConnorBeasley 2 49
(Noel Wilson) *dwlt: hld up in rr: rdn over 2f out: kpt on fnl f* **25/1**

5-40 **7** nk **Glaceon (IRE)**[18] 3297 4-8-8 **53** ConnorMurtagh(5) 4 46
(Tina Jackson) *in tch on inner: rdn over 2f out: wknd over 1f out* **9/1**

1305 **8** 5 **Thunder Buddy**[47] 2349 4-9-8 **62** (v) CliffordLee 10 41
(K R Burke) *midfield: rdn over 4f out: wknd 2f out* **8/1**

0-00 **9** 1 ½ **Al Suil Eile (FR)**[19] 3249 3-9-9 **72** (t) JasonHart 11 44
(John Quinn) *trckd ldrs: rdn over 2f out: wknd over 1f out* **11/2**[3]

5000 **10** 19 **Mountain Of Stars**[22] 3144 4-8-9 **49** oh4 (t) PaddyMathers 3
(Suzzanne France) *dwlt: hld up in midfield: rdn 3f out: wknd over 1f out* **100/1**

1m 28.05s (0.45) **Going Correction** +0.10s/f (Good)
WFA 3 from 4yo+ 9lb **10 Ran SP% 114.8**
Speed ratings (Par 103): **101,99,95,95,95 94,94,88,87,65**
CSF £93.00 CT £448.29 TOTE £4.30: £1.60, £7.60, £1.90; EX 89.50 Trifecta £449.30.
Owner Mrs Sarah Bryan **Bred** Drumlin Bloodstock **Trained** Malton, N Yorks

FOCUS
Add 10yds. This was very slightly quicker than the first division. The first two raced nearer to the inside rail than most, and finished clear. A turf pb from the winner.

3971 RACINGTV.COM H'CAP 6f
3:20 (3:21) (Class 4) (0-85,89) 3-Y-O+
£6,986 (£2,079; £1,038; £519; £300; £300) **Stalls** Centre

Form RPR

1-46 **1** **Royal Prospect (IRE)**[147] 353 4-9-9 **81** GrahamLee 7 91
(Julie Camacho) *midfield: racd quite keenly: pushed along and hdwy to chse ldrs over 1f out: rdn and kpt on fnl f: led towards fin* **8/1**

3-01 **2** nk **Came From The Dark (IRE)**[10] 3590 3-9-2 **81** LiamKeniry 3 88+
(Ed Walker) *midfield: smooth hdwy 2f out: pushed into ld appr fnl f: edgd rt and sn rdn: kpt on but hdd towards fin* **2/1**[1]

2-50 **3** 1 ¾ **Gin In The Inn (IRE)**[41] 2526 6-9-11 **83** PaulHanagan 2 86
(Richard Fahey) *prom: pushed into ld over 1f out: hdd appr fnl f: sn carried rt by ldr: rdn and one pce fnl 110yds* **7/1**

3606 **4** nk **Sheepscar Lad (IRE)**[8] 3658 5-8-11 **74** FayeMcManoman(5) 4 76
(Nigel Tinkler) *dwlt: hld up: pushed along over 2f out: swtchd lft appr fnl f: rdn and kpt on* **13/2**[3]

-400 **5** nk **Russian Realm**[49] 2247 9-8-11 **72** BenRobinson(3) 1 73
(Paul Midgley) *hld up: rdn 2f out: kpt on fnl f* **14/1**

-003 **6** 3 **Lucky Lucky Man (IRE)**[18] 3309 4-9-6 **83** ConnorMurtagh(5) 9 74
(Richard Fahey) *dwlt: sn trckd ldr: rdn over 2f out: wknd fnl f (jockey said gelding missed the break)* **11/2**[2]

0040 **7** 2 **Henley**[33] 2775 7-9-9 **81** CamHardie 6 66
(Tracy Waggott) *led: rdn and hdd over 1f out: wknd fnl f* **20/1**

1101 **8** nk **Pennsylvania Dutch**[9] 3636 5-10-0 **89** 5ex SeanDavis(3) 8 73
(Kevin Ryan) *dwlt: hld up in tch: rdn over 2f out: wknd fnl f* **11/2**[2]

000- **9** 1 ¼ **Arcavallo (IRE)**[239] 8481 4-9-12 **84** (p) AndrewMullen 5 64
(Michael Dods) *trckd ldrs: racd keenly: rdn 2f out: sn wknd* **25/1**

1m 12.46s (-0.34) **Going Correction** +0.10s/f (Good)
WFA 3 from 4yo+ 7lb **9 Ran SP% 116.3**
Speed ratings (Par 105): **106,105,103,102,102 98,95,95,93**
CSF £24.57 CT £121.10 TOTE £7.20: £2.10, £1.30, £2.30; EX 37.90 Trifecta £322.20.
Owner Geoff & Sandra Turnbull **Bred** Highpark Bloodstock Ltd **Trained** Norton, N Yorks

■ Stewards' Enquiry : Liam Keniry two-day ban: interference & careless riding (Jun 23, Jul 2)

FOCUS
Decent sprint handicap form, in a time under 2sec outside standard. The winner has been rated back to form, with the third and fourth a bit below.

3972 FOLLOW @RACINGTV ON TWITTER / EBF STALLIONS NOVICE STKS 7f
3:55 (3:59) (Class 5) 3-Y-O+
£4,851 (£1,443; £721; £360) **Stalls** Low

Form RPR

3-32 **1** **Current Option (IRE)**[21] 3184 3-9-2 84 PaulHanagan 12 82+
(William Haggas) *prom on outer: t.k.h early: pushed into ld wl over 1f out: rdn clr ins fnl f: pushed out fnl 50yds* **5/4**[2]

0 **2** 2 ½ **Siglo Six**[68] 1723 3-9-2 0 (h) JackMitchell 8 75
(Hugo Palmer) *hld up: pushed along and hdwy 2f out: rdn and kpt on fnl f: wnt 2nd fnl 75yds: no ch w wnr* **14/1**

31 **3** 1 ½ **Alkaraama (USA)**[28] 2938 3-9-9 0 DaneO'Neill 9 78
(Sir Michael Stoute) *trckd ldrs: pushed along over 2f out: drvn to chse ldr appr fnl f: edgd lft and one pce: lost 2nd 75yds out: no ex* **11/10**[1]

65 **4** shd **Dawaaween (IRE)**[26] 3013 3-8-11 0 KieranShoemark 3 66
(Owen Burrows) *trckd ldrs: pushed along and edgd lft over 1f out: n.m.r 110yds out: kpt on fnl 75yds (jockey said filly ran green)* **7/1**[3]

6 **5** hd **Rudy Lewis (IRE)**[18] 3324 3-9-2 0 StevieDonohoe 7 70
(Charlie Fellowes) *midfield: pushed along over 2f out: rdn ins fnl f: kpt on fnl 150yds* **25/1**

26 **6** ¾ **Kind Review**[12] 3517 3-9-2 0 CamHardie 1 68?
(Tracy Waggott) *led narrowly: pushed along over 2f out: edgd lft and hdd wl over 1f out: sn drvn: no ex fnl 100yds* **50/1**

0 **7** 6 **Hurricane Ali (IRE)**[12] 3510 3-9-2 0 AndrewMullen 2 52
(John Mackie) *dwlt: hld up: pushed along over 2f out: kpt on ins fnl f: nvr threatened (jockey said gelding hung left turning in)* **25/1**

0-0 **8** ½ **General Mischief (IRE)**[19] 3247 3-9-2 0 ConnorBeasley 4 51
(Michael Dods) *in tch: pushed along 3f out: sn outpcd and btn* **66/1**

06 **9** ½ **Ripon Spa**[12] 3510 3-8-13 0 JaneElliott(3) 11 50
(Jedd O'Keeffe) *hld up: rdn and outpcd over 3f out: plugged on ins fnl f* **50/1**

0-0 **10** 4 **Coco Motion (IRE)**[29] 2912 3-9-2 0 RobbieDowney 5 39
(Michael Dods) *dwlt: a towards rr* **66/1**

0- **11** 9 **Kyllachy Castle**[232] 8698 3-8-13 0 ConorMcGovern(3) 10 14
(Lynn Siddall) *midfield: rdn 3f out: wknd 2f out* **150/1**

1m 28.17s (0.57) **Going Correction** +0.10s/f (Good) **11 Ran SP% 126.5**
Speed ratings (Par 103): **100,97,95,95,95 94,87,86,86,81 71**
CSF £20.43 TOTE £2.30: £1.10, £2.80, £1.10; EX 19.70 Trifecta £33.50.
Owner Bernard Kantor **Bred** Grangecon Holdings Ltd **Trained** Newmarket, Suffolk

FOCUS
Add 10yds. An interesting novice event with a useful winner. The level is a bit fluid in behind the winner, but the fourth has been rated close to her previous runs for now.

3973 THEAKSTON LEGENDARY ALES PALE ALE H'CAP 1m 4f 8y
4:35 (4:35) (Class 4) (0-80,85) 4-Y-O+
£7,309 (£2,175; £1,087; £543; £300; £300) **Stalls** High

Form RPR

0-10 **1** **Buckland Boy (IRE)**[32] 2793 4-8-9 **68** StevieDonohoe 6 77
(Charlie Fellowes) *midfield: hdwy 3f out: rdn to ld appr fnl f: drvn and edgd lft: styd on* **7/2**[2]

-061 **2** 1 ¼ **Dragons Voice**[8] 3663 5-9-5 **85** 5ex Pierre-LouisJamin(7) 7 92
(David Menuisier) *s.i.s: hld up in rr: rdn along over 3f out: drvn and hdwy 2f out: styd on to go 2nd 75yds out: nvr getting to wnr* **3/1**[1]

5661 **3** ½ **Ingleby Hollow**[15] 3415 7-9-3 **76** (t) DavidNolan 5 82
(David O'Meara) *midfield: hdwy over 3f out: rdn to chal 2f out: drvn ins fnl f: one pce fnl 110yds* **11/1**

4210 **4** 4 **Royal Cosmic**[4] 3816 5-9-1 **74** PaulHanagan 2 74
(Richard Fahey) *trckd ldrs: pushed along over 3f out: sn outpcd: plugged on ins fnl f but no threat* **10/1**

003- **5** ¾ **Statuario**[37] 8486 4-9-6 **79** KieranShoemark 4 77
(Richard Spencer) *prom: rdn over 2f out: led wl over 1f out: hdd appr fnl f: wknd ins fnl f* **8/1**

6-51 **6** 3 ¾ **Follow Intello (IRE)**[32] 2793 4-9-2 **75** GeorgeWood 3 67
(Chris Wall) *trckd ldrs: rdn along 3f out: wknd over 1f out (trainer's rep said gelding was unsuited by the ground (good to soft, soft in places) on this occasion and would prefer a quicker surface)* **5/1**[3]

-040 **7** 2 **Alfa McGuire (IRE)**[43] 2479 4-9-6 **79** SamJames 1 68
(Phillip Makin) *led: rdn over 2f out: hdd wl over 1f out: sn wknd* **18/1**

5-03 **8** shd **Rashdan (FR)**[58] 1971 4-9-4 **77** (v) JackMitchell 10 66
(Hugo Palmer) *prom on outer: rdn along 3f out: wknd over 1f out* **6/1**

45-6 **9** 2 **Contrebasse**[31] 2819 4-8-6 **65** DuranFentiman 8 51
(Tim Easterby) *midfield: rdn over 3f out: wknd over 1f out* **20/1**

12/0 **10** 16 **Ennjaaz (IRE)**[12] 3502 5-9-5 **78** NathanEvans 9 38
(Marjorie Fife) *dwlt: hld up: rdn 3f out: sn wknd* **66/1**

2m 38.36s (-1.64) **Going Correction** +0.10s/f (Good) **10 Ran SP% 118.2**
Speed ratings (Par 105): **109,108,107,105,104 102,100,100,99,88**
CSF £14.68 CT £105.31 TOTE £4.60: £1.80, £1.50, £2.40; EX 16.10 Trifecta £162.90.
Owner P S McNally **Bred** Thomas Hassett **Trained** Newmarket, Suffolk

FOCUS
Add 27yds. The initial pace didn't appear to be overly strong, but all the first three came from the rear half of the field. They finished clear. The third has been rated close to his best.

3974 EVERY RACE LIVE ON RACING TV / EBF FILLIES' NOVICE STKS 7f 218y
5:10 (5:16) (Class 5) 3-Y-0+ **£4,851** (£1,443; £721; £360) **Stalls Centre**

Form RPR

1-2 **1** **Loolwah (IRE)**[16] 3372 3-9-4 .... DaneO'Neill 6 87
(Sir Michael Stoute) *trckd ldrs: hrd drvn into narrow ld appr fnl f: carried hd bit awkwardly but styd on to assert towards fin* **7/4**[1]

5 **2** *½* **Incredulous**[12] 3517 3-8-11 .... PaulHanagan 8 79
(William Haggas) *trckd ldrs: pushed along to chal strly over 2f out: rdn over 1f out: drvn and edgd lft ins fnl f: one pce fnl 50yds* **9/2**[3]

5-3 **3** *4* **Shaqwar**[45] 2420 3-8-11 .... JasonHart 2 70
(Kevin Ryan) *led: rdn and strly pressed over 2f out: hdd appr fnl f: wknd* **11/4**[2]

4 *¾* **Amber Star (IRE)** 3-8-11 .... ShaneGray 4 68+
(David O'Meara) *dwlt: hld up: pushed along 3f out: nvr threatened* **10/1**

6 **5** *8* **Casting Spells**[25] 3050 3-8-11 .... CliffordLee 7 50
(Tom Dascombe) *prom: pushed along over 3f out: wknd over 1f out* **7/1**

1m 42.4s (0.70) **Going Correction** +0.10s/f (Good) **5 Ran SP% 102.8**
Speed ratings (Par 100): **100,99,95,94,86**
CSF £7.78 TOTE £2.00: £1.60, £2.00; EX 7.20 Trifecta £11.30.Lady Amelia was withdrawn. Price at time of withdrawal 16-1. Rule 4 does not apply.

Owner Hamdan Al Maktoum **Bred** Shadwell Estate Company Limited **Trained** Newmarket, Suffolk

■ Happy Face (10/1) was withdrawn. Rule 4 applies to bets struck prior to withdrawal but not SP bets. Deduction - 5p in the £. New market formed. Lope Scholar (4/1) was withdrawn Rule 4 applies to all bets - Deduction 20p in the £

FOCUS
Add 10yds. This field of inexperienced fillies took a long time to load and three of them were withdrawn after giving trouble. The first pair finished clear. The third has been rated close to her latest.

3975 SCOUTING FOR GIRLS - LIVE @THIRSKRACES 16TH AUGUST H'CAP 5f
5:45 (5:46) (Class 6) (0-65,66) 3-Y-0+
£3,398 (£1,011; £505; £300; £300; £300) **Stalls Centre**

Form RPR

0220 **1** **Gamesome (FR)**[35] 2709 8-9-7 **65** .... ConnorMurtagh(5) 6 72
(Paul Midgley) *dwlt: hld up towards far side: smooth hdwy 2f out: jnd ldrs gng wl 1f out: pushed into ld ins fnl f: drvn out fnl 110yds (trainer said, regarding the improved form shown, the gelding may have benefited from being able to get cover from a better draw on this occasion)* **8/1**[3]

5045 **2** *½* **B Fifty Two (IRE)**[1] 3928 10-9-4 **60** ....(vt) JaneElliott(3) 1 65
(Marjorie Fife) *dwlt: midfield towards far side: swtchd rt and hdwy over 1f out: rdn to chal jst ins fnl f: kpt on* **12/1**

0-26 **3** *shd* **Debawtry (IRE)**[13] 3470 4-9-13 **66** .... SamJames 19 71+
(Phillip Makin) *dwlt: hld up towards stands' side: pushed along and hdwy over 1f out: rdn and r.o wl fnl f* **9/2**[2]

26R **4** *1¼* **Piazon**[12] 3518 8-9-4 **57** ....(be) NathanEvans 10 57
(Julia Brooke) *racd centre: led: rdn 2f out: edgd rt appr fnl f: drvn and hdd ins fnl f: one pce fnl 110yds* **33/1**

-026 **5** *1* **Bronze Beau**[20] 3227 12-9-9 **62** ....(tp) ShaneGray 7 59
(Linda Stubbs) *racd towards far side: w ldr: rdn 2f out: no ex fnl 110yds* **33/1**

2246 **6** *nk* **Always Amazing**[5] 3772 5-9-4 **57** .... JasonHart 8 53
(Derek Shaw) *trckd ldrs centre: rdn over 1f out: no ex ins fnl f* **11/1**

5041 **7** *½* **Optimickstickhill**[12] 3518 4-8-11 **50** ....(b) KieranO'Neill 5 44
(Scott Dixon) *chsd ldrs towards far side: rdn over 2f out: edgd rt over 1f out: no ex fnl f* **8/1**[3]

-400 **8** *shd* **Raffle King (IRE)**[12] 3518 5-8-8 **50** ....(b[1]) JamieGormley(3) 2 44
(Ruth Carr) *chsd ldrs far side: rdn 2f out: wknd fnl 110yds* **20/1**

10-4 **9** *¾* **Burtonwood**[148] 347 7-9-4 **64** .... VictorSantos(7) 9 55
(Julie Camacho) *chsd ldrs centre: rdn 2f out: wknd ins fnl f* **25/1**

5252 **10** *¾* **Shepherd's Purse**[8] 3658 7-9-9 **62** .... JamesSullivan 15 50
(Ruth Carr) *racd towards stands' side: prom: rdn over 2f out: wknd ins fnl f* **3/1**[1]

0050 **11** *hd* **Celerity (IRE)**[3] 3846 5-8-0 **46** oh1 ....(p) ElishaWhittington(7) 13 33
(Lisa Williamson) *hld up centre: nvr threatened* **40/1**

-000 **12** *nk* **Swiss Miss**[7] 3697 3-7-11 **47** .... AndrewBreslin(5) 3 31
(John Gallagher) *racd towards far side: hld up: rdn over 2f out: nvr involved* **33/1**

0333 **13** *1¼* **Le Manege Enchante (IRE)**[15] 3425 6-8-7 **46** ....(v) PaddyMathers 14 28
(Derek Shaw) *dwlt: hld up towards centre: rdn over 2f out: wknd over 1f out* **14/1**

043- **14** *nse* **Little Miss Lola**[179] 9668 5-8-4 **48** .... PaulaMuir(5) 11 30
(Lynn Siddall) *hld up towards centre: nvr threatened* **25/1**

3600 **15** *nk* **Twentysvnthlancers**[12] 3518 6-9-1 **57** .... BenRobinson(3) 17 38
(Paul Midgley) *racd towards stands' side: hld up: rdn over 2f out: wknd over 1f out (jockey said gelding stopped quickly)* **20/1**

-000 **16** *1¼* **Vimy Ridge**[50] 2206 7-9-5 **65** ....(t) JessicaCooley(7) 4 41
(Alan Bailey) *dwlt: racd towards far side and a in rr* **20/1**

06-0 **17** *11* **Pritty Livvy**[50] 2197 3-8-1 **46** oh1 ....(w) DuranFentiman 12
(Noel Wilson) *trckd ldrs centre: racd quite keenly: rdn 2f out: wknd* **100/1**

59.83s (0.43) **Going Correction** +0.10s/f (Good)
WFA 3 from 4yo+ 6lb **17 Ran SP% 122.3**
Speed ratings (Par 101): **100,99,99,97,95 94,94,94,92,91 91,90,88,88,88 86,68**
CSF £87.17 CT £508.56 TOTE £9.30: £2.40, £3.50, £1.30, £5.60; EX 133.10 Trifecta £774.80.

Owner M Hammond & P T Midgley **Bred** Jean-Pierre Deroubaix **Trained** Westow, N Yorks

■ Tick Tock Croc was withdrawn. Price at time of withdrawal 16/1. Rule 4 does not apply.

FOCUS
Low-grade sprint form. Six of the first eight home came from a group of seven who raced towards the far side, the exceptions being the third and fourth. The likes of the third help set the level.
T/Plt: £61.40 to a £1 stake. Pool: £42,685.42 - 507.35 winning units. T/Qpdt: £7.60 to a £1 stake. Pool: £4,689.05 - 451.92 winning units. **Andrew Sheret**

3976 - 4011a (Foreign Racing) - See Raceform Interactive

3948 ROYAL ASCOT (R-H)
Wednesday, June 19

OFFICIAL GOING: Straight course - good to soft; round course - soft (good to soft in places; stands' 8.2, ctr 8.4, far 8.2, rnd 7.2) changing to soft on both courses af
Almost NilRain, clearing after race 3

3983 QUEEN MARY STKS (GROUP 2) (FILLIES) 5f
2:30 (2:32) (Class 1) 2-Y-O
£62,381 (£23,650; £11,836; £5,896; £2,959; £1,485) **Stalls Centre**

Form RPR

21 **1** **Raffle Prize (IRE)**[25] 3071 2-9-0 0 .... FrankieDettori 25 106
(Mark Johnston) *athletic; looked wl; racd nr side: chsd ldrs: drvn and chsd ldr jst over 1f out: styd on wl u.p to ld wl ins fnl f: hld on gamely cl home: 1st of 16 in gp* **18/1**

2 *hd* **Kimari (USA)**[55] 2-9-0 0 ....(b) JohnRVelazquez 18 105
(Wesley A Ward, U.S.A) *str; racd nr side: sn led: rdn over 1f out: drvn and hdd wl ins fnl f: rallied gamely u.p towards fin: hld cl home: 2nd of 16 in gp* **13/2**[2]

1 **3** *1* **Final Song (IRE)**[40] 2565 2-9-0 0 .... ChristopheSoumillon 23 102
(Saeed bin Suroor) *athletic; racd nr side: hld up in tch in midfield: swtchd lft and hdwy u.p over 1f out: chsd ldrs 1f out: styd on wl: nvr quite enough pce to threaten ldrs: 3rd of 16 in gp* **6/1**[1]

11 **4** *1¼* **Liberty Beach**[11] 3564 2-9-0 0 .... JasonHart 6 97+
(John Quinn) *tall; racd far side: stdd after s: t.k.h: hld up in midfield: effrt and hdwy over 1f out: rdn to ld gp and chsd ldrs ins fnl f: styd on but nvr threatened ldrs: 1st of 8 in gp* **16/1**

2 **5** *¾* **Al Raya**[14] 3469 2-9-0 0 .... AndreaAtzeni 24 94
(Simon Crisford) *str; racd nr side: hld up in midfield: effrt ent fnl 2f: hdwy over 1f out: kpt on wl ins fnl f: no threat to ldrs: 4th of 16 in gp* **14/1**

22 **6** *nk* **Mighty Spirit (IRE)**[33] 2805 2-9-0 0 .... PJMcDonald 11 93+
(Richard Fahey) *str; racd far side: chsd ldrs in gp but midfield overall: hdwy to ld gp 2f: rdn over 1f out: kpt on same pce ins fnl f: 2nd of 8 in gp* **20/1**

1 **7** *shd* **Flaming Princess (IRE)**[14] 3469 2-9-0 0 .... BarryMcHugh 27 93
(Richard Fahey) *compact; racd nr side: hld up in midfield: effrt ent fnl 2f: hdwy over 1f out: edgd rt and kpt on ins fnl f: no threat to ldrs: 5th of 16 in gp* **33/1**

311 **8** *nk* **Flippa The Strippa (IRE)**[27] 3023 2-9-0 0 .... JamesMcDonald 14 92
(Charles Hills) *compact; racd nr side: hld up in midfield: effrt jst over 2f out: hdwy u.p over 1f out: kpt on ins fnl f: nvr trbld ldrs: 6th of 16 in gp* **20/1**

9 *shd* **Tango (IRE)**[11] 3606 2-9-0 0 .... RyanMoore 2 92+
(A P O'Brien, Ire) *str; sltly on toes; racd far side: dwlt: in rr: rdn jst over 2f out: hdwy u.p ent fnl f: styd on: nvr trbld ldrs: 3rd of 8 in gp* **9/1**

11 **10** *1½* **Lambeth Walk**[48] 2316 2-9-0 0 .... OisinMurphy 20 86
(Archie Watson) *compact; racd nr side: broke wl: sn restrained and in tch in midfield: over 2f out: sn struggling: lost pl and wl hld over 1f out: no threat to ldrs but kpt on again ins fnl f: 7th of 16 in gp* **14/1**

1 **11** *¾* **Theory Of Time (IRE)**[30] 2915 2-9-0 0 .... JamesDoyle 16 84
(Charlie Appleby) *compact; racd nr side: in tch in midfield: effrt 2f out: sn drvn and unable qck over 1f out: wknd ins fnl f: 8th of 16 in gp* **7/1**[3]

3 **12** *hd* **Multiply By Eight (FR)**[20] 3259 2-9-0 0 .... SilvestreDeSousa 26 83
(Tom Dascombe) *str; racd nr side: bhd: rdn over 2f out: nt clr run over 1f out: kpt on to pass btn horses ins fnl f: nvr trbld ldrs: 9th of 16 in gp* **33/1**

1 **13** *nk* **Shadn (IRE)**[14] 3461 2-9-0 0 .... DavidProbert 12 82
(Andrew Balding) *athletic; racd nr side: dwlt: hld up in rr: effrt jst over 2f out: swtchd rt over 1f out: swtchd rt again and kpt on to pass btn horses ins fnl f: nvr trbld ldrs: 10th of 16 in gp* **40/1**

1 **14** *½* **Divine Spirit**[30] 2918 2-9-0 0 .... KerrinMcEvoy 17 80
(Charlie Appleby) *athletic; racd nr side: in tch in midfield: lost pl u.p over 1f out: wknd ins fnl f: 11th of 16 in gp* **13/2**[2]

06 **15** *nk* **Too Shy Shy (IRE)**[14] 3461 2-9-0 0 .... JasonWatson 7 79+
(Richard Spencer) *tall; sltly on toes; racd far side: broke wl: gp ldr but midfield overall: lost gp ld and no ex u.p over 1f out: wknd ins fnl f: 4th of 8 in gp* **100/1**

16 *nse* **Anna's Fast (USA)**[56] 2-9-0 0 ....(bt) TylerGaffalione 22 79
(Wesley A Ward, U.S.A) *str; ponied to s: racd nr side: chsd ldr tl over 1f out: no ex u.p and hung rt: wknd ins fnl f: 12th of 16 in gp* **16/1**

2 **17** *nk* **Ventura Flame (IRE)**[8] 3679 2-9-0 0 .... PaulMulrennan 1 78+
(Keith Dalgleish) *str; racd far side: dwlt: in rr: u.p over 2f out: wandered rt ent fnl f: kpt on ins fnl f: nvr involved: 5th of 8 in gp* **100/1**

18 *½* **Isabeau (IRE)**[19] 3326 2-9-0 0 ....(b) LeighRoche 15 76
(M D O'Callaghan, Ire) *str; racd nr side: chsd ldrs: unable qck u.p and lost pl over 1f out: wknd ins fnl f: 13th of 16 in gp* **40/1**

22 **19** *hd* **Partridge (IRE)**[13] 3507 2-9-0 0 .... PatDobbs 21 75
(Richard Hannon) *workmanlike; racd nr side: hld up towards rr: effrt 2f out: no prog: nvr involved: 14th of 16 in gp* **33/1**

20 *½* **Love Bracelet (USA)**[26] 3059 2-9-0 0 .... DonnachaO'Brien 8 73+
(A P O'Brien, Ire) *str; racd far side: midfield overall: rdn over 2f out: drvn over 1f out: wnt rt and no imp ins fnl f: 6th of 8 in gp* **25/1**

44 **21** *¾* **American Lady (IRE)**[31] 2881 2-9-0 0 .... ChrisHayes 28 71
(J A Stack, Ire) *athletic; racd nr side: bhd: rdn over 2f out: drvn over 1f out: nvr involved: 15th of 16 gp* **50/1**

1 **22** *3* **Applecross (IRE)**[26] 3033 2-9-0 0 .... HayleyTurner 4 60
(Michael Bell) *compact; racd far side: in rr: swtchd rt and effrt u.p ent fnl 2f: no imp over 1f out: sn wknd and bhd ins fnl f: 7th of 8 in gp* **66/1**

1 **23** *shd* **Brand New Day (IRE)**[11] 2-9-0 0 ....(p[1]) AntoineHamelin 5 59
(Matthieu Palussiere, France) *str; racd far side: prom in gp but midfield overall: u.p and lost pl ent fnl 2f: wknd fnl f: 8th of 8 in gp* **33/1**

24 *2½* **Daughter In Law (IRE)**[25] 3101 2-9-0 0 ....(b) JimCrowley 19 50
(Kieran P Cotter, Ire) *athletic; racd nr side: chsd ldrs: rdn 2f out: sn struggling and lost pl: fdd ins fnl f: 16th of 16 in gp* **25/1**

1 **R** **Ickworth (IRE)**[44] 2491 2-9-0 0 .... WJLee 3
(W McCreery, Ire) *leggy; rrd as stalls opened and sat on haunches: rdr unbalanced: tk no part* **11/1**

1m 1.58s (0.88) **Going Correction** +0.475s/f (Yiel) **25 Ran SP% 141.4**
Speed ratings (Par 102): **112,111,110,108,106 106,106,105,105,103 102,101,101,100,99 99,99,98,98,97 96,91,91,87,**
CSF £127.61 CT £837.05 TOTE £16.90: £5.05, £3.25, £4.00; EX 330.60 Trifecta £2864.70.

Owner Sheikh Hamdan bin Mohammed Al Maktoum **Bred** Godolphin **Trained** Middleham Moor, N Yorks

■ Stewards' Enquiry : John R Velazquez nine-day ban: used whip above the permitted level (Jul 3-11)

FOCUS

As was the case on the opening day the running rail on the round course was positioned 3yds out from approx 9f out to the home straight. The course avoided heavy overnight rain, with just 1mm recorded, but it hammered down in the hour leading up to the opening race. Afterwards riders James Doyle and David Probert said: 'It's soft but wet and they're getting through it'. This year's Group 2 Queen Mary saw the biggest field size in recent memory even with three defections. With two US raiders drawn high not surprisingly the stands' side proved the place to be and the principals were a little way clear at the finish. It was something of a slow-motion finish, with the going playing its part, although the winning time did suggest the official assessment to be correct. The opening level is slightly fluid but has been rated in line with the race par for now.

3984 QUEEN'S VASE (GROUP 2) 1m 6f 34y

3:05 (3:06) (Class 1) 3-Y-O

£127,597 (£48,375; £24,210; £12,060; £6,052; £3,037) **Stalls Low**

Form RPR

0-23 **1** **Dashing Willoughby**[42] 2523 3-9-0 102........................ OisinMurphy 6 106
(Andrew Balding) *prom: led after 2f tl hdd after 3f: continued to trck ldrs: rdn to chal 2f out: led ins fnl f: styd on gamely and edgd lft towards fin* **6/1**[2]

2 ½ **Barbados (IRE)**[13] 3523 3-9-0 98........................ WayneLordan 12 105
(A P O'Brien, Ire) *prom on outer: chsd ldr after 3f: rdn to ld jst over 2f out: hrd pressed: hdd ins fnl f: continued to chal: styd on for press: hld towards fin* **20/1**

-165 **3** ½ **Nayef Road (IRE)**[18] 3341 3-9-0 104........................ AndreaAtzeni 8 104
(Mark Johnston) *pushed along early: prom after nrly 2f: led after 3f: rdn and hdd jst over 2f out: hung lft whn stl ev ch over 1f out: edgd rt fnl 100yds whn stl chalng: kpt on for press: hld towards fin* **16/1**

-113 **4** 2 ½ **Moonlight Spirit (IRE)**[24] 3120 3-9-0 99........................ KerrinMcEvoy 7 100
(Charlie Appleby) *midfield: effrt on outer 3f out: hdwy 2f out: chsd ldrs over 1f out: kpt on ins fnl f: nvr able to chal front trio* **17/2**

5 1 **Eminent Authority (IRE)**[13] 3523 3-9-0 0........................(t) JamieSpencer 3 99
(Joseph Patrick O'Brien, Ire) *ly; s.i.s: midfield: nt clr run over 3f: drvn and angled out on bnd wl over 2f out: lugged rt fr 2f out: no imp tl styd on ins fnl f: nvr able to rch ldrs* **11/1**

6 ½ **Harpo Marx (IRE)**[15] 3460 3-9-0 86........................(b[1]) SeamieHeffernan 10 98
(A P O'Brien, Ire) *hld up: drvn over 2f: nt clr run briefly wl over 1f out: hdwy u.p sn after: styd on ins fnl f: nvr able to trble ldrs* **25/1**

121 **7** 1 ¼ **Almost Midnight**[32] 2845 3-9-0 90........................ JamesMcDonald 13 96
(David Simcock) *str; hld up in rr: drvn and hdwy 2f out: chsd ldrs but no imp over 1f out: one pce ins fnl f* **50/1**

1202 **8** 1 **Themaxwecan (IRE)**[18] 3337 3-9-0 94........................ SilvestreDeSousa 2 95
(Mark Johnston) *looked wl; midfield: rdn on inner to cl over 2f out: chsd ldrs: no further imp over 1f out: no ex fnl 150yds* **20/1**

4-20 **9** *nse* **Norway (IRE)**[18] 3345 3-9-0 107........................ RyanMoore 4 95
(A P O'Brien, Ire) *sweating; hld up: sme hdwy u.p over 1f out: kpt on wout threatening: eased fnl 100yds* **11/4**[1]

13-3 **10** 3 ¾ **Nate The Great**[39] 2619 3-9-0 101........................ HollieDoyle 11 90
(Archie Watson) *prom: dropped to midfield after 3f: rdn over 3f out: outpcd over 2f out: wknd over 1f out* **9/1**

-302 **11** 4 ½ **Pythion (FR)**[32] 2853 3-9-0 100........................ ColinKeane 1 83
(G M Lyons, Ire) *str; led early: in tch: rdn to chse ldrs over 2f out: wknd over 1f out* **33/1**

-251 **12** 22 **Western Australia (IRE)**[32] 2853 3-9-0 107........................ DonnachaO'Brien 5 52
(A P O'Brien, Ire) *looked wl; hld up: rdn over 3f out: edgd rt u.p whn no imp wl over 1f out: sn eased whn wl btn (trainer's rep could offer no explanation for the colt's performance)* **6/1**[2]

2-11 **13** 10 **Jalmoud**[46] 2426 3-9-0 103........................ JamesDoyle 9 38
(Charlie Appleby) *racd keenly: sn led: hdd after 2f: trckd ldrs after 3f: rdn over 2f out: sn wknd: eased whn wl btn over 1f out (jockey said colt ran too free)* **7/1**[3]

3m 7.86s (3.56) **Going Correction** +0.475s/f (Yiel) **13 Ran SP% 120.8**
Speed ratings (Par 111): **108,107,107,106,105 105,104,103,103,101 99,86,80**
CSF £127.44 CT £1839.44 TOTE £6.90: £2.15, £8.40, £5.60; EX 151.30 Trifecta £1952.00.
Owner Mick and Janice Mariscotti **Bred** Meon Valley Stud **Trained** Kingsclere, Hants

FOCUS

Add 11yds. A race that's throw to top performers in Stradivarius and Kew Gardens since being reduced in distance to 1m6f, but it was unsatisfactory race this time around, with the pace slowing right down after a couple of furlongs and the first three were in the leading trio throughout. Those held up never stood a chance so not form to take much notice of moving forward as a result. The third has been rated close to form.

3985 PRINCE OF WALES'S STKS (GROUP 1) (BRITISH CHAMPIONS SERIES) 1m 1f 212y

3:40 (3:40) (Class 1) 4-Y-O+

£425,325 (£161,250; £80,700; £40,200; £20,175; £10,125) **Stalls Low**

Form RPR

2-11 **1** **Crystal Ocean**[32] 2827 5-9-0 125........................ FrankieDettori 6 128
(Sir Michael Stoute) *looked wl; awkward leaving stalls: sn prom tl chsd ldr 8f out: clsd to press ldr 3f out: rdn to ld 2f out: edgd lft u.p over 1f out: sn edging bk rt u.p: styd on strly ins fnl f* **3/1**[2]

-111 **2** 1 ¼ **Magical (IRE)**[24] 3114 4-8-11 123........................ RyanMoore 1 123
(A P O'Brien, Ire) *sn prom: chsd ldr after 1f tl 8f out: chsd ldng pair after: rdn to chse wnr and swtchd lft over 1f out: sn swtchd bk rt: drvn and carried rt ins fnl f: kpt on but a hld* **13/8**[1]

55-1 **3** 3 ¼ **Waldgeist**[52] 2168 5-9-0 122........................ Pierre-CharlesBoudot 8 119+
(A Fabre, France) *hld up in last trio: swtchd lft and effrt over 2f out: hdwy and hung rt 2f out: styd and chsd clr ldng pair 100yds out: nvr a threat* **4/1**[3]

-344 **4** 2 **Hunting Horn (IRE)**[39] 2646 4-9-0 108........................ DonnachaO'Brien 7 115
(A P O'Brien, Ire) *led: rdn and pressed 3f out: hdd 2f out: 3rd and outpcd over 1f out: wknd and lost 3rd 100yds out* **25/1**

112- **5** 2 ¼ **Sea Of Class (IRE)**[255] 8026 4-8-11 122........................ JamesDoyle 5 108+
(William Haggas) *nudged leaving stalls: hld up in last pair: swtchd lft and wd bnd over 2f out: hdwy into 5th over 1f out: pushed along and no imp after* **5/1**

32-4 **6** 4 ½ **Deirdre (JPN)**[52] 2178 5-8-11 113........................ YutakaTake 3 99
(Mitsuru Hashida, Japan) *chsd ldr for 1f: in tch in midfield after: jst getting outpcd u.p whn squeezed for room 2f out: sn wknd* **33/1**

2-11 **7** 16 **Zabeel Prince (IRE)**[24] 3122 6-9-0 117........................ AndreaAtzeni 2 70
(Roger Varian) *looked wl; hld up in midfield: shortlived effrt over 2f out: sn btn: wl bhd and eased ins fnl f* **9/1**

1-30 **8** 3 ½ **Desert Encounter (IRE)**[81] 1446 7-9-0 118........................(h) JimCrowley 4 63
(David Simcock) *stdd and wnt lft s: hld up in rr: effrt towards inner over 2f out: sn btn: wl bhd and eased ins fnl f* **66/1**

2m 10.25s (2.55) **Going Correction** +0.475s/f (Yiel) **8 Ran SP% 118.0**
Speed ratings (Par 117): **108,107,104,102,101 97,84,81**
CSF £8.51 CT £19.26 TOTE £4.10: £1.25, £1.15, £1.55; EX 9.50 Trifecta £32.50.
Owner Sir Evelyn De Rothschild **Bred** Southcourt Stud **Trained** Newmarket, Suffolk

FOCUS

Billed as the race of the week by most, this year's Prince of Wales's Stakes was run in driving rain. An uneven pace definitely helped those racing handily, but the form is still outstanding. Add 11yds. The third has been rated close to form.

3986 DUKE OF CAMBRIDGE STKS (GROUP 2) (F&M) 1m (S)

4:20 (4:22) (Class 1) 4-Y-O+

£99,242 (£37,625; £18,830; £9,380; £4,707; £2,362) **Stalls Centre**

Form RPR

222- **1** **Move Swiftly**[230] 8769 4-9-0 104........................ DanielTudhope 11 115
(William Haggas) *n.m.r and checked after nrly 1f: hld up: smooth hdwy ent fnl 2f: rdn to chal over 1f out: r.o to ld fnl 110yds: kpt on wl nr fin* **9/1**

1-32 **2** *nk* **Rawdaa**[34] 2776 4-9-0 109........................ FrankieDettori 3 114
(Sir Michael Stoute) *looked wl; in tch: effrt to ld narrowly over 1f out: hrd pressed: hdd fnl 110yds: kpt on wl but hld nr fin* **4/1**[2]

-062 **3** 1 ¾ **I Can Fly**[25] 3105 4-9-3 110........................ RyanMoore 2 113
(A P O'Brien, Ire) *hld up: rdn 2f out: hdwy over 1f out: chalng ins fnl f: outpcd by front two fnl 50yds* **7/2**[1]

6-43 **4** 1 **Veracious**[18] 3342 4-9-0 108........................(t) OisinMurphy 12 108
(Sir Michael Stoute) *racd keenly: prom: rdn to chal over 1f out: unable qck fnl 110yds: styd on same pce towards fin* **8/1**

51-0 **5** 1 ½ **Di Fede (IRE)**[25] 3069 4-9-0 103........................ HarryBentley 5 104
(Ralph Beckett) *in tch: effrt over 1f out: sn drvn and cl up: styd on same pce fnl 175yds* **20/1**

-021 **6** 2 ¾ **Anna Nerium**[18] 3342 4-9-0 107........................ TomMarquand 4 98
(Richard Hannon) *hld up: pushed along over 4f out: hdwy u.p over 1f out: styd on ins fnl f: nt pce to trble ldrs* **14/1**

-240 **7** 1 **Nyaleti (IRE)**[18] 3342 4-9-0 107........................ PJMcDonald 8 96
(Mark Johnston) *prom: led over 5f out: rdn and edgd rt over 1f out: sn hdd: no ex ins fnl f* **33/1**

06-3 **8** ¾ **Red Tea**[25] 3105 6-9-0 107........................ DonnachaO'Brien 6 94
(Joseph Patrick O'Brien, Ire) *midfield: rdn 2f out: styd on fnl 150yds: nvr able to rch ldrs* **14/1**

2-41 **9** *nk* **Shenanigans (IRE)**[28] 2961 5-9-0 96........................ AndreaAtzeni 9 93
(Roger Varian) *trckd ldrs: rdn 2f out: outpcd over 1f out: fdd ins fnl f* **33/1**

3-01 **10** 1 ½ **Indian Blessing**[18] 3359 5-9-0 105........................ JamieSpencer 17 90
(Ed Walker) *racd alone towards nrside: prom: rdn and lost pl over 1f out: kpt on same pce and n.d ins fnl f* **33/1**

25-1 **11** *hd* **Agrotera (IRE)**[60] 1941 4-9-0 102........................ GeraldMosse 14 89
(Ed Walker) *ponied to s: racd keenly: hld up: rdn over 2f out: sme hdwy over 1f out: kpt on and edgd rt ins fnl f: nvr a threat (trainer could offer no explanation for the filly's performance)* **8/1**

543- **12** 1 ¼ **Threading (IRE)**[266] 7662 4-9-0 104........................ SilvestreDeSousa 13 86
(Mark Johnston) *hld up: pushed along and angled lft over 2f out: no imp over 1f out: one pce* **28/1**

21-1 **13** *nk* **Pretty Baby (IRE)**[39] 2621 4-9-0 106........................ JamesDoyle 1 86
(William Haggas) *looked wl; chsd ldrs: rdn over 2f out and outpcd: wknd over 1f out* **7/1**[3]

35-2 **14** 1 **Preening**[60] 1941 4-9-0 99........................ KerrinMcEvoy 7 83
(James Fanshawe) *led: hdd over 5f out: remained prom: u.p to hold pl whn n.m.r and checked over 1f out: wknd ins fnl f* **20/1**

0-24 **15** ½ **Hand On Heart (IRE)**[13] 3521 4-9-0 99........................ ChrisHayes 10 82
(J A Stack, Ire) *hld up in midfield: rdn over 2f out and outpcd: wknd over 1f out* **28/1**

1-54 **16** ¾ **Bella Ragazza**[18] 3342 4-9-0 97........................ DavidProbert 15 81
(Hughie Morrison) *racd keenly: trckd ldrs: rdn over 2f out: wknd over 1f out* **50/1**

4-22 **17** ½ **Dan's Dream**[12] 3557 4-9-0 104........................ RonanWhelan 16 79
(Mick Channon) *hld up: rdn over 2f out: no imp over 1f out: wl btn ins fnl f* **33/1**

1m 42.63s (1.23) **Going Correction** +0.475s/f (Yiel) **17 Ran SP% 130.4**
Speed ratings (Par 115): **112,111,109,108,107 104,103,102,102,101 100,99,99,98,97 97,96**
CSF £42.52 CT £164.35 TOTE £11.05: £4.20, £1.95, £2.10; EX 61.40 Trifecta £418.40.
Owner Sheikh Rashid Dalmook Al Maktoum **Bred** Mrs K E Collie **Trained** Newmarket, Suffolk

FOCUS

The going was officially changed to soft all over after the third. They went a solid pace down the middle in this ultra-competitive edition of this Group 2 prize for fillies. The second has been rated as matching her 1m2f latest, and the fourth similar to her latest.

3987 ROYAL HUNT CUP (HERITAGE H'CAP) 1m (S)

5:00 (5:01) (Class 2) 3-Y-O+

£108,937 (£32,620; £16,310; £8,155; £4,077; £2,047) **Stalls Centre**

Form RPR

630- **1** **Afaak**[263] 7773 5-9-3 **103**........................ JimCrowley 21 113
(Charles Hills) *racd nr side: t.k.h: chsd ldrs tl led 2f out: sn rdn: forged ahd u.p ins fnl f: pressed wl ins fnl f: kpt on and jst hld on 1st of 14 in gp* **20/1**

5-10 **2** *nse* **Clon Coulis (IRE)**[61] 1918 5-8-13 **99**........................(h) JamieSpencer 18 109
(David Barron) *racd nr side: hld up in rr: clsd and nt clrest of runs 2f out: hdwy to chse ldrs ent fnl f: chsd wnr and drvn ins fnl f: styd on wl and clsd on wnr fnl 100yds: jst hld: 2nd of 14 in gp* **16/1**

16-4 **3** 2 **Raising Sand**[39] 2609 7-9-3 **103**........................ NicolaCurrie 32 108
(Jamie Osborne) *racd nr side: stdd and wnt rt s: t.k.h: hld up in tch in midfield: nt clr run ent fnl 2f: sn rdn: hdwy and wnt between rivals 1f out: swtchd lft and r.o strly: nt rch ldrs: 3rd of 14 in gp* **8/1**[2]

10-5 **4** *hd* **Stylehunter**[11] 3605 4-8-13 **99**........................(b) RobertHavlin 25 104+
(John Gosden) *looked wl; racd nr side: s.i.s: in rr: clsd and swtchd rt jst over 2f out: nt clr run over 1f out: sn swtchd rt and hdwy 1f out: r.o wl u.p: nt rch ldrs: 4th of 14 in gp* **22/1**

5-22 **5** *hd* **Kynren (IRE)**[39] 2609 5-9-1 **101**........................ RobertWinston 3 105
(David Barron) *racd centre to far side: in tch in midfield: clsd to trck gp ldrs 2f out: rdn to ld gp and chsd ldrs overall over 1f out: drvn and no ex ins fnl f: outpcd fnl 100yds: 1st of 14 in gp* **11/2**[1]

0-34 **6** *nk* **Roc Angel (FR)**[21] 5-9-3 **103** 5ex........................ ChristopheSoumillon 6 106
(F Chappet, France) *racd centre to far side: hld up in midfield: clsd whn nt clr run and switching lft and trying to get through over 1f out: hdwy u.p to chse ldrs overall ins fnl f: outpcd fnl 100yds: 2nd of 14 in gp* **33/1**

404- **7** *hd* **Vale Of Kent (IRE)**[256] 7977 4-8-13 **99**.......................... PJMcDonald 29 102
(Mark Johnston) *racd nr side: chsd ldrs: effrt 2f out: hrd drvn over 1f out: kpt on same pce ins fnl f: 5th of 14 in gp* **33/1**

2633 **8** *3/4* **Red Starlight**[18] 3359 4-9-0 **100**.......................... TomMarquand 13 101
(Richard Hannon) *racd centre to far side: in tch in midfield: effrt over 2f out: drvn and clsng whn barging match w rival over 1f out: chsd overall ldrs 1f out: no ex and wknd towards fin: 3rd of 14 in gp* **33/1**

-342 **9** *hd* **So Beloved**[25] 3094 9-9-5 **105**..........................(h) DanielTudhope 4 106
(David O'Meara) *racd centre to far side: t.k.h: restrained to rr sn after s: clsd and swtchd rt wl over 1f out: rdn to chse ldrs overall 1f out: no ex and wknd towards fin: 4th of 14 in gp* **33/1**

2-15 **10** *1/2* **Mordin (IRE)**[18] 3343 5-9-6 **106**..........................(p) PatCosgrave 22 106
(Simon Crisford) *racd nr side: in tch in midfield: effrt and edgd rt 2f out: unable qck u.p over 1f out: kpt on same pce ins fnl f: 6th of 14 in gp* **14/1**

1251 **11** *1/2* **War Glory (IRE)**[11] 3581 6-8-13 **99** 5ex.......................... SeanLevey 20 97
(Richard Hannon) *racd nr side: hld up in tch in midfield: clsd to trck ldrs 2f out: sn rdn and chal over 1f out: no ex 1f out: wknd ins fnl f: 7th of 14 in gp* **50/1**

0-31 **12** *3/4* **What's The Story**[34] 2778 5-9-0 **100**..........................(p) PaulMulrennan 26 97
(Keith Dalgleish) *racd nr side: chsd overall ldr tl rdn to ld over 2f out: sn hdd and unable qck over 1f out: wknd ins fnl f: 8th of 14 in gp* **12/1**[3]

-315 **13** *nse* **Beringer**[34] 2778 4-8-13 **99**..........................(p[1]) AndreaAtzeni 2 96
(Alan King) *racd centre to far side: hld up in tch in midfield: clsd to and wl in tch whn nt clr run over 1f out: edgd out lft and effrt 1f out: little rspnse and no imp ins fnl f: 5th of 14 in gp* **18/1**

0-63 **14** *3/4* **Chief Ironside**[18] 3343 4-9-4 **104**.......................... JasonWatson 28 99
(William Jarvis) *racd nr side: hld up in tch in midfield: nt clr run and swtchd rt ent fnl 2f: effrt over 1f out: kpt on same pce and no threat to ldrs ins fnl f: 9th of 14 in gp* **33/1**

0400 **15** *1 1/4* **Key Victory (IRE)**[111] 961 4-9-5 **105**..........................(p) JamesDoyle 17 97
(Charlie Appleby) *racd nr side: hld up towards rr: hdwy 1/2-way: rdn ent fnl 2f: no prog u.p over 1f out: wknd ins fnl f: 10th of 14 in gp* **25/1**

1040 **16** *hd* **Zwayyan**[54] 2085 6-9-0 **100**.......................... SilvestreDeSousa 31 92
(Andrew Balding) *racd nr side: bmpd and short of room s: t.k.h: hld up towards rr: clsd and swtchd rt jst over 2f out: sn rdn and clsd to chse ldrs: hung lft over 1f out: wknd ins fnl f: 11th of 14 in gp (vet said gelding lost its left-hind shoe)* **22/1**

-545 **17** *nse* **Mitchum Swagger**[11] 3588 7-9-2 **107**............ ThoreHammerHansen(5) 8 98
(Ralph Beckett) *racd centre to far side: hld up in tch in midfield: nt clr run over 1f out: effrt 1f out: sn drvn: no prog and plugged on same pce fnl f: 6th of 14 in gp* **20/1**

004- **18** *3* **Chilean**[270] 7567 4-9-1 **101**.......................... RobHornby 9 86
(Martyn Meade) *looked wl; racd centre to far side: chsd ldrs: rdn jst over 2f out: pressing gp ldrs but struggling to qckn whn edgd rt 1f out: sn wknd: 7th of 14 in gp* **25/1**

12-1 **19** *1/2* **New Graduate (IRE)**[53] 2116 4-9-5 **105**.......................... FrankieDettori 1 88
(James Tate) *looked wl; racd centre to far side: chsd ldrs: effrt over 2f out: drvn to ld gp and chsd ldrs overall over 1f out: sn struggling to qckn and edgd lft: wknd ins fnl f: 8th of 14 in gp* **11/2**[1]

0030 **20** *nk* **Robin Of Navan (FR)**[32] 2832 6-9-5 **105**.......................... OisinMurphy 15 88
(Harry Dunlop) *looked wl; racd centre to far side: stdd s: hld up in rr: swtchd lft and clsd jst over 2f out: rdn and clsd to chse overall ldrs over 1f out: no ex 1f out: sn wknd: 9th of 14 in gp* **12/1**[3]

0001 **21** *1* **Circus Couture (IRE)**[14] 3472 7-9-2 **102** 5ex..........................(v) JFEgan 24 82
(Jane Chapple-Hyam) *racd nr side: nt clrest of runs over 2f out: sn swtchd rt and rdn 2f out: unable qck and wknd ins fnl f: 12th of 14 in gp* **25/1**

0000 **22** *2 1/4* **Comin' Through (AUS)**[19] 3315 5-9-2 **107**..........................(t) DylanHogan(5) 5 82
(George Scott) *racd centre to far side: stdd s: hld up in rr: shortlived effrt ent fnl 2f: sn btn and wknd ins fnl f: 10th of 14 in gp* **100/1**

00-3 **23** *1/2* **Zhui Feng (IRE)**[27] 3009 6-9-4 **104**..........................(p) PatDobbs 14 78
(Amanda Perrett) *racd centre to far side: led gp and chsd ldrs overall: rdn and losing pl whn n.m.r jst over 1f out: wknd ins fnl f: 11th of 14 in gp* **40/1**

-114 **24** *1 1/4* **Petrus (IRE)**[32] 2832 4-9-0 **100**..........................(p) MartinDwyer 16 71
(Brian Meehan) *racd centre to far side: in tch in midfield: effrt over 2f out: unable qck u.p and btn over 1f out: wknd fnl f: 12th of 14 in gp* **22/1**

03 **25** *hd* **King's Field (IRE)**[31] 2879 4-9-3 **103**.......................... DonnachaO'Brien 11 74
(Joseph Patrick O'Brien, Ire) *racd centre to far side: chsd ldrs: rdn 2f out: struggling to qckn u.p and losing pl whn squeezed for room 1f out: wknd fnl f: 13th of 14 in gp* **25/1**

0301 **26** *2 1/2* **Cardsharp**[25] 3094 4-9-11 **111**.......................... JasonHart 33 76
(Mark Johnston) *mounted in the chute: racd nr side: overall ldr tl rdn and hdd over 2f out: sn dropped out and bhd ins fnl f: 13th of 14 in gp* **50/1**

-000 **27** *hd* **Settle For Bay (FR)**[13] 3521 5-9-5 **105**..........................(t) WJLee 7 70
(David Marnane, Ire) *racd centre to far side: chsd gp ldr and wl in tch tl over 2f out: sn u.p and lost pl 2f out: bhd ins fnl f: 14th of 14 in gp* **20/1**

-230 **28** *27* **Glendevon (USA)**[25] 3074 4-9-2 **102**..........................(h[1]) ShaneKelly 19 4
(Richard Hughes) *mounted in the chute: racd nr side: stdd s: t.k.h: hld up: bhd 2f out: eased over 1f out: t.o: 14th of 14 in gp* **66/1**

1m 42.36s (0.96) **Going Correction** +0.475s/f (Yiel) **28** Ran SP% **143.4**
Speed ratings (Par 109): **114,113,111,111,111 111,111,110,110,109 109,108,108,107,106 106,106,103,102,102 101,99,98,97,9**
CSF £283.41 CT £2843.26 TOTE £31.60: £7.00, £5.30, £2.50, £6.95; EX 511.70 Trifecta £9617.20.
Owner Hamdan Al Maktoum **Bred** Shadwell Estate Company Limited **Trained** Lambourn, Berks
■ Stewards' Enquiry : Jim Crowley two-day ban: used whip above the permitted level (Jul 3-4)
Robert Winston two-day ban: used whip above the permitted level (Jun 23, Jul 3)

FOCUS
A typical edition of the race, although the soft ground clearly wouldn't have suited some, they raced in two groups and those stands' side came out on top, being responsible for the first four home. A pb from the second, with the third giving a good line to the form.

3988 WINDSOR CASTLE STKS (LISTED RACE) 5f
5:35 (5:44) (Class 1) 2-Y-O

£51,039 (£19,350; £9,684; £4,824; £2,421; £1,215) **Stalls** Centre

Form RPR

1 **Southern Hills (IRE)**[18] 3362 2-9-3 0.......................... RyanMoore 24 101
(A P O'Brien, Ire) *str; looked wl; hld up nrside: hdwy over 2f out: rdn to ld over 1f out: r.o gamely ins fnl f* **7/1**[2]

21 **2** *1/2* **Platinum Star (IRE)**[22] 3194 2-9-3 0.......................... ChristopheSoumillon 22 99
(Saeed bin Suroor) *compact; hld up: hdwy over 2f out: rdn to chal jst over 1f out: r.o ins fnl f: nt quite pce of wnr towards fin* **8/1**[3]

21 **3** *hd* **Glasvegas (IRE)**[33] 2783 2-9-3 0.......................... PaulMulrennan 23 98
(Keith Dalgleish) *athletic; in rr: pushed along and outpcd over 2f out: rdn and hdwy over 1f out: running on whn nt clr run and swtchd rt fnl 75yds: gaining at fin* **25/1**

1 **4** *hd* **Symbolize (IRE)**[34] 2767 2-9-3 0.......................... DavidProbert 11 98+
(Andrew Balding) *leggy; athletic; carried rt early on: chsd ldrs: rdn 2f out: edgd lft fnl 150yds whn running on to chal: run flattened out towards fin* **6/1**[1]

221 **5** *1* **Illusionist (GER)**[12] 3530 2-9-3 0..........................(b) OisinMurphy 19 94
(Archie Watson) *compact; midfield: effrt to chse ldrs 2f out: bmpd over 1f out: styd on ins fnl f: nt quite pce to get to ldrs* **12/1**

31 **6** *hd* **Summer Sands**[11] 3566 2-9-3 0.......................... BarryMcHugh 9 93+
(Richard Fahey) *str; midfield: rdn 2f out: hdwy wl over 1f out: r.o for press ins fnl f and edgd lft: fin wl* **10/1**

1164 **7** *1 1/4* **Electric Ladyland (IRE)**[27] 3023 2-8-12 0.......................... LukeMorris 20 85
(Archie Watson) *leggy; chsd ldrs: rdn over 2f out: outpcd whn nt clr run over 1f out: styd on ins fnl f: no imp towards fin* **66/1**

221 **8** *1 1/4* **Taxiwala (IRE)**[12] 3534 2-9-3 0..........................(b) HollieDoyle 12 84
(Archie Watson) *workmanlike; carried rt early on: midfield: rdn over 1f out: kpt on ins fnl f: nt pce to rch ldrs (vet said colt had lost its left-hind shoe)* **33/1**

9 *1/2* **Red Epaulette (IRE)**[31] 2878 2-9-3 0..........................(b) LeighRoche 4 83
(M D O'Callaghan, Ire) *str; prom displaying gd pce: rdn and ev ch over 1f out: unable to go w ldrs ins fnl f: no ex fnl 150yds* **28/1**

1 **10** *1/2* **Rayong**[30] 2892 2-9-3 0.......................... SilvestreDeSousa 14 94+
(K R Burke) *compact; towards rr: pushed along over 2f out: rdn and hdwy whn n.m.r and hmpd over 1f out: kpt on ins fnl f whn no ch* **8/1**[3]

11 *1* **Wheels On Fire (FR)**[20] 2-9-3 0..........................(p[1]) AntoineHamelin 1 77+
(Matthieu Palussiere, France) *str; gd spd to ld on far side: rdn over 2f out: hdd over 1f out: stl there tl fdd fnl 75yds* **50/1**

1 **12** *3/4* **Bill Neigh**[18] 3355 2-9-3 0.......................... CierenFallon 7 75+
(John Ryan) *str; midfield: rdn and hdwy 2f out: edgd rt ins fnl f: one pce* **33/1**

11 **13** *1 3/4* **Temple Of Heaven**[32] 2830 2-9-3 0.......................... SeanLevey 10 68
(Richard Hannon) *str; hld up: rdn over 2f out: swtchd rt ent fnl f: coasted home ins fnl f: nvr able to get involved (jockey said colt was never travelling)* **6/1**[1]

21 **14** *nk* **Dylan De Vega**[44] 2475 2-9-3 0.......................... TonyHamilton 3 70+
(Richard Fahey) *tall; looked wl; chsd ldrs: drvn and wl there ent fnl 2f: sn hung rt: fdd ins fnl f* **18/1**

15 *hd* **Karak (USA)**[25] 2-8-12 0..........................(b) TylerGaffalione 18 61
(Wesley A Ward, U.S.A) *str; wnt rt early on: displayed gd pce and prom: rdn and hung rt over 1f out: sn wknd* **10/1**

1 **16** *1 1/2* **Iffraaz (IRE)**[19] 3290 2-9-3 0.......................... FrankieDettori 8 61+
(Mark Johnston) *str; ly; hld up: rdn over 2f out: no imp: eased whn wl hld fnl 150yds* **8/1**[3]

12 **17** *hd* **Iva Reflection (IRE)**[42] 2520 2-9-3 0.......................... RichardKingscote 2 60+
(Tom Dascombe) *str; midfield: rdn 2f out: wknd over 1f out* **50/1**

31 **18** *1* **Charlemaine (IRE)**[60] 1931 2-9-3 0.......................... RaulDaSilva 21 57
(Paul Cole) *ly; midfield: drvn and wandered 2f out: wknd over 1f out* **50/1**

2323 **19** *hd* **Paper Star**[10] 3634 2-8-12 0.......................... NicolaCurrie 15 51
(George Baker) *leggy; carried rt early on: chsd ldrs tl rdn and lost pl over 2f out: sn bhd* **100/1**

20 *3/4* **Foolish Humor (USA)**[48] 2-8-12 0..........................(bt) JohnRVelazquez 5 48
(Wesley A Ward, U.S.A) *compact; ponied to s: displayed gd pce and prom: rdn and hmpd over 1f out: sn wknd* **20/1**

1 **21** *13* **Better The Devil (USA)**[7] 3717 2-9-3 0.......................... EdwardGreatrex 13 7
(Archie Watson) *str; looked wl; carried rt early on: in tch: rdn over 2f out: wknd ent fnl 2f: eased whn btn fnl f (jockey said colt stopped quickly)* **25/1**

1m 3.05s (2.35) **Going Correction** +0.475s/f (Yiel) **21** Ran SP% **135.7**
Speed ratings (Par 101): **100,99,98,98,96 96,94,92,91,91 89,88,85,84,84 82,81,80,80,78 58**
CSF £60.90 CT £912.63 TOTE £6.85: £2.00, £3.60, £9.65; EX 77.80 Trifecta £1272.70.
Owner Mrs John Magnier & Michael Tabor & Derrick Smith **Bred** Coolmore **Trained** Cashel, Co Tipperary
■ Show Me Show Me was withdrawn. Price at time of withdrawal 50/1. Rule 4 does not apply
■ Stewards' Enquiry : Paul Mulrennan two-day ban: used whip above the permitted level (Jun 25, Jul 4)

FOCUS
Two of the more fancied runners came to the fore in this wide-open Listed juvenile sprint and it saw a clean sweep for the top three stalls racing stands' side. They raced in one big group, with the exception of Wheels On Fire, who stayed on his own more far side from stall one. It's been rated as a lesser renewal.
T/Jkpt: Not Won. T/Plt: £890.90 to a £1 stake. Pool: £548,775.15 - 449.63 winning units T/Qpdt: £22.00 to a £1 stake. Pool: £46,018.77 - 1,542.82 winning units **Steve Payne & Darren Owen**

3578 CHELMSFORD (A.W) (L-H)
Wednesday, June 19

OFFICIAL GOING: Polytrack: standard

3989 BET TOTESCOOP6 AT TOTESPORT.COM H'CAP (DIV I) 7f (P)
5:40 (5:41) (Class 6) (0-55,60) 3-Y-O+

£3,428 (£1,020; £509; £300; £300; £300) **Stalls** Low

Form RPR

3661 **1** **Captain Dion**[9] 3656 6-9-12 **60** 5ex..........................(b) GabrieleMalune(3) 3 74+
(Ivan Furtado) *mde all: kicked 3 l clr 2f out: sn rdn: 4 l ld 1f out: in command and eased fnl f* **9/4**[1]

60-0 **2** *4 1/2* **Prince Rock (IRE)**[23] 3144 4-9-1 **46** oh1..........................(h) NickyMackay 13 46
(Simon Dow) *hld up: drvn and hdwy 1 1/2f out: 5th 1f out: rdn 1/2f out: r.o into 2nd last 50yds: nvr nr wnr* **20/1**

0006 **3** *nk* **Brigand**[35] 2740 4-9-6 **51**.......................... AdamKirby 6 51
(John Butler) *hld up: drvn in 6th 2f out: racd wd 1 1/2f out: sn rdn: kpt on into 3rd wl ins fnl f* **11/4**[2]

40-0 **4** *1/2* **Come On Bear (IRE)**[30] 2900 4-9-2 **47**..........................(v) JoeyHaynes 12 45
(Alan Bailey) *bhd: drvn and hdwy on inner over 2f out: rdn into 2nd ent fnl f: no ex and lost two pls last 50yds* **50/1**

05-5 **5** *4 1/2* **Kafoo**[62] 1880 6-9-12 **57**..........................(v) AlistairRawlinson 1 44
(Michael Appleby) *chsd ldr: drvn in 3 l 2nd 2f out: sn rdn: lost 2nd ent fnl f: wknd (jockey said gelding hung right-handed)* **7/1**

3053 **6** *1 1/2* **Cristal Pallas Cat (IRE)**[27] 3007 4-9-2 **47**.......................... FergusSweeney 11 30
(Roger Ingram) *chsd ldr: drvn and lost pl 2f out: sn rdn: no ex fnl f (starter reported that the gelding was the subject of a third criteria failure; trainer was informed that the gelding could not run until the day after passing a stalls test)* **12/1**

5502 **7** *nk* **Mezmaar**[8] 3687 10-9-6 **54**..........................(p) GaryMahon(3) 8 36
(Mark Usher) *mid-div on outer: drvn 2f out: racd wd 1 1/2f out: sn rdn: one pce* **10/1**

6000 **8** 6 **Black Truffle (FR)**[14] [3476] 9-8-8 **46** oh1..............(p) EllieMacKenzie(7) 7 12
(Mark Usher) *hld up: drvn 2f out: no imp* **33/1**
000 **9** 3/4 **Hooriya**[16] [3431] 3-9-1 **55**..............................(b1) DanielMuscutt 2 16
(Marco Botti) *mid-div: drvn 2f out: rdn 1 1/2f out: wknd and eased fnl f* **20/1**
0006 **10** shd **The Special One (IRE)**[60] [1936] 6-8-11 **49**..........(t) GraceMcEntee(7) 14 13
(Phil McEntee) *chsd ldr: rdn and lost pl 2f out: sn wknd* **33/1**
00-0 **11** 5 **Catalogue**[19] [3299] 3-8-12 **52**.............................. EoinWalsh 10
(Christine Dunnett) *a bhd* **100/1**
-650 **12** shd **Beg For Mercy**[16] [3410] 3-8-7 **47**..............................(v1) CharlieBennett 5
(Michael Attwater) *mid-div: drvn and lost pl over 2f out: wknd* **50/1**
1203 **13** nk **Simba Samba**[6] [3775] 3-8-13 **53**..............................(t) DannyBrock 9
(Philip McBride) *mid-div: drvn and lost pl over 2f out: rdn over 1f out: sn eased: dropped to last nr fin (jockey said gelding stopped quickly)* **5/1**[3]

1m 25.8s (-1.40) **Going Correction** -0.225s/f (Stan)
WFA 3 from 4yo+ 9lb **13 Ran SP% 123.7**
Speed ratings (Par 101): **99,93,93,92,87 86,85,78,78,77 72,72,71**
CSF £55.83 CT £141.30 TOTE £2.60: £1.10, £6.40, £1.30; EX 66.20 Trifecta £366.90.
Owner Daniel Macauliffe & Anoj Don **Bred** Miss R J Dobson **Trained** Wiseton, Nottinghamshire

FOCUS
The first division of a moderate handicap. The favourite didn't see another rival after breaking well and getting clear at the top of the home straight. The winner has been rated as backing up his recent win.

3990 BET TOTEPLACEPOT AT TOTESPORT.COM EBF NOVICE AUCTION STKS 7f (P)
6:10 (6:12) (Class 5) 2-Y-O **£4,527** (£1,347; £673; £336) **Stalls** Low

Form RPR
5 **1** **Governor Of Punjab (IRE)**[8] [3702] 2-9-5 0.............................. AdamKirby 10 74+
(Mark Johnston) *mde all: drvn in narrow ld 2f out: rdn over 1f out: asserted wl ins fnl f: on top nr fin* **6/4**[1]
0 **2** 3/4 **Milltown Star**[20] [3245] 2-9-2 0.............................. DavidEgan 6 69
(Mick Channon) *trckd ldr: drvn into cl 2nd 2f out: rdn and ev ch over 1f out: r.o: no ex as wnr asserted wl ins fnl f* **12/1**
0 **3** 2 1/2 **Banmi (IRE)**[32] [2840] 2-8-9 0.............................. SeamusCronin(5) 1 61+
(Mohamed Moubarak) *awkward leaving stalls: bhd: pushed along and plenty to do 2f out: drvn and hdwy on inner over 1f out: rdn fnl f: r.o wl: tk 3rd last stride* **66/1**
043 **4** nse **Bacchalot (IRE)**[16] [3405] 2-8-12 0.............................. FergusSweeney 4 58
(Richard Hannon) *mid-div: pushed along and hdwy on inner 2f out: rdn in 3rd over 1f out: one pce fnl f: lost 3rd last stride* **14/1**
5 hd **Gladice** 2-8-12 0.............................. HayleyTurner 11 58
(Marco Botti) *chsd ldrs: drvn and cl up on outer 2f out: rdn over 1f out: one pce fnl f* **20/1**
00 **6** 1/2 **Sparkling Diamond**[13] [3491] 2-8-11 0.............................. DannyBrock 7 56
(Philip McBride) *mid-div: pushed along 2f out: rdn to chse ldrs over 1f out: one pce fnl f* **33/1**
7 3/4 **Galispeed (FR)** 2-9-5 0.............................. JackMitchell 2 62
(Archie Watson) *hld up: pushed along 2f out: rdn fnl f: no imp* **9/2**[3]
0 **8** 1/2 **Jungle Book (GER)**[34] [2761] 2-9-2 0.............................. StevieDonohoe 3 57
(Jonathan Portman) *hld up: pushed along 2f out: no imp* **11/4**[2]
0 **9** 1 **Pilsdon Pen**[33] [2792] 2-9-2 0.............................. LiamKeniry 9 55
(Joseph Tuite) *hld up: drvn 2f out: rdn fnl f: no imp* **50/1**
00 **10** 2 1/4 **Mac McCarthy (IRE)**[13] [3491] 2-9-0 0.............................. FinleyMarsh(3) 5 50
(Richard Hughes) *a bhd* **16/1**
11 3 1/4 **Star Of St Louis (FR)** 2-9-2 0.............................. EoinWalsh 13 40
(Denis Quinn) *prom: drvn and lost pl 2f out: rdn and wknd over 1f out* **100/1**
0 **12** 2 **Indra Dawn (FR)**[20] [3245] 2-9-5 0.............................. AdamMcNamara 8 38
(Archie Watson) *mid-div on outer: drvn over 2f out: sn rdn and wknd: dropped to last and eased fnl f* **12/1**

1m 27.74s (0.54) **Going Correction** -0.225s/f (Stan) **12 Ran SP% 124.9**
Speed ratings (Par 93): **87,86,83,83,83 82,81,81,79,77 73,71**
CSF £23.05 TOTE £2.10: £1.20, £2.90, £20.90; EX 21.70 Trifecta £515.80.
Owner Rob Ferguson **Bred** Mrs Joan Murphy **Trained** Middleham Moor, N Yorks

FOCUS
An ordinary juvenile novice contest in terms of prior form but Capla Temptress, a subsequent Canadian Grade 1 winner on firm at Woodbine, won this race on debut in 2017. It appeared to be a tactical gallop and it proved hard to make up much ground from off the pace.

3991 BET TOTEEXACTA AT TOTESPORT.COM H'CAP 7f (P)
6:40 (6:43) (Class 3) (0-95,95) 4-Y-O+ **£9,703** (£2,887; £1,443; £721) **Stalls** Low

Form RPR
440- **1** **Ambassadorial (USA)**[293] [6732] 5-9-7 **95**.............................. DavidEgan 7 108
(Jane Chapple-Hyam) *hld up: pushed along 2f out: drvn and hdwy on outer 1 1/2f out: sn rdn: str run to ld 1/2f out: sn clr: pushed out nr fin* **8/1**
6-44 **2** 3 1/2 **Charles Molson**[26] [3040] 8-9-7 **95**.............................. DanielMuscutt 2 99
(Patrick Chamings) *mid-div: pushed along 2f out: drvn and hdwy over 1f out: sn rdn: r.o fnl f: tk 2nd 100yds out* **10/1**
63/1 **3** nk **That Is The Spirit**[13] [3496] 8-8-1 **80**.............................. TheodoreLadd(5) 9 83
(Michael Appleby) *led: pushed along in 1 l ld 2f out: rdn 1 1/2f out: 2 l ld 1f out: hdd 1/2f out: no ex and lost 2nd 100yds out* **7/1**
000/ **4** 1 **Mustarrid (IRE)**[137] [572] 5-8-11 **85**.............................. KieranShoemark 4 85+
(Ian Williams) *detached in rr: drvn and plenty to do in last 2f out: rdn over 1f out: r.o wl fnl f: tk 4th last stride: nvr nrr* **25/1**
5260 **5** nse **Areen Heart (FR)**[18] [3347] 5-9-5 **93**..............................(h) LiamKeniry 6 93
(David O'Meara) *hld up: pushed along and hdwy over 1f out: rdn fnl f: kpt on* **25/1**
00-3 **6** nk **Papa Stour (USA)**[23] [3147] 4-8-2 **76**.............................. HayleyTurner 3 75
(Andrew Balding) *hld up: pushed along 2f out: sn rdn: effrt over 1f out: kpt on fnl f* **5/1**[3]
-000 **7** 1 3/4 **Never Back Down (IRE)**[118] [843] 4-9-7 **95**.............................. JackMitchell 10 89
(Hugo Palmer) *mid-div: drvn and rn wd 1 1/2f out: sn rdn and wknd (jockey said gelding hung right-handed throughout)* **16/1**
3014 **8** 2 **Laieth**[19] [3308] 4-9-7 **95**..............................(p1) AdamKirby 1 84
(Saeed bin Suroor) *chsd ldrs: drvn 2f out: sn rdn: wknd fnl f (trainer's rep said gelding ran flat)* **7/2**[1]
-113 **9** 1/2 **Walk On Walter (IRE)**[33] [2791] 4-9-7 **95**..............................(h) StevieDonohoe 5 83
(Jonathan Portman) *hld up: drvn 2f out: rdn fnl f: no imp* **8/1**
-051 **10** 4 1/2 **Sword Exceed (GER)**[23] [3147] 5-8-2 **79**.............................. GabrieleMalune(3) 11 54
(Ivan Furtado) *chsd ldr: rdn and lost pl over 1f out: wknd fnl f* **14/1**
114- **11** 1 **Maaward (IRE)**[270] [7525] 4-9-7 **95**.............................. DaneO'Neill 8 68
(Richard Hannon) *chsd ldrs: drvn 2f out: sn rdn and wknd: dropped to last and eased fnl f (jockey said gelding was never travelling)* **9/2**[2]

1m 24.03s (-3.17) **Going Correction** -0.225s/f (Stan) **11 Ran SP% 121.1**
Speed ratings (Par 107): **109,105,104,103,103 103,101,98,98,93 91**
CSF £88.05 CT £600.89 TOTE £9.60: £2.60, £3.00, £2.20; EX 117.10 Trifecta £1048.40.
Owner Mrs Jane Chapple-Hyam **Bred** Darley **Trained** Dalham, Suffolk

FOCUS
A good handicap. The clear-cut winner's time was by far the quickest of the first three 7f races on the card. The third has been rated close to his latest.

3992 BET TOTEQUADPOT AT TOTESPORT.COM H'CAP 1m 2f (P)
7:10 (7:12) (Class 2) (0-100,101) 4-Y-O+ **£16,172** (£4,812; £2,405; £1,202) **Stalls** Low

Form RPR
2 **1** **Indeed**[67] [1753] 4-9-4 **96**.............................. LiamKeniry 11 105
(Dominic Ffrench Davis) *prom: 1 l 2nd 2f out: drvn to ld over 1f out: sn rdn: r.o wl fnl f* **6/1**[3]
1234 **2** 3/4 **Desert Fire (IRE)**[61] [1927] 4-9-9 **101**..............................(p1) PatCosgrave 6 109
(Saeed bin Suroor) *trckd ldrs: pushed along in 4th 2f out: rdn over 1f out: wnt 2nd 100yds out: kpt on but a hld by wnr* **5/2**[2]
2042 **3** 3/4 **Exec Chef (IRE)**[27] [3005] 4-9-6 **98**.............................. OisinMurphy 1 104
(Jim Boyle) *chsd ldrs: pushed along over 1f out: 1/2 l 2nd ent fnl f: one pce and lost 2nd 100yds out* **2/1**[1]
4043 **4** 2 3/4 **Michele Strogoff**[62] [1882] 6-8-4 **87**.............................. TheodoreLadd(5) 5 88
(Michael Appleby) *led: pushed along in 1 l ld 2f out: rdn and hdd over 1f out: wknd fnl f* **33/1**
0032 **5** nk **Ventura Knight (IRE)**[11] [3605] 4-9-6 **98**.............................. SilvestreDeSousa 10 98
(Mark Johnston) *hld up: drvn on outer 2f out: rdn over 1f out: kpt on fnl f* **14/1**
-115 **6** 1 **Simoon (IRE)**[25] [3072] 5-8-5 **83**.............................. HayleyTurner 2 81
(Andrew Balding) *mid-div: pushed along 2f out: sn rdn: no imp* **8/1**
30-4 **7** 1 1/2 **Highbrow**[27] [3005] 4-9-4 **96**.............................. StevieDonohoe 3 91
(David Simcock) *hld up: pushed along 2f out: drvn over 1f out: rdn fnl f: no imp* **9/1**
1-60 **8** 1/2 **Dukhan**[40] [2574] 4-9-2 **94**.............................. JackMitchell 8 88
(Hugo Palmer) *hld up in rr: drvn 2f out: rdn fnl f: nvr a factor* **16/1**
1160 **9** 3 1/4 **Petite Jack**[29] [1917] 6-9-7 **99**.............................. AdamKirby 4 86
(Neil King) *hld up: pushed along 2f out: rdn over 1f out: no rspnse* **40/1**
6-50 **10** 3/4 **Plutonian (IRE)**[34] [2778] 5-9-6 **98**.............................. KieranShoemark 9 84
(Charles Hills) *mid-div: drvn 2f out: sn rdn and wknd: lost shoe (vet said gelding lost its left fore shoe)* **22/1**

2m 4.19s (-4.41) **Going Correction** -0.225s/f (Stan) **10 Ran SP% 119.6**
Speed ratings (Par 109): **108,107,106,104,104 103,102,101,99,98**
CSF £21.60 CT £41.52 TOTE £6.60: £2.10, £1.20, £1.10; EX 23.40 Trifecta £136.00.
Owner Marchwood Aggregates **Bred** Juddmonte Farms Ltd **Trained** Lambourn, Berks

FOCUS
A good handicap. The winner did well to assert in the final furlong from an always prominent pitch in another good comparative time. The third has been rated to form.

3993 BET TOTETRIFECTA AT TOTESPORT.COM H'CAP 5f (P)
7:40 (7:40) (Class 2) (0-105,104) 3-Y-O+ **£16,172** (£4,812; £2,405; £1,202) **Stalls** Low

Form RPR
3402 **1** **Tropics (USA)**[11] [3582] 11-9-6 **103**..............................(h) SophieRalston(7) 3 111
(Dean Ivory) *chsd ldr: 1 l 2nd 2f out: sn drvn: rdn in cl 3rd 1f out: r.o to ld 1/2f out: drvn clr* **7/2**[1]
0505 **2** 1 1/4 **Royal Birth**[11] [3582] 8-9-8 **98**..............................(t) OisinMurphy 2 102
(Stuart Williams) *chsd ldrs: drvn 1 1/2f out: rdn to ld jst ins fnl f: hdd 1/2f out: no ex* **7/2**[1]
1315 **3** 1/2 **Embour (IRE)**[11] [3602] 4-8-12 **93**.............................. SeamusCronin(5) 9 95
(Richard Hannon) *hld up: pushed along on inner 2f out: drvn and effrt 1 1/2f out: sn rdn: kpt on into 3rd fnl f* **9/2**[2]
-001 **4** 1/2 **Lord Riddiford (IRE)**[11] [3582] 4-9-3 **93**.............................. JasonHart 5 93
(John Quinn) *mid-div: drvn in 4th 2f out: rdn 1 1/2f out: kpt on fnl f* **7/2**[1]
6510 **5** 1 **Just That Lord**[18] [3344] 6-8-11 **87**.............................. CharlieBennett 1 83
(Michael Attwater) *led: 1 l ld 2f out: rdn in narrow ld 1f out: hdd jst ins fnl f: sn wknd* **8/1**[3]
103/ **6** 5 **Unabated (IRE)**[682] [5684] 5-10-0 **104**..............................(e1) DavidEgan 4 82
(Jane Chapple-Hyam) *hld up: pushed along in 6th 2f out: racd wd 1 1/2f out: sn drvn and lost tch* **9/1**
-403 **7** 3 3/4 **Spoof**[17] [3375] 4-9-3 **93**..............................(h) KieranShoemark 8 58
(Charles Hills) *rrd up leaving stalls: a in rr: lost tch fr 2f out (jockey said gelding reared leaving the stalls)* **11/1**

57.99s (-2.21) **Going Correction** -0.225s/f (Stan) **7 Ran SP% 114.3**
Speed ratings (Par 109): **108,106,105,104,102 94,88**
CSF £15.82 CT £54.82 TOTE £4.30: £2.10, £2.00; EX 18.50 Trifecta £66.40.
Owner Dean Ivory **Bred** D Konecny, S Branch & A Branch **Trained** Radlett, Herts

FOCUS
A good sprint handicap. A veteran sprinter, and one of the three co-favourites, won well in a quick time. The winner has been rated to his C&D best, with the third a bit below his latest.

3994 TOTEPOOL QUEEN CHARLOTTE FILLIES' STKS (LISTED RACE) 7f (P)
8:10 (8:11) (Class 1) 4-Y-O+
£42,532 (£16,125; £8,070; £4,020; £2,017; £1,012) **Stalls** Low

Form RPR
5-30 **1** **Billesdon Brook**[32] [2829] 4-9-0 107.............................. SeanLevey 2 105
(Richard Hannon) *mid-div: hdwy to trck ldrs over 1f out: rdn to chal 1f out: led 1/2f out: sn clr* **5/1**[3]
0150 **2** 1 **Crossing The Line**[25] [3069] 4-9-0 100.............................. SilvestreDeSousa 9 103
(Andrew Balding) *hld up: pushed along 2f out: drvn and hdwy over 1f out: sn rdn: swtchd and r.o wl fnl f: tk 2nd 50yds out* **7/1**
13-2 **3** 1/2 **Solar Gold (IRE)**[25] [3085] 4-9-0 96.............................. TomMarquand 12 102+
(William Haggas) *hld up: pushed along: hdwy and looking for room over 1f out: in clr and rdn fnl f: r.o wl to take 3rd nr fin (jockey said filly was denied a clear run)* **9/2**[2]
04-2 **4** nk **Comedia Eria (FR)**[38] [2670] 7-9-0 96..............................(t1) DavidEgan 1 101
(P Monfort, France) *trckd ldrs: pushed into ld over 1f out: sn rdn: hdd 1/2f out: wknd last 100yds* **33/1**
1226 **5** shd **Island Of Life (USA)**[25] [3085] 5-9-0 100..............................(tp) DanielTudhope 14 101+
(William Haggas) *hld up: plenty to do 2f out: pushed along: hdwy and nt clr run over 1f out: in clr ins fnl f: r.o wl (jockey said mare was denied a clear run)* **8/1**
1154 **6** 3/4 **Tiger Eye (IRE)**[46] [2404] 4-9-0 94.............................. OisinMurphy 4 99
(James Fanshawe) *hld up: pushed along and swtchd to outer over 1f out: rdn fnl f: kpt on* **6/1**
2060 **7** 3/4 **Pattie**[4] [3857] 5-9-0 94.............................. CallumShepherd 11 97
(Mick Channon) *hld up: pushed along and hdwy on inner over 1f out: rdn and one pce fnl f* **50/1**
5-13 **8** nk **Heavenly Holly (IRE)**[25] [3085] 4-9-0 97.............................. JackMitchell 8 97
(Hugo Palmer) *chsd ldrs: pushed along 1 1/2f out: rdn and wknd fnl f* **7/1**
0365 **9** 3 **Vivianite (IRE)**[18] [3342] 4-9-0 94..............................(p1) HollieDoyle 5 90
(Archie Watson) *disp ld tl led on own over 2f out: rdn and hdd over 1f out: wknd fnl f* **50/1**

0-00 **10** *1½* **Rock On Baileys**[39] 2627 4-9-0 93.............................(p) LewisEdmunds 3 86
(Amy Murphy) *mid-div: drvn on outer 1 1/2f out: sn rdn and wknd* **66/1**

-232 **11** *nse* **Goodnight Girl (IRE)**[13] 3492 4-9-0 92.........................(p) KieranShoemark 10 86
(Jonathan Portman) *chsd ldrs: drvn 2f out: rdn and wknd over 1f out* **33/1**

1-31 **12** *½* **Belated Breath**[23] 3164 4-9-0 88.. GeraldMosse 13 85
(Hughie Morrison) *trckd across fr wd draw to dispute ld: pushed along and hdd over 2f out: rdn and wknd 1 1/2f out* **33/1**

0511 **13** *2¼* **Victory Wave (USA)**[13] 3494 5-9-0 104.............................(h) PatCosgrave 7 80
(Saeed bin Suroor) *hld up: drvn over 1f out: reminder fnl f: no rspnse (jockey said mare was never travelling; vet said mare was lame left fore)* **11/4**[1]

5226 **14** *10* **Yusra**[50] 2252 4-9-0 78.. GeorgeWood 6 57
(Marco Botti) *mid-div on outer: drvn and lost pl 2f out: dropped to last over 1f out: eased fnl f* **66/1**

1m 23.81s (-3.39) **Going Correction** -0.225s/f (Stan) **14** Ran SP% **127.6**
Speed ratings (Par 108): **110,108,108,107,107 106,106,105,102,100 100,100,97,86**
CSF £41.07 TOTE £5.10: £1.90, £2.40, £2.20; EX 50.30 Trifecta £644.60.
Owner Pall Mall Partners & Mrs R J McCreery **Bred** Stowell Hill Partners **Trained** East Everleigh, Wilts

■ Stewards' Enquiry : Callum Shepherd one-day ban: started from wrong stall (Jul 3)
Kieran Shoemark one-day ban: started from wrong stall (Jul 3)

FOCUS
The feature race was a good quality Listed fillies' contest and the shock 2018 1000 Guineas winner notched her first win since in a good comparative time. The fourth looks the key to the form.

3995 CELEBRATE JUNE'S HERO LOUISE ELTON FILLIES' H'CAP 1m 6f (P)
8:40 (8:42) (Class 2) (0-105,104) 4-Y-O+ **£29,110** (£8,662; £4,329; £2,164) **Stalls** Low

Form RPR

2113 **1** **Bayshore Freeway (IRE)**[25] 3096 4-9-4 **101**........... SilvestreDeSousa 5 107
(Mark Johnston) *led after 1f: mde rest: pushed along in 1 l ld 2f out: sn drvn: rdn in 1 1/2 l ld 1f out: r.o wl fnl f* **2/1**[1]

0-03 **2** *1* **Lady Bergamot (FR)**[32] 2822 5-8-5 **88**........................... GeorgeWood 3 92
(James Fanshawe) *led 1f: trckd ldrs whn hdd: drvn in 3rd 2f out: rdn over 1f out: disp 2nd thrght fnl f: r.o to secure 2nd last stride* **4/1**[3]

251- **3** *nse* **Highgarden**[264] 7733 4-9-7 **104**.. RobertHavlin 4 108
(John Gosden) *prom: drvn in 1 l 2nd 2f out: rdn over 1f out: disp 2nd thrght fnl f: kpt on: pipped for 2nd last stride* **7/2**[2]

6-44 **4** *2* **White Chocolate (IRE)**[5] 3800 5-8-2 **88**...................... RosieJessop(3) 2 89
(David Simcock) *hld up: drvn in 4th 2f out: sn rdn: one pce fnl f* **10/1**

6-16 **5** *2¼* **Jedhi**[11] 3586 4-8-2 **85**... HollieDoyle 7 83
(Hughie Morrison) *hld up in rr: pushed into 5th 2f out: rdn over 1f out: no imp* **6/1**

0-05 **6** *14* **Maid Up**[25] 3096 4-9-5 **102**.. RobHornby 1 80
(Andrew Balding) *hld up: rdn and dropped to last 2f out: sn lost tch* **7/1**

2m 56.9s (-6.30) **Going Correction** -0.225s/f (Stan) **6** Ran SP% **111.4**
Speed ratings (Par 96): **109,108,108,107,105 97**
CSF £10.06 TOTE £2.50: £1.60, £2.10; EX 9.70 Trifecta £29.10.
Owner Kingsley Park Owners Club **Bred** Lynch Bages Ltd **Trained** Middleham Moor, N Yorks

FOCUS
A good staying fillies' handicap. The favourite gamely dictated her own increasing tempo under a fine front-running ride by Silvestre de Sousa. The second has been rated close to her AW form, with the third to last year's Listed win.

3996 BET TOTESCOOP6 AT TOTESPORT.COM H'CAP (DIV II) 7f (P)
9:10 (9:22) (Class 6) (0-55,57) 3-Y-O+
£3,428 (£1,020; £509; £300; £300; £300) **Stalls** Low

Form RPR

1223 **1** **Magicinthemaking (USA)**[19] 3304 5-9-8 **53**.................... HollieDoyle 10 62
(John E Long) *hld up: hdwy on outer 2f out: rdn 1 1/2f out: str run ent fnl f: led last 50yds: won gng away* **3/1**[1]

1344 **2** *1* **Tarseekh**[19] 3304 6-9-5 **50**...(b) DavidEgan 8 56
(Charlie Wallis) *led: disp ld after 2f: led on own over 2f out: rdn in 2 l ld 1f out: hdd last 50yds: no ex* **9/2**[2]

00-1 **3** *3¼* **Quick Monet (IRE)**[19] 3304 6-9-4 **49**.............................. JoeyHaynes 5 47
(Shaun Harris) *hld up: pushed along 2f out: rdn 1 1/2f out: hdwy fnl f: r.o to take 3rd nr fin* **9/2**[2]

6046 **4** *nk* **Ventriloquist**[16] 3430 7-9-12 **57**................................... TomMarquand 7 54
(Simon Dow) *hld up: drvn 2f out: rdn on outer over 1f out: r.o into 4th fnl f* **6/1**

-434 **5** *1¼* **Es Que Magic (IRE)**[70] 1678 3-9-2 **56**............................ LiamKeniry 4 47
(Alex Hales) *hld up: hdwy into 3rd 2f out: sn rdn: wknd fnl f* **5/1**[3]

6044 **6** *2* **Diamond Pursuit**[16] 3410 4-8-12 **46** oh1.............(p) GabrieleMalune(3) 13 35+
(Ivan Furtado) *prom: disp ld after 2f: hdd over 2f out: sn rdn and wknd* **12/1**

1635 **7** *nk* **Mr Potter**[27] 3007 6-9-10 **55**..(v) PhilipPrince 1 43
(Richard Guest) *t.k.h: chsd ldrs: drvn in 4th 2f out: rdn over 1f out: wknd fnl f* **8/1**

5000 **8** *3½* **Malaysian Boleh**[14] 3475 9-8-8 **46** oh1..............(be) GraceMcEntee(7) 15 25
(Phil McEntee) *chsd ldrs: drvn in 5th 2f out: sn rdn and wknd* **25/1**

00 **9** *¾* **Cala Sveva (IRE)**[19] 3299 3-7-13 **46** oh1..........(p¹) IsobelFrancis(7) 2 20
(Mark Usher) *hld up: pushed along 2f out: sn rdn: no imp* **25/1**

0000 **10** *5* **Reformed Character (IRE)**[18] 3352 3-8-12 **52**............... EoinWalsh 12 13
(Lydia Pearce) *bhd: drvn over 2f out: reminder over 1f out: no imp (jockey said colt was never travelling)* **16/1**

0-00 **11** *3¾* **Tattenhams**[20] 3277 3-8-9 **49**..................................... CharlieBennett 3
(Adam West) *chsd ldrs: rdn and lost pl over 2f out: wknd* **66/1**

6-00 **12** *1½* **Could Be Gold (IRE)**[12] 3533 5-8-10 **46** oh1........(h) DarraghKeenan(5) 9
(John Butler) *hld up: drvn over 2f out: dropped to last over 1f out* **66/1**

1m 25.83s (-1.37) **Going Correction** -0.225s/f (Stan)
WFA 3 from 4yo+ 9lb **12** Ran SP% **127.7**
Speed ratings (Par 101): **98,96,93,92,91 89,88,84,83,78 73,72**
CSF £17.33 CT £63.81 TOTE £3.30: £1.40, £1.70, £1.90; EX 16.90 Trifecta £48.60.
Owner Martin J Gibbs & R D John **Bred** Janice Woods **Trained** Brighton, East Sussex

■ Cool Echo and Jonathans Girl were withdrawn. Prices at time of withdrawal were 10/1 & 50/1 respectively. Rule 4 applies to board prices prior to withdrawal - deduction 5p in the pound. New market formed

FOCUS
The second division of a moderate handicap. The favourite's winning time was marginally slower.
T/Plt: £61.20 to a £1 stake. Pool: £43,512.32 - 518.90 winning units T/Qpdt: £26.60 to a £1 stake. Pool: £6,481.48 - 179.95 winning units **Keith McHugh**

3716 HAMILTON (R-H)
Wednesday, June 19

OFFICIAL GOING: Good to firm (good in places; 8.0)
Wind: Almost nil Weather: Fine, dry

3997 HAMILTON PARK SUPPORTING RACING TO SCHOOL NOVICE AUCTION STKS (PLUS 10 RACE) (£20K BB SERIES QUAL) 5f 7y
1:50 (1:51) (Class 4) 2-Y-O **£5,433** (£1,617; £808; £404) **Stalls** High

Form RPR

243 **1** **Dandizette (IRE)**[15] 3451 2-8-11 0................................ AndrewMullen 7 72
(Adrian Nicholls) *mde all: rdn and edgd lft over 1f out: hrd pressed fnl f: hld on gamely towards fin* **10/3**[2]

0 **2** *nk* **Teenar**[13] 3498 2-8-13 0...................................... SeanDavis(3) 5 76
(Richard Fahey) *in tch: effrt over 1f out: squeezed through and ev ch against stands' rail ins fnl f: kpt on: hld nr fin* **28/1**

3 *1¾* **Rose Bandit (IRE)** 2-8-11 0... ShaneGray 2 65
(Stef Keniry) *hld up in tch on outside: effrt and edgd rt over 1f out: kpt on same pce ins fnl f* **33/1**

2 **4** *nse* **Hidden Spell (IRE)**[9] 3652 2-8-11 0................................ BenCurtis 1 64
(K R Burke) *trckd ldrs on outside: effrt and cl 2nd over 2f out to over 1f out: rdn and one pce fnl f* **13/8**[1]

5 *1* **Auckland Lodge (IRE)** 2-8-6 0................................ HarrisonShaw(5) 6 61
(Ben Haslam) *dwlt: hld up: n.m.r briefly over 1f out: sn pushed along: kpt on fnl f: nt pce to chal* **28/1**

1322 **6** *1¼* **Birkenhead**[21] 3212 2-9-3 0..................................(v) FayeMcManoman(5) 3 69
(Les Eyre) *prom: nt clr run over 2f out to over 1f out: sn rdn and outpcd: btn fnl f* **4/1**

12 **7** *7* **Probable Cause**[18] 3350 2-9-3 0.................................... PaulHanagan 4 37
(Archie Watson) *t.k.h: pressed wnr to over 2f out: losing pl whn n.m.r over 1f out: sn wknd* **7/2**[3]

59.88s (-0.52) **Going Correction** -0.125s/f (Firm) **7** Ran SP% **113.2**
Speed ratings (Par 95): **99,98,95,95,94 92,80**
CSF £79.98 TOTE £3.40: £1.30, £11.40; EX 84.80 Trifecta £696.30.
Owner Ne-Chance **Bred** L Lynch & R Sherrard **Trained** Sessay, N Yorks

FOCUS
Rail movements added 15 yds to races 4,5,6,7 and 8. A fair novice run at a sound pace. The winner has been rated to her mark.

3998 BRITISH STALLION STUDS EBF MAIDEN STKS (PLUS 10 RACE) (£20,000 BB FOODSERVICE 2YO SERIES QUAL) 6f 6y
2:20 (2:28) (Class 4) 2-Y-O **£5,433** (£1,617; £808; £404) **Stalls** High

Form RPR

62 **1** **The New Marwan**[25] 3071 2-9-2 0.......................... SeanDavis(3) 1 82
(Richard Fahey) *hld up: pushed along 1/2-way: hdwy on outside over 1f out: edgd lft and led ins fnl f: drvn out* **9/4**[1]

2 *½* **One Hart (IRE)** 2-9-2 0... FrannyNorton 3 77+
(Mark Johnston) *green in preliminaries: t.k.h: pressed ldr: effrt and disp ld over 1f out to ins fnl f: kpt on: hld nr fin* **5/1**

4 **3** *2¾* **Matera**[13] 3507 2-9-5 0.. KevinStott 7 72
(Kevin Ryan) *led: rdn: edgd rt and hrd pressed over 1f out: kpt on same pce ins fnl f* **4/1**[3]

502 **4** *1¾* **Corndavon Lad (IRE)**[17] 3371 2-9-5 0.............................. PaulHanagan 2 67
(Richard Fahey) *chsd ldrs: rdn and effrt 2f out: wknd ins fnl f* **9/1**

5 *¾* **Haldane (IRE)** 2-9-2 0.. SamJames 4 62
(Phillip Makin) *slowly away: hld up: pushed along 2f out: no imp fnl f* **7/2**[2]

6 *nse* **Aberama Gold** 2-9-2 0.. ShaneGray 6 61+
(Keith Dalgleish) *dwlt: t.k.h: in tch: n.m.r over 2f out: sn rdn: outpcd fr over 1f out* **8/1**

1m 12.82s (0.12) **Going Correction** -0.125s/f (Firm) **6** Ran SP% **110.8**
Speed ratings (Par 95): **94,93,89,87,86 86**
CSF £13.36 TOTE £3.20: £2.00, £1.90; EX 12.00 Trifecta £29.10.
Owner Dr Marwan Koukash **Bred** Saeed Nasser Al Romaithi **Trained** Musley Bank, N Yorks

■ Bad Rabbit was withdrawn. Price at time of withdrawal 66/1. Rule 4 does not apply

FOCUS
Not a bad maiden run at a solid pace. The winner has been rated in line with his Chester run.

3999 SAM COLLINGWOOD-CAMERON H'CAP 6f 6y
2:55 (2:57) (Class 5) (0-75,74) 3-Y-O+
£4,140 (£1,232; £615; £307; £300; £300) **Stalls** High

Form RPR

-542 **1** **Jordan Electrics**[7] 3719 3-8-9 **65**.........................(h) BenRobinson(3) 5 70
(Linda Perratt) *mde all against stands' rail: rdn over 1f out: hld on wl fnl f* **9/2**[2]

0210 **2** *¾* **Epeius (IRE)**[21] 3221 6-9-10 **70**.................................(v) AndrewMullen 3 75
(Ben Haslam) *dwlt: sn pushed along in rr: hdwy and angled rt ins fnl f: kpt on to take 2nd last stride* **5/1**[3]

-513 **3** *shd* **Friendly Advice (IRE)**[28] 2960 3-9-7 **74**........................ ShaneGray 1 77
(Keith Dalgleish) *hld up bhd ldng gp: stdy hdwy to trck ldrs over 1f out: sn pushed along: angled rt and kpt on ins fnl f* **11/2**

006 **4** *hd* **Mr Wagyu (IRE)**[33] 2788 4-9-9 **69**.................................(v) KevinStott 8 73
(John Quinn) *trckd ldrs: effrt and rdn over 1f out: kpt on same pce wl ins fnl f* **5/1**[3]

2212 **5** *¾* **Sczueme**[8] 3706 5-9-11 **71**...(h) SamJames 4 76+
(Phillip Makin) *trckd wnr to over 2f out: cl up: nt clr run over 1f out: effrt and keeping on whn no room last 50yds: nt rcvr (jockey said gelding was denied a clear run 1f out)* **9/4**[1]

0006 **6** *shd* **Requinto Dawn (IRE)**[18] 3360 4-9-6 **69**.......................(p) SeanDavis(3) 7 70
(Richard Fahey) *t.k.h: prom: wnt 2nd over 2f out: effrt and rdn over 1f out: edgd lft and no ex ins fnl f (jockey said gelding hung left under pressure)* **14/1**

61-1 **7** *6* **Highly Focussed (IRE)**[33] 2789 5-9-8 **68**..................... PaulHanagan 2 50
(Ann Duffield) *slowly away: bhd and outpcd: rdn and wknd over 1f out* **14/1**

1m 11.19s (-1.51) **Going Correction** -0.125s/f (Firm)
WFA 3 from 4yo+ 7lb **7** Ran SP% **111.0**
Speed ratings (Par 103): **105,104,103,103,102 102,94**
CSF £25.33 CT £119.75 TOTE £7.60: £3.00, £3.10; EX 32.40 Trifecta £162.00.
Owner Brian Jordan, B Jordan & Stephen Jordan **Bred** T J Cooper **Trained** East Kilbride, S Lanarks

FOCUS
A fair handicap run at a decent pace. Ordinary form.

4000 FOLLOW @HAMILTONPARKRC ON TWITTER H'CAP 1m 68y
3:30 (3:31) (Class 5) (0-70,72) 3-Y-O

£4,140 (£1,232; £615; £307; £300; £300) **Stalls Low**

Form RPR
5406 **1** **Five Helmets (IRE)**[30] 2897 3-8-11 **63**..................(p) JamieGormley(3) 11 73
(Iain Jardine) *s.i.s: hld up: hdwy on outside over 2f out: edgd rt and led over 1f out: rdn clr fnl f (trainer said, regarding the apparent improvement in form, gelding has been working well at home recently, and may have appreciated the step up in trip to 1 mile ½ a furlong on this occasion)* **6/1**[3]

6621 **2** *3* **Ivory Charm**[21] 3223 3-9-0 **66**.................................... SeanDavis(3) 1 69
(Richard Fahey) *hld up in midfield: effrt and angled lft over 2f out: drvn: edgd rt and chsd wnr over 1f out: kpt on same pce fnl f* **9/4**[1]

66-5 **3** *4* **Eesha's Smile (IRE)**[50] 2253 3-9-9 **72**.......................... DavidNolan 4 66
(Ivan Furtado) *led: rdn over 2f out: hdd over 1f out: sn outpcd* **4/1**[2]

-600 **4** *1* **Startego**[11] 3580 3-9-4 **67**..(p[1]) PaulHanagan 9 59
(Archie Watson) *hld up: stdy hdwy 3f out: rdn and outpcd wl over 1f out: kpt on fnl f: nt pce to chal* **10/1**

-000 **5** *2* **Gremoboy**[13] 3516 3-8-9 **58**.. DuranFentiman 6 45
(Tim Easterby) *chsd ldrs: rdn over 2f out: wknd over 1f out* **16/1**

6040 **6** *½* **Euro No More (IRE)**[8] 3709 3-8-10 **59**..........................(p) ShaneGray 3 45
(Keith Dalgleish) *s.i.s: hld up: rdn along over 2f out: angled lft and kpt on fnl f: nvr able to chal* **14/1**

63-6 **7** *5* **Castle Quarter (IRE)**[39] 2630 3-9-0 **66**....................... BenRobinson(3) 10 40
(Seb Spencer) *sn pressing ldr: drvn and ch over 2f out: wknd over 1f out (jockey said gelding hung left home straight)* **14/1**

5443 **8** *shd* **Fiction Writer (USA)**[29] 2933 3-9-2 **70**.................... AndrewBreslin(5) 8 44
(Mark Johnston) *hld up in midfield: rdn along over 3f out: hung rt and wknd over 2f out* **4/1**[2]

56-0 **9** *1 ½* **Delectable**[20] 3270 3-8-8 **57**.. AndrewMullen 2 28
(Adrian Nicholls) *chsd ldrs: drvn along 3f out: wknd fr 2f out* **33/1**

1m 46.49s (-1.91) **Going Correction** -0.125s/f (Firm) 9 Ran **SP% 116.3**
Speed ratings (Par 99): **104,101,97,96,94 93,88,88,86**
CSF £20.04 CT £61.53 TOTE £6.50: £1.60, £1.50, £1.50; EX 24.20 Trifecta £105.30.
Owner Brendan Keogh **Bred** Ms Natalie Cleary **Trained** Carrutherstown, D'fries & G'way

FOCUS
Rail movements added 15yds. The pace was sound for this fair handicap. The winner has been rated back to his 2yo best.

4001 BOTHWELL CASTLE H'CAP 1m 68y
4:05 (4:05) (Class 4) (0-80,81) 3-Y-O+

£8,021 (£2,387; £1,192; £596; £300; £300) **Stalls Low**

Form RPR
1 **1** **Southern Rock (IRE)**[45] 2438 3-9-2 **78**............................ DavidNolan 2 86+
(David O'Meara) *cl up: led after 2f: hdd over 2f out: sn outpcd: rallied and regained ld ins fnl f: kpt on strly* **2/1**[1]

5626 **2** *1 ½* **Four Kingdoms (IRE)**[26] 3046 5-8-12 **69**................. BenSanderson(5) 8 76
(R Mike Smith) *hld up: pushed along over 2f out: hdwy and hung rt over 1f out: chsd wnr ins fnl f: r.o* **12/1**

-310 **3** *¾* **Wild Hope**[20] 3249 3-9-5 **81**... KevinStott 4 84
(Kevin Ryan) *led 2f: cl up: effrt over 2f out: ev ch ins fnl f: hld towards fin* **7/2**[3]

3613 **4** *2 ½* **Jacob Black**[30] 2898 8-9-9 **75**..(v) ShaneGray 1 75
(Keith Dalgleish) *dwlt: t.k.h: sn prom: led gng wl over 2f out: rdn and hdd ins fnl f: sn wknd* **10/1**

0442 **5** *¾* **Harvey Dent**[8] 3683 3-9-2 **78**.. PaulHanagan 6 74+
(Archie Watson) *t.k.h: cl up: effrt over 2f out: wknd ins fnl f* **5/2**[2]

0-00 **6** *3 ¾* **Indian Sounds (IRE)**[27] 2997 3-9-0 **81**..................... AndrewBreslin(5) 3 68
(Mark Johnston) *cl up: ev ch over 3f out to over 2f out: wknd over 1f out* **14/1**

100- **7** *15* **Morticia**[277] 7307 4-9-8 **77**.. SeanDavis(3) 5 32
(Keith Dalgleish) *hld up: rdn 3f out: wknd fr over 2f out: eased whn no ch over 1f out* **25/1**

1m 46.24s (-2.16) **Going Correction** -0.125s/f (Firm)
WFA 3 from 4yo+ 10lb 7 Ran **SP% 111.4**
Speed ratings (Par 105): **105,103,102,100,99 95,80**
CSF £25.22 CT £76.50 TOTE £2.40: £1.70, £6.60; EX 27.10 Trifecta £100.10.
Owner O T I Racing & Middleham Park Racing Vi **Bred** Godolphin **Trained** Upper Helmsley, N Yorks

FOCUS
Rail movements added 15yds. A fair handicap. The third has been rated in line with his Carlisle win.

4002 SAINTS & SINNERS RACENIGHT NEXT WEEK H'CAP (DIV I) 1m 1f 35y
4:45 (4:47) (Class 6) (0-60,61) 3-Y-O+

£3,493 (£1,039; £519; £300; £300; £300) **Stalls Low**

Form RPR
-424 **1** **Hector's Here**[20] 3270 3-9-0 **59**.................................. TrevorWhelan 7 66+
(Ivan Furtado) *hld up in midfield: hdwy to ld over 1f out: kpt on wl fnl f* **5/1**

5-44 **2** *2 ¼* **Don't Be Surprised**[103] 1083 4-9-4 **55**...................... BenRobinson(3) 8 59
(Seb Spencer) *w ldr: led 3f out to over 1f out: edgd rt: kpt on same pce fnl f* **14/1**

5-60 **3** *½* **Move In Faster**[16] 3415 4-9-12 **60**.................................... AndrewMullen 12 63
(Michael Dods) *prom: rdn over 2f out: ev ch briefly over 1f out: sn one pce* **25/1**

6144 **4** *1 ½* **Allux Boy (IRE)**[14] 3473 5-9-3 **56**......................... FayeMcManoman(5) 6 56
(Nigel Tinkler) *trckd ldrs: effrt and rdn whn n.m.r briefly over 1f out: sn one pce* **7/2**[2]

3641 **5** *½* **Three Castles**[8] 3684 3-9-2 **61** 6ex.................................... ShaneGray 2 59
(Keith Dalgleish) *hld up: pushed along and outpcd over 2f out: rallied over 1f out: edgd lft ins fnl f: nvr rchd ldrs* **10/3**[1]

2-64 **6** *2* **Broctune Red**[21] 3224 4-9-1 **49**.. PhilDennis 1 44
(Gillian Boanas) *led to 3f out: cl up tl rdn and wknd over 1f out* **8/1**

6303 **7** *½* **I Am Dandy (IRE)**[21] 3225 4-9-2 **50**.................................(t[1]) KevinStott 3 44
(James Ewart) *hld up in tch on ins: drvn along and outpcd over 2f out: n.d after* **9/2**[3]

6052 **8** *1 ¾* **Highwayman**[19] 3297 6-8-9 **46** oh1.................................. JamieGormley(3) 5 36
(David Thompson) *hld up: stdy hdwy over 3f out: rdn and wknd fr 2f out* **8/1**

0-50 **9** *¾* **Happy Hannah (IRE)**[48] 2337 3-8-3 **48**..........................(h[1]) CamHardie 10 36
(John Davies) *hld up: rdn and struggling over 2f out: sn btn* **33/1**

1m 59.15s (0.15) **Going Correction** -0.125s/f (Firm)
WFA 3 from 4yo+ 11lb 9 Ran **SP% 115.8**
Speed ratings (Par 101): **94,92,91,90,89 88,87,86,85**
CSF £71.73 CT £1588.45 TOTE £5.00: £1.60, £3.70, £6.60; EX 59.90 Trifecta £1005.40.
Owner John Marriott & Giggle Factor **Bred** Bredon Hill Bloodstock Ltd **Trained** Wiseton, Nottinghamshire

FOCUS
Rail movements added 15yds. A modest handicap. The third has been rated to his Newcastle mark.

4003 SAINTS & SINNERS RACENIGHT NEXT WEEK H'CAP (DIV II) 1m 1f 35y
5:20 (5:20) (Class 6) (0-60,60) 3-Y-O+

£3,493 (£1,039; £519; £300; £300; £300) **Stalls Low**

Form RPR
4000 **1** **Restive (IRE)**[7] 3721 6-9-9 **60**.. BenRobinson(3) 2 69
(Jim Goldie) *hld up: hdwy and prom over 1f out: rdn to ld ins fnl f: r.o wl* **9/2**[2]

-532 **2** *1 ¾* **Neileta**[13] 3513 3-8-11 **56**...(p[1]) DuranFentiman 1 61+
(Tim Easterby) *t.k.h: chsd ldr: effrt and rdn over 2f out: led over 1f out to ins fnl f: kpt on same pce* **2/1**[1]

-000 **3** *3 ½* **Mi Laddo (IRE)**[42] 2531 3-8-4 **49**..................................(t[1]) ShaneGray 12 47
(Oliver Greenall) *hld up: hdwy on outside to ld briefly 2f out: edgd rt: outpcd ins fnl f* **33/1**

4564 **4** *nk* **You Little Beauty**[8] 3684 3-8-1 **46** oh1.............................. CamHardie 6 43
(Ann Duffield) *hld up: rdn and outpcd over 3f out: rallied over 1f out: kpt on fnl f: nt pce to chal* **14/1**

0404 **5** *hd* **Followme Followyou (IRE)**[16] 3409 3-8-13 **58**............ FrannyNorton 4 55
(Mark Johnston) *hld up on ins: rdn over 2f out: no imp over 1f out* **6/1**

5662 **6** *9* **Optima Petamus**[15] 3448 7-9-2 **50**..................................(b) PhilDennis 8 30
(Liam Bailey) *t.k.h: prom: ev ch briefly 2f out: sn rdn: wknd fnl f* **11/1**

2233 **7** *¾* **Splash Of Verve (IRE)**[21] 3224 7-8-9 **50**.......................... TobyEley(7) 10 28
(David Thompson) *t.k.h: sn cl up: lost pl over 2f out: n.d after (jockey said gelding ran too free)* **6/1**

3000 **8** *nk* **Crazy Tornado (IRE)**[7] 3721 6-9-3 **56**..................(h) BenSanderson(5) 5 33+
(Keith Dalgleish) *led: clr 1/2-way: rdn and hdd 2f out: sn wknd* **5/1**[3]

1m 56.99s (-2.01) **Going Correction** -0.125s/f (Firm)
WFA 3 from 4yo+ 11lb 8 Ran **SP% 114.7**
Speed ratings (Par 101): **103,101,98,98,97 89,89,88**
CSF £13.98 CT £259.83 TOTE £5.10: £1.80, £1.10, £10.50; EX 17.00 Trifecta £356.80.
Owner Johnnie Delta Racing **Bred** Epona Bloodstock Ltd **Trained** Uplawmoor, E Renfrews

FOCUS
Rail movements added 15yds. A strongly run handicap. The winner has been rated to last year's 1m6f form.

4004 HAMILTON-PARK.CO.UK APPRENTICE H'CAP 1m 4f 15y
5:55 (5:56) (Class 6) (0-60,61) 4-Y-O+

£3,493 (£1,039; £519; £300; £300; £300) **Stalls High**

Form RPR
0-65 **1** **Ninepin Bowler**[7] 3718 5-9-9 **57**................................... HarrisonShaw(3) 8 64
(Ann Duffield) *plld hrd early: cl up: led after 2f: mde rest: rdn clr over 1f out: hung lft ins fnl f: r.o wl* **6/1**[3]

3131 **2** *1 ¾* **Cold Harbour**[22] 3209 4-9-13 **61**...(t) PaulaMuir(3) 9 65
(Robyn Brisland) *plld hrd early: prom: wnt 2nd after 3f to over 3f out: effrt over 2f out: regained 2nd ins fnl f: nt rch wnr* **9/4**[1]

0-40 **3** *2* **Life Knowledge (IRE)**[15] 3447 7-9-3 **53**................(p) JonathanFisher(5) 6 54
(Liam Bailey) *t.k.h: hld up: hdwy on outside and ev ch over 3f out to over 2f out: edgd rt over 1f out: no ex and lost 2nd pl ins fnl f* **13/2**

5301 **4** *¾* **Dew Pond**[8] 3705 7-9-8 **56** 4ex.......................................(bt) DannyRedmond(3) 5 56+
(Tim Easterby) *rrd in stalls: hld up: stdy hdwy over 3f out: effrt and rdn 2f out: kpt on fnl f: nt pce to chal* **9/4**[1]

2604 **5** *4* **Pammi**[13] 3500 4-9-3 **55**..(p[1]) CoreyMadden(7) 3 48
(Jim Goldie) *hld up: rdn and outpcd over 3f out: rallied and edgd rt 2f out: sn no imp* **5/1**[2]

00-0 **6** *1* **Kissesforeveryone**[23] 3162 4-9-0 **45**................................ RowanScott 1 37
(Andrew Crook) *in tch: drvn and outpcd over 3f out: n.d after* **50/1**

00 **7** *7* **Go Guarantor**[22] 3175 5-8-11 **45**................................(tp) AndrewBreslin(3) 4 25
(R Mike Smith) *dwlt: hld up: outpcd over 4f out: nvr on terms* **33/1**

0-00 **8** *nk* **Mullion Dreams**[20] 3248 5-9-0 **45**...................................... BenRobinson 2 25
(James Ewart) *led 2f: prom tl rdn and wknd over 3f out* **28/1**

0-00 **9** *nk* **Judith Gardenier**[82] 1398 7-9-0 **45**.........................(tp) ConorMcGovern 7 24
(R Mike Smith) *t.k.h: prom: rdn over 3f out: wknd fr 2f out* **50/1**

2m 40.06s (1.46) **Going Correction** -0.125s/f (Firm) 9 Ran **SP% 116.1**
Speed ratings (Par 101): **90,88,87,87,84 83,79,78,78**
CSF £19.63 CT £90.35 TOTE £5.30: £1.90, £1.10, £2.10; EX 22.80 Trifecta £97.00.
Owner Ramscove Ltd **Bred** B Buckley **Trained** Constable Burton, N Yorks

FOCUS
Rail movements added 15yds. A modest handicap. The winner has been rated within 2lb of his best.
T/Plt: £586.00 to a £1 stake. Pool: £40,663.69 - 50.65 winning units T/Qpdt: £56.80 to a £1 stake. Pool: £4,812.76 - 62.69 winning units **Richard Young**

3512 RIPON (R-H)
Wednesday, June 19

OFFICIAL GOING: Soft (7.1)
Wind: light largely across Weather: sunny

4005 MIDDLEHAM RACING BREAKS APPRENTICE (S) H'CAP 1m 1f 170y
6:50 (6:50) (Class 5) (0-75,64) 3-6-Y-O

£4,075 (£1,212; £606; £303; £300; £300) **Stalls Low**

Form RPR
0-06 **1** **Myklachi (FR)**[20] 3246 3-8-11 **57**.................................(h) GeorgeBass 4 63
(David O'Meara) *midfield: pushed along over 3f out: rdn and hdwy 2f out: styd on to ld fnl 50yds* **7/1**[3]

-444 **2** *1 ¼* **Ventura Bay (IRE)**[14] 3478 3-9-4 **64**.................................. JoeBradnam 2 68
(Richard Fahey) *prom: led 3f out: pushed along over 1f out: one pce ins fnl f and hdd 50yds out* **11/8**[1]

-003 **3** *¾* **Slaithwaite (IRE)**[13] 3513 3-8-6 **52**.................................. OwenPayton 8 54
(Roger Fell) *trckd ldrs: rdn and outpcd over 3f out: rallied over 1f out: kpt on same pce fnl f* **7/1**[3]

0-00 **4** *3 ¼* **Amy Blair**[7] 3720 6-9-2 **50**... LukeBacon 5 46
(Stef Keniry) *sn led: hdd over 3f out: wknd fnl f* **9/1**

50-0 **5** 2½ **Arms Of The Angel (GER)**[2] 3926 3-9-1 **64** AidanRedpath(3) 9 55
(Mark Johnston) *sn trckd ldrs: rdn along over 3f out: wknd over 1f out* **6/1**[2]
0020 **6** 2¼ **Amity Island**[15] 3447 4-9-2 **50** (b) IzzyClifton 6 37
(Ollie Pears) *midfield: rdn over 2f out: wknd over 1f out* **14/1**
6250 **7** 5 **Simon's Smile (FR)**[13] 3513 3-9-4 **64** (p) GianlucaSanna 3 41
(K R Burke) *hld up in midfield: rdn over 3f out: sn btn* **17/2**
4-00 **8** 31 **X Rated (IRE)**[16] 3429 5-9-11 **62** AidenSmithies(3) 7
(Mark Johnston) *a in rr: t.o fnl 3f* **20/1**
040 **9** 16 **Heldtoransom**[14] 3463 3-8-0 **46** oh1 (h) MolliePhillips 1
(Joseph Tuite) *a in rr: t.o fnl 4f* **50/1**
2m 9.84s (5.24) **Going Correction** +0.30s/f (Good)
WFA 3 from 4yo+ 12lb **9** Ran SP% **115.3**
Speed ratings: **92,91,90,87,85 84,80,55,42**
CSF £16.98 CT £71.33 TOTE £6.90: £2.50, £1.10, £1.80; EX 22.40 Trifecta £183.80.There was no bid for the winner. Ventura Bay was the subject of a friendly claim by Mr R. A. Fahey £6,000
Owner Middleham Park Racing XCVII **Bred** Pierre Cadec **Trained** Upper Helmsley, N Yorks
FOCUS
Add 6yds. Soft but drying ground, and a time 9.54sec slower than standard with a suspicion that the leaders went off too fast. This was a very modest event indeed, confined to apprentices who hadn't ridden a winner before Sunday. It produced a 1-2 with 3yos for owners Middleham Park Racing. The winner has been rated back to his best.

4006 MONDAY NIGHT MADNESS 8TH JULY MAIDEN FILLIES' STKS (PLUS 10 RACE) 5f
7:20 (7:20) (Class 5) 2-Y-O **£3,881** (£1,155; £577; £288) **Stalls** High

Form RPR
2 **1** **Pink Sands (IRE)**[30] 2918 2-9-0 0 LiamJones 10 82+
(William Haggas) *mde all: pushed clr appr fnl f: readily* **4/9**[1]
2 3¾ **Felicia Blue** 2-8-9 0 ConnorMurtagh(5) 5 66
(Richard Fahey) *trckd ldr: pushed along and outpcd in 2nd appr fnl f: kpt on ins fnl f but no ch w wnr* **12/1**
3 ¾ **Living In The Past (IRE)** 2-9-0 0 BenCurtis 4 66+
(K R Burke) *dwlt: swtchd lft sn after s and shied at rail: hld up: pushed along 2f out: kpt on ins fnl f to go 3rd towards fin (jockey said filly veered sharply left after leaving the stalls losing several lengths)* **8/1**[3]
4 ¾ **Aryaaf (IRE)** 2-9-0 0 KieranO'Neill 3 60
(Simon Crisford) *slowly away: hld up: hdwy and in tch on outside 3f out: rdn and edgd rt 2f out: continued to edgd rt and no ex fnl 110yds: lost 3rd towards fin* **5/1**[2]
0 **5** 1¼ **Orlaith (IRE)**[20] 3244 2-9-0 0 JamesSullivan 8 56
(Iain Jardine) *chsd ldr: pushed along over 1f out: grad wknd ins fnl f* **33/1**
000 **6** 2½ **Ice Skate**[16] 3411 2-9-0 0 DavidAllan 9 47
(Tim Easterby) *in tch tl wknd over 1f out* **25/1**
7 20 **Luckyforsome (IRE)** 2-9-0 0 TomEaves 2
(Eric Alston) *hld up: wknd and bhd fnl 2f* **50/1**
1m 0.62s (1.22) **Going Correction** +0.30s/f (Good) **7** Ran SP% **113.5**
Speed ratings (Par 90): **102,96,94,93,91 87,55**
CSF £6.98 TOTE £1.20: £1.10, £3.40; EX 7.00 Trifecta £25.30.
Owner Bermuda Thoroughbred Racing Limited **Bred** Lynchbages Edgeridge Ltd & Glenvale Stud **Trained** Newmarket, Suffolk
FOCUS
Easy for the favourite, in a race containing some green opponents.

4007 TOPSPORT EQUISAND FILLIES' H'CAP 1m 1f 170y
7:50 (7:50) (Class 4) (0-85,81) 3-Y-O+ **£5,692** (£1,694; £846; £423; £300) **Stalls** Low

Form RPR
30-2 **1** **Amber Spark (IRE)**[18] 3336 3-8-10 **78** SeanDavis(3) 1 87
(Richard Fahey) *trckd ldr: pushed into ld over 2f out: 2 l clr over 1f out: rdn out fnl f* **3/1**[2]
245 **2** 2¼ **Lady Alavesa**[20] 3276 4-8-10 **63** (p) JosephineGordon 2 67
(Gay Kelleway) *hld up in tch: hdwy and trckd ldrs 3f out: rdn to go 2nd over 1f out: styd on but a hld* **6/1**
-002 **3** 2½ **Existential (IRE)**[22] 3192 4-9-13 **80** HectorCrouch 4 79
(Clive Cox) *led: rdn and hdd over 2f out: no ex over 1f out* **4/1**[3]
-313 **4** nk **Black Lotus**[18] 3338 4-10-0 **81** DavidAllan 3 79
(Chris Wall) *trckd ldr: rdn over 2f out: no ex over 1f out* **15/8**[1]
12-4 **5** 16 **Camelot Rakti (IRE)**[14] 3468 3-8-13 **78** TomEaves 5 43
(James Tate) *dwlt: hld up: rdn 3f out: wknd 2f out (trainer's rep could offer no explanation for the filly's performance)* **5/1**
2m 7.41s (2.81) **Going Correction** +0.30s/f (Good)
WFA 3 from 4yo 12lb **5** Ran SP% **110.7**
Speed ratings (Par 102): **102,100,98,97,85**
CSF £19.93 TOTE £2.80: £1.80, £2.50; EX 16.90 Trifecta £59.20.
Owner Nick Bradley Racing 9 & Sohi And Partner **Bred** Sandra Russell **Trained** Musley Bank, N Yorks
FOCUS
Add 6yds. Fair fillies' form, but not a strongly run race. The winner has been rated as at least matching last year's French form, with the second close to form.

4008 WELLS MEMORIAL CHALLENGE TROPHY H'CAP 5f
8:20 (8:20) (Class 3) (0-90,85) 3-Y-O
£9,337 (£2,796; £1,398; £699; £349; £175) **Stalls** High

Form RPR
2221 **1** **Moss Gill (IRE)**[18] 3339 3-9-0 **78** PaulHanagan 7 87+
(James Bethell) *dwlt: in tch: pushed along and hdwy to chal ent fnl f: rdn to ld ins fnl f: kpt on pushed out: shade cosily* **6/4**[1]
0650 **2** 1 **Good Luck Fox (IRE)**[12] 3531 3-9-1 **79** RossaRyan 3 84
(Richard Hannon) *chsd ldrs towards outer: rdn along 2f out: drvn to chal jst ins fnl f: kpt on* **16/1**
3253 **3** 1 **Tenax (IRE)**[9] 3654 3-8-12 **81** FayeMcManoman(5) 1 83
(Nigel Tinkler) *dwlt: hld up: pushed along and hdwy over 1f out: kpt on ins fnl f (jockey said gelding reared as stalls opened)* **9/2**[2]
1011 **4** 1½ **Mark's Choice (IRE)**[14] 3479 3-9-5 **83** JamesSullivan 6 80
(Ruth Carr) *in tch: rdn along and outpcd over 1f out: kpt on same pce ins fnl f* **8/1**
5-11 **5** ½ **Chitra**[11] 3596 3-9-2 **80** KieranO'Neill 4 75
(Daniel Kubler) *led narrowly: rdn 2f out: edgd rt over 1f out: hdd ins fnl f: wknd* **6/1**[3]
3113 **6** 1¾ **Look Out Louis**[14] 3479 3-9-7 **85** DavidAllan 5 75
(Tim Easterby) *chsd ldrs: rdn to chal over 1f out: wknd ins fnl f (jockey said gelding hung right final 2f)* **9/2**[2]
242 **7** 6 **Scale Force**[13] 3508 3-8-6 **70** (v) JosephineGordon 2 41
(Gay Kelleway) *pressed ldr: rdn and edgd rt 2f out: sn wknd* **16/1**
59.92s (0.52) **Going Correction** +0.30s/f (Good) **7** Ran SP% **113.5**
Speed ratings (Par 103): **107,105,103,101,100 97,88**
CSF £27.73 TOTE £2.20: £1.30, £8.80; EX 39.00 Trifecta £121.80.
Owner G Van Cutsem & Partner **Bred** Camas Park & Lynch Bages **Trained** Middleham Moor, N Yorks
FOCUS
Decent sprint handicap form, with a very likeable winner. The third has been rated close to form.

4009 IT'S RIPON RACES LADIES DAY TOMORROW H'CAP 1m 4f 10y
8:50 (8:50) (Class 5) (0-75,75) 4-Y-O+
£4,075 (£1,212; £606; £303; £300; £300) **Stalls** Centre

Form RPR
0044 **1** **Appointed**[5] 3816 5-9-5 **73** (t) DavidAllan 6 84+
(Tim Easterby) *led for 2f: trckd ldr: pushed along to ld again 2f out: sn clr: eased fnl 75yds* **13/8**[1]
4-46 **2** 3¾ **Remember The Days (IRE)**[16] 3415 5-9-7 **75** TomEaves 3 77
(Jedd O'Keeffe) *hld up in tch: rdn and hdwy to chse ldr over 2f out: plugged on in modest 2nd fr over 1f out: no ch w wnr* **6/1**[3]
0-22 **3** 7 **Albert Boy (IRE)**[23] 3155 6-8-6 **60** KieranO'Neill 1 51
(Scott Dixon) *trckd ldr: rdn to ld narrowly over 2f out: hdd 2f out: wknd over 1f out* **6/1**[3]
634- **4** 2 **Card High (IRE)**[268] 7600 9-9-1 **69** (t) NathanEvans 5 57
(Wilf Storey) *hld up in rr: pushed along over 3f out: sn no imp and btn* **25/1**
0006 **5** 2¾ **Mapped (USA)**[14] 3467 4-9-5 **73** (p) PaulHanagan 4 56
(Iain Jardine) *trckd ldr: racd keenly and led 10f out: hung persistently rt fr over 3f out: hdd over 2f out: wknd (jockey said gelding hung right throughout)* **6/1**[3]
2512 **6** ½ **Francophilia**[16] 3415 4-9-5 **73** AndrewMullen 7 55
(Mark Johnston) *hld up in tch: rdn along over 4f out: wknd over 2f out (jockey said filly was never travelling)* **5/2**[2]
2m 40.44s (4.14) **Going Correction** +0.30s/f (Good) **6** Ran SP% **113.4**
Speed ratings (Par 103): **98,95,90,89,87 87**
CSF £12.18 TOTE £2.40: £1.80, £2.60; EX 13.20 Trifecta £38.20.
Owner Martyn MacLeod Racing **Bred** Lady Jennifer Green **Trained** Great Habton, N Yorks
FOCUS
Add 6yds. Probably not the sturdiest form. The second has been rated to his reappearance run.

4010 FUN FOR LEGO FANS 5TH AUGUST MAIDEN STKS 6f
9:20 (9:22) (Class 5) 3-Y-O **£3,881** (£1,155; £577; £288) **Stalls** High

Form RPR
4232 **1** **Abate**[16] 3416 3-9-5 75 AndrewMullen 2 77
(Adrian Nicholls) *mde all: rdn clr over 1f out: kpt on* **5/4**[1]
5 **2** 2¾ **Attorney General**[30] 2900 3-9-5 0 BenCurtis 6 68
(Ed Vaughan) *dwlt: hld up: pushed along and hdwy over 1f out: rdn to go 2nd ins fnl f: kpt on but no ch w wnr* **11/2**[3]
3 2 **Springwood Drive** 3-9-0 0 DavidAllan 15 57+
(Tim Easterby) *dwlt: hld up in rr: pushed along and hdwy over 2f out: swtchd rt 2f out: n.m.r over 1f out: kpt on wl to go 3rd ins fnl f: bttr for r* **25/1**
4 3 **Rangefield Express (IRE)**[238] 8555 3-9-5 62 SamJames 14 52
(Geoffrey Harker) *chsd ldrs: rdn over 2f out: wknd ins fnl f* **40/1**
6-02 **5** hd **Molaaheth**[53] 2098 3-9-5 72 (t) RossaRyan 12 52
(Richard Hannon) *midfield: rdn and hdwy to chse ldrs 2f out: wknd ins fnl f (jockey said colt had no more to give)* **4/1**[2]
6 1 **Gorgeous Gobolina** 3-8-7 0 HarryRussell(7) 1 43
(Susan Corbett) *midfield on outside: rdn over 2f out: no imp* **100/1**
-42 **7** 4 **Chil Chil**[12] 3532 3-9-0 0 JosephineGordon 7 31
(Andrew Balding) *prom: rdn over 2f out: wknd over 1f out* **11/2**[3]
60-4 **8** 2¼ **Baldwin (IRE)**[44] 2477 3-9-5 68 TomEaves 4 28
(Kevin Ryan) *prom: rdn over 2f out: wknd over 1f out* **17/2**
0400 **9** 1¾ **Slieve Donard**[23] 3158 3-8-12 45 (v1) CianMacRedmond(7) 5 23
(Noel Wilson) *v.s.a: a in rr (jockey said gelding fly leapt as the stalls opened)* **150/1**
10 11 **Bluetta** 3-9-0 0 CamHardie 11
(Robyn Brisland) *s.i.s: a towards rr* **66/1**
0 **11** ¾ **Key Choice**[13] 3510 3-9-5 0 JackGarritty 8
(Eric Alston) *trckd ldrs: stmbld bdly 5f out: rdr lost irons: eased and bhd fnl 3f* **33/1**
1m 14.22s (1.72) **Going Correction** +0.30s/f (Good) **11** Ran SP% **118.1**
Speed ratings (Par 99): **100,96,93,89,89 88,82,79,77,62 61**
CSF £8.31 TOTE £2.30: £1.10, £1.70, £3.90; EX 8.90 Trifecta £119.70.
Owner Malih L Al Basti **Bred** Malih L Al Basti **Trained** Sessay, N Yorks
FOCUS
A very ordinary sprint maiden. The winner has been rated in line with the better view of his C&D form.
T/Plt: £64.40 to a £1 stake. Pool: £57,352.43 - 650.06 winning units T/Qpdt: £31.20 to a £1 stake. Pool: £4,969.10 - 117.53 winning units **Andrew Sheret**

4011a (Foreign Racing) - See Raceform Interactive

3983 **ROYAL ASCOT** (R-H)
Thursday, June 20

OFFICIAL GOING: Soft (good to soft in places; str 7.0, rnd 5.7) changing to good to soft (soft in places on round course) after race 4 (4.20)
Wind: LIGHT, HALF AGAINST Weather: FINE

4012 NORFOLK STKS (GROUP 2) 5f

2:30 (2:32) (Class 1) 2-Y-O

£56,710 (£21,500; £10,760; £5,360; £2,690; £1,350) **Stalls** Centre

Form RPR

2 **1** **A'Ali (IRE)**[15] [3477] 2-9-1 0 FrankieDettori 9 107
(Simon Crisford) *athletic; sn dropped to midfield: rdn and hdwy over 1f out: r.o to ld ent fnl f: pushed out towards fin: a in control* **5/1**[2]

11 **2** *nk* **Ventura Rebel**[50] [2267] 2-9-1 0 PaulHanagan 11 106+
(Richard Fahey) *looked wl; no bttr than midfield tl effrt whn nt clr run wl over 1f out: hdwy sn after: swtchd rt ent fnl f: sn chsd wnr and edgd rt: r.o and gaining towards fin: nvr gng to get there (vet said colt lost left-hind shoe)* **16/1**

21 **3** *2¾* **Dubai Station**[14] [3507] 2-9-1 0 JamieSpencer 3 96
(K R Burke) *unfurnished; hld up: swtchd rt and hdwy wl over 1f out: r.o for press fnl 100yds: gng on at fin: nt rch front two* **14/1**

13 **4** *nk* **Strive For Glory (USA)**[28] [3023] 2-9-1 0 RichardKingscote 4 95
(Robert Cowell) *workmanlike; prom: rdn wl over 1f out: unable qck ins fnl f: styd on same pce fnl 50yds* **50/1**

1 **5** *1¼* **Emten (IRE)**[52] [2205] 2-8-12 0 NicolaCurrie 15 87
(Jamie Osborne) *str; hld up towards nrside: rdn over 2f out: prog for press ins fnl f: edgd rt and styd on towards fin: nvr nrr* **80/1**

2 **6** *nk* **King Neptune (USA)**[27] [3060] 2-9-1 0 DonnachaO'Brien 1 89
(A P O'Brien, Ire) *str; looked wl; midfield: sltly bmpd over 2f out: sn rdn: effrt over 1f out: styd on u.p: one pce fnl 100yds* **20/1**

313 **7** *shd* **Misty Grey (IRE)**[20] [3312] 2-9-1 0 SilvestreDeSousa 14 89
(Mark Johnston) *chsd ldrs: rdn over 2f out: unable qck over 1f out: one pce ins fnl f* **16/1**

8 *nk* **Sunday Sovereign**[16] [3455] 2-9-1 0 WJLee 10 88
(P Twomey, Ire) *str; looked wl; prom: led over 1f out: sn rdn: hdd ent fnl f: sn bmpd: wknd fnl 50yds (trainer said colt ran too free)* **13/8**[1]

1 **9** *¾* **Expressionist (IRE)**[40] [2610] 2-9-1 0 JamesDoyle 6 85+
(Charlie Appleby) *compact; missed break: hld up: rdn and hdwy over 1f out: nt clr run and angled lft ins fnl f: kpt on: nvr able to get involved (jockey said colt was slowly away)* **11/1**

16 **10** *hd* **Firepower (FR)**[33] [2830] 2-9-1 0 AdamKirby 2 85
(Clive Cox) *str; midfield: angled rt whn nt clr run over 2f out and sltly bmpd rival: rdn over 1f out: no imp* **33/1**

11 *nk* **Mount Fuji (IRE)**[29] [2979] 2-9-1 0 RyanMoore 13 83
(A P O'Brien, Ire) *athletic; racd towards nrside: niggled along towards rr: drvn to go pce 3f out: nvr able to get on terms w ldrs* **7/1**[3]

2 **12** *¾* **Cool Sphere (USA)**[23] [3190] 2-9-1 0 JamesMcDonald 7 83
(Robert Cowell) *compact; led: hdd over 1f out: sn rdn: fdd ins fnl f: eased whn wl hld fnl 100yds (jockey said colt hung left-handed and ran green)* **80/1**

13 *¾* **Air Force Jet**[19] [3362] 2-9-1 0 OisinMurphy 8 78+
(Joseph Patrick O'Brien, Ire) *compact; sweating; midfield: pushed along over 2f out: outpcd over 1f out: eased fnl 50yds: nvr a threat* **8/1**

1 **14** *1½* **Real Appeal (GER)**[20] [3333] 2-9-1 0 (b) AntoineHamelin 12 73
(Matthieu Palussiere, France) *leggy; hld up: drvn wl over 1f out: outpcd after: nvr a threat* **25/1**

1m 1.9s (1.20) **Going Correction** +0.275s/f (Good) **14** Ran SP% **121.1**
Speed ratings (Par 105): **101,100,96,95,93 93,93,92,91,91 90,89,88,85**
CSF £77.35 CT £1098.97 TOTE £6.85: £2.25, £3.60, £5.10; EX 87.30 Trifecta £1034.60.
Owner Shaikh Duaij Al Khalifa **Bred** Tally-Ho Stud **Trained** Newmarket, Suffolk

FOCUS
All distances as advertised. The ground was given as soft, good to soft in places after no overnight rain - (GoingStick: Stands' side, Centre and Far side: 7.0. Round 5.7). The round course was changed to good to soft, soft in places after the Gold Cup. False rail removed on the round course from 9f to the home bend to open up fresh ground. This renewal looked well up to scratch with plenty of depth to it, and it went to a maiden for the first time since 1990. The fourth has been rated to his Sandown effort.

4013 HAMPTON COURT STKS (GROUP 3) 1m 1f 212y

3:05 (3:05) (Class 1) 3-Y-O

£51,039 (£19,350; £9,684; £4,824; £2,421; £1,215) **Stalls** Low

Form RPR

14-3 **1** **Sangarius**[28] [3026] 3-9-0 105 (t) FrankieDettori 8 114+
(Sir Michael Stoute) *looked wl; t.k.h: chsd ldr early: styd chsng ldrs: nt clr run and trying to switch lft over 2f out: gap opened and qcknd to ld over 1f out: clr and rn strly fnl f: readily* **13/2**

13 **2** *2¼* **Fox Chairman (IRE)**[42] [2558] 3-9-0 0 SilvestreDeSousa 4 112+
(Andrew Balding) *squeezed for room leaving stalls: sn rcvrd and t.k.h in midfield: nt clr run over 2f out: swtchd lft over 1f out: sltly impeded and edgd lft 1f out: r.o strly u.p to snatch 2nd last strides: no threat to wnr* **7/2**[1]

0-14 **3** *nk* **King Ottokar (FR)**[43] [2523] 3-9-0 106 JamesDoyle 6 108
(Charlie Fellowes) *nudged lft leaving stalls: hld up in tch towards rr on outer: effrt over 2f out: hdwy u.p to chse wnr ent fnl f: kpt on but no imp: lost 2nd last strides* **5/1**[3]

-312 **4** *1* **Eightsome Reel**[33] [2833] 3-9-0 99 JamesMcDonald 9 106
(Michael Bell) *looked wl; hld up in tch in last quintet: swtchd lft and effrt over 2f out: hdwy and edgd rt 1f out: kpt on ins fnl f: no threat to wnr* **25/1**

312 **5** *¾* **Roseman (IRE)**[28] [3026] 3-9-0 105 AndreaAtzeni 13 105+
(Roger Varian) *bmpd leaving stalls: t.k.h: and styd wd early: hld up in rr: effrt over 2f out: hdwy 1f out: styd on strly ins fnl f: nvr trbld ldrs* **11/1**

-562 **6** *shd* **Arthur Kitt**[10] [3646] 3-9-0 106 RichardKingscote 14 104
(Tom Dascombe) *wnt rt leaving stalls: chsd ldr after 1f: drvn to chal ent fnl 2f tl unable to match pce of wnr over 1f out: shifted lft 1f out: kpt on same pce fnl f* **25/1**

1-24 **7** *2* **Cap Francais**[40] [2619] 3-9-0 103 JamieSpencer 2 100
(Ed Walker) *in tch in midfield: rdn over 3f out: outpcd over 2f out: rallying u.p whn pushed lft 1f out: no threat to ldrs but kpt on ins fnl f: eased cl home* **12/1**

-261 **8** *¾* **Getchagetchagetcha**[10] [3646] 3-9-0 95 AdamKirby 12 99
(Clive Cox) *squeezed for room leaving stalls: hld up in tch in last quintet: effrt 2f out: nt clrest of runs over 1f out: swtchd lft and kpt on ins fnl f: nvr trbld ldrs* **40/1**

1105 **9** *hd* **Golden Spectrum**[32] [2889] 3-9-0 104 GeraldMosse 3 98
(Gay Kelleway) *nudged lft leaving stalls: in tch in midfield on outer: rdn and hdwy to chse ldrs ent fnl 2f: unable qck and short of room jst over 1f out: wknd ins fnl f* **100/1**

3-14 **10** *nk* **Cape Of Good Hope (IRE)**[18] [3390] 3-9-0 110 RyanMoore 1 98
(A P O'Brien, Ire) *trckd ldrs on inner: swtchd lft and waiting for gap over 2f out: rdn to chal 2f out tl unable qck over 1f out: wknd ins fnl f (trainer could offer no explanation for the colt's performance)* **4/1**[2]

-203 **11** *1½* **Great Scot**[32] [2889] 3-9-0 110 JimCrowley 10 95
(Tom Dascombe) *t.k.h: chsd ldrs on outer: effrt u.p to press ldrs 2f out: outpcd over 1f out and losing pl whn bmpd and hmpd 1f out: wknd* **14/1**

3-0 **12** *1¼* **Old Glory (IRE)**[13] [3558] 3-9-0 102 SeamieHeffernan 15 92
(A P O'Brien, Ire) *str; stdd and dropped in bhd after s: hld up in tch in rr: effrt 2f out: no imp and edgd rt over 1f out: nvr involved (jockey said colt hung right-handed in the straight)* **16/1**

-100 **13** *hd* **Kick On**[18] [3390] 3-9-0 109 OisinMurphy 11 92
(John Gosden) *sweating; led: rdn over 2f out: hdd over 1f out and sn lost pl: wknd fnl f* **7/1**

2m 8.36s (0.66) **Going Correction** +0.275s/f (Good) **13** Ran SP% **124.4**
Speed ratings (Par 109): **108,106,105,105,104 104,102,102,102,101 100,99,99**
CSF £29.94 CT £129.07 TOTE £8.15: £2.95, £1.65, £2.05; EX 34.30 Trifecta £238.70.
Owner K Abdullah **Bred** Juddmonte Farms Ltd **Trained** Newmarket, Suffolk
■ Stewards' Enquiry : James McDonald two-day ban: used whip above permitted level (Jul 4-5)

FOCUS
Perhaps not the strongest edition of the race, but a taking winner who looks bound for bigger things. Having gone a steady enough gallop early, the pace increased a fair way out and the closers came into it late, but the winner had already flown.

4014 RIBBLESDALE STKS (GROUP 2) (FILLIES) 1m 3f 211y

3:40 (3:40) (Class 1) 3-Y-O

£121,926 (£46,225; £23,134; £11,524; £5,783; £2,902) **Stalls** Low

Form RPR

6-13 **1** **Star Catcher**[33] [2831] 3-9-0 98 FrankieDettori 6 109
(John Gosden) *midfield: hdwy over 2f out: sn rdn: led ent fnl 2f: r.o wl and stretched out nicely fnl 50yds* **4/1**[2]

1-03 **2** *1½* **Fleeting (IRE)**[20] [3316] 3-9-0 110 RyanMoore 9 107
(A P O'Brien, Ire) *hld up: rdn and hdwy whn nt clr run over 2f out: r.o ins fnl f to take 2nd fnl 130yds: sn swtchd rt whn nt clr run: no imp on wnr towards fin* **7/4**[1]

1-10 **3** *1¼* **Sparkle Roll (FR)**[36] [2745] 3-9-0 92 OisinMurphy 5 104
(John Gosden) *str; racd keenly: hld up in no bttr than midfield: hdwy 3f out: rdn on outer over 2f out: tried to chal over 1f out: r.o u.p: nt pce of front two and styd on same pce fnl 50yds* **11/1**

1-21 **4** *1¼* **Queen Power (IRE)**[33] [2831] 3-9-0 100 SilvestreDeSousa 8 102+
(Sir Michael Stoute) *looked wl; edgy; racd keenly: trckd ldrs: led jst over 2f out: rdn and hdd ent fnl 2f: sn edgd rt: nt pce of wnr ins fnl f: styd on same pce fnl 100yds* **9/2**[3]

1103 **5** *1¾* **Love So Deep (JPN)**[28] [3012] 3-9-0 95 JFEgan 10 99
(Jane Chapple-Hyam) *hld up: rdn over 2f out: hdwy on wd outer over 1f out: styd on ins fnl f: nt pce to rch ldrs* **66/1**

1-26 **6** *nk* **Frankellina**[20] [3316] 3-9-0 105 JamesDoyle 4 99
(William Haggas) *looked wl; racd keenly: trckd ldrs: lost pl over 2f out: sn swtchd lft whn nt clr run: one pce and no imp after* **6/1**

544 **7** *¾* **Fresnel**[36] [2745] 3-9-0 98 GaryHalpin 11 98
(Jack W Davison, Ire) *compact; looked wl; hld up in rr: rdn over 2f out: swtchd lft to outer over 1f out: kpt on ins fnl f: nvr able to trble ldrs* **33/1**

0-22 **8** *4½* **Shambolic (IRE)**[28] [3012] 3-9-0 100 RobertHavlin 7 91
(John Gosden) *in tch: chsd ldr after 3f: rdn and ev ch over 2f out: outpcd by ldrs over 1f out: wknd ins fnl f* **25/1**

2-13 **9** *6* **Fanny Logan (IRE)**[43] [2521] 3-9-0 94 AndreaAtzeni 3 81
(John Gosden) *racd keenly: led early: chsd ldr tl after 3f: trckd ldrs after: rdn and outpcd over 2f out: wknd wl over 1f out* **11/1**

-402 **10** *13* **Peach Tree (IRE)**[6] [3820] 3-9-0 102 SeamieHeffernan 2 60
(A P O'Brien, Ire) *sn led: rdn and hdd jst over 2f out: wknd over 1f out* **33/1**

5 **11** *24* **Altair (IRE)**[22] [3230] 3-9-0 93 (p[1]) DonnachaO'Brien 1 22
(Joseph Patrick O'Brien, Ire) *hld up in no bttr than midfield: pushed along over 3f out: wknd over 2f out: t.o (trainer said filly was unsuited by the soft, good to soft in places ground and would prefer a quicker surface)* **40/1**

2m 33.52s (0.92) **Going Correction** +0.275s/f (Good) **11** Ran SP% **119.2**
Speed ratings (Par 108): **107,106,105,104,103 102,102,99,95,86 70**
CSF £11.08 CT £72.34 TOTE £5.95: £1.90, £1.30, £3.25; EX 15.50 Trifecta £128.50.
Owner A E Oppenheimer **Bred** Hascombe And Valiant Studs **Trained** Newmarket, Suffolk

FOCUS
This was our first glimpse of the Oaks form, and while it wasn't let down, the race instead was won by a rapidly improving filly who had 12lb to find with the runner-up on official ratings coming into the race. It was John Gosden's third win following Michita and Coronet. The pace was far from frantic. The second set the standard but has been rated below her Oaks level.

4015 GOLD CUP (GROUP 1) (BRITISH CHAMPIONS SERIES) 2m 3f 210y

4:20 (4:20) (Class 1) 4-Y-O+

£283,550 (£107,500; £53,800; £26,800; £13,450; £6,750) **Stalls** Low

Form RPR

11-1 **1** **Stradivarius (IRE)**[34] [2807] 5-9-2 120 FrankieDettori 2 121+
(John Gosden) *trckd ldrs: stl travelling strly and nt clr run wl over 2f out: swtchd lft and effrt over 1f out: rdn and hdwy to ld 1f out: in command and styd on wl fnl f: pushed out towards fin* **1/1**[1]

3-11 **2** *1* **Dee Ex Bee**[28] [3024] 4-9-1 115 SilvestreDeSousa 8 119
(Mark Johnston) *looked wl; led: rdn 3f out: hdd 2f out and sn drvn: unable to match pce of wnr 1f out: a hld after but kpt on gamely and wnt 2nd again on post* **7/2**[2]

50-1 **3** *nse* **Master Of Reality (IRE)**[34] [2814] 4-9-1 108 WayneLordan 9 119
(Joseph Patrick O'Brien, Ire) *looked wl; pressed ldr: upsides and travelling bttr wl over 2f out: pushed to ld 2f out: sn rdn: hdd and nt match pce of wnr 1f out: a hld after but kpt on gamely: lost 2nd on post* **66/1**

21-1 **4** *¾* **Cross Counter**[82] [1441] 4-9-1 118 JamesDoyle 4 118
(Charlie Appleby) *sweating; stdd s: hld up in last trio: clsd wl over 2f out: hdwy u.p to chse ldng trio over 1f out: styd on wl: nvr quite getting on terms* **4/1**[3]

-222 **5** *5* **Flag Of Honour (IRE)**[25] [3114] 4-9-1 117 RyanMoore 5 113
(A P O'Brien, Ire) *hld up in tch in midfield: effrt 3f out: unable qck u.p and btn over 1f out: wknd ins fnl f* **11/1**

40-5 **6** *1 ¼* **Capri (IRE)**[34] 2814 5-9-2 113.................................... DonnachaO'Brien 7 112
(A P O'Brien, Ire) *chsd ldrs: rdn wl over 2f out and stl pressing ldrs 2f out: sn outpcd and btn 1f out: wknd ins fnl f* **16/1**

-623 **7** *nk* **Raymond Tusk (IRE)**[33] 2827 4-9-1 111............................ JamieSpencer 10 111
(Richard Hannon) *stdd and dropped in bhd after s: hld up in rr: clsd over 2f out: swtchd lft and effrt over 1f out: edgd rt and plugged on same pce fnl f* **40/1**

2-31 **8** *½* **Called To The Bar (IRE)**[25] 3123 5-9-2 113................(t) OisinMurphy 1 111
(Mme Pia Brandt, France) *hld up in midfield: clsd run on inner wl over 2f out: swtchd and effrt 2f out: edgd rt and no hdwy over 1f out: wknd ins fnl f* **20/1**

10-3 **9** *3* **Magic Circle (IRE)**[42] 2560 7-9-2 114.............................. JimCrowley 6 108
(Ian Williams) *hld up in midfield: nt clrest of runs briefly over 2f out: no imp u.p and btn over 1f out: wknd fnl f* **25/1**

12-2 **10** *45* **Thomas Hobson**[39] 2666 9-9-2 112.................................... AndreaAtzeni 3 63
(W P Mullins, Ire) *t.k.h: hld up in tch in midfield: clsd on inner to chse ldrs over 3f out: rdn over 2f out: sn btn and wknd over 1f out: virtually p.u ins fnl f: t.o (jockey said gelding ran too free)* **25/1**

6-50 **11** *19* **Cypress Creek (IRE)**[20] 3314 4-9-1 107................(p) SeamieHeffernan 11 44
(A P O'Brien, Ire) *hld up in last trio: lost tch over 2f out: virtually p.u ins fnl f* **66/1**

4m 30.88s (8.88) **Going Correction** +0.275s/f (Good)
WFA 4 from 5yo+ 1lb **11** Ran SP% **124.3**
Speed ratings (Par 117): **93,92,92,92,90 89,89,89,88,70 62**
CSF £4.58 CT £147.24 TOTE £1.80: £1.20, £1.60, £21.30; EX 6.40 Trifecta £223.90.
Owner B E Nielsen **Bred** Bjorn Nielsen **Trained** Newmarket, Suffolk

FOCUS
A race that firmly revolved around the favourite and defending champion Stradivarius, even more so given Dettori's previous achievements on the day, and neither horse nor rider disappointed despite a brief scare having been boxed in. Although a massive outsider filled third, he was massively overpriced and it has to rate top-notch staying form. The early pace was steady and with a circuit to race the first three home were in the leading trio, but as always it still proved a thorough test of stamina and the non-stayers were exposed.

4016 BRITANNIA STKS (HERITAGE H'CAP) (C&G) 1m (S)
5:00 (5:03) (Class 2) (0-105,105) 3-Y-O

£74,700 (£22,368; £11,184; £5,592; £2,796; £1,404) **Stalls** Centre

Form RPR

112 **1** **Biometric**[19] 3351 3-8-8 92.. HarryBentley 29 104
(Ralph Beckett) *racd in nrside gp: hld up: hdwy 2f out: drvn whn hung rt wl over 1f out: chsd ldr over 1f out: r.o to ld fnl 60yds: wl in command nr fin: 1st of 19 fr gp* **28/1**

-035 **2** *1 ¼* **Turgenev**[35] 2777 3-9-4 102.. FrankieDettori 22 111
(John Gosden) *racd in nrside gp: prom: led over 2f out and overall ldr: rdn abt 3 l clr over 1f out: worn down and hdd fnl 60yds: no ex nr fin: 2nd of 19 fr gp* **7/2**[1]

-104 **3** *2* **Fanaar (IRE)**[26] 3075 3-9-0 98................................(b) DaneO'Neill 18 102
(William Haggas) *looked wl; hmpd s: racd in nrside gp: hld up: hdwy whn nt clr run over 2f out and swtchd rt: sn rdn: chsd ldrs over 1f out: styd on ins fnl f: no further imp fnl 75yds: 3rd of 19 fr gp* **50/1**

-201 **4** *2 ¼* **Awe**[12] 3599 3-8-10 94.. KerrinMcEvoy 5 93+
(William Haggas) *racd in far side gp: midfield: hdwy over 2f out: chsd ldrs over 1f out: edgd lft and styd on ins fnl f: nt pce of front three: 1st of 9 fr gp* **14/1**

3 **5** *2* **Numerian (IRE)**[106] 1049 3-9-0 98........................... DonnachaO'Brien 31 98+
(Joseph Patrick O'Brien, Ire) *racd in nrside gp: hld up in rr: nt clr run 3f out and swtchd rt: nt clr run again over 2f out: hdwy whn hung rt over 1f out: r.o ins fnl f: gng on at fin: 4th of 19 fr gp* **50/1**

4034 **6** *nk* **Victory Command (IRE)**[19] 3341 3-8-8 92.......................... FrannyNorton 3 86
(Mark Johnston) *racd in far side gp: hld up: rdn and hdwy over 2f out: sn edgd lft: kpt on ins fnl f: nt pce to chal: 2nd of 9 fr gp* **50/1**

-221 **7** *1 ½* **Migration (IRE)**[35] 2766 3-8-6 90.................................. JasonWatson 24 80
(David Menuisier) *racd in nrside gp: chsd ldrs: drifted rt 2f out: unable qck over 1f out: outpcd by ldrs ins fnl f: no ex fnl 75yds: 5th of 19 fr gp* **7/1**[3]

-304 **8** *nk* **Dark Vision (IRE)**[28] 3026 3-9-7 105.............................. JamieSpencer 1 95+
(Mark Johnston) *racd in far side gp: hld up in rr: rdn over 2f out: hdwy over 1f out: styd on ins fnl f: nt pce of ldrs: one pce fnl 110yds: 3rd of 9 fr gp* **18/1**

2-25 **9** *½* **Glorious Lover (IRE)**[33] 2834 3-9-0 98........................... GeraldMosse 14 87
(Ed Walker) *racd in nrside gp: midfield: effrt over 2f out: chsd ldrs over 1f out: styd on same pce ins fnl f: 6th of 19 fr gp* **40/1**

2-31 **10** *hd* **Hero Hero (IRE)**[26] 3067 3-8-11 95........................ SilvestreDeSousa 25 83
(Andrew Balding) *racd in nrside gp: led gp: rdn over 3f out: hdd over 2f out: sn edgd rt u.p: outpcd by ldr over 1f out: styd on same pce ins fnl f: 7th of 19 fr gp* **16/1**

6-32 **11** *hd* **Tulfarris**[47] 2395 3-8-9 93.. StevieDonohoe 13 81
(Charlie Fellowes) *racd in nrside gp: hld up in midfield: rdn and hdwy whn carried rt over 2f out: carried rt again over 1f out: styd on ins fnl f: nt pce to trble ldrs: 8th of 19 fr gp* **25/1**

0401 **12** *1 ¼* **Finoah (IRE)**[12] 3591 3-8-4 91................................(v) JaneElliott[(3)] 28 76
(Tom Dascombe) *sweating; racd in nrside gp: handy: rdn over 3f out: sn lost pl: rdn and hung rt over 2f out: one pce ins fnl f: 9th of 19 fr gp* **66/1**

2-50 **13** *2 ¾* **Mordred (IRE)**[47] 2414 3-8-2 91...................... ThoreHammerHansen[(5)] 2 70+
(Richard Hannon) *racd in far side gp: midfield: rdn over 3f out: outpcd over 1f out: edgd rt u.p ins fnl f: no imp after: 4th of 9 fr gp* **100/1**

-564 **14** *hd* **Certain Lad**[26] 3082 3-9-0 98.. RonanWhelan 11 76+
(Mick Channon) *sweating; racd in far side gp: led gp: rdn over 2f out: hdd wl over 1f out and outpcd by overall ldr: no ex ins fnl f: 5th of 9 fr gp* **66/1**

0-41 **15** *1* **Beatboxer (USA)**[26] 3082 3-9-4 102..............................(t) RobertHavlin 27 78
(John Gosden) *racd in nrside gp: hld up: nt clr run over 3f out: rdn over 2f out: no imp: one pce ins fnl f: 10th of 19 fr gp* **16/1**

3-11 **16** *1* **Motafaawit (IRE)**[41] 2570 3-9-5 103.................................. JimCrowley 4 76+
(Richard Hannon) *racd in far side gp: in tch: effrt over 2f out: no imp over 1f out: one pce ins fnl f: 6th of 9 fr gp* **12/1**

2-22 **17** *nk* **King Ademar (USA)**[15] 3471 3-8-9 93..........................(p[1]) OisinMurphy 16 66
(Martyn Meade) *wnt lft s: racd in nrside gp: hld up: sme hdwy 3f out: pushed along and no imp over 2f out: outpcd over 1f out: wl btn ins fnl f: 11th of 19 fr gp* **15/2**

6-35 **18** *1 ½* **Barristan The Bold**[26] 3082 3-8-6 90........................ RichardKingscote 6 59+
(Tom Dascombe) *racd in far side gp: chsd ldrs: rdn over 3f out: lost pl over 2f out: n.d after: 7th of 9 fr gp* **16/1**

-610 **19** *½* **Pogo (IRE)**[32] 2889 3-9-2 100.. KieranShoemark 26 68
(Charles Hills) *racd in nrside gp: chsd ldrs: nt clr run and lost pl over 2f out: sn rdn and hmpd wl over 1f out: wl hld after: 12th of 19 fr gp* **33/1**

1-13 **20** *shd* **Dubai Legacy (USA)**[26] 3075 3-9-0 98.............................. PatCosgrave 10 66+
(Saeed bin Suroor) *racd in far side gp: chsd ldrs: rdn over 2f out and unable qck: wknd over 1f out: 8th of 9 fr gp* **33/1**

0-11 **21** *1 ¾* **Davydenko**[17] 3412 3-8-6 90.. DavidProbert 15 54
(Sir Michael Stoute) *sweating; racd in nrside gp: in tch: rdn over 2f out: wknd over 1f out: 13th of 19 fr gp* **10/1**

4 **22** *½* **Dunkirk Harbour (USA)**[39] 2660 3-9-3 101..................(b) RyanMoore 30 64
(A P O'Brien, Ire) *racd in nrside gp: hld up: pushed along over 2f out: sn nt clr run and hung rt: wl btn over 1f out: 14th fr 19 in gp (jockey said colt suffered interference in running)* **20/1**

6-05 **23** *nk* **Dark Jedi (IRE)**[42] 2558 3-8-11 95................................ TomMarquand 19 57
(Charles Hills) *sweating; racd in nrside gp: midfield: rdn over 3f out: wknd 2f out: 15th of 19 fr gp* **50/1**

1032 **24** *2 ¼* **Sameem (IRE)**[21] 3262 3-8-7 91...................................... PJMcDonald 21 48
(James Tate) *racd in nrside gp: chsd ldrs: rdn and lost pl over 3f out: bhd fnl 2f: 16th of 19 in gp* **50/1**

4-00 **25** *nk* **Dunkerron**[26] 3075 3-9-2 100.. DavidEgan 32 56
(Alan King) *looked wl; racd in nrside gp: in tch: chsd ldrs over 3f out: rdn and wknd over 2f out: 17th of 19 fr gp* **66/1**

2-11 **26** *½* **Velorum (IRE)**[21] 3277 3-8-12 96...................................... JamesDoyle 7 51+
(Charlie Appleby) *looked wl; racd in far side gp: prom: rdn and ev ch 2f out: wl there and unable qck over 1f out: wknd ent fnl f: sn eased: 9th of 9 fr gp (jockey said colt stopped quickly; vet said a post-race examination of the colt revealed it to be displaying signs of a prolonged recovery)* **6/1**[2]

1-00 **27** *1* **Hot Team (IRE)**[12] 3581 3-8-13 97...........................(v) JamesMcDonald 33 50
(Hugo Palmer) *looked wl; racd in nrside gp: hld up in midfield: rdn 3f out: wknd 2f out: 18th of 19 fr gp* **66/1**

3-52 **28** *2* **Eclipse Storm**[45] 2492 3-8-11 98........................... ConorMaxwell[(3)] 12 46
(J A Stack, Ire) *racd in nrside gp: chsd ldrs: rdn over 2f out: sn lost pl: wknd over 1f out: 19th of 19 fr gp* **66/1**

1m 41.25s (-0.15) **Going Correction** +0.275s/f (Good) **28** Ran SP% **145.8**
Speed ratings (Par 105): **111,109,107,105,103 103,101,101,100,100 100,99,96,96,95 94,94,92,92,91 90,89,89,87,86 86,85,8**
CSF £128.07 CT £5226.61 TOTE £56.45: £9.20, £1.65, £17.95, £4.30; EX 455.00 Trifecta £13539.50.
Owner K Abdullah **Bred** Juddmonte Farms Ltd **Trained** Kimpton, Hants

■ Aweedram was withdrawn. Price at time of withdrawal 14-1. Rule 4 applies to all bets struck prior to withdrawal, but not to SP bets. Deduction - 5p in the pound. New market formed.

■ Stewards' Enquiry : Harry Bentley two-day ban: used whip above permitted level (4-5 Jul)

FOCUS
The going was changed to Good to Soft, Soft in places on the round course, and Good to Soft on the straight course prior to this contest. A hugely open contest as per normal, although the betting did have an unusual look to it courtesy of Turgenev and the Frankie factor. The winner and runner-up were both drawn high and came down the stands' side. The time was reasonable. It's been rated around the race standard for now.

4017 KING GEORGE V STKS (H'CAP) 1m 3f 211y
5:35 (5:35) (Class 2) (0-105,105) 3-Y-O

£56,025 (£16,776; £8,388; £4,194; £2,097; £1,053) **Stalls** Low

Form RPR

1 **South Pacific**[40] 2643 3-8-10 94 ow1........................ SeamieHeffernan 8 103+
(A P O'Brien, Ire) *hld up in midfield: swtchd lft and effrt over 2f out: hdwy and hung rt 1f out: stl hanging rt but r.o strly to ld wl ins fnl f: pushed out nr fin* **22/1**

3-1 **2** *nk* **Constantinople (IRE)**[27] 3063 3-9-7 105........................ RyanMoore 18 113+
(A P O'Brien, Ire) *compact; wnt rt s: hld up in tch in midfield: nt clr run over 2f out: rdn and hdwy to chse ldrs over 1f out: led ent fnl f: hdd wl ins fnl f: kpt on but hld cl home* **11/2**

- **3** *1 ¾* **Eminence (IRE)**[40] 2643 3-8-7 91.................................. WayneLordan 19 96
(A P O'Brien, Ire) *s.i.s: hld up towards rr: hdwy and nt clr run jst over 2f out: swtchd rt over 1f out and squeezed through ins fnl f: styd on wl to snatch 3rd last strides* **25/1**

-334 **4** *nk* **Persian Moon (IRE)**[27] 3042 3-9-2 100........................ FrannyNorton 20 105
(Mark Johnston) *looked wl; t.k.h: wl in tch in midfield: hdwy to chse ldrs over 3f out: rdn to chse ldr wl over 1f out tl 3rd: edgd lft and unable qck 1f out: kpt on same pce ins fnl f* **33/1**

41-0 **5** *¾* **Almania (IRE)**[35] 2777 3-8-11 95.............................. JamesMcDonald 21 99
(Sir Michael Stoute) *looked wl; in tch in midfield on outer: swtchd lft and effrt over 2f out: chsng ldrs but nt qcknng whn edgd rt 1f out: stl edging rt and kpt on same pce ins fnl f* **16/1**

310 **6** *hd* **Severance**[40] 2619 3-8-9 92 ow1..............................(h) RonanWhelan 15 96
(Mick Channon) *bmpd s: sn rcvrd and t.k.h in midfield: clsd to chse ldrs and short of room 2f out: edgd rt u.p and kpt on same pce fnl f* **20/1**

2210 **7** *4 ½* **Majestic Dawn (IRE)**[33] 2828 3-8-6 90............................ DavidProbert 14 86+
(Paul Cole) *t.k.h: chsd ldrs tl wnt 2nd 6f out: led over 2f out: hdd and no ex u.p ent fnl f: wknd qckly ins fnl f* **20/1**

-212 **8** *3 ½* **Sinjaari (IRE)**[33] 2828 3-8-13 97...................................... JamesDoyle 22 87
(William Haggas) *looked wl; styd v wd for 4f: in tch in midfield: clsd to chse ldrs over 2f out: sn rdn and edgd rt: edgd lft and unable qck over 1f out: wknd ins fnl f* **4/1**[2]

6-11 **9** *1 ¼* **Fox Premier (IRE)**[21] 3262 3-8-12 96........................ SilvestreDeSousa 2 84
(Andrew Balding) *looked wl; hld up in midfield: impeded after 2f: nt clr run and swtchd lft ent fnl 2f: drifting rt and no imp u.p over 1f out: wl btn fnl f* **9/1**

1-13 **10** *½* **Good Birthday (IRE)**[33] 2828 3-8-12 96........................... OisinMurphy 7 84
(Andrew Balding) *hld up towards rr: pushed along and swtchd lft wl over 2f out: nvr threatened to get on terms* **12/1**

204 **11** *2 ¼* **Antilles (USA)**[27] 3063 3-9-2 100............................ DonnachaO'Brien 13 84
(A P O'Brien, Ire) *hld up in rr: effrt over 2f out: drifting rt over 1f out: nvr involved* **50/1**

-113 **12** *hd* **Summer Moon**[19] 3337 3-8-11 95...................................... PJMcDonald 3 79
(Mark Johnston) *t.k.h: chsd ldrs: unable qck u.p ent fnl 2f: sn outpcd: wknd over 1f out* **20/1**

4-11 **13** *shd* **Sir Ron Priestley**[26] 3086 3-8-10 94.............................. AndreaAtzeni 10 78
(Mark Johnston) *led tl over 2f out: sn u.p and lost pl over 1f out: wknd fnl f* **9/2**[3]

122 **14** *28* **Questionare**[24] 3152 3-8-10 94..........................(t[1]) FrankieDettori 5 33
(John Gosden) *s.i.s: a bhd: eased fnl f: t.o (trainer's rep said colt got upset in the preliminaries and may benefit from being gelded)* **7/2**[1]

-211 **15** *7* **Babbo's Boy (IRE)**[31] 2905 3-8-7 91.............................. JasonWatson 1 19
(Michael Bell) *sn pushed ldr for 6f: rdn and struggling over 2f out: wknd over 1f out: bhd and eased ins fnl f: t.o* **18/1**

0-06 **16** *2* **Kuwait Currency (USA)**[55] 2084 3-9-0 **98**........................(t) PatDobbs 9 22
(Richard Hannon) *midfield and swtchd rt after 2f: rdn over 3f out: sn dropped to rr: eased ins fnl f: t.o* **66/1**

2m 32.74s (0.14) **Going Correction** +0.275s/f (Good) **16** Ran SP% **133.5**
Speed ratings (Par 105): **110,109,108,108,107 107,104,102,101,101 99,99,99,80,76 74**
CSF £140.13 CT £3149.13 TOTE £42.80: £5.95, £1.50, £7.30, £7.05; EX 209.50 Trifecta £1269.00.
Owner Derrick Smith & Mrs John Magnier & Michael Tabor **Bred** Skymarc Farm Inc And Ecurie Des Monceaux **Trained** Cashel, Co Tipperary

FOCUS
Always an ultra-competitive handicap, there was no hanging around and the race very much set up for the closers. It was a remarkable one-two-three for Aidan O'Brien, although given the trainer's dominance in the 3yo middle-distance division perhaps it wasn't a surprise at all. It's been rated around the fourth, fifth and sixth.
T/Jkpt: Not won. T/Plt: £353.30 to a £1 stake. Pool: £544,785.61 - 1,125.44 winning units
T/Qpdt: £38.60 to a £1 stake. Pool: £36,081.39 - 689.95 winning units
Darren Owen/Steve Payne

3989 CHELMSFORD (A.W) (L-H)

Thursday, June 20

OFFICIAL GOING: Polytrack: standard
Wind: Light across Weather: Overcast

4018 LOVE THAT HAT EBF MAIDEN AUCTION STKS — 6f (P)

1:50 (1:51) (Class 5) 2-Y-O — **£5,822** (£1,732; £865; £432) **Stalls** Centre

Form — RPR

5 **1** **Hard Nut (IRE)**[10] 3660 2-9-5 0.................................. SeanLevey 8 71
(Richard Hannon) *racd keenly in 2nd: shkn up to ld over 1f out: rdn and edgd lft ins fnl f: styd on* **7/2**[2]

324 **2** *nk* **My Motivate Girl (IRE)**[10] 3644 2-8-9 0.............(v) ThomasGreatrex(5) 2 65+
(Archie Watson) *s.s: hld up: swtchd rt and hdwy over 1f out: rdn and edgd lft ins fnl f: r.o wl* **11/2**[3]

03 **3** *1* **Ossco**[12] 3579 2-9-0 0.................................. SeamusCronin(5) 1 67
(Mohamed Moubarak) *hld up: nt clr run over 1f out: n.m.r and r.o ins fnl f: wnt 3rd nr fin* **7/1**

03 **4** *1/2* **Zain Storm (FR)**[24] 3141 2-9-5 0.................................. HollieDoyle 5 66
(John Butler) *led at stdy pce: qcknd over 2f out: rdn and hdd over 1f out: styd on same pce wl ins fnl f* **8/1**

5 *hd* **Exciting Days (USA)** 2-9-5 0.................................. LukeMorris 4 65
(Robert Cowell) *chsd ldrs: rdn and edgd lft over 1f out: edgd rt ins fnl f: styd on* **7/2**[2]

6 **6** *1 1/2* **Under Your Spell (IRE)**[7] 3767 2-9-5 0.................................. DougieCostello 9 60
(Jamie Osborne) *hld up in tch: shkn up over 2f out: edgd lft over 1f out: styd on same pce ins fnl f* **20/1**

7 *hd* **Thomas Lanfiere (FR)** 2-9-0 0.................................. DylanHogan(5) 3 60
(David Simcock) *chsd ldrs: shkn up over 1f out: no ex ins fnl f* **5/2**[1]

5 **8** *1 1/2* **Chateau Peapod**[16] 3441 2-9-0 0.................................. BrettDoyle 6 50
(Lydia Pearce) *s.i.s: hld up: shkn up over 2f out: nvr on terms* **66/1**

9 *9* **Conker** 2-9-5 0.................................. RossaRyan 7 28
(Charlie Wallis) *s.i.s: hld up on outer: plld hrd: hung rt over 2f out: wknd wl over 1f out* **50/1**

1m 15.85s (2.15) **Going Correction** -0.275s/f (Stan) **9** Ran SP% **120.2**
Speed ratings (Par 93): **74,73,72,71,71 69,69,67,55**
CSF £23.85 TOTE £4.30: £1.50, £1.90, £2.40; EX 15.10 Trifecta £68.70.
Owner Mrs J K Powell & Mrs A Doyle **Bred** Springwell Stud **Trained** East Everleigh, Wilts
■ Stewards' Enquiry : Thomas Greatrex two-day ban: used whip above the permitted level (Jul 4-5)

FOCUS
An ordinary juvenile maiden. They went a modest gallop and two horses towards the head of the betting with the benefit of experience came to the fore.

4019 ESSEX LIFE MAGAZINE H'CAP — 2m (P)

2:20 (2:22) (Class 5) (0-75,77) 4-Y-0+ — **£5,498** (£1,636; £817; £408; £300; £300) **Stalls** Low

Form — RPR

3-65 **1** **Jumping Cats**[19] 3334 4-9-3 **70**..................................(p[1]) JackMitchell 5 83
(Chris Wall) *a.p: chsd ldr over 2f out: rdn to ld over 1f out: styd on wl* **5/2**[1]

1/06 **2** *4* **Remember The Man (IRE)**[40] 2626 6-8-11 **67**.....(p) CameronNoble(3) 6 75
(Michael Bell) *chsd ldr tl led over 4f out: rdn and hdd over 1f out: no ex ins fnl f* **6/1**[3]

2333 **3** *12* **Alabaster**[24] 3145 5-9-9 **76**.................................. LukeMorris 3 70
(Sir Mark Prescott Bt) *hld up: hdwy over 2f out: rdn and hung lft over 1f out: wknd fnl f* **5/2**[1]

4551 **4** *3* **Carvelas (IRE)**[14] 3497 10-8-5 **58**.................................. NickyMackay 4 48
(J R Jenkins) *hld up: hdwy over 5f out: rdn over 3f out: wknd over 1f out* **8/1**

2660 **5** *2 3/4* **Demophon**[23] 3205 5-8-2 **55** oh10.................................. RaulDaSilva 2 42
(Steve Flook) *chsd ldrs: pushed along 1/2-way: lost pl over 5f out: hdwy u.p over 2f out: wknd over 1f out* **50/1**

0601 **6** *3/4* **Eye Of The Storm (IRE)**[31] 2901 9-9-10 **77**.................... HayleyTurner 1 63
(Conor Dore) *hld up: racd keenly: hdwy over 7f out: chsd ldr over 3f out tl shkn up over 2f out: wknd over 1f out* **10/1**

00-0 **7** *3 1/4* **Conkering Hero (IRE)**[127] 700 5-9-7 **74**.....................(v) JasonHart 9 56
(Joseph Tuite) *hld up: rdn on outer over 3f out: wknd over 2f out* **25/1**

3-P5 **8** *2* **Paddy A (IRE)**[15] 3467 5-9-10 **77**.....................(v) GeorgeDowning 8 57
(Ian Williams) *led: hdd over 4f out: rdn and wknd over 2f out (jockey said gelding stopped quickly)* **9/2**[2]

466/ **9** *38* **Winter Spice (IRE)**[16] 1223 8-9-3 **70**.....................(h) KieranO'Neill 7 4
(Johnny Farrelly) *sn pushed along into mid-div: rdn: hung lft and lost pl over 8f out: wknd 5f out* **33/1**

3m 27.38s (-2.62) **Going Correction** -0.275s/f (Stan) **9** Ran SP% **118.6**
Speed ratings (Par 103): **95,93,87,85,84 83,82,81,62**
CSF £18.57 CT £41.55 TOTE £3.20: £1.30, £2.10, £1.10; EX 21.50 Trifecta £91.10.
Owner Des Thurlby **Bred** New England Stud, Myriad & T Vestey **Trained** Newmarket, Suffolk

FOCUS
A fair staying handicap. One of the joint-favourites won going away from off a modest gallop. A pb from the winner, and the form could be rated higher if the runner-up confirms it.

4020 AUSTRALIAN GOLD SUMMER H'CAP — 1m (P)

2:55 (2:56) (Class 3) (0-95,97) 4-Y-O+ — **£10,350** (£3,080; £1,539; £769) **Stalls** Low

Form — RPR

0-00 **1** **Via Serendipity**[26] 3094 5-9-7 **95**..................................(t) DanielMuscutt 5 107
(Stuart Williams) *mde all: rdn clr over 1f out: eased nr fin (trainer could offer no explanation for the gelding's performance other than the gelding had benefited from an easy lead having made the running on this occasion)* **6/1**

2430 **2** *5* **Masham Star (IRE)**[5] 3857 5-9-6 **94**.................................. JasonHart 1 95
(Mark Johnston) *s.i.s: rcvrd to chse ldr 7f out: rdn over 1f out: styd on same pce fnl f* **10/3**[2]

4430 **3** *1 1/4* **Cliffs Of Capri**[112] 961 5-9-9 **97**..................................(p) DougieCostello 4 95
(Jamie Osborne) *hld up in tch: shkn up over 2f out: rdn over 1f out: styd on same pce fnl f* **7/1**

-003 **4** *3/4* **Qaysar (FR)**[12] 3563 4-9-2 **90**.................................. SeanLevey 8 86
(Richard Hannon) *hld up: ct wd over 4f out: pushed along and swtchd lft over 2f out: styd on fr over 1f out: nt trble ldrs* **3/1**[1]

0-14 **5** *nk* **Enigmatic (IRE)**[34] 2803 5-8-11 **90**.......................... DarraghKeenan(5) 3 85
(Alan Bailey) *chsd ldr 1f: remained handy: rdn over 2f out: no ex fnl f* **8/1**

0611 **6** *1/2* **Ballard Down (IRE)**[17] 3423 6-9-1 **92**.....................(v) FinleyMarsh(3) 2 86
(David Pipe) *s.s: hld up: swtchd rt over 1f out: r.o ins fnl f: nvr nrr (jockey said gelding hung left-handed travelling up the home straight)* **10/1**

41-3 **7** *1* **Tahreek**[14] 3496 4-8-12 **86**.................................. ShaneKelly 7 78
(Sir Michael Stoute) *plld hrd early: hld up: rdn on outer over 1f out: edgd lft ins fnl f: nvr on terms* **9/2**[3]

/4-0 **8** *7* **Domagnano (IRE)**[28] 3005 4-8-11 **92**.....................(t[1]) StefanoCherchi(7) 6 68
(Marco Botti) *s.i.s: plld hrd and sn prom: shkn up over 2f out: wknd over 1f out* **40/1**

1m 36.62s (-3.28) **Going Correction** -0.275s/f (Stan) **8** Ran SP% **115.7**
Speed ratings (Par 107): **105,100,98,98,97 97,96,89**
CSF £26.66 CT £144.90 TOTE £6.10: £1.90, £1.50, £2.00; EX 28.90 Trifecta £184.30.
Owner Happy Valley Racing & Breeding Limited **Bred** R Shaykhutdinov **Trained** Newmarket, Suffolk

FOCUS
A good handicap. The clear-cut winner made all in a decent comparative time. The second has been rated close to his recent effort, but the level is fluid.

4021 JOHN LEWIS AND PARTNERS PERSONAL STYLING H'CAP — 1m 2f (P)

3:30 (3:31) (Class 3) (0-95,97) 4-Y-O+ — **£10,350** (£3,080; £1,539; £769) **Stalls** Low

Form — RPR

2204 **1** **Star Of Southwold (FR)**[34] 2800 4-8-12 **85**............ AlistairRawlinson 8 92
(Michael Appleby) *mde virtually all: qcknd 3f out: rdn and edgd rt over 1f out: all out* **14/1**

1-10 **2** *hd* **Lexington Empire**[29] 2969 4-9-2 **89**.................................(b) ShaneKelly 1 96
(David Lanigan) *hld up in tch: shkn up over 2f out: rdn to chse wnr wl ins fnl f: r.o* **7/1**

1246 **3** *1/2* **Nonios (IRE)**[28] 3005 7-9-1 **93**..................................(h) DylanHogan(5) 3 99
(David Simcock) *s.i.s: hld up: shkn up and swtchd rt over 1f out: r.o ins fnl f: wnt 3rd post: nt quite rch ldrs* **14/1**

0030 **4** *nk* **Rufus King**[20] 3313 4-9-3 **90**.................................. LukeMorris 10 95
(Mark Johnston) *s.i.s: rcvrd to chse wnr after 1f: rdn over 2f out: lost 2nd wl ins fnl f: styd on u.p* **16/1**

0-20 **5** *1 1/2* **Mistiroc**[34] 2808 8-9-4 **91**..................................(v) JasonHart 6 93
(John Quinn) *hld up: swtchd rt and hdwy over 1f out: r.o: nt rch ldrs* **16/1**

0311 **6** *1/2* **Fayez (IRE)**[14] 3515 5-9-10 **97**..................................(p) ShaneGray 5 98
(David O'Meara) *s.i.s: hld up: nt clr run and r.o ins fnl f: nt rch ldrs* **12/1**

-113 **7** *1 1/2* **El Ghazwani (IRE)**[49] 2320 4-9-6 **93**..................................(t) JackMitchell 4 91
(Hugo Palmer) *pushed along to chse ldrs: rdn over 2f out: edgd rt and no ex wl ins fnl f* **4/1**[3]

5526 **8** *6* **Fennaan (IRE)**[24] 3160 4-9-1 **88**..................................(h) SamJames 9 74
(Phillip Makin) *broke wl: sn stdd and lost pl: rdn on outer over 2f out: n.d* **9/1**

-012 **9** *hd* **Shareef Star**[24] 3168 4-9-0 **87**..................................(b[1]) LouisSteward 7 73
(Sir Michael Stoute) *chsd ldrs: rdn and edgd rt over 1f out: wknd fnl f (jockey said gelding was never travelling; trainer's rep said gelding was unsuited by the application of first-time blinkers)* **10/3**[2]

122- **10** *1/2* **Spanish Archer (FR)**[266] 7697 4-9-7 **94**.................................. DanielMuscutt 2 79
(James Fanshawe) *hld up: rdn and edgd rt over 1f out: sn wknd (jockey said gelding stopped quickly)* **3/1**[1]

2m 2.7s (-5.90) **Going Correction** -0.275s/f (Stan) **10** Ran SP% **123.4**
Speed ratings (Par 107): **112,111,111,111,110 109,108,103,103,103**
CSF £114.69 CT £1428.17 TOTE £11.80: £3.60, £2.50, £4.80; EX 118.00 Trifecta £1406.60.
Owner Middleham Park Racing XXXIII **Bred** S C Snig Elevage **Trained** Oakham, Rutland

FOCUS
A good handicap. The winner was all out to marginally make most and had dipped under standard time. The third has been rated close to form.

4022 STRAWBERRY LIPO AT THE BEAUTY CENTRE FILLIES' NOVICE MEDIAN AUCTION STKS — 1m 2f (P)

4:05 (4:08) (Class 4) 3-4-Y-O — **£6,145** (£1,828; £913; £456) **Stalls** Low

Form — RPR

1 **1** **Kirstenbosch**[31] 2912 3-9-3 0.................................. DanielMuscutt 8 99+
(James Fanshawe) *trckd ldrs: wnt 2nd over 3f out: led over 2f out: rdn clr fnl f* **5/4**[1]

24 **2** *5* **Inference**[35] 2770 3-8-11 0.................................. NickyMackay 2 83
(John Gosden) *hld up in tch: chsd wnr over 2f out: rdn over 1f out: styd on same pce* **13/8**[2]

-33P **3** *8* **Cabarita**[40] 2612 3-8-11 76.................................. RobHornby 7 67
(Ralph Beckett) *hld up: hdwy to go 3rd over 2f out: sn outpcd* **5/1**[3]

05 **4** *8* **Zappiness (USA)**[30] 2925 3-8-11 0.................................. HayleyTurner 10 51
(Peter Chapple-Hyam) *s.i.s: hld up: hdwy to go 4th over 1f out: nvr on terms* **50/1**

00 **5** *4 1/2* **Postie**[21] 3263 3-8-11 0..................................(h) RyanTate 1 42
(James Eustace) *s.i.s: hld up: rdn over 3f out: nvr on terms* **50/1**

0- **6** *5* **Prodigious**[251] 8150 3-8-11 0.................................. LouisSteward 5 32
(Sir Michael Stoute) *hld up: shkn up over 3f out: sn wknd* **10/1**

52 **7** *hd* **Narina (IRE)**[27] 3035 3-8-11 0.................................. LiamJones 9 32
(William Haggas) *s.i.s: hdwy over 6f out: rdn over 3f out: sn wknd* **10/1**

0 **8** *12* **Resurrected (IRE)**[41] 2581 3-8-11 0.................................. DannyBrock 3 8
(Philip McBride) *led 1f: chsd ldrs: rdn and wknd over 2f out* **66/1**

6 **9** *nk* **Emerald Fox**[64] 1849 4-9-4 0 .... SeamusCronin(5) 6 7
(Robyn Brisland) *plld hrd: w ldrs tl settled into 2nd over 8f out: lost 2nd over 3f out: hung rt and wknd over 2f out (vet said filly lost its left fore shoe)* **50/1**

0 **10** *4* **Astral Girl**[14] 3495 3-8-8 0 .... MitchGodwin(3) 4
(Hughie Morrison) *led after 1f: rdn and hdd over 2f out: sn wknd* **40/1**

2m 3.63s (-4.97) **Going Correction** -0.275s/f (Stan)
WFA 3 from 4yo 12lb **10** Ran SP% **127.2**
Speed ratings (Par 102): **108,104,97,91,87 83,83,73,73,70**
CSF £3.88 TOTE £2.30: £1.10, £1.10, £1.70; EX 4.50 Trifecta £13.60.
Owner Fittocks Stud **Bred** Fittocks Stud **Trained** Newmarket, Suffolk

FOCUS
A fair fillies' novice contest. The favourite dismissed the well-backed second-favourite in smart fashion and this field finished strung out across Essex.

4023 LIFEHOUSE SPA DAY FILLIES' H'CAP 6f (P)
4:45 (4:46) (Class 3) (0-95,96) 3-Y-O+ £10,350 (£3,080; £1,539; £769) **Stalls** Centre

Form RPR

5-11 **1** **Shimmering Dawn (IRE)**[34] 2787 3-9-1 **84** .... TomEaves 6 96+
(James Tate) *s.i.s: hld up: swtchd rt over 1f out: rdn and str run ins fnl f to ld towards fin: comf* **5/1**[3]

16-1 **2** *1* **Furious**[17] 3427 3-9-0 **88** .... DylanHogan(5) 4 94
(David Simcock) *hmpd s: sn prom: chsd ldr over 1f out: rdn to ld wl ins fnl f: hdd towards fin* **6/1**

-312 **3** *¾* **Isaan Queen (IRE)**[32] 2874 3-9-13 **96** .... EdwardGreatrex 2 100+
(Archie Watson) *hld up in tch: rdn over 1f out: r.o: wnt 3rd nr fin* **5/1**[3]

1151 **4** *½* **Probability (IRE)**[26] 3068 3-9-6 **89** .... HollieDoyle 10 91
(Archie Watson) *led 5f out: rdn over 1f out: hdd wl ins fnl f* **12/1**

35-4 **5** *¾* **Restless Rose**[38] 2687 4-9-4 **80** .... DanielMuscutt 9 82
(Stuart Williams) *prom: chsd ldr over 4f out tl rdn over 1f out: styd on same pce ins fnl f* **16/1**

0-03 **6** *nk* **Porcelain Girl (IRE)**[12] 3583 3-8-9 **78** .... HayleyTurner 5 77
(Michael Bell) *s.i.s: hld up: rdn over 1f out: r.o ins fnl f: nt trble ldrs (vet said filly lost its right hind shoe)* **20/1**

41-0 **7** *¾* **Accommodate (IRE)**[34] 2809 3-8-12 **81** .... KieranO'Neill 7 78
(Sir Michael Stoute) *sn led: hdd 5f out: chsd ldrs: rdn over 1f out: styd on same pce ins fnl f* **10/1**

-340 **8** *¾* **Indian Tygress**[40] 2627 4-9-9 **85** .... GeorgeWood 3 81
(James Fanshawe) *edgd rt s: hld up: hdwy over 1f out: no ex wl ins fnl f* **7/2**[1]

12/0 **9** *1* **Lady Of Aran (IRE)**[61] 1955 4-9-0 **76** .... RossaRyan 8 69
(Charlie Fellowes) *s.i.s: hld up: rdn over 1f out: n.d* **25/1**

-210 **10** *nk* **Alhakmah (IRE)**[26] 3075 3-9-0 **83** .... SeanLevey 1 73
(Richard Hannon) *hld up in tch: rdn over 1f out: wknd ins fnl f* **9/2**[2]

1m 10.89s (-2.81) **Going Correction** -0.275s/f (Stan)
WFA 3 from 4yo 7lb **10** Ran SP% **119.3**
Speed ratings (Par 104): **107,105,104,104,103 102,101,100,99,98**
CSF £36.03 CT £160.45 TOTE £5.60: £1.70, £1.80, £2.20; EX 23.30 Trifecta £95.00.
Owner Sheikh Juma Dalmook Al Maktoum **Bred** Cloneymore Farm Ltd **Trained** Newmarket, Suffolk

FOCUS
A good fillies' handicap. One of the joint-third favourites produced a remarkable display, coming from last to first in the straight to win eased-down in the final 25 yards. The third has been rated as matching her C&D Listed win.

4024 BETSI H'CAP 1m 6f (P)
5:20 (5:20) (Class 4) (0-85,83) 3-Y-O £8,991 (£2,675; £1,337; £668; £300) **Stalls** Low

Form RPR

6-00 **1** **Manton Warrior (IRE)**[20] 3311 3-8-2 **64** oh1 .... HayleyTurner 5 70
(Charlie Fellowes) *a.p: chsd ldr over 10f out: shkn up over 3f out: led over 2f out: rdn over 1f out: edgd lft ins fnl f: styd on* **7/2**[3]

6214 **2** *1½* **Withoutdestination**[49] 2317 3-9-0 **76** ....(b) ShaneKelly 4 81
(Marco Botti) *chsd ldrs: rdn to chse wnr over 1f out: styd on same pce towards fin* **12/1**

5255 **3** *1¼* **Mr Zoom Zoom**[12] 3604 3-8-5 **67** .... KieranO'Neill 2 69
(Luke McJannet) *s.s: hld up: nt clr run fr over 3f out tl swtchd rt over 2f out: hdwy u.p over 1f out: sn hung lft: styd on same pce ins fnl f* **10/3**[2]

4522 **4** *6* **Message**[13] 3538 3-8-1 **68** .... AndrewBreslin(5) 1 62
(Mark Johnston) *sn chsng ldr: lost 2nd over 10f out: pushed along 9f out: rdn over 2f out: no ex fnl f* **10/3**[2]

2151 **5** *17* **Lord Lamington**[21] 3260 3-9-7 **83** .... JasonHart 3 53
(Mark Johnston) *led: rdn and hdd over 2f out: wknd over 1f out (trainer could offer no explanation for the gelding's performance)* **2/1**[1]

2m 58.49s (-4.71) **Going Correction** -0.275s/f (Stan) **5** Ran SP% **109.4**
Speed ratings (Par 101): **102,101,100,97,87**
CSF £36.34 TOTE £4.30: £1.90, £4.00; EX 51.10 Trifecta £208.20.
Owner Second Chancers **Bred** Glashare House Stud **Trained** Newmarket, Suffolk

FOCUS
A fair 3yo staying handicap. The favourite failed to dominate off his own modest tempo and an AW newcomer won with a bit in hand. The winner has been rated in line with the better view of last year's Pontefract form.
T/Plt: £91.70 to a £1 stake. Pool: £30,435.86 - 331.59 winning units T/Qpdt: £32.90 to a £1 stake. Pool: £2,729.94 - 82.73 winning units **Colin Roberts**

3687 LINGFIELD (L-H)
Thursday, June 20

OFFICIAL GOING: Polytrack: standard
Wind: Fresh, half behind Weather: Fine but cloudy

4025 VISIT ATTHERACES.COM H'CAP 6f 1y(P)
5:50 (5:51) (Class 6) (0-58,59) 3-Y-O+
£3,105 (£924; £461; £300; £300; £300) **Stalls** Low

Form RPR

1-02 **1** **Papa Delta**[19] 3352 5-9-7 **58** .... GeorgeDowning 11 65
(Tony Carroll) *trckd ldng trio: clsng whn nt clr run and swtchd rt 1f out: styd on strly fnl f to ld last strides* **5/1**[3]

3005 **2** *½* **Red Tycoon (IRE)**[13] 3527 7-9-6 **57** .... AdamKirby 2 62
(Ken Cunningham-Brown) *trckd ldng pair: rdn to ld towards inner 1f out: drvn and hdd last strides* **9/2**[2]

3222 **3** *hd* **Daring Guest (IRE)**[24] 3143 5-9-6 **57** ....(vt[1]) LukeMorris 4 61
(Tom Clover) *trckd ldrs in 5th: swtchd ins and drvn over 1f out: styd on fnl f and nrly snatched 2nd* **7/2**[1]

0431 **4** *nk* **Billyoakes (IRE)**[24] 3144 7-9-6 **57** ....(p) JackMitchell 8 60
(Charlie Wallis) *pressed ldr: rdn to chal over 1f out: nt qckn fnl f and a hld after: kpt on* **14/1**

0-51 **5** *nk* **Napping**[8] 3738 6-9-5 **59** 5ex .... GabrieleMalune(3) 3 61
(Amy Murphy) *hld up towards rr: rdn and prog over 1f out: styd on fnl f: pressed for a pl nr fin (jockey said mare was slowly away)* **7/2**[1]

0600 **6** *3¼* **Tavener**[17] 3430 7-9-7 **58** ....(p) PhilDennis 1 50
(David C Griffiths) *led: rdn and hdd 1f out: wknd qckly* **8/1**

3F00 **7** *shd* **Mercers**[61] 1930 5-9-5 **56** ....(b) JoeyHaynes 5 48
(Paddy Butler) *towards rr: pushed along 1/2-way: effrt u.p over 1f out: kpt on but nvr a threat* **66/1**

1-00 **8** *2¼* **Cuban Spirit**[99] 1179 4-9-5 **56** .... LiamKeniry 7 41
(Lee Carter) *slowly away: pushed along in rr: no significant prog fnl 2f* **33/1**

40-0 **9** *¾* **Kingsley Klarion (IRE)**[70] 1715 6-9-3 **57** .... TimClark(3) 10 40
(John Butler) *heavily restrained s: detached in last pair: no prog and nvr remotely in it (jockey said gelding jumped awkwardly)* **8/1**

5524 **10** *4½* **Maazel (IRE)**[23] 3187 5-9-5 **56** .... RobertWinston 6 26
(Lee Carter) *slowly away: mostly detached in last pair: nvr a factor (jockey said gelding was never traveling)* **5/1**[3]

1m 11.03s (-0.87) **Going Correction** -0.10s/f (Stan) **10** Ran SP% **129.3**
Speed ratings (Par 101): **101,100,100,99,99 94,94,91,90,84**
CSF £31.19 CT £96.04 TOTE £6.60: £2.90, £2.10, £1.30; EX 44.40 Trifecta £267.60.
Owner Paul Downing **Bred** W G H Barrons & Qatar Bloodstock Ltd **Trained** Cropthorne, Worcs

FOCUS
An ordinary sprint handicap and they finished in a heap. Straightforward limited form.

4026 KOMFORT PARTITIONING AND KNAUF AMF (S) STKS 5f 6y(P)
6:25 (6:25) (Class 6) 3-Y-O+
£3,105 (£924; £461; £300; £300; £300) **Stalls** High

Form RPR

6022 **1** **Green Door (IRE)**[16] 3443 8-9-2 82 ....(v) LukeMorris 3 78
(Robert Cowell) *mde virtually all: def advantage 1/2-way: urged clr over 1f out: eased last 50yds* **1/3**[1]

-600 **2** *5* **Sir Hector (IRE)**[52] 2206 4-9-6 64 ....(h[1]) JackMitchell 6 62
(Charlie Wallis) *in tch: pushed along 1/2-way: rdn to chse clr wnr over 1f out: no imp* **5/1**[2]

4000 **3** *nk* **Avon Green**[53] 2153 4-9-1 53 .... CharlesBishop 4 56
(Joseph Tuite) *hld up: prog to press for 2nd 1f out: no ch w wnr and nt qckn nr fin* **14/1**

0504 **4** *2½* **Deer Song**[9] 3688 6-8-13 45 ....(b) CierenFallon(7) 2 52
(John Bridger) *w wnr to 1/2-way: lost 2nd and fdd over 1f out* **100/1**

05-0 **5** *¾* **Raise A Little Joy**[15] 3475 4-8-11 42 ....(p) DannyBrock 5 40
(J R Jenkins) *a in rr: drvn and no real prog 2f out* **50/1**

030- **6** *½* **Staffa (IRE)**[180] 9681 6-8-4 56 .... MichaelPitt(7) 1 38
(Denis Coakley) *a in last pair: no ch fnl 2f* **25/1**

-000 **7** *2½* **Sylvia's Mother**[14] 3508 3-8-13 64 ....(b) LiamKeniry 7 35
(Joseph Tuite) *pressed ldrs: rdn 2f out: wknd wl over 1f out* **7/1**[3]

58.27s (-0.53) **Going Correction** -0.10s/f (Stan)
WFA 3 from 4yo+ 6lb **7** Ran SP% **117.6**
Speed ratings (Par 101): **100,92,91,87,86 85,81**
CSF £2.71 TOTE £1.30: £1.10, £1.60; EX 2.90 Trifecta £10.30.The winner was bought in for £6,000.
Owner Bottisham Heath Stud **Bred** Mrs Sue Lenehan **Trained** Six Mile Bottom, Cambs

FOCUS
This proved easy pickings for the odds-on favourite, who had plenty in hand at the weights.

4027 HAPPY 50TH BIRTHDAY DR CLAIRE JACKSON H'CAP 5f 6y(P)
7:00 (7:02) (Class 6) (0-65,65) 4-Y-O+
£3,105 (£924; £461; £300; £300; £300) **Stalls** High

Form RPR

0302 **1** **Brogans Bay (IRE)**[17] 3425 4-8-8 **52** .... JFEgan 4 58
(Simon Dow) *mde all: sent for home wl over 1f out: kpt on fnl f and a in command* **7/1**

-663 **2** *¾* **Exceedingly Diva**[2] 3961 4-9-3 **61** .... CharlesBishop 8 64
(George Baker) *s.i.s: hld up in last trio: prog on inner wl over 1f out: rdn and styd on to take 2nd last strides (trainer said filly did not handle the bend)* **7/2**[2]

2200 **3** *½* **Archimedes (IRE)**[23] 3206 6-9-6 **64** ....(tp) PhilDennis 6 66
(David C Griffiths) *chsd wnr: rdn 2f out: nt qckn and no imp fnl f* **8/1**

3130 **4** *¾* **Time To Reason (IRE)**[49] 2318 6-9-7 **65** ....(p) JackMitchell 1 64
(Charlie Wallis) *chsd ldng pair: rdn 2f out: nt qckn over 1f out: lost 3rd ins fnl f* **3/1**[1]

02-0 **5** *¾* **Roundabout Magic (IRE)**[16] 3443 5-9-7 **65** .... NickyMackay 9 61
(Simon Dow) *hld up in last trio: sme prog whn rn into trble over 1f out and swtchd rt: shkn up and r.o fnl f: too late* **10/1**

0124 **6** *½* **Hurricane Alert**[17] 3404 7-8-0 **51** oh3 .... AledBeech(7) 10 45
(Mark Hoad) *racd on outer: in tch: rdn and no prog 2f out: one pce after (vet said gelding was struck into its left hind)* **16/1**

2000 **7** *nse* **Come On Dave (IRE)**[17] 3404 10-9-2 **60** ....(b) DanielMuscutt 7 54
(John Butler) *slowly away: rcvrd into midfield: rdn and no prog wl over 1f out (jockey said gelding jumped awkwardly)* **5/1**[3]

/33- **8** *1¾* **L'Age D'Or**[369] 3842 4-8-12 **56** .... LukeMorris 2 44
(Robert Cowell) *chsd ldrs: rdn 2f out: lost pl and fdd over 1f out (vet said filly lost its right fore shoe)* **6/1**

3656 **9** *1¼* **Pharoh Jake**[58] 2010 11-8-1 **52** oh3 ow1 .... CierenFallon(7) 3 35
(John Bridger) *a towards rr: no prog over 1f out* **16/1**

-605 **10** *5* **Ask The Guru**[30] 2924 9-8-8 **52** oh5 ow1 ....(p) KierenFox 5 17
(Michael Attwater) *reluctant to enter stall: racd wd: a bhd (jockey said gelding hung badly right-handed; starter reported that the gelding was reluctant to enter the stalls; trainer was informed that the gelding could not run until the day after passing a stalls test)* **25/1**

58.06s (-0.74) **Going Correction** -0.10s/f (Stan) **10** Ran SP% **126.5**
Speed ratings (Par 101): **101,99,99,97,96 95,95,92,90,82**
CSF £34.63 CT £211.65 TOTE £8.50: £1.90, £2.10, £3.20; EX 34.30 Trifecta £529.80.
Owner Richard A Murray **Bred** M Morrissey **Trained** Epsom, Surrey

FOCUS
A modest affair controlled from the front.

4028 REMEMBERING BRENDA'S 60 YEARS OF LINGFIELD RACING H'CAP 1m 1y(P)
7:30 (7:31) (Class 5) (0-70,70) 4-Y-0+
£3,752 (£1,116; £557; £300; £300; £300) Stalls High

Form RPR
-630 1 **Nawar**28 3022 4-9-7 70 ....(t) GeorgeWood 4 79
(Martin Bosley) *trckd ldng trio: rdn and clsd over 1f out: led jst ins fnl f: drvn out* 12/1
2304 2 1 1/4 **Subliminal**17 3429 4-9-1 64 ....(b) LukeMorris 11 70
(Simon Dow) *slowly away: towards rr: drvn and prog over 1f out: r.o to take 2nd last 100yds: nvr able to chal* 5/1[2]
2304 3 1 **Tamerlane (IRE)**20 3305 4-9-5 68 ....(vt) AdamKirby 3 72
(Clive Cox) *s.i.s: towards rr: urged along 2f out: prog and drvn jst over 1f out: styd on to take 3rd nr fin* 2/1[1]
3253 4 1/2 **Pendo**40 2617 8-9-2 65 .... KierenFox 7 68
(John Best) *s.i.s: t.k.h: hld up in rr: shkn up over 1f out: styd on fnl f to take 4th last strides: too late* 7/1[3]
0634 5 1 **Militry Decoration (IRE)**28 3002 4-8-12 64 .... JoshuaBryan(3) 10 64
(Dr Jon Scargill) *chsd ldr: rdn 2f out: led briefly 1f out: wknd last 100yds* 8/1
3-U0 6 1 3/4 **Angel Islington (IRE)**29 2971 4-9-3 66 .... DavidProbert 5 62
(Andrew Balding) *fractious to post: hld up in rr: rdn 2f out: passed rivals last 150yds but nvr a threat* 20/1
20-0 7 1/2 **Momentarily**12 3572 4-8-13 67 ....(h) ScottMcCullagh(5) 9 62
(Mick Channon) *led: stl gng strly 2f out: hdd & wknd 1f out* 25/1
24-0 8 nk **Flora Tristan**50 2297 4-8-13 65 ....(h) GabrieleMalune(3) 2 59
(Ivan Furtado) *plld hrd: chsd ldng pair to over 1f out: wknd ins fnl f* 50/1
6603 9 1/2 **Ruby Gates (IRE)**15 3468 6-9-2 70 .... DarraghKeenan(5) 1 63
(John Butler) *trckd ldrs on inner: pushed along 2f out: no prog against rail 1f out: lost pls after* 8/1
0105 10 1 1/2 **Full Intention**15 3462 5-9-7 70 ....(p) JackMitchell 6 60
(Lydia Pearce) *nvr bttr than midfield: rdn 3f out: lost pl and struggling wl over 1f out* 8/1
0-00 11 1/2 **Connaught Ranger (IRE)**37 2714 4-9-2 65 .... CharlesBishop 12 54
(Denis Coakley) *hld up in last: pushed along over 2f out: no prog and nvr in it (jockey said gelding hung left-handed throughout)* 14/1
5460 12 7 **The Warrior (IRE)**28 3002 7-9-5 68 .... RobertWinston 8 41
(Lee Carter) *wl in rr: effrt on wd outside over 3f out: v wd bnd 2f out and wknd* 14/1

1m 36.45s (-1.75) **Going Correction** -0.10s/f (Stan) 12 Ran SP% 127.4
Speed ratings (Par 103): **104,102,101,101,100 98,98,97,97,95 95,88**
CSF £75.09 CT £179.75 TOTE £12.90: £4.20, £2.10, £1.40; EX 104.30 Trifecta £497.90.
Owner Quartet Racing **Bred** Saleh Al Homaizi & Imad Al Sagar **Trained** Chalfont St Giles, Bucks

FOCUS
A modest affair, but competitive enough.

4029 RACING WELFARE H'CAP 1m 1y(P)
8:00 (8:02) (Class 6) (0-55,55) 3-Y-0
£3,105 (£924; £461; £300; £300; £300) Stalls High

Form RPR
0004 1 **Mitigator**7 3780 3-9-6 55 ....(b) BrettDoyle 9 62
(Lydia Pearce) *dwlt: rcvrd into midfield: rdn and prog on outer over 2f out: clsd on ldng pair 1f out: styd on u.p to ld last 50yds* 8/1
0530 2 1/2 **Dark Poet**9 3697 3-9-6 55 .... AdamKirby 8 61
(Clive Cox) *mostly chsd ldr: rdn to ld wl over 1f out: idled sltly in front: hdd and no ex last 50yds (jockey said gelding hung right-handed in the closing stages)* 7/2[2]
-410 3 2 1/4 **Poetic Motion**21 3256 3-9-2 51 .... CharlieBennett 5 52
(Jim Boyle) *led after 100yds: rdn and hdd wl over 1f out: one pce fnl f* 7/1[3]
0000 4 3 1/4 **Islay Mist**16 3442 3-9-2 51 ....(t) RobertWinston 7 44
(Lee Carter) *chsd ldrs: drvn over 2f out: outpcd over 1f out: n.d fnl f* 25/1
-065 5 2 1/4 **Smith (IRE)**17 3409 3-9-6 55 ....(p) CharlesBishop 6 43
(Eve Johnson Houghton) *sn in rr: dropped to last 1/2-way: drvn 3f out: no prog tl fnlly r.o last 200yds* 12/1
6003 6 1/2 **Luna Princess**9 3684 3-9-0 52 ....(p[1]) JaneElliott(3) 2 39
(Michael Appleby) *cl up on inner: rdn 2f out: outpcd over 1f out: fdd* 10/1
3006 7 1 **Hanbury Dreams**21 3258 3-9-6 55 ....(p[1]) LukeMorris 10 40
(Tom Clover) *hld up in last trio: pushed along and no prog 2f out: no ch whn rdn fnl f: nvr in it* 25/1
0-36 8 3/4 **Daniel Dravot**17 3409 3-9-6 55 ....(h) CallumShepherd 11 38
(Michael Attwater) *nvr beyond midfield: u.p and struggling wl over 2f out* 25/1
3-60 9 2 1/2 **Keep It Country Tv**17 3410 3-8-13 51 .... PaddyBradley(3) 12 28
(Pat Phelan) *racd v wd early: prog to trck ldrs over 3f out: wknd 2f out* 12/1
0412 10 3 1/2 **Crazy Spin**23 3204 3-9-3 52 ....(p) SilvestreDeSousa 4 21
(Ivan Furtado) *led 100yds: qckly lost pl and in midfield: lost further grnd fr 1/2-way: wl in rr 2f out: eased whn no ch fnl f (jockey said filly stopped quickly)* 7/4[1]
500- 11 hd **Ocean Rouge**295 6681 3-9-6 55 .... DavidProbert 3 24
(Tony Carroll) *a towards rr: rdn and no prog wl over 2f out* 16/1
0-00 12 2 1/2 **Yes Can Do (USA)**36 2735 3-9-4 53 .... RobertHavlin 1 16
(Ed Dunlop) *mostly in last trio: shkn up and no prog over 2f out* 33/1

1m 37.59s (-0.61) **Going Correction** -0.10s/f (Stan) 12 Ran SP% 127.0
Speed ratings (Par 97): **99,98,96,93,90 90,89,88,86,82 82,79**
CSF £37.36 CT £217.89 TOTE £8.70: £2.60, £1.60, £2.30; EX 47.20 Trifecta £248.50.
Owner W Prosser **Bred** Adweb Ltd & Mrs R J Gallagher **Trained** Newmarket, Suffolk

FOCUS
The winner did well to win this. The third has been rated close to her pre-race mark.

4030 INJURED JOCKEYS FUND NOVICE STKS 6f 1y(P)
8:30 (8:31) (Class 5) 2-Y-0
£3,752 (£1,116; £557; £278) Stalls Low

Form RPR
5 1 **Will To Win (GER)**12 3601 2-9-5 .... SilvestreDeSousa 7 78
(Simon Crisford) *mde all: rdn over 1f out: styd on wl and firmly in command fnl f* 10/11[1]
2 2 3/4 **Harlequin** 2-9-5 .... DanielMuscutt 5 70
(Luke Dace) *sn chsd wnr: rdn 2f out: no imp over 1f out but kpt on (jockey said colt hung left-handed in the final furlong)* 25/1
02 3 1/2 **Indian Creak (IRE)**17 3419 2-9-5 .... PatDobbs 4 71
(Mick Channon) *sn chsd ldng pair: rdn over 1f out: no threat to wnr but kpt on to press for 2nd nr fin* 4/1[3]
4 1 1/2 **Top Class Angel (IRE)** 2-9-0 .... RossaRyan 3 59+
(Richard Hannon) *settled in midfield: outpcd 2f out: tk modest 4th jst over 1f out: r.o wl fnl f: nrst fin* 5/1
0 5 6 **Broughtons Compass**21 3257 2-9-5 .... JoeyHaynes 2 46+
(Mark Hoad) *hld up in last pair: sme prog on inner 2f out: no ch whn sltly impeded over 1f out* 100/1
06 6 3/4 **Mungo's Quest (IRE)**12 3579 2-9-5 .... NickyMackay 1 44
(Simon Dow) *fractious bef ent stalls: chsd ldrs outpcd in 4th 2f out: fdd fnl f* 50/1
0 7 1 1/4 **Beat The Breeze**14 3491 2-9-5 .... JFEgan 8 40
(Simon Dow) *hld up in last pair: lft bhd over 2f out: shkn up briefly over 1f out: nvr in it* 20/1
8 6 **Cherokee Mist (CAN)** 2-9-5 .... BrettDoyle 6 22
(Charlie Appleby) *racd on outer: in tch: dropped to last pair 1/2-way and struggling: sn bhd* 9/4[2]
0 9 16 **Power Of Love**17 3419 2-9-5 .... CharlesBishop 9
(George Baker) *prom to 1/2-way: wknd rapidly: t.o* 33/1

1m 11.85s (-0.05) **Going Correction** -0.10s/f (Stan) 9 Ran SP% 134.3
Speed ratings (Par 93): **96,92,91,89,81 80,79,71,49**
CSF £38.18 TOTE £1.70: £1.10, £7.50, £1.40; EX 42.10 Trifecta £117.70.
Owner Mohammed Al Suboosi **Bred** Stiftung Gestut Fahrhof **Trained** Newmarket, Suffolk

FOCUS
A gamble was landed on the favourite, who had been as big as 5-1 the previous day and around 3-1 in the morning.

4031 WITHEFORD EQUINE BARRIER TRIALS 2ND JULY H'CAP 1m 4f (P)
9:00 (9:00) (Class 5) (0-70,72) 3-Y-O
£3,752 (£1,116; £557; £300; £300; £300) Stalls Low

Form RPR
6-33 1 **Mondain**60 1972 3-9-7 70 .... FrannyNorton 3 75+
(Mark Johnston) *trckd ldng pair: rdn whn pce lifted over 2f out: clsd over 1f out: led ins fnl f: drvn out* 5/2[2]
-215 2 3/4 **Natsovia**96 1233 3-9-8 71 .... NicolaCurrie 4 74
(Jamie Osborne) *dwlt: hld up in last: outpcd whn pce lifted over 2f out and plenty to do: gd prog on inner over 1f out: chal ins fnl f: no ex last 100yds* 8/1
55-6 3 shd **Young Merlin (IRE)**47 2407 3-9-9 72 .... JasonWatson 5 75
(Roger Charlton) *led after 1f tl after 4f: led again 2f out and drvn for home: hdd and one pce ins fnl f* 4/1[3]
0-35 4 hd **Sawasdee (IRE)**35 2769 3-9-5 68 ....(p[1]) SilvestreDeSousa 2 70
(Andrew Balding) *t.k.h early: led 1f: settled bhd ldrs: outpcd over 2f out: drvn over 1f out: styd on fnl f but too late to chal* 7/4[1]
-010 5 1/2 **Twenty Years On**6 3809 3-9-1 67 ....(p[1]) FinleyMarsh(3) 7 69
(Richard Hughes) *hld up in 5th: outpcd over 2f out and wd bnd sn after: styd on fnl f but too late* 5/1
4-40 6 3 3/4 **Fares Alpha (USA)**49 2336 3-9-0 70 .... CierenFallon(7) 6 66
(Marco Botti) *led after 4f: tried to kick on over 2f out but sn hdd: wknd over 1f out* 12/1

2m 32.14s (-0.86) **Going Correction** -0.10s/f (Stan) 6 Ran SP% 120.4
Speed ratings (Par 99): **98,97,97,96 94**
CSF £23.83 TOTE £3.70: £1.80, £2.10; EX 27.00 Trifecta £64.50.
Owner Sheikh Hamdan bin Mohammed Al Maktoum **Bred** Godolphin **Trained** Middleham Moor, N Yorks

FOCUS
A bit of a tactical affair and they were well bunched at the finish.
T/Plt: £45.90 to a £1 stake. Pool: £50,437.54 - 800.64 winning units T/Qpdt: £23.60 to a £1 stake. Pool: £6,914.82 - 216.64 winning units **Jonathan Neesom**

4005 RIPON (R-H)
Thursday, June 20

OFFICIAL GOING: Good to soft (7.2)
Wind: fresh half behind Weather: fine

4032 THESECRETSPA.NET EBF NOVICE STKS 6f
2:10 (2:11) (Class 5) 2-Y-0
£3,881 (£1,155; £577; £288) Stalls High

Form RPR
5 1 **Silver Mission (IRE)**31 2892 2-9-2 .... TonyHamilton 6 72
(Richard Fahey) *hld up: pushed along over 3f out: hdwy 2f out: drvn to chse ldrs appr fnl f: kpt on wl: led 25yds out* 11/4[2]
1 2 nk **Coastal Mist (IRE)**21 3265 2-9-3 .... SeanDavis(3) 8 75
(John Quinn) *prom: rdn to ld appr fnl f: sn drvn: kpt on but hdd 25yds out* 7/4[1]
203 3 1 **What A Business (IRE)**22 3212 2-9-2 .... PaulMulrennan 5 68
(Roger Fell) *led narrowly: rdn 2f out: hdd appr fnl f: kpt on same pce* 7/1[3]
4 1 1/2 **National League (IRE)** 2-9-2 .... PaddyMathers 4 64+
(Richard Fahey) *dwlt: hld up: pushed along over 2f out: swtchd rt to outer over 1f out: kpt on ins fnl f* 14/1
2 5 6 **Just Jean (IRE)**14 3512 2-8-11 .... AndrewMullen 7 41
(Micky Hammond) *chsd ldrs: rdn along 3f out: wknd over 1f out* 7/1[3]
36 6 2 1/2 **Constitutional (IRE)**38 2686 2-9-2 .... BenCurtis 2 38
(K R Burke) *chsd ldrs on outer: rdn over 2f out: wknd fnl f* 17/2
25 7 8 **Kilig**14 3507 2-9-2 ....(t[1]) DavidAllan 9 14
(Tim Easterby) *pressed ldr tl wknd over 1f out* 20/1
8 7 **William Alexander** 2-9-2 .... BarryMcHugh 3
(Les Eyre) *wnt rt s and slowly away: sn swtchd lft to rail: a in rr* 50/1

1m 15.06s (2.56) **Going Correction** +0.25s/f (Good) 8 Ran SP% 111.9
Speed ratings (Par 93): **92,91,90,88,80 76,66,56**
CSF £7.58 TOTE £4.00: £1.60, £1.10, £1.20; EX 8.20 Trifecta £43.00.
Owner Sheikh Hamed Dalmook Al Maktoum **Bred** Yeomanstown Stud **Trained** Musley Bank, N Yorks

FOCUS
Good to soft going, the ground having already been drying out during Wednesday night's card here. The opener was 4.56sec outside standard and it's fair novice form. The second has been rated to his debut form.

4033 TOPSPORT EQUISAND H'CAP 5f
2:45 (2:46) (Class 5) (0-70,70) 3-Y-O
£4,075 (£1,212; £606; £303; £300; £300) **Stalls** High

Form RPR
3-42 **1** **Ginvincible**[19] 3339 3-8-13 **62** BarryMcHugh 3 68
(James Given) *pressed ldr: rdn into narrow ld appr fnl f: sn edgd rt: drvn all out* **10/1**
3315 **2** *hd* **Timetodock**[9] 3709 3-9-1 **64** (b) DavidAllan 6 69
(Tim Easterby) *led narrowly: drvn and hdd appr fnl f: remained chalng: kpt on* **3/1**[2]
0264 **3** *1* **Dancing Mountain (IRE)**[17] 3417 3-8-6 **55** BenCurtis 5 56
(Roger Fell) *chsd ldrs: rdn 2f out: kpt on* **6/1**[3]
000 **4** *¾* **Montalvan (IRE)**[24] 3159 3-8-8 **57** ow1 (p[1]) CliffordLee 2 56
(Roger Fell) *chsd ldrs: rdn 2f out: kpt on same pce* **12/1**
0041 **5** *2½* **Dancing Rave**[9] 3709 3-9-7 **70** 6ex DanielTudhope 7 60
(David O'Meara) *hld up: pushed along 3f out: drvn over 1f out: no imp (jockey said filly ran flat)* **5/4**[1]
3405 **6** *9* **Muhallab (IRE)**[23] 3202 3-7-12 **54** LauraCoughlan(7) 1 11
(Adrian Nicholls) *prom on outer: rdn over 2f out: wknd over 1f out* **8/1**

1m 0.26s (0.86) **Going Correction** +0.25s/f (Good) **6** Ran SP% **111.6**
Speed ratings (Par 99): **103,102,101,99,95 81**
CSF £39.31 TOTE £8.20: £3.50, £1.60; EX 46.30 Trifecta £132.90.
Owner Roy Tozer & Team Given 2 **Bred** D R Botterill **Trained** Willoughton, Lincs

FOCUS
A modest sprint handicap. The winner has been rated in line with her winter AW form, and the second to form.

4034 SLINGSBY GIN H'CAP 1m 4f 10y
3:20 (3:22) (Class 4) (0-80,82) 3-Y-O **£5,692** (£1,694; £846; £423; £300) **Stalls** Centre

Form RPR
65-4 **1** **Faylaq**[43] 2524 3-9-6 **73** DanielTudhope 2 95+
(William Haggas) *hld up in tch: hdwy and trckd ldr over 6f out: led on bit 3f out: cruised clr over 1f out: v easily* **8/15**[1]
1-41 **2** *4½* **Battle Of Wills (IRE)**[18] 3373 3-10-1 **82** DavidAllan 3 91
(James Tate) *in tch: rdn over 3f out: drvn to go 2nd 2f out: kpt on but no ch w wnr (jockey said colt hung right-handed)* **4/1**[2]
-405 **3** *2* **Mister Chiang**[15] 3474 3-9-6 **73** ConnorBeasley 1 78
(Mark Johnston) *hld up: rdn along 4f out: drvn over 2f out: plugged on to go modest 3rd ins fnl f* **13/2**[3]
0011 **4** *2¼* **Agravain**[22] 3219 3-8-6 **59** JamesSullivan 5 60
(Tim Easterby) *sn led: rdn and hdd 3f out: wknd over 1f out* **12/1**
-216 **5** *16* **Cuban Sun**[30] 2935 3-9-7 **74** BarryMcHugh 4 50
(James Given) *chsd ldr: rdn over 3f out: wknd over 1f out* **25/1**

2m 39.13s (2.83) **Going Correction** +0.25s/f (Good) **5** Ran SP% **110.1**
Speed ratings (Par 101): **100,97,95,94,83**
CSF £3.00 TOTE £1.40: £1.30, £1.30; EX 3.20 Trifecta £7.30.
Owner Hamdan Al Maktoum **Bred** Teruya Yoshida **Trained** Newmarket, Suffolk

FOCUS
Add 6yds. This fair handicap turned into a procession. The second has been rated to form, and the third to this year's turf form.

4035 RIPON RACES LADIES DAY H'CAP 1m 1f 170y
3:55 (3:55) (Class 3) (0-90,91) 4-Y-O+
£9,337 (£2,796; £1,398; £699; £349; £175) **Stalls** Low

Form RPR
-340 **1** **Borodin (IRE)**[20] 3315 4-9-7 **90** (p) PaddyMathers 9 101
(Richard Fahey) *trckd ldrs: rdn to ld 2f out: drvn fnl f: jnd 110yds out: fnd ex* **11/2**
5-50 **2** *nk* **Gulf Of Poets**[68] 1753 7-8-13 **89** JoshQuinn(7) 5 99
(Michael Easterby) *hld up: angled lft towards outer and hdwy 2f out: rdn to chse ldr appr fnl f: drvn and jnd ldr 110yds out: one pce towards fin* **33/1**
4001 **3** *3½* **Dutch Uncle**[7] 3766 7-8-3 **75** 4ex (p) SeanDavis(3) 8 78
(Tom Clover) *hld up: hdwy on outer over 3f out: rdn to chse ldr 2f out: no ex ins fnl f* **22/1**
6032 **4** *½* **Mutamaded (IRE)**[5] 3862 6-9-0 **83** JamesSullivan 2 85
(Ruth Carr) *trckd ldrs: n.m.r towards inner 2f out tl appr fnl f: rdn and kpt on ins fnl f* **10/3**[2]
-550 **5** *nk* **Kharbetation (IRE)**[37] 2710 6-8-5 **74** (p) CamHardie 6 75
(David O'Meara) *dwlt: hld up in rr: rdn and sme hdwy on outside over 1f out: kpt on ins fnl f* **33/1**
113- **6** *2* **Ummalnar**[274] 7445 4-9-8 **91** DanielTudhope 7 88+
(William Haggas) *midfield: pushed along over 2f out: n.m.r over 1f out tl 1f out: lot to do after: eased towards fin* **7/4**[1]
0-05 **7** *2¼* **Thomas Cranmer (USA)**[24] 3160 5-8-6 **78** RowanScott(3) 4 71
(Tina Jackson) *prom: rdn over 2f out: wknd ins fnl f* **14/1**
3011 **8** *½* **Harbour Breeze (IRE)**[29] 2969 4-9-5 **88** GrahamLee 1 80
(Lucy Wadham) *led: rdn and hdd 2f out: sn wknd (jockey said colt ran too free)* **5/1**[3]
5411 **9** *½* **Mulligatawny (IRE)**[19] 3356 6-9-1 **89** (p) BenSanderson(5) 3 80
(Roger Fell) *midfield on inner: n.m.r 4f out: lost pl over 2f out and swtchd lft to outer: rdn and no imp* **12/1**

2m 5.02s (0.42) **Going Correction** +0.25s/f (Good) **9** Ran SP% **116.1**
Speed ratings (Par 107): **109,108,105,105,105 103,101,101,101**
CSF £168.71 CT £3620.19 TOTE £5.50: £2.00, £6.30, £4.80; EX 132.20 Trifecta £2612.10.
Owner Sir Robert Ogden **Bred** Sir Robert Ogden **Trained** Musley Bank, N Yorks

FOCUS
Add 6yds. Good handicap form, with the first two clear. The third has been rated a bit below his shaky Newbury win.

4036 QUILTER PRIVATE CLIENT ADVISERS LADIES' DERBY H'CAP (FOR LADY AMATEUR RIDERS) 1m 4f 10y
4:35 (4:35) (Class 6) (0-65,66) 4-Y-O+
£3,306 (£1,025; £512; £300; £300; £300) **Stalls** Centre

Form RPR
2223 **1** **Nevada**[52] 2202 6-10-8 **66** (p) MissJoannaMason 8 76
(Steve Gollings) *trckd ldrs: rdn to ld over 1f out: styd on wl* **10/3**[1]
0342 **2** *1¾* **Mr Carbonator**[9] 3681 4-10-1 **59** MissAmieWaugh 6 66
(Philip Kirby) *trckd ldrs: led over 2f out: rdn and hdd over 1f out: styd on same pce* **11/2**
3050 **3** *hd* **Be Perfect (USA)**[17] 3415 10-10-0 **63** MissEmilyBullock(5) 1 70
(Ruth Carr) *midfield: hdwy and trckd ldrs 3f out: rdn 2f out: kpt on* **7/1**
0-03 **4** *2½* **Iolani (GER)**[14] 3511 7-10-5 **63** MissEmmaSayer 5 66
(Dianne Sayer) *midfield: hdwy on outer over 2f out: rdn to chal over 1f out: no ex ins fnl f* **9/2**[2]
5551 **5** *4* **Thorntoun Care**[14] 3511 8-10-2 **65** (p) MissAmyCollier(5) 7 62
(Karen Tutty) *hld up: pushed along and hdwy over 2f out: no further imp fr over 1f out (jockey said the saddle slipped approaching the final furlong)* **8/1**
0505 **6** *4½* **Lafilia (GER)**[37] 2720 4-10-2 **60** (p[1]) MissBrodieHampson 2 51
(Archie Watson) *led narrowly: rdn and hdd over 2f out: wknd over 1f out* **14/1**
4602 **7** *1½* **Earthly (USA)**[14] 3511 5-9-8 **52** (tp) MissSerenaBrotherton 10 40
(Bernard Llewellyn) *hld up in midfield on inner: rdn along over 2f out: wknd over 1f out* **5/1**[3]
50-0 **8** *11* **Graceful Act**[24] 3163 11-8-11 **47** oh1 SophieSmith(5) 11 18
(Ron Barr) *prom: wknd over 2f out (trainer said mare was found to have struck into herself)* **50/1**
0005 **9** *16* **Belabour**[81] 1463 6-10-5 **63** MissBeckyBrisbourne 3 11
(Kevin Frost) *hld up: wknd and bhd fnl 4f* **18/1**
-036 **10** *15* **Lucy's Law (IRE)**[16] 3449 5-10-4 **62** MissAbbieMcCain 9
(Tom Tate) *pressed ldr: wknd qckly 3f out: t.o* **18/1**

2m 40.68s (4.38) **Going Correction** +0.25s/f (Good) **10** Ran SP% **116.1**
Speed ratings (Par 101): **95,93,93,92,89 86,85,78,67,57**
CSF £21.52 CT £120.67 TOTE £3.60: £1.20, £2.60, £2.00; EX 19.40 Trifecta £147.30.
Owner Northern Bloodstock Racing **Bred** Good Breed **Trained** Scamblesby, Lincs

FOCUS
Add 6yds. A modest handicap, but pretty competitive as a 'Derby' ought to be.

4037 STRAY FM CELEBRATING LADIES DAY H'CAP 6f
5:10 (5:10) (Class 5) (0-70,71) 4-Y-O+
£4,075 (£1,212; £606; £303; £300; £300) **Stalls** High

Form RPR
4502 **1** **Cupid's Arrow (IRE)**[7] 3771 5-7-13 **50** JamieGormley(3) 3 59
(Ruth Carr) *mde all: rdn over 1f out: drvn and kpt on fnl f* **5/2**[1]
0024 **2** *¾* **Mutabaahy (IRE)**[9] 3706 4-9-7 **69** CamHardie 6 75
(Antony Brittain) *prom: rdn over 2f out: drvn fnl f: kpt on but a hld* **5/1**[2]
6065 **3** *2¾* **Meshardal (GER)**[3] 3921 9-8-2 **52** oh2 (p) AndrewMullen 5 47
(Ruth Carr) *hld up in tch: rdn over 1f out: kpt on to go 3rd fnl 50yds: no threat to ldng pair* **7/1**
0422 **4** *nk* **Tadaany (IRE)**[7] 3772 7-8-5 **53** (p) JamesSullivan 1 49
(Ruth Carr) *wnt rt s: sn chsd ldrs towards outer: rdn over 2f out: no ex ins fnl f: lost 3rd fnl 50yds* **11/2**[3]
-300 **5** *½* **Point Of Woods**[14] 3518 6-8-3 **58** SophieRalston(7) 7 53
(Tina Jackson) *chsd ldrs: rdn over 2f out: outpcd appr fnl f* **25/1**
5036 **6** *2¼* **Danehill Desert (IRE)**[13] 3550 4-8-5 **56** (p) SeanDavis(3) 9 43
(Richard Fahey) *hld up: rdn along 3f out: drvn 2f out: nvr threatened* **16/1**
-002 **7** *hd* **Shortbackandsides (IRE)**[13] 3549 4-9-3 **65** DavidAllan 10 52
(Tim Easterby) *hld up: pushed along over 2f out: nvr threatened* **5/2**[1]
0304 **8** *5* **Astrophysics**[22] 3227 7-8-6 **57** ConorMcGovern(3) 8 28
(Lynn Siddall) *chsd ldrs: rdn over 2f out: hung rt over 1f out and wknd* **20/1**

1m 12.94s (0.44) **Going Correction** +0.25s/f (Good) **8** Ran SP% **116.2**
Speed ratings (Par 103): **107,106,102,101,101 98,98,91**
CSF £15.72 CT £77.34 TOTE £3.20: £1.40, £1.50, £2.10; EX 22.00 Trifecta £95.40.
Owner Miss Vanessa Church **Bred** Liam Foley **Trained** Huby, N Yorks

FOCUS
A routine sprint handicap. The second has been rated to his recent effort.

4038 INN AT SOUTH STAINLEY H'CAP (DIV I) 1m 4f 10y
5:45 (5:46) (Class 6) (0-60,62) 3-Y-O
£3,428 (£1,020; £509; £300; £300; £300) **Stalls** Centre

Form RPR
4033 **1** **Stone Cougar (USA)**[2] 3965 3-9-5 **57** ConnorBeasley 7 69
(Mark Johnston) *in tch: hdwy to press ldr after 2f: led 3f out: rdn and r.o strly fnl 2f* **7/2**[2]
0-14 **2** *2½* **Gold Arch**[17] 3418 3-9-9 **61** (b[1]) PaulMulrennan 6 69
(David Lanigan) *dwlt: bhd and pushed along whn stmbld after 1f: hdwy and prom after 3f: effrt and chsd wnr whn hung persistently rt fr over 1f out: one pce ins fnl f (jockey said gelding stumbled twice in the first 2 furlongs and ran in snatches)* **3/1**[1]
60-0 **3** *14* **Amber Rock (USA)**[82] 1417 3-8-8 **46** ow1 BarryMcHugh 4 32
(Les Eyre) *hld up: rdn along 3f out: hdwy over 1f out: tk modest 3rd wl ins fnl f: no imp* **6/1**[3]
06-5 **4** *½* **Fame N Fortune**[12] 3594 3-9-4 **56** KevinStott 9 41
(Joseph Tuite) *led: rdn and hdd 3f out: wknd over 1f out* **17/2**
4050 **5** *hd* **Tunky**[7] 3777 3-8-12 **50** (b[1]) JamesSullivan 8 34
(James Given) *t.k.h in midfield: hdwy and prom over 3f out: rdn and wknd over 1f out* **25/1**
3454 **6** *2¼* **Kensington Art**[14] 3505 3-9-10 **62** (p[1]) TonyHamilton 3 43
(Richard Fahey) *hld up on ins: effrt and angled lft over 3f out: hung rt and outpcd fnl 2f* **3/1**[1]
2542 **7** *1½* **Picture Poet (IRE)**[20] 3299 3-9-7 **59** BenCurtis 5 37
(Henry Spiller) *chsd ldrs early: in tch: drvn and outpcd over 3f out: btn fnl 2f* **12/1**
-050 **8** *6* **Preservation**[22] 3226 3-8-5 **46** RowanScott(3) 2 15
(Jedd O'Keeffe) *in tch on ins: nt clr run over 4f out to over 3f out: sn rdn and outpcd: btn fnl 2f* **12/1**
0000 **9** *17* **Yasmin From York**[23] 3198 3-8-7 **45** CamHardie 1
(Brian Rothwell) *pressed ldr 3f: prom tl rdn and wknd over 3f out* **100/1**

2m 41.18s (4.88) **Going Correction** +0.25s/f (Good) **9** Ran SP% **117.3**
Speed ratings (Par 97): **93,91,82,81,81 80,79,75,63**
CSF £14.71 CT £60.98 TOTE £3.70: £1.90, £1.60, £1.80; EX 16.30 Trifecta £93.60.
Owner Sheikh Hamdan bin Mohammed Al Maktoum **Bred** Godolphin **Trained** Middleham Moor, N Yorks

The Form Book Flat 2019, Raceform Ltd, Newbury, RG14 5SJ

FOCUS
Add 6yds. The first two finished well clear in this low-grade handicap, which was the slower division by 1.54sec.

4039 INN AT SOUTH STAINLEY H'CAP (DIV II) 1m 4f 10y
6:20 (6:20) (Class 6) (0-60,61) 3-Y-O

£3,428 (£1,020; £509; £300; £300; £300) **Stalls** Centre

Form RPR

034 **1** **Theatro (IRE)**[32] 2875 3-9-7 **58** GrahamLee 3 77+
(Jedd O'Keeffe) *sn pushed along in tch: stdy hdwy to chse clr ldng pair 1/2-way: wnt 2nd 4f out: shkn up to ld 2f out: sn clr: eased last 100yds: readily* **5/2**[1]

0-00 **2** *12* **Langholm (IRE)**[31] 2913 3-8-6 **50**.....(t) CianMacRedmond(7) 4 46
(Declan Carroll) *led at decent gallop: clr over 4f out to over 3f out: hdd 2f out: no ch w v easy wnr* **13/2**

5-00 **3** *6* **Play It By Ear (IRE)**[23] 3198 3-9-10 **61**.....(t[1]) DanielTudhope 9 50
(David O'Meara) *hld up: pushed along and effrt 3f out: hung rt and chsd clr ldng pair 2f out: nvr able to chal* **7/2**[2]

0-65 **4** *2* **Geyser**[23] 3198 3-8-4 **46** ow1.....ConnorMurtagh(5) 1 29
(Barry Murtagh) *hld up: hdwy to chse clr ldng pair 3f out: sn edgd rt: outpcd fr 2f out* **12/1**

-002 **5** *5* **Ritchie Star (IRE)**[21] 3246 3-9-6 **57**.....AndrewMullen 2 32
(Ben Haslam) *t.k.h early: chsd clr ldng pair to 1/2-way: sn outpcd: rallied over 3f out: wknd over 2f out* **6/1**

6400 **6** *15* **Golden Grenade (FR)**[43] 2530 3-8-2 **46**.....RPWalsh(7) 5
(Ian Williams) *slowly away: bhd: drvn and struggling over 3f out: sn btn: t.o* **16/1**

2202 **7** *4 ½* **Rich Cummins**[23] 3198 3-9-10 **61**.....(b[1]) ConnorBeasley 7
(Mark Johnston) *pressed ldr and sn clr of rest: drvn and lost 2nd 4f out: wknd fr 3f out: t.o (trainer's rep could offer no explanation for the gelding's performance)* **4/1**[3]

6000 **8** *4 ½* **Amourie**[21] 3246 3-8-11 **48**.....CliffordLee 8
(Ray Craggs) *hld up: outpcd and rn wd bnd over 4f out: sn struggling: t.o* **28/1**

2m 39.64s (3.34) **Going Correction** +0.25s/f (Good) 8 Ran SP% **115.4**
Speed ratings (Par 97): **98,90,86,84,81 71,68,65**
CSF £19.60 CT £56.61 TOTE £3.80: £1.90, £1.60, £2.00; EX 20.10 Trifecta £76.00.
Owner Geoff & Sandra Turnbull **Bred** Elwick Stud **Trained** Middleham Moor, N Yorks

FOCUS
Add 6yds. The quicker division by 1.54sec, and again they finished well stretched out.
T/Plt: £37.30 to a £1 stake. Pool: £49,237.79 - 936.62 winning units T/Qpdt: £17.10 to a £1 stake. Pool: £4,385.48 - 189.75 winning units **Andrew Sheret**

4040 - 4047a (Foreign Racing) - See Raceform Interactive

4012
ROYAL ASCOT (R-H)
Friday, June 21

OFFICIAL GOING: Good to soft (soft in places on round course) changing to good (good to soft in places on round course) after race 3 (3.40)
Wind: Light, against Weather: Fine

4048 ALBANY STKS (GROUP 3) (FILLIES) 6f
2:30 (2:35) (Class 1) 2-Y-O

£51,039 (£19,350; £9,684; £4,824; £2,421; £1,215) **Stalls** Centre

Form RPR

1 **1** **Daahyeh**[34] 2836 2-9-0 0.....DavidEgan 14 105+
(Roger Varian) *athletic; looked wl; racd nr side: hld up in tch: clsd and swtchd rt ent fnl 2f: rdn to ld over 1f out: drvn 1f out: forged ahd and styd on strly wl ins fnl f: 1st of 18 in gp* **4/1**[1]

3 **2** *1 ½* **Celtic Beauty (IRE)**[33] 2881 2-9-0 0.....WJLee 16 100
(K J Condon, Ire) *leggy; racd nr side: hld up in tch in midfield: clsd travelling strly over 2f out: upsides wnr over 1f out: drvn 1f out: no ex and outpcd wl ins fnl f: 2nd of 18 in gp* **25/1**

424 **3** *1* **Aroha (IRE)**[28] 3033 2-9-0 0.....HarryBentley 3 97
(Brian Meehan) *leggy; racd far side: hld up in rr: effrt jst over 2f out: hdwy u.p to ld gp and chsd overall ldrs jst over 1f out: kpt on wl: 1st of 7 in gp* **100/1**

2 **4** *1* **Alabama Whitman**[25] 3165 2-9-0 0.....AdamKirby 17 94
(Richard Spencer) *unfurnished; racd nr side: hld up towards rr: swtchd rt and hdwy u.p over 1f out: kpt on wl ins fnl f: nt rch ldrs: 3rd of 18 in gp* **50/1**

5 *2 ¾* **Precious Moments (IRE)**[28] 3059 2-9-0 0.....RyanMoore 7 86+
(A P O'Brien, Ire) *athletic; racd far side: prom in gp and chsd ldrs overall: effrt ent fnl 2f: chsd gp ldr and drvn over 1f out: no imp fnl f: 2nd of 7 in gp* **10/1**

6 *shd* **Lil Grey (IRE)**[14] 3554 2-9-0 0.....RobbieColgan 25 85
(Ms Sheila Lavery, Ire) *leggy; racd nr side: hld up in midfield: swtchd rt over 2f out: chsd ldrs and hung rt 1f out: kpt on same pce ins fnl f: 4th of 18 in gp* **9/1**

7 *¾* **Lorelei Rock (IRE)**[17] 3455 2-9-0 0.....LeighRoche 15 83
(M D O'Callaghan, Ire) *str; racd nr side: in tch in midfield: rdn over 2f out: keeping on whn swtchd lft ins fnl f: kpt on but no threat to ldrs: 5th of 18 in gp* **66/1**

1 **8** *1 ½* **Silent Wave**[27] 3076 2-9-0 0.....JamesDoyle 10 79+
(Charlie Appleby) *racd nr side: chsd ldrs tl clsd and upsides ldr ent fnl 2f: unable qck over 1f out: wknd ins fnl f: 6th of 18 in gp* **14/1**

1 **9** *½* **Diligent Deb (IRE)**[11] 3660 2-9-0 0.....JasonWatson 4 77
(William Muir) *unfurnished; racd nr side: s.i.s: swtchd lft to join main gp and wl bhd: hdwy 1/2-way: no imp u.p over 1f out: 7th of 18 in gp* **66/1**

10 *hd* **Back To Brussels (IRE)**[28] 3060 2-9-0 0.....JamieSpencer 23 77
(J A Stack, Ire) *tall; racd nr side: stdd s: hld up in rr: clsd ent fnl 2f: u.p and no imp whn wnt lft 1f out: nvr involved: 8th of 18 in gp* **20/1**

5 **11** *hd* **So Wonderful (USA)**[33] 2881 2-9-0 0.....DonnachaO'Brien 21 77
(A P O'Brien, Ire) *str; looked wl; racd nr side: in tch in midfield: unable qck and outpcd over 1f out: btn whn short of room 1f out: 9th of 18 in gp* **10/1**

12 *nk* **Chili Petin (USA)**[65] 2-9-0 0.....(bt) JohnRVelazquez 11 75+
(Wesley A Ward, U.S.A) *str; ponied to s: racd nr side: overall ldr tl rdn and hdd over 1f out: wknd ins fnl f: 10th of 18 in gp* **22/1**

13 *nk* **Nayibeth (USA)**[65] 2-9-0 0.....(b) JoelRosario 1 74+
(Wesley A Ward, U.S.A) *tall; str; racd far side: gp ldr and chsd overall ldrs: rdn wl over 1f out: lost gp ld and btn jst over 1f out: sn btn and wknd ins fnl f: 3rd of 7 in gp* **8/1**[3]

4 **14** *nk* **Galadriel**[35] 2805 2-9-0 0.....AndreaAtzeni 22 73+
(Kevin Ryan) *compact; racd nr side: chsd ldrs tl lost pl u.p 2f out: sn btn and wknd fnl f: 11th of 18 in gp* **10/1**

261 **15** *hd* **Separate**[20] 3350 2-9-0 0.....SeanLevey 9 73
(Richard Hannon) *racd nr side: in tch in midfield: clsd u.p to chse ldrs 2f out: sn outpcd and wknd ins fnl f: 12th of 18 in gp* **33/1**

10 **16** *shd* **Fleeting Princess**[35] 2805 2-9-0 0.....JamesMcDonald 6 72
(Charles Hills) *compact; racd far side: midfield and in tch: effrt and swtchd lft over 1f out: fnd little and btn 1f out: wknd ins fnl f: 4th of 7 in gp* **80/1**

12 **17** *nk* **Exclusively**[54] 2138 2-9-0 0.....OisinMurphy 12 72+
(Archie Watson) *workmanlike; looked wl; racd nr side: chsd ldrs: unable qck u.p and outpcd over 1f out: wknd ins fnl f: 13th of 18 in gp* **16/1**

31 **18** *1 ¼* **Kemble (IRE)**[39] 2686 2-9-0 0.....PatDobbs 2 68
(Richard Hannon) *compact; racd far side: in tch in midfield: effrt ent fnl 2f: sn hung rt and outpcd over 1f out: wknd ins fnl f: 5th of 7 in gp* **25/1**

1 **19** *1* **Exceptional**[22] 3244 2-9-0 0.....TonyHamilton 24 65
(Richard Fahey) *str; racd nr side: a towards rr: nvr involved: 14th of 18 in gp* **20/1**

01 **20** *4* **Seraphinite (IRE)**[30] 2968 2-9-0 0.....NicolaCurrie 5 53
(Jamie Osborne) *leggy; racd far side: in tch in midfield: effrt u.p 2f out: sn no imp and wknd ins fnl f: 6th of 7 in gp* **100/1**

0 **21** *½* **Get The Look (IRE)**[17] 3441 2-9-0 0.....(p[1]) LukeMorris 26 51?
(J S Moore) *workmanlike; racd nr side: s.i.s: a in rr: wl bhd and hung rt over 2f out: 15th of 18 in gp* **150/1**

1 **22** *½* **Graceful Magic**[22] 3259 2-9-0 0.....CharlesBishop 18 50
(Eve Johnson Houghton) *workmanlike; racd nr side: in tch in midfield: u.p 1/2-way: lost pl and bhd ins fnl f: 16th of 18 in gp* **100/1**

22 **23** *shd* **Jm Jackson (IRE)**[29] 3023 2-9-0 0.....SilvestreDeSousa 20 49+
(Mark Johnston) *str; racd nr side: chsd ldrs: rdn 2f out: sn struggling and lost pl: bhd ins fnl f: 17th of 18 in gp* **14/1**

3 **24** *¾* **Moon Of Love (IRE)**[13] 3564 2-9-0 0.....BarryMcHugh 8 47
(Richard Fahey) *workmanlike; racd far side: t.k.h: chsd gp ldr and prom overall: lost pl wl over 1f out: bhd ins fnl f: 7th of 7 in gp* **33/1**

1 **25** *2 ¾* **Last Surprise (IRE)**[17] 3441 2-9-0 0.....FrankieDettori 19 39+
(Simon Crisford) *leggy; athletic; racd nr side: chsd ldr tl over 2f out: lost pl over 1f out: bhd ins fnl f: 18th of 18 in gp (jockey said filly stopped quickly)* **6/1**[2]

1m 14.05s (0.35) **Going Correction** +0.05s/f (Good) **25** Ran SP% **139.1**
Speed ratings (Par 100): **99,97,95,94,90 90,89,87,86,86 86,85,85,85,84 84,84,82,81,76 75,74,74,73,69**
CSF £119.18 CT £8930.57 TOTE £4.90: £2.40, £7.00, £44.20; EX 155.90 Trifecta £12546.20.
Owner H H SH Nasser Bin Hamad Al Khalifa **Bred** D J And Mrs Deer **Trained** Newmarket, Suffolk

FOCUS
There was 10mm of rain on Wednesday but it had been mainly dry since and it was a sunny, reasonably warm day. A huge field for this year's Albany - the biggest in the race's history, dating back to 2002 - and they split into two groups, with the larger bunch, middle to stands' side, having the edge over those far side. The second, third, fourth and fifth were maidens coming into this so it's hard to get excited by the form, but the winner is smart and there are some promising types among the beaten runners.

4049 KING EDWARD VII STKS (GROUP 2) (C&G) 1m 3f 211y
3:05 (3:05) (Class 1) 3-Y-O

£127,597 (£48,375; £24,210; £12,060; £6,052; £3,037) **Stalls** Low

Form RPR

1-43 **1** **Japan**[20] 3345 3-9-0 **117**.....RyanMoore 2 120+
(A P O'Brien, Ire) *sweating; hld up: hdwy on outer over 3f out: led wl over 1f out: sn edgd rt: powered clr fnl f: r.o wl* **6/4**[1]

-110 **2** *4 ½* **Bangkok (IRE)**[20] 3345 3-9-0 **104**.....SilvestreDeSousa 5 112
(Andrew Balding) *hld up in last: hdwy on inner 3f out: nt clr run jst after: effrt over 2f out: sn ev ch: nt gng pce of wnr over 1f out: kpt on same pce ins fnl f whn no ch: jst doing enough cl home to hold 2nd* **10/1**

-216 **3** *nk* **Eagles By Day (IRE)**[41] 2619 3-9-0 **93**.....DanielTudhope 4 111
(Michael Bell) *str; looked wl; hld up: nt clr run briefly over 3f out: rdn and hdwy over 2f out: swtchd rt: drvn to chse ldrs over 1f out: tk 3rd fnl 150yds: styng on whn swtchd lft fnl 75yds: clsd on 2nd towards fin (vet reported colt lost its left-fore shoe)* **25/1**

-111 **4** *2 ½* **Private Secretary**[28] 3042 3-9-0 **106**.....FrankieDettori 3 107
(John Gosden) *midfield: hdwy over 3f out: effrt on outer over 2f out: sn led: hdd wl over 1f out: outpcd by ldrs ins fnl f: styd on same pce whn no ch* **9/2**[3]

1-22 **5** *1 ¼* **Pablo Escobarr (IRE)**[41] 2619 3-9-0 **103**.....(t) JamesDoyle 6 105
(William Haggas) *sweating; trckd ldrs: pushed along over 3f out: effrt on outer sn after: rdn and ev ch 2f out: unable qck over 1f out: kpt on same pce ins fnl f* **13/2**

411 **6** *9* **Pondus**[22] 3263 3-9-0 **98**.....OisinMurphy 8 91
(James Fanshawe) *str; racd keenly: prom: chsd ldr after 3f: rdn to ld wl over 2f out: sn hdd: wknd over 1f out (jockey said colt ran too free)* **4/1**[2]

1-10 **7** *1 ¼* **Humanitarian (USA)**[20] 3345 3-9-0 **107**.....RobertHavlin 1 89
(John Gosden) *looked wl; racd keenly: prom: plld off inner rail 1/2-way: n.m.r and lost pl over 3f out: bhd fr over 2f out* **12/1**

8 *33* **Jack Yeats (IRE)**[53] 2225 3-9-0 **92**.....DonnachaO'Brien 7 36
(A P O'Brien, Ire) *str; led: rdn and hdd wl over 2f out: sn wknd: eased whn wl btn over 1f out* **16/1**

2m 29.16s (-3.44) **Going Correction** +0.05s/f (Good) **8** Ran SP% **118.0**
Speed ratings (Par 111): **113,110,109,108,107 101,100,78**
CSF £19.11 CT £275.83 TOTE £1.95: £1.01, £3.05, £6.45; EX 16.20 Trifecta £202.60.
Owner Derrick Smith & Mrs John Magnier & Michael Tabor **Bred** Newsells Park Stud **Trained** Cashel, Co Tipperary
■ Stewards' Enquiry : Frankie Dettori three-day ban: careless riding (tba)

FOCUS
They went a good gallop and finished in roughly the opposite order to that they raced. The favourite put up a commanding performance and the form looks solid.

4050 COMMONWEALTH CUP (GROUP 1) (BRITISH CHAMPIONS SERIES) 6f
3:40 (3:43) (Class 1) 3-Y-O

£283,550 (£107,500; £53,800; £26,800; £13,450; £6,750) **Stalls** Centre

Form RPR

12-0 **1** **Advertise**[48] 2411 3-9-3 **119**.....(b[1]) FrankieDettori 4 121
(Martyn Meade) *looked wl; hld up in tch: clsd jst over 2f out: rdn to chal and edgd lft over 1f out: led jst ins fnl f: styd on strly* **8/1**

0-51 **2** *1 ½* **Forever In Dreams (IRE)**[27] 3085 3-9-0 **98**.....OisinMurphy 5 113
(Aidan F Fogarty, Ire) *bmpd leaving stalls: chsd ldr: rdn to ld over 1f out: hdd jst ins fnl f: no ex and outpcd towards fin* **20/1**

1-41 **3** *hd* **Hello Youmzain (FR)**[27] 3083 3-9-3 113 KevinStott 6 116
(Kevin Ryan) *looked wl; restless in stalls: in tch in last trio: pushed along and clsd 2f out: drvn and chsd ldrs 1f out: kpt on u.p ins fnl f* **6/1**[3]

11-5 **4** *¾* **Ten Sovereigns (IRE)**[48] 2411 3-9-3 120 RyanMoore 3 113
(A P O'Brien, Ire) *looked wl; wl in tch in midfield: niggled along 1/2-way: drvn to chse ldng trio and swtchd rt 1f out: kpt on ins fnl f but nvr enough pce to rch ldrs: swtchd rt towards fin* **1/1**[1]

2-43 **5** *6* **Royal Intervention (IRE)**[27] 3083 3-9-0 99 GeraldMosse 1 91
(Ed Walker) *led: shkn up 2f out: rdn and hdd over 1f out: no ex and wknd ins fnl f* **50/1**

12-1 **6** *nk* **Jash (IRE)**[34] 2834 3-9-3 118 JimCrowley 9 93
(Simon Crisford) *looked wl; in tch in last trio: effrt 2f out: no imp over 1f out and outpcd whn hung rt 1f out: wl hld fnl f* **5/1**[2]

11-1 **7** *1¼* **Khaadem (IRE)**[34] 2826 3-9-3 107 DaneO'Neill 8 89
(Charles Hills) *mounted in chute: in rr: effrt 2f out: no imp u.p over 1f out: wl btn fnl f* **7/1**

6-30 **8** *nk* **Konchek**[34] 2826 3-9-3 100 (t[1]) AdamKirby 2 88
(Clive Cox) *edgy; chsd ldng pair: effrt 2f out: sn outpcd and btn whn hung lft jst over 1f out: wknd ins fnl f* **50/1**

103- **9** *3¼* **Rumble Inthejungle (IRE)**[265] 7772 3-9-3 110 JamesDoyle 7 78
(Richard Spencer) *broke wl: restrained: wnt rt and bmpd leaving stalls: wl in tch in midfield and t.k.h: nt qckn u.p: lost pl and btn whn hung rt over 1f out: wknd fnl f* **16/1**

1m 11.88s (-1.82) **Going Correction** +0.05s/f (Good) **9** Ran SP% **119.1**
Speed ratings (Par 113): **114,112,111,110,102 102,100,100,95**
CSF £148.76 CT £1030.66 TOTE £8.75: £2.20, £4.30, £1.90; EX 152.90 Trifecta £962.70.
Owner Phoenix Thoroughbred Limited 1 **Bred** Cheveley Park Stud Ltd **Trained** Manton, Wilts

FOCUS
The ground on the straight track was upgraded to good following this race. Now in its fifth year, this was the smallest field yet for the Commonwealth Cup, with Calyx a notable absentee, but it was still a solid enough edition featuring two previous Group 1 winners. They all raced up the middle.

4051 CORONATION STKS (GROUP 1) (BRITISH CHAMPIONS SERIES) (FILLIES) 7f 213y(R)
4:20 (4:20) (Class 1) 3-Y-O

£283,550 (£107,500; £53,800; £26,800; £13,450; £6,750) Stalls Low

Form RPR

1-16 **1** **Watch Me (FR)**[40] 2669 3-9-0 104 Pierre-CharlesBoudot 9 117
(F-H Graffard, France) *str; trckd ldrs: led over 1f out: edgd rt ins fnl f: r.o wl: rdn out* **20/1**

2-11 **2** *1½* **Hermosa (IRE)**[26] 3115 3-9-0 118 RyanMoore 10 113
(A P O'Brien, Ire) *chsd ldr: rdn to draw level over 2f out: led briefly wl over 1f out: kpt on u.p ins fnl f but nt pce of wnr* **1/1**[1]

-11 **3** *1* **Jubiloso**[35] 2794 3-9-0 101 JamesMcDonald 5 111
(Sir Michael Stoute) *str; looked wl; midfield: hdwy 2f out: effrt to chse ldrs over 1f out: nvr able to chal wnr: styd on same pce fnl 100yds* **9/2**[2]

-212 **4** *1* **Twist 'N' Shake**[35] 2806 3-9-0 104 FrankieDettori 1 109
(John Gosden) *midfield: pushed along over 2f out: effrt over 1f out: kpt on u.p ins fnl f: nvr able to chal* **7/1**

11 **5** *¾* **Castle Lady (IRE)**[40] 2669 3-9-0 111 MickaelBarzalona 8 107
(H-A Pantall, France) *compact; hld up: pushed along over 2f out: hung rt u.p fr over 1f out: kpt on ins fnl f: nvr able to trble ldrs* **6/1**[3]

21 **6** *2* **Happen (USA)**[46] 2493 3-9-0 103 (t) DonnachaO'Brien 4 102
(A P O'Brien, Ire) *str; looked wl; hld up in rr: pushed along over 2f out: rdn over 1f out: kpt on towards fin: nvr able to get competitive* **16/1**

43-2 **7** *½* **Pretty Pollyanna**[26] 3115 3-9-0 116 SilvestreDeSousa 3 101
(Michael Bell) *looked wl; led: rdn and jnd over 2f out: hdd wl over 1f out: wknd ins fnl f* **10/1**

4-60 **8** *4* **Just Wonderful (USA)**[26] 3115 3-9-0 109 SeamieHeffernan 6 92
(A P O'Brien, Ire) *hld up: pushed along over 1f out: nvr threatened: eased whn wl hld fnl 100yds* **20/1**

3-01 **9** *6* **Main Edition (IRE)**[26] 3119 3-9-0 107 OisinMurphy 7 78
(Mark Johnston) *trckd ldrs: rdn over 2f out: wknd over 1f out (starter reported the filly was the subject of a third criteria failure; trainer was informed that the filly could not run until the day after passing a stalls test)* **33/1**

1m 39.61s (-0.99) **Going Correction** +0.05s/f (Good) **9** Ran SP% **122.4**
Speed ratings (Par 110): **106,104,103,102,101 99,99,95,89**
CSF £42.19 CT £123.19 TOTE £33.35: £5.15, £1.05, £1.75; EX 82.10 Trifecta £506.60.
Owner Alexander Tamagni **Bred** Mme A Tamagni & Cocheese Bloodstock Anstalt **Trained** France

FOCUS
This was run at a fair gallop and looks sound enough form. It's been rated as an average renewal.

4052 SANDRINGHAM STKS (H'CAP) (FILLIES) 1m (S)
5:00 (5:01) (Class 2) (0-105,105) 3-Y-O

£56,025 (£16,776; £8,388; £4,194; £2,097; £1,053) Stalls Centre

Form RPR

5-22 **1** **Thanks Be**[31] 2935 3-8-0 84 oh4 HayleyTurner 4 92
(Charlie Fellowes) *hld up in rr: clsd and nt clr run over 1f out: swtchd lft and hdwy to ld jst over 1f out: hld on wl u.str.p towards fin* **33/1**

64-1 **2** *nk* **Magnetic Charm**[35] 2806 3-9-7 105 JamesDoyle 11 112
(William Haggas) *looked wl; hld up in tch in midfield: effrt whn nudged rt and then swtchd rt 2f out: swtchd rt again over 1f out: clsd to chal u.p 1f out: pressing wnr and kpt on wl fnl 150yds* **7/1**[2]

311 **3** *1¼* **Hotsy Totsy (IRE)**[30] 2967 3-8-7 91 ow1 JamieSpencer 18 95
(Ed Walker) *looked wl; heavily restrained leaving stalls: hld up in rr: clsd and nt clr run 2f out: effrt and swtchd lft over 1f out: sn hung rt but r.o wl ins fnl f to go 3rd last strides: nvr getting to ldrs* **7/1**[2]

1-00 **4** *hd* **Coral Beach (IRE)**[26] 3115 3-9-2 100 (t) RyanMoore 28 103
(A P O'Brien, Ire) *in rr: effrt ent fnl 2f: hdwy u.p over 1f out: styd on wl ins fnl f to chse ldng pair wl ins fnl f: nvr getting to ldrs and lost 3rd last strides* **10/1**

4-54 **5** *1* **Model Guest**[41] 2608 3-8-7 91 BarryMcHugh 26 92
(George Margarson) *hld up towards rr: effrt over 2f out: hdwy u.p over 1f out: kpt on ins fnl f: nvr getting on terms w ldrs* **50/1**

061- **6** *½* **California Love**[218] 9065 3-8-3 87 JosephineGordon 23 87+
(Richard Spencer) *chsd ldrs: ev ch u.p over 1f out: led 1f out: sn hdd: no ex and wknd wl ins fnl f* **66/1**

21-1 **7** *¾* **Desirous**[28] 3041 3-8-4 88 HarryBentley 25 86
(Ralph Beckett) *hld up in tch in midfield: swtchd lft and effrt over 2f out: sn u.p and hung rt: clsd to chse ldrs 1f out: no ex and wknd wl ins fnl f* **11/2**[1]

0-31 **8** *½* **Whimbrel (IRE)**[15] 3495 3-8-0 84 oh4 DavidEgan 5 81+
(John Gosden) *in tch in midfield: effrt over 2f out: clsd u.p to chse ldrs 1f out: no ex and outpcd ins fnl f* **16/1**

4 **9** *1¾* **Aim Power (IRE)**[31] 2934 3-8-6 90 SilvestreDeSousa 6 83+
(Richard Hannon) *in tch in midfield: effrt 2f out: nt clr run and swtchd rt over 1f out: sme prog u.p 1f out: sn no imp and one pce ins fnl f* **40/1**

21-6 **10** *½* **Spanish Aria**[16] 3468 3-8-0 84 oh2 NickyMackay 7 76
(John Gosden) *hld up in midfield: effrt 2f out: styd on ins fnl f: no threat to ldrs* **25/1**

0-02 **11** *½* **No Way Jose (IRE)**[24] 3193 3-8-3 87 FrannyNorton 3 78
(Brian Meehan) *in tch in midfield: effrt over 2f out: clsd u.p to chse ldrs over 1f out: no ex 1f out and wknd ins fnl f* **50/1**

-635 **12** *½* **Modern Millie**[35] 2806 3-8-10 94 RonanWhelan 1 84
(Mick Channon) *hld up towards rr: swtchd rt and nt clr run 2f out: swtchd lft over 1f out: rdn and kpt on and wnt between rivals ins fnl f: nvr trbld ldrs* **40/1**

2221 **13** *½* **Maamora (IRE)**[15] 3517 3-8-4 88 WayneLordan 9 76
(Simon Crisford) *t.k.h: w ldrs: rdn and ev ch over 1f out: no ex 1f out: sn wknd* **14/1**

1512 **14** *shd* **I'm Available (IRE)**[42] 2569 3-8-3 87 MartinDwyer 12 75
(Andrew Balding) *w ldrs tl led over 5f out: rdn wl over 1f out: hdd jst over 1f out: sn wknd* **8/1**[3]

1-20 **15** *hd* **Kimblewick (IRE)**[34] 2831 3-8-0 84 KieranO'Neill 10 72
(John Gosden) *str; looked wl; trckd ldrs: effrt 2f out: struggling to qckn whn pushed rt over 1f out: no prog and wl hld after* **50/1**

3-10 **16** *½* **Ice Gala**[20] 3359 3-8-11 95 JamesMcDonald 17 82
(William Haggas) *in tch in midfield: effrt wl over 1f out: no imp and btn 1f out: wknd ins fnl f* **16/1**

3-03 **17** *1¾* **Gypsy Spirit**[46] 2498 3-8-11 95 LukeMorris 21 77
(Tom Clover) *bmpd s: in tch in midfield: effrt 2f out: no prog u.p and btn whn short of room over 1f out: wknd ins fnl f* **25/1**

-124 **18** *1¾* **Star Of War (USA)**[43] 2552 3-8-0 84 oh2 JimmyQuinn 2 62
(Richard Hannon) *in tch in midfield: effrt over 2f out: unable qck and btn over 1f out: wknd ins fnl f* **66/1**

22-0 **19** *nse* **Stay Classy (IRE)**[69] 1751 3-9-0 98 (h) AdamKirby 27 76
(Richard Spencer) *hld up towards rr: clsd and nt clr run 2f out: no prog u.p over 1f out: wknd ins fnl f* **25/1**

2-10 **20** *2¼* **El Gumryah (IRE)**[35] 2806 3-8-7 91 MickaelBarzalona 14 64
(Simon Crisford) *led for over 2f: styd pressing ldrs: ev ch and rdn ent fnl 2f: sn outpcd* **66/1**

0-11 **21** *nk* **Invitational**[66] 1838 3-8-8 92 AndreaAtzeni 19 64
(Roger Varian) *str; looked wl; in tch in midfield: effrt 2f out: sn outpcd and wl btn over 1f out* **12/1**

14-1 **22** *nk* **Lady Madison (IRE)**[53] 2210 3-8-7 91 ShaneKelly 16 63
(Richard Hughes) *sweating; hld up in tch: clsd: nt clrest of runs and edgd rt ent fnl 2f: no hdwy u.p over 1f out: wknd fnl f* **14/1**

0-46 **23** *1* **Concello (IRE)**[20] 3359 3-8-7 91 (b) HollieDoyle 24 60
(Archie Watson) *t.k.h: chsd ldrs tl over 2f out: sn dropped out: bhd fnl f* **100/1**

411 **24** *3½* **Nonchalance**[13] 3603 3-8-7 91 RobertHavlin 13 52
(John Gosden) *compact; trckd ldrs: effrt 2f out: unable qck and btn over 1f out: eased ins fnl f (trainer said filly may be suited by a return to 7f)* **8/1**[3]

-16 **25** *5* **Flighty Almighty**[35] 2806 3-8-0 87 (p[1]) JaneElliott(3) 8 37
(Tom Dascombe) *chsd ldrs tl over 2f out: sn dropped out u.p: bhd fnl f* **33/1**

6-01 **26** *nk* **Layaleena (IRE)**[31] 2934 3-8-7 91 JimCrowley 15 40
(Sir Michael Stoute) *in tch in midfield: shortlived effrt over 2f out: sn btn and eased ins fnl f (trainer could offer no explanation for the filly's performance)* **10/1**

1-05 **27** *4½* **Garrel Glen**[29] 3012 3-8-8 92 RichardKingscote 22 31
(Mark H Tompkins) *wnt rt s: in tch in midfield: rdn over 2f out: sn lost pl: bhd over 1f out* **50/1**

1m 39.61s (-1.79) **Going Correction** +0.05s/f (Good) **27** Ran SP% **149.2**
Speed ratings (Par 102): **110,109,108,108,107 106,106,105,103,103 102,102,101,101,101 100,99,97,97,95 94,94,93,90,85 84**
CSF £268.17 CT £1905.11 TOTE £45.95: £8.85, £2.30, £2.15, £2.70; EX 349.50 Trifecta £4166.00.
Owner Mrs Emma Capon **Bred** Deveron Limited **Trained** Newmarket, Suffolk
■ Stewards' Enquiry : James Doyle two-day ban: used whip in incorrect place
Hayley Turner £1,600 fine & nine-day ban: used whip above permitted level (Jul 5-13)

FOCUS
This race lost its Listed status last year but still attracted loads of runners and was tremendously competitive. There were two groups early but the field soon merged, with the main action up the middle, and it set up for those ridden patiently. The winner rates as a big improver.

4053 DUKE OF EDINBURGH STKS (H'CAP) 1m 3f 211y
5:35 (5:37) (Class 2) (0-105,105) 3-Y-O+

£56,025 (£16,776; £8,388; £4,194; £2,097; £1,053) Stalls Low

Form RPR

1-31 **1** **Baghdad (FR)**[47] 2440 4-9-8 104 RyanMoore 12 114
(Mark Johnston) *midfield: hdwy over 3f out: rdn over 2f out: led over 1f out: styd on and edgd rt ins fnl f: all out towards fin: gamely jst hld on* **7/2**[1]

033- **2** *shd* **Ben Vrackie**[252] 8149 4-9-8 104 FrankieDettori 14 113+
(John Gosden) *looked wl; missed break: hld up in rr: rdn and hdwy on outer over 2f out: styd on strly ins fnl f: edgd rt: tk 2nd fnl 75yds: clsd on wnr towards fin: jst failed* **7/1**[3]

1-12 **3** *1½* **Fujaira Prince (IRE)**[37] 2742 5-9-3 99 AndreaAtzeni 11 106
(Roger Varian) *prom early: lost pl after 4f: in tch: pushed along over 3f out: nt clr run and swtchd lft 3f out: sn rdn: swtchd rt ent fnl 2f: chsd ldrs over 1f out: styd on u.p: nt pce of front two fnl 75yds* **4/1**[2]

26-3 **4** *1¼* **Corgi**[37] 2742 4-9-3 99 JimCrowley 9 104
(Hughie Morrison) *in tch: effrt over 2f out: rdn and ev ch over 1f out: unable qck ins fnl f: styd on same pce fnl 100yds* **7/1**[3]

0-14 **5** *nk* **Collide**[37] 2742 4-9-3 99 (t) JamesMcDonald 2 104
(Hugo Palmer) *looked wl; hld up: rdn and hdwy over 2f out: chsd ldrs over 1f out: styd on towards fin* **14/1**

660- **6** *½* **Downdraft (IRE)**[27] 3106 4-9-3 99 (t) DavidEgan 3 103
(Joseph Patrick O'Brien, Ire) *dwlt: towards rr: hdwy on inner over 2f out: sn nt clr run and swtchd lft: styd on ins fnl f: nvr able to chal* **28/1**

2010 **7** *1* **Aquarium**[20] 3346 4-9-7 103 FrannyNorton 18 105
(Mark Johnston) *hld up: nt clr run and hdwy over 2f out: sn angled lft: styd on ins fnl f: nvr able to rch ldrs* **40/1**

1-02 **8** *nse* **Byron Flyer**[20] 3346 8-9-9 **105** (v[1]) MickaelBarzalona 22 107
(Ian Williams) *sn led: rdn and hdd over 1f out: nt pce of ldrs ins fnl f: styd on same pce fnl 100yds* **25/1**

0- **9** *3/4* **Arthurian Fame (IRE)**[35] 2816 4-9-4 **100** DonnachaO'Brien 4 101
(Joseph Patrick O'Brien, Ire) *midfield: hdwy whn forced wd on bnd wl over 2f out: chsd ldrs styng on for press over 1f out: no ex fnl 75yds* **14/1**

-452 **10** *1/2* **Lucius Tiberius (IRE)**[35] 2808 4-9-6 **102** BrettDoyle 20 102
(Charlie Appleby) *prom early: chsd ldrs after: nt clr run whn swtchd lft and lost pl 3f out: rallied over 2f out: wl there over 1f out: no ex fnl 100yds* **25/1**

040- **11** *3 1/2* **Lethal Steps**[24] 7347 4-9-6 **102** JamieSpencer 16 96
(Gordon Elliott, Ire) *hld up: rdn over 2f out: hdwy whn nt clr run over 1f out: swtchd rt ent fnl f: styd on wout troubling ldrs* **33/1**

351/ **12** *2* **Secret Advisor (FR)**[664] 6445 5-9-7 **103** JamesDoyle 1 94
(Charlie Appleby) *midfield: rdn over 2f out: no imp: edgd lft ins fnl f: nvr a danger* **12/1**

13 *2* **Johnny Drama (IRE)**[39] 2700 4-9-2 **98** ColinKeane 8 86
(G M Lyons, Ire) *broke wl: handy: trckd ldrs after 4f: effrt over 2f out: unable qck: wknd over 1f out (trainer said colt may have been unsuited by the step up in trip)* **10/1**

30-5 **14** *nk* **Top Tug (IRE)**[34] 2827 8-9-5 **101** TomMarquand 17 89
(Alan King) *looked wl; midfield: pushed along over 3f out: rdn over 2f out: one pce fr over 1f out: no imp* **20/1**

1-23 **15** *3 1/2* **Spark Plug (IRE)**[63] 1917 8-9-7 **103** (p) OisinMurphy 7 85
(Brian Meehan) *midfield: rdn over 2f out: no imp* **33/1**

060- **16** *13* **Temple Church (IRE)**[223] 9005 5-9-2 **98** RichardKingscote 6 59
(Hughie Morrison) *midfield: pushed along over 3f out: effrt to chse ldrs over 2f out: wknd over 1f out* **66/1**

01- **17** *1 3/4* **Kasperenko**[228] 8883 5-9-2 **98** (b) AdamKirby 10 56
(Clive Cox) *in rr: sn pushed along: swtchd lft u.p over 2f out: hung rt over 1f out: nvr a threat* **20/1**

-664 **18** *9* **Pivoine (IRE)**[34] 2827 5-9-8 **104** (v) SilvestreDeSousa 5 48
(Andrew Balding) *prom: rdn and wknd 2f out: eased whn wl btn over 1f out* **33/1**

00-0 **19** *17* **Sevenna Star (IRE)**[35] 2807 4-9-6 **102** (t) GeraldMosse 15 19
(John Ryan) *chsd ldrs: rdn and losing pl whn n.m.r and hmpd over 3f out: bhd fnl 2f* **100/1**

2m 30.57s (-2.03) **Going Correction** +0.05s/f (Good) **19** Ran SP% **131.7**
Speed ratings (Par 109): **108,107,106,106,105 105,104,104,104,104 101,100,99,98,96 87,86,80,69**
CSF £25.78 CT £110.16 TOTE £4.70: £1.60, £2.45, £1.70, £1.75; EX 32.90 Trifecta £146.90.
Owner Mohammed Bin Hamad Khalifa Al Attiya **Bred** S C E A Haras De Saint Pair Et Al **Trained** Middleham Moor, N Yorks

FOCUS
The right horses came to the fore in this competitive handicap. The first two and fifth are all sired by Frankel, who has a good record with his runners on the Round course here. This rates a pb from the winner, a minor Group-class performance on the figures.
T/Jkpt: Not Won T/Plt: £173.50 to a £1 stake. Pool: £554,519.27 - 2,332.05 winning units T/Qpdt: £24.20 to a £1 stake. Pool: £38,948.97 - 1,189.65 winning units **Steve Payne/Darren Owen**

3175 **AYR** (L-H)
Friday, June 21

OFFICIAL GOING: Good (good to firm in places; 8.0)
Wind: Breezy, half against in sprints and in over 3f of home straight in races on the round course Weather: Fine, dry

4054 ISLE OF JURA AMATEUR RIDERS' H'CAP — 1m 2f
5:55 (5:57) (Class 6) (0-65,67) 4-Y-O+
£2,994 (£928; £464; £400; £400; £400) **Stalls High**

Form RPR

2-04 **1** **Remember Rocky**[24] 3181 10-10-9 **58** (b) MissAbbieMcCain 1 65
(Lucy Normile) *trckd ldrs: effrt and wnt 2nd over 1f out: led ins fnl f: kpt on wl* **25/1**

1311 **2** *nk* **Jackhammer (IRE)**[10] 3682 5-11-0 **63** 5ex (bt) MissEmmaSayer 10 69
(Dianne Sayer) *t.k.h: prom: smooth hdwy to ld over 2f out: pushed along and edgd lft over 1f out: hdd ins fnl f: one pce* **6/4**[1]

51-0 **3** *3/4* **Firby (IRE)**[15] 3511 4-10-11 **67** MissRachelTaylor(7) 8 74
(Michael Dods) *dwlt: t.k.h: hld up: stdy hdwy whn n.m.r: stmbld and nrly uns rdr over 1f out: angled rt: nudged along and kpt on wl fnl f: unlucky (jockey said gelding was denied a clear run and clipped heels 2f out)* **10/1**

0060 **4** *1 3/4* **Remmy D (IRE)**[17] 3448 4-10-10 **59** (p) MrJamesHarding 13 61
(Jim Goldie) *hld up in midfield on outside: effrt over 2f out: edgd lft over 1f out: kpt on same pce ins fnl f* **18/1**

0150 **5** *1 3/4* **King Of Naples**[13] 3568 6-10-7 **61** (h) MissEmilyBullock(5) 12 60
(Ruth Carr) *t.k.h: hld up: hdwy and prom over 2f out: rdn over 1f out: edgd lft and one pce ins fnl f* **8/1**

6436 **6** *1/2* **Home Before Dusk**[10] 3705 4-10-4 **60** MrEireannCagney(7) 2 58
(Keith Dalgleish) *dwlt: sn midfield: effrt and pushed along over 2f out: kpt on same pce fnl f* **7/1**[3]

00-3 **7** *3/4* **Bollin Ted**[23] 3217 5-10-12 **61** MrWilliamEasterby 11 58
(Tim Easterby) *prom: pushed along over 2f out: edgd lft and outpcd ins fnl f* **11/2**[2]

-005 **8** *1 1/4* **Haymarket**[24] 3181 10-10-1 **50** (t) MrsCarolBartley 5 44
(R Mike Smith) *led to over 2f out: rdn and wknd over 1f out* **14/1**

3560 **9** *2 3/4* **Testa Rossa (IRE)**[30] 2963 9-11-0 **63** MissCatherineWalton 4 52
(Jim Goldie) *sn bhd: outpcd over 2f out: nvr rchd ldrs* **12/1**

-000 **10** *2 1/2* **Let Right Be Done**[30] 2963 7-9-10 **45** (p[1]) MissBeckySmith 3 30
(Linda Perratt) *trckd ldr: ev ch over 2f out: rdn and wknd fnl f* **40/1**

-000 **11** *5* **Judith Gardenier**[2] 4004 7-9-10 **45** (tp) MissAmieWaugh 7 21
(R Mike Smith) *hld up: pushed along and struggling over 2f out: sn btn (vet said mare lost its left fore shoe)* **66/1**

0P-0 **12** *8* **Indie Groove (IRE)**[23] 3225 4-9-8 **48** MissAmyCollier(5) 6 9
(Linda Perratt) *slowly away: bhd: struggling over 3f out: btn fnl 2f* **100/1**

2m 9.86s (-2.54) **Going Correction** -0.35s/f (Firm) **12** Ran SP% **116.5**
Speed ratings (Par 101): **96,95,95,93,92 91,91,90,88,86 82,75**
CSF £61.10 CT £430.54 TOTE £25.30: £6.60, £1.10, £2.80; EX 76.10 Trifecta £600.70.
Owner The Silver Tops **Bred** Cherry Park Stud **Trained** Duncrievie, Perth & Kinross

FOCUS
Add 15 yards. Not a bad renewal of this amateur riders' handicap.

4055 GUINNESS NOVICE STKS — 1m 1f 20y
6:30 (6:31) (Class 5) 3-Y-O+
£3,752 (£1,116; £557; £278) **Stalls High**

Form RPR

30/ **1** **Match Maker (IRE)**[727] 4068 4-9-13 0 (t) GrahamLee 1 82+
(Simon Crisford) *sn in tch on ins: effrt over 2f out: led 1f out: kpt on wl* **6/4**[1]

13 **2** *nk* **Alright Sunshine (IRE)**[16] 3482 4-10-4 0 ShaneGray 10 86+
(Keith Dalgleish) *sn trcking ldr: led over 2f out: sn pushed along and hung lft: hdd 1f out: rallied: hld nr fin* **7/4**[2]

6-6 **3** *3/4* **Memphis Bleek**[62] 1956 3-9-2 0 (p[1]) DavidNolan 8 78
(Ivan Furtado) *prom: effrt and rdn over 2f out: kpt on ins fnl f* **20/1**

433 **4** *1 1/2* **Noble Prospector (IRE)**[23] 3218 3-9-2 76 PaulHanagan 4 78+
(Richard Fahey) *t.k.h early: trckd ldrs: effrt and ev ch over 2f out to over 1f out: 3rd and one pce whn short of room wl ins fnl f* **3/1**[3]

30 **5** *12* **Clovenstone**[22] 3248 3-8-13 0 JamieGormley(3) 6 49
(Alistair Whillans) *bhd: rdn over 3f out: hdwy fnl f: nvr rchd ldrs* **20/1**

0-0 **6** *1/2* **Philyaboots**[22] 3248 3-9-2 0 TomEaves 3 48
(Donald McCain) *bhd: pushed along and hdwy wl over 1f out: sn hung lft: no imp fnl f* **100/1**

-050 **7** *2 3/4* **Wontgetfooledagen (IRE)**[106] 1066 3-9-2 38 (t) PaddyMathers 2 41
(Rebecca Menzies) *midfield: drvn and outpcd over 2f out: sn btn* **100/1**

60 **8** *1/2* **Tanaawol**[22] 3248 3-8-11 0 AndrewBreslin(5) 7 40
(Mark Johnston) *t.k.h: led to over 2f out: sn rdn and wknd (jockey said colt hung right)* **33/1**

0 **9** *7* **Indiaro**[15] 3499 3-9-2 0 JamesSullivan 5 25
(Linda Perratt) *hld up: drvn and outpcd over 2f out: sn btn* **100/1**

00 **10** *22* **Ayr Poet**[10] 3680 4-9-13 0 (h) PhilDennis 9
(Jim Goldie) *s.i.s: bhd: struggling over 3f out: t.o* **100/1**

1m 55.97s (-4.23) **Going Correction** -0.35s/f (Firm)
WFA 3 from 4yo 11lb **10** Ran SP% **117.8**
Speed ratings (Par 103): **104,103,103,101,91 90,88,87,81,61**
CSF £4.24 TOTE £2.40: £1.10, £1.30, £3.70; EX 5.00 Trifecta £31.20.
Owner Mrs Doreen Tabor **Bred** Lofts Hall Stud **Trained** Newmarket, Suffolk
■ Stewards' Enquiry : Shane Gray two-day ban: interference & careless riding (Jul 5, 7)

FOCUS
Add 15 yards. An informative race and the first four pulled a long way clear. The winner has been rated close to his debut form.

4056 COCA COLA H'CAP — 1m 7f
7:05 (7:05) (Class 5) (0-70,72) 4-Y-O+
£3,752 (£1,116; £557; £400; £400; £400) **Stalls High**

Form RPR

336 **1** **Trautmann (IRE)**[121] 803 5-9-5 **68** (tp) AlistairRawlinson 4 75
(Rebecca Menzies) *dwlt: hld up: hdwy on outside to ld over 2f out: hrd pressed and edgd lft over 1f out: kpt on wl fnl f* **11/2**[2]

6441 **2** *1* **The Resdev Way**[30] 2974 6-8-10 **64** PaulaMuir(5) 7 69
(Philip Kirby) *slowly away: hld up: hdwy on outside over 2f out: effrt and ev ch over 1f out: one pce ins fnl f* **5/1**[1]

3005 **3** *2* **Hugoigo**[71] 1718 5-8-2 **51** oh6 PaddyMathers 1 54
(Jim Goldie) *hld up in midfield: drvn along over 2f out: hdwy over 1f out: kpt on to take 3rd pl wl ins fnl f: r.o* **10/1**

4-00 **4** *1 1/4* **Question Of Faith**[21] 3294 8-9-9 **72** PaulHanagan 8 74
(Martin Todhunter) *hld up in midfield: hdwy and prom over 2f out: rdn and edgd lft over 1f out: kpt on same pce fnl f* **7/1**[3]

04-5 **5** *3/4* **Buyer Beware (IRE)**[16] 3481 7-8-12 **61** (p[1]) SamJames 9 62
(Liam Bailey) *in tch: effrt and rdn over 2f out: edgd rt over 1f out: one pce fnl f* **5/1**[1]

6045 **6** *1 1/2* **Pammi**[2] 4004 4-7-13 **55** KieranSchofield(7) 2 54
(Jim Goldie) *in tch: rdn along and effrt over 2f out: outpcd fnl f* **11/2**[2]

-300 **7** *5* **Tomorrow's Angel**[10] 3686 4-8-12 **64** JamieGormley(3) 3 57
(Iain Jardine) *missed break: hld up: rdn over 4f out: nvr rchd ldrs (jockey said filly hung right under pressure; trainer said filly had a breathing problem)* **10/1**

-400 **8** *5* **Spark Of War (IRE)**[13] 3568 4-8-9 **58** (v[1]) TomEaves 5 45
(Keith Dalgleish) *t.k.h: cl up: rdn and lost pl over 2f out: sn btn* **14/1**

6-00 **9** *1 1/2* **Golden Jeffrey (SWI)**[12] 3511 6-9-5 **68** (b) GrahamLee 11 53
(Iain Jardine) *led at decent gallop: rdn and hdd over 2f out: sn wknd* **10/1**

0000 **10** *10* **Enemy Of The State (IRE)**[17] 3447 5-8-4 **53** oh6 ow2 (p) PhilDennis 6 26
(Jason Ward) *cl up tl drvn and wknd over 2f out (jockey said gelding hung left)* **16/1**

3m 16.41s (-10.59) **Going Correction** -0.35s/f (Firm) **10** Ran SP% **116.4**
Speed ratings (Par 103): **114,113,112,111,111 110,107,105,104,99**
CSF £33.12 CT £269.54 TOTE £5.20: £2.20, £1.70, £3.50; EX 28.50 Trifecta £371.80.
Owner David Slater **Bred** Butlersgrove Stud **Trained** Mordon, Durham

FOCUS
Add 15 yards. A moderate handicap. The winner has been rated to his winter AW form.

4057 WHYTE & MACKAY H'CAP — 1m 2f
7:40 (7:40) (Class 4) (0-85,87) 3-Y-O+
£5,530 (£1,645; £822; £411; £400; £400) **Stalls High**

Form RPR

35-2 **1** **Asian Angel (IRE)**[11] 3647 3-8-2 **75** AndrewBreslin(5) 2 89+
(Mark Johnston) *pressed ldr: rdn to ld over 1f out: edgd lft: drew clr fnl f: readily* **5/4**[1]

0120 **2** *5* **Never Be Enough**[17] 3449 4-9-8 **78** TomEaves 1 81
(Keith Dalgleish) *stdd s: t.k.h: hld up: hdwy over 2f out: chsd (clr) wnr over 1f out: kpt on: no imp* **8/1**[3]

056- **3** *1* **Glasses Up (USA)**[252] 8164 4-10-0 **84** PaddyMathers 6 85
(R Mike Smith) *hld up: drvn and outpcd over 2f out: rallied over 1f out: kpt on fnl f: nt pce to chal* **8/1**[3]

0-40 **4** *nk* **Gworn**[6] 3867 9-8-5 **66** PaulaMuir(5) 3 66
(R Mike Smith) *chsd ldrs: drvn along over 2f out: one pce fr over 1f out* **10/1**

0/00 **5** *2* **Shrewd**[17] 3450 9-10-0 **84** GrahamLee 8 80
(Iain Jardine) *hld up: pushed along over 2f out: kpt on fnl f: nvr able to chal* **33/1**

6-45 **6** *hd* **Royal Regent**[24] 3180 7-8-13 **74** ConnorMurtagh(5) 4 70
(Lucy Normile) *t.k.h: led: clr 1/2-way to over 2f out: hdd over 1f out: sn outpcd* **16/1**

00-1 **7** *28* **Briardale (IRE)**[28] 3046 7-9-3 **73**.. PaulHanagan 7 13
(James Bethell) *in tch: stdy hdwy over 2f out: sn rdn: wknd over 1f out (jockey said gelding lost its action approaching the final furlong)* **5/2**[2]

2m 7.91s (-4.49) **Going Correction** -0.35s/f (Firm)
WFA 3 from 4yo+ 12lb **7 Ran SP% 113.2**
Speed ratings (Par 105): **103,99,98,97,96 96,73**
CSF £12.03 CT £56.32 TOTE £2.60: £1.70, £2.60; EX 10.10 Trifecta £34.00.
Owner Dr J Walker **Bred** Skymarc Farm **Trained** Middleham Moor, N Yorks

FOCUS
Add 15 yards. This wasn't the deepest 0-85 you'll see but there was an awful lot to like about the performance of the winner.

4058 TENNENT'S LAGER H'CAP 7f 50y
8:10 (8:10) (Class 4) (0-85,84) 4-Y-0+
£6,080 (£1,809; £904; £452; £400; £400) **Stalls** High

Form RPR

-664 **1** **Lamloom (IRE)**[32] 2894 5-9-6 **83**.. DavidNolan 3 92
(David O'Meara) *t.k.h: mde all at decent gallop: sn clr: rdn over 1f out: kpt on wl fnl f: unchal* **5/1**[3]

3654 **2** *2 1/4* **Logi (IRE)**[11] 3657 5-8-6 **69**..(b) PhilDennis 7 72
(Rebecca Bastiman) *prom: effrt over 2f out: chsd (clr) wnr over 1f out: kpt on fnl f: nt pce to chal* **10/1**

4200 **3** *nk* **Strong Steps**[4] 3922 7-8-2 **68**..(p) JamieGormley(3) 5 70
(Jim Goldie) *cl up: effrt and rdn over 2f out: kpt on u.p ins fnl f* **5/1**[3]

5100 **4** *1 3/4* **Florenza**[17] 3450 6-9-7 **84**.. MichaelStainton 4 81
(Chris Fairhurst) *hld up towards rr: drvn along over 2f out: kpt on fnl f: nvr able to chal* **7/1**

2251 **5** *shd* **Tommy G**[24] 3179 6-9-2 **79**.. AlistairRawlinson 2 76
(Jim Goldie) *hld up: rdn along over 2f out: hdwy over 1f out: no imp fnl f* **3/1**[1]

6134 **6** *2 1/2* **Jacob Black**[2] 4001 8-8-12 **75**..(v) ShaneGray 8 65
(Keith Dalgleish) *dwlt: hld up: rdn over 2f out: sn n.d* **4/1**[2]

0632 **7** *1 3/4* **Lucky Violet (IRE)**[24] 3178 7-8-2 **65**..(h) PaddyMathers 1 51
(Linda Perratt) *t.k.h: cl up: drvn over 2f out: wknd over 1f out* **13/2**

1m 28.54s (-3.96) **Going Correction** -0.35s/f (Firm) **7 Ran SP% 113.3**
Speed ratings (Par 105): **108,105,105,103,102 100,98**
CSF £50.70 CT £260.68 TOTE £5.90: £4.50, £3.70; EX 51.40 Trifecta £303.70.
Owner Hamad Rashed Bin Ghedayer **Bred** M Duffy **Trained** Upper Helmsley, N Yorks

FOCUS
Add 15 yards. This was strongly run and the winner dominated. The runner-up/third have been rated close to this year's form.

4059 GORDON'S PINK GIN H'CAP 5f
8:45 (8:49) (Class 5) (0-70,71) 3-Y-0+
£3,752 (£1,116; £557; £400; £400; £400) **Stalls** High

Form RPR

2520 **1** **Shepherd's Purse**[3] 3975 7-9-4 **62**.. JamesSullivan 6 72
(Ruth Carr) *rrd s: hld up: hdwy 1/2-way: effrt and wnt 2nd over 1f out: sustained run fnl f to ld cl home* **7/2**[1]

4-04 **2** *hd* **Vee Man Ten**[13] 3590 3-9-6 **70**.. PaulHanagan 2 77
(Ivan Furtado) *led: rdn and clr over 1f out: kpt on fnl f: hdd cl home* **9/2**[2]

-200 **3** *1 1/2* **Suwaan (IRE)**[24] 3206 5-9-10 **68**.. TomEaves 7 72
(Ruth Carr) *chsd wnr to over 1f out: rdn and one pce ins fnl f* **14/1**

3060 **4** *nse* **Amazing Grazing (IRE)**[15] 3504 5-9-12 **70**.. LewisEdmunds 13 74
(Rebecca Bastiman) *hld up: rdn along 1/2-way: hdwy over 1f out: kpt on fnl f: nvr able to chal* **15/2**

-144 **5** *1* **Northern Society (IRE)**[15] 3516 3-9-3 **67**.. ShaneGray 11 65
(Keith Dalgleish) *hld up: rdn along 1/2-way: kpt on fnl f: no imp* **12/1**

-046 **6** *1/2* **Jeffrey Harris**[47] 2433 4-8-13 **57**..(h) AlistairRawlinson 12 55
(Jim Goldie) *fly-jmpd s: bhd: rdn 1/2-way: kpt on fnl f: nvr rchd ldrs* **28/1**

-600 **7** *nk* **Lexington Palm (IRE)**[18] 3414 3-8-6 **56**.. RoystonFfrench 14 51
(Keith Dalgleish) *midfield: drvn and outpcd 1/2-way: rallied fnl f: no imp* **25/1**

0300 **8** *3/4* **Jessie Allan (IRE)**[30] 2958 8-8-8 **52**.. PaddyMathers 8 47
(Jim Goldie) *bhd: drvn 1/2-way: sme late hdwy: nvr rchd ldrs* **40/1**

2460 **9** *nk* **Burmese Blazer (IRE)**[34] 2841 4-9-5 **63**..(h) PhilDennis 3 56
(Jim Goldie) *in tch: effrt over 1f out: no ex fnl f* **8/1**

-210 **10** *3/4* **Super Julius**[21] 3328 5-9-0 **65**..(b[1]) KieranSchofield(7) 9 56
(S Donohoe, Ire) *prom: rdn over 2f out: wknd over 1f out* **10/1**

0320 **11** *3/4* **Prestbury Park (USA)**[10] 3706 4-9-12 **70**.. GrahamLee 5 58
(Paul Midgley) *midfield: drvn over 2f out: wknd over 1f out* **5/1**[3]

5-40 **12** *3* **Brendan (IRE)**[30] 2958 6-8-4 **51** oh3.. JamieGormley(3) 1 28
(Jim Goldie) *in tch: rdn 1/2-way: wknd over 1f out (vet said gelding bled from the nose)* **28/1**

-140 **13** *4 1/2* **Our Place In Loule**[49] 2368 6-9-13 **71**..(b) DavidNolan 4 32
(Noel Wilson) *hld up in midfield: rdn over 2f out: wknd wl over 1f out (jockey said gelding slipped leaving the stalls)* **20/1**

58.27s (-1.73) **Going Correction** -0.35s/f (Firm)
WFA 3 from 4yo+ 6lb **13 Ran SP% 121.3**
Speed ratings (Par 103): **99,98,96,96,94 93,93,92,91,90 89,84,77**
CSF £17.62 CT £202.13 TOTE £4.30: £1.80, £2.10, £5.10; EX 23.00 Trifecta £256.60.
Owner The Chancers And Mrs R Carr **Bred** F Stribbling **Trained** Huby, N Yorks

FOCUS
This was strongly run and represents solid form for the grade. The runner-up led everywhere bar the line.

4060 MAGNERS ROSE H'CAP 7f 50y
9:15 (9:24) (Class 6) (0-65,69) 3-Y-0+
£3,105 (£924; £461; £400; £400; £400) **Stalls** High

Form RPR

6061 **1** **Mujassam**[4] 3928 7-10-1 **69** 4ex..(v) DavidNolan 12 77
(David O'Meara) *hld up in tch: effrt and rdn over 1f out: hdwy to ld ins fnl f: kpt on strly* **3/1**[1]

2300 **2** *1* **Sir Ottoman (FR)**[14] 3549 6-9-4 **65**..(p) KieranSchofield(7) 3 71
(Ivan Furtado) *led at decent gallop: rdn over 1f out: hdd ins fnl f: kpt on same pce* **16/1**

0025 **3** *nk* **Forever A Lady (IRE)**[10] 3685 6-9-4 **58**.. ShaneGray 14 63
(Keith Dalgleish) *chsd ldrs: effrt and rdn 2f out: ev ch briefly ins fnl f: sn one pce* **12/1**

-561 **4** *1/2* **Pudding Chare (IRE)**[24] 3177 5-8-13 **58**..(t) AndrewBreslin(5) 5 62
(R Mike Smith) *chsd ldr: rdn and edgd lft 2f out: kpt on same pce ins fnl f* **12/1**

1104 **5** *hd* **Colour Contrast (IRE)**[24] 3178 6-9-4 **61**..(b) JamieGormley(3) 13 64
(Iain Jardine) *hld up: effrt and edgd lft 2f out: kpt on fnl f: nt pce to chal* **8/1**[3]

64-6 **6** *1 3/4* **Royal Duchess**[24] 3178 9-9-2 **61**.. ConnorMurtagh(5) 10 60
(Lucy Normile) *hld up on outside: rdn over 2f out: sn outpcd: kpt on fnl f: nvr able to chal* **13/2**[2]

6000 **7** *shd* **Desai**[3] 3969 5-9-7 **61**..(t) JamesSullivan 9 59
(Noel Wilson) *s.i.s: hld up: rdn over 2f out: hdwy over 1f out: nvr rchd ldrs* **40/1**

0000 **8** *1 3/4* **Insurplus (IRE)**[21] 3305 6-9-6 **60**.. PhilDennis 7 54
(Jim Goldie) *in tch: drvn over 2f out: wknd over 1f out* **14/1**

2020 **9** *3/4* **Roaring Forties (IRE)**[8] 3781 6-9-8 **62**..(p) LewisEdmunds 8 54
(Rebecca Bastiman) *missed break: hld up: drvn along over 2f out: n.d* **11/1**

0410 **10** *1 1/4* **Robben Rainbow**[24] 3178 5-9-2 **56**.. RoystonFfrench 2 45
(Katie Scott) *dwlt: sn midfield: rdn over 2f out: wknd over 1f out* **20/1**

5-00 **11** *1 3/4* **Naples Bay**[35] 2788 5-9-4 **58**.. GrahamLee 6 43
(Katie Scott) *t.k.h in midfield: drvn and outpcd over 2f out: n.d after* **16/1**

1m 29.61s (-2.89) **Going Correction** -0.35s/f (Firm) **11 Ran SP% 98.8**
Speed ratings (Par 101): **102,100,100,99,99 97,97,95,94,93 91**
CSF £36.60 CT £263.78 TOTE £2.60: £2.10, £3.40, £2.60; EX 34.70 Trifecta £346.00.
Owner Thoroughbred British Racing **Bred** Bumble Bs, D F Powell & S Nicholls **Trained** Upper Helmsley, N Yorks

■ Aliento was withdrawn. Price at time of withdrawal 100-30. Rule 4 applies to all bets - deduction 20p in the pound

FOCUS
Add 15 yards. This concluding handicap was run minus recent Thirsk winner Aliento, who was withdrawn after breaking through the stalls. Straightforward form.
T/Plt: £46.30 to a £1 stake. Pool: £43,785.90 - 688.94 winning units T/Qpdt: £20.60 to a £1 stake. Pool: £5,190.72 - 186.46 winning units **Richard Young**

3797 GOODWOOD (R-H)
Friday, June 21

OFFICIAL GOING: Good (good to soft in places)
Wind: Slight cross wind Weather: Warm and sunny

4061 NOW TV APPRENTICE H'CAP 7f
5:50 (5:51) (Class 4) (0-85,87) 4-Y-0+
£6,404 (£1,905; £952; £476; £400; £400) **Stalls** Low

Form RPR

33-1 **1** **De Vegas Kid (IRE)**[24] 3185 5-9-3 **75**.. DarraghKeenan 5 83
(Tony Carroll) *restrained in last: stl gng wl in last 2f out: pushed along into 3rd 1f out: sn rdn and qcknd up wl to ld cl home* **9/2**

3061 **2** *1/2* **Quick Breath**[16] 3462 4-9-5 **80**.. TylerSaunders(3) 3 87
(Jonathan Portman) *racd in midfield: clsd gng wl 2f out: rdn to ld 1f out: kpt on wl but unable to match wnr whn hdd clsng stages* **5/2**[1]

0-00 **3** *2 1/4* **Jackpot Royale**[8] 3763 4-10-1 **87**.. TheodoreLadd 2 88
(Michael Appleby) *racd in midfield: rdn along and unable qck over 2f out: kpt on one pce u.p fnl f* **5/1**

4422 **4** *3/4* **Salt Whistle Bay (IRE)**[14] 3529 5-9-7 **79**.. WilliamCox 1 78
(Rae Guest) *trckd ldr: rdn along and upsides ldr 2f out: sn wknd ins fnl f* **3/1**[2]

0-04 **5** *1* **Robsdelight (IRE)**[24] 3183 4-8-9 **74**..(p) GraceMcEntee(7) 6 70
(Gay Kelleway) *led: pushed along to maintain short ld 2f out: rdn along and hdd 1f out: wknd fnl f* **20/1**

-524 **6** *nk* **Elysium Dream**[15] 3494 4-9-8 **80**..(b) ThoreHammerHansen 4 75
(Richard Hannon) *hld up: rdn along and little rspnse over 2f out: plugged on one pce fnl f* **4/1**[3]

1m 29.89s (3.19) **Going Correction** +0.35s/f (Good) **6 Ran SP% 113.2**
Speed ratings (Par 105): **95,94,91,89 89**
CSF £16.40 TOTE £4.30: £2.20, £1.50; EX 16.80 Trifecta £81.20.
Owner The Rebelle Boys **Bred** Miriam O'Donnell & Kevin F O'Donnell **Trained** Cropthorne, Worcs

FOCUS
Warm, drying weather had improved conditions from good to soft, soft in places of two days previously. The stalls were on the inner for this reasonable apprentice handicap, in which the winner passed them all up the straight.

4062 DISCIPLES NOVICE AUCTION STKS (PLUS 10 RACE) 6f
6:20 (6:29) (Class 4) 2-Y-O **£6,727** (£2,002; £1,000; £500) **Stalls** High

Form RPR

1 **Sovereign Beauty (IRE)** 2-9-0 0.. HectorCrouch 3 72
(Clive Cox) *settled in 4th: little green 1/2-way: rdn along to ld on outer 2f out: rdn out fnl f: jst prevailed* **6/1**[3]

2 *shd* **Smuggler** 2-9-5 0.. PatDobbs 4 77+
(Marcus Tregoning) *hld up: improving on rail whn short of room over 1f out: rdn and styd on strly once in clr fnl f: jst failed* **10/1**

52 **3** *1/2* **Flash Henry**[11] 3644 2-9-5 0.. CharlesBishop 6 75
(George Scott) *trckd ldr: forced way between rivals over 1f out: rdn along and ev ch 1f out: no ex fnl f* **8/15**[1]

4 *9* **Too Hard To Hold (IRE)** 2-9-5 0.. PJMcDonald 5 48
(Mark Johnston) *led: rdn along and hdd 2f out: wknd fnl f* **7/2**[2]

0 **5** *1 1/4* **Depeche Toi (IRE)**[25] 3165 2-9-0 0.. TrevorWhelan 2 39
(Jonathan Portman) *trckd ldr: rdn along and outpcd 2f out: wknd fnl f* **18/1**

1m 15.21s (3.11) **Going Correction** +0.35s/f (Good) **5 Ran SP% 116.1**
Speed ratings (Par 95): **93,92,92,80,78**
CSF £55.91 TOTE £6.60: £1.80, £3.30; EX 41.10 Trifecta £95.70.
Owner The Free Flyers **Bred** C F Harrington **Trained** Lambourn, Berks

FOCUS
Stalls on the stands' side for this juvenile sprint, delayed for nearly ten minutes whilst Quarrystreetmagic was first reshod and ultimately withdrawn. The winner raced widest throughout. The third has been rated to his ordinary debut form.

4063 KENNELS H'CAP 1m 3f 218y
6:55 (7:01) (Class 3) (0-95,85) 3-Y-O **£12,602** (£3,772; £1,886; £944; £470) **Stalls** High

Form RPR

-332 **1** **Never Do Nothing (IRE)**[27] 3073 3-9-3 **83**.. DavidProbert 2 92
(Andrew Balding) *hld up in last: smooth prog on outer to go 2nd 2f out: rdn to ld wl over 1f out: rdn out* **10/1**

0211 **2** *1 3/4* **Just Benjamin**[20] 3358 3-9-2 **82**.. LiamJones 4 92+
(William Haggas) *hld up: pushed along and bdly hmpd whn clsng on rail 2f out: sn rdn whn gap appeared and styd on wl: nt rch wnr* **15/8**[1]

3-53 **3** *2* **Aspire Tower (IRE)**[20] 3358 3-9-3 **83**.. PJMcDonald 1 86
(Steve Gollings) *led: rdn to maintain short ld 2f out: drvn and hdd wl over 1f out: kpt on one pce fnl f* **9/1**

2-12 **4** *1* **Laafy (USA)**[35] 2811 3-9-5 **85**.............................. PatDobbs 3 86
(Sir Michael Stoute) *midfield: pushed along 3f out: drvn over 1f out: one pce fnl f* **5/2**[2]

21-1 **5** *3 ¾* **Brasca**[29] 2999 3-9-4 **84**.............................. HarryBentley 6 79
(Ralph Beckett) *midfield: rdn along and no imp over 2f out: sn drvn and no prog over 1f out: one pce after* **6/1**

41-5 **6** *4 ½* **Ginistrelli (IRE)**[67] 1824 3-9-2 **82**.............................. HectorCrouch 5 70
(Ed Walker) *trckd ldr: pushed along 3f out: rdn and outpcd 2f out: plugged on* **4/1**[3]

2m 41.09s (1.49) **Going Correction** +0.35s/f (Good) **6** Ran SP% **116.7**
Speed ratings (Par 103): **109,107,106,105,103 100**
CSF £30.66 TOTE £7.20: £2.90, £1.30; EX 27.20 Trifecta £183.00.
Owner A Brooke-Rankin & Partner **Bred** B Kennedy & Mrs Ann Marie Kennedy **Trained** Kingsclere, Hants

FOCUS
Stalls on outer. On the face of it not the strongest event for the grade, with the topweight all of 10lb below the ratings ceiling, but many of these still remain on fair marks or otherwise of interest. The second didn't get a run so has been rated up with the winner.

4064 WELLBEING OF WOMEN FILLIES' H'CAP 1m 3f 218y
7:30 (7:35) (Class 4) (0-85,87) 3-Y-0+ **£8,668** (£2,579; £1,289) **Stalls High**

Form RPR
0-04 **1** **Wannie Mae (IRE)**[14] 3553 3-8-0 **67** oh1.............................. NicolaCurrie 1 73
(William Haggas) *settled in last: effrt on outer to chse ldng pair 3f out: wnt 2nd 2f out: drvn and wandered briefly ins fnl f bef styng on strly to ld cl home* **7/2**[2]

201 **2** *nk* **Sneaky Peek**[24] 3200 3-8-11 **78**.............................. DavidProbert 3 83
(Andrew Balding) *trckd ldr: led gng wl over 2f out: rdn and strly pressed by wnr over 1f out: kpt on wl but hdd by wnr cl home* **4/1**[3]

3221 **3** *7* **Sapa Inca (IRE)**[8] 3765 3-9-2 **83** 6ex.............................. PJMcDonald 4 77
(Mark Johnston) *led: rdn along and hdd over 2f out: kpt on one pce fnl f (trainer could offer no explanation for the filly's performance)* **2/5**[1]

2m 41.04s (1.44) **Going Correction** +0.35s/f (Good)
WFA 3 from 4yo 14lb **3** Ran SP% **113.7**
Speed ratings (Par 102): **109,108,104**
CSF £13.12 TOTE £4.70; EX 14.60 Trifecta £14.00.
Owner Bjarne Minde **Bred** Churchtown House Stud **Trained** Newmarket, Suffolk

FOCUS
Stalls on outer. Just a three-runner affair after Dono Di Dio unseated and ran loose on the way down, but still won in a time 0.05 seconds faster than the preceding 0-95. The level is a bit fluid with the favourite disappointing.

4065 NOW TV H'CAP 1m
8:00 (8:04) (Class 4) (0-85,87) 3-Y-0 **£8,668** (£2,579; £1,289; £644; £400) **Stalls Low**

Form RPR
15-5 **1** **Sophosc (IRE)**[29] 3011 3-9-2 **78**.............................. CharlesBishop 5 84
(Joseph Tuite) *hld up: pushed along to cl 2f out: rdn to ld 1f out: drvn and hdd briefly ins fnl f: rallied to ld again cl home* **10/1**

45-0 **2** *nk* **Hawridge Storm (IRE)**[16] 3465 3-9-1 **77**.............................. PJMcDonald 4 82
(Rod Millman) *dwlt and racd in last: hdwy to chal on ldr 2f out: sn rdn and led briefly ins fnl f: styd on wl but hdd by wnr cl home* **14/1**

25-1 **3** *6* **Kodiac Pride**[23] 3218 3-9-7 **83**.............................. OisinMurphy 1 74
(William Haggas) *led: pushed along w short ld 2f out: sn rdn and hdd by wnr 1f out: wknd fnl f* **1/1**[1]

2523 **4** *4 ½* **Reeves**[20] 3357 3-9-11 **87**..............................(p) RaulDaSilva 3 68
(Robert Cowell) *midfield: hdwy u.p to press ldr 3f out: sn rdn and no imp 2f out: wknd fnl f* **7/4**[2]

221- **5** *2 ¼* **Water Diviner (IRE)**[246] 8336 3-9-5 **81**.............................. PatDobbs 2 57
(Richard Hannon) *trckd ldr: rdn and outpcd 2f out: wknd fnl f* **9/1**[3]

1m 41.55s (2.35) **Going Correction** +0.35s/f (Good) **5** Ran SP% **112.1**
Speed ratings (Par 101): **102,101,95,91,88**
CSF £107.85 TOTE £11.00: £2.50, £4.30; EX 50.60 Trifecta £275.10.
Owner The Harefield Racing Club **Bred** Birchill Stables **Trained** Lambourn, Berks

FOCUS
Stalls on inner. The early pace was contested and the first two home sat furthest back initially - they have been rated as improving.

4066 LEVIN DOWN MAIDEN STKS 1m 6f
8:35 (8:36) (Class 4) 3-Y-0+ **£5,822** (£1,732; £865; £432) **Stalls Low**

Form RPR
24 **1** **Make My Day (IRE)**[10] 3699 3-8-12 0..............................(p[1]) KieranO'Neill 5 89
(John Gosden) *mde all: rdn w short ld 2f out: sn drvn and kpt on strly fnl f: a doing enough* **7/2**[3]

2 *1 ¼* **December Second (IRE)**[25] 5-10-0 0.............................. PJMcDonald 4 87
(Philip Kirby) *dwlt and racd in rr: hdwy to chse wnr 2f out: kpt on wl u.p fnl f: nt rch wnr* **6/1**

223 **3** *¾* **Cape Cavalli (IRE)**[25] 3152 3-8-12 87.............................. OisinMurphy 8 86
(Simon Crisford) *trckd ldr: pushed along to chse wnr over 2f out: sn drvn and kpt on one pce fnl f* **1/1**[1]

2 **4** *nk* **Caravan Of Hope (IRE)**[22] 3247 3-8-12 0.............................. HarryBentley 9 85
(Hugo Palmer) *hld up: rdn along and no imp over 2f out: drvn 1f out: kpt on same pce fnl f* **5/2**[2]

5 *8* **Black Kalanisi (IRE)**[33] 6-10-0 0.............................. CharlesBishop 2 73
(Joseph Tuite) *in rr of midfield: rdn along and no imp 2f out: kpt on one pce for press fnl f* **20/1**

05 **6** *11* **Lyrical Waters**[7] 3802 3-8-5 0.............................. GeorgiaDobie[(7)] 7 59
(Eve Johnson Houghton) *midfield on outer: effrt on outer 3f out: rdn and wknd over 1f out* **33/1**

03 **7** *7* **Spirit Of Nicobar**[53] 2195 3-8-7 0.............................. DavidProbert 1 44
(Andrew Balding) *racd in midfield: rdn along and no hdwy 2f out: wknd whn btn fnl f* **16/1**

00 **8** *30* **Prime Approach (IRE)**[35] 2795 3-8-9 0..............................(v[1]) WilliamCox[(3)] 6 7
(Brett Johnson) *trckd wnr: pushed along and lost pl 4f out: rdn in rr 3f out: sn detached (jockey said gelding weakened quickly; vet said gelding was lame right hind)* **50/1**

3m 7.76s (4.06) **Going Correction** +0.35s/f (Good)
WFA 3 from 5yo+ 16lb **8** Ran SP% **130.6**
Speed ratings (Par 105): **102,101,100,100,96 89,85,68**
CSF £28.06 TOTE £4.60: £1.40, £1.60, £1.50; EX 25.70 Trifecta £58.20.
Owner John Gunther & Tanya Gunther **Bred** Sahara Group Holdings **Trained** Newmarket, Suffolk

FOCUS
Stalls on inner. A good maiden and the winner has been rated as improving.
T/Plt: £6,287.90 to a £1 stake. Pool: £42,895.79 - 4.98 winning units T/Qpdt: £321.70 to a £1 stake. Pool: £5,453.16 - 12.54 winning units **Mark Grantham**

3599 NEWMARKET (R-H)
Friday, June 21

OFFICIAL GOING: Good to soft (good in places; 7.0)
Wind: Light half-behind Weather: Cloudy

4067 WELCOME TO NEWMARKET NIGHTS APPRENTICE H'CAP 1m
5:05 (5:08) (Class 5) (0-75,77) 4-Y-0+
£4,528 (£1,347; £673; £400; £400; £400) **Stalls High**

Form RPR
5-60 **1** **Mountain Rescue (IRE)**[51] 2273 7-9-11 **77**..............(p[1]) SeamusCronin 5 87
(Michael Attwater) *w ldr tl led over 5f out: overall ldr over 2f out: rdn over 1f out: edgd lft wl ins fnl f: styd on (trainer said, regarding the apparent improvement in form, that gelding had benefitted from the application of first time cheekpieces)* **12/1**

-231 **2** *1 ½* **Marshal Dan (IRE)**[36] 2774 4-9-2 **73**.............................. StefanoCherchi[(5)] 4 80
(Heather Main) *hld up in tch: edgd rt 3f out: rdn to chse wnr over 1f out: styd on* **11/4**[1]

4-06 **3** *4 ½* **Trulee Scrumptious**[24] 3185 10-8-3 **58**..............(v) AledBeech[(3)] 14 55
(Peter Charalambous) *racd alone far side: overall ldr tl over 2f out: sn rdn: no ex fnl f* **11/1**

53-0 **4** *3 ¼* **Nordic Flight**[39] 2690 4-8-10 **67**.............................. LukeCatton[(5)] 13 56
(James Eustace) *hld up: styd on u.p appr fnl f: nt trble ldrs* **20/1**

0-00 **5** *nk* **Kyllachys Tale (IRE)**[38] 2714 5-8-7 **62**..............(p) CierenFallon[(3)] 7 50
(Roger Teal) *s.i.s: pushed along and hdwy over 6f out: rdn and wknd over 1f out* **14/1**

50-6 **6** *1 ¾* **The Throstles**[45] 2516 4-9-2 **73**.............................. SeanKirrane[(5)] 12 57
(Kevin Frost) *w ldrs tl rdn over 2f out: wknd over 1f out* **10/1**

3346 **7** *2 ½* **Guvenor's Choice (IRE)**[14] 3541 4-9-5 **71**..............(t) HarrisonShaw 11 50
(Marjorie Fife) *s.i.s: hld up: rdn over 2f out: n.d* **25/1**

1201 **8** *½* **Zodiakos (IRE)**[9] 3730 6-9-10 **76** 5ex..............(p) BenSanderson 3 54
(Roger Fell) *s.i.s: sn pushed along in rr: rdn and hung lft over 2f out: n.d* **11/2**[3]

0-05 **9** *¾* **Gulland Rock**[8] 3781 8-7-11 **54** oh9.............................. IsobelFrancis[(5)] 1 30
(Anthony Carson) *prom: pushed along and lost pl over 5f out: n.d after* **50/1**

62-2 **10** *3* **Al Reeh (IRE)**[168] 54 5-9-7 **73**..............(p) SebastianWoods 8 42
(Marco Botti) *prom: rdn and hung lft over 2f out: wknd over 1f out (trainer could offer no explanation for the poor form shown; vet said gelding had post-race heat stress)* **9/2**[2]

5520 **11** *shd* **Lacan (IRE)**[35] 2797 8-8-10 **69**.............................. JoeBradnam[(7)] 6 38
(Michael Bell) *s.i.s: pushed along over 2f out: a in rr* **8/1**

5055 **12** *nse* **Me Too Nagasaki (IRE)**[8] 3766 5-8-13 **70**..............(vt[1]) MarcoGhiani[(5)] 2 39
(Stuart Williams) *led main gp tl over 5f out: remained handy: hmpd 3f out: sn rdn and hung lft: wknd wl over 1f out* **15/2**

1m 37.85s (-2.15) **Going Correction** 0.0s/f (Good) **12** Ran SP% **125.5**
Speed ratings (Par 103): **110,108,104,100,100 98,96,95,94,91 91,91**
CSF £46.85 CT £403.31 TOTE £18.70: £4.20, £1.70, £2.20; EX 89.70 Trifecta £552.40.
Owner The Attwater Partnership **Bred** Lady Richard Wellesley **Trained** Epsom, Surrey

FOCUS
Far side course. Stalls: far side, except 1m2f: centre. A drying day and the ground was given officially given as 'good to soft, good in places'. Rail movements meant the 1m 2f races were extended by 30yds. No more than a fair apprentice handicap which not many got into.

4068 HEATH COURT "IT MUST BE LOVE" H'CAP 1m 2f
5:40 (5:42) (Class 4) (0-85,86) 3-Y-0
£7,762 (£2,310; £1,154; £577; £400; £400) **Stalls Centre**

Form RPR
221 **1** **American Graffiti (FR)**[121] 804 3-9-7 **85**.............................. KerrinMcEvoy 2 96
(Charlie Appleby) *chsd ldr tl shkn up to ld over 1f out: rdn and r.o wl* **9/2**[3]

0-12 **2** *3* **Takumi (IRE)**[33] 2872 3-9-5 **83**.............................. JackMitchell 8 88
(Roger Varian) *s.i.s: hld up: hdwy on outer over 2f out: chsd wnr over 1f out: sn ev ch and edgd rt: rdn: hung lft and rt ins fnl f: nt run on* **3/1**[1]

12-1 **3** *½* **Universal Order**[28] 3035 3-9-8 **86**.............................. StevieDonohoe 7 90
(David Simcock) *s.i.s: hld up: hdwy over 1f out: rdn and nt clr run ins fnl f: styd on* **14/1**

-330 **4** *½* **Politicise (IRE)**[20] 3341 3-8-13 **84**..............(p) CierenFallon[(7)] 6 87
(William Haggas) *chsd ldrs: ev ch over 1f out: sn rdn: hung rt and styd on same pce ins fnl f* **7/2**[2]

5145 **5** *2* **Elisheba (IRE)**[27] 3099 3-9-4 **82**.............................. KieranShoemark 5 81
(John Gosden) *hld up: nt clr run fr over 3f out tl 1f out: nvr trbld ldrs (jockey said filly was denied a clear run)* **14/1**

-260 **6** *hd* **Deebee**[19] 3373 3-8-9 **73**.............................. JasonWatson 1 72
(Declan Carroll) *led: rdn and hdd over 1f out: wknd ins fnl f* **10/1**

0-21 **7** *nk* **Edmond Dantes (IRE)**[7] 3797 3-8-3 **67**.............................. JFEgan 4 65
(David Menuisier) *hld up: racd keenly: hdwy on outer over 4f out: rdn and ev ch over 2f out: wknd ins fnl f (jockey said gelding became unbalanced in the dip)* **3/1**[1]

2-10 **8** *1 ½* **Robert L'Echelle (IRE)**[63] 1911 3-8-11 **75**.............................. CharlieBennett 3 70
(Hughie Morrison) *chsd ldrs: shkn up over 1f out: wknd ins fnl f* **25/1**

2m 7.34s (0.24) **Going Correction** 0.0s/f (Good) **8** Ran SP% **116.7**
Speed ratings (Par 101): **99,96,96,95,94 94,93,92**
CSF £18.86 CT £175.37 TOTE £4.60: £1.60, £1.40, £3.30; EX 23.80 Trifecta £80.90.
Owner Godolphin **Bred** Dayton Investments Limited **Trained** Newmarket, Suffolk

FOCUS
An above-average 3yo handicap, with the first two rated as improving and third/fourth close to form. Add 30yds.

4069 HEATH COURT HOTEL CELEBRATING #SUFFOLKDAY NOVICE STKS (PLUS 10 RACE) 6f
6:10 (6:10) (Class 4) 2-Y-0 **£5,175** (£1,540; £769; £384) **Stalls High**

Form RPR
1 **King's Command** 2-9-5 0.............................. KerrinMcEvoy 7 83+
(Charlie Appleby) *led: shkn up and hdd over 2f out: nt clr run over 1f out: rallied and hung lft ins fnl f: r.o to ld post (vet said colt lost right hind shoe)* **2/1**[2]

3 **2** *nk* **Al Namir (IRE)**[22] 3274 2-9-5 0.............................. RossaRyan 2 80
(Richard Hannon) *chsd ldr tl led over 2f out: rdn and hung lft over 1f out: hdd wl ins fnl f: r.o* **6/1**[3]

22 **3** *nse* **Electrical Storm**[47] 2444 2-9-5 0.............................. PatCosgrave 4 80
(Saeed bin Suroor) *hmpd s: sn chsng ldrs: rdn to ld wl ins fnl f: hdd post* **1/1**[1]

4 ½ **Royal Commando (IRE)** 2-9-5 0 KieranShoemark 6 79
(Charles Hills) *hld up: hdwy and hung lft over 1f out: nt clr run and swtchd rt ins fnl f: r.o* 11/1

5 3 ¼ **The City's Phantom** 2-9-5 0 SeanLevey 3 71+
(Richard Spencer) *wnt lft s: chsd ldrs: shkn up over 2f out: rdn and hung lft fr over 1f out: no ex ins fnl f (jockey said colt hung left-handed)* 33/1

6 2 ¾ **Atheeb** 2-9-5 0 LouisSteward 5 60
(Sir Michael Stoute) *hmpd s: hld up: shkn up over 2f out: outpcd fr over 1f out* 16/1

7 8 **Rochford (IRE)** 2-9-5 0 JFEgan 1 36
(Henry Spiller) *s.i.s: hld up: shkn up over 2f out: wknd over 1f out* 33/1

1m 13.58s (1.48) **Going Correction** 0.0s/f (Good) **7** Ran SP% **117.7**
Speed ratings (Par 95): **90,89,89,88,84 80,70**
CSF £15.26 TOTE £3.00: £1.60, £2.20; EX 14.10 Trifecta £27.00.
Owner Godolphin **Bred** Godolphin **Trained** Newmarket, Suffolk

FOCUS
Invincible Army took this in 2017 and the 121-rated Quorto in 2018, so this renewal has a lot to live up to. They finished in a bunch, with a rallying winner who looks promising.

4070 HEATH COURT HOTEL "HOUSE OF FUN" H'CAP (DIV I) 1m
6:45 (6:46) (Class 5) (0-70,72) 3-Y-O
£4,528 (£1,347; £673; £400; £400; £400) **Stalls** High

Form RPR

-040 1 **Potenza (IRE)**[22] 3246 3-8-0 **52** GabrieleMalune(3) 5 64
(Stef Keniry) *sn w ldrs: led over 5f out: shkn up and hdd over 3f out: led again over 1f out: rdn clr (trainer said, regarding the improved form shown, the gelding appreciated the ground)* 5/1

565 2 3 ¾ **Osho**[54] 2140 3-9-0 **63** SeanLevey 1 66
(Richard Hannon) *s.i.s: hld up: rdn over 1f out: r.o to go 2nd wl ins fnl f: no ch w wnr* 9/2[3]

-244 3 1 ¾ **Maqaadeer**[50] 2336 3-9-8 **71** PatCosgrave 4 70
(Ed Dunlop) *hld up in tch: nt clr run over 2f out: rdn to chse wnr over 1f out: edgd rt and no ex ins fnl f* 5/1

006 4 1 **Sandy Steve**[49] 2366 3-8-7 **56** JasonWatson 9 53
(Stuart Williams) *hld up: hdwy over 3f out: rdn over 1f out: no ex fnl f* 16/1

060 5 2 ½ **Raha**[13] 3603 3-9-4 **67** CharlieBennett 8 58
(Julia Feilden) *racd alone far side and up w the pce: rdn over 1f out: wknd ins fnl f* 20/1

5300 6 ½ **Shaleela's Dream**[55] 2125 3-9-2 **65** JFEgan 2 55
(Jane Chapple-Hyam) *broke wl: sn stdd and lost pl: hld up: hdwy over 2f out: rdn over 1f out: hung lft and wknd ins fnl f* 8/1

00-0 7 1 **Lynchpin (IRE)**[11] 3665 3-8-13 **69** CierenFallon(7) 7 56
(Lydia Pearce) *w ldrs: rdn over 2f out: wknd ins fnl f* 20/1

-003 8 2 **House Deposit**[13] 3570 3-9-3 **66** (t) KerrinMcEvoy 6 49
(Declan Carroll) *led: hdd over 5f out: led again over 3f out: rdn and hdd over 1f out: wknd ins fnl f* 4/1[2]

1-03 9 5 **My Boy Lewis (IRE)**[22] 3249 3-9-9 **72** KieranShoemark 11 43
(Roger Fell) *s.i.s: hld up: hdwy over 3f out: rdn over 1f out: wknd and eased fnl f (jockey said gelding lost its action when travelling into the dip and he ran flat)* 7/2[1]

0000 10 28 **Rock Up In Style**[11] 3665 3-9-5 **68** StevieDonohoe 3
(Clare Ellam) *s.i.s: hdwy to join ldrs over 6f out tl shkn up over 3f out: sn wknd (jockey said gelding stopped quickly)* 33/1

1m 39.16s (-0.84) **Going Correction** 0.0s/f (Good) **10** Ran SP% **123.2**
Speed ratings (Par 99): **104,100,98,97,95 94,93,91,86,58**
CSF £28.78 CT £122.73 TOTE £5.90: £2.10, £2.00, £2.20; EX 35.10 Trifecta £193.40.
Owner Kristian Strangeway **Bred** Angelo Robiati **Trained** Middleham, N Yorks

FOCUS
The first division of a modest handicap with an easy, well-backed winner who has been rated as improving plenty.

4071 HEATH COURT HOTEL "HOUSE OF FUN" H'CAP (DIV II) 1m
7:15 (7:18) (Class 5) (0-70,71) 3-Y-O
£4,528 (£1,347; £673; £400; £400; £400) **Stalls** High

Form RPR

4-33 1 **Akwaan (IRE)**[27] 3093 3-9-6 **69** (p[1]) DaneO'Neill 6 79
(Simon Crisford) *s.i.s and hmpd s: hld up: racd keenly: hdwy over 1f out: rdn to ld ins fnl f: r.o wl* 10/1

3211 2 2 **Antico Lady (IRE)**[22] 3271 3-9-3 **69** BenRobinson(3) 2 74
(Brian Ellison) *led: rdn over 1f out: hdd ins fnl f: styd on same pce* 11/4[1]

60-2 3 3 **Rock The Cradle (IRE)**[25] 3170 3-9-8 **71** ShaneKelly 5 69
(Ed Vaughan) *hmpd s: sn chsng ldrs: rdn over 2f out: no ex ins fnl f* 5/1[2]

523- 4 hd **Li Kui**[177] 9708 3-9-7 **70** (p[1]) RossaRyan 3 68
(Paul Cole) *hld up: hdwy over 1f out: sn rdn and hung lft: styd on same pce fnl f* 10/1

3642 5 2 ¾ **Kingdom Of Dubai (FR)**[30] 2965 3-9-5 **68** (b) JackMitchell 11 59
(Roger Varian) *hld up: hdwy over 1f out: sn rdn: wknd ins fnl f* 6/1[3]

4360 6 ½ **Margaret J**[9] 3741 3-7-9 **51** oh5 (p) SophieRalston(7) 9 41
(Phil McEntee) *w ldr 6f: sn rdn: wknd fnl f* 25/1

00-1 7 1 ¾ **Pushmi Pullyu (IRE)**[8] 3780 3-8-13 **65** 6ex RowanScott(3) 4 51
(Jane Chapple-Hyam) *s.i.s: hld up: rdn over 1f out: n.d (trainer could offer no explanation for the filly's performance other than the race may have possibly come too soon)* 11/4[1]

4226 8 1 ½ **Redemptive**[25] 3154 3-9-2 **65** JFEgan 7 48
(John Butler) *edgd rt s: sn chsng ldrs: rdn and ev ch wl over 1f out: wknd ins fnl f (jockey said filly had no more to give)* 16/1

5-51 9 ¾ **Kahina (IRE)**[31] 2930 3-8-7 **56** (p) JasonWatson 8 37
(Hugo Palmer) *prom: racd keenly: rdn over 2f out: wknd fnl f* 10/1

1m 39.86s (-0.14) **Going Correction** 0.0s/f (Good) **9** Ran SP% **121.3**
Speed ratings (Par 99): **100,98,95,94,92 91,89,88,87**
CSF £39.72 CT £162.08 TOTE £11.10: £3.00, £1.80, £1.60; EX 53.40 Trifecta £366.20.
Owner Hamdan Al Maktoum **Bred** John O'Connor **Trained** Newmarket, Suffolk

FOCUS
The second division looked stronger on paper but it's still no more than modest form. They were 0.7 seconds slower, with the early pace not looking as strong.

4072 HEATH COURT "OUR HOUSE' FILLIES" H'CAP 7f
7:50 (7:50) (Class 3) (0-95,87) 3-Y-O+ **£9,703** (£2,887; £1,443; £721) **Stalls** High

Form RPR

51-3 1 **Breathtaking Look**[35] 2809 4-9-8 **81** KerrinMcEvoy 6 95
(Stuart Williams) *trckd ldrs: racd keenly: shkn up over 2f out: chal over 1f out: rdn to ld ins fnl f: r.o (jockey said filly lost left hind shoe)* 5/1[3]

-212 2 3 **Agincourt (IRE)**[15] 3494 4-10-0 **87** DanielTudhope 3 93
(David O'Meara) *hld up: hdwy over 2f out: led over 1f out: rdn and hdd ins fnl f: styd on same pce* 9/4[1]

104- 3 1 ¼ **Dupioni (IRE)**[210] 9224 3-9-2 **84** ShaneKelly 2 84
(Rae Guest) *s.i.s: hld up: hdwy over 1f out: styd on* 16/1

-005 4 1 ¼ **Octave (IRE)**[15] 3494 3-9-1 **83** JasonWatson 9 79
(Mark Johnston) *led: rdn: hung lft and hdd over 1f out: no ex ins fnl f* 10/1

-324 5 2 **Heritage**[25] 3151 3-9-1 **83** LiamKeniry 8 74
(Clive Cox) *chsd ldr tl shkn up over 1f out: wknd ins fnl f* 6/1

11-3 6 3 **Gold Arrow**[21] 3293 3-9-1 **83** RobHornby 5 66
(Ralph Beckett) *hld up: rdn over 2f out: wknd over 1f out* 9/2[2]

3020 7 2 ¼ **Starlight Romance (IRE)**[21] 3308 5-10-0 **87** TonyHamilton 4 67
(Richard Fahey) *s.s: a bhd (jockey said mare was slowly away and never travelling early, before staying on toward the finish)* 6/1

0-65 8 5 **Ajrar**[24] 3193 3-9-2 **84** SeanLevey 7 47
(Richard Hannon) *chsd ldrs: rdn over 2f out: wknd over 1f out* 12/1

1m 23.7s (-2.00) **Going Correction** 0.0s/f (Good)
WFA 3 from 4yo+ 9lb **8** Ran SP% **116.9**
Speed ratings (Par 107): **111,107,106,104,102 99,96,90**
CSF £17.10 CT £170.13 TOTE £5.00: £1.60, £1.30, £5.00; EX 15.80 Trifecta £113.60.
Owner J W Parry **Bred** Ellis Stud And Bellow Hill Stud **Trained** Newmarket, Suffolk

FOCUS
The feature was a fair fillies' handicap. This rates a step forward from the winner, with the runner-up close to form.

4073 PALACE HOUSE NEWMARKET BRITISH EBF NOVICE STKS (PLUS 10 RACE) 1m 2f
8:25 (8:26) (Class 4) 3-Y-O **£5,822** (£1,732; £865; £432) **Stalls** Centre

Form RPR

1 1 **Logician**[35] 2795 3-9-8 0 RobertHavlin 6 93+
(John Gosden) *chsd ldr: shkn up over 2f out: rdn to ld over 1f out: styd on (trainer's rep said colt lost right hind shoe)* 2/9[1]

2 1 ¾ **Away He Goes (IRE)** 3-9-2 0 SeanLevey 2 83
(Ismail Mohammed) *s.i.s: sn chsng ldrs: swtchd lft over 2f out: rdn over 1f out: edgd lft and styd on to go 2nd wl ins fnl f* 20/1[3]

3 3 shd **Persuading (IRE)**[127] 723 3-9-2 0 KerrinMcEvoy 1 82
(Charlie Appleby) *led: shkn up and edgd lft over 2f out: hdd over 1f out: styd on same pce wl ins fnl f* 6/1[2]

05 4 4 ½ **Earth And Sky (USA)**[14] 3553 3-8-11 0 PatCosgrave 5 68+
(George Scott) *hld up in tch: shkn up over 2f out: sn outpcd: styd on ins fnl f* 20/1[3]

5 ¾ **Look Closely** 3-9-2 0 JackMitchell 3 72
(Roger Varian) *s.s: hdwy over 5f out: rdn over 2f out: wkng whn hung rt ins fnl f* 6/1[2]

64 6 11 **Noble Account**[22] 3277 3-9-2 0 (h[1]) CharlieBennett 4 50
(Julia Feilden) *hld up: plld hrd early: shkn up over 2f out: sn wknd* 25/1

00 7 2 ¼ **Aide Memoire (IRE)**[35] 2802 3-8-11 0 JFEgan 7 40
(Neil King) *s.i.s and wnt lft s: hld up: plld hrd early: shkn up and wknd over 2f out* 66/1

2m 9.32s (2.22) **Going Correction** 0.0s/f (Good) **7** Ran SP% **125.3**
Speed ratings (Par 101): **91,89,89,85,85 76,74**
CSF £12.52 TOTE £1.10: £1.10, £5.30; EX 12.40 Trifecta £49.10.
Owner K Abdullah **Bred** Juddmonte Farms Ltd **Trained** Newmarket, Suffolk

FOCUS
An uncompetitive novice that was taken in 2018 by the subsequent Group-2 winning Loxley. The winner probably didn't need to improve from his debut. Add 30yds.

4074 HEATH COURT "WINGS OF A DOVE" FILLIES' H'CAP 5f
8:55 (8:56) (Class 5) (0-70,68) 4-Y-O+
£4,528 (£1,347; £673; £400; £400; £400) **Stalls** High

Form RPR

3-32 1 **Princess Keira (IRE)**[29] 3020 4-9-0 **61** PatCosgrave 5 67
(Mick Quinn) *hld up: hdwy 1/2-way: chsd ldr over 1f out: rdn to ld ins fnl f: r.o* 5/1[3]

0-32 2 nse **Lethal Angel**[35] 2804 4-9-7 **68** (b) KerrinMcEvoy 4 74
(Stuart Williams) *chsd ldr tl led over 1f out: rdn and hdd ins fnl f: r.o* 4/1[2]

0060 3 1 ¼ **The Special One (IRE)**[2] 3989 6-7-9 **49** (t) SophieRalston(7) 7 51
(Phil McEntee) *broke wl: sn pushed along and outpcd: hdwy over 1f out: r.o* 12/1

0151 4 1 ½ **Precious Plum**[29] 3001 5-9-1 **62** (p) JackMitchell 2 59
(Charlie Wallis) *hld up: hung lft fr 1/2-way: rdn and hdwy over 1f out: nt trble ldrs* 7/1

2220 5 ½ **Honey Gg**[24] 3206 4-8-12 **66** CianMacRedmond(7) 3 62
(Declan Carroll) *chsd ldrs: rdn over 1f out: no ex ins fnl f* 9/4[1]

304 6 2 ¼ **Spenny's Lass**[25] 3144 4-8-9 **56** (p) BrettDoyle 1 44
(John Ryan) *s.i.s: nvr nrr* 10/1

366- 7 nk **Global Rose (IRE)**[292] 6836 4-8-7 **61** (p) CierenFallon(7) 6 48
(Gay Kelleway) *chsd ldrs: rdn 1/2-way: hung rt over 1f out: wknd ins fnl f* 12/1

2-30 8 8 **Invisible Storm**[137] 597 4-8-6 **53** (b) JFEgan 8 15
(William Stone) *led: rdn: hung rt and hdd over 1f out: wknd fnl f* 8/1

00 9 3 ¼ **Alaskan Bay (IRE)**[29] 3001 4-8-5 **52** LukeMorris 9 3
(Rae Guest) *s.i.s: a in rr: wknd over 1f out (jockey said filly jumped awkwardly leaving stalls)* 20/1

59.63s (0.93) **Going Correction** 0.0s/f (Good) **9** Ran SP% **120.3**
Speed ratings (Par 100): **92,91,89,87,86 83,82,69,64**
CSF £26.51 CT £233.34 TOTE £5.50: £1.60, £1.60, £2.80; EX 16.10 Trifecta £271.80.
Owner Kenny Bruce **Bred** B & C Equine **Trained** Newmarket, Suffolk

FOCUS
A cracking finish to this modest fillies' handicap
T/Plt: £82.50 to a £1 stake. Pool: £44,412.32 - 392.98 winning units T/Qpdt: £25.90 to a £1 stake. Pool: £5,261.56 - 150.01 winning units **Colin Roberts**

3196 REDCAR (L-H)
Friday, June 21

OFFICIAL GOING: Good to soft (good in places; 7.3)
Wind: light against Weather: Fine

4075 START YOUR RACING TV FREE TRIAL NOW (S) STKS 7f
1:40 (1:44) (Class 5) 2-Y-O
£3,823 (£1,137; £568; £300; £300; £300) **Stalls** Centre

Form RPR

000 1 **Rain Cap**[7] 3812 2-8-12 0 BenCurtis 5 60
(Mick Channon) *chsd ldr: rdn along to press ldr over 2f out: drvn over 1f out: kpt on to ld 50yds out* 4/1[2]

640 **2** *1 1/4* **Classy Lady**[7] 3812 2-8-7 0 RoystonFfrench 3 52
(Ollie Pears) *led: pushed along and pressed over 2f out: rdn over 1f out: hdd 50yds out: no ex* **8/1**
0 **3** *2 1/2* **Our Dave**[10] 3703 2-8-12 0 JasonHart 1 50
(John Quinn) *s.i.s: hld up: pushed along and hdwy to chse ldrs 2f out: rdn over 1f out: kpt on same pce* **11/4[1]**
05 **4** *1 1/2* **Six Gun**[50] 2331 2-8-12 0 EdwardGreatrex 7 46
(Archie Watson) *chsd ldrs: rdn over 2f out: drvn over 1f out: one pce* **10/1**
60 **5** *3 1/2* **The Trendy Man (IRE)**[7] 3812 2-8-9 0 (p) ConorMcGovern(3) 2 37
(David O'Meara) *in tch: rdn along 3f out: outpcd over 1f out* **6/1[3]**
0 **6** *3/4* **Susie Javea**[46] 2475 2-8-7 0 CamHardie 10 30
(Ollie Pears) *dwlt: hld up: rdn along 3f out: nvr threatened* **66/1**
0 **7** *1* **Fulbeck Rose**[24] 3196 2-8-7 0 (t[1]) AndrewMullen 4 28
(Nigel Tinkler) *slowly away: hld up: pushed along and hdwy over 2f out: wknd ins fnl f* **25/1**
04 **8** *2 1/4* **Not Another Word**[23] 3212 2-8-2 0 FayeMcManoman(5) 11 22
(Nigel Tinkler) *hld up: rdn over 3f out: nvr involved* **28/1**
00 **9** *hd* **Dream Isle (IRE)**[11] 3644 2-8-5 0 (p[1]) TobyEley(7) 9 26
(Steph Hollinshead) *midfield: rdn 3f out: wknd over 1f out (jockey said colt was never travelling)* **50/1**
0605 **10** *6* **Birkie Queen (IRE)**[10] 3714 2-8-0 0 LauraCoughlan(7) 8 6
(J S Moore) *chsd ldrs: rdn 3f out: wknd 2f out* **6/1[3]**
005 **11** *22* **Brown Eyes Blue (IRE)**[14] 3562 2-8-4 0 (b) SeanDavis(3) 6
(J S Moore) *hld up: wknd and bhd over 2f out* **7/1**

1m 25.84s (0.44) **Going Correction** 0.0s/f (Good) 11 Ran SP% **118.7**
Speed ratings (Par 93): **97,95,92,91,87 86,85,82,82,75 50**
CSF £35.28 TOTE £5.60: £1.70, £2.30, £1.60; EX 34.40 Trifecta £126.20.There was no bid for the winner.
Owner M Channon **Bred** Mike Channon Bloodstock Limited **Trained** West Ilsley, Berks

FOCUS
A modest seller which was also one of the first 7f juvenile races of the year. It rates as par for the grade.

4076 TRIAL RACING TV FOR FREE NOW NOVICE STKS — 1m 2f 1y
2:10 (2:13) (Class 5) 3-Y-O+ **£4,528** (£1,347; £673; £336) **Stalls** Low

Form RPR
2-22 **1** **Audarya (FR)**[22] 3277 3-8-11 81 DanielMuscutt 5 90+
(James Fanshawe) *in tch: trckd ldr 4f out: led 3f out: sn pushed clr: kpt on: easily* **1/2[1]**
0 **2** *3 3/4* **Medal Winner (FR)**[42] 2581 3-9-2 0 EdwardGreatrex 7 82+
(Archie Watson) *hld up in tch: rdn and hdwy 3f out: wnt 2nd 2f out: kpt on but no ch w easy wnr* **16/1[3]**
5-1 **3** *9* **Proton (IRE)**[22] 3248 3-9-9 0 PaulMulrennan 2 71
(Jedd O'Keeffe) *dwlt but sn led: rdn along and hdd 3f out: wknd 2f out* **3/1[2]**
0 **4** *3 1/2* **Nataleena (IRE)**[33] 2875 3-8-11 0 CamHardie 6 52
(Ben Haslam) *hld up: pushed along over 4f out: nvr threatened* **80/1**
0/0 **5** *2* **Howbaar (USA)**[22] 3247 4-10-0 0 AndrewElliott 8 53
(James Bethell) *pressed ldr: hung lft and lost pl over 3f out: wknd over 2f out* **100/1**
60 **6** *4 1/2* **Shamitsar**[41] 2634 5-10-0 0 ConnorBeasley 4 44
(Ray Craggs) *hld up in tch: rdn over 3f out: sn wknd* **100/1**
31- **7** *1* **Artois**[287] 7022 3-9-9 0 BenCurtis 3 49
(Hugo Palmer) *trckd ldrs: rdn 3f out: wknd qckly* **3/1[2]**

2m 6.66s (-0.24) **Going Correction** 0.0s/f (Good)
WFA 3 from 4yo+ 12lb 7 Ran SP% **125.8**
Speed ratings (Par 103): **100,97,89,87,85 81,81**
CSF £14.39 TOTE £1.10: £1.10, £5.10; EX 18.10 Trifecta £31.80.
Owner Mrs A M Swinburn **Bred** Haras D'Ecouves **Trained** Newmarket, Suffolk
■ Laulloir was withdrawn. Price at time of withdrawal 25-1. Rule 4 does not apply.

FOCUS
This looked an interesting novice event and the winner rates as an improver.

4077 CELEBRATE THE LIFE OF JOE NEWTON H'CAP — 1m 2f 1y
2:45 (2:45) (Class 4) (0-80,81) 3-Y-O
£6,663 (£1,982; £990; £495; £300; £300) **Stalls** Low

Form RPR
-055 **1** **Production**[21] 3307 3-9-3 **76** BenCurtis 5 83
(Richard Hannon) *prom: rdn over 2f out: drvn to ld appr fnl f: kpt on* **7/1**
2213 **2** *1 3/4* **Highwaygrey**[15] 3505 3-8-10 **69** DavidAllan 3 72
(Tim Easterby) *hld up in tch: hdwy 3f out and sn trckd ldrs: rdn 2f out: kpt on same pce: wnt 2nd post* **4/1[2]**
2-21 **3** *hd* **Cape Victory (IRE)**[39] 2677 3-9-7 **80** PaulMulrennan 1 83
(James Tate) *dwlt but sn led: pushed along over 2f out: hdd appr fnl f: drvn and sn one pce: lost 2nd post* **9/4[1]**
10-0 **4** *3/4* **Ride The Monkey (IRE)**[32] 2895 3-9-2 **75** ConnorBeasley 7 76
(Michael Dods) *hld up: rdn along over 3f out: styd on fnl f* **28/1**
4534 **5** *1 3/4* **Itchingham Lofte (IRE)**[15] 3513 3-8-11 **70** RobbieDowney 6 68
(David Barron) *hld up in tch: rdn along over 2f out: edgd lft over 1f out: no imp* **9/1**
6-40 **6** *shd* **Flint Hill**[55] 2096 3-9-0 **73** (p[1]) AndrewMullen 2 70
(Michael Dods) *trckd ldrs: rdn along 3f out: sn outpcd and no threat after* **9/2[3]**
2-10 **7** *11* **Dancin Boy**[20] 3358 3-9-8 **81** JackGarritty 4 56
(Michael Dods) *trckd ldrs: rdn 3f out: wknd 2f out* **4/1[2]**

2m 7.15s (0.25) **Going Correction** 0.0s/f (Good) 7 Ran SP% **114.9**
Speed ratings (Par 101): **99,97,97,96,95 95,86**
CSF £35.20 TOTE £8.00: £3.70, £2.80; EX 32.20 Trifecta £109.10.
Owner The Royal Ascot Racing Club **Bred** Sun Kingdom Pty Ltd **Trained** East Everleigh, Wilts

FOCUS
Mainly unexposed sorts in this handicap for 3yos, which was run at just a fair gallop. Less than 5l covered the first six but the winner rates as an improver.

4078 WATCH RACING TV IN STUNNING HD CLAIMING STKS — 7f
3:20 (3:20) (Class 5) 3-Y-O+
£4,075 (£1,212; £606; £303; £300; £300) **Stalls** Centre

Form RPR
-233 **1** **Tukhoom (IRE)**[3] 3957 6-9-9 70 (b[1]) JasonHart 6 79
(Michael Herrington) *mde all: rdn over 1f out: kpt on wl* **2/1[1]**
0-40 **2** *4* **Imperial State**[15] 3503 6-9-9 81 (v) PaulMulrennan 3 69
(Michael Easterby) *hld up in midfield: rdn and hdwy 2f out: wnt 2nd jst ins fnl f: kpt on but no ch w wnr* **5/2[2]**
60-6 **3** *1 1/4* **Roller**[54] 2151 6-9-5 77 (p[1]) NathanEvans 5 61
(Michael Easterby) *hld up: rdn and hdwy over 1f out: kpt on fnl f: wnt 3rd towards fin (jockey said gelding slipped leaving stalls)* **11/4[3]**
5402 **4** *3/4* **Robero**[29] 3018 7-9-11 76 (p) BenCurtis 15 65
(Gay Kelleway) *prom: rdn over 2f out: lost 2nd jst ins fnl f: no ex and lost 3rd towards fin* **9/1**
5646 **5** *5* **Mutarakez (IRE)**[10] 3704 7-9-6 68 (b) SeanDavis(3) 12 50
(Ruth Carr) *chsd ldrs: rdn over 2f out: wknd appr fnl f* **14/1**
2060 **6** *3/4* **Thedevilinneville**[11] 3651 3-8-7 48 (p[1]) RoystonFfrench 10 38
(Adam West) *midfield: rdn over 2f out: hung lft and no imp* **80/1**
0-06 **7** *1 1/2* **Our Secret (IRE)**[53] 2197 3-8-3 47 ow1 AndrewMullen 13 31
(Liam Bailey) *midfield: rdn over 2f out: no imp* **50/1**
5000 **8** *3/4* **Dasheen**[9] 3721 6-9-2 59 (p) GemmaTutty(3) 14 39
(Karen Tutty) *hld up: nvr threatened* **66/1**
0000 **9** *1 3/4* **Lord Rob**[25] 3163 8-8-9 44 TobyEley(7) 2 31
(David Thompson) *slowly away and in rr: nvr involved* **100/1**
4-00 **10** *3/4* **Itsupforgrabsnow (IRE)**[25] 3158 4-8-7 43 (h) RussellHarris(7) 7 27
(Susan Corbett) *midfield: rdn 3f out: wknd over 1f out* **125/1**
000- **11** *2* **Barney Bullet (IRE)**[206] 9273 4-8-10 42 HarryRussell(7) 4 25
(Noel Wilson) *chsd ldrs tl wknd over 2f out* **100/1**
440- **12** *hd* **Cotton Socks (IRE)**[188] 9559 4-9-5 42 DavidAllan 11 26
(Ann Duffield) *midfield: rdn over 2f out: wknd over 1f out* **100/1**
0-0 **13** *4* **Neigh Dramas**[41] 2633 3-8-10 0 AndrewElliott 16 13
(Bryan Smart) *wnt rt s: a towards rr* **100/1**
032/ **14** *hd* **Kalk Bay (IRE)**[782] 2184 12-9-0 80 JoshQuinn(7) 8 17
(Michael Easterby) *v.s.a: a wl bhd (jockey said gelding jumped awkwardly leaving the stalls and was slowly away)* **33/1**
60 **15** *31* **Melwood**[24] 3200 3-8-7 0 CamHardie 1
(Antony Brittain) *chsd ldrs tl wknd qckly over 2f out: t.o* **100/1**
6/04 **P** **Graphite (IRE)**[50] 2335 5-9-6 65 (b[1]) ConnorBeasley 9
(Geoffrey Harker) *midfield: wnt wrong and p.u over 5f out* **11/1**

1m 23.03s (-2.37) **Going Correction** 0.0s/f (Good)
WFA 3 from 4yo+ 9lb 16 Ran SP% **126.9**
Speed ratings (Par 103): **108,103,102,101,95 94,92,92,90,89 86,86,82,81,46**
CSF £7.35 TOTE £3.00: £1.50, £1.10, £1.50; EX 9.20 Trifecta £28.40.
Owner Mark A Leatham **Bred** Kabansk Ltd & Rathbarry Stud **Trained** Cold Kirby, N Yorks

FOCUS
A wide range of abilities in this claimer, in which the first four finished clear and few featured. The winner has been rated around last year's best.

4079 RACING TV FREE FOR A MONTH STRAIGHT MILE SERIES H'CAP (RACING TV STRAIGHT MILE SERIES QUALIFIER) — 7f 219y
3:55 (3:55) (Class 3) (0-90,90) 3-Y-O+ **£7,762** (£2,310; £1,154; £577) **Stalls** Centre

Form RPR
2125 **1** **On The Line (IRE)**[62] 1945 3-9-1 **87** (bt) BenCurtis 7 95
(Hugo Palmer) *dwlt sltly: hld up: rdn and hdwy 2f out: drvn to chal strly fnl f: kpt on: led post* **7/1[3]**
2050 **2** *shd* **Weld Al Emarat**[15] 3502 7-9-0 **76** PaulMulrennan 3 86
(Michael Easterby) *trckd ldrs: pushed along 2f out: rdn to ld appr fnl f: sn strly pressed: kpt on but hdd post* **7/2[2]**
4502 **3** *3* **Dawaaleeb (USA)**[35] 2803 5-10-0 **90** (v) JasonHart 1 93
(Les Eyre) *led narrowly: rdn and hdd 2f out: kpt on same pce fnl f* **3/1[1]**
5-06 **4** *nk* **Calvados Spirit**[83] 1413 6-9-2 **81** SeanDavis(3) 5 83
(Richard Fahey) *half-rrd s: sn midfield: pushed along and chsd ldrs over 2f out: rdn and outpcd over 1f out: plugged on ins fnl f* **8/1**
0230 **5** *nk* **Swift Emperor (IRE)**[7] 3811 7-9-4 **80** RobbieDowney 4 82
(David Barron) *slowly away: hld up: rdn and hdwy to chse ldrs on outer 2f out: no ex ins fnl f* **10/1**
-000 **6** *3/4* **Tricorn (IRE)**[25] 3160 5-9-13 **89** JackGarritty 6 89
(Ruth Carr) *hld up: rdn along over 2f out: kpt on ins fnl f: nvr involved* **14/1**
1600 **7** *1/2* **Give It Some Teddy**[6] 3867 5-9-6 **82** DuranFentiman 9 81
(Tim Easterby) *hld up: pushed along over 2f out: nvr involved* **11/1**
0-5 **8** *nse* **Donncha (IRE)**[104] 1097 8-9-10 **86** DavidAllan 8 85
(Seb Spencer) *trckd ldrs: rdn over 2f out: outpcd and btn over 1f out* **9/1**
30-0 **9** *1 1/2* **Gymkhana**[13] 3589 6-9-11 **90** ConorMcGovern(3) 2 85
(David O'Meara) *prom: rdn to ld 2f out: hdd appr fnl f: wknd* **40/1**
2603 **10** *1 1/4* **Reggae Runner (FR)**[10] 3683 3-8-12 **84** AndrewMullen 10 74
(Mark Johnston) *chsd ldrs: rdn over 2f out: wknd fnl f* **7/1[3]**

1m 36.86s (0.26) **Going Correction** 0.0s/f (Good)
WFA 3 from 5yo+ 10lb 10 Ran SP% **119.9**
Speed ratings (Par 107): **98,97,94,94,94 93,93,93,91,90**
CSF £32.68 CT £93.38 TOTE £8.40: £2.90, £1.30, £2.50; EX 37.40 Trifecta £237.80.
Owner V I Araci **Bred** Biddestone Stud Ltd **Trained** Newmarket, Suffolk

FOCUS
This wasn't the strongest of 0-90 handicaps as not many came into it in much form. The pace was just fair, and though the first two were clear, the others were in a bit of a heap.

4080 WATCH RACING TV WITH FREE TRIAL NOW H'CAP — 7f
4:35 (4:35) (Class 5) (0-70,71) 3-Y-O
£4,075 (£1,212; £606; £303; £300; £300) **Stalls** Centre

Form RPR
-503 **1** **Leo Davinci (USA)**[11] 3665 3-9-5 **67** (t) BenCurtis 6 77+
(George Scott) *midfield: rdn and hdwy 2f out: led 1f out: kpt on wl* **10/3[1]**
5232 **2** *2 1/4* **Beryl The Petal (IRE)**[13] 3569 3-9-6 **71** (v[1]) ConorMcGovern(3) 7 74
(David O'Meara) *prom: led over 2f out: drvn and hdd 1f out: one pce* **11/2[3]**
6-04 **3** *1/2* **Olivia R (IRE)**[11] 3650 3-9-4 **66** (h[1]) RobbieDowney 2 68
(David Barron) *slowly away: hld up: rdn over 2f out: hdwy over 1f out: kpt on fnl f* **4/1[2]**
-643 **4** *1* **Reasoned (IRE)**[30] 2965 3-9-1 **63** RyanTate 9 62
(James Eustace) *trckd ldrs: rdn over 2f out: kpt on same pce* **11/1**
0254 **5** *3/4* **Ey Up Its Mick**[10] 3709 3-8-10 **58** (b) JasonHart 15 55
(Tony Coyle) *slowly away: hld up: pushed along over 2f out: kpt on ins fnl f: nrst fin* **20/1**
560- **6** *shd* **Dreamseller (IRE)**[291] 6875 3-8-8 **56** DuranFentiman 11 53
(Tim Easterby) *prom: rdn over 2f out: outpcd over 1f out: plugged on fnl f* **33/1**
5000 **7** *3/4* **Parion**[18] 3413 3-8-9 **57** NathanEvans 13 52
(Richard Fahey) *hld up: rdn over 2f out: hdwy over 1f out: no further imp fnl f* **25/1**
0-13 **8** *hd* **Aghast**[31] 2937 3-9-1 **63** AndrewMullen 10 57
(Kevin Ryan) *midfield: rdn along 2f out: swtchd lft ins fnl f: kpt on: nvr threatened* **10/1**
020- **9** *2* **Ugo Gregory**[258] 7988 3-9-2 **64** DavidAllan 12 53
(Tim Easterby) *in tch: pushed along and lost pl over 2f out: no threat after* **20/1**
50 **10** *1* **Chains Of Love (IRE)**[39] 2689 3-9-7 **69** (p) CliffordLee 3 55
(K R Burke) *hld up: nvr threatened* **10/1**

30-2 **11** *nk* **Micronize (IRE)**[151] 341 3-8-4 **55** SeanDavis(3) 4 40
(Richard Fahey) *led narrowly: hdd over 2f out: rdn and sn hung lft: wknd fnl f* **14/1**
-300 **12** *1* **Sophia Maria**[25] 3146 3-9-3 **65** AndrewElliott 8 47
(James Bethell) *w ldr: rdn over 2f out: wknd over 1f out* **28/1**
5-00 **13** *1 1/4* **Axe Axelrod (USA)**[21] 3307 3-9-9 **71** (p) ConnorBeasley 14 50
(Michael Dods) *prom: rdn over 2f out: wknd over 1f out* **10/1**
0-03 **14** *1 3/4* **Abie's Hollow**[13] 3569 3-9-1 **63** (p1) DougieCostello 1 37
(Tony Coyle) *midfield: rdn over 2f out: wknd over 1f out (jockey said gelding hung left-handed under pressure)* **10/1**
1m 24.54s (-0.86) **Going Correction** 0.0s/f (Good) **14** Ran SP% **129.6**
Speed ratings (Par 99): **104,101,100,99,98 98,97,97,95,94 93,92,91,89**
CSF £21.53 CT £81.37 TOTE £4.40: £1.50, £2.30, £2.00; EX 23.60 Trifecta £90.00.
Owner Excel Racing & Keith Breen II **Bred** H Sexton, S Sexton & Silver Fern Farm **Trained** Newmarket, Suffolk
■ Olympic Spirit was withdrawn. Price at time of withdrawal 33-1. Rule 4 \n\x\x does not appl
FOCUS
Straightforward form to an ordinary 3yo handicap, with the winner progressing again, rated around the second, third and fourth.

4081 RACINGTV.COM MAIDEN H'CAP 5f
5:10 (5:13) (Class 5) (0-75,70) 3-Y-O+
£4,075 (£1,212; £606; £303; £300; £300) **Stalls Centre**

Form RPR
0056 **1** **Dream House**[4] 3921 3-8-10 **59** DavidAllan 4 65
(Tim Easterby) *chsd ldrs: rdn to chal ent fnl f: led 110yds out: kpt on* **9/4**[1]
5560 **2** *nk* **Hard Solution**[11] 3645 3-8-12 **61** CamHardie 2 66
(David O'Meara) *chsd ldrs: sn pushed along: rdn over 1f out: ev ch ins fnl f: kpt on* **14/1**
0552 **3** *3/4* **Tie A Yellowribbon**[24] 3189 3-9-2 **65** BenCurtis 5 67
(James Bethell) *led: rdn over 1f out: drvn and hdd 110yds out: one pce* **5/2**[2]
202 **4** *3/4* **Sound Of Iona**[24] 3176 3-9-0 **70** CoreyMadden(7) 1 70
(Jim Goldie) *hld up: pushed along and hdwy on outer over 1f out: rdn and kpt on fnl f* **8/1**
560 **5** *1 3/4* **Skeetah**[15] 3508 3-9-2 **65** JasonHart 6 58
(John Quinn) *prom: rdn over 1f out: wknd ins fnl f* **8/1**
3423 **6** *1 1/4* **Brigadier**[20] 3339 3-9-0 **66** (v1) SeanDavis(3) 3 55
(Robert Cowell) *prom: rdn over 2f out: hung lft over 1f out: wknd ins fnl f (jockey said gelding lost right fore shoe)* **12/1**
-003 **7** *nse* **Global Hope (IRE)**[20] 3351 4-8-11 **61** (p) TobyEley(7) 7 52
(Gay Kelleway) *chsd ldrs: rdn 2f out: wknd ins fnl f (jockey said gelding was never travelling)* **4/1**[3]
58.58s (0.08) **Going Correction** 0.0s/f (Good)
WFA 3 from 4yo+ 6lb **7** Ran SP% **115.9**
Speed ratings (Par 103): **99,98,97,96,93 91,91**
CSF £34.42 CT £84.84 TOTE £4.20: £2.00, £7.40; EX 33.60 Trifecta £133.00.
Owner Ontoawinner, SDH Project Services Ltd 2 **Bred** Whitsbury Manor Stud **Trained** Great Habton, N Yorks
FOCUS
A maiden handicap and unlikely to be a strong race.
T/Plt: £21.60 to a £1 stake. Pool: £36,426.83 - 1,225.96 winning units T/Qpdt: £7.70 to a £1 stake. Pool: £3,783.39 - 360.5 winning units **Andrew Sheret**

4082 - 4090a (Foreign Racing) - See Raceform Interactive

4048
ROYAL ASCOT (R-H)
Saturday, June 22

OFFICIAL GOING: Good (good to firm in places; stands' 8.2, ctr 8.4, far 8.1, rnd 6.7) changing to good to firm on straight course after race 2 (3.05)
Wind: virtually nil Weather: fine

4091 CHESHAM STKS (LISTED RACE) 7f
2:30 (2:33) (Class 1) 2-Y-O
£51,039 (£19,350; £9,684; £4,824; £2,421; £1,215) **Stalls Centre**

Form RPR
11 **1** **Pinatubo (IRE)**[22] 3312 2-9-3 0 JamesDoyle 7 111+
(Charlie Appleby) *midfield: pushed along and hdwy 2f out: swtchd rt wl over 1f out: edgd lft over 1f out: sn led: r.o strly to draw clr fnl 100yds: impressive* **3/1**[2]
2 *3 1/4* **Lope Y Fernandez (IRE)**[15] 3555 2-9-3 0 RyanMoore 13 103+
(A P O'Brien, Ire) *trckd ldrs: rdn to ld wl over 1f out: sn edgd rt: hdd jst over 1f out: outpcd by wnr fnl 100yds* **5/4**[1]
1 **3** *1 1/4* **Highland Chief (IRE)**[71] 1733 2-9-3 0 RaulDaSilva 10 99
(Paul Cole) *trckd ldrs: rdn 2f out: unable qck whn checked over 1f out: edgd lft ins fnl f: kpt on but nt pce of front two* **14/1**
51 **4** *2 1/4* **Sun Power (FR)**[19] 3426 2-9-3 0 SilvestreDeSousa 5 93
(Richard Hannon) *hld up in rr: hdwy and swtchd lft over 2f out: styng on whn edgd rt over 1f out: styd on towards fin: no imp on ldrs* **33/1**
5 *hd* **Harpocrates (IRE)**[29] 3060 2-9-3 0 DonnachaO'Brien 14 93
(A P O'Brien, Ire) *racd keenly: prom: led over 2f out: rdn and hdd wl over 1f out: outpcd by ldrs whn intimidated over 1f out: styd on same pce ins fnl f* **12/1**
2 **6** *hd* **Heaven Forfend**[36] 2792 2-9-3 0 OisinMurphy 1 92
(Sir Michael Stoute) *hld up: pushed along 3f out: hdwy whn nt clr run over 1f out: sn drifted rt: styd on ins fnl f: nt pce to trble ldrs* **20/1**
7 *1 1/2* **Year Of The Tiger (IRE)**[15] 3554 2-9-3 0 SeamieHeffernan 16 89
(A P O'Brien, Ire) *midfield: rdn over 2f out: effrt over 1f out: nt pce of ldrs: intimidated ent fnl f: kpt on same pce after* **10/1**
4112 **8** *2 3/4* **Rose Of Kildare (IRE)**[14] 3564 2-8-12 0 FrankieDettori 2 76
(Mark Johnston) *in tch: rdn over 2f out: unable qck over 1f out: wknd ins fnl f* **8/1**[3]
4 **9** *1* **United Front (USA)**[14] 3607 2-9-3 0 WayneLordan 6 79
(A P O'Brien, Ire) *hld up: rdn over 2f out: checked whn nt clr run briefly over 1f out: kpt on ins fnl f: nvr able to trble ldrs* **50/1**
22 **10** *3/4* **Clay Regazzoni**[11] 3703 2-9-3 0 DanielTudhope 17 77
(Keith Dalgleish) *stdd s: hld up: hdwy over 3f out: rdn whn in tch over 2f out: wknd over 1f out* **66/1**
4 **11** *3/4* **Zmile**[29] 3049 2-8-12 0 JamesMcDonald 8 70
(Michael Bell) *trckd ldrs tl rdn and wknd over 1f out: eased whn wl btn fnl 100yds* **66/1**
12 *2* **Montanari** 2-9-3 0 DavidProbert 9 70
(Andrew Balding) *dwlt: hld up: rdn over 2f out: hmpd whn u.p and outpcd over 1f out: wl hld after* **66/1**
1 **13** *1 1/4* **Ardenlee Star (USA)**[11] 3702 2-9-3 0 TonyHamilton 12 66
(Richard Fahey) *midfield: rdn over 2f out: wknd over 1f out* **80/1**
2 **14** *hd* **Dramatic Sands (IRE)**[23] 3274 2-9-3 0 EdwardGreatrex 11 66+
(Archie Watson) *mounted on crse: led: rdn and hdd over 2f out: n.m.r and hmpd whn u.p over 1f out: sn wknd* **25/1**
1m 25.73s (-1.77) **Going Correction** 0.0s/f (Good) 2y crse rec **14** Ran SP% **123.2**
Speed ratings (Par 101): **110,106,104,102,102 101,100,96,95,94 94,91,90,90**
CSF £6.81 CT £47.91 TOTE £3.90: £1.35, £1.20, £3.75; EX 8.80 Trifecta £69.30.
Owner Godolphin **Bred** Godolphin **Trained** Newmarket, Suffolk
FOCUS
The ground had dried to good, good to firm in places and would only have been getting faster on a warm, sunny day, as evidenced by the fact the juvenile course record fell in this opening Listed event. It was, of course, partly to do with the fact Pinatubo is a high-class 2yo also and the form looks strong. There had been a tweak to race conditions, with horses whose sire or dam (previously just sire) had won over at least 1m2f now eligible. They raced in one group down the centre.

4092 JERSEY STKS (GROUP 3) 7f
3:05 (3:08) (Class 1) 3-Y-O
£51,039 (£19,350; £9,684; £4,824; £2,421; £1,215) **Stalls Centre**

Form RPR
-230 **1** **Space Traveller**[14] 3621 3-9-1 102 DanielTudhope 8 114
(Richard Fahey) *stdd s: hld up in last trio: effrt u.p and swtchd rt 2f out: clsd to chse ldrs 1f out: str run u.p to ld wl ins fnl f* **25/1**
4211 **2** *hd* **Space Blues (IRE)**[22] 3317 3-9-1 110 JamesDoyle 7 113
(Charlie Appleby) *stdd s: hld up in tch in midfield: clsd and nt clrest of runs 2f out: trcking ldrs whn nt clr run and swtchd lft 1f out: drvn and hdwy to ld ins fnl f: hdd wl ins fnl f* **5/2**[1]
-344 **3** *1 1/2* **Angel's Hideaway (IRE)**[22] 3317 3-8-12 109 RobertHavlin 4 106
(John Gosden) *hld up in tch in midfield: clsd to chse ldrs and swtchd rt over 1f out: drvn and clsd to chal 1f out: no ex and outpcd fnl 100yds* **14/1**
-302 **4** *1* **Urban Icon**[22] 3317 3-9-1 108 TomMarquand 11 106
(Richard Hannon) *in tch in midfield: pushed along briefly 4f out: effrt u.p 2f out: nt clr run and edgd out lft over 1f out: kpt on wl u.p ins fnl f: nvr getting on terms w ldrs* **7/1**
-350 **5** *nk* **Duke Of Hazzard (FR)**[28] 3082 3-9-1 104 (t) ChristopheSoumillon 9 105
(Paul Cole) *trckd ldrs: clsd travelling strly ent fnl 2f: rdn to ld over 1f out: drvn and hdd ins fnl f: no ex and sn outpcd* **25/1**
2-20 **6** *3/4* **Momkin (IRE)**[49] 2411 3-9-1 108 (b1) AndreaAtzeni 13 106+
(Roger Charlton) *s.i.s: sn in tch: hdwy into midfield 4f out: nt clr run 2f out: effrt and hung rt over 1f out: squeezed for room 1f out: kpt on same pce after (vet said colt had lost its right-fore shoe)* **9/1**
-131 **7** *nk* **Happy Power (IRE)**[8] 3814 3-9-1 112 SilvestreDeSousa 1 103
(Andrew Balding) *t.k.h: chsd ldrs: clsd and rdn to press ldrs 2f out: drvn and ev ch over 1f out tl no ex ins fnl f: wknd towards fin* **6/1**[3]
5443 **8** *2 1/4* **Marie's Diamond (IRE)**[22] 3317 3-9-1 104 FrankieDettori 3 97
(Mark Johnston) *led: rdn and hdd over 1f out: sn drvn and no ex 1f out: wknd ins fnl f* **14/1**
3-31 **9** *nk* **So Perfect (USA)**[34] 2882 3-9-1 110 RyanMoore 10 96
(A P O'Brien, Ire) *stdd after s: hld up in tch in midfield: clsd to trck ldrs and nt clr run 2f out: edgd out rt and effrt over 1f out: nt qckning pushed lft and hmpd 1f out: swtchd rt and no prog after* **4/1**[2]
-110 **10** *3/4* **Masaru**[28] 3082 3-9-1 97 PatDobbs 12 94
(Richard Hannon) *chsd ldrs: nt clrest of runs and edgd out lft over 1f out: unable qck and wknd ins fnl f* **50/1**
4-65 **11** *3/4* **Dubai Dominion**[14] 3621 3-9-1 98 (b) JamieSpencer 2 92
(Ed Vaughan) *stdd s: hld up in tch in midfield: swtchd rt and effrt 2f out: no imp and hung rt over 1f out: wknd ins fnl f* **66/1**
56 **12** *nk* **I Am Superman (IRE)**[28] 3104 3-9-1 107 LeighRoche 5 91
(M D O'Callaghan, Ire) *t.k.h: pressed ldr tl unable qck over 1f out: wknd ins fnl f (jockey said colt had no more to give)* **16/1**
-114 **13** *2 1/4* **Bye Bye Hong Kong (USA)**[21] 3343 3-9-1 112 OisinMurphy 15 85
(Andrew Balding) *chsd ldrs: rdn and struggling to qckn whn edgd rt and nudged 2f out: sn outpcd: wl btn fnl f* **16/1**
1625 **14** *1 3/4* **No Nonsense**[37] 2779 3-9-1 102 GeraldMosse 18 80
(David Elsworth) *in tch in midfield: lost pl u.p over 2f out: n.d after* **50/1**
0-0 **15** *3/4* **On A Session (USA)**[20] 3383 3-9-1 94 (p1) WayneLordan 14 78
(Aidan F Fogarty, Ire) *in tch in midfield: lost pl u.p over 2f out: no ch after* **50/1**
-054 **16** *1 3/4* **Fire Fly (IRE)**[9] 3786 3-8-12 101 SeamieHeffernan 17 70
(A P O'Brien, Ire) *s.i.s: a in rr: swtchd lft and effrt over 2f out: no prog u.p: wl btn after* **66/1**
5000 **17** *1/2* **Air Hair Lair (IRE)**[12] 3651 3-9-1 62 KierenFox 6 72?
(Sheena West) *a towards rr: rdn 3f out: sn struggling and no ch fnl 2f* **100/1**
4 **18** *3 3/4* **Western Frontier (USA)**[34] 2882 3-9-1 96 DonnachaO'Brien 16 62
(A P O'Brien, Ire) *chsd ldrs: rdn 1/2-way: lost pl over 2f out: bhd and eased ins fnl f* **33/1**
1m 24.57s (-2.93) **Going Correction** 0.0s/f (Good) **18** Ran SP% **130.9**
Speed ratings (Par 109): **116,115,114,112,112 111,111,108,108,107 106,106,103,101,100 98,98,94**
CSF £88.69 CT £992.36 TOTE £48.35: £11.00, £1.45, £5.80; EX 202.70 Trifecta £2988.40.
Owner Clipper Logistics **Bred** El Catorce Partnership **Trained** Musley Bank, N Yorks
■ Stewards' Enquiry : James Doyle two-day ban: used whip above the permitted level (Jul 8-9); two-day ban: interference & careless riding (Jul 10-11)
FOCUS
The top eight rated runners were separated by just 5lb in a solid and competitive edition. Its recent roll of honour featured subsequent Group/Grade 1 winners Ribchester and Expert Eye. They went an even pace and raced in one big group down the centre of the track. The winner was a surprise improver, rating 10lb+ up on anything he'd achieved before.

4093 HARDWICKE STKS (GROUP 2) 1m 3f 211y
3:40 (3:40) (Class 1) 4-Y-O+
£127,597 (£48,375; £24,210; £12,060; £6,052; £3,037) **Stalls Low**

Form RPR
-421 **1** **Defoe (IRE)**[22] 3314 5-9-1 118 AndreaAtzeni 7 121
(Roger Varian) *hld up in midfield: hdwy on outer over 2f out: edgd rt wl over 1f out: sn led: edgd rt again 1f out: kpt on wl: a doing enough towards fin* **11/4**[1]
44-3 **2** *1/2* **Nagano Gold**[49] 2428 5-9-1 105 (t1) ChristopheSoumillon 3 120
(Vaclav Luka Jr, Czech Republic) *bdly hmpd s: hld up in last pl: nt clr run 2f out: hdwy whn carried rt over 1f out: sn rdn: r.o to chse wnr wl ins fnl f: clsng towards fin but nr gng to get there* **25/1**

20-1 **3** *1* **Mirage Dancer**[28] 3077 5-9-1 116........................ PatDobbs 9 118
(Sir Michael Stoute) *racd in cl 2nd pl: travelling wl and led jst over 2f out: rdn and hdd over 1f out: carried rt by wnr 1f out: styd on same pce fnl 75yds* **6/1**

1-10 **4** *3* **Morando (FR)**[22] 3314 6-9-1 117........................ SilvestreDeSousa 8 113
(Andrew Balding) *racd keenly: trckd ldrs: rdn and unable qck 2f out: nt clr run and carried rt over 1f out: sn swtchd rt: kpt on u.p after but no imp* **12/1**

131- **5** *nk* **Masar (IRE)**[385] 3358 4-9-1 121........................ JamesDoyle 5 113
(Charlie Appleby) *stmbld bdly and nrly uns rdr s: hld up: hdwy on outer wl over 2f out: edgd rt whn chsng ldrs and cl up over 1f out: nt pce of front three ins fnl f: no ex fnl 100yds (jockey said colt stumbled leaving the stalls)* **3/1[2]**

0-32 **6** *3 ½* **Southern France (IRE)**[36] 2807 4-9-1 113........................ RyanMoore 1 107
(A P O'Brien, Ire) *hld up in midfield: rdn over 2f out: u.p whn nt clr run and checked sltly over 1f out: no imp and one pce ins fnl f* **9/2[3]**

0-13 **7** *¾* **Salouen (IRE)**[22] 3314 5-9-1 116........................ OisinMurphy 6 106
(Sylvester Kirk) *led: rdn and hdd jst over 2f out: unable to go w ldrs over 1f out: sn wknd* **8/1**

-014 **8** *12* **Communique (IRE)**[22] 3314 4-9-1 114........................ FrannyNorton 2 87
(Mark Johnston) *trckd ldrs: rdn and unable qck over 2f out: wknd over 1f out (vet said colt lost its right-fore shoe)* **14/1**

2m 31.09s (-1.51) **Going Correction** 0.0s/f (Good) **8** Ran SP% **113.5**
Speed ratings (Par 115): **105,104,104,102,101 99,98,90**
CSF £66.98 CT £381.16 TOTE £3.30: £1.15, £6.25, £2.00; EX 68.70 Trifecta £406.20.
Owner Sheikh Mohammed Obaid Al Maktoum **Bred** Darley **Trained** Newmarket, Suffolk
■ Stewards' Enquiry : Andrea Atzeni two-day ban: interference & careless riding (Jul 7-8)

FOCUS
The older horse scene over 1m4f has been a pretty weak one in the first part of the season, with Enable tucked away in her box and the likes of Crystal Ocean and Sea Of Class trying their hand, successfully in the former's case, at 1m2f. Defoe emerged as the best of the bunch in the Coronation Cup and backed that win, although there's a strong argument to be made that the 105-rated Czech runner in second was unlucky. They didn't go overly fast, with the pace just an even one. The third looked to run his race and sets the standard, but the runner-up was a big improver.

4094 DIAMOND JUBILEE STKS (GROUP 1) (BRITISH CHAMPIONS SERIES) 6f
4:20 (4:21) (Class 1) 4-Y-O+

£340,260 (£129,000; £64,560; £32,160; £16,140; £8,100) **Stalls** Centre

Form RPR

1111 **1** **Blue Point (IRE)**[4] 3950 5-9-3 120........................ JamesDoyle 9 122
(Charlie Appleby) *taken down early: chsd ldr for 2f: styd prom in chsng gp and travelled strly: wnt 2nd and clsd on ldr over 1f out: rdn to ld 1f out and kicked clr: drvn ins fnl f: all out cl home but a jst holding o* **6/4[1]**

0-11 **2** *hd* **Dream Of Dreams (IRE)**[33] 2916 5-9-3 111........................ DanielTudhope 11 121
(Sir Michael Stoute) *stdd s: hld up in rr: clsd over 1f out: swtchd rt and hdwy ent fnl f: str run to chse wnr wl ins fnl f: clsng qckly cl home: nt quite get to wnr* **12/1**

-115 **3** *2 ½* **Kachy**[28] 3084 6-9-3 112........................ RichardKingscote 10 113
(Tom Dascombe) *broke v fast: led and clr: rdn and jnd over 1f out: hdd 1f out and nt match pce of wnr: lost 2nd wl ins fnl f: hung on gamely for 3rd towards fin* **33/1**

00-2 **4** *¾* **Speak In Colours**[28] 3103 4-9-3 111........................(t) DonnachaO'Brien 16 111
(Joseph Patrick O'Brien, Ire) *midfield: effrt 2f out: kpt on u.p ins fnl f: nvr enough pce to get on terms w ldrs* **50/1**

-355 **5** *¾* **Le Brivido (FR)**[4] 3948 5-9-3 114........................ RyanMoore 14 108
(A P O'Brien, Ire) *stdd s: hld up in rr: effrt wl over 1f out: hdwy u.p 1f out: styd on ins fnl f: nvr trbld ldrs* **8/1**

10-3 **6** *hd* **The Tin Man**[33] 2916 7-9-3 117........................ OisinMurphy 17 108
(James Fanshawe) *s.i.s: towards rr: effrt 2f out: hdwy whn nt clr run and swtchd lft 1f out: styd on ins fnl f: nvr trbld ldrs* **8/1**

0-11 **7** *¾* **Invincible Army (IRE)**[38] 2744 4-9-3 115........................ PJMcDonald 13 105
(James Tate) *prom in chsng gp: effrt 2f out: kpt on press and chsd ldrs whn edgd rt 1f out: no imp fnl f* **7/1[3]**

0- **8** *2 ¼* **Lim's Cruiser (AUS)**[28] 6-9-3 114........................(b) VladDuric 12 98
(Stephen Gray, Singapore) *midfield: effrt over 1f out: unable qck and wknd ins fnl f* **66/1**

520- **9** *nk* **City Light (FR)**[57] 2089 5-9-3 114........................ ChristopheSoumillon 7 97
(S Wattel, France) *hld up in midfield: effrt over 1f out: sn drvn and unable qck: edgd lft and wknd ins fnl f* **6/1[2]**

16-0 **10** *½* **Projection**[38] 2744 6-9-3 110........................ JasonWatson 3 95
(Roger Charlton) *taken down early and led rdrless most of the way to s: hld up in midfield: clsd and nt clr run 2f out: effrt over 1f out: nt clr run hmpd 1f out: swtchd rt and kpt on ins fnl f* **40/1**

406- **11** *½* **Tip Two Win**[182] 9688 4-9-3 116........................ DavidProbert 18 94
(Roger Teal) *midfield: sn pushed along and dropped to rr: sme modest late hdwy: n.d* **50/1**

-101 **12** *½* **Keystroke**[66] 1853 7-9-3 110........................(t) AdamKirby 2 92
(Stuart Williams) *stdd after s: hld up towards rr: swtchd rt and effrt u.p over 1f out: no prog and wknd ins fnl f* **50/1**

0/3- **13** *1 ½* **Bound For Nowhere (USA)**[77] 5-9-3 115........................(t[1]) TylerGaffalione 1 87
(Wesley A Ward, U.S.A) *ponied to s: prom in chsng gp: edgd lft u.p and unable qck over 1f out: wknd ins fnl f* **12/1**

0-23 **14** *3* **Yafta**[38] 2744 4-9-3 109........................ JimCrowley 4 78
(Richard Hannon) *midfield: u.p ent fnl 2f: lost pl over 1f out: wknd fnl f* **40/1**

0 **15** *½* **Enzo's Lad (AUS)**[4] 3950 6-9-3 113........................(b) FergusSweeney 5 76
(Michael Pitman, New Zealand) *midfield: rdn 2f out: sn lost pl and bhd fnl f* **66/1**

1-63 **16** *3* **Sands Of Mali (FR)**[16] 3501 4-9-3 118........................(t[1]) JamesMcDonald 6 67
(Richard Fahey) *midfield: effrt over 1f out: sn btn and wknd ins fnl f (vet said colt had lost its right-fore shoe)* **16/1**

33-2 **17** *3* **Emblazoned (IRE)**[42] 2614 4-9-3 109........................(b[1]) FrankieDettori 8 57
(John Gosden) *wnt rt sn after leaving stalls: chse ldr after 2f tl over 1f out: sn btn and eased ins fnl f (jockey said colt stopped quickly)* **20/1**

1m 11.42s (-2.28) **Going Correction** 0.0s/f (Good) **17** Ran SP% **131.7**
Speed ratings (Par 117): **115,114,111,110,109 109,108,105,104,104 103,102,100,96,96 92,88**
CSF £21.99 CT £484.29 TOTE £2.10: £1.15, £5.25, £14.30; EX 34.20 Trifecta £1256.10.
Owner Godolphin **Bred** Oak Lodge Bloodstock **Trained** Newmarket, Suffolk

FOCUS
A superb renewal of this top quality sprint featured runners from six different countries. Favourite Blue Point became just the third horse to complete the King's Stand Stakes - Diamond Jubilee double. He rates up to standard, albeit a bit below his King's Stand win.

4095 WOKINGHAM STKS (HERITAGE H'CAP) 6f
5:00 (5:00) (Class 2) (0-110,108) 3-Y-O+

£108,937 (£32,620; £16,310; £8,155; £4,077; £2,047) **Stalls** Centre

Form RPR

20-1 **1** **Cape Byron**[42] 2609 5-9-9 **107**........................ AndreaAtzeni 10 118
(Roger Varian) *racd in centre of trck: chsd ldrs: effrt to ld overall over 1f out: rdn out and r.o ins fnl f: 1st of 20 in gp* **7/2[1]**

-404 **2** *1 ½* **Tis Marvellous**[29] 3043 5-9-3 **101**........................(t) AdamKirby 13 107
(Clive Cox) *racd in centre of trck: chsd ldrs: effrt 2f out: rdn and ev ch over 1f out: r.o u.p ins fnl f: nt pce of wnr: 2nd of 20 in gp* **14/1**

05-1 **3** *hd* **Danzeno**[20] 3375 8-9-4 **102** 5ex........................ FrankieDettori 17 107
(Michael Appleby) *racd in centre of trck: hld up: rdn and hdwy over 1f out: continued to prog ins fnl f: r.o towards fin: nrst fin: 3rd of 20 in gp* **7/1[2]**

2226 **4** *nk* **Raucous**[30] 3009 6-8-8 **99**........................(tp) CierenFallon[(7)] 12 103
(Robert Cowell) *racd in centre of trck: midfield: drvn and hdwy over 2f out: chsd ldrs over 1f out: styd on ins fnl f: nt pce of wnr fnl 100yds: 4th of 20 in gp* **50/1**

0-22 **5** *1* **Summerghand (IRE)**[48] 2442 5-9-2 **100**........................ DanielTudhope 15 101
(David O'Meara) *racd in centre of trck: hld up: rdn over 2f out: hdwy over 1f out: styd on ins fnl f: run flattened out towards fin: 5th of 20 in gp* **12/1**

0-54 **6** *nse* **Gunmetal (IRE)**[28] 3097 6-9-5 **103**........................ OisinMurphy 6 104
(David Barron) *racd far side: trckd ldrs: rdn over 1f out: r.o to ld gp fnl 75yds: nt quite pce of overall ldrs: kpt on nr fin: 1st of 6 fr gp* **12/1**

1-20 **7** *hd* **Perfection**[28] 3085 4-9-3 **101**........................(p) GeraldMosse 23 104+
(David O'Meara) *racd nrside: hld up: nt clr run over 2f out: swtchd rt and hdwy over 1f out: sn nt clr run: r.o ins fnl f: nt rch ldrs: 6th of 20 in gp* **28/1**

0312 **8** *nk* **Lake Volta (IRE)**[21] 3347 4-9-5 **103**........................ FrannyNorton 16 102
(Mark Johnston) *racd in centre of trck: prom: rdn and ev ch 2f out: unable qck over 1f out: styd on same pce ins fnl f: 7th of 20 in gp* **20/1**

2-25 **9** *nk* **Hey Jonesy (IRE)**[38] 2744 4-9-8 **106**........................(p) KevinStott 18 104
(Kevin Ryan) *racd in centre of trck early: chsd ldrs: rdn over 2f out: edgd lft and unable qck over 1f out: kpt on u.p ins fnl f: kpt on same pce towards fin: 8th of 20 fr gp* **17/2[3]**

0-15 **10** *½* **Vanbrugh (USA)**[42] 2615 4-9-10 **108**........................ JamesMcDonald 3 105
(Charles Hills) *racd far side: prom: led gp 3f out: rdn over 1f out: r.o u.p: nt pce of overall ldrs wl ins fnl f: hdd in gp fnl 75yds: no ex towards fin: 2nd of 6 in gp* **16/1**

0045 **11** *¾* **Intisaab**[38] 2743 8-9-5 **103**........................(p) JamieSpencer 22 97
(David O'Meara) *swtchd rt early: racd in centre of trck: hld up: rdn wl over 1f out: kpt on ins fnl f: nvr able to chal: 9th of 20 in gp* **25/1**

1411 **12** *½* **Watchable**[21] 3347 9-9-0 **98** 5ex........................(p) JasonWatson 11 91
(David O'Meara) *racd in centre of trck: led overall: rdn 2f out: hdd over 1f out: nt pce of wnr ins fnl f: fdd fnl 100yds: 10th of 20 in gp* **20/1**

2000 **13** *hd* **Stone Of Destiny**[21] 3347 4-9-4 **102**........................ SilvestreDeSousa 27 94
(Andrew Balding) *racd nrside: hld up: nt clr run 2f out: swtchd rt over 1f out: styd on ins fnl f: nvr able to rch ldrs: 11th of 20 in gp* **16/1**

14 *nk* **Southern Horse (ARG)**[149] 3-9-6 **104**........................ KevinManning 19 95
(J S Bolger, Ire) *racd in centre of trck: midfield: rdn over 2f out: no imp on ldrs: eased fnl 100yds: 12th of 20 in gp* **16/1**

53-5 **15** *shd* **Spring Loaded (IRE)**[33] 2916 7-9-1 **104**........................ DylanHogan[(5)] 24 95
(Paul D'Arcy) *racd nrside: midfield: rdn over 2f out: hdwy and edgd lft over 1f out: wl there: outpcd ins fnl 150yds: 13th of 20 in gp* **16/1**

1-64 **16** *hd* **Foxtrot Lady**[33] 2916 4-9-2 **100**........................ DavidProbert 1 90
(Andrew Balding) *racd far side: chsd ldrs: rdn and unable qck over 1f out: styd on same pce ins fnl f: 3rd of 6 fr gp* **20/1**

53-1 **17** *½* **Sir Maximilian (IRE)**[49] 2396 10-8-11 **95**........................(v) FergusSweeney 31 84
(Ian Williams) *racd nrside: midfield: rdn over 2f out: nt clr run wl over 1f out: nt clr run again and swtchd rt fnl 150yds: gng on at fin: 14th of 20 fr gp* **50/1**

3-65 **18** *nk* **Fighting Irish (IRE)**[16] 3501 4-8-13 **97**........................(p) RichardKingscote 7 85
(Harry Dunlop) *racd far side: led gp: rdn and hdd 3f out: outpcd by ldrs over 1f out: kpt on same pce ins fnl f: 4th of 6 fr gp* **50/1**

1501 **19** *½* **Soldier's Minute**[38] 2743 4-9-2 **100**........................ PatDobbs 29 86
(Keith Dalgleish) *racd nrside: chsd ldrs: rdn 2f out: unable qck over 1f out: no ex fnl 100yds: 15th of 20 fr gp* **22/1**

-260 **20** *1 ¾* **Cenotaph (USA)**[65] 1891 7-9-2 **100**........................ RyanMoore 8 81
(Jeremy Noseda) *racd far side: hld up: rdn over 2f out: one pce fnl f: eased whn wl hld fnl 50yds: 5th fr 6 in gp* **20/1**

0030 **21** *1 ½* **Marnie James**[28] 3097 4-9-3 **104**........................(t) JamieGormley[(3)] 25 80
(Iain Jardine) *racd nrside: prom: rdn and n.m.r over 1f out: sn lost pl: n.d whn hmpd and snatched up fnl 100yds: 16th of 20 in gp (jockey said gelding was denied a clear run)* **66/1**

400- **22** *shd* **Bacchus**[245] 8405 5-9-10 **108**........................ JimCrowley 21 83
(Brian Meehan) *racd in centre of trck: midfield: rdn over 2f out: no imp 1f out: wknd fnl 100yds: 17th of 20 in gp* **12/1**

2200 **23** *1 ½* **Straight Right (FR)**[42] 2609 5-9-2 **103**........................ JoshuaBryan[(3)] 14 74
(Andrew Balding) *s.i.s: racd in centre of trck: hld up: drvn over 2f out: no imp over 1f out: outpcd fnl f: 18th of 20 in gp* **50/1**

1-56 **24** *nk* **Baron Bolt**[33] 2916 6-9-7 **105**........................(p) PJMcDonald 26 75
(Paul Cole) *racd nrside: hld up: pushed along over 2f out: outpcd over 1f out: 19th of 20 in gp* **33/1**

-660 **25** *2 ¼* **Gifted Master (IRE)**[48] 2442 6-9-9 **107**........................(p[1]) JamesDoyle 30 69
(Hugo Palmer) *racd nrside: prom: pushed along whn n.m.r and hmpd wl over 1f out: sn lost pl: nvr rcvrd: eased ins fnl f: 20th of 20 in gp (jockey said gelding suffered interference)* **20/1**

2031 **26** *21* **Corinthia Knight (IRE)**[67] 1839 4-8-11 **100**........................ ThomasGreatrex[(5)] 4
(Archie Watson) *racd far side: hld up in tch: lost pl 3f out: outpcd over 2f out: lft bhd fr over 1f out: eased whn wl btn fnl f: 6th of 6 in gp (jockey said gelding stopped quickly; vet said a post-race examination of the gelding found him to be suffering from an irregular heartbeat)* **66/1**

1m 11.72s (-1.98) **Going Correction** 0.0s/f (Good)
WFA 3 from 4yo+ 7lb **26** Ran SP% **147.7**
Speed ratings (Par 109): **113,111,110,110,109 108,108,108,107,107 106,105,105,104,104 104,103,103,102,100 98,98,96,95,92**
CSF £50.29 CT £370.06 TOTE £4.70: £2.00, £3.90, £2.15, £13.50; EX 59.90 Trifecta £1048.60.
Owner Sheikh Mohammed Obaid Al Maktoum **Bred** Darley **Trained** Newmarket, Suffolk
■ Stewards' Enquiry : Dylan Hogan seven-day ban: interference & careless riding (Jul 6-12)

FOCUS
Not as competitive as the field size suggested, with the favourite potentially a cut above, and so it proved. There was a group of six racing more towards the far side, but it paid to race with the bulk of the field centre-to-stands' side.

4096 QUEEN ALEXANDRA STKS (CONDITIONS RACE) 2m 5f 143y
5:35 (5:35) (Class 2) 4-Y-0+

£56,025 (£16,776; £8,388; £4,194; £2,097; £1,053) **Stalls** Low

Form RPR
3-36 1 **Cleonte (IRE)**[43] 2575 6-9-2 105 .... SilvestreDeSousa 10 105
(Andrew Balding) *t.k.h: hld up in tch in midfield: effrt to chse ldrs over 2f out: rdn to ld over 1f out: drvn clr ins fnl f: styd on* **7/2**[2]
/10- 2 1 1/4 **Pallasator**[36] 2814 10-9-5 105 .... OisinMurphy 8 107
(Gordon Elliott, Ire) *mounted on crse: hld up in last trio: effrt on outer bnd over 2f out: hdwy to chse ldrs and hung rt over 2f out: chsd wnr ins fnl f: styd on* **10/1**
260- 3 4 **Max Dynamite (FR)**[237] 8667 9-9-2 110 .... RyanMoore 5 101
(W P Mullins, Ire) *t.k.h: trckd ldrs: swtchd lft 3f out: rdn and clsd to ld 2f out: drvn and hdd over 1f out: outpcd and lost 2nd ins fnl f* **10/3**[1]
4201 4 3 1/4 **Lucky Deal**[28] 3081 4-9-1 104 .... FrannyNorton 2 97
(Mark Johnston) *hmpd sn after s: hld up in last quartet: nt clr run 4f out: effrt u.p over 2f out: 7th 2f out: styd on wout threatening ldrs (vet said colt was suffering from mild post-race ataxia)* **11/2**[3]
00/1 5 3 **Paddys Motorbike (IRE)**[8] 3799 7-9-2 89 .... LiamKeniry 7 95
(Nigel Twiston-Davies) *taken down down early: t.k.h: chsd ldr for 5f out: styd handy: swtchd rt and drvn over 2f out: sn outpcd: wknd fnl f* **25/1**
-030 6 3 1/4 **Jukebox Jive (FR)**[4] 3952 5-9-2 93 .... (t) DougieCostello 12 92
(Jamie Osborne) *stdd and dropped in after s: hld up in last pair: effrt and drvn over 3f out: no imp but plugged on to pass btn rivals fnl f* **33/1**
31-2 7 1 1/2 **Corelli (USA)**[48] 2440 4-9-4 97 .... (t[1]) FrankieDettori 11 93
(John Gosden) *t.k.h: hld up in midfield: swtchd lft away fr rivals after 4f: hdwy to press ldr 5f out: rdn to ld over 2f out: hdd 2f out: sn btn and wknd fnl f (vet said gelding was suffering from mild post-race ataxia)* **11/2**[3]
8 4 **Black Corton (FR)**[56] 8-9-2 0 .... (t) MeganNicholls 9 87
(Paul Nicholls) *led: jnd 5f out: rdn and hdd over 2f out: sn outpcd and wknd over 1f out* **10/1**
0/U4 9 11 **Pilansberg**[42] 2607 7-9-2 100 .... (bt) GeorgeDowning 6 77
(Mark Gillard) *hld up in last pair: rdn 4f out: outpcd and lost tch over 2f out* **125/1**
00-1 10 1/2 **Coeur Blimey (IRE)**[71] 1735 8-9-2 89 .... DavidProbert 1 77
(Sue Gardner) *hld up in midfield: hmpd sn after s: rdn 4f out: outpcd and struggling whn hmpd over 2f out: eased: dismntd sn after fin (vet said gelding was dismounted on the course, appeared to be lame on pulling up and showing signs of heat-stress)* **16/1**
11 7 **Younevercall (IRE)**[56] 8-9-2 0 .... (tp) JamesDoyle 13 92
(Kim Bailey) *t.k.h: racd away fr rivals for 5f: midfield tl chsd ldr after 5f: lost 2nd 5f out and losing pl u.p whn hung rt over 2f out: sn eased (jockey said gelding hung right-handed throughout)* **11/2**[3]

4m 51.22s (7.62) **Going Correction** 0.0s/f (Good)
WFA 4 from 5yo+ 1lb 11 Ran SP% 123.1
Speed ratings (Par 109): **86,85,84,82,81 80,80,78,74,74 71**
CSF £40.13 CT £131.01 TOTE £4.90: £1.70, £4.05, £1.55; EX 44.50 Trifecta £226.20.
Owner King Power Racing Co Ltd **Bred** Societe Civile Ecurie De Meautry **Trained** Kingsclere, Hants

FOCUS
The longest race on the Flat calendar. It developed from a relatively early stage and suited those with stamina already proven. The winner did not need to improve, with the third below form, and runner-up has been rated to the same mark as when winning this the previous year.
T/Jkpt: £68,194.10 to a £1 stake. 1 winning unit T/Plt: £25.40 to a £1 stake. Pool: £547,990.17 - 15,747.44 winning units T/Qpdt: £11.90 to a £1 stake. Pool: £33,629.76 - 2,081.42 winning units
Steve Payne & Darren Owen

4054 AYR (L-H)
Saturday, June 22

OFFICIAL GOING: Good (good to firm in places; 7.9)
Wind: Breezy, half against in sprints and in over 3f of home straight in races on the round course Weather: Cloudy, dry

4097 JW GRANT BUILDERS MERCHANTS H'CAP (FOR THE JOHNSTONE ROSE BOWL) 1m
2:00 (2:01) (Class 2) (0-100,98) 4-Y-0+

£18,675 (£5,592; £2,796; £1,398; £699; £351) **Stalls** High

Form RPR
-451 1 **Club Wexford (IRE)**[23] 3268 8-8-5 82 ow1 .... BenCurtis 2 93
(Roger Fell) *mde all: rdn clr 2f out: kpt on wl fnl f: unchal* **14/1**
6015 2 2 1/2 **Waarif (IRE)**[16] 3515 6-9-5 96 .... CamHardie 9 100
(David O'Meara) *chsd wnr thrght: rdn 2f out: kpt on fnl f: nt pce to chal* **17/2**
-412 3 nk **Game Player (IRE)**[30] 3009 4-9-4 95 .... ColmO'Donoghue 4 104+
(Roger Varian) *hld up: stdy hdwy against far rail whn nt clr run over 2f out to ent fnl f: kpt on wl fnl f: one to nte (jockey said gelding was denied a clear run 1 1/2f out)* **4/1**[2]
-110 4 hd **Universal Gleam**[16] 3515 4-8-12 89 .... PaulHanagan 11 92
(Keith Dalgleish) *hld up in midfield on outside: hdwy on outside over 2f out: edgd lft and disp 2nd pl over 1f out to ins fnl f: one pce* **10/1**
2015 5 2 **Sha La La La Lee**[28] 3069 4-9-2 93 .... AlistairRawlinson 8 92
(Tom Dascombe) *missed break: hld up: rdn over 2f out: hdwy on outside over 1f out: nvr rchd ldrs (jockey said gelding was slowly away)* **10/1**
5304 6 nse **Nicholas T**[26] 3160 7-8-6 83 .... BarryMcHugh 7 81
(Jim Goldie) *hld up: stdy hdwy whn n.m.r over 2f out to over 1f out: rdn and r.o fnl f: nvr able to chal* **7/1**
1165 7 shd **Hortzadar**[22] 3313 4-9-4 95 .... ShaneGray 5 93
(David O'Meara) *prom: rdn over 2f out: outpcd fr over 1f out* **11/2**[3]
-362 8 1 3/4 **Just Hiss**[16] 3515 6-8-12 89 .... (p) RachelRichardson 10 83
(Tim Easterby) *cl up: drvn and outpcd over 2f out: n.d after* **10/1**
04-0 9 nk **Banksea**[43] 2574 6-9-5 96 .... (h) JamesSullivan 3 89
(Marjorie Fife) *t.k.h in midfield: pushed along over 2f out: outpcd fr over 1f out* **40/1**
0-60 10 1 3/4 **Carry On Deryck**[34] 2873 7-9-4 98 .... BenRobinson(3) 6 87
(Ollie Pears) *hld up in tch: drvn and outpcd over 2f out: n.d after* **66/1**
14-6 11 20 **Blue Mist**[42] 2609 4-9-5 96 .... AdamMcNamara 1 39
(Roger Charlton) *prom: rdn over 2f out: wknd over 1f out: eased whn no ch fnl f (jockey said gelding stopped quickly)* **3/1**[1]

1m 37.44s (-5.36) **Going Correction** -0.375s/f (Firm) 11 Ran SP% 121.3
Speed ratings (Par 109): **111,108,108,108,106 105,105,104,103,102 82**
CSF £131.79 CT £585.59 TOTE £15.50: £4.10, £2.70, £2.50; EX 150.10 Trifecta £1277.00.
Owner C Varley **Bred** J S Bolger **Trained** Nawton, N Yorks

FOCUS
Add 15 yards. The ground was on the fast side of good, and though this appeared to be competitive handicap few got into it and the two market leaders didn't run up to their best. The winner posted his best figure since he was a 2yo.

4098 EBF O'NEIL GAS & PLUMBING MAIDEN STKS (PLUS 10 RACE) 6f
2:35 (2:37) (Class 4) 2-Y-O

£4,787 (£1,424; £711; £355) **Stalls** High

Form RPR
545 1 **Gobi Sunset**[15] 3542 2-9-5 0 .... JasonHart 8 80
(Mark Johnston) *mde all against stands' rail: rdn 2f out: hld on wl fnl f* **7/2**[2]
2 3/4 **Byline** 2-9-5 0 .... TomEaves 3 78+
(Kevin Ryan) *dwlt: bhd and green: rdn and outpcd 1/2-way: gd hdwy on outside over 1f out: chsd wnr ins fnl f: kpt on: improve* **3/1**[1]
6 3 nk **Aberama Gold**[3] 3998 2-9-5 0 .... ShaneGray 5 77
(Keith Dalgleish) *dwlt: hld up: stdy hdwy 2f out: rdn and r.o wl fnl f* **12/1**
4 2 1/2 **The Peckhampouncer (IRE)**[47] 2490 2-9-5 0 .... ColmO'Donoghue 7 69
(D Broad, Ire) *trckd ldrs: effrt and ev ch over 1f out: outpcd whn n.m.r wl ins fnl f* **9/2**[3]
5 1 3/4 **Jamais Assez (USA)** 2-9-5 0 .... BenCurtis 4 64+
(K R Burke) *w ldr to over 2f out: rdn and outpcd fr over 1f out* **8/1**
6 1 3/4 **Kuwait Shield** 2-9-5 0 .... PaulHanagan 2 59+
(Richard Fahey) *in tch: pushed along and green over 2f out: outpcd fr over 1f out* **6/1**
7 nk **Cotai Again (IRE)** 2-9-5 0 .... GrahamLee 6 58+
(Charles Hills) *t.k.h: in tch: lost pl over 2f out: n.d after* **11/2**
66 8 4 **Van Dijk**[28] 3098 2-9-5 0 .... CamHardie 1 46
(Antony Brittain) *chsd ldrs on outside tl rdn and wknd over 1f out* **22/1**

1m 12.04s (-1.06) **Going Correction** -0.375s/f (Firm) 8 Ran SP% 118.2
Speed ratings (Par 95): **92,91,90,87,84 82,82,76**
CSF £15.05 TOTE £4.40: £1.60, £1.30, £3.20; EX 17.30 Trifecta £129.70.
Owner N Browne,I Boyce, S Frosell & S Richards **Bred** Lordship Stud **Trained** Middleham Moor, N Yorks

FOCUS
Four of the eight runners in this juvenile maiden were newcomers. The winner was the most experienced in the field and has been rated just above his pre-race mark.

4099 BOB VALENTINE 80TH BIRTHDAY CELEBRATION H'CAP 7f 50y
3:10 (3:12) (Class 3) (0-90,88) 3-Y-O

£9,337 (£2,796; £1,398; £699; £349; £175) **Stalls** High

Form RPR
0-15 1 **Irreverent**[21] 3340 3-8-13 80 .... PaulHanagan 4 91
(Richard Fahey) *hld up: effrt on outside over 1f out: edgd lft and led ent fnl f: pushed clr: readily* **11/2**[3]
-043 2 2 3/4 **Fastman (IRE)**[38] 2746 3-9-6 87 .... BenCurtis 3 91
(David O'Meara) *in tch: effrt and rdn over 1f out: chsd wnr ins fnl f: sn one pce* **2/1**[1]
0-35 3 1 1/4 **Celebrity Dancer (IRE)**[21] 3357 3-9-6 87 .... TomEaves 1 88
(Kevin Ryan) *dwlt: hld up on ins: n.m.r over 2f out: effrt and edgd rt over 1f out: r.o fnl f* **11/1**
1114 4 hd **Shanghai Grace**[73] 1685 3-9-4 85 .... GrahamLee 8 85
(Charles Hills) *hld up: effrt and pushed along whn n.m.r over 1f out: kpt on fnl f: nt pce to chal* **10/1**
3631 5 nk **Howzer Black (IRE)**[33] 2896 3-9-0 81 .... (p) ShaneGray 10 80
(Keith Dalgleish) *hld up: hdwy on outside to ld over 1f out: rdn and hdd ent fnl f: sn one pce* **9/1**
53-0 6 2 **Daafr (IRE)**[108] 1035 3-9-7 88 .... CamHardie 6 82
(Antony Brittain) *hld up: rdn and effrt on outside over 1f out: kpt on fnl f: no imp* **50/1**
2-04 7 1 **Theatre Of War (IRE)**[5] 3930 3-8-11 78 .... JasonHart 7 69
(Keith Dalgleish) *led tl rdn and hdd over 1f out: sn wknd* **5/1**[2]
5126 8 1 **Obee Jo (IRE)**[12] 3654 3-8-8 75 .... JamesSullivan 5 63
(Tim Easterby) *plld hrd: cl up: rdn and ev ch over 1f out: hung lft and sn wknd* **9/1**
3-30 9 1 1/2 **Woodside Wonder**[44] 2559 3-8-11 83 .... (p) BenSanderson(5) 2 67
(Keith Dalgleish) *trckd ldrs: rdn over 2f out: wknd over 1f out* **18/1**
2210 10 1 3/4 **Regular**[14] 3599 3-8-11 78 .... (p) ColmO'Donoghue 9 58
(Michael Bell) *t.k.h: prom on outside: lost pl whn checked over 1f out: sn eased (jockey said gelding suffered interference 2f out)* **9/1**

1m 28.38s (-4.12) **Going Correction** -0.375s/f (Firm) 10 Ran SP% 120.0
Speed ratings (Par 103): **108,104,103,103,102 100,99,98,96,94**
CSF £17.41 CT £117.95 TOTE £6.90: £1.90, £1.20, £3.60; EX 19.80 Trifecta £188.80.
Owner Mr & Mrs N Wrigley **Bred** Mr & Mrs N Wrigley **Trained** Musley Bank, N Yorks

FOCUS
Quite a competitive 7f handicap run over 15 yards further than advertised. The pace was strong and, those that set it up, dropped out of contention. A clear pb from the winner.

4100 BRIDGEND MOTOR GROUP H'CAP 5f
3:45 (3:49) (Class 4) (0-85,87) 4-Y-O+

£5,530 (£1,645; £822; £411; £300; £300) **Stalls** High

Form RPR
6221 1 **Lathom**[12] 3658 6-8-13 77 .... GrahamLee 2 89
(Paul Midgley) *prom: effrt and rdn over 1f out: led ins fnl f: pushed out: comf* **4/1**[2]
2331 2 1 3/4 **Jabbarockie**[16] 3509 6-9-7 85 .... TomEaves 4 91
(Eric Alston) *chsd ldrs: rdn to ld over 1f out: hdd ins fnl f: kpt on same pce (vet said gelding had lost its right front shoe)* **9/2**[3]
0-64 3 1 1/2 **Excessable**[35] 2841 6-9-1 79 .... RachelRichardson 8 80
(Tim Easterby) *prom: effrt and rdn 2f out: kpt on same pce ins fnl f* **7/1**
5103 4 nk **Canford Bay (IRE)**[16] 3509 5-9-3 81 .... CamHardie 9 81
(Antony Brittain) *hld up bhd ldng gp: effrt and drvn along over 1f out: kpt on fnl f: nt pce to chal* **10/1**
6462 5 1/2 **Primo's Comet**[21] 3360 4-8-12 76 .... AlistairRawlinson 11 74
(Jim Goldie) *hld up: rdn along over 1f out: kpt on fnl f: nvr rchd ldrs* **17/2**
0066 6 3/4 **Harome (IRE)**[21] 3344 5-9-8 86 .... BenCurtis 3 81
(Roger Fell) *t.k.h: chsd ldr to 2f out: wknd fnl f* **5/2**[1]

0-00 **7** 3/4 **Longroom**[35] 2841 7-9-0 **78**........................ JasonHart 7 70
(Noel Wilson) *dwlt: bhd: rdn along 1/2-way: sme late hdwy: nvr on terms* **20/1**

0050 **8** 1/2 **Bashiba (IRE)**[35] 2841 8-7-13 **70**........................ IzzyClifton(7) 5 61
(Nigel Tinkler) *hld up: effrt and pushed along over 2f out: edgd lft and no imp fr over 1f out* **22/1**

0-00 **9** 2 3/4 **Cox Bazar (FR)**[20] 3375 5-9-9 **87**........................(h[1]) PaulHanagan 1 68
(Ivan Furtado) *rn wout declared tongue-tie: led at decent gallop: rdn and hdd over 1f out: sn wknd* **40/1**

55 **10** 1 1/2 **Secretinthepark**[35] 2841 9-8-12 **76**........................(b) JamesSullivan 6 51
(Michael Mullineaux) *dwlt: bhd: rdn along over 2f out: nvr on terms* **25/1**

57.6s (-2.40) **Going Correction** -0.375s/f (Firm) **10** Ran SP% **114.3**
Speed ratings (Par 105): **104,101,98,98,97 96,95,94,89,87**
CSF £19.83 CT £108.34 TOTE £4.70: £1.40, £1.90, £2.40; EX 16.50 Trifecta £127.90.
Owner David W Armstrong **Bred** T G Lane **Trained** Westow, N Yorks
■ Royal Brave was withdrawn. Price at time of withdrawal 12/1. Rule 4 applies to all bets - deduction 5p in the pound

FOCUS
A competitive 5f handicap run at a decent gallop. There was no draw or pace bias and the form should work out. The winner posted his best figure since he was a 3yo, with the runner-up to form.

4101 BRITISH STALLION STUDS EBF LAND O'BURNS FILLIES' STKS (LISTED RACE) 5f
4:25 (4:35) (Class 1) 3-Y-O+
£28,355 (£10,750; £5,380; £2,680; £1,345; £675) **Stalls High**

Form RPR

116- **1** **Rebecca Rocks**[364] 4113 5-9-4 89........................ PaulHanagan 1 96
(Henry Candy) *cl up far side gp: led gng wl 1f out: sn rdn: hld on wl cl home: 1st of 7 in gp* **11/1**

6-05 **2** nk **Glass Slippers**[28] 3085 3-8-12 92........................ TomEaves 10 93+
(Kevin Ryan) *hld up in tch on outside of stands' side gp: hdwy to ld that gp over 1f out: rdn and edgd lft ins fnl f: kpt on: jst hld by far side wnr: 1st of 7 in gp* **10/1**

1-10 **3** 1/2 **Queen Of Desire (IRE)**[49] 2409 4-9-7 97........................ ColmO'Donoghue 8 96
(Roger Varian) *bhd far side: rdn over 2f out: hdwy over 1f out: kpt on ins fnl f: 2nd of 7 in gp* **9/1**

006- **4** 1 1/4 **Little Kim**[252] 8214 3-8-12 95........................ BenCurtis 5 87
(K R Burke) *replated at s: in tch far side: effrt and rdn over 2f out: kpt on ins fnl f: 3rd of 7 in gp* **10/1**

-536 **5** hd **Merry Banter**[33] 2910 5-9-4 83........................ BenRobinson 6 88
(Paul Midgley) *led and overall ldr far side gp: hdd 1f out: sn outpcd: 4th of 7 in gp* **28/1**

00-4 **6** shd **Deia Glory**[37] 2779 3-8-12 95........................ JasonHart 7 86
(Michael Dods) *in tch far side: rdn over 2f out: kpt on ins fnl f: nt pce to chal: 5th of 7 in gp* **22/1**

0620 **7** nk **Yolo Again (IRE)**[22] 3293 3-8-12 86........................ LewisEdmunds 4 85
(Roger Fell) *hld up far side: rdn and outpcd over 2f out: rallied and edgd lft fnl f: r.o: 6th of 7 in gp* **40/1**

1210 **8** hd **Gold Filigree (IRE)**[28] 3085 4-9-4 97........................ FinleyMarsh 12 86
(Richard Hughes) *cl up stands' side gp: led that gp over 2f out to over 1f out: sn outpcd: 2nd of 7 in gp* **15/2**

-312 **9** 1/2 **She Can Boogie (IRE)**[7] 3844 3-8-12 93........................ AlistairRawlinson 2 82
(Tom Dascombe) *prom far side: rdn along over 2f out: kpt on same pce fr over 1f out: last of 7 in gp* **5/1[2]**

4-40 **10** 2 1/4 **Blame Roberta (USA)**[51] 2319 3-8-12 89........................ CamHardie 17 74
(Robert Cowell) *led stands' side gp to over 2f out: rdn and outpcd fr over 1f out: 3rd of 7 in gp* **40/1**

-060 **11** nse **One Last Night (IRE)**[14] 3587 4-9-4 88........................(p[1]) GrahamLee 16 76
(Robert Cowell) *dwlt: bhd stands' side: rdn over 2f out: sme late hdwy: nvr rchd ldrs: 4th of 7 in gp* **50/1**

6160 **12** shd **Rose Berry**[19] 3427 5-9-4 85........................(h) BarryMcHugh 14 75
(Charlie Wallis) *in tch stands' side: outpcd over 2f out: n.d after: 5th of 7 in gp* **100/1**

0106 **13** 1/2 **Midnight Malibu (IRE)**[25] 3201 6-9-4 86........................ RachelRichardson 9 74
(Tim Easterby) *racd centre: in tch: outpcd over 2f out: btn over 1f out* **50/1**

0-04 **14** nk **Ocelot**[28] 3085 5-9-4 92........................ ShaneGray 15 73
(Robert Cowell) *hld up stands' side: rdn over 2f out: sn no imp: 6th of 7 in gp* **20/1**

45-1 **15** 2 1/4 **Maid In India (IRE)**[14] 3587 5-9-7 100........................ JamesSullivan 13 67
(Eric Alston) *w ldr to over 2f out: rdn and wknd over 1f out: last of 7 in gp (trainer said mare was found to have an infected foot post-race)* **3/1[1]**

00-3 **P** **Heartwarming**[64] 1913 3-8-12 94........................ HectorCrouch 3
(Clive Cox) *bhd far side: broke down bdly over 3f out (jockey said he pulled up the filly as she had lost her action and he felt as though something was amiss)* **13/2[3]**

57.79s (-2.21) **Going Correction** -0.375s/f (Firm)
WFA 3 from 4yo+ 6lb **16** Ran SP% **125.6**
Speed ratings (Par 108): **102,101,100,98,98 98,97,97,96,93 92,92,92,91,87**
CSF £111.70 TOTE £13.20: £3.80, £3.40, £3.60; EX 174.20 Trifecta £2013.70.
Owner Hunscote Stud Limited **Bred** Hunscote Stud **Trained** Kingston Warren, Oxon
■ Shumookhi was withdrawn. Price at time of withdrawal 25/1. Rule 4 does not apply

FOCUS
A big field for this Listed sprint for fillies and mares which has thrown up some smart winners like Marsha and Margot Did in the past. This didn't look a vintage running as the highest rated was 100. It won't prove the best of form guides as the pace and the finish concerned those drawn low who raced on the far side and the stand side group could never get into it.

4102 WELLINGTON BAR PAISLEY H'CAP (FOR THE WINTON CUP) 1m 5f 26y
5:05 (5:14) (Class 2) (0-100,98) 4-Y-O+ **£25,876** (£7,700; £3,848; £1,924) **Stalls High**

Form RPR

0-40 **1** **Island Brave (IRE)**[64] 1927 5-9-5 **96**........................ AlistairRawlinson 12 104
(Heather Main) *hld up: rdn over 2f out: hdwy on outside over 1f out: edgd lft and led ins fnl f: kpt on strly* **12/1**

-206 **2** 3/4 **Kelly's Dino (FR)**[63] 1947 6-9-4 **95**........................(p w) BenCurtis 13 102
(K R Burke) *in tch: hdwy on outside to ld over 1f out: hdd ins fnl f: rallied: hld nr fin* **10/1**

1-10 **3** 3/4 **Crystal King**[38] 2742 4-9-0 **91**........................ LouisSteward 11 98+
(Sir Michael Stoute) *hld up in midfield: rdn over 2f out: hdwy over 1f out: chsng ldrs whn checked ins fnl f: r.o fin (jockey said gelding ran too free)* **9/2[1]**

2-16 **4** 1/2 **Hareeq**[36] 2801 4-8-8 **88**........................(p) FinleyMarsh(3) 5 93
(Richard Hughes) *in tch: effrt and rdn 2f out: edgd lft: kpt on same pce ins fnl f* **18/1**

2411 **5** nse **Charles Kingsley**[19] 3408 4-9-7 **98**........................ JasonHart 8 103
(Mark Johnston) *hld up in midfield: drvn and outpcd over 2f out: n.d after* **6/1[3]**

-060 **6** hd **Manjaam (IRE)**[37] 2781 6-8-8 **85**........................(p) PaulHanagan 7 89
(Ian Williams) *hld up towards rr: rdn along 3f out: hdwy over 1f out: kpt on fnl f: nvr able to chal* **11/1**

4145 **7** hd **Grandee (IRE)**[21] 3346 5-8-7 **89**........................ BenSanderson(5) 6 93
(Roger Fell) *prom: drvn along over 2f out: kpt on same pce appr fnl f* **13/2**

0-26 **8** 1 1/4 **Indianapolis (IRE)**[38] 2742 4-9-5 **96**........................ BarryMcHugh 4 99
(James Given) *cl up: led over 2f out to over 1f out: drvn and outpcd fnl f* **13/2**

3210 **9** 1 **Theglasgowwarrior**[14] 3600 5-8-11 **91**........................ BenRobinson(3) 2 92
(Jim Goldie) *hld up: rdn along 3f out: sme late hdwy: nvr rchd ldrs* **10/1**

4-23 **10** 3/4 **Sleeping Lion (USA)**[31] 2969 4-9-0 **91**........................ HectorCrouch 15 91
(James Fanshawe) *s.i.s: bhd: rdn along over 3f out: kpt on fnl f: n.d* **5/1[2]**

0003 **11** 1 1/4 **My Reward**[12] 3655 7-8-13 **90**........................ ShaneGray 10 88
(Tim Easterby) *led to over 2f out: rdn and wknd over 1f out* **33/1**

0426 **12** 4 **Fire Fighting (IRE)**[21] 3346 8-9-4 **95**........................ ColmO'Donoghue 9 87
(Mark Johnston) *missed break: sn pushed along in rr: struggling over 2f out: nvr on terms* **20/1**

0533 **13** 6 **Dragon Mountain**[24] 3222 4-8-2 **79** oh4........................ JamesSullivan 14 62
(Keith Dalgleish) *pressed ldr: rdn over 2f out: wknd over 1f out* **40/1**

-600 **14** 34 **Maifalki (FR)**[128] 730 6-9-4 **95**........................ GrahamLee 1 27
(Jason Ward) *hld up towards rr: struggling over 2f out: sn btn: t.o* **40/1**

2m 47.02s (-7.38) **Going Correction** -0.375s/f (Firm) **14** Ran SP% **127.9**
Speed ratings (Par 109): **111,110,110,109,109 109,109,108,108,107 106,104,100,79**
CSF £130.51 CT £637.62 TOTE £13.80: £4.50, £3.80, £1.70; EX 170.70 Trifecta £1621.20.
Owner Donald M Kerr **Bred** Tally-Ho Stud **Trained** Kingston Lisle, Oxon

FOCUS
A valuable 1m5f handicap run over 15 yards further than advertised. The pace was sound and the form should work out, with the winner matching his AW best.

4103 DEBRA CHARITY H'CAP 6f
5:40 (5:44) (Class 4) (0-80,80) 3-Y-O+
£5,530 (£1,645; £822; £411; £300; £300) **Stalls High**

Form RPR

0002 **1** **Boy In The Bar**[28] 3079 8-9-13 **79**........................(v) PaulHanagan 4 87
(Ian Williams) *hld up: hdwy on outside of gp over 1f out: led and hrd pressed ins fnl f: hld on wl cl home* **4/1[1]**

-000 **2** nk **Upstaging**[7] 3868 7-9-9 **75**........................ BarryMcHugh 8 82
(Noel Wilson) *dwlt: hld up: hdwy over 1f out: rdn to chal ins fnl f: kpt on: hld cl home* **20/1**

3434 **3** 1 1/4 **Atholblair Boy (IRE)**[35] 2824 6-9-6 **79**........................ IzzyClifton(7) 3 82
(Nigel Tinkler) *fly-jmpd and wnt lft s: bhd and sn angled to stands' rail: rdn and hdwy over 1f out: kpt on fnl f: nt pce to chal* **15/2[3]**

3050 **4** 1 1/2 **Another Angel (IRE)**[7] 3868 5-9-8 **74**........................ CamHardie 9 72
(Antony Brittain) *led: rdn over 1f out: hdd ins fnl f: kpt on same pce* **16/1**

0165 **5** 1 1/2 **Oriental Lilly**[22] 3309 5-9-8 **77**........................ BenRobinson(3) 5 70
(Jim Goldie) *hld up in tch: effrt and rdn over 1f out: kpt on same pce fnl f* **7/1[2]**

-252 **6** 1/2 **Glorious Emaraty (FR)**[14] 3590 3-9-4 **77**........................ HectorCrouch 6 67
(Clive Cox) *prom: rdn along 2f out: outpcd fnl f* **4/1[1]**

3002 **7** 1 3/4 **Sir Ottoman (FR)**[1] 4060 6-8-13 **65**........................(bt[1]) TomEaves 7 51
(Ivan Furtado) *chsd ldrs: effrt and rdn 2f out: wknd fnl f* **8/1**

1-01 **8** 1/2 **Gullane One (IRE)**[11] 3706 4-9-4 **70**........................(t) JasonHart 10 55
(Tim Easterby) *blindfold slow to remove: sn chsng ldrs: drvn and outpcd wl over 1f out: btn fnl f (jockey said gelding hung both ways)* **4/1[1]**

0043 **9** 1 3/4 **Uncle Jerry**[12] 3659 3-9-4 **80**........................(b) FinleyMarsh(3) 11 57
(Richard Hughes) *hld up bhd ldng gp: pushed along and edgd lft wl over 1f out: sn outpcd: btn fnl f* **12/1**

-005 **10** 4 1/2 **Mutafarrid (IRE)**[15] 3549 4-9-7 **73**........................ GrahamLee 1 38
(Paul Midgley) *fly-jmpd and wnt bdly lft s: sn wl bhd: nvr on terms (jockey said gelding fly-leapt and jumped left leaving the stalls resulting in the gelding being slowly away)* **12/1**

1m 10.33s (-2.77) **Going Correction** -0.375s/f (Firm)
WFA 3 from 4yo+ 7lb **10** Ran SP% **121.4**
Speed ratings (Par 105): **103,102,100,98,96 96,93,93,90,84**
CSF £95.79 CT £605.86 TOTE £3.80: £1.30, £6.30, £2.80; EX 129.30 Trifecta £744.50.
Owner Allwins Stables **Bred** Brinkley Stud S R L **Trained** Portway, Worcs

FOCUS
A fair 6f 61-80 handicap and though the first two finished in the middle of the track there didn't seem quite the same bias as in the Listed race earlier in the card.
T/Plt: £318.50 to a £1 stake. Pool: £57,911.96 - 132.71 winning units T/Qpdt: £42.30 to a £1 stake. Pool: £4,844.73 - 84.69 winning units **Richard Young**

3724 HAYDOCK (L-H)
Saturday, June 22

OFFICIAL GOING: Good to soft (good in places; 6.8)
Wind: faint breeze Weather: sunny and warm, light cloud

4104 EVERY RACE LIVE ON RACING TV MAIDEN STKS 1m 3f 175y
6:30 (6:30) (Class 5) 3-Y-O+ **£5,175** (£1,540; £769; £384) **Stalls Centre**

Form RPR

44 **1** **Space Walk**[55] 2142 3-9-0 0........................(t) StevieDonohoe 2 87
(William Haggas) *mde all: pushed along in narrow ld 3f out: rdn over 2f out: jnd 1 1/2f out: led ins fnl f: r.o stoutly* **6/5[1]**

3 **2** 1/2 **Paths Of Glory**[12] 3664 4-10-0 0........................(t) RossaRyan 1 86
(Hugo Palmer) *trckd ldr: 3rd 5f out: hdwy gng wl 3f out: drvn to dispute ld 1 1/2f out: sn rdn: hdd ins fnl f: no ex nr fin* **6/1[2]**

33 **3** 8 **Swift Wing**[10] 3724 3-9-0 0........................(b[1]) NickyMackay 5 73
(John Gosden) *t.k.h: prom: 2nd 5f out: drvn and cl up 3f out: dropped to 3rd over 2f out: reminder over 1f out: no rspnse: wknd fnl f* **6/5[1]**

4 14 **Gabriel Oak** 3-9-0 0........................ PaulMulrennan 3 51
(Donald McCain) *t.k.h: prom early: sn hld up in last: wnt 4th 5f out: rdn and lost grnd on front three 4f out: no ch fr over 2f out* **14/1[3]**

00 **5** 71 **Piccolo Ramoscello**[15] 3553 6-9-2 0........................(p[1]) ElishaWhittington(7) 4
(Lisa Williamson) *t.k.h: hld up: dropped to last and drvn 5f out: lost tch 4f out* **66/1**

2m 29.94s (-3.36) **Going Correction** -0.25s/f (Firm)
WFA 3 from 4yo+ 14lb **5** Ran SP% **113.4**
Speed ratings (Par 103): **101,100,95,86,38**
CSF £9.74 TOTE £2.00: £1.20, £1.90; EX 7.70 Trifecta £8.30.
Owner The Queen **Bred** The Queen **Trained** Newmarket, Suffolk

FOCUS
The going was given as good to soft, good in places (Going Stick 6.8) and all races were run on the stands' side home straight. Add 10yds. They went fairly steady in the early stages but the first two pulled well clear in the end.

4105 INTRODUCING RACING TV EBF FILLIES' H'CAP (JOCKEY CLUB GRASSROOTS FLAT SPRINT QUALIFIER) 5f
7:00 (7:00) (Class 4) (0-85,82) 4-Y-O+
£7,115 (£2,117; £1,058; £529; £400; £400) **Stalls** Centre

Form — RPR

5334 **1** **Seen The Lyte (IRE)**[7] 3868 4-8-13 **79**............(h) FayeMcManoman(5) 9 — 87
(Nigel Tinkler) *dwlt: bhd and drvn along: rcvrd to r in mid-div 1/2-way: pushed along 2f out: shkn up over 1f out: drvn and str run fnl f: led last stride* **9/2**[3]

1442 **2** *shd* **Boundary Lane**[16] 3509 4-9-5 **80**.................................. PaulMulrennan 6 — 87
(Julie Camacho) *trckd ldr: pushed along to chal 1 1/2f out: led 1f out: rdn fnl f: 1 l ld 1/2f out: sn clsd down by wnr: hdd last stride* **6/5**[1]

-000 **3** *1* **Quench Dolly**[13] 3636 5-9-1 **79**..............................(b[1]) GeorgeBuckell(3) 8 — 82
(John Gallagher) *prom: pushed along 2f out: rdn 1 1/2f out: 3rd ent fnl f: kpt on* **17/2**

-004 **4** *1 1/4* **Lydiate Lady**[16] 3518 7-7-11 **63** oh3.............................. RhiainIngram(5) 4 — 62
(Eric Alston) *led: narrow ld 2f out: rdn and hdd 1f out: wknd fnl f* **11/1**

0611 **5** *1 3/4* **Peggie Sue**[42] 2625 4-9-0 **82**.. TobyEley(7) 2 — 75
(Adam West) *mid-div: drvn 2f out: sn lost pl and rdn: one pce fnl f* **7/2**[2]

1006 **6** *nse* **Bellevarde (IRE)**[14] 3576 5-8-10 **74**.............................. JaneElliott(3) 7 — 66
(Richard Price) *prom: pushed along 2f out: rdn and lost pl over 1f out: wknd* **12/1**

56-2 **7** *1/2* **Peace Dreamer (IRE)**[29] 3037 5-8-13 **77**........................ SeanDavis(3) 5 — 68
(Robert Cowell) *bhd: pushed along 1/2-way: sn drvn: no imp* **11/1**

0500 **8** *1/2* **Celerity (IRE)**[4] 3975 5-7-9 **63** oh18...................(p) ElishaWhittington(7) 3 — 52
(Lisa Williamson) *bhd: pushed along 1/2-way: rdn over 1f out: no imp* **50/1**

58.99s (-1.41) **Going Correction** -0.25s/f (Firm) — **8** Ran SP% **122.7**
Speed ratings (Par 102): **101,100,99,97,94 94,93,92**
CSF £11.16 CT £47.13 TOTE £5.80: £1.60, £1.10, £2.40; EX 12.10 Trifecta £101.10.
Owner Boys Of Buckley **Bred** Highest Praise Syndicate **Trained** Langton, N Yorks
■ Stewards' Enquiry : Paul Mulrennan two-day ban: used whip above the permitted level (Jul 7-8)

FOCUS
They dipped under the standard time on drying ground. A small pb from the winner.

4106 WATCH RACING TV NOW MAIDEN STKS (PLUS 10 RACE) 7f 37y
7:30 (7:31) (Class 4) 2-Y-O **£6,469** (£1,925; £962; £481) **Stalls** Low

Form — RPR

1 **Mystery Power (IRE)** 2-9-5 0.. RossaRyan 8 — 87+
(Richard Hannon) *mid-div: disp 3rd 3f out: drvn to chal and rn green 2f out: led 1f out: rdn fnl f: r.o wl* **4/1**[2]

2 **2** *1* **Subjectivist**[15] 3551 2-9-5 0.. PaulMulrennan 4 — 85
(Mark Johnston) *led 1f: chsd ldr whn hdd: led 2f out: rdn 1 1/2f out: hdd 1f out: kpt on fnl f: nt pce of wnr* **4/11**[1]

3 *3/4* **Valdermoro (USA)** 2-9-5 0.. TonyHamilton 3 — 83+
(Richard Fahey) *chsd ldrs: disp 3rd 3f out: pushed along 2f out: trying to chal between rivals whn nt clr run over 1f out: kpt on fnl f* **8/1**[3]

40 **4** *9* **We Owen A Dragon**[7] 3841 2-9-2 0.............................. JaneElliott(3) 9 — 60
(Tom Dascombe) *prom: led after 1f: 4 l clr whn racd awkwardly over 4f out: rdn and hdd 2f out: wknd (jockey said gelding ran greenly)* **10/1**

5 *1/2* **Thunder King (FR)** 2-9-5 0.. StevieDonohoe 5 — 59
(Amy Murphy) *hld up: drvn in 6th 3f out: reminder over 1f out: no imp* **14/1**

6 *2 3/4* **Phoenix Approach (IRE)** 2-9-5 0.............................. DuranFentiman 2 — 52+
(Tim Easterby) *hld up on inner: 5th 3f out: pushed along and n.m.r 2f out: sn wknd* **20/1**

00 **7** *5* **Must Dream**[37] 2780 2-9-5 0.. AndrewElliott 7 — 40
(Seb Spencer) *rrd leaving stalls: bhd: rdn and no ch fr 3f out* **33/1**

8 *11* **Loretta Lass** 2-8-7 0.. TobyEley(7) 1 — 7
(Adam West) *slowly away: a bhd (jockey said filly was slowly away and ran greenly)* **33/1**

1m 28.85s (-2.55) **Going Correction** -0.25s/f (Firm) — **8** Ran SP% **130.8**
Speed ratings (Par 95): **104,102,102,91,91 88,82,69**
CSF £6.64 TOTE £6.00: £1.30, £1.10, £2.00; EX 7.50 Trifecta £27.70.
Owner King Power Racing Co Ltd **Bred** Ms Siobhan O'Rahilly **Trained** East Everleigh, Wilts

FOCUS
A bit of a turn-up but this has been rated positively.

4107 RACINGTV.COM H'CAP 1m 37y
8:00 (8:00) (Class 4) (0-85,87) 3-Y-O **£7,439** (£2,213; £1,106; £553; £400) **Stalls** Low

Form — RPR

3113 **1** **Mayfair Spirit (IRE)**[20] 3373 3-8-12 **74**......................(t) StevieDonohoe 1 — 79+
(Charlie Fellowes) *racd in 3rd: dropped to 4th 3f out: pushed along 2f out: swtchd to outer over 1f out: hdwy ent fnl f: sn rdn and r.o wl: led last few strides* **9/4**[1]

-135 **2** *hd* **Hesslewood (IRE)**[35] 2821 3-9-7 **83**............................ PaulMulrennan 3 — 87
(James Bethell) *hld up: hdwy on outer into 3rd 3f out: pushed along 2f out: drvn to ld 1f out: rdn in narrow ld ins fnl f: r.o: hdd last few strides* **4/1**

0041 **3** *1/2* **Amadeus Grey (IRE)**[11] 3683 3-9-5 **81**......................(t) DuranFentiman 4 — 84
(Tim Easterby) *led: pushed along in narrow ld 3f out: sn drvn: rdn and hdd 1f out: kpt on fnl f* **11/4**[2]

6035 **4** *4 1/2* **Kuwait Station (IRE)**[5] 3930 3-9-5 **81**............................ DavidNolan 5 — 74
(David O'Meara) *trckd ldr: pushed along to chal 3f out: drvn and ev ch 2f out: lost pl over 1f out: wknd fnl f* **7/2**[3]

6540 **5** *1* **Sir Victor (IRE)**[17] 3471 3-8-12 **77**............................ JaneElliott(3) 2 — 67
(Tom Dascombe) *hld up in last: pushed along and lost grnd on rest of field 3f out: sn drvn: no imp* **11/2**

1m 43.37s (-1.53) **Going Correction** -0.25s/f (Firm) — **5** Ran SP% **115.0**
Speed ratings (Par 101): **97,96,96,91,90**
CSF £12.03 TOTE £2.70: £1.70, £2.10; EX 10.50 Trifecta £30.10.
Owner J Soiza **Bred** Ringfort Stud Ltd **Trained** Newmarket, Suffolk

FOCUS
This was tightly fought and there wasn't much to choose between the first three at the line. The winner progressed again.

4108 RACING TV H'CAP 1m 37y
8:30 (8:31) (Class 4) (0-85,86) 4-Y-O+
£7,439 (£2,213; £1,106; £553; £400; £400) **Stalls** Low

Form — RPR

0000 **1** **Arcanada (IRE)**[7] 3867 6-9-3 **82**..................................(p) JaneElliott(3) 1 — 90
(Tom Dascombe) *down on nose leaving stalls: sn rcvrd to r in mid-div: looking for room and nt clr run 2f out: swtchd to outer: rdn and hdwy over 1f out: led 1/2f out: r.o wl (jockey said gelding hung left-handed under pressure; trainer's rep said, regarding the improved form shown, the gelding had benefitted from the back drop in trip to a mile and contesting what in his opinion was a less competitive race)* **11/2**[2]

415 **2** *1/2* **Kripke (IRE)**[34] 2873 4-9-5 **81**.. TonyHamilton 2 — 88
(David Barron) *chsd ldrs: drvn to chal 2f out: led over 1f out: rdn and hdd 1/2f out: kpt on wl* **9/2**[1]

5420 **3** *2 1/4* **Lawmaking**[22] 3315 6-9-0 **83**..(b) TobyEley(7) 7 — 85
(Michael Scudamore) *slowly away: bhd: pushed along and hdwy on inner over 2f out: rdn 1 1/2f out: swtchd ent fnl f: r.o into 3rd fnl 50yds* **11/2**[2]

3424 **4** *2 1/4* **Newmarket Warrior (IRE)**[53] 2246 8-8-7 **69**.............(p) NickyMackay 5 — 66
(Iain Jardine) *hld up: pushed along and swtchd to outer 1 1/2f out: rdn and r.o fnl f: tk 4th nr fin (jockey said gelding as denied a clear run for some distance approaching 1 1/2f out)* **25/1**

3600 **5** *nk* **Critical Thinking (IRE)**[116] 914 5-8-4 **73**......(tp w) LauraCoughlan(7) 10 — 69
(David Loughnane) *chsd ldrs: pushed along in 3rd 3f out: drvn to chal 2f out: rdn over 1f out: wknd fnl f (jockey said gelding ran too freely)* **25/1**

-203 **6** *3/4* **Redgrave (IRE)**[5] 3944 5-8-12 **77**................................ SeanDavis(3) 8 — 71
(Joseph Tuite) *hld up: pushed along and looking for room 2f out: nt clr run over 1f out: sn in clr and rdn: one pce fnl f* **6/1**[3]

-030 **7** *3* **Calder Prince (IRE)**[7] 3846 6-9-5 **81**............................ PaulMulrennan 4 — 68
(Tom Dascombe) *hld up: pushed along and hdwy on outer 2f out: rdn and wknd over 1f out* **11/2**[2]

3204 **8** *1/2* **Confrontational (IRE)**[7] 3845 5-9-3 **79**........................(p) DavidNolan 11 — 65
(Jennie Candlish) *prom: rdn and lost pl 2f out: sn wknd* **10/1**

-350 **9** *nk* **Make Me**[5] 3922 4-8-9 **71**..(p) DuranFentiman 3 — 56
(Tim Easterby) *led: drvn in narrow ld 2f out: sn rdn: hdd over 1f out: wknd fnl f* **7/1**

33-0 **10** *2 1/4* **Bertog**[25] 3179 4-8-10 **72**.. RossaRyan 9 — 52
(John Mackie) *mid-div: pushed along in 5th 3f out: drvn and lost pl 2f out: sn rdn and wknd* **12/1**

0-30 **11** *1 3/4* **Labrega**[42] 2608 4-9-10 **86**..(h) StevieDonohoe 6 — 62
(Hugo Palmer) *hld up in rr: drvn fr 3f out: no rspnse* **12/1**

1m 41.25s (-3.65) **Going Correction** -0.25s/f (Firm) — **11** Ran SP% **123.3**
Speed ratings (Par 105): **108,107,105,103,102 101,98,98,98,95 94**
CSF £32.11 CT £147.63 TOTE £5.70: £2.30, £2.10, £2.30; EX 33.60 Trifecta £239.40.
Owner The Arcanada Partnership **Bred** C J Foy **Trained** Malpas, Cheshire

FOCUS
A competitive handicap but the first two finished nicely clear.

4109 JOIN RACING TV NOW H'CAP 1m 2f 100y
9:00 (9:01) (Class 5) (0-70,72) 3-Y-O+
£5,175 (£1,540; £769; £400; £400; £400) **Stalls** Centre

Form — RPR

604 **1** **Corncrake**[37] 2769 3-9-3 **68**.. RossaRyan 9 — 78
(Richard Hannon) *hld up: drvn on outer 3f out: hdwy 2f out: rdn to ld 1f out: r.o wl to assert fnl f* **3/1**[1]

6025 **2** *1 3/4* **Dark Devil (IRE)**[7] 3845 6-9-11 **67**............................(p) SeanDavis(3) 7 — 74
(Richard Fahey) *hld up: pushed along and hdwy over 2f out: swtchd 2f out: drvn to ld 1 1/2f out: sn rdn: hdd 1f out: no ex as wnr asserted fnl f* **6/1**[3]

0055 **3** *2* **Manfadh (IRE)**[19] 3429 4-9-12 **65**.............................. PaulMulrennan 6 — 68
(Kevin Frost) *chsd ldrs: pushed along 3f out: rdn and lost pl 2f out: r.o ins fnl f: tk 3rd last 100yds* **8/1**

022 **4** *3/4* **Universal Effect**[22] 3324 3-9-3 **68**.............................. StevieDonohoe 4 — 70
(David Lanigan) *chsd ldrs: pushed along 3f out: drvn to chal 2f out: lost pl over 1f out: rdn fnl f: no ex* **3/1**[1]

4014 **5** *3/4* **Motahassen (IRE)**[11] 3681 5-8-12 **58**...............(t) CianMacRedmond(7) 8 — 58
(Declan Carroll) *hld up in rr: pushed along and effrt on outer 3f out: rdn over 2f out: one pce* **7/2**[2]

15-0 **6** *2 1/2* **Our Rodney (IRE)**[21] 2101 3-8-10 **68**............................ EllaMcCain(7) 1 — 64
(Donald McCain) *led: pushed along and hdd 3f out: sn rdn: grad wknd* **16/1**

0-04 **7** *3/4* **So You Thought (USA)**[10] 3718 5-9-7 **60**........................ AndrewElliott 5 — 54
(Simon West) *prom: drvn to ld 3f out: sn rdn: hdd 1 1/2f out: wknd* **8/1**

4R-0 **R** **Duck Egg Blue (IRE)**[46] 2509 5-10-0 **72**....................(p) PaulaMuir(5) 2
(Liam Bailey) *ref to leave stalls (starter reported that the mare had refused to race; trainer was informed that any future similar behaviour from the mare may result in being reported to the Head Office of the BHA)* **20/1**

2m 13.43s (-3.17) **Going Correction** -0.25s/f (Firm)
WFA 3 from 4yo+ 12lb — **8** Ran SP% **119.4**
Speed ratings (Par 103): **102,100,99,98,97 95,95,**
CSF £22.63 CT £133.60 TOTE £3.80: £1.50, £2.00, £2.50; EX 22.70 Trifecta £118.70.
Owner Exors Of The Late Lady Rothschild **Bred** The Rt Hon Lord Rothschild **Trained** East Everleigh, Wilts

FOCUS
A modest handicap that went the way of one of the two newcomers to this sphere, with the winner finding plenty of improvement.
T/Plt: £13.70 to a £1 stake. Pool: £61,551.33 - 3259.00 winning units T/Qpdt: £7.00 to a £1 stake. Pool: £6,179.61 - 648.84 winning units **Keith McHugh**

4025 LINGFIELD (L-H)

Saturday, June 22

OFFICIAL GOING: Good to soft (good in places; 7.1) changing to good (good to soft in places) after race 1 (5.45)

Wind: Moderate, across Weather: Fine, warm

4110 VISIT ATTHERACES.COM FILLIES' H'CAP — 1m 2f

5:45 (5:47) (Class 5) (0-75,76) 3-Y-O

£3,752 (£1,116; £557; £400; £400; £400) **Stalls** Low

Form — RPR

644 **1** **Specialise**[33] 2919 3-9-8 **76**.................................. CharlieBennett 11 93+
(Roger Varian) sn chsd ldrs but forced to r wd: prog over 2f out: rdn to chal wl over 1f out: led ins fnl f: styd on wl **3/1[2]**

11-3 **2** 1¾ **Hallalulu**[23] 3264 3-9-7 **75**.................................. TomMarquand 4 88+
(William Haggas) cl up: rdn to ld over 2f out: hrd pressed over 1f out: hdd and one pce ins fnl f **7/4[1]**

543 **3** 1½ **Moll Davis (IRE)**[16] 3495 3-9-4 **72**.................................. HayleyTurner 9 82+
(George Scott) sn trckd ldr: led over 3f out: rdn and hdd over 2f out: styd on same pce after **5/1[3]**

2501 **4** 6 **Colony Queen**[22] 3310 3-8-13 **67**.................................. RobertHavlin 2 65
(Steve Gollings) hld up in midfield: effrt to chse ldrs 3f out: steadily wknd 2f out **10/1**

6415 **5** nk **Patchouli**[9] 3762 3-9-2 **75**.................................. ScottMcCullagh(5) 6 72
(Mick Channon) dwlt: hld up in last: rdn wl over 2f out: sme prog after but nvr on terms **10/1**

04-3 **6** 1¼ **Innocent (IRE)**[77] 1594 3-9-7 **75**.................................. HarryBentley 1 70
(Ralph Beckett) cl up on inner: rdn over 2f out: wknd wl over 1f out **11/1**

3302 **7** 1 **Bolt N Brown**[10] 3741 3-8-5 **66**..................................(t) GraceMcEntee(7) 3 59
(Gay Kelleway) pushed along early: mostly in midfield: lft bhd over 2f out: no ch after **12/1**

44-0 **8** 2¼ **Guroor**[53] 2253 3-9-5 **73**..................................(h) ShaneKelly 5 61
(Marco Botti) dwlt: hld up in last pair: rdn and no real prog over 2f out (jockey said filly was slowly away) **33/1**

-600 **9** 2¼ **The Meter**[26] 3146 3-8-6 **65**..................................(t[1]) DarraghKeenan(5) 8 49
(Mohamed Moubarak) in tch towards rr: rdn and wknd over 2f out **50/1**

030- **10** 27 **Give Me Breath**[206] 9291 3-9-4 **72**.................................. JimmyQuinn 7
(Sir Michael Stoute) in tch to over 3f out: wknd qckly: t.o **20/1**

3-46 **11** 19 **Parish Poet (IRE)**[16] 3495 3-9-2 **70**.................................. RaulDaSilva 10
(Paul Cole) led to over 3f out: wknd rapidly: t.o (vet said filly had bled from the nose) **16/1**

2m 7.02s (-5.18) **Going Correction** -0.075s/f (Good) 11 Ran SP% **127.8**
Speed ratings (Par 96): **103,101,100,95,95 94,93,91,89,68 53**
CSF £9.36 CT £27.59 TOTE £4.50: £1.40, £1.20, £2.10; EX 11.90 Trifecta £56.80.
Owner Saif Ali **Bred** Newsells Park Stud **Trained** Newmarket, Suffolk

FOCUS
The ground continued to dry out and was now good to soft, good in places (from good to soft, soft in places). GoingStick: 7.1. There was a cutaway at the 3f marker in the home straight. The first three came clear and the first two have been rated as improving.

4111 MCMILLAN WILLIAMS SOLICITORS H'CAP — 1m 3f 133y

6:15 (6:17) (Class 6) (0-55,55) 3-Y-O+

£3,105 (£924; £461; £400; £400; £400) **Stalls** High

Form — RPR

0351 **1** **Kingfast (IRE)**[14] 3571 4-9-10 **55**..................................(p) HarryBentley 5 65+
(David Dennis) hld up in rr: outpcd and shkn up over 4f out: gd prog 3f out to cl on ldrs 2f out: drvn to ld 1f out: drew clr **3/1[2]**

-000 **2** 3¾ **Iballisticvin**[32] 2928 6-9-10 **55**..................................(p[1]) ShaneKelly 4 59
(Gary Moore) prom: trckd ldr 4f out: rdn to ld over 2f out: hdd and outpcd 1f out: hld on for 2nd **8/1**

0222 **3** nk **Mistress Nellie**[10] 3740 4-9-0 **48**.................................. GabrieleMalune(3) 8 52
(William Stone) trckd ldrs: outpcd and pushed along over 4f out: prog 3f out: clsd on ldrs 2f out: one pce over 1f out **11/4[1]**

0-54 **4** nk **Peace Prevails**[23] 3276 4-9-10 **55**..................................(p) CharlieBennett 10 58
(Jim Boyle) trckd ldr: led 5f out: rdn and hdd over 2f out: one pce after **7/1**

2-01 **5** 3¼ **Champs Inblue**[23] 3252 4-9-5 **50**.................................. CharlesBishop 7 48
(Chris Gordon) s.i.s and pushed along early: in tch: outpcd over 4f out: rdn and tried to cl on ldrs 3f out: no imp fnl 2f **5/1[3]**

0052 **6** 3¼ **Tilsworth Lukey**[9] 3774 6-9-4 **49**.................................. TomMarquand 6 41
(J R Jenkins) hld up in last pair: bdly outpcd over 4f out: rdn and prog over 2f out: no hdwy over 1f out: fdd **7/1**

0001 **7** 4½ **Loving Your Work**[11] 3700 8-9-5 **53**.................................. WilliamCox(3) 2 38
(Ken Cunningham-Brown) prom: rdn and wknd wl over 2f out **14/1**

0200 **8** 3¼ **Boycie**[14] 3571 6-9-0 **50**..................................(b) PoppyBridgwater(5) 11 29
(Adrian Wintle) s.s: t.k.h and sn rcvrd: pressed ldrs 1/2-way: wknd over 3f out **20/1**

40-0 **9** 14 **Guardiola (USA)**[30] 2998 4-9-3 **48**..................................(t) RobertHavlin 3
(Bernard Llewellyn) s.i.s: a wl in rr: t.o **25/1**

0-00 **10** 10 **Widnes**[31] 2975 5-9-3 **53**..................................(v) DarraghKeenan(5) 1
(Alan Bailey) in tch tl wknd 4f out: t.o **25/1**

46-0 **11** 14 **Bay Dude**[30] 3017 4-9-7 **55**.................................. PaddyBradley(3) 9
(Brett Johnson) led to 5f out: wknd rapidly over 3f out: t.o **33/1**

2m 30.61s (-3.39) **Going Correction** -0.075s/f (Good) 11 Ran SP% **126.5**
Speed ratings (Par 101): **94,91,91,91,88 86,83,81,72,65 56**
CSF £28.37 CT £77.38 TOTE £3.80: £1.50, £2.80, £1.70; EX 45.40 Trifecta £146.80.
Owner G Saville, G Brandrick & Partner **Bred** D Veitch & B Douglas **Trained** Hanley Swan, Worcestershire

FOCUS
The going was changed to good, good to soft in places before this race. A moderate handicap with a clear-cut winner.

4112 WATCH SKY SPORTS RACING IN HD H'CAP — 1m 5f

6:45 (6:51) (Class 5) (0-75,76) 4-Y-O+

£3,752 (£1,116; £557; £400; £400; £400) **Stalls** Centre

Form — RPR

5233 **1** **Berrahri (IRE)**[15] 3545 8-9-7 **75**.................................. KierenFox 4 83
(John Best) mde all: rdn over 2f out: hrd pressed fnl f: hld on gamely nr fin **7/2[2]**

-042 **2** nk **Blazing Saddles**[21] 3349 4-9-6 **74**..................................(b) HarryBentley 1 81
(Ralph Beckett) hld up in midfield: prog over 2f out: chsd wnr over 1f out: hrd rdn and str chal ins fnl f: jst hld nr fin **3/1[1]**

4-40 **3** 2 **Cacophonous**[15] 3545 4-9-1 **69**.................................. JasonWatson 7 73
(David Menuisier) racd wd: in tch: rdn 3f out: tried to cl on ldrs 2f out: kpt on same pce u.p to take 3rd last strides **9/2[3]**

6-62 **4** shd **Nabhan**[28] 2901 7-8-13 **70**..................................(tp) JoshuaBryan(3) 2 73
(Bernard Llewellyn) prom: rdn to dispute 2nd over 2f out: nt qckn over 1f out: kpt on same pce after **14/1**

0034 **5** ¾ **El Borracho (IRE)**[13] 3633 4-9-5 **73**..................................(h) TomMarquand 8 75
(Simon Dow) prom: rdn to chse wnr over 2f out: hanging and nt qckn over 1f out: sn lost 2nd and one pce after **6/1**

310- **6** 2½ **Pepper Street (IRE)**[26] 7466 4-8-9 **63**..................................(p[1]) GeorgeWood 9 62
(Amy Murphy) chsd wnr to over 2f out: steadily fdd **25/1**

1U3/ **7** nk **Tobougaloo**[660] 6610 8-8-8 **65**.................................. WilliamCox(3) 6 63
(Stuart Kittow) hld up in rr: rdn 3f out: sme prog 2f out: one pce and no hdwy over 1f out **33/1**

6042 **8** 4½ **Dagueneau (IRE)**[20] 3377 4-9-8 **76**..................................(v[1]) RobertHavlin 10 67
(Ed Dunlop) hld up towards rr: shkn up 3f out: no prog **10/1**

31-0 **9** ½ **Dance To Paris**[17] 3467 4-9-7 **75**..................................(b) HayleyTurner 3 66
(Lucy Wadham) hld up in last pair: outpcd over 4f out: shkn up and no prog 3f out **8/1**

0/-0 **10** 30 **Navajo War Dance**[36] 2793 6-9-1 **69**.................................. CharlesBishop 5 15
(Ali Stronge) a in rr: lost tch 5f out: sn t.o: eased over 1f out **10/1**

2m 49.81s 10 Ran SP% **122.4**
CSF £15.31 CT £49.77 TOTE £4.50: £1.60, £1.70, £2.10; EX 20.20 Trifecta £85.80.
Owner White Turf Racing UK **Bred** Kilnamoragh Stud **Trained** Oad Street, Kent

FOCUS
Just a fair staying handicap and it paid to be handy, but all credit to the game winner who posted his best figure since early last year.

4113 SKY SPORTS RACING ON SKY 415 FILLIES' H'CAP — 7f 135y

7:15 (7:18) (Class 4) (0-85,92) 4-Y-O+

£5,530 (£1,645; £822; £411; £400; £400) **Stalls** Centre

Form — RPR

-160 **1** **Daddies Girl (IRE)**[20] 3374 4-9-2 **87**.................................. OliverSearle(7) 3 94
(Rod Millman) racd alone towards nr side: on terms w main gp: overall ldr 3f out: pushed along and kpt on steadily fnl 2f **6/1**

600- **2** 2 **Nkosikazi**[268] 7701 4-9-7 **85**.................................. TomMarquand 4 87
(William Haggas) led main gp in centre and overall ldr to 3f out: rdn over 2f out: kpt on one pce over 1f out **4/1[2]**

-231 **3** nse **Infanta Isabella**[9] 3763 5-9-7 **92**..................................(t) CierenFallon(7) 1 94
(George Baker) trckd ldrs in centre: shkn up 3f out: chal over 1f out: kpt on but nt on terms w wnr **10/11[1]**

-200 **4** 2 **Zoraya (FR)**[112] 992 4-8-11 **75**..................................(t w) RaulDaSilva 5 72
(Paul Cole) racd towards nr side early then swtchd to centre: hld up: shkn up 3f out: effrt 2f out: kpt on same pce **14/1**

3112 **5** 2½ **Chica De La Noche**[6] 3892 5-8-10 **74**..................................(p) HarryBentley 6 65
(Simon Dow) pressed ldr in centre to over 2f out: steadily wknd **5/1[3]**

3240 **6** ¾ **Roman Spinner**[103] 1143 4-8-13 **77**..................................(t) ShaneKelly 2 66
(Rae Guest) racd centre: hld up in last: shkn up 3f out: no prog and one pce after **25/1**

1m 31.82s (0.12) **Going Correction** -0.075s/f (Good) 6 Ran SP% **113.8**
Speed ratings (Par 102): **101,99,98,96,94 93**
CSF £30.28 TOTE £5.30: £2.00, £2.40; EX 37.10 Trifecta £64.70.
Owner Daddies Girl Partnership **Bred** William Blake **Trained** Kentisbeare, Devon

FOCUS
Not a bad fillies' handicap and a fascinating tactical battle, with the winner the only one to take the stands' rail route - the form has been rated around her.

4114 WITHEFORD EQUINE BARRIER TRIALS MAIDEN AUCTION STKS — 7f

7:45 (7:50) (Class 6) 2-Y-O

£3,105 (£924; £461; £230) **Stalls** Centre

Form — RPR

432 **1** **Miss Matterhorn**[23] 3257 2-8-1 **0**.................................. GeorgiaDobie(7) 11 66+
(Eve Johnson Houghton) racd towards nr side: mde virtually all: rdn and pressed over 1f out: edgd lft fnl f: kpt on wl **5/4[1]**

2 1¼ **Mrs Dukesbury (FR)** 2-8-12 **0**.................................. OisinMurphy 4 67
(Archie Watson) prom in centre: chsd wnr over 2f out: drvn to chal fnl f: no ex fnl 100yds **9/2[3]**

3 ¾ **Sweet Sixteen (GER)** 2-8-12 **0**.................................. GeorgeWood 8 65
(Amy Murphy) trckd ldrs towards nr side: shkn up over 2f out: outpcd over 1f out: styd on again fnl f to take 3rd nr fin **14/1**

06 **4** ½ **Craigburn**[52] 2282 2-9-1 **0**.................................. HarryBentley 2 66
(Tom Clover) cl up in centre: drvn to chse ldrs 2f out: one pce ins fnl f **25/1**

5 nk **Wallaby (IRE)** 2-8-5 **0**.................................. WilliamCox(3) 6 58
(Jonathan Portman) dwlt: sn chsd ldrs: effrt in centre 2f out: kpt on same pce over 1f out **25/1**

6 ½ **Manap** 2-9-1 **0**.................................. EdwardGreatrex 10 64+
(Archie Watson) difficult to load: rn green: outpcd and wl bhd in last: sed to pick up over 2f out: shkn up and styd on fnl f: nrst fin (jockey said gelding ran green early on) **7/1**

7 1¼ **Forus** 2-8-13 **0**.................................. ThoreHammerHansen(5) 3 64
(Jamie Osborne) dwlt: wl off the pce in rr: sme prog over 2f out: rdn and kpt on same pce over 1f out (vet said colt lost its right hind shoe) **25/1**

56 **8** 3 **Kahpehlo**[11] 3695 2-8-7 **0** ow2.................................. MitchGodwin(3) 9 48
(John Bridger) prom in centre tl wknd u.p 2f out **50/1**

9 1½ **Halfacrown (IRE)** 2-9-1 **0**.................................. NicolaCurrie 1 49
(Jamie Osborne) wl in rr: rdn and sme prog over 2f out: wknd over 1f out (jockey said colt hung right-handed in the latter stages) **16/1**

4 **10** ¾ **Moontide (IRE)**[19] 3405 2-9-0 **0**.................................. JosephineGordon 7 46
(J S Moore) cl up tl wknd over 2f out (vet said gelding lost its right fore shoe) **50/1**

11 4 **Premium Bond** 2-8-13 **0**.................................. TomMarquand 12 34
(Richard Hannon) pressed wnr towards nr side tl wknd u.p over 2f out **7/2[2]**

12 8 **Gifted Dreamer (IRE)** 2-8-13 **0**.................................. RyanTate 5 12
(Mark Usher) sn struggling in rr: nvr a factor **40/1**

1m 26.34s (2.04) **Going Correction** -0.075s/f (Good) 12 Ran SP% **127.8**
Speed ratings (Par 91): **90,88,87,87,86 86,84,81,79,78 74,65**
CSF £7.23 TOTE £2.10: £1.10, £1.70, £4.00; EX 9.10 Trifecta £74.20.
Owner The Ascot Colts & Fillies Club **Bred** Eve Johnson Houghton **Trained** Blewbury, Oxon

FOCUS
A modest maiden auction event with previous experience and a high draw proving key.

4115 SKY SPORTS RACING ON VIRGIN 535 H'CAP — 7f
8:15 (8:19) (Class 6) (0-60,60) 4-Y-0+
£3,105 (£924; £461; £400; £400; £400) Stalls Centre

Form — RPR

0055 1 **Fighting Temeraire (IRE)**[57] 2076 6-9-6 **59** ... MartinDwyer 15 — 71+
(Dean Ivory) *hld up towards nr side: waiting for a gap 3f out: swtchd lft and rdn to chse clr ldr 2f out: styd on wl fnl f to ld fnl 50yds* **9/4**[1]

0050 2 *nk* **Magical Ride**[25] 3208 4-9-2 **55** ... HarryBentley 13 — 66
(Richard Spencer) *mde most and racd towards nr side: rdn clr 2f out: kpt on but worn down fnl 50yds* **6/1**[2]

-546 3 *6* **Zefferino**[51] 2318 5-9-7 **60** ... (t) GeorgeWood 17 — 55
(Martin Bosley) *chsd ldrs towards nr side: rdn over 2f out: hanging lft after but kpt on to take 3rd ins fnl f* **8/1**

2003 4 *3* **Chikoko Trail**[15] 3539 4-9-7 **60** ... (tp) ShaneKelly 12 — 47
(Gary Moore) *chsd ldrs towards nr side: rdn and outpcd 2f out: one pce after* **14/1**

050 5 *¾* **Ubla (IRE)**[38] 2740 6-8-7 **53** ... CierenFallon(7) 18 — 38
(Gay Kelleway) *cl up towards nr side: rdn and outpcd 2f out: one pce after* **10/1**

123 6 *nse* **Atalanta Queen**[10] 3730 4-8-13 **52** ... (v) NicolaCurrie 11 — 37
(Robyn Brisland) *chsd ldrs towards nr side: pushed along 1/2-way: outpcd u.p 2f out: kpt on* **7/1**[3]

0-35 7 *9* **Secret Glance**[141] 530 7-8-8 **52** ... PoppyBridgwater(5) 7 — 12
(Adrian Wintle) *racd centre: on terms w wnr to over 2f out: wknd* **25/1**

-505 8 *¾* **Quick Recovery**[30] 3020 4-9-4 **57** ... CharlieBennett 4 — 15
(Jim Boyle) *taken down early: racd centre: hld up: nvr on terms: passed a few wkng rivals fnl f* **14/1**

-022 9 *nse* **Fiery Breath**[70] 1766 4-9-7 **60** ... (h) TomMarquand 10 — 18
(Robert Eddery) *pressed ldrs towards nr side tl wknd over 2f out* **10/1**

0-00 10 *1* **Mister Freeze (IRE)**[51] 2349 5-8-12 **51** ... (vt) JoeyHaynes 14 — 7
(Patrick Chamings) *dwlt: racd towards nr side: rdn and struggling in rr 3f out: no prog* **33/1**

3000 11 *½* **Mrs Benson (IRE)**[42] 2617 4-9-7 **60** ... CharlesBishop 8 — 14
(Michael Blanshard) *prom in centre over 4f: wknd* **20/1**

0200 12 *¾* **Letmestopyouthere (IRE)**[10] 3716 5-8-10 **56** ... (p) KateLeahy(7) 3 — 8
(Archie Watson) *racd centre: a in rr: hung lft fnl 2f (jockey said gelding stopped quickly)* **9/1**

0000 13 *½* **Tebay (IRE)**[17] 3481 4-9-1 **54** ... (b[1]) EoinWalsh 5 — +
(Luke McJannet) *slowly away: rcvrd to be prom in centre: wknd over 2f out (jockey said gelding reared as the stalls opened and stopped quickly)* **25/1**

010- 14 *1¼* **Counterfeit**[316] 5973 4-8-13 **52** ... (p) KierenFox 9
(Paul George) *nvr beyond midfield: wknd over 2f out* **33/1**

0-56 15 *½* **Lily Of Year (FR)**[38] 2728 4-8-10 **54** ... ScottMcCullagh(5) 1
(Denis Coakley) *taken down early: racd centre: nvr on terms: no ch fnl 2f* **14/1**

1m 22.84s (-1.46) **Going Correction** -0.075s/f (Good) **15** Ran SP% **135.2**
Speed ratings (Par 101): **107,106,99,96,95 95,85,84,84,83 82,81,81,79,79**
CSF £15.81 CT £99.57 TOTE £3.20: £1.60, £2.90, £3.40; EX 26.50 Trifecta £156.60.
Owner Michael & Heather Yarrow **Bred** Hot Ticket Partnership **Trained** Radlett, Herts

FOCUS
A big field for this moderate handicap and a dramatic race, with the favourite getting out of jail.

4116 FOLLOW AT THE RACES ON TWITTER NOVICE STKS — 6f
8:45 (8:51) (Class 5) 3-Y-0+ £3,752 (£1,116; £557; £278) Stalls Centre

Form — RPR

0-3 1 **Lapidary**[17] 3463 3-8-3 ... EllieMacKenzie(7) 12 — 77
(Heather Main) *t.k.h: mde all and racd towards nr side: hrd pressed fnl f: edgd lft but hld on wl* **8/1**

-502 2 *1* **Real Smooth (IRE)**[28] 3090 3-9-1 77 ... SeanLevey 6 — 79+
(Richard Hannon) *racd centre: w ldrs: rdn to chal over 1f out: ev ch ins fnl f: nt qckn nr fin* **6/5**[1]

1/5- 3 *3* **Springbourne**[385] 3367 5-9-8 ... RyanWhile(5) 15 — 76
(Bill Turner) *chsd ldrs towards nr side: outpcd and rdn 2f out: kpt on to take 3rd ins fnl f* **33/1**

4 4 *3* **Kodiak Attack (IRE)**[22] 3302 3-9-1 ... EdwardGreatrex 10 — 60
(Sylvester Kirk) *pressed ldrs: outpcd by ldng pair 2f out: fdd and lost 3rd ins fnl f* **16/1**

5 5 *nk* **Annexation (FR)**[28] 3090 3-9-1 ... RobertHavlin 11 — 59+
(Ed Dunlop) *uns rdr and rn off bef s: hld up in rr towards nr side: shkn up and sme prog 2f out: styd on fnl f: nvr nrr* **6/1**[3]

22-4 6 *nk* **Ricochet (IRE)**[19] 3421 3-9-1 79 ... NicolaCurrie 7 — 58
(Jamie Osborne) *prom in centre: shkn up over 2f out: fdd over 1f out* **7/1**

52 7 *2¾* **Alliseeisnibras (IRE)**[19] 3421 3-8-10 ... OisinMurphy 1 — 44
(Ismail Mohammed) *prom in centre: pushed along 2f out: nt on terms after: fdd* **5/1**[2]

0- 8 *1* **Forthwith**[197] 9442 3-8-10 ... HayleyTurner 3 — 41
(Tony Carroll) *stdd s: hld up in rr: pushed along 2f out: sme prog and shkn up over 1f out: kpt on: nt disgracd* **50/1**

00-0 9 *6* **Aegean Legend**[47] 2483 4-9-5 50 ... (p[1]) MitchGodwin(3) 9 — 29
(John Bridger) *chsd ldrs tl wknd over 2f out* **66/1**

/050 10 *hd* **Angelical Eve (IRE)**[31] 2972 5-9-3 39 ... KierenFox 2 — 23
(Dai Williams) *racd centre: a in rr: no ch fnl 2f* **66/1**

00 11 *¾* **Dutch Story**[12] 3661 3-9-1 ... ShaneKelly 16 — 24
(Amanda Perrett) *prom early nr side: struggling and in rr by 1/2-way* **33/1**

0-03 12 *2¾* **Gambon (GER)**[19] 3421 3-9-1 77 ... CharlesBishop 13 — 15
(Eve Johnson Houghton) *awkward s: chsd ldrs towards nr side: wknd over 2f out: eased* **7/1**

00 13 *shd* **Vallachy**[12] 3661 4-9-8 ... JasonWatson 14 — 17
(William Muir) *in tch towards nr side tl wknd over 2f out* **50/1**

0 14 *6* **Hidden Dream (FR)**[12] 3661 4-8-10 60 ... MorganCole(7) 5
(John Butler) *racd centre: hld up in rr: wknd 2f out* **66/1**

04- 15 *7* **Layla's Dream**[292] 6866 3-8-11 ow1 ... TomMarquand 4
(Tony Carroll) *nvr on terms: bhd fnl 2f* **50/1**

6 16 *7* **Glory Street**[77] 1587 3-9-1 ... JoeyHaynes 8
(Paddy Butler) *sn t.o* **80/1**

1m 11.14s (-0.36) **Going Correction** -0.075s/f (Good)
WFA 3 from 4yo+ 7lb **16** Ran SP% **135.9**
Speed ratings (Par 103): **104,102,98,94,94 93,90,88,80,80 79,75,75,67,58 49**
CSF £19.48 TOTE £10.20: £2.90, £1.20, £18.90; EX 24.20 Trifecta £782.90.
Owner Andrew Knott & Wetumpka Racing **Bred** Trebles Holford Farm Thoroughbreds **Trained** Kingston Lisle, Oxon

FOCUS
A big field for this novice, but few could be seriously fancied and they finished well spread out. Prominent racers were favoured and this rates a pb from the winner.
T/Plt: £16.00 to a £1 stake. Pool: £57,513.80 - 2,607.98 winning units T/Qpdt: £10.60 to a £1 stake. Pool: £7,280.18 - 506.52 winning units **Jonathan Neesom**

4067 NEWMARKET (R-H)
Saturday, June 22

OFFICIAL GOING: Good (7.5)
Wind: Light across Weather: Sunny spells

4117 HEATH COURT HOTEL BRITISH EBF NOVICE STKS (PLUS 10 RACE) — 7f
1:40 (1:44) (Class 4) 2-Y-0 £5,175 (£1,540; £769; £384) Stalls Low

Form — RPR

4 1 **Saqqara King (USA)**[21] 3335 2-9-5 0 ... KerrinMcEvoy 5 — 81
(Charlie Appleby) *s.i.s: sn prom: lost pl over 5f out: swtchd lft 1/2-way: hdwy over 2f out: rdn to ld 1f out: styd on* **4/6**[1]

5 2 *½* **Mass Media**[23] 3274 2-9-5 0 ... KieranO'Neill 4 — 80
(John Gosden) *w ldr tl led 1/2-way: rdn and hdd 1f out: styd on (vet said colt lost its left fore shoe)* **9/2**[3]

3 *½* **Moolhim (FR)** 2-9-5 0 ... JackMitchell 2 — 78+
(Simon Crisford) *s.i.s: hdwy over 5f out: nt clr run over 1f out: rdn and ev ch sn after: kpt on* **4/1**[2]

0 4 *1¼* **Arthur's Court (IRE)**[31] 2973 2-9-5 0 ... PatCosgrave 8 — 75
(Hugo Palmer) *chsd ldrs: rdn and ev ch over 1f out: styd on same pce wl ins fnl f* **10/1**

0 5 *3¾* **Selsey Sizzler**[23] 3274 2-9-5 0 ... CallumShepherd 9 — 65
(William Knight) *sn led: hdd 1/2-way: rdn over 1f out: sn outpcd* **50/1**

6 *1½* **Game Over (IRE)** 2-9-5 0 ... SeanLevey 6 — 62
(Richard Hannon) *s.i.s: hld up: shkn up over 1f out: sn outpcd* **12/1**

7 *12* **Astroman** 2-9-5 0 ... DanielMuscutt 7 — 30
(Mark H Tompkins) *hld up: shkn up over 2f out: wknd over 1f out* **100/1**

1m 28.14s (2.44) **Going Correction** +0.20s/f (Good) **7** Ran SP% **117.9**
Speed ratings (Par 95): **94,93,92,91,87 85,71**
CSF £4.48 TOTE £1.50: £1.10, £2.40; EX 4.20 Trifecta £10.50.
Owner Godolphin **Bred** Aaron & Marie Jones Llc **Trained** Newmarket, Suffolk
■ Archie Bear was withdrawn. Price at time of withdrawal 100/1. Rule 4 does not apply

FOCUS
The far side course was used. Stalls: all races stands' side. The ground had continued to dry out following Friday evening's card. After the first, Kerrin McEvoy said: " It's lovely ground," and Jack Mitchell's take was: "It's like a carpet." A fairly good novice, with no anchor to the form.

4118 HEATH COURT HOTEL BESTWESTERN.CO.UK H'CAP — 1m 6f
2:10 (2:17) (Class 4) (0-85,87) 4-Y-0+
£7,762 (£2,310; £1,154; £577; £300; £300) Stalls Low

Form — RPR

333- 1 **Victoria Drummond (IRE)**[184] 9639 4-9-9 **87** ... HarryBentley 3 — 94
(Mark Johnston) *s.i.s: rcvrd to ld after 1f: shkn up over 3f out: rdn over 1f out: rdr dropped whip ins fnl f: styd on gamely* **3/1**[1]

25-6 2 *nk* **Potters Lady Jane**[23] 3269 7-8-6 **70** ... HayleyTurner 8 — 76
(Lucy Wadham) *stdd s: hld up: nt clr run over 2f out: hdwy and n.m.r over 1f out: rdn and ev ch ins fnl f: styd on* **8/1**[3]

2142 3 *hd* **Vampish**[26] 3145 4-8-9 **73** ... PhilDennis 4 — 79+
(Philip McBride) *edgd lft s: hld up: nt clr run fr over 2f out tl swtchd rt and hdwy over 1f out: rdn and ev ch whn n.m.r ins fnl f: styd on (jockey said filly was denied a clear run)* **5/1**[2]

0060 4 *3¾* **Battle Of Marathon (USA)**[21] 3361 7-8-10 **74** ... BrettDoyle 6 — 74
(John Ryan) *s.i.s and hmpd s: hld up: hdwy on outer over 2f out: rdn and ev ch whn hung rt fr over 1f out: no ex ins fnl f* **33/1**

-122 5 *3½* **Orin Swift (IRE)**[13] 3635 5-9-8 **86** ... RobHornby 9 — 81
(Jonathan Portman) *led 1f: chsd wnr: rdn and ev ch over 1f out: wknd ins fnl f* **3/1**[1]

-001 6 *nk* **Swordbill**[21] 3334 4-8-5 **69** ... (p) KerrinMcEvoy 10 — 63
(Ian Williams) *chsd ldrs: rdn over 1f out: wknd ins fnl f* **3/1**[1]

4-06 7 *10* **Sunblazer (IRE)**[28] 3091 9-8-9 **73** ... (t) LukeMorris 5 — 53
(Kim Bailey) *s.i.s and hmpd s: hld up: hdwy over 3f out: rdn over 2f out: wknd fnl f* **40/1**

646- 8 *nk* **Darksideoftarnside (IRE)**[183] 9156 5-9-5 **83** ... (p) KieranShoemark 1 — 63
(Ian Williams) *hld up: rdn over 2f out: sn wknd* **14/1**

6-50 9 *nk* **Great Hall**[14] 3600 9-9-5 **83** ... PatCosgrave 2 — 63
(Mick Quinn) *chsd ldrs: rdn over 3f out: wknd over 1f out* **20/1**

3m 3.9s (4.00) **Going Correction** +0.20s/f (Good) **9** Ran SP% **119.6**
Speed ratings (Par 105): **96,95,95,93,91 91,85,85,85**
CSF £29.13 CT £119.21 TOTE £3.60: £1.50, £1.80, £2.80; EX 26.70 Trifecta £140.40.
Owner P F M D Carmo **Bred** Mrs Renata Coleman **Trained** Middleham Moor, N Yorks
■ Amourice (6-1) was withdrawn. Rule 4 applies to all bets struck prior to withdrawal, but not to SP bets. Deduction - 10p in the pound. New market formed.
■ Stewards' Enquiry : Brett Doyle four-day ban: used whip above the permitted level (Jun 7-10)

FOCUS
Add 30yds. Ordinary fillies' form, rated around the second and third.

4119 HEATH COURT HOTEL FILLIES' H'CAP — 1m
2:45 (2:47) (Class 4) (0-85,82) 3-Y-0 £7,762 (£2,310; £1,154; £577; £300) Stalls Low

Form — RPR

41-3 1 **She's Got You**[51] 2340 3-9-6 **81** ... KieranO'Neill 1 — 88
(John Gosden) *awkward leaving stalls: hld up: carried hd to one side: pushed along and hdwy on outer over 2f out: rdn over 1f out: led ins fnl f: drvn out* **15/8**[2]

005- 2 *2* **Aubretia (IRE)**[231] 8834 3-8-10 **71** ... MartinDwyer 2 — 73
(Richard Hannon) *chsd ldr: rdn and ev ch over 1f out: styd on same pce u.p ins fnl f: wnt 2nd nr fin* **14/1**

-260 3 *½* **Zofelle (IRE)**[36] 2809 3-9-6 **81** ... (t[1]) PatCosgrave 4 — 82
(Hugo Palmer) *sn chsng ldrs: shkn up to ld over 1f out: rdn and edgd rt sn after: hdd ins fnl f: no ex towards fin* **10/1**

33-1 4 *9* **Ascended (IRE)**[19] 3431 3-9-7 **82** ... KerrinMcEvoy 5 — 61
(William Haggas) *led: racd keenly: rdn and hdd over 1f out: wknd ins fnl f (jockey said filly ran too freely)* **6/4**[1]

66-1 5 *7* **Mulan (IRE)**[25] 3193 3-9-2 **77** ... KieranShoemark 3 — 39
(Sir Michael Stoute) *prom: stdd and lost pl over 5f out: rdn over 2f out: wknd over 1f out* **7/2**[3]

1m 39.83s (-0.17) **Going Correction** +0.20s/f (Good) **5** Ran SP% **112.8**
Speed ratings (Par 98): **108,106,105,96,89**
CSF £24.23 TOTE £3.00: £1.50, £5.90; EX 22.20 Trifecta £95.60.

Owner John Gunther & Tanya Gunther **Bred** John Gunther **Trained** Newmarket, Suffolk
■ Stewards' Enquiry : Kieran O'Neill two-day ban: used whip above the permitted level (Jul 7-8)

FOCUS
Fair fillies' form, with the winner progressing again and a pb from the second.

4120 HEATH COURT DINING CLUB BRITISH EBF NOVICE STKS (PLUS 10 RACE) (DIV I) 1m
3:20 (3:24) (Class 4) 3-Y-O **£5,822** (£1,732; £865; £432) **Stalls** Low

Form RPR
3- **1** **Cadre Du Noir (USA)**[234] 8739 3-9-2 0 RobHornby 6 88+
(Martyn Meade) *hld up: hdwy on outer over 3f out: rdn to ld and edgd rt over 1f out: r.o wl: comf* **11/4**[2]
0-1 **2** 1¼ **Wings Of Time**[141] 534 3-9-8 0 KerrinMcEvoy 5 90
(Charlie Appleby) *sn led: hdd over 5f out: led again 3f out: rdn and hdd over 1f out: styd on same pce wl ins fnl f* **4/1**[3]
53 **3** 1¾ **Society Guest (IRE)**[15] 3546 3-8-11 0 CallumShepherd 4 75
(Mick Channon) *stdd s: hld up: racd keenly: hdwy over 2f out: shkn up over 1f out: styd on same pce ins fnl f* **25/1**
4 1¼ **Going Places** 3-9-2 0 JackMitchell 9 77+
(Roger Varian) *racd keenly: prom: nt clr run over 2f out: shkn up over 1f out: styd on same pce fnl f (vet said colt lost its right hind shoe)* **10/1**
54 **5** 1¾ **San Sebastian (IRE)**[20] 3372 3-9-2 0 DanielMuscutt 10 73
(Ed Dunlop) *hld up: hdwy over 4f out: shkn up over 1f out: no ex ins fnl f* **20/1**
6 5 **Ghanim (IRE)** 3-9-2 0 CharlesBishop 1 61
(Conrad Allen) *s.i.s: hld up: racd keenly: shkn up over 2f out: nt trble ldrs* **50/1**
5 **7** 1 **Majaalis (FR)**[36] 2790 3-9-2 0 DaneO'Neill 8 58
(William Haggas) *s.i.s: hld up: hdwy over 4f out: rdn and ev ch wl over 1f out: wknd fnl f* **6/4**[1]
6- **8** 4 **Colonel Slade (IRE)**[323] 5683 3-9-2 0 (t[1]) PatCosgrave 7 49
(Brian Meehan) *s.i.s: sn prom: nt clr run and lost pl over 4f out: wknd over 1f out* **28/1**
00 **9** 1½ **Starlight**[53] 2250 3-8-4 0 SaraDelFabbro(7) 3 40
(Michael Bell) *s.i.s: hld up: shkn up on outer over 2f out: wknd over 1f out* **100/1**
10 1¾ **Eventura** 3-8-11 0 BrettDoyle 2 36
(Tony Carroll) *chsd ldrs: nt clr run and lost pl over 3f out: wknd over 1f out* **100/1**
6- **11** 15 **Arabian King**[316] 5968 3-9-2 0 (w) LukeMorris 11 5
(David Elsworth) *s.i.s: plld hrd and sn prom: led over 5f out: hdd 3f out: sn rdn: wknd wl over 1f out (jockey said colt ran too freely)* **9/1**

1m 40.93s (0.93) **Going Correction** +0.20s/f (Good) **11 Ran SP% 121.8**
Speed ratings (Par 101): **103,101,100,98,97 92,91,87,85,83 68**
CSF £13.98 TOTE £3.20: £1.60, £1.30, £5.70; EX 15.00 Trifecta £180.30.
Owner Phoenix Thoroughbred Limited **Bred** Sf Bloodstock Llc, D Andrews Et Al **Trained** Manton, Wilts

FOCUS
Division one of this novice event, which was the quicker of the two divisions by 0.37sec.

4121 HEATH COURT DINING CLUB BRITISH EBF NOVICE STKS (PLUS 10 RACE) (DIV II) 1m
4:00 (4:01) (Class 4) 3-Y-O **£5,822** (£1,732; £865; £432) **Stalls** Low

Form RPR
5-23 **1** **Moqtarreb**[21] 3340 3-9-5 85 DaneO'Neill 5 94
(Roger Varian) *chsd ldrs: shkn up to ld and hung lft fr over 1f out: rdn clr ins fnl f* **7/2**[3]
3 **2** 4 **Reynolds**[36] 2790 3-9-5 0 CharlesBishop 7 84
(Eve Johnson Houghton) *led: rdn and hdd over 1f out: styng on same pce whn hung lft ins fnl f* **15/8**[1]
43- **3** 2¼ **Light And Dark**[241] 8548 3-9-5 0 CallumShepherd 11 79
(Saeed bin Suroor) *stmbld s: sn prom: rdn and ev ch over 1f out: hung lft and no ex ins fnl f (jockey said colt stumbled leaving the stalls)* **3/1**[2]
4 3½ **Frontman** 3-9-5 0 (p[1]) KieranO'Neill 4 70
(John Gosden) *s.i.s: racd keenly and sn prom: rdn over 2f out: wknd over 1f out: hung lft ins fnl f* **7/1**
5 ¾ **Sea Wings** 3-9-5 0 KerrinMcEvoy 6 68
(William Haggas) *s.i.s: hld up: hdwy over 2f out: rdn and wknd over 1f out* **7/1**
24 **6** 2¼ **Bardo Contiguo (IRE)**[28] 3067 3-9-5 0 JackMitchell 10 63
(Roger Varian) *chsd ldr tl shkn up over 2f out: wknd over 1f out* **9/1**
7 nk **Your Thoughts (FR)** 3-9-0 0 MartinDwyer 3 57
(Paul Webber) *s.s and wnt rt s: hld up: shkn up over 2f out: nvr on terms* **100/1**
6 **8** ¾ **Ecstasea (IRE)**[30] 3019 3-9-0 0 LukeMorris 9 55
(Rae Guest) *prom: rdn over 2f out: wknd over 1f out* **100/1**
0- **8** dht **Asensio**[227] 8931 3-9-5 0 SeanLevey 8 60
(Mohamed Moubarak) *rrd s: hld up: rdn over 2f out: sn wknd* **80/1**
00 **10** 1¼ **Fountain Of Life**[23] 3277 3-9-5 0 PhilDennis 12 57
(Philip McBride) *s.i.s: hld up: wknd over 2f out* **100/1**
0-0 **11** 14 **Heartbreak Hotel (IRE)**[12] 3648 3-9-0 0 JosephineGordon 1 19
(Michael Bell) *hld up: wknd over 2f out* **50/1**
0 **12** 28 **Isaac Murphy (USA)**[14] 3584 3-9-5 0 DanielMuscutt 2
(Mark H Tompkins) *hld up: wknd over 2f out* **100/1**

1m 41.3s (1.30) **Going Correction** +0.20s/f (Good) **12 Ran SP% 124.2**
Speed ratings (Par 101): **101,97,94,91,90 88,87,87,87,85 71,43**
CSF £11.13 TOTE £5.10: £1.60, £1.30, £1.40; EX 13.20 Trifecta £32.60.
Owner Hamdan Al Maktoum **Bred** Shadwell Estate Company Limited **Trained** Newmarket, Suffolk

FOCUS
The slower division by 0.37sec. This time they raced in the centre of the track, with the principals ending up nearer the far rail.

4122 HEATH COURT HOTEL H'CAP 5f
4:40 (4:40) (Class 2) (0-105,101) 3-Y-O **£12,938** (£3,850; £1,924; £962) **Stalls** Low

Form RPR
5160 **1** **Wedding Date**[7] 3865 3-8-1 86 ThoreHammerHansen(5) 3 93
(Richard Hannon) *chsd ldrs: rdn over 1f out: str run to ld wl ins fnl f* **9/2**[2]
6-10 **2** 1 **Street Parade**[7] 3855 3-9-7 101 (t) KerrinMcEvoy 4 104
(Stuart Williams) *hld up: racd keenly: hdwy over 1f out: r.o* **11/1**[3]
211 **3** nk **Philipine Cobra**[8] 3815 3-8-3 83 LukeMorris 2 85
(Phil McEntee) *chsd ldr: led 2f out: shkn up and edgd rt over 1f out: hdd wl ins fnl f* **9/2**[2]
0-04 **4** 1 **Alfie Solomons (IRE)**[36] 2810 3-8-5 85 MartinDwyer 5 83
(Richard Spencer) *chsd ldrs: rdn over 1f out: styd on same pce wl ins fnl f* **9/2**[2]
66-1 **5** 1¼ **Semoum (USA)**[48] 2434 3-9-5 99 JackMitchell 6 93+
(Roger Varian) *s.i.s: hld up: hdwy over 1f out: sn rdn: no ex wl ins fnl f* **13/8**[1]
120 **6** ¾ **Fen Breeze**[51] 2319 3-8-2 82 oh1 KieranO'Neill 7 73
(Rae Guest) *prom: stdd and lost pl over 3f out: pushed along and hdwy on outer 2f out: no ex fnl f* **11/1**[3]
3200 **7** 1¾ **Chapelli**[28] 3075 3-8-9 94 AndrewBreslin(5) 1 79
(Mark Johnston) *led: edgd lft 1/2-way: hdd 2f out: wknd ins fnl f* **14/1**

59.09s (0.39) **Going Correction** +0.20s/f (Good) **7 Ran SP% 116.0**
Speed ratings (Par 105): **104,102,101,100,98 97,94**
CSF £51.91 TOTE £5.30: £2.30, £4.10; EX 65.90 Trifecta £246.40.
Owner Middleham Park Racing CXIV **Bred** Llety Farms **Trained** East Everleigh, Wilts

FOCUS
A good sprint handicap run in a time only 1.59sec outside standard. A pb from the winner under her 5lb claimer.

4123 PARK REGIS KRIS KIN HOTEL DUBAI H'CAP 6f
5:15 (5:17) (Class 4) (0-85,87) 3-Y-O+ **£7,762** (£2,310; £1,154; £577; £300; £300) **Stalls** Low

Form RPR
0404 **1** **Suzi's Connoisseur**[15] 3550 8-9-0 71 (v) JFEgan 11 80
(Jane Chapple-Hyam) *hld up: hdwy 1/2-way: chsd ldr over 1f out: rdn and r.o to ld wl ins fnl f* **8/1**
3162 **2** 1 **Ballyquin (IRE)**[42] 2611 4-9-9 80 RobHornby 5 86
(Andrew Balding) *led main gp: overall ldr 2f out: rdn and edgd rt over 1f out: hdd wl ins fnl f* **4/1**[2]
1133 **3** 1¼ **Martineo**[29] 3043 4-9-10 81 SeanLevey 10 83
(John Butler) *hld up: nt clr run and swtchd rt over 2f out: hdwy over 1f out: sn rdn: styd on same pce wl ins fnl f* **3/1**[1]
0-52 **4** ½ **Revich (IRE)**[29] 3048 3-9-7 85 LukeMorris 3 83
(Richard Spencer) *chsd ldrs: rdn over 1f out: styd on same pce ins fnl f* **7/1**
0-35 **5** ½ **Motagally**[43] 2567 3-9-2 80 DaneO'Neill 8 77
(Charles Hills) *s.i.s: hld up: racd keenly: nt clr run over 2f out: sn rdn: r.o ins fnl f: nvr nrr* **10/1**
5204 **6** nk **Vegas Boy (IRE)**[14] 3597 4-10-0 85 (t) NicolaCurrie 9 83
(Jamie Osborne) *chsd ldr tl rdn over 1f out: no ex wl ins fnl f* **10/1**
6000 **7** ½ **Don Armado (IRE)**[35] 2835 3-9-9 87 KieranShoemark 4 81
(Robert Cowell) *prom: sn stdd and lost pl: hdwy over 1f out: sn rdn: no ex ins fnl f* **16/1**
0544 **8** 1 **Foreign Legion (IRE)**[9] 3781 4-8-9 66 oh4 (b) KieranO'Neill 1 59
(Luke McJannet) *racd alone stands' side: overall ldr 4f: sn rdn: hung lft and no ex fnl f* **20/1**
0-06 **9** 8 **Hart Stopper**[26] 3164 5-9-13 84 (p[1]) KerrinMcEvoy 2 51
(Stuart Williams) *hld up: nt clr run and hmpd over 2f out: nvr on terms* **14/1**
1111 **10** 27 **Camachess (IRE)**[10] 3742 3-8-13 77 PhilDennis 6
(Philip McBride) *s.i.s: hld up: hdwy 1/2-way: rdn and hung rt over 2f out: sn wknd: eased over 1f out (jockey said filly lugged right-handed throughout)* **6/1**[3]
3-60 **11** 5 **Breaking Records (IRE)**[91] 1290 4-9-13 84 (h) PatCosgrave 7
(Hugo Palmer) *chsd ldrs: pushed along 1/2-way: wknd and eased over 1f out* **25/1**

1m 13.02s (0.92) **Going Correction** +0.20s/f (Good)
WFA 3 from 4yo+ 7lb **11 Ran SP% 122.2**
Speed ratings (Par 105): **101,99,98,97,96 96,95,94,83,47 40**
CSF £41.69 CT £124.09 TOTE £9.30: £2.80, £1.70, £1.70; EX 55.50 Trifecta £258.40.
Owner Mrs Jane Chapple-Hyam **Bred** Greenstead Hall Racing Ltd **Trained** Dalham, Suffolk
■ Stewards' Enquiry : J F Egan two-day ban: used whip above the permitted level (Jul 7-8)

FOCUS
The first three in this competitive handicap all made the frame in a similar race won by Molls Memory at Ascot last month and this rates straightforward form.

4124 "SADDLE UP" ART TRAIL H'CAP 7f
5:50 (5:52) (Class 4) (0-85,85) 3-Y-O **£7,762** (£2,310; £1,154; £577; £300; £300) **Stalls** Low

Form RPR
4-32 **1** **Jaleel**[29] 3051 3-9-2 80 JackMitchell 10 87
(Roger Varian) *hld up: hdwy over 2f out: rdn and hung lft over 1f out: sn wnt rt: led and flashed tail ins fnl f: hung rt: drvn out* **15/2**[3]
6535 **2** nk **Dirty Rascal (IRE)**[17] 3465 3-9-7 85 (b[1]) SeanLevey 5 91
(Richard Hannon) *chsd ldr 6f out: led over 1f out: rdn and hdd ins fnl f: styd on* **4/1**[2]
5-42 **3** ½ **Majestic Mac**[32] 2927 3-8-12 76 RobHornby 11 81+
(Hughie Morrison) *s.i.s: hld up: hdwy over 1f out: sn rdn: r.o* **9/1**
220- **4** nk **Jadeerah**[191] 9522 3-9-1 79 (h[1]) DaneO'Neill 3 83
(John Gosden) *trckd ldrs: racd keenly: rdn over 1f out: r.o* **8/1**
203 **5** 1¾ **Gentlewoman (IRE)**[19] 3431 3-9-1 79 (h) KieranO'Neill 2 78
(John Gosden) *chsd ldrs: shkn up over 2f out: nt clr run and swtchd rt over 1f out: sn rdn: styd on* **10/1**
24-1 **6** 2¼ **Make A Wish (IRE)**[33] 2909 3-9-4 82 KerrinMcEvoy 1 75
(Simon Crisford) *led 6f out: rdn: hung lft and hdd over 1f out: no ex ins fnl f* **3/1**[1]
0040 **7** 1¼ **Battle Of Waterloo (IRE)**[21] 3357 3-9-0 78 LukeMorris 7 68
(John Ryan) *hld up: hdwy 1/2-way: rdn over 1f out: no ex fnl f* **22/1**
0200 **8** 7 **Azor Ahai**[22] 3307 3-8-13 77 CallumShepherd 4 48
(Mick Channon) *hld up: rdn and hung lft over 1f out: n.d* **33/1**
5200 **9** ½ **Songkran (IRE)**[29] 3051 3-8-13 77 DanielMuscutt 9 46
(David Elsworth) *prom: lost pl over 5f out: hdwy over 1f out: sn rdn: wknd ins fnl f (jockey said colt jumped left-handed when leaving the stalls)* **20/1**
3462 **10** 1¼ **Facethepuckout (IRE)**[8] 3805 3-8-10 74 (p) BrettDoyle 8 40
(John Ryan) *led 1f: remained handy: rdn and wknd over 1f out* **25/1**
-314 **11** 1¼ **Jilbaab**[14] 3580 3-8-12 76 MartinDwyer 12 39
(Brian Meehan) *s.i.s: hld up: rdn and hung lft over 2f out: wknd over 1f out* **10/1**
04-1 **12** 2 **Heroic**[21] 3353 3-8-12 76 KieranShoemark 6 33
(Charles Hills) *chsd ldrs: rdn over 2f out: wknd over 1f out* **14/1**
0-64 **13** ½ **Bullington Boy (FR)**[12] 3675 3-8-11 75 JFEgan 13 31
(Jane Chapple-Hyam) *hld up: racd keenly: hdwy 1/2-way: rdn over 2f out: hung lft and wknd over 1f out (jockey said colt lost its action)* **12/1**

1m 26.31s (0.61) **Going Correction** +0.20s/f (Good) **13 Ran SP% 126.3**
Speed ratings (Par 101): **104,103,103,102,100 98,96,88,88,86 85,83,82**
CSF £37.97 CT £295.64 TOTE £8.30: £2.80, £1.90, £2.70; EX 39.90 Trifecta £344.60.
Owner Abdullatif M Al-Abdulrazzaq **Bred** Jane Allison **Trained** Newmarket, Suffolk

FOCUS
They raced towards the stands' side in this fair handicap, and those positioned nearest the fence in the first half of the contest came out on top. The winner progressed again.
T/Plt: £68.30 to a £1 stake. Pool: £51,696.75 - 551.87 winning units T/Qpdt: £39.50 to a £1 stake. Pool: £3,676.79 - 68.86 winning units **Colin Roberts**

4075 REDCAR (L-H)
Saturday, June 22

OFFICIAL GOING: Good (8.0)
Wind: Moderate across Weather: Cloudy with sunny periods

4125 CHIC HATS EBF NOVICE STKS — 5f 217y
1:35 (1:36) (Class 5) 2-Y-O — **£4,528** (£1,347; £673; £336) **Stalls** Centre

Form	Pos	Btn	Horse / details	Jockey	RPR
31	1		**War Storm**[28] 3098 2-9-6 0 (Archie Watson) *prom: cl up 1/2-way: chal over 1f out and sn rdn: drvn to ld wl ins fnl f: kpt on* 8/15[1]	(p[1]) HollieDoyle 3	81
3	2	nk	**Cruising**[23] 3265 2-9-2 0 (David Brown) *sn slt ld: pushed along 2f out: sn rdn: drvn 1f out: hdd wl ins fnl f: kpt on* 9/1[3]	PaulMulrennan 5	76
	3	1 1/4	**Saint Of Katowice (IRE)** 2-9-2 0 (Richard Fahey) *towards rr: hdwy 1/2-way: chsd ldrs 2f out: sn rdn: kpt on same pce fnl f* 11/2[2]	DavidNolan 1	72
4	4	1	**Zuckerberg (IRE)**[25] 3190 2-9-2 0 (Ivan Furtado) *in tch: hdwy to trck ldrs over 2f out: rdn wl over 1f out: drvn and no imp fnl f* 12/1	TrevorWhelan 4	69
56	5	6	**Out Of Here (IRE)**[23] 3265 2-9-2 0 (Kevin Ryan) *dwlt and in rr: hdwy over 2f out: rdn wl over 1f out: kpt on fnl f: nvr trble ldrs* 18/1	AndrewMullen 2	50+
	6	1 1/2	**Araka Li (IRE)** 2-9-2 0 (Tim Easterby) *dwlt: t.k.h and sn in tch: trckd ldrs 1/2-way: rdn along 2f out: kpt on same pce* 40/1	DuranFentiman 6	46
	7	1 3/4	**Kendred Soul (IRE)** 2-8-12 0 ow1 (Jedd O'Keeffe) *t.k.h: chsd ldrs: rdn along over 2f out: grad wknd* 33/1	JackGarritty 8	36
	8	1	**Abbey Wharf (IRE)** 2-8-6 0 (Nigel Tinkler) *trckd ldrs: rdn along outpcd wl over 2f out: styng on whn n.m.r over 1f out: kpt on same pce* 100/1	FayeMcManoman(5) 12	32
	9	shd	**Hi Harry (IRE)** 2-9-2 0 (Declan Carroll) *prom on outer: rdn along over 2f out: sn drvn and wknd* 14/1	NathanEvans 11	37
0	10	3/4	**Chocoholic**[66] 1843 2-8-9 0 (Bryan Smart) *cl up: rdn along wl over 2f out: sn wknd* 50/1	HarryRussell(7) 7	35
644	11	nk	**King Lenox**[34] 2869 2-8-13 0 (Nigel Tinkler) *trckd ldrs: pushed along 1/2-way: sn rdn and wknd* 28/1	RowanScott(3) 10	34
0	12	2	**Tiltilys Rock (IRE)**[11] 3702 2-9-2 0 (Andrew Crook) *cl up: rdn along 1/2-way: drvn and wknd wl over 2f out* 100/1	AndrewElliott 9	28
5	13	5	**Wots The Wifi Code**[23] 3265 2-8-13 0 (Tony Coyle) *a towards rr: outpcd and bhd fnl 2f* 50/1	SeanDavis(3) 13	12

1m 11.0s (-0.80) **Going Correction** -0.15s/f (Firm) **13** Ran SP% **125.0**
Speed ratings (Par 93): **103,102,100,99,91 89,87,85,85,84 84,81,75**
CSF £6.47 TOTE £1.30: £1.02, £2.40, £2.20; EX 6.40 Trifecta £27.60.
Owner Saeed Bin Mohammed Al Qassimi **Bred** Gary Hodson & Peter Moule **Trained** Upper Lambourn, W Berks

FOCUS
A fairly decent juvenile novice contest. The odds-on favourite made his experience count in defying a small penalty.

4126 BETTY LEIGH BOUTIQUE FASHION SHOW H'CAP — 1m 5f 218y
2:05 (2:05) (Class 6) (0-60,60) 4-Y-O+ — **£3,823** (£1,137; £568; £300; £300; £300) **Stalls** Low

Form	Pos	Btn	Horse / details	Jockey	RPR
-000	1		**Nearly There**[18] 3447 6-8-13 **52** (Wilf Storey) *hld up in rr: stdy hdwy on outer over 3f out: chsd ldrs over 2f out: rdn to chal wl over 1f out: drvn to ld ins fnl f: kpt on wl* 12/1	(t) HollieDoyle 7	60
6231	2	1/2	**Angel Gabrial (IRE)**[17] 3481 10-9-7 **60** (Patrick Morris) *trckd ldr: hdwy to ld over 2f out: rdn along wl over 1f out: drvn and hdd ins fnl f: kpt on* 13/2	(p) PaulMulrennan 12	67
60-4	3	2 1/4	**Muftakker**[40] 2695 5-9-5 **58** (John Norton) *in tch: hdwy to trck ldrs over 4f out: rdn along over 2f out: drvn over 1f out: kpt on same pce fnl f* 8/1	JackGarritty 5	62
3-04	4	1/2	**Jan De Heem**[18] 3447 9-8-7 **51** (Tina Jackson) *hld up: stdy hdwy over 3f out: trckd ldrs 2f out: effrt over 1f out: sn rdn and kpt on same pce* 16/1	(p) ConnorMurtagh(5) 8	55
0-64	5	3/4	**Up Ten Down Two (IRE)**[54] 2217 10-9-6 **59** (Michael Easterby) *hld up in rr: hdwy 3f out: rdn along wl over 1f out: styd on fnl f: nrst fin* 9/1	(t) NathanEvans 9	62
54/4	6	shd	**Another Lincolnday**[23] 3272 8-9-2 **55** (Rebecca Menzies) *trckd ldrs on inner: hdwy 4f out: pushed along 3f out: rdn over 2f out: drvn wl over 1f out: kpt on same pce* 7/2[2]	StevieDonohoe 1	58
0000	7	nk	**Miss Ranger (IRE)**[6] 3886 7-9-1 **59** (Roger Fell) *hld up towards rr: hdwy 4f out: pushed along whn sltly outpcd and n.m.r over 2f out: swtchd rt to outer wl over 1f out: styd on wl fnl f: nrst fin* 16/1	(b[1]) PaulaMuir(5) 3	61
/0-4	8	1/2	**Big Time Dancer (IRE)**[21] 3334 6-9-7 **60** (Jennie Candlish) *trckd ldrs: hdwy 4f out: cl up 3f out: rdn along and ev ch 2f out: sn drvn and wknd wl over 1f out (vet said an endoscopic examination revealed the gelding had bled)* 3/1[1]	(p) DavidNolan 10	62
0-05	9	3	**Point Of Honour (IRE)**[11] 3705 4-8-11 **50** (Ruth Carr) *led: rdn along over 3f out: hdd wl over 2f out: sn wknd* 5/1[3]	AndrewMullen 4	48
02-0	10	8	**Midnight Warrior**[26] 3162 9-8-12 **54** (Ron Barr) *prom: rdn along over 3f out: sn wknd (trainer said gelding lost its tongue tie during the race and in his opinion, materially affected the gelding's performance)* 25/1	(t) RowanScott(3) 6	41
0-0	11	8	**Zenafire**[16] 3511 10-9-4 **60** (Sarah Hollinshead) *towards rr: effrt and sme hdwy on outer over 3f out: sn rdn and wknd* 33/1	(p) JaneElliott(3) 11	37

3m 1.73s (-5.27) **Going Correction** -0.15s/f (Firm) **11** Ran SP% **124.6**
Speed ratings (Par 101): **109,108,107,107,106 106,106,106,104,99 95**
CSF £93.25 CT £682.20 TOTE £25.30: £4.60, £2.20, £2.70; EX 177.00 Trifecta £1129.50.
Owner Geegeez.co.uk 1 **Bred** Raymond Clive Tooth **Trained** Muggleswick, Co Durham

FOCUS
Seemingly straightforward form with the winner rated back to his Tapeta peak from last year.

4127 H JARVIS 141ST ANNIVERSARY H'CAP — 7f
2:40 (2:40) (Class 3) (0-95,95) 4-Y-O+ — **£7,762** (£2,310; £1,154; £577) **Stalls** Centre

Form	Pos	Btn	Horse / details	Jockey	RPR
0-00	1		**Raydiance**[70] 1753 4-9-2 **90** (K R Burke) *trckd ldrs: hdwy over 2f out: rdn to ld appr fnl f: kpt on strly (trainer's rep said, regarding the improved form shown, the gelding had freshened up for a 70-day break and was working well at home)* 9/1	CliffordLee 7	98
3-03	2	3/4	**Ulshaw Bridge (IRE)**[18] 3450 4-8-11 **88** (James Bethell) *towards rr: pushed along wl over 2f out: hdwy wl over 1f out: rdn and ev ch ins fnl f: kpt on* 6/1[3]	(p) SeanDavis(3) 2	94
531-	3	nk	**Bambino Lola**[355] 4469 4-9-5 **93** (Adam West) *trckd ldng pair: hdwy and cl up 2f out: rdn wl over 1f out: drvn and ev ch ent fnl f: kpt on* 9/1	RoystonFfrench 5	98
1-02	4	1/2	**Byron's Choice**[14] 3563 4-9-5 **93** (Michael Dods) *trckd ldrs: hdwy and cl up 2f out: rdn over 1f out: ev ch ent fnl f: sn drvn and kpt on same pce* 4/1[1]	PaulMulrennan 1	97
00-5	5	1/2	**Wahoo**[49] 2393 4-8-13 **87** (Michael Dods) *cl up: rdn along wl over 1f out: drvn and kpt on same pce fnl f* 16/1	ConnorBeasley 10	89
-540	6	3/4	**Hajjam**[42] 2609 5-9-4 **92** (David O'Meara) *trckd ldrs: hdwy 2f out: rdn over 1f out: drvn and one pce fnl f* 9/2[2]	DavidNolan 9	92
3-30	7	hd	**Presidential (IRE)**[42] 2609 5-8-12 **89** (Roger Fell) *hld up in rr: hdwy 2f out: rdn over 1f out: ch appr fnl f: sn drvn and btn* 7/1	CameronNoble(3) 8	89
-000	8	nk	**Parys Mountain (IRE)**[18] 3450 5-8-12 **86** (Tim Easterby) *led: rdn along 2f out: hdd and drvn over 1f out: grad wknd* 22/1	(h) DuranFentiman 4	85
2026	9	shd	**Danielsflyer (IRE)**[7] 3863 5-9-3 **91** (Michael Dods) *in tch: rdn along over 2f out: sn drvn and one pce* 10/1	(p) AndrewMullen 11	90
-006	10	hd	**Shady McCoy (USA)**[22] 3318 9-9-7 **95** (Ian Williams) *trckd ldrs: effrt 2f out: sn rdn: drvn and n.m.r ent fnl f: sn one pce* 8/1	PaddyMathers 3	93
-000	11	hd	**Von Blucher (IRE)**[49] 2396 6-8-13 **87** (Rebecca Menzies) *in tch: rdn along 2f out: drvn and wknd over 1f out* 25/1	(p) StevieDonohoe 6	85
-001	12	1 1/2	**Citron Major**[28] 3100 4-8-12 **89** (Nigel Tinkler) *dwlt: hld up: a in rr* 12/1	RowanScott(3) 12	83

1m 22.46s (-2.94) **Going Correction** -0.15s/f (Firm) **12** Ran SP% **126.9**
Speed ratings (Par 107): **110,109,108,108,107 106,106,106,106,105 105,103**
CSF £66.77 CT £526.29 TOTE £11.80: £3.10, £2.70, £3.80; EX 88.40 Trifecta £1208.50.
Owner Ontoawinner 14 & Mrs E Burke **Bred** Hungerford Park Stud **Trained** Middleham Moor, N Yorks
■ Stewards' Enquiry : Sean Davis two-day ban: used whip above the permitted level (Jul 7-8)

FOCUS
The feature contest was a fairly good handicap. The winner proved far too strong towards the near rail in the final furlong in a good comparative time - he has been rated close to his 3yo form.

4128 MARKET CROSS JEWELLERS H'CAP — 5f
3:15 (3:16) (Class 4) (0-80,81) 3-Y-O — **£6,663** (£1,982; £990; £495; £300; £300) **Stalls** Centre

Form	Pos	Btn	Horse / details	Jockey	RPR
206-	1		**Get The Rhythm**[266] 7751 3-9-1 **78** (Richard Fahey) *sn outpcd and bhd: gd hdwy 2f out: rdn to chse ldrs appr fnl f: styd on strly to ld nr fin* 13/2[2]	ConnorMurtagh(5) 8	84
1-30	2	1/2	**True Hero**[56] 2121 3-9-2 **79** (Nigel Tinkler) *prom: cl up over 2f out: led wl over 1f out: sn rdn: drvn and edgd lft jst ins fnl f: hdd and no ex towards fin* 8/1	FayeMcManoman(5) 6	83
10-0	3	1/2	**Que Amoro (IRE)**[70] 1762 3-9-9 **81** (Michael Dods) *chsd ldrs: hdwy 2f out: rdn and ev ch ins fnl f: kpt on* 12/1	(p) PaulMulrennan 9	83
3022	4	1	**Enchanted Linda**[15] 3531 3-9-4 **76** (Richard Hannon) *awkward s and t.k.h: trckd ldrs: hdwy 2f out: chal jst over 1f out: rdn and ev ch whn hung lft ins fnl f: kpt on same pce (jockey said filly hung left)* 7/4[1]	(h) HollieDoyle 4	74
-401	5	2 1/2	**Fizzy Feet (IRE)**[81] 1492 3-9-6 **78** (David Loughnane) *towards rr: rdn along 1/2-way: hdwy wl over 1f out: kpt on fnl f: n.d (jockey said filly was never travelling)* 15/2	TrevorWhelan 1	67
1-20	6	1 3/4	**Dragon Beat (IRE)**[152] 342 3-8-7 **70** (Michael Appleby) *in tch: hdwy 2f out: rdn to chse ldrs over 1f out: sn drvn and btn* 7/1[3]	TheodoreLadd(5) 3	53
2520	7	shd	**Kyllachy Warrior (IRE)**[26] 3159 3-9-1 **73** (Lawrence Mullaney) *in tch: hdwy on outer over 2f out: rdn to chse ldrs over 1f out: sn drvn and wknd* 14/1	ConnorBeasley 10	56
4015	8	1	**Key To Power**[10] 3742 3-9-4 **76** (Mark Johnston) *dwlt and hmpd s: rdn along 1/2-way: a bhd (jockey said filly missed the break)* 8/1	AndrewElliott 7	55
-140	9	4	**Lille**[12] 3659 3-8-13 **71** (Kevin Ryan) *cl up: rdn along 2f out: hung bdly lft over 1f out: sn wknd* 14/1	(t[1]) AndrewMullen 2	36
306-	10	4 1/2	**Packington Lane**[234] 8741 3-8-12 **70** (Tim Easterby) *led: rdn along over 2f out: hdd wl over 1f out: sn wknd* 33/1	(p) DuranFentiman 5	19

57.49s (-1.01) **Going Correction** -0.15s/f (Firm) **10** Ran SP% **120.2**
Speed ratings (Par 101): **102,101,100,98,94 92,91,90,83,76**
CSF £59.45 CT £619.71 TOTE £9.10: £2.50, £2.80, £2.90; EX 66.80 Trifecta £244.00.
Owner P Timmins & A Rhodes Haulage **Bred** D Curran **Trained** Musley Bank, N Yorks

FOCUS
A fair 3yo sprint handicap. The action developed centrally and the second-favourite burst through to win well in just above standard time.

4129 ROCKLIFFE HALL NOVICE MEDIAN AUCTION STKS — 5f 217y
3:50 (3:52) (Class 5) 3-5-Y-O — **£4,528** (£1,347; £673; £336) **Stalls** Centre

Form	Pos	Btn	Horse / details	Jockey	RPR
3	1		**Fashionesque (IRE)**[31] 2976 3-8-12 0 (Rae Guest) *midfield: swtchd rt and hdwy over 2f out: chsd ldrs over 1f out: chal ent fnl f: sn led and drvn: jst hld on* 5/1[2]	ConnorBeasley 10	64
4-53	2	nse	**Quirky Gertie (IRE)**[14] 3574 3-8-12 65 (Mick Channon) *towards rr: hdwy over 2f out: chsd ldrs and swtchd lft ent fnl f: sn rdn and ev ch: jst hld* 5/4[1]	HollieDoyle 7	63+
10	3	1 1/4	**Metal Exchange**[110] 1020 3-9-5 0 (Kevin Ryan) *cl up: rdn along wl over 1f out: drvn and kpt on same pce fnl f* 12/1	SamJames 6	66

15 **4** *1* **Melrose Way**[51] 2334 3-9-5 0.............................. CliffordLee 11 63
(James Bethell) *prom: led 2f out: rdn over 1f out: drvn and hdd ins fnl f: kpt on same pce* **8/1**

0 **5** *3 1/4* **Hawk In The Sky**[74] 1665 3-9-3 0.............................. NathanEvans 4 50
(Richard Whitaker) *chsd ldrs: rdn along 2f out: drvn and one pce fr over 1f out* **33/1**

0605 **6** *nse* **Arriba De Toda (IRE)**[51] 2325 3-8-10 44.............. KieranSchofield(7) 12 50
(Brian Ellison) *chsd ldrs: rdn along over 2f out: drvn wl over 1f out: kpt on one pce* **40/1**

20-0 **7** *shd* **Musical Sky**[42] 2635 3-8-12 67..............................(w) AndrewMullen 13 45
(Michael Dods) *slt ld: rdn along and hdd 2f out: cl up and ev ch over 1f out: drvn and wknd ent fnl f* **12/1**

43 **8** *nse* **Raksha (IRE)**[19] 3416 3-8-12 0.............................. RobbieDowney 8 45
(David O'Meara) *t.k.h: chsd ldrs: rdn along over 2f out: sn drvn and wknd* **13/2**

5 **9** *1 1/2* **Cominginonmonday (IRE)**[21] 3339 4-8-12 0.............. SeanKirrane(7) 1 42
(Robyn Brisland) *towards rr: hdwy over 2f out: sn rdn along and n.d* **33/1**

2-3 **10** *1 1/2* **Jungle Secret (IRE)**[172] 1 3-8-7 0.............. ConnorMurtagh(5) 3 35
(Richard Fahey) *v s.i.s and lost six l s: a bhd (jockey said filly reared as the stalls opened and was slowly away)* **11/2[3]**

050- **11** *1/2* **Wearraah**[206] 9283 3-9-3 39.............................. DavidNolan 9 39
(Alan Brown) *a in rr* **50/1**

6 **12** *nk* **Final Legacy**[7] 3836 3-8-12 0.............................. PaddyMathers 5 33
(Derek Shaw) *t.k.h: in tch: rdn along 1/2-way: sn outpcd* **66/1**

1m 10.98s (-0.82) **Going Correction** -0.175s/f (Firm)
WFA 3 from 4yo 7lb **12 Ran SP% 128.1**
Speed ratings (Par 103): **102,101,100,98,94 94,94,94,92,90 89,89**
CSF £12.31 TOTE £5.70: £1.90, £1.30, £3.70; EX 14.30 Trifecta £146.30.
Owner Miss V Markowiak **Bred** Miss Victoria Markowiak **Trained** Newmarket, Suffolk

FOCUS
A modest novice. The winner improved, with the standard set by the runner-up on this year's form.

4130 TRIAL RACING TV FOR FREE NOW MAIDEN H'CAP (DIV I) 7f 219y
4:35 (4:37) (Class 5) (0-70,72) 4-Y-0+
£4,075 (£1,212; £606; £303; £300; £300) **Stalls Centre**

Form RPR

4 **1** **Spiorad (IRE)**[66] 1849 4-9-11 72.............................. DavidNolan 10 84
(David O'Meara) *trckd ldrs: hdwy 3f out: led 2f out: rdn clr ent fnl f: kpt on strly* **6/1[3]**

0-26 **2** *3 1/4* **Red Seeker**[17] 3473 4-8-10 57..............................(t) PaddyMathers 3 62
(Tim Easterby) *cl up: led after 1 1/2f: rdn along and hdd 2f out: drvn over 1f out: kpt on same pce* **10/3[1]**

-000 **3** *1 1/4* **Seek The Moon (USA)**[19] 3414 4-8-11 58..............................(h) CliffordLee 4 60
(Lawrence Mullaney) *trckd ldrs: hdwy 3f out: rdn 2f out: cl up and drvn over 1f out: kpt on same pce fnl f* **10/1**

4-02 **4** *3* **Farhh Away**[53] 2246 4-9-7 68..............................(p) ConnorBeasley 1 63
(Michael Dods) *t.k.h: hld up towards rr: hdwy 3f out: rdn along to chse ldrs wl over 1f out: sn drvn and no imp* **7/2[2]**

4 **5** *hd* **Bidding War**[129] 697 4-8-2 54.............................. TheodoreLadd(5) 8 49
(Michael Appleby) *led 1 1/2f: cl up: rdn along wl over 2f out: wknd wl over 1f out* **8/1**

0-40 **6** *3 3/4* **Elysee Star**[12] 3657 4-8-2 49 oh1.............................. AndrewMullen 2 35
(Ben Haslam) *towards rr: sme hdwy over 2f out: sn rdn and n.d* **8/1**

0030 **7** *4* **Anchises**[14] 3567 4-9-5 66.............................. JackGarritty 9 43
(Rebecca Menzies) *dwlt: hld up: a towards rr* **6/1[3]**

00-0 **8** *nk* **Bevsboy (IRE)**[11] 3681 5-7-12 50 oh4 ow1.............................. PaulaMuir(5) 6 26
(Lynn Siddall) *chsd ldrs: rdn along wl over 3f out: sn outpcd* **50/1**

0-50 **9** *3/4* **Pretty Passe**[54] 2183 5-8-8 55.............................. NathanEvans 12 30
(Martin Todhunter) *in tch on outer: rdn along wl over 2f out: sn drvn and wknd* **28/1**

00-6 **10** *1 1/4* **Mystical Mac (IRE)**[11] 3682 4-8-4 51..............................(p) HollieDoyle 5 23
(Iain Jardine) *chsd ldrs: rdn along 1/2-way: sn outpcd* **8/1**

5006 **11** *4 1/2* **Henrietta's Dream**[33] 2912 5-8-4 51 oh4 ow2..........(p) RoystonFfrench 7 12
(John Wainwright) *a in rr* **66/1**

1m 36.37s (-0.23) **Going Correction** -0.15s/f (Firm) **11 Ran SP% 123.2**
Speed ratings (Par 103): **95,91,90,87,87 83,79,79,78,77 72**
CSF £27.43 CT £207.80 TOTE £5.50: £2.00, £1.60, £3.10; EX 26.70 Trifecta £255.20.
Owner Hambleton Racing Ltd XXXVII **Bred** Irish National Stud **Trained** Upper Helmsley, N Yorks
■ Geneva Trumpet was withdrawn. Price at time of withdrawal 100/1. Rule 4 does not apply

FOCUS
The first division of an ordinary maiden handicap. One of the joint-third favourites proved far too good from the near side of the pack in a notably quicker time than the following contest. The winner has been rated as improving, with the second to form.

4131 TRIAL RACING TV FOR FREE NOW MAIDEN H'CAP (DIV II) 7f 219y
5:10 (5:12) (Class 5) (0-70,69) 4-Y-0+
£4,075 (£1,212; £606; £303; £300; £300) **Stalls Centre**

Form RPR

-400 **1** **Glaceon (IRE)**[4] 3970 4-8-5 53.............................. NathanEvans 1 58
(Tina Jackson) *trckd ldrs: hdwy 3f out: rdn to ld ent fnl f: drvn out* **4/1[2]**

4-04 **2** *nk* **Show The Money**[38] 2740 4-8-11 59.............................. TrevorWhelan 9 63
(Ivan Furtado) *hld up in rr: hdwy on outer over 2f out: rdn to chse ldrs over 1f out: styd on strly fnl f (jockey said gelding hung left)* **9/1**

522/ **3** *1* **Flying Raconteur**[568] 9030 5-9-3 68..............................(t) RowanScott(3) 6 70
(Nigel Tinkler) *hld up in tch: effrt over 1f out and sn rdn: styng on whn n.m.r ins fnl f: sn swtchd lft and fin strly (jockey said gelding was denied a clear run approaching 2f out and again approaching the final furlong)* **10/1**

-605 **4** *nse* **Fard**[10] 3721 4-8-4 57.............................. PaulaMuir(5) 11 59
(Roger Fell) *hld up: hdwy over 3f out: chsd ldrs 2f out: rdn and slt ld over 1f out: hdd ent fnl f: kpt on same pce towards fin* **8/1**

5002 **5** *nk* **Kingdom Brunel**[11] 3704 4-9-7 69..............................(p) DavidNolan 7 70
(David O'Meara) *hld up: hdwy 2f out: rdn to chse ldrs ent fnl f: sn drvn and kpt on* **11/4[1]**

0500 **6** *1/2* **Tarnhelm**[26] 3163 4-7-9 50.............................. IsobelFrancis(7) 10 50
(Wilf Storey) *in tch: hdwy on outer to ld over 3f out: rdn along over 2f out: hdd over 1f out: cl up ent fnl f: sn wandered: kpt on same pce* **33/1**

00-0 **7** *1 1/2* **Sunstorm**[25] 3203 4-8-6 54.............................. PaddyMathers 3 50
(Stef Keniry) *chsd ldrs: rdn along wl over 2f out: sn drvn and kpt on one pce* **5/1[3]**

0000 **8** *2* **Lord Rob**[1] 4078 8-8-4 52 oh5 ow2.............................. RoystonFfrench 8 44
(David Thompson) *dwlt: a in rr* **33/1**

-006 **9** *2* **Sunbright (IRE)**[22] 3304 4-7-13 52 oh5 ow2.............................. TheodoreLadd(5) 4 39
(Michael Appleby) *prom: hdwy along 3f out: sn drvn and wknd fnl 2f (vet said filly finished lame on its right fore)* **16/1**

0300 **10** *3 1/4* **Prince Consort (IRE)**[11] 3682 4-8-3 51 oh5 ow1......(p) AndrewMullen 5 31
(John Wainwright) *prom: cl up 3f out: rdn along 2f out: drvn and ev ch over 1f out: wkng whn lost action and eased ins fnl f (vet said gelding lost its action in the closing stages)* **66/1**

0/0- **11** *22* **Salsa Verde (IRE)**[430] 1891 4-8-8 56.............................. HollieDoyle 2
(Ed de Giles) *t.k.h: sn led: pushed along and hdd 2f out: sn rdn and wknd: bhd and eased fnl 2f (jockey said gelding ran too freely and stopped quickly; vet said gelding to be slightly lame on its right fore)* **5/1[3]**

1m 37.18s (0.58) **Going Correction** -0.15s/f (Firm) **11 Ran SP% 123.5**
Speed ratings (Par 103): **91,90,89,89,89 88,87,85,83,80 58**
CSF £41.74 CT £354.35 TOTE £4.50: £1.70, £2.30, £3.50; EX 48.00 Trifecta £424.60.
Owner Peter Jeffers & Howard Thompson **Bred** J Connolly **Trained** Liverton, Cleveland
■ Stewards' Enquiry : Nathan Evans two-day ban: used whip above the permitted level (Jul 7-8)

FOCUS
The second division of an ordinary maiden handicap. This has been rated negatively.

4132 RACING TV FREE FOR A MONTH H'CAP 5f
5:55 (5:56) (Class 6) (0-60,62) 4-Y-0+
£3,823 (£1,137; £568; £300; £300; £300) **Stalls Centre**

Form RPR

0032 **1** **Cuppacoco**[24] 3213 4-9-5 55.............................. JackGarritty 14 61
(Ann Duffield) *trckd ldrs: hdwy 2f out: rdn to chal over 1f out: led ins fnl f: edgd lft and drvn out* **6/1[3]**

26R4 **2** *1/2* **Piazon**[4] 3975 8-9-7 57..............................(be) NathanEvans 10 61
(Julia Brooke) *prom: cl up 2f out: rdn and ev ch ins fnl f: drvn and no ex towards fin* **12/1**

0-54 **3** *nse* **I'll Be Good**[10] 3723 10-8-8 49.............................. ConnorMurtagh(5) 12 53
(Alan Berry) *cl up: led 2f out: rdn over 1f out: hung lft ent fnl f: sn drvn and hdd: no ex towards fin (jockey said gelding hung left under pressure)* **25/1**

0330 **4** *nse* **Atyaaf**[42] 2632 4-9-3 53.............................. PaddyMathers 13 57
(Derek Shaw) *hld up towards rr: hdwy wl over 1f out: sn rdn: styd on strly fnl f* **20/1**

0 **5** *3/4* **War Ensign (IRE)**[24] 3225 4-8-11 47.............................. ConnorBeasley 11 48
(Tim Easterby) *in tch: hdwy to chse ldrs over 1f out: rdn and n.m.r ins fnl f: kpt on (jockey said gelding was denied a clear run in the closing stages)* **12/1**

2-60 **6** *3/4* **Paco Escostar**[42] 2632 4-8-13 56..............................(v[1]) VictorSantos(7) 15 54
(Julie Camacho) *in tch on wd outside: hdwy 2f out: rdn over 1f out: kpt on u.p fnl f* **16/1**

3531 **7** *shd* **Groundworker (IRE)**[10] 3723 8-9-3 53.............................. HollieDoyle 1 51
(Paul Midgley) *wnt rt s: hld up in tch: hdwy to trck ldrs 2f out: pushed along over 1f out: rdn and no imp ins fnl f (jockey said gelding hung right throughout)* **3/1[1]**

2605 **8** *nk* **Someone Exciting**[10] 3723 6-8-10 51..............................(b[1]) HarrisonShaw(5) 6 48
(David Thompson) *towards rr: hdwy over 1f out: sn rdn and kpt on fnl f* **11/2[2]**

00-0 **9** *hd* **Whigwham**[171] 28 5-8-9 45.............................. AndrewMullen 5 41
(Gary Sanderson) *towards rr tl styd on fnl f* **50/1**

50-0 **10** *1* **Mightaswellsmile**[5] 3933 5-8-6 45.............................. RowanScott(3) 9 38
(Ron Barr) *cl up: rdn along and ev ch over 1f out: edgd lft ent fnl f: sn wknd* **25/1**

0060 **11** *2 1/2* **One Boy (IRE)**[10] 3723 8-9-3 53.............................. RobbieDowney 2 37
(Paul Midgley) *hmpd s: a towards rr* **12/1**

0265 **12** *1/2* **Bronze Beau**[4] 3975 12-9-12 62..............................(tp) SamJames 8 44
(Linda Stubbs) *slt ld towards far side: rdn along and hdd 2f out: sn drvn and grad wknd appr fnl f* **9/1**

63/0 **13** *3* **Mr Greenlight**[70] 1760 4-9-7 62.............................. DannyRedmond(5) 4 33
(Tim Easterby) *in tch: hdwy to chse ldrs 2f out: sn rdn and wknd appr fnl f* **8/1**

0353 **14** *4 1/2* **Glyder**[14] 3577 5-8-9 45..............................(p) RoystonFfrench 3
(John Holt) *chsd ldrs: rdn along 2f out: sn drvn and wknd (jockey said mare stopped quickly; vet said a post-race examination revealed the mare to be suffering from atrial fibrillation)* **17/2**

57.92s (-0.58) **Going Correction** -0.15s/f (Firm) **14 Ran SP% 129.7**
Speed ratings (Par 101): **98,97,97,97,95 94,94,94,93,92 88,87,82,75**
CSF £79.08 CT £1732.82 TOTE £6.40: £2.40, £4.30, £3.90; EX 89.40 Trifecta £1638.00.
Owner C A Gledhill **Bred** Llety Farms **Trained** Constable Burton, N Yorks

FOCUS
A straightforward low-grade handicap.
T/Plt: £242.00 to a £1 stake. Pool: £46,743.04 - 140.98 winning units T/Qpdt: £44.50 to a £1 stake. Pool: £3,996.17 - 66.38 winning units **Joe Rowntree**

4133 - 4135a (Foreign Racing) - See Raceform Interactive

3326 DOWN ROYAL (R-H)
Saturday, June 22

OFFICIAL GOING: Round course - yielding (yielding to soft in places); straight course - good to yielding

4136a MAGNERS ULSTER DERBY (PREMIER H'CAP) 1m 4f 150y
3:25 (3:26) 3-Y-O
£53,153 (£17,117; £8,108; £3,603; £1,801; £900)

RPR

1 **Dadoozdart**[42] 2643 3-9-7 89.............................. ShaneFoley 6 96+
(Noel Meade, Ire) *w.w towards rr: tk clsr order in 9th after 1/2-way and impr to dispute 6th 4f out: prog on outer 3f out: rdn in 2nd 2f out and clsd u.p ins fnl f to ld narrowly nr fin* **11/2[3]**

2 *nk* **King's Vow (FR)**[41] 2664 3-9-8 90..............................(bt) DeclanMcDonogh 10 97
(Joseph Patrick O'Brien, Ire) *dwlt sltly and pushed along early: sn settled in rr of mid-div: 7th 1/2-way: prog on outer after 1/2-way: hdwy in 4th 4f out to ld over 3f out: strly pressed ins fnl f and hdd narrowly nr fin* **13/2**

3 *2 1/2* **Future Investment**[17] 3482 3-9-7 89.............................. GaryCarroll 1 93
(Ralph Beckett) *sn settled bhd ldrs: 5th 1/2-way: n.m.r briefly bhd ldrs over 3f out: rdn in 3rd over 2f out and clsd u.p to chal briefly 1f out: no imp on ldrs wl ins fnl f: kpt on same pce* **7/2[1]**

4 *2 1/2* **Halimi (IRE)**[8] 3822 3-8-10 78.............................. RoryCleary 4 77
(J S Bolger, Ire) *mid-div: 6th 1/2-way: rdn in 7th 3f out and no imp on ldrs u.p 2f out: wnt mod 4th over 1f out: kpt on nr fin: nvr trbld ldrs* **7/1**

5 *hd* **Millswyn (IRE)**[42] 2643 3-9-5 87.............................. NGMcCullagh 5 86
(Joseph Patrick O'Brien, Ire) *dwlt and in rr: tk clsr order in 9th over 4f out: rdn in 8th over 3f out and sme hdwy u.p nr side under 2f out into mod 5th over 1f out: kpt on nr fin: nvr trbld ldrs* **20/1**

6 8 ½ **A Wave Of The Sea (IRE)**[22] 3331 3-8-11 **84**......... ShaneCrosse(5) 11 69
(Joseph Patrick O'Brien, Ire) *chsd ldrs: 3rd 1/2-way: rdn bhd ldrs over 3f out and sn wknd* **4/1**[2]

7 ½ **Metier (IRE)**[12] 3670 3-8-2 **75**.................................. AndrewSlattery(5) 7 59
(Andrew Slattery, Ire) *sn led: rdn and hdd over 3f out: wknd qckly: mod 8th 1f out: n.m.r and swtchd lft ins fnl f: kpt on again nr fin* **11/1**

8 ½ **Fujimoto Flyer (JPN)**[32] 2951 3-8-5 **73**............................ ChrisHayes 8 56
(Emmet Mullins, Ire) *dismntd bef s: cl up bhd ldr: 2nd 1/2-way: rdn between horses over 3f out and sn no ex in 2nd: wknd over 2f out* **12/1**

9 32 **Zander**[76] 1621 3-9-12 **94**...................................(b[1]) ColinKeane 2 26
(G M Lyons, Ire) *in rr of mid-div: 8th 1/2-way: pushed along in 8th 4f out and sn wknd: eased under 3f out: nvr a factor* **20/1**

10 5 ½ **Hiroshima**[21] 3345 3-9-11 **93**.. GaryHalpin 9 16
(John Ryan) *towards rr thrght: pushed along and reminder bef 1/2-way: no imp u.p in rr under 5f out: eased over 3f out: lame (vet said colt was found to be lame on his off hind post race)* **12/1**

11 75 **Kashagan**[35] 2845 3-9-0 **82**... DavidEgan 3
(Archie Watson) *hooded to load: prom tl sn settled bhd ldrs: drvn in 4th and reminder 6f out: no ex and wknd qckly under 5f out: eased under 4f out: lame (jockey said colt never travelled; vet said colt was slightly lame on its off fore)* **16/1**

2m 54.9s **11 Ran SP% 122.6**
CSF £43.12 CT £144.16 TOTE £4.90: £2.20, £2.30, £1.40; DF 45.50 Trifecta £239.80.
Owner Mrs M Cahill **Bred** Godolphin **Trained** Castletown, Co Meath
■ Stewards' Enquiry : Shane Foley one-day ban: use of whip (tba)
Gary Carroll one-day ban: use of whip (tba)

FOCUS
The one-two have been rated as improving, with the next three helping to set the standard.

4137 - 4141a (Foreign Racing) - See Raceform Interactive

3652
PONTEFRACT (L-H)
Sunday, June 23

OFFICIAL GOING: Good (good to soft in places: 7.4)
Wind: Light half against Weather: Cloudy with sunny periods

4142 JOHN EDWARD'S 50TH BIRTHDAY CELEBRATION EBF FILLIES' NOVICE STKS (PLUS 10 RACE) 6f
2:20 (2:21) (Class 5) 2-Y-O **£4,528** (£1,347; £673; £336) **Stalls** Low

Form RPR

1 **Soffika (IRE)** 2-9-0 0.. RyanMoore 7 82+
(Sir Michael Stoute) *dwlt: green in rr: hdwy over 2f out: rdn to chse ldng pair over 1f out: sn chal: led last 100yds: kpt on strly* **5/1**

4 2 2 ¼ **Heavens Open**[12] 3679 2-9-0 0.. TonyHamilton 6 76
(Richard Fahey) *t.k.h early: led 1 1/2f: trckd ldr: hdwy and cl up 2f out: rdn to chal over 1f out: slt ld ent fnl f: sn drvn: hdd last 100yds: kpt on same pce* **7/2**[2]

422 3 ½ **Inyamazane (IRE)**[16] 3534 2-9-0 0.................................. DavidEgan 8 74
(Mick Channon) *dwlt: t.k.h and hdwy to ld after 1 1/2f: pushed along 2f out: sn jnd and rdn: hdd and drvn ent fnl f: kpt on same pce* **9/2**[3]

4 nk **Cloudea (IRE)** 2-8-11 0... SeanDavis(3) 1 73
(Richard Fahey) *t.k.h: trckd ldrs: green and pushed along over 2f out: effrt and n.m.r wl over 1f out: swtchd rt to outer and kpt on fnl f* **6/1**

5 5 2 ¼ **Ebony Legend**[13] 3652 2-9-0 0.. JasonHart 4 66
(John Quinn) *chsd ldrs: rdn along over 2f out: sn drvn and wknd over 1f out* **16/1**

6 6 ½ **Guipure**[17] 3506 2-9-0 0.. BenCurtis 2 65+
(K R Burke) *dwlt: green and sn pushed along: a towards rr* **11/4**[1]

7 11 **Schumli** 2-9-0 0.. DanielTudhope 5 32
(David O'Meara) *t.k.h: cl up on inner: pushed along 2f out: rdn wl over 1f out: sn wknd* **12/1**

1m 18.55s (1.45) **Going Correction** -0.075s/f (Good) **7 Ran SP% 111.6**
Speed ratings (Par 90): **87,84,83,82,79 79,64**
CSF £21.64 TOTE £4.20: £2.60, £3.00; EX 13.80 Trifecta £36.20.
Owner Sir Evelyn De Rothschild **Bred** Southcourt Stud **Trained** Newmarket, Suffolk

FOCUS
Add 8yds to all race distances. The going dried out to good, good to soft in places, ahead of the first. An open novice sprint in which they finished bunched up, though the winner won snugly enough.

4143 FARMER COPLEYS GFF FARM-SHOP-OF-THE-YEAR NOVICE STKS (PLUS 10 RACE) 1m 4f 5y
2:55 (2:56) (Class 3) 3-Y-O **£9,703** (£2,887; £1,443; £721) **Stalls** Low

Form RPR

32 1 **Dubai Tradition (USA)**[18] 3482 3-9-2 0......................... HectorCrouch 3 89+
(Saeed bin Suroor) *mde all: rdn clr over 1f out: kpt on wl towards fin* **1/1**[1]

41 2 2 ¾ **Grenadier Guard (IRE)**[11] 3724 3-9-8 0......................... FrannyNorton 2 88
(Mark Johnston) *trckd ldng pair: green and pushed along 7f out: hdwy and hung rt home turn: sn rdn: edgd lft ins fnl f: kpt on wl towards fin* **7/2**[3]

3 3 ½ **Dante's View (IRE)**[15] 3584 3-9-2 0................................... RyanMoore 5 81
(Sir Michael Stoute) *trckd wnr: effrt over 2f out: sn rdn along: drvn over 1f out: kpt on same pce* **7/4**[2]

06 4 61 **Ozark**[36] 2845 3-8-11 0... JamesSullivan 4
(Jennie Candlish) *a in rr: rdn along 1/2-way: outpcd and bhd fnl 4f* **100/1**

2m 37.05s (-4.05) **Going Correction** -0.075s/f (Good) **4 Ran SP% 109.6**
Speed ratings (Par 103): **110,108,107,67**
CSF £4.94 TOTE £1.70; EX 4.20 Trifecta £5.30.
Owner Godolphin **Bred** Godolphin **Trained** Newmarket, Suffolk

FOCUS
Add 8yds. An interesting novice featuring several promising types, and the winner set a good gallop.

4144 MAM & DAD REUNITED LOVE TEAM WOOD H'CAP 1m 2f 5y
3:25 (3:26) (Class 3) (0-90,91) 3-Y-O+ **£9,238** (£2,781; £1,390; £693; £348; £175) **Stalls** Low

Form RPR

2-14 1 **Derevo**[52] 2321 3-8-10 **83**.. RyanMoore 2 101
(Sir Michael Stoute) *mde all: rdn clr 2f out: styd on strly* **11/10**[1]

1-12 2 5 **Hats Off To Larry**[24] 3250 5-9-7 **82**............................ CallumShepherd 3 90
(Mick Channon) *hld up towards rr: hdwy on inner and n.m.r wl over 1f out: swtchd rt and rdn ent fnl f: kpt on: no ch w wnr* **11/2**

1-61 3 2 ½ **Victory Chime (IRE)**[26] 3192 4-9-8 **83**..........................(p) HarryBentley 1 86
(Ralph Beckett) *reminders s: rn in snatches: sn trcking ldng pair: pushed along on inner over 4f out: rdn 3f out: drvn along 2f out: one pce* **5/1**[3]

2022 4 ½ **Addis Ababa (IRE)**[9] 3811 4-10-0 **89**............................(v) DanielTudhope 4 91
(David O'Meara) *trckd ldrs: effrt and hdwy on outer 3f out: rdn along wl over 1f out: sn btn* **9/2**[2]

P023 5 hd **Ayutthaya (IRE)**[15] 3605 4-10-0 **89**.................................. ShaneGray 5 91
(Kevin Ryan) *trckd wnr: pushed along 3f out: rdn over 2f out: drvn wl over 1f out: kpt on one pce* **8/1**

11/5 6 20 **Shargiah (IRE)**[169] 87 6-9-11 **91**.............................. TheodoreLadd(5) 6 53
(Michael Appleby) *hld up: a in rr* **33/1**

2m 10.52s (-4.48) **Going Correction** -0.075s/f (Good)
WFA 3 from 4yo+ 12lb **6 Ran SP% 111.9**
Speed ratings (Par 107): **114,110,108,107,107 91**
CSF £7.61 TOTE £1.80: £1.10, £2.60; EX 6.90 Trifecta £17.50.
Owner K Abdullah **Bred** Juddmonte Farms Ltd **Trained** Newmarket, Suffolk

FOCUS
Add 8yds. A decent middle-distance handicap. Last year's winner, Rainbow Rebel, followed-up in the valuable Old Newton Cup, bucking the trend of previous winners who failed to win next time out. The winner set only a modest tempo in making all.

4145 PONTEFRACT CASTLE FILLIES' STKS (LISTED RACE) 1m 4f 5y
4:00 (4:00) (Class 1) 4-Y-O+ **£28,010** (£10,665; £5,340; £2,665; £1,335; £670) **Stalls** Low

Form RPR

1131 1 **Bayshore Freeway (IRE)**[4] 3995 4-9-0 101.................... FrannyNorton 5 101
(Mark Johnston) *trckd ldrs: effrt wl over 1f out and sn n.m.r: rdn and hdwy to chse ldng pair ent fnl f: styd on wl to ld last 50yds* **7/4**[1]

6-15 2 ½ **Dance Legend**[15] 3586 4-9-0 95.. LukeMorris 4 100
(Rae Guest) *trckd ldng pair on inner: hdwy over 2f out: swtchd rt and rdn to ld jst over 1f out: jnd and drvn ins fnl f: hdd and no ex last 50yds* **12/1**

0521 3 1 ¾ **Tamreer**[19] 3449 4-9-0 81...(h) BenCurtis 3 97
(Roger Fell) *trckd ldr: hdwy to ld 2f out: sn rdn and hdd jst over 1f out: drvn and kpt on fnl f* **40/1**

00-1 4 2 ¼ **Spirit Of Appin**[31] 3010 4-9-0 95...................................... HarryBentley 7 94
(Brian Meehan) *hld up in rr: hdwy on inner over 2f out: rdn over 1f out: kpt on fnl f* **5/1**[3]

-301 5 2 ¾ **Hulcote**[11] 3726 4-9-0 87.. HollieDoyle 8 89
(Clive Cox) *hld up: hdwy over 2f out: rdn along to chse ldrs over 1f out: sn drvn and no imp* **12/1**

2115 6 3 **Makawee (IRE)**[8] 3862 4-9-0 89..................................... DanielTudhope 1 84
(David O'Meara) *sn led: pushed along and qcknd 3f out: rdn and hdd wl over 1f out: sn drvn and wknd* **4/1**[2]

10-5 7 1 **Crystal Moonlight**[50] 2401 4-9-0 90................................... RyanMoore 6 83
(Sir Michael Stoute) *trckd ldng pair: hdwy on outer over 3f out: rdn to chal 2f out: drvn over 1f out: sn wknd (vet said filly lost right hind shoe)* **10/1**

11-1 8 shd **Hameem**[38] 2763 4-9-0 94.. DaneO'Neill 9 87
(John Gosden) *in tch: effrt on outer 3f out: rdn along 2f out: sn drvn and n.d (jockey said filly ran too freely being unable to get cover from a wide draw)* **7/1**

2m 36.43s (-4.67) **Going Correction** -0.075s/f (Good) **8 Ran SP% 112.4**
Speed ratings (Par 108): **112,111,110,109,107 105,104,104**
CSF £23.93 TOTE £2.20: £1.10, £3.60, £6.90; EX 22.10 Trifecta £359.30.
Owner Kingsley Park Owners Club **Bred** Lynch Bages Ltd **Trained** Middleham Moor, N Yorks

FOCUS
Add 8yds. A fair Listed event featuring numerous recent winners, but they didn't go flat out.

4146 STEPHANE OSBORNE PONTEFRACT CUP H'CAP (ROUND 4 OF THE PONTEFRACT STAYERS CHAMPIONSHIP 2019) 2m 2f 2y
4:35 (4:36) (Class 4) (0-85,84) 4-Y-O+ **£6,469** (£1,925; £962; £481; £400; £400) **Stalls** Low

Form RPR

220- 1 **Becky The Thatcher**[29] 7466 6-8-3 **66**.........................(p) FrannyNorton 5 73
(Micky Hammond) *trckd ldng pair: hdwy over 2f out: rdn over 1f out: chal ent fnl f: drvn to ld last 110yds: kpt on wl* **5/2**[1]

000- 2 nk **Forewarning**[187] 9595 5-8-2 **65**.......................................(w) CamHardie 4 71
(Julia Brooke) *hld up in tch: hdwy 3f out: rdn to chse ldrs over 1f out: drvn to chse wnr ins fnl f: kpt on wl nr fin* **12/1**

1114 3 3 ½ **Champarisi**[38] 2781 4-8-13 **76**.. SamJames 2 80
(Grant Tuer) *trckd ldng pair: hdwy on outer 3f out: rdn to ld wl over 1f out: drvn ent fnl f: hdd last 110yds: kpt on same pce* **7/2**[2]

6/60 4 1 ¼ **Norab (GER)**[40] 2718 8-8-2 **65** oh7...............................(b) HollieDoyle 1 66?
(Bernard Llewellyn) *led: rdn along over 2f out: hdd wl over 1f out: drvn and rallied to have ev ch ent fnl f: grad wknd* **20/1**

-204 5 3 ¾ **Suegioo (FR)**[8] 3847 10-9-7 **84**....................................(v) RyanMoore 3 82
(Ian Williams) *dwlt and reminders s: rn in snatches and sn detached in rr: tk clsr order 1/2-way: rdn along and outpcd 4f out: drvn 3f out: bhd and swtchd rt to outer 2f out: plugged on fnl f: n.d* **5/2**[1]

5-10 6 5 **Handiwork**[38] 2781 9-9-7 **84**...(p) DanielTudhope 7 77
(Steve Gollings) *trckd ldr: cl up over 5f out: rdn along 3f out: sn wknd* **11/2**[3]

55-0 7 14 **Arty Campbell (IRE)**[29] 2578 9-8-12 **75**..........................(p) LukeMorris 6 54
(Bernard Llewellyn) *in tch: effrt and sme hdwy on outer 4f out: rdn along 3f out: sn wknd* **20/1**

4m 5.35s (-2.35) **Going Correction** -0.075s/f (Good) **7 Ran SP% 112.0**
Speed ratings (Par 105): **102,101,100,99,98 95,89**
CSF £31.81 TOTE £2.80: £2.00, £4.30; EX 36.80 Trifecta £156.60.
Owner Mcgoldrick Racing **Bred** D R Botterill **Trained** Middleham, N Yorks

FOCUS
Add 8yds. Last year's first two returned for this staying handicap, but it was the 2018 runner-up who came out best this time around. They went a fair pace and four held a chance at the furlong pole.

4147 JOSH CAYGILL 30TH BIRTHDAY FILLIES' H'CAP 1m 6y
5:05 (5:08) (Class 3) (0-90,83) 3-Y-O **£9,337** (£2,796; £1,398; £699) **Stalls** Low

Form RPR

341 1 **Bighearted**[34] 2919 3-9-0 **79**.. CameronNoble(3) 1 90
(Michael Bell) *mde all: jnd and pushed along 2f out: rdn over 1f out: drvn ins fnl f: hld on gamely towards fin* **7/4**[1]

3-23 2 nk **Pennywhistle (IRE)**[30] 3041 3-9-7 **83**...........................(p[1]) RyanMoore 4 93
(John Gosden) *trckd wnr: hdwy and cl up 2f out: sn chal: rdn over 1f out: drvn and ev ch ins fnl f: kpt on* **15/8**[2]

4631 3 10 **Venusta (IRE)**[13] 3665 3-8-10 **72**.................................... DavidEgan 2 59
(Mick Channon) *trckd ldng pair: pushed along 3f out: sn rdn and outpcd fnl 2f* **5/2**[3]

633 **4** 3/4 **Summer Bride (IRE)**[15] 3565 3-8-5 **67**........................ DuranFentiman 3 53
(Tim Easterby) *trckd ldng pair: rdn along 3f out: one pce fnl 2f* **11/1**

1m 44.86s (-1.04) **Going Correction** -0.075s/f (Good) 4 Ran SP% **108.1**
Speed ratings (Par 100): **102,101,91,90**
CSF £5.33 TOTE £2.60; EX 6.30 Trifecta £8.80.
Owner M E Perlman **Bred** R Frisby **Trained** Newmarket, Suffolk

FOCUS
Add 8yds. A small fillies' handicap in which the first two in the betting had it to themselves in pulling clear.

4148 ROGERTHORPE MANOR HOTEL H'CAP (DIV I) 6f
5:40 (5:41) (Class 5) (0-70,70) 3-Y-O+
£4,528 (£1,347; £673; £400; £400; £400) **Stalls** Low

Form RPR

2312 **1** **Tricky Dicky**[6] 3928 6-9-13 **69**.. BenCurtis 10 78
(Roger Fell) *cl up: rdn to chal wl over 1f out: drvn to ld ins fnl f: kpt on wl towards fin* **9/4[2]**

3100 **2** 3/4 **Highly Sprung (IRE)**[8] 3868 6-9-9 **70**...................... HarrisonShaw(5) 11 77
(Les Eyre) *trckd ldng pair: hdwy 2f out: rdn over 1f out: drvn to chse wnr wl ins fnl f: kpt on* **16/1**

6611 **3** 1/2 **Captain Dion**[4] 3989 6-9-10 **69** 5ex........................(b) GabrieleMalune(3) 1 74
(Ivan Furtado) *qckly away and led: rdn along wl over 1f out: drvn and hdd ins fnl f: kpt on u.p* **6/4[1]**

-640 **4** 1 **Uncle Charlie (IRE)**[13] 3656 5-9-6 **62**........................ FrannyNorton 8 64
(Ann Duffield) *chsd ldrs: swtchd lft and rdn along wl over 1f out: drvn ins fnl f: kpt on* **10/1[3]**

4010 **5** 3 1/2 **Kentuckyconnection (USA)**[34] 2898 6-9-5 **68**.......... HarryRussell(7) 12 59
(Bryan Smart) *towards rr: rdn along on outer and wd st: drvn over 1f out: fin strly* **16/1**

5-02 **6** 1/2 **Mosseyb (IRE)**[13] 3656 4-8-9 **51** oh1.............................. KevinStott 9 40
(Paul Midgley) *dwlt and towards rr: pushed along over 2f out: rdn to chse ldrs wl over 1f out: drvn and no imp fnl f* **20/1**

1000 **7** 1 1/4 **The Right Choice (IRE)**[17] 3503 4-9-12 **68**.............(p[1]) TonyHamilton 2 53
(Richard Fahey) *chsd ldrs on inner: rdn along 2f out: sn drvn and wknd over 1f out* **10/1[3]**

000- **8** 1/2 **Dawn Breaking**[236] 8720 4-8-10 **52**.................................. PhilDennis 5 35
(Richard Whitaker) *a towards rr* **33/1**

6000 **9** 1 **Primeiro Boy (IRE)**[17] 3508 3-8-10 **62**........................ SeanDavis(3) 6 40
(Richard Fahey) *dwlt: a in rr* **50/1**

3205 **10** 2 **Gunmaker (IRE)**[13] 3656 5-9-9 **65**.............................. JamesSullivan 4 39
(Ruth Carr) *chsd ldrs on inner: rdn along over 2f out: sn wknd* **11/1**

0000 **11** 6 **Intense Pleasure (IRE)**[12] 3704 4-9-0 **56**.................... JackGarritty 7 11
(Ruth Carr) *dwlt: a in rr* **33/1**

1m 17.05s (-0.05) **Going Correction** -0.075s/f (Good) 11 Ran SP% **121.7**
WFA 3 from 4yo+ 7lb
Speed ratings (Par 103): **97,96,95,94,89 88,87,86,85,82 74**
CSF £38.09 CT £72.96 TOTE £3.10: £1.30, £4.40, £1.10; EX 42.30 Trifecta £121.70.
Owner Eight Gents and a Lady **Bred** Onslow, Stratton & Parry **Trained** Nawton, N Yorks
■ Stewards' Enquiry : Gabriele Malune four-day ban: used whip above permitted level (Jul 7-10)

FOCUS
Add 8yds. The first division of the sprint handicap was run at a good lick, though the trio of speedsters who forced it kept those positions throughout and came down the middle. Not much got into it.

4149 ROGERTHORPE MANOR HOTEL H'CAP (DIV II) 6f
6:10 (6:11) (Class 5) (0-70,69) 3-Y-O+
£4,528 (£1,347; £673; £400; £400; £400) **Stalls** Low

Form RPR

5026 **1** **Penny Pot Lane**[13] 3657 6-9-8 **63**..............................(p[1]) LewisEdmunds 4 71
(Richard Whitaker) *trckd ldrs: hdwy wl over 1f out: rdn to chal ins fnl f: sn drvn: kpt on wl to ld last 50yds (trainer said, regarding improved form, mare was suited by the application of first-time cheek pieces)* **10/1**

2002 **2** 1/2 **Inexes**[11] 3722 7-9-13 **68**..(p) JasonHart 2 74
(Ivan Furtado) *trckd ldrs on inner: hdwy 2f out: rdn over 1f out: led ins fnl f: drvn and hdd last 50yds: no ex* **3/1[1]**

5023 **3** 1 1/2 **Black Salt**[37] 2788 5-10-0 **69**.. RobbieDowney 8 71+
(David Barron) *in tch: hdwy wl over 1f out: rdn and edgd lft ins fnl f: styd on wl towards fin* **7/2[2]**

0-55 **4** shd **Stewardess (IRE)**[13] 3658 4-10-0 **69**............................ DavidNolan 7 70
(Richard Fahey) *cl up: rdn and ev ch over 1f out: drvn and kpt on same pce fnl f: lost 3rd nr line* **9/1**

6004 **5** 3/4 **Vallarta (IRE)**[20] 3413 9-8-11 **52**.............................. JamesSullivan 1 51
(Ruth Carr) *led: rdn along wl over 1f out: drvn and hdd ins fnl f: grad wknd* **16/1**

0004 **6** nse **Valley Of Fire**[37] 2804 7-9-11 **66**..............................(b) BenCurtis 3 65
(Les Eyre) *chsd ldrs: rdn along wl over 1f out: drvn and no imp fnl f* **7/1[3]**

-001 **7** 3/4 **Carlovian**[10] 3772 6-9-0 **55**......................................(v) DougieCostello 10 51
(Mark Walford) *dwlt and towards rr: styd on on fnl f (jockey said gelding anticipated start and banged head on stalls causing it to be slowly away)* **25/1**

00-0 **8** 2 1/4 **Arogo**[43] 2635 3-9-1 **63**.. TomEaves 6 50
(Kevin Ryan) *t.k.h in midfield: pushed along over 2f out: sn rdn and n.d* **10/1**

-005 **9** nk **Uncle Norman (FR)**[13] 3650 3-8-8 **56**..................(b) RachelRichardson 12 42
(Tim Easterby) *dwlt and towards rr: rdn along and sme hdwy on outer 1/2-way: drvn 2f out: n.d* **25/1**

2060 **10** hd **Jan Van Hoof (IRE)**[40] 2709 8-9-13 **68**........................ BarryMcHugh 5 56
(Michael Herrington) *hld up in rr: effrt and sme hdwy on inner over 1f out: sn rdn and n.d* **12/1**

3630 **11** nk **Exchequer (IRE)**[50] 2418 8-10-0 **69**..........................(p) PhilipPrince 9 56
(Richard Guest) *cl up: rdn along over 2f out: sn wknd* **25/1**

0505 **12** nk **Coastal Drive**[20] 3413 4-9-0 **55**.................................... KevinStott 11 41
(Paul Midgley) *dwlt: a in rr* **16/1**

1m 17.49s (0.39) **Going Correction** -0.075s/f (Good) 12 Ran SP% **118.9**
WFA 3 from 4yo+ 7lb
Speed ratings (Par 103): **94,93,91,91,90 90,89,86,85,85 85,84**
CSF £39.24 CT £128.42 TOTE £11.90: £2.80, £1.60, £1.80; EX 49.40 Trifecta £324.70.
Owner A Melville **Bred** Hellwood Stud Farm & G P Clarke **Trained** Scarcroft, W Yorks

FOCUS
Add 8yds. The second division was run in a 0.44s slower time and the winner came down the middle.
T/Plt: £144.40 to a £1 stake. Pool: £67,113.77 - 339.08 winning units T/Qpdt: £35.40 to a £1 stake. Pool: £6,089.22 - 126.99 winning units **Joe Rowntree**

4150 - 4156a (Foreign Racing) - See Raceform Interactive

3288 DORTMUND (R-H)
Sunday, June 23

OFFICIAL GOING: Turf: good

4157a 32ND GROSSER PREIS DER WIRTSCHAFT (GROUP 3) (3YO+) (TURF) 1m 165y
2:10 3-Y-O+
£28,828 (£10,810; £5,405; £2,702; £1,801)

RPR

1 **Potemkin (GER)**[224] 9028 8-9-5 0.............................. EduardoPedroza 1 105
(A Wohler, Germany) *mde all: broke wl and led: shkn up under 2 1/2f out and kicked for home: rdn w 1 1/2f to run: styd on wl: a holding runner-up* **2/1[2]**

2 1/2 **Palace Prince (GER)**[24] 3287 7-9-1 0..........................(p) FilipMinarik 4 101
(Jean-Pierre Carvalho, Germany) *trckd ldr: drvn to try and chal wl over 1 1/2f out: styd on u.p: a jst hld by wnr* **43/5**

3 hd **Kronprinz (GER)**[24] 3287 4-9-3 0.............................. AndraschStarke 5 102
(P Schiergen, Germany) *disp 3rd on inner: drvn and sing to cl whn nt clr run over 1 1/2f out: swtchd outside and began to pick up again 1f out: styd on u.p fnl f: nvr quite on terms* **41/5**

4 3/4 **Volfango (IRE)**[24] 3287 5-9-3 0.............................. AurelienLemaitre 3 102
(F Vermeulen, France) *w.w in rr: rdn and prog on outer 2f fr home: styd on fnl f: nt pce to chal* **9/5[1]**

5 1 1/4 **Folie De Louise (FR)**[24] 3288 5-9-0 0............................ TonyPiccone 6 97
(Carmen Bocskai, Germany) *disp 3rd on outer: rdn but nt qckn fr 2f out: kpt on at one pce* **6/1[3]**

6 nk **Melodino (GER)**[24] 3287 4-9-1 0..........................(p) MarcoCasamento 7 98
(K Demme, Germany) *settled in fnl trio on outer: drvn and sme late prog: nvr in contention* **29/1**

7 1 1/4 **Degas (GER)**[24] 3287 5-9-3 0.. AdriedeVries 2 99
(Markus Klug, Germany) *racd in fnl trio on inner: drvn 2f out but no imp: one pce fnl f: nvr trbld ldrs* **81/10**

1m 47.46s 7 Ran SP% **118.9**
PARI-MUTUEL (all including 1 euro stake): WIN 3.00 PLACE: 3.00, 4.40; SF: 19.70.
Owner Klaus Allofs & Stiftung Gestut Fahrhof **Bred** Siftung Gestut Fahrhof **Trained** Germany

4158 - 4169a (Foreign Racing) - See Raceform Interactive

3643 SAN SIRO (R-H)
Sunday, June 23

OFFICIAL GOING: Turf: good to soft

4170a PREMIO PAOLO MEZZANOTTE (LISTED RACE) (4YO+ FILLIES & MARES) (GRANDE COURSE) (TURF) 1m 3f
3:40 4-Y-O+
£17,567 (£7,729; £4,216; £2,108)

RPR

1 **Shailene (IRE)**[21] 3374 4-8-11 0.............................. SilvestreDeSousa 9 97+
(Andrew Balding) *hld up towards rr: shkn up and clsd fr 2 1/2f out: chsd ldr u.p wl over 1f out: sustained run to ld fnl 75yds: won gng away* **76/100[1]**

2 1 1/4 **Close Your Eyes (ITY)**[42] 4-8-11 0..............................(h) DarioVargiu 7 95
(A Botti, Italy) **885/100**

3 1 1/2 **Lapulced'acqua (IRE)**[378] 3659 4-8-11 0......................(t) SilvanoMulas 8 92+
(Grizzetti Galoppo SRL, Italy) **123/10**

4 3/4 **La Base (IRE)**[224] 9025 4-8-11 0..............................(t) FabioBranca 3 91
(A Botti, Italy) **19/5[2]**

5 3 **Great Aventura (IRE)**[239] 8666 5-8-11 0.......................... CarloFiocchi 6 86
(Cristiano Davide Fais, Italy) **16/1**

6 1 1/2 **Key Master (IRE)**[378] 3659 4-8-11 0..................(tp) AndreaMezzatesta 1 83
(R Biondi, Italy) **137/10**

7 1/2 **Light My Fire (FR)**[87] 4-8-11 0.................................. CristianDemuro 10 82
(Karoly Kerekes, Germany) **97/20[3]**

8 1/2 **Prigioniera (IRE)** 4-8-11 0..............................(b) DarioDiTocco 5 81
(Marco Gasparini, Italy) **115/10**

9 6 **Lovelett (IRE)**[24] 3288 5-8-11 0..............................(b) LucaManiezzi 4 70
(M Figge, Germany) **151/10**

10 2 1/2 **Pizzo Carbonara (IRE)** 6-8-11 0.................................. FedericoBossa 2 66
(Valentina Oglialoro, Italy) **53/1**

2m 18.1s (-0.50) 10 Ran SP% **141.2**
PARI-MUTUEL (all including 1 euro stake): WIN 1.77; PLACE 1.24, 2.03, 2.24; DF 8.45.
Owner George Strawbridge **Bred** George Strawbridge **Trained** Kingsclere, Hants

4171a OAKS D'ITALIA (GROUP 2) (3YO FILLIES) (GRANDE COURSE) (TURF) 1m 3f
4:30 3-Y-O
£166,666 (£73,333; £40,000; £20,000)

RPR

1 **Lamaire (IRE)**[28] 3-8-11 0.. FabioBranca 7 101+
(Riccardo Santini, Italy) *dwlt: hld up towards rr: nt clr run whn pushed along over 2f out: swtchd and rdn 2f out: sn making gd hdwy: hung rt fnl f: styd on wl to ld last stride* **151/10**

2 shd **Must Be Late (IRE)**[28] 3-8-11 0..............................(b) CristianDemuro 6 100
(A Botti, Italy) *trckd ldrs: rdn to ld under 3f out: drvn over 2f out: kpt on wl tl no ex clsng stages: hdd last stride* **102/10**

3 3/4 **Call Me Love**[35] 2887 3-8-11 0.. DarioVargiu 1 99
(A Botti, Italy) *in tch: rdn under 3f out: drvn and pressed ldr 1f out: kpt on wl tl squeezed and nt clr run clsng stages* **37/20[1]**

4 1 1/2 **Apadanah (GER)**[28] 3-8-11 0.. AntoineHamelin 11 96
(Waldemar Hickst, Germany) *veered lft leaving stalls and s.v.s: towards rr: hdwy fr 3f out: rdn 2 1/2f out: swvd rt and bmpd rival whn drvn 1 1/2f out: styd on fnl f* **114/10**

5 3 **Elisa Again**[28] 3-8-11 0..............................(tp) AndreaMezzatesta 2 91
(R Biondi, Italy) *midfield: rdn and hdwy to chse ldrs 3f out: wknd fnl f* **67/10**

6 1 1/2 **Cima Fire (FR)**[224] 3-8-11 0..............................(t) SilvanoMulas 10 88
(Grizzetti Galoppo SRL, Italy) *midfield on inner: rdn and outpcd under 3f out: sme hdwy appr fnl f: one pce ins fnl f* **28/1**

7 1 1/2 **Malevra (FR)**[21] 3391 3-8-11 0.. AndreaAtzeni 4 85
(G Botti, France) *led: rdn over 3f out: hdd under 3f out: wknd 1 1/2f out* **204/100[2]**

8 3/4 **Bunora De L'Alguer (IRE)** 3-8-11 0 ....(t) NinoMurru 3 84
(Gian Marco Pala, Italy) *towards rr: rdn under 4f out: hung rt over 1f out: kpt on fnl f: nvr in contention* **113/1**
9 1 **Spietata**[78] 3-8-11 0 ....(p) SergioUrru 5 82
(Nicolo Simondi, Italy) *midfield: rdn and effrt 3f out: bmpd 1 1/2f out: wknd ins fnl f: eased fnl 125yds* **42/1**
10 4 **King Power**[43] 2618 3-8-11 0 .... SilvestreDeSousa 8 75
(Andrew Balding) *w ldr: rdn 3f out: lost pl 2f out: wkng whn nt clr run over 1f out: sn btn* **53/20**[3]
11 12 **Zolushka (IRE)** 3-8-11 0 .... DarioDiTocco 9 53
(Marco Gasparini, Italy) *a towards rr: eased fnl 1 1/2f* **39/1**
2m 13.5s (-5.10) **11 Ran SP% 140.7**
PARI-MUTUEL (all including 1 euro stake): WIN 16.12; PLACE 3.20, 3.07, 1.60; DF 150.14.
Owner Razza Dormello Olgiata Di Citai SPA **Bred** Razza Dormello Olgiata and CITAI **Trained** Italy

4172a PREMIO PRIMI PASSI (GROUP 3) (2YO) (DRITTA II COURSE) (TURF) 6f
5:10 2-Y-O **£31,531** (£13,873; £7,567; £3,783)

RPR
1 **Malotru**[27] 3141 2-8-11 0 .... AndreaAtzeni 10 100
(Marco Botti) *hld up towards rr: smooth hdwy fr 3f out: rdn to ld 1f out: kpt on strly and drew clr fnl f: readily* **282/100**[2]
2 2 1/2 **Sicomoro (ITY)**[39] 2-8-11 0 .... SergioUrru 1 93
(Nicolo Simondi, Italy) *t.k.h in midfield: rdn and styd on wl fr over 1f out: wnt 2nd cl home: no ch w wnr* **83/10**
3 1/2 **Golden Air Force (ITY)**[53] 2-8-11 0 ....(t) FabioBranca 7 91
(F Boccardelli, Italy) *chsd ldrs: led travelling wl over 2f out: rdn 1 1/2f out: hdd 1f out: no ex and lost 2nd cl home* **152/10**
4 3 **I Love Thisgame (IRE)** 2-8-11 0 ....(t) SamueleDiana 8 82
(Annalisa Umbre, Italy) *in tch: rdn and effrt under 2f out: wknd ins fnl f* **596/100**
5 3/4 **Aisa Dream (IRE)**[14] 2-8-8 0 ....(t) CarloFiocchi 6 77
(V Fazio, Italy) *dwlt: in rr: rdn and kpt on fr 2f out: n.d* **35/4**
6 1/2 **Caballero Chopper** 2-8-11 0 ....(t) SilvanoMulas 5 78
(Grizzetti Galoppo SRL, Italy) *towards rr: tk clsr order appr 2f out: rdn and outpcd over 1f out* **29/1**
7 shd **Lovely Smile (ITY)**[25] 2-8-11 0 .... CristianDemuro 9 78
(A Botti, Italy) *racd keenly towards rr of midfield: gd hdwy appr 2f out: pressed ldr whn rdn 1 1/2f out: wknd qckly fnl f* **11/2**
8 2 1/2 **Gerardino Jet (IRE)**[14] 2-8-11 0 .... PierantonioConvertino 4 70
(Mario Marcialis, Italy) *chsd ldr: rdn and outpcd 1 1/2f: wknd qckly 1f out: eased fnl 100yds* **11/5**[1]
9 4 1/2 **Adelinda (IRE)**[35] 2-8-8 0 .... DarioVargiu 2 54
(A Botti, Italy) *led: hdd over 2f out: rdn 2f out: wknd over 1f out: eased ins fnl f* **79/20**[3]
10 7 **Batellik (IRE)**[14] 2-8-11 0 ....(t) AntonioFresu 3 36
(A Peraino, Italy) *midfield: rdn and lost pl 2f out: sn struggling: eased fnl f* **31/1**
1m 9.7s (-2.10) **10 Ran SP% 141.0**
PARI-MUTUEL (all including 1 euro stake): WIN 3.82; PLACE 2.05, 3.54, 5.63; DF 41.91.
Owner Les Boyer Partnership 1 **Bred** Wattlefield Stud Ltd & Partner **Trained** Newmarket, Suffolk

4173a GRAN PREMIO DI MILANO (GROUP 2) (3YO+) (GRANDE COURSE) (TURF) 1m 4f
5:45 3-Y-O+ **£82,882** (£36,468; £19,891; £9,945)

RPR
1 **Assiro**[35] 2885 4-9-6 0 ....(tp) AndreaMezzatesta 2 109
(R Biondi, Italy) *hld up: rdn and hdwy fr 3f out: drvn under 2f out: led under 1f out: kpt on wl and grad asserted* **17/5**[3]
2 3/4 **Crowned Eagle**[57] 2119 5-9-6 0 .... SilvestreDeSousa 5 108
(Marco Botti) *led: rdn 3f out: drvn 2f out: hdd under 1f out: kpt on wl* **6/4**[1]
3 1 **Keep On Fly (IRE)**[35] 2887 3-8-7 0 ....(b) DarioVargiu 1 107
(A Botti, Italy) *in tch: rdn under 3f out: drvn and ev ch 1f out: no ex fnl 100yds* **17/10**[2]
4 6 **Being Alive**[14] 3-8-7 0 .... FabioBranca 3 97
(A Botti, Italy) *in tch: rdn and outpcd over 3f out: sn dropped to rr and no imp* **558/100**
5 2 1/2 **Presley (ITY)**[35] 2885 6-9-6 0 ....(t) CristianDemuro 4 92
(A Botti, Italy) *racd keenly: chsd ldr: rdn 3f out: wknd 1 1/2f out: eased ins fnl f* **596/100**
2m 27.0s (-4.50)
WFA 3 from 4yo+ 14lb **5 Ran SP% 129.3**
PARI-MUTUEL (all including 1 euro stake): WIN 4.39; PLACE 2.28, 1.76; DF 11.81.
Owner Luigi Roveda **Bred** Gestut Zur Kuste Ag **Trained** Italy

3640 LES LANDES
Friday, June 21

4174a JERSEY RACE CLUB H'CAP (TURF) 7f
7:05 (7:05) 3-Y-O+ **£1,780** (£640; £380)

RPR
1 **Relaxed Boy (FR)**[40] 6-10-12 .... MrFrederickTett 69
(Mrs A Malzard, Jersey) **11/4**[3]
2 1/2 **Masquerade Bling (IRE)**[18] 3430 5-9-11 .... PhilipDonovan 53
(Neil Mulholland) **4/5**[1]
3 1 1/2 **Sing Something**[12] 3641 6-9-12 ....(v) MattieBatchelor 50
(Mrs C Gilbert, Jersey) **11/4**[3]
4 2 **Salve Helena (IRE)**[12] 4-9-0 .... ChristopherGrosbois 32
(T Le Brocq, Jersey) **18/1**
5 2 **Limelite (IRE)**[12] 3641 5-9-9 .... PhilipPrince 36
(K Kukk, Jersey) **11/1**
6 4 **Fruit Salad**[12] 3641 6-10-2 .... MarkQuinlan 32
(K Kukk, Jersey) **9/4**[2]

Owner P G Somers **Bred** Mme P Ades-Hazan & M Henochsberg **Trained** St Ouen, Jersey

4175a MARJE MERICK H'CAP ON BEHALF OF THE JSPCA JERSEY 1m 100y
8:15 (8:15) (0-50,) 3-Y-O+ **£1,780** (£640; £380)

RPR
1 **Molliana**[12] 3642 4-10-12 .... SamTwiston-Davies 49
(Neil Mulholland) **2/5**[1]
2 2 **Mendacious Harpy (IRE)**[12] 3642 8-9-9 ....(p) VictoriaMalzard 28
(Mrs A Malzard, Jersey) **6/1**[3]
3 2 **Kalani Rose**[25] 3174 5-9-3 ....(v) MissSerenaBrotherton 17
(Mrs A Corson, Jersey) **12/1**
4 5 **Drummer Jack (IRE)**[25] 3174 3-10-1 ....(t) MarkQuinlan 26
(K Kukk, Jersey) **17/2**
5 8 **Frivolous Prince (IRE)**[12] 3640 6-10-3 ....(t) MattieBatchelor 3
(Mrs C Gilbert, Jersey) **12/1**
6 8 **Lucifers Shadow (IRE)**[12] 10-10-10 ....(v) MrFrederickTett
(Mrs C Gilbert, Jersey) **5/2**[2]

Owner Dajam Ltd **Bred** Norman Court Stud **Trained** Limpley Stoke, Wilts

3571 CHEPSTOW (L-H)
Monday, June 24

OFFICIAL GOING: Good (5.9)
Wind: Slight half against Weather: Hazy sunshine

4176 PETE SMITH CAR SALES H'CAP 1m 2f
2:00 (2:01) (Class 5) (0-70,70) 3-Y-O
£3,752 (£1,116; £557; £300; £300; £300) **Stalls Low**

Form RPR
5-45 1 **El Picador (IRE)**[45] 2582 3-9-7 **70** ....(v1) KieranShoemark 8 78
(Sir Michael Stoute) *prom: led after 4f: 3 l clr whn shkn up 2f out: drvn 1f out: hld on wl* **8/1**
0-52 2 3/4 **Starczewski (USA)**[30] 3093 3-9-1 **69** .... DylanHogan(5) 7 75
(David Simcock) *s.s: t.k.h in rr: hdwy on inner 4f out: rdn 3f out: wnt 2nd ins fnl f: styd on: nt rch wnr* **6/4**[1]
005 3 1 1/2 **Unplugged (IRE)**[14] 3664 3-9-6 **69** .... DavidProbert 6 72
(Andrew Balding) *midfield: hdwy to press wnr after 4f: rdn over 2f out: unable qck and lost 2nd ins fnl f* **5/2**[2]
0-05 4 7 **Renardeau**[14] 3665 3-9-4 **67** ....(p) TomMarquand 2 56
(Ali Stronge) *prom: rdn over 3f out: wknd over 1f out* **10/1**
3441 5 3 1/4 **Lieutenant Conde**[48] 2517 3-9-1 **64** .... CharlieBennett 5 47
(Hughie Morrison) *chsd ldrs: rdn over 2f out: sn outpcd: wknd fnl f* **10/1**
-036 6 shd **Greeley (IRE)**[14] 3647 3-9-6 **69** ....(b1) KieranO'Neill 1 51
(Rod Millman) *uns rdr bef s and briefly rn loose: towards rr: sltly outpcd and rdn along 5f out: drvn and nt qckn 3f out: no threat* **11/2**[3]
0-04 7 10 **Crackaway (FR)**[17] 3538 3-8-12 **64** ....(p) MitchGodwin(3) 4 26
(Harry Dunlop) *led 4f: chsd ldng pair: rdn over 3f out: sn wknd* **33/1**
0-00 8 11 **Pourmorechampagne**[22] 3372 3-7-11 **51** oh6 .... SophieRalston(5) 3
(Paul Webber) *bmpd s: t.k.h in rr: rdn 3f out: sn wknd (trainer said gelding did not handle the undulations of the track)* **66/1**
2m 7.97s (-4.83) **Going Correction** -0.15s/f (Firm) **8 Ran SP% 117.7**
Speed ratings (Par 99): **104,103,102,96,94 93,85,77**
CSF £21.12 CT £40.34 TOTE £8.40: £2.20, £1.10, £1.30; EX 25.20 Trifecta £56.70.
Owner Niarchos Family **Bred** Niarchos Family **Trained** Newmarket, Suffolk

FOCUS
The tempo increased a long way out courtesy of the winner and the first three have been rated as improving.

4177 ALAN BUSHELL ON COURSE BOOKMAKER NOVICE STKS 1m 2f
2:30 (2:31) (Class 5) 3-Y-O+ **£3,752** (£1,116; £557; £278) **Stalls Low**

Form RPR
3 1 **Saffran (IRE)**[22] 3372 3-9-2 0 .... DaneO'Neill 3 79+
(Simon Crisford) *prom: rdn to ld over 1f out: r.o strly: eased cl home* **1/1**[1]
1 2 4 1/2 **Train To Georgia (USA)**[101] 1217 3-9-9 0 .... DavidProbert 1 74
(Joseph Tuite) *trckd ldr tl led after 3f: rdn over 2f out: hdd over 1f out: kpt on but no ch w wnr* **9/2**[3]
34 3 4 **Dilmun Dynasty (IRE)**[16] 3584 3-9-2 0 .... KieranShoemark 7 59
(Sir Michael Stoute) *chsd ldrs on outer tl reined bk after 2f and hld up: clsd over 3f out: wnt modest 4th and drvn over 2f out: hung lft over 1f out: styd on wl to go 3rd ins fnl f: nvr nrr* **11/8**[2]
00-0 4 1 1/2 **Ocean Reach**[27] 3204 3-8-11 40 .... TomMarquand 9 51?
(Richard Price) *led 3f: remained prom: drvn 3f out: kpt on tl no ex and lost 3rd ins fnl f* **100/1**
00 5 4 **Dancing Lilly**[40] 2731 4-9-4 0 .... RachealKneller(5) 8 43
(Matthew Salaman) *towards rr: hdwy over 5f out: nt clr run over 3f out: sn drvn and outpcd by ldrs: styd on fnl f* **100/1**
0-0 6 2 1/2 **Para Queen (IRE)**[20] 3445 3-8-4 0 .... EllieMacKenzie(7) 5 38
(Heather Main) *s.i.s: towards rr: hdwy to chse ldrs after 3f: rdn over 3f out: sn outpcd and no threat* **66/1**
00 7 shd **Arcadienne**[20] 3445 3-8-11 0 .... HarryBentley 4 38
(Ralph Beckett) *chsd ldrs: rdn 3f out: wknd over 1f out* **10/1**
0 8 1/2 **Zaydanides (FR)**[56] 2208 7-10-0 0 .... JoeyHaynes 6 42
(Tim Pinfield) *dwlt: effrt over 2f out: a in rr* **100/1**
00 9 3 1/2 **Limited Reserve (IRE)**[7] 3946 7-10-0 0 .... FergusSweeney 2 35
(Christian Williams) *s.i.s: rdn over 2f out: a in rr* **40/1**
2m 7.45s (-5.35) **Going Correction** -0.15s/f (Firm)
WFA 3 from 4yo+ 12lb **9 Ran SP% 126.3**
Speed ratings (Par 103): **106,102,99,98,94 92,92,92,89**
CSF £7.23 TOTE £1.80: £1.10, £1.20, £1.10; EX 9.10 Trifecta £12.90.
Owner Mohammed Ali al Tajir **Bred** Hadi Al-Tajir **Trained** Newmarket, Suffolk

FOCUS
A novice that looked a match between two fair maidens, but it proved rather uncompetitive with the Stoute runner never in the race. They went little pace and racing up prominently was an advantage, as evidence by the 40-rated Ocean Reach, who made the running early, only just losing out on a place. Questionable form.

4178 COUNTY MARQUEES NOVICE STKS 1m 14y
3:00 (3:03) (Class 5) 3-Y-O+ **£3,752** (£1,116; £557; £278) **Stalls Centre**

Form RPR
23-2 1 **Red Armada (IRE)**[38] 2790 3-9-2 **85** ....(p1) HectorCrouch 6 84+
(Clive Cox) *racd keenly: cl up: led 3f out: pressed whn shkn up over 1f out: r.o wl ins fnl f* **4/7**[1]

2- **2** 1 3/4 **Bint Soghaan**[245] 8469 3-8-11 0........ DaneO'Neill 3 75
(Richard Hannon) *swished tail early: chsd ldrs: rdn and ev ch over 1f out: nt pce of wnr fnl 100yds* **7/1**[3]

05 **3** 2 3/4 **Eddie Cochran (IRE)**[42] 2690 3-9-2 0........ SeanLevey 4 74
(Richard Hannon) *hld up: rdn and hdwy over 2f out: styd on to go 3rd nr fin* **20/1**

66 **4** nk **Recondite (IRE)**[38] 2802 3-9-2 0........ HarryBentley 5 73
(Ralph Beckett) *t.k.h: prom: rdn over 2f out: outpcd by ldng pair appr fnl f: lost 3rd nr fin (jockey said colt was restless in stalls)* **7/2**[2]

4 **5** nk **Soft Cover**[35] 2909 3-8-11 0........ TomMarquand 7 67
(William Haggas) *chsd ldrs: rdn over 2f out: kpt on same pce fnl f* **9/1**

03 **6** 1 3/4 **Helian (IRE)**[11] 3768 3-9-2 0........ GeorgeWood 10 68+
(Ed Dunlop) *hld up: rdn over 2f out: styd on: nvr able to threaten ldrs* **20/1**

00 **7** 16 **Mottaham (FR)**[7] 3946 4-9-12 0........ FergusSweeney 2 33
(Christian Williams) *towards rr on outer: rdn over 2f out: sn wknd* **200/1**

8 16 **Midas Spirit** 3-9-2 0........ DavidProbert 9
(Ed Walker) *s.i.s: racd keenly in midfield: rdn over 2f out: wknd qckly: t.o: fin 9th: plcd 8th* **40/1**

00 **D** 6 **Yet Another (IRE)**[13] 3696 4-9-5 0........ KeelanBaker(7) 8 20
(Grace Harris) *led: lost weight cloth 1/2-way: hdd 3f out: rdn and sn wknd: fin 8th - disqualified and plcd last* **200/1**

60 **P** **Kung Fu**[44] 2634 3-9-2 0........(v[1]) KieranShoemark 1
(Simon Crisford) *dropped in and hld up: pushed along and sme hdwy whn p.u over 1f out: fatally injured* **20/1**

1m 34.8s (-1.20) **Going Correction** -0.15s/f (Firm) **10 Ran SP% 126.1**
WFA 3 from 4yo 10lb
Speed ratings (Par 103): **100,98,95,95,94 93,77,55,71,**
CSF £5.75 TOTE £1.40: £1.10, £1.80, £4.10; EX 6.60 Trifecta £44.20.
Owner China Horse Club International Limited **Bred** Castle Paddock Bloodstock Ltd **Trained** Lambourn, Berks

FOCUS
They raced centre-field in an ordinary novice and the winner probably didn't need to be at his best.

4179 BMC, THE BUCKET MANUFACTURING COMPANY CLASSIFIED STKS — 1m 14y
3:30 (3:32) (Class 6) 3-Y-O
£3,169 (£943; £471; £300; £300; £300) **Stalls** Centre

Form RPR

-300 **1** **Starlight Red (IRE)**[24] 3311 3-9-0 65........ RobertWinston 5 68
(Charles Hills) *swtchd lft sn after s: hld up in tch: hdwy 3f out: drvn 2f out: led over 1f out: edgd rt ins fnl f: rdn out* **7/1**

-616 **2** 1 3/4 **Orliko (IRE)**[13] 3697 3-9-0 62........(t) RossaRyan 2 64
(Richard Hannon) *racd keenly: led narrowly tl hdd after 3f: remained cl up: rdn over 2f out: ev ch whn hung lft and bmpd jst ins fnl f: carried sltly rt sn after: unable qck (jockey said gelding hung left-handed throughout)* **5/1**[3]

-543 **3** 1 1/2 **Ballet Red (FR)**[31] 3034 3-8-11 65........ MitchGodwin(3) 1 62
(Harry Dunlop) *w ldr tl led after 3f: drvn: hung lft and hdd over 1f out: cl 3rd whn hmpd jst ins fnl f: no ex* **3/1**[2]

-600 **4** 3/4 **Miss Communicate**[75] 1678 3-9-0 50........ DavidProbert 8 59
(Lydia Pearce) *hld up: rdn over 2f out: hdwy to chse ldrs over 1f out: disp hld 3rd ins fnl f tl nr fin* **50/1**

4-00 **5** 1 1/4 **Almokhtaar (USA)**[38] 2795 3-9-0 65........ DaneO'Neill 7 56
(Owen Burrows) *hld up in tch: rdn over 2f out: wknd fnl f* **2/1**[1]

005 **6** 1 **Mystical Jadeite**[23] 3354 3-9-0 60........ LiamJones 4 54
(Grace Harris) *towards rr: rdn 3f out: outpcd and btn 2f out* **16/1**

3-00 **7** 4 **Canavese**[39] 2760 3-9-0 62........ CharlesBishop 3 45
(Eve Johnson Houghton) *prom: rdn 3f out: wknd appr fnl f* **7/1**

5-00 **8** 15 **Antidote (IRE)**[70] 1825 3-9-0 62........ ShaneKelly 6 12
(Richard Hughes) *t.k.h: trckd ldrs: rdn and outpcd wl over 2f out: wknd over 1f out: eased towards fin: t.o* **11/1**

1m 36.69s (0.69) **Going Correction** -0.15s/f (Firm) **8 Ran SP% 116.2**
Speed ratings (Par 97): **90,88,86,86,84 83,79,64**
CSF £42.43 TOTE £9.30: £2.20, £1.80, £1.60; EX 45.70 Trifecta £169.40.
Owner R Whitehand,D James,S Jenkins & Partners **Bred** Bloomsbury Stud **Trained** Lambourn, Berks

FOCUS
Moderate 3yo form but the winner came back to something like her best. They raced centre-to-stands' side.

4180 PICKWICK ON COURSE BOOKMAKER H'CAP — 7f 16y
4:00 (4:02) (Class 6) (0-60,61) 3-Y-O
£3,105 (£924; £461; £300; £300; £300) **Stalls** Centre

Form RPR

-323 **1** **Glamorous Crescent**[13] 3697 3-9-1 54........ JimmyQuinn 7 60
(Grace Harris) *wnt to post early: a.p: led over 2f out: edgd lft ins fnl f: drvn out* **4/1**[1]

000 **2** 1/2 **Immoral (IRE)**[16] 3565 3-9-7 60........(b[1]) ShaneKelly 3 65
(Ed Walker) *chsd ldrs: rdn over 2f out: r.o fnl f: wnt 2nd nr fin* **16/1**

3-50 **3** 3/4 **Aigiarne (IRE)**[62] 2018 3-9-8 61........(h[1]) HectorCrouch 6 64
(Clive Cox) *wnt to post early: a.p: chsd wnr 2f out: kpt on u.p tl no ex and lost 2nd nr fin* **10/1**

0005 **4** 1/2 **Quarto Cavallo**[21] 3410 3-8-7 46 oh1........ RoystonFfrench 11 48
(Adam West) *chsd ldrs: rdn and sltly outpcd over 2f out: r.o fnl f (trainer informed filly can't run until day after stalls test)* **25/1**

0-00 **5** 1 1/4 **Grey Hare**[8] 3887 3-8-9 48........(t[1]) JoeyHaynes 10 47
(Tony Carroll) *hld up: rdn over 3f out: swtchd rt and hdwy over 1f out: r.o fnl f* **66/1**

1500 **6** shd **Brother Bentley**[14] 3650 3-9-1 54........(b) DavidProbert 12 52
(Ronald Harris) *towards rr: hdwy 1/2-way: drvn and disp 2nd over 2f out: no ex fnl f* **14/1**

0-54 **7** 1 1/4 **Boorowa**[25] 3258 3-9-3 56........ RossaRyan 8 51
(Ali Stronge) *midfield: rdn over 2f out: styd on fnl f: nvr able to chal* **11/2**[3]

00-6 **8** 1/2 **Sharqeyya (IRE)**[16] 3603 3-9-8 61........ DaneO'Neill 4 55
(Owen Burrows) *s.i.s: towards rr: rdn over 2f out: hdwy over 1f out: no further imp fnl f* **7/1**

6-50 **9** 3 3/4 **Old Red Eyes (USA)**[14] 3650 3-9-7 60........ KieranShoemark 5 45
(Joseph Tuite) *s.i.s: sn in midfield: rdn over 2f out: edgd lft and sme prog over 1f out: no ex fnl f* **13/2**

0300 **10** 2 1/4 **Dark Glory (IRE)**[13] 3697 3-9-7 60........(b) HarryBentley 9 39
(Brian Meehan) *prom: rdn over 3f out: wknd over 1f out (jockey could offer no explanation for colt's performance)* **9/2**[2]

0-00 **11** 3/4 **Power Seeker (IRE)**[40] 2734 3-8-7 46 oh1........(b) KieranO'Neill 14 23
(Rod Millman) *led trio on stands' side and chsd ldrs overall: rdn over 2f out: wandered over 1f out: sn wknd* **50/1**

0-04 **12** 1 **Bonny Blue**[16] 3574 3-9-7 60........ CharlieBennett 1 35
(Rod Millman) *in rr: hung lft and racd alone on far side fr 1/2-way: rdn 3f out: sn no ch (jockey said filly hung badly left-handed)* **10/1**

0000 **13** 1 3/4 **Rakastava (IRE)**[9] 3839 3-9-4 57........(v[1]) CallumShepherd 2 27
(Mick Channon) *led tl rdn and hdd over 2f out: wknd over 1f out* **16/1**

3000 **14** 1 1/2 **Zaula**[11] 3780 3-8-12 56........ ScottMcCullagh(5) 16 22
(Mick Channon) *racd in stands'-side trio tl swtchd lft to join main gp over 5f out: rdn over 2f out: a towards rr* **16/1**

-005 **15** 5 **Little Anxious**[32] 2995 3-8-7 46 oh1........(h) LiamJones 13
(Grace Harris) *s.s: racd alone towards stands' side: in rr: rdn 3f out: wknd 2f out* **25/1**

0-00 **16** 12 **Dancing Jaquetta (IRE)**[138] 620 3-8-7 46 oh1........ AndrewMullen 15
(Mark Loughnane) *racd in trio on stands' side: rdn over 2f out: a in rr* **66/1**

1m 23.46s (-0.44) **Going Correction** -0.15s/f (Firm) **16 Ran SP% 134.5**
Speed ratings (Par 97): **96,95,94,94,92 92,91,90,86,83 82,81,79,77,72 58**
CSF £75.35 CT £637.89 TOTE £4.70: £1.40, £4.50, £2.90, £6.20; EX 109.40 Trifecta £1662.60.
Owner Robert & Nina Bailey **Bred** Robert & Mrs Nina Bailey **Trained** Shirenewton, Monmouthshire

FOCUS
The fourth and fifth limit the form in an ordinary race.

4181 GEORGE SMITH HORSE BOXES H'CAP — 6f 16y
4:30 (4:36) (Class 6) (0-65,65) 3-Y-O+
£3,105 (£924; £461; £300; £300; £300) **Stalls** Centre

Form RPR

3103 **1** **Somewhere Secret**[7] 3921 5-9-10 61........(p) AndrewMullen 11 67
(Michael Mullineaux) *a.p: rdn over 2f out: led 1f out: hung lft ins fnl f: kpt on* **6/1**[2]

R000 **2** 1/2 **Gold Hunter (IRE)**[30] 3089 9-9-10 61........(tp) JosephineGordon 7 66
(Steve Flook) *hld up towards rr: rdn and plenty to do over 2f out: hdwy over 1f out: r.o wl fnl f: wnt 2nd cl home* **20/1**

0-05 **3** shd **Kinglami**[16] 3576 10-9-12 63........(p) RossaRyan 2 67
(John O'Shea) *chsd ldrs: rdn over 2f out: swtchd lft over 1f out: r.o fnl f: tk 3rd cl home* **16/1**

6052 **4** 1/2 **Princely**[13] 3701 4-9-6 64........ JessicaCooley(7) 8 67
(Tony Newcombe) *prom: rdn to ld over 2f out: hdd 1f out: kpt on: lost 2 pls cl home* **7/1**[3]

0104 **5** 1 1/2 **Jaganory (IRE)**[16] 3577 7-9-1 57........(v) SophieRalston(5) 12 55
(Christopher Mason) *chsd ldrs: rdn over 2f out: kpt on same pce fnl f* **25/1**

00-6 **6** 1 3/4 **Hellovaqueen**[14] 3645 4-9-11 62........(b[1]) ShaneKelly 13 55
(Richard Hughes) *midfield: rdn over 2f out: no imp on ldrs fnl f* **28/1**

4431 **7** nk **Jungle Juice (IRE)**[8] 3887 3-8-13 64........ GeorgeBass(7) 10 54
(Mick Channon) *midfield: rdn over 2f out: nt clr run and swtchd rt over 1f out: r.o ins fnl f: nvr able to chal* **4/1**[1]

0130 **8** nk **Air Of York (IRE)**[16] 3575 7-9-9 65........(p) ScottMcCullagh(5) 14 57+
(John Flint) *s.i.s: in rr: rdn over 2f out: nt clr run and swtchd rt early ins fnl f: r.o wl: nrst fin* **14/1**

-00U **9** hd **Pastfact**[17] 3527 5-9-8 59........ FergusSweeney 15 50
(Malcolm Saunders) *hld up in rr: rdn and sme hdwy over 2f out: outpcd by ldrs over 1f out* **12/1**

-400 **10** hd **Swanton Blue (IRE)**[16] 3576 6-9-9 65........ PoppyBridgwater(5) 5 55
(Ed de Giles) *w ldr: rdn 1/2-way: sn lost 2nd: fdd fnl f* **7/1**[3]

-203 **11** 1 **Trotter**[14] 3645 5-9-7 58........(b) DaneO'Neill 3 45
(Stuart Kittow) *s.s: in rr: rdn over 3f out: no prog tl kpt on ins fnl f* **9/1**

6200 **12** 1 **Who Told Jo Jo (IRE)**[17] 3527 5-9-8 59........ KieranShoemark 4 43
(Joseph Tuite) *towards rr: rdn over 2f out: no imp* **40/1**

004 **13** 1/2 **Fantasy Justifier (IRE)**[17] 3527 8-9-2 53........(p) DavidProbert 9 35
(Ronald Harris) *t.k.h in midfield: rdn over 2f out: wknd fnl f* **14/1**

5-00 **14** 6 **Mabo**[21] 3430 4-9-3 54........(p) LiamJones 16 18
(Grace Harris) *rdn over 3f out: a in rr* **40/1**

2563 **15** 1 3/4 **Hey Ho Let's Go**[14] 3651 3-9-6 64........ HectorCrouch 6 21
(Clive Cox) *led tl rdn and hdd over 2f out: wknd over 1f out* **7/1**[3]

000 **16** 1 1/2 **Alfie's Angel (IRE)**[17] 3543 5-9-3 54........(p) KieranO'Neill 17 9
(Milton Bradley) *midfield: rdn and edgd lft over 4f out: wknd over 2f out* **16/1**

1m 11.34s (-0.16) **Going Correction** -0.15s/f (Firm) **16 Ran SP% 131.5**
WFA 3 from 4yo+ 7lb
Speed ratings (Par 101): **95,94,94,93,91 89,88,88,88,87 86,85,84,76,74 72**
CSF £134.46 CT £1955.39 TOTE £6.70: £1.80, £4.90, £4.20, £2.00; EX 173.40 Trifecta £2686.70.
Owner Mia Racing **Bred** Mia Racing **Trained** Alpraham, Cheshire

FOCUS
Moderate sprint form.

4182 ALAN BUSHELL ON COURSE BOOKMAKER H'CAP — 5f 16y
5:00 (5:05) (Class 6) (0-55,56) 3-Y-O+
£3,105 (£924; £461; £300; £300; £300) **Stalls** Centre

Form RPR

-045 **1** **Broadhaven Dream (IRE)**[9] 3839 3-9-1 55........ KieranO'Neill 2 65+
(Ronald Harris) *wnt lft s: racd alone on far rail: chsd ldrs tl led after 2f: rdn 2f out: r.o wl* **7/2**[1]

-500 **2** 2 1/4 **Aquadabra (IRE)**[31] 3036 4-8-12 46........ CallumShepherd 9 50
(Christopher Mason) *midfield: hdwy over 1f out: rdn ent fnl f: wnt 2nd 150yds out: no imp on wnr* **16/1**

0-30 **3** 1 1/4 **Wild Flower (IRE)**[79] 1595 7-9-2 50........(b) EoinWalsh 4 50
(Jimmy Fox) *chsd ldrs: rdn and chsd wnr wl over 1f out: no imp: lost 2nd 150yds out* **12/1**

0000 **4** 1 3/4 **Swiss Miss**[6] 3975 3-8-6 46 oh1........ RoystonFfrench 13 38+
(John Gallagher) *s.i.s and hmpd s: in rr and sn rdn along: hdwy over 1f out: r.o wl fnl f* **14/1**

-023 **5** 1 **Arnoul Of Metz**[28] 3144 4-9-2 55........(p[1]) DylanHogan(5) 6 45
(Henry Spiller) *midfield: rdn and clsd 1/2-way: sltly hmpd over 1f out: kpt on same pce* **13/2**[3]

0003 **6** nk **John Joiner**[11] 3772 7-8-12 46 oh1........(v) JosephineGordon 8 35
(Shaun Keightley) *cl up: rdn over 1f out: fdd ins fnl f* **12/1**

0002 **7** 1/2 **Bluella**[7] 3933 4-8-12 46 oh1........(v) DavidProbert 16 33
(Robyn Brisland) *led narrowly tl hdd after 2f: drvn 2f out: fdd ins fnl f* **9/1**

0050 **8** 1/2 **Burauq**[17] 3527 7-8-7 46 oh1........(v) PoppyBridgwater(5) 11 31
(Milton Bradley) *chsd ldrs: rdn and sltly outpcd 1/2-way: kpt on same pce fnl f* **25/1**

4000 **9** nk **Tally's Song**[17] 3527 6-8-12 46 oh1........(p) JimmyQuinn 12 30
(Grace Harris) *sltly hmpd s: in rr: rdn 2f out: r.o fnl f* **33/1**

000/ **10** hd **Picc And Go**[645] 7190 6-8-7 46 oh1........ RachealKneller(5) 7 29
(Matthew Salaman) *prom tl rdn and lost pl 2f out: wknd fnl f* **50/1**

-0U0 **11** *2 ½* **Red Allure**[7] 3921 4-8-12 **46**.. AndrewMullen 10 20
(Michael Mullineaux) *s.s: hld up: rdn 1/2-way: sme hdwy over 1f out: wknd fnl f* **5/1**[2]

0000 **12** *2 ¼* **Stoneyford Lane (IRE)**[17] 3550 5-8-12 **53**.....................(v) TobyEley[(7)] 1 19
(Steph Hollinshead) *carried lft and hmpd leaving stalls: sn rdn along: a in rr* **7/2**[1]

0300 **13** *1 ¼* **Swendab (IRE)**[65] 1952 11-8-5 **46**..............................(b) KateLeahy[(7)] 14 8
(John O'Shea) *half-rrdand wnt lft s: sn rcvrd to chse ldrs: rdn 2f out: wknd over 1f out* **22/1**

0-00 **14** *hd* **Hellofagame**[16] 3577 4-8-5 **46** oh1........................... EllieMacKenzie[(7)] 3 7
(Richard Price) *awkward s and slowly away: rdn 1/2-way: a in rr (jockey said gelding was slowly away)* **40/1**

58.8s (-0.60) **Going Correction** -0.15s/f (Firm)
WFA 3 from 4yo+ 6lb **14** Ran SP% **127.9**
Speed ratings (Par 101): **98,94,92,89,88 87,86,85,85,85 81,77,75,75**
CSF £65.28 CT £654.14 TOTE £4.40: £1.90, £6.30, £3.50; EX 74.80 Trifecta £665.20.
Owner M Doocey, S Doocey & P J Doocey **Bred** Ms Sinead Maher **Trained** Earlswood, Monmouths

FOCUS
After those who raced nearer the far rail came out on top in the previous sprint, the winner this time raced on the far rail from his low draw.
T/Plt: £16.20 to a £1 stake. Pool: £74,921.43 - 3,371.39 winning units T/Qpdt: £12.90 to a £1 stake. Pool: £6,788.35 - 388.89 winning units **Richard Lowther**

3941 WINDSOR (R-H)

Monday, June 24

OFFICIAL GOING: Good (good to firm in places; 7.5)
Wind: Almost nil Weather: Fine but cloudy, humid

4183 VISIT MARATHONBET.CO.UK H'CAP 5f 21y
5:40 (5:41) (Class 6) (0-65,66) 3-Y-O

£3,105 (£924; £461; £300; £300; £300) **Stalls** Centre

Form RPR

1001 **1** **Ever Rock (IRE)**[9] 3839 3-8-6 **57**.............................. LauraCoughlan[(7)] 5 64+
(J S Moore) *pushed along in last trio: prog on wd outside 1/2-way: clsd on ldrs over 1f out: led last 100yds: styd on wl* **10/1**

00-1 **2** *1* **Celsius (IRE)**[18] 3508 3-9-8 **66**..................................(t) MartinDwyer 6 69
(Tom Clover) *mde most: rdn over 1f out: hung bdly lft fnl f: hdd and no ex last 100yds (jockey said gelding hung left-handed under pressure)* **9/4**[1]

050 **3** *¾* **Sweet Forgetme Not (IRE)**[14] 3650 3-8-4 **48** ow1...........(bt[1]) JFEgan 2 48
(Samuel Farrell, Ire) *racd in last trio: prog on wd outside 1/2-way: clsd on ldrs over 1f out: trying to chal whn carried lft and impeded ins fnl f: kpt on* **28/1**

50 **4** *1* **Mayfair Madame**[10] 3801 3-9-1 **59**.................................. JasonWatson 10 56
(Stuart Kittow) *mostly in midfield: rdn 2f out: no hdwy tl styd on last 150yds: nrst fin* **9/1**

-035 **5** *shd* **Mrs Worthington (IRE)**[10] 3801 3-9-5 **63**........................ RobHornby 8 60
(Jonathan Portman) *racd in last trio: prog on wd outside 1/2-way: hanging lft but clsd on ldrs over 1f out: trying to mount a chal whn squeezed out ins fnl f* **5/1**[2]

6364 **6** *shd* **Valentino Sunrise**[18] 3508 3-9-1 **59**.............................. NicolaCurrie 11 55
(Mick Channon) *chsd ldrs: rdn 2f out: cl up and ch whn impeded 1f out: kpt on same pce after* **5/1**[2]

-004 **7** *1 ¼* **Sarsaparilla Kit**[28] 3148 3-8-10 **54**.............................. OisinMurphy 12 45
(Stuart Williams) *chsd ldrs: rdn 2f out: fdd over 1f out* **11/1**

-046 **8** *nk* **Aquarius (IRE)**[12] 3742 3-9-4 **62**..........................(v[1]) AlistairRawlinson 9 52
(Michael Appleby) *nvr beyond midfield: rdn and no prog 2f out* **14/1**

65-0 **9** *1 ¼* **Fancy Flyer**[20] 3440 3-9-0 **65**.. LukeBacon[(7)] 1 51
(Dean Ivory) *racd towards nr side: nvr on terms w ldrs: no ch fnl f* **7/1**[3]

0040 **10** *1* **Starchant**[31] 3045 3-8-8 **57** ow1................................ KatherineBegley[(5)] 4 39
(John Bridger) *w ldr to over 1f out: wknd* **20/1**

1600 **11** *nk* **Sister Of The Sign (IRE)**[45] 2592 3-9-0 **58**.................. BarryMcHugh 3 39
(James Given) *racd against nr side rail: nvr beyond midfield: struggling over 1f out* **33/1**

-050 **12** *1 ¾* **Dark Impulse (IRE)**[31] 3045 3-7-11 **46** oh1................. RhiainIngram[(5)] 7 21
(John Bridger) *a towards rr: nvr a factor* **100/1**

59.9s (-0.20) **Going Correction** -0.025s/f (Good) **12** Ran SP% **122.8**
Speed ratings (Par 97): **100,98,97,95,95 95,93,92,90,89 88,85**
CSF £32.98 CT £646.82 TOTE £10.20: £2.80, £1.40, £7.30; EX 37.50 Trifecta £971.00.
Owner Ever Equine & J S Moore **Bred** Tom Twomey **Trained** Upper Lambourn, Berks
■ Stewards' Enquiry : Martin Dwyer caution; careless riding

FOCUS
An overcast and muggy evening. A low-grade but competitive sprint handicap, and despite the quicker ground, four of the first five home came up the far side in what proved to be a messy race, after the favourite drifted markedly left in the final 1f.

4184 DOWNLOAD THE MARATHONBET APP "NEWCOMERS" EBF MAIDEN STKS (HORSES WHICH HAVE NEVER RUN) 6f 12y
6:10 (6:15) (Class 5) 2-Y-O **£3,752** (£1,116; £557; £278) **Stalls** Centre

Form RPR

1 **Knight Shield (IRE)** 2-9-5 0.. PatDobbs 8 75
(William Haggas) *wl in tch: pushed along and prog jst over 2f out: shkn up to chse ldr 1f out: styd on to ld last stride* **5/1**[3]

2 *shd* **Tambourine Girl** 2-9-0 0.. JasonWatson 7 70
(Roger Charlton) *mde most: shkn up wl over 1f out: kpt on fnl f but hdd last stride* **7/1**

3 *1 ¼* **Irish Acclaim (IRE)** 2-9-5 0....................................... AdamKirby 2 71
(Clive Cox) *chsd ldrs and racd against rail: urged along and no prog 2f out: styd on fnl f to take 3rd last strides* **4/1**[2]

4 *hd* **Commit No Nuisance (IRE)** 2-9-5 0............................ DavidEgan 1 70
(William Knight) *in tch in midfield: shkn up over 1f out: prog fnl f to take 3rd brief nr fin* **50/1**

5 *¾* **Batchelor Boy (IRE)** 2-9-5 0...................................... RobertHavlin 9 68
(Marco Botti) *in tch in midfield: shkn up 2f out: sme prog over 1f out: kpt on but n.d* **10/3**[1]

6 *shd* **Shadow Glen** 2-9-5 0... CharlesBishop 6 68
(Eve Johnson Houghton) *racd against rail: mostly chsd ldr to 1f out: wknd* **12/1**

7 *shd* **Tiritomba (IRE)** 2-9-0 0.. TomMarquand 5 63+
(Richard Hannon) *slowly away: pushed along in last trio: rdn 2f out: stl only 10th 1f out: styd on wl last 100yds* **6/1**

8 *1* **Kyllwind** 2-9-5 0.. RobHornby 12 65
(Martyn Meade) *dwlt: in rr: pushed along 2f out: nvr a threat but kpt on same pce fnl f* **14/1**

9 *1 ¾* **Sir Arthur Dayne (IRE)** 2-9-5 0.................................. OisinMurphy 4 59
(Mick Channon) *slowly away: mostly in last trio and sn urged along: no prog tl styd on last 100yds (jockey said colt was slowly away)* **11/1**

10 *nse* **Bowling Russian (IRE)** 2-9-5 0................................. PatCosgrave 10 59
(George Baker) *pressed ldrs: shkn up 2f out: wknd jst over 1f out* **20/1**

11 *2 ¾* **Sterling Stamp (IRE)** 2-9-5 0..................................... RaulDaSilva 11 51
(Paul Cole) *racd on outer: in tch but green: wknd over 1f out* **25/1**

12 *32* **Mr Jack Daniels** 2-9-5 0... RyanTate 3
(John Spearing) *uns rdr on way to post: chsd ldrs 2f: sn bhd: t.o* **50/1**

1m 13.27s (1.17) **Going Correction** -0.025s/f (Good) **12** Ran SP% **121.8**
Speed ratings (Par 93): **91,90,89,88,87 87,87,86,84,83 80,37**
CSF £39.67 TOTE £5.40: £1.90, £2.50, £1.80; EX 45.00 Trifecta £209.30.
Owner M M Stables **Bred** M P & R J Coleman **Trained** Newmarket, Suffolk

FOCUS
An interesting newcomers' maiden, and there was not much between them. The first two home came up the middle-to-stands' side. This has been rated to the lower end of the race averages.

4185 MARATHONBET LIVE CASINO H'CAP 6f 12y
6:40 (6:44) (Class 5) (0-75,75) 3-Y-O

£3,752 (£1,116; £557; £300; £300; £300) **Stalls** Centre

Form RPR

5-42 **1** **Revolutionise (IRE)**[20] 3440 3-9-5 **73**.............................. DavidEgan 9 83+
(Roger Varian) *towards rr: prog on outer 1/2-way: rdn 2f out: chsd ldr fnl f: hrd drvn to ld last 75yds: hld on* **6/5**[1]

-050 **2** *hd* **Baby Steps**[24] 3307 3-9-3 **71**.. OisinMurphy 6 80
(David Loughnane) *pressed ldr: led 1/2-way: rdn 2f out: hdd last 75yds: kpt on wl but jst hld* **9/1**[3]

-120 **3** *1 ¾* **Spirit Of May**[15] 3638 3-9-5 **73**...................................... JasonWatson 8 76
(Roger Teal) *racd against rail: led to 1/2-way: pressed ldr to 1f out: one pce last 100yds* **7/1**[2]

0-35 **4** *1 ¼* **Mykindofsunshine (IRE)**[40] 2730 3-9-4 **72**...................... AdamKirby 5 71
(Clive Cox) *t.k.h early: hld up bhd ldrs: shkn up and nt qckn 2f out: styd on again last 100yds* **14/1**

0112 **5** *½* **Pink Flamingo**[17] 3535 3-9-7 **75**................................... CharlieBennett 11 73
(Michael Attwater) *trckd ldrs: on terms over 1f out in ldng quartet: fdd ins fnl f* **18/1**

P044 **6** *½* **River Dawn**[14] 3661 3-8-8 **62**.. RaulDaSilva 4 58
(Paul Cole) *wl in rr: rdn over 2f out: nvr a threat but styd on fnl f: nrst fin* **9/1**[3]

-350 **7** *2 ½* **Phoenix Star (IRE)**[51] 2421 3-9-6 **74**......................... SilvestreDeSousa 13 62
(Amy Murphy) *dwlt: mostly in last pair: taken to outer and drvn over 2f out: nvr on terms but plugged on (jockey said gelding hung right-handed)* **20/1**

40-0 **8** *1 ½* **Drumnadrochit**[39] 2772 3-8-8 **62**................................(b) NicolaCurrie 2 45
(Charles Hills) *prom against rail to 1/2-way: struggling in midfield 2f out: n.d after* **25/1**

0000 **9** *1* **Aegean Mist**[10] 3801 3-8-6 **60**....................................... FrannyNorton 14 40
(John Bridger) *racd on outer: nvr beyond midfield: no prog 2f out: wknd over 1f out* **50/1**

10-6 **10** *½* **Red Saree (IRE)**[55] 2255 3-9-6 **74**..................................(b[1]) JFEgan 1 53
(Michael Wigham) *hld up towards rr: shkn up briefly 2f out: no prog and nvr in it: eased last 100yds* **33/1**

45-0 **11** *3 ¼* **Requited (IRE)**[16] 3590 3-8-11 **72**............................ JosephLyons[(7)] 3 40
(Hughie Morrison) *t.k.h: trckd ldrs: nt clr run 2f out and rdn: wknd over 1f out (jockey said gelding ran too free)* **33/1**

-413 **12** *hd* **Devils Roc**[31] 3045 3-9-1 **69**... RobHornby 12 37
(Jonathan Portman) *pressed ldrs 4f: wknd qckly over 1f out* **10/1**

600 **13** *2 ¾* **Trust Me (IRE)**[19] 3464 3-8-9 **63**..................................... MartinDwyer 10 22
(Dean Ivory) *dwlt: a in last pair: pushed along and no prog 2f out* **16/1**

1m 11.62s (-0.48) **Going Correction** -0.025s/f (Good) **13** Ran SP% **121.3**
Speed ratings (Par 99): **102,101,99,97,97 96,93,91,89,89 84,84,80**
CSF £11.67 CT £59.73 TOTE £1.70: £1.10, £3.00, £2.60; EX 14.70 Trifecta £65.80.
Owner A D Spence **Bred** Ballylinch Stud **Trained** Newmarket, Suffolk

FOCUS
Competitive for the grade and a strongly run affair. The form looks solid.

4186 MARATHONBET SPORTSBOOK H'CAP (WINDSOR SPRINT SERIES QUALIFIER) 6f 12y
7:10 (7:11) (Class 3) (0-95,96) 3-Y-O+

£7,158 (£2,143; £1,071; £535; £267; £134) **Stalls** Centre

Form RPR

3500 **1** **Open Wide (USA)**[23] 3344 5-9-11 **92**..........................(b) PatDobbs 12 100
(Amanda Perrett) *hld up in last: swtchd lft and shkn up jst over 1f out: prog on wd outside fnl f: wl-timed run to ld last 75yds* **7/1**[3]

-60 **2** *½* **Sunsprite (IRE)**[16] 3599 3-9-7 **95**.................................. ShaneKelly 11 99
(Richard Hughes) *dwlt: in tch in rr: prog and shkn up 2f out: drvn to chal and upsides ins fnl f: jst outpcd nr fin* **7/1**[3]

-512 **3** *nk* **Louie De Palma**[16] 3602 7-10-1 **96**................................ AdamKirby 2 101
(Clive Cox) *mde most and racd against nr side rail: rdn 2f out: edgd lft u.p fnl f: hdd last 75yds* **3/1**[1]

0-60 **4** *¾* **Oeil De Tigre (FR)**[17] 3531 8-8-5 **79**.................. ElishaWhittington[(7)] 1 82
(Tony Carroll) *hld up in tch and racd against nr side rail: shkn up 2f out: no imp on ldrs tl styd on last 150yds: unable to chal* **33/1**

4300 **5** *1* **Green Power**[31] 3043 4-9-11 **95**................................ GeorgeBuckell[(3)] 3 98+
(John Gallagher) *dwlt: sn chsd ldrs: rdn wl over 1f out: stl v cl up whn hmpd ins fnl f: nt rcvr* **6/1**[2]

-462 **6** *hd* **Naughty Rascal (IRE)**[21] 3422 3-9-1 **89**...................... TomMarquand 8 86
(Richard Hannon) *prom on outer: first one rdn over 2f out: nt qckn u.p over 1f out: one pce and lost pls fnl f* **3/1**[1]

-210 **7** *nse* **Daschas**[23] 3344 5-9-2 **83**...(t) OisinMurphy 7 82
(Stuart Williams) *racd towards outer: w ldr to jst ins fnl f: fdd* **7/1**[3]

-006 **8** *½* **Count Otto (IRE)**[18] 3492 4-9-5 **86**........................(b) RobertHavlin 6 83
(Amanda Perrett) *hld up bhd ldrs: gng strly and poised to chal 2f out: nt clr run briefly and lost pl over 1f out: ch gone* **20/1**

2-00 **9** *2 ¼* **Mountain Peak**[23] 3347 4-9-5 **86**.................................... LiamKeniry 5 76
(Ed Walker) *wl there: rdn 2f out: no rspnse over 1f out: wknd fnl f* **12/1**

1m 10.93s (-1.17) **Going Correction** -0.025s/f (Good)
WFA 3 from 4yo+ 7lb **9** Ran SP% **117.2**
Speed ratings (Par 107): **106,105,104,103,102 102,102,101,98**
CSF £55.91 CT £180.47 TOTE £8.40: £2.00, £1.90, £1.80; EX 59.80 Trifecta £211.40.
Owner George Materna & John McInerney **Bred** Moyglare Stud **Trained** Pulborough, W Sussex
■ Stewards' Enquiry : Adam Kirby caution; careless riding

FOCUS
A decent sprint and, while they finished in a heap, this appears sound form. A small pb from the winner, rated around the third.

4187 OLBG APP FOR BEST RACING TIPSTERS H'CAP — 1m 3f 99y
7:40 (7:40) (Class 4) (0-80,82) 3-Y-O
£5,530 (£1,645; £822; £411; £300; £300) Stalls Low

Form RPR
60-3 **1** **Fox Vardy (USA)**[13] 3699 3-9-7 77 .... SilvestreDeSousa 7 84
(Martyn Meade) *pressed ldr: led 4f out: racd awkwardly and hanging lft after: hrd rdn 2f out: styd on to assert fnl f (jockey said colt ran green and hung left-handed under pressure)* **11/8[1]**
35-6 **2** 1 1/4 **Zoffee**[31] 3051 3-9-5 75 .... AdamKirby 6 80
(Tom Dascombe) *hld up in 5th: gng strly over 3f out: brought to chal over 2f out and racd alone towards nr side: drvn and nt qckn over 1f out: hld fnl f* **12/1**
5-21 **3** 1 **Asian Angel (IRE)**[3] 4057 3-9-12 82 6ex .... FrannyNorton 8 85
(Mark Johnston) *w ldrs 3f: styd in tch: pushed along 4f out: drvn to chal on outer wl over 1f out: one pce after* **15/8[2]**
5303 **4** nse **The Pink'n**[10] 3808 3-9-6 76 .... RobHornby 5 79
(Seamus Mullins) *hld up in last: rdn and prog on outer 3f out: chal wl over 1f out: nt qckn and hld fnl f* **10/1**
511 **5** 9 **Earl Of Harrow**[18] 3505 3-9-4 74 .... OisinMurphy 3 62
(Mick Channon) *trckd ldrs: rdn to chal whn bmpd by wnr wl over 1f out: wknd sn after* **5/1[3]**
035 **6** 11 **Desert Mission (IRE)**[18] 3495 3-8-9 68 .... (p[1]) MeganNicholls(3) 1 37
(Simon Crisford) *led to 4f out: wknd qckly over 2f out (vet said filly was lame on it's right fore)* **25/1**
2m 27.76s (-1.94) **Going Correction** -0.025s/f (Good) 6 Ran SP% **114.2**
Speed ratings (Par 101): **106,105,104,104,97 89**
CSF £19.08 CT £31.59 TOTE £2.20: £1.20, £6.30; EX 21.60 Trifecta £56.50.
Owner King Power Racing Co Ltd **Bred** J D Gunther, Cudney Stables & S Irwin **Trained** Manton, Wilts

FOCUS
Rail re-alignment added 23 yards to the distance of this ordinary handicap and, while the pace was indifferent, the winner is a likely improver.

4188 OLBG APP FOR BEST RACING TIPS H'CAP — 1m 2f
8:15 (8:26) (Class 4) (0-85,86) 3-Y-O
£5,530 (£1,645; £822; £411; £300; £300) Stalls Low

Form RPR
-103 **1** **Korcho**[17] 3548 3-9-4 81 .... OisinMurphy 3 92
(Hughie Morrison) *trckd ldng pair: shkn up against rail to ld jst over 1f out: sn rdn clr: comf* **9/4[2]**
341- **2** 5 **Alnadir (USA)**[257] 8108 3-9-9 86 .... (h[1]) AdamKirby 6 87
(Simon Crisford) *led: tried to kick on 3f out: hdd u.p jst over 1f out: no ch w wnr after* **2/1[1]**
32-6 **3** 1 **Baryshnikov**[32] 3011 3-9-2 79 .... LiamKeniry 8 78
(Ed Walker) *trckd ldr: rdn over 2f out: nt qckn and lost 2nd over 1f out: outpcd after* **7/2[3]**
1555 **4** hd **Eardley Road (IRE)**[25] 3261 3-8-11 74 .... (t[1]) PatDobbs 7 73
(Clive Cox) *trckd ldng trio: rdn over 2f out: one pce and outpcd fnl f* **12/1**
-520 **5** 9 **Entertaining (IRE)**[24] 3307 3-8-12 75 .... SilvestreDeSousa 5 56
(Richard Hannon) *dwlt: hld up in last: outpcd 3f out: shkn up over 2f out: nvr in it but fin quite wl (jockey said gelding was never travelling)* **5/1**
525 **6** hd **Guandi (USA)**[18] 3510 3-8-12 75 .... FrannyNorton 4 55
(Tom Dascombe) *dropped to last pair after 4f and sn pushed along: outpcd 3f out: no ch after* **8/1**
-110 **7** nk **Renegade Master**[25] 3261 3-9-4 81 .... NicolaCurrie 2 61
(George Baker) *a in last trio: outpcd 3f out: no ch after* **33/1**
2m 9.35s (0.35) **Going Correction** -0.025s/f (Good) 7 Ran SP% **124.7**
Speed ratings (Par 101): **97,93,92,92,84 84,84**
CSF £8.16 CT £16.07 TOTE £2.60: £1.40, £1.70; EX 7.80 Trifecta £24.10.
Owner M Kerr-Dineen, M Hughes & W Eason **Bred** Jeremy Green And Sons **Trained** East Ilsley, Berks
■ Albert Finney was withdrawn. Price at time of withdrawal 9-2. Rule 4 \n\x\x applies to board prices prior to withdrawal but not to SP bets - deduction 15p in the pound. New market formed

FOCUS
Rail re-alignment added 23 yards to the distance. There was a delay to the start of this decent handicap when Albert Finney broke the stalls, unshipped Rab Havlin and was withdrawn. They went no great tempo early but the winner did it nicely and improved again, with the second, third and fourth rated close to form.

4189 MARATHONBET OFFICIAL GLOBAL PARTNER OF MANCHESTER CITY NOVICE STKS — 1m 31y
8:45 (8:59) (Class 5) 3-Y-O+
£3,752 (£1,116; £557; £278) Stalls Low

Form RPR
34 **1** **Assembled**[24] 3306 3-9-2 0 .... PatCosgrave 14 77+
(Hugo Palmer) *s.i.s: sn prom: trckd ldr 1/2-way: led 3f out: sent for home 2f out: rdn out to hold on fnl f* **3/1[1]**
6-3 **2** 3/4 **Jack D'Or**[23] 3353 3-9-2 0 .... LiamKeniry 9 73
(Ed Walker) *wl in tch: prog to chse wnr wl over 1f out: steadily clsd fnl f but a hld* **8/1[3]**
3 3 1/4 **War Princess (IRE)** 3-8-11 0 .... CallumShepherd 11 61+
(Alan King) *uns rdr bef ent stall: dwlt: hld up towards rr: prog over 2f out: shkn up to take 3rd 1f out: no threat to ldng pair* **33/1**
04 **4** 3 **Molotov (IRE)**[11] 3768 3-9-2 0 .... NicolaCurrie 8 59
(Jamie Osborne) *fractious bef s: led: hung lft bnd 5f out: hdd 3f out: fdd over 1f out* **50/1**
0- **5** 1 1/4 **Lady Navarra (IRE)**[233] 8832 3-8-11 0 .... ShaneKelly 13 51
(Gay Kelleway) *reluctant to enter stall: hld up in rr: lft bhd over 2f out: pushed along and kpt on steadily over 1f out* **100/1**
6 2 1/4 **Teemlucky** 3-8-11 0 .... MartinDwyer 12 46
(Ian Williams) *in tch: effrt on outer over 2f out: rn green and fdd wl over 1f out* **33/1**
7 2 1/4 **Extrodinair**[130] 4-9-9 0 .... RowanScott(3) 3 47
(Jane Chapple-Hyam) *dwlt: t.k.h in rr: hanging lft bnd 5f out: nvr on terms* **100/1**
0 **8** 2 1/2 **If At Sea**[32] 3013 3-8-11 0 .... (h) RobertHavlin 1 35
(Amanda Perrett) *chsd ldrs: shkn up and wknd over 2f out* **50/1**
9 2 1/2 **My Footsteps**[23] 4-9-12 0 .... TomMarquand 4 36
(Paul D'Arcy) *prom tl wknd qckly 2f out* **100/1**
10 1 **Squelch** 3-8-8 0 .... (h[1]) GeorgiaCox(3) 10 27
(William Haggas) *taken down early: restless in stalls: rn green and detached in last early: nvr a factor* **7/1[2]**
1m 46.47s (1.97) **Going Correction** -0.025s/f (Good) 10 Ran SP% **61.4**
WFA 3 from 4yo 10lb
Speed ratings (Par 103): **89,88,85,82,80 78,76,73,71,70**
CSF £5.10 TOTE £1.90: £1.10, £1.20, £3.00; EX 5.10 Trifecta £28.60.
Owner V I Araci & Partners **Bred** Aston House Stud **Trained** Newmarket, Suffolk
■ Brute Force, Clarion Lady, Desert Lion and Hat Yai were withdrawn. Prices at times of withdrawal 50-1, 100-1, 10-11f & 8-1 respectively. Rule 4 applies to all bets - deduction 60p in the pound

FOCUS
Add 23 yards to the distance. An eventful novice, and a lengthy delay with four withdrawn at the start, including the favourite, who reared up and got his foreleg over his stall, which unsettled others. The first two came clear of the remainder in a race that appeared to lack depth.
T/Jkpt: Not Won. T/Plt: £26.90 to a £1 stake. Pool: £83,359.90 - 2261.75 winning units T/Qpdt: £5.60 to a £1 stake. Pool: £9,087.68 - 1,181.84 winning units **Jonathan Neesom**

3425 WOLVERHAMPTON (A.W) (L-H)
Monday, June 24

OFFICIAL GOING: Tapeta: standard
Wind: Almost nil Weather: Overcast

4190 VISIT ATTHERACES.COM AMATEUR RIDERS' (S) STKS — 1m 4f 51y (Tp)
6:00 (6:01) (Class 6) 4-Y-O+
£2,994 (£928; £464; £300; £300; £300) Stalls Low

Form RPR
2000 **1** **Shovel It On (IRE)**[32] 3017 4-10-9 42 .... (bt) BenJones(3) 5 53
(Steve Flook) *a.p: shkn up to ld over 1f out: rdn out (trainers' rep said, regarding apparent improvement in form, gelding had been working well at home and had benefitted from the re-application of a tongue strap)* **50/1**
0004 **2** 2 1/4 **Fern Owl**[21] 3428 7-10-9 56 .... (p) MissAliceHaynes(3) 3 49
(John Butler) *chsd ldrs: shkn up and ev ch over 1f out: edgd rt ins fnl f: styd on same pce: eased nr fin* **10/1**
0-45 **3** 5 **Hayward Field (IRE)**[28] 3163 6-10-12 46 .... (e) MissBeckySmith 12 41
(Noel Wilson) *hld up: hdwy over 2f out: styd on same pce fnl f: wnt 3rd nr fin* **16/1**
64 **4** 3/4 **Meagher's Flag (IRE)**[35] 2902 4-11-1 76 .... (tp) BryanCarver(3) 6 46
(Paul Nicholls) *racd keenly in 2nd: wnt upsides over 8f out: led over 6f out: rdn and hdd over 1f out: wknd wl ins fnl f* **4/1[2]**
-550 **5** 6 **Torch**[44] 2626 6-10-7 45 .... (p) MissAntoniaPeck(5) 7 31
(Laura Morgan) *s.i.s: in rr: hdwy over 2f out: wknd over 1f out* **40/1**
000- **6** 3/4 **Splash Around**[221] 9067 5-10-5 62 .... (b) MissJessicaLlewellyn(7) 8 29
(Bernard Llewellyn) *hld up: shkn up over 2f out: nvr on terms* **33/1**
350- **7** 1 3/4 **Chant (IRE)**[289] 7074 9-10-12 69 .... MissJoannaMason 2 27
(Ann Duffield) *led: hdd over 6f out: chsd ldr: ev ch 2f out: sn rdn: wknd fnl f* **4/1[2]**
0510 **8** 3 1/4 **Hussar Ballad (USA)**[11] 3769 10-11-4 56 .... MissSerenaBrotherton 4 27
(Antony Brittain) *hld up in tch: pushed along over 3f out: wknd wl over 1f out* **9/2[3]**
4-05 **9** 4 **River Rule**[82] 1519 4-10-0 44 .... (p[1]) MrRobertLaw-Eadie(7) 1 10
(Adrian Wintle) *hld up: hdwy over 3f out: hung rt and wknd over 2f out* **100/1**
/560 **10** 2 3/4 **Uncle Bernie (IRE)**[56] 2217 9-10-5 64 .... (p) MrSeanHawkins(7) 9 11
(Sarah Hollinshead) *s.s: hdwy on outer over 7f out: pushed along 4f out: wknd 3f out* **25/1**
5633 **11** 1 3/4 **Dream Magic (IRE)**[21] 3428 5-11-4 66 .... (b) MrSimonWalker 11 14
(Mark Loughnane) *prom: racd on outer: pushed along and wknd over 2f out (trainer said, regarding the poor form shown, that gelding had been caught wide without cover from a high draw and has been unable to dominate on this occasion)* **2/1[1]**
-010 **12** 1 3/4 **Our Manekineko**[17] 1769 9-11-4 49 .... (bt) MrJamesKing 10 11
(Stephen Michael Hanlon, Ire) *hld up: nt clr run and wknd over 2f out* **33/1**
2m 39.94s (-0.86) **Going Correction** -0.10s/f (Stan) 12 Ran SP% **121.6**
Speed ratings (Par 101): **98,96,93,92,88 88,87,84,82,80 79,78**
CSF £482.16 TOTE £120.90: £15.50, £3.10, £5.40; EX 1264.80 Trifecta £3137.70.There was no bid for the winner. Meagher's Flag was claimed by Mrs S. V. O. Leech for £6,000
Owner S Flook **Bred** Dylan Finucane **Trained** Leominster, Herefordshire

FOCUS
A weak seller, although it's possible this could be rated a bit higher.

4191 FOLLOW AT THE RACES ON TWITTER NOVICE STKS (PLUS 10 RACE) — 5f 21y (Tp)
6:30 (6:31) (Class 4) 2-Y-O
£4,787 (£1,424; £711; £355) Stalls Low

Form RPR
54 **1** **Dazzling Des (IRE)**[40] 2747 2-9-4 .... DanielTudhope 8 81
(David O'Meara) *sn chsng ldrs: rdn to ld ins fnl f: r.o* **9/2[3]**
3 **2** nk **Sermon (IRE)**[18] 3507 2-9-4 .... RichardKingscote 3 80
(Tom Dascombe) *led: shkn up and hung lft over 1f out: rdn and hdd ins fnl f: r.o (jockey said colt ran greenly under pressure)* **5/4[1]**
222 **3** 1 1/2 **Quiet Place (IRE)**[20] 3441 2-8-13 .... TomQueally 2 70
(Saeed bin Suroor) *chsd ldrs: shkn up over 1f out: swtchd rt ins fnl f: sn rdn: r.o* **2/1[2]**
10 **4** 4 1/2 **Exclusive (IRE)**[16] 3564 2-9-5 .... LukeMorris 1 59
(Archie Watson) *w ldr: ev ch 2f out: sn rdn: nt clr run over 1f out: edgd rt and no ex ins fnl f* **14/1**
0 **5** 1 1/4 **Forgetful Agent**[14] 3660 2-9-4 .... HayleyTurner 6 54
(Eve Johnson Houghton) *hld up plld hrd: rdn and hung lft over 1f out: no ex fnl f* **10/1**
05 **6** 3 1/4 **Come On Girl**[16] 3573 2-8-13 .... GeorgeDowning 7 37
(Tony Carroll) *hld up: pushed along and edgd rt 1/2-way: wknd over 1f out* **100/1**
0 **7** 1/2 **Pacific Coast**[25] 3265 2-9-4 .... CamHardie 4 40
(Antony Brittain) *hld up: pushed along 1/2-way: wknd over 1f out* **66/1**
1m 1.52s (-0.38) **Going Correction** -0.10s/f (Stan) 7 Ran SP% **114.2**
Speed ratings (Par 95): **99,98,96,88,86 81,80**
CSF £10.53 TOTE £4.80: £2.00, £1.40; EX 10.50 Trifecta £21.20.
Owner Evan M Sutherland **Bred** Tom Foley **Trained** Upper Helmsley, N Yorks

The Form Book Flat 2019, Raceform Ltd, Newbury, RG14 5SJ

FOCUS
A fair novice.

4192 GRAND THEATRE WOLVERHAMPTON H'CAP 5f 21y (Tp)
7:00 (7:00) (Class 5) (0-70,70) 3-Y-O

£3,752 (£1,116; £557; £300; £300; £300) **Stalls** Low

Form / RPR

5124 **1** **Superseded (IRE)**22 3376 3-9-3 **66**.................. RobertWinston 4 72
(John Butler) *hmpd s: hld up: swtchd rt and hdwy over 1f out: r.o to ld nr fin* **5/2**1

2420 **2** *nk* **Scale Force**5 4008 3-9-0 **70**..........................(b) CierenFallon(7) 3 75
(Gay Kelleway) *hmpd s: sn chsng ldrs: rdn to ld ins fnl f: hdd nr fin (jockey said gelding ran too freely)* **5/2**1

1200 **3** *1 1/4* **Miss Enigma (IRE)**9 3839 3-8-5 **61**..........................(b) AngusVilliers(7) 2 62
(Richard Hughes) *wnt rt s: prom: hmpd and lost pl 1/2-way: rdn over 1f out: r.o ins fnl f: wnt 3rd nr fin* **13/2**3

-040 **4** *nk* **Jill Rose**18 3516 3-8-13 **62**..........................(p1) PhilDennis 6 61
(Richard Whitaker) *hmpd s: sn chsng ldrs: rdn over 1f out: styd on same pce ins fnl f* **6/1**2

3-03 **5** *2 1/4* **Awarded**28 3148 3-8-5 **54**..........................(p) LukeMorris 8 45
(Robert Cowell) *chsd ldr tl led 2f out: rdn over 1f out: hdd and no ex ins fnl f* **16/1**

4000 **6** *hd* **Griggy (IRE)**20 3442 3-8-3 **57**.................. DarraghKeenan(5) 7 48
(John Butler) *hmpd sn after s: hld up: r.o ins fnl f: nvr nrr* **10/1**

34-4 **7** *4* **Society Star**16 3596 3-9-1 **64**.................. BrettDoyle 5 40
(Robert Cowell) *hmpd s: sn prom: pushed along 1/2-way: rn wd and lost pl wl over 1f out: edgd lft and eased ins fnl f (jockey said filly hung right-handed throughout)* **7/1**

5300 **8** *5* **Not So Shy**104 1167 3-8-3 **52**.................. CamHardie 1 10
(Lisa Williamson) *led 3f: sn rdn: wknd fnl f* **40/1**

1m 1.55s (-0.35) **Going Correction** -0.10s/f (Stan) **8** Ran SP% **114.7**
Speed ratings (Par 99): **98,97,95,95,91 91,84,76**
CSF £8.33 CT £34.61 TOTE £2.80: £1.30, £1.20, £2.10; EX 10.10 Trifecta £51.20.
Owner Northumbria Leisure Ltd **Bred** Eimear Mulhern **Trained** Newmarket, Suffolk

FOCUS
An ordinary sprint. The leaders went off fast enough and it set up for the closers.

4193 JESS GLYNNE - LIVE AT LADIES DAY CLAIMING STKS 6f 20y (Tp)
7:30 (7:30) (Class 5) 3-Y-O

£3,752 (£1,116; £418; £300; £300) **Stalls** Low

Form / RPR

1204 **1** **Swiss Pride (IRE)**17 3535 3-8-11 **74**.................. AngusVilliers(7) 4 76
(Richard Hughes) *sn pushed along to join ldr: led over 1f out: shkn up and edgd rt ins fnl f: r.o (trainers' rep said, regarding apparent improvement in form, gelding appreciated the drop in grade from handicap company to a claimer and also benefitted from the removal of blinker, having worn them on it's previous two starts)* **11/4**2

-023 **2** *1 1/2* **Journey Of Life**28 3167 3-9-0 **72**..........................(h) CierenFallon(7) 7 75
(Gary Moore) *chsd ldrs on outer: shkn up and hung lft fr over 1f out: chsd wnr ins fnl f: styd on* **5/2**1

0030 **3** *1/2* **Freedom And Wheat (IRE)**20 3440 3-8-11 **64**..........................(v) ShaneGray 6 63
(Mark Usher) *s.i.s: hld up: r.o ins fnl f: nt rch ldrs (jockey said gelding was slowly away and hung right-handed)* **9/2**

5-00 **3** *dht* **Pegasus Bridge**13 3697 3-8-4 **55**..........................(b) GeorgiaDobie(7) 2 63
(Eve Johnson Houghton) *chsd ldrs: rdn over 1f out: styd on* **20/1**

2161 **5** *1/2* **Ollivander (IRE)**16 3569 3-9-4 **70**..........................(v) ConorMcGovern(3) 3 72
(David O'Meara) *led: rdn and hdd over 1f out: no ex wl ins fnl f* **3/1**3

0064 **6** *5* **Sussudio**20 3442 3-8-3 **57**..........................(p) LukeMorris 1 39
(Richard Spencer) *trckd ldrs: racd keenly: drvn along 2f out: wknd u.p wl ins fnl f* **7/1**

0-00 **7** *1 3/4* **Rock N Roll Queen**36 2871 3-8-3 **52**..........................(p1) JimmyQuinn 5 33
(John Mackie) *s.i.s: pushed along early in rr: rdn over 2f out: n.d* **50/1**

660- **8** *5* **Willett**255 8154 3-8-8 **50**..........................(p) GabrieleMalune(3) 9 26
(Sarah Hollinshead) *hld up: rdn and wknd over 2f out (jockey said gelding stopped quickly)* **100/1**

6- **9** *13* **Little Thornton**233 8826 3-8-6 **0**.................. CamHardie 10
(Stella Barclay) *broke wl: sn stdd and lost pl: hld up: plld hrd: rdn over 1f out: eased ins fnl f* **100/1**

1m 13.69s (-0.81) **Going Correction** -0.10s/f (Stan) **9** Ran SP% **119.6**
Speed ratings (Par 99): **101,99,98,98,97 91,88,82,64**
WIN: 3.50 Swiss Pride; PL: 1.40 Journey Of Life 1.40 Swiss Pride 0.70 Freedom And Wheat 3.30 Pegasus Bridge; EX: 11.10; CSF: 10.36; TF: SP&JOF&FAW: 19.10, SP&JOL&PB: 49.70 CSF £10.36 TOTE £3.50: £1.40, £1.40, £0.70; EX 11.10 Trifecta £19.10.
Owner Don Churston & Ray Greatorex **Bred** Edward Lynam & John Cullinan **Trained** Upper Lambourn, Berks

FOCUS
Quite a competitive claimer on paper, but the winner was entitled to take this at the weights.

4194 COME TO GENTLEMAN'S EVENING - 16TH NOVEMBER H'CAP 1m 142y (Tp)
8:00 (8:01) (Class 6) (0-65,65) 4-Y-O+

£3,105 (£924; £461; £300; £300; £300) **Stalls** Low

Form / RPR

0221 **1** **Street Poet (IRE)**21 3429 6-9-4 **65**.................. PhilDennis 4 71
(Michael Herrington) *chsd ldrs: wnt 2nd over 2f out: led and hung rt fr over 1f out: sn rdn: jst hld on* **13/2**

6230 **2** *hd* **Ghazan (IRE)**21 3429 4-9-3 **64**..........................(p1) RossaRyan 2 70
(Kevin Frost) *broke wl: lost pl after 1f: hdwy over 5f out: rdn and nt clr run over 1f out: hung rt ins fnl f: r.o* **20/1**

6031 **3** *3/4* **Celtic Artisan (IRE)**42 2692 8-9-3 **64**..........................(bt) StevieDonohoe 11 68
(Rebecca Menzies) *s.i.s: hld up: rdn and r.o wl ins fnl f: wnt 3rd nr fin: nt rch ldrs* **10/1**

202 **4** *3/4* **Billy Roberts (IRE)**35 2902 6-9-2 **63**.................. JasonHart 13 65
(Richard Whitaker) *sn led: rdn: hdd and hung rt over 1f out: styd on same pce wl ins fnl f* **6/1**

5545 **5** *1/2* **Arlecchino's Leap**32 3002 7-9-3 **64**..........................(p) ShaneGray 8 65
(Mark Usher) *prom: edgd lft and lost pl over 7f out: hld up: rdn and nt clr run over 1f out: r.o ins fnl f* **16/1**

5-00 **6** *1 1/4* **Bhodi (IRE)**16 3567 4-9-1 **65**.................. JoshuaBryan(3) 10 64
(Kevin Frost) *prom: chsd ldr on outer 7f out tl rdn over 2f out: hung lft and no ex ins fnl f* **100/1**

3042 **7** *1/2* **Subliminal**4 4028 4-9-3 **64**..........................(b) LukeMorris 5 62
(Simon Dow) *chsd ldrs: rdn and hung rt over 1f out: no ex ins fnl f (jockey said colt ran flat)* **3/1**1

1504 **8** *3/4* **Grey Destiny**42 2692 9-9-2 **63**..........................(p) CamHardie 1 59
(Antony Brittain) *s.i.s: hld up: hdwy 2f out: rdn and nt clr run ins fnl f: styd on same pce* **20/1**

1103 **9** *1/2* **Citta D'Oro**31 3046 4-9-3 **64**..........................(p) RichardKingscote 12 59
(James Unett) *hld up: shkn up over 1f out: nt trble ldrs* **4/1**2

464 **10** *nse* **Whatwouldyouknow (IRE)**6 3960 4-9-3 **64**.................. PhilipPrince 9 59
(Richard Guest) *prom: lost pl over 7f out: rdn and nt clr run over 1f out: n.d after (vet said gelding lost it's left fore shoe)* **8/1**

00 **11** *1/2* **Bated Beauty (IRE)**19 3463 4-9-4 **65**.................. TomQueally 3 59
(John Butler) *hld up: hmpd over 7f out: pushed along on outer over 2f out: nvr on terms* **9/2**3

04-0 **12** *nk* **Dark Crocodile (IRE)**19 3462 4-9-3 **64**..........................(t) HayleyTurner 7 57
(Seamus Durack) *s.i.s: shkn up over 2f out: edgd rt fnl f: n.d* **100/1**

0250 **13** *9* **Gonzaga**17 3543 4-8-13 **65**.................. RachealKneller(5) 6 39
(James Bennett) *prom: racd keenly: pushed along over 3f out: wknd and eased over 1f out (jockey said gelding lost it's action in the home straight)* **50/1**

1m 48.56s (-1.54) **Going Correction** -0.10s/f (Stan) **13** Ran SP% **130.4**
Speed ratings (Par 101): **102,101,101,100,100 98,98,97,97,97 96,96,88**
CSF £141.45 CT £1358.11 TOTE £8.30: £2.70, £5.30, £2.70; EX 130.30 Trifecta £575.00.
Owner Mrs H Lloyd-Herrington **Bred** Mrs C Regalado-Gonzalez **Trained** Cold Kirby, N Yorks
■ Stewards' Enquiry : Shane Gray four-day ban: careless riding (Jul 8-11)

FOCUS
A modest but competitive heat. It paid to race fairly handily. The runner-up helps to pin a straightforward level to the form.

4195 VISIT THE BLACK COUNTRY H'CAP 7f 36y (Tp)
8:35 (8:36) (Class 6) (0-60,60) 3-Y-O+

£3,105 (£924; £461; £300; £300; £300) **Stalls** High

Form / RPR

2104 **1** **Poet's Pride**37 2846 4-9-6 **60**..........................(w) RobertWinston 7 72+
(David Barron) *hld up in tch: shkn up to ld ins fnl f: r.o: comf* **9/4**1

00-0 **2** *2 1/2* **Sherzy Boy**37 2846 4-9-2 **56**..........................(t1) NathanEvans 9 59
(Jacqueline Coward) *hld up: swtchd rt and hdwy over 1f out: rdn and r.o to go 2nd wl ins fnl f: no ch w wnr* **8/1**

6245 **3** *2* **Rockesbury**21 3430 4-8-12 **59**..........................(b) LauraCoughlan(7) 1 57
(David Loughnane) *led: shkn up over 2f out: rdn over 1f out: hdd ins fnl f: styd on same pce* **8/1**

5-55 **4** *1/2* **Kafoo**5 3989 6-8-12 **57**..........................(b) TheodoreLadd(5) 8 54
(Michael Appleby) *s.i.s: hld up: swtchd rt wl over 1f out: rdn and r.o ins fnl f: nt rch ldrs* **11/1**

4060 **5** *nk* **Elusif (IRE)**13 3701 4-8-11 **58**.................. GavinAshton(7) 6 54
(Shaun Keightley) *hld up: swtchd rt and hdwy over 1f out: styd on same pce ins fnl f* **20/1**

6356 **6** *nk* **Christmas Night**26 3215 4-9-0 **57**.................. BenRobinson(3) 5 52
(Ollie Pears) *chsd ldrs: rdn over 2f out: no ex ins fnl f (jockey said gelding hung left-handed throughout. Vet said gelding lost it's right fore shoe)* **7/1**

4040 **7** *nse* **The King's Steed**42 2692 6-9-2 **56**..........................(bt) JosephineGordon 3 51
(Shaun Lycett) *pushed along to join ldr: rdn and ev ch fr over 1f out tl ins fnl f: wknd towards fin* **13/2**3

60-4 **8** *1/2* **Gold Flash**21 3430 7-9-5 **59**.................. RichardKingscote 12 53
(Rod Millman) *hld up: swtchd lft over 6f out: rdn over 1f out: nvr on terms* **5/1**2

2635 **9** *1 1/4* **Sooqaan**34 2944 8-9-5 **59**..........................(p) CamHardie 4 50
(Antony Brittain) *prom: rdn over 2f out: wknd ins fnl f* **16/1**

-006 **10** *6* **Lagenda**12 3730 6-9-6 **60**..........................(b) ShaneGray 11 36
(Liam Bailey) *hld up: shkn up on outer over 2f out: eased whn no ch fnl f* **50/1**

1m 27.95s (-0.85) **Going Correction** -0.10s/f (Stan) **10** Ran SP% **116.4**
Speed ratings (Par 101): **100,97,94,94,93 93,93,92,91,84**
CSF £20.86 CT £127.27 TOTE £1.80: £1.10, £2.10, £2.80; EX 23.40 Trifecta £186.70.
Owner Laurence O'Kane/Harrowgate BloodstockLtd **Bred** Swettenham Stud Bloodstock Ltd **Trained** Maunby, N Yorks

FOCUS
They finished in a heap behind the first two. This rates a pb from the winner.

4196 SKY SPORTS RACING ON SKY 415 NOVICE STKS 7f 36y (Tp)
9:05 (9:07) (Class 5) 3-Y-O+ **£3,752** (£1,116; £557; £278) **Stalls** High

Form / RPR

2 **1** **Mutamaasik**19 3464 3-9-1 **0**.................. JackMitchell 1 85
(Roger Varian) *sn chsng ldr: shkn up to ld over 1f out: rdn and hung lft ins fnl f: r.o* **4/5**1

45- **2** *1 1/2* **Aluqair (IRE)**235 8783 3-9-1 **0**..........................(h1) RyanPowell 3 81
(Simon Crisford) *led: rdn and hdd over 1f out: nt clr run ins fnl f: styd on same pce* **6/1**3

02 **3** *6* **Military Tactic (IRE)**44 2634 3-9-1 **0**..........................(p1) HayleyTurner 9 65
(Saeed bin Suroor) *hld up in tch: shkn up over 2f out: styd on to go 3rd ins fnl f: nt trble ldrs* **5/2**2

5 **4** *1* **Clifton**24 3324 3-9-1 **0**.................. NathanEvans 6 62
(Michael Easterby) *chsd ldrs: rdn over 1f out: wknd ins fnl f* **50/1**

-45 **5** *hd* **My Style (IRE)**22 3372 3-8-8 **0**.................. GeorgiaDobie(7) 12 62+
(Eve Johnson Houghton) *s.i.s: hld up: rdn over 1f out: r.o ins fnl f: nvr nrr* **16/1**

6 **6** *1 1/4* **Mogsy (IRE)**30 3067 3-9-1 **0**.................. RichardKingscote 11 58+
(Tom Dascombe) *s.i.s: hld up: styd on ins fnl f: nvr nrr* **33/1**

03 **7** *2* **Colonelle (USA)**16 3598 3-8-10 **0**.................. JimmyQuinn 4 48
(Ed Vaughan) *chsd ldrs: rdn over 2f out: wknd fnl f (jockey said filly lugged right-handed in the home straight)* **25/1**

8 *nk* **Sharp Talk (IRE)** 3-9-1 **0**.................. JosephineGordon 5 52
(Shaun Keightley) *s.i.s: hld up: nvr on terms* **80/1**

0-0 **9** *shd* **Dream Model (IRE)**156 316 3-8-10 **0**.................. CamHardie 10 47
(Mark Loughnane) *hld up: rdn over 2f out: no ch whn hung lft over 1f out* **100/1**

0 **10** *1/2* **Set Point Charlie (IRE)**19 3464 3-9-1 **0**.................. TomQueally 2 50
(Seamus Durack) *hld up: shkn up over 2f out: n.d* **100/1**

0/ **11** *12* **Come On Sal**583 8849 4-9-5 **0**.................. RossaRyan 8 16
(Kevin Frost) *hld up: shkn up and hung lft over 2f out: wknd wl over 1f out* **100/1**

1m 28.12s (-0.68) **Going Correction** -0.10s/f (Stan)
WFA 3 from 4yo 9lb **11** Ran SP% **117.2**
Speed ratings (Par 103): **99,97,90,89,89 87,85,85,84,84 70**
CSF £6.05 TOTE £1.40: £1.10, £1.20, £1.30; EX 6.90 Trifecta £11.90.
Owner Hamdan Al Maktoum **Bred** Shadwell Estate Company Limited **Trained** Newmarket, Suffolk
■ Aljari was withdrawn. Price at time of withdrawal 11-1. Rule 4 applies to all bets - deduction 5p in the pound

FOCUS
This was steadily run and the first two had it between them from the turn in. This has been rated around the runner-up's 2yo debut but could be worth more.
T/Plt: £872.90 to a £1 stake. Pool: £71,159.36 - 59.51 winning units T/Qpdt: £11.20 to a £1 stake. Pool: £9,925.16 - 654.12 winning units **Colin Roberts**

4197 - 4203a (Foreign Racing) - See Raceform Interactive

3878 MAISONS-LAFFITTE (R-H)
Monday, June 24

OFFICIAL GOING: Turf: good

4204a PRIX TABOUN (MAIDEN) (3YO) (TURF) 5f 110y
2:00 3-Y-O £11,261 (£4,504; £3,378; £2,252; £1,126)

RPR
1 **Exalted Angel (FR)**[66] 1924 3-9-3 0 ow1 .... BenCurtis 3 81
(K R Burke) *wl into stride: disp ld early: pushed into clr ld over 2f out: rdn to hold advantage over 1f out: drvn and hung lft towards rail ins fnl f: kpt on strly* **3/1**[2]
2 *2* **Morning Basma (FR)**[13] 3713 3-9-0 0 ow1 .... CristianDemuro 7 71
(E J O'Neill, France) **23/10**[1]
3 *snk* **Roseya (FR)**[32] 3-9-0 0 ow1 .... ChristopheSoumillon 4 71
(A De Royer-Dupre, France) **9/2**
4 *1 1/4* **Celtic (IRE)**[32] 3-9-0 0 ow1 .... MaximeGuyon 5 66
(A Fabre, France) **16/5**[3]
5 *7* **Shawaf**[246] 8447 3-9-3 0 ow1 .... AurelienLemaitre 2 46
(F Head, France) *trckd ldrs: urged along over 2f out: rdn w limited rspnse over 1f out: no ex ins fnl f* **48/10**
6 *12* **Fear And Fire (FR)**[26] 3-8-10 0 ow1 .... MlleCoraliePacaut(4) 6 4
(Mme G Rarick, France) **44/1**
7 *15* **Printemps D'Avril (FR)**[316] 3-8-10 0 ow1 .... DelphineSantiago(4) 1
(J-P Perruchot, France) **34/1**

1m 4.14s (-3.16) 7 Ran SP% 119.6
PARI-MUTUEL (all including 1 euro stake): WIN 4.00; PLACE 1.70, 1.70; SF 11.80.
Owner Pau-Perth Partnership & Mrs E Burke **Bred** Tirnaskea Stud **Trained** Middleham Moor, N Yorks

4205a PRIX HAMPTON (LISTED RACE) (3YO+) (TURF) 5f
3:10 3-Y-O+ £23,423 (£9,369; £7,027; £4,684; £2,342)

RPR
1 **Shades Of Blue (IRE)**[39] 2779 3-8-8 0 ow1 .... HollieDoyle 8 104
(Clive Cox) *sn prom: trckd ldrs: urged along 2f out: rdn to chal over 1f out: strly drvn and hung lft ins fnl f: kpt on wl u.p fnl 100yds to ld on post* **11/10**[1]
2 *shd* **Forza Capitano (FR)**[43] 2667 4-9-3 0 ow1 .... VincentCheminaud 1 109
(H-A Pantall, France) **11/1**
3 *2* **Ken Colt (IRE)**[43] 2667 4-9-3 0 ow1 .... Pierre-CharlesBoudot 4 101
(F Chappet, France) **48/10**[3]
4 *1 3/4* **Lady In France**[16] 3587 3-8-8 0 ow1 .... BenCurtis 3 90
(K R Burke) *qckly into stride: chsd ldrs: rdn and ev ch over 1f out: no ex ins fnl f* **15/2**
5 *5* **Son Cesio (FR)**[236] 8755 8-9-3 0 ow1 .... MaximeGuyon 6 77
(F Chappet, France) **18/1**
6 *6* **Sexy Metro (FR)**[46] 2564 3-8-11 0 ow1 .... CristianDemuro 5 53
(D Guillemin, France) **22/5**[2]
7 *7* **Pirandello**[9] 5-9-3 0 ow1 .... MickaelBarzalona 7 30
(A Fabre, France) *dwlt bdly: in rr and adrift early: nvr on terms and eased once ch had gone* **76/10**

57.97s
WFA 3 from 4yo+ 6lb 7 Ran SP% 120.4
PARI-MUTUEL (all including 1 euro stake): WIN 2.10; PLACE 1.20, 2.00, 1.50; DF 12.60.
Owner Miss A Jones **Bred** Newtown Stud **Trained** Lambourn, Berks

3954 BEVERLEY (R-H)
Tuesday, June 25

OFFICIAL GOING: Good (6.3) changing to good to soft after race 1 (2.00) changing to soft after race 5 (4.00)
Wind: Fresh across Weather: Heavy cloud and rain

4206 PURE BROADBAND NOVICE STKS 7f 96y
2:00 (2:00) (Class 5) 2-Y-O £4,463 (£1,328; £663; £331) Stalls Low

Form RPR
2 1 **Walk In Marrakesh (IRE)**[19] 3506 2-9-0 0 .... FrannyNorton 2 79+
(Mark Johnston) *mde all: pushed along over 1f out: kpt on strly* **1/2**[1]
4 2 *1 1/4* **Frasard**[26] 3245 2-9-5 0 .... GrahamLee 6 79
(Bryan Smart) *trckd ldrs: hdwy on inner over 2f out: swtchd lft and rdn to chse wnr ent fnl f: sn drvn and no imp* **3/1**[2]
03 3 *6* **Breguet Man (IRE)**[10] 3841 2-9-5 0 .... ShaneGray 3 64
(Keith Dalgleish) *trckd wnr: pushed along 2f out: sn rdn: drvn over 1f out: kpt on same pce* **11/2**[3]
4 *4 1/2* **Impression** 2-9-0 0 .... BenCurtis 5 48
(Amy Murphy) *trckd ldng pair: pushed along over 2f out: rdn wl over 1f out: edgd rt and wknd over 1f out* **14/1**
0 5 *5* **Road Rage (IRE)**[73] 1758 2-9-5 0 .... TomEaves 8 41
(Michael Dods) *in tch: sme hdwy 3f out: rdn along 2f out: n.d* **16/1**
0 6 *nk* **Majarra (IRE)**[24] 3335 2-9-0 0 .... AndrewMullen 7 35
(Adrian Nicholls) *a towards rr* **50/1**
7 *7* **Cersei Lannister (IRE)** 2-9-0 0 .... ConnorBeasley 1 18+
(Adrian Nicholls) *v s.i.s and lost 10 l s: clsd up to join field 1/2-way: rdn along over 2f out: sn wknd (jockey said filly was slowly away)* **20/1**
0 8 *10* **Richard Of Cambria**[7] 3954 2-9-5 0 .... BarryMcHugh 4
(Adrian Nicholls) *a towards rr: outpcd and bhd fr over 2f out* **80/1**

1m 36.05s (3.45) **Going Correction** +0.35s/f (Good) 8 Ran SP% 127.6
Speed ratings (Par 93): **94,92,85,80,74 74,66,55**
CSF £2.81 TOTE £1.40: £1.02, £1.10, £2.00; EX 3.40 Trifecta £7.00.
Owner Merriebelle Irish Farm Limited **Bred** Merriebelle Irish Farm Ltd **Trained** Middleham Moor, N Yorks

FOCUS
The going was given as good (Going Stick 6.3) prior to racing but soon changed to good to soft after the first race. The inside rail around the bottom bend was out to provide fresh ground. Add 7yds. This proved fairly uncompetitive.

4207 FLAT OUT MORE RACING ON RACINGTV H'CAP 7f 96y
2:30 (2:30) (Class 5) (0-75,74) 3-Y-O+
£4,599 (£1,376; £688; £344; £300; £300) Stalls Low

Form RPR
04-1 1 **Keepup Kevin**[27] 3215 5-9-12 **72** .... CallumShepherd 9 80
(Pam Sly) *wnt lft sn after s: trckd ldr: hdwy and cl up 3f out: slt ld 2f out: rdn over 1f out: drvn ins fnl f: kpt on wl towards fin* **3/1**[1]
1321 2 *1/2* **Waqt (IRE)**[18] 3539 5-9-12 **72** .... (p[1]) RossaRyan 4 78
(Alexandra Dunn) *trckd ldng pair on inner: hdwy over 2f out: rdn over 1f out: drvn to chal ins fnl f: kpt on same pce towards fin* **6/1**[3]
0-05 3 *hd* **Coviglia (IRE)**[28] 3199 5-9-3 **63** .... KieranO'Neill 12 68
(Jacqueline Coward) *t.k.h early: trckd ldng pair: effrt 2f out: rdn over 1f out: drvn and ch ins fnl f: kpt on same pce towards fin* **14/1**
5232 4 *2 1/4* **Donnelly's Rainbow (IRE)**[8] 3924 6-8-11 **57** .... LewisEdmunds 7 56+
(Rebecca Bastiman) *t.k.h early: hld up in rr: hdwy wl over 2f out: chsd ldrs over 1f out and sn rdn: drvn ins fnl f: no imp towards fin* **5/1**[2]
0-04 5 *1* **Final Frontier (IRE)**[32] 3053 6-9-6 **66** .... (b) JamesSullivan 5 63
(Ruth Carr) *towards rr: hdwy 3f out: rdn along and in tch 2f out: sn drvn: swtchd lft ent fnl f: kpt on towards fin* **9/1**
546- 6 *hd* **Allen A Dale (IRE)**[196] 9490 3-9-4 **73** .... PaulHanagan 2 66
(Richard Fahey) *midfield: hdwy on inner over 2f out: swtchd lft and rdn to chse ldrs over 1f out: kpt on fnl f* **6/1**[3]
0-00 7 *1 3/4* **Relight My Fire**[27] 3215 9-8-12 **58** .... (p) DavidAllan 6 49
(Tim Easterby) *chsd ldrs: rdn along 2f out: sn drvn and one pce* **22/1**
1513 8 *1/2* **Space War**[13] 3716 12-8-5 **58** .... (t) JoshQuinn(7) 14 48
(Michael Easterby) *hld up in rr: sme hdwy on outer fnl 2f: n.d* **33/1**
64-0 9 *1/2* **Great Shout (IRE)**[160] 251 3-9-1 **70** .... (t[1] w) GeorgeWood 8 56
(Amy Murphy) *chsd ldrs: rdn along wl over 2f out: sn drvn and wknd* **16/1**
00/0 10 *3/4* **Echo Of Lightning**[10] 3868 9-9-9 **74** .... (p) PaulaMuir(5) 13 61
(Roger Fell) *qckly away and led: sn crossed to inner rail and clr after 2f: rdn along over 2f out: sn hdd: drvn and wknd over 1f out* **33/1**
3000 11 *1 3/4* **Proceeding**[8] 3924 4-8-10 **56** .... CamHardie 10 38
(Tracy Waggott) *hmpd s: a in rr (jockey said gelding was hampered leaving the stalls)* **40/1**
0-00 12 *nk* **Bahuta Acha**[33] 2997 4-10-0 **74** .... BenCurtis 1 55
(David Loughnane) *a towards rr (jockey said gelding hung left throughout)* **11/1**
064 13 *nse* **Intense Style (IRE)**[9] 3880 7-9-9 **74** .... FayeMcManoman(5) 11 55
(Les Eyre) *midfield: rdn along 3f out: sn wknd* **8/1**

1m 34.42s (1.82) **Going Correction** +0.35s/f (Good)
WFA 3 from 4yo+ 9lb 13 Ran SP% 124.9
Speed ratings (Par 103): **103,102,102,99,98 98,96,95,95,94 92,91,91**
CSF £20.83 CT £238.35 TOTE £3.10: £1.10, £2.80, £5.80; EX 25.00 Trifecta £407.30.
Owner W Robinson & P M Sly **Bred** Mrs P M Sly **Trained** Thorney, Cambs
■ Stewards' Enquiry : Faye McManoman five-day ban; careless riding (July 9-13)

FOCUS
Add 7yds. A competitive handicap, but it didn't pay to be too far off the pace, the first three racing in second, third and fourth early on. A small pb from the winner.

4208 RACING TV'S BIGGEST EVER FLAT SEASON H'CAP 1m 4f 23y
3:00 (3:00) (Class 5) (0-75,76) 4-Y-O+
£4,599 (£1,376; £688; £344; £300; £300) Stalls Low

Form RPR
6-05 1 **Celestial Force (IRE)**[53] 2374 4-9-9 **76** .... (v[1]) PJMcDonald 8 83
(Tom Dascombe) *sn led and set stdy pce: pushed along and qcknd over 2f out: rdn over 1f out: drvn ins fnl f: kpt on gamely* **3/1**[1]
-063 2 *1 1/4* **Qawamees (IRE)**[10] 3845 4-9-7 **74** .... (bt) KieranO'Neill 5 79
(Michael Easterby) *in rr and pushed along early stages: hld up: gd hdwy over 2f out: rdn to chal ent fnl f: sn drvn and ev ch: edgd rt and kpt on same pce towards fin* **7/1**
3014 3 *1/2* **Dew Pond**[6] 4004 7-8-2 **55** .... (bt) DuranFentiman 7 59
(Tim Easterby) *trckd ldng pair: hdwy over 2f out: cl up 1 1/2f out: sn rdn and ev ch ins fnl f: sn drvn and kpt on same pce last 75yds* **13/2**[3]
1433 4 *1 1/4* **Sioux Frontier (IRE)**[8] 3925 4-9-4 **71** .... LewisEdmunds 2 74+
(Iain Jardine) *trckd ldrs: hdwy over 2f out: chsd ldrs over 1f out: rdn and ev ch ent fnl f: drvn and hld whn n.m.r last 75yds* **3/1**[1]
4061 5 *3 3/4* **Zihaam**[7] 3959 5-8-9 **67** 5ex .... (p) BenSanderson(5) 6 63
(Roger Fell) *hld up towards rr: hdwy 3f out: chsd ldrs 2f out: sn rdn and n.d* **9/2**[2]
-062 6 *2* **Low Profile**[32] 3054 4-9-1 **68** .... (p) DanielTudhope 3 61
(Rebecca Bastiman) *trckd wnr: hdwy over 2f out: rdn and ev ch over 1f out: sn drvn and wknd ent fnl f (trainer said gelding was unsuited by the ground and would prefer a faster surface)* **9/2**[2]
6515 7 *7* **Star Ascending (IRE)**[25] 3321 7-8-11 **64** .... (p) AndrewMullen 1 46
(Jennie Candlish) *trckd ldng pair on inner: pushed along 3f out: rdn over 2f out: sn drvn and wknd* **16/1**

2m 41.73s (2.93) **Going Correction** +0.35s/f (Good) 7 Ran SP% 118.1
Speed ratings (Par 103): **104,103,102,102,99 98,93**
CSF £25.86 CT £129.05 TOTE £4.00: £1.50, £4.00; EX 25.60 Trifecta £129.40.
Owner John Dance **Bred** Sunderland Holdings Inc **Trained** Malpas, Cheshire
■ Stewards' Enquiry : Kieran O'Neill two-day ban; careless riding (July 9-10)

FOCUS
Add 7yds. The winner had the run of things out in front and this rates his best since early 3yo form.

4209 BEVERLEY ANNUAL BADGEHOLDERS H'CAP 1m 1f 207y
3:30 (3:30) (Class 4) (0-80,82) 4-Y-O+
£6,868 (£2,055; £1,027; £514; £300; £300) Stalls Low

Form RPR
3422 1 **Bit Of A Quirke**[10] 3845 6-8-11 **67** .... (v) AndrewMullen 3 77
(Mark Walford) *mde all: rdn and qcknd clr over 2f out: kpt on strly* **11/4**[2]
0000 2 *2 3/4* **Regal Mirage (IRE)**[11] 3816 5-9-0 **70** .... DavidAllan 4 75
(Tim Easterby) *hld up: hdwy over 3f out: rdn along 2f out: sn chsng wnr: drvn and no imp fnl f* **9/1**
4113 3 *2 3/4* **Archie Perkins (IRE)**[11] 3811 4-9-8 **81** .... RowanScott(3) 8 80
(Nigel Tinkler) *t.k.h: hld up towards rr: effrt and nt clr run on inner 2f out: rdn over 1f out: kpt on fnl f* **15/8**[1]
056 4 *2 1/2* **Moxy Mares**[36] 2894 4-9-6 **76** .... PJMcDonald 9 70
(Mark Loughnane) *hld up: towards rr 1/2-way: hdwy over 2f out: sn rdn: kpt on fnl f* **10/1**

5512 **5** *nk* **Global Art**[33] 3004 4-9-7 **82** .... DylanHogan(5) 6 75
(Ed Dunlop) *sn trcking wnr: pushed along over 2f out: rdn wl over 1f out: sn drvn and grad wknd* **9/1**

6341 **6** *4 ½* **Winged Spur (IRE)**[24] 3349 4-9-11 **81** .... FrannyNorton 2 65
(Mark Johnston) *a in rr* **7/1**[3]

2231 **7** *1 ¼* **Gendarme (IRE)**[17] 3572 4-9-6 **76** ....(b) GeorgeWood 5 58
(Alexandra Dunn) *trckd ldrs: hdwy on outer 3f out: rdn along 2f out: sn drvn and wknd (trainers' rep said, regarding the poor form shown, that gelding was unsuited by the ground and would prefer a faster surface)* **11/1**

505/ **8** *2 ¼* **Cross Step (USA)**[194] 5-9-5 **75** .... ConnorBeasley 1 52
(Adrian Nicholls) *chsd ldrs: rdn along wl over 2f out: sn wknd (vet said gelding lost it's right hind shoe)* **33/1**

2m 8.73s (3.03) **Going Correction** +0.35s/f (Good) **8 Ran SP% 114.3**
Speed ratings (Par 105): **101,98,96,94,94 90,89,87**
CSF £27.53 CT £56.14 TOTE £2.90: £1.10, £2.50, £1.30; EX 24.10 Trifecta £88.00.
Owner A Quirke & Mrs G B Walford **Bred** Dr A Gillespie **Trained** Sherriff Hutton, N Yorks

FOCUS
Add 7yds. Another front-running winner and he rates back to his best.

4210 RACING TV EXTRA ON RACINGTV.COM H'CAP 1m 1f 207y
4:00 (4:01) (Class 6) (0-65,66) 3-Y-O
£3,493 (£1,039; £519; £300; £300; £300) **Stalls** Low

Form RPR

-002 **1** **Langholm (IRE)**[5] 4039 3-8-7 **50** ....(t) PaulHanagan 12 61
(Declan Carroll) *mde all: rdn 2f out: clr ent fnl f: kpt on strly* **11/2**[3]

0544 **2** *3 ¼* **One To Go**[27] 3226 3-9-5 **62** ....(b) DavidAllan 8 67
(Tim Easterby) *trckd ldrs: hdwy 3f out: chsd wnr 2f out and sn rdn: drvn over 1f out: no imp fnl f* **9/4**[1]

0U04 **3** *hd* **Northern Lyte**[8] 3947 3-9-0 **62** .... FayeMcManoman(5) 11 66+
(Nigel Tinkler) *hld up in tch: hdwy 2f out: rdn to chse ldng pair over 1f out: drvn and kpt on fnl f* **13/2**

0043 **4** *5* **Tails I Win (CAN)**[8] 3938 3-9-0 **57** ....(h) BenCurtis 7 52+
(Roger Fell) *hld up: hdwy over 2f out: rdn wl over 1f out: sn drvn and nvr rching ldrs* **5/2**[2]

5050 **5** *5* **Biz Markee (IRE)**[8] 3931 3-8-12 **60** ....(b[1]) BenSanderson(5) 5 45+
(Roger Fell) *dwlt and in rr: hdwy 3f out: rdn along over 2f out: kpt on: n.d* **25/1**

0-50 **6** *hd* **Rodney After Dave (IRE)**[14] 3684 3-8-7 **50** .... NathanEvans 9 35+
(Marjorie Fife) *towards rr tl sme late hdwy* **40/1**

0-00 **7** *4* **Angel Sarah (IRE)**[26] 3271 3-8-4 **47** .... PaddyMathers 14 24
(Richard Fahey) *in tch: hdwy on wd outside over 2f out: sn rdn and wknd wl over 1f out* **25/1**

5-00 **8** *1 ½* **Seven For A Pound (USA)**[17] 3594 3-8-12 **58** .... SeanDavis(3) 2 33+
(Richard Fahey) *a towards rr* **12/1**

00-4 **9** *1* **Pinkie Pie (IRE)**[8] 3938 3-7-11 **45** .... AndrewBreslin(5) 3 18
(Andrew Crook) *nvr bttr than midfield* **20/1**

5365 **10** *2 ½* **Curfewed (IRE)**[19] 3513 3-9-7 **64** ....(p) CamHardie 15 32
(Tracy Waggott) *chsd ldrs: rdn along over 3f out: sn wknd* **10/1**

0-00 **11** *nk* **Hard Knock Life**[29] 3157 3-8-2 **45** .... DuranFentiman 10 12
(Tim Easterby) *chsd ldrs: rdn along 3f out: sn wknd* **33/1**

0500 **12** *15* **Gloryella**[13] 3721 3-8-2 **45** .... JamesSullivan 6
(Ruth Carr) *in tch on inner: rdn along 3f out: sn wknd* **66/1**

00-0 **13** *1 ¾* **George's Law**[26] 3270 3-8-10 **53** .... RachelRichardson 13
(Tim Easterby) *trckd wnr: pushed along over 3f out: rdn over 2f out: sn wknd* **28/1**

2m 9.95s (4.25) **Going Correction** +0.35s/f (Good) **13 Ran SP% 127.6**
Speed ratings (Par 97): **97,94,94,90,86 86,82,81,80,78 78,66,65**
CSF £18.25 CT £88.92 TOTE £7.10: £2.60, £1.30, £2.90; EX 20.60 Trifecta £105.00.
Owner Steve Ryan & M J Tedham **Bred** Yeomanstown Stud **Trained** Malton, N Yorks

FOCUS
Add 7yds. Another all-the-way winner, the fourth from the first five races on the card.

4211 MORE FLAT RACING ON RACING TV MEDIAN AUCTION MAIDEN STKS 1m 100y
4:30 (4:30) (Class 5) 3-Y-O **£4,599** (£1,376; £688; £344; £171) **Stalls** Low

Form RPR

3 **1** **Muhaarar's Nephew**[25] 3324 3-9-5 0 .... DaneO'Neill 4 73
(Owen Burrows) *cl up: led after 3f: rdn 2f out: drvn ent fnl f: kpt on gamely towards fin* **13/8**[2]

2 *½* **Five Diamonds** 3-9-0 0 .... DanielTudhope 1 67+
(William Haggas) *dwlt and in rr: hdwy 1/2-way: chsd ldrs on outer 2f out: rdn over 1f out: styd on wl to chal ins fnl f: kpt on* **5/4**[1]

02 **3** *¾* **Elena**[17] 3598 3-9-0 0 .... PJMcDonald 5 65
(Charles Hills) *led 3f: cl up: rdn along 2f out: drvn and ev ch over 1f out: kpt on same pce ins fnl f* **7/2**[3]

6 **4** *1 ¼* **Oblate**[118] 930 3-9-0 0 .... KieranO'Neill 6 62?
(Robyn Brisland) *trckd ldrs: hdwy 3f out: chsd ldng pair wl over 1f out: sn rdn: drvn and kpt on same pce fnl f* **66/1**

64 **5** *5* **Cuba Ruba**[8] 3932 3-9-5 0 .... DavidAllan 3 56
(Tim Easterby) *hld up in rr: hdwy 3f out: rdn along over 2f out: kpt on same pce* **25/1**

04 **6** *1 ¾* **Heart In Havana**[22] 3412 3-9-5 0 .... NathanEvans 7 52
(Michael Easterby) *hld up towards rr: pushed along and hdwy 3f out: rdn and kpt on same pce fnl 2f* **50/1**

0 **7** *10* **Reine Magnifique (FR)**[25] 3324 3-9-0 0 .... GeorgeWood 2 24
(James Fanshawe) *t.k.h: chsd ldng pair: rdn along over 2f out: sn wknd (jockey said filly ran green)* **20/1**

1m 51.78s (5.38) **Going Correction** +0.35s/f (Good) **7 Ran SP% 116.8**
Speed ratings (Par 99): **87,86,85,84,79 77,67**
CSF £4.07 TOTE £2.50: £1.10, £1.40; EX 4.70 Trifecta £9.20.
Owner Hadi Al-Tajir **Bred** Shadwell Estate Company Limited **Trained** Lambourn, Berks

FOCUS
Add 7yds. The going was changed to soft before this race. Although the winner didn't quite make all like the majority of previous winners on the card, he was in the lead on the rail most of the way - he's been rated similarly to his debut.

4212 GO RACING IN YORKSHIRE FUTURE STARS APPRENTICE H'CAP 5f
5:00 (5:01) (Class 6) (0-65,64) 3-Y-O+
£3,428 (£1,020; £509; £300; £300; £300) **Stalls** Low

Form RPR

3413 **1** **Ginger Jam**[38] 2846 4-9-5 **64** .... IzzyClifton(7) 14 71+
(Nigel Tinkler) *midfield on outer: hdwy over 1f out: str run ent fnl f: led last 50yds* **11/2**[2]

2025 **2** *1 ½* **Pearl Noir**[8] 3933 9-9-2 **54** ....(b) TheodoreLadd 10 56
(Scott Dixon) *led: rdn along wl over 1f out: drvn ent fnl f: hdd and no ex last 50yds (vet said gelding lost it's left hind shoe)* **16/1**

3040 **3** *hd* **Astrophysics**[5] 4037 7-9-5 **57** .... BenSanderson 15 58
(Lynn Siddall) *swtchd rt s and in tch: hdwy to chse ldrs over 2f out: rdn over 1f out: drvn and ev ch jst ins fnl f: kpt on* **20/1**

0630 **4** *nk* **Raquelle (IRE)**[22] 3417 3-8-1 **45** ....(p) RhiainIngram 11 43
(Tim Easterby) *prom: cl up 2f out: rdn over 1f out: drvn and ev ch ins fnl f: kpt on same pce towards fin* **33/1**

3330 **5** *¾* **Le Manege Enchante (IRE)**[7] 3975 6-8-5 **46** ....(v) AledBeech(3) 8 43
(Derek Shaw) *in rr and sn rdn along: hdwy wl over 1f out: kpt on u.p fnl f* **25/1**

4312 **6** *½* **Viking Way (IRE)**[13] 3738 4-8-7 **52** .... LukeCatton(7) 4 47
(Olly Williams) *in tch: effrt 2f out and sn rdn: drvn and kpt on fnl f: n.d* **5/2**[1]

3005 **7** *shd* **One One Seven (IRE)**[29] 3159 3-8-6 **53** .... KieranSchofield(3) 3 46
(Antony Brittain) *midfield on inner: rdn along and hdwy wl over 1f out: kpt on fnl f* **7/1**

0410 **8** *hd* **Optimickstickhill**[7] 3975 4-8-12 **50** ....(b) DylanHogan 5 44
(Scott Dixon) *chsd ldrs: rdn along wl over 1f out: drvn and kpt on same pce fnl f* **13/2**

-561 **9** *nk* **Oriental Splendour (IRE)**[27] 3213 7-8-10 **48** ....(p) ConnorMurtagh 2 41
(Ruth Carr) *prom: cl up 2f out: rdn and ev ch over 1f out: drvn ent fnl f: wknd* **6/1**[3]

053- **10** *hd* **Alotabottle**[251] 8323 3-8-13 **64** .... ZakWheatley(7) 6 54
(Declan Carroll) *towards rr: hdwy 2f out: rdn along over 1f out: drvn and no imp ent fnl f* **9/1**

0-00 **11** *½* **Shall We Begin (IRE)**[38] 2823 3-8-6 **50** .... AndrewBreslin 9 39
(Michael Easterby) *dwlt and hmpd s: bhd: hdwy 2f out: sn rdn: kpt on fnl f (jockey said filly missed the break)* **25/1**

-654 **12** *shd* **Newgate Angel**[36] 2908 3-7-10 **47** ....(p) LukeBacon(7) 12 35
(Tony Coyle) *wnt lft s: chsd ldrs on outer: rdn along 2f out: wknd appr fnl f* **25/1**

00-5 **13** *½* **Robbian**[82] 1554 8-8-3 **46** .... RhonaPindar(5) 1 34
(Charles Smith) *chsd ldrs on inner: rdn along wl over 1f out: wknd ent fnl f (jockey said gelding was denied a clear run in the closing stages)* **25/1**

0000 **14** *5* **Bagatino**[7] 3969 3-7-9 **46** ....(t) JessicaAnderson(7) 7 14
(Declan Carroll) *in rr: rdn along stmbld 2f out: nvr a factor* **50/1**

1330 **15** *4 ½* **Encoded (IRE)**[13] 3723 6-8-9 **47** .... PaulaMuir 13 1
(Lynn Siddall) *a towards rr* **50/1**

1m 4.2s (1.30) **Going Correction** +0.35s/f (Good)
WFA 3 from 4yo+ 6lb **15 Ran SP% 127.0**
Speed ratings (Par 101): **103,100,100,99,98 97,97,97,96,96 95,95,94,86,79**
CSF £84.53 CT £1674.72 TOTE £7.00: £2.90, £4.10, £7.40; EX 89.80 Trifecta £1749.30.
Owner Walter Veti **Bred** Bearstone Stud Ltd **Trained** Langton, N Yorks

FOCUS
An ordinary sprint handicap, and a rare winner from off the pace on the card.
T/Plt: £12.70 to a £1 stake. Pool: £66,342.99 - 3,802.41 winning units. T/Qpdt: £7.30 to a £1 stake. Pool: £5,311.15 - 533.77 winning units. **Joe Rowntree**

3961

BRIGHTON (L-H)
Tuesday, June 25

OFFICIAL GOING: Good to soft (good in places; 7.1)
Wind: light, across Weather: warm, muggy

4213 DAVE & DEB 25TH ANNIVERSARY H'CAP 5f 60y
2:15 (2:15) (Class 4) (0-80,80) 3-Y-O+
£5,530 (£1,645; £822; £411; £300; £300) **Stalls** Centre

Form RPR

-564 **1** **Whataguy**[10] 3838 3-9-0 **77** ....(p[1]) MeganNicholls(3) 3 82
(Paul Nicholls) *dwlt: towards rr: rdn over 2f out: hung lft but clsd to chse ldrs and swtchd rt 1f out: styd on wl to ld fnl 75yds (jockey said gelding hung left-handed)* **5/1**

0531 **2** *1 ¼* **A Sure Welcome**[17] 3576 5-9-10 **78** ....(p) RyanTate 7 81
(John Spearing) *midfield: effrt over 2f out: styd on wl u.p ins fnl f: wnt 2nd last strides* **11/4**[1]

4130 **3** *hd* **Shamshon (IRE)**[7] 3963 8-9-12 **80** .... JasonWatson 6 82
(Stuart Williams) *chsd clr ldng pair: effrt over 2f out: clsd and hung lft over 1f out: clsd to chse ldrs ins fnl f: kpt on (jockey said gelding hung left-handed down the camber)* **3/1**[2]

2003 **4** *nk* **Archimedes (IRE)**[5] 4027 6-8-7 **61** oh2 ....(tp) PhilDennis 8 62
(David C Griffiths) *broke fast: led tl over 4f out: styd w ldr and clr tl led again over 2f out: rdn 2f out: hdd and no ex 75yds out: lost 2 pls last strides* **10/1**

0003 **5** *2 ¼* **Crystal Deauville (FR)**[7] 3967 4-8-4 **65** ....(v) CierenFallon(7) 1 58
(Gay Kelleway) *taken down early: sn w ldr and led over 4f out: hdd over 2f out and sn rdn: no ex jst ins fnl f: wknd wl ins fnl f* **10/3**[3]

-405 **6** *3 ¾* **Jashma (IRE)**[21] 3443 5-9-11 **79** ....(b) ShaneKelly 5 59
(Richard Hughes) *s.i.s: a in rr: effrt over 2f out: hung lft u.p and no hdwy over 1f out: wknd ins fnl f* **9/1**

1m 2.27s (-0.73) **Going Correction** +0.025s/f (Good)
WFA 3 from 4yo+ 6lb **6 Ran SP% 110.5**
Speed ratings (Par 105): **106,104,103,103,99 93**
CSF £18.45 CT £44.61 TOTE £6.30: £3.10, £2.80; EX 20.90 Trifecta £85.30.
Owner Heal, Nicholls & Osborne **Bred** James Patton **Trained** Ditcheat, Somerset

FOCUS
A competitive sprint handicap in which the pair who disputed an overly strong pace eventually set things up for a trio of closers. The winner rates back to his 2yo best.

4214 PHILIP BYRNE 70TH BIRTHDAY CELEBRATION NOVICE AUCTION STKS 5f 215y
2:45 (2:46) (Class 5) 2-Y-O **£3,752** (£1,116; £557; £278) **Stalls** Centre

Form RPR

2 **1** **Bredenbury (IRE)**[12] 3776 2-8-12 0 .... StevieDonohoe 3 80+
(David Simcock) *travelled strly thrght: sn led: shkn up: rn green but readily asserted wl over 1f out: r.o strly: v easily* **8/11**[1]

31 **2** *3 ½* **Faldetta**[22] 3405 2-8-12 .... GeorgiaDobie(7) 1 74
(Eve Johnson Houghton) *led early: sn hdd and trckd ldrs after 2f: n.m.r over 2f out: sn swtchd rt and rdn: chsd wnr clr over 1f out: kpt on but no imp* **11/4**[2]

0 **3** *7* **Luscifer**[17] 3595 2-9-3 0 .... ShaneKelly 2 49
(Richard Hughes) *stdd s: t.k.h: hld up wl in tch in midfield: rdn 2f out: sn outpcd and wl btn 1f out: snatched modest 3rd last strides* **14/1**

5 4 nk **Al Verde**[14] 3695 2-9-3 0 TomMarquand 5 48
(Ali Stronge) *t.k.h: chsd ldrs tl clsd to press ldr over 4f out: rdn over 2f out: outpcd: lost 2nd and btn over 1f out: wknd ins fnl f* **5/1**[3]

1m 12.19s (1.09) **Going Correction** +0.025s/f (Good) 4 Ran SP% **107.9**
Speed ratings (Par 93): **93,88,79,78**
CSF £2.96 TOTE £1.50; EX 2.90 Trifecta £8.80.
Owner The Khat Partnership **Bred** Rabbah Bloodstock Limited **Trained** Newmarket, Suffolk

FOCUS
A steadily run novice in which the winner was in command from a long way out.

4215 NATALIE NAYLOR MEMORIAL H'CAP 1m 1f 207y
3:15 (3:16) (Class 6) (0-65,64) 3-Y-O+
£3,105 (£924; £461; £300; £300; £300) **Stalls** High

Form RPR

0310 **1** **Couldn't Could She**[26] 3276 4-9-11 **60** CharlieBennett 5 70
(Adam West) *hld up in last pair: hdwy over 4f out: trckd ldrs and edgd out rt over 2f out: drvn to ld over 1f out: kpt on wl ins fnl f* **16/1**

-121 **2** 1 1/4 **Seaborn (IRE)**[8] 3941 5-9-6 **62** WilliamCarver(7) 6 70
(Patrick Chamings) *chsd ldrs: effrt and chsd wnr over 2f out: ev ch u.p over 1f out: chsd wnr and kpt on same pce ins fnl f* **6/4**[1]

5151 **3** 4 **Tigerfish (IRE)**[18] 3537 5-9-7 **63** (p) MarcoGhiani(7) 9 63
(William Stone) *in tch in midfield: clsd 5f out: pressed ldr 4f out tl led and hung lft over 2f out: hdd and no ex u.p over 1f out: wknd ins fnl f* **6/1**[3]

-562 **4** 3 1/2 **Tartlette**[22] 3407 3-9-0 **61** RobertHavlin 11 54
(Hughie Morrison) *dwlt: sn rcvrd and in tch in midfield: clsd to chse ldrs over 2f out: outpcd u.p over 1f out: wl hld and plugged on same pce fnl f* **3/1**[2]

4-22 **5** 1 1/2 **Light Of Air (FR)**[56] 2233 6-9-6 **62** (b) LouisGaroghan(7) 2 53
(Gary Moore) *hld up in last pair: outpcd and swtchd rt 3f out: shkn up and hung lft over 2f out: plugged on but no threat to ldrs after* **7/1**

1550 **6** nse **Contingency Fee**[12] 3778 4-9-6 **62** (p) GraceMcEntee(7) 8 52
(Phil McEntee) *chsd ldr tl led 4f out: hdd and rdn over 2f out: sn outpcd and wl hld over 1f out* **20/1**

3106 **7** 1 3/4 **Fenjal (IRE)**[18] 3538 3-9-2 **63** (b) ShaneKelly 1 50
(Gay Kelleway) *led: hdd 4f out: losing pl and hung rt 3f out: wl hld fnl 2f* **50/1**

0060 **8** 1 1/4 **Dutch Melody**[25] 3296 5-8-3 **45** VictorSantos(7) 10 30
(Lucinda Egerton) *in tch in midfield tl dropped to last pair over 4f out: swtchd rt and no rspnse to press over 2f out: wl hld fnl 2f (trainer said mare was unsuited by the ground and would prefer a faster surface)* **66/1**

4-40 **9** 2 1/2 **Irish Art (IRE)**[17] 3594 3-9-3 **64** (b[1]) StevieDonohoe 7 44
(David Lanigan) *in tch towards rr: struggling u.p and outpcd over 2f out: wl hld fnl 2f (vet said gelding lost its left-fore shoe)* **12/1**

0/00 **10** 39 **Machiavelian Storm (IRE)**[32] 3038 7-8-10 **45** (p) HollieDoyle 4
(Richard Mitchell) *chsd ldrs tl 5f out: sn lost pl and bhd 3f out: t.o (jockey said mare stopped quickly)* **100/1**

2m 4.15s (-0.85) **Going Correction** +0.025s/f (Good)
WFA 3 from 4yo+ 12lb 10 Ran SP% **114.6**
Speed ratings (Par 101): **104,103,99,97,95 95,94,93,91,60**
CSF £39.30 CT £169.12 TOTE £20.70: £3.60, £1.30, £1.30; EX 59.60 Trifecta £265.20.
Owner Ross Deacon & Partners **Bred** D R Botterill & E Boumans **Trained** Epsom, Surrey

FOCUS
There was a fair pace on in this moderate handicap, and the form seems sound enough, with the winner rated back to last year's level.

4216 MERCI POUR L'AVENTURE XAVIER DE CARNIERE AMATEUR RIDERS' H'CAP 1m 3f 198y
3:45 (3:51) (Class 6) (0-65,64) 4-Y-O+ **£2,994** (£928; £464; £300; £300) **Stalls** High

Form RPR

3254 **1** **Sigrid Nansen**[17] 3571 4-9-6 **45** (p) MissHannahWelch(3) 5 59
(Alexandra Dunn) *mounted on the crse: prom in chsng gp: clsd to trck ldrs 1/2-way: led on inner and travelling strly over 2f out: readily wnt clr and styd on wl ins fnl f: v easily* **13/2**[3]

5606 **2** 6 **Orobas (IRE)**[25] 3297 7-10-9 **59** (v) MrSimonWalker 11 63
(Lucinda Egerton) *pressed ldr and clr of field tl 1/2-way: rdn and ev ch over 2f out: outpcd by wnr and edgd lft over 1f out: pluged on same pce ins fnl f* **12/1**

5465 **3** 1 1/4 **Roy Rocket (FR)**[18] 3537 9-10-9 **59** MrRossBirkett 6 61+
(John Berry) *stdd after s: hld up in rr: clsd and swtchd rt over 2f out: styd on u.p fr over 1f out: wnt 3rd wl ins fnl f: no threat to wnr* **7/1**

300- **4** 1/2 **Rose Crown**[259] 8079 5-10-7 **62** MissNellMcCann(5) 8 64
(Mick Channon) *midfield: clsd and wl in tch 1/2-way: chsd ldrs over 4f out: pushed along and unable qck over 1f out: no ch w wnr and one pce fnl f* **10/1**

4600 **5** 1 1/4 **Ezanak (IRE)**[38] 2819 6-11-0 **64** (vt) MissSerenaBrotherton 2 64
(Michael Appleby) *t.k.h: chsd clr ldng pair tl clsd to trck ldrs 1/2-way: effrt and shifted lft over 1f out: outpcd over 1f out: no ch w wnr and plugged on fnl f* **4/1**[1]

5336 **5** dht **Seventii**[8] 3941 5-9-4 **45** MrGeorgeEddery(5) 3 45
(Robert Eddery) *midfield: clsd and wl in tch 1/2-way: effrt u.p over 2f out: sn outpcd: wl hld and plugged on same pce fr over 1f out* **4/1**[1]

0003 **7** 3 3/4 **Happy Ending (IRE)**[10] 3834 4-9-9 **50** (p[1]) MrMatthewFielding(5) 4 44
(Seamus Mullins) *dwlt and pushed along early: midfield: clsd and wl in tch 1/2-way: u.p and outpcd over 2f out: sn wl btn* **6/1**[2]

-006 **8** 4 1/2 **Mahna Mahna (IRE)**[28] 3186 5-9-4 **45** MissAntoniaPeck(5) 9 31
(David W Drinkwater) *led tl rdn and hdd over 2f out: sn btn and wknd over 1f out* **33/1**

6620 **9** 6 **Strictly Art (IRE)**[28] 3175 6-10-4 **61** MissEmmaJack(7) 12 38
(Alan Bailey) *racd wd: midfield: clsd and wl in tch 1/2-way: lost pl over 4f out: bhd and no ch whn hung lft 1f out* **10/1**

00 **10** 9 **Thunderhooves**[7] 3966 4-9-3 **46** (t) MrThomasMiles(7) 10 8
(John Ryan) *dwlt: a towards rr: clsd and wl in tch 1/2-way: u.p and struggling 3f out: wl bhd fnl 2f* **50/1**

3000 **11** 3 1/2 **Punkawallah**[19] 3511 5-10-5 **62** (tp) MrTambyWelch(7) 7 19
(Alexandra Dunn) *midfield: clsd and wl in tch midfield: lost pl u.p 3f out: wl bhd fnl 2f: burst blood vessel (vet said gelding bled from the nose)* **16/1**

424/ **12** 22 **Los Cerritos (SWI)**[47] 1196 7-9-10 **53** (tp w) MrsDawnScott(7) 1
(Milton Harris) *a last trio: clsd and in tch 1/2-way: struggling 5f out: t.o fnl 2f* **50/1**

2m 35.69s (-0.31) **Going Correction** +0.025s/f (Good) 12 Ran SP% **118.7**
Speed ratings (Par 101): **102,98,97,96,96 96,93,90,86,80 78,63**
CSF £81.24 CT £565.21 TOTE £6.60: £2.10, £3.80, £2.10; EX 83.00 Trifecta £814.20.
Owner West Buckland Bloodstock Ltd **Bred** Hunscote Stud **Trained** West Buckland, Somerset

FOCUS
They went an uneven pace in this weak amateur riders' handicap. The winner rates near last year's peak.

4217 DOVES LIVE HERE 26 JULY H'CAP 7f 211y
4:15 (4:18) (Class 6) (0-55,55) 3-Y-O+
£3,105 (£924; £461; £300; £300; £300) **Stalls** Centre

Form RPR

/50- **1** **Miss Recycled**[250] 8335 4-9-2 **47** TomMarquand 7 53
(Michael Madgwick) *hld up in tch last quartet: effrt over 2f out: hdwy u.p over 1f out: chsd wnr ins fnl f: r.o to ld last stride* **100/1**

0302 **2** shd **Joyful Dream (IRE)**[22] 3410 5-8-12 **46** (b) MeganNicholls(3) 14 52
(John Butler) *hld up in tch in midfield: swtchd rt and hdwy over 2f out: pushed into ld and hung lft 1f out: sn rdn and hung to inner rail: kpt on u.p: hdd last stride* **7/2**[1]

0026 **3** 1 3/4 **Princess Florence (IRE)**[7] 3964 3-8-0 **48** ow1 CierenFallon(7) 3 48
(John Ryan) *stdd after s: hld up in last quartet: clsd whn short of room over 2f out: hung lft over 1f out: hdwy and edgd out rt 1f out: kpt on u.p ins fnl f (jockey said filly ran too free in the early stages, hung left-handed in the straight and was denied a clear run approximately 2f out)* **16/1**

0000 **4** 1 1/4 **Middlescence (IRE)**[13] 3716 5-9-1 **53** (b[1]) VictorSantos(7) 6 52
(Lucinda Egerton) *chsd ldr tl rdn to ld wl over 1f out: hdd 1f out: no ex and wknd ins fnl f* **14/1**

2-03 **5** 2 **Luxford**[33] 3006 5-9-5 **50** HectorCrouch 2 45
(Gary Moore) *t.k.h early: chsd ldrs: effrt on inner over 2f out: drvn and pressing ldrs 2f out: short of room 1f out: sn outpcd and wknd ins fnl f* **9/2**[3]

3040 **6** 1 **Sweet Nature (IRE)**[28] 3187 4-9-10 **55** LiamJones 10 48
(Laura Mongan) *in tch in midfield: effrt over 2f out: nt clr run and swtchd rt over 1f out: kpt on u.p ins fnl f but no threat to ldrs* **33/1**

2310 **7** 1/2 **Rock In Society (IRE)**[25] 3304 4-9-4 **54** DarraghKeenan(5) 1 45
(John Butler) *sn pushed into ld: rdn jst over 2f out: hdd wl over 1f out: no ex 1f out and wknd ins fnl f* **8/1**

00-0 **8** 1 **Harbour Times (IRE)**[41] 2734 3-8-7 **48** JoeyHaynes 8 35
(Patrick Chamings) *in tch in midfield: effrt ent fnl 2f: unable qck and no imp over 1f out: wknd ins fnl f* **20/1**

0504 **9** shd **Jailbreak (IRE)**[14] 3697 3-8-8 **49** RoystonFfrench 9 36
(Richard Hughes) *in tch in midfield: effrt and edgd rt over 2f out: carried lft and no imp over 1f out: wl hld and plugged on same pce ins fnl f* **4/1**[2]

-004 **10** 1 1/2 **Hidden Stash**[7] 3966 5-9-1 **46** oh1 (p) HollieDoyle 5 31+
(William Stone) *midfield: pushed along 5f out: no imp and wl hld whn nt clr run and hmpd over 1f out: swtchd rt and no imp fnl f* **7/1**

000 **11** 3 **Inspirational (IRE)**[31] 3080 3-8-11 **52** LiamKeniry 15 28
(Ed Dunlop) *racd in last quartet: effrt ent fnl 2f: no rspnse and wl hld over 1f out* **25/1**

200- **12** 1 **Duke Of Yorkie (IRE)**[262] 7995 3-8-11 **52** CharlieBennett 13 26
(Adam West) *a in rr: pushed along over 4f out: outpcd over 2f out: no ch fnl 2f* **33/1**

0002 **13** 1 3/4 **Song Of Summer**[12] 3781 4-8-8 **46** oh1 (tp) GraceMcEntee(7) 16 18
(Phil McEntee) *wd: in tch in midfield: rdn and nudged rt over 2f out: sn struggling: bhd ins fnl f* **33/1**

0040 **14** 17 **Cat Royale (IRE)**[25] 3298 6-9-4 **49** (b) DannyBrock 12
(John Butler) *midfield: u.p and edgd rt over 2f out: lost pl and wl bhd whn eased ins fnl f* **16/1**

1m 36.76s (-0.14) **Going Correction** +0.025s/f (Good)
WFA 3 from 4yo+ 10lb 14 Ran SP% **120.9**
Speed ratings (Par 101): **101,100,99,97,95 94,94,93,93,91 88,87,86,69**
CSF £413.27 CT £6165.05 TOTE £137.50: £24.80, £1.60, £4.40; EX 748.80.
Owner Recycled Products Limited **Bred** Recycled Products Limited **Trained** Denmead, Hants

FOCUS
This ordinary handicap was run to suit the closers and there was a shock, improved winner.

4218 RAG'N'BONE MAN LIVE HERE 27 JULY H'CAP 6f 210y
4:45 (4:48) (Class 5) (0-70,70) 3-Y-O
£3,752 (£1,116; £557; £300; £300; £300) **Stalls** Centre

Form RPR

4061 **1** **Global Destination (IRE)**[12] 3764 3-9-6 **69** GeraldMosse 2 73+
(Ed Dunlop) *led for 1f: trckd ldrs: ev ch over 2f out: rdn to ld wl over 1f out: styd on and a doing enough ins fnl f: pushed out towards fin* **11/10**[1]

3204 **2** 3/4 **Tarrzan (IRE)**[15] 3645 3-8-4 **53** ow1 LiamJones 3 54
(John Gallagher) *t.k.h: swtchd rt 5f out and sn chsng ldr: rdn and ev ch over 2f out: kpt on u.p but a hld ins fnl f* **20/1**

320 **3** 3/4 **Moveonup (IRE)**[9] 3884 3-9-0 **70** CierenFallon(7) 6 69
(Gay Kelleway) *t.k.h: led after 1f: rdn over 2f out: hdd wl over 1f out: kpt on same pce u.p ins fnl f (jockey said gelding ran too free in the early stages)* **13/2**[3]

432- **4** nse **Just Later**[187] 9636 3-9-6 **69** TomMarquand 4 68
(Amy Murphy) *stmbld leaving stalls: wl in tch: effrt over 2f out: kpt on u.p ins fnl f: nt quite enough pce to threaten ldrs (jockey said gelding stumbled badly leaving the stalls)* **5/1**[2]

-043 **5** 1/2 **Miss Elsa**[18] 3532 3-8-13 **69** GeorgiaDobie(7) 5 66
(Eve Johnson Houghton) *t.k.h: effrt ent fnl 2f: edgd lft u.p over 1f out: kpt on ins fnl f: nt enough pce to threaten (vet said filly sustained a laceration to her left-hind pastern)* **7/1**

0-30 **6** nse **So Claire**[14] 3697 3-8-8 **57** HollieDoyle 7 54
(William Muir) *in tch in rr: pushed along over 4f out: drvn over 2f out: kpt on ins fnl f: nvr threatened ldrs* **13/2**[3]

1m 24.25s (0.45) **Going Correction** +0.025s/f (Good) 6 Ran SP% **108.2**
Speed ratings (Par 99): **98,97,96,96,95 95**
CSF £22.48 TOTE £1.80: £1.40, £3.00; EX 15.90 Trifecta £60.00.
Owner Dr Johnny Hon **Bred** Norelands Bloodstock **Trained** Newmarket, Suffolk

FOCUS
A steady pace meant that they finished bunched and those held up weren't seen to best effect, but there's little doubt the winner was full value for it and this rates another slight step up.

4219 SKY SPORTS RACING ON SKY 415 H'CAP 5f 215y
5:15 (5:15) (Class 6) (0-60,57) 3-Y-O+
£3,105 (£924; £461; £300; £300; £300) **Stalls** Centre

Form RPR

6005 **1** **Nervous Nerys (IRE)**[15] 3645 3-8-0 **45** AmeliaGlass(7) 8 49
(Alex Hales) *in tch in midfield: effrt and hdwy over 1f out: pushed along and chsd ldr ins fnl f: kpt on wl to ld towards fin: hld on* **20/1**

2304 **2** shd **Pearl Spectre (USA)**[13] 3744 8-9-5 **57** (v) GraceMcEntee(7) 7 63
(Phil McEntee) *in tch in midfield: effrt u.p over 2f out: hdwy u.p to chse ldrs 1f out: ev ch towards fin: kpt on: jst hld* **6/1**[3]

6-30 **3** ½ **Cool Strutter (IRE)**[35] 2924 7-9-4 **49**....(p) RyanTate 1 53
(John Spearing) *led: rdn 2f out and kicked on: drvn over 1f out: hdd and no ex towards fin* **8/1**

0452 **4** ¾ **Toolatetodelegate**[18] 3527 5-8-13 **47**....(tp) MeganNicholls(3) 10 49
(Brian Barr) *hld up in tch in midfield: effrt over 2f out: hdwy and edging lft over 1f out: chsng ldrs whn nt clr run and swtchd rt ins fnl f: kpt on u.p towards fin* **7/2[2]**

00-3 **5** 2½ **Alyx Vance**[10] 3836 3-8-12 **57**.... MarcoGhiani(7) 14 49
(Lydia Pearce) *racd in last quartet: effrt over 2f out: no imp tl styd on wl to pass btn horses ins fnl f: nvr trbld ldrs* **28/1**

0640 **6** ½ **Knockout Blow**[92] 1328 4-9-10 **55**.... HectorCrouch 3 48
(John E Long) *chsd ldng trio: swtchd rt and effrt to chse ldr 2f out: no imp u.p 1f out: lost 2nd ins fnl f: wknd towards fin* **13/2**

00-R **7** 1 **Free Talkin**[158] 293 4-9-0 **45**.... HollieDoyle 13 35
(Michael Attwater) *mounted on crse: s.i.s: racd in last quartet: effrt ent fnl 2f: sme hdwy and edgd lft over 1f out: kpt on ins fnl f: nvr trbld ldrs* **50/1**

4003 **8** 1 **Camanche Grey (IRE)**[13] 3723 8-8-9 **47**....(b) VictorSantos(7) 4 34
(Lucinda Egerton) *mounted on the crse and taken down early: chsd ldrs: c towards centre and rdn over 2f out: hung lft and lost pl over 1f out: wknd ins fnl f* **16/1**

040- **9** ¾ **Clipsham Tiger (IRE)**[209] 9284 3-8-7 **45**.... RoystonFfrench 5 27
(Michael Appleby) *chsd ldr tl 2f out: unable qck u.p over 1f out: wknd ins fnl f* **10/1**

0000 **10** 2¾ **Hornby**[22] 3404 4-9-0 **45**.... CharlieBennett 12 21
(Michael Attwater) *taken down early: racd in last quartet: nvr involved* **66/1**

00-0 **11** 1 **Birthday Girl (IRE)**[28] 3187 4-8-7 **45**....(b[1]) CierenFallon(7) 2 18
(Amanda Perrett) *midfield but nvr on terms: u.p wl over 2f out: no prog: lost pl and bhd fnl f* **25/1**

-126 **12** 1¼ **Olaudah**[18] 3527 5-9-4 **56**.... GeorgiaDobie(7) 11 25
(Henry Candy) *taken down early: in tch in midfield: effrt jst over 2f out: hung lft and no hdwy over 1f out: wknd fnl f* **3/1[1]**

400 **13** 14 **Kiowa**[47] 2550 3-8-9 **47** ow2.... DannyBrock 6
(Philip McBride) *s.i.s: a bhd: lost tch over 2f out: eased (jockey said gelding moved poorly)* **16/1**

1m 11.12s (0.02) **Going Correction** +0.025s/f (Good)
WFA 3 from 4yo+ 7lb **13** Ran SP% **122.3**
Speed ratings (Par 101): **100,99,99,98,94 94,92,91,90,86 85,83,65**
CSF £133.82 CT £1100.42 TOTE £20.50: £4.90, £2.70, £2.00; EX 148.30 Trifecta £1658.00.
Owner Equinox Racing **Bred** Mrs B Gardiner **Trained** Edgcote, Northamptonshire

FOCUS
A low-grade sprint in which the tight finish was dominated by a pair that came wide and late from off a strong pace. The third, who was in front for most of the way, shaped best.
T/Plt: £126.70 to a £1 stake. Pool: £70,661.12 - 406.96 winning units. T/Qpdt: £33.00 to a £1 stake. Pool: £8,517.69 - 190.56 winning units. **Steve Payne**

3760 NEWBURY (L-H)
Tuesday, June 25

OFFICIAL GOING: Good to soft (7.0)
Wind: Light, behind Weather: Cloudy becoming bright, humid

4220 INDZINE APPRENTICE H'CAP 1m 3f
4:55 (4:57) (Class 5) (0-70,70) 4-Y-0+
£3,752 (£1,116; £557; £300; £300; £300) **Stalls Low**

Form RPR

2021 **1** **Gas Monkey**[56] 2259 4-9-5 **68**....(h) SeanKirrane(5) 4 84
(Julia Feilden) *trckd ldrs gng wl: clsd to ld 2f out: pushed along and sn drew rt away* **11/2[2]**

144 **2** 8 **Banksy's Art**[18] 3537 4-9-0 **63**....(p[1]) GeorgeBass(5) 11 65
(Mick Channon) *hld up in rr: rdn and prog over 2f out: styd on over 1f out to take 2nd ins fnl f: no ch w wnr* **14/1**

0003 **3** 1¼ **Gawdawpalin (IRE)**[12] 3766 6-9-10 **68**.... SebastianWoods 6 68
(Sylvester Kirk) *trckd ldr: led 3f out: sn rdn: hdd wl over 1f out: no ch w wnr sn after: lost 2nd ins fnl f* **10/1**

650 **4** ½ **Lawyersgunsn'money**[64] 1989 4-9-3 **61**.... SeamusCronin 13 60
(Roger Teal) *hld up wl in rr: promising hdwy gng wl 3f out: rdn w ch of a pl over 1f out: one pce after* **33/1**

0642 **5** 2 **Barca (USA)**[34] 2970 5-8-12 **59**.... JonathanFisher(3) 1 55
(Marcus Tregoning) *wl in tch: rdn over 2f out: one pce and nvr able to chal* **5/1[1]**

2011 **6** 2½ **Rail Dancer**[41] 2738 7-9-3 **66**....(v) GavinAshton(5) 15 57
(Shaun Keightley) *hld up in midfield: prog 3f out: rdn over 2f out: no imp on ldrs over 1f out: fdd* **7/1[3]**

0-24 **7** 1¾ **Champs De Reves**[41] 2732 4-9-12 **70**.... PoppyBridgwater 3 58
(Michael Blake) *t.k.h: hld up in tch: rdn and effrt over 2f out: sn no prog* **9/1**

26-0 **8** 1½ **Principia**[45] 2626 4-9-2 **63**.... Pierre-LouisJamin(3) 14 49
(Adam West) *disp 2nd pl to 3f out: sn rdn and steadily wknd* **33/1**

1-42 **9** 1 **Love And Be Loved**[17] 3572 5-9-6 **67**.... ScottMcCullagh(3) 8 51
(John Flint) *had to be led to post and mounted at s: led to 3f out: wknd 2f out* **9/1**

23-6 **10** 1¼ **Go Fox**[56] 2259 4-9-2 **67**.... GianlucaSanna(7) 2 49
(Tom Clover) *chsd ldrs: urged along and wknd over 2f out* **12/1**

2140 **11** ¾ **Affluence (IRE)**[29] 2617 4-8-8 **59**.... JacobClark(7) 16 40
(Martin Smith) *hld up in rr: shkn up and no real prog on outer over 2f out* **12/1**

0-40 **12** 2¼ **Kismat**[26] 3267 4-8-13 **60**.... TobyEley(3) 9 37
(Alan King) *chsd ldrs: rdn over 3f out: sn lost pl and btn (jockey said filly suffered interference leaving the stalls)* **20/1**

-00R **13** 29 **Camakasi (IRE)**[14] 3700 8-9-2 **65**.... AngusVilliers(5) 5
(Ali Stronge) *v rel to r: ct up after 4f: wknd 4f out: t.o* **50/1**

30-1 **P** **Raven's Raft (IRE)**[64] 1988 4-9-1 **62**.... LauraCoughlan(3) 10
(David Loughnane) *in tch: sddle slipped bdly and p.u 4f out (jockey said saddle slipped)* **11/1**

2m 20.27s (-2.93) **Going Correction** -0.05s/f (Good) **14** Ran SP% **116.6**
Speed ratings (Par 103): **108,102,101,100,99 97,96,95,94,93 93,91,70,**
CSF £74.51 CT £752.57 TOTE £5.20: £2.40, £4.00, £3.40; EX 84.30 Trifecta £573.70.
Owner Newmarket Equine Tours Racing Club **Bred** Julia Feilden **Trained** Exning, Suffolk

FOCUS
1mm of rain overnight resulted in the ground being changed to good to soft from good to firm, good, and it looked to be riding just on the easy side. One-way traffic in this modest apprentice handicap, as the winner improved again.

4221 WIN RACES WITH JONATHAN PORTMAN FILLIES' NOVICE AUCTION STKS (PLUS 10 RACE) (DIV I) 6f
5:30 (5:31) (Class 4) 2-Y-O
£4,787 (£1,424; £711; £355) **Stalls High**

Form RPR

1 **Special Secret** 2-8-10 0.... CharlesBishop 5 80+
(Eve Johnson Houghton) *wl in tch: plld out and pushed along 2f out: clsd to ld jst over 1f out: shkn up and drew clr fnl f* **9/2[2]**

2 4½ **Mild Illusion (IRE)** 2-8-8 0.... RobHornby 7 65+
(Jonathan Portman) *dwlt: pushed along to stay in tch in rr: gng bttr fr 1/2-way: prog over 1f out: styd on steadily to take 2nd last 75yds* **12/1**

4631 **3** 1¾ **Ocasio Cortez (IRE)**[17] 3595 2-8-13 0.... SeamusCronin(5) 4 69
(Richard Hannon) *trckd ldrs: gng easily 2f out: rdn to ld briefly over 1f out: sn outpcd by wnr: one pce and lost 2nd last 75yds* **2/1[1]**

4 **4** nk **Hashtagmetoo (USA)**[17] 3578 2-9-0 0.... NicolaCurrie 2 64
(Jamie Osborne) *in tch: pushed along and dropped to last pair 2f out: prog over 1f out: styd on fnl f and nrly snatched 3rd* **10/1[3]**

5 1¾ **Carmel** 2-8-8 0.... OisinMurphy 6 53
(Archie Watson) *pressed ldrs tl fdd over 1f out* **2/1[1]**

6 **6** 2 **Hollywood Waltz**[15] 3652 2-8-8 0.... SilvestreDeSousa 11 47
(Mick Channon) *led against nr side rail: hdd over 1f out: sn wknd* **14/1**

0 **7** 1½ **Lightning Bug (IRE)**[17] 3578 2-8-8 0.... JasonWatson 3 43
(Suzy Smith) *dwlt: rn green: in tch: outpcd 2f out: no ch over 1f out* **50/1**

8 nse **The Red Witch** 2-8-2 0 ow1.... TobyEley(7) 9 43
(Steph Hollinshead) *sn pushed along to chse ldrs: steadily lft bhd fnl 2f (jockey said filly ran green and received a slight bump approx 2f out)* **50/1**

04 **9** 3¾ **Whispering Leaves (IRE)**[14] 3695 2-8-9 0.... WilliamCox(3) 10 35
(Clive Cox) *prom over 3f: wknd 2f out* **33/1**

10 16 **Jane Victoria** 2-8-8 0.... EoinWalsh 1
(Adam West) *prom on outer to 1/2-way: wknd qckly: t.o* **50/1**

1m 14.33s (1.13) **Going Correction** -0.05s/f (Good) **10** Ran SP% **117.1**
Speed ratings (Par 92): **90,84,81,81,78 76,74,74,69,47**
CSF £55.18 TOTE £4.90: £1.60, £3.40, £1.60; EX 54.00 Trifecta £170.60.
Owner H Frost **Bred** Aston House Stud **Trained** Blewbury, Oxon

FOCUS
The first leg of a modest juvenile novice, it was won in taking style by one of the newcomers. They raced stands' side.

4222 WIN RACES WITH JONATHAN PORTMAN FILLIES' NOVICE AUCTION STKS (PLUS 10 RACE) (DIV II) 6f
6:05 (6:06) (Class 4) 2-Y-O
£4,787 (£1,424; £711; £355) **Stalls High**

Form RPR

034 **1** **Twice As Likely**[17] 3573 2-8-10 0.... ShaneKelly 6 72
(Richard Hughes) *disp ld 1f: sn pushed along: reminder over 3f out: prog to ld jst over 2f out: rdn over 1f out: kpt on wl* **8/1[3]**

50 **2** 1¼ **Chromium**[19] 3491 2-8-8 0.... NicolaCurrie 3 66
(Mark Usher) *wl in tch: rdn and prog to chse wnr over 1f out: styd on but nvr able to chal* **50/1**

0 **3** 1¾ **I Had A Dream**[15] 3644 2-8-8 0.... LukeMorris 4 62
(Tom Clover) *dwlt: carried lft and hmpd s: sn in tch: drvn on outer over 2f out: kpt on u.p to win battle for 3rd* **8/1[3]**

05 **4** nse **Lethal Talent**[19] 3491 2-8-8 0.... RobHornby 5 61
(Jonathan Portman) *wnt lft s: in tch: shkn up 2f out: kpt on steadily to press for 3rd ins fnl f* **8/1[3]**

5 nse **Pretty Pickle (IRE)** 2-9-0 0.... PatDobbs 9 67+
(William Haggas) *trckd ldrs: waiting for a gap over 2f out to over 1f out: rdn to chse ldng pair fnl f: no imp and lost 2 pls nr fin* **6/4[1]**

3 **6** 3¾ **Gert Lush (IRE)**[32] 3033 2-9-0 0.... DavidProbert 8 56
(Roger Teal) *dwlt: sn urged along in last: sme prog 2f out: pushed along and no hdwy fnl f* **6/1[2]**

00 **7** 2¾ **Lafontaine (FR)**[14] 3694 2-8-8 0.... DavidEgan 7 41
(Sylvester Kirk) *trckd ldrs: shkn up over 2f out: wknd over 1f out* **40/1**

0 **8** ½ **Summer Lake**[14] 3695 2-8-8 0.... JasonWatson 10 40
(Roger Charlton) *a towards rr: struggling whn short of room over 1f out* **16/1**

9 1½ **Intimate Moment** 2-8-10 0.... SilvestreDeSousa 1 37
(Philip McBride) *disp ld 1f: chsd ldr: chal and upsides 2f out: wknd qckly over 1f out* **10/1**

4 **10** 6 **The Blue Bower (IRE)**[19] 3491 2-8-9 ow1.... KierenFox 2 18
(Suzy Smith) *impeded s: rcvrd to ld after 1f and racd against nr side rail: hdd jst over 2f out: wkng qckly whn short of room over 1f out* **8/1[3]**

1m 14.48s (1.28) **Going Correction** -0.05s/f (Good) **10** Ran SP% **118.1**
Speed ratings (Par 92): **89,87,85,84,84 79,76,75,73,65**
CSF £323.39 TOTE £7.50: £1.80, £8.20, £2.20; EX 282.70 Trifecta £4141.90.
Owner Ms H N Pinniger **Bred** Horizon Bloodstock Limited **Trained** Upper Lambourn, Berks

FOCUS
Again they raced stands' side. This rates a step forward from the winner but it looks ordinary form for the track.

4223 EQUINE PRODUCTIONS EBF FILLIES' NOVICE STKS (PLUS 10 RACE) 7f (S)
6:35 (6:41) (Class 4) 2-Y-O
£4,787 (£1,424; £711; £355) **Stalls High**

Form RPR

46 **1** **Picture Frame**[20] 3469 2-9-0 0.... HarryBentley 2 82+
(Saeed bin Suroor) *trckd ldrs and racd on outer: clsd to ld over 2f out: signs of inexperience but stretched clr in decent style over 1f out* **2/1[1]**

0 **2** 4½ **Willa**[38] 2836 2-9-0 0.... SeanLevey 10 71+
(Richard Hannon) *w ldrs: racd alone against nr side rail fr 3f out: rt on terms over 2f out: chsd wnr after: styd on but readily outpcd* **12/1**

5 **3** 3¼ **Zulu Girl**[20] 3461 2-9-0 0.... CharlesBishop 1 63
(Eve Johnson Houghton) *in tch: shkn up over 2f out: outpcd by ldrs but prog over 1f out: styd on one pce to take 3rd last strides* **13/2[3]**

6 **4** hd **Golden Lips (IRE)**[32] 3049 2-9-0 0.... OisinMurphy 5 62
(Harry Dunlop) *taken down early: led to over 2f out: sn outpcd: fdd fnl f and lost 3rd last strides* **16/1**

5 shd **Onassis (IRE)** 2-9-0 0.... StevieDonohoe 8 62
(Charlie Fellowes) *trckd ldrs: looked poised to chal over 2f out: shkn up and nt qckn wl over 1f out: kpt on same pce fnl f to press for 3rd nr fin* **9/4[2]**

6 5 **Incognito (IRE)** 2-9-0 0 .... PatDobbs 11 49
(Mick Channon) *fractious preliminaries and difficult to load: a in rr: struggling by 1/2-way: no ch fnl 2f* **25/1**

7 1 1/2 **Pearl Beach** 2-9-0 0 .... JasonWatson 3 46
(William Knight) *dwlt and then impeded shortly after s: t.k.h: trckd ldrs: wknd 2f out* **40/1**

8 3 1/4 **Staycee** 2-9-0 0 .... DavidEgan 4 38
(Rod Millman) *w ldrs on outer tl wknd qckly over 2f out* **20/1**

9 5 **Little Tipsy** 2-9-0 0 .... NicolaCurrie 7 25
(Adam West) *a in last and sn struggling* **66/1**

1m 27.19s (0.19) **Going Correction** -0.05s/f (Good) **9** Ran SP% **103.6**
Speed ratings (Par 92): **96,90,87,86,86 81,79,75,69**
CSF £19.17 TOTE £2.60: £1.80, £2.40, £1.60; EX 21.00 Trifecta £78.00.
Owner Godolphin **Bred** Whitsbury Manor Stud And Mrs M E Slade **Trained** Newmarket, Suffolk
■ Star Spirit was withdrawn. Price at time of withdrawal 11/2. Rule 4 applies to all bets - deduction 15p in the £.

FOCUS
A fairly ordinary fillies' novice, made more winnable after Star Spirit refused to enter the stalls, they raced stands' side and the favourite won in good style.

4224 PEGASUS PUMPS LTD H'CAP 1m 4f
7:10 (7:10) (Class 3) (0-90,92) 3-Y-O+ **£7,439** (£2,213; £1,106; £553) **Stalls** Low

Form RPR

5-54 1 **Frontispiece**[11] 3806 5-9-6 **82** .... KieranShoemark 4 91
(Amanda Perrett) *t.k.h: led after 1f after nthing else wanted to: mde rest: rdn over 2f out: jnd over 1f out: jst prevailed nr fin* **8/1**[3]

-140 2 shd **Mackaar (IRE)**[38] 2828 3-9-2 **92** .... DavidEgan 3 101+
(Roger Varian) *reluctant ldr 1f: trckd wnr after: rdn over 2f out: chal and upsides over 1f out: jst hld last strides: sddle slipped (jockey said saddle slipped back)* **3/1**[1]

02-5 3 1 1/4 **Western Duke (IRE)**[34] 2969 5-9-8 **84** .... (p) StevieDonohoe 8 91
(Ian Williams) *trckd ldrs: rdn wl over 2f out: styd on wl fnl f to take 3rd nr fin* **16/1**

115- 4 3/4 **Saroog**[312] 6241 5-10-0 **90** .... SilvestreDeSousa 9 96
(Simon Crisford) *trckd ldng pair: rdn over 2f out to try to chal: racd awkwardly and nt qckn over 1f out: lost 3rd nr fin* **3/1**[1]

4032 5 1 **Perfect Illusion**[22] 3408 4-9-2 **78** .... (p) OisinMurphy 2 82
(Andrew Balding) *trckd ldrs: rdn over 2f out: nvr pce to chal: kpt on* **9/2**[2]

-140 6 2 1/2 **Get Back Get Back (IRE)**[15] 3663 4-9-8 **84** .... AdamKirby 10 84
(Clive Cox) *hld up in last pair: urged along 3f out: kpt on fnl 2f but ldrs nt stopping* **8/1**[3]

4-00 7 5 **Rock Force (IRE)**[15] 3663 4-9-2 **78** .... (v[1]) DavidProbert 12 70
(Alan King) *t.k.h: hld up in last pair: rdn 3f out: brief prog 2f out: sn no hdwy and btn* **20/1**

5500 8 1 1/2 **Galactic Spirit**[20] 3467 4-8-13 **75** .... RaulDaSilva 6 65
(James Evans) *hld up towards rr: prog 4f out: rdn 3f out: sn no hdwy: wknd wl over 1f out* **50/1**

/0-0 9 2 **Torcello (IRE)**[20] 3466 5-9-3 **86** .... ElishaWhittington(7) 11 73
(Shaun Lycett) *hld up towards rr: rdn 3f out: dropped to last and wl btn 2f out* **50/1**

360- 10 1 3/4 **Seaport**[382] 3553 8-9-6 **82** .... (t w) TomQueally 7 66
(Seamus Durack) *nvr bttr than midfield: no prog 3f out: wknd 2f out* **50/1**

5266 P **Seafarer (IRE)**[20] 3466 5-9-13 **89** .... (v) MartinDwyer 1
(Marcus Tregoning) *t.k.h: hld up in midfield: rdn and wknd rapidly over 4f out: sn t.o and p.u (vet said gelding bled from the nose and has an irregular heartbeat)* **10/1**

2m 36.24s (-1.76) **Going Correction** -0.05s/f (Good)
WFA 3 from 4yo+ 14lb **11** Ran SP% **116.0**
Speed ratings (Par 107): **103,102,102,101,100 99,95,94,93,92**
CSF £30.98 CT £373.25 TOTE £8.50: £2.20, £2.80, £4.10; EX 39.30 Trifecta £359.00.
Owner Frontispiece Partnership **Bred** The Queen **Trained** Pulborough, W Sussex

FOCUS
One significant non-runner in Infrastructure, who would likely have been sent off favourite, but still a good-quality handicap and the right horses came to the fore. The pace was a steady one, though, with nothing wanting to lead and the winner made most - and he has been rated close to his best.

4225 JUNG PUMPEN & PUMP TECHNOLOGY H'CAP 1m
7:40 (7:43) (Class 5) (0-70,70) 3-Y-O
£4,140 (£1,232; £615; £307; £300; £300) **Stalls** Low

Form RPR

0365 1 **City Wanderer (IRE)**[16] 3638 3-9-3 **66** .... SilvestreDeSousa 4 74
(Mick Channon) *trckd ldng pair: led 2f out: rdn and hrd pressed sn after: styd on wl and in command ins fnl f* **7/2**[1]

-223 2 1 3/4 **Image Of The Moon**[59] 2125 3-9-7 **70** .... AdamKirby 8 74
(Shaun Keightley) *trckd ldrs in 5th: rdn over 2f out: clsd to chse wnr jst over 1f out: kpt on but no imp fnl f* **7/1**[2]

056 3 nse **Strict (IRE)**[14] 3696 3-8-13 **62** .... (p[1]) OisinMurphy 12 66
(Andrew Balding) *trckd ldr: rdn over 2f out: nt qckn wl over 1f out: kpt on to press for 2nd fnl f* **8/1**[3]

050- 4 1 **Bruyere (FR)**[246] 8468 3-9-3 **66** .... (h[1]) RobertWinston 1 68
(Dean Ivory) *heavily restrained s: t.k.h and hld up in last: prog over 2f out: cajoled along and racd awkwardly after: rchd 4th fnl f: kpt on* **10/1**

4-04 5 2 **Corrida De Toros (IRE)**[14] 3696 3-9-7 **70** .... PatCosgrave 3 67
(Ed de Giles) *trckd ldrs in 6th: prog to chal and w wnr wl over 1f out: wknd sn after* **7/2**[1]

036 6 nk **Cool Possibility (IRE)**[15] 3648 3-9-5 **68** .... KieranShoemark 2 64
(Charles Hills) *dwlt and sltly impeded s: hld up in rr: rdn and sme prog jst over 2f out: no hdwy over 1f out* **8/1**[3]

54-6 7 nk **Reconnaissance**[59] 2114 3-9-4 **67** .... LukeMorris 9 63
(Tom Clover) *trckd ldng trio: hrd rdn over 2f out: lost pl and btn over 1f out* **7/1**[2]

554 8 2 1/4 **Foxes Flyer (IRE)**[19] 3517 3-9-2 **70** .... (t) JamieJones(5) 7 60
(Luke McJannet) *sltly awkward s: hld up in 7th: rdn and no real prog over 2f out: wl btn whn hung rt over 1f out* **20/1**

42-0 9 3/4 **Max Guevara (IRE)**[29] 3170 3-9-5 **68** .... DavidEgan 6 57
(William Muir) *led at gd pce to 2f out: wknd* **12/1**

5465 10 9 **Lethal Lover**[29] 3154 3-8-13 **62** .... DavidProbert 11 30
(Clive Cox) *a in rr: shkn up over 3f out: sn struggling* **25/1**

1m 39.22s (-1.28) **Going Correction** -0.05s/f (Good) **10** Ran SP% **117.1**
Speed ratings (Par 99): **104,102,102,101,99 98,98,96,95,86**
CSF £28.31 CT £187.96 TOTE £4.30: £1.60, £1.80, £2.30; EX 29.90 Trifecta £162.20.
Owner George Materna & Roger Badley **Bred** Kildaragh Stud **Trained** West Ilsley, Berks

FOCUS
Modest form, they headed centre-field in the straight. The winner rates as an improver.

4226 PUMP TECHNOLOGY H'CAP 7f (S)
8:15 (8:17) (Class 5) (0-75,75) 3-Y-O+
£3,752 (£1,116; £557; £300; £300; £300) **Stalls** High

Form RPR

6540 1 **Swift Approval (IRE)**[15] 3649 7-9-12 **73** .... JasonWatson 8 83
(Stuart Williams) *mde all: rdn wl over 1f out: pressed ins fnl f but a looked in control: kpt on wl* **7/1**

1432 2 1/2 **Sir Roderic (IRE)**[8] 3944 6-9-11 **72** .... (v[1]) GeraldMosse 12 80
(Rod Millman) *wl plcd bhd ldrs: rdn over 1f out: chal fnl f: styd on but a hld* **7/1**

6063 3 1 1/4 **Balata Bay**[16] 3638 3-9-3 **73** .... PatDobbs 6 75
(Richard Hannon) *dwlt: sn in midfield: rdn 2f out: styd on fr over 1f out to take 3rd nr fin* **10/1**

00-3 4 1/2 **Eligible (IRE)**[36] 2900 3-9-5 **75** .... AdamKirby 1 75
(Clive Cox) *prom on outer of gp: rdn 2f out: nt qckn over 1f out: kpt on same pce and lost 3rd nr fin* **9/2**[1]

3-05 5 nk **Bounty Pursuit**[34] 2971 7-9-3 **67** .... MitchGodwin(3) 17 69+
(Michael Blake) *hld up wl in rr: rdn and prog towards nr side wl over 1f out: styd on fnl f: nrst fin* **50/1**

0010 6 hd **Nezar (IRE)**[15] 3649 8-9-7 **73** .... SophieRalston(5) 7 75
(Dean Ivory) *hld up wl in rr: prog wl over 1f out: styd on fnl f but nvr able to chal* **12/1**

0-00 7 shd **Fortune And Glory (USA)**[20] 3462 6-9-5 **66** .... RossaRyan 14 68
(Joseph Tuite) *stmbld s: sn in midfield: rdn 2f out: styd on fnl f but nvr able to chal* **33/1**

200- 8 2 **Gerry The Glover (IRE)**[237] 8733 7-9-2 **63** .... (h) SeanLevey 16 59+
(Lee Carter) *stdd s: hld up in last trio: gd prog over 1f out: shkn up and no real hdwy ins fnl f: nvr really in it* **50/1**

0-00 9 1/2 **Another Boy**[17] 3575 6-8-13 **60** .... (p) HarryBentley 5 55
(Ralph Beckett) *mostly chsd wnr to over 1f out: fdd* **20/1**

14P- 10 1 1/4 **Danecase**[199] 9462 6-10-0 **75** .... (t) DavidProbert 10 67
(David Dennis) *stdd s: hld up in last trio: prog over 1f out: rdn and no hdwy ins fnl f* **40/1**

1-20 11 nk **Vixen (IRE)**[12] 3763 5-9-6 **72** .... ThomasGreatrex(5) 13 63
(Emma Lavelle) *trckd ldrs: rdn over 2f out: lost pl and btn over 1f out* **33/1**

140 12 hd **Native Silver**[15] 3664 3-9-1 **71** .... LukeMorris 20 58
(Robert Eddery) *racd nr side first 2f: prom whn jnd main gp: rdn over 2f out: steadily wknd* **50/1**

60-3 13 3/4 **Keeper's Choice (IRE)**[39] 2797 5-9-13 **74** .... OisinMurphy 9 62
(Denis Coakley) *mostly in midfield: rdn over 2f out: lost pl and btn over 1f out* **5/1**[2]

4-26 14 1/2 **Bbob Alula**[34] 2977 4-9-7 **72** .... (t) RyanWhile(5) 19 60
(Bill Turner) *racd nr side first 2f: in tch in rr whn jnd main gp: rdn and no prog 2f out* **33/1**

3-03 15 nk **Knightshayes**[28] 3193 3-9-1 **74** .... (p[1]) MeganNicholls(3) 3 57
(Paul George) *on terms w ldrs to over 2f out: sn wknd* **16/1**

00-0 16 11 **Bombastic (IRE)**[25] 3305 4-9-11 **72** .... PatCosgrave 2 28
(Ed de Giles) *stdd s: t.k.h: sn chsd ldrs: wknd over 2f out: t.o* **6/1**[3]

0-13 17 2 1/2 **Filles De Fleur**[46] 2597 3-9-2 **72** .... SilvestreDeSousa 18 19
(George Scott) *wl in rr: hung rt to r against nr side over 2f out: sn eased: t.o (jockey said filly hung right-handed)* **11/1**

/P-0 P **Kestrel Dot Com**[34] 2977 7-10-0 **75** .... (b) DavidEgan 4
(Charlie Wallis) *wl in tch tl lost pl rapidly over 2f out: t.o whn p.u over 1f out (vet said gelding bled from the nose)* **66/1**

1m 26.09s (-0.91) **Going Correction** -0.05s/f (Good)
WFA 3 from 4yo+ 9lb **18** Ran SP% **128.5**
Speed ratings (Par 103): **103,102,101,100,100 99,99,97,96,95 95,94,94,93,93 80,77,**
CSF £53.33 CT £510.69 TOTE £7.60: £2.30, £2.40, £2.30, £2.40; EX 68.00 Trifecta £507.90.
Owner JLM Racing **Bred** Mrs Jean Brennan **Trained** Newmarket, Suffolk

FOCUS
Modest form. The winner, with the run of the race in front, took advantage of a reduced mark.

4227 LEE SAN MARINE SANITATION H'CAP 6f
8:45 (8:48) (Class 5) (0-70,71) 3-Y-O+
£4,140 (£1,232; £615; £307; £300; £300) **Stalls** High

Form RPR

4104 1 **Rasheeq (IRE)**[18] 3549 6-9-7 **68** .... (p) SeamusCronin(5) 11 82
(Mohamed Moubarak) *racd centre: hld up: prog over 2f out gng wl: led wl over 1f out: rdn out and wl in command fnl f* **9/1**

3-01 2 3 1/4 **Rose Hip**[20] 3470 4-9-11 **67** .... SeanLevey 5 71
(Tony Carroll) *t.k.h: prom in centre: rdn to chal 2f out: hanging and awkward after: chsd wnr but nvr able to land a blow* **5/1**[2]

0241 3 nk **Eye Of The Water (IRE)**[14] 3697 3-9-6 **69** .... DavidProbert 13 70+
(Ronald Harris) *prom on gp towards nr side: lost pl over 2f out: drvn over 1f out: rallied sn after: styd on to take 3rd nr fin* **8/1**

6-41 4 1/2 **Raincall**[31] 3089 4-10-0 **70** .... HarryBentley 16 71+
(Henry Candy) *racd nr side: prom but nt on terms w centre ldrs sn after 1/2-way: drvn and styd on fr over 1f out: nvr nrr but no ch* **7/2**[1]

5624 5 hd **Cent Flying**[12] 3772 4-9-7 **63** .... (t[1]) OisinMurphy 3 63
(William Muir) *racd centre: trckd ldr: led 1/2-way: rdn and hdd wl over 1f out: one pce fnl f* **7/1**[3]

234- 6 1/2 **Q Twenty Boy (IRE)**[305] 6478 4-9-2 **58** .... (p[1]) JasonWatson 14 57+
(Mark Usher) *dwlt: racd on outer of gp towards nr side: rdn and moved across to join centre gp 2f out: tried to chal over 1f out: fdd fnl f* **33/1**

4-40 7 1/2 **Yimou (IRE)**[20] 3462 4-10-0 **70** .... MartinDwyer 18 67
(Dean Ivory) *t.k.h: racd against nr side rail: prom but nt on terms w centre gp sn after 1/2-way: drvn and kpt on* **10/1**

2206 8 shd **Wiff Waff**[10] 3856 4-9-12 **68** .... ShaneKelly 2 65
(Chris Gordon) *restless stalls: chsd ldrs in centre: rdn over 2f out: no imp over 1f out* **25/1**

5-40 9 1 3/4 **Arctic Flower (IRE)**[14] 3687 6-8-4 **51** oh6 .... SophieRalston(5) 15 42
(John Bridger) *racd towards nr side: in tch in that gp but nt on terms w centre ldrs 2f out: fdd* **20/1**

-000 10 2 1/4 **Vincenzo Coccotti (USA)**[31] 3089 7-8-12 **54** .... (p) PatDobbs 12 38
(Ken Cunningham-Brown) *chsd ldrs in centre: rdn 2f out: fdd over 1f out* **25/1**

-000 11 nk **Field Of Vision (IRE)**[18] 3543 6-9-5 **66** .... (p) ScottMcCullagh(5) 8 49
(John Flint) *racd centre: a in rr and struggling fr 1/2-way* **14/1**

24-6 12 nse **Lilbourne Star (IRE)**[20] 3464 4-9-13 **69** .... AdamKirby 9 52
(Clive Cox) *led in centre to 1/2-way: wknd 2f out* **16/1**

-300 **13** *1/2* **Poet's Magic**[15] 3665 3-8-7 **63**............................ TobyEley(7) 7 42
(Jonathan Portman) *awkward s: racd centre: nvr gng wl and a bhd (jockey said filly dropped it's head as the stalls opened and was slowly away)* **11/1**

-600 **14** *2 3/4* **Porto Ferro (IRE)**[33] 3020 5-9-7 **63**............................ NicolaCurrie 17 36
(John Bridger) *racd towards nr side: in tch but nt on terms w centre ldrs 2f out: wknd* **50/1**

1m 13.11s (-0.09) **Going Correction** -0.05s/f (Good)
WFA 3 from 4yo+ 7lb **14** Ran SP% **119.8**
Speed ratings (Par 103): **98,93,93,92,92 91,91,90,88,85 85,85,84,80**
CSF £50.01 CT £393.69 TOTE £9.70: £6.70, £1.50, £2.70; EX 65.90 Trifecta £413.60.
Owner David Fremel **Bred** Rabbah Bloodstock Limited **Trained** Newmarket, Suffolk

FOCUS
The right horses came to the fore in this modest sprint and the winner has been rated to his 2018 best.
T/Jkpt: Not Won. T/Plt: £104.00 to a £1 stake. Pool: £65,460.56 - 459.44 winning units. T/Qpdt: £29.50 to a £1 stake. Pool: £9,236.35 - 231.09 winning units. **Jonathan Neesom**

LE CROISE-LAROCHE
Tuesday, June 25
OFFICIAL GOING: Turf: good to firm

4228a PRIX DU JOCKEY-CLUB DE BELGIQUE (CLAIMER) (2YO) (TURF) 5f 110y
5:47 2-Y-O £6,756 (£2,702; £2,027; £1,351; £675)

RPR

1 **Lost In France (IRE)**[50] 2-9-0 0 ow1............................ EddyHardouin 2 67
(Matthieu Palussiere, France) **39/10[3]**

2 *1 3/4* **Shiso (IRE)** 2-9-2 0 ow1............................ MickaelBerto 9 63
(R Rohne, Germany) **23/1**

3 *shd* **Lalacelle (FR)**[14] 3714 2-8-7 0 ow1............................ MlleLeaBails(9) 3 63
(M Boutin, France) **33/10[1]**

4 *3/4* **Vereny Ka (FR)**[14] 3714 2-8-9 0 ow1............................ FabriceVeron 7 54
(C Lerner, France) **7/1**

5 *1/2* **Panthera Tigris**[14] 3714 2-8-4 0 ow1............................(b) HugoBesnier(5) 1 52
(Jo Hughes, France) *prom on inner: pushed along to chse ldr 1 1/2f out: sn rdn: nt qckn and kpt on same pce ins fnl f* **37/1**

6 *1* **Aban (IRE)** 2-9-2 0 ow1............................ ClementLecoeuvre 4 56
(Henk Grewe, Germany) **13/2**

7 *3/4* **Diva Du Dancing (FR)**[14] 3714 2-9-1 0 ow1............ TeddyHautbois(5) 5 57
(T Castanheira, France) **7/2[2]**

8 *1 1/2* **Ekaitzana (FR)**[14] 3714 2-8-13 0 ow2............................ MlleCoraliePacaut(4) 8 49
(Andrea Marcialis, France) **51/10**

9 *6* **Coply (FR)**[39] 2-8-13 0 ow2............................ JeromeClaudic 6 25
(Matthieu Palussiere, France) **23/1**

1m 4.7s **9** Ran SP% **119.1**
PARI-MUTUEL (all including 1 euro stake): WIN 4.10 (Coupled with Coply) ; PLACE 2.20, 5.20, 1.60; DF 44.50.
Owner Mrs Theresa Marnane **Bred** C Marnane **Trained** France

4229a PRIX D'OSTENDE (CLAIMER) (3YO) (TURF) 5f 110y
6:22 3-Y-O £6,756 (£2,702; £2,027; £1,351; £675)

RPR

1 **Hit The Track Jack**[17] 3-8-13 0 ow2............................ JeremieMonteiro 1 59
(N Caullery, France) **5/1[3]**

2 *nse* **Velvet Vixen (IRE)**[14] 3713 3-8-13 0 ow2............................ HugoBesnier 8 59
(Jo Hughes, France) *prom on outer: pushed along 2f out: sn rdn to chse ldr 1 1/2f out: responded for press ins fnl f: r.o wl: jst denied* **14/1**

3 *2* **Baylagan (FR)**[10] 3878 3-9-5 0 ow1............................(b) KoenClijmans 13 58
(Mme G Rarick, France) **31/10[1]**

4 *3/4* **Grand Secret (FR)**[17] 3-9-3 0 ow1............................(b) MlleAlisonMassin(3) 4 57
(M Boutin, France) **5/1[3]**

5 *2 1/2* **Deluree (FR)**[17] 3-8-9 0 ow1............................(b) EmmanuelEtienne 3 38
(N Caullery, France) **24/1**

6 *2* **Philippine Cobra (FR)**[35] 2954 3-8-13 0 ow2............................(p) PierreBazire 10 35
(G Botti, France) **6/1**

7 *1 1/2* **Wild Emotion (GER)**[64] 1990 3-8-13 0 ow2............ BertrandFlandrin 12 30
(Andreas Suborics, Germany) **33/10[2]**

8 *7* **Tosen Ciara (IRE)**[17] 3-8-9 0 ow1............................ YanisAouabed 7 3
(J-C Bertin, France) **11/1**

9 *nk* **Flying Dandy (IRE)**[291] 3-8-9 0 ow1............................ MlleSaraVermeersch(3) 2 5
(R Ducasteele, France) **54/1**

10 *nk* **Melody D'Amour (FR)**[47] 3-9-2 0 ow1............................(b) MirkoSanna 5 8
(E Kurdu, Germany) **38/1**

11 *snk* **Disque Rouge (FR)**[314] 6173 3-8-9 0 ow1............................ ClementGuitraud 9
(J-M Capitte, France) **88/1**

1m 3.4s **11** Ran SP% **119.8**
PARI-MUTUEL (all including 1 euro stake): WIN 6.00; PLACE 1.90, 3.10, 1.70; DF 36.00.
Owner Julien Caullery **Bred** Ftp Equine Holdings Ltd **Trained** France

3834 BATH (L-H)
Wednesday, June 26
OFFICIAL GOING: Good (good to firm in places; 7.7)
Wind: Fresh behind Weather: Cloudy with sunny spells

4230 BEST FREE TIPS AT VALUERATER.CO.UK H'CAP (BATH SUMMER SPRINT SERIES QUALIFIER) 5f 10y
6:10 (6:12) (Class 5) (0-70,72) 4-Y-O+
£3,752 (£1,116; £557; £300; £300; £300) **Stalls** Centre

Form RPR

0402 **1** **Big Lachie**[11] 3838 5-9-5 **71**............................ GeorgiaCox(3) 3 80
(Mark Loughnane) *s.i.s: outpcd: swtchd rt over 1f out: gd hdwy fnl f: edgd lft and r.o to ld nr fin* **8/1**

6-56 **2** *1* **Edged Out**[18] 3577 9-8-3 **55**............................ WilliamCox(3) 8 60
(Christopher Mason) *chsd ldrs: rdn to ld over 1f out: hdd nr fin* **50/1**

5230 **3** *shd* **Powerful Dream (IRE)**[19] 3531 6-9-2 **65**............................(p) DavidProbert 13 70
(Ronald Harris) *mid-div: sn pushed along: hdwy over 1f out: r.o* **14/1**

-643 **4** *nk* **Our Oystercatcher**[11] 3856 5-9-9 **72**............................ HectorCrouch 14 76
(Mark Pattinson) *chsd ldrs: led 2f out: rdn and hdd over 1f out: edgd lft ins fnl f: styd on same pce towards fin* **5/1[2]**

3105 **5** *1 1/2* **Secret Potion**[43] 2717 5-9-0 **63**............................ FrannyNorton 12 61
(Ronald Harris) *mid-div: sn pushed along: rdn over 1f out: r.o ins fnl f: nt rch ldrs* **10/1**

5-43 **6** *1/2* **Three Little Birds**[18] 3596 4-9-4 **70**............................ GaryMahon(3) 17 66
(Sylvester Kirk) *prom on outer: rdn over 1f out: edgd lft and styd on same pce ins fnl f* **25/1**

0P03 **7** *1/2* **Look Surprised**[11] 3838 6-8-9 **63**............................ SophieRalston(5) 1 58+
(Roger Teal) *prom: hmpd and lost pl over 4f out: swtchd rt and r.o ins fnl f: nt trble ldrs* **7/1[3]**

1020 **8** *1 1/4* **Coronation Cottage**[19] 3531 5-9-6 **69**............................ TomQueally 9 59
(Malcolm Saunders) *s.i.s: sn prom: rdn over 1f out: hung lft and no ex ins fnl f* **14/1**

6432 **9** *1* **David's Beauty (IRE)**[18] 3577 6-8-11 **60**............................(b) LukeMorris 16 46
(Brian Baugh) *chsd ldrs: rdn 1/2-way: wknd ins fnl f* **25/1**

550 **10** *nk* **Delagate This Lord**[11] 3856 5-9-6 **69**............................ CharlieBennett 4 57
(Michael Attwater) *mid-div: pushed along 1/2-way: hdwy u.p over 1f out: edgd lft and nt clr run ins fnl f: nt trble ldrs* **9/1**

40-0 **11** *3/4* **Silverrica (IRE)**[54] 2358 9-9-2 **65**............................ FergusSweeney 11 48
(Malcolm Saunders) *led 3f: wknd ins fnl f* **50/1**

-522 **12** *shd* **Ghepardo**[23] 3404 4-9-3 **66**............................(t) TomMarquand 7 48
(Patrick Chamings) *s.i.s: swtchd rt 1/2-way: sn rdn: n.d* **28/1**

6441 **13** *nse* **Storm Melody**[19] 3527 6-9-4 **67**............................(p) RobHornby 6 49+
(Ali Stronge) *s.i.s: hld up: hdwy over 1f out: nt clr run ins fnl f: n.d (jockey said gelding was denied a clear run)* **4/1[1]**

0600 **14** *2* **Bahamian Sunrise**[11] 3856 7-9-1 **64**............................(b) RichardKingscote 5 43
(John Gallagher) *edgd rt s: sn pushed along to chse ldrs: rdn 1/2-way: wknd and eased ins fnl f* **10/1**

0003 **15** *5* **Desert Ace (IRE)**[16] 3658 8-9-8 **71**............................ PatDobbs 2 28
(Paul Midgley) *chsd ldrs: edgd rt over 4f out: lost pl over 3f out: no ch whn eased over 1f out (jockey said gelding moved poorly throughout)* **12/1**

1m 0.95s (-1.05) **Going Correction** -0.05s/f (Good) **15** Ran SP% **124.5**
Speed ratings (Par 103): **106,104,104,103,101 100,99,97,96,95 94,94,94,91,83**
CSF £384.86 CT £5540.47 TOTE £9.30: £4.50, £9.90, £3.60; EX 575.80 Trifecta £1422.40.
Owner Big Lachie Syndicate **Bred** Mrs C Lloyd **Trained** Rock, Worcs
■ Stewards' Enquiry : Rob Hornby two-day ban: careless riding (30 Jun & 10 Jul)

FOCUS
A modest sprint handicap.

4231 VALUE RATER RACING CLUB H'CAP (BATH SUMMER STAYERS' SERIES QUALIFIER) 1m 5f 11y
6:40 (6:40) (Class 5) (0-75,75) 3-Y-O+
£3,752 (£1,116; £557; £300; £300; £300) **Stalls** High

Form RPR

6-26 **1** **Sufi**[17] 3633 5-9-10 **71**............................ PatDobbs 6 78
(Ken Cunningham-Brown) *chsd ldrs: rdn and hung lft over 2f out: edgd lft ins fnl f: styd on to ld nr fin* **8/1**

-163 **2** *hd* **Hermocrates (FR)**[51] 2485 3-8-0 **67**.......(b[1]) ThoreHammerHansen(5) 11 73
(Richard Hannon) *edgd lft s: rcvrd to join ldr after 1f: led over 9f out: clr over 6f out tl rdn over 2f out: pressed over 1f out: hdd nr fin* **9/1**

2122 **3** *nk* **Singing The Blues (IRE)**[15] 3700 4-9-12 **73**............................ RobHornby 7 78
(Rod Millman) *led: hdd over 9f out: chsd ldr who wnt clr over 6f out: shkn up to take clsr order over 2f out: rdn and ev ch over 1f out: bmpd ins fnl f: styd on* **7/2[2]**

60-6 **4** *2 1/4* **Rosie Royale (IRE)**[18] 3571 7-8-12 **59**............................ SilvestreDeSousa 14 61
(Roger Teal) *s.i.s: hld up: swtchd rt over 2f out: hdwy u.p over 1f out: styd on: nt rch ldrs* **20/1**

5-30 **5** *1 1/4* **Surrey Warrior (USA)**[21] 3474 3-8-4 **73**.........(b) Pierre-LouisJamin(7) 13 73
(Archie Watson) *chsd ldrs: rdn over 2f out: hung lft over 1f out: no ex ins fnl f* **50/1**

24-3 **6** *1/2* **Tidal Watch (IRE)**[39] 119 5-9-10 **71**............................ LiamKeniry 12 70
(Jonjo O'Neill) *hld up: hdwy u.p and hung lft over 1f out: nt trble ldrs* **10/1**

-043 **7** *hd* **Enhanced**[26] 3311 3-8-10 **72**............................ TomMarquand 2 71
(Hughie Morrison) *s.i.s: hld up: hdwy over 7f out: rdn over 2f out: styd on same pce fnl f* **13/8[1]**

634- **8** *2 1/4* **Ourmullion**[39] 9609 5-9-4 **68**............................(tp) FinleyMarsh(3) 10 64
(David Pipe) *s.i.s and hmpd s: hld up: rdn over 2f out: nt trble ldrs* **33/1**

136/ **9** *1/2* **Borak (IRE)**[12] 6279 7-9-11 **75**............................(p) JoshuaBryan(3) 3 70
(Bernard Llewellyn) *hld up: hdwy u.p over 1f out: no ex ins fnl f* **50/1**

020 **10** *6* **Moghram (IRE)**[15] 3699 3-8-5 **67**............................ FrannyNorton 1 53
(Marcus Tregoning) *hld up in tch: lost pl over 7f out: n.d after* **5/1[3]**

340 **11** *15* **Famous Dynasty (IRE)**[19] 3545 5-9-0 **61**............................ DavidProbert 4 24
(Michael Blanshard) *hld up: hdwy over 2f out: rdn and wknd over 1f out: eased fnl f* **40/1**

0060 **12** *17* **Mouchee (IRE)**[18] 3571 4-8-12 **62**............................(p) MitchGodwin(3) 8
(Michael Blake) *hld up: hdwy on outer 5f out: rdn and wknd over 2f out: eased over 1f out* **100/1**

2m 51.0s (-1.80) **Going Correction** -0.05s/f (Good)
WFA 3 from 4yo+ 15lb **12** Ran SP% **122.2**
Speed ratings (Par 103): **103,102,102,101,100 100,100,98,98,94 85,75**
CSF £75.56 CT £304.23 TOTE £10.20: £2.80, £2.60, £1.30; EX 98.00 Trifecta £412.60.
Owner John Pearl **Bred** Lady Bamford **Trained** Danebury, Hants

FOCUS
A fair staying handicap, and a small pb from the winner.

4232 SKY SPORTS RACING SKY 415 H'CAP 1m 2f 37y
7:10 (7:13) (Class 6) (0-55,55) 3-Y-O+
£3,105 (£924; £461; £300; £300; £300) **Stalls** Low

Form RPR

-605 **1** **Confils (FR)**[23] 3407 3-8-12 **55**............................ PatCosgrave 14 66
(George Baker) *s.i.s: hld up: hdwy on outer over 2f out: rdn to ld over 1f out: r.o wl* **6/1[2]**

405- **2** *3 1/4* **Frantical**[268] 7834 7-8-12 **50**............................ ElishaWhittington(7) 9 55
(Tony Carroll) *hld up: hdwy on outer over 1f out: rdn to chse wnr and edgd lft ins fnl f: styd on* **25/1**

0005 **3** *2 1/4* **Prerogative (IRE)**[29] 3186 5-9-2 **47**............................(b) TomMarquand 2 48
(Tony Carroll) *sn prom: led wl over 1f out: sn rdn and hdd: no ex ins fnl f* **7/1[3]**

06-0 **4** *3* **Allofmelovesallofu**[25] 3348 5-9-1 **46**............................ PatDobbs 8 41
(Ken Cunningham-Brown) *hld up: hdwy over 1f out: nt rch ldrs* **8/1**

00-0 **5** 3/4 **Delirium (IRE)**27 3267 5-9-8 **53**..........(p) RichardKingscote 11 46
(Ed de Giles) *led early: lost pl over 8f out: hdwy u.p over 2f out: styd on same pce fnl f* **7/2**1

0-66 **6** 1/2 **Just Right**34 2998 4-8-13 **47**.......... WilliamCox(3) 3 39
(John Flint) *chsd ldrs: rdn and outpcd over 2f out: styd on ins fnl f* **16/1**

1600 **7** 2 **My Brother Mike (IRE)**60 2112 5-9-10 **55**.......... TrevorWhelan 13 44
(Kevin Frost) *prom: rdn and ev ch over 1f out: wknd ins fnl f (jockey said gelding stopped quickly)* **20/1**

6600 **8** shd **Acadian Angel (IRE)**21 3473 5-9-2 **54**..........(p1) TobyEley(7) 5 42
(Steph Hollinshead) *s.i.s: hld up: hdwy u.p and hung rt over 2f out: hung lft over 1f out: wnt rt again ins fnl f: nt trble ldrs (jockey said mare hung both left and right-handed)* **33/1**

0-00 **9** 1 **Guardiola (USA)**4 4111 4-9-0 **48**..........(bt1) JoshuaBryan(3) 7 35
(Bernard Llewellyn) *sn led: rdn and hdd wl over 1f out: wknd ins fnl f* **25/1**

3-64 **10** nk **Howardian Hills (IRE)**17 3640 6-9-5 **50**..........(b1) LukeMorris 6 36
(Victor Dartnall) *chsd ldr after 1f: rdn over 2f out: sn ev ch: wknd ins fnl f* **8/1**

0-00 **11** 1 3/4 **Windsorlot (IRE)**26 3325 6-9-7 **52**.......... GeorgeDowning 1 37
(Tony Carroll) *s.i.s: hdwy over 8f out: rdn and nt clr run over 1f out: wknd fnl f (jockey said gelding was denied a clear run)* **16/1**

1160 **12** 28 **Arlecchino's Arc (IRE)**17 3633 4-9-10 **55**..........(v) DavidProbert 10
(Mark Usher) *s.i.s: sn pushed along in rr: hdwy on outer over 6f out: wknd over 2f out: eased over 1f out (jockey said gelding hung both left and right-handed and stopped quickly)* **8/1**

6-00 **13** 3 **Summa Force (IRE)**13 3777 3-8-12 **55**..........(b1) FergusSweeney 4
(Richard Hannon) *s.i.s: sn pushed along to go handy: lost pl over 8f out: bhd fr 1/2-way* **25/1**

0-60 **14** 2 **Golden Deal (IRE)**15 3687 4-9-3 **48**.......... TomQueally 12
(Richard Phillips) *s.i.s: sn prom: wknd over 3f out: eased wl over 1f out* **22/1**

2m 11.47s (0.37) **Going Correction** -0.05s/f (Good) **14 Ran SP% 117.7**
WFA 3 from 4yo+ 12lb
Speed ratings (Par 101): **96,93,91,89,88 88,86,86,85,85 84,61,59,57**
CSF £155.41 CT £1077.12 TOTE £5.20: £1.70, £6.30, £3.20; EX 193.30 Trifecta £961.20.
Owner Confidence Partnership **Bred** E A R L Haras De Mandore **Trained** Chiddingfold, Surrey

FOCUS
A moderate handicap. An improving 3yo filly made full use of her significant weight-for-age allowance despite coming off a stacking, muddling gallop.

4233 BONITI/BRITISH EBF FILLIES' NOVICE STKS (PLUS 10 RACE) 5f 160y

7:40 (7:42) (Class 4) 2-Y-O **£4,662** (£1,395; £697; £349; £173) **Stalls** Centre

Form RPR

1 **Raheeq** 2-9-0.......... JimCrowley 7 89+
(Roger Varian) *hld up in tch: chsd ldr over 2f out: led 2f out: shkn up over 1f out: pushed clr fnl f: impressive* **11/8**1

4 **2** 4 1/2 **Allez Sophia (IRE)**64 2020 2-9-0.......... CharlesBishop 1 74
(Eve Johnson Houghton) *s.i.s: hld up: swtchd rt and hdwy over 2f out: chsd wnr over 1f out: no ex ins fnl f* **4/1**

341 **3** 3/4 **Know No Limits (IRE)**11 3841 2-9-3.......... RichardKingscote 4 75
(Tom Dascombe) *led: hdd over 4f out: pushed along 1/2-way: styd on same pce fnl f* **7/2**3

32 **4** 1 1/4 **Love Love**15 3689 2-9-0.......... SilvestreDeSousa 8 68
(Richard Hannon) *chsd ldr: led over 4f out: rdn and hdd 2f out: wknd ins fnl f* **3/1**2

5 9 **Diva Rock** 2-9-0.......... PatCosgrave 3 38
(George Baker) *s.i.s: sn prom: chsd ldr over 3f out tl rdn over 2f out: wknd over 1f out* **33/1**

0 **6** 9 **Ohnotanotherone**18 3573 2-8-11.......... WilliamCox(3) 2 8
(Stuart Kittow) *s.i.s: hdwy over 4f out: rdn and wknd over 2f out* **100/1**

0 **7** 12 **Hot Poppy**15 3689 2-8-11.......... GeorgeBuckell(3) 5
(John Gallagher) *s.i.s: sn pushed along in rr: hung rt and lost tch 3f out* **66/1**

1m 9.97s (-1.13) **Going Correction** -0.05s/f (Good) **7 Ran SP% 114.8**
Speed ratings (Par 92): **105,99,98,96,84 72,56**
CSF £7.47 TOTE £1.80: £1.10, £1.90; EX 6.80 Trifecta £17.90.
Owner Hamdan Al Maktoum **Bred** Shadwell Estate Company Limited **Trained** Newmarket, Suffolk

FOCUS
A fair juvenile fillies' novice contest. The favourite won in taking fashion on debut in a good comparative time, and the third has been rated to close to her Chester win.

4234 SKY SPORTS RACING SKY 415 MAIDEN STKS 1m 3f 137y

8:10 (8:11) (Class 5) 3-Y-O+ **£3,752** (£1,116; £557; £278) **Stalls** Low

Form RPR

4 **1** **Monaafasah (IRE)**41 2771 3-8-9 0.......... JimCrowley 5 83
(Marcus Tregoning) *chsd ldr tl over 10f out: wnt 2nd again 7f out: shkn up over 2f out: rdn to ld wl over 1f out: drvn clr fnl f* **2/1**2

0-23 **2** 7 **Shrewdness**17 3637 3-8-9 75.......... TomMarquand 3 72
(William Haggas) *led: shkn up over 2f out: rdn and hdd wl over 1f out: no ex ins fnl f* **5/4**1

4 **3** 4 1/2 **Imperium (IRE)**47 2566 3-9-0 0.......... TrevorWhelan 2 70
(Roger Charlton) *prom: sn pushed along: shkn up over 2f out: styd on same pce fr over 1f out (jockey said gelding was never travelling)* **9/4**3

4 5 **More Buck's (IRE)**63 9-9-11 0..........(t) JoshuaBryan(3) 4 62
(Peter Bowen) *s.i.s: sn prom: chsd ldr over 10f out tl 7f out: rdn over 3f out: wknd over 1f out* **20/1**

0 **5** 6 **Mr Nice Guy (IRE)**40 2795 3-8-11 0.......... GaryMahon(3) 6 52
(Sylvester Kirk) *broke wl: sn lost pl and bhd* **33/1**

2m 31.27s (0.47) **Going Correction** -0.05s/f (Good) **5 Ran SP% 116.3**
WFA 3 from 9yo 14lb
Speed ratings (Par 103): **96,91,88,85,81**
CSF £5.26 TOTE £2.70: £1.60, £1.10; EX 6.10 Trifecta £7.90.
Owner Hamdan Al Maktoum **Bred** Shadwell Estate Company Limited **Trained** Whitsbury, Hants

FOCUS
A fair middle-distance maiden and the winner rates a big improver.

4235 QUEENS SQUARE WEALTH MANAGEMENT H'CAP 1m

8:40 (8:40) (Class 5) (0-70,70) 3-Y-O+
£3,752 (£1,116; £557; £300; £300; £300) **Stalls** Low

Form RPR

1 **Magic Shuffle (IRE)**27 3280 3-8-11 **63**.......... TomMarquand 10 70
(Barry Brennan) *broke wl enough: sn lost pl: bhd and drvn along over 5f out: hdwy on outer over 1f out: edgd lft and r.o u.p to ld wl ins fnl f* **50/1**

1044 **2** 3/4 **Takeonefortheteam**35 2978 4-9-6 **62**.......... RichardKingscote 6 69
(Mark Loughnane) *s.i.s: hld up: hdwy over 2f out: led over 1f out: rdn and hdd wl ins fnl f* **6/1**2

5303 **3** 2 1/2 **Accomplice**19 3533 5-9-2 **58**.......... CharlesBishop 14 59
(Michael Blanshard) *s.i.s: hld up: hdwy and nt clr run over 1f out: r.o to go 3rd nr fin (jockey said mare was denied a clear run)* **7/1**3

4460 **4** nk **Gates Pass**34 2998 4-9-8 **64**..........(t1) TrevorWhelan 1 65+
(Brian Barr) *sn led: rdn and hdd over 1f out: styd on same pce ins fnl f* **25/1**

00-3 **5** 1/2 **Lady Mazie (IRE)**23 3409 3-8-4 **56**.......... LukeMorris 4 53
(Dominic Ffrench Davis) *trckd ldrs: plld hrd: rdn and ev ch over 1f out: no ex ins fnl f* **10/1**

-053 **6** 1 1/2 **Mister Musicmaster**33 3038 10-9-6 **62**.......... DavidProbert 3 58
(Ron Hodges) *mid-div: hdwy over 3f out: rdn over 2f out: no ex ins fnl f* **14/1**

1320 **7** nk **Purple Paddy**59 2145 4-8-4 **51**.......... ThoreHammerHansen(5) 2 46
(Jimmy Fox) *s.i.s: hld up: hdwy over 2f out: rdn over 1f out: no ex ins fnl f* **14/1**

00-4 **8** nk **Outer Space**34 2994 8-9-10 **66**..........(p) RobHornby 7 61
(John Flint) *hld up: hdwy and nt clr run over 1f out: nt trble ldrs* **20/1**

6610 **9** 3 1/4 **Brockagh Cailin**19 3533 4-9-3 **59**.......... LiamKeniry 13 46
(J S Moore) *s.i.s: hld up: hdwy on outer over 2f out: sn rdn: wknd over 1f out* **16/1**

5463 **10** 3/4 **Espresso Freddo (IRE)**123 886 5-9-3 **64**..........(t1 w) PoppyBridgwater(5) 12 49
(Robert Stephens) *hld up in tch: plld hrd: rdn over 2f out: wknd fnl f* **10/1**

310 **11** 3 1/4 **Bayston Hill**34 3022 5-9-11 **70**..........(p) GaryMahon(3) 11 48
(Mark Usher) *s.i.s: sn rcvrd into mid-div: pushed along on outer 5f out: rdn and lost pl over 3f out: n.d after* **12/1**

63-1 **12** 2 1/4 **Freckles**56 2277 4-9-10 **66**.......... NicolaCurrie 8 39
(Marcus Tregoning) *s.i.s: plld hrd and sn w ldr tl shkn up over 2f out: rdn and edgd rt over 1f out: sn wknd (jockey said filly ran too free)* **13/8**1

650- **13** 1 **Buzz Lightyere**260 8070 6-9-7 **63**..........(p) CharlieBennett 5 33
(Patrick Chamings) *chsd ldrs: rdn over 3f out: wknd wl over 1f out* **25/1**

1m 40.54s (-1.16) **Going Correction** -0.05s/f (Good) **13 Ran SP% 124.4**
WFA 3 from 4yo+ 10lb
Speed ratings (Par 103): **103,102,99,99,98 97,97,96,93,92 89,87,86**
CSF £332.83 CT £2509.84 TOTE £23.10: £19.40, £1.70, £3.00; EX 853.30 Trifecta £1412.20.
Owner F J Brennan **Bred** T Kimura **Trained** Upper Lambourn, Berks

FOCUS
A modest handicap. A rank outsider benefited from a pace-collapse up front and became another winner on the night to make the most of his significant 3yo allowance. This has been rated around the runner-up to a better view of his form.

4236 HAPPY BIRTHDAY PAUL H'CAP 5f 160y

9:10 (9:13) (Class 4) (0-85,87) 3-Y-O+
£5,387 (£1,612; £806; £403; £300; £300) **Stalls** Centre

Form RPR

0405 **1** **Beyond Equal**13 3770 4-9-10 **83**.......... RobHornby 3 98+
(Stuart Kittow) *trckd ldrs: led over 1f out: rdn clr fnl f: eased nr fin* **11/2**2

-004 **2** 2 **Blaine**17 3636 9-9-4 **77**.......... TrevorWhelan 2 82
(Brian Barr) *hld up: pushed along and hdwy 1/2-way: styd on to go 2nd wl ins fnl f* **16/1**

0010 **3** nk **Red Alert**30 3164 5-9-3 **81**..........(p) DarraghKeenan(5) 5 85
(Tony Carroll) *hld up: hdwy over 1f out: edgd lft and r.o to go 3rd wl ins fnl f* **20/1**

-011 **4** 1 **Dark Shadow (IRE)**23 3422 3-9-5 **85**.......... HectorCrouch 6 84
(Clive Cox) *broke wl: nt clr run and lost pl sn after s: hdwy over 1f out: sn rdn: no ex wl ins fnl f* **6/1**3

3341 **5** 1 1/4 **Little Boy Blue**8 3963 4-9-9 **87** 5ex..........(h) RyanWhile(5) 8 84
(Bill Turner) *chsd ldrs: rdn and edgd rt over 1f out: styng on same pce whn edgd lft and nt clr run wl ins fnl f* **11/4**1

-003 **6** 2 1/4 **Iconic Knight (IRE)**17 3636 4-9-5 **78**.......... LiamKeniry 12 67
(Ed Walker) *hld up: nt clr run and swtchd rt over 1f out: rdn and edgd lft ins fnl f: nt trble ldrs* **8/1**

4330 **7** shd **Global Academy (IRE)**48 2556 4-8-11 **77**.......... TobyEley(7) 1 66
(Gay Kelleway) *led: rdn and hdd over 1f out: wknd ins fnl f (jockey said gelding hung right-handed)* **25/1**

-056 **8** 3 3/4 **Helvetian**25 3347 4-9-12 **85**.......... DavidProbert 11 61
(Mick Channon) *hld up: hdwy 1/2-way: rdn and edgd rt over 1f out: wknd ins fnl f* **7/1**

1362 **9** 7 **Major Blue**42 2730 3-8-6 **72**.......... LukeMorris 9 23
(James Eustace) *s.i.s: hdwy 1/2-way: sn rdn: wknd fnl f* **14/1**

2160 **10** 2 3/4 **The Daley Express (IRE)**19 3531 5-9-13 **86**..........(p1) FrannyNorton 7 30
(Ronald Harris) *prom: racd freely: jnd ldr over 3f out tl 1/2-way: wknd over 1f out (jockey said gelding ran too free)* **10/1**

5305 **11** 1/2 **Champion Brogie (IRE)**23 3420 3-8-4 **70**.......... NicolaCurrie 10 11
(J S Moore) *rrd s: outpcd (jockey said gelding was never travelling)* **25/1**

-000 **12** 6 **He'Zanarab (IRE)**39 2835 3-9-6 **86**.......... TomMarquand 4 7
(Richard Hannon) *s.i.s: sn prom: nt clr run over 4f out: rdn and wknd over 2f out* **11/1**

1m 9.48s (-1.62) **Going Correction** -0.05s/f (Good) **12 Ran SP% 122.4**
WFA 3 from 4yo+ 7lb
Speed ratings (Par 105): **108,105,104,103,101 98,98,93,84,80 80,72**
CSF £90.42 CT £1644.40 TOTE £6.60: £2.20, £5.60, £7.10; EX 107.60 Trifecta £1982.80.
Owner Stuart Wood & Partner **Bred** Redgate Bloodstock Ltd **Trained** Blackborough, Devon

FOCUS
The feature contest was a decent sprint handicap and the winner looked to improve again.
T/Jkpt: Not Won T/Plt: £607.00 to a £1 stake. Pool: £67,489.42 - 81.16 winning units T/Qpdt: £34.80 to a £1 stake. Pool: £8,289.00 - 175.92 winning units **Colin Roberts**

3919 CARLISLE (R-H)

Wednesday, June 26

OFFICIAL GOING: Good to firm (good in places; 7.6)
Wind: Breezy, half behind in over 2f of home straight Weather: Fine, dry

4237 BOOK YOUR CHRISTMAS PARTY AT CARLISLE RACECOURSE MAIDEN AUCTION STKS 5f

2:00 (2:02) (Class 5) 2-Y-O **£4,204** (£1,251; £625; £312) **Stalls** Low

Form RPR

5 **1** **Auckland Lodge (IRE)**7 3997 2-8-9 0.......... HarrisonShaw(5) 8 74
(Ben Haslam) *mde all: rdn and edgd lft over 1f out: hld on wl fnl f* **15/2**2

2 **2** nk **Asmund (IRE)**12 3810 2-9-5 0.......... BenCurtis 5 78
(K R Burke) *trckd ldrs: wnt 2nd over 2f out: sn rdn: kpt on fnl f: jst hld* **1/5**1

30 **3** 6 **Dancinginthesand (IRE)**23 3411 2-9-5 0.......... GrahamLee 2 56
(Bryan Smart) *trckd wnr to over 2f out: sn pushed along: outpcd by first two fr over 1f out* **10/1**

4 1 **Woven Quality (IRE)** 2-9-5 0 .... TomEaves 4 53+
(Donald McCain) *noisy in paddock: chsd ldng gp: rn green and outpcd over 2f out: rallied fnl f: nrst fin* **50/1**

5 nk **Midnight Mimosa (IRE)** 2-9-0 0 .... DavidAllan 1 47
(Tim Easterby) *missed break: bhd and outpcd: hdwy over 1f out: kpt on fnl f: no imp* **10/1**

6 3/4 **Ralphy Boy Two (IRE)** 2-9-5 0 .... PaulMulrennan 7 49
(Alistair Whillans) *chsd clr ldng trio: pushed along over 2f out: green and wandered over 1f out: wknd ins fnl f* **28/1**

0 7 1 1/4 **Aiden's Reward (IRE)**[15] 3703 2-9-5 0 .... AndrewMullen 3 45
(Ben Haslam) *hld up: pushed along over 2f out: sn no imp: btn over 1f out* **40/1**

64 8 1 3/4 **Pearlwood (IRE)**[14] 3717 2-8-11 0 .... SeanDavis(3) 6 33
(Richard Fahey) *bhd: shkn up 2f out: sn n.d: btn fnl f* **9/1**[3]

1m 1.64s (-0.46) **Going Correction** -0.15s/f (Firm) **8** Ran SP% **131.1**
Speed ratings (Par 93): **97,96,86,85,84 83,81,78**
CSF £10.85 TOTE £12.30: £1.80, £1.02, £2.10; EX 21.00 Trifecta £102.40.
Owner The Auckland Lodge Partnership **Bred** R Galway **Trained** Middleham Moor, N Yorks

FOCUS
After the first the riders were complimentary about the going, and the winning time suggested there was plenty of 'good' in it. The first pair dominated this ordinary 2yo maiden, sticking to the centre of the home straight, and there was a turn-up. The winner rates a clear improver.

4238 BRITISH STALLION STUDS EBF NOVICE STKS (PLUS 10 RACE) 5f 193y
2:30 (2:31) (Class 4) 2-Y-O £5,175 (£1,540; £769; £384) Stalls Low

Form RPR

32 1 **Keep Busy (IRE)**[9] 3927 2-9-0 0 .... JasonHart 6 73
(John Quinn) *t.k.h: prom: effrt and chsd ldr over 1f out: sn rdn and hung rt: led wl ins fnl f: r.o* **10/3**[2]

2 1/2 **Alix James** 2-9-5 0 .... JamieGormley 10 76+
(Iain Jardine) *trckd ldrs: rdn and outpcd 2f out: rallied fnl f: wnt 2nd towards fin* **13/2**

53 3 nk **Endowed**[32] 3071 2-9-5 0 .... RossaRyan 1 75
(Richard Hannon) *trckd ldr: led over 2f out: rdn and edgd rt over 1f out: hdd and no ex wl ins fnl f* **7/4**[1]

0 4 1 1/4 **One Bite (IRE)**[27] 3245 2-9-5 0 .... ShaneGray 2 71
(Keith Dalgleish) *sn pushed along in midfield: effrt and in tch over 1f out: rdn and kpt on ins fnl f: lost front shoe (vet said gelding lost it's right front shoe)* **12/1**

0 5 6 **Street Life**[22] 3451 2-9-5 0 .... PaulHanagan 5 52
(Richard Fahey) *prom: rdn over 2f out: hung rt and outpcd over 1f out: n.d after* **9/2**[3]

6 hd **Honnold** 2-9-5 0 .... GrahamLee 3 52
(Donald McCain) *missed break: hld up on ins: pushed along over 2f out: no imp over 1f out* **66/1**

7 shd **Elpheba (IRE)** 2-9-0 0 .... DavidEgan 11 46
(David Loughnane) *led to over 2f out: rdn and wknd over 1f out* **33/1**

6 8 1 1/2 **Jazz Style (IRE)**[24] 3371 2-9-5 0 .... PaulMulrennan 7 46
(David Brown) *bhd: drvn and outpcd over 2f out: sn btn* **50/1**

9 1 1/4 **Grand Pianola** 2-9-5 0 .... RachelRichardson 9 42
(Tim Easterby) *hld up: rdn along over 2f out: nvr on terms* **66/1**

10 2 1/2 **Joe's Way** 2-9-5 0 .... DavidAllan 8 34
(Tim Easterby) *missed break: bhd: struggling over 2f out: nvr on terms* **16/1**

1m 14.51s (-0.09) **Going Correction** -0.15s/f (Firm) **10** Ran SP% **112.4**
Speed ratings (Par 95): **94,93,92,91,83 83,82,80,79,75**
CSF £23.78 TOTE £3.10: £1.10, £2.60, £1.10; EX 24.60 Trifecta £83.50.
Owner Altitude Racing **Bred** Hackcanter Ltd & Mr P Gleeson **Trained** Settrington, N Yorks

FOCUS
This didn't look a bad 2yo novice event and it was run at a solid pace, although the time was only modest. A step forward from the winner and this race could be a bit better than rated.

4239 CARLISLE BELL CONSOLATION RACE H'CAP 7f 173y
3:00 (3:02) (Class 4) (0-80,83) 3-Y-O+ £7,439 (£2,213; £1,106; £553; £300; £300) Stalls Low

Form RPR

3112 1 **Jackhammer (IRE)**[5] 4054 5-9-0 65 .... (bp) JamesSullivan 11 74
(Dianne Sayer) *hld up in midfield: hdwy and prom 2f out: rdn to ld ins fnl f: kpt on wl* **7/1**

60-2 2 nk **Zoravan (USA)**[37] 2899 6-8-13 64 .... (v) TomEaves 5 72
(Keith Dalgleish) *hld up in midfield: hdwy on outside to ld over 1f out: edgd rt: hdd ins fnl f: rallied: hld nr fin* **20/1**

1346 3 2 1/2 **Jacob Black**[5] 4058 8-9-10 75 .... (v) ShaneGray 6 77
(Keith Dalgleish) *hld up: hdwy whn nt clr run over 2f out to over 1f out: chsd clr ldng pair wl ins fnl f: r.o* **16/1**

00-6 4 nk **Inner Circle (IRE)**[8] 3969 5-9-6 71 .... (p) BenCurtis 7 73
(Roger Fell) *trckd ldrs: led over 2f out to over 1f out: no ex ins fnl f* **8/1**

0011 5 1 **Redarna**[9] 3922 5-9-12 77 5ex .... (p) PaulMulrennan 14 76
(Dianne Sayer) *cl up on outside: rdn and edgd lft 2f out: sn outpcd: no imp fnl f (vet said gelding was suffering from post-race heat stress)* **3/1**[1]

1133 6 1/2 **Ventura Gold (IRE)**[18] 3568 4-9-7 75 .... SeanDavis(3) 12 73
(Richard Fahey) *hld up: effrt and drvn along over 2f out: kpt on fnl f: nt pce to chal* **16/1**

036- 7 hd **Mango Chutney**[231] 8924 6-9-7 72 .... (p) SamJames 2 70
(John Davies) *hld up on ins: effrt over 2f out: hung rt and no imp over 1f out* **50/1**

100 8 2 3/4 **Paparazzi**[26] 3305 4-9-5 70 .... CamHardie 3 61
(Tracy Waggott) *missed break: bhd: rdn over 2f out: kpt on fnl f: nvr rchd ldrs (jockey said gelding was slowly away)* **20/1**

0-06 9 3/4 **Irish Minister (USA)**[9] 3922 4-9-3 68 .... AndrewElliott 9 58
(David Thompson) *s.i.s: bhd tl sme late hdwy: nvr on terms* **66/1**

001 10 1/2 **Storm Ahead (IRE)**[10] 3880 6-9-11 76 5ex .... (b) DavidAllan 10 64+
(Tim Easterby) *hld up: effrt whn nt clr run fr over 2f out to 1f out: nt rcvr (jockey said gelding was denied a clear run approaching the final furlong)* **5/1**[3]

5040 11 4 **Burj**[21] 3471 3-9-8 83 .... DavidEgan 1 60
(Saeed bin Suroor) *in tch: hdwy over 2f out: edgd lft and wknd over 1f out (trainers' rep could offer no explanation for the poor performance)* **9/2**[2]

1240 12 4 1/2 **Barasti Dancer (IRE)**[10] 3885 3-8-10 71 .... (p[1]) CliffordLee 13 38
(K R Burke) *prom: hung rt and lost pl over 2f out: sn btn* **20/1**

4501 13 4 **Smugglers Creek (IRE)**[37] 2899 5-9-2 67 .... (p) JamieGormley 8 27
(Iain Jardine) *led to over 2f out: rdn and wknd over 1f out (jockey said gelding had no more to give)* **16/1**

1m 39.02s (-0.98) **Going Correction** -0.15s/f (Firm) **13** Ran SP% **118.8**
WFA 3 from 4yo+ 10lb
Speed ratings (Par 105): **98,97,95,94,93 93,93,90,89,89 85,80,76**
CSF £145.09 CT £2225.12 TOTE £7.80: £2.10, £5.00, £4.70; EX 129.60 Trifecta £1546.30.
Owner Mrs Dianne Sayer **Bred** F Dunne **Trained** Hackthorpe, Cumbria

FOCUS
Predictably they didn't hang around in this solid consolidation handicap.

4240 AGMA STABLEMATE CARLISLE BELL H'CAP 7f 173y
3:30 (3:31) (Class 4) (0-85,90) 3-Y-O+ £19,407 (£5,775; £2,886; £1,443; £300; £300) Stalls Low

Form RPR

0-46 1 **Rousayan (IRE)**[18] 3563 8-9-7 82 .... (h) DavidEgan 4 94
(Roger Fell) *hld up in midfield: hdwy 3f out: chsng ldrs over 1f out: rdn to ld ins fnl f: kpt on wl* **14/1**

2041 2 2 1/4 **Star Of Southwold (FR)**[6] 4021 4-9-10 90 5ex .... TheodoreLadd(5) 9 97
(Michael Appleby) *led 2f: pressed ldr: regained ld over 2f out: hdd ins fnl f: kpt on same pce* **7/1**[3]

-510 3 2 1/4 **Algaffaal (USA)**[22] 3450 4-8-13 77 .... (p[1]) BenRobinson(3) 17 79
(Brian Ellison) *dwlt: hld up: rdn and hdwy over 2f out: chsd clr ldng pair ins fnl f: r.o* **40/1**

3112 4 3/4 **Saisons D'Or (IRE)**[39] 2842 4-9-5 80 .... JackGarritty 8 80
(Jedd O'Keeffe) *prom: effrt and edgd lft 2f out: kpt on same pce fnl f* **10/1**

4511 5 nk **Club Wexford (IRE)**[4] 4097 8-9-10 85 4ex .... BenCurtis 6 84
(Roger Fell) *pressed ldr: led after 2f to over 2f out: drvn and outpcd fnl f* **9/2**[1]

-026 6 3/4 **Dark Intention (IRE)**[12] 3813 6-9-1 81 .... (p[1]) PaulaMuir(5) 12 79
(Lawrence Mullaney) *hld up bhd ldng bunch: drvn and outpcd over 2f out: rallied fnl f: r.o* **11/1**

0205 7 1/2 **Tough Remedy (IRE)**[22] 3450 4-9-8 83 .... PJMcDonald 2 79
(Keith Dalgleish) *hld up on ins: outpcd 3f out: rallied fnl f: nvr rchd ldrs* **11/1**

-045 8 1/2 **Mikmak**[12] 3811 6-9-7 82 .... (p) JasonHart 16 77+
(Tim Easterby) *hld up: no room fr over 3f out to ins fnl f: kpt on fin: nvr able to chal (jockey said gelding was denied a clear run continually from 2f out)* **8/1**

0661 9 nk **Brother McGonagall**[18] 3567 5-9-8 83 .... DavidAllan 3 78
(Tim Easterby) *hld up in midfield on ins: effrt over 2f out: no imp fr over 1f out* **7/1**[3]

6-55 10 nk **Al Erayg (IRE)**[39] 2844 6-9-8 83 .... RachelRichardson 5 77
(Tim Easterby) *hld up towards rr: drvn along 3f out: no imp fr over 1f out* **6/1**[2]

-060 11 1/2 **New Look (FR)**[12] 3813 4-9-3 78 .... (p[1]) PhilDennis 1 71
(Tim Easterby) *towards rr: effr whn nt clr run briefly over 2f out: no imp fr over 1f out* **25/1**

00-0 12 1 1/4 **Dream Walker (FR)**[12] 3813 10-9-6 81 .... CamHardie 14 71
(Brian Ellison) *towards rr: drvn and outpcd over 3f out: n.d after* **66/1**

0-26 13 1/2 **The Navigator**[27] 3250 4-9-2 77 .... PaulMulrennan 15 66
(Dianne Sayer) *hld up: shortlived effrt on outside over 2f out: sn btn* **25/1**

3301 14 4 1/2 **Tadaawol**[37] 2894 6-9-2 82 .... (p) BenSanderson(5) 11 60
(Roger Fell) *trckd ldrs tl rdn and wknd fr 2f out* **12/1**

000 15 5 **My Amigo**[12] 3813 6-9-3 78 .... (tp) JamesSullivan 10 45
(Marjorie Fife) *in tch: drvn along over 3f out: wknd over 2f out* **40/1**

6641 16 7 **Lamloom (IRE)**[5] 4058 5-9-13 88 5ex .... DanielTudhope 13 39
(David O'Meara) *cl up on outside tl rdn and wknd qckly fr over 2f out (trainer said, regarding poor form shown, that gelding ran too freely from the wide draw on this occasion)* **8/1**

1m 38.17s (-1.83) **Going Correction** -0.15s/f (Firm) **16** Ran SP% **133.9**
Speed ratings (Par 105): **103,100,98,97,97 96,96,95,95,95 94,93,92,88,83 76**
CSF £115.18 CT £4058.81 TOTE £16.40: £3.80, £2.30, £11.30, £2.60; EX 140.80 Trifecta £1772.50.
Owner The Roses Partnership **Bred** Haras De Son Altesse L'Aga Khan Scea **Trained** Nawton, N Yorks

FOCUS
Another highly competitive edition of this age-old handicap and there was a strong pace on.

4241 CUMBERLAND PLATE H'CAP 1m 3f 39y
4:00 (4:03) (Class 4) (0-85,84) 3-Y-O+ £19,407 (£5,775; £2,886; £1,443; £300; £300) Stalls High

Form RPR

-413 1 **Where's Jeff**[11] 3862 4-9-5 77 .... NathanEvans 6 84
(Michael Easterby) *cl up: rdn and led over 1f out: kpt on gamely fnl f* **5/1**[1]

35-5 2 nk **Groveman**[12] 2080 4-9-6 78 .... PJMcDonald 9 84
(Jedd O'Keeffe) *trckd ldrs: effrt and rdn over 1f out: pressed wnr ins fnl f: hld nr fin* **8/1**

02-4 3 hd **Volcanic Sky**[21] 3466 4-9-11 83 .... CallumShepherd 17 89+
(Saeed bin Suroor) *prom: effrt and rdn over 1f out: ev ch ins fnl f: kpt on: hld nr fin* **7/1**[3]

0324 4 1/2 **Mutamaded (IRE)**[6] 4035 6-9-12 84 .... JamesSullivan 14 89
(Ruth Carr) *hld up: rdn over 2f out: hdwy on outside over 1f out: kpt on fnl f: nrst fin* **16/1**

0441 5 3/4 **Appointed**[7] 4009 5-9-5 77 5ex .... (t) DavidAllan 13 81
(Tim Easterby) *led: rdn over 2f out: hdd over 1f out: no ex ins fnl f* **6/1**[2]

0-24 6 shd **Chingachgook**[46] 2629 4-9-2 74 .... (bt[1]) ConnorBeasley 3 77
(Tristan Davidson) *t.k.h: hld up: nt clr run over 2f out: effrt and edgd rt over 1f out: r.o ins fnl f (jockey said gelding was denied a clear run 2f out)* **10/1**

00/0 7 1 **Top Notch Tonto (IRE)**[12] 3811 9-9-4 79 .... BenRobinson(3) 15 81
(Brian Ellison) *s.i.s: bhd: rdn and plenty to do bnd over 2f out: kpt on wl fnl f: nvr rchd ldrs (jockey said gelding was slowly away)* **33/1**

0020 8 nk **Armandihan (IRE)**[28] 3222 5-9-10 82 .... (p) KevinStott 5 83
(Kevin Ryan) *hld up: effrt on outside over 2f out: kpt on same pce fnl f* **18/1**

5300 9 nk **Desert Ruler**[32] 3073 6-9-9 81 .... JackGarritty 7 82
(Jedd O'Keeffe) *t.k.h in midfield: n.m.r briefly over 2f out: effrt whn blkd over 1f out: one pce fnl f* **40/1**

-061 10 hd **Rake's Progress**[17] 3633 5-9-5 77 .... DavidEgan 1 77
(Heather Main) *midfield on ins: effrt and pushed along over 2f out: no imp fr over 1f out* **15/2**

1641 11 3/4 **Regular Income (IRE)**[11] 3845 4-9-9 81 .... (p) JimmyQuinn 4 80
(Adam West) *midfield on outside: effrt and rdn 2f out: outpcd fnl f* **18/1**

4-30 12 3/4 **Dance King**[32] 3073 9-9-11 83 .... (tp) PaulMulrennan 2 81
(Tim Easterby) *hld up: effrt whn nt clr run briefly over 2f out: drvn and no further imp over 1f out* **20/1**

-403 13 1 3/4 **Benadalid**[20] 3514 4-9-10 82 .... MichaelStainton 11 77
(Chris Fairhurst) *prom on outside tl rdn and wknd wl over 1f out* **16/1**

-000 14 3 **Multellie**[11] 3862 7-9-10 82 .... JasonHart 10 72
(Tim Easterby) *hld up on outside: drvn along over 2f out: wknd over 1f out* **33/1**

15 2 **Sea Of Mystery (IRE)**[53] 5094 6-9-3 75 AlistairRawlinson 8 61
(Michael Appleby) s.i.s: hld up: rdn and struggling over 2f out: sn btn 33/1

4630 16 21 **Employer (IRE)**[30] 3160 4-9-9 81 DanielTudhope 12 32
(Jim Goldie) t.k.h: hld up in midfield on outside: hdwy and cl up 1/2-way: rdn and wkng whn short of room wl over 1f out: sn eased (trainers' rep could offer no explanation for the poor performance other than the gelding ran too free) 11/1

210- 17 12 **Dagian (IRE)**[120] 8308 4-9-5 77 (p) PaulHanagan 16 7
(James Moffatt) bhd: struggling over 4f out: t.o 50/1

2m 25.07s (-4.63) **Going Correction** -0.15s/f (Firm) 17 Ran SP% 124.0
Speed ratings (Par 105): **110,109,109,109,108 108,107,107,107,107 106,106,104,102,101 86,77**
CSF £41.20 CT £289.85 TOTE £5.00: £1.90, £2.00, £2.10, £3.20; EX 43.90 Trifecta £183.90.
Owner A G Pollock, Golden Ratio & J Sissons **Bred** Lucky 5 Partnership & Stittenham Racing **Trained** Sheriff Hutton, N Yorks

FOCUS
One had to be handy in this year's Cumberland Plate and it saw a blanket finish.

4242 BRITISH STALLION STUDS EBF ETERNAL STKS (LISTED RACE) (FILLIES) 6f 195y
4:30 (4:33) (Class 1) 3-Y-O
£22,684 (£8,600; £4,304; £2,144; £1,076; £540) Stalls Low

Form RPR

221 1 **Tapisserie**[15] 3696 3-9-0 88 PaulHanagan 8 102+
(William Haggas) dwlt: bhd: outpcd over 4f out: last and plenty to do 3f out: drvn and gd hdwy on outside over 1f out: hung lft and led ins fnl f: kpt on wl 5/1[2]

-304 2 1 1/4 **Cava (IRE)**[25] 3359 3-9-0 97 JimmyQuinn 12 99
(Joseph Patrick O'Brien, Ire) hld up: stdy hdwy whn nt clr run over 2f out: effrt over 1f out: chsd wnr ins fnl f: r.o: lost front shoe (vet said filly lost it's right fore shoe) 12/1

20-0 3 3/4 **Viadera**[33] 3061 3-9-0 101 ColinKeane 2 97+
(G M Lyons, Ire) trckd ldr: led 2f out to ins fnl f: kpt on same pce 15/8[1]

-002 4 1 1/4 **Impulsion (IRE)**[18] 3583 3-9-0 88 (p[1]) DavidEgan 7 94
(Roger Varian) hld up: effrt and swtchd lft 2f out: kpt on fnl f: nvr able to chal 14/1

2000 5 1 3/4 **Chapelli**[4] 4122 3-9-0 94 ConnorBeasley 11 89
(Mark Johnston) midfield on outside: effrt and rdn 2f out: no imp fnl f 25/1

-005 6 1/2 **Come On Leicester (IRE)**[46] 2627 3-9-0 89 RossaRyan 5 88
(Richard Hannon) midfield: effrt over 2f out: wnt lft over 1f out: sn no imp 33/1

-046 7 2 1/2 **Sunday Star**[26] 3317 3-9-0 97 JasonHart 3 81
(Ed Walker) t.k.h early: prom: nt clr run over 2f out: effrt and rdn over 1f out: wknd ins fnl f 7/1

151- 8 3/4 **Summer Daydream (IRE)**[263] 7988 3-9-3 96 ShaneGray 4 82
(Keith Dalgleish) hld up: drvn and outpcd over 2f out: n.d after 20/1

-511 9 1 **Neon Sea (FR)**[18] 3583 3-9-0 89 PJMcDonald 10 76
(Sir Michael Stoute) in tch: effrt and rdn 2f out: wknd ins fnl f 13/2[3]

-460 10 3 **Concello (IRE)**[5] 4052 3-9-0 91 (b) BenCurtis 1 68
(Archie Watson) led 2f: pressed ldr to over 2f out: wknd over 1f out 40/1

2311 11 7 **Astrologer**[19] 3552 3-9-0 87 DanielTudhope 9 49
(David O'Meara) t.k.h early: led after 2f: rdn and hdd 2f out: sn wknd 8/1

1m 25.95s (-2.05) **Going Correction** -0.15s/f (Firm) 11 Ran SP% 116.7
Speed ratings (Par 104): **105,103,102,101,99 98,95,95,93,90 82**
CSF £59.58 TOTE £5.20: £1.80, £2.70, £1.50; EX 61.20 Trifecta £258.70.
Owner Isa Salman **Bred** Newsells Park Stud **Trained** Newmarket, Suffolk

FOCUS
A mixed bag of fillies took in this Listed race. The strong pace collapsed a furlong out.

4243 BRITISH STALLION STUDS EBF FILLIES' H'CAP 6f 195y
5:00 (5:01) (Class 4) (0-85,73) 3-Y-O-£7,439 (£2,213; £1,106; £553; £300) Stalls Low

Form RPR

2-21 1 **Caustic Love (IRE)**[9] 3921 3-9-2 71 6ex ShaneGray 4 78
(Keith Dalgleish) trckd ldrs: wnt 2nd over 4f out: rdn to ld over 1f out: edgd rt ins fnl f: kpt on wl 6/4[1]

2-12 2 3/4 **Polyphony (IRE)**[15] 3685 4-9-8 68 (h) JasonHart 3 75
(John Mackie) trckd ldr to over 4f out: cl up: effrt and rdn over 1f out: chsd wnr ins fnl f: r.o 11/4[2]

-213 3 2 3/4 **Harvest Day**[18] 3567 4-9-13 73 (t) NathanEvans 5 73
(Michael Easterby) t.k.h: led to over 1f out: drvn and outpcd ins fnl f 8/1

4130 4 1/2 **Javelin**[30] 3147 4-9-7 67 DanielTudhope 1 65
(William Muir) in tch: rdn over 2f out: hung rt over 1f out: kpt on fnl f: no imp 11/2

1322 5 20 **Supaulette (IRE)**[23] 3414 4-9-8 68 (bt) DavidAllan 2 12
(Tim Easterby) hld up in last pl: rdn over 2f out: wknd over 1f out: eased whn no ch ins fnl f 5/1[3]

1m 26.95s (-1.05) **Going Correction** -0.15s/f (Firm) 5 Ran SP% 109.8
WFA 3 from 4yo 9lb
Speed ratings (Par 102): **100,99,96,95,72**
CSF £5.81 TOTE £2.30: £1.60, £1.30; EX 5.30 Trifecta £23.20.
Owner Weldspec Glasgow Limited **Bred** Mrs C Holohan **Trained** Carluke, S Lanarks

FOCUS
This modest little fillies' handicap proved tactical.
T/Plt: £53.60 to a £1 stake. Pool: £68,134.31 - 927.28 winning units T/Qpdt: £52.00 to a £1 stake. Pool: £5,265.17 - 74.88 winning units **Richard Young**

3461 KEMPTON (A.W) (R-H)
Wednesday, June 26

OFFICIAL GOING: Polytrack: standard to slow (watered)
Wind: windy Weather: bright

4244 RACING TV APPRENTICE H'CAP 7f (P)
5:15 (5:17) (Class 6) (0-55,57) 3-Y-O
£3,105 (£924; £461; £300; £300; £300) Stalls Low

Form RPR

0124 1 **Comeonfeeltheforce (IRE)**[27] 3264 3-9-5 56 (t) GeorgiaDobie(3) 6 72+
(Lee Carter) bhd ldrs: travelling wl whn shkn up to ld wl over 1f out: qckn and sn bounded clr: v easily 15/8[1]

00-0 2 7 **Lady Morpheus**[36] 2926 3-8-9 48 LouisGaroghan(5) 4 45+
(Gary Moore) sluggish s: rcvrd and sn in rr-div: effrt 2f out: sustained run fr over 1f out to take 2nd cl home in bunch fin for placings: no ch w wnr 20/1

4005 3 nse **Jeanette May**[29] 3182 3-8-9 46 oh1 JonathanFisher(3) 3 43
(William Stone) mid-div on inner: rdn bhd ldng trio 2f out: stuck on fr over 1f out to grab 3rd in bunch fin for placings 10/1

252 4 nse **Valley Belle (IRE)**[22] 3442 3-9-4 57 GraceMcEntee(5) 10 54
(Phil McEntee) cl up bhd ldrs a bit wd: rdn 2f out and ev ch: sn lft bhd by wnr: plugged on ins fnl f in bunch fin for placings 8/1[3]

064- 5 nse **Meraki**[245] 8540 3-8-13 50 (b[1]) RhonaPindar(3) 2 47
(Tim Pinfield) racd in last: swtchd to outer over 2f out and rdn: no real imp tl picked up wl over 1f out: keeping on ins fnl f to chal in bunch fin for placings 16/1

-600 6 hd **Seafaring Girl (IRE)**[27] 3271 3-8-9 46 SeanKirrane(3) 1 42
(Mark Loughnane) bhd ldr: rdn and ev ch 2f out: sn lft bhd by wnr: stuck on in 2nd ent fnl f: one pce last 150yds 16/1

00P0 7 hd **Gonbutnotforgotten (FR)**[27] 3277 3-9-5 53 DylanHogan 8 49
(Philip McBride) in rr-div and niggled along at 1/2-way: rdn wl over 2f out: no imp tl kpt on one pce fr over 1f out 20/1

0022 8 1/2 **The Big House (IRE)**[16] 3650 3-9-0 51 LauraCoughlan(3) 14 45
(Adrian Nicholls) in rr: swtchd to outer over 2f out: sn rdn: kpt on fr over 1f out: styng on wl fnl f (jockey said gelding ran too free) 4/1[2]

6-00 9 3/4 **Fanny Chenal**[23] 3421 3-8-10 49 IsobelFrancis(5) 11 41
(Jim Boyle) mid-div on outer: rdn over 2f out: plugged on fr over 1f out 10/1

0-50 10 1 **Dance To Freedom**[42] 2735 3-9-2 55 (t) MarcoGhiani(5) 13 45
(Stuart Williams) in rr-div and sltly hmpd after 2f: effrt wl over 2f out: no imp sn after 20/1

0004 11 2 1/4 **Islay Mist**[6] 4029 3-9-0 51 (t) WilliamCarver(3) 7 34
(Lee Carter) led: rdn over 2f out: hdd wl over 1f out: fdd sn after 12/1

0-00 12 2 1/4 **Grandad's Legacy**[25] 3354 3-9-3 54 (h) CierenFallon(3) 9 31
(Ali Stronge) edgy bhd stalls: racd cl up bhd ldrs: niggled along to hold pl 4f out: rdn wl over 3f out: fdd over 1f out (jockey said gelding was never travelling) 12/1

500 13 1 1/2 **Katie O'Hara (IRE)**[29] 3182 3-8-9 46 oh1 JessicaCooley(3) 5 19
(Samuel Farrell, Ire) mid-div on inner: pushed along wl over 3f out: no ex over 1f out (vet said filly lost left-fore shoe) 66/1

1m 25.94s (-0.06) **Going Correction** 0.0s/f (Stan) 13 Ran SP% 127.0
Speed ratings (Par 97): **100,92,91,91,91 91,91,90,89,88 86,83,81**
CSF £52.24 CT £331.65 TOTE £2.80: £1.20, £5.50, £3.40; EX 63.70 Trifecta £517.30.
Owner Kestonracingclub **Bred** Thomas & Seamus Whelan & David Harrison **Trained** Epsom, Surrey

FOCUS
An ordinary handicap but this has to rate a significant pb from the winner.

4245 32RED.COM - BRITISH STALLION STUDS EBF FILLIES' NOVICE STKS (PLUS 10 RACE) 7f (P)
5:50 (5:51) (Class 4) 2-Y-O £5,822 (£1,732; £865; £432) Stalls Low

Form RPR

1 **Wren** 2-9-0 0 JasonWatson 3 79+
(Roger Charlton) acted up in paddock: threw hd in the air and ct jockey on face: last to post: racd in 3rd on inner: pushed along over 2f out: chsd ldr ent fnl f: sustained effrt fnl 150yds to ld last strides: snug at fin 8/1

4 2 nk **Daily Times**[18] 3601 2-9-0 0 NickyMackay 2 78
(John Gosden) trckd ldr and t.k.h thrght: drvn 2f out: led over 1f out: sltly green in front: kpt on ent fnl f: ct last strides 2/1[1]

3 3 **Queen Of The Sea (IRE)** 2-9-0 0 GeorgeWood 1 70+
(Saeed bin Suroor) s.s: hld up in 5th on inner: effrt over 2f out: kpt on fr over 1f out: one pce fnl f and tk 3rd fnl 110yds (jockey said filly was slowly away) 9/4[2]

03 4 1 1/4 **Fashion Free**[22] 3441 2-9-0 0 HollieDoyle 6 67
(Archie Watson) led: rdn over 2f out: hdd over 1f out: stuck on tl lost 2nd jst ins fnl f: no ex and lost 3rd sn after (jockey said filly hung left-handed throughout) 16/1

3 5 2 1/4 **Topkapi Star**[10] 3881 2-9-0 0 JackMitchell 7 61
(Roger Varian) hld up in last: rdn over 2f out: plugged on 5/1[3]

0 6 15 **Little Lulu (IRE)**[15] 3689 2-8-11 0 JaneElliott(3) 5 20+
(Archie Watson) racd in 3rd: pushed along 4f out: lost pl 3f out: dropped to last over 2f out: eased over 1f out: t.o 50/1

P **Love Powerful (IRE)** 2-9-0 0 SeanLevey 4
(Richard Hannon) wnt lft leaving stalls: in last whn wnt amiss and p.u after 2f: dismntd (jockey said he felt filly go amiss) 5/1[3]

1m 27.37s (1.37) **Going Correction** 0.0s/f (Stan) 7 Ran SP% 116.4
Speed ratings (Par 92): **92,91,88,86,84 67,**
CSF £25.26 TOTE £10.70: £4.90, £1.20; EX 31.70 Trifecta £108.30.
Owner Exors Of The Late Lady Rothschild **Bred** Kincorth Investments Inc **Trained** Beckhampton, Wilts

FOCUS
They went fairly steady early on in this fillies' novice. The level is fluid.

4246 32RED CASINO / EBFSTALLIONS.COM NOVICE STKS (PLUS 10 RACE) 6f (P)
6:20 (6:24) (Class 4) 2-Y-O £5,822 (£1,732; £865; £432) Stalls Low

Form RPR

1 **Aussie Showstopper (FR)** 2-9-5 0 ShaneKelly 4 75+
(Richard Hughes) w ldr: led after 3f: rdn 2f out: kicked clr over 1f out: stuck on wl fnl f and jst hld on 12/1

2 nse **Great Ambassador** 2-9-5 0 HarryBentley 7 75
(Ralph Beckett) pushed along leaving stalls: in rr: rdn 3f out and swtchd wd wl over 2f out: no immediate imp over 1f out: styd on strly ent fnl f: gaining on wnr w ev stride fnl 110yds: jst failed 5/2[1]

3 1/2 **Hector Loza** 2-9-5 0 NickyMackay 1 73+
(Simon Dow) bhd ldrs and sltly keen: smooth prog over 2f out: rdn 2f out: kpt on wl and tk 2nd 1f out: clsng on wnr but lost 2nd cl home 25/1

4 3/4 **Qaaddim (IRE)** 2-9-5 0 JackMitchell 5 71
(Roger Varian) hld up in rr: shkn up and tk clsr order over 2f out: rdn 2f out: styd on wl fr over 1f out 7/2[2]

5 1 **Zingaro Boy (IRE)** 2-9-5 0 HollieDoyle 6 68
(Hugo Palmer) in rr-div: swtchd to outer over 2f out: rdn 2f out: kpt on fr over 1f out 9/1

6 3/4 **Striding Edge (IRE)** 2-9-5 0 OisinMurphy 3 66
(Mark Johnston) cl up in mid-div on inner: rdn over 2f out: kpt on over 1f out: one pce fnl f 10/1

2 7 hd **Red Sun (IRE)**[19] 3530 2-9-5 0 KieranShoemark 2 65
(Charles Hills) uns rdr gng to post and got loose: in rr-div on inner: rdn 2f out: kpt on one pce 4/1[3]

0 8 1/2 **Winnetka (IRE)**[9] 3943 2-9-5 0 SeanLevey 10 64
(Richard Hannon) wl away fr wd draw and sn w ldrs on outer: rdn over 2f out: no ex 2f out 10/1

The Form Book Flat 2019, Raceform Ltd, Newbury, RG14 5SJ

9 3 **Modern British Art (IRE)** 2-9-5 0 JasonWatson 9 55
(Michael Bell) *racd in mid-div: niggled along at 1/2-way: rdn over 2f out: briefly qcknd over 1f out: no ex ent fnl f* 9/1

10 9 **Last Date** 2-9-2 0 GabrieleMalune(3) 8 28
(Ivan Furtado) *led tl narrowly hdd after 2f: styd w ldr: rdn over 2f out: no ex sn after* 50/1

1m 13.35s (0.25) **Going Correction** 0.0s/f (Stan) **10** Ran SP% **122.5**
Speed ratings (Par 95): **98,97,97,96,94 93,93,93,89,77**
CSF £44.38 TOTE £12.30: £2.90, £1.60, £6.10; EX 51.70 Trifecta £672.20.
Owner Peter Cook **Bred** S A R L Eds Stud Ltd **Trained** Upper Lambourn, Berks

FOCUS
The two who had already had a run didn't set a high standard and the race was dominated by the newcomers, so the level is fluid.

4247 100% PROFIT AT 32REDSPORT.COM FILLIES' H'CAP (DIV I) 7f (P)
6:50 (6:53) (Class 5) (0-70,72) 3-Y-0+
£3,752 (£1,116; £557; £300; £300; £300) **Stalls** Low

Form RPR

5-06 1 **Delilah Park**[19] 3549 5-9-13 **69** JackMitchell 5 81
(Chris Wall) *taken off heels early: sn trckd ldr: rdn between horses 2f out: led wl over 1f out: sn clr* 4/1[2]

1243 2 3 1/2 **Chloellie**[35] 2971 4-10-1 **71** OisinMurphy 10 74
(J R Jenkins) *bhd ldrs: rdn 2f out and briefly led: kpt on chsng wnr fnl f* 5/1[3]

5632 3 2 1/2 **Seraphim**[30] 3146 3-8-12 **66** (t) GabrieleMalune(3) 7 59
(Marco Botti) *cl up in mid-div: rdn over 2f out: kpt on ins fnl f to jst take 3rd post* 9/1

-114 4 nse **Fantastic Flyer**[30] 3146 4-9-5 **61** MartinDwyer 12 57
(Dean Ivory) *bhd ldrs on outer: rdn 2f out: ev ch over 1f out: plugged on fnl f and lost 3rd post* 9/1

321- 5 2 **Wild Dancer**[326] 5744 6-9-10 **66** JoeyHaynes 2 56
(Patrick Chamings) *in rr on inner: effrt to cl over 3f out: rdn over 2f out: styd on fr over 1f out* 20/1

45-2 6 2 **Gaslight**[35] 2967 3-9-5 **70** (t) GeorgeWood 1 52
(James Fanshawe) *mid-div on inner and sn squeezed up: rdn over 2f out: plugged on fr over 1f out* 7/1

4103 7 hd **Met By Moonlight**[21] 3462 5-10-0 **70** (b) JasonWatson 4 54
(Ron Hodges) *mid-div between horses: rdn wl over 2f out: one pce over 1f out (jockey said mare moved poorly)* 3/1[1]

23-5 8 2 1/4 **Shellebeau (IRE)**[54] 2356 3-9-4 **72** MeganNicholls(3) 8 47
(Paul Nicholls) *hld up in rr: rdn over 2f out: styd on one pce* 12/1

000 9 2 **Ainne**[30] 3142 4-8-2 **51** oh3 (tp) ElinorJones(7) 9 24
(Sylvester Kirk) *racd in rr-div: racd wd bnd: effrt over 2f out: no ex over 1f out* 50/1

3555 10 3/4 **Canford Dancer**[18] 3598 3-9-3 **68** (b[1]) ShaneKelly 6 36
(Richard Hughes) *led: shkn up jst under 2f out: hdd & wknd sn after* 10/1

3065 11 4 **Lady Schannell (IRE)**[27] 3258 3-8-11 **62** (bt[1]) AndreaAtzeni 3 19
(Marco Botti) *in rr-div: scrubbed along wl over 3f out: no imp fr 2f out* 14/1

4520 12 1 1/4 **Naralsaif (IRE)**[65] 1986 5-8-13 **55** (v) PaddyMathers 11 12
(Derek Shaw) *missed break and sn struggling in detached last: sme prog in st* 25/1

1m 25.7s (-0.30) **Going Correction** 0.0s/f (Stan)
WFA 3 from 4yo+ 9lb **12** Ran SP% **128.2**
Speed ratings (Par 100): **101,97,94,94,91 89,89,86,84,83 79,77**
CSF £26.15 CT £183.02 TOTE £4.80: £1.90, £1.60, £3.00; EX 29.50 Trifecta £222.60.
Owner Mr & Mrs De & J Cash And P Turner **Bred** Derra Park Stud **Trained** Newmarket, Suffolk

FOCUS
The quicker of the two divisions by 0.45sec, but few got into it, with it paying to be close to the pace. A pb from the winner.

4248 100% PROFIT AT 32REDSPORT.COM FILLIES' H'CAP (DIV II) 7f (P)
7:20 (7:22) (Class 5) (0-70,72) 3-Y-0+
£3,752 (£1,116; £557; £300; £300; £300) **Stalls** Low

Form RPR

-032 1 **Crystal Casque**[41] 2774 4-9-13 **68** OisinMurphy 8 75
(Rod Millman) *w ldr: drvn over 2f out: rdn 2f out: styd on wl ent fnl f to ld cl home* 3/1[2]

1404 2 1/2 **Gregorian Girl**[13] 3764 3-8-11 **61** MartinDwyer 5 64
(Dean Ivory) *trckd ldrs on inner: rdn 2f out and styd to inner: kpt on wl fr over 1f out to take 2nd cl home* 7/1

53-1 3 hd **Local History**[35] 2976 3-9-6 **70** KieranShoemark 4 72
(James Tate) *led: rdn 2f out: kpt on and one l advantage ent fnl f: chal both sides 110yds out: hdd cl home* 6/1[3]

2-44 4 hd **Regal Banner**[15] 3685 3-9-8 **72** AndreaAtzeni 9 74+
(Roger Varian) *hld up in rr-div: swtchd to outer over 2f out: shkn up 2f out: outpcd over 1f out: styd on fnl f* 11/4[1]

5540 5 1 1/2 **Huddle**[33] 3041 3-8-13 **63** JasonWatson 6 61
(William Knight) *bhd ldrs between horses: rdn 2f out: tk false step wl over 1f out: plugged on* 16/1

-100 6 1/2 **Kodiac Lass (IRE)**[26] 3323 3-9-7 **71** HarryBentley 2 68
(Marco Botti) *hld up in rr-div: rdn over 2f out: plugged on fr over 1f out* 8/1

025 7 2 3/4 **Sonnet Rose (IRE)**[14] 3744 5-9-6 **61** (bt) NickyMackay 11 53
(Conrad Allen) *bhd ldrs on outer: rdn over 2f out: fdd wl over 1f out* 20/1

5604 8 1/2 **Alba Del Sole (IRE)**[34] 3020 4-8-12 **56** (b[1]) GabrieleMalune(3) 7 47
(Ivan Furtado) *in rr: effrt 2f out: no imp* 8/1

4420 9 15 **Ventura Blues (IRE)**[102] 1234 5-10-2 **71** (p) GeorgeWood 1 21
(Alexandra Dunn) *a in rr: effrt wl over 2f out: sn hld: t.o* 16/1

1m 26.15s (0.15) **Going Correction** 0.0s/f (Stan)
WFA 3 from 4yo+ 9lb **9** Ran SP% **117.2**
Speed ratings (Par 100): **99,98,98,97,96 95,92,91,74**
CSF £24.86 CT £120.31 TOTE £3.30: £1.30, £2.00, £2.40; EX 25.20 Trifecta £153.10.
Owner The Dirham Partnership **Bred** Mrs J E Laws **Trained** Kentisbeare, Devon

FOCUS
They went fairly steady early on, the time was 0.45sec slower than the first division, and it paid to be on the pace. The winner has been rated in line with her best.

4249 32RED H'CAP (LONDON MILE SERIES QUALIFIER) 1m (P)
7:50 (7:51) (Class 4) (0-80,80) 3-Y-0+
£6,469 (£1,443; £481; £300; £300) **Stalls** Low

Form RPR

210- 1 **Kings Highway (IRE)**[239] 8729 4-9-7 **76** SeanLevey 2 84
(Ivan Furtado) *bhd ldr: rdn on inner 2f out: kpt on wl fr over 1f out: led 110yds out: stuck on best in three-way: jst hld on* 6/1[3]

-010 2 shd **Directory**[35] 2966 4-9-9 **78** RyanTate 9 85
(James Eustace) *led: rdn 2f out: kpt on wl tl hdd 110yds out: rallied cl home in three-way fin* 12/1

-402 2 dht **Kingston Kurrajong**[29] 3185 6-9-4 **73** JasonWatson 1 80
(William Knight) *racd in mid-div on inner: clsr whn rdn 2f out: briefly outpcd over 1f out: stuck on wl ent fnl f: styd on in three-way fin cl home: jst failed* 4/1[1]

0-60 4 3 **Arigato**[26] 3313 4-9-11 **80** (p) JosephineGordon 5 80
(William Jarvis) *between horses bhd ldrs: rdn over 2f out: kpt on fr over 1f out* 10/1

/21- 5 nk **Let Rip (IRE)**[180] 9732 5-9-10 **79** KieranShoemark 14 78+
(Henry Candy) *bhd ldr on outer: rdn over 2f out: plugged on* 7/1

-022 6 1 **Ragstone View (IRE)**[34] 2994 4-9-2 **71** (h) JackMitchell 10 68+
(Rod Millman) *s.s and in rr: rdn over 2f out: kpt on fr over 1f out* 16/1

1450 7 1/2 **Harbour Vision**[12] 3813 4-9-6 **75** PaddyMathers 13 71+
(Derek Shaw) *hld up in rr: rdn over 2f out: one pce* 9/1

6306 8 1/2 **Magic Mirror**[40] 2797 6-9-4 **73** (p) HollieDoyle 7 68
(Mark Rimell) *in rr-div: shkn up on outer over 2f out: shuffled along w a bit to do fr over 1f out* 10/1

5-20 9 3/4 **Just Brilliant (IRE)**[58] 2207 4-9-11 **80** OisinMurphy 8 73
(Peter Chapple-Hyam) *w ldr: rdn 2f out: wknd sn after* 9/2[2]

0656 10 2 1/4 **Jellmood**[13] 3763 4-9-7 **76** ShaneKelly 11 64
(Chris Gordon) *racd in mid-div: effrt over 2f out: plugged on one pce (jockey said gelding hung left-handed rounding the bend)* 14/1

535- 11 5 **Fronsac**[261] 8055 4-9-6 **75** RobertWinston 12 51
(Daniel Kubler) *a towards rr* 12/1

100- 12 10 **Seven Clans (IRE)**[377] 3772 7-9-10 **79** (b) JFEgan 3 32
(Neil Mulholland) *in rr-div: rdn over 2f out: sn hld* 33/1

50-0 13 3 3/4 **Chai Chai (IRE)**[32] 3072 4-9-7 **76** (t) HarryBentley 6 21
(Tom Dascombe) *bhd ldrs: rdn wl over 2f out and lost pl: wknd over 1f out* 25/1

0000 14 37 **Margie's Choice (GER)**[27] 3264 4-9-3 **72** (v) GeorgeWood 4
(Michael Madgwick) *racd in mid-div: rdn over 2f out: no ex sn after and eased (jockey said filly was never travelling)* 25/1

1m 38.62s (-1.18) **Going Correction** 0.0s/f (Stan) **14** Ran SP% **131.7**
Speed ratings (Par 105): **105,104,104,101,101 100,100,99,98,96 91,81,77,40**WIN: 8.30 Kings Highway; PL: 4.30 Directory, 1.60 Kingston Kurrajong, 3.10 Kings Highway; Exacta: KH/D - 54.70, KH/KK - 19.90; CSF: KH/D - 41.17, KH/KK - 16.30; Tricast: KH/D/KK - 172.75, KH/KK/D - 153.40; Trifecta: KH/D/KK - 240.60, KH/KK/D - 150.20;: £27, £Owner, £A Graham - Bankruptcy Trustee M Stanley, £BredCentury Farms Trained Trifecta £Wiseton, Nottinghamshire.

FOCUS
A good battle between the first three, and they pulled clear of the rest. The winner found a bit of improvement.

4250 32RED ON THE APP STORE H'CAP (LONDON MIDDLE DISTANCE SERIES QUALIFIER) 1m 2f 219y(P)
8:20 (8:21) (Class 4) (0-85,87) 4-Y-0+
£6,469 (£1,925; £962; £481; £300; £300) **Stalls** Low

Form RPR

1-30 1 **The Pinto Kid (FR)**[41] 2763 4-8-13 **77** (t) GeorgeWood 1 86+
(James Fanshawe) *racd in mid-div on inner: shkn up over 2f out and smooth prog: rdn wl over 1f out: qcknd and led 1f out: styd on wl cl home to fend off runner-up* 9/2[2]

-500 2 nk **Fairy Tale (IRE)**[37] 3136 4-9-7 **85** ShaneKelly 8 92
(Gay Kelleway) *hld up in rr: shkn up over 2f out and prog fr 2f out: rdn w a bit to do over 1f out: kpt on strly fnl f: nvr nrr* 66/1

0-04 3 1 **Oh It's Saucepot**[34] 3004 5-8-13 **77** JackMitchell 5 83
(Chris Wall) *hld up in rr: clsr whn rdn over 2f out: kpt on wl fr over 1f out* 12/1

4-45 4 nk **Autumn War (IRE)**[46] 2606 4-9-7 **85** RobertWinston 9 90
(Charles Hills) *in rr-div tl prog on outer appr first bnd: sn bhd ldrs on outer: shkn up over 3f out and c wd into st: rdn over 2f out: kpt on fr over 1f out: nt disgrac* 4/1[1]

3634 5 1 1/2 **Wimpole Hall**[35] 2969 6-9-1 **79** (b[1]) JasonWatson 2 81
(William Jarvis) *led and t.k.h: hdd on first bnd and sn bhd ldr: gng wl and pressed ldr fr over 2f out: rdn to ld 2f out: kpt on wl tl hdd 1f out: wknd qckly sn after* 8/1

20-3 6 1 3/4 **You're Hired**[40] 2800 6-9-9 **87** KieranShoemark 3 86
(Amanda Perrett) *racd in mid-div and t.k.h: rdn over 2f out: plugged on fr over 1f out (jockey said gelding hung left-handed)* 11/2[3]

0023 7 1/2 **Petrastar**[23] 3424 4-9-1 **79** OisinMurphy 6 77
(Clive Cox) *s.s and in rr: rapid prog on outer gng into first bnd and sn led: hdd over 1f out: stuck on tl wknd qckly fnl 150yds (jockey said gelding was slowly away)* 6/1

5-00 8 2 **Orange Suit (IRE)**[35] 2966 4-8-7 **71** HollieDoyle 7 66
(Ed de Giles) *bhd ldrs on inner: rdn 2f out: outpcd over 1f out: plugged on* 10/1

21-3 9 hd **Mainsail Atlantic (USA)**[64] 2022 4-9-4 **82** AndreaAtzeni 4 76
(James Fanshawe) *in rr-div: rdn over 2f out: kpt on fr over 1f out (trainer's rep said colt was unsuited by the slow pace)* 4/1[1]

-310 10 2 3/4 **Tralee Hills**[12] 3806 5-9-0 **78** (p[1]) JosephineGordon 10 67
(Peter Hedger) *a in rr and outpcd: sme prog fr over 1f out* 33/1

2330 11 nk **Paco's Prince**[12] 3816 4-8-0 **71** AledBeech(7) 12 60
(Nick Littmoden) *bhd ldr on outer: rdn over 2f out and losing pl: no ex sn after (jockey said gelding stopped quickly)* 33/1

2m 20.55s (-0.45) **Going Correction** 0.0s/f (Stan) **11** Ran SP% **123.1**
Speed ratings (Par 105): **104,103,103,102,101 100,100,98,98,96 96**
CSF £284.26 CT £3375.17 TOTE £5.40: £1.90, £20.10, £4.40; EX 206.10 Trifecta £4056.10.
Owner Fred Archer Racing - Bruce **Bred** Petra Bloodstock Agency Ltd **Trained** Newmarket, Suffolk

FOCUS
Something of a muddling race but the winner has been rated as improving.

4251 FAREWELL LAUREN GOLDSMITH & GOOD LUCK H'CAP 1m 7f 218y(P)
8:50 (8:50) (Class 6) (0-65,65) 4-Y-0+
£3,105 (£924; £461; £300; £300; £300) **Stalls** Low

Form RPR

3105 1 **Thresholdofadream (IRE)**[34] 3017 4-8-10 **54** JasonWatson 5 62+
(Amanda Perrett) *hld up in rr-div: shkn up and smooth prog fr over 2f out: rdn wl over 1f out: led ent fnl f: kpt on* 10/1

5515 2 1 3/4 **Bird For Life**[58] 2217 5-8-9 **60** (p) EllieMacKenzie(7) 4 66
(Mark Usher) *hld up in rr-div: rapid prog in bk st to ld 7f out: rdn over 2f out: drifted to nrside over 1f out: hdd ent fnl f and plugged on (jockey said mare hung badly left-handed)* 6/1[3]

2652 **3** 2 **Nafaayes (IRE)**[22] 3444 5-9-4 **62**..........................(p) MartinDwyer 7 66
(Jean-Rene Auvray) *hld up in rr-div: rapid prog in bk st to press ldr 7f out: rdn over 2f out: carried to nrside by runner-up over 1f out: stuck on one pce fnl f* **6/1**[3]

5600 **4** 2 1/4 **Akavit (IRE)**[36] 2936 7-9-2 **63**.......................... JaneElliott(3) 8 64
(Ed de Giles) *bmpd leaving stalls: t.k.h in rr: rdn wl over 2f out: kpt on wl fr over 1f out* **16/1**

0035 **5** 1 1/4 **Fitzwilly**[22] 3444 9-8-13 **62**.......................... ScottMcCullagh(5) 6 61
(Mick Channon) *in rr-div tl rapid prog on outer after 5f to briefly ld after 6f: rdn over 2f out: outpcd wl over 1f out: kpt on again ent fnl f* **16/1**

6000 **6** 1/2 **Mood For Mischief**[34] 3015 4-8-5 **54**..........................(p) RachealKneller(5) 1 53
(James Bennett) *racd in mid-div on outer: tk clsr order in bk st: rdn over 2f out: kpt on* **40/1**

00/3 **7** 4 1/2 **Daghash**[43] 2718 10-9-0 **58**.......................... OisinMurphy 3 51
(Stuart Kittow) *in rr: tk clsr order over 3f out: rdn on inner over 2f out: plugged on* **12/1**

0-03 **8** 5 **The Fiddler**[27] 3272 4-8-7 **51**.......................... GeorgeWood 14 38
(Chris Wall) *racd in mid-div on outer: rdn wl over 3f out: plugged on* **11/2**[2]

5511 **9** 1/2 **Greenview Paradise (IRE)**[64] 2014 5-8-9 **53**.......................... KieranO'Neill 2 40
(Jeremy Scott) *bhd ldrs: shkn up gng okay over 3f out: rdn over 2f out: one pce* **13/2**

512- **10** 2 **Deebaj (IRE)**[89] 3200 7-9-7 **65**.......................... ShaneKelly 12 49
(Gary Moore) *mid-div tl prog fr 5f to sit bhd ldrs 6f: lost pl sn after: pushed along in mid-div in bk st: rdn over 4f out: no ex fr 2f out* **8/1**

1305 **11** 1/2 **Double Legend (IRE)**[42] 2733 4-9-4 **62**.......................... KieranShoemark 10 46
(Amanda Perrett) *cl up in mid-div: rdn wl over 4f out: plugged on in st* **5/1**[1]

-506 **12** 1 1/2 **Looking For Carl**[15] 3686 4-9-3 **64**..........................(p) MeganNicholls(3) 13 46
(Mark Loughnane) *sn led: briefly hdd after 6f: hdd 7f out: remained bhd ldr: rdn wl over 3f out: wknd fr 2f out* **12/1**

0-02 **13** 108 **Ness Of Brodgar**[20] 3497 4-8-8 **52**..........................(t) JFEgan 11
(Mark H Tompkins) *in rr-div: wknd over 4f out: t.o fr 3f out (trainer's rep said filly had a breathing problem)* **25/1**

3m 30.11s (0.01) **Going Correction** 0.0s/f (Stan) **13 Ran SP% 127.6**
Speed ratings (Par 101): **100,99,98,97,96 96,93,91,91,90 89,89,**
CSF £73.72 CT £408.13 TOTE £9.40: £2.80, £2.90, £2.40; EX 75.80 Trifecta £816.90.
Owner D M James & Woodcote Stud **Bred** Woodcote Stud **Trained** Pulborough, W Sussex
■ Stewards' Enquiry : Ellie MacKenzie two-day ban: interference & careless riding (Jul 7, 11)

FOCUS
A modest affair and a bit of a messy one from a pace perspective.
T/Plt: £144.50 to a £1 stake. Pool: £44,347.51 - 223.97 winning units T/Qpdt: £35.00 to a £1 stake. Pool: £6,894.69 - 145.64 winning units **Cathal Gahan**

3887 SALISBURY (R-H)
Wednesday, June 26

OFFICIAL GOING: Good to firm (8.2)
Wind: light behind Weather: sunny

4252 WHITSBURY MANOR STUD BRITISH EBF BLAGRAVE MAIDEN STKS (PLUS 10 RACE) 6f 213y
2:20 (2:22) (Class 4) 2-Y-O **£5,110** (£1,520; £759; £379) **Stalls High**

Form RPR

1 **Positive** 2-9-5 0.......................... AdamKirby 1 94+
(Clive Cox) *mid-div: trckd ldrs after 2f: carried lft whn mounting chal over 1f out: sn led: qcknd clr: readily* **6/4**[1]

6 **2** 5 **Hexagon (IRE)**[23] 3419 2-9-5 0.......................... JasonWatson 2 79
(Roger Charlton) *led: hung lft u.p over 1f out: sn hdd: nt pce of wnr fnl f (jockey said gelding hung left-handed)* **10/1**

4 **3** 3 3/4 **Owney Madden**[19] 3542 2-9-5 0.......................... RobHornby 5 69
(Martyn Meade) *prom: rdn whn carried lft over 1f out: sn hld: kpt on same pce fnl f* **11/2**[3]

5 **4** hd **Vulcan (IRE)**[12] 3804 2-9-2 0.......................... MitchGodwin(3) 10 69
(Harry Dunlop) *hld up in last trio: shkn up and prog over 2f out: kpt on ins fnl f but nt pce to get on terms* **20/1**

5 3 1/4 **Dyami (FR)** 2-9-5 0.......................... PatCosgrave 11 60
(George Baker) *mid-div: rdn over 2f out: kpt on ins fnl f wout ever threatening to get involved (jockey said colt hung left-handed)* **50/1**

2 **6** 1/2 **Wightman (IRE)**[10] 3890 2-9-5 0.......................... RyanMoore 8 59
(Mick Channon) *trckd ldrs: rdn over 2f out: sn one pce* **10/3**[2]

7 2 **Mon Choix** 2-9-5 0.......................... OisinMurphy 3 54
(Andrew Balding) *mid-div: rdn over 2f out: little imp: wknd fnl f* **12/1**

8 9 **Raadea** 2-9-5 0.......................... JimCrowley 6 30
(Marcus Tregoning) *rn green: struggling in last pair wl over 3f out: wknd over 1f out* **18/1**

9 7 **Today Power (IRE)** 2-9-5 0.......................... SilvestreDeSousa 9
(Richard Hannon) *s.i.s: rn green: sn outpcd in detached last: nvr on terms* **10/1**

1m 26.87s (-1.83) **Going Correction** -0.175s/f (Firm) **9 Ran SP% 116.3**
Speed ratings (Par 95): **103,97,93,92,89 88,86,75,67**
CSF £18.38 TOTE £2.40: £1.10, £2.50, £2.50; EX 17.10 Trifecta £71.10.
Owner A D Spence **Bred** Cheveley Park Stud Ltd **Trained** Lambourn, Berks

FOCUS
The market spoke strongly in favour of the winner overnight and during the day. He got the job done impressively and the form is probably fair in behind him, although the level is fluid.

4253 INSPIRE FOUNDATION VETERANS' H'CAP 5f
2:50 (2:52) (Class 4) (0-80,82) 6-Y-O+ **£5,692** (£1,694; £846; £423; £300; £300) **Stalls High**

Form RPR

63U3 **1** **Zac Brown (IRE)**[20] 3492 8-9-1 **70**..........................(t) JoshuaBryan(3) 7 77
(Charlie Wallis) *pressed ldr: str chal u.p fr 2f out: rdr dropped rein ins fnl f: kpt on: led cl home* **7/1**

2325 **2** hd **Harry Hurricane**[16] 3662 7-10-1 **81**..........................(p) JosephineGordon 1 87
(George Baker) *led: rdn whn strly chal fr 2f out: kpt on: hdd cl home* **3/1**[1]

0444 **3** 1/2 **Pettochside**[10] 3893 10-9-0 **73**.......................... CieranFallon(7) 5 77
(John Bridger) *hld up bhd ldrs: rdn and prog over 2f out: kpt on fnl 120yds (jockey said gelding hung right-handed)* **13/2**

5-05 **4** 1/2 **Dr Doro (IRE)**[34] 2997 6-9-4 **70**..........................(v) JimCrowley 2 73
(Ian Williams) *rousted along to chse ldng pair: hanging rt but keeping on ins fnl f whn nt clr run between front pair fnl 120yds: swtchd lft: r.o cl home (jockey said mare hung right-handed and was denied a clear run)* **7/2**[2]

2501 **5** 1 1/4 **Foxy Forever (IRE)**[19] 3531 9-10-2 **82**..........................(bt) JFEgan 4 80
(Michael Wigham) *chsd ldrs: rdn 2f out: fdd fnl 100yds (jockey said gelding ran flat)* **7/2**[2]

-565 **6** 1/2 **La Fortuna**[18] 3596 6-9-2 **68**..........................(t) RichardKingscote 6 64
(Charlie Wallis) *last pair: rdn over 2f out: nt pce to get on terms* **12/1**

-013 **7** 1 1/2 **Waseem Faris (IRE)**[19] 3531 10-10-2 **82**.......................... PatDobbs 3 73
(Ken Cunningham-Brown) *last pair: rdn 2f out: nt pce to threaten (jockey said gelding anticipated the start)* **6/1**[3]

1m 0.21s (-0.29) **Going Correction** -0.175s/f (Firm) **7 Ran SP% 117.3**
Speed ratings: **95,94,93,93,91 90,87**
CSF £29.40 TOTE £8.20: £3.40, £1.90; EX 29.40 Trifecta £163.60.
Owner Porterhouse Ltd J Goddard **Bred** Tally-Ho Stud **Trained** Ardleigh, Essex

FOCUS
The whole field finished close up and it produced a tight finish. This has been rated around the runner-up to the balance of this year's form.

4254 HUNT FOREST GROUP/JOHN DEERE AUCTION STKS (PLUS 10 RACE) 6f
3:20 (3:23) (Class 3) 2-Y-O **£7,115** (£2,117; £1,058; £529) **Stalls High**

Form RPR

02 **1** **Milltown Star**[7] 3990 2-8-7 0.......................... FrannyNorton 7 81
(Mick Channon) *disp ld tl clr ldr 3f out: r.o strly ins fnl f: comf* **6/1**

2 **2** 2 1/4 **Sword Beach (IRE)**[15] 3695 2-8-13 0.......................... TomMarquand 5 80
(Eve Johnson Houghton) *trckd ldrs: rdn over 2f out: kpt on ins fnl f but nt pce of wnr* **11/4**[2]

3 **3** 1 **Atmospheric**[32] 3076 2-8-9 0.......................... HollieDoyle 2 73+
(Clive Cox) *trckd ldrs: rdn 2f out: kpt on but nt pce to get on terms* **13/8**[1]

43 **4** 5 **Fantom Force (IRE)**[8] 3962 2-9-1 0.......................... RyanMoore 4 64
(Richard Hannon) *disp ld tl 3f out: sn rdn: wknd ent fnl f* **7/2**[3]

5 10 **Parker's Boy** 2-8-5 0.......................... NicolaCurrie 1 24
(Brian Barr) *in tch: rdn over 2f out: nt pce to get on terms: wknd over 1f out* **66/1**

6 8 **Intercessor** 2-8-7 0.......................... RoystonFfrench 3 2
(John Gallagher) *s.i.s: sn outpcd in last pair: nvr on terms* **33/1**

7 nk **Majestic Ace** 2-8-6 0.......................... KieranO'Neill 6
(Richard Hannon) *rn green: sn outpcd in last pair: nvr on terms (jockey said colt ran green)* **16/1**

1m 14.13s (-0.37) **Going Correction** -0.175s/f (Firm) **7 Ran SP% 111.6**
Speed ratings (Par 97): **95,92,90,84,70 60,59**
CSF £21.72 TOTE £5.40: £2.40, £2.20; EX 18.60 Trifecta £48.40.
Owner Hunscote Stud Limited And Partner **Bred** Hunscote Stud **Trained** West Ilsley, Berks

FOCUS
This may not be as good a race as the grade would suggest but the winner rates a clear improver however viewed.

4255 MOLSON COORS H'CAP 1m
3:50 (3:55) (Class 2) (0-100,97) 3-Y-O+ **£12,450** (£3,728; £1,864; £932; £466; £234) **Stalls High**

Form RPR

1-20 **1** **Power Of Darkness**[53] 2408 4-9-10 **91**.......................... AndreaAtzeni 5 98+
(Marcus Tregoning) *dwlt: bhd: hdwy in centre fr over 2f out: kpt on wl ins fnl f: drifted rt: led towards fin (jockey said gelding hung right-handed under pressure)* **5/2**[1]

1-03 **2** 1/2 **Nicklaus**[18] 3581 4-9-12 **93**.......................... RyanMoore 6 99
(William Haggas) *led: rdn over 1f out: kpt on but no ex whn hdd towards fin* **4/1**[2]

0050 **3** 3/4 **Hors De Combat**[26] 3313 8-10-0 **95**.......................... OisinMurphy 7 99
(Denis Coakley) *hld up in last pair: rdn 3f out: stl last pair ent fnl f: fin strly: snatched 3rd cl home* **8/1**

0250 **4** nk **Swift Rose (IRE)**[42] 2745 3-9-6 **97**.......................... HarryBentley 9 99
(Saeed bin Suroor) *trckd ldr: rdn over 2f out: kpt on ins fnl f but nt pce to get on terms: lost 3rd fnl strides* **10/1**

2-10 **5** 1 **King's Slipper**[53] 2419 4-9-10 **91**.......................... AdamKirby 10 92
(Clive Cox) *slowly away: mid-div: hdwy over 2f out: sn rdn: briefly short of room over 1f out: kpt on but nt pce to chal fnl f* **11/1**

3566 **6** hd **Wahash (IRE)**[26] 3313 5-9-11 **92**.......................... SeanLevey 8 93
(Richard Hannon) *trckd ldr: wnt 2nd over 4f out: rdn over 2f out: kpt on tl no ex ins fnl f* **6/1**[3]

1303 **7** 1 3/4 **Pactolus (IRE)**[68] 1921 8-9-6 **87**..........................(t) RichardKingscote 1 84
(Stuart Williams) *trckd ldr: rdn over 2f out: kpt on same pce fnl f* **9/1**

1203 **8** 1/2 **Family Fortunes**[23] 3423 5-9-3 **89**.......................... ScottMcCullagh(5) 2 85
(Michael Madgwick) *trckd ldrs: rdn over 2f out: one pce fnl f* **22/1**

-000 **9** 2 1/2 **George Of Hearts (FR)**[34] 3009 4-9-4 **85**.......................... PatDobbs 3 75
(Richard Hannon) *last trio: rdn over 2f out: no imp and wknd ent fnl f* **15/2**

1m 40.9s (-2.60) **Going Correction** -0.175s/f (Firm) **9 Ran SP% 117.5**
WFA 3 from 4yo+ 10lb
Speed ratings (Par 109): **106,105,104,104,103 103,101,101,98**
CSF £12.56 CT £69.92 TOTE £3.30: £1.30, £1.80, £2.20; EX 14.40 Trifecta £107.50.
Owner R C C Villers **Bred** Mrs C R Philipson & Lofts Hall Stud **Trained** Whitsbury, Hants
■ Stewards' Enquiry : Andrea Atzeni caution; careless riding

FOCUS
A really competitive handicap for useful types and the winner is still on the upgrade.

4256 WHITSBURY MANOR STUD BIBURY CUP H'CAP 1m 4f 5y
4:20 (4:21) (Class 3) (0-95,94) 3-Y-O **£14,006** (£4,194; £2,097; £1,048; £524; £263) **Stalls Low**

Form RPR

413 **1** **Desert Icon (FR)**[40] 2802 3-8-12 **85**.......................... RyanMoore 3 98+
(William Haggas) *hld up in last trio: hdwy 3f out: led over 1f out: enough in hand and a holding on fnl f: rdn out* **11/4**[1]

-621 **2** nk **Kiefer**[40] 2796 3-8-9 **82** ow1.......................... CharlesBishop 7 94+
(Eve Johnson Houghton) *hld up in last pair: hdwy over 2f out: rdn over 1f out: sn hanging rt: styd on wl ins fnl f: clsng on wnr at fin* **9/2**[3]

2-51 **3** 1 **Apparate**[41] 2764 3-8-10 **83**.......................... AndreaAtzeni 9 93
(Roger Varian) *mid-div: hdwy 3f out: ev ch briefly whn rdn 2f out: styd on same pce fnl f: lost 2nd towards fin* **9/2**[3]

631 **4** 5 **Great Example**[38] 2875 3-9-4 **91**.......................... OisinMurphy 8 93
(Saeed bin Suroor) *chsd ldng pair: led 2f out: sn rdn and hdd: no ex ins fnl f* **4/1**[2]

-306 **5** 2 **Kaloor**[33] 3042 3-9-2 **94**.......................... ThomasGreatrex(5) 5 93
(Brian Meehan) *chsd ldng pair: rdn over 2f out: sn hld: fdd fnl f* **22/1**

5-21 **6** 1 1/2 **Buriram (IRE)**[26] 3295 3-8-11 **84**.......................... SilvestreDeSousa 1 81
(Ralph Beckett) *chsd clr ldr: led over 3f out: rdn and hdd 2f out: wknd fnl f* **7/1**

2313 **7** *1 1/2* **Gantier**[40] 2796 3-9-2 **89**......(b) RobertHavlin 6 83
(John Gosden) *slowly away: sn rousted along in last: kpt on fnl 2f but nvr gng pce to get involved* **8/1**

11-4 **8** *27* **Jersey Wonder (IRE)**[27] 3262 3-8-12 **85**......(b[1]) NicolaCurrie 2 36
(Jamie Osborne) *racd freely: led: sn clr: hdd over 3f out: wknd over 2f out (jockey said gelding ran too free)* **22/1**

2m 32.55s (-5.05) **Going Correction** -0.175s/f (Firm) **8** Ran SP% **115.3**
Speed ratings (Par 103): **109,108,108,104,103 102,101,83**
CSF £15.46 CT £51.81 TOTE £3.60: £1.40, £1.70, £1.90; EX 15.90 Trifecta £69.80.

Owner Sheikh Juma Dalmook Al Maktoum **Bred** Ecurie Des Charmes **Trained** Newmarket, Suffolk

FOCUS
This can often produce good horses, even if they don't pass the post first. For instance, Mekong was second last year and he went on to finish second in a Group 3, while Redicean (sixth in 2017) and Master Blueyes (third in 2016) both went on to land Grade 2 hurdle events. In 2015, the race was taken by Simple Verse, who, eventually after an appeal, was the St Leger winner later that year. This was run at a good gallop and the first three, held up, rate as improvers, with the winner and second up with the race standard.

4257 H S LESTER MEMORIAL H'CAP — 1m 6f 44y
4:50 (4:50) (Class 4) (0-85,86) 4-Y-0+

£5,692 (£1,694; £846; £423; £300; £300) **Stalls** High

Form RPR

5154 **1** **Master Grey (IRE)**[15] 3700 4-8-4 **68**...... KieranO'Neill 76
(Rod Millman) *racing keenly in midfield early: settled in last pair after 3f: hdwy over 2f out: sn rdn: drifting rt ent fnl f: led fnl 120yds: styd on wl* **9/2[3]**

2122 **2** *1 3/4* **Dono Di Dio**[34] 3010 4-8-12 **81**...... ScottMcCullagh[(5)] 86
(Michael Madgwick) *mid-div: hdwy fr 3f out: sn rdn: kpt on to chal ent fnl f: sn tight for room: styd on* **4/1[2]**

1-22 **3** *nk* **General Zoff**[15] 3693 4-8-6 **70**...... JFEgan 74
(William Muir) *trckd ldrs: chal over 3f out: sn rdn: styd on w ev ch ins fnl f: no ex nring fin* **5/1**

-542 **4** *2 1/2* **Ravenous**[32] 3070 8-8-12 **76**...... DaneO'Neill 77
(Luke Dace) *trckd ldr: led narrowly over 3f out: sn rdn: hld on wl tl hdd fnl 120yds: no ex* **8/1**

-335 **5** *2 3/4* **Running Cloud (IRE)**[41] 2781 4-9-0 **78**......(v) RyanMoore 75
(Alan King) *mid-div: hdwy 3f out: sn rdn: one pce fnl 2f* **3/1[1]**

50-0 **6** *1 1/4* **Universal Command**[36] 1757 4-8-13 **77**......(h[1]) RobertHavlin 72
(Jack R Barber) *mid-div: effrt over 2f out: sn one pce* **40/1**

1-06 **7** *2* **Brancaster (IRE)**[15] 3700 5-8-3 **67**...... NicolaCurrie 59
(David Elsworth) *hld up: pushed along over 4f out: rdn over 3f out: nvr any imp* **10/1**

600/ **8** *13* **She's Gina (GER)**[22] 6-9-7 **85**......(b) RaulDaSilva 59
(Seamus Mullins) *hld up in last trio: struggling over 5f out: wknd over 2f out* **9/1**

6 **9** *12* **Dawn Trouper (IRE)**[32] 3070 4-9-6 **84**......(t) AdamKirby 41
(Nigel Hawke) *set decent pce: hdd 3f out: sn wknd (jockey said gelding had no more to give in the final 2f)* **12/1**

3m 2.42s (-4.18) **Going Correction** -0.175s/f (Firm) **9** Ran SP% **120.2**
Speed ratings (Par 105): **104,103,102,101,99 99,97,90,83**
CSF £23.94 CT £95.52 TOTE £4.90: £1.50, £2.00, £1.90; EX 27.80 Trifecta £151.50.

Owner David Little The Links Partnership **Bred** Summerhill & J Osborne **Trained** Kentisbeare, Devon

FOCUS
No stalls were used. Ordinary staying form, with the second and third setting the standard.

4258 RADCLIFFE & CO 60TH ANNIVERSARY BRITISH EBF MAIDEN STKS — 1m 1f 201y
5:20 (5:22) (Class 4) 3-Y-0+ **£5,660** (£1,684; £841; £420) **Stalls** Low

Form RPR

22- **1** **Gifts Of Gold (IRE)**[247] 8478 4-9-9...... ThomasGreatrex[(5)] 2 96+
(Saeed bin Suroor) *in tch: hdwy over 4f out: disp 2nd over 2f out: led over 1f out: kpt on wl: comf* **11/4[3]**

34-3 **2** *3 1/4* **Scentasia**[61] 2087 3-8-11 79...... RobertHavlin 3 84
(John Gosden) *sn trcking ldr: led over 2f out: rdn and hdd over 1f out: kpt on but sn hld by wnr* **5/4[1]**

0 **3** *8* **Ned Pepper (IRE)**[18] 3584 3-9-2...... NicolaCurrie 5 73
(Alan King) *trckd ldrs: rdn to dispute 2nd over 2f out: styd on but nt pce of front pair* **50/1**

0 **4** *2 1/4* **Hindaam (USA)**[20] 3495 3-8-11...... GeraldMosse 8 64
(Owen Burrows) *led after 2f: rdn and hdd over 2f out: sn one pce* **16/1**

5 *15* **Soldier Of War (USA)**[47] 4-10-0...... AdamKirby 6 39
(Ben Pauling) *s.i.s: last: struggling 5f out: nvr any threat* **50/1**

6 *13* **So Strictly** 3-9-2......(w) RaulDaSilva 7 13
(Paul Cole) *led for 2f: trckd ldr: rdn over 3f out: wknd over 2f out* **14/1**

00 **7** *17* **Aleatoric (IRE)**[47] 2566 3-9-2...... EoinWalsh 4
(Martin Smith) *hld up: hdwy over 5f out: rdn over 3f out: sn btn: t.o (jockey said gelding ran green)* **150/1**

22 **8** *13* **Al Hadeer (USA)**[52] 2438 3-9-2...... DaneO'Neill 1 51
(William Haggas) *trckd ldrs: rdn 3f out: sn wknd: t.o (trainers' rep said colt had a breathing problem)* **7/4[2]**

2m 7.58s (-2.92) **Going Correction** -0.175s/f (Firm)
WFA 3 from 4yo 12lb **8** Ran SP% **124.6**
Speed ratings (Par 105): **104,101,95,93,81 70,57,46**
CSF £7.31 TOTE £3.50: £1.40, £1.10, £8.70; EX 8.50 Trifecta £160.40.

Owner Godolphin **Bred** Paul Hyland **Trained** Newmarket, Suffolk

FOCUS
The betting only suggested three had any chance, each representing major Newmarket stables, and two of them pulled well clear. The winner rates a nice improver, with the runner-up to her latest form, although the level is a bit fluid.

T/Plt: £31.10 to a £1 stake. Pool: £56,631.40 - 1,325.80 winning units T/Qpdt: £7.60 to a £1 stake. Pool: £5,685.63 - 548.35 winning units **Tim Mitchell**

4259 - 4273a (Foreign Racing) - See Raceform Interactive

3997
HAMILTON (R-H)
Thursday, June 27

OFFICIAL GOING: Good to firm (watered; 8.5)
Wind: Light, half against in sprints and in over 4f of home straight in races on the round course Weather: Sunny, hot

4274 PLAN.COM SAINTS & SINNERS AMATEUR RIDERS' H'CAP (FOR THE SAINTS & SINNERS CHALLENGE CUP) — 1m 5f 16y
6:05 (6:07) (Class 5) (0-70,72) 4-Y-0+

£3,992 (£1,238; £618; £309; £300; £300) **Stalls** High

Form RPR

0503 **1** **Be Perfect (USA)**[7] 4036 10-10-2 **63**...... MissEmilyBullock[(5)] 8 73
(Ruth Carr) *t.k.h: hld up bhd ldng gp: hdwy over 3f out: led over 2f out: hung rt over 1f out: kpt on strly* **7/2[2]**

320- **2** *3 1/2* **Calliope**[29] 8079 6-10-5 **61**......(t) MissEmmaSayer 3 66
(Dianne Sayer) *chsd ldrs: drvn along over 3f out: rallied and chsd wnr over 1f out: no imp fnl f* **6/1[3]**

0-06 **3** *2 1/2* **Duke Of Yorkshire**[21] 3511 9-10-4 **60**......(p) MissEmilyEasterby 2 61
(Tim Easterby) *t.k.h: pressed ldr: led 1/2-way to over 2f out: sn outpcd: rallied fnl f: no imp* **7/1**

3-53 **4** *2 1/2* **Donnachies Girl (IRE)**[30] 3175 6-9-10 **59**...... MrConnorWood[(7)] 7 57
(Alistair Whillans) *prom: rdn and outpcd 2f out: hung rt: rallied ins fnl f: nt pce to chal* **3/1[1]**

0245 **5** *1/2* **Corton Lad**[10] 3925 9-10-7 **70**......(tp) MrEireannCagney[(7)] 4 67
(Keith Dalgleish) *led to 1/2-way: w ldr to over 2f out: sn rdn: wknd fnl f* **8/1**

-403 **6** *1* **Life Knowledge (IRE)**[8] 4004 7-9-11 **53**......(b) MissCatherineWalton 1 48
(Liam Bailey) *s.s: hld up: hdwy over 3f out: rdn: hung rt and wknd over 1f out* **15/2**

0-66 **7** *4* **Carbon Dating (IRE)**[12] 3873 7-10-11 **72**......(b) MrMatthewEnnis[(5)] 5 61
(Andrew Hughes, Ire) *slowly away: bhd: rdn over 3f out: wknd fr 2f out* **11/1**

433- **8** *29* **JJ's Journey (IRE)**[241] 8711 4-10-12 **68**...... MrLJMcGuinness 6 14
(Andrew Hughes, Ire) *hld up: drvn and struggling over 4f out: lost tch over 2f out: t.o* **12/1**

2m 49.72s (-4.98) **Going Correction** -0.30s/f (Firm) **8** Ran SP% **112.9**
Speed ratings (Par 103): **103,100,99,97,97 96,94,76**
CSF £24.06 CT £136.90 TOTE £4.50: £1.90, £1.80, £1.70; EX 25.70 Trifecta £109.70.

Owner The Beer Stalkers & Ruth Carr **Bred** Joseph Allen **Trained** Huby, N Yorks

FOCUS
Rail movements added 15yds to the race distance. A modest amateur riders' handicap, but a clear-cut success for a centurion. The form's rated around the third.

4275 BB FOODSERVICE EBF MAIDEN STKS (PLUS 10 RACE) (A £20,000 BB FOODSERVICE 2YO SERIES QUALIFIER) — 6f 6y
6:35 (6:36) (Class 4) 2-Y-0 **£5,433** (£1,617; £808; £404) **Stalls** High

Form RPR

2 **1** **One Hart (IRE)**[8] 3998 2-9-5 0...... FrannyNorton 8 84+
(Mark Johnston) *trckd ldr: led over 2f out: pushed clr fnl f: readily* **1/1[1]**

05 **2** *5* **Navajo Dawn (IRE)**[22] 3469 2-8-9 0...... SeamusCronin[(5)] 6 64
(Robyn Brisland) *t.k.h: led to over 2f out: rdn and hung rt over 1f out: kpt on same pce* **16/1**

3 *2* **Alwaatn Sound (IRE)** 2-9-5 0...... KevinStott 7 63
(Kevin Ryan) *trckd ldrs: effrt and rdn over 1f out: veered lft and no ex ins fnl f: bttr for r* **13/8[2]**

4 *1 3/4* **Feel Good Factor** 2-9-0 0...... TonyHamilton 5 53
(Richard Fahey) *dwlt and wnt rt s: hld up in tch: pushed along and outpcd by first three 2f out: n.d after* **7/1[3]**

5 *3 1/4* **Romintheglomin (IRE)** 2-8-11 0...... RowanScott[(3)] 3 43
(Andrew Hughes, Ire) *missed break: bhd: rdn and struggling over 2f out: sn btn* **40/1**

6 *1/2* **Grimbold** 2-9-0 0...... HarrisonShaw[(5)] 1 47
(K R Burke) *dwlt: hld up: rdn and outpcd 3f out: btn fnl 2f* **28/1**

1m 11.53s (-1.17) **Going Correction** -0.30s/f (Firm) **6** Ran SP% **112.4**
Speed ratings (Par 95): **95,88,85,83,79 78**
CSF £18.48 TOTE £1.70: £1.10, £4.70; EX 12.70 Trifecta £15.70.

Owner Middleham Park Racing CVI **Bred** Jennifer & Evelyn Cullen **Trained** Middleham Moor, N Yorks

FOCUS
Some major yards were represented in this juvenile maiden but only three mattered in the betting. Experience counted this time and the winner scored decisively. He looks sure to do better still.

4276 NINE WHOLESALE, FREE TO PERFORM (S) H'CAP — 5f 7y
7:05 (7:09) (Class 6) (0-60,61) 3-Y-0+

£3,493 (£1,039; £519; £300; £300; £300) **Stalls** Centre

Form RPR

5602 **1** **Hard Solution**[6] 4081 3-9-3 **59**...... DavidNolan 8 67
(David O'Meara) *cl up: led 1/2-way: drvn over 1f out: kpt on wl fnl f* **5/2[2]**

0001 **2** *1 3/4* **Ninjago**[24] 3413 9-9-10 **60**......(v) BenCurtis 3 64
(Paul Midgley) *prom: angled lft sn after s: effrt and chsd wnr over 1f out: kpt on fnl f: nt pce to chal* **85/40[1]**

0452 **3** *nk* **B Fifty Two (IRE)**[9] 3975 10-9-7 **60**......(vt) JaneElliott[(3)] 10 63
(Marjorie Fife) *hld up in tch: effrt and rdn 2f out: edgd rt ins fnl f* **6/1[3]**

6000 **4** *3 1/4* **Thorntoun Lady (USA)**[15] 3716 9-8-7 **46** oh1......(p) SeanDavis[(3)] 2 37
(Jim Goldie) *bhd: rdn and outpcd 1/2-way: r.o fnl f: nrst fin* **25/1**

4056 **5** *nk* **Muhallab (IRE)**[7] 4033 3-8-12 **54**...... ConnorBeasley 9 42
(Adrian Nicholls) *led to 1/2-way: rallied: drvn and outpcd over 1f out: btn ins fnl f* **8/1**

-553 **6** *1/2* **Amazing Alba**[25] 3376 3-9-5 **61**...... KevinStott 11 47
(Alistair Whillans) *cl up: rdn 1/2-way: outpcd fr over 1f out* **9/1**

4100 **7** *6* **Gunnabedun (IRE)**[24] 3417 3-8-12 **54**......(b) JamieGormley 5 18
(Iain Jardine) *midfield: hung rt and outpcd 2f out: sn btn* **16/1**

00-0 **8** *nse* **Nifty Niece (IRE)**[24] 3413 5-8-10 **46** oh1...... FrannyNorton 6 12
(Ann Duffield) *rrd s: bhd and outpcd: nvr on terms* **33/1**

050/ **9** *7* **Ya Boy Sir (IRE)**[1063] 4834 12-8-5 **46** oh1......(p) AndrewBreslin[(5)] 1
(Alistair Whillans) *dwlt and veered rt s: bhd and a outpcd* **66/1**

000- **10** *3/4* **Heidiava**[292] 7082 3-8-10 **52** ow2...... TomEaves 7
(Chris Grant) *in tch: drvn and struggling over 2f out: sn btn* **50/1**

0 11 3/4 **Born Fighting (IRE)**[28] 3283 3-8-4 46 oh1......................(b[1]) ShaneGray 4
(Andrew Hughes, Ire) *prom: hmpd and lost pl sn after s: struggling fr 1/2-way* 20/1

58.56s (-1.84) **Going Correction** -0.30s/f (Firm) 11 Ran SP% **116.9**
WFA 3 from 5yo+ 6lb
Speed ratings (Par 101): **102,99,98,93,93 92,82,82,71,70 68**
CSF £7.67 CT £28.21 TOTE £3.10: £1.20, £1.20, £2.20; EX 7.60 Trifecta £29.40.The winner was bought in for £4,800.
Owner D O'Meara **Bred** Whitsbury Manor Stud **Trained** Upper Helmsley, N Yorks
■ Stewards' Enquiry : Ben Curtis four-day ban: misuse of the whip (30 Jun & 15-17 Jul)

FOCUS
A moderate selling handicap in which the market leaders came clear in a pretty good time.

4277 THISTLE BLOODSTOCK MAIDEN STKS 1m 1f 35y
7:35 (7:40) (Class 5) 3-Y-O+ £4,140 (£1,232; £615; £307) **Stalls** Low

Form RPR
03 1 **Sendeed (IRE)**[21] 3510 3-9-3 0.................................. KevinStott 1 76+
(Saeed bin Suroor) *mde all: shkn up 2f out: rdn clr fnl f: easily* 1/6[1]

03 2 6 **Philip's Wish**[16] 3707 3-9-3 0.....................(h) ShaneGray 6 63
(Keith Dalgleish) *plld hrd early: chsd ldrs: effrt and wnt 2nd over 2f out: rdn and one pce fr over 1f out* 7/1[2]

0 3 7 **Mirabelle Plum (IRE)**[37] 2932 3-8-7 0.................. SeamusCronin(5) 4 43
(Robyn Brisland) *in tch: drvn and outpcd over 2f out: n.d after* 22/1

6 4 shd **Twentysixthstreet (IRE)**[21] 3499 3-9-0 0.................. RowanScott(3) 7 47
(Andrew Hughes, Ire) *chsd wnr to 2f out: rdn and wknd over 1f out* 10/1[3]

60 5 3/4 **At Peace (IRE)**[16] 3707 3-8-12 0.................................. AndrewMullen 3 41
(John Quinn) *slowly away: hld up: struggling over 2f out: sn btn* 20/1

1m 59.92s (0.92) **Going Correction** -0.30s/f (Firm) 5 Ran SP% **116.4**
WFA 3 from 7yo 11lb
Speed ratings (Par 103): **83,77,71,71,70**
CSF £2.46 TOTE £1.10: £1.02, £2.20; EX 2.50 Trifecta £10.10.
Owner Godolphin **Bred** Godolphin **Trained** Newmarket, Suffolk
■ Echo Express was withdrawn, price at time of withdrawal 20/1. Rule 4 does not apply.

FOCUS
Rail movements added 15yds to the race distance. An uncompetitive maiden won easily by the long odds-on favourite. The runner-up is rated close to his debut run.

4278 CAPTAIN J C STEWART FILLIES' H'CAP 1m 68y
8:05 (8:07) (Class 4) (0-80,78) 3-Y-O+ £8,021 (£2,387; £1,192; £596; £300; £300) **Stalls** Low

Form RPR
1202 1 **Never Be Enough**[6] 4057 4-10-0 78.................................. TomEaves 3 89+
(Keith Dalgleish) *stdd in last pl: smooth hdwy on outside to ld over 1f out: drvn out fnl f* 5/2[2]

354 2 2 **Outside Inside (IRE)**[12] 3843 4-9-11 75.................................. FrannyNorton 6 80
(Mark Johnston) *sn chsng ldr: led 2f out to over 1f out: edgd lft ins fnl f: kpt on same pce* 5/1[3]

6320 3 1 1/4 **Lucky Violet (IRE)**[6] 4058 7-9-1 65.....................(h) DavidNolan 5 67
(Linda Perratt) *t.k.h: in tch: effrt whn nt clr run briefly over 2f out: effrt and hdwy over 1f out: kpt on ins fnl f* 16/1

4532 4 1/2 **Queen Penn**[12] 3843 4-9-8 75.....................(p) SeanDavis(3) 8 76
(Richard Fahey) *hld up in tch on outside: effrt and drvn along over 2f out: no imp fr over 1f out* 5/1[3]

0-05 5 1/2 **Ladies First**[12] 3867 5-9-12 76.....................(t) DavidAllan 4 76
(Michael Easterby) *hld up on ins: effrt whn nt clr run over 2f out to over 1f out: kpt on fnl f: nvr rchd ldrs (jockey said mare was slowly away and denied a clear run app 2f out)* 15/8[1]

0550 6 1 **Set In Stone (IRE)**[21] 3502 5-9-5 72.....................(b[1]) RowanScott(3) 2 70
(Andrew Hughes, Ire) *cl up: rdn over 2f out: no ex fr over 1f out* 18/1

5400 7 3/4 **Grey Berry (IRE)**[24] 3414 3-8-2 62.................................. DuranFentiman 7 56
(Tim Easterby) *led to over 2f out: rallied: wknd ins fnl f* 40/1

00-0 8 18 **Morticia**[8] 4001 4-9-13 77.................................. ShaneGray 9 31
(Keith Dalgleish) *sn prom: shortlived effrt over 2f out: sn wknd: lost tch and eased fnl f* 33/1

1m 46.0s (-2.40) **Going Correction** -0.30s/f (Firm) 8 Ran SP% **113.2**
WFA 3 from 4yo+ 10lb
Speed ratings (Par 102): **100,98,96,96,95 94,94,76**
CSF £15.16 CT £160.17 TOTE £3.50: £1.30, £1.50, £3.30; EX 14.80 Trifecta £83.00.
Owner Straightline Bloodstock **Bred** J L Skinner **Trained** Carluke, S Lanarks

FOCUS
Rail movements added 15yds to the race distance. Quite a competitive fillies' handicap in which the market leaders had contrasting fortunes with their runs. The form's taken at face value.

4279 PATERSONS OF GREENOAKHILL H'CAP 5f 7y
8:35 (8:36) (Class 4) (0-80,81) 3-Y-O+ £8,021 (£2,387; £1,192; £596; £300; £300) **Stalls** Centre

Form RPR
6041 1 **Dapper Man (IRE)**[34] 3056 5-9-4 75.....................(b) BenCurtis 5 93
(Roger Fell) *mde all: shkn up and clr over 1f out: edgd rt ins fnl f: kpt on strly: unchal* 4/1[2]

1-01 2 6 **Spirit Of Wedza (IRE)**[53] 2433 7-8-11 75.................. VictorSantos(7) 6 71
(Julie Camacho) *chsd wnr thrght: effrt and rdn 2f out: kpt on fnl f: no ch w ready wnr* 5/1[3]

0-64 3 1/2 **Only Spoofing (IRE)**[17] 3658 5-8-13 73.................. SeanDavis(3) 3 68
(Jedd O'Keeffe) *dwlt: hld up in tch: rdn and effrt 2f out: kpt on same pce ins fnl f* 7/2[1]

-065 4 nk **Move In Time**[21] 3509 11-9-8 79.................................. KevinStott 7 73
(Paul Midgley) *missed break: hld up: effrt over 2f out: edgd rt and hdwy over 1f out: no imp fnl f* 7/1

3205 5 2 **Wrenthorpe**[21] 3504 4-8-12 76.................................. HarryRussell(7) 1 62
(Bryan Smart) *bhd: drvn and outpcd 1/2-way: rallied over 1f out: sn no imp (jockey said gelding stumbled leaving stalls)* 4/1[2]

1400 6 2 1/4 **Bossipop**[12] 3846 6-9-10 81.....................(b) DavidAllan 2 59
(Tim Easterby) *chsd ldrs: rdn along 1/2-way: wknd over 1f out* 17/2

0-10 7 4 **Zig Zag Zyggy (IRE)**[21] 3503 4-9-7 81.....................(v) RowanScott(3) 4 45
(Andrew Hughes, Ire) *hld up in tch: rdn 1/2-way: wknd over 1f out* 11/2

57.2s (-3.20) **Going Correction** -0.30s/f (Firm) course record 7 Ran SP% **117.3**
Speed ratings (Par 105): **113,103,102,102,98 95,88**
CSF £25.12 TOTE £3.80: £2.00, £2.60; EX 14.40 Trifecta £35.70.
Owner Colne Valley Racing & Partner **Bred** William Joseph Martin **Trained** Nawton, N Yorks

FOCUS
This sprint handicap was run 1.36secs faster than the earlier seller and lowered the track record. The form could have been rated a few pounds higher on time.

4280 RACING TV PROFITS RETURNED TO RACING H'CAP 6f 6y
9:05 (9:06) (Class 5) (0-75,74) 3-Y-O+ £4,140 (£1,232; £615; £307; £300; £300) **Stalls** Centre

Form RPR
5133 1 **Friendly Advice (IRE)**[8] 3999 3-9-7 74.....................(p[1]) ShaneGray 8 79
(Keith Dalgleish) *prom: effrt and rdn over 1f out: led wl ins fnl f: hld on wl* 11/2

2102 2 shd **Epeius (IRE)**[8] 3999 6-9-10 70.....................(v) AndrewMullen 5 76
(Ben Haslam) *missed break: hld up: hdwy over 1f out: chal and blkd ins fnl f: edgd lft cl home: jst hld* 9/2[3]

0611 3 nse **Mujassam**[6] 4060 7-9-13 73 8ex.....................(b) DavidNolan 3 79
(David O'Meara) *prom: effrt and ev ch over 1f out: led briefly ins fnl f: sn edgd rt: keeping on whn bmpd cl home* 9/4[1]

-600 4 nk **Autumn Flight (IRE)**[19] 3590 3-8-13 66.....................(p[1]) DavidAllan 6 69
(Tim Easterby) *led: rdn over 1f out: hdd ins fnl f: kpt on: hld towards fin* 9/1

35-4 5 4 **Zebzardee (IRE)**[15] 3719 3-8-13 69.................. ConnorMurtagh(3) 1 59
(Richard Fahey) *in tch on outside: drvn along and outpcd over 2f out: rallied over 1f out: sn no imp* 12/1

064 6 1 **Mr Wagyu (IRE)**[8] 3999 4-9-9 69.....................(b[1]) KevinStott 2 58
(John Quinn) *dwlt: sn cl up: rdn along 1/2-way: wknd fnl f* 4/1[2]

60-1 7 3/4 **Roys Dream**[43] 2729 5-10-0 74.....................(p) FrannyNorton 4 60
(Paul Collins) *cl up tl rdn and wknd over 1f out* 9/1

-501 8 17 **Archies Lad**[30] 3191 3-8-10 63.................................. BenCurtis 7
(R Mike Smith) *sn bhd: struggling 1/2-way: sn btn: t.o* 25/1

1m 10.37s (-2.33) **Going Correction** -0.30s/f (Firm) 8 Ran SP% **115.9**
WFA 3 from 4yo+ 7lb
Speed ratings (Par 103): **103,102,102,102,97 95,94,72**
CSF £30.84 CT £72.06 TOTE £6.80: £1.60, £1.30, £1.60; EX 31.00 Trifecta £110.30.
Owner A R M Galbraith **Bred** A R M Galbraith **Trained** Carluke, S Lanarks
■ Stewards' Enquiry : David Nolan two-day ban: caused interference (30 Jun & 11 Jul)

FOCUS
This modest handicap was run well over a second faster than the earlier juvenile maiden. A bunch finish with the third the best guide.
T/Plt: £11.00 to a £1 stake. Pool: £51,316.76 - 3,385.57 winning units T/Qpdt: £4.60 to a £1 stake. Pool: £6,985.06 - 1,105.36 winning units **Richard Young**

3644 LEICESTER (R-H)
Thursday, June 27

OFFICIAL GOING: Good to soft (good in places) changing to good (good to soft in places) after race 2 (6.25)
Wind: Light across Weather: Fine

4281 LANGHAM LADIES' H'CAP (FOR LADY AMATEUR RIDERS) 7f
5:55 (5:57) (Class 5) (0-70,75) 3-Y-O+ £3,618 (£1,122; £560; £300; £300; £300) **Stalls** High

Form RPR
0-14 1 **Fieldsman (USA)**[42] 2774 7-9-12 66.................. MissSarahBowen(5) 4 74
(Tony Carroll) *chsd ldr tl over 3f out: wnt 2nd again over 2f out: rdn to ld over 1f out: styd on* 4/1[2]

5031 2 1/2 **Leo Davinci (USA)**[6] 4080 3-10-3 75 6ex......(t) MissSerenaBrotherton 13 82+
(George Scott) *carried lft sn after s: hld up: hdwy and nt clr run over 1f out: sn swtchd lft: r.o wl ins fnl f: wnt 2nd towards fin: nt rch wnr (jockey said gelding hung right throughout)* 7/2[1]

004- 3 1 **Ballymount**[241] 8697 4-10-5 68.....................(p) MissJoannaMason 3 72
(Michael Easterby) *s.i.s: sn prom: rdn 1/2-way: styd on same pce ins fnl f* 11/2

6333 4 1/2 **Evening Attire**[14] 3781 8-9-9 63.................. MissAntoniaPeck(5) 6 66
(William Stone) *led: rdn and hdd over 1f out: no ex wl ins fnl f* 8/1

-165 5 1/2 **Zafaranah (USA)**[127] 812 5-10-7 70.................. MissBeckySmith 2 71
(Pam Sly) *hld up: hdwy over 1f out: sn rdn: styd on* 5/1[3]

4630 6 2 1/2 **Winklemann (IRE)**[48] 2580 7-9-5 61.....................(p) MissImogenMathias(7) 1 56
(John Flint) *s.s: sn pushed along in rr: hdwy u.p over 2f out: hung rt and no ex ins fnl f* 8/1

-103 7 shd **Incentive**[22] 3470 5-9-8 62.....................(b) MissMillieWonnacott(5) 5 56
(Stuart Kittow) *chsd ldrs: rdn over 1f out: no ex ins fnl f* 25/1

0656 8 3/4 **Peachey Carnehan**[10] 3924 5-9-11 60........(v) MissMichelleMullineaux 7 52
(Michael Mullineaux) *s.i.s: sn pushed along in rr: swtchd rt over 1f out: styd on ins fnl f: nvr nrr* 25/1

0-00 9 6 **Sayesse**[14] 3781 5-9-9 63.................................. MissAmyCollier(5) 12 39
(Lisa Williamson) *hmpd and stmbld sn after s: sn outpcd: r.o ins fnl f: nvr nrr* 50/1

-136 10 nk **Gottardo (IRE)**[12] 3838 4-10-1 69.................................. SophieSmith(5) 16 44
(Ed Dunlop) *hld up: edgd rt sn after s: plld hrd: rdn over 2f out: n.d* 28/1

3400 11 1/2 **Mr Minerals**[94] 1329 5-10-6 72.....................(t) MissHannahWelch(3) 10 46
(Alexandra Dunn) *s.i.s: sn prom: lost pl over 3f out: wknd over 2f out* 22/1

00-0 12 2 3/4 **De Bruyne Horse**[44] 2714 4-9-11 67..........(b) MissJessicaLlewellyn(7) 8 33
(Bernard Llewellyn) *wnt lft after s: chsd ldrs: rdn over 2f out: wknd over 1f out (vet said gelding lost left hind shoe)* 50/1

4026 13 6 **The Lamplighter (FR)**[9] 3967 4-9-11 67.........(tp) MissShaeEdwards(7) 15 17
(George Baker) *s.i.s: hdwy over 4f out: chsd ldr over 3f out tl over 2f out: wknd over 1f out* 20/1

4-00 14 14 **The Lacemaker**[12] 3838 5-9-9 65.....................(p) MrsDawnScott(7) 14
(Milton Harris) *s.i.s: a in rr: wknd over 2f out* 66/1

1m 26.87s (1.17) **Going Correction** +0.05s/f (Good) 14 Ran SP% **122.2**
WFA 3 from 4yo+ 9lb
Speed ratings (Par 103): **95,94,93,92,92 89,89,88,81,81 80,77,70,54**
CSF £16.83 CT £81.78 TOTE £5.00: £1.90, £2.90, £2.70; EX 21.70 Trifecta £105.50.
Owner Sf Racing Club **Bred** H Sexton, S Sexton & Silver Fern Farm **Trained** Cropthorne, Worcs

FOCUS
A modest handicap in which the field came down the middle of the track. Straightforward form.

4282 BRITISH STALLION STUDS EBF NOVICE STKS (PLUS 10 RACE) 7f
6:25 (6:25) (Class 4) 2-Y-O £5,757 (£1,713; £856; £428) **Stalls** High

Form RPR
0 1 **Fred**[36] 2957 2-9-2 0.................................. PJMcDonald 3 80
(Mark Johnston) *mde all: shkn up and qckند over 1f out: sn rdn: jst hld on* 5/1[3]

2 nse **Law Of Peace** 2-9-2 0 KerrinMcEvoy 4 80+
(Charlie Appleby) *chsd ldrs: shkn up to chse wnr over 2f out: rdn over 1f out: r.o wl* 2/1[2]

1 3 1 ½ **Mottrib (IRE)**[14] 3760 2-9-8 0 DavidEgan 7 82+
(Roger Varian) *broke wl: plld hrd: stdd and lost pl after 1f: sddle slipped: hdwy over 2f out: shkn up over 1f out: styd on (jockey said saddle slipped in early stages)* 4/5[1]

4 4 ½ **Itkaann (IRE)** 2-9-2 0 DavidProbert 2 64
(Owen Burrows) *s.i.s: hld up: hdwy over 2f out: wknd fnl f* 14/1

0 5 11 **Leg It Lenny (IRE)**[17] 3644 2-9-2 0 TomQueally 1 36
(Robert Cowell) *chsd wnr over 4f: wknd over 1f out* 25/1

0401 6 14 **Show Me Heaven**[13] 3798 2-9-0 70 JimmyQuinn 8
(Bill Turner) *s.s: hdwy over 4f out: wknd over 2f out* 25/1

5 7 4 **Dark Moonlight (IRE)**[11] 3890 2-9-2 0 RichardKingscote 6
(Charles Hills) *s.i.s: racd keenly: hdwy over 5f out: lost pl over 4f out: wknd over 2f out* 33/1

0 8 16 **Break Cover**[33] 3098 2-9-2 0 DanielMuscutt 5
(Mark H Tompkins) *hld up: pushed along over 3f out: wknd over 2f out* 100/1

1m 25.97s (0.27) **Going Correction** +0.05s/f (Good) 8 Ran SP% 123.8
Speed ratings (Par 95): **100,99,98,93,80 64,59,41**
CSF £16.51 TOTE £5.10: £1.40, £1.40, £1.10; EX 22.00 Trifecta £45.50.
Owner The Burke Family **Bred** Normandie Stud Ltd **Trained** Middleham Moor, N Yorks

FOCUS
A decent novice stakes, but the favourite was unable to give his true running. The winner left his debut form well behind.

4283 VIS-A-VIS SYMPOSIUMS H'CAP 1m 2f
6:55 (6:56) (Class 5) (0-75,80) 4-Y-0+

£4,075 (£1,212; £606; £303; £300; £300) Stalls Low

Form RPR

-233 1 **Stormingin (IRE)**[18] 3633 6-9-6 74 AdamKirby 3 82
(Gary Moore) *broke wl: sn stdd and lost pl: hld up: rdn over 2f out: hdwy over 1f out: sn swtchd lft: edgd lft and r.o u.p to ld wl ins fnl f* 6/1[2]

30-6 2 ½ **Junderstand**[59] 2207 4-9-6 74 DavidProbert 7 81
(Alan King) *trckd ldrs: led over 2f out: rdn and edgd lft fr over 1f out: hdd wl ins fnl f* 22/1

-011 3 2 ½ **Lucky's Dream**[22] 3473 4-9-2 70 KerrinMcEvoy 10 72
(Ian Williams) *prom: led over 8f out: rdn and hdd over 2f out: styd on same pce wl ins fnl f* 8/1

2644 4 ¾ **High Acclaim (USA)**[41] 2797 5-9-4 72 (p) PJMcDonald 4 73
(Roger Teal) *s.i.s: hld up: rdn over 2f out: r.o ins fnl f: nt rch ldrs* 8/1

5-66 5 nk **Escape The City**[16] 3698 4-9-7 75 (t) RobertWinston 8 75
(Hughie Morrison) *sn prom: rdn over 2f out: no ex wl ins fnl f* 7/1[3]

-04 6 hd **Horatio Star**[20] 3545 4-8-13 72 ThomasGreatrex(5) 5 72
(Brian Meehan) *sn pushed along and prom: rdn over 2f out: styd on same pce ins fnl f* 4/1[1]

223- 7 ¾ **Glorious Jem**[241] 8703 4-9-4 72 DanielMuscutt 9 70
(David Lanigan) *prom: chsd ldr over 8f out: sn rdn and ev ch: wknd wl ins fnl f* 6/1[2]

0-10 8 5 **Nightingale Valley**[22] 3468 6-9-9 77 TomQueally 1 65
(Stuart Kittow) *led: racd keenly: hdd over 8f out: rdn over 2f out: wknd over 1f out* 20/1

2021 9 ¾ **Stringybark Creek**[9] 3957 5-9-5 80 5ex LauraCoughlan(7) 6 67
(David Loughnane) *s.i.s: hld up: hdwy on outer over 3f out: rdn and wknd over 1f out (regarding the run, trainer said gelding had failed to stay the 1 mile 2 furlongs on this occasion, having raced 9 days previously)* 4/1[1]

554- 10 4 ½ **Trade Talks**[206] 9380 4-9-4 72 GeorgeWood 2 50
(Chris Wall) *hld up: hdwy over 4f out: rdn and wknd over 2f out* 16/1

2m 8.55s (-0.65) **Going Correction** +0.05s/f (Good) 10 Ran SP% 118.3
Speed ratings (Par 103): **104,103,101,101,100 100,100,96,95,91**
CSF £128.73 CT £1068.23 TOTE £6.10: £1.90, £6.00, £2.10; EX 158.40 Trifecta £1375.60.
Owner Mrs Catherine Reed **Bred** Kilnamoragh Stud **Trained** Lower Beeding, W Sussex

FOCUS
Fair handicap form. The winner's been rated to his best.

4284 NUCLEUSHR H'CAP 1m 53y
7:25 (7:26) (Class 6) (0-65,64) 3-Y-0

£3,428 (£1,020; £509; £300; £300; £300) Stalls Low

Form RPR

0401 1 **Potenza (IRE)**[6] 4070 3-8-12 58 6ex GabrieleMalune(3) 4 69+
(Stef Keniry) *hld up: hdwy and edgd rt fr over 2f out: sn rdn and hmpd: chsd ldr over 1f out: drvn to ld ins fnl f: r.o wl: comf* 11/10[1]

0-00 2 2 ¼ **Jimmy Greenhough (IRE)**[30] 3195 3-8-13 56 PaddyMathers 14 60
(Richard Fahey) *led: hdd over 6f out: chsd ldr tl led again 3f out: rdn and edgd lft fr over 1f out: hdd ins fnl f: styd on same pce* 14/1

03-2 3 2 ½ **Mac Ailey**[19] 3570 3-9-6 63 RachelRichardson 13 63
(Tim Easterby) *chsd ldrs: rdn over 2f out: nt clr run over 1f out: no ex ins fnl f* 20/1

054 4 1 ¼ **Canasta**[29] 3218 3-9-6 63 (h) DanielMuscutt 7 59
(James Fanshawe) *hld up: rdn over 2f out: styd on fr over 1f out: nt rch ldrs* 12/1

-004 5 1 **Sukalia**[31] 3154 3-9-1 58 DavidProbert 2 53
(Alan King) *hld up: hdwy: edgd lft and hmpd over 2f out: sn rdn: wknd ins fnl f* 25/1

3-50 6 1 ¾ **Padura Brave**[17] 3665 3-9-7 64 (p) NicolaCurrie 5 54
(Mark Usher) *prom: rdn over 2f out: wknd ins fnl f (jockey said filly suffered interference approximately 2 1/2f out)* 25/1

0-04 7 ¾ **City Master**[23] 3440 3-9-2 59 PatDobbs 8 47
(Ralph Beckett) *s.s: hld up: rdn over 2f out: nvr nrr* 5/1[2]

0-62 8 1 **Purgatory**[14] 3780 3-9-2 59 GeorgeWood 11 45
(Chris Wall) *hld up: rdn over 2f out: hung rt fr over 1f out: n.d* 8/1[3]

360 9 11 **Sweet Poem**[17] 3665 3-9-5 62 AdamKirby 12 24
(Clive Cox) *prom: lost pl 6f out: sn pushed along: rdn: hung rt and wknd over 2f out* 20/1

3240 10 3 ¾ **Elikapeka (FR)**[17] 3650 3-9-4 61 DougieCostello 1 14
(Kevin Ryan) *prom: rdn over 3f out: wknd 2f out* 25/1

5103 11 3 ¼ **Um Shama (IRE)**[141] 614 3-9-7 64 HollieDoyle 10 10
(David Loughnane) *hld up: a in rr: shkn up over 2f out: sn wknd* 25/1

040 12 2 ¼ **Jaidaa**[19] 3584 3-9-5 62 JackMitchell 6 3
(Simon Crisford) *chsd ldr tl led over 6f out: rdn and hdd 3f out: wknd wl over 1f out* 14/1

1m 45.05s (-1.25) **Going Correction** +0.05s/f (Good) 12 Ran SP% 121.3
Speed ratings (Par 97): **108,105,103,102,101 99,98,97,86,82 79,77**
CSF £16.43 CT £198.26 TOTE £1.90: £1.10, £3.80, £5.60; EX 19.80 Trifecta £254.30.
Owner Kristian Strangeway **Bred** Angelo Robiati **Trained** Middleham, N Yorks

FOCUS
Comfortable for the favourite in this modest handicap, which was run at what appeared to be a decent gallop. It was 1.73sec quicker than the other race over the trip, a Class 5 event for fillies. The form looks straightforward.

4285 KINGS NORTON FILLIES' H'CAP 1m 53y
7:55 (7:56) (Class 5) (0-70,71) 3-Y-0+

£4,075 (£1,212; £606; £303; £300; £300) Stalls Low

Form RPR

-424 1 **Al Messila**[34] 3041 3-9-8 71 PatDobbs 4 80
(Richard Hannon) *prom: lost pl 6f out: hdwy and nt clr run over 1f out: rdn to ld ins fnl f: r.o wl* 3/1[1]

4512 2 2 ½ **Remembering You (IRE)**[17] 3665 3-9-3 66 AdamKirby 11 69
(Clive Cox) *chsd ldrs: rdn over 2f out: styd on u.p* 4/1[3]

-606 3 nk **Diviner (IRE)**[21] 3513 3-9-3 66 PJMcDonald 3 68
(Mark Johnston) *chsd ldr over 6f out: led wl over 2f out: rdn over 1f out: hdd ins fnl f: styd on same pce* 7/1

40-5 4 1 **Heavenly Bliss**[27] 3306 3-9-3 66 KerrinMcEvoy 1 67
(Sir Michael Stoute) *hld up in tch: shkn up and nt clr run over 2f out: swtchd lft over 1f out: styd on same pce ins fnl f* 7/2[2]

4-64 5 shd **Tarbeyah (IRE)**[28] 3247 4-10-0 67 JackMitchell 5 69
(Kevin Frost) *hld up: rdn over 2f out: r.o ins fnl f: nt rch ldrs* 10/1

05-0 6 nk **Winterkoenigin**[38] 2904 3-9-3 66 (p[1]) DanielMuscutt 2 68+
(David Lanigan) *hld up: nt clr run over 1f out: swtchd rt and r.o ins fnl f: nt rch ldrs (jockey said filly was denied a clear run approximately 2f out)* 16/1

-404 7 shd **Bob's Girl**[29] 3217 4-8-9 48 oh3 (b) JimmyQuinn 6 49
(Michael Mullineaux) *hld up: plld hrd: hdwy over 3f out: rdn over 1f out: styd on (jockey said filly hung right)* 33/1

2-03 8 1 ½ **Solfeggio (IRE)**[31] 3154 3-9-6 69 (h) GeorgeWood 7 64
(Chris Wall) *prom: plld hrd: rdn over 2f out: hmpd over 1f out: no ex fnl f* 8/1

005 9 nk **Misty**[20] 3546 3-8-11 60 JosephineGordon 9 55
(Ralph Beckett) *s.i.s: hdwy on outer over 6f out: sn pushed along and lost pl: rdn over 3f out: hung rt ins fnl f: nt trble ldrs* 20/1

565- 10 1 **Lady Scatterley (FR)**[297] 6859 3-9-6 69 RachelRichardson 8 61
(Tim Easterby) *plld hrd and prom: hmpd and lost pl over 6f out: effrt on outer over 2f out: hung rt over 1f out: nt trble ldrs* 50/1

504- 11 9 **Intricate**[197] 9498 3-9-6 69 (p[1]) HollieDoyle 10 41
(Archie Watson) *sn led: shkn up and hdd wl over 2f out: wknd over 1f out (jockey said filly jumped right handed from the stalls and stopped quickly)* 25/1

1m 46.78s (0.48) **Going Correction** +0.05s/f (Good)
WFA 3 from 4yo 10lb 11 Ran SP% 119.3
Speed ratings (Par 100): **99,96,96,95,95 94,94,93,92,91 82**
CSF £14.62 CT £79.92 TOTE £3.70: £1.40, £2.70, £1.80; EX 16.40 Trifecta £103.40.
Owner Al Shaqab Racing **Bred** Lofts Hall Stud & B Sangster **Trained** East Everleigh, Wilts

FOCUS
Quite a messy race and modest form. Improvement from the winner with the next two rated to their latest form. The time was 1.73sec slower than the preceding Class 6 event.

4286 COLD OVERTON H'CAP 6f
8:25 (8:26) (Class 5) (0-70,70) 3-Y-0

£4,075 (£1,212; £606; £303; £300; £300) Stalls High

Form RPR

6600 1 **Gold At Midnight**[59] 2204 3-9-4 67 HollieDoyle 10 75
(William Stone) *w ldrs: shkn up to ld wl over 1f out: rdn and hdd ins fnl f: rallied to ld towards fin* 10/1

223 2 ½ **Lofty**[56] 2334 3-9-7 70 RobertWinston 9 77
(David Barron) *hld up: hdwy to chse wnr over 1f out: rdn to ld ins fnl f: hdd towards fin* 7/2[1]

5-50 3 2 ¾ **Molly's Game**[28] 3273 3-9-7 70 HayleyTurner 3 68
(David Elsworth) *prom: rdn over 2f out: styd on same pce ins fnl f* 14/1

0-06 4 1 ¼ **Brawny**[13] 3805 3-9-5 68 RichardKingscote 8 62
(Charles Hills) *chsd ldrs: rdn over 2f out: styd on same pce wl ins fnl f* 9/1

346 5 1 ¾ **Tulloona**[14] 3764 3-9-5 68 (t[1]) LukeMorris 11 56
(Tom Clover) *s.i.s: sn pushed along in rr: drvn along 1/2-way: styd on u.p fnl f: nvr nrr* 11/1

5546 6 1 ½ **Gunnison**[14] 3771 3-8-9 58 PaddyMathers 2 42
(Richard Fahey) *s.i.s: in rr and pushed along over 4f out: sme hdwy fnl f: wknd towards fin* 15/2[2]

-040 7 1 ¼ **Jack Randall**[28] 3246 3-8-6 55 RachelRichardson 7 35
(Tim Easterby) *sn led: rdn and hdd wl over 1f out: wknd ins fnl f* 8/1[3]

-400 8 1 **Invincible One (IRE)**[26] 3354 3-8-13 62 PJMcDonald 5 38
(Sylvester Kirk) *stmbld s: sn prom: lost pl after 1f: bhd fr 1/2-way* 10/1

46-2 9 ½ **Swinging Eddie**[11] 3884 3-9-3 66 DougieCostello 1 41
(Kevin Ryan) *hld up: racd keenly: hdwy 2f out: sn rdn: wknd fnl f (trainer could offer no explanation for the gelding's performance)* 7/2[1]

5-63 10 1 **Grandstand (IRE)**[153] 401 3-9-0 63 DavidEgan 6 35
(Richard Price) *w ldrs: rdn and ev ch wl over 1f out: wknd ins fnl f* 18/1

0-04 11 11 **Quanah (IRE)**[63] 2055 3-8-12 61 (bt[1]) DanielMuscutt 4
(Mark H Tompkins) *s.i.s: racd keenly and hdwy 5f out: rdn and wknd over 1f out: eased (jockey said gelding ran too freely)* 25/1

1m 13.35s (1.25) **Going Correction** +0.05s/f (Good) 11 Ran SP% 119.6
Speed ratings (Par 99): **93,92,88,87,84 82,81,79,79,77 63**
CSF £45.74 CT £513.14 TOTE £12.30: £3.90, £1.50, £3.80; EX 61.10 Trifecta £524.00.
Owner Mrs Denis Haynes **Bred** Wretham Stud **Trained** West Wickham, Cambs

FOCUS
The first two finished clear in this modest event. The winner got back to her 2yo form.

4287 BRUNTINGTHORPE H'CAP 1m 3f 179y
8:55 (8:55) (Class 6) (0-60,60) 4-Y-0+

£3,105 (£924; £461; £300; £300; £300) Stalls Low

Form RPR

-004 1 **Becky Sharp**[35] 3017 4-8-7 46 (b) CharlieBennett 13 55
(Jim Boyle) *pushed along to ld over 10f out: rdn over 1f out: styd on wl* 25/1

606 2 2 ¼ **Ekayburg (FR)**[17] 3664 5-9-4 60 (t) FinleyMarsh(3) 5 65
(David Pipe) *hld up in tch: rdn over 2f out: carried hd high fr over 1f out: styd on to go 2nd wl ins fnl f: nt rch wnr* 4/1[3]

0504 3 2 ½ **Normandy Blue**[21] 3497 4-8-13 52 JimmyQuinn 9 53
(Louise Allan) *prom: lost pl after 1f: hdwy u.p over 2f out: swtchd lft ins fnl f: r.o* 50/1

3511 **4** *nse* **Kingfast (IRE)**[5] 4111 4-9-7 **60** 5ex.............................(p) DougieCostello 11 61
(David Dennis) *s.i.s: hld up: hdwy 5f out: rdn over 2f out: no ex ins fnl f*
7/2[2]

0412 **5** *1* **Kodi Koh (IRE)**[23] 3447 4-8-9 **48**.............................. LukeMorris 16 48
(Simon West) *hld up: hdwy over 3f out: chsd wnr over 2f out: sn rdn: hung rt fr over 1f out: no ex ins fnl f (jockey said filly hung badly right and was unsteerable under pressure)* **12/1**

4356 **6** *1 ¼* **Don't Do It (IRE)**[14] 3774 4-8-13 **52**..................(v) AlistairRawlinson 17 50
(Michael Appleby) *hld up: hdwy u.p over 2f out: nt trble ldrs* **16/1**

0-32 **7** *4* **Maroon Bells (IRE)**[16] 3705 4-9-7 **60**............................ DavidEgan 8 51
(David Menuisier) *prom: chsd ldr over 8f out tl rdn over 2f out: wknd ins fnl f* **13/8**[1]

060 **8** *1 ½* **Incredible Dream (IRE)**[12] 3834 6-9-2 **55**.................(p) MartinDwyer 18 44
(Conrad Allen) *s.s: hld up: rdn over 2f out: hung rt over 1f out: n.d (jockey said gelding was slowly away)* **14/1**

6000 **9** *1* **Chantresse (IRE)**[22] 3473 4-8-7 **53**.....................(p) EllieMacKenzie(7) 10 40
(Mark Usher) *hld up in tch: rdn over 2f out: wknd over 1f out* **25/1**

4353 **10** *4* **Be Thankful**[16] 3691 4-9-7 **60**..................................(h) TomQueally 3 41
(Martin Keighley) *chsd ldrs: rdn over 3f out: wknd over 1f out* **25/1**

-630 **11** *2 ½* **Vanity Vanity (USA)**[73] 1826 4-9-5 **58**............................ DavidProbert 4 35
(Denis Coakley) *s.s: rdn over 2f out: n.d* **16/1**

0-00 **12** *3* **Roser Moter (IRE)**[15] 3740 4-8-6 **50**.......................... TheodoreLadd(5) 14 22
(Michael Appleby) *prom: lost pl after 1f: hdwy over 3f out: sn rdn: wknd wl over 1f out* **66/1**

4206 **13** *7* **Qayed (CAN)**[27] 3321 4-8-9 **48**.. JackMitchell 12 9
(Kevin Frost) *s.i.s: bhd fnl 4f* **20/1**

00-0 **14** *17* **Genuine Approval (IRE)**[48] 2595 6-9-1 **57** ow1.................. TimClark(3) 7
(John Butler) *led 1f: remained handy: rdn over 3f out: wknd over 2f out* **25/1**

30-0 **15** *33* **Mythological (IRE)**[16] 3700 4-9-4 **57**.......................(t[1]) RobertWinston 6
(Louise Allan) *led after 1f: hdd over 10f out: chsd ldrs: hung lft and rdn over 4f out: sn wknd (jockey said gelding hung badly left)* **40/1**

500- **16** *33* **Roodeparis**[252] 8349 4-8-13 **52**.................................(p) JosephineGordon 1
(Mark Usher) *mid-div: lost pl 9f out: bhd fnl 6f (vet said gelding bled from nose)* **40/1**

2m 34.81s (-0.19) **Going Correction** +0.05s/f (Good) **16** Ran SP% **134.9**
Speed ratings (Par 101): **102,100,98,98,98 97,94,93,92,90 88,86,81,70,48 26**
CSF £125.63 CT £5153.50 TOTE £39.80: £5.60, £1.40, £8.70, £1.40; EX 241.60.
Owner Harrier Racing 1 **Bred** Mildmay Bloodstock Ltd **Trained** Epsom, Surrey

FOCUS
Very modest form. The winner cashed in on a good mark.
T/Jkpt: Not Won. T/Plt: £36.00 to a £1 stake. Pool: £55,610.75 - 1,125.17 winning units T/Qpdt: £19.00 to a £1 stake. Pool: £5,365.29 - 208.05 winning units **Colin Roberts**

3447 NEWCASTLE (A.W) (L-H)

Thursday, June 27

OFFICIAL GOING: Tapeta: standard changing to standard to slow after race 1 (1:50)
Wind: Moderate across Weather: Fine and dry

4288 COOPERS MARQUEES H'CAP 7f 14y (Tp)

1:50 (1:52) (Class 5) (0-75,75) 3-Y-O
£3,752 (£1,116; £557; £300; £300; £300) **Stalls** Centre

Form RPR

-361 **1** **Defence Treaty (IRE)**[17] 3650 3-9-5 **73**..................(p) DanielTudhope 12 83
(Richard Fahey) *hld up towards rr: hdwy towards stands' side 2f out: rdn to chse ldrs and edgd lft jst over 1f out: styd on strly fnl f to ld fnl 50yds* **4/1**[1]

5-44 **2** *1* **Sense Of Belonging (FR)**[18] 3638 3-9-1 **69**...................... TomEaves 3 76
(Kevin Ryan) *hld up towards rr: stdy hdwy on inner over 3f out: sn trcking ldrs: effrt to ld over 1f out: rdn ins fnl f: hdd and no ex fnl 50yds* **12/1**

-000 **3** *3* **Axe Axelrod (USA)**[6] 4080 3-9-3 **71**............................ ConnorBeasley 13 70
(Michael Dods) *hld up in rr: gd hdwy nr stands' rail 2f out: sn rdn: styd on wl fnl f* **16/1**

0056 **4** *nk* **Jem Scuttle (USA)**[27] 3307 3-9-3 **71**.............................(t) DavidNolan 5 69
(Declan Carroll) *cl up: pushed along over 2f out: rdn and ev ch over 1f out: sn drvn and kpt on one pce* **4/1**[1]

4-14 **5** *nse* **Daring Venture (IRE)**[19] 3603 3-9-7 **75**....................... AndreaAtzeni 1 73+
(Roger Varian) *trckd ldrs: led 5f out: pushed along 2f out: sn rdn and hdd over 1f out: wknd fnl f* **9/2**[2]

-440 **6** *7* **Jack Berry House**[47] 2630 3-9-5 **73**.........................(t) StevieDonohoe 4 52
(Charlie Fellowes) *chsd ldrs: rdn along 3f out: sn drvn and outpcd fnl 2f* **14/1**

-354 **7** *hd* **Edgewood**[56] 2333 3-9-7 **75**..(p[1]) GrahamLee 10 54
(James Bethell) *cl up: rdn along over 2f out: sn wknd* **9/1**

-005 **8** *3 ¾* **Barbarosa (IRE)**[35] 3018 3-9-0 **68**.................................. ShaneGray 8 36
(Michael Herrington) *towards rr: hdwy 3f out: rdn along over 2f out: sn outpcd* **28/1**

-133 **9** *2 ¾* **Gale Force Maya**[15] 3719 3-9-0 **68**.............................. PaulMulrennan 9 29
(Michael Dods) *chsd ldrs: rdn along over 2f out: sn wknd* **6/1**[3]

6564 **10** *3 ¾* **Serengeti Song (IRE)**[19] 3565 3-8-13 **72**.................. HarrisonShaw(5) 7 33
(K R Burke) *t.k.h: trckd ldrs: pushed along over 2f out: sn rdn and wknd wl over 1f out (vet said gelding bled from nose)* **14/1**

550- **11** *1 ¼* **Epaulini**[261] 8073 3-8-10 **64** ow1................................ RobbieDowney 14 11
(Michael Dods) *prom: rdn along wl over 2f out: sn wknd* **66/1**

6324 **12** *1 ¼* **Puzzle**[38] 2912 3-9-5 **73**...(p[1]) ShaneKelly 11 17
(Richard Hughes) *trckd ldrs: pushed along wl over 2f out: sn rdn and wknd* **33/1**

1m 28.02s (1.82) **Going Correction** +0.325s/f (Slow) **12** Ran SP% **117.3**
Speed ratings (Par 99): **102,100,97,97,97 89,88,84,81,77 75,74**
CSF £51.56 CT £707.07 TOTE £5.30: £1.70, £5.60, £5.90; EX 68.70 Trifecta £537.50.
Owner Clipper Logistics **Bred** Michael Rogers **Trained** Musley Bank, N Yorks

FOCUS
A fair 3yo handicap. One of the joint-favourites came through late towards the near rail to win well. The first pair were clear with the winner backing up his latest form. The Tapeta going description was changed from standard to standard to slow after this race.

4289 WINGATE SIGNS SUPPORTING #SUPERJOSH CHARITY NOVICE MEDIAN AUCTION STKS 7f 14y (Tp)

2:25 (2:27) (Class 5) 2-Y-O **£3,752** (£1,116; £557; £278) **Stalls** Centre

Form RPR

33 **1** **Gallaside (FR)**[28] 3245 2-9-5 0.. HollieDoyle 3 82
(Archie Watson) *trckd ldr: effrt 2f out: sn pushed along and edgd lft: rdn to ld over 1f out and sn hung rt: clr ins fnl f: kpt on* **5/4**[1]

2 *2 ¾* **Reclaim Victory (IRE)** 2-8-11 0.............................. BenRobinson(3) 6 70
(Brian Ellison) *hld up in rr: hdwy towards stands' side 2f out: rdn to chse ldrs over 1f out: styd on wl fnl f: tk 2nd nr line* **20/1**

3 *nse* **You're My Rock** 2-9-5 0.. PaulHanagan 8 75+
(Richard Fahey) *dwlt and towards rr: hdwy over 2f out: chsd ldrs wl over 1f out: sn rdn and chsd wnr ins fnl f: lost 2nd nr line* **8/1**[3]

003 **4** *3* **The Lazy Monkey (IRE)**[19] 3578 2-9-0 68.............. SilvestreDeSousa 7 62
(Mark Johnston) *led: rdn along over 2f out: sn edgd lft: drvn and hdd over 1f out: sn hung bdly bdly lft to inner rail and grad wknd (jockey said filly hung left-handed)* **17/2**

2 **5** *1* **Northern Hope**[9] 3954 2-9-5 0... DanielTudhope 4 65
(David O'Meara) *prom: pushed along 2f out: sn rdn and wandered over 1f out: kpt on same pce fnl f (jockey said colt hung left-handed throughout)* **11/8**[2]

0 **6** *6* **Trickydickysimpson**[9] 3954 2-9-5 0............................... TonyHamilton 5 50
(Richard Fahey) *hld up in rr: pushed along 3f out: rdn over 2f out: sme late hdwy* **20/1**

7 *5* **Thomas Hawk** 2-9-5 0.. DavidNolan 2 37
(Alan Brown) *chsd ldrs: rdn along wl over 2f out: sn wknd* **125/1**

8 *1* **Full Strength** 2-9-5 0... AndrewMullen 1 35
(Ivan Furtado) *dwlt: sn trcking ldrs on inner: rdn along 3f out: sn wknd* **40/1**

1m 30.72s (4.52) **Going Correction** +0.325s/f (Slow) **8** Ran SP% **120.9**
Speed ratings (Par 93): **87,83,83,80,79 72,66,65**
CSF £31.67 TOTE £2.20: £1.10, £4.30, £2.00; EX 29.20 Trifecta £163.60.
Owner Apple Tree Stud **Bred** Safsaf Canarias Srl & Mme Felix Miranda-Suarez **Trained** Upper Lambourn, W Berks

FOCUS
A fair juvenile novice contest. It turned into something of a sprint and the favourite's winning time was nearly three seconds slower than the opening C&D handicap. There's more to come from the winner.

4290 BETFAIR CASINO NOVICE STKS (PLUS 10 RACE) 6f (Tp)

3:00 (3:02) (Class 4) 2-Y-O **£4,787** (£1,424; £711; £355) **Stalls** Centre

Form RPR

1 **1** **Oti Ma Boati**[17] 3652 2-9-3 0... TonyHamilton 6 78
(Richard Fahey) *in rr: pushed along wl over 2f out: rdn and hdwy wl over 1f out: drvn ins fnl f: kpt on wl to ld nr fin* **12/1**[3]

2 *½* **Spreadsheet (IRE)** 2-9-5 0.. AndreaAtzeni 4 79+
(Roger Varian) *dwlt and green in rr: hdwy 2f out: pushed along nr stands' rail and cl up over 1f out: rdn to take slt ld ins fnl f: hdd and no ex nr fin* **8/11**[1]

6 **3** *shd* **Pentewan**[16] 3702 2-9-0 0... SamJames 1 73
(Phillip Makin) *cl up on inner: pushed along 2f out: rdn over 1f out: drvn and ev ch ins fnl f: no ex nr fin* **40/1**

63 **4** *5* **Welcome Surprise (IRE)**[24] 3426 2-9-5 0..................... DanielTudhope 3 63
(Saeed bin Suroor) *trckd ldr: hdwy 2f out and sn chal: sn rdn and ev ch: wknd fnl f* **9/4**[2]

5 **5** *1 ¾* **Interrupted Dream**[15] 3739 2-9-5 0........................... SilvestreDeSousa 2 58
(Mark Johnston) *led: jnd and rdn wl over 1f out: drvn ent fnl f: sn hdd & wknd (jockey said colt ran green)* **14/1**

6 *3 ¼* **Dandy Dancer** 2-9-5 0.. ShaneKelly 7 48
(Richard Hughes) *chsd ldrs: rdn along over 2f out: wknd over 1f out* **40/1**

1m 15.11s (2.61) **Going Correction** +0.325s/f (Slow) **6** Ran SP% **107.9**
Speed ratings (Par 95): **95,94,94,87,85 80**
CSF £19.91 TOTE £8.10: £2.50, £1.20; EX 25.10 Trifecta £274.50.
Owner R A Fahey **Bred** Bearstone Stud **Trained** Musley Bank, N Yorks

FOCUS
A fair juvenile novice contest. The only previous winner in the race won gamely in a quicker comparative time than the previous juvenile contest. It's tricky to pin the level of the form and time will tell.

4291 SKY SPORTS RACING ON SKY 415 H'CAP 1m 4f 98y (Tp)

3:30 (3:30) (Class 5) (0-75,76) 3-Y-O
£3,816 (£1,135; £567; £300; £300; £300) **Stalls** High

Form RPR

000 **1** **Samba Saravah (USA)**[41] 2802 3-8-10 **62**...............(t[1]) StevieDonohoe 2 71
(Charlie Fellowes) *awkward and dwlt s: pushed along in rr 1/2-way: hdwy over 3f out: rdn to chse ldrs wl over 1f out: kpt on to ld jst ins fnl f: styd on strly* **16/1**

0-03 **2** *3 ¾* **Frankadore (IRE)**[34] 3052 3-9-2 **68**...............(p) SilvestreDeSousa 5 71
(Tom Dascombe) *racd wd early: trckd ldr: led after 2f: pushed along over 3f out: rdn 2f out: drvn ent fnl f: sn hdd and kpt on one pce* **6/1**

3-52 **3** *¾* **Tammooz**[23] 3446 3-9-10 **76**... AndreaAtzeni 3 78
(Roger Varian) *trckd ldrs: hdwy 3f out: rdn to chse ldr 2f out: ev ch over 1f out: sn drvn and kpt on one pce* **11/4**[1]

-623 **4** *¾* **London Eye (USA)**[27] 3295 3-9-7 **73**................................. DavidAllan 4 74
(Sir Michael Stoute) *trckd ldng pair: hdwy over 3f out: pushed along wl over 2f out: sn rdn: drvn over 1f out: one pce* **3/1**[2]

3-34 **5** *7* **Dubai Philosopher (FR)**[28] 3254 3-9-6 **72**..............(p[1]) DanielTudhope 6 66
(Michael Bell) *hld up in tch: hdwy 4f out: rdn along over 2f out: sn wknd* **5/1**

0341 **6** *5* **Theatro (IRE)**[7] 4039 3-8-12 **64** 6ex.................................. GrahamLee 1 51
(Jedd O'Keeffe) *trckd ldr: pushed along 5f out: rdn over 3f out: sn wknd (regarding the performance, trainer said race may have come too soon)* **10/3**[3]

2m 43.56s (2.46) **Going Correction** +0.325s/f (Slow) **6** Ran SP% **111.6**
Speed ratings (Par 99): **104,101,101,100,95 92**
CSF £102.08 TOTE £19.20: £6.90, £3.00; EX 141.80 Trifecta £846.90.
Owner Mrs Susan Roy **Bred** Santa Rosa Partners **Trained** Newmarket, Suffolk

FOCUS
A fair 3yo handicap. A strong pace collapsed from 2f out. The winner was a notable improver with the form taken at face value.

4292 BETFAIR EXCHANGE SEATON DELAVAL H'CAP 1m 5y (Tp)
4:05 (4:05) (Class 2) (0-105,103) 4-Y-O+
£19,920 (£5,964; £2,982; £1,491; £745; £374) **Stalls** Centre

Form RPR
2-10 **1** **Military Law**[75] 1757 4-8-8 **90** NickyMackay 8 101
(John Gosden) *trckd ldng pair: cl up 1/2-way: led over 3f out: rdn wl over 1f out: drvn ent fnl f: kpt on gamely* **11/1**
-232 **2** 1 1/4 **Qaroun**[19] 3581 4-8-8 **90** DavidAllan 2 98
(Sir Michael Stoute) *trckd ldrs: hdwy and cl up over 2f out: rdn to chal over 1f out: drvn and ev ch ent fnl f: kpt on same pce fnl 100yds* **7/1**
0325 **3** 1 3/4 **Ventura Knight (IRE)**[8] 3992 4-9-2 **98** SilvestreDeSousa 7 102
(Mark Johnston) *chsd ldrs: rdn along over 2f out: drvn and kpt on fnl f (starter reported that the gelding was the subject of a third criteria failure; trainer was informed that the gelding could not run until the day after passing a stalls test)* **20/1**
-402 **4** 1 1/4 **Seniority**[27] 3313 5-9-6 **102** PaulHanagan 5 103
(William Haggas) *hld up towards rr: hdwy over 2f out: sn rdn: styd on fnl f: nrst fin* **6/1**[3]
5662 **5** *nk* **Bedouin's Story**[23] 3450 4-8-13 **95** HectorCrouch 12 95
(Saeed bin Suroor) *trckd ldr: cl up 1/2-way: rdn along 2f out: ev ch tl drvn and wknd appr fnl f* **13/2**
1-25 **6** 4 **Glengarry**[30] 3179 6-8-2 **84** ShaneGray 4 75
(Keith Dalgleish) *wnt violently lft s: in rr: pushed along 3f out: styd on fnl 2f: n.d* **33/1**
1/31 **7** 8 **Bowerman**[59] 2187 5-9-7 **103** AndreaAtzeni 10 81
(Roger Varian) *in tch: hdwy over 2f out: rdn wl over 1f out: sn btn and eased ins fnl f (vet said finished slightly lame on its right-fore)* **5/2**[1]
236 **8** 1 1/4 **Trevithick**[36] 2959 4-8-9 **91** ow2 GrahamLee 3 61
(Bryan Smart) *led: hdd over 3f out: sn rdn along and wknd wl over 1f out (vet said gelding bled from the nose)* **50/1**
4-22 **9** 28 **Baltic Baron (IRE)**[12] 3857 4-9-1 **97** DanielTudhope 11 3
(David O'Meara) *a towards rr (jockey said colt behaved in a coltish manner and became upset in the preliminaries and at the start)* **10/1**
2300 **10** 8 **Glendevon (USA)**[8] 3987 4-9-6 **102** (h) ShaneKelly 1
(Richard Hughes) *dwlt and hmpd s: a towards rr* **40/1**
2120 **P** **Rey Loopy (IRE)**[58] 2242 5-8-2 **84** AndrewMullen 6
(Ben Haslam) *in rr: pushed along bef 1/2-way: detached and lost action over 2f out: sn p.u (vet said gelding bled from the nose)* **33/1**
4151 **U** **Crownthorpe**[23] 3450 4-8-9 **94** SeanDavis(3) 9
(Richard Fahey) *stmbld and uns rdr s* **11/2**[2]

1m 39.71s (1.11) **Going Correction** +0.325s/f (Slow) **12 Ran SP% 116.5**
Speed ratings (Par 109): **107,105,104,102,102 98,90,89,61,53 ,**
CSF £80.06 CT £1545.47 TOTE £12.70: £3.60, £2.60, £5.20; EX 85.40 Trifecta £667.50.
Owner Qatar Racing Limited **Bred** Qatar Bloodstock Ltd **Trained** Newmarket, Suffolk

FOCUS
The feature contest was a good handicap. The front-runner faded to finish eighth off his own strong gallop centrally and two horses from the next wave were able to gamely outstay their opponents towards the far rail. Solid form, the third helping with the standard.

4293 PHOBIA HALLOWEEN EVENT NEWCASTLE RACECOURSE H'CAP 1m 5y (Tp)
4:40 (4:41) (Class 6) (0-60,60) 3-Y-O+
£3,105 (£924; £461; £300; £300; £300) **Stalls** Centre

Form RPR
4366 **1** **Home Before Dusk**[6] 4054 4-9-10 **58** (v[1]) DanielTudhope 10 71
(Keith Dalgleish) *dwlt and towards rr: hdwy into midfield 5f out: chsd ldrs towards stands' side 2f out: rdn to take slt ld appr fnl f: sn drvn and kpt on wl towards fin* **6/1**[3]
4400 **2** *nk* **Toro Dorado**[28] 3256 3-9-1 **59** SilvestreDeSousa 3 69
(Ed Dunlop) *in tch: hdwy over 2f out: cl up and rdn over 1f out: drvn and ev ch ins fnl f: kpt on same pce towards fin (jockey said gelding hung right-handed)* **4/1**[2]
4205 **3** 10 **Rebel State (IRE)**[15] 3720 6-9-1 **56** (v) OwenPayton(7) 5 46
(Jedd O'Keeffe) *trckd ldrs: rdn along over 2f out: drvn over 1f out: sn one pce* **14/1**
0040 **4** 5 **Im Dapper Too**[10] 3922 8-9-7 **55** (p) SamJames 7 34
(John Davies) *hld up towards rr: hdwy over 2f out: rdn wl over 1f out: kpt on fnl f* **18/1**
0-02 **5** 1 **Sherzy Boy**[3] 4195 4-9-8 **56** (tp) NathanEvans 1 33
(Jacqueline Coward) *racd alone nr far rail: in tch: hdwy over 2f out: chsd ldrs and rdn wl over 1f out: sn drvn and kpt on one pce* **7/2**[1]
3004 **6** 1/2 **Adventureman**[15] 3730 7-9-5 **53** (b) JamesSullivan 11 29
(Ruth Carr) *led: pushed along 3f out: rdn over 2f out: hdd and rdr dropped whip wl over 1f out: sn wknd* **20/1**
5453 **7** 1/2 **Roman De Brut (IRE)**[61] 2124 7-9-9 **60** BenRobinson(3) 12 35
(Rebecca Menzies) *trckd ldr: pushed along over 3f out: rdn over 2f out: sn drvn and wknd (vet said gelding finished lame left fore)* **7/1**
000- **8** 10 **Jessinamillion**[230] 8980 5-8-12 **53** (p) VictoriaSanchez(7) 14 6
(James Bethell) *prom: rdn along wl over 2f out: sn wknd* **66/1**
-000 **9** *hd* **Khitaamy (IRE)**[9] 3969 5-9-4 **52** (tp) PaulHanagan 8 5
(Tina Jackson) *a towards rr* **66/1**
-050 **10** 2 3/4 **Joyful Star**[30] 3177 9-9-2 **50** PaulMulrennan 6
(Fred Watson) *a in rr* **40/1**
6626 **11** 5 **Optima Petamus**[8] 4003 7-8-11 **50** (b) FayeMcManoman(5) 2
(Liam Bailey) *rdn along sn after s: a in rr (jockey said gelding was slowly away)* **28/1**
00-0 **12** 2 3/4 **Symbolic Star (IRE)**[27] 3296 7-9-3 **54** (p) ConnorMurtagh(3) 9
(Barry Murtagh) *in tch: rdn along wl over 3f out: sn wknd* **50/1**
02/ **13** 7 **Paved With Gold (IRE)**[279] 7503 6-9-4 **57** BenSanderson(5) 13
(Tristan Davidson) *chsd ldrs: rdn along over 3f out: sn wknd* **7/2**[1]

1m 41.21s (2.61) **Going Correction** +0.325s/f (Slow)
WFA 3 from 4yo+ 10lb **13 Ran SP% 118.8**
Speed ratings (Par 101): **99,98,88,83,82 82,81,71,71,68 63,61,54**
CSF £28.43 CT £334.45 TOTE £7.50: £2.40, £1.60, £3.20; EX 37.00 Trifecta £378.90.
Owner G R Leckie **Bred** G L S Partnership **Trained** Carluke, S Lanarks

FOCUS
A modest handicap. The fourth and third-favourites came clear of this field in a fair time for the grade. The 1-2 are rated back near their respective bests.

4294 SKY SPORTS RACING ON VIRGIN 535 H'CAP 5f (Tp)
5:10 (5:11) (Class 4) (0-85,92) 3-Y-O
£5,530 (£1,645; £822; £411; £300; £300) **Stalls** Centre

Form RPR
6200 **1** **Yolo Again (IRE)**[5] 4101 3-9-12 **86** DanielTudhope 5 91
(Roger Fell) *trckd ldr: cl up 2f out: rdn over 1f out: drvn ins fnl f: kpt on wl to ld nr fin* **11/4**[2]
-302 **2** *nk* **True Hero**[5] 4128 3-9-0 **79** FayeMcManoman(5) 7 83
(Nigel Tinkler) *led: pushed along 2f out: rdn over 1f out: hdd nr fin* **9/4**[1]
0-00 **3** 1 1/4 **Prince Of Rome (IRE)**[33] 3075 3-9-13 **87** (t) ShaneKelly 4 87
(Richard Hughes) *trckd ldrs: hdwy 2f out: rdn over 1f out: drvn to chal and ev ch ins fnl f: kpt on same pce fnl 50yds* **7/2**[3]
0-03 **4** 1 1/2 **Que Amoro (IRE)**[5] 4128 3-9-7 **81** (p) PaulMulrennan 2 75
(Michael Dods) *hld up in tch: hdwy 2f out: rdn along over 1f out: ch jst ins fnl f: sn drvn and kpt on same pce* **6/1**
042- **5** 1/2 **Almurr (IRE)**[260] 8107 3-9-7 **81** SamJames 1 73
(Phillip Makin) *bhd: hdwy 2f out: rdn to chse ldrs ins fnl f: kpt on same pce towards fin* **10/1**
-000 **6** 1 3/4 **Little Legs**[27] 3293 3-9-3 **80** BenRobinson(3) 8 66
(Brian Ellison) *trckd ldr: cl up over 2f out: sn rdn and wknd wl over 1f out* **12/1**

1m 1.09s (1.59) **Going Correction** +0.325s/f (Slow) **6 Ran SP% 110.7**
Speed ratings (Par 101): **100,99,97,95,94 91**
CSF £9.09 CT £19.36 TOTE £2.90: £1.40, £2.10; EX 9.50 Trifecta £35.00.
Owner Nick Bradley Racing 12 & Partner **Bred** The Suite Partnership **Trained** Nawton, N Yorks

FOCUS
A decent 3yo sprint handicap. The second-favourite's winning time was comparatively modest from off a slow gallop. Slight improvement from the winner.
T/Plt: £4,387.90 to a £1 stake. Pool: £65,218.52 - 10.85 winning units T/Qpdt: £228.70 to a £1 stake. Pool: £6,589.80 - 21.32 winning units **Joe Rowntree**

4117 NEWMARKET (R-H)
Thursday, June 27

OFFICIAL GOING: Good (7.6)
Wind: Light, against Weather: Sunny

4295 BLACK TYPE ACCOUNTANCY NOVICE AUCTION STKS (PLUS 10 RACE) 6f
2:10 (2:10) (Class 4) 2-Y-O
£5,175 (£1,540; £769; £384) **Stalls** High

Form RPR
3 **1** **Tomfre**[10] 3943 2-9-2 0 HarryBentley 8 85
(Ralph Beckett) *trckd ldrs: nt clr run briefly over 2f out: effrt to chse ldr wl over 1f out: styd on u.p ins fnl f to ld last strides* **6/5**[1]
523 **2** *hd* **Flash Henry**[6] 4062 2-9-4 0 (p[1]) OisinMurphy 9 86
(George Scott) *led: rdn and kicked on wl over 1f out: hrd pressed ins fnl f: kpt on u.p but hdd last strides* **9/4**[2]
3 3 1/2 **Ananya** 2-8-11 0 BrettDoyle 7 69
(Peter Chapple-Hyam) *chsd ldrs: rdn and unable qck over 1f out: kpt on same pce ins fnl f* **28/1**
6 **4** 1 1/2 **Broken Rifle**[26] 3335 2-9-5 0 SeanLevey 2 72
(Ivan Furtado) *in tch: hdwy to chse ldr over 2f out tl unable qck wl over 1f out: wknd ins fnl f* **9/1**
6 **5** 2 1/4 **Dubai Avenue (IRE)**[17] 3644 2-9-4 0 JamieSpencer 1 65+
(Clive Cox) *hld up in tch: effrt and swtchd lft over 2f out: outpcd over 1f out: wl hld and wnt rt ins fnl f* **5/1**[3]
0 **6** 7 **Thomas Lanfiere (FR)**[7] 4018 2-9-5 0 CallumShepherd 5 45
(David Simcock) *hld up in tch in rr: outpcd ent fnl 2f: wl bhd ins fnl f* **16/1**
7 2 3/4 **Surrajah (IRE)** 2-9-5 0 LukeMorris 4 36
(Tom Clover) *chsd ldr tl over 2f out: sn struggling: wl bhd ins fnl f* **33/1**
8 1/2 **Wizardry (FR)** 2-9-4 0 HayleyTurner 6 34
(George Scott) *s.i.s: rn green and a towards rr: rdn 1/2-way: wl bhd ins fnl f* **25/1**

1m 13.33s (1.23) **Going Correction** +0.125s/f (Good) **8 Ran SP% 119.0**
Speed ratings (Par 95): **96,95,91,89,86 76,73,72**
CSF £4.17 TOTE £1.80: £1.10, £1.20, £5.60; EX 4.30 Trifecta £62.60.
Owner Mrs Philip Snow & Partners **Bred** Mrs P Snow & Partners **Trained** Kimpton, Hants

FOCUS
It was a sunny day, although the winning time of the opener suggested there was still some moisture underfoot.\n\x\x The first pair dominated the finish of this modest novice event, keeping to the far side. The winner ran to a similar level to his debut.

4296 CHEMTEST ENVIRONMENTAL LABORATORIES H'CAP 1m 4f
2:45 (2:47) (Class 5) (0-75,79) 3-Y-O+
£4,528 (£1,347; £673; £336; £300; £300) **Stalls** High

Form RPR
5-41 **1** **Faylaq**[7] 4034 3-9-6 **79** 6ex JimCrowley 5 99+
(William Haggas) *t.k.h early: hld up in midfield: clsd and trcking ldrs and travelling strly 3f out: led over 1f out: sn clr and in command: v easily* **1/3**[1]
0041 **2** 6 **West Newton**[27] 3311 3-8-7 **66** (p) HayleyTurner 6 71
(Roger Charlton) *led for 1f: chsd ldr tl led again 3f out: sn rdn: hdd and immediately brushed aside by wnr over 1f out: kpt on same pce fnl f* **6/1**[2]
336 **3** 1 1/4 **Isolate (FR)**[16] 3699 3-9-1 **74** RobHornby 2 77
(Martyn Meade) *chsd ldrs: effrt and ev ch ent fnl 2f: outpcd by wnr and btn over 1f out: plugged on same pce fnl f (starter reported that colt was the subject of a third criteria failure; trainer was informed that the colt could not run until the day after passing a stalls test)* **6/1**[2]
06-0 **4** 8 **Paddy The Chef (IRE)**[30] 3192 4-9-10 **69** (p[1]) OisinMurphy 3 59
(Ian Williams) *hld up in midfield: effrt over 2f out: outpcd over 1f out: sn wknd* **16/1**[3]
00 **5** 4 1/2 **The Corporal (IRE)**[42] 2766 3-8-13 **72** TomMarquand 4 55
(Chris Wall) *hld up in last pair: effrt jst over 2f out: outpcd whn rt and wnt sharply lft wl over 1f out: sn wl btn* **20/1**
6350 **6** 11 **Makambe (IRE)**[18] 3633 4-9-8 **67** JamieSpencer 7 32
(Paul Howling) *hld up in last pair: effrt wl over 2f out: sn struggling and wl btn over 1f out: eased ins fnl f* **25/1**

The Form Book Flat 2019, Raceform Ltd, Newbury, RG14 5SJ

4-20 **7** *15* **French Riviera (FR)**[20] 3545 4-10-0 73 .... HarryBentley 8 14
(Ralph Beckett) *t.k.h: led after 1f and sn clr: hdd 3f out: sn dropped out and bhd: eased ins fnl f* **20/1**

2m 33.97s (0.07) **Going Correction** +0.125s/f (Good)
WFA 3 from 4yo 14lb **7** Ran SP% **122.8**
Speed ratings (Par 103): **104,100,99,93,90 83,73**
CSF £3.42 CT £6.95 TOTE £1.20: £1.10, £2.50; EX 3.40 Trifecta £8.90.
Owner Hamdan Al Maktoum **Bred** Teruya Yoshida **Trained** Newmarket, Suffolk
■ Sea Battle was withdrawn, price at time of withdrawal 33/1. Rule 4 does not apply.

FOCUS
This went the way the market strongly suggested it would. The winner's way ahead of his mark. Add 30yds.

4297 TRM "EXCELLENCE IN EQUINE NUTRITION" H'CAP 6f
3:20 (3:20) (Class 4) (0-80,80) 3-Y-O
£6,469 (£1,925; £721; £300; £300) **Stalls** High

Form RPR
-206 **1** **The Night Watch**[19] 3590 3-9-7 80 .... RyanMoore 5 85
(William Haggas) *in tch in last pair: effrt over 2f out: hdwy u.p to press ldrs 1f out: led ins fnl f: sn in command and r.o wl* **7/2**[2]

3-54 **2** *1 3/4* **Mrs Discombe**[20] 3532 3-8-13 72 .... TomMarquand 7 72
(Mick Quinn) *led: rdn 2f out: sn drvn and hdd 1f out: chsd wnr and kpt on same pce wl ins fnl f* **33/1**

-060 **3** *hd* **Tin Hat (IRE)**[35] 2997 3-9-6 79 .... CharlesBishop 4 78
(Eve Johnson Houghton) *chsd ldrs: effrt over 1f out: kpt on and pressing ldrs whn squeezed for room wl ins fnl f: one pce towards fin* **12/1**

0342 **3** *dht* **Triple Distilled**[17] 3654 3-9-4 77 .... OisinMurphy 6 84+
(Nigel Tinkler) *hld up in tch: clsd to trck ldrs and nt clr run over 1f out: continually denied a run: squeezed for room: hmpd and swtchd rt wl ins fnl f: r.o wl towards fin* **15/8**[1]

0-10 **5** *1 1/4* **Tone The Barone**[21] 3508 3-8-3 62 .... (t) MartinDwyer 3 57
(Stuart Williams) *t.k.h: sn w ldr: rdn and ev ch over 1f out: drvn to ld 1f out: sn hung lft and hdd ins fnl f: wknd towards fin* **9/2**[3]

0-60 **6** *hd* **Three Card Trick**[41] 2810 3-9-5 78 .... (b[1]) JamieSpencer 1 72
(Kevin Ryan) *stdd s: racd away fr rivals in centre: chsd ldrs: effrt over 1f out: unable qck and btn whn pushed rt wl ins fnl f* **8/1**

-012 **7** *1 1/2* **Queen Of Burgundy**[21] 3516 3-8-13 77 .... DarraghKeenan(5) 2 67
(Christine Dunnett) *t.k.h early: in tch: swtchd towards rr: no imp over 1f out: keeping on same pce whn hmpd wl ins fnl f* **5/1**

000 **8** *8* **Walkman (IRE)**[12] 3838 3-9-1 74 .... (p) JimCrowley 8 38
(Mark Usher) *outpcd and rdn early: wl bhd ins fnl f* **20/1**

1m 12.69s (0.59) **Going Correction** +0.125s/f (Good) **8** Ran SP% **118.4**
Speed ratings (Par 101): **101,98,98,98,96 96,94,83**
WIN: 4.50 The Night Watch; PL: 1.90 Tin Hat, 0.50 Triple Distilled, 5.80 Mrs Discombe, 1.40 The Night Watch; EX: 91.70; CSF: 103.83; TC: TNW/MD/TH 632.61, TNW/MD/TD 140.55; TF: TNW/MD/TH 289.60, TNW/MD/TD 143.90;.
Owner Nicholas Jones **Bred** Coln Valley Stud **Trained** Newmarket, Suffolk
■ Stewards' Enquiry : Oisin Murphy caution: careless riding

FOCUS
Again the far side was favoured in this 3yo sprint handicap and it proved messy. The form's a bit fluid.

4298 TRM KURASYN 360X MAIDEN STKS 7f
3:50 (3:52) (Class 4) 3-Y-O+ **£5,822** (£1,732; £865; £432) **Stalls** High

Form RPR
3 **1** **Nazeef**[19] 3603 3-9-0 0 .... JimCrowley 3 81+
(John Gosden) *trckd ldrs tl pushed into ld over 1f out: rdn and kpt on ins fnl f: pushed out towards fin* **4/6**[1]

0- **2** *1 1/4* **Ghalyoon**[327] 5715 4-10-0 0 .... MartinDwyer 5 86+
(Marcus Tregoning) *t.k.h: hld up wl in tch in midfield: effrt to chse ldrs: rn green and drifted rt jst over 1f out: chsd wnr ins fnl f: kpt on wl for clr 2nd but a hld (jockey said gelding ran too free)* **20/1**

4-22 **3** *6* **Lyndon B (IRE)**[15] 3727 3-9-5 82 .... HarryBentley 7 67
(George Scott) *dwlt and rousted along leaving stalls: sn rcvrd to press ldr: drvn over 1f out and nt match pce of wnr 1f out: lost 2nd and wknd ins fnl f* **2/1**[2]

0- **4** *2* **Threefeetfromgold (IRE)**[237] 8796 3-9-5 0 .... (h[1]) EoinWalsh 4 61
(Martin Smith) *t.k.h: led: rdn and hdd over 1f out: sn outpcd: edgd rt and wknd ins fnl f* **66/1**

5 *1 1/2* **Critical Time** 3-9-0 0 .... RyanMoore 6 52
(William Haggas) *in tch in last pair: hdwy 1/2-way: rdn and outpcd 2f out: sn btn and wknd ins fnl f* **13/2**[3]

00 **6** *2 1/4* **Exning Queen (IRE)**[19] 3603 3-8-7 0 .... SeanKirrane(7) 2 46?
(Julia Feilden) *in tch: rdn over 2f out: sn hung lft and outpcd: wknd over 1f out* **100/1**

00- **7** *5* **Ketts Hill**[229] 8993 3-9-0 0 .... (t[1]) JamieJones(5) 1 38
(Mohamed Moubarak) *stdd and dropped in bhd after s: a towards rr: lost tch over 1f out* **100/1**

1m 26.13s (0.43) **Going Correction** +0.125s/f (Good) **7** Ran SP% **114.9**
WFA 3 from 4yo 9lb
Speed ratings (Par 105): **102,100,93,91,89 87,81**
CSF £17.25 TOTE £1.50: £1.10, £5.40; EX 14.80 Trifecta £26.70.
Owner Hamdan Al Maktoum **Bred** Shadwell Estate Company Limited **Trained** Newmarket, Suffolk

FOCUS
The first pair came clear off a muddling pace in this interesting maiden. The winner's sure to do better but the bare form is limited by the fourth and sixth.

4299 TRM CALPHORMIN H'CAP 7f
4:25 (4:27) (Class 2) (0-100,100) 3-Y-O+ **£12,938** (£3,850; £1,924; £962) **Stalls** High

Form RPR
251 **1** **Land Of Legends (IRE)**[22] 3464 3-8-10 91 .... CallumShepherd 5 96+
(Saeed bin Suroor) *chsd ldrs: rdn to ld over 1f out: styd on wl and a doing enough ins fnl f* **5/2**[1]

1044 **2** *1/2* **Reputation (IRE)**[19] 3602 6-9-10 96 .... BarryMcHugh 3 102
(Ruth Carr) *stdd s: hld up in rr: swtchd lft to far rail over 2f out: nt clr run wl over 1f out: swtchd rt jst ins fnl f: r.o strly to go 2nd last strides: nvr getting to wnr* **14/1**

0410 **3** *nk* **Apex King (IRE)**[19] 3581 5-9-4 90 .... LukeMorris 13 95
(David Loughnane) *in tch in midfield: chsd ldrs 3f out: edgd lft u.p over 1f out: drvn and chsd wnr ins fnl f: kpt on: lost 2nd last strides* **8/1**

00-0 **4** *3/4* **Medahim (IRE)**[40] 2832 5-9-10 96 .... SeanLevey 4 99
(Ivan Furtado) *in tch in midfield: hdwy over 2 out: drvn to chse ldrs over 1f out: kpt on same pce ins fnl f* **12/1**

000- **5** *hd* **George William**[432] 1962 6-9-8 94 .... LiamKeniry 8 97
(Ed Walker) *hld up in tch in midfield: n.m.r 2f out: effrt over 1f out: rdn ins fnl f: kpt on towards fin* **40/1**

0100 **6** *3/4* **Kimifive (IRE)**[34] 3062 4-9-7 93 .... OisinMurphy 1 94
(Joseph Tuite) *in tch towards rr: effrt ent fnl 2f: kpt on u.p ins fnl f* **5/1**[2]

6210 **7** *3/4* **Pettifogger (IRE)**[27] 3308 4-9-1 87 .... (h) GeraldMosse 9 86
(Marco Botti) *led: rdn 2f out: hdd over 1f out: no ex and outpcd ins fnl f* **16/1**

50-5 **8** *3/4* **Makzeem**[35] 3009 6-10-0 100 .... (t) RyanMoore 10 97+
(Roger Charlton) *in tch in midfield: effrt whn squeezed for room over 1f out: pushed along and no imp ins fnl f (jockey said gelding was denied a clear run)* **7/1**[3]

-300 **9** *1/2* **Presidential (IRE)**[5] 4127 5-9-0 89 .... CameronNoble(3) 7 84
(Roger Fell) *in tch in last quartet: effrt 2f out: rdn over 1f out: swtchd rt 1f out: kpt on same pce ins fnl f* **8/1**

4310 **10** *hd* **Love Dreams (IRE)**[12] 3863 5-9-13 99 .... (v) JimCrowley 12 94
(Mark Johnston) *chsd ldr tl unable qck u.p over 1f out: wknd ins fnl f* **10/1**

5641 **11** *15* **Corazon Espinado (IRE)**[27] 3318 4-8-12 84 .... TomMarquand 2 38
(Simon Dow) *chsd ldrs tl over 2f out: sn lost pl u.p: wl bhd and eased ins fnl f* **8/1**

-000 **12** *1/2* **Taurean Star (IRE)**[18] 3632 6-8-12 84 .... HarryBentley 6 37
(Ralph Beckett) *hld up in last trio: shkn up 2f out: sn btn and wl bhd whn eased ins fnl f* **20/1**

1m 24.68s (-1.02) **Going Correction** +0.125s/f (Good)
WFA 3 from 4yo+ 9lb **12** Ran SP% **121.3**
Speed ratings (Par 109): **110,109,109,108,108 107,106,105,104,104 87,86**
CSF £40.81 CT £604.94 TOTE £2.90: £1.60, £3.20, £5.90; EX 34.50 Trifecta £947.70.
Owner Godolphin **Bred** Godolphin **Trained** Newmarket, Suffolk

FOCUS
Competitive stuff. They predictably went far side, at a fair pace, and there was a tight finish. Good form, the winner confirming the potential of his debut run.

4300 TRM KURASYN "ART OF MOVEMENT" H'CAP 1m
5:00 (5:02) (Class 4) (0-85,85) 3-Y-O+
£6,469 (£1,925; £962; £481; £300; £300) **Stalls** High

Form RPR
-211 **1** **Ouzo**[13] 3805 3-9-4 85 .... SeanLevey 6 95+
(Richard Hannon) *stdd after s: hld up in tch towards rr: effrt ent fnl 2f: rdn and hdwy to ld over 1f out: clr and r.o strly ins fnl f* **13/8**[1]

42-1 **2** *2 1/2* **Balgair**[43] 2739 5-10-0 85 .... (h) LukeMorris 13 91
(Tom Clover) *stdd after s: hld up in rr: clsd and swtchd lft over 2f out: nt clr run and swtchd rt over 1f out: edging lft u.p but chsd clr wnr ins fnl f: no imp* **12/1**

4223 **3** *nk* **Regimented (IRE)**[14] 3763 4-9-8 79 .... RyanMoore 3 84
(Richard Hannon) *hld up in tch towards rr: effrt over 2f out: hdwy u.p over 1f out: chsd ldrs: flashing tail and kpt on same pce ins fnl f* **8/1**[2]

-533 **4** *2 1/2* **Medieval (IRE)**[41] 2803 5-9-11 82 .... (t) RaulDaSilva 1 82
(Paul Cole) *wl in tch in midfield: effrt to chse ldrs u.p over 1f out: hung lft and nt match pce of wnr 1f out: wknd and lost 2 pls ins fnl f* **8/1**[2]

42-5 **5** *2 1/4* **Monaadhil (IRE)**[21] 3496 5-9-11 82 .... JimCrowley 10 76
(Marcus Tregoning) *t.k.h: hld up in tch in midfield: nt clr run 2f out: effrt over 1f out: kpt on but no threat to ldrs ins fnl f* **9/1**[3]

0005 **6** *hd* **Rampant Lion (IRE)**[36] 2966 4-9-8 79 .... (p) GeraldMosse 12 73
(William Jarvis) *wl in tch in midfield: hdwy to chse ldrs 3f out: swtchd rt and rdn to ld jst over 2f out: hdd over 1f out: sn outpcd and wknd ins fnl f* **12/1**

3314 **7** *2 1/4* **Strawberry Jack**[19] 3569 3-8-13 80 .... (vt) HarryBentley 8 67
(George Scott) *in tch in midfield: lost pl and bmpd over 2f out: sn drvn: no ch w ldrs but plugged on to pass btn horses ins fnl f (jockey said gelding suffered interference in running)* **14/1**

0-50 **8** *1* **Data Protection**[14] 3763 4-9-6 77 .... (t) NicolaCurrie 2 63
(William Muir) *hld up in tch in midfield: effrt ent fnl 2f: no imp u.p over 1f out: wl hld fnl f* **14/1**

4410 **9** *2 3/4* **Chevallier**[10] 3944 7-9-11 82 .... RobHornby 11 62
(Michael Attwater) *chsd ldrs: pushed along ent fnl 2f: u.p and outpcd over 1f out: wknd ins fnl f* **40/1**

6060 **10** *6* **Ghayadh**[27] 3313 4-9-9 80 .... (t) MartinDwyer 9 46
(Stuart Williams) *led: rdn and hdd jst over 2f out: losing pl whn hung rt and hmpd over 1f out: no ch and eased ins fnl f (jockey said gelding hung right-handed)* **33/1**

1000 **11** *3/4* **Capriolette (IRE)**[76] 1727 4-9-6 77 .... LiamKeniry 7 42
(Ed Walker) *t.k.h: chsd ldrs: rdn ent fnl 2f: sn struggling and lost pl over 1f out: wknd fnl f* **33/1**

0-05 **12** *3* **Colonel Frank**[17] 3649 5-9-6 77 .... CharlesBishop 14 35
(Mick Quinn) *t.k.h: chsd ldr: rdn ent fnl 2f: sn outpcd and wknd fnl f* **25/1**

0-00 **13** *15* **Indian Viceroy**[19] 3591 3-8-10 77 .... OisinMurphy 5
(Hughie Morrison) *t.k.h: chsd ldrs tl lost pl and bmpd over 2f out: wl bhd fnl f (jockey said gelding stopped quickly)* **9/1**[3]

1m 39.03s (-0.97) **Going Correction** +0.125s/f (Good)
WFA 3 from 4yo+ 10lb **13** Ran SP% **121.2**
Speed ratings (Par 105): **109,106,106,103,101 101,99,98,95,89 88,85,70**
CSF £22.17 CT £134.50 TOTE £2.30: £1.20, £3.00, £2.90; EX 17.20 Trifecta £52.90.
Owner Michael Kerr-Dineen & Martin Hughes **Bred** Equine Breeding Limited **Trained** East Everleigh, Wilts

FOCUS
This teed up for the closers and it's solid form for the class. The winner continues to improve.

4301 TRM SPEEDXCELL H'CAP 5f
5:30 (5:30) (Class 4) (0-85,85) 3-Y-O+
£6,469 (£1,925; £962; £481; £300; £300) **Stalls** High

Form RPR
5354 **1** **Jack The Truth (IRE)**[84] 1551 5-8-12 69 .... HarryBentley 10 80
(George Scott) *in tch: clsd to chse ldrs 2f out: nt clrest of over 1f out: rdn and hdwy to chal 1f out: led ins fnl f: r.o wl* **7/1**

5203 **2** *1/2* **Nibras Again**[38] 2910 5-9-4 75 .... OisinMurphy 8 84
(Paul Midgley) *chsd ldrs: effrt to chal over 1f out: led ent fnl f: hdd ins fnl f: kpt on but hld towards fin* **7/2**[1]

-514 **3** *1* **Burford Brown**[25] 3375 4-9-12 83 .... JimCrowley 9 88
(Robert Cowell) *chsd ldrs tl wnt 2nd 1/2-way: ev ch u.p over 1f out: no ex and one pce ins fnl f* **13/2**

0000 **4** *1 1/2* **Leo Minor (USA)**[20] 3536 5-9-0 76 .... (p) DylanHogan(5) 5 76+
(Robert Cowell) *in tch in rr: nt clr run 2f out: swtchd rt over 1f out: styd on ins fnl f: nvr trbld ldrs* **8/1**

0332 **5** *hd* **Hawaam (IRE)**[10] 3936 4-9-3 77 .... (p) CameronNoble(3) 7 76
(Roger Fell) *led: rdn and wandered 2f out: hdd ent fnl f: no ex and wknd ins fnl f* **9/2**[2]

2402 **6** 3/4 **Enthaar**[35] 3021 4-9-1 72 (t) SeanLevey 6 69
(Stuart Williams) *in tch towards rr: hdwy u.p to chse ldrs over 1f out: sn drvn and wknd ins fnl f* **11/2**[3]

-000 **7** 2 1/2 **Soie D'Leau**[19] 3589 7-10-0 85 (p) HayleyTurner 2 73
(Linda Stubbs) *chsd ldrs: unable qck u.p over 1f out: wknd ins fnl f* **7/1**

0-15 **8** 7 **Grandfather Tom**[35] 3021 4-9-1 72 LukeMorris 1 34
(Robert Cowell) *wnt rt leaving stalls: sn rcvrd and in tch in midfield: rdn 1/2-way: struggling whn pushed rt over 1f out: sn wknd (jockey said gelding jumped awkwardly)* **12/1**

1-50 **9** 1/2 **Gifted Zebedee (IRE)**[37] 2940 3-8-8 71 (t[1]) EoinWalsh 4 30
(Anthony Carson) *chsd ldr tl 1/2-way: sn rdn and lost pl over 1f out: wknd fnl f (trainer said gelding had a breathing problem)* **25/1**

59.04s (0.34) **Going Correction** +0.125s/f (Good)
WFA 3 from 4yo+ 6lb **9** Ran SP% **116.8**
Speed ratings (Par 105): **102,101,99,97,96 95,91,80,79**
CSF £32.12 CT £151.51 TOTE £8.60: £2.40, £1.60, £2.00; EX 44.60 Trifecta £156.30.
Owner Jack Stephenson **Bred** Michael G Daly **Trained** Newmarket, Suffolk

FOCUS
Not a bad sprint handicap. The winner is rated pretty much to his best turf form.
T/Plt: £6.50 to a £1 stake. Pool: £63,951.79 - 7,110.18 winning units T/Qpdt: £5.80 to a £1 stake. Pool: £4,752.10 - 602.12 winning units **Steve Payne**

3934 NOTTINGHAM (L-H)
Thursday, June 27

OFFICIAL GOING: Good to soft (good in places)
Wind: Light breeze, against in home straight Weather: Sunny with light cloud, pleasant

4302 MANSIONBET MEDIAN AUCTION MAIDEN STKS 6f 18y
2:00 (2:01) (Class 5) 2-Y-O **£3,881** (£1,155; £577; £288) **Stalls** Centre

Form RPR

3 **1** **Be Prepared**[37] 2931 2-9-5 0 KerrinMcEvoy 7 87+
(Simon Crisford) *trckd ldrs: pushed along and hdwy to chal over 1f out: drvn to ld ent fnl f: sn pushed clr: easily* **1/2**[1]

3 **2** 6 **Second Love (IRE)**[21] 3491 2-9-5 0 CliffordLee 9 67
(K R Burke) *chsd ldrs: cl up and drvn 2f out: rdn in 3rd 1f out: kpt on fnl f: tk 2nd nr fin (jockey said colt hung left under pressure)* **7/1**[3]

6 **3** 1/2 **Saras Hope**[21] 3507 2-9-5 0 PJMcDonald 4 66
(John Gallagher) *led: drvn and hdd ent fnl f: sn rdn and no ex: lost 2nd nr fin* **50/1**

62 **4** 1 1/2 **Star Of St James (GER)**[28] 3265 2-9-5 0 JackGarritty 1 61
(Richard Fahey) *chsd ldrs: drvn 2f out: sn rdn: one pce fnl f* **5/2**[2]

5 2 1/4 **Poetic Lilly** 2-9-0 0 DavidEgan 10 49
(David Menuisier) *racd on own on stands' side: bhd: drvn 2f out: reminders over 1f out: kpt on fnl f* **22/1**

6 **6** 8 **Contract Kid (IRE)**[69] 1910 2-9-5 0 JasonWatson 6 30
(Mark Loughnane) *bhd and sn pushed along: drvn 1/2-way: no imp* **100/1**

7 1 1/2 **Red Hottie** 2-9-0 0 AlistairRawlinson 5 21
(Michael Appleby) *chsd ldrs: drvn and lost pl 2f out: wknd* **16/1**

8 3 1/4 **Camacho Man (IRE)** 2-9-5 0 RossaRyan 3 16
(Jennie Candlish) *slowly away: bhd and sn pushed along: drvn and lost tch 1/2-way* **33/1**

0 **9** nk **Lethal Sensation**[12] 3835 2-9-0 0 DaneO'Neill 8 10
(Paul Webber) *mid-div: rdn and wknd 2f out* **100/1**

10 90 **Youarefullofchat** 2-9-0 0 JosephineGordon 2
(Robyn Brisland) *dwlt: sn wl bhd and hung lft: t.o* **50/1**

1m 14.79s (0.99) **Going Correction** +0.075s/f (Good) **10** Ran SP% **126.8**
Speed ratings (Par 93): **96,88,87,85,82 71,69,65,64,**
CSF £5.77 TOTE £1.40: £1.02, £3.30, £15.30; EX 7.80 Trifecta £84.40.
Owner Abdulla Al Mansoori **Bred** Glebe Farm Stud **Trained** Newmarket, Suffolk

FOCUS
Outer track. Rail set out 8yds on the stands bend, adding 24yds to the 5.20. There wasn't much depth to this maiden and, as expected, the favourite won comfortably.

4303 MANSIONBET H'CAP 6f 18y
2:35 (2:37) (Class 4) (0-80,80) 3-Y-O+
£6,469 (£1,925; £962; £481; £300; £300) **Stalls** Centre

Form RPR

-400 **1** **Spring Romance (IRE)**[56] 2339 4-9-4 72 JoeyHaynes 3 81
(Dean Ivory) *led: drvn and hdd 2f out: rdn to ld 1f out: drifted rt fnl f: r.o to repel rivals either side (jockey said gelding hung right under pressure)* **25/1**

2025 **2** nk **Zumurud (IRE)**[12] 3868 4-9-9 77 AdamKirby 11 85
(Rebecca Bastiman) *prom: drvn to ld 2f out: rdn and hdd 1f out: carried rt by wnr ins fnl f: r.o: jst hld* **9/2**[2]

52-6 **3** nk **Zeyzoun (FR)**[40] 2824 5-9-8 76 (h) GeorgeWood 2 83
(Chris Wall) *mid-div: drvn and hdwy 2f out: sn rdn: 3rd 1f out: r.o fnl f* **7/2**[1]

3140 **4** 2 3/4 **Stoney Lane**[13] 3813 4-9-8 76 LewisEdmunds 1 74
(Richard Whitaker) *prom: drvn and lost pl 2f out: sn rdn: one pce fnl f* **7/2**[1]

0030 **5** 1/2 **Global Hope (IRE)**[6] 4081 4-8-7 61 (vt[1]) DavidEgan 6 58
(Gay Kelleway) *chsd ldrs: drvn 2f out: rdn over 1f out: one pce fnl f* **20/1**

2200 **6** 3/4 **Saluti (IRE)**[13] 3813 5-9-12 80 PatDobbs 8 74
(Paul Midgley) *bhd: rdn and effrt over 1f out: one pce fnl f* **16/1**

5-40 **7** hd **Across The Sea**[27] 3293 3-8-12 73 PJMcDonald 5 65
(James Tate) *mid-div: drvn 2f out: rdn over 1f out: wknd fnl f* **8/1**

0461 **8** 1 1/2 **Miracle Garden**[12] 3838 7-8-9 63 (v) KerrinMcEvoy 12 52
(Ian Williams) *bhd: rdn 2f out: no imp (trainer's rep could offer no explanation for the gelding's performance)* **16/1**

4-25 **9** 3/4 **Great Midge**[17] 3661 4-9-7 75 DavidProbert 4 61
(Henry Candy) *mid-div: drvn 2f out: sn rdn and wknd* **13/2**[3]

300- **10** 1 3/4 **Militia**[259] 8132 4-9-9 77 (w) JackGarritty 9 58
(Richard Fahey) *t.k.h: hld up: trckd ldrs 1/2-way: pushed along 2f out: rdn and wknd over 1f out* **25/1**

6650 **11** 10 **Bengali Boys (IRE)**[21] 3509 4-9-8 76 GeorgeDowning 13 25
(Tony Carroll) *mid-div on stands' side: drvn and lost pl over 2f out: sn wl bhd (jockey said gelding hung left)* **50/1**

000 **12** 33 **Case Key**[20] 3550 6-8-13 67 RoystonFfrench 7
(Michael Appleby) *mid-div: pushed along and dropped away bef 1/2-way: eased over 1f out (jockey said gelding stopped quickly)* **50/1**

1m 13.52s (-0.28) **Going Correction** +0.075s/f (Good)
WFA 3 from 4yo+ 7lb **12** Ran SP% **115.2**
Speed ratings (Par 105): **104,103,103,99,98 97,97,95,94,92 78,34**
CSF £125.52 CT £505.62 TOTE £27.80: £7.00, £2.00, £1.70; EX 96.20 Trifecta £2507.60.

Owner Solario Racing (Berkhamsted) **Bred** Zalim Bifov **Trained** Radlett, Herts
■ Stewards' Enquiry : Joey Haynes two-day ban: caused interference (Jul 11, 15)

FOCUS
This fair handicap had an open feel to it and while the winner was something of a surprise result he did have some good back form. The form's rated around the third. It paid to race prominently.

4304 MANSIONBET NOVICE STKS 1m 2f 50y
3:10 (3:11) (Class 5) 3-Y-O+ **£3,881** (£1,155; £577; £288) **Stalls** Low

Form RPR

43 **1** **Tatweej**[11] 3889 3-8-11 DavidProbert 8 73
(Owen Burrows) *prom: drvn to ld 2f out: rdn over 1f out: r.o wl and a holding on fnl f* **25/1**

54 **2** nk **Skerryvore**[45] 2690 3-9-2 DanielMuscutt 5 77
(James Fanshawe) *hld up: pushed along and hdwy to chse ldrs 2f out: drvn into 2nd over 1f out: rdn and r.o wl fnl f: a hld* **12/1**

1-0 **3** 2 **Power Of States (IRE)**[76] 1737 3-9-7 PatCosgrave 7 79+
(Hugo Palmer) *mid-div: hdwy into 3rd 3f out: drvn: nt clr run and bmpd over 1f out: reminder fnl f: kpt on* **11/1**

0-32 **4** nk **Infuse (IRE)**[34] 3050 3-8-11 76 (p[1]) JasonWatson 2 68
(Roger Charlton) *t.k.h: mid-div: drvn over 2f out: sn rdn: kpt on fnl f over 1f out* **5/2**[2]

5 1 3/4 **Point Taken (IRE)**[40] 8751 5-10-2 TheodoreLadd[(5)] 6 76
(Michael Appleby) *slowly away: bhd: drvn in last 3f out: hdwy on inner 2f out: swtchd over 1f out: no ex fnl f (jockey said gelding hung left under pressure)* **25/1**

0 **6** 4 1/2 **The Cruix (IRE)**[28] 3263 4-10-0 JoeyHaynes 4 60
(Dean Ivory) *prom: sn lost pl: drvn in 7th 3f out: sn rdn: no imp* **66/1**

02 **7** 3 1/4 **Wild Animal**[17] 3664 3-9-2 DavidEgan 1 54
(Saeed bin Suroor) *led: drvn in narrow ld 2f out: sn hdd & wknd (vet said colt lost left fore shoe)* **2/1**[1]

41 **8** 10 **Mohtarrif (IRE)**[96] 1293 3-9-9 DaneO'Neill 3 41
(Marcus Tregoning) *t.k.h: chsd ldrs: pushed along in 4th 3f out: sn rdn and lost pl: dropped to last over 1f out (jockey said colt ran too free)* **11/4**[3]

2m 15.55s (2.15) **Going Correction** +0.075s/f (Good)
WFA 3 from 4yo+ 12lb **8** Ran SP% **113.8**
Speed ratings (Par 103): **94,93,92,91,90 86,84,76**
CSF £280.81 TOTE £20.00: £4.30, £2.80, £2.80; EX 214.10 Trifecta £2191.70.
Owner Hamdan Al Maktoum **Bred** Highclere Stud And Floors Farming **Trained** Lambourn, Berks

FOCUS
An interesting novice event and something of a Placepot buster with all the fancied contenders disappointing and out of the frame. Improvement from the 1-2 but form with a few question marks over it.

4305 DOWNLOAD THE MANSIONBET APP NOVICE STKS 1m 75y
3:40 (3:42) (Class 4) 3-Y-O+ **£6,469** (£1,925; £962; £481) **Stalls** Centre

Form RPR

1- **1** **Honest Albert**[218] 9172 3-9-5 0 RobertHavlin 8 93+
(John Gosden) *chsd ldrs: drvn in 3rd 2f out: sn rdn: hdwy over 1f out: led jst ins fnl f: sn clr: readily* **4/1**[2]

1-3 **2** 1 1/2 **Bayroot (IRE)**[69] 1926 3-9-7 0 DavidEgan 1 91+
(Roger Varian) *trckd ldr: disp ld 4f out: led over 2f out: rdn 1f out: hdd jst ins fnl f: one pce* **8/11**[1]

13 **3** 1 **Freerolling**[16] 3680 4-10-3 0 KieranShoemark 2 90
(Charlie Fellowes) *led: jnd 4f out: drvn and hdd over 2f out: sn rdn: one pce fnl f* **6/1**

4-3 **4** 1 3/4 **Alandalos**[72] 1834 3-8-9 0 DaneO'Neill 9 72
(Charles Hills) *reluctant to load: mid-div: pushed along in 4th 3f out: rdn 2f out: no imp* **8/1**

30 **5** 8 **Edaraat**[41] 2802 3-9-0 0 JackMitchell 5 59
(Roger Varian) *hld up: pushed along and effrt over 2f out: reminder 1 1/2f out: wknd* **11/2**[3]

6 6 **Olympic Conqueror (IRE)** 3-9-0 0 DanielMuscutt 6 45
(James Fanshawe) *slowly away: in rr: pushed along 3f out: no imp fr over 2f out (jockey said gelding was slowly away and ran green)* **25/1**

0 **7** nse **Pearl Jam**[38] 2909 3-8-9 0 GeorgeWood 4 40
(James Fanshawe) *hld up: pushed along 3f out: drvn and wknd 2f out* **50/1**

00 **8** 5 **Thespinningwheel (IRE)**[10] 3946 4-9-10 0 CharlieBennett 3 35
(Adam West) *mid-div: pushed along 4f out: reminders and wknd over 3f out* **150/1**

P0-0 **9** 1/2 **Gavi Di Gavi (IRE)**[17] 3648 4-9-10 0 TomQueally 7 34
(Alan King) *hld up: pushed along and effrt on outer 3f out: wknd over 2f out* **100/1**

1m 46.42s (-0.28) **Going Correction** +0.075s/f (Good)
WFA 3 from 4yo 10lb **9** Ran SP% **126.1**
Speed ratings (Par 105): **104,102,101,99,91 85,85,80,80**
CSF £8.02 TOTE £6.10: £1.70, £1.10, £1.90; EX 10.20 Trifecta £30.20.
Owner Ms Rachel D S Hood **Bred** Rachel D S Hood **Trained** Newmarket, Suffolk

FOCUS
Plenty of interesting types in this and the form will probably work out. The first four were clear of the remainder, the pace modest.

4306 MANSIONBET H'CAP 1m 75y
4:15 (4:16) (Class 5) (0-75,77) 3-Y-O
£3,881 (£1,155; £577; £300; £300; £300) **Stalls** Centre

Form RPR

1625 **1** **Prince Of Harts**[19] 3580 3-9-9 76 PJMcDonald 2 86+
(Rod Millman) *mid-div: trckd ldrs 4f out: pushed into 3rd over 2f out: chal on inner 2f out: shkn up to ld over 1f out: qcknd clr fnl f: easily* **11/4**[2]

55-5 **2** 2 1/2 **Skyman**[28] 3247 3-9-5 72 JasonWatson 4 76
(Roger Charlton) *chsd ldrs: tk clsr order 4f out: pushed along to ld 2 1/2f out: rdn and hdd over 1f out: no ex fnl f* **8/1**

663- **3** 1 3/4 **Motawaj**[244] 8593 3-9-7 74 DavidEgan 6 74
(Roger Varian) *mid-div: pushed along 3f out: sn drvn: rdn 2f out: 5th 1f out: r.o to take 3rd ins fnl f* **9/4**[1]

2-05 **4** 1/2 **Crimewave (IRE)**[19] 3584 3-9-10 77 (p[1]) JackMitchell 10 76
(Tom Clover) *hld up: hdwy on outer 3f out: drvn 2f out: rdn over 1f out: no ex fnl f* **5/1**[3]

3-30 **5** 1 **Penrhos**[22] 3464 3-9-5 72 KieranShoemark 7 70
(Charles Hills) *prom: led 3f out: sn drvn: hdd 2 1/2f out: wknd fr 2f out* **16/1**

340 **6** 4 1/2 **Noble Fox**[22] 3463 3-9-5 72 AdamKirby 8 58
(Clive Cox) *hld up: pushed along on inner 3f out: rdn and wknd 2f out* **12/1**

1010 **7** *4* **Love Your Work (IRE)**[28] 3278 3-9-6 **73**.................. CharlieBennett 9 50
(Adam West) *rrd leaving stalls and slowly away losing several l: bhd: rdn over 2f out: no impression (jockey said gelding reared as the stalls opened and was slowly away as a result)* **18/1**

66-6 **8** *18* **Miss Pollyanna (IRE)**[169] 141 3-8-2 **60**.................. RhiainIngram(5) 1
(Roger Ingram) *led: pushed along and hdd 3f out: sn drvn and wknd: eased fnl f* **66/1**

6200 **9** *17* **Whenapoet**[48] 2582 3-8-2 **60**..........................(p) TheodoreLadd(5) 5
(Michael Appleby) *t.k.h: hld up: pushed along 3f out: drvn 2f out: sn dropped to last: eased fnl f: lame (vet said colt was lame right hind)* **10/1**

1m 46.97s (0.27) **Going Correction** +0.075s/f (Good) **9** Ran SP% **114.6**
Speed ratings (Par 99): **101,98,96,96,95 90,86,68,51**
CSF £24.95 CT £56.43 TOTE £3.50: £1.20, £1.90, £1.40; EX 23.10 Trifecta £71.80.
Owner Perfect Match 2 **Bred** Harts Farm Stud **Trained** Kentisbeare, Devon

FOCUS
Only a fair handicap but there's good reason to think the winner may go on to better things.

4307 DOWNLOAD THE MANSIONBET APP H'CAP — 5f 8y
4:50 (4:53) (Class 5) (0-70,70) 4-Y-O+
£3,881 (£1,155; £577; £300; £300; £300) **Stalls** Centre

Form — RPR

0300 **1** **Show Palace**[21] 3509 6-9-6 **69**..........................(p[1]) RossaRyan 1 81
(Jennie Candlish) *mde all: drvn in 1 l ld 1f out: rdn fnl f: hld on wl (regarding the apparent improvement in form, trainer said gelding benefitted from the first-time application of cheekpieces on this occasion)* **7/1**[2]

2400 **2** *1* **Johnny Cavagin**[12] 3868 10-9-7 **70**.................. PatDobbs 2 77
(Paul Midgley) *trckd ldrs: rdn to chal over 1f out: chsd wnr fnl f: kpt on but no imp* **10/3**[1]

0010 **3** *½* **Afandem (IRE)**[20] 3550 5-9-2 **70**..........................(p) DannyRedmond(5) 4 75
(Tim Easterby) *restless in stalls: hld up: drvn and hdwy over 1f out: rdn and r.o into 3rd fnl f* **14/1**

0410 **4** *nk* **Boudica Bay (IRE)**[29] 3213 4-8-7 **56**.................. RachelRichardson 3 60
(Eric Alston) *prom: drvn in 2nd 2f out: rdn over 1f out: no ex fnl f* **8/1**[3]

3304 **5** *1* **Atyaaf**[5] 4132 4-8-4 **53**.................. PaddyMathers 7 54
(Derek Shaw) *chsd ldrs: drvn 2f out: rdn fnl f: no ex* **8/1**[3]

0020 **6** *3* **Ladweb**[9] 3961 9-9-2 **65**.................. RoystonFfrench 8 55
(John Gallagher) *bhd: drvn 1/2-way: rdn fnl f: no imp (jockey said gelding was slowly away)* **12/1**

2030 **7** *½* **Kraka (IRE)**[12] 3868 4-9-4 **67**..........................(v) AdamKirby 10 55
(Christine Dunnett) *prom on stands' side: rdn and lost pl over 2f out: wknd* **7/1**[2]

441 **8** *½* **Prominna**[10] 3936 9-8-8 **57** 4ex.................. JoeyHaynes 11 43
(Tony Carroll) *hld up: pushed along and effrt 1/2-way: rdn and wknd over 1f out (jockey said gelding hung left)* **12/1**

4530 **9** *¾* **Seamster**[17] 3658 12-8-3 **59**..........................(t) LauraCoughlan(7) 6 42
(David Loughnane) *slowly away: bhd: rdn and effrt 2f out: no further prog (jockey said gelding was slowly away)* **10/1**

000- **10** *15* **Undercover Brother**[215] 9251 4-9-2 **65**.................. LewisEdmunds 9
(John Balding) *slowly away: a bhd: eased fnl f (jockey said gelding was never travelling and hung left throughout)* **40/1**

59.59s (-0.61) **Going Correction** +0.075s/f (Good) **10** Ran SP% **103.9**
Speed ratings (Par 103): **107,105,104,104,102 97,96,96,94,70**
CSF £24.83 CT £201.42 TOTE £5.70: £2.20, £1.50, £3.70; EX 24.10 Trifecta £168.90.
Owner P and Mrs G A Clarke **Bred** M C Humby **Trained** Basford Green, Staffs

■ Foxtrot Knight was withdrawn, price at time of withdrawal 8/1. Rule 4 applies to all bets. Deduction of 10p in the pound.

FOCUS
This was a modest event, and while it had an open look to it, nothing really got into it as the winner made all.

4308 MANSIONBET "HANDS N HEELS" APPRENTICE H'CAP (RACING EXCELLENCE INITIATIVE) — 1m 6f
5:20 (5:23) (Class 5) (0-75,76) 4-Y-O+
£3,881 (£1,155; £577; £300; £300; £300) **Stalls** Low

Form — RPR

14/3 **1** **Tawseef (IRE)**[16] 3686 11-8-12 **60**..........................(p) EllaMcCain 7 70
(Donald McCain) *mde all: pushed into 8 l ld 4f out: 10 l ld 2f out: advantage reduced ins fnl f but nvr in any danger* **8/1**

3333 **2** *4 ½* **Alabaster**[7] 4019 5-10-0 **76**..........................(v) GavinAshton 8 79
(Sir Mark Prescott Bt) *chsd ldr: pushed along in 8 l 2nd 4f out: continued to chse ldr: cut into wnr's ld ins fnl f but nvr able to mount a chal* **4/1**[2]

60-6 **3** *¾* **Aria Rose**[36] 2970 4-8-4 **55** oh2.................. GeorgeBass(3) 3 57
(David Arbuthnot) *chsd ldrs: drvn in 3rd 3f out: one pce fnl 2f* **8/1**

50-0 **4** *6* **Bartholomew J (IRE)**[30] 3192 5-9-5 **72**.................. MorganCole(5) 4 66
(Lydia Pearce) *hld up: drvn in distant 6th 3f out: styd on into 4th fr 2f out* **22/1**

0604 **5** *1 ½* **Battle Of Marathon (USA)**[5] 4118 7-9-9 **74**.................. GraceMcEntee(3) 2 65
(John Ryan) *hld up: drvn and one pce fr 3f out* **7/1**

24-0 **6** *11* **Jawshan (USA)**[40] 2819 4-9-4 **66**.................. JessicaCooley 5 42
(Ian Williams) *mid-div: drvn in 4th 3f out: sn wknd and drifted rt (jockey said gelding hung badly right)* **12/1**

22-1 **7** *15* **Imperial Court (IRE)**[14] 3778 4-9-8 **70**..........................(h) CianMacRedmond 1 25
(David Simcock) *slowly away losing several l: a bhd (jockey said gelding was slowly away and ran flat)* **2/1**[1]

4412 **8** *1 ¾* **The Resdev Way**[6] 4056 6-8-11 **64**.................. NickBarratt-Atkin(5) 6 17
(Philip Kirby) *hld up: drvn and wknd 3f out (jockey said gelding hung right home straight)* **13/2**[3]

3m 7.8s (1.40) **Going Correction** +0.075s/f (Good) **8** Ran SP% **113.4**
Speed ratings (Par 103): **99,96,96,92,91 85,76,75**
CSF £39.30 CT £264.88 TOTE £7.80: £2.10, £2.50, £3.00; EX 40.10 Trifecta £305.00.
Owner D McCain Jnr **Bred** Shadwell Estate Company Limited **Trained** Cholmondeley, Cheshire

FOCUS
Add 24yds. A fair handicap to end proceedings and it went to the oldest member of the field who was giving the runner-up six years in age. There wasn't much depth to this.

T/Plt: £159.10 to a £1 stake. Pool: £44,684.64 - 204.93 winning units T/Qpdt: £52.00 to a £1 stake. Pool: £4,713.40 - 67.06 winning units **Keith McHugh**

4309 - 4312a (Foreign Racing) - See Raceform Interactive

3554 CURRAGH (R-H)
Thursday, June 27

OFFICIAL GOING: Straight course - good to yielding; round course - good

4313a TOTE ROCKINGHAM H'CAP (PREMIER HANDICAP) — 5f
7:45 (7:53) 3-Y-O+
£66,441 (£21,396; £10,135; £4,504; £2,252; £1,126) **Stalls** Centre

RPR

1 **El Astronaute (IRE)**[13] 3818 6-9-13 **106**.................. JasonHart 14 111
(John Quinn) *hooded to load: sn led nr side and mde rest: stl gng wl w narrow advantage under 2f out: rdn out ins fnl f: comf* **7/1**[1]

2 *1* **Manshood (IRE)**[12] 3868 6-8-4 **83** oh4..........................(v) KillianLeonard 13 85
(Paul Midgley) *chsd ldrs nr side: rdn 2f out and no imp on wnr u.p disputing 2nd ins fnl f: kpt on wl in 2nd nr fin* **20/1**

3 *¾* **Rapid Reaction (IRE)**[13] 3818 4-8-6 **90**.................. AndrewSlattery(5) 16 89
(J F Grogan, Ire) *cl up nr side: rdn nr side over 1f out and no imp on wnr u.p in 3rd wl ins fnl f: kpt on wl* **16/1**

4 *nk* **Orvar (IRE)**[33] 3097 6-8-12 **91**.................. LeighRoche 11 89
(Paul Midgley) *w.w: drvn towards rr under 2f out and sme hdwy over 1f out where n.m.r briefly and swtchd rt: rdn and r.o between horses wl ins fnl f into nvr nrr 4th cl home* **10/1**

5 *nk* **Lord Riddiford (IRE)**[8] 3993 4-8-9 **93**.................. ShaneCrosse(5) 3 90+
(John Quinn) *chsd ldrs far side: rdn 2f out and no imp on wnr u.p disputing 2nd ins fnl f: no ex nr fin where dropped to 5th* **12/1**

6 *nk* **Maarek**[10] 3945 12-8-4 **83** oh4.................. MarkGallagher 17 79
(Miss Evanna McCutcheon, Ire) *hooded to load: dwlt: towards rr: rdn 2f out and sme late hdwy u.p nr side ins fnl f: nvr nrr* **33/1**

7 *hd* **Smash Williams (IRE)**[13] 3818 6-9-11 **104**..........................(t) KevinManning 9 99
(J S Bolger, Ire) *dwlt and pushed along towards rr early: r.o u.p nr side ins fnl f: nvr nrr* **7/1**[1]

8 *nk* **Venturous (IRE)**[19] 3582 6-8-7 **86**.................. ChrisHayes 2 80
(David Barron) *got upset in stalls: w.w far side early: prog 2f out: rdn disputing 3rd ins fnl f and sn no ex: wknd nr fin* **12/1**

9 *1 ½* **Duke Of Firenze**[11] 3883 10-8-11 **90**.................. PhilDennis 5 79
(David C Griffiths) *chsd ldrs far side: drvn under 2f out and n.m.r briefly between horses ent fnl f: sn wknd* **12/1**

10 *hd* **True Blue Moon (IRE)**[23] 3457 4-8-8 **87**..........................(t) WayneLordan 4 75
(Joseph Patrick O'Brien, Ire) *hld up towards rr far side: pushed along after 1/2-way and swtchd rt: rdn over 1f out and sme late hdwy: nvr nrr* **33/1**

11 *hd* **Ardhoomey (IRE)**[13] 3818 7-9-10 **103**..........................(t) ColinKeane 6 90
(G M Lyons, Ire) *hooded to load: prom early tl sn settled bhd ldrs far side: pushed along in mid-div under 2f out and no imp under hands and heels ins fnl f* **10/1**

12 *1* **Dash D'or (IRE)**[13] 3819 6-7-11 **83** oh6.................. AdamFarragher(7) 8 67
(Kieran P Cotter, Ire) *towards rr down centre: rdn after 1/2-way and no imp 1 1/2f out where nt clr run briefly: kpt on u.p ins fnl f: nvr a factor* **20/1**

13 *hd* **Dark Shot**[26] 3344 6-8-10 **89**..........................(p) KieranO'Neill 15 72
(Scott Dixon) *cl up nr side: rdn 2f out and no ex u.p over 1f out: wknd* **9/1**[3]

14 *1 ½* **Nitro Boost (IRE)**[20] 3559 3-8-6 **98**.................. NathanCrosse(7) 12 73
(W McCreery, Ire) *cl up: rdn down centre 2f out and sn wknd* **8/1**[2]

15 *1 ¼* **Just Glamorous (IRE)**[17] 3662 6-8-8 **87** ow1.................. SeamieHeffernan 7 59
(Grace Harris) *dwlt sltly: sn chsd ldrs: cl 3rd far side bef 1/2-way: rdn under 2f out and sn wknd* **16/1**

16 *3 ½* **Hathiq (IRE)**[26] 3344 5-8-13 **92**..........................(t) RoryCleary 1 52
(Denis Gerard Hogan, Ire) *chsd ldrs far side: rdn after 1/2-way and no ex u.p over 1f out: wknd* **7/1**[1]

59.3s (-1.10) **Going Correction** +0.225s/f (Good) **16** Ran SP% **127.0**
WFA 3 from 4yo+ 6lb
Speed ratings: **115,113,112,111,111 110,110,109,107,107 106,105,105,102,100 95**
CSF £153.27 CT £1364.64 TOTE £5.30: £2.00, £5.60, £3.10, £3.00; DF 214.40 Trifecta £2801.00.
Owner Ross Harmon Racing **Bred** T Jones **Trained** Settrington, N Yorks

FOCUS
One for the visitors, renewing a trend evident in this event between 2011 and 2015 when there were four British-trained winners in five years. Between them, John Quinn and Paul Midgley provided four of the first five, a notable feat. The high numbers dominated comprehensively. The winner is rated in line with his latest form.

4314 - 4315a (Foreign Racing) - See Raceform Interactive

3841 CHESTER (L-H)
Friday, June 28

OFFICIAL GOING: Good
Wind: Fairly strong, behind in straight of over 1f Weather: Sunny

4316 WHITE OAK UK SILK SERIES LADY RIDERS' H'CAP — 7f 127y
5:50 (5:50) (Class 4) (0-80,81) 3-Y-O
£6,404 (£1,905; £952; £476; £400; £400) **Stalls** Low

Form — RPR

2-32 **1** **Sezim**[15] 3779 3-10-5 **78**.................. NicolaCurrie 9 84+
(Roger Varian) *s.i.s: hld up: hdwy on inner over 1f out: sn swtchd rt: r.o to ld fnl 100yds: pushed out towards fin* **3/1**[2]

4425 **2** *nk* **Harvey Dent**[9] 4001 3-10-6 **79**.................. HollieDoyle 1 84
(Archie Watson) *led at stdy pce: rdn over 1f out: hrd pressed ins fnl f: hdd fnl 100yds: hld towards fin* **9/4**[1]

2100 **3** *1* **Pacino**[27] 3357 3-10-4 **80**.................. MeganNicholls(3) 5 82
(Richard Fahey) *chsd ldrs: wnt 2nd over 1f out: chalng ins fnl f: styd on same pce towards fin* **8/1**

0323 **4** *hd* **Lightning Attack**[12] 3885 3-10-2 **75**..........................(p) JosephineGordon 8 77
(Richard Fahey) *midfield: hdwy to go prom over 4f out: rdn over 2f out: chalng ins fnl f: unable qck fnl 100yds: no ex towards fin* **9/2**[3]

1400 **5** *shd* **Oloroso (IRE)**[23] 3465 3-10-0 **76**.................. PageFuller(3) 6 77+
(Andrew Balding) *racd keenly: hld u: hdwy on outer 2f out: chsd ldrs over 1f out: kpt on same pce fnl 100yds* **5/1**

5040 **6** *1 ¾* **Bay Of Naples (IRE)**[20] 3580 3-9-11 **73**.................. JaneElliott(3) 10 70
(Mark Johnston) *in tch: pushed along 3f out: drvn and no imp over 1f out: edgd lft and one pce fnl 150yds* **16/1**

4300 **7** *2 ½* **Any Smile (IRE)**[32] 3154 3-9-5 **64**.................. HayleyTurner 4 55
(Michael Bell) *chsd ldr: pushed along over 2f out: lost 2nd over 1f out: edgd lft and wknd fnl 150yds* **25/1**

The Form Book Flat 2019, Raceform Ltd, Newbury, RG14 5SJ

1154 **8** *1 ¼* **Plumette**[21] 3552 3-9-6 **72**....................(t) LauraCoughlan(7) 2 60
(David Loughnane) *missed break and awkward s: in rr: pushed along over 1f out: nvr able to get competitive* **10/1**

-000 **9** *4 ½* **Caramel Curves**[40] 2870 3-8-9 **61** oh11.................... SophieRalston(7) 3 37
(Lisa Williamson) *midfield: pushed along and lost pl 4f out: outpcd over 2f out: lft bhd over 1f out* **50/1**

1m 34.88s (-0.82) **Going Correction** -0.10s/f (Good) 9 Ran SP% **122.5**
Speed ratings (Par 101): **100,99,98,98,98 96,94,92,88**
CSF £10.94 CT £50.92 TOTE £4.60: £1.80, £1.80, £2.40; EX 14.70 Trifecta £81.10.
Owner Nurlan Bizakov **Bred** Hesmonds Stud Ltd **Trained** Newmarket, Suffolk

FOCUS
Add 13 yards. A competitive handicap for lady riders and it saw something of a bunch finish. The race is rated around the second, third and fourth.

4317 MBNA MAIDEN AUCTION STKS (PLUS 10 RACE) 7f 1y
6:20 (6:20) (Class 4) 2-Y-O

£6,162 (£1,845; £922; £461; £230; £115) **Stalls** Low

Form RPR

2 **1** **Sesame Birah (IRE)**[11] 3934 2-9-0 **0**.................... DanielTudhope 8 77+
(Richard Hannon) *w ldr: rdn to ld narrowly over 1f out: hung lft and bmpd rival ins fnl f: continued to hang lft and a doing enough towards fin* **7/2**[2]

4 **2** *hd* **King's Caper**[14] 3804 2-9-5 **0**.................... FrannyNorton 3 81
(Mark Johnston) *led: rdn and hdd narrowly over 1f out: bmpd by wnr ins fnl f: r.o u.p and continued to chal: a hld towards fin* **1/2**[1]

065 **3** *8* **G For Gabrial (IRE)**[13] 3841 2-9-2 **66**.................... SeanDavis(3) 5 59
(Richard Fahey) *hld up: rdn to go pce over 2f out: kpt on to chse clr front pair over 1f out: nvr any ch* **7/1**[3]

4 *½* **Precision Storm** 2-9-5 **0**.................... NicolaCurrie 4 58
(Mark Loughnane) *hld up: rdn and outpcd over 2f out: edgd let and kpt on ins fnl f: nvr trbld ldrs* **20/1**

5 *1 ¾* **Anniemation (IRE)** 2-9-5 **0**.................... JackGarritty 2 53
(Stella Barclay) *hld up in rr: rdn over 2f out: swtchd lft wl ins fnl f: kpt on towards fin: nvr a threat* **33/1**

00 **6** *1* **Eileen's Magic**[13] 3841 2-8-7 **0**.................... GavinAshton(7) 1 45
(Lisa Williamson) *chsd ldrs: rdn over 2f out: outpcd and no ch w front two over 1f out: wknd ins fnl f* **66/1**

5 **7** *1* **Saoirse's Gift (IRE)**[21] 3551 2-9-5 **0**.................... TonyHamilton 6 48
(Tim Easterby) *chsd ldrs: rdn over 2f out: wknd over 1f out* **16/1**

1m 28.0s (0.50) **Going Correction** -0.10s/f (Good) 7 Ran SP% **116.5**
Speed ratings (Par 95): **93,92,83,83,81 79,78**
CSF £5.74 TOTE £4.10: £2.30, £1.10; EX 7.30 Trifecta £14.90.
Owner Middleham Park Racing XXIV **Bred** Rathasker Stud **Trained** East Everleigh, Wilts

FOCUS
Add 13 yards. This lacked depth and big two had it between themselves for the length of the straight. The winner drifted into the runner-up under pressure and had to survive a stewards' enquiry. He has the scope to do better than the bare form.

4318 EDWARD BRYAN JONES MEMORIAL EBF BREEDERS' SERIES FILLIES' H'CAP 1m 2f 70y
6:55 (6:55) (Class 3) (0-90,87) 3-Y-O+

£11,827 (£3,541; £1,770; £885; £442; £222) **Stalls** High

Form RPR

4613 **1** **Ocala**[22] 3502 4-9-13 **81**.................... RobHornby 4 89
(Andrew Balding) *chsd ldr: rdn over 1f out: led ins fnl f: r.o: a doing enough towards fin* **5/1**[3]

1-12 **2** *½* **Nearooz**[38] 2934 3-9-5 **85**.................... JackMitchell 5 92+
(Roger Varian) *in rr: effrt whn nt clr run and bmpd rival over 1f out: sn swtchd lft and hdwy: r.o to chse wnr fnl 110yds: ev ch towards fin but a hld* **13/8**[1]

6123 **3** *2* **Bell Heather (IRE)**[13] 3843 6-8-9 **66**....................(p) SeanDavis(3) 6 69
(Patrick Morris) *racd keenly: led: rdn over 1f out: hdd ins fnl f: kpt on u.p: no ex towards fin* **25/1**

1-50 **4** *1 ½* **Red Hot (FR)**[27] 3341 3-9-7 **87**.................... DanielTudhope 3 87
(Richard Fahey) *trckd ldrs: rdn and unable qck whn bmpd over 1f out: styd on same pce ins fnl f* **9/4**[2]

-513 **5** *1 ½* **Geetanjali (IRE)**[27] 3336 4-9-10 **78**....................(p) HayleyTurner 2 75
(Michael Bell) *hld up: effrt on inner over 1f out: cl up ins fnl f: one pce fnl 150yds* **8/1**

1-63 **6** *1 ½* **Romola**[22] 3494 3-9-1 **81**.................... ColmO'Donoghue 7 75
(Sir Michael Stoute) *hld up: rdn and outpcd over 1f out: nvr able to threaten (trainer's rep said filly had been unsuited by the tight track)* **6/1**

2m 12.17s (-2.13) **Going Correction** -0.10s/f (Good)
WFA 3 from 4yo+ 12lb 6 Ran SP% **114.8**
Speed ratings (Par 104): **104,103,102,100,99 98**
CSF £14.06 TOTE £6.40: £3.20, £1.20; EX 13.90 Trifecta £121.10.
Owner George Strawbridge **Bred** George Strawbridge **Trained** Kingsclere, Hants

FOCUS
Add 14 yards. This was steadily run and things failed to pan out for the unfortunate runner-up. The winner backed up her Chepstow win with the third rated to form.

4319 ESL GROUP CLAIMING STKS 7f 127y
7:30 (7:31) (Class 4) 4-Y-O+

£6,404 (£1,905; £952; £476; £400; £400) **Stalls** Low

Form RPR

4000 **1** **Aces (IRE)**[13] 3863 7-9-12 **90**.................... FrannyNorton 7 94
(Ian Williams) *chsd ldrs: rdn to chse ldr over 2f out: r.o to ld narrowly ins fnl f: hld on gamely fin* **7/2**[2]

4331 **2** *nse* **Call Out Loud**[18] 3649 7-8-13 **78**....................(vt) TheodoreLadd(5) 4 86
(Michael Appleby) *racd keenly: led: kicked on 2f out: hdd narrowly ins fnl f: rallied towards fin: jst denied* **7/2**[2]

0-63 **3** *1 ½* **Roller**[7] 4078 6-9-0 **77**....................(p) NathanEvans 3 78+
(Michael Easterby) *missed break: hld up: rdn and swtchd rt off rail wl over 2f out: hdwy on outer over 1f out: styd on ins fnl f: gng on at fin: nvr able to trble front pair* **11/2**[3]

0-00 **4** *¾* **Gymkhana**[7] 4079 6-9-12 **90**....................(v[1]) DanielTudhope 9 88
(David O'Meara) *chsd ldrs: rdn over 1f out: chalng ins fnl f: no ex fnl 75yds* **16/1**

0530 **5** *1 ½* **Gabrial (IRE)**[13] 3863 10-9-12 **99**.................... TonyHamilton 1 85
(Richard Fahey) *midfield: rdn and hdwy wl over 1f out: chsd ldrs ins fnl f: one pce fnl 100yds* **6/4**[1]

-402 **6** *1 ½* **Imperial State**[7] 4078 6-9-2 **81**....................(v) HayleyTurner 10 74
(Michael Easterby) *missed break: in rr: rdn over 2f out: n.m.r and hmpd over 1f out: sn swtchd rt: kpt on towards fin* **10/1**

32/0 **7** *3 ¾* **Kalk Bay (IRE)**[7] 4078 12-8-7 **80**.................... JoshQuinn(7) 2 59
(Michael Easterby) *hld up: rdn wl over 2f out: edgd lft over 1f out whn no real imp: wknd ins fnl f* **50/1**

4-00 **8** *8* **Domagnano (IRE)**[8] 4020 4-9-7 **92**.................... ColmO'Donoghue 8 46
(Marco Botti) *chsd ldr: drvn 3f out: lost 2nd over 2f out: wknd over 1f out* **33/1**

0000 **9** *10* **Mr Wing (IRE)**[32] 3158 4-9-0 **17**.................... JackGarritty 6 14
(John Wainwright) *towards rr: struggling 2f out: nvr a threat* **100/1**

60-0 **10** *7* **Zizum**[48] 2633 4-8-8 **37**.................... EllaMcCain(7) 5
(Alan Berry) *midfield: pushed along and wkng whn sltly hmpd wl over 2f out: sn bhd* **100/1**

1m 32.85s (-2.85) **Going Correction** -0.10s/f (Good) 10 Ran SP% **121.7**
Speed ratings (Par 105): **110,109,108,107,106 104,100,92,82,75**
CSF £16.93 TOTE £5.20: £1.10, £1.20, £3.00; EX 19.50 Trifecta £81.80.Roller claimed by Mark Loughnane for £6000
Owner Paul Wildes **Bred** Viscountess Brookeborough **Trained** Portway, Worcs

FOCUS
Add 13 yards. A good-quality claimer with four of the runners rated 90 and above. It was strongly run and the judge took some time to separate the first two. The form's rated around them.

4320 CLOSE BROTHERS H'CAP 7f 1y
8:05 (8:06) (Class 4) (0-85,84) 3-Y-O+

£6,404 (£1,905; £952; £476; £400; £400) **Stalls** Low

Form RPR

0564 **1** **Penwortham (IRE)**[13] 3846 6-9-9 **79**.................... TonyHamilton 14 88
(Richard Fahey) *in rr: rdn and hdwy whn swtchd lft over 1f out: gd run on inner ins fnl f: led fnl 75yds: in command nr fin* **16/1**

1630 **2** *¾* **Candelisa (IRE)**[14] 3813 6-9-7 **77**....................(t) HollieDoyle 7 84
(David Loughnane) *dwlt: towards rr: hdwy on outer 3f out: styd on to ld ins fnl f: hdd fnl 75yds: hld towards fin* **6/1**

0413 **3** *2 ½* **Gabrial The Tiger (IRE)**[13] 3846 7-8-13 **69**.................... JackGarritty 3 69
(Richard Fahey) *led: rdn over 2f out: hdd ins fnl f: styd on same pce fnl 100yds* **7/2**[1]

-621 **4** *shd* **Luzum (IRE)**[10] 3969 4-9-0 **70** 5ex.................... NathanEvans 6 70
(Michael Easterby) *chsd ldrs: rdn over 1f out: ev ch ins fnl f: nt pce of front two fnl 100yds* **11/2**[3]

-564 **5** *nk* **Sparklealot (IRE)**[20] 3591 3-9-4 **83**....................(p[1]) TrevorWhelan 9 79
(Ivan Furtado) *pressed ldr: rdn over 2f out: ev ch ins fnl f: styd on same pce fnl 100yds* **5/1**[2]

6005 **6** *½* **Critical Thinking (IRE)**[6] 4108 5-8-10 **73**....................(tp) LauraCoughlan(7) 4 71
(David Loughnane) *hld up towards rr: rdn and hdwy on inner over 1f out: styd on ins fnl f: nvr able to chal (jockey said gelding was denied a clear run in the home straight)* **16/1**

-304 **7** *nk* **Queen's Sargent (FR)**[19] 3632 4-9-11 **81**....................(p[1]) SamJames 1 78
(Kevin Ryan) *chsd ldrs: rdn over 2 out: nt pce of ldrs over 1f out: one pce ins fnl f: n.m.r cl home* **5/1**[2]

-005 **8** *hd* **Dragons Tail (IRE)**[13] 3846 4-9-10 **83**....................(p) JaneElliott(3) 8 79
(Tom Dascombe) *pushed along most of way: midfield: lost pl and outpcd over 3f out: styd on fnl 150yds: nvr able to rch ldrs* **14/1**

0-06 **9** *¾* **Maggies Angel (IRE)**[14] 3815 4-9-7 **80**.................... SeanDavis(3) 2 74
(Richard Fahey) *midfield: pushed along over 3f out: rdn and hdwy whn swtchd lft over 1f out: chsng ldrs u.p whn n.m.r and lost pl fnl 150yds: n.d after: eased towards fin* **16/1**

0222 **10** *¾* **Turanga Leela**[13] 3846 5-9-0 **70**....................(b) FrannyNorton 11 62
(John Mackie) *midfield: pushed along and lost pl whn nt clr run over 1f out: nvr a threat* **14/1**

2-40 **11** *2* **Intransigent**[36] 3009 10-9-13 **83**....................(v) RobHornby 5 70
(Andrew Balding) *midfield: rdn over 1f out: sn btn* **14/1**

1444 **12** *¾* **Oneovdem**[53] 2472 5-9-1 **76**.................... TheodoreLadd(5) 10 61
(Tim Pinfield) *chsd ldrs: pushed along over 3f out: wknd 2f out* **25/1**

1m 26.35s (-1.15) **Going Correction** -0.10s/f (Good)
WFA 3 from 4yo+ 9lb 12 Ran SP% **126.7**
Speed ratings (Par 105): **102,101,98,98,97 97,96,96,95,94 92,91**
CSF £116.62 CT £434.08 TOTE £24.80: £5.20, £2.60, £1.20; EX 164.00 Trifecta £786.90.
Owner Dr Marwan Koukash **Bred** Kilfeacle Stud **Trained** Musley Bank, N Yorks

FOCUS
Add 13 yards. This competitive handicap was run at a furious early pace and was set up perfectly for the closers. The winner's rated in line with this year's form.

4321 CHESTER BET H'CAP 1m 2f 70y
8:40 (8:40) (Class 4) (0-85,84) 3-Y-O

£6,404 (£1,905; £952; £476; £400; £400) **Stalls** High

Form RPR

2-31 **1** **Mokammal**[29] 3266 3-9-7 **84**.................... ColmO'Donoghue 3 91
(Sir Michael Stoute) *chsd ldr: rdn 2f out: led ins fnl f: r.o towards fin* **9/2**[3]

-131 **2** *1 ¼* **Conundrum**[31] 3195 3-9-0 **77**.................... JackGarritty 5 81
(Jedd O'Keeffe) *led: rdn over 1f out: hdd ins fnl f: no ex towards fin* **3/1**[2]

3514 **3** *½* **Gabrial The One (IRE)**[13] 3842 3-9-4 **81**.................... TonyHamilton 4 84
(Richard Fahey) *chsd ldrs: rdn over 1f out: kpt on towards fin: nvr able to chal* **11/2**

6212 **4** *1 ¼* **Ivory Charm**[9] 4000 3-8-0 **66**.................... SeanDavis(3) 1 67
(Richard Fahey) *in tch: pushed along over 2f out: rdn over 1f out: hung rt ins fnl f: kpt on towards fin: nt pce to trble ldrs* **10/1**

1504 **5** *¾* **Blood Eagle (IRE)**[18] 3647 3-8-10 **73**.................... RobHornby 7 72
(Andrew Balding) *hld up in rr: rdn over 1f out: kpt on u.p ins fnl f: nvr able to get involved* **9/1**

2134 **6** *hd* **Sparkle In His Eye**[29] 3261 3-9-4 **81**....................(p[1]) DanielTudhope 2 80
(William Haggas) *in tch: rdn over 2f out: one pce ins fnl f (jockey said colt hung right-handed throughout)* **2/1**[1]

-340 **7** *2 ¼* **Guildhall**[42] 2796 3-9-1 **78**.................... JosephineGordon 6 72
(Ralph Beckett) *towards rr: pushed along early: u.p again over 3f out: outpcd over 1f out* **16/1**

2m 12.69s (-1.61) **Going Correction** -0.10s/f (Good) 7 Ran SP% **116.9**
Speed ratings (Par 101): **102,101,100,99,99 98,97**
CSF £19.11 TOTE £2.60: £2.50, £1.20; EX 22.80 Trifecta £89.40.
Owner Hamdan Al Maktoum **Bred** G R Bailey Ltd **Trained** Newmarket, Suffolk

FOCUS
Add 14 yards. They appeared to go steadily and the first two were up there throughout. The form's rated around the third.

T/Plt: £28.70 to a £1 stake. Pool: £67,972.27 - 1,723.22 winning units T/Qpdt: £19.80 to a £1 stake. Pool: £5,816.46 - 216.38 winning units **Darren Owen**

3880 DONCASTER (L-H)

Friday, June 28

OFFICIAL GOING: Good to soft (good in places) changing to good after race 1 (2.10)

Weather: Sunny

4322 TOPSPORT EQUISAND H'CAP — 7f 213y(R)

2:10 (2:12) (Class 5) (0-75,77) 3-Y-O+

£3,752 (£1,116; £557; £300; £300; £300) **Stalls High**

Form — RPR

0453 **1** **Star Shield**[18] 3649 4-9-12 73 .... DanielTudhope 5 87
(David O'Meara) *hld up: hdwy on outer over 2f out: chsd ldr over 1f out: rdn to chal ent fnl f: sn drvn: kpt on wl to ld nr fin* **7/2**[1]

-102 **2** *nse* **Anna Bunina (FR)**[23] 3478 3-9-0 71 .... JackGarritty 6 83
(Jedd O'Keeffe) *led: hdd 3f out: cl up and led again over 2f out: rdn over 1f out: sn jnd: drvn ins fnl f: hdd nr fin* **7/2**[1]

4506 **3** *2 ½* **Mickey (IRE)**[34] 3072 6-10-2 77 ....(v) RichardKingscote 9 85
(Tom Dascombe) *trckd ldrs: hdwy over 2f out: chsd ldng pair over 1f out and sn rdn: drvn and no imp fnl f* **14/1**

3-11 **4** *2 ½* **De Vegas Kid (IRE)**[7] 4061 5-9-7 75 .... ElishaWhittington(7) 3 77
(Tony Carroll) *hld up: hdwy on inner over 2f out: chsd ldrs over 1f out: sn rdn and no imp fnl f* **8/1**[3]

30-6 **5** *hd* **Mustaqbal (IRE)**[20] 3567 7-9-13 74 .... PaulMulrennan 4 76
(Michael Dods) *hld up towards rr: hdwy 3f out: chsd ldrs wl over 1f out: sn rdn and kpt on same pce fnl f (jockey said gelding was slowly away)* **25/1**

0113 **6** *3* **Hammer Gun (USA)**[12] 3880 6-9-10 71 ....(v) PaddyMathers 2 66
(Derek Shaw) *dwlt and in rr tl styd on fnl 2f* **14/1**

0216 **7** *¾* **Verdigris (IRE)**[16] 3743 4-9-7 68 .... TomEaves 13 61
(Ruth Carr) *stdd s: t.k.h and hld up in rr: sme hdwy 2f out: kpt on: n.d* **10/1**

6340 **8** *½* **Highlight Reel (IRE)**[20] 3567 4-9-12 73 .... LewisEdmunds 11 65
(Rebecca Bastiman) *cl up: led briefly 3f out: rdn and hdd over 2f out: grad wknd (vet said gelding finished lame on its right fore)* **12/1**

5005 **9** *1 ¾* **God Willing**[57] 2335 8-8-13 60 ....(t) KevinStott 1 48
(Declan Carroll) *trckd ldrs: pushed along 3f out: rdn over 2f out: sn drvn and wknd* **12/1**

3315 **10** *hd* **Lothario**[11] 3944 5-9-11 72 .... RobertWinston 10 60
(Dean Ivory) *trckd ldrs: hdwy over 3f out: rdn along 2f out: sn drvn and btn (jockey said gelding ran flat)* **15/2**[2]

20-0 **11** *½* **Dawn Treader (IRE)**[29] 3261 3-9-6 77 .... PatDobbs 12 62
(Richard Hannon) *chsd ldrs: rdn along over 3f out: sn wknd* **33/1**

-000 **12** *14* **Desert Dream**[10] 3957 5-9-3 64 ....(t) NathanEvans 7 18
(Michael Easterby) *dwlt: t.k.h early: hld up: a in rr (vet said gelding was found to have an irregular heart rhythm)* **16/1**

1m 38.95s (-1.85) **Going Correction** -0.15s/f (Firm) — 12 Ran SP% **117.8**

WFA 3 from 4yo+ 10lb

Speed ratings (Par 103): **103,102,100,97,97 94,94,93,91,91 91,77**

CSF £13.61 CT £153.39 TOTE £3.60: £1.60, £1.90, £4.50; EX 17.50 Trifecta £218.20.

Owner Middleham Park Racing XXIX **Bred** Mildmay Bloodstock Ltd **Trained** Upper Helmsley, N Yorks

FOCUS

The two joint-favourites contested the finish of this modest handicap, in which the field came down the middle of the track once in line for home. Improvement from the first two, and the form could be rated a little higher.

4323 NAPOLEONS CASINO, RESTAURANT & BAR SHEFFIELD EBF FILLIES' NOVICE STKS (PLUS 10 RACE) — 6f 2y

2:45 (2:46) (Class 5) 2-Y-O

£3,752 (£1,116; £557; £278) **Stalls High**

Form — RPR

221 **1** **Go Well Spicy (IRE)**[11] 3934 2-9-4 0 .... CallumShepherd 2 76
(Mick Channon) *cl up: led after 1f: rdn along wl over 1f out: drvn and edgd rt ent fnl f: kpt on wl towards fin* **7/2**[2]

65 **2** *2 ¼* **Divine Covey**[13] 3835 2-9-0 0 .... PatDobbs 3 65+
(Richard Hannon) *trckd ldrs: hdwy over 2f out: chsd wnr over 1f out: rdn and ch ent fnl f: sn n.m.r and kpt on same pce* **7/1**[3]

4 **3** *3 ½* **Sabaaya (IRE)**[13] 3835 2-9-0 0 .... JimCrowley 1 55
(Charles Hills) *wnt lft s: t.k.h: trckd ldng pair: hdwy 2f out: rdn over 1f out: kpt on same pce* **7/2**[2]

6 **4** *4 ½* **Capp It All (IRE)**[31] 3194 2-9-0 0 .... JasonHart 4 41
(David Loughnane) *sn pushed along in rr: rdn and outpcd fr 1/2-way* **17/2**

5 *2 ¾* **Sushi Power (IRE)** 2-9-0 0 .... SilvestreDeSousa 5 33+
(Tim Easterby) *broke wl and led for 1f: cl up tl green and pushed along 1/2-way: sn rdn and wknd over 2f out* **6/4**[1]

1m 13.95s (1.25) **Going Correction** -0.15s/f (Firm) — 5 Ran SP% **107.5**

Speed ratings (Par 90): **85,82,77,71,67**

CSF £24.26 TOTE £4.50: £1.30, £3.30; EX 17.60 Trifecta £35.40.

Owner Six Or Sticks **Bred** Grangemore Stud **Trained** West Ilsley, Berks

■ Gelsmoor Bay was withdrawn. Price at time of withdrawal 50-1. Rule 4 does not apply

FOCUS

The official ground description became Good all over prior to this race. The previous three runnings of this event were all won by fillies who went on to make their mark in Group/Listed events, but this looked a lesser renewal. It's hard to rate the form any higher.

4324 LEGAL DIRECTOR NOVICE STKS (PLUS 10 RACE) — 7f 6y

3:20 (3:25) (Class 4) 2-Y-O

£4,787 (£1,424; £711; £355) **Stalls High**

Form — RPR

1 **Thunderous (IRE)** 2-9-2 0 .... JasonHart 2 80+
(Mark Johnston) *mde most: rdn wl over 1f out: drvn clr ins fnl f: kpt on wl* **5/1**[2]

14 **2** *2 ¼* **Dancinginthewoods**[28] 3312 2-9-5 0 .... JoeyHaynes 3 77
(Dean Ivory) *trckd ldrs: hdwy over 2f out: sn pushed along: rdn to chse wnr wl over 1f out: chal appr fnl f: sn drvn and ev ch: kpt on same pce* **5/1**[2]

3 *3 ¼* **Breathalyze (FR)** 2-9-2 0 .... RichardKingscote 6 66
(Tom Dascombe) *trckd ldrs: pushed along over 2f out: rdn wl over 1f out: kpt on u.p fnl f* **14/1**

0 **4** *shd* **Bad Rabbit (IRE)**[35] 3047 2-9-2 0 .... JasonWatson 5 65
(David Loughnane) *cl up: disp ld 1/2-way: rdn wl over 2f out: drvn wl over 1f out: kpt on same pce* **66/1**

5 *¾* **Cipango** 2-9-2 0 .... LukeMorris 8 63
(Marco Botti) *dwlt and in rr: hdwy over 2f out: green and rdn along: kpt on fnl f* **33/1**

6 *nk* **Imperial Empire** 2-9-2 0 .... KerrinMcEvoy 4 63
(Charlie Appleby) *dwlt: towards rr: hdwy 3f out: green: rdn along and sltly outpcd wl over 1f out: kpt on fnl f* **4/6**[1]

7 *2 ½* **Grouseman** 2-9-2 0 .... GrahamLee 7 56
(Pam Sly) *dwlt and towards rr: green and pushed along over 2f out: sme late hdwy* **25/1**

8 *1 ¼* **Green Book (FR)** 2-9-2 0 .... TomEaves 9 53
(Brian Ellison) *chsd ldng pair: rdn along wl over 2f out: sn wknd* **40/1**

9 *4 ½* **Always Fearless (IRE)** 2-9-2 0 .... SilvestreDeSousa 1 41
(Richard Hannon) *in tch: hdwy on outer 3f out: chsd ldrs over 2f out: sn rdn along and wknd over 1f out* **8/1**[3]

1m 26.64s (0.24) **Going Correction** -0.15s/f (Firm) — 9 Ran SP% **121.8**

Speed ratings (Par 95): **92,89,85,85,84 84,81,80,74**

CSF £30.96 TOTE £5.80: £1.40, £1.10, £2.70; EX 27.20 Trifecta £161.20.

Owner Highclere T'Bred Racing - George Stubbs **Bred** Rabbah Bloodstock Limited **Trained** Middleham Moor, N Yorks

FOCUS

This looked a decent little novice event, and the winner looks a useful recruit. The form's rated around the runner-up.

4325 ROMERO INSURANCE BROKERS H'CAP — 7f 213y(R)

3:50 (3:52) (Class 3) (0-95,89) 3-Y-O

£7,762 (£2,310; £1,154; £577) **Stalls High**

Form — RPR

0211 **1** **Global Gift (FR)**[16] 3728 3-9-3 85 ....(h) GeraldMosse 5 93
(Ed Dunlop) *hld up in rr: gd hdwy on outer 3f out: chal wl over 1f out: rdn to ld ent fnl f: kpt on wl* **10/1**

0242 **2** *1 ½* **Ginger Fox**[12] 3885 3-8-7 76 ....(p) JasonWatson 7 81
(Ian Williams) *trckd ldrs: hdwy 3f out: rdn to take slt ld wl over 1f out: sn jnd: drvn and hdd ent fnl f: no ex last 100yds* **9/2**[2]

-216 **3** *2 ½* **Emirates Knight (IRE)**[29] 3262 3-9-5 87 .... KerrinMcEvoy 6 86
(Roger Varian) *cl up: rdn along over 2f out: drvn over 1f out: kpt on same pce fnl f* **7/1**[3]

21-6 **4** *nk* **House Of Kings (IRE)**[48] 2616 3-9-3 85 .... HectorCrouch 4 84
(Clive Cox) *trckd ldng pair on inner: hdwy 3f out: rdn along 2f out: drvn over 1f out: kpt on same pce (jockey said gelding was denied a clear run approaching 1f out)* **12/1**

214 **5** *7* **Archaeology**[17] 3683 3-9-2 84 .... AntonioFresu 2 66
(Jedd O'Keeffe) *hld up: effrt 3f out: rdn along over 2f out: sn btn* **9/2**[2]

1431 **6** *3 ½* **Fox Leicester (IRE)**[29] 3261 3-9-7 89 .... SilvestreDeSousa 3 63
(Andrew Balding) *sn led: pushed along 3f out: rdn over 2f out: hdd wl over 1f out: sn wknd (trainer's rep could offer no explanation for the colt's poor performance)* **5/4**[1]

1m 38.36s (-2.44) **Going Correction** -0.15s/f (Firm) — 6 Ran SP% **110.1**

Speed ratings (Par 103): **106,104,102,101,94 91**

CSF £51.03 TOTE £7.30: £3.20, £1.80; EX 31.60 Trifecta £148.90.

Owner Dr Johnny Hon **Bred** Ecurie Des Monceaux, Lordship Stud Et Al **Trained** Newmarket, Suffolk

FOCUS

A good handicap, although with the favourite not running his race the form isn't as solid as it might have been. They went what looked a sound pace and the time was 2.56sec outside standard. This time they stayed on the inside in the home straight. The winner continued on the upgrade with the second rated to his latest form.

4326 PLANET PLATFORMS LTD SUPERLATIVE FILLIES' NOVICE STKS — 1m 2f 43y

4:25 (4:25) (Class 5) 3-Y-O+

£3,752 (£1,116; £557; £278) **Stalls High**

Form — RPR

1 **Sweet Promise** 3-8-12 0 .... GeorgeWood 7 93+
(James Fanshawe) *hld up: stdy hdwy over 4f out: chsd ldrs over 2f out: chal over 1f out: rdn to ld ent fnl f: styd on strly* **25/1**

2 **2** *3 ½* **The Very Moon**[43] 2771 3-8-12 0 .... RichardKingscote 4 86
(Sir Michael Stoute) *led: clr 1/2-way: pushed along over 2f out: rdn wl over 1f out: hdd and drvn ent fnl f: kpt on same pce* **8/11**[1]

2 **3** *8* **Merry Vale**[19] 3637 3-8-12 0 .... KieranO'Neill 2 70
(John Gosden) *trckd ldrs: hdwy to chse ldr over 3f out: rdn along 2f out: sn drvn and kpt on one pce* **2/1**[2]

43 **4** *2* **J Gaye (IRE)**[56] 2361 3-8-12 0 .... GrahamLee 8 66
(Richard Phillips) *in tch: hdwy on outer to chse ldrs over 3f out: rdn along over 2f out: drvn wl over 1f out: one pce* **25/1**

5 *¾* **Vibrance** 3-8-12 0 .... DanielMuscutt 3 65+
(James Fanshawe) *hld up: hdwy and in tch 4f out: rdn along 3f out: kpt on one pce fnl 2f* **20/1**

50 **6** *1 ¼* **Love Explodes**[36] 3012 3-8-12 0 .... KerrinMcEvoy 10 62
(Ed Vaughan) *hld up in rr: hdwy 1/2-way: chsd ldrs on outer 3f out: rdn along 2f out: sn wknd* **9/1**[3]

4 **7** *6* **Walk It Talk It**[52] 2505 3-8-12 0 ....(h) JasonHart 9 50
(Chris Wall) *a in rr* **16/1**

00 **8** *17* **Quiet Shy (FR)**[21] 3553 4-9-10 0 .... DougieCostello 11 16
(Michael Scudamore) *a in rr* **100/1**

-46 **9** *2* **Sweet Dreamer**[16] 3724 3-8-5 0 .... RhonaPindar(7) 1 12
(K R Burke) *chsd ldng pair: rdn along over 4f out: sn wknd* **66/1**

10 *14* **We've Got The Love (IRE)** 3-8-12 0 .... HectorCrouch 5
(Clive Cox) *a in rr* **40/1**

35 **11** *4* **Caen Na Coille (USA)**[13] 3860 3-8-12 0 .... JasonWatson 6
(Ed Dunlop) *trckd ldr: rdn along over 4f out: wknd over 3f out* **50/1**

2m 9.1s (-3.20) **Going Correction** -0.15s/f (Firm) — 11 Ran SP% **126.5**

WFA 3 from 4yo 12lb

Speed ratings (Par 100): **106,103,96,95,94 93,88,75,73,62 59**

CSF £45.84 TOTE £40.90: £6.70, £1.10, £1.10; EX 112.40 Trifecta £208.90.

Owner A Boyd-Rochfort **Bred** Mr & Mrs G Middlebrook **Trained** Newmarket, Suffolk

FOCUS

Add 12yds. Again, they remained on the inside once in line for home. This decent novice event was run at what seemed to be a true pace, and the first two pulled clear. A fine start from the winner with the second rated up a little on her debut form.

4327 BELIEVE MONEY GROUP H'CAP — 1m 6f 115y

5:00 (5:03) (Class 4) (0-85,83) 3-Y-O

£5,530 (£1,645; £822; £411; £300; £300) **Stalls High**

Form — RPR

0-04 **1** **Calculation**[24] 3446 3-8-7 69 ....(v[1]) KerrinMcEvoy 1 86+
(Sir Michael Stoute) *dwlt: hld up in rr: hdwy 3f out: rdn to chal over 1f out: led appr fnl f: sn clr: styd on strly* **5/1**

3343 **2** 4 ½ **Rochester House (IRE)**[16] 3729 3-9-6 **82** .... JasonHart 5 88
(Mark Johnston) *trckd ldr: cl up over 5f out: led over 4f out: rdn along over 2f out: hdd and drvn appr fnl f: kpt on same pce* **9/2**[3]

5-64 **3** 3 ¼ **Divine Gift (IRE)**[16] 3729 3-9-7 **83** .... RichardKingscote 6 84
(Charlie Fellowes) *trckd ldng pair: effrt over 3f out and sn pushed along: rdn over 2f out: drvn wl over 1f out: kpt on one pce* **9/2**[3]

1-55 **4** ¾ **Skymax (GER)**[27] 3337 3-9-7 **83** .... PatDobbs 2 83
(Ralph Beckett) *led: pushed along and hdd over 4f out: sn rdn and outpcd fnl 3f (jockey said gelding hung right throughout)* **4/1**[2]

430 **5** 9 **Arthur Pendragon (IRE)**[17] 3699 3-9-2 **78** ....(p[1]) MartinDwyer 4 65
(Brian Meehan) *a in rr* **25/1**

-413 **6** 16 **Great Bear**[20] 3604 3-9-5 **81** .... JasonWatson 3 46
(Roger Charlton) *trckd ldng pair on inner: effrt and hdwy over 4f out: rdn along 3f out: sn drvn and wknd (trainer's rep could offer no explanation for the colt's performance)* **2/1**[1]

3m 8.45s (-3.15) **Going Correction** -0.15s/f (Firm) **6** Ran SP% **110.2**
Speed ratings (Par 101): **102,99,97,97,92 84**
CSF £26.09 TOTE £4.90: £2.10, £2.00; EX 17.40 Trifecta £77.90.
Owner The Queen **Bred** The Queen **Trained** Newmarket, Suffolk

FOCUS
Add 12yds. An interesting little staying handicap, in which they remained on the inside up the home straight. Big improvement from the winner with the form rated around the next two.

4328 ELLGIA RECYCLING ZERO TO LANDFILL H'CAP 6f 2y
5:35 (5:36) (Class 6) (0-60,60) 3-Y-O
£3,105 (£924; £461; £300; £300; £300) **Stalls** High

Form RPR

663 **1** **Victory Rose**[38] 2938 3-9-7 **60** .... AndrewElliott 12 70+
(Lydia Pearce) *bmpd s and in rr: hdwy 2f out: swtchd rt towards stands' side and chsd ldrs over 1f out: rdn to chal ins fnl f: led last 100yds* **10/1**

0004 **2** ½ **Montalvan (IRE)**[8] 4033 3-8-12 **56** .... BenSanderson(5) 19 63
(Roger Fell) *prom towards stands' side: hdwy and cl up over 2f out: rdn to ld wl over 1f out: jnd and drvn ins fnl f: hdd last 100yds: kpt on same pce* **10/1**

0555 **3** 2 ¼ **Ghost Buy (FR)**[12] 3884 3-9-5 **58** ....(t) DougieCostello 8 58
(Ivan Furtado) *chsd ldrs centre: hdwy 2f out: rdn over 1f out: drvn and kpt on fnl f* **8/1**[3]

430 **4** ½ **Senorita Grande (IRE)**[22] 3499 3-9-5 **58** ....(v[1]) JasonHart 13 57
(John Quinn) *towards rr: pushed along and hdwy over 2f out: rdn wl over 1f out: styd on wl fnl f* **10/1**

-000 **5** 1 ¼ **Furyan**[53] 2482 3-8-12 **54** ....(v[1]) RowanScott(3) 10 49
(Nigel Tinkler) *dwlt and in rr: hdwy wl over 1f out: sn rdn and kpt on wl fnl f* **22/1**

0211 **6** 1 **Lincoln Red**[15] 3775 3-9-2 **58** .... ConnorMurtagh(3) 4 50
(Olly Williams) *in tch centre: hdwy to chse ldrs 2f out: rdn over 1f out: swtchd rt and drvn ent fnl f: kpt on same pce* **8/1**[3]

4306 **7** ¾ **Sharrabang**[13] 3839 3-9-2 **55** .... GrahamLee 7 45
(Stella Barclay) *midfield centre: rdn along and sltly outpcd 2f out: kpt on fnl f* **22/1**

6033 **8** 1 ½ **Chop Chop (IRE)**[13] 3839 3-9-3 **56** ....(b) JasonWatson 9 41
(Roger Charlton) *wnt lft s and towards rr: hdwy to ld in centre after 2f: rdn 2f out: hdd and hung lft wl over 1f out: sn drvn and wknd* **7/2**[1]

243 **9** 1 ¼ **Tizwotitiz**[32] 3158 3-8-13 **59** .... TobyEley(7) 14 41
(Steph Hollinshead) *chsd ldrs towards stands' side: rdn along 2f out: grad wknd (jockey said gelding ran too freely)* **18/1**

1424 **10** 2 **Ascot Dreamer**[31] 3202 3-9-4 **57** ....(t[1]) PatDobbs 18 33
(David Brown) *a towards rr* **7/1**[2]

0-40 **11** ½ **Deptford Mick (IRE)**[13] 3839 3-9-7 **60** .... KieranO'Neill 11 34
(Rae Guest) *a towards rr* **12/1**

-315 **12** nk **Frosted Lass**[25] 3417 3-9-5 **58** .... RobbieDowney 20 31
(David Barron) *racd towards stands' side: led 2f: chsd ldr: rdn along 2f out: sn wknd* **12/1**

0-00 **13** 2 ½ **Secret Treaties**[48] 2623 3-9-2 **55** .... LewisEdmunds 6 21
(Christine Dunnett) *midfield: rdn along over 2f out: sn wknd* **25/1**

0030 **14** nk **Vino Rosso (IRE)**[13] 3839 3-9-4 **57** .... CharlieBennett 16 22
(Michael Blanshard) *a towards rr* **50/1**

060- **15** ¾ **Stainforth Swagger**[233] 8922 3-9-2 **55** .... MartinDwyer 15 17
(Ronald Thompson) *a in rr* **50/1**

0500 **16** ½ **The Thorny Rose**[28] 3292 3-9-4 **57** .... AndrewMullen 5 18
(Michael Dods) *t.k.h: a towards rr* **40/1**

5000 **17** nk **Raypeteafterme**[20] 3604 3-9-4 **57** ....(t) TomEaves 3 17
(Declan Carroll) *t.k.h: hld up: a in rr* **20/1**

1m 12.36s (-0.34) **Going Correction** -0.15s/f (Firm) **17** Ran SP% **128.5**
Speed ratings (Par 97): **96,95,92,91,90 88,87,85,84,81 80,80,76,76,75 74,74**
CSF £103.21 CT £891.64 TOTE £10.90: £2.70, £3.70, £2.60, £2.90; EX 131.10 Trifecta £1437.10.
Owner Bulent Eskitutuncu **Bred** M E Broughton **Trained** Newmarket, Suffolk

FOCUS
A low-grade sprint but very well contested, and it went to the top weight. She can progress.
T/Plt: £93.90 to a £1 stake. Pool: £82,189.65 - 638.88 winning units T/Qpdt: £18.20 to a £1 stake. Pool: £7,342.39 - 298.53 winning units **Joe Rowntree**

4288 NEWCASTLE (A.W) (L-H)
Friday, June 28

OFFICIAL GOING: Tapeta: standard to slow
Wind: Breezy, half behind in races on the straight course and in over 3f of home straight in races on the Weather: Fine, dry

4329 COOPERS MARQUEES H'CAP 1m 5y (Tp)
5:30 (5:32) (Class 4) (0-80,82) 3-Y-O+
£5,530 (£1,645; £616; £400; £400) **Stalls** Centre

Form RPR

5134 **1** **Liliofthelamplight (IRE)**[14] 3807 3-9-3 **76** .... PJMcDonald 5 81
(Mark Johnston) *prom: effrt and hdwy over 1f out: led ins fnl f: hld on wl cl home* **25/1**

000 **2** nk **Paparazzi**[2] 4239 4-10-0 **77** .... KevinStott 4 83+
(Tracy Waggott) *missed break: hld up: gd hdwy to press ldr over 1f out: hung lft and led briefly ins fnl f: rallied: hld nr fin* **13/2**

051- **3** ½ **Elamirr (IRE)**[182] 9730 3-9-8 **81** .... AndreaAtzeni 7 84
(Roger Varian) *hld up in midfield: drvn over 2f out: hdwy over 1f out: kpt on fnl f: nrst fin* **11/4**[1]

3-46 **3** dht **Najashee (IRE)**[13] 3867 5-9-7 **70** .... BenCurtis 11 75
(Roger Fell) *prom: rdn and sltly outpcd over 1f out: rallied ins fnl f: r.o* **5/1**[3]

2112 **5** shd **Antico Lady (IRE)**[7] 4071 3-8-8 **70** .... BenRobinson(3) 1 73
(Brian Ellison) *chsd ldr to over 1f out: drvn and rallied ins fnl f: r.o* **10/3**[2]

4244 **6** ½ **Newmarket Warrior (IRE)**[6] 4108 8-9-6 **69** ....(p) DavidAllan 9 72
(Iain Jardine) *hld up: pushed along over 2f out: hdwy over 1f out: r.o fnl f* **17/2**

4-00 **7** ½ **Pickett's Charge**[13] 3868 6-9-7 **70** ....(p) CamHardie 3 72
(Brian Ellison) *hld up in tch: drvn along 2f out: kpt on same pce ins fnl f* **28/1**

102- **8** ¾ **Monsieur Jimmy**[269] 7868 7-9-7 **77** .... KieranSchofield(7) 6 78
(Brian Ellison) *led: clr over 2f out: hdd ins fnl f: sn btn* **50/1**

-400 **9** 1 ½ **Metatron (IRE)**[50] 2559 3-9-9 **82** .... AlistairRawlinson 10 77
(Tom Dascombe) *midfield: rdn and outpcd over 2f out: n.d after* **16/1**

5600 **10** 1 ¼ **Testa Rossa (IRE)**[7] 4054 9-9-0 **63** ....(b) PhilDennis 8 57
(Jim Goldie) *hld up: drvn and outpcd over 2f out: sn btn* **14/1**

32-0 **11** 2 ½ **Falathaat (USA)**[39] 2909 3-9-5 **78** ....(p[1]) PaulHanagan 2 65
(Saeed bin Suroor) *hld up: drvn and struggling over 2f out: sn wknd* **20/1**

1m 40.59s (1.99) **Going Correction** +0.15s/f (Slow)
WFA 3 from 4yo+ 10lb **11** Ran SP% **116.8**
Speed ratings (Par 105): **96,95,95,95,95 94,94,93,91,90 88**
WIN: 27.30 Liliofthelamplight; PL: 2.60 Paparazzi 0.70 Elamirr 1.00 Najashee 5.60 Liliofthelamplight; EX: 247.00; CSF: 173.04; TC: L/P/N: 300.93, L/P/E 489.06; TF: L/P/N 870.90, L/P/E 574.20.
Owner Garrett J Freyne **Bred** L Montgomery **Trained** Middleham Moor, N Yorks

FOCUS
Not too many interesting types, with one obvious exception in Elamirr, but he was weak in the market all day which spelt trouble. The winner still has some upside but they finished in a heap and the form looks no more than ordinary even for the grade.

4330 WINGATE SIGNS SUPPORTING #SUPERJOSH CHARITY FILLIES' H'CAP 5f (Tp)
6:00 (6:02) (Class 5) (0-75,77) 3-Y-O+
£3,752 (£1,116; £557; £400; £400; £400) **Stalls** Centre

Form RPR

0105 **1** **Dandy's Beano (IRE)**[17] 3706 4-9-11 **70** ....(h) KevinStott 8 85
(Kevin Ryan) *mde all: rdn along over 1f out: drew clr ins fnl f: unchal* **6/1**

1-02 **2** 3 ¼ **Mercenary Rose (IRE)**[32] 3167 3-9-12 **77** .... PJMcDonald 4 78
(Paul Cole) *pressed ldrs: wnt 2nd 1/2-way: effrt and rdn over 1f out: one pce fnl f* **9/2**[2]

3103 **3** 2 **Lady Calcaria**[11] 3935 3-9-12 **77** .... DuranFentiman 10 71
(Tim Easterby) *chsd wnr to 1/2-way: sn drvn along: kpt on same pce fr over 1f out* **11/2**[3]

1655 **4** ¾ **Oriental Lilly**[6] 4103 5-9-11 **77** .... CoreyMadden(7) 6 70
(Jim Goldie) *s.i.s: hld up: hdwy over 1f out: kpt on fnl f: nvr able to chal* **7/2**[1]

1414 **5** ½ **Everkyllachy (IRE)**[22] 3504 5-9-1 **65** ....(v) PaulaMuir(5) 3 57
(Karen McLintock) *towards rr: drvn and outpcd 1/2-way: rallied over 1f out: kpt on ins fnl f: nt pce to chal* **9/2**[2]

3016 **6** 1 ¼ **Klopp**[22] 3508 3-9-2 **67** ....(h) CamHardie 1 52
(Antony Brittain) *prom: rdn along 1/2-way: wknd over 1f out* **8/1**

1652 **7** 1 ¼ **Santafiora**[28] 3291 5-8-4 **56** .... VictorSantos(7) 5 39
(Julie Camacho) *s.i.s: t.k.h: hld up on outside: drvn and outpcd 1/2-way: n.d after* **14/1**

2125 **8** 3 ¼ **Hanati (IRE)**[98] 1275 3-8-11 **65** ....(p[1]) BenRobinson(3) 2 34
(Brian Ellison) *hld up bhd ldng gp: drvn and struggling 1/2-way: sn btn* **33/1**

3464 **9** shd **Epona**[11] 3923 3-9-2 **67** .... ShaneGray 7 36
(Keith Dalgleish) *t.k.h: in tch: rdn and outpcd 1/2-way: btn over 1f out* **16/1**

59.11s (-0.39) **Going Correction** +0.15s/f (Slow)
WFA 3 from 4yo+ 6lb **9** Ran SP% **114.9**
Speed ratings (Par 100): **109,103,100,99,98 96,94,89,89**
CSF £32.95 CT £158.21 TOTE £8.20: £2.30, £1.80, £2.60; EX 43.60 Trifecta £239.00.
Owner Hambleton Racing Ltd XLVII **Bred** Ruskerne Ltd **Trained** Hambleton, N Yorks

FOCUS
An ordinary enough handicap dominated from the front by the winner. She's rated back to the form she showed when second in this race last year.

4331 BETFAIR EXCHANGE GOSFORTH PARK CUP H'CAP 5f (Tp)
6:35 (6:36) (Class 2) (0-105,105) 3-Y-O+
£31,125 (£9,320; £4,660; £2,330; £1,165; £585) **Stalls** Centre

Form RPR

-603 **1** **Fool For You (IRE)**[12] 3883 4-8-9 **88** .... PJMcDonald 11 97
(Richard Fahey) *hld up in midfield in centre of gp: rdn and hdwy over 1f out: led ins fnl f: hung lft: kpt on strly* **14/1**

2130 **2** ¾ **Copper Knight (IRE)**[27] 3344 5-9-12 **105** ....(t) DavidAllan 10 111
(Tim Easterby) *cl up in centre of gp: led over 1f out to ins fnl f: kpt on: hld towards fin* **10/3**[1]

0243 **3** nk **El Hombre**[92] 1388 5-8-13 **92** .... PaulHanagan 9 97
(Keith Dalgleish) *in tch in centre of gp: rdn over 2f out: effrt and edgd lft over 1f out: kpt on ins fnl f* **20/1**

0404 **4** hd **Eeh Bah Gum (IRE)**[27] 3344 4-8-9 **88** .... JamieGormley 1 92
(Tim Easterby) *racd on far side jst away fr main gp: cl up: rdn and ev ch over 1f out to ins fnl f: kpt on same pce towards fin* **10/1**

100- **5** 1 **Dakota Gold**[244] 8632 5-9-4 **97** .... ConnorBeasley 3 98
(Michael Dods) *led at decent gallop in centre of gp to over 1f out: rallied: one pce wl ins fnl f* **16/1**

2500 **6** hd **Line Of Reason (IRE)**[27] 3344 9-8-9 **88** .... BarryMcHugh 2 88+
(Paul Midgley) *s.i.s: swtchd rt s: hld up in centre of gp: rdn over 2f out: r.o fnl f: nrst fin* **20/1**

1302 **7** ¾ **Foolaad**[43] 2775 8-9-6 **99** ....(t) RobertWinston 14 96
(Roy Bowring) *prom on nr side of gp: drvn along 1/2-way: rallied: one pce fnl f* **4/1**[2]

-303 **8** hd **Tarboosh**[20] 3587 6-9-4 **97** .... KevinStott 8 93
(Paul Midgley) *dwlt: hld up in centre of gp: rdn and hdwy over 1f out: kpt on fnl f: nt pce to chal (vet said gelding received treatment for post race heat stress)* **10/1**

4534 **9** ½ **Blue De Vega (GER)**[18] 3662 6-8-12 **91** ....(t[1]) JimCrowley 6 86
(Robert Cowell) *hld up on far side of gp: rdn and hdwy over 1f out: no imp ins fnl f* **18/1**

-121 **10** 1 ¾ **Makanah**[27] 3360 4-9-3 **96** .... PaulMulrennan 12 84
(Julie Camacho) *hld up in midfield on nr side of gp: drvn and outpcd over 2f out: n.d after* **9/1**[3]

6603 **11** ¾ **Encore D'Or**[20] 3582 7-9-5 **103** DylanHogan(5) 5 89
(Robert Cowell) *hld up in midfield on far side of gp: rdn over 2f out: wknd over 1f out* **12/1**

0310 **12** ¾ **Merhoob (IRE)**[20] 3602 7-9-9 **102** BenCurtis 4 85
(John Ryan) *hld up on far side of gp: drvn along 1/2-way: sn btn* **9/1**[3]

1310 **13** 2¼ **Moonraker**[130] 786 7-9-2 **95** AlistairRawlinson 13 70
(Michael Appleby) *hld up on nr side of gp: struggling over 2f out: sn btn* **28/1**

58.6s (-0.90) **Going Correction** +0.15s/f (Slow) **13** Ran SP% **119.7**
Speed ratings (Par 109): **113,111,111,111,109 109,107,107,106,103 102,101,97**
CSF £58.77 CT £964.81 TOTE £13.60: £3.70, £1.20, £4.70; EX 82.20 Trifecta £1335.20.
Owner John Dance **Bred** Serdal Adali **Trained** Mulsey Bank, N Yorks
■ Stewards' Enquiry : David Allan two-day ban: used whip above the permitted level (Jul 15-16)

FOCUS
A really competitive sprint handicap run at a strong gallop and there were no obvious excuses in terms of track/positional bias.

4332 BETFAIR CASINO HOPPINGS FILLIES' STKS (GROUP 3) 1m 2f 42y (Tp)
7:05 (7:10) (Class 1) 3-Y-O+
£34,026 (£12,900; £6,456; £3,216; £1,614; £810) **Stalls** High

Form RPR

6-31 **1** **Sun Maiden**[26] 3374 4-9-5 100 JimCrowley 1 110
(Sir Michael Stoute) *t.k.h early: trckd ldrs: shkn up to ld over 1f out: drvn out fnl f* **11/8**[1]

2400 **2** ½ **Nyaleti (IRE)**[9] 3986 4-9-5 107 PJMcDonald 9 109
(Mark Johnston) *pressed ldr: rdn and chal over 1f out: kpt on fnl f: hld nr fin* **11/1**[3]

-410 **3** 3½ **Shenanigans (IRE)**[9] 3986 5-9-5 96 AndreaAtzeni 2 102
(Roger Varian) *prom: effrt over 2f out: rdn and chsd ldng pair over 1f out: kpt on fnl f: nt pce to chal* **4/1**[2]

-056 **4** 1¼ **Rasima**[26] 3374 4-9-5 98 (p[1]) DavidEgan 4 100
(Roger Varian) *hld up: rdn over 2f out: hdwy over 1f out: kpt on fnl f: no imp* **11/1**[3]

2-33 **5** 1 **Glance**[26] 3387 3-8-7 100 HarryBentley 7 98
(Ralph Beckett) *hld up in tch on outside: rdn and outpcd over 2f out: rallied ins fnl f: no imp* **4/1**[2]

0553 **6** nk **Queen Of Time**[26] 3374 5-9-5 94 (p) BenCurtis 6 97
(Henry Candy) *led at modest gallop: rdn and hdd over 1f out: sn outpcd: btn fnl f* **25/1**

31-3 **7** 7 **Rainbow Heart (IRE)**[69] 1939 3-8-7 95 PaulHanagan 8 83
(William Haggas) *s.i.s: plld hrd in last pl: rdn over 2f out: sn no imp: btn over 1f out* **11/1**[3]

06-0 **8** 2¼ **Dancing Brave Bear (USA)**[69] 1941 4-9-5 93 ShaneKelly 3 78
(Ed Vaughan) *t.k.h: hld up in tch on ins: rdn 2f out: sn wknd* **33/1**

2m 12.57s (2.17) **Going Correction** +0.15s/f (Slow) **8** Ran SP% **113.9**
WFA 3 from 4yo+ 12lb
Speed ratings (Par 110): **97,96,93,92,92 91,86,84**
CSF £18.37 TOTE £2.00: £1.50, £1.70, £1.60; EX 16.90 Trifecta £73.00.
Owner K Abdullah **Bred** Juddmonte Farms Ltd **Trained** Newmarket, Suffolk

FOCUS
Not a particularly deep Group 3 and they crawled round, rendering the form fairly flimsy at best. The winner is rated as better than ever.

4333 KELTEK MANAGED WATER SOLUTIONS H'CAP 1m 2f 42y (Tp)
7:40 (7:40) (Class 5) (0-75,77) 4-Y-O+
£3,752 (£1,116; £557; £400; £400; £400) **Stalls** High

Form RPR

-453 **1** **Autretot (FR)**[32] 3161 4-9-10 **77** ShaneGray 6 88+
(David O'Meara) *t.k.h early: trckd ldrs: led gng wl over 1f out: rdn and edgd rt ins fnl f: r.o* **5/1**[3]

006 **2** 1¼ **Trinity Star (IRE)**[22] 3502 8-9-0 **67** (v) PJMcDonald 7 73
(Karen McLintock) *dwlt: hld up: pushed along over 2f out: hdwy over 1f out: chsd wnr ins fnl f: kpt on nt pce to chal* **16/1**

4-0R **3** ¾ **First Flight (IRE)**[20] 3567 8-9-3 **73** BenRobinson(3) 2 78
(Brian Ellison) *t.k.h: in tch: hdwy to chse wnr over 1f out to ins fnl f: one pce* **10/1**

-351 **4** 5 **Granite City Doc**[24] 3448 6-8-8 **66** PaulaMuir(5) 9 61
(Lucy Normile) *cl up: effrt and ev ch over 2f out to over 1f out: rdn and wknd ins fnl f* **4/1**[1]

0-33 **5** 1¼ **Archippos**[49] 2577 6-9-7 **74** PhilDennis 3 66
(Michael Herrington) *in tch: drvn along over 2f out: edgd rt and wknd over 1f out* **9/2**[2]

020- **6** 2½ **Elhafei (USA)**[371] 4075 4-9-7 **74** AlistairRawlinson 12 61
(Michael Appleby) *s.i.s: sn in tch: drvn over 2f out: wknd over 1f out* **12/1**

-025 **7** hd **Bahkit (IRE)**[59] 2244 5-8-10 **63** PaulHanagan 1 50
(Philip Kirby) *led: rdn over 2f out: hdd over 1f out: wknd ins fnl f* **15/2**

6050 **8** 1¼ **Thawry**[14] 3816 4-8-13 **66** (b) CamHardie 8 50
(Antony Brittain) *hld up: rdn along over 2f out: no imp fr over 1f out* **12/1**

-000 **9** ½ **Blacklooks (IRE)**[58] 2297 4-9-2 **69** DavidAllan 5 52
(Ivan Furtado) *t.k.h in midfield: rdn and outpcd over 2f out: n.d after* **25/1**

0302 **10** 6 **Elixsoft (IRE)**[24] 3449 4-9-6 **73** BenCurtis 11 44
(Roger Fell) *midfield: drvn and outpcd over 2f out: wknd over 1f out (trainer's rep could offer no explanation for the filly's performance)* **6/1**

4020 **11** 14 **Seaborough (IRE)**[16] 3718 4-8-9 **62** ow1 (p) ConnorBeasley 10 5
(David Thompson) *t.k.h: hld up: drvn and struggling 3f out: sn btn* **33/1**

2m 10.53s (0.13) **Going Correction** +0.15s/f (Slow) **11** Ran SP% **118.0**
Speed ratings (Par 103): **105,104,103,99,98 96,96,95,94,90 78**
CSF £82.34 CT £776.90 TOTE £5.10: £1.50, £3.50, £2.50; EX 75.90 Trifecta £1172.00.
Owner Craig Miller **Bred** S A Franklin Finance & Elisabeth Vidal **Trained** Upper Helmsley, N Yorks

FOCUS
Mostly exposed performers in this ordinary contest. They looked to go pretty steady but still clocked a 2 secs quicker time than the Group 3 contest 35 mins earlier. The front three came clear and the winner is value for a bit further.

4334 VERTEM - VERY DIFFERENT STOCKBROKERS NOVICE STKS 7f 14y (Tp)
8:15 (8:16) (Class 5) 3-Y-O+ **£3,752** (£1,116; £557; £278) **Stalls** Centre

Form RPR

11- **1** **Turjomaan (USA)**[248] 8502 3-9-8 0 JimCrowley 1 84+
(Roger Varian) *mde virtually all: shkn up and asserted over 1f out: kpt on strly fnl f* **1/3**[1]

3 **2** 2¾ **Hour Of The Dawn (IRE)**[18] 3661 3-9-1 0 ShaneKelly 2 70
(Ed Vaughan) *in tch: rdn over 2f out: hdwy to chse wnr ins fnl f: kpt on: nt pce to chal* **20/1**

62 **3** hd **Grab And Run (IRE)**[11] 3932 3-9-1 0 PaulHanagan 5 69
(Richard Fahey) *hld up in tch: effrt and angled rt over 1f out: rdn and kpt on fnl f: no imp* **25/1**

42 **4** ½ **Double Honour**[28] 3306 3-9-1 0 PJMcDonald 7 68
(James Bethell) *hld up in tch: hdwy to chse wnr over 1f out to ins fnl f: kpt on same pce* **8/1**[3]

5-1 **5** 3¼ **Gometra Ginty (IRE)**[11] 3920 3-9-3 0 ShaneGray 4 61
(Keith Dalgleish) *cl up: rdn over 2f out: wknd over 1f out* **33/1**

6 1¾ **Shark (FR)** 3-9-1 0 DanielMuscutt 3 54
(James Fanshawe) *dwlt: hld up: stdy hdwy over 2f out: rdn over 1f out: sn wknd* **11/2**[2]

0-0 **7** 19 **Irish Charm (FR)**[122] 913 5-9-3 0 (p[1]) KieranSchofield(7) 6 6
(Ivan Furtado) *disp ld to 1/2-way: rdn and wknd 2f out: lost tch and eased ins fnl f (jockey said gelding hung left-handed)* **80/1**

1m 26.86s (0.66) **Going Correction** +0.15s/f (Slow) **7** Ran SP% **114.3**
WFA 3 from 5yo 9lb
Speed ratings (Par 103): **102,98,98,98,94 92,70**
CSF £12.41 TOTE £1.20: £1.40, £4.90; EX 8.00 Trifecta £59.70.
Owner Hamdan Al Maktoum **Bred** Shadwell Farm LLC **Trained** Newmarket, Suffolk

FOCUS
Probably no more than an ordinary novice event and Turjomaan, who brought the best form to the table, proved much the best despite carrying a penalty. He didn't need to improve.

4335 TITANIUM RACING CLUB H'CAP 6f (Tp)
8:50 (8:52) (Class 5) (0-70,70) 3-Y-O+
£3,752 (£1,116; £557; £400; £400; £400) **Stalls** Centre

Form RPR

6603 **1** **Kapono**[22] 3508 3-9-6 **69** (p) BenCurtis 7 82
(Roger Fell) *midfield in centre of gp: smooth hdwy over 2f out: led over 1f out: rdn clr and edgd rt ins fnl f: kpt on strly: eased towards fin* **15/2**

2300 **2** 2¾ **Lucky Lodge**[21] 3549 9-9-7 **70** (b) KieranSchofield(7) 5 76
(Antony Brittain) *led towards far side of gp: rdn and hdd over 1f out: rallied and chsd (clr) wnr ins fnl f: r.o* **14/1**

1501 **3** 2 **Decision Maker (IRE)**[24] 3452 5-9-4 **60** RobertWinston 9 60
(Roy Bowring) *t.k.h: cl up in centre of gp: disp ld over 1f out: rdn and outpcd ins fnl f* **9/1**

-312 **4** 1 **Fairy Stories**[20] 3596 3-9-2 **68** ConnorMurtagh(3) 11 62
(Richard Fahey) *dwlt: hld up in centre of gp: hdwy and in tch over 1f out: rdn and one pce fnl f* **13/2**[3]

-044 **5** 1¼ **Kodicat (IRE)**[18] 3656 5-9-1 **57** (p) KevinStott 2 49
(Kevin Ryan) *cl up on far side of gp: rdn over 2f out: no ex fr over 1f out* **22/1**

4432 **6** shd **Gleeful**[14] 3801 3-9-7 **70** AndreaAtzeni 10 60
(Roger Varian) *hld up towards rr: pushed along over 2f out: hdwy over 1f out: kpt on fnl f: nvr rchd ldrs* **9/2**[1]

3000 **7** 1 **Chaplin Bay (IRE)**[16] 3716 7-10-0 **70** (b) JamesSullivan 1 59
(Ruth Carr) *dwlt: bhd on far side of gp: drvn along over 2f out: kpt on fnl f: nvr rchd ldr* **18/1**

4526 **8** shd **Avenue Of Stars**[22] 3503 6-9-10 **66** (v) PJMcDonald 6 55
(Karen McLintock) *towards rr on far side of gp: drvn along over 2f out sn no imp* **9/1**

0242 **9** ½ **Mutabaahy (IRE)**[8] 4037 4-9-12 **68** CamHardie 3 55
(Antony Brittain) *in tch towards far side of gp: rdn along over 2f out: no ex fr over 1f out (jockey said gelding fly-leapt leaving the stalls)* **13/2**[3]

00-0 **10** ½ **Swiss Connection**[53] 2477 3-8-11 **67** HarryRussell(7) 13 50
(Bryan Smart) *t.k.h: in tch on nr side of gp: effrt and rdn over 2f out: wknd over 1f out* **25/1**

2600 **11** ¾ **Duke Cosimo**[60] 2183 9-9-7 **63** PhilDennis 14 46
(Michael Herrington) *hld up on nr side of gp: drvn along over 2f out: sn n.d* **20/1**

5046 **12** ½ **Rockley Point**[11] 3933 6-9-1 **57** JamieGormley 8 38
(Katie Scott) *hld up in centre of gp: drvn along over 2f out: nvr on terms* **40/1**

3500 **13** 2½ **Deeds Not Words (IRE)**[18] 3656 8-9-4 **60** AndrewMullen 4 33
(Tracy Waggott) *bhd in centre of gp: drvn 1/2-way: nvr on terms (jockey said gelding clipped heels shortly after the start)* **40/1**

0004 **14** 4 **Dirchill (IRE)**[11] 3921 5-9-6 **62** (b) ConnorBeasley 12 23
(David Thompson) *in tch in centre of gp: drvn and lost pl 2f out: sn wknd (jockey said gelding ran too free)* **6/1**[2]

1m 12.37s (-0.13) **Going Correction** +0.15s/f (Slow) **14** Ran SP% **120.7**
WFA 3 from 4yo+ 7lb
Speed ratings (Par 103): **106,102,99,98,96 96,95,95,94,93 92,92,88,83**
CSF £100.83 CT £964.93 TOTE £8.80: £2.90, £4.10, £3.40; EX 121.20 Trifecta £768.20.
Owner Sabah Mubarak Al Sabah **Bred** Mr & Mrs S Bosley **Trained** Nawton, N Yorks

FOCUS
A wide open heat on paper but it was won in good style by one of the three-year-olds that are open to improvement. The form is rated around the runner-up.
T/Jkpt: Not Won. T/Plt: £72.50 to a £1 stake. Pool: £67,704.37 - 680.97 winning units T/Qpdt: £20.50 to a £1 stake. Pool: £8,398.18 - 302.79 winning units **Richard Young**

4295 NEWMARKET (R-H)
Friday, June 28

OFFICIAL GOING: Good (good to firm in places)
Wind: nil Weather: hot and sunny; 24 degrees

4336 MONTAZ RESTAURANT H'CAP 1m
5:40 (5:40) (Class 5) (0-70,71) 3-Y-O+
£4,528 (£1,347; £673; £400; £400; £400) **Stalls** Low

Form RPR

-533 **1** **Angel's Whisper (IRE)**[29] 3279 4-9-8 **60** DavidProbert 11 75
(Amy Murphy) *trckd ldrs on outer: rdn over 2f out: led over 1f out: steadily pushed clr* **5/1**

34-1 **2** 5 **Scoffsman**[44] 2740 4-9-7 **62** JoshuaBryan(3) 6 66
(Kevin Frost) *plld hrd: 2nd tl led 2f out: rdn and hdd over 1f out: edgd rt: one pce and wnr sn clr* **9/4**[1]

2416 **3** 1¾ **Coverham (IRE)**[23] 3462 5-10-5 **71** RyanTate 7 71
(James Eustace) *towards rr: rdn and effrt 2f out: wnt 3rd 1f out: n.m.r and swtchd lft: nvr got in a blow* **6/1**

-023 **4** 2 **Beguiling Charm (IRE)**[23] 3478 3-9-7 **69** LiamKeniry 9 62
(Ed Walker) *in rr and rdn 1/2-way: rdn and sme prog in 4th over 1f out: edgd lft: no imp and n.d* **9/2**[3]

-063 **5** *1 ¾* **Trulee Scrumptious**[7] 4067 10-9-6 **58**.........................(v) JimmyQuinn 4 49
(Peter Charalambous) *racd freely: led tl rdn and hdd 2f out: fdd tamely after nt getting much room over 1f out (jockey said mare suffered interference)* **7/2**[2]

-000 **6** *6* **Ishallak**[15] 3774 4-8-3 **48**.......................................(v) EllieMacKenzie(7) 12 25
(Mark Usher) *prom: rdn over 3f out: racd awkwardly and fdd wl over 1f out* **25/1**

0000 **7** *3 ¼* **Malaysian Boleh**[9] 3996 9-8-2 **47** oh2.................(p) GraceMcEntee(7) 13 17
(Phil McEntee) *tk a grip early: chsd ldrs: urged along over 2f out: nt keen and sn btn* **50/1**

5503 **8** *10* **Boxatricks (IRE)**[16] 3744 4-8-11 **49**................................ CharlesBishop 3
(Julia Feilden) *wnt rt s and dwlt: sn chsng ldrs: rdn 1/2-way: sn btn: t.o and eased (jockey said gelding hung right handed)* **14/1**

05 **9** *1* **Rotherhithe**[59] 2261 4-9-13 **65**.. PatCosgrave 8 9
(Henry Spiller) *taken down early and hrd to restrain: stdd s: keen and sn towards rr: rdn 1/2-way: sn lost pl: t.o and eased* **33/1**

6-00 **10** *17* **Masai Spirit**[43] 2762 3-8-1 **56**... AliceBond(7) 10
(Philip McBride) *rdr lost iron by 1/2-way: completely unbalanced and sn t.o after (jockey said filly had lost her stirrup and was unable to regain it)* **33/1**

1m 39.73s (-0.27) **Going Correction** +0.075s/f (Good)
WFA 3 from 4yo+ 10lb **10** Ran SP% **120.5**
Speed ratings (Par 103): **104,99,97,95,93 87,84,74,73,56**
CSF £16.80 CT £72.81 TOTE £6.00: £1.80, £1.20, £2.50; EX 20.60 Trifecta £79.80.

Owner Box Clever Display & Shepherd Global **Bred** Paul & Billy McEnery **Trained** Newmarket, Suffolk

FOCUS
There was 4mm of water added after racing the previous day; good/fast ground on a warm evening. An interesting race for the grade, and they raced near side. This was a pb from the winner, in line with her debut promise, and the runner-up was close to his Yarmouth figure.

4337 TECHTRAK BRITISH EBF MAIDEN FILLIES' STKS (PLUS 10 RACE) 6f
6:10 (6:11) (Class 4) 2-Y-O **£5,175** (£1,540; £769; £384) **Stalls** Low

Form RPR

1 **Ultra Violet** 2-9-0 0.. KieranShoemark 1 95+
(Ed Vaughan) *lost 4 l s: t.k.h in rr: rdn 2f out: str run after: led fnl 200yds and sn strode clr: impressive* **10/1**

2 *8* **Game And Set** 2-9-0 0.. DavidProbert 7 71
(Andrew Balding) *chsd ldrs: rdn 2f out: sn hanging bdly lft: kpt on to go 2nd fnl 100yds: no ch w v easy wnr (jockey said filly hung left-handed)* **8/1**

3 *1 ¾* **Airbrush (IRE)** 2-9-0 0.. OisinMurphy 4 66
(Richard Hannon) *led: rdn 2f out: hdd jst ins fnl f: nt qckn and lost 2nd 100yds out* **4/1**[2]

4 *¾* **Rachel Wall (IRE)** 2-9-0 0.. CharlesBishop 2 64
(Henry Candy) *chsd ldrs: drvn and rn green and racd awkwardly over 2f out: btn over 1f out: wnt 4th ins fnl f* **2/1**[1]

0 **5** *1 ½* **With Virtue**[23] 3469 2-9-0 0.. PatCosgrave 5 59
(James Tate) *t.k.h: prom alone in centre: rdn 2f out: sn btn: fdd to lose 4th ins fnl f* **14/1**

6 *1* **Perfect Inch** 2-9-0 0.. StevieDonohoe 6 56
(Charlie Fellowes) *lost 6 l s: rn green in rr: rdn and btn over 2f out* **13/2**

7 *6* **Oribi** 2-8-11 0.. GeorgiaCox(3) 3 38+
(William Haggas) *chsd ldrs: drvn over 2f out: sn btn: t.o and eased* **9/2**[3]

50 **8** *¾* **Luna Wish**[41] 2836 2-9-0 0.. TomQueally 9 36
(George Margarson) *sn racing v awkwardly in rr: drvn and btn 1/2-way: t.o and eased* **50/1**

1m 13.51s (1.41) **Going Correction** +0.075s/f (Good) **8** Ran SP% **113.7**
Speed ratings (Par 92): **93,82,80,79,77 75,67,66**
CSF £84.96 TOTE £13.00: £3.30, £1.80, £1.60; EX 94.90 Trifecta £569.50.

Owner Sheikh Hamed Dalmook Al Maktoum **Bred** Christopher Humber **Trained** Newmarket, Suffolk

FOCUS
Not much worthwhile form to go on as only two of these had run before - the fifth and eighth - and have yet to show much, and the runner-up was wayward, but the winner was in a different league. The main action was near side.

4338 JIGSAW SPORTS BRANDING H'CAP 7f
6:45 (6:45) (Class 4) (0-80,80) 3-Y-O
£6,469 (£1,925; £962; £481; £400; £400) **Stalls** Low

Form RPR

11 **1** **Nahaarr (IRE)**[27] 3351 3-8-13 **75**........................ GeorgiaCox(3) 4 100+
(William Haggas) *racd stands' side: mde all: drew clr 2f out: hands and heels fnl f: impressive* **4/6**[1]

-046 **2** *5* **I Am A Dreamer**[27] 3357 3-9-4 **77**.............. SilvestreDeSousa 3 84
(Mark Johnston) *chsd wnr in stands' gp: rdn and outpcd by him wl over 1f out but a clr of rest* **11/2**[2]

3-20 **3** *4 ½* **Chatham House**[62] 2094 3-9-7 **80**.. SeanLevey 7 75+
(Richard Hannon) *stdd and t.k.h: 3rd of four in centre: rdn and c rt to stands' rails 2f out: wnt mod 3rd ins fnl f: veered lft cl home* **14/1**

000 **4** *1* **Deira Surprise**[28] 3323 3-9-6 **79**.. PatCosgrave 5 71
(Hugo Palmer) *stdd s: in last of four on stands' side: rdn and outpcd wl over 1f out: jst won r for mod 4th* **40/1**

6420 **5** *hd* **Greek Kodiac (IRE)**[15] 3779 3-9-4 **77**..............................(p[1]) TomQueally 6 69
(Mick Quinn) *2nd in centre gp: rdn over 2f out: sn btn* **33/1**

-230 **6** *nk* **Attainment**[23] 3465 3-9-6 **79**..............................(p[1]) OisinMurphy 1 70
(James Tate) *chsd ldrs stands' side: rdn over 2f out: sn wknd* **11/2**[2]

-001 **7** *2 ¾* **Broughtons Flare (IRE)**[42] 2798 3-8-11 **70**................ StevieDonohoe 8 53
(Philip McBride) *led centre quartet but sn bhd stands' side gp: rdn and btn over 2f out* **10/1**[3]

224 **8** *hd* **Assimilation (IRE)**[35] 3051 3-9-3 **76**.................................. LiamKeniry 9 59
(Ed Walker) *in last of four racing in centre: rdn and coming rt and btn wl over 2f out* **12/1**

1m 25.08s (-0.62) **Going Correction** +0.075s/f (Good) **8** Ran SP% **119.6**
Speed ratings (Par 101): **106,100,95,94,93 93,90,90**
CSF £5.23 CT £30.17 TOTE £1.60: £1.20, £1.30, £2.50; EX 5.70 Trifecta £31.50.

Owner Sheikh Ahmed Al Maktoum **Bred** Rossenarra Bloodstock Limited **Trained** Newmarket, Suffolk

FOCUS
The field split into two even groups early on but there was more pace in the near-side group, so those up the middle had no chance, and the race fell apart behind the first two finishers. The winner built on recent promise and the runner-up has been rated to his York form two starts ago.

4339 LETTERGOLD H'CAP (JOCKEY CLUB GRASSROOTS FLAT STAYERS' SERIES QUALIFIER) 1m 5f
7:20 (7:20) (Class 4) (0-80,80) 3-Y-O **£9,703** (£2,887; £1,443; £721; £400) **Stalls** Low

Form RPR

3411 **1** **Glutnforpunishment**[24] 3446 3-8-8 **67**.................. SilvestreDeSousa 3 75
(Nick Littmoden) *mde all: pushed along 2f out: a holding rivals fr over 1f out* **7/1**

0123 **2** *2 ¼* **Smarter (IRE)**[57] 2317 3-9-7 **80**.. JamieSpencer 6 85
(William Haggas) *t.k.h in last pair: rdn 3f out: wnt 2nd 2f out: sn hung rt and nvr making any imp on wnr* **15/8**[2]

-002 **3** *8* **Monsieur Lambrays**[39] 2914 3-9-2 **75**..............................(p) LukeMorris 4 68
(Tom Clover) *racd in last pair: rdn 5f out: racing v awkwardly and twice hung bdly lft fr over 2 out: wnt poor 3rd over 1f out* **7/2**[3]

1261 **4** *7* **Cafe Espresso**[29] 3253 3-9-7 **80**..............................(b) JoeyHaynes 2 63
(Paul Howling) *t.k.h pressing ldrs: rdn over 2f out: sn struggling* **33/1**

40-1 **5** *2 ¾* **Green Etoile**[27] 2343 3-8-9 **68**.. DavidProbert 5 46
(Alan King) *pressed ldr: drvn 3f out: fdd tamely 2f out: t.o and eased (trainer's rep said gelding may not have liked the ground (good, good to firm in places) and may benefit from a slower surface; vet said gelding had lost his right hind shoe)* **7/4**[1]

2m 51.08s (5.18) **Going Correction** +0.075s/f (Good) **5** Ran SP% **108.8**
Speed ratings (Par 101): **87,85,80,76,74**
CSF £20.06 TOTE £5.90: £2.20, £1.60; EX 23.80 Trifecta £64.30.

Owner A A Goodman **Bred** Rabbah Bloodstock Limited **Trained** Newmarket, Suffolk

FOCUS
Add 30yds. Only the first two were really still running on at the line, with the third horse being wayward and the favourite just not himself, so not a deep race, but the winner continued his progress.

4340 COATES & SEELY BLANC DE BLANCS FILLIES' H'CAP 6f
7:55 (7:55) (Class 3) (0-90,91) 3-Y-O+ **£9,703** (£2,887; £1,443; £721) **Stalls** Low

Form RPR

16 **1** **Emily Goldfinch**[21] 3536 6-9-5 **81**..............................(p) SilvestreDeSousa 4 97
(Phil McEntee) *mde all: rdn 2f out: clr over 1f out: kpt on wl* **15/2**

-022 **2** *5* **Be Like Me (IRE)**[34] 3068 3-9-2 **85**.................................. GeraldMosse 1 83
(Marco Botti) *bhd: rdn and effrt 2f out: chsd wnr over 1f out: nvr making any imp* **10/3**[2]

5-45 **3** *¾* **Restless Rose**[8] 4023 4-9-4 **80**.. KerrinMcEvoy 6 78
(Stuart Williams) *chsd ldrs: rdn and outpcd in last over 2f out: sme prog ins fnl f: unable to chal* **4/1**[3]

0-30 **4** *nk* **Firelight (FR)**[13] 3865 3-9-8 **91**.. OisinMurphy 7 86
(Andrew Balding) *t.k.h: pressed ldr: drvn 2f out: hung rt and fdd over 1f out* **15/8**[1]

0-00 **5** *3* **Zain Hana**[34] 3085 4-9-4 **87**.. CierenFallon(7) 3 74
(John Butler) *racd in last pair: effrt 1/2-way: chsd ldrs briefly: rdn and wknd over 1f out* **12/1**

2020 **6** *¾* **Treasure Me**[20] 3587 4-10-0 **90**.. StevieDonohoe 5 75
(Charlie Fellowes) *chsd ldrs: rdn 2f out: wknd over 1f out* **5/1**

1m 12.07s (-0.03) **Going Correction** +0.075s/f (Good)
WFA 3 from 4yo+ 7lb **6** Ran SP% **114.0**
Speed ratings (Par 104): **103,96,95,94,90 89**
CSF £33.04 TOTE £7.40: £3.70, £2.40; EX 28.40 Trifecta £159.90.

Owner Miss R McEntee & J Paxton **Bred** J M Paxton & Mrs S J Wrigley **Trained** Newmarket, Suffolk

FOCUS
They soon headed to the middle of the track but ended up more near side, and the winner got the run of the race in front, posting a pb.

4341 COATES & SEELY BRUT RESERVE FILLIES' NOVICE STKS 1m
8:30 (8:31) (Class 4) 3-Y-O+ **£5,822** (£1,732; £865; £432) **Stalls** Low

Form RPR

5-3 **1** **Fabulist**[77] 1739 3-8-11 0.. RobertHavlin 9 88+
(John Gosden) *chsd ldrs: effrt 2f out: rdn to ld over 1f out: styd on wl* **9/4**[1]

2 *2 ¼* **Whispering Beauty (USA)** 3-8-11 0.................................. JFEgan 3 81
(William Haggas) *lost 6 l s: bhd: rdn and gd prog on outer 2f out: wnt 2nd ins fnl f: nt rch wnr* **25/1**

6 **3** *1 ½* **Magical Rhythms (USA)**[39] 2919 3-8-11 0................ NickyMackay 11 77
(John Gosden) *prom: led over 2f out: hdd over 1f out: edgd rt and lost 2nd and no ex ins fnl f* **7/2**[3]

00 **4** *1* **Daryana**[23] 3463 3-8-11 0.. CharlesBishop 5 75
(Eve Johnson Houghton) *rdn after 3f: bhd: str run ins fnl f: promising* **66/1**

3 **5** *½* **Ojooba**[72] 1855 3-8-11 0.. DaneO'Neill 8 76+
(Owen Burrows) *led 2f: chsd ldrs: rdn over 3f out: outpcd wl over 1f out: kpt on again ins fnl f (jockey said filly was denied a clear run in the closing stages)* **11/4**[2]

0 **6** *hd* **Squelch**[4] 4189 3-8-8 0..............................(h) GeorgiaCox(3) 4 73
(William Haggas) *chsd ldrs: rdn over 2f out: 4th 1f out: wknd ins fnl f* **50/1**

31- **7** *¾* **Inhale**[217] 9225 3-9-4 0.. KerrinMcEvoy 6 78
(Amanda Perrett) *taken down early: led 2f: chsd ldrs: rdn and nt qckn wl over 1f out* **7/1**

0-4 **8** *1 ¼* **Mina Vagante**[12] 3889 3-8-11 0.. PatCosgrave 7 68
(Hugo Palmer) *rdn over 3f out: nvr looked like troubling ldrs after* **33/1**

5 **9** *1 ½* **Visionara**[20] 3603 3-8-11 0.. SilvestreDeSousa 2 65
(Simon Crisford) *t.k.h: chsd ldrs: rdn 2f out: n.d after* **6/1**

36 **10** *6* **Powerful Star (IRE)**[25] 3431 3-8-11 0.................................. StevieDonohoe 10 50
(David Lanigan) *bhd: rdn and racd awkwardly 3f out: struggling after* **25/1**

11 *72* **Troisouni (FR)** 3-8-4 0..............................(t[1]) CierenFallon(7) 1
(Conrad Allen) *bhd: rdn 1/2-way: sn bdly t.o: lost action (jockey said filly lost her action)* **66/1**

1m 39.48s (-0.52) **Going Correction** +0.075s/f (Good) **11** Ran SP% **122.0**
Speed ratings (Par 102): **105,102,101,100,99 99,98,97,96,90 18**
CSF £67.99 TOTE £3.30: £1.90, £3.40, £1.40; EX 58.20 Trifecta £238.50.

Owner B E Nielsen **Bred** Bjorn Nielsen **Trained** Newmarket, Suffolk

FOCUS
This looked a good fillies' novice although the pace seemed quite fast. The action was towards the near side.

4342 YORK THOROUGHBRED RACING H'CAP — 1m 2f
9:00 (9:00) (Class 2) (0-100,100) 3-Y-O+ £12,938 (£3,850; £1,924; £962) Stalls Low

Form — RPR

/144 1 **Setting Sail**[28] 3315 4-9-9 95 .... KerrinMcEvoy 3 104
(Charlie Appleby) *led 1f: 2nd or 3rd tl led again over 2f out: sn rdn: a holding rivals after* **10/3**[2]

36-1 2 1 1/2 **Rise Hall**[79] 1694 4-9-7 93 .... (b) OisinMurphy 1 99
(Martyn Meade) *midfield: hdwy 3f out: rdn and chsd wnr over 2f out: no imp fnl f* **9/4**[1]

13-4 3 nk **Prejudice**[42] 2796 3-8-2 86 .... LukeMorris 7 91
(David Simcock) *bhd: rdn 4f out: wnt 3rd over 1f out: kpt on steadily wout threatening wnr* **7/2**[3]

4-00 4 1 1/4 **First Sitting**[32] 3160 8-9-13 99 .... GeraldMosse 4 102
(Chris Wall) *towards rr early: rdn and effrt 3f out: 4th and unable qck fnl f* **25/1**

-452 5 4 1/2 **Leroy Leroy**[32] 3160 3-9-0 98 .... SilvestreDeSousa 6 92
(Richard Hannon) *t.k.h towards rr: effrt 3f out: 3rd and rdn over 2f out: sn racing reluctantly: btn wl over 1f out* **7/2**[3]

-005 6 2 1/4 **Original Choice (IRE)**[120] 961 5-9-11 100 .... JoshuaBryan(3) 5 89
(Nick Littmoden) *rrd and lost 8 l s: bhd: rdn and struggling 4f out (jockey said gelding reared as stalls opened and was slowly away)* **33/1**

-206 7 10 **The Emperor Within (FR)**[42] 2808 4-9-7 93 .... HectorCrouch 2 62
(Martin Smith) *pressed ldr: drvn 4f out: wknd tamely over 2f out: t.o* **20/1**

-601 8 2 1/4 **Finniston Farm**[34] 3087 4-9-9 95 .... (p) RichardKingscote 8 60
(Tom Dascombe) *wnt rt s: t.k.h: led after 1f: drvn and hdd over 2f out: lost pl rapidly: t.o (jockey said gelding ran too freely)* **16/1**

150 9 35 **Creationist (USA)**[27] 3341 3-8-10 94 .... KieranShoemark 10
(Roger Charlton) *chsd ldrs to 1/2-way: last and drvn 4f out: sn bdly t.o: eased: lost action (jockey said colt lost his action)* **33/1**

2m 6.2s (-0.90) **Going Correction** +0.075s/f (Good)
WFA 3 from 4yo+ 12lb — 9 Ran SP% 118.7
Speed ratings (Par 109): **106,104,104,103,99 98,90,88,60**
CSF £11.12 CT £27.13 TOTE £4.30: £1.40, £1.30, £1.50; EX 13.00 Trifecta £36.60.
Owner Godolphin **Bred** Godolphin **Trained** Newmarket, Suffolk

FOCUS
Add 30yds. Another interesting race, a good handicap, and they raced near side. The first three have been rated as improving.
T/Plt: £52.90 to a £1 stake. Pool: £56,813.20 - 783.02 winning units T/Qpdt: £9.80 to a £1 stake. Pool: £6,462.28 - 484.38 winning units **Iain Mackenzie**

3775 YARMOUTH (L-H)
Friday, June 28

OFFICIAL GOING: Good to firm (good in places; 6.9)
Wind: light to medium, across Weather: fine

4343 STRICTLY FUN RACING CLUB H'CAP — 5f 42y
2:00 (2:01) (Class 5) (0-75,76) 3-Y-O
£3,752 (£1,116; £557; £300; £300; £300) Stalls Centre

Form — RPR

-242 1 **Texting**[16] 3742 3-8-11 67 .... SeamusCronin(5) 7 78+
(Mohamed Moubarak) *hld up in tch: clsd to chse ldrs and travelling strly whn nt clr run over 1f out: swtchd rt ent fnl f: pushed along and qcknd to ld ins fnl f: sn clr: easily* **9/4**[1]

3326 2 2 **Mr Buttons (IRE)**[12] 3884 3-9-8 76 .... (p[1]) CameronNoble(3) 3 79
(Linda Stubbs) *chsd ldr: rdn 1/2-way: sn drvn: led over 1f out: hdd and nt match pce of wnr ins fnl f* **4/1**[3]

-004 3 1 1/4 **Cookupastorm (IRE)**[16] 3742 3-8-6 64 .... (b[1]) SeanKirrane(7) 5 63
(Richard Spencer) *hld up wl in tch in midfield: effrt 2f out: chsd ldrs and rdn over 1f out: nt match ldng pair and outpcd ins fnl f: kpt on* **12/1**

6-56 4 nk **Invincible Larne (IRE)**[53] 2489 3-9-2 67 .... PatCosgrave 4 64
(Mick Quinn) *hld up wl in tch in midfield: effrt 2f out: hdwy u.p to chse ldrs over 1f out: no ex and outpcd by ldng pair ins fnl f* **13/2**

0000 5 nk **Sandridge Lad (IRE)**[18] 3659 3-9-7 72 .... StevieDonohoe 6 68
(John Ryan) *chsd ldrs: rdn ent fnl 2f: drvn and unable qck jst over 1f out: kpt on same pce ins fnl f* **33/1**

2553 6 1/2 **Hanakotoba (USA)**[16] 3742 3-8-5 63 .... (t) MarcoGhiani(7) 1 58
(Stuart Williams) *chsd ldrs: effrt 2f out: unable qck u.p 1f out: wknd ins fnl f* **8/1**

4202 7 3 **Scale Force**[4] 4192 3-8-12 70 .... (b) CierenFallon(7) 2 54
(Gay Kelleway) *led: rdn 2f out: hdd and no ex u.p over 1f out: wknd ins fnl f* **3/1**[2]

360- 8 3/4 **Emily's Sea (IRE)**[223] 9130 3-8-10 66 .... ThoreHammerHansen(5) 8 47
(Nick Littmoden) *wnt rt leaving stalls: sn dropped in bhd and hld up in tch: effrt 2f out: c nr stands and no imp u.p over 1f out: wknd ins fnl f* **22/1**

1m 0.76s (-1.14) **Going Correction** -0.10s/f (Good) — 8 Ran SP% 115.2
Speed ratings (Par 99): **105,101,99,99,98 98,93,92**
CSF £11.63 CT £87.05 TOTE £2.30: £1.10, £1.40, £2.80; EX 13.40 Trifecta £193.00.
Owner M Moubarak **Bred** Laundry Cottage Stud Farm **Trained** Newmarket, Suffolk

FOCUS
Modest sprinting form, although quite a decisive winner. The form's rated around the fifth.

4344 BRITISH STALLION STUDS EBF NOVICE MEDIAN AUCTION STKS (PLUS 10 RACE) — 6f 3y
2:30 (2:32) (Class 4) 2-Y-O £5,175 (£1,540; £769; £384) Stalls Centre

Form — RPR

53 1 **Otago**[16] 3739 2-9-5 .... TomMarquand 4 77
(Michael Bell) *trckd ldrs tl clsd to press ldr jst over 2f out: rdn and led over 1f out: kpt on wl ins fnl f* **9/4**[2]

43 2 3/4 **Born To Destroy**[34] 3088 2-9-5 .... AdamKirby 2 75
(Richard Spencer) *wnt lft leaving stalls: sn led: rdn 2f out: drvn and hdd over 1f out: kpt on u.p but a hld ins fnl f* **11/8**[1]

3242 3 1 1/2 **My Motivate Girl (IRE)**[8] 4018 2-9-0 72 .... (v) OisinMurphy 3 65
(Archie Watson) *wl in tch in midfield: effrt u.p over 1f out: chsd ldrs and kpt on same pce ins fnl f* **11/4**[3]

4 2 1/2 **Time Force (IRE)** 2-9-5 .... CliffordLee 5 63
(K R Burke) *in tch in last pair: clsd jst over 2f out: rdn and chsd ldrs over 1f out: no ex: edgd lft and wknd ins fnl f* **11/1**

00 5 3 **Sir Rodneyredblood**[11] 3943 2-9-5 .... DannyBrock 6 54
(J R Jenkins) *stdd s: t.k.h: hld up in rr: swtchd lft after 1f: effrt and swtchd lft over 1f out: sn u.p and no imp: wknd ins fnl f* **66/1**

03 6 1 1/4 **Boston Girl (IRE)**[11] 3934 2-9-0 .... RobertHavlin 1 45
(Ed Dunlop) *led: sn hdd and chsd ldr tl jst over 2f out: lost pl u.p and bhd 1f out: wknd ins fnl f* **25/1**

1m 12.71s (0.11) **Going Correction** -0.10s/f (Good) — 6 Ran SP% 113.2
Speed ratings (Par 95): **95,94,92,88,84 83**
CSF £5.84 TOTE £2.70: £1.40, £1.40; EX 6.40 Trifecta £11.20.
Owner The Queen **Bred** The Queen **Trained** Newmarket, Suffolk

FOCUS
Average juvenile form, although a couple of these could do okay in nurseries. The third and fifth suggest this form can't be rated any higher.

4345 C A DESIGN SERVICES 35TH ANNIVERSARY H'CAP — 1m 6f 17y
3:05 (3:06) (Class 6) (0-65,65) 3-Y-O
£3,105 (£924; £461; £300; £300; £300) Stalls High

Form — RPR

-602 1 **Funny Man**[10] 3965 3-9-0 58 .... (b) LiamJones 9 64+
(William Haggas) *stdd s: hld up in last pair: effrt 2f out: hdwy to chse ldr and hung lft ent fnl f: styd on wl to ld 50yds out* **7/2**[1]

4133 2 1/2 **Victoriano (IRE)**[11] 3931 3-9-7 65 .... (b) OisinMurphy 7 70
(Archie Watson) *chsd ldrs: hmpd and swtchd rt after 1f: sn led: rdn over 2f out: drvn over 1f out: hdd and one pce 50yds out* **7/2**[1]

-550 3 2 3/4 **No Thanks**[16] 3741 3-8-13 57 .... KieranShoemark 6 58
(William Jarvis) *taken down early: hld up in last trio: effrt ent fnl 2f: swtchd rt over 1f out: styd on to go 3rd ins fnl f: no threat to ldng pair* **25/1**

6054 4 1 **Spring Run**[14] 3809 3-8-13 57 .... PatCosgrave 5 57
(Jonathan Portman) *chsd ldrs: hmpd after 1f: chsd ldr over 5f out: rdn over 2f out: drvn 2f out: lost 2nd ent fnl f: one pce after* **9/1**

0624 5 2 3/4 **Thomas Cubitt (FR)**[30] 3219 3-9-4 62 .... (p[1]) TomMarquand 4 59
(Michael Bell) *in tch in midfield: effrt and edgd lft over 2f out: drvn and chsd ldrs 2f out: unable qck over 1f out: wknd ins fnl f* **5/1**[3]

0041 6 1 **Lock Seventeen (USA)**[21] 3528 3-8-13 57 .... StevieDonohoe 8 52
(Charlie Fellowes) *sn led and crossed to inner rail: hdd over 12f out: chsd ldr tl over 5f out: rdn over 2f out: sn drvn and unable qck over 1f out: wknd ins fnl f* **9/2**[2]

0-03 7 16 **New Expo (IRE)**[29] 3275 3-8-3 47 oh1 ow1 .... RoystonFfrench 2 21
(Julia Feilden) *led: sn hdd and impeded after 1f: in tch in midfield after: rdn and dropped to rr over 3f out: lost tch 2f out (jockey said gelding was never travelling)* **14/1**

-404 8 99 **Battle Of Pembroke (USA)**[31] 3198 3-9-2 60 .... JamieSpencer 3
(David Simcock) *stdd s: hld up in last pair: shkn up over 2f out: sn eased and t.o (jockey said colt lost its action)* **9/2**[2]

3m 3.68s (-1.02) **Going Correction** -0.10s/f (Good) — 8 Ran SP% 118.0
Speed ratings (Par 97): **98,97,96,95,94 93,84,27**
CSF £16.36 CT £266.12 TOTE £4.00: £1.10, £1.60, £7.80; EX 15.30 Trifecta £254.00.
Owner Apple Tree Stud **Bred** Apple Tree Stud **Trained** Newmarket, Suffolk
■ Stewards' Enquiry : Stevie Donohoe four-day ban: interference & careless riding (Jul 15-18)

FOCUS
The two market leaders pulled away from the rest late on in what was a moderate staying handicap for 3yos. The bare form is limited.

4346 CLIFF HOTEL OF GORLESTON H'CAP — 1m 2f 23y
3:40 (3:41) (Class 6) (0-60,59) 3-Y-O+
£3,105 (£924; £461; £300; £300; £300) Stalls Low

Form — RPR

0002 1 **Elsie Violet (IRE)**[20] 3593 3-8-9 57 .... (p) AledBeech(7) 2 64
(Robert Eddery) *mde all and sn clr: c bk to field and rdn 2f out: kpt on u.p and a doing enough ins fnl f: rdn out* **7/1**

6334 2 1 3/4 **Red Archangel (IRE)**[16] 3741 3-8-6 54 .... (p) SeanKirrane(7) 1 58
(Richard Spencer) *prom in chsng gp: clsd on wnr over 2f out: 3rd and rdn over 1f out: kpt on to chse wnr ins fnl f: no imp fnl 75yds* **5/1**[3]

0006 3 1/2 **Cedar**[25] 3410 3-8-8 49 ow3 .... (t[1]) KierenFox 3 52
(Mohamed Moubarak) *prom in chsng gp: chsd wnr over 3f out: clsd and rdn ent fnl 2f: drvn over 1f out: kpt on same pce and lost 2nd ins fnl f* **33/1**

5300 4 1 **Homesick Boy (IRE)**[21] 3538 3-9-3 58 .... RobertHavlin 4 59
(Ed Dunlop) *midfield: clsd to go prom in chsng gp and in tch 2f out: hung lft and one pce ins fnl f* **12/1**

0623 5 hd **Fair Power (IRE)**[21] 3537 5-9-13 56 .... AdamKirby 10 56
(John Butler) *midfield: clsd to chse ldrs jst over 2f out: 4th and swtchd lft jst over 1f out: kpt on same pce ins fnl f* **9/2**[2]

-454 6 1 1/2 **Swiss Peak**[29] 3256 3-9-4 59 .... JamieSpencer 14 57
(Michael Bell) *stdd s: hld up in rr: clsd ent fnl 2f: nt clr run and sltly impeded ent fnl f: drvn and kpt on same pce ins fnl f* **5/2**[1]

-605 7 hd **Doctor Wonderful**[23] 3473 4-10-0 57 .... (p) CliffordLee 5 54
(Kevin Frost) *hld up towards rr: clsd over 2f out: sn u.p: nvr getting on terms w ldrs and one pce ins fnl f* **12/1**

6430 8 1 1/4 **Merdon Castle (IRE)**[32] 3142 7-8-11 45 .... SeamusCronin(5) 11 40
(Frank Bishop) *midfield: clsd over 2f out: swtchd and no imp u.p over 1f out: plugged on same pce fnl f* **33/1**

0340 9 nse **Telekinetic**[37] 2975 4-9-3 46 .... RoystonFfrench 7 41
(Julia Feilden) *s.i.s: towards rr: clsd over 2f out: sn rdn: nt clrest of runs 1f out: kpt on but no ch ins fnl f (jockey said filly was slowly away)* **10/1**

3300 10 3 **Break The Silence**[11] 3939 5-9-0 50 .... (p) CierenFallon(7) 8 39
(Scott Dixon) *chsd clr ldr tl over 3f out: unable qck u.p and lost pl 2f out: wknd ins fnl f* **14/1**

0-00 11 8 **Ice Cool Cullis (IRE)**[93] 1362 4-9-2 45 .... (t) JohnFahy 13 19
(Mark Loughnane) *stdd s: midfield: effrt and swtchd rt over 2f out: sn struggling and wknd over 1f out* **50/1**

000- 12 4 **Sexy Secret**[256] 8281 8-9-3 53 .... (p) MorganCole(7) 6 19
(Lydia Pearce) *midfield: struggling and losing pl whn bmpd over 2f out: no ch after* **25/1**

4330 13 hd **Hidden Dream (IRE)**[28] 3298 4-9-2 45 .... (v[1]) EoinWalsh 12 11
(Christine Dunnett) *stdd s: t.k.h: racd wd and hung rt thrght: midfield: c to stands' side over 3f out: effrt over 2f out: no prog and wl btn over 1f out: wknd (jockey said filly hung badly right throughout)* **16/1**

0065 14 14 **Stay In The Light**[17] 3691 4-8-11 45 .... (t[1]) RhiainIngram(5) 9
(Roger Ingram) *v.s.a: a in rr: lost tch over 2f out: t.o (jockey said filly was slowly away and never travelling thereafter)* **66/1**

2m 7.97s (-0.83) **Going Correction** -0.10s/f (Good)
WFA 3 from 4yo+ 12lb — 14 Ran SP% 126.1
Speed ratings (Par 101): **99,97,97,96,96 95,94,93,93,91 85,81,81,70**
CSF £42.46 CT £1124.29 TOTE £5.20: £1.80, £1.70, £14.60; EX 46.80 Trifecta £704.40.
Owner Edwin S Phillips **Bred** Irish National Stud **Trained** Newmarket, Suffolk
■ Stewards' Enquiry : Kieren Fox two-day ban: used whip above the permitted level (Jul 15-16)

FOCUS
Lowly handicap form and no surprise to see the 3yos dominate. They went a good gallop, courtesy of the winner, who was soon clear. Those coming from off the pace never featured.

4347 MOULTON NURSERIES H'CAP — 1m 3y
4:10 (4:14) (Class 2) (0-105,92) 3-Y-O **£12,291** (£3,657; £1,827; £913) **Stalls** Centre

Form — RPR

1103 **1** **Oasis Prince**[16] 3728 3-9-6 **91** .... JamieSpencer 1 100
(Mark Johnston) *chsd ldr tl led 2f out: sn rdn and edgd rt over 1f out: hdd ent fnl f: battled bk gamely u.p to ld again towards fin* **5/1**

-512 **2** *nk* **Destination**[23] 3463 3-9-1 **86** .... TomMarquand 2 94
(William Haggas) *trckd ldrs: clsd and upsides ldrs ent fnl 2f: sn rdn and led ent fnl f: r.o u.p: hdd and no ex towards fin* **7/4**[1]

2-01 **3** *3 ½* **Wiretap (FR)**[15] 3779 3-8-12 **83** .... OisinMurphy 4 83
(David Simcock) *stdd s: t.k.h: hld up in tch in last pair: effrt over 1f out: drvn and no imp 1f out: outpcd ins fnl f* **3/1**[3]

-116 **4** *1 ¾* **Aweedram (IRE)**[34] 3082 3-9-7 **92** .... AdamKirby 3 88
(Alan King) *stdd s: hld up in last pair: swtchd lft and effrt ent fnl 2f: unable qck u.p and btn 1f out: wknd ins fnl f* **5/2**[2]

3-00 **5** *4 ½* **Mistress Of Love (USA)**[18] 3677 3-9-1 **86** .... CliffordLee 5 72
(K R Burke) *led tl hdd and rdn 2f out: unable qck and lost pl over 1f out: wknd ins fnl f* **16/1**

1m 36.48s (-1.72) **Going Correction** -0.10s/f (Good) **5 Ran SP% 112.5**
Speed ratings (Par 105): **104,103,100,98,93**
CSF £14.56 TOTE £5.50: £2.30, £2.20; EX 16.90 Trifecta £35.20.
Owner J David Abell **Bred** Highclere Stud And Floors Farming **Trained** Middleham Moor, N Yorks

FOCUS
Just the five runners, but a really useful 3yo handicap and two pulled clear late. Both progressed from their previous starts.

4348 ASL MAKING WORK FLOW H'CAP — 7f 3y
4:45 (4:46) (Class 3) (0-90,90) 3-Y-O **£7,246** (£2,168; £1,084; £542; £270) **Stalls** Centre

Form — RPR

212- **1** **Marhaba Milliar (IRE)**[300] 6793 3-9-3 **90** .... RobertHavlin 3 96+
(John Gosden) *wnt rt leaving stalls: trckd ldr: clsd and shkn up over 1f out: rdn to ld ins fnl f: r.o wl* **6/4**[1]

1-1 **2** *nk* **Motakhayyel**[28] 3306 3-9-2 **89** .... DaneO'Neill 1 94
(Richard Hannon) *t.k.h: hld up in tch: shkn up 2f out: rdn and clsd to press ldrs 1f out: sustained chal but a hld fnl 100yds* **13/8**[2]

2-00 **3** *1 ¼* **Blonde Warrior (IRE)**[55] 2414 3-9-3 **90** ....(p[1]) TomMarquand 2 92
(Hugo Palmer) *led: rdn over 1f out: hdd ins fnl f: no ex and one pce after* **11/2**[3]

03 **4** *1 ½* **Givinitsum (SAF)**[59] 2260 3-9-5 **90** .... GeorgiaDobie(7) 5 91
(Eve Johnson Houghton) *t.k.h: chsd ldrs: effrt ent fnl 2f: unable qck u.p 1f out: kpt on same pce ins fnl f* **20/1**

0032 **5** *¾* **Ultimate Avenue (IRE)**[28] 3301 5-9-9 **87** ....(h) JamieSpencer 4 86
(David Simcock) *stdd and sltly impeded leaving stalls: t.k.h: hld up in rr: clsd: swtchd rt and effrt over 1f out: kpt on ins fnl f: nvr getting terms* **7/1**

1m 23.48s (-1.62) **Going Correction** -0.10s/f (Good)
WFA 3 from 5yo 9lb **5 Ran SP% 110.7**
Speed ratings (Par 107): **105,104,103,101,100**
CSF £4.29 TOTE £2.10: £1.10, £1.60; EX 4.40 Trifecta £14.20.
Owner Jaber Abdullah **Bred** Rabbah Bloodstock Limited **Trained** Newmarket, Suffolk

FOCUS
The right pair came to the fore in this fair handicap. The 1-2 arrived unexposed and the third's the best guide.

4349 WARNERS LEISURE HOLIDAYS EAST COAST H'CAP — 1m 3y
5:20 (5:20) (Class 6) (0-55,55) 4-Y-O+
£3,105 (£924; £461; £300; £300; £300) **Stalls** Centre

Form — RPR

0502 **1** **Magical Ride**[6] 4115 4-9-7 **55** .... AdamKirby 6 66+
(Richard Spencer) *chsd ldr tl rdn to ld over 1f out: clr and styd on strly ins fnl f: comf* **6/4**[1]

2001 **2** *3 ¼* **Sir Jamie**[37] 2972 6-9-4 **52** ....(b) TomMarquand 8 56
(Tony Carroll) *stdd s: hld up in rr: clsd and nt clr run 2f out: nvr much room tl hdwy u.p 1f out: chsd clr wnr ins fnl f: r.o: nvr threat* **8/1**

00 **3** *1 ¾* **Enzo (IRE)**[59] 2256 4-9-7 **55** .... RobertHavlin 12 55
(John Butler) *t.k.h: hld up in tch in midfield: clsd to chse ldrs 2f out: drvn and no imp over 1f out: briefly chsd clr wnr ins fnl f: 3rd and kpt on same pce fnl 100yds* **9/1**

-002 **4** *2* **Coachella (IRE)**[10] 3966 5-8-13 **52** ....(b) SeamusCronin(5) 9 47
(Ed de Giles) *stdd s: hld up towards rr: clsd 2f out: nt clr run and swtchd rt over 1f out: sn rdn and styd on ins fnl f: no ch w wnr* **14/1**

4243 **5** *½* **Port Soif**[57] 2350 5-9-3 **51** ....(p) CliffordLee 5 45
(Scott Dixon) *led: rdn ent fnl 2f: hdd over 1f out: sn outpcd and wknd ins fnl f* **25/1**

3012 **6** *nk* **King Oswald (USA)**[37] 2972 6-9-7 **55** ....(tp) LiamJones 7 48
(James Unett) *towards rr: clsd over 2f out: swtchd lft and hdwy and u.p over 1f out: sn no imp and wknd ins fnl f* **7/1**[3]

5052 **7** *1 ¾* **Red Gunner**[21] 3533 5-9-4 **52** .... JohnFahy 1 41
(Mark Loughnane) *s.i.s: towards rr: swtchd lft and hdwy over 2f out: no imp u.p over 1f out: wknd ins fnl f* **20/1**

0-41 **8** *1 ¼* **Billie Beane**[17] 3687 4-9-7 **55** .... KierenFox 11 41
(Dr Jon Scargill) *wl in tch in midfield: clsd to chse ldrs 1/2-way: rdn ent fnl 2f: unable qck and btn over 1f out: wknd ins fnl f* **16/1**

-3F0 **9** *1* **Spanish Mane (IRE)**[37] 2972 4-8-13 **54** .... SeanKirrane(7) 3 38
(Julia Feilden) *t.k.h: hld up in tch in midfield: effrt jst over 2f out: no prog u.p over 1f out: wknd ins fnl f* **20/1**

0000 **10** *½* **Aljunood (IRE)**[11] 3939 5-9-1 **49** .... RoystonFfrench 14 32
(John Norton) *t.k.h: hld up in tch in midfield: effrt over 2f out: sn drvn and lost pl: wl hld and swtchd lft over 1f out: plugged on* **50/1**

-000 **11** *1 ¾* **Viento De Condor (IRE)**[15] 3774 4-8-13 **50** ......(b[1]) CameronNoble(3) 13 29
(Tom Clover) *rn wout the declared tongue-strap: chsd ldrs: rdn over 2f out: sn struggling and lost pl over 1f out: wknd ins fnl f* **33/1**

0256 **12** *2 ¼* **Khazix (IRE)**[31] 3187 4-9-1 **52** .... WilliamCox(3) 4 26
(Daniele Camuffo) *chsd ldrs tl u.p and struggling over 2f out: wl btn over 1f out* **25/1**

-524 **13** *hd* **Hi Ho Silver**[29] 3279 5-9-0 **53** .... SebastianWoods(5) 16 26
(Chris Wall) *t.k.h: hld up in tch in midfield: effrt jst over 2f out: drvn and no hdwy over 1f out: wknd ins fnl f (trainer's rep could offer no explanation for the gelding's performance)* **5/1**[2]

000 **14** *13* **Emojie**[29] 3277 5-9-2 **50** .... BrettDoyle 2
(Jane Chapple-Hyam) *dwlt: towards rr: hdwy 1/2-way: struggling u.p over 2f out: bhd over 1f out: wknd fnl f* **33/1**

1m 36.5s (-1.70) **Going Correction** -0.10s/f (Good) **14 Ran SP% 127.4**
Speed ratings (Par 101): **104,100,99,97,96 96,94,93,92,91 89,87,87,74**
CSF £13.51 CT £92.39 TOTE £2.30: £1.20, £2.40, £4.10; EX 20.70 Trifecta £308.10.
Owner The Magic Horse Syndicate **Bred** Highclere Stud **Trained** Newmarket, Suffolk

FOCUS
Moderate handicap form and one-way traffic for the favourite. The winner backed up his recent improvement.
T/Plt: £25.90 to a £1 stake. Pool: £65,374.20 - 1,838.17 winning units T/Qpdt: £12.80 to a £1 stake. Pool: £5,236.16 - 300.76 winning units **Steve Payne**

4350 - (Foreign Racing) - See Raceform Interactive

4309 CURRAGH (R-H)
Friday, June 28

OFFICIAL GOING: Good (good to firm in places on round course)

4351a COMER GROUP INTERNATIONAL CURRAGH CUP (GROUP 2) — 1m 6f
3:45 (3:52) 3-Y-O+
£79,729 (£25,675; £12,162; £5,405; £2,702; £1,351)

RPR

1 **Twilight Payment (IRE)**[42] 2814 6-9-11 109 ....(p) KevinManning 7 111
(J S Bolger, Ire) *disp early tl sn led: over 3 l clr bef 1/2-way: stl gng wl w reduced ld 3f out: sn pushed along and pressed clly: rdn and jnd over 1f out: sn regained advantage and styd on wl nr fin* **7/1**[3]

2 *nk* **Latrobe (IRE)**[10] 3953 4-9-11 112 .... DonnachaO'Brien 6 111
(Joseph Patrick O'Brien, Ire) *disp ld early tl sn settled bhd ldr in 2nd: effrt nr side under 2f out: rdn to dispute ld over 1f out tl sn hdd: kpt on wl wout matching wnr clsng stages* **5/2**[2]

3 *2 ¾* **Raa Atoll**[21] 3561 4-9-11 110 .... FrankieDettori 3 107
(Luke Comer, Ire) *led and disp early tl sn hdd and settled bhd ldrs: rdn in 3rd over 2f out and no imp on wnr ins fnl f: kpt on same pce to hold 3rd* **14/1**

4 *nk* **Southern France (IRE)**[6] 4093 4-9-11 113 .... RyanMoore 9 106+
(A P O'Brien, Ire) *hld up in rr of mid-div: 7th 3f out: rdn and sme hdwy 1 1/2f out: rdn into 4th ins fnl f where no imp on ldrs: kpt on same pce* **15/8**[1]

5 *hd* **Mustajeer**[33] 3114 6-9-11 108 ....(h) ColinKeane 4 106+
(G M Lyons, Ire) *in rr of mid-div: 8th 3f out: pushed along over 2f out: swtchd lft in 8th over 1f out and sn rdn: sme late hdwy ins fnl f: r.o: nrst fin* **14/1**

6 *2 ¼* **Masaff (IRE)**[41] 2853 3-8-10 105 .... ChrisHayes 5 105
(D K Weld, Ire) *mid-div: drvn in 5th into st and no imp on ldrs u.p under 2f out: kpt on one pce in 7th wl ins fnl f into 6th on line* **10/1**

7 *nse* **Western Australia (IRE)**[9] 3984 3-8-10 105 .... SeamieHeffernan 2 105
(A P O'Brien, Ire) *chsd ldrs: drvn in 4th under 3f out and no ex u.p in 4th over 1f out: wknd ins fnl f: denied 6th on line* **10/1**

8 *½* **Cimeara (IRE)**[61] 2158 4-9-8 102 .... ShaneCrosse 1 99
(Joseph Patrick O'Brien, Ire) *mid-div: 6th 3f out: drvn over 2f out and no ex u.p over 1f out: sn wknd* **25/1**

9 *hd* **The King (IRE)**[21] 3558 4-9-11 110 ....(t) ShaneFoley 8 102
(Mrs John Harrington, Ire) *s.i.s and in rr: tk clsr order in 9th fr 5f out: pushed along in 9th into st: rdn nr side and no ex over 1f out* **12/1**

10 *8* **Heaven On Earth (IRE)**[7] 4086 3-8-7 81 .... WayneLordan 10 90
(A P O'Brien, Ire) *a bhd: dropped to rr fr 5f out: drvn and no imp into st: no ex over 2f out where rdn briefly: wknd: nvr a factor* **50/1**

3m 3.83s (-4.07) **Going Correction** +0.075s/f (Good)
WFA 3 from 4yo+ 16lb **10 Ran SP% 120.9**
Speed ratings: **112,111,110,110,109 108,108,108,108,103**
CSF £25.80 TOTE £8.40: £2.40, £1.30, £3.10; DF 27.30 Trifecta £349.10.
Owner Mrs J S Bolger **Bred** J S Bolger **Trained** Coolcullen, Co Carlow

FOCUS
A really tough performance from the winner to gain a well-merited success at this level. A tight finish for the distance in a race where the placed horses are rated broadly in line with par figures.

4352a AIRLIE STUD STKS (GROUP 2) (FILLIES) — 6f
4:15 (4:26) 2-Y-O
£69,099 (£22,252; £10,540; £4,684; £2,342; £1,171) **Stalls** Centre

RPR

1 **Albigna (IRE)**[35] 3059 2-9-0 0 .... ShaneFoley 10 107+
(Mrs John Harrington, Ire) *towards rr: 8th 1/2-way: drvn after 1/2-way and hdwy 1 1/2f out: u.p in 5th ent fnl f: rdn into 3rd ins fnl f and r.o strly nr side to ld fnl strides* **5/2**[1]

2 *½* **Precious Moments (IRE)**[7] 4048 2-9-0 0 .... RyanMoore 12 106
(A P O'Brien, Ire) *chsd ldrs: 5th 1/2-way: hdwy nr side 2f out to ld over 1f out: rdn and extended advantage briefly ins fnl f tl reduced advantage nr fin and hdd fnl strides* **5/1**[3]

3 *1 ½* **Peace Charter**[40] 2881 2-9-0 0 .... ColinKeane 11 101
(G M Lyons, Ire) *cl up bhd ldr in 2nd: rdn under 2f out and led briefly 1 1/2f out tl sn hdd: no ex wl ins fnl f where dropped to 3rd* **4/1**[2]

4 *4 ½* **Lorelei Rock (IRE)**[7] 4048 2-9-0 0 .... LeighRoche 9 88
(M D O'Callaghan, Ire) *chsd ldrs: disp 3rd at 1/2-way: effrt over 2f out: sn sltly impeded between horses and rdn 1 1/2f out: no imp on ldrs in 6th ins fnl f: kpt on into 4th cl home* **20/1**

5 *nse* **Yesterdayoncemore (IRE)**[40] 2881 2-9-0 0 .... ChrisHayes 3 87
(J A Stack, Ire) *w.w: 7th 1/2-way: rdn and sme hdwy far side over 1f out: no imp on ldrs disputing 4th wl ins fnl f: dropped to 5th cl home* **50/1**

6 *nk* **Tango (IRE)**[9] 3983 2-9-0 0 .... DonnachaO'Brien 1 86
(A P O'Brien, Ire) *chsd ldrs far side early tl settled towards rr bef 1/2-way: last at 1/2-way: pushed along and prog far side 2f out: rdn over 1f out and no imp on ldrs disputing 4th wl ins fnl f: dropped to 6th cl home* **4/1**[2]

7 *1 ¼* **Blissful (IRE)**[22] 3519 2-9-0 0 .... SeamieHeffernan 8 83
(A P O'Brien, Ire) *hld up in rr: racd keenly: 9th 1/2-way: rdn in 9th 1 1/2f out and kpt on nr side ins fnl f: nvr nrr* **16/1**

8 *1 ¾* **Ickworth (IRE)**[9] 3983 2-9-0 0 .... WJLee 2 77
(W McCreery, Ire) *mid-div: 6th 1/2-way: tk clsr order bhd ldrs after 1/2-way gng wl: rdn almost on terms far side 1 1/2f out and sn no ex in 3rd: wknd ins fnl f* **13/2**

9 *shd* **Windham Belle (IRE)**[40] 2878 2-9-0 0 .... RonanWhelan 4 77
(W McCreery, Ire) *led and rn freely early: narrow advantage at 1/2-way: drvn and hdd 1 1/2f out: wknd qckly* **50/1**

10 2 1/4 **A New Dawn (IRE)**[2] 4259 2-9-0 0 WayneLordan 5 70
(Joseph Patrick O'Brien, Ire) *chsd ldrs: disp 3rd at 1/2-way: pushed along bhd ldrs after 1/2-way and wknd 2f out: eased in rr ins fnl f* **10/1**

1m 12.9s (-1.30) **Going Correction** +0.075s/f (Good) **10** Ran SP% **122.2**
Speed ratings: **111,110,108,102,102 101,100,97,97,94**
CSF £15.92 TOTE £3.70: £1.50, £1.60, £1.90; DF 16.20 Trifecta £75.00.
Owner Niarchos Family **Bred** Niarchos Family **Trained** Moone, Co Kildare

FOCUS
This race has been upgraded this year. The winner produced an explosive burst to land it, and emphasised what a good bunch of fillies the trainer has this season. The first three came clear. A slightly positive view has been taken of the form.

4353a FINLAY VOLVO CARS SUMMER FILLIES H'CAP (PREMIER HANDICAP) 7f
4:50 (4:56) 3-Y-0+
£53,153 (£17,117; £8,108; £3,603; £1,801; £900)

RPR

1 **Crafty Madam (IRE)**[22] 3522 5-8-4 **78** oh2 (t) NGMcCullagh 5 84
(K J Condon, Ire) *mid-div: disp 6th at 1/2-way: swtchd lft 2f out and prog over 1f out: rdn in 2nd ins fnl f and kpt on wl to dispute ld nr side cl home and led on line* **8/1**[3]

2 shd **Surrounding (IRE)**[22] 3521 6-9-12 **100** (t) RonanWhelan 3 106
(M Halford, Ire) *chsd ldrs: 5th 1/2-way: gng wl bhd ldrs over 2f out where sn swtchd lft and prog: rdn to ld over 1f out: jnd u.p far side cl home and hdd on line* **6/1**[2]

3 5 **Sonaiyla (IRE)**[35] 3064 3-7-11 **87** oh8 AdamFarragher(7) 4 80+
(M Halford, Ire) *mid-div early: 9th 1/2-way: hdwy far side under 2f out to chse ldrs over 1f out where n.m.r briefly: r.o in 5th between horses ins fnl f into nvr threatening 3rd cl home* **6/1**[2]

4 3/4 **Mia Mento (IRE)**[40] 2882 3-8-6 **89** LeighRoche 8 76
(Thomas Mullins, Ire) *trckd ldr: cl 2nd at 1/2-way: rdn almost on terms 1 1/2f out and sn no ex u.p in 4th: kpt on same pce nr fin* **11/1**

5 nse **Bungee Jump (IRE)**[20] 3575 4-9-3 **91** RossaRyan 2 81
(Grace Harris) *broke wl to ld: narrow advantage at 1/2-way: drvn under 3f out and hdd u.p over 1f out: no ex in 3rd and wknd wl ins fnl f* **12/1**

6 3/4 **Innamorare (IRE)**[33] 3116 4-8-4 **78** oh1 (v[1]) ChrisHayes 9 66
(Gavin Cromwell, Ire) *chsd ldrs: disp 3rd at 1/2-way: rdn bhd ldrs 2f out and no imp u.p in 7th ins fnl f: kpt on one pce in 6th nr fin* **5/1**[1]

7 1 **I Remember You (IRE)**[15] 3786 3-8-4 **87** oh2 WayneLordan 1 70
(A P O'Brien, Ire) *w.w towards rr: pushed along over 2f out and sme hdwy: sn rdn and no ex u.p in 6th ins fnl f: one pce nr fin* **12/1**

8 shd **Silver Service (IRE)**[5] 4152 3-7-13 **87** oh3 (t) AndrewSlattery(5) 11 69
(Michael Mulvany, Ire) *hld up towards rr: pushed along in 10th fr 1/2-way and no imp u.p 1 1/2f out where bmpd sltly: kpt on one pce ins fnl f* **25/1**

9 nk **Thiswaycadeaux (IRE)**[54] 2449 5-8-2 **83** (b[1]) NathanCrosse(7) 13 68
(W McCreery, Ire) *dwlt and in rr: last at 1/2-way: drvn after 1/2-way and sme hdwy under 2f out where sn wandered sltly and sltly bmpd rival: one pce fnl f* **9/1**

10 1 1/4 **Crotchet**[33] 3116 4-9-5 **93** (t[1]) DonnachaO'Brien 12 74
(Joseph Patrick O'Brien, Ire) *mid-div: disp 6th at 1/2-way: pushed along over 2f out: bmpd and hmpd 1 1/2f out: no imp after and sn eased (jockey said filly received a bump from behind in the closing stages)* **5/1**[1]

11 4 3/4 **Shekiba (IRE)**[13] 3875 4-9-3 **91** (b) GaryCarroll 6 59
(Joseph G Murphy, Ire) *chsd ldrs: disp 3rd at 1/2-way: rdn under 3f out and sn wknd* **16/1**

12 1 **Solar Wave (IRE)**[14] 3828 4-9-0 **88** KevinManning 10 54
(J S Bolger, Ire) *mid-div: disp 6th at 1/2-way: rdn 3f out and wknd u.p to rr 2f out* **33/1**

1m 23.87s (-1.13) **Going Correction** +0.075s/f (Good)
WFA 3 from 4yo+ 9lb **12** Ran SP% **119.4**
Speed ratings: **109,108,103,102,102 101,100,100,99,98 92,91**
CSF £55.86 CT £314.50 TOTE £6.90: £2.20, £2.10, £2.50; DF 45.80 Trifecta £415.80.
Owner Con Harrington **Bred** Con Harrington **Trained** Rathbride, Co Kildare

FOCUS
The winner would have been an unlucky loser and will be on the search for black type. The first three all ran pbs.

4354a JUDDMONTE PRETTY POLLY STKS (GROUP 1) (F&M) 1m 2f
5:25 (5:27) 3-Y-0+ **£159,459** (£51,351; £24,324; £10,810; £5,405)

RPR

1 **Iridessa (IRE)**[33] 3115 3-8-12 107 WayneLordan 3 114+
(Joseph Patrick O'Brien, Ire) *trckd ldr early tl dropped to 3rd after 1f: gng wl bhd ldrs over 2f out: sn swtchd lft and prog to chal gng best over 1f out: led ins fnl f and rdn: hung sltly rt nr fin where extended ld* **8/1**

2 2 1/4 **Magic Wand (IRE)**[10] 3953 4-9-10 106 DonnachaO'Brien 6 111
(A P O'Brien, Ire) *led tl hdd after 2f: cl 2nd at 1/2-way: gng wl bhd ldr into st and pushed along to ld under 2f out: sn rdn and hdd ins fnl f: hld whn short of room and checked sltly on inner nr fin* **9/2**[3]

3 1 1/4 **Pink Dogwood (IRE)**[28] 3316 3-8-12 112 RyanMoore 1 107
(A P O'Brien, Ire) *w.w in 4th: tk clsr order in 3rd over 2f out: sn pushed along and no imp on ldrs ins fnl f where rdn briefly: kpt on same pce* **11/10**[1]

4 1 1/4 **Wild Illusion**[33] 3122 4-9-10 115 (p) JamesDoyle 7 105
(Charlie Appleby) *trckd ldrs early tl wnt 2nd after 1f and led after 2f: narrow advantage at 1/2-way: rdn and strly pressed into st: hdd under 2f out and sn no ex u.p in 4th 1f out: kpt on same pce* **7/2**[2]

5 14 **Worth Waiting**[54] 2441 4-9-10 111 FrankieDettori 5 77
(David Lanigan) *in rr thrght: rdn and no imp on ldrs over 3f out: eased fnl f (jockey said filly was leaning right from 6f out)* **7/1**

2m 6.46s (-5.04) **Going Correction** +0.075s/f (Good)
WFA 3 from 4yo 12lb **5** Ran SP% **111.6**
Speed ratings: **118,116,115,114,103**
CSF £41.64 TOTE £12.60: £3.30, £2.00; DF 38.50 Trifecta £96.30.
Owner Mrs C C Regalado-Gonzalez **Bred** Whisperview Trading Ltd **Trained** Owning Hill, Co Kilkenny

FOCUS
The Joseph O'Brien-trained winner bounced right back to her best and the couple of furlongs further than the Guineas suited her extremely well. The leading contenders didn't bring their best but the winner didn't have to be at full stretch to oblige. The second helps with the standard.

4355- 4356a (Foreign Racing) - See Raceform Interactive

CLAIREFONTAINE (R-H)
Friday, June 28

OFFICIAL GOING: Turf: good to soft changing to good after race 5 (3.06)

4357a PRIX EQUURES-EAU & ENERGIES-RESPECT DES RESSOURCES & ENERGIES RENOUVELABLE (CLAIMER) (3YO) (TURF) 1m
3:06 3-Y-0 **£10,360** (£4,144; £3,108; £2,072; £1,036)

RPR

1 **Paradoxal (FR)**[25] 3-9-6 0 ow1 VincentCheminaud 4 66
(H-A Pantall, France) **58/10**[3]

2 snk **Addicted Love (FR)**[63] 2090 3-8-9 0 ow1 ChristopherGrosbois 1 55
(F Foucher, France) **11/1**

3 snk **La Regle Du Jeu (FR)**[25] 3-8-13 0 ow2 ChristopheSoumillon 3 58
(Y Barberot, France) **29/10**[2]

4 3/4 **Lovely Miss (FR)**[59] 2265 3-8-9 0 ow1 (p) TonyPiccone 2 53
(H De Nicolay, France) **63/10**

5 1 1/4 **Just Proud (FR)**[25] 3-8-13 0 ow2 (b) TheoBachelot 11 54
(S Wattel, France) **23/10**[1]

6 2 1/2 **Grandee Daisy**[36] 3028 3-8-9 0 ow1 (b) Louis-PhilippeBeuzelin 8 44
(Jo Hughes, France) *hld up towards rr: prog into mid-div over 1/2-way: effrt on nr side rail fr 3f out: rdn 2f out: kpt on same pce ins fnl f: n.d* **34/1**

7 snk **Estibere (FR)**[237] 8840 3-8-13 0 ow2 AntoineHamelin 10 48
(Edouard Thueux, France) **63/1**

8 shd **Will Ness (IRE)**[20] 3-8-9 0 ow1 DelphineSantiago(3) 6 46
(D Allard, France) **28/1**

9 3/4 **Visionary Dreamer (FR)**[59] 3-8-4 0 ow1 (p) MllePerrineCheyer(8) 9 45
(Matthieu Palussiere, France) **15/1**

10 10 **Rum Lad**[13] 3878 3-8-13 0 ow2 CristianDemuro 7 23
(Jo Hughes, France) *racd a little keenly: in tch: pushed along to chal 3f out: sn rdn: unable to go w ldrs and wknd fr over 1f out: eased clsng stages* **17/1**

11 6 **Hedidit**[40] 3-9-2 0 ow1 FabriceVeron 5 12
(C Lerner, France) **11/1**

1m 40.3s **11** Ran SP% **120.7**
PARI-MUTUEL (all including 1 euro stake): WIN 6.70; PLACE 2.40, 2.80, 2.30; DF 33.10.
Owner Jacques Cygler **Bred** D Clee **Trained** France

4316 CHESTER (L-H)
Saturday, June 29

OFFICIAL GOING: Good to firm (good in places; 7.8)
Wind: Fairly strong, across in straight of over 1f Weather: Overcast

4358 PIMM'S NOVICE STKS 7f 127y
2:00 (2:03) (Class 4) 3-Y-0+
£6,162 (£1,845; £922; £461; £230; £115) **Stalls Low**

Form RPR

0644 1 **Symphony (IRE)**[39] 2943 3-8-10 48 HayleyTurner 6 50
(James Unett) *checked s: hld up: swtchd rt and hdwy over 2f out: rdn to chse ldrs over 1f out: r.o ins fnl f to ld towards fin* **7/1**[3]

-000 2 3/4 **Isabella Ruby**[129] 809 4-8-13 44 (h) GavinAshton(7) 14 50
(Lisa Williamson) *in tch: effrt 2f out: edgd lft over 1f out: led fnl 150yds: hdd and hld towards fin* **50/1**

/5-0 3 3/4 **Highcastle (IRE)**[67] 2014 4-9-11 48 (p[1]) JFEgan 10 53
(Lisa Williamson) *hld up: nt clr run over 2f out: sn rdn: hdwy on outer over 1f out: styd on towards fin: nt quite pce to chal* **80/1**

4 hd **Red Derek** 3-9-1 0 CamHardie 12 51
(Lisa Williamson) *dwlt: towards rr: pushed along and outpcd: hdwy 3f out: proged ins fnl f: fin wl (jockey said gelding was denied a clear run approaching the home turn)* **50/1**

42 5 hd **Puerto Banus**[23] 3499 3-9-1 0 RobHornby 11 50
(Andrew Balding) *midfield on outer: rdn 3f out: no imp on ldrs over 1f out tl kpt on for press towards fin (trainer's rep said colt ran greenly and was unsuited by the track)* **4/5**[1]

0060 6 shd **Henrietta's Dream**[7] 4130 5-9-3 43 ConorMcGovern(3) 1 47
(John Wainwright) *wnt rt s: led: rdn 2f out: hdd fnl 150yds: no ex towards fin* **66/1**

7 2 1/4 **Hide Your Heart (IRE)**[120] 975 3-8-10 50 (p[1]) AndrewMullen 4 39
(David Loughnane) *chsd ldrs: rdn and cl up on inner over 1f out: styd on same pce ins fnl f* **18/1**

6-2 8 shd **Ambersand (IRE)**[18] 3707 3-8-10 0 PaddyMathers 8 39
(Richard Fahey) *chsd ldr: pushed along 3f out: rdn and hung lft fr over 2f out: lost 2nd over 1f out: no ex fnl 150yds (jockey said filly hung left-handed throughout and he had difficulty steering the filly)* **2/1**[2]

-000 9 3/4 **Eternal Destiny**[16] 3774 4-9-6 41 JosephineGordon 2 39
(Ian Williams) *wnt lft s and sn hmpd: bhd and pushed along: hdwy over 3f out: rdn into midfield over 1f out: nvr able to trble ldrs* **20/1**

0-00 10 12 **Hilbre Lake (USA)**[143] 621 3-8-8 44 HarryRussell(7) 3 12
(Lisa Williamson) *wnt lft s: bhd: rdn over 2f out: nvr able to get involved* **66/1**

0000 11 shd **Mr Wing (IRE)**[1] 4319 4-9-11 17 JamieGormley 13 14
(John Wainwright) *midfield: pushed along over 2f out: wknd over 1f out* **100/1**

005 12 3 3/4 **Piccolo Ramoscello**[7] 4104 6-8-13 10 ElishaWhittington(7) 5
(Lisa Williamson) *a towards rr: pushed along over 3f out: nvr able to get on terms* **100/1**

6-00 13 15 **Pritty Livvy**[11] 3975 3-8-10 37 BarryMcHugh 9
(Noel Wilson) *racd keenly: chsd ldrs: lost pl 3f out: sn wknd* **66/1**

14 13 **Alltami (IRE)** 3-9-1 0 RoystonFfrench 7
(Steph Hollinshead) *midfield: pushed along 5f out: lost pl 4f out: eased whn bhd over 1f out* **10/1**

1m 36.38s (0.68) **Going Correction** -0.075s/f (Good)
WFA 3 from 4yo+ 10lb **14** Ran SP% **132.1**
Speed ratings (Par 105): **93,92,91,91,91 91,88,88,87,75 75,72,57,44**
CSF £327.09 TOTE £7.90: £2.00, £16.10, £39.50; EX 578.80.
Owner Paul Steadman And Partner **Bred** Rathasker Stud **Trained** Wolverhampton, West Midlands

FOCUS
The rail between the 6f and 1 1/2f was moved out by three yards after racing on Friday. Add 24 yards. Those with a rating set a lowly standard and, with the first three home all rated in the 40s, this has to be considered one of the weakest novice races ever run. Even at this low level the form is far from solid.

4359 MARTINI H'CAP — 5f 15y
2:35 (2:35) (Class 3) (0-95,93) 3-Y-O+

£8,715 (£2,609; £1,304; £652; £326; £163) **Stalls** Low

Form — RPR

0024 **1** **Gabrial The Saint (IRE)**[35] 3069 4-9-7 **87**.................... PaddyMathers 1 — 95
(Richard Fahey) *hld up: rdn and hdwy over 1f out: sn swtchd lft to chal: led fnl 150yds: r.o* **2/1**[1]

1006 **2** ½ **Abel Handy (IRE)**[27] 3375 4-9-9 **89**.......................... JFEgan 4 — 95
(Declan Carroll) *led: rdn over 1f out: hdd fnl 150yds: kpt on but hld after (jockey said gelding hung right-handed throughout; vet said gelding lost its left fore shoe)* **10/1**

4422 **3** nk **Boundary Lane**[7] 4105 4-9-3 **83**..........................(p[1]) BarryMcHugh 7 — 88
(Julie Camacho) *hld up in rr: nt clr run over 1f out: sn rdn and hdwy: r.o towards fin* **7/1**

3120 **4** 2 ¾ **She Can Boogie (IRE)**[7] 4101 3-9-7 **93**........................ LiamJones 8 — 86
(Tom Dascombe) *chsd ldr tl rdn over 1f out: hung lft whn no ex fnl 150yds* **7/1**

-011 **5** nk **Angel Alexander (IRE)**[14] 3844 3-9-5 **91**.................... JackMitchell 10 — 83+
(Tom Dascombe) *chsd ldrs: effrt over 1f out: lugged lft and unable qck ent fnl f: lugged lft and no ex fnl 150yds* **9/2**[3]

-400 **6** hd **Wild Edric**[21] 3590 3-8-6 **78**................................ HayleyTurner 2 — 69
(Tom Dascombe) *trckd ldrs: effrt on inner over 2f out: unable qck over 1f out: styd on same pce ins fnl f* **7/2**[2]

3004 **7** ¾ **Confessional**[13] 3883 12-9-4 **84**..........................(e) JamieGormley 5 — 75
(Tim Easterby) *hld up: outpcd and bhd over 2f out: kpt on u.p ins fnl f but nvr threatened* **9/1**

1m 0.06s (-2.04) **Going Correction** -0.075s/f (Good)
WFA 3 from 4yo+ 6lb — **7 Ran SP% 117.8**
Speed ratings (Par 107): **113,112,111,107,106 106,105**
CSF £24.34 CT £121.11 TOTE £2.80: £1.60, £4.30; EX 24.90 Trifecta £104.40.
Owner Dr Marwan Koukash **Bred** Tally-Ho Stud **Trained** Musley Bank, N Yorks

FOCUS
Add 20 yards. Three notable absentees lessened the strength of this 0-95 somewhat, though it was strongly run and looks solid enough sprinting form. The form's rated around the second.

4360 MATTHEW CLARK H'CAP — 7f 1y
3:10 (3:10) (Class 2) (0-100,102) 3-Y-O

£11,827 (£3,541; £1,770; £885; £442; £222) **Stalls** Low

Form — RPR

0214 **1** **Gabrial The Wire**[21] 3599 3-8-9 **83**.......................... BarryMcHugh 2 — 92
(Richard Fahey) *chsd ldrs: waited for a run on inner 2f out: produced to ld jst over 1f out: sn clr: r.o wl: eased towards fin* **9/2**[3]

-350 **2** 2 ½ **Barristan The Bold**[9] 4016 3-9-1 **89**........................ HayleyTurner 5 — 91+
(Tom Dascombe) *midfield: rdn over 1f out: hdwy ent fnl f: styd on to take 2nd fnl 150yds: no ch w wnr* **7/2**[2]

1421 **3** 1 ¾ **Mawakib**[24] 3465 3-9-0 **88**..................................... JackMitchell 4 — 86
(Roger Varian) *towards rr: hdwy into midfield over 2f out: styd on ins fnl f: tk 3rd towards fin: nvr able to chal* **6/4**[1]

1003 **4** ½ **Pacino**[1] 4316 3-8-6 **80**.. PaddyMathers 1 — 76
(Richard Fahey) *w ldr: rdn over 2f out: led over 1f out: sn hdd: no ex fnl 100yds* **8/1**

60-0 **5** ½ **Athmad (IRE)**[21] 3599 3-9-3 **91**................................ LiamJones 7 — 86
(Brian Meehan) *in rr: pushed along most of way: hdwy wl ins fnl f: kpt on towards fin* **25/1**

-300 **6** nk **Woodside Wonder**[7] 4099 3-8-4 **78**......................(v[1]) JosephineGordon 6 — 72
(Keith Dalgleish) *chsd ldrs: rdn over 2f out: unable qck over 1f out: styd on same pce ins fnl f* **28/1**

-026 **7** hd **Jack's Point**[21] 3599 3-9-7 **95**.................................. JFEgan 3 — 88
(William Muir) *led: rdn and hdd over 1f out: nt pce of ldrs ins fnl f: wknd fnl 75yds (starter reported that the gelding was the subject of a third criteria failure; trainer was informed that the gelding could not run until the day after passing a stalls test)* **6/1**

4-10 **8** nk **Forseti**[51] 2559 3-8-6 **80**...(h) RobHornby 10 — 73
(Andrew Balding) *stdd s: hld up: rdn over 1f out: kpt on ins fnl f: nvr able to chal* **20/1**

-220 **9** 7 **Blown By Wind**[14] 3865 3-10-0 **102**.......................... RoystonFfrench 11 — 76
(Mark Johnston) *midfield on outer: lost pl 3f out: bhd over 2f out* **14/1**

1m 26.08s (-1.42) **Going Correction** -0.075s/f (Good) — **9 Ran SP% 124.5**
Speed ratings (Par 105): **105,102,100,99,99 98,98,98,90**
CSF £21.95 CT £35.69 TOTE £5.20: £1.40, £1.60, £1.10; EX 20.20 Trifecta £57.00.
Owner Dr Marwan Koukash **Bred** S Emmet And Miss R Emmet **Trained** Musley Bank, N Yorks
■ Stewards' Enquiry : Jack Mitchell two-day ban: misuse of the whip (Jul 15-16)

FOCUS
Add 24 yards. They went a good pace in this feature handicap and it brought about a personal best from the ready winner, who progressed again.

4361 CCE SIGNATURE MIXERS EBF NOVICE STKS (PLUS 10 RACE) — 5f 15y
3:45 (3:46) (Class 4) 2-Y-O — **£6,162** (£1,845; £922; £461; £230) **Stalls** Low

Form — RPR

02 **1** **Lincoln Blue**[17] 3739 2-9-2 0.. JFEgan 2 — 79
(Jane Chapple-Hyam) *chsd ldrs: sn nudged along: effrt on inner over 1f out: r.o towards fin to ld post (jockey said colt hung right-handed throughout)* **7/2**[3]

32 **2** nse **Sermon (IRE)**[5] 4191 2-9-2 0... LiamJones 7 — 79
(Tom Dascombe) *w ldr: rdn over 1f out: led narrowly wl ins fnl f: hdd post* **9/4**[1]

4 **3** nk **Upstate New York (IRE)**[16] 3767 2-9-2 0...................... BarryMcHugh 5 — 78
(Richard Fahey) *missed break: bhd: sn outpcd: hdwy over 1f out: r.o and ev ch wl ins fnl f: hld towards fin (jockey said colt missed the break)* **5/2**[2]

1225 **4** nk **Rodnee Tee**[21] 3566 2-9-2 80.................................. ConorMcGovern(3) 1 — 80
(David O'Meara) *led: rdn over 1f out: hdd narrowly wl ins fnl f: nt quite pce of front three towards fin* **9/2**

2431 **5** 2 **Dandizette (IRE)**[10] 3997 2-9-0 70............................... AndrewMullen 6 — 67
(Adrian Nicholls) *chsd ldrs: rdn over 1f out: nt pce to chal and styd on same pce ins fnl f* **5/1**

1m 2.08s (-0.02) **Going Correction** -0.075s/f (Good) — **5 Ran SP% 116.4**
Speed ratings (Par 95): **97,96,96,95,92**
CSF £12.50 TOTE £3.60: £2.30, £1.60; EX 13.50 Trifecta £24.20.
Owner Gordon Li **Bred** Mr & Mrs Sandy Orr **Trained** Dalham, Suffolk

FOCUS
Add 20 yards. They went a furious early pace here and it's probably form to be a bit cautious of. A compressed finish.

4362 BEEFEATER ORIGINAL H'CAP — 1m 4f 63y
4:20 (4:20) (Class 4) (0-80,82) 3-Y-O+

£6,404 (£1,905; £952; £476; £300; £300) **Stalls** Low

Form — RPR

-366 **1** **Cape Islay (FR)**[22] 3548 3-9-4 **82**............................. JackMitchell 5 — 90
(Mark Johnston) *chsd ldr: upsides 2f out: rdn to ld over 1f out: kpt on wl (trainer's rep could offer no explanation for the filly's improved form)* **6/1**[3]

02-6 **2** ½ **Overhaugh Street**[31] 3222 6-8-13 **63**........................ BarryMcHugh 4 — 70
(Ed de Giles) *led: jnd 2f out: rdn and hdd over 1f out: kpt on u.p ins fnl f and continued to chal but a hld* **20/1**

2224 **3** 3 ¾ **Paradise Boy (FR)**[21] 3585 3-8-13 **77**........................ RobHornby 7 — 78+
(Andrew Balding) *chsd ldrs: rdn over 1f out: hung lft ins fnl f: kpt on ins fnl f: no imp* **7/2**[2]

0-1P **4** 2 **Raven's Raft (IRE)**[4] 4220 4-8-12 **62**...................... AndrewMullen 1 — 60
(David Loughnane) *chsd ldrs: rdn over 2f out: one pce over 1f out and no imp* **14/1**

5143 **5** hd **Gabrial The One (IRE)**[1] 4321 3-9-3 **81**.................. PaddyMathers 2 — 78
(Richard Fahey) *in tch: pushed along 3f out: outpcd over 2f out: kpt on ins fnl f: nt pce to trble ldrs (jockey said gelding hung left-handed)* **11/8**[1]

6-03 **6** 6 **James Park Woods (IRE)**[30] 3247 3-9-0 **78**............ JosephineGordon 3 — 66
(Ralph Beckett) *in rr: pushed along for most of way after 4f: nvr able to get involved (jockey said gelding was never travelling)* **7/2**[2]

3156 **7** 15 **Heart Of Soul (IRE)**[14] 3847 4-9-13 **82**..............(p) BenSanderson(5) 6 — 46
(Ian Williams) *hld up: pushed along over 5f out: outpcd over 2f out: nvr a threat* **8/1**

2m 38.46s (-3.74) **Going Correction** -0.075s/f (Good)
WFA 3 from 4yo+ 14lb — **7 Ran SP% 123.4**
Speed ratings (Par 105): **109,108,106,104,104 100,90**
CSF £113.95 CT £493.60 TOTE £6.00: £3.50, £2.50; EX 119.40 Trifecta £791.00.
Owner N Browne,I Boyce, S Frosell & S Richards **Bred** S N C Scuderia Micolo Di Nocola Galliec **Trained** Middleham Moor, N Yorks

FOCUS
Add 38 yards. Very few figured here and it developed into a match in the home straight. The form's rated around the second.

4363 LAURENT PERRIER H'CAP — 1m 7f 196y
4:55 (4:55) (Class 4) (0-85,76) 4-Y-O+

£6,404 (£1,905; £952; £476; £300; £300) **Stalls** Low

Form — RPR

2312 **1** **Angel Gabrial (IRE)**[7] 4126 10-8-7 **62**......................(p) BarryMcHugh 4 — 69
(Patrick Morris) *racd keenly: chsd ldrs: led after 7f: mde rest: rdn over 1f out: styd on wl: comf* **5/2**[1]

3/24 **2** ½ **Red Royalist**[22] 480 5-9-7 **76**...................................(p) CamHardie 6 — 81
(Stuart Edmunds) *hld up: rdn and hdwy over 1f out: carried hd to one side: styd on to take 2nd fnl 150yds: clsd on wnr towards fin* **3/1**[2]

6-02 **3** 1 ¾ **Iconic Belle**[30] 3269 5-9-7 **76**..................................... PhilDennis 3 — 79
(Philip Kirby) *chsd ldr: rdn over 2f out: chalng over 1f out: unable qck jst ins fnl f: lost 2nd and no ex fnl 150yds* **6/1**[3]

6-10 **4** ¾ **Charlie D (USA)**[35] 3073 4-9-7 **76**...........................(tp) LiamJones 2 — 78
(Tom Dascombe) *s.i.s: rn in snatches: in tch: rdn over 2f out and outpcd: hung lft ins fnl f: kpt on towards fin* **7/1**

1/1- **5** ½ **Noble Behest**[541] 42 5-9-7 **76**..................................... PaddyMathers 1 — 77
(Ian Williams) *led: hdd after 7f: trckd ldrs after: rdn and outpcd over 1f out: kpt on same pce ins fnl f* **3/1**[2]

3520 **6** 1 ¼ **Ebqaa (IRE)**[18] 3708 5-8-12 **67**.............................(p) JosephineGordon 5 — 67
(James Unett) *hld up: rdn over 2f out: nvr able to get involved* **7/1**

3m 30.21s (-1.69) **Going Correction** -0.075s/f (Good) — **6 Ran SP% 117.9**
Speed ratings (Par 105): **101,100,99,99,99 98**
CSF £11.00 TOTE £2.60: £1.50, £3.10; EX 9.10 Trifecta £30.40.
Owner Dr Marwan Koukash **Bred** K And Mrs Cullen **Trained** Prescot, Merseyside
■ Stewards' Enquiry : Liam Jones two-day ban: used whip with his arm above shoulder height (Jul 15-16)

FOCUS
Add 70 yards. A good effort from the veteran Angel Gabrial, who made it three wins on the card for his owner. The third's the best guide.

4364 MAGNERS H'CAP — 5f 15y
5:30 (5:32) (Class 4) (0-85,82) 4-Y-O+

£6,404 (£1,905; £952; £476; £300; £300) **Stalls** Low

Form — RPR

1034 **1** **Canford Bay (IRE)**[7] 4100 5-9-4 **79**............................ CamHardie 12 — 88+
(Antony Brittain) *chsd ldrs: effrt to take 2nd 2f out: led over 1f out: edgd lft ins fnl f: kpt on wl* **11/1**

-500 **2** ¾ **Powerallied (IRE)**[14] 3846 6-9-5 **80**......................... PaddyMathers 3 — 87
(Richard Fahey) *chsd ldrs: wnt 2nd over 1f out: styd on ins fnl f: nt quite pce of wnr* **9/4**[1]

0420 **3** ¾ **Zapper Cass (FR)**[16] 3770 6-8-12 **73**.......................(v) LiamJones 1 — 77
(Michael Appleby) *midfield: rdn and hdwy over 1f out: edgd rt ins fnl f: styd on towards fin* **7/1**

1562 **4** shd **King Robert**[14] 3856 6-9-2 **77**................................. JackMitchell 8 — 81
(Charlie Wallis) *hld up towards rr: nt clr run over 1f out: sn swtchd rt and hdwy: styd on ins fnl f: nt quite get to ldrs* **10/3**[3]

-605 **5** 2 ½ **Billy Dylan (IRE)**[39] 2940 4-9-4 **82**..................(p) ConorMcGovern(3) 5 — 77
(David O'Meara) *led: rdn 2f out: hdd over 1f out: outpcd by ldrs ins fnl f: edgd rt and no ex fnl 100yds* **10/1**

2250 **6** nk **Qaaraat**[19] 3658 4-8-8 **69**.. RobHornby 9 — 63
(Antony Brittain) *chsd ldr tl 2f out: rdn and outpcd over 1f out: no ex ins fnl f* **12/1**

0400 **7** ¾ **Brandy Station (IRE)**[23] 3509 4-7-9 **63**............... ElishaWhittington(7) 4 — 54
(Lisa Williamson) *chsd ldrs: rdn over 1f out: one pce ins fnl f* **25/1**

24-0 **8** nse **Computable**[36] 3056 5-8-7 **68**..............................(p) JamieGormley 10 — 59
(Tim Easterby) *hld up: rdn over 2f out: kpt on towards fin: nvr a threat* **20/1**

0002 **9** nk **Upstaging**[7] 4103 7-9-3 **78**....................................... BarryMcHugh 2 — 68
(Noel Wilson) *bhd: outpcd over 2f out: kpt on ins fnl f: nvr able to trble ldrs* **3/1**[2]

10-0 **10** 2 ½ **Quantum Dot (IRE)**[57] 2358 8-8-10 **71**..............(b) JosephineGordon 14 — 52
(Ed de Giles) *hld up: rdn over 1f out: nvr able to get involved* **33/1**

5100 **11** *2½* **Alsvinder**[57] 2368 6-9-6 **81**..........(w) JFEgan 6 53
(Philip Kirby) *midfield: rdn and no imp over 1f out: wknd ins fnl f: sn eased (jockey said horse had no more to give)* **25/1**

1m 1.11s (-0.99) **Going Correction** -0.075s/f (Good) **11** Ran SP% **131.9**
Speed ratings (Par 105): **104,102,101,101,97 96,95,95,95,91 87**
CSF £39.06 CT £208.62 TOTE £12.90: £3.60, £2.40, £2.40; EX 59.00 Trifecta £594.20.
Owner Northgate Racing **Bred** R McCulloch **Trained** Warthill, N Yorks
■ Stewards' Enquiry : Paddy Mathers two-day ban: used whip in the incorrect place (Jul 15-16)

FOCUS
Add 20 yards. This was fast and furious and the winner can be upgraded, given he came from stall 12. It was probably a pb from him.
T/Plt: £9,191.90 to a £1 stake. Pool: £69,380.24 - 5.51 winning units T/Qpdt: £64.30 to a £1 stake. Pool: £6,515.54 - 74.91 winning units **Darren Owen**

4322 DONCASTER (L-H)
Saturday, June 29

OFFICIAL GOING: Straight course - good to firm: round course - good (good to firm in places)
Wind: Light half-against Weather: Fine

4365 CONSTRUCTION INDEX H'CAP — 7f 6y
5:25 (5:28) (Class 4) (0-80,80) 4-Y-O+
£5,530 (£1,645; £822; £411; £400; £400) **Stalls** Centre

Form RPR

4343 **1** **Athollblair Boy (IRE)**[7] 4103 6-8-13 **79**.......... IzzyClifton(7) 11 87
(Nigel Tinkler) *hld up: swtchd rt and hdwy over 1f out: rdn into ld and edgd lft wl ins fnl f: r.o* **9/1**

12-2 **2** *½* **Lucky Louie**[29] 3305 6-9-1 **74**..........(p) RobertWinston 10 81
(Roger Teal) *hld up: hdwy over 2f out: led 1f out: edgd lft and hdd wl ins fnl f: kpt on* **4/1**[2]

-400 **3** *5* **Private Matter**[20] 3636 5-9-6 **79**..........(b1) JasonHart 6 72
(Amy Murphy) *racd keenly in 2nd tl led over 5f out: rdn and hdd 1f out: no ex ins fnl f* **20/1**

-200 **4** *1¼* **Knowing Glance (IRE)**[19] 3649 4-8-11 **70**.......... TonyHamilton 4 60
(Richard Fahey) *s.i.s: hld up: pushed along and hdwy over 2f out: rdn over 1f out: styd on same pce fnl f (jockey said gelding was restless in the stalls)* **7/1**[3]

0-14 **5** *1* **Wind In My Sails**[26] 3423 7-9-0 **80**.......... TobyEley(7) 8 67
(Ed de Giles) *s.i.s: hld up: rdn and hung lft fr over 1f out: styd on: nt trble ldrs (jockey said gelding missed the break)* **8/1**

04-2 **6** *¾* **Envisaging (IRE)**[38] 2977 5-9-2 **75**..........(t) GeorgeWood 9 60
(James Fanshawe) *prom: rdn over 1f out: wknd ins fnl f* **4/1**[2]

2122 **7** *3¼* **Rock Of Estonia (IRE)**[21] 3575 4-9-5 **78**.......... CharlieBennett 3 54
(Charles Hills) *trckd ldrs: plld hrd: wnt 2nd 3f out: rdn over 1f out: wknd ins fnl f* **7/2**[1]

-450 **8** *1* **Deansgate (IRE)**[15] 3813 6-8-13 **72**.......... TomEaves 5 46
(Julie Camacho) *s.i.s: hld up: sme hdwy over 1f out: wknd ins fnl f* **14/1**

0000 **9** *4* **Big Storm Coming**[21] 3563 9-9-5 **78**.......... DougieCostello 12 41
(John Quinn) *s.i.s: sn prom: rdn over 2f out: wknd over 1f out* **14/1**

0400 **10** *½* **Staplegrove (IRE)**[36] 3046 4-8-5 **64**.......... JimmyQuinn 13 25
(Philip Kirby) *sn led: hdd over 5f out: rdn over 2f out: sn wknd* **16/1**

-000 **11** *28* **Black Isle Boy (IRE)**[14] 3868 5-9-1 **74**..........(t1) ShaneGray 2
(David O'Meara) *hld up: rdn 1/2-way: wknd over 2f out: eased over 1f out (vet said gelding lost its left fore shoe)* **25/1**

1m 23.2s (-3.20) **Going Correction** -0.25s/f (Firm) **11** Ran SP% **123.7**
Speed ratings (Par 105): **108,107,101,100,99 98,94,93,88,88 56**
CSF £47.33 CT £728.58 TOTE £10.60: £2.90, £1.80, £6.00; EX 58.30 Trifecta £810.90.
Owner The Geezaaah Partnership **Bred** Ms Ashley O'Leary **Trained** Langton, N Yorks

FOCUS
A fair handicap. The 6yo winner came through late to defeat one of the market leaders in about a second outside of standard time. The first two finished clear, with the winner rated to his best.

4366 PANELCRAFT SUPERIOR ACCESS PANELS EBF FILLIES' NOVICE MEDIAN AUCTION STKS (PLUS 10 RACE) — 7f 6y
5:55 (5:59) (Class 5) 2-Y-O **£3,752** (£1,116; £557; £278) **Stalls** Centre

Form RPR

6 **1** **Little Bird (IRE)**[44] 2761 2-9-0.......... TomMarquand 1 71
(Richard Hannon) *mde all: set stdy pce tl shkn up and qcknd over 2f out: rdn over 1f out: styd on* **5/6**[1]

52 **2** *¾* **Blausee (IRE)**[21] 3578 2-9-0.......... JasonHart 5 69
(Philip McBride) *trckd ldrs: shkn up over 1f out: rdn to chse wnr ins fnl f: r.o* **3/1**[2]

4 **3** *1¼* **Lady Red Moon**[16] 3776 2-8-11.......... AaronJones(3) 4 66
(Marco Botti) *s.i.s: hld up: shkn up over 2f out: rdn: hung lft and r.o ins fnl f: nt rch ldrs* **11/1**

4 *½* **Dancing Feet (IRE)** 2-9-0.......... ShaneGray 3 65
(David O'Meara) *s.i.s: sn prom: chsd wnr over 2f out: rdn over 1f out: edgd lft and styd on same pce wl ins fnl f* **7/1**[3]

5 *1½* **City Escape (IRE)** 2-9-0.......... TonyHamilton 2 61
(Rae Guest) *s.i.s: hld up: shkn up over 2f out: nt trble ldrs* **20/1**

3 **6** *7* **It's Not My Fault (IRE)**[17] 3725 2-9-0.......... TomEaves 6 42
(Tom Dascombe) *sn chsng wnr: rdn and lost 2nd over 2f out: wknd over 1f out* **9/1**

1m 26.77s (0.37) **Going Correction** -0.25s/f (Firm) **6** Ran SP% **115.2**
Speed ratings (Par 90): **87,86,84,84,82 74**
CSF £3.72 TOTE £1.70: £1.20, £1.40; EX 4.30 Trifecta £21.40.
Owner Michael Pescod & Justin Dowley **Bred** Springbank Way Stud **Trained** East Everleigh, Wilts

FOCUS
An ordinary juvenile fillies' novice contest. The odds-on favourite produced a controlled victory from the front. Her winning time was over three seconds slower than the opening C&D handicap.

4367 GILKS FENCING "HAPPY BIRTHDAY CHILD OF 69" MAIDEN STKS — 6f 2y
6:30 (6:33) (Class 5) 3-Y-O+ **£3,752** (£1,116; £557; £278) **Stalls** Centre

Form RPR

1 **Ejtilaab (IRE)** 3-9-5.......... CharlieBennett 8 85+
(Roger Varian) *restless in stalls: sn chsng ldrs: rdn over 1f out: r.o to ld nr fin* **6/4**[1]

00-2 **2** *nk* **Crantock Bay**[19] 3661 3-9-5 82.......... HayleyTurner 4 84
(George Scott) *chsd ldrs tl led over 1f out: rdn and edgd rt wl ins fnl f: hdd towards fin* **9/4**[2]

0-5 **3** *5* **Debonair Don Juan (IRE)**[24] 3463 3-9-5.......... StevieDonohoe 9 68
(Ed Vaughan) *restless in stalls: s.i.s: hld up: rdn and hung lft over 1f out: r.o to go 3rd towards fin: nt trble ldrs* **10/3**[3]

32 **4** *1* **Diamond Shower (IRE)**[12] 3920 3-9-0.......... TonyHamilton 1 60
(Richard Fahey) *chsd ldr to 1/2-way: remained handy: rdn over 1f out: styd on same pce ins fnl f* **6/1**

6 **5** *hd* **Gorgeous Gobolina**[10] 4010 3-8-7.......... HarryRussell(7) 2 59
(Susan Corbett) *led: rdn and hdd over 1f out: no ex ins fnl f* **40/1**

6 *5* **Friday Fizz (IRE)** 3-9-0.......... AndrewMullen 6 43
(Mark Loughnane) *hld up in tch: plld hrd: rdn over 2f out: wknd over 1f out* **14/1**

0-0 **7** *2* **Kyllachy Castle**[11] 3972 3-9-5.......... JackGarritty 5 42
(Lynn Siddall) *s.i.s: hld up: plld hrd: wknd over 2f out* **150/1**

50 **8** *4½* **Cominginonmonday (IRE)**[7] 4129 4-9-7.......... RobertWinston 11 24
(Robyn Brisland) *wnt rt s: hld up: hung rt over 2f out: nvr nr to chal (jockey said filly hung right)* **33/1**

00 **9** *7* **Doncaster Star**[42] 2823 4-9-7..........(t1) TomEaves 10 2
(Ivan Furtado) *s.i.s: a in rr: bhd fr 1/2-way* **66/1**

10 *2¼* **Jeans Maite** 3-9-0.......... LewisEdmunds 7
(Roy Bowring) *s.s: racd keenly and hdwy over 4f out: chsd ldr 1/2-way tl rdn: hung lft and wknd over 1f out (jockey said filly ran green)* **50/1**

40-0 **11** *8* **Sandytown (IRE)**[117] 1016 4-9-12 55..........(w) DougieCostello 3
(David C Griffiths) *prom: rdn and lost pl over 3f out: wknd over 2f out* **50/1**

1m 11.76s (-0.94) **Going Correction** -0.25s/f (Firm)
WFA 3 from 4yo 7lb **11** Ran SP% **126.3**
Speed ratings (Par 103): **96,95,88,87,87 80,78,72,62,59 49**
CSF £5.44 TOTE £2.30: £1.20, £1.10, £1.30; EX 5.60 Trifecta £15.50.
Owner Hamdan Al Maktoum **Bred** Tom & Cathy Burns **Trained** Newmarket, Suffolk

FOCUS
A fair maiden. The favourite, and winning debutant, got the hang of what was required in the final furlong to run down the form horse in the closing stages in a fair comparative time. The winner looks sure to do better.

4368 GO INTERIORS & FGF FACADES H'CAP — 5f 143y
7:00 (7:02) (Class 4) (0-85,84) 3-Y-O
£5,530 (£1,645; £822; £411; £400; £400) **Stalls** Centre

Form RPR

0354 **1** **Princess Power (IRE)**[24] 3479 3-9-5 **82**..........(v1) TomEaves 3 91
(Nigel Tinkler) *hld up in tch: nt clr run and swtchd lft over 1f out: rdn to ld ins fnl f: r.o* **8/1**

-123 **2** *1¼* **Whelans Way (IRE)**[21] 3590 3-9-2 **79**.......... RobertWinston 1 84
(Roger Teal) *hld up in tch: shkn up to ld over 1f out: rdn: edgd rt and hdd ins fnl f: styd on same pce* **9/4**[1]

4064 **3** *nk* **Coolagh Magic**[14] 3844 3-8-12 **75**..........(p) StevieDonohoe 7 79
(Richard Fahey) *chsd ldr to 1/2-way: rdn and edgd lft over 1f out: r.o* **16/1**

0114 **4** *½* **Mark's Choice (IRE)**[10] 4008 3-9-6 **83**.......... JackGarritty 8 85
(Ruth Carr) *hld up: racd keenly: rdn and edgd rt over 1f out: r.o: nt rch ldrs* **11/2**

5-00 **5** *½* **Nicki's Angel (IRE)**[14] 3865 3-9-7 **84**.......... TonyHamilton 5 85
(Richard Fahey) *s.i.s: hld up: hdwy over 1f out: sn rdn: styd on same pce wl ins fnl f* **20/1**

2514 **6** *2* **Show Me The Bubbly**[36] 3045 3-8-5 **71**.......... JaneElliott(3) 2 65
(John O'Shea) *chsd ldrs: wnt 2nd 1/2-way: rdn and ev ch over 1f out: no ex ins fnl f* **14/1**

2321 **7** *2* **Abate**[10] 4010 3-8-12 **75**.......... AndrewMullen 6 62
(Adrian Nicholls) *led: rdn and hdd over 1f out: n.m.r sn after: hmpd and wknd ins fnl f* **5/2**[2]

-623 **8** *2¾* **Thegreatestshowman**[26] 3422 3-9-2 **79**..........(p) DougieCostello 9 57
(Amy Murphy) *s.i.s: hdwy 1/2-way: rdn and wknd over 1f out* **9/2**[3]

1m 6.01s (-2.09) **Going Correction** -0.25s/f (Firm) **8** Ran SP% **121.3**
Speed ratings (Par 101): **103,101,100,100,99 96,94,90**
CSF £28.14 CT £297.50 TOTE £8.70: £2.40, £1.10, £4.70; EX 29.30 Trifecta £321.60.
Owner A Killoran **Bred** Roundhill Stud **Trained** Langton, N Yorks

FOCUS
A decent 3yo sprint handicap. One of the three fillies in the race won a shade cosily in a good comparative time. The form's rated through the runner-up.

4369 JORDAN ROAD SURFACING H'CAP — 6f 2y
7:30 (7:31) (Class 4) (0-85,86) 4-Y-O+
£5,530 (£1,645; £822; £411; £400; £400) **Stalls** Centre

Form RPR

3600 **1** **Cartmell Cleave**[14] 3868 7-8-12 **76**.......... JamesSullivan 3 89
(Ruth Carr) *wnt lft s: hld up: hdwy u.p over 2f out: rdn to ld and hung lft ins fnl f: r.o* **7/2**[2]

0006 **2** *1½* **Gabrial The Devil (IRE)**[14] 3846 4-9-1 **82**.......... ConnorMurtagh(3) 8 90
(Richard Fahey) *chsd ldrs: rdn to ld over 1f out: hdd ins fnl f: styd on same pce* **8/1**

0060 **3** *2* **Roundhay Park**[24] 3480 4-9-2 **85**.......... FayeMcManoman(5) 6 87
(Nigel Tinkler) *s.i.s: sn chsng ldrs: rdn over 1f out: styd on same pce ins fnl f* **11/2**

0-35 **4** *2¼* **Normal Equilibrium**[26] 3404 9-7-13 **66** oh3..........(p) JaneElliott(3) 5 61
(Ivan Furtado) *led: rdn and hdd over 1f out: no ex ins fnl f (jockey said gelding hung left under pressure)* **25/1**

4031 **5** *nk* **Galloway Hills**[14] 3868 4-9-2 **83**..........(p) SeanDavis(3) 11 77
(Phillip Makin) *hdwy over 4f out: chsd ldr over 3f out tl rdn over 1f out: no ex ins fnl f* **3/1**[1]

0520 **6** *1¼* **Buccaneers Vault (IRE)**[14] 3868 7-9-1 **79**.......... GrahamLee 1 69
(Paul Midgley) *hmpd sn after s: hld up: rdn over 2f out: nt trble ldrs* **10/1**

-003 **7** *nk* **Captain Jameson (IRE)**[16] 3770 4-9-7 **85**.......... JasonHart 9 74
(John Quinn) *hld up: rdn over 2f out: n.d (trainer's rep said gelding was unsuited by the going and would prefer an easier surface)* **4/1**[3]

0036 **8** *1¼* **Lucky Lucky Man (IRE)**[11] 3971 4-9-3 **81**.......... TonyHamilton 7 66
(Richard Fahey) *s.i.s: nvr on terms* **11/1**

0-60 **9** *nk* **Barton Mills**[14] 3868 4-8-9 **73**.......... NathanEvans 4 57
(Michael Easterby) *chsd ldr tl pushed along over 3f out: rdn and wknd over 1f out* **40/1**

100 **10** *14* **Erissimus Maximus (FR)**[13] 3883 5-9-8 **86**..........(b) LewisEdmunds 2 25
(Amy Murphy) *stmbld and hmpd s: pushed along over 3f out: sn wknd (jockey said gelding stumbled leaving the stalls)* **16/1**

1m 10.17s (-2.53) **Going Correction** -0.25s/f (Firm) **10** Ran SP% **123.3**
Speed ratings (Par 105): **106,104,101,98,97 96,95,94,93,75**
CSF £33.94 CT £160.35 TOTE £4.20: £1.40, £2.60, £2.20; EX 32.30 Trifecta £216.60.
Owner G D C Jewell **Bred** D R Tucker **Trained** Huby, N Yorks

FOCUS
The feature contest was a good handicap. The second-favourite's winning time was notably quicker than the earlier C&D maiden. The winner found a bit on this year's form.

4370 SHIRETOILETHIRE.CO.UK H'CAP 1m 3f 197y
8:00 (8:00) (Class 5) (0-70,70) 4-Y-0+
£3,752 (£1,116; £557; £400; £400; £400) **Stalls** High

Form RPR
230 **1** **Trailboss (IRE)**[30] 3263 4-9-4 **67**....................(b[1]) StevieDonohoe 13 76+
(Ed Vaughan) *s.i.s: hld up: hdwy over 3f out: led over 2f out: rdn over 1f out: styd on wl* **4/1**[2]
5-60 **2** *2* **Contrebasse**[11] 3973 4-9-0 **63**.................... DavidAllan 4 69
(Tim Easterby) *hld up: hdwy over 3f out: rdn over 2f out: styd on* **6/1**[3]
0524 **3** *hd* **Agent Gibbs**[46] 2718 7-8-7 **63**.................... KateLeahy(7) 12 68
(John O'Shea) *led: clr 7f out tl 3f out: hdd over 2f out: rdn and hung rt ins fnl f: styd on* **8/1**
030- **4** *½* **Visor**[217] 9249 4-9-1 **64**....................(h) DanielMuscutt 1 69
(James Fanshawe) *chsd ldrs: rdn over 2f out: hmpd ins fnl f: styd on same pce* **6/1**[3]
06-0 **5** *½* **Jetstream (IRE)**[92] 1399 4-8-10 **59**....................(t) HayleyTurner 9 63
(D J Jeffreys) *stmbld s: sn hld up in tch: tk clsr order over 3f out: rdn over 1f out: edgd lft ins fnl f: styd on same pce* **10/1**
0056 **6** *½* **Flower Power**[11] 3955 8-9-1 **64**....................(p) JasonHart 8 67
(Tony Coyle) *hld up: hdwy over 2f out: rdn over 1f out: styd on same pce ins fnl f* **14/1**
-000 **7** *3* **Ad Libitum**[21] 3568 4-9-7 **70**.................... LewisEdmunds 3 68
(Roger Fell) *prom: rdn over 2f out: edgd rt and no ex ins fnl f* **8/1**
3-23 **8** *17* **Sweet Marmalade (IRE)**[32] 3200 4-9-0 **68**........ FayeMcManoman(5) 11 39
(Lawrence Mullaney) *s.i.s: hld up: rdn over 2f out: n.d* **12/1**
040- **9** *½* **Princess Nearco (IRE)**[261] 8136 5-8-7 **56**.................... PhilDennis 6 26
(Liam Bailey) *s.i.s: rdn over 3f out: n.d* **25/1**
-062 **10** *15* **Roof Garden**[26] 3429 4-9-2 **65**.................... DougieCostello 2 11
(Mark H Tompkins) *hld up in tch: lost pl over 3f out: sn wknd* **25/1**
1312 **11** *33* **Cold Harbour**[10] 4004 4-8-7 **61**....................(t) SeamusCronin(5) 7
(Robyn Brisland) *w ldr over 4f: rdn over 3f out: wknd wl over 2f out (trainer could offer no explanation for the gelding's performance)* **3/1**[1]

2m 33.18s (-3.42) **Going Correction** -0.25s/f (Firm) **11** Ran SP% **126.9**
Speed ratings (Par 103): **101,99,99,99,98 98,96,85,84,74 52**
CSF £30.97 CT £190.19 TOTE £4.70: £2.50, £2.20, £2.90; EX 24.00 Trifecta £226.00.
Owner The Open Range **Bred** Camas Park, Lynch Bages & Summerhill **Trained** Newmarket, Suffolk
■ Stewards' Enquiry : Kate Leahy two-day ban: interference & careless riding (Jul 15-16)

FOCUS
12 yards added. An ordinary middle-distance handicap, with the third as good a guide as any.

4371 THECONSTRUCTIONINDEX.CO.UK FILLIES' H'CAP 1m 2f 43y
8:30 (8:30) (Class 5) (0-70,71) 4-Y-0+
£3,752 (£1,116; £557; £400; £400; £400) **Stalls** High

Form RPR
-050 **1** **Bollin Joan**[21] 3568 4-9-0 **63**....................(p) DavidAllan 7 74
(Tim Easterby) *hld up: hdwy over 3f out: led over 1f out: rdn out (trainer said, regarding the improved form shown, the filly appreciated the return to a sounder surface)* **14/1**
6500 **2** *¾* **Destinys Rock**[24] 3473 4-8-5 **57**....................(p) GeorgiaCox(3) 3 66
(Mark Loughnane) *hld up: hdwy on outer over 2f out: rdn to chse wnr fnl f: styd on* **25/1**
1414 **3** *4* **Kilbaha Lady (IRE)**[11] 3957 5-9-4 **70**.................... RowanScott(3) 11 71
(Nigel Tinkler) *hld up: hdwy over 2f out: rdn over 1f out: styd on same pce ins fnl f* **5/1**[3]
3-54 **4** *nk* **First Dance (IRE)**[30] 3267 5-9-3 **66**.................... JamesSullivan 10 66
(Tom Tate) *s.i.s: hld up: styd on u.p fr over 1f out: nt rch ldrs* **4/1**[2]
0003 **5** *1¼* **Seek The Moon (USA)**[7] 4130 4-8-8 **57**....................(h) GrahamLee 5 55
(Lawrence Mullaney) *chsd ldrs: rdn over 2f out: styd on same pce fnl f* **9/1**
-020 **6** *3¾* **Kwanza**[40] 2911 4-8-10 **59**.................... JasonHart 12 49
(Mark Johnston) *chsd ldrs: swtchd lft 4f out: led over 2f out: rdn and hdd over 1f out: wknd ins fnl f* **8/1**
2204 **7** *2* **Ideal Candy (IRE)**[21] 3568 4-9-5 **71**.................... GemmaTutty(3) 4 57
(Karen Tutty) *led: hdd over 2f out: wknd over 1f out* **3/1**[1]
-005 **8** *nk* **Inflexiball**[11] 3959 7-8-2 **51** oh4.................... JimmyQuinn 8 37
(John Mackie) *s.i.s: hld up: hdwy over 3f out: rdn and wknd over 1f out* **33/1**
00-5 **9** *2½* **Classified (IRE)**[18] 3687 5-8-2 **54**.................... JaneElliott(3) 9 35
(Ed de Giles) *hld up: rdn and wknd over 2f out* **6/1**
3366 **10** *1¼* **Velvet Vision**[16] 3778 4-9-2 **65**.................... DougieCostello 2 43
(Mark H Tompkins) *s.s: hld up: pushed along on outer over 3f out: wknd 2f out (jockey said filly was slowly away)* **10/1**
-406 **11** *20* **Malaspina (ITY)**[128] 840 7-9-6 **69**....................(p) TomEaves 1 7
(Ivan Furtado) *chsd ldr tl over 3f out: wknd over 2f out* **22/1**
0-40 **12** *99* **Last Enchantment (IRE)**[23] 2685 4-9-7 **70**....................(t) StevieDonohoe 6
(Neil Mulholland) *prom: lost pl over 4f out: eased (jockey said filly lost its action turning into the home straight; vet said a post-race examination revealed the filly to have post race heat stress)* **20/1**

2m 8.67s (-3.63) **Going Correction** -0.25s/f (Firm) **12** Ran SP% **128.7**
Speed ratings (Par 100): **104,103,100,99,98 95,94,94,92,91 75,**
CSF £341.05 CT £2016.73 TOTE £17.70: £3.70, £8.80, £1.80; EX 573.90 Trifecta £734.20.
Owner Richard Taylor & Philip Hebdon **Bred** Habton Farms **Trained** Great Habton, N Yorks

FOCUS
12 yards added. An ordinary fillies' handicap. The winner looks back to her best.
T/Plt: £64.60 to a £1 stake. Pool: £70,846.90 - 799.63 winning units T/Qpdt: £12.60 to a £1 stake. Pool: £9,675.07 - 566.65 winning units **Colin Roberts**

4110 LINGFIELD (L-H)
Saturday, June 29

OFFICIAL GOING: Good to firm (good in places; watered)
Wind: light, behind Weather: very hot

4372 MATT HODGES STAG DO CELEBRATIONS FILLIES' H'CAP 1m 3f 133y
5:45 (5:49) (Class 5) (0-70,71) 3-Y-0
£3,752 (£1,116; £557; £400; £400; £400) **Stalls** High

Form RPR
000- **1** **Whistler Bowl**[224] 9122 3-8-8 **57**.................... JoeyHaynes 7 67
(Gary Moore) *chsd ldr tl 8f out: styd trcking ldrs tl effrt to ld and hung lft 2f out: r.o wl and drew clr fnl f: comf (trainer said, regarding the improved form shown, the filly benefitted from a break and strengthening over the winter)* **16/1**
0003 **2** *3¾* **Born Leader (FR)**[21] 3593 3-8-5 **54**.................... HollieDoyle 1 58
(Hughie Morrison) *restless in stalls: chsd ldrs: effrt and ev ch ent fnl 2f: sltly impeded 2f out and unable to match pce of wnr over 1f out: no ch w wnr but kpt on to go 2nd again ins fnl f* **3/1**[2]
533- **3** *¾* **Fearlessly (IRE)**[226] 9074 3-9-8 **71**.................... OisinMurphy 4 74
(Roger Varian) *in tch in midfield: effrt on inner to chal ent fnl 2f: sltly impeded sn after and unable to match wnr over 1f out: kpt on same pce and lost 2nd ins fnl f* **15/8**[1]
0331 **4** *2¾* **Stone Cougar (USA)**[9] 4038 3-9-1 **64**.................... ConnorBeasley 8 62
(Mark Johnston) *restless in stalls: in tch in midfield: effrt in centre ent fnl 3f: styd on ins fnl f: nvr trbld ldrs* **3/1**[2]
0120 **5** *½* **Vin D'Honneur (IRE)**[16] 3777 3-8-7 **59**....................(t[1]) WilliamCox(3) 2 57
(Stuart Williams) *led: rdn: hdd and sltly impeded 2f out: sn outpcd and wl hld 4th 1f out: wknd ins fnl f* **25/1**
640- **6** *shd* **Hidden Pearl**[194] 9590 3-9-7 **70**.................... LiamKeniry 10 67
(Ed Walker) *t.k.h: chsd ldrs: effrt over 2f out: unable qck and btn over 1f out: plugged on* **20/1**
-600 **7** *nse* **Petits Fours**[21] 3594 3-8-8 **60**....................(h) FinleyMarsh(3) 6 57
(Charlie Fellowes) *hld up in last trio: effrt over 2f out: racd awkwardly and no imp: kpt on ins fnl f: nvr trbld ldrs* **9/1**[3]
456- **8** *10* **Accredited**[255] 8311 3-9-3 **66**.................... JohnFahy 9 47
(David Flood) *wd in midfield: hdwy to chse ldr 8f out tl over 2f out: sn lost pl u.p: wknd over 1f out* **40/1**
6600 **9** *nse* **Matilda Bay (IRE)**[29] 3299 3-8-2 **51** oh3....................(b[1]) NicolaCurrie 5 32
(Jamie Osborne) *s.i.s: a in rr: rdn and struggling on downhill run over 3f out: no ch fnl 2f* **50/1**
500 **10** *4½* **Plissken**[27] 3372 3-8-12 **61**....................(h) KieranO'Neill 3 35
(Tom Clover) *a towards rr: rdn 3f out: sn btn and bhd over 1f out* **14/1**

2m 29.42s (-4.58) **Going Correction** -0.275s/f (Firm) **10** Ran SP% **120.3**
Speed ratings (Par 96): **104,101,101,99,98 98,98,92,92,89**
CSF £63.92 CT £138.17 TOTE £20.30: £4.00, £1.50, £1.10; EX 122.70 Trifecta £445.30.
Owner Chris Stedman **Bred** C E Stedman **Trained** Lower Beeding, W Sussex

FOCUS
Add 3yds. A drying day and the going was changed to good to firm, good in places. An uneven tempo to this fillies' handicap but with three unexposed sorts drawing clear it is probably form to take a positive view of. The race has been rated at face value.

4373 VISIT ATTHERACES.COM EBF NOVICE STKS 4f 217y
6:15 (6:20) (Class 5) 2-Y-0 **£3,752** (£1,116; £557; £278) **Stalls** Centre

Form RPR
32 **1** **Raahy**[12] 3943 2-9-5 .... PatCosgrave 8 87+
(George Scott) *mde all: shkn up and asserted over 1f out: r.o wl: comf* **5/6**[1]
2 *4* **X Force (IRE)** 2-9-5 .... OisinMurphy 7 75+
(Archie Watson) *chsd ldrs: effrt to chse wnr wl over 1f out: sn outpcd and kpt on same pce fnl f* **9/4**[2]
20 **3** *1¼* **Cool Sphere (USA)**[9] 4012 2-9-5 .... LouisSteward 3 71+
(Robert Cowell) *hld up in tch in midfield: effrt ent fnl 2f: wnt 3rd 1f out: nvr any ch w wnr and one pce after* **4/1**[3]
001 **4** *2¼* **Shani**[20] 3634 2-9-0 66.................... KieranO'Neill 9 60
(John Bridger) *chsd ldrs: rdn: outpcd and hung lft jst over 2f out: no ch w wnr but plugged on fnl f* **25/1**
05 **5** *1¼* **Prissy Missy (IRE)**[18] 3679 2-9-0 .... DavidProbert 4 56
(David Loughnane) *chsd ldr: shkn up and hung lft ent fnl f: sn lost pl and wknd fnl f* **50/1**
6 *8* **Glamorous Force** 2-9-5 .... EoinWalsh 2 37
(Ronald Harris) *rn green: in tch in midfield: struggling and hung lft over 2f out: sn btn and fdd ins fnl f* **40/1**
05 **7** *2½* **Crime Of Passion (IRE)**[30] 3259 2-9-0 .... NicolaCurrie 10 24
(Jamie Osborne) *sn outpcd: no ch 1/2-way (jockey said filly was never travelling)* **20/1**
8 *2* **Itoldyoutobackit (IRE)** 2-9-5 .... LiamKeniry 6 23
(Jonjo O'Neill) *v s.i.s: rn green and nvr on terms* **20/1**
60 **9** *3¼* **Shaun's Delight (IRE)**[18] 3695 2-9-5 .... NickyMackay 1 14
(Ronald Harris) *broke on terms but sn struggling: outpcd over 3f out: no ch 1/2-way* **100/1**

56.94s (-1.76) **Going Correction** -0.275s/f (Firm) **9** Ran SP% **124.1**
Speed ratings (Par 93): **103,96,94,91,89 76,72,69,63**
CSF £3.01 TOTE £1.80: £1.10, £1.20, £1.20; EX 3.90 Trifecta £7.00.
Owner Fawzi Abdulla Nass **Bred** Haddenham Stud Farm Ltd **Trained** Newmarket, Suffolk
■ Dark Side Prince was withdrawn. Price at time of withdrawal 100/1. Rule 4 does not apply

FOCUS
A drying day and the going was changed to good to firm, good in places.\n\x\x Only three mattered in the betting and the race itself was one-way traffic, the favourite coming home clear from a favourable draw. Straightforward form, the winner rated a minor improver.

4374 DARSEY CELEBRATION H'CAP 4f 217y
6:45 (6:49) (Class 5) (0-75,75) 3-Y-0+
£3,752 (£1,116; £557; £400; £400; £400) **Stalls** Centre

Form RPR
0150 **1** **Key To Power**[7] 4128 3-9-6 **75**.................... ConnorBeasley 1 81
(Mark Johnston) *chsd ldr: rdn and clsd to ld ent fnl f: hrd pressed 100yds out: hld on gamely u.p towards fin* **5/1**[3]
-055 **2** *nk* **Secretfact**[14] 3856 6-9-9 **72**.................... FergusSweeney 3 79
(Malcolm Saunders) *t.k.h: hld up in tch in last trio: clsd: nt clr run and hmpd over 1f out: swtchd lft and hdwy 1f out: sn chsng wnr and str chal 100yds out: hld towards fin* **7/1**

-111 **3** *1½* **Spanish Star (IRE)**[22] 3543 4-9-12 **75** ... LiamKeniry 8 77+
(Patrick Chamings) *stdd s: hld up in tch in rr: clsd on stands' rail over 1f out: nt clr run and swtchd lft ins fnl f: r.o strly fnl 100yds: nvr getting to ldrs* **2/1**[1]

2-05 **4** *hd* **Roundabout Magic (IRE)**[9] 4027 5-9-1 **64** ... NickyMackay 5 65
(Simon Dow) *stdd s: hld up in tch in last trio: swtchd lft and effrt 2f out: hdwy and rdn to chse ldrs whn hung rt 1f out: no ex and one pce fnl 100yds* **16/1**

0-00 **5** *nse* **Silverrica (IRE)**[3] 4230 9-9-2 **65** ... (t[1]) DavidProbert 6 66
(Malcolm Saunders) *broke wl: sn restrained and chsd ldrs: effrt wl over 1f out: chsd ldrs 1f out: no ex and one pce ins fnl f* **16/1**

4026 **6** *1* **Enthaar**[2] 4301 4-9-2 **72** ... (t) MarcoGhiani(7) 4 69
(Stuart Williams) *midfield: lost pl 1/2-way: swtchd lft and effrt wl over 1f out: swtchd rt again and kpt on ins fnl f* **3/1**[2]

0-00 **7** *¾* **Flowing Clarets**[11] 3961 6-8-7 **56** oh3 ... HollieDoyle 9 50
(John Bridger) *taken down early: chsd ldrs tl unable qck and edgd lft over 1f out: hld and one pce fnl f* **28/1**

6606 **8** *2* **Arzaak (IRE)**[60] 2227 5-9-11 **74** ... (b) OisinMurphy 2 61
(Charlie Wallis) *in tch in midfield: effrt 2f out: chsng ldrs but struggling to qckn whn squeezed for room and hmpd 1f out: n.d after* **12/1**

60-0 **9** *shd* **Country Rose (IRE)**[26] 3422 3-9-6 **75** ... (h) KieranO'Neill 7 60
(Ronald Harris) *sn led: rdn and hdd ent fnl f: no ex and wknd ins fnl f* **12/1**

56.98s (-1.72) **Going Correction** -0.275s/f (Firm)
WFA 3 from 4yo+ 6lb **9** Ran **SP% 118.1**
Speed ratings (Par 103): **102,101,99,98,98 97,95,92,92**
CSF £40.77 CT £93.60 TOTE £2.80: £2.50, £2.40, £1.20; EX 49.50 Trifecta £177.70.
Owner Sheikh Hamdan bin Mohammed Al Maktoum **Bred** Godolphin **Trained** Middleham Moor, N Yorks

FOCUS
A drying day and the going was changed to good to firm, good in places.\n\x\x A run of the mill sprint handicap, run at a strong early pace, and the winner did well to overcome stall 1. She's rated back to her Brighton win.

4375 SILK SERIES LADY RIDERS' H'CAP (PRO-AM LADY RIDERS) 4f 217y

7:15 (7:15) (Class 4) (0-85,84) 3-Y-O+ **£4,690** (£1,395; £697; £348) **Stalls** Centre

Form RPR

6115 **1** **Peggie Sue**[7] 4105 4-10-5 **82** ... NicolaCurrie 2 87
(Adam West) *chsd ldng pair: effrt over 1f out: hdwy to chse ldr 1f out: led wl ins fnl f: styd on strly* **11/2**[3]

2420 **2** *1¼* **Bowson Fred**[40] 2910 7-9-10 **78** ... MissJoannaMason(5) 5 79
(Michael Easterby) *mounted on crse and taken down early: w ldr and sn clr: led 1/2-way: shkn up 2f out: rdn over 1f out: hdd and no ex wl ins fnl f* **11/4**[2]

-315 **3** *2* **Shining**[26] 3422 3-9-3 **79** ... IsobelFrancis(7) 3 70
(Jim Boyle) *sn led and clr w runner-up: hdd 1/2-way: hung lft and unable qck over 1f out: hld and one pce fnl f* **9/1**

1211 **4** *3¾* **Inspired Thought (IRE)**[17] 3719 3-10-1 **84** ... HollieDoyle 4 62
(Archie Watson) *s.i.s: bhd and niggled along: effrt 2f out: no imp over 1f out: wl hld and edgd lft ins fnl f (jockey said filly was never travelling)* **4/5**[1]

57.07s (-1.63) **Going Correction** -0.275s/f (Firm)
WFA 3 from 4yo+ 6lb **4** Ran **SP% 107.6**
Speed ratings (Par 105): **102,100,96,90**
CSF £19.47 TOTE £5.60; EX 16.60 Trifecta £29.10.
Owner West Racing Partnership **Bred** Sean Gollogly **Trained** Epsom, Surrey

FOCUS
A drying day and the going was changed to good to firm, good in places.\n\x\x A modest race for the grade and with the odds-on favourite underperforming, this doesn't look form to take a strong view of. The winner's rated to a better view of her Nottingham win.

4376 D-DAY 75 CLASSIFIED STKS 6f

7:45 (7:52) (Class 6) 3-Y-O+
£3,105 (£924; £461; £400; £400; £400) **Stalls** Centre

Form RPR

0545 **1** **Hello Girl**[17] 3738 4-9-7 50 ... OisinMurphy 7 59
(Nigel Tinkler) *chsd ldr: effrt to chse ldr over 1f out: rdn to ld ent fnl f: styd on* **6/4**[1]

-000 **2** *1¼* **Gold Club**[47] 2693 8-9-0 49 ... GeorgiaDobie(7) 17 55
(Lee Carter) *chsd ldrs tl led 2f out: hung lft over 1f out: hdd ent fnl f: kpt on same pce ins fnl f* **16/1**

6560 **3** *3¾* **Pharoh Jake**[9] 4027 11-9-7 48 ... KieranO'Neill 2 44
(John Bridger) *racd in centre: midfield: rdn over 2f out: chsd clr ldng pair 1f out: no imp but hung on for 3rd wl ins fnl f* **40/1**

0603 **4** *½* **The Special One (IRE)**[8] 4074 6-9-0 48 ... (t) GraceMcEntee(7) 15 44
(Phil McEntee) *in tch in rr: effrt u.p over 1f out: nt clr run and hmpd 1f out: styd on fnl 100yds: nvr trbld ldrs* **12/1**

4303 **5** *shd* **Three C's (IRE)**[28] 3352 5-9-7 50 ... (p) HollieDoyle 16 42
(Adrian Wintle) *chsd ldr tl jst over 2f out: unable qck u.p over 1f out: wl hld and kpt on same pce ins fnl f* **3/1**[2]

0606 **6** *nk* **Thedevilinneville**[8] 4078 3-9-0 46 ... (p) EoinWalsh 18 39
(Adam West) *led rdrless to post: dwlt and early reminder: towards rr: hdwy u.p and hung lft 1f out: kpt on but no ch w ldrs* **16/1**

05-0 **7** *1¾* **Sandkissed (IRE)**[24] 3475 4-9-4 46 ... (p) GabrieleMalune(3) 8 36
(Amy Murphy) *led: rdn: hung lft and hdd 2f out: edgd rt and no ex over 1f out: wknd ins fnl f (jockeys said filly hung both ways under pressure)* **16/1**

00 **8** *½* **Breathoffreshair**[29] 3304 5-9-7 47 ... (tp) PhilipPrince 14 35
(Richard Guest) *midfield: losing pl whn squeezed for room over 3f out: in rr and rdn 1/2-way: modest late hdwy but no ch w ldrs* **20/1**

3640 **9** *nk* **Classy Cailin (IRE)**[28] 3352 4-9-7 50 ... (p[1]) DavidProbert 13 34
(Pam Sly) *taken down early: hld up in tch: clsd whn nt clr run 2f out: edgd out lft and hdwy u.p over 1f out: no imp 150yds out and sn wknd* **5/1**[3]

00-0 **10** *nk* **Crimson Princess**[28] 3352 4-9-7 44 ... JohnFahy 3 33
(Nikki Evans) *racd in centre: midfield: rdn ent fnl 2f: no imp: nvr involved* **66/1**

-000 **11** *2* **Solesmes**[29] 3319 3-9-0 50 ... DaneO'Neill 12 28
(Tony Newcombe) *mounted in chute: hld up in tch: clsd whn nt clr run and hmpd 2f out: effrt over 1f out: no prog: wl hld and eased wl ins fnl f* **25/1**

00-0 **12** *shd* **Loving Life (IRE)**[11] 3964 3-9-0 41 ... LiamKeniry 5 24
(Martin Bosley) *hld up towards rr: nt clr run 2f out: pushed along over 1f out: reminder and no imp ins fnl f* **40/1**

0040 **13** *14* **Anglesey Penny**[13] 3887 3-9-0 43 ... (v[1]) DannyBrock 10
(J R Jenkins) *chsd ldrs: struggling whn hung lft ent fnl 2f: sn lost pl: bhd and virtually p.u wl ins fnl f* **40/1**

4000 **R** **Dandilion (IRE)**[29] 3320 6-9-7 50 ... (t[1]) NicolaCurrie 9
(Alex Hales) *ref to r* **16/1**

1m 10.22s (-1.28) **Going Correction** -0.275s/f (Firm)
WFA 3 from 4yo+ 7lb **14** Ran **SP% 130.3**
Speed ratings (Par 101): **97,95,90,89,89 89,86,86,85,85 82,82,63,**
CSF £31.35 TOTE £2.40: £1.30, £5.40, £8.60; EX 41.50 Trifecta £2314.00.
Owner A Chapman **Bred** Max Weston **Trained** Langton, N Yorks

FOCUS
A drying day and the going was changed to good to firm, good in places.\n\x\x Low-grade fare, with the well-backed favourite obliging with the minimum of fuss. Not really a race to be making excuses for those in behind.

4377 WITHEFORD EQUINE BARRIER TRIALS 2ND JULY NOVICE MEDIAN AUCTION STKS 7f

8:15 (8:20) (Class 6) 3-5-Y-O **£3,105** (£924; £461; £230) **Stalls** Centre

Form RPR

2-36 **1** **Alfred Boucher**[24] 3465 3-9-1 80 ... DavidProbert 7 79
(Henry Candy) *led tl over 5f out: pressed ldr tl led again 2f out: edgd rt u.p over 1f out: forged ahd ins fnl f: styd on wl* **5/6**[1]

-422 **2** *1* **Voltaic**[28] 3353 3-9-1 75 ... RaulDaSilva 6 76
(Paul Cole) *trckd ldrs: squeezed through on stands' rail 2f out and chsd wnr: drvn and ev ch 1f out: no ex and jst outpcd fnl 100yds* **6/1**[3]

31 **3** *3¾* **Tabassor (IRE)**[39] 2932 3-9-2 0 ... DaneO'Neill 9 67
(Charles Hills) *w ldr tl led over 5f out: hdd: edgd rt and jostled 2f out: 3rd and outpcd over 1f out: wl hld and one pce fnl f* **5/2**[2]

6-5 **4** *1¼* **Young Bernie**[24] 3464 4-9-7 0 ... WilliamCox(3) 3 66
(Andrew Balding) *stdd s: t.k.h: hld up in last pair: clsd over 2f out: 4th and no imp over 1f out: wl hld and one pce fnl f* **20/1**

1 **5** *4½* **Elzaam's Dream (IRE)**[19] 3645 3-8-10 0 ... (h) KieranO'Neill 5 45
(Ronald Harris) *t.k.h: hld up wl in tch in midfield: edgd out lft and effrt jst over 2f out: sn struggling and wl btn over 1f out* **33/1**

6 *7* **Crochet (USA)** 3-8-10 0 ... OisinMurphy 4 26
(Hugo Palmer) *s.i.s: rn green and pushed along early: in tch in last pair: rdn jst over 2f out: sn outpcd and wknd over 1f out* **8/1**

00- **7** *11* **And Yet She Moves (IRE)**[382] 3700 3-8-10 0 ... EoinWalsh 2
(Adam West) *chsd ldrs tl 3f out: sn u.p: edgd lft and lost pl: wl bhd over 1f out* **100/1**

1m 22.15s (-2.15) **Going Correction** -0.275s/f (Firm)
WFA 3 from 4yo 9lb **7** Ran **SP% 117.2**
Speed ratings (Par 101): **101,99,95,94,89 81,68**
CSF £6.93 TOTE £1.60: £1.20, £2.50; EX 6.20 Trifecta £11.60.
Owner Robert Allcock **Bred** Robert Allcock **Trained** Kingston Warren, Oxon

FOCUS
A drying day and the going was changed to good to firm, good in places.\n\x\x Little depth in this novice auction race and the well-backed favourite obliged at the sixth time of asking.

4378 RACING WELFARE RACING STAFF WEEK H'CAP 7f

8:45 (8:50) (Class 6) (0-65,65) 3-Y-O+
£3,105 (£924; £461; £400; £400; £400) **Stalls** Centre

Form RPR

000- **1** **Kendergarten Kop (IRE)**[255] 8317 4-9-10 **59** ... DavidProbert 5 65
(David Flood) *hld up in tch in midfield: effrt ent fnl 2f: clsd u.p to chse ldrs 1f out: styd on to ld last strides: all out* **16/1**

5440 **2** *nse* **Foreign Legion (IRE)**[7] 4123 4-9-13 **62** ... (p) NickyMackay 14 68
(Luke McJannet) *chsd ldr: rdn over 2f out: drvn and pressing ldr over 1f out: ev ch and maintained chal ins fnl f: jst hld on post* **8/1**

0-60 **3** *hd* **Flying Sakhee**[28] 3352 6-8-11 **46** ... (v[1]) KieranO'Neill 12 51
(John Bridger) *hld up in tch: effrt and hdwy over 2f out: drvn to ld over 1f out: kpt on u.p tl hdd and lost 2 pls last strides* **50/1**

2132 **4** *¾* **Your Mothers' Eyes**[11] 3964 3-9-0 **63** ... (p) DarraghKeenan(5) 16 63
(Alan Bailey) *chsd ldrs: rdn to ld 2f out: sn hdd: pressing ldrs and kpt on same pce ins fnl f* **3/1**[1]

000- **5** *½* **Captain Sedgwick (IRE)**[220] 9180 5-8-12 **47** ... RyanTate 8 49
(John Spearing) *taken down early: effrt over 2f out: clsd u.p over 1f out: chsd ldrs and kpt on same pce ins fnl f* **33/1**

6202 **6** *½* **Stay Forever (FR)**[13] 3887 3-9-7 **65** ... OisinMurphy 18 63
(Andrew Balding) *wl in tch in midfield: effrt ent fnl 2f: kpt on same pce u.p ins fnl f* **7/2**[2]

0-01 **7** *2½* **Song Of The Isles (IRE)**[28] 3354 3-8-13 **64** ... EllieMacKenzie(7) 10 55
(Heather Main) *chsd ldrs: effrt jst over 2f out: no ex u.p 1f out: wknd ins fnl f* **9/2**[3]

0300 **8** *1¼* **Swiss Cross**[26] 3410 12-8-10 **45** ... (tp) HollieDoyle 3 35
(Phil McEntee) *towards rr: effrt jst over 2f out: hdwy u.p over 1f out: kpt on ins fnl f: nvr trbld ldrs* **33/1**

200/ **9** *1¼* **Miss Icon**[589] 8818 5-9-7 **56** ... LiamKeniry 7 43
(Patrick Chamings) *in tch in midfield: u.p over 2f out: drvn and no imp over 1f out: kpt on same pce ins fnl f* **25/1**

5 **10** *2¾* **War Advocate (IRE)**[27] 3382 4-9-5 **61** ... (bt) CierenFallon(7) 6 41
(Adrian Paul Keatley, Ire) *hld up towards rr: effrt jst over 2f out: hung lft u.p over 1f out: sme late hdwy: nvr involved (jockey said gelding was never travelling)* **11/1**

0003 **11** *¾* **Stand Firm (IRE)**[18] 3687 4-8-12 **47** ... (v) RaulDaSilva 15 25
(Robert Cowell) *sn outpcd and detached in last: hung lft across the crse over 2f out: sme late hdwy: nvr involved (jockey said gelding was slowly away and never travelling)* **12/1**

5050 **12** *nk* **More Salutes (IRE)**[70] 1933 4-8-7 **45** ... WilliamCox(3) 1 22
(Michael Attwater) *midfield: u.p over 2f out: unable qck and btn over 1f out: wknd ins fnl f* **66/1**

0000 **13** *5* **Air Hair Lair (IRE)**[7] 4092 3-9-4 **62** ... KierenFox 11 22
(Sheena West) *midfield: rdn wl over 2f out: sn struggling and lost pl: wl hld over 1f out: wknd ins fnl f* **8/1**

2300 **14** *½* **Amor Kethley**[41] 2870 3-8-13 **60** ... (bt[1]) GabrieleMalune(3) 13 19
(Amy Murphy) *led: hdd and drvn 2f out: sn outpcd and wknd ins fnl f* **25/1**

550- **15** *10* **Capala (IRE)**[212] 9307 3-9-3 **61** ... EoinWalsh 17
(Adam West) *midfield: lost pl and bhd over 2f out: wl bhd and eased ins fnl f (trainer's rep said gelding was unsuited by the going and would prefer an easier surface)* **25/1**

5-05 **16** *21* **Raise A Little Joy**[9] 4026 4-8-10 **45** ... (p) DannyBrock 9
(J R Jenkins) *tch in rdn over 2f out: sn struggling and lost pl: wl bhd and eased ins fnl f* **50/1**

1m 22.55s (-1.75) **Going Correction** -0.275s/f (Firm)
WFA 3 from 4yo+ 9lb **16** Ran **SP% 132.4**
Speed ratings (Par 101): **99,98,98,97,97 96,93,92,91,87 87,86,80,80,68 44**
CSF £140.87 CT £6498.90 TOTE £16.90: £4.10, £2.50, £7.60, £1.20; EX 187.00 Trifecta £1949.20.
Owner Mrs Anne Cowley **Bred** Kildaragh Stud **Trained** Chiseldon, Wiltshire

■ Stewards' Enquiry : Ryan Tate two-day ban: used whip without time to respond (Jul 15-16)
Nicky Mackay two-day ban: used whip above the permitted level (Jul 15-16)

FOCUS

A drying day and the going was changed to good to firm, good in places.\n\x\x A big field to round off proceedings and a slow-motion ending, the winner scrambling home in a blanket finish.
T/Plt: £70.30 to a £1 stake. Pool: £62,666.12 - 649.94 winning units T/Qpdt: £41.30 to a £1 stake. Pool: £7,139.22 - 127.79 winning units **Steve Payne**

4329 **NEWCASTLE (A.W)** (L-H)

Saturday, June 29

OFFICIAL GOING: Tapeta: standard to slow

Wind: Breezy, half behind in races on the straight course and in over 3f of home straight in races on the Weather: Overcast, humid

4379 BETFAIR EXCHANGE H'CAP — 6f (Tp)

1:50 (1:51) (Class 2) (0-100,97) 3-Y-0+

£15,562 (£4,660; £2,330; £1,165; £582; £292) **Stalls** Centre

Form / RPR

3000 **1** **Staxton**[14] 3863 4-9-12 **95**.........(p) DuranFentiman 10 105
(Tim Easterby) *cl up towards centre of gp: rdn to ld over 1f out: kpt on strly fnl f* **15/2**

5-24 **2** 1 ½ **Cosmic Law (IRE)**[14] 3865 3-9-7 **97**......... PJMcDonald 13 100
(Richard Fahey) *hld up on nr side of gp: rdn over 2f out: hdwy over 1f out: chsd wnr ins fnl f: r.o* **5/1**[1]

1610 **3** ½ **Katheefa (USA)**[18] 3706 5-8-10 **84**......... HarrisonShaw(5) 7 87
(Ruth Carr) *dwlt: sn trcking ldrs on far side of gp: effrt and rdn over 1f out: kpt on same pce ins fnl f* **18/1**

3654 **4** ½ **Giogiobbo**[23] 3492 6-9-4 **87**.........(b) BenCurtis 6 89
(Nick Littmoden) *led in centre of gp: drvn and hdd over 1f out: kpt on same pce ins fnl f* **16/1**

0516 **5** *hd* **Brian The Snail (IRE)**[16] 3770 5-9-8 **91**......... PaulHanagan 1 92
(Richard Fahey) *towards rr on far side of gp: drvn and outpcd 1/2-way: rallied over 1f out: kpt on fnl f: nt pce to chal* **11/1**

0000 **6** 1 ¼ **Von Blucher (IRE)**[7] 4127 6-9-1 **84**.........(b[1]) CliffordLee 4 81
(Rebecca Menzies) *hld up in centre of gp: drvn along over 2f out: kpt on fnl f: nvr able to chal* **9/1**

2040 **7** ¾ **Deep Intrigue**[35] 3075 3-9-3 **93**......... SilvestreDeSousa 14 86
(Mark Johnston) *hld up on nr side of gp: rdn and outpcd over 2f out: n.d after* **11/2**[2]

0-00 **8** 1 ¼ **Arecibo (FR)**[45] 2743 4-9-11 **94**......... JasonWatson 8 85
(David O'Meara) *cl up in centre of gp: rdn over 2f out: wknd over 1f out* **18/1**

1340 **9** *shd* **Mokaatil**[28] 3344 4-9-3 **86**......... KerrinMcEvoy 12 76
(Ian Williams) *towards rr on nr side of gp: struggling over 2f out: sn btn* **12/1**

-031 **10** 2 ¼ **Dalton**[16] 3770 5-9-4 **87**......... GrahamLee 9 70
(Julie Camacho) *midfield in centre of gp: outpcd over 2f out: sn btn* **6/1**[3]

-011 **11** *nk* **Air Raid**[17] 3722 4-9-12 **95**......... JackGarritty 3 77
(Jedd O'Keeffe) *prom on far side of gp tl rdn and wknd over 1f out (trainer said gelding was unsuited by the slow surface)* **6/1**[3]

36-0 **12** 1 ½ **Fuente**[14] 3865 3-9-2 **92**......... KieranShoemark 2 67
(Keith Dalgleish) *dwlt: bhd on far side of gp: struggling 1/2-way: nvr on terms (jockey said colt lost his action)* **28/1**

1m 11.24s (-1.26) **Going Correction** +0.175s/f (Slow)
WFA 3 from 4yo+ 7lb **12 Ran SP% 118.3**
Speed ratings (Par 109): **115,113,112,111,111 109,108,107,106,103 103,101**
CSF £44.70 CT £669.02 TOTE £7.80: £2.20, £2.40, £4.20; EX 42.30 Trifecta £582.60.
Owner Ontoawinner 10 & Partner **Bred** B & B Equine Limited **Trained** Great Habton, N Yorks

FOCUS

In baking hot conditions the track was described as standard to slow; it had been rolled & 'Gallopmastered' three times the previous day and again before racing, and after the fifth race, to assist in tightening up the surface. The top weights in this opening sprint were rated 7lb below the race ceiling and, with the pace not looking strong, few got into it. The runner-up is rated close to his solid latest form.

4380 BETFAIR EXCHANGE CHIPCHASE STKS (GROUP 3) — 6f (Tp)

2:25 (2:25) (Class 1) 3-Y-0+

£39,697 (£15,050; £7,532; £3,752; £1,883; £945) **Stalls** Centre

Form / RPR

-110 **1** **Invincible Army (IRE)**[7] 4094 4-9-8 115......... PJMcDonald 2 118
(James Tate) *mde all: pushed along over 1f out: kpt on strly fnl f* **10/11**[1]

4-43 **2** 2 ¼ **Laugh A Minute**[49] 2614 4-9-3 105......... AndreaAtzeni 6 106
(Roger Varian) *hld up in tch: effrt over 2f out: chsd wnr over 1f out: kpt on fnl f: nt pce to chal* **5/1**[2]

2265 **3** ½ **Island Of Life (USA)**[10] 3994 5-9-0 99.........(tp) KerrinMcEvoy 4 101
(William Haggas) *hld up: rdn and outpcd over 2f out: rallied fnl f: kpt on: nrst fin* **8/1**[3]

01-0 **4** 1 **Encrypted**[71] 1919 4-9-3 105......... BenCurtis 7 101
(Hugo Palmer) *pressed wnr to over 1f out: drvn and no ex fnl f* **16/1**

0000 **5** 1 ½ **Above The Rest (IRE)**[14] 3863 8-9-3 107.........(h) CliffordLee 1 96
(David Barron) *chsd ldrs: rdn over 2f out: wknd over 1f out* **11/1**

12-1 **6** *nse* **Mr Lupton (IRE)**[35] 3103 6-9-8 111......... PaulHanagan 3 101
(Richard Fahey) *hld up: rdn and outpcd over 2f out: n.d after* **5/1**[2]

1m 11.33s (-1.17) **Going Correction** +0.175s/f (Slow) **6 Ran SP% 111.0**
Speed ratings (Par 113): **114,111,110,109,107 106**
CSF £5.66 TOTE £1.60: £1.30, £1.80; EX 5.90 Trifecta £23.50.
Owner Saeed Manana **Bred** Rabbah Bloodstock Limited **Trained** Newmarket, Suffolk

FOCUS

There were no confirmed front-runners in this small field so the winner was able to set a steady looking early pace and the final time was 0.09sec slower than the preceding handicap. The form looks straightforward.

4381 BETFAIR EXCHANGE NORTHUMBERLAND VASE H'CAP (CONSOLATION RACE FOR THE NORTHUMBERLAND PLATE) — 2m 56y (Tp)

3:00 (3:00) (Class 2) 3-Y-0+

£46,687 (£13,980; £6,990; £3,495; £1,747; £877) **Stalls** Low

Form / RPR

-211 **1** **Carnwennan (IRE)**[33] 3145 4-9-3 **87**......... StevieDonohoe 5 99+
(Charlie Fellowes) *hld up in tch: smooth hdwy to ld over 2f out: clr and pushed along whn edgd lft over 1f out: kpt on strly fnl f* **7/2**[1]

-310 **2** 3 ½ **Rare Groove (IRE)**[45] 2742 4-9-10 **94**......... PJMcDonald 10 101
(Jedd O'Keeffe) *hld up in midfield: rdn over 3f out: hung lft and hdwy to chse (clr) wnr over 1f out: kpt on fnl f: nt pce to chal* **6/1**[3]

-215 **3** 1 ¾ **Coeur De Lion**[11] 3952 6-9-4 **93**.........(p) ThoreHammerHansen(5) 7 98
(Alan King) *hld up on outside: rdn and outpcd over 3f out: rallied on outside 2f out: kpt on fnl f: nrst fin* **7/1**

04/0 **4** ½ **Seamour (IRE)**[71] 1927 8-9-6 **93**......... BenRobinson(3) 4 97
(Brian Ellison) *hld up on ins: gd hdwy to chse ldrs 2f out: kpt on same pce ins fnl f* **16/1**

2100 **5** 1 ¾ **Theglasgowwarrior**[7] 4102 5-9-7 **91**......... AlistairRawlinson 9 93
(Jim Goldie) *hld up: rdn along over 2f out: hdwy over 1f out: kpt on fnl f: nvr able to chal* **12/1**

1356 **6** 1 ¾ **Busy Street**[35] 3081 7-9-5 **94**......... TheodoreLadd(5) 6 94
(Michael Appleby) *in tch: drvn along over 2f out: wknd over 1f out* **14/1**

0-32 **7** 1 ¼ **Always Resolute**[24] 3481 8-8-4 **74**.........(v) DuranFentiman 1 73
(Ian Williams) *hld up: rdn over 3f out: hdwy over 1f out: no imp* **25/1**

260 **8** 2 **Glan Y Gors (IRE)**[19] 3653 7-8-10 **80** ow3.........(b) CliffordLee 3 76
(David Thompson) *plld hrd in midfield: drvn along 3f out: no imp fr 2f out* **50/1**

14-0 **9** ¾ **Canford Heights (IRE)**[24] 3466 4-9-6 **90**......... TomMarquand 12 85
(William Haggas) *led to over 2f out: rdn and wknd over 1f out* **9/2**[2]

-410 **10** 4 **Lissitzky (IRE)**[21] 3600 4-9-1 **85**......... SilvestreDeSousa 8 76
(Andrew Balding) *hld up: drvn and outpcd over 3f out: n.d after* **6/1**[3]

-041 **11** ¾ **Michael's Mount**[19] 3653 6-9-1 **85** 5ex......... KerrinMcEvoy 15 75
(Ian Williams) *trckd ldr tl lost pl over 2f out: sn struggling* **12/1**

/334 **12** 42 **Desert Point (FR)**[23] 3514 7-9-0 **84**......... KieranShoemark 14 23
(Keith Dalgleish) *hld up in midfield on outside: rdn 4f out: wknd over 2f out: lost tch and eased over 1f out: t.o* **28/1**

-240 **13** 32 **Exceeding Power**[24] 3466 8-9-8 **92**......... LukeMorris 13
(Martin Bosley) *prom tl rdn and wknd over 1f out: lost tch and eased over 1f out: t.o* **50/1**

1300 **14** 18 **Stamford Raffles**[43] 2801 6-9-4 **91**......... PaddyBradley(3) 11
(Jane Chapple-Hyam) *chsd ldrs tl lost pl over 2f out: sn struggling: lost tch and eased over 1f out: t.o (jockey said gelding stopped quickly)* **25/1**

2045 **P** **Suegioo (FR)**[6] 4146 10-9-1 **85**.........(v) PaulHanagan 2
(Ian Williams) *slowly away: rel to r and sn t.o: p.u after 2f* **33/1**

3m 32.97s (-2.03) **Going Correction** +0.175s/f (Slow) **15 Ran SP% 127.4**
Speed ratings (Par 109): **112,110,109,109,108 107,106,105,105,103 103,82,66,57,**
CSF £23.84 CT £146.93 TOTE £4.10: £1.70, £2.60, £2.90; EX 27.00 Trifecta £133.00.
Owner Dr Vincent K F Kong **Bred** Brian Williamson **Trained** Newmarket, Suffolk
■ Stewards' Enquiry : Ben Robinson two-day ban: used whip above the permitted level (Jul 15-16)

FOCUS

A straightforward running of this consolation race for the Northumberland Plate. The bare time was a length faster than the plate, and the winner continues on the upgrade.

4382 BETFAIR EXCHANGE NORTHUMBERLAND PLATE H'CAP (HERITAGE HANDICAP) — 2m 56y (Tp)

3:35 (3:37) (Class 2) 3-Y-0+

£92,385 (£27,810; £13,905; £6,930; £3,480; £1,755) **Stalls** Low

Form / RPR

3-32 **1** **Who Dares Wins (IRE)**[50] 2575 7-9-1 **101**.........(p) TomMarquand 7 108
(Alan King) *hld up in midfield: rdn along over 2f out: hdwy u.p over 1f out: sustained run fnl f to ld towards fin* **12/1**

342- **2** *hd* **Dubawi Fifty**[375] 3965 6-9-0 **100**.........(p) LukeMorris 8 107
(Karen McLintock) *chsd ldrs: led gng wl over 2f out: rdn and edgd lft over 1f out: kpt on fnl f: hdd and no ex towards fin* **14/1**

-603 **3** 1 **Proschema (IRE)**[21] 3600 4-9-0 **103**......... JaneElliott(3) 17 109+
(Tom Dascombe) *bhd: last and plenty to do 3f out: gd hdwy on outside over 1f out: wnt 3rd towards fin* **11/1**

1-21 **4** ¾ **Bartholomeu Dias**[71] 1927 4-8-12 **98**......... KieranShoemark 6 103
(Charles Hills) *led 2f: cl up: ev ch over 2f out: rdn and edgd lft over 1f out: no ex ins fnl f* **14/1**

2430 **5** *nk* **Cosmelli (ITY)**[11] 3952 6-8-10 **96**.........(b) DanielMuscutt 1 101
(Gay Kelleway) *hld up in tch: smooth hdwy over 2f out: effrt and ev ch over 1f out: sn edgd rt: no ex ins fnl f* **33/1**

1111 **6** *nk* **King's Advice**[35] 3078 5-9-1 **101**......... PJMcDonald 18 105+
(Mark Johnston) *hld up in rr: rdn and hdwy on outside over 2f out: kpt on fnl f: nt pce to chal* **5/1**[2]

1146 **7** *nk* **Making Miracles**[14] 3864 4-9-8 **108**......... BenCurtis 16 112
(Mark Johnston) *dwlt: bhd: rdn along 3f out: hdwy over 1f out: kpt on fnl f: nvr rchd ldrs* **28/1**

2001 **8** 1 **Red Galileo**[21] 3600 8-9-4 **109** 5ex.........(h) ThomasGreatrex(5) 4 113+
(Saeed bin Suroor) *in tch: pushed along over 6f out: outpcd 3f out: rallied over 1f out: n.m.r briefly ins fnl f: no imp* **12/1**

1034 **9** ½ **Austrian School (IRE)**[14] 3864 4-9-10 **110**......... SilvestreDeSousa 19 112
(Mark Johnston) *hld up towards rr: rdn and effrt on outside over 2f out: no imp fr over 1f out* **10/1**

000- **10** 1 ½ **Stratum**[32] 8860 6-9-2 **102**.........(h) LeighRoche 3 102
(W P Mullins, Ire) *cl up: ev ch over 2f out to over 1f out: sn checked and outpcd: no ex fnl f* **9/2**[1]

0-55 **11** 2 **Desert Skyline (IRE)**[14] 3864 5-9-4 **107**.........(p) JoshuaBryan(3) 20 105
(David Elsworth) *hld up in tch: drvn along 3f out: wknd over 1f out* **40/1**

3455 **12** 2 ¾ **Fearsome**[37] 3024 5-8-13 **99**......... GrahamLee 14 94
(Nick Littmoden) *hld up towards rr: rdn along over 2f out: nvr able to chal* **80/1**

41-P **13** ½ **Shabeeb (USA)**[50] 2575 6-8-12 **98**......... PaulHanagan 9 92
(Ian Williams) *hld up towards rr: drvn along 3f out: no imp fr 2f out* **33/1**

1460 **14** *shd* **Aircraft Carrier (IRE)**[43] 2807 4-9-0 **100**.........(v[1]) BrettDoyle 11 94
(John Ryan) *t.k.h in midfield: drvn and hung lft over 2f out: sn wknd* **40/1**

-003 **15** 1 ¼ **Time To Study (FR)**[11] 3952 5-8-10 **96**......... KerrinMcEvoy 15 88
(Ian Williams) *hld up: rdn and effrt over 2f out: sn n.d* **9/1**[3]

1160 **16** 13 **Mootasadir**[22] 3561 4-9-7 **112**......... DylanHogan(5) 2 89
(Hugo Palmer) *slowly away: sn pushed into midfield on ins: drvn and struggling over 2f out: sn btn* **20/1**

6602 **17** 2 ½ **Speedo Boy (FR)**[21] 3600 5-8-10 **96**......... JasonWatson 13 70
(Ian Williams) *led after 2f: rdn and hdd over 2f out: hung rt and wknd over 1f out: bit slipped (jockey said gelding hung right-handed throughout and the bit slipped through the gelding's mouth)* **11/1**

0/45 **18** 64 **Cohesion**[19] 3646 6-8-13 **99**......... StevieDonohoe 12
(David Bridgwater) *cl up tl lost pl 3f out: sn lost tch: t.o (jockey said gelding stopped quickly)* **66/1**

131/ **P** **Gibbs Hill (GER)**[724] 4498 6-9-5 **105** .... AndreaAtzeni 5
(Roger Varian) *reluctant to enter stalls: t.k.h in midfield: rdn and struggling 3f out: sn lost pl: last and no ch whn p.u and dismntd over 1f out (jockey said gelding stopped quickly)* **5/1**[2]

3m 33.14s (-1.86) **Going Correction** +0.175s/f (Slow) **19 Ran SP% 137.7**
Speed ratings (Par 109): **111,110,110,110,109 109,109,109,108,108 107,105,105,105,104 98,97,65,**
CSF £177.44 CT £1956.61 TOTE £12.10: £2.40, £3.40, £3.70, £4.10; EX 157.30 Trifecta £8945.80.
Owner HP Racing Who Dares Wins **Bred** Mount Coote Stud **Trained** Barbury Castle, Wilts

FOCUS
A really competitive Northumberland Plate with the runners spread across the track in the straight and loads of them still in with a chance until late on. The time was 0.17sec slower than the preceding consolation race. A small pb from Who Dares Wins.

4383 BETFAIR H'CAP — 1m 4f 98y (Tp)
4:10 (4:10) (Class 4) (0-80,80) 4-Y-0+
£5,530 (£1,645; £822; £411; £300; £300) **Stalls** High

Form | | | | RPR
5126 **1** **Francophilia**[10] 4009 4-9-0 **73** .... SilvestreDeSousa 3 80
(Mark Johnston) *sn trcking ldr: shkn up to ld over 2f out: rdn and r.o wl fnl f* **5/1**[3]
563/ **2** 3/4 **The Blues Master (IRE)**[519] 6210 5-8-7 **66** .... JasonWatson 6 72
(Alan King) *hld up in midfield: effrt on outside over 2f out: chsd wnr ins fnl f: kpt on: hld towards fin* **10/1**
2410 **3** nk **Houlton**[56] 2398 4-9-3 **76** ....(tp) AndreaAtzeni 7 81
(Marco Botti) *cl up: rdn over 2f out: edgd lft and outpcd wl over 1f out: rallied ins fnl f: r.o* **9/2**[2]
14-4 **4** 1 **Snookered (IRE)**[49] 2628 5-8-13 **72** ....(p) KerrinMcEvoy 9 75
(Brian Ellison) *led: rdn and hdd over 2f out: pressed wnr to ins fnl f: no ex* **13/2**
-030 **5** 6 **Rashdan (FR)**[11] 3973 4-9-2 **75** ....(b) BenCurtis 8 68
(Hugo Palmer) *t.k.h: prom: drvn and outpcd over 2f out: n.d after* **4/1**[1]
-530 **6** hd **Zabeel Star (IRE)**[15] 3811 7-9-7 **80** ....(p[1]) LukeMorris 10 73
(Karen McLintock) *missed break: hld up: rdn and outpcd over 2f out: nvr rchd ldrs (jockey said gelding missed the break)* **20/1**
0400 **7** 1/2 **Alfa McGuire (IRE)**[11] 3973 4-9-3 **76** ....(h[1]) PaulHanagan 5 68
(Phillip Makin) *stdd s: hld up: drvn and outpcd over 2f out: sn btn* **10/1**
0/00 **8** 1 1/4 **Top Notch Tonto (IRE)**[3] 4241 9-9-3 **79** .... BenRobinson(3) 1 69
(Brian Ellison) *hld up towards rr: drvn along over 2f out: sn outpcd: nvr on terms (jockey said gelding was never travelling)* **5/1**[3]
1110 **9** 14 **Archive (FR)**[35] 3095 9-8-3 **69** .... KieranSchofield(7) 2 37
(Brian Ellison) *hld up: drvn and struggling over 2f out: sn btn* **12/1**
/20- **10** 47 **Orsino (IRE)**[291] 7150 5-9-2 **75** .... PJMcDonald 4
(Seb Spencer) *hld up in tch on ins: struggling 3f out: sn lost tch and eased: t.o* **25/1**

2m 44.22s (3.12) **Going Correction** +0.175s/f (Slow) **10 Ran SP% 119.3**
Speed ratings (Par 105): **96,95,95,94,90 90,90,89,80,48**
CSF £55.51 CT £244.66 TOTE £6.00: £1.90, £3.10, £1.90; EX 78.90 Trifecta £288.90.
Owner Miss K Rausing **Bred** Miss K Rausing **Trained** Middleham Moor, N Yorks

FOCUS
Few got into this modest handicap which has been rated around the fourth.

4384 BETFAIR CASINO EBF NOVICE STKS (PLUS 10 RACE) — 5f (Tp)
4:45 (4:45) (Class 3) 2-Y-O **£7,561** (£2,263; £1,131; £566; £282) **Stalls** Centre

Form | | | | RPR
1 **Hurcle (IRE)** 2-9-4 .... BenCurtis 5 79
(Archie Watson) *trckd ldr: led gng wl over 1f out: rdn: edgd lft and kpt on wl fnl 100yds* **5/2**[2]
16 **2** 1 **Mrs Bouquet**[14] 3841 2-9-5 .... SilvestreDeSousa 3 76
(Mark Johnston) *led to over 1f out: rallied and ev ch ins fnl f: one pce fnl 100yds* **9/4**[1]
02 **3** 3/4 **Teenar**[10] 3997 2-9-4 .... PaulHanagan 6 72
(Richard Fahey) *prom: rdn and outpcd over 2f out: rallied ins fnl f: r.o* **5/1**
03 **4** 1/2 **Paddy Elliott (IRE)**[77] 1758 2-9-1 .... BenRobinson(3) 1 71
(Brian Ellison) *trckd ldrs: rdn over 2f out: kpt on same pce fnl f* **16/1**
25 **5** 3 1/4 **Olcan**[15] 3810 2-9-4 .... JasonWatson 7 59
(David O'Meara) *chsd ldng gp: drvn and outpcd over 2f out: n.d after* **9/2**[3]
6 5 **Aysar (IRE)** 2-9-4 .... PJMcDonald 4 41
(Ed Dunlop) *s.i.s: bhd: struggling 1/2-way: sn btn* **8/1**
4 **7** 26 **Flowing Magic (IRE)**[17] 3739 2-9-4 ....(t[1]) LukeMorris 2
(George Scott) *s.i.s: sn wl bhd: t.o (jockey said colt was never travelling)* **16/1**

59.99s (0.49) **Going Correction** +0.175s/f (Slow) **7 Ran SP% 117.1**
Speed ratings (Par 97): **103,101,100,99,94 86,44**
CSF £8.96 TOTE £3.20: £1.60, £1.70; EX 10.10 Trifecta £33.60.
Owner The Hurcle Syndicate **Bred** Mattock Stud **Trained** Upper Lambourn, W Berks

FOCUS
This looked a fair 2yo novice. The form's been given a token rating around the second and third.

4385 BETFAIR CASINO H'CAP — 7f 14y (Tp)
5:15 (5:16) (Class 2) (0-105,99) 3-Y-0+ **£16,172** (£4,812; £2,405; £1,202) **Stalls** Centre

Form | | | | RPR
2-12 **1** **Mubhij (IRE)**[20] 3632 4-9-6 **91** .... AndreaAtzeni 9 102+
(Roger Varian) *pressed ldr: shkn up to ld over 1f out: edgd lft ins fnl f: kpt on strly* **2/1**[1]
-204 **2** 1 3/4 **Woven**[23] 3493 3-8-12 **92** .... KerrinMcEvoy 4 95
(David Simcock) *led at ordinary gallop: rdn and hdd over 1f out: rallied: kpt on same pce ins fnl f* **14/1**
-001 **3** nk **Raydiance**[7] 4127 4-9-8 **93** .... CliffordLee 5 98
(K R Burke) *hld up in tch: hdwy and cl up over 4f out: rdn and outpcd over 2f out: rallied to chse ldng pair ins fnl f: r.o* **13/2**
5406 **4** 1 1/2 **Hajjam**[7] 4127 5-9-5 **90** .... JasonWatson 1 91
(David O'Meara) *prom: drvn along 3f out: rallied: kpt on same pce fr over 1f out* **12/1**
-105 **5** hd **Name The Wind**[21] 3581 3-9-3 **97** .... PJMcDonald 2 94
(James Tate) *t.k.h: hld up bhd ldng gp: drvn and outpcd over 2f out: rallied ins fnl f: no imp* **4/1**[2]
2-51 **6** nk **Diocles Of Rome (IRE)**[29] 3308 4-9-2 **87** .... BenCurtis 8 87
(Ralph Beckett) *t.k.h: in tch: rdn over 2f out: no imp fr over 1f out (jockey said gelding ran too free)* **5/1**[3]
4506 **7** 2 1/4 **Gallipoli (IRE)**[35] 3100 6-9-5 **90** ....(v) PaulHanagan 6 84
(Richard Fahey) *plld hrd: hld up bhd ldng gp: drvn and outpcd over 2f out: sn wknd* **16/1**

04-0 **8** 1 1/2 **Vale Of Kent (IRE)**[10] 3987 4-10-0 **99** .... SilvestreDeSousa 7 88
(Mark Johnston) *missed break: t.k.h and sn prom: rdn and outpcd over 2f out: wknd over 1f out* **7/1**

1m 27.1s (0.90) **Going Correction** +0.175s/f (Slow)
WFA 3 from 4yo+ 9lb **8 Ran SP% 116.1**
Speed ratings (Par 109): **101,99,98,96,96 96,93,92**
CSF £33.17 CT £158.47 TOTE £2.70: £1.50, £3.60, £1.50; EX 30.90 Trifecta £407.70.
Owner Hamdan Al Maktoum **Bred** S V Schilcher **Trained** Newmarket, Suffolk

FOCUS
The early pace looked steady and the first two more or less raced in the top two spots, in the other order, for much of the way. The winner progressed again.

4386 BETFAIR CASINO ALWAYS A CHANCE H'CAP — 1m 2f 42y (Tp)
5:50 (5:52) (Class 4) (0-85,87) 4-Y-O+
£5,530 (£1,645; £822; £411; £300; £300) **Stalls** High

Form | | | | RPR
042 **1** **Anythingtoday (IRE)**[23] 3514 5-9-12 **87** ....(p) SilvestreDeSousa 1 101
(David O'Meara) *prom: smooth hdwy to ld wl over 1f out: drvn clr* **9/2**[3]
110- **2** 3 3/4 **Howman (IRE)**[330] 5673 4-9-6 **81** .... AndreaAtzeni 5 87
(Roger Varian) *t.k.h: early ldr: pressed ldr: led gng wl over 2f out: rdn and hdd wl over 1f out: kpt on same pce fnl f* **6/4**[1]
4203 **3** 1 3/4 **Lawmaking**[7] 4108 6-9-7 **82** ....(b) JasonWatson 3 85
(Michael Scudamore) *hld up bhd ldng gp: drvn and outpcd over 2f out: rallied over 1f out: kpt on fnl f: nt pce to chal* **4/1**[2]
4063 **4** nk **Windsor Cross (IRE)**[43] 2784 4-9-0 **75** .... PaulHanagan 7 77
(Richard Fahey) *dwlt: sn led and dictated modest gallop: rdn and hdd over 2f out: kpt on same pce fr over 1f out* **12/1**
1-04 **5** 1 3/4 **Time Change**[42] 2822 4-9-5 **80** .... BenCurtis 9 78
(Ralph Beckett) *in tch: hdwy and ev ch over 2f out: drvn and outpcd over 1f out: btn ins fnl f* **10/1**
6016 **6** 1 1/4 **Eye Of The Storm (IRE)**[9] 4019 9-9-0 **75** .... PJMcDonald 4 71
(Conor Dore) *s.i.s: hld up: rdn along over 2f out: no imp over 1f out* **28/1**
31-6 **7** 3/4 **Thaayer**[92] 1401 4-9-5 **80** ....(t) AlistairRawlinson 10 74
(Rebecca Menzies) *hld up in last pl: rdn and outpcd over 2f out: sn n.d (jockey said gelding ran too free)* **16/1**
10-6 **8** 5 **Rose Tinted Spirit**[28] 3356 4-9-3 **78** .... LukeMorris 2 62
(Karen McLintock) *t.k.h: hld up on ins: drvn and outpcd 3f out: sn btn* **16/1**
-4P5 **9** 24 **Bobby K (IRE)**[28] 3338 4-9-12 **87** ....(p) KerrinMcEvoy 6 23
(Simon Crisford) *t.k.h: prom: rdn over 2f out: wknd over 1f out: eased whn no ch ins fnl f* **17/2**

2m 12.12s (1.72) **Going Correction** +0.175s/f (Slow) **9 Ran SP% 120.7**
Speed ratings (Par 105): **100,97,95,95,93 92,92,88,69**
CSF £12.22 CT £30.25 TOTE £5.00: £1.80, £1.10, £1.60; EX 10.30 Trifecta £52.30.
Owner Woodhurst Construction Ltd **Bred** T Whitehead **Trained** Upper Helmsley, N Yorks

FOCUS
There wasn't much pace on but the winner did this well. He was not far off his 3yo best.
T/Plt: £96.10 to a £1 stake. Pool: £135,644.59 - 1,029.92 winning units T/Qpdt: £29.00 to a £1 stake. Pool: £11,407.96 - 290.20 winning units **Richard Young**

4336 NEWMARKET (R-H)
Saturday, June 29

OFFICIAL GOING: Good to firm (good in places; 7.6)
Wind: nil Weather: very hot and sunny; 28 degrees

4387 RANDOX HEALTH EMPRESS FILLIES' STKS (LISTED RACE) — 6f
2:05 (2:05) (Class 1) 2-Y-O
£17,013 (£6,450; £3,228; £1,608; £807; £405) **Stalls** High

Form | | | | RPR
1 **1** **Summer Romance (IRE)**[16] 3776 2-9-0 0 .... JamesDoyle 5 107+
(Charlie Appleby) *racd enthusiastically: cl up and gng easily: led wl over 1f out: sn pushed clr: v emphatic* **5/6**[1]
1 **2** 6 **Ursulina (IRE)**[17] 3725 2-9-0 0 .... RichardKingscote 4 89
(Tom Dascombe) *trckd ldrs: rdn and outpcd over 2f out: 4th 1f out: styd on wl to go 2nd fnl 100yds: no ch w easy wnr* **14/1**
103 **3** 1 3/4 **Companion**[18] 3689 2-9-0 **83** .... FrankieDettori 7 84
(Mark Johnston) *pressed ldr: rdn 2f out: chsd her vainly fr over 1f out tl lost 2nd fnl 100yds* **10/1**
41 **4** 1/2 **Rosadora (IRE)**[18] 3689 2-9-0 0 .... HarryBentley 1 83
(Ralph Beckett) *bhd: last and rdn wl over 2f out: kpt on stoutly ins fnl f: promising* **8/1**[3]
31 **5** 6 **Star Alexander**[14] 3835 2-9-0 0 .... AdamKirby 6 65
(Clive Cox) *led tl rdn and hdd wl over 1f out: wknd rapidly* **7/2**[2]
301 **6** 1 1/2 **Shammah (IRE)**[12] 3942 2-9-0 **80** .... SeanLevey 3 60
(Richard Hannon) *taken down early: bhd: rdn and btn wl over 2f out* **10/1**
4301 **7** 1 1/4 **Amnaa**[15] 3812 2-9-0 **72** .... ConnorBeasley 2 56
(Adrian Nicholls) *t.k.h: chsd ldrs: rdn 1/2-way: sn outpcd* **50/1**

1m 12.23s (0.13) **Going Correction** +0.125s/f (Good) **7 Ran SP% 114.7**
Speed ratings (Par 98): **104,96,93,93,85 83,81**
CSF £15.00 TOTE £1.50: £1.20, £5.20; EX 12.30 Trifecta £77.80.
Owner Godolphin **Bred** Roundhill Stud **Trained** Newmarket, Suffolk

FOCUS
An uncompetitive 2yo fillies' Listed race but it was won impressively by a filly who can rate a lot higher. She looks a lot better than the usual winners of this event.

4388 COATES & SEELY BLANC DE BLANCS NOVICE STKS (PLUS 10 RACE) — 7f
2:40 (2:40) (Class 4) 2-Y-O **£5,175** (£1,540; £769; £384) **Stalls** High

Form | | | | RPR
1 **Al Dabaran** 2-9-5 0 .... JamesDoyle 1 85+
(Charlie Appleby) *dwlt: sn rcvrd to press ldr: rdn to ld over 1f out: readily forged clr* **9/4**[1]
2 2 1/2 **Ursa Minor (IRE)** 2-9-5 0 .... RobertHavlin 5 78
(John Gosden) *awkward leaving stalls: towards rr: 4th and rdn and outpcd 1f out: rallied and styd on wl after: snatched 2nd but nt rch wnr* **9/4**[1]
0 **3** nse **Gold Souk (IRE)**[16] 3760 2-9-5 0 .... HarryBentley 3 78
(Mark Johnston) *led: rdn and hdd over 1f out: sn outpcd by wnr and pipped for 2nd* **11/4**[2]
4 1 1/2 **Manigordo (USA)** 2-9-5 0 .... SeanLevey 4 74
(Richard Hannon) *awkward leaving stalls: sn rcvrd to chse ldrs: 3rd and rdn and outpcd 1f out: lost 3rd fnl 100yds* **11/2**[3]

0 **5** *6* **King's View (IRE)**[16] 3760 2-9-5 0........................ DaneO'Neill 2 58
(Richard Hannon) *towards rr: rdn and lost tch wl over 1f out* **16/1**

6 *3 ½* **Aldrich Bay (IRE)** 2-9-5 0........................ DavidEgan 6 48
(William Knight) *chsd ldrs to 1/2-way: rdn and struggling in last wl over 2f out* **40/1**

1m 27.27s (1.57) **Going Correction** +0.125s/f (Good) **6 Ran SP% 111.9**
Speed ratings (Par 95): **96,93,93,91,84 80**
CSF £7.55 TOTE £2.90: £1.40, £1.70; EX 7.20 Trifecta £15.30.
Owner Godolphin **Bred** Godolphin **Trained** Newmarket, Suffolk

FOCUS
Probably an above-average novice event. The form's likely to work out although time will tell the full worth.

4389 RANDOX HEALTH CRITERION STKS (GROUP 3) 7f
3:15 (3:15) (Class 1) 3-Y-O+
£34,026 (£12,900; £6,456; £3,216; £1,614; £810) **Stalls High**

Form RPR

10-4 **1** **Limato (IRE)**[45] 2744 7-9-10 113........................ HarryBentley 5 119
(Henry Candy) *t.k.h trcking ldrs: travelled smoothly: wnt 2nd 2f out: rdn to ld over 1f out: hrd pressed fnl 100yds but hld on gamely* **11/4**[1]

0-02 **2** *nk* **Glorious Journey**[40] 2916 4-9-5 108........................ JamesDoyle 7 113
(Charlie Appleby) *trckd ldrs: wnt 3rd 2f out: sustained chal to go 2nd ins fnl f: drvn and tried hrd but a jst hld cl home* **7/2**[2]

-442 **3** *½* **Suedois (FR)**[21] 3588 8-9-5 110........................ DanielTudhope 2 112
(David O'Meara) *t.k.h: stdd s: bhd early: effrt to go 4th 2f out: rdn and tried to chal ins fnl f: no imp last 100yds* **7/2**[2]

0-20 **4** *1* **Larchmont Lad (IRE)**[49] 2615 5-9-5 107........................ SeanLevey 6 109
(Joseph Tuite) *pressed ldr: led and rdn over 2f out: hdd over 1f out: no ex fnl 100yds* **16/1**

0-30 **5** *2 ¾* **Breton Rock (IRE)**[21] 3588 9-9-5 105........................ CharlesBishop 1 102
(David Simcock) *outpcd in last tl 1/2-way: rdn and kpt on steadily fr over 1f out: nt rch ldrs* **40/1**

11-4 **6** *4* **Tabarrak (IRE)**[59] 2271 6-9-5 110........................ DaneO'Neill 3 91
(Richard Hannon) *towards rr: rdn and outpcd 2f out* **6/1**

3010 **7** *5* **Cardsharp**[10] 3987 4-9-5 110........................ FrankieDettori 4 77
(Mark Johnston) *t.k.h and prom: rdn 1/2-way: wknd 2f out: eased clsng stages* **4/1**[3]

0544 **8** *15* **Salateen**[35] 3094 7-9-5 100........................(tp) AdamKirby 8 37
(David O'Meara) *led: rdn 1/2-way: hdd over 2f out: dropped out rapidly: eased and t.o* **28/1**

1m 24.51s (-1.19) **Going Correction** +0.125s/f (Good) **8 Ran SP% 117.2**
Speed ratings (Par 113): **111,110,110,108,105 101,95,78**
CSF £12.98 TOTE £3.40: £1.30, £1.50, £1.20; EX 13.80 Trifecta £40.60.
Owner Paul G Jacobs **Bred** Seamus Phelan **Trained** Kingston Warren, Oxon

FOCUS
A solid edition of this Group 3 prize, which was run at an even tempo. A smart effort from Limato, who's rated in line with last year's form.

4390 RANDOX HEALTH FRED ARCHER STKS (LISTED RACE) 1m 4f
3:50 (3:52) (Class 1) 4-Y-O+
£22,684 (£8,600; £4,304; £2,144) **Stalls Low**

Form RPR

614- **1** **Wells Farhh Go (IRE)**[311] 6427 4-9-0 112........................ DavidAllan 1 113
(Tim Easterby) *led after 1f: pushed clr gng best over 1f out: styd on stoutly* **5/4**[1]

30-3 **2** *4* **Walton Street**[135] 730 5-9-0 107........................(p) JamesDoyle 4 106
(Charlie Appleby) *2nd mostly: rdn over 2f out: no match for wnr fnl f* **13/8**[2]

2-33 **3** *1 ½* **Barsanti (IRE)**[35] 3077 7-9-0 109........................(p[1]) DavidEgan 2 104
(Roger Varian) *led 1f: disp 2nd after: rdn over 2f out: 3rd and outpcd by wnr over 1f out* **7/2**[3]

3321 **4** *2* **Birch Grove (IRE)**[33] 3169 4-8-9 76........................ HarryBentley 3 95?
(David Simcock) *a last: keen early: rdn 3f out: kpt on same pce whn wl hld fnl 2f* **28/1**

2m 32.17s (-1.73) **Going Correction** +0.125s/f (Good) **4 Ran SP% 108.2**
Speed ratings (Par 111): **110,107,106,105**
CSF £3.59 TOTE £2.10; EX 3.50 Trifecta £4.00.
Owner S A Heley & Partner **Bred** Ms Maria Marron **Trained** Great Habton, N Yorks

FOCUS
A small yet select bunch for this Listed contest. Predictably it proved tactical. The fourth will sure ly prove to have been flattered. Add 30yds.

4391 RANDOX HEALTH FILLIES' H'CAP 1m 4f
4:25 (4:25) (Class 3) (0-95,93) 3-Y-O+
£9,703 (£2,887; £1,443; £721) **Stalls Low**

Form RPR

5-25 **1** **Lady Of Shalott**[28] 3336 4-9-8 87........................(h) HarryBentley 4 96+
(David Simcock) *settled in last pl tl over 3f out: shkn up over 2f out: smooth run to ld over 1f out: easily drew clr* **9/4**[2]

1-01 **2** *1 ¾* **Manorah (IRE)**[39] 2935 3-8-1 80........................ DavidEgan 5 84
(Roger Varian) *sn settled in 3rd pl: effrt 4f out: led and drvn 2f out tl wnr breezed past over 1f out: plugged on same pce after* **11/10**[1]

02-4 **3** *10* **Miss Mumtaz (IRE)**[33] 3169 4-8-9 74........................ RichardKingscote 1 62
(Ian Williams) *t.k.h: sn chsng clr ldr: clsd 5f out: led and drvn over 3f out: hdd 2f out: nt run on: mod 3rd fnl f* **11/2**

-030 **4** *61* **Mazzuri (IRE)**[28] 3346 4-10-0 93........................(v) JamesDoyle 2
(Amanda Perrett) *led and plld much too hrd: wnt str gallop: 8 l clr for 5f: rdn and hdd over 3f out: dropped out immediately: bdly t.o and eased (jockey said filly ran too free and stopped quickly)* **5/1**[3]

2m 33.7s (-0.20) **Going Correction** +0.125s/f (Good) **4 Ran SP% 110.4**
WFA 3 from 4yo 14lb
Speed ratings (Par 104): **105,103,97,56**
CSF £5.28 TOTE £2.80; EX 6.60 Trifecta £14.10.
Owner Khalifa Dasmal **Bred** Mr & Mrs R & P Scott **Trained** Newmarket, Suffolk

FOCUS
This was a fair little fillies' handicap with the second setting the level. The winner looks improved. The pace was sound. Add 30yds.

4392 COATES & SEELY BRUT RESERVE H'CAP (JOCKEY CLUB GRASSROOTS MIDDLE DISTANCE SERIES QUALIFIER) 1m 2f
5:00 (5:01) (Class 4) (0-80,80) 3-Y-O+
£6,469 (£1,925; £962; £481; £300; £300) **Stalls Low**

Form RPR

3112 **1** **Cardano (USA)**[15] 3797 3-9-2 79........................(p[1]) RichardKingscote 7 86+
(Ian Williams) *prom: rdn to ld 2f out: a doing jst enough thrght fnl f* **5/2**[1]

36-4 **2** *shd* **Dramatic Device**[32] 3192 4-10-0 79........................ JamesDoyle 8 85
(Chris Wall) *settled towards rr: effrt wd 4f out: chal 2f out: hrd drvn and ev ch fnl f: btn on nod* **6/1**[3]

-045 **3** *1* **Shir Khan**[39] 2942 3-9-3 80........................ RossaRyan 2 84
(Paul Cole) *t.k.h towards rr: rdn and swtchd lft and effrt 2f out: outpcd over 1f out: styng on again cl home (jockey said colt was denied a clear run)* **6/1**[3]

4021 **4** *5* **Silkstone (IRE)**[13] 3885 3-9-1 78........................ ShaneKelly 4 72
(Pam Sly) *led at stdy pce: rdn and hdd 2f out: outpcd by ldng trio fnl f* **13/2**

2-03 **5** *¾* **Starfighter**[32] 3195 3-8-11 74........................ DavidEgan 10 67
(Ed Walker) *t.k.h: w ldr tl rdn 2f out: wknd over 1f out* **4/1**[2]

0021 **6** *3* **Tangramm**[12] 3937 7-9-6 71........................(p) RyanTate 9 58
(Dean Ivory) *midfield: effrt to chse ldrs on outer 5f out: rdn and wknd over 2f out* **20/1**

31-2 **7** *1* **Cornborough**[34] 2628 8-9-11 76........................(v) AdamKirby 3 61
(Mark Walford) *midfield: rdn 3f out: btn 2f out* **9/1**

3-00 **8** *1 ¼* **Midnight Wilde**[50] 2577 4-9-12 77........................ RobertHavlin 5 59
(John Ryan) *n.m.r s: a towards rr: rdn and btn wl over 2f out* **20/1**

00-P **9** *1* **Tribal Commander**[27] 3373 3-8-3 73........................ RPWalsh[(7)] 1 53
(Ian Williams) *plld hrd in rr: rdn and struggling over 2f out* **33/1**

-340 **10** *5* **Sweet Charity**[30] 3264 4-9-9 74........................ CharlesBishop 6 44
(Denis Coakley) *edgd rt s: plld hrd towards rr: rdn and fdd over 2f out: t.o and eased (jockey said filly ran too free)* **11/1**

2m 9.19s (2.09) **Going Correction** +0.125s/f (Good)
WFA 3 from 4yo+ 12lb **10 Ran SP% 121.3**
Speed ratings (Par 105): **96,95,95,91,90 88,87,86,85,81**
CSF £18.14 CT £84.74 TOTE £3.10: £1.40, £2.80, £2.70; EX 23.80 Trifecta £210.20.
Owner Sohi & Sohi **Bred** Mt Brilliant Broodmares II Llc **Trained** Portway, Worcs

FOCUS
They went an ordinary pace in this modest handicap and the first pair came clear. The winner is rated in line with his Ripon form. Add 30yds.

4393 RANDOX HEALTH BRITISH EBF FILLIES' H'CAP 1m
5:35 (5:37) (Class 3) (0-95,92) 3-Y-O+
£9,703 (£2,887; £1,443; £721) **Stalls High**

Form RPR

5-20 **1** **Clara Peeters**[24] 3468 3-8-9 83 ow1........................ RossaRyan 5 88
(Gary Moore) *t.k.h towards rr: effrt 2f out: rdn to ld over 1f out: hld on wl* **15/2**

1-34 **2** *1* **Gallic**[42] 2821 3-8-11 85........................ ShaneKelly 2 87
(Ed Walker) *bhd: rdn and hdwy over 1f out: chsd wnr ins fnl f: kpt on but a hld* **7/2**[2]

4-63 **3** *½* **Hunni**[17] 3743 4-8-12 76........................ CharlesBishop 8 81+
(Tom Clover) *racd keenly pressing ldrs: rdn 1/2-way: hmpd and lost several l 2f out: nt rcvr but rallied and clsng again ins fnl f (jockey said filly was denied a clear run)* **5/1**[3]

43-2 **4** *hd* **Pure Shores**[175] 81 5-9-1 79........................ RichardKingscote 6 87+
(Ian Williams) *bhd on far rails: bdly checked over 2f out: rdn and swtchd rt and rallied fnl f: kpt on gamely: unlucky (jockey said mare was denied a clear run)* **5/1**[3]

4-00 **5** *3 ½* **Akvavera**[28] 3342 4-10-0 92........................ HarryBentley 1 86
(Ralph Beckett) *t.k.h and prom: led over 2f out: rdn and hdd over 1f out: sn lost pl* **11/1**

00-0 **6** *5* **Marilyn**[38] 2977 5-8-13 77........................(p) RobertHavlin 3 60
(Shaun Keightley) *t.k.h: pressed ldr tl rdn and wknd tamely over 2f out* **33/1**

231 **7** *6* **Ocean Paradise**[16] 3768 3-8-7 81........................(h) DavidEgan 7 48
(Charles Hills) *too free to s and in r: led tl hdd and dropped out v rapidly over 2f out: t.o and eased (jockey said filly ran too free to post and in the early stages of the race)* **13/8**[1]

1m 39.73s (-0.27) **Going Correction** +0.125s/f (Good)
WFA 3 from 4yo+ 10lb **7 Ran SP% 116.7**
Speed ratings (Par 104): **106,105,104,104,100 95,89**
CSF £34.95 CT £146.19 TOTE £9.40: £3.40, £2.00; EX 41.50 Trifecta £199.20.
Owner R A Green **Bred** G R Bailey Ltd **Trained** Lower Beeding, W Sussex

FOCUS
A fair fillies' handicap, run to suit the closers. Rather a messy race.
T/Plt: £84.60 to a £1 stake. Pool: £68,146.17 - 587.90 winning units. T/Qpdt: £45.60 to a £1 stake. Pool: £4,699.30 - 76.20 winning units. **Iain Mackenzie**

4183 WINDSOR (R-H)
Saturday, June 29

OFFICIAL GOING: Good (good to firm in places; watered; 7.4) changing to good to firm (good in places) after race 1 (1.40)
Wind: Inconsequential breeze Weather: Hot, sunny

4394 GENTINGBET CASINOS NOVICE STKS 6f 12y
1:40 (1:42) (Class 5) 2-Y-O
£3,752 (£1,116; £557; £278) **Stalls Centre**

Form RPR

42 **1** **Homespin (USA)**[26] 3426 2-9-5........................ FrannyNorton 7 79
(Mark Johnston) *trckd ldr: shkn up to ld over 1f out: hdd ins fnl f: drvn to ld again last 75yds* **6/4**[1]

3 **2** *½* **Hubert (IRE)**[12] 3942 2-9-2........................ GaryMahon[(3)] 3 78
(Sylvester Kirk) *slowly away: rn green but sn in midfield: nt clr run and swtchd rt over 2f out: rdn and prog over 1f out: burst between rivals to ld ins fnl f: hdd and nt qckn last 75yds* **16/1**

3 **3** *1 ½* **Good Earth (IRE)**[22] 3542 2-9-5........................ NicolaCurrie 10 73
(Jamie Osborne) *pressed ldng pair: rdn to chal over 1f out: one pce ins fnl f* **9/1**

4 *1* **One Step Beyond (IRE)** 2-9-5........................ HollieDoyle 11 70+
(Richard Spencer) *coltish preliminaries: slowly away: wl in rr and rn green: shkn up 2f out: styd on steadily over 1f out: nrst fin (jockey said colt was slowly away)* **8/1**[3]

5 *1* **Kingsholm (IRE)** 2-9-5........................ OisinMurphy 2 67
(Archie Watson) *led and r against rail: hdd over 1f out: wknd fnl f* **2/1**[2]

05 **6** *¾* **Ebony Adams**[19] 3644 2-9-0........................ PatCosgrave 6 60
(Brian Meehan) *chsd ldrs: drvn 2f out: one pce and no prog over 1f out* **25/1**

5345 **7** *2* **Fact Or Fable (IRE)**[20] 3634 2-9-5 60........................(b[1]) LiamKeniry 9 59
(J S Moore) *towards rr: rdn 2f out: no real prog* **50/1**

00 **8** *2 ¾* **Pilsdon Pen**[10] 3990 2-9-5........................ LouisSteward 4 51
(Joseph Tuite) *hld up and sn in last pair: pushed along 1/2-way: bhd over 1f out: kpt on steadily fnl f* **100/1**

5 **9** *shd* **Subutai (IRE)**[37] 3008 2-9-5........................(p[1]) HectorCrouch 1 50
(Clive Cox) *chsd ldrs 4f: wknd* **12/1**

0 **10** *4 ½* **Hares Rocket (IRE)**[12] 3943 2-9-5........................ KieranO'Neill 14 37
(Joseph Tuite) *spd on outer to 1/2-way: wknd qckly* **100/1**

The Form Book Flat 2019, Raceform Ltd, Newbury, RG14 5SJ

11 3/4 **Quarrystreetmagic (IRE)** 2-9-0 .... SebastianWoods(5) 8 35
(Brian Meehan) *spd on outer to 1/2-way: wknd qckly* **33/1**

12 *nse* **Winning Streak** 2-9-5 .... DavidProbert 13 35
(Stuart Williams) *s.s: rn green and mostly in last: a bhd (jockey said colt was slowly away)* **20/1**

60 13 7 **Secret Cecil (FR)**[36] 3039 2-9-5 .... RobbieDowney 5 14
(Joseph Tuite) *spd 2f: sn dropped to rr: wknd 2f out: t.o* **100/1**

1m 13.06s (0.96) **Going Correction** -0.20s/f (Firm) **13 Ran SP% 124.5**
Speed ratings (Par 93): **85,84,82,81,79 78,76,72,72,66 65,65,55**
CSF £29.04 TOTE £2.40: £1.10, £3.70, £3.00; EX 26.20 Trifecta £132.40.
Owner Sheikh Hamdan bin Mohammed Al Maktoum **Bred** Godolphin **Trained** Middleham Moor, N Yorks

FOCUS
On a very hot day the ground had dried out to good, good to firm in places with a stick reading of 7.4. il was inevitably changed to good to firm after the first and the first race was obviously run on good to firm. The market principals had this between them from the outset. The winner came from a good Nottingham race.

4395 GENTINGBET SPORTSBOOK H'CAP — 1m 3f 99y
2:15 (2:16) (Class 2) (0-100,97) 4-Y-O+ £12,450 (£3,728; £1,864; £932; £466) **Stalls Low**

Form RPR

2-14 1 **Sextant**[28] 3346 4-9-7 **97** .... LouisSteward 4 103+
(Sir Michael Stoute) *dwlt: hld up in 4th: shkn up 3f out: grad clsd on outer fr 2f out: drvn to chal fnl f: styd on dourly to ld nr fin* **6/4**[1]

-451 2 *hd* **Oasis Fantasy (IRE)**[37] 3016 8-8-12 **88** .... PatCosgrave 3 93
(David Simcock) *led: rdn 2f out: hung lft over 1f out: continued to edge lft but kpt on u.p: hdd nr fin* **15/2**

0012 3 *nse* **Speed Company (IRE)**[15] 3816 6-8-13 **89** .... DavidProbert 1 94
(Ian Williams) *hld up in last: prog to trck ldr 2f out and sn chalng: upsides fnl f: jst pipped in tight fin* **9/2**[3]

-003 4 1 1/4 **Banditry (IRE)**[33] 3168 7-9-4 **94** .... PatDobbs 5 98
(Ian Williams) *trckd ldng pair: shkn up 2f out: swtchd lft and trying to chal whn hmpd over 1f out: nt rcvr but styd on again last 100yds* **14/1**

022 5 6 **Big Kitten (USA)**[24] 3466 4-9-5 **95** .... OisinMurphy 6 87
(William Haggas) *chsd ldr to 2f out: wknd over 1f out* **15/8**[2]

2m 24.45s (-5.25) **Going Correction** -0.20s/f (Firm) **5 Ran SP% 111.4**
Speed ratings (Par 109): **111,110,110,109,105**
CSF £12.96 TOTE £2.30: £1.40, £2.80; EX 12.00 Trifecta £31.30.
Owner The Queen **Bred** The Queen **Trained** Newmarket, Suffolk

FOCUS
A winner not far from home for the Queen with a progressive four-year-old. The form's rated around the runner-up.

4396 CELEBRATION NOVICE STKS — 5f 21y
2:50 (2:53) (Class 5) 3-Y-O+ £3,752 (£1,116; £557; £278) **Stalls Centre**

Form RPR

2502 1 **Khafooq**[14] 3836 3-9-4 68 .... PatDobbs 3 73
(Robert Cowell) *mde all: gng far bttr than rest fr 1/2-way: shkn up over 1f out: styd on: unchal* **4/1**[3]

6 2 2 3/4 **Great Suspense**[19] 3661 3-9-4 .... FrannyNorton 4 63+
(William Jarvis) *awkward s and slowly away: hanging lft thrght: in rr tl rdn and prog 1/2-way: chsd wnr over 1f out: kpt on but no imp* **11/10**[1]

44 3 2 **Kodiak Attack (IRE)**[7] 4116 3-9-4 .... OisinMurphy 1 56
(Sylvester Kirk) *stmbld s: chsd ldrs: rdn 1/2-way: kpt on one pce over 1f out: no threat* **2/1**[2]

260- 4 1 3/4 **Devil Or Angel**[271] 7832 4-9-5 52 ....(h) KieranO'Neill 5 47
(Bill Turner) *chsd wnr: rdn 1/2-way: lost 2nd and wknd over 1f out* **28/1**

0040 5 2 3/4 **Sarsaparilla Kit**[5] 4183 3-8-6 54 ....(p[1]) MarcoGhiani(7) 2 35
(Stuart Williams) *n.m.r over 3f out and snatched up: in tch to 2f out: wknd* **12/1**

0- 6 10 **Diamond Cara**[260] 8150 3-8-13 .... DavidProbert 7
(Stuart Williams) *hung lft thrght: sn in rr: t.o* **33/1**

59.59s (-0.51) **Going Correction** -0.20s/f (Firm) **6 Ran SP% 115.0**
WFA 3 from 4yo 6lb
Speed ratings (Par 103): **96,91,88,85,81 65**
CSF £9.18 TOTE £4.10: £1.40, £1.20; EX 10.90 Trifecta £14.80.
Owner Mrs J Morley **Bred** J Channon **Trained** Six Mile Bottom, Cambs

FOCUS
A small-field novice for older horses with no great standard being set, but the winner was the most exposed. The winner's rated back to his best.

4397 GENTINGBET MIDSUMMER STKS (LISTED RACE) — 1m 31y
3:25 (3:27) (Class 1) 3-Y-O+
£20,801 (£7,918; £3,962; £1,975; £991; £499) **Stalls Low**

Form RPR

1220 1 **Matterhorn (IRE)**[11] 3948 4-9-6 110 .... FrannyNorton 7 115
(Mark Johnston) *mde virtually all: had rest hrd at work over 2f out: rdn over 1f out: styd on strly* **11/8**[1]

2-10 2 2 **New Graduate (IRE)**[10] 3987 4-9-6 105 .... OisinMurphy 6 110
(James Tate) *trckd ldng pair: rdn to chse wnr 2f out: styd on but no real imp fnl f* **5/2**[2]

403- 3 1 3/4 **Khafoo Shememi (IRE)**[411] 2707 5-9-6 105 .... LouisSteward 3 106
(Sir Michael Stoute) *awkward s: hld up in last trio: shkn up over 2f out: prog on outer over 1f out: drvn to take 3rd ins fnl f: n.d* **7/1**

-564 4 *hd* **Arbalet (IRE)**[13] 3891 4-9-6 102 ....(t) PatCosgrave 1 106
(Hugo Palmer) *hld up in midfield: tk false step bnd 5f out: rdn over 2f out: one pce and no imp after (jockey said colt clipped heels on the bend turning into the home straight)* **20/1**

0-30 5 *hd* **Zhui Feng (IRE)**[10] 3987 6-9-6 103 .... NicolaCurrie 2 105
(Amanda Perrett) *chsd wnr: shkn up 3f out: lost 2nd 2f out and one pce after* **12/1**

6223 6 1/2 **Oh This Is Us (IRE)**[15] 3814 6-9-6 111 .... PatDobbs 5 104
(Richard Hannon) *hld up in last: pushed along over 2f out: one pce and no ch whn rdn fnl f* **9/2**[3]

1-00 7 1/2 **Isole Canarie (IRE)**[48] 2670 4-9-4 97 .... HectorCrouch 4 101
(Gavin Hernon, France) *in tch in last trio: rdn 3f out: no prog 2f out: n.d after* **50/1**

1m 39.47s (-5.03) **Going Correction** -0.20s/f (Firm) course record **7 Ran SP% 115.8**
Speed ratings (Par 111): **117,115,113,113,112 112,111**
CSF £5.14 TOTE £2.30: £1.10, £1.90; EX 5.50 Trifecta £24.50.
Owner Sheikh Hamdan bin Mohammed Al Maktoum **Bred** Barronstown Stud **Trained** Middleham Moor, N Yorks

FOCUS
An interesting Listed contest with some very different profiles among the principals. This rates a turf best from Matterhorn.

4398 LONGINES IRISH CHAMPIONS' WEEKEND EBF FILLIES' CONDITIONS STKS (PLUS 10 RACE) — 5f 21y
4:00 (4:03) (Class 2) 2-Y-O £11,205 (£3,355; £1,677; £838; £419) **Stalls Centre**

Form RPR

1 **Hand On My Heart** 2-8-12 .... HectorCrouch 1 84+
(Clive Cox) *mde all and racd against nr side rail: hrd pressed thrght: rdn jst over 1f out: kpt on wl and asserted ins fnl f* **5/1**[3]

2610 2 1/2 **Separate**[8] 4048 2-9-3 82 .... PatDobbs 3 87
(Richard Hannon) *sn pushed along in last but in tch: styd on fnl f: tk 2nd last 75yds: nt rch wnr* **6/1**

1134 3 3/4 **Lady Kermit (IRE)**[29] 3333 2-9-5 89 .... OisinMurphy 4 86
(Archie Watson) *w wnr: rdn over 1f out: jst hld ins fnl f and lost 2nd last 75yds* **1/1**[1]

4223 4 1 3/4 **Inyamazane (IRE)**[6] 4142 2-9-0 .... DavidProbert 6 75
(Mick Channon) *in tch: hanging lft fr 1/2-way: rdn 2f out: nt qckn over 1f out: fdd ins fnl f* **16/1**

10 5 *nse* **Last Surprise (IRE)**[8] 4048 2-9-3 .... PatCosgrave 2 78
(Simon Crisford) *trckd ldrs: plld out and effrt 2f out: rdn and nt qckn over 1f out: fdd ins fnl f* **3/1**[2]

59.55s (-0.55) **Going Correction** -0.20s/f (Firm) **5 Ran SP% 111.8**
Speed ratings (Par 96): **96,95,94,91,91**
CSF £32.43 TOTE £6.40: £3.00, £2.80; EX 30.00 Trifecta £62.20.
Owner Hot To Trot Racing V **Bred** Whitsbury Manor Stud **Trained** Lambourn, Berks

FOCUS
A small field 2yo conditions race but four realistic contenders and form to take seriously. The winner will be one to respect up in grade.

4399 CHARTWELL ANNIVERSARY (A H'CAP) — 1m 31y
4:35 (4:36) (Class 2) (0-105,98) 3-Y-O £12,450 (£3,728; £1,864; £932; £466) **Stalls Low**

Form RPR

0152 1 **Waarif (IRE)**[7] 4097 6-9-12 **96** .... RobbieDowney 6 103
(David O'Meara) *trckd ldr: shkn up over 2f out: sustained effrt u.p to ld last 100yds: hld on* **3/1**[1]

0-04 2 1/2 **Bless Him (IRE)**[21] 3581 5-9-9 **93** ....(h) PatCosgrave 4 99
(David Simcock) *hld up in last: stl there over 1f out: cajoled along to cl on ldrs fnl f: hanging lft but styd on to take 2nd nr fin* **10/3**[2]

4221 3 *nk* **Spirit Warning**[23] 3493 3-8-8 **88** .... DavidProbert 3 91
(Andrew Balding) *led: rdn against nr side rail over 1f out: hdd last 100yds: one pce and lost 2nd nr fin* **7/2**[3]

2121 4 2 1/2 **Kodiac Harbour (IRE)**[33] 3149 4-9-0 **87** .... MeganNicholls(3) 5 87
(Paul George) *trckd ldng pair: plld out and effrt 2f out: rdn and nt qckn over 1f out: wl hld after* **3/1**[1]

2510 5 1 1/4 **War Glory (IRE)**[10] 3987 6-10-0 **98** .... PatDobbs 1 95
(Richard Hannon) *trckd ldng pair: shkn up 2f out: no rspnse over 1f out: fdd fnl f* **5/1**

1m 41.63s (-2.87) **Going Correction** -0.20s/f (Firm) **5 Ran SP% 112.0**
WFA 3 from 4yo+ 10lb
Speed ratings (Par 109): **106,105,105,102,101**
CSF £13.36 TOTE £5.20: £2.00, £1.80; EX 13.40 Trifecta £37.10.
Owner Middleham Park Racing XLIX **Bred** Joseph Stewart Investments **Trained** Upper Helmsley, N Yorks

■ Stewards' Enquiry : Robbie Downey two-day ban: used whip above the permitted level (Jul 15-16)

FOCUS
A tight small-field handicap and a tight finish. Good form.

4400 DOWNLOAD THE GENTINGBET APP APPRENTICE H'CAP — 1m 3f 99y
5:10 (5:13) (Class 6) (0-60,60) 3-Y-O
£3,105 (£924; £461; £300; £300; £300) **Stalls Low**

Form RPR

1 1 **Champagne Terri (IRE)**[15] 3824 3-9-4 **60** .... CierenFallon(3) 6 70+
(Adrian Paul Keatley, Ire) *trckd ldrs: gng easily whn chalng over 3f out: led over 2f out: rdn clr over 1f out: readily* **7/2**[1]

0660 2 3 3/4 **Watch And Learn**[22] 3528 3-8-12 **54** .... WilliamCarver(3) 2 58
(Andrew Balding) *dwlt: sn in midfield: prog 3f out: rdn to chal whn hung bdly lft jst over 2f out: chsd wnr after: kpt on but no imp* **12/1**

52 3 1 1/4 **Miss Green Dream**[30] 3275 3-8-3 **47** .... SeanKirrane(5) 11 49
(Julia Feilden) *trckd ldrs: tried to chal over 2f out: rdn and one pce fnl 2f* **4/1**[2]

0655 4 *hd* **Smith (IRE)**[9] 4029 3-8-9 **51** ....(v[1]) GeorgiaDobie(3) 14 53
(Eve Johnson Houghton) *wl in rr: pushed along and prog 3f out: rdn to chse ldrs 2f out: kpt on same pce after (jockey said gelding suffered interference on the bend)* **16/1**

-650 5 4 **Moon Artist (FR)**[58] 2343 3-8-7 **46** oh1 .... DarraghKeenan 4 42
(Michael Blanshard) *trckd ldrs: stl cl up whn impeded jst over 2f out: fdd over 1f out* **50/1**

1250 6 2 **Mr Fox**[26] 3407 3-9-0 **60** .... AngusVilliers(7) 9 52
(Michael Attwater) *sn in last and pushed along: prog on wd outside over 2f out: kpt on but nvr any ch* **12/1**

05-5 7 2 **Crystal Tiara**[16] 3777 3-8-7 **53** .... GeorgeBass(7) 7 42
(Mick Channon) *trckd ldng pair: cl up 3f out: wknd 2f out* **14/1**

-360 8 1 1/2 **Daniel Dravot**[9] 4029 3-8-8 **50** ....(h) AledBeech(3) 5 36
(Michael Attwater) *wl in rr: struggling 4f out: passed a few late on but nvr a factor* **25/1**

3004 9 1/2 **Mi Manchi (IRE)**[16] 3777 3-8-9 **55** ....(p) StefanoCherchi(7) 10 41
(Marco Botti) *wl in tch tl wknd over 2f out (jockey said filly hung left handed)* **10/1**

103 10 7 **Heatherdown (IRE)**[70] 1957 3-9-2 **60** ....(p) TristanPrice(5) 1 34
(Ian Williams) *mde most to over 2f out: wknd rapidly* **9/1**

2535 11 2 **Brinkleys Katie**[26] 3418 3-8-12 **51** ....(v) RhiainIngram 8 22
(Paul George) *trckd ldr to 3f out: wknd rapidly (jockey said filly hung right-handed)* **9/1**

-660 12 2 1/4 **Darwin Dream**[29] 3311 3-9-7 **60** ....(p) PoppyBridgwater 3 28
(Sophie Leech) *dwlt: a wl in rr: struggling 4f out (jockey said gelding was never travelling)* **20/1**

000 13 1 3/4 **Video Diva (IRE)**[22] 3553 3-8-8 **54** .... LorenzoAtzori(7) 15 19
(James Fanshawe) *dwlt: in rr: urged along and effrt over 3f out: sn wknd* **5/1**[3]

0600 14 5 **Tribune**[11] 3965 3-8-6 **52** .... ElinorJones(7) 13 9
(Sylvester Kirk) *racd wd in midfield: unbalanced 3f out and wknd* **50/1**

The Form Book Flat 2019, Raceform Ltd, Newbury, RG14 5SJ

000 15 *88* **I'm Brian**[39] 2925 3-8-12 **51** SebastianWoods 12
(Julia Feilden) *unruly to post: in tch to 5f out: sn in last and rel to r: t.o (jockey said gelding jumped left handed out of the stalls and his saddle slipped)* **20/1**

2m 26.41s (-3.29) **Going Correction** -0.20s/f (Firm) **15** Ran SP% **133.2**
Speed ratings (Par 97): **103,100,99,99,96 94,93,92,91,86 85,83,82,78,14**
CSF £48.94 CT £187.45 TOTE £4.30: £2.40, £3.60, £2.10; EX 55.60 Trifecta £434.40.
Owner Mrs B Keatley **Bred** John R Jeffers **Trained** Rossmore Cottage, Co Kildare

FOCUS
A large but modest field under apprentices to end things, and an Irish raider made no mistake.
T/Plt: £70.40 to a £1 stake. Pool: £54,643.46 - 566.0 winning units T/Qpdt: £18.80 to a £1 stake. Pool: £4,226.16 - 165.86 winning units **Jonathan Neesom**

[3862] YORK (L-H)
Saturday, June 29

OFFICIAL GOING: Good to firm (stands' 7.3, ctr 7.3, far 7.4)
Wind: Light across Weather: Fine and dry

4401 SUN RACING AVAILABLE IN APP STORE NOVICE STKS (PLUS 10 RACE) 6f
2:10 (2:12) (Class 3) 2-Y-O **£9,703** (£2,887; £1,443; £721) **Stalls** Low

Form RPR

1 **1** **Al Aakif (IRE)**[27] 3371 2-9-8 0 ColmO'Donoghue 3 93
(William Haggas) *bmpd s: trckd ldrs: hdwy over 2f out: chal over 1f out: sn rdn: led ins fnl f: kpt on wl* **11/8**[1]

3 **2** *1 ½* **Clareyblue (IRE)**[21] 3601 2-9-2 0 PaulMulrennan 5 83
(Martyn Meade) *cl up: led over 3f out: jnd and rdn over 1f out: drvn and hdd ins fnl f: kpt on* **4/1**[3]

3 *6* **Treble Treble (IRE)** 2-9-2 0 TomEaves 1 65+
(Kevin Ryan) *slt ld: hdd over 3f out: rdn along 2f out: sn edgd rt and kpt on same pce* **14/1**

03 **4** *4* **Good Night Mr Tom (IRE)**[18] 3679 2-9-2 0 JimmyQuinn 4 53
(Mark Johnston) *chsd ldng pair: rdn along over 2f out: sn drvn and kpt on same pce* **8/1**

50 **5** *1 ½* **International Lion**[14] 3866 2-9-2 0 TonyHamilton 2 48
(Richard Fahey) *in rr and awkward path after 200yds: reminders and sn detached: rdn along 1/2-way: styd on fnl 2f* **25/1**

6 *2 ½* **Plymouth Rock (IRE)** 2-9-2 0 JasonHart 7 41+
(John Quinn) *dwlt and wnt rt s: sn trcking ldrs: pushed along wl over 2f out: rdn wl over 1f out: sn wknd* **7/2**[2]

3 **7** *3 ¼* **Mischief Star**[18] 3703 2-9-2 0 DavidNolan 6 31
(David O'Meara) *in tch: rdn along wl over 2f out: sn outpcd* **9/1**

1m 11.39s (-0.21) **Going Correction** 0.0s/f (Good) **7** Ran SP% **116.0**
Speed ratings (Par 97): **101,99,91,85,83 80,76**
CSF £7.38 TOTE £2.20: £1.60, £2.40; EX 7.50 Trifecta £65.10.
Owner Hamdan Al Maktoum **Bred** Rathbarry Stud **Trained** Newmarket, Suffolk

FOCUS
The rail was out six metres around the home bend from 1m1f to the entrance to the home straight. The first two pulled clear and look above average. This form could easily have been rated a little higher.

4402 SUN RACING H'CAP 6f
2:45 (2:47) (Class 2) (0-105,103) 3-Y-O+
£31,125 (£9,320; £4,660; £2,330; £1,165; £585) **Stalls** Low

Form RPR

0034 **1** **Gulliver**[12] 3945 5-9-2 **95** (tp) JasonHart 4 105
(David O'Meara) *midfield: pushed along 1/2-way: hdwy over 2f out: rdn to ld over 1f out: drvn ins fnl f: kpt on strly* **20/1**

0045 **2** *1 ½* **Growl**[21] 3589 7-8-9 **91** ConnorMurtagh(3) 20 96
(Richard Fahey) *hld up towards rr: hdwy 2f out: rdn over 1f out: styd on to chal ins fnl f: sn drvn and kpt on same pce towards fin* **16/1**

0005 **3** *½* **Golden Apollo**[14] 3863 5-8-12 **91** JamesSullivan 1 95
(Tim Easterby) *in tch: hdwy to chse ldrs 2f out: rdn over 1f out: drvn ins fnl f: kpt on* **7/1**[1]

0450 **4** *shd* **Intisaab**[7] 4095 8-9-8 **101** (p) DavidNolan 2 104
(David O'Meara) *midfield: hdwy over 2f out: rdn to chse ldrs over 1f out: kpt on fnl f* **10/1**

5226 **5** *1 ¾* **Wentworth Falls**[21] 3602 7-9-1 **94** SamJames 10 95
(Geoffrey Harker) *hld up towards rr: hdwy 2f out: rdn over 1f out: kpt on fnl f* **9/1**[3]

3-10 **6** *nk* **Sir Maximilian (IRE)**[7] 4095 10-9-2 **95** (p) ColmO'Donoghue 14 92
(Ian Williams) *hld up on outer: hdwy over 2f out: rdn and edgd lft over 1f out: kpt on u.p fnl f* **12/1**

1206 **7** *¾* **George Bowen (IRE)**[13] 3891 7-9-3 **103** (v) RussellHarris(7) 8 97
(Richard Fahey) *dwlt and in rr: hdwy wl over 1f out: sn rdn and kpt on fnl f* **12/1**

0004 **8** *nk* **Flying Pursuit**[14] 3863 6-9-1 **94** (p) RachelRichardson 12 87
(Tim Easterby) *wnt lft s: cl up: rdn along wl over 2f out: sn wknd* **25/1**

-320 **9** *shd* **Jawwaal**[42] 2843 4-8-5 **89** PaulaMuir(5) 19 84
(Michael Dods) *sltly hmpd s: hld up towards rr: hdwy 2f out: styng on whn hmpd over 1f out: sn swtchd rt and kpt on fnl f* **16/1**

-033 **10** *1* **Great Prospector (IRE)**[14] 3863 4-9-1 **94** TonyHamilton 6 84
(Richard Fahey) *midfield: pushed along over 2f out: sn rdn and n.d (jockey said gelding was denied a clear run approaching the final furlong)* **8/1**[2]

5010 **11** *1 ¼* **Soldier's Minute**[7] 4095 4-9-6 **99** ShaneGray 5 85
(Keith Dalgleish) *led: rdn along and hdd wl over 1f out: wknd fnl f* **7/1**[1]

40-0 **12** *nk* **Justanotherbottle (IRE)**[44] 2775 5-9-6 **99** TomQueally 13 84
(Declan Carroll) *prom: rdn along wl over 2f out: sn wknd* **20/1**

5-10 **13** *shd* **Ventura Ocean (IRE)**[14] 3865 3-8-2 **91** SeanDavis(3) 15 74
(Richard Fahey) *swtchd lft s: hld up: a towards rr* **25/1**

3120 **14** *hd* **Lake Volta (IRE)**[7] 4095 4-9-4 **102** AndrewBreslin(5) 7 86
(Mark Johnston) *chsd ldrs: rdn along 1/2-way: sn wknd* **8/1**[2]

6210 **15** *hd* **Hyperfocus (IRE)**[14] 3863 5-8-12 **91** PaulMulrennan 18 74
(Tim Easterby) *in tch: rdn along over 2f out: grad wknd* **25/1**

1413 **16** *2 ½* **Paddy Power (IRE)**[13] 3893 6-8-1 **83** NoelGarbutt(3) 17 58
(Richard Fahey) *a towards rr* **20/1**

-040 **17** *2 ¾* **Savalas (IRE)**[21] 3589 4-8-13 **92** TomEaves 11 58
(Kevin Ryan) *sltly hmpd s: cl up: rdn along over 2f out: wknd wl over 1f out* **9/1**[3]

0000 **18** *99* **Don Armado (IRE)**[7] 4123 3-8-0 **86** oh1 JimmyQuinn 9
(Robert Cowell) *towards rr: lost action over 4f out: sn eased and wl bhd (jockey said colt lost its action; vet said colt to be lame on its left hind)* **50/1**

1m 10.09s (-1.51) **Going Correction** 0.0s/f (Good)
WFA 3 from 4yo+ 7lb **18** Ran SP% **131.2**
Speed ratings (Par 109): **110,108,107,107,104 104,103,103,102,101 99,99,99,99,98 95,91,**
CSF £305.61 CT £2558.17 TOTE £33.60: £6.40, £3.90, £2.30, £2.90; EX 488.70 Trifecta £5996.10.
Owner Withernsea Thoroughbred Limited **Bred** S A Douch **Trained** Upper Helmsley, N Yorks

FOCUS
A typically competitive sprint handicap. The winner scored decisively, but several of those in behind are worth keeping an eye on. Sound form, with a turf pb from the winner.

4403 VISIT SUNRACING.CO.UK FOR TOP TIPS H'CAP 7f 192y
3:20 (3:22) (Class 3) (0-90,92) 3-Y-O+ **£9,703** (£2,887; £1,443; £721) **Stalls** Low

Form RPR

-502 **1** **Irv (IRE)**[26] 3412 3-8-0 **72** JamesSullivan 2 82
(Micky Hammond) *hld up towards rr: hdwy into midfield 4f out: chsd ldrs 2f out: rdn and n.m.r jst over 1f out: drvn to ld jst ins fnl f: kpt on strly* **11/1**

0223 **2** *2* **Markazi (FR)**[14] 3867 5-9-11 **87** (p) DavidNolan 1 94
(David O'Meara) *trckd ldrs: smooth hdwy on inner 3f out: cl up 2f out: rdn and ev ch over 1f out: drvn ins fnl f: kpt on same pce towards fin* **9/2**[1]

0004 **3** *1* **King's Pavilion (IRE)**[23] 3515 6-9-12 **88** NathanEvans 14 93
(Jason Ward) *stdd and swtchd lft s: hld up and bhd: hdwy 2f out: rdn to chse ldrs 1 1/2f out: styng on whn n.m.r and swtchd rt ins fnl f: kpt on wl towards fin* **25/1**

1064 **4** *½* **Juanito Chico (IRE)**[39] 2927 5-9-1 **77** (t) CallumShepherd 9 81
(Stuart Williams) *hld up in rr: hdwy over 3f out: chsd ldrs wl over 1f out: sn rdn: styd on fnl f* **33/1**

-300 **5** *shd* **International Man**[46] 2710 4-8-9 **74** ConnorMurtagh(3) 3 77
(Richard Fahey) *cl up: led wl over 2f out: rdn wl over 1f out: drvn and hdd jst ins fnl f: hld whn rdr dropped whip fnl 100yds* **20/1**

5351 **6** *1 ¾* **Poet's Dawn**[14] 3867 4-9-8 **84** RachelRichardson 11 83
(Tim Easterby) *cl up: rdn along and ev ch 2f out: sn drvn and grad wknd* **9/1**

4152 **7** *½* **Furzig**[14] 3867 4-9-3 **79** TonyHamilton 10 77
(Richard Fahey) *hld up towards rr: hdwy wl over 2f out: rdn wl over 1f out: kpt on: n.d* **7/1**[3]

5626 **8** *hd* **Humble Gratitude**[14] 3845 4-9-4 **80** (p) ColmO'Donoghue 4 78
(Ian Williams) *chsd ldrs: hdwy on outer 3f out: sn cl up: ev ch 2f out: sn rdn and grad wknd* **16/1**

041 **9** *1* **Greek Hero**[18] 3707 3-8-6 **78** SamJames 6 71
(Declan Carroll) *hld up: a towards rr* **14/1**

6000 **10** *nk* **Give It Some Teddy**[8] 4079 5-9-4 **80** JasonHart 15 75
(Tim Easterby) *hld up: a in rr* **12/1**

-242 **11** *hd* **King Of Tonga (IRE)**[28] 3357 3-9-0 **89** SeanDavis(3) 13 81
(Richard Fahey) *in tch on outer: rdn along 3f out: sn wknd* **6/1**[2]

2310 **12** *hd* **Kaeso**[14] 3863 5-9-11 **92** FayeMcManoman(5) 12 86
(Nigel Tinkler) *hld up: a in rr* **7/1**[3]

2130 **13** *2* **Hayadh**[14] 3863 6-10-1 **91** LewisEdmunds 5 80
(Rebecca Bastiman) *chsd ldrs: pushed along over 3f out: sn rdn and wknd* **7/1**[3]

2006 **14** *4 ½* **Commander Han (FR)**[21] 3581 4-9-10 **86** TomEaves 7 65
(Kevin Ryan) *slt ld: rdn along over 3f out: hdd wl over 2f out: sn wknd* **11/1**

1m 36.62s (-0.88) **Going Correction** 0.0s/f (Good)
WFA 3 from 4yo+ 10lb **14** Ran SP% **128.4**
Speed ratings (Par 107): **104,102,101,100,100 98,98,97,96,96 96,96,94,89**
CSF £62.62 CT £1294.20 TOTE £15.40: £4.50, £2.10, £11.40; EX 81.30 Trifecta £3126.50.
Owner Irvine Lynch **Bred** Mrs Marion Emerson **Trained** Middleham, N Yorks

FOCUS
Add 17yds. Plenty of viable contenders in this, but the winner scored with authority. The form's rated around the second.

4404 VISIT SUNRACING.CO.UK FOR TOP BOOKMAKER OFFERS H'CAP 2m 56y
3:55 (3:56) (Class 4) (0-80,82) 4-Y-O+
£8,927 (£2,656; £1,327; £663; £300; £300) **Stalls** Low

Form RPR

1212 **1** **True Destiny**[19] 3653 4-9-7 **79** TrevorWhelan 13 89+
(Roger Charlton) *hld up towards rr: smooth hdwy 4f out: sn trcking ldrs: led wl over 2f out: rdn and edgd rt wl over 1f out: drvn and hung rt to stands' rail ins fnl f: kpt on* **7/4**[1]

/-00 **2** *1 ¼* **Aldreth**[15] 3816 8-9-6 **78** (p) NathanEvans 2 84
(Michael Easterby) *in tch: hdwy to trck ldrs over 4f out: smooth hdwy and cl up over 2f out: rdn and ev ch whn sltly hmpd and swtchd lft over 1f out: sn drvn and kpt on* **25/1**

4-55 **3** *nk* **Buyer Beware (IRE)**[8] 4056 7-8-2 **63** ow3 (p) AaronJones(3) 14 68
(Liam Bailey) *trckd ldrs: hdwy on outer 3f out: rdn along 2f out: drvn over 1f out: kpt on wl u.p fnl f* **25/1**

2220 **4** *nk* **Shine Baby Shine**[13] 3886 5-8-4 **65** ConnorMurtagh(3) 10 70
(Philip Kirby) *hld up in rr: hdwy over 4f out: chsd ldrs and rdn over 2f out: cl up and carried rt ent fnl f: drvn and styng on whn nt clr run nr stands' rail last 75yds: swtchd lft and kpt on* **14/1**

-365 **5** *1 ¾* **October Storm**[20] 3635 6-9-5 **77** CallumShepherd 8 80
(Mick Channon) *towards rr: pushed along over 4f out: hdwy 3f out: sn rdn: chsd ldrs over 1f out: sn drvn and kpt on* **13/2**[2]

1-46 **6** *3 ½* **Graceful Lady**[33] 3145 6-9-0 **77** AndrewBreslin(5) 4 76
(Robert Eddery) *dwlt and bhd: hdwy on inner over 4f out: rdn along 3f out: plugged on fnl 2f: n.d* **10/1**

2-21 **7** *¾* **Auxiliary**[15] 3816 6-8-7 **72** (p) JonathanFisher(7) 5 70
(Liam Bailey) *hld up towards rr: hdwy over 3f out: in tch and rdn along over 2f out: sn drvn and n.d* **9/1**

-004 **8** *2 ½* **Stormin Tom (IRE)**[24] 3481 7-9-0 **72** RachelRichardson 11 67
(Tim Easterby) *trckd ldng pair: led after 3f: pushed along 4f out: rdn over 3f out: hdd wl over 2f out: sn drvn and wknd* **10/1**

1-00 **9** *12* **Waiting For Richie**[19] 3653 6-9-1 **73** JamesSullivan 6 53
(Tom Tate) *prom: trckd ldr 7f out: pushed along 4f out: rdn over 3f out: sn wknd* **16/1**

504- **10** *¾* **Liva (IRE)**[70] 8045 4-8-11 **72** SeanDavis(3) 3 52
(Stef Keniry) *led 3f: chsd ldr: rdn along 4f out: sn wknd* **12/1**

361 **11** *nk* **Trautmann (IRE)**[8] 4056 5-8-12 **70** (tp) PaulMulrennan 9 49
(Rebecca Menzies) *dwlt: a in rr* **8/1**[3]

/040 **12** *1 ¾* **Red Tornado (FR)**[44] 2781 7-9-3 **75** MichaelStainton 7 52
(Chris Fairhurst) *trckd ldrs: effrt 5f out: rdn along 4f out: sn wknd* **25/1**

The Form Book Flat 2019, Raceform Ltd, Newbury, RG14 5SJ

066- **13** *33* **Mercer's Troop** (IRE)[51] 5796 4-9-1 **73**............................ TomQueally 12 10
(Alistair Whillans) *in tch: pushed along 6f out: rdn 5f out: sn lost pl and bhd* **33/1**

3m 32.55s (-1.35) **Going Correction** 0.0s/f (Good) 13 Ran SP% **123.7**
Speed ratings (Par 105): **103,102,102,102,101 99,99,97,91,91 91,90,73**
CSF £61.69 CT £882.83 TOTE £2.30: £1.30, £8.40, £10.50; EX 64.90 Trifecta £501.70.

Owner Exors Of The Late Sultan Ahmad Sha **Bred** M J & L A Taylor Llp **Trained** Beckhampton, Wilts

■ Stewards' Enquiry : Trevor Whelan two-day ban: interference & careless riding (Jul 15-16)

FOCUS
Add 22yds. An eventful staying handicap with the progressive winner hanging right across the course, but having enough in reserve to prevail. He can continue on the upgrade.

4405 FOLLOW SUN RACING ON INSTAGRAM BRITISH EBF FILLIES' NOVICE STKS (PLUS 10 RACE) 7f

4:30 (4:32) (Class 3) 3-Y-O **£9,703** (£2,887; £1,443; £721) **Stalls** Low

Form RPR

4- **1** **Mubtasimah**[307] 6589 3-9-0 0............................ ColmO'Donoghue 4 94
(William Haggas) *hld up in rr: smooth hdwy 3f out: cl up 2f out: shkn up to ld wl over 1f out: sn clr: easily* **4/6**[1]

533 **2** *9* **Society Guest** (IRE)[7] 4120 3-9-0 75............................ CallumShepherd 2 73
(Mick Channon) *trckd ldr: hdwy and cl up over 2f out: sn rdn: drvn over 1f out: kpt on same pce* **4/1**[3]

0 **3** *7* **Alnaseem**[78] 1740 3-9-0 0............................ PaulMulrennan 3 51
(Owen Burrows) *sn led: pushed along over 2f out: rdn and hdd wl over 1f out: sn wknd* **7/2**[2]

4 *7* **Angel Lane** (FR) 3-9-0 0............................ MichaelStainton 1 32
(K R Burke) *t.k.h: trckd ldng pair: effrt on inner 3f out: rdn along over 2f out: sn outpcd* **9/1**

1m 23.42s (-1.18) **Going Correction** 0.0s/f (Good) 4 Ran SP% **112.2**
Speed ratings (Par 100): **106,95,87,79**
CSF £3.93 TOTE £1.40; EX 3.00 Trifecta £5.30.

Owner Sheikh Juma Dalmook Al Maktoum **Bred** Panda Bloodstock **Trained** Newmarket, Suffolk

FOCUS
An easy task for the winner and she did it in fine style. The form's been rated at face value around the runner-up.

4406 FOLLOW SUN RACING ON TWITTER "JUMP JOCKEYS' NUNTHORPE" H'CAP (PROFESSIONAL JUMP JOCKEYS) 5f

5:05 (5:08) (Class 3) (0-90,91) 4-Y-O+

£15,562 (£4,660; £2,330; £1,165; £582; £292) **Stalls** Low

Form RPR

2032 **1** **Nibras Again**[2] 4301 5-10-8 **75**............................ JoshuaMoore 18 85
(Paul Midgley) *racd towards stands' side: in tch: hdwy 2f out: rdn over 1f out: led ins fnl f: drvn out* **8/1**[2]

-643 **2** *¾* **Excessable**[7] 4100 6-10-11 **78**............................ JamieHamilton 19 85
(Tim Easterby) *racd towards stands' side: prom: led 2f out: rdn over 1f out: drvn and hdd ins fnl f: kpt on* **12/1**

5006 **3** *nk* **Line Of Reason** (IRE)[1] 4331 9-11-7 **88**............................ AlainCawley 17 94+
(Paul Midgley) *hld up towards rr nr stands' side: hdwy 2f out: swtchd rt wl over 1f out: rdn to chse ldrs and swtchd lft ent fnl f: sn drvn: fin strly* **16/1**

50 **4** *¾* **Secretinthepark**[7] 4100 9-10-7 **74**............................(b) KielanWoods 13 77
(Michael Mullineaux) *prom: centre: cl up 2f out: rdn and ev ch over 1f out: drvn ins fnl f and kpt on same pce* **50/1**

-120 **5** *½* **Fendale**[44] 2775 7-11-5 **86**............................ ConnorKing 8 87
(Bryan Smart) *hld up towards rr centre: hdwy 2f out: rdn over 1f out: styd on wl fnl f* **7/1**[1]

0-66 **6** *¾* **War Whisper** (IRE)[57] 2368 6-10-13 **80**............................ TomScudamore 9 79
(Paul Midgley) *chsd ldrs centre: hdwy and cl up over 2f out: rdn wl over 1f out: drvn ent fnl f: kpt on same pce* **16/1**

6064 **7** *1¼* **Sheepscar Lad** (IRE)[11] 3971 5-10-5 **72**............................ AndrewTinkler 3 66
(Nigel Tinkler) *hld up: swtchd to centre and hdwy 2f out: rdn to chse ldrs whn nt clr run 1f out: styd on towards fin* **10/1**[3]

002 **8** *½* **Roman River**[72] 1892 4-11-10 **91**............................ LeightonAspell 15 83
(Martin Smith) *racd towards stands' side: in tch: hdwy to chse ldrs 2f out: rdn over 1f out: n.m.r and carried lft 1f out: kpt on same pce after* **8/1**[2]

6140 **9** *¾* **Musharrif**[18] 3706 7-10-7 **74**............................ NickScholfield 6 64
(Declan Carroll) *racd towards far side: led: rdn along and hdd 2f out: drvn over 1f out: grad wknd* **16/1**

-503 **10** *2¼* **Gin In The Inn** (IRE)[11] 3971 6-11-2 **83**............................ DarylJacob 1 65
(Richard Fahey) *racd towards far side: chsd ldrs: rdn along 2f out: wknd over 1f out* **8/1**[2]

0000 **11** *hd* **Captain Colby** (USA)[21] 3589 7-11-6 **87**............................ SamTwiston-Davies 12 72
(Paul Midgley) *a towards rr* **25/1**

0106 **12** *¾* **Poyle Vinnie**[21] 3582 9-11-6 **87**............................ HarryCobden 7 65
(Ruth Carr) *chsd ldrs centre: rdn along 2f out: sn wknd* **16/1**

0505 **13** *1* **Boom The Groom** (IRE)[13] 3893 8-11-3 **84**............................(p[1]) HarryBannister 10 59
(Tony Carroll) *chsd ldrs centre: rdn along 2f out: sn wknd* **12/1**

423- **14** *1* **Rosina**[198] 9525 6-10-11 **78**............................(p) BryonyFrost 5 49
(Ann Duffield) *chsd ldrs: rdn along over 2f out: sn wknd* **25/1**

-045 **15** *nk* **Consequences** (IRE)[13] 3883 4-10-12 **79**............................(t) AidanColeman 11 49
(Ian Williams) *sltly hmpd s: a towards rr* **16/1**

1205 **16** *½* **Pea Shooter**[113] 1082 10-10-8 **75**............................ HenryBrooke 4 43
(Brian Ellison) *racd towards far side: a towards rr* **50/1**

0120 **17** *3¼* **East Street Revue**[14] 3868 6-10-9 **76**............................(p) JamesBowen 2 32
(Tim Easterby) *racd towards far side: a in rr* **10/1**[3]

12-4 **18** *½* **Lomu** (IRE)[23] 3501 5-11-8 **89**............................ BrianHughes 14 44
(Keith Dalgleish) *t.k.h: racd towards stands' side: chsd ldrs: rdn along over 2f out: sn wknd* **7/1**[1]

3412 **19** *18* **Music Society** (IRE)[14] 3868 4-10-10 **77**............................(p[1]) BrendanPowell 16
(Tim Easterby) *dwlt: a bhd (jockey said he was slow to remove the blindfold due to the gelding being restless in the stalls)* **10/1**[3]

58.44s (0.24) **Going Correction** 0.0s/f (Good) 19 Ran SP% **142.0**
Speed ratings (Par 107): **98,96,96,95,94 93,91,90,89,85 85,84,82,80,80 79,74,73,44**
CSF £112.33 CT £982.92 TOTE £11.80: £2.70, £4.10, £4.40, £12.00; EX 143.90 Trifecta £1579.10.

Owner Peedeetee Syndicate, TA Stephenson & TWM **Bred** Cheveley Park Stud Ltd **Trained** Westow, N Yorks

FOCUS
Plenty of top jump jockeys on show and they served up an exciting race. The winner did it well on ground he likes and was given a fine ride by Josh Moore. Another pb from the winner.

4407 SUN RACING ANDROID APP VISIT SUNRACING.CO.UK APPRENTICE H'CAP 1m 3f 188y

5:40 (5:40) (Class 3) (0-90,89) 4-Y-O+ **£9,703** (£2,887; £1,443; £721) **Stalls** Centre

Form RPR

663 **1** **Gossip Column** (IRE)[14] 3847 4-9-6 **83**............................ CameronNoble 5 92
(Ian Williams) *hld up towards rr: stdy hdwy on outer 3f out: cl up 2f out: rdn to chal and edgd lft jst over 1f out: drvn to take slt advantage ins fnl f: hld on wl towards fin* **7/2**[2]

06-6 **2** *shd* **Doctor Cross** (IRE)[23] 3514 5-8-7 **73**............................ ConnorMurtagh(3) 1 81
(Richard Fahey) *trckd ldng pair: hdwy on inner 3f out: rdn to ld 1 1/2f out: sn jnd: drvn and hdd narrowly ins fnl f: rallied gamely and kpt on wl towards fin* **7/1**

6-34 **3** *4* **Pirate King**[35] 3081 4-9-7 **84**............................ MitchGodwin 3 86
(Harry Dunlop) *trckd ldrs: hdwy 3f out: rdn along 2f out: drvn over 1f out: kpt on same pce fnl f* **11/2**

-050 **4** *1¾* **Thomas Cranmer** (USA)[9] 4035 5-8-12 **75**............................ RowanScott 4 74
(Tina Jackson) *led: pushed along 3f out: rdn over 2f out: hdd 1 1/2f out: sn drvn: hld whn n.m.r ent fnl f: one pce after* **9/2**[3]

3136 **5** *3* **Claire Underwood** (IRE)[19] 3655 4-9-9 **86**............................ SeanDavis 7 80
(Richard Fahey) *cl up: pushed along 3f out: rdn 2f out: sn drvn and wknd* **11/4**[1]

1-41 **6** *6* **My Boy Sepoy**[37] 3022 4-8-13 **79**............................ DylanHogan(3) 9 63
(Stuart Williams) *trckd ldrs: hdwy on outer 4f out: cl up 3f out: sn rdn along and wknd fnl 2f* **9/2**[3]

440/ **7** *13* **Percy** (IRE)[359] 4591 5-9-8 **88**............................ SeamusCronin(3) 8 52
(Frank Bishop) *s.i.s and bhd: tk clsr order over 5f out: rdn along over 3f out: sn wknd* **16/1**

2m 31.1s (-2.10) **Going Correction** 0.0s/f (Good) 7 Ran SP% **119.0**
Speed ratings (Par 107): **107,106,104,103,101 97,88**
CSF £29.36 CT £134.73 TOTE £3.70: £2.10, £3.30; EX 29.20 Trifecta £133.20.

Owner Dr Marwan Koukash **Bred** Peter Reynolds & Robert Dore **Trained** Portway, Worcs

FOCUS
Add 22yds. A thrilling finish to a competitive middle-distance handicap. The form should stand up but it's ordinary for the grade.
T/Jkpt: Not won. T/Plt: £170.70 to a £1 stake. Pool: £120,964.32 - 517.30 winning units T/Qpdt: £41.40 to a £1 stake. Pool: £9,032.32 - 161.12 winning units **Joe Rowntree**

4408 - 4410a (Foreign Racing) - See Raceform Interactive

4350 CURRAGH (R-H)

Saturday, June 29

OFFICIAL GOING: Good (good to firm in places on round course)

4411a DUBAI DUTY FREE FULL OF SURPRISES INTERNATIONAL STKS (GROUP 3) 1m 2f

3:30 (3:30) 3-Y-O+ **£39,864** (£12,837; £6,081; £2,702; £1,351; £675)

RPR

1 **Buckhurst** (IRE)[36] 3063 3-8-12 104............................ WayneLordan 4 108+
(Joseph Patrick O'Brien, Ire) *settled bhd ldrs: 3rd 1/2-way: gng wl in 3rd into st: effrt nr side 1 1/2f out where disp ld and sn led gng best: rdn ins fnl f where pressed and edgd sltly lft briefly: kpt on wl to assert nr fin* **2/1**[1]

2 *1½* **Blenheim Palace** (IRE)[27] 3390 3-8-12 106............................ RyanMoore 1 105
(A P O'Brien, Ire) *pushed along briefly fr s: sn led and disp: hdd after 2f: rdn in cl 2nd over 2f out and disp ld briefly 1 1/2f out tl sn hdd: no imp on wnr nr fin: kpt on same pce* **3/1**[3]

3 *nk* **Georgeville**[47] 2699 3-8-12 97............................ OisinOrr 7 104
(D K Weld, Ire) *w.w: 6th 1/2-way: gng wl in 5th 3f out: clsr in 4th 2f out: rdn and ev ch nr side over 1f out: no imp on wnr u.p in 3rd nr fin: kpt on same pce* **9/4**[2]

4 *¾* **Lady Wannabe** (IRE)[36] 3061 3-8-9 83............................ ChrisHayes 2 100
(J A Stack, Ire) *towards rr tl tk clsr order and disp 4th after 1f: pushed along in 4th into st: n.m.r fr over 2f out: rdn bhd ldrs in 5th over 1f out and no imp on wnr u.p in 4th wl ins fnl f: kpt on same pce* **20/1**

5 *¾* **Global Giant**[11] 3953 4-9-9 104............................ GeraldMosse 5 100
(Ed Dunlop) *in rr early tl tk clsr order and disp 4th after 1f: 5th 1/2-way: pushed along in 6th into st: rdn under 2f out and u.p in 6th 1f out: kpt on same pce into 5th nr fin: nvr trbld ldrs* **9/1**

6 *1¾* **Zihba** (IRE)[11] 3953 4-9-9 104............................(t[1]) WJLee 3 97
(J A Stack, Ire) *led and disp early: led after 2f: rdn under 2f out where sn jnd and hdd: no ex bhd ldrs over 1f out: wknd* **8/1**

7 *3* **Zabriskie** (IRE)[28] 3343 4-9-9 95............................(t[1]) ColinKeane 8 91
(Luke Comer, Ire) *cl up early tl sn settled bhd ldrs and dropped to rr after 1f: drvn in rr into st and no imp u.p 2f out: one pce after* **50/1**

2m 7.74s (-3.76) **Going Correction** +0.075s/f (Good) 7 Ran SP% **116.9**
WFA 3 from 4yo+ 12lb
Speed ratings: **114,112,112,111,111 109,107**
CSF £8.77 TOTE £2.80: £1.50, £1.70; DF 7.90 Trifecta £20.40.

Owner Lloyd J Williams **Bred** Denford Stud Ltd **Trained** Owning Hill, Co Kilkenny

FOCUS
The absence of Addeybb opened up this race, the winner saw it out in very taking fashion.

4412a (Foreign Racing) - See Raceform Interactive

4413a GAIN RAILWAY STKS (GROUP 2) 6f

4:40 (4:40) 2-Y-O **£69,099** (£22,252; £10,540; £4,684; £2,342) **Stalls** Centre

RPR

1 **Siskin** (USA)[36] 3060 2-9-3 103............................ ColinKeane 2 115+
(G M Lyons, Ire) *led briefly tl sn settled bhd ldrs in 3rd: tk clsr order travelling wl far side 2f out and led 1 1/2f out: rdn clr 1f out and sn in command: eased cl home: easily* **4/6**[1]

2 *2½* **Monarch Of Egypt** (USA)[77] 1772 2-9-3 0............................ RyanMoore 3 107
(A P O'Brien, Ire) *hld up bhd ldrs in 4th: prog far side fr 2f out into 2nd over 1f out: sn rdn and no imp on easy wnr ins fnl f: kpt on same pce* **7/2**[2]

3 *2¼* **Fort Myers** (USA)[11] 3949 2-9-3 105............................ DonnachaO'Brien 4 100
(A P O'Brien, Ire) *sltly awkward s: sn led and disp: narrow advantage at 1/2-way: drvn and hdd nr side 1 1/2f out: sn no imp on easy wnr in 3rd: jnd for 3rd briefly wl ins fnl f: kpt on into 3rd fnl stride* **7/2**[2]

4 *hd* **Real Force**[9] 4040 2-9-3 83............................ NGMcCullagh 5 99
(Gerard O'Leary, Ire) *dwlt: in rr: last at 1/2-way: tk clsr order and rdn between horses ent fnl f: disp 3rd briefly far side wl ins fnl f where no imp on ldrs: 4th fnl stride* **66/1**

5 *8 1/2* **Romero (IRE)**[42] 2820 2-9-3 0............................ KevinStott 1 74
(Kevin Ryan) *sn led and disp: cl 2nd at 1/2-way: pushed along in 2nd over 2f out and sn no ex in 3rd: wknd to rr 1f out: eased clsng stages* **12/1**[3]

1m 13.02s (-1.18) **Going Correction** +0.075s/f (Good) **5 Ran SP% 113.6**
Speed ratings: **110,106,103,103,92**
CSF £3.59 TOTE £1.50: £1.02, £2.20; DF 3.70 Trifecta £5.90.
Owner K Abdullah **Bred** Juddmonte Farms Inc **Trained** Dunsany, Co Meath

FOCUS
Strongly supported before the off, \bSiskin\p maintained his unbeaten record and he did it in style. He would appear to be the best two-year-old to have run in Ireland thus far this season and should be hard to beat in the Phoenix Stakes. He's rated in line with the best winner of this in the past 20 years and looks nailed on to do better again.

4414a DUBAI DUTY FREE IRISH DERBY (GROUP 1) (ENTIRE COLTS & FILLIES) 1m 4f
5:20 (5:21) 3-Y-O
£770,270 (£256,756; £121,621; £54,054; £27,027; £13,513)

RPR

1 **Sovereign (IRE)**[28] 3345 3-9-0 105............................ PBBeggy 2 117
(A P O'Brien, Ire) *disp early tl sn led and mde rest: 2 l clr of nrest rival and clr of remainder at 1/2-way: stl gng wl into st: rdn briefly and clr 1 1/2f out: styd on strly under hands and heels ins fnl f: easily (trainer said, regarding the improved form shown, the colt has shown plenty of ability in the past and appeared to appreciate the front running tactics and he stayed the trip very well)* **33/1**

2 *6* **Anthony Van Dyck (IRE)**[28] 3345 3-9-0 118.................. RyanMoore 4 109+
(A P O'Brien, Ire) *sweated up befhand: chsd ldrs in 3rd early tl settled in 4th after 1f: mod 4th bef 1/2-way: pushed along into st and no imp on clr ldrs: rdn into 2nd ins fnl f and kpt on wl: nt trble easy wnr* **5/4**[1]

3 *2 1/2* **Norway (IRE)**[10] 3984 3-9-0 104.............................(p) SeamieHeffernan 7 103
(A P O'Brien, Ire) *disp ld early tl sn settled in 2nd: 2 l bhd ldr and clr of remainder at 1/2-way: pushed along in 2nd over 3f out and no imp on easy wnr: u.p 2f out: dropped to 3rd ins fnl f: jst hld 3rd* **16/1**[3]

4 *shd* **Madhmoon (IRE)**[28] 3345 3-9-0 117............................ ChrisHayes 1 103+
(Kevin Prendergast, Ire) *w.w: mod 5th after 4f: disp mod 5th at 1/2-way: drvn 2f out and no imp on clr ldrs: rdn into 4th over 1f out and kpt on u.p: jst failed for 3rd: nt trble easy wnr* **5/2**[2]

5 *2* **Guaranteed (IRE)**[22] 3558 3-9-0 107............................(t) KevinManning 5 100+
(J S Bolger, Ire) *chsd ldrs in 4th early tl impr into 3rd after 1f: mod 3rd bef 1/2-way: pushed along into st where no imp on clr ldrs and lost pl u.p 2f out: dropped to 5th over 1f out and one pce after* **50/1**

6 *4 1/2* **Broome (IRE)**[28] 3345 3-9-0 117............................ DonnachaO'Brien 8 93+
(A P O'Brien, Ire) *s.i.s and in rr early: tk clsr order after 1f: mod 6th after 4f: disp mod 5th at 1/2-way: drvn into st and no imp on clr ldrs in mod 6th: kpt on one pce fnl 2f* **5/2**[2]

7 *2 3/4* **Il Paradiso (USA)**[48] 2665 3-9-0 87............................(p[1]) WayneLordan 6 88+
(A P O'Brien, Ire) *hld up towards rr: mod 7th at 1/2-way: bmpd sltly under 4f out: sn rdn and no imp in rr into st: swtchd lft under 2f out and rdn into mod 7th over 1f out: kpt on one pce* **40/1**

8 *9 1/2* **Rakan**[23] 3523 3-9-0 102............................ JimCrowley 3 73+
(D K Weld, Ire) *a bhd: last at 1/2-way: short of room briefly under 4f out where edgd lft and sltly bmpd rival: pushed along in mod 7th under 3f out and no ex: rdn 1 1/2f out and sn wknd to rr* **18/1**

2m 31.5s (-7.20) **Going Correction** +0.075s/f (Good) **8 Ran SP% 120.1**
Speed ratings: **103,99,97,97,95 92,91,84**
CSF £78.50 CT £766.02 TOTE £43.30: £6.40, £1.02, £3.00; DF 120.70 Trifecta £771.90.
Owner Mrs John Magnier & Michael Tabor & Derrick Smith **Bred** Barronstown Stud **Trained** Cashel, Co Tipperary

FOCUS
A shock result which left many scratching their head. The winner showed bits and pieces of form and, while he is an uncomplicated stayer who gallops for fun, he'd posted nothing to suggest he was capable of providing an upset of this magnitude. He was provided with plenty of rope and was good enough to capitalise on the opportunity. Whether this form proves to be rock-solid remains to be seen but there have to be some question marks given the winner seemed to get away from them. A step forward in any case from Sovereign, with Norway given his biggest beating of the year. Anthony Van Dyck is rated 11lb off his Epsom figure.

4415a (Foreign Racing) - See Raceform Interactive

4089
CHANTILLY (R-H)
Saturday, June 29
OFFICIAL GOING: Turf: good to soft

4416a ARQANA PRIX CHLOE (GROUP 3) (3YO FILLIES) (TURF) 1m 1f
6:45 3-Y-O
£36,036 (£14,414; £10,810; £7,207; £3,603)

RPR

1 **Suphala (FR)**[19] 3677 3-8-13 0 ow2.................. Pierre-CharlesBoudot 6 107+
(A Fabre, France) *prom: angled out w more than 1 1/2f to run: sustained prog to ld fnl 80yds: drvn out* **19/5**[3]

2 *nk* **Romanciere (IRE)**[43] 3-8-13 0 ow2............................ MaximeGuyon 7 106
(A Fabre, France) *trckd ldr on outer: drvn but nt qckn ent fnl 2f: styd on u.p fnl f: tk 2nd cl home* **21/1**

3 *1 1/4* **Imperial Charm**[34] 3121 3-8-13 0 ow2.................. MickaelBarzalona 8 104
(Simon Crisford) *led: sn swtchd to ins rail fr wd draw: drvn for home wl over 1 1/2f out: rallied u.p: hdd last 80yds: no ex: lost 2nd cl home* **8/5**[1]

4 *1 3/4* **Matematica (GER)**[27] 3387 3-8-13 0 ow2.................. OlivierPeslier 5 100
(C Laffon-Parias, France) *racd keenly: chsd ldrs on inner: cl 3rd and drvn 1 1/2f out: kpt on at same pce* **9/1**

5 *1* **Ashtara (USA)**[31] 3-8-13 0 ow2.................. ChristopheSoumillon 4 98
(A De Royer-Dupre, France) *w.w in fnl trio: drvn and began to cl over 2f out: in tch over 1f out: no further imp fnl f* **14/5**[2]

6 *4* **Volskha (FR)**[40] 3137 3-8-13 0 ow2.................. CristianDemuro 9 90
(Simone Brogi, France) *racd keenly: hld up in fnl pair: kpt on past btn horses fnl f: nvr in contention* **10/1**

7 *3/4* **Iconic Choice**[34] 3119 3-8-13 0 ow2.................. TonyPiccone 3 88
(Tom Dascombe) *hld up in fnl pair: rdn and no imp over 2f out: sn btn* **10/1**

8 *6* **Pietra Della Luna (IRE)**[28] 3-8-13 0 ow2.................. AntoineHamelin 1 75
(M Figge, Germany) *hld up towards rr on inner: rdn and no imp 2f out: wknd more than 1f out* **39/1**

1m 50.06s (-1.04) **8 Ran SP% 120.8**
PARI-MUTUEL (all including 1 euro stake): WIN 4.80; PLACE 1.70, 3.10, 1.30; DF 36.20.
Owner Lady Bamford **Bred** Haras D'Etreham & Riviera Equine S.A.R.L. **Trained** Chantilly, France

4417a CONNOLLY'S REDMILLS PRIX DU BOIS (GROUP 3) (2YO) (TURF) 5f
7:45 2-Y-O
£36,036 (£14,414; £10,810; £7,207; £3,603)

RPR

1 **Maven (USA)**[71] 2-9-1 0 ow1............................(b) MickaelBarzalona 6 106
(Wesley A Ward, U.S.A) *mde virtually all: sn w ldrs: led bef end of 1f: mde rest: 2 l clr and hrd rdn over 1f out: styd on u.p: jst hld on* **21/10**[2]

2 *hd* **Jolie (FR)**[29] 3333 2-8-11 0 ow1............................ MaximeGuyon 1 101
(Andrea Marcialis, France) *sn in rr: shkn up and hdwy 1 1/2f out: r.o fnl f: jst failed* **11/1**

3 *3* **Kenlova (FR)**[43] 2-8-11 0 ow1............................ ChristopheSoumillon 4 90
(P Bary, France) *prom bhd front rnk: drvn but nt qckn immediately over 1 1/2f out: styd on u.p ins fnl f: tk 3rd cl home* **10/1**[3]

4 *1/2* **Fan Club Rules (IRE)**[29] 3333 2-9-1 0 ow1............................ AntoineHamelin 7 93
(Matthieu Palussiere, France) *chsd ldr: rdn in 2nd but no imp ins fnl 2f: began to labour last 150yds and dropped two pls* **40/1**

5 *1 1/4* **Great Dame (IRE)**[29] 3333 2-8-11 0 ow1............................ AlexisBadel 3 84
(David O'Meara) *away wl enough: sn in fnl trio on inner: drvn to cl fr after 1/2-way: one pce u.p fnl f: nvr trbld ldrs* **32/1**

6 *3 1/2* **Sound Machine (GER)**[13] 2-8-11 0 ow1............................ IoritzMendizabal 5 71
(Mario Hofer, Germany) *chsd front rnk on inner: rdn but no imp fr over 1 1/2f out: wl hld fnl f* **29/1**

7 *nse* **Hurricane Ivor (IRE)**[43] 2-9-1 0 ow1.................. Pierre-CharlesBoudot 2 75
(F Chappet, France) *s.i.s: sn rcvrd to be chsng front rnk bef 1/2-way: rdn and btn wl over 1f out* **4/5**[1]

8 *2 1/2* **Salerne**[24] 2-8-13 0 ow3............................ OlivierPeslier 8 64
(D Guillemin, France) *chsd ldng pair on outer: bmpd and then wknd 1 1/2f out* **20/1**

58.36s (0.06) **8 Ran SP% 118.8**
PARI-MUTUEL (all including 1 euro stake): WIN 3.10; PLACE 2.60, 3.20, 4.30; DF 13.60.
Owner Richard Ravin **Bred** Wesley Ward **Trained** North America

FOCUS
Probably not the deepest race for the grade.

LA ZARZUELA (R-H)
Saturday, June 29
OFFICIAL GOING: Turf: good

4418a CENTENARIO DEL GRAN PREMIO DE MADRID (CONDITIONS) (3YO+) (TURF) 1m 4f 110y
8:10 3-Y-O+
£45,045 (£18,018; £9,009; £4,504)

RPR

1 **Hipodamo De Mileto (FR)**[89] 1490 5-9-10 0..........(p) ClementCadel 12 98
(J Calderon, Spain) **5/2**[1]

2 *1* **Zascandil (FR)**[616] 5-9-10 0............................ BorjaFayosMartin 6 96
(C Delcher-Sanchez, France) **17/5**[2]

3 *3/4* **Putumayo (FR)** 4-9-10 0............................ JoeyMartinez 4 95
(J-M Osorio, Spain) **84/10**

4 *hd* **Genetics (FR)**[28] 3346 5-9-10 0............................ MartinDwyer 2 95
(Andrew Balding) *racd keenly: led under restraint: drvn turning for home 2 1/2f out: rdn and hdd over 1 1/2f out: styd on again u.p ins fnl f* **169/10**

5 *hd* **Almorox**[35] 3109 7-9-10 0............................ JulienAuge 7 95
(C Ferland, France) **48/10**[3]

6 *3/4* **Le Rafale (FR)** 4-9-10 0............................(h) JoseLuisBorrego 8 93
(J C Rosell, Spain) **38/1**

7 *hd* **Parsifal (SPA)**[121] 959 6-9-10 0............................(h) VaclavJanacek 3 93
(G Arizkorreta Elosegui, Spain) **36/1**

8 *4 3/4* **Karlsburg (FR)**[769] 5-9-10 0............................ JulienGrosjean 13 85
(Carlos Fernandez-Balcones, Spain) **34/1**

9 *1 3/4* **Armorial (FR)**[230] 9028 4-9-10 0.................. FranciscoJimenezAlvarez 5 83
(Enrique Leon Penate, Spain) **55/1**

10 *2* **Qatar River (FR)**[213] 4-9-10 0............................ EmilienRevolte 10 79
(Leyla Ennouni, Spain) **52/1**

11 *5 3/4* **Tuvalu**[251] 7-9-10 0............................(h) JaimeGelabertBautista 1 70
(J-M Osorio, Spain) **58/10**

12 *2 1/4* **Atty Persse (IRE)**[203] 9463 5-9-10 0............................ RicardoSousa 9 67
(Enrique Leon Penate, Spain) **8/1**

13 *10 1/4* **Intaglio (POR)**[562] 6-9-10 0.................. MrIgnacioMelgarejoLoring 11 50
(Andre Vale, Spain) **43/1**

Owner Cuadra Nanina **Bred** E Beca Borrego **Trained** Spain

OVREVOLL (R-H)
Saturday, June 29
OFFICIAL GOING: Turf: good

4419a OSLO CUP (GROUP 3) (3YO+) (TURF) 1m 4f
7:10 3-Y-O+
£31,731 (£13,599; £6,527; £4,351; £2,719)

RPR

1 **Square De Luynes (FR)**[307] 4-9-4............................ RafaelSchistl 2 100
(Niels Petersen, Norway) *plld hrd: restrained in 2nd: led over 2f out: clr ins fnl f: easily* **8/5**[1]

2 *4 1/2* **Baltic Eagle (GER)**[23] 5-9-4 0............................ SandroDePaiva 9 93
(Wido Neuroth, Norway) *settled in midfield on outer: 6th and drvn over 1f out: styd on wl ins fnl f: tk 2nd cl home: no ch w wnr* **159/10**

3 *3/4* **Cockney Cracker (FR)**[716] 4825 8-9-4 0............................ OliverWilson 6 92
(Niels Petersen, Norway) *hld up in fnl trio: plenty to do 3 1/2f out: began to make grnd w 2 1/2f to run: styd on wl fr 1 1/2f out: wnt 2nd last 100yds: run flattened out: dropped to 3rd cl home* **223/10**

The Form Book Flat 2019, Raceform Ltd, Newbury, RG14 5SJ

4 nse **Bokan (FR)**[236] 7-9-4 0 .... Per-AndersGraberg 1 92
(Wido Neuroth, Norway) *a.p on inner: drvn to press ldr 2f out: kpt on at same pce fnl f* **174/10**

5 hd **Trouble Of Course (FR)**[56] 5-9-4 0 .... JacobJohansen 3 92
(Niels Petersen, Norway) *w.w in fnl trio: plenty to do 3 1/2f out: drvn and clsd 2 1/2f out: kpt on fnl f: nt pce to chal* **235/10**

6 1/2 **Ginmann (IRE)**[13] 3902 5-9-4 0 .... NikolajStott 7 91
(Bolette Rosenlund, Denmark) *outpcd in rr: plenty to do 1/2-way: began to make hdwy 2f out: styd on fnl f: nvr nrr* **13/2**

7 nse **Pas De Secrets (IRE)**[236] 6-9-4 0 .... Jan-ErikNeuroth 5 91
(Wido Neuroth, Norway) *towards rr on inner: sme prog 3 1/2f out: drvn to chse ldng gp 2f out: one pce u.p fnl f* **58/10**[3]

8 nk **High As A Kite (FR)**[13] 5-9-1 0 .... DaleSwift 8 87
(Jan Bjordal, Norway) *racd in midfield: outpcd and drvn fr 2 1/2f out: styd on fnl f: nvr trbld ldrs* **164/10**

9 8 1/2 **Alberone (IRE)**[279] 7590 5-9-4 0 ....(p) CarlosLopez 4 77
(Bent Olsen, Denmark) *prom early: dropped into midfield wl bef 1/2-way: bhd fr 2f out* **104/10**

10 1 1/4 **Our Last Summer (IRE)**[13] 3902 6-9-6 0 .... ManuelGMartinez 10 77
(Niels Petersen, Norway) *led: drvn whn pressed 3f out: hdd over 2f out: sn wknd* **89/20**[2]

11 2 3/4 **Silver Falcon (IRE)**[671] 5-9-4 0 .... ElioneChaves 11 70
(Cathrine Erichsen, Norway) *sweated up bdly: cl up on outer: rdn and wknd ins fnl 2f* **135/10**

2m 30.1s (-4.00) 11 Ran SP% 126.0

Owner Stall Power Girls **Bred** Jacques Beres **Trained** Norway

4394 WINDSOR (R-H)

Sunday, June 30

OFFICIAL GOING: Good to firm (watered; 7.6)
Wind: Quite fresh, half behind Weather: Fine but cloudy

4420 JAMES COOK 90TH BIRTHDAY H'CAP 6f 12y

2:10 (2:12) (Class 4) (0-85,85) 3-Y-O **£4,820** (£1,442; £721; £361; £179) **Stalls** Centre

Form RPR

1215 1 **Second Collection**[23] 3544 3-9-1 **79** ....(h) DavidEgan 2 87
(Tony Carroll) *hld up in 8th: pushed along and prog over 2f out: rdn and swtchd lft 1f out: urged along to ld last 75yds: hld on* **7/1**

12U0 2 shd **Dominus (IRE)**[13] 3945 3-9-4 **82** .... OisinMurphy 7 90
(Brian Meehan) *dwlt: sn pressed ldrs on outer: clsd 2f out: drvn to ld jst ins fnl f: hdd last 75yds: styd on but jst denied* **9/4**[1]

5023 3 2 **Nefarious (IRE)**[15] 3858 3-9-4 **82** .... DavidProbert 9 84
(Henry Candy) *led: rdn over 1f out: hdd and one pce jst ins fnl f* **10/3**[2]

2235 4 3/4 **Tinto**[43] 2835 3-9-3 **81** .... RobertHavlin 8 80
(Amanda Perrett) *trckd ldrs: gng strly whn squeezed for room wl over 1f out: carried lft jst ins fnl f: kpt on but nvr able to rcvr* **10/1**

21-6 5 3/4 **Golden Force**[37] 3048 3-9-0 **78** .... HollieDoyle 6 75
(Clive Cox) *taken down early: pressed ldr: drvn over 2f out: lost pl over 1f out: one pce after* **6/1**[3]

-161 6 3/4 **Benny And The Jets (IRE)**[40] 2937 3-9-5 **83** ....(t) RobHornby 4 77
(Sylvester Kirk) *trckd ldrs and r against rail: rdn 2f out: one pce over 1f out* **6/1**[3]

6400 7 2 3/4 **Fares Kodiac (IRE)**[37] 3048 3-9-7 **85** ....(t[1]) ShaneKelly 10 71
(Marco Botti) *sltly awkward s: sn prom: edgd rt u.p 2f out: wknd jst over 1f out* **22/1**

0245 8 hd **Cotubanama**[14] 3892 3-8-11 **75** .... NicolaCurrie 1 60
(Mick Channon) *outpcd and pushed along in detached last: nvr on terms (jockey said filly was never travelling)* **33/1**

005 9 2 3/4 **Oberyn Martell**[34] 3166 3-9-5 **83** .... CharlesBishop 5 59
(Eve Johnson Houghton) *chsd ldrs: shoved along 1/2-way: wknd wl over 1f out* **33/1**

1m 11.4s (-0.70) **Going Correction** -0.15s/f (Firm) 9 Ran SP% **114.2**
Speed ratings (Par 101): **98,97,95,94,93 92,88,88,84**
CSF £22.45 CT £61.86 TOTE £7.20: £2.10, £1.20, £1.40; EX 30.00 Trifecta £147.10.
Owner A A Byrne **Bred** Anthony Byrne **Trained** Cropthorne, Worcs
■ Fly The Nest was withdrawn. Price at time of withdrawal 66-1. Rule 4 does not apply

FOCUS
The rail has been moved all the way back to inside line. This wasn't a bad 3yo sprint handicap. It proved pretty rough and the first pair came clear down the middle.

4421 AUGUST 11TH WINDSOR'S ICE CREAM FESTIVAL NOVICE STKS 6f 12y

2:45 (2:46) (Class 5) 3-4-Y-O **£3,169** (£943; £471; £235) **Stalls** Centre

Form RPR

1 1 **Drummond Warrior (IRE)**[27] 3421 3-9-9 0 .... ShaneKelly 1 84
(Pam Sly) *mde all: rdn over 1f out: wandered after w hd high but readily drew clr fnl f* **5/1**[3]

2 4 1/2 **Grisons (FR)** 3-9-2 0 .... HollieDoyle 4 63
(Clive Cox) *t.k.h: chsd wnr: hung lft fr 1/2-way: shkn up 2f out: outpcd over 1f out (jockey said colt hung left-handed)* **3/1**[2]

3 1 **Mofaaji** 3-9-2 0 ....(p[1]) JackMitchell 5 59
(Simon Crisford) *t.k.h: hld up: prog 1/2-way: shkn up to chse ldng pair and carried sltly lft 2f out: outpcd over 1f out* **1/1**[1]

55 4 3/4 **Annexation (FR)**[8] 4116 3-9-2 0 .... RobertHavlin 2 57
(Ed Dunlop) *hld up in tch: outpcd 2f out: pushed along and kpt on steadily fnl f: could do bttr* **10/1**

5 7 **Peggotty** 3-8-11 0 .... TomMarquand 6 30
(Tony Carroll) *in tch to over 2f out: wknd* **40/1**

6 1/2 **Strathspey Stretto (IRE)** 4-9-4 0 .... HayleyTurner 3 30
(Marcus Tregoning) *dwlt: rcvrd to chse ldrs: pushed along and wknd over 2f out* **12/1**

7 7 **Disey's Edge** 3-8-11 0 .... TrevorWhelan 7 6
(Christopher Mason) *spd 1f: dropped rapidly to rr and sn t.o: no prog after (jockey said filly ran green)* **66/1**

1m 11.83s (-0.27) **Going Correction** -0.15s/f (Firm) 7 Ran SP% **112.4**
WFA 3 from 4yo 7lb
Speed ratings (Par 103): **95,89,87,86,77 76,67**
CSF £19.63 TOTE £4.50: £1.60, £1.70; EX 17.40 Trifecta £30.00.
Owner G A Libson & Mrs P M Sly **Bred** Ronan Fitzpatrick **Trained** Thorney, Cambs

FOCUS
There was something of a slow-motion finish to this modest novice sprint.

4422 WATCH SKY SPORTS RACING IN HD H'CAP 5f 21y

3:15 (3:15) (Class 3) (0-95,97) 3-Y-O **£7,470** (£2,236; £1,118; £559; £279) **Stalls** Centre

Form RPR

6251 1 **Amplify (IRE)**[36] 3090 3-8-13 **81** .... OisinMurphy 2 87
(Brian Meehan) *led after 1f and racd against rail: mde rest: drvn and hrd pressed fnl f: styd on wl* **6/5**[1]

00-0 2 1/2 **Junius Brutus (FR)**[43] 2826 3-9-8 **97** .... CierenFallon[(7)] 5 101
(Ralph Beckett) *chsd ldrs: shkn up 2f out: tk 2nd 1f out and sn drvn to chal: nt qckn last 75yds (jockey said gelding hung right-handed)* **5/1**[3]

4630 3 1/2 **Kinks**[20] 3654 3-9-7 **89** .... NicolaCurrie 4 91
(Mick Channon) *pushed along in last after 2f and outpcd: stl last whn swtchd rt and rdn jst over 1f out: styd on wl last 150yds: gaining at fin* **6/1**

6-02 4 3/4 **More Than Likely**[27] 3427 3-8-5 **80** .... GeorgeRooke[(7)] 6 80
(Richard Hughes) *led 1f: pressed wnr: rdn and edgd lft over 1f out: sn lost 2nd and one pce* **8/1**

216- 5 1 1/2 **Swiss Air**[317] 6242 3-8-12 **80** ....(t) TomMarquand 3 74
(William Haggas) *chsd ldrs: pushed along 1/2-way: edgd lft u.p over 1f out: fdd fnl f* **3/1**[2]

58.37s (-1.73) **Going Correction** -0.15s/f (Firm) 5 Ran SP% **112.5**
Speed ratings (Par 103): **107,106,105,104,101**
CSF £7.85 TOTE £2.20: £1.40, £1.90; EX 8.10 Trifecta £24.70.
Owner Manton Thoroughbreds III **Bred** Drumlin Bloodstock **Trained** Manton, Wilts

FOCUS
This fair sprint was run at a solid pace and it saw a good winning time.

4423 ROYAL WINDSOR RACECOURSE PANORAMIC 1866 RESTAURANT NOVICE STKS 1m 31y

3:50 (3:50) (Class 4) 3-5-Y-O **£4,820** (£1,442; £721; £361; £179) **Stalls** Low

Form RPR

2-32 1 **Vasiliev**[20] 3648 3-9-5 **89** .... AdamKirby 1 85
(Clive Cox) *mde all: hanging lft most of way: hung lft whn shkn up 2f out but sn drew clr: comf* **4/9**[1]

6- 2 3 1/4 **Al Battar (IRE)**[200] 9499 3-9-5 ....(p[1]) OisinMurphy 4 78
(Ed Vaughan) *chsd wnr: shkn up over 2f out: outpcd over 1f out* **11/4**[2]

3 1 1/2 **Fiery Mission (USA)** 3-9-5 .... RichardKingscote 6 74
(Sir Michael Stoute) *s.i.s: hld up in 4th: shkn up over 2f out: tk 3rd wl over 1f out: styd on same pce after* **10/1**[3]

0-5 4 3 3/4 **Closer Than Close**[19] 3696 3-9-5 ....(h) RobHornby 5 65
(Jonathan Portman) *chsd ldng pair to wl over 1f out: fdd* **50/1**

04 5 5 **Uncertain Smile (IRE)**[23] 3546 3-9-0 .... HollieDoyle 2 49
(Clive Cox) *hld up in 5th and off the pce: pushed along over 2f out: no prog and nvr in it* **40/1**

6 30 **The Pastoral Bear** 3-8-7 .... IsobelFrancis[(7)] 3
(Mark Pattinson) *s.s: a bhd: t.o (jockey said filly was slowly away and ran green)* **100/1**

1m 42.6s (-1.90) **Going Correction** -0.15s/f (Firm) 6 Ran SP% **110.4**
Speed ratings (Par 105): **103,99,98,94,89 59**
CSF £1.82 TOTE £1.40: £1.10, £1.10; EX 1.80 Trifecta £3.40.
Owner Cheveley Park Stud **Bred** Cheveley Park Stud Ltd **Trained** Lambourn, Berks

FOCUS
An uncompetitive little novice event.

4424 PERFUME SHOP, SCENTING THE NATION FILLIES' H'CAP 1m 31y

4:25 (4:25) (Class 5) (0-75,76) 3-Y-O+ **£3,169** (£943; £471; £235) **Stalls** Low

Form RPR

4-32 1 **Itizzit**[31] 3266 3-9-5 **74** .... OisinMurphy 5 83
(Hughie Morrison) *trckd ldr after 2f: led wl over 2f out and sent for home: clr over 1f out: rdn out: decisively* **9/2**[2]

0012 2 2 3/4 **Emma Point (USA)**[31] 3264 3-9-4 **73** ....(h) DavidEgan 1 76
(Marco Botti) *trckd ldr 2f: styd prom: rdn over 2f out: chsd wnr wl over 1f out: kpt on but no imp* **3/1**[1]

4016 3 1 1/4 **Amorously (IRE)**[17] 3779 3-9-5 **74** .... RossaRyan 8 74
(Richard Hannon) *hld up towards rr: rdn and prog over 2f out: kpt on u.p to take 3rd ins fnl f* **10/1**

0000 4 1/2 **Toybox**[20] 3665 3-8-12 **67** .... RobHornby 3 66
(Jonathan Portman) *trckd ldrs: rdn wl over 2f out and sn outpcd: kpt on again at same pce over 1f out* **14/1**

30-3 5 nse **I'lletyougonow**[61] 2251 3-9-5 **74** .... CharlesBishop 4 73
(Mick Channon) *trckd ldrs: rdn over 2f out: racd awkwardly and nt qckn over 1f out: wl hld after* **7/1**

1062 6 2 **Pytilia (USA)**[25] 3468 3-9-7 **76** .... ShaneKelly 10 70
(Richard Hughes) *hld up in 6th: rdn on outer over 2f out: no prog over 1f out: wknd* **7/1**

2004 7 1 1/4 **Zoraya (FR)**[8] 4113 4-9-13 **72** ....(t) DavidProbert 9 65
(Paul Cole) *stdd s: hld up in last: sme prog on outer over 3f out: rdn and no real hdwy 2f out: wknd fnl f* **11/1**

3-53 8 1/2 **Arctic Spirit**[48] 2689 3-9-1 **70** .... RobertHavlin 11 60
(Ed Dunlop) *hld up in last trio: shkn up and no real prog 2f out: nvr in it* **8/1**

0332 9 hd **Choral Music**[25] 3462 4-10-0 **73** .... HollieDoyle 7 65
(John E Long) *a towards rr: rdn and no prog over 2f out: n.d after* **13/2**[3]

00-5 10 3 1/2 **Bint Dandy (IRE)**[39] 2977 8-10-0 **76** ....(p) JoshuaBryan[(3)] 2 60
(Charlie Wallis) *led to wl over 2f out: wknd qckly wl over 1f out* **33/1**

0500 11 13 **Angelical Eve (IRE)**[8] 4116 5-8-6 **54** oh9 ....(t[1]) NoelGarbutt[(3)] 6 8
(Dai Williams) *s.i.s: a in last pair: rdn and wknd over 3f out: t.o* **100/1**

1m 40.65s (-3.85) **Going Correction** -0.15s/f (Firm) 11 Ran SP% **120.6**
WFA 3 from 4yo+ 10lb
Speed ratings (Par 100): **111,108,107,106,106 104,103,102,102,99 86**
CSF £18.91 CT £134.11 TOTE £5.50: £2.40, £1.40, £2.80; EX 22.70 Trifecta £214.60.
Owner Hot To Trot Racing 1 **Bred** Moyns Park Estate And Stud Ltd **Trained** East Ilsley, Berks

FOCUS
Few landed a serious blow in this ordinary fillies' handicap.

4425 FOLLOW AT THE RACES ON TWITTER H'CAP 1m 3f 99y

5:00 (5:03) (Class 4) (0-85,84) 4-Y-O+ **£4,820** (£1,442; £721; £361; £179) **Stalls** Low

Form RPR

0345 1 **El Borracho (IRE)**[8] 4112 4-8-2 **72** ....(h) LeviWilliams[(7)] 1 79
(Simon Dow) *hld up in last: stl there 2f out: swtchd lft to outer jst over 1f out: qckly clsd to ld ins fnl f: pushed out* **14/1**

-225 2 3/4 **C'Est No Mour (GER)**[15] 3861 6-9-2 **79** .... TomMarquand 4 85
(Peter Hedger) *trckd ldng pair: urged along 3f out: grad clsd u.p to ld over 1f out: hdd and outpcd ins fnl f* **5/2**[2]

0536 **3** 1 1/4 **C Note (IRE)**[16] 3806 6-9-6 **83**.............................. CharlesBishop 2 87
(Heather Main) *trckd ldng pair: stl gng strly 3f out: hanging lft over 2f out: sn rdn: tried to chal over 1f out but fnd little: one pce after* **10/3**[3]

2-53 **4** nse **Western Duke (IRE)**[5] 4224 5-9-7 **84**..................(p) AdamKirby 5 88
(Ian Williams) *awkward to post: led: urged along over 3f out: hrd rdn 2f out: hdd and nt qckn over 1f out* **2/1**[1]

-401 **5** 1/2 **Tiar Na Nog (IRE)**[48] 2685 7-8-10 **73**.................. OisinMurphy 3 76
(Denis Coakley) *trckd ldr: rdn to chal over 2f out: upsides over 1f out but nt qckn: one pce fnl f* **4/1**

2m 27.3s (-2.40) **Going Correction** -0.15s/f (Firm) 5 Ran SP% **111.7**
Speed ratings (Par 105): **102,101,100,100,100**
CSF £48.87 TOTE £14.70: £4.10, £1.70; EX 45.20 Trifecta £132.70.
Owner Robert Moss **Bred** Christopher Maye **Trained** Epsom, Surrey

FOCUS
A tight-looking handicap and it was run at a steady pace, resulting in a blanket finish.

4426 VISIT ATTHERACES.COM H'CAP — 1m 2f
5:35 (5:39) (Class 5) (0-70,72) 4-Y-O+
£3,752 (£1,116; £557; £400; £400; £400) **Stalls** Low

Form RPR

-141 **1** **Junoesque**[19] 3691 5-8-11 **60**..................(p) HectorCrouch 14 71
(John Gallagher) *chsd ldr and clr in ldng trio: rdn to ld wl over 1f out: drvn rt out* **10/1**

0-0 **2** 1 **Blue Medici**[37] 3046 5-9-0 **63**.................. RichardKingscote 5 72
(Mark Loughnane) *dwlt: hld up in rr and off the pce: rdn and prog over 2f out: styd on to take 2nd ins fnl f: nt rch wnr* **16/1**

-214 **3** 2 **Broad Appeal**[13] 3941 5-8-8 **64**.................. TylerSaunders(7) 1 69
(Jonathan Portman) *chsd clr ldng trio: rdn and clsd over 2f out: tk 2nd briefly ins fnl f: one pce after* **6/1**[2]

3-30 **4** 1 3/4 **Cogital**[38] 3022 4-9-5 **68**..................(h) KieranShoemark 13 70
(Amanda Perrett) *hld up in last trio and wl off the pce: swtchd lft to outer over 2f out and drvn: kpt on after and tk 4th nr fin: nvr on terms* **10/1**

4222 **5** 3/4 **Dashing Poet**[19] 3691 5-8-9 **65**.................. EllieMacKenzie(7) 8 65
(Heather Main) *t.k.h: led and set str pce: drvn over 2f out: hdd wl over 1f out: fdd fnl f* **7/1**

3152 **6** 1 1/2 **Mullarkey**[25] 3473 5-8-11 **60**..................(t) KierenFox 3 57
(John Best) *trckd ldr and clr in ldng trio: rdn over 2f out: wknd steadily over 1f out* **9/1**

166- **7** 1/2 **Midnight Mood**[284] 7427 6-8-7 **56**.................. HollieDoyle 9 52
(Dominic Ffrench Davis) *stmbld bdly s: wl off the pce in rr: rdn wl over 2f out: plugged on but nvr a threat* **20/1**

-120 **8** 1 1/2 **Perfect Refuge**[131] 793 4-9-9 **72**.................. AdamKirby 6 65
(Clive Cox) *s.s: a in rr: rdn and no great prog 3f out* **10/1**

3-04 **9** 2 **Jumping Jack (IRE)**[17] 3766 5-9-7 **70**..................(p) CharlesBishop 12 59
(Chris Gordon) *dwlt: urged along to rch midfield: u.p 4f out: sn btn* **16/1**

1111 **10** 1 1/2 **Jai Hanuman (IRE)**[85] 1591 5-9-7 **70**..................(t) FrannyNorton 2 56
(Michael Wigham) *hld up towards rr and off the pce: shkn up over 2f out: no real prog and nvr in it: eased ins fnl f* **11/2**[1]

00-2 **11** 3/4 **Le Maharajah (FR)**[31] 3276 4-9-4 **67**.................. LukeMorris 4 52
(Tom Clover) *in tch in midfield: rdn 3f out: wknd 2f out* **13/2**[3]

62 **12** 2 1/2 **Brecqhou Island**[18] 3744 4-7-9 **51** oh2.................. IsobelFrancis(7) 11 31
(Mark Pattinson) *mostly in last and a wl bhd (jockey said gelding was unsuited by the good to firm going on this occasion and would prefer an easier surface)* **33/1**

00-0 **13** 30 **Bakht A Rawan (IRE)**[23] 3541 7-9-0 **70**.................. CierenFallon(7) 10
(Roger Teal) *a in rr: rdn and struggling 4f out: eased over 1f out: t.o* **50/1**

2m 5.43s (-3.57) **Going Correction** -0.15s/f (Firm) 13 Ran SP% **114.2**
Speed ratings (Par 103): **108,107,105,104,103 102,102,100,99,98 97,95,71**
CSF £142.68 CT £907.47 TOTE £11.40: £3.80, £5.00, £2.20; EX 177.90 Trifecta £997.80.
Owner The Juniper Racing Club Ltd **Bred** Adweb Ltd **Trained** Chastleton, Oxon
■ Miss Blondell was withdrawn. Price at time of withdrawal 10-1. Rule 4 \n\x\x applies to all bets - deduction 5p in the poun

FOCUS
This looked wide open and they were soon strung out.
T/Plt: £42.40 to a £1 stake. Pool: £93,730.99 - 1,613.06 winning units T/Qpdt: £11.10 to a £1 stake. Pool: £7,757.27 - 515.57 winning units **Jonathan Neesom**

HAMBURG (R-H)
Sunday, June 30
OFFICIAL GOING: Turf: good

4427a PFERDEWETTEN.DE GROSSER HANSA PREIS (GROUP 2) (3YO+) (TURF) — 1m 4f
4:05 3-Y-0+
£36,036 (£13,963; £7,207; £3,603; £2,252)

RPR

1 **French King**[56] 2455 4-9-6 0.................. OlivierPeslier 1 114+
(H-A Pantall, France) *midfield on inner: angled out and smooth prog to ld wl over 1f out: sn clr: pushed out* **8/5**[1]

2 2 1/2 **Royal Youmzain (FR)**[28] 3386 4-9-6 0.................. EduardoPedroza 5 110
(A Wohler, Germany) *chsd ldr: rdn to chal 1 1/2f out: styd on u.p but no match for wnr* **2/1**[2]

3 1 **Colomano**[42] 5-9-6 0.................. AdriedeVries 3 108
(Markus Klug, Germany) *midfield on outer: lost pl bef 1/2-way: last and scrubbed along 3f out: styd on fr over 1f out: nvr on terms* **66/10**

4 1/2 **Oriental Eagle (GER)**[28] 3386 5-9-6 0.................. FilipMinarik 6 107
(J Hirschberger, Germany) *led: racd alone towards centre of trck tl cut ins to rail first bnd: c wd into home st: hdd wl over 1f out: grad dropped away* **249/10**

5 3 1/4 **Skyful Sea (FR)**[28] 3385 3-8-5 0 ow1.................. AndraschStarke 4 101
(P Schiergen, Germany) *w.w in fnl pair: rdn but no imp over 2f out: kpt on ins fnl f but nvr in contention* **18/5**[3]

6 3/4 **Alounak (FR)**[28] 3386 4-9-6 0.................. MichaelCadeddu 2 101
(Waldemar Hickst, Germany) *hld up in fnl pair: rdn and no imp 2f out: kpt on at same pce: nvr able to get involved* **113/10**

2m 29.61s (-4.94)
WFA 3 from 4yo+ 14lb 6 Ran SP% **118.7**
PARI-MUTUEL (all including 1 euro stake): WIN 2.60 PLACE: 1.40, 1.40; SF: 4.70.
Owner H H Sheikh Abdulla Bin Khalifa Al Thani **Bred** Umm Qarn Farms **Trained** France

3171
SAINT-CLOUD (L-H)
Sunday, June 30
OFFICIAL GOING: Turf: good to soft

4428a PRIX DE SAINT-PATRICK (LISTED RACE) (3YO COLTS & GELDINGS) (TURF) — 1m
1:00 3-Y-0
£24,774 (£9,909; £7,432; £4,954; £2,477)

RPR

1 **Art Du Val**[136] 727 3-9-3 0 ow1.................. JamesDoyle 4 106+
(Charlie Appleby) *broke wl and led: sn hdd and chsd ldr: eased into ld 1 1/2f out: sn drvn whn pressed: r.o fnl f: a holding runner-up under hands and heels: comf* **1/1**[1]

2 3/4 **Tantpispoureux (IRE)**[27] 3-9-3 0 ow1.................. RonanThomas 1 104
(F-H Graffard, France) **23/10**[3]

3 6 **Boardman**[60] 3-9-3 0 ow1.................. Pierre-CharlesBoudot 3 90
(P Bary, France) **11/5**[2]

4 2 **Tel Aviv (FR)**[15] 3-9-3 0 ow1.................. CristianDemuro 2 86
(Andrea Marcialis, France) **9/1**

1m 38.94s (-8.56) 4 Ran SP% **121.6**
PARI-MUTUEL (all including 1 euro stake): WIN 2.00; PLACE 1.10, 1.30; SF 4.10.
Owner Godolphin **Bred** D J And Mrs Deer **Trained** Newmarket, Suffolk

FOCUS
This turned into a 300m sprint. The winner's rated in line with a best view of his Meydan form.

4429a PRIX DE MALLERET (GROUP 2) (3YO FILLIES) (TURF) — 1m 4f
3:25 3-Y-0
£66,756 (£25,765; £12,297; £8,198; £4,099)

RPR

1 **Mehdaayih**[30] 3316 3-8-13 0 ow1.................. FrankieDettori 3 108+
(John Gosden) *w.w in fnl pair: in last and travelling nicely 1/2-way: began to cl on outer 2 1/2f out: drvn and styd on 1 1/2f out: led ins fnl f: sn clr: comf* **4/5**[1]

2 2 **Edisa (USA)**[20] 3676 3-8-13 0 ow1.................. ChristopheSoumillon 6 103
(A De Royer-Dupre, France) *settled in midfield: smooth prog to chse ldrs 2f out: drvn to chal 1 1/2f out: sn outpcd by eventual wnr: kpt on at same pce* **18/5**[2]

3 snk **Merimbula (USA)**[35] 3121 3-8-13 0 ow1.................. AurelienLemaitre 5 103
(F Head, France) *led: drvn and lened over 2f out: hdd ins fnl f: kpt on at same pce* **11/1**

4 5 **Villa D'Amore (IRE)**[41] 3137 3-8-13 0 ow1.................. Pierre-CharlesBoudot 7 95
(A Fabre, France) *trckd ldr on outer: pushed along but nt qckn over 2f out: lost pl appr 1 1/2f out: wl hld fnl f* **61/10**[3]

5 nk **Moonoon (FR)**[27] 3-8-13 0 ow1.................. JulienAuge 1 95
(C Ferland, France) *w.w in rr: tk clsr order 1/2-way: swtchd towards outer 2f out: sn pushed along: kpt on at one pce: nvr on terms* **11/1**

6 hd **Sakura Zensen (FR)**[60] 3-8-13 0 ow1..................(b) GregoryBenoist 4 94
(Hiroo Shimizu, France) *trckd ldr on inner: outpcd and rdn w more than 1 1/2f to run: wl btn fnl f* **14/1**

7 7 **High Ball (FR)**[22] 3-8-13 0 ow1.................. MaximeGuyon 2 83
(F Vermeulen, France) *settled towards rr: last and rdn 2 1/2f out: wknd fnl 1 1/2f* **17/1**

2m 28.69s (-11.71) 7 Ran SP% **120.3**
PARI-MUTUEL (all including 1 euro stake): WIN 1.80; PLACE 1.30, 1.70; SF 5.30.
Owner Emirates Park Pty Ltd **Bred** Rabbah Bloodstock Limited **Trained** Newmarket, Suffolk

4430a GRAND PRIX DE SAINT-CLOUD (GROUP 1) (4YO+) (TURF) — 1m 4f
4:00 4-Y-0+
£205,909 (£82,378; £41,189; £20,576; £10,306)

RPR

1 **Coronet**[57] 2410 5-9-0 0 ow1.................. FrankieDettori 1 114+
(John Gosden) *w.w in midfield on inner: chsd ldng pair fr 1/2-way: drvn 2f out: sustained run u.p fr 1 1/2f out: grad wore down ldr: led cl home* **11/5**[2]

2 snk **Ziyad**[28] 3389 4-9-3 0 ow1.................. MaximeGuyon 6 117
(C Laffon-Parias, France) *led: kicked for home whn drvn 2f out: rallied gamely u.p whn chal fnl f: hdd cl home* **14/1**

3 shd **Lah Ti Dar**[30] 3314 4-9-0 0 ow1.................. RyanMoore 3 114+
(John Gosden) *a cl up: drvn to try and chal fr 2 1/2f out: nt go on w ldr 1 1/2f out: styd on u.p fnl f: jst missed 2nd* **47/10**[3]

4 3 1/2 **Aspetar (FR)**[28] 3389 4-9-3 0 ow1.................. JasonWatson 5 111
(Roger Charlton) *racd keenly: midfield on outer: pushed along over 2f out: styd on u.p wl over 1f out: nt must pce to trble ldrs* **14/1**

5 hd **Marmelo**[30] 3314 6-9-3 0 ow1.................. ChristopheSoumillon 4 111
(Hughie Morrison) *settled in fnl pair on outer: outpcd and drvn in last 2 1/2f out: began to cl ins fnl 1 1/2f: styd on wl fnl f: nvr nrr* **83/10**

6 hd **Morgan Le Faye**[41] 3138 5-9-0 0 ow1.................. MickaelBarzalona 7 108
(A Fabre, France) *racd in 3rd: 4th and pushed along less than 2f fr home: no imp on ldrs and plugged on at same pce* **13/10**[1]

7 1 1/4 **Thundering Blue (USA)**[36] 3074 6-9-3 0 ow1.................. SeanLevey 2 109
(David Menuisier) *w.w in fnl pair on inner: rdn and no imp 2f out: kpt on fnl f but nvr in contention* **22/1**

2m 28.66s (-11.74) 7 Ran SP% **120.7**
PARI-MUTUEL (all including 1 euro stake): WIN 3.20; PLACE 2.10, 4.50; SF 38.10.
Owner Denford Stud **Bred** Denford Stud Ltd **Trained** Newmarket, Suffolk

FOCUS
The likes of Montjeu, Youmzain, Sarafina and Treve have won this Group 1 since the turn of the millennium, but this edition didn't have anything of that calibre with all seven runners looking for a first Group 1 success. Five of the field were trained in England and it was the one with the most solid form at this level that came out on top.

4431a PRIX EUGENE ADAM (GROUP 2) (3YO) (TURF) — 1m 2f
4:35 3-Y-0
£66,756 (£25,765; £12,297; £8,198; £4,099)

RPR

1 **Headman**[43] 2828 3-9-1 0 ow1.................. JasonWatson 6 117+
(Roger Charlton) *waited in w in 2nd trio: swtchd outside and hdwy 2f out: drvn to ld 1 1/2f out: sn clr: drvn out* **11/5**[2]

2 3 **Jalmoud**[11] 3984 3-9-1 0 ow1.................. JamesDoyle 3 110
(Charlie Appleby) *led after 1f: wnt 3 l clr wl over 2 1/2f out: drvn 2f out: hdd 1 1/2f out: sn outpcd by wnr but unchal for 2nd* **23/5**[3]

3 3 1/2 **Flop Shot (IRE)**[55] 2499 3-9-1 0 ow1.................. MaximeGuyon 2 103
(A Fabre, France) *racd keenly: hld up bhd ldng pair: nt qckn u.p wl over 1 1/2f out: kpt on to take 3rd last 125yds but no match for front pair* **13/10**[1]

4 1 1/4 **Flambeur (USA)**[11] 3-9-1 0 ow1.................... ThierryThulliez 1 101
(C Laffon-Parias, France) *led early: hdd after 1f: remained cl up: rdn and dropped away fr 1 1/2f out* **23/1**

5 1 3/4 **Skazino (FR)**[26] 3-9-1 0 ow1.................... ChristopheSoumillon 5 97
(Cedric Rossi, France) *racd in 2nd trio: rdn and effrt 2f out: sn btn* **8/1**

6 *dist* **Montviette (FR)**[35] 3121 3-8-11 0 ow1.................... CristianDemuro 4
(J-C Rouget, France) *in rr: lost tch fr 2f out: eased and t.o* **10/1**

2m 2.66s (-13.34) **6 Ran SP% 117.0**
PARI-MUTUEL (all including 1 euro stake): WIN 3.20; PLACE 2.50, 2.80; SF 14.00.
Owner K Abdullah **Bred** Juddmonte Farms (east) Ltd **Trained** Beckhampton, Wilts

4170 **SAN SIRO** (R-H)
Sunday, June 30

OFFICIAL GOING: Turf: good

4432a PREMIO DEL GIUBILEO (GROUP 3) (3YO+) (GRANDE COURSE) (TURF) 1m 1f
7:40 3-Y-O+ **£29,279** (£12,882; £7,027; £3,513)

RPR

1 **Lapulced'acqua (IRE)**[7] 4170 4-9-1 0....................(t) SilvanoMulas 3 97
(Grizzetti Galoppo SRL, Italy) *racd keenly: chsd ldr on inner under restraint: shkn up to chal over 1 1/2f out: led appr fnl f: styd on u.p* **28/1**

2 1/2 **Time To Choose**[21] 3643 6-9-6 0....................(t) DarioVargiu 6 101
(A Botti, Italy) *midfield on outer: clsd to chse ldrs fr 2f out: styd on u.p fnl f: nt pce to reel in wnr* **14/5**[2]

3 *nk* **Out Of Time (ITY)**[21] 3643 3-8-9 0.................... FabioBranca 5 99
(A Botti, Italy) *plld hrd: hld up in fnl pair on inner: swtchd outside and hdwy 2f out: styd on u.p but nt pce to chal* **27/20**[1]

4 *snk* **Cherisy (FR)**[43] 4-9-1 0.................... PierantonioConvertino 7 95
(Cedric Rossi, France) *hld up in fnl pair on outer: drvn but no imp over 2f out: styd on fnl f: nvr quite on terms* **109/20**

5 1 3/4 **Fulminix (ITY)**[21] 3643 4-9-4 0....................(t) AntonioFresu 2 94
(Endo Botti, Italy) *midfield on inner: nt clr run over 2f out: angled out and effrt wl over 1f out: run flattened out last half f* **79/20**[3]

6 1 1/2 **Frutireu (IRE)**[35] 4-9-4 0.................... SalvatoreSulas 1 91
(A Botti, Italy) *led: rdn 1 1/2f out: hdd appr fnl f: sn btn and eased last 100yds* **133/10**

7 17 **Dersu Uzala (IRE)**[435] 6-9-4 0.................... DarioDiTocco 4 55
(Marco Gasparini, Italy) *chsd ldr on outer: drvn 2 1/2f out: lost pl fr 2f out: bhd whn eased ins fnl f* **56/10**

1m 49.3s (-8.60) **7 Ran SP% 130.2**
WFA 3 from 4yo+ 11lb
PARI-MUTUEL (all including 1 euro stake): WIN 29.44; PLACE 9.56, 2.63; DF 61.45.
Owner Leonardo Ciampoli **Bred** Anfonso Litta **Trained** Italy

3927 **CATTERICK** (L-H)
Monday, July 1

OFFICIAL GOING: Good to firm (watered; 8.8)
Wind: Fairly strong, half against in straight of over 2f Weather: Fine

4433 JOHANNA BRITTON (MY SISTER JO)/EBF NOVICE STKS 5f
6:00 (6:01) (Class 5) 2-Y-O **£4,140** (£1,232; £615; £307) **Stalls Low**

Form RPR

5 1 **Mia Diva**[73] 1923 2-8-11 0.................... JasonHart 3 72+
(John Quinn) *chsd ldrs: wnt 2nd jst over 2f out: rdn over 1f out: led ins fnl f: r.o* **3/1**[2]

00 2 1 1/4 **Ellenor Gray (IRE)**[13] 3968 2-8-11 0.................... PaulHanagan 1 68
(Richard Fahey) *wnt rt s: chsd ldrs: pushed along and outpcd 1/2-way: angled out and hdwy over 1f out: styd on to take 2nd towards fin: nvr able to chal wnr* **12/1**[3]

31 3 3/4 **Tom Tulliver**[19] 3739 2-9-9 0.................... DavidNolan 11 77
(Declan Carroll) *led: rdn whn pressed over 1f out: hdd ins fnl f: no ex towards fin* **3/1**[2]

05 4 1 **Orlaith (IRE)**[12] 4006 2-8-11 0.................... JamieGormley 6 61+
(Iain Jardine) *dwlt: hld up: hdwy 2f out: shkn up 1f out: styd on ins fnl f under hand ride: nt rch ldrs (enquiry held into the running and riding of the filly which jumped on terms and was considerably handled in midfield before staying on to finish fourth, beaten by 3 lengths, under a hands and heels ride. Jockey said his instructions were to keep the fi* **16/1**

31 5 3 1/2 **Bushtucker Trial (IRE)**[42] 2903 2-9-6 0.................... HayleyTurner 12 58
(Michael Bell) *wnt to post early: chsd ldr tl jst over 2f out: outpcd after* **5/4**[1]

00 6 3 **Tiltilys Rock (IRE)**[9] 4125 2-9-2 0.................... AndrewElliott 8 43
(Andrew Crook) *hld up: pushed along and outpcd 1/2-way: sme hdwy whn hung lft over 1f out: green: nvr able to trble ldrs* **100/1**

0 7 1 1/2 **Samsar (IRE)**[35] 3156 2-9-2 0.................... AndrewMullen 4 38
(Adrian Nicholls) *dwlt: chsd ldrs: pushed along 1/2-way: wknd over 1f out* **40/1**

00 8 2 **Pacific Coast**[7] 4191 2-9-2 0.................... CamHardie 5 30
(Antony Brittain) *dwlt: towards rr: pushed along and sn outpcd: plugged on fnl f: nvr a threat* **100/1**

55 9 6 **Stone Princess (IRE)**[58] 2415 2-8-8 0....................(h[1]) BenRobinson[(3)] 13
(Brian Ellison) *chsd ldrs: rdn 1/2-way: sn wknd* **28/1**

10 8 **Packet Racket** 2-9-2 0.................... RoystonFfrench 2
(Ann Duffield) *dwlt: bhd and outpcd: nvr on terms* **40/1**

11 12 **Nice One Too** 2-8-11 0.................... DavidAllan 10
(David C Griffiths) *green to post: towards rr: bhd and outpcd 3f out: nvr on terms* **33/1**

1m 1.2s (0.70) **Going Correction** -0.15s/f (Firm) **11 Ran SP% 121.3**
Speed ratings (Par 94): **88,86,84,83,77 72,70,67,57,44 25**
CSF £37.13 TOTE £3.90: £1.60, £1.90, £1.40; EX 35.10 Trifecta £139.20.
Owner Phoenix Thoroughbred Limited **Bred** Rabbah Bloodstock Limited **Trained** Settrington, N Yorks
■ Stewards' Enquiry : Jamie Gormley ten-day ban; failure to achieve best possible placing (July 15-24)

FOCUS
Ordinary juvenile form, but the winner could go on to be useful. The third has been rated to his Yarmouth form.

4434 RACING WELFARE RACING STAFF WEEK (S) STKS 5f 212y
6:30 (6:30) (Class 6) 3-Y-O+ **£3,105** (£924; £461; £300; £300; £300) **Stalls Low**

Form RPR

6021 1 **Hard Solution**[4] 4276 3-9-0 64.................... DanielTudhope 11 66+
(David O'Meara) *chsd ldrs: effrt to ld 1f out: kpt on wl fnl f* **6/5**[1]

5-00 2 3/4 **Extrasolar**[14] 3928 9-9-10 60....................(tp) SamJames 5 68
(Geoffrey Harker) *midfield: hdwy 2f out: angled out over 1f out: styd on ins fnl f: tk 2nd fnl strides: nvr able to chal wnr* **10/1**

4523 3 *nk* **B Fifty Two (IRE)**[4] 4276 10-9-3 61....................(tp) JaneElliott[(3)] 7 63
(Marjorie Fife) *midfield: hdwy 2f out: tried to chal 1f out: unable qck ins fnl f: kpt on same pce towards fin* **7/1**[2]

5030 4 1/2 **Alfred The Grey (IRE)**[14] 3921 3-8-10 52.................... CamHardie 1 56
(Tracy Waggott) *led: rdn and hdd 1f out: stl ev ch ins fnl f: no ex towards fin* **8/1**[3]

100- 5 1/2 **Adam's Ale**[283] 7481 10-9-1 83....................(p) FayeMcManoman[(5)] 9 60
(Marjorie Fife) *wnt to post early: chsd ldrs: rdn over 1f out: jinked rt fnl 110yds: nt pce to chal* **8/1**[3]

5050 6 3/4 **Coastal Drive**[8] 4149 4-9-2 55.................... KevinStott 10 54
(Paul Midgley) *racd keenly: rdn and lost 2nd over 1f out: kpt on same pce ins fnl f* **8/1**[3]

0560 7 1 **Soldier Blue (FR)**[31] 3325 5-8-13 46....................(p) BenRobinson[(3)] 3 51
(Brian Ellison) *towards rr: rdn and sme hdwy 2f out: no imp on ldrs fnl f (jockey said gelding was slowly away)* **28/1**

6050 8 4 **Someone Exciting**[9] 4132 6-8-10 50....................(b) HarrisonShaw[(5)] 4 38
(David Thompson) *midfield: rdn 2f out: outpcd after (jockey said mare hung right throughout)* **16/1**

4000 9 3/4 **Slieve Donard**[12] 4010 3-8-11 45 ow1....................(v) ConnorBeasley 8 36
(Noel Wilson) *dwlt: a bhd: u.p 2f out: nvr got involved* **125/1**

3-00 10 1/2 **Dothraki (IRE)**[32] 3271 3-8-10 49.................... AndrewElliott 12 34
(Ronald Thompson) *in rr: u.p 2f out: nvr a threat* **80/1**

6200 11 6 **Windforpower (IRE)**[27] 3452 9-9-10 44....................(v) BarryMcHugh 2 25
(Tracy Waggott) *hld up: rdn over 1f out: outpcd after* **66/1**

1m 12.47s (-1.13) **Going Correction** -0.15s/f (Firm) **11 Ran SP% 113.2**
WFA 3 from 4yo+ 6lb
Speed ratings (Par 101): **101,100,99,98,98 97,95,90,89,88 80**
CSF £13.37 TOTE £1.80: £1.10, £3.20, £1.80; EX 14.10 Trifecta £74.90.The winner was bought in for £7,500.
Owner D O'Meara **Bred** Whitsbury Manor Stud **Trained** Upper Helmsley, N Yorks

FOCUS
No surprise to see this seller fall to one of the 3yos. The winner has been rated as repeating his latest win.

4435 BUY BOSCH APPLIANCES AT MAXWELLS NORTHALLERTON H'CAP 1m 5f 192y
7:00 (7:00) (Class 6) (0-55,55) 3-Y-O+ **£3,105** (£924; £461; £300; £300; £300) **Stalls Low**

Form RPR

0354 1 **Robeam (IRE)**[14] 3931 3-8-8 51.................... PaddyMathers 11 59
(Richard Fahey) *in tch: rdn and outpcd by ldrs over 2f out: rallying whn nt clr run: checked and lost momentum 1f out: plld out towards fin and styd on to ld post* **7/2**[2]

0143 2 *shd* **Dew Pond**[6] 4208 7-9-12 55....................(bt) DavidAllan 7 61
(Tim Easterby) *hld up: hdwy on outer over 2f out: rdn to ld ins fnl f: hdd post* **3/1**[1]

-044 3 3/4 **Jan De Heem**[9] 4126 9-9-4 50....................(p) ConnorMurtagh[(3)] 8 55
(Tina Jackson) *chsd ldrs: wnt 2nd travelling wl 2f out: led over 1f out: sn edgd rt u.p: hdd ins fnl f: hld towards fin* **17/2**

-050 4 3 3/4 **Point Of Honour (IRE)**[9] 4126 4-9-5 48.................... JamesSullivan 1 48
(Ruth Carr) *led: rdn and hdd over 1f out: no ex fnl 100yds* **8/1**

5-02 5 1 1/2 **Artic Nel**[18] 3769 5-9-3 46 oh1.................... PaulHanagan 6 44
(Ian Williams) *midfield: rdn over 2f out: hdwy over 1f out: styd on ins fnl f: nvr able to trble ldrs* **4/1**[3]

-250 6 3/4 **Betancourt (IRE)**[81] 1718 9-9-8 54.................... GabrieleMalune[(3)] 5 51+
(Stef Keniry) *hld up in rr: rdn and outpcd 3f out: styd on ins fnl f: gng on at fin* **12/1**

2-00 7 *nk* **Midnight Warrior**[9] 4126 9-9-4 50....................(t) RowanScott[(3)] 10 47
(Ron Barr) *chsd ldr: rdn over 3f out: lost 2nd 2f out: one pce u.p fr over 1f out* **40/1**

-000 8 *hd* **Richard Strauss (IRE)**[25] 3511 5-9-9 52....................(p) KevinStott 15 49
(Philip Kirby) *midfield: reminder over 4f out: rdn over 2f out: hdwy on outer over 1f out: one pce fnl 100yds (jockey said gelding hung left throughout)* **11/1**

240- 9 3/4 **Rockliffe**[44] 5581 6-9-5 48....................(p) GrahamLee 9 44
(Micky Hammond) *in tch: rdn and outpcd over 3f out: no imp after* **25/1**

606 10 1 1/2 **Shamitsar**[10] 4076 5-9-8 51.................... ConnorBeasley 12 45
(Ray Craggs) *chsd ldrs: rdn over 3f out: outpcd over 2f out: wknd over 1f out* **33/1**

/000 11 12 **About Glory**[20] 3705 5-9-9 52.................... JamieGormley 4 30
(Iain Jardine) *midfield: rdn and lost pl over 3f out: bhd fnl 2f* **50/1**

0100 12 8 **Rajapur**[40] 2196 6-8-12 46....................(b) HarrisonShaw[(5)] 14 14
(David Thompson) *dwlt: hld up: rdn over 3f out: bhd over 1f out: nvr on terms* **50/1**

3m 3.0s (-4.60) **Going Correction** -0.15s/f (Firm) **12 Ran SP% 118.0**
WFA 3 from 4yo+ 14lb
Speed ratings (Par 101): **107,106,106,104,103 103,102,102,102,101 94,90**
CSF £13.72 CT £81.99 TOTE £4.30: £1.70, £1.60, £2.00; EX 10.10 Trifecta £85.70.
Owner Amie Canham I **Bred** Val & Angela Leeson **Trained** Musley Bank, N Yorks

FOCUS
The first three came clear in this moderate staying handicap. It's been rated around the principals.

4436 MILLBRY HILL H'CAP 5f
7:30 (7:31) (Class 5) (0-70,75) 3-Y-O **£4,075** (£1,212; £606; £303; £300; £300) **Stalls Low**

Form RPR

3152 1 **Timetodock**[11] 4033 3-9-3 66....................(b) DavidAllan 2 73
(Tim Easterby) *wnt rt s: chsd ldr: rdn 2f out: r.o ins fnl f: led towards fin and wl in command* **4/1**[2]

611 2 1 1/2 **The Defiant**[28] 3417 3-9-7 70.................... KevinStott 1 72
(Paul Midgley) *racd keenly: led: rdn over 1f out: hdd towards fin and outpcd by wnr* **9/2**[3]

5523 **3** 3/4 **Tie A Yellowribbon**[10] 4081 3-9-2 **65**..........(p) DanielTudhope 6 64
(James Bethell) *chsd ldrs: rdn and unable qck over 1f out: styd on towards fin* **5/1**

-000 **4** hd **Shall We Begin (IRE)**[6] 4212 3-8-2 **51** oh1.......... JamesSullivan 8 49
(Michael Easterby) *midfield: rdn and hung lft fr 2f out: hdwy over 1f out to chse ldrs: styd on: n.m.r and snatched up post: nvr able to chal* **14/1**

0050 **5** 3/4 **One One Seven (IRE)**[6] 4212 3-8-4 **53**.......... CamHardie 7 49
(Antony Brittain) *towards rr: pushed along 1/2-way: hdwy wl ins fnl f: styd on towards fin: nvr able to trble ldrs: lame (vet said gelding finished lame on it's right fore and lost it's right fore shoe)* **14/1**

0460 **6** 2 1/4 **Aquarius (IRE)**[7] 4183 3-8-8 **62**..........(v) TheodoreLadd(5) 3 49
(Michael Appleby) *wnt to post early: hmpd s: hld up: rdn over 1f out: nvr able to get involved* **16/1**

6031 **7** shd **Kapono**[3] 4335 3-9-12 **75** 6ex..........(p) BenCurtis 9 62
(Roger Fell) *chsd ldrs: rdn 1/2-way: wknd 1f out (jockey said gelding was outpaced throughout)* **7/4**[1]

10-0 **8** 7 **Legal Tender (IRE)**[72] 1954 3-8-11 **67**..........(h) HarryRussell(7) 4 29
(Bryan Smart) *wnt to post early: in rr: rdn 2f out: hung lft u.p over 1f out: nvr on terms* **66/1**

59.91s (-0.59) **Going Correction** -0.15s/f (Firm) **8 Ran SP% 111.9**
Speed ratings (Par 100): **98,95,94,94,92 89,89,77**
CSF £21.32 CT £89.57 TOTE £4.10: £1.10, £1.80, £1.30; EX 23.00 Trifecta £86.00.
Owner E A Brook & Partner **Bred** Crossfields Bloodstock Ltd **Trained** Great Habton, N Yorks

FOCUS
This ordinary 3yo sprint handicap was run at a frantic pace. The third has been rated close to form.

4437 KC ETHICAL BRITISH CAVIAR H'CAP — 1m 4f 13y
8:00 (8:00) (Class 4) (0-85,87) 4-Y-O+ **£6,663** (£1,982; £990; £495; £300) **Stalls Low**

Form — RPR

1044 **1** **New Show (IRE)**[21] 3663 4-10-4 **87**.......... PJMcDonald 7 92
(Michael Bell) *hld up: hdwy over 2f out: wnt 2nd over 1f out: led fnl 120yds: kpt on wl* **5/2**[1]

-511 **2** 1/2 **Grand Inquisitor**[14] 3929 7-10-3 **86**..........(v) BenCurtis 4 90
(Ian Williams) *led at stdy pce: rdn over 1f out: hdd fnl 120yds: hld towards fin* **10/3**[3]

6613 **3** nk **Ingleby Hollow**[13] 3973 7-9-7 **76**..........(t) DanielTudhope 5 79
(David O'Meara) *hld up in rr: rdn and hdwy over 1f out: styd on towards fin: nvr able to mount serious chal* **3/1**[2]

355- **4** 5 **Final**[182] 9775 7-10-3 **86**.......... FrannyNorton 6 81
(Mark Johnston) *prom: rdn over 2f out: lost pl and outpcd over 1f out: wl hld fnl 100yds* **9/2**

4050 **5** 3/4 **Framley Garth (IRE)**[17] 3816 7-8-12 **72**.......... PaulaMuir(5) 3 66
(Liam Bailey) *racd keenly: prom: rdn 2f out: sn lost pl: edgd rt and outpcd over 1f out: n.d after* **6/1**

2m 38.25s (-2.35) **Going Correction** -0.15s/f (Firm) **5 Ran SP% 109.1**
Speed ratings (Par 105): **101,100,100,97,96**
CSF £10.78 TOTE £2.80: £1.30, £1.90; EX 12.40 Trifecta £28.40.
Owner Edward J Ware **Bred** Rabbah Bloodstock Limited **Trained** Newmarket, Suffolk

FOCUS
This feature handicap was run at a fair pace. The third has been rated to his recent form.

4438 BRITISH EBF FILLIES' H'CAP — 7f 6y
8:30 (8:30) (Class 4) (0-80,78) 4-Y-O+
£6,404 (£1,905; £952; £476; £300; £300) **Stalls Low**

Form — RPR

-061 **1** **Rux Ruxx (IRE)**[20] 3685 4-9-2 **73**.......... PaulMulrennan 1 82
(Tim Easterby) *dwlt: in rr for 1f: hld up: rdn and hdwy 2f out: led 1f out: pushed out towards fin* **9/4**[1]

6041 **2** 1 1/4 **Eponina (IRE)**[16] 3843 5-8-2 **64**.......... TheodoreLadd(5) 4 70
(Michael Appleby) *led: rdn over 1f out: sn hdd: kpt on same pce towards fin* **11/4**[2]

060 **3** 1 **Bibbidibobbidiboo (IRE)**[23] 3567 4-8-6 **63**.......... FrannyNorton 6 66
(Ann Duffield) *pushed along thrght: in rr after 1f: drvn over 1f out: effrt whn nt clr and swtchd rt fnl 150yds: styd on towards fin* **9/2**[3]

231- **4** nk **Arabian Jazz (IRE)**[304] 6756 4-9-4 **78**..........(h) CameronNoble(3) 3 80
(Michael Bell) *hld up in tch: effrt over 2f out: unable qck over 1f out: kpt on ins fnl f: nt pce to mount serious chal* **6/1**

0/00 **5** 3/4 **Betsey Trotter (IRE)**[20] 3706 4-9-1 **72**..........(p[1]) DanielTudhope 7 72
(David O'Meara) *chsd ldr after 1f: rdn and ev ch fr over 1f out: stl there ins fnl f: wknd fnl 50yds (jockey said filly hung right in the straight)* **6/1**

-000 **6** 2 **Rose Marmara**[14] 3928 6-8-8 **68**..........(tp) ConnorMurtagh(3) 2 63
(Brian Rothwell) *chsd ldr for 1f: remained handy: drvn over 2f out: one pce ins fnl f: eased fnl 75yds* **12/1**

1m 24.9s (-2.50) **Going Correction** -0.15s/f (Firm) **6 Ran SP% 111.9**
Speed ratings (Par 102): **108,106,105,105,104 101**
CSF £8.62 CT £23.57 TOTE £3.90: £1.80, £1.40; EX 9.60 Trifecta £39.90.
Owner King Power Racing Co Ltd **Bred** Yeomanstown Stud **Trained** Great Habton, N Yorks

FOCUS
This modest fillies' handicap looked trappy and it saw a bunched finish, but the form is solid enough. The second has been rated close to form.

4439 TRIAL RACING TV FOR FREE NOW NOVICE STKS — 7f 6y
9:00 (9:00) (Class 5) 3-Y-O+ **£4,140** (£1,232; £615; £307) **Stalls Low**

Form — RPR

1-1 **1** **I Could Do Better (IRE)**[42] 2895 3-9-13 **95**.......... DanielTudhope 4 90+
(Keith Dalgleish) *prom: led after nrly 2f: mde rest travelling strly: v easily* **1/12**[1]

3 **2** 2 3/4 **Springwood Drive**[12] 4010 3-8-9 **0** ow1.......... DavidAllan 3 56
(Tim Easterby) *sn dropped to rr: rdn over 2f out: hdwy wl over 1f out: kpt on to take 2nd fnl 110yds: no ch w wnr* **4/1**[2]

0 **3** 2 **Little Miss Muffin**[20] 3707 3-8-8 **0**.......... CamHardie 5 50
(Sam England) *in tch: prom 4f out: wnt 2nd 3f out: rdn and unable to go w wnr 2f out: kpt on same pce: lost 2nd fnl 110yds* **66/1**

00-0 **4** 3 1/4 **Just A Rumour (IRE)**[43] 2871 3-8-8 **45**.......... JamesSullivan 1 41
(Noel Wilson) *prom for 2f: in tch: rdn over 1f out: kpt on one pce and edgd lft whn no ch ins fnl f (vet said filly lost it's right hind shoe)* **50/1**

0556 **5** 2 1/4 **Biscuit Queen**[23] 3569 3-8-7 **46** ow2..........(b) BenRobinson(3) 2 37
(Brian Ellison) *led for nrly 2f: remained prom: drvn and unable to go w wnr over 2f out: wknd 1f out* **25/1**[3]

00 **6** 16 **Olivia On Green**[33] 3218 3-8-8 **0**.......... AndrewElliott 6
(Ronald Thompson) *s.i.s: hld up: u.p and lft bhd over 2f out* **125/1**

1m 25.81s (-1.59) **Going Correction** -0.15s/f (Firm) **6 Ran SP% 120.4**
Speed ratings (Par 103): **103,99,97,93,91 73**
CSF £1.16 TOTE £1.10: £1.02, £1.40; EX 1.20 Trifecta £6.70.
Owner Paul & Clare Rooney **Bred** Minch Bloodstock **Trained** Carluke, S Lanarks

FOCUS
This was all about the smart winner.
T/Jkpt: £10,739.90 to a £1 stake. Pool: £75,179.37 - 7.0 winning units T/Plt: £20.70 to a £1 stake. Pool: £76,565.36 - 2,692.46 winning units T/Qpdt: £7.70 to a £1 stake. Pool: £7,624.28 - 729.87 winning units **Darren Owen**

4142 PONTEFRACT (L-H)
Monday, July 1

OFFICIAL GOING: Good to firm (good in places; 8.2)
Wind: strong half behind Weather: Cloudy with blustery with sunny periods

4440 GEOFFREY OLDROYD - A LIFETIME IN RACING H'CAP — 6f
2:00 (2:02) (Class 5) (0-75,77) 3-Y-O+
£3,557 (£1,058; £529; £300; £300; £300) **Stalls Low**

Form — RPR

4420 **1** **Magical Effect (IRE)**[17] 3813 7-9-12 **74**.......... JamesSullivan 3 82
(Ruth Carr) *trckd ldrs: swtchd rt to outer and hdwy wl over 1f out: cl up and rdn ins fnl f: styd on wl to ld towards fin* **17/2**

3121 **2** nk **Tricky Dicky**[8] 4148 6-10-1 **77** 5ex.......... BenCurtis 5 84
(Roger Fell) *trckd ldr: cl up 2f out: rdn to ld wl over 1f out: drvn ins fnl f: hdd and no ex towards fin (vet said gelding lost right fore shoe)* **11/4**[1]

6113 **3** 3/4 **Mujassam**[4] 4280 7-9-12 **74**..........(b) DanielTudhope 10 79
(David O'Meara) *trckd ldng pair: hdwy 2f out: rdn to chal ins fnl f: sn drvn and ev ch: kpt on same pce towards fin* **5/1**[3]

2125 **4** 1 **Scuzeme**[12] 3999 5-9-10 **72**..........(h) SamJames 1 74
(Phillip Makin) *trckd ldng pair: hdwy 2f out: rdn over 1f out: ev ch ins fnl f: drvn and wknd towards fin* **9/2**[2]

4000 **5** 2 **Round The Island**[21] 3656 6-8-9 **57**.......... PhilDennis 9 52
(Richard Whitaker) *hld up towards rr: hdwy 2f out: n.m.r on inner wl over 1f out: sn rdn: swtchd rt over 1f out: kpt on u.p fnl f (jockey said gelding was continually denied a clear run from 2f to 1f out)* **14/1**

0261 **6** 1/2 **Penny Pot Lane**[8] 4149 6-9-6 **68** 5ex..........(p) LewisEdmunds 7 62
(Richard Whitaker) *hld up towards rr: hdwy 2f out: rdn over 1f out: kpt on fnl f* **16/1**

-010 **7** 3 1/2 **Gullane One (IRE)**[9] 4103 4-9-8 **70**..........(t[1]) DavidAllan 2 53
(Tim Easterby) *led: rdn along over 2f out: hdd wl over 1f out: sn drvn and grad wknd* **11/1**

0050 **8** 1/2 **Mutafarrid (IRE)**[9] 4103 4-9-11 **73**.......... GrahamLee 6 54
(Paul Midgley) *hld up: a towards rr* **40/1**

-646 **9** nk **Princess Palliser (IRE)**[19] 3719 3-8-11 **65**.......... JasonHart 4 44
(John Quinn) *chsd ldrs: rdn along 2f out: sn wknd* **25/1**

6360 **10** 1 **Mr Orange (IRE)**[20] 3706 6-9-11 **73**..........(p) KevinStott 8 50
(Paul Midgley) *hld up towards rr: hdwy on outer 2f out: rdn along over 1f out: n.d* **10/1**

0030 **11** 3/4 **Cosmic Chatter**[14] 3921 9-8-7 **55**..........(p) AndrewMullen 11 29
(Ruth Carr) *dwlt: a in rr (jockey said gelding was slowly away)* **33/1**

1505 **12** 6 **Mystical Moon (IRE)**[60] 2318 4-8-7 **55** oh2.......... FrannyNorton 13 10
(David C Griffiths) *a towards rr* **50/1**

-230 **13** 1/2 **John Clare (IRE)**[14] 3930 3-9-4 **72**..........(p[1]) CallumShepherd 12 25
(Pam Sly) *chsd ldrs: rdn along 2f out: sn wknd (jockey said gelding had no more to give)* **16/1**

1m 15.62s (-1.48) **Going Correction** -0.10s/f (Good)
WFA 3 from 4yo+ 6lb **13 Ran SP% 119.1**
Speed ratings (Par 103): **105,104,103,102,99 98,94,93,93,91 90,82,82**
CSF £31.00 CT £137.81 TOTE £8.80: £2.20, £1.50, £2.60; EX 35.70 Trifecta £264.20.
Owner Miss Vanessa Church **Bred** W Maxwell Ervine **Trained** Huby, N Yorks

FOCUS
Following light watering the day before racing, the going was good to firm, good in places. There was a false running rail approximately 15 feet out from the permanent rail, adding 8yds to all races. A competitive sprint handicap run at a good gallop. The third has been rated to his recent form.

4441 BRITISH STALLION STUDS EBF SPINDRIFTER CONDITIONS STKS (PLUS 10 RACE) — 6f
2:30 (2:30) (Class 2) 2-Y-O **£12,450** (£3,728; £1,864) **Stalls Low**

Form — RPR

321 **1** **Hurstwood**[17] 3810 2-9-2 **82**.......... DavidAllan 3 90
(Tim Easterby) *chsd ldr: rdn along 2f out: sn cl up: slt ld over 1f out: drvn ins fnl f: kpt on wl towards fin* **13/2**[3]

51 **2** 1 **Toro Strike (USA)**[28] 3411 2-9-2 **0**.......... TonyHamilton 4 87
(Richard Fahey) *trckd ldng pair: effrt 2f out: rdn along and n.m.r over 1f out: sn swtchd rt and hdwy ent fnl f: sn ev ch: edgd lft and kpt on same pce last 100yds* **7/2**[2]

210 **3** 3/4 **Monoski (USA)**[13] 3949 2-9-2 **97**.......... PJMcDonald 1 85
(Mark Johnston) *led: rdn along and jnd 2f out: drvn and hdd over 1f out: kpt on same pce fnl f* **2/5**[1]

1m 16.56s (-0.54) **Going Correction** -0.10s/f (Good) **3 Ran SP% 107.0**
Speed ratings (Par 100): **99,97,96**
CSF £20.89 TOTE £4.80; EX 12.40 Trifecta £12.90.
Owner David W Armstrong **Bred** Highfield Farm Llp **Trained** Great Habton, N Yorks

FOCUS
Add 8yds. Only three runners following the defection of Lord Of The Lodge and it was the outsider of them who prevailed. There seemed to be no fluke about the result. The second has been rated to his debut figure.

4442 NAPOLEONS CASINO BRADFORD FILLIES' H'CAP — 6f
3:00 (3:04) (Class 3) (0-90,89) 3-Y-O+
£9,337 (£2,796; £1,398; £699; £349; £175) **Stalls Low**

Form — RPR

-203 **1** **Cale Lane**[19] 3722 4-8-11 **72**.......... GrahamLee 3 79
(Julie Camacho) *hld up in tch: hdwy on outer wl over 1f out: rdn to chal ins fnl f: drvn and kpt on wl to ld nr line* **3/1**[1]

0-55 **2** nk **Hells Babe**[17] 3815 6-9-12 **87**.......... AlistairRawlinson 1 93
(Michael Appleby) *chsd ldr: hdwy 2f out: rdn over 1f out: drvn to ld last 75yds: hdd and no ex nr line* **3/1**[1]

0002 **3** hd **Daffy Jane**[17] 3815 4-8-13 **79**.......... FayeMcManoman(5) 4 84
(Nigel Tinkler) *trckd ldrs: hdwy wl over 1f out: rdn ins fnl f: ev ch: kpt on* **11/2**[3]

4-40 **4** 1 1/4 **Dizzy G (IRE)**[31] 3309 4-9-3 **78**.......... CliffordLee 6 79
(K R Burke) *sn led and clr: rdn along over 1f out: drvn ins fnl f: hdd and no ex last 75yds* **15/2**

5406 **5** 2 3/4 **Chynna**[31] 3293 3-9-8 **89**.......... FrannyNorton 2 81
(Mick Channon) *in rr: outpcd and rdn along 1/2-way: hdwy 2f out: rdn wl over 1f out: no imp fnl f* **11/2**[3]

12-0 **6** *9* **Princes Des Sables**[21] 3654 3-9-6 **87**.................................. TomEaves 5 50
(Kevin Ryan) *trckd ldng pair: rdn along over 2f out: wknd wl over 1f out* **4/1**[2]

1m 15.71s (-1.39) **Going Correction** -0.10s/f (Good) **6** Ran SP% **112.5**
WFA 3 from 4yo+ 6lb
Speed ratings (Par 104): **105,104,104,102,99 87**
CSF £12.20 TOTE £3.30: £1.70, £2.20; EX 12.30 Trifecta £58.30.
Owner David W Armstrong **Bred** Highfield Farm Llp **Trained** Norton, N Yorks

FOCUS
Add 8yds. They went a fair clip in this fillies' sprint handicap and the winner only settled matters in the last stride. The form has been rated at face value, with the third to her latest.

4443 WAYNE CONWAY MEMORIAL H'CAP — 1m 4f 5y
3:30 (3:30) (Class 5) (0-70,71) 3-Y-O **£3,557** (£1,058; £529; £300; £300) **Stalls** Low

Form RPR
4053 **1** **Mister Chiang**[11] 4034 3-9-10 **71**.................................(b[1]) FrannyNorton 2 75+
(Mark Johnston) *trckd ldng pair on inner: hdwy 2f out: effrt and n.m.r jst over 1f out: rdn to chal ins fnl f: drvn and hung rt 75yds out: styd on wl to ld nr fin* **1/1**[1]

4344 **2** *nk* **Fayetta**[13] 3955 3-9-7 **68**.................................(b[1]) HollieDoyle 1 71
(David Loughnane) *set stdy pce: pushed along and qcknd over 2f out: rdn over 1f out: drvn ins fnl f: hdd and no ex nr fin* **5/1**[3]

4-06 **3** *3 ¼* **Burnage Boy (IRE)**[33] 3219 3-8-4 **51**................................ AndrewMullen 3 49
(Micky Hammond) *hld up in rr: hdwy over 2f out: rdn along wl over 1f out: chsd ldrs ent fnl f: sn drvn and kpt on same pce* **16/1**

0005 **4** *½* **Menin Gate (IRE)**[14] 3926 3-9-0 **61**................................ TonyHamilton 4 58
(Richard Fahey) *trckd ldr: cl up 3f out: rdn along to chal 2f out: drvn over 1f out: wknd ins fnl f* **11/2**

04-0 **5** *10* **Strindberg**[21] 3664 3-9-7 **68**................................ BenCurtis 5 49
(Marcus Tregoning) *trckd ldng pair on outer: pushed along 3f out: rdn over 2f out: sn wknd* **7/2**[2]

2m 41.82s (0.72) **Going Correction** -0.10s/f (Good) **5** Ran SP% **110.2**
Speed ratings (Par 100): **93,92,90,90,83**
CSF £6.43 TOTE £1.40: £1.10, £1.80; EX 4.70 Trifecta £24.70.
Owner The Originals **Bred** Miss K Rausing **Trained** Middleham Moor, N Yorks

FOCUS
Add 8yds. Ordinary fare, but the winner scored despite doing quite a bit wrong and may have had a little bit up his sleeve. It's been rated around the second.

4444 17TH WILFRED UNDERWOOD MEMORIAL CLASSIFIED STKS — 6f
4:00 (4:01) (Class 5) 3-Y-O **£4,204** (£1,251; £625; £312; £300) **Stalls** Low

Form RPR
2322 **1** **Beryl The Petal (IRE)**[10] 4080 3-9-0 71....................(v) DanielTudhope 3 82
(David O'Meara) *mde all: rdn clr wl over 1f out: readily* **11/4**[3]

0-23 **2** *1 ¾* **Northernpowerhouse**[34] 3202 3-9-0 73................................ GrahamLee 1 76
(Bryan Smart) *trckd ldng pair on inner: hdwy 2f out: n.m.r and swtchd rt jst ins fnl f: sn drvn and kpt on: no ch w wnr* **6/4**[1]

2000 **3** *nk* **Azor Ahai**[9] 4124 3-9-0 74................................ FrannyNorton 4 75
(Mick Channon) *chsd wnr: rdn along 2f out: drvn and edgd lft jst ins fnl f: kpt on same pce* **10/1**

0-53 **4** *1* **Dream Of Honour (IRE)**[38] 3058 3-9-0 75......................(p) DavidAllan 2 72
(Tim Easterby) *hld up in rr: hdwy 2f out and sn rdn: drvn ent fnl f: no imp* **5/2**[2]

461 **5** *9* **Raspberry**[34] 3176 3-8-11 75................................ ConnorMurtagh(3) 5 43
(Olly Williams) *wnt rt s: sn trcking ldng pair on outer: pushed along wl over 2f out: rdn wl over 1f out: sn wknd* **14/1**

1m 15.91s (-1.19) **Going Correction** -0.10s/f (Good) **5** Ran SP% **111.0**
Speed ratings (Par 100): **103,100,100,98,86**
CSF £7.39 TOTE £4.50: £2.60, £1.30; EX 8.50 Trifecta £37.40.
Owner N D Crummack Ltd & A Rhodes And Partner **Bred** Pigeon Park Stud **Trained** Upper Helmsley, N Yorks

FOCUS
Add 8yds. Easy pickings for the winner, who was allowed to set the fractions and scored without turning a hair. A clear pb from the winner, with the second rated a bit below his recent form.

4445 JOHN QUINN RACING H'CAP — 1m 6y
4:30 (4:30) (Class 4) (0-85,86) 3-Y-O+ **£6,145** (£1,828; £913; £456; £300; £300) **Stalls** Low

Form RPR
-461 **1** **Rousayan (IRE)**[5] 4240 8-10-1 **86** 4ex.......................(h) BenCurtis 7 95
(Roger Fell) *hld up towards rr: hdwy on outer wl over 1f out: rdn and str run to ld ins fnl f: kpt on wl* **7/2**[2]

6040 **2** *1 ¼* **Mont Kinabalu (IRE)**[13] 3957 4-9-2 **73**................................ TomEaves 1 78
(Kevin Ryan) *dwlt and bhd: hdwy over 2f out: rdn along on outer wl over 1f out: styd on to chse wnr ins fnl f: no imp towards fin* **14/1**

41 **3** *2 ¾* **Spiorad (IRE)**[9] 4130 4-9-8 **79**................................ DanielTudhope 3 78+
(David O'Meara) *trckd ldrs on inner: hdwy over 2f out: effrt whn n.m.r wl over 1f out and again ent fnl f: sn rdn and kpt on same pce* **15/8**[1]

3-56 **4** *nk* **Kheros**[30] 3341 3-9-3 **83**................................ HollieDoyle 2 79
(Archie Watson) *led: pushed along over 2f out: rdn wl over 1f out: drvn and hdd ins fnl f: grad wknd* **5/1**[3]

0010 **5** *2 ½* **Ghalib (IRE)**[17] 3811 7-9-10 **81**................................ LewisEdmunds 6 73
(Rebecca Bastiman) *trckd ldr: hdwy and cl up over 2f out: sn chal and rdn: drvn appr fnl f: wknd* **25/1**

-141 **6** *hd* **Smile A Mile (IRE)**[38] 3051 3-9-5 **85**................................ FrannyNorton 5 75
(Mark Johnston) *trckd ldrs: pushed along over 3f out: sn rdn and wknd wl over 2f out* **5/1**[3]

-040 **7** *1 ½* **Frankelio (FR)**[16] 3867 4-9-8 **79**................................(p[1]) GrahamLee 4 67
(Micky Hammond) *hld up in rr: effrt and sme hdwy on inner whn nt clr run wl over 1f out: n.d* **11/1**

1023 **8** *½* **Casement (IRE)**[42] 2902 5-9-6 **77**................................ AlistairRawlinson 8 64
(Michael Appleby) *trckd ldrs: hdwy on outer 3f out: rdn along 2f out: sn drvn and btn* **20/1**

1m 43.77s (-2.13) **Going Correction** -0.10s/f (Good) **8** Ran SP% **113.9**
WFA 3 from 4yo+ 9lb
Speed ratings (Par 105): **106,104,102,101,99 99,97,97**
CSF £49.71 CT £117.35 TOTE £4.50: £2.30, £3.00, £1.10; EX 43.80 Trifecta £172.40.
Owner The Roses Partnership **Bred** Haras De Son Altesse L'Aga Khan Scea **Trained** Nawton, N Yorks

FOCUS
Add 8yds. This looked competitive on paper, but the winner scored decisively and supplemented his success of five days earlier. The second has been rated to his April C&D win.

4446 GUIDE DOGS FOR THE BLIND SUPPORTING PONTEFRACT H'CAP (FOR LADY AMATEUR RIDERS) — 1m 2f 5y
5:00 (5:04) (Class 5) (0-70,71) 3-Y-O+
£3,431 (£1,064; £531; £300; £300; £300) **Stalls** Low

Form RPR
5512 **1** **Edgar Allan Poe (IRE)**[14] 3922 5-10-5 **68**........ MissSerenaBrotherton 7 76
(Rebecca Bastiman) *hld up in midfield: hdwy and chsd ldrs whn n.m.r and swtchd lft to inner over 1f out: sn rdn: styd on strly to ld last 75yds* **9/1**

0313 **2** *1 ½* **Celtic Artisan (IRE)**[7] 4194 8-9-10 **64**..............(bt) MissEmilyBullock(5) 5 69
(Rebecca Menzies) *hld up in rr: stdy hdwy on wd outside over 3f out: chsd ldng pair wl over 1f out: rdn to ld jst ins fnl f: hdd and no ex last 75yds* **7/1**[3]

0244 **3** *nk* **Beverley Bullet**[14] 3922 6-9-12 **66**......................(p) MissSarahBowen(5) 3 70
(Lawrence Mullaney) *led: pushed along over 2f out: rdn wl over 1f out: drvn and hdd appr fnl f: kpt on wl u.p towards fin* **7/1**[3]

5515 **4** *nk* **Thorntoun Care**[11] 4036 8-9-11 **65**......................(p) MissAmyCollier(5) 10 68
(Karen Tutty) *hld up in rr: hdwy 3f out: rdn to chse ldrs over 1f out: swtchd lft ins fnl f: kpt on wl towards fin* **20/1**

0002 **5** *½* **Regal Mirage (IRE)**[6] 4209 5-10-2 **70**............ MissJessicaGillam(5) 4 72
(Tim Easterby) *cl up: chal 2f out: rdn to ld jst over 1f out: drvn and hdd ins fnl f: kpt on same pce* **11/2**[2]

6005 **6** *3 ¾* **Ezanak (IRE)**[6] 4216 6-9-8 **64**..........................(vt) MissSarahWilliams(7) 2 59
(Michael Appleby) *t.k.h: trckd ldrs on inner: pushed along 3f out: rdn 2f out grad wknd* **14/1**

0430 **7** *shd* **Quoteline Direct**[24] 3547 6-10-3 **66**........................(h) MissBeckySmith 8 61
(Micky Hammond) *hld up in rr: effrt and hdwy on inner whn nt clr run wl over 1f out: sn swtchd rt and rdn: styd on fnl f: n.d (jockey said gelding was denied a clear run)* **7/1**[3]

-445 **8** *1 ¼* **Grandscape**[24] 3541 4-10-3 **71**................................ SophieSmith(5) 1 63
(Ed Dunlop) *in tch on inner: pushed along over 4f out: s rdn over 3f out: sn wknd* **5/1**[1]

0-52 **9** *nk* **Agar's Plough**[67] 2056 4-10-5 **68**................................ MissJoannaMason 6 60
(Michael Easterby) *trckd ldrs: hdwy over 3f out: rdn along 2f out: sn drvn and wknd* **5/1**[1]

6-05 **10** *3* **Correggio**[25] 3511 9-9-2 **51**................................(p) MissCatherineWalton 11 37
(Micky Hammond) *hld up: a towards rr* **25/1**

6-40 **11** *2 ½* **Salam Zayed**[14] 3926 3-9-4 **63**................................ MrsCarolBartley 9 45
(Richard Fahey) *trckd ldng pair on outer: pushed along over 3f out: rdn along over 2f out: sn wknd* **16/1**

2m 13.98s (-1.02) **Going Correction** -0.10s/f (Good) **11** Ran SP% **117.4**
WFA 3 from 4yo+ 10lb
Speed ratings (Par 103): **100,98,98,98,97 94,94,93,93,91 89**
CSF £70.56 CT £472.32 TOTE £9.60: £2.80, £2.90, £2.10; EX 50.90 Trifecta £305.40.
Owner I B Barker / P Bastiman **Bred** Paul, Ben & Charlie Cartan **Trained** Cowthorpe, N Yorks

FOCUS
Add 8yds. A decent lady amateur riders' handicap in which the winner got a dream run up the inner and scored nicely. It's been rated around the third, and the second in line with his better AW form over the past year.
T/Plt: £75.80 to a £1 stake. Pool: £63,560.52 - 611.62 winning units T/Qpdt: £5.60 to a £1 stake. Pool: £7,612.14 - 1,005.73 winning units **Joe Rowntree**

4420 WINDSOR (R-H)
Monday, July 1

OFFICIAL GOING: Good to firm (watered; 7.8)
Wind: Quite fresh, behind Weather: Cloudy

4447 VISITMARATHONBET.CO.UK FILLIES' H'CAP — 1m 3f 99y
5:45 (5:45) (Class 5) (0-70,72) 3-Y-O+
£3,428 (£1,020; £509; £300; £300; £300) **Stalls** Low

Form RPR
5411 **1** **Cherry Cola**[18] 3777 3-9-3 **65**................................ TrevorWhelan 6 73+
(Sheena West) *dwlt: hld up in midfield: smooth prog over 2f out: rdn to ld jst over 1f out: kpt on wl* **5/2**[1]

350 **2** *1 ¼* **Scenesetter (IRE)**[25] 3495 3-9-2 **64**......................(p[1]) SilvestreDeSousa 1 70
(Marco Botti) *led: sent for home 3f out: drvn and hdd jst over 1f out: one pce (jockey said filly ran green)* **7/1**

6-35 **3** *1 ¾* **Lightening Dance**[39] 3010 5-10-7 **72**..........................(b) RobertHavlin 7 74
(Amanda Perrett) *trckd ldrs: rdn to try to chal 2f out: nt qckn over 1f out: one pce after* **9/2**

0-50 **4** *shd* **Spice Of Life**[55] 2505 3-8-8 **56**................................ HarryBentley 5 59
(Ralph Beckett) *prom: chsd ldr over 4f out to over 1f out: nt qckn and wl hld after* **4/1**[3]

4-31 **5** *4* **Miss M (IRE)**[16] 3834 5-10-0 **65**................................ MartinDwyer 4 60
(William Muir) *dwlt: t.k.h: hld up in rr: shkn up over 2f out: nvr on terms w ldrs* **11/4**[2]

00-0 **6** *½* **Delta Bravo (IRE)**[60] 2341 3-8-5 **53**................................ KieranO'Neill 2 48
(J S Moore) *chsd ldr to over 4f out: rdn over 3f out: steadily fdd* **25/1**

0-40 **7** *nk* **Maiden Navigator**[130] 836 3-8-6 **57**..........................(h) RosieJessop(3) 3 52
(David Simcock) *t.k.h: hld up towards rr: stl keen 4f out: pushed along and no prog over 2f out* **33/1**

340- **8** *1 ½* **Full Suit**[226] 9128 5-9-0 **56**................................ SeamusCronin(5) 8 47
(Ralph J Smith) *broke wl but sn hld up in last: effrt on outer wl over 2f out: no prog over 1f out: sn wknd* **50/1**

-350 **9** *19* **Mary Elise (IRE)**[27] 3444 4-9-6 **60**................................ MitchGodwin(3) 9 19
(Michael Blake) *dwlt: a in last pair: t.o* **50/1**

2m 28.9s (-0.80) **Going Correction** -0.05s/f (Good) **9** Ran SP% **116.6**
WFA 3 from 4yo+ 11lb
Speed ratings (Par 100): **100,99,97,97,94 94,94,93,79**
CSF £20.17 CT £74.20 TOTE £3.80: £1.80, £1.70, £1.30; EX 21.70 Trifecta £70.50.
Owner Ashley Head **Bred** Norman Court Stud **Trained** Falmer, E Sussex

FOCUS
A modest enough fillies' handicap, it was run at a steady gallop and saw the in-form favourite complete a hat-trick. Add nine yards. The third has been rated close to her C&D form earlier this year.

4448 BRITISH EBF MEDIAN AUCTION MAIDEN FILLIES' STKS (PLUS 10 RACE) 5f 21y
6:15 (6:18) (Class 5) 2-Y-O £3,881 (£1,155; £577; £288) Stalls Centre

Form RPR
433 1 **Dream Kart (IRE)**[17] 3803 2-9-0 71 SilvestreDeSousa 3 81+
(Mark Johnston) *mde all: shkn up and drew rt away fnl f: comf* 10/3[3]
52P 2 6 **Sneaky**[14] 3927 2-9-0 0 OisinMurphy 8 60
(Archie Watson) *pressed ldrs: rdn to chse wnr wl over 1f out and tried to chal: nt qckn and sn wl outpcd* 11/4[1]
2444 3 nk **Beignet (IRE)**[22] 3634 2-9-0 63 SeanLevey 1 58
(Richard Hannon) *chsd ldrs: pushed along over 2f out: hung lft whn rdn fnl f but kpt on to take 3rd nr fin* 12/1
452 4 ½ **Microscopic (IRE)**[23] 3595 2-9-0 65 AndreaAtzeni 7 56
(David Simcock) *pressed wnr to wl over 1f out: sn outpcd* 3/1[2]
5 hd **Quaint (IRE)** 2-9-0 0 CharlieBennett 9 56+
(Hughie Morrison) *s.i.s: sltly outpcd in 8th: pushed along after 2f: kpt on steadily over 1f out: nvr nrr* 16/1
6 6 2 ¼ **Queen Aya**[20] 3689 2-9-0 0 LiamKeniry 6 47
(Ed Walker) *chsd ldrs: shkn up 2f out: no prog over 1f out* 20/1
7 2 ¼ **Blue Venture** 2-9-0 0 BrettDoyle 4 39
(Tony Carroll) *w ldrs to 2f out: hung lft and wknd over 1f out* 40/1
000 8 ¾ **Love My Life (IRE)**[14] 3943 2-9-0 0 NicolaCurrie 5 37
(Jamie Osborne) *s.i.s: bdly outpcd and pushed along: nvr on terms but kpt on fnl f* 50/1
9 3 ¼ **Bockos Amber (IRE)** 2-9-0 0 JackMitchell 10 25
(Roger Teal) *in tch: pushed along and no prog 2f out: wknd over 1f out* 11/2
10 67 **Ivamonet (IRE)** 2-9-0 0 PatCosgrave 2
(Michael Wigham) *s.s: sn wl t.o* 33/1

59.58s (-0.52) **Going Correction** -0.05s/f (Good) **10 Ran SP% 115.8**
Speed ratings (Par 91): **102,92,91,91,90 87,83,82,77,**
CSF £12.37 TOTE £4.20: £1.50, £1.50, £3.00; EX 12.90 Trifecta £62.00.
Owner John O'Connor & Partner **Bred** John O'Connor **Trained** Middleham Moor, N Yorks

FOCUS
Modest juvenile form, but a dominant winner.

4449 DOWNLOAD THE MARATHONBET APP (S) STKS 6f 12y
6:45 (6:45) (Class 6) 3-Y-O+ £2,781 (£827; £413; £300; £300) Stalls Centre

Form RPR
0305 1 **Tomily (IRE)**[23] 3597 5-9-3 77 SeanLevey 6 79
(Richard Hannon) *hld up: smooth prog 1/2-way: led wl over 1f out and sn in command: rdn out* 1/1[1]
2062 2 4 ½ **Upavon**[20] 3688 9-9-3 64 AdamKirby 3 66
(Tony Carroll) *hld up: rdn over 2f out: prog to chse wnr over 1f out: kpt on but nvr able to chal* 8/1[3]
-650 3 10 **Time For Bed (IRE)**[18] 3764 3-8-6 69 KieranO'Neill 7 31
(Richard Hannon) *w ldrs: led 3f out to wl over 1f out: wknd qckly* 11/8[2]
300- 4 nk **Jeopardy John**[206] 9441 4-8-12 55 ScottMcCullagh(5) 2 35
(Michael Attwater) *led to 1/2-way: sn btn* 20/1
/000 5 38 **Whirl Me Round**[71] 1969 5-8-12 54 (v) SeamusCronin(5) 4
(Robyn Brisland) *restless stalls: awkward s: w ldr to 1/2-way: wknd rapidly: t.o and eased over 1f out (vet said gelding bled from the nose)* 40/1

1m 11.75s (-0.35) **Going Correction** -0.05s/f (Good)
WFA 3 from 4yo+ 6lb **5 Ran SP% 110.4**
Speed ratings (Par 101): **100,94,80,80,29**
CSF £9.62 TOTE £1.90: £1.30, £2.60; EX 7.30 Trifecta £13.00.The winner was sold to Mr Colm Sharkey for £14,500.
Owner Des Anderson **Bred** D J Anderson **Trained** East Everleigh, Wilts

FOCUS
An uncompetitive seller won readily by the standout candidate.

4450 MARATHONBET SPORTSBOOK H'CAP 1m 2f
7:15 (7:15) (Class 3) (0-90,89) 3-Y-O+ £7,561 (£2,263; £1,131; £566; £282) Stalls Low

Form RPR
4100 1 **Stealth Fighter (IRE)**[25] 3515 4-9-13 88 OisinMurphy 1 96
(Saeed bin Suroor) *sn led and set mod pce: hdd 3f out: led again 2f out against rail and drvn: styd on and jst hld on* 7/2[2]
-122 2 nk **Takumi (IRE)**[10] 4068 3-8-13 84 (p[1]) AndreaAtzeni 6 91+
(Roger Varian) *hld up in midfield: boxed in whn pce lifted over 2f out: fnd room over 1f out: drvn and r.o to take 2nd last 75yds: too late and jst hld* 11/8[1]
3021 3 nk **Grapevine (IRE)**[14] 3944 6-9-4 79 (p) KieranShoemark 5 85+
(Charles Hills) *hld up in last: waiting for room 2f out: prog over 1f out to chse wnr fnl f: styd on but nt qckn and lost 2nd last 75yds* 11/1
5330 4 1 ¼ **Al Jellaby**[53] 2563 4-9-13 88 (h) AdamKirby 3 92
(Clive Cox) *t.k.h: trckd ldng pair: rdn over 2f out: wandered sltly over 1f out: tried to cl fnl f but one pce* 9/2[3]
3-03 5 ¾ **Rotherwick (IRE)**[17] 3806 7-9-5 85 (t) DylanHogan(5) 8 87
(Paul Cole) *hld up in last trio: rdn on outer over 2f out: cl enough over 1f out: no imp after* 14/1
0413 6 1 ¼ **Uther Pendragon (IRE)**[39] 3022 4-9-1 76 (p) LiamKeniry 7 76
(J S Moore) *hld up in last trio: shkn up and effrt on outer over 2f out: cl enough over 1f out: nt qckn* 14/1
-003 7 1 **Madeleine Bond**[20] 3698 5-9-1 76 HarryBentley 4 74
(Henry Candy) *mostly chsd wnr: led 3f out to 2f out: lost 2nd and wknd fnl f* 9/1
04-0 8 1 **Maratha (IRE)**[28] 3423 5-9-2 77 (t) SeanLevey 9 73
(Stuart Williams) *trckd ldng trio: rdn over 2f out: wandered over 1f out: wknd fnl f* 66/1

2m 7.7s (-1.30) **Going Correction** -0.05s/f (Good)
WFA 3 from 4yo+ 10lb **8 Ran SP% 115.7**
Speed ratings (Par 107): **103,102,102,101,100 99,99,98**
CSF £8.81 CT £45.98 TOTE £4.10: £1.40, £1.10, £2.20; EX 11.70 Trifecta £92.50.
Owner Godolphin **Bred** B Kennedy & Mrs Ann Marie Kennedy **Trained** Newmarket, Suffolk

FOCUS
Add nine yards. A decent handicap and the winner just did enough having enjoyed the run of the race. The second and third have been rated as progressing a little from their latest efforts.

4451 SKY SPORTS RACING ON VIRGIN 535 H'CAP (SKY BET WINDSOR SPRINT SERIES QUALIFIER) 6f 12y
7:45 (7:45) (Class 2) (0-105,97) 3-Y-O+
£12,450 (£3,728; £1,864; £932; £466; £234) Stalls Centre

Form RPR
3153 1 **Embour (IRE)**[12] 3993 4-9-8 92 SeanLevey 3 100
(Richard Hannon) *trckd ldng trio: clsd 2f out: rdn to take narrow ld jst over 1f out: drvn out* 7/2[2]
2012 2 ½ **Equitation**[14] 3945 5-9-2 86 (t) OisinMurphy 5 92
(Stuart Williams) *dwlt: hld up in last trio: rdn and prog over 1f out: styd on to take 2nd last 75yds: a jst hld* 11/4[1]
6026 3 ½ **Ice Age (IRE)**[21] 3662 6-9-13 97 CharlesBishop 2 101
(Eve Johnson Houghton) *fast away: led against nr side rail: drvn 2f out: narrowly hdd jst over 1f out: stl ev ch 100yds out: no ex* 5/1[3]
66-4 4 ½ **Show Stealer**[42] 2917 6-9-2 86 (p) SilvestreDeSousa 8 89
(Rae Guest) *hld up in last pair: rdn on wd outside 2f out: clsd fnl f: nt quite pce to chal after but kpt on* 5/1[3]
1130 5 shd **Walk On Walter (IRE)**[12] 3991 4-9-11 95 RobHornby 1 97
(Jonathan Portman) *trckd ldr: rdn 2f out: tried to chal over 1f out but hanging sltly: one pce fnl f* 11/2
45-6 6 1 ¾ **Polybius**[37] 3094 8-9-11 95 AndreaAtzeni 6 92
(David Simcock) *stdd s: hld up in last pair: pushed along 2f out: kpt on but whn rdn fnl f but nvr in it* 8/1
0-40 7 ½ **Victory Angel (IRE)**[42] 2917 5-9-6 90 TomMarquand 4 85
(Robert Cowell) *trckd ldrs: rdn 2f out: chal over 1f out: fdd fnl f* 16/1

1m 10.75s (-1.35) **Going Correction** -0.05s/f (Good) **7 Ran SP% 114.6**
Speed ratings (Par 109): **107,106,105,105,104 102,101**
CSF £13.64 CT £46.79 TOTE £4.60: £2.30, £1.50; EX 14.10 Trifecta £41.10.
Owner Sullivanb'Stock,Ruxleyholdings,Mrs Doyle **Bred** Carpet Lady Partnership **Trained** East Everleigh, Wilts

FOCUS
A useful little sprint won by a progressive 4yo. The second has been rated to his best, and the fourth close to her latest.

4452 RITA ORA LIVE AT WINDSOR RACECOURSE MAIDEN STKS 1m 31y
8:15 (8:18) (Class 5) 3-Y-O+ £3,428 (£1,020; £509; £254) Stalls Low

Form RPR
03 1 **Rum Baba**[27] 3445 3-9-5 0 RichardKingscote 1 80
(Charlie Fellowes) *wl away fr ins draw: led 2f: trckd ldr: rdn to ld again 2f out: hrd pressed fnl f: hld on* 6/5[1]
4 2 nk **Frontman**[9] 4121 3-9-5 0 (p) RobertHavlin 4 79
(John Gosden) *chsd ldng pair: rdn over 2f out: wnt 2nd fnl f and sn chal: nt qckn last 75yds* 2/1[2]
35 3 1 ½ **Moftris**[100] 1293 3-9-5 0 TomMarquand 14 76
(William Haggas) *wl away fr wdst draw and led after 2f: rdn and hdd 2f out: one pce fnl f* 5/1[3]
0 4 6 **Bear Force One**[20] 3696 3-9-5 0 JackMitchell 8 62
(Roger Teal) *prom in chsng gp: wnt 4th over 3f out: rdn and no imp on clr ldng trio after* 28/1
6-0 5 5 **Colonel Slade (IRE)**[9] 4120 3-9-5 0 (t) MartinDwyer 3 51
(Brian Meehan) *prom in chsng gp: shkn up 3f out and no imp: fdd 2f out* 33/1
0 6 nk **Petite Malle (USA)**[39] 3003 3-9-0 0 GeorgeWood 10 45
(James Fanshawe) *towards rr: 9th 1/2-way: shkn up 3f out: passed a few after but nvr a factor* 25/1
65 7 ¾ **Wild Cat**[18] 3761 3-9-0 0 JasonWatson 9 43
(Roger Charlton) *hld up in midfield: shkn up and rchd 5th over 2f out: no prog after and wknd over 1f out* 8/1
0 8 ½ **Cinzento (IRE)**[21] 3648 3-9-5 0 CallumShepherd 12 47
(Stuart Williams) *dwlt: wl in rr: pushed along 3f out: nvr a factor but passed sme rivals late on* 100/1
0- 9 3 ¾ **Dark Seraphim (IRE)**[357] 4753 4-10-0 0 (w) KieranShoemark 6 40
(Charles Hills) *nvr beyond midfield: shkn up and brief effrt 3f out: wknd 2f out* 28/1
5 10 2 ¾ **Soldier Of War (USA)**[5] 4258 4-10-0 0 AdamKirby 13 34
(Ben Pauling) *dwlt: a in rr: rdn and struggling wl over 3f out* 66/1
11 1 ¼ **Sea Sister (IRE)**[192] 9674 3-9-0 0 KieranO'Neill 5 24
(Olly Murphy) *s.i.s: wl in rr: rdn and no prog 4f out* 100/1
12 ½ **Colourful Sky (FR)** 3-9-0 0 LiamKeniry 2 23
(J S Moore) *s.i.s: a in rr: struggling 4f out* 100/1
0 13 1 ¼ **Capricorn Prince**[45] 2795 3-9-5 0 HectorCrouch 11 25
(Gary Moore) *prom in chsng gp to 1/2-way: sn wknd* 100/1
14 3 ½ **Angels Chant** 3-9-0 0 CharlieBennett 7 12
(Jim Boyle) *dwlt: mostly in last and a bhd* 100/1

1m 41.95s (-2.55) **Going Correction** -0.05s/f (Good)
WFA 3 from 4yo 9lb **14 Ran SP% 126.7**
Speed ratings (Par 103): **110,109,108,102,97 96,96,95,91,89 87,87,86,82**
CSF £3.71 TOTE £2.10: £1.10, £1.10, £1.90; EX 4.20 Trifecta £13.10.
Owner Normandie Stud Ltd **Bred** Normandie Stud Ltd **Trained** Newmarket, Suffolk
■ Stewards' Enquiry : Robert Havlin 13-day ban; misuse of whip (July 15-27)

FOCUS
Add nine yards. The market leaders dominated this modest maiden. The winner has been rated in line with his AW latest.

4453 VISIT ATTHERACES.COM H'CAP 1m 31y
8:45 (8:48) (Class 5) (0-70,72) 3-Y-O+
£3,428 (£1,020; £509; £300; £300; £300) Stalls Low

Form RPR
6055 1 **Black Medick**[26] 3468 3-9-5 70 LiamJones 2 73
(Laura Mongan) *trckd ldrs: rdn and clsd to ld wl over 1f out: drvn and hrd pressed fnl f: hung lft nr fin: hld on (jockey said filly hung badly left-handed)* 33/1
00-0 2 ½ **Sir Magnum**[13] 3966 4-8-10 52 BrettDoyle 3 56
(Tony Carroll) *wl in tch: rdn and prog 2f out: chsd wnr jst over 1f out: chal fnl f: hld whn carried lft nr fin* 40/1
6-66 3 ¾ **Tally's Son**[39] 2994 5-8-9 51 oh3 (b[1]) RobHornby 9 53+
(Grace Harris) *slowly away: towards rr: prog into midfield over 3f out: nt clr run 2f out: impeded over 1f out: rdn and styd on to take 3rd ins fnl f: hmpd last stride* 25/1

The Form Book Flat 2019, Raceform Ltd, Newbury, RG14 5SJ

2-60 **4** *hd* **Copal**[26] 3471 3-9-7 **72**................................ HarryBentley 7 72+
(Ralph Beckett) *trckd ldng pair: waiting for a gap over 2f out: sn rdn: nt clr run over 1f out: kpt on one pce u.p fnl f* **2/1**[1]

6162 **5** *nse* **Orliko (IRE)**[7] 4179 3-8-11 **62**.......................(bt) RossaRyan 8 62
(Richard Hannon) *led: rdn and hdd wl over 1f out: lost 2nd jst over 1f out: one pce fnl f (jockey said gelding hung left-handed)* **11/2**[3]

-560 **6** *hd* **Shifting Gold (IRE)**[23] 3594 3-8-6 **57**.......................... DavidEgan 1 56
(William Knight) *wl in tch in midfield: trckd ldrs 2f out and waiting for room: rdn and kpt on same pce fnl f* **10/1**

316 **7** *nse* **Rakematiz**[100] 1292 5-9-11 **72**...................... ScottMcCullagh(5) 13 73
(Brett Johnson) *hld up in last: pushed along 2f out: styd on steadily ins fnl f: nrst fin but nvr in it* **20/1**

2-21 **8** *1 ½* **Delicate Kiss**[150] 516 5-10-1 **71**........................(b) KieranO'Neill 10 69
(John Bridger) *hld up in last pair: shkn up over 2f out: only modest late prog* **7/1**

-526 **9** *½* **Maximum Power (FR)**[117] 1038 4-9-5 **61**..................... MartinDwyer 12 57
(Tim Pinfield) *trckd ldr to 2f out: drvn whn swtchd lft over 1f out: wknd fnl f* **14/1**

-055 **10** *4 ½* **Bounty Pursuit**[6] 4226 7-9-8 **67**........................ MitchGodwin(3) 11 53
(Michael Blake) *sn in last trio on outer: shkn up and no prog 3f out: nvr a factor* **5/1**[2]

-302 **11** *2 ½* **Monsieur Fox**[108] 1215 4-9-0 **56**...................(p[1]) RichardKingscote 5 36
(Lydia Richards) *in tch: rdn 1/2-way: sn struggling (trainer said gelding was unsuited by the undulating track)* **14/1**

1m 43.95s (-0.55) **Going Correction** -0.05s/f (Good)
WFA 3 from 4yo+ 9lb **11** Ran SP% **114.3**
Speed ratings (Par 103): **100,99,98,98,98 98,98,96,96,91 89**
CSF £844.51 CT £22146.62 TOTE £32.10: £6.30, £17.50, £7.10; EX 1348.70.
Owner Mrs P J Sheen **Bred** Rockcliffe Stud **Trained** Epsom, Surrey
■ Fleeting Freedom was withdrawn. Price at time of withdrawal was 8/1. Rule 4 applies to all bets. Deduction - 10p in the pound.

FOCUS
Add nine yards. This moderate handicap was a messy affair. The winner has been rated back to form, and the fifth close to form.
T/Plt: £5.80 to a £1 stake. Pool: £99,541.52 - 12,362.89 winning units T/Qpdt: £2.40 to a £1 stake. Pool: £10,497.26 - 3,211.51 winning units **Jonathan Neesom**

4190 WOLVERHAMPTON (A.W) (L-H)

Monday, July 1

OFFICIAL GOING: Tapeta: standard
Wind: Fresh across Weather: Overcast

4454 SMARTVETMEDS.COM CLASSIFIED STKS 7f 36y (Tp)
2:15 (2:15) (Class 6) 3-Y-O
£2,781 (£827; £413; £300; £300; £300) **Stalls High**

Form RPR

0000 **1** **Primeiro Boy (IRE)**[8] 4148 3-8-11 **62**...................... SeanDavis(3) 6 68
(Richard Fahey) *hld up: rdn over 2f out: hdwy over 1f out: edgd lft ins fnl f: r.o u.p to ld nr fin (regarding the apparent improvement in form, trainer's rep said gelding had appreciated the step up in trip to 7 furlongs and also benefitted from the drop into class 6 company on this occasion)* **33/1**

2616 **2** *½* **In Trutina**[17] 3801 3-9-0 **64**.............................. LukeMorris 5 67
(Archie Watson) *led: hdd over 5f out: chsd ldr: rdn to ld ins fnl f: hdd nr fin* **7/1**

0000 **3** *1* **Desert Lantern (USA)**[23] 3570 3-8-9 **65**............... AndrewBreslin(5) 3 64
(Mark Johnston) *hld up: hdwy and nt clr run over 1f out: r.o to go 3rd nr fin* **6/1**

3104 **4** *nk* **Molly Mai**[18] 3779 3-8-9 **65**............................ DylanHogan(5) 1 64
(Philip McBride) *prom: rdn over 2f out: swtchd rt over 1f out: sn hung lft: nt clr run ins fnl f: styd on* **3/1**[1]

665 **5** *nse* **Charlie Arthur (IRE)**[87] 1570 3-9-0 **64**..................(h) ShaneKelly 8 63
(Richard Hughes) *chsd ldrs: led over 5f out: rdn over 1f out: hdd and hung lft ins fnl f: styd on same pce* **9/1**

5-23 **6** *¾* **Leopardina (IRE)**[24] 3535 3-9-0 **63**..................(h[1]) StevieDonohoe 2 62
(David Simcock) *chsd ldrs: shkn up and edgd lft over 1f out: rdn and edgd rt ins fnl f: styd on same pce* **9/1**

0303 **7** *1 ½* **Freedom And Wheat (IRE)**[7] 4193 3-9-0 **64**..........(v) DavidProbert 9 58
(Mark Usher) *swtchd lft sn after s: hld up: rdn and hung lft fr over 1f out: nvr on terms (jockey said gelding was never travelling)* **9/2**[3]

0065 **R** **Greybychoice (IRE)**[27] 3440 3-8-9 **62**.............. PoppyBridgwater(5) 7
(Nick Littmoden) *ref to r* **7/2**[2]

1m 29.34s (0.54) **Going Correction** 0.0s/f (Stan) **8** Ran SP% **115.1**
Speed ratings (Par 98): **96,95,94,93,93 93,91,**
CSF £246.45 TOTE £32.60: £6.40, £2.50, £2.20; EX 317.10 Trifecta £2018.60.
Owner Bardsley, Hyde & Tattersall **Bred** McCracken Farms **Trained** Musley Bank, N Yorks

FOCUS
A moderate race. The winner has been rated back to his best.

4455 SMARTVETMEDS.COM APPRENTICE CLAIMING STKS 7f 36y (Tp)
2:45 (2:45) (Class 6) 4-Y-O+
£2,781 (£827; £413; £300; £300; £300) **Stalls High**

Form RPR

2332 **1** **Mister Music**[60] 2346 10-8-13 **84**..................... ElishaWhittington(7) 5 73+
(Tony Carroll) *s.i.s: hld up: hdwy over 1f out: rdn and r.o to ld towards fin* **9/4**[1]

2440 **2** *¾* **Sarasota (IRE)**[86] 1586 4-8-11 **61**.......................... AndrewBreslin 7 62
(Alexandra Dunn) *chsd ldr: carried lft 6f out: led 2f out: rdn and edgd lft ins fnl f: hdd towards fin* **20/1**

-000 **3** *shd* **Art Echo**[18] 3781 6-8-9 **62**..............................(vt) TobyEley(3) 8 63
(John Mackie) *s.i.s: hld up: hdwy 1/2-way: nt clr run over 1f out: rdn and hung lft ins fnl f: r.o (jockey said gelding hung right)* **13/2**[3]

3016 **4** *2* **Motajaasid (IRE)**[20] 3701 4-9-7 **76**..............(tp) AngusVilliers(7) 12 74
(Richard Hughes) *edgd lft s: sn led: edgd lft again 6f out: racd keenly: shkn up and hdd 2f out: styd on same pce wl ins fnl f (jockey said gelding jumped left leaving stalls)* **5/1**[2]

2040 **5** *1 ½* **The Groove**[24] 3543 6-9-3 **69**.......................... GeorgiaDobie(3) 2 62
(David Evans) *hld up: rdn over 1f out: styd on ins fnl f: nt trble ldrs* **5/1**[2]

5040 **6** *nse* **Grey Destiny**[7] 4194 9-8-13 **63**..................(p) KieranSchofield(3) 9 58
(Antony Brittain) *s.i.s: hld up: hdwy over 1f out: styd on: nt trble ldrs* **13/2**[3]

0-00 **7** *1 ¼* **Dark Side Dream**[26] 3462 7-9-2 **73**................ ThoreHammerHansen 3 55
(Charlie Wallis) *chsd ldrs: hmpd 6f out: rdn and edgd rt over 1f out: wknd ins fnl f* **12/1**

633 **8** *¾* **Secondo (FR)**[48] 2717 9-9-0 **59**...................(v) PoppyBridgwater 4 51
(Robert Stephens) *prom: hmpd 6f out: rdn over 1f out: styd on same pce* **8/1**

-400 **9** *nk* **Dark Confidant (IRE)**[28] 3413 6-8-5 **43**..................(t[1]) EllaMcCain(5) 11 46
(Donald McCain) *s.i.s: hld up: racd keenly and hung rt: n.d (jockey said gelding hung right)* **100/1**

0450 **10** *¾* **Caledonian Gold**[16] 3843 6-8-7 **44**............................ WilliamCox 6 41
(Lisa Williamson) *chsd ldrs: hmpd 6f out: rdn over 2f out: wknd fnl f* **100/1**

-000 **11** *14* **Royal Rattle**[35] 3158 4-8-7 **43**.................... CianMacRedmond(5) 1 11
(John Norton) *s.i.s: hld up: rdn and wknd over 2f out* **100/1**

1m 28.84s (0.04) **Going Correction** 0.0s/f (Stan) **11** Ran SP% **117.3**
Speed ratings (Par 101): **99,98,98,95,94 93,92,91,91,90 74**
CSF £52.95 TOTE £2.90: £2.00, £3.90, £1.90; EX 52.60 Trifecta £316.80.
Owner A Sergent & Partner **Bred** Longview Stud & Bloodstock Ltd **Trained** Cropthorne, Worcs

FOCUS
The winner didn't have to be at his best to take this ordinary claimer. The second, third and ninth's recent form set the opening level.

4456 SMARTVETMEDS.COM EBF NOVICE STKS 7f 36y (Tp)
3:15 (3:17) (Class 5) 2-Y-O
£3,428 (£1,020; £509; £254) **Stalls High**

Form RPR

54 **1** **Rich Belief**[20] 3702 2-9-5 0.............................. RobertWinston 4 76
(James Bethell) *chsd ldr: shkn up over 2f out: rdn to ld and hung lft over 1f out: styd on wl* **9/2**[2]

52 **2** *2 ½* **Dark Kris (IRE)**[24] 3542 2-9-5 0............................ ShaneKelly 3 70
(Richard Hughes) *led at stdy pce: racd keenly: shkn up and qckned over 2f out: rdn: hung lft and hdd over 1f out: flashed tail and no ex ins fnl f* **4/7**[1]

3 *1* **Breck's Selection (FR)** 2-9-5 0.............................. LukeMorris 2 67+
(Mark Johnston) *s.i.s: sn pushed along: hdwy over 5f out: drvn along over 2f out: swtchd rt over 1f out: styd on* **8/1**[3]

0 **4** *2 ¾* **Cherokee Mist (CAN)**[11] 4030 2-9-5 0........................ BrettDoyle 5 60
(Charlie Appleby) *uns rdr to post: hacked arnd for 4f: chsd ldrs: pushed along 1/2-way: rdn and hung lft over 1f out: styd on same pce fnl f* **12/1**

5 *1 ½* **Danking** 2-9-5 0... TomMarquand 6 57
(Alan King) *s.s: hdwy to latch on to bk of field over 5f out: shkn up over 2f out: no ex fnl f (jockey said colt was slowly away)* **9/1**

1m 29.53s (0.73) **Going Correction** 0.0s/f (Stan) **5** Ran SP% **110.6**
Speed ratings (Par 94): **95,92,91,87,86**
CSF £7.66 TOTE £5.10: £1.30, £1.40; EX 7.90 Trifecta £27.60.
Owner Clarendon Thoroughbred Racing **Bred** Phillistown House Ltd **Trained** Middleham Moor, N Yorks

FOCUS
The first two had already shown fair ability.

4457 SMARTVETMEDS.COM ONLINE PHARMACY H'CAP 6f 20y (Tp)
3:45 (3:47) (Class 6) (0-65,65) 3-Y-O
£2,781 (£827; £413; £300; £300; £300) **Stalls Low**

Form RPR

0-20 **1** **Micronize (IRE)**[10] 4080 3-8-7 **54**....................... SeanDavis(3) 12 59
(Richard Fahey) *broke wl: chsd ldr: led and edgd rt over 1f out: rdn and edgd lft ins fnl f: styd on* **25/1**

4065 **2** *nk* **Alicia Darcy (IRE)**[15] 3887 3-9-2 **60**....................... LukeMorris 10 64+
(Archie Watson) *broke wl: sn pushed along and lost pl: hdwy over 2f out: rdn over 1f out: nt clr run and swtchd rt ins fnl f: r.o to go 2nd nr fin* **10/1**

6506 **3** *½* **Miss Gargar**[15] 3887 3-8-10 **54**........................(v[1]) GeorgeWood 7 57
(Harry Dunlop) *pushed along to chse ldrs: rdn over 2f out: hung lft over 1f out: styd on: carried rt towards fin* **20/1**

-340 **4** *nse* **Tease Maid**[20] 3709 3-9-2 **60**.............................. RobbieDowney 1 62
(John Quinn) *sn led: rdn and hdd over 1f out: ev ch ins fnl f: no ex towards fin* **14/1**

3054 **5** *½* **Deconso**[18] 3775 3-8-9 **53**..................................... ShaneKelly 11 54
(Christopher Kellett) *sn chsng ldrs: rdn and hung lft over 1f out: styd on* **16/1**

0533 **6** *1* **Under Curfew**[28] 3406 3-9-3 **61**............................ TomMarquand 8 59+
(Tony Carroll) *hld up: hdwy and hung lft fr over 1f out: sn rdn: r.o: nt rch ldrs* **9/2**[2]

2003 **7** *½* **Miss Enigma (IRE)**[7] 4192 3-9-0 **61**....................(b) FinleyMarsh(3) 9 57+
(Richard Hughes) *hld up in tch: rdn over 1f out: styd on same pce ins fnl f* **11/2**

524 **8** *1 ¼* **Valley Belle (IRE)**[5] 4244 3-8-13 **57**.................... JosephineGordon 3 50
(Phil McEntee) *broke wl: sn pushed along: lost pl after 1f: rdn over 1f out: r.o ins fnl f* **4/1**[1]

0163 **9** *1 ½* **Sepahi**[20] 3709 3-8-13 **62**................................(p) DylanHogan(5) 5 50+
(Henry Spiller) *s.i.s: r.o towards fin: nvr nrr* **14/1**

55-0 **10** *nk* **Scottish Blade (IRE)**[64] 2139 3-9-3 **61**................... KieranShoemark 2 48+
(Charles Hills) *s.i.s: hld up: shkn up over 1f out: nvr on terms* **5/1**[3]

4324 **11** *6* **Bequest**[56] 2474 3-9-7 **65**................................. DavidProbert 4 34
(Ron Hodges) *sn pushed along in rr: rdn over 2f out: n.d* **7/1**

3000 **12** *1 ¼* **Not So Shy**[7] 4192 3-8-1 **52**........................ ElishaWhittington(7) 6 18
(Lisa Williamson) *chsd ldrs: pushed along over 3f out: n.m.r over 2f out: sn wknd* **80/1**

1m 14.58s (0.08) **Going Correction** 0.0s/f (Stan) **12** Ran SP% **120.9**
Speed ratings (Par 98): **99,98,97,97,97 95,95,93,91,91 83,81**
CSF £257.80 CT £5116.49 TOTE £23.50: £5.60, £3.00, £4.90; EX 163.40 Trifecta £2704.50.
Owner Nick Bradley Racing 43 & Partner **Bred** Nick Bradley Bloodstock **Trained** Musley Bank, N Yorks
■ Stewards' Enquiry : Sean Davis one-day ban: failed to keep straight from stalls (19- Jul); two-day ban: careless riding (17-18 Jul)

FOCUS
A moderate handicap. The winner has been rated to his previous best, with the fourth among those who help set the level.

4458 SMARTVETMEDS.COM H'CAP 5f 21y (Tp)
4:15 (4:15) (Class 4) (0-85,86) 3-Y-O+
£5,207 (£1,549; £774; £387; £300; £300) **Stalls Low**

Form RPR

3051 **1** **Harry's Bar**[27] 3443 4-9-9 **81**............................ GeorgeWood 8 90+
(James Fanshawe) *s.i.s: hdwy on outer over 3f out: shkn up to chse ldr over 1f out: rdn to ld and edgd rt wl ins fnl f* **7/4**[1]

5105 **2** *¾* **Just That Lord**[12] 3993 6-10-0 **86**.......................... LukeMorris 7 92
(Michael Attwater) *led 4f out: rdn over 1f out: sn hung rt: hdd wl ins fnl f* **7/2**[2]

4015 **3** *nk* **Fizzy Feet (IRE)**[9] 4128 3-9-0 **77**.......................... TomMarquand 4 80
(David Loughnane) *chsd ldrs: pushed along 1/2-way: chsd ldr 2f out tl rdn and swtchd lft over 1f out: styd on* **9/1**

4123 **4** *3/4* **Cappananty Con**[27] 3443 5-9-1 **76**.......................... JoshuaBryan(3) 1 78
(Charlie Wallis) *hood removed late: s.i.s: hld up: swtchd rt over 3f out: rdn over 1f out: r.o ins fnl f: nt rch ldrs* **11/2**

6251 **5** *hd* **You're Cool**[31] 3303 7-9-11 **83**..........................(t) JasonWatson 3 85
(John Balding) *led 1f: chsd ldr: hmpd over 3f out: lost 2nd 2f out: sn rdn: styd on same pce wl ins fnl f* **10/1**

2506 **6** *hd* **Qaaraat**[2] 4364 4-8-4 **69**.......................... KieranSchofield(7) 2 70
(Antony Brittain) *chsd ldrs: nt clr run and lost pl over 3f out: rdn over 1f out: r.o ins fnl f* **4/1**[3]

1m 0.91s (-0.99) **Going Correction** 0.0s/f (Stan)
WFA 3 from 4yo+ 5lb **6** Ran SP% **113.1**
Speed ratings (Par 105): **107,105,105,104,103 103**
CSF £8.21 CT £40.44 TOTE £2.20: £1.50, £2.70; EX 10.40 Trifecta £41.60.
Owner Jan and Peter Hopper **Bred** Jan & Peter Hopper **Trained** Newmarket, Suffolk

FOCUS
Solid form and it's likely there's more to come from the improving winner. The second has been rated back to the level of his February C&D win.

4459 SMARTVETMEDS.COM NOVICE MEDIAN AUCTION STKS 1m 4f 51y (Tp)
4:45 (4:47) (Class 6) 3-4-Y-0 £2,781 (£827; £413; £206) **Stalls Low**

Form RPR

15 **1** **Moment Of Hope (IRE)**[44] 2838 3-9-2 0.......................... SeanDavis(3) 3 78+
(David Simcock) *hld up: racd keenly: hdwy over 1f out: rdn to ld ins fnl f: styd on* **8/1**

04 **2** *nk* **Lord Halifax (IRE)**[21] 3664 3-9-3 0.......................... StevieDonohoe 8 75+
(Charlie Fellowes) *s.i.s: pushed along and hdwy to go prom after 1f: rdn to ld 1f out: hdd ins fnl f: styd on* **11/4**[2]

4322 **3** *2 1/2* **Luck Of Clover**[17] 3809 3-8-12 65.......................... DavidProbert 5 66
(Andrew Balding) *led 1f: chsd ldr tl led again over 2f out: rdn and hdd 1f out: no ex wl ins fnl f* **5/1**[3]

0-60 **4** *3/4* **Star Talent (IRE)**[23] 3584 3-9-3 68.......................... ShaneKelly 6 69
(Gay Kelleway) *hld up: hdwy over 2f out: rdn and edgd lft fr over 1f out: styd on same pce ins fnl f* **16/1**

03-0 **5** *2 3/4* **Avenue Foch**[29] 3373 3-9-3 71.......................... DanielMuscutt 7 65
(James Fanshawe) *hld up: rdn on outer over 2f out: hung lft fr over 1f out: nt rch ldrs* **6/4**[1]

6 *5* **Allocated (IRE)** 3-9-0 0.......................... JoshuaBryan(3) 2 57
(John Butler) *led after 1f tl rdn and hdd over 2f out: wknd fnl f* **33/1**

7 *7* **Jukebox Blues (FR)** 3-9-3 0.......................... LukeMorris 1 46
(Mark Johnston) *chsd ldrs: rdn over 3f out: wknd 2f out* **15/2**

P **Hurry Kane** 3-8-12 0..........................(h[1]) RhiainIngram(5) 4
(Paul George) *hld up: hung rt and lost tch over 6f out: sn p.u* **50/1**

2m 43.41s (2.61) **Going Correction** 0.0s/f (Stan) **8** Ran SP% **117.0**
Speed ratings (Par 101): **91,90,89,88,86 83,78,**
CSF £31.09 TOTE £8.50: £2.20, £1.50, £1.50; EX 32.20 Trifecta £108.80.
Owner Saeed Jaber **Bred** Rabbah Bloodstock Limited **Trained** Newmarket, Suffolk

FOCUS
An ordinary novice but good going from the winner to defy a penalty.

4460 SMARTVETMEDS.COM AMATEUR RIDERS' H'CAP 1m 142y (Tp)
5:15 (5:16) (Class 6) (0-55,55) 3-Y-0+
£2,682 (£832; £415; £300; £300; £300) **Stalls Low**

Form RPR

0623 **1** **Luna Magic**[62] 2259 5-11-0 **55**.......................... MissBrodieHampson 12 67
(Archie Watson) *sn chsng ldr: wnt upsides over 5f out: led over 3f out: rdn over 1f out: edgd rt ins fnl f: styd on* **7/2**[2]

1444 **2** *1 1/4* **Allux Boy (IRE)**[12] 4002 5-11-0 **55**..........................(p) MrSimonWalker 6 64
(Nigel Tinkler) *prom: chsd wnr over 2f out: rdn and edgd rt over 1f out: styd on* **6/4**[1]

4663 **3** *6* **Pike Corner Cross (IRE)**[31] 3322 7-10-6 **54**....... MrPhilipThomas(7) 10 51
(David Evans) *s.i.s: sn prom: nt clr run and lost pl over 3f out: hrd rdn and hdwy on outer over 1f out: hung lft ins fnl f: styd on same pce* **6/1**[3]

26-0 **4** *5* **Dutch Artist (IRE)**[13] 3959 7-10-6 **54**.......................... MissBelindaJohnson(7) 2 40
(Nigel Tinkler) *s.i.s: hld up: pushed along over 3f out: r.o ins fnl f: nvr nrr* **28/1**

400 **5** *1/2* **Showdance Kid**[28] 3430 5-10-7 **53**.......................... MrMAGalligan(5) 13 38
(Kevin Frost) *hld up: rdn over 2f out: r.o ins fnl f: nvr nrr* **33/1**

2006 **6** *nk* **Misu Pete**[31] 3325 7-10-6 **54**..........................(p) MrCiaranJones(7) 11 39
(Mark Usher) *prom: rdn over 3f out: wknd over 1f out* **33/1**

3100 **7** *1/2* **Limerick Lord (IRE)**[23] 3592 7-10-11 **52**..........................(p) MrRossBirkett 9 36
(Julia Feilden) *led: hdd over 3f out: rdn over 1f out: wknd fnl f* **16/1**

1400 **8** *1/2* **Irish Times**[18] 3774 4-10-7 **55**..........................(p[1]) MrEireannCagney(7) 5 37
(Henry Spiller) *chsd ldrs: rdn over 2f out: wknd over 1f out* **25/1**

660 **9** *nse* **Rosin Box (IRE)**[14] 3924 6-10-7 **55**..........................(t[1]) MissSallyDavison(7) 1 37
(Tristan Davidson) *awkward s: prom: nt clr run and lost pl wl over 7f out: hdwy and hit rails over 5f out: hmpd over 3f out: wknd 2f out* **14/1**

6000 **10** *1/2* **Rock Warbler (IRE)**[20] 3705 6-10-8 **49**..........................(h) MissMichelleMullineaux 4 30
(Michael Mullineaux) *hld up: a in rr* **40/1**

2324 **11** *nk* **Snooker Jim**[14] 3939 4-10-5 **53**..........................(t) MrLiamHamblett(7) 3 34
(Steph Hollinshead) *hld up in tch: rdn and nt clr run over 1f out: wknd fnl f* **14/1**

0001 **12** *3 1/4* **Mime Dance**[23] 3592 8-10-8 **52**.......................... MissAliceHaynes(3) 7 26
(John Butler) *hld up: nt clr run and lost pl over 6f out: n.d after* **28/1**

0420 **13** *6* **Diamond Reflection (IRE)**[40] 2970 7-10-7 **51**(tp) MissHannahWelch(3) 8 12
(Alexandra Dunn) *s.i.s: sn swtchd lft nt clr run over 7f out: pushed along over 3f out: wknd over 2f out* **12/1**

1m 49.84s (-0.26) **Going Correction** 0.0s/f (Stan) **13** Ran SP% **122.5**
Speed ratings (Par 101): **101,99,94,90,89 89,88,88,88,88 87,84,79**
CSF £8.62 CT £32.91 TOTE £4.70: £1.80, £1.10, £2.30; EX 10.60 Trifecta £51.30.
Owner Marco Polo **Bred** Lady Jennifer Green **Trained** Upper Lambourn, W Berks

FOCUS
Few got into this moderate handicap for amateur riders.

T/Plt: £131.10 to a £1 stake. Pool: £75,336.57 - 419.37 winning units T/Qpdt: £20.40 to a £1 stake. Pool: £9,276.16 - 335.14 winning units **Colin Roberts**

4427 HAMBURG (R-H)
Monday, July 1

OFFICIAL GOING: Turf: good

4461a 100 JAHRE HUGO PHOHE-RENNEN (GROUP 3) (3YO+ FILLIES & MARES) (TURF) 1m
6:30 3-Y-0+ £28,828 (£10,810; £5,405; £2,702; £1,801)

RPR

1 **Axana (GER)**[36] 3119 3-8-9 0.......................... EduardoPedroza 6 106
(A Wohler, Germany) *racd keenly: restrained bhd ldr: angled out and drvn between horses to chal 1 1/2f out: led appr fnl f: r.o: readily* **6/5**[1]

2 *1 1/2* **Shalona (FR)**[36] 3119 3-8-7 0.......................... LukasDelozier 7 101
(Henk Grewe, Germany) *towards rr: hdwy ins fnl 2f: r.o ins fnl f: nt rch wnr* **37/10**[2]

3 *nk* **Madita (GER)**[32] 3288 4-9-2 0.......................... BauyrzhanMurzabayev 8 102
(S Smrczek, Germany) *dwlt: hld up in fnl pair: hdwy over 1 1/2f out: styd on wl fnl f: nvr nrr* **26/5**[3]

4 *2 1/2* **Emerita (GER)**[32] 3288 4-9-0 0.......................... MarcoCasamento 5 95
(H-J Groschel, Germany) *settled in midfield: tk clsr order 3f out: cl 4th and rdn 1 1/2f out: one pce fnl f* **188/10**

5 *1* **Best On Stage (GER)**[36] 3119 3-8-7 0.......................... AndraschStarke 11 92
(P Schiergen, Germany) *midfield on outer: edgd lft over 2f out and sltly impeded over 1 1/2f out: kpt on ins fnl f: nvr trbld ldrs* **104/10**

6 *hd* **Peace Of Paris (GER)**[70] 1990 3-8-7 0.......................... MartinSeidl 10 92
(Markus Klug, Germany) *racd keenly: v wd into and out of first bnd: sn cl up on outer under restraint: drvn to chal and ev ch 1 1/2f out: sn rdn and dropped away fnl f* **184/10**

7 *1* **Caesara**[21] 4-9-0 0.......................... FilipMinarik 2 90
(Jean-Pierre Carvalho, Germany) *led: hdd appr fnl f: sn wknd* **30/1**

8 *1 1/4* **Akua'rella (GER)**[21] 4-9-0 0.......................... WladimirPanov 3 87
(D Moser, Germany) *prom on inner: lost pl 1/2-way: rdn and btn 1 1/2f out* **188/10**

9 *1 3/4* **Seaside Song**[15] 5-9-2 0.......................... CarlosLopez 9 85
(Cathrine Erichsen, Norway) *racd in fnl pair: rdn and no imp 2f out: wl hld fnl f* **182/10**

10 *nse* **Cabarita (GER)**[21] 4-9-0 0.......................... BayarsaikhanGanbat 4 82
(H-J Groschel, Germany) *slow to stride: towards rr on inner: unable to cl whn asked over 2f out: nvr in contention* **26/1**

1m 35.45s
WFA 3 from 4yo+ 9lb **10** Ran SP% **119.0**
PARI-MUTUEL (all including 1 euro stake): WIN 2.20 PLACE: 1.30, 1.60, 1.60; SF: 5.30.
Owner Team Valor **Bred** S Penner **Trained** Germany

4462 - 4471a (Foreign Racing) - See Raceform Interactive

4213 BRIGHTON (L-H)
Tuesday, July 2

OFFICIAL GOING: Good to firm (watered; 7.8) changing to good to firm (firm in places) after race 2 (2.30)
Wind: virtually nil Weather: warm and sunny

4472 RACING STAFF WEEK 2019 H'CAP 6f 210y
2:00 (2:11) (Class 6) (0-60,61) 3-Y-0+
£2,781 (£827; £413; £300; £300; £300) **Stalls Centre**

Form RPR

0623 **1** **Hedging (IRE)**[14] 3966 5-9-2 **57**..........................(b) GeorgiaDobie(7) 6 65
(Eve Johnson Houghton) *racd in midfield: hdwy u.p to chse ldr over 1f out: rdn to ld 1f out: styd on wl* **7/2**[3]

4311 **2** *1 1/2* **Confrerie (IRE)**[29] 3410 4-9-13 **61**.......................... PatCosgrave 9 65
(George Baker) *racd in rr of midfield: effrt on outer to chse ldr 2f out: rdn and gd hdwy over 1f out: kpt on wl fnl f: nt rch wnr* **10/3**[2]

050 **3** *1* **Avorisk Et Perils (FR)**[25] 3546 4-9-9 **57**.......................... HectorCrouch 5 58
(Gary Moore) *hld up: rdn along to cl 2f out: kpt on wl u.p ins fnl f to take 3rd cl home* **40/1**

3-03 **4** *1/2* **Harlequin Rose (IRE)**[29] 3410 5-8-12 **46** oh1..........(v) TomMarquand 7 46
(Patrick Chamings) *hld up: pushed along on outer over 2f out: rdn and no immediate imp over 1f out: kpt on fnl f* **8/1**

0004 **5** *1 3/4* **Middlescence (IRE)**[7] 4217 5-8-12 **53**..........................(bt) VictorSantos(7) 4 48
(Lucinda Egerton) *chsd ldr tl led 3f out: rdn along and hdd by wnr 1f out: wknd fnl f* **8/1**

3042 **6** *3 1/2* **Pearl Spectre (USA)**[7] 4219 8-9-9 **57**..........................(v) OisinMurphy 1 43
(Phil McEntee) *led tl hdd 3f out: sn rdn along and no imp 2f out: plugged on one pce fnl f* **3/1**[1]

0220 **7** *2 1/4* **Fiery Breath**[10] 4115 4-9-9 **57**..........................(h) DavidProbert 3 37
(Robert Eddery) *cl up: pushed along on inner 2f out: rdn and ev ch over 1f out: wknd fnl f* **12/1**

0210 **8** *1 1/4* **Blessed To Empress (IRE)**[42] 2929 4-9-5 **60**............ CierenFallon(7) 8 36
(Amy Murphy) *prom in 3rd: rdn and no imp 2f out: wknd ins fnl f* **8/1**

-600 **9** *14* **Two Faced**[42] 2924 3-8-4 **46** oh1.......................... KieranO'Neill 2
(Lydia Pearce) *racd in rr: rdn along and detached 2f out: nvr on terms (vet said filly lost it's left-hind shoe)* **80/1**

1m 21.84s (-1.96) **Going Correction** -0.275s/f (Firm)
WFA 3 from 4yo+ 8lb **9** Ran SP% **115.0**
Speed ratings (Par 101): **100,98,97,96,94 90,88,86,70**
CSF £15.54 CT £392.57 TOTE £4.70: £1.60, £1.90, £6.20; EX 17.00 Trifecta £440.10.
Owner Eden Racing Club **Bred** Old Carhue & Graeng Bloodstock **Trained** Blewbury, Oxon
■ Stewards' Enquiry : Georgia Dobie two-day ban; misuse of whip (tba)

FOCUS
5 yards added. A moderate handicap. The second has been rated to his latest effort.

4473 FOLLOW @RACINGWELFARE ON INSTAGRAM H'CAP 7f 211y
2:30 (2:38) (Class 6) (0-65,67) 3-Y-0+
£2,781 (£827; £413; £300; £300; £300) **Stalls Centre**

Form RPR

6062 **1** **Orobas (IRE)**[7] 4216 7-9-3 **59**..........................(v) VictorSantos(7) 8 69
(Lucinda Egerton) *settled in midfield: gd hdwy to chse ldr 3f out: pushed along to ld wl over 2f out: sn clr and hung lft to far rail 1f out: kpt on strly: readily* **7/1**

0006 **2** 6 **My Lady Claire**[18] 3797 3-9-2 **60** .... JackMitchell 5 54+
(Ed Walker) *racd in midfield: rdn along to hold position 1/2-way: no imp u.str.p 2f out: drvn and mde gd late hdwy to take remote 2nd ins fnl f* **8/1**

0-00 **3** 1/2 **Momentarily**[12] 4028 4-10-0 **63** .... TomMarquand 4 58
(Mick Channon) *chsd ldr: rdn to ld 3f out: sn hdd by wnr and readily outpcd: kpt on one pce fnl f* **17/2**

-U06 **4** 1 1/4 **Angel Islington (IRE)**[12] 4028 4-10-0 **63** ....(p[1]) DavidProbert 3 55
(Andrew Balding) *racd promly: swtchd lft and effrt on inner 2f out: sn rdn over 1f out: kpt on one pce fnl f* **9/1**

0020 **5** hd **Brother In Arms (IRE)**[14] 3966 5-8-12 **47** .... BrettDoyle 6 39
(Tony Carroll) *racd in rr: rdn along and outpcd 2f out: kpt on passed btn horses ins fnl f* **12/1**

6004 **6** 1/2 **Startego**[13] 4000 3-9-7 **65** ....(p) OisinMurphy 2 54
(Archie Watson) *led: rdn along and hdd 3f out: kpt on wl for press tl 1f out: no ex fnl f* **7/2**[1]

5056 **7** 2 **Precision Prince (IRE)**[21] 3684 3-9-0 **58** ....(p[1]) JasonWatson 10 42
(Mark Loughnane) *dwlt and racd in rr: rdn along over 2f out and no hdwy: nvr on terms* **13/2**[3]

-433 **8** 3/4 **Kachumba**[35] 3185 4-10-4 **67** .... DaneO'Neill 9 51
(Rae Guest) *racd in tch: rdn to chse wnr 2f out: wknd ins fnl f* **4/1**[2]

4505 **9** 6 **Dukes Meadow**[41] 2972 8-8-5 **45** .... RhiainIngram(5) 7 15
(Roger Ingram) *hld up: rdn along over 2f out: a bhd* **40/1**

3-40 **10** 1 3/4 **Aye Aye Skipper (IRE)**[39] 3038 9-8-12 **47** ....(p) KieranO'Neill 1 13
(Ken Cunningham-Brown) *racd in rr of midfield: rdn along 3f out: sn bhd* **22/1**

1m 34.43s (-2.47) **Going Correction** -0.275s/f (Firm) **10** Ran SP% **114.2**
WFA 3 from 4yo+ 9lb
Speed ratings (Par 101): **101,95,94,93,93 92,90,89,83,82**
CSF £60.50 CT £482.21 TOTE £7.60: £2.60, £2.60, £3.40; EX 65.30 Trifecta £468.90.
Owner Northern Belles **Bred** Ciaran Mac Ferran **Trained** Malton, N Yorks

FOCUS
5 yards added. A modest handicap. The going was changed to good to firm, firm in places after this race on another hot afternoon.

4474 JANES SOLICITORS NO WIN NO FEE MAIDEN STKS 1m 1f 207y
3:00 (3:04) (Class 5) 3-Y-O+
£3,428 (£1,020; £509; £254) **Stalls** High

Form RPR

02 **1** **Medal Winner (FR)**[11] 4076 3-9-2 .... OisinMurphy 3 89
(Archie Watson) *hld up in last: clsd gng wl 2f out: rdn to ld wl over 1f out: hung lft to far rail 1f out: sn wl clr: readily* **10/1**

-262 **2** 6 **Damon Runyon**[17] 3860 3-9-2 80 ....(b) RobertHavlin 4 77
(John Gosden) *led: rdn along and hdd by wnr wl over 1f out: plugged on for remote 2nd* **7/2**[3]

46 **3** 3 1/2 **Meqdam (IRE)**[30] 3372 3-9-2 ....(p[1]) HectorCrouch 2 70
(Saeed bin Suroor) *settled wl in 3rd: almost upsides ldr and ev ch over 2f out: sn rdn and fnd little: wknd fnl f* **10/3**[2]

42 **4** 13 **Clarion**[25] 3546 3-8-11 .... JasonWatson 1 39
(Sir Michael Stoute) *stmbld bdly leaving stalls and almost uns: sn rcvrd to chse ldr: pushed along over 2f out: sn rdn and lft bhd by wnr: wknd fnl f (jockey said filly stumbled badly leaving the stalls. Trainers' rep said filly was unsuited by the ground and would prefer an easier surface)* **8/11**[1]

1m 59.44s (-5.56) **Going Correction** -0.275s/f (Firm) **4** Ran SP% **112.3**
Speed ratings (Par 103): **111,106,103,93**
CSF £41.00 TOTE £10.70; EX 32.00 Trifecta £45.50.
Owner Qatar Racing Limited **Bred** E A R L Haras De Mandore **Trained** Upper Lambourn, W Berks

FOCUS
5 yards added. Effectively, a fairly decent little 3yo maiden. The weakest horse in the betting won readily in a good comparative time.

4475 RACING WITH PRIDE H'CAP 1m 1f 207y
3:30 (3:34) (Class 6) (0-55,56) 4-Y-0+
£2,781 (£827; £413; £300; £300; £300) **Stalls** High

Form RPR

0050 **1** **Altaira**[31] 3348 8-8-12 **46** oh1 ....(p) TomMarquand 3 52
(Tony Carroll) *racd in midfield: clsd gng wl over 2f out: sn rdn and styd on wl to ld wl ins fnl f: won gng away (trainer could offer no explanation for the apparent improvement in form)* **8/1**

0036 **2** 1 1/2 **Clive Clifton (IRE)**[29] 3429 6-8-12 **46** oh1 .... StevieDonohoe 5 49
(Kevin Frost) *led: rdn along and strly pressed by rivals over 1f out: drvn and hdd by wnr wl ins fnl f: kpt on* **7/1**[3]

5300 **3** hd **With Approval (IRE)**[14] 3966 7-9-5 **53** ....(p) HectorCrouch 10 56
(Laura Mongan) *racd in midfield: effrt on outer to take clsr order 3f out: sn rdn and upsides ldr 2f out: kpt on wl fnl f but unable to match wnr (vet said gelding lost it's left-fore shoe)* **9/1**

0060 **4** 2 3/4 **Rainbow Jazz (IRE)**[15] 3941 4-9-1 **56** ....(be) Pierre-LouisJamin(7) 4 54
(Adam West) *racd in midfield on inner: niggled along to hold position 3f out: rdn and hdwy 2f out: kpt on one pce ins fnl f* **13/2**[2]

-200 **5** 3 1/2 **Sussex Girl**[35] 3186 5-9-2 **50** ....(p[1]) DaneO'Neill 7 41
(John Berry) *in rr of midfield: gd hdwy gng wl 2f out: sn rdn and no imp over 1f out: effrt flattened out fnl f* **7/1**[3]

5000 **6** 1/2 **Rocksette**[15] 3941 5-9-1 **49** ....(p) TomQueally 13 39+
(Gary Moore) *dwlt bdly and immediately swtchd lft in rr: hdwy u.p in amongst rivals 2f out: sn rdn and no further imp over 1f out* **3/1**[1]

-000 **7** 1/2 **Rebel Cause (IRE)**[20] 3720 6-9-6 **54** .... RoystonFfrench 6 43
(John Holt) *trckd ldr: rdn upsides ldr and ev ch 2f out: drvn along 1f out: wknd fnl f* **8/1**

-000 **8** 3 1/4 **Takiah**[124] 940 4-8-12 **46** oh1 .... KieranO'Neill 12 29
(Peter Hiatt) *hld up: rdn along in rr over 2f out: n.d* **18/1**

0600 **9** 2 1/4 **Dutch Melody**[7] 4215 5-8-5 **46** oh1 .... VictorSantos(7) 2 25
(Lucinda Egerton) *trckd ldr: rdn along and lost pl 2f out: wknd fnl f* **25/1**

005- **10** 1 1/4 **Kennerton Green (IRE)**[315] 6377 4-9-2 **50** ....(w) AndrewElliott 14 26
(Lydia Pearce) *racd in rr: rdn 3f out: nvr a factor* **16/1**

-000 **11** 1 3/4 **Interrogation (FR)**[20] 3740 4-8-5 **46** oh1 ....(b[1]) CierenFallon(7) 9 19
(Alan Bailey) *hld up: effrt on outer 3f out: sn rdn and fnd little: nvr on terms* **50/1**

0-R0 **12** nk **Duhr (IRE)**[17] 3834 5-8-12 **49** .... MeganNicholls(3) 8 21
(Ralph J Smith) *dwlt bdly and rel to r: sn detached* **50/1**

0-00 **13** 15 **Imminent Approach**[17] 3834 4-9-7 **55** ....(p[1]) EoinWalsh 11
(Tony Newcombe) *racd promly: rdn along and lost pl over 2f out: eased whn btn ins fnl f (trainer said filly was unsuited by the ground and would prefer an easier surface)* **28/1**

2m 2.51s (-2.49) **Going Correction** -0.275s/f (Firm) **13** Ran SP% **117.9**
Speed ratings (Par 101): **98,96,96,94,91 91,90,88,86,85 84,83,71**
CSF £60.35 CT £517.35 TOTE £8.90: £2.60, £2.20, £2.30; EX 63.40 Trifecta £425.20.
Owner Mrs Susan Keable **Bred** Skymarc Farm Inc **Trained** Cropthorne, Worcs

FOCUS
5 yards added. A moderate handicap. The winning time was over three seconds slower that the proceeding C&D maiden. Limited, straightforward form, rated around the principals.

4476 BRIGHTON SUPPORTS RACING STAFF WEEK H'CAP 1m 1f 207y
4:00 (4:03) (Class 6) (0-65,66) 3-Y-O
£2,781 (£827; £413; £300; £300; £300) **Stalls** High

Form RPR

0001 **1** **Crystal Tribe (IRE)**[24] 3594 3-9-9 **66** ....(b) TomMarquand 8 82+
(William Haggas) *restrained in rr: gd hdwy on outer over 2f out: rdn to ld 1f out: qcknd away readily ins fnl f: comf* **6/5**[1]

0055 **2** 4 1/2 **Garrison Commander (IRE)**[25] 3538 3-9-7 **64** ....(b) OisinMurphy 6 68
(Eve Johnson Houghton) *trckd ldr on inner: clsd gng wl over 2f out: pushed along to ld 2f out: sn rdn and hdd by wnr 1f out: kpt on but no match for easy wnr* **9/2**[3]

0550 **3** 4 **Four Mile Bridge (IRE)**[35] 3195 3-9-4 **61** .... FergusSweeney 7 57
(Mark Usher) *racd in midfield: hdwy to chse ldr 2f out: sn rdn and kpt on one pce fnl f* **16/1**

0444 **4** 1/2 **Winter Snowdrop (IRE)**[29] 3407 3-7-11 **45** .... SophieRalston(5) 1 40
(Julia Feilden) *led: rdn along and hdd 2f out: kpt on wl for press ins fnl f* **28/1**

5652 **5** 3/4 **Osho**[11] 4070 3-9-6 **63** .... SeanLevey 2 57
(Richard Hannon) *stmbld shortly after s: racd in midfield: effrt to cl on ldrs over 2f out: sn rdn and no imp over 1f out: one pce after (jockey said colt stumbled shortly after leaving the stalls)* **11/4**[2]

060 **6** 1 1/2 **Iris's Spirit**[97] 1358 3-8-2 **45** .... KieranO'Neill 10 36
(Tony Carroll) *racd in rr of midfield: rdn along to chse ldr over 2f out: sn drvn and no imp over 1f out: plugged on* **40/1**

005 **7** 1/2 **Sibylline**[21] 3690 3-8-10 **56** .... RosieJessop(3) 4 46
(David Simcock) *hld up in last: rdn along in rr 3f out: nvr on terms* **25/1**

000- **8** 2 3/4 **Maykir**[287] 7376 3-8-10 **53** .... JasonWatson 5 38
(Amanda Perrett) *trckd ldr: pushed along to chse ldr 3f out: sn rdn 2f out: wknd fnl f* **25/1**

2m 1.18s (-3.82) **Going Correction** -0.275s/f (Firm) **8** Ran SP% **109.8**
Speed ratings (Par 98): **104,100,97,96,96 95,94,92**
CSF £5.99 CT £45.57 TOTE £1.70: £1.10, £1.30, £3.00; EX 6.80 Trifecta £35.10.
Owner Lord Lloyd-Webber **Bred** Watership Down Stud **Trained** Newmarket, Suffolk
■ Circle Of Stars was withdrawn. Price at time of withdrawal 10-1. Rule 4 applies to all bets - deduction 5p in the pound.

FOCUS
5 yards added. A modest 3yo handicap. The favourite's winning time was notably quicker than the proceeding C&D handicap. The second has been rated to the best of this year's form.

4477 #RACINGSTAFFWEEK H'CAP 6f 210y
4:30 (4:30) (Class 6) (0-60,60) 3-Y-O
£2,781 (£827; £413; £300; £300; £300) **Stalls** Centre

Form RPR

0263 **1** **Princess Florence (IRE)**[7] 4217 3-8-1 **47** .... CierenFallon(7) 7 53
(John Ryan) *hld up: hdwy on outer to chse ldr 2f out: sn rdn and led over 1f out: hung lft to far rail 1f out but sn wl in command: rdn out (jockey said filly hung left-handed)* **11/2**

6004 **2** 1 3/4 **Melo Pearl**[42] 2926 3-8-7 **46** oh1 ....(v) RoystonFfrench 1 47
(Mrs Ilka Gansera-Leveque) *hld up in last: rdn and stl last 2f out: drvn and styd on strly down the outside to go 2nd fnl f: nt rch wnr* **16/1**

-025 **3** 2 **Approve The Dream (IRE)**[19] 3780 3-8-10 **56** .... SeanKirrane(7) 9 52
(Julia Feilden) *hld up: drvn along and hdd by wnr over 1f out: kpt on one pce fnl f* **7/2**[2]

-012 **4** 1/2 **Sonnetina**[21] 3697 3-9-6 **59** .... TomQueally 4 54
(Denis Coakley) *racd promly: clsd gng wl over 2f out: rdn and ev ch over 1f out: no match for wnr and outpcd fnl f* **9/4**[1]

00-0 **5** 1 1/4 **Lewis Slack**[82] 1723 3-8-13 **59** ....(t[1]) WilliamCarver(7) 3 50
(Richard J Bandey) *hld up: making hdwy amongst rivals whn short of room 2f out: sn rdn and no further imp 1f out: one pce after* **25/1**

-003 **6** 1 **Pegasus Bridge**[8] 4193 3-8-9 **55** ....(b) GeorgiaDobie(7) 6 43
(Eve Johnson Houghton) *racd in midfield: rdn along and outpcd 2f out: one pce fnl f* **4/1**[3]

05-5 **7** 3/4 **Haitian Spirit**[157] 438 3-9-7 **60** .... HectorCrouch 8 46
(Gary Moore) *chsd ldr on inner: rdn and outpcd 2f out: wknd fnl f* **12/1**

6066 **8** 1/2 **Thedevilinneville**[3] 4376 3-8-7 **46** ....(p) AndrewElliott 2 31
(Adam West) *trckd ldr on inner: rdn along 2f and no prog 2f out: sn wknd fnl f* **9/1**

1m 22.55s (-1.25) **Going Correction** -0.275s/f (Firm) **8** Ran SP% **115.8**
Speed ratings (Par 98): **96,94,91,91,89 88,87,87**
CSF £86.66 CT £355.70 TOTE £5.20: £1.80, £3.10, £1.80; EX 43.10 Trifecta £228.10.
Owner Bb Thoroughbreds **Bred** Tally-Ho Stud **Trained** Newmarket, Suffolk

FOCUS
5 yards added. A moderate 3yo handicap. The winner has been rated back near her best.

4478 SKY SPORTS RACING ON SKY 415 H'CAP 5f 60y
5:00 (5:00) (Class 5) (0-75,76) 3-Y-O+
£3,428 (£1,020; £509; £300; £300; £300) **Stalls** Centre

Form RPR

1125 **1** **Pink Flamingo**[8] 4185 3-9-0 **75** .... CierenFallon(7) 2 83
(Michael Attwater) *trckd ldr: pushed along to ld over 1f out: sn rdn and styd on wl* **7/2**[3]

4021 **2** 2 **Big Lachie**[6] 4230 5-9-10 **76** 5ex .... GeorgiaCox(3) 4 79
(Mark Loughnane) *slowly away and racd in last: rdn and hdwy between rivals over 1f out: styd on wl fnl f: nt rch wnr* **9/4**[1]

0034 **3** 1 1/4 **Archimedes (IRE)**[7] 4213 6-8-9 **58** ....(tp) PhilDennis 6 57
(David C Griffiths) *led: rdn along and hdd by wnr over 1f out: kpt on one pce fnl f* **7/2**[3]

-210 **4** 3/4 **All Back To Mine**[18] 3801 3-8-12 **66** .... OisinMurphy 5 60
(Joseph Tuite) *settled in 4th: rdn along to chse wnr and hung lft over 1f out: one pce fnl f* **6/1**

2132 **5** 1 1/2 **Essaka (IRE)**[14] 3961 7-8-13 **67** .... SophieRalston(5) 7 58
(Tony Carroll) *trckd ldr: upsides and ev ch over 1f out: sn rdn and unable qck 1f out: no ex* **10/3**[2]

0030 **6** 1 1/4 **Camanche Grey (IRE)**[7] 4219 8-8-0 **56** oh9 .... VictorSantos(7) 1 42
(Lucinda Egerton) *racd keenly in 5th: rdn and little rspnse over 1f out: sn btn* **40/1**

1m 1.48s (-1.52) **Going Correction** -0.275s/f (Firm) **6** Ran SP% **115.0**
WFA 3 from 4yo+ 5lb
Speed ratings (Par 103): **101,97,95,94,92 90**
CSF £12.24 TOTE £4.20: £1.90, £1.40; EX 16.10 Trifecta £56.10.
Owner Dare To Dream Racing **Bred** Lowther Racing **Trained** Epsom, Surrey

FOCUS
Five yards added. An ordinary sprint handicap. One of the joint-third favourites won well in a pretty good comparative time. The second has been rated a bit below his Bath win.
T/Plt: £1,426.80 to a £1 stake. Pool: £79,260.04 - 40.55 winning units T/Qpdt: £77.50 to a £1 stake. Pool: £8,462.86 - 80.79 winning units **Mark Grantham**

4176 CHEPSTOW (L-H)
Tuesday, July 2

OFFICIAL GOING: Good (good to firm in places; watered; 6.0)
Wind: Slight breeze, behind Weather: Sunny spells

4479 FLOYDS TURFCARE AND WEEDCARE SOLUTIONS H'CAP — 7f 16y
6:00 (6:01) (Class 5) (0-70,72) 3-Y-O+
£3,428 (£1,020; £509; £300; £300; £300) Stalls Centre

Form / RPR
4310 **1** **Jungle Juice (IRE)**[8] 4181 3-9-3 **67** CallumShepherd 13 76
(Mick Channon) *prom: drvn over 2f out: led on stands' rail over 1f out: sltly hmpd by loose horse ins fnl f: in command whn swtchd lft towards fin* **8/1**
4205 **2** 2 **Dancingwithwolves (IRE)**[16] 3885 3-9-7 **71** DanielMuscutt 3 74
(Ed Dunlop) *led: drvn over 2f out: hdd over 1f out: one pce* **11/2**[2]
-032 **3** 3 ½ **Masquerade Bling (IRE)**[11] 4174 5-9-2 **58** (p) LukeMorris 9 52
(Neil Mulholland) *hld up: rdn and hdwy to chse ldrs over 2f out: edgd lft and kpt on same pce fnl f* **20/1**
0120 **4** 1 ¾ **De Little Engine (IRE)**[25] 3540 5-9-11 **67** (p) RossaRyan 2 56
(Alexandra Dunn) *prom: drvn over 2f out: kpt on same pce* **8/1**
1300 **5** 1 ¾ **Air Of York (IRE)**[8] 4181 7-9-4 **65** (p) ScottMcCullagh(5) 12 48
(John Flint) *dwlt sltly: in rr: rdn 3f out: stl last over 1f out: r.o fnl f: nvr nrr* **10/1**
4630 **6** nk **Espresso Freddo (IRE)**[6] 4235 5-9-3 **64** (tp) PoppyBridgwater(5) 4 46
(Robert Stephens) *hld up in tch on outer: drvn and hdwy over 2f out: no imp appr fnl f* **14/1**
0006 **7** ¾ **Reshaan (IRE)**[15] 3939 4-8-4 **51** oh1 ThoreHammerHansen(5) 8 31
(Alexandra Dunn) *prom: rdn 3f out: wknd wl over 1f out* **20/1**
02 **8** 1 ¾ **The Establishment**[49] 2717 4-10-0 **70** CharlesBishop 11 44
(David Evans) *t.k.h early: prom over 1f: hld up after: rdn and hdwy over 2f out: wknd over 1f out* **11/2**[2]
6035 **9** 2 ¼ **Spiritual Star (IRE)**[64] 2215 10-8-9 **51** (t) JFEgan 5 18
(Paul George) *midfield: rdn and outpcd 3f out: wknd fnl f* **25/1**
-006 **10** 6 **Watchmyeverymove (IRE)**[16] 3885 3-9-8 **72** (vt[1]) JimCrowley 7 17
(Stuart Williams) *chsd ldrs: drvn 1/2-way: wknd over 2f out* **9/2**[1]
0002 **U** **Gold Hunter (IRE)**[8] 4181 9-9-5 **61** (tp) RaulDaSilva 6
(Steve Flook) *rrd and uns rdr leaving stalls* **6/1**[3]

1m 21.87s (-2.03) **Going Correction** -0.175s/f (Firm)
WFA 3 from 4yo+ 8lb — 11 Ran SP% **114.6**
Speed ratings (Par 103): **104,101,97,95,93 93,92,90,87,81**
CSF £48.66 CT £866.13 TOTE £6.60: £2.40, £2.30, £4.40; EX 43.70 Trifecta £701.30.
Owner Insignia Racing (ribbon) **Bred** Ballybrennan Stud Ltd **Trained** West Ilsley, Berks

FOCUS
A drying day and the ground was officially good, good to firm in places. A competitive opener, with drama at the start as Gold Hunter reared and unseated his rider. Not much got into it, with two of the 3yos dominating. The second has been rated to form for now.

4480 BETTINGSITES.LTD.UK MEDIAN AUCTION MAIDEN STKS — 7f 16y
6:30 (6:35) (Class 6) 2-Y-O
£2,781 (£827; £413; £206) Stalls Centre

Form / RPR
20 **1** **Dramatic Sands (IRE)**[10] 4091 2-9-5 0 HollieDoyle 5 77
(Archie Watson) *w ldr tl led 3f out: rdn over 2f out: hung lft and narrowly hdd over 1f out: rallied to ld again nr fin* **5/4**[1]
0 **2** hd **Overpriced Mixer**[33] 3257 2-9-5 0 NicolaCurrie 11 76
(Jamie Osborne) *prom: rdn and briefly outpcd by ldrs 3f out: led narrowly over 1f out: drifted lft fnl f: hdd nr fin* **16/1**
05 **3** 2 ¾ **London Calling (IRE)**[33] 3257 2-9-5 0 KieranShoemark 9 69+
(Richard Spencer) *t.k.h: chsd ldrs: rdn and sltly outpcd over 2f out: clsd again over 1f out: wnt 3rd fnl 100yds* **14/1**
4 1 ½ **Cloud Drift** 2-9-5 0 JimCrowley 4 65+
(Michael Bell) *s.i.s: sn chsng ldrs on outer: drvn 3f out: ev ch 2f out: outpcd by ldng pair appr fnl f: lost 3rd fnl 100yds* **7/2**[2]
5 2 ½ **Punchbowl Flyer (IRE)** 2-9-5 0 CharlesBishop 3 62+
(Eve Johnson Houghton) *chsd ldrs tl rn green: outpcd and reminders after 3f: rdn and clsd over 1f out: kpt on* **12/1**
6 hd **Don't Stop Dancing (IRE)** 2-9-5 0 LukeMorris 6 58
(Ronald Harris) *dwlt: in rr: sn running green and pushed along: hung lft fr 1/2-way: hdwy over 1f out: no imp fnl f* **66/1**
0 **7** 1 ¼ **Sir Arthur Dayne (IRE)**[8] 4184 2-9-5 0 FrannyNorton 10 54
(Mick Channon) *s.i.s: in tch in midfield: rdn over 2f out: styd on fnl f: nvr a threat* **9/2**[3]
00 **8** 1 ¼ **Port Noir**[35] 3194 2-9-0 0 RossaRyan 1 46
(Grace Harris) *prom: rdn over 2f out: wknd over 1f out* **100/1**
9 4 **Party Potential (USA)** 2-9-5 0 CallumShepherd 7 40
(Alan King) *s.i.s: sn pushed along in rr: rdn 1/2-way: no imp* **33/1**
10 7 **Lets Go Lucky** 2-9-0 0 JFEgan 2 16
(David Evans) *led 4f: sn rdn: wknd 2f out* **20/1**
11 34 **Gypsy Rosaleen** 2-9-0 0 LiamJones 8
(David Evans) *dwlt bdly: a bhd: t.o* **50/1**

1m 22.96s (-0.94) **Going Correction** -0.175s/f (Firm) — 11 Ran SP% **117.2**
Speed ratings (Par 92): **98,97,94,92,90 89,88,86,82,74 35**
CSF £24.45 TOTE £1.90: £1.10, £3.60, £2.70; EX 20.80 Trifecta £117.00.
Owner Hambleton Racing XLV & Partner **Bred** Tullamaine Castle Stud And Partners **Trained** Upper Lambourn, W Berks

FOCUS
A range of abilities on show in this maiden auction event and two runners with experience pulled clear.

4481 COMPAREBETTINGSITES.COM BEST BETTING SITE H'CAP — 6f 16y
7:00 (7:04) (Class 6) (0-55,54) 3-Y-O+
£2,781 (£827; £413; £300; £300; £300) Stalls Centre

Form / RPR
00-0 **1** **Castlerea Tess**[176] 116 6-9-1 **48** (p) RobHornby 3 55
(Sarah Hollinshead) *a.p: rdn to ld over 2f out: drvn out fnl f* **25/1**
0-00 **2** 1 ¼ **Billiebrookedit (IRE)**[53] 2595 4-8-12 **45** RossaRyan 14 48
(Kevin Frost) *a.p: rdn over 2f out: r.o to go 2nd towards fin* **9/2**[2]
0006 **3** nse **Jupiter**[42] 2930 4-8-12 **50** (b[1]) SebastianWoods(5) 17 53
(Alexandra Dunn) *led tl rdn and hdd over 2f out: swtchd lft over 1f out: sn lost 2nd and continued to drift lft u.p: r.o fnl f* **10/1**
5002 **4** nk **Aquadabra (IRE)**[8] 4182 4-8-13 **46** CallumShepherd 12 48
(Christopher Mason) *t.k.h early: trckd ldrs: rdn to go 2nd over 1f out: unable qck ins fnl f: lost 2 pls towards fin* **7/1**[3]
-303 **5** 1 **Wild Flower (IRE)**[8] 4182 7-9-3 **50** (b) KieranShoemark 16 49
(Jimmy Fox) *chsd ldrs: rdn over 2f out: hung lft over 1f out: r.o fnl f* **8/1**
0040 **6** nk **Fantasy Justifier (IRE)**[8] 4181 8-9-6 **53** (p) DavidProbert 10 51+
(Ronald Harris) *s.i.s: hld up: rdn 2f out: hdwy over 1f out: r.o ins fnl f: nvr nrr* **12/1**
2000 **7** 1 ¾ **Letmestopyouthere (IRE)**[10] 4115 5-9-7 **54** (b[1]) HollieDoyle 13 47
(Archie Watson) *s.i.s: towards rr: rdn over 3f out: hdwy over 2f out: kpt on same pce fnl f (jockey said gelding was never travelling)* **7/2**[1]
0004 **7** dht **Jacksonfire**[27] 3475 7-8-8 **46** (p) FayeMcManoman(5) 8 39
(Michael Mullineaux) *in rr: rdn over 2f out: carried lft over 1f out: r.o* **20/1**
404 **9** ½ **Shesadabber**[60] 2357 3-8-6 **45** (p[1]) JFEgan 15 36
(Brian Baugh) *s.i.s: sn prom: rdn over 2f out: wknd ins fnl f* **16/1**
6600 **10** ½ **Indian Affair**[36] 3144 9-8-5 **45** (bt) TobyEley(7) 5 35
(Milton Bradley) *towards rr: rdn over 3f out: no hdwy tl r.o ins fnl f* **20/1**
6054 **11** ½ **Seaforth (IRE)**[50] 2693 7-9-1 **51** FinleyMarsh(3) 4 40
(Adrian Wintle) *wnt to post early: towards rr: rdn over 2f out: edgd lft over 1f out: nvr able to chal* **20/1**
0505 **12** 1 **Kyllachy Princess**[32] 3319 3-8-7 **46** (b) NicolaCurrie 1 31
(David Loughnane) *midfield: rdn over 2f out: wknd over 1f out* **33/1**
3060 **13** 1 ½ **Poppy Jag (IRE)**[27] 3475 4-8-9 **45** (b) JaneElliott(3) 6 26
(Kevin Frost) *midfield: rdn 1/2-way: wknd over 1f out* **33/1**
000 **14** 1 ½ **Alfie's Angel (IRE)**[8] 4181 5-9-7 **54** FrannyNorton 9 31
(Milton Bradley) *midfield: rdn 3f out: wknd over 1f out* **25/1**
00/0 **15** 7 **Picc And Go**[8] 4182 6-8-7 **45** RachealKneller(5) 7 1
(Matthew Salaman) *w ldr over 2f: remained prom: rdn 2f out: sn wknd (jockey said mare stopped quickly)* **66/1**
-020 **16** 1 ½ **Spirit Of Ishy**[25] 3527 4-8-12 **45** (b) HayleyTurner 2
(Stuart Kittow) *s.i.s: sn swtchd rt: rdn over 2f out: a in rr* **33/1**
5006 **17** 23 **Brother Bentley**[8] 4180 3-9-1 **54** (b) LukeMorris 11
(Ronald Harris) *towards rr: rdn and trying to cl whn stmbld wl over 2f out: sn eased: t.o (jockey said gelding stumbled five furlongs out and clipped heels three furlongs out)* **11/1**

1m 10.47s (-1.03) **Going Correction** -0.175s/f (Firm)
WFA 3 from 4yo+ 6lb — 17 Ran SP% **127.3**
Speed ratings (Par 101): **99,97,97,96,95 95,92,92,92,91 90,89,87,85,76 74,43**
WIN: 35.00 Castlerea Tess; PL: 2.40 Jupiter 6.30 Castlerea Tess 2.00 Aquadabra 1.80 Billiebrookedit; EX: 320.10; CSF: 126.22; TC: 1290.49; TF: 3417.20 CSF £126.22 CT £1290.49 TOTE £35.00: £6.30, £1.80, £2.40, £2.00; EX 320.10 Trifecta £3417.20.
Owner John Graham & Sarah Hollinshead **Bred** Graham Brothers Racing Partnership **Trained** Upper Longdon, Staffs
■ Stewards' Enquiry : Sebastian Woods two-day ban; misuse of whip (July 16-17)

FOCUS
A big field for this low-grade sprint and very little got into it, the winner the only one of the first seven home to be drawn in single figures. It's been rated as straightforward limited form.

4482 COMPAREBETTINGSITES.COM EBF STALLIONS MAIDEN STKS (PLUS 10 RACE) — 6f 16y
7:30 (7:31) (Class 4) 2-Y-O
£4,851 (£1,443; £721; £360) Stalls Centre

Form / RPR
3 **1** **Huboor (IRE)**[19] 3776 2-9-0 0 JimCrowley 4 76+
(Mark Johnston) *trckd ldrs: drvn to ld 2f out: edgd lft ins fnl f: r.o* **9/4**[1]
2 1 ½ **Fleeting Prince (IRE)** 2-9-5 0 KieranShoemark 5 77
(Charles Hills) *s.i.s: t.k.h and hld up: hdwy 2f out: sn rdn: edgd lft and chsd wnr jst ins fnl f: r.o (jockey said colt ran green)* **4/1**
3 **3** nk **Swinley Forest (IRE)**[19] 3760 2-9-5 0 MartinDwyer 2 76
(Brian Meehan) *dwlt sltly: rcvrd to ld after 100yds: rdn and hdd 2f out: lost 2nd jst ins fnl f: kpt on* **3/1**[3]
4 **4** nk **Stone Circle (IRE)**[29] 3419 2-9-5 0 HayleyTurner 6 75
(Michael Bell) *led 100yds: trckd ldr over 2f: rdn over 2f out: styd on fnl f* **5/2**[2]
5 30 **Numinous (IRE)** 2-9-5 0 DavidProbert 1
(Henry Candy) *prom tl rdn and outpcd over 4f out: lost tch over 2f out: t.o* **20/1**

1m 11.06s (-0.44) **Going Correction** -0.175s/f (Firm) — 5 Ran SP% **109.1**
Speed ratings (Par 96): **95,93,92,92,52**
CSF £11.18 TOTE £3.80: £1.30, £3.40; EX 9.30 Trifecta £23.00.
Owner Hamdan Al Maktoum **Bred** China Horse Club **Trained** Middleham Moor, N Yorks

FOCUS
A fair maiden in which the winner further advertised the merits of the unbeaten Godolphin filly Summer Romance. The level is hard to pin down.

4483 COMPAREBETTINGSITES.COM H'CAP — 2m
8:00 (8:00) (Class 5) (0-75,76) 4-Y-O+
£3,428 (£1,020; £509; £300; £300; £300) Stalls Low

Form / RPR
2364 **1** **So Near So Farhh**[21] 3693 4-8-10 **64** FrannyNorton 6 73
(Mick Channon) *hld up: hdwy after 4f: rdn to ld over 2f out: sn hrd pressed: narrowly hdd over 1f out: carried lft ins fnl f: kpt on to ld nr fin* **9/2**[2]
30R0 **2** shd **Jacob Cats**[27] 3467 10-9-0 **68** (v) CallumShepherd 8 77
(William Knight) *hld up: hdwy on outer over 3f out: pressed ldr 2f out: led narrowly over 1f out: hung lft ins fnl f: hdd nr fin* **16/1**
6004 **3** 8 **Akavit (IRE)**[6] 4251 7-8-6 **63** JaneElliott(3) 9 62
(Ed de Giles) *t.k.h: prom: led after 3f: rdn over 3f out: hdd over 2f out: outpcd by ldng pair appr fnl f* **7/2**[1]
3426 **4** ¾ **Knight Commander**[42] 2936 6-8-4 **58** (t) RaulDaSilva 7 56
(Steve Flook) *led 3f: remained prom: drvn 4f out: outpcd by ldrs over 2f out: styd on but no threat* **10/1**
5-00 **5** ½ **Arty Campbell (IRE)**[9] 4146 9-9-7 **75** DanielMuscutt 1 73
(Bernard Llewellyn) *hld up towards rr: hdwy 5f out: drvn over 3f out: one pce fnl 2f* **25/1**
25-0 **6** 2 **Early Summer (IRE)**[23] 3635 4-9-8 **76** CharlieBennett 2 71
(Hughie Morrison) *prom 3f: hld up after: rdn and clsd 3f out: wknd over 1f out* **5/1**[3]
/604 **7** 2 ½ **Norab (GER)**[9] 4146 8-8-4 **58** (b) HollieDoyle 4 50
(Bernard Llewellyn) *prom: lost pl 1/2-way: towards rr whn rdn 4f out: styd on fnl f* **7/1**
1/05 **8** 5 **Mere Anarchy (IRE)**[21] 3693 8-8-6 **65** (v) PoppyBridgwater(5) 3 51
(Robert Stephens) *midfield: hdwy to chse ldrs after 7f: drvn over 2f out: nt run on and grad wknd* **10/1**

3606 **9** *4* **Gang Warfare**[27] 3481 8-9-7 **75**........................(bt) RossaRyan 5 57
(Alexandra Dunn) *s.i.s: in rr: hdwy to chse ldrs after 5f: rdn over 3f out: wknd over 2f out (jockey said gelding was slowly away)* **25/1**

1446 **10** *4* **Moon Of Baroda**[67] 2080 4-9-7 **75**........................(b) KieranShoemark 10 52
(Charles Hills) *chsd ldrs tl lost pl 6f out: clsd again over 3f out: wknd over 2f out (jockey said gelding lost it's action)* **11/2**

3m 33.65s (-8.45) **Going Correction** -0.45s/f (Firm) **10** Ran SP% **116.7**
Speed ratings (Par 103): **103,102,98,98,98 97,96,93,91,89**
CSF £73.65 CT £277.46 TOTE £4.90: £1.10, £5.50, £1.90; EX 75.60 Trifecta £388.50.
Owner Mrs Nicola Murray **Bred** Whitwell Bloodstock **Trained** West Ilsley, Berks

FOCUS
A messy staying handicap, with a stop-start early gallop, and the front two did well to pull so far clear in the circumstances. The winner has been rated back to her reappearance level.

4484 COUNTY MARQUEES CHEPSTOW H'CAP — 1m 4f
8:30 (8:30) (Class 6) (0-65,66) 3-Y-O
£2,781 (£827; £413; £300; £300; £300) **Stalls Low**

Form — RPR

520 **1** **Narina (IRE)**[12] 4022 3-9-6 **64**........................ LiamJones 1 73
(William Haggas) *s.s and chsd along early: hdwy to ld over 10f out: mde rest: drvn 3f out: styd on wl u.p* **10/1**

5224 **2** *2* **Message**[12] 4024 3-9-8 **66**........................ FrannyNorton 3 72
(Mark Johnston) *midfield: rdn and clsd over 3f out: chsd wnr ins fnl f: styd on but a being hld* **11/4**[2]

4-62 **3** *2* **Sinndarella (IRE)**[25] 3528 3-8-2 **49**........................ NoelGarbutt(3) 5 52
(Sarah Hollinshead) *midfield: hdwy and prom over 5f out: pressed wnr 4f out tl no ex and lost 2nd ins fnl f* **10/1**

0-00 **4** *5* **Barb's Prince (IRE)**[30] 3373 3-8-10 **54**........................(p[1]) MartinDwyer 2 49
(Ian Williams) *prom: trckd wnr over 10f out tl lost 2nd 4f out: kpt on same pce fnl 2f* **40/1**

0013 **5** *hd* **Admirals Bay (GER)**[19] 3765 3-9-4 **62**........................ RobHornby 6 56
(Andrew Balding) *chsd ldrs: rdn and outpcd over 3f out: styd on same pce fnl 2f* **9/4**[1]

0452 **6** *8* **Sea Art**[16] 3888 3-9-7 **65**........................(v) DavidProbert 4 46
(William Knight) *t.k.h: led over 1f: chsd ldrs tl lost pl 1/2-way: drvn 4f out: wknd wl over 1f out* **13/2**

000- **7** *2* **Waterproof**[215] 9308 3-9-0 **58**........................ NicolaCurrie 7 36
(Jamie Osborne) *hld up: detached last after 4f: rdn 5f out: limited prog over 2f out* **16/1**

040 **8** *13* **Perique**[138] 723 3-9-2 **60**........................ DanielMuscutt 10 17
(Ed Dunlop) *rdn over 5f out: a towards rr* **33/1**

0446 **9** *46* **Robert Fitzroy (IRE)**[16] 3888 3-9-7 **65**........................(p) ShaneKelly 8
(Michael Bell) *s.s: in rr and early reminders: hdwy and prom after 3f: rdn and lost pl over 5f out: wknd 3f out: t.o (jockey said gelding was never travelling)* **11/2**[3]

2m 36.59s (-3.71) **Going Correction** -0.45s/f (Firm) **9** Ran SP% **115.6**
Speed ratings (Par 98): **94,92,91,88,87 82,81,72,41**
CSF £37.78 CT £288.45 TOTE £10.30: £3.00, £1.40, £2.50; EX 38.60 Trifecta £458.90.
Owner Jon and Julia Aisbitt **Bred** Jon And Julia Aisbitt **Trained** Newmarket, Suffolk

FOCUS
A low-grade event but run at a good pace, the winner getting to the front despite a tardy start and keeping on strongly. It's been rated around the second and third.

4485 BETTINGSITES.LTD.UK ONLINE H'CAP — 1m 2f
9:00 (9:02) (Class 6) (0-55,55) 3-Y-O
£2,781 (£827; £413; £300; £300; £300) **Stalls Low**

Form — RPR

-050 **1** **Hammy End (IRE)**[136] 765 3-9-4 **52**........................(h) NicolaCurrie 1 57
(William Muir) *chsd ldrs tl drvn and lost pl over 3f out: swtchd rt and hdwy over 1f out: stl only 5th 1f out: r.o to ld fnl 75yds (trainers' rep said, regards apparent improvement in form, gelding was the slow maturing type and has now learned to settle)* **33/1**

0-03 **2** *3/4* **Nabvutika (IRE)**[63] 2262 3-9-3 **51**........................ TomQueally 2 55
(John Butler) *midfield: hdwy 3f out: rdn over 2f out: wnt 2nd over 1f out: led briefly 110yds out: sn hdd and unable qck* **7/2**[1]

0-00 **3** *nk* **Sari Mareis**[48] 2734 3-9-1 **49**........................ CharlesBishop 10 52
(Denis Coakley) *s.i.s: in rr: rdn and hdwy 3f out: sltly impeded 1f out: ev ch ins fnl f: unable qck (jockey said filly was slowly away)* **20/1**

000 **4** *2 3/4* **All Right**[28] 3445 3-9-4 **52**........................ DavidProbert 15 50
(Henry Candy) *chsd ldng pair: rdn to ld over 2f out: hdd 110yds out: no ex* **9/2**[2]

0003 **5** *1 3/4* **Mi Laddo (IRE)**[13] 4003 3-8-13 **47**........................(tp) KieranShoemark 4 42
(Oliver Greenall) *s.i.s: in rr: rdn 3f out: hdwy 2f out: nt clr run over 1f out: r.o ins fnl f (jockey said gelding was denied a clear run)* **12/1**

5050 **6** *2 1/2* **Chakrii (IRE)**[24] 3593 3-9-2 **50**........................(p) HollieDoyle 12 40
(Henry Spiller) *hld up: rdn 3f out: hdwy over 1f out: styd on same pce fnl f* **8/1**

000 **7** *1/2* **Starlight**[10] 4120 3-8-12 **46** oh1........................ HayleyTurner 9 35
(Michael Bell) *towards rr: pushed along and sme prog over 3f out: styd on steadily fnl 2f* **8/1**

060 **8** *1 3/4* **Society Sweetheart (IRE)**[22] 3664 3-9-4 **52**........................ CallumShepherd 7 38
(J S Moore) *chsd ldrs: rdn over 3f out: one pce fnl 2f* **50/1**

-540 **9** *1 1/2* **Parknacilla (IRE)**[33] 3275 3-8-11 **50**........................ PoppyBridgwater(5) 8 33
(Henry Spiller) *midfield: rdn over 2f out: chsd ldrs over 1f out: wknd ins fnl f* **11/1**

5040 **10** *4 1/2* **Jailbreak (IRE)**[7] 4217 3-9-1 **49**........................ ShaneKelly 13 23
(Richard Hughes) *towards rr: rdn 4f out: wknd over 2f out* **7/1**[3]

0400 **11** *3* **Frenchmans Creek (IRE)**[29] 3407 3-9-2 **50**........................(h[1]) RaulDaSilva 14 19+
(Seamus Durack) *led 3f: w ldr: rdn and ev ch 3f out: sn wknd* **22/1**

-000 **12** *3* **Lucky Circle**[24] 3593 3-8-12 **46** oh1........................ JFEgan 5 9
(David Evans) *chsd ldrs: rdn over 3f out: wknd over 2f out* **16/1**

4-00 **13** *10* **No Trouble (IRE)**[20] 3741 3-9-7 **55**........................(v[1]) DanielMuscutt 11 +
(Stuart Williams) *trckd ldr tl led after 3f: rdn over 2f out: wknd qckly* **9/1**

2m 8.5s (-4.30) **Going Correction** -0.45s/f (Firm) **13** Ran SP% **121.0**
Speed ratings (Par 98): **99,98,98,95,94 92,92,90,89,85 83,81,73**
CSF £143.39 CT £2455.45 TOTE £37.30: £7.30, £1.80, £5.50; EX 198.70 Trifecta £1982.50.
Owner John O'Mulloy **Bred** Grangecon Holdings Ltd **Trained** Lambourn, Berks

FOCUS
A drying day and the ground was officially good, good to firm in places. A low-grade finale but run at a strong pace and the fourth emerges with plenty of credit. A minor pb from the third.
T/Jkpt: Not won. T/Plt: £85.90 to a £1 stake. Pool: 93,982.13 - 798.23 winning units T/Qpdt: £12.50 to a £1 stake. Pool: £12,491.60 - 735.59 winning units **Richard Lowther**

4274 HAMILTON (R-H)
Tuesday, July 2

OFFICIAL GOING: Good (good to firm in places; 7.9)
Wind: Breezy, across Weather: Fine, dry

4486 BB FOODSERVICE NOVICE AUCTION STKS (PLUS 10 RACE) (£20,000 BB FOODSERVICE 2YO SERIES QUALIFIER) — 6f 6y
2:15 (2:15) (Class 4) 2-Y-O
£5,433 (£1,617; £808; £404) **Stalls High**

Form — RPR

525 **1** **Dragon Command**[32] 3312 2-9-2 76........................(p[1]) BenCurtis 4 80
(George Scott) *trckd ldr: rdn to ld over 1f out: drvn: edgd lft and kpt on strly fnl f* **5/1**[3]

4 **2** *2 3/4* **National League (IRE)**[12] 4032 2-9-2 0........................ TonyHamilton 5 72
(Richard Fahey) *prom: effrt and drvn along 2f out: chsd wnr ins fnl f: r.o: nt pce to chal* **3/1**[2]

12 **3** *3* **Coastal Mist (IRE)**[12] 4032 2-9-8 0........................ JasonHart 7 69
(John Quinn) *t.k.h: trckd ldrs: rdn over 2f out: outpcd over 1f out: rallied ins fnl f: tk 3rd last stride* **7/4**[1]

4 **4** *shd* **Too Hard To Hold (IRE)**[11] 4062 2-9-2 0........................ PJMcDonald 1 62
(Mark Johnston) *led: crossed to stands' rail after 1f: rdn and hdd over 1f out: outpcd ins fnl f* **8/1**

4 **5** *shd* **Don Ramiro (IRE)**[43] 2906 2-9-2 0........................ TomEaves 2 62
(Kevin Ryan) *hld up in tch on outside: stdy hdwy and cl up over 2f out: rdn over 1f out: kpt on same pce fnl f* **8/1**

4 **6** *3 1/4* **Sir Havelock (IRE)**[15] 3919 2-8-13 0........................ SeanDavis(3) 8 52
(Richard Fahey) *s.i.s: hld up: pushed along 2f out: no imp fnl f* **20/1**

06 **7** *3 1/2* **Congratulate**[33] 3245 2-8-11 0........................ DavidAllan 3 37
(Tim Easterby) *slowly away: bhd: struggling over 2f out: sn btn* **25/1**

8 *hd* **Yorkshire Grey (IRE)** 2-9-2 0........................(h[1]) ShaneGray 9 41
(Ann Duffield) *trckd ldrs: drvn along over 2f out: wknd over 1f out* **33/1**

1m 12.3s (-0.40) **Going Correction** -0.025s/f (Good) **8** Ran SP% **111.8**
Speed ratings (Par 96): **101,97,93,93,93 88,84,83**
CSF £19.32 TOTE £3.50: £1.40, £1.40, £1.10; EX 20.30 Trifecta £33.00.
Owner The Black Dragon **Bred** Saleh Al Homaizi & Imad Al Sagar **Trained** Newmarket, Suffolk

FOCUS
The Loop rail was out 5yds. This opening juvenile sprint was run at a solid pace on the near side. The winning time backed up an official assessment of good ground. The winner's Carlisle form could be rated this high.

4487 FERNIEGAIR H'CAP (DIV I) — 1m 68y
2:45 (2:46) (Class 6) (0-60,62) 3-Y-O
£3,493 (£1,039; £519; £300; £300; £300) **Stalls Low**

Form — RPR

1 **Blackstone Cliff (IRE)**[29] 3435 3-8-8 **45**........................ JamesSullivan 2 54+
(Adrian Murray, Ire) *plld hrd early: in tch: hdwy and rdn over 1f out: led ins fnl f: edgd rt: pushed out: comf (trainer said, regards apparent improvement in form, gelding benefitted from the step up in trip and a better draw on this occasion)* **5/1**[3]

0050 **2** *1 1/2* **Temple Of Wonder (IRE)**[15] 3924 3-9-7 **58**........................ DavidNolan 1 62
(Liam Bailey) *hld up: stdy hdwy 3f out: effrt and rdn over 1f out: kpt on wl fnl f to take 2nd nr fin: no ch w wnr* **25/1**

0100 **3** *nk* **Jazz Hands (IRE)**[31] 3348 3-9-0 **51**........................ TonyHamilton 8 54
(Richard Fahey) *cl up: led over 2f out to ins fnl f: one pce and lost 2nd towards fin* **11/1**

0033 **4** *nk* **Brutalab**[15] 3926 3-9-1 **52**........................ DavidAllan 9 54
(Tim Easterby) *t.k.h: prom: ev ch over 2f out: rdn along over 1f out: kpt on same pce fnl f* **9/4**[1]

-000 **5** *hd* **Somewhat Sisyphean**[82] 1721 3-8-5 **45**........................ SeanDavis(3) 7 47
(Wilf Storey) *s.s: hld up: hdwy on outside over 2f out: sn rdn: kpt on wl fnl f: nrst fin* **50/1**

000B **6** *1* **Harperelle**[20] 3720 3-8-10 **50**........................ ConnorMurtagh(3) 6 50
(Alistair Whillans) *led 2f: cl up: drvn along 2f out: one pce fnl f* **40/1**

004- **7** *1/2* **Lady Rouda (IRE)**[257] 8351 3-8-10 **47**........................ CliffordLee 3 46
(Philip Kirby) *hld up in tch: rdn along over 2f out: one pce appr fnl f* **22/1**

60-4 **8** *nk* **Donnago (IRE)**[24] 3570 3-8-13 **53**........................ BenRobinson(3) 13 51
(Brian Ellison) *hld up: rdn along 3f out: kpt on fnl f: nvr able to chal* **20/1**

2013 **9** *nk* **Fitzy**[20] 3721 3-9-6 **57**........................ PJMcDonald 10 54
(David Brown) *cl up: led after 2f: rdn and hdd over 2f out rallied: wknd ins fnl f* **4/1**[2]

-034 **10** *3/4* **Treasured Company (IRE)**[55] 2531 3-8-8 **45**........................(e) PhilipPrince 11 41
(Richard Guest) *t.k.h: hld up on outside: effrt over 2f out: sn hung rt: no imp over 1f out* **20/1**

5062 **11** *nk* **Zalmi Angel**[22] 3651 3-8-9 **51**........................ PaulaMuir(5) 5 46
(Adrian Nicholls) *missed break: t.k.h: hld up towards rr: rdn along over 2f out: sn no imp* **9/1**

000- **12** *4* **My Little Orphan**[258] 8330 3-9-11 **62**........................ ShaneGray 14 48
(Keith Dalgleish) *s.i.s: hld up: rdn and outpcd over 2f out: sn btn* **16/1**

0 **13** *1/2* **Scarlet Skis**[76] 1863 3-9-4 **55**........................ TomEaves 12 40
(Stef Keniry) *hld up in midfield on outside: drvn along over 2f out: wknd over 1f out* **25/1**

1m 49.31s (0.91) **Going Correction** -0.025s/f (Good) **13** Ran SP% **117.6**
Speed ratings (Par 98): **94,92,92,91,91 90,90,89,89,88 88,84,84**
CSF £126.95 CT £1366.58 TOTE £5.80: £2.10, £6.20, £3.20; EX 116.50 Trifecta £1656.20.
Owner Adrian Murray **Bred** James Wallace **Trained** Rathowen, Co. Westmeath

FOCUS
A moderate 3yo handicap, run at a sound pace. Add 15yds. The form could be rated a bit higher through the second and third.

4488 FERNIEGAIR H'CAP (DIV II) — 1m 68y
3:15 (3:18) (Class 6) (0-60,62) 3-Y-O
£3,493 (£1,039; £519; £300; £300; £300) **Stalls Low**

Form — RPR

-065 **1** **Mecca's Gift (IRE)**[27] 3478 3-9-7 **60**........................(b[1]) ConnorBeasley 2 72+
(Michael Dods) *t.k.h early: in tch: hdwy to ld over 1f out: drvn clr fnl f: eased nr fin* **5/1**[3]

4646 **2** *7* **Monsieur Piquer (FR)**[20] 3721 3-8-13 **57**........................(v) HarrisonShaw(5) 11 53
(K R Burke) *hld up: hdwy on outside over 2f out: chsd (clr) wnr over 1f out: kpt on fnl f: no imp* **10/1**

5-46 **3** *shd* **God Of Dreams**[34] 3226 3-9-9 **62**........................ JamieGormley 10 58
(Iain Jardine) *hld up in midfield: effrt over 2f out: disp 2nd pl ins fnl f: kpt on: no imp* **14/1**

-622 **4** 1 3/4 **Juniors Fantasy (IRE)**[21] 3684 3-9-3 **56**.................... DuranFentiman 3 51
(Tim Easterby) *hld up on ins: effrt whn nt clr run over 2f out to over 1f out: nt clr run ent fnl f: kpt on towards fin: nvr able to chal (jockey said gelding was continually denied a clear run in the final two furlongs)* **3/1**[1]

-606 **5** 1 1/4 **Keska**[19] 3777 3-8-4 **46** oh1..(v[1]) SeanDavis(3) 13 35
(Richard Fahey) *cl up: led after 2f: rdn and hdd over 1f out: wknd ins fnl f (vet said filly lost it's right fore shoe)* **25/1**

00-0 **6** hd **Be Proud (IRE)**[61] 2325 3-8-10 **52**.................... BenRobinson(3) 5 41
(Jim Goldie) *t.k.h: hld up in tch: effrt over 2f out: wknd fnl f* **14/1**

-635 **7** 3 1/4 **Royal Countess**[21] 3684 3-8-2 **46**.................... PaulaMuir(5) 7 28
(Lucy Normile) *s.i.s: bhd: rdn along over 2f out: kpt on fnl f: nvr able to chal* **8/1**

0006 **8** 3 **Kimberley Girl**[35] 3208 3-8-12 **51**.................... CamHardie 6 26
(Michael Easterby) *led 2f: cl up: rdn over 2f out: wknd over 1f out* **18/1**

0-06 **9** 4 1/2 **Philyaboots**[11] 4055 3-8-10 **49**.................... TomEaves 1 14
(Donald McCain) *t.k.h: hld up: rdn 3f out: hung lft and wknd over 1f out* **16/1**

000- **10** 2 3/4 **Lady Mayhem (IRE)**[251] 8540 3-8-11 **50**.................... BenCurtis 4 9
(Roger Fell) *bhd: struggling 1/2-way: nvr on terms* **12/1**

50-0 **11** 5 **Wearraah**[10] 4129 3-8-7 **46** oh1.................... ShaneGray 9
(Alan Brown) *cl up tl rdn and wknd fr 2f out* **66/1**

0220 **U** **The Big House (IRE)**[6] 4244 3-8-12 **51**.................... AndrewMullen 8
(Adrian Nicholls) *t.k.h: sn midfield: stmbld and uns rdr after 1f* **7/2**[2]

1m 47.79s (-0.61) **Going Correction** -0.025s/f (Good) 12 Ran SP% **121.6**
Speed ratings (Par 98): **102,95,94,93,91 91,88,85,80,78 73,**
CSF £56.00 CT £680.76 TOTE £5.60: £1.70, £2.60, £3.50; EX 53.20 Trifecta £999.90.
Owner D J Metcalfe & M Dods **Bred** Doc Bloodstock **Trained** Denton, Co Durham

FOCUS
This second division of the moderate 3yo handicap was 1.52secs quicker than the first. Add 15yds. The second and third help set a modest level.

4489 RACINGTV.COM NOVICE STKS 6f 6y
3:45 (3:47) (Class 5) 3-Y-O+ **£4,140** (£1,232; £615; £307) **Stalls** Centre

Form RPR

3-1 **1** **Last Empire**[26] 3499 3-9-5 0.................... DanielTudhope 8 76+
(Kevin Ryan) *trckd ldrs: led gng wl over 2f out: shkn up and qcknd clr fnl f: readily* **4/7**[1]

0-32 **2** 2 1/2 **Delachance (FR)**[41] 2976 3-8-12 74....................(h) DylanHogan(5) 4 64
(David Simcock) *trckd ldrs: rdn: carried hd high and wnt 2nd over 1f out: kpt on fnl f: nt pce to chal* **9/4**[2]

3 2 **Belvelly Boy (IRE)** 3-9-3 0.................... DavidNolan 6 58
(David O'Meara) *dwlt: bhd: drvn along over 2f out: hdwy over 1f out: kpt on fnl f: nvr able to chal* **11/1**

00 **4** hd **Indiaro**[11] 4055 3-9-3 0.................... JamesSullivan 5 57?
(Linda Perratt) *chsd ldng gp: drvn along 1/2-way: kpt on fnl f: no imp* **100/1**

0- **5** 1 1/2 **See My Baby Jive**[258] 8322 3-8-12 0.................... JasonHart 2 47?
(Donald Whillans) *dwlt: t.k.h: hld up in tch: rdn and hung rt 2f out: wknd fnl f* **50/1**

64 **6** 3 3/4 **Perfect Charm**[15] 3920 3-8-12 0.................... BenCurtis 7 35
(Archie Watson) *led to over 2f out: rdn and wknd over 1f out* **11/2**[3]

-006 **7** 4 1/2 **Trulove**[57] 2481 6-8-11 41.................... HarryRussell(7) 1 22
(John David Riches) *racd on outside: prom tl rdn and wknd over 1f out* **100/1**

64- **8** 2 1/4 **Jordan's Chris (IRE)**[348] 5133 3-8-9 0....................(h[1]) BenRobinson(3) 3 14
(Linda Perratt) *slowly away: bhd and outpcd: nvr on terms* **80/1**

1m 12.28s (-0.42) **Going Correction** -0.025s/f (Good)
WFA 3 from 6yo 6lb 8 Ran SP% **123.3**
Speed ratings (Par 103): **101,97,95,94,92 87,81,78**
CSF £2.45 TOTE £1.30: £1.10, £1.10, £2.20; EX 2.70 Trifecta £8.50.
Owner Clipper Logistics **Bred** Mrs G S Rees And Douglas McMahon **Trained** Hambleton, N Yorks

FOCUS
An uncompetitive novice event.

4490 ALMADA MILE H'CAP (FOR THE WATSON MEMORIAL CUP) 1m 68y
4:15 (4:15) (Class 2) (0-100,96) 3-Y-O+
£18,675 (£5,592; £2,796; £1,398; £699; £351) **Stalls** Low

Form RPR

0346 **1** **Victory Command (IRE)**[12] 4016 3-9-2 **91**.................... PJMcDonald 2 97
(Mark Johnston) *trckd ldrs: n.m.r over 2f out: shkn up and hdwy to ld over 1f out: edgd rt ins fnl f: rdn and r.o wl* **15/8**[1]

3046 **2** 3/4 **Nicholas T**[10] 4097 7-8-12 **81**.................... BenRobinson(3) 3 90+
(Jim Goldie) *hld up: hdwy whn nt clr run fr over 2f out: hmpd over 1f out: swtchd rt and hdwy to chse (clr) wnr ins fnl f: str run to cl nr fin* **8/1**

2021 **3** 2 1/2 **Never Be Enough**[5] 4278 4-9-3 **83** 5ex.................... TomEaves 1 84
(Keith Dalgleish) *hld up: effrt on outside over 1f out: kpt on ins fnl f: nt pce to chal* **4/1**[2]

6610 **4** 1/2 **Brother McGonagall**[6] 4240 5-9-3 **83**.................... DavidAllan 5 83
(Tim Easterby) *t.k.h: mde most to over 1f out: kpt on same pce ins fnl f* **15/2**

0450 **5** 1/2 **Mikmak**[6] 4240 6-9-2 **82**....................(p) JasonHart 8 81
(Tim Easterby) *pressed ldr: ev ch over 2f out to over 1f out: no ex ins fnl f* **7/1**

3311 **6** 3/4 **Coolagh Forest (IRE)**[60] 2369 3-9-4 **96**.................... SeanDavis(3) 6 91
(Richard Fahey) *chsd ldrs: rdn along over 2f out: wknd ins fnl f* **6/1**[3]

2463 **7** 1 1/4 **Nonios (IRE)**[12] 4021 7-9-0 **85**....................(h) DylanHogan(5) 7 79
(David Simcock) *hld up: hdwy on outside over 2f out: rdn and wknd over 1f out* **16/1**

1m 47.65s (-0.75) **Going Correction** -0.025s/f (Good)
WFA 3 from 4yo+ 9lb 7 Ran SP% **110.3**
Speed ratings (Par 109): **102,101,100,100,99 99,97**
CSF £16.26 CT £49.45 TOTE £2.60: £1.50, £4.30; EX 15.30 Trifecta £61.20.
Owner Kingsley Park 10 **Bred** J Higgins **Trained** Middleham Moor, N Yorks

FOCUS
Not the strongest race for the class and it was run at an average pace. Add 15yds. The winner has been rated as finding a bit on his 3yo form.

4491 HAMILTON PARK SUPPORTING RACING STAFF WEEK H'CAP 1m 5f 16y
4:45 (4:45) (Class 5) (0-75,74) 3-Y-O+ **£4,787** (£1,424; £711; £355; £300) **Stalls** Low

Form RPR

-331 **1** **Mondain**[12] 4031 3-8-13 **72**.................... PJMcDonald 6 81+
(Mark Johnston) *chsd clr ldr: clsd over 3f out: led over 2f out: rdn and clr ins fnl f: kpt on strly* **11/10**[1]

0632 **2** 3 **Qawamees (IRE)**[7] 4208 4-10-0 **74**....................(bt) JamesSullivan 1 78
(Michael Easterby) *t.k.h: hld up in last pl: pushed along over 2f out: chsd (clr) wnr ins fnl f: kpt on: no imp* **7/2**[2]

1120 **3** nk **Echo (IRE)**[22] 3653 4-10-0 **74**....................(b) JackGarritty 5 77
(Jedd O'Keeffe) *chsd ldrs: rdn over 2f out: sn outpcd: rallied ins fnl f: tk 3rd cl home: no imp* **7/2**[2]

2455 **4** 1/2 **Corton Lad**[5] 4274 9-9-9 **69**....................(tp) ShaneGray 2 71
(Keith Dalgleish) *led and clr to over 3f out: hdd over 2f out: rallied: no ex and lost two pls last 100yds* **7/1**[3]

-004 **5** 11 **Question Of Faith**[11] 4056 8-9-11 **71**.................... DavidNolan 7 57
(Martin Todhunter) *slowly away: in tch: rdn over 2f out: wknd over 1f out* **14/1**

2m 53.0s (-1.70) **Going Correction** -0.025s/f (Good)
WFA 3 from 4yo+ 13lb 5 Ran SP% **111.2**
Speed ratings (Par 103): **104,102,101,101,94**
CSF £5.32 TOTE £1.80: £1.10, £1.80; EX 6.30 Trifecta £12.50.
Owner Sheikh Hamdan bin Mohammed Al Maktoum **Bred** Godolphin **Trained** Middleham Moor, N Yorks

FOCUS
This fair handicap was run at a muddling pace. Add 15yds. The second has been rated to his recent form, and the third close to form.

4492 JOIN RACING TV NOW H'CAP 6f 6y
5:15 (5:16) (Class 4) (0-85,83) 3-Y-O **£6,727** (£2,002; £1,000; £500; £300) **Stalls** Centre

Form RPR

0021 **1** **Firmdecisions (IRE)**[43] 2893 9-9-9 **83**.................... RowanScott(3) 4 90
(Nigel Tinkler) *chsd ldr: rdn and effrt over 1f out: led ins fnl f: hld on wl* **4/1**[3]

5421 **2** 3/4 **Jordan Electrics**[13] 3999 3-8-6 **69**....................(h) CamHardie 3 72
(Linda Perratt) *led at ordinary gallop: rdn over 1f out: hung lft and hdd ins fnl f: rallied: hld nr fin (jockey said gelding hung left-handed under pressure)* **3/1**[2]

4130 **3** nk **Paddy Power (IRE)**[3] 4402 6-9-9 **83**.................... SeanDavis(3) 5 86
(Richard Fahey) *in tch: shkn up over 2f out: rdn and outpcd over 1f out: rallied ins fnl f: kpt on fin* **5/2**[1]

6315 **4** 1 3/4 **Howzer Black (IRE)**[10] 4099 3-9-4 **81**....................(p) ShaneGray 2 77
(Keith Dalgleish) *trckd ldrs: effrt and rdn over 1f out: edgd rt and no ex ins fnl f* **5/2**[1]

00-6 **5** 4 1/2 **Yes You (IRE)**[20] 3722 5-9-8 **79**.................... JamieGormley 1 59
(Iain Jardine) *dwlt: hld up in last pl: struggling over 2f out: sn btn* **12/1**

1m 11.2s (-1.50) **Going Correction** -0.025s/f (Good)
WFA 3 from 5yo+ 6lb 5 Ran SP% **109.8**
Speed ratings (Par 105): **109,108,107,105,99**
CSF £15.99 TOTE £4.60: £2.20, £1.40; EX 16.30 Trifecta £33.50.
Owner White Bear Racing **Bred** Thomas O'Meara **Trained** Langton, N Yorks

FOCUS
This was run at a routine pace and saw a tight finish. The winner has been rated in line with last year's form.

4493 EVERY RACE LIVE ON RACING TV H'CAP 5f 7y
5:45 (5:47) (Class 6) (0-55,55) 3-Y-O+
£3,493 (£1,039; £519; £300; £300; £300) **Stalls** Centre

Form RPR

4- **1** **Rego Park Lady (IRE)**[45] 2851 4-9-7 **55**....................(p) JamesSullivan 6 62+
(Adrian Murray, Ire) *hld up bhd ldng gp: hdwy whn nt clr run over 2f out to over 1f out: led ins fnl f: hld on wl* **3/1**[2]

4050 **2** hd **Picks Pinta**[61] 2329 8-8-6 **47** ow1....................(b) HarryRussell(7) 8 52
(John David Riches) *hld up: rdn along over 2f out: hdwy and angled lft over 1f out: kpt on wl fnl f to take 2nd cl home: jst hld* **20/1**

1030 **3** nk **Red Stripes (USA)**[17] 3846 7-9-5 **53**....................(b) PJMcDonald 7 57
(Lisa Williamson) *cl up: led over 1f out to ins fnl f: kpt on: no ex and lost 2nd nr fin (vet said gelding lost it's left fore shoe)* **8/1**[3]

-030 **4** 1 3/4 **Funkadelic**[26] 3518 4-8-9 **48**.................... HarrisonShaw(5) 11 46
(Ben Haslam) *cl up stands' side: rdn along over 2f out: edgd rt: kpt on fnl f* **8/1**[3]

033U **5** 1/2 **Popping Corks (IRE)**[32] 3292 3-8-12 **54**.................... BenRobinson(3) 1 48
(Linda Perratt) *hmpd s: bhd: rdn and hdwy on wd outside 2f out: kpt on same pce ins fnl f* **14/1**

6304 **6** shd **Raquelle (IRE)**[7] 4212 3-8-7 **46** oh1....................(p) DuranFentiman 2 40
(Tim Easterby) *wnt rt s: hld up: hdwy on wd outside and ev ch over 1f out: edgd lft and no ex ins fnl f* **10/1**

0-00 **7** 1 3/4 **Lady Joanna Vassa (IRE)**[15] 3933 6-8-12 **46** oh1........(v) PhilipPrince 3 35
(Richard Guest) *trckd ldrs: effrt and ev ch briefly over 1f out: wknd ins fnl f* **66/1**

1000 **8** 1/2 **Gunnabedun (IRE)**[5] 4276 3-9-1 **54**....................(b) CamHardie 12 40
(Iain Jardine) *bhd and outpcd stands' side: hdwy fnl f: nvr able to chal* **22/1**

-543 **9** 1 1/2 **I'll Be Good**[10] 4132 10-8-12 **49**.................... ConnorMurtagh(3) 4 31
(Alan Berry) *t.k.h: led to over 1f out: wknd fnl f* **9/1**

5000 **10** 1 3/4 **Corton Lass**[20] 3723 4-8-12 **46** oh1.................... ShaneGray 5 22
(Keith Dalgleish) *chsd ldrs: rdn over 2f out: wknd over 1f out* **28/1**

2643 **11** 1/2 **Dancing Mountain (IRE)**[12] 4033 3-9-1 **54**.................... BenCurtis 10 26+
(Roger Fell) *rrd s: bhd and outpcd: nvr on terms (jockey said filly fly-leapt leaving the stalls)* **11/4**[1]

43-0 **12** 1 1/4 **Little Miss Lola**[14] 3975 5-8-8 **47**.................... PaulaMuir(5) 9 17
(Lynn Siddall) *chsd ldrs stands' side tl rdn and wknd fr 2f out (vet said mare bled from the nose)* **12/1**

1m 0.6s (0.20) **Going Correction** -0.025s/f (Good)
WFA 3 from 4yo+ 5lb 12 Ran SP% **121.4**
Speed ratings (Par 101): **97,96,96,93,92 92,89,88,86,83 82,80**
CSF £68.91 CT £452.30 TOTE £4.60: £1.90, £5.50, £2.40; EX 70.00 Trifecta £802.30.
Owner A F McLoughlin & C Higgins & H Murray **Bred** Miss Jessica Leahy **Trained** Rathowen, Co. Westmeath

FOCUS
The main action developed down the centre in this weak sprint handicap. Ordinary form.
T/Plt: £43.80 to a £1 stake. Pool: £71,334.56 - 1187.54 winning units T/Qpdt: £12.60 to a £1 stake. Pool: £8,239.58 - 482.30 winning units **Richard Young**

4230 BATH (L-H)

Wednesday, July 3

OFFICIAL GOING: Firm (9.3)
Wind: virtually nil Weather: sunny

4494 BEST FREE TIPS AT VALUERATER.CO.UK H'CAP (VALUE RATER RACING CLUB BATH SUMMER SPRINT SERIES) 5f 160y

6:10 (6:11) (Class 6) (0-65,67) 4-Y-0+

£2,781 (£827; £413; £300; £300; £300) Stalls Centre

Form RPR

4410 **1** **Storm Melody**[7] 4230 6-9-11 **67**..................(p) TomMarquand 7 77
(Ali Stronge) *racd in last trio: hdwy over 2f out: led over 1f out: kpt on wl* **11/4**[1]

0 **2** *2* **Coffeemeanscoffee (IRE)**[7] 4260 4-8-3 **45**..................(p) KieranO'Neill 3 48
(W J Martin, Ire) *in tch: outpcd 3f out: swtchd rt 2f out: hdwy over 1f out: chsd wnr ent fnl f: kpt on but a being hld* **10/1**

0106 **3** *3¾* **My Town Chicago (USA)**[42] 2971 4-9-6 **62**..................(bt[1]) RossaRyan 2 52
(Kevin Frost) *prom: rdn to ld jst over 2f out: hdd over 1f out: lost 2nd ent fnl f: no ex* **10/1**

1045 **4** *hd* **Jaganory (IRE)**[9] 4181 7-8-10 **57**..................(v) PoppyBridgwater(5) 6 47
(Christopher Mason) *chsd ldrs: rdn over 2f out: kpt on same pce fnl f* **14/1**

0-30 **5** *1* **Bayards Cove**[20] 3771 4-8-3 **45**.................. HayleyTurner 11 31
(Stuart Kittow) *outpcd in detached least early: hdwy 2f out: kpt on ins fnl f: wnt 4th towards fin* **25/1**

35U4 **6** *¾* **Mooroverthebridge**[39] 3089 5-9-0 **56**.................. JimmyQuinn 1 40
(Grace Harris) *trckd ldrs: rdn over 2f out: nt quite pce to chal: no ex ins fnl f* **10/1**

32-0 **7** *½* **Compton Poppy**[50] 2717 5-9-2 **58**.................. GeorgeDowning 5 40
(Tony Carroll) *s.i.s: sn trckd ldrs: rdn over 2f out: one pce fnl f* **20/1**

0343 **8** *2* **Archimedes (IRE)**[1] 4478 6-9-2 **58**..................(tp) FrannyNorton 4 33
(David C Griffiths) *led: rdn and hdd jst over 2f out: wknd fnl f* **3/1**[2]

P030 **9** *1½* **Look Surprised**[7] 4230 6-9-7 **63**.................. HollieDoyle 12 33
(Roger Teal) *sn chsng ldrs: rdn over 2f out: wknd ent fnl f (jockey said mare ran flat)* **7/2**[3]

0500 **10** *2½* **Burauq**[9] 4182 7-8-3 **45**..................(v) JosephineGordon 10 7
(Milton Bradley) *outpcd in last pair: nvr on terms* **50/1**

1m 9.71s (-1.39) **Going Correction** -0.175s/f (Firm) **10 Ran SP% 118.4**
Speed ratings (Par 101): **102,99,94,94,92 91,91,88,86,83**
CSF £30.96 CT £249.54 TOTE £3.60: £1.60, £3.20, £3.50; EX 28.70 Trifecta £215.20.
Owner Shaw Racing Partnership 2 **Bred** Selwood B/S, Hoskins & Jonason **Trained** Eastbury, Berks

FOCUS
A modest sprint handicap.

4495 SARSAS LISTENING BELIEVING AND SUPPORTING "CONFINED" H'CAP (FOR HORSES THAT HAVE NOT WON IN 2019) 5f 160y

6:40 (6:42) (Class 4) (0-80,81) 3-Y-0+

£5,207 (£1,549; £774; £387; £300; £300) Stalls Centre

Form RPR

500 **1** **Delagate This Lord**[7] 4230 5-9-2 **69**.................. CharlieBennett 9 77
(Michael Attwater) *trckd ldrs: led over 1f out: kpt on wl whn strly chal ins fnl f: hld on* **12/1**

1-06 **2** *shd* **Cool Reflection (IRE)**[41] 2997 3-9-6 **79**..................(p[1]) TomMarquand 3 85
(Paul Cole) *trckd ldrs: rdn for str chal jst ins fnl f: kpt on: hld cl home* **10/1**

6-20 **3** *3* **Peace Dreamer (IRE)**[11] 4105 5-9-4 **76**.................. DylanHogan(5) 4 73
(Robert Cowell) *mid-div: hdwy 2f out: sn swtchd rt: kpt on ins fnl f but nt pce to get on terms* **12/1**

-060 **4** *1¾* **Mutawaffer (IRE)**[26] 3531 3-9-7 **80**.................. RichardKingscote 2 71
(Charles Hills) *racd freely: led: rdn and hdd over 1f out: no ex fnl f (jockey said gelding ran too free)* **3/1**[1]

0042 **5** *hd* **Blaine**[7] 4236 9-9-10 **77**.................. TrevorWhelan 6 68
(Brian Barr) *last pair: sn nudged along: hdwy 2f out: kpt on ins fnl f: nrly snatched 4th fnl stride* **5/1**[2]

3252 **6** *¾* **Harry Hurricane**[7] 4253 7-10-0 **81**..................(p) JosephineGordon 8 70
(George Baker) *pressed ldr: rdn over 1f out: fdd fnl f* **11/2**[3]

2303 **7** *2¾* **Powerful Dream (IRE)**[7] 4230 6-8-12 **65**..................(p) KieranO'Neill 1 44
(Ronald Harris) *chsd ldrs: rdn over 2f out: wknd fnl f* **11/2**[3]

00-0 **8** *10* **Our Lord**[17] 3893 7-8-12 **72**.................. CierenFallon(7) 5 18
(Michael Attwater) *in tch for over 1f out: rdn in last trio wl over 2f out: eased whn btn ent fnl f (jockey said gelding lost its action)* **20/1**

-445 **9** *9* **Jack Taylor (IRE)**[26] 3536 4-8-12 **72**..................(b) AngusVilliers(7) 7
(Richard Hughes) *rrd bdly stalls: nvr rcvrd: a bhd (jockey said gelding reared leaving stalls)* **13/2**

1m 9.1s (-2.00) **Going Correction** -0.175s/f (Firm)
WFA 3 from 4yo+ 6lb **9 Ran SP% 115.0**
Speed ratings (Par 105): **106,105,101,99,99 98,94,81,69**
CSF £124.14 CT £1478.44 TOTE £14.10: £4.30, £4.30, £3.70; EX 179.60 Trifecta £1692.80.
Owner Mrs M S Teversham **Bred** Mrs Monica Teversham **Trained** Epsom, Surrey

FOCUS
A fair sprint handicap in which the narrow winner dipped under standard time. The second has been rated up there with the best view of his previous form.

4496 SKY SPORTS RACING VIRGIN 535 MAIDEN STKS 5f 10y

7:10 (7:13) (Class 4) 3-Y-0+ £5,207 (£1,549; £774; £387) Stalls Centre

Form RPR

3245 **1** **Heritage**[12] 4072 3-9-0 81..................(p[1]) LiamKeniry 4 84+
(Clive Cox) *mde all: pushed clr over 1f out: comf* **1/4**[1]

22 **2** *7* **Vandella (IRE)**[161] 370 3-9-0.................. JFEgan 5 59
(David Evans) *pressed wnr tl rdn over 2f out: sn hld but kpt on for clr 2nd* **11/4**[2]

-040 **3** *11* **Bonny Blue**[9] 4180 3-9-0 60.................. CharlieBennett 2 19
(Rod Millman) *chsd ldng pair: outpcd over 2f out: no threat after* **14/1**[3]

6000 **4** *2¾* **Dutch Melody**[1] 4475 5-8-12 44.................. VictorSantos(7) 3 11
(Lucinda Egerton) *sn rousted along to chse ldrs: outpcd over 2f out: wknd fnl f* **50/1**

00-6 **5** *17* **Isla Skye (IRE)**[25] 3598 3-8-7 30.................. LauraCoughlan(7) 1
(Barry Brennan) *chsd ldrs: outpcd over 2f out: wknd over 1f out* **100/1**

59.71s (-2.29) **Going Correction** -0.175s/f (Firm)
WFA 3 from 5yo 5lb **5 Ran SP% 116.3**
Speed ratings (Par 105): **111,99,82,77,50**
CSF £1.48 TOTE £1.20: £1.10, £1.10; EX 1.50 Trifecta £2.00.
Owner Cheveley Park Stud **Bred** Cheveley Park Stud Ltd **Trained** Lambourn, Berks

FOCUS
An uncompetitive little maiden. The odds-on favourite won easing down by a wide margin from the right filly in second, dipping nearly a second under standard time. It's been rated around the winner.

4497 POMMERY CHAMPAGNE BLAYTHWAYT PLATE H'CAP 1m

7:40 (7:40) (Class 3) (0-90,85) 3-Y-0 £7,876 (£2,357; £1,178; £590) Stalls Low

Form RPR

6030 **1** **Reggae Runner (FR)**[12] 4079 3-9-4 **82**.................. FrannyNorton 5 88
(Mark Johnston) *led: edgd rt over 1f out: slt bump whn narrowly hdd sn after: drvn bk in front ins fnl 120yds: game* **3/1**[2]

1-61 **2** *nk* **Listen To The Wind (IRE)**[34] 3278 3-9-0 **85**.................. CierenFallon(7) 4 90
(William Haggas) *trckd ldrs: drifting lft and bmpd whn taking narrow advantage over 1f out: sn drvn: hdd ins fnl 120yds: no ex cl home* **5/4**[1]

1144 **3** *2* **Shanghai Grace**[11] 4099 3-9-7 **85**.................. RichardKingscote 3 85
(Charles Hills) *trckd wnr: rdn 2f out: ev ch ent fnl f: kpt on same pce fnl 120yds* **5/1**

41-2 **4** *¾* **Hold Still (IRE)**[34] 3261 3-9-3 **81**.................. TomMarquand 2 79
(William Muir) *trckd ldrs: wnt 2nd over 5f out: chal over 2f out: rdn and hld whn tight for room briefly over 1f out: kpt on same pce fnl f* **7/2**[3]

1m 43.54s (1.84) **Going Correction** -0.175s/f (Firm) **4 Ran SP% 108.3**
Speed ratings (Par 104): **83,82,80,79**
CSF £7.20 TOTE £3.20; EX 8.90 Trifecta £19.30.
Owner Hugh Hart **Bred** Hugh Hart **Trained** Middleham Moor, N Yorks
■ Stewards' Enquiry : Franny Norton two-day ban: used whip without giving time to respond (17-18 Jul)

FOCUS
The feature contest was a decent 3yo handicap. The second-favourite attempted to dominate off his own modest, stop-start gallop and proved thoroughly resolute in the finish. A small pb from the second, with the third rated to his latest.

4498 VALUE RATER RACING CLUB H'CAP (VALUE RATER RACING CLUB BATH SUMMER STAYERS' SERIES) 1m 3f 137y

8:10 (8:14) (Class 6) (0-55,61) 3-Y-0+

£2,781 (£827; £413; £300; £300; £300) Stalls Low

Form RPR

2541 **1** **Sigrid Nansen**[8] 4216 4-8-13 **50** 5ex..................(p) CierenFallon(7) 3 63
(Alexandra Dunn) *trckd ldrs: led over 2f out: styd on strly to assert ins fnl f: rdn out* **7/2**[2]

6051 **2** *5* **Confils (FR)**[7] 4232 3-9-5 **61** 6ex.................. PatCosgrave 2 67
(George Baker) *mid-div: nudged along to hold pl over 5f out: hdwy 3f out: sn rdn: chal 2f out: kpt on w ev ch tl no ex ins fnl f* **11/8**[1]

6050 **3** *2¾* **Dimmesdale**[41] 2998 4-9-10 **54**.................. LiamJones 12 54
(John O'Shea) *mid-div: hdwy on outer over 3f out: rdn to dispute 3rd jst over 2f out: edgd lft: kpt on same pce* **14/1**

06-0 **4** *½* **Kay Sera**[51] 2698 11-9-2 **46**.................. EoinWalsh 4 45
(Tony Newcombe) *hld up towards rr: hdwy fr 3f out: rdn over 2f out: hld 5th whn nt clr run and hmpd ins fnl f: sn swtchd rt: r.o fnl 120yds* **66/1**

-403 **5** *¾* **Filament Of Gold (USA)**[49] 2733 8-9-5 **49**..................(b) JFEgan 1 47
(Roy Brotherton) *mid-div: hdwy fr 3f out: rdn to dispute 3rd jst over 2f out: edgd lft: no ex fnl 120yds* **8/1**[3]

-666 **6** *8* **Just Right**[7] 4232 4-9-0 **47**.................. WilliamCox(3) 9 32
(John Flint) *prom: rdn and ev ch over 2f out: wknd over 1f out* **16/1**

00-0 **7** *2* **Mamnoon (IRE)**[41] 2998 6-9-1 **45**..................(b) KieranO'Neill 11 27
(Roy Brotherton) *led: rdn and hdd jst over 2f out: wknd over 1f out* **40/1**

60-0 **8** *3¼* **Innstigator**[41] 2998 5-9-1 **45**.................. CallumShepherd 5 21
(Sue Gardner) *hld up towards rr: rdn over 2f out: little imp* **25/1**

9 *¾* **Cape Agulhas (IRE)**[61] 2382 5-9-2 **51**..................(t[1]) DylanHogan(5) 10 26
(W J Martin, Ire) *trckd ldrs: rdn 3f out: sn btn (trainer said gelding was unsuited by the track)* **16/1**

0504 **10** *3½* **Sellingallthetime (IRE)**[18] 3834 8-8-11 **48**..................(v) EllieMacKenzie(7) 8 17
(Mark Usher) *dwlt: bhd: hdwy to trck ldrs over 6f out: rdn 3f out: wknd 2f out* **9/1**

000- **11** *hd* **Eben Dubai (IRE)**[275] 7834 7-9-1 **45**..................(p) RossaRyan 6 14
(John Flint) *mid-div: rdn over 3f out: wknd 2f out* **33/1**

000- **12** *3¾* **Celtic Classic (IRE)**[188] 9725 3-8-6 **48**..................(p[1]) CharlieBennett 13 12
(Paul Cole) *trckd ldrs for 3f: grad lost pl: bhd fnl 2f* **14/1**

0000 **13** *2* **Phobos**[34] 3252 4-9-1 **45**.................. HayleyTurner 7 4
(Michael Blanshard) *a towards rr* **50/1**

2m 29.27s (-1.53) **Going Correction** -0.175s/f (Firm)
WFA 3 from 4yo+ 12lb **13 Ran SP% 123.2**
Speed ratings (Par 101): **98,94,92,92,92 86,85,83,82,80 80,77,76**
CSF £8.59 CT £62.79 TOTE £4.00: £3.20, £1.30, £4.80; EX 8.60 Trifecta £84.50.
Owner West Buckland Bloodstock Ltd **Bred** Hunscote Stud **Trained** West Buckland, Somerset

FOCUS
A moderate middle-distance handicap. The winner confirmed her Brighton level.

4499 P & N PROPERTY SOLUTIONS FILLIES' H'CAP 1m 2f 37y

8:40 (8:41) (Class 6) (0-65,65) 3-Y-0+

£2,781 (£827; £413; £300; £300; £300) Stalls Low

Form RPR

0-41 **1** **Sadlers Beach (IRE)**[40] 3034 3-8-12 **54**..................(h) HayleyTurner 7 66+
(Marcus Tregoning) *trckd ldrs: chal over 2f out: sn rdn: kpt on to ld ins fnl f: rdn out* **15/8**[1]

6-60 **2** *nk* **Perfect Grace**[137] 761 3-9-4 **60**.................. HollieDoyle 3 71+
(Archie Watson) *trckd ldr: led over 2f out: sn rdn and strly chal: kpt on: hdd towards fin* **12/1**

0-04 **3** *3½* **Whimsical Dream**[152] 532 3-8-5 **47**.................. KieranO'Neill 6 51
(Michael Bell) *trckd ldrs: rdn over 2f out: sn chsng ldng pair: kpt on same pce fnl f* **16/1**

0-05 **4** *4* **Delirium (IRE)**[7] 4232 5-9-7 **53**..................(p) PatCosgrave 4 49
(Ed de Giles) *untidily away: towards rr: hdwy over 2f out: rdn to press for 4th over 1f out: kpt on same pce fnl f* **9/2**[3]

3101 **5** *1* **Couldn't Could She**[8] 4215 4-9-12 **65** 5ex.................. TobyEley(7) 2 59
(Adam West) *in tch: tk clsr order over 2f out: sn rdn in 4th: nt pce to chal: no ex fnl 120yds (jockey said filly was unsuited by the going and would prefer an easier surface)* **5/1**

6100 **6** *3¼* **Brockagh Cailin**[7] 4235 4-9-13 **59**.................. JosephineGordon 5 47
(J S Moore) *hld up in last pair: hdwy over 2f out: sn rdn: wknd ent fnl f* **16/1**

6300 **7** *2¼* **Vanity Vanity (USA)**[6] 4287 4-9-7 **58**.................. ScottMcCullagh(5) 8 41
(Denis Coakley) *hld up: rdn and hdwy over 2f out: nvr threatened: wknd over 1f out* **20/1**

0-25 **8** 2 ¾ **Cwynar**[25] 3572 4-9-13 **59**.......................... RichardKingscote 1 37
(Rebecca Curtis) *led tl rdn over 2f out: sn wknd* **4/1**[2]

2m 8.27s (-2.83) **Going Correction** -0.175s/f (Firm)
WFA 3 from 4yo+ 10lb **8** Ran SP% **113.9**
Speed ratings (Par 98): **104,103,100,97,96 94,92,90**
CSF £26.33 CT £276.39 TOTE £2.80: £1.10, £2.60, £5.60; EX 30.90 Trifecta £183.50.
Owner R Kingston **Bred** Ken Carroll **Trained** Whitsbury, Hants

FOCUS
A modest fillies' handicap. The favourite refused to be denied on the quick ground close home.

4500 BRAKES CLASSIFIED STKS 5f 10y

9:10 (9:10) (Class 6) 3-Y-0+

£3,428 (£1,020; £509; £300; £300; £300) **Stalls** Centre

Form RPR

4524 **1** **Toolatetodelegate**[8] 4219 5-9-5 47..........(tp) TrevorWhelan 2 55
(Brian Barr) *hld up: hdwy over 2f out: led ent fnl f: r.o wl: rdn out* **2/1**[1]

503 **2** 1 ½ **Sweet Forgetme Not (IRE)**[9] 4183 3-9-0 47......(bt) JosephineGordon 7 48
(Samuel Farrell, Ire) *in tch: pushed along over 2f out: hdwy over 1f out: r.o wl fnl f: wnt 2nd cl home* **5/1**[3]

0306 **3** ¾ **Camanche Grey (IRE)**[1] 4478 8-8-12 47.................... VictorSantos(7) 5 47
(Lucinda Egerton) *led: rdn over 2f out: hdd ent fnl f: no ex* **8/1**

-303 **4** 2 ¼ **Cool Strutter (IRE)**[8] 4219 7-9-5 49.........................(p) LiamKeniry 6 39
(John Spearing) *prom: rdn over 2f out: ev ch over 1f out: no ex ent fnl f* **5/1**[3]

0555 **5** 4 ½ **Ar Saoirse**[15] 3961 4-9-5 47.......................................(b) RichardKingscote 4 23
(Clare Hobson) *trckd ldrs: rdn over 2f out: wknd ent fnl f* **3/1**[2]

/00- **6** 4 ½ **Regal Miss**[475] 1211 7-9-5 44.. CharlieBennett 9 7
(Patrick Chamings) *trckd ldrs: squeezed up over 2f out: rdn over 1f out: wknd ent fnl f* **33/1**

3000 **7** 10 **Swendab (IRE)**[9] 4182 11-8-12 46..................................(b) KateLeahy(7) 8
(John O'Shea) *a towards rr* **20/1**

5060 **8** 2 ¼ **Shackled N Drawn (USA)**[83] 1716 7-9-5 48.................(vt) LiamJones 3 +
(Peter Hedger) *slowly away: racd in last pair: hdwy over 2f out: sn rdn: wknd ent fnl f (jockey said gelding was slowly away)* **20/1**

1m 1.52s (-0.48) **Going Correction** -0.175s/f (Firm)
WFA 3 from 4yo+ 5lb **8** Ran SP% **115.2**
Speed ratings (Par 101): **96,93,92,88,81 74,58,54**
CSF £12.16 TOTE £3.60: £1.60, £1.40, £2.10; EX 11.70 Trifecta £64.70.
Owner Brian Barr Racing Club **Bred** D R Tucker **Trained** Longburton, Dorset

FOCUS
A moderate classified stakes. The strong favourite burst between rivals over 1f out to win well.
T/Plt: £248.50 to a £1 stake. Pool: £70,112.34. 205.89 winning units. T/Qpdt: £17.20 to a £1 stake. Pool: £7,561.59. 324.47 winning units. **Tim Mitchell**

4244 KEMPTON (A.W) (R-H)

Wednesday, July 3

OFFICIAL GOING: Polytrack: standard to slow
Wind: Quite fresh, across (towards stands) Weather: Sunny, warm

4501 JOCKEY CLUB SUPPORTING RACING STAFF WEEK APPRENTICE H'CAP 6f (P)

5:50 (5:51) (Class 5) (0-70,71) 4-Y-0+

£3,752 (£1,116; £557; £300; £300; £300) **Stalls** Low

Form RPR

-420 **1** **Soar Above**[42] 2971 4-9-9 **67**..........................(p) DarraghKeenan 4 80
(John Butler) *trckd ldng trio gng wl: clsd to ld wl over 1f out: sn clr: rdn out* **5/2**[1]

0440 **2** 2 ¾ **Grey Galleon (USA)**[18] 3838 5-9-8 **71**..................(p) AmeliaGlass(5) 6 75+
(Clive Cox) *sn outpcd in rr gp: brought v wd in st and ended against nr side rail: styd on fr 2f out: tk 2nd last 75yds: no ch w wnr (jockey said gelding hung right)* **3/1**[2]

4551 **3** ½ **Perfect Symphony (IRE)**[37] 3143 5-9-0 **63**............(p) IsobelFrancis(5) 7 66
(Mark Pattinson) *chsd clr ldng quartet and sn clr of rest: prog on inner 2f out: chsd clr wnr jst ins fnl f: no imp and lost 2nd last 75yds* **12/1**

000 **4** hd **Hollander**[53] 2286 5-8-11 **55**..........................(t[1]) SebastianWoods 8 57
(Alexandra Dunn) *sn outpcd in rr gp: drvn and hung lft towards nr side over 2f out: styd on after: pressed for a pl nr fin* **20/1**

0605 **5** 2 **Elusif (IRE)**[9] 4195 4-8-9 **58**.................................... GavinAshton(5) 1 54
(Shaun Keightley) *sn outpcd in rr gp: clsd over 2f out: ch of a pl 1f out: one pce after* **4/1**[3]

00-0 **6** 5 **Jonnysimpson (IRE)**[84] 1682 4-8-7 **54**........................ GeorgiaDobie(3) 5 34
(Lee Carter) *awkward s: sn outpcd in rr gp: passed wkng rivals fnl f but nvr a factor* **50/1**

3021 **7** ½ **Brogans Bay (IRE)**[13] 4027 4-8-7 **56**........................ LeviWilliams(5) 2 34
(Simon Dow) *t.k.h: trckd ldng pair: led briefly 2f out: sn no ch w wnr: lost 2nd and wknd qckly jst ins fnl f* **10/1**

0000 **8** 1 **Black Truffle (FR)**[14] 3989 9-8-0 **51** oh6...................(p) EllaBoardman(7) 9 26
(Mark Usher) *sn outpcd in rr gp: nvr a factor* **80/1**

21/0 **9** ¾ **Gustavo Fring (IRE)**[37] 3147 5-9-7 **70**........................ SeanKirrane(5) 12 42
(Richard Spencer) *spd fr wd draw to press ldr: rdn over 2f out: wknd qckly over 1f out (vet said gelding had laceration to right hind)* **10/1**

4330 **10** 2 **Catapult**[21] 3738 4-8-0 **51**.......................................(p) MorganCole(7) 3 17
(Shaun Keightley) *led to 2f out: wknd rapidly* **8/1**

60-0 **11** 7 **Dutiful Son (IRE)**[42] 2971 9-9-4 **65**........................ WilliamCarver(3) 10 9
(Emma Owen) *sn outpcd in rr gp: wknd over 2f out* **66/1**

1m 12.37s (-0.73) **Going Correction** 0.0s/f (Stan) **11** Ran SP% **120.0**
Speed ratings (Par 103): **104,100,99,99,96 90,89,88,87,84 75**
CSF £10.02 CT £76.75 TOTE £3.10: £1.20, £1.40, £2.90; EX 11.50 Trifecta £87.40.
Owner J Butler **Bred** Cheveley Park Stud Ltd **Trained** Newmarket, Suffolk

FOCUS
A warm summer's evening and the Polytrack had been watered. It was officially given as standard to slow. A good pace to this modest apprentice handicap. The third has been rated close to his Chelmsford latest.

4502 BRITISH STALLION STUDS EBF FILLIES' NOVICE STKS (PLUS 10 RACE) 7f (P)

6:20 (6:27) (Class 5) 2-Y-0

£3,881 (£1,155; £577; £288) **Stalls** Low

Form RPR

1 **Cressida** 2-9-0 0.. RobertHavlin 6 82+
(John Gosden) *dwlt: t.k.h early: rn green but chsd ldng quartet: pushed along and clsd qckly to ld wl over 1f out: more than a l ahd ins fnl f: ld dwindled nr fin but a in charge* **9/2**

2 nk **Wasaayef (IRE)** 2-9-0 0.. DaneO'Neill 4 82+
(John Gosden) *trckd ldng pair: shkn up over 2f out: chsd wnr over 1f out: styd on but no imp tl clsd fnl 75yds: a hld* **3/1**[3]

03 **3** 5 **Banmi (IRE)**[14] 3990 2-8-9 0.................................. SeamusCronin(5) 5 68
(Mohamed Moubarak) *trckd ldng pair: pushed along over 2f out: sn outpcd: no ch after but kpt on to take modest 3rd ins fnl f* **14/1**

02 **4** nk **Willa**[8] 4223 2-9-0 0.. PatDobbs 3 67
(Richard Hannon) *pressed ldr: shkn up and nt qckn over 2f out: sn lost pl and outpcd: one pce after* **2/1**[1]

5 ½ **Dramatista (IRE)** 2-9-0 0.. LukeMorris 1 66
(Archie Watson) *led: rdn over 2f out: hdd wl over 1f out and sn outpcd: n.d after* **11/4**[2]

6 12 **Divine Connection** 2-9-0 0.. RobHornby 2 33+
(Jonathan Portman) *restless stalls: slowly away: a bhd: t.o (jockey said filly ran green)* **16/1**

55 **7** 6 **Ride And Prejudice**[58] 2469 2-8-7 0.............................. SeanKirrane(7) 8 17
(Julia Feilden) *unruly and reluctant to enter stall: in tch on outer 3f: sn bhd: t.o (starter reported that the filly was reluctant to enter stalls; trainer was informed hat the filly could not run until the day after passing a stalls test)* **125/1**

0 **8** 3 ¾ **Lily Bonnette**[48] 2761 2-8-9 0.................................... SophieRalston(5) 7
(Julia Feilden) *a bhd: t.o* **125/1**

1m 26.48s (0.48) **Going Correction** 0.0s/f (Stan) **8** Ran SP% **117.3**
Speed ratings (Par 91): **97,96,90,90,90 76,69,65**
CSF £18.97 TOTE £5.70: £1.40, £1.20, £3.20; EX 17.70 Trifecta £119.70.

Owner K Abdullah **Bred** Juddmonte Farms Ltd **Trained** Newmarket, Suffolk

FOCUS
Three smart fillies' have taken this race, Urban Fox (peak RPR of 115) in 2016, 1000 Guineas winner Billesdon Brook (115) in 2017 and Look Around (99) in 2018. This didn't look competitive, they were down at the start for a while and it was an eventual John Gosden one-two. The opening level is fluid.

4503 100% PROFIT BOOST AT 32REDSPORT.COM FILLIES' NOVICE STKS 1m 3f 219y(P)

6:50 (6:52) (Class 3) 3-Y-0+

£9,703 (£2,887; £1,443; £721) **Stalls** Low

Form RPR

2 **1** **Illumined (IRE)**[58] 2481 3-9-0 0.................................. RobertHavlin 2 80
(John Gosden) *mde all: pushed along and drew clr over 2f out: rdn out fnl f* **4/6**[1]

0 **2** 6 **Rewrite The Stars (IRE)**[44] 2919 3-9-0 0........................ JamieSpencer 1 70
(James Tate) *trckd ldng pair: shkn up to chse wnr over 3f out: rn green after and no imp but clr of rest fnl 2f* **16/1**[3]

61 **3** 5 **Hereby (IRE)**[19] 3802 3-9-6 0...................................... HarryBentley 5 68
(Ralph Beckett) *trckd wnr: rdn and lost pl qckly over 3f out: toiling u.p over 2f out: plugged on to take 3rd ins fnl f* **9/4**[2]

0 **4** 1 ¾ **Persepone**[61] 2361 3-9-0 0.. OisinMurphy 7 60
(Hugo Palmer) *s.s: rcvrd to chse ldng trio: wnt 3rd over 3f out: outpcd by ldng pair sn after: wknd ins fnl f* **16/1**[3]

5 ¾ **Pensee** 3-9-0 0.. JasonWatson 4 58
(Roger Charlton) *t.k.h: a in last trio: pushed along 5f out: struggling after but plugged on fnl 2f* **20/1**

0 **6** 1 **Giving Back**[27] 3495 5-9-12 0...................................... TomQueally 6 56
(Alan King) *hld up in last: no ch fr 3f out: pushed along and kpt on one pce fnl 2f* **66/1**

0/0 **7** 20 **Bird To Love**[23] 3664 5-9-12 0...................................... RyanTate 3 24
(Mark Usher) *dwlt: a in rr: wknd 2f out: t.o* **200/1**

2m 33.9s (-0.60) **Going Correction** 0.0s/f (Stan)
WFA 3 from 5yo 12lb **7** Ran SP% **109.3**
Speed ratings (Par 104): **102,98,94,93,93 92,79**
CSF £12.32 TOTE £1.70: £1.30, £3.90; EX 11.10 Trifecta £19.80.

Owner George Strawbridge **Bred** Forenaghts Stud & Tinnakill Bloodstock **Trained** Newmarket, Suffolk

FOCUS
The market had this pegged as a two-horse race, but the winner proved much the best. The level is a bit fluid, but the third has been rated below her Goodwood form.

4504 32RED H'CAP 1m 3f 219y(P)

7:20 (7:22) (Class 3) (0-95,94) 4-Y-0+

£9,337 (£2,796; £1,398; £699; £349; £175) **Stalls** Low

Form RPR

/11- **1** **Deja (FR)**[254] 8476 4-9-6 **93**...................................... AndreaAtzeni 3 106+
(Peter Chapple-Hyam) *t.k.h and sn hld up: pushed along 4f out: rdn and clsd on ldrs 2f out: sustained effrt to ld 1f out: styd on wl and drew clr* **5/1**[2]

-511 **2** 3 ½ **Soto Sizzler**[32] 3346 4-9-5 **92**...................................... OisinMurphy 4 99
(William Knight) *pushed along early: chsd ldr 3f: styd in tch: rdn and prog to ld wl over 1f out: hdd 1f out: no ex and lft bhd by wnr after* **1/1**[1]

2550 **3** 2 ¾ **Al Hamdany (IRE)**[28] 3466 5-9-7 **94**.............................. DavidEgan 2 97
(Marco Botti) *hld up in last trio: pushed along 4f out: prog between rivals to chal 2f out: on terms over 1f out: fdd fnl f* **10/1**

0-40 **4** 3 **Highbrow**[14] 3992 4-9-6 **93**.. JamieSpencer 6 91
(David Simcock) *hld up in last: drvn 2f out: tk 4th over 1f out but nt on terms: no imp after* **8/1**

4-10 **5** 3 ¼ **Point In Time (IRE)**[18] 3861 4-8-3 **76**.......................... NicolaCurrie 5 69
(Mark Usher) *t.k.h: prog to chse ldr after 3f to over 2f out: sn btn* **20/1**

121 **6** 4 **Lawn Ranger**[30] 3424 4-9-2 **89**...................................... KierenFox 7 75
(Michael Attwater) *led at gd pce: drvn and hdd wl over 1f out: immediately wknd (jockey said gelding stopped quickly)* **16/1**

1130 **7** 27 **El Ghazwani (IRE)**[13] 4021 4-9-5 **92**........................(t) JamesDoyle 1 35
(Hugo Palmer) *t.k.h: trckd ldrs: rdn to dispute 2nd briefly over 2f out: sn wknd rapidly: eased and t.o (jockey said gelding stopped quickly)* **7/1**[3]

2m 31.17s (-3.33) **Going Correction** 0.0s/f (Stan) **7** Ran SP% **110.0**
Speed ratings (Par 107): **111,108,106,104,102 100,82**
CSF £9.60 TOTE £3.70: £1.90, £1.80; EX 11.70 Trifecta £67.10.

Owner Phoenix Thoroughbred Limited **Bred** Laurent Dulong & Yannick Dulong **Trained** Newmarket, Suffolk

FOCUS
Just a small field but the majority had recent winning form, the time was good and it looked an up-to-scratch class 3.

4505 32RED ON THE APP STORE H'CAP — 1m 7f 218y(P)
7:50 (7:52) (Class 3) (0-90,91) 4-Y-O+

£9,337 (£2,796; £1,398; £699; £349; £175) **Stalls** Low

Form				RPR
0-00	**1**		**Artarmon (IRE)**[47] 2801 4-9-4 **85**..................(v) StevieDonohoe 1	94
			(Michael Bell) *trckd ldng pair: rdn and clsd to ld 2f out: clr fnl f: styd on wl (trainer said, regarding the improved form shown, the gelding benefited from the reapplication of visors)* **28/1**
-100	**2**	*3*	**Al Kout**[18] 3847 5-9-5 **86**.................. DavidEgan 3	91
			(Heather Main) *led: rdn and hdd 2f out: outpcd by wnr over 1f out and dropped to 3rd: kpt on to take 2nd again last strides* **14/1**
0-04	**3**	*nk*	**Master Archer (IRE)**[24] 3635 5-9-7 **88**..................(v) DavidProbert 6	92
			(James Fanshawe) *hld up in last trio: prog on inner over 2f out: drvn to chse wnr jst over 1f out: no imp: lost 2nd last strides* **8/1**
5313	**4**	*3/4*	**Sassie (IRE)**[23] 3653 4-8-13 **80**.................. OisinMurphy 9	83+
			(Sylvester Kirk) *hld up in last trio: stl there jst over 2f out: taken to outer and prog over 1f out: kpt on but nvr cl enough to chal* **7/2**[2]
2	**5**	*2*	**Superb Story (IRE)**[28] 3467 8-9-1 **82**.................. JamieSpencer 8	83+
			(Harry Fry) *stdd s and hld up in last: stl there over 2f out: taken wd and drvn sn after: plugged on to take 5th last 100yds: no hope of being a threat* **13/8**[1]
1631	**6**	*1 1/4*	**Seinesational**[18] 3861 4-9-0 **81**..................(v) JasonWatson 4	81
			(William Knight) *t.k.h: trckd ldrs: rdn and hanging over 2f out: sn outpcd by ldrs: n.d after* **11/2**[3]
0/4-	**7**	*1 1/4*	**Talent To Amuse (IRE)**[54] 6190 6-8-10 **77**..................(vt[1]) RobertHavlin 2	75
			(Emma Lavelle) *dwlt: tended to run in snatches: towards rr: effrt over 2f out: sn no prog and btn* **50/1**
-610	**8**	*5*	**Cayirli (FR)**[74] 1943 7-9-10 **91**.................. FergusSweeney 7	83
			(Seamus Durack) *hld up towards rr: rdn and briefly clsd on ldrs over 2f out: sn wknd* **16/1**
22-0	**9**	*15*	**Maquisard (FR)**[24] 3635 7-9-5 **86**.................. CharlesBishop 5	60
			(Chris Gordon) *racd wd: in tch: rdn and wknd over 3f out: t.o* **25/1**
3-23	**10**	*1/2*	**Mandalayan (IRE)**[62] 2342 4-9-5 **86**.................. RobHornby 10	59
			(Jonathan Portman) *pressed ldr tl wknd rapidly over 2f out: t.o* **10/1**

3m 27.32s (-2.78) **Going Correction** 0.0s/f (Stan) **10 Ran SP% 117.7**
Speed ratings (Par 107): **106,104,104,103,102 102,101,99,91,91**
CSF £369.43 CT £3416.49 TOTE £42.30: £8.80, £2.30, £2.40; EX 383.40 Trifecta £2079.30.
Owner OTI Racing 1 **Bred** Glenvale Stud & Edgeridge Ltd **Trained** Newmarket, Suffolk

FOCUS
Decent staying form, although it looked a marked advantage to race prominently and there was a shock winner. Muddling form, but it's been rated around the second, with the winner back to his best.

4506 32RED CASINO H'CAP (LONDON MILE SERIES QUALIFIER) — 1m (P)
8:20 (8:22) (Class 4) (0-80,82) 3-Y-O+

£6,469 (£1,925; £962; £481; £300; £300) **Stalls** Low

Form				RPR
-404	**1**		**Harbour Spirit (FR)**[27] 3526 3-9-3 **78**.................. ShaneKelly 5	87
			(Richard Hughes) *hld up in midfield: hanging whn asked for effrt over 2f out: picked up over 1f out and gd prog to ld jst ins fnl f: sn rdn clr* **10/1**
3043	**2**	*2 3/4*	**Tamerlane (IRE)**[13] 4028 4-9-2 **68**..................(vt) HectorCrouch 7	73
			(Clive Cox) *s.s: hld up in last pair: rdn and prog on outer 2f out: styd on fnl f to take 2nd last strides: no ch w wnr* **7/1**[3]
0102	**3**	*1*	**Directory**[7] 4249 4-9-12 **78**.................. RyanTate 10	81
			(James Eustace) *sn led: rdn 2f out: edgd rt to rail over 1f out: hdd and outpcd jst ins fnl f: lost 2nd last strides* **7/2**[1]
3-60	**4**	*3/4*	**Mazyoun**[34] 3268 5-9-11 **82**..................(v) SebastianWoods(5) 2	83
			(Hugo Palmer) *hld up in rr: shkn up over 2f out: trying to make prog whn nt clr run briefly over 1f out: styd on fnl f: nvr able to threaten* **5/1**[2]
4056	**5**	*1*	**Letsbe Avenue (IRE)**[16] 3944 4-9-2 **75**.................. LukeCatton(7) 8	77+
			(Richard Hannon) *cl up: chsd ldr 2f out: trying to chal against rail whn hmpd jst over 1f out: lost pl and nt rcvr (jockey said gelding was denied a clear run)* **18/1**
430-	**6**	*1/2*	**Wingreen (IRE)**[277] 7776 3-9-1 **76**.................. HarryBentley 12	72
			(Ralph Beckett) *mostly chsd ldr to 2f out: wknd jst over 1f out* **12/1**
-004	**7**	*1 3/4*	**Plunger**[16] 3944 4-10-0 **80**..................(b) RaulDaSilva 3	76+
			(Paul Cole) *broke wl but restrained into midfield and t.k.h: effrt over 2f out: no great prog and wl hld whn hmpd jst ins fnl f* **11/1**
53-0	**8**	*5*	**Sing Out Loud (IRE)**[19] 3806 4-10-1 **81**..................(p[1]) CharlesBishop 11	63
			(Chris Gordon) *prom tl wknd 2f out* **33/1**
-101	**9**	*1*	**La Maquina**[40] 3040 4-10-2 **82**..................(t) NicolaCurrie 1	87+
			(George Baker) *hld up in last: sme prog on inner over 1f out: keeping on but no ch of winning whn nt clr run and then bdly hmpd 100yds out: eased* **7/2**[1]
0100	**10**	*8*	**Love Your Work (IRE)**[6] 4306 3-9-2 **77**..................(b) JasonWatson 6	36
			(Adam West) *awkward s and slowly away: t.k.h: prog on outer fr rr 5f out to press ldrs over 3f out: wknd rapidly over 2f out: t.o (jockey said gelding lost its action and hung right)* **10/1**

1m 39.14s (-0.66) **Going Correction** 0.0s/f (Stan)
WFA 3 from 4yo+ 9lb **10 Ran SP% 116.0**
Speed ratings (Par 105): **103,100,99,98,97 97,95,90,89,81**
CSF £77.80 CT £296.74 TOTE £11.90: £3.10, £3.70, £1.40; EX 90.90 Trifecta £202.10.
Owner The Heffer Syndicate **Bred** S A R L Haras D'Etreham Et Al **Trained** Upper Lambourn, Berks
■ Stewards' Enquiry : Luke Catton seven-day ban: interference & careless riding (Jul 17-23)

FOCUS
A typically wide-open London Mile qualifier but there wasn't much pace and it got very messy in the straight. It's been rated around the second to his recent form.

4507 32RED.COM H'CAP (JOCKEY CLUB GRASSROOTS FLAT SPRINT SERIES QUALIFIER) — 6f (P)
8:50 (8:51) (Class 5) (0-75,77) 3-Y-O

£3,752 (£1,116; £557; £300; £300; £300) **Stalls** Low

Form				RPR
45-0	**1**		**Mendoza (IRE)**[33] 3302 3-9-5 **73**..................(h) RyanTate 8	78
			(James Eustace) *trckd ldr: rdn to chal 2f out: led jst over 1f out: hrd pressed fnl f: drvn and hld on wl* **33/1**
0614	**2**	*nk*	**Di Matteo**[30] 3427 3-9-0 **68**.................. ShaneKelly 1	72
			(Marco Botti) *trckd ldrs: prog over 1f out: drvn to chal fnl f: upsides 100yds out: nt qckn nr fin* **6/1**[3]
4013	**3**	*1 3/4*	**Stallone (IRE)**[17] 3887 3-9-2 **70**..................(v) HarryBentley 4	68
			(Richard Spencer) *dwlt then hmpd s: racd in last pair and pushed along fr 1/2-way: drvn and prog over 1f out: styd on wl to take 3rd last 75yds* **11/2**[2]
4-00	**4**	*1 1/4*	**Excelled (IRE)**[40] 3048 3-9-9 **77**.................. DanielMuscutt 6	71
			(James Fanshawe) *hld up towards rr: rdn on outer 2f out: styd on over 1f out to take 4th nr fin: n.d* **13/2**
1105	**5**	*1/2*	**Solar Park (IRE)**[71] 2024 3-9-8 **76**.................. OisinMurphy 9	69
			(James Tate) *led: tried to go for home 2f out: hdd and fdd jst over 1f out* **8/1**
0-30	**6**	*nk*	**Abanica**[49] 2730 3-8-11 **65**..................(b[1]) PatDobbs 5	57
			(Amanda Perrett) *hld up in midfield: pushed along 2f out: no imp on ldrs whn rdn fnl f* **20/1**
0232	**7**	*1 1/2*	**Journey Of Life**[9] 4193 3-9-4 **72**.................. JasonWatson 7	59
			(Gary Moore) *t.k.h: trapped out wd in midfield: shkn up over 2f out: no prog over 1f out: wknd (jockey said gelding hung left early stages)* **5/1**[1]
-025	**8**	*1/2*	**Molaaheth**[14] 4010 3-9-3 **71**..................(t) DaneO'Neill 10	58
			(Richard Hannon) *trckd ldrs: shkn up over 2f out: nt qckn over 1f out: wknd fnl f* **16/1**
32-5	**9**	*1 3/4*	**Evolutionary (IRE)**[72] 1985 3-9-2 **70**.................. JamieSpencer 3	50
			(James Tate) *heavily restrained s and hld up in last: drvn 2f out: nvr any prog (jockey said filly jumped awkwardly from stalls)* **11/2**[2]
10-6	**10**	*2 3/4*	**Lively Lydia**[43] 2937 3-9-5 **73**..................(v[1]) CharlesBishop 2	44
			(Eve Johnson Houghton) *nvr bttr than midfield: rdn 2f out: fnd nil wl over 1f out: wknd* **5/1**[1]

1m 13.2s (0.10) **Going Correction** 0.0s/f (Stan) **10 Ran SP% 116.4**
Speed ratings (Par 100): **99,98,96,94,93 93,91,90,88,84**
CSF £220.15 CT £1304.50 TOTE £33.80: £6.50, £1.40, £2.00; EX 437.70 Trifecta £2291.00.
Owner The MacDougall Two **Bred** Gortskagh House Stud & Tally Ho Stud **Trained** Newmarket, Suffolk

FOCUS
An ordinary sprint for 3yos. The winner has been rated back to his 2yo form, and the second to form.
T/Plt: £127.40 to a £1 stake. Pool: £62,310.47. 356.89 winning units. T/Qpdt: £30.20 to a £1 stake. Pool: £7,293.10. 178.26 winning units. **Jonathan Neesom**

3355 MUSSELBURGH (R-H)
Wednesday, July 3

OFFICIAL GOING: Good to firm (9.6)
Wind: Breezy, half against in sprints and in approximately 4f of home straight in races on the round cours Weather: Fine, dry

4508 REWARDING OWNERSHIP WITH THE RACEHORSE OWNERS ASSOCIATION H'CAP — 5f 1y
2:00 (2:02) (Class 6) (0-60,61) 3-Y-O

£2,911 (£866; £432; £300; £300; £300) **Stalls** High

Form				RPR
0-05	**1**		**Alisia R (IRE)**[36] 3191 3-8-0 **46** oh1.................. IzzyClifton(7) 10	49+
			(Les Eyre) *sn bhd: hdwy over 1f out: hung rt and led ins fnl f: kpt on wl towards fin (trainers' rep said, regards apparent improvement in form, filly benefitted from the drop back in trip)* **25/1**
2-30	**2**	*nk*	**Jungle Secret (IRE)**[11] 4129 3-9-2 **55**..................(h[1]) TonyHamilton 9	57
			(Richard Fahey) *unruly bef s: t.k.h: sn trcking ldrs: effrt over 1f out: rdn and pressed wnr ins fnl f: r.o* **8/1**
5536	**3**	*1 1/4*	**Amazing Alba**[6] 4276 3-9-8 **61**..................(h) KevinStott 5	58
			(Alistair Whillans) *pressed ldr: effrt and ev ch over 1f out: led briefly ins fnl f: sn one pce* **5/1**
0206	**4**	*nk*	**Brahma Kamal**[30] 3417 3-8-7 **46** oh1.................. ShaneGray 7	42
			(Keith Dalgleish) *led: rdn and hrd pressed over 1f out: hdd ins fnl f: no ex* **4/1**[3]
6540	**5**	*2 1/4*	**Newgate Angel**[8] 4212 3-8-5 **47**..................(p) SeanDavis(3) 1	35
			(Tony Coyle) *bhd: pushed along over 2f out: hdwy over 1f out: no imp fnl f* **10/1**
430	**6**	*1 1/2*	**Raksha (IRE)**[11] 4129 3-9-7 **60**.................. DavidNolan 8	43
			(David O'Meara) *trckd ldrs: rdn along over 1f out: wknd ins fnl f* **11/4**[1]
4-00	**7**	*6*	**Lady Kinsale**[30] 3417 3-8-7 **46** oh1.................. RachelRichardson 2	7
			(Eric Alston) *dwlt and blkd s: hld up: hdwy on outside and prom 1/2-way: rdn and wknd fnl f* **40/1**
345-	**8**	*nk*	**Haighfield**[196] 9612 3-9-7 **60**.................. GrahamLee 4	20
			(Paul Midgley) *wnt rt s: in tch: rdn: hung rt and wknd over 1f out (jockey said filly hung right-handed throughout)* **7/2**[2]
5400	**9**	*1 3/4*	**Swiss Chime**[27] 3508 3-8-8 **52**.................. HarrisonShaw(5) 6	6
			(Alan Berry) *bhd: drvn and struggling 1/2-way: nvr on terms* **40/1**

59.84s (0.14) **Going Correction** -0.05s/f (Good) **9 Ran SP% 114.5**
Speed ratings (Par 98): **96,95,93,93,89 87,77,76,74**
CSF £206.63 CT £1176.35 TOTE £25.30: £6.10, £1.90, £2.10; EX 180.30 Trifecta £1159.30.
Owner M Rozenbroek **Bred** M J Rozenbroek **Trained** Catwick, N Yorks

FOCUS
The official distances were as advertised. There was a false rail on the stands' rail from the dog leg (3f) to 1m 1/2f then a drop in. The opener was a moderate sprint. The second has been rated as improving a fraction.

4509 ROA BRITISH STALLION STUDS EBF NOVICE MEDIAN AUCTION STKS — 5f 1y
2:30 (2:32) (Class 5) 2-Y-O

£3,557 (£1,058; £529; £264) **Stalls** High

Form				RPR
10	**1**		**Bill Neigh**[14] 3988 2-9-9 0.................. CamHardie 6	84+
			(John Ryan) *trckd ldrs: effrt and rdn over 1f out: kpt on wl fnl f to ld cl home* **13/8**[2]
20	**2**	*nse*	**Ventura Flame (IRE)**[14] 3983 2-8-11 0.................. ShaneGray 3	72
			(Keith Dalgleish) *led: rdn over 1f out: rdr dropped rt-side rein ins fnl f: kpt on wl: hdd cl home* **1/1**[1]
5	**3**	*2 1/4*	**Arriba Arriba (IRE)**[28] 3477 2-9-2 0.................. GrahamLee 1	69
			(Rebecca Menzies) *pressed ldr: drvn along over 1f out: edgd rt and outpcd ins fnl f* **20/1**
4	*1*	**Lady Celia** 2-8-11 0.................. TonyHamilton 4	60
			(Richard Fahey) *dwlt: hld up in last pl: stdy hdwy over 2f out: effrt and hung rt over 1f out: outpcd ins fnl f* **10/1**[3]
4	**5**	*2 1/4*	**Time Force (IRE)**[5] 4344 2-9-2 0.................. CliffordLee 5	57
			(K R Burke) *dwlt: sn prom: effrt and rdn over 1f out: wknd ins fnl f* **11/1**

1m 0.02s (0.32) **Going Correction** -0.05s/f (Good) **5 Ran SP% 110.3**
Speed ratings (Par 94): **95,94,91,89,86**
CSF £3.60 TOTE £2.40: £1.10, £1.40; EX 3.70 Trifecta £14.20.
Owner Gerry McGladery **Bred** Selwood Bloodstock Ltd **Trained** Newmarket, Suffolk

FOCUS
A small field but a really tight finish. It's been rated around the second to her debut effort.

4510 ROA OWNERS JACKPOT H'CAP 1m 7f 217y
3:00 (3:01) (Class 6) (0-60,60) 4-Y-O+

£3,428 (£1,020; £509; £300; £300; £300) **Stalls** High

Form RPR

133- **1** **Lever Du Soleil (FR)**[72] 4602 4-9-1 **54** CliffordLee 10 62+
(Gavin Cromwell, Ire) *in tch: stdy hdwy 3f out: led and hung rt over 1f out: drvn out fnl f* **5/6**[1]

-026 **2** *2 ½* **Urban Spirit (IRE)**[51] 2695 5-9-2 **55** ShaneGray 12 59
(Karen McLintock) *chsd ldr: led over 3f out: rdn and hdd whn blkd over 1f out: kpt on same pce ins fnl f* **8/1**[2]

2323 **3** *1 ½* **Siyahamba (IRE)**[36] 3205 5-8-7 **46** (p[1]) CamHardie 11 48
(Bryan Smart) *t.k.h: trckd ldrs: effrt and rdn over 2f out: hung rt over 1f out: kpt on same pce fnl f* **11/1**[3]

3030 **4** *¾* **Elite Icon**[21] 3718 5-8-10 **49** (v) PhilDennis 8 50
(Jim Goldie) *in tch: effrt and drvn along over 2f out: kpt on same pce fr over 1f out: lost hind shoe (vet said gelding lost it's right hind shoe)* **25/1**

3000 **5** *nk* **Tomorrow's Angel**[12] 4056 4-9-7 **60** (vt) JamieGormley 14 61
(Iain Jardine) *t.k.h: hld up on outside: effrt over 2f out: rdn and edgd rt over 1f out: no imp fnl f* **33/1**

25-5 **6** *1* **Kitty's Cove**[34] 3251 4-8-9 **48** DavidAllan 2 49
(Tim Easterby) *t.k.h: hld up in midfield: effrt whn nt clr run briefly over 2f out: no imp over 1f out* **25/1**

4-00 **7** *2* **Bogardus (IRE)**[40] 3046 8-9-7 **60** DavidNolan 13 57
(Liam Bailey) *hld up: pushed along over 2f out: no imp fr over 1f out* **50/1**

0053 **8** *1 ¼* **Hugoigo**[12] 4056 5-8-3 **49** CoreyMadden(7) 6 45
(Jim Goldie) *bhd: rdn over 4f out: hdwy over 1f out: kpt on: nt pce to chal* **12/1**

0000 **9** *2 ½* **Miss Ranger (IRE)**[11] 4126 7-9-3 **56** (b) RachelRichardson 5 49
(Roger Fell) *hld up: rdn and outpcd over 3f out: btn fr 2f out* **33/1**

4041 **10** *1 ¾* **Rock N'Stones (IRE)**[51] 2684 8-8-9 **48** KevinStott 7 39
(Gillian Boanas) *hld up in midfield: rdn over 3f out: wknd over 2f out* **12/1**

0404 **11** *nk* **St Andrews (IRE)**[23] 3653 6-9-2 **55** (v) DuranFentiman 4 45
(Gillian Boanas) *slowly away: bhd: struggling over 4f out: nvr on terms* **14/1**

4/46 **12** *16* **Another Lincolnday**[11] 4126 8-9-0 **53** (p) GrahamLee 1 24
(Rebecca Menzies) *led to over 3f out: rdn and wknd over 2f out: t.o* **8/1**[2]

506- **13** *20* **Slipper Satin (IRE)**[5] 7396 9-8-2 **46** oh1 (t) AndrewBreslin(5) 3
(Simon West) *sn midfield: pushed along and struggling fr 1/2-way: btn fnl 4f: t.o (jockey said mare was never travelling)* **66/1**

3m 27.37s (-4.13) **Going Correction** -0.05s/f (Good) **13** Ran SP% **124.2**
Speed ratings (Par 101): **108,106,106,105,105 104,103,103,102,101 101,93,83**
CSF £7.65 CT £52.32 TOTE £1.80: £1.10, £2.50, £2.20; EX 8.50 Trifecta £60.20.
Owner Sunrise Partnership **Bred** S C E A Haras De La Perelle **Trained** Navan, Co. Meath

FOCUS
A modest-looking staying event run at what looked a solid pace, although the first three home were second, third and fourth in the early part of the contest. It's been rated around the second to his best recent (AW) form.

4511 ROA REWARDS MEMBERS H'CAP 7f 33y
3:30 (3:34) (Class 3) (0-90,87) 4-Y-O+

£8,092 (£2,423; £1,211; £605; £302; £152) **Stalls** Low

Form RPR

114- **1** **Tribal Warrior**[375] 4135 4-9-2 **82** DavidAllan 2 95+
(James Tate) *t.k.h: hld up in tch: nt clr run over 2f out tl gap appeared and chsd clr ldr over 1f out: rdn and qcknd ins fnl f: led towards fin: snugly* **3/1**[2]

2503 **2** *1* **Raselasad (IRE)**[33] 3308 5-9-7 **87** RoystonFfrench 1 94
(Tracy Waggott) *led: shkn up and clr wl over 1f out: rdn ins fnl f: hdd and no ex towards fin* **9/4**[1]

2515 **3** *4* **Tommy G**[12] 4058 6-8-5 **78** CoreyMadden(7) 5 74
(Jim Goldie) *hld up: effrt on outside over 2f out: chsd clr ldng pair ins fnl f: r.o* **12/1**

0350 **4** *1* **How Bizarre**[36] 3199 4-7-11 **68** AndrewBreslin(5) 7 62
(Liam Bailey) *t.k.h: cl up: effrt and rdn over 2f out: edgd rt and one pce fnl f* **20/1**

-256 **5** *1* **Glengarry**[6] 4292 6-9-1 **84** SeanDavis(3) 6 75
(Keith Dalgleish) *dwlt: hld up in tch: effrt and drvn along over 2f out: outpcd fnl f* **13/2**[3]

0000 **6** *1* **Parys Mountain (IRE)**[11] 4127 5-9-4 **84** (t) DuranFentiman 3 72
(Tim Easterby) *chsd ldr: drvn over 2f out: wknd fnl f* **6/1**

3463 **7** *1 ¼* **Jacob Black**[7] 4239 8-8-8 **74** (v) ShaneGray 4 59
(Keith Dalgleish) *dwlt: hld up pushed along over 2f out: wknd over 1f out* **8/1**

101- **8** *60* **Pepys**[261] 8263 5-8-13 **79** GrahamLee 8
(Bryan Smart) *dwlt: bhd: drvn and struggling over 3f out: sn lost tch: t.o: b.b.v (vet said gelding bled from the nose)* **8/1**

1m 26.14s (-2.86) **Going Correction** -0.05s/f (Good) **8** Ran SP% **111.5**
Speed ratings (Par 107): **112,110,106,105,104 102,101,32**
CSF £9.61 CT £65.00 TOTE £3.50: £1.40, £1.20, £2.90; EX 10.20 Trifecta £101.00.
Owner Saeed Manana **Bred** Rabbah Bloodstock Limited **Trained** Newmarket, Suffolk

FOCUS
A fair race for the level, and the winner looks sure to hold his own in better company. The second has been rated back to his C&D reappearance form.

4512 BENEFITS FOR ROA MEMBERS AT ROA.CO.UK H'CAP (DIV I) 1m 2y
4:00 (4:01) (Class 6) (0-60,61) 4-Y-O+

£2,911 (£866; £432; £300; £300; £300) **Stalls** Low

Form RPR

6564 **1** **Be Bold**[21] 3721 7-8-11 **49** (b) DavidAllan 5 55
(Rebecca Bastiman) *hld up in tch: effrt and chsd ldr over 1f out: kpt on wl fnl f to ld towards fin* **6/1**

0253 **2** *¾* **Forever A Lady (IRE)**[12] 4060 6-9-7 **59** ShaneGray 8 63
(Keith Dalgleish) *pressed ldr: led over 2f out: rdn and drifted rt over 1f out: kpt on fnl f: hdd and no ex towards fin* **5/1**[3]

-455 **3** *1* **Foxy Rebel**[16] 3939 5-8-7 **45** JamesSullivan 10 47
(Ruth Carr) *t.k.h: led: rdn and hdd over 2f out: kpt on same pce fnl f* **10/1**

00-0 **4** *nk* **Barney Bullet (IRE)**[12] 4078 4-8-7 **45** (e[1]) PhilDennis 7 46
(Noel Wilson) *plld hrd: hld up towards rr: effrt and hdwy over 1f out: kpt on ins fnl f* **40/1**

2000 **5** *¾* **Captain Peaky**[21] 3730 6-8-2 **45** AndrewBreslin(5) 11 45
(Liam Bailey) *missed break: hld up: effrt on outside 2f out: rdn and no imp fnl f* **28/1**

2306 **6** *1 ¼* **Corked (IRE)**[18] 3843 6-9-0 **55** (p[1]) RowanScott(3) 3 54
(Alistair Whillans) *hld up: effrt whn nt clr run over 2f out and over 1f out: no imp fnl f (jockey said mare was denied a clear run approaching the final furlong)* **9/1**

2053 **7** *½* **Rebel State (IRE)**[6] 4293 6-8-11 **56** (v) OwenPayton(7) 1 52
(Jedd O'Keeffe) *s.i.s: t.k.h: sn cl up: rdn over 2f out: wknd over 1f out (jockey said gelding missed the break)* **5/2**[1]

-000 **8** *1* **Relight My Fire**[8] 4207 9-9-6 **58** (p) RachelRichardson 2 51
(Tim Easterby) *prom: drvn along over 2f out: wknd over 1f out* **10/1**

6324 **9** *1 ¼* **Lukoutoldmakezebak**[21] 3720 6-8-8 **46** (b[1]) JamieGormley 6 36
(David Thompson) *in tch on outside: rdn over 2f out: hung rt and wknd over 1f out* **4/1**[2]

00-0 **10** *4* **Dark Crystal**[21] 3721 8-9-0 **52** CamHardie 12 33
(Linda Perratt) *bhd: struggling over 2f out: sn btn* **50/1**

1m 39.76s (-0.24) **Going Correction** -0.05s/f (Good) **10** Ran SP% **115.6**
Speed ratings (Par 101): **99,98,97,96,96 94,94,93,92,88**
CSF £35.25 CT £296.10 TOTE £6.40: £2.20, £1.80, £2.50; EX 38.10 Trifecta £300.30.
Owner N Barber & Partner **Bred** Simon Balding **Trained** Cowthorpe, N Yorks

FOCUS
The first division of a modest mile handicap. It's been rated around the winner to last year's best and the second to her better recent form.

4513 BENEFITS FOR ROA MEMBERS AT ROA.CO.UK H'CAP (DIV II) 1m 2y
4:30 (4:32) (Class 6) (0-60,60) 4-Y-O+

£2,911 (£866; £432; £300; £300; £300) **Stalls** Low

Form RPR

1 **Lappet (IRE)**[17] 3897 4-9-1 **54** GrahamLee 4 62
(Gavin Cromwell, Ire) *mde virtually all: hrd pressed fr over 1f out: kpt on gamely towards fin (trainer said, regards apparent improvement in form, filly was suited by being able to make the running on this occasion)* **4/1**[2]

301 **2** *nk* **Cliff Bay (IRE)**[16] 3924 5-8-10 **49** ShaneGray 11 56
(Keith Dalgleish) *hld up in tch: rdn and hdwy over 2f out: hung rt and disp ld over 1f out to ins fnl f: hld towards fin* **9/2**[3]

2324 **3** *1 ¾* **Donnelly's Rainbow (IRE)**[8] 4207 6-9-4 **57** DavidAllan 8 62+
(Rebecca Bastiman) *hld up on ins: no room fr 3f out to ent fnl f: angled lft and sn chsng ldng pair: kpt on fin (jockey said gelding was continually denied a clear run from two furlongs out)* **5/2**[1]

0000 **4** *1 ½* **Let Right Be Done**[12] 4054 7-8-7 **46** oh1 (b) CamHardie 1 47
(Linda Perratt) *prom: drvn along over 2f out: one pce whn hmpd appr fnl f* **50/1**

00-5 **5** *2* **Prosecute (FR)**[22] 3681 6-8-7 **46** oh1 RoystonFfrench 10 41
(Sean Regan) *t.k.h: pressed wnr: ev ch over 2f out to over 1f out: wknd ins fnl f (jockey said gelding ran too free)* **25/1**

4100 **6** *1 ¼* **Robben Rainbow**[12] 4060 5-8-12 **56** BenSanderson(5) 5 48
(Katie Scott) *in tch: rdn over 2f out: edgd rt over 1f out: wknd ins fnl f* **14/1**

0306 **7** *nse* **My Valentino (IRE)**[21] 3716 6-8-7 **46** (bt) JamieGormley 2 38
(Dianne Sayer) *hld up: rdn along over 2f out: no imp fr over 1f out (jockey said gelding was slowly away)* **4/1**[2]

1505 **8** *1* **King Of Naples**[12] 4054 6-9-7 **60** (h) JamesSullivan 12 50
(Ruth Carr) *hld up: stdy hdwy gng wl over 2f out: rdn over 1f out: fnd little* **10/1**

00-0 **9** *1* **Newspeak (IRE)**[35] 3224 7-8-7 **46** oh1 (p) DuranFentiman 9 34
(Fred Watson) *hld up: drvn along over 2f out: nvr rchd ldrs* **80/1**

0000 **10** *1* **Desai**[12] 4060 5-9-5 **58** (t) PhilDennis 3 43
(Noel Wilson) *prom: rdn along over 2f out: wknd over 1f out* **20/1**

-646 **P** **Broctune Red**[14] 4002 4-8-5 **47** SeanDavis(3) 7
(Gillian Boanas) *t.k.h: prom: broke down and lost pl 2f out: p.u and dismntd ins fnl f (jockey said gelding lost it's action. Vet said gelding was lame left hind)* **12/1**

1m 40.35s (0.35) **Going Correction** -0.05s/f (Good) **11** Ran SP% **122.0**
Speed ratings (Par 101): **96,95,93,92,90 89,89,88,87,86**
CSF £22.62 CT £56.32 TOTE £4.80: £1.70, £1.50, £1.40; EX 27.30 Trifecta £134.60.
Owner Thomas Mitchell **Bred** Gerry Flannery Developments Ltd **Trained** Navan, Co. Meath

FOCUS
The second division of the mile handicap saw an exciting finish.

4514 FRIDGE SPARES WHOLESALE (S) STKS 5f 1y
5:00 (5:01) (Class 5) 4-Y-O+ **£3,493** (£1,039; £519; £300; £300) **Stalls** High

Form RPR

0030 **1** **Desert Ace (IRE)**[7] 4230 8-9-9 71 KevinStott 4 69+
(Paul Midgley) *fly-jmpd s: hld up in tch: stdy hdwy to press ldr over 1f out: effrt and carried rt ins fnl f: led towards fin: snugly* **9/2**[3]

-000 **2** *½* **Longroom**[11] 4100 7-9-1 75 DannyRedmond(5) 1 65+
(Noel Wilson) *w ldrs: led 1/2-way: rdn over 1f out: hung rt ins fnl f: hdd and no ex towards fin* **5/2**[2]

0000 **3** *3 ¾* **Robot Boy (IRE)**[16] 3928 9-9-2 67 JamesSullivan 2 47
(Marjorie Fife) *led to 1/2-way: pushed along whn short of room over 1f out: sn one pce* **7/1**

000- **4** *2 ¼* **Raise A Billion**[315] 6410 8-8-11 33 HarrisonShaw(5) 3 39
(Alan Berry) *in tch: drvn along and outpcd after 2f: edgd rt and outpcd fr over 1f out* **80/1**

6055 **5** *½* **Billy Dylan (IRE)**[4] 4364 4-9-9 82 (p) DavidNolan 5 44
(David O'Meara) *w ldrs to 2f out: sn rdn and edgd rt: wknd fnl f* **1/1**[1]

59.58s (-0.12) **Going Correction** -0.05s/f (Good) **5** Ran SP% **110.5**
Speed ratings (Par 103): **98,97,91,87,86**
CSF £16.04 TOTE £5.50: £1.80, £1.10; EX 13.70 Trifecta £50.00.There was no bid for the winner.
Owner M Hammond, Mad For Fun & Partners **Bred** Kildaragh Stud **Trained** Westow, N Yorks
■ Stewards' Enquiry : Danny Redmond three-day ban; careless riding (July 17-19)

FOCUS
This probably isn't going to be reliable form in the coming weeks, as the market leader was well below his best. The fourth limits the level, and the winner has been rated as just matching this year's form.

4515 ROA: A VOICE FOR RACEHORSE OWNERS H'CAP 1m 4f 104y
5:35 (5:36) (Class 6) (0-60,56) 4-Y-O+

£3,428 (£1,020; £509; £300; £300; £300) **Stalls** Low

Form RPR

0-00 **1** **Strategic (IRE)**[22] 3682 4-8-11 **46** (h) RachelRichardson 4 52
(Eric Alston) *hld up in tch on outside: hdwy over 2f out: effrt over 1f out: led wl ins fnl f: r.o* **16/1**

60-5 **2** *hd* **Melabi (IRE)**[29] 3447 6-8-11 **46** CamHardie 7 53
(Stella Barclay) *t.k.h in midfield: effrt and hanging rt whn nt clr run fr over 2f out to over 1f out: rdn and r.o wl fnl f: jst hld* **12/1**

4000 3 shd **Spark Of War (IRE)**[12] 4056 4-9-7 **56**..............................(v) ShaneGray 10 62
(Keith Dalgleish) *cl up: led over 2f out: rdn over 1f out: hdd wl ins fnl f: kpt on: jst hld* **5/1**[3]
4012 4 1 ½ **Sosian**[21] 3718 4-8-11 **49**..............................(b) SeanDavis(3) 5 52
(Richard Fahey) *hld up towards rr: rdn over 2f out: angled lft and styd on wl fnl f: nt pce to chal* **7/2**[2]
-453 5 nse **Hayward Field (IRE)**[9] 4190 6-8-11 **46**..............................(e) PhilDennis 1 49
(Noel Wilson) *prom: effrt and ev ch over 1f out: kpt on same pce ins fnl f* **7/1**
0456 6 nk **Pammi**[12] 4056 4-9-4 **53**..............................(p) JamieGormley 2 56
(Jim Goldie) *led to 1/2-way: cl up: rdn over 2f out: one pce fnl f* **6/1**
4125 7 6 **Kodi Koh (IRE)**[6] 4287 4-8-10 **48**.............................. RowanScott(3) 11 41
(Simon West) *hld up towards rr: hdwy on outside over 2f out: rdn and hung rt over 1f out: sn outpcd* **3/1**[1]
0000 8 nk **Enemy Of The State (IRE)**[12] 4056 5-8-10 **45**.......(p) RoystonFfrench 8 37
(Jason Ward) *hld up: rdn along over 2f out: nvr rchd ldrs* **14/1**
000 9 ½ **Kaizer**[22] 3680 4-9-7 **56**..............................(h[1]) GrahamLee 6 48
(Alistair Whillans) *cl up: led 1/2-way to over 2f out: wknd over 1f out* **14/1**
5003 10 nk **Fillydelphia (IRE)**[16] 3929 8-8-5 **45**..............................(b) AndrewBreslin(5) 3 36
(Liam Bailey) *awkward s: hld up: rdn and effrt over 2f out: sn wknd* **33/1**
2m 42.77s (-1.73) **Going Correction** -0.05s/f (Good) **10** Ran SP% **120.5**
Speed ratings (Par 101): **103,102,102,101,101 101,97,97,97,96**
CSF £199.11 CT £1113.60 TOTE £18.00: £3.50, £3.50, £1.90; EX 245.80 Trifecta £2961.60.
Owner Paul Buist & John Thompson **Bred** Pat Fullam **Trained** Longton, Lancs

FOCUS
A moderate middle-distance contest to finish the meeting with. Limited form.
T/Plt: £20.90 to a £1 stake. Pool: £54,376.48. 1,898.64 winning units. T/Qpdt: £6.00 to a £1 stake. Pool: £5,159.75. 633.9 winning units. **Richard Young**

3968 **THIRSK** (L-H)
Wednesday, July 3

OFFICIAL GOING: Good to firm
Wind: Light, largely across Weather: sunny

4516 SRI LANKA UNBOWED EBF NOVICE AUCTION STKS (DIV I) 6f
2:10 (2:10) (Class 5) 2-Y-O **£3,881** (£1,155; £577; £288) **Stalls** Centre

Form RPR
2 1 **Harry Love (IRE)**[22] 3702 2-8-9 0.............................. BenRobinson(3) 13 75
(Ollie Pears) *dwlt: sn prom: pushed along 2f out: rdn to ld ins fnl f: kpt on wl* **11/4**[1]
5 2 ½ **Spygate**[22] 3703 2-9-2 0.............................. DanielTudhope 5 78
(Richard Fahey) *led narrowly: rdn over 1f out: drvn and hdd ins fnl f: kpt on same pce* **3/1**[2]
3 3 1 ¾ **Kayewhykelly (IRE)**[22] 3702 2-8-8 0.............................. JasonHart 9 64
(Julie Camacho) *chsd ldrs: pushed along 2f out: rdn and kpt on same pce fnl f* **6/1**[3]
02 4 1 ¾ **Moonlighting**[16] 3919 2-8-7 0.............................. SamJames 3 58
(Kevin Ryan) *prom: rdn 2f out: no ex fnl f* **20/1**
0 5 ½ **Singe Anglais (IRE)**[18] 3866 2-8-10 0.............................. FayeMcManoman(5) 8 65
(Nigel Tinkler) *chsd ldrs: rdn along 2f out: no ex fnl f* **33/1**
6 shd **Naseeb (IRE)** 2-8-13 0.............................. PaulHanagan 7 62
(Richard Fahey) *s.i.s: hld up: pushed along and hdwy over 1f out: hung lft and one pce ins fnl f (jockey said colt hung left under pressure)* **8/1**
1 7 5 **Commanche Falls**[22] 3703 2-9-7 0.............................. ConnorBeasley 4 56
(Michael Dods) *chsd ldrs: pushed along over 3f out: hmpd over 1f out: sn wknd (jockey said gelding was never travelling and trainer could offer no explanation for the poor performance)* **11/4**[1]
0 8 ½ **Newsical**[22] 3702 2-9-0 0.............................. DougieCostello 11 47
(Mark Walford) *wnt lft s: hld up: nvr threatened* **100/1**
9 2 ½ **Ontheradar (IRE)** 2-8-13 0.............................. AndrewElliott 2 38
(Ronald Thompson) *slowly away: sn pushed along and a towards rr* **100/1**
10 1 **Jay Me Lo (IRE)** 2-8-9 0.............................. LewisEdmunds 1 31
(Lawrence Mullaney) *hld up: sn pushed along: nvr threatened* **50/1**
0 11 1 **The Works (IRE)**[15] 3968 2-8-10 0.............................. TomEaves 6 31
(Declan Carroll) *dwlt: hld up in tch: racd quite keenly: pushed along whn hmpd and carried lft over 1f out: nvr involved* **28/1**
5 12 9 **Hot Heir (IRE)**[61] 2367 2-8-10 0..............................(w) AndrewMullen 12
(Adrian Nicholls) *prom tl hung bdly lft over 1f out and wknd (jockey said filly hung left throughout)* **50/1**
1m 11.51s (-1.29) **Going Correction** -0.275s/f (Firm) **12** Ran SP% **120.8**
Speed ratings (Par 94): **97,96,94,91,91 90,84,83,80,78 77,65**
CSF £10.91 TOTE £3.20: £1.30, £1.90, £1.80; EX 14.50 Trifecta £58.20.
Owner Ownaracehorse Ltd & Ollie Pears **Bred** Kenneth Purcell & Lawman Syndicate **Trained** Norton, N Yorks

FOCUS
Home (wood) bend was dolled out by 3m and the away (stables) bend also out by 5m. The first four in the market in this modest novice event ran at the previous meeting here 22 days earlier. Straightforward form in behind the first two.

4517 SRI LANKA UNBOWED EBF NOVICE AUCTION STKS (DIV II) 6f
2:40 (2:41) (Class 5) 2-Y-O **£3,881** (£1,155; £577; £288) **Stalls** Centre

Form RPR
1 1 **Magical Max**[18] 3866 2-9-6 0.............................. AndrewMullen 7 82
(Mark Walford) *mde all: pushed along and pressed over 1f out: rdn and edgd lft ins fnl f: hld on wl* **5/4**[1]
2 nk **Sweet Joanna (IRE)** 2-8-11 0.............................. PaulHanagan 13 72
(Richard Fahey) *trckd ldr: pushed along over 1f out: rdn fnl f: edgd lft: kpt on fnl 50yds* **10/1**
22 3 2 ¼ **Spring Bloom**[21] 3717 2-9-0 0.............................. BenCurtis 5 68
(K R Burke) *chsd ldr: rdn to chal strly over 1f out: edgd lft and no ex fnl 110yds* **3/1**[2]
2033 4 5 **What A Business (IRE)**[13] 4032 2-8-13 68.............................. DanielTudhope 4 52
(Roger Fell) *in tch: rdn along 2f out: wknd fnl f* **9/2**[3]
5 1 ½ **Imperial Eagle (IRE)** 2-8-2 0.............................. PaulaMuir(5) 11 42
(Lawrence Mullaney) *slowly away: hld up: sn pushed along along: hdwy and in tch 3f out: rdn 2f out: wknd fnl f* **28/1**
0 6 ¾ **Schumli**[10] 4142 2-8-9 0.............................. RobbieDowney 3 42
(David O'Meara) *stdd s: hld up in tch: racd keenly: rdn along 2f out: nvr threatened* **66/1**
0 7 1 ¾ **Inductive**[34] 3245 2-8-13 0.............................. ConnorBeasley 9 40
(Michael Dods) *chsd ldrs: pushed along over 2f out: wknd over 1f out* **20/1**
8 3 ½ **Azure World** 2-8-10 0.............................. TomEaves 10 27
(Kevin Ryan) *dwlt: a towards rr* **20/1**
25 9 1 ¼ **Just Jean (IRE)**[13] 4032 2-8-8 0.............................. PJMcDonald 12 21
(Micky Hammond) *midfield: sn pushed along: wknd 2f out* **22/1**
00 10 ¾ **Jakodobro**[62] 2331 2-8-6 0 ow1.............................. HarryRussell(7) 1 24
(Bryan Smart) *in tch: outpcd and lost pl over 3f out: wknd over 1f out* **100/1**
11 2 **Hands Down (IRE)** 2-8-4 0.............................. FayeMcManoman(5) 6 14
(Nigel Tinkler) *slowly away: a towards rr (jockey said filly was slowly away)* **50/1**
0 12 2 ½ **Mr Bowjangles**[21] 3739 2-9-0 0.............................. JasonHart 8 11
(Gay Kelleway) *prom: pushed along and wknd 2f out* **50/1**
1m 11.07s (-1.73) **Going Correction** -0.275s/f (Firm) **12** Ran SP% **120.4**
Speed ratings (Par 94): **100,99,96,89,87 86,84,79,78,77 74,71**
CSF £14.40 TOTE £2.10: £1.20, £2.80, £1.10; EX 17.30 Trifecta £39.60.
Owner Mrs E Holmes, M Johnson & Mrs Walford **Bred** Poole, Trickledown & The Late Mrs Poole **Trained** Sheriff Hutton, N Yorks

FOCUS
This second division of the 2yo novice sprint was 0.44secs quicker than the opener. The winner has been rated in line with his York debut.

4518 INAUGURAL 6 REGIMENT RLC REGIMENTAL DAY (S) H'CAP 7f 218y
3:10 (3:11) (Class 6) (0-60,59) 3-5-Y-O
£3,074 (£914; £457; £300; £300; £300) **Stalls** Centre

Form RPR
4540 1 **Blyton Lass**[37] 3142 4-9-5 **48**.............................. BarryMcHugh 3 54
(James Given) *midfield: rdn and hdwy over 1f out: kpt on to ld nr fin* **10/1**
2220 2 hd **Loose Chippings (IRE)**[49] 2738 5-9-9 **52**..............(p[1]) DougieCostello 16 57
(Ivan Furtado) *trckd ldrs: rdn to ld wl over 1f out: sn edgd lft: drvn and one pce ins fnl f: hdd nr fin* **15/2**[2]
6056 3 hd **Arriba De Toda (IRE)**[11] 4129 3-8-2 **47**.............. KieranSchofield(7) 2 50
(Brian Ellison) *midfield towards inner: rdn over 2f out: hdwy appr fnl f: sn chsd ldr: swtchd lft 75yds out: kpt on* **12/1**
6006 4 2 **Seafaring Girl (IRE)**[7] 4244 3-8-8 **46**.............................. AndrewMullen 6 44
(Mark Loughnane) *in tch: drvn to chse ldr 2f out: no ex fnl 75yds* **22/1**
0-05 5 shd **Silk Mill Blue**[35] 3215 5-9-7 **50**.............................. BenCurtis 12 49
(Richard Whitaker) *hld up in midfield: rdn over 2f out: hdwy over 1f out: kpt on same pce fnl f* **6/1**[1]
4005 6 4 **Spiritual Boy (IRE)**[34] 3271 3-8-12 **53**..............(p) ConorMcGovern(3) 11 39
(David O'Meara) *hld up: rdn 2f out: hdwy appr fnl f: kpt on: nvr threatened ldrs* **6/1**[1]
1300 7 ½ **Lexikon**[25] 3569 3-9-1 **53**.............................. JasonHart 4 38
(Ollie Pears) *trckd ldrs: rdn over 2f out: wknd fnl f* **10/1**
6-00 8 ½ **Secret Magic (IRE)**[34] 3270 3-8-5 **46**.............................. JaneElliott(3) 9 30
(Mark Loughnane) *hld up in rr: rdn over 2f out: sme hdwy on outside over 1f out: nvr threatened* **40/1**
-600 9 ¾ **Lethal Guest**[34] 3271 3-9-4 **59**..............(h[1] w) BenRobinson(3) 10 41
(Ollie Pears) *hld up: rdn over 2f out: nvr threatened* **25/1**
0005 10 1 ¾ **Smashing Lass (IRE)**[25] 3569 3-8-12 **50**..............(p) PaddyMathers 1 27
(Ollie Pears) *dwlt: hld up: rdn over 2f out: nvr threatened* **20/1**
0-00 11 hd **French Flyer (IRE)**[67] 2111 4-9-9 **52**.............................. LewisEdmunds 5 30
(Rebecca Bastiman) *in tch: rdn over 2f out: drvn over 1f out: wknd fnl f* **14/1**
0405 12 3 ½ **Sulafaat (IRE)**[29] 3448 4-9-6 **49**..............................(p) PaulHanagan 7 18
(Rebecca Menzies) *midfield: rdn over 2f out: wknd over 1f out* **8/1**[3]
0000 13 1 ½ **Duba Plains**[16] 3932 4-9-3 **46**..............................(p[1]) PaulMulrennan 14 11
(Kenny Johnson) *prom: led 3f out: rdn and hdd wl over 1f out: sn wknd* **50/1**
0350 14 2 ¾ **Tommycole**[28] 3473 4-9-9 **52**.............................. JackMitchell 15 10
(Olly Williams) *hld up: rdn over 3f out: sn btn* **11/1**
50-0 15 shd **Royal Liberty**[37] 3163 4-9-5 **48**.............................. ConnorBeasley 8 5
(Geoffrey Harker) *led: rdn and hdd 3f out: wknd* **18/1**
5565 16 3 ½ **Biscuit Queen**[2] 4439 3-8-5 **46**..............................(b) ConnorMurtagh(3) 13
(Brian Ellison) *midfield on outer: rdn over 2f out: sn wknd* **12/1**
1m 39.43s (-2.27) **Going Correction** -0.275s/f (Firm)
WFA 3 from 4yo+ 9lb **16** Ran SP% **122.6**
Speed ratings (Par 101): **100,99,99,97,97 93,93,92,91,90 89,86,84,82,81 78**
CSF £78.42 CT £963.97 TOTE £11.80: £2.30, £2.30, £2.60, £6.80; EX 111.80 Trifecta £1462.30.There was no bid for the winner.
Owner Andy Clarke **Bred** Mrs V J Lovelace **Trained** Willoughton, Lincs

FOCUS
They went hard early on in this selling handicap. Add 10yds. It's been rated as straightforward form around the balance of the first three.

4519 RESOLUTE AND BEAUTIFUL SRI LANKA H'CAP 6f
3:40 (3:42) (Class 6) (0-65,65) 3-Y-O+
£3,752 (£1,116; £557; £300; £300; £300) **Stalls** Centre

Form RPR
-050 1 **Related**[23] 3657 9-9-10 **65**..............................(b) DanielTudhope 9 75
(Paul Midgley) *led after 1f: mde rest: pushed along 2f out: drvn appr fnl f: kpt on wl (trainer said, regards apparent improvement in form, gelding was suited by the return to a quicker surface and benefitted from a drop in class)* **5/1**[1]
0104 2 1 ½ **Indian Pursuit (IRE)**[16] 3928 6-9-9 **64**..............................(v) RobbieDowney 8 70
(John Quinn) *led for 1f: chsd ldrs: drvn to chal appr fnl f: kpt on same pce* **18/1**
0352 3 hd **Bedtime Bella (IRE)**[22] 3709 3-9-2 **63**..............................(v) PJMcDonald 12 67
(K R Burke) *half-rrd s: rcvrd to press ldr after 1f: rdn 2f out: kpt on same pce fnl f* **8/1**[3]
-000 4 nse **Fumbo Jumbo (IRE)**[23] 3658 6-9-4 **59**.............................. LewisEdmunds 10 64
(Rebecca Bastiman) *chsd ldrs: rdn over 2f out: kpt on fnl f* **50/1**
0006 5 1 **Mr Strutter (IRE)**[23] 3656 5-9-8 **63**.............................. AndrewElliott 13 66
(Ronald Thompson) *hld up in midfield: pushed along over 2f out: hdwy whn n.m.r appr fnl f: kpt on fnl 110yds: nrst fin* **16/1**
4004 6 shd **Spirit Of Zebedee (IRE)**[16] 3933 6-8-11 **52**..............................(v) JasonHart 2 54
(John Quinn) *chsd ldrs: rdn over 2f out: kpt on same pce fnl f* **16/1**
-450 7 hd **Sfumato**[23] 3656 5-9-5 **60**.............................. AndrewMullen 19 61
(Adrian Nicholls) *dwlt and swtchd lft s: hld up: pushed along and n.m.r over 1f out: sn swtchd rt: kpt on ins fnl f* **9/1**
-000 8 1 ¼ **Suitcase 'N' Taxi**[23] 3658 5-9-6 **61**.............................. ConnorBeasley 6 58
(Tim Easterby) *midfield: rdn 2f out: no imp* **16/1**
0010 9 nse **Carlovian**[10] 4149 6-9-0 **55**..............................(v) DougieCostello 14 52
(Mark Walford) *prom: rdn over 2f out: no ex ins fnl f* **33/1**
0-40 10 1 ½ **Burtonwood**[15] 3975 7-9-0 **62**.............................. HarryRussell(7) 15 55
(Julie Camacho) *chsd ldrs: rdn over 2f out: wknd ins fnl f* **20/1**

006- **11** *nk* **Charlie's Boy (IRE)**[250] 8593 3-9-0 **61** PaulMulrennan 7 52
(Michael Dods) *hld up: nvr threatened* **16/1**
4240 **12** *½* **Ascot Dreamer**[5] 4328 3-8-10 **57** (t) PaulHanagan 4 46
(David Brown) *nvr bttr than midfield* **10/1**
0-40 **13** *¾* **Baldwin (IRE)**[14] 4010 3-9-4 **65** (v[1]) TomEaves 5 52
(Kevin Ryan) *dwlt: hld up: nvr threatened* **18/1**
3126 **14** *¾* **Viking Way (IRE)**[8] 4212 4-8-11 **52** (b) JackMitchell 18 38
(Olly Williams) *midfield: rdn over 2f out: wknd over 1f out (trainer said gelding returned with a stone wedged under it's right fore shoe)* **13/2**[2]
0554 **15** *nk* **Cliff (IRE)**[21] 3738 9-8-5 **51** (p) FayeMcManoman(5) 3 36
(Nigel Tinkler) *stmbld s and slowly away: a towards rr* **12/1**
4224 **16** *1½* **Tadaany (IRE)**[13] 4037 7-8-13 **54** (p) JackGarritty 16 34
(Ruth Carr) *midfield: rdn over 2f out: wknd over 1f out* **14/1**
-065 **17** *hd* **Separable**[25] 3570 3-8-4 **51** oh1 (b) PaddyMathers 17 30
(Tim Easterby) *midfield: sn rdn along: drvn over 2f out: wknd over 1f out* **20/1**
0-40 **18** *nse* **Pearl's Calling (IRE)**[16] 3932 4-8-7 **51** oh5 JaneElliott(3) 1 31
(Ron Barr) *midfield: rdn and outpcd 3f out: sn wknd (jockey said saddle slipped in the closing stages)* **80/1**

1m 10.93s (-1.87) **Going Correction** -0.275s/f (Firm)
WFA 3 from 4yo+ 6lb **18** Ran SP% **124.3**
Speed ratings (Par 101): **101,99,98,98,97 97,96,95,95,93 92,92,91,90,89 87,87,87**
CSF £91.68 CT £729.20 TOTE £6.50: £1.80, £4.60, £1.90, £11.80; EX 117.40 Trifecta £1820.60.
Owner Taylor's Bloodstock Ltd **Bred** Laundry Cottage Stud Farm **Trained** Westow, N Yorks

FOCUS
The middle was the place to be in this moderate sprint handicap. The second has been rated near this year's win.

4520 SRI LANKA WONDER OF ASIA EBF NOVICE STKS 7f 218y
4:10 (4:15) (Class 5) 3-Y-0+ **£4,851** (£1,443; £721; £360) **Stalls** Centre

Form RPR
0- **1** **Ghaziyah**[250] 8591 3-9-0 DanielTudhope 6 81+
(William Haggas) *hld up in tch: pushed along and hdwy on outer over 2f out: led over 1f out: rdn and edgd lft ins fnl f: kpt on wl: shade cosily* **5/4**[1]
02 **2** *¾* **Siglo Six**[15] 3972 3-9-5 (h) JackMitchell 3 84
(Hugo Palmer) *hld up in tch: hdwy over 2f out: rdn to chal over 1f out: drvn fnl f: kpt on but a hld* **3/1**[2]
3 *4* **Eva Maria** 3-9-0 PaulHanagan 2 70+
(Richard Fahey) *trckd ldrs: pushed along over 2f out: kpt on ins fnl f: wnt 3rd ins towards fin* **9/1**
4 **4** *¾* **Amber Star (IRE)**[15] 3974 3-9-0 RobbieDowney 4 68
(David O'Meara) *trckd ldrs: rdn to chal 2f out: wknd ins fnl f: lost 3rd towards fin* **20/1**
624 **5** *2¼* **Royal Welcome**[30] 3431 3-9-0 76 PJMcDonald 1 63
(James Tate) *led: rdn over 2f out: hdd over 1f out: sn wknd (trainers' rep could offer no explanation for the poor performance)* **7/2**[3]
02 **6** *8* **International Guy (IRE)**[69] 2058 3-9-5 BarryMcHugh 8 50
(Richard Fahey) *dwlt: hld up: rdn over 2f out: hung lft over 1f out: wknd* **14/1**
02-4 **7** *9* **Coup De Gold (IRE)**[93] 1484 3-9-5 73 (h) JasonHart 7 29
(David Thompson) *trckd ldrs: rdn over 2f out: sn wknd* **50/1**
0 **8** *7* **Lady Sebastian**[35] 3218 3-8-11 (h[1]) ConorMcGovern(3) 5 8
(Jason Ward) *prom: rdn 3f out: wknd 2f out* **100/1**

1m 39.74s (-1.96) **Going Correction** -0.275s/f (Firm) **8** Ran SP% **116.0**
Speed ratings (Par 103): **98,97,93,92,90 82,73,66**
CSF £5.20 TOTE £2.10: £1.10, £1.10, £2.10; EX 5.60 Trifecta £26.50.
Owner Sheikh Juma Dalmook Al Maktoum **Bred** Denford Stud Ltd **Trained** Newmarket, Suffolk

FOCUS
The first pair came clear in this ordinary novice event. Add 10yds. The second has been rated as building on his latest form.

4521 SRI LANKA STAYING STRONG H'CAP 6f
4:40 (4:41) (Class 3) (0-95,94) 3-Y-0+ **£9,703** (£2,887; £1,443; £721) **Stalls** Centre

Form RPR
1010 **1** **Pennsylvania Dutch**[15] 3971 5-9-4 **86** TomEaves 2 96
(Kevin Ryan) *pressed ldr: rdn 2f out: drvn into narrow ld appr fnl f: edgd rt ins fnl f: kpt on* **12/1**
6610 **2** *¾* **Muscika**[39] 3097 5-9-8 **90** (v) DanielTudhope 5 97
(David O'Meara) *trckd ldrs: drvn to chal strly appr fnl f: edgd rt 75yds out: one pce* **7/2**[2]
2265 **3** *1¼* **Wentworth Falls**[4] 4402 7-9-12 **94** (p) SamJames 9 97
(Geoffrey Harker) *dwlt: hld up: hdwy on outer over 2f out: rdn and edgd lft over 1f out: sn chsd ldrs: edgd lft again fnl 110yds: no ex towards fin* **3/1**[1]
-104 **4** *¾* **The Armed Man**[20] 3770 6-8-11 **84** PaulaMuir(5) 7 86
(Chris Fairhurst) *chsd ldrs: rdn over 1f out: keeping on whn hmpd 75yds out and swtchd lft* **7/1**
2000 **5** *1¾* **Pipers Note**[28] 3480 9-9-7 **89** JackGarritty 3 84
(Ruth Carr) *chsd ldrs: rdn 2f out: no ex fnl f* **28/1**
6041 **6** *¾* **Moon Trouble (IRE)**[27] 3492 6-9-9 **91** AlistairRawlinson 8 84
(Michael Appleby) *trckd ldrs: rdn 2f out: wknd ins fnl f* **6/1**[3]
-510 **7** *1½* **Dark Defender**[25] 3589 6-9-6 **88** (b) LewisEdmunds 4 83
(Rebecca Bastiman) *led narrowly: rdn and hdd over 1f out: no ex whn bmpd 50yds out: eased (jockey said gelding suffered interference in the final furlong)* **16/1**
-461 **8** *2½* **Royal Prospect (IRE)**[15] 3971 4-9-3 **85** PaulMulrennan 1 65
(Julie Camacho) *slowly away: hld up: hdwy and chsd ldrs over 2f out: rdn over 1f out: wknd ins fnl f (jockey said gelding was restless in the stalls and jumped awkwardly)* **7/2**[2]
3400 **9** *1¼* **Gracious John (IRE)**[78] 1839 6-9-6 **88** AndrewMullen 6 64
(David Evans) *dwlt: hld up: nvr threatened (jockey said gelding slipped leaving the stalls and didn't move fluently)* **28/1**

1m 10.47s (-2.33) **Going Correction** -0.275s/f (Firm) **9** Ran SP% **116.7**
Speed ratings (Par 107): **104,103,101,100,98 97,95,91,90**
CSF £54.43 CT £161.18 TOTE £14.70: £3.80, £1.70, £1.20; EX 61.90 Trifecta £348.00.
Owner K&J Bloodstock Ltd **Bred** Lael Stables **Trained** Hambleton, N Yorks

FOCUS
Once again the centre was favoured in this feature sprint handicap. The second has been rated to his best and the third as close to form.

4522 JOHN HOPKINSON MEMORIAL CLAIMING STKS 1m 4f 8y
5:10 (5:10) (Class 5) 3-Y-0+ **£4,075** (£1,212; £606; £303; £300) **Stalls** High

Form RPR
5062 **1** **Lexington Law (IRE)**[30] 3428 6-9-7 85 (v) DanielTudhope 3 87
(Alan King) *trckd ldr: led 5f out: rdn along 2f out: edgd rt over 1f out: jnd ins fnl f: drvn and fnd ex towards fin* **4/1**[2]
5112 **2** *½* **Grand Inquisitor**[2] 4437 7-9-11 86 (v) BenCurtis 2 90
(Ian Williams) *trckd ldr: rdn over 2f out: drvn to join ldr ins fnl f: one pce towards fin* **5/6**[1]
0500 **3** *8* **Mirsaale**[16] 3929 9-9-7 84 (p) JasonHart 1 73
(Keith Dalgleish) *hld up in tch: rdn along 4f out: sn struggling: wnt poor 3rd 2f out* **12/1**[3]
0250 **4** *7* **Royal Flag**[16] 3940 9-9-2 64 BenRobinson(3) 5 60
(Brian Ellison) *hld up in tch: rdn along over 4f out: sn btn* **16/1**
-011 **5** *14* **Izvestia (IRE)**[37] 3150 3-8-3 80 (b) JaneElliott(3) 4 38
(Archie Watson) *led: hdd 5f out: rdn along and sn outpcd in 3rd: wknd 2f out (jockey said filly ran flat)* **4/1**[2]

2m 34.81s (-5.19) **Going Correction** -0.275s/f (Firm)
WFA 3 from 6yo+ 12lb **5** Ran SP% **108.1**
Speed ratings (Par 103): **106,105,100,95,86**
CSF £7.55 TOTE £3.60: £1.90, £1.10; EX 7.40 Trifecta £28.00.Grand Inquisitor was claimed by Conor Dore for £19,000.
Owner Middleham Park Racing XXXIX **Bred** Mary Kinsella & Brian O'Connor **Trained** Barbury Castle, Wilts

FOCUS
The first pair dominated the finish of this fair little claimer. Add 27yds. A token rating has been given.

4523 SUPPORT SRI LANKA H'CAP 7f
5:40 (5:40) (Class 5) (0-70,69) 3-Y-0+ **£4,398** (£1,309; £654; £327; £300; £300) **Stalls** Low

Form RPR
0-64 **1** **Inner Circle (IRE)**[7] 4239 5-9-12 **69** (p) BenCurtis 11 78
(Roger Fell) *hld up towards inner: angled rt towards outer 2f out: pushed along and hdwy over 1f out: rdn to ld 100yds out: kpt on wl* **4/1**[1]
1651 **2** *1¾* **Thornaby Nash**[22] 3704 8-9-7 **67** (b) ConorMcGovern(3) 3 71
(Jason Ward) *in tch: rdn over 2f out: sn chsd ldrs: chal strly 1f out: one pce fnl 110yds* **12/1**
5240 **3** *¾* **Dandy Highwayman (IRE)**[22] 3704 5-9-3 **63** (tp) BenRobinson(3) 5 65
(Ollie Pears) *pressed ldr: rdn into narrow ld 2f out: drvn and hdd 110yds out: no ex* **33/1**
2332 **4** *hd* **Atletico (IRE)**[27] 3496 7-9-8 **65** (v) AndrewMullen 10 66
(David Evans) *dwlt sltly and rdn along leaving s: hld up in midfield: pushed along over 2f out: rdn over 1f out: swtchd rt ent fnl f: kpt on* **9/2**[2]
10-0 **5** *½* **Shamaheart (IRE)**[36] 3199 9-9-4 **61** (tp) SamJames 12 61
(Geoffrey Harker) *midfield: rdn along 2f out: kpt on fnl f* **50/1**
0105 **6** *nk* **Kentuckyconnection (USA)**[10] 4148 6-9-4 **68** HarryRussell(7) 6 67
(Bryan Smart) *dwlt: hld up: rdn over 2f out: sme hdwy on outside over 1f out: kpt on fnl f* **8/1**
6054 **7** *shd* **Fard**[11] 4131 4-8-8 **56** PaulaMuir(5) 13 55
(Roger Fell) *hld up in rr: rdn over 2f out: sme hdwy over 1f out: kpt on ins fnl f* **12/1**
0-50 **8** *1* **Groupie**[15] 3969 5-9-4 **61** TomEaves 8 57
(Tom Tate) *hld up in midfield: rdn and hdwy 2f out: no ex fnl 1f* **25/1**
5-45 **9** *½* **Zebzardee (IRE)**[6] 4280 3-9-1 **69** ConnorMurtagh(3) 9 61
(Richard Fahey) *midfield: pushed along over 2f out: no imp: n.m.r ins fnl f* **25/1**
5054 **10** *nk* **Our Charlie Brown**[15] 3969 5-9-3 **60** (p) JasonHart 7 54
(Tim Easterby) *trckd ldrs: rdn over 2f out: wknd ins fnl f* **6/1**[3]
4003 **11** *hd* **Mudawwan (IRE)**[15] 3969 5-9-9 **66** (p) PaulHanagan 4 60
(James Bethell) *led narrowly: rdn and hdd 2f out: wknd fnl f* **14/1**
0-00 **12** *2¼* **Hitman**[60] 2418 6-9-8 **65** LewisEdmunds 14 53
(Rebecca Bastiman) *hld up in rr: rdn on wd outside over 2f out: nvr threatened* **25/1**
0555 **13** *nk* **Explain**[44] 2899 7-9-10 **67** (b) JackGarritty 2 54
(Ruth Carr) *trckd ldrs: rdn over 2f out: wknd over 1f out* **16/1**
-063 **14** *2¼* **I Know How (IRE)**[15] 3970 4-9-6 **63** PJMcDonald 1 44
(Julie Camacho) *chsd ldrs: rdn along over 2f out: wknd appr fnl f* **11/1**

1m 25.25s (-2.35) **Going Correction** -0.275s/f (Firm)
WFA 3 from 4yo+ 8lb **14** Ran SP% **116.3**
Speed ratings (Par 103): **102,100,99,98,98 98,97,96,96,95 95,93,92,90**
CSF £47.08 CT £1421.91 TOTE £3.70: £1.50, £2.60, £10.90; EX 55.10 Trifecta £1506.70.
Owner MPR, Ventura Racing 6 & Partner **Bred** Anthony Morris **Trained** Nawton, N Yorks

FOCUS
This modest handicap was wide open. It was run at a sound pace and the second sets the level. Add 10yds. The winner has been rated close to last year's best, with the second to his recent C&D form and the third close to form.
T/Jkpt: Not won. T/Plt: £33.40 to a £1 stake. Pool: £66,433.57. 1,447.92 winning units. T/Qpdt: £21.60 to a £1 stake. Pool: £5,885.72. 201.53 winning units. **Andrew Sheret**

4524 - 4531a (Foreign Racing) - See Raceform Interactive

977
DEAUVILLE (R-H)
Wednesday, July 3

OFFICIAL GOING: Polytrack: standard; turf: good

4532a PRIX DU CANAL DE RETOUR D'EAU (CLAIMER) (4YO+) (ALL-WEATHER TRACK) (POLYTRACK) 6f 110y(P)
11:25 4-Y-0+ **£7,207** (£2,882; £2,162; £1,441; £720)

RPR
1 **Chef Oui Chef (FR)**[43] 9-9-5 0 (p) SebastienMaillot 10 71
(M Boutin, France) **13/5**[1]
2 *2½* **Wooldix (FR)**[31] 4-9-4 0 (p) MarcNobili 11 63
(Mlle Stephanie Penot, France) **10/1**
3 *1* **La Belle Mayson**[43] 4-8-8 0 (b) ClementGuitraud 4 50
(P Monfort, France) **35/1**
4 *1½* **Duquesa Penguin**[43] 7-8-11 0 BertrandFlandrin 5 49
(Sofie Lanslots, France) **30/1**
5 *½* **Ali Spirit (IRE)**[12] 4090 6-9-4 0 (p) PierreBazire 2 54
(Elias Mikhalides, France) **18/5**[2]
6 *nk* **Get Even**[22] 3715 4-9-1 0 Louis-PhilippeBeuzelin 1 50
(Jo Hughes, France) *settled towards rr: urged along over 2f out: rdn over 1f out: styd on same pce fnl f* **18/5**[2]
7 *shd* **Eva Glitters (FR)**[22] 3715 4-8-13 0 JeffersonSmith 8 48
(P Demercastel, France) **22/1**
8 *hd* **Mangaia (FR)**[676] 6455 5-8-11 0 HugoBesnier 9 45
(Vaclav Luka Jr, Czech Republic) **12/1**
9 *2½* **Artplace (IRE)**[12] 9-9-2 0 (b) FrankPanicucci 7 43
(F Rossi, France) **53/10**[3]

The Form Book Flat 2019, Raceform Ltd, Newbury, RG14 5SJ

10 2 **Shot In The Dark (FR)**[81] 6-9-1 0 GlenBraem 6 36
(C Boutin, France) **44/1**

11 4 ½ **Bombetta (FR)**[27] 4-8-8 0 MlleAlisonMassin(3) 3 19
(Rosine Bouckhuyt, Belgium) **30/1**

1m 17.83s **11** Ran SP% **119.7**
PARI-MUTUEL (all including 1 euro stake): WIN 3.60; PLACE 1.80, 3.10, 7.00; DF 17.80.
Owner Ecurie Rogier **Bred** Mlle F Perree **Trained** France

4533a PRIX DE FIRFOL (MAIDEN) (UNRACED 2YO FILLIES) (ROUND COURSE) (TURF) 7f

11:55 2-Y-O £12,162 (£4,864; £3,648; £2,432; £1,216)

RPR

1 **Mageva** 2-9-0 0 StephanePasquier 3 75
(F Chappet, France) **69/10**[3]

2 snk **Vienne (IRE)** 2-9-0 0 CristianDemuro 10 75
(J-C Rouget, France) **19/10**[2]

3 hd **La Pentola (FR)** 2-8-8 0 QuentinPerrette(6) 4 74
(F Belmont, France) **48/1**

4 1 ¾ **Anobar (FR)** 2-9-0 0 MaximeGuyon 12 69
(Andrea Marcialis, France) **29/1**

5 snk **Actee (IRE)** 2-9-0 0 GregoryBenoist 5 69
(R Le Dren Doleuze, France) **31/1**

6 1 ¼ **Angela (FR)** 2-9-0 0 AlexisBadel 11 66
(Miss V Haigh, France) **59/1**

7 nse **Ordalie Jem (FR)** 2-9-0 0 EddyHardouin 6 65
(S Jesus, France) **53/1**

8 ¾ **Miss Lara (IRE)** 2-9-0 0 Pierre-CharlesBoudot 8 63
(A Fabre, France) **8/5**[1]

9 3 **Diamonds Forever (FR)** 2-9-0 0 TheoBachelot 7 55
(L Gadbin, France) **31/1**

10 hd **Circe (FR)** 2-9-0 0 MickaelBarzalona 9 55
(J-M Beguigne, France) **9/1**

11 3 ½ **Rose Diamant (FR)** 2-9-0 0 JulienAuge 2 45
(E J O'Neill, France) **14/1**

12 10 **Goodbye To Jane (FR)** 2-9-0 0 Louis-PhilippeBeuzelin 1 18
(Jo Hughes, France) *dwlt: rcvrd to r in midfield: pushed along over 2f out: fnd little and eased over 1f out* **46/1**

1m 28.35s (0.05) **12** Ran SP% **119.5**
PARI-MUTUEL (all including 1 euro stake): WIN 7.90; PLACE 2.40, 1.50, 8.80; DF 11.10.
Owner Hubert Guy **Bred** E.A.R.L. Haras Saint-James **Trained** France

4461 **HAMBURG** (R-H)
Wednesday, July 3

OFFICIAL GOING: Turf: good

4534a SPARKASSE HOLSTEIN CUP (GROUP 3) (3YO+) (TURF) 6f

7:00 3-Y-O+ **£28,828** (£10,810; £5,405; £2,702; £1,801)

RPR

1 **Waldpfad (GER)**[17] 3907 5-9-2 0 WladimirPanov 3 102
(D Moser, Germany) *w.w towards rr: hdwy appr 1 1/2f out: r.o wl fnl f: led last 50yds: won gng away* **17/10**[1]

2 1 ½ **Ambiance (IRE)**[17] 8-9-2 0 Per-AndersGraberg 6 97
(Roy Arne Kvisla, Sweden) *led: kicked nrly 2 l clr ins fnl 2f: styd on u.p fnl f: hdd fnl 50yds: no ex* **13/2**

3 ¾ **Clear For Take Off**[23] 5-8-10 0 AdriedeVries 7 89
(D Moser, Germany) *in rr: began to cl 1 1/2f out: styd on wl u.p last 150yds: nvr on terms* **83/10**

4 2 **Iron Duke (GER)**[32] 3369 3-8-8 0 FilipMinarik 1 85
(P Schiergen, Germany) *plld hrd: chsd ldr: no imp whn asked over 1 1/2f out: kpt on at same pce* **43/5**

5 shd **Suprimo (GER)**[52] 3-8-8 0 AndraschStarke 4 85
(P Schiergen, Germany) *cl up on outer: 3rd and drvn 2f out but no imp: one pce fnl f* **9/2**[3]

6 2 ½ **McQueen (FR)**[32] 3369 7-9-2 0 MichaelCadeddu 2 80
(Yasmin Almenrader, Germany) *trckd ldr: outpcd and drvn ins fnl 2f: dropped away fnl f* **7/2**[2]

7 nk **Power Zone (IRE)**[23] 3-8-5 0 JozefBojko 5 73
(A Wohler, Germany) *squeezed out between horses leaving stalls: lit up and plld hrd: restrained in fnl pair: rdn and nt qckn 2f out: mde up sme grnd late on but nvr in contention* **134/10**

1m 11.42s (-1.27)
WFA 3 from 5yo+ 6lb **7** Ran SP% **118.9**
PARI-MUTUEL (all including 1 euro stake): WIN 2.70 PLACE: 1.40, 2.80, 2.00; SF: 18.10.
Owner Gestut Brummerhof **Bred** Gestut Brummerhof **Trained** Germany

4535 - 4542a (Foreign Racing) - See Raceform Interactive

3341 **EPSOM** (L-H)
Thursday, July 4

OFFICIAL GOING: Good (good to firm in places; watered; 7.3)
Wind: Almost nil Weather: Fine, warm

4543 TAPIS LIBRE & JOANNA MASON LADIES' DERBY H'CAP (FOR LADY AMATEUR RIDERS) 1m 4f 6y

6:05 (6:09) (Class 4) (0-80,81) 4-Y-O+
£5,927 (£1,838; £918; £459; £300; £300) **Stalls** Centre

Form RPR

-624 1 **Nabhan**[12] 4112 7-9-4 69 (tp) MissJessicaLlewellyn(7) 8 76
(Bernard Llewellyn) *s.i.s: hld up: 8th and plenty to do st: prog and swtchd rt 2f out: rdn to chse ldr fnl f: styd on wl to ld nr fin* **16/1**

1130 2 nk **French Mix (USA)**[19] 3862 5-10-1 76 MissHannahWelch(3) 9 82
(Alexandra Dunn) *trckd ldrs: 4th st: smooth prog to ld over 2f out: pushed along over 1f out: kpt on but hdd nr fin* **12/1**

5031 3 1 **Be Perfect (USA)**[7] 4274 10-9-4 67 4ex MissEmilyBullock(5) 2 71
(Ruth Carr) *dwlt: in tch: 6th st: prog over 2f out: rdn to chse ldr wl over 1f out to fnl f: kpt on* **5/1**

3036 4 ½ **Gravity Wave (IRE)**[37] 3175 5-8-11 62 (p) MissImogenMathias(7) 5 65
(John Flint) *awkward s: detached in last tl v modest 9th st: urged along and gd prog over 2f out: tried to cl on ldrs 1f out: kpt on same pce after* **20/1**

0650 5 6 **Archimento**[19] 3861 6-10-9 81 MissBrodieHampson 10 75
(William Knight) *hld up: 8th st: prog to chse ldrs 2f out: wknd jst over 1f out (jockey said gelding hung left-handed)* **12/1**

0046 6 1 **Tapis Libre**[19] 3862 11-10-0 72 (p) MissJoannaMason 6 64
(Jacqueline Coward) *narrow ld after 1f: rdn and hdd over 2f out: steadily wknd* **9/2**[3]

3-04 7 1 ¼ **Polish**[19] 3861 4-10-4 81 SophieSmith(5) 1 71
(John Gallagher) *led 1f: chsd ldrs: 5th and losing pl st: sn struggling: tried to rally over 1f out: no ch whn hmpd nr fin* **7/1**

5000 8 4 **River Dart (IRE)**[62] 2353 7-9-1 64 MissSarahBowen(5) 3 48
(Tony Carroll) *dwlt: in tch to 1/2-way: sn lost pl: last and bhd st: no ch after* **33/1**

3514 9 12 **King Of The Sand (IRE)**[34] 3321 4-10-7 79 MissBeckySmith 4 43
(Gary Moore) *stmbld s: rcvrd to press ldr after 1f to over 2f out: wknd rapidly: t.o (jockey said gelding stumbled leaving the stalls)* **7/2**[1]

0422 10 ½ **Blazing Saddles**[12] 4112 4-10-3 75 (b) MissSerenaBrotherton 7 39
(Ralph Beckett) *prom: 3rd st: lost pl over 2f out: sn wknd: t.o* **4/1**[2]

2m 37.92s (-2.88) **Going Correction** -0.125s/f (Firm) **10** Ran SP% **118.5**
Speed ratings (Par 105): **104,103,103,102,98 98,97,94,86,86**
CSF £196.04 CT £1110.42 TOTE £18.70: £4.30, £3.60, £1.20; EX 173.70 Trifecta £960.40.

Owner Gethyn Mills & Alex James **Bred** Rabbah Bloodstock Limited **Trained** Fochriw, Caerphilly

■ Stewards' Enquiry : Miss Joanna Mason caution; careless riding

FOCUS
Rail movements added 3yds to the race distance. The Ladies' Derby was named in honour of the four-time winner, who took part again. However, the leaders probably went too fast early and the first three came from the rear. The third and fourth have been rated close to their recent form.

4544 BRITISH STALLION STUDS EBF MEDIAN AUCTION MAIDEN STKS (PLUS 10 RACE) 7f 3y

6:40 (6:44) (Class 4) 2-Y-O £4,787 (£1,424; £711; £355) **Stalls** Low

Form RPR

023 1 **Indian Creak (IRE)**[14] 4030 2-9-5 77 PatDobbs 8 80
(Mick Channon) *mde all: pushed along and in command fr 2f out: shkn up ins fnl f: unchal* **5/1**[3]

32 2 3 **Diva Kareem (IRE)**[20] 3798 2-9-0 0 DavidProbert 5 67
(George Baker) *in tch: 5th st: prog over 2f out: disp 2nd wl over 1f out: no ch w wnr: kpt on* **2/1**[1]

3 nse **Lawaa (FR)** 2-9-5 0 TonyHamilton 2 72
(Richard Fahey) *trckd ldrs: 3rd st: chsd clr wnr wl over 1f out: no imp and jst lost out in battle for 2nd* **9/2**[2]

4 4 ¾ **Chairlift Chat (IRE)**[23] 3694 2-9-5 0 RobHornby 4 70
(Eve Johnson Houghton) *chsd ldrs: 4th st: shkn up on outer over 2f out: kpt on same pce and nvr able to threaten* **9/2**[2]

00 5 nk **Winnetka (IRE)**[8] 4246 2-9-0 0 ThoreHammerHansen(5) 7 69
(Richard Hannon) *in tch: 6th st: effrt on outer over 2f out: rdn and kpt on same pce over 1f out* **14/1**

2 6 1 ½ **Mrs Dukesbury (FR)**[12] 4114 2-9-0 0 LukeMorris 1 60
(Archie Watson) *trckd wnr: rdn 3f out: lost 2nd and fdd wl over 1f out* **6/1**

7 4 **Buy Nice Not Twice (IRE)** 2-9-0 0 TomMarquand 3 50
(Richard Hannon) *a in last pair: nt on terms st: no prog* **9/1**

8 6 **Bad Company** 2-9-5 0 CharlieBennett 9 39
(Jim Boyle) *rn green and sn pushed along: hung bdly rt 4f out: bhd after (jockey said colt hung right-handed on the bend)* **50/1**

1m 24.34s (0.94) **Going Correction** -0.125s/f (Firm) **8** Ran SP% **119.3**
Speed ratings (Par 96): **89,85,85,84,84 82,78,71**
CSF £16.19 TOTE £5.60: £1.60, £1.30, £1.70; EX 16.30 Trifecta £78.10.

Owner Peter Taplin & Susan Bunney **Bred** Mount Coote Stud & New England Stud **Trained** West Ilsley, Berks

■ Austin Taetious was withdrawn. Price at time of withdrawal 100/1. Rule 4 does not apply.

FOCUS
Rail movements added 2yds to the race distance. A fair looking auction maiden for juveniles that produced a clear-cut winner.

4545 SIR MICHAEL PICKARD H'CAP 6f 3y

7:15 (7:18) (Class 3) (0-95,90) 3-Y-O+
£7,470 (£2,236; £1,118; £559; £279; £140) **Stalls** High

Form RPR

0060 1 **Count Otto (IRE)**[10] 4186 4-9-8 86 (h) PatDobbs 4 94
(Amanda Perrett) *w.w in 6th: pushed along and prog on outer 2f out: rdn and r.o to ld last 100yds* **5/1**[3]

3415 2 ½ **Little Boy Blue**[8] 4236 4-9-7 90 (h) RyanWhile(5) 5 96
(Bill Turner) *trckd ldr: rdn to ld 1f out: hdd u.p last 100yds: kpt on* **3/1**[2]

46-0 3 1 ¼ **Ashpan Sam**[33] 3347 10-9-6 84 (p) LukeMorris 2 86
(David W Drinkwater) *trckd ldng trio: clsd 2f out: rdn to chal jst over 1f out: nt qckn* **12/1**

4560 4 nse **Highland Acclaim (IRE)**[19] 3846 8-8-13 77 (h) DavidProbert 3 79
(David O'Meara) *hld up in 5th: shkn up and no rspnse 2f out: kpt on ins fnl f but n.d* **11/4**[1]

0106 5 nk **Harrogate (IRE)**[30] 3443 4-9-0 78 (b) CharlieBennett 1 79
(Jim Boyle) *led: drvn and hdd 1f out: fdd* **10/1**

1501 6 ¾ **Poetic Force (IRE)**[27] 3529 5-9-1 79 (t) GeorgeDowning 7 78
(Tony Carroll) *dwlt: mostly detached in last: rdn 2f out: no prog tl r.o last 100yds: nrst fin* **5/1**[3]

2315 7 nk **Handytalk (IRE)**[19] 3838 6-8-13 77 (b) RobHornby 6 75
(Rod Millman) *trckd ldng pair: shkn up and lost pl 2f out: one pce over 1f out* **7/1**

1m 7.89s (-2.01) **Going Correction** -0.125s/f (Firm) **7** Ran SP% **114.3**
Speed ratings (Par 107): **108,107,105,105,105 104,103**
CSF £20.34 TOTE £5.70: £2.50, £1.90; EX 22.60 Trifecta £162.90.

Owner Count Otto Partnership **Bred** Noel Finegan **Trained** Pulborough, W Sussex

FOCUS
Rail movements added 1yd to the race distance. The feature contest and a decent sprint handicap featuring a couple of multiple course winners. However, a pair with younger legs saw it out better. The winner has been rated to his best.

4546 RACING WELFARE FOR ALL RACING'S WORKFORCE H'CAP — 7f 3y
7:45 (7:48) (Class 4) (0-85,85) 3-Y-O+

£5,498 (£1,636; £817; £408; £300; £300) **Stalls** Low

Form				RPR
-524	1		**Revich (IRE)**[12] [4123] 3-9-6 **84** .... LukeMorris 3 (Richard Spencer) *mde all at gd clip: urged along over 1f out: kpt on wl whn pressed ins fnl f* **9/2**[2]	91
-541	2	3/4	**Sir Busker (IRE)**[25] [3638] 3-9-7 **85** ....(v) CallumShepherd 5 (William Knight) *trckd ldng pair: shkn up to chse wnr 2f out: rdn to chal fnl f: nt qckn last 100yds* **9/4**[1]	90
4553	3	1 1/4	**Luis Vaz De Torres (IRE)**[20] [3813] 7-9-8 **78**........(h) TonyHamilton 2 (Richard Fahey) *in tch: disp 3rd st: shkn up 2f out: nt qckn over 1f out: kpt on same pce fnl f* **8/1**[3]	83
-423	4	1/2	**Majestic Mac**[12] [4124] 3-8-13 **77**........ CharlieBennett 6 (Hughie Morrison) *taken down early: hld up in 5th: prog on outer over 2f out: rdn and looked a threat over 1f out: effrt petered out fnl f* **9/4**[1]	78
-036	5	2	**Al Barg (IRE)**[38] [3149] 4-10-0 **84**........(b) PatDobbs 4 (Richard Hannon) *dwlt: hld up in last: pushed along and tk 5th over 1f out: no hdwy after and nvr remotely in it (jockey said gelding hung badly left-handed)* **8/1**[3]	82
441-	6	6	**Headland**[301] [6996] 3-9-5 **83**........ RobHornby 1 (Martyn Meade) *chsd wnr to 2f out: wknd* **8/1**[3]	62

1m 22.12s (-1.28) **Going Correction** -0.125s/f (Firm)
WFA 3 from 4yo+ 8lb — **6** Ran SP% **113.1**
Speed ratings (Par 105): **102,101,99,99,96 90**
CSF £15.28 TOTE £4.80: £2.20, £1.70; EX 15.90 Trifecta £90.40.
Owner Middleham Park Lxvii & Phil Cunningham **Bred** T Jones **Trained** Newmarket, Suffolk

FOCUS
Rail movements added 2yds to the race distance. This run of the mill handicap was run 2.22secs faster than the earlier 2yo race. The second has been rated in line with his Goodwood win, and the third close to his York latest.

4547 ASD CONTRACTS H'CAP — 1m 4f 6y
8:20 (8:27) (Class 6) (0-65,67) 3-Y-O+

£3,557 (£1,058; £529; £300; £300; £300) **Stalls** Centre

Form				RPR
-544	1		**Peace Prevails**[12] [4111] 4-9-3 **54**........(p) CharlieBennett 8 (Jim Boyle) *hld up in midfield: 6th st: prog on outer over 2f out and briefly edgd lft: rdn to ld over 1f out: clr fnl f: styd on wl* **7/1**	63
5333	2	3	**Queen's Soldier (GER)**[20] [3797] 3-8-13 **62**........ DavidProbert 13 (Andrew Balding) *hld up: 7th st: prog 2f out: drvn to chse wnr fnl f: no imp and jst hld on for 2nd* **10/3**[1]	67
0005	3	nse	**Esspeegee**[17] [3941] 6-9-2 **60**........(p) CierenFallon(7) 12 (Alan Bailey) *s.s: hld up: 8th st: prog whn short of room 2f out: drvn and hdwy over 1f out: styd on fnl f: nrly snatched 2nd (jockey said gelding was slowly away and was denied a clear run)* **12/1**	64
6156	4	shd	**Ignatius (IRE)**[35] [3275] 3-8-6 **54** ow1........ KierenFox 4 (John Best) *s.i.s: hld up: prog and 5th st: nt clr run and swtchd rt jst over 2f out: drvn and hdwy over 1f out: chal for 2nd fnl f: no ch w wnr (jockey said gelding was slowly away and denied a clear run)* **13/2**	61
-463	5	3 1/2	**Foresee (GER)**[37] [3209] 6-9-6 **57**........(h) TomMarquand 6 (Tony Carroll) *led early: chsd ldr after 2f: rdn and edgd rt over 2f out: wknd over 1f out* **6/1**[3]	55
1632	6	1/2	**Hermocrates (FR)**[8] [4231] 3-9-4 **67**........(b) PatDobbs 10 (Richard Hannon) *led early: settled bhd ldrs: 4th st: effrt whn nowhere to go over 2f out: lost pl and momentum: nt rcvr (jockey said gelding was denied a clear run and hung left-handed)* **4/1**[2]	67
0604	7	shd	**Rainbow Jazz (IRE)**[2] [4475] 4-9-5 **56**........(p) RoystonFfrench 2 (Adam West) *led after 2f and set gd pce: hdd & wknd over 1f out* **16/1**	53
0604	8	3/4	**Ideal Grace**[18] [3888] 3-8-7 **56**........ JosephineGordon 9 (Eve Johnson Houghton) *chsd ldrs: lost pl bdly downhill and 9th st: no ch after but kpt on over 1f out* **8/1**	53+
-322	9	3 3/4	**Il Sicario (IRE)**[27] [3537] 5-9-9 **65**........(h) RyanWhile(5) 11 (Bill Turner) *a in rr: 10th st: rdn and no real prog over 2f out* **14/1**	55
1314	10	8	**Muraaqeb**[34] [3298] 5-9-1 **52**........(p) LukeMorris 3 (Milton Bradley) *chsd ldrs but chivvied along at times: 3rd st: wknd qckly 2f out* **20/1**	29
06/3	11	76	**Onomatopoeia**[23] [3690] 5-9-11 **67**........ RobJFitzpatrick(5) 5 (Camilla Poulton) *prom early: wknd rapidly over 5f out: t.o (trainers' rep said mare was unsuited by the undulations at Epsom)* **33/1**	

2m 37.62s (-3.18) **Going Correction** -0.125s/f (Firm)
WFA 3 from 4yo+ 12lb — **11** Ran SP% **122.3**
Speed ratings (Par 101): **105,103,102,102,100 100,100,99,97,91 41**
CSF £31.84 CT £286.52 TOTE £7.80: £2.70, £1.80, £2.90; EX 33.20 Trifecta £370.30.
Owner Epsom Equine Spa Partnership **Bred** W A Tinkler **Trained** Epsom, Surrey
■ Amangiri was withdrawn. Price at time of withdrawal 22/1. Rule 4 does not apply.

FOCUS
Rail movements added 3yds to the race distance. This modest handicap was run three tenths of a second faster than the earlier amateur riders' handicap over the same trip. A small step up from the fourth.

4548 LANGLEY VALE H'CAP (JOCKEY CLUB GRASSROOTS FLAT MIDDLE DISTANCE SERIES QUALIFIER) — 1m 2f 17y
8:50 (8:57) (Class 4) (0-80,82) 4-Y-O+

£5,498 (£1,636; £817; £408; £300) **Stalls** Low

Form				RPR
0230	1		**Mr Scaramanga**[20] [3806] 5-9-11 **82**........ TomMarquand 6 (Simon Dow) *mde all: stretched 2 l clr wl over 1f out: drvn out to hold on nr fin* **11/4**[2]	90
-230	2	1/2	**Allegiant (USA)**[20] [3806] 4-8-13 **70**........ CallumShepherd 2 (Stuart Williams) *hld up in 5th: trapped bhd rivals over 2f out to over 1f out: drvn and prog to chse wnr last 100yds: gaining at fin* **9/2**[3]	78+
-151	3	1 1/4	**Ashazuri**[35] [3264] 5-9-1 **72**........(h) RobHornby 3 (Jonathan Portman) *trckd wnr 2f: 3rd st: shkn up over 2f out: styd on to take 2nd v briefly ins fnl f: nt pce to chal* **11/2**	76
03-5	4	2 1/2	**Statuario**[16] [3973] 4-9-7 **78**........ DavidProbert 5 (Richard Spencer) *trckd wnr after 2f: rdn and nt qckn 2f out: lost 2nd and wknd ins fnl f* **5/2**[1]	77
2540	5	2 1/2	**Delph Crescent (IRE)**[20] [3811] 4-9-6 **77**........(p) TonyHamilton 4 (Richard Fahey) *t.k.h: trckd ldng trio: shkn up over 2f out: nt qckn and no imp: wknd fnl f* **7/1**	71
2054	6	2 1/2	**Narjes**[27] [3539] 5-8-13 **70**........(h) LukeMorris 1 (Laura Mongan) *awkward s: a in last pair: rdn and no prog over 2f out* **16/1**	59
-222	7	10	**Hackbridge**[87] [1655] 4-9-4 **75**........(v) CharlieBennett 7 (Pat Phelan) *a in last pair: rdn and struggling over 3f out: sn no ch (trainer could offer no explanation for the poor form shown other than the gelding may have been unsuited by the undulations at Epsom)* **12/1**	44

2m 6.72s (-3.28) **Going Correction** -0.125s/f (Firm) — **7** Ran SP% **114.9**
Speed ratings (Par 105): **108,107,106,104,102 100,92**
CSF £15.71 CT £62.74 TOTE £3.30: £2.20, £3.10; EX 20.70 Trifecta £83.00.
Owner Robert Moss **Bred** Lordship Stud **Trained** Epsom, Surrey
■ Pendo was withdrawn not under orders. Rule 4 does not apply

FOCUS
Rail movements added 3yds to the race distance. A fair handicap but an all the way winner. The second has been rated close to last year's course form.
T/Jkpt: Not won. T/Plt: £191.00 to a £1 stake. Pool: £75,749.58 - 289.48 winning units T/Qpdt: £19.70 to a £1 stake. Pool: £9,523.68 - 356.22 winning units **Jonathan Neesom**

4104 HAYDOCK (L-H)
Thursday, July 4

OFFICIAL GOING: Good to firm (watered; 7.7)
Wind: faint breeze Weather: sunny and warm, turning overcast later

4549 FIT SHOW 12TH - 14TH MAY 2020 H'CAP — 1m 3f 175y
2:00 (2:01) (Class 4) (0-80,82) 3-Y-O

£7,115 (£2,117; £1,058; £529; £300; £300) **Stalls** Centre

Form				RPR
3-05	1		**State Of Affair (USA)**[63] [2336] 3-9-1 **74**........ AndreaAtzeni 4 (Ed Walker) *trckd ldrs: pushed along and tk clsr order 3f out: drvn to ld 2f out: rdn over 1f out: strly chal by runner-up ins fnl f: r.o wl: jst hld on* **16/1**	81
-522	2	nse	**Starczewski (USA)**[10] [4176] 3-8-10 **69**........ StevieDonohoe 3 (David Simcock) *hld up: pushed along and hdwy 3f out: drvn 2f out: sn rdn: chal wnr and hung rt ins fnl f: r.o last 100yds: jst hld* **9/2**	76
1-32	3	1 1/2	**Hallalulu**[12] [4110] 3-9-0 **80**........ CierenFallon(7) 1 (William Haggas) *hld up: 4 l last 4f out: pushed along 3f out: drvn and hdwy 2f out: rdn in cl 2nd over 1f out: one pce and dropped to 3rd fnl f* **9/4**[1]	85
-412	4	2 1/4	**Battle Of Wills (IRE)**[14] [4034] 3-9-9 **82**........ PJMcDonald 2 (James Tate) *trckd ldrs: pushed along and lost pl 3f out: rdn and hdwy between ldrs over 1f out: no ex fnl f* **7/2**[2]	83
1203	5	3/4	**Fraser Island (IRE)**[40] [3086] 3-9-8 **81**........ JasonHart 5 (Mark Johnston) *led: pushed along in narrow ld 3f out: sn rdn: hdd 2f out: no ex* **6/1**	81
032	6	10	**Frankadore (IRE)**[7] [4291] 3-8-9 **68**........ RichardKingscote 6 (Tom Dascombe) *prom: pushed along in cl 2nd 3f out: rdn over 2f out: sn wknd and dropped to last* **4/1**[3]	52

2m 29.55s (-3.75) **Going Correction** -0.075s/f (Good) — **6** Ran SP% **111.3**
Speed ratings (Par 102): **109,108,107,106,105 99**
CSF £82.50 TOTE £17.90: £6.30, £1.60; EX 91.60 Trifecta £230.50.
Owner Mrs Fitri Hay **Bred** Forging Oaks Farm Llc **Trained** Upper Lambourn, Berks

FOCUS
All races on stands' side home straight. Add 24yds. They stayed on the inside up the home straight in this good little handicap. A surprise pb from the winner, with the fifth rated similar to his C&D latest.

4550 DUTEMANN "EXCEEDS EXPECTATIONS" EBF STALLIONS MAIDEN STKS (PLUS 10 RACE) — 6f
2:30 (2:30) (Class 4) 2-Y-O

£6,469 (£1,925; £962; £481) **Stalls** Centre

Form				RPR
2	1		**Buhturi (IRE)**[42] [3008] 2-9-5 0........ JimCrowley 3 (Charles Hills) *mde all: pushed along 2f out: rdn in 1/2 l ld over 1f out: r.o wl and asserted fnl f* **4/9**[1]	83
	2	1	**Feelinlikeasomeone** 2-9-0 0........ PJMcDonald 1 (Mark Johnston) *chsd ldr: pushed along 2f out: drvn in 1/2 l 2nd over 1f out: sn rdn: kpt on wl fnl f but nt pce of wnr* **10/1**[3]	75
	3	1 1/4	**Red Treble** 2-9-0 0........ CamHardie 2 (Rebecca Menzies) *slowly away: bhd: hdwy gng quite wl over 2f out: rdn over 1f out: r.o into 3rd fnl f* **50/1**	71+
	4	6	**Grand Rock (IRE)** 2-9-5 0........ JamesDoyle 4 (William Haggas) *trckd ldrs: drvn and lost grnd 2f out: sn wknd: lost 3rd and eased ins fnl f* **3/1**[2]	58
03	5	1 3/4	**Javea Magic (IRE)**[29] [3477] 2-9-5 0........ RichardKingscote 5 (Tom Dascombe) *hld up: pushed along over 2f out: sn drvn and wknd* **16/1**	53

1m 14.51s (0.61) **Going Correction** -0.075s/f (Good) — **5** Ran SP% **111.2**
Speed ratings (Par 96): **92,90,89,81,78**
CSF £6.15 TOTE £1.20: £1.10, £3.50; EX 5.60 Trifecta £39.00.
Owner Hamdan Al Maktoum **Bred** Shadwell Estate Company Limited **Trained** Lambourn, Berks

FOCUS
Quite useful juvenile form.

4551 DISTINCTION DOORS EBF NOVICE STKS (PLUS 10 RACE) — 7f 37y
3:00 (3:00) (Class 4) 2-Y-O

£6,469 (£1,925; £962; £481) **Stalls** Low

Form				RPR
32	1		**Path Of Thunder (IRE)**[43] [2973] 2-9-5 0........ JamesDoyle 2 (Charlie Appleby) *prom: rdn to ld over 1f out: reminder and drvn fnl f: r.o wl* **5/4**[1]	86
	2	1	**Encipher** 2-9-5 0........ RobertHavlin 5 (John Gosden) *hld up in rr: hdwy 2f out: rdn in 3rd over 1f out: r.o wl into 2nd fnl f* **6/4**[2]	83+
	3	hd	**Kingbrook** 2-9-5 0........ JasonHart 3 (Mark Johnston) *t.k.h: trckd ldrs: pushed along 3f out: sn drvn: reminders ent fnl 2f and 1f out: drvn and kpt on wl into 3rd fnl f* **7/1**[3]	83
	4	2 1/4	**Boomer** 2-9-0 0........ RichardKingscote 1 (Tom Dascombe) *led: drvn 2f out: hdd over 1f out: rdn and wknd fnl f* **10/1**	72

3 **5** *2* **Glory Maker (FR)**[28] 3498 2-9-5 0 .... BenCurtis 4 72
(K R Burke) *t.k.h: chsd ldrs: pushed along 3f out: sn drvn: dropped to last and rdn 2f out: no ex* **25/1**

1m 31.37s (-0.03) **Going Correction** -0.075s/f (Good) **5** Ran SP% **109.9**
Speed ratings (Par 96): **97,95,95,93,90**
CSF £3.38 TOTE £2.00: £1.10, £1.10; EX 3.90 Trifecta £8.40.
Owner Godolphin **Bred** Rabbah Bloodstock Limited **Trained** Newmarket, Suffolk

FOCUS
Add 6yds. Fairly useful juvenile form, with a 1-2 for Godolphin.

4552 PILKINGTON GLASS H'CAP — 7f 37y
3:30 (3:32) (Class 5) (0-75,77) 3-Y-O+
£4,851 (£1,443; £721; £360; £300; £300) **Stalls** Low

Form RPR

5063 **1** **Mickey (IRE)**[6] 4322 6-10-2 **77** ....(v) RichardKingscote 10 86
(Tom Dascombe) *mid-div: hdwy on outer over 2f out: rdn to chal over 1f out: led 1/2f out: drvn out nr fin* **11/2**[3]

2164 **2** *1* **Global Spirit**[22] 3722 4-9-11 **72** .... BenCurtis 1 79+
(Roger Fell) *mid-div: pushed along over 2f out: rdn and hdwy over 1f out: briefly n.m.r ins fnl f: sn in clr: r.o wl* **9/2**[2]

2/00 **3** *½* **Lady Of Aran (IRE)**[14] 4023 4-9-11 **72** .... StevieDonohoe 9 77
(Charlie Fellowes) *hld up: drvn and hdwy over 1f out: rdn and r.o wl ins fnl f: tk 3rd nr fin* **14/1**

-135 **4** *nk* **Ramesses**[23] 3683 3-9-4 **73** .... PaddyMathers 12 74
(Richard Fahey) *led: drvn in narrow ld 2f out: rdn in 1/2 l ld 1f out: hdd 1/2f out: wknd* **9/1**

2331 **5** *¾* **Tukhoom (IRE)**[13] 4078 6-10-2 **77** ....(b) DanielTudhope 6 79
(David O'Meara) *prom: drvn in cl 2nd 2f out: sn rdn: 1/2 l 2nd 1f out: wknd fnl f* **11/4**[1]

046 **6** *1 ¼* **Valley Of Fire**[11] 4149 7-9-5 **66** .... LewisEdmunds 4 68+
(Les Eyre) *hld up on inner: pushed along and hdwy over 2f out: chsd ldrs 1f out and sn nt clr run: position accepted fr 1/2f out (jockey said gelding was denied a clear run in the final furlong)* **22/1**

-503 **7** *1 ¾* **Punjab Mail**[34] 3307 3-9-4 **73** .... PJMcDonald 5 64
(Ian Williams) *trckd ldrs: rdn 2f out: sn wknd* **9/2**[2]

-000 **8** *nk* **Bahuta Acha**[9] 4207 4-9-13 **74** ....(p) TrevorWhelan 3 67
(David Loughnane) *mid-div: drvn 2f out: rdn over 1f out: no imp* **50/1**

5405 **9** *1* **Sir Victor (IRE)**[12] 4107 3-9-5 **74** .... AlistairRawlinson 13 61
(Tom Dascombe) *hld up in rr: drvn 2f out: effrt whn nt clr run over 1f out: one pce fnl f (jockey said gelding hung left in the home straight)* **25/1**

-011 **10** *1* **Fitzrovia**[17] 3939 4-9-7 **68** .... BarryMcHugh 7 56
(Ed de Giles) *hld up: drvn on outer 2f out: no imp* **8/1**

-000 **11** *2 ¼* **Sayesse**[7] 4281 5-9-2 **63** ....(p[1]) CamHardie 8 44
(Lisa Williamson) *hld up: drvn 3f out: no rspnse* **66/1**

1000 **12** *3 ½* **Liberation Day**[41] 3048 3-9-4 **76** ....(p) JaneElliott(3) 2 45
(Tom Dascombe) *chsd ldrs: drvn and wknd over 2f out* **50/1**

1m 29.97s (-1.43) **Going Correction** -0.075s/f (Good) **12** Ran SP% **119.8**
WFA 3 from 4yo+ 8lb
Speed ratings (Par 103): **105,103,103,102,102 100,98,98,97,96 93,89**
CSF £29.52 CT £341.49 TOTE £6.20: £2.30, £1.90, £4.40; EX 30.80 Trifecta £312.00.
Owner Mrs Janet Lowe & Tom Dascombe **Bred** Viscountess Brookeborough **Trained** Malpas, Cheshire

FOCUS
Add 6yds. A modest handicap and something of a messy race. Again they stayed on the inner up the home straight. The second has been rated back to form, with the third stepping back towards her 2yo form.

4553 BOHLE MASTERTRACK H'CAP — 1m 2f 100y
4:00 (4:02) (Class 3) (0-90,90) 3-Y-O **£10,997** (£3,272; £1,635; £817) **Stalls** High

Form RPR

51-1 **1** **Dal Horrisgle**[32] 3372 3-9-7 **90** .... JamesDoyle 3 104+
(William Haggas) *hld up in rr: hdwy on outer 3f out: pushed into ld over 2f out: rdn and drifted lft in 1 l ld 1f out: readily drew clr fnl f* **1/1**[1]

11 **2** *3* **Southern Rock (IRE)**[15] 4001 3-9-0 **83** .... DanielTudhope 2 89
(David O'Meara) *hld up: pushed along and tk clsr order 3f out: rdn 2f out: kpt on into 2nd fnl f: no ch w wnr* **11/4**[2]

61-3 **3** *½* **Mubariz**[19] 3859 3-9-6 **89** ....(p[1]) JasonWatson 4 94
(Roger Charlton) *led: hdd 3f out: rdn 2f out: 1 l 2nd 1f out: no ex and lost 2nd ins fnl f: lost shoe (vet said colt lost it's left hind shoe)* **9/2**[3]

3123 **4** *nk* **Albert Finney**[35] 3262 3-9-1 **84** .... RobertHavlin 1 88
(John Gosden) *trckd ldrs: dropped to last and pushed along over 2f out: rdn in 4th on outer over 1f out: one pce fnl f* **6/1**

-540 **5** *9* **Lola's Theme**[19] 3842 3-8-4 **76** ....(p[1]) JaneElliott(3) 5 63
(Tom Dascombe) *prom: pushed along and tk narrow ld 3f out: rdn and hdd over 2f out: sn wknd and dropped to last* **25/1**

2m 12.39s (-4.21) **Going Correction** -0.075s/f (Good) **5** Ran SP% **113.0**
Speed ratings (Par 104): **113,110,110,109,102**
CSF £4.18 TOTE £1.80: £1.10, £1.40; EX 4.50 Trifecta £10.90.
Owner St Albans Bloodstock Limited **Bred** St Albans Bloodstock Ltd **Trained** Newmarket, Suffolk

FOCUS
Add 14yds. An impressive winner of this good handicap. The second and third have been rated as progressing, with the fourth rated to his Windsor run.

4554 TUFFX GLASS FILLIES' H'CAP — 1m 37y
4:30 (4:32) (Class 5) (0-75,76) 3-Y-O+ **£4,851** (£1,443; £721; £360; £300) **Stalls** Low

Form RPR

3332 **1** **Saikung (IRE)**[17] 3923 3-9-3 **69** .... JamesDoyle 4 80
(Charles Hills) *t.k.h: hld up in rr: hdwy over 3f out: eased out fr rail 2f out: rdn over 1f out: str chal u.p fnl f: led 1/2f out: drvn out nr fin* **13/8**[1]

55-3 **2** *¾* **Just My Type**[40] 3080 3-9-7 **73** .... AndreaAtzeni 3 82
(Roger Varian) *led: 1/2 l ld 3f out: pushed along in 1 l ld 2f out: rdn fnl f: hdd 1/2f out: no ex* **13/8**[1]

5200 **3** *6* **This Girl**[55] 2577 4-10-5 **76** .... RichardKingscote 2 73
(Tom Dascombe) *trckd ldrs: wnt 2nd and pushed along 3f out: rdn 2f out: sn wknd* **3/1**[2]

5320 **4** *3 ¾* **Lady Lavinia**[31] 3414 3-8-3 **55** .... CamHardie 6 42
(Michael Easterby) *hld up: pushed along 3f out: drvn and hdwy on outer 2f out: rdn and wknd over 1f out* **16/1**[3]

00-0 **5** *½* **Longville Lilly**[50] 2731 4-8-4 **52** oh7 .... SophieRalston(5) 5 39
(Trevor Wall) *prom: drvn 3f out: rdn and lost pl over 2f out: sn wknd and drifted lft to rail (jockey said filly ran green)* **66/1**

1m 46.04s (1.14) **Going Correction** -0.075s/f (Good) **5** Ran SP% **108.6**
WFA 3 from 4yo 9lb
Speed ratings (Par 100): **91,90,84,80,80**
CSF £4.36 TOTE £2.40: £1.30, £1.30; EX 4.50 Trifecta £6.30.
Owner Kangyu International Racing (HK) Limited **Bred** M Fahy **Trained** Lambourn, Berks

FOCUS
Add 6yds. A weakly contested fillies' handicap in which two went clear. The pace was a steady one. The level is a bit fluid, but the first two have been rated as progressing.

4555 SUPALITE SKY EDGE APPRENTICE TRAINING SERIES H'CAP (PART OF THE RACING EXCELLENCE INITIATIVE) — 5f
5:00 (5:01) (Class 5) (0-75,80) 3-Y-O+
£4,851 (£1,443; £721; £360; £300; £300) **Stalls** Centre

Form RPR

0411 **1** **Dapper Man (IRE)**[7] 4279 5-10-0 **80** 5ex ....(b) AngusVilliers(5) 9 92
(Roger Fell) *mde all on stands' side: drvn over 1f out: rdn fnl f: pushed clr fr 1/2f out: comf* **10/11**[1]

5000 **2** *3 ¾* **Celerity (IRE)**[12] 4105 5-8-6 **56** oh11 ....(p) GavinAshton(3) 10 54
(Lisa Williamson) *hld up: pushed along and hdwy 2f out: rdn over 1f out: r.o wl fnl f: tk 2nd last two strides* **100/1**

0303 **3** *hd* **Red Stripes (USA)**[2] 4493 7-8-9 **56** oh3 ....(b) KieranSchofield 2 53
(Lisa Williamson) *prom on far side: drvn 2f out: rdn 1 1/2f out: 2nd ent fnl f: kpt on: lost 2nd last two strides* **16/1**

1400 **4** *½* **Musharrif**[5] 4406 7-9-8 **74** ....(t[1]) ZakWheatley(5) 4 69
(Declan Carroll) *mid-div in centre: drvn 1/2-way: sn rdn: kpt on fnl f* **6/1**[3]

3160 **5** *nse* **Toni's A Star**[93] 1507 7-8-9 **61** .... ElishaWhittington(5) 11 56
(Tony Carroll) *chsd ldr on stands' side: rdn and effrt over 1f out: sn drifted lft to centre of crse: 4th 1/2f out: no ex* **25/1**

4104 **6** *1* **Boudica Bay (IRE)**[7] 4307 4-8-6 **56** .... EllaMcCain(3) 1 48
(Eric Alston) *prom on far side: ev ch 1f out: 3rd ent fnl f: sn wknd (jockey said filly hung left)* **9/2**[2]

4000 **7** *2 ¾* **Brandy Station (IRE)**[5] 4364 4-9-2 **63** .... WilliamCarver 8 45
(Lisa Williamson) *chsd ldrs: drvn 1/2-way: rdn 2f out: wknd over 1f out* **20/1**

34-6 **8** *nk* **Q Twenty Boy (IRE)**[9] 4227 4-8-8 **58** .... CianMacRedmond(3) 5 39
(Mark Usher) *slowly away: bhd: drvn over 2f out: effrt over 1f out: no ex fnl f* **7/1**

0461 **9** *3* **Economic Crisis (IRE)**[17] 3933 10-8-10 **60** .... HarryRussell(3) 7 30
(Alan Berry) *prom: drvn over 2f out: sn rdn and wknd* **16/1**

0000 **10** *5* **Lambrini Lullaby**[19] 3846 4-8-6 **56** oh11 .... RussellHarris(3) 6 8
(Lisa Williamson) *mid-div: drvn and wknd over 2f out* **100/1**

0000 **11** *10* **Not So Shy**[3] 4457 3-8-4 **56** oh4 ....(p) LauraCoughlan 3
(Lisa Williamson) *restless in stalls: mid-div on far side: drvn and lost grnd 1/2-way: sn dropped to rr and rdn: drifted lft fnl f (jockey said filly was restless in the stalls)* **100/1**

1m 0.47s (0.07) **Going Correction** -0.075s/f (Good) **11** Ran SP% **120.7**
WFA 3 from 4yo+ 5lb
Speed ratings (Par 103): **96,90,89,88,88 87,82,82,77,69 53**
CSF £185.63 CT £1018.85 TOTE £1.70: £1.10, £23.50, £4.00; EX 142.30 Trifecta £1362.30.
Owner Colne Valley Racing & Partner **Bred** William Joseph Martin **Trained** Nawton, N Yorks

FOCUS
Ordinary form, but a very dominant winner. The winner has been rated similar to his Hamilton win.
T/Plt: £27.40 to a £1 stake. Pool: £58,345.21 - 1,549.43 winning units T/Qpdt: £4.40 to a £1 stake. Pool: £5,410.96 - 907.39 winning units **Keith McHugh**

4220 NEWBURY (L-H)
Thursday, July 4

OFFICIAL GOING: Good to firm (watered; 7.7)
Wind: virtually nil Weather: sunny

4556 BILLY MCKENZIE APPRENTICE H'CAP — 5f 34y
5:45 (5:45) (Class 5) (0-70,74) 3-Y-O+
£3,428 (£1,020; £509; £300; £300; £300) **Stalls** Centre

Form RPR

3541 **1** **Jack The Truth (IRE)**[7] 4301 5-10-4 **74** 5ex .... SeamusCronin 4 85
(George Scott) *travelled wl: hld up: smooth hdwy over 2f out: shkn up to ld ins fnl f: r.o: readily* **11/8**[1]

-562 **2** *2* **Edged Out**[8] 4230 9-8-13 **55** .... PoppyBridgwater 8 59
(Christopher Mason) *led: rdn over 1f out: hdd ins fnl f: kpt on but nt pce of wnr* **8/1**

4130 **3** *2 ¾* **Devils Roc**[10] 4185 3-9-5 **69** .... TylerSaunders(3) 3 61
(Jonathan Portman) *outpcd in detached last: hdwy ent fnl f: fin strly to snatch 3rd cl home* **9/2**[2]

0004 **4** *½* **Firenze Rosa (IRE)**[16] 3961 4-8-6 **51** oh4 .... Pierre-LouisJamin(3) 1 43
(John Bridger) *chsd ldrs: rdn over 1f out: kpt on same pce fnl f: lost 3rd cl home* **16/1**

26-4 **5** *1 ½* **Kath's Lustre**[50] 2729 4-9-7 **68** ....(b) GeorgeRooke(5) 2 55
(Richard Hughes) *disp ld: rdn and hdd jst over 1f out: sn no ex* **7/1**[3]

0043 **6** *½* **Cookupastorm (IRE)**[6] 4343 3-9-0 **64** ....(b) ScottMcCullagh(3) 5 47
(Richard Spencer) *chsd ldrs: rdn over 2f out: sn one pce* **15/2**

0066 **7** *shd* **Mawde (IRE)**[18] 3893 3-9-1 **67** .... OliverSearle(5) 9 50
(Rod Millman) *trckd ldrs: rdn over 1f out: one pce fnl f* **12/1**

30-6 **8** *2 ¼* **Staffa (IRE)**[14] 4026 6-8-4 **53** .... MichaelPitt(7) 7 30
(Denis Coakley) *little slowly away: in last pair: rdn over 2f out: nvr any imp* **33/1**

-000 **9** *5* **Flowing Clarets**[5] 4374 6-8-8 **53** .... TobyEley(3) 6 12
(John Bridger) *chsd ldrs: rdn over 2f out: wknd over 1f out (jockey said mare was never travelling)* **20/1**

1m 0.85s (-0.65) **Going Correction** -0.15s/f (Firm) **9** Ran SP% **116.9**
WFA 3 from 4yo+ 5lb
Speed ratings (Par 103): **99,95,91,90,88 87,87,83,75**
CSF £13.47 CT £41.34 TOTE £2.20: £1.10, £1.80, £1.20; EX 11.30 Trifecta £34.90.
Owner Jack Stephenson **Bred** Michael G Daly **Trained** Newmarket, Suffolk

FOCUS
A modest sprint contest for apprentice riders. A pb from the winner, with the second rated close to her latest.

4557 PREMIER FOOD COURTS EBF FILLIES' NOVICE STKS (PLUS 10 RACE) — 6f
6:20 (6:20) (Class 4) 2-Y-O **£5,110** (£1,520; £759; £379) **Stalls** Centre

Form RPR

1 **So Sharp** 2-9-0 0 .... HollieDoyle 2 80+
(Archie Watson) *sn led: qcknd up wl over 1f out: drifted sharply rt ins fnl f but a in command: comf* **11/10**[1]

2 *1* **Dark Lady** 2-9-0 0 .... SeanLevey 5 77+
(Richard Hannon) *hld up: ducked lft after 1f: hdwy over 2f out: rdn to chse wnr over 1f out: kpt on wl fnl f but a being hld* **6/1**[3]

3 1¼ **Vividly** 2-9-0 0 .... KieranShoemark 6 75+
(Charles Hills) *hld up: nt clr run and swtchd rt over 1f out: kpt on nicely fnl f: wnt 3rd toward fin: improve* 14/1

4 ¾ **Miss Paxman** 2-9-0 0 .... OisinMurphy 4 71+
(Martyn Meade) *trckd ldrs: rdn over 1f out: kpt on fnl f but nt pce of front pair: lost 3rd cl home* 15/2

2 5 2¾ **Fair Pass (IRE)**[29] 3461 2-9-0 0 .... ShaneKelly 9 63
(Marco Botti) *racd keenly: hld up: hdwy 2f out: sn rdn: nt pce to get on terms* 7/2[2]

6 1½ **Jouska** 2-9-0 0 .... MartinDwyer 7 58
(Henry Candy) *racd keenly: prom tl outpcd over 1f out: fdd fnl f* 10/1

00 7 shd **Aust Ferry**[19] 3835 2-9-0 0 .... CharlesBishop 3 58
(Eve Johnson Houghton) *in tch: nt clrest of runs 2f out: sn rdn: nt pce to get involved* 28/1

8 1½ **Final Deal** 2-9-0 0 .... NicolaCurrie 1 53
(Mark Usher) *trckd ldrs: rdn over 1f out: wknd fnl f* 100/1

0 9 1½ **The Red Witch**[9] 4221 2-8-7 0 .... TobyEley(7) 8 49
(Steph Hollinshead) *trckd ldrs tl over 2f out: wknd over 1f out* 100/1

1m 13.6s (0.40) **Going Correction** -0.15s/f (Firm) 9 Ran SP% **117.1**
Speed ratings (Par 93): **91,89,88,87,83 81,81,79,77**
CSF £8.45 TOTE £1.90: £1.10, £1.60, £3.40; EX 8.90 Trifecta £50.00.
Owner Sheikh Rashid Dalmook Al Maktoum **Bred** Mildmay Bloodstock & D H Caslon **Trained** Upper Lambourn, W Berks

FOCUS
Amazingly, all three previous winners of this novice event have yet to add another success to their profile. The early pace didn't appear strong.

4558 COMPTON BEAUCHAMP ESTATES LTD NOVICE STKS (PLUS 10 RACE) (C&G) 6f
6:55 (6:57) (Class 4) 2-Y-O £6,145 (£1,828; £913; £456) **Stalls** Centre

Form RPR

1 **Man Of The Night (FR)** 2-9-0 0 .... SeanLevey 5 80+
(Richard Hannon) *mid-div: pushed along for stdy prog fr 2f out: rdn to ld jst ins fnl f: r.o wl* 4/6[1]

2 1¼ **Ethic** 2-9-0 0 .... KerrinMcEvoy 12 76+
(William Haggas) *hld up in last trio: hdwy fr 2f out: sn drifting lft: wnt 2nd fnl 120yds: kpt on nicely wout threatening wnr* 8/1[2]

0 3 1 **Dark Silver (IRE)**[24] 3660 2-9-0 0 .... LiamKeniry 7 73
(Ed Walker) *hld up in last trio: hdwy whn nt clr run over 1f out: r.o wl whn clr ins fnl f: wnt 3rd towards fin* 25/1

20 4 1 **Red Sun (IRE)**[8] 4246 2-9-0 0 .... KieranShoemark 2 70
(Charles Hills) *prom: rdn and ev ch ent fnl f: sn outpcd by wnr: kpt on but no ex whn losing 2 pls fnl 120yds* 10/1[3]

5 ¾ **Outtake** 2-9-0 0 .... HollieDoyle 10 69+
(Richard Hannon) *mid-div: disputing 4th and running on whn squeezed out ent fnl f: kpt on but no threat after (jockey said colt was tight for room inside the final furlong)* 40/1

04 6 hd **Pitcher**[18] 3890 2-8-9 0 .... SeamusCronin(5) 3 67
(Richard Hannon) *led: rdn over 1f out: hdd jst ins fnl f: sn no ex* 14/1

7 1¾ **Bermuda Schwartz** 2-9-0 0 .... ShaneKelly 6 62+
(Richard Hughes) *s.i.s: in last trio: rdn over 1f out: nt pce to get involved* 50/1

8 nse **Speed Merchant (IRE)** 2-9-0 0 .... OisinMurphy 8 62
(Brian Meehan) *trckd ldrs: rdn 2f out: wknd fnl f* 20/1

9 4½ **Raabeh** 2-9-0 0 .... JimCrowley 9 48
(Brian Meehan) *trckd ldrs: rdn over 2f out: wkng whn hmpd jst over 1f out* 14/1

1m 13.59s (0.39) **Going Correction** -0.15s/f (Firm) 9 Ran SP% **106.5**
Speed ratings (Par 96): **91,89,88,86,85 85,83,83,77**
CSF £4.75 TOTE £1.30: £1.02, £2.20, £4.70; EX 5.20 Trifecta £66.30.
Owner Saeed Manana **Bred** Jean-Pierre Dubois **Trained** East Everleigh, Wilts
■ Impressor and Shadow Glen were withdrawn. Prices at time of withdrawal 33/1 & 8/1 respectively. Rule 4 applies to all bets - deduction 10p in the £.

FOCUS
There had been lots of money for the market leader after the bookmakers priced this race up the night before and he won in decent style. Much like the previous contest, which was run in an identical time, the early fractions didn't seem that quick. The time was slow and the field was compressed, so the bare form can't be rated too highly, but it's been rated on the positive side.

4559 RANCHO ZABACO H'CAP 1m 4f
7:25 (7:28) (Class 3) (0-90,90) 3-Y-O £8,086 (£2,406; £1,202; £601) **Stalls** Low

Form RPR

11 1 **Logician**[13] 4073 3-9-7 90 .... FrankieDettori 2 109+
(John Gosden) *trckd ldng trio: stdy prog to ld wl over 2f out: sn pushed clr: easily* 1/5[1]

-561 2 4½ **Natty Night**[23] 3692 3-8-6 75 .... MartinDwyer 1 82
(William Muir) *led: rdn and hdd wl over 2f out: sn hld by wnr: kpt on same pce* 14/1[3]

0-64 3 2½ **Just Hubert (IRE)**[56] 2562 3-8-11 80 .... KerrinMcEvoy 3 84
(William Muir) *trckd ldrs: rdn over 2f out: wnt hld 3rd over 1f out: kpt on same pce* 14/1[3]

2212 4 6 **Agent Basterfield (IRE)**[23] 3692 3-8-10 79 .... OisinMurphy 4 72
(Andrew Balding) *trckd ldr: chalng whn rdn wl over 2f out: sn hld: wknd over 1f out* 6/1[2]

2-66 5 22 **Massam**[47] 2821 3-9-5 88 .... JimCrowley 5 59
(David Simcock) *s.i.s: last of the 5: effrt over 3f out: wknd over 2f out* 16/1

2m 29.35s (-8.65) **Going Correction** -0.15s/f (Firm) 5 Ran SP% **116.8**
Speed ratings (Par 104): **110,107,105,101,86**
CSF £5.44 TOTE £1.10: £1.10, £4.50; EX 4.30 Trifecta £15.70.
Owner K Abdullah **Bred** Juddmonte Farms Ltd **Trained** Newmarket, Suffolk

FOCUS
A one-sided race when looking at the betting and those who invested at short odds had few worries.

4560 CHURCHILL RETIREMENT LIVING BRITISH EBF FILLIES' H'CAP 6f
8:00 (8:04) (Class 4) (0-85,85) 3-Y-O+ £5,919 (£1,761; £880; £440; £300; £300) **Stalls** Centre

Form RPR

-166 1 **Shorter Skirt**[31] 3427 3-8-11 74 .... CharlesBishop 6 83
(Eve Johnson Houghton) *hld up: swtchd rt and gd hdwy ent fnl f: sn rdn: led fnl 90yds: r.o wl* 8/1

-322 2 3 **Lethal Angel**[13] 4074 4-8-13 70 .... (b) KerrinMcEvoy 2 70
(Stuart Williams) *led: rdn and hdd ins fnl f: nt pce of wnr* 4/1[3]

0033 3 ½ **Lady Dancealot (IRE)**[20] 3815 4-10-0 85 .... GeraldMosse 4 84
(David Elsworth) *hld up: hdwy over 2f out: rdn on 3rd wl over 1f out: kpt on same pce fnl f* 15/8[1]

1234 4 ½ **With Caution (IRE)**[26] 3583 3-9-6 83 .... OisinMurphy 3 79
(James Tate) *trckd ldr: rdn over 1f out: nt pce to chal: lost 3rd cl home* 7/2[2]

3115 5 2 **Always A Drama (IRE)**[31] 3427 4-9-5 76 .... KieranShoemark 1 67
(Charles Hills) *trckd ldng pair: rdn 2f out: kpt on same pce fnl f* 8/1

240- 6 3¼ **Sweet Pursuit**[274] 7909 5-9-4 78 .... FinleyMarsh(3) 8 58
(Rod Millman) *trckd ldrs: rdn whn sltly outpcd over 2f out: fdd ins fnl f* 25/1

054 7 49 **Dr Doro (IRE)**[8] 4253 6-8-13 70 .... (v) JasonWatson 5
(Ian Williams) *virtually ref to r: a wl bhd* 8/1

1m 11.67s (-1.53) **Going Correction** -0.15s/f (Firm)
WFA 3 from 4yo+ 6lb 7 Ran SP% **114.2**
Speed ratings (Par 102): **104,100,99,98,96 91,26**
CSF £39.58 CT £84.95 TOTE £9.70: £4.30, £2.20; EX 46.10 Trifecta £200.70.
Owner Hot To Trot Racing - Shorter Skirt **Bred** P T Tellwright **Trained** Blewbury, Oxon

FOCUS
A fair-looking sprint for fillies, that seemed to be run at a decent pace. The winner has been rated back to her 2yo form, with the second close to form.

4561 LUMBER'S BARTHOLOMEW GIN DISTILLERY H'CAP 1m 2f
8:30 (8:33) (Class 5) (0-75,74) 4-Y-O+ £3,428 (£1,020; £509; £300; £300; £300) **Stalls** Low

Form RPR

0050 1 **Prevent**[34] 3305 4-9-7 74 .... (p) JimCrowley 11 81
(Ian Williams) *mid-div: hdwy fr 3f out: rdn over 1f out: styd on wl fnl f: led fnl stride* 16/1

0155 2 nse **Carp Kid (IRE)**[27] 3545 4-9-3 73 .... (p) FinleyMarsh(3) 1 80
(John Flint) *led: jnd 4f out: sn rdn: edgd rt over 1f out: kpt on v gamely to edge ahd fnl 120yds: hdd fnl stride* 5/1[3]

132 3 ½ **Anif (IRE)**[27] 3541 5-9-5 72 .... KerrinMcEvoy 4 78
(David Evans) *trckd ldrs: disp ld 2f out: sn rdn: kpt on tl hdd ins fnl f: no ex cl home* 9/2[2]

1-35 4 1 **Sudona**[42] 3022 4-9-7 74 .... OisinMurphy 8 78
(Hugo Palmer) *hld up: sme prog 2f out: sn rdn: styd on ins fnl f: snatched 4th cl home* 11/2

6444 5 hd **High Acclaim (USA)**[7] 4283 5-9-5 72 .... JasonWatson 9 76
(Roger Teal) *s.i.s: sn mid-div: hdwy over 3f out: rdn and ev ch 2f out tl ent fnl f: kpt on same pce* 7/1

2400 6 nk **The Lords Walk**[26] 3571 6-8-2 62 .... (p) GeorgeRooke(7) 2 65
(Bill Turner) *s.i.s: sn in tch: rdn to chse ldrs 2f out but nt clrest of runs: kpt on same pce ins fnl f* 11/1

0-44 7 ¾ **Dangerous Ends**[90] 1566 5-9-1 73 .... (p) SeamusCronin(5) 6 75
(Brett Johnson) *hld up: hdwy 2f out but nt best of runs: swtchd lft and sn rdn: nt pce to get on terms* 25/1

3-04 8 hd **Nordic Flight**[13] 4067 4-8-12 65 .... RyanTate 10 66
(James Eustace) *hld up last: swtchd to centre wl over 2f out: rdn over 1f out: no imp tl r.o ins fnl f but nvr any threat (vet said gelding lost both hind shoes)* 20/1

-304 9 2½ **Cogital**[4] 4426 4-9-1 68 .... (h) KieranShoemark 7 64
(Amanda Perrett) *hld up last quartet: rdn in last pair over 2f out: sme prog but hanging lft ent fnl f: wknd fnl 120yds* 4/1[1]

3-30 10 2 **Balmoral Castle**[27] 3541 10-9-0 74 .... TylerSaunders(7) 5 66
(Jonathan Portman) *trckd ldr: disp ld 4f out tl rdn 2f out: wknd ent fnl f* 20/1

60-3 11 1 **Shufoog**[36] 1183 6-8-6 66 .... EllieMacKenzie(7) 3 56
(Mark Usher) *in tch: hdwy 6f out: disp ld 4f out tl rdn over 2f out: wknd over 1f out* 8/1

2m 7.29s (-2.41) **Going Correction** -0.15s/f (Firm) 11 Ran SP% **121.4**
Speed ratings (Par 103): **103,102,102,101,101 101,100,100,98,97 96**
CSF £94.70 CT £433.93 TOTE £21.50: £6.30, £2.10, £1.80; EX 100.10 Trifecta £644.80.
Owner Sohi & Sohi **Bred** Juddmonte Farms Ltd **Trained** Portway, Worcs

FOCUS
Lots of these had a chance entering the final stages, so this may not be reliable form. Ordinary form rated around the second and third.

4562 RAYNER BOSCH CAR SERVICE H'CAP 1m (S)
9:00 (9:02) (Class 5) (0-75,75) 3-Y-O £3,428 (£1,020; £509; £300; £300; £300) **Stalls** Centre

Form RPR

-345 1 **Canal Rocks**[24] 3647 3-9-4 72 .... JasonWatson 9 80
(Henry Candy) *trckd ldr: led over 1f out: r.o wl fnl f: rdn out* 7/2[1]

033- 2 2 **Quarry Beach**[250] 8630 3-9-2 70 .... CharlesBishop 8 73
(Henry Candy) *hld up: hdwy whn nt clr run 2f out: r.o to chse wnr jst ins fnl f: a being hld* 13/2[3]

-441 3 1 **Rambaldi (IRE)**[44] 2933 3-9-4 72 .... (t) ShaneKelly 5 73
(Marco Botti) *hld up: rdn and hdwy over 1f out: r.o wl fnl f: wnt 3rd towards fin* 6/1[2]

0-44 4 ¾ **Trelinney (IRE)**[20] 3797 3-8-8 62 .... MartinDwyer 10 61
(Marcus Tregoning) *hld up: hdwy after 3f: rdn 2f out: wnt 4th ent fnl f: kpt on same pce* 7/1

1115 5 shd **Capofaro**[38] 3170 3-9-7 75 .... NicolaCurrie 11 74
(Jamie Osborne) *led: rdn and hdd over 1f out: kpt on same pce fnl f* 12/1

0-04 6 3 **Elegant Love**[24] 3665 3-8-13 67 .... KieranShoemark 7 59
(David Evans) *cl up: rdn over 2f out: sn one pce* 20/1

0-03 7 ½ **Rosamour (IRE)**[21] 3764 3-8-12 69 .... FinleyMarsh(3) 2 60
(Richard Hughes) *trckd ldrs: rdn 2f out: sn outpcd* 8/1

0633 8 1¼ **Balata Bay**[9] 4226 3-9-0 73 .... KatherineBegley(5) 3 61
(Richard Hannon) *cl up: effrt 2f out: wknd fnl f (jockey said colt hung left-handed under pressure)* 6/1[2]

3402 9 nk **John Betjeman**[21] 3764 3-9-0 73 .... SeamusCronin(5) 4 60
(Mark Gillard) *hld up: swtchd lft and hdwy wl over 1f out: wknd fnl f* 13/2[3]

1m 37.4s (-2.50) **Going Correction** -0.15s/f (Firm) 9 Ran SP% **113.5**
Speed ratings (Par 100): **106,104,103,102,102 99,98,97,97**
CSF £25.68 CT £130.44 TOTE £5.10: £2.60, £1.70, £1.50; EX 17.50 Trifecta £134.30.
Owner The Earl Cadogan **Bred** The Earl Cadogan **Trained** Kingston Warren, Oxon

FOCUS
The field raced as a bunch down the middle of the track. The early gallop didn't appear strong. The third has been rated close to his Nottingham latest.
T/Plt: £22.10 to a £1 stake. Pool: £57,274.94 - 1,890.31 winning units. T/Qpdt: £8.80 to a £1 stake. Pool: £6,117.11 - 512.53 winning units. **Tim Mitchell**

4343 YARMOUTH (L-H)

Thursday, July 4

OFFICIAL GOING: Good to firm (watered; 7.2)

Wind: light, across Weather: sunny and warm

4563 MANSIONBET BEATEN BY A HEAD H'CAP 5f 42y

2:20 (2:20) (Class 6) (0-60,61) 3-Y-O+

£2,781 (£827; £413; £300; £300; £300) **Stalls** Centre

Form RPR

6003 **1** **Tilsworth Rose**17 3933 5-8-10 **45**..........(b) NickyMackay 8 51
(J R Jenkins) *hld up in tch: nt clr run 2f out: swtchd rt and hdwy over 1f out: r.o u.p to ld wl ins fnl f: rdn out* **14/1**

2650 **2** 1 ½ **Bronze Beau**12 4132 12-9-7 **59**..........(tp) CameronNoble(3) 5 60
(Linda Stubbs) *taken down early: led: rdn over 1f out: hdd and one pce wl ins fnl f* **8/1**

0043 **3** ¾ **Tina Teaspoon**31 3404 5-8-10 **45**..........(h) JoeyHaynes 6 43
(Derek Shaw) *stdd s: hld up in tch in last trio: clsd jst over 2f out: swtchd rt and effrt over 1f out: hdwy to chse ldrs and jinked jst ins fnl f: kpt on to go 3rd wl ins fnl f* **16/1**

1514 **4** 1 ½ **Precious Plum**13 4074 5-9-12 **61**..........(p) DavidEgan 4 54
(Charlie Wallis) *taken down early: t.k.h: hld up wl in tch in midfield: clsd over 2f out: stl clsd ldr wl over 1f out: sn u.p and pressed wnr tl no ex 150yds out: wknd wl ins fnl f* **9/4**1

0-00 **5** 1 ½ **Haveoneyerself (IRE)**46 2876 4-9-4 **58**.......... DarraghKeenan(5) 1 45
(John Butler) *chsd ldrs: effrt over 1f out: unable qck u.p 1f out: wl hld whn hung rt towards fin (jockey said gelding hung right-handed and was never travelling)* **7/2**2

0646 **6** 1 **Sussudio**10 4193 3-8-10 **57**..........(p) SeanKirrane(7) 2 39
(Richard Spencer) *stdd after s: hld up in tch in last trio: swtchd lft jst over 2f out: effrt wl over 1f out: no imp u.p and wl hld ins fnl f* **6/1**3

44-5 **7** nse **Swell Song**32 3376 3-8-13 **53**.......... TomQueally 7 34
(Robert Cowell) *chsd ldrs: unable qck u.p and 1f out: wknd ins fnl f* **12/1**

-040 **8** ¾ **Quanah (IRE)**7 4286 3-9-7 **61**..........(b) DougieCostello 3 40
(Mark H Tompkins) *taken down early: hld up in tch in last trio: shkn up to cl and nt clr run over 1f out: nvr enough room and no prog ins fnl f (vet said gelding lost it's left hind shoe)* **33/1**

-043 **9** 1 **Awake In Asia**129 906 3-9-6 **60**..........(p) LukeMorris 10 35
(Charlie Wallis) *wl in tch in midfield: unable qck and lost pl u.p over 1f out: wknd ins fnl f (vet said gelding lost it's right hind shoe)* **33/1**

40-0 **10** 2 **Clipsham Tiger (IRE)**9 4219 3-8-0 **45**..........(p1) TheodoreLadd(5) 9 13
(Michael Appleby) *chsd ldr tl wl over 1f out: sn lost pl u.p and bhd 1f out: wknd ins fnl f* **7/1**

1m 2.51s (0.61) **Going Correction** +0.10s/f (Good)
WFA 3 from 4yo+ 5lb 10 Ran SP% **117.0**
Speed ratings (Par 101): **99,96,95,93,90 89,88,87,86,82**
CSF £121.56 CT £1809.19 TOTE £17.80: £4.00, £2.40, £3.20; EX 123.30 Trifecta £1619.90.

Owner M Ng **Bred** Michael Ng **Trained** Royston, Herts

FOCUS

An extremely weak sprint handicap won by a ten-race maiden, although she does look to be on the improve now. She's been rated as running a pb.

4564 BRITISH STALLION STUDS EBF NOVICE STKS (PLUS 10 RACE) 6f 3y

2:50 (2:52) (Class 4) 2-Y-O **£4,851** (£1,443; £721; £360) **Stalls** Centre

Form RPR

10 **1** **Iffraaz (IRE)**15 3988 2-9-8 0.......... FrannyNorton 9 84+
(Mark Johnston) *chsd ldrs: effrt ent fnl 2f: chsd ldr over 1f out: drvn to chal 1f out: edgd lft and led ins fnl f: styd on wl and gng away at fin* **7/4**1

4 **2** 2 **Incinerator**16 3962 2-9-2 0..........(t1) PatCosgrave 5 72
(Hugo Palmer) *racd keenly: led: rdn over 1f out: edgd lft and hdd ins fnl f: no ex and outpcd towards fin* **6/1**3

3 ½ **Villain's Voice** 2-9-2 0.......... DavidEgan 2 71+
(Roger Varian) *hld up in tch in midfield: clsd to chse ldrs and swtchd lft over 1f out: pressing ldng pair whn sltly impeded and swtchd lft ins fnl f: kpt on but nt pce of wnr towards fin* **15/8**2

0 **4** 1 **Order Of St John**35 3274 2-9-2 0.......... GeraldMosse 8 68
(John Ryan) *t.k.h: hld up wl in tch in midfield: clsd nt clrest of runs over 1f out: rdn and hdwy ent fnl f: kpt on wout threatening wnr* **16/1**

5 1 ¾ **Kassab** 2-9-2 0.......... TomQueally 7 62+
(Peter Chapple-Hyam) *dwlt: in tch in last trio: pushed along and rn green at times: clsd and nt clr run 2f out: swtchd rt and effrt over 1f out: kpt on ins fnl f: nvr trbld ldrs* **14/1**

6 ¾ **Golden Dragon (IRE)** 2-9-2 0.......... JFEgan 10 60
(Stuart Williams) *chsd ldr: rdn: unable qck and lost 2nd over 1f out: wknd ins fnl f* **25/1**

6 **7** 2 ¼ **Little Brown Trout**26 3601 2-8-13 0.......... GabrieleMalune(3) 1 53
(William Stone) *stdd s: hld up in tch in last trio: effrt ent fnl 2f: no imp and btn over 1f out: wknd ins fnl f* **12/1**

0 **8** 3 **Star Of St Louis (FR)**15 3990 2-9-2 0.......... KieranO'Neill 11 44
(Denis Quinn) *in tch in midfield: outpcd and hung lft over 1f out: wknd ins fnl f* **100/1**

5 **9** 1 **Exciting Days (USA)**14 4018 2-9-2 0.......... LukeMorris 3 41
(Robert Cowell) *t.k.h: chsd ldrs: rdn over 2f out: sn struggling and lost pl: bhd ins fnl f* **20/1**

10 hd **Just Norman** 2-9-2 0.......... DanielMuscutt 6 41
(Paul D'Arcy) *chsd ldrs: rdn: unable qck and lost pl over 1f out: wknd ins fnl f* **100/1**

06 **11** 1 **Thomas Lanfiere (FR)**7 4295 2-9-2 0.......... JamieSpencer 4 38
(David Simcock) *stdd after s: hld up in rr: shkn up 2f out: no prog and sn outpcd: bhd ins fnl f (vet said colt lost it's right fore shoe)* **25/1**

1m 13.22s (0.62) **Going Correction** +0.10s/f (Good) 11 Ran SP% **120.1**
Speed ratings (Par 96): **99,96,95,94,92 91,88,84,82,82 81**
CSF £12.57 TOTE £2.10: £1.10, £2.00, £1.20; EX 13.00 Trifecta £40.30.

Owner Sheikh Hamdan bin Mohammed Al Maktoum **Bred** Godolphin **Trained** Middleham Moor, N Yorks

FOCUS

Probably no more than ordinary novice form at this stage but the winner looks a colt going places. The time and those down the field suggest the bare form can't be much better than rated.

4565 GROSVENOR CASINO OF GREAT YARMOUTH H'CAP 1m 3y

3:20 (3:23) (Class 4) (0-80,80) 3-Y-O

£5,207 (£1,549; £774; £387; £300; £300) **Stalls** Centre

Form RPR

-331 **1** **Akwaan (IRE)**13 4071 3-9-3 **76**..........(p) DaneO'Neill 3 87+
(Simon Crisford) *s.i.s: c to stands' side 6f out: hld up in last pair: effrt and rdn over 2f out: clsd to ld and edgd rt over 1f out: in command and styd on wl ins fnl f* **11/4**2

2223 **2** 2 **You Little Ripper (IRE)**50 2736 3-9-4 **77**.......... JackMitchell 7 82
(Peter Chapple-Hyam) *stdd s: sn c to stands' side and hld up in rr: clsd over 2f out: nt clr run swtchd lft and jostling over 1f out: chsd wnr jst ins fnl f: kpt on but a hld* **3/1**3

0354 **3** 2 ¾ **Kuwait Station (IRE)**12 4107 3-9-6 **79**.......... DavidNolan 5 78
(David O'Meara) *stdd s: t.k.h: c to stands' side 6f out: chsd gp ldr: clsd over 1f out: rdn and pressing ldrs whn nt clr run and swtchd lft over 1f out: kpt on same pce ins fnl f* **9/1**

-213 **4** ½ **Cape Victory (IRE)**13 4077 3-9-7 **80**.......... JamieSpencer 8 78
(James Tate) *sn c to stands' side: chsd overall ldr: j. path over 5f out: clsd over 2f out: rdn and pressing ldr whn squeezed for room over 1f out: unable qck and lost 2nd jst ins fnl f: sn wknd* **9/4**1

0400 **5** ¾ **Battle Of Waterloo (IRE)**12 4124 3-9-3 **76**.......... GeraldMosse 6 72
(John Ryan) *hld up in midfield: c to stands' side 6f out: clsd but dropped to rr whn nt clr run over 1f out: swtchd lft 1f out: no imp and wl hld fnl f (jockey said gelding was denied a clear run)* **6/1**

0060 **6** 4 ½ **Watchmyeverymove (IRE)**2 4479 3-8-6 **72**..........(vt) MarcoGhiani(7) 4 57
(Stuart Williams) *led and styd towards far side: clr over 5f out: grad c over to r against stands' rail 3f out: rdn 2f out: hdd over 1f out: sn outpcd: wknd ins fnl f (jockey said gelding hung badly right-handed)* **22/1**

1m 39.27s (1.07) **Going Correction** +0.10s/f (Good) 6 Ran SP% **111.1**
Speed ratings (Par 102): **98,96,93,92,92 87**
CSF £11.14 CT £59.45 TOTE £3.30: £1.70, £1.60; EX 10.40 Trifecta £36.20.

Owner Hamdan Al Maktoum **Bred** John O'Connor **Trained** Newmarket, Suffolk

FOCUS

An open-looking 3yo handicap in which the stands'-side group ignored tearaway leader Watchmyeverymove on the far side. Things got a bit tight as the main group bunched together but the winner is on the up now and he cleared away to win decisively.

4566 MICKEY T 70TH BIRTHDAY H'CAP 1m 3y

3:50 (3:52) (Class 5) (0-75,78) 3-Y-O+

£3,428 (£1,020; £509; £300; £300; £300) **Stalls** Centre

Form RPR

-104 **1** **Coastline (IRE)**35 3273 3-9-2 **73**.......... JamieSpencer 8 81
(James Tate) *stdd s: hld up in last pair: clsd and swtchd rt 2f out: hdwy jst over 1f out: chsd ldr ins fnl f: r.o wl to ld towards fin* **8/1**

4531 **2** ½ **Star Shield**6 4322 4-10-2 **78** 5ex.......... DavidNolan 1 87
(David O'Meara) *in tch in midfield: clsd and nt clrest of runs ent fnl 2f: swtchd lft and hdwy to ld over 1f out: rdn and wandered lft ins fnl f: wandered bk rt and hdd towards fin* **5/2**2

0312 **3** 3 ¼ **Leo Davinci (USA)**7 4281 3-9-2 **73**..........(t) HayleyTurner 5 73
(George Scott) *stdd s: in tch towards rr: clsd over 2f out: effrt to chse ldrs over 1f out: 2nd but outpcd by wnr whn hung lft 1f out: wl hld and one pce ins fnl f* **9/4**1

4-00 **4** ½ **Maratha (IRE)**3 4450 5-10-1 **77**..........(t) DanielMuscutt 2 77
(Stuart Williams) *chsd ldrs: effrt ent fnl 2f: stl pressing ldrs but unable qck over 1f out: outpcd ins fnl f* **16/1**

3212 **5** 1 ¼ **Waqt (IRE)**9 4207 5-9-10 **72**..........(p) RossaRyan 6 70
(Alexandra Dunn) *trckd ldrs: effrt ent fnl 2f: drvn and no ex over 1f out: wknd ins fnl f* **13/2**

5121 **6** nk **Oud Metha Bridge (IRE)**22 3743 5-9-4 **73**.......... SeanKirrane(7) 7 70
(Julia Feilden) *racd keenly: led for over 5f out: styd upsides ldr tl led again over 2f out: hdd and unable to match pce of wnr over 1f out: wknd ins fnl f* **6/1**3

0204 **7** 4 **Glory Awaits (IRE)**22 3743 9-9-9 **76**..........(b) DylanHogan(5) 4 64
(David Simcock) *racd keenly: w ldr tl led over 5f out: hdd over 2f out and sn edging lft: outpcd over 1f out: wknd ins fnl f* **14/1**

5200 **8** 14 **Lacan (IRE)**13 4067 8-8-11 **66**.......... JoeBradnam(7) 3 21
(Michael Bell) *s.i.s: a bhd* **25/1**

1m 37.79s (-0.41) **Going Correction** +0.10s/f (Good)
WFA 3 from 4yo+ 9lb 8 Ran SP% **114.5**
Speed ratings (Par 103): **106,105,102,101,100 100,96,82**
CSF £28.42 CT £60.94 TOTE £9.60: £2.70, £1.30, £1.10; EX 37.00 Trifecta £148.40.

Owner Sheikh Juma Dalmook Al Maktoum **Bred** Gerry Flannery Developments **Trained** Newmarket, Suffolk

FOCUS

The front two came clear in the closing stages and the bang in-form runner-up helps give the form a solid enough feel for the level. They appeared to go a reasonable gallop.

4567 DOWNLOAD THE MANSIONBET APP H'CAP 7f 3y

4:20 (4:22) (Class 6) (0-65,64) 3-Y-O+

£2,781 (£827; £413; £300; £300; £300) **Stalls** Centre

Form RPR

5021 **1** **Magical Ride**6 4349 4-9-9 **64** 5ex.......... SeanKirrane(7) 3 71+
(Richard Spencer) *sn chsng ldrs: clsd to chse ldr 2f out: sn rdn and chalng: clr w ldr 1f out: edgd rt but kpt on wl to ld towards fin* **8/13**1

250 **2** nk **Sonnet Rose (IRE)**8 4248 5-9-8 **61**..........(bt) SebastianWoods(5) 8 67
(Conrad Allen) *chsd ldrs tl trckd ldr 5f out: shkn up to ld 2f out: sn rdn and clr w wnr 1f out: hdd and one pce towards fin* **14/1**

3006 **3** 1 ¾ **Shaleela's Dream**13 4070 3-9-6 **62**.......... JFEgan 13 60
(Jane Chapple-Hyam) *in tch in rr: swtchd rt and effrt 2f out: hdwy u.p to chse ldng pair ent fnl f: kpt on but nvr threatening ldng pair* **12/1**3

6003 **4** 1 ½ **Global Acclamation**16 3964 3-9-0 **56**..........(p) TomQueally 10 51+
(Ed Dunlop) *hld up in tch: nt clr run 2f out: edgd out lft and rdn ent fnl f: styd on: nvr threatened ldrs* **14/1**

5-40 **5** ½ **Salmon Fishing (IRE)**24 3651 3-9-5 **61**..........(t1) RossaRyan 6 54
(Mohamed Moubarak) *hld up in tch in midfield: effrt and edgd lft over 1f out: kpt on but no imp ins fnl f* **8/1**2

-003 **6** nk **Penarth Pier (IRE)**23 3688 3-9-7 **63**.......... FrannyNorton 9 55
(Christine Dunnett) *chsd ldrs: shuffled bk and nt clr run wl over 1f out: rallied and kpt on ins fnl f: no threat to ldrs* **33/1**

-060 **7** *hd* **Parisean Artiste (IRE)**38 3154 3-8-11 **60**................. GeorgiaDobie(7) 2 52
(Eve Johnson Houghton) *hld up in tch: effrt ent fnl 2f: hdwy to chse ldrs over 1f out: sn u.p and unable qck: wknd ins fnl f* **25/1**

4600 **8** *1 1/4* **Laqab (IRE)**26 3567 6-9-10 **58**................................ JoeyHaynes 5 50
(Derek Shaw) *s.i.s: hld up in rr: clsd over 2f out: rdn and unable qck over 1f out: wknd ins fnl f (jockey said gelding was slowly away)* **33/1**

-046 **9** *1 3/4* **Agent Of Fortune**38 3146 4-9-12 **60**............................ KieranO'Neill 11 47
(Christine Dunnett) *in tch in midfield: hdwy over 2f out: chsd ldrs and hung lft u.p over 1f out: wknd ins fnl f* **16/1**

0100 **10** *2 3/4* **Caledonia Laird**44 2944 8-9-8 **56**....................(p) DanielMuscutt 4 36
(Gay Kelleway) *hld up in tch: effrt over 1f out: sn btn and wknd ins fnl f* **40/1**

41/0 **11** *4* **Tom Dooley (IRE)**35 3279 8-8-11 **45**............................ JimmyQuinn 7 15
(Philip Kirby) *t.k.h: led for 1f: chsd ldr tl 5f out: steadily lost pl: bhd ins fnl f* **50/1**

-515 **12** *2* **Napping**14 4025 6-9-9 **60**.................................... GabrieleMalune(3) 1 24
(Amy Murphy) *chsd ldrs: rdn over 2f out: unable qck and lost pl over 1f out: wknd fnl f (jockey said mare stopped quickly. Trainers' rep said mare would prefer an easier surface)* **8/1**2

-500 **13** *5* **Quduraat**36 3213 3-8-10 **57**................................. TheodoreLadd(5) 12 5
(Michael Appleby) *t.k.h: hdwy to ld 5f out: hdd 2f out: sn rdn and dropped out: bhd and wknd 1f out* **40/1**

1m 25.58s (0.48) **Going Correction** +0.10s/f (Good)
WFA 3 from 4yo+ 8lb **13** Ran SP% **127.6**
Speed ratings (Par 101): **101,100,98,96,96 96,95,94,92,89 84,82,76**
CSF £11.60 CT £77.31 TOTE £1.40: £1.10, £3.80, £4.00; EX 10.90 Trifecta £108.50.
Owner The Magic Horse Syndicate **Bred** Highclere Stud **Trained** Newmarket, Suffolk

FOCUS
Good recent form was thin on the ground here, barring the obvious exception of last week's course winner Magical Ride who was extremely well backed to follow up. It's been rated as straightforward form.

4568 MANSIONBET WIN H'CAP 1m 2f 23y
4:50 (4:52) (Class 6) (0-60,63) 3-Y-O+

£2,781 (£827; £413; £300; £300; £300) **Stalls** Low

Form RPR

1400 **1** **Affluence (IRE)**9 4220 4-10-0 **59**..............................(p) EoinWalsh 4 66
(Martin Smith) *hld up in midfield: clsd 3f out: swtchd lft and effrt to chse ldrs over 1f out: rdn to chse ldr ent fnl f: styd on to ld towards fin (trainer said, regards apparent improvement in form, gelding appreciated the faster surface)* **6/1**

3300 **2** *1/2* **Hidden Dream (IRE)**6 4346 4-9-0 **45**......................(p) KieranO'Neill 5 51
(Christine Dunnett) *chsd ldrs tl wnt 2nd over 3f out: rdn to ld and hung rt over 1f out: drvn ins fnl f: hdd and one pce towards fin (jockey said filly hung right-handed)* **10/1**

0-05 **3** *3/4* **Cheng Gong**35 3275 3-8-7 **48**.............................(p) GeorgeWood 6 54
(Tom Clover) *chsd ldrs: shuffled bk over 2f out and n.m.r: swtchd lft and rdn over 1f out: hdwy and kpt on wl ins fnl f (jockey said gelding was never travelling)* **3/1**1

0021 **4** *1* **Elsie Violet (IRE)**6 4346 3-9-3 **63** 6ex...............(p) DarraghKeenan(5) 11 67
(Robert Eddery) *sn led: rdn 2f out: sn hdd and unable qck: kpt on same pce ins fnl f* **7/2**2

-060 **5** *1 1/4* **Pinchpoint (IRE)**16 3966 4-9-8 **53**.............................(h) DavidEgan 8 53
(John Butler) *hld up off the pce in midfield: clsd over 4f out: unable qck u.p over 1f out: kpt on same pce ins fnl f* **9/1**

4546 **6** *hd* **Swiss Peak**6 4346 3-9-1 **59**...............................(b1) CameronNoble(3) 12 60
(Michael Bell) *stdd and dropped in after s: t.k.h: hld up off the pce in last pair: clsd over 3f out: effrt over 1f out: drvn and one pce ins fnl f* **9/2**3

5514 **7** *1 1/4* **Carvelas (IRE)**14 4019 10-9-10 **55**.............................. NickyMackay 2 53
(J R Jenkins) *chsd ldrs: rdn 3f out: outpcd u.p 2f out: kpt on same pce fnl f* **20/1**

0000 **8** *4* **George Formby**17 3938 3-8-12 **53**..............................(h) PatCosgrave 9 44
(Hugo Palmer) *stdd s: hld up off the pce in last trio: clsd over 3f out: no prog u.p over 1f out: wknd ins fnl f* **16/1**

-000 **9** *3/4* **Canavese**10 4179 3-9-0 **62**..................................(p1) GeorgiaDobie(7) 7 52
(Eve Johnson Houghton) *t.k.h: chsd ldr tl over 3f out: styd chsng ldrs tl no ex u.p over 1f out: wknd ins fnl f* **25/1**

-060 **10** *5* **Achaeus (GER)**34 3311 3-9-1 **56**.................................. TomQueally 10 36
(Ed Dunlop) *t.k.h: hld up in midfield on outer: clsd and effrt 2f out: sn drvn and unable qck: wknd ins fnl f* **40/1**

000 **11** *4 1/2* **I'm Brian**5 4400 3-8-5 **51**.. TheodoreLadd(5) 3 22
(Julia Feilden) *stdd after s: hld up off the pce in rr: swtchd rt and effrt over 2f out: sn wl btn* **16/1**

5-00 **12** *30* **Ocean Spray**35 3279 4-9-0 **45**.. JohnFahy 1
(Eugene Stanford) *off the pce in last quartet: dropped to rr and lost tch over 3f out: t.o* **100/1**

2m 8.98s (0.18) **Going Correction** +0.10s/f (Good)
WFA 3 from 4yo+ 10lb **12** Ran SP% **122.6**
Speed ratings (Par 101): **103,102,102,101,100 100,99,95,95,91 87,63**
CSF £64.71 CT £220.04 TOTE £6.40: £1.80, £3.50, £1.30; EX 68.10 Trifecta £306.50.
Owner The Affluence Partnership **Bred** Mrs Michelle Smith **Trained** Newmarket, Suffolk
■ Stewards' Enquiry : Kieran O'Neill two-day ban; careless riding (July 18-19)

FOCUS
Add 10yds. Modest stuff even for the grade but they looked to go a good gallop. The winner has been rated to this year's AW form.

4569 MANSIONBET "HANDS AND HEELS" APPRENTICE H'CAP (PART OF THE RACING EXCELLENCE INITIATIVE) 1m 3f 104y
5:20 (5:20) (Class 5) (0-75,73) 4-Y-O+

£3,428 (£1,020; £509; £300; £300; £300) **Stalls** Low

Form RPR

3-33 **1** **Percy Prosecco**63 2344 4-8-7 **59**............................ KateLeahy(3) 4 65
(Archie Watson) *sn led and mde rest: pushed along 2f out: kpt on wl ins fnl f* **9/4**1

6045 **2** *nk* **Battle Of Marathon (USA)**7 4308 7-9-7 **73**............ LauraPearson(3) 2 78
(John Ryan) *stdd s: hld up in rr: clsd over 3f out: shifted rt and effrt over 1f out: hdwy ins fnl f: styd on strly to go 2nd last strides: nt quite rch wnr* **7/1**

5-62 **3** *hd* **Potters Lady Jane**12 4118 7-9-3 **71**........................ JoeBradnam(5) 1 76
(Lucy Wadham) *led: sn hdd but pressed wnr thrght: pushed along over 1f out: kpt on wl but a jst hld ins fnl f: lost 2nd last strides* **3/1**2

5056 **4** *2 1/2* **Brittanic (IRE)**90 1566 5-9-9 **72**........................... SeanKirrane 5 73
(David Simcock) *stdd s: hld up off the pce in last pair: clsd 4f out: rdn over 2f out: kpt on same pce ins fnl f* **8/1**

0-04 **5** *1 3/4* **Bartholomew J (IRE)**7 4308 5-9-4 **72**...................... MorganCole(5) 3 70
(Lydia Pearce) *off the pce in midfield: clsd 4f out: effrt on inner over 2f out: one pce and no imp fnl f* **15/2**

442 **6** *nk* **Banksy's Art**9 4220 4-8-11 **63**..............................(p) GeorgeBass(3) 6 61
(Mick Channon) *cl up in 3rd: effrt over 2f out: unable qck over 1f out: hld and kpt on same pce fnl f* **4/1**3

2m 29.68s (1.88) **Going Correction** +0.10s/f (Good) **6** Ran SP% **111.1**
Speed ratings (Par 103): **97,96,96,94,93 93**
CSF £17.80 TOTE £2.30: £1.10, £2.80; EX 16.00 Trifecta £49.60.
Owner The Real Quiz **Bred** Clive Dennett **Trained** Upper Lambourn, W Berks

FOCUS
Add 10yds. A small field but they looked to go a decent gallop and were well strung out from an early stage.
T/Plt: £185.20 to a £1 stake. Pool: £70,324.66 - 277.13 winning units T/Qpdt: £13.60 to a £1 stake. Pool: £8,955.29 - 484.88 winning units **Steve Payne**

4570 - 4579a (Foreign Racing) - See Raceform Interactive

4150 TIPPERARY (L-H)
Thursday, July 4

OFFICIAL GOING: Flat course - good to firm changing to good to firm (firm in places) after race 1 (5.05); jumps course - good (watered)

4580a COOLMORE US NAVY FLAG TIPPERARY STKS (LISTED RACE) 5f
6:45 (6:46) 2-Y-O

£25,247 (£8,130; £3,851; £1,711; £855; £427)

RPR

1 **Strive For Glory (USA)**14 4012 2-9-3 0.............................. WJLee 6 101
(Robert Cowell) *awkward leaving stalls and racd in mid-div: prog on outer into 3rd appr fnl f: styd on wl for press to ld fnl 100yds: kpt on wl* **9/4**1

2 *3/4* **Air Force Jet**14 4012 2-9-3 94.......................... DonnachaO'Brien 1 98
(Joseph Patrick O'Brien, Ire) *broke wl and disp on inner tl led 2f out: strly pressed fnl f: hdd fnl 100yds: kpt on wl* **7/2**2

3 *1/2* **Isabeau (IRE)**15 3983 2-8-12 0...................................(b) LeighRoche 3 92
(M D O'Callaghan, Ire) *chsd ldrs: 5th at 1/2-way: gd prog appr fnl f on inner into 3rd: kpt on wl fnl 100yds in clr 3rd* **6/1**

4 *2 1/2* **American Lady (IRE)**15 3983 2-8-12 88........................... ChrisHayes 7 83
(J A Stack, Ire) *broke wl and trckd ldrs in 3rd tl appr fnl f: sn no ex w principals: kpt on same pce* **12/1**

5 *1 1/2* **Royal Affair (IRE)**20 3817 2-8-12 0..................... SeamieHeffernan 5 77
(Joseph Patrick O'Brien, Ire) *racd in rr tl late prog ins fnl f into 5th cl home: nvr nrr* **16/1**

6 *1/2* **Invincible Diva (IRE)**12 4133 2-8-12 0.........................(t) ShaneFoley 4 75
(Mrs John Harrington, Ire) *chsd ldrs: 4th at 1/2-way: pushed along and nt qckn over 1f out: kpt on one pce and dropped to 6th cl home* **6/1**

7 *3 1/2* **Illusionist (GER)**15 3988 2-9-3 96..........................(b) GaryCarroll 2 68
(Archie Watson) *sn disp tl hdd 2f out: wknd qckly appr fnl f: coughing (vet said colt was coughing post race)* **9/2**3

57.64s (-1.36) **7** Ran SP% **113.3**
CSF £10.05 TOTE £3.40: £1.70, £2.40; DF 11.10 Trifecta £30.80.
Owner T W Morley **Bred** Michael Feuerborn & Amy Feuerborn **Trained** Six Mile Bottom, Cambs

FOCUS
The British-trained winner produced a pretty smart effort. The second has been rated in line with his pre-Ascot form.

3789 LONGCHAMP (R-H)
Thursday, July 4

OFFICIAL GOING: Turf: good

4581a PRIX DE LA PORTE MAILLOT (GROUP 3) (3YO+) (NEW COURSE: 2ND POST) (TURF) 7f
6:35 3-Y-O+ **£36,036** (£14,414; £10,810; £7,207; £3,603)

RPR

1 **Polydream (IRE)**35 3289 4-8-13 0........................... MaximeGuyon 5 109
(F Head, France) *hld up in rr: tk clsr order 2f out: rdn to chse ldr over 1f out: drvn to ld ins fnl f: kpt on wl* **4/5**1

2 *1/2* **Marianafoot (FR)**35 3289 4-9-2 0................... Pierre-CharlesBoudot 6 111
(J Reynier, France) *hld up in 5th: pushed along 2f out: rdn and ev ch over 1f out: kpt on ins fnl f but a being hld* **7/2**2

3 *1 1/2* **Spinning Memories (IRE)**35 3289 4-8-13 0...... ChristopheSoumillon 1 104
(P Bary, France) *trckd ldrs: shkn up 2f out: rdn to ld over 1f out: drvn and hdd ins fnl f: no ex fnl 100yds* **39/10**3

4 *7 1/2* **Tornibush (IRE)**35 3289 5-9-2 0........................... OlivierPeslier 4 87
(P Decouz, France) *chsd ldr: rdn along 2f out: sn btn and no ex fnl f* **11/1**

5 *4 1/2* **Trois Mille (FR)**26 3-8-8 0.. AlexisBadel 3 72
(S Cerulis, France) *led: pushed along over 2f out: rdn and hdd over 1f out: wknd fnl f* **15/2**

6 *2* **Repercussion**38 6-9-2 0...................................(p) CristianDemuro 2 69
(Gavin Hernon, France) *settled in 3rd: urged along over 2f out: rdn w limited rspnse over 1f out: wknd fnl f* **27/1**

1m 19.35s (-1.35)
WFA 3 from 4yo+ 8lb **6** Ran SP% **121.9**
PARI-MUTUEL (all including 1 euro stake): WIN 1.80; PLACE 1.20, 1.50; SF 4.70.
Owner Wertheimer & Frere **Bred** Wertheimer Et Frere **Trained** France

FOCUS
The winner and third help set the level.

4206 **BEVERLEY** (R-H)

Friday, July 5

OFFICIAL GOING: Good to firm (watered; 7.9)

Wind: light half against Weather: Sunny

4582 PURE BROADBAND (S) STKS — 7f 96y

6:10 (6:12) (Class 6) 3-Y-O+

£3,105 (£924; £461; £400; £400; £400) Stalls Low

Form	Pos	Dist	Horse / Comment	RPR
1634	1		**Muatadel**[60] 2478 6-9-6 65...(p) DanielTudhope 7 (Roger Fell) *trckd ldrs: pushed along to chse ldr over 1f out: rdn and kpt on fnl f: led towards fin* 5/2[2]	68+
6465	2	1/2	**Mutarakez (IRE)**[14] 4078 7-9-2 64...(p) JamesSullivan 12 (Ruth Carr) *led: pushed along 2f out: rdn ins fnl f: one pce and hdd towards fin* 4/1[3]	63+
3000	3	6	**Prince Consort (IRE)**[13] 4131 4-9-2 43...(p) PaulMulrennan 2 (John Wainwright) *chsd ldrs: rdn over 2f out: outpcd in 3rd fr appr fnl f* 200/1	48
-650	4	2	**Ajrar**[14] 4072 3-8-3 80...MartinDwyer 6 (Richard Hannon) *racd keenly in tch: pushed along and sme hdwy on outer over 2f out: rdn over 1f out: hung lft and sn btn (jockey said filly hung left throughout)* 11/8[1]	36
0050	5	nk	**God Willing**[7] 4322 8-8-9 60...(bt) ZakWheatley(7) 1 (Declan Carroll) *midfield on inner: short of room and stmbld after 1f out: rdn along over 2f out: no imp* 7/1	43
0-00	6	nk	**George's Law**[10] 4210 3-8-8 53...(h[1]) DavidAllan 3 (Tim Easterby) *rrd s and slowly away: in rr tl sme late hdwy (jockey said gelding reared as stalls opened)* 33/1	39+
00	7	1 3/4	**Resurrected (IRE)**[15] 4022 3-8-0 0...(t[1]) NoelGarbutt(3) 8 (Philip McBride) *hld up: nvr threatened* 50/1	30
3050	8	4 1/2	**Thunder Buddy**[17] 3970 4-9-3 58...(p) JonathanFisher(7) 5 (K R Burke) *hld up: rdn over 2f out: wknd over 1f out* 16/1	35
0000	9	12	**Bagatino**[10] 4212 3-8-9 45 ow1...(t) TomEaves 9 (Declan Carroll) *dwlt: hld up: wknd and bhd fnl 2f* 100/1	
0446	10	13	**Diamond Pursuit**[16] 3996 4-8-4 44...(p) KieranSchofield(7) 11 (Ivan Furtado) *prom: rdn 3f out: wknd 2f out (vet said filly bled from the nose)* 33/1	

1m 32.79s (0.19) **Going Correction** 0.0s/f (Good) 10 Ran SP% **118.4**

WFA 3 from 4yo+ 8lb

Speed ratings (Par 101): **98,97,90,88,87 87,85,80,66,51**

CSF £13.00 TOTE £3.60: £2.70, £1.90, £16.70; EX 12.60 Trifecta £544.00.The winner was bought in for £6,500. Ajrar was claimed by Mr Guy O'Callaghan for £6,000.

Owner R G Fell **Bred** Lofts Hall Stud & B Sangster **Trained** Nawton, N Yorks

FOCUS

A dry run up to a meeting staged on watered ground. Rail movements added approximately 7yds to races on the round course. A modest event in which eight of the runners were having their first run in selling company. The gallop was sound but not many figured and, although the first two pulled clear in the last furlong, the proximity of the third holds down the form. The runners raced into a light headwind in the straight.

4583 WILLIAM JACKSON FOOD GROUP BRITISH EBF FILLIES' NOVICE STKS (PLUS 10 RACE) — 5f

6:40 (6:44) (Class 4) 2-Y-O

£5,607 (£1,678; £839; £420; £209) Stalls Low

Form	Pos	Dist	Horse / Comment	RPR
3	1		**Living In The Past (IRE)**[16] 4006 2-9-0 0...DanielTudhope 2 (K R Burke) *led for 1f: remained cl up: led again over 2f out: pushed along and pressed over 1f out: kpt on wl to assert fnl 110yds* 5/1[2]	94
226	2	1 1/2	**Mighty Spirit (IRE)**[16] 3983 2-9-0 93...PJMcDonald 1 (Richard Fahey) *trckd ldrs: pushed along to chal over 1f out: drvn fnl f: one pce fnl 110yds* 1/3[1]	88
63	3	4 1/2	**Pentewan**[8] 4290 2-9-0 0...SamJames 6 (Phillip Makin) *midfield: pushed along over 2f out: hdwy over 1f out: kpt on to go 3rd ins fnl f* 25/1	72
4	4	2	**Aryaaf (IRE)**[16] 4006 2-9-0 0...DaneO'Neill 4 (Simon Crisford) *chsd ldrs: pushed along 2f out: rdn over 1f out: wknd ins fnl f* 6/1[3]	65
	5	3/4	**Dearly Beloved (IRE)** 2-8-11 0...SeanDavis(3) 7 (Keith Dalgleish) *hld up in rr: pushed along over 2f out: rdn over 2f out: kpt on ins fnl f* 20/1	62+
66	6	1/2	**Secret Identity**[17] 3968 2-9-0 0...JackGarritty 9 (Jedd O'Keeffe) *stdd s: hld up in rr: rdn over 2f out: kpt on ins fnl f: nvr involved (jockey said filly was restless in stalls)* 50/1	60
50	7	2 3/4	**Wafrah**[24] 3679 2-8-11 0...(v[1]) ConorMcGovern(3) 3 (David O'Meara) *hld up: rdn along 2f out: nvr threatened* 66/1	50
060	8	6	**Too Shy Shy (IRE)**[16] 3983 2-9-0 82...MartinDwyer 11 (Richard Spencer) *led after 1f: hdd over 2f out: sn rdn: wknd appr fnl f (jockey said filly stopped quickly)* 12/1	29
0	9	4	**Dublin Rocker (IRE)**[29] 3506 2-9-0 0...TomEaves 5 (Kevin Ryan) *chsd ldrs tl hung lft and wknd 2f out* 22/1	14

1m 2.52s (-0.38) **Going Correction** 0.0s/f (Good) 9 Ran SP% **130.1**

Speed ratings (Par 93): **103,100,93,90,89 88,83,74,67**

CSF £7.76 TOTE £9.70: £2.10, £1.20, £3.50; EX 11.90 Trifecta £98.00.

Owner Clipper Logistics **Bred** Newlands House Stud & Mrs A M Burns **Trained** Middleham Moor, N Yorks

FOCUS

Not too much in the way of strength in depth and a race that didn't take as much winning as seemed likely with the short-priced market leader underperforming to a degree. However the first two pulled clear and the winner looks a useful prospect.

4584 JACKSON'S YORKSHIRE CHAMPION BREAD H'CAP — 7f 96y

7:15 (7:17) (Class 6) (0-60,60) 3-Y-O+

£3,105 (£924; £461; £400; £400; £400) Stalls Low

Form	Pos	Dist	Horse / Comment	RPR
-045	1		**Kodimoor (IRE)**[29] 3518 6-8-12 46 oh1...(p) DougieCostello 1 (Mark Walford) *dwlt sltly: led after 1f: mde rest: drvn appr fnl f: strly pressed fnl 150yds: all out* 20/1	52
-000	2	nse	**Rosy Ryan (IRE)**[32] 3414 9-9-0 48...CamHardie 3 (Tina Jackson) *midfield: rdn and hdwy over 1f out: drvn to chal strly fnl 150yds: kpt on* 9/1	54
-555	3	hd	**Dominannie (IRE)**[35] 3296 6-8-12 46 oh1...(p[1]) AndrewMullen 2 (Ron Barr) *dwlt: sn trckd ldrs racing keenly: rdn over 1f out: chal strly fnl 110yds: kpt on* 14/1	51
60-6	4	1/2	**Dreamseller (IRE)**[14] 4080 3-8-12 54...DavidAllan 6 (Tim Easterby) *midfield on inner: pushed along and n.m.r bhd ldrs over 1f out tl ent fnl f: rdn and kpt on (jockey said gelding was denied a clear run inside final furlong)* 4/1[1]	56
0000	5	1 3/4	**Parion**[14] 4080 3-8-8 53...SeanDavis(3) 14 (Richard Fahey) *hld up in rr: pushed along 2f out: rdn and kpt on fnl f: nrst fin* 10/1	50
00-5	6	3/4	**Mr Cool Cash**[35] 3297 7-8-12 46 oh1...(t) SamJames 12 (John Davies) *hld up: n.m.r 2f out: swtchd rt ent fnl f: rdn and kpt on* 16/1	45+
4003	7	nk	**Muraadef**[18] 3924 4-9-2 50...JamesSullivan 11 (Ruth Carr) *hld up: racd keenly: n.m.r over 1f out and swtchd lft to wd outside: kpt on ins fnl f (jockey said gelding missed break)* 10/1	47+
0-05	8	1/2	**Make On Madam (IRE)**[37] 3214 7-9-7 55...LewisEdmunds 4 (Les Eyre) *prom: rdn over 2f out: wknd ins fnl f* 9/2[2]	51
00-0	9	1/2	**Dawn Breaking**[12] 4148 4-9-4 52...PhilDennis 9 (Richard Whitaker) *chsd ldrs: rdn over 2f out: wknd ins fnl f* 20/1	47
0200	10	1/2	**Roaring Forties (IRE)**[14] 4060 6-9-12 60...(b) DanielTudhope 5 (Rebecca Bastiman) *midfield: rdn 2f out: wknd ins fnl f* 11/2[3]	54
-500	11	3/4	**Happy Hannah (IRE)**[16] 4002 3-8-4 46 oh1...RoystonFfrench 13 (John Davies) *midfield on wd outside: dropped to rr after 1f: rdn along 2f out: nvr threatened* 28/1	35
00-0	12	3 1/2	**Destination Aim**[18] 3924 12-9-0 48...TonyHamilton 8 (Fred Watson) *in tch: rdn over 2f out: wknd appr fnl f* 25/1	31
000-	13	3 3/4	**Grimsdyke**[280] 7719 3-8-4 46 oh1...RachelRichardson 10 (Tim Easterby) *dwlt: midfield on outer: rdn along over 2f out: wknd over 1f out* 20/1	17
-000	14	1 1/4	**Legend Island (FR)**[18] 3938 3-8-12 54...(b[1]) RossaRyan 7 (Ed Walker) *led for 1f: prom: rdn over 2f out: wknd wl over 1f out (jockey said gelding hung left on the bend)* 9/1	22

1m 33.14s (0.54) **Going Correction** 0.0s/f (Good) 14 Ran SP% **125.9**

WFA 3 from 4yo+ 8lb

Speed ratings (Par 101): **96,95,95,95,93 92,91,91,90,90 89,85,81,79**

CSF £186.04 CT £1641.17 TOTE £23.10: £6.10, £3.50, £4.40; EX 232.40 Trifecta £546.80.

Owner Ursa Major Racing & Partner **Bred** Tally-Ho Stud **Trained** Sherriff Hutton, N Yorks

FOCUS

Exposed performers in a moderate handicap in which rail movements added approximately 7yds to the official distance. The pace was reasonable and the first four finished in a heap. The winner has been rated back near last year's best.

4585 GEMMA PLATTEN MEMORIAL H'CAP — 1m 100y

7:45 (7:48) (Class 5) (0-75,77) 3-Y-O

£4,347 (£1,301; £650; £400; £400; £400) Stalls Low

Form	Pos	Dist	Horse / Comment	RPR
1022	1		**Anna Bunina (FR)**[7] 4322 3-9-4 71...JackGarritty 2 (Jedd O'Keeffe) *in tch: pushed along to chse ldr 2f out: led 1f out: rdn and wandered: edgd rt and bmpd into 2nd 50yds out: kpt on* 11/10[1]	80
4241	2	nk	**Hector's Here**[16] 4002 3-8-12 65...(p[1]) TrevorWhelan 1 (Ivan Furtado) *in tch: pushed along to chse ldrs 1f out: rdn and edgd lft 110yds out: chal and bmpd by wnr 50yds out: kpt on* 7/1[3]	73
1615	3	2 3/4	**Ollivander (IRE)**[11] 4193 3-9-3 70...(v) DanielTudhope 6 (David O'Meara) *chsd ldr: rdn to ld narrowly over 1f out: sn hdd: no ex fnl 75yds* 7/1[3]	72
-050	4	1/2	**Flying Dragon (FR)**[43] 3011 3-9-6 73...RossaRyan 4 (Richard Hannon) *hld up in rr: rdn over 1f out: kpt on same pce fnl f: nvr threatened* 3/1[2]	74
6-41	5	3 1/4	**Hunterwali**[27] 3570 3-9-7 74...PaulMulrennan 3 (Michael Dods) *hld up: rdn over 2f out: bit clsr 2f out: wknd ins fnl f* 15/2	68
	6	1/2	**Vivacious Spirit**[21] 3827 3-8-12 65...SamJames 7 (Phillip Makin) *led: 4 l clr 4f out: rdn and reduced ld 2f out: hdd over 1f out: sn wknd* 16/1	58

1m 44.96s (-1.44) **Going Correction** 0.0s/f (Good) 6 Ran SP% **115.3**

Speed ratings (Par 100): **107,106,103,103,100 99**

CSF £10.08 TOTE £1.90: £1.40, £3.40; EX 9.50 Trifecta £43.60.

Owner Highbeck Racing 3 **Bred** Dermot Cantillon **Trained** Middleham Moor, N Yorks

■ Stewards' Enquiry : Jack Garritty two-day ban: used whip above the shoulder inside final furlong (tba)

FOCUS

A fair handicap in which the official distance was increased by approximately 7yds. The gallop was reasonable and this form should prove reliable. The winner has been rated close to her latest Doncaster second, and the third in line with his recent form.

4586 FERGUSON FAWSITT ARMS H'CAP — 5f

8:20 (8:24) (Class 6) (0-65,65) 3-Y-O+

£3,493 (£1,039; £519; £400; £400; £400) Stalls Low

Form	Pos	Dist	Horse / Comment	RPR
4131	1		**Ginger Jam**[10] 4212 4-9-4 64...IzzyClifton(7) 8 (Nigel Tinkler) *hld up: swtchd lft to outer 2f out: sn hdwy: rdn to ld ins fnl f: kpt on wl* 6/4[1]	75+
3/00	2	2	**Mr Greenlight**[13] 4132 4-9-5 58...DavidAllan 6 (Tim Easterby) *midfield towards inner: swtchd lft and hdwy to chse ldr ent fnl f: rdn and kpt on* 20/1	62
1042	3	1 1/4	**Indian Pursuit (IRE)**[2] 4519 6-9-11 64...(v) RobbieDowney 10 (John Quinn) *chsd ldrs: rdn to ld over 1f out: hdd ins fnl f: one pce* 7/1	64
4543	4	1	**Gorgeous General**[67] 2183 4-9-5 58...DanielTudhope 1 (Lawrence Mullaney) *chsd ldrs: rdn 2f out: kpt on same pce* 6/1[3]	54
6000	5	1 1/2	**Classic Pursuit**[18] 3928 8-9-12 65...(v) SamJames 12 (Marjorie Fife) *led narrowly: rdn and hdd over 1f out: no ex ins fnl f* 66/1	56
6000	6	3/4	**Twentysvnthlancers**[17] 3975 6-9-2 55...PaulMulrennan 17 (Paul Midgley) *midfield on outer: rdn 2f out: hdwy and chsd ldrs appr fnl f: no ex fnl 110yds* 33/1	43
0565	7	1 1/4	**Muhallab (IRE)**[8] 4276 3-8-7 51...AndrewMullen 11 (Adrian Nicholls) *midfield: rdn 2f out: kpt on same pce and nvr threatened* 40/1	32
3300	8	1/2	**Encoded (IRE)**[10] 4212 6-8-5 47...ConorMcGovern(3) 2 (Lynn Siddall) *dwlt: hld up: pushed along and sme hdwy on inner over 1f out: rdn and one pce fnl f* 40/1	29
4120	9	nk	**Tomahawk Ridge (IRE)**[29] 3508 3-9-5 63...PJMcDonald 3 (John Gallagher) *hld up: rdn 2f out: sme hdwy appr fnl f: one pce ins fnl f* 5/1[2]	41
260-	10	1	**Gleaming Arch**[238] 8981 5-9-7 60...TonyHamilton 7 (Fred Watson) *hld up in rr: kpt on ins fnl f: nvr threatened* 50/1	37
0000	11	2 3/4	**Raypeteafterme**[7] 4328 3-8-13 57...(t) TomEaves 5 (Declan Carroll) *dwlt: hld up: nvr threatened* 33/1	22

0-00 **12** 1 ¾ **Mightaswellsmile**[13] 4132 5-8-7 **46** oh1 .... JamieGormley 14
(Ron Barr) *prom: rdn 2f out: wknd ins fnl f (jockey said mare hung left under pressure)* **50/1**
4000 **13** 2 ½ **Raffle King (IRE)**[17] 3975 5-8-9 **48** ....(b) JamesSullivan 4
(Ruth Carr) *midfield: rdn over 2f out: wknd fnl f* **9/1**
0252 **14** *hd* **Pearl Noir**[10] 4212 9-8-7 **53** ....(b) KieranSchofield(7) 9
(Scott Dixon) *chsd ldrs: rdn 2f out: wknd* **14/1**
0321 **15** 2 ½ **Cuppacoco**[13] 4132 4-9-4 **57** .... JackGarritty 16
(Ann Duffield) *racd on outside: w ldr: rdn 2f out: wknd over 1f out (jockey said filly hung left)* **14/1**
0404 **16** ½ **Jill Rose**[11] 4192 3-9-4 **62** ....(p) PhilDennis 13
(Richard Whitaker) *prom: rdn over 2f out: wknd fnl f* **22/1**

1m 2.41s (-0.49) **Going Correction** 0.0s/f (Good)
WFA 3 from 4yo+ 5lb **16** Ran SP% **132.1**
Speed ratings (Par 101): **103,99,97,96,93 92,90,89,89,87 83,80,76,76,72 71**
CSF £43.28 CT £193.42 TOTE £2.20: £1.20, £4.20, £2.00, £1.60; EX 46.30 Trifecta £206.70.
Owner Walter Veti **Bred** Bearstone Stud Ltd **Trained** Langton, N Yorks
■ Stewards' Enquiry : Sam James four-day ban: interference & careless riding (Jul 19-22)

FOCUS
A modest handicap in which the gallop was sound throughout and this form should prove reliable. A minor turf pb from the fourth.

4587 CELEBRATING RACING STAFF WEEK H'CAP (BEVERLEY MIDDLE DISTANCE SERIES) 1m 4f 23y
8:50 (8:55) (Class 6) (0-60,60) 3-Y-0+
£3,105 (£924; £461; £400; £400; £400) **Stalls** Low

Form RPR
0114 **1** **Agravain**[15] 4034 3-9-1 **59** .... DavidAllan 9 69+
(Tim Easterby) *mde all: pushed clr over 1f out: kpt on: comf* **2/1**[1]
4546 **2** 2 ¼ **Kensington Art**[15] 4038 3-9-1 **59** ....(p) TonyHamilton 6 64
(Richard Fahey) *trckd ldrs: rdn over 2f out: kpt on same pce in 2nd fnl f: no ch w wnr* **4/1**[3]
0-05 **3** 1 ¼ **Arms Of The Angel (GER)**[16] 4005 3-8-9 **60** .... AidanRedpath(7) 2 63
(Mark Johnston) *slowly away: hld up: pushed along and hdwy on inner over 1f out: kpt on to go 3rd 110yds out (jockey said filly missed break)* **11/1**
3466 **4** 1 **Tabou Beach Boy**[38] 3198 3-8-10 **54** .... PJMcDonald 1 56
(Michael Easterby) *midfield: pushed along over 3f out: rdn over 2f out: styd on same pce fnl f* **4/1**[3]
-651 **5** 2 **Ninepin Bowler**[16] 4004 5-10-0 **60** .... DanielTudhope 5 58
(Ann Duffield) *prom: rdn over 2f out: wknd ins fnl f* **5/2**[2]
0505 **6** 1 ½ **Biz Markee (IRE)**[10] 4210 3-8-6 **55** ....(b) BenSanderson(5) 12 51
(Roger Fell) *midfield: trckd ldrs 5f out: rdn 2f out: wknd appr fnl f* **25/1**
-665 **7** 1 **Size Matters**[17] 3960 5-9-1 **47** .... JamesSullivan 11 41
(Mike Sowersby) *hld up in rr: sme hdwy 2f out: sn rdn: wknd ins fnl f* **33/1**
0663 **8** 10 **Jagerbond**[36] 3246 3-8-3 **47** ....(p) CamHardie 3 26
(Andrew Crook) *hld up: hdwy into midfield 5f out: rdn 3f out: wknd over 1f out* **20/1**

2m 40.79s (1.99) **Going Correction** 0.0s/f (Good)
WFA 3 from 5yo+ 12lb **8** Ran SP% **121.8**
Speed ratings (Par 101): **93,91,90,90,88 87,87,80**
CSF £11.06 CT £73.47 TOTE £2.80: £1.10, £1.50, £2.90; EX 13.10 Trifecta £89.00.
Owner Geoff & Sandra Turnbull **Bred** Elwick Stud **Trained** Great Habton, N Yorks

FOCUS
A moderate handicap run at a distance approximately 7yds further than advertised. A steady gallop suited those up with the pace and this bare form may not be entirely reliable. Straightforward form behind the winner.
T/Plt: £78.40 to a £1 stake. Pool: £61,090.62 - 568.71 winning units T/Qpdt: £32.00 to a £1 stake. Pool: £5,843.24 - 134.81 winning units **Andrew Sheret**

4018
CHELMSFORD (A.W) (L-H)
Friday, July 5

OFFICIAL GOING: Polytrack: standard
Wind: Light, across Weather: Sunny and warm

4588 BET TOTEPLACEPOT AT TOTESPORT.COM EBF NOVICE STKS (PLUS 10 RACE) 7f (P)
5:25 (5:27) (Class 4) 2-Y-O
£7,439 (£2,213; £1,106; £553) **Stalls** Low

Form RPR
22 **1** **Subjectivist**[13] 4106 2-9-5 0 .... JasonHart 4 87+
(Mark Johnston) *trckd ldng pair: swtchd rt and effrt to press ldr whn hung rt bnd wl over 1f out: sn led and readily wnt clr: v easily* **4/11**[1]
2 7 **Lost In Time** 2-9-5 0 .... JosephineGordon 5 68+
(Saeed bin Suroor) *wnt rt leaving stalls: rn green: chsd ldr: rdn 4f out: hung rt bnd wl over 2f out: 3rd and unable qck 2f out: chsd clr wnr 1f out: no imp* **9/4**[2]
0 **3** 4 **Rochford (IRE)**[14] 4069 2-9-5 0 .... JFEgan 2 57
(Henry Spiller) *awkward leaving stalls: hld up in rr: pushed along and outpcd over 1f out: no ch after: wnt modest 3rd ins fnl f* **50/1**
6 **4** 5 **Red Jasper**[29] 3512 2-9-5 0 .... GeraldMosse 3 44
(Michael Appleby) *led: rdn and hdd over 1f out: sn btn and wknd fnl f* **25/1**[3]

1m 26.98s (-0.22) **Going Correction** -0.175s/f (Stan) **4** Ran SP% **109.9**
Speed ratings (Par 96): **94,86,81,75**
CSF £1.50 TOTE £1.20; EX 1.50 Trifecta £6.30.
Owner Dr J Walker **Bred** Mascalls Stud **Trained** Middleham Moor, N Yorks

FOCUS
A fair little juvenile novice contest. The odds-on favourite won pretty much as he liked despite some wayward tendencies through lack of experience. The third and fourth will be the key to the level.

4589 BET TOTEEXACTA AT TOTESPORT.COM H'CAP 7f (P)
6:00 (6:05) (Class 6) (0-55,55) 4-Y-O+
£3,493 (£1,039; £519; £400; £400; £400) **Stalls** Low

Form RPR
0063 **1** **Brigand**[16] 3989 4-9-3 **51** .... OisinMurphy 1 59
(John Butler) *trckd ldr for 2f: styd trcking ldrs: effrt on inner to chal jst over 1f out: led 150yds out: kpt on* **9/4**[1]
3442 **2** 1 **Tarseekh**[16] 3996 6-9-3 **51** ....(b) JackMitchell 14 56
(Charlie Wallis) *broke fast to ld fr wd draw: rdn over 1f out: hdd 150yds out: one pce after* **5/1**[3]
0-02 **3** 1 ¼ **Prince Rock (IRE)**[16] 3989 4-8-12 **46** oh1 ....(h) NickyMackay 4 48
(Simon Dow) *t.k.h: chsd ldrs tl wnt 2nd 5f out: 3rd and unable qck jst over 1f out: kpt on same pce ins fnl f (vet said gelding lost right fore shoe)* **9/2**[2]
0-04 **4** ½ **Come On Bear (IRE)**[16] 3989 4-8-12 **46** ....(v) JoeyHaynes 5 47+
(Alan Bailey) *s.i.s and wnt lft leaving stalls: early reminder and wl off the pce in rr: clsd and swtchd rt 3f out: hdwy over 1f out: styd on strly ins fnl f: nt rch ldrs (jockey said filly was slowly away)* **16/1**
0454 **5** 1 ½ **Shyarch**[121] 1032 5-8-13 **47** ....(p) KieranO'Neill 13 44
(Christine Dunnett) *rousted along leaving stalls: midfield tl hdwy to chse ldrs over 5f out: 4th and drvn over 2f out: unable qck over 1f out: kpt on same pce fnl f (vet said gelding lost right fore shoe)* **14/1**
0464 **6** 3 **Ventriloquist**[16] 3996 7-9-7 **55** .... JFEgan 2 43
(Simon Dow) *awkward leaving stalls and dwlt: sn rcvrd and in tch in midfield: 5th and unable qck over 2f out: wknd ins fnl f* **5/1**[3]
-000 **7** *nk* **Out Of The Ashes**[23] 3738 6-8-12 **46** oh1 ....(t) RaulDaSilva 6 34
(Mohamed Moubarak) *midfield: rdn and lost pl over 3f out: edging lft but kpt on to pass btn horses ins fnl f: no threat to ldrs* **33/1**
-000 **8** 1 ¼ **Good Luck Charm**[28] 3540 10-9-6 **54** ....(b) LiamKeniry 8 38
(Gary Moore) *hld up in midfield: shuffled bk bhd a wkng rivals and towards rr over 2f out: effrt on inner over 1f out: kpt on but nvr getting involved* **25/1**
-554 **9** 1 ¾ **Kafoo**[11] 4195 6-9-7 **55** ....(v) GeraldMosse 3 35
(Michael Appleby) *midfield: u.p and struggling to qckn over 2f out: wl hld over 1f out: wknd ins fnl f (jockey said gelding was never travelling)* **7/1**
4500 **10** *hd* **Caledonian Gold**[4] 4455 6-8-5 **46** oh1 .... GavinAshton(7) 10 25
(Lisa Williamson) *taken down early: short of room sn after s: in tch: rdn and struggling over 2f out: wl hld over 1f out: wknd ins fnl f (jockey said mare stumbled leaving stalls)* **40/1**
006 **11** 2 ¼ **Plucky Dip**[65] 2298 8-8-5 **46** oh1 ....(p) LauraPearson(7) 7 19
(John Ryan) *midfield: losing pl u.p over 2f out: wl btn over 1f out: wknd fnl f* **33/1**
000/ **12** ¾ **Lady Carduros (IRE)**[106] 8984 5-8-7 **46** oh1 .... TheodoreLadd(5) 12 17
(Michael Appleby) *s.i.s: a towards rr (jockey said mare ran green)* **33/1**
000 **13** 3 ½ **Vallachy**[13] 4116 4-9-0 **48** .... JasonHart 9 9
(William Muir) *wnt lft sn after s: sn outpcd in rr: nvr involved (vet said gelding lost left fore shoe)* **33/1**
000- **14** 7 **Patienceisavirtue**[240] 8919 4-8-12 **46** oh1 ....(p) RyanPowell 11
(Christine Dunnett) *midfield: hdwy on outer to chse ldrs 5f out: rdn and lost pl over 2f out: wl bhd fnl f* **66/1**

1m 26.4s (-0.80) **Going Correction** -0.175s/f (Stan) **14** Ran SP% **126.9**
Speed ratings (Par 101): **97,95,94,93,92 88,88,86,84,84 82,81,77,69**
CSF £13.23 CT £51.84 TOTE £2.50: £1.30, £2.10, £1.70; EX 17.60 Trifecta £59.30.
Owner Power Geneva Ltd **Bred** D R Tucker **Trained** Newmarket, Suffolk
■ Stewards' Enquiry : Gerald Mosse two-day ban: used whip above permitted level (19-20 Jul)

FOCUS
A moderate handicap. The favourite's winning time was marginally quicker than the previous C&D juvenile contest.

4590 BET TOTEQUADPOT AT TOTESPORT.COM MAIDEN STKS 7f (P)
6:30 (6:35) (Class 5) 3-Y-O+
£4,948 (£1,472; £735; £367) **Stalls** Low

Form RPR
-322 **1** **Qutob (IRE)**[42] 3058 3-9-5 81 .... OisinMurphy 10 88
(Charles Hills) *chsd ldr tl led and hung lft over 1f out: in command and kpt on ins fnl f (vet said gelding lost right fore shoe)* **6/4**[1]
22-0 **2** 2 **Dubrava**[36] 3264 3-9-0 73 .... JackMitchell 4 77
(Roger Varian) *chsd ldrs: effrt over 2f out: chsd wnr ins fnl f: swtchd rt and styd on towards fin* **4/1**[3]
45-2 **3** 1 ½ **Aluqair (IRE)**[11] 4196 3-9-5 0 ....(h) RyanPowell 3 78
(Simon Crisford) *led: rdn and hdd over 1f out: unable qck and hung lft 1f out: lost 2nd and plugged on same pce ins fnl f* **15/8**[2]
40 **4** 2 ¾ **Undercolours (IRE)**[35] 3324 3-8-12 0 .... StefanoCherchi(7) 2 70
(Marco Botti) *chsd ldrs: effrt ent fnl 2f: shifting rt and outpcd ent fnl f: hung rt and plugged on same pce ins fnl f* **25/1**
45 **5** ½ **Soft Cover**[11] 4178 3-8-7 0 .... GianlucaSanna(7) 5 64
(William Haggas) *hld up in tch in midfield: effrt over 1f out: unable qck and impeded ent fnl f: plugged on same pce and carried rt ins fnl f* **7/1**
0 **6** 3 ¾ **Midas Spirit**[11] 4178 3-9-5 0 .... LiamKeniry 6 59
(Ed Walker) *in tch in midfield: effrt and outpcd ent fnl 2f: wl hld whn rn green and hung lft over 1f out: lame (vet said colt was lame on its right-hind leg)* **50/1**
0 **7** 8 **Interrogator (IRE)**[45] 2932 3-9-5 0 .... JoeyHaynes 7 37
(Alan Bailey) *dwlt: in tch in rr of main gp: rdn wl over 2f out: sn struggling and outpcd 2f out: no ch after* **66/1**
0 **8** 3 **Sterling Price**[45] 2938 3-9-5 0 .... RyanTate 8 29
(James Eustace) *in tch in midfield: rdn over 2f out: sn struggling and outpcd: wl btn over 1f out: lame (vet said gelding was lame left fore)* **50/1**
9 6 **Maryellen** 3-9-0 0 .... JosephineGordon 9 8
(Alan Bailey) *awkward leaving stalls and wnt lft: v green and bucking early: towards rr: nvr involved (jockey said filly jumped awkwardly from the stalls and ran green)* **50/1**
10 58 **Ed Cuvee** 3-9-5 0 .... KieranO'Neill 1
(Christine Dunnett) *slowly away: rn green and a bhd: t.o fnl 2f: lame (jockey said gelding was slowly away; vet said gelding was lame left hind)* **100/1**

1m 25.64s (-1.56) **Going Correction** -0.175s/f (Stan) **10** Ran SP% **119.5**
Speed ratings (Par 103): **101,98,97,93,93 89,79,76,69,3**
CSF £8.05 TOTE £2.10: £1.10, £1.30, £1.10; EX 9.00 Trifecta £22.40.
Owner Hamdan Al Maktoum **Bred** Max Morris **Trained** Lambourn, Berks
■ Stewards' Enquiry : Stefano Cherchi two-day ban: careless riding (19-20 Jul)

FOCUS
A fair, effectively 3yo maiden. The favourite's winning time was notably quicker than the previous two 7f contests. The second and fourth help set the level.

4591 BET TOTETRIFECTA AT TOTESPORT.COM H'CAP 7f (P)
7:05 (7:05) (Class 5) (0-75,81) 3-Y-O
£5,175 (£1,540; £769; £400) **Stalls** Low

Form RPR
111 **1** **Nahaarr (IRE)**[7] 4338 3-9-10 **81** 6ex .... GeorgiaCox(3) 6 101+
(William Haggas) *wnt rt leaving stalls: in rr: hdwy to ld over 4f out: readily wnt clr over 1f out: v easily* **1/10**[1]
-550 **2** 6 **Sonja Henie (IRE)**[36] 3278 3-9-6 **74** ....(t[1]) GeraldMosse 4 74
(Marco Botti) *chsd ldr tl over 4f out: cl up in 4th whn nt clr run over 2f out: sn swtchd rt: chsd clr wnr over 1f out: no imp* **12/1**[2]
4620 **3** 7 **Facethepuckout (IRE)**[13] 4124 3-8-12 **73** ....(p) CierenFallon(7) 3 54
(John Ryan) *chsd ldrs: rdn and sltly outpcd 4f out: clsd on inner over 2f out: wnt 2nd but wnr gng clr 2f out: wl btn 3rd 1f out: wknd* **16/1**[3]

4236 **4** 24 **Brigadier**[14] 4081 3-8-10 **64** KieranO'Neill 5
(Robert Cowell) *wnt rt leaving stalls: led: hdd over 4f out: rdn over 2f out: dropped to rr over 1f out: sn wknd: t.o* **33/1**

1m 25.13s (-2.07) **Going Correction** -0.175s/f (Stan) 4 Ran SP% **107.4**
Speed ratings (Par 100): **104,97,89,61**
CSF £2.09 TOTE £1.10; EX 2.20 Trifecta £4.10.
Owner Sheikh Ahmed Al Maktoum **Bred** Rossenarra Bloodstock Limited **Trained** Newmarket, Suffolk

FOCUS
A fair, if uncompetitive, 3yo handicap. The long odds-on favourite had something of a solo from over 2f out in a notably quicker time than the previous three 7f contests. The second has been rated to her AW handicap form.

4592 BET TOTESWINGER AT TOTESPORT.COM FILLIES' NOVICE STKS 1m (P)
7:35 (7:37) (Class 4) 3-5-Y-O **£7,697** (£2,290; £858) **Stalls** Low

Form RPR

20-4 **1** **Jadeerah**[13] 4124 3-9-0 79 (h) KieranO'Neill 11 87+
(John Gosden) *t.k.h: chsd ldr: rdn to ld jst over 1f out: r.o strly* **2/1[2]**

2 **2** 4 1/2 **Beauty Of Deira (IRE)**[22] 3761 3-9-0 0 OisinMurphy 2 77
(Hugo Palmer) *w ldr early: sn restrained and chsd ldrs: effrt over 2f out: swtchd rt and rdn over 1f out: kpt on same pce and no threat to wnr ins fnl f: wnt 2nd cl home* **7/4[1]**

0- **3** 1/2 **Aladaala (IRE)**[204] 9522 3-8-11 0 GeorgiaCox(3) 3 76
(William Haggas) *t.k.h: hld up in tch in midfield: hdwy into midfield over 3f out: effrt over 1f out: no ch w wnr but kpt on ins fnl f* **14/1**

2035 **3** dht **Gentlewoman (IRE)**[13] 4124 3-9-0 78 (h) RobertHavlin 9 76
(John Gosden) *sn led: rdn over 1f out: sn hdd and nt match pce of wnr: lost 2nd cl home* **4/1[3]**

5 2 1/2 **Lope Scholar (IRE)** 3-9-0 0 HarryBentley 10 70
(Ralph Beckett) *midfield: 6th and outpcd wl over 1f out: no threat to wnr and kpt on same pce after* **7/1**

6 3 3/4 **Midas Girl (FR)** 3-9-0 0 LiamKeniry 1 61
(Ed Walker) *chsd ldrs: unable qck u.p and btn over 1f out: wknd ins fnl f* **25/1**

0-5 **7** 1 1/4 **Lady Navarra (IRE)**[11] 4189 3-9-0 0 JasonHart 4 59
(Gay Kelleway) *midfield: struggling whn hung rt 3f out: no ch after* **50/1**

0- **8** 18 **Miss Firecracker (IRE)**[284] 7607 3-9-0 0 JFEgan 6 17
(Dr Jon Scargill) *awkward leaving stalls: a towards rr* **100/1**

00 **9** 6 **Shawwaslucky**[45] 2938 3-8-7 0 AledBeech(7) 8 3
(Derek Shaw) *a towards rr: wl bhd fnl 2f (jockey said filly hung right-handed throughout)* **100/1**

10 17 **Annakonda (IRE)** 3-9-0 0 BrettDoyle 7
(Peter Chapple-Hyam) *s.i.s: a towards rr: lost tch 2f out: t.o* **25/1**

1m 37.84s (-2.06) **Going Correction** -0.175s/f (Stan) 10 Ran SP% **120.5**
Speed ratings (Par 102): **103,98,98,98,95 91,90,72,66,49**
TF: J/BOD/G 6.40, J/BOD/A 21.90; CSF £5.96 TOTE £2.60: £1.10, £1.10, £1.70, £0.70; EX 6.40.
Owner Hamdan Al Maktoum **Bred** Shadwell Estate Company Limited **Trained** Newmarket, Suffolk

FOCUS
A fairly decent, effectively 3yo fillies' novice contest. The second-favourite won decisively in a good comparative time.

4593 BET TOTESCOOP6 AT TOTESPORT.COM H'CAP 5f (P)
8:10 (8:10) (Class 4) (0-80,82) 4-Y-O+ **£8,021** (£2,387; £1,192; £596; £400; £400) **Stalls** Low

Form RPR

4111 **1** **Dapper Man (IRE)**[1] 4555 5-9-5 75 5ex (b) AndreaAtzeni 2 93
(Roger Fell) *sn led and mde rest: pushed and drifted rt over 1f out: r.o strly and wl in command ins fnl f: easily* **10/11[1]**

0216 **2** 5 **Big Time Maybe (IRE)**[17] 3961 4-8-12 73 (p) ScottMcCullagh(5) 1 73
(Michael Attwater) *sn in rr: hdwy 1f out: kpt on u.p ins fnl f: snatched 2nd on post: no ch w wnr* **25/1**

6506 **3** nse **Something Lucky (IRE)**[18] 3936 7-9-2 72 (v) AlistairRawlinson 4 72
(Michael Appleby) *sn rdn in midfield: effrt on inner over 1f out: chsd clr wnr ins fnl f: no imp and lost 2nd on post* **8/1[3]**

3U31 **4** 1 1/2 **Zac Brown (IRE)**[9] 4253 8-9-8 81 4ex (t) JoshuaBryan(3) 5 75
(Charlie Wallis) *chsd wnr: unable qck u.p over 1f out: lost 2nd and wknd wl ins fnl f* **14/1**

1051 **5** 1/2 **Dandy's Beano (IRE)**[7] 4330 4-9-5 75 5ex (h) HarryBentley 6 68
(Kevin Ryan) *wd in midfield: hung rt bnd 3f out: wknd ins fnl f* **3/1[2]**

3300 **6** 4 **Global Academy (IRE)**[9] 4236 4-9-5 82 (p) CierenFallon(7) 7 60
(Gay Kelleway) *taken down early: in tch: effrt over 1f out: no imp: wknd and hung lft fnl f (jockey said gelding hung right-handed)* **16/1**

1225 **7** 1/2 **Warrior's Valley**[79] 1860 4-9-5 75 (tp) OisinMurphy 3 51
(David C Griffiths) *taken down early: t.k.h: chsd ldrs: unable qck u.p and swtchd rt 1f out: wknd fnl f (jockey said gelding moved poorly)* **8/1[3]**

58.35s (-1.85) **Going Correction** -0.175s/f (Stan) 7 Ran SP% **116.0**
Speed ratings (Par 105): **107,99,98,96,95 89,88**
CSF £29.28 TOTE £1.50: £1.40, £5.00; EX 23.30 Trifecta £141.80.
Owner Colne Valley Racing & Partner **Bred** William Joseph Martin **Trained** Nawton, N Yorks

FOCUS
The feature contest was a fairly decent sprint handicap. The odds-on favourite completed a decisive four-timer in clearly the best comparative time on the night. The second has been rated close to form.

4594 RACING STAFF WEEK 2019 H'CAP 1m 6f (P)
8:40 (8:43) (Class 6) (0-60,59) 3-Y-O+ **£3,493** (£1,039; £519; £400; £400; £400) **Stalls** Low

Form RPR

0621 **1** **Champagne Marengo (IRE)**[18] 3931 3-8-13 58 (p) AndreaAtzeni 13 64
(Ian Williams) *midfield and pushed along early: hdwy to chse ldr after 2f: led over 3f out: rdn ent fnl 2f: kpt on u.p to forge ahd nr fin: a holding on cl home* **4/1[3]**

0-23 **2** nk **Spargrove**[21] 3809 3-8-13 58 OisinMurphy 7 64
(Hughie Morrison) *hld up in midfield: nt clr run wl over 2f out: effrt to chse ldrs 2f out: drvn over 1f out: styd on wl ins fnl f: wnt 2nd cl home: nt quite rch wnr* **11/8[1]**

-020 **3** 1/2 **Ness Of Brodgar**[9] 4251 4-9-7 52 (t) DanielMuscutt 11 56
(Mark H Tompkins) *led: sn hdd and trckd ldrs: swtchd rt and pressed wnr ent fnl 3f: rdn and ev ch over 1f out: kpt on u.p: no ex nr fin and lost 2nd cl home: lame (vet said filly was lame right fore)* **40/1**

/060 **4** nse **Beau Knight**[56] 2593 7-8-11 47 SebastianWoods(5) 4 52
(Alexandra Dunn) *trckd ldrs: short of room and impeded after over 1f: effrt to chal over 1f out: kpt on u.p: no ex towards fin* **33/1**

1113 **5** 2 3/4 **Croeso Cymraeg**[29] 3497 5-10-0 59 RaulDaSilva 12 59+
(James Evans) *stdd and dropped in bhd after s: hld up in rr: stl last and nt clr run wl over 2f out: swtchd sharply rt wl over 1f out: sn rdn and hdwy: r.o ins fnl f: no ch of rching ldrs* **7/2[2]**

006 **6** 5 **Peripherique**[31] 3445 3-8-10 55 RyanTate 5 50
(James Eustace) *hld up in last quartet: rdn briefly 6f out: effrt over 2f out: sme prog over 1f out: nvr a threat to ldrs* **8/1**

0001 **7** 3 1/2 **Shovel It On (IRE)**[11] 4190 4-8-12 50 5ex (bt) CierenFallon(7) 2 39
(Steve Flook) *mounted on crse: hld up in midfield: short of room and hmpd after over 1f: shuffled bk over 2f out: swtchd lft and sme prog u.p over 1f out: no ch w ldrs* **16/1**

030 **8** 6 **Spirit Of Nicobar**[14] 4066 3-9-0 59 DavidProbert 3 41
(Andrew Balding) *stdd s: hld up in last quartet: effrt over 2f out: nt clr run and swtchd lft over 1f out: no imp and wl btn fnl f* **16/1**

2000 **9** 8 **Tilsworth Sammy**[31] 3444 4-9-2 47 (p[1]) NickyMackay 9 18
(J R Jenkins) *midfield on outer: reminder 6f out: more reminders 4f out: drvn and struggling over 2f out: wknd over 1f out* **33/1**

0-00 **10** 1/2 **Roue De Charrette**[23] 3740 4-9-0 45 (b[1]) JosephineGordon 10 15
(Amy Murphy) *t.k.h: chsd ldrs: rdn over 2f out: sn outpcd and wknd over 1f out* **50/1**

060- **11** 1/2 **Awesome Rock (IRE)**[75] 4860 10-9-0 45 RobertHavlin 6 15
(Roger Ingram) *uns rdr coming onto the crse and cantered loose to s: stdd s: hld up in last pair: hdwy 4f out: effrt over 2f out: sn struggling and wknd over 1f out* **80/1**

0-00 **12** 11 **Mythological (IRE)**[8] 4287 4-9-12 57 (v[1]) BrettDoyle 8 12
(Louise Allan) *t.k.h: hld up wl in tch in midfield: rdn over 2f out: sn struggling and wknd: t.o* **66/1**

65-0 **13** 30 **Oyster Card**[92] 1548 6-8-9 45 (v) TheodoreLadd(5) 14
(Michael Appleby) *sn led: hdd and rdn over 3f out: dropped out rapidly over 2f out: t.o (jockey said gelding stopped quickly)* **50/1**

4-30 **14** 26 **Bigshotte**[51] 2738 4-10-0 59 (t) KieranO'Neill 1
(Luke Dace) *t.k.h: hld up up in tch in midfield: short of room and hmpd after over 1f: rdn jst over 3f: sn eased: t.o (trainer said gelding did not stay)* **20/1**

3m 0.55s (-2.65) **Going Correction** -0.175s/f (Stan)
WFA 3 from 4yo+ 14lb 14 Ran SP% **126.9**
Speed ratings (Par 101): **100,99,99,99,97 95,93,89,85,84 84,78,61,46**
CSF £9.86 CT £209.35 TOTE £4.80: £1.70, £1.20, £17.20; EX 14.50 Trifecta £285.30.
Owner Champagne Charlies Club **Bred** Helen Lyons **Trained** Portway, Worcs
■ Stewards' Enquiry : Daniel Muscutt three-day ban: careless riding (Jul 19-21)

FOCUS
A modest staying handicap. The finish was dominated by two 3yos in receipt of 14lb in weight-for-age over this sort of trip at this time of year. They went a muddling gallop and the winning time was over six seconds above standard.
T/Plt: £3.10 to a £1 stake. Pool: £36,732.50 - 8,560.33 winning units T/Qpdt: £1.80 to a £1 stake. Pool: £3,019.14 - 1,211.67 winning units **Steve Payne**

4365 DONCASTER (L-H)
Friday, July 5

OFFICIAL GOING: Good to firm (watered; 8.1)
Wind: Moderate against Weather: Cloudy with sunny periods

4595 JOLLYS JEWELLERS FILLIES' H'CAP 5f 3y
2:00 (2:01) (Class 4) (0-80,82) 3-Y-O+ **£5,207** (£1,549; £774; £387; £300; £300) **Stalls** Low

Form RPR

-020 **1** **Queens Gift (IRE)**[21] 3815 4-9-13 81 PaulMulrennan 3 96
(Michael Dods) *stdd s and hld up towards rr: hdwy on outer over 2f out: rdn to chse ldr jst over 1f out: sn chal: led last 100yds: drvn out (trainer said, regarding the improved form shown, the filly appreciated the quicker ground)* **4/1[1]**

-104 **2** hd **Lufricia**[28] 3544 3-9-8 81 DavidEgan 8 93
(Roger Varian) *trckd ldng pair: hdwy over 2f out: rdn to ld 1 1/2f out: jnd and drvn ent fnl f: hdd last 100yds: kpt on* **9/2[2]**

0224 **3** 5 **Enchanted Linda**[13] 4128 3-8-12 76 (h) ThoreHammerHansen(5) 7 70
(Richard Hannon) *awkward s and towards rr: rapid hdwy to trck ldr after 1f: sn cl up: rdn to ld briefly 2f out: sn hdd and drvn: edgd lft and kpt on same pce fnl f* **4/1[1]**

2-16 **4** 3/4 **Lorna Cole (IRE)**[165] 342 3-9-1 74 MartinDwyer 2 66
(William Muir) *prom: rdn along 2f out: drvn over 1f out: kpt on same pce* **8/1**

-440 **5** nk **Society Queen (IRE)**[21] 3815 3-9-6 79 TonyHamilton 5 70
(Richard Fahey) *hld up: hdwy to chse ldrs 2f out: sn rdn and no imp* **11/2**

0006 **6** 3/4 **Rose Marmara**[4] 4438 6-8-11 68 (bt) ConnorMurtagh(3) 9 58
(Brian Rothwell) *led: rdn along 1/2-way: sn hdd and grad wknd* **25/1**

1206 **7** nk **Fen Breeze**[13] 4122 3-9-7 80 TomMarquand 4 67
(Rae Guest) *chsd ldrs: rdn along 2f out: sn wknd (vet said a post-race examination revealed the filly to be lame left hind)* **5/1[3]**

31-0 **8** 1/2 **Raheeb (IRE)**[64] 2319 3-9-9 82 DaneO'Neill 6 67
(Owen Burrows) *chsd ldrs: rdn along 1/2-way: sn wknd* **11/1**

59.22s (-0.38) **Going Correction** -0.125s/f (Firm)
WFA 3 from 4yo+ 5lb 8 Ran SP% **113.5**
Speed ratings (Par 102): **98,97,89,88,88 86,86,85**
CSF £21.75 CT £75.65 TOTE £5.20: £2.30, £1.90, £1.60; EX 28.60 Trifecta £119.90.
Owner Geoff & Sandra Turnbull **Bred** Old Carhue & Graeng Bloodstock **Trained** Denton, Co Durham

FOCUS
The going was good to firm (GoingStick: 8.1). Round course railed out from about 1m2f until the round meets the straight. Add 12yds to the three 1m4f races. This was a wide-open fillies' sprint handicap according to the market and a strongly run affair. The first two pulled well clear. The second has been rated back to the level of her Newcastle win.

4596 TAKE PAYMENTS BRIGHT AWARDS MAIDEN STKS 6f 111y
2:30 (2:31) (Class 5) 2-Y-O **£3,428** (£1,020; £509; £254) **Stalls** Low

Form RPR

4 **1** **Royal Commando (IRE)**[14] 4069 2-9-5 0 KieranShoemark 1 89+
(Charles Hills) *trckd ldng pair: hdwy to ld over 2f out: rdn clr wl over 1f out: readily* **6/4[2]**

4 **2** 3 1/4 **Imperial Gloriana (IRE)**[17] 3968 2-9-0 0 DanielTudhope 2 75
(David O'Meara) *t.k.h: trckd ldng pair: swtchd rt and hdwy over 2f out: sn chsng wnr: rdn over 1f out: no imp* **9/2[3]**

3 3/4 **Written Broadcast (IRE)** 2-9-5 0 PatDobbs 4 78
(Richard Hannon) *trckd ldr: cl up 3f out: rdn along and ev ch 2f out: sn drvn and kpt on same pce* **12/1**

The Form Book Flat 2019, Raceform Ltd, Newbury, RG14 5SJ

02 **4** 2½ **Baadirr**[22] 3760 2-9-5 0............ TomMarquand 3 71
(William Haggas) *set stdy pce: pushed along and qcknd 1/2-way: sn rdn and hdd over 2f out: wknd (trainer said colt was unsuited by the ground on this occasion and would prefer an easier surface)* 5/4[1]

1m 20.58s (0.98) **Going Correction** -0.125s/f (Firm) 4 Ran SP% **110.3**
Speed ratings (Par 94): **89,85,84,81**
CSF £8.23 TOTE £2.50; EX 8.90 Trifecta £29.00.
Owner Ziad A Galadari **Bred** Mountarmstrong Stud **Trained** Lambourn, Berks

FOCUS
A small-field maiden taken apart by the winner. The second has been rated as building slightly on her Thirsk debut.

4597 BLOOMFIELDS HORSEBOXES FILLIES' NOVICE STKS 7f 6y
3:05 (3:06) (Class 5) 3-Y-O+ **£3,428** (£1,020; £509; £254) **Stalls** Low

Form RPR
5- **1** **Lyzbeth (FR)**[301] 7007 3-8-11............ RobHornby 6 89+
(Martyn Meade) *trckd ldr: cl up 1/2-way: chal 2f out: rdn to ld ent fnl f: edgd lft and kpt on wl* 9/1

1- **2** 2¼ **Lady Lawyer (USA)**[256] 8469 3-9-4............ FrankieDettori 4 91+
(John Gosden) *led: pushed along and jnd 2f out: rdn over 1f out: hdd ent fnl f: kpt on same pce* 11/10[1]

06-4 **3** 1½ **Posted**[49] 2790 3-8-11 85............(h) TomMarquand 3 79
(Richard Hannon) *trckd ldr: cl up 1/2-way: rdn along 2f out: sn drvn and kpt on one pce* 5/2[2]

2-2 **4** hd **Bint Soghaan**[11] 4178 3-8-11............ DaneO'Neill 5 78
(Richard Hannon) *trckd ldrs: pushed along and sltly outpcd 1/2-way: rdn over 2f out: kpt on u.p fnl f* 4/1[3]

5 3 **Rapture (FR)** 3-8-11............ DanielTudhope 1 70
(Archie Watson) *dwlt: sn trcking ldrs: pushed along 3f out: rdn over 1f out: sn wknd* 16/1

6 17 **Amber Jet (IRE)** 3-8-11............ JimmyQuinn 2 24
(John Mackie) *a in rr: outpcd fnl 2f* 66/1

1m 25.18s (-1.22) **Going Correction** -0.125s/f (Firm) 6 Ran SP% **113.6**
Speed ratings (Par 100): **101,98,96,96,93 73**
CSF £19.97 TOTE £11.00: £3.20, £1.30; EX 28.90 Trifecta £105.20.
Owner Mantonbury Stud **Bred** S A S Elevage Du Haras De Bourgeauville **Trained** Manton, Wilts

FOCUS
An interesting fillies' novice and a nice performance by the winner. The third has been rated close to her reappearance figure, with the fourth helping to set the level.

4598 BETFAIR CASINO CLASSIFIED STKS 7f 6y
3:35 (3:35) (Class 3) 4-Y-O+ **£7,762** (£2,310; £1,154; £577) **Stalls** Low

Form RPR
-236 **1** **Insurgence**[104] 1294 4-9-5 84............(p) DanielMuscutt 1 94
(James Fanshawe) *hld up in rr: effrt 2f out: nt clr run over 1f out: squeezed through to take slt ld ent fnl f: sn drvn: kpt on wl towards fin* **7/1**

-124 **2** 2 **Jalaad (IRE)**[29] 3496 4-9-5 87............(h[1]) KevinStott 2 89
(Saeed bin Suroor) *trckd ldng pair: pushed along and sltly outpcd over 2f out: rdn over 1f out: chal ins fnl f: sn drvn and ev ch: kpt on same pce last 75yds* 5/4[1]

-205 **3** 2½ **Whinmoor**[35] 3308 4-9-2 87............ RowanScott(3) 3 82
(Nigel Tinkler) *sn trcking ldr: cl up 3f out: rdn along wl over 1f out: sn edgd lft and drvn: kpt on same pce* 13/8[2]

4012 **4** 2¼ **Key Player**[28] 3536 4-9-5 84............ CharlesBishop 4 76
(Eve Johnson Houghton) *led: pushed along over 2f out: jnd and rdn wl over 1f out: edgd rt appr fnl f: sn drvn: hdd & wknd (jockey said gelding hung right-handed under pressure)* 11/2[3]

1m 25.14s (-1.26) **Going Correction** -0.125s/f (Firm) 4 Ran SP% **110.4**
Speed ratings (Par 107): **102,99,96,94**
CSF £16.58 TOTE £8.10; EX 18.80 Trifecta £23.90.
Owner Dr Catherine Wills & Frederik Tylicki **Bred** St Clare Hall Stud **Trained** Newmarket, Suffolk

FOCUS
A tight little classified event, with 3lb covering the four runners, and the quartet were in a line across the track coming to the last furlong. The winner has been rated as matching his AW best.

4599 BETFAIR EXCHANGE BRITISH EBF FILLIES' H'CAP 1m 3f 197y
4:10 (4:10) (Class 4) (0-85,82) 3-Y-O+ **£6,080** (£1,809; £904; £452) **Stalls** Low

Form RPR
-031 **1** **Arctic Ocean (IRE)**[17] 3955 3-8-7 72............ JimmyQuinn 2 83+
(Sir Michael Stoute) *trckd ldng pair: hdwy on inner over 2f out: rdn to ld appr fnl f: kpt on strly* 5/2[3]

5213 **2** 1 **Tamreer**[12] 4145 4-10-0 81............(h) DavidEgan 4 88
(Roger Fell) *trckd ldng pair: hdwy on outer over 2f out: rdn to chal over 1f out: ev ch: drvn and edgd lft and rt ins fnl f: kpt on same pce* 13/8[1]

-416 **3** 3¾ **Dorah**[23] 3729 3-9-3 82............ DanielTudhope 1 84
(Archie Watson) *led: pushed along over 2f out: sn rdn: drvn and hdd jst over 1f out: sn one pce* 9/4[2]

0-13 **4** 5 **Eesha My Flower (USA)**[39] 3169 3-8-9 74 ow1......(p[1]) TomMarquand 3 71
(Marco Botti) *trckd ldr: cl up 3f out: rdn along 2f out: sn drvn and wknd over 1f out* 7/1

2m 32.65s (-3.95) **Going Correction** -0.125s/f (Firm)
WFA 3 from 4yo 12lb 4 Ran SP% **109.9**
Speed ratings (Par 102): **102,101,98,95**
CSF £7.05 TOTE £2.90; EX 7.10 Trifecta £8.40.
Owner Qatar Racing Limited **Bred** Martin White **Trained** Newmarket, Suffolk

FOCUS
Add 12yds to race distance. This small-field fillies' handicap was run at a modest early pace and the tempo didn't increase until coming to the last 2f. The quartet came up the centre after turning in. The second has been rated to her Newcastle win.

4600 MARTYN BALDWIN 60TH BIRTHDAY PARTY NOVICE STKS 1m 3f 197y
4:45 (4:47) (Class 4) 3-Y-O+ **£5,207** (£1,549; £774; £387) **Stalls** Low

Form RPR
3 **1** **Promissory (IRE)**[43] 3013 3-8-9 0............ FrankieDettori 1 85+
(John Gosden) *trckd ldng pair: hdwy to ld 3f out: sn pushed clr: styd on strly: readily* 1/3[1]

2 **2** 5 **December Second (IRE)**[14] 4066 5-9-12 0............ DanielTudhope 7 81+
(Philip Kirby) *trckd ldrs: hdwy on outer over 3f out: chsd wnr fr wl over 2f out: rdn wl over 1f out: no imp fnl f* 9/4[2]

06 **3** 13 **The Cruix (IRE)**[8] 4304 4-9-12 0............(p[1]) RobHornby 4 60
(Dean Ivory) *led: pushed along 4f out: rdn and hdd 3f out: drvn and kpt on one pce fnl 2f* 25/1

0 **4** ¾ **Hazm (IRE)**[25] 3664 4-9-12 0............(w) DougieCostello 2 59
(Tim Vaughan) *in tch: hdwy 4f out: rdn along 3f out: plugged on fnl 2f: n.d* 16/1

0 **5** nk **Albanderi**[29] 3495 3-8-9 0............ JimmyQuinn 5 55
(Sir Michael Stoute) *t.k.h: trckd ldr: green: pushed along and outpcd over 3f out: sn rdn: kpt on appr fnl f* 13/2[3]

0 **6** ½ **Champ Ayr**[20] 3860 3-9-0 0............ KieranShoemark 8 59
(David Menuisier) *a towards rr* 25/1

0 **7** 6 **Jesse Jude (IRE)**[59] 2505 6-9-12 0............ AndrewElliott 6 48
(Simon West) *in tch: rdn along over 5f out: sn outpcd* 33/1

0- **8** 2 **I Think So (IRE)**[337] 5657 4-9-0 0............ LauraCoughlan(7) 3 40
(David Loughnane) *a in rr* 66/1

2m 32.63s (-3.97) **Going Correction** -0.125s/f (Firm)
WFA 3 from 4yo+ 12lb 8 Ran SP% **137.1**
Speed ratings (Par 105): **102,98,90,89,89 88,84,83**
CSF £2.00 TOTE £1.20: £1.10, £1.10, £4.10; EX 1.70 Trifecta £12.60.
Owner HRH Princess Haya Of Jordan **Bred** T R G Vestey **Trained** Newmarket, Suffolk

FOCUS
Add 12yds to race distance. This was basically a match between the two market leaders and the pair pulled a long way clear of the rest. The third has been rated to his Nottingham latest.

4601 LYCETTS INSURANCE BROKERS H'CAP 1m 3f 197y
5:15 (5:15) (Class 5) (0-70,69) 4-Y-O+
£3,428 (£1,020; £509; £300; £300; £300) **Stalls** Low

Form RPR
0211 **1** **Gas Monkey**[10] 4220 4-8-13 68............(h) SeanKirrane(7) 5 84+
(Julia Feilden) *trckd ldrs: smooth hdwy 3f out: led wl over 1f out: sn rdn clr: easily* 8/13[1]

0305 **2** 6 **Mobham (IRE)**[24] 3700 4-9-0 62............(p[1]) BarryMcHugh 7 67
(J R Jenkins) *hld up towards rr: hdwy 4f out: chsd ldrs 2f out: rdn to chse wnr over 1f out: sn drvn and no imp (vet said gelding lost its right hind shoe)* 12/1

0566 **3** 2¾ **Flower Power**[6] 4370 8-9-2 64............(p) DougieCostello 4 65
(Tony Coyle) *trckd ldrs: hdwy over 3f out: sn pushed along: rdn over 2f out: sn drvn and kpt on same pce (jockey said mare lugged left-handed in the closing stages)* 10/1

-314 **4** 2¼ **Majestic Stone (IRE)**[18] 3925 5-7-12 53 oh1 ow3....... VictorSantos(7) 6 50
(Julie Camacho) *t.k.h: hld up: pulling hrd and rapid hdwy to ld 5f out: hdd wl over 1f out: grad wknd (jockey said gelding ran too freely)* 8/1[3]

2032 **5** ½ **Movie Star (GER)**[18] 3941 4-9-1 63............ GeorgeWood 3 59
(Amy Murphy) *chsd ldng pair: rdn along 3f out: drvn and one pce fnl 2f* 7/1[2]

0030 **6** 1 **Airplane (IRE)**[34] 3334 4-8-13 61............ RachelRichardson 1 56
(Tim Easterby) *led: hdd 5f out: rdn along over 3f out: sn wknd* 16/1

-223 **7** nk **Albert Boy (IRE)**[16] 4009 6-8-5 60............ WilliamCarver(7) 8 54
(Scott Dixon) *trckd ldr: rdn along 4f out: drvn and wknd 3f out* 8/1[3]

5150 **8** shd **Star Ascending (IRE)**[10] 4208 7-8-13 64............(p) SeanDavis(3) 9 58
(Jennie Candlish) *hld up: a in rr* 25/1

002- **9** 99 **Doctor Jazz (IRE)**[48] 7325 4-9-7 69............(t[1]) AndrewMullen 2
(Donald McCain) *midfield: rdn along 5f out: sn outpcd and wl bhd fnl 3f* 22/1

2m 32.18s (-4.42) **Going Correction** -0.125s/f (Firm) 9 Ran SP% **127.5**
Speed ratings (Par 103): **103,99,97,95,95 94,94,94,28**
CSF £11.87 CT £53.95 TOTE £1.50: £1.10, £3.30, £2.10; EX 12.30 Trifecta £63.90.
Owner Newmarket Equine Tours Racing Club **Bred** Julia Feilden **Trained** Exning, Suffolk

FOCUS
Add 12yds to race distance. An ordinary handicap and one-way traffic. The second and third have been rated close to their latest efforts.
T/Plt: £247.00 to a £1 stake. Pool: £57,618.42 - 170.24 winning units T/Qpdt: £53.50 to a £1 stake. Pool: £3,278.17 - 45.28 winning units **Joe Rowntree**

4549
HAYDOCK (L-H)
Friday, July 5

OFFICIAL GOING: Good to firm (watered; 8.1)
Wind: Moderate, against in straight of over 4f Weather: Sunny

4602 THREE SISTERS H'CAP 1m 2f 100y
5:50 (5:51) (Class 5) (0-70,72) 3-Y-O+
£4,851 (£1,443; £721; £400; £400; £400) **Stalls** High

Form RPR
1021 **1** **Mr Coco Bean (USA)**[39] 3162 5-9-9 65............ PatDobbs 5 75+
(David Barron) *hld up: hdwy over 2f out: led over 1f out: styd on ins fnl f: a doing enough towards fin* 4/1[2]

-433 **2** 1 **Little India (FR)**[35] 3310 3-9-6 72............ CliffordLee 10 77+
(K R Burke) *chsd ldr: led over 2f out: rdn and hdd over 1f out: kpt on ins fnl f: rallied towards fin but a hld* 7/1

0-66 **3** ½ **The Throstles**[14] 4067 4-10-0 70............ DavidNolan 4 73
(Kevin Frost) *hld up in rr: drvn and hdwy over 2f out: angled rt fr over 1f out: chsd ldrs fnl f: styd on towards fin: nt pce to chal* 14/1

3460 **4** 4 **Guvenor's Choice (IRE)**[14] 4067 4-9-11 67............(t) HollieDoyle 1 62
(Marjorie Fife) *hld up in midfield: rdn and hdwy 3f out: plld rt whn chsng ldrs over 1f out: one pce ins fnl f* 25/1

0-36 **5** 3½ **Pioneering (IRE)**[21] 3811 5-9-11 67............ BenCurtis 2 56
(Roger Fell) *hld up: rdn and hdwy 2f out: no imp fr over 1f out: one pce* 9/4[1]

-300 **6** nk **Maghfoor**[42] 3046 5-9-9 65............ LukeMorris 8 53
(Eric Alston) *trckd ldrs: ev ch over 2f out: rdn and wknd over 1f out* 18/1

-306 **7** 1¾ **Artistic Streak**[36] 3264 3-9-4 70............ RichardKingscote 3 56
(Tom Dascombe) *hld up: rdn over 2f out: nvr able to trble ldrs* 5/1[3]

0 **8** 16 **Gennaro (IRE)**[65] 2299 3-8-13 65............(t) PaulHanagan 6 20
(Ivan Furtado) *wnt to post early: led: rdn and hdd over 2f out: sn wknd* 8/1

-550 **9** 2½ **The Gingerbreadman**[22] 3772 4-8-4 51 oh6............ PaulaMuir(5) 11 1
(Chris Fairhurst) *racd keenly on outer wout cover: in tch: rdn and wknd 4f out (jockey said gelding hung right around top bend)* 66/1

2450 **10** 13 **Smoki Smoka (IRE)**[57] 2562 3-9-0 66............(p) GrahamLee 9
(Donald McCain) *trckd ldrs: rdn 4f out: wknd over 3f out: sn bhd* 40/1

-213 **11** 1¼ **Glorious Dane**[21] 3415 3-8-13 68............(p[1]) GabrieleMalune(3) 7
(Stef Keniry) *midfield: rdn and wknd 4f out: eased whn wl btn ins fnl f (jockey said gelding was restless in stalls)* 11/1

2m 13.44s (-3.16) **Going Correction** -0.05s/f (Good)
WFA 3 from 4yo+ 10lb 11 Ran SP% **119.1**
Speed ratings (Par 103): **110,109,109,106,103 102,101,88,86,76 75**
CSF £32.27 CT £362.46 TOTE £3.50: £2.00, £2.10, £4.40; EX 28.80 Trifecta £355.60.
Owner S Raines **Bred** Stewart Larkin Armstrong **Trained** Maunby, N Yorks

The Form Book Flat 2019, Raceform Ltd, Newbury, RG14 5SJ

FOCUS
All races on stands' side home straight. Add 14yds. A competitive opener run at a fair pace, the winner and third held up well off the pace in the early stages.

4603 EVERY RACE LIVE ON RACINGTV H'CAP 6f
6:20 (6:22) (Class 4) (0-80,80) 3-Y-O
£7,115 (£2,117; £1,058; £529; £400; £400) Stalls Centre

Form RPR
2533 1 **Tenax (IRE)**[16] 4008 3-9-2 **80** FayeMcManoman(5) 6 88
(Nigel Tinkler) *bmpd s: hld up in rr: rdn and hdwy over 2f out: led over 1f out: r.o wl: pushed out towards fin* **9/2**
2-15 2 3/4 **Pendleton**[27] 3590 3-9-7 **80** GrahamLee 5 85
(Michael Dods) *bmpd s: hld up: hdwy 1/2-way: led briefly wl over 1f out: kpt on ins fnl f: nt pce of wnr* **11/4**[2]
0310 3 5 **Kapono**[4] 4436 3-9-2 **75** 6ex (p) BenCurtis 4 64
(Roger Fell) *chsd ldrs: effrt over 2f out: ch wl over 1f out: outpcd fnl f* **7/2**[3]
6004 4 5 **Autumn Flight (IRE)**[8] 4280 3-8-7 **66** (p) DuranFentiman 3 39
(Tim Easterby) *prom: rdn and lost pl over 2f out: wknd over 1f out* **14/1**
10-0 5 1 1/2 **Michaels Choice**[70] 2086 3-9-5 **78** RichardKingscote 2 46
(William Jarvis) *prom: drvn and lost pl 1/2-way: n.d after* **16/1**
-221 6 1 1/2 **Magical Spirit (IRE)**[29] 3516 3-9-5 **78** PaulHanagan 7 41
(Kevin Ryan) *wnt lft s: led: rdn and edgd lft ent fnl 2f: sn hdd: wknd over 1f out (jockey said gelding hung left throughout)* **9/4**[1]
-610 7 nse **Manana Chica (IRE)**[35] 3307 3-9-3 **76** HectorCrouch 1 39
(Clive Cox) *in tch: rdn and outpcd over 2f out: wknd wl over 1f out* **22/1**

1m 14.33s (0.43) **Going Correction** -0.05s/f (Good) **7** Ran SP% **114.7**
Speed ratings (Par 102): **95,94,87,80,78 76,76**
CSF £17.42 TOTE £5.40: £3.10, £2.20; EX 23.30 Trifecta £132.00.
Owner James Marshall & Chris Marshall **Bred** Eimear Mulhern & Abbeville Stud **Trained** Langton, N Yorks

FOCUS
A fair sprint handicap with the winner gaining compensation of a series of good runs in 2019.

4604 WATCH IRISH RACING ON RACINGTV H'CAP 5f
6:55 (6:56) (Class 4) (0-80,81) 3-Y-O
£7,115 (£2,117; £1,058; £529; £400; £400) Stalls Centre

Form RPR
0-12 1 **Celsius (IRE)**[11] 4183 3-8-13 **66** (t) LukeMorris 5 75+
(Tom Clover) *awkward s: in rr: effrt whn nt clr run wl over 1f out: swtchd lft whn nt clr run again ent fnl f: r.o to ld fnl 175yds: rdn out* **7/2**[2]
06-0 2 1 1/2 **Diamonique**[68] 2149 3-9-6 **73** RichardKingscote 7 76
(Keith Dalgleish) *in tch: effrt over 1f out: edgd lft ins fnl f: styd on towards fin: nt pce of wnr* **13/2**
3262 3 nk **Mr Buttons (IRE)**[7] 4343 3-9-4 **74** (p) CameronNoble(3) 6 76
(Linda Stubbs) *in tch: effrt over 1f out: edgd lft ins fnl f: styd on: run flattened out towards fin (jockey said gelding hung both ways)* **9/2**[3]
0561 4 2 **Dream House**[14] 4081 3-8-10 **63** DuranFentiman 1 58
(Tim Easterby) *chsd ldrs: effrt whn carried lft ent fnl f: styd on same pce fnl 100yds* **8/1**
022 5 1 **True Hero**[8] 4294 3-9-9 **81** (p[1]) FayeMcManoman(5) 4 72
(Nigel Tinkler) *racd keenly: chsd ldr: led over 1f out: sn edgd lft: hdd fnl 175yds: no ex* **9/2**[3]
-042 6 4 1/2 **Vee Man Ten**[14] 4059 3-9-6 **73** PaulHanagan 2 57
(Ivan Furtado) *awkward s: led: rdn and hdd over 1f out: stl there but rdn whn n.m.r and hmpd ent fnl f: nt rcvr* **11/4**[1]
4000 7 9 **Swiss Chime**[2] 4508 3-7-12 **56** oh3 ow1 PaulaMuir(5) 3
(Alan Berry) *in rr: bhd and outpcd 1/2-way: nvr a threat* **100/1**

1m 1.77s (1.37) **Going Correction** -0.05s/f (Good) **7** Ran SP% **110.7**
Speed ratings (Par 102): **87,84,84,80,79 72,57**
CSF £24.33 TOTE £3.90: £4.90, £3.40; EX 24.20 Trifecta £112.60.
Owner J Collins, C Fahy & S Piper **Bred** Owenstown Stud **Trained** Newmarket, Suffolk
■ Stewards' Enquiry : Faye McManoman three-day ban: careless riding (19-21 Jul)

FOCUS
This looked an interesting race beforehand and they went a strong pace, the winner confirming himself a much-improved performer this year. Sound form, with the third helping to set the level.

4605 LONGINES IRISH CHAMPIONS WEEKEND EBF FILLIES' NOVICE STKS (PLUS 10 RACE) 7f 37y
7:25 (7:26) (Class 4) 2-Y-O £7,115 (£2,117; £1,058; £529) Stalls Low

Form RPR
1 **West End Girl** 2-9-0 0 FrannyNorton 5 83+
(Mark Johnston) *hld up: rdn over 3f out: hdwy over 2f out: led ins fnl f: kpt on wl towards fin* **17/2**
2 1 1/4 **Fraternity (IRE)** 2-9-0 0 PaddyMathers 2 80
(Richard Fahey) *dwlt: racd on inner: chsd ldrs: rdn over 2f out: chalng ins fnl f: outpcd by wnr towards fin (jockey said filly ran green)* **12/1**
4 3 3 **Anfield Girl (IRE)**[29] 3506 2-9-0 0 RichardKingscote 1 72
(Tom Dascombe) *led: rdn over 2f out: hdd ins fnl f: no ex fnl 100yds* **9/4**[2]
4 4 nk **Top Class Angel (IRE)**[15] 4030 2-9-0 0 PatDobbs 8 71
(Richard Hannon) *in rr: hdwy over 2f out: chsd ldrs over 1f out: styd on under hand ride towards fin: nvr trbld ldrs* **9/2**[3]
2 5 3 1/2 **Lola Paige (IRE)**[19] 3881 2-9-0 0 PaulHanagan 4 63
(William Haggas) *chsd ldr: rdn and ev ch over 1f out: unable qck ins fnl f: wknd fnl 150yds (jockey said filly stopped quickly)* **6/4**[1]
6 1 3/4 **Gloryana** 2-9-0 0 HollieDoyle 7 58
(Archie Watson) *hld up: sme hdwy for press on outer over 2f out: nvr rchd ldrs: one pce over 1f out* **16/1**
7 1 **Rhyme Scheme (IRE)** 2-9-0 0 CallumShepherd 3 56
(Mick Channon) *in tch: pushed along over 3f out: outpcd whn n.m.r and hmpd over 2f out: n.d after* **40/1**
66 8 3 1/2 **Guipure**[12] 4142 2-9-0 0 BenCurtis 6 47
(K R Burke) *chsd ldrs: rdn and losing pl whn n.m.r and hmpd over 2f out: n.d after* **33/1**

1m 31.09s (-0.31) **Going Correction** -0.05s/f (Good) **8** Ran SP% **118.4**
Speed ratings (Par 93): **99,97,94,93,89 87,86,82**
CSF £105.84 TOTE £7.00: £2.20, £2.20, £1.20; EX 69.50 Trifecta £320.70.
Owner A D Spence & M B Spence **Bred** Car Colston Hall Stud **Trained** Middleham Moor, N Yorks
■ Stewards' Enquiry : Pat Dobbs caution: careless riding

FOCUS
Add 6yds. This looked a fair race beforehand and with two newcomers pulling clear of one who'd shown promise, it's form to take a positive view of. The winner was providing Golden Horn with his first winner as a sire.

4606 RACING WELFARE RACING STAFF WEEK H'CAP 7f 37y
8:00 (8:01) (Class 5) (0-70,70) 3-Y-O
£4,851 (£1,443; £721; £400; £400; £400) Stalls Low

Form RPR
1664 1 **Warning Fire**[17] 3967 3-9-7 **70** FrannyNorton 3 84
(Mark Johnston) *mde all: qcknd 2f out: drew clr over 1f out: r.o wl: comf* **9/4**[1]
-500 2 3 1/2 **Golden Parade**[19] 3885 3-8-12 **61** (p[1]) DuranFentiman 9 65
(Tim Easterby) *in tch: effrt over 2f out: wnt 2nd wl over 1f out: no imp on wnr: all out to hold on to 2nd* **10/1**
0-40 3 hd **Ifton**[25] 3650 3-9-0 **63** BenCurtis 5 66
(Ruth Carr) *dwlt: hld up: nt clr run over 2f out: hdwy over 1f out: chsd ldrs ins fnl f: styd on towards fin: no ch w wnr* **6/1**[3]
0564 4 4 **Jem Scuttle (USA)**[8] 4288 3-9-1 **64** (t) DavidNolan 10 57
(Declan Carroll) *midfield: hdwy over 2f out: rdn over 1f out: kpt on ins fnl f: one pce fnl 100yds* **7/2**[2]
4006 5 8 **Call Him Al (IRE)**[22] 3780 3-8-9 **58** PaulHanagan 11 29
(Richard Fahey) *chsd ldrs: rdn over 2f out: outpcd over 1f out: n.d after* **12/1**
4050 6 1 3/4 **Rich Approach (IRE)**[27] 3569 3-9-3 **66** RichardKingscote 7 32
(James Bethell) *hld up: rdn and no imp over 2f out: wknd over 1f out* **6/1**[3]
-060 7 3/4 **Benji**[17] 3969 3-8-5 **54** PaddyMathers 6 18
(Richard Fahey) *wnt to post early: midfield: pushed along over 3f out: outpcd over 2f out: nvr a threat* **33/1**
00-0 8 2 1/2 **Cavalry Park**[50] 2772 3-9-0 **63** HollieDoyle 4 21
(Charlie Fellowes) *chsd ldr: rdn over 2f out: lost 2nd wl over 1f out: sn wknd* **8/1**
040 9 11 **Guiding Spirit (IRE)**[96] 1458 3-8-11 **60** HectorCrouch 1
(Clive Cox) *chsd ldrs: rdn over 2f out: wknd over 1f out* **12/1**
0-0 10 1/2 **Liberty Diva (IRE)**[64] 2327 3-7-12 **52** oh6 ow1 PaulaMuir(5) 8
(Alan Berry) *dwlt: in rr: struggling and edgd lft over 2f out: nvr a threat* **125/1**

1m 29.48s (-1.92) **Going Correction** -0.05s/f (Good) **10** Ran SP% **120.9**
Speed ratings (Par 100): **108,104,103,99,90 88,87,84,71,71**
CSF £27.69 CT £127.36 TOTE £3.00: £1.40, £3.60, £2.20; EX 32.20 Trifecta £163.20.
Owner Sheikh Hamdan bin Mohammed Al Maktoum **Bred** Godolphin **Trained** Middleham Moor, N Yorks

FOCUS
Add 6yds. This looked competitive beforehand but it was anything but in the closing stages, the winner having things sewn up some way from home. The second has been rated close to this year's form.

4607 RACINGTV.COM H'CAP 1m 37y
8:30 (8:33) (Class 3) (0-95,96) 3-Y-O+ £10,350 (£3,080; £1,539; £769) Stalls Low

Form RPR
5640 1 **Certain Lad**[15] 4016 3-9-11 **96** CallumShepherd 4 102
(Mick Channon) *wnt to post early: chsd ldr: rdn to ld over 1f out: kpt on gamely ins fnl f* **7/2**[1]
2422 2 1/2 **Ginger Fox**[7] 4325 3-8-7 **78** (p) PaulHanagan 8 83
(Ian Williams) *midfield: rdn and hdwy over 1f out: r.o to take 2nd fnl 110yds: hld towards fin* **4/1**[2]
0304 3 1 **Rufus King**[15] 4021 4-10-0 **90** FrannyNorton 2 95
(Mark Johnston) *racd keenly: trckd ldrs: rdn 2f out: unable qck 1f out: kpt on ins fnl f: hld fnl 75yds* **13/2**
0442 4 nse **Reputation (IRE)**[6] 4299 6-10-6 **96** BarryMcHugh 3 100
(Ruth Carr) *s.s: hld up in rr: rdn and hdwy over 1f out: styd on ins fnl f: one pce towards fin* **6/1**
-134 5 3/4 **Absolutio (FR)**[20] 3859 3-8-12 **83** (h) BenCurtis 5 84
(K R Burke) *led: rdn over 2f out: hdd over 1f out: nt pce of ldrs ins fnl f: no ex fnl 75yds* **9/2**[3]
3202 6 1 1/4 **Ambient (IRE)**[23] 3743 4-8-9 **76** SeamusCronin(5) 7 77
(Mohamed Moubarak) *hld up: rdn and hdwy over 1f out: chsd ldrs ins fnl f: one pce fnl 75yds and eased* **16/1**
0001 7 1 3/4 **Arcanada (IRE)**[13] 4108 6-9-7 **86** (p) JaneElliott(3) 6 83
(Tom Dascombe) *hld up in midfield: effrt on inner over 2f out: n.m.r whn no real imp fnl 175yds: n.d after (jockey said gelding was denied a clear run inside the final furlong)* **10/1**
0300 8 1 **Calder Prince (IRE)**[13] 4108 6-9-3 **79** RichardKingscote 1 75
(Tom Dascombe) *chsd ldrs: rdn over 2f out: unable qck over 1f out: losing pl whn n.m.r ins fnl f: eased fnl 100yds (jockey said gelding jumped right from the stalls and was denied a clear run inside the final furlong)* **7/1**

1m 42.28s (-2.62) **Going Correction** -0.05s/f (Good)
WFA 3 from 4yo+ 9lb **8** Ran SP% **115.5**
Speed ratings (Par 107): **111,110,109,109,108 107,105,104**
CSF £17.82 CT £87.27 TOTE £4.60: £1.40, £1.80, £2.40; EX 20.10 Trifecta £203.30.
Owner C R Hirst **Bred** Barry Walters **Trained** West Ilsley, Berks
■ Stewards' Enquiry : Callum Shepherd four-day ban: used whip above permitted level (19-22 Jul)

FOCUS
Add 6yds. The feature race on the card, run at a fair pace, and the well-backed winner capitalised on a drop in grade. The winner has been rated in line with his 2yo best, with the third helping to set the level on his recent form.

4608 INTRODUCING RACING TV NOVICE STKS 1m 37y
9:00 (9:03) (Class 5) 3-Y-O+ £4,851 (£1,443; £721; £360) Stalls Low

Form RPR
1 1 **Vitralite (IRE)**[29] 3510 3-9-9 0 BenCurtis 6 94
(K R Burke) *mde all: rdn and edgd lft over 1f out: r.o wl to draw clr ins fnl f* **7/2**[2]
2 3 1/4 **Dubai Future** 3-9-2 0 CallumShepherd 1 80
(Saeed bin Suroor) *chsd ldrs: wnt 2nd over 2f out: plld off rail over 1f out: outpcd by wnr and no ch fnl f* **9/2**[3]
4 3 1 1/2 **Joyful Mission (USA)**[78] 1886 3-9-2 0 RichardKingscote 2 76
(Sir Michael Stoute) *hld up: rdn over 2f out: sn chsd ldrs: styd on same pce fnl f: nt pce to chal* **4/6**[1]
0- 4 7 **Imajorblush**[342] 5476 3-8-11 0 PaulaMuir(5) 5 59
(Philip Kirby) *hld up: effrt on outer over 2f out: edgd lft and outpcd over 1f out: n.d after* **100/1**
6 5 1/2 **Laurier (USA)**[30] 3463 3-8-11 0 KevinStott 3 53
(Kevin Ryan) *chsd ldrs: effrt and cl up over 2f out: wknd over 1f out* **7/1**

0 6 15 **Juniors Dream (IRE)**[20] 3860 3-8-13 0..................... GabrieleMalune(3) 4 22
(Ivan Furtado) *chsd wnr tl over 2f out: sn lost pl: rdn whn hung lft and wknd over 1f out: eased whn wl btn ins fnl f (jockey said gelding ran too free)* **66/1**

1m 46.23s (1.33) **Going Correction** -0.05s/f (Good)
WFA 3 from 5yo 9lb **6** Ran SP% **115.4**
Speed ratings (Par 103): **91,87,86,79,78 63**
CSF £20.01 TOTE £4.00: £2.10, £1.60; EX 18.60 Trifecta £26.90.
Owner S P C Woods **Bred** Donnchadh Higgins **Trained** Middleham Moor, N Yorks

FOCUS
Add 6yds. A steadily run novice event to round off the card but even allowing for the winner getting things his own way, it was still a taking performance to defy a penalty and maintain his unbeaten record. The third has been rated close to his debut run for now.
T/Plt: £355.10 to a £1 stake. Pool: £64,619.42 - 132.84 winning units T/Qpdt: £43.20 to a £1 stake. Pool: £6,226.16 - 106.5 winning units **Darren Owen**

3855 SANDOWN (R-H)
Friday, July 5

OFFICIAL GOING: Good to firm (watered; 7.8)
Wind: Almost nil Weather: Sunny, very warm

4609 SANDOWN PARK SUPPORTS RACING STAFF WEEK H'CAP 5f 10y
1:50 (1:50) (Class 3) (0-95,91) 3-Y-0+
£10,582 (£3,168; £1,584; £792; £396; £198) **Stalls** Low

Form RPR
0-45 1 **Jumira Bridge**[162] 389 5-9-9 **88**..............................(w) KerrinMcEvoy 4 98
(Robert Cowell) *on toes; sweating; in tch: smooth prog on outer to ld wl over 1f out: sn 2 l ahd: pressed ins fnl f: rdn out nr fin* **14/1**

2354 2 ¾ **Tinto**[5] 4420 3-8-11 **81**.............................. RobertHavlin 5 86
(Amanda Perrett) *dwlt: racd in last pair: prog wl over 1f out w bandage unravelling: chsd wnr fnl f: styd on wl but a hld* **7/1**[3]

0004 3 4 ½ **Leo Minor (USA)**[8] 4301 5-8-11 **76**..............................(p) JasonWatson 6 67+
(Robert Cowell) *in tch: effrt whn stmbld wl over 1f out: kpt on to take 3rd ins fnl f but ldng pair clr (jockey said gelding suffered interference in running)* **8/1**

30-2 4 ¾ **Miracle Of Medinah**[49] 2791 8-9-12 **91**....................... FergusSweeney 7 79
(Mark Usher) *dwlt: mostly in last: pushed along 2f out: no prog tl passed wkng rivals fnl f* **9/1**

25-0 5 1 ½ **Swiss Knight**[27] 3602 4-9-6 **85**..............................(t) OisinMurphy 3 68
(Stuart Williams) *chsd ldng pair to 2f out: wknd over 1f out* **7/2**[2]

4051 6 ½ **Beyond Equal**[9] 4236 4-9-9 **88** 5ex.............................. ShaneKelly 1 69
(Stuart Kittow) *looked wl; racd against rail: pressed ldr: upsides 1/2-way to wl over 1f out: wknd fnl f* **5/2**[1]

-231 7 1 ¼ **Exalted Angel (FR)**[11] 4204 3-8-11 **81** 6ex.......................(p) BenCurtis 2 56
(K R Burke) *mde most to wl over 1f out: wknd (trainer said gelding was unsuited by the going and would prefer an easier surface)* **7/2**[2]

1m 0.63s (-0.67) **Going Correction** +0.025s/f (Good)
WFA 3 from 4yo+ 5lb **7** Ran SP% **113.3**
Speed ratings (Par 107): **106,104,97,96,94 93,91**
CSF £103.10 TOTE £18.50: £7.20, £3.00; EX 90.30 Trifecta £470.80.
Owner Mrs J Morley **Bred** Cheveley Park Stud Ltd **Trained** Six Mile Bottom, Cambs

FOCUS
Fast ground on a very warm day. This decent sprint handicap was won in a time just over a second outside the standard. The winner has been rated to last year's turf best, and the second to his best.

4610 CHASEMORE FARM DRAGON STKS (LISTED RACE) 5f 10y
2:20 (2:22) (Class 1) 2-Y-0
£17,013 (£6,450; £3,228; £1,608; £807; £405) **Stalls** Low

Form RPR
114 1 **Liberty Beach**[16] 3983 2-8-11 97.............................. JasonHart 2 104+
(John Quinn) *trckd ldrs: clsd over 1f out: led jst ins fnl f and qcknd smartly clr: pushed out firmly: impressive* **9/4**[1]

13 2 3 ¼ **Dream Shot (IRE)**[27] 3566 2-9-2 0.............................. JamieSpencer 4 96
(James Tate) *sweating; sltly s.i.s: off the pce in rr: prog wl over 1f out: drvn and styd on fnl f to take 2nd last strides* **12/1**

10 3 nk **Rayong**[16] 3988 2-9-2 0.............................. OisinMurphy 1 95
(K R Burke) *in tch in midfield: pushed along in 5th 2f out: prog over 1f out: drvn and styd on to take 3rd last strides* **7/1**

25 4 ½ **Al Raya**[16] 3983 2-8-11 0.............................. AndreaAtzeni 8 88+
(Simon Crisford) *prom: chsd ldr over 3f out: led over 1f out and gng wl enough: hdd jst ins fnl f and qckly outpcd: lost 2 pls nr fin (jockey said filly jumped left leaving the stalls)* **4/1**[2]

10 5 1 ½ **Expressionist (IRE)**[15] 4012 2-9-2 0.............................. KerrinMcEvoy 6 88
(Charlie Appleby) *looked wl; chsd ldr to over 3f out: struggling to hold pl fr 1/2-way: one pce over 1f out* **9/2**[3]

1 6 ½ **Aussie Showstopper (FR)**[9] 4246 2-9-2 0.............................. ShaneKelly 10 86
(Richard Hughes) *str; looked wl; swvd bdly lft s: mostly in last: pushed along and trying to make prog on inner whn nt clr run 150yds out: swtchd lft and r.o nr fin (jockey said colt jumped badly left leaving the stalls and inside the final furlong and he had to take a precautionary check and switch left around a weakening colt)* **40/1**

101 7 2 **Bill Neigh**[2] 4509 2-9-2 0.............................. CierenFallon 5 79
(John Ryan) *a in rr and off the pce: pushed along and no prog 2f out* **20/1**

541 8 ¾ **Dazzling Des (IRE)**[11] 4191 2-9-2 0.............................. HarryBentley 9 76
(David O'Meara) *workmanlike; sltly impeded s: a in rr and off the pce: pushed along and no prog 2f out* **25/1**

51 9 ½ **Wentworth Amigo (IRE)**[21] 3803 2-9-2 0.............................. NicolaCurrie 3 74
(Jamie Osborne) *looked wl; chsd ldrs 2f: sn dropped to rr and struggling* **33/1**

210 10 1 ½ **Makyon (IRE)**[17] 3949 2-9-2 96.............................. RyanMoore 7 69+
(Mark Johnston) *led to over 1f out: wknd qckly* **9/2**[3]

1m 0.52s (-0.78) **Going Correction** +0.025s/f (Good) **10** Ran SP% **121.3**
Speed ratings (Par 102): **107,101,101,100,98 97,94,92,92,89**
CSF £31.86 TOTE £3.10: £1.30, £3.20, £2.20; EX 35.20 Trifecta £254.60.
Owner Philip Wilkins **Bred** Phillip Wilkins **Trained** Settrington, N Yorks

FOCUS
A competitive Listed event featuring runners from four Royal Ascot events. The three principals were drawn low this time but only raced on the rail for the first half or so of the race. The time was 0.11sec quicker than the Class 3 handicap.

4611 IRISH STALLION FARMS EBF NOVICE STKS (PLUS 10 RACE) 7f
2:55 (2:55) (Class 4) 2-Y-0
£6,598 (£1,963; £981; £490) **Stalls** Low

Form RPR
1 **Laser Show (IRE)** 2-9-5 0.............................. TomQueally 2 87+
(Saeed bin Suroor) *athletic; trckd ldng pair: effrt 2f out: reminder to chse ldr 1f out: pushed along and clsd steadily: led last strides: cleverly* **14/1**

2 2 nk **Riot (IRE)**[21] 3804 2-9-5 0.............................. OisinMurphy 5 86
(John Gosden) *looked wl; trckd ldr: led jst over 2f out gng wl: 2 l clr over 1f out: pressed and rdn ins fnl f: styd on but hdd last strides* **4/6**[1]

3 3 5 **Moolhim (FR)**[13] 4117 2-9-5 0.............................. KerrinMcEvoy 4 73
(Simon Crisford) *compact; led to jst over 2f out: sn outpcd by wnr: lost 2nd 1f out and wknd* **3/1**[2]

4 1 ¼ **Fahad** 2-9-5 0.............................. AndreaAtzeni 6 69
(Roger Varian) *str; s.i.s: racd in last pair: pushed along over 2f out: lft bhd wl over 1f out* **8/1**[3]

5 ½ **Morisco (IRE)** 2-9-5 0.............................. AlistairRawlinson 1 68
(Tom Dascombe) *str; bit bkward; s.s: racd in last pair: pushed along over 2f out: lft bhd wl over 1f out* **50/1**

6 hd **What An Angel** 2-9-5 0.............................. RyanMoore 3 67
(Richard Hannon) *workmanlike; chsd ldng pair: pushed along 3f out: lft bhd fr 2f out* **12/1**

1m 29.71s (0.41) **Going Correction** +0.025s/f (Good) **6** Ran SP% **112.4**
Speed ratings (Par 96): **98,97,91,90,89 89**
CSF £24.38 TOTE £15.10: £4.90, £1.10; EX 30.40 Trifecta £67.60.
Owner Godolphin **Bred** Godolphin **Trained** Newmarket, Suffolk

FOCUS
Add 8yds. The two divisions of this last year were won by King Of Comedy and Arctic Sound, both of whom have made up into Group performers, while the beaten runners included Phoenix Of Spain, Line Of Duty and Persian Moon. The first two came clear this time, showing useful form.

4612 DAVIES INSURANCE SERVICES GALA STKS (LISTED RACE) 1m 1f 209y
3:25 (3:25) (Class 1) 3-Y-0+
£22,684 (£8,600; £4,304; £2,144; £1,076; £540) **Stalls** Low

Form RPR
-413 1 **Elarqam**[17] 3953 4-9-10 111.............................. JimCrowley 7 115
(Mark Johnston) *looked wl; t.k.h: trckd ldng pair: rdn to chal over 1f out: led jst ins fnl f: hrd pressed after: drvn and hld on wl* **11/10**[1]

-235 2 hd **Extra Elusive**[41] 3074 4-9-7 106.............................. RyanMoore 4 111
(Roger Charlton) *s.i.s: hld up in last pair: pushed along over 2f out: prog on outer over 1f out: chsd wnr ins fnl f and sn chalng: edgd clsr nr fin: jst hld* **15/2**

1350 3 1 **First Nation**[17] 3953 5-9-7 106.............................. KerrinMcEvoy 1 109
(Charlie Appleby) *hld up in last pair: pushed along over 2f out: trying to make prog whn nt clr run over 1f out: r.o to take 3rd last 80yds: unable to rch ldng pair* **12/1**

311- 4 1 ¾ **Royal Line**[237] 9005 5-9-7 111.............................. RobertHavlin 3 106
(John Gosden) *sweating; led at mod pce: pressed and tried to kick on over 2f out: drvn and hdd jst ins fnl f: fdd* **5/1**[2]

413 5 nk **Fifth Position (IRE)**[42] 3042 3-8-11 100.............................. AndreaAtzeni 6 106
(Roger Varian) *sn trckd ldr: chal over 2f out: hanging sltly and nt qckn over 1f out: fdd ins fnl f* **6/1**[3]

-630 6 1 ¼ **Chief Ironside**[16] 3987 4-9-7 108.............................. JamieSpencer 5 102
(William Jarvis) *hld up in tch: pushed along over 2f out: tried to cl on ldrs over 1f out: fdd ins fnl f* **12/1**

-150 7 ¾ **Oasis Charm**[17] 3953 5-9-7 106..............................(p) BrettDoyle 2 101
(Charlie Appleby) *t.k.h: sn hld up bhd ldrs: pushed along over 2f out: no prog and hanging 1f out: fdd* **11/1**

2m 7.11s (-3.09) **Going Correction** +0.025s/f (Good)
WFA 3 from 4yo+ 10lb **7** Ran SP% **114.1**
Speed ratings (Par 111): **113,112,112,110,110 109,108**
CSF £10.07 TOTE £1.90: £1.40, £3.40; EX 9.30 Trifecta £62.00.
Owner Hamdan Al Maktoum **Bred** Floors Farming **Trained** Middleham Moor, N Yorks

FOCUS
Add 8yds. A competitive edition of this Listed race, which was won last year by Lockinge winner and Eclipse runner Mustashry. It's been rated around the second and third, with the latter close to his Dubai form.

4613 GEORGE LINDON-TRAVERS MEMORIAL H'CAP 1m 1f 209y
4:00 (4:01) (Class 2) (0-100,98) 3-Y-0+
£24,744 (£7,416; £3,712; £1,848; £928; £468) **Stalls** Low

Form RPR
1-22 1 **Jazeel (IRE)**[35] 3315 4-9-6 **92**.............................. JamieSpencer 3 100
(Jedd O'Keeffe) *t.k.h: hld up in midfield: prog 2f out: rdn to chal fnl f: drvn ahd last 75yds: hrd pressed after: won on the nod* **7/2**[2]

3150 2 shd **Beringer**[16] 3987 4-9-12 **98**..............................(p) AndreaAtzeni 2 106
(Alan King) *looked wl; t.k.h: hld up and sn in midfield: prog on outer 2f out: rdn and clsd on ldrs fnl f: chal last strides: jst failed* **11/2**[3]

6132 3 nse **Hyanna**[21] 3800 4-8-10 **89**.............................. GeorgiaDobie(7) 10 97
(Eve Johnson Houghton) *hld up in tch: prog over 2f out: led over 1f out: hdd last 75yds: rallied fnl strides: jst failed* **12/1**

0423 4 1 ¾ **Exec Chef (IRE)**[16] 3992 4-9-12 **98**.............................. PatCosgrave 9 103+
(Jim Boyle) *trckd ldr to 1/2-way: styd cl up: lost pl on inner over 1f out and nt clr run sn after: styd on again ins fnl f* **11/2**[3]

-122 5 shd **Hats Off To Larry**[12] 4144 5-8-12 **84** oh2.............................. NicolaCurrie 1 88
(Mick Channon) *tk v t.k.h: hld up bhd ldrs: effrt over 2f out: rdn and stl cl up over 1f out: outpcd after but kpt on (jockey said gelding was denied a clear run)* **14/1**

3-10 6 ¾ **Elector**[35] 3315 4-9-9 **95**.............................. RyanMoore 6 99+
(Sir Michael Stoute) *led: pressed over 2f out: rdn and hdd over 1f out: wknd ins fnl f* **5/2**[1]

0110 7 3 **Harbour Breeze (IRE)**[15] 4035 4-9-2 **88**..............................(t[1]) JasonWatson 5 85
(Lucy Wadham) *t.k.h: hld up in last trio: rdn and no prog over 2f out: nvr able to threaten after (jockey said colt ran too free)* **16/1**

3030 8 3 **Pactolus (IRE)**[9] 4255 8-9-1 **87**..............................(t) KerrinMcEvoy 8 78
(Stuart Williams) *prom: trckd ldr 1/2-way: chal over 2f out: lost 2nd over 1f out: wkng whn impeded ins fnl f* **33/1**

5- 9 2 **Mutaabeq (IRE)**[266] 8174 4-9-5 **91**.............................. JimCrowley 4 78
(Marcus Tregoning) *awkward s: tk v t.k.h: hld up in last trio: pushed along 2f out: no prog (jockey said gelding ran too free)* **20/1**

1511 **10** *2* **Badenscoth**[21] 3806 5-9-7 **93**........................ RobertWinston 7 76
(Dean Ivory) *hld up and sn detached in last: pushed along 3f out: no prog whn drvn 2f out* **9/1**
2m 8.17s (-2.03) **Going Correction** +0.025s/f (Good) **10** Ran SP% **119.5**
Speed ratings (Par 109): **109,108,108,107,107 106,104,102,100,98**
CSF £23.89 CT £211.97 TOTE £4.10: £1.60, £2.10, £3.50; EX 24.10 Trifecta £315.90.
Owner Quantum **Bred** Mrs Joan Murphy **Trained** Middleham Moor, N Yorks
■ Stewards' Enquiry : Pat Cosgrave two-day ban: interference & careless riding (Jul 19-20)

FOCUS
Add 8yds. A valuable and competitive handicap with a tight finish. Sound form. The winner has been rated as finding a bit on his latest effort.

4614 SEQUEL H'CAP — 1m 6f
4:35 (4:36) (Class 4) (0-85,87) 3-Y-O+
£6,145 (£1,828; £913; £456; £300; £300) **Stalls** Low

Form RPR

1220 **1** **Knight Crusader**[30] 3467 7-9-11 **81**........................ LiamJones 3 89
(John O'Shea) *hld up in 7th: pushed along and prog over 2f out: rdn to chse ldr over 1f out: led jst ins fnl f: drvn out and hld on* **10/1**

4-40 **2** *½* **Machine Learner**[41] 3070 6-10-0 **84**........................ SeanLevey 8 91
(Joseph Tuite) *t.k.h: hld up in 8th: stdy prog jst over 2f out: shkn up over 1f out: chsd wnr and rdn last 100yds: clsd at fin: too late* **12/1**

40-6 **3** *1 ¼* **Imphal**[26] 3635 5-10-0 **84**........................ RyanMoore 7 89
(Gary Moore) *s.i.s: mostly in last pair: shkn up 3f out and no prog: styd on u.p over 1f out: fin wl to take 3rd last strides* **7/1**

2402 **4** *½* **Emenem**[25] 3663 5-9-10 **80**........................ HarryBentley 9 84
(Simon Dow) *wl plcd bhd ldrs: shkn up over 2f out: tried to cl over 1f out: one pce fnl f* **11/2**[2]

/62- **5** *¾* **Gwafa (IRE)**[508] 690 8-10-3 **87**........................(w) FergusSweeney 2 90
(Paul Webber) *wl in tch: effrt to chse ldr jst over 2f out: hanging and nt qckn over 1f out: lost 2nd sn after and one pce* **20/1**

031- **6** *1 ¼* **Beer With The Boys**[256] 8479 4-9-1 **71**........................ AndreaAtzeni 5 73
(Mick Channon) *wl in tch: effrt over 2f out: rdn and nt qckn wl over 1f out: no imp on ldrs after* **6/1**[3]

0441 **7** *nk* **Unit Of Assessment (IRE)**[28] 3545 5-9-11 **81**.........(vt) JasonWatson 6 82
(William Knight) *led 3f: styd in ldng trio: led wl over 2f out and dashed for home: hdd & wknd jst ins fnl f* **8/1**

3-12 **8** *2 ½* **Ship Of The Fen**[21] 3799 4-10-3 **87**........................ KerrinMcEvoy 4 85
(Ian Williams) *looked wl; swift prog to ld after 3f: hdd wl over 2f out: sn lost pl and btn (trainer's rep said gelding may have been unsuited by racing without cover)* **6/4**[1]

010- **9** *2* **Toshima (IRE)**[11] 8582 4-9-12 **82**........................(t) PatCosgrave 1 77
(Robert Stephens) *hld up in last pair: rdn 3f out and no prog: wl bhd over 1f out: kpt on last 150yds* **33/1**

-600 **10** *11* **Medburn Cutler**[42] 3044 9-9-8 **78**........................(p w) ShaneKelly 10 57
(Peter Hedger) *mostly chsd ldr to 3f out: wknd qckly: t.o* **50/1**

3m 5.34s (-0.66) **Going Correction** +0.025s/f (Good) **10** Ran SP% **119.7**
Speed ratings (Par 105): **102,101,101,100,100 99,99,97,96,90**
CSF £123.04 CT £905.23 TOTE £13.00: £2.90, £3.60, £2.10; EX 169.00 Trifecta £1116.80.
Owner S P Bloodstock **Bred** Steven & Petra Wallace **Trained** Elton, Gloucs

FOCUS
Add 8yds. This was run at what appeared to be a decent gallop, and the first three all raced in the last quartet. Straightforward form, with the third rated to his best and the fourth to his recent efforts.

4615 COPPAFEEL 10 YEAR ANNIVERSARY H'CAP (FOR LADY AMATEUR RIDERS) — 1m
5:05 (5:08) (Class 5) (0-70,71) 4-Y-O+
£4,679 (£1,451; £725; £363; £300; £300) **Stalls** Low

Form RPR

0055 **1** **Biotic**[38] 3192 8-10-7 **69**........................ MissJoannaMason 8 79
(Rod Millman) *dwlt: wl off a v str pce in 9th: prog over 2f out: shkn up to chal over 1f out: rdn to ld ins fnl f: edgd lft after: hld on* **4/1**[1]

6-01 **2** *½* **Club Tropicana**[36] 3279 4-10-5 **67**........................(t) MissGinaAndrews 12 76
(Richard Spencer) *hld up wl off the str pce in 8th: smooth prog 3f out: led wl over 1f out: sn pressed: shkn up and hdd ins fnl f: carried lft after: a hld* **4/1**[1]

00-0 **3** *5* **Gerry The Glover (IRE)**[10] 4226 7-9-8 **63**(h) MissSuzannahStevens(7) 10 61
(Lee Carter) *stdd s: hld up in last pair and virtually t.o: stl long way adrift over 2f out: styd on after: passed toiling rivals to take modest 3rd last 75yds* **10/1**

5220 **4** *1 ¾* **Baashiq (IRE)**[100] 1355 5-10-3 **65**........................(p) MissLillyPinchin 3 58
(Peter Hiatt) *blindfold off sltly late and dwlt: sn chsd ldrs: prog to ld over 2f out: hdd wl over 1f out: wknd fnl f* **14/1**

0500 **5** *½* **Chetan**[28] 3540 7-9-7 **62**........................ MissSarahBowen(5) 2 54
(Tony Carroll) *mounted on crse: chsd ldrs at v str pce: nt clr run briefly and swtchd rt over 2f out: nvr able to chal: wknd fnl f* **15/2**

4-55 **6** *1* **Tajdeed (IRE)**[36] 3248 4-10-3 **65**........................ MissBeckySmith 6 55
(Michael Appleby) *prom in r run at str pce: chal over 2f out: sn lost pl and btn: wknd ins fnl f (vet said gelding lost its left hind shoe)* **9/2**[2]

1462 **7** *shd* **Lunar Deity**[36] 3279 10-9-5 **60**........................ MissJuliaEngstrom(7) 13 50
(Stuart Williams) *s.s: virtually t.o in last pair: nvr any hope but passed sme wkng rivals fnl f* **11/1**

0003 **8** *2* **Sir Plato (IRE)**[28] 3529 5-10-4 **71**........................(b) MissMillieWonnacott(5) 9 56
(Rod Millman) *prom in r run at v str pce: rdn and lost pl over 2f out: sn btn* **7/1**[3]

0050 **9** *1 ½* **Tobacco Road (IRE)**[43] 3006 9-9-4 **55**........................(t) MissHannahWelch(3) 1 37
(Mark Pattinson) *chsd ldrs: u.p by 1/2-way: wl btn over 2f out* **14/1**

0-04 **10** *2 ¾* **Ad Valorem Queen (IRE)**[86] 1683 4-8-13 **52**........................ SophieSmith(5) 7 27
(William Knight) *chsd clr ldr at v str pce to over 2f out: wknd* **33/1**

-400 **11** *½* **Kismat**[10] 4220 4-9-5 **60**........................(p[1]) MissGeorgiaKing(7) 11 34
(Alan King) *hld up in last trio and long way bhd: briefly threatened to make sme prog 2f out: nudged along and wknd fnl f* **25/1**

0600 **12** *8* **Golconda Prince (IRE)**[23] 3740 5-9-0 **53**..(v[1]) MissRosieMargarson(5) 5 9
(Mark Pattinson) *led at frntic pce and had field wl strung out: hdd & wknd rapidly over 2f out* **40/1**

13 *21* **Daubney's Dream (IRE)**[224] 9232 4-9-9 **64**...(tp) MissMeganTrainor(7) 4
(Paddy Butler) *dwlt: a wl in rr: t.o* **50/1**

1m 43.05s (-0.25) **Going Correction** +0.025s/f (Good) **13** Ran SP% **124.4**
Speed ratings (Par 103): **102,101,96,94,94 93,93,91,89,86 86,78,57**
CSF £19.90 CT £156.48 TOTE £4.60: £1.90, £1.80, £3.70; EX 23.70 Trifecta £200.30.
Owner Mrs B Sumner & B R Millman **Bred** Mette Campbell-Andenaes **Trained** Kentisbeare, Devon
■ Stewards' Enquiry : Miss Joanna Mason two-day ban: interference & careless riding (Jul 19-20)

FOCUS
Add 8yds. This ladies' handicap was run at a very strong gallop and they were soon strung out. The first two finished clear, and there was a stewards' enquiry before the result was allowed to stand. The winner has been rated close to his best form over the past two years, with the second to her 3yo best.
T/Jkpt: Not won. T/Plt: £361.20 to a £1 stake. Pool: £84,863.62 - 171.50 winning units T/Qpdt: £18.70 to a £1 stake. Pool: £5,845.31 - 231.13 winning units **Jonathan Neesom**

4616 - 4620a (Foreign Racing) - See Raceform Interactive

4204 MAISONS-LAFFITTE (R-H)
Friday, July 5
OFFICIAL GOING: Turf: good to soft

4621a PRIX AMANDINE (LISTED RACE) (3YO FILLIES) (TURF) — 7f
3:05 3-Y-O **£24,774** (£9,909; £7,432; £4,954; £2,477)

RPR

1 **Rose Flower (GER)**[45] 2954 3-8-13 0 ow2........................ AlexisBadel 1 101
(G Botti, France) **26/1**

2 *1 ¼* **Gypsy Spirit**[14] 4052 3-8-13 0 ow2........................ TonyPiccone 14 97
(Tom Clover) *racd keenly bhd ldr: led on inner after 1f: drvn 1 1/2f out and rallied: hdd fnl 100yds: no ex* **12/1**

3 *hd* **Nooramunga (FR)**[25] 3-8-13 0 ow2........................ VincentCheminaud 2 97
(M Delzangles, France) **89/10**

4 *1* **Adelante (FR)**[25] 3-8-13 0 ow2........................ TheoBachelot 4 94
(George Baker) *a cl up: rdn and nt qckn ins fnl 1 1/2f: styd on at same pce* **29/1**

5 *hd* **Devant (FR)**[27] 3621 3-8-13 0 ow2........................ Pierre-CharlesBoudot 12 93
(H-A Pantall, France) **83/10**

6 *3* **Madeleine Must (FR)**[25] 3677 3-8-13 0 ow2........................ RonanThomas 5 85
(H-A Pantall, France) **67/10**[2]

7 *1 ¼* **Aviatress (IRE)**[25] 3677 3-8-13 0 ow2........................ ChristopheSoumillon 11 82
(A De Royer-Dupre, France) **3/1**[1]

8 *½* **Simplicity (FR)**[25] 3677 3-8-13 0 ow2........................(b) CristianDemuro 6 81
(F Chappet, France) **79/10**[3]

9 *shd* **Zenagh (USA)**[35] 3-8-13 0 ow2........................ MaximeGuyon 10 80
(A Fabre, France) **10/1**

10 *1 ¾* **Flaming Star (FR)**[27] 3621 3-8-13 0 ow2........................ JulienGuillochon 8 76
(H-A Pantall, France) **15/1**

11 *4* **Jet Setteuse (FR)**[49] 3-8-13 0 ow2........................ StephanePasquier 3 65
(F Rohaut, France) **9/1**

12 *1 ¾* **Etruria**[60] 2498 3-8-13 0 ow2........................ MickaelBarzalona 9 60
(A Fabre, France) *towards rr: rdn and no imp 2f out: sn btn* **17/1**

13 *1 ½* **Jojo (IRE)**[24] 3712 3-8-13 0 ow2........................ Louis-PhilippeBeuzelin 13 56
(Jo Hughes, France) *prom on outer: outpcd and drvn 2f out: sn wknd* **54/1**

14 *dist* **La Belle De Mai (FR)**[243] 3-8-13 0 ow2........................ AntoineHamelin 7
(I Endaltsev, Czech Republic) **74/1**

1m 23.24s (-4.76) **14** Ran SP% **118.9**
PARI-MUTUEL (all including 1 euro stake): WIN 27.20; PLACE 6.90, 4.50, 3.50; DF 112.10.
Owner G Botti **Bred** Gestut Karlshof **Trained** France

FOCUS
The second, fourth and ninth potentially limit the form, but the winner was impressive.

4534 HAMBURG (R-H)
Friday, July 5
OFFICIAL GOING: Turf: good

4622a GROSSER PREIS VON LOTTO HAMBURG (GROUP 3) (3YO+) (TURF) — 1m 2f
6:55 3-Y-O+ **£28,828** (£10,810; £5,405; £2,702; £1,801)

RPR

1 **King David (DEN)**[19] 3902 4-9-2 0........................ OliverWilson 6 107
(Marc Stott, Denmark) *hld up in rr: shkn up and hdwy over 2f out: led appr fnl f: sn clr: comfortably* **69/10**

2 *2 ½* **Nikkei (GER)**[25] 3678 4-9-4 0........................ AndraschStarke 2 104
(P Schiergen, Germany) *cl up on outer: pressed ldr 3f out: drvn to ld 2 1/2f out: hdd appr fnl f: sn outpcd by wnr but kpt on for 2nd* **58/10**[3]

3 *½* **Amorella (IRE)**[36] 4-8-13 0........................ AdriedeVries 3 98
(Markus Klug, Germany) *racd keenly: chsd ldr on inner: rdn and no imp 2f out: styd on same pce u.p* **42/10**[2]

4 *nk* **Itobo (GER)**[33] 3386 7-9-6 0........................ MarcoCasamento 4 104
(H-J Groschel, Germany) *settled in 2nd trio: 4th and pushed along 3f out: rdn and no imp over 1 1/2f out: kpt on at same pce u.p: nvr able to chal* **1/1**[1]

5 *nse* **Stex (IRE)**[26] 3639 3-8-5 0 ow2........................ WladimirPanov 1 100
(R Dzubasz, Germany) *broke wl and led: hdd 2 1/2f out: kpt on for press: outpcd by ldrs fnl f* **43/5**

6 *4 ½* **Serena (GER)**[25] 4-8-13 0........................ BauyrzhanMurzabayev 5 88
(H-J Groschel, Germany) *racd keenly: hld up in 2nd trio on outer: rdn and wknd 1 1/2f out* **15/2**

2m 8.36s **6** Ran SP% **118.8**
WFA 3 from 4yo+ 10lb
PARI-MUTUEL (all including 1 euro stake): WIN: 7.90; PLACE: 4.70, 3.00; SF: 50.20.
Owner Mme M Fernande **Bred** Stutterie Stork **Trained** Denmark

4582 BEVERLEY (R-H)
Saturday, July 6
OFFICIAL GOING: Good to firm (watered; 7.7)
Wind: Moderate behind Weather: Clpoudy with sunny periods

4623 DANDPHAULAGE.CO.UK NOVICE AUCTION STKS — 7f 96y
2:00 (2:00) (Class 5) 2-Y-O **£4,095** (£1,225; £612; £306; £152) **Stalls** Low

Form RPR

42 **1** **King's Caper**[8] 4317 2-9-3 0........................ ConnorBeasley 2 87
(Mark Johnston) *trckd ldng pair: hdwy to chse ldr 2f out: rdn over 1f out: drvn to chal over 1f out: kpt on wl u.p fnl f to ld last 50yds* **1/2**[1]

42 **2** ¾ **Frasard**[11] 4206 2-9-2 0........................ GrahamLee 9 84
(Bryan Smart) *trckd ldr: cl up 3f out: led wl over 2f out: rdn over 1f out: sn jnd and drvn: hdd and no ex last 50yds* **3/1**[2]

4 **3** 13 **Typsy Toad**[30] 3498 2-8-12 0........................ SeanDavis(3) 7 51
(Richard Fahey) *sn led: pushed along 3f out: sn rdn and hdd wl over 2f out: drvn wl over 1f out: sn one pce* **14/1**[3]

4 nk **Lion's Vigil (USA)** 2-9-4 0........................ TonyHamilton 10 53
(Richard Fahey) *chsd ldrs on outer: rdn along wl over 2f out: sn one pce* **14/1**[3]

5 1¼ **King's Charisma (IRE)** 2-9-5 0........................ DavidNolan 1 51+
(David O'Meara) *dwlt: sn in tch: chsd ldrs 1/2-way: rdn along on inner 3f out: sn outpcd* **16/1**

0 **6** ¾ **Carriesmatic**[18] 3968 2-8-9 0........................ AndrewMullen 6 40
(David Barron) *a towards rr* **66/1**

7 ½ **Harswell Approach (IRE)** 2-9-1 0........................ PaulMulrennan 8 44
(Liam Bailey) *in rr: pushed along on outer 3f out: sn rdn and plugged on fnl f* **66/1**

05 **8** nk **Little Ted**[18] 3954 2-9-4 0........................ DavidAllan 5 47
(Tim Easterby) *a in rr* **20/1**

03 **9** 1½ **Our Dave**[15] 4075 2-9-1 0........................ RobbieDowney 3 40
(John Quinn) *a towards rr* **16/1**

0 **10** 2¼ **Teasel's Rock (IRE)**[37] 3245 2-8-11 0........................ DuranFentiman 4 30
(Tim Easterby) *t.k.h: chsd ldrs: pushed along bef 1/2-way: sn rdn and wknd* **100/1**

1m 32.73s (0.13) **Going Correction** -0.05s/f (Good) **10** Ran **SP%** **125.5**
Speed ratings (Par 94): **97,96,81,80,79 78,78,77,76,73**
CSF £2.46 TOTE £1.40: £1.10, £1.10, £3.20; EX 2.60 Trifecta £15.50.
Owner Kingsley Park 13 **Bred** Highclere Stud **Trained** Middleham Moor, N Yorks

FOCUS
A bright, warm afternoon. Rail realignment added 7yds to the distance. All bar three of these had experience and the well-supported favourite prevailed off a decent pace. The first two drew clear of the remainder. Fair form.

4624 D&P PALLET DISTRIBUTION EBF MAIDEN STKS 5f
2:35 (2:36) (Class 5) 2-Y-O
£4,204 (£1,251; £625; £312) **Stalls** Low

Form RPR

3 **1** **Istanbul (IRE)**[30] 3512 2-9-5 0........................ TonyHamilton 9 80
(Richard Fahey) *chsd ldr: effrt 2f out: rdn wl over 1f out: drvn to chal over 1f out: styd on u.p to ld ins fnl f* **5/2**[1]

33 **2** 1¾ **She Looks Like Fun**[35] 3355 2-9-0 0........................ CliffordLee 5 69
(K R Burke) *led: rdn along wl over 1f out: jnd over 1f out and sn drvn: hdd ins fnl f: no ex* **4/1**[3]

3 1¾ **Point Of Order** 2-9-5 0........................ AndrewMullen 1 67
(Archie Watson) *chsd ldng pair: rdn along 2f out: drvn over 1f out: kpt on same pce fnl f* **3/1**[2]

4 2¾ **Rapid Russo** 2-9-5 0........................ TomEaves 4 58+
(Michael Dods) *chsd ldrs: rdn along and sltly outpcd wl over 1f out: kpt on fnl f* **12/1**

5 ½ **Sombra De Mollys** 2-8-11 0........................ BenRobinson(3) 3 51
(Brian Ellison) *chsd ldrs on inner: swtchd lft and rdn along 2f out: styd on same pce* **25/1**

023 **6** 3¼ **Bezzas Lad (IRE)**[53] 2706 2-9-5 74........................ PaulMulrennan 10 44
(Phillip Makin) *chsd ldrs: rdn along 2f out: sn drvn and wknd* **11/2**

55 **7** 2½ **Ebony Legend**[13] 4142 2-9-0 0........................ RobbieDowney 6 30
(John Quinn) *a in rr* **16/1**

8 2 **Northern Celt (IRE)** 2-9-5 0........................ DavidAllan 2 28
(Tim Easterby) *a in rr* **8/1**

9 3 **Tenbobmillionaire** 2-9-5 0........................ DuranFentiman 7 17
(Tim Easterby) *green: sn rdn along and a in rr* **40/1**

10 nk **Speedymining (IRE)** 2-9-5 0........................ GrahamLee 11 16
(Bryan Smart) *wnt lft s: green and a bhd (jockey said gelding ran green)* **33/1**

1m 2.64s (-0.26) **Going Correction** -0.05s/f (Good) **10** Ran **SP%** **122.9**
Speed ratings (Par 94): **100,97,94,90,89 84,80,76,72,71**
CSF £13.36 TOTE £3.30: £2.20, £1.30, £1.30; EX 14.00 Trifecta £35.00.
Owner D O'Callaghan **Bred** Equine Breeding Limited **Trained** Musley Bank, N Yorks

FOCUS
An interesting maiden with six newcomers. Very few got into it.

4625 D&P WAREHOUSING H'CAP 5f
3:10 (3:10) (Class 4) (0-82,83) 3-Y-O+
£8,758 (£2,621; £1,310; £656; £326; £300) **Stalls** Low

Form RPR

-643 **1** **Only Spoofing (IRE)**[9] 4279 5-9-1 71........................ GrahamLee 4 82
(Jedd O'Keeffe) *cl up on inner: led wl over 1f out: jnd and rdn ent fnl f: sn drvn and kpt on strly* **3/1**[1]

-666 **2** 1¼ **War Whisper (IRE)**[7] 4406 6-9-9 79........................ PaulMulrennan 3 85
(Paul Midgley) *trckd ldrs on inner: swtchd lft and hdwy over 1f out: rdn to chal ent fnl f: sn drvn and ev ch: kpt on same pce last 75yds* **3/1**[1]

1200 **3** 3¼ **East Street Revue**[7] 4406 6-9-5 75........................ DuranFentiman 6 69
(Tim Easterby) *trckd ldrs: pushed along and sltly outpcd 2f out: rdn over 1f out: swtchd rt and kpt on fnl f* **15/2**

5201 **4** ½ **Shepherd's Purse**[15] 4059 7-8-10 66........................ JamesSullivan 1 59
(Ruth Carr) *in tch on inner: rdn along and hdwy 2f out: drvn over 1f out: kpt on fnl f* **7/2**[2]

00-0 **5** 1 **Arcavallo (IRE)**[18] 3971 4-9-12 82........................(p) TomEaves 5 71
(Michael Dods) *slt ld: rdn along 2f out: sn hdd: drvn over 1f out: grad wknd* **18/1**

3341 **6** ¾ **Seen The Lyte (IRE)**[14] 4105 4-9-8 83........................(h) FayeMcManoman(5) 9 69
(Nigel Tinkler) *dwlt and hmpd s: in rr: hdwy 2f out: rdn over 1f out: no imp fnl f (jockey said filly was denied a clear run approaching the final furlong)* **12/1**

4-00 **7** 1¾ **Computable**[7] 4364 5-8-10 66........................(p) DavidAllan 8 46
(Tim Easterby) *wnt bdly lft s: a towards rr* **22/1**

00-0 **8** 3½ **Choosey (IRE)**[36] 3309 4-9-5 75........................ CamHardie 7 42
(Michael Easterby) *chsd ldrs: rdn along 2f out: sn drvn and wknd* **33/1**

0066 **9** ½ **Requinto Dawn (IRE)**[17] 3999 4-8-9 68........................(p) SeanDavis(3) 2 34
(Richard Fahey) *dwlt: a in rr (jockey said gelding missed the break)* **6/1**[3]

1m 1.37s (-1.53) **Going Correction** -0.05s/f (Good) **9** Ran **SP%** **118.5**
Speed ratings (Par 105): **110,108,102,102,100 99,96,90,90**
CSF £12.44 CT £62.03 TOTE £3.40: £1.20, £1.40, £2.80; EX 13.40 Trifecta £99.30.
Owner Mrs H Mannion, B Carter & F Durbin **Bred** Limestone And Tara Studs **Trained** Middleham Moor, N Yorks

FOCUS
Competitive for the grade and the winner made most of the running, with the first two drawing a little way clear of the remainder.

4626 D&P PALLETWAYS DELIVERY FILLIES' H'CAP 1m 100y
3:45 (3:48) (Class 3) (0-90,85) 3-Y-O+ **£16,172** (£4,812; £2,405; £1,202) **Stalls** Low

Form RPR

3411 **1** **Bighearted**[13] 4147 3-9-4 85........................ CameronNoble(3) 5 92+
(Michael Bell) *mde all: rdn over 1f out: drvn ins fnl f: kpt on strly towards fin* **2/1**[2]

0004 **2** 2½ **Deira Surprise**[8] 4338 3-8-13 77........................ DavidAllan 4 78
(Hugo Palmer) *sn trcking wnr: pushed along over 2f out: rdn wl over 1f out: drvn and kpt on fnl f* **10/1**

133 **3** nk **Harvest Day**[10] 4243 4-9-3 72........................(t) PhilDennis 1 74
(Michael Easterby) *trckd ldrs: hdwy on inner 2f out: sn n.m.r: effrt and nt clr run over 1f out: swtchd lft and rdn ent fnl f: sn chsng wnr and drvn: kpt on same pce towards fin* **9/2**[3]

1113 **4** 3½ **Kylie Rules**[29] 3552 4-9-13 82........................ JamesSullivan 3 76
(Ruth Carr) *t.k.h: hld up in tch: hdwy to trck ldrs 1/2-way: pushed along wl over 2f out: rdn wl over 1f out: sn drvn and btn* **6/4**[1]

1341 **5** ¾ **Liliofthelamplight (IRE)**[8] 4329 3-9-0 78........................ ConnorBeasley 2 69
(Mark Johnston) *hld up in rr: hdwy on inner 2 1/2f out: rdn wl over 1f out: sn drvn and n.d* **6/1**

4-50 **6** 2 **Sootability (IRE)**[21] 3862 3-8-6 73........................ SeanDavis(3) 6 59
(Richard Fahey) *wnt lft s: a in rr* **16/1**

1m 46.52s (0.12) **Going Correction** -0.05s/f (Good)
WFA 3 from 4yo 9lb **6** Ran **SP%** **120.8**
Speed ratings (Par 104): **97,94,94,90,89 87**
CSF £23.32 TOTE £3.20: £2.10, £5.40; EX 31.20 Trifecta £127.00.
Owner M E Perlman **Bred** R Frisby **Trained** Newmarket, Suffolk

FOCUS
Add 7yds to the distance. A decent prize for this competitive, small-field fillies' handicap and the winner made all off an initial steady pace. The third has been rated in line with her best turf form.

4627 D&P UK AND EUROPEAN DISTRIBUTION H'CAP 1m 1f 207y
4:20 (4:22) (Class 5) (0-75,75) 4-Y-O+
£6,301 (£1,886; £943; £472; £300; £300) **Stalls** Low

Form RPR

024 **1** **Billy Roberts (IRE)**[12] 4194 6-8-12 66........................ ConnorBeasley 4 74
(Richard Whitaker) *sn cl up: led 1 1/2f out: sn rdn: drvn and kpt on wl fnl f* **9/2**[2]

3422 **2** 1¾ **Mr Carbonator**[16] 4036 4-8-6 60........................ PhilDennis 3 64
(Philip Kirby) *trckd ldng pair: hdwy 2f out: rdn over 1f out: sn chsng wnr: drvn and no imp towards fin* **5/1**[3]

2046 **3** 1¾ **Placebo Effect (IRE)**[28] 3568 4-8-12 69........................ BenRobinson(3) 5 70
(Ollie Pears) *hld up in rr: hdwy 3f out: rdn to chse ldrs over 1f out: drvn and kpt on fnl f: tk 3rd on line* **5/1**[3]

0505 **4** shd **Indomeneo**[28] 3568 4-9-4 75........................ SeanDavis(3) 6 75
(Richard Fahey) *trckd ldrs: pushed along and hdwy wl over 2f out: rdn over 1f out: chsd ldng pair and drvn ent fnl f: kpt on same pce: lost 3rd on line* **7/1**

0501 **5** 7 **Bollin Joan**[7] 4371 4-9-0 68........................(p) DavidAllan 1 54
(Tim Easterby) *led: rdn along 2f out: hdd and drvn 1 1/2f out: sn wknd* **9/4**[1]

4143 **6** 12 **Kilbaha Lady (IRE)**[7] 4371 5-8-11 70........................(p) FayeMcManoman(5) 7 32
(Nigel Tinkler) *s.i.s: sn in tch: rdn along over 2f out: sn wknd (jockey said mare hung left on the bend)* **13/2**

2-43 **7** 11 **Miss Mumtaz (IRE)**[7] 4391 4-9-1 72........................(p) CameronNoble(3) 2 12
(Ian Williams) *in tch: pushed along over 3f out: sn rdn: lost pl and bhd fr wl over 2f out (vet said filly was lame on its left fore)* **8/1**

2m 4.15s (-1.55) **Going Correction** -0.05s/f (Good) **7** Ran **SP%** **119.2**
Speed ratings (Par 103): **104,102,101,101,95 85,77**
CSF £28.61 TOTE £5.80: £3.00, £2.10; EX 26.40 Trifecta £148.30.
Owner R M Whitaker **Bred** Burgage Stud **Trained** Scarcroft, W Yorks

FOCUS
Rail realignment added 7yds to the distance of this modest race for the grade. The winner was always up with the pace. The winner has been rated to his best over the past two years, and the second close to his recent form.

4628 D&P HAULAGE CONTRACT DISTRIBUTION FILLIES' H'CAP 1m 1f 207y
4:55 (4:57) (Class 5) (0-70,72) 3-Y-O
£5,292 (£1,584; £792; £396; £300; £300) **Stalls** Low

Form RPR

U043 **1** **Northern Lyte**[11] 4210 3-8-7 61........................ FayeMcManoman(5) 7 70
(Nigel Tinkler) *hld up towards rr: smooth hdwy on outer 3f out: led 2f out and sn hung rt: rdn clr over 1f out: kpt on strly* **5/2**[1]

65-0 **2** 2½ **Lady Scatterley (FR)**[9] 4285 3-9-4 67........................ DavidAllan 4 71
(Tim Easterby) *hld up in rr: hdwy wl over 2f out: rdn along wl over 1f out: styd on wl to chse wnr ins fnl f: no imp towards fin* **16/1**

6-53 **3** 4 **Eesha's Smile (IRE)**[17] 4000 3-9-4 70........................ BenRobinson(3) 5 66
(Ivan Furtado) *prom: effrt over 2f out and sn cl up: rdn along wl over 1f out: drvn and one pce fnl f* **9/2**[3]

2124 **4** 2 **Ivory Charm**[8] 4321 3-9-2 68........................ SeanDavis(3) 3 60
(Richard Fahey) *trckd ldrs: pushed along wl over 2f out: rdn wl over 1f out: plugged on one pce* **3/1**[2]

3440 **5** ¾ **Osmosis**[25] 3708 3-8-13 65........................ ConorMcGovern(3) 8 56
(Jason Ward) *sn led: rdn along 3f out: hdd 2f out and sn wknd* **8/1**

055 **6** 5 **Canoodling**[18] 3958 3-9-2 68........................ CameronNoble(3) 1 49
(Ian Williams) *midfield: rdn along over 3f out: n.d* **5/1**

0-54 **7** 6 **Thakaa (USA)**[27] 3637 3-9-9 72........................ GrahamLee 9 41
(Charles Hills) *chsd ldrs on outer: rdn along 3f out: hld whn hmpd 2f out: sn wknd* **7/1**

003 **8** 9 **Kostantina**[20] 3882 3-8-6 55........................ PhilDennis 6 6
(Olly Williams) *sn cl up: rdn along 3f out: wkng whn hmpd 2f out* **33/1**

000 **9** 10 **Initial Approach (IRE)**[116] 1165 3-8-2 51 oh6........................ DuranFentiman 2
(Alan Brown) *a in rr: bhd fnl 3f* **50/1**

2m 6.24s (0.54) **Going Correction** -0.05s/f (Good) **9** Ran **SP%** **122.8**
Speed ratings (Par 97): **95,93,89,88,87 83,78,71,63**
CSF £47.86 CT £180.56 TOTE £3.40: £1.30, £3.80, £1.70; EX 43.80 Trifecta £286.10.
Owner Exors Of The Late Miss C Wright **Bred** The Glanvilles Stud **Trained** Langton, N Yorks

FOCUS
Add 7yds to the distance. A weak fillies' handicap for the grade, the first two came from off the pace and they finished strung out. A length pb from the winner.

4629 D&P EXPRESS PALLET DELIVERY NOVICE STKS 5f
5:30 (5:30) (Class 5) 3-Y-O+ £4,662 (£1,395; £697; £349; £173) Stalls Low

Form RPR
05 1 **Hawk In The Sky**[14] 4129 3-9-5 0 ConnorBeasley 2 71
(Richard Whitaker) *trckd ldng pair: rdn along wl over 1f out: chsd wnr and drvn ent fnl f: kpt on wl to ld nr fin* **4/1[2]**
-534 2 ½ **Dream Of Honour (IRE)**[5] 4444 3-9-5 75 (b[1]) DavidAllan 5 69
(Tim Easterby) *sn led: pushed clr wl over 1f out: shkn up and rdn ins fnl f: sn drvn: hdd and no ex nr fin* **2/11[1]**
06 3 6 **Dilly Dilly (IRE)**[35] 3339 3-8-11 0 BenRobinson(3) 1 42
(John Wainwright) *chsd ldrs: rdn along 2f out: kpt on same pce* **10/1[3]**
00-0 4 8 **Ganton Eagle**[28] 3565 3-8-12 43 JoshQuinn(7) 4 19
(Michael Easterby) *a in rr* **22/1**
6-0 5 2 ¼ **Little Thornton**[12] 4193 3-8-7 0 VictorSantos(7) 3 6
(Stella Barclay) *chsd ldr: rdn along over 2f out: sn wknd* **50/1**
1m 2.85s (-0.05) **Going Correction** -0.05s/f (Good) **5 Ran SP% 120.0**
Speed ratings (Par 103): **98,97,87,74,71**
CSF £5.71 TOTE £6.70: £1.60, £1.10; EX 7.20 Trifecta £13.10.
Owner Michael Hawkins **Bred** R C Dollar & Hellwood Stud Farm **Trained** Scarcroft, W Yorks

FOCUS
A terribly weak novice sprint which saw a hotpot turned over. The second has been rated close to his recent form.
T/Plt: £42.70 to a £1 stake. Pool: £58,640.03 - 1,000.27 winning units T/Qpdt: £36.90 to a £1 stake. Pool: £3,326.64 - 66.60 winning units **Joe Rowntree**

4237 CARLISLE (R-H)
Saturday, July 6

OFFICIAL GOING: Good to firm (good in places; watered; 7.6)
Wind: Almost nil Weather: Hot, sunny

4630 GRETNA GATEWAY APPRENTICE H'CAP (JOCKEY CLUB GRASSROOTS SPRINT SERIES QUALIFIER) 5f 193y
6:00 (6:03) (Class 5) (0-70,68) 4-Y-O+
£4,204 (£1,251; £625; £400; £400; £400) Stalls Low

Form RPR
5006 1 **Tarnhelm**[14] 4131 4-8-2 49 oh2 RhonaPindar(5) 2 61
(Wilf Storey) *s.s: sn pushed along in detached last: gd hdwy over 1f out: led ins fnl f: sn clr* **20/1**
0022 2 2 ½ **Ventura Secret (IRE)**[19] 3921 5-9-0 56 (tp) PaulaMuir 6 60
(Michael Dods) *trckd ldrs: effrt and rdn over 1f out: ev ch briefly ins fnl f: nt pce of wnr* **5/2[1]**
0000 3 1 ¼ **Suitcase 'N' Taxi**[3] 4519 5-9-5 61 DannyRedmond 7 61
(Tim Easterby) *led: rdn and wandered over 1f out: hdd ins fnl f: kpt on same pce (jockey said gelding hung left-handed in the final furlong)* **5/1**
-002 4 2 ¼ **Extrasolar**[5] 4434 9-8-13 60 (tp) ZakWheatley(5) 5 53
(Geoffrey Harker) *hld up in tch: pushed along over 2f out: hdwy over 1f out: no imp fnl f* **9/2[3]**
0266 5 2 ¾ **Cameo Star (IRE)**[19] 3930 4-9-11 67 (p) ConnorMurtagh 4 51
(Richard Fahey) *dwlt: hld up: rdn over 2f out: sme late hdwy: nvr rchd ldrs (jockey said gelding missed the break)* **4/1[2]**
3200 6 ½ **Prestbury Park (USA)**[15] 4059 4-9-7 68 CianMacRedmond(5) 8 50
(Paul Midgley) *pressed ldr: rdn 2f out: wknd fnl f* **6/1**
3510 7 1 ½ **Mansfield**[31] 3475 6-8-13 58 KieranSchofield(3) 1 36
(Stella Barclay) *t.k.h: trckd ldrs: rdn over 2f out: wknd fnl f* **7/1**
0-00 8 14 **Bevsboy (IRE)**[14] 4130 5-8-2 49 oh4 EllaMcCain(5) 3
(Lynn Siddall) *chsd ldng gp: drvn and struggling over 3f out: lost tch fnl 2f: t.o* **50/1**
1m 13.24s (-1.36) **Going Correction** -0.10s/f (Good) **8 Ran SP% 116.9**
Speed ratings (Par 103): **105,101,100,97,93 92,90,72**
CSF £71.65 CT £304.82 TOTE £26.80: £5.00, £1.40, £2.00; EX 102.70 Trifecta £887.70.
Owner H S Hutchinson & W Storey **Bred** Theobalds Stud **Trained** Muggleswick, Co Durham

FOCUS
The winner came from well back in this very modest handicap, suggesting the pace up front was a strong one. The time, on a sound surface, was 2.24sec outside standard. The second has been rated to his C&D latest.

4631 GATEWAY GALLOP NOVICE MEDIAN AUCTION STKS 5f
6:30 (6:36) (Class 5) 2-Y-O £4,204 (£1,251; £625; £312) Stalls Low

Form RPR
63 1 **Aberama Gold**[14] 4098 2-9-5 0 ShaneGray 1 77
(Keith Dalgleish) *trckd ldrs: led over 1f out: drvn and kpt on wl fnl f* **3/1[2]**
32 2 ½ **Cruising**[14] 4125 2-9-5 0 PaulMulrennan 5 75
(David Brown) *unruly bef s: pressed ldr: led over 2f out to over 1f out: rallied and ev ch to ins fnl f: one pce towards fin* **5/2[1]**
3 5 **Ma Boy Harris (IRE)** 2-9-5 0 BenCurtis 3 57+
(Phillip Makin) *dwlt: sn trcking ldrs: pushed along over 2f out: rdn and hung rt over 1f out: sn outpcd* **5/1[3]**
40 4 2 ¾ **Red Hot Streak**[21] 3841 2-9-5 0 JackGarritty 4 47
(Tim Easterby) *led to over 2f out: rdn and wknd over 1f out* **12/1**
5 42 **Zakher Alain** 2-9-5 0 AndrewMullen 2 +
(Adrian Nicholls) *missed break: a wl bhd: eased fr 1/2-way* **20/1**
1m 1.66s (-0.44) **Going Correction** -0.10s/f (Good) **5 Ran SP% 82.7**
Speed ratings (Par 94): **99,98,90,85,18**
CSF £5.94 TOTE £2.90: £1.60, £1.20; EX 5.60 Trifecta £10.30.
Owner Weldspec Glasgow Limited **Bred** Mrs J McMahon **Trained** Carluke, S Lanarks
■ Felicia Blue was withdrawn. Price at time of withdrawal 2/1F. Rule 4 applies to all bets - deduction 30p in the pound

FOCUS
A fair novice event, although it was weakened when Felicia Blue declined to enter the stalls. It's been rated around the previous form of the first two.

4632 GRETNA GATEWAY DREAM H'CAP 5f
7:00 (7:04) (Class 5) (0-70,69) 3-Y-O+
£4,204 (£1,251; £625; £400; £400; £400) Stalls Low

Form RPR
2201 1 **Gamesome (FR)**[18] 3975 8-9-8 68 ConnorMurtagh(3) 9 75
(Paul Midgley) *hld up: gd hdwy on wd outside appr fnl f: kpt on wl to ld cl home* **14/1**
0103 2 hd **Afandem (IRE)**[9] 4307 5-9-7 69 (p) DannyRedmond(5) 3 75
(Tim Easterby) *prom: effrt and rdn over 1f out: kpt on to take 2nd cl home* **10/1**
4320 3 hd **David's Beauty (IRE)**[10] 4230 6-9-1 58 (b) PaulMulrennan 4 63
(Brian Baugh) *led: rdn over 1f out: hung rt ins fnl f: hdd and no ex towards fin* **16/1**
2003 4 nk **Suwaan (IRE)**[15] 4059 5-9-10 67 (h[1]) JamesSullivan 1 71
(Ruth Carr) *trckd ldrs: effrt and shkn up over 1f out: hd high and ev ch ins fnl f: hld nr fin* **7/1[3]**
0233 5 ¾ **Black Salt**[13] 4149 5-9-12 69 RobbieDowney 10 71
(David Barron) *hld up: hdwy on outside to chse ldrs over 1f out: no ex ins fnl f* **4/1[2]**
-263 6 nk **Debawtry (IRE)**[18] 3975 4-9-10 67 BenCurtis 5 73+
(Phillip Makin) *hld up in midfield: n.m.r over 2f out to over 1f out: sn rdn: keeping on whn n.m.r thrght fnl f: nt rcvr (jockey said filly was also denied a clear run approaching the line)* **15/8[1]**
1445 7 ½ **Northern Society (IRE)**[15] 4059 3-9-3 65 ShaneGray 2 62
(Keith Dalgleish) *hld up in midfield on ins: effrt and rdn over 1f out: kpt on same pce ins fnl f* **12/1**
0604 8 shd **Amazing Grazing (IRE)**[15] 4059 5-9-12 69 LewisEdmunds 6 67
(Rebecca Bastiman) *in tch: drvn and outpcd 2f out: sme late hdwy: nvr rchd ldrs* **7/1[3]**
4-06 9 1 ¼ **Beechwood Izzy (IRE)**[45] 2960 3-9-7 69 TomEaves 7 61
(Keith Dalgleish) *pressed ldr: rdn and ev ch over 1f out: wknd ins fnl f* **20/1**
05-0 10 hd **Dahik (IRE)**[19] 3921 4-9-0 57 CamHardie 11 50
(Michael Easterby) *missed break: bhd: drvn over 2f out: nvr on terms* **50/1**
1-10 11 2 **Highly Focussed (IRE)**[17] 3999 5-9-10 67 JackGarritty 8 53
(Ann Duffield) *hld up: rdn and outpcd over 2f out: nvr on terms* **25/1**
1m 1.32s (-0.78) **Going Correction** -0.10s/f (Good)
WFA 3 from 4yo+ 5lb **11 Ran SP% 119.7**
Speed ratings (Par 103): **102,101,101,100,99 99,98,98,96,95 92**
CSF £145.72 CT £2323.10 TOTE £13.30: £3.90, £3.50, £3.70; EX 145.30 Trifecta £1618.90.
Owner M Hammond & P T Midgley **Bred** Jean-Pierre Deroubaix **Trained** Westow, N Yorks

FOCUS
A bunch finish to this modest sprint handicap. The winner has been rated as backing up his latest win, the runner-up rated to his C&D win, and the third and fourth close to form.

4633 ANDERSONS (DENTON HOME) H'CAP 1m 1f
7:30 (7:30) (Class 6) (0-60,64) 4-Y-O+
£3,105 (£924; £461; £400; £400; £400) Stalls Low

Form RPR
0001 1 **Dutch Coed**[18] 3960 7-8-13 55 RowanScott(3) 7 62
(Nigel Tinkler) *hld up in midfield: hdwy to ld over 1f out: rdn and r.o wl fnl f* **7/1[3]**
1211 2 1 **Betty Grable (IRE)**[38] 3224 5-8-7 53 RhonaPindar(7) 8 58
(Wilf Storey) *hld up in midfield: hdwy to dispute ld over 1f out: kpt on same pce wl ins fnl f* **5/1[2]**
0-00 3 nk **Graceful Act**[16] 4036 11-8-2 46 oh1 (p) PaulaMuir(5) 6 50
(Ron Barr) *prom: effrt and drvn along over 1f out: kpt on same pce ins fnl f* **66/1**
3240 4 2 ½ **Lukoutoldmakezebak**[3] 4512 6-8-7 46 (p) JamieGormley 9 45
(David Thompson) *led: rdn and hdd over 1f out: outpcd ins fnl f* **11/1**
3661 5 1 ¼ **Home Before Dusk**[9] 4293 4-9-11 64 (v) ShaneGray 14 61
(Keith Dalgleish) *s.i.s: hld up: rdn over 2f out: hdwy over 1f out: kpt on fnl f: nt pce to chal* **5/1[2]**
5600 6 1 ½ **Captain Scott (IRE)**[19] 3941 4-9-6 59 (b) AlistairRawlinson 11 53
(Heather Main) *cl up: drvn and hung rt over 1f out: sn wknd* **14/1**
6004 7 3 ¼ **John Caesar (IRE)**[18] 3959 8-8-0 46 oh1 (p) KieranSchofield(7) 4 33
(Rebecca Bastiman) *hld up towards rr: drvn along over 2f out: no imp fr over 1f out* **33/1**
00-0 8 2 ½ **Maldonado (FR)**[19] 3939 5-9-7 60 PaulMulrennan 5 42
(Michael Easterby) *hld up towards rr: rdn over 2f out: nvr rchd ldrs* **33/1**
-262 9 nse **Red Seeker**[14] 4130 4-9-4 57 (t) PaddyMathers 13 39
(Tim Easterby) *chsd ldrs: drvn along over 2f out: wknd over 1f out* **7/2[1]**
00-3 10 1 ¾ **Millie The Minx (IRE)**[25] 3681 5-8-8 47 (t[1]) JamesSullivan 15 26
(Dianne Sayer) *prom tl rdn and wknd over 1f out* **5/1[2]**
-006 11 hd **Pumaflor (IRE)**[45] 2978 7-8-12 54 (p) ConnorMurtagh(3) 10 33
(Philip Kirby) *awkward s: hld up towards rr: shkn up whn checked over 2f out: nvr on terms* **33/1**
4040 12 2 ¾ **Bob's Girl**[9] 4285 4-8-9 48 oh1 ow2 (b) TomEaves 12 21
(Michael Mullineaux) *hld up towards rr: drvn and outpcd over 2f out: sn btn* **33/1**
2330 13 nk **Splash Of Verve (IRE)**[17] 4003 7-8-3 49 (p) TobyEley(7) 3 21
(David Thompson) *dwlt: bhd and outpcd: nvr on terms* **18/1**
0520 14 2 ¼ **Highwayman**[17] 4002 6-8-7 46 oh1 (h) CamHardie 16 14
(David Thompson) *hld up: drvn and struggling over 2f out: sn btn* **25/1**
000P 15 44 **Rock Island Line**[40] 3162 5-8-9 48 (b) AndrewMullen 1
(Mark Walford) *plld hrd in midfield: struggling 4f out: t.o (jockey said gelding ran too free and stopped quickly)* **20/1**
1m 56.56s (-2.44) **Going Correction** -0.10s/f (Good) **15 Ran SP% 126.9**
Speed ratings (Par 101): **106,105,104,102,101 100,97,95,95,93 93,90,90,88,49**
CSF £41.03 CT £2208.79 TOTE £8.60: £2.80, £2.00, £18.30; EX 54.10 Trifecta £572.80.
Owner Ms Sara Hattersley **Bred** Sara Hattersley **Trained** Langton, N Yorks

FOCUS
Add 14yds. A low-grade handicap in which the principals came from the first half of the field. The winner has been rated to last year's form.

4634 DESIGNER DISCOUNTS AT GRETNA GATEWAY H'CAP 7f 173y
8:00 (8:00) (Class 4) (0-80,82) 3-Y-O+
£7,439 (£2,213; £1,106; £553; £400; £400) Stalls Low

Form RPR
4252 1 **Harvey Dent**[8] 4316 3-9-7 80 DanielTudhope 5 89
(Archie Watson) *mde all: shkn up over 1f out: kpt on strly fnl f: unchal* **2/1[1]**
3205 2 1 ¾ **Ghayyar (IRE)**[18] 3957 5-9-5 69 (tp) JackGarritty 3 76
(Tim Easterby) *prom: std hdwy to chse wnr over 2f out: effrt and rdn over 1f out: edgd rt and one pce ins fnl f* **11/2[3]**
3010 3 3 **Tadaawol**[10] 4240 6-10-4 82 (p) LewisEdmunds 10 82
(Roger Fell) *hld up on outside: effrt and rdn over 2f out: kpt on same pce fnl f* **12/1**
0-22 4 shd **Zoravan (USA)**[10] 4239 6-9-4 68 TomEaves 4 68+
(Keith Dalgleish) *hld up: nt clr run over 2f out to over 1f out: shkn up and kpt on steadily fnl f: nvr nrr (jockey said gelding was denied a clear run)* **6/1**

1212 **5** *2* **Abushamah (IRE)**[18] [3957] 8-9-2 **66** .... JamesSullivan 1 61
(Ruth Carr) *in tch: rdn over 2f out: edgd rt over 1f out: sn outpcd* **12/1**

60 **6** *1* **Irish Minister (USA)**[10] [4239] 4-9-1 **65** .... AndrewElliott 6 58
(David Thompson) *s.i.s: hld up: effrt and drvn over 2f out: no further imp over 1f out* **33/1**

2312 **7** *½* **Marshal Dan (IRE)**[15] [4067] 4-9-11 **75** .... AlistairRawlinson 2 67
(Heather Main) *hld up on ins: rdn 2f out: edgd rt appr fnl f: nvr rchd ldrs (jockey said gelding failed to handle the track and ran flat)* **9/4[2]**

6200 **8** *1¼* **Mustadun**[20] [3885] 3-9-0 **73** .... FrannyNorton 7 60
(Mark Johnston) *trckd ldrs: rdn and outpcd over 1f out: hld whn checked ins fnl f* **10/1**

05/0 **9** *6* **Cross Step (USA)**[11] [4209] 5-9-6 **70** .... AndrewMullen 8 45
(Adrian Nicholls) *pressed wnr to over 2f out: rdn and wknd over 1f out* **50/1**

1m 38.87s (-1.13) **Going Correction** -0.10s/f (Good)
WFA 3 from 4yo+ 9lb **9** Ran SP% **123.2**
Speed ratings (Par 105): **101,99,96,96,94 93,92,91,85**
CSF £14.86 CT £112.42 TOTE £2.80: £1.10, £1.80, £2.80; EX 16.70 Trifecta £139.20.
Owner Saxon Thoroughbreds **Bred** Mrs D O Joly **Trained** Upper Lambourn, W Berks

FOCUS
Add 11yds. Just a fair handicap. The second has been rated to this year's form.

4635 NEW VISION NEW VILLAGE AT GRETNA GATEWAY H'CAP 6f 195y
8:30 (8:31) (Class 4) (0-85,87) 3-Y-O **£7,439** (£2,213; £1,106; £553; £400) **Stalls** Low

Form RPR

0462 **1** **I Am A Dreamer**[8] [4338] 3-9-2 **79** .... FrannyNorton 3 86
(Mark Johnston) *mde virtually all: rdn and hrd pressed fr over 1f out: hld on gamely towards fin* **5/4[1]**

63-2 **2** *hd* **Enough Already**[30] [3510] 3-9-5 **82** .... KevinStott 7 88
(Kevin Ryan) *prom: smooth hdwy over 2f out: effrt and disp ld fr over 1f out: hung rt ins fnl f: kpt on: hld cl home* **5/2[2]**

266 **3** *2¾* **Kind Review**[18] [3972] 3-8-4 **67** .... CamHardie 2 66
(Tracy Waggott) *in tch: smooth hdwy over 2f out: rdn over 1f out: edgd lft and one pce ins fnl f* **16/1**

1020 **4** *8* **Havana Ooh Na Na**[20] [3884] 3-8-4 **67** ....(p) AndrewMullen 4 44
(K R Burke) *cl up tl rdn and wknd over 1f out* **9/1**

1-36 **5** *3¼* **Gold Arrow**[15] [4072] 3-9-4 **81** .... BenCurtis 5 50
(Ralph Beckett) *disp ld to wl over 1f out: sn rdn and wknd* **10/3[3]**

1m 26.91s (-1.09) **Going Correction** -0.10s/f (Good) **5** Ran SP% **112.0**
Speed ratings (Par 102): **102,101,98,89,85**
CSF £4.76 TOTE £2.00: £1.10, £1.70; EX 5.00 Trifecta £33.10.
Owner M Doyle **Bred** Bearstone Stud Ltd **Trained** Middleham Moor, N Yorks

FOCUS
Not a particularly well contested race of its type. The winner has been rated back to his best.

4636 GRETNA GATEWAY DREAMS MAIDEN STKS 1m 3f 39y
9:00 (9:02) (Class 5) 3-Y-O+ **£4,204** (£1,251; £625; £312) **Stalls** High

Form RPR

1 **Yellow Tiger (FR)**[46] 3-9-3 83 .... FrannyNorton 2 83+
(Mark Johnston) *pressed ldr: led 2f out: idled wl ins fnl f: hld on* **5/2[2]**

2 *nk* **Roman Stone (USA)** 3-9-3 0 .... PaulMulrennan 4 79
(Keith Dalgleish) *chsd ldrs: rdn and outpcd fnl f: rallied to chse wnr ins fnl f: clsng at fin* **10/1**

33 **3** *1½* **Dante's View (IRE)**[13] [4143] 3-9-3 0 .... DanielTudhope 5 76
(Sir Michael Stoute) *led to 2f out: drvn and one pce fnl f* **4/11[1]**

4 *1¾* **Baladio (IRE)** 3-8-12 0 .... TonyHamilton 6 68
(Richard Fahey) *prom: drvn along over 2f out: kpt on same pce fr over 1f out* **8/1[3]**

0 **5** *9* **Ezzrah**[24] [3724] 3-9-3 0 .... AndrewMullen 1 57
(Mark Walford) *s.i.s: t.k.h in tch: rdn and outpcd over 2f out: btn over 1f out* **16/1**

00/ **6** *17* **Abouttimeyoutoldme**[990] [7458] 5-10-0 0 .... JackGarritty 7 25
(Alistair Whillans) *t.k.h early: stdd in rr: rdn and struggling over 3f out: sn btn: t.o* **50/1**

7 *8* **Hunters Step** 3-9-3 0 .... LewisEdmunds 3 12
(Noel Wilson) *s.i.s: hld up: struggling over 3f out: btn fnl 2f: t.o* **33/1**

8 *2½* **Ingleby George** 5-9-11 0 .... ConorMcGovern(3) 9 6
(Jason Ward) *v.s.a: bhd: struggling 4f out: t.o (jockey said gelding was slowly away)* **50/1**

2m 28.63s (-1.07) **Going Correction** -0.10s/f (Good)
WFA 3 from 5yo+ 11lb **8** Ran SP% **134.8**
Speed ratings (Par 103): **99,98,97,96,89 77,71,69**
CSF £32.51 TOTE £4.10: £1.10, £2.50, £1.10; EX 40.20 Trifecta £51.80.
Owner Jaber Abdullah **Bred** Nicolas De Chambure **Trained** Middleham Moor, N Yorks

FOCUS
Add 14yds. The winner of this ordinary maiden was value for a bit further. The winner has been rated as running to a figure in line with his French official rating.
T/Plt: £68.80 to a £1 stake. Pool: £62,570.26 - 663.05 winning units T/Qpdt: £48.30 to a £1 stake. Pool: £6,870.79 - 105.06 winning units **Richard Young**

4588 CHELMSFORD (A.W) (L-H)
Saturday, July 6

OFFICIAL GOING: Polytrack: standard
Wind: light, across Weather: overcast

4637 BET AT TOTESPORT.COM NURSERY H'CAP 6f (P)
1:40 (1:43) (Class 2) 2-Y-O **£12,938** (£3,850; £1,924; £962) **Stalls** Centre

Form RPR

2221 **1** **Bettys Hope**[44] [2996] 2-8-4 **75** .... HollieDoyle 1 76
(Rod Millman) *mde all: rdn over 1f out: drifted rt ins fnl f: hld on wl towards fin (jockey said filly hung right-handed)* **8/1[3]**

122 **2** *nk* **Oh Purple Reign (IRE)**[28] [3566] 2-9-10 **95** .... SeanLevey 2 95
(Richard Hannon) *trckd ldrs: swtchd lft and effrt over 1f out: sn drvn and clsd: ev ch ins fnl f: styd on* **8/15[1]**

124 **3** *1½* **Xcelente**[28] [3566] 2-9-0 **85** .... JackMitchell 3 81
(Mark Johnston) *t.k.h: hld up in tch: rdn and clsd to press ldrs ent fnl 2f: kpt on same pce ins fnl f* **6/1[2]**

010 **4** *¾* **Seraphinite (IRE)**[15] [4048] 2-8-5 **76** .... NicolaCurrie 6 69
(Jamie Osborne) *stdd and dropped in bhd after s: hld up in tch in last pair: swtchd rt and effrt over 1f out: kpt on same pce ins fnl f* **8/1[3]**

033 **5** *hd* **Ossco**[16] [4018] 2-8-0 **71** .... RaulDaSilva 5 64
(Mohamed Moubarak) *hld up in tch in last pair: nt clr run ent fnl 2f: effrt on inner and hdwy to chse ldrs 1f out: no ex and wknd wl ins fnl f* **33/1**

3114 **6** *1¾* **Zulu Zander (IRE)**[66] [2267] 2-8-12 **83** .... PJMcDonald 4 70
(David Evans) *t.k.h: pressed ldr: rdn over 1f out: struggling to qckn and squeezed for room 1f out: wknd ins fnl f* **14/1**

1m 12.82s (-0.88) **Going Correction** -0.225s/f (Stan) **6** Ran SP% **111.3**
Speed ratings (Par 100): **96,95,93,92,92 90**
CSF £12.67 TOTE £8.00: £2.50, £1.10; EX 13.00 Trifecta £44.80.
Owner Mrs Louise Millman **Bred** Llety Farms **Trained** Kentisbeare, Devon

FOCUS
A valuable nursery in which odds-on backers got their fingers burned. The second has been rated to form.

4638 TOTEPOOL CASHBACK CLUB AT TOTESPORT.COM H'CAP 6f (P)
2:15 (2:15) (Class 3) (0-95,88) 3-Y-O **£9,703** (£2,887; £1,443; £721) **Stalls** Centre

Form RPR

313 **1** **Alkaraama (USA)**[18] [3972] 3-9-4 **85** .... ColmO'Donoghue 6 92+
(Sir Michael Stoute) *travelled strly: chsd ldr: effrt over 1f out: rdn and sustained chal ins fnl f to ld towards fin* **7/2[2]**

1-01 **2** *nk* **Heath Charnock**[36] [3302] 3-9-2 **83** .... KieranO'Neill 7 89
(Michael Dods) *wnt rt leaving stalls: sn led: rdn wl over 1f out: kpt on wl u.p tl hdd and no ex towards fin* **8/1**

-163 **3** *hd* **Intuitive (IRE)**[40] [3151] 3-9-2 **83** .... PJMcDonald 3 88+
(James Tate) *in tch in last pair: effrt and wanting to hang lft over 1f out: hdwy ins fnl f: styd on strly fnl 100yd: nt quite rch ldrs* **9/4[1]**

1-13 **4** *1* **San Carlos**[30] [3493] 3-9-5 **86** .... ShaneKelly 2 88
(Shaun Keightley) *chsd ldrs: effrt wl over 1f out: drvn and unable qck 1f out: wknd wl ins fnl f* **5/1[3]**

2-11 **5** *1¾* **Celtic Manor (IRE)**[20] [3884] 3-8-12 **79** .... LiamJones 4 76
(William Haggas) *t.k.h: wl in tch in midfield: effrt u.p over 1f out: no imp and wknd ins fnl f* **6/1**

1-00 **6** *½* **Luxor**[21] [3865] 3-9-2 **88** .... CierenFallon(5) 5 83
(William Haggas) *stdd s: hld up in tch in rr: effrt on inner over 1f out: nvr threatened to get on terms and one pce ins fnl f* **6/1**

2-00 **7** *½* **Roxy Art (IRE)**[65] [2319] 3-9-4 **85** .... SeanLevey 1 78
(Ed Dunlop) *hld up in midfield: short of room over 4f out: effrt and drvn over 1f out: no imp and wknd ins fnl f* **33/1**

1m 11.74s (-1.96) **Going Correction** -0.225s/f (Stan) **7** Ran SP% **112.3**
Speed ratings (Par 104): **104,103,103,102,99 99,98**
CSF £29.66 TOTE £3.60: £1.90, £3.80; EX 27.20 Trifecta £324.10.
Owner Hamdan Al Maktoum **Bred** Frank Hutchinson **Trained** Newmarket, Suffolk

FOCUS
A warm 3yo sprint handicap and a tight finish between the first three. The second has been rated in line with the best view of his previous C&D win.

4639 EXTRA PLACES AT TOTESPORT.COM H'CAP 1m (P)
2:50 (2:53) (Class 3) (0-90,92) 3-Y-O+ **£9,703** (£2,887; £1,443; £721) **Stalls** Low

Form RPR

1-53 **1** **Dalaalaat (IRE)**[31] [3471] 3-8-9 **84** .... CierenFallon(5) 1 93
(William Haggas) *pressed ldr tl led on inner 4f out: rdn over 1f out: sustained duel w runner-up after: styd on and asserted towards fin* **5/2[1]**

1-45 **2** *¾* **Felix The Poet**[29] [3548] 3-9-1 **85** ....(b[1]) HollieDoyle 6 92
(Archie Watson) *sn led: hdd 4f out but styd pressing wnr: rdn and sustained duel w wnr after: no ex and jst outpcd towards fin* **10/1**

3151 **3** *1¼* **Solar Heights (IRE)**[28] [3580] 3-9-0 **84** ....(v) ShaneKelly 4 88
(James Tate) *short of room leaving stalls: in tch in midfield: effrt in 5th ent fnl 2f: drvn over 1f out: styd on ins fnl f to go 3rd towards fin* **6/1[3]**

2612 **4** *¾* **Fields Of Athenry (USA)**[30] [3493] 3-9-8 **92** .... PJMcDonald 2 94
(James Tate) *chsd ldrs: drvn and unable qck whn shifted lft over 1f out: kpt on same pce ins fnl f: lost 3rd towards fin* **7/2[2]**

1-10 **5** *1* **Noble Lineage (IRE)**[71] [2088] 3-9-1 **85** .... RobHornby 10 85+
(James Tate) *dropped in bhd after s: swtchd rt and effrt over 1f out: sn edging lft: kpt on ins fnl f: nvr trbld ldrs* **9/1**

1-02 **6** *hd* **Turn 'n Twirl (USA)**[33] [3431] 3-8-13 **88** .... SeamusCronin(5) 13 88
(Simon Crisford) *chsd ldrs: rdn ent fnl 2f: unable qck 1f out: wknd wl ins fnl f* **16/1**

1303 **7** *shd* **Merchant Of Venice**[45] [2966] 4-9-10 **85** .... GeorgeWood 8 86
(James Fanshawe) *hld up in tch in last quartet: hdwy over 3f out: effrt u.p and shifted lft over 1f out: kpt on ins fnl f: nvr threatened ldrs* **8/1**

0-42 **8** *2½* **Secret Return (IRE)**[23] [3763] 6-9-1 **79** .... MeganNicholls(3) 11 75
(Paul George) *in tch in midfield on outer: effrt 2f out: drvn and unable qck over 1f out: wl hld and plugged on same pce ins fnl f* **33/1**

40-0 **9** *1½* **Mushtaq (IRE)**[84] [1757] 4-9-9 **84** .... SeanLevey 9 76
(Richard Hannon) *hld up in last quartet: rdn 3f out: nvr trbld ldrs* **20/1**

006- **10** *nk* **Surrey Hope (USA)**[329] [6012] 5-10-0 **89** .... GeraldMosse 3 80
(Hughie Morrison) *midfield: no imp over 1f out: wl hld and eased ins fnl f* **8/1**

653- **11** *12* **Dyagilev**[282] [7692] 4-8-11 **72** .... JackMitchell 5 36
(Lydia Pearce) *a in rr: lost tch 2f out* **66/1**

31-0 **12** *1½* **Artois**[15] [4076] 3-9-1 **85** ....(b[1]) PatCosgrave 7 43
(Hugo Palmer) *rousted along leaving stalls: sn rcvrd and keen in midfield: rdn and losing pl over 2f out: bhd fnl f* **33/1**

1m 36.9s (-3.00) **Going Correction** -0.225s/f (Stan)
WFA 3 from 4yo+ 9lb **12** Ran SP% **124.4**
Speed ratings (Par 107): **106,105,104,103,102 102,101,99,97,97 85,84**
CSF £29.63 CT £146.20 TOTE £3.00: £1.10, £3.90, £2.50; EX 35.10 Trifecta £197.10.
Owner Hamdan Al Maktoum **Bred** Shadwell Estate Co Ltd **Trained** Newmarket, Suffolk

FOCUS
A warm handicap, but a race in which you had to be handy with the front pair dominating throughout. It's been rated slightly positively, with the fourth to his C&D latest.

4640 IRISH LOTTO AT TOTESPORT.COM BRITISH EBF FILLIES' H'CAP 1m 2f (P)
3:25 (3:29) (Class 3) (0-95,91) 3-Y-O+ **£9,703** (£2,887; £1,443; £721) **Stalls** Low

Form RPR

316- **1** **Naqaawa (IRE)**[273] [7986] 4-10-0 **89** .... PJMcDonald 2 98
(William Haggas) *hld up wl in tch in rr: swtchd rt and effrt over 1f out: rdn and clsd to chal ins fnl f: led wl ins fnl f: r.o wl* **6/1[3]**

6441 **2** *1* **Specialise**[14] [4110] 3-9-0 **85** .... JackMitchell 1 93+
(Roger Varian) *trckd ldrs: effrt 2f out: nt clr run and swtchd rt 1f out: rallied strly u.p fnl 100yds: wnt 2nd last strides* **7/4[2]**

11-0 **3** *nk* **Cantiniere (USA)**[182] [97] 4-9-6 **81** .... HectorCrouch 3 87
(Saeed bin Suroor) *sn pressing ldr: rdn over 2f out: sustained chal u.p tl nt match pce of wnr wl ins fnl f* **7/1**

-311 **4** *nk* **Vivion**[35] 3336 3-9-6 **91**.............................. ColmO'Donoghue 4 96
(Sir Michael Stoute) *led: rdn over 1f out: drvn 1f out: hdd and no ex wl ins fnl f* **6/5**[1]

2m 4.83s (-3.77) **Going Correction** -0.225s/f (Stan)
WFA 3 from 4yo 10lb 4 Ran SP% **108.6**
Speed ratings (Par 104): **106,105,104,104**
CSF £16.63 TOTE £5.90; EX 16.30 Trifecta £43.10.
Owner Miss Yvonne Jacques **Bred** Shadwell Estate Company Limited **Trained** Newmarket, Suffolk

FOCUS
A tight fillies' handicap despite the small field and a game of cat and mouse. Muddling form, and hard to rate too positively.

4641 BET IN PLAY AT TOTESPORT.COM FILLIES' NOVICE STKS 1m 2f (P)
4:00 (4:03) (Class 4) 3-Y-O+ **£5,822** (£1,732; £865; £432) **Stalls** Low

Form RPR

1 **Last Look (IRE)** 3-8-11 0.............................. GeorgeWood 8 91+
(Saeed bin Suroor) *dwlt: sn rcvrd and in tch in midfield: effrt and hdwy over 2f out: clsd u.p to ld 1f out: r.o v strly and drew wl clr ins fnl f* **5/1**[3]

2 **2** *5* **Jomrok**[20] 3889 3-8-11 0.............................. GeraldMosse 4 81
(Owen Burrows) *chsd ldrs: effrt in 3rd ent fnl 2f: unable qck over 1f out: no ch w wnr but kpt on same pce to go 2nd ins fnl f* **13/8**[1]

3 *1/2* **Fly The Flag** 3-8-11 0.............................. KieranO'Neill 2 80+
(John Gosden) *s.i.s: hld up in last trio: effrt over 2f out: swtchd rt over 1f out: no ch w wnr but kpt on wl ins fnl f* **12/1**

6 **4** *2 3/4* **Gallatin**[28] 3584 3-8-11 0.............................. RobHornby 9 75
(Andrew Balding) *chsd ldr over 8f out: rdn jst over 2f out: unable qck ent fnl f: wknd ins fnl f* **16/1**

242 **5** *hd* **Inference**[16] 4022 3-8-11 87.............................. NickyMackay 3 74
(John Gosden) *led over 8f out: rdn 2f out: hdd 1f out: sn outpcd and wknd ins fnl f* **15/8**[2]

0- **6** *1/2* **Honfleur (IRE)**[233] 9068 3-8-11 0.............................. ColmO'Donoghue 11 73
(Sir Michael Stoute) *dwlt: in tch in last quartet: rdn 3f out: sltly impeded and no imp over 1f out: wl hld but kpt on steadily ins fnl f* **14/1**

6 **7** *1* **Ela Katrina**[51] 2771 3-8-11 0.............................. JackMitchell 6 71
(Roger Varian) *t.k.h: hld up in last quartet: effrt 3f out: no imp over 1f out: wl hld and one pce fnl f* **25/1**

06 **8** *5* **Eagle Queen**[20] 3889 3-8-8 0.............................. WilliamCox(3) 7 61
(Andrew Balding) *wnt rt leaving stalls: stdd and hld up in last pair: rdn jst over 2f out: sn btn and bhd* **50/1**

9 *3 1/4* **Roving Mission (USA)** 3-8-11 0.............................. HectorCrouch 5 55
(Ralph Beckett) *t.k.h: midfield: rdn and losing pl over 2f out: bhd fnl f* **25/1**

0-0 **10** *38* **Galileo Jade (IRE)**[23] 3761 3-8-11 0.............................. SeanLevey 1
(Richard Hannon) *led tl over 8f out: prom tl lost pl rapidly 3f out: t.o* **66/1**

2m 4.04s (-4.56) **Going Correction** -0.225s/f (Stan)
WFA 3 from 4yo 10lb 10 Ran SP% **120.9**
Speed ratings (Par 102): **109,105,104,102,102 101,101,97,94,64**
CSF £13.74 TOTE £6.20: £2.00, £1.10, £3.00; EX 14.20 Trifecta £130.20.
Owner Godolphin **Bred** Godolphin **Trained** Newmarket, Suffolk

FOCUS
Several big stables were represented in this fillies' novice, but it was taken apart by one of the newcomers. It's been rated around the second to her debut form.

4642 DOUBLE DELIGHT HAT-TRICK HEAVEN AT TOTESPORT.COM H'CAP 1m (P)
4:35 (4:39) (Class 6) (0-60,67) 3-Y-O

£3,105 (£924; £461; £300; £300; £300) **Stalls** Low

Form RPR

0365 **1** **Lethal Laura**[19] 3938 3-8-7 **46** oh1..............................(p) PJMcDonald 12 55
(James Given) *sn prom: chsd ldr after 1f tl 4f out: styd chsng ldrs tl effrt to chse ldr again wl over 1f out: rdn to ld 1f out: r.o strly* **20/1**

4103 **2** *2 1/2* **Poetic Motion**[16] 4029 3-8-11 **50**.............................. PatCosgrave 6 54
(Jim Boyle) *led: rdn over 1f out: hdd 1f out and nt match pce of wnr fnl f* **4/1**[1]

-220 **3** *hd* **Lonicera**[26] 3651 3-9-7 **60**.............................. JackMitchell 10 63
(Henry Candy) *hld up in midfield: swtchd rt and hdwy 5f out: chsd ldr 4f out: rdn and outpcd in 3rd over 1f out: kpt on same pce ins fnl f* **8/1**

6434 **4** *1 3/4* **Reasoned (IRE)**[15] 4080 3-9-2 **62**.............................. LukeCatton(7) 4 61
(James Eustace) *chsd ldrs: 4th and rdn 2f out: no imp and kpt on same pce ins fnl f* **10/1**

6-04 **5** *3/4* **Classic Star**[26] 3651 3-9-3 **61**.............................. SophieRalston(5) 1 59+
(Dean Ivory) *hld up in midfield: short of room and hmpd on inner over 6f out: effrt on inner over 1f out: kpt on ins fnl f: nvr trbld ldrs* **9/2**[2]

1241 **6** *1/2* **Comeonfeeltheforce (IRE)**[10] 4244 3-9-7 **67**.......(t) GeorgiaDobie(7) 14 63
(Lee Carter) *t.k.h: chsd ldrs: unable qck u.p over 1f out: wl hld and kpt on same pce ins fnl f* **6/1**

000 **7** *nk* **Break Of Day**[28] 3603 3-9-0 **53**..............................(b[1]) LiamJones 5 49
(William Haggas) *s.i.s and sn rdn: in rr: kpt on to pass btn horses ins fnl f: nvr trbld ldrs* **14/1**

6000 **8** *1/2* **The Meter**[14] 4110 3-9-2 **60**..............................(t) SeamusCronin(5) 11 55
(Mohamed Moubarak) *chsd ldr for 1f: wl in tch after: unable qck u.p over 1f out: kpt on same pce and hung lft ins fnl f* **33/1**

-040 **9** *1/2* **City Master**[9] 4284 3-9-4 **57**.............................. RobHornby 3 51
(Ralph Beckett) *t.k.h: hld up in tch in midfield: u.p and no imp over 1f out: kpt on same pce ins fnl f* **5/1**[3]

0000 **10** *1 1/4* **Piccolita**[37] 3271 3-8-7 **46** oh1..............................(b[1]) GeorgeWood 13 37
(Hughie Morrison) *in rr: rdn over 3f out: no imp and wl hld whn hung lft 1f out* **50/1**

3460 **11** *2 3/4* **Kadiz (IRE)**[26] 3665 3-9-0 **56**..............................(p) MeganNicholls(3) 2 41
(Paul George) *midfield: rdn and no hdwy over 1f out: wknd ins fnl f* **25/1**

1625 **12** *1 1/2* **Orliko (IRE)**[5] 4453 3-9-10 **63**..............................(bt) SeanLevey 8 45
(Richard Hannon) *wnt rt leaving stalls: t.k.h: hld up in tch in midfield: hrd drvn and btn over 1f out: wknd fnl f* **8/1**

00-0 **13** *19* **Duke Of Yorkie (IRE)**[11] 4217 3-8-6 **50**.............................. CierenFallon(5) 9
(Adam West) *s.i.s and short of room leaving stalls: racd on outer and nvr bttr than midfield: lost pl and bhd over 1f out* **25/1**

620- **P** **Roca Magica**[292] 7365 3-9-2 **55**.............................. ColmO'Donoghue 7
(Ed Dunlop) *t.k.h: hld up in rr: eased 3f out: p.u over 1f out (jockey said he pulled up the filly as he felt the filly go amiss)* **50/1**

1m 38.54s (-1.36) **Going Correction** -0.225s/f (Stan) 14 Ran SP% **126.4**
Speed ratings (Par 98): **97,94,94,92,91 91,91,90,90,88 86,84,65,**
CSF £98.08 CT £743.56 TOTE £25.40: £7.70, £1.50, £3.10; EX 189.30 Trifecta £1035.30.
Owner C G Rowles Nicholson **Bred** Limestone And Tara Studs **Trained** Willoughton, Lincs

FOCUS
A modest handicap and another race where it was an advantage to be handy. The winner has been rated back to her best.

4643 RACING WELFARE H'CAP 7f (P)
5:10 (5:10) (Class 4) (0-80,82) 3-Y-O+

£5,692 (£1,694; £846; £423; £300; £300) **Stalls** Low

Form RPR

3040 **1** **Astonished (IRE)**[20] 3880 4-10-0 **80**.............................. PJMcDonald 4 89
(James Tate) *chsd ldrs: wnt 2nd and effrt over 2f out: drvn to press ldr 1f out: led 100yds out: hld on towards fin* **9/2**[1]

5140 **2** *nk* **Buckingham (IRE)**[31] 3465 3-9-1 **82**.............................. GeorgiaDobie(7) 8 87
(Eve Johnson Houghton) *racd in last quartet: clsd and swtchd rt wl over 1f out: drvn and clsd to press ldrs ins fnl f: str chal wl ins fnl f: hld towards fin* **9/2**[1]

21-5 **3** *2* **Water Diviner (IRE)**[15] 4065 3-9-0 **79**.............................. SeamusCronin(5) 12 79
(Richard Hannon) *chsd ldrs early: sn settled bk into midfield: clsd again and rdn to chse ldrs 2f out: drvn over 1f out: no ex ins fnl f: wknd towards fin* **10/1**

3-10 **4** *1 1/4* **Scat King (IRE)**[31] 3465 3-9-8 **82**.............................. ShaneKelly 1 79
(Richard Hughes) *chsd ldrs: effrt wl over 1f out: drvn 1f out: no imp ins fnl f* **5/1**[2]

6306 **5** *nse* **Philamundo (IRE)**[44] 3004 4-9-7 **78**..................(b) ScottMcCullagh(5) 2 77
(Richard Spencer) *stdd after s and off the pce in last pair: swtchd rt and hdwy on wd outside over 2f out: kpt on ins fnl f: nvr trbld ldrs* **8/1**[3]

1050 **6** *nse* **Full Intention**[16] 4028 5-9-3 **69**..............................(p) PatCosgrave 9 68
(Lydia Pearce) *broke wl: sn stdd bk and hld up in midfield: nt clrest of runs 2f out: effrt over 1f out: kpt on same pce ins fnl f* **14/1**

0510 **7** *1/2* **Sword Exceed (GER)**[17] 3991 5-9-13 **79**.............................. LiamJones 10 77
(Ivan Furtado) *sn led: hdd over 5f out but styd w ldr tl led again over 2f out: drvn over 1f out: hdd 100yds out: wknd towards fin* **12/1**

3542 **8** *1/2* **Outside Inside (IRE)**[9] 4278 4-9-4 **75**.............................. CierenFallon(5) 3 72
(Mark Johnston) *racd in last trio: rdn 3f out: kpt on u.p ins fnl f: nvr trbld ldrs* **5/1**[2]

0-06 **9** *2 3/4* **Marilyn**[7] 4393 5-9-1 **72**..............................(v[1]) SebastianWoods(5) 6 61
(Shaun Keightley) *wnt lft: awkward leaving stalls and rdr briefly lost an iron: in rr: swtchd rt and effrt over 2f out: no prog over 1f out: wknd ins fnl f* **25/1**

1104 **P** **Nahham (IRE)**[29] 3529 4-9-11 **77**.............................. SeanLevey 5
(Richard Hannon) *welt lft leaving stalls: sn rcvrd and w ldr: led over 5f out: hdd over 2f out: sn dropped out: eased and p.u ins fnl f: burst blood vessel (vet said gelding had bled from the nose)* **5/1**[2]

1m 24.44s (-2.76) **Going Correction** -0.225s/f (Stan)
WFA 3 from 4yo+ 8lb 10 Ran SP% **124.8**
Speed ratings (Par 105): **106,105,103,101,101 101,100,100,97,**
CSF £26.60 CT £205.04 TOTE £5.70: £1.90, £2.20, £3.00; EX 30.80 Trifecta £541.60.
Owner Saeed Manana **Bred** Michael Ryan **Trained** Newmarket, Suffolk

FOCUS
A fair handicap to end and there was no hanging about. The third has been rated close to form.
T/Plt: £555.50 to a £1 stake. Pool: £42,316.32 - 55.60 winning units T/Qpdt: £127.60 to a £1 stake. Pool: £3,326.61 - 19.28 winning units **Steve Payne**

4602 HAYDOCK (L-H)
Saturday, July 6

OFFICIAL GOING: Good to firm (watered; 7.3)
Wind: light breeze Weather: overcast, sunny intervals, warm

4644 BET365 H'CAP 1m 6f
2:05 (2:05) (Class 2) 3-Y-O

£62,250 (£18,640; £9,320; £4,660; £2,330; £1,170) **Stalls** Low

Form RPR

-110 **1** **Sir Ron Priestley**[16] 4017 3-9-6 **94**.............................. FrannyNorton 5 103
(Mark Johnston) *prom: sn trcking ldrs: pushed along and cl up 3f out: drvn over 2f out: 1 l 2nd 1f out: rdn fnl f: r.o wl: led last 25yds* **15/8**[1]

3-11 **2** *1/2* **Mind The Crack (IRE)**[28] 3585 3-9-1 **89**.............................. RichardKingscote 2 97
(Mark Johnston) *trckd ldrs: lost pl 1/2-way: hdwy on inner 3f out: led 2 1/2f out: 1 l ld 1f out: r.o fnl f: hdd last 25yds* **7/2**[2]

6-23 **3** *2* **Prefontaine (IRE)**[21] 3842 3-8-13 **87**..............................(b[1]) DavidEgan 6 92
(Roger Varian) *hld up: pushed along 3f out: drvn and hdwy 2f out: tried to chal between horses over 1f out: swtchd to outer and rdn fnl f: one pce* **10/1**

1130 **4** *4 1/2* **Summer Moon**[16] 4017 3-9-7 **95**.............................. BenCurtis 1 94
(Mark Johnston) *led: drvn 3f out: hdd 2 1/2f out: rdn and no ex* **6/1**

2020 **5** *1 3/4* **Themaxwecan (IRE)**[17] 3984 3-9-6 **94**.............................. DanielTudhope 3 90
(Mark Johnston) *hld up: pushed along 3f out: drvn over 2f out: rdn 1 1/2f out: no imp: lost shoe (vet said colt lost its left fore shoe)* **4/1**[3]

6111 **6** *5* **Arctic Fox**[21] 3862 3-9-0 **88**.............................. PaddyMathers 4 77
(Richard Fahey) *hld up: pushed along on outer 3f out: hdwy 2f out: rdn and wknd over 1f out* **10/1**

5332 **7** *nk* **Tidal Point (IRE)**[24] 3729 3-8-0 **74**..............................(p[1]) RoystonFfrench 7 63
(Steph Hollinshead) *prom: cl up and rdn 3f out: wknd over 2f out* **25/1**

3m 5.77s (1.17) **Going Correction** +0.05s/f (Good) 7 Ran SP% **113.3**
Speed ratings (Par 106): **98,97,96,94,93 90,89**
CSF £8.40 TOTE £2.70: £1.60, £2.20; EX 9.50 Trifecta £55.00.
Owner Paul Dean **Bred** Mascalls Stud **Trained** Middleham Moor, N Yorks

FOCUS
All races on stands' side home straight. Add 48yds. With four of the seven runners in this £100,000 handicap trained by Mark Johnston, it was difficult beforehand to know how this might work out from a tactical perspective, and they looked to go pretty steady on the front end, which probably explains the slow time. The third has been rated to his best.

4645 BET365 LANCASHIRE OAKS (GROUP 2) (F&M) 1m 3f 175y
2:40 (2:41) (Class 1) 3-Y-O+

£52,740 (£19,995; £10,006; £4,984; £2,501; £1,255) **Stalls** High

Form RPR

4-12 **1** **Enbihaar (IRE)**[42] 3096 4-9-5 **105**.............................. DaneO'Neill 1 112
(John Gosden) *chsd ldr: pushed along 3f out: rdn in cl 2nd 2f out: led ent fnl f: r.o wl: a holding runner-up* **5/2**[2]

1-01 **2** *nk* **Dramatic Queen (USA)**[42] 3096 4-9-5 **106**.............. RichardKingscote 3 111
(William Haggas) *led: pushed along in 1 l ld 3f out: drvn 2f out: rdn in narrow ld 1 1/2f out: hdd ent fnl f: kpt on wl: a jst hld* **4/1**[3]

2-21 **3** *4* **Klassique**28 3586 4-9-5 107 DanielTudhope 2 104
(William Haggas) *hld up: pushed along and hdwy 3f out: drvn 2f out: rdn over 1f out: one pce fnl f* **13/8**1

4002 **4** *3* **Nyaleti (IRE)**8 4332 4-9-5 105 FrannyNorton 6 99
(Mark Johnston) *chsd ldr: cl up 3f out: drvn and lost pl 2f out: rdn over 1f out: no ex* **9/1**

6621 **5** *1 1/4* **Shailene (IRE)**13 4170 4-9-5 98 DavidProbert 4 97
(Andrew Balding) *t.k.h: hld up: gng wl on outer 3f out: pushed along: reminder and lost grnd over 2f out: sn rdn and drifted lft: no ex* **28/1**

51-3 **6** *3/4* **Highgarden**17 3995 4-9-5 104 (p1) RobertHavlin 5 96
(John Gosden) *hld up in rr: drvn 3f out: rdn and no ch fr 2f out* **9/1**

2m 30.63s (-2.67) **Going Correction** +0.05s/f (Good) **6** Ran SP% **110.1**
Speed ratings (Par 115): **110,109,107,105,104 103**
CSF £12.30 TOTE £3.00: £1.40, £2.20; EX 10.30 Trifecta £15.50.
Owner Hamdan Al Maktoum **Bred** Haras Du Mezeray **Trained** Newmarket, Suffolk

FOCUS
Add 29yds. Very little between all bar Shailene on official ratings and this this didn't look the strongest of renewals. The gallop looked fairly steady and it was all to play for entering the home straight, but the front two came away in the closing stages, just as they did at York.

4646 BET365 OLD NEWTON CUP H'CAP 1m 3f 175y
3:15 (3:17) (Class 2) 4-Y-0+
£62,250 (£18,640; £9,320; £4,660; £2,330; £1,170) **Stalls** High

Form RPR

2062 **1** **Kelly's Dino (FR)**14 4102 6-8-12 97 (p) BenCurtis 18 108
(K R Burke) *prom: drvn to ld 2f out: sn rdn: 1/2 l ld ent fnl f: r.o wl: on top nr fin* **14/1**3

4520 **2** *1* **Lucius Tiberius (IRE)**15 4053 4-9-2 101 BrettDoyle 1 110
(Charlie Appleby) *led: pushed along 3f out: drvn and hdd 2f out: sn rdn: 1/2 l 2nd ent fnl f: kpt on wl and ev ch ins fnl f: hld nr fin* **14/1**3

-120 **3** *1/2* **Epaulement (IRE)**40 3160 4-8-13 98 RichardKingscote 4 106
(Tom Dascombe) *mid-div on inner: pushed along and hdwy 3f out: rdn over 2f out: kpt on fnl f: gng on at fin* **10/1**2

-260 **4** *2 1/4* **Indianapolis (IRE)**14 4102 4-8-10 95 BarryMcHugh 2 100
(James Given) *hld up: pushed along and hdwy on inner over 2f out: sn drvn: rdn over 1f out: kpt on wl to take 4th ins fnl f* **14/1**3

2313 **5** *nse* **Eddystone Rock (IRE)**35 3346 7-8-7 92 KierenFox 13 97
(John Best) *slowly away: bhd: pushed along and hdwy 3f out: rdn 2f out: weaved way into 5th on to inner ins fnl f: kpt on (jockey said gelding was slowly away)* **33/1**

401 **6** *1/2* **Island Brave (IRE)**14 4102 5-9-0 99 AlistairRawlinson 12 103
(Heather Main) *hld up: drvn and hdwy on outer over 2f out: sn rdn: r.o fnl f* **18/1**

4-32 **7** *1* **Koeman**45 2969 5-8-11 96 JFEgan 10 98
(Mick Channon) *hld up: sweeping move on outer over 4f out: pushed into 5th 3f out: sn rdn: no ex fnl f* **16/1**

3205 **8** *1 1/4* **Everything For You (IRE)**26 3655 5-8-6 91 (p) ShaneGray 11 91
(Kevin Ryan) *trckd ldrs: drvn 3f out: sn rdn: wknd fnl f* **33/1**

0-00 **9** *1 1/4* **Melting Dew**28 3600 5-8-12 97 PatDobbs 3 97+
(Sir Michael Stoute) *hld up: drvn over 2f out: rdn 2f out: btn whn nt clr run ins fnl f* **20/1**

2520 **10** *1* **Society Red**40 3160 5-8-6 91 PaddyMathers 7 88
(Richard Fahey) *hld up: drvn 2f out: sn rdn: no imp: lost shoe (vet said gelding lost its left fore shoe)* **50/1**

13-1 **11** *2 3/4* **First Eleven**52 2742 4-9-10 109 (t) RobertHavlin 17 101
(John Gosden) *hld up: slipped on home bnd over 4f out: drvn and hdwy on outer over 3f out: rdn 2f out: wknd fnl f (jockey said colt slipped on the bend)* **7/2**1

4115 **12** *shd* **Charles Kingsley**14 4102 4-8-13 98 DavidEgan 14 90
(Mark Johnston) *trckd ldrs: drvn and lost pl 3f out: sn rdn: no ex* **14/1**3

3-53 **13** *1 1/4* **Bombyx**26 3646 4-8-13 98 (v1) DanielMuscutt 5 88
(James Fanshawe) *broke wl and prom: sn trcking ldrs: drvn over 2f out: sn rdn and wknd* **14/1**3

2-40 **14** *1* **Restorer**28 3600 7-8-13 98 PaulHanagan 6 89+
(Ian Williams) *mid-div: pushed along 3f out: drvn 2f out: wknd fnl f* **20/1**

0100 **15** *4* **Aquarium**15 4053 4-9-4 103 FrannyNorton 9 85
(Mark Johnston) *slowly away: bhd: slipped on home bnd over 4f out: pushed along 3f out: drvn 2f out: no imp (jockey said colt slipped on the bend)* **10/1**2

-020 **16** *3 3/4* **Byron Flyer**15 4053 8-9-5 104 (v) DavidProbert 15 80
(Ian Williams) *slowly away: sn prom on outer: drvn and lost pl over 3f out* **25/1**

4-51 **17** *6* **Al Muffrih (IRE)**40 3160 4-8-12 97 (h) DanielTudhope 19 63
(William Haggas) *mid-div on outer: slipped on home bnd and lost pl over 4 out: sn dropped to rr: eased 3f out (jockey said gelding slipped on the bend causing the gelding to reach and his surcingle to snap)* **7/2**1

2m 30.2s (-3.10) **Going Correction** +0.05s/f (Good) **17** Ran SP% **128.3**
Speed ratings (Par 109): **112,111,111,109,109 109,108,107,106,106 104,104,103,102,100 97,93**
CSF £189.97 CT £2079.45 TOTE £25.30: £3.80, £3.50, £2.90, £3.50; EX 445.20 Trifecta £5362.00.
Owner Liam Kelly & Mrs E Burke **Bred** S C E A De Maulepaire **Trained** Middleham Moor, N Yorks

FOCUS
Add 29yds. As competitive a handicap as you could wish to see. Four-year-olds have a really good recent record in the race, winning over 50% of renewals in the last 40 years. Horses of that age dominated the top of the market, but things didn't work out at all for both in what turned into quite a messy race. The gallop looked no more than steady and the first two home both raced prominently. The second has been rated in line with his better form.

4647 BET365 NURSERY H'CAP 6f
3:50 (3:53) (Class 4) (0-80,82) 2-Y-0
£12,161 (£3,619; £1,808; £904; £300; £300) **Stalls** High

Form RPR

321 **1** **Keep Busy (IRE)**10 4238 2-9-2 73 DanielTudhope 7 77
(John Quinn) *hld up: trckd ldrs 2f out: pushed into ld on stands' rail 1 1/2f out: sn drvn: rdn out fnl f* **7/4**1

6034 **2** *3/4* **Lexi The One (IRE)**21 3841 2-8-6 63 PaddyMathers 5 65
(Richard Fahey) *hld up: drvn and hdwy in centre 1 1/2f out: rdn in 2nd fnl f: kpt on wl* **20/1**

5024 **3** *3/4* **Corndavon Lad (IRE)**17 3998 2-9-2 73 PaulHanagan 1 73
(Richard Fahey) *chsd ldrs in centre: drvn and hdwy 2f out: sn rdn: 3rd ent fnl f: kpt on* **22/1**

541 **4** *5* **Havana Dawn**18 3968 2-8-13 70 SamJames 6 55
(Phillip Makin) *nodded leaving stalls: prom: cl up and drvn 1 1/2f out: sn rdn: one pce fnl f* **5/1**3

4212 **5** *3/4* **Lili Wen Fach (IRE)**22 3812 2-9-0 71 DavidEgan 3 54
(David Evans) *prom in centre: rdn over 2f out: wknd 1f out* **7/1**

2211 **6** *4* **Go Well Spicy (IRE)**8 4323 2-9-7 78 FrannyNorton 8 49
(Mick Channon) *prom: pushed along 2f out: sn lost pl and wknd* **7/2**2

4301 **7** *nk* **Dark Optimist (IRE)**42 3088 2-9-10 81 (t) JFEgan 4 51
(David Evans) *mid-div in centre: drvn 1/2-way: rdn and wknd 2f out* **14/1**

120 **8** *2 1/4* **Iva Reflection (IRE)**17 3988 2-9-4 82 PoppyFielding(7) 2 45
(Tom Dascombe) *slowly away: bhd on far side: reminder over 1f out: no imp* **12/1**

064 **9** *1/2* **Craigburn**14 4114 2-8-12 69 DavidProbert 10 30
(Tom Clover) *led on stands' side: pushed along in narrow ld 2f out: hdd 1 1/2f out: sn rdn and wknd: lost shoe (vet said lost its right fore shoe)* **28/1**

425 **10** *4 1/2* **Gin Gembre (FR)**57 2586 2-9-1 72 BenCurtis 9 20
(K R Burke) *prom on stands' side: rdn and lost pl over 2f out: wknd* **12/1**

1m 14.93s (1.03) **Going Correction** +0.05s/f (Good) **10** Ran SP% **122.4**
Speed ratings (Par 96): **95,94,93,86,85 80,79,76,75,69**
CSF £46.72 CT £631.20 TOTE £2.50: £1.10, £5.00, £7.40; EX 42.10 Trifecta £597.90.
Owner Altitude Racing **Bred** Hackcanter Ltd & Mr P Gleeson **Trained** Settrington, N Yorks

FOCUS
A wide open nursery featuring six previous winners but contenders thinned out at the business end and the front three came well clear. The third has been rated as repeating his Nottingham form.

4648 BET365 CONDITIONS STKS 6f
4:25 (4:25) (Class 2) 3-Y-0+ **£14,006** (£4,194; £2,097; £1,048; £524) **Stalls** High

Form RPR

5-13 **1** **Danzeno**14 4095 8-9-5 105 AlistairRawlinson 4 108
(Michael Appleby) *prom: pushed into ld 1 1/2f out: rdn in narrow ld 1f out: hld on wl fnl f* **6/5**1

50-5 **2** *1/2* **Enjazaat**43 3043 4-9-5 100 DaneO'Neill 3 106
(Owen Burrows) *slowly away: racd in rr: swtchd to outer and hdwy 2f out: cl 2nd and rdn 1f out: r.o wl fnl f but a hld* **9/2**3

-225 **3** *3/4* **Summerghand (IRE)**14 4095 5-9-5 100 DanielTudhope 1 104
(David O'Meara) *hld up: pushed along 2f out: rdn in 3rd 1f out: kpt on fnl f* **15/8**2

-000 **4** *4 1/2* **Dunkerron**16 4016 3-8-13 95 (v1) TomQueally 2 88
(Alan King) *trckd ldrs: pushed along 2f out: sn drvn and dropped to last: rdn into 4th 1f out: no ex fnl f* **20/1**

0000 **5** *6* **Never Back Down (IRE)**17 3991 4-9-9 93 (b) RobertHavlin 5 74
(Hugo Palmer) *led: pushed along 2f out: drvn and hdd 1 1/2f out: sn wknd: dropped to last 1f out* **14/1**

1m 12.89s (-1.01) **Going Correction** +0.05s/f (Good)
WFA 3 from 4yo+ 6lb **5** Ran SP% **109.8**
Speed ratings (Par 109): **108,107,106,100,92**
CSF £7.01 TOTE £2.00: £1.10, £2.20; EX 5.90 Trifecta £9.40.
Owner A M Wragg **Bred** A M Wragg **Trained** Oakham, Rutland

FOCUS
A decent enough sprint but the winner had stand-out credentials on these terms and he duly obliged without needing to be at his best. It's been rated around the third to his recent solid handicap form.

4649 CASH OUT AT BET365 H'CAP 6f
5:00 (5:02) (Class 4) (0-85,87) 3-Y-0+
£12,161 (£3,619; £1,808; £904; £300; £300) **Stalls** High

Form RPR

0062 **1** **Gabrial The Devil (IRE)**7 4369 4-9-12 82 PaulHanagan 6 90
(Richard Fahey) *trckd ldrs: hdwy to ld over 1f out: pushed into 1/2 l ld 1f out: rdn and strly pressed fnl f: hld on wl* **11/4**1

0603 **2** *hd* **Roundhay Park**7 4369 4-9-10 83 RowanScott(3) 9 90
(Nigel Tinkler) *mid-div: weaved way through to cl on ldrs over 1f out: rdn to chal fnl f: r.o wl: jst denied* **4/1**2

0550 **3** *1 1/2* **Normandy Barriere (IRE)**19 3945 7-9-10 87 (p) IzzyClifton(7) 3 90
(Nigel Tinkler) *hld up: pushed along and hdwy on outer over 2f out: sn rdn and cl up: 2nd ent fnl f: no ex last 100yds* **14/1**

2121 **4** *2* **Equiano Springs**49 2824 5-9-11 81 DanielTudhope 11 79+
(Tom Tate) *mid-div on rails: looking for room 2f out: in clr and hdwy 1f out: tk 4th fnl f: nvr nr ldrs* **11/4**1

2006 **5** *1 1/4* **Saluti (IRE)**9 4303 5-9-8 78 PatDobbs 12 70
(Paul Midgley) *prom: drvn 1 1/2f out: wknd fnl f* **10/1**3

3063 **6** *3/4* **Madrinho (IRE)**29 3549 6-9-4 74 FrannyNorton 1 64
(Tony Carroll) *chsd ldrs: pushed along 2f out: sn drvn: no ex fnl f* **18/1**

000 **7** *1/2* **Double Up**27 3636 8-9-12 82 (v) RobertHavlin 7 70
(Ian Williams) *mid-div: drvn and hmpd 1f out: rdn and no ex fnl f* **25/1**

5206 **8** *nse* **Buccaneers Vault (IRE)**7 4369 7-9-7 77 KevinStott 8 65
(Paul Midgley) *hld up: pushed along 2f out: sn drvn: no imp* **18/1**

351 **9** *hd* **Last Page**70 2107 4-9-7 84 LauraCoughlan(7) 10 71
(David Loughnane) *slowly away: bhd drvn over 1f out: nvr a threat* **12/1**

-164 **10** *3/4* **Nick Vedder**127 964 5-9-13 83 (b) DavidEgan 5 68
(Michael Wigham) *hld up: drvn and effrt over 1f out: wknd fnl f* **12/1**

42-5 **11** *2* **Almurr (IRE)**9 4294 3-9-5 81 SamJames 4 59
(Phillip Makin) *c across fr wd draw to ld on stands' side: pushed along 2f out: hdd over 1f out: sn rdn and wknd* **28/1**

0055 **12** *6* **Englishman**29 3543 9-8-10 66 JFEgan 2 25
(Milton Bradley) *prom: drvn and reminder 2f out: sn wknd and eased* **33/1**

1m 13.14s (-0.76) **Going Correction** +0.05s/f (Good)
WFA 3 from 4yo+ 6lb **12** Ran SP% **125.2**
Speed ratings (Par 105): **107,106,104,102,100 99,98,98,98,97 94,86**
CSF £14.05 CT £140.63 TOTE £3.40: £1.40, £1.90, £3.70; EX 14.70 Trifecta £119.60.
Owner Dr Marwan Koukash **Bred** Austin Curran **Trained** Musley Bank, N Yorks
■ Stewards' Enquiry : Sam James two-day ban: interference & careless riding (Jul 23-24); one-day ban: failure to ride to their draw (Jul 25)

FOCUS
A wide-open sprint handicap but the market seemed to know a big run was coming from Gabriel The Devil (6-1 into 11-4) and he didn't disappoint. The winner has been rated close to his 6f best.

4650 BET365.COM H'CAP 7f 37y
5:35 (5:35) (Class 2) (0-105,101) 3-Y-0+ **£16,172** (£4,812; £2,405; £1,202) **Stalls** Low

Form RPR

1041 **1** **Beat Le Bon (FR)**42 3075 3-9-7 101 PatDobbs 7 108+
(Richard Hannon) *hld up: hdwy on outer 2f out: drvn into 3rd over 1f out: rdn fnl f: chal last 50yds: led last stride* **6/4**1

1006 **2** *nse* **Kimifive (IRE)**9 4299 4-9-6 92 DavidEgan 4 101
(Joseph Tuite) *hld up: hdwy on inner over 3f out: wnt 2nd 2f out: rdn in 1 1/2 l 2nd 1f out: led 1/2f out: chal last 50yds: hdd last stride* **11/2**3

416 **3** *1/2* **Lincoln Park**27 3632 3-8-9 89 JFEgan 3 94+
(Michael Appleby) *involved in early scrimagging in bid to ld: drvn in 3 l ld 2f out: rdn over 1f out: 1 1/2 l ld 1f out: hdd 1/2f out: no ex* **16/1**

00/4 **4** 1 ¾ **Mustarrid (IRE)**[17] 3991 5-8-12 **84**........................ PaulHanagan 6 87
(Ian Williams) *hld up: drvn over 2f out: rdn over 1f out: one pce fnl f* **10/1**

3100 **5** 2 ½ **Love Dreams (IRE)**[9] 4299 5-9-12 **98**........................(v) FrannyNorton 5 94
(Mark Johnston) *chsd ldrs: drvn and lost pl 2f out: hmpd 1 1/2f out: no ex* **7/1**

1040 **6** 1 ¾ **Three Saints Bay (IRE)**[21] 3863 4-10-0 **100**.................. DanielTudhope 2 91
(David O'Meara) *hld up: pushed along 2f out: rdn 1f out: no imp* **8/1**

311 **7** nk **Mutaraffa (IRE)**[44] 3019 3-8-13 **93**........................(h) DaneO'Neill 1 81
(Charles Hills) *t.k.h: involved in early scrimmaging for ld: chsd ldr: 2 l 2nd 3f out: sn drvn and wknd* **7/2**[2]

1m 30.12s (-1.28) **Going Correction** +0.05s/f (Good) **7 Ran SP% 116.2**
WFA 3 from 4yo+ 8lb
Speed ratings (Par 109): **109,108,108,106,103 101,101**
CSF £10.62 TOTE £2.30: £1.40, £2.90; EX 10.10 Trifecta £83.00.
Owner Sullivan B'Stock/ Merriebelle Irish Farm **Bred** Gestut Zur Kuste Ag **Trained** East Everleigh, Wilts

FOCUS
Add 14yds. They went hard here so no surprise to see the finish was dominated by horses who came from off the pace. The second has been rated in line with his Goodwood form, and the third to his best.
T/Plt: £353.50 to a £1 stake. Pool: £125,486.13 - 259.09 winning units T/Qpdt: £87.10 to a £1 stake. Pool: £10,923.99 - 92.80 winning units **Keith McHugh**

4281 LEICESTER (R-H)
Saturday, July 6

OFFICIAL GOING: Good to firm (good in places; watered; 9.0)
Wind: Light across Weather: Light rain clearing

4651 TAP'NSHOWER.COM FILLIES' H'CAP — 6f
1:55 (1:56) (Class 5) (0-70,72) 3-Y-O+
£4,075 (£1,212; £606; £303; £300; £300) **Stalls High**

Form / RPR

3-02 **1** **Foxy Femme**[21] 3839 3-8-11 **61**........................(h) JoeyHaynes 4 69
(John Gallagher) *hld up: pushed along 1/2-way: swtchd rt and hdwy 2f out: rdn and hung lft fr over 1f out: led ins fnl f: r.o wl (jockey said filly hung left-handed)* **8/1**

6001 **2** 2 ½ **Gold At Midnight**[9] 4286 3-9-8 **72**........................ TomMarquand 9 73
(William Stone) *stmbld s: sn rcvrd to ld rdn over 1f out: hdd ins fnl f: hmpd sn after: styd on same pce* **4/1**[2]

0011 **3** 1 ¼ **Ever Rock (IRE)**[12] 4183 3-8-5 **62**........................ LauraCoughlan(7) 8 58
(J S Moore) *chsd ldrs: rdn over 2f out: styd on* **12/1**

353- **4** nse **Backstreet Girl (IRE)**[191] 9727 3-9-2 **66**........................ CharlieBennett 7 62
(Roger Varian) *hld up: hdwy u.p over 1f out: nt rch ldrs* **9/4**[1]

0435 **5** 2 **Miss Elsa**[11] 4218 3-9-3 **67**........................ CharlesBishop 3 58
(Eve Johnson Houghton) *prom: nt clr run and lost pl over 5f out: hld up: hdwy over 2f out: rdn and ev ch over 1f out: nt clr run sn after: no ex ins fnl f (jockey said filly was slightly hampered just after the 5f marker)* **5/1**[3]

0-04 **6** 2 ¼ **Nostrovia (IRE)**[28] 3598 3-8-13 **70**........................(v[1]) SeanKirrane(7) 1 52
(Richard Spencer) *wnt lft s: sn chsng ldrs: rdn over 1f out: wknd ins fnl f (jockey said filly jumped left from the stalls)* **10/1**

-063 **7** 1 ½ **Cardaw Lily (IRE)**[23] 3771 4-8-7 **51** oh6........................ JosephineGordon 10 29
(Ruth Carr) *chsd ldr: rdn over 2f out: lost 2nd over 1f out: nt clr run and wknd ins fnl f* **22/1**

-424 **8** 2 **Sarasota Bay**[22] 3801 3-9-3 **67**........................ DougieCostello 5 38
(John Quinn) *hld up: hdwy over 2f out: sn rdn: nt clr run over 1f out: wknd fnl f (jockey said filly was slightly hampered one furlong out)* **8/1**

0060 **9** ¾ **Knockabout Queen**[21] 3839 3-8-9 **59**........................ EoinWalsh 2 28
(Tony Carroll) *s.i.s and hmpd s: hld up: rdn over 2f out: sme hdwy over 1f out: wknd fnl f (jockey said filly was slowly away)* **20/1**

00-0 **10** 8 **The Last Party**[56] 2635 3-9-6 **70**........................ LewisEdmunds 6 13
(James Given) *hld up: rdn over 2f out: wknd over 1f out* **33/1**

1m 12.03s (-0.07) **Going Correction** -0.025s/f (Good) **10 Ran SP% 118.5**
WFA 3 from 4yo 6lb
Speed ratings (Par 100): **99,95,94,93,91 88,86,83,82,71**
CSF £39.74 CT £397.66 TOTE £8.10: £1.90, £2.30, £3.40; EX 33.40 Trifecta £345.10.
Owner Mrs C Clifford **Bred** Mrs Caryl Clifford **Trained** Chastleton, Oxon

FOCUS
A modest but quite competitive fillies' handicap that got a bit rough in the closing stages. The second has been rated close to her C&D latest.

4652 H.A.C. GROUP MEDICAL GAS DIVISION (S) STKS — 6f
2:30 (2:32) (Class 5) 2-Y-O
£4,075 (£1,212; £606; £303; £300; £300) **Stalls High**

Form / RPR

3136 **1** **Calippo (IRE)**[22] 3812 2-8-5 76........................(p) Pierre-LouisJamin(7) 5 68
(Archie Watson) *sn prom: rdn to ld and hung rt fr over 1f out: styd on wl* **7/4**[1]

2450 **2** 3 ½ **Out Of Breath**[22] 3812 2-9-0 67........................(b) KieranShoemark 3 60
(Jamie Osborne) *chsd ldrs: rdn to ld wl over 1f out: sn hdd: no ex ins fnl f* **9/1**

620 **3** 4 ½ **Sir Gordon**[22] 3812 2-9-0 69........................ CallumShepherd 4 46
(Mick Channon) *chsd ldrs: rdn over 2f out: styd on same pce fr over 1f out: wnt 3rd nr fin* **9/2**[3]

056 **4** nk **Come On Girl**[12] 4191 2-8-9 42........................ GeorgeDowning 2 40
(Tony Carroll) *sn led: rdn and hdd wl over 1f out: wknd ins fnl f* **50/1**

036 **5** ½ **Bob's Oss (IRE)**[38] 3220 2-9-0 66........................(p[1]) DougieCostello 1 44
(John Quinn) *s.i.s: hdwy over 2f out: rdn over 1f out: wknd ins fnl f* **16/1**

0 **6** 7 **Sooty's Return (IRE)**[27] 3634 2-9-0 0........................ TrevorWhelan 8 23
(J S Moore) *s.i.s: sn outpcd (jockey said gelding was slowly away and never travelled; vet said gelding lost his right-hind shoe)* **50/1**

7 ¾ **Leo's Luckyman** 2-9-0 0........................ LukeMorris 7 20
(David Flood) *s.i.s: outpcd* **9/2**[3]

4 **8** 1 **Dorchester Dom (IRE)**[98] 1416 2-9-0 0........................ LiamKeniry 6 17
(David Evans) *racd keenly: sn jnd ldr tl shkn up over 2f out: rdn and wknd over 1f out (jockey said gelding hung right-handed)* **11/4**[2]

1m 12.98s (0.88) **Going Correction** -0.025s/f (Good) **8 Ran SP% 119.2**
Speed ratings (Par 94): **93,88,82,81,81 71,70,69**
CSF £20.11 TOTE £2.70: £1.30, £2.70, £1.50; EX 15.70 Trifecta £49.70.The winner was bought in for £8,500.
Owner Marco Polo **Bred** Padraig Williams **Trained** Upper Lambourn, W Berks

FOCUS
Not a bad juvenile seller and the time was 0.95secs slower than the preceding fillies' handicap. The winner has been rated to her best.

4653 EBF/TAP'NSHOWER.COM FILLIES' H'CAP — 1m 2f
3:05 (3:05) (Class 5) (0-75,76) 3-Y-O+ **£4,133** (£1,237; £618; £309; £300) **Stalls Low**

Form / RPR

5-35 **1** **Chicago Doll**[37] 3264 3-9-2 **71**........................ TomMarquand 5 78
(Alan King) *chsd ldrs: pushed along and outpcd over 5f out: hdwy over 2f out: sn rdn: led and wandered ins fnl f: styd on* **9/4**[2]

0-61 **2** 1 **Railport Dolly**[37] 3267 4-10-0 **73**........................(h) LiamKeniry 1 78
(David Barron) *chsd ldrs: wnt 2nd over 2f out: rdn to ld and flashed tail fr over 1f out: hdd ins fnl f: styd on same pce* **5/4**[1]

6-00 **3** 2 ¼ **Principia**[11] 4220 4-9-1 **60**........................ CharlieBennett 3 61
(Adam West) *s.i.s: hld up: shkn up over 3f out: r.o ins fnl f: nvr nrr* **12/1**

0434 **4** 1 ¼ **Tails I Win (CAN)**[11] 4210 3-8-3 **58**........................(h) JimmyQuinn 2 56
(Roger Fell) *s.i.s: sn rcvrd to go 2nd: racd keenly: led over 5f out: clr over 3f out tl 2f out: rdn and hdd over 1f out: no ex ins fnl f* **7/2**[3]

3200 **5** 18 **Lady Cosette (FR)**[44] 3012 3-9-7 **76**........................(b) LukeMorris 4 38
(Harry Dunlop) *led at stdy pce tl over 5f out: chsd ldr: rdn over 3f out: lost 2nd over 2f out: wknd over 1f out* **11/1**

2m 8.81s (-0.39) **Going Correction** -0.025s/f (Good) **5 Ran SP% 113.5**
WFA 3 from 4yo 10lb
Speed ratings (Par 100): **100,99,97,96,82**
CSF £5.69 TOTE £2.80: £1.80, £1.20; EX 5.30 Trifecta £18.50.
Owner Hunscote Stud Limited **Bred** Bredon Hill Bloodstock Ltd **Trained** Barbury Castle, Wilts

FOCUS
An ordinary fillies' handicap and just modest form. It's been rated around the second.

4654 H.A.C. GROUP OF COMPANIES H'CAP — 7f
3:40 (3:45) (Class 3) (0-95,94) 3-Y-O+ **£12,938** (£3,850; £1,924; £962) **Stalls High**

Form / RPR

-620 **1** **Blackheath**[36] 3318 4-9-4 **84**........................ LiamKeniry 9 96
(Ed Walker) *hld up: hdwy over 2f out: rdn to ld ins fnl f: edgd rt: styd on* **9/1**

-305 **2** ¾ **Graphite Storm**[27] 3632 5-9-1 **81**........................ KieranShoemark 11 91
(Clive Cox) *s.i.s: hld up: swtchd rt and hdwy over 1f out: rdn to chse wnr ins fnl f: styd on* **8/1**

-102 **3** 1 ½ **Admirality**[21] 3863 5-9-9 **94**........................ BenSanderson(5) 6 100
(Roger Fell) *chsd ldrs: led wl over 1f out: sn rdn: hdd ins fnl f: styd on same pce* **5/2**[1]

1111 **4** ¾ **Glenn Coco**[50] 2799 5-9-5 **85**........................(t) CallumShepherd 4 89
(Stuart Williams) *led 1f: chsd ldrs: rdn and ev ch over 1f out: styd on same pce ins fnl f* **7/1**[3]

22-4 **5** 1 **Monsieur Noir**[42] 3090 3-8-11 **85**........................ CharlieBennett 2 83
(Roger Varian) *w ldrs over 1f: remained handy: rdn and ev ch over 1f out: no ex ins fnl f* **6/1**[2]

0400 **6** ¾ **Deep Intrigue**[7] 4379 3-8-12 **91**........................ AndrewBreslin(5) 1 87
(Mark Johnston) *led 6f out: rdn and hdd wl over 1f out: no ex ins fnl f* **8/1**

5666 **7** nk **Wahash (IRE)**[10] 4255 5-9-10 **90**........................ TomMarquand 5 88
(Richard Hannon) *s.i.s: hld up: hdwy over 2f out: sn rdn: styd on same pce fnl f (jockey said gelding pulled up lame; vet said gelding was lame on his right-fore)* **7/1**[3]

-550 **8** hd **Al Erayg (IRE)**[10] 4240 6-9-0 **80**........................ RachelRichardson 10 78
(Tim Easterby) *hld up: rdn over 2f out: nt trble ldrs* **15/2**

2603 **9** 2 ¾ **Zofelle (IRE)**[14] 4119 3-8-6 **80**........................(t) LukeMorris 3 67
(Hugo Palmer) *hld up in tch: rdn over 2f out: wknd ins fnl f* **14/1**

-000 **10** 9 **Cox Bazar (FR)**[14] 4100 5-9-3 **83**........................(e[1]) TrevorWhelan 8 49
(Ivan Furtado) *s.s: hld up: plld hrd: wknd over 1f out (jockey said gelding ran to free)* **66/1**

1m 23.39s (-2.31) **Going Correction** -0.025s/f (Good) **10 Ran SP% 120.0**
WFA 3 from 4yo+ 8lb
Speed ratings (Par 107): **112,111,109,108,107 106,106,106,102,92**
CSF £81.26 CT £237.75 TOTE £11.40: £3.10, £3.00, £1.30; EX 80.20 Trifecta £455.50.
Owner Matthew Cottis **Bred** Rangefield Bloodstock **Trained** Upper Lambourn, Berks

FOCUS
The feature race and a decent prize produced a good competitive handicap and the field were quite closely bunched behind the first two. Sound form.

4655 TAP'NSHOWER.COM BATHROOM PRODUCTS LTD/EBF BREEDERS BACKING RACING RATING RELATED MAIDEN STKS — 7f
4:15 (4:16) (Class 5) 3-Y-O+
£4,851 (£1,443; £721; £360) **Stalls High**

Form / RPR

-030 **1** **Gambon (GER)**[14] 4116 3-9-0 75........................ CharlesBishop 2 80+
(Eve Johnson Houghton) *s.i.s: hld up: hdwy on outer over 2f out: shkn up to ld over 1f out: edgd lft: pushed out (trainer said, regarding the improved form shown, the gelding was upset in the stalls last time out and that he had settled much better in the preliminary stages today)* **12/1**

4-03 **2** ¾ **Desert Land (IRE)**[25] 3696 3-9-0 75........................ StevieDonohoe 7 76
(David Simcock) *plld hrd and sn prom: rdn and ev ch over 1f out: styd on (jockey said colt ran too free)* **10/3**[2]

-223 **3** 4 **Rhossili Down**[19] 3920 3-9-0 75........................ KieranShoemark 5 65
(Charles Hills) *s.i.s: hld up: hdwy 1/2-way: ev ch over 2f out: sn rdn: nt run on: eased nr fin* **4/1**[3]

3-46 **4** 2 ¾ **Woods (IRE)**[141] 733 3-9-0 74........................(p[1]) TomMarquand 8 58
(William Haggas) *hld up in tch: rdn over 2f out: hung rt over 1f out: wknd ins fnl f* **5/2**[1]

5332 **5** 2 ½ **Society Guest (IRE)**[7] 4405 3-9-0 75........................ CallumShepherd 4 51
(Mick Channon) *led: hdd over 5f out: chsd ldrs: rdn over 1f out: wknd fnl f* **5/1**

2-46 **6** 1 **Ricochet (IRE)**[14] 4116 3-9-0 75........................ NicolaCurrie 1 48
(Jamie Osborne) *w ldrs: led over 5f out: rdn and hdd over 1f out: wknd fnl f* **6/1**

-253 **7** 3 ¾ **Sirius Slew**[33] 3420 3-9-0 74........................(p[1]) JoeyHaynes 3 38
(Alan Bailey) *hld up: rdn over 2f out: wknd over 1f out* **11/1**

1m 25.3s (-0.40) **Going Correction** -0.025s/f (Good) **7 Ran SP% 118.6**
Speed ratings (Par 103): **101,100,95,92,89 88,84**
CSF £54.26 TOTE £14.30: £4.80, £2.00; EX 64.20 Trifecta £131.80.
Owner Anthony Pye-Jeary **Bred** Stiftung Gestut Fahrhof **Trained** Blewbury, Oxon

FOCUS
This rating related maiden was a competitive event but was run nearly two seconds slower than the preceding Class 3 handicap.

4656 H.A.C. PIPELINE SUPPLIES LTD H'CAP — 1m 3f 179y
4:50 (4:50) (Class 5) (0-70,72) 3-Y-O £4,075 (£1,212; £606; £303; £300) Stalls Low

Form — RPR

456 1 **Global Falcon**[64] 2354 3-9-9 71 .... KieranShoemark 3 78
(Charles Hills) *led at stdy pce: qcknd 4f out: hdd 3f out: sn rdn: rallied to ld over 1f out: styd on* 9/1

2242 2 ½ **Message**[4] 4484 3-8-13 66 .... AndrewBreslin(5) 2 72
(Mark Johnston) *chsd ldrs: shkn up over 3f out: rdn and hung rt wl over 1f out: chsd wnr jst over 1f out: r.o* 9/4[2]

-503 3 5 **Fragrant Belle**[18] 3955 3-9-5 72 .... ThoreHammerHansen(5) 5 70
(Ralph Beckett) *w ldr tl shkn up to ld 3f out: rdn and hdd over 1f out: no ex ins fnl f* 3/1[3]

0-01 4 1 **Cambric**[20] 3888 3-9-7 69 .... AdamMcNamara 1 65
(Roger Charlton) *s.i.s: sn chsng ldrs: nt clr run and swtchd lft over 3f out: rdn over 2f out: styd on same pce fr over 1f out* 7/4[1]

2426 5 nk **Hummdinger (FR)**[22] 3809 3-9-2 64 .... TomMarquand 4 60
(Alan King) *hld up: rdn over 2f out: nvr trbld ldrs* 8/1

2m 34.67s (-0.33) **Going Correction** -0.025s/f (Good) 5 Ran SP% 113.2
Speed ratings (Par 100): **100,99,96,95,95**
CSF £30.13 TOTE £10.60: £3.40, £1.90; EX 33.50 Trifecta £59.90.
Owner Dr Johnny Hon **Bred** G R Bailey Ltd **Trained** Lambourn, Berks

FOCUS
A small field for this 3yo handicap and it developed into a 3f sprint. The second has been rated to his Chepstow latest.

4657 TAPN'SHOWER.COM NATIONWIDE DELIVERIES H'CAP — 1m 53y
5:25 (5:25) (Class 6) (0-65,65) 3-Y-O+ £3,493 (£1,039; £519; £300; £300; £300) Stalls Low

Form — RPR

-020 1 **Cape Cyclone (IRE)**[52] 2740 4-8-5 49 .... MarcoGhiani(7) 5 57
(Stuart Williams) *a.p: chsd ldr over 3f out: rdn to ld ins fnl f: styd on* 11/1

0-21 2 1½ **Princess Way (IRE)**[29] 3533 5-9-5 61 .... (v) RhiainIngram(5) 2 66
(Paul George) *chsd ldr: led 6f out: rdn and hdd ins fnl f: styd on same pce: edgd rt towards fin* 9/2[2]

3235 3 1¼ **Straight Ash (IRE)**[28] 3567 4-9-7 65 .... HarryRussell(7) 6 67
(Ollie Pears) *mid-div: pushed along over 4f out: hdwy u.p and hung rt fr over 1f out: r.o to go 3rd post: nt rch ldrs* 5/1[3]

0050 4 hd **Little Choosey**[31] 3473 9-8-9 46 oh1 .... (tp) JohnFahy 4 48+
(Roy Bowring) *hld up: rdn and hdwy over 1f out: r.o to go 4th post: nt rch ldrs* 25/1

2302 5 shd **Ghazan (IRE)**[12] 4194 4-10-0 65 .... (p) RossaRyan 3 66
(Kevin Frost) *sn prom: rdn over 1f out: styd on same pce wl ins fnl f* 7/1

4402 6 1 **Foreign Legion (IRE)**[7] 4378 4-9-12 63 .... (p) EoinWalsh 14 62
(Luke McJannet) *mid-div: hdwy over 4f out: rdn over 2f out: styd on u.p* 5/1[3]

6000 7 ¾ **False Id**[18] 3959 6-9-13 64 .... (b) TrevorWhelan 11 61
(David Loughnane) *dwlt: hld up: hdwy u.p over 2f out: no ex wl ins fnl f (jockey said gelding was slowly away)* 12/1

0442 8 1 **Takeonefortheteam**[10] 4235 4-9-5 63 .... SeanKirrane(7) 10 58
(Mark Loughnane) *s.s: hld up: hdwy u.p over 1f out: no ex wl ins fnl f (jockey said gelding was slowly away)* 7/2[1]

36-0 9 4½ **Vicky Cristina (IRE)**[24] 3721 4-8-9 46 oh1 .... RoystonFfrench 12 31
(John Holt) *chsd ldrs: rdn over 2f out: wknd fnl f* 28/1

-000 10 shd **My Society (IRE)**[31] 3476 4-9-2 53 .... (tp) StevieDonohoe 13 38
(David Dennis) *led 2f: chsd ldr tl over 3f out: rdn over 2f out: wknd fnl f* 20/1

00-0 11 3¼ **Summer Angel (IRE)**[184] 37 4-8-9 46 oh1 .... NicolaCurrie 1 24
(Michael Appleby) *mid-div: shkn up over 3f out: rdn and hung rt over 1f out: sn wknd* 25/1

0054 12 2¾ **Quarto Cavallo**[12] 4180 3-8-0 46 .... JimmyQuinn 9 16
(Adam West) *s.i.s: hld up: hdwy over 3f out: rdn over 1f out: sn wknd* 12/1

-000 13 6 **Dancing Jaquetta (IRE)**[12] 4180 3-7-11 46 oh1 .... NoelGarbutt(3) 8 3
(Mark Loughnane) *prom: rdn over 4f out: wknd over 2f out* 50/1

0 14 6 **Dragon Girl (IRE)**[123] 1021 4-9-6 57 .... (p) LiamKeniry 7 3
(Roy Brotherton) *s.i.s: a in rr: wknd over 2f out* 33/1

1m 45.64s (-0.66) **Going Correction** -0.025s/f (Good) 14 Ran SP% 130.8
WFA 3 from 4yo+ 9lb
Speed ratings (Par 101): **102,100,99,99,98 97,97,96,91,91 88,85,79,73**
CSF £60.69 CT £295.20 TOTE £15.70: £4.40, £2.20, £1.80; EX 118.90 Trifecta £818.70.
Owner Anthony Lyons **Bred** Rabbah Bloodstock Limited **Trained** Newmarket, Suffolk

FOCUS
A big field in this low-grade handicap, but it paid to race close to the pace. It's been rated around the balance of the second and third.
T/Plt: £87.80 to a £1 stake. Pool: £44,168.15 - 367.09 winning units T/Qpdt: £19.40 to a £1 stake. Pool: £3,296.06 - 125.71 winning units **Colin Roberts**

4302 NOTTINGHAM (L-H)
Saturday, July 6

OFFICIAL GOING: Good (good to soft in places; watered)
Weather: Warm, dry

4658 GENTING CASINO NOTTINGHAM H'CAP (FOR LADY AMATEUR RIDERS) — 1m 2f 50y
5:40 (5:42) (Class 6) (0-65,65) 4-Y-O+ £2,807 (£870; £435; £400; £400; £400) Stalls Low

Form — RPR

-02 1 **Blue Medici**[6] 4426 5-10-5 63 .... MissBeckySmith 12 78
(Mark Loughnane) *hld up: hdwy 3f: wnt 2nd 2f: rdn to ld 1f: r.o: comf* 3/1[2]

6231 2 2¼ **Luna Magic**[5] 4460 5-10-2 60 5ex .... MissEmmaSayer 8 71
(Archie Watson) *led: hdd 8f: remained prom: regained ld wl over 2f out: hdd 1f: sn rdn: kpt on* 11/8[1]

0000 3 3½ **Contrast (IRE)**[19] 3941 5-9-11 60 .... MissAmyCollier(5) 6 64
(Michael Easterby) *hld up: rdn 3f out: styd on fr 2f out: no ch w front two* 20/1

-000 4 5 **Windsorlot (IRE)**[10] 4232 6-9-2 51 .... MissSarahBowen(5) 5 46
(Tony Carroll) *mid-div: rdn wl over 2f out: styd on: nvr nrr* 20/1

5000 5 ½ **Angelical Eve (IRE)**[6] 4424 5-8-11 46 oh1 .... SophieSmith(5) 7 40
(Dai Williams) *trckd ldrs wd: rdn 3f out: kpt on* 80/1

0-44 6 ½ **Misty Breese (IRE)**[24] 3740 4-8-11 46 oh1 .... MissAntoniaPeck(5) 1 39
(Sarah Hollinshead) *t.k.h: trckd ldrs: hdwy to ld 6f: hdd wl over 2f out: sn rdn and one pce* 16/1

0-30 7 ½ **Bollin Ted**[15] 4054 5-10-2 60 .... MissEmilyEasterby 11 52
(Tim Easterby) *prom: lost pl over 4f out: rdn 3f out: one pce* 6/1[3]

1550 8 nk **Glacier Fox**[18] 3959 4-10-7 65 .... MissSerenaBrotherton 2 56
(Tom Tate) *prom: led 8f out: hdd 6f out: rdn 3f out: sn wknd* 11/1

0-55 9 1¼ **Prosecute (FR)**[3] 4513 6-9-2 46 oh1 .... MissAmieWaugh 9 35
(Sean Regan) *slowly away: a towards rr: rdn 3f out: one pce* 25/1

0201 10 ¾ **Spirit Of Sarwan (IRE)**[24] 3721 5-9-12 61 .... (p) MissKellyAdams(5) 3 48
(Stef Keniry) *dwlt: a towards rr: n.d (jockey said gelding was slowly away and never travelling)* 16/1

6-04 11 5 **Dutch Artist (IRE)**[5] 4460 7-9-6 57 ow3 .... MissBelindaJohnson(7) 10 35
(Nigel Tinkler) *mid-div: wd and lost pl 8f out: rdn 3f out: n.d* 25/1

030 12 22 **Sunshineandbubbles**[21] 3834 6-9-8 52 .... (b[1]) MissJoannaMason 4
(Jennie Candlish) *trckd ldrs: rdn 3f out: sn wknd* 25/1

2m 14.23s (0.83) **Going Correction** +0.15s/f (Good) 12 Ran SP% 123.8
Speed ratings (Par 101): **102,100,97,93,93 92,92,91,90,90 86,68**
CSF £7.09 CT £72.89 TOTE £4.50: £1.90, £1.20, £7.20; EX 11.00 Trifecta £167.20.
Owner Laurence Bellman **Bred** Kirtlington Stud Ltd **Trained** Rock, Worcs
■ Stewards' Enquiry : Miss Sarah Bowen two-day ban: interference & careless riding (Jul 20-21)

FOCUS
Outer track in use. The rail was out 2yds on the home bend and 4yds on the stands' bend. Add 6yds. The ground had been watered - 10mm on Monday, Wednesday and Friday, and there was a further 5mm of rain on raceday morning, leaving the ground officially good, good to soft in places. The big two in the market had this between them from a furlong and a half out.

4659 DOWNLOAD THE DG TAXI APP FILLIES' NOVICE STKS (PLUS 10 RACE) — 5f 8y
6:10 (6:10) (Class 5) 2-Y-O £3,881 (£1,155; £577; £288) Stalls Low

Form — RPR

1 **Never In Paris (IRE)** 2-9-0 0 .... CliffordLee 4 83+
(K R Burke) *hld up in rr: rdn 2f out: drvn to ld 110yds: sn in command: won gng away* 6/1[3]

120 2 2¼ **Exclusively**[15] 4048 2-9-7 85 .... HollieDoyle 3 82
(Archie Watson) *led: rdn 2f out: hdd 110yds: kpt on* 4/6[1]

3 ¾ **What Is Life (IRE)** 2-9-0 0 .... DavidNolan 2 72
(Richard Fahey) *hld up in tch: rdn wl over 2f out: hdwy to chal briefly 1f: sn no ex* 6/1[3]

4 3½ **Dana Forever (IRE)** 2-9-0 0 .... RichardKingscote 1 60
(Tom Dascombe) *prom: rdn 2f out: wknd fnl 1f* 7/2[2]

5 1¼ **Hyba** 2-9-0 0 .... LukeMorris 5 55
(Robert Cowell) *wnt rt s: trckd ldr: rdn wl over 2f out: sn btn* 33/1

1m 1.77s (1.57) **Going Correction** +0.15s/f (Good) 5 Ran SP% 113.7
Speed ratings (Par 91): **93,89,88,82,80**
CSF £11.05 TOTE £8.00: £3.10, £1.10; EX 11.40 Trifecta £34.90.
Owner Ontoawinner, A Marsh And E Burke **Bred** A R W Marsh **Trained** Middleham Moor, N Yorks

FOCUS
The favourite set a fair standard for the newcomers to aim at in this fillies' novice. It's been rated around the balance of the second's form to date.

4660 GENTING ELECTRONIC GAMING H'CAP — 6f 18y
6:40 (6:40) (Class 5) (0-75,77) 3-Y-O+ £3,557 (£1,058; £529; £400; £400; £400) Stalls Low

Form — RPR

-554 1 **Stewardess (IRE)**[13] 4149 4-9-8 68 .... DavidNolan 6 76
(Richard Fahey) *hld up: rdn and hdwy 3f: led 1f: r.o: cosily* 11/4[1]

0120 2 1½ **Queen Of Burgundy**[9] 4297 3-9-11 77 .... JoeyHaynes 7 79
(Christine Dunnett) *hld up: rdn and hdwy 3f: led wl over 1f out: hdd 1f: kpt on (jockey said filly hung left-handed under pressure)* 11/4[1]

-000 3 12 **Mostahel**[49] 2824 5-9-11 71 .... LukeMorris 5 36
(Paul Midgley) *rrd s and wnt rt: in rr: rdn 3f out: kpt on through btn horses fnl 2f (jockey said gelding jumped awkwardly when leaving the stalls, resulting in the gelding being slowly away)* 5/1[3]

0101 4 ¾ **King Crimson**[18] 3961 7-9-6 71 .... DarraghKeenan(5) 2 33
(John Butler) *led: drew clr 3f out: rdn 2f out: sn hdd & wknd* 11/2

-064 5 shd **Brawny**[9] 4286 3-9-0 66 .... (b[1]) KieranShoemark 4 27
(Charles Hills) *prom: rdn and hung lft 2f: grad wknd (jockey said gelding hung left-handed under pressure)* 10/1

2550 6 24 **Field Gun (USA)**[30] 3492 4-9-12 72 .... (vt) RichardKingscote 3
(Stuart Williams) *trckd ldrs: rdn 3f out: sn wknd: eased whn btn (trainer's rep said gelding did not face the visor on this occasion)* 9/2[2]

1m 15.64s (1.84) **Going Correction** +0.15s/f (Good) 6 Ran SP% 112.7
WFA 3 from 4yo+ 6lb
Speed ratings (Par 103): **93,91,75,74,73 41**
CSF £10.46 TOTE £2.90: £1.50, £3.90; EX 9.70 Trifecta £38.60.
Owner Five Plus One Syndicate **Bred** Austin Lyons **Trained** Musley Bank, N Yorks

FOCUS
The leader ensured this was run at a strong gallop. The winner has been rated back close to her 3yo form, and the second close to form.

4661 MY GENTING REWARDS H'CAP (JOCKEY CLUB GRASSROOTS STAYERS SERIES QUALIFIER) — 1m 6f
7:10 (7:11) (Class 5) (0-70,70) 4-Y-O+ £3,557 (£1,058; £529; £400; £400; £400) Stalls Low

Form — RPR

0-32 1 **Goscote**[44] 2999 4-9-5 68 .... DavidProbert 2 79+
(Henry Candy) *trckd ldrs: hdwy to ld over 2f out: drvn 1f: kpt on wl: a doing enough* 6/1

/112 2 nk **Maid In Manhattan (IRE)**[20] 3886 5-8-3 57 .... (h) HarrisonShaw(5) 5 66
(Rebecca Menzies) *hld up: gd hdwy 4f: led 3f tl hdd over 2f out: sn drvn and kpt on u.p: a jst hld* 5/1[3]

0-34 3 1½ **Fields Of Fortune**[23] 3778 5-9-3 66 .... TomMarquand 10 73
(Alan King) *hld up towards rr: hdwy 3f: drvn 2f: styd on same pce* 6/1

0-43 4 1¼ **Motaraabet**[44] 2999 4-9-7 70 .... StevieDonohoe 11 75
(Owen Burrows) *trckd ldrs: hdwy 3f: sn drvn: no ex fnl 1f* 7/2[1]

600- 5 2¼ **Bazooka (IRE)**[110] 9721 8-9-6 69 .... (t) HollieDoyle 4 71
(David Flood) *hld up in rr: hdwy to chse ldrs 3f: rdn 2f out: kpt on same pce (vet said gelding lost its left hind shoe)* 16/1

-140 6 ½ **Valkenburg**[26] 3653 4-9-4 67 .... (b) RichardKingscote 12 68
(Harriet Bethell) *hld up: rdn 3f out: kpt on u.p tl wknd fnl 100yds* 12/1

2506 7 7 **Betancourt (IRE)**[5] 4435 9-8-2 54 .... (p) GabrieleMalune(3) 6 46
(Stef Keniry) *mid-div: rdn 3f out: one pce* 20/1

35-5 8 2 **Wind Place And Sho**[26] 3653 7-9-7 70 .... RyanTate 9 59
(James Eustace) *mid-div: rdn 6f out: one pce fnl 4f* 12/1

The Form Book Flat 2019, Raceform Ltd, Newbury, RG14 5SJ

0016 **9** *1* **Swordbill**[14] 4118 4-9-6 **69**....................(p) JasonHart 7 56
(Ian Williams) *mid-div: rdn 4f out: grad wknd* **9/2**[2]

3020 **10** *17* **The Detainee**[30] 3511 6-9-5 **68**....................(p) LukeMorris 8 32
(Neil Mulholland) *mid-div: rdn 3f out: sn wknd* **28/1**

2461 **11** *19* **Banta Bay**[44] 3017 5-8-2 **51**.................... JosephineGordon 1
(John Best) *chsd ldr: rdn 3f out: sn wknd* **10/1**

0000 **12** *¾* **Miss Ranger (IRE)**[3] 4510 7-8-7 **56**....................(b) CliffordLee 3
(Roger Fell) *led: sn wl clr: rdn 4f out: hdd 3f: sn btn and wknd (jockey said mare ran too freely and had no more to give when under pressure)* **20/1**

3m 7.64s (1.24) **Going Correction** +0.15s/f (Good) **12** Ran SP% **129.0**
Speed ratings (Par 103): **102,101,100,100,98 98,94,93,92,83 72,71**
CSF £38.53 CT £198.53 TOTE £7.30: £2.40, £1.80, £2.50; EX 27.30 Trifecta £108.70.
Owner Major M G Wyatt **Bred** Dunchurch Lodge Stud Company **Trained** Kingston Warren, Oxon

FOCUS
Add 18yds. The early leader went off too fast but ensured it was a proper test at the trip. The third helps set the level.

4662 DG EXECUTIVE CARS H'CAP (JOCKEY CLUB GRASSROOTS MIDDLE DISTANCE SERIES QUALIFIER) 1m 75y
7:40 (7:40) (Class 4) (0-85,86) 3-Y-O+ **£6,145** (£1,828; £913; £456; £400) **Stalls** Centre

Form RPR

6-21 **1** **Chance**[44] 2995 3-8-12 **72**.................... JackMitchell 4 86+
(Simon Crisford) *hld up: hdwy 4f: led over 1f out: qckly asserted: pushed out: comf* **11/10**[1]

-211 **2** *4* **Lethal Missile (IRE)**[40] 3170 3-9-6 **80**.................... HectorCrouch 5 82
(Clive Cox) *hld up: briefly in rr in 4f: rdn wl over 2f out: styd on fnl 1f: no ch w wnr* **3/1**[2]

0434 **3** *½* **Michele Strogoff**[17] 3992 6-10-7 **86**.................... TheodoreLadd 1 89
(Michael Appleby) *led: rdn 3f out: hdd over 1f out: kpt on same pce* **13/2**

0644 **4** *2¼* **Juanito Chico (IRE)**[7] 4403 5-9-11 **76**....................(t[1]) DanielMuscutt 3 74
(Stuart Williams) *trckd ldr: rdn to chal 2f out: sn drvn and one pce* **9/2**[3]

5246 **5** *8* **Elysium Dream**[15] 4061 4-9-13 **78**....................(v[1]) TomMarquand 2 57
(Richard Hannon) *prom: lost pl 5f: rdn 4f out: sn wknd* **12/1**

1m 46.61s (-0.09) **Going Correction** +0.15s/f (Good)
WFA 3 from 4yo+ 9lb **5** Ran SP% **111.8**
Speed ratings (Par 105): **106,102,101,99,91**
CSF £4.75 TOTE £1.70: £1.10, £1.40; EX 2.90 Trifecta £17.00.
Owner Khalifa Saeed Sulaiman **Bred** Haras D'Etreham & Eric De Chambure **Trained** Newmarket, Suffolk

FOCUS
Add 6yds. The favourite finished well on top here and is progressing quickly. It's been rated around the third to his recent AW form.

4663 DS DERBY SALON CLASSIFIED STKS 1m 2f 50y
8:10 (8:10) (Class 5) 3-Y-O
£3,881 (£1,155; £577; £400; £400; £400) **Stalls** Low

Form RPR

6041 **1** **Corncrake**[14] 4109 3-9-0 **73**.................... RossaRyan 5 88+
(Richard Hannon) *hld up: hdwy 4f: drvn to ld over 1f out: sn clr: easily* **7/2**[2]

-451 **2** *4* **El Picador (IRE)**[12] 4176 3-9-1 **76**....................(v) KieranShoemark 7 78
(Sir Michael Stoute) *hld up: hdwy 3f: drvn over 1f out: styd on wl: no ch w wnr* **3/1**[1]

3-34 **3** *1¼* **Fragrant Dawn**[39] 3195 3-9-0 **73**.................... RichardKingscote 6 75
(Charles Hills) *prom: led 8f: rdn 3f out: drvn 2f: hdd over 1f out: kpt on* **7/1**[3]

0-30 **4** *1¼* **Kingson (IRE)**[18] 3957 3-9-0 **75**.................... DavidNolan 1 72
(Richard Fahey) *hld up in rr: hdwy 3f: swtchd to inner to chal over 1f out: kpt on same pce fnl 1f* **14/1**

3-44 **5** *4* **Vexed**[47] 2914 3-9-0 **72**.................... StevieDonohoe 2 64
(David Simcock) *trckd ldrs: rdn 3f out: grad wknd fnl 2f* **7/2**[2]

204 **6** *4* **Fly Lightly**[32] 3445 3-9-0 **75**.................... LukeMorris 3 56
(Robert Cowell) *led: hdd 8f: remained prom drvn 3f: sn wknd* **16/1**

5340 **7** *7* **Wanaasah**[59] 2521 3-9-0 **71**....................(p) JasonHart 8 42
(David Loughnane) *t.k.h: trckd ldrs: rdn 3f out: sn wknd (jockey said filly ran too freely)* **20/1**

2-53 **8** *22* **Tronada**[23] 3773 3-9-0 **74**.................... TomMarquand 4
(Alan King) *trckd ldrs: rdn 4f out: sn btn (trainer's rep could offer no explanation for the poor form shown)* **7/2**[2]

2m 13.0s (-0.40) **Going Correction** +0.15s/f (Good) **8** Ran SP% **121.5**
Speed ratings (Par 100): **107,103,102,101,98 95,89,72**
CSF £15.54 TOTE £4.40: £1.50, £1.50, £2.40; EX 12.70 Trifecta £58.50.
Owner Exors Of The Late Lady Rothschild **Bred** The Rt Hon Lord Rothschild **Trained** East Everleigh, Wilts

FOCUS
Add 6yds. A tight race on the ratings, but the winner won with a nice bit in hand. The second and third have been rated to their latest form.

4664 GREAT NIGHT OUT AT GENTING NOTTINGHAM H'CAP 1m 2f 50y
8:40 (8:40) (Class 5) (0-70,70) 3-Y-O
£3,557 (£1,058; £529; £400; £400; £400) **Stalls** Low

Form RPR

2443 **1** **Maqaadeer**[15] 4070 3-9-7 **70**.................... KieranShoemark 2 77
(Ed Dunlop) *led: pushed along 3f: drvn and hung lft 1f: kpt on gamely u.p: hld on* **3/1**[2]

6454 **2** *nk* **Lady Mascara**[46] 2933 3-9-5 **68**.................... GeorgeWood 3 74
(James Fanshawe) *hld up towards rr: hdwy 3f: rdn 2f out: drvn to chal 1f: kpt on: jst hld* **5/2**[1]

5-20 **3** *3* **Kings Royal Hussar (FR)**[28] 3580 3-9-7 **70**.................... TomMarquand 6 70
(Alan King) *stdd s: hld up: rdn 3f out: hdwy to chse ldr wl over 1f out: sn drvn: no ex fnl 100yds* **5/2**[1]

00-0 **4** *3* **Sephton**[45] 2965 3-8-13 **62**.................... DavidProbert 5 56
(Alan King) *prom: rdn 3f out: one pce fr wl over 1f out* **10/1**

5426 **5** *12* **Smeaton (IRE)**[30] 3505 3-8-12 **66**.................... BenSanderson[(5)] 4 36
(Roger Fell) *t.k.h: trckd ldr: rdn 3f out: sn wknd* **4/1**[3]

1125 **6** *3* **Dolly Dupree**[93] 1549 3-8-1 **55**....................(b) TheodoreLadd[(5)] 1 19
(Paul D'Arcy) *dwlt: in rr: rdn 4f out: n.d (jockey said filly jumped awkwardly when leaving the stalls)* **20/1**

2m 15.59s (2.19) **Going Correction** +0.15s/f (Good) **6** Ran SP% **116.0**
Speed ratings (Par 100): **97,96,94,91,82 79**
CSF £11.45 TOTE £3.50: £2.30, £1.60; EX 8.50 Trifecta £23.60.
Owner Hamdan Al Maktoum **Bred** Miss G Abbey **Trained** Newmarket, Suffolk

FOCUS
Add 6yds. A modest handicap.

T/Plt: £6.90 to a £1 stake. Pool: £46,964.51 - 4,931.77 winning units T/Qpdt: £3.80 to a £1 stake. Pool: £5,202.18 - 996.33 winning units **Jonathan Doidge**

4609 SANDOWN (R-H)
Saturday, July 6

OFFICIAL GOING: Good to firm (watered; 7.7)
Wind: Light, half against Weather: Fine but cloudy, warm

4665 CORAL CHARGE (GROUP 3) (REGISTERED AS THE SPRINT STKS) 5f 10y
1:50 (1:53) (Class 1) 3-Y-O+
£39,697 (£15,050; £7,532; £3,752; £1,883; £945) **Stalls** Low

Form RPR

-201 **1** **Kurious**[21] 3855 3-8-9 **96**.................... HarryBentley 6 105
(Henry Candy) *wl away: racd against rail: on terms w ldr in centre: rdn over 1f out: responded wl to ld last 150yds: styd on strly* **6/1**

4-11 **2** *¾* **Garrus (IRE)**[51] 2779 3-8-12 **109**.................... JamesDoyle 9 106
(Charles Hills) *dwlt: in tch on outer: rdn and prog 2f out: chal fnl f: chsd wnr last 120yds: styd on but readily hld* **10/3**[2]

0-60 **3** *1* **Caspian Prince (IRE)**[35] 3344 10-9-3 **111**....................(t) OisinMurphy 8 104
(Michael Appleby) *racd wd: mde most: rdn over 1f out: hdd last 150yds: sn lost 2nd and one pce after (jockey said gelding hung right-handed)* **11/1**

10-0 **4** *nk* **Poetry**[58] 2564 3-8-9 **98**.................... JamieSpencer 10 98
(Michael Bell) *dwlt and stdd s: hld up in last pair and swtchd to r against rail: effrt gng strly over 1f out: keeping on but no ch of winning whn nt clr run nr fin* **33/1**

1602 **5** *nk* **The Cruising Lord**[21] 3855 3-8-12 **98**.................... JasonWatson 3 100
(Michael Attwater) *mostly in last pair: outpcd and struggling sn after 1/2-way: styd on strly last 150yds: gaining at fin* **20/1**

-140 **6** *nse* **Sergei Prokofiev (CAN)**[18] 3950 3-8-12 **110**.................... RyanMoore 2 100
(A P O'Brien, Ire) *dwlt: chsd ldrs against rail: eased out and drvn over 1f out: styd on same pce fnl f and nvr able to chal* **5/2**[1]

03-0 **7** *1* **Rumble Inthejungle (IRE)**[15] 4050 3-8-12 **108**.................... FrankieDettori 1 96
(Richard Spencer) *w ldrs: upsides over 1f out: lost pl and n.m.r briefly ins fnl f: one pce after* **9/1**

00-5 **8** *½* **Muthmir (IRE)**[35] 3344 9-9-3 **105**....................(p) JimCrowley 5 96
(William Haggas) *chsd ldrs: rdn and nt qckn over 1f out: kpt on same pce fnl f: n.d* **11/2**[3]

244 **9** *11* **Pocket Dynamo (USA)**[42] 3084 3-8-12 **104**.................... AndreaAtzeni 4 55
(Robert Cowell) *chsd ldrs 3f: wknd qckly: t.o (jockey said colt stopped quickly)* **14/1**

59.23s (-2.07) **Going Correction** -0.125s/f (Firm)
WFA 3 from 9yo+ 5lb **9** Ran SP% **114.0**
Speed ratings (Par 113): **111,109,108,107,107 107,105,104,87**
CSF £25.95 TOTE £7.00: £2.10, £1.50, £2.60; EX 26.00 Trifecta £266.20.
Owner Hot To Trot Racing 2 **Bred** Mrs B A Matthews **Trained** Kingston Warren, Oxon

FOCUS
Round Course rail at innermost with all distances as advertised. Sprint Course at full width. The official going description was unchanged from the previous day as good to firm all round. A good renewal of this Group 3 in which it paid to race prominently. The second has been rated close to form, and the fourth to her 2yo form for now.

4666 CORAL CHALLENGE (H'CAP) 1m
2:25 (2:26) (Class 2) 3-Y-O+
£46,192 (£13,905; £6,952; £3,465; £1,740; £877) **Stalls** Low

Form RPR

110/ **1** **Mojito (IRE)**[637] 7807 5-9-8 **101**.................... FrankieDettori 8 113+
(William Haggas) *led after 1f: mde rest: stl gng strly 2f out and bttr than the rest: shkn up over 1f out: styd on wl: decisively* **4/1**[1]

000 **2** *1¼* **Escobar (IRE)**[51] 2778 5-9-5 **98**....................(t) AndreaAtzeni 9 106
(David O'Meara) *blindfold off sltly late and dwlt: sn in midfield: rdn and prog on inner 2f out: chsd wnr jst ins fnl f: styd on but nvr able to chal* **12/1**

1140 **3** *½* **Petrus (IRE)**[17] 3987 4-9-6 **99**....................(p) OisinMurphy 7 106
(Brian Meehan) *racd on outer in midfield: shkn up over 2f out: styd on fnl f to take 3rd last strides* **12/1**

4000 **4** *hd* **Key Victory (IRE)**[17] 3987 4-9-10 **103**....................(p) JamesDoyle 3 109
(Charlie Appleby) *trckd ldrs in 6th: shkn up over 2f out: prog to press for 2nd pl over 1f out: styd on same pce fnl f* **10/1**

4134 **5** *½* **Greenside**[21] 3857 8-9-1 **94**.................... HarryBentley 4 99
(Henry Candy) *hld up towards rr: rdn over 2f out: sme prog u.p over 1f out: styd on but nvr enough pce to threaten* **15/2**

-001 **6** *¾* **Via Serendipity**[16] 4020 5-9-4 **97**....................(t) KerrinMcEvoy 6 101
(Stuart Williams) *trckd ldrs: 1f: chsd wnr to 1/2-way: styd cl up: rdn over 2f out: stl pressing for 2nd 1f out: fdd nr fin* **8/1**

0301 **7** *½* **History Writer (IRE)**[21] 3857 4-9-4 **97**....................(t) JasonWatson 11 99
(David Menuisier) *hld up in last pair: rdn on outer over 2f out: laboured prog over 1f out: kpt on: n.d* **7/1**[3]

-120 **8** *1¼* **Salute The Soldier (GER)**[49] 2832 4-9-3 **96**.................... AdamKirby 1 95
(Clive Cox) *trckd ldrs in 5th: rdn over 2f out: nt qckn and lost pl over 1f out: fdd nr fin* **16/1**

-305 **9** *¾* **Zhui Feng (IRE)**[7] 4397 6-9-8 **101**.................... JimCrowley 10 101
(Amanda Perrett) *stmbld s: sn prom: chsd wnr 1/2-way to over 1f out: wknd ins fnl f* **25/1**

6-03 **10** *nse* **Rum Runner**[27] 3632 4-8-5 **84**.................... MartinDwyer 12 82
(Richard Hannon) *s.s: t.k.h and hld up in last trio: rdn and no prog over 2f out: no ch after* **25/1**

351 **11** *½* **Breden (IRE)**[49] 2832 9-9-7 **100**.................... RobertWinston 5 97
(Linda Jewell) *broke on terms but restrained into last trio: rdn and no prog over 2f out: no ch after* **33/1**

2322 **12** *¾* **Qaroun**[9] 4292 4-9-0 **93**.................... RyanMoore 2 93
(Sir Michael Stoute) *trckd ldng trio: rdn over 2f out: chsd wnr jst over 1f out to jst ins fnl f: wknd and heavily eased last 100yds* **6/1**[2]

-316 **13** *½* **Lush Life (IRE)**[32] 3450 4-9-1 **94**.................... JamieSpencer 14 88
(Jamie Osborne) *hld up in rr: rdn over 2f out: no prog over 1f out: wl btn after: eased nr fin* **7/1**[3]

1m 40.83s (-2.47) **Going Correction** -0.125s/f (Firm) **13** Ran SP% **123.2**
Speed ratings (Par 109): **107,105,105,105,104 103,103,102,101,101 100,100,99**
CSF £54.33 CT £547.30 TOTE £4.80: £2.40, £4.10, £4.30; EX 60.10 Trifecta £854.30.
Owner Ms Fiona Carmichael **Bred** Earl Ecurie Du Grand Chene **Trained** Newmarket, Suffolk

The Form Book Flat 2019, Raceform Ltd, Newbury, RG14 5SJ

FOCUS
A hugely competitive handicap, but the winner did it nicely from the front following a lengthy absence from the track. The third, fourth and fifth help set a solid standard, and the winner looks a Group horse in the making.

4667 CORAL DISTAFF (LISTED RACE) (FILLIES) 1m
3:00 (3:00) (Class 1) 3-Y-O

£22,684 (£8,600; £4,304; £2,144; £1,076; £540) **Stalls** Low

Form RPR

5-44 **1** **Hidden Message (USA)**[34] 3387 3-9-0 99........................ OisinMurphy 7 106
(William Haggas) *trckd ldrs: wnt 2nd over 1f out and sn rdn to ld: in command fnl f though advantage dwindled nr fin* **9/4**[1]

2 **2** ¾ **Encapsulation (IRE)**[69] 2157 3-9-0 100........................ JimCrowley 1 104
(Andrew Balding) *trckd ldr 3f: pushed along in 4th 3f out: swtchd lft and rallied over 1f out: styd on wl to take 2nd last 75yds: nt rch wnr* **7/1**

-014 **3** 2 **Muchly**[44] 3012 3-9-0 101........................ FrankieDettori 3 99
(John Gosden) *led: kicked on 2f out: rdn and hdd jst over 1f out: one pce and lost 2nd last 75yds* **10/3**[2]

160- **4** 5 **Beyond Reason (IRE)**[267] 8148 3-9-0 107........................ JamesDoyle 6 88
(Charlie Appleby) *trckd ldr after 3f: poised to chal 2f out: shkn up and no rspnse over 1f out: sn wknd* **7/2**[3]

6350 **5** ½ **Modern Millie**[15] 4052 3-9-0 92........................ AndreaAtzeni 2 86
(Mick Channon) *mostly in same pl: rdn and no prog over 2f out: steadily wknd* **14/1**

1-10 **6** 1 **Desirous**[15] 4052 3-9-0 88........................ HarryBentley 5 84
(Ralph Beckett) *nvr gng wl: sn pushed along in last pair: rdn 3f out: no prog* **5/1**

0540 **7** 1 ½ **Al Hayette (USA)**[98] 1443 3-9-0 90........................ KerrinMcEvoy 8 81
(Ismail Mohammed) *hld up in last: shkn up and no prog wl over 2f out* **50/1**

1m 40.11s (-3.19) **Going Correction** -0.125s/f (Firm) 7 Ran SP% **113.9**
Speed ratings (Par 105): **110,109,107,102,101 100,99**
CSF £18.59 TOTE £2.80: £1.70, £2.90; EX 21.10 Trifecta £70.60.
Owner Qatar Racing Limited **Bred** Frank Hutchinson **Trained** Newmarket, Suffolk

FOCUS
A fillies' Listed event, in which a couple of progressive performers came to the fore. A clear pb from the winner, with the third rated to form.

4668 CORAL-ECLIPSE (GROUP 1) (BRITISH CHAMPIONS SERIES) 1m 1f 209y
3:35 (3:40) (Class 1) 3-Y-O+

£425,325 (£161,250; £80,700; £40,200; £20,175; £10,125) **Stalls** Low

Form RPR

111- **1** **Enable**[245] 8848 5-9-4 125........................ FrankieDettori 8 124+
(John Gosden) *trckd ldr: led over 2f out: shkn up over 1f out: styd on strly and nvr in serious danger fnl f* **4/6**[1]

1112 **2** ¾ **Magical (IRE)**[17] 3985 4-9-4 123........................ RyanMoore 7 122
(A P O'Brien, Ire) *trckd ldng pair: shkn up over 2f out: rdn to chse wnr wl over 1f out: styd on wl but nvr able to seriously threaten* **11/4**[2]

3-31 **3** 2 **Regal Reality**[44] 3025 4-9-7 116........................ KerrinMcEvoy 4 121
(Sir Michael Stoute) *fractious on to crse and taken whole lap of trck to post: dwlt: hld up in last trio: prog over 2f out: rdn to chse ldng pair over 1f out: styd on same pce after (vet said colt lost its right fore shoe)* **17/2**[3]

-131 **4** 2 ½ **Danceteria (FR)**[26] 3678 4-9-7 110........................ JamieSpencer 1 116
(David Menuisier) *hld up and sn in last: rdn and detached over 2f out: styd on fnl f to take 4th last strides* **50/1**

-310 **5** hd **Mustashry**[18] 3948 6-9-7 121........................ JimCrowley 5 116
(Sir Michael Stoute) *hld up in last trio: gng strly 3f out: rdn and nt qckn 2f out: one pce after* **12/1**

3444 **6** nk **Hunting Horn (IRE)**[17] 3985 4-9-7 114........................ PBBeggy 3 115
(A P O'Brien, Ire) *led at str pce: stdd 1/2-way: rdn and hdd over 2f out: steadily wknd* **33/1**

2110 **7** 2 ¼ **Telecaster**[35] 3345 3-8-11 115........................ OisinMurphy 6 111
(Hughie Morrison) *failed to parade: trckd ldrs in 5th shkn up over 2f out: no rspnse and dropped to last fnl f* **10/1**

-110 **8** nk **Zabeel Prince (IRE)**[17] 3985 6-9-7 117........................ AndreaAtzeni 2 109
(Roger Varian) *trckd ldng trio: rdn over 2f out: wknd over 1f out* **20/1**

2m 4.77s (-5.43) **Going Correction** -0.125s/f (Firm)
WFA 3 from 4yo+ 10lb 8 Ran SP% **123.6**
Speed ratings (Par 117): **116,115,113,111,111 111,109,109**
CSF £3.01 CT £9.14 TOTE £1.50: £1.10, £1.20, £2.50; EX 3.10 Trifecta £10.50.
Owner K Abdullah **Bred** Juddmonte Farms Ltd **Trained** Newmarket, Suffolk

FOCUS
Sadly there wasn't a strong 3yo presence in one of the mid-summer highlights of the Flat season, and the race revolved around whether the market leader, and winner of the previous two runnings of the Prix de l'Arc de Triomphe, was at her best on seasonal return over a trip short of her best. The gallop seemed at least fair early, slackened on the bend before quickening on entering the home straight. The winner has been rated close to her best, with the second close to form.

4669 SMART MONEY'S ON CORAL H'CAP 7f
4:10 (4:13) (Class 3) (0-90,91) 3-Y-O

£9,337 (£2,796; £1,398; £699; £349; £175) **Stalls** Low

Form RPR

4-16 **1** **Make A Wish (IRE)**[14] 4124 3-8-11 80........................ KerrinMcEvoy 1 91
(Simon Crisford) *led after 1f: mde rest: rdn and hrd pressed fnl f: styd on wl and a fending off chalr* **7/2**[2]

2163 **2** nk **Magical Wish (IRE)**[21] 3865 3-9-8 91........................ RyanMoore 2 101
(Richard Hannon) *cl up: rdn over 2f out: drvn to chse wnr on inner over 1f out: str chal fnl f: styd on but a hld (vet said colt lost its right fore shoe)* **7/4**[1]

4115 **3** 3 ½ **Cristal Breeze (IRE)**[21] 3859 3-9-0 83........................ JamesDoyle 7 84
(William Haggas) *hld up in 6th: rdn and prog over 2f out: chsd wnr wl over 1f out and tried to chal: lost 2nd sn after and outpcd fnl f* **9/2**[3]

-605 **4** nk **Sheila's Showcase**[21] 3858 3-8-9 78........................ JasonWatson 6 78
(Denis Coakley) *hld up in 7th: rdn over 2f out: styd on over 1f out to press for 3rd nr fin* **16/1**

4010 **5** ¾ **Finoah (IRE)**[16] 4016 3-9-4 90........................(v) JaneElliott[(3)] 3 88
(Tom Dascombe) *taken down early: t.k.h: trckd ldrs: rdn and nt qckn 2f out: n.d over 1f out* **11/1**

0-05 **6** shd **Athmad (IRE)**[7] 4360 3-9-5 88........................ MartinDwyer 9 86
(Brian Meehan) *taken down early: hld up in 8th: shkn up over 2f out: no prog tl kpt on fnl f: no ch* **12/1**

-506 **7** ½ **Fintas**[30] 3493 3-9-7 90........................(t[1]) AdamKirby 5 87
(David O'Meara) *stdd s: hld up in last: rdn over 2f out: no prog tl styd on quite wl last 150yds* **20/1**

0005 **8** 2 ¼ **Chapelli**[10] 4242 3-9-5 88........................ FrankieDettori 4 78
(Mark Johnston) *led 1f: chsd wnr: rdn over 2f out: lost 2nd wl over 1f out and wknd* **7/1**

4-66 **9** nk **Indomitable (IRE)**[28] 3591 3-8-8 77........................ OisinMurphy 10 67
(Andrew Balding) *trckd ldrs: rdn and lost pl over 2f out: steadily dropped away* **10/1**

1m 27.32s (-1.98) **Going Correction** -0.125s/f (Firm) 9 Ran SP% **125.0**
Speed ratings (Par 104): **106,105,101,101,100 100,99,97,96**
CSF £11.00 CT £29.84 TOTE £4.40: £1.50, £1.30, £1.60; EX 11.80 Trifecta £44.30.
Owner Michael Tabor **Bred** Chelston Ireland **Trained** Newmarket, Suffolk

FOCUS
A useful 3yo handicap and solid form, with the two principals pulling nicely clear of the rest. The third has been rated to form and the fourth close to his C&D latest.

4670 CORAL MARATHON (LISTED RACE) (REGISTERED AS THE ESHER STKS) 2m 50y
4:45 (4:45) (Class 1) 4-Y-O+ £22,684 (£8,600; £4,304; £2,144; £1,076) **Stalls** Centre

Form RPR

3- **1** **Falcon Eight (IRE)**[50] 2814 4-9-0 109........................(p[1]) FrankieDettori 3 114
(D K Weld, Ire) *trckd ldr to 6f out: shkn up 3f out: tk 2nd again 2f out: sustained chal over 1f out: drvn to ld last strides* **10/11**[1]

2-20 **2** hd **Mekong**[21] 3864 4-9-0 110........................ RyanMoore 1 113
(Sir Michael Stoute) *s.v.s: sn in tch in rr: swift move to press ldr 6f out: rdn to ld over 2f out: hrd pressed over 1f out: stirring duel and fought on wl: hdd last strides* **9/4**[2]

-361 **3** 4 ½ **Cleonte (IRE)**[14] 4096 6-9-0 105........................ OisinMurphy 2 108
(Andrew Balding) *trckd ldng pair to 6f out: rdn over 2f out: tk 3rd again over 1f out: nt pce to chal and lft bhd by ldng pair fnl f* **4/1**[3]

0 **4** 6 **Hermoso Mundo (SAF)**[113] 1230 6-9-0 100........................ JamesDoyle 5 100
(Hughie Morrison) *hld up and last after 4f: rdn 3f out: steadily lft bhd: tk modest 4th fnl f* **50/1**

211- **5** 6 **Jackfinbar (FR)**[307] 6847 4-9-0 107........................ JimCrowley 6 93
(Harry Dunlop) *led: rdn and hdd over 2f out: sn wknd* **20/1**

3m 32.55s (-5.35) **Going Correction** -0.125s/f (Firm) 5 Ran SP% **109.9**
Speed ratings (Par 111): **108,107,105,102,99**
CSF £3.19 TOTE £1.70: £1.10, £1.30; EX 3.00 Trifecta £4.20.
Owner Moyglare Stud Farm **Bred** Moyglare Stud Farm Ltd **Trained** Curragh, Co Kildare

FOCUS
This smart staying even produced a magnificent finish, with two pulling nicely away from the third. The second and third have been rated to form.

4671 CORAL DON'T BET SILLY BET SAVVY H'CAP 1m 1f 209y
5:20 (5:21) (Class 4) (0-80,81) 3-Y-O

£6,469 (£1,925; £962; £481; £300; £300) **Stalls** Low

Form RPR

41-3 **1** **Marronnier (IRE)**[23] 3779 3-9-4 77........................(t) AdamKirby 7 87
(Stuart Williams) *trckd ldr: led over 2f out: sent for home and sn at least 2 l clr: rdn out fnl f* **9/1**

06-1 **2** ¾ **Dreamweaver (IRE)**[63] 2406 3-8-8 67........................ AndreaAtzeni 10 75
(Ed Walker) *hld up in last trio: rdn over 2f out: hanging sltly but prog over 1f out: r.o to take 2nd last 50yds: nt rch wnr* **11/4**[1]

0-61 **3** nk **Light Up Our Stars (IRE)**[53] 2715 3-9-7 80........................ KerrinMcEvoy 1 87
(Richard Hughes) *trckd ldng pair: drvn to chse wnr wl over 1f out: kpt on but nvr able to chal: lost 2nd last 50yds* **16/1**

0551 **4** 3 ½ **Production**[15] 4077 3-9-8 81........................ RyanMoore 2 81
(Richard Hannon) *trckd ldrs in 5th: rdn over 2f out: tk 3rd briefly 1f out but nvr able to chal: one pce after* **8/1**

0-P0 **5** hd **Tribal Commander**[7] 4392 3-8-11 70........................ MartinDwyer 11 70
(Ian Williams) *hld up in last: shkn up over 3f out: no prog u.p 2f out: styd on fnl f: nvr nrr* **33/1**

4-52 **6** 1 ¼ **Madeeh**[18] 3958 3-9-5 78........................ JimCrowley 6 75
(Sir Michael Stoute) *hld up in 6th: shkn up and nt qckn over 2f out: no real prog after* **4/1**[3]

3-01 **7** 1 ¼ **Amjaady (USA)**[26] 3647 3-9-6 79........................ JamesDoyle 4 76
(Owen Burrows) *trckd ldng trio: shkn up over 2f out: lost pl and btn over 1f out* **5/1**

0214 **8** 1 **Pempie (IRE)**[25] 3698 3-9-0 73........................ OisinMurphy 3 66
(Andrew Balding) *led: pushed along and hdd over 2f out: wknd over 1f out* **3/1**[2]

4614 **9** nk **Navigate By Stars (IRE)**[36] 3310 3-8-13 75........................(p) JaneElliott[(3)] 5 67
(Tom Dascombe) *hld up in last trio: rdn over 2f out: nt qckn and no prog (jockey said filly was denied clear run)* **25/1**

2m 7.67s (-2.53) **Going Correction** -0.125s/f (Firm) 9 Ran SP% **122.1**
Speed ratings (Par 102): **105,104,104,101,101 100,99,98,98**
CSF £36.08 CT £408.88 TOTE £9.70: £2.70, £1.60, £3.40; EX 50.20 Trifecta £1059.90.
Owner GG Thoroughbreds III **Bred** Skymarc Farm **Trained** Newmarket, Suffolk

FOCUS
Four last-time-out winners took their chance in this competitive-looking 3yo handicap, but none of them could follow up their recent success. This is usually a good race and it's been rated as such.
T/Jkpt: £7,789.50 to a £1 stake. Pool: £49,370.23 - 4.50 winning units T/Plt: £25.10 to a £1 stake. Pool: £207632.32 - 6030.66 winning units T/Qpdt: £2.90 to a £1 stake. Pool: £17192.92 - 4327.68 winning units **Jonathan Neesom**

4672 - 4678a (Foreign Racing) - See Raceform Interactive

4357
CLAIREFONTAINE (R-H)
Saturday, July 6

OFFICIAL GOING: Turf: good to soft

4679a PRIX MENUISERIE DUVERNOIS (CLAIMER) (2YO) (TURF) 7f
4:42 2-Y-O £12,162 (£4,864; £3,648; £2,432; £1,216)

RPR

1 **Soliers (FR)**[24] 2-8-9 0........................(b[1]) AlexandreChesneau[(6)] 9 70
(G Botti, France) **32/1**

2 nk **Kongastet (FR)**[23] 2-8-6 0........................(b) ThomasTrullier[(5)] 10 65
(S Wattel, France) **66/10**

3 hd **Moontide (IRE)**[14] 4114 2-8-11 0........................ MickaelBarzalona 3 64
(J S Moore) *disp early: settled in mid-div: pushed along to chse ldrs over 2f out: sn rdn: swtchd lft over 1f out: kpt on wl ins fnl f: nt quite pce to rch wnr* **12/1**

4 1 ¼ **The Nile Song (FR)**[111] 1240 2-8-4 0........................ ClementGuitraud[(7)] 4 61
(Y Barberot, France) **21/1**

5 nk **Fact Or Fable (IRE)**[7] 4394 2-8-11 0.............................. HugoJourniac 2 60
(J S Moore) *racd in fnl trio: pushed along 2f out: sn drvn: swtchd rt between rivals 1 1/2f out: unable qck w ldrs ins fnl f: one pce clsng stages* **27/1**

6 nk **Carmague (IRE)**[25] 3714 2-8-11 0.............................. GregoryBenoist 7 60
(J S Moore) *cl up on outer: pushed along to keep tabs on ldr 3f out: rdn jst under 2f out: unable to go w ldrs fr 1f out: kpt on same pce ins fnl f* **22/1**

7 1 1/4 **Stelvio (FR)**[24] 2-8-10 0.............................. MlleAudeDuporte(9) 5 64
(A Giorgi, Italy) **48/10**[2]

8 1 1/4 **Another Planet (FR)** 2-9-1 0..............................(b) EddyHardouin 6 57
(Matthieu Palussiere, France) **15/2**

9 snk **Pic Cel (FR)** 2-8-11 0.............................. MlleCoraliePacaut(4) 1 57
(J-C Rouget, France) **17/10**[1]

10 1/2 **Zo Lane (FR)**[24] 2-8-11 0.............................. ThierryThulliez 8 51
(F Rossi, France) **5/1**[3]

1m 27.0s **10** Ran SP% **119.1**

PARI-MUTUEL (all including 1 euro stake): WIN: 32.60; PLACE: 7.50, 3.20, 4.20; DF: 68.30.

Owner Elia Tanghetti & G Botti **Bred** Franklin Finance S.A., Mme Ribard & S Vidal **Trained** France

4680 - 4682a (Foreign Racing) - See Raceform Interactive

4622 HAMBURG (R-H)

Saturday, July 6

OFFICIAL GOING: Turf: good

4683a MEHL MULHENS TROPHY (GROUP 3) (3YO FILLIES) (TURF) 1m 3f

2:45 3-Y-O £28,828 (£10,810; £5,405; £2,702; £1,801)

RPR

1 **Durance (GER)**[21] 3877 3-9-2 0..............................(p) AndraschStarke 2 99
(P Schiergen, Germany) *prom on inner: swtchd to nr side and pushed along 2f out: prog to chal ent fnl f: kpt on strly u.p: led fnl 110yds* **31/10**[3]

2 1 1/4 **Anna Pivola (GER)**[27] 3639 3-9-2 0.............................. AdriedeVries 3 96
(Markus Klug, Germany) *in tch on outer: asked for effrt over 2f out: sltly outpcd and lost position ent st: rdn 1 1/2f out: kpt on wl into 2nd ins fnl f: nt match pce of wnr* **3/1**[2]

3 3/4 **Shining Pass (GER)**[27] 3639 3-9-2 0.............................. EduardoPedroza 4 95
(A Wohler, Germany) *restrained towards rr of mid-div: pushed along and prog fr 2f out: rdn to ld narrowly 1 1/2f out: hdd fnl 110yds: kpt on but no ex towards fin* **32/5**

4 1/2 **Liberty London (GER)** 3-9-2 0.............................. WladimirPanov 1 94
(H-J Groschel, Germany) *trckd ldr: pushed along 2f out: rdn to chal ldr over 1 1/2f out: ev ch ent fnl f: nt quite able to qckn and kpt on same pce clsng stages* **15/2**

5 1 1/2 **Whispering Angel (GER)**[27] 3639 3-9-2 0.............................. MartinSeidl 5 91
(Markus Klug, Germany) *hld up in fnl trio: asked to improve between rivals over 2f out: rdn over 1 1/2f out: kpt on same pce ins fnl f: nvr threatened* **27/10**[1]

6 1 1/2 **Sharoka (IRE)**[41] 3119 3-9-2 0.............................. MaximPecheur 6 89
(Markus Klug, Germany) *hld up in last pair: pushed along over 2f out: limited rspnse and sn rdn: unable qck and kpt on one pce fr over 1f out* **108/10**

7 2 **Wildbeere (GER)** 3-9-2 0.............................. MarcoCasamento 7 85
(Waldemar Hickst, Germany) *led: asked to qckn over 2f out: rdn whn hrd pressed over 1 1/2f out: sn hdd: grad wknd ins fnl f: no ex* **243/10**

8 2 1/2 **Wish You Well (GER)**[50] 3-9-2 0.............................. FilipMinarik 8 81
(Jean-Pierre Carvalho, Germany) *a in rr* **202/10**

2m 22.94s (-1.76) **8** Ran SP% **118.8**

PARI-MUTUEL (all including 1 euro stake): WIN: 4.10; PLACE: 1.50, 1.40, 2.10; SF: 9.80.

Owner Gestut Ebbesloh **Bred** Gestut Ebbesloh **Trained** Germany

4174 LES LANDES

Friday, July 5

OFFICIAL GOING: Firm

4684a WILSONS ESTATE AGENT H'CAP (TURF) 7f

6:30 (6:30) (0-50,0) 3-Y-O+ £1,780 (£640; £190; £190)

RPR

1 **Swiss Cross**[6] 4378 12-10-9 0..............................(tp) SamTwiston-Davies 53
(Phil McEntee) *mde all: c over to stand's rail st: drvn out* **11/8**[1]

2 3 1/2 **Mendacious Harpy (IRE)**[14] 4175 8-9-7 0..............................(p) MrFrederickTett 28
(Mrs A Malzard, Jersey) *mid-div: 5th into st: kpt on to go 2nd ins fnl f* **6/1**[3]

3 3 1/2 **Brown Velvet**[26] 7-10-4 0.............................. MattieBatchelor 30
(Mrs C Gilbert, Jersey) *mid-div: 4th into st: kpt on ins fnl f to share 3rd post* **12/1**

3 dht **Tidal's Baby**[211] 9433 10-10-8 0.............................. JordanNailor 34
(John O'Neill) *hld up: 7th into st: kpt on to go 3rd cl home* **7/1**

5 nk **Drummer Jack (IRE)**[14] 4175 3-9-12 0..............................(t) MarkQuinlan 28
(K Kukk, Jersey) *trckd ldr: wnt 2nd after 1f: ev ch over 1f out: sn wknd* **10/1**

6 1 1/4 **Coastguard Watch (FR)**[39] 3174 3-10-2 0.............................. TimClark 28
(Natalie Lloyd-Beavis) *outpcd in rr: last into st: mod late hdwy* **16/1**

7 shd **Kalani Rose**[14] 4175 5-9-0 0..............................(v) MissSerenaBrotherton 7
(Mrs A Corson, Jersey) *trckd ldrs: wnt 3rd after 1f: wknd fr 1f out* **14/1**

8 2 **Mr Potter**[16] 3996 6-10-12 0..............................(v) PhilipPrince 28
(Richard Guest) *t.k.h trcking ldr tl blew turn after 1f: 6th into st: wknd* **2/1**[2]

9 9 **Snejinska (FR)**[14] 5-10-4 0..............................(h) MorganRaine
(Mrs C Gilbert, Jersey) *a bhd: 9th into st: n.d* **20/1**

10 5 **Spanish Bounty**[39] 3173 14-10-6 0.............................. VictoriaMalzard
(Mrs A Malzard, Jersey) *reluctant to line up: hld up: 8th into st: n.d* **20/1**

Owner Steve Jakes **Bred** Lordship Stud **Trained** Newmarket, Suffolk

4685a MILLBROOK H'CAP SPRINT (TURF) 5f 100y

7:05 (7:05) 3-Y-O+ £1,780 (£640; £380)

RPR

1 **Man Of The Sea (IRE)**[26] 3641 3-10-0 0..............................(tp) SamTwiston-Davies 62
(Neil Mulholland) *chsd ldrs: 3rd into st: drvn to ld wl ins fnl f: all out* **6/4**[1]

2 3/4 **Relaxed Boy (FR)**[14] 4174 6-10-12 0..............................(t) MrFrederickTett 69
(Mrs A Malzard, Jersey) *outpcd in rr: last into st: styd on strly fnl f: nrst fin* **9/2**

3 1/2 **Fruit Salad**[14] 4174 6-10-0 0.............................. MarkQuinlan 55
(K Kukk, Jersey) *chsd ldrs: 6th into st: styng on w ch whn n.m.r wl ins fnl f: no ex cl home* **4/1**[3]

4 hd **Sing Something**[14] 4174 6-9-9 0..............................(p) MattieBatchelor 49
(Mrs C Gilbert, Jersey) *outpcd: 7th into st: kpt on one pce fnl f* **5/1**

5 1/2 **Lady Joanna Vassa (IRE)**[3] 4493 6-8-5 0 oh4..............................(v) PhilipPrince 30
(Richard Guest) *chsd ldrs: 4th into st: wnt 2nd and ev ch wl ins fnl f: wknd and lost pls last few strides* **7/1**

6 2 1/4 **Doctor Parkes**[39] 3173 13-9-7 0.............................. TimClark 38
(Natalie Lloyd-Beavis) *s.s: sn chsd ldrs: 5th into st: one pced* **5/1**

7 hd **Limelite (IRE)**[14] 4174 5-9-4 0..............................(p) MissSerenaBrotherton 34
(K Kukk, Jersey) *broke best: hdd after 1f: wnt on again 3f out: hdd wl ins fnl f: wknd rapidly* **10/1**

8 1 **Country Blue (FR)**[26] 3641 10-9-9 0..............................(p) DarraghKeogh 36
(Mrs A Malzard, Jersey) *led after 1f: hdd again 3f out: wknd fnl f* **7/2**[2]

9 1 **Honcho (IRE)**[14] 7-9-13 0.............................. VictoriaMalzard 37
(Mrs A Malzard, Jersey) *outpcd and a bhd: 8th into st: n.d* **9/1**

Owner Dajam Ltd **Bred** Stephanie Hanly **Trained** Limpley Stoke, Wilts

4686a PLANTAGENET H'CAP (TURF) 1m 2f

8:15 (8:15) 3-Y-O+ £1,780 (£640; £380)

RPR

1 **Wolf Hunter (IRE)**[14] 3-10-6 0..............................(b) CorentinSmeulders 71
(J Moon, Jersey) *trckd ldrs: 3rd into st: wnt on over 1f out: drvn out* **13/8**[1]

2 nk **Contingency Fee**[10] 4215 4-9-12 0..............................(p) GraceMcEntee 51
(Phil McEntee) *a.p: disp ld tl wnt on 6f out: hdd over 1f out: kpt on one pce* **9/4**[2]

3 3 **Ice Royal (IRE)**[26] 6-10-6 0..............................(t) MrFrederickTett 53
(Mrs A Malzard, Jersey) *mid-div: 5th into st: wnt 2nd and ev ch over 1f out: wknd and lost 2nd cl home* **6/1**

4 4 **Aussie Lyrics (FR)**[312] 9-10-12 0.............................. MattieBatchelor 51
(Mrs C Gilbert, Jersey) *hld up in rr: hdwy fr 4f out: 6th into st: kpt on one pce* **13/2**

5 hd **Captain James (FR)**[14] 9-9-5 0.............................. MorganRaine 30
(Mrs C Gilbert, Jersey) *hld up: 8th into st: late hdwy but nvr able to chal* **12/1**

6 hd **Hard To Handel**[26] 7-10-1 0.............................. MissSerenaBrotherton 39
(Mrs A Malzard, Jersey) *trckd ldrs: rdn and 4th into st: sn wknd* **5/2**[3]

7 1 **William Booth (IRE)**[14] 5-8-11 0..............................(v) GeorgeRooke 19
(Mrs C Gilbert, Jersey) *hld up: last into st: n.d* **12/1**

8 2 3/4 **Benoordenhout (IRE)**[14] 8-9-12 0 ow1..............................(p) MarkQuinlan 29
(T Le Brocq, Jersey) *disp ld tl 6f out: drvn along fr 3f out: wkd rapidly* **8/1**

9 1 **St Ouen (IRE)**[14] 3-9-0 0..............................(t) PhilipPrince 26
(K Kukk, Jersey) *mid-div: drvn and 7th into st: wknd* **16/1**

Owner D Moon & Mrs Caroline Michel **Bred** Tally-Ho Stud **Trained** St-Martin, Jersey

4687a MOST BEAUTIFUL SUNSET H'CAP (TURF) 1m 6f

8:50 (8:50) (0-60,0) 3-Y-O+ £1,780 (£640; £380)

RPR

1 **Kenoughty (FR)**[14] 3-9-2 0.............................. GeorgeRooke 48
(J Moon, Jersey) *dwlt: hld up: hdwy fr 3f out: c over to stand's rail st: led ins fnl f: push out* **10/3**[3]

2 5 **Safira Menina**[14] 7-10-12 0.............................. MrFrederickTett 50
(Mrs A Malzard, Jersey) *rel to r: hld up: hdwy fr 3f out: rdn to ld over 1f out: no ex whn hdd ins fnl f* **5/2**[2]

3 2 3/4 **Frivolous Prince (IRE)**[14] 4175 6-9-3 0..........(p) MissSerenaBrotherton 23
(Mrs C Gilbert, Jersey) *prom: wnt 2nd 6f out: ev ch over 1f out: one pced* **18/1**

4 1 **Fourni (IRE)**[14] 10-9-10 0..............................(p) VictoriaMalzard 29
(Mrs A Malzard, Jersey) *hld up: hdwy fr 4f out: ev ch 1f out: one pced* **11/2**

5 6 **Gabster (IRE)**[14] 6-10-11 0.............................. MarkQuinlan 35
(K Kukk, Jersey) *led: hdd over 1f out: wknd rapidly* **7/4**[1]

6 3 1/2 **Rainbow Charlie**[14] 2502 8-8-6 0 oh11 ow1..............................(v) GraceMcEntee
(Mrs A Corson, Jersey) *trckd ldr to 6f out: wknd fr 2f out* **28/1**

7 1 1/4 **Salve Helena (IRE)**[14] 4174 4-10-2 0.............................. SamTwiston-Davies 20
(T Le Brocq, Jersey) *mid-div: brief effrt fr over 2f out: sn wknd* **11/2**

8 3 1/2 **Grey Gem (IRE)**[14] 5987 8-8-13 0.............................. DarraghKeogh
(K Kukk, Jersey) *trckd ldrs: bhd fr 2f out* **20/1**

9 65 **Fintech (IRE)**[37] 5742 5-10-10 0..............................(t) PhilipPrince
(Colin Heard) *trckd ldrs: drvn and wknd fr 4f out: t.o* **7/2**

Owner Moya & Co **Bred** Petra Bloodstock Agency Ltd **Trained** St-Martin, Jersey

4097 AYR (L-H)

Sunday, July 7

OFFICIAL GOING: Good to firm (watered; 8.5)

Wind: Breezy, half against in sprints and in over 3f of home straight in races on the round course Weather: Fine, dry

4688 EBF MAIDEN STKS 6f

2:00 (2:01) (Class 5) 2-Y-O £3,428 (£1,020; £509; £254) Stalls Centre

Form RPR

1 **Macho Time (IRE)** 2-9-5 0.............................. CliffordLee 2 77
(K R Burke) *prom on outside: led over 2f out: sn rn green: rdn and r.o wl fr over 1f out: improve* **4/1**[3]

6 2 1 3/4 **Streaker**[46] 2957 2-9-5 0.............................. TomEaves 4 71
(Kevin Ryan) *wnt rt s: cl up: ev ch over 2f out to over 1f out: kpt on fnl f: nt pce of wnr* **12/1**

3 1 1/2 **Magic Twist (USA)** 2-9-0 0.............................. FrannyNorton 6 62
(Mark Johnston) *t.k.h to post: cl up: pushed along 2f out: kpt on ins fnl f* **3/1**[1]

4 *hd* **Dick Datchery (IRE)** 2-9-5 0 DanielTudhope 5 66+
(David O'Meara) *noisy in paddock: dwlt and checked s: hld up bhd ldng gp: effrt 2f out: rdn and one pce ins fnl f: bttr for r* **3/1**[1]

45 **5** *1 3/4* **Spanish Time**[37] [3290] 2-9-5 0 JasonHart 7 61
(Keith Dalgleish) *led to over 2f out: rdn and outpcd fr over 1f out* **9/1**

6 *hd* **Light The Fuse (IRE)** 2-9-5 0 (w) BenCurtis 1 60+
(K R Burke) *slowly away: rn green in rr: hdwy over 1f out: no further imp fnl f* **7/2**[2]

6 **7** *2 1/4* **Ralphy Boy Two (IRE)**[11] [4237] 2-9-5 0 GrahamLee 3 54
(Alistair Whillans) *prom: rdn and outpcd over 2f out: btn over 1f out* **25/1**

1m 12.28s (-0.82) **Going Correction** -0.25s/f (Firm) **7** Ran SP% **113.8**
Speed ratings (Par 94): **95,92,90,90,88 87,84**
CSF £47.96 TOTE £5.20: £2.00, £4.50; EX 40.60 Trifecta £196.20.
Owner J C Fretwell **Bred** Denis McDonnell **Trained** Middleham Moor, N Yorks

FOCUS
Those with previous experience set a very moderate standard, so this appeared to revolve around the four newcomers. Punters struggled to find a favourite and the form is probably nothing out of the ordinary. The opening level is fluid.

4689 AYRGOLDCUP.CO.UK H'CAP 1m 2f
2:30 (2:31) (Class 4) (0-80,83) 3-Y-O+
£5,272 (£1,568; £784; £400; £400; £400) **Stalls** Low

Form RPR

4061 **1** **Five Helmets (IRE)**[18] [4000] 3-8-10 **72** (p) JamieGormley 4 79
(Iain Jardine) *hld up: effrt on outside over 2f out: sustained run fnl f to ld cl home* **9/2**[3]

420/ **2** *nk* **Wild Shot**[47] [2950] 5-8-11 **63** (t) JamesSullivan 9 69
(Noel C Kelly, Ire) *cl up: wnt 2nd 1/2-way: led gng wl over 2f out: rdn over 1f out: kpt on fnl f: hdd cl home* **14/1**

0025 **3** *nk* **Regal Mirage (IRE)**[6] [4446] 5-9-4 **70** PaulHanagan 6 75
(Tim Easterby) *prom: hdwy and ev ch over 2f out to ins fnl f: kpt on: hld cl home* **10/1**

6262 **4** *3/4* **Four Kingdoms (IRE)**[18] [4001] 5-8-13 **70** AndrewBreslin(5) 3 74
(R Mike Smith) *led 1f: chsd ldr to 1/2-way: cl up: outpcd over 2f out: rallied over 1f out: kpt on ins fnl f* **12/1**

04 **5** *1* **Cockalorum (IRE)**[22] [3867] 4-9-13 **79** (p) BenCurtis 5 81
(Roger Fell) *midfield on ins: angled rt and effrt over 2f out: kpt on same pce ins fnl f* **3/1**[1]

-045 **6** *nse* **Dark Lochnagar (USA)**[36] [3358] 3-9-1 **77** JasonHart 2 79
(Keith Dalgleish) *s.i.s: hld up: n.m.r over 2f out: stdy hdwy fr over 1f out: kpt on: nrst fin (jockey said colt was denied a clear run on several occasions from 2f out)* **5/1**

5505 **7** *3/4* **Kharbetation (IRE)**[17] [4035] 6-9-7 **73** (p) DavidNolan 10 73
(David O'Meara) *led after 1f: rdn and hdd over 2f out: rallied: no ex ins fnl f (jockey said gelding had no more to give having made the running)* **20/1**

4531 **8** *3/4* **Autretot (FR)**[9] [4333] 4-10-3 **83** DanielTudhope 1 81
(David O'Meara) *hld up in tch: stdy hdwy whn n.m.r over 2f out: rdn over 1f out: sn no ex* **10/3**[2]

311/ **9** *1* **Pete So High (GER)**[366] [6723] 5-10-0 **80** (w) GrahamLee 11 76
(Julia Brooke) *hld up: pushed along over 2f out: no imp fr over 1f out* **33/1**

0001 **10** *3* **Restive (IRE)**[18] [4003] 6-8-11 **66** BenRobinson(3) 7 56
(Jim Goldie) *s.i.s: hld up: rdn along over 2f out: nvr able to chal* **25/1**

2/00 **11** *8* **Ennjaaz (IRE)**[19] [3973] 5-9-5 **74** ConnorMurtagh(3) 8 48
(Marjorie Fife) *hld up in midfield: drvn and outpcd over 2f out: sn btn* **66/1**

2m 7.66s (-4.74) **Going Correction** -0.25s/f (Firm)
WFA 3 from 4yo+ 10lb **11** Ran SP% **119.4**
Speed ratings (Par 105): **108,107,107,106,106 106,105,104,104,101 95**
CSF £63.37 CT £607.66 TOTE £5.00: £1.70, £3.80, £2.80; EX 76.00 Trifecta £871.30.
Owner Brendan Keogh **Bred** Ms Natalie Cleary **Trained** Carrutherstown, D'fries & G'way

FOCUS
Add 9 yards. A fair handicap and it produced a close finish. The third has been rated to his recent 1m2f best.

4690 ISABEL NECESSARY ON A BIKE H'CAP 1m 2f
3:05 (3:07) (Class 6) (0-60,60) 3-Y-O+
£2,781 (£827; £413; £400; £400; £400) **Stalls** Low

Form RPR

5322 **1** **Neileta**[18] [4003] 3-9-4 **58** (p) DuranFentiman 5 64
(Tim Easterby) *plld hrd early: cl up: led over 2f out: rdn and hld on wl fnl f* **3/1**[2]

-0 **2** *1/2* **Greengage (IRE)**[38] [3251] 4-9-9 **53** (h[1]) JasonHart 8 57+
(Tristan Davidson) *hld up: effrt whn nt clr run over 2f out to appr fnl f: kpt on wl to take 2nd cl home (jockey said filly was denied a clear run inside 2f out and again in the final furlong)* **15/2**

4045 **3** *nse* **Followme Followyou (IRE)**[18] [4003] 3-9-1 **55** FrannyNorton 2 60
(Mark Johnston) *hld up in tch: effrt and rdn 2f out: chsd wnr ins fnl f tl towards fin: no ex* **7/1**[3]

-061 **4** *1* **Myklachi (FR)**[18] [4005] 3-9-6 **60** (h) DanielTudhope 7 63
(David O'Meara) *hld up in midfield: rdn over 2f out: hdwy fnl f: kpt on fin* **5/2**[1]

0-00 **5** *1* **Doon Star**[26] [3705] 4-9-6 **50** AlistairRawlinson 11 50
(Jim Goldie) *in tch: rdn and hdwy to chse ldrs over 1f out: kpt on same pce ins fnl f (jockey said filly hung left in the straight)* **22/1**

0604 **6** *2 3/4* **Remmy D (IRE)**[16] [4054] 4-9-11 **58** (p) BenRobinson(3) 13 53
(Jim Goldie) *dwlt: sn rcvrd and pressed ldr after 1f: ev ch over 2f out to over 1f out: wknd ins fnl f* **9/1**

0050 **7** *nk* **Haymarket**[16] [4054] 10-8-13 **48** AndrewBreslin(5) 10 42
(R Mike Smith) *dwlt: gd hdwy to ld after 1f: hdd over 2f out: rallied: wknd fnl f (jockey said gelding reared as the gates opened and was slowly away; vet said gelding lost its right fore shoe)* **16/1**

056- **8** *shd* **Exclusive Waters (IRE)**[51] [2815] 9-9-8 **52** (b) BenCurtis 1 46
(Garvan Donnelly, Ire) *missed break: hld up: effrt on ins 2f out: kpt on fnl f: nvr able to chal (jockey said gelding was slowly away)* **7/1**[3]

-000 **9** *nse* **Morley Gunner (IRE)**[25] [3718] 4-9-1 **45** RobbieDowney 9 39
(S Donohoe, Ire) *hld up: effrt on outside 2f out: kpt on fnl f: no imp* **50/1**

-400 **10** *1 3/4* **Eyreborn (IRE)**[46] [2964] 5-9-1 **45** TomEaves 14 36
(Keith Dalgleish) *prom: drvn along over 2f out: wknd over 1f out* **50/1**

400 **11** *hd* **Lizzie Loch**[25] [3721] 3-8-10 **50** JamesSullivan 12 41
(Alistair Whillans) *s.i.s: hld up: rdn over 2f out: nvr able to chal* **40/1**

0-64 **12** *1/2* **Clayton Hall (IRE)**[26] [3705] 6-9-3 **47** (p) GrahamLee 6 36
(John Wainwright) *hld up towards rr: drvn and outpcd over 2f out: sn btn* **33/1**

13 *2* **Another Dressin (IRE)**[23] [3831] 4-9-1 **45** (p) LewisEdmunds 3 31
(Garvan Donnelly, Ire) *hld up on ins: drvn and outpcd over 2f out: sn btn* **25/1**

0066 **14** *3 3/4* **Just Heather (IRE)**[26] [3681] 5-9-1 **45** (p) PaulHanagan 4 23
(John Wainwright) *led 1f: cl up tl rdn and wknd over 2f out* **66/1**

2m 9.08s (-3.32) **Going Correction** -0.25s/f (Firm)
WFA 3 from 4yo+ 10lb **14** Ran SP% **125.2**
Speed ratings (Par 101): **103,102,102,101,100 98,98,98,98,97 96,96,94,91**
CSF £25.57 CT £153.68 TOTE £4.10: £1.70, £3.30, £2.70; EX 30.20 Trifecta £237.80.
Owner E A Brook & Partner **Bred** Howard J A Russell **Trained** Great Habton, N Yorks

FOCUS
Add 9 yards. Very moderate stuff, though another competitive race with less than a length separating the first three home. The winner dwarfed his rivals and looks sure to go jumping before long. The fourth has been rated to his latest effort.

4691 BOOK SCOTTISH SUN LADIES NIGHT H'CAP 5f 110y
3:35 (3:38) (Class 4) (0-85,85) 4-Y-O+ **£5,272** (£1,568; £784; £400; £400) **Stalls** Centre

Form RPR

0666 **1** **Harome (IRE)**[15] [4100] 5-9-7 **85** BenCurtis 5 96+
(Roger Fell) *dwlt: sn prom: shkn up and hdwy to ld 1f out: kpt on wl fnl f: eased nr fin* **5/4**[1]

0321 **2** *1* **Nibras Again**[8] [4406] 5-9-2 **80** GrahamLee 3 86
(Paul Midgley) *led: rdn and hdd 1f out: kpt on: nt pce of wnr* **7/4**[2]

4625 **3** *1 3/4* **Primo's Comet**[15] [4100] 4-8-11 **75** AlistairRawlinson 2 75
(Jim Goldie) *t.k.h: cl up: effrt and edgd lft over 1f out: kpt on same pce ins fnl f* **11/2**[3]

1400 **4** *3/4* **Our Place In Loule**[16] [4059] 6-8-5 **69** PhilDennis 1 66
(Noel Wilson) *dwlt: hld up in tch: effrt and rdn over 1f out: no imp fnl f* **25/1**

240- **5** *1 3/4* **Prince Ahwahnee**[329] [6054] 4-9-7 **85** SamJames 4 76
(Phillip Makin) *chsd ldr to 1/2-way: wknd over 1f out* **8/1**

1m 5.32s (-1.18) **Going Correction** -0.25s/f (Firm) **5** Ran SP% **111.1**
Speed ratings (Par 105): **97,95,93,92,90**
CSF £3.76 TOTE £2.00: £1.30, £1.10; EX 4.20 Trifecta £8.40.
Owner Middleham Park Racing LXXI & Partner **Bred** Limestone & Tara Studs **Trained** Nawton, N Yorks

FOCUS
A small field and not as much depth as you'd generally associate with a sprint handicap at this level. The winner won readily and could well reappear back here under a penalty on Monday. The second has been rated to his York win.

4692 MONDAY 15 JULY IS FAMILY DAY H'CAP 1m
4:10 (4:12) (Class 3) (0-95,97) 3-Y-O+ **£9,056** (£2,695; £1,346; £673) **Stalls** Low

Form RPR

0462 **1** **Nicholas T**[5] [4490] 7-8-12 **81** BenRobinson(3) 2 88+
(Jim Goldie) *hld up: effrt and hdwy over 1f out: led ins fnl f: kpt on strly* **7/4**[1]

1416 **2** *nk* **Smile A Mile (IRE)**[6] [4445] 3-8-10 **85** FrannyNorton 4 89
(Mark Johnston) *pressed ldr: rdn and sltly outpcd over 1f out: rallied and pressed wnr wl ins fnl f: jst hld* **9/2**[3]

-064 **3** *3/4* **Calvados Spirit**[16] [4079] 6-8-13 **79** TonyHamilton 7 83
(Richard Fahey) *t.k.h: led at ordinary gallop: rdn over 1f out: hdd ins fnl f: kpt on same pce* **5/1**

3116 **4** *1* **Fayez (IRE)**[17] [4021] 5-10-3 **97** (p) DanielTudhope 1 99+
(David O'Meara) *hld up in last pl: effrt and pushed along over 1f out: kpt on fnl f: nt pce to chal* **7/2**[2]

56-3 **5** *1* **Glasses Up (USA)**[16] [4057] 4-9-3 **83** PaddyMathers 3 82
(R Mike Smith) *t.k.h: prom: rdn 2f out: kpt on same pce ins fnl f* **12/1**

4-00 **6** *1 1/2* **Banksea**[15] [4097] 6-9-12 **92** (h) JamesSullivan 6 88
(Marjorie Fife) *dwlt: t.k.h: hld up in tch: effrt and edgd lft over 1f out: no imp fnl f* **18/1**

51-0 **7** *nk* **Summer Daydream (IRE)**[11] [4242] 3-9-6 **95** PaulHanagan 5 88
(Keith Dalgleish) *prom: drvn along over 2f out: wknd over 1f out* **11/1**

1m 41.06s (-1.74) **Going Correction** -0.25s/f (Firm)
WFA 3 from 4yo+ 9lb **7** Ran SP% **114.7**
Speed ratings (Par 107): **98,97,96,95,94 93,93**
CSF £10.03 TOTE £2.20: £1.10, £2.60; EX 9.00 Trifecta £29.40.
Owner James Callow & J S Goldie **Bred** W M Johnstone **Trained** Uplawmoor, E Renfrews

FOCUS
Add 9 yards. A decent enough edition of this feature handicap and a good effort from the winner, who overcame an unsatisfactory slow early pace. The third has been rated to this year's form.

4693 AYR FLOWER SHOW @AYR RACECOURSE H'CAP 7f 50y
4:40 (4:41) (Class 5) (0-75,77) 3-Y-O+
£3,428 (£1,020; £509; £400; £400; £400) **Stalls** High

Form RPR

1642 **1** **Global Spirit**[3] [4552] 4-10-0 **72** (p) BenCurtis 5 81+
(Roger Fell) *hld up: hdwy over 1f out: rdn to ld ins fnl f: r.o* **11/8**[1]

0320 **2** *1/2* **Esprit De Corps**[23] [3813] 5-10-0 **72** DanielTudhope 2 79
(David Barron) *hld up: smooth hdwy against far rail to ld over 1f out: rdn and hdd ins fnl f: kpt on: hld nr fin* **7/2**[2]

5614 **3** *1 1/2* **Pudding Chare (IRE)**[16] [4060] 5-8-11 **60** (t) AndrewBreslin(5) 7 63+
(R Mike Smith) *dwlt: hld up: rdn over 2f out: hdwy to chse ldng pair ins fnl f: r.o* **20/1**

3203 **4** *3* **Lucky Violet (IRE)**[10] [4278] 7-9-6 **64** (h) DavidNolan 6 59
(Linda Perratt) *hld up: hdwy on outside over 1f out: rdn and no imp ins fnl f* **10/1**

-504 **5** *2 1/4* **Welcoming (FR)**[20] [3935] 3-9-11 **77** FrannyNorton 9 63
(Mark Johnston) *prom: effrt and rdn 2f out: wknd ins fnl f (jockey said filly slipped on the bend)* **7/1**[3]

-045 **6** *3/4* **Final Frontier (IRE)**[12] [4207] 6-9-7 **65** (b) JamesSullivan 10 53
(Ruth Carr) *prom: rdn and outpcd over 2f out: n.d after* **16/1**

5010 **7** *2* **Smugglers Creek (IRE)**[11] [4239] 5-9-9 **67** (p) JamieGormley 3 49
(Iain Jardine) *chsd ldr: rdn over 2f out: wknd fnl f* **20/1**

2003 **8** *nk* **Strong Steps**[16] [4058] 7-9-8 **66** (p) AlistairRawlinson 4 53
(Jim Goldie) *hld up in midfield: effrt whn nt clr run fr over 2f out to ins fnl f: nvr able to chal (jockey said gelding was denied a clear run on several occasions in the home straight)* **11/1**

-040 **9** *1/2* **Theatre Of War (IRE)**[15] [4099] 3-9-11 **77** (p[1]) TomEaves 8 54
(Keith Dalgleish) *led to over 1f out: sn rdn and wknd* **11/1**

5600 **10** *5* **Usain Boat (IRE)**[27] [3645] 3-8-13 **65** GrahamLee 1 29
(Noel C Kelly, Ire) *hld up: drvn and outpcd over 2f out: sn btn* **50/1**

1m 28.7s (-3.80) **Going Correction** -0.25s/f (Firm)
WFA 3 from 4yo+ 8lb **10** Ran SP% **120.0**
Speed ratings (Par 103): **111,110,108,105,102 101,99,99,98,92**
CSF £6.00 CT £69.61 TOTE £2.00: £1.10, £2.00, £4.80; EX 7.70 Trifecta £76.60.
Owner Arthington Barn Racing **Bred** Car Colston Hall Stud **Trained** Nawton, N Yorks

FOCUS
Add 9 yards. This featured some largely consistent sorts, though the combined records of the first and second favourites was just 2-38. The market got it spot on and it was furlong for the furlong, the quickest comparable time of the afternoon. The second has been rated to form.

4694 ENTER NOW FOR THE AYR CLASSIC RUN AMATEUR RIDERS' H'CAP 5f

5:15 (5:19) (Class 6) (0-65,67) 4-Y-O+ **£2,682** (£832; £415; £400; £400) **Stalls** Centre

Form RPR

0003 1 **Robot Boy (IRE)**[4] 4514 9-11-4 **67**.................... MissCatherineWalton 2 74
(Marjorie Fife) *cl up far side: rdn to ld over 1f out: edgd rt: kpt on wl fnl f* **12/1**

6006 2 1 1/2 **Teepee Time**[37] 3291 6-9-12 **47**..................(b) MissMichelleMullineaux 9 49
(Michael Mullineaux) *wnt lft s: racd centre: chsd ldr to over 2f out: sn hung lft and outpcd: rallied to regain 2nd towards fin* **33/1**

0466 3 1/2 **Jeffrey Harris**[16] 4059 4-10-6 **55**........................ MrJamesHarding 13 55
(Jim Goldie) *hld up on nr side: rdn and hdwy over 1f out: kpt on fnl f to take 3rd pl cl home: nt pce to chal* **10/1**

5233 4 nse **B Fifty Two (IRE)**[6] 4434 10-10-11 **60**..............(vt) MissJoannaMason 7 60
(Marjorie Fife) *prom centre: effrt and pushed along over 1f out: wnt 2nd ins fnl f: no ex and lost two pls towards fin* **6/1**

3333 5 1 1/4 **National Glory (IRE)**[20] 3936 4-11-0 **63**..............(b) MissEmmaSayer 6 58
(Archie Watson) *led in centre to over 1f out: rdn and one pce fnl f* **9/2**[2]

/002 5 dht **Mr Greenlight**[2] 4586 4-10-9 **58**.......................... MissEmilyEasterby 12 53
(Tim Easterby) *in tch in centre: effrt and pushed along over 1f out: one pce fnl f* **7/2**[1]

5610 7 nk **Oriental Splendour (IRE)**[12] 4212 7-9-8 **48**.....(p) MissEmilyBullock[(5)] 4 42
(Ruth Carr) *in tch towards far side: effrt and ch over 1f out: no ex fnl f* **7/1**

-400 8 nk **Brendan (IRE)**[16] 4059 6-9-5 **47**........................ MissShannonWatts[(7)] 1 40
(Jim Goldie) *dwlt: bhd far side: effrt over 1f out: nvr rchd ldrs* **25/1**

660- 9 shd **Red Forever**[214] 9415 8-9-7 **45**..................(p[1]) MissHelenCuthbert[(3)] 14 38
(Helen Cuthbert) *fly-jmpd s: bhd nr side tl hdwy fnl f: nrst fin (jockey said gelding missed the break and jumped awkwardly)* **66/1**

4600 10 3/4 **Burmese Blazer (IRE)**[16] 4059 4-10-12 **61**..............(h) MrsCarolBartley 5 51
(Jim Goldie) *bhd centre: pushed along and shortlived effrt over 1f out: sn no imp (jockey said gelding missed the break)* **11/2**[3]

-330 11 2 **Mr Shelby (IRE)**[46] 2958 5-10-0 **54**..................(p) MrMatthewEnnis[(5)] 15 37
(S Donohoe, Ire) *hld up nr side: rdn over 2f out: wknd over 1f out* **9/1**

0-00 12 1/2 **Zizum**[9] 4319 4-9-3 **45**.. MrEireannCagney[(7)] 3 26
(Alan Berry) *bhd towards far side: rdn along 1/2-way: nvr rchd ldrs* **100/1**

00-4 13 hd **Raise A Billion**[4] 4514 8-9-3 **45**......................... MrLiamHamblett[(7)] 11 25
(Alan Berry) *midfield nr side: struggling 2f out: sn btn* **66/1**

6344 14 1 1/2 **Fast Track**[134] 883 8-10-9 **63**............................. MissCharlotteCrane[(5)] 8 38
(Marjorie Fife) *midfield in centre: rdn and outpcd over 2f out: sn btn* **28/1**

50/0 15 7 **Ya Boy Sir (IRE)**[10] 4276 12-9-3 **45**..................(p) MrConnorWood[(7)] 10
(Alistair Whillans) *dwlt: bhd centre: struggling 1/2-way: nvr on terms* **80/1**

58.57s (-1.43) **Going Correction** -0.25s/f (Firm) **15 Ran SP% 124.8**
Speed ratings (Par 101): **101,98,97,97,95 95,95,94,94,93 90,89,89,86,75**
CSF £372.28 CT £4165.94 TOTE £15.30: £4.80, £11.50, £2.90; EX 471.20 Trifecta £4255.30.
Owner Unrefined Racing **Bred** Corduff Stud Ltd **Trained** Stillington, N Yorks

FOCUS
A competitive and strongly run edition of this amateur riders' handicap. Marjorie Fife made it three wins in the race in the space of four years. The winner has been rated to this year's best, and the form looks straightforward in behind.
T/Jkpt: £2,222.20 to a £1 stake. Pool: £14,084.51 - 4.5 winning units T/Plt: £80.80 to a £1 stake. Pool: £101,169.43 - 913.16 winning units T/Qpdt: £3.80 to a £1 stake. Pool: £12,489.65 - 2,404.27 winning units **Richard Young**

4695 - 4702a (Foreign Racing) - See Raceform Interactive

4532
DEAUVILLE (R-H)
Sunday, July 7

OFFICIAL GOING: Polytrack: standard; turf: good

4703a QATAR PRIX KISTENA (LISTED RACE) (3YO) (STRAIGHT COURSE) (TURF) 6f

1:35 3-Y-O **£24,774** (£9,909; £7,432; £4,954; £2,477)

RPR

1 **Far Above (IRE)**[27] 3661 3-8-13 0.......................... PJMcDonald 2 100
(James Tate) *racd keenly: restrained in share of 3rd: drvn to chse ldr wl over 1f out: styd on wl to ld last 100yds: hld on fr fast-fining 2nd* **32/5**[2]

2 snk **Duhail (IRE)**[31] 3-8-13 0.......................... VincentCheminaud 5 100
(A Fabre, France) **9/10**[1]

3 shd **We Go (FR)**[29] 3621 3-8-13 0.......................... Pierre-CharlesBoudot 3 100
(H-A Pantall, France) **22/1**

4 1 1/4 **Milord's Song (FR)**[29] 3621 3-8-13 0.......................... CristianDemuro 6 96
(S Wattel, France) **14/1**

5 1 1/2 **Eagleway (FR)**[29] 3621 3-9-3 0.......................... ChristopheSoumillon 9 95
(Andrea Marcialis, France) **87/10**

6 nse **Epic Hero (FR)**[70] 2166 3-8-13 0.......................... MickaelBarzalona 8 91
(A Fabre, France) *chsd ldng pair outside: pushed along and edgd rt wl over 1f out: dropped away fnl f* **13/2**[3]

7 snk **Shafran Mnm (IRE)**[27] 3-9-0 0.......................... FrankieDettori 7 91
(Andrea Marcialis, France) **79/10**

8 hd **Happy Odyssey (IRE)**[59] 2564 3-8-9 0.......................... StephanePasquier 4 86
(N Clement, France) **23/1**

9 7 **Reticent Angel (IRE)**[22] 3855 3-8-9 0..................(p) GeraldMosse 1 63
(Clive Cox) *hld up towards rr: niggled along sn after 1/2-way: rdn and btn fr 1 1/2f out* **28/1**

1m 8.73s (-2.27) **9 Ran SP% 119.7**
PARI-MUTUEL (all including 1 euro stake): WIN 7.40; PLACE 2.20, 1.50, 3.60; DF 6.90.
Owner Sheikh Rashid Dalmook Al Maktoum **Bred** Mohamed Abdul Malik **Trained** Newmarket, Suffolk

4704a QATAR GRAND H'CAP DE NORMANDIE (4YO+) (ROUND COURSE) (TURF) 1m (R)

2:15 4-Y-O+
£31,531 (£11,981; £8,828; £5,045; £2,522; £1,891)

RPR

1 **Sandyssime (FR)**[48] 3136 4-8-3 0.......................... AlexandreChesneau 2 82
(G Botti, France) **97/10**

2 nk **Dark American (FR)**[31] 5-8-11 0..................(b) ChristopheSoumillon 5 89
(V Sartori, France) **19/5**[1]

3 1/2 **Larno (FR)**[52] 5-8-4 0.......................... EddyHardouin 1 81
(M Boutin, France) **18/1**

4 nk **Gloria**[39] 4-8-4 0.......................... AlexisBadel 3 80
(Mme M Bollack-Badel, France) **12/1**

5 nk **Teston (FR)**[48] 3136 4-8-13 0.......................... AurelienLemaitre 7 89
(P Bary, France) **12/1**

6 hd **Diwan Senora (FR)**[22] 3879 6-9-4 0..................(p) JeromeCabre 6 93
(Y Barberot, France) **11/1**

7 3/4 **Jumpin' Jack Flash (FR)**[16] 5-8-13 0.......................... MickaelBarzalona 8 86
(T Lemer, France) **14/1**

7 dht **Walec**[31] 7-8-8 0.......................... MaximeGuyon 4 81
(N Caullery, France) **13/2**[2]

9 2 1/2 **French Pegasus (FR)**[52] 2782 4-8-6 0.......................... IoritzMendizabal 9 74
(Y Barberot, France) **9/1**[3]

10 3/4 **Wetrov (FR)**[41] 4-8-5 0.......................... MickaelBerto 10 71
(R Rohne, Germany) **45/1**

11 shd **Uther Pendragon (IRE)**[6] 4450 4-8-5 0..................(p) AnthonyCrastus 14 71
(J S Moore) *sn prom: chsd ldr after 2f: 2nd and pushed along over 2f out: wknd ins fnl f* **28/1**

12 nk **Millfield (FR)**[47] 6-9-4 0.......................... CristianDemuro 11 83
(D Smaga, France) **14/1**

13 nse **Ziveri (FR)**[48] 3136 4-8-6 0..................(b) StephanePasquier 15 71
(F Rossi, France) **14/1**

14 hd **Esperitum (FR)**[21] 5-8-4 0.......................... DelphineSantiago 12 68
(Carina Fey, France) **24/1**

15 6 **Rayon Vert (FR)**[31] 5-9-6 0.......................... FabriceVeron 16 71
(Laurent Loisel, France) **20/1**

16 snk **George The Prince (FR)**[31] 5-8-7 0..................(b) VincentCheminaud 13 57
(G Doleuze, France) **27/1**

1m 39.47s (-1.33) **16 Ran SP% 120.4**
PARI-MUTUEL (all including 1 euro stake): WIN 10.70; PLACE 3.50, 2.20, 4.70; DF 23.60.
Owner Moreno Meiohas & Simone Carnevali **Bred** D Malingue **Trained** France

4705a QATAR PRIX JEAN PRAT (GROUP 1) (3YO COLTS & FILLIES) (STRAIGHT COURSE) (TURF) 7f

2:52 3-Y-O **£205,909** (£82,378; £41,189; £20,576; £10,306)

RPR

1 **Too Darn Hot**[19] 3951 3-9-2 0.......................... FrankieDettori 10 125
(John Gosden) *trckd ldrs in far side gp: rdn under 2f out: led 1 1/2f out: kpt on strly and drew clr fnl f: comf* **4/5**[1]

2 3 **Space Blues (IRE)**[15] 4092 3-9-2 0.......................... JamesDoyle 5 116
(Charlie Appleby) *hld up in far side gp: tk clsr order as gps merged 2f out: rdn under 2f out: styd on fnl f: wnt 2nd 150yds out: no imp on comfortable wnr* **31/10**[2]

3 2 **Fox Champion (IRE)**[19] 3951 3-9-2 0.......................... OisinMurphy 11 111
(Richard Hannon) *led far side gp: rdn over 2f out: overall ldr as gps merged 2f out: hdd 1 1/2f out: kpt on same pce* **24/1**

4 1 1/2 **Munitions (USA)**[56] 2668 3-9-2 0.......................... MickaelBarzalona 2 107
(A Fabre, France) *hld up towards rr of midfield in nrside gp: rdn and kpt on fr 2f out* **13/1**

5 snk **Namos (GER)**[36] 3369 3-9-2 0.......................... WladimirPanov 1 107
(D Moser, Germany) *hld up in rr of nrside gp: rdn 2f out: kpt on fnl f* **24/1**

6 nse **Watan**[50] 2834 3-9-2 0.......................... ChristopheSoumillon 3 106
(Richard Hannon) *led nrside gp: rdn to chse ldr as gps merged 2f out: wknd fnl f* **32/1**

7 1 3/4 **Pretty Boy (IRE)**[29] 3621 3-9-2 0.......................... MaximeGuyon 6 102
(Mme Pia Brandt, France) *chsd ldr in nrside gp: rdn 2 1/2f out: wknd steadily fr under 2f out: sltly hmpd 1f out* **51/1**

8 nk **Graignes (FR)**[56] 2668 3-9-2 0.......................... CristianDemuro 9 101
(Y Barberot, France) *hld up in far side gp: tk clsr order as gps merged 2f out: sn rdn and outpcd: wknd fnl f* **10/1**[3]

9 1 3/4 **Pure Zen (FR)**[35] 3387 3-8-13 0.......................... StephanePasquier 8 93
(Gianluca Bietolini, France) *midfield in nrside gp: rdn and no imp fr over 2f out: wknd fnl f* **22/1**

10 1 3/4 **Urwald**[38] 3289 3-9-2 0.......................... Pierre-CharlesBoudot 4 91
(A Fabre, France) *dwlt: hld up in nrside gp: a towards rr* **27/1**

11 2 **Azano**[21] 3903 3-9-2 0.......................... RobertHavlin 12 86
(John Gosden) *dwlt: chsd ldr in far side gp: rdn 2 1/f out: outpcd appr 2f out: wknd over 1f out* **31/1**

12 3/4 **Royal Marine (IRE)**[19] 3951 3-9-2 0.......................... AdamKirby 7 84
(Saeed bin Suroor) *trckd ldrs in nrside gp: rdn 2 1/2f out: wknd under 2f out: sn btn* **60/1**

1m 21.29s (-7.01) **12 Ran SP% 121.8**
PARI-MUTUEL (all including 1 euro stake): WIN 1.90; PLACE 1.20, 1.70, 2.80; DF 3.20.
Owner Lord Lloyd-Webber **Bred** Watership Down Stud **Trained** Newmarket, Suffolk

FOCUS
This Group 1 contest can often go to a decent colt, with subsequent dual Dubai World Cup winner Thunder Snow the most notable recent winner. The field split into two groups on leaving the stalls, one kept to the stands' side and the other stayed in the middle. Being towards the centre early seemed key, although wherever the market leader had been drawn you suspect he'd have collected. The going was said to have been really quick by the winner's trainer.

4706a QATAR PRIX DE LA CALONNE - FONDS EUROPEEN DE L'ELEVAGE (LISTED RACE) (4YO+ FILLIES & MARES) (STR) 1m (R)

3:30 4-Y-O+ **£21,621** (£8,648; £6,486; £4,324; £2,162)

RPR

1 **Joplin (GER)**[27] 5-8-11 0.......................... FrankieDettori 7 102
(D Fechner, Germany) **9/1**

2 1/2 **Silvery Mist (FR)**[56] 2670 4-8-11 0.......................... StephanePasquier 9 101
(F Chappet, France) **9/1**

3 1 3/4 **Di Fede (IRE)**[18] 3986 4-9-1 0.......................... HarryBentley 5 101
(Ralph Beckett) *cl up in stands' side gp: 4th and rdn w 1 1/2f to run: swtchd ins to rail and kpt on fnl f: nt pce of front two* **14/5**[1]

4 1 **Cherry Lady (GER)**[21] 3907 4-9-1 0.......................... WladimirPanov 1 98
(P Schiergen, Germany) **38/1**

5 snk **Zavrinka (FR)**[31] 4-8-11 0.......................... CristianDemuro 6 94
(V Sartori, France) **83/10**

6 1/2 **Contrive (IRE)**[36] 3342 4-8-11 0.......................... OisinMurphy 4 93
(Roger Varian) *trckd ldr on stands' side: shkn up to press ldr 2 1/2f out: led and scrubbed along more than 2f out: hdd appr fnl f: plugged on at one pce* **89/10**

7 2 **Richmond Avenue (IRE)**[22] 4-8-11 0.......................... MickaelBarzalona 3 88
(A Fabre, France) *racd keenly: hld up in middle of stands' side gp: sltly impeded: lost pl and in last wl over 2f out: styd on past btn horses last 125yds* **29/10**[2]

8 ¾ **Dathanna (IRE)**[38] 3288 4-8-11 0 JamesDoyle 2 87
(Charlie Appleby) *led stands' side gp of eight: pushed along whn pressed 2 1/2f out: hdd more than 2f out: grad dropped away last 1 1/2f* **71/10**[3]

9 2 ½ **Pure Shores**[8] 4393 5-8-11 0 GeraldMosse 10 81
(Ian Williams) *tacked ins fr wd draw: in rr of stands' side gp: angled out and drvn but no imp fnl 1 1/2f: nvr in contention* **17/1**

10 1 **Shepherd Market (IRE)**[29] 3588 4-9-1 0 AdamKirby 8 82
(Clive Cox) *led pair in centre of crse: 3rd overall and drvn 3f out: wl hld fnl 1 1/2f* **16/1**

1m 36.08s (-4.72) **10 Ran SP% 119.2**
PARI-MUTUEL (all including 1 euro stake): WIN 10.00; PLACE 2.70, 2.60, 2.00; DF 31.60.
Owner Stall Captain's Friends **Bred** Gestut Karlshof **Trained** Baden-Baden, Germany

4683 HAMBURG (R-H)
Sunday, July 7

OFFICIAL GOING: Turf: good

4707a IDEE 150TH DEUTSCHES DERBY (GROUP 1) (3YO COLTS & FILLIES) (TURF) 1m 4f
3:50 3-Y-0 **£351,351** (£117,117; £70,270; £35,135; £11,711)

RPR

1 **Laccario (GER)**[27] 3674 3-9-2 0 EduardoPedroza 4 113
(A Wohler, Germany) *in tch in midfield: trckd ldrs 3 1/2f out: swtchd to ins rail on turn into st over 2f out and sn rdn: led 1 1/2f out: kpt on strly fnl f: rdn out* **2/1**[1]

2 1 ¼ **Django Freeman (GER)**[27] 3674 3-9-2 0 LukasDelozier 3 111
(Henk Grewe, Germany) *midfield: smooth hdwy fr 3f out: rdn to chse ldrs 2f out: led briefly under 2f out: hdd 1 1/2f out: kpt on fnl f: no imp on wnr* **33/10**[3]

3 1 ¼ **Accon (GER)**[35] 3385 3-9-2 0 JanPalik 11 109
(Markus Klug, Germany) *midfield: rdn over 2f out: styd on wl fnl f: nrst fin* **172/10**

4 nk **Quest The Moon (GER)**[42] 3120 3-9-2 0 AndraschStarke 15 109
(Frau S Steinberg, Germany) *racd keenly: in tch: wd into st: rdn and ev ch 2f out: kpt on same pce fnl f* **31/10**[2]

5 1 ½ **Surrey Thunder (FR)**[35] 3385 3-9-2 0 JasonWatson 1 106
(Joseph Tuite) *trckd ldrs: rdn to ld over 2f out: hdd under 2f out: drvn and no ex fnl f* **227/10**

6 ½ **Dschingis First (GER)**[27] 3674 3-9-2 0 AdriedeVries 9 105
(Markus Klug, Germany) *towards rr of midfield on outside: v wd into st: rdn 2f out: styd on fnl f: nrst fin* **104/10**

7 nk **Moonlight Man (GER)**[35] 3385 3-9-2 0 MaximPecheur 10 105
(Markus Klug, Germany) *towards rr of midfield: hdwy appr 2f out: rdn 2f out: no ex fnl f* **34/1**

8 2 ½ **Andoro (GER)**[27] 3674 3-9-2 0 JackMitchell 13 101
(R Dzubasz, Germany) *hld up in rr: rdn and kpt on fr 2f out: n.d* **85/1**

9 hd **So Chivalry (GER)**[27] 3674 3-9-2 0 FilipMinarik 8 101
(Jean-Pierre Carvalho, Germany) *hld up towards rr: rdn 2 1/2f out: kpt on fnl f: n.d* **30/1**

10 5 ½ **Ormuz (GER)**[22] 3877 3-8-13 0 BauyrzhanMurzabayev 12 89
(A Wohler, Germany) *hld up in rr: rdn 2 1/2f out: kpt on steadily fnl f: nvr in contention* **44/1**

11 ½ **Sibelius (GER)**[27] 3674 3-9-2 0 MartinSeidl 5 91
(Markus Klug, Germany) *midfield: rdn and effrt on inner over 2f out: wknd over 1f out* **38/1**

12 1 **Beam Me Up (GER)**[14] 3-9-2 0 DarioVargiu 14 89
(Markus Klug, Germany) *midfield on outside: rdn 2 1/2f out: wd into st: wknd 1 1/2f out* **29/1**

13 2 ½ **Mojano (FR)**[14] 3-9-2 0 BayarsaikhanGanbat 6 85
(S Richter, Germany) *a towards rr* **117/1**

14 3 **Amiro (GER)**[27] 3-9-2 0 (b) PatCosgrave 2 81
(M Figge, Germany) *led: rdn and hdd over 2f out: wknd under 2f out* **40/1**

15 8 **Magadan (GER)**[13] 3-9-2 0 FabianXaverWeissmeier 16 68
(J M Snackers, Germany) *t.k.h: w ldr: rdn over 2f out: wknd qckly under 2f out: sn struggling* **146/1**

2m 29.95s (-4.60) **15 Ran SP% 118.8**
PARI-MUTUEL (all including 1 euro stake): WIN 3.00 PLACE: 1.70, 1.90, 4.10; SF: 7.90.
Owner Gestut Ittlingen **Bred** Gestut Hof Ittlingen **Trained** Germany

4708 - 4718a (Foreign Racing) - See Raceform Interactive

4688 AYR (L-H)
Monday, July 8

OFFICIAL GOING: Good to firm (watered; 8.5)
Wind: Light, half against in sprints and in over 3f of home straight in races on the round course Weather: Overcast, dry

4719 TOTEPLACEPOT EBF STALLIONS MAIDEN STKS 6f
2:00 (2:01) (Class 5) 2-Y-O **£3,428** (£1,020; £509; £254) **Stalls Centre**

Form RPR

1 **Volatile Analyst (USA)** 2-9-5 0 DanielTudhope 1 79+
(Keith Dalgleish) *noisy in paddock: cl up: led over 1f out: rdn and veered lft ins fnl f: kpt on wl: eased nr fin: promising* **4/1**[3]

3 2 1 ¼ **Saint Of Katowice (IRE)**[16] 4125 2-9-5 0 TonyHamilton 3 74
(Richard Fahey) *cl up: effrt and chsd wnr over 1f out: kpt on fnl f: nt pce of wnr* **2/1**[1]

3 ½ **Baltic State (IRE)** 2-9-5 0 KevinStott 2 72
(Kevin Ryan) *t.k.h: led to over 1f out: kpt on same pce ins fnl f* **7/2**[2]

4 4 ½ **Ainsdale** 2-9-5 0 BenCurtis 4 58
(K R Burke) *prom: rdn over 2f out: hung lft and wknd over 1f out* **2/1**[1]

0 5 38 **Packet Racket**[7] 4433 2-9-5 0 RoystonFfrench 5
(Ann Duffield) *slowly away: bhd and detached: lost tch fr 1/2-way: t.o* **100/1**

1m 12.34s (-0.76) **Going Correction** -0.275s/f (Firm) **5 Ran SP% 109.9**
Speed ratings (Par 94): **94,92,91,85,35**
CSF £12.36 TOTE £4.20: £2.20, £1.10; EX 11.60 Trifecta £25.50.
Owner Anthony F O'Callaghan **Bred** Pollock Farms Et Al **Trained** Carluke, S Lanarks

FOCUS
They kept to the middle of the track in this fair little 2yo maiden, and it has been rated around the runner-up's debut.

4720 TOTEEXACTA H'CAP 6f
2:30 (2:33) (Class 6) (0-55,55) 3-Y-O+
£2,781 (£827; £413; £300; £300; £300) **Stalls Centre**

Form RPR

1 **Kinch (IRE)**[16] 4135 3-8-11 **54** DonaghO'Connor(3) 4 64
(G M Lyons, Ire) *hld up: rdn 1/2-way: hdwy on far side of gp over 1f out: kpt on wl fnl f to ld cl home (trainer's rep had no explanation for the apparent improvement in form, other than, it had been a frustrating gelding and had found it difficult to be competitive in Ireland)* **9/1**

0445 2 shd **Kodicat (IRE)**[10] 4335 5-9-7 **55** (p) KevinStott 3 64
(Kevin Ryan) *cl up far side of gp: led over 2f out: rdn and edgd rt over 1f out: kpt on fnl f: hdd cl home* **13/2**[3]

-420 3 1 **Perfect Swiss**[28] 3651 3-9-0 **54** DavidAllan 14 59
(Tim Easterby) *led in centre of gp: hdd over 2f out: rallied: kpt on ins fnl f* **7/1**

0046 4 1 ½ **Spirit Of Zebedee (IRE)**[5] 4519 6-9-4 **52** (v) JasonHart 2 53
(John Quinn) *midfield: drvn along on far side of gp over 2f out: hdwy over 1f out: r.o fnl f* **5/1**[2]

2535 5 ½ **Macs Blessings (IRE)**[39] 3270 3-8-11 **54** (v[1]) SeanDavis(3) 9 53+
(Stef Keniry) *stmbld bdly s: hld up: rdn over 2f out: hdwy on nr side of gp over 1f out: kpt on: nvr able to chal (jockey said gelding stumbled badly leaving the stalls)* **14/1**

5451 6 1 **Hello Girl**[9] 4376 4-9-3 **54** RowanScott(3) 13 50
(Nigel Tinkler) *in tch in centre of gp: drvn along 2f out: kpt on same pce fnl f* **7/2**[1]

3046 7 nk **Leeshaan (IRE)**[26] 3723 4-8-12 **46** LewisEdmunds 10 41
(Rebecca Bastiman) *t.k.h: hld up in centre of gp: rdn over 2f out: hdwy and angled rt over 1f out: kpt on: no imp* **20/1**

33U5 8 shd **Popping Corks (IRE)**[6] 4493 3-8-11 **54** BenRobinson(3) 8 48
(Linda Perratt) *bhd: rdn on far side over 2f out: hdwy over 1f out: kpt on fnl f: no imp* **20/1**

1600 9 2 ½ **Star Cracker (IRE)**[26] 3723 7-8-13 **47** (p) PhilDennis 5 34
(Jim Goldie) *cl up in centre of gp tl rdn and wknd over 1f out* **50/1**

3000 10 ½ **Jessie Allan (IRE)**[17] 4059 8-8-8 **49** CoreyMadden(7) 11 35
(Jim Goldie) *hld up on nr side of gp: rdn over 2f out: nvr rchd ldrs* **25/1**

00-0 11 ¾ **Palavicini Run (IRE)**[67] 2328 6-8-12 **46** oh1 JamieGormley 7 29
(Linda Perratt) *in tch in centre of gp: drvn along over 2f out: wknd over 1f out (jockey said mare was denied a clear run approaching the final furlong)* **100/1**

0045 12 1 **Vallarta (IRE)**[15] 4149 9-9-2 **50** JamesSullivan 12 30
(Ruth Carr) *towards rr: rdn along and outpcd over 2f out: n.d after* **9/1**

050/ 13 ½ **Night Law**[308] 6889 5-8-7 **46** oh1 BenSanderson(5) 17 24
(Katie Scott) *in tch on nr side of gp: hdwy to join ldr over 3f out: rdn and wknd over 1f out* **33/1**

6430 14 1 ¾ **Dancing Mountain (IRE)**[6] 4493 3-9-0 **54** BenCurtis 16 26
(Roger Fell) *in tch on nr side of gp: rdn over 2f out: wknd over 1f out* **12/1**

6000 15 ¾ **Lexington Palm (IRE)**[17] 4059 3-8-13 **53** ShaneGray 15 22
(Keith Dalgleish) *midfield in centre of gp: drvn along over 2f out: wknd over 1f out* **16/1**

0606 16 nk **Henrietta's Dream**[9] 4358 5-8-12 **46** oh1 (b) TomEaves 1 15
(John Wainwright) *bhd: drvn and struggling over 2f out: sn btn* **50/1**

1m 11.22s (-1.88) **Going Correction** -0.275s/f (Firm)
WFA 3 from 4yo+ 6lb **16 Ran SP% 126.2**
Speed ratings (Par 101): **101,100,99,97,96 95,95,95,91,91 90,88,88,85,84 84**
CSF £64.44 CT £465.11 TOTE £9.40: £2.10, £1.80, £2.90, £1.50; EX 61.40 Trifecta £596.80.
Owner David Spratt & Sean Jones & Mrs Lynne Lyons **Bred** Cavalier Bloodstock **Trained** Dunsany, Co Meath

FOCUS
Again the middle was initially favoured in this ordinary sprint handicap, although the main action developed nearer the stands' side. The winner has been rated back to his early Irish 2yo form.

4721 TOTEQUADPOT H'CAP 6f
3:00 (3:03) (Class 5) (0-70,76) 3-Y-O+
£3,428 (£1,020; £509; £300; £300; £300) **Stalls Centre**

Form RPR

- 1 **Nigg Bay (IRE)**[38] 3328 5-9-7 **69** (v) DonaghO'Connor(3) 3 75
(J F Levins, Ire) *wnt sltly rt s: prom: effrt and rdn over 1f out: led ins fnl f: hld on wl* **11/2**[3]

6641 2 hd **Warning Fire**[3] 4606 3-9-11 **76** 6ex JasonHart 2 80
(Mark Johnston) *pressed ldr: led over 1f out: rdn and hdd ins fnl f: rallied: hld nr fin* **1/1**[1]

6000 3 nk **Burmese Blazer (IRE)**[1] 4694 4-8-13 **61** (h) SeanDavis(3) 4 65
(Jim Goldie) *carried rt and blkd s: t.k.h: hld up: hdwy over 1f out: effrt and disp ld ins fnl f: kpt on: hld cl home* **20/1**

6040 4 ¾ **Chookie Dunedin**[40] 3221 4-9-9 **68** TomEaves 1 70
(Keith Dalgleish) *chsd ldrs: drvn along 2f out: kpt on ins fnl f* **8/1**

2334 5 1 ¼ **B Fifty Two (IRE)**[1] 4694 10-8-12 **60** (tp) JaneElliott(3) 5 58
(Marjorie Fife) *blkd s: hld up in tch: rdn over 2f out: edgd lft over 1f out: kpt on ins fnl f: nt pce to chal* **16/1**

4212 6 3 ¾ **Jordan Electrics**[6] 4492 3-9-1 **69** (h) BenRobinson(3) 6 54
(Linda Perratt) *blkd s: led: rdn and hdd over 1f out: sn wknd* **7/2**[2]

1m 10.79s (-2.31) **Going Correction** -0.275s/f (Firm)
WFA 3 from 4yo+ 6lb **6 Ran SP% 109.4**
Speed ratings (Par 103): **104,103,103,102,100 95**
CSF £10.91 TOTE £4.40: £2.50, £1.10; EX 12.30 Trifecta £78.50.
Owner David Spratt & J M O'Riordan **Bred** Mrs C R Philipson & Lofts Hall Stud **Trained** The Curragh, Co Kildare
■ Stewards' Enquiry : Donagh O'Connor two-day ban: used whip above the permitted level (Jul 24-25)

FOCUS
This saw a fair winning time for the class and has been rated around the fourth.

4722 TOTETRIFECTA H'CAP 5f
3:30 (3:31) (Class 3) (0-90,91) 3-Y-O+ **£9,703** (£2,887; £1,443; £721) **Stalls Centre**

Form RPR

-000 1 **Arecibo (FR)**[9] 4379 4-10-3 **91** DanielTudhope 2 99
(David O'Meara) *unruly in paddock: hld up in tch: hdwy over 1f out: rdn to ld ins fnl f: kpt on wl* **7/1**[3]

6661 2 nk **Harome (IRE)**[1] 4691 5-10-2 **90** 5ex BenCurtis 3 97
(Roger Fell) *chsd clr ldr: clsd over 1f out: effrt and ev ch ins fnl f: kpt on: hld nr fin* **6/4**[1]

1100 **3** *hd* **Venturous (IRE)**[11] [4313] 6-9-12 **86**........................ RobbieDowney 5 92
(David Barron) *hld up: effrt and hdwy over 1f out: rdn and kpt on wl fnl f* **4/1**[2]

5365 **4** *1* **Merry Banter**[16] [4101] 5-9-6 **83**........................ BenRobinson(3) 7 86
(Paul Midgley) *led and clr against stands' rail to over 2f out: hdd ins fnl f: one pce* **4/1**[2]

6554 **5** *hd* **Oriental Lilly**[10] [4330] 5-9-1 **75**........................(p[1]) PhilDennis 6 77
(Jim Goldie) *in tch: rdn along over 2f out: kpt on fnl f: nt pce to chal* **12/1**

601- **6** *shd* **Evasive Power (USA)**[15] [4152] 3-9-1 **80**........................ GaryHalpin 4 80
(Denis Gerard Hogan, Ire) *dwlt: hld up: rdn along over 2f out: kpt on fnl f: no imp* **18/1**

2024 **7** *4* **Sound Of Iona**[17] [4081] 3-8-4 **69**........................ JamieGormley 1 54
(Jim Goldie) *hld up in tch on outside: drvn and struggling 2f out: sn btn* **20/1**

58.28s (-1.72) **Going Correction** -0.275s/f (Firm)
WFA 3 from 4yo+ 5lb **7 Ran SP% 110.2**
Speed ratings (Par 107): **102,101,101,99,99 99,92**
CSF £16.67 TOTE £6.40: £2.60, £1.50; EX 19.00 Trifecta £75.90.
Owner George Turner & Clipper Logistics **Bred** Wertheimer Et Frere **Trained** Upper Helmsley, N Yorks

FOCUS
This feature sprint handicap was run to suit the closers. The winner had dropped to a good mark.

4723 TOTEPOOL H'CAP 1m
4:00 (4:00) (Class 4) (0-85,82) 3-Y-O+
£5,272 (£1,568; £784; £392; £300; £300) **Stalls Low**

Form RPR
3103 **1** **Wild Hope**[19] [4001] 3-9-4 **81**........................ KevinStott 3 86
(Kevin Ryan) *cl up: led after 1f and maintained modest gallop: rdn 2f out: hld on wl fnl f* **11/4**[1]

0103 **2** *nk* **Tadaawol**[2] [4634] 6-9-9 **82**........................(p) BenSanderson(5) 1 88
(Roger Fell) *prom on ins: rdn 2f out: chsd wnr ins fnl f: r.o* **12/1**

0413 **3** *hd* **Amadeus Grey (IRE)**[16] [4107] 3-9-4 **81**........................(t) DavidAllan 7 85
(Tim Easterby) *chsd ldrs: effrt and chsd wnr over 2f out to ins fnl f: kpt on* **10/3**[2]

4 *shd* **Excelcius (USA)**[25] [3784] 3-8-11 **77**........................(t) DonaghO'Connor(3) 8 80
(G M Lyons, Ire) *hld up: rdn over 2f out: hdwy on outside over 1f out: r.o fnl f: nrst fin* **4/1**[3]

2034 **5** *½* **Lucky Violet (IRE)**[1] [4693] 7-8-7 **64**........................(h) BenRobinson(3) 5 68
(Linda Perratt) *t.k.h: prom: rdn over 2f out: effrt over 1f out: one pce ins fnl f* **14/1**

0643 **6** *¾* **Calvados Spirit**[1] [4692] 6-9-8 **79**........................ SeanDavis(3) 4 81
(Richard Fahey) *t.k.h: hld up: nt clr run briefly over 2f out: kpt on same pce ins fnl f* **6/1**

6300 **7** *1 ¾* **Employer (IRE)**[12] [4241] 4-9-12 **80**........................ AlistairRawlinson 2 78
(Jim Goldie) *t.k.h: hld up: effrt on outside over 2f out: no imp fr over 1f out* **18/1**

-006 **8** *½* **Indian Sounds (IRE)**[19] [4001] 3-9-0 **77**........................ BenCurtis 6 72
(Mark Johnston) *led 1f: pressed wnr to over 2f out: wknd over 1f out* **12/1**

1m 39.51s (-3.29) **Going Correction** -0.275s/f (Firm)
WFA 3 from 4yo+ 9lb **8 Ran SP% 111.3**
Speed ratings (Par 105): **105,104,104,104,103 103,101,100**
CSF £34.39 CT £109.80 TOTE £3.40: £1.40, £3.00, £1.40; EX 30.20 Trifecta £174.50.
Owner Hambleton Racing Ltd XLIV **Bred** Watership Down Stud **Trained** Hambleton, N Yorks

FOCUS
Add 9yds. A competitive affair and it looks straightforward form.

4724 TOTEPLACEPOT H'CAP 1m 5f 26y
4:30 (4:31) (Class 5) (0-70,70) 4-Y-O+
£3,428 (£1,020; £509; £300; £300; £300) **Stalls Low**

Form RPR
33-1 **1** **Lever Du Soleil (FR)**[5] [4510] 4-8-10 **59** 5ex........................ CliffordLee 7 74
(Gavin Cromwell, Ire) *hld up: hdwy over 2f out: effrt and pressed wnr over 1f out: led wl ins fnl f: styd on wl* **4/6**[1]

212- **2** *nk* **Sbraase**[14] [4202] 8-8-12 **61**........................ JamesSullivan 6 75
(Noel C Kelly, Ire) *dwlt: hld up: hdwy 3f out: led over 1f out to wl ins fnl f: rallied: jst hld* **10/1**[3]

-534 **3** *7* **Donnachies Girl (IRE)**[11] [4274] 6-8-6 **58**........................(v) RowanScott(3) 10 61
(Alistair Whillans) *s.i.s: hld up: rdn over 2f out: hdwy over 1f out: wnt 3rd towards fin: no ch w first two* **16/1**

4566 **4** *nk* **Pammi**[5] [4515] 4-8-4 **53**........................(p) PhilDennis 9 56
(Jim Goldie) *hld up: hdwy over 2f out: chsd clr ldng pair ins fnl f: no ex towards fin* **33/1**

4554 **5** *2 ½* **Corton Lad**[6] [4491] 9-9-5 **68**........................(tp) KevinStott 2 67
(Keith Dalgleish) *led to 5f out: cl up: ev ch over 2f out: wknd ins fnl f* **14/1**

10-0 **6** *6* **Sarvi**[75] [1503] 4-9-6 **69**........................ AlistairRawlinson 1 59
(Jim Goldie) *hld up in tch: effrt and drvn along over 2f out: wknd over 1f out* **40/1**

0000 **7** *¾* **Ad Libitum**[9] [4370] 4-9-4 **67**........................(p) BenCurtis 5 56
(Roger Fell) *chsd clr ldng pair: rdn and effrt over 2f out: wknd over 1f out* **10/1**[3]

3-50 **8** *1* **Reassurance**[27] [3708] 4-9-2 **65**........................(p) DavidAllan 11 53
(Tim Easterby) *hld up towards rr: drvn along over 2f out: sn btn* **14/1**

3 **9** *3 ¾* **Machiavelli**[14] [4202] 4-9-0 **63**........................(b) GaryHalpin 8 45
(Denis Gerard Hogan, Ire) *prom: effrt and rdn over 2f out: wknd over 1f out* **9/1**[2]

0065 **10** *1 ½* **Mapped (USA)**[19] [4009] 4-9-7 **70**........................(b) JamieGormley 3 50
(Iain Jardine) *sn pressing ldr: led 5f out to over 2f out: wknd over 1f out (jockey said gelding ran too freely)* **12/1**

0004 **11** *32* **Dr Richard Kimble (IRE)**[21] [3929] 4-9-4 **70**........................(p[1]) JaneElliott(3) 4 2
(Marjorie Fife) *hld up in tch: drvn and struggling over 3f out: sn btn: eased whn no ch ins fnl f* **66/1**

2m 49.59s (-4.81) **Going Correction** -0.275s/f (Firm) **11 Ran SP% 122.0**
Speed ratings (Par 103): **103,102,98,98,96 93,92,92,89,88 69**
CSF £8.79 CT £68.63 TOTE £1.60: £1.20, £1.90, £3.00; EX 10.00 Trifecta £56.70.
Owner Sunrise Partnership **Bred** S C E A Haras De La Perelle **Trained** Navan, Co. Meath

FOCUS
Add 15yds. A frantic pace collapsed in this weak staying handicap and two came right away.

4725 COLLECT TOTEPOOL WINNINGS APPRENTICE H'CAP (DIV I) 7f 50y
5:00 (5:05) (Class 6) (0-60,60) 3-Y-O+
£2,781 (£827; £413; £300; £300; £300) **Stalls High**

Form RPR
6143 **1** **Pudding Chare (IRE)**[1] [4693] 5-10-0 **60**........................(t) SeanDavis 5 71
(R Mike Smith) *mde all: qcknd 1/2-way: clr over 1f out: kpt on wl fnl f: unchal* **11/2**[2]

0-64 **2** *2 ½* **Dreamseller (IRE)**[3] [4584] 3-9-0 **54**........................ DannyRedmond 10 55
(Tim Easterby) *prom: rdn over 2f out: chsd (clr) wnr over 1f out: kpt on: nt pce to chal* **5/2**[1]

4-04 **3** *1 ¼* **Retirement Beckons**[47] [2964] 4-8-9 **46** oh1........(h) CianMacRedmond(5) 3 47
(Linda Perratt) *slowly away: bhd: hdwy 2f out: kpt on fnl f: nrst fin (jockey said gelding missed the break)* **10/1**

2020 **4** *hd* **Firsteen**[21] [3921] 3-9-1 **55**........................ RowanScott 1 52
(Alistair Whillans) *midfield: effrt and rdn over 2f out: kpt on fnl f: nvr able to chal* **9/1**

430- **5** *1 ¾* **My Ukulele (IRE)**[220] [9325] 3-9-5 **59**........................ BenRobinson 12 52
(John Quinn) *hld up towards rr: rdn over 2f out: hdwy over 1f out: no imp fnl f* **10/1**

0-06 **6** *2 ½* **Gilmer (IRE)**[35] [3413] 8-9-9 **55**........................ HarrisonShaw 9 44
(Stef Keniry) *in tch: drvn and outpcd over 2f out: n.d after* **20/1**

2004 **7** *hd* **Milton Road**[21] [3924] 4-9-8 **54**........................(p[1]) PhilDennis 7 43
(Rebecca Bastiman) *chsd wnr to over 1f out: wknd ins fnl f* **7/1**[3]

0000 **8** *1* **Insurplus (IRE)**[17] [4060] 6-9-4 **57**........................(p[1]) CoreyMadden(7) 11 43
(Jim Goldie) *hld up: drvn along over 2f out: sme late hdwy: nvr on terms* **12/1**

3120 **9** *nk* **La Cumparsita (IRE)**[26] [3716] 5-9-6 **52**........................ BenSanderson 4 37
(Tristan Davidson) *prom: drvn along over 2f out: wknd over 1f out* **9/1**

0450 **10** *1 ½* **Saltie Girl**[21] [3921] 3-9-3 **57**........................ JaneElliott 6 35
(David Barron) *hld up in midfield: drvn and outpcd over 2f out: n.d after (jockey said filly moved poorly)* **9/1**

0060 **11** *2 ¾* **Kimberley Girl**[6] [4488] 3-8-8 **51**........................ JoshQuinn(3) 2 22
(Michael Easterby) *reluctant to enter stalls: towards rr: drvn and struggling over 2f out: sn btn* **25/1**

6-05 **12** *3 ¼* **Bareed (USA)**[47] [2964] 4-9-0 **46** oh1........................(h) PaulaMuir 8 12
(Linda Perratt) *hld up: rdn and outpcd over 2f out: sn btn (jockey said gelding ran flat)* **20/1**

1m 29.55s (-2.95) **Going Correction** -0.275s/f (Firm)
WFA 3 from 4yo+ 8lb **12 Ran SP% 125.7**
Speed ratings (Par 101): **105,102,100,100,98 95,95,94,93,92 89,85**
CSF £20.27 CT £144.59 TOTE £5.20: £1.60, £1.60, £4.20; EX 18.30 Trifecta £255.20.
Owner Ayr Racecourse Club **Bred** Mrs Eleanor Kent **Trained** Galston, E Ayrshire

FOCUS
Add 9yds. They were soon strung out in this moderate handicap, and a pb from the winner with the runner-up to form.

4726 COLLECT TOTEPOOL WINNINGS APPRENTICE H'CAP (DIV II) 7f 50y
5:30 (5:36) (Class 6) (0-60,60) 3-Y-O+
£2,781 (£827; £413; £300; £300; £300) **Stalls High**

Form RPR
4-66 **1** **Royal Duchess**[17] [4060] 9-10-0 **59**........................ ConnorMurtagh 8 66
(Lucy Normile) *cl up: rdn to ld over 1f out: edgd rt: edgd lft ins fnl f: kpt on wl towards fin* **7/2**[2]

0004 **2** *½* **Let Right Be Done**[5] [4513] 7-9-0 **45**........................(b) BenRobinson 7 50
(Linda Perratt) *led: rdn and hdd over 1f out: rallied: kpt on same pce towards fin* **9/1**

5466 **3** *½* **Gunnison**[11] [4286] 3-9-2 **55**........................ SeanDavis 3 56
(Richard Fahey) *prom: rdn over 2f out: hdwy and edgd lft over 1f out: kpt on ins fnl f* **10/1**

641- **4** *2* **Burning Lake (IRE)**[39] [3283] 3-9-7 **60**........................ DonaghO'Connor 1 56
(J F Levins, Ire) *hld up on ins: effrt and hdwy over 2f out: rdn and no imp fr over 1f out* **10/3**[1]

146- **5** *½* **Darwina**[201] [9613] 3-9-5 **58**........................(h) RowanScott 9 52
(Alistair Whillans) *reluctant to enter stalls: missed break: bhd: rdn on outside over 2f out: kpt on wl fnl f: nrst fin* **33/1**

0004 **6** *1* **Thorntoun Lady (USA)**[11] [4276] 9-8-7 **45**........................ CoreyMadden(7) 4 40
(Jim Goldie) *s.i.s: hld up: rdn over 2f out: kpt on fnl f: nvr rchd ldrs* **14/1**

-000 **7** *1* **Naples Bay**[17] [4060] 5-9-11 **56**........................ BenSanderson 5 48
(Katie Scott) *t.k.h: hld up: rdn and effrt 2f out: no imp fnl f* **12/1**

50-5 **8** *½* **Cambeleza (IRE)**[28] [3651] 3-9-2 **55**........................ HarrisonShaw 2 43
(Kevin Ryan) *hld up on ins: effrt over 2f out: no imp fr over 1f out* **5/1**[3]

9 *1 ¼* **Shamalov (IRE)**[14] [4197] 3-9-4 **57**........................(p) JaneElliott 11 41
(Denis Gerard Hogan, Ire) *midfield: rdn and outpcd over 2f out: n.d after* **11/1**

6-65 **10** *¾* **Milabella**[41] [3176] 3-8-6 **45**........................ PaulaMuir 10 28
(R Mike Smith) *in tch on outside: drvn along over 2f out: wknd over 1f out* **40/1**

0-00 **11** *½* **Princess Apollo**[21] [3933] 5-9-0 **45**........................ DannyRedmond 12 29
(Donald Whillans) *chsd ldrs: drvn along over 2f out: wknd over 1f out* **66/1**

0-00 **12** *nk* **Dark Crystal**[5] [4512] 8-9-2 **52**........................ CianMacRedmond(5) 13 35
(Linda Perratt) *hld up in midfield on outside: rdn along over 2f out: edgd lft and sn wknd* **33/1**

-000 **13** *½* **Wensley**[26] [3716] 4-9-10 **55**........................ PhilDennis 6 37
(Rebecca Bastiman) *t.k.h: prom tl rdn and wknd over 2f out (jockey said gelding ran too freely)* **16/1**

1m 30.98s (-1.52) **Going Correction** -0.275s/f (Firm) **13 Ran SP% 119.4**
WFA 3 from 4yo+ 8lb
Speed ratings (Par 101): **97,96,95,93,93 91,90,90,88,87 87,86,86**
CSF £34.33 CT £293.88 TOTE £5.20: £2.70, £2.40, £3.00; EX 33.90 Trifecta £327.30.
Owner Steve Dick **Bred** Steve Dick **Trained** Duncrievie, Perth & Kinross

FOCUS
Add 9yds. This second division of the moderate 7f handicap was 1.43secs slower than the preceding heat; muddling form.
T/Jkpt: Not Won. T/Plt: £18.40 to a £1 stake. Pool: £66,652.83 - 2,638.40 winning units T/Qpdt: £3.80 to a £1 stake. Pool: £6,449.42 - 1,241.49 winning units **Richard Young**

4032

RIPON (R-H)

Monday, July 8

OFFICIAL GOING: Good to firm (good in places; watered; 8.3)

Wind: virtually nil Weather: overcast

4727 RIPON RACES GENTLEMAN'S EVENING 6TH AUGUST FILLIES' NOVICE AUCTION STKS (PLUS 10 RACE) 6f

6:40 (6:40) (Class 5) 2-Y-O **£3,881** (£1,155; £577; £288) **Stalls** High

Form RPR

1 **Under The Stars (IRE)** 2-9-0 0 .... PJMcDonald 5 87+
(James Tate) *dwlt: hld up: sn pushed along: swtchd rt over 2f out: sn hdwy: led over 1f out: kpt on wl and sn clr: eased towards fin* **7/4**[1]

5 **2** 3 **Requiems Dream (IRE)**[21] 3919 2-9-0 0 .... FrannyNorton 3 75
(Mark Johnston) *pressed ldr: led narrowly over 3f out: rdn 2f out: edgd lft and hdd over 1f out: one pce and sn no ch w wnr (jockey said filly hung left-handed)* **7/1**

0 **3** 1 ½ **Kendred Soul (IRE)**[16] 4125 2-9-0 0 .... JackGarritty 6 70
(Jedd O'Keeffe) *led narrowly: hdd over 3f out: remained cl up: rdn in 3rd whn short of room on rail appr fnl f and swtchd rt: one pce ins fnl f* **16/1**

355 **4** 1 ½ **Knightcap**[49] 2906 2-9-0 71 .... RachelRichardson 2 65
(Tim Easterby) *chsd ldrs: rdn over 2f out: sn one pce* **17/2**

2423 **5** 1 ¾ **My Motivate Girl (IRE)**[10] 4344 2-8-9 70 ....(v) ThomasGreatrex(5) 4 60
(Archie Watson) *dwlt and wnt lft s: sn outpcd in rr: minor hdwy over 1f out: nvr involved (trainer rep said filly became unbalanced by undulations at Ripon on this occasion)* **9/4**[2]

6 3 **Ghost Of Alcatraz (IRE)** 2-9-0 0 .... PaulHanagan 7 50
(Richard Fahey) *chsd ldrs: rdn over 2f out: wknd over 1f out* **9/2**[3]

7 29 **Wrongroadtomayo** 2-8-11 0 .... ConorMcGovern(3) 1
(Fred Watson) *v.s.a: a outpcd in rr (jockey said filly was slowly away)* **150/1**

1m 11.83s (-0.67) **Going Correction** -0.275s/f (Firm) **7 Ran SP% 114.9**
Speed ratings (Par 91): **93,89,87,85,82 78,40**
CSF £15.01 TOTE £1.90: £2.10, £3.70; EX 14.60 Trifecta £134.90.
Owner Saeed Manana **Bred** Rabbah Bloodstock Limited **Trained** Newmarket, Suffolk

FOCUS
The stalls were on the stands' side for this opening fillies' juvenile novice auction stakes, in which the winning favourite wisely declined the contested early pace.

4728 MIDDLEHAM TRAINERS ASSOCIATION H'CAP 1m

7:10 (7:11) (Class 5) (0-70,72) 3-Y-0+
£3,752 (£1,116; £557; £300; £300; £300) **Stalls** Low

Form RPR

402 **1** **Ascot Week (USA)**[41] 3177 5-9-11 67 ....(v) JasonHart 12 76
(John Quinn) *hld up in midfield on inner: pushed along 3f out: swtchd lft to outer over 1f out: rdn and kpt on wl: led towards fin* **10/1**

-035 **2** ¾ **Kannapolis (IRE)**[38] 3305 4-10-0 70 .... GrahamLee 6 77
(Michael Easterby) *in tch: rdn 3f out: hdwy 2f out: drvn to ld appr fnl f: one pce and hdd towards fin* **7/2**[1]

3300 **3** 1 **Fume (IRE)**[41] 3202 3-9-4 69 ....(w) PJMcDonald 14 72
(James Bethell) *midfield: rdn over 2f out: hdwy and chsd ldrs over 1f out: kpt on* **14/1**

22/3 **4** nk **Flying Raconteur**[16] 4131 5-9-7 68 .... FayeMcManoman(5) 13 72
(Nigel Tinkler) *midfield: rdn along and bit outpcd over 3f out: angled lft towards outer 2f out: kpt on wl fnl f* **8/1**[3]

3504 **5** ½ **How Bizarre**[5] 4511 4-9-12 68 .... DavidNolan 10 71
(Liam Bailey) *trckd ldrs: rdn to ld narrowly wl over 1f out: hdd appr fnl f: no ex fnl 110yds* **9/1**

3-23 **6** 1 ¼ **Mac Ailey**[11] 4284 3-8-12 63 .... RachelRichardson 5 61
(Tim Easterby) *rrd s and slowly away: hld up in rr: pushed along and hdwy on outer 2f out: kpt on fnl f: nrst fin (jockey said gelding reared as stalls opened which resulted the gelding in being slowly away)* **8/1**[3]

4404 **7** ½ **Twin Appeal (IRE)**[30] 3567 8-9-13 72 ....(b) GemmaTutty(3) 8 71
(Karen Tutty) *midfield: rdn along over 2f out: n.m.r over 1f out: kpt on fnl f* **10/1**

4001 **8** ½ **Glaceon (IRE)**[16] 4131 4-8-12 54 .... CamHardie 3 52
(Tina Jackson) *trckd ldrs on inner: persistently short of room 2f out tl 1f out: kpt on same pce (jockey said filly was denied a clear run approaching fnl f)* **18/1**

36-2 **9** 2 ½ **Ventura Royal (IRE)**[20] 3960 4-9-7 63 ....(h) DanielTudhope 2 55
(David O'Meara) *led narrowly: rdn over 2f out: hdd wl over 1f out: sn wknd* **9/2**[2]

4-00 **10** 2 ¼ **Watheer**[22] 3880 4-10-0 70 ....(b) DavidEgan 4 57
(Roger Fell) *pressed ldr: rdn over 2f out: wknd over 1f out* **16/1**

0046 **11** nk **Adventureman**[11] 4293 7-8-9 51 .... AndrewMullen 7 37
(Ruth Carr) *dwlt: sn midfield: rdn over 2f out: wknd fnl f* **33/1**

-055 **12** 1 ¾ **Silk Mill Blue**[5] 4518 5-8-9 50 oh1 ....(p) PaulHanagan 1 33
(Richard Whitaker) *a towards rr* **11/1**

2440 **13** 2 ½ **Tagur (IRE)**[82] 1859 5-10-0 70 ....(p) TomEaves 11 47
(Kevin Ryan) *a towards rr* **50/1**

0-05 **14** nse **Magic Ship (IRE)**[26] 3730 4-8-6 45 oh6 .... ConorMcGovern(3) 9 27
(John Norton) *in tch on outer: rdn along over 3f out: wknd over 1f out (trainer said gelding was unsuited by Good to Firm, Good in places going on this occasion and would prefer an easier surface)* **80/1**

1m 38.46s (-2.54) **Going Correction** -0.275s/f (Firm)
WFA 3 from 4yo+ 9lb **14 Ran SP% 123.1**
Speed ratings (Par 103): **101,100,99,98,98 97,96,96,93,91 91,89,86,86**
CSF £45.53 CT £524.42 TOTE £12.10: £3.20, £2.10, £4.70; EX 63.60 Trifecta £972.80.
Owner JJ Quinn Racing Ltd **Bred** Hadi Al Tajir **Trained** Settrington, N Yorks

FOCUS
Stalls on inner. A pretty competitive mile event, in which the winner swooped late down the middle of the track and he has been rated in line with an Ayr race that's worked out really well.

4729 SKY SPORTS RACING VIRGIN 535 H'CAP 1m 4f 10y

7:40 (7:40) (Class 4) (0-80,80) 3-Y-O **£5,369** (£1,597; £798; £399; £300) **Stalls** Centre

Form RPR

-643 **1** **Just Hubert (IRE)**[4] 4559 3-9-7 80 .... DanielTudhope 5 85+
(William Muir) *hld up in rr: pushed along over 4f out: rdn and sme hdwy 2f out: 2 l down in 3rd 1f out: drvn and styd on wl: led post* **5/4**[1]

-040 **2** hd **Ideological (IRE)**[33] 3468 3-9-7 80 .... FrannyNorton 1 84
(Mark Johnston) *trckd ldrs: chal over 1f out: pushed into narrow ld jst ins fnl f: styd on: hdd post* **11/1**

354 **3** nse **Euro Implosion (IRE)**[21] 3926 3-8-3 62 .... DavidEgan 6 66
(Keith Dalgleish) *prom: pushed into ld 2f out: rdn and pressed over 1f out: hdd jst ins fnl f: remained chalng: styd on* **6/1**

-001 **4** 10 **Manton Warrior (IRE)**[18] 4024 3-8-9 68 .... StevieDonohoe 2 56
(Charlie Fellowes) *in tch: pushed along over 4f out: rdn 3f out: sn wknd (trainer rep said gelding became unbalanced by the undulations at Ripon on this occasion)* **11/4**[2]

1141 **5** ½ **Agravain**[3] 4587 3-8-6 65 6ex .... DuranFentiman 4 52
(Tim Easterby) *dwlt sltly: sn led: rdn and hdd 2f out: sn wknd (jockey said gelding ran flat)* **9/2**[3]

2m 31.04s (-5.26) **Going Correction** -0.275s/f (Firm) course record **5 Ran SP% 111.9**
Speed ratings (Par 102): **106,105,105,99,98**
CSF £15.43 TOTE £2.00: £1.40, £2.10; EX 14.80 Trifecta £67.60.
Owner Foursome Thoroughbreds **Bred** Ringfort Stud **Trained** Lambourn, Berks

FOCUS
Stalls in centre. The second and third set an ordinary standard.

4730 RIPON, YORKSHIRE'S GARDEN RACECOURSE H'CAP 1m 1f 170y

8:10 (8:10) (Class 3) (0-90,92) 3-Y-0+
£9,337 (£2,796; £1,398; £699; £349; £175) **Stalls** Low

Form RPR

0320 **1** **Sameem (IRE)**[18] 4016 3-9-2 90 .... PJMcDonald 5 101
(James Tate) *mde most: pushed along 2f out: rdn appr fnl f: kpt on wl* **7/4**[1]

4505 **2** 2 ½ **Mikmak**[6] 4490 6-9-4 82 ....(p) DuranFentiman 3 87
(Tim Easterby) *in tch: rdn over 2f out: drvn in 3rd over 1f out: kpt on fnl f: wnt 2nd post* **8/1**

3043 **3** hd **Rufus King**[3] 4607 4-9-12 90 .... FrannyNorton 6 94
(Mark Johnston) *prom: rdn over 2f out: kpt on same pce fnl f: lost 2nd post* **3/1**[2]

4030 **4** 6 **Benadalid**[12] 4241 4-9-2 80 .... MichaelStainton 4 72
(Chris Fairhurst) *trckd ldrs: rdn over 2f out: wknd fnl f* **9/1**

0224 **5** 2 **Addis Ababa (IRE)**[15] 4144 4-9-10 88 ....(v) DanielTudhope 8 76
(David O'Meara) *hld up in tch: racd keenly: pushed along over 4f out: sme hdwy 3f out: rdn over 2f out: hung rt and sn btn* **4/1**[3]

0043 **6** 7 **King's Pavilion (IRE)**[9] 4403 6-9-7 88 .... ConorMcGovern(3) 7 62
(Jason Ward) *hld up in rr: rdn along 4f out: sn btn (trainer said gelding became unbalanced by undulations at Ripon on this occasion)* **12/1**

-600 **7** 13 **Carry On Deryck**[16] 4097 7-9-7 92 .... HarryRussell(7) 2 39
(Ollie Pears) *trckd ldrs: rdn over 3f out: wknd over 1f out* **25/1**

1m 59.23s (-5.37) **Going Correction** -0.275s/f (Firm)
WFA 3 from 4yo+ 10lb **7 Ran SP% 114.0**
Speed ratings (Par 107): **110,108,107,103,101 95,85**
CSF £16.62 CT £39.35 TOTE £2.30: £1.50, £3.10; EX 15.90 Trifecta £41.10.
Owner Sultan Ali **Bred** Rabbah Bloodstock Limited **Trained** Newmarket, Suffolk

FOCUS
Stalls on inner. A reasonable turnout for the evening's feature and the winner maintained his progress.

4731 TOPSPORT EQUISAND H'CAP 6f

8:40 (8:49) (Class 5) (0-70,65) 3-Y-O
£3,752 (£1,116; £557; £300; £300; £300) **Stalls** High

Form RPR

-230 **1** **Pinarella (FR)**[38] 3292 3-9-2 60 .... AndrewMullen 5 69
(Ben Haslam) *mde all: rdn 2f out: strly pressed appr fnl f: hung persistently rt but kpt on wl (trainer rep said, regarding improved form, filly appreciated the Good to Firm, Good in places going on this occasion, having finished unplaced on Soft ground last time out)* **16/1**

0042 **2** 1 **Montalvan (IRE)**[10] 4328 3-9-2 60 ....(p) DavidEgan 4 66
(Roger Fell) *prom on outer: pushed along 2f out: chal strly appr fnl f: sn drvn: one pce towards fin* **11/4**[1]

5032 **3** 1 ¼ **Josiebond**[25] 3775 3-8-10 54 .... LewisEdmunds 10 56
(Rebecca Bastiman) *midfield: pushed along over 2f out: rdn to chse ldrs appr fnl f: kpt on* **14/1**

2503 **4** 2 **Joey Boy (IRE)**[47] 2958 3-8-13 57 ....(p) ShaneGray 13 53
(Kevin Ryan) *chsd ldrs: rdn 2f out: one pce* **14/1**

-066 **5** hd **Supreme Dream**[30] 3570 3-8-4 48 .... PaddyMathers 11 43
(Ollie Pears) *chsd ldrs: rdn over 2f out: one pce* **25/1**

-400 **6** 1 **Baldwin (IRE)**[5] 4519 3-9-7 65 .... KevinStott 2 57
(Kevin Ryan) *hld up: pushed along over 3f out: rdn over 1f out: kpt on ins fnl f* **6/1**[3]

4 **7** shd **Rangefield Express (IRE)**[19] 4010 3-9-2 60 .... SamJames 7 51
(Geoffrey Harker) *prom: rdn over 2f out: no ex ins fnl f* **18/1**

0005 **8** ½ **Furyan**[10] 4328 3-8-1 52 ....(v) IzzyClifton(7) 3 42
(Nigel Tinkler) *hld up: rdn over 2f out: kpt on ins fnl f: nvr threatened* **8/1**

0050 **9** hd **Uncle Norman (FR)**[15] 4149 3-8-10 54 ....(b) DuranFentiman 14 43
(Tim Easterby) *hld up: sn pushed along: nvr threatened* **16/1**

0-44 **10** 7 **Kodiac Dancer (IRE)**[35] 3416 3-8-10 54 .... GrahamLee 9 21
(Julie Camacho) *prom: racd keenly: rdn 2f out: wknd appr fnl f* **14/1**

0000 **11** 1 ¾ **Dream Chick (IRE)**[30] 3570 3-8-9 53 .... TomEaves 6 14
(Kevin Ryan) *midfield: rdn over 2f out: wknd fnl f* **20/1**

00-6 **12** 7 **Allsfineandandy (IRE)**[38] 3292 3-8-5 49 .... CamHardie 12
(Lynn Siddall) *a in rr: hung bdly rt over 2f out (jockey said gelding became unbalanced by undulations a Ripon on this occasion)* **40/1**

1222 **13** ½ **Fairy Fast (IRE)**[35] 3417 3-9-6 64 ....(b) DanielTudhope 8
(David O'Meara) *midfield on outside: rdn over 2f out: hung rt and sn btn: eased ins fnl f (jockey said filly was slowly away)* **7/2**[2]

1m 11.3s (-1.20) **Going Correction** -0.275s/f (Firm) **13 Ran SP% 122.4**
Speed ratings (Par 100): **97,95,94,91,91 89,89,88,88,79 77,67,67**
CSF £59.97 CT £688.18 TOTE £18.00: £4.70, £1.70, £3.20; EX 87.80 Trifecta £1381.30.
Owner Ontoawinner, B Haslam & K Nicol **Bred** Thierry De La Heronniere & Jedburgh Stud **Trained** Middleham Moor, N Yorks

FOCUS
Stalls on stands' side. A moderate sprint handicap and this rates a pb from the winner. The race was delayed for nine minutes whilst the winner was led to post.

4732 FUN FOR LEGO FANS 5TH AUGUST MAIDEN STKS 1m

9:10 (9:15) (Class 5) 3-Y-0+ **£3,881** (£1,155; £577; £288) **Stalls** Low

Form RPR

2-0 **1** **Stagehand**[83] 1828 3-9-0 0 .... KieranShoemark 3 79
(Charles Hills) *prom: pushed into ld appr fnl f: kpt on wl* **2/1**[2]

33 **2** 2 ¾ **Morning Duel (IRE)**[21] 3932 3-9-5 0 ....(t[1]) DanielTudhope 4 79
(David O'Meara) *led: rdn and hdd appr fnl f: one pce and sn hld in 2nd* **6/4**[1]

003 **3** *7* **Power Player**[26] 3727 3-9-5 72 PJMcDonald 5 62+
(K R Burke) *trckd ldrs: rdn along 3f out: sn outpcd and btn* **9/2**[3]

6 **4** *3/4* **Ghanim (IRE)**[16] 4120 3-9-5 0 TomEaves 7 60
(Conrad Allen) *in tch: rdn along 3f out: sn outpcd and btn* **10/1**

5/ **5** *3 1/2* **Ningaloo (GER)**[1051] 5676 5-10-0 0 LewisEdmunds 1 54
(Rebecca Bastiman) *slowly away: hld up in rr: pushed along and sme hdwy over 2f out: nvr involved (jockey said gelding was slowly away)* **20/1**

\- **6** *4* **Abwab (IRE)** 3-9-5 0 JamesSullivan 2 43
(Michael Easterby) *dwlt: hld up: rdn along over 3f out: wknd over 2f* **14/1**

0-04 **7** *20* **Ganton Eagle**[2] 4629 3-9-5 43 CamHardie 6
(Michael Easterby) *hld up: rdn over 3f out: sn wknd* **150/1**

1m 38.81s (-2.19) **Going Correction** -0.275s/f (Firm) 7 Ran SP% **112.7**
WFA 3 from 5yo 9lb
Speed ratings (Par 103): **99,96,89,88,85 81,61**
CSF £5.20 TOTE £3.00: £1.70, £1.10; EX 6.70 Trifecta £12.90.
Owner K Abdullah **Bred** Juddmonte Farms Ltd **Trained** Lambourn, Berks

FOCUS
Stalls on inner. A modest maiden and the first two have been rated in line with their respective debut races. The winning time was 0.85 seconds slower than that of the earlier 0-70 handicap.
T/Plt: £25.70 to a £1 stake. Pool: £74,477.12 - 2108.95 winning units T/Qpdt: £7.60 to a £1 stake. Pool: £ 7,898.41 - 763.05 winning units **Andrew Sheret**

4447 WINDSOR (R-H)
Monday, July 8

OFFICIAL GOING: Good to firm (watered; 7.5)
Wind: Almost nil Weather: Fine becoming cloudy, warm

4733 HORSE GUARDS LONDON DRY GIN SAUL APPRENTICE H'CAP 6f 12y
5:50 (5:54) (Class 6) (0-65,64) 4-Y-O+
£2,781 (£827; £413; £300; £300; £300) **Stalls** Centre

Form RPR

0650 **1** **Top Boy**[42] 3147 9-9-12 **64** DarraghKeenan 6 73
(Tony Carroll) *taken down early: racd centre: trckd ldrs: led wl over 1f out: rdn and styd on after: wl in command fnl f* **9/2**[2]

4000 **2** *1 1/4* **Swanton Blue (IRE)**[14] 4181 6-9-11 **63** PoppyBridgwater 11 68
(Ed de Giles) *racd centre: w ldr: upsides 2f out: chsd wnr over 1f out: kpt on but no imp: jst hld on for 2nd* **11/1**

0305 **3** *nse* **Global Hope (IRE)**[11] 4303 4-9-4 **59** (tp) CierenFallon(3) 12 64
(Gay Kelleway) *dwlt: sltly: racd centre: towards rr: rdn and prog over 1f out: styd on fnl f and nrly snatched 2nd* **7/2**[1]

-005 **4** *1 1/4* **Harry Beau**[44] 3089 5-9-9 **64** (vt) ScottMcCullagh(3) 1 65
(David Evans) *racd nr side: w ldrs: nt qckn and lost pl wl over 1f out: kpt on one pce fnl f* **9/1**

6245 **5** *hd* **Cent Flying**[13] 4227 4-9-7 **62** (t) Pierre-LouisJamin(3) 13 62
(William Muir) *racd centre: in tch: rdn 2f out: tried to cl over 1f out: one pce fnl f* **8/1**

-053 **6** *3/4* **Kinglami**[14] 4181 10-9-5 **64** (p) KateLeahy(7) 3 62
(John O'Shea) *chsd ldrs towards nr side: no prog 2f out: one pce after* **9/1**

-321 **7** *shd* **Princess Keira (IRE)**[17] 4074 4-9-12 **64** SeamusCronin 4 64+
(Mick Quinn) *hld up in centre: trckd ldrs fr 1/2-way: waiting to chal whn gap clsd over 1f out: nt rcvr and no prog fnl f (jockey said filly denied clear run)* **6/1**[3]

0220 **8** *nse* **Dalness Express**[33] 3476 6-8-11 **49** (bt) TheodoreLadd 2 46
(John O'Shea) *racd towards nr side: mde most to wl over 1f out: wknd fnl f (vet said gelding lost left hind shoe)* **10/1**

0400 **9** *2 3/4* **The King's Steed**[14] 4195 6-8-8 **53** (bt) GeorgeRooke(7) 9 42
(Shaun Lycett) *towards rr: rdn over 2f out: no great prog* **12/1**

-000 **10** *5* **Cuban Spirit**[18] 4025 4-8-13 **54** (p[1]) GeorgiaDobie(3) 7 27
(Lee Carter) *dwlt: a in rr: no ch over 1f out (jockey said gelding was never travelling)* **40/1**

-000 **11** *8* **Hellofagame**[14] 4182 4-8-4 **45** AledBeech(3) 8
(Richard Price) *towards rr: wknd over 2f out: t.o* **100/1**

000- **12** *2* **Hold Your Breath**[235] 9079 4-8-2 **45** ElishaWhittington(5) 10
(Tony Carroll) *t.k.h early: struggling in last 1/2-way: t.o* **33/1**

1m 12.07s (-0.03) **Going Correction** +0.025s/f (Good) 12 Ran SP% **117.3**
Speed ratings (Par 101): **101,99,99,97,97 96,96,96,92,85 75,72**
CSF £52.26 CT £196.44 TOTE £4.90: £2.20, £5.50, £1.90; EX 42.40 Trifecta £210.20.
Owner D Allen **Bred** Mrs C R Philipson & Mrs H G Lascelle **Trained** Cropthorne, Worcs

FOCUS
Moderate sprint form, the main action unfolded away from the stands' rail. The winner was handily weighted on his best.

4734 MARATHONBET "BETTER ODDS MEAN BIGGER WINNINGS" EBF NOVICE STKS 6f 12y
6:20 (6:21) (Class 5) 2-Y-O
£3,428 (£1,020; £509; £254) **Stalls** Centre

Form RPR

1 **Old News** 2-9-5 0 ShaneKelly 8 77
(Richard Hughes) *trckd ldrs: pushed along on outer and clsd over 1f out: rdn to chse ldr ins fnl f: led fnl 75yds: readily* **33/1**

33 **2** *nk* **Good Earth (IRE)**[9] 4394 2-9-5 0 NicolaCurrie 2 76
(Jamie Osborne) *wl away: led and racd against nr side rail: rdn fnl f: hdd fnl 75yds: styd on* **11/2**[3]

3 *1 3/4* **Smokey Bear (IRE)** 2-9-5 0 JasonWatson 1 70
(Roger Charlton) *trckd ldrs against nr side rail: rdn and stl cl up 1f out: one pce after* **10/1**

3 **4** *1/2* **Irish Acclaim (IRE)**[14] 4184 2-9-5 0 AdamKirby 7 70
(Clive Cox) *mostly trckd ldr: rdn over 1f out: lost 2nd and one pce ins fnl f* **10/11**[1]

6 **5** *3 1/2* **Ecclesiastical**[21] 3943 2-9-5 0 RobHornby 10 58
(Martyn Meade) *pressed ldrs: stl ch jst over 1f out: wknd ins fnl f* **3/1**[2]

0 **6** *1 3/4* **Boy George**[32] 3491 2-9-5 0 LiamKeniry 5 52
(Dominic Ffrench Davis) *wl in rr: outpcd 1/2-way: reminders 2f out: nvr in it but kpt on steadily over 1f out* **66/1**

0 **7** *nse* **Camacho Man (IRE)**[11] 4302 2-9-5 0 RossaRyan 4 52
(Jennie Candlish) *nvr beyond midfield: rdn and outpcd sn after 1/2-way: no imp on ldrs after* **100/1**

00 **8** *3 1/2* **Beat The Breeze**[18] 4030 2-9-5 0 JFEgan 6 41
(Simon Dow) *wl in rr: outpcd 1/2-way: no ch after (trainer said colt had breathing problem)* **66/1**

9 *3/4* **Timon (IRE)** 2-9-5 0 CallumShepherd 9 38
(Mick Channon) *spd to chse ldrs to 1/2-way: sn wknd* **20/1**

00 **10** *1* **Hares Rocket (IRE)**[9] 4394 2-9-5 0 DavidProbert 11 35
(Joseph Tuite) *nvr beyond midfield: outpcd 1/2-way: sn no ch (jockey said gelding was slowly away)* **100/1**

0 **11** *5* **Jochi Khan (USA)**[36] 3371 2-9-5 0 OisinMurphy 3 19
(Robert Cowell) *a in last: bhd fnl 2f* **16/1**

1m 12.76s (0.66) **Going Correction** +0.025s/f (Good) 11 Ran SP% **120.4**
Speed ratings (Par 94): **96,95,93,92,87 85,85,80,79,78 71**
CSF £205.34 TOTE £36.40: £6.00, £1.70, £2.70; EX 207.20 Trifecta £1375.50.
Owner The Queens **Bred** Biddestone Stud Ltd **Trained** Upper Lambourn, Berks

FOCUS
Bit of a turn up in this juvenile novice with the market leaders disappointing. It has been rated around the runner-up and fourth.

4735 HORSE GUARDS LONDON DRY GIN PHIPPS CLAIMING STKS 1m 2f
6:50 (6:50) (Class 5) 3-Y-O
£3,428 (£1,020; £509; £300; £300; £300) **Stalls** Low

Form RPR

6554 **1** **Smith (IRE)**[9] 4400 3-8-8 51 (v) GeorgiaDobie(7) 3 57
(Eve Johnson Houghton) *hld up in last pair: shkn up and prog on outer jst over 2f out: chsd ldr over 1f out: led ins fnl f: styd on wl (jockey said gelding hung both ways)* **5/1**[2]

0115 **2** *1 3/4* **Izvestia (IRE)**[5] 4522 3-9-0 80 (b) OisinMurphy 6 52
(Archie Watson) *trckd ldr: shkn up to ld over 3f out: racd against rail after: u.p 2f out: hdd and nt qckn ins fnl f* **2/5**[1]

0 **3** *1 1/2* **Beechwood James (FR)**[95] 1550 3-9-0 0 ThoreHammerHansen(5) 2 54
(Richard Hannon) *trckd ldrs: rdn wl over 2f out: cl enough over 1f out: one pce* **8/1**[3]

00-0 **4** *3* **Maykir**[6] 4476 3-9-1 53 RobertHavlin 5 44
(Amanda Perrett) *in tch: shkn up 3f out: u.p whn nt clr run briefly over 1f out: wknd after* **25/1**

1030 **5** *shd* **Um Shama (IRE)**[11] 4284 3-8-5 63 LauraCoughlan(7) 9 41
(David Loughnane) *t.k.h: hld up in last pair: prog on outer 1/2-way: chal and w ldr over 3f out to 2f out: wknd (jockey said filly ran too free)* **11/1**

00 **6** *3/4* **Cala Sveva (IRE)**[19] 3996 3-8-3 41 (v[1]) WilliamCox(3) 4 33
(Mark Usher) *led to over 3f out: steadily wknd* **50/1**

2m 10.45s (1.45) **Going Correction** +0.025s/f (Good) 6 Ran SP% **113.3**
Speed ratings (Par 100): **95,93,92,90,89 89**
CSF £7.57 TOTE £5.90: £1.60, £1.40; EX 8.20 Trifecta £19.10.
Owner Anthony Pye-Jeary **Bred** John Connaughton **Trained** Blewbury, Oxon

FOCUS
Add 18yds. A weak, muddling race, but the winner has been rated to form.

4736 DOWNLOAD THE MARATHONBET APP H'CAP (SKY BET WINDSOR SPRINT SERIES QUALIFIER) 5f 21y
7:20 (7:20) (Class 3) (0-90,90) 3-Y-O
£7,439 (£2,213; £1,106; £553) **Stalls** Centre

Form RPR

1106 **1** **Free Love**[23] 3844 3-8-12 **86** TheodoreLadd(5) 1 92
(Michael Appleby) *hld up in tch: prog to ld wl over 1f out: sn rdn: hung lft after and jnd nr fin: hld on wl (jockey said filly hung left-handed under pressure)* **7/2**[2]

0114 **2** *nk* **Dark Shadow (IRE)**[12] 4236 3-9-1 **84** HectorCrouch 6 89
(Clive Cox) *trckd ldrs: led briefly 2f out: pressed wnr after: wnt lft fnl f: upsides nr fin: nt qckn last strides* **5/2**[1]

1601 **3** *1 3/4* **Wedding Date**[16] 4122 3-9-2 **90** ThoreHammerHansen(5) 5 89
(Richard Hannon) *hld up in last: effrt on outer 2f out: chsd ldng pair jst over 1f out: no imp ins fnl f: eased last strides* **5/2**[1]

-055 **4** *1 1/2* **Pink Iceburg (IRE)**[28] 3659 3-8-4 **73** JimmyQuinn 2 66
(Peter Crate) *racd against rail: disp ld to 2f out: lost pl and sn btn* **33/1**

4334 **5** *nk* **Pass The Gin**[24] 3815 3-8-11 **80** OisinMurphy 4 72
(Andrew Balding) *disp ld to 2f out: lost pl and btn over 1f out* **7/2**[2]

6623 **6** *4* **Jungle Inthebungle (IRE)**[41] 3191 3-8-4 **73** ow1 JosephineGordon 3 51
(Mick Channon) *chsd ldrs to 1/2-way: dropped to last and struggling over 1f out* **14/1**[3]

59.46s (-0.64) **Going Correction** +0.025s/f (Good) 6 Ran SP% **111.2**
Speed ratings (Par 104): **106,105,102,100,99 93**
CSF £12.41 TOTE £5.00: £2.50, £2.00; EX 14.40 Trifecta £37.40.
Owner The North South Syndicate **Bred** Brendan Boyle Bloodstock Ltd **Trained** Oakham, Rutland

FOCUS
Ordinary form for the grade, with the winner back to her Nottingham win, rated around the runner-up.

4737 VISIT MARATHONBET.CO.UK H'CAP 1m 2f
7:50 (7:50) (Class 5) (0-70,70) 3-Y-O+
£3,428 (£1,020; £509; £300; £300; £300) **Stalls** Low

Form RPR

2505 **1** **Arctic Sea**[31] 3539 5-10-0 **70** RossaRyan 2 74
(Paul Cole) *trckd ldr 2f: prom after: styd against nr side rail in st: rdn 2f out: clsd to ld ins fnl f: hung lft after and drvn out (jockey said gelding hung left-handed in final furlong)* **4/1**[2]

4405 **2** *nk* **Grange Walk (IRE)**[46] 3015 4-9-4 **63** PaddyBradley(3) 1 66
(Pat Phelan) *dwlt: sn wl in tch: cl up bhd ldrs 2f out: produced between them to chal fnl f: w wnr after: jst hld* **5/1**[3]

1 **3** *1 1/4* **Magic Shuffle (IRE)**[12] 4235 3-9-0 **66** TomMarquand 4 66
(Barry Brennan) *hld up in last pair: urged along 3f out: prog on outer 2f out: drvn to chal 1f out: nt qckn fnl f (jockey said gelding hung right-handed under pressure)* **7/2**[1]

1010 **4** *3/4* **Run After Genesis (IRE)**[20] 3964 3-9-2 **68** DanielMuscutt 8 67
(Brett Johnson) *trckd ldr after 2f: led 2f out: drvn over 1f out: hdd & wknd ins fnl f* **8/1**

46-0 **5** *nk* **Peggy McKay**[30] 3603 4-9-9 **65** OisinMurphy 5 64
(Andrew Balding) *trckd ldrs: cl up and rdn 2f out: nt qckn over 1f out: no prog fnl f* **4/1**[2]

0366 **6** *3/4* **Cool Possibility (IRE)**[13] 4225 3-8-8 **65** (t[1]) CierenFallon(5) 7 61
(Charles Hills) *dwlt: hld up in last pair: urged along 3f out: edgd lft whn rdn 2f out: no prog* **4/1**[2]

0340 **7** *1/2* **Natch**[117] 1183 4-9-1 **57** (p) CharlieBennett 3 52
(Michael Attwater) *led: rdn and hdd 2f out: steadily wknd over 1f out* **14/1**

2m 9.83s (0.83) **Going Correction** +0.025s/f (Good)
WFA 3 from 4yo+ 10lb 7 Ran SP% **116.7**
Speed ratings (Par 103): **97,96,95,95,94 94,93**
CSF £24.97 CT £76.69 TOTE £4.70: £2.90, £2.70; EX 24.10 Trifecta £115.80.
Owner P F I Cole Ltd **Bred** Waratah Thoroughbreds Pty Ltd **Trained** Whatcombe, Oxon

FOCUS
Add 18yds. Modest form but the winner rates close to his best.

4738 HORSE GUARDS LONDON DRY GIN MCINTYRE NOVICE STKS 1m 31y
8:20 (8:21) (Class 5) 3-4-Y-O £3,428 (£1,020; £509; £254) Stalls Low

Form RPR
1 nse **Global Hunter (IRE)** 3-9-5 0 .... JosephineGordon 5 85+
(Saeed bin Suroor) *dwlt: off the pce in rr: pushed along in 8th bef 1/2-way: prog over 3f out: drvn to chse clr ldr over 1f out: styd on fnl f: clsng whn impeded last 2 strides: jst failed: fin 2nd: awrdd the r* **7/2[2]**
-220 2 **King Ademar (USA)**[18] 4016 3-9-5 95 ....(p) OisinMurphy 9 87+
(Martyn Meade) *mde all: clr over 2f out: rdn over 1f out: hung bdly lft u.p fnl 50yds: jst hld on: fin 1st: disqualified and plcd 2nd* **1/3[1]**
6-0 3 6 **Nantucket (IRE)**[73] 2087 3-9-0 0 .... DavidProbert 3 66
(Sir Michael Stoute) *chsd ldr: rdn and no imp over 2f out: lost 2nd and btn over 1f out* **8/1**
02- 4 4 **Waterfront (IRE)**[242] 8956 3-9-5 0 .... AdamKirby 8 62
(Simon Crisford) *chsd ldng pair: no imp over 2f out: sn lost 3rd and fdd* **5/1[3]**
6 5 1 1/4 **So Strictly**[12] 4258 3-9-5 0 .... RossaRyan 4 59
(Paul Cole) *chsd ldrs: rdn to dispute 3rd over 2f out but no further prog: fdd over 1f out* **50/1**
6 6 1 1/4 **Teemlucky**[14] 4189 3-9-0 0 .... MartinDwyer 2 51
(Ian Williams) *dwlt: rn green in last pair and wl off the pce: nvr a factor but kpt on fnl 2f* **33/1**
00 7 1 1/4 **Set Point Charlie (IRE)**[14] 4196 3-9-5 0 .... TomQueally 6 53
(Seamus Durack) *dwlt: wl off the pce in rr: shkn up over 3f out: nvr a factor* **100/1**
06- 8 1 **Time Trialist**[340] 5637 3-9-2 0 .... PaddyBradley(3) 1 51
(Pat Phelan) *taken down early: a wl off the pce towards rr: nvr on terms w ldrs* **100/1**
0 9 1 1/4 **Eventura**[16] 4120 3-9-0 0 .... TomMarquand 10 43
(Tony Carroll) *chsd ldrs in 5th tl wknd over 3f out* **100/1**
00 10 17 **Red Moon Lady**[35] 3421 3-9-0 0 .... JoeyHaynes 7 4
(Dean Ivory) *a off the pce in rr: wknd 3f out: t.o* **100/1**

1m 42.55s (-1.95) **Going Correction** +0.025s/f (Good) **10 Ran SP% 133.9**
Speed ratings (Par 103): **109,110,103,99,98 97,96,95,93,76**
CSF £5.94 TOTE £5.70: £1.02, £1.20, £1.80; EX 8.60 Trifecta £23.40.
Owner Godolphin **Bred** Mrs Clodagh McStay **Trained** Newmarket, Suffolk
■ Stewards' Enquiry : Oisin Murphy caution: careless riding

FOCUS
Add 18yds. Drama in this novice with the 1-3 favourite King Ademar, who appeared to have the race in the bag from a fair way out, hanging violently left late on and just holding on. The stewards' deemed the interference he caused the runner-up was enough to reverse the result, however. Weak novice form.

4739 HORSE GUARDS LONDON DRY GIN FALLS H'CAP 1m 3f 99y
8:50 (8:50) (Class 4) (0-85,86) 3-Y-O
£5,207 (£1,549; £774; £387; £300; £300) Stalls Low

Form RPR
1-40 1 **Jersey Wonder (IRE)**[12] 4256 3-9-7 **85** .... TomMarquand 3 92
(Jamie Osborne) *chsd clr ldr and clr of rest tl field clsd 1/2-way: shkn up 3f out: clsd 2f out: drvn to ld over 1f out: hanging lft after but hld on wl* **12/1**
1-26 2 3/4 **Queen Constantine (GER)**[39] 3260 3-8-9 **73** ....(h) DavidProbert 1 78
(William Jarvis) *hld up in last pair: prog 3f out to chal 2f out: nt qckn over 1f out: chsd wnr fnl f: carried sltly lft but a hld* **10/1**
-336 3 2 1/4 **Fearless Warrior (FR)**[23] 3842 3-9-2 **80** ....(b[1]) OisinMurphy 5 81
(Ralph Beckett) *hld up in last trio: shkn up 3f out: tried to cl on outer 2f out: sn nt qckn: one pce after* **7/2[3]**
41-2 4 hd **Alnadir (USA)**[14] 4188 3-9-8 **86** ....(p) AdamKirby 2 87
(Simon Crisford) *led and clr: stdd 1/2-way: kicked on again 3f out and styd against rail: hdd and fdd over 1f out* **5/2[2]**
542 5 hd **Johnny Kidd**[24] 3802 3-8-11 **75** .... RobHornby 6 75
(Andrew Balding) *chsd clr ldng pair: in tch 1/2-way: pushed along and lost pl 3f out: brief rally 2f out: wknd fnl f* **8/1**
0-22 6 nk **Group Stage (GER)**[25] 3765 3-8-7 **71** .... JasonWatson 4 71
(Alan King) *hld up in last trio: shkn up 3f out: one pce and no imp on ldrs fnl 2f* **2/1[1]**

2m 29.08s (-0.62) **Going Correction** +0.025s/f (Good) **6 Ran SP% 112.0**
Speed ratings (Par 102): **103,102,100,100,100 100**
CSF £113.13 TOTE £14.20: £5.30, £1.80; EX 168.40 Trifecta £460.90.
Owner A Taylor **Bred** Camas Park, Lynch Bages & Summerhill **Trained** Upper Lambourn, Berks

FOCUS
Add 18yds. An ordinary handicap that fell apart somewhat with the market leaders disappointing and the two outsiders coming to the fore, but this still rates a pb from the winner.
T/Plt: £118.30 to a £1 stake. Pool: £89,25.17 - 550.71 winning units T/Qpdt: £7.80 to a £1 stake. Pool: £10,517.66 - 988.07 winning units **Jonathan Neesom**

4740 - 4744a (Foreign Racing) - See Raceform Interactive

3666 ROSCOMMON (R-H)
Monday, July 8

OFFICIAL GOING: Good

4745a LENEBANE STKS (LISTED RACE) 1m 3f 175y
8:30 (8:30) 3-Y-O+ £31,891 (£10,270; £4,864; £2,162)

RPR
1 **Downdraft (IRE)**[17] 4053 4-9-11 98 ....(t) DonnachaO'Brien 2 100+
(Joseph Patrick O'Brien, Ire) *trckd ldr in 2nd: clsr travelling wl 2f out: rdn to ld 1f out: edgd sltly lft fnl 150yds and again fnl 50yds where pressed: kpt on wl clsng stages* **6/4[1]**
2 1/2 **Massif Central (IRE)**[11] 4311 5-9-11 98 .... ColinKeane 4 99+
(M Halford, Ire) *rrd sltly leaving stalls: sn settled in 3rd: pushed along under 2f out: kpt on wl into 2nd fnl 150yds: nt quite rch wnr* **5/2[3]**
3 1 3/4 **Masaff (IRE)**[10] 4351 3-9-0 105 ....(h[1]) ChrisHayes 5 98
(D K Weld, Ire) *led: shkn up 2f out: hdd ent fnl f and no ex in 3rd fnl 100yds: kpt on same pce* **15/8[2]**
4 1/2 **Dream Ascot**[9] 4412 4-9-6 83 .... LeighRoche 1 90
(J A Stack, Ire) *a in rr: rdn and no imp 2f out: kpt on fnl f: nvr nrr* **14/1**

2m 39.6s (-3.70)
WFA 3 from 4yo+ 12lb **4 Ran SP% 110.0**
CSF £5.64 TOTE £2.50; DF 5.30 Trifecta £8.70.
Owner O T I Racing **Bred** Airlie Stud **Trained** Owning Hill, Co Kilkenny

FOCUS
Only four runners and it did turn tactical but the winner was the best horse in the race.

4746 - (Foreign Racing) - See Raceform Interactive

4703 DEAUVILLE (R-H)
Monday, July 8

OFFICIAL GOING: Polytrack: standard; turf: good

4747a PRIX DU COTENTIN (H'CAP) (4YO+) (ROUND COURSE) (TURF) 1m (R)
12:50 4-Y-O+
£23,423 (£8,900; £6,558; £3,747; £1,873; £1,405)

RPR
1 **A Head Ahead (GER)**[42] 5-9-4 0 ....(b) CyrilleStefan 4 83
(S Smrczek, Germany) **26/1**
2 snk **Geonpi (IRE)**[22] 8-8-11 0 .... AlexandreRoussel 8 76
(N Bellanger, France) **43/5**
3 3/4 **Keravnos (FR)**[32] 9-9-5 0 .... TheoBachelot 6 82
(Y Barberot, France) **12/1**
4 snk **Nosdargent (FR)**[32] 4-9-4 0 .... FabriceVeron 13 81
(D & P Prod'Homme, France) **13/1**
5 shd **Plantlove (FR)**[25] 4-9-2 0 .... HugoJourniac 9 79
(M Nigge, France) **83/10[3]**
6 hd **El Indio (FR)**[49] 3136 4-9-3 0 .... StephanePasquier 15 79
(H-A Pantall, France) **9/1**
7 2 **Smart Move (FR)**[32] 4-8-10 0 .... MlleAlisonMassin 2 68
(D & P Prod'Homme, France) **46/1**
8 snk **Look Back (FR)**[49] 4-9-0 0 .... VincentCheminaud 12 71
(H-A Pantall, France) **44/5**
9 1 1/4 **Cape Greco (USA)**[69] 2264 4-8-10 0 .... MlleCoraliePacaut 1 64
(Jo Hughes, France) *trckd ldrs: urged along 2f out: rdn w limited rspnse over 1f out: kpt on same pce fnl f* **19/1**
10 3/4 **Latinius (FR)**[49] 4-8-13 0 .... MickaelBarzalona 7 66
(J-M Beguigne, France) **31/5[2]**
11 hd **Calaf (FR)**[53] 7-9-0 0 .... AurelienLemaitre 10 66
(H Fortineau, France) **20/1**
12 1 1/4 **Dixit Confucius (FR)**[32] 4-8-11 0 .... TonyPiccone 5 60
(F Chappet, France) **41/10[1]**
13 3/4 **Mascalino (GER)**[32] 5-9-6 0 .... AnthonyCrastus 3 68
(H Blume, Germany) **29/1**
14 1 **Magic Song (FR)**[67] 5-8-8 0 .... CristianDemuro 16 53
(S Kobayashi, France) **13/1**
15 6 **Aprilios (FR)**[67] 7-9-3 0 .... IoritzMendizabal 14 49
(Georgios Alimpinisis, France) **23/1**

1m 39.8s (-1.00) **15 Ran SP% 119.9**
PARI-MUTUEL (all including 1 euro stake): WIN 26.60; PLACE 7.70, 3.90, 4.90; DF 97.10.
Owner Stall 3 Musketiere **Bred** Nicolas Ferrand **Trained** Germany

4748a PRIX DE GASSARD (CLAIMER) (4YO+) (ROUND COURSE) (TURF) 1m 7f
4:20 4-Y-O+ £8,558 (£3,423; £2,567; £1,711; £855)

RPR
1 **Vienna Woods (FR)**[32] 5-8-8 0 .... GregoryBenoist 11 72
(Y Barberot, France) **67/10**
2 1 **Tres Rush (IRE)**[85] 5-8-11 0 ....(b) MlleMarylineEon(4) 1 77
(Mme Pia Brandt, France) **12/1**
3 2 **Vaudou Des Ongrais (FR)**[62] 10-8-11 0 ....(b) EmmanuelEtienne 3 71
(P Chemin & C Herpin, France) **26/1**
4 1 **Foxboro (GER)**[262] 4-8-11 0 .... TheoBachelot 4 70
(P Schiergen, Germany) **13/1**
5 snk **Culmination**[17] 4089 7-9-4 0 .... MickaelBarzalona 7 77
(Jo Hughes, France) *Disputed ld early: settled to trck ldrs on outer: pushed along to chal over 2f out: rdn and ev ch over 1f out: drvn but no ex ins fnl f* **14/5[1]**
6 3/4 **Combat Des Trente (FR)**[39] 6-9-4 0 .... MaximeGuyon 10 76
(C Lotoux, France) **53/10[3]**
7 snk **Le Pin (FR)**[75] 6-9-2 0 ....(p) ChristopheSoumillon 2 74
(F Vermeulen, France) **29/10[2]**
8 4 **Ajmany (IRE)**[26] 9-8-13 0 .... MlleCoraliePacaut(3) 5 69
(J-M Baudrelle, France) **9/1**
9 13 **Insider (FR)**[16] 7-8-8 0 ....(p) AlexandreChesneau(3) 8 48
(Alex Fracas, France) **11/1**
10 8 **Elecktric Cafe (FR)**[23] 8-8-11 0 ....(p) DelphineSantiago(4) 9 43
(J Carayon, France) **45/1**
11 dist **Oulmes Dream (FR)**[26] 4-8-6 0 .... MaixentRemy(5) 6
(Mme E Siavy-Julien, France) **87/1**

3m 12.3s (-6.80) **11 Ran SP% 121.0**
PARI-MUTUEL (all including 1 euro stake): WIN 7.70; PLACE 2.90, 3.60, 5.60; DF 26.70.
Owner Ecurie Billon **Bred** Le Thenney S.A. & Edy S.R.L. **Trained** France

4472 BRIGHTON (L-H)
Tuesday, July 9

OFFICIAL GOING: Good to firm (firm in places; watered; 9.0)
Wind: Virtually nil Weather: Warm and sunny

4749 EXEATS CRICKET CLUB BRIGHTON TOUR (S) H'CAP 5f 215y
5:40 (5:40) (Class 6) (0-60,61) 3-Y-O+
£2,781 (£827; £413; £300; £300; £300) Stalls Centre

Form RPR
6406 1 **Knockout Blow**[14] 4219 4-9-5 **53** ....(p) HectorCrouch 2 60
(John E Long) *led after 1f and mde rest: rdn along w short ld over 1f out: drvn and kpt on strly fnl f* **7/1**
-034 2 2 **Red Snapper**[69] 2287 4-8-4 **45** ....(p) MarcoGhiani(7) 7 46
(William Stone) *led for 1f then trckd wnr: rdn and briefly outpcd over 1f out: drvn and kpt on again ins fnl f* **16/1**
4402 3 nk **Sarasota (IRE)**[8] 4455 4-9-8 **61** .... CierenFallon(5) 4 61
(Alexandra Dunn) *midfield on outer: rdn along and no immediate imp 2f out: sn drvn and kpt on fnl f to snatch 3rd cl home* **7/2[2]**

005 **4** *nk* **Showdance Kid**[8] 4460 5-9-2 **53**........................(p) JoshuaBryan(3) 3 52
(Kevin Frost) *trckd ldrs: effrt to chse wnr over 1f out: drvn and kpt on one pce fnl f: lost 3rd fnl strides* **10/3**[1]

0052 **5** *1* **Red Tycoon (IRE)**[19] 4025 7-9-10 **58**........................(p[1]) PatDobbs 8 54
(Ken Cunningham-Brown) *towards rr: clsd on wnr gng wl 2f out: sn rdn and fnd little: one pce after* **4/1**[3]

60-4 **6** *nk* **Devil Or Angel**[10] 4396 4-8-11 **52**........................ GeorgeRooke(7) 5 47
(Bill Turner) *dwlt and hld up: rdn along and hung lft to far rail over 1f out: one pce fnl f* **14/1**

000 **7** *1 1/4* **Little Tipple**[26] 3775 3-8-0 **45**........................ DarraghKeenan(5) 1 35
(John Ryan) *racd in midfield: pushed along to chse wnr 2f out: sn rdn and no rspnse: no ex fnl f* **22/1**

6034 **8** *1* **The Special One (IRE)**[10] 4376 6-8-13 **47**........................(t) DavidEgan 6 35
(Phil McEntee) *hld up: rdn along on outer 2f out: wknd whn btn fnl f* **9/2**

1m 10.1s (-1.00) **Going Correction** -0.20s/f (Firm) **8 Ran SP% 112.9**
WFA 3 from 4yo+ 6lb
Speed ratings (Par 101): **98,95,94,94,93 92,91,89**
CSF £104.75 CT £458.37 TOTE £8.40: £1.60, £3.00, £1.50; EX 94.50 Trifecta £339.80.There was no bid for the winner.
Owner Mrs S Colville **Bred** Christopher & Annabelle Mason **Trained** Brighton, East Sussex

FOCUS
Add 6yds. Lowly sprinting form, they were spread centre-to-far side in the straight and the winner made most. The runner-up has been rated to this year's form.

4750 J&D BAND NOVICE STKS 6f 210y
6:10 (6:10) (Class 5) 2-Y-O **£3,428** (£1,020; £509; £254) **Stalls** Centre

Form RPR

51 **1** **Governor Of Punjab (IRE)**[20] 3990 2-9-6 **0**........................ FrannyNorton 4 84+
(Mark Johnston) *mde virtually all: pushed along w 1 l ld 2f out: rdn w reduced advantage 1f out: drvn and strly pressed by rivals cl home: kpt on gamely* **9/4**[1]

3 **2** *nse* **Mensen Ernst (IRE)**[26] 3767 2-8-11 **0**........................ SeamusCronin(5) 1 79+
(Richard Hannon) *dwlt and racd in rr: hdwy u.p 2f out: rdn and hung lft to far rail 1f out: kpt on strly fnl f: jst failed* **7/2**[2]

31 **3** *3/4* **World Title (IRE)**[21] 3954 2-9-6 **0**........................ AdamMcNamara 2 81
(Archie Watson) *in tch in midfield: pushed along 3f out: rdn to chse wnr over 1f out: kpt on wl fnl f: nt rch wnr* **7/2**[2]

30 **4** *7* **Dorset Blue (IRE)**[31] 3601 2-9-2 **0**........................ PatDobbs 3 58
(Richard Hannon) *trckd wnr: rdn along to chse wnr over 1f out: carried lft by rival jst ins fnl f: no ex after* **6/1**

01 **5** *4* **Big City**[26] 3767 2-9-9 **0**........................ AdamKirby 5 54
(Saeed bin Suroor) *trckd wnr: rdn along to chse wnr 2f out: hung lft u.p over 1f out: wknd fnl f* **9/2**[3]

0 **6** *4 1/2* **Farhhmorecredit**[22] 3943 2-9-2 **0**........................ JFEgan 6 35
(Michael Attwater) *midfield: pushed along and outpcd over 2f out: sn rdn and no imp over 1f out: plugged on* **150/1**

7 *3 1/2* **Now I'm A Believer** 2-8-11 **0**........................ CallumShepherd 7 21
(Mick Channon) *dwlt and racd in last: a in rr (jockey said filly ran green)* **25/1**

1m 22.92s (-0.88) **Going Correction** -0.20s/f (Firm) **7 Ran SP% 112.2**
Speed ratings (Par 94): **97,96,96,88,83 78,74**
CSF £9.96 TOTE £2.60: £1.10, £2.20; EX 11.90 Trifecta £35.00.
Owner Rob Ferguson **Bred** Mrs Joan Murphy **Trained** Middleham Moor, N Yorks

FOCUS
Add 6yds. A fair novice, as in the opener the winner made most. The front three finished clear.

4751 STREAMLINE TAXIS 202020 FILLIES' H'CAP 6f 210y
6:40 (6:40) (Class 5) (0-70,69) 3-Y-O+
£3,428 (£1,020; £509; £300; £300; £300) **Stalls** Centre

Form RPR

4330 **1** **Kachumba**[7] 4473 4-9-12 **67**........................ AdamKirby 6 76
(Rae Guest) *dwlt and pushed along to rcvr into midfield: pushed along and gd hdwy to ld on outer 2f out: rdn and sn clr 1f out: kpt on strly* **5/2**[1]

66-0 **2** *3 1/4* **Global Rose (IRE)**[18] 4074 4-8-12 **58**........................ CierenFallon(5) 4 58
(Gay Kelleway) *hld up and racd a little keenly: effrt and swtchd lft between rivals to chse wnr over 1f out: kpt on wl fnl f but no match for wnr* **9/1**

0003 **3** *4* **Desert Lantern (USA)**[8] 4454 3-9-2 **65**........................ FrannyNorton 1 51
(Mark Johnston) *s.i.s and racd in last: pushed along in rr over 2f out: rdn and kpt on passed btn horses into 3rd 1f out* **11/4**[2]

-003 **4** *5* **Momentarily**[7] 4473 4-9-8 **63**........................ CallumShepherd 3 39
(Mick Channon) *disp ld tl led after 3f: drvn and hdd by wnr 2f out: wknd fnl f* **3/1**[3]

0-00 **5** *4 1/2* **Summer Angel (IRE)**[3] 4657 4-8-4 **50** oh5........................ TheodoreLadd(5) 2 14
(Michael Appleby) *disp ld for 3f then trckd ldr: rdn along and readily outpcd 2f out: one pce after* **16/1**

-204 **6** *1 1/4* **Dreaming Of Paris**[28] 3691 5-10-0 **69**........................(p[1]) LiamKeniry 5 29
(Patrick Chamings) *disp ld for 3f then trckd ldr: rdn and lost pl 2f out: wknd fnl f* **11/2**

1m 22.22s (-1.58) **Going Correction** -0.20s/f (Firm) **6 Ran SP% 111.5**
WFA 3 from 4yo+ 8lb
Speed ratings (Par 100): **101,97,92,87,81 80**
CSF £24.08 TOTE £3.00: £1.20, £3.40; EX 25.20 Trifecta £91.50.
Owner The Bucket List Racing Syndicate **Bred** Brook Stud Bloodstock Ltd **Trained** Newmarket, Suffolk

FOCUS
Add 6yds. The pace didn't hold up in this moderate fillies' sprint, the front two drawing right away late. The winner has been rated back to her best.

4752 GREEN PEOPLE H'CAP 1m 3f 198y
7:10 (7:10) (Class 4) (0-85,85) 4-Y-O+ **£5,207** (£1,549; £774; £387) **Stalls** High

Form RPR

0325 **1** **Perfect Illusion**[14] 4224 4-8-7 **78**........................(p) WilliamCarver(7) 3 88
(Andrew Balding) *settled wl in 3rd: upsides gng wl 2f out: pushed along to ld 1f out and readily asserted: pushed out: comf* **2/1**[2]

0-36 **2** *3 1/2* **You're Hired**[13] 4250 6-9-7 **85**........................ PatDobbs 2 89
(Amanda Perrett) *led: rdn along and hdd by wnr 1f out: one pce fnl f (vet said gelding was showing signs of a prolonged recovery)* **3/1**[3]

2355 **3** *11* **Hollywood Road (IRE)**[47] 3016 6-9-2 **80**........................ HectorCrouch 1 67
(Gary Moore) *hld up: drvn along in last over 3f out: rdn and no imp over 1f out: plugged on for poor 3rd (vet said gelding was lame on it's left-fore leg)* **8/1**

1261 **4** *2 1/2* **Francophilia**[10] 4383 4-8-12 **76**........................ FrannyNorton 4 59
(Mark Johnston) *dwlt sltly and pushed up to trck ldr: rdn along and outpcd by ldng pair 2f out: wknd fr 1f out (trainers' rep could offer no explanation for the poor performance)* **11/8**[1]

2m 29.24s (-6.76) **Going Correction** -0.20s/f (Firm) **4 Ran SP% 111.5**
Speed ratings (Par 105): **114,111,104,102**
CSF £8.32 TOTE £2.90; EX 5.80 Trifecta £13.80.
Owner Mr & Mrs R Gorell/N Botica & Partner **Bred** James Ortega Bloodstock Ltd **Trained** Kingsclere, Hants

FOCUS
Add 6yds. Just the four of them and the favourite failed to give her running but the winner, under his claimer, has been rated back to his best.

4753 JOHN TERNOUTH 70TH BIRTHDAY H'CAP 7f 211y
7:40 (7:42) (Class 6) (0-55,62) 3-Y-O+ **£2,264** (£673; £336; £168) **Stalls** Centre

Form RPR

-034 **1** **Harlequin Rose (IRE)**[7] 4472 5-8-8 **46** oh1........................(v) WilliamCarver(7) 15 54
(Patrick Chamings) *midfield on outer: effrt to chse ldr 2f out: rdn along to ld wl over 1f out: drvn and kpt on wl fnl f* **15/2**[3]

2050 **2** *nk* **Sharp Operator**[21] 3966 6-9-5 **55**........................(h) TheodoreLadd(5) 11 62
(Charlie Wallis) *towards rr: hdwy u.p to chse wnr 2f out: sn rdn and edgd lft u.p 1f out: styd on wl fnl f: nt rch wnr* **8/1**

3054 **3** *3 1/4* **N Over J**[28] 3687 4-9-7 **52**........................(v) DavidEgan 12 52
(William Knight) *trckd ldrs: drvn along and outpcd by wnr wl over 1f out: kpt on one pce fnl f* **8/1**

6231 **4** *1* **Hedging (IRE)**[7] 4472 5-9-10 **62** 5ex........................(b) GeorgiaDobie(7) 2 60
(Eve Johnson Houghton) *trckd ldrs: pushed along over 2f out: rdn and no imp over 1f out: plugged on one pce* **5/2**[1]

3022 **5** *1* **Joyful Dream (IRE)**[14] 4217 5-8-11 **47**........................(p) DarraghKeenan(5) 4 42
(John Butler) *trckd ldrs: rdn and sltly impeded by wnr as tempo qckned 2f out: drvn 1f out: one pce fnl f (jockey said mare suffered interference)* **6/1**[2]

-044 **6** *2 1/4* **Come On Bear (IRE)**[4] 4589 4-9-1 **46**........................(v) JoeyHaynes 9 36
(Alan Bailey) *dwlt and racd in rr: pushed along in rr over 2f out: rdn and no imp over 1f out: kpt on (jockey said filly was slowly away)* **12/1**

50-1 **7** *3/4* **Miss Recycled**[14] 4217 4-8-13 **49**........................ CierenFallon(5) 1 37
(Michael Madgwick) *hld up: rdn and struggling over 2f out: kpt on passed btn horses fnl f* **12/1**

-040 **8** *2 3/4* **Solveig's Song**[70] 2231 7-9-8 **53**........................(p) AdamKirby 8 35
(Steve Woodman) *midfield: rdn and no imp 2f out: kpt on one pce fnl f* **25/1**

4300 **9** *nk* **Merdon Castle (IRE)**[11] 4346 7-8-10 **46** oh1........................(b[1]) SeamusCronin(5) 3 28
(Frank Bishop) *led: rdn along and hdd by wnr wl over 1f out: wknd fnl f (jockey said gelding hung left-handed)* **25/1**

0040 **10** *1/2* **Hidden Stash**[14] 4217 5-9-1 **46** oh1........................(b[1]) JFEgan 6 26
(William Stone) *chsd ldr: rdn along and lost pl wl over 1f out: wknd fnl f* **16/1**

-000 **11** *nk* **Padmavati**[31] 3593 3-8-13 **53**........................(b[1]) LiamKeniry 10 30
(Ed Walker) *midfield: effrt to chse ldrs over 2f out: rdn and no imp over 1f out: n.d* **20/1**

-035 **12** *30* **Luxford**[14] 4217 5-9-4 **49**........................ HectorCrouch 7
(Gary Moore) *midfield: rdn along in rr over 2f out: nvr on terms* **8/1**

00-0 **13** *3 1/4* **Davina**[145] 724 4-8-8 **46** oh1........................ GeorgeRooke(7) 5
(Bill Turner) *hld up: rdn and detached 1/2-way: a bhd* **66/1**

1m 34.58s (-2.32) **Going Correction** -0.20s/f (Firm) **13 Ran SP% 123.2**
WFA 3 from 4yo+ 9lb
Speed ratings (Par 101): **103,102,99,98,97 95,94,91,91,90 90,60,57**
CSF £65.73 CT £379.59 TOTE £9.20: £3.10, £3.00, £3.10; EX 78.00 Trifecta £632.30.
Owner G E Bassett & P R Chamings **Bred** Langton Stud **Trained** Baughurst, Hants

FOCUS
Add 6yds. The front two pulled away late in what was a moderate handicap.

4754 MARATHONBET FESTIVAL OF RACING 7TH-9TH AUGUST H'CAP 6f 210y
8:10 (8:10) (Class 6) (0-60,60) 3-Y-O
£2,781 (£827; £413; £300; £300; £300) **Stalls** Centre

Form RPR

0446 **1** **River Dawn**[15] 4185 3-9-7 **60**........................ KieranShoemark 5 69+
(Paul Cole) *mde all: pushed along whn chal 2f out: sn rdn and asserted again over 1f out: styd on strly* **15/8**[1]

2042 **2** *2 1/2* **Tarrzan (IRE)**[14] 4218 3-9-0 **53**........................ LiamJones 7 54
(John Gallagher) *towards rr: hmpd by rival over 4f out: effrt to cl over 2f out: swtchd arnd rival and rdn over 1f out: styd on wl fnl f (vet said gelding lost it's left hind shoe)* **12/1**

6030 **3** *nk* **Spirit Of Lucerne (IRE)**[26] 3780 3-8-3 **49** ow1........................ GraceMcEntee(7) 2 49
(Phil McEntee) *hld up: gd hdwy on outer to chse ldr over 2f out: rdn and hung lft over 1f out: kpt on sltly awkwardly ins fnl f* **33/1**

-306 **4** *2* **So Claire**[14] 4218 3-9-1 **54**........................ MartinDwyer 9 49
(William Muir) *trckd wnr: rdn and outpcd by wnr 2f out: kpt on one pce u.p fnl f* **8/1**

4606 **5** *3/4* **Aquarius (IRE)**[8] 4436 3-9-1 **59**........................(v) TheodoreLadd(5) 8 52
(Michael Appleby) *racd in midfield v keenly: hung lft and hmpd rivals over 4f out: rdn along 2f out: sn drvn and no imp 1f out: plugged on* **10/1**

0-35 **6** *1/2* **Alyx Vance**[14] 4219 3-9-2 **55**........................ RoystonFfrench 1 46
(Lydia Pearce) *chsd wnr: rdn and outpcd by wnr wl over 1f out: one pce fnl f* **20/1**

2631 **7** *3/4* **Princess Florence (IRE)**[7] 4477 3-8-9 **53** 6ex........................ CierenFallon(5) 6 42
(John Ryan) *racd in midfield: clsd into 4th 3f out: upsides wnr wl 2f out: sn rdn and fnd little: wknd fnl f (jockey said filly ran too free early)* **5/1**[3]

-005 **8** *hd* **Grey Hare**[15] 4180 3-8-7 **46** oh1........................(t) JoeyHaynes 4 35
(Tony Carroll) *hld up: hmpd by rival over 4f out: rdn on outer in rr over 2f out: nvr able to get on terms (jockey said gelding suffered interference)* **16/1**

-065 **9** *3 1/2* **Forty Four Sunsets (FR)**[38] 3348 3-8-8 **52**........................(b[1]) SeamusCronin(5) 3 45+
(Richard Hannon) *midfield on inner: bdly hmpd against the rails over 4f out: sn bhd* **3/1**[2]

1m 23.33s (-0.47) **Going Correction** -0.20s/f (Firm) **9 Ran SP% 117.9**
Speed ratings (Par 98): **94,91,90,88,87 87,86,86,82**
CSF £27.24 CT £576.66 TOTE £2.60: £1.70, £2.60, £8.30; EX 23.10 Trifecta £390.60.
Owner Mrs Fitri Hay **Bred** Biddestone Stud Ltd **Trained** Whatcombe, Oxon
■ Stewards' Enquiry : Theodore Ladd four-day ban; careless riding (July 23-26)

The Form Book Flat 2019, Raceform Ltd, Newbury, RG14 5SJ

FOCUS
Add 6yds. A step up from the winner, with the runner-up close to this year's form.

4755 SKY SPORTS RACING ON SKY 415 H'CAP 5f 215y
8:40 (8:41) (Class 6) (0-60,62) 3-Y-O

£2,781 (£827; £413; £300; £300; £300) **Stalls** Centre

Form RPR
0652 **1** **Alicia Darcy (IRE)**[8] 4457 3-9-7 60..........(b[1]) AdamMcNamara 7 68
(Archie Watson) *trckd ldr: rdn along to ld over 1f out: sn in command and styd on strly fnl f (vet said filly bled from the nose)* **4/1[3]**
-004 **2** 2 **Miss Liberty Belle (AUS)**[21] 3964 2-9-4 57.......... KieranShoemark 2 59
(William Jarvis) *slowly away and racd in last: rdn along in last over 1f out: picked up wl ins fnl f: nt rch wnr* **9/4[2]**
6525 **3** 1 1/4 **Urban Highway (IRE)**[26] 3764 3-9-4 62 DarraghKeenan(5) 1 60
(Tony Carroll) *midfield on inner: rdn along and ev ch on inner 1f out: nt pce of wnr fnl 100yds* **7/4[1]**
0000 **4** 1 **Zaula**[15] 4180 3-8-12 51.......... DavidEgan 3 45
(Mick Channon) *midfield: rdn along to chse wnr over 1f out: one pce fnl f* **16/1**
4000 **5** 1 3/4 **Kiowa**[14] 4219 3-8-7 46 oh1.......... DannyBrock 6 35
(Philip McBride) *led: rdn along and hdd by wnr wl over 1f out: wknd fnl f* **10/1**
00-0 **6** 11 **Willa's Wish (IRE)**[24] 3839 3-8-7 46 oh1.......... JoeyHaynes 4
(Tony Carroll) *chsd ldr: pushed along to chse ldr over 2f out: rdn and ev ch over 1f out: wknd fnl f* **22/1**

1m 10.82s (-0.28) **Going Correction** -0.20s/f (Firm) **6** Ran SP% **106.5**
Speed ratings (Par 98): **93,90,88,87,85 70**
CSF £11.74 TOTE £4.50: £2.00, £1.50; EX 13.30 Trifecta £25.40.
Owner Boadicea Bloodstock **Bred** Tally-Ho Stud **Trained** Upper Lambourn, W Berks
■ Nervous Nerys was withdrawn, price at time of withdrawal 8/1. Rule 4 applies to all bets. Deduction of 10p in the pound.

FOCUS
Add 6yds. Lowly 3yo sprint form but the winner built on her latest run.
T/Plt: £189.60 to a £1 stake. Pool: £72,172.90 - 277.8 winning units T/Qpdt: £61.20 to a £1 stake. Pool: £7,694.19 - 93.00 winning units **Mark Grantham**

4440 PONTEFRACT (L-H)
Tuesday, July 9

OFFICIAL GOING: Good to firm (good in places; watered; 7.9)
Wind: Virtually nil Weather: Cloudy

4756 DIANNE NURSERY H'CAP 6f
2:15 (2:16) (Class 5) (0-70,70) 2-Y-O

£5,498 (£1,636; £817; £408; £300; £300) **Stalls** Low

Form RPR
450 **1** **Ambyfaeirvine (IRE)**[52] 2820 2-8-11 60.......... DavidAllan 10 70
(Ivan Furtado) *prom: led over 2f out: rdn over 1f out: styd on wl fnl f* **14/1**
2100 **2** 1 1/2 **Infinite Grace**[22] 3927 2-9-7 70.......... DanielTudhope 6 75
(David O'Meara) *trckd ldrs on inner: swtchd rt and hdwy wl over 1f out: sn chsng ldng pair: rdn to chse wnr ins fnl f: sn drvn: no imp towards fin* **5/1[2]**
034 **3** 1 **Fashion Free**[13] 4245 2-9-2 65.......... HollieDoyle 13 67
(Archie Watson) *trckd ldrs: smooth hdwy over 2f out: sn cl up: chal wl over 1f out: sn rdn and edgd lft: drvn ent fnl f: kpt on same pce (jockey said filly hung left in the home straight)* **8/1**
605 **4** 2 **Lexington Quest (IRE)**[26] 3767 2-9-3 66.......... SeanLevey 4 61+
(Richard Hannon) *towards rr: pushed along 1/2-way: hdwy 2f out: sn swtchd rt and rdn: n.m.r and swtchd lft over 1f out: styd on wl fnl f* **8/1**
456 **5** 1 1/4 **Callipygian**[31] 3578 2-9-1 64.......... BarryMcHugh 12 55
(James Given) *chsd ldrs: rdn along 2f out: sn drvn and kpt on one pce* **16/1**
055 **6** 1/2 **Stormy Bay**[33] 3498 2-8-6 55..........(p[1]) AndrewMullen 11 45
(Keith Dalgleish) *in tch on outer: hdwy to chse ldrs 1/2-way: rdn along 2f out: sn one pce* **20/1**
560 **7** 3 1/4 **Mystic Knight (IRE)**[51] 2869 2-8-5 54.......... DuranFentiman 7 33
(Tim Easterby) *chsd ldrs: rdn along over 2f out: sn drvn and wknd* **16/1**
640 **8** nk **Pearlwood (IRE)**[13] 4237 2-8-6 58.......... SeanDavis(3) 5 36
(Richard Fahey) *a towards rr* **20/1**
606 **9** nk **The Ginger Bullet**[52] 2820 2-8-13 62.......... PaulHanagan 2 39
(Richard Fahey) *t.k.h in midfield: effrt over 2f out and sn rdn along: n.m.r and drvn over 1f out: sn btn* **10/3[1]**
660 **10** 3/4 **Van Dijk**[17] 4098 2-8-6 62..........(b[1]) KieranSchofield(7) 3 37
(Antony Brittain) *s.i.s: a in rr* **14/1**
000 **11** 2 1/2 **Bosun's Chair**[21] 3954 2-8-6 55.......... RachelRichardson 15 22
(Tim Easterby) *dwlt: a in rr* **40/1**
0034 **12** 2 1/2 **The Lazy Monkey (IRE)**[12] 4289 2-9-3 66.......... PJMcDonald 9 25
(Mark Johnston) *sn led: pushed along 1/2-way: rdn and hdd over 2f out: sn wknd* **11/1**
000 **13** 3 1/2 **Beautrix**[25] 3812 2-8-3 52.......... JamesSullivan 1
(Michael Dods) *hld up towards rr: effrt on inner and sme hdwy 2f out: rdn and nt clr run wl over 1f out: n.d (jockey said filly was denied a clear run approaching the final furlong and stumbled on a few occasions. vet reported filly lost her right hind shoe)* **13/2[3]**

1m 19.41s (2.31) **Going Correction** +0.175s/f (Good) **13** Ran SP% **120.7**
Speed ratings (Par 94): **91,89,87,85,83 82,78,77,77,76 73,69,65**
CSF £81.50 CT £635.61 TOTE £17.50: £5.70, £2.00, £2.50; EX 106.90 Trifecta £1540.70.
Owner From The Front Racing 1 **Bred** Owenstown Bloodstock Ltd **Trained** Wiseton, Nottinghamshire

FOCUS
A false running rail was out approximately 15ft from the permanent rail, adding approximately 8yds to all races. Plenty of unknowns in this ordinary nursery but a clear pb from the winner.

4757 STEVE EVANS MEMORIAL SOCHALL SMITH CHARTERED ACCOUNTANTS H'CAP 5f 3y
2:45 (2:45) (Class 5) (0-75,76) 3-Y-O £3,557 (£1,058; £529) **Stalls** Low

Form RPR
3620 **1** **Major Blue**[13] 4236 3-9-6 71..........(b[1]) HollieDoyle 3 76
(James Eustace) *sn led: rdn and qcknd clr 2f out: kpt on wl fnl f* **2/1[2]**
-606 **2** 3 1/4 **Three Card Trick**[12] 4297 3-9-11 76.......... JamieSpencer 1 69
(Kevin Ryan) *rrd and lost 4 l s: chsd ldng pair: hdwy over 2f out: rdn wl over 1f out: sn chsng wnr: drvn and no imp fnl f (jockey said gelding reared as the stalls opened and missed the break)* **4/5[1]**
06-0 **3** 1 1/2 **Packington Lane**[17] 4128 3-9-2 67.......... DavidAllan 2 55
(Tim Easterby) *trckd wnr: pushed along over 2f out: sn rdn and kpt on same pce* **5/1[3]**

1m 4.34s (0.44) **Going Correction** +0.175s/f (Good) **3** Ran SP% **105.6**
Speed ratings (Par 100): **103,97,95**
CSF £3.96 TOTE £2.30; EX 3.40 Trifecta £4.10.
Owner J C Smith **Bred** Littleton Stud **Trained** Newmarket, Suffolk

FOCUS
Add 8yds. A trappy little 3yo sprint handicap and the winner looked to improve.

4758 WEATHERBYS TBA PIPALONG STKS (LISTED RACE) (F&M) 1m 6y
3:15 (3:15) (Class 1) 4-Y-O+

£28,010 (£10,665; £5,340; £2,665; £1,335; £670) **Stalls** Low

Form RPR
-024 **1** **Exhort**[37] 3374 4-9-0 93.......... PaulHanagan 10 101
(Richard Fahey) *hld up: pushed along and sltly outpcd 2f out: hdwy wl over 1f out: sn n.m.r and swtchd lft: rdn to chse ldrs and swtchd rt ins fnl f: styd on strly to ld nr fin* **25/1**
-301 **2** 3/4 **Billesdon Brook**[20] 3994 4-9-3 107.......... SeanLevey 4 102
(Richard Hannon) *trckd ldrs: hdwy on outer over 2f out: rdn to chal over 1f out: drvn ins fnl f: led fnl 50yds: hdd and no ex nr fin* **3/1[2]**
2122 **3** 1/2 **Agincourt (IRE)**[18] 4072 4-9-0 87.......... DanielTudhope 3 98
(David O'Meara) *led: pushed along over 2f out: rdn over 1f out: drvn ins fnl f: hdd fnl 50yds: no ex* **8/1[3]**
0-45 **4** 1 1/4 **New Day Dawn (IRE)**[38] 3359 4-9-0 92.......... RichardKingscote 2 95
(Tom Dascombe) *trckd ldrs: hdwy over 2f out: sn rdn along: drvn over 1f out: kpt on u.p fnl f* **12/1**
-102 **5** nse **Clon Coulis (IRE)**[20] 3987 5-9-0 103..........(h) JamieSpencer 8 95
(David Barron) *dwlt and hld up in rr: hdwy on outer over 2f out: rdn to chse ldrs over 1f out: drvn ins fnl f: no imp towards fin* **9/4[1]**
6-52 **6** nse **Wisdom Mind (IRE)**[10] 4410 4-9-0 98..........(t) GaryHalpin 9 95
(Joseph Patrick O'Brien, Ire) *trckd ldrs: hdwy over 2f out: rdn along wl over 1f out: drvn and kpt on same pce fnl f* **25/1**
0213 **7** 1/2 **Never Be Enough**[7] 4490 4-9-0 83.......... TomEaves 5 94?
(Keith Dalgleish) *hld up in rr: hdwy 2f out: rdn over 1f out: kpt on fnl f* **50/1**
43-0 **8** 3 **Threading (IRE)**[20] 3986 4-9-0 102.......... PJMcDonald 1 87
(Mark Johnston) *chsd ldrs on inner: rdn along over 2f out: sn wknd* **3/1[2]**
0600 **9** 1 1/2 **Pattie**[20] 3994 5-9-0 93.......... BenCurtis 7 83
(Mick Channon) *rrd s and slowly away: a in rr (jockey said mare jumped awkwardly leaving the stalls)* **25/1**
056- **10** 1 **Dance Diva**[276] 7990 4-9-0 96.......... TonyHamilton 12 81
(Richard Fahey) *stdd and swtchd lft s: hld up: hdwy over 2f out: rdn along wl over 1f out: sn drvn and wknd* **66/1**
3650 **11** 4 **Vivianite (IRE)**[20] 3994 4-9-0 93..........(p) HollieDoyle 6 72
(Archie Watson) *t.k.h: trckd ldr: pushed along over 2f out: sn rdn and wknd (jockey said filly stopped quickly)* **40/1**

1m 45.39s (-0.51) **Going Correction** +0.175s/f (Good) **11** Ran SP% **117.0**
Speed ratings (Par 111): **109,108,107,106,106 106,105,102,101,100 96**
CSF £94.79 TOTE £32.10: £5.20, £1.10, £2.30; EX 104.70 Trifecta £1359.40.
Owner Cheveley Park Stud **Bred** Cheveley Park Stud Ltd **Trained** Musley Bank, N Yorks

FOCUS
Add 8yds. They went a sound pace in this fillies' Listed event and the winner has been rated to her best.

4759 KING RICHARD III H'CAP 6f
3:45 (3:46) (Class 3) (0-90,90) 3-Y-O+

£9,337 (£2,796; £1,398; £699; £349; £175) **Stalls** Low

Form RPR
4004 **1** **Musharrif**[5] 4555 7-8-4 73..........(t) ZakWheatley(7) 2 85
(Declan Carroll) *trckd ldrs: hdwy 2f out: chal over 1f out: sn led and rdn: clr whn rdr lost whip jst ins fnl f: kpt on strly* **17/2**
-100 **2** 3 3/4 **Ventura Ocean (IRE)**[10] 4402 3-9-5 90.......... SeanDavis(3) 8 89
(Richard Fahey) *stdd and swtchd lft s: hld up in rr: hdwy 2f out: rdn to chse ldrs over 1f out: drvn ins fnl f: kpt on: no ch w wnr* **13/2[3]**
1400 **3** 3/4 **Reflektor (IRE)**[31] 3589 6-10-0 90.......... RichardKingscote 7 88
(Tom Dascombe) *prom: cl up 2f out: rdn to take slt ld 1 1/2f out: sn hdd and drvn: kpt on same pce* **14/1**
0302 **4** shd **Tommy Taylor (USA)**[39] 3308 5-9-13 89.......... KevinStott 5 86
(Kevin Ryan) *dwlt: sn pushed along and bhd: hdwy and wd st: rdn wl over 1f out: styd on wl u.p fnl f* **9/4[1]**
1501 **5** 4 **Key To Power**[10] 4374 3-8-11 79.......... ConnorBeasley 3 62
(Mark Johnston) *led: pushed along over 2f out: rdn and hdd 1 1/2f out: sn drvn and wknd* **9/1**
0-00 **6** 5 **Ower Fly**[80] 1944 6-9-9 85..........(w) JamesSullivan 6 53
(Ruth Carr) *trckd ldrs: pushed along over 2f out: rdn wl over 1f out: sn btn* **8/1**
0006 **7** 8 **Von Blucher (IRE)**[10] 4379 6-9-6 82..........(b) PJMcDonald 4 25
(Rebecca Menzies) *dwlt and wnt rt s: a in rr (vet reported gelding lost its right hind shoe)* **7/2[2]**
-400 **8** 30 **Sandra's Secret (IRE)**[55] 2743 6-10-0 90..........(v[1]) LewisEdmunds 1
(Les Eyre) *cl up on inner: rdn along over 2f out: sn wknd (jockey said mare lost its action in the closing stages)* **10/1**

1m 17.54s (0.44) **Going Correction** +0.175s/f (Good)
WFA 3 from 5yo+ 6lb **8** Ran SP% **113.7**
Speed ratings (Par 107): **104,99,98,97,92 85,75,35**
CSF £61.40 CT £773.64 TOTE £9.40: £2.50, £2.80, £4.20; EX 64.50 Trifecta £753.40.
Owner Ray Flegg & John Bousfield **Bred** Mr & Mrs J Davis & P Mitchell B'Stock **Trained** Malton, N Yorks

FOCUS
Add 8yds. They went a solid pace in this good-quality sprint handicap and the winner has been rated close to his best.

4760 BEN AND MARY HIBBERT MEMORIAL MAIDEN STKS 1m 2f 5y
4:15 (4:16) (Class 5) 3-Y-O+ £4,204 (£1,251; £625; £312) **Stalls** Low

Form RPR
22 **1** **Harrovian**[35] 3445 3-9-4 0.......... RobertHavlin 1 84+
(John Gosden) *mde all: rdn clr wl over 1f out: kpt on strly* **4/5[1]**
2 7 **Gazton** 3-9-4 0..........(h[1]) SeanLevey 4 70
(Ivan Furtado) *hld up in tch: hdwy 4f out: rdn along over 2f out: styd on to take 2nd ent fnl f: kpt on: no ch w wnr* **33/1**
-423 **3** 4 **Alhaazm**[31] 3585 3-9-4 82.......... JimCrowley 3 65
(Sir Michael Stoute) *trckd wnr: pushed along over 2f out: rdn wl over 1f out: sn drvn and one pce* **6/4[2]**

4 1 1/4 **Sible Hedingham** 3-8-13 0 ... HollieDoyle 2 55
(James Eustace) *green in rr: pushed along and outpcd 3f out: sn rdn: styd on fr over 1f out: n.d* **50/1**

3 5 8 **Beyond The Clouds**[21] 3958 6-10-0 0 ... TomEaves 6 43
(Kevin Ryan) *trckd ldng pair: pushed along 3f out: rdn 2f out: sn wknd* **17/2[3]**

45 6 31 **Nineteenrbo'Malley**[23] 3882 7-10-0 0 ... AndrewMullen 5
(Robyn Brisland) *trckd ldrs: lost pl 1/2-way: bhd fnl 3f* **100/1**

2m 16.18s (1.18) **Going Correction** +0.175s/f (Good)
WFA 3 from 6yo+ 10lb **6 Ran SP% 112.0**
Speed ratings (Par 103): **102,96,93,92,85 61**
CSF £26.19 TOTE £1.60: £1.10, £10.50; EX 35.50 Trifecta £72.90.
Owner HH Sheikh Zayed bin Mohammed Racing **Bred** Miss K Rausing **Trained** Newmarket, Suffolk

FOCUS
Add 8yds. They finished well strung out in this maiden and it's hard to know the true worth of the form.

4761 ATLAS LEISURE HOMES LTD H'CAP 1m 6y
4:45 (4:45) (Class 5) (0-70,71) 3-Y-O
£4,204 (£1,251; £625; £312; £300; £300) **Stalls Low**

Form RPR

23-4 1 **Li Kui**[18] 4071 3-9-6 **69** ... (t[1]) RossaRyan 4 76
(Paul Cole) *trckd ldrs: hdwy over 2f out: rdn to ld over 1f out: drvn ins fnl f: kpt on wl towards fin* **5/1[2]**

5442 2 *nk* **One To Go**[14] 4210 3-8-12 **61** ... (b) DavidAllan 1 67
(Tim Easterby) *led 1f: trckd ldr: led again on inner 2f out: rdn and hdd over 1f out: drvn and rallied ins fnl f: ev ch tl no ex towards fin* **4/1[1]**

064- 3 2 **Alfa Dawn (IRE)**[276] 7989 3-9-7 **70** ... SamJames 2 72
(Phillip Makin) *hld up towards rr: hdwy over 3f out: rdn to chse ldng pair over 1f out: drvn and kpt on fnl f* **16/1**

0552 4 7 **Garrison Commander (IRE)**[7] 4476 3-9-1 **64** ... (b) HollieDoyle 3 50
(Eve Johnson Houghton) *cl up: led after 1f: rdn along over 2f out: sn hdd and drvn: grad wknd* **4/1[1]**

-030 5 4 **My Boy Lewis (IRE)**[18] 4070 3-9-8 **71** ... BenCurtis 7 47
(Roger Fell) *towards rr: hdwy on inner 3f out: rdn over 2f out: drvn wl over 1f out: nvr nr ldrs* **9/1**

-650 6 8 **The Rutland Rebel (IRE)**[33] 3513 3-9-2 **65** ... GrahamLee 6 23
(Micky Hammond) *a in rr* **25/1**

-002 7 1/2 **Jimmy Greenhough (IRE)**[12] 4284 3-8-9 **58** ... PaddyMathers 10 15
(Richard Fahey) *chsd ldrs: rdn along 3f out: sn wknd* **15/2[3]**

0005 8 18 **Gremoboy**[20] 4000 3-8-5 **54** ... (b[1]) DuranFentiman 8
(Tim Easterby) *prom: rdn along 3f out: sn wknd* **33/1**

3001 9 11 **Starlight Red (IRE)**[15] 4179 3-9-5 **68** ... PaulHanagan 5
(Charles Hills) *a towards rr: rdn along 3f out: sn outpcd and bhd* **16/1**

0651 10 1 1/4 **Mecca's Gift (IRE)**[7] 4488 3-9-3 **66** 6ex ... (b) ConnorBeasley 9
(Michael Dods) *trckd ldrs: pushed along 3f out: rdn over 2f out: sn drvn and btn: eased fr wl over 1f out* **4/1[1]**

1m 46.53s (0.63) **Going Correction** +0.175s/f (Good) **10 Ran SP% 117.0**
Speed ratings (Par 100): **103,102,100,93,89 81,81,63,52,50**
CSF £25.43 CT £252.82 TOTE £5.60: £2.00, £1.40, £5.90; EX 20.80 Trifecta £294.30.
Owner Hurun UK Racing **Bred** Ms J Allison **Trained** Whatcombe, Oxon

FOCUS
Add 8yds. A modest 3yo handicap in which two came clear, and this rates a pb from the winner.

4762 "WELL DONE US" RIP STEVE APPRENTICE H'CAP 1m 2f 5y
5:15 (5:16) (Class 5) (0-75,73) 3-Y-O+
£3,557 (£1,058; £529; £300; £300; £300) **Stalls Low**

Form RPR

5121 1 **Edgar Allan Poe (IRE)**[8] 4446 5-10-1 **73** 5ex ... PhilDennis 1 81
(Rebecca Bastiman) *trckd ldrs: smooth hdwy over 2f out: led over 1f out: sn rdn: drvn and kpt on wl towards fin* **5/2[1]**

00-4 2 1/2 **Rose Crown**[14] 4216 5-8-9 **60** ... GeorgeBass(7) 3 67
(Mick Channon) *t.k.h: hld up in rr: hdwy 2f out: rdn to chse wnr ins fnl f: sn drvn and ev ch: no ex towards fin* **8/1**

0406 3 3 1/4 **Bay Of Naples (IRE)**[11] 4316 3-9-3 **71** ... JaneElliott 5 72
(Mark Johnston) *led at stdy pce: pushed along 2f out: rdn wl over 1f out: sn hdd: drvn and kpt on same pce fnl f* **7/1[3]**

4300 4 1/2 **Quoteline Direct**[8] 4446 6-9-5 **66** ... (h) HarrisonShaw(3) 2 66+
(Micky Hammond) *hld up in tch: hdwy on inner 2f out: effrt and nt clr run over 1f out and ins fnl f: swtchd rt and rdn fnl 100yds: styd on strly* **9/2[2]**

062 5 1/2 **Trinity Star (IRE)**[11] 4333 8-9-6 **69** ... (v) LauraCoughlan(5) 7 68
(Karen McLintock) *t.k.h: cl up: rdn along 2f out: wknd appr fnl f* **9/2[2]**

2610 6 1 1/4 **Champagne Rules**[25] 3816 8-9-11 **72** ... ConnorMurtagh(3) 4 68
(Sharon Watt) *t.k.h: prom: rdn along and wd st: drvn over 1f out: one pce* **7/1[3]**

0025 7 11 **Kingdom Brunel**[17] 4131 4-9-10 **68** ... (p) ConorMcGovern 6 42
(David O'Meara) *hld up in tch: pushed along wl over 2f out: sn rdn and wknd* **9/1**

2m 16.35s (1.35) **Going Correction** +0.175s/f (Good)
WFA 3 from 4yo+ 10lb **7 Ran SP% 111.0**
Speed ratings (Par 103): **101,100,98,97,97 96,87**
CSF £21.64 TOTE £3.10: £1.90, £3.80; EX 18.00 Trifecta £129.50.
Owner I B Barker / P Bastiman **Bred** Paul, Ben & Charlie Cartan **Trained** Cowthorpe, N Yorks

FOCUS
Add 8yds. This run-of-the-mill handicap was run at a muddling pace and the winner proved better than ever.
T/Jkpt: Not Won. T/Plt: £514.90 to a £1 stake. Pool: £65,219.03 - 92.45 winning units T/Qpdt: £44.80 to a £1 stake. Pool: £9,522.47 - 157.18 winning units **Joe Rowntree**

4454 WOLVERHAMPTON (A.W) (L-H)
Tuesday, July 9

OFFICIAL GOING: Tapeta: standard
Wind: Light behind Weather: Overcast

4763 OUR CHARMING FABRICATORS TRICKS OF THE TRADE H'CAP 6f 20y (Tp)
2:00 (2:02) (Class 6) (0-60,60) 3-Y-O+
£2,781 (£827; £413; £300; £300; £300) **Stalls Low**

Form RPR

1260 1 **Olaudah**[14] 4219 5-9-10 **60** ... DavidProbert 3 67+
(Henry Candy) *trckd ldrs: racd keenly: shkn up to ld and hung lft over 1f out: drvn out* **9/2[2]**

00-1 2 *nk* **Kennocha (IRE)**[35] 3442 3-9-3 **59** ... (t) SilvestreDeSousa 2 64
(Amy Murphy) *chsd ldr tl over 4f out: remained handy: rdn and nt clr run over 1f out: swtchd rt: r.o u.p* **3/1[1]**

6520 3 1/2 **Santafiora**[11] 4330 5-9-5 **55** ... CamHardie 9 60
(Julie Camacho) *s.i.s: hld up: hdwy over 1f out: rdn and r.o to go 3rd nr fin: nt rch ldrs (jockey said mare was slowly away)* **11/1**

3404 4 3/4 **Tease Maid**[8] 4457 3-9-4 **60** ... JasonHart 6 61
(John Quinn) *hld up in tch: rdn over 1f out: nt clr run and swtchd rt ins fnl f: running on whn nt clr run towards fin* **5/1[3]**

010 5 *nse* **Lysander Belle (IRE)**[24] 3839 3-9-3 **59** ... StevieDonohoe 13 60
(Sophie Leech) *prom: shkn up over 2f out: r.o* **14/1**

3046 6 3/4 **Spenny's Lass**[18] 4074 4-9-4 **54** ... (p) LukeMorris 11 54
(John Ryan) *chsd ldrs: sn pushed along and lost pl: r.o u.p ins fnl f* **14/1**

40-3 7 1/2 **Haze**[164] 438 3-9-4 **60** ... (b[1]) JasonWatson 10 57
(Paul Cole) *sn led: rdn and hdd over 1f out: no ex wl ins fnl f: n.m.r towards fin (jockey said filly was tight of room on the run to the line)* **14/1**

000 8 2 **Impressionable**[36] 3431 3-9-1 **57** ... (b[1]) ShaneKelly 1 48
(Marco Botti) *free to post: s.i.s: racd keenly and sn prom: pushed along 1/2-way: no ex fnl f* **14/1**

0-61 9 1/2 **Sovereign State**[31] 3577 4-9-5 **55** ... RossaRyan 12 45
(Tony Newcombe) *broke wl: sn stdd and lost pl: n.d after* **25/1**

560 10 *nse* **Peachey Carnehan**[12] 4281 5-9-8 **58** ... (v) PhilDennis 8 48
(Michael Mullineaux) *s.i.s: rdn over 2f out: n.d (jockey said gelding never travelled)* **6/1**

430 11 1 3/4 **Tizwotitiz**[11] 4328 3-8-8 **57** ... TobyEley(7) 7 40
(Steph Hollinshead) *sn pushed along in rr: nvr on terms (jockey said gelding ran too freely; vet reported gelding lost its left fore shoe)* **20/1**

6000 12 3 3/4 **Jorvik Prince**[22] 3933 5-9-6 **56** ... JackGarritty 4 28
(Julia Brooke) *chsd ldr over 4f out tl over 1f out: wknd fnl f* **20/1**

1m 14.73s (0.23) **Going Correction** +0.025s/f (Slow)
WFA 3 from 4yo+ 6lb **12 Ran SP% 122.5**
Speed ratings (Par 101): **99,98,97,96,96 95,95,92,91,91 89,84**
CSF £18.47 CT £147.49 TOTE £5.90: £2.40, £1.30, £3.10; EX 21.40 Trifecta £190.70.
Owner A Davis **Bred** D R Tucker **Trained** Kingston Warren, Oxon

FOCUS
An ordinary sprint handicap rated around the third, fourth and fifth.

4764 FIT FITTERS MITRE & SAWS CLASSIFIED CLAIMING STKS 6f 20y (Tp)
2:30 (2:31) (Class 5) 3-Y-O+
£3,428 (£1,020; £509; £300; £300; £300) **Stalls Low**

Form RPR

0405 1 **The Groove**[8] 4455 6-9-4 69 ... HarryBentley 1 68
(David Evans) *chsd ldrs: nt clr run over 1f out: rdn to ld ins fnl f: all out* **7/4[1]**

6000 2 *nse* **Duke Cosimo**[11] 4335 9-9-0 61 ... PhilDennis 7 64
(Michael Herrington) *rrd s: sn lost pl: hdwy over 1f out: sn rdn: r.o* **6/1**

031 3 1 1/2 **Creek Harbour (IRE)**[28] 3688 4-9-2 70 ... LukeMorris 6 61
(Milton Bradley) *sn led at stdy pce: racd keenly: qcknd 2f out: rdn over 1f out: hdd ins fnl f: styd on same pce* **10/1**

-201 4 1 1/4 **Micronize (IRE)**[8] 4457 3-9-2 54 ... DavidNolan 4 62
(Richard Fahey) *s.i.s: sn chsng ldrs: rdn over 1f out: no ex wl ins fnl f* **7/2[3]**

3002 5 8 **Lucky Lodge**[11] 4335 9-9-12 70 ... (v) CamHardie 3 41
(Antony Brittain) *s.i.s: hld up: nt clr run over 3f out: nvr on terms* **9/4[2]**

-500 6 3 **Lope De Loop (IRE)**[73] 2128 4-8-13 42 ... (t w) SophieRalston(5) 8 24
(Aytach Sadik) *prom on outer tl wknd over 1f out* **150/1**

-000 7 9 **Spoken Words**[123] 1085 10-7-13 38 ... (p) ElishaWhittington(7) 2
(John David Riches) *chsd ldrs: pushed along over 2f out: wknd over 1f out* **150/1**

1m 14.32s (-0.18) **Going Correction** +0.025s/f (Slow)
WFA 3 from 4yo+ 6lb **7 Ran SP% 114.1**
Speed ratings (Par 103): **102,101,99,98,87 83,71**
CSF £13.01 TOTE £2.50: £1.20, £3.90; EX 13.80 Trifecta £99.90.
Owner Dave & Emma Evans **Bred** Cheveley Park Stud Ltd **Trained** Pandy, Monmouths

FOCUS
A competitive claimer. The fourth looks the key to the form.

4765 GUILLOTINERS ARMS H'CAP 5f 21y (Tp)
3:00 (3:00) (Class 6) (0-55,54) 3-Y-O+
£2,781 (£827; £413; £300; £300; £300) **Stalls Low**

Form RPR

0024 1 **Aquadabra (IRE)**[7] 4481 4-8-13 **46** ... TomMarquand 10 54
(Christopher Mason) *chsd ldr out wd tl swtchd lft 4f out: shkn up to ld over 1f out: sn rdn: jst hld on* **15/2**

0235 2 *shd* **Arnoul Of Metz**[15] 4182 4-9-6 **53** ... (p) DavidProbert 9 60
(Henry Spiller) *chsd ldrs: swtchd lft over 1f out: rdn to chse wnr ins fnl f: sn ev ch: r.o* **7/2[1]**

3305 3 *hd* **Le Manege Enchante (IRE)**[14] 4212 6-8-5 **45** ... (v) AledBeech(7) 2 51
(Derek Shaw) *chsd ldrs: rdn over 1f out: r.o* **10/1**

2466 4 1 1/4 **Always Amazing**[21] 3975 5-9-7 **54** ... TomQueally 8 56
(Derek Shaw) *hld up: hdwy u.p over 1f out: r.o* **9/2[2]**

0003 5 2 **Avon Green**[19] 4026 4-9-6 **53** ... OisinMurphy 5 48
(Joseph Tuite) *hld up: hdwy 1/2-way: rdn over 1f out: styd on same pce ins fnl f* **5/1[3]**

5522 6 1 **Angel Eyes**[68] 2324 4-8-8 **48** ... HarryRussell(7) 7 39
(John David Riches) *led: rdn and hdd over 1f out: no ex ins fnl f* **5/1[3]**

2650 7 1/2 **Dandy Lad (IRE)**[47] 2995 3-9-2 **54** ... LukeMorris 4 41
(Natalie Lloyd-Beavis) *edgd rt s: sn chsng ldrs: drvn along 1/2-way: styd on same pce fr over 1f out (vet reported gelding lost its left hind shoe)* **50/1**

0002 8 *nk* **Celerity (IRE)**[5] 4555 5-8-5 **45** ... (p) ElishaWhittington(7) 11 33
(Lisa Williamson) *s.i.s: styd on ins fnl f: nvr nrr* **25/1**

0000 9 1 1/4 **Furni Factors**[22] 3933 4-9-4 **51** ... (b) AndrewElliott 3 35
(Ronald Thompson) *s.i.s: nvr on terms* **8/1**

0000 10 5 **Alfie's Angel (IRE)**[7] 4481 5-9-3 **50** ... (b) JackMitchell 6 16
(Milton Bradley) *chsd ldrs: lost pl after 1f: drvn along 3f out: n.d after* **12/1**

1m 1.95s (0.05) **Going Correction** +0.025s/f (Slow)
WFA 3 from 4yo+ 5lb **10 Ran SP% 119.2**
Speed ratings (Par 101): **100,99,99,97,94 92,91,91,89,81**
CSF £34.75 CT £276.78 TOTE £9.80: £2.60, £1.60, £3.30; EX 54.10 Trifecta £404.10.
Owner Brian Hicks **Bred** Rathasker Stud **Trained** Caewent, Monmouthshire

FOCUS
This looks straightforward, with the one-two-three pretty much to their marks.

4766 CADS & ESTIMATORS MAIDEN AUCTION STKS 7f 36y (Tp)
3:30 (3:32) (Class 6) 2-Y-O £2,781 (£827; £413; £206) Stalls High

Form RPR

1 **Come On My Son** 2-9-5 0 OisinMurphy 8 76+
(Mark Loughnane) *prom: lost pl 1/2-way: hdwy over 1f out: rdn and r.o to ld nr fin* **10/1**

2 shd **Nirodha (IRE)** 2-9-0 0 TomMarquand 2 70
(Amy Murphy) *prom: pushed along 1/2-way: nt clr run over 2f out: led over 1f out: sn rdn and edgd lft: hdd nr fin* **20/1**

5 3 2 3/4 **Gladice**[20] 3990 2-9-0 0 ShaneKelly 3 63
(Marco Botti) *s.i.s: hdwy over 5f out: shkn up over 1f out: styd on same pce ins fnl f* **7/1**[3]

0 4 hd **Forus**[17] 4114 2-9-0 0 ThoreHammerHansen(5) 7 67
(Jamie Osborne) *sn led: hdd 6f out: led again over 5f out: hdd over 3f out: rdn over 1f out: edgd lft and styd on same pce ins fnl f* **10/1**

00 5 1 1/2 **Jungle Book (GER)**[20] 3990 2-9-5 0 RobHornby 6 63
(Jonathan Portman) *hld up: hdwy over 1f out: nt rch ldrs* **10/1**

3 6 4 **Breck's Selection (FR)**[8] 4456 2-9-5 0 SilvestreDeSousa 9 52
(Mark Johnston) *racd on outer: led 6f out: sn hdd: led again and edgd lft over 3f out: rdn and hdd over 1f out: wknd ins fnl f (jockey said gelding hung left under pressure)* **1/1**[1]

7 6 **Grace Note** 2-9-0 0 LukeMorris 1 31
(Archie Watson) *s.i.s: sn chsng ldrs: shkn up over 2f out: edgd lft and wknd over 1f out* **9/2**[2]

03 8 1 **Luscifer**[14] 4214 2-9-2 0 FinleyMarsh(3) 4 33
(Richard Hughes) *prom: nt clr run and lost pl over 6f out: pushed along and hdwy on outer 4f out: rdn and wknd over 1f out: hung lft fnl f* **22/1**

0 9 nse **Gifted Dreamer (IRE)**[17] 4114 2-9-5 0 FergusSweeney 10 33
(Mark Usher) *s.i.s: sn pushed along and a in rr* **150/1**

1m 30.49s (1.69) **Going Correction** +0.025s/f (Slow) 9 Ran SP% **117.7**
Speed ratings (Par 92): **91,90,87,87,85 81,74,73,73**
CSF £183.74 TOTE £12.60: £3.40, £5.40, £1.40; EX 202.80 Trifecta £574.40.
Owner Excel Racing, R Gray & Partners **Bred** Ron Hull **Trained** Rock, Worcs

FOCUS
There was a disputed lead and the first two came through from off the pace. The level is set around the third, fourth and fifth.

4767 GRIND IT, BEND IT, WELD IT H'CAP 7f 36y (Tp)
4:00 (4:01) (Class 5) (0-70,70) 3-Y-O+
£3,428 (£1,020; £509; £300; £300; £300) Stalls High

Form RPR

2211 1 **Street Poet (IRE)**[15] 4194 6-9-11 **67** JasonHart 4 75
(Michael Herrington) *mde virtually all: set stdy pce tl qcknd over 2f out: rdn and edgd rt over 1f out: styd on* **11/2**[3]

-455 2 1 **Take Fright**[21] 3970 3-9-3 **67** (p[1]) OisinMurphy 2 69
(Hugo Palmer) *trckd ldrs: rdn over 1f out: chsd wnr wl ins fnl f: styd on* **14/1**

0406 3 1/2 **Grey Destiny**[8] 4455 9-9-6 **62** (p) CamHardie 10 66
(Antony Brittain) *s.i.s: hld up: rdn and r.o ins fnl f: nt rch ldrs* **33/1**

1041 4 shd **Poet's Pride**[15] 4195 4-9-11 **67** RobertWinston 9 71
(David Barron) *prom: racd keenly: ct out wd: rdn to chse wnr over 1f out tl wl ins fnl f: styd on same pce* **5/2**[2]

0000 5 1/2 **Chaplin Bay (IRE)**[11] 4335 7-9-12 **68** JackGarritty 12 70
(Ruth Carr) *hld up: hdwy over 1f out: r.o: nt rch ldrs* **25/1**

-045 6 shd **Corrida De Toros (IRE)**[14] 4225 3-9-5 **69** PatCosgrave 1 68
(Ed de Giles) *prom: rdn over 1f out: styd on same pce wl ins fnl f* **15/2**

0056 7 1 1/4 **Critical Thinking (IRE)**[11] 4320 5-10-0 **70** (tp) StevieDonohoe 5 69
(David Loughnane) *hld up in tch: shkn up and nt clr run over 1f out: styd on same pce ins fnl f* **10/1**

2000 8 2 1/2 **Viola Park**[49] 2944 5-9-0 **56** (p) DavidProbert 6 48
(Ronald Harris) *w wnr tl shkn up over 2f out: wknd ins fnl f* **33/1**

5644 9 4 1/2 **Jem Scuttle (USA)**[4] 4606 3-9-6 **70** (bt[1]) DavidNolan 7 47
(Declan Carroll) *plld hrd and prom: rdn over 2f out: wknd fnl f (jockey said colt was too keen)* **2/1**[1]

60-0 10 5 **Kings Academy**[22] 3939 5-9-6 **62** (v[1]) JimmyQuinn 3 28
(John Mackie) *stall opened fractionally late: s.i.s: nvr on terms* **50/1**

1-20 11 57 **Pushkin Museum (IRE)**[71] 2194 8-9-7 **63** DanielMuscutt 11
(John Butler) *s.i.s: a in rr: shkn up 1/2-way: sn wknd: eased over 1f out (jockey said gelding was never travelling)* **40/1**

6162 12 51 **In Trutina**[8] 4454 3-9-0 **64** LukeMorris 8
(Archie Watson) *rrd s: a bhd (jockey said filly reared in the stalls)* **14/1**

1m 28.93s (0.13) **Going Correction** +0.025s/f (Slow)
WFA 3 from 4yo+ 8lb 12 Ran SP% **125.6**
Speed ratings (Par 103): **100,98,98,98,97 97,96,93,88,82 17,**
CSF £79.91 CT £2404.06 TOTE £5.40: £1.70, £3.10, £5.50; EX 76.50 Trifecta £2089.30.
Owner Mrs H Lloyd-Herrington **Bred** Mrs C Regalado-Gonzalez **Trained** Cold Kirby, N Yorks

FOCUS
They went steady early and the winner was always in pole position, rated close to last year's best.

4768 THE LADIES, THE DUCHESS & THE ACCOUNTANT FILLIES' NOVICE STKS 1m 1f 104y (Tp)
4:30 (4:33) (Class 5) 3-4-Y-O £3,428 (£1,020; £509; £254) Stalls Low

Form RPR

52 1 **Incredulous**[21] 3974 3-9-0 0 TomMarquand 5 77
(William Haggas) *sn led at stdy pce: hung rt bnd 7f out: shkn up and qcknd over 2f out: rdn and edgd lft ins fnl f: styd on* **6/4**[1]

4 2 1/2 **Orchidia (IRE)**[73] 2102 3-9-0 0 JasonWatson 10 76
(Roger Charlton) *wnt 2nd and racd keenly after 1f: lost 2nd over 5f out: rdn to chse wnr over 1f out: n.m.r ins fnl f: styd on* **5/2**[2]

3 3 3 **Abr Al Hudood (JPN)**[63] 2518 3-9-0 0 OisinMurphy 12 70
(Hugo Palmer) *s.i.s and edgd rt s: hdwy over 7f out: chsd wnr over 5f out tl rdn over 1f out: styd on same pce ins fnl f* **4/1**[3]

4 3/4 **Voice Of Calm** 3-9-0 0 GeorgeWood 6 68
(Harry Dunlop) *sn prom: shkn up and hung lft fr over 1f out: styd on same pce ins fnl f* **100/1**

33 5 2 **Corinthian Girl (IRE)**[34] 3464 3-9-0 0 StevieDonohoe 4 64+
(David Lanigan) *prom: lost pl 7f out: hdwy over 4f out: shkn up over 2f out: nt trble ldrs* **15/2**

4-5 6 1/2 **Alma Linda**[36] 3431 3-9-0 0 LukeMorris 3 63
(Sir Mark Prescott Bt) *hld up in tch: racd keenly: outpcd over 2f out: hdwy and hung lft fr over 1f out: nt trble ldrs* **12/1**

7 nk **Shining Sea (IRE)** 3-9-0 0 RyanTate 11 63+
(Sir Mark Prescott Bt) *hld up: pushed along over 3f out: r.o ins fnl f: nvr nrr* **33/1**

8 2 3/4 **Hermosura** 3-9-0 0 HarryBentley 7 57
(Ralph Beckett) *s.i.s: in rr and pushed along 6f out: hung lft and styd on ins fnl f: nvr nrr* **8/1**

36- 9 5 **Scheme**[221] 9323 3-9-0 0 DavidProbert 2 46
(Sir Mark Prescott Bt) *prom: n.m.r and lost pl after 1f: styd on appr fnl f* **22/1**

0- 10 3/4 **Compassionate**[294] 7383 3-9-0 0 CharlesBishop 8 45
(Eve Johnson Houghton) *led early: chsd ldrs: rdn over 2f out: wknd over 1f out* **66/1**

0 11 9 **Sharqi (IRE)**[23] 3889 3-9-0 0 (t) TomQueally 13 26
(Jean-Rene Auvray) *hld up: racd keenly: bhd fnl 3f* **200/1**

04 12 2 1/4 **Lady Muk**[28] 3680 3-8-7 0 (p) TobyEley(7) 1 21
(Steph Hollinshead) *s.i.s: sn pushed along: bhd fnl 3f* **100/1**

0- 13 99 **Tulipe Angelique (FR)**[237] 9048 3-9-0 0 ShaneKelly 9
(Paul Webber) *s.i.s: sme hdwy on outer 7f out: lost pl over 5f out: wknd over 3f out* **150/1**

1m 59.6s (-1.20) **Going Correction** +0.025s/f (Slow) 13 Ran SP% **131.1**
Speed ratings (Par 100): **106,105,102,102,100 99,97,92,92 84,82,**
CSF £5.86 TOTE £2.50: £1.10, £1.60, £2.20; EX 10.10 Trifecta £32.90.
Owner Cheveley Park Stud **Bred** Cheveley Park Stud Ltd **Trained** Newmarket, Suffolk

FOCUS
The pace was controlled by the winner and it proved hard to make up ground. Ordinary form, with the winner rated close to her latest.

4769 TOP MAN ALAN'S 40 YEAR RACE H'CAP 1m 4f 51y (Tp)
5:00 (5:04) (Class 5) (0-70,70) 3-Y-O
£3,428 (£1,020; £509; £300; £300; £300) Stalls Low

Form RPR

-142 1 **Gold Arch**[19] 4038 3-9-1 **64** (b) DanielMuscutt 7 72
(David Lanigan) *unruly to post: s.i.s: drvn along early in rr: hdwy on outer over 10f out: shkn up to ld over 1f out: rdn and hung lft ins fnl f: jst hld on* **4/1**[2]

2322 2 hd **Gold Fleece**[21] 3955 3-9-6 **69** (p) JackMitchell 8 76
(Hugo Palmer) *hld up in tch: shkn up over 2f out: swtchd rt over 1f out: rdn and r.o wl* **5/1**[3]

2-43 3 shd **Swansdown**[27] 3741 3-9-3 **66** (p[1]) TomMarquand 4 73
(William Haggas) *prom: lost pl 10f out: hld up: hdwy over 1f out: sn rdn: r.o wl* **3/1**[1]

00-4 4 3 1/2 **Percy's Prince**[39] 3299 3-8-5 **54** LukeMorris 9 55
(Sir Mark Prescott Bt) *chsd ldr after 1f tl led over 3f out: rdn and hdd over 1f out: styd on same pce ins fnl f* **13/2**

0-03 5 2 **Bartimaeus (IRE)**[31] 3594 3-9-1 **64** CharlesBishop 2 62
(Denis Coakley) *chsd ldrs: rdn and nt clr run over 1f out: no ex ins fnl f* **17/2**

3442 6 1 1/4 **Fayetta**[8] 4443 3-9-5 **68** (b) OisinMurphy 5 64
(David Loughnane) *sn led at stdy pce: hdd over 3f out: rdn and ev ch over 1f out: wknd ins fnl f* **9/1**

504 7 2 1/4 **So Hi Cardi (FR)**[25] 3802 3-8-13 **62** JasonWatson 6 54
(Roger Charlton) *hld up: rdn over 1f out: n.d* **25/1**

4415 8 2 **Lieutenant Conde**[15] 4176 3-9-1 **64** CharlieBennett 10 53
(Hughie Morrison) *dwlt: hld up: rdn over 2f out: n.d* **20/1**

4410 9 3/4 **Torolight**[35] 3446 3-9-7 **70** (p[1]) ShaneKelly 12 58
(Richard Hughes) *hld up in tch: racd keenly: tk clsr order over 5f out: shkn up and hung lft over 1f out: wknd fnl f* **11/1**

6606 10 shd **Blue Beirut (IRE)**[22] 3938 3-8-8 **57** HarryBentley 1 45
(William Muir) *s.i.s: rdn over 3f out: a in rr* **50/1**

400 11 shd **Second Sight**[31] 3584 3-9-2 **65** StevieDonohoe 3 53
(Charlie Fellowes) *pushed along early in rr: hdwy over 9f out: rdn over 3f out: wknd over 1f out* **16/1**

2m 40.2s (-0.60) **Going Correction** +0.025s/f (Slow) 11 Ran SP% **120.3**
Speed ratings (Par 100): **103,102,102,100,99 98,96,95,94,94 94**
CSF £24.49 CT £69.55 TOTE £4.40: £1.30, £1.80, £1.80; EX 21.20 Trifecta £82.30.
Owner Middleham Park, Ventura, Delaney & Black **Bred** Trinity Park Stud **Trained** Newmarket, Suffolk

FOCUS
The first three finished nicely clear and look ones to keep on side in this sphere.
T/Plt: £729.20 to a £1 stake. Pool: £73,771.49 - 73.85 winning units T/Qpdt: £102.70 to a £1 stake. Pool: £8,610.93 - 62.00 winning units **Colin Roberts**

4770a- (Foreign Racing) - See Raceform Interactive

4494 BATH (L-H)
Wednesday, July 10

OFFICIAL GOING: Firm (10.0)
Wind: Light breeze, across Weather: sunny

4771 SKY SPORTS RACING SKY 415 H'CAP 1m 2f 37y
6:00 (6:00) (Class 6) (0-60,60) 3-Y-O+
£2,781 (£827; £413; £300; £300; £300) Stalls Low

Form RPR

-602 1 **Perfect Grace**[7] 4499 3-9-4 **60** HollieDoyle 1 74+
(Archie Watson) *mde all: rdn clr over 1f out: comf* **4/5**[1]

063 2 2 3/4 **War Of Succession**[71] 2233 5-9-3 **56** JessicaCooley(7) 3 63
(Tony Newcombe) *slowly away: bhd: hdwy fr 2f out: sn rdn but hanging lft: chsd wnr over 1f out: styd on but a being comf hld (jockey said gelding hung left and right-handed)* **8/1**[3]

0053 3 5 **Prerogative (IRE)**[14] 4232 5-9-0 **46** oh1 (t[1]) TomMarquand 10 43
(Tony Carroll) *hld up towards rr: rdn wl over 2f out: hdwy over 1f out: chsd ldng pair ent fnl f: nt pce to get on terms: jst hld on for 3rd* **7/2**[2]

50-0 4 shd **Buzz Lightyere**[14] 4235 6-10-0 **60** (v[1]) CharlieBennett 6 57
(Patrick Chamings) *trckd ldrs early: midfield 5f out: rdn over 2f out: no imp tl r.o fnl f: nrly snatched 3rd fnl stride* **25/1**

00-0 5 2 1/4 **Ramatuelle**[43] 3204 3-8-9 **51** JosephineGordon 8 44
(Sir Mark Prescott Bt) *midfield: struggling in last 4f out: styd on fnl 2f but nvr threat to ldrs* **9/1**

0-00 6 3/4 **Mamnoon (IRE)**[7] 4498 6-9-0 **46** oh1 (b) KieranO'Neill 4 37
(Roy Brotherton) *pressed wnr tl rdn over 2f out: wknd ent fnl f (vet said gelding bled from nose)* **25/1**

0024 7 4 1/2 **Coachella (IRE)**[12] 4349 5-9-7 **53** (b) KieranShoemark 2 35
(Ed de Giles) *mid-div: hdwy 6f out to trck ldrs: rdn over 2f out: wknd over 1f out* **12/1**

0-60 **8** 3½ **Lyn's Secret (IRE)**[22] 2345 4-9-11 **57**........................ TrevorWhelan 7 32
(Seamus Mullins) *chsd ldrs: rdn over 2f out: wknd over 1f out* **50/1**

24/0 **9** 38 **Los Cerritos (SWI)**[15] 4216 7-9-4 **50**..................(vt) RobertWinston 5
(Milton Harris) *chsd ldrs tl 5f out: sn pushed along: wknd and eased over 2f out (trainer said gelding was unsuited by the firm going and would prefer a slower surface)* **50/1**

2m 9.49s (-1.61) **Going Correction** 0.0s/f (Good)
WFA 3 from 4yo+ 10lb **9** Ran SP% **118.2**
Speed ratings (Par 101): **106,103,99,99,97 97,93,90,60**
CSF £8.16 CT £16.23 TOTE £1.80: £1.10, £2.00, £1.20; EX 9.90 Trifecta £20.70.
Owner Dr Bridget Drew & R A Farmiloe **Bred** Mildmay Bloodstock Ltd **Trained** Upper Lambourn, W Berks

FOCUS
A sunny evening with temperatures around 20C. A modest contest and the pace was genuine. The winner was well in and progressed.

4772 BEST FREE TIPS AT VALUERATER.CO.UK H'CAP (VALUE RATER RACING CLUB BATH SUMMER SPRINT SERIES QUAL) 5f 10y
6:30 (6:30) (Class 6) (0-60,60) 3-Y-0+
£2,781 (£827; £413; £300; £300; £300) **Stalls** Centre

Form RPR

0021 **1** **Thegreyvtrain**[44] 3148 3-9-2 **56**........................ KieranO'Neill 1 63
(Ronald Harris) *led: rdn and narrowly hdd over 2f out: kpt on gamely to regain advantage ent fnl f: edgd sltly rt: asserting towards fin (jockey said filly hung right-handed)* **5/1**[2]

5622 **2** 1¾ **Edged Out**[6] 4556 9-9-1 **55**........................ PoppyBridgwater(5) 6 59
(Christopher Mason) *pressed wnr: tk narrow advantage over 2f out: sn rdn: hdd ent fnl f: sn carried sltly rt: no ex towards fin* **5/6**[1]

-060 **3** 1¾ **Spot Lite**[33] 3527 4-9-3 **52**..................(p[1]) CharlieBennett 5 48
(Rod Millman) *pressed front pair tl rdn over 2f out: kpt on same pce fnl f* **11/2**[3]

006 **4** 1½ **Midnight Guest (IRE)**[65] 2473 4-9-10 **59**..................(v) HollieDoyle 8 50
(David Evans) *last pair: hdwy over 2f out: sn rdn: kpt on fnl f but nvr gng pce to get on terms* **12/1**

0640 **5** 1½ **Terri Rules (IRE)**[65] 2473 4-9-0 **56**........................ GeorgiaDobie(7) 2 42
(Lee Carter) *s.i.s: sn outpcd in last: wnt 5th fnl f but nvr gng pce to get involved (jockey was slow to remove blindfold and filly was slowly away; vet said filly lost right-hind shoe)* **10/1**

04-0 **6** ¾ **Layla's Dream**[18] 4116 3-9-6 **60**........................ TomMarquand 7 41
(Tony Carroll) *chsd ldng trio: rdn over 2f out: nvr threatened to get on terms: wknd fnl f* **33/1**

0105 **7** 2¼ **Lysander Belle (IRE)**[1] 4763 3-9-5 **59**........................ TrevorWhelan 4 32
(Sophie Leech) *chsd ldng trio tl rdn over 2f out: wknd ent fnl f* **10/1**

1m 2.22s (0.22) **Going Correction** 0.0s/f (Good)
WFA 3 from 4yo+ 5lb **7** Ran SP% **115.4**
Speed ratings (Par 101): **98,95,92,90,87 86,82**
CSF £9.78 CT £23.43 TOTE £5.20: £1.90, £2.00; EX 10.80 Trifecta £33.80.
Owner Ridge House Stables Ltd **Bred** David C Mead **Trained** Earlswood, Monmouths

FOCUS
A weak sprint handicap and the first two had it to themselves throughout.

4773 DEREK BRAITHWAITE MEMORIAL H'CAP 1m
7:00 (7:00) (Class 4) (0-85,73) 3-Y-O **£5,207** (£1,549; £774) **Stalls** Low

Form RPR

0-36 **1** **Conspiritor**[31] 3638 3-9-5 **71**........................ KieranShoemark 3 74
(Charles Hills) *pressed ldr: rdn over 2f out: led ent fnl f: kpt on wl* **2/1**[2]

3016 **2** ¾ **Creek Island (IRE)**[22] 3957 3-9-7 **73**........................ FrannyNorton 1 74
(Mark Johnston) *led: rdn over 1f out: edgd rt whn hdd ent fnl f: kpt on (jockey said colt hung right-handed)* **1/1**[1]

0366 **3** nk **Greeley (IRE)**[16] 4176 3-9-1 **67**..................(p[1]) CharlieBennett 4 67
(Rod Millman) *trckd ldng pair: rdn w ch 2f out: kpt on fnl f* **3/1**[3]

1m 41.04s (-0.66) **Going Correction** 0.0s/f (Good) **3** Ran SP% **108.3**
Speed ratings (Par 102): **103,102,101**
CSF £4.42 TOTE £2.30; EX 3.10 Trifecta £5.20.
Owner D M James **Bred** D M James **Trained** Lambourn, Berks

FOCUS
Uncompetitive for the grade with all three participants 12lb or more below the ceiling, yet there was little between them. The early pace was modest. The first two have been rated pretty much to form.

4774 KAREN HOWELL NOVICE STKS 1m
7:30 (7:31) (Class 5) 3-Y-0+ **£3,428** (£1,020; £509; £254) **Stalls** Low

Form RPR

24 **1** **Desert Lion**[72] 2198 3-9-0 0........................ TrevorWhelan 2 67+
(David Simcock) *trckd ldrs: led jst over 1f out: briefly edgd rt u.p: r.o (jockey said gelding wandered under pressure)* **30/100**[1]

6-05 **2** ¾ **Colonel Slade (IRE)**[9] 4452 3-9-0 0..................(t) TomMarquand 1 64
(Brian Meehan) *led: rdn and hdd jst over 1f out: kpt on but nt pce of wnr* **7/2**[2]

00 **3** 1¼ **Honey Bear (IRE)**[103] 1400 3-8-9 0........................ FrannyNorton 5 56
(Mark Johnston) *trckd ldrs: chsd ldng pair over 1f out: kpt on but nt quite pce to chal fnl f* **7/1**[3]

4 10 **Lady Of Mercia** 3-8-9 0........................ KieranO'Neill 7 32
(John Flint) *s.i.s: racd in last pair: hdwy over 4f out: rdn to chse ldrs over 2f out: wknd fnl f* **50/1**

000 **5** 2 **Yet Another (IRE)**[16] 4178 4-9-2 0........................ KeelanBaker(7) 3 34
(Grace Harris) *trckd ldr tl rdn wl over 2f out: wknd ent fnl f* **66/1**

0 **6** 11 **Lambristo (IRE)**[35] 3463 3-9-0 0........................ JosephineGordon 6 6
(J S Moore) *in tch: struggling in last pair over 4f out: wknd 2f out* **100/1**

7 1¼ **Just Champion** 3-8-11 0........................ WilliamCox(3) 4 3
(John Flint) *s.i.s: sn struggling in last pair: wknd over 2f out (jockey said gelding was slowly away)* **50/1**

1m 41.43s (-0.27) **Going Correction** 0.0s/f (Good)
WFA 3 from 4yo 9lb **7** Ran SP% **118.0**
Speed ratings (Par 103): **101,100,99,89,87 76,74**
CSF £1.93 TOTE £1.20: £1.10, £1.70; EX 2.00 Trifecta £3.00.
Owner Qatar Racing Ltd & Partners **Bred** The Sorella Bella Partnership **Trained** Newmarket, Suffolk

FOCUS
A weak novice and the first three drew clear.

4775 AMBER FOUNDATION H'CAP 5f 10y
8:00 (8:00) (Class 5) (0-75,75) 3-Y-0+ **£3,428** (£1,020; £509) **Stalls** Centre

Form RPR

-012 **1** **Rose Hip**[15] 4227 4-9-4 **67**........................ TomMarquand 1 78
(Tony Carroll) *trckd ldr: led jst over 1f out: sn shkn up: r.o wl: readily* **11/10**[1]

0212 **2** 2¼ **Big Lachie**[8] 4478 5-9-9 **75**........................ GeorgiaCox(3) 3 78
(Mark Loughnane) *trckd ldng pair: rdn to chse wnr jst ins fnl f: nt pce to get on terms* **6/4**[2]

0035 **3** 2¾ **Crystal Deauville (FR)**[15] 4213 4-8-12 **64**..................(b) WilliamCox(3) 4 57
(Gay Kelleway) *led: rdn and hdd jst over 1f out: no ex ins fnl f* **7/2**[3]

1m 1.31s (-0.69) **Going Correction** 0.0s/f (Good) **3** Ran SP% **109.8**
Speed ratings (Par 103): **105,101,97**
CSF £3.14 TOTE £1.90; EX 3.50 Trifecta £2.80.
Owner Lady Whent **Bred** Lady Whent **Trained** Cropthorne, Worcs

FOCUS
The early tempo was modest although it was far from tactical. The winner quickened up smartly and has been rated as improving.

4776 SKY SPORTS RACING VIRGIN 535 H'CAP 5f 160y
8:30 (8:30) (Class 6) (0-55,57) 3-Y-0+
£2,781 (£827; £413; £300; £300; £300) **Stalls** Centre

Form RPR

5220 **1** **Holdenhurst**[33] 3527 4-9-4 **57**........................ RyanWhile(5) 7 69
(Bill Turner) *trckd ldrs: rdn to ld over 1f out: sn clr: comf (vet said gelding lost left fore shoe)* **13/2**

4000 **2** 4½ **Sugar Plum Fairy**[33] 3527 4-8-12 **46** oh1........................ TomMarquand 5 43
(Tony Carroll) *last trio: sltly hmpd after 2f: hdwy 3f out: sn rdn: chsd wnr jst ins fnl f: nt pce to get on terms* **11/2**

0454 **3** ¾ **Jaganory (IRE)**[7] 4494 7-9-3 **56**..................(v) PoppyBridgwater(5) 2 51
(Christopher Mason) *disp ld tl over 1f out: kpt on same pce fnl f* **9/2**[3]

5050 **4** nse **Quick Recovery**[18] 4115 4-9-7 **55**..................(b[1]) CharlieBennett 6 50
(Jim Boyle) *disp ld tl over 1f out: kpt on same pce fnl f* **7/2**[2]

0200 **5** 1½ **Spirit Of Ishy**[8] 4481 4-8-12 **46** oh1........................ HollieDoyle 9 36
(Stuart Kittow) *outpcd in last: hdwy 2f out: kpt on fnl f but nt pce to get involved* **28/1**

5241 **6** 2¾ **Toolatetodelegate**[7] 4500 5-9-4 **52** 5ex..................(tp) TrevorWhelan 1 32
(Brian Barr) *hld up: hdwy into 4th 3f out: sn rdn: nvr threatened: wknd ent fnl f (jockey said mare ran flat)* **2/1**[1]

0-00 **7** 7 **Birthday Girl (IRE)**[15] 4219 4-8-12 **46** oh1..........(bt) JosephineGordon 8 3
(Amanda Perrett) *last trio: rdn 3f out: nvr threatened* **50/1**

0433 **8** 15 **Tina Teaspoon**[6] 4563 5-8-12 **46** oh1..................(h) FrannyNorton 3
(Derek Shaw) *plld v hrd and hung bdly rt bhd ldrs: swtchd rt after 2f: wknd over 1f out (jockey said mare ran too free)* **9/1**

1m 10.59s (-0.51) **Going Correction** 0.0s/f (Good)
WFA 3 from 4yo+ 6lb **8** Ran SP% **117.9**
Speed ratings (Par 101): **103,97,96,95,93 90,80,60**
CSF £43.24 CT £181.33 TOTE £8.40: £2.20, £2.40, £1.30; EX 54.40 Trifecta £287.10.
Owner Ansells Of Watford **Bred** Southill Stud **Trained** Sigwells, Somerset

FOCUS
Fairly competitive for the grade and the winner has been rated back to around his 2yo level.

4777 VALUE RATER RACING CLUB H'CAP (VALUE RATER RACING CLUB BATH SUMMER STAYERS' SERIES QUALIFIER) 1m 5f 11y
9:00 (9:00) (Class 6) (0-60,58) 4-Y-0+
£2,781 (£827; £413; £300; £300; £300) **Stalls** High

Form RPR

50-0 **1** **Street Jester**[32] 3571 5-8-10 **47**........................ JosephineGordon 8 53
(Robert Stephens) *rousted along leaving stalls: sn trcking ldr: rdn to ld over 2f out: fnd more whn strly chal ent fnl f: styd on strly (jockey said gelding slipped on the bend)* **8/1**

4035 **2** ¾ **Filament Of Gold (USA)**[7] 4498 8-8-12 **49**..................(b) KieranO'Neill 1 54
(Roy Brotherton) *in tch: rdn and hdwy over 2f out: str chal ins fnl f: styd on but no ex towards fin* **11/4**[2]

5056 **3** nk **Lafilia (GER)**[20] 4036 4-9-7 **58**..................(b[1]) HollieDoyle 7 62
(Archie Watson) *pushed along leaving stalls: led after 1f: rdn and hdd over 2f out: styd on but no ex ins fnl f (jockey said filly slipped on the bend)* **5/2**[1]

6033 **4** 2¼ **Butterfield (IRE)**[49] 2974 6-9-0 **51**..................(p) EoinWalsh 2 52
(Tony Carroll) *trckd ldrs: rdn over 2f out: styd on same pce fnl f* **7/2**[3]

1020 **5** 1½ **Sea's Aria (IRE)**[41] 3252 8-8-10 **47**........................ KieranShoemark 6 46
(Mark Hoad) *in tch: rdn over 2f out: styd on same pce* **6/1**

300/ **6** 1 **Delaire**[19] 4087 7-8-8 **45**..................(tp) JohnFahy 5 42
(N Dooly, Ire) *hld up: rdn over 2f out: little imp* **20/1**

6605 **7** ¾ **Demophon**[20] 4019 5-8-5 **45**........................ WilliamCox(3) 3 41
(Steve Flook) *led for 1f: trckd ldrs: rdn over 2f out: wknd over 1f out* **8/1**

2m 52.54s (-0.26) **Going Correction** 0.0s/f (Good) **7** Ran SP% **118.7**
Speed ratings (Par 101): **100,99,99,97,97 96,95**
CSF £31.91 CT £72.99 TOTE £9.30: £5.30, £1.90; EX 52.70 Trifecta £121.40.
Owner R U Miles **Bred** R U Miles **Trained** Penhow, Newport

■ Oborne Lady was withdrawn. Price at time of withdrawal 4-1. Rule 4 only applies to bets prior to withdrawal - deduction 20p in the pound. New market formed.

FOCUS
Weak for the grade. The winner has been rated to last year's C&D success.
T/Plt: £24.80 to a £1 stake. Pool: £65,815.35. 1,931.21 winning units. T/Qpdt: £14.80 to a £1 stake. Pool: £4,581.00. 228.90 winning units. **Tim Mitchell**

4433 CATTERICK (L-H)
Wednesday, July 10

OFFICIAL GOING: Good to firm (good in places; 8.5)
Wind: fresh largely across Weather: overcast

4778 EVERY RACE LIVE ON RACING TV CLAIMING STKS 5f
2:00 (2:02) (Class 6) 2-Y-O
£3,105 (£924; £461; £300; £300; £300) **Stalls** Low

Form RPR

530 **1** **Blitzle**[23] 3927 2-8-13 65........................ BenRobinson(3) 5 64
(Ollie Pears) *prom: rdn into narrow ld over 1f out: drvn out fnl f* **11/10**[1]

000 **2** ½ **Flight Of Thunder (IRE)**[30] 3644 2-8-12 55........................ KevinStott 3 58
(Kevin Ryan) *led narrowly: rdn and hdd over 1f out: kpt on but a hld* **11/4**[2]

06 **3** 4½ **Two Hearts**[28] 3717 2-8-12 0........................ JamesSullivan 8 42
(Grant Tuer) *sn chsd ldrs: rdn 2f out: one pce in 3rd ins fnl f* **20/1**

060 **4** 1¾ **Comeatchoo (IRE)**[53] 2820 2-9-7 62........................ DavidAllan 1 45
(Tim Easterby) *chsd ldrs: rdn over 2f out: wknd ins fnl f* **11/2**[3]

0 **5** 1¼ **Starfield Song (IRE)**[29] 3679 2-8-9 0........................ JamieGormley 6 28
(Iain Jardine) *dwlt: outpcd in rr tl sme late hdwy* **33/1**

60 **6** *1* **South Light (IRE)**[43] 3196 2-8-9 0........................(t[1]) KieranSchofield(7) 7 32
(Antony Brittain) *dwlt: hld up: rdn and sme hdwy on outside 2f out: edgd lft and wknd fnl f* **33/1**

00 **7** *2* **Queen Moya (IRE)**[26] 3812 2-8-9 0.................................. RowanScott(3) 2 20
(Nigel Tinkler) *sn outpcd and a towards rr* **12/1**

600 **8** *3 1/2* **Secret Cecil (FR)**[11] 4394 2-9-1 54.........................(v[1]) RobbieDowney 4 11
(Joseph Tuite) *midfield: rdn along over 3f out: sn outpcd and btn* **16/1**

59.91s (-0.59) **Going Correction** -0.20s/f (Firm) **8** Ran SP% **113.9**
Speed ratings (Par 92): **96,95,88,85,83 81,78,72**
CSF £4.02 TOTE £1.70: £1.10, £1.70, £3.90; EX 4.80 Trifecta £35.40.

Owner Np Racing Syndicate & Ollie Pears **Bred** John Jackson **Trained** Norton, N Yorks

FOCUS
The rail on the bend turning into home straight was dolled out 2yds. This weak 2yo claimer was dominated by the pacesetters and it wasn't a bad time for the level. The winner has been rated to form, with the runner-up improving.

4779 NFRC MEDIAN AUCTION MAIDEN STKS 1m 4f 13y
2:30 (2:30) (Class 5) 3-4-Y-O **£4,140** (£1,232; £615; £307) **Stalls** Low

Form RPR
5345 **1** **Itchingham Lofte (IRE)**[19] 4077 3-9-2 69.................. RobbieDowney 2 75+
(David Barron) *trckd ldr: pushed along to ld 2f out: rdn clr over 1f out: eased towards fin* **5/1**[2]

6-22 **2** *2 3/4* **Whiskey And Water**[19] 2323 3-8-13 74.................. BenRobinson(3) 6 69
(Brian Ellison) *led: rdn and hdd 2f out: sn outpcd by wnr: edgd rt ins fnl f: styd on* **5/6**[1]

-604 **3** *hd* **Star Talent (IRE)**[9] 4459 3-9-2 68.................................. JasonHart 5 69
(Gay Kelleway) *hld up in tch: rdn along and sme hdwy 2f out: forced way through gap to dispute 2nd 150yds out: kpt on same pce* **15/2**[3]

-305 **4** *2* **Surrey Warrior (USA)**[14] 4231 3-9-2 68..........................(b) BenCurtis 7 66
(Archie Watson) *trckd ldrs: rdn and edgd lft 2f out: disputing 2nd whn bmpd 150yds out: no ex* **5/1**[2]

-230 **5** *6* **Sweet Marmalade (IRE)**[11] 4370 4-9-9 65.................. GrahamLee 1 50
(Lawrence Mullaney) *hld up in tch: rdn 3f out: sn wknd* **25/1**

6 *17* **Stevie Smith** 3-8-11 0.. KevinStott 3 24
(Amy Murphy) *hld up: wknd and bhd fnl 3f* **40/1**

0 **7** *3 3/4* **Jukebox Blues (FR)**[9] 4459 3-9-2 0.................................. JoeFanning 4 23
(Mark Johnston) *slowly away: rcvrd and prom after 1f: rdn over 2f out: wknd* **16/1**

2m 39.38s (-1.22) **Going Correction** -0.20s/f (Firm)
WFA 3 from 4yo 12lb **7** Ran SP% **111.8**
Speed ratings (Par 103): **96,94,94,92,88 77,74**
CSF £9.13 TOTE £5.40: £2.60, £1.10; EX 11.70 Trifecta £49.10.

Owner Miss N J Barron **Bred** Sean Madigan **Trained** Maunby, N Yorks

FOCUS
Add 6yds. A moderate maiden, run at a fair enough pace. The winner looked improved, with the runner-up to form.

4780 ST TERESA'S HOSPICE FILLIES' NURSERY H'CAP 5f 212y
3:00 (3:00) (Class 4) (0-85,79) 2-Y-O **£5,433** (£1,617; £808; £404) **Stalls** Low

Form RPR
162 **1** **Mrs Bouquet**[11] 4384 2-9-7 77.. JoeFanning 3 83+
(Mark Johnston) *mde all: pushed along 2f out: rdn and pressed over 1f out: edgd rt 1f out: kpt on wl* **11/8**[1]

104 **2** *1 3/4* **Baileys In Bloom (FR)**[23] 3927 2-9-3 73.................. PaulHanagan 4 73
(Richard Fahey) *prom: pushed along to chal strly over 1f out: edgd rt jst ins fnl f: one pce fnl 75yds* **13/8**[2]

046 **3** *1 1/4* **Rusalka (IRE)**[29] 3703 2-8-5 61.................................. RachelRichardson 5 57
(Tim Easterby) *dwlt: hld up in tch: rdn along 2f out: kpt on to go 3rd ins fnl f: no threat to ldng pair* **14/1**

415 **4** *1 1/2* **Bella Brazil (IRE)**[32] 3564 2-9-4 74.................................. TomEaves 2 65
(David Barron) *in tch: rdn 2f out: wknd ins fnl f* **4/1**[3]

1m 13.63s (0.03) **Going Correction** -0.20s/f (Firm) **4** Ran SP% **106.9**
Speed ratings (Par 93): **91,88,87,85**
CSF £3.84 TOTE £1.60; EX 4.00 Trifecta £13.10.

Owner Garrett J Freyne **Bred** Hatford Enterprises **Trained** Middleham Moor, N Yorks

FOCUS
Add 6yds. This wasn't a bad little fillies' nursery, but it proved tactical and the winner dictated. The winner improved, with the runner-up to form.

4781 LOOKERS VOLKSWAGEN H'CAP 7f 6y
3:30 (3:30) (Class 5) (0-75,77) 3-Y-O
£4,140 (£1,232; £615; £307; £300; £300) **Stalls** Low

Form RPR
3221 **1** **Beryl The Petal (IRE)**[9] 4444 3-9-9 77 6ex....................(v) DavidNolan 8 85
(David O'Meara) *hld up: rdn and hdwy over 1f out: drvn to ld 110yds out: kpt on wl* **7/2**[1]

3006 **2** *2 1/2* **Woodside Wonder**[11] 4360 3-9-4 75..........................(p) SeanDavis(3) 3 76
(Keith Dalgleish) *prom: rdn to chal strly over 1f out: one pce ins fnl f* **8/1**

-001 **3** *1/2* **Bumbledom**[23] 3932 3-9-0 68.......................................(p) ConnorBeasley 1 68
(Michael Dods) *led: drvn and strly pressed over 1f out: hdd 110yds out: no ex* **6/1**

6203 **4** *1/2* **Stronsay (IRE)**[23] 3930 3-9-4 72.......................................(p[1]) GrahamLee 7 70
(Bryan Smart) *chsd ldrs: rdn 2f out: kpt on same pce* **4/1**[2]

0-00 **5** *8* **Evie Speed (IRE)**[51] 2896 3-9-4 72.................................. JackGarritty 6 49
(Jedd O'Keeffe) *hld up in tch: rdn over 2f out: wknd over 1f out* **5/1**[3]

-144 **6** *1 1/4* **Socru (IRE)**[24] 3884 3-9-5 73.. PaulMulrennan 5 46
(Michael Easterby) *dwlt: hld up in tch: rdn and outpcd 3f out: wknd over 1f out (trainers' rep said gelding was never travelling)* **7/2**[1]

1060 **7** *3/4* **Bugler Bob (IRE)**[24] 3884 3-9-5 73.......................................(v[1]) JasonHart 4 44
(John Quinn) *dwlt: sn chsd ldrs: rdn and outpcd over 2f out: wknd over 1f out* **12/1**

1m 26.16s (-1.24) **Going Correction** -0.20s/f (Firm) **7** Ran SP% **114.2**
Speed ratings (Par 100): **99,96,95,95,85 84,83**
CSF £31.30 CT £161.60 TOTE £3.20: £2.10, £4.10; EX 23.10 Trifecta £87.20.

Owner N D Crummack Ltd & A Rhodes And Partner **Bred** Pigeon Park Stud **Trained** Upper Helmsley, N Yorks

FOCUS
Add 6yds. An ordinary 3yo handicap, run at a sound pace, and the winner improved again.

4782 RACINGTV.COM H'CAP (FOR THE TURMERIC CHALLENGE TROPHY) 1m 7f 189y
4:00 (4:00) (Class 4) (0-85,84) 3-Y-O+
£6,727 (£2,002; £1,000; £500; £300; £300) **Stalls** Low

Form RPR
3-11 **1** **Lever Du Soleil (FR)**[2] 4724 4-8-9 65 10ex........................ CliffordLee 5 81+
(Gavin Cromwell, Ire) *hld up in tch: smooth hdwy 3f out: led on bit 2f out: cruised clr* **10/11**[1]

1515 **2** *11* **Lord Lamington**[20] 4024 3-8-10 83.................................. JoeFanning 2 81
(Mark Johnston) *trckd ldrs: rdn over 2f out: wnt 2nd over 1f out: plugged on but no ch w wnr* **5/1**[2]

-651 **3** *nk* **Jumping Cats**[20] 4019 4-9-8 78..(p) DavidAllan 6 77
(Chris Wall) *trckd ldrs: wnt in snatches: rdn along over 4f out: outplcd and dropped to 5th 3f out: plugged on ins fnl f* **6/1**[3]

0040 **4** *2* **Stormin Tom (IRE)**[11] 4404 7-9-0 70........................ RachelRichardson 7 67
(Tim Easterby) *prom: narrow ld after 2f out: rdn along 3f out: hdd 2f out: wknd fnl f* **16/1**

20-4 **5** *3 1/2* **Trouble And Strife (IRE)**[37] 3408 4-9-12 82..............(p) AndrewElliott 4 74
(Sir Mark Prescott Bt) *led for 2f: remained cl up: rdn over 2f out: wknd fnl f* **7/1**

-106 **6** *25* **Handiwork**[17] 4146 9-10-0 84..(p) PJMcDonald 1 46
(Steve Gollings) *v.s.a: a in rr (jockey said gelding slipped leaving the stalls and was therefore slowly away)* **14/1**

3m 27.92s (-8.08) **Going Correction** -0.20s/f (Firm)
WFA 3 from 4yo+ 17lb **6** Ran SP% **108.4**
Speed ratings (Par 105): **112,106,106,105,103 91**
CSF £5.26 TOTE £1.60: £1.10, £1.80; EX 6.00 Trifecta £15.40.

Owner Sunrise Partnership **Bred** S C E A Haras De La Perelle **Trained** Navan, Co. Meath

FOCUS
Add 12yds. This feature staying handicap was run at a solid early pace. The runner-up has been rated close to form.

4783 JOIN RACING TV NOW FILLIES' H'CAP 5f
4:30 (4:30) (Class 5) (0-75,77) 3-Y-O **£4,140** (£1,232; £615; £307; £300) **Stalls** Low

Form RPR
2243 **1** **Enchanted Linda**[5] 4595 3-9-13 76..................................(h) JasonHart 3 83
(Michael Herrington) *led narrowly: rdn and hdd over 2f out: drvn over 1f out: led again ins fnl f: kpt on wl* **3/1**[2]

5146 **2** *3/4* **Show Me The Bubbly**[11] 4368 3-9-7 70.............................. BenCurtis 4 74
(John O'Shea) *pressed ldr: led over 2f out: sn rdn: hdd ins fnl f: one pce (jockey said filly hung right)* **9/2**[3]

-022 **3** *1 3/4* **Mercenary Rose (IRE)**[12] 4330 3-10-0 77..........................(t[1]) PJMcDonald 1 75
(Paul Cole) *chsd ldrs: rdn to chal strly over 1f out: no ex fnl 110yds* **5/4**[1]

4040 **4** *2* **Jill Rose**[5] 4586 3-8-11 60..(p) PhilDennis 5 51
(Richard Whitaker) *chsd ldrs: rdn over 2f out: outpcd and btn appr fnl f* **16/1**

-421 **5** *nse* **Ginvincible**[20] 4033 3-9-2 65.. BarryMcHugh 6 56
(James Given) *chsd ldrs: rdn along 2f out: no ex ins fnl f: eased briefly towards fin and lost 4th post* **9/2**[3]

59.21s (-1.29) **Going Correction** -0.20s/f (Firm) **5** Ran SP% **111.7**
Speed ratings (Par 97): **102,100,98,94,94**
CSF £16.42 TOTE £4.70: £2.70, £2.80; EX 17.40 Trifecta £35.60.

Owner Middleham Park Racing LXXXII **Bred** M E Broughton **Trained** Cold Kirby, N Yorks

■ Stewards' Enquiry : Barry McHugh four-day ban; failure to ride out (July 24-26,28)

FOCUS
A tight 3yo fillies' sprint handicap, and a small pb from the winner.

4784 RACING AGAIN 17TH JULY H'CAP (DIV I) 7f 6y
5:00 (5:02) (Class 6) (0-65,70) 3-Y-O+
£3,105 (£924; £461; £300; £300; £300) **Stalls** Low

Form RPR
5355 **1** **Macs Blessings (IRE)**[2] 4720 3-8-4 54................(v) HarrisonShaw(5) 15 60
(Stef Keniry) *chsd ldrs on outer: rdn 2f out: chal over 1f out: edgd lft 1f out: sn led: drvn out* **7/1**[3]

603 **2** *1/2* **Bibbidibobbidiboo (IRE)**[9] 4438 4-9-12 63.................. JoeFanning 14 70
(Ann Duffield) *prom: rdn to ld over 1f out: drvn and hdd ins fnl f: kpt on same pce* **17/2**

3243 **3** *hd* **Donnelly's Rainbow (IRE)**[7] 4513 6-9-5 56.................. DavidAllan 13 62
(Rebecca Bastiman) *chsd ldrs: rdn along over 2f out: kpt on fnl 75yds* **4/1**[2]

0540 **4** *1 1/2* **Our Charlie Brown**[7] 4523 5-9-9 60.............................. DuranFentiman 6 62
(Tim Easterby) *prom: rdn along 2f out: n.m.r ins fnl f: one pce fnl 110yds (jockey said gelding was denied a clear run 1f out)* **4/1**[2]

6/00 **5** *1* **Eldelbar (SPA)**[51] 2898 5-9-9 60..................................(h) ConnorBeasley 3 59+
(Geoffrey Harker) *hld up: rdn 2f out: kpt on ins fnl f: nrst fin* **25/1**

1 **6** *1 1/4* **Lappet (IRE)**[7] 4513 4-9-8 59 5ex.................................. GrahamLee 11 55
(Gavin Cromwell, Ire) *sn led: rdn and hdd over 1f out: wknd ins fnl f* **5/2**[1]

1006 **7** *2 3/4* **Robben Rainbow**[7] 4513 5-9-5 56.................................. PhilDennis 12 44
(Katie Scott) *hld up: rdn over 2f out: nvr threatened* **20/1**

2050 **8** *1/2* **Gunmaker (IRE)**[17] 4148 5-9-11 62.............................. JamesSullivan 10 49
(Ruth Carr) *dwlt: hld up in midfield: rdn over 2f out: no imp* **12/1**

0000 **9** *nk* **Khitaamy (IRE)**[13] 4293 5-8-10 47..............................(vt[1]) PaulHanagan 1 33
(Tina Jackson) *dwlt: hld up: rdn over 2f out: nvr threatened* **66/1**

0660 **10** *43* **Dancing Speed (IRE)**[22] 3969 3-9-2 61.............................. DavidNolan 4
(Marjorie Fife) *midfield on inner: rdn over 2f out: wknd over 1f out: eased (vet said gelding bled from the nose)* **14/1**

1m 26.49s (-0.91) **Going Correction** -0.20s/f (Firm)
WFA 3 from 4yo+ 8lb **10** Ran SP% **116.1**
Speed ratings (Par 101): **97,96,96,94,93 91,88,88,87,38**
CSF £63.20 CT £230.05 TOTE £7.20: £1.60, £2.10, £2.10; EX 75.50 Trifecta £263.70.

Owner Central Racing Ltd And Stef Keniry **Bred** Miss Jill Finegan **Trained** Middleham, N Yorks

■ Stewards' Enquiry : Joe Fanning caution; careless riding

FOCUS
Add 6yds. This moderate handicap was hit by non-runners. It paid to be handy, and the winner has been rated pretty much to his best.

4785 RACING AGAIN 17TH JULY H'CAP (DIV II) 7f 6y
5:30 (5:30) (Class 6) (0-65,63) 3-Y-O+
£3,105 (£924; £461; £300; £300; £300) Stalls Low

Form RPR
0065 1 **Mr Strutter (IRE)**[7] 4519 5-10-0 63 AndrewElliott 7 72
(Ronald Thompson) *hld up: rdn along over 2f out: gd hdwy on outside over 1f out: kpt on wl to ld towards fin* 9/1
4500 2 ¾ **Sfumato**[7] 4519 5-9-8 60 SeanDavis(3) 13 67
(Adrian Nicholls) *in tch: rdn over 2f out: hdwy 2f out: drvn into narrow ld 1f out: hdd 110yds out: kpt on* 10/1
05-1 3 ½ **Aliento**[37] 3414 4-10-0 63 TomEaves 15 69
(Michael Dods) *midfield: rdn along 2f out: angled rt to outer over 1f out: sn hdwy: drvn into narrow ld 110yds out: hdd towards fin: no ex* 4/1[1]
0540 4 2¾ **Fard**[7] 4523 4-9-7 56 (p) BenCurtis 11 54
(Roger Fell) *dwlt: hld up: rdn and hdwy over 1f out: kpt on fnl f (jockey said gelding hung right)* 7/1
0065 5 ¾ **Call Him Al (IRE)**[5] 4606 3-9-1 58 PaddyMathers 8 51
(Richard Fahey) *chsd ldrs: rdn and hung lft over 1f out: no ex ins fnl f* 16/1
0000 6 hd **Wensley**[2] 4726 4-9-6 55 PhilDennis 12 51
(Rebecca Bastiman) *slowly away: hld up in rr: rdn 2f out: kpt on fnl f: nrst fin* 40/1
6404 7 1 **Uncle Charlie (IRE)**[17] 4148 5-9-12 61 PaulMulrennan 10 54
(Ann Duffield) *in tch: rdn 2f out: one pce* 9/2[2]
0450 8 1 **Super Florence (IRE)**[23] 3930 4-9-11 60 (h) JamieGormley 3 50
(Iain Jardine) *led: rdn over 2f out: drvn and hdd 1f out: sn wknd* 20/1
3204 9 hd **Lady Lavinia**[6] 4554 3-8-10 53 CamHardie 6 40
(Michael Easterby) *midfield: rdn along over 3f out: no imp* 20/1
0000 10 1 **Intense Pleasure (IRE)**[17] 4148 4-9-3 52 (h) JamesSullivan 5 39
(Ruth Carr) *hld up in midfield: nvr threatened* 25/1
0040 11 1¼ **Fingal's Cave (IRE)**[23] 3922 7-9-7 56 (p) PaulHanagan 1 40
(Philip Kirby) *trckd ldrs: rdn over 2f out: wknd fnl f* 10/1
-022 12 2¾ **Tom's Anna (IRE)**[23] 3939 9-8-12 47 MichaelStainton 2 23
(Sean Regan) *in tch: rdn over 2f out: wknd over 1f out (jockey said mare was denied a clear run approaching the final furlong)* 28/1
0600 13 1 **Chickenfortea (IRE)**[23] 3921 5-9-7 56 RachelRichardson 4 30
(Eric Alston) *fly leapt s: prom: rdn over 2f out: wknd appr fnl f (jockey said gelding flyleapt then stumbled leaving the stalls)* 6/1[3]
000- 14 4½ **Moonlight Escapade**[246] 8904 3-8-9 52 JasonHart 9 10
(John Quinn) *midfield: rdn over 2f out: wknd over 1f out* 33/1

1m 26.07s (-1.33) **Going Correction** -0.20s/f (Firm) 14 Ran SP% 121.2
WFA 3 from 4yo+ 8lb
Speed ratings (Par 101): **99,98,97,94,93 93,92,91,90,89 88,85,83,78**
CSF £87.55 CT £434.10 TOTE £9.80: £2.50, £3.20, £2.90; EX 102.40 Trifecta £350.90.
Owner Mrs Amanda Harrison **Bred** Wardstown Stud Ltd **Trained** Stainforth, S Yorks

FOCUS
Add 6yds. A decent early pace collapsed in this second division of the moderate 7f handicap. The winner has been rated close to his best.
T/Plt: £39.00 to a £1 stake. Pool: £46,830.30. 875.86 winning units. T/Qpdt: £23.00 to a £1 stake. Pool: £3,221.71. 103.39 winning units. **Andrew Sheret**

4501 KEMPTON (A.W) (R-H)
Wednesday, July 10

OFFICIAL GOING: Polytrack: standard to slow
Wind: Moderate, across (away from stands) Weather: Fine, very warm

4786 32RED ON THE APP STORE APPRENTICE H'CAP 7f (P)
5:15 (5:15) (Class 4) (0-80,82) 4-Y-O+
£6,469 (£1,925; £962; £481; £300; £300) Stalls Low

Form RPR
4201 1 **Soar Above**[7] 4501 4-8-12 72 5ex (p) MorganCole(7) 5 82
(John Butler) *trckd ldr: chal 2f out: pushed into the ld over 1f out: styd on steadily: comf* 10/3[2]
0612 2 1 **Quick Breath**[19] 4061 4-10-1 82 TylerSaunders 1 89
(Jonathan Portman) *trckd ldng pair: clsd and shkn up to ld 2f out: hdd over 1f out: styd on but no real threat to wnr fnl f* 6/4[1]
4402 3 1 **Grey Galleon (USA)**[7] 4501 5-9-1 71 (p) AmeliaGlass(3) 7 75
(Clive Cox) *led: wd bnd 3f out: hdd 2f out: one pce after (jockey said gelding hung left throughout)* 15/2
2406 4 1¼ **Roman Spinner**[18] 4113 4-9-2 74 (t) StefanoCherchi(5) 2 75
(Rae Guest) *hld up in tch: clsd on ldrs 2f out: ch over 1f out: one pce after* 6/1
0-00 5 1¾ **The Gates Of Dawn (FR)**[74] 2107 4-9-9 76 ScottMcCullagh 6 72
(George Baker) *hld up in last pair: effrt 2f out: no prog and btn over 1f out* 40/1
4-10 6 1½ **Briyouni (FR)**[169] 355 6-8-8 68 CharlotteBennett(7) 3 60
(Ralph Beckett) *dwlt and stdd s: hld up in last pair: rdn on inner 2f out: no prog over 1f out: fdd* 16/1
2233 7 hd **Regimented (IRE)**[13] 4300 4-9-7 79 LukeCatton(5) 4 71
(Richard Hannon) *chsd ldng trio: lost pl jst over 2f out: no prog and wl btn over 1f out* 11/2[3]

1m 26.53s (0.53) **Going Correction** +0.025s/f (Slow) 7 Ran SP% 112.8
Speed ratings (Par 105): **98,96,95,94,92 90,90**
CSF £8.50 TOTE £4.30: £1.90, £1.10; EX 9.70 Trifecta £33.90.
Owner J Butler **Bred** Cheveley Park Stud Ltd **Trained** Newmarket, Suffolk

FOCUS
A fairly decent apprentice riders' handicap. The first two are on the upgrade.

4787 WISE BETTING AT RACINGTV.COM H'CAP 1m (P)
5:45 (5:48) (Class 6) (0-65,65) 3-Y-O+
£3,105 (£924; £461; £300; £300; £300) Stalls Low

Form RPR
-000 1 **Fortune And Glory (USA)**[15] 4226 6-9-11 64 DavidEgan 3 79
(Joseph Tuite) *trckd ldrs: clsd qckly on inner to ld wl over 1f out: sn clr: easily* 11/4[1]
5-60 2 3½ **Recuerdame (USA)**[77] 2035 3-9-3 65 HarryBentley 5 70
(Simon Dow) *hld up in midfield on inner: eased out over 2f out: rdn and prog over 1f out: chsd wnr fnl f: styd on but no ch* 5/1[2]
0406 3 2¼ **Sweet Nature (IRE)**[15] 4217 4-9-7 60 (p) HectorCrouch 1 62
(Laura Mongan) *trckd ldr to 2f out: rdn to go 2nd again over 1f out but no ch w wnr: one pce and dropped to 3rd fnl f* 16/1
0540 4 1¾ **Cashel (IRE)**[74] 2106 4-9-12 65 AlistairRawlinson 11 63
(Michael Appleby) *nt that wl away: wl in rr and pushed along early: rdn over 2f out: no prog tl styd on over 1f out to take 4th last 100yds (jockey said gelding stumbled leaving stalls)* 8/1
6345 5 2 **Militry Decoration (IRE)**[20] 4028 4-9-6 62 JoshuaBryan(3) 10 55
(Dr Jon Scargill) *racd on outer: trckd ldrs: rdn and nt qckn 2f out: sn outpcd: one pce after* 13/2[3]
3000 6 ¾ **Golden Nectar**[22] 3967 5-9-9 62 (p[1]) LiamKeniry 9 53
(Laura Mongan) *wl in tch: rdn 2f out: sn outpcd: n.d over 1f out* 33/1
0310 7 ½ **Mans Not Trot (IRE)**[48] 3006 4-9-0 56 (p) MeganNicholls(3) 7 46
(Brian Barr) *led to 2f out: sn btn* 16/1
0-00 8 2 **Lynchpin (IRE)**[19] 4070 3-9-2 64 AdrianMcCarthy 8 48
(Lydia Pearce) *nvr bttr than midfield: no prog 2f out* 66/1
06-0 9 ½ **Mr Spirit (IRE)**[71] 2238 3-8-13 64 (bt[1]) AaronJones(3) 4 47
(Marco Botti) *wl in rr: rdn over 2f out: no significant prog* 25/1
0-36 10 ½ **Flying Moon (GER)**[57] 2715 3-9-3 65 (b[1]) AdamKirby 14 46
(Jonathan Portman) *racd on outer: nvr beyond midfield: rdn and no prog over 2f out* 16/1
0301 11 ½ **Classic Charm**[61] 2585 4-9-8 61 MartinDwyer 6 43
(Dean Ivory) *chsd ldr: led briefly 2f out: wknd qckly over 1f out* 15/2
400 12 nk **Confab (USA)**[35] 3464 3-9-3 65 PatCosgrave 2 45
(George Baker) *nt that wl away: a in rr: shkn up over 2f out: no prog* 22/1
00-0 13 11 **Alexandria**[64] 2507 4-9-5 58 GeorgeWood 13 14
(Charlie Fellowes) *dwlt: a in rr: wknd 2f out: t.o* 16/1

1m 39.6s (-0.20) **Going Correction** +0.025s/f (Slow) 13 Ran SP% 115.7
WFA 3 from 4yo+ 9lb
Speed ratings (Par 101): **102,98,96,94,92 91,91,89,88,88 87,87,76**
CSF £14.13 CT £164.94 TOTE £2.80: £1.30, £2.10, £4.20; EX 14.50 Trifecta £221.20.
Owner Richard J Gurr **Bred** Dromoland Farm **Trained** Lambourn, Berks

FOCUS
A modest handicap. The favourite picked up really well from off the pace to win with ease and has been rated back to his best.

4788 32RED CASINO H'CAP (LONDON MILE SERIES QUALIFIER) (DIV I) 1m (P)
6:15 (6:17) (Class 5) (0-75,77) 3-Y-O
£3,752 (£1,116; £557; £300; £300; £300) Stalls Low

Form RPR
63-3 1 **Motawaj**[13] 4306 3-9-6 74 DavidEgan 6 87+
(Roger Varian) *hld up in tch: shkn up and swift prog on outer to ld 2f out: sn clr: edgd rt over 1f out: pushed out fnl f* 9/4[1]
0-34 2 3½ **Eligible (IRE)**[15] 4226 3-9-7 75 AdamKirby 5 80+
(Clive Cox) *hld up in tch: waiting for room over 2f out: prog wl over 1f out: drvn to chse clr ldng pair fnl f: styd on to take 2nd nr fin but no ch to threaten wnr* 7/2[2]
0-26 3 ¾ **Francisco Bay**[26] 3808 3-9-0 68 PatCosgrave 7 71
(Ed de Giles) *hld up in last: rdn and gd prog on outer 2f out to chse wnr over 1f out: styd on but no imp and lost 2nd nr fin* 12/1
-030 4 3½ **Solfeggio (IRE)**[13] 4285 3-8-12 66 (h) GeorgeWood 3 61
(Chris Wall) *hld up in tch: waiting for room over 2f out: shkn up and prog over 1f out: kpt on to take 4th nr fin: too late* 7/1[3]
-640 5 ½ **Bullington Boy (FR)**[18] 4124 3-9-5 73 JFEgan 4 67
(Jane Chapple-Hyam) *t.k.h: hld up bhd ldrs: waiting briefly for a gap over 2f out: tried to chal sn after but outpcd by ldng pair: wknd fnl f* 8/1
003 6 4 **Forbidden Dance**[27] 3761 3-9-6 74 OisinMurphy 8 59
(Hughie Morrison) *disp ld to 2f out: sn wknd* 9/1
053 7 5 **Eddie Cochran (IRE)**[16] 4178 3-9-6 74 SeanLevey 9 47
(Richard Hannon) *prom: rdn 3f out: wknd 2f out* 20/1
-310 8 1¼ **Pacificadora (USA)**[56] 2731 3-9-2 70 NickyMackay 2 41
(Simon Dow) *cl up on inner tl wknd wl over 1f out* 12/1
0460 9 ½ **Azets**[26] 3797 3-8-8 62 (b) HarryBentley 10 31
(Amanda Perrett) *disp ld to 2f out: wknd qckly* 20/1

1m 39.17s (-0.63) **Going Correction** +0.025s/f (Slow) 9 Ran SP% 111.5
Speed ratings (Par 100): **104,100,99,96,95 91,86,85,85**
CSF £9.32 CT £71.29 TOTE £2.50: £1.40, £1.50, £2.80; EX 10.60 Trifecta £78.20.
Owner Sheikh Ahmed Al Maktoum **Bred** Godolphin **Trained** Newmarket, Suffolk

FOCUS
The first division of a fair 3yo handicap. The favourite improved to win with authority and his time was quicker than the previous C&D handicap despite a modest gallop.

4789 32RED CASINO H'CAP (LONDON MILE SERIES QUALIFIER) (DIV II) 1m (P)
6:45 (6:46) (Class 5) (0-75,75) 3-Y-O
£3,752 (£1,116; £557; £300; £300; £300) Stalls Low

Form RPR
305 1 **Edaraat**[13] 4305 3-9-6 74 JimCrowley 3 88+
(Roger Varian) *nt that wl away: sn in midfield: prog 2f out: rdn to chal whn swvd bdly lft 1f out and ended against nr side rail: stl led ins fnl f and in command nr fin (jockey said gelding veered violently left away from the whip)* 3/1[2]
4-62 2 1¾ **Fares Poet (IRE)**[50] 2942 3-9-7 75 (h) ShaneKelly 10 80
(Marco Botti) *led: drvn and pressed 2f out: kpt on but hdd and outpcd ins fnl f* 10/1
6-32 3 2 **Jack D'Or**[16] 4189 3-9-7 75 LiamKeniry 9 75
(Ed Walker) *hld up in last trio: rdn over 2f out: no prog tl styd on wl fnl f to take 3rd last stride* 11/1
-506 4 shd **Padura Brave**[13] 4284 3-8-8 62 (p) DavidProbert 1 62
(Mark Usher) *trckd ldng pair: wnt 2nd 2f out and tried to chal: nt qckn over 1f out: one pce fnl f and lost 3rd last stride* 12/1
321 5 ½ **In The Cove (IRE)**[36] 3440 3-9-5 73 SeanLevey 7 72
(Richard Hannon) *pressed ldr to 2f out: outpcd over 1f out: kpt on fnl f* 6/1[3]
5-52 6 hd **Skyman**[13] 4306 3-9-5 73 JasonWatson 4 72+
(Roger Charlton) *hld up towards rr: rdn over 2f out: nvr gng pce to threaten but kpt on fnl f* 9/4[1]
-130 7 1¼ **Filles De Fleur**[15] 4226 3-9-4 72 (h[1]) HarryBentley 2 68
(George Scott) *nt that wl away but sn in midfield: rdn and no prog over 2f out* 20/1
2000 8 3 **Songkran (IRE)**[18] 4124 3-9-6 74 SilvestreDeSousa 8 63
(David Elsworth) *hld up in last trio: shkn up on inner 2f out: no prog* 13/2

2-00 **9** 2½ **Max Guevara (IRE)**[15] 4225 3-8-11 **65**............................ DavidEgan 5 48
(William Muir) *trckd ldng trio on outer: rdn and lost pl 2f out: steadily wknd* **33/1**

2406 **10** *nk* **Thunderoad**[36] 3446 3-9-0 **68**.................................. GeorgeDowning 11 50
(Tony Carroll) *hld up in last trio: rdn and no prog over 2f out* **50/1**

1m 40.55s (0.75) **Going Correction** +0.025s/f (Slow) **10** Ran SP% **118.2**
Speed ratings (Par 100): **97,95,93,93,92 92,91,88,85,85**
CSF £32.94 CT £301.89 TOTE £3.80: £1.20, £3.20, £3.60; EX 38.20 Trifecta £372.30.
Owner Hamdan Al Maktoum **Bred** Shadwell Estate Company Limited **Trained** Newmarket, Suffolk

FOCUS
The second division of a fair 3yo handicap with a dramatic ending and the wayward second-favourite's time was notably slower than the previous two 1m contests. Still, this rates improved form.

4790 32RED/BRITISH STALLION STUDS EBF FILLIES' NOVICE STKS (PLUS 10 RACE) 6f (P)
7:15 (7:15) (Class 4) 2-Y-O **£5,822** (£1,732; £865; £216) **Stalls** Low

Form RPR

2 **1** **Hot Touch**[22] 3968 2-9-0 0.................................. JackMitchell 2 81+
(Hugo Palmer) *chsd ldrs in 6th: shkn up 2f out: clsd and rdn 1f out: led last 100yds: styd on wl* **11/4**[2]

2 1¼ **Breath Of Joy** 2-9-0 0.................................. SilvestreDeSousa 11 77
(Amy Murphy) *trckd ldr: chal 2f out: upsides whn wnr wnt past 100yds out: styd on* **16/1**

2 **3** 1¼ **Tambourine Girl**[16] 4184 2-9-0 0.................................. JasonWatson 3 73
(Roger Charlton) *led: hrd pressed fr 2f out: hdd and no ex last 100yds* **11/10**[1]

10 **4** ½ **Graceful Magic**[19] 4048 2-9-7 0.................................. CharlesBishop 7 78
(Eve Johnson Houghton) *trckd ldrs: shkn up 2f out: no imp over 1f out: styd on ins fnl f* **14/1**

4 *dht* **Predictable Tully (IRE)** 2-9-0 0.................................. HectorCrouch 9 71
(Clive Cox) *trckd ldrs on outer: shkn up 2f out: no imp over 1f out: styd on ins fnl f* **20/1**

6 1¼ **Clegane** 2-9-0 0.................................. RichardKingscote 4 67+
(Ed Walker) *dwlt: sn in midfield: pushed along 2f out: kpt on steadily over 1f out: nt disgracd (vet said filly lost right fore shoe)* **20/1**

3 **7** ¾ **Airbrush (IRE)**[12] 4337 2-9-0 0.................................. OisinMurphy 1 65
(Richard Hannon) *pressed ldng pair: chal 2f out: stl nrly upsides jst over 1f out: wknd fnl f* **7/1**[3]

8 3½ **Miarka (FR)** 2-9-0 0.................................. JimCrowley 8 54
(Harry Dunlop) *a in rr: rdn and lft bhd 2f out* **25/1**

0 **9** 1 **Oribi**[12] 4337 2-9-0 0.................................. StevieDonohoe 12 51
(William Haggas) *hld up in last: rdn over 2f out: sn lft bhd by ldrs* **33/1**

10 10 **Havana Princess** 2-9-0 0.................................. KierenFox 6 19
(Dr Jon Scargill) *a in rr: bhd over 1f out* **100/1**

45 **11** ½ **Silent Agenda**[22] 3962 2-9-0 0.................................. AdamMcNamara 5 17
(Archie Watson) *a in rr: rdn and wknd 2f out: sn bhd* **16/1**

1m 13.0s (-0.10) **Going Correction** +0.025s/f (Slow) **11** Ran SP% **122.5**
Speed ratings (Par 93): **101,99,97,97,97 95,94,89,88,75 74**
CSF £44.00 TOTE £3.60: £1.30, £5.00, £1.20; EX 59.10 Trifecta £126.70.
Owner Dr Ali Ridha **Bred** The Stroll Patrol Partnership **Trained** Newmarket, Suffolk

FOCUS
A fair juvenile fillies' novice contest. The second-favourite won well in a good comparative time, improving from her debut.

4791 BET AT RACINGTV.COM H'CAP 1m 7f 218y(P)
7:45 (7:46) (Class 5) (0-75,75) 4-Y-O+ **£3,752** (£1,116; £557; £300; £300; £300) **Stalls** Low

Form RPR

12-0 **1** **Encryption (IRE)**[54] 2793 4-9-4 **72**.................................. StevieDonohoe 5 78+
(David Simcock) *dwlt: hld up towards rr: plenty to do 4f out once pce lifted: gd prog on inner over 2f out: drvn to chse ldr fnl f: led last 100yds: hld on* **7/1**

-100 **2** *nk* **Le Torrent**[107] 1330 7-9-5 **73**.................................. AdamKirby 4 78+
(Emma Lavelle) *hld up in midfield: plenty to do once pce lifted 4f out: rdn and prog on outer over 2f out: drvn and styd on fnl f to take 2nd last strides: jst too late* **11/1**

0053 **3** ½ **Gavlar**[38] 3377 8-9-5 **73**..................................(v) CallumShepherd 11 77
(William Knight) *trckd ldrs: moved up to 2nd 5f out and sn forced pce to increase: drvn to ld 3f out: clung on tl hdd last 100yds* **16/1**

0-00 **4** 2 **Conkering Hero (IRE)**[20] 4019 5-9-4 **72**..................................(v) OisinMurphy 10 74
(Joseph Tuite) *a.p: drvn to chse ldng pair over 2f out: nvr quite able to chal over 1f out: fdd last 100yds* **25/1**

1154 **5** ½ **Blazon**[35] 3467 6-9-1 **69**..................................(p) SilvestreDeSousa 13 70+
(Kim Bailey) *hld up in last trio: lot to do once pce lifted 4f out: rdn and prog on outer over 2f out: styd on fnl f: nrst fin but too late to chal* **4/1**[2]

2501 **6** ¾ **Atomic Jack**[29] 3693 4-9-1 **69**.................................. NicolaCurrie 2 70
(George Baker) *led: briefly hdd 10f out: jnd 5f out and forced to up the pce: hdd 3f out: tried to rally 2f out but fdd fnl f* **5/2**[1]

-403 **7** 14 **Cacophonous**[18] 4112 4-9-0 **68**.................................. JasonWatson 6 56
(David Menuisier) *hld up in midfield: swift move to press ldr and led briefly 10f out: lost 2nd 5f out: rdn over 3f out: wknd over 1f out: heavily eased* **11/2**[3]

432- **8** 2¼ **True North (IRE)**[277] 8002 4-9-1 **69**..................................(p) RyanTate 7 53
(Sir Mark Prescott Bt) *trckd ldrs: urged along over 3f out and in tch: wknd 2f out* **8/1**

0-2P **9** 1½ **Continuum**[56] 559 10-8-13 **67**..................................(v) CharlesBishop 12 46
(Peter Hedger) *s.s: a in rr: lft bhd 4f out: no ch after* **50/1**

0 **10** 1¾ **Sea Of Mystery (IRE)**[14] 4241 6-9-5 **73**..................................(p) AlistairRawlinson 14 50
(Michael Appleby) *trckd ldr 6f: styd prom tl wknd over 3f out* **50/1**

-P50 **11** 10 **Paddy A (IRE)**[20] 4019 5-9-7 **75**..................................(p) JimCrowley 9 40
(Ian Williams) *a in rr: lft bhd 4f out: no ch after: t.o* **12/1**

02-0 **12** 8 **Ardamir (FR)**[176] 84 7-8-12 **66**.................................. LiamJones 8 22
(Laura Mongan) *hld up in last: lft bhd 4f out: no ch after: t.o* **50/1**

225 **13** 49 **High Command (IRE)**[63] 2528 6-8-5 **62**..................................(b) MeganNicholls(3) 3
(Brian Barr) *chsd ldrs tl wknd rapidly over 4f out: t.o (trainer's rep said gelding had a breathing problem)* **50/1**

3m 28.29s (-1.81) **Going Correction** +0.025s/f (Slow) **13** Ran SP% **121.2**
Speed ratings (Par 103): **105,104,104,103,103 102,95,94,94,93 88,84,59**
CSF £79.91 CT £1185.83 TOTE £7.90: £2.50, £3.80, £5.00; EX 93.50 Trifecta £1151.80.
Owner A Olesen **Bred** Lynch Bages & Rjb Bloodstock **Trained** Newmarket, Suffolk

FOCUS
A fair staying handicap with a busy finish. The third helps set the standard.

4792 32RED H'CAP (LONDON MIDDLE DISTANCE SERIES QUALIFIER) 1m 2f 219y(P)
8:15 (8:18) (Class 4) (0-85,87) 3-Y-O+ **£6,469** (£1,925; £962; £481; £300; £300) **Stalls** Low

Form RPR

2-04 **1** **Galileo Silver (IRE)**[25] 3860 4-9-11 **80**.................................. JimCrowley 10 89+
(Alan King) *rn in snatches in midfield: drvn and outpcd over 3f out: styd on 2f out: clsd to take 2nd ins fnl f: fin wl to ld last strides* **8/1**

0-46 **2** ½ **Zzoro (IRE)**[28] 3726 6-9-7 **76**.................................. JasonWatson 13 84
(Amanda Perrett) *trckd ldr: led wl over 2f out and dashed for home: 3 l clr fnl f: worn down last strides* **14/1**

1406 **3** 1¼ **Get Back Get Back (IRE)**[15] 4224 4-10-0 **83**.................................. AdamKirby 6 89
(Clive Cox) *chsd ldrs: outpcd and rdn over 3f out: styd on fr 2f out: tk 3rd nr fin but unable to chal* **2/1**[1]

-540 **4** 2 **Noble Gift**[26] 3806 9-9-13 **82**.................................. CallumShepherd 8 84
(William Knight) *won battle for ld then set mod pce: kicked on over 3f out: hdd wl over 2f out: lost 2nd and one pce ins fnl f* **20/1**

613 **5** 1½ **Victory Chime (IRE)**[17] 4144 4-9-13 **82**..................................(b[1]) HarryBentley 5 82
(Ralph Beckett) *chsd ldng pair: rdn over 3f out: no imp 2f out: fdd fnl f* **3/1**[2]

6 1 **Walter White (FR)**[363] 4-9-7 **76**.................................. DavidProbert 7 74
(Alan King) *hld up in last pair: lft bhd over 3f out: pushed along and passed wkng rivals fnl 2f: nvr in it (jockey said gelding was slowly away and denied a clear run)* **16/1**

3205 **7** 2 **Loch Ness Monster (IRE)**[25] 3857 3-9-7 **87**.................................. AlistairRawlinson 12 83
(Michael Appleby) *in tch on outer: outpcd over 3f out: n.d fnl 2f out: plugged on* **6/1**[3]

00-1 **8** 2¼ **Bombero (IRE)**[23] 3925 5-9-1 **70**.................................. PatCosgrave 3 61
(Ed de Giles) *in tch: rdn over 3f out: sn outpcd: wknd 2f out* **14/1**

0166 **9** *nse* **Eye Of The Storm (IRE)**[11] 4386 9-9-5 **74**.................................. NicolaCurrie 1 65
(Conor Dore) *slow to get gng and racd in last: outpcd over 3f out: no ch after (jockey said gelding was slow into stride)* **33/1**

116 **10** 3¾ **Rail Dancer**[15] 4220 7-9-0 **69**..................................(v) ShaneKelly 11 54
(Shaun Keightley) *chsd ldrs on outer: outpcd and rdn over 3f out: wknd 2f out* **16/1**

0-00 **11** ¾ **Accessor (IRE)**[40] 3321 4-8-11 **66**.................................. JFEgan 9 49
(Michael Wigham) *a in rr: outpcd over 3f out: no ch after* **50/1**

0-00 **12** 1¼ **Torcello (IRE)**[15] 4224 5-9-10 **82**.................................. MeganNicholls(3) 2 63
(Shaun Lycett) *a in rr: outpcd over 3f out: no ch after* **66/1**

2m 21.26s (0.26) **Going Correction** +0.025s/f (Slow)
WFA 3 from 4yo+ 11lb **12** Ran SP% **120.0**
Speed ratings (Par 105): **103,102,101,100,99 98,97,95,95,92 92,91**
CSF £111.70 CT £312.71 TOTE £8.60: £2.40, £4.00, £1.10; EX 84.00 Trifecta £314.60.
Owner Walters Plant Hire & Potter Group **Bred** Mt Brilliant Broodmares Ii, Llc **Trained** Barbury Castle, Wilts

FOCUS
A decent middle-distance handicap. The pace was muddling, so the form has been set around the well-placed runner-up.

4793 32RED.COM H'CAP 7f (P)
8:45 (8:47) (Class 4) (0-85,85) 3-Y-O **£6,469** (£1,925; £962; £481; £300; £300) **Stalls** Low

Form RPR

03-2 **1** **Molivaliente (USA)**[62] 2550 3-8-10 **74**.................................. KierenFox 4 82+
(John Best) *t.k.h: trckd ldrs: rdn to go 2nd over 1f out: sustained chal to ld narrowly 75yds out: hld on* **3/1**[2]

0233 **2** *shd* **Nefarious (IRE)**[10] 4420 3-9-7 **85**.................................. DavidProbert 5 92
(Henry Candy) *led: drvn for home over 2f out: narrowly hdd 75yds out: kpt on wl but jst hld* **7/2**[3]

-041 **3** ¾ **Maid For Life**[40] 3323 3-9-2 **80**..................................(h) GeorgeWood 1 85
(Charlie Fellowes) *hld up: waiting for room 2f out: rdn and prog over 1f out: tk 3rd last 100yds: clsng at fin* **11/2**

-421 **4** 1½ **Revolutionise (IRE)**[16] 4185 3-9-0 **78**.................................. DavidEgan 7 79
(Roger Varian) *t.k.h: cl up: tk 2nd and pressed ldr 2f out: hanging and nt qckn over 1f out: one pce fnl f (jockey said gelding ran too free)* **11/4**[1]

1-00 **5** 1 **Hackle Setter (USA)**[35] 3465 3-8-13 **77**.................................. JasonWatson 3 75
(Sylvester Kirk) *hld up in last: outpcd and rdn over 2f out: styd on fnl f: nvr nrr but no ch* **20/1**

0-05 **6** 2 **Red Bravo (IRE)**[32] 3591 3-9-0 **78**.................................. RichardKingscote 8 71
(Charles Hills) *pressed ldr to 2f out: wknd fnl f* **11/1**

3104 **7** 2½ **Global Warning**[35] 3465 3-9-6 **84**.................................. GeraldMosse 6 70
(Ed Dunlop) *dwlt: in tch in rr: rdn and no prog over 2f out: wknd over 1f out* **12/1**

-440 **8** 6 **Converter (IRE)**[35] 3479 3-9-2 **80**.................................. DanielMuscutt 2 50
(John Butler) *prom on inner: rdn 2f out: wknd rapidly over 1f out* **50/1**

1m 26.33s (0.33) **Going Correction** +0.025s/f (Slow) **8** Ran SP% **112.0**
Speed ratings (Par 102): **99,98,98,96,95 92,90,83**
CSF £13.34 CT £53.19 TOTE £4.10: £1.50, £1.50, £1.10; EX 14.40 Trifecta £67.50.
Owner A Graham - Bankruptcy Trustee M Stanley **Bred** Green Lantern Stables Llc **Trained** Oad Street, Kent

FOCUS
A decent 3yo handicap and the winner improved.
T/Jkpt: £1,666.60 to a £1 stake. Pool: £10,000.00. 6 winning units. T/Plt: £58.50 to a £1 stake. Pool: £63,377.77. 790.22 winning units. T/Qpdt: £19.70 to a £1 stake. Pool: £11,110.74. 415.8 winning units. **Jonathan Neesom**

4372 LINGFIELD (L-H)
Wednesday, July 10

OFFICIAL GOING: Good to firm (firm in places on round course; 9.8)
Wind: Virtually nil Weather: Fine

4794 DOWNLOAD THE STAR SPORTS APP NOW! H'CAP 1m 1f
2:10 (2:11) (Class 6) (0-60,59) 3-Y-O **£2,781** (£827; £413; £300; £300; £300) **Stalls** Low

Form RPR

0246 **1** **Dear Miriam (IRE)**[22] 3965 3-9-7 **59**.................................. SilvestreDeSousa 9 65
(Mick Channon) *led: rdn over 2f out: hdd over 1f out: rallied to ld ins fnl f: styd on* **5/2**[1]

-000 **2** *nk* **Tattenhams**[21] 3996 3-8-3 **46**.................................. ThoreHammerHansen(5) 1 51
(Adam West) *chsd ldrs: rdn and swtchd rt 2f out: chsd wnr wl ins fnl f: styd on* **50/1**

5050 **3** 2¼ **Cromwell**[27] 3764 3-9-4 **56**..........................(t) FergusSweeney 7 57
(Luke Dace) *a.p: chsd wnr over 2f out: led over 1f out: rdn and hdd ins fnl f: styd on same pce* **8/1**[3]

0-00 **4** ¾ **Ragstone Cowboy (IRE)**[39] 3354 3-9-6 **58**.......................... LiamKeniry 5 57+
(Gary Moore) *trckd ldrs: rdn over 1f out: styd on* **7/1**[2]

-032 **5** 2¾ **Nabvutika (IRE)**[8] 4485 3-8-13 **51**.......................... ShaneKelly 12 44
(John Butler) *hld up on outer: rdn over 2f out: styd on fnl f: nt rch ldrs* **5/2**[1]

0045 **6** ½ **Sukalia**[13] 4284 3-9-4 **56**..........................(p[1]) DavidProbert 6 48
(Alan King) *hld up: racd keenly: rdn over 2f out: styd on fnl f: nt rch ldrs* **8/1**[3]

-020 **7** ¾ **Bumblekite**[29] 3684 3-8-6 **51**.......................... TobyEley[(7)] 2 42
(Steph Hollinshead) *hld up: hdwy u.p over 1f out: nt trble ldrs (jockey said filly suffered interference)* **20/1**

005 **8** ¾ **Risk Mitigation (USA)**[106] 1344 3-9-3 **55**..........................(v[1]) JFEgan 8 44
(David Evans) *s.i.s: hld up: rdn over 2f out: nvr on terms* **16/1**

-500 **9** 1 **Dance To Freedom**[14] 4244 3-9-0 **52**..........................(t) OisinMurphy 10 39
(Stuart Williams) *chsd wnr tl rdn over 2f out: wknd fnl f* **14/1**

4000 **10** 6 **Invincible One (IRE)**[13] 4286 3-9-6 **58**.......................... JasonWatson 3 32
(Sylvester Kirk) *hld up: a in rr* **16/1**

6-00 **11** 2 **London Pride**[23] 3947 3-9-7 **59**.......................... TrevorWhelan 4 29
(Jonathan Portman) *hld up in tch: rdn over 2f out: sn wknd* **20/1**

00-0 **12** ¾ **King Of The Ring**[29] 3696 3-8-7 **45**.......................... NicolaCurrie 11 14
(Paul Nicholls) *a in rr (jockey said gelding was never travelling)* **33/1**

1m 52.39s (-4.51) **Going Correction** -0.45s/f (Firm) course record **12** Ran SP% **124.7**
Speed ratings (Par 98): **102,101,99,99,96 96,95,94,93,88 86,86**
CSF £189.91 CT £943.75 TOTE £3.50: £1.60, £12.50, £2.00; EX 167.30 Trifecta £1803.90.
Owner T P Radford **Bred** P & B Bloodstock **Trained** West Ilsley, Berks
■ Stewards' Enquiry : Thore Hammer Hansen two-day ban; misuse of whip (July 24-25)

FOCUS
Add 4yds. Moderate 3yo form, little got into it from off the pace with the winner making most.

4795 STARSPORTS.BET H'CAP 1m 3f 133y
2:40 (2:41) (Class 5) (0-70,72) 3-Y-O+ **£3,428** (£1,020; £509; £300; £300) **Stalls** High

Form RPR

4-06 **1** **Baasem (USA)**[43] 3195 3-9-6 **72**.......................... JimCrowley 3 84
(Owen Burrows) *mde all: racd keenly: shkn up over 2f out: rdn clr fnl f* **2/1**[2]

-354 **2** 7 **Sawasdee (IRE)**[20] 4031 3-9-1 **67**..........................(p) SilvestreDeSousa 1 68
(Andrew Balding) *s.i.s: sn rcvrd to chse wnr: rdn over 2f out: edgd lft and no ex fnl f* **5/4**[1]

22-0 **3** 1¾ **Ban Shoof**[33] 3541 6-10-0 **68**..........................(b) HectorCrouch 4 66
(Gary Moore) *chsd ldrs: rdn over 3f out: no ex fnl f* **16/1**

4111 **4** 1½ **Cherry Cola**[9] 4447 3-9-5 **71** 6ex.......................... TrevorWhelan 2 67
(Sheena West) *hood removed late: s.s: hld up: hdwy over 2f out: rdn over 1f out: no ex fnl f (jockey said blindfold was tucking in tightly to the bridle and took two attempts to remove it)* **3/1**[3]

400 **5** 17 **Famous Dynasty (IRE)**[14] 4231 5-9-4 **58**.......................... DavidProbert 5 25
(Michael Blanshard) *broke wl: sn lost pl: rdn 4f out: wknd wl over 1f out: eased* **25/1**

2m 26.35s (-7.65) **Going Correction** -0.45s/f (Firm) **5** Ran SP% **112.5**
WFA 3 from 5yo+ 12lb
Speed ratings (Par 103): **107,102,101,100,88**
CSF £5.04 TOTE £2.90: £1.40, £1.30; EX 5.20 Trifecta £22.10.
Owner Hamdan Al Maktoum **Bred** Shadwell Farm LLC **Trained** Lambourn, Berks

FOCUS
Add 4yds. Modest 3yo form, the winner dominated at his own tempo and bolted up, posting a clear pb.

4796 READ SILVESTRE DE SOUSA'S EXCLUSIVE BLOG STARSPORTSBET.CO.UK H'CAP 2m 68y
3:10 (3:13) (Class 6) (0-60,60) 4-Y-O+
£2,781 (£827; £413; £300; £300; £300) **Stalls** Centre

Form RPR

0355 **1** **Fitzwilly**[14] 4251 9-9-7 **60**.......................... OisinMurphy 9 68
(Mick Channon) *s.i.s: hdwy 13f out: shkn up over 4f out: rdn over 2f out: led ins fnl f: styd on wl* **9/4**[2]

23-6 **2** 3½ **Royal Hall (FR)**[41] 3252 7-8-8 **47**.......................... SilvestreDeSousa 3 51
(Gary Moore) *chsd ldr: wnt upsides 5f out: rdn over 2f out: led over 1f out: hdd and no ex ins fnl f* **13/8**[1]

500- **3** 1¾ **Danglydontask**[257] 8613 8-8-10 **49** ow1..........................(p) RossaRyan 1 51
(Mike Murphy) *led at stdy pce tl hdd 5f out: remained handy: rdn over 2f out: styd on same pce fr over 1f out: wnt 3rd towards fin* **18/1**

-530 **4** 1½ **Sauchiehall Street (IRE)**[44] 1826 4-9-6 **59**.......................... DavidProbert 7 59
(Noel Williams) *hld up: hdwy to ld 5f out: rdn: edgd rt and hdd over 1f out: wknd wl ins fnl f* **6/1**[3]

0-03 **5** 1¾ **Essgee Nics (IRE)**[48] 3017 6-8-7 **46** oh1..........................(p) KierenFox 5 44
(Paul George) *hld up: outpcd over 4f out: rdn over 2f out: r.o ins fnl f: nvr nrr* **8/1**

0006 **6** 1 **Mood For Mischief**[14] 4251 4-8-7 **51**..........................(p) RachealKneller[(5)] 4 48
(James Bennett) *chsd ldrs: pushed along 4f out: outpcd fnl 3f* **25/1**

0440 **7** 1¼ **Millie May**[56] 2733 5-8-2 **46**.......................... ThoreHammerHansen[(5)] 6 41
(Jimmy Fox) *s.i.s: in rr: pushed along and stmbld bnd ent st: nvr on terms* **16/1**

4653 **8** 3 **Roy Rocket (FR)**[15] 4216 9-9-5 **58**.......................... JFEgan 2 50
(John Berry) *prom: lost pl over 12f out: hdwy over 4f out: rdn over 2f out: wknd over 1f out* **14/1**

3m 32.38s (-3.62) **Going Correction** -0.45s/f (Firm) **8** Ran SP% **115.9**
Speed ratings (Par 101): **91,89,88,87,86 86,85,84**
CSF £6.40 CT £48.33 TOTE £3.20: £1.10, £1.10, £4.40; EX 7.60 Trifecta £80.10.
Owner Peter Taplin & Partner **Bred** Imperial & Mike Channon Bloodstock Ltd **Trained** West Ilsley, Berks

FOCUS
Add 4yds. The right horses came to the fore in this lowly staying handicap and the winner has been rated close to form, with the runner-up to his latest.

4797 DOWNLOAD THE STAR SPORTS APP NOW! (S) H'CAP 7f
3:40 (3:41) (Class 6) (0-65,66) 3-Y-O+
£2,781 (£827; £413; £300; £300; £300) **Stalls** Centre

Form RPR

0034 **1** **Chikoko Trail**[18] 4115 4-9-9 **58**..........................(vt[1]) HectorCrouch 4 69
(Gary Moore) *mde all against nr side rails: shkn up over 1f out: r.o wl: eased nr fin* **7/2**[2]

0000 **2** 5 **Vincenzo Coccotti (USA)**[15] 4227 7-8-13 **51**..........(p) FinleyMarsh[(3)] 7 49
(Ken Cunningham-Brown) *stdd s: hld up: hdwy over 2f out: rdn and edgd lft over 1f out: styd on to go 2nd ins fnl f: no ch w wnr* **6/1**

4320 **3** ¾ **Lippy Lady (IRE)**[41] 3256 3-8-12 **55**..........................(h) JFEgan 3 47
(Paul George) *s.s: hdwy on outer over 4f out: rdn and edgd lft over 2f out: styd on same pce fnl f* **9/4**[1]

P05 **4** ¾ **Kafeel (USA)**[107] 1328 8-9-7 **56**..........................(p) RossaRyan 6 49
(Alexandra Dunn) *chsd ldrs: wnt 2nd 3f out tl rdn over 1f out: no ex fnl f* **12/1**

0544 **5** 2¾ **Edge (IRE)**[33] 3541 8-9-9 **58**..........................(b) DavidProbert 2 44
(Bernard Llewellyn) *s.i.s: rdn over 2f out: styd on fr over 1f out: nt trble ldrs (jockey said gelding was never travelling)* **9/2**[3]

-260 **6** 1¼ **Satchville Flyer**[146] 717 8-10-3 **66**..........................(v) OisinMurphy 8 49
(David Evans) *chsd ldrs: rdn over 1f out: no ex* **10/1**

0-00 **7** 1¼ **De Bruyne Horse**[13] 4281 4-9-11 **63**..........................(b) JoshuaBryan[(3)] 9 42
(Bernard Llewellyn) *s.i.s: outpcd: edgd lft 1/2-way: nvr nrr* **12/1**

0000 **8** 1¾ **Malaysian Boleh**[12] 4336 9-8-3 **45**..........................(be) GraceMcEntee[(7)] 5 20
(Phil McEntee) *prom: stmbld and lost pl over 4f out: n.d after* **33/1**

00-4 **9** 23 **Jeopardy John**[9] 4449 4-9-1 **55**..........................(v[1]) ScottMcCullagh[(5)] 1
(Michael Attwater) *w ldr tl over 4f out: lost 2nd 3f out: sn rdn and hung lft: wknd 2f out (jockey said gelding stopped quickly)* **20/1**

1m 21.13s (-3.17) **Going Correction** -0.45s/f (Firm) **9** Ran SP% **117.6**
WFA 3 from 4yo+ 8lb
Speed ratings (Par 101): **100,94,93,92,89 88,86,84,58**
CSF £25.42 CT £57.53 TOTE £4.40: £1.50, £2.20, £1.50; EX 26.10 Trifecta £79.20.There was no bid for the winner. De Bruyne Horse was claimed by Mr D. Griffiths for £6,400.
Owner M Albon **Bred** G Hedley & Mike Channon Bloodstock Ltd **Trained** Lower Beeding, W Sussex

FOCUS
One-way traffic in this selling handicap and the winner seemed back to something like his best.

4798 CALL STAR SPORTS ON 08000 521 321 NOVICE MEDIAN AUCTION STKS 6f
4:10 (4:12) (Class 5) 2-Y-O **£3,428** (£1,020; £509; £254) **Stalls** Centre

Form RPR

0 **1** **Company Minx (IRE)**[51] 2918 2-9-0 0.......................... HectorCrouch 1 77+
(Clive Cox) *chsd ldrs on outer: rdn over 2f out: carried lft ins fnl f: r.o to ld nr fin* **33/1**

2 nse **Laikaparty (IRE)** 2-9-5 0.......................... OisinMurphy 5 81
(Archie Watson) *chsd ldrs: shkn up to ld and bmpd wl over 1f out: rdn and hung lft ins fnl f: hdd nr fin* **3/1**[1]

3334 **3** 4 **Audio**[47] 3039 2-9-5 76..........................(b) RossaRyan 10 68
(Richard Hannon) *led: rdn: hung lft and hdd wl over 1f out: continued to hang lft: no ex ins fnl f* **9/2**[2]

4 4½ **Gypsy Whisper** 2-9-0 0.......................... JasonWatson 9 49+
(David Menuisier) *sn pushed along in rr: swtchd lft over 2f out: hdwy over 1f out: nt rch ldrs* **15/2**

5 1 **Burniston Rocks** 2-9-5 0.......................... StevieDonohoe 6 50+
(Ed Vaughan) *s.i.s: outpcd: r.o ins fnl f: nvr nrr* **14/1**

0 **6** nk **New Jack Swing (IRE)**[37] 3419 2-9-5 0.......................... SeanLevey 8 49
(Richard Hannon) *chsd ldrs: rdn and hung lft over 1f out: wknd fnl f* **5/1**[3]

6 **7** 1¼ **Souter Johnnie (IRE)**[29] 3694 2-9-5 0.......................... ShaneKelly 4 45
(Richard Hughes) *s.i.s: pushed along and hdwy over 2f out: wknd fnl f* **11/2**

50 **8** 1½ **Ask Siri (IRE)**[51] 2918 2-8-11 0.......................... MitchGodwin[(3)] 2 36
(John Bridger) *chsd ldrs: rdn: hung lft and flashed tail over 1f out: wknd fnl f* **100/1**

9 ½ **Quimerico** 2-9-5 0.......................... KierenFox 11 39
(John Best) *edgd lft s: sn pushed along towards rr: n.d* **25/1**

10 3 **Rushcutters Bay** 2-9-5 0.......................... JimCrowley 7 29
(Hugo Palmer) *s.i.s: hdwy on outer over 2f out: wknd fnl f* **11/2**

4 **11** 4½ **Krishmaya (IRE)**[26] 3798 2-8-9 0.......................... ThoreHammerHansen[(5)] 13 10
(Adam West) *s.i.s: hdwy over 4f out: rdn over 2f out: wknd over 1f out* **16/1**

5 **12** 7 **Numinous (IRE)**[8] 4482 2-9-5 0.......................... DavidProbert 12
(Henry Candy) *chsd ldrs: rdn over 2f out: wknd wl over 1f out* **20/1**

0 **13** 3¾ **Helluvasunset**[23] 3942 2-9-0 0.......................... FergusSweeney 3
(Mark Usher) *awkward s: hld up in tch: wknd over 2f out* **100/1**

1m 9.41s (-2.09) **Going Correction** -0.45s/f (Firm) 2y crse rec **13** Ran SP% **128.5**
Speed ratings (Par 94): **95,94,89,83,82 81,80,78,77,73 67,58,53**
CSF £136.29 TOTE £57.50: £9.20, £1.30, £1.80; EX 363.20 Trifecta £5882.30.
Owner Mrs Olive Shaw **Bred** Mrs O A Shaw **Trained** Lambourn, Berks

FOCUS
Two came clear in this average maiden and there was a bit of a turn up, with the winner rating a big improver.

4799 WATCH THE £BETTINGPEOPLE VIDEOS STARSPORTSBET.CO.UK NURSERY H'CAP 4f 217y
4:40 (4:40) (Class 5) (0-75,77) 2-Y-O **£3,428** (£1,020; £509; £300) **Stalls** Centre

Form RPR

120 **1** **Probable Cause**[21] 3997 2-9-12 **76**..........................(b[1]) OisinMurphy 5 80
(Archie Watson) *chsd ldrs: rdn and hung rt over 1f out: r.o to ld nr fin* **6/1**[2]

4331 **2** shd **Dream Kart (IRE)**[9] 4448 2-9-13 **77** 6ex.......................... SilvestreDeSousa 3 80
(Mark Johnston) *stmbld s: led: hung lft 1/2-way: sn rdn: hung rt over 1f out: wandered ins fnl f: hdd nr fin (jockey said filly hung badly both ways)* **30/100**[1]

3230 **3** 3 **Paper Star**[21] 3988 2-9-1 **65**.......................... NicolaCurrie 2 57
(George Baker) *sn outpcd: r.o ins fnl f: nt trble ldrs (jockey said filly was outpaced early on)* **7/1**[3]

443 **4** 4 **Bartat**[70] 2275 2-9-1 **65**.......................... CallumShepherd 1 43
(Mick Channon) *chsd ldrs: rdn and hung lft fr 1/2-way: eased whn btn ins fnl f* **16/1**

57.38s (-1.32) **Going Correction** -0.45s/f (Firm) **4** Ran SP% **109.6**
Speed ratings (Par 94): **92,91,87,80**
CSF £8.74 TOTE £5.60; EX 10.40 Trifecta £13.80.
Owner Blackbriar Racing **Bred** Whatton Manor Stud **Trained** Upper Lambourn, W Berks

FOCUS
Bit of a turn up in this small-field nursery, with the favourite costing himself victory by wandering under pressure. The raced centre-field.

4800 FIRST FOR INDUSTRY JOBS VISIT STARRECRUITMENT.BET NOVICE MEDIAN AUCTION STKS 7f
5:10 (5:10) (Class 6) 3-5-Y-O **£2,781** (£827; £413; £206) **Stalls** Centre

Form RPR

52 **1** **Attorney General**[21] 4010 3-9-5 0.......................... ShaneKelly 4 71
(Ed Vaughan) *hmpd s: sn led: rdn over 1f out: styd on wl* **7/4**[2]

4222 **2** 1½ **Voltaic**[11] 4377 3-9-5 75.......................... DavidProbert 1 67
(Paul Cole) *chsd wnr: rdn over 1f out: styd on same pce wl ins fnl f* **4/7**[1]

The Form Book Flat 2019, Raceform Ltd, Newbury, RG14 5SJ

0-4 **3** *2 ¼* **Threefeetfromgold (IRE)**[13] 4298 3-9-5 0......................(h) EoinWalsh 7 61
(Martin Smith) *hld up: plld hrd: hdwy 5f out: shkn up over 1f out: styd on same pce ins fnl f (jockey said gelding ran too free)* **16/1**[3]

0 **4** *9* **Sharp Talk (IRE)**[16] 4196 3-9-5 0.......................... FergusSweeney 3 37
(Shaun Keightley) *s.i.s and hmpd s: hld up: nvr nr to chal* **25/1**

00 **5** *25* **If At Sea**[16] 4189 3-8-9 0.................................. RhiainIngram(5) 5
(Amanda Perrett) *plld hrd and prom: pushed along 1/2-way: hung lft over 2f out: sn wknd: eased fnl f* **50/1**

6 *9* **Squizzy Boy (IRE)** 3-9-5 0.. LiamJones 2
(Laura Mongan) *wnt rt s: plld hrd: lost pl over 4f out: wknd 1/2-way* **50/1**

1m 21.51s (-2.79) **Going Correction** **-0.45s/f (Firm)** **6** Ran SP% **113.7**
Speed ratings (Par 101): **97,95,92,82,53 43**
CSF £3.10 TOTE £2.80: £1.10, £1.10; EX 3.30 Trifecta £6.80.
Owner Khalifa Dasmal **Bred** K A Dasmal **Trained** Newmarket, Suffolk

FOCUS
A modest and uncompetitive novice, the odds-on favourite was turned over. This rates a small pb from the winner.
T/Plt: £54.60 to a £1 stake. Pool: £62,422.14. 833.39 winning units. T/Qpdt: £18.20 to a £1 stake. Pool: £6,215.67. 251.84 winning units. **Colin Roberts**

4563 YARMOUTH (L-H)
Wednesday, July 10

OFFICIAL GOING: Good to firm (7.2)
Wind: Virtually nil Weather: Light shower, muggy

4801 HAVEN SEASHORE HOLIDAY PARK H'CAP 1m 3y
2:20 (2:21) (Class 6) (0-65,69) 3-Y-O+
£2,781 (£827; £413; £300; £300; £300) **Stalls Centre**

Form RPR

0002 **1** **Immoral (IRE)**[16] 4180 3-9-4 **63**......................(b) LukeMorris 4 69
(Ed Walker) *in tch in midfield: effrt and rdn over 2f out: drvn and kpt on to chal whn hung lft u.p 1f out: led ins fnl f: rdn out* **13/2**[3]

5-06 **2** *1* **Winterkoenigin**[13] 4285 3-9-6 **65**......................(p) DanielMuscutt 1 69
(David Lanigan) *rrd as stalls opened and swtchd rt sn after s: hld up in tch in last pair: clsd to trck ldrs 2f out: effrt over 1f out: kpt on u.p ins fnl f: wnt 2nd towards fin (jockey said filly reared when leaving the stalls)* **10/1**

0336 **3** *¾* **Catch My Breath**[28] 3741 3-8-13 **63**.................... CierenFallon(5) 7 65
(John Ryan) *dwlt: sn rcvrd and wl in tch in midfield: trckd ldrs 1/2-way: clsd to press ldr over 2f out: drvn over 1f out: kpt on same pce ins fnl f* **3/1**[2]

0211 **4** *nk* **Magical Ride**[6] 4567 4-9-12 **69** 5ex.......................... SeanKirrane(7) 6 72
(Richard Spencer) *led: rdn over 2f out: drvn over 1f out: hdd and one pce ins fnl f* **10/11**[1]

4042 **5** *4 ½* **Percy Toplis**[44] 3142 5-8-9 **45**..........................(b) JimmyQuinn 3 38
(Christine Dunnett) *s.i.s: hld up in rr: clsd and shkn up 2f out: sn drvn and no imp: wl hld fnl f (jockey said gelding was slowly away)* **33/1**

0620 **6** *5* **Roof Garden**[11] 4370 4-9-10 **60**............................ DougieCostello 5 41
(Mark H Tompkins) *t.k.h: pressed ldr tl over 2f out: rdn and lost pl over 1f out: wknd ins fnl f* **33/1**

3606 **7** *8* **Margaret J**[19] 4071 3-7-10 **46**..........................(p) SophieRalston(5) 2 7
(Phil McEntee) *chsd ldrs tl 1/2-way: bhd fnl 2f* **22/1**

1m 38.74s (0.54) **Going Correction** **+0.025s/f (Good)**
WFA 3 from 4yo+ 9lb **7** Ran SP% **110.0**
Speed ratings (Par 101): **98,97,96,95,91 86,78**
CSF £58.79 TOTE £6.60: £2.80, £4.20; EX 72.90 Trifecta £191.20.
Owner Highclere Thoroughbred Racing -Syonhouse **Bred** Tom & Cathy Burns **Trained** Upper Lambourn, Berks

FOCUS
A moderate event in which the early pace didn't seem overly strong.

4802 BRITISH STALLION STUDS EBF NOVICE AUCTION STKS 5f 42y
2:50 (2:50) (Class 5) 2-Y-O **£3,428** (£1,020; £509; £254) **Stalls Centre**

Form RPR

0 **1** **Intimate Moment**[15] 4222 2-8-10 1 ow1........................ RobHornby 5 79
(Philip McBride) *t.k.h: hld up wl in tch in midfield: effrt ent fnl 2f: hdwy to ld over 1f out: flashing tail u.p but r.o strly ins fnl f: readily* **33/1**

3 **2** *3* **Bubbly Splash (IRE)**[28] 3717 2-8-12 0.................... DanielTudhope 8 70+
(David O'Meara) *stmbld as stalls opened and slowly away: in tch in rr: swtchd rt and rn green over 2f out: rdn over 1f out: drvn and hdwy to chse wnr ins fnl f: styd on but no imp (jockey said colt stumbled leaving the stalls)* **9/4**[1]

10 **3** *1 ¾* **Better The Devil (USA)**[21] 3988 2-9-7 0.................... LukeMorris 3 73
(Archie Watson) *led tl over 3f out: rdn jst over 2f out: stl pressing ldrs and drvn over 1f out: 3rd and kpt on same pce ins fnl f* **9/2**[2]

100 **4** *1 ¼* **Fleeting Princess**[19] 4048 2-9-2 **80**.......................... GeraldMosse 2 64
(Charles Hills) *t.k.h: chsd ldrs: clsd to chal and rdn ent fnl 2f: edgd lft u.p over 1f out: wknd ins fnl f* **9/4**[1]

43 **5** *½* **Dynamighty**[39] 3350 2-8-4 0.................................. SeanKirrane(7) 1 57
(Richard Spencer) *wl in tch in midfield: effrt ent fnl 2f: chsd ldrs and rdn over 1f out: no ex and wknd ins fnl f* **9/1**[3]

6 **6** *¾* **Dreamy Rascal (IRE)**[86] 1821 2-8-11 0........................ AndreaAtzeni 4 54
(Richard Hannon) *t.k.h: chsd ldr tl led over 3f out: rdn and hung lft over 1f out: sn hdd & wknd ins fnl f* **9/2**[2]

406 **7** *8* **Dark Side Division**[28] 3739 2-8-9 **60**.................... CierenFallon(5) 6 28
(John Ryan) *chsd ldrs tl lost pl over 2f out: bhd over 1f out* **50/1**

0 **8** *4 ½* **Conker**[20] 4018 2-8-11 0.................................... TheodoreLadd(5) 7 14
(Charlie Wallis) *in tch in last pair: rdn ent fnl 2f: sn struggling and bhd over 1f out* **150/1**

1m 2.46s (0.56) **Going Correction** **+0.025s/f (Good)** **8** Ran SP% **113.5**
Speed ratings (Par 94): **96,91,88,86,85 84,71,64**
CSF £105.52 TOTE £43.70: £6.40, £1.50, £1.10; EX 172.80 Trifecta £1530.40.
Owner PMRacing **Bred** Dukes Stud & Overbury Stallions Ltd **Trained** Newmarket, Suffolk

FOCUS
The winner was clearly a big improver from her debut, but the level is a bit fluid.

4803 JME LTD ADVANCED INSPECTION SERVICES H'CAP 1m 6f 17y
3:20 (3:20) (Class 5) (0-75,73) 3-Y-O
£3,428 (£1,020; £509; £300; £300; £300) **Stalls High**

Form RPR

00-4 **1** **Land Of Oz**[43] 3197 3-8-6 **58**.................................... LukeMorris 8 70+
(Sir Mark Prescott Bt) *midfield on outer whn impeded and dropped to rr bnd 13f out: effrt and hdwy 4f out: led 2f out: sn hung lft: rn green and wandered jst over 1f out: styd on and doing enough ins fnl f: rdn out* **9/2**[3]

025 **2** *1 ¼* **Australis (IRE)**[52] 2875 3-9-6 **72**............................ AndreaAtzeni 6 82+
(Roger Varian) *s.i.s and rousted along early: hld up in last trio: hdwy on inner over 3f out: drvn to chse wnr over 1f out: pressing wnr 1f out: kpt on but a hld ins fnl f* **10/3**[1]

-242 **3** *3 ½* **Palladium**[35] 3474 3-9-7 **73**.................................... RobHornby 3 78
(Martyn Meade) *led: rdn and hdd jst over 2f out: unable qck over 1f out: kpt on same pce ins fnl f* **7/2**[2]

-420 **4** *1 ¼* **L'Un Deux Trois (IRE)**[39] 3358 3-9-2 **71**.................. CameronNoble(3) 1 74
(Michael Bell) *chsd ldr tl 12f out: styd prom: rdn to ld jst over 2f out: sn hdd and unable qck over 1f out: wl hld and plugged on same pce fnl f* **10/1**

2422 **5** *2 ¾* **Message**[4] 4656 3-9-0 **66**.. JimmyQuinn 7 65
(Mark Johnston) *shifted rt bnd 13f out: racd in last trio: dropped to last and rdn over 5f out: sme prog over 1f out: nvr threatened ldrs and no imp fnl f (vet said colt lost it's left fore shoe)* **6/1**

5-63 **6** *4 ½* **Young Merlin (IRE)**[20] 4031 3-9-6 **72**.................... AdamMcNamara 2 65
(Roger Charlton) *chsd ldrs tl chsd ldr 12f out: pushed along 5f out: rdn 3f out: lost 2nd and struggling to qckn over 2f out: hung lft and btn over 1f out: wknd fnl f (jockey said gelding hung left-handed throughout)* **18/1**

0002 **7** *3 ¼* **Soloist (IRE)**[23] 3926 3-9-3 **69**..............................(p) DanielTudhope 4 58
(William Haggas) *in tch in midfield: squeezed for room over 12f out: hdwy to chse ldrs 10f out: rdn over 2f out: sn struggling to qckn and btn over 1f out: wknd fnl f* **9/2**[3]

40-6 **8** *5* **Hidden Pearl**[11] 4372 3-9-1 **67**................................ GeraldMosse 5 49
(Ed Walker) *in tch in midfield: struggling whn n.m.r over 2f out: sn btn: eased fnl f* **25/1**

0400 **9** *21* **Perique**[8] 4484 3-8-8 **60**......................................(t[1]) RobertHavlin 9 12
(Ed Dunlop) *dwlt: swtchd lft sn after s: sn rcvrd and in tch in midfield: lost pl and racd awkwardly over 2f out: sn wl bhd: eased fnl f: t.o* **100/1**

3m 3.92s (-0.78) **Going Correction** **+0.025s/f (Good)** **9** Ran SP% **115.1**
Speed ratings (Par 100): **103,102,100,99,98 95,93,90,78**
CSF £19.84 CT £57.94 TOTE £5.20: £1.40, £1.70, £1.50; EX 15.80 Trifecta £78.30.
Owner John Brown & Megan Dennis **Bred** Stetchworth & Middle Park Studs Ltd **Trained** Newmarket, Suffolk

FOCUS
Add 10yds. This was an interesting staying handicap for 3yos, and two horses pulled well clear - they are on the upgrade. It provided Sir Mark Prescott with his first winner since January.

4804 PALM COURT HOTEL OF YARMOUTH FILLIES' H'CAP 1m 2f 23y
3:50 (3:51) (Class 5) (0-70,72) 3-Y-O+
£3,428 (£1,020; £509; £300; £300; £300) **Stalls Low**

Form RPR

33-3 **1** **Fearlessly (IRE)**[11] 4372 3-9-11 **71**.......................... AndreaAtzeni 6 84
(Roger Varian) *mde all and styd wd early: clr 5f out: c bk to field 4f out: pushed along and asserted over 1f out: r.o strly and drew clr ins fnl f: easily* **5/4**[1]

552 **2** *6* **Sweet Celebration (IRE)**[50] 2932 3-9-12 **72**.............. DanielMuscutt 5 73
(Marco Botti) *hld up in tch: shkn up 3f out: sn rdn and outpcd 2f out: rallied u.p and kpt on ins fnl f to snatch 2nd on post: no ch w wnr* **9/1**

41-0 **3** *nse* **Minnelli**[55] 2765 3-9-6 **66**.. RobHornby 3 67
(Philip McBride) *chsd wnr tl 4f out: drvn and outpcd 2f out: rallied u.p ins fnl f to chse clr wnr towards fin: no imp and lost 2nd on post* **16/1**

4-12 **4** *1* **Eve Harrington (USA)**[160] 500 3-9-7 **67**.................... LukeMorris 2 66
(Sir Mark Prescott Bt) *chsd ldrs tl chsd wnr 4f out: shkn up jst over 2f out: unable to match pce of wnr over 1f out: plugged on same pce and lost 2 pls towards fin* **4/1**[3]

030 **5** *1 ½* **Colonelle (USA)**[16] 4196 3-9-2 **62**............................ JimmyQuinn 1 58
(Ed Vaughan) *stdd s: hld up in rr: clsd 3f out: unable qck u.p and btn over 1f out: wknd ins fnl f* **16/1**

4-63 **6** *1 ½* **Poetic Era**[41] 3266 3-9-7 **67**.................................... DanielTudhope 4 60
(David Simcock) *t.k.h: hld up in tch in midfield: hung lft and effrt over 2f out: chsd ldrs 2f out: sn drvn and unable qck: wknd ins fnl f (jockey said filly hung left-handed. Trainer said filly did not stay the trip on this occasion)* **3/1**[2]

2m 9.29s (0.49) **Going Correction** **+0.025s/f (Good)** **6** Ran SP% **111.2**
Speed ratings (Par 100): **99,94,94,93,92 90**
CSF £13.23 TOTE £1.70: £1.10, £4.10; EX 8.00 Trifecta £48.10.
Owner Saif Ali **Bred** Nafferty Stud **Trained** Newmarket, Suffolk

FOCUS
Add 10yds. The winner dictated matter from the front and came away from her rivals in the latter stages.

4805 MOULTON NURSERIES OF ACLE OPTIONAL CLAIMING H'CAP 6f 3y
4:20 (4:20) (Class 2) 4-Y-O+ **£19,407** (£5,775; £2,886; £1,443) **Stalls Centre**

Form RPR

2264 **1** **Raucous**[18] 4095 6-9-9 **100**..............................(tp) CierenFallon(5) 3 110
(Robert Cowell) *broke wl: sn hdd and chsd ldr tl over 4f out: styd wl in tch: clsd to trck ldrs 2f out: rdn to ld over 1f out: edgd rt but kpt on wl ins fnl f* **10/3**[2]

-060 **2** *1 ¼* **Hart Stopper**[18] 4123 5-8-9 **81**..............................(t) AndreaAtzeni 6 87
(Stuart Williams) *hld up in tch in last pair: n.m.r wl over 1f out: rdn and hdwy jst over 1f out: chsd wnr jst ins fnl f: kpt on but a hld* **7/1**

1/45 **3** *1 ¾* **Indian Raj**[38] 3375 5-8-2 **74**..............................(t[1]) RaulDaSilva 8 74
(Stuart Williams) *in tch in midfield: effrt wl over 1f out: kpt on same pce u.p ins fnl f* **7/2**[3]

6102 **4** *½* **Muscika**[7] 4521 5-9-4 **90**......................................(v) DanielTudhope 9 89
(David O'Meara) *led: rdn and hdd over 1f out: no ex and outpcd ins fnl f* **2/1**[1]

6-44 **5** *2 ¼* **Show Stealer**[9] 4451 6-9-0 **86**..............................(p) LukeMorris 5 78
(Rae Guest) *dwlt: in tch in last pair: effrt jst over 2f out: swtchd lft and drvn to chse ldrs over 1f out: edgd lft 1f out: wknd ins fnl f* **9/1**

0000 **6** *9* **Comin' Through (AUS)**[21] 3987 5-10-0 **100**..................(t) GeraldMosse 1 63
(George Scott) *sn rousted along: in tch in midfield: clsd to chse ldrs over 3f out tl lost pl 2f out: bhd and eased ins fnl f* **12/1**

03/6 **7** *2* **Unabated (IRE)**[21] 3993 5-9-4 **93**..............................(e) PaddyBradley(3) 2 49
(Jane Chapple-Hyam) *in tch: hdwy to chse ldr over 4f out tl shkn up 2f out: unable qck and lost pl over 1f out: bhd and eased ins fnl f* **14/1**

1m 10.89s (-1.71) **Going Correction** **+0.025s/f (Good)** **7** Ran SP% **115.5**
Speed ratings (Par 109): **112,110,108,107,104 92,89**
CSF £27.01 CT £86.35 TOTE £2.80: £1.30, £3.70; EX 30.40 Trifecta £93.70.
Owner T W Morley **Bred** Saleh Al Homaizi & Imad Al Sagar **Trained** Six Mile Bottom, Cambs
■ Stewards' Enquiry : Raul Da Silva two-day ban; misuse of whip (Jul 24-25)

FOCUS
This was the first optional claiming handicap of the year, but only Unabated could have been claimed afterwards. These contests were introduced the previous year so connections can handicap their horses subject to a claiming price being stated. The winner has been rated back to his best.

4806 GARY & SONIA COOPER WEDDING ANNIVERSARY MAIDEN STKS — 1m 3y
4:50 (4:50) (Class 5) 3-Y-O — £3,428 (£1,020; £509; £254) Stalls Centre

Form — RPR
-253 1 **New Jazz (USA)**[32] 3580 3-9-0 76........................ RobertHavlin 2 79
(John Gosden) *mde all: urged along over 1f out: 2 l clr 1f out: r.o wl: unchal* 13/8[2]
5 2 2 1/4 **Critical Time**[13] 4298 3-9-0 0........................ DanielTudhope 4 74+
(William Haggas) *hld up in tch in rr: shkn up 2f out: rdn and hdwy to chse ldrs over 1f out: chsd wnr and edgd lft jst ins fnl f: no imp* 10/1[3]
-545 3 2 1/4 **Model Guest**[19] 4052 3-9-0 91........................ TomQueally 7 68
(George Margarson) *trckd wnr: edgd out lft and effrt ent fnl 2f: drvn and unable qck over 1f out: lost 2nd jst ins fnl f: wknd towards fin* 8/11[1]
00 4 3 **Global Rock (FR)**[41] 3247 3-9-0 0........................ CierenFallon(5) 3 66
(Ed Dunlop) *trckd ldng pair: shkn up 2f out: rdn and outpcd over 1f out: wl hld and one pce ins fnl f* 40/1
0-0 5 1 1/4 **Asensio**[18] 4121 3-9-0 0........................ SeamusCronin(5) 1 63
(Mohamed Moubarak) *stdd and dropped in after s: hld up in tch: effrt over 1f out: sn outpcd and btn* 33/1

1m 40.87s (2.67) **Going Correction** +0.025s/f (Good) — 5 Ran SP% 110.5
Speed ratings (Par 100): **87,84,82,79,78**
CSF £16.57 TOTE £2.60: £1.20, £3.10; EX 12.00 Trifecta £15.50.
Owner HH Sheikha Al Jalila Racing **Bred** Blackstone Farm Llc **Trained** Newmarket, Suffolk
FOCUS
A modest maiden with the favourite disappointing, rated around the front-running winner.

4807 GREAT YARMOUTH SUPPORTS RACING WELFARE H'CAP — 7f 3y
5:20 (5:22) (Class 6) (0-65,65) 3-Y-O+
£2,781 (£827; £413; £300; £300; £300) Stalls Centre

Form — RPR
502 1 **Sonnet Rose (IRE)**[6] 4567 5-9-4 59........................(bt) SebastianWoods(5) 4 67
(Conrad Allen) *mostly trckd ldr: rdn ent fnl 2f: drvn over 1f out: kpt on u.p to ld last strides* 7/4[1]
5000 2 hd **Essential**[37] 3428 5-8-4 45........................(b) DarraghKeenan(5) 2 52
(Olly Williams) *led: shkn up 2f out: rdn over 1f out: drvn ins fnl f: grad worn down and hdd last strides* 20/1
0000 3 1 3/4 **Letmestopyouthere (IRE)**[8] 4481 5-9-4 54........................(p) LukeMorris 3 56
(Archie Watson) *in tch in midfield: effrt over 2f out: chsd ldrs over 1f out: kpt on u.p ins fnl f: nvr getting on terms w ldrs* 8/1
0460 4 1 3/4 **Agent Of Fortune**[6] 4567 4-9-10 60........................(p[1]) JimmyQuinn 5 58
(Christine Dunnett) *s.i.s: hld up in last pair: effrt and hdwy over 1f out: kpt on u.p ins fnl f: wnt 4th last strides: nvr threatened ldrs* 12/1
0220 5 nk **Holy Tiber (IRE)**[44] 3143 4-9-9 59........................ JoeyHaynes 1 56
(Paul Howling) *stdd s: hld up in last pair: hdwy to chse ldrs and edgd lft 2f out: no imp u.p over 1f out: wknd ins fnl f* 14/1
2116 6 3 3/4 **Lincoln Red**[12] 4328 3-9-0 58........................ RobertHavlin 10 42
(Olly Williams) *hld up in tch in last trio: effrt over 1f out: rdn and no imp ins fnl f: nvr involved* 7/1[3]
6323 7 1 1/4 **Seraphim**[14] 4247 3-9-7 65........................(t) AndreaAtzeni 9 45
(Marco Botti) *in tch in midfield: rdn ent fnl 2f: sn drvn and outpcd: wknd ins fnl f (trainer was filly was unsuited by the ground on this occasion and would prefer a slightly easier surface)* 7/2[2]
3000 8 4 **Any Smile (IRE)**[12] 4316 3-9-0 61........................(v[1]) CameronNoble(3) 8 30
(Michael Bell) *t.k.h: sn prom: lost pl and rdn 2f out: sn wl btn: wknd fnl f* 16/1
5000 9 3/4 **Mochalov**[56] 2741 4-9-2 55........................(e[1]) PaddyBradley(3) 7 25
(Jane Chapple-Hyam) *in tch in midfield: j. path over 5f out: u.p and dropped to rr 2f out: bhd fnl f* 40/1

1m 25.01s (-0.09) **Going Correction** +0.025s/f (Good)
WFA 3 from 4yo+ 8lb — 9 Ran SP% 109.6
Speed ratings (Par 101): **101,100,98,96,96 92,90,86,85**
CSF £37.13 CT £192.64 TOTE £1.90: £1.10, £6.20, £2.10; EX 44.00 Trifecta £290.30.
Owner John C Davies **Bred** J C Davies **Trained** Newmarket, Suffolk
■ Shyarch was withdrawn. Price at time of withdrawal 10-1. Rule 4 applies to all bets - deduction 5p in the pound.
FOCUS
A moderate handicap run at an even gallop early. The field went towards the inside of the track. The winner was well in and has been rated similarly to last time.
T/Plt: £198.60 to a £1 stake. Pool: £64,246.47. 236.06 winning units. T/Qpdt: £17.20 to a £1 stake. Pool: £6,731.94. 289.45 winning units. **Steve Payne**

4808 - 4816a (Foreign Racing) - See Raceform Interactive

4630
CARLISLE (R-H)
Thursday, July 11

OFFICIAL GOING: Good to firm (watered; 8.0)
Wind: Breezy, half against in over 2f of home straight Weather: Overcast, dry

4817 RACHAEL BELL WEALTH MANAGEMENT H'CAP — 1m 3f 39y
2:00 (2:00) (Class 5) (0-75,75) 3-Y-O+
£4,204 (£1,251; £625; £312; £300; £300) Stalls High

Form — RPR
0615 1 **Zihaam**[16] 4208 5-8-11 65........................(p) BenSanderson(5) 4 69
(Roger Fell) *prom: rdn over 2f out: hdwy over 1f out: led ins fnl f: hld on wl cl home* 5/1
-260 2 hd **The Navigator**[15] 4240 4-9-12 75........................ JamesSullivan 6 78
(Dianne Sayer) *s.i.s: t.k.h: hld up in tch: gd hdwy on outside to ld over 2f out: rdn over 1f out: hdd ins fnl f: rallied: hld cl home* 10/1
-462 3 1 **Remember The Days (IRE)**[22] 4009 5-9-11 74........................ GrahamLee 3 75
(Jedd O'Keeffe) *pressed ldr: chal 1/2-way to over 2f out: sn rdn: rallied: one pce ins fnl f* 5/2[1]
2005 4 1 3/4 **Sempre Presto (IRE)**[27] 3816 4-9-5 68........................ PaulHanagan 2 66
(Richard Fahey) *trckd ldrs: drvn along 2f out: edgd rt: no ex ins fnl f* 7/2[2]
-006 5 3/4 **Diodorus (IRE)**[27] 3816 5-9-3 73........................ LauraCoughlan(7) 5 70
(Karen McLintock) *hld up in tch: rdn and outpcd over 2f out: rallied ins fnl f: no imp* 4/1[3]
-000 6 2 **Orange Suit (IRE)**[15] 4250 4-9-5 68........................(p[1]) AdamMcNamara 1 62
(Ed de Giles) *led: jnd 1/2-way: hdd over 2f out: wknd over 1f out* 5/1

2m 28.04s (-1.66) **Going Correction** -0.10s/f (Good) — 6 Ran SP% 113.2
Speed ratings (Par 103): **102,101,101,99,99 97**
CSF £50.17 TOTE £5.60: £1.60, £4.10; EX 56.30 Trifecta £181.50.
Owner Nick Bradley Racing 29 & Partner **Bred** Cheveley Park Stud Ltd **Trained** Nawton, N Yorks
FOCUS
Rail movements added 13yds to the opener, just an ordinary middle-distance handicap. The winner has been rated close to his best, with the second and third to recent form.

4818 BRITISH STALLION STUDS EBF NOVICE STKS — 7f 173y
2:35 (2:39) (Class 5) 3-4-Y-O — £4,204 (£1,251; £625; £312) Stalls Low

Form — RPR
44 1 **Amber Star (IRE)**[8] 4520 3-8-11 0........................ RobbieDowney 1 56+
(David O'Meara) *chsd ldr: pushed along over 2f out: rdn to ld over 1f out: kpt on wl fnl f* 1/6[1]
00 2 1 1/2 **Key Choice**[22] 4010 3-9-2 0........................ RachelRichardson 4 58
(Eric Alston) *rn wout front shoe: led: rdn and hdd over 1f out: edgd rt: kpt on same pce ins fnl f* 9/1[2]
00 3 7 **Simul Amicis**[143] 785 3-8-11 0........................ JamesSullivan 3 36
(Dianne Sayer) *dwlt: sn chsng ldrs: rdn along over 2f out: wknd over 1f out* 33/1
5-03 4 39 **Highcastle (IRE)**[12] 4358 4-9-11 48........................(p) CamHardie 5
(Lisa Williamson) *hld up in tch: rdn 4f out: struggling over 2f out: lost tch and eased fnl f (trainer's rep could offer no explanation for the gelding's performance)* 10/1[3]

1m 40.86s (0.86) **Going Correction** -0.10s/f (Good)
WFA 3 from 4yo 9lb — 4 Ran SP% 107.7
Speed ratings (Par 103): **91,89,82,43**
CSF £2.28 TOTE £1.10; EX 2.50 Trifecta £7.20.
Owner Sir Robert Ogden **Bred** Sir Robert Ogden **Trained** Upper Helmsley, N Yorks
■ Taaldara was withdrawn. Price at time of withdrawal 12-1. Rule 4 applies to all bets - deduction 5p in the pound.
■ Stewards' Enquiry : Robbie Downey two-day ban: used whip with excessive frequency (tba)
FOCUS
Add 9yds. A weak novice. The runner-up is the key to the form.

4819 BRITISH STALLION STUDS EBF FILLIES' NOVICE STKS (PLUS 10 RACE) — 6f 195y
3:10 (3:14) (Class 5) 2-Y-O — £3,881 (£1,155; £577; £288) Stalls Low

Form — RPR
24 1 **Alabama Whitman**[20] 4048 2-9-0 0........................ PaulMulrennan 4 78+
(Richard Spencer) *trckd ldrs: shkn up to ld over 1f out: edgd lft ins fnl f: pushed out: comf* 4/7[1]
2 1 **Tulip Fields** 2-9-0 0........................ AndrewMullen 2 75
(Mark Johnston) *t.k.h: led: rdn and hung lft over 1f out: sn hdd: rallied: kpt on same pce ins fnl f (jockey said filly hung left throughout)* 11/2[3]
3 1 3/4 **Christmas Diamond** 2-8-11 0........................ BenRobinson(3) 6 70
(Ollie Pears) *hld up in tch on outside: hdwy and ev ch briefly over 1f out: edgd rt ins fnl f: one pce* 40/1
4 1 **Diamond Sparkles (USA)** 2-9-0 0........................ PaddyMathers 8 67+
(Richard Fahey) *hld up: effrt whn nt clr run briefly 2f out: kpt on fnl f: nt pce to chal* 5/1[2]
5 3 1/2 **Bye Bye Euro (IRE)** 2-9-0 0........................ GrahamLee 1 58
(Keith Dalgleish) *hld up on ins: pushed along over 2f out: short-lived effrt over 1f out: sn btn* 10/1
6 3 **Secret Passion** 2-9-0 0........................ AdamMcNamara 5 50
(Archie Watson) *t.k.h pressed ldr to over 1f out: sn rdn and wknd* 7/1
64 7 3 **Capp It All (IRE)**[13] 4323 2-9-0 0........................ CamHardie 9 42
(David Loughnane) *t.k.h: prom: rdn over 2f out: wknd over 1f out* 50/1
0 8 4 1/2 **Cersei Lannister (IRE)**[16] 4206 2-9-0 0........................ ConnorBeasley 3 30
(Adrian Nicholls) *slowly away: hld up: rdn over 3f out: wknd fr 2f out* 50/1

1m 29.5s (1.50) **Going Correction** -0.10s/f (Good) — 8 Ran SP% 123.7
Speed ratings (Par 91): **87,85,83,82,78 75,71,66**
CSF £5.00 TOTE £1.40: £1.02, £1.80, £6.50; EX 4.10 Trifecta £82.60.
Owner Rebel Racing III **Bred** Robert Pocock **Trained** Newmarket, Suffolk
■ Half Of Seven was withdrawn. Price at time of withdrawal 40-1. Rule 4 \n\x\x does not apply
FOCUS
Add 9yds. The winner didn't need to get near her Ascot form and this level is fluid.

4820 IONE'S VINGT ET UN MAIDEN H'CAP — 6f 195y
3:45 (3:46) (Class 5) (0-70,70) 3-Y-O+
£4,204 (£1,251; £625; £312; £300; £300) Stalls Low

Form — RPR
3060 1 **Sharrabang**[13] 4328 3-8-2 52........................ CamHardie 5 58
(Stella Barclay) *mde virtually all: hrd pressed fr 2f out: hld on gamely towards fin* 20/1
5404 2 shd **Fard**[1] 4785 4-8-9 56........................ PaulaMuir(5) 4 64
(Roger Fell) *hld up in tch: hdwy on outside to chal fr 2f out: kpt on fnl f: jst hld* 5/1[3]
3200 3 3 **Blindingly (GER)**[33] 3567 4-10-0 70........................(v[1]) AndrewMullen 9 70
(Ben Haslam) *dwlt: t.k.h and sn chsng wnr: rdn over 2f out: one pce fr over 1f out* 10/1
-043 4 1 1/2 **Olivia R (IRE)**[20] 4080 3-9-1 65........................(h) RobbieDowney 2 58
(David Barron) *dwlt: hld up: rdn over 2f out: hdwy over 1f out: kpt on fnl f: nt pce to chal* 9/2[2]
0-00 5 1/2 **Musical Sky**[19] 4129 3-8-11 61 ow1........................ PaulMulrennan 8 53
(Michael Dods) *t.k.h: prom: effrt and edgd lft 2f out: sn checked and outpcd: n.d after* 20/1
463 6 1 **God Of Dreams**[9] 4488 3-8-12 62........................ JamieGormley 3 51
(Iain Jardine) *in tch: effrt and pushed along whn short of room and lost pl 2f out: n.d after (jockey said gelding was denied a clear run 2f out)* 10/1
6334 7 hd **Summer Bride (IRE)**[18] 4147 3-9-1 65........................ GrahamLee 12 53
(Tim Easterby) *hld up on outside: effrt over 2f out: wknd over 1f out* 14/1
-403 7 dht **Ifton**[6] 4606 3-8-13 63........................ JamesSullivan 1 51
(Ruth Carr) *t.k.h: hld up on ins: rdn and hdwy over 2f out: wknd over 1f out (jockey said gelding hung left)* 85/40[1]
6-06 9 1/2 **Iron Mike**[70] 2336 3-9-2 66........................ PaulHanagan 6 53
(Keith Dalgleish) *dwlt: hld up: rdn and outpcd over 2f out: hung rt and btn over 1f out* 13/2
420- 10 12 **Dixieland (IRE)**[342] 5671 3-9-3 70........................ BenRobinson(3) 7 25
(Marjorie Fife) *bhd: struggling over 2f out: sn btn* 50/1

1m 27.72s (-0.28) **Going Correction** -0.10s/f (Good)
WFA 3 from 4yo 8lb — 10 Ran SP% 116.5
Speed ratings (Par 103): **97,96,93,91,91 90,89,89,89,75**
CSF £114.91 CT £1103.11 TOTE £26.80: £5.50, £2.70, £2.00; EX 156.00 Trifecta £2226.80.

Owner The Bounty Hunters **Bred** The Bounty Hunters **Trained** Garstang, Lancs
FOCUS
Add 9yds. A moderate event The first pair came clear, racing in the centre of the track in the latter stages.

4821 WATCH RACING TV NOW H'CAP 5f
4:15 (4:16) (Class 4) (0-80,78) 3-Y-O+

£7,115 (£2,117; £1,058; £529; £300; £300) **Stalls** Low

Form				RPR
6431	1		**Only Spoofing (IRE)**[5] 4625 5-9-10 **76** 5ex GrahamLee 1 (Jedd O'Keeffe) *t.k.h: mde virtually all: rdn over 1f out: kpt on gamely fnl f* **2/1**[2]	87
1032	2	½	**Afandem (IRE)**[5] 4632 5-8-12 **69** (p) DannyRedmond(5) 4 (Tim Easterby) *prom: effrt and rdn along 2f out: chsd wnr fnl f: r.o* **5/1**[3]	78
-200	3	1	**Red Pike (IRE)**[30] 3706 8-8-13 **72** HarryRussell(7) 5 (Bryan Smart) *prom: rdn along 2f out: kpt on same pce ins fnl f* **20/1**	78
5411	4	1 ½	**Jack The Truth (IRE)**[7] 4556 5-9-8 **74** ConnorBeasley 7 (George Scott) *hld up: hdwy whn nt clr run over 1f out and ins fnl f: no imp towards fin (jockey said gelding was denied a clear run approaching the final furlong, and again 1/2f out)* **13/8**[1]	82+
-012	5	nse	**Spirit Of Wedza (IRE)**[14] 4279 7-9-2 **75** VictorSantos(7) 3 (Julie Camacho) *plld hrd: w wnr to over 1f out: rdn and outpcd fnl f* **10/1**	75
0400	6	6	**Henley**[23] 3971 7-9-12 **78** CamHardie 8 (Tracy Waggott) *racd wout hind shoes: t.k.h: w ldrs on outside: rdn over 2f out: wknd over 1f out* **33/1**	56
23-0	7	8	**Rosina**[12] 4406 6-9-10 **76** (p) PaulMulrennan 6 (Ann Duffield) *hld up: rdn and outpcd over 2f out: sn btn (jockey said mare was never travelling)* **25/1**	26

1m 0.65s (-1.45) **Going Correction** -0.10s/f (Good)
WFA 3 from 4yo+ 5lb **7** Ran SP% **108.7**
Speed ratings (Par 105): **107,106,104,102,102 92,79**
CSF £10.88 CT £129.52 TOTE £2.90: £1.60, £2.00; EX 12.50 Trifecta £110.90.
Owner Mrs H Mannion, B Carter & F Durbin **Bred** Limestone And Tara Studs **Trained** Middleham Moor, N Yorks
FOCUS
A fair sprint handicap, run only 0.85sec slower than standard, and the winner rates back to his best.

4822 BRITISH STALLION STUDS EBF FILLIES' H'CAP 5f 193y
4:50 (4:52) (Class 4) (0-80,78) 3-Y-O+

£7,115 (£2,117; £1,058; £529; £300; £300) **Stalls** Low

Form				RPR
1330	1		**Gale Force Maya**[14] 4288 3-8-12 **68** PaulMulrennan 6 (Michael Dods) *prom: hdwy to ld over 1f out: pushed out fnl f (trainer's rep said, regarding the apparent improvement in form, the filly may have appreciated the return to turf)* **11/2**[3]	80
315	2	1 ¾	**Mina Velour**[35] 3499 3-8-11 **67** (h) GrahamLee 8 (Bryan Smart) *s.i.s: t.k.h in rr: hdwy and angled lft over 1f out: chsd wnr ins fnl f: r.o* **8/1**	73
1/0-	3	1 ¼	**Kindly**[258] 8614 6-9-7 **78** JoshQuinn(7) 2 (Michael Easterby) *cl up in chsng gp: effrt and ev ch briefly over 1f out: nt qckn ins fnl f* **16/1**	81
-211	4	2 ¼	**Caustic Love (IRE)**[15] 4243 3-9-7 **77** PaulHanagan 9 (Keith Dalgleish) *hld up in tch: effrt and pushed along over 2f out: outpcd fr over 1f out* **1/1**[1]	72
1033	5	1 ¾	**Lady Calcaria**[13] 4330 3-9-7 **77** RachelRichardson 3 (Tim Easterby) *chsd clr ldr: rdn over 2f out: edgd rt and wknd over 1f out* **4/1**[2]	66
21-5	6	¾	**Essenza (IRE)**[24] 3935 3-8-12 **68** PaddyMathers 4 (Richard Fahey) *hld up bhd ldng gp: drvn along over 2f out: no imp over 1f out* **22/1**	55
3225	7	1	**Supaulette (IRE)**[15] 4243 4-9-4 **68** (bt) CamHardie 7 (Tim Easterby) *hld up: drvn and outpcd over 2f out: sn btn* **16/1**	53
10	8	1 ¼	**Roys Dream**[14] 4280 5-9-2 **73** (v[1]) HarryRussell(7) 1 (Paul Collins) *led: clr over 3f out: rdn and hdd over 1f out: sn btn: fin lame (vet said mare finished lame right fore)* **18/1**	54

1m 12.44s (-2.16) **Going Correction** -0.10s/f (Good)
WFA 3 from 4yo+ 6lb **8** Ran SP% **117.9**
Speed ratings (Par 102): **110,107,106,103,100 99,98,96**
CSF £49.88 CT £672.56 TOTE £5.60: £1.50, £2.20, £3.20; EX 40.30 Trifecta £524.00.
Owner Frank Lowe **Bred** Mrs J Imray **Trained** Denton, Co Durham
FOCUS
A fair fillies' handicap and this rates a clear step forward from the winner.

4823 EVERY RACE LIVE ON RACING TV H'CAP (DIV I) 5f 193y
5:20 (5:22) (Class 6) (0-60,60) 3-Y-O+

£3,234 (£962; £481; £300; £300; £300) **Stalls** Low

Form				RPR
0012	1		**Ninjago**[14] 4276 9-9-7 **60** (v) BenRobinson(3) 3 (Paul Midgley) *trckd ldrs: effrt and wnt 2nd over 1f out: rdn to ld ins fnl f: kpt on wl* **11/4**[1]	71
00	2	1 ¼	**Fox Hill**[30] 3685 3-8-8 **55** HarrisonShaw(5) 1 (Eric Alston) *led to over 4f out: chsd ldr: regained ld wl over 1f out to ins fnl f: kpt on same pce towards fin* **20/1**	61
0460	3	1 ¼	**Leeshaan (IRE)**[3] 4720 4-8-10 **46** LewisEdmunds 10 (Rebecca Bastiman) *hld up: rdn and hdwy over 1f out: chsd ldng pair ins fnl f: r.o* **4/1**[2]	49
0502	4	2 ¾	**Picks Pinta**[9] 4493 8-8-6 **49** ow3 (b) HarryRussell(7) 4 (John David Riches) *hld up bhd ldng gp: effrt and rdn over 1f out: kpt on fnl f: nt pce to chal* **5/1**[3]	43
0100	5	½	**Carlovian**[8] 4519 6-9-5 **55** (v) DougieCostello 13 (Mark Walford) *cl up: led over 4f out to over 1f out: sn drvn and outpcd* **8/1**	48
50-0	6	hd	**Epaulini**[14] 4288 3-9-4 **60** ConnorBeasley 14 (Michael Dods) *hld up on outside: drvn along over 2f out: edgd rt and no imp over 1f out* **12/1**	51
00-0	7	½	**Grimsdyke**[6] 4584 3-8-4 **46** oh1 RachelRichardson 9 (Tim Easterby) *in tch: drvn along over 2f out: outpcd fr over 1f out* **28/1**	35
4630	8	shd	**Roaring Rory**[59] 2678 6-9-2 **52** (p) JamieGormley 11 (Ollie Pears) *slowly away: bhd: rdn over 2f out: nvr rchd ldrs (jockey said gelding was slowly away)* **11/1**	42
5	9	5	**De Latour**[70] 2327 3-8-11 **56** ConorMcGovern(3) 2 (Jason Ward) *hld up on ins: rdn over 2f out: hung rt and wknd over 1f out* **18/1**	29
4-40	R		**Erastus**[41] 3304 4-8-10 **46** JamesSullivan 12 (Ruth Carr) *ref to r* **8/1**	

1m 13.38s (-1.22) **Going Correction** -0.10s/f (Good)
WFA 3 from 4yo+ 6lb **10** Ran SP% **115.1**
Speed ratings (Par 101): **104,102,100,97,96 96,95,95,88,**
CSF £60.97 CT £224.78 TOTE £2.90: £1.20, £6.20, £1.80; EX 71.60 Trifecta £606.10.
Owner Taylor's Bloodstock Ltd & P T Midgley **Bred** Newsells Park Stud **Trained** Westow, N Yorks
FOCUS
Modest form, and the slightly slower division.

4824 EVERY RACE LIVE ON RACING TV H'CAP (DIV II) 5f 193y
5:55 (5:55) (Class 6) (0-60,60) 3-Y-O+

£3,234 (£962; £481; £300; £300; £300) **Stalls** Low

Form				RPR
0061	1		**Tarnhelm**[5] 4630 4-8-4 **47** RhonaPindar(7) 14 (Wilf Storey) *s.s: hld up on outside: effrt over 2f out: hdwy fr over 1f out to ld ins fnl f: hrd pressed: hld on wl cl home* **11/10**[1]	54
0-00	2	hd	**Prince Of Time**[71] 2298 7-8-6 **47** oh1 ow1 BenSanderson(5) 8 (Stella Barclay) *hld up in tch: rdn and hdwy over 1f out: disp ld ins fnl f: kpt on: jst hld* **40/1**	53
3345	3	2 ¼	**B Fifty Two (IRE)**[3] 4721 10-9-7 **60** (vt) JaneElliott(3) 4 (Marjorie Fife) *trckd ldrs: wnt 2nd 1/2-way to ins fnl f: sn no ex* **7/1**	59
6632	4	¾	**The Bull (IRE)**[29] 3723 4-9-5 **55** (p) AndrewMullen 12 (Ben Haslam) *hld up: pushed along over 2f out: hdwy over 1f out: kpt on fnl f: nt pce to chal* **9/2**[2]	52
-606	5	1 ¼	**Paco Escostar**[19] 4132 4-9-4 **54** (v) CamHardie 10 (Julie Camacho) *led: rdn over 1f out: hdd ins fnl f: sn btn* **10/1**	47
2000	6	1 ¾	**Who Told Jo Jo (IRE)**[17] 4181 5-9-7 **57** RobbieDowney 3 (Joseph Tuite) *chsd ldr to 1/2-way: cl up tl rdn and wknd over 1f out* **11/1**	44
0630	7	1	**Cardaw Lily (IRE)**[5] 4651 4-8-10 **46** oh1 JamesSullivan 13 (Ruth Carr) *s.i.s and wnt lft s: bhd: rdn over 2f out: btn fnl f* **6/1**[3]	30
0004	8	1 ½	**Swiss Miss**[17] 4182 3-8-4 **46** oh1 RoystonFfrench 7 (John Gallagher) *hld up in tch on outside: drvn over 2f out: wknd wl over 1f out* **20/1**	24
6-00	9	20	**Hop Maddocks (IRE)**[24] 3921 4-9-2 **52** (v) PaulMulrennan 6 (Fred Watson) *in tch: rdn and struggling over 2f out: lost tch over 1f out (jockey said gelding hung left throughout)* **66/1**	

1m 13.22s (-1.38) **Going Correction** -0.10s/f (Good)
WFA 3 from 4yo+ 6lb **9** Ran SP% **118.7**
Speed ratings (Par 101): **105,104,101,100,99 96,95,93,66**
CSF £65.97 CT £239.59 TOTE £2.00: £1.10, £12.70, £1.80; EX 86.60 Trifecta £256.80.
Owner H S Hutchinson & W Storey **Bred** Theobalds Stud **Trained** Muggleswick, Co Durham
FOCUS
Slightly the quicker of the two divisions but the winner has been rated below the level of her last-time-out success.
T/Plt: £255.60 to a £1 stake. Pool: £26,370.42 - 103.16 winning units. T/Qpdt: £41.60 to a £1 stake. Pool: £3,242.13 - 77.93 winning units. **Richard Young**

4595 DONCASTER (L-H)
Thursday, July 11

OFFICIAL GOING: Good to firm (watered; 8.2)
Wind: Light against Weather: Cloudy

4825 JOHN KAYE BUILDING & CONSTRUCTION AMATEUR RIDERS' H'CAP 2m 109y
1:40 (1:40) (Class 5) (0-70,70) 4-Y-O+

£3,306 (£1,025; £512; £300; £300; £300) **Stalls** Low

Form				RPR
04-1	1		**Perla Blanca (USA)**[44] 3175 5-10-6 **67** SophieSmith(5) 4 (Ed Dunlop) *hld up in rr: stdy hdwy 1/2-way: trckd ldrs over 4f out: cl up 2f out: led over 1f out: rdn and edgd lft ins fnl f: kpt on strly* **7/2**[2]	75
4040	2	2 ¾	**St Andrews (IRE)**[8] 4510 6-9-13 **55** MissEmmaTodd 8 (Gillian Boanas) *hld up: hdwy over 3f out: pushed along to chse ldrs over 2f out: styng on whn n.m.r and swtchd rt ins fnl f: sn chsng wnr: no imp towards fin* **14/1**	59
-063	3	½	**Duke Of Yorkshire**[14] 4274 9-10-3 **59** (p) MissEmilyEasterby 6 (Tim Easterby) *trckd ldrs: hdwy over 4f out: cl up over 3f out: led wl over 1f out: sn rdn and hdd: kpt on same pce fnl f* **25/1**	62
0530	4	3 ¾	**Hugoigo**[8] 4510 5-9-2 **51** oh2 (p) MissShannonWatts(7) 3 (Jim Goldie) *hld up in rr: hdwy 3f out: rdn along 2f out: sn swtchd rt to outer and kpt on fnl f: nvr nr ldrs* **20/1**	50
-331	5	6	**Percy Prosecco**[7] 4569 4-10-3 **59** MissBeckySmith 11 (Archie Watson) *led: pushed along 3f out: rdn over 2f out: hdd wl over 1f out: sn drvn and wknd* **2/1**[1]	51
0050	6	6	**Belabour**[21] 4036 6-10-6 **62** MissBeckyBrisbourne 9 (Kevin Frost) *t.k.h: trckd ldr: rdn along wl over 3f out: sn wknd* **40/1**	47
3441	7	6	**Colwood**[37] 3444 5-10-7 **68** (p) MrGeorgeEddery(5) 7 (Robert Eddery) *in tch: pushed along 5f out: rdn wl over 3f out: sn wknd* **11/2**[3]	45
-553	8	4 ½	**Buyer Beware (IRE)**[12] 4404 7-10-7 **63** (p) MissSerenaBrotherton 1 (Liam Bailey) *t.k.h: trckd ldr on inner: pushed along 4f out: rdn over 3f out: sn wknd (jockey said gelding slipped final bend)* **13/2**	35
-645	P		**Up Ten Down Two (IRE)**[19] 4126 10-10-1 **57** (t) MissJoannaMason 2 (Michael Easterby) *trckd ldrs: lost action and p.u 1/2-way (vet said gelding was lame right fore)* **7/1**	

3m 39.41s (-0.99) **Going Correction** -0.05s/f (Good) **9** Ran SP% **114.5**
Speed ratings (Par 103): **100,98,98,96,93 90,87,85,**
CSF £48.46 CT £1052.91 TOTE £3.90: £1.50, £4.80, £4.00; EX 49.30 Trifecta £541.90.
Owner Mrs C L Smith **Bred** Ted Folkerth Et Al **Trained** Newmarket, Suffolk
FOCUS
Round course railed out from about 1m2f until the round meets the straight. Add 12yds. Sand was applied to the entrance to the home straight after a rider reported her mount had slipped there during the first race. A clear-cut victory with the winner following up her win in this race last season, and this rates a pb. The winning time was moderate.

4826 STEELPHALT EBF MAIDEN STKS 6f 2y
2:10 (2:14) (Class 5) 2-Y-O **£3,428** (£1,020; £509; £254) **Stalls** High

Form				RPR
53	1		**St Ives**[26] 3866 2-9-5 0 LiamJones 7 (William Haggas) *t.k.h early: hld up in tch: hdwy and nt clr run wl over 1f out: rdn to chal ent fnl f: sn drvn: edgd lft and kpt on to ld nr fin* **15/8**[1]	77+

2 shd	**Mr Jones And Me** 2-9-5 0 RichardKingscote 5	76+
	(Tom Dascombe) *dwlt and towards rr: hdwy over 2f out: swtchd lft and effrt to chse ldrs over 1f out: rdn ins fnl f: ev ch: no ex nr fin* **28/1**	
3 hd	**Soaring Star (IRE)** 2-9-5 0 KevinStott 4	75+
	(Kevin Ryan) *in tch: pushed along and sltly outpcd wl over 1f out: rdn and n.m.r appr fnl f: styd on wl towards fin* **16/1**	
4 nk	**Shoot To Kill (IRE)** 2-9-5 0 DanielMuscutt 15	74
	(George Scott) *prom: hdwy on outer to ld over 1f out: sn rdn: jnd and drvn ins fnl f: hdd and no ex nr fin (jockey said colt ran green)* **33/1**	
5 1 ½	**Hostelry** 2-9-0 0 KieranO'Neill 14	64
	(Michael Dods) *trckd ldrs: pushed along wl over 1f out: sn rdn and kpt on fnl f* **28/1**	
6 ¾	**Powertrain (IRE)** 2-9-5 0 BenCurtis 2	67
	(Hugo Palmer) *cl up: led 1/2-way: rdn along 2f out: drvn and hdd over 1f out: edgd lft and wknd ins fnl f (jockey said colt ran green and hung both ways)* **9/2**[3]	
0 7 1 ¾	**Kyllwind**[17] 4184 2-9-5 0 RobHornby 3	62
	(Martyn Meade) *prom: cl up 2f out: sn rdn: drvn and hld whn hmpd jst ins fnl f: kpt on same pce after* **14/1**	
4 8 ¾	**One Step Beyond (IRE)**[12] 4394 2-9-5 0 AdamKirby 9	62+
	(Richard Spencer) *cl up: pushed along over 2f out: rdn wl over 1f out: drvn and hld whn n.m.r ins fnl f (vet said colt was lame right hind)* **10/3**[2]	
9 1	**Cheat (IRE)** 2-9-5 0 RossaRyan 12	56
	(Richard Hannon) *midfield: hdwy 2f out: sn rdn along and n.d* **14/1**	
0 10 nse	**Rebel Redemption**[30] 3702 2-9-5 0 JasonHart 1	56+
	(John Quinn) *t.k.h: led: hdd 1/2-way: rdn along 2f out: wkng whn n.m.r and hmpd ent fnl f* **33/1**	
11 1 ¼	**Redzone** 2-9-5 0 JackGarritty 8	51
	(Bryan Smart) *dwlt: a towards rr (jockey said colt hung left)* **33/1**	
12 1	**Trevie Fountain** 2-9-5 0 TonyHamilton 10	48
	(Richard Fahey) *a towards rr (vet said colt lost its left fore shoe)* **25/1**	
46 13 2	**Sir Havelock (IRE)**[9] 4486 2-9-2 0 ConnorMurtagh(3) 13	42
	(Richard Fahey) *a towards rr* **66/1**	
6 14 ½	**Araka Li (IRE)**[19] 4125 2-9-5 0 DaneO'Neill 11	40
	(Tim Easterby) *t.k.h: in tch: pushed along 1/2-way: sn rdn and wknd 2f out (jockey said colt was tightened for room 3f out)* **66/1**	
15 8	**Khalaty** 2-9-0 0 BarryMcHugh 16	10
	(James Given) *dwlt: a towards rr* **150/1**	

1m 13.55s (0.85) **Going Correction** -0.05s/f (Good) **15 Ran SP% 118.5**
Speed ratings (Par 94): **92,91,91,91,89 88,85,84,83,83 81,80,77,77,66**
CSF £69.15 TOTE £2.60: £1.40, £7.50, £6.10; EX 51.40 Trifecta £496.80.
Owner G Smith-Bernal **Bred** Seamus Burns Esq **Trained** Newmarket, Suffolk

FOCUS
The bare form is probably ordinary, rated around the winner.

4827 PJP GROUP BARNSLEY NOVICE STKS 6f 2y
2:45 (2:47) (Class 5) 3-Y-0+ **£3,428** (£1,020; £509; £254) **Stalls High**

Form			RPR
50	1	**Majaalis (FR)**[19] 4120 3-9-2 0 DaneO'Neill 7	84+
		(William Haggas) *dwlt and hld up in rr: hdwy towards stands' side 2f out: rdn to ld nr stands' rail jst ins fnl f: jst hld on* **7/2**[3]	
0-22	2 shd	**Crantock Bay**[12] 4367 3-9-2 82 BenCurtis 5	82
		(George Scott) *trckd ldrs centre: hdwy to chal ent fnl f: sn rdn and ev ch whn hung rt ins fnl f: drvn and kpt on: jst hld* **6/4**[1]	
41-	3 4 ½	**Thirlmere**[244] 8976 4-9-10 0 JasonHart 4	71
		(Julie Camacho) *t.k.h: cl up: rdn to ld 1 1/2f out: drvn ent fnl f: sn hdd: kpt on same pce* **20/1**	
51	4 nse	**Tipperary Jack (USA)**[36] 3463 3-9-9 0 KierenFox 6	74
		(John Best) *trckd ldrs: hdwy 2f out: rdn over 1f out: swtchd rt and drvn ins fnl f: kpt on same pce* **11/4**[2]	
	5 ½	**Gleniffer** 3-8-9 0 CoreyMadden(7) 3	66
		(Jim Goldie) *dwlt and in rr: hdwy wl over 1f out: sn rdn and kpt on wl fnl f* **100/1**	
04	6 ¾	**George Thomas**[26] 3836 3-9-2 0 JackMitchell 8	63
		(Mick Quinn) *cl up: rdn and ev ch 1 1/2f out: sn drvn and wknd appr fnl f* **100/1**	
2	7 1 ¼	**Grisons (FR)**[11] 4421 3-9-2 0 AdamKirby 1	59
		(Clive Cox) *racd centre: led: pushed along 2f out: rdn and hdd 1 1/2f out: sn wknd* **6/1**	
	8 5	**Blank Canvas** 3-8-11 0 JoeFanning 2	38
		(Keith Dalgleish) *t.k.h centre: prom: rdn along 2f out: sn wknd* **28/1**	
65	9 3 ½	**Gorgeous Gobolina**[12] 4367 3-8-11 0 RaulDaSilva 10	27
		(Susan Corbett) *racd towards stands' rail: chsd ldrs: rdn along over 2f out: sn wknd* **80/1**	

1m 12.52s (-0.18) **Going Correction** -0.05s/f (Good)
WFA 3 from 4yo 6lb **9 Ran SP% 114.6**
Speed ratings (Par 103): **99,98,92,92,92 91,89,82,78**
CSF £8.87 TOTE £4.40: £1.20, £1.10, £4.50; EX 10.90 Trifecta £91.30.
Owner Hamdan Al Maktoum **Bred** Jean-Philippe Dubois **Trained** Newmarket, Suffolk

FOCUS
An informative novice event and the winner, who built on his debut promise, could be useful. The front two pulled well clear.

4828 STAFF FINDERS RECRUITMENT YORKSHIRE FILLIES' H'CAP 1m (S)
3:20 (3:21) (Class 4) (0-85,84) 3-Y-0+
£5,207 (£1,549; £774; £387; £300; £300) **Stalls High**

Form			RPR
1-43	1	**Duneflower (IRE)**[51] 2934 3-9-6 84 KieranO'Neill 4	95+
		(John Gosden) *trckd ldrs: pushed along over 2f out: hdwy to ld over 1f out: sn rdn and qcknd clr: edgd rt ins fnl f: readily* **9/5**[1]	
-461	2 1	**Sufficient**[27] 3807 3-9-0 78 (h) DanielMuscutt 5	86
		(Rod Millman) *trckd ldrs on outer: smooth hdwy over 2f out: led wl over 1f out: sn rdn and hung bdly rt to stands' rail: hdd appr fnl f: kpt on u.p* **12/1**	
4311	3 2 ¾	**La Sioux (IRE)**[52] 2911 5-8-13 68 TonyHamilton 7	72
		(Richard Fahey) *trckd ldr: pushed along and sltly outpcd 2f out: sn rdn: n.m.r ins fnl f: kpt on* **12/1**	
2422	4 nk	**Nooshin**[27] 3807 3-8-11 75 DaneO'Neill 8	76
		(Charles Hills) *t.k.h: trckd ldr: cl up 3f out: rdn along 2f out: drvn over 1f out: kpt on same pce* **7/1**	
05-2	5 nse	**Aubretia (IRE)**[19] 4119 3-8-2 71 ThoreHammerHansen(5) 1	72
		(Richard Hannon) *sn led: pushed along 1/2-way: hdd 3f out: rdn over 2f out: drvn wl over 1f out: kpt on same pce* **4/1**[3]	
-633	6 2	**Hunni**[12] 4393 4-9-7 76 BenCurtis 3	74
		(Tom Clover) *cl up: led 3f out: rdn along over 2f out: hdd 1 1/2f out: sn wknd (jockey said filly slipped leaving the stalls)* **7/2**[2]	
1004	7 2 ¾	**Florenza**[20] 4058 6-10-0 83 MichaelStainton 6	75
		(Chris Fairhurst) *in tch: pushed along 3f out: rdn over 2f out: n.d* **12/1**	

1m 38.76s (-1.44) **Going Correction** -0.05s/f (Good)
WFA 3 from 4yo+ 9lb **7 Ran SP% 113.5**
Speed ratings (Par 102): **105,104,101,100,100 98,96**
CSF £24.53 CT £200.18 TOTE £2.50: £1.70, £5.90; EX 26.70 Trifecta £103.20.
Owner HRH Princess Haya Of Jordan **Bred** Godolphin **Trained** Newmarket, Suffolk

FOCUS
This race had an open feel to it beforehand but was won comfortably by the favourite, who progressed.

4829 PPM H'CAP 5f 3y
3:55 (3:56) (Class 5) (0-70,74) 3-Y-0+
£3,428 (£1,020; £509; £300; £300; £300) **Stalls High**

Form			RPR
-121	1	**Celsius (IRE)**[6] 4604 3-9-11 74 6ex (t) BenCurtis 1	83+
		(Tom Clover) *awkward and dwlt s: in rr: swtchd rt to stands' side and hdwy 2f out: rdn over 1f out: styd on strly fnl f to ld nr fin* **7/5**[1]	
0-00	2 nk	**Han Solo Berger (IRE)**[44] 3206 4-9-11 69 (p) GeorgeWood 9	76
		(Chris Wall) *trckd ldrs: hdwy wl over 1f out: rdn to chal ent fnl f and sn edgd lft: drvn to ld ins fnl 100yds: hdd and no ex nr fin* **7/1**[3]	
0500	3 1	**Bashiba (IRE)**[19] 4100 8-9-6 67 (t) RowanScott(3) 3	71
		(Nigel Tinkler) *trckd ldrs on outer: hdwy 2f out: rdn to ld over 1f out: edgd rt ent fnl f: drvn and hdd last 100yds: kpt on same pce* **9/2**[2]	
00-0	4 nk	**Young Tiger**[43] 3213 6-8-7 51 oh4 (h) JoeFanning 2	56+
		(Tom Tate) *hld up towards rr: hdwy 2f out: rdn to chse ldrs over 1f out: n.m.r ent fnl f: sn drvn and kpt on same pce (jockey said gelding was denied a clear run approaching the final furlong)* **14/1**	
4500	5 ¾	**Alqaab**[41] 3291 4-9-4 62 (h[1]) JackGarritty 7	62
		(Ruth Carr) *trckd ldrs: hdwy 2f out: rdn over 1f out: drvn and kpt on same pce fnl f* **22/1**	
3033	6 2 ¾	**Red Stripes (USA)**[7] 4555 7-8-2 53 (b) KieranSchofield(7) 5	45
		(Lisa Williamson) *cl up: rdn and ev ch wl over 1f out: sn drvn and wknd ent fnl f* **12/1**	
500-	7 3	**Ebitda**[194] 9748 5-9-11 69 KieranO'Neill 8	51
		(Scott Dixon) *prom: rdn along 2f out: sn drvn and wkng whn n.m.r ent fnl f* **33/1**	
0100	8 hd	**Gullane One (IRE)**[10] 4440 4-9-12 70 (bt[1]) JasonHart 4	51
		(Tim Easterby) *slt ld: rdn 2f out: drvn and hdd over 1f out: hld whn n.m.r and hmpd ent fnl f* **15/2**	
-206	9 17	**Dragon Beat (IRE)**[19] 4128 3-9-5 68 AdamKirby 6	
		(Michael Appleby) *dwlt: a in rr (jockey said filly slipped leaving stalls)* **10/1**	

58.82s (-0.78) **Going Correction** -0.05s/f (Good)
WFA 3 from 4yo+ 5lb **9 Ran SP% 114.9**
Speed ratings (Par 103): **104,103,101,101,100 95,91,90,63**
CSF £11.59 CT £35.75 TOTE £2.20: £1.20, £1.90, £1.70; EX 14.10 Trifecta £50.90.
Owner J Collins, C Fahy & S Piper **Bred** Owenstown Stud **Trained** Newmarket, Suffolk

FOCUS
Only a modest handicap but an improving winner who did well to his third race in four starts. The time was sound.

4830 BARTON STORAGE SYSTEMS H'CAP 1m 2f 43y
4:25 (4:25) (Class 4) (0-85,85) 3-Y-0 **£5,207** (£1,549; £774; £387) **Stalls High**

Form			RPR
0411	1	**Corncrake**[5] 4663 3-9-1 79 6ex RossaRyan 5	86+
		(Richard Hannon) *hld up: hdwy to trck ldng pair 3f out: pushed along 2f out: rdn to chal over 1f out: drvn to take slt ld ins fnl f: kpt on wl towards fin* **5/6**[1]	
5-51	2 ½	**Sophosc (IRE)**[20] 4065 3-9-4 82 RobHornby 3	87
		(Joseph Tuite) *led: pushed along 2f out: jnd and rdn over 1f out: drvn ent fnl f: sn hdd narrowly: kpt on gamely u.p tl no ex towards fin* **12/1**	
-223	3 ¾	**Al Mureib (IRE)**[31] 3648 3-9-7 85 HectorCrouch 2	88
		(Saeed bin Suroor) *hld up: hdwy 2f out: chal over 1f out: ev ch and rdn ins fnl f: kpt on same pce towards fin* **9/4**[2]	
2-40	4 14	**Felix**[34] 3548 3-9-7 85 (t) ColmO'Donoghue 4	60
		(Sir Michael Stoute) *trckd ldr: pushed along over 2f out: rdn wl over 1f out: sn wknd* **5/1**[3]	

2m 10.91s (-1.39) **Going Correction** -0.05s/f (Good) **4 Ran SP% 109.7**
Speed ratings (Par 102): **103,102,102,90**
CSF £10.39 TOTE £1.50; EX 8.90 Trifecta £13.60.
Owner Exors Of The Late Lady Rothschild **Bred** The Rt Hon Lord Rothschild **Trained** East Everleigh, Wilts

FOCUS
Add 12yds. A fair handicap and an intriguing one despite the lack of numbers. The front three pulled a long way clear. The winner was close to his last-time-out Nottingham figure, another pb from the second.

4831 PJP GROUP BARNSLEY FILLIES' H'CAP 7f 6y
5:00 (5:02) (Class 5) (0-75,76) 3-Y-0+
£3,428 (£1,020; £509; £300; £300; £300) **Stalls High**

Form			RPR
6412	1	**Warning Fire**[3] 4721 3-9-10 76 6ex JoeFanning 5	83+
		(Mark Johnston) *mde all: rdn and qcknd clr over 1f out: kpt on strly* **11/10**[1]	
5201	2 1 ¾	**Arletta Star**[24] 3923 3-8-13 65 JasonHart 7	67
		(Tim Easterby) *trckd wnr: pushed along 2f out: rdn wl over 1f out: drvn and kpt on same pce fnl f* **5/1**[3]	
5	3 hd	**Bidding War**[19] 4130 4-8-4 53 oh1 TheodoreLadd(5) 2	57
		(Michael Appleby) *trckd ldrs: hdwy wl over 1f out: sn rdn: drvn and kpt on same pce fnl f* **16/1**	
1655	4 nk	**Zafaranah (USA)**[14] 4281 5-9-11 69 RobHornby 4	72
		(Pam Sly) *hld up in tch: hdwy wl over 1f out: sn rdn: drvn and n.m.r ins fnl f: kpt on* **3/1**[2]	
1006	5 ½	**Kodiac Lass (IRE)**[15] 4248 3-9-3 69 (p[1]) DanielMuscutt 3	68
		(Marco Botti) *trckd wnr: rdn along 2f out: drvn over 1f out: kpt on same pce* **25/1**	
333	6 2 ¾	**Harvest Day**[5] 4626 4-9-9 72 (t) ScottMcCullagh(5) 1	66
		(Michael Easterby) *hld up in rr: hdwy 2f out: sn rdn and n.d* **6/1**	

1m 25.44s (-0.96) **Going Correction** -0.05s/f (Good)
WFA 3 from 4yo+ 8lb **6 Ran SP% 113.3**
Speed ratings (Par 100): **103,101,100,100,99 96**
CSF £7.29 TOTE £1.70: £1.30, £2.10; EX 5.80 Trifecta £39.40.
Owner Sheikh Hamdan bin Mohammed Al Maktoum **Bred** Godolphin **Trained** Middleham Moor, N Yorks

FOCUS
The market suggested this would be one-sided and that is how it proved.
T/Plt: £27.90 to a £1 stake. Pool: £60,829.36 - 1,588.02 winning units. T/Qpdt: £5.60 to a £1 stake. Pool: £5,999.76 - 787.98 winning units. **Joe Rowntree**

4543 EPSOM (L-H)
Thursday, July 11

OFFICIAL GOING: Good to firm (good in places; watered; 7.5)
Wind: virtually nil Weather: warm with bright sunny spells

4832 BRITISH STALLION STUDS EBF NOVICE STKS (PLUS 10 RACE) 7f 3y
6:00 (6:01) (Class 4) 2-Y-O £4,905 (£1,543; £830) **Stalls** Low

Form RPR
01 **1** **Grove Ferry (IRE)**[30] 3695 2-9-6 0 DavidProbert 4 88
(Andrew Balding) *trckd ldr: effrt to cl on ldr whn sltly unbalanced over 1f out: sn rdn and styd on wl to ld fnl 75yds* **7/2**[2]
31 **2** *¾* **Be Prepared**[14] 4302 2-9-6 0 OisinMurphy 1 86
(Simon Crisford) *led and travelled wl thrght: rdn whn pressed by wnr 1f out: kpt on but hdd by wnr fnl 75yds* **2/9**[1]
00 **3** *4* **Sir Arthur Dayne (IRE)**[9] 4480 2-9-2 0 CallumShepherd 3 71
(Mick Channon) *dwlt sltly and racd in last: rdn and outpcd by front pair over 2f out: kpt on one pce fnl f (jockey said colt reared as stalls opened)* **22/1**[3]
P0 **P** **Austin Taetious**[31] 3644 2-8-11 0 RhiainIngram(5) 2
(Adam West) *lost action and qckly p.u sn after s (jockey said she felt the gelding go amiss shortly after leaving the stalls so pulled the gelding up)* **100/1**
1m 23.04s (-0.36) **Going Correction** -0.125s/f (Firm) 4 Ran SP% **109.4**
Speed ratings (Par 96): **97,96,91,**
CSF £4.88 TOTE £4.10; EX 6.30 Trifecta £6.60.
Owner Martin & Valerie Slade & Partner **Bred** Skymarc Farm **Trained** Kingsclere, Hants

FOCUS
The rail was out up to 5yds from 1m to the winning post. Add 7yds. This 2yo novice event proved tactical, but they still lowered the course record. It's tricky to know the exact worth of the form.

4833 RUBBING HOUSE H'CAP 7f 3y
6:30 (6:30) (Class 5) (0-75,77) 4-Y-O+ £4,528 (£1,347; £673; £336; £300; £300) **Stalls** Low

Form RPR
0000 **1** **Big Storm Coming**[12] 4365 9-9-1 **73** CierenFallon(5) 4 83
(John Quinn) *racd in midfield: effrt whn briefly short of room 2f out: rdn once in the clr 1f out: styd on wl to ld wl ins fnl f: won gng away (trainer said, regarding the apparent improvement in form, that gelding appreciated a return to Epsom)* **4/1**[3]
1133 **2** *2½* **Mujassam**[10] 4440 7-9-7 **74** (v) OisinMurphy 7 77
(David O'Meara) *racd in midfield on outer: pushed along on outer over 2f out: sn rdn and no immediate imp over 1f out: kpt on to snatch 2nd post* **9/4**[1]
2003 **3** *shd* **Dream Catching (IRE)**[23] 3963 4-9-9 **76** (v) DavidProbert 6 79
(Andrew Balding) *trckd ldr: clsd gng wl over 2f out: pushed into ld 2f out: sn rdn and hdd by wnr wl ins fnl f: lost 2nd fnl strides* **4/1**[3]
-302 **4** *1¼* **Seprani**[23] 3967 5-9-1 **71** GabrieleMalune(3) 2 70
(Amy Murphy) *hld up: effrt to cl on outer over 2f out: rdn along and ev ch over 1f out: one pce fnl f (vet said mare lost right-fore shoe)* **7/2**[2]
4100 **5** *2¼* **Chevallier**[14] 4300 7-9-10 **77** (p) LukeMorris 1 70
(Michael Attwater) *hld up: rdn and outpcd 2f out: drvn and no imp over 1f out: no ex* **12/1**
5513 **6** *1* **Perfect Symphony (IRE)**[8] 4501 5-8-3 **63** (p) IsobelFrancis(7) 5 54
(Mark Pattinson) *chsd ldr tl led 3f out: drvn along and hdd 2f out: wknd fnl f (jockey said gelding hung left-handed in straight)* **14/1**
6006 **7** *2* **Tavener**[21] 4025 7-8-3 **56** (p) FrannyNorton 3 41
(David C Griffiths) *led: rdn along and lost pl 3f out: sn struggling* **12/1**
1m 22.81s (-0.59) **Going Correction** -0.125s/f (Firm) 7 Ran SP% **115.0**
Speed ratings (Par 103): **98,95,95,93,91 89,87**
CSF £13.63 TOTE £4.90: £2.10, £1.60; EX 19.00 Trifecta £59.80.
Owner Fishlake Commercial Motors Ltd **Bred** Bearstone Stud Ltd **Trained** Settrington, N Yorks

FOCUS
Add 7yds. This modest handicap was run at an average pace.

4834 THE WORSHIPFUL COMPANY OF LORINERS H'CAP 1m 4f 6y
7:05 (7:10) (Class 6) (0-60,60) 3-Y-O £3,881 (£1,155; £577; £300; £300; £300) **Stalls** Centre

Form RPR
000- **1** **Blame It On Sally (IRE)**[237] 9104 3-9-5 **58** LukeMorris 10 66+
(Sir Mark Prescott Bt) *mde virtually all: pushed along w short ld 2f out: sn drvn and responded generously 1f out: kpt on gamely* **7/1**[3]
-053 **2** *1* **Arms Of The Angel (GER)**[6] 4587 3-9-7 **60** FrannyNorton 11 66
(Mark Johnston) *chsd ldr: clsd up gng wl 2f out: sn rdn and ev ch 1f out: kpt on but unable to get by wnr fnl f* **11/4**[1]
4315 **3** *1½* **Highway Robbery**[23] 3965 3-8-4 **48** (p) SophieRalston(5) 3 52
(Julia Feilden) *racd in midfield: stl gng wl amongst horses 3f out: sn rdn 2f out: kpt on wl fnl f: nt rch ldrs* **12/1**
6602 **4** *½* **Watch And Learn**[12] 4400 3-9-2 **55** OisinMurphy 8 58
(Andrew Balding) *racd in midfield: hdwy into 3rd 3f out: sn drvn to chse ldng pair 2f out: one pce fnl f* **7/2**[2]
1564 **5** *2¾* **Ignatius (IRE)**[7] 4547 3-9-1 **54** KierenFox 5 53
(John Best) *hld up: effrt into midfield 3f out: rdn and wnt 5th 2f out: kpt on fnl f (jockey said gelding was slowly into stride and never travelling)* **7/2**[2]
5-50 **6** *5* **Crystal Tiara**[12] 4400 3-8-11 **50** CallumShepherd 6 41
(Mick Channon) *racd in midfield: drvn on outer to cl 3f out: hung lft u.p 2f out: one pce after* **16/1**
5-00 **7** *½* **Loving Pearl**[29] 3741 3-8-13 **59** GeorgiaDobie(7) 2 49
(John Berry) *in rr of midfield: rdn over 2f out: drvn and no imp over 1f out: no ex* **20/1**
3600 **8** *1½* **Daniel Dravot**[12] 4400 3-8-7 **46** (h) CharlieBennett 4 34
(Michael Attwater) *settled wl in midfield: effrt to chse ldng pair 3f out: rdn and no imp 2f out: nvr on terms* **33/1**
6-00 **9** *9* **Arbuckle**[38] 3418 3-8-5 **49** CierenFallon(5) 7 22
(Michael Madgwick) *trckd ldr: rdn and outpcd 3f out: sn lost pl and bhd 2f out (trainer said gelding was unsuited by the camber)* **50/1**
056 **10** *1½* **Lyrical Waters**[20] 4066 3-9-7 **60** DavidProbert 1 31
(Eve Johnson Houghton) *trckd ldr: rdn and outpcd over 2f out: wknd fr over 1f out* **20/1**
0400 **11** *4* **Moonlit Sea**[87] 1825 3-9-4 **60** PaddyBradley(3) 9 24
(Pat Phelan) *hld up: rdn and sn bhd 3f out* **20/1**
-605 **12** *45* **Alramz**[27] 3809 3-9-0 **53** RobertWinston 12
(Lee Carter) *racd in last: racd awkwardly 1/2-way: sn detached (jockey said gelding was never travelling early and hung left-handed)* **18/1**
2m 39.28s (-1.52) **Going Correction** -0.125s/f (Firm) 12 Ran SP% **121.6**
Speed ratings (Par 98): **100,99,98,98,96 92,92,91,85,84 81,51**
CSF £25.39 CT £237.04 TOTE £5.00: £2.00, £1.60, £2.60; EX 33.30 Trifecta £332.10.
Owner Mr & Mrs John Kelsey-Fry **Bred** John Kelsey-Fry **Trained** Newmarket, Suffolk

FOCUS
Add 14yds. It paid to be prominent in this moderate 3yo handicap. The first two are progressive, and also small pbs from the third and fourth.

4835 HIGHLAND ACCLAIM H'CAP 6f 3y
7:35 (7:39) (Class 4) (0-85,84) 3-Y-O+ £7,115 (£2,117; £1,058; £529; £300; £300) **Stalls** High

Form RPR
1065 **1** **Harrogate (IRE)**[7] 4545 4-9-5 **77** (b) CharlieBennett 1 83
(Jim Boyle) *mde all: rdn along to maintain short ld 2f out: drvn and strly pressed fnl f: kpt on wl* **13/2**
6-03 **2** *½* **Ashpan Sam**[7] 4545 10-9-12 **84** (p) LukeMorris 3 88
(David W Drinkwater) *trckd wnr: rdn to chse wnr over 1f out: drvn and kpt on wl fnl f: nt rch wnr* **6/1**[3]
5604 **3** *nse* **Highland Acclaim (IRE)**[7] 4545 8-9-5 **77** (h) DavidProbert 7 81
(David O'Meara) *chsd wnr: drvn to chse wnr over 1f out: kpt on fnl f: lost 2nd last strides* **3/1**[2]
0560 **4** *1* **Helvetian**[15] 4236 4-9-10 **82** OisinMurphy 2 83
(Mick Channon) *settled in midfield: stl gng wl over 2f out: pushed along but lugging in bhd rivals over 1f out: sn rdn once in clr and kpt on wl fnl f* **11/4**[1]
00-4 **5** *1¼* **Clear Spring (IRE)**[45] 3164 11-9-5 **77** FrannyNorton 5 74
(John Spearing) *hld up: pushed along and hdwy on outer 2f out: sn rdn and no further imp 1f out: one pce fnl f* **6/1**[3]
1512 **6** *2¾* **Diamond Lady**[23] 3963 8-9-7 **79** ShaneKelly 4 67
(William Stone) *racd in midfield: pushed along 3f out: sn rdn and outpcd 2f out: no ex fnl f* **7/1**
2154 **7** *6* **Real Estate (IRE)**[23] 3963 4-8-12 **70** (p) CallumShepherd 6 51
(Michael Attwater) *restrained and racd in last: rdn along 3f out: sn struggling (jockey said colt had no more to give)* **8/1**
1m 9.22s (-0.68) **Going Correction** -0.125s/f (Firm) 7 Ran SP% **117.2**
Speed ratings (Par 105): **99,98,98,96,95 91,83**
CSF £46.03 TOTE £7.10: £3.20, £2.90; EX 43.80 Trifecta £143.00.
Owner Goff, Walsh & Zerdin **Bred** P O'Rourke **Trained** Epsom, Surrey

FOCUS
Add 4yds. Few got into this feature sprint handicap; ordinary form.

4836 80'S NYE PARTY AT EPSOM DOWNS H'CAP 1m 2f 17y
8:10 (8:11) (Class 5) (0-70,71) 3-Y-O £4,528 (£1,347; £673; £336; £300; £300) **Stalls** Low

Form RPR
5642 **1** **Teodora De Vega (IRE)**[28] 3773 3-9-7 **68** HarryBentley 6 74
(Ralph Beckett) *settled in midfield: hdwy u.p over 2f out: rdn and clsd qckly to ld 1f out: sn jnd by rival: drvn and styd on strly* **10/3**[3]
0036 **2** *¾* **Isle Of Wolves**[24] 3947 3-9-3 **64** PatCosgrave 5 68
(Jim Boyle) *hld up: hdwy between rivals to chse ldr over 2f out: hmpd by rival over 1f out: sn rdn and ev ch whn disputing ld ins fnl f: nt match wnr last 100yds* **2/1**[1]
4002 **3** *3* **Toro Dorado**[14] 4293 3-9-2 **63** OisinMurphy 3 61
(Ed Dunlop) *led briefly then chsd ldr: pushed along to ld 2f out: rdn and hung lft to rail over 1f out: drvn and hdd by wnr 1f out: no ex fnl f* **3/1**[2]
4444 **4** *2¼* **Winter Snowdrop (IRE)**[9] 4476 3-7-11 **49** oh4 SophieRalston(5) 1 43
(Julia Feilden) *trckd ldrs bef being restrained to rr: effrt on outer 3f out: rdn and no imp 2f out: one pce after (jockey said filly hung right-handed)* **28/1**
34-0 **5** *5* **Slade King (IRE)**[68] 2406 3-9-10 **71** DavidProbert 7 55
(Gary Moore) *midfield on outer: rdn along over 1f out: wknd ins fnl f* **8/1**
0063 **6** *2¼* **Cedar**[13] 4346 3-8-2 **49** (t) FrannyNorton 2 28
(Mohamed Moubarak) *chsd ldr: rdn along 2f out: sn wknd over 1f out* **8/1**
00-4 **7** *3¾* **Limelighter**[68] 2407 3-9-4 **65** KierenFox 4 37
(Sheena West) *sn led: rdn along and hdd 2f out: wknd fnl f* **10/1**
2m 8.08s (-1.92) **Going Correction** -0.125s/f (Firm) 7 Ran SP% **116.2**
Speed ratings (Par 100): **102,101,99,97,93 91,88**
CSF £10.79 TOTE £3.90: £2.10, £1.90; EX 13.40 Trifecta £39.50.
Owner Waverley Racing **Bred** Norelands Stud & Lofts Hall Stud **Trained** Kimpton, Hants

FOCUS
Add 14yds. They went a fair pace in this ordinary 3yo handicap and this rates straightforward form.

4837 CHRISTMAS PARTIES AT EPSOM DOWNS H'CAP 1m 113y
8:40 (8:41) (Class 4) (0-80,82) 3-Y-O- £7,115 (£2,117; £1,058; £529; £300) **Stalls** Low

Form RPR
12-5 **1** **Grey Spirit (IRE)**[41] 3300 4-9-11 **76** LukeMorris 2 88+
(Sir Mark Prescott Bt) *hld up: hdwy on outer gng wl 2f out: pushed alongside ldr 1f out: nudged out to ld under hands and heels ins fnl f to win cosily* **3/1**[3]
-604 **2** *2¼* **Arigato**[15] 4249 4-10-0 **79** (p) JosephineGordon 4 86
(William Jarvis) *led: rdn along and strly pressed by wnr 1f out: kpt on but no match for wnr once hdd ins fnl f* **5/2**[2]
-500 **3** *2* **Data Protection**[14] 4300 4-9-9 **74** (t) HarryBentley 3 77
(William Muir) *trckd ldr: rdn along and briefly short of room 2f out: one pce fnl f* **6/1**
1156 **4** *shd* **Simoon (IRE)**[22] 3992 5-10-3 **82** OisinMurphy 5 84
(Andrew Balding) *trckd ldr: effrt to chse ldr 2f out: sn rdn and readily outpcd by wnr 1f out: one pce after* **13/8**[1]
4600 **5** *9* **The Warrior (IRE)**[21] 4028 7-8-8 **66** GeorgiaDobie(7) 1 49
(Lee Carter) *hld up: rdn in last over 2f out: nvr on terms* **20/1**
1m 44.14s (-2.26) **Going Correction** -0.125s/f (Firm) 5 Ran SP% **110.7**
Speed ratings (Par 105): **105,103,101,101,93**
CSF £10.91 TOTE £3.20: £1.50, £1.60; EX 10.30 Trifecta £37.40.
Owner Philip Bamford - Osborne House **Bred** Michael Doyle **Trained** Newmarket, Suffolk

FOCUS
Add 14yds. This looked like a tight handicap, but the finish was dominated by the first pair. The winner resumed his 3yo progress.
T/Plt: £352.70 to a £1 stake. Pool: £54,525.51 - 112.84 winning units. T/Qpdt: £36.80 to a £1 stake. Pool: £7,820.90 - 157.10 winning units. **Mark Grantham**

4556 NEWBURY (L-H)

Thursday, July 11

OFFICIAL GOING: Good to firm (watered; 7.7)

Wind: light against Weather: sunny periods

4838 NEWBURY NUFFIELD HEALTH GYM AMATEUR RIDERS' H'CAP 1m (S)

5:40 (5:42) (Class 5) (0-75,80) 3-Y-O+

£3,306 (£1,025; £512; £300; £300; £300) Stalls Centre

Form RPR

0226 1 **Ragstone View (IRE)**[15] 4249 4-10-10 71..........(h) MrPatrickMillman 3 80
(Rod Millman) *s.i.s: towards rr: stdy prog fr over 2f out: rdn into 3rd ent fnl f: r.o wl to ld towards fin* 11/1

2312 2 ¾ **Luna Magic**[5] 4658 5-9-13 60 5ex.......................... MissBeckySmith 6 67
(Archie Watson) *prom: led 3f out: rdn over 1f out: kpt on but no ex whn hdd towards fin* 7/4[1]

-054 3 1 ¼ **Crimewave (IRE)**[14] 4306 3-10-0 75..........................(p) MrCharlesClover(5) 4 77
(Tom Clover) *trckd ldrs: rdn to chse ldr jst over 1f out: kpt on same pce ins fnl f* 7/1

646 4 1 ¾ **Noble Account**[20] 4073 3-9-11 67..........................(h) MrRossBirkett 8 65
(Julia Feilden) *wnt rt s: sn mid-div: rdn over 2f out: kpt on ins fnl f: wnt 4th towards fin* 20/1

-225 5 2 **Light Of Air (FR)**[16] 4215 6-9-7 61.......................(b) MissKatyBrooks(7) 2 57
(Gary Moore) *trckd ldrs: rdn over 2f out: nt pce to chal: fdd fnl 75yds* 20/1

4-66 6 5 **William Hunter**[31] 3663 7-10-5 73..........................(t) MrJamieNeild(7) 10 57
(Nigel Twiston-Davies) *slowly away: towards rr: hdwy 2f out: sn rdn: nt pce to get on terms: fdd fnl 120yds (jockey said he was slow to remove blindfold)* 28/1

1323 7 1 ¾ **Anif (IRE)**[7] 4561 5-10-4 72.......................... MrPhilipThomas(7) 1 52
(David Evans) *disp ld tl rdn 3f out: kpt on tl wknd ins fnl f* 6/1[3]

4060 8 3 ¾ **First Link (USA)**[25] 3892 4-10-4 65.......................... MrJamesHarding 11 37
(Jean-Rene Auvray) *awkwardly away: a towards rr* 66/1

-321 9 1 **Itizzit**[11] 4424 3-10-10 80 6ex.......................... MissSerenaBrotherton 5 47
(Hughie Morrison) *racd keenly: disp ld tl rdn 3f out: sn hld: wknd over 1f out* 7/2[2]

0565 10 4 **Letsbe Avenue (IRE)**[8] 4506 4-11-0 75.......................... MrSimonWalker 9 35
(Richard Hannon) *trckd ldrs: rdn over 3f out: wknd over 2f out (vet said gelding lost right fore shoe)* 12/1

04-0 11 3 ¼ **Extreme Force (IRE)**[68] 2406 3-9-9 72.......................... MrAnthonyO'Neill(7) 12 23
(Jonjo O'Neill) *prom tl over 3f out* 66/1

000 12 1 ¾ **Thunderhooves**[16] 4216 4-9-2 56 oh11..........................(t[1]) MrThomasMiles(7) 7 5
(John Ryan) *dwlt: a bhd* 150/1

1m 39.71s (-0.19) **Going Correction** -0.05s/f (Good) 12 Ran SP% **118.0**

WFA 3 from 4yo+ 9lb

Speed ratings (Par 103): **98,97,96,94,92 87,85,81,80,76 73,71**

CSF £28.97 CT £152.36 TOTE £11.20: £2.80, £1.10, £2.70; EX 42.50 Trifecta £380.50.

Owner Rioja Raiders 04 **Bred** Peter Henley **Trained** Kentisbeare, Devon

FOCUS

Little gallop on here in a modest amateur riders' handicap. The raced centre-field. Straightforward form and this rates a pb from the winner.

4839 MIRAGE SIGNS EBF NOVICE AUCTION STKS (C&G) 6f

6:10 (6:11) (Class 5) 2-Y-O £3,428 (£1,020; £509; £254) Stalls Centre

Form RPR

51 1 **Hard Nut (IRE)**[21] 4018 2-9-4 0.......................... SeanLevey 7 85+
(Richard Hannon) *a.p: led over 1f out: sn rdn: r.o strly: readily* 7/1

4 2 1 ½ **Commit No Nuisance (IRE)**[17] 4184 2-8-7 0.......................... JasonWatson 3 69
(William Knight) *in tch: tk clsr order 2f out: sn rdn: drifted rt jst over 1f out: kpt on to chse wnr fnl 120yds but nt pce to threaten* 5/1[3]

4 3 1 ¼ **Centurion Song (IRE)**[24] 3943 2-8-9 0.......................... MartinDwyer 8 67
(Brian Meehan) *in tch: hdwy 2f out: sn rdn: disp 2nd ent fnl f: kpt on same pce* 13/8[1]

0 4 1 **Max's Thunder (IRE)**[30] 3694 2-8-11 0.......................... RobertHavlin 9 66+
(Jamie Osborne) *hld up: hdwy over 1f out: sn rdn: kpt on fnl f* 28/1

5 hd **Master Spy (IRE)** 2-8-11 0.......................... FergusSweeney 5 65+
(Paul Cole) *unsettled stalls: in tch: lost pl whn outpcd 2f out: no threat after but kpt on nicely ins fnl f* 20/1

02 6 hd **Jim 'N' Tomic (IRE)**[55] 2792 2-9-0 0.......................... LiamKeniry 1 68
(Dominic Ffrench Davis) *prom: led 2f out: sn rdn and hdd: fdd fnl 120yds* 3/1[2]

7 2 **Lin Chong** 2-9-0 0.......................... PatDobbs 10 61
(Paul Cole) *wnt rt s and slowly away: towards rr: sme prog over 1f out: wknd ins fnl f* 11/1

8 1 ½ **Colonel Whitehead (IRE)** 2-8-4 0.......................... WilliamCox(3) 2 49
(Heather Main) *in tch: effrt 2f out: wknd fnl f* 20/1

9 14 **Born For Fun (IRE)** 2-8-9 0.......................... HollieDoyle 4 7
(Ali Stronge) *rrd leaving stalls: racd keenly: sn led: hdd 2f out: wknd (jockey said gelding reared as the stalls opened and ran too free)* 50/1

1m 14.22s (1.02) **Going Correction** -0.05s/f (Good) 9 Ran SP% **115.5**

Speed ratings (Par 94): **91,89,87,86,85 85,82,80,62**

CSF £39.61 TOTE £7.10: £1.70, £1.80, £1.10; EX 41.30 Trifecta £120.20.

Owner Mrs J K Powell & Mrs A Doyle **Bred** Springwell Stud **Trained** East Everleigh, Wilts

FOCUS

Ordinary novice form but this rates a clear step up from the winner.

4840 CALDERS & GRANDIDGE EBF FILLIES' NOVICE AUCTION STKS (PLUS 10 RACE) 6f

6:40 (6:42) (Class 5) 2-Y-O £3,428 (£1,020; £509; £254) Stalls Centre

Form RPR

1 **Odyssey Girl (IRE)** 2-8-9 0.......................... JasonWatson 6 72
(Richard Spencer) *in tch: hdwy fr 2f out: rdn to ld jst ins fnl f: edgd lft: r.o wl* 14/1

2 ½ **Fromnowon (IRE)** 2-8-11 0.......................... SeanLevey 12 72+
(Richard Hannon) *hld up towards rr: hdwy over 1f out: drifted lft u.p ins fnl f but r.o wl: rdr dropped whip whn gng 2nd nring fin* 14/1

3 hd **Elegant Erin (IRE)** 2-8-9 0.......................... FergusSweeney 9 69
(Richard Hannon) *s.i.s: towards rr: hdwy over 2f out: 5th ent fnl f: kpt on wl: wnt 3rd cl home* 20/1

4 hd **Mitty's Smile (IRE)** 2-8-9 0.......................... HollieDoyle 1 69
(Archie Watson) *mid-div: hdwy over 2f out: rdn in cl 4th ent fnl f: kpt on* 8/1[3]

44 5 hd **Hashtagmetoo (USA)**[16] 4221 2-8-11 0.......................... NicolaCurrie 2 70
(Jamie Osborne) *led: rdn and hdd jst ins fnl f: squeezed up whn no ex towards fin* 14/1

6 1 ¼ **Angel Grey (IRE)** 2-9-0 0.......................... MartinDwyer 13 72+
(Andrew Balding) *hld up towards rr: hdwy under hands and heels fr over 1f out: running on but hld whn nt clr run fnl 120yds* 20/1

1 7 ¾ **Special Secret**[16] 4221 2-9-0 0.......................... CharlesBishop 11 70+
(Eve Johnson Houghton) *mid-div: hdwy 2f out: sn rdn: running on but hld whn bdly hmpd fnl 120yds* 11/10[1]

1 8 2 **Sovereign Beauty (IRE)**[20] 4062 2-8-11 0.......................... AmeliaGlass(7) 4 70+
(Clive Cox) *prom: ev ch 2f out: sn rdn: fading whn bdly hmpd fnl 120yds* 4/1[2]

06 9 4 **Candid (IRE)**[27] 3798 2-8-9 0.......................... RobertHavlin 8 42
(Jonathan Portman) *trckd ldrs: rdn 2f out: sn wknd* 40/1

05 10 hd **Depeche Toi (IRE)**[20] 4062 2-8-4 0.......................... WilliamCox(3) 3 40
(Jonathan Portman) *trckd ldrs: rdn over 2f out: wknd over 1f out* 50/1

00 11 8 **Summer Lake**[16] 4222 2-8-4 0.......................... MeganNicholls(3) 7 14
(Roger Charlton) *mid-div: rdn over 2f out: sn wknd* 50/1

5 12 6 **Pink Tulip**[33] 3578 2-8-11 0.......................... StevieDonohoe 10
(David Simcock) *s.i.s: a towards rr (jockey said filly stumbled 1/2f out)* 20/1

13 7 **Goodman Square** 2-8-7 0.......................... EoinWalsh 5
(Mark Usher) *s.i.s: hung lft fr over 2f out: a towards rr (jockey said filly ran green and hung left-handed)* 100/1

1m 13.4s (0.20) **Going Correction** -0.05s/f (Good) 13 Ran SP% **120.4**

Speed ratings (Par 91): **96,95,95,94,94 92,91,89,83,83 72,64,55**

CSF £181.00 TOTE £13.00: £3.10, £3.20, £6.50; EX 256.70 Trifecta £2307.40.

Owner Mrs Emma Cunningham **Bred** Guy O'Callaghan **Trained** Newmarket, Suffolk

FOCUS

With the market leaders disappointing this ordinary fillies' novice was dominated by newcomers.

4841 THE NEWBURY WEEKLY NEWS H'CAP 1m 2f

7:15 (7:15) (Class 4) (0-80,82) 3-Y-O+

£6,404 (£1,905; £952; £476; £300; £300) Stalls Low

Form RPR

30/1 1 **Match Maker (IRE)**[20] 4055 4-10-0 80..........................(t) JamesDoyle 9 89+
(Simon Crisford) *hld up: hdwy over 3f out: shkn up over 2f out: led jst over 1f out: sn rdn: kpt on wl* 9/2[2]

-035 2 ¾ **Starfighter**[12] 4392 3-8-11 73.......................... RichardKingscote 10 79
(Ed Walker) *hld up: pushed along and stdy prog 3f out: swtchd rt whn nt clr run 2f out: rdn and r.o ins fnl f: drifted lft: wnt 2nd towards fin* 7/1[3]

204- 3 1 ¼ **Miss Blondell**[217] 9431 6-9-1 67.......................... NicolaCurrie 5 70
(Marcus Tregoning) *hld up: hdwy over 2f out: sn rdn: ev ch ent fnl f: kpt on but no ex fnl 100yds* 33/1

1552 4 hd **Carp Kid (IRE)**[7] 4561 4-9-4 73..........................(p) FinleyMarsh(3) 8 76
(John Flint) *led: rdn and hdd jst over 1f out: kpt on same pce fnl f* 10/1

1240 5 nk **Star Of War (USA)**[20] 4052 3-9-6 82.......................... SeanLevey 6 84
(Richard Hannon) *s.i.s: towards rr: hdwy over 3f out: nt clr run over 2f out: swtchd rt over 1f out: sn rdn: chalng for hld 4th whn tight for room and snatched up fnl 120yds* 16/1

046 6 2 **Horatio Star**[14] 4283 4-9-4 70..........................(p[1]) PJMcDonald 2 68
(Brian Meehan) *trckd ldrs: rdn over 2f out: nt quite pce to chal: fdd fnl 120yds* 11/1

-665 7 nse **Escape The City**[14] 4283 4-9-8 74.......................... TomMarquand 3 72
(Hughie Morrison) *mid-div: hdwy over 4f out: rdn and ev ch 2f: stl chalng ent fnl f: sn no ex* 16/1

23-3 8 ½ **Ambling (IRE)**[54] 2838 3-9-2 78..........................(h) RobertHavlin 1 77
(John Gosden) *mid-div: hdwy fr 4f out: rdn and ev ch over 1f out: sn hld: one pce whn hmpd and snatched up ins fnl f* 7/1[3]

0-21 9 31 **My Dear Friend**[148] 698 3-9-0 76.......................... SilvestreDeSousa 7 12
(Ralph Beckett) *trckd ldrs: rdn and ev ch 3f out: wknd 2f out: eased (jockey said gelding stopped quickly)* 12/1

3-32 10 3 **Rhythmic Intent (IRE)**[27] 3808 3-9-5 81.......................... JasonWatson 4 11+
(Stuart Williams) *in tch: hmpd and lost pl over 3f out: rdn whn hmpd again 2f out: no ch after and eased* 7/4[1]

2m 8.74s (-0.96) **Going Correction** -0.05s/f (Good) 10 Ran SP% **119.4**

WFA 3 from 4yo+ 10lb

Speed ratings (Par 105): **101,100,99,99,99 97,97,96,72,69**

CSF £37.06 CT £938.39 TOTE £4.40: £1.70, £2.10, £7.30; EX 39.40 Trifecta £894.90.

Owner Mrs Doreen Tabor **Bred** Lofts Hall Stud **Trained** Newmarket, Suffolk

FOCUS

Add 26yds. A fair handicap, there wasn't much pace on and several of these raced keenly. The winner built on his Ayr success.

4842 KENNET CENTRE NOVICE STKS 1m 2f

7:45 (7:47) (Class 5) 3-Y-O £3,428 (£1,020; £382) Stalls Low

Form RPR

2 1 **Away He Goes (IRE)**[20] 4073 3-9-2 0.......................... SeanLevey 1 91+
(Ismail Mohammed) *mid-div: hdwy over 3f out: travelling wl bhd ldrs but nt clr run fr 2f out tl over 1f out: qcknd up wl fnl 120yds: led cl home* 8/1

2 ½ **Passion And Glory (IRE)** 3-9-2 0.......................... TomQueally 4 90
(Saeed bin Suroor) *trckd ldrs: rdn to ld wl over 2f out: styd on but no ex whn hdd cl home* 11/1

6-25 3 1 **High Commissioner (IRE)**[45] 3152 3-9-2 85.......................... SilvestreDeSousa 11 88
(Paul Cole) *led: rdn and hdd wl over 1f out: kpt on tl no ex clsng stages (jockey said gelding ran green)* 4/1[2]

21 3 dht **Hamish**[24] 3946 3-9-9 0.......................... JamesDoyle 5 95
(William Haggas) *trckd ldr: rdn in cl 3rd 2f out: styd on same pce fnl f* 4/7[1]

61- 5 ½ **Kosciuszko (IRE)**[300] 7257 3-9-9 0.......................... RobertHavlin 2 94
(John Gosden) *mid-div: hdwy over 3f out: rdn in 5th over 2f out: styd on same pce fnl f* 5/1[3]

43 6 9 **Imperium (IRE)**[15] 4234 3-9-2 0.......................... TrevorWhelan 6 69
(Roger Charlton) *mid-div: rdn over 2f out: little imp: wknd fnl f* 33/1

03 7 6 **Ned Pepper (IRE)**[15] 4258 3-9-2 0.......................... TomMarquand 10 57
(Alan King) *towards rr of midfield: rdn and hung lft over 2f out: nvr any imp* 50/1

8 ½ **Cochise** 3-9-2 0.......................... JasonWatson 9 56
(Roger Charlton) *a towards rr* 33/1

0 9 1 **Mini Milk**[25] 3889 3-8-11 0.......................... RichardKingscote 7 49
(Jonathan Portman) *trckd ldrs: rdn over 2f out: sn wknd* 100/1

6 10 8 **Brass (FR)**[90] 1738 3-8-11 0.......................... FergusSweeney 3 33
(Paul Webber) *awkwardly away: a towards rr* 150/1

The Form Book Flat 2019, Raceform Ltd, Newbury, RG14 5SJ

11 11 **Misread** 3-8-11 0 .... LiamKeniry 8 11
(Geoffrey Deacon) *a towards rr* **200/1**

2m 7.89s (-1.81) **Going Correction** -0.05s/f (Good) **11** Ran SP% **129.8**
Speed ratings (Par 100): **105,104,103,103,103 96,91,91,90,83 75**
WIN: 10.90 Away He Goes; PL: 2.20 Away He Goes, 0.70 High Commissioner, 3.00 Passion And Glory, 0.50 Hamish; EX: 109.10; CSF: 95.48; TF: AHG/PAG/H: 136.80, AHG/PAG/HC: 226.20;.
Owner Khalifa Saeed Sulaiman **Bred** Rabbah Bloodstock Limited **Trained** Newmarket, Suffolk
FOCUS
Add 26yds. A strong novice rated around the front-running third.

4843 BOMBAY SAPPHIRE H'CAP — 1m 5f 61y
8:20 (8:20) (Class 5) (0-70,68) 3-Y-O+ **£3,428** (£1,020; £509; £300; £300) **Stalls** Low

Form — RPR

34-0 1 **Highland Sky (IRE)**[51] 2928 4-10-0 **67** ....(h) StevieDonohoe 6 73
(David Simcock) *hld up 5th: hdwy over 3f out: rdn to chal 2f out: led jst over 1f out: styd on: drvn out* **10/1**

-453 2 ½ **Tamachan**[34] 3538 3-9-2 **68** .... JasonWatson 4 73
(Roger Charlton) *sn led: rdn whn chal 2f out: hdd jst over 1f out: styd on: hld towards fin* **11/10**[1]

0-30 3 ¾ **Brooklyn Boy**[38] 3418 3-8-7 **59** .... HollieDoyle 1 63
(Harry Dunlop) *hld up 4th: rdn over 2f out: sn drifted lft: hdwy over 1f out: chsd ldng pair ins fnl f: styd on* **15/2**

0105 4 1½ **Twenty Years On**[21] 4031 3-8-11 **66** ....(p) FinleyMarsh(3) 3 68
(Richard Hughes) *trckd ldr tl rdn 2f out: kpt on same pce fnl f* **3/1**[2]

-040 5 2½ **Taurean Dancer (IRE)**[30] 3700 4-9-9 **62** .... PJMcDonald 5 60
(Roger Teal) *trckd ldrs: rdn 3f out: wknd ent fnl f* **5/1**[3]

2m 55.72s (1.32) **Going Correction** -0.05s/f (Good)
WFA 3 from 4yo 13lb **5** Ran SP% **110.1**
Speed ratings (Par 103): **93,92,92,91,89**
CSF £21.88 TOTE £9.10: £3.30, £1.10; EX 23.20 Trifecta £98.30.
Owner Mrs Fitri Hay **Bred** Healing Music Partnership **Trained** Newmarket, Suffolk
FOCUS
Add 26yds. Bit of a turn up in this with the 3yos denied by the back-to-form top weight. They went just a steady gallop.

4844 DONNINGTON GROVE VETERINARY GROUP H'CAP — 6f
8:50 (8:50) (Class 5) (0-75,75) 3-Y-O+
£3,428 (£1,020; £509; £300; £300; £300) **Stalls** Centre

Form — RPR

-400 1 **Yimou (IRE)**[16] 4227 4-9-5 **68** .... MartinDwyer 9 83+
(Dean Ivory) *mde all: kpt on wl: readily* **9/2**[2]

-400 2 1½ **Across The Sea**[14] 4303 3-9-2 **71** ....(v[1]) PJMcDonald 6 79
(James Tate) *trckd ldrs: wnt 2nd wl over 1f out: sn edgd lft: rdn ent fnl f: kpt on but nt pce to chal* **9/2**[2]

-436 3 2¼ **Three Little Birds**[15] 4230 4-9-5 **68** .... TomMarquand 1 70
(Sylvester Kirk) *hld up in tch: hdwy over 1f out: rdn into 3rd ent fnl f: nt pce to get on terms* **13/2**

1113 4 2 **Spanish Star (IRE)**[12] 4374 4-9-12 **75** .... LiamKeniry 4 70
(Patrick Chamings) *hld up: rdn and hdwy over 1f out: kpt on same pce fnl f* **7/2**[1]

4443 5 hd **Pettochside**[15] 4253 10-9-9 **72** .... HollieDoyle 8 67
(John Bridger) *trckd wnr: rdn 2f out: sn one pce (jockey said gelding hung right-handed)* **10/1**

0113 6 1¾ **Ever Rock (IRE)**[5] 4651 3-8-4 **62** .... MeganNicholls(3) 2 50
(J S Moore) *sn pushed along in last: sme late prog: n.d* **7/1**

2060 7 6 **Wiff Waff**[16] 4227 4-9-3 **66** .... CharlesBishop 3 36
(Chris Gordon) *cl up tl wknd over 1f out* **20/1**

4P-0 8 ¾ **Danecase**[16] 4226 6-9-10 **73** ....(t[1]) SilvestreDeSousa 5 41
(David Dennis) *hld up: effrt over 2f out: nt pce to get on terms: wknd over 1f out* **11/2**[3]

1m 11.66s (-1.54) **Going Correction** -0.05s/f (Good)
WFA 3 from 4yo+ 6lb **8** Ran SP% **113.7**
Speed ratings (Par 103): **108,106,103,100,100 97,89,88**
CSF £24.70 CT £130.78 TOTE £7.20: £1.70, £1.60, £2.10; EX 30.20 Trifecta £157.40.
Owner Andrew L Cohen **Bred** Alexander Bloodstock **Trained** Radlett, Herts
FOCUS
Little got involved with the winner making all. The runner-up has been rated to this year's form.
T/Plt: £256.60 to a £1 stake. Pool: £65,655.17 - 186.76 winning units. T/Qpdt: £135.00 to a £1 stake. Pool: £7,456.94 - 40.85 winning units. **Tim Mitchell**

4387 NEWMARKET (R-H)
Thursday, July 11
OFFICIAL GOING: Good to firm (watered; ovr 8.1; stands' 8.2, ctr 8.0, far 7.9)
Wind: virtually nil Weather: fine, warm

4845 BAHRAIN TROPHY STKS (GROUP 3) — 1m 5f
1:50 (1:51) (Class 1) 3-Y-O
£99,242 (£37,625; £18,830; £9,380; £4,707; £2,362) **Stalls** High

Form — RPR

1-52 1 **Spanish Mission (USA)**[48] 3042 3-9-1 103 .... JamieSpencer 1 113
(David Simcock) *stdd s: hld up in last trio: hdwy into midfield 4f out: rdn to press ldr and edgd rt ent fnl f: led ins fnl f: styd on strly: readily* **13/2**

1653 2 4 **Nayef Road (IRE)**[22] 3984 3-9-1 103 .... SilvestreDeSousa 6 107
(Mark Johnston) *midfield: clsd to go prom in chsng gp 4f out: clsd over 2f out: rdn to ld wl over 1f out: sn edgd rt: edgd lft and hdd ins fnl f: nt match pce of wnr after but kpt on for clr 2nd* **3/1**[2]

3-30 3 3¾ **Nate The Great**[22] 3984 3-9-1 100 .... HollieDoyle 5 101
(Archie Watson) *prom in chsng gp: rdn over 3f out: lost pl: nt clrest of runs and swtchd rt over 1f out: plugged on into 3rd ins fnl f: no ch w ldng pair* **20/1**

2 4 2 **Barbados (IRE)**[22] 3984 3-9-1 103 .... RyanMoore 8 98
(A P O'Brien, Ire) *chsd clr ldr: rdn over 3f out: sn edgd lft but ev ch 2f out: no ex and outpcd over 1f out: wknd ins fnl f* **4/1**[3]

115 5 1¾ **Ranch Hand**[61] 2619 3-9-1 94 .... OisinMurphy 4 95
(Andrew Balding) *midfield: rdn over 3f out: lost pl u.p and impeded over 1f out: no ch w ldrs but plugged on to pass btn rivals ins fnl f* **16/1**

24-5 6 1¼ **Waldstern**[26] 3842 3-9-1 98 .... FrankieDettori 7 94
(John Gosden) *s.i.s: hld up in rr: effrt jst over 2f out: swtchd lft 2f out: racd awkwardly u.p and btn over 1f out: wknd ins fnl f* **11/1**

5-34 7 ¾ **Boerhan**[63] 2553 3-9-1 97 ....(b[1]) JamesDoyle 9 92
(William Haggas) *stdd after s: hld up in last trio: clsd over 3f out: swtchd lft jst over 2f out: no imp u.p and btn over 1f out: wknd ins fnl f* **14/1**

2163 8 shd **Eagles By Day (IRE)**[20] 4049 3-9-1 108 .... DanielTudhope 2 92
(Michael Bell) *prom in chsng gp: clsd over 3f out and sn rdn: unable qck and outpcd whn nt clrest of runs over 1f out: sn btn and wknd ins fnl f: burst blood vessel (trainer could offer no explanation for the colt's performance; vet said colt bled from nose)* **2/1**[1]

3106 9 12 **Severance**[21] 4017 3-9-1 93 ....(h) KerrinMcEvoy 3 74
(Mick Channon) *racd keenly: led and sn wnt clr: c bk to field 3f out: hdd wl over 1f out: sn dropped out: bhd and eased ins fnl f (jockey said colt ran too free)* **20/1**

2m 39.96s (-5.94) **Going Correction** -0.125s/f (Firm) course record **9** Ran SP% **122.1**
Speed ratings (Par 110): **113,110,108,107,105 105,104,104,97**
CSF £27.97 TOTE £9.30: £2.50, £1.30, £5.00; EX 40.50 Trifecta £390.10.
Owner Honorable Earle Mack & Team Valor LLC **Bred** St Elias Stables LLC **Trained** Newmarket, Suffolk
FOCUS
Plenty of good horses have landed this staying event down the years, notably Masked Marvel in 2011 and subsequent top Australian performer Hartnell in 2014. This was a proper test even though they let the leader go around 20l clear at one stage, and it saw a course record time. The winner rates an improver, with the runner-up to form.

4846 TATTERSALLS JULY STKS (GROUP 2) (C&G) — 6f
2:25 (2:25) (Class 1) 2-Y-O
£45,368 (£17,200; £8,608; £4,288; £2,152; £1,080) **Stalls** High

Form — RPR

0 1 **Royal Lytham (FR)**[23] 3949 2-9-0 0 .... WayneLordan 8 107
(A P O'Brien, Ire) *dwlt: hld up wl in tch in last pair: swtchd lft and effrt over 1f out: pressing ldrs and carried lft 1f out: sn chalng and maintained effrt u.p: carried lft towards fin: led last strides: hld on* **11/1**

212 2 shd **Platinum Star (IRE)**[22] 3988 2-9-0 99 .... HarryBentley 3 107
(Saeed bin Suroor) *dwlt: hld up wl in tch in last pair: effrt 2f out: hdwy u.p and str chal jst ins fnl f: battled on wl: wnt 2nd last strides: jst hld* **10/1**[3]

1 3 hd **Visinari (FR)**[33] 3601 2-9-0 0 .... FrankieDettori 1 106
(Mark Johnston) *sn pressing ldr: rdn to ld over 1f out: hrd pressed and drvn jst ins fnl f: battled on wl u.p tl edgd lft: hdd: no ex and lost 2 pls last strides* **4/6**[1]

13 4 2 **Guildsman (FR)**[23] 3949 2-9-0 0 .... OisinMurphy 4 99+
(Archie Watson) *wl in tch in midfield: effrt to chse ldrs and nt clrest of runs over 1f out: kpt on u.p ins fnl f wout threatening ldrs* **7/2**[2]

26 5 1 **King Neptune (USA)**[21] 4012 2-9-0 0 .... RyanMoore 2 96
(A P O'Brien, Ire) *led: rdn 2f out: hdd over 1f out: drvn and outpcd 1f out: wknd ins fnl f* **14/1**

1 6 ½ **Classy Moon (USA)**[30] 3679 2-9-0 0 .... CliffordLee 6 94
(K R Burke) *t.k.h: w ldr early: styd prom: edgd lft u.p and unable qck 1f out: wknd ins fnl f* **11/1**

3211 7 2¼ **Hurstwood**[10] 4441 2-9-0 82 .... DavidAllan 7 87
(Tim Easterby) *chsd ldrs: rdn 2f out: sn struggling and outpcd: wknd ins fnl f* **33/1**

1m 11.16s (-0.94) **Going Correction** -0.125s/f (Firm) **7** Ran SP% **117.6**
Speed ratings (Par 106): **101,100,100,97,96 95,92**
CSF £114.07 TOTE £12.70: £3.70, £3.40; EX 100.10 Trifecta £236.70.
Owner Michael Tabor & Derrick Smith & Mrs John Magnier **Bred** S A R L Haras Du Logis Saint Germain **Trained** Cashel, Co Tipperary
■ Stewards' Enquiry : Frankie Dettori caution: careless riding
FOCUS
This race saw the third and seventh from the Coventry, and the runner-up from the Windsor Castle, taking on impressive first-time-out winner Visinari. There was little to choose between the first three at the line and they have all been rated as improving, but with the fourth below his Coventry level.

4847 BET365 H'CAP — 6f
3:00 (3:01) (Class 2) (0-105,102) 3-Y-O
£62,250 (£18,640; £9,320; £4,660; £2,330; £1,170) **Stalls** High

Form — RPR

01 1 **Pass The Vino (IRE)**[121] 1168 3-8-4 **85** .... DavidEgan 20 94
(Paul D'Arcy) *far side gp: wl in tch: clsd to chse ldrs 2f out: rdn to ld ent fnl f: styd on: jst hld on: 1st of 11 in gp* **25/1**

2211 2 shd **Moss Gill (IRE)**[22] 4008 3-8-3 **84** .... NicolaCurrie 1 92+
(James Bethell) *nr side gp: t.k.h: hld up in rr: effrt 2f out: hdwy over 1f out: edgd lft but drvn and chsd wnr ins fnl f: styd on strly towards fin: jst failed: 1st of 9 in gp* **8/1**[3]

-216 3 1 **Dazzling Dan (IRE)**[26] 3865 3-9-3 **98** .... DavidProbert 14 102
(Pam Sly) *far side gp: chsd ldrs: effrt wl over 1f out: sn drvn and pressing ldrs: unable qck and jst outpcd fnl 100yds: 2nd of 11 in gp* **7/1**[2]

3541 4 ½ **Princess Power (IRE)**[12] 4368 3-8-6 **87** ....(v) PJMcDonald 5 90
(Nigel Tinkler) *nr side gp: hld up in tch in midfield: effrt over 1f out: nt clr run over 1f out: swtchd lft and kpt on wl u.p ins fnl f: 2nd of 9 in gp* **10/1**

6400 5 hd **Barbill (IRE)**[26] 3865 3-9-3 **98** .... JFEgan 19 100
(Mick Channon) *far side gp: towards rr: rdn 3f out: hdwy u.p to chse ldrs 1f out: kpt on ins fnl f: 3rd of 11 in gp* **33/1**

4241 6 hd **Aplomb (IRE)**[24] 3935 3-8-7 **88** .... TomMarquand 8 90+
(William Haggas) *nr side gp: in tch in midfield: effrt 2f out: edgd lft and kpt on u.p ins fnl f: 3rd of 9 in gp* **10/1**

2113 7 nk **Philipine Cobra**[19] 4122 3-8-2 **83** .... JosephineGordon 6 84
(Phil McEntee) *nr side gp: racd keenly: overall ldr tl edgd lft and hdd over 1f out: no ex and wknd wl ins fnl f: 4th of 9 in gp* **25/1**

-044 8 ¾ **Alfie Solomons (IRE)**[19] 4122 3-8-3 **84** ....(t[1]) LukeMorris 13 82
(Richard Spencer) *far side gp: in tch in midfield: effrt 2f out: hrd drvn over 1f out: swtchd rt and kpt on same pce ins fnl f: 4th of 11 in gp* **25/1**

1152 9 shd **Top Breeze (IRE)**[45] 3166 3-8-11 **92** .... ShaneKelly 15 90
(Richard Hughes) *far side gp: gp ldr and w overall ldr: rdn to ld over 1f out: sn hdd: no ex u.p and wknd wl ins fnl f: 5th of 11 in gp* **16/1**

2141 10 nk **Gabrial The Wire**[12] 4360 3-8-7 **91** .... SeanDavis(3) 16 88
(Richard Fahey) *far side gp: towards rr: swtchd lft and hdwy u.p over 1f out: nt clr run and hmpd ins fnl f: swtchd rt and kpt on wl ins fnl f: 6th of 11 in gp* **25/1**

6303 11 ½ **Kinks**[11] 4422 3-8-8 **89** .... AndreaAtzeni 11 84
(Mick Channon) *far side gp: dwlt and squeezed for room leaving stalls: wl in tch in midfield: effrt 2f out: unable qck u.p over 1f out: wknd ins fnl f: 7th of 11 in gp* **14/1**

1632 12 ½ **Magical Wish (IRE)**[5] 4669 3-8-10 **91** .... SilvestreDeSousa 2 85
(Richard Hannon) *nr side gp: chsd ldrs: rdn 2f out: unable qck and outpcd over 1f out: kpt on same pce ins fnl f: 5th of 9 in gp (jockey said colt was never travelling)* **7/2**[1]

0260 **13** *1 ½* **Jack's Point**[12] 4360 3-8-13 **94** .... DanielTudhope 3 83
(William Muir) *nr side gp: in tch in midfield: unable qck u.p over 1f out: wknd ins fnl f: 6th of 9 in gp* **16/1**

2042 **14** *hd* **Woven**[12] 4385 3-8-12 **93** .... JamieSpencer 18 81
(David Simcock) *far side gp: hld up in rr: effrt over 1f out: sme hdwy and swtchd rt 1f out: sn drvn and no imp: 8th of 11 in gp* **16/1**

2200 **15** *½* **Blown By Wind**[12] 4360 3-9-7 **102** .... JamesDoyle 9 89
(Mark Johnston) *nr side gp: restless in stalls: chsd ldrs: rdn 2f out: unable qck and struggling over 1f out: wknd ins fnl f: 7th of 9 in gp (starter reported that the colt was the subject of a third criteria failure; trainer was informed that the colt could not run until the day after passing a stalls test)* **16/1**

3-35 **16** *1 ¼* **Almufti**[68] 2412 3-8-11 **92** .... OisinMurphy 4 75
(Hugo Palmer) *nr side gp: hld up in tch: nt clr run 2f out: swtchd lft and effrt over 1f out: no prog: wknd ins fnl f: 8th of 9 in gp* **20/1**

-102 **17** *1* **Street Parade**[19] 4122 3-9-6 **101** ....(t) KerrinMcEvoy 17 81
(Stuart Williams) *far side gp: hld up towards rr: effrt over 1f out: no prog: wknd ins fnl f: 9th of 11 in gp* **25/1**

1616 **18** *5* **Benny And The Jets (IRE)**[11] 4420 3-8-2 **83** .... NickyMackay 7 47
(Sylvester Kirk) *nr side gp: chsd ldrs: rdn 2f out: losing pl whn squeezed for room over 1f out: wknd ins fnl f: 9th of 9 in gp* **33/1**

-110 **19** *6* **Rathbone**[26] 3865 3-8-13 **94** .... TomEaves 10 38
(Kevin Ryan) *far side gp: in tch in midfield: rdn 2f out: sn btn and bhd ins fnl f: 10th of 11 in gp* **12/1**

1136 **20** *8* **Look Out Louis**[22] 4008 3-8-4 **85** .... DuranFentiman 12 4
(Tim Easterby) *far side gp: chsd ldrs tl over 2f out: sn rdn and losing pl: wl bhd ins fnl f: 11th of 11 in gp (vet said gelding had mild colic)* **33/1**

1m 10.0s (-2.10) **Going Correction** -0.125s/f (Firm) **20** Ran SP% **134.7**
Speed ratings (Par 106): **109,108,107,106,106 106,105,104,104,104 103,103,101,100,100 98,97,90,82,71**
CSF £208.98 CT £1621.41 TOTE £22.00: £4.10, £2.50, £2.30, £3.30; EX 409.70 Trifecta £4574.10.
Owner Rowley Racing **Bred** Dr D Harron **Trained** Newmarket, Suffolk

FOCUS
They raced in two groups initially before merging around halfway. The first two finished wide apart and the time was 1.16sec faster than the July Stakes. This has been rated close to standard and the winner was a surprise improver.

4848 PRINCESS OF WALES'S TATTERSALLS STKS (GROUP 2) 1m 4f
3:35 (3:35) (Class 1) 3-Y-O+

£56,710 (£21,500; £10,760; £5,360; £2,690; £1,350) **Stalls** High

Form RPR

0140 **1** **Communique (IRE)**[19] 4093 4-9-9 114 .... SilvestreDeSousa 1 117
(Mark Johnston) *trckd ldr tl clsd to press ldr 4f out: led over 2f out and sn rdn: styd on wl ins fnl f and in command ins fnl f* **11/1**

0-13 **2** *1 ¾* **Mirage Dancer**[19] 4093 5-9-6 116 .... RyanMoore 3 111
(Sir Michael Stoute) *t.k.h: wl in tch in midfield: nt clr run 2f out tl rdn to chse wnr ent fnl f: kpt on same pce and a hld after* **10/3**[2]

-300 **3** *½* **Desert Encounter (IRE)**[22] 3985 7-9-6 116 ....(h) HarryBentley 5 110
(David Simcock) *t.k.h: hld up in tch in last pair: nt clr run over 2f out: swtchd lft and hdwy over 1f out: 3rd and kpt on same pce ins fnl f* **25/1**

-231 **4** *½* **Dashing Willoughby**[22] 3984 3-8-11 104 .... OisinMurphy 2 113
(Andrew Balding) *led and set stdy gallop: hdd and rdn over 2f out: unable qck u.p: edgd lft and kpt on same pce ins fnl f* **10/1**

-311 **5** *2* **Baghdad (FR)**[20] 4053 4-9-6 109 .... AndreaAtzeni 4 106
(Mark Johnston) *hld up in tch in last pair: effrt ent fnl 3f: unable qck and no imp over 1f out: wl hld and one pce ins fnl f* **11/2**[3]

31-5 **6** *¾* **Masar (IRE)**[19] 4093 4-9-6 119 .... JamesDoyle 6 105
(Charlie Appleby) *t.k.h early: trckd ldrs: effrt ent fnl 2f: unable qck over 1f out and btn 1f out: wknd ins fnl f (jockey said colt ran too free)* **5/6**[1]

2m 28.63s (-5.27) **Going Correction** -0.125s/f (Firm)
WFA 3 from 4yo+ 12lb **6** Ran SP% **114.3**
Speed ratings (Par 115): **112,110,110,110,108 108**
CSF £48.11 TOTE £11.10: £4.10, £1.70; EX 40.50 Trifecta £363.80.
Owner Sheikh Hamdan bin Mohammed Al Maktoum **Bred** Godolphin **Trained** Middleham Moor, N Yorks

FOCUS
This was run at a steady early pace and it was an advantage to be handy. The winner was well positioned to capitalise, and he lowered the course record by 0.74sec. Muddling form.

4849 BRITISH STALLION STUDS EBF MAIDEN FILLIES' STKS (PLUS 10 RACE) 6f
4:05 (4:06) (Class 2) 2-Y-O **£12,938** (£3,850; £1,924; £962) **Stalls** High

Form RPR

46 **1** **Miss Lucy (IRE)**[24] 3927 2-9-0 0 .... CliffordLee 4 81
(K R Burke) *restless in stalls: hld up in tch in midfield: effrt over 1f out: hdwy to chse ldr ent fnl f: edgd lft but styd on wl to ld 50yds out* **20/1**

42 **2** *¾* **Daily Times**[15] 4245 2-9-0 0 .... FrankieDettori 7 79
(John Gosden) *led: rdn over 1f out: drvn 1f out: hdd 50yds out: no ex towards fin* **7/2**[2]

3 *½* **East Of Eden (IRE)** 2-9-0 0 .... RyanMoore 5 77+
(Hugo Palmer) *t.k.h: hld up wl in tch in midfield: clsd to chse ldrs 1/2-way: rdn to press ldrs 1f out: n.m.r and one pce towards fin* **8/1**[3]

4 *2 ¼* **Dubai Paradise (IRE)** 2-9-0 0 .... JamesDoyle 9 70
(Charlie Appleby) *chsd ldrs: effrt over 1f out: unable qck 1f out: wknd ins fnl f* **10/11**[1]

46 **5** *hd* **Falconidae (IRE)**[54] 2836 2-9-0 0 .... TomMarquand 3 70?
(Richard Hannon) *chsd ldr: rdn over 1f out: unable qck and lost 2nd ent fnl f: wknd ins fnl f* **16/1**

6 *1 ¾* **Led Astray** 2-9-0 0 .... DanielTudhope 1 64+
(Michael Bell) *dwlt: rn green in rr: swtchd rt over 2f out: effrt over 1f out: kpt on ins fnl f: nvr threatened ldrs* **8/1**[3]

7 *¾* **Fast And Free** 2-9-0 0 .... KerrinMcEvoy 8 62
(William Haggas) *in tch in midfield: struggling to hold pl 1/2-way: rdn and no imp over 1f out: wl hld and one pce ins fnl f* **12/1**

8 *1 ½* **Farewell Kiss (IRE)** 2-9-0 0 .... JamieSpencer 6 57
(Michael Bell) *stdd after s: hld up in tch in last trio: effrt over 1f out: sn outpcd and wknd ins fnl f* **20/1**

9 *½* **Sea Willow** 2-9-0 0 .... JFEgan 10 55
(Henry Spiller) *in tch in last trio: effrt wl over 1f out: sn struggling and outpcd: wknd ins fnl f* **66/1**

1m 12.28s (0.18) **Going Correction** -0.125s/f (Firm) **9** Ran SP% **121.4**
Speed ratings (Par 97): **93,92,91,88,88 85,84,82,82**
CSF £91.90 TOTE £23.60: £4.20, £1.40, £2.30; EX 154.20 Trifecta £1126.80.
Owner Nick Bradley 28, A O'Callaghan & Burke **Bred** Iadora Farm & Tally-Ho Stud **Trained** Middleham Moor, N Yorks

FOCUS
Lumiere, in one of the divisions in 2015, is the last horse to have won another race after landing this. The winner rates a surprise improver, with the runner-up to her latest form.

4850 EDMONDSON HALL SOLICITORS SIR HENRY CECIL STKS (LISTED RACE) 1m
4:40 (4:40) (Class 1) 3-Y-O

£28,355 (£10,750; £5,380; £2,680; £1,345; £675) **Stalls** High

Form RPR

3505 **1** **Duke Of Hazzard (FR)**[19] 4092 3-9-3 105 ....(b[1]) PJMcDonald 5 113
(Paul Cole) *broke wl: sn restrained and t.k.h in midfield: chsng ldrs whn nt clr run and swtchd lft over 1f out: rdn and qcknd to ld ins fnl f: sn clr and r.o strly* **10/1**

-206 **2** *2 ½* **Momkin (IRE)**[19] 4092 3-9-3 108 ....(b) AndreaAtzeni 1 107
(Roger Charlton) *trckd ldrs: effrt 2f out: ev ch and drvn ent fnl f: jst getting outpcd whn hung lft u.p ins fnl f: kpt on same pce after: wnt 2nd nr fin* **7/2**[3]

3024 **3** *½* **Urban Icon**[19] 4092 3-9-3 108 .... TomMarquand 4 106
(Richard Hannon) *sn trcking ldr: effrt 2f out: drvn to ld ent fnl f: hdd and nt match pce of wnr ins fnl f: kpt on same pce and lost 2nd nr fin* **3/1**[2]

0352 **4** *1 ¾* **Turgenev**[21] 4016 3-9-3 108 .... FrankieDettori 3 104
(John Gosden) *sn led: rdn over 1f out: sn hdd: struggling and outpcd whn squeezed for room ins fnl f: sn wknd* **11/8**[1]

-110 **5** *hd* **Motafaawit (IRE)**[21] 4016 3-9-3 103 .... JimCrowley 6 101
(Richard Hannon) *hld up wl in tch: effrt 2f out: drvn and clsd to chse ldrs over 1f out: no ex 1f out: wknd ins fnl f* **10/1**

1-60 **6** *1 ¼* **Bell Rock**[23] 3951 3-9-3 98 .... GeraldMosse 2 98
(Andrew Balding) *hld up wl in tch in rr: effrt 2f out: no imp whn hung lft over 1f out: wl hld and kpt on same pce ins fnl f* **12/1**

1m 36.98s (-3.02) **Going Correction** -0.125s/f (Firm) **6** Ran SP% **115.2**
Speed ratings (Par 108): **110,107,107,105,105 103**
CSF £45.73 TOTE £8.90: £3.20, £2.10; EX 55.50 Trifecta £112.40.
Owner Mrs Fitri Hay **Bred** Runnymede Farm Inc & Catesby W Clay **Trained** Whatcombe, Oxon

FOCUS
A decent field for the level and this rates a surprising pb from the winner.

4851 JOHN DEERE & BEN BURGESS H'CAP 1m
5:10 (5:12) (Class 3) (0-90,92) 3-Y-O+ **£12,938** (£3,850; £1,924; £962) **Stalls** High

Form RPR

0-12 **1** **Wings Of Time**[19] 4120 3-9-5 **90** .... JamesDoyle 1 100+
(Charlie Appleby) *racd in centre to nr side thrght: prom: ev ch and drifted to stands' rail over 1f out: styd on wl u.p to ld nr fin* **6/1**

00-2 **2** *nk* **Nkosikazi**[19] 4113 4-9-6 **85** .... DanielTudhope 7 96
(William Haggas) *led: pressed 3f out: rdn 2f out: drvn and kpt on wl ins fnl f: hdd nr fin* **17/2**

-032 **3** *3* **Ulshaw Bridge (IRE)**[19] 4127 4-9-13 **89** ....(p) PJMcDonald 11 93
(James Bethell) *hld up in tch in last trio: hdwy over 2f out: drvn over 1f out: kpt on ins fnl f: wnt 3rd towards fin: no threat to ldng pair* **10/1**

-231 **4** *½* **Moqtarreb**[19] 4121 3-9-7 **92** .... JimCrowley 10 93
(Roger Varian) *hld up wl in tch in midfield: effrt and clsd 2f out: drvn and pressing ldrs over 1f out: no ex and wknd ins fnl f: lost 3rd towards fin (trainer said colt was unsuited by the good to firm ground and would prefer a slower surface)* **15/8**[1]

-145 **5** *hd* **Enigmatic (IRE)**[21] 4020 5-9-8 **89** .... DarraghKeenan[(5)] 9 91
(Alan Bailey) *chsd ldrs: rdn wl over 2f out: drvn and unable qck over 1f out: kpt on same pce ins fnl f* **20/1**

-500 **6** *1 ¼* **Mordred (IRE)**[21] 4016 3-9-3 **88** .... RyanMoore 3 86
(Richard Hannon) *bmpd s: in tch in midfield: effrt over 2f out: unable qck over 1f out: wl hld and kpt on same pce ins fnl f* **16/1**

3116 **7** *1 ¾* **Artistic Rifles (IRE)**[26] 3858 3-9-2 **87** .... SilvestreDeSousa 5 81
(Charles Hills) *wnt rt leaving stalls: sn chsng ldr: rdn and clsd to press ldr 3f out: unable qck and outpcd over 1f out: wknd ins fnl f* **9/2**[2]

2-12 **8** *3 ¾* **Balgair**[14] 4300 5-9-10 **86** ....(h) AndreaAtzeni 2 73
(Tom Clover) *stdd and bmpd s: t.k.h: hld up in tch in midfield: swtchd to r bhd wnr 5f out: hung lft to rejoin main gp and in rr over 1f out: wl btn after (jockey said gelding hung left-handed under pressure)* **11/2**[3]

1333 **9** *½* **Martineo**[19] 4123 4-9-5 **81** .... JamieSpencer 4 67
(John Butler) *stdd s: hld up in tch in last trio: swtchd rt 2f out: no hdwy over 1f out: wl btn fnl f* **16/1**

0-35 **10** *¾* **Leader Writer (FR)**[28] 3763 7-9-7 **83** ....(p) TomMarquand 6 67
(David Elsworth) *s.i.s: hld up in rr: effrt 2f out: sn struggling and no hdwy over 1f out: bhd ins fnl f* **22/1**

1m 37.03s (-2.97) **Going Correction** -0.125s/f (Firm)
WFA 3 from 4yo+ 9lb **10** Ran SP% **123.1**
Speed ratings (Par 107): **109,108,105,105,105 103,102,98,97,97**
CSF £59.47 CT £525.46 TOTE £5.00: £2.10, £2.80, £3.00; EX 53.90 Trifecta £771.10.
Owner Godolphin **Bred** Godolphin **Trained** Newmarket, Suffolk

FOCUS
A decent handicap in which plenty of the field came into it off a good performance. Unfortunately, the first two were separated by almost the width of the track, making reading the form tricky. The first two have been rated as improving, with the third close to his latest.
T/Jkpt: Not Won. T/Plt: £1,457.40 to a £1 stake. Pool: £156,351.35 - 78.31 winning units. T/Qpdt: £49.80 to a £1 stake. Pool: £18,552.98 - 275.22 winning units. **Steve Payne**

4852 - 4855a (Foreign Racing) - See Raceform Interactive

4040 LEOPARDSTOWN (L-H)
Thursday, July 11

OFFICIAL GOING: Good to firm (good in places; watered)

4856a IRISH STALLION FARMS EBF STANERRA STKS (GROUP 3) (F&M) 1m 6f
7:55 (7:55) 3-Y-O+

£39,864 (£12,837; £6,081; £2,702; £1,351; £675)

RPR

1 **Peach Tree (IRE)**[21] 4014 3-8-9 100 .... WayneLordan 8 100
(A P O'Brien, Ire) *trckd early ldr in 2nd: sn chsd ldrs in 3rd: wnt 2nd under 2f out: rdn to ld narrowly ins fnl f: kpt on wl clsng stages (trainer said, regarding apparent improvement in form, filly appeared to appreciate a drop back in class from Group 2 to Group 3)* **7/1**

2 *½* **Moteo (IRE)**[27] 3820 4-9-9 96 .... RonanWhelan 2 98+
(John M Oxx, Ire) *hld up in 6th: clsr on outer to chse ldrs in 3rd ent fnl f: kpt on wl into 2nd clsng stages: nt rch wnr* **10/1**

3 1 **Cimeara (IRE)**[13] 4351 4-9-9 101................ DonnachaO'Brien 1 97
(Joseph Patrick O'Brien, Ire) *led for 4f: trckd ldr in 2nd: bk on terms over 3f out and led 2f out: hdd ins fnl f: no ex in 3rd fnl 50yds* **6/1**[2]

4 hd **South Sea Pearl (IRE)**[8] 4531 3-8-9 92................ SeamieHeffernan 3 97
(A P O'Brien, Ire) *chsd ldrs in 4th: pushed along over 2f out: kpt on wl ins fnl f whn short of room fnl 75yds: styd on wl again cl home (jockey said filly was short of room closing stages)* **13/2**[3]

5 2 **Simply Beautiful (IRE)**[15] 4265 3-8-9 78................ KillianHennessy 5 95
(A P O'Brien, Ire) *racd in rr: pushed along over 2f out: prog towards inner over 1f out in 5th: no imp fnl 100yds: kpt on same pce* **20/1**

6 9 **Flowering Peach (IRE)**[15] 4263 3-8-9 84................ MichaelHussey 4 82
(A P O'Brien, Ire) *hld up in 5th: pushed along over 2f out and sn dropped to rr: no imp over 1f out* **25/1**

7 12 **True Self (IRE)**[33] 3586 6-9-9 108................ ColinKeane 7 64
(W P Mullins, Ire) *trckd ldrs in 3rd on outer tl led after 4f: hdd 2f out and wknd qckly over 1f out: sn eased* **8/11**[1]

3m 2.08s (-1.12) **Going Correction** +0.075s/f (Good)
WFA 3 from 4yo+ 14lb 7 Ran SP% **115.7**
Speed ratings: **106,105,105,105,103 98,91**
CSF £72.88 TOTE £8.20: £2.90, £3.40; DF 57.20 Trifecta £206.80.
Owner Michael Tabor & Derrick Smith & Mrs John Magnier **Bred** Pikaboo Syndicate **Trained** Cashel, Co Tipperary

FOCUS
A competitive contest, the winner looked capable of winning such a race.

4857 - 4858a (Foreign Racing) - See Raceform Interactive

4581
LONGCHAMP (R-H)
Thursday, July 11

OFFICIAL GOING: Turf: good

4859a PRIX DE LA DAME BLANCHE (H'CAP) (4YO+ FILLIES & MARES) (MOYENNE COURSE: 2ND POST) (TURF) 1m 3f 55y
4:15 4-Y-O+ £11,711 (£4,684; £3,513; £2,342; £1,171)

RPR
1 **Elara**[31] 5-9-1 0................ MlleAlisonMassin(3) 12 82
(S Wattel, France) **77/10**

2 2½ **Zawadi (GER)**[237] 6-8-6 0................ MlleCoraliePacaut(3) 7 68
(Frau V Henkenjohann, Germany) **9/1**

3 1¼ **Sissi Doloise (FR)**[31] 5-8-7 0................(b) StephanePasquier 13 64
(A Bonin, France) **33/10**[1]

4 snk **Kailyn (GER)**[44] 6-9-6 0................(p) MaximeGuyon 11 76
(M Krebs, France) **16/1**

5 ¾ **Rebecamille (FR)**[17] 6-8-7 0................(p) AnthonyCrastus 10 62
(Mme A Rosa, France) **13/1**

6 ½ **Sans Regret (FR)**[31] 4-9-2 0................ MorganDelalande 8 70
(S Wattel, France) **22/1**

7 snk **Winfola (FR)**[60] 5-9-8 0................(p) GuillaumeGuedj-Gay(6) 4 82
(X Thomas-Demeaulte, France) **56/10**[2]

8 nk **Merci Capucine**[31] 4-9-2 0................ ThomasTrullier(3) 14 72
(S Wattel, France) **14/1**

9 6½ **Rosamunde (FR)**[14] 5-8-2 0................ MlleLeaBails(6) 5 50
(Mme N Verheyen, Belgium) **15/1**

10 4½ **Soala (IRE)**[31] 4-9-3 0................ RonanThomas 9 51
(J E Hammond, France) **20/1**

11 nk **Donna Leon (FR)**[413] 4-9-2 0................ EddyHardouin 6 49
(Werner Glanz, Germany) **40/1**

12 nk **Luminosa (FR)**[11] 4-9-0 0................(b) CristianDemuro 3 47
(D Smaga, France) **13/2**[3]

13 11 **Chiavari (IRE)**[74] 2160 5-9-4 0................ AlexisBadel 2 31
(Alexandra Dunn) *wl into stride: led: urged along over 2f out: rdn and hdd over 1f out: wknd qckly and eased* **38/1**

14 1 **Midgrey (IRE)**[31] 4-9-7 0................(p) MickaelBarzalona 1 32
(F-X Belvisi, France) **14/1**

PARI-MUTUEL (all including 1 euro stake): WIN 8.70; PLACE 2.50, 2.80, 1.70; DF 26.70.
Owner Capt A Pratt **Bred** Rabbah Bloodstock Limited **Trained** France

4860a PRIX DE L'ODEON (CLAIMER) (4YO+) (MOYENNE COURSE) (TURF) 1m
6:35 4-Y-O+ £8,558 (£3,423; £2,567; £1,711; £855)

RPR
1 **Song Of Life**[20] 4090 5-8-7 0................ MlleLeaBails(9) 3 85
(Andrea Marcialis, France) **27/10**[2]

2 2½ **Ascot Angel (FR)**[73] 2226 5-9-5 0................(p) MickaelBarzalona 2 82
(X Thomas-Demeaulte, France) **17/10**[1]

3 ½ **Rogue**[20] 4090 4-9-1 0................ MlleCoraliePacaut(3) 7 80
(Alexandra Dunn) *led: shkn up over 2f out: rdn and hdd over 1f out: kpt on same pce fnl f* **67/10**

4 2 **Shutterbug (FR)**[20] 4090 7-8-13 0................(p) JeremieMonteiro(5) 8 75
(W Mongil, Germany) **84/10**

5 1½ **Waleed (FR)**[43] 5-8-13 0................ MathieuPelletan(5) 1 72
(M Delcher Sanchez, France) **5/1**[3]

6 ½ **Unguja (FR)**[28] 4-8-11 0................ JeromeClaudic 4 64
(E Lyon, France) **30/1**

7 3½ **Kinetic Cross**[371] 5-8-9 0................ GuillaumeGuedj-Gay(6) 6 60
(Werner Glanz, Germany) **25/1**

8 2 **Alberobello (FR)**[56] 6-8-4 0................ Joseph-MathieuMighty(7) 5 51
(M Delcher Sanchez, France) **16/1**

9 dist **Blue Mariposa (FR)**[376] 4-8-8 0................ FabienLefebvre 9
(Mme E Siavy-Julien, France) **56/1**

1m 40.09s (1.69) 9 Ran SP% **119.1**
PARI-MUTUEL (all including 1 euro stake): WIN 3.70; PLACE 1.30, 1.20, 1.70; DF 4.90.
Owner Mme Eleonora Marcialis **Bred** Genesis Green Stud **Trained** France

4091
ASCOT (R-H)
Friday, July 12

OFFICIAL GOING: Good to firm (good in places on round course; watered; rnd 7.2, str 8.4)
Wind: Light, against Weather: Fine, warm

4861 KNIGHTS NURSERY H'CAP 6f
2:15 (2:15) (Class 3) (0-90,88) 2-Y-O **£7,762** (£2,310; £1,154; £577) **Stalls** High

Form RPR
031 1 **Eton College (IRE)**[24] 3962 2-9-1 **82**................ AdamKirby 6 86
(Mark Johnston) *mde all: pushed along 2f out: rdn to assert 1f out: drvn out whn pressed nr fin* **5/4**[1]

0355 2 ½ **Return To Senders (IRE)**[28] 3812 2-8-7 **74**................(b[1]) NicolaCurrie 3 76
(Jamie Osborne) *rousted early then t.k.h in last: prog on outer over 2f out: rdn wl over 1f out: chsd wnr ins fnl f and tried to chal: nt qckn nr fin* **8/1**

312 3 1¾ **Faldetta**[17] 4214 2-8-9 **76**................ CharlesBishop 4 72
(Eve Johnson Houghton) *trckd ldrs against rail: shkn up 2f out: nvr gng pce to threaten but kpt on fnl f* **8/1**

0341 4 ¾ **Twice As Likely**[17] 4222 2-8-4 **71**................ MartinDwyer 2 65
(Richard Hughes) *pressed wnr: shkn up over 2f out: stl chalng over 1f out: lost 2nd and fdd ins fnl f* **5/1**[3]

310 5 ½ **Kemble (IRE)**[21] 4048 2-9-7 **88**................ SeanLevey 5 80
(Richard Hannon) *tk v t.k.h early: hld up in tch: effrt 2f out: nt qckn over 1f out and no prog after* **9/4**[2]

1m 15.5s (1.80) **Going Correction** +0.10s/f (Good) 5 Ran SP% **114.1**
Speed ratings (Par 98): **92,91,89,88,87**
CSF £12.18 TOTE £2.10: £1.40, £2.80; EX 11.90 Trifecta £53.70.
Owner Sheikh Hamdan bin Mohammed Al Maktoum **Bred** Godolphin **Trained** Middleham Moor, N Yorks

FOCUS
A decent nursery. The favourite successfully dictated his own tempo up the stands' rail and his winning time was around three seconds outside of standard. The winner's Brighton win could be rated almost as high as this.

4862 SIGNATURE CAPITAL H'CAP 1m 7f 209y
2:50 (2:50) (Class 4) (0-85,84) 3-Y-O **£6,727** (£2,002; £1,000; £500; £300) **Stalls** Low

Form RPR
6211 1 **Champagne Marengo (IRE)**[7] 4594 3-7-11 **65** 6ex(p) ThoreHammerHansen(5) 1 75
(Ian Williams) *hld up in last: pushed along briefly 1/2-way: shkn up and prog on outer over 2f out: rdn to ld over 1f out: styd on wl and sn clr* **9/2**[3]

3223 2 5 **Luck Of Clover**[11] 4459 3-8-2 **65**................ MartinDwyer 4 69
(Andrew Balding) *trckd ldr: led wl over 2f out and sent for home: hdd over 1f out: sn outpcd* **9/1**

412 3 2¼ **Grenadier Guard (IRE)**[19] 4143 3-9-6 **83**................ AdamKirby 2 84
(Mark Johnston) *dropped to 4th pl after 5th and nvr looked to be gng wl after: urged along over 4f out: drvn into 3rd over 1f out but sn outpcd (trainer could offer no explanation for the colt's performance)* **1/1**[1]

1-15 4 2¼ **Brasca**[21] 4063 3-9-7 **84**................ HarryBentley 5 83
(Ralph Beckett) *in tch: trckd ldng pair after 5f: rdn over 2f out: cl enough but nt qckn over 1f out: fdd* **3/1**[2]

4305 5 2¼ **Arthur Pendragon (IRE)**[14] 4327 3-8-13 **76**................(b[1]) JasonWatson 3 72
(Brian Meehan) *sn led and set brisk pce early: rdn and hdd wl over 2f out: wknd over 1f out* **14/1**

3m 30.53s (-2.77) **Going Correction** +0.10s/f (Good) 5 Ran SP% **109.8**
Speed ratings (Par 102): **110,107,106,105,104**
CSF £38.04 TOTE £4.00: £1.80, £2.40; EX 28.50 Trifecta £45.60.
Owner Champagne Charlies Club **Bred** Helen Lyons **Trained** Portway, Worcs

FOCUS
20 yards added. A decent 3yo staying handicap and there is no denying the third-favourite's superiority over this 2m trip. The second has been rated to form.

4863 CLOSE BROTHERS PROPERTY FINANCE H'CAP 1m 1f 212y
3:25 (3:25) (Class 3) (0-95,94) 3-Y-O+ **£9,703** (£2,887; £1,443; £721) **Stalls** Low

Form RPR
6-15 1 **Duckett's Grove (USA)**[49] 3042 3-9-2 **92**................ HectorCrouch 6 105
(Ed Walker) *mde all: set mod pce tl stretched on over 2f out: drvn clr over 1f out: in n.d after* **11/4**[2]

34-0 2 4½ **Wafy (IRE)**[90] 1753 4-9-10 **90**................ DaneO'Neill 2 94
(Charles Hills) *chsd ldng pair: shkn up over 2f out: nvr any ch w wnr but kpt on to take 2nd ins fnl f* **12/1**

2211 3 nk **American Graffiti (FR)**[21] 4068 3-9-4 **94**................ BrettDoyle 4 97
(Charlie Appleby) *chsd wnr: pushed along over 3f out: no rspnse whn wnr upped the pce over 2f out: lost 2nd ins fnl f* **6/4**[1]

15-0 4 1½ **Breath Caught**[41] 3346 4-9-13 **93**................ JasonWatson 5 93
(David Simcock) *hld up in last: rdn and effrt on outer over 2f out: one pce and nvr able to threaten* **6/1**

1650 5 1½ **Hortzadar**[20] 4097 4-9-13 **93**................ HarryBentley 3 90
(David O'Meara) *hld up in 4th: pushed along over 3f out: no prog 2f out: fdd* **11/2**[3]

-1P0 6 1¾ **He's Amazing (IRE)**[28] 3806 4-9-4 **84**................ LiamKeniry 7 78
(Ed Walker) *hld up in 5th: shkn up 3f out: no prog 2f out: wknd (jockey said gelding was never travelling)* **12/1**

2m 7.5s (-0.20) **Going Correction** +0.10s/f (Good)
WFA 3 from 4yo+ 10lb 6 Ran SP% **111.7**
Speed ratings (Par 107): **104,100,100,98,97 96**
CSF £32.27 CT £63.76 TOTE £3.70: £2.10, £4.50; EX 37.30 Trifecta £71.80.
Owner P K Siu **Bred** Silver Springs Stud, Llc **Trained** Upper Lambourn, Berks

FOCUS
17 yards added. A fairly good handicap. The second-favourite dominated from start to finish under an excellent front-running ride from Hector Crouch. It's been rated at face value, with the second to form.

4864 ALVARIUM BRITISH EBF FILLIES' H'CAP 1m 3f 211y
4:00 (4:03) (Class 3) (0-95,94) 3-Y-O+ **£12,938** (£3,850; £1,924; £962) **Stalls** Low

Form RPR
-111 1 **Bella Vita**[31] 3698 3-8-9 **87**................ CharlesBishop 3 97+
(Eve Johnson Houghton) *hld up: pushed along over 3f out: rdn and clsd qckly fr 2f out to ld over 1f out: hung lft fnl f but styd on wl* **5/2**[1]

3214 2 1½ **Birch Grove (IRE)**[13] 4390 4-8-10 **76**................ HarryBentley 5 84
(David Simcock) *hld up: rdn over 2f out: prog over 1f out: chsd wnr fnl f: styd on but readily hld* **7/2**[2]

2012 **3** 1 1/4 **Sneaky Peek**[21] 4064 3-8-2 **80** .... MartinDwyer 1 86
(Andrew Balding) *trckd ldng pair: rdn and nt qckn 2f out: sn lost pl: kpt on to take 3rd again nr fin* **7/2**[2]

1-10 **4** 1/2 **Hameem**[19] 4145 4-10-0 **94** .... DaneO'Neill 2 99
(John Gosden) *trckd ldr: rdn over 2f out: lost 2nd over 1f out: one pce fnl f* **7/1**

-444 **5** 2 1/4 **White Chocolate (IRE)**[23] 3995 5-9-6 **86** ....(p[1]) AdamKirby 7 87
(David Simcock) *hld up in last: rdn and no prog over 2f out: sn detached and no ch after* **7/1**

3661 **6** hd **Cape Islay (FR)**[13] 4362 3-8-8 **86** .... JasonWatson 6 87
(Mark Johnston) *led: rdn over 2f out: hdd over 1f out: wknd qckly fnl f* **9/2**[3]

2m 32.43s (-0.17) **Going Correction** +0.10s/f (Good) **6 Ran SP% 116.2**
WFA 3 from 4yo+ 12lb
Speed ratings (Par 104): **104,103,102,101,100 100**
CSF £12.06 TOTE £2.80: £1.80, £2.40; EX 12.30 Trifecta £39.50.
Owner Mrs Heather Raw **Bred** Shoreham Stud **Trained** Blewbury, Oxon
■ Dono di Dio was withdrawn. Price at time of withdrawal 12-1. Rule 4 \n\x\x applies to board prices prior to withdrawal, but not to SP bets. Deduction 5p in the pound. New market forme

FOCUS
17 yards added. The feature contest was a good middle-distance fillies' handicap. The favourite picked up strongly to complete a four-timer in the home straight. The fourth has been rated in line with her reappearance win.

4865 SAVILLS H'CAP 7f 213y(R)
4:35 (4:37) (Class 3) (0-90,91) 3-Y-O **£9,703** (£2,887; £1,443; £721) **Stalls Low**

Form RPR

3-21 **1** **Red Armada (IRE)**[18] 4178 3-9-4 **85** ....(p) AdamKirby 4 93
(Clive Cox) *hld up in midfield: rdn and prog to chse ldr over 1f out and sn chalng: narrow ld ins fnl f: edgd lft and drvn out* **11/4**[1]

3-13 **2** hd **Muraad (IRE)**[50] 3003 3-9-7 **88** .... DaneO'Neill 1 95
(Owen Burrows) *mde most: rdn 2f out: narrowly hdd ins fnl f: kpt on wl but jst hld* **6/1**

251 **3** 1 1/4 **Prince Of Harts**[15] 4306 3-9-2 **83** .... DanielMuscutt 6 87
(Rod Millman) *hld up in last pair: rdn and prog jst over 2f out: kpt on u.p fnl f to win battle for 3rd* **8/1**

2-63 **4** shd **Baryshnikov**[18] 4188 3-8-10 **77** .... LiamKeniry 3 81
(Ed Walker) *sn pressed ldr: shkn up over 2f out: lost 2nd over 1f out: kpt on same pce* **9/1**

4222 **5** hd **Ginger Fox**[7] 4607 3-8-11 **78** ....(v[1]) JasonWatson 5 81
(Ian Williams) *hld up in tch: shkn up over 2f out and briefly nt clr run sn after: kpt on to press for a pl ins fnl f but nvr able to chal* **9/2**[3]

41-1 **6** shd **Pesto**[27] 3858 3-9-10 **91** .... SeanLevey 2 94
(Richard Hannon) *hld up in last pair: rdn over 2f out: styd on over 1f out to press for a pl nr fin: nvr nrr* **3/1**[2]

51-3 **7** 10 **Elamirr (IRE)**[14] 4329 3-9-0 **81** .... CharlesBishop 8 61
(Roger Varian) *t.k.h: pressed ldrs on outer: shkn up over 2f out: sn lost pl and btn* **14/1**

4-10 **8** 8 **Lady Madison (IRE)**[21] 4052 3-9-10 **91** .... ShaneKelly 7 53
(Richard Hughes) *broke wl: t.k.h and sn restrained into rr: shkn up and no prog over 2f out: wknd over 1f out: eased* **20/1**

1m 40.89s (0.29) **Going Correction** +0.10s/f (Good) **8 Ran SP% 116.7**
Speed ratings (Par 104): **102,101,100,100,100 100,90,82**
CSF £20.20 CT £119.46 TOTE £3.50: £1.60, £2.00, £2.30; EX 20.20 Trifecta £111.00.
Owner China Horse Club International Limited **Bred** Castle Paddock Bloodstock Ltd **Trained** Lambourn, Berks

FOCUS
11 yards added. A decent 3yo handicap with a busy finish, but the favourite narrowly fended off an equally resolute runner-up in one of the better comparative times. The third helps set the level, while the fourth has been rated to his best.

4866 LONG HARBOUR DEREK LUCIE-SMITH MEMORIAL H'CAP 6f
5:10 (5:13) (Class 3) (0-95,96) 3-Y-O+ **£9,703** (£2,887; £1,443; £721) **Stalls High**

Form RPR

223- **1** **Swindler**[275] 8106 3-8-9 **82** .... LiamKeniry 4 94+
(Ed Walker) *stdd s: hld up in last pair: smooth prog wl over 1f out: pushed into the ld jst ins fnl f: won decisively* **9/4**[1]

5503 **2** 3/4 **Normandy Barriere (IRE)**[6] 4649 7-8-13 **87** ....(p) IzzyClifton[(7)] 5 91
(Nigel Tinkler) *trckd ldrs: tried to chal over 1f out: bmpd along and nt qckn fnl f: styd on to take 3rd nr fin: fin 3rd: plcd 2nd* **9/2**[2]

5123 **3** 1 **Louie De Palma**[18] 4186 7-10-1 **96** .... AdamKirby 2 97
(Clive Cox) *trckd ldr: led wl over 1f out: rdn and hdd jst ins fnl f: one pce after: fin 4th: plcd 3rd* **5/1**[3]

0646 **4** 1 1/4 **Lightning Charlie**[24] 3963 7-8-11 **78** .... PatDobbs 6 75
(Amanda Perrett) *hld up towards rr: pushed along over 1f out: kpt on steadily fnl f: no threat and nvr in it: fin 5th: plcd 4th* **20/1**

-050 **5** 1 1/4 **Concierge (IRE)**[69] 2412 3-9-7 **94** .... HarryBentley 1 86
(George Scott) *hld up towards rr: prog on outer 2f out: chsd ldrs over 1f out: fdd ins fnl f fin 6th: plcd 5th* **20/1**

5-66 **6** 1 3/4 **Polybius**[11] 4451 8-10-0 **95** .... JasonWatson 3 82
(David Simcock) *s.i.s: hld up in last: pushed along 2f out: passed a few fnl f but nvr a factor: fin 7th: plcd 6th* **14/1**

2046 **7** 1/2 **Vegas Boy (IRE)**[20] 4123 4-9-2 **83** ....(t) NicolaCurrie 8 69
(Jamie Osborne) *t.k.h: hld up bhd ldrs: shkn up 2f out: wknd jst over 1f out: fin 8th: plcd 7th* **6/1**

0006 **8** 1/2 **Doc Sportello (IRE)**[25] 3945 7-8-4 **76** oh2..........(p) DarraghKeenan[(5)] 7 60
(Tony Carroll) *led to wl over 1f out: wkng whn short of room sn after: fin 9th: plcd 8th* **33/1**

2-15 **9** hd **Margub**[64] 2551 4-10-0 **95** .... DaneO'Neill 9 79
(Marcus Tregoning) *t.k.h: trckd ldrs: shkn up and sing to lose pl whn short of room over 1f out: wknd: fin 10th: plcd 9th* **8/1**

-602 **D** 1 3/4 **Sunsprite (IRE)**[18] 4186 3-9-9 **96** ....(p[1]) ShaneKelly 10 102
(Richard Hughes) *hld up in midfield: shkn up and prog over 1f out: tk 2nd ins fnl f: styd on but no ch w wnr: fin 2nd: disqualified - jockey failed to draw correct weight* **8/1**

1m 12.93s (-0.77) **Going Correction** +0.10s/f (Good) **10 Ran SP% 121.3**
WFA 3 from 4yo+ 6lb
Speed ratings (Par 107): **109,105,104,102,101 98,98,97,97,106**
CSF £12.41 CT £47.72 TOTE £3.20: £1.50, £1.70, £2.00; EX 15.10 Trifecta £67.00.
Owner B E Nielsen **Bred** Bjorn Nielsen **Trained** Upper Lambourn, Berks

FOCUS
A good sprint handicap. The favourite came there swinging from off the pace and asserted in pretty taking fashion in easily the best comparative time on the card.

4867 CMS REAL DEAL APPRENTICE H'CAP 1m (S)
5:45 (5:46) (Class 4) (0-85,87) 4-Y-O+ **£6,727** (£2,002; £1,000; £500; £300; £300) **Stalls High**

Form RPR

5312 **1** **Star Shield**[8] 4566 4-9-0 **78** .... ScottMcCullagh[(5)] 11 86+
(David O'Meara) *stdd s: hld up in last: prog over 1f out and burst between rivals sn after: led jst ins fnl f: r.o wl* **3/1**[1]

2160 **2** 1/2 **Masked Identity**[27] 3867 4-9-2 **78** .... SebastianWoods[(3)] 6 85
(Shaun Keightley) *trckd ldrs: waiting to chal over 1f out: rdn fnl f: sn chsd wnr: r.o but a hld* **11/1**

-005 **3** 1/2 **Breanski**[28] 3813 5-9-7 **80** .... FinleyMarsh 1 86
(Jedd O'Keeffe) *hld up towards rr: shkn up and gd prog on outer 2f out: chal and upsides 1f out: outpcd last 100yds* **7/2**[2]

5016 **4** 1/2 **Poetic Force (IRE)**[8] 4545 5-9-3 **79** ....(t) DarraghKeenan[(3)] 4 84
(Tony Carroll) *hld up in rr: prog over 1f out gng wl: asked for effrt fnl f: r.o but nt pce to chal* **6/1**[3]

-200 **5** 1 **Top Mission**[36] 3496 5-9-3 **83** .... StefanoCherchi[(7)] 5 85
(Marco Botti) *hld up in midfield: shkn up 2f out: styd on fnl f but nvr gng pce to threaten* **20/1**

-601 **6** nk **Mountain Rescue (IRE)**[21] 4067 7-9-7 **83** ....(p) SeamusCronin[(3)] 8 85
(Michael Attwater) *led: rdn 2f out: hdd over 1f out: outpcd jst ins fnl f* **10/1**

2232 **7** 3/4 **Markazi (FR)**[13] 4403 5-10-0 **87** ....(p) WilliamCox 9 87
(David O'Meara) *hld up in midfield: effrt on nr side over 1f out: one pce and n.d* **7/1**

3321 **8** 2 1/2 **Mister Music**[11] 4455 10-9-1 **81** 4ex........................ ElishaWhittington[(7)] 10 75
(Tony Carroll) *stdd s: hld up in rr: pushed along and no real prog over 1f out* **20/1**

0-36 **9** 2 1/4 **Papa Stour (USA)**[23] 3991 4-9-2 **75** .... JoshuaBryan 2 64
(Andrew Balding) *in tch in midfield: pushed along and no prog over 1f out: wknd fnl f* **8/1**

-003 **10** shd **Jackpot Royale**[21] 4061 4-9-9 **85** .... TheodoreLadd[(3)] 3 74
(Michael Appleby) *pressed ldr to over 1f out: wknd fnl f* **16/1**

0035 **11** 6 **Pour La Victoire (IRE)**[24] 3963 9-8-13 **75** .... PoppyBridgwater[(3)] 7 50
(Tony Carroll) *t.k.h: pressed ldr to 2f out: sn wknd* **33/1**

1m 40.93s (-0.47) **Going Correction** +0.10s/f (Good) **11 Ran SP% 120.9**
Speed ratings (Par 105): **106,105,105,104,103 103,102,99,97,97 91**
CSF £37.22 CT £125.63 TOTE £3.50: £1.60, £4.20, £1.90; EX 61.20 Trifecta £291.50.
Owner Middleham Park Racing XXIX **Bred** Mildmay Bloodstock Ltd **Trained** Upper Helmsley, N Yorks

FOCUS
A decent apprentice riders' handicap. The favourite burst through late to win in one of the better comparative times on the card. The second has been rated to his AW best, and the fourth in line with his turf best.
T/Plt: £325.30 to a £1 stake. Pool: £63,935.11 - 143.44 winning units. T/Qpdt: £19.00 to a £1 stake. Pool: £9,370.40 - 363.22 winning units. **Jonathan Neesom**

4479 CHEPSTOW (L-H)
Friday, July 12

OFFICIAL GOING: Good to firm (watered; 6.1)
Weather: Fine

4868 ITS APPRENTICE TRAINING H'CAP (PART OF THE RACING EXCELLENCE INITIATIVE) 1m 4f
6:00 (6:00) (Class 6) (0-55,57) 4-Y-O+ **£2,781** (£827; £413; £400; £400; £400) **Stalls Low**

Form RPR

5411 **1** **Sigrid Nansen**[9] 4498 4-9-9 **57** 5ex........................(p) CierenFallon 6 67+
(Alexandra Dunn) *led: hdd over 8f out: chsd ldrs: led again 3f out: clr 2f out: easily* **11/10**[1]

0-30 **2** 2 **Das Kapital**[27] 3834 4-9-1 **49** .... WilliamCarver 5 52+
(John Berry) *s.i.s: hld up: hdwy over 3f out: rdn to chse wnr and hung lft fr over 1f out: styd on same pce fnl f (jockey said gelding hung left)* **4/1**[2]

00-0 **3** 3 3/4 **Carnage**[51] 1102 4-9-4 **52** .... GeorgiaDobie 8 49
(Nikki Evans) *chsd ldrs: rdn over 3f out: styd on same pce fr over 1f out* **9/2**[3]

6003 **4** hd **The Wire Flyer**[63] 2593 4-8-12 **46** oh1........................(p) SeanKirrane 12 43
(John Flint) *hld up in tch: shkn up over 3f out: edgd lft over 1f out: no ex ins fnl f* **10/1**

15-0 **5** 5 **Purple Jazz (IRE)**[27] 3834 4-9-7 **55** ....(t) AledBeech 4 44
(Jeremy Scott) *s.s: hld up: pushed along over 3f out: nvr nrr (jockey said gelding was slow away)* **16/1**

0000 **6** 2 1/2 **Interrogation (FR)**[10] 4475 4-8-9 **46** oh1..............(b) JessicaCooley[(3)] 10 31
(Alan Bailey) *s.i.s: sn chsng ldrs: led over 8f out tl over 7f out: led again over 3f out: sn hdd: wknd over 1f out* **100/1**

0/60 **7** 4 **Cougar Kid (IRE)**[23] 2733 8-8-7 **46** oh1........................(b) KateLeahy[(5)] 9 24
(John O'Shea) *hld up: pushed along over 3f out: n.d (jockey said gelding suffered interference on the bend)* **14/1**

-000 **8** 1/2 **Ice Cool Cullis (IRE)**[14] 4346 4-8-5 **46** oh1..........(p[1]) MolliePhillips[(7)] 1 23
(Mark Loughnane) *plld hrd and prom: jinked lft over 9f out: led over 7f out: hdd over 3f out: wknd wl over 1f out (jockey said gelding ran too freely; vet said gelding lost it's right fore-shoe)* **66/1**

35-0 **9** 9 **Crindle Carr (IRE)**[114] 619 5-8-10 **49** ....(p) LukeCatton[(5)] 3 15+
(John Flint) *hld up in tch: hmpd and lost pl wl over 6f out: wknd over 3f out* **14/1**

2m 37.94s (-2.36) **Going Correction** -0.25s/f (Firm) **9 Ran SP% 116.6**
Speed ratings (Par 101): **97,95,93,93,89 88,85,85,79**
CSF £5.67 CT £14.35 TOTE £2.00: £1.10, £1.80, £1.70; EX 5.80 Trifecta £25.80.
Owner West Buckland Bloodstock Ltd **Bred** Hunscote Stud **Trained** West Buckland, Somerset

FOCUS
A low-grade apprentice handicap, but a hat-trick for the progressive top weight. The second has been rated to his recent form.

4869 BMC "CONFINED" FILLIES" H'CAP (NOT WON A RACE IN 2019) 1m 4f
6:30 (6:32) (Class 5) (0-70,70) 4-Y-O+

£3,428 (£1,020; £509; £400; £400; £400) **Stalls** Low

Form RPR

0-64 **1** **Rosie Royale (IRE)**[16] 4231 7-8-9 **58**........................ RossaRyan 8 64
(Roger Teal) *chsd ldr: rdn over 2f out: edgd lft over 1f out: styd on to ld wl ins fnl f* **7/2**[2]

0563 **2** 1/2 **Lafilia (GER)**[2] 4777 4-8-9 **58**........................(b) AdamMcNamara 5 63
(Archie Watson) *led: rdn over 2f out: hdd wl ins fnl f* **6/1**

0-42 **3** 1 1/2 **Rose Crown**[3] 4762 5-8-4 **60**........................ GeorgeBass(7) 4 63
(Mick Channon) *s.i.s: sn chsng ldrs: rdn and nt clrest of runs fr over 2f out: styd on same pce ins fnl f* **15/8**[1]

-400 **4** 1/2 **Last Enchantment (IRE)**[13] 4371 4-9-2 **70**........................(t) BenCoen(5) 9 72
(Neil Mulholland) *hld up: hdwy over 2f out: sn rdn: styd on same pce ins fnl f* **25/1**

-054 **5** 4 1/2 **Delirium (IRE)**[9] 4499 5-7-13 **51**........................(p) JaneElliott(3) 7 46
(Ed de Giles) *s.i.s: hld up: hdwy on outer over 2f out: shkn up over 1f out: edgd lft and no ex fnl f* **17/2**

-530 **6** 5 **Ripley (IRE)**[129] 1024 4-8-5 **59**........................(t) CierenFallon(5) 6 46
(Charles Hills) *hld up in tch: rdn over 3f out: wknd over 1f out* **12/1**

420 **7** 18 **Cherries At Dawn (IRE)**[36] 3495 4-9-0 **70**........................ GeorgiaDobie(7) 1 28
(Dominic Ffrench Davis) *hld up in tch: plld hrd early: rdn over 3f out: wknd wl over 1f out (trainer said filly was unsuited by the good to firm going and would prefer a slower surface in his opinion and also failed to handle the track)* **16/1**

0005 **8** 6 **Tomorrow's Angel**[9] 4510 4-8-11 **60**........................(v) OisinMurphy 3 8
(Iain Jardine) *rn wout declared tongue strap: s.i.s: sn prom: rdn over 3f out: wknd over 2f out* **9/2**[3]

2m 37.24s (-3.06) **Going Correction** -0.25s/f (Firm) **8** Ran SP% **117.4**
Speed ratings (Par 103): **100,99,98,98,95 92,80,76**
CSF £25.53 CT £50.59 TOTE £4.30: £2.30, £2.30, £1.10; EX 24.80 Trifecta £92.30.
Owner The Idle B's **Bred** Fergus Cousins **Trained** Lambourn, Berks

FOCUS
This modest fillies' handicap was run 0.7sec faster than the opening race. It paid to race close to the pace. It's been rated at face value around the second.

4870 DAVID BAKER AND CO 50TH ANNIVERSARY FILLIES' H'CAP 1m 14y
7:05 (7:07) (Class 5) (0-70,69) 3-Y-O+

£3,428 (£1,020; £509; £400; £400; £400) **Stalls** Centre

Form RPR

-005 **1** **Kyllachys Tale (IRE)**[21] 4067 5-9-1 **59**........................ CierenFallon(5) 6 65
(Roger Teal) *s.i.s: sn trcking ldrs: nt clr run over 1f out: sn rdn: r.o to ld nr fin* **4/1**[2]

-010 **2** nk **Song Of The Isles (IRE)**[13] 4378 3-8-9 **64**........................ EllieMacKenzie(7) 3 67
(Heather Main) *racd keenly: w ldrs: shkn up over 1f out: led ins fnl f: hdd nr fin* **5/1**

350 **3** 1/2 **Caen Na Coille (USA)**[14] 4326 3-9-6 **68**........................ OisinMurphy 5 70
(Ed Dunlop) *w ldrs: rdn to ld over 1f out: edgd lft and hdd ins fnl f: styd on same pce towards fin* **9/1**

5405 **4** 1 1/2 **Huddle**[16] 4248 3-9-0 **62**........................ LiamJones 1 61
(William Knight) *racd freely: w ldrs: led 5f out: rdn: edgd rt and hdd over 1f out: no ex wl ins fnl f* **9/1**

-645 **5** 3/4 **Tarbeyah (IRE)**[15] 4285 4-10-0 **67**........................ RossaRyan 9 66+
(Kevin Frost) *s.i.s: hld up: pushed along over 3f out: rdn: hung lft and r.o ins fnl f: nt rch ldrs (trainer said filly was unsuited by the Good to Firm going, and would prefer a slower surface in their opinion)* **7/2**[1]

0000 **6** hd **Cooperess**[66] 2513 6-8-6 **48** oh3........................ JaneElliott(3) 7 47
(Adrian Wintle) *w ldrs over 3f: remained handy: rdn over 1f out: styd on same pce ins fnl f* **25/1**

3033 **7** 2 1/4 **Accomplice**[16] 4235 5-9-5 **58**........................ DanielMuscutt 10 51
(Michael Blanshard) *s.i.s: hld up: hdwy over 1f out: sn rdn: no ex ins fnl f* **9/2**[3]

5U46 **8** 1/2 **Mooroverthebridge**[9] 4494 5-9-3 **56**........................ TrevorWhelan 8 48
(Grace Harris) *prom: rdn over 2f out: no ex ins fnl f* **12/1**

0/0- **9** 4 **Skylark Lady (IRE)**[225] 4502 6-8-4 **48** oh3........................(p) SophieRalston(5) 4 31
(Nikki Evans) *prom: sn pushed along and lost pl: nvr on terms after* **100/1**

3-50 **10** 11 **Shellebeau (IRE)**[16] 4247 3-9-4 **69**........................ MeganNicholls(3) 2 25
(Paul Nicholls) *w ldrs 3f: rdn over 2f out: wknd over 1f out (trainer rep said filly was unsuited by the track and in their opinion would prefer a less undulating surface)* **9/1**

1m 33.78s (-2.22) **Going Correction** -0.25s/f (Firm)
WFA 3 from 4yo+ 9lb **10** Ran SP% **119.6**
Speed ratings (Par 100): **101,100,100,98,97 97,95,95,91,80**
CSF £25.13 CT £173.13 TOTE £4.90: £1.70, £2.60, £2.40; EX 26.20 Trifecta £241.10.
Owner Barry Kitcherside And Darren Waterer **Bred** Old Carhue Stud **Trained** Lambourn, Berks

FOCUS
Another ordinary fillies' handicap but it produced a good finish. The second has been rated in line with her Lingfield win, and the fourth to her latest.

4871 HOTSPRING HOT TUBS SPLASH & DASH MAIDEN STKS 5f 16y
7:35 (7:36) (Class 5) 2-Y-O **£3,428** (£1,020; £509; £254) **Stalls** Centre

Form RPR

06 **1** **Glamorous Anna**[27] 3835 2-8-11 0........................ MitchGodwin(3) 7 78
(Christopher Mason) *prom: jnd ldr 1/2-way: led and hung lft over 1f out: rdn clr* **33/1**

2 **2** 4 1/2 **X Force (IRE)**[13] 4373 2-9-5 0........................ OisinMurphy 6 67
(Archie Watson) *led 4f out: hdd over 1f out: edgd lft and no ex ins fnl f (jockey said colt lost its action)* **1/3**[1]

5 **3** 1/2 **Outtake**[8] 4558 2-9-5 0........................ RossaRyan 5 65
(Richard Hannon) *chsd ldrs: hung lft fr over 3f out: rdn over 1f out: styd on same pce fnl f (jockey said colt hung left)* **7/2**[2]

4 **4** 1 **Tilly Tamworth**[60] 2686 2-9-0 0........................ DanielMuscutt 1 56
(Rod Millman) *led 1f: rdn and hung lft over 1f out: no ex fnl f* **11/1**[3]

6 **5** 5 **Dandy Dancer**[15] 4290 2-8-12 0........................ GeorgeRooke(7) 2 43
(Richard Hughes) *chsd ldrs: outpcd fr over 3f out: hung rt fnl f* **20/1**

6 **6** 8 **Glamorous Force**[13] 4373 2-9-5 0........................ EoinWalsh 3 15
(Ronald Harris) *s.s: outpcd: hung rt ins fnl f (jockey said colt ran green)* **33/1**

58.6s (-0.80) **Going Correction** -0.25s/f (Firm) **6** Ran SP% **116.2**
Speed ratings (Par 94): **96,88,88,86,78 65**
CSF £47.13 TOTE £33.60: £7.80, £1.10; EX 73.20 Trifecta £224.50.
Owner Robert & Nina Bailey **Bred** Robert & Mrs Nina Bailey **Trained** Caewent, Monmouthshire

FOCUS
An uncompetitive juvenile maiden that appeared a match on paper, but didn't turn out that way with one of the outsiders bolting up. The level is fluid.

4872 SILK SERIES LADY RIDERS' H'CAP (PRO-AM LADY RIDERS' RACE) 6f 16y
8:10 (8:10) (Class 4) (0-80,80) 3-Y-O+

£5,433 (£1,617; £808; £404; £400; £400) **Stalls** Centre

Form RPR

3103 **1** **Major Valentine**[31] 3701 7-9-7 **73**........................ KateLeahy(7) 3 87
(John O'Shea) *w ldr tl led over 4f out: pushed clr fnl 2f: comf (trainer was informed that the gelding could not run until the day after passing a stalls test)* **13/2**

0524 **2** 4 **Princely**[18] 4181 4-8-12 **64**........................ JessicaCooley(7) 9 65
(Tony Newcombe) *stdd s: hld up: hdwy over 1f out: r.o to go 2nd wl ins fnl f: no ch w wnr* **4/1**[1]

-604 **3** 1 3/4 **Oeil De Tigre (FR)**[18] 4186 8-9-12 **78**........................ MissSophieColl(7) 2 74
(Tony Carroll) *prom: chsd wnr over 3f out: rdn over 1f out: styd on same pce: lost 2nd wl ins fnl f* **6/1**[3]

0536 **4** hd **Kinglami**[4] 4733 10-9-2 **64**........................(p) JaneElliott(3) 1 59
(John O'Shea) *hld up: hdwy over 1f out: r.o: nt rch ldrs* **6/1**[3]

6502 **5** 4 **Good Luck Fox (IRE)**[23] 4008 3-9-10 **80**........................(p[1]) KatherineBegley(5) 6 61
(Richard Hannon) *sn chsng ldrs: pushed along 1/2-way: rdn over 1f out: wknd fnl f* **4/1**[1]

0510 **6** 3 **Mama Africa (IRE)**[35] 3541 5-9-0 **66**........................(p) MissImogenMathias(7) 7 39
(John Flint) *prom: pushed along 1/2-way: rdn and wknd over 1f out* **16/1**

3140 **7** 4 **Strawberry Jack**[15] 4300 3-9-10 **78**........................(vt) GeorgiaCox(3) 8 37
(George Scott) *s.i.s and wnt lft s: outpcd (jockey said gelding was slowly away and was never travelling)* **9/2**[2]

3123 **8** 3/4 **Joegogo (IRE)**[146] 763 4-10-4 **80**........................ MeganNicholls(3) 5 37
(David Evans) *led: hdd over 4f out: rdn over 2f out: wknd over 1f out* **10/1**

1m 9.11s (-2.39) **Going Correction** -0.25s/f (Firm)
WFA 3 from 4yo+ 6lb **8** Ran SP% **115.1**
Speed ratings (Par 105): **105,99,97,97,91 87,82,81**
CSF £32.86 CT £165.96 TOTE £7.40: £1.90, £1.70, £2.20; EX 36.90 Trifecta £201.70.
Owner Pete Smith **Bred** J R Salter **Trained** Elton, Gloucs

FOCUS
The feature race and a pro-am lady riders' sprint. It was an open betting market but there was only one winner from some way out. Not the most solid of form.

4873 CARDIFF SPORTS ORTHOPAEDIC H'CAP 7f 16y
8:40 (8:44) (Class 6) (0-60,62) 3-Y-O+

£2,781 (£827; £413; £400; £400; £400) **Stalls** Centre

Form RPR

002U **1** **Gold Hunter (IRE)**[10] 4479 9-10-1 **62**........................(tp) RaulDaSilva 15 77
(Steve Flook) *hdwy 4f out: led 3f out: rdn over 1f out: r.o wl* **11/2**[2]

00-1 **2** 5 **Kendergarten Kop (IRE)**[13] 4378 4-10-0 **61**........................ OisinMurphy 16 63
(David Flood) *chsd ldrs: lft 2nd 3f out: rdn and hung lft fr over 1f out: no ex fnl f* **9/4**[1]

0536 **3** 1/2 **Mister Musicmaster**[16] 4235 10-9-11 **61**........................ MeganNicholls(3) 12 61
(Ron Hodges) *s.i.s: sn pushed along in rr: r.o ins fnl f: wnt 3rd nr fin: nt rch ldrs* **9/1**

-305 **4** nk **Bayards Cove**[9] 4494 4-8-9 **45**........................ JaneElliott(3) 11 44
(Stuart Kittow) *hld up in tch: rdn over 1f out: styd on same pce fnl f* **25/1**

1-2 **5** 3/4 **Captain Dan (IRE)**[44] 3234 5-9-10 **62**........................(p) ScottMcCullagh(5) 7 59
(John James Feane, Ire) *prom: rdn over 1f out: styd on same pce fnl f* **6/1**[3]

6330 **6** 1 1/4 **Secondo (FR)**[11] 4455 9-9-7 **59**........................(v) PoppyBridgwater(5) 3 53
(Robert Stephens) *hld up: hmpd wl over 5f out: hdwy over 1f out: wknd wl ins fnl f* **14/1**

1-54 **7** 1/2 **Langley Vale**[35] 3533 10-8-12 **50**........................ CierenFallon(5) 10 43+
(Roger Teal) *led hmpd by loose horse over 3f out: sn hdd: rdn and nt clr run over 1f out: wknd ins fnl f* **9/1**

0-40 **8** 3/4 **Gold Flash**[18] 4195 7-9-3 **57**........................(v) AledBeech(7) 13 48
(Rod Millman) *chsd ldrs: pushed along 1/2-way: rdn and edgd rt over 1f out: wknd fnl f* **9/1**

2200 **9** 1 1/4 **Dalness Express**[4] 4733 6-9-2 **49**........................(t) LiamJones 14 36
(John O'Shea) *s.i.s: hdwy over 2f out: wknd ins fnl f* **10/1**

-650 **10** hd **Silvington**[29] 3774 4-8-5 **45**........................(b) SeanKirrane(7) 9 32
(Mark Loughnane) *s.i.s and rdr lost iron leaving stalls: n.d* **50/1**

0000 **11** 1 **Tally's Song**[18] 4182 6-8-12 **45**........................(p) TrevorWhelan 6 29
(Grace Harris) *chsd ldrs: rdn over 2f out: wknd over 1f out* **50/1**

0540 **12** 1 **Seaforth (IRE)**[10] 4481 7-9-1 **51**........................ FinleyMarsh(3) 2 32
(Adrian Wintle) *chsd ldrs: rdn 1/2-way: wknd over 1f out* **33/1**

6000 **U** **Indian Affair**[10] 4481 9-8-5 **45**........................(bt) WilliamCarver(7) 5
(Milton Bradley) *prom: clipped heels: stmbld and uns rdr wl over 5f out* **25/1**

1m 21.59s (-2.31) **Going Correction** -0.25s/f (Firm) **13** Ran SP% **120.8**
Speed ratings (Par 101): **103,97,96,96,95 94,93,92,91,91 89,88,**
CSF £17.53 CT £108.25 TOTE £6.00: £2.40, £1.40, £3.10; EX 21.40 Trifecta £368.10.
Owner Chasing Charlie Syndicate **Bred** Airlie Stud And Sir Thomas Pilkington **Trained** Leominster, Herefordshire

■ Rising Sunshine was withdrawn. Price at time of withdrawal 50-1. Rule \n\x\x 4 does not appl

FOCUS
A moderate handicap but rather messy with one of the runners unseating due to clipping heels, and then causing mayhem amongst the leaders after halfway.

4874 PETE SMITH CAR SALES COLEFORD H'CAP 7f 16y
9:10 (9:14) (Class 5) (0-70,72) 3-Y-O

£3,428 (£1,020; £509; £400; £400; £400) **Stalls** Centre

Form RPR

3101 **1** **Jungle Juice (IRE)**[10] 4479 3-9-6 **72** 6ex........................ ScottMcCullagh(5) 9 81
(Mick Channon) *s.i.s: hdwy over 2f out: shkn up to ld and hung lft fr over 1f out: rdn out* **5/2**[2]

2052 **2** 2 3/4 **Dancingwithwolves (IRE)**[10] 4479 3-9-10 **71**........................ DanielMuscutt 3 73
(Ed Dunlop) *edgd lft s: sn w ldrs: led over 4f out: rdn: edgd rt and hdd over 1f out: edgd lft and styd on same pce ins fnl f (jockey said gelding hung right)* **11/4**[3]

3231 **3** 3/4 **Glamorous Crescent**[18] 4180 3-8-12 **59**........................ OisinMurphy 4 59
(Grace Harris) *w ldrs: rdn and ev ch over 1f out: no ex wl ins fnl f* **9/4**[1]

0545 **4** 3 1/4 **Deconso**[11] 4457 3-8-6 **53**........................ LiamJones 1 44
(Christopher Kellett) *edgd lft s: pushed along early in rr: hdwy 1/2-way: rdn over 2f out: hung rt and wknd wl ins fnl f* **25/1**

32-4 **5** ½ **Just Later**[17] 4218 3-9-7 **68**........................ AdamMcNamara 6 58
(Amy Murphy) *led: bmpd over 6f out: hdd over 5f out: chsd ldrs: rdn over 2f out: wknd ins fnl f* **7/1**

0-00 **6** 1½ **Dawn Treader (IRE)**[14] 4322 3-9-4 **72**........................ LukeCatton(7) 2 58
(Richard Hannon) *chsd ldrs: lost pl 4f out: n.d after* **11/1**

000- **7** 1 **Swiper (IRE)**[268] 8330 3-9-5 **66**........................ RossaRyan 8 49
(John O'Shea) *prom: rdn over 2f out: wknd over 1f out (trainer said gelding was unsuited by the Good to Firm going, and would prefer a slower surface in their opinion)* **20/1**

03-0 **8** nse **Atty's Edge**[57] 2772 3-9-1 **62**........................ TrevorWhelan 5 45
(Christopher Mason) *racd freely: w ldrs: edgd rt over 6f out: led over 5f out tl over 4f out: nt clr run over 3f out: wknd over 1f out* **33/1**

1m 22.44s (-1.46) **Going Correction** -0.25s/f (Firm) **8** Ran SP% **118.4**
Speed ratings (Par 100): **98,94,94,90,89 88,86,86**
CSF £10.02 CT £17.39 TOTE £3.40: £1.30, £1.40, £1.30; EX 9.40 Trifecta £27.80.
Owner Insignia Racing (ribbon) **Bred** Ballybrennan Stud Ltd **Trained** West Ilsley, Berks

FOCUS
This 3yo handicap was run 0.85sec slower than the preceding contest, but the winner scored comfortably. The second has been rated to form, and the third to her latest C&D win.
T/Plt: £13.60 to a £1 stake. Pool: £57,511.37 - 3,086.93 winning units. T/Qpdt: £10.20 to a £1 stake. Pool: £6,291.77 - 455.73 winning units. **Colin Roberts**

4358 **CHESTER** (L-H)
Friday, July 12
OFFICIAL GOING: Good (good to soft in places; 6.5)
Wind: Moderate, against in straight of over 1f Weather: Fine

4875 KNIGHTS PLC H'CAP (FOR LADY AMATEUR RIDERS) 7f 127y
5:50 (5:51) (Class 4) (0-80,80) 3-Y-O+
£5,864 (£1,818; £908; £454; £400; £400) **Stalls Low**

Form RPR

-400 **1** **Salam Zayed**[11] 4446 3-8-9 **63**........................ MrsCarolBartley 12 68
(Richard Fahey) *midfield: hdwy 2f out: led over 1f out: edgd lft ins fnl f: kpt on wl (trainer said regarding apparent improvement in from that the gelding appreciated the drop in trip from 1m 2f to 7f on this occasion)* **28/1**

0115 **2** 1 **Redarna**[16] 4239 5-10-5 **78**........................(p) MissEmmaSayer 1 83
(Dianne Sayer) *trckd ldrs: rdn and unable qck over 1f out: styd on to take 2nd towards fin: nt gng pce to chal wnr* **3/1**[1]

1233 **3** hd **Bell Heather (IRE)**[14] 4318 6-9-7 **66**........................(p) MsLO'Neill 5 70
(Patrick Morris) *trckd ldrs: effrt on inner over 1f out: wnt 2nd ins fnl f: sn n.m.r and checked: swtchd rt and kpt on towards fin* **9/2**[3]

-053 **4** ½ **Coviglia (IRE)**[17] 4207 5-9-6 **65**........................ MissJoannaMason 8 68
(Jacqueline Coward) *in tch: clsd 3f out: led wl over 1f out: sn hdd: nt pce of wnr ins fnl f: styd on same pce towards fin* **7/2**[2]

6260 **5** 2¼ **Humble Gratitude**[13] 4403 4-10-5 **78**........................(v[1]) MissEmmaTodd 10 75+
(Ian Williams) *in rr: pushed along and hdwy 2f out: kpt on ins fnl f: nvr able to trble ldrs* **10/1**

2453 **6** ½ **Rockesbury**[18] 4195 4-9-2 **61** oh3........................(b) MissMichelleMullineaux 3 57
(David Loughnane) *led: rdn and hdd wl over 1f out: fdd wl ins fnl f* **14/1**

04-3 **7** nse **Ballymount**[15] 4281 4-9-9 **68**........................(p) MissSerenaBrotherton 11 64
(Michael Easterby) *towards rr: pushed along over 4f out: hdwy u.p 2f out: nvr able to trble ldrs (vet said gelding lost its left hind shoe)* **8/1**

0-00 **8** ¾ **Capton**[41] 3338 6-10-2 **80**........................ MissAmyCollier(5) 7 74
(Michael Easterby) *hld up in midfield: rdn and outpcd over 2f out: n.d after* **25/1**

0/00 **9** 3½ **Echo Of Lightning**[17] 4207 9-9-13 **72**........................(p) MissBeckySmith 9 57
(Roger Fell) *prom on outer: chsd ldr over 4f out: ev ch 2f out: sn lost 2nd: wknd over 1f out* **25/1**

0000 **10** ¾ **Rock Warbler (IRE)**[11] 4460 6-9-2 **61** oh12........................ MissAlysonDeniel 2 44
(Michael Mullineaux) *nvr bttr than midfield: lost pl 4f out: nvr a threat* **66/1**

0000 **11** 1½ **My Amigo**[16] 4240 6-10-1 **74**........................(tp) MissCatherineWalton 6 54
(Marjorie Fife) *s.i.s: in rr: niggled along over 2f out: nvr a threat* **9/1**

02-0 **12** 13 **Baltic Prince (IRE)**[49] 3040 9-10-0 **78**........................ MissSarahBowen(5) 4 25
(Tony Carroll) *chsd ldr tl over 4f out: pushed along over 2f out: sn wknd* **20/1**

1m 39.48s (3.78) **Going Correction** +0.65s/f (Yiel)
WFA 3 from 4yo+ 9lb **12** Ran SP% **119.7**
Speed ratings (Par 105): **107,106,105,105,103 102,102,101,98,97 96,83**
CSF £107.07 CT £478.99 TOTE £42.10: £9.00, £2.00, £2.20; EX 339.40 Trifecta £2683.60.
Owner Dr Marwan Koukash **Bred** Newsells Park Stud **Trained** Musley Bank, N Yorks

FOCUS
After 5mm of rain overnight the ground was just on the easy side. This was a handicap for women amateurs run over 37 yards further than advertised. It featured mainly exposed sorts and the pace. The second, third and fourth set the level.

4876 MBNA EBF NOVICE AUCTION STKS (PLUS 10 RACE) 6f 17y
6:20 (6:20) (Class 4) 2-Y-O
£5,851 (£1,752; £876; £438; £219; £109) **Stalls Low**

Form RPR

42 **1** **National League (IRE)**[10] 4486 2-9-2 0........................ PaddyMathers 3 78
(Richard Fahey) *pushed along early: no bttr than midfield: pushed along again over 3f out: outpcd over 2f out: plenty of work to do u.p in 4th over 1f out: styd on strly wl ins fnl f: led towards fin* **11/4**[3]

10 **2** ¾ **Coase**[24] 3949 2-9-8 0........................ PatCosgrave 2 82
(Hugo Palmer) *led: rdn over 1f out: worn down and hdd towards fin: nt pce of wnr* **13/8**[1]

4 **3** ¾ **Woven Quality (IRE)**[16] 4237 2-9-2 0........................ AndrewMullen 1 74
(Donald McCain) *chsd ldrs: rdn over 2f out: plld off the rail whn struggling to qckn over 1f out: kpt on u.p towards fin: nt pce of wnr* **20/1**

2 **4** ¾ **Feelinlikeasomeone**[8] 4550 2-8-11 0........................ FrannyNorton 4 66
(Mark Johnston) *chsd ldr: rdn over 2 out: unable qck over 1f out: edgd lft ent fnl f: lost 2nd fnl 75yds: no ex towards fin* **7/4**[2]

36 **5** 7 **It's Not My Fault (IRE)**[13] 4366 2-8-11 0........................ RichardKingscote 5 44
(Tom Dascombe) *chsd ldrs: rdn and outpcd over 2f out: wknd wl over 1f out* **20/1**

6 7 **Cappella Fella (IRE)** 2-9-2 0........................ RobHornby 8 26
(Sarah Hollinshead) *hld up towards rr: pushed along and outpcd over 2f out: nvr a threat* **50/1**

006 **7** 1½ **Eileen's Magic**[14] 4317 2-8-11 47........................ NathanEvans 7 17
(Lisa Williamson) *hld up: pushed along and outpcd over 2f out: wnt rt over 1f out: nvr a threat* **150/1**

1m 19.32s (3.82) **Going Correction** +0.65s/f (Yiel) **7** Ran SP% **113.3**
Speed ratings (Par 96): **100,99,98,97,87 78,76**
CSF £7.44 TOTE £3.00: £1.50, £2.30; EX 7.70 Trifecta £52.80.
Owner R A Fahey **Bred** Rockhart Trading Ltd **Trained** Musley Bank, N Yorks

FOCUS
A juvenile novice auction run over 37 yard further than advertised. The pace was strong, the winner came from some way back and the first four were clear. The second and fourth could back the form being rated higher.

4877 TOGETHER COMMERCIAL FINANCE H'CAP 1m 3f 75y
6:55 (6:55) (Class 3) (0-95,93) 3-Y-O+
£9,337 (£2,097; £2,097; £699; £349; £175) **Stalls Low**

Form RPR

66-4 **1** **Infrastructure**[34] 3605 4-9-9 **90**........................ RobHornby 6 96
(Martyn Meade) *in tch: effrt over 1f out: r.o to ld and edgd lft fnl 75yds: in command nr fin* **4/1**[2]

1003 **2** 1¼ **Lunar Jet**[30] 3726 5-9-12 **93**........................ JimmyQuinn 4 98+
(John Mackie) *hld up: hdwy whn pushed along and nt clr run over 1f out: sn swtchd rt: running on to chal whn n.m.r between horses and hmpd fnl 75yds: nt rcvr: fin dead-heat 3rd: originally plcd 2nd: later dead-heat 2nd (vet said gelding lost its left hind shoe)* **9/1**

-025 **2** dht **Vivid Diamond (IRE)**[27] 3877 3-9-0 **92**........................ FrannyNorton 3 95
(Mark Johnston) *led: rdn over 1f out: sn hrd pressed: hdd ins fnl f: kpt on same pce towards fin: fin dead-heat 3rd: originally plcd 4th: later dead-heat 2nd* **4/1**[2]

0530 **4** ¾ **Dark Red (IRE)**[30] 3726 7-9-9 **90**........................(b) BenCurtis 1 95
(Ed Dunlop) *trckd ldrs: plld out over 1f out: sn chalng: led ins fnl f: hdd and edgd rt fnl 75yds: hld towards fin: fin 2nd: disqualified and originally plcd 3rd: subsequently plcd 4th* **13/2**[3]

-205 **5** 1¼ **Mistiroc**[22] 4021 8-9-9 **90**........................(v) JasonHart 7 90
(John Quinn) *w ldr: pushed along over 2f out: rdn to chal over 1f out: unable qck ins fnl f: kpt on same pce fnl 75yds* **10/1**

3-15 **6** ¾ **Mugatoo (IRE)**[28] 3799 4-9-8 **89**........................ JamieSpencer 2 88
(David Simcock) *hld up in rr: effrt and hdwy on outer 2f out: no imp over 1f out: one pce ins fnl f* **4/1**[2]

6631 **7** nk **Gossip Column (IRE)**[13] 4407 4-9-5 **86**........................ RichardKingscote 5 85
(Ian Williams) *hld up: pushed along to go pce 2f out: nvr able to trble ldrs (jockey said gelding was slowly away)* **10/3**[1]

2m 33.68s (6.28) **Going Correction** +0.65s/f (Yiel)
WFA 3 from 4yo+ 11lb **7** Ran SP% **115.5**
Speed ratings (Par 107): **103,102,101,101,100 100,99**
CSF £39.27 TOTE £6.10: £2.20, £4.60; EX 37.40 Trifecta £274.80.
Owner Sefton Syndicate **Bred** Lane Stud Farms Ltd **Trained** Manton, Wilts

FOCUS
A 0-95 handicap which was run over 57 yards further than advertised. The pace was moderate and things got tight late on so it wouldn't be the most reliable of form guides. The winner has been rated to form and the second close to his recent best.

4878 ESL GROUP NURSERY H'CAP 7f 1y
7:25 (7:28) (Class 4) (0-85,85) 2-Y-O
£6,080 (£1,809; £904; £452; £400; £400) **Stalls Low**

Form RPR

3413 **1** **Know No Limits (IRE)**[16] 4233 2-9-0 **78**........................ RichardKingscote 3 87
(Tom Dascombe) *wnt rt s and bmpd rival: mde all: kicked clr over 1f out: r.o wl* **11/4**[2]

033 **2** 2¾ **Breguet Man (IRE)**[17] 4206 2-8-3 **67**........................ ShaneGray 5 69
(Keith Dalgleish) *hld up: hdwy on outer 3f out: chsd wnr 1f out: no imp ins fnl f* **16/1**

621 **3** 2 **The New Marwan**[23] 3998 2-9-4 **82**........................ PaulHanagan 4 79
(Richard Fahey) *bmpd s: prom: rdn to chse wnr over 2f out: hung lft whn unable qck over 1f out: sn lost 2nd: no ex fnl 100yds* **2/1**[1]

311 **4** ¾ **War Storm**[20] 4125 2-9-7 **85**........................(p) LukeMorris 1 80+
(Archie Watson) *chsd ldrs: pushed along 3f out: one pce u.p over 1f out: nvr able to chal* **4/1**[3]

0653 **5** ½ **G For Gabrial (IRE)**[14] 4317 2-8-1 **65**........................ PaddyMathers 2 58
(Richard Fahey) *sn pushed along: no bttr than midfield: kpt on u.p fnl 100yds: nvr able to trble ldrs* **12/1**

450 **6** 5 **Dark Of Night (IRE)**[43] 3274 2-8-13 77........................(p[1]) GeorgeWood 7 57
(Saeed bin Suroor) *dwlt: hld up: effrt on outer over 1f out: nvr threatened* **12/1**

5622 **7** 12 **Vardon Flyer**[27] 3866 2-9-3 **81**........................ NathanEvans 6 28
(Michael Easterby) *racd keenly: prom: chsd wnr fr 5f out tl over 2f out: checked whn outpcd under 2f out: wknd over 1f out* **6/1**

1m 32.42s (4.92) **Going Correction** +0.65s/f (Yiel) **7** Ran SP% **115.6**
Speed ratings (Par 96): **97,93,91,90,90 84,70**
CSF £44.14 TOTE £5.50: £1.80, £6.90; EX 109.60 Trifecta £535.20.
Owner Fdcholdings Hedges Nolan Rutherford **Bred** Ballyreddin Stud **Trained** Malpas, Cheshire

FOCUS
Add 37 yards. This wasn't the most competitive of nurseries and a couple met trouble. In addition it was run at a bit of a stop-start gallop with the winning rider dictating matters.

4879 TOGETHER, LENDING FOR THE NEW NORMAL, H'CAP 7f 1y
8:00 (8:00) (Class 4) (0-80,82) 3-Y-O+
£5,851 (£1,752; £876; £438; £400; £400) **Stalls Low**

Form RPR

4133 **1** **Gabrial The Tiger (IRE)**[14] 4320 7-9-3 **69**........................ PaulHanagan 12 78
(Richard Fahey) *wnt to post early: mde all: rdn over 1f out: r.o ins fnl f* **9/1**

2-63 **2** 1¼ **Zeyzoun (FR)**[15] 4303 5-9-11 **77**........................(h) GeorgeWood 6 83
(Chris Wall) *racd keenly: in tch: rdn over 1f out to chse ldrs: wnt 2nd and edgd rt ins fnl f: styd on towards fin: nt trble wnr* **5/1**[2]

0410 **3** 1½ **John Kirkup**[27] 3868 4-9-11 **77**........................(p) ConnorBeasley 9 79
(Michael Dods) *chsd wnr: rdn over 1f out: lost 2nd ins fnl f: kpt on same pce fnl 100yds* **20/1**

6542 **4** 1½ **Logi (IRE)**[21] 4058 5-9-2 **68**........................(b) LewisEdmunds 5 66
(Rebecca Bastiman) *midfield: rdn over 2f out: hdwy over 1f out: kpt on ins fnl f to chse ldrs: nvr able to chal* **11/1**

6302 **5** shd **Candelisa (IRE)**[14] 4320 6-10-0 **80**........................(t) BenCurtis 11 78
(David Loughnane) *midfield: rdn and hdwy over 1f out: chsd ldrs fnl f: one pce and no imp fnl 100yds* **13/2**[3]

-224 **6** ¾ **Zoravan (USA)**[6] 4634 6-9-2 **68**........................ ShaneGray 1 64
(Keith Dalgleish) *hld up: rdn and hdwy over 1f out: kpt on u.p ins fnl f: nvr able to get involved* **7/1**

4610 **7** *1 3/4* **Miracle Garden**[15] 4303 7-8-11 **63**..............................(v) PaddyMathers 2 54
(Ian Williams) *pushed along and bhd: styd on ins fnl f: nvr nrr* **25/1**

2220 **8** *1/2* **Turanga Leela**[14] 4320 5-9-4 **70**..............................(b) FrannyNorton 4 60
(John Mackie) *chsd ldrs: rdn over 2f out: wknd ins fnl f* **7/1**

-000 **9** *nk* **Start Time (IRE)**[27] 3868 6-9-7 **73**.............................. LukeMorris 10 62
(Paul Midgley) *chsd ldrs: unable qck looking awkward over 1f out: wknd ins fnl f* **16/1**

6522 **10** *2 3/4* **Proud Archi (IRE)**[28] 3813 5-10-2 **82**.............................. AndrewMullen 3 63
(Michael Dods) *chsd ldrs: dropped to midfield 5f out: rdn and wknd 2f out (trainer could offer no explanation for the gelding's performance)* **4/1**[1]

0020 **11** *3 3/4* **Upstaging**[13] 4364 7-9-12 **78**.............................. BarryMcHugh 7 49
(Noel Wilson) *s.i.s: in rr: rdn over 2f out: nvr a threat* **40/1**

/53- **P** **Brigham Young**[249] 8882 4-9-11 **77**.............................. RichardKingscote 8
(Ed Walker) *hld up: rdn over 2f out: eased over 1f out: p.u ins fnl f (jockey said gelding lost its action app 1 1/2f out)* **13/2**[3]

1m 31.47s (3.97) **Going Correction** +0.65s/f (Yiel) **12 Ran SP% 123.6**
Speed ratings (Par 105): **103,101,99,98,98 97,95,94,94,91 86,**
CSF £54.81 CT £916.13 TOTE £7.00: £2.80, £2.20, £8.40; EX 65.60 Trifecta £1469.90.
Owner Dr Marwan Koukash **Bred** Kenneth Heelan **Trained** Musley Bank, N Yorks

FOCUS
Mostly exposed sorts in this handicap which was run over 37 yards further than advertised. The pace was ordinary and it was an advantage to race handy so the form is unlikely to prove reliable. The winner has been rated close to his best over the past two years, with the second to form.

4880 EUROGOLD H'CAP 5f 110y
8:30 (8:34) (Class 4) (0-80,81) 4-Y-0+

£6,080 (£1,809; £904; £452; £400; £400) **Stalls** Low

Form RPR

5002 **1** **Powerallied (IRE)**[13] 4364 6-9-8 **81**.............................. PaulHanagan 5 88
(Richard Fahey) *chsd ldrs: pushed along over 3f out: effrt on inner over 1f out: swtchd rt ins fnl f: r.o towards fin to ld post* **11/4**[1]

0066 **2** *shd* **Bellevarde (IRE)**[20] 4105 5-9-0 **73**.............................. PatCosgrave 8 79
(Richard Price) *chsd ldrs: rdn and wnt 2nd over 1f out: led ins fnl f: hdd post* **20/1**

0336 **3** *1 3/4* **Red Stripes (USA)**[1] 4829 7-8-3 **62** oh8 ow1..........(b) AndrewMullen 13 62?
(Lisa Williamson) *led: rdn over 1f out: hdd ins fnl f: no ex fnl 50yds* **66/1**

4006 **4** *nk* **Bossipop**[15] 4279 6-9-7 **80**..............................(b) RobHornby 2 79
(Tim Easterby) *midfield: lost pl 3f out: hdwy over 1f out: r.o ins fnl f: gng on at fin* **4/1**[3]

0020 **5** *1/2* **Celerity (IRE)**[3] 4765 5-7-13 **61** oh16..............................(p) NoelGarbutt(3) 7 58?
(Lisa Williamson) *in tch: rdn 2f out: no imp over 1f out: styd on same pce ins fnl f* **100/1**

4030 **6** *3/4* **Redrosezorro**[35] 3549 5-8-8 **67**..............................(h) RachelRichardson 14 62+
(Eric Alston) *hld up in rr: rdn and hdwy ent fnl f: styd on towards fin: nvr able to rch ldrs* **18/1**

U314 **7** *1 1/2* **Zac Brown (IRE)**[7] 4593 8-8-12 **71**..............................(t) RichardKingscote 4 61+
(Charlie Wallis) *stmbld bdly s and missed break: sn in midfield: nt clr run over 1f out: sn swtchd lft: kpt on ins fnl f: one pce fnl 75yds* **3/1**[2]

0636 **8** *3/4* **Madrinho (IRE)**[6] 4649 6-9-1 **74**.............................. FrannyNorton 12 61+
(Tony Carroll) *s.i.s: in rr: rdn over 1f out: nt clr run ins fnl f: kpt on: nvr able to trble ldrs* **7/1**

1000 **9** *3/4* **Alsvinder**[13] 4364 6-9-6 **79**.............................. BenCurtis 3 64
(Philip Kirby) *chsd ldr tl rdn over 1f out and unable qck: wknd ins fnl f* **20/1**

4202 **10** *1* **Bowson Fred**[13] 4375 7-9-5 **78**.............................. PhilDennis 6 59
(Michael Easterby) *wnt to post early: chsd ldrs: rdn 2f out: wknd ins fnl f* **7/1**

0-00 **11** *1 3/4* **Quantum Dot (IRE)**[13] 4364 8-8-10 **69**..............................(b) BarryMcHugh 11 44
(Ed de Giles) *racd off the pce: sn pushed along: nvr able to get on terms* **66/1**

5000 **12** *3 3/4* **Caledonian Gold**[7] 4589 6-8-4 **63** oh16 ow2.............................. NathanEvans 10 25
(Lisa Williamson) *wnt to post early: s.i.s: in rr: nvr a threat: wnt rt towards fin* **100/1**

0301 **13** *2 1/4* **Desert Ace (IRE)**[9] 4514 8-9-1 **74** 4ex.............................. LukeMorris 9 29+
(Paul Midgley) *in tch: rdn over 1f out: outpcd whn n.m.r over 1f out: eased whn btn fnl 150yds (jockey said gelding lost its action)* **25/1**

1m 10.62s (1.62) **Going Correction** +0.65s/f (Yiel) **13 Ran SP% 120.3**
Speed ratings (Par 105): **113,112,110,110,109 108,106,105,104,103 100,95,92**
CSF £63.92 CT £3058.88 TOTE £3.20: £1.40, £5.10, £8.30; EX 76.30 Trifecta £2805.30.
Owner Dr Marwan Koukash **Bred** John R Jeffers **Trained** Musley Bank, N Yorks

FOCUS
Add 33yds. The pace held up pretty well here. The third has been rated to his best turf form for two years.

4881 AMBER ENERGY FILLIES' H'CAP 1m 7f 196y
9:00 (9:02) (Class 4) (0-85,82) 3-Y-0+

£6,080 (£1,809; £904; £452; £400; £400) **Stalls** Low

Form RPR

6523 **1** **Nafaayes (IRE)**[16] 4251 5-8-10 **62**..............................(p) PaulHanagan 8 69
(Jean-Rene Auvray) *hld up: hdwy over 3f out: led over 1f out: edgd lft ins fnl f: sn clr: styd on wl* **10/1**

0000 **2** *3* **Miss Ranger (IRE)**[6] 4661 7-7-13 **56**..............................(b) PaulaMuir(5) 6 59
(Roger Fell) *racd keenly: chsd ldrs: upsides 3f out: rdn and stl ev ch over 1f out: unable qck ins fnl f: styd on same pce after* **25/1**

1-63 **3** *2 1/4* **Miss Latin (IRE)**[43] 3269 4-9-9 **75**.............................. PatCosgrave 5 75
(David Simcock) *hld up: rdn over 2f out: hdwy over 1f out: styd on to chse front two wl ins fnl f: nvr able to chal* **7/2**[3]

3641 **4** *1 1/4* **So Near So Farhh**[10] 4483 4-9-3 **69** 5ex.............................. FrannyNorton 4 68
(Mick Channon) *w ldr: led after 3f: rdn and hdd over 1f out: no ex fnl 150yds* **15/8**[1]

1-00 **5** *2 1/2* **Dance To Paris**[20] 4112 4-9-8 **74**..............................(b) RichardKingscote 3 70
(Lucy Wadham) *in tch: pushed along over 2f out: no imp over 1f out* **13/2**

4163 **6** *6* **Dorah**[7] 4599 3-8-13 **82**.............................. LukeMorris 1 72
(Archie Watson) *led: hdd after 3f: remained handy: rdn and lost pl over 2f out: wknd wl over 1f out: lame (vet said filly was lame on its right hind)* **3/1**[2]

2-06 **7** *5* **Perfect Summer (IRE)**[26] 3886 9-9-3 **69**..............................(v) BenCurtis 7 52
(Ian Williams) *prom: pushed along 6f out: drvn over 4f out: wknd 3f out: lft bhd over 2f out (jockey said mare hung left)* **11/1**

3m 43.81s (11.91) **Going Correction** +0.65s/f (Yiel)
WFA 3 from 4yo+ 17lb **7 Ran SP% 116.6**
Speed ratings (Par 102): **96,94,93,92,91 88,86**
CSF £203.98 CT £1050.50 TOTE £8.90: £4.20, £13.40; EX 167.00 Trifecta £751.90.
Owner Nigel Kelly & Stuart McPhee **Bred** Shadwell Estate Company Limited **Trained** Calne, Wilts

FOCUS
A staying handicap run over 72 yards further than advertised for fillies and mares run at a fair gallop. Although the winner won well the form is unlikely to be strong with several underperforming. It's been rated on the negative side, with the winner in line with her AW best.
T/Plt: £393.20 to a £1 stake. Pool: £68,345.26 - 126.88 winning units. T/Qpdt: £111.10 to a £1 stake. Pool: £6,326.95 - 42.14 winning units. **Darren Owen**

4845 NEWMARKET (R-H)
Friday, July 12

OFFICIAL GOING: Good to firm (watered; ovr 8.4; stands' 8.6, ctr 8.4, far 8.3)
Wind: light, behind Weather: mostly fine, clouding over and shower race 4

4882 BET365 H'CAP 1m 2f
1:50 (1:53) (Class 2) (0-105,105) 3-Y-O

£49,800 (£14,912; £7,456; £3,728; £1,864; £936) **Stalls** Centre

Form RPR

-225 **1** **Walkinthesand (IRE)**[50] 3026 3-9-7 **105**.............................. RyanMoore 6 114
(Richard Hannon) *wl in tch in midfield: effrt 2f out: rdn to chal over 1f out: led ins fnl f: styd on wl: rdn out* **9/1**

1031 **2** *1* **Korcho**[18] 4188 3-8-6 **90**.............................. KerrinMcEvoy 4 97
(Hughie Morrison) *hld up in tch in midfield: clsd to chse ldrs 2f out: rdn over 1f out: chsd wnr ins fnl f: kpt on but no imp fnl 100yds* **12/1**

2100 **3** *nk* **Majestic Dawn (IRE)**[22] 4017 3-8-5 **89**.............................. JosephineGordon 13 95
(Paul Cole) *led and sn crossed to inner rail: rdn 2f out: drvn over 1f out: hdd and one pce ins fnl f* **12/1**

3040 **4** *1/2* **Dark Vision (IRE)**[22] 4016 3-9-5 **103**.............................. JamesDoyle 10 108
(Mark Johnston) *hld up in midfield: clsd and nt clr run 2f out: rdn and hdwy 1f out: styd on wl ins fnl f: nvr trbld ldrs* **8/1**[3]

-130 **5** *3/4* **Good Birthday (IRE)**[22] 4017 3-8-11 **95**.............................. SilvestreDeSousa 12 99+
(Andrew Balding) *stdd s: t.k.h: hld up in last pair: hdwy on outer over 2f out: chsng ldrs whn veered lft u.p over 1f out: kpt on same pce ins fnl f* **13/2**[1]

1031 **6** *nk* **Oasis Prince**[14] 4347 3-8-12 **96**.............................. JamieSpencer 1 99
(Mark Johnston) *chsd ldrs for 3f: wl in tch in midfield after: nt clr run and swtchd rt over 1f out: kpt on u.p ins fnl f: no threat to ldrs* **10/1**

2210 **7** *2 1/4* **Migration (IRE)**[22] 4016 3-8-6 **90**.............................. AndreaAtzeni 8 89
(David Menuisier) *stdd s: hld up in last quartet: effrt nrest stands' rail 2f out: rdn over 1f out: kpt on ins fnl f: nvr trbld ldrs* **9/1**

1-42 **8** *1/2* **Almashriq (USA)**[50] 3003 3-8-4 **88**.............................. ChrisHayes 16 86
(John Gosden) *stdd after s: hld up in last quartet: effrt 3f out: hdwy in centre to chse ldrs 2f out: struggling to qckn whn hmpd over 1f out: wl hld and kpt on same pce fnl f* **9/1**

-320 **9** *nk* **Tulfarris**[22] 4016 3-8-8 **92**.............................. StevieDonohoe 3 89
(Charlie Fellowes) *hld up in tch in midfield: effrt and nt clrest of runs over 1f out: rdn and no imp ins fnl f* **14/1**

-252 **10** *2 1/4* **The Trader (IRE)**[41] 3341 3-8-9 **93**.............................. JoeFanning 9 86
(Mark Johnston) *chsd ldr tl 3f out: stl cl up and rdn over 1f out: sn edgd lft and unable qck: wknd ins fnl f* **15/2**[2]

1-10 **11** *3/4* **Solid Stone (IRE)**[55] 2828 3-8-6 **90**.............................. PJMcDonald 15 81
(Sir Michael Stoute) *hld up in tch in midfield: rdn and hdwy to chse ldrs 2f out: unable qck and outpcd whn impeded jst over 1f out: wknd ins fnl f* **8/1**[3]

1164 **12** *1* **Aweedram (IRE)**[14] 4347 3-8-7 **91**.............................. DavidEgan 14 80
(Alan King) *stdd s: t.k.h: hld up in last pair: clsd and nt clrest of runs 2f out: drifting rt and no imp over 1f out: edgd lft u.p 1f out: wknd ins fnl f* **25/1**

2223 **13** *3/4* **Alkaamel**[41] 3341 3-8-5 **89**.............................. LiamJones 7 77
(William Haggas) *t.k.h: chsd ldrs: clsd to press ldr and rdn 3f out: drvn and no ex over 1f out: sn outpcd and wknd ins fnl f (jockey said gelding ran too free)* **16/1**

31-6 **14** *60* **Allmankind**[64] 2558 3-8-6 **90** ow1.............................. CliffordLee 5
(Michael Bell) *taken down early: plld hrd: hld up in tch in midfield: clsd to chse ldrs 6f out tl lost pl qckly 3f out: sn bhd: t.o (jockey said colt ran too free)* **12/1**

2m 0.61s (-6.49) **Going Correction** -0.30s/f (Firm) course record **14 Ran SP% 125.9**
Speed ratings (Par 106): **113,112,111,111,110 110,108,108,108,106 105,105,104,56**
CSF £117.96 CT £1328.17 TOTE £10.00: £3.20, £5.10, £4.00; EX 149.70 Trifecta £3061.40.
Owner Saeed Suhail **Bred** Churchtown House Stud **Trained** East Everleigh, Wilts

FOCUS
Lightening fast ground and a tailwind on day two of the July Festival. Going Stick reading 8.4 at 9:00am. An ultra-competitive and wide-open edition of this 3yo handicap, which was won last year by subsequent Group 2 Princess of Wales's Stakes scorer Communique. Three of the first five home had contested the London Gold Cup at Newbury in May and the first three have been rated as improving. They lowered the track record by over a second. It's been rated around the race averages, with the fourth to his reappearance form.

4883 DUCHESS OF CAMBRIDGE STKS (SPONSORED BY BET365) (GROUP 2) (FILLIES) 6f
2:25 (2:25) (Class 1) 2-Y-O

£45,368 (£17,200; £8,608; £4,288; £2,152; £1,080) **Stalls** Low

Form RPR

211 **1** **Raffle Prize (IRE)**[23] 3983 2-9-3 104.............................. FrankieDettori 1 113
(Mark Johnston) *sn led and mde rest: shkn up over 1f out: rdn 1f out: sn asserted and r.o strly ins fnl f: readily* **9/2**[3]

11 **2** *1 3/4* **Daahyeh**[21] 4048 2-9-0 109.............................. DavidEgan 3 104
(Roger Varian) *in tch in midfield: swtchd lft 2f out: hdwy u.p over 1f out: styd on ins fnl f but nvr matching pce of wnr: wnt 2nd cl home* **5/4**[1]

13 **3** *hd* **Final Song (IRE)**[23] 3983 2-9-0 0.............................. RyanMoore 6 103
(Saeed bin Suroor) *chsd ldrs: effrt to press wnr over 1f out: drvn and unable to match pce of wnr 1f out: kpt on same pce and lost 2nd cl home* **10/3**[2]

110 **4** *2 1/4* **Lambeth Walk**[23] 3983 2-9-0 88.............................. OisinMurphy 5 96
(Archie Watson) *w wnr tl unable qck and outpcd over 1f out: wknd ins fnl f: lame (vet said filly was lame on its right fore)* **25/1**

10 **5** *1/2* **Divine Spirit**[23] 3983 2-9-0 0.............................. JamesDoyle 2 94
(Charlie Appleby) *t.k.h: trckd ldrs: effrt 2f out: unable qck u.p over 1f out: wknd ins fnl f* **8/1**

21 **6** *3 1/2* **Bredenbury (IRE)**[17] 4214 2-9-0 0.............................. JamieSpencer 7 83
(David Simcock) *dropped in bhd after s: hld up in last pair: effrt wl over 1f out: no imp and sn outpcd: wknd ins fnl f* **33/1**

32 **7** *hd* **Celtic Beauty (IRE)**[21] 4048 2-9-0 0 .... WJLee 4 82
(K J Condon, Ire) *hld up in last pair: effrt wl over 1f out: sn struggling and outpcd: wknd ins fnl f* **9/1**

1m 9.09s (-3.01) **Going Correction** -0.30s/f (Firm) 2y crse rec **7** Ran SP% **113.6**
Speed ratings (Par 103): **108,105,105,102,101 97,96**
CSF £10.41 TOTE £4.90: £2.40, £1.30; EX 9.80 Trifecta £25.60.
Owner Sheikh Hamdan bin Mohammed Al Maktoum **Bred** Godolphin **Trained** Middleham Moor, N Yorks

FOCUS
The winners of the Queen Mary and Albany finished one-two in that order, so a good standard, although the winner was able to dictate at close to the ideal tempo, and on fast ground the all-age course record was lowered by 0.02sec. The action was near side. The second has been rated close to her Ascot form.

4884 BET365 TROPHY (HERITAGE H'CAP) 1m 6f
3:00 (3:03) (Class 2) 4-Y-O+
£74,700 (£22,368; £11,184; £5,592; £2,796; £1,404) **Stalls** Low

Form RPR

1116 **1** **King's Advice**[13] 4382 5-9-4 **101** .... JoeFanning 3 112
(Mark Johnston) *led for 1f: styd chsng ldrs tl rdn to ld again 2f out: styd on strly and drew clr ins fnl f: readily* **10/1**

0-51 **2** *2 ½* **Te Akau Caliburn (IRE)**[32] 3655 4-9-0 **97** .... SilvestreDeSousa 17 104
(Andrew Balding) *hld up in tch in midfield: hdwy and rdn to chal 3f out tl unable to match pce of wnr 1f out: kpt on same pce ins fnl f* **13/2[3]**

-550 **3** *¾* **Desert Skyline (IRE)**[13] 4382 5-9-10 **107** ....(p) GeraldMosse 18 113
(David Elsworth) *hld up in rr: hdwy and rdn ent fnl 3f: styd on u.p ins fnl f: no threat to wnr* **33/1**

0-04 **4** *hd* **Not So Sleepy**[32] 3655 7-8-9 **92** ....(t) PJMcDonald 11 99+
(Hughie Morrison) *t.k.h: hld up in tch in midfield: nt clr run wl over 2f out: effrt over 1f out: hdwy and swtchd rt jst ins fnl f: styd on wl fnl 100yds: no threat to wnr* **40/1**

1450 **5** *¾* **Grandee (IRE)**[20] 4102 5-8-6 **89** .... DavidEgan 16 94
(Roger Fell) *chsd ldrs: effrt 3f out: nt clr run wl over 1f out: swtchd lft and squeezed through ent fnl f: kpt on u.p* **16/1**

111- **6** *1* **Outbox**[21] 4089 4-9-5 **102** .... AndreaAtzeni 6 105
(Simon Crisford) *t.k.h early: hld up in tch in midfield: clsd and rdn to chse ldrs 3f out: unable qck u.p over 1f out: wknd ins fnl f* **9/2[2]**

3135 **7** *nk* **Eddystone Rock (IRE)**[6] 4646 7-8-9 **92** .... KierenFox 4 95
(John Best) *short of room sn after s: hld up towards rr: swtchd lft and effrt ent fnl 3f: hdwy and chsd ldrs u.p over 1f out: no ex 1f out and wknd ins fnl f* **25/1**

0606 **8** *½* **Manjaam (IRE)**[20] 4102 6-8-2 **85** ....(p) KieranO'Neill 8 87
(Ian Williams) *w wnr tl led after 1f: rdn and hrd pressed 3f out: hdd 2f out: edgd lft and no ex 1f out: wknd ins fnl f* **25/1**

50-6 **9** *2* **Platitude**[48] 3078 6-9-0 **97** .... KieranShoemark 7 96
(Amanda Perrett) *taken down early: hld up in tch in midfield: effrt over 2f out: unable qck u.p over 1f out: btn whn nt clr run ins fnl f: sn wknd* **33/1**

-024 **10** *2 ½* **What A Welcome**[34] 3600 5-9-3 **100** .... JoeyHaynes 14 96
(Patrick Chamings) *t.k.h: wl in tch in midfield: effrt and rdn to press ldrs 3f out tl 2f out: outpcd and lost pl over 1f out: wknd ins fnl f* **20/1**

-301 **11** *hd* **Desert Wind (IRE)**[37] 3466 4-9-1 **98** .... StevieDonohoe 1 94
(Ed Vaughan) *hld up in tch in midfield: nt clr run and swtchd lft over 2f out: effrt over 1f out: no prog and wknd ins fnl f* **10/1**

51/0 **12** *1 ½* **Secret Advisor (FR)**[21] 4053 5-9-6 **103** .... JamesDoyle 2 96
(Charlie Appleby) *in tch in midfield: effrt over 2f out: unable qck and btn over 1f out: hung lft and eased ins fnl f (jockey said gelding had no more to give)* **8/1**

33-2 **13** *1 ¾* **Ben Vrackie**[21] 4053 4-9-7 **104** .... FrankieDettori 5 95
(John Gosden) *s.i.s: hld up in rr: effrt over 2f out: no imp over 1f out: wl hld whn nt clr run and eased ins fnl f (trainer said colt was unsuited by the going and would prefer an easier surface)* **3/1[1]**

-006 **14** *nk* **Never Surrender (IRE)**[28] 3799 5-8-0 **83** oh3 ....(p) RaulDaSilva 9 74
(Charles Hills) *hld up in rr: nt clr run and swtchd rt 2f out: hung lft and no prog over 1f out: stl hanging and wl btn ins fnl f* **50/1**

-145 **15** *¾* **Collide**[21] 4053 4-9-2 **99** ....(t) OisinMurphy 12 89
(Hugo Palmer) *t.k.h: chsd ldrs: rdn and ev ch 3f out: struggling 2f out and lost pl over 1f out: wknd ins fnl f* **10/1**

0030 **16** *15* **Time To Study (FR)**[13] 4382 5-8-13 **96** .... JimCrowley 10 65
(Ian Williams) *chsd ldrs tl 4f out: bhd and eased ins fnl f* **22/1**

4100 **17** *19* **Lissitzky (IRE)**[13] 4381 4-8-2 **85** .... JosephineGordon 13 27
(Andrew Balding) *hld up towards rr: rdn ent fnl 4f: bhd 2f out: virtually p.u ins fnl f* **50/1**

2m 53.53s (-6.37) **Going Correction** -0.30s/f (Firm) course record **17** Ran SP% **129.8**
Speed ratings (Par 109): **106,104,104,104,103 103,102,102,101,100 99,99,98,97,97 88,78**
CSF £69.99 CT £2125.22 TOTE £11.10: £2.70, £2.10, £7.70, £8.60; EX 82.70 Trifecta £3524.30.

Owner Saeed Jaber **Bred** Rabbah Bloodstock Limited **Trained** Middleham Moor, N Yorks

FOCUS
The inaugural running of this staying handicap was won 12 month's ago by subsequent Group 3 Geoffrey Freer Stakes winner Hamada. This renewal looked well up to scratch and it represents rock solid handicap form. It was won with some authority by the prolific King's Advice, who resumed his progress, and was the third race in succession where the track record was broken. The second confirmed his Pontefract win, with the third close to his best.

4885 TATTERSALLS FALMOUTH STKS (GROUP 1) (BRITISH CHAMPIONS SERIES) (F&M) 1m
3:35 (3:36) (Class 1) 3-Y-O+
£113,420 (£43,000; £21,520; £10,720; £5,380; £2,700) **Stalls** Low

Form RPR

-434 **1** **Veracious**[23] 3986 4-9-7 108 ....(t) OisinMurphy 4 116
(Sir Michael Stoute) *mde all: rdn 2f out: hrd pressed and drvn jst ins fnl f: hld on gamely fnl 100yds: all out* **6/1**

0-43 **2** *nk* **One Master**[24] 3948 5-9-7 113 .... JamesDoyle 2 115
(William Haggas) *hld up in last pair: clsd over 2f out: swtchd lft and effrt over 1f out: chal and edgd rt jst ins fnl f: r.o wl but hld towards fin* **10/3[2]**

0623 **3** *2 ¾* **I Can Fly**[23] 3986 4-9-7 110 .... RyanMoore 6 109
(A P O'Brien, Ire) *in tch in midfield: edgd out lft and drvn over 1f out: unable qck and kpt on same pce ins fnl f* **5/2[1]**

-130 **4** *1 ¾* **Qabala (USA)**[47] 3115 3-8-12 109 .... AndreaAtzeni 1 103
(Roger Varian) *chsd ldng pair: effrt ent fnl 2f: unable qck u.p ent fnl f: wknd ins fnl f* **10/3[2]**

51-1 **5** *1* **Beshaayir**[48] 3105 4-9-7 109 ....(t) FrankieDettori 5 102
(William Haggas) *chsd wnr: effrt wl over 1f out: unable qck u.p ent fnl f: wknd ins fnl f* **9/2[3]**

1-20 **6** *2 ½* **Mot Juste (USA)**[68] 2443 3-8-12 103 .... DavidEgan 3 95
(Roger Varian) *hld up in last pair: effrt over 2f out: no imp u.p over 1f out: wknd ins fnl f* **16/1**

1m 35.89s (-4.11) **Going Correction** -0.30s/f (Firm) course record **6** Ran SP% **113.1**
WFA 3 from 4yo+ 9lb
Speed ratings (Par 117): **108,107,104,103,102 99**
CSF £26.39 TOTE £8.10: £3.00, £1.90; EX 29.40 Trifecta £90.70.
Owner Cheveley Park Stud **Bred** Cheveley Park Stud Ltd **Trained** Newmarket, Suffolk

FOCUS
There was a rain shower before and during this race. Only one of these - the runner-up - had won at the top level and the winner was allowed a surprisingly easy lead on the near rail, with the others initially shunning the fence, before soon joining her, and she set a steady pace. Still, another course record. It's been rated at face value for now, with the second to her Ascot form.

4886 WEATHERBYS BRITISH EBF MAIDEN STKS (PLUS 10 RACE) (C&G) 7f
4:10 (4:11) (Class 3) 2-Y-O
£7,762 (£2,310; £1,154; £577) **Stalls** Low

Form RPR

1 **Al Madhar (FR)** 2-9-0 0 .... JimCrowley 7 88+
(Richard Hannon) *chsd ldrs: rdn over 2f out: clsd to press ldrs over 1f out: edgd lft 1f out: sustained effrt u.p and styd on wl to ld last strides* **8/1**

2 *nk* **Al Suhail** 2-9-0 0 .... JamesDoyle 12 87+
(Charlie Appleby) *hld up in tch in midfield: clsd to press ldrs and travelling strly 2f out: rdn to ld and edgd rt 1f out: sn hrd pressed but kpt on u.p: hdd last strides* **10/3[2]**

3 *1 ¼* **First Receiver** 2-9-0 0 .... OisinMurphy 3 84+
(Sir Michael Stoute) *bmpd s: hld up in tch in midfield: nt clr run and swtchd rt 2f out: effrt over 1f out: rdn and kpt on wl ins fnl f* **14/1**

4 *¾* **Tsar** 2-9-0 0 .... FrankieDettori 14 82+
(John Gosden) *v.s.a: hld up in tch in last trio: clsd over 2f out: rdn and hdwy over 1f out: kpt on ins fnl f* **13/2[3]**

5 *1* **Kipling (IRE)**[35] 3555 2-9-0 0 .... RyanMoore 13 79
(A P O'Brien, Ire) *led: rdn 2f out: hdd 1f out: no ex: edgd lft and wknd wl ins fnl f* **7/4[1]**

6 *2 ¼* **Dulas (IRE)** 2-9-0 0 .... KieranShoemark 8 73
(Charles Hills) *t.k.h: hld up wl in tch in midfield: effrt and rn green over 1f out: unable qck u.p and wnt lft 1f out: wknd ins fnl f* **33/1**

7 *½* **Eshaasy** 2-9-0 0 .... ChrisHayes 9 71+
(John Gosden) *v.s.a: in tch in last trio: effrt over 1f out: shifting rt but hdwy ent fnl f: kpt on wl ins fnl f: nvr trbld ldrs* **22/1**

8 *nk* **Tammani** 2-9-0 0 .... KerrinMcEvoy 5 71+
(William Haggas) *hld up in tch in last quartet: clsd over 2f out: effrt and unable qck over 1f out: rdn and wknd ins fnl f* **33/1**

52 **9** *¾* **Mass Media**[20] 4117 2-9-0 0 .... RobertHavlin 10 69
(John Gosden) *w ldr: rdn over 1f out: sn struggling to qckn and edgd lft: wknd ins fnl f* **9/1**

10 *3* **Wild Hero (IRE)** 2-9-0 0 .... SilvestreDeSousa 2 61
(Andrew Balding) *wnt lft leaving stalls: sn rcvrd and in tch in midfield: effrt over 1f out: no imp whn squeezed for room wl over 1f out: wknd fnl f* **33/1**

11 *1 ½* **Celtic Art (FR)** 2-9-0 0 .... PJMcDonald 11 56
(Paul Cole) *chsd ldrs: shkn up 2f out: unable qck and losing pl whn impeded 1f out: sn wknd* **20/1**

12 *2* **Stepney Causeway** 2-9-0 0 .... TomMarquand 6 51
(Michael Bell) *in tch in midfield: rdn over 2f out: sn struggling and towards rr whn wandered rt over 1f out: wknd fnl f* **50/1**

13 *½* **Union Spirit** 2-9-0 0 .... JamieSpencer 4 50
(Peter Chapple-Hyam) *squeezed for room leaving stalls: hld up in last trio: outpcd and shkn up 2f out: sn btn and wknd fnl f* **66/1**

14 *7* **Anglo Saxon (IRE)** 2-9-0 0 .... StevieDonohoe 1 31
(Charlie Fellowes) *midfield: rdn over 2f out: lost pl and bhd whn hung lft over 1f out: wknd fnl f* **50/1**

1m 23.76s (-1.94) **Going Correction** -0.30s/f (Firm) **14** Ran SP% **123.9**
Speed ratings (Par 98): **99,98,97,96,95 92,92,91,90,87 85,83,82,74**
CSF £33.25 TOTE £9.00: £2.30, £1.80, £3.50; EX 48.10 Trifecta £627.40.
Owner Hamdan Al Maktoum **Bred** Robin Geffen **Trained** East Everleigh, Wilts

FOCUS
Traditionally a strong maiden, this latest running has been rated in line with the race standard, with the fifth close to his debut form.

4887 PORSCHE CENTRE CAMBRIDGE H'CAP 7f
4:45 (4:46) (Class 3) (0-90,92) 3-Y-O+ **£16,172** (£4,812; £2,405; £1,202) **Stalls** Low

Form RPR

43-3 **1** **Light And Dark**[20] 4121 3-8-13 **82** .... CallumShepherd 1 94+
(Saeed bin Suroor) *hld up in tch in midfield: nt clr run jst over 2f out: swtchd lft and squeezed through over 1f out: rdn to ld 1f out: r.o strly and sn clr: readily* **6/1[3]**

1010 **2** *3* **La Maquina**[9] 4506 4-9-7 **82** ....(t) JimCrowley 3 89+
(George Baker) *taken down early: hld up in last pair: swtchd lft and nt clr run 2f out: swtchd lft and hdwy u.p 1f out: chsd clr wnr ins fnl f: kpt on but nvr a threat* **14/1**

5352 **3** *1 ¼* **Dirty Rascal (IRE)**[20] 4124 3-9-4 **87** ....(b) TomMarquand 4 88
(Richard Hannon) *chsd ldrs: effrt wl over 1f out: wnt 2nd but wnr gng clr whn edgd lft 1f out: edgd bk rt: one pce and lost 2nd ins fnl f* **11/2[2]**

1006 **4** *1 ¾* **Maksab (IRE)**[70] 2363 4-9-10 **85** .... SilvestreDeSousa 5 84
(Mick Channon) *led for 1f: chsd ldrs tl shuffled bk and rdn 2f out: swtchd rt over 1f out: no threat to ldrs but kpt on u.p ins fnl f* **25/1**

3024 **5** *½* **Tommy Taylor (USA)**[3] 4759 5-10-0 **89** .... RyanMoore 8 87
(Kevin Ryan) *restless in stalls: hld up in tch in midfield: clsd to chse ldrs 2f out: sn rdn and unable qck ent fnl f: wknd ins fnl f* **8/1**

5334 **6** *½* **Medieval (IRE)**[15] 4300 5-9-4 **79** ....(b) PJMcDonald 6 75
(Paul Cole) *hld up in tch towards rr: hdwy over 2f out: drvn over 1f out: sn swtchd lft and no ex: wknd ins fnl f* **7/1**

1-31 **7** *¾* **Breathtaking Look**[21] 4072 4-9-13 **88** .... KerrinMcEvoy 10 82
(Stuart Williams) *wl in tch in midfield: clsd to chse ldrs over 2f out: hld and unable qck over 1f out: wknd ins fnl f: nudged lft and wknd ins fnl f* **9/2[1]**

0056 **8** *3 ½* **Rampant Lion (IRE)**[15] 4300 4-9-1 **76** ....(p) GeraldMosse 12 61
(William Jarvis) *chsd ldrs: wnt 2nd 5f out: rdn and ev ch 2f out: led and edgd lft over 1f out: hdd 1f out: sn outpcd and wknd ins fnl f* **25/1**

-321 **9** *3 ½* **Jaleel**[20] 4124 3-9-0 **83** .... AndreaAtzeni 2 55
(Roger Varian) *dwlt and short of room sn after s: hld up in tch in rr: effrt 2f out: no imp and wl hld whn nt clr run and swtchd lft 1f out: wknd ins fnl f (jockey said gelding stopped quickly)* **9/2[1]**

2100 **10** *1* **Portledge (IRE)**[103] 1457 5-9-4 **79** ....(b) FrankieDettori 7 52
(James Bethell) *led after 1f and c across to stands' rail: rdn and hdd over 1f out: sn btn and wknd ins fnl f* **25/1**

0060 **11** *1* **Shady McCoy (USA)**[20] 4127 9-10-3 **92**.................. JamesDoyle 13 62
(Ian Williams) *wl in tch in midfield: struggling to qckn u.p whn nudged lft over 1f out: sn btn and wknd fnl f* **20/1**

-030 **12** *1 1/2* **Rum Runner**[6] 4666 4-9-9 **84**.................. TomQueally 9 50
(Richard Hannon) *hld up in tch in midfield: effrt ent fnl 2f: sn struggling and outpcd: wknd fnl f* **16/1**

4621 **13** *4* **I Am A Dreamer**[6] 4635 3-9-2 **85** 6ex.................. JoeFanning 11 37
(Mark Johnston) *midfield: rdn 3f out: sn struggling and bhd over 1f out* **10/1**

1m 21.78s (-3.92) **Going Correction** -0.30s/f (Firm) course record
WFA 3 from 4yo+ 8lb **13** Ran SP% **127.6**
Speed ratings (Par 107): **110,106,105,103,102 102,101,97,93,92 90,89,84**
CSF £88.50 CT £382.62 TOTE £5.60: £2.40, £5.80, £2.20; EX 131.20 Trifecta £1298.70.
Owner Godolphin **Bred** Godolphin **Trained** Newmarket, Suffolk

FOCUS
On a day when the near rail looked favoured the first four were drawn 1-3-4-5, although the field became spread out in the closing stages. Another track record. The winner rates a big improver and the second is on the upgrade.

4888 JFD H'CAP 5f
5:20 (5:20) (Class 2) (0-100,95) 3-Y-O+ **£16,172** (£4,812; £2,405; £1,202) **Stalls** Low

Form RPR
-000 **1** **Mountain Peak**[18] 4186 4-9-2 **83**.................. AndreaAtzeni 6 94
(Ed Walker) *pressed ldr tl rdn to ld over 1f out: clr and in command ins fnl f: r.o wl* **6/1**

0400 **2** *1 3/4* **Savalas (IRE)**[13] 4402 4-9-8 **89**..................(p) RyanMoore 7 94
(Kevin Ryan) *wl in tch in last pair: effrt over 1f out: kpt on u.p ins fnl f: wnt 2nd towards fin but no threat to wnr* **9/2**[3]

1303 **3** *shd* **Shamshon (IRE)**[17] 4213 8-8-13 **80**.................. JimCrowley 2 84
(Stuart Williams) *wl in tch in midfield: swtchd lft and effrt over 1f out: rdn and chsd wnr ins fnl f: no imp and one pce after: lost 2nd towards fin* **11/1**

2100 **4** *1 1/4* **Saaheq**[34] 3582 5-9-10 **91**.................. AlistairRawlinson 1 91
(Michael Appleby) *chsd ldng pair: effrt over 1f out: wnt 2nd briefly 1f out but wnr gng clr: sn lost 2nd and wknd fnl 100yds* **9/2**[3]

004 **5** *1* **Orvar (IRE)**[15] 4313 6-9-10 **91**.................. PJMcDonald 5 87
(Paul Midgley) *stmbld leaving stalls: hld up wl in tch in rr: effrt 2f out: no imp and kpt on same pce ins fnl f* **7/2**[2]

0145 **6** *1/2* **Lord Riddiford (IRE)**[15] 4313 4-9-12 **93**.................. FrankieDettori 4 87
(John Quinn) *led: rdn and hdd over 1f out: unable qck and wknd ins fnl f (jockey said gelding moved poorly)* **9/4**[1]

57.31s (-1.39) **Going Correction** -0.30s/f (Firm) course record **6** Ran SP% **112.0**
Speed ratings (Par 109): **99,96,96,94,92 91**
CSF £32.14 TOTE £7.20: £3.30, £2.20; EX 36.80 Trifecta £282.10.
Owner Ebury Racing **Bred** Mrs Hugh Maitland-Jones **Trained** Upper Lambourn, Berks

FOCUS
They shunned the near rail, racing more up the middle. Not many runners but still fair form. This was the sixth course record from seven races. The second and third have been rated close to form.
T/Jkpt: Not Won. T/Plt: £946.00 to a £1 stake. Pool: £166,847.82 - 128.75 winning units. T/Qpdt: £116.60 to a £1 stake. Pool: £16,271.91 - 103.24 winning units. **Steve Payne**

4401 YORK (L-H)
Friday, July 12

OFFICIAL GOING: Good to firm (watered; ovr 7.4; far 7.4, ctr 7.3, stands' 7.3)
Wind: Light against Weather: cloudy with sunny periods

4889 ACTURIS IRISH STALLION FARMS EBF NOVICE STKS (PLUS 10 RACE) 5f 89y
2:05 (2:05) (Class 3) 2-Y-O **£9,703** (£2,887; £1,443; £721) **Stalls** Low

Form RPR
41 **1** **Spartan Fighter**[37] 3477 2-9-8 0.................. DanielTudhope 5 90
(Declan Carroll) *trckd ldng pair: hdwy 2f out: led over 1f out: sn rdn and edgd lft: readily* **1/2**[1]

2 *1* **Fanzone (IRE)** 2-9-2 0.................. HollieDoyle 1 80+
(Archie Watson) *dwlt: t.k.h: trckd ldrs: hdwy 2f out: n.m.r and swtchd rt over 1f out: sn rdn: styd on wl fnl f: tk 2nd nr line* **8/1**[3]

56 **3** *hd* **She Can Dance**[28] 3810 2-8-11 0.................. KevinStott 2 74
(Kevin Ryan) *wnt rt s: trckd ldr: cl up over 2f out: rdn and ev ch over 1f out: drvn and kpt on same pce fnl f* **16/1**

51 **4** *3 3/4* **Auckland Lodge (IRE)**[16] 4237 2-8-12 0.................. HarrisonShaw[(5)] 3 67
(Ben Haslam) *led: rdn along 2f out: drvn and hdd over 1f out: grad wknd* **12/1**

3 **5** *10* **Galactic Glow (IRE)**[76] 2093 2-9-2 0.................. DavidProbert 4 31
(William Jarvis) *dwlt: t.k.h and trckd ldrs: pushed along 2f out: rdn and hung bdly lft 1 1/2f out: sn wknd (jockey said colt was restless in the stalls and ran too free in the early stages)* **5/1**[2]

1m 5.33s (1.73) **Going Correction** +0.225s/f (Good) **5** Ran SP% **108.0**
Speed ratings (Par 98): **95,93,93,87,71**
CSF £4.87 TOTE £1.40: £1.10, £2.50; EX 5.00 Trifecta £18.40.
Owner Clipper Logistics **Bred** Cheveley Park Stud Ltd **Trained** Malton, N Yorks

FOCUS
The going was given as good to firm (Going Stick 7.4); Home straight - far side 7.4; centre 7.3; stands' side 7.3. After riding in the opener Kevin Stott said: "It's fast ground" and Danny Tudhope said: "It's good to firm, lovely ground." The rail was out 10m from its innermost line on the home bend from 1m1f to the entrance to the home straight. The short-priced favourite set a decent standard and got the job done cosily, but there were one or two promising efforts in behind as well. The level will depend on how much the third has improved.

4890 WILLIAM HILL LEADING RACECOURSE BOOKMAKER H'CAP 1m 3f 188y
2:40 (2:40) (Class 3) (0-95,94) 3-Y-O+ **£12,450** (£3,728; £1,864; £932; £466; £234) **Stalls** Centre

Form RPR
421 **1** **Anythingtoday (IRE)**[13] 4386 5-10-0 **94**..................(p) DanielTudhope 9 102+
(David O'Meara) *trckd ldng pair: hdwy 3f out: cl up 2f out: led 1 1/2f out and sn rdn clr: readily* **2/1**[1]

0123 **2** *1 1/4* **Speed Company (IRE)**[13] 4395 6-9-9 **89**.................. BenCurtis 6 93
(Ian Williams) *hld up in tch: hdwy over 3f out: chsd ldrs 2f out: rdn over 1f out: drvn and kpt on fnl f* **2/1**[1]

6000 **3** *shd* **Maifalki (FR)**[20] 4102 6-9-11 **91**.................. GrahamLee 7 95
(Jason Ward) *hld up in rr: hdwy over 2f out: rdn over 1f out: drvn and kpt on wl fnl f* **33/1**

22-3 **4** *4 1/2* **Final Rock**[41] 3349 4-9-1 **81**..................(v[1]) LukeMorris 2 78
(Sir Mark Prescott Bt) *trckd ldr: hdwy over 3f out: pushed along wl over 2f out: sn rdn: drvn wl over 1f out: sn wknd* **6/1**[3]

-300 **5** *nk* **Dance King**[16] 4241 9-9-1 **81**..................(tp) PaulMulrennan 1 77
(Tim Easterby) *hld up: hdwy 3f out: rdn along 2f out: n.d* **10/1**

4512 **6** *nk* **Oasis Fantasy (IRE)**[13] 4395 8-9-5 **88**.................. SeanDavis[(3)] 4 84
(David Simcock) *led: styd alone nr far rail in st: pushed along 3f out: rdn 2f out: hdd wl over 1f out: sn drvn and grad wknd* **4/1**[2]

2m 34.21s (1.01) **Going Correction** +0.225s/f (Good)
WFA 3 from 4yo+ 12lb **6** Ran SP% **113.0**
Speed ratings (Par 107): **105,104,104,101,100 100**
CSF £6.17 CT £88.42 TOTE £2.60: £1.60, £2.00; EX 6.00 Trifecta £91.20.
Owner Woodhurst Construction Ltd **Bred** T Whitehead **Trained** Upper Helmsley, N Yorks

FOCUS
Add 32yds. They raced in single file into the straight, at which point the leader stayed on the far rail and dropped out to finish last, while the rest came up the middle of the track. The second has been rated to his recent best.

4891 WILLIAM HILL SUMMER STKS (GROUP 3) (F&M) 6f
3:15 (3:18) (Class 1) 3-Y-O+
£36,861 (£13,975; £6,994; £3,484; £1,748; £877) **Stalls** Low

Form RPR
-435 **1** **Royal Intervention (IRE)**[21] 4050 3-8-12 **99**.................. PaulHanagan 9 109
(Ed Walker) *racd centre: mde all: rdn wl over 1f out: drvn ins fnl f: edgd lft and hld on wl towards fin* **6/1**[3]

-321 **2** *nk* **Shades Of Blue (IRE)**[18] 4205 3-8-12 **103**.................. HollieDoyle 3 108
(Clive Cox) *prom centre: chsd wnr 2f out: rdn to chal over 1f out: drvn and ev ch ins fnl f: no ex nr fin* **3/1**[1]

010- **3** *3 3/4* **Red Balloons**[279] 7988 3-8-12 **95**.................. BarryMcHugh 1 96
(Richard Fahey) *racd towards far side: hld up towards rr: hdwy on inner over 2f out: chsd ldrs wl over 1f out: sn rdn: styd on wl fnl f* **16/1**

-052 **4** *1 1/2* **Glass Slippers**[20] 4101 3-8-12 **96**.................. TomEaves 8 91
(Kevin Ryan) *chsd ldrs centre: hdwy 2f out: rdn over 1f out: drvn and kpt on same pce fnl f* **14/1**

2-00 **5** *nk* **Stay Classy (IRE)**[21] 4052 3-8-12 **95**.................. PaulMulrennan 10 90
(Richard Spencer) *awkward s and towards rr: hdwy into midfield centre after 2f: effrt to chse ldrs and rdn wl over 1f out: kpt on fnl f* **25/1**

-103 **6** *1 1/2* **Queen Of Desire (IRE)**[20] 4101 4-9-4 **97**.................. DanielTudhope 15 86
(Roger Varian) *racd towards stands' side: hld up: hdwy 2f out: swtchd rt and rdn over 1f out: kpt on fnl f (starter reported that the filly was the subject of a third criteria failure; trainer was informed that the filly could not run until the day after passing a stalls test)* **12/1**

-640 **7** *hd* **Foxtrot Lady**[20] 4095 4-9-4 **98**.................. DavidProbert 11 86
(Andrew Balding) *prom centre: pushed along 2f out: sn rdn: drvn and wknd fnl f* **7/1**

5-43 **8** *nse* **Fairy Falcon**[24] 3956 4-9-4 **86**.................. GrahamLee 14 86
(Bryan Smart) *racd towards stands' side: in tch: rdn along to chse ldrs 2f out: sn edgd lft and drvn: no imp* **50/1**

111 **9** *nk* **Archer's Dream (IRE)**[26] 3891 3-8-12 **100**.................. GeorgeWood 5 84
(James Fanshawe) *prom centre: pushed along over 2f out: rdn wl over 1f out: sn drvn and wknd (trainer's rep said filly was unsuited by the going and would prefer a slower surface)* **7/2**[2]

2653 **10** *1* **Island Of Life (USA)**[13] 4380 5-9-4 **95**..................(tp) TonyHamilton 2 81
(William Haggas) *dwlt and in rr tl styd on fnl 2f* **12/1**

-040 **11** *hd* **Ocelot**[20] 4101 5-9-4 **90**.................. KevinStott 4 81
(Robert Cowell) *awkward s: hld up: n.d* **40/1**

0024 **12** *2* **Impulsion (IRE)**[16] 4242 3-8-12 **90**..................(p) JackMitchell 12 73
(Roger Varian) *a towards rr* **33/1**

06-4 **13** *1* **Little Kim**[20] 4101 3-8-12 **94**.................. BenCurtis 6 70
(K R Burke) *in tch centre: pushed along over 2f out: sn rdn and wknd* **25/1**

0-0 **14** *2 1/2* **Fille De Reve**[56] 2791 4-9-4 **93**.................. ColmO'Donoghue 13 63
(Ed Walker) *nvr bttr than midfield* **33/1**

0-60 **15** *6* **Miss Bar Beach (IRE)**[146] 756 4-9-4 **90**.................. ShaneGray 17 44
(Keith Dalgleish) *stdd and swtchd lft s: racd towards stands' side and hld up in rr: sme hdwy 1/2-way: sn rdn along and n.d* **100/1**

3123 **16** *3/4* **Isaan Queen (IRE)**[22] 4023 3-8-12 **96**.................. LukeMorris 16 41
(Archie Watson) *racd towards stands' side: in tch: rdn along wl over 2f out: sn wknd (jockey said filly was never travelling)* **33/1**

1m 10.42s (-1.18) **Going Correction** +0.225s/f (Good)
WFA 3 from 4yo+ 6lb **16** Ran SP% **123.8**
Speed ratings (Par 113): **116,115,110,108,108 106,105,105,105,104 103,101,99,96,88 87**
CSF £22.82 TOTE £6.80: £2.70, £1.50, £5.00; EX 31.10 Trifecta £392.20.
Owner Lord Lloyd Webber And W S Farish **Bred** Exciting Times Partnership **Trained** Upper Lambourn, Berks

FOCUS
A competitive Group 3 on paper but the first two pulled clear of the rest. A clear pb from the winner, with the second rated in line with the better view of her form, and the third close to last year's win here.

4892 30 YEAR CURZON CLUB YORK ANNIVERSARY H'CAP 1m 2f 56y
3:45 (3:48) (Class 4) (0-85,85) 3-Y-O+
£9,962 (£2,964; £1,481; £740; £300; £300) **Stalls** Low

Form RPR
1133 **1** **Archie Perkins (IRE)**[17] 4209 4-9-6 **80**.................. RowanScott[(3)] 5 89
(Nigel Tinkler) *prom: trckd ldr after 2f: cl up over 3f out: slt ld 2f out: sn rdn: drvn ins fnl f: hld on gamely towards fin (starter reported that the gelding was the subject of a third criteria failure; trainer was informed that the gelding could not run until the day after passing a stalls test)* **4/1**[1]

1520 **2** *nk* **Furzig**[13] 4403 4-9-4 **78**.................. SeanDavis[(3)] 14 86
(Richard Fahey) *stdd and swtchd lft s: hld up towards rr: hdwy over 2f out: rdn over 1f out: drvn and styd on to chal last 100yds ev ch tl no ex nr fin* **8/1**

3161 **3** *1 1/4* **Music Seeker (IRE)**[28] 3811 5-9-5 **83**..........(t) ClanMacRedmond[(7)] 13 88
(Declan Carroll) *hld up in tch: hdwy over 3f out: cl up over 2f out: rdn wl over 1f out: drvn and ev ch ent fnl f: kpt on same pce towards fin* **11/1**

0504 **4** *shd* **Thomas Cranmer (USA)**[13] 4407 5-9-2 **73**.................. CamHardie 8 78
(Tina Jackson) *trckd ldrs: hdwy over 3f out: pushed along 2f out: rdn and ev ch over 1f out: drvn and kpt on same pce fnl f* **11/2**[3]

1/56 **5** *3/4* **Shargiah (IRE)**[19] 4144 6-10-0 **85**.................. LukeMorris 11 88
(Michael Appleby) *t.k.h: led after 1f: jnd and pushed along over 3f out: rdn and hdd 2f out: cl up and ev ch over 1f out: sn drvn and kpt on same pce* **40/1**

-544 **6** ¾ **First Dance (IRE)**[13] 4371 5-8-9 **66** oh1........................ JamesSullivan 7 68
(Tom Tate) *hld up and bhd: hdwy 3f out: rdn along 2f out: styd on appr fnl f: nrst fin* **16/1**

0266 **7** ½ **Dark Intention (IRE)**[16] 4240 6-9-9 **80**........................ DanielTudhope 3 81
(Lawrence Mullaney) *in tch on inner: hdwy 3f out: chsd ldrs 2f out: rdn over 1f out: drvn and no imp fnl f (vet said mare returned lame on its right fore)* **5/1**[2]

2443 **8** shd **Beverley Bullet**[11] 4446 6-8-9 **66**........................(p) GrahamLee 12 67
(Lawrence Mullaney) *trckd ldrs: hdwy over 3f out: pushed along 2f out: sn rdn and grad wknd* **20/1**

0211 **9** nk **Mr Coco Bean (USA)**[7] 4602 5-8-13 **70** 5ex........................ TomEaves 9 70
(David Barron) *hld up towards rr: hdwy 3f out: effrt to chse ldrs on outer 2f out: sn rdn: drvn and wknd ent fnl f* **15/2**

1-20 **10** 5 **Cornborough**[13] 4392 8-9-5 **76**........................(t[1]) DougieCostello 6 66
(Mark Walford) *hld up in rr: rdn along 3f out and sn outpcd* **40/1**

0200 **11** ¾ **Armandihan (IRE)**[16] 4241 5-9-9 **80**........................(p) KevinStott 10 69
(Kevin Ryan) *led 1f: trckd ldng pair: hdwy and cl up 3f out: rdn along over 2f out: wknd wl over 1f out* **12/1**

-463 **12** 3 **Najashee (IRE)**[14] 4329 5-8-13 **70**........................ BenCurtis 2 53
(Roger Fell) *trckd ldrs on inner: hdwy and cl up 3f out: ev ch 2f out: sn rdn and wknd over 1f out* **7/1**

2m 10.98s (0.68) **Going Correction** +0.225s/f (Good) **12 Ran SP% 119.0**
WFA 3 from 4yo+ 10lb
Speed ratings (Par 105): **106,105,104,104,104 103,103,103,102,98 98,95**
CSF £35.53 CT £327.49 TOTE £4.50: £1.90, £2.80, £3.10; EX 40.50 Trifecta £294.30.
Owner J Raybould & S Perkins **Bred** Helen Lyons **Trained** Langton, N Yorks

FOCUS
Add 32yds. The early gallop wasn't that strong and they finished in a bit of a heap. Straightforward form, with the second and third rated as running as well as ever.

4893 GARBUTT AND ELLIOTT NURSERY H'CAP 5f
4:20 (4:20) (Class 3) (0-95,86) 2-Y-O **£9,703** (£2,887; £1,443; £721) **Stalls Low**

Form RPR

1621 **1** **Mrs Bouquet**[2] 4780 2-9-4 **83** 6ex........................ ConnorBeasley 1 90
(Mark Johnston) *mde all: rdn over 1f out: drvn ins fnl f: kpt on wl towards fin* **5/2**[1]

210 **2** 1½ **Dylan De Vega**[23] 3988 2-9-7 **86**........................ TonyHamilton 5 88
(Richard Fahey) *trckd ldng pair: effrt 2f out and sn cl up: rdn and ev ch ins fnl f: sn drvn and kpt on same pce* **11/4**[2]

0130 **3** 3¼ **Manolith**[53] 2903 2-8-12 **77**........................ DanielTudhope 3 67
(David O'Meara) *dwlt: sn outpcd and bhd: pushed along 1/2-way: rdn 2f out: hdwy over 1f out: kpt on wl fnl f* **10/1**

1043 **4** hd **Iva Go (IRE)**[25] 3927 2-8-10 **75**........................ DavidAllan 6 65
(Tim Easterby) *trckd ldrs: hdwy on outer over 2f out: sn cl up: rdn and ev ch over 1f out: drvn ent fnl f: grad wknd* **3/1**[3]

010 **5** 7 **Harswell (IRE)**[58] 2747 2-8-8 **76**........................ SeanDavis(3) 4 40
(Liam Bailey) *chsd ldrs: rdn along 2f out: drvn and wknd over 1f out* **16/1**

3016 **6** nk **Shammah (IRE)**[13] 4387 2-9-1 **80**........................ FergusSweeney 2 43
(Richard Hannon) *cl up: rdn along 2f out: sn wknd (trainer's rep could offer no explanation for the filly's performance)* **5/1**

59.57s (1.37) **Going Correction** +0.225s/f (Good) **6 Ran SP% 111.9**
Speed ratings (Par 98): **98,95,90,90,78 78**
CSF £9.62 TOTE £3.10: £1.70, £1.60; EX 10.10 Trifecta £49.00.
Owner Garrett J Freyne **Bred** Hatford Enterprises **Trained** Middleham Moor, N Yorks

FOCUS
Nothing could get past the leader in this small-field nursery. The second has been rated to form.

4894 IRISH THOROUGHBRED MARKETING H'CAP 5f
4:55 (4:58) (Class 4) (0-85,85) 3-Y-O+
£9,962 (£2,964; £1,481; £740; £300; £300) **Stalls Low**

Form RPR

04 **1** **Secretinthepark**[13] 4406 9-8-9 **73**........................(b) CianMacRedmond(7) 11 83
(Michael Mullineaux) *blind removed late and dwlt: bhd: rdn along 2f out: hdwy towards stands' side over 1f out: rdn and styd on strly fnl f: led nr line* **22/1**

3312 **2** hd **Jabbarockie**[20] 4100 6-10-0 **85**........................ PhilDennis 13 94
(Eric Alston) *racd towards stands' side: cl up: led 2f out: rdn clr over 1f out: drvn ins fnl f: hdd and no ex nr line* **6/1**[2]

1220 **3** ¾ **Acclaim The Nation (IRE)**[48] 3097 6-10-0 **85**........................(p[1]) TomEaves 10 91
(Eric Alston) *racd centre: led: rdn along and hdd 2f out: drvn over 1f out: kpt on u.p fnl f* **12/1**

0-00 **4** ½ **Holmeswood**[48] 3097 5-9-13 **84**........................(w) PaulMulrennan 3 89+
(Julie Camacho) *in tch: hdwy 2f out: rdn to chse ldrs over 1f out: drvn and edgd lft ins fnl f: kpt on same pce* **6/1**[2]

0341 **5** 1½ **Canford Bay (IRE)**[13] 4364 5-9-12 **83**........................ CamHardie 1 82
(Antony Brittain) *towards rr: rdn along over 2f out: hdwy wl over 1f out: sn chsng ldrs: kpt on fnl f* **12/1**

2100 **6** 1 **Daschas**[18] 4186 5-9-11 **82**........................(t) DanielTudhope 8 78
(Stuart Williams) *hld up towards rr: hdwy 2f out: rdn along to chse ldrs over 1f out: no imp fnl f* **7/1**[3]

2211 **7** 2¼ **Lathom**[20] 4100 6-9-13 **84**........................ GrahamLee 7 71
(Paul Midgley) *chsd ldrs: rdn along 2f out: sn drvn and grad wknd* **9/2**[1]

6432 **8** ½ **Excessable**[13] 4406 6-9-9 **80**........................ RachelRichardson 2 66
(Tim Easterby) *prom towards far side: rdn along 2f out: grad wknd* **7/1**[3]

00-0 **9** ¾ **Militia**[15] 4303 4-9-1 **75**........................ SeanDavis(3) 6 58
(Richard Fahey) *chsd ldrs: rdn along 2f out: sn wknd* **25/1**

1241 **10** ¾ **Superseded (IRE)**[18] 4192 3-8-8 **70**........................ DavidProbert 12 48
(John Butler) *racd towards stands' side: chsd ldrs: rdn along 2f out: sn wknd* **33/1**

2055 **11** 1¼ **Wrenthorpe**[15] 4279 4-8-11 **75**........................ HarryRussell(7) 4 51
(Bryan Smart) *prom centre: rdn along over 2f out: sn wknd* **14/1**

-005 **12** 7 **Nicki's Angel (IRE)**[13] 4368 3-9-6 **82**........................ TonyHamilton 9 31
(Richard Fahey) *chsd ldrs centre: rdn along over 2f out: sn lost pl and bhd* **16/1**

58.36s (0.16) **Going Correction** +0.225s/f (Good) **12 Ran SP% 110.8**
WFA 3 from 4yo+ 5lb
Speed ratings (Par 105): **107,106,105,104,102 100,97,96,95,93 91,80**
CSF £130.59 CT £1004.10 TOTE £24.40: £5.90, £2.20, £3.90; EX 174.30 Trifecta £1629.40.
Owner Mia Racing **Bred** Mia Racing **Trained** Alpraham, Cheshire

■ Music Society was withdrawn. Price at time of withdrawal 10-1. Rule 4 applies to all bets - deduction 5p in the pound.
■ Stewards' Enquiry : Cian MacRedmond two-day ban: used whip above the permitted level (Jul 26, 28)

FOCUS
A competitive sprint in which the winner came from last to first, but the placed horses were prominent throughout. The second has been rated as running as well as ever.

4895 COOPERS MARQUEES APPRENTICE H'CAP 7f
5:30 (5:30) (Class 3) (0-90,88) 3-Y-O **£9,703** (£2,887; £1,443; £721) **Stalls Low**

Form RPR

3423 **1** **Triple Distilled**[15] 4297 3-9-1 **77**........................ RowanScott 2 86
(Nigel Tinkler) *trckd ldrs: hdwy on inner 2f out: rdn to ld 1f out: kpt on strly* **10/3**[2]

113 **2** 1½ **Sandret (IRE)**[56] 2787 3-9-0 **79**........................ HarrisonShaw(3) 1 83
(Ben Haslam) *t.k.h on inner: hld up in rr: effrt whn n.m.r and swtchd markedly lft wl over 1f out: rdn and chsd ldrs whn edgd rt ins fnl f: kpt on* **15/2**

-151 **3** nk **Irreverent**[20] 4099 3-9-12 **88**........................ SeanDavis 8 91
(Richard Fahey) *trckd ldrs: effrt on outer 2f out: rdn and ev ch whn edgd lft jst over 1f out: sn drvn and kpt on same pce ins fnl f* **3/1**[1]

0432 **4** ¾ **Fastman (IRE)**[20] 4099 3-9-12 **88**........................ ConorMcGovern 3 89
(David O'Meara) *t.k.h: trckd ldrs: hdwy and cl up over 2f out: rdn to ld wl over 1f out: hdd and drvn 1f out: kpt on same pce* **7/2**[3]

5030 **5** nk **Punjab Mail**[8] 4552 3-8-12 **74**........................ CameronNoble 7 74
(Ian Williams) *t.k.h: hld up: hdwy on outer 2f out: rdn over 1f out: kpt on fnl f* **16/1**

0410 **6** hd **Greek Hero**[13] 4403 3-8-7 **76**........................ CianMacRedmond(7) 5 76+
(Declan Carroll) *dwlt: hld up in rr: hdwy 2f out: effrt and n.m.r over 1f out: rdn and kpt on ins fnl f (jockey said gelding was denied a clear run in the final furlong)* **16/1**

3-06 **7** 4½ **Daafr (IRE)**[20] 4099 3-9-5 **86**........................ KieranSchofield(5) 4 74
(Antony Brittain) *chsd ldrs: rdn along over 2f out: drvn whn n.m.r over 1f out: sn wknd* **33/1**

41-0 **8** 2¾ **Absolute Dream (IRE)**[104] 1424 3-9-0 **76**........................(w) ConnorMurtagh 6 56
(Richard Fahey) *cl up: rdn to ld briefly 2f out: sn hdd and drvn: wknd over 1f out* **20/1**

-353 **9** 3 **Celebrity Dancer (IRE)**[20] 4099 3-9-8 **87**........................ ThomasGreatrex(3) 10 59
(Kevin Ryan) *wnt rt s: sn led: pushed along 3f out: rdn and hdd 2f out: sn wknd (trainer's rep could offer no explanation for the gelding's performance)* **11/2**

1m 26.05s (1.45) **Going Correction** +0.225s/f (Good) **9 Ran SP% 116.9**
Speed ratings (Par 104): **100,98,97,97,96 96,91,88,84**
CSF £29.01 CT £83.18 TOTE £3.80: £1.40, £2.40, £1.60; EX 27.30 Trifecta £115.20.
Owner John R Saville **Bred** Copgrove Hall Stud **Trained** Langton, N Yorks

FOCUS
A messy race, in which the early pace was steady, and it resulted in a bit of dash for home. The winner and third have been rated to their latest efforts.
T/Plt: £47.30 to a £1 stake. Pool: £93,993.31 - 1,449.43 winning units. T/Qpdt: £22.30 to a £1 stake. Pool: £7,740.52 - 255.80 winning units. **Joe Rowntree**

4861 ASCOT (R-H)
Saturday, July 13

OFFICIAL GOING: Good to firm (watered; rnd 7.2, str 8.4)
Wind: Light, across Weather: Fine but cloudy

4896 BETFRED HERITAGE H'CAP 5f
1:45 (1:47) (Class 2) 3-Y-O+
£62,250 (£18,640; £9,320; £4,660; £2,330; £1,170) **Stalls High**

Form RPR

4042 **1** **Tis Marvellous**[21] 4095 5-9-8 **103**........................(t) AdamKirby 20 114
(Clive Cox) *trckd ldrs: shkn up and clsd nr side to ld jst over 1f out: sn rdn clr: decisively* **9/2**[1]

5001 **2** 2½ **Open Wide (USA)**[19] 4186 5-9-0 **95**........................(b) CharlesBishop 15 97
(Amanda Perrett) *rrd sltly s: hld up towards rr: swtchd lft to nr side over 1f out: prog after: styd on fnl f to take 2nd nr fin* **12/1**

6612 **3** nk **Harome (IRE)**[5] 4722 5-8-10 **91** 6ex........................ NicolaCurrie 8 92
(Roger Fell) *t.k.h: mde most to jst over 1f out: sn outpcd by wnr: lost 2nd nr fin* **16/1**

1531 **4** 1 **Embour (IRE)**[12] 4451 4-9-0 **95**........................ PatDobbs 7 92+
(Richard Hannon) *wl in tch: rdn over 1f out: styd on fnl f to take 4th nr fin* **14/1**

5165 **5** shd **Brian The Snail (IRE)**[14] 4379 5-8-9 **90**........................ JosephineGordon 16 87+
(Richard Fahey) *broke wl but stdd into midfield: dropped to rr and rdn over 1f out: styd on wl fnl f: nrly snatched 4th* **22/1**

0000 **6** hd **Stone Of Destiny**[21] 4095 4-9-5 **100**........................ SilvestreDeSousa 6 96
(Andrew Balding) *pressed ldrs: stl cl enough and rdn over 1f out: one pce after* **9/1**[3]

5340 **7** hd **Blue De Vega (GER)**[15] 4331 6-8-9 **90**........................(tp) JasonWatson 3 86
(Robert Cowell) *s.i.s and sltly impeded s: hld up: last 2f out: prog nr side over 1f out: styd on fnl f: nrst fin* **16/1**

4110 **8** nk **Watchable**[21] 4095 9-9-3 **98**........................(p) JoeFanning 17 92
(David O'Meara) *pressed ldr to over 1f out: fdd fnl f* **10/1**

6031 **9** hd **Fool For You (IRE)**[15] 4331 4-8-11 **92**........................ PJMcDonald 9 86
(Richard Fahey) *towards rr: rdn 2f out: kpt on same pce: n.d (starter reported that the filly was the subject of a third criteria failure; trainer was informed that the filly could not run until the day after passing a stalls test)* **16/1**

0-50 **10** ½ **Muthmir (IRE)**[7] 4665 9-9-9 **104**........................(b) TomMarquand 4 96
(William Haggas) *wnt rt s: wl in rr: rdn 2f out: styd on fnl f: nvr nrr (jockey said gelding was denied a clear run)* **12/1**

0241 **11** hd **Gabrial The Saint (IRE)**[14] 4359 4-8-10 **91**........................ RoystonFfrench 14 82
(Richard Fahey) *dwlt: nvr beyond midfield: rdn and one pce over 1f out* **16/1**

4044 **12** hd **Eeh Bah Gum (IRE)**[15] 4331 4-8-7 **88**........................ JamieGormley 10 78
(Tim Easterby) *pressed ldrs: rdn and stl cl enough over 1f out: fdd fnl f* **8/1**[2]

0063 **13** ½ **Line Of Reason (IRE)**[14] 4406 9-8-8 **89**........................ LukeMorris 13 78
(Paul Midgley) *dwlt: towards rr: rdn 2f out: nvr enough pce to threaten* **14/1**

5052 **14** hd **Royal Birth**[24] 3993 8-8-5 **86**........................(t) KieranO'Neill 18 74
(Stuart Williams) *chsd ldrs: rdn 2f out: no prog over 1f out: wl hld after* **14/1**

00-5 **15** ½ **Koditime (IRE)**[49] 3097 4-8-12 **93**........................ DavidProbert 11 79
(Clive Cox) *hld up in rr: stl gng wl enough 2f out: shkn up over 1f out: one pce and no real prog* **16/1**

0300 **16** ½ **Marnie James**[21] 4095 4-9-5 **103**........................(t) BenRobinson(3) 5 87
(Iain Jardine) *chsd ldrs tl wknd over 1f out* **28/1**

The Form Book Flat 2019, Raceform Ltd, Newbury, RG14 5SJ

0452 **17** *nk* **Growl**[14] 4402 7-8-6 **92** BenSanderson(5) 1 75
(Richard Fahey) *v awkward s and slowly away: wl in rr: effrt on wd outside 2f out: no prog over 1f out* **12/1**

1-01 **18** *1 ½* **Machree (IRE)**[46] 3201 4-8-5 **86** ConorHoban 19 64
(Declan Carroll) *pressed ldr to wl over 1f out: sn wknd* **33/1**

-010 **19** *2 ¾* **Moyassar**[56] 2826 3-9-7 **107** JimCrowley 2 73
(Richard Hannon) *nvr on terms w ldrs on outer: wknd over 1f out* **14/1**

58.92s (-1.78) **Going Correction** +0.05s/f (Good)
WFA 3 from 4yo+ 5lb **19 Ran SP% 138.3**
Speed ratings (Par 109): **116,112,111,109,109 109,109,108,108,107 107,106,106,105,104 104,103,101,96**
CSF £62.94 CT £872.21 TOTE £4.30: £1.40, £4.50, £4.80, £3.70; EX 92.60 Trifecta £844.30.
Owner Miss J Deadman & S Barrow **Bred** Crossfields Bloodstock Ltd **Trained** Lambourn, Berks

FOCUS
A good quality sprint handicap. The confirmed front-runners had high draws and the action developed stands' side. The favourite had a dream tow into the race and won in emphatic fashion. Three of the jockeys reportedly concurred with the good to firm going description. A clear pb from the winner, and the second and third's best could back this form being rated a bit better.

4897 RUDDY NOVICE AUCTION STKS (PLUS 10 RACE) 7f
2:15 (2:19) (Class 3) 2-Y-O **£6,469** (£1,925; £962; £481) **Stalls** High

Form RPR

3 **1** **Kingbrook**[9] 4551 2-9-5 0 JoeFanning 8 86+
(Mark Johnston) *pressed ldr: led jst over 2f out: rdn over 1f out: hdd ins fnl f: rallied to ld again nr fin* **7/4**[1]

4 **2** *nk* **Manigordo (USA)**[14] 4388 2-9-5 0 PatDobbs 4 85+
(Richard Hannon) *trckd ldrs: wnt 2nd wl over 1f out gng strly: clsd to ld ins fnl f: shkn up and hdd nr fin* **4/1**[3]

53 **3** *5* **Zulu Girl**[18] 4223 2-9-0 0 CharlesBishop 1 66
(Eve Johnson Houghton) *in tch: pushed along and prog over 2f out: rdn to chse clr ldng pair over 1f out: no imp but hld on for 3rd* **16/1**

4 *nk* **Berkshire Rocco (FR)** 2-9-5 0 SilvestreDeSousa 6 70+
(Andrew Balding) *dwlt: wl in rr: pushed along bef 1/2-way: wandered u.p 2f out: sed to pick up over 1f out: r.o fnl f: nrly snatched 3rd* **11/4**[2]

04 **5** *4 ½* **Bad Rabbit (IRE)**[15] 4324 2-9-5 0 JasonWatson 7 58
(David Loughnane) *led to jst over 2f out: wknd over 1f out* **25/1**

24 **6** *1 ¼* **Miss Villanelle**[40] 3426 2-9-0 0 DavidProbert 9 50
(Charles Hills) *chsd ldrs: shkn up over 2f out: wknd over 1f out* **12/1**

7 *shd* **Kentucky Hardboot (IRE)** 2-9-5 0 KerrinMcEvoy 2 54
(Mick Channon) *dwlt: outpcd in last and pushed along: stl last jst over 2f out: styd on on fnl f: nvr nrr* **16/1**

8 *nk* **Hermano Bello (FR)** 2-9-5 0 FergusSweeney 10 54
(Richard Hannon) *nvr beyond midfield: lft bhd by ldrs fr 2f out* **25/1**

0 **9** *1 ½* **Speed Merchant (IRE)**[9] 4558 2-9-5 0 JimCrowley 11 50
(Brian Meehan) *chsd ldrs tl rdn and wknd 2f out* **33/1**

10 *nk* **Twittering (IRE)** 2-9-5 0 NicolaCurrie 12 49
(Jamie Osborne) *dwlt: wl in rr: nvr a factor* **22/1**

11 *2 ½* **Clever Candy** 2-9-0 0 TomMarquand 5 37
(Michael Bell) *a towards rr: shkn up and struggling over 2f out* **18/1**

12 *11* **Mr Nutherputt (IRE)** 2-9-5 0 LukeMorris 3 12
(William Knight) *dwlt: in tch: pushed along 1/2-way: wknd over 2f out* **33/1**

1m 27.62s (0.12) **Going Correction** +0.05s/f (Good) **12 Ran SP% 125.7**
Speed ratings (Par 98): **101,100,94,94,89 88,87,87,85,85 82,70**
CSF £8.84 TOTE £2.40: £1.10, £1.80, £3.60; EX 10.10 Trifecta £90.20.
Owner R S Brookhouse **Bred** Ashbrittle Stud **Trained** Middleham Moor, N Yorks

FOCUS
A decent juvenile novice auction contest which divided in 2017 and both winners had useful 1m handicap form at three. The two colts with the best form fought out an engaging tussle in the final furlong. The third has been rated in line with her turf latest.

4898 TRANT ENGINEERING FILLIES' H'CAP 1m (S)
2:50 (2:51) (Class 3) (0-90,92) 3-Y-O+ **£12,938** (£3,850; £1,924; £962) **Stalls** High

Form RPR

13-6 **1** **Ummalnar**[23] 4035 4-10-0 **90** TomMarquand 4 104
(William Haggas) *n.m.r s: sn prom: rdn over 2f out: led over 1f out: styd on wl and sn clr* **7/2**[2]

1-55 **2** *4* **Mums Hope**[36] 3552 3-8-6 **77** HollieDoyle 7 80
(Hughie Morrison) *hld up in rr: prog 2f out: rdn to take 2nd over 1f out: styd on and clr of rest but no ch w wnr* **20/1**

3400 **3** *3 ½* **Sweet Charity**[14] 4392 4-8-10 **72** CharlesBishop 8 69
(Denis Coakley) *hld up in rr: shkn up and outpcd in last pair 2f out: kpt on fnl f to take modest 3rd last strides* **33/1**

1-21 **4** *½* **Loolwah (IRE)**[25] 3974 3-9-0 **85** JimCrowley 2 79
(Sir Michael Stoute) *hld up in tch: effrt 3f out: rdn and outpcd 2f out: kpt on to press for a pl nr fin* **7/2**[2]

31 **5** *nk* **Fabulist**[15] 4341 3-8-12 **83** KerrinMcEvoy 1 76
(John Gosden) *led: stl gng strly over 2f out: hdd & wknd tamely over 1f out: lost pls nr fin* **7/4**[1]

4-21 **6** *nk* **Be More**[36] 3546 3-8-12 **83** DavidProbert 6 75
(Andrew Balding) *in tch: rdn and hanging over 2f out: kpt on one pce fnl f to press for a pl nr fin* **6/1**[3]

-102 **7** *17* **Quick**[32] 3696 3-8-10 **81** PatDobbs 5 34
(Richard Hannon) *t.k.h: trckd ldr over 2f: wknd over 2f out: t.o* **25/1**

3505 **8** *2 ½* **Modern Millie**[7] 4667 3-9-7 **92** SilvestreDeSousa 3 40
(Mick Channon) *prom: mostly trckd ldr over 5f out to over 2f out: wknd qckly: eased and t.o* **7/1**

1m 39.15s (-2.25) **Going Correction** +0.05s/f (Good)
WFA 3 from 4yo 9lb **8 Ran SP% 119.1**
Speed ratings (Par 104): **113,109,105,105,104 104,87,84**
CSF £70.51 CT £2020.06 TOTE £4.20: £1.60, £3.50, £7.30; EX 87.50 Trifecta £2389.70.
Owner Mohammed Jaber **Bred** Rabbah Bloodstock Limited **Trained** Newmarket, Suffolk

FOCUS
A good fillies' handicap won last year by subsequent Group 2 winner Beshaayir. The previous five renewals went to 3yos, but one of the two 4yos won in particularly decisive fashion. A clear pb from the winner, with the second rated as running as well as ever.

4899 FRESH AIR HELICOPTERS H'CAP 1m 6f 34y
3:25 (3:25) (Class 3) (0-95,97) 3-Y-O+ **£9,703** (£2,887; £1,443; £721) **Stalls** Low

Form RPR

15-4 **1** **Saroog**[18] 4224 5-9-9 **90** KerrinMcEvoy 4 101+
(Simon Crisford) *dwlt: hld up in last trio and wl off the pce: rdn and prog 3f out: clsd on outer to chse ldrs 1f out: sustained effrt to ld fnl 75yds* **9/4**[1]

3566 **2** *nk* **Busy Street**[14] 4381 7-9-0 **86** TheodoreLadd(5) 6 96
(Michael Appleby) *trckd clr ldng pair and wl ahd of rest: rdn to cl and led jst over 2f out: drvn and edgd lft fnl f: hdd and jst hld last 75yds* **14/1**

-051 **3** *5* **Celestial Force (IRE)**[18] 4208 4-8-12 **79** (v) PJMcDonald 7 82
(Tom Dascombe) *led at str pce and sn had field wl strung out: drvn and hdd jst over 2f out: lost 2nd 1f out: tired but clung on for 3rd* **15/2**

-120 **4** *1 ¾* **Ship Of The Fen**[8] 4614 4-9-6 **87** JimCrowley 2 88
(Ian Williams) *hld up in 6th and wl off the pce: rdn 3f out: tried to cl fr 2f out: no imp over 1f out* **13/2**[3]

-043 **5** *nk* **Master Archer (IRE)**[10] 4505 5-9-7 **88** (v) DavidProbert 5 88
(James Fanshawe) *racd in 5th and sme way off the pce: rdn to cl 3f out: drvn and cl enough over 1f out: fdd fnl f* **12/1**

-001 **6** *3 ¾* **Artarmon (IRE)**[10] 4505 4-9-9 **90** (v) SilvestreDeSousa 9 85
(Michael Bell) *chsd clr ldng trio and wl ahd of rest: drvn and no prog over 2f out: wknd over 1f out (jockey said gelding stopped quickly)* **8/1**

222P **7** *7* **Ulster (IRE)**[25] 3952 4-9-12 **93** HollieDoyle 8 78
(Archie Watson) *tried to ld but unable to: pressed ldr at str pce: lost 2nd and wknd over 2f out (jockey said gelding ran flat)* **9/2**[2]

5002 **8** *¾* **Fairy Tale (IRE)**[17] 4250 4-9-6 **87** DanielMuscutt 10 71
(Gay Kelleway) *hld up in 7th and wl off the pce: rdn and no prog 3f out* **14/1**

1-P0 **9** *11* **Shabeeb (USA)**[14] 4382 6-10-0 **95** AdamKirby 1 64
(Ian Williams) *dwlt: hld up in last trio and wl off the pce: shkn up over 2f out and no prog (jockey said gelding had no more to give)* **14/1**

0-00 **10** *7* **Nakeeta**[49] 3081 8-10-2 **97** (t) RoystonFfrench 3 56
(Linda Jewell) *s.s: hld up in last and long way off the pce: rdn and no prog over 3f out: t.o (jockey said gelding was slowly away)* **14/1**

3m 3.85s (-0.45) **Going Correction** +0.05s/f (Good) **10 Ran SP% 119.5**
Speed ratings (Par 107): **103,102,99,98,98 96,92,92,85,81**
CSF £38.04 CT £211.16 TOTE £2.90: £1.40, £4.40, £2.80; EX 28.70 Trifecta £194.40.
Owner Abdulla Al Mansoori **Bred** Ammerland Verwaltung Gmbh & Co Kg **Trained** Newmarket, Suffolk

FOCUS
Add 20 yards. A good staying handicap. The favourite came through powerfully from off a strung out field to grab the new leader centrally in the closing stages. The second has been rated in line with his turf best, and the third close to his latest.

4900 FRED COWLEY MBE MEMORIAL SUMMER MILE STKS (GROUP 2) 7f 213y(R)
4:00 (4:01) (Class 1) 4-Y-O+
£79,394 (£30,100; £15,064; £7,504; £3,766; £1,890) **Stalls** Low

Form RPR

-102 **1** **Beat The Bank**[25] 3948 5-9-4 116 SilvestreDeSousa 5 120
(Andrew Balding) *t.k.h early: trckd ldrs: urged along 3f out: rdn and cl 2f out: chal over 1f out: drvn into narrow ld last 75yds: lost action last stride and jst hld on: fatally injured (vet said gelding was lame on its left hind)* **2/1**[1]

0-11 **2** *nse* **Zaaki**[42] 3343 4-9-1 112 KerrinMcEvoy 1 116
(Sir Michael Stoute) *hld up in 6th: smooth prog on outer over 2f out: rdn to ld jst over 1f out: hdd last 75yds: kpt on wl and jst failed* **11/4**[2]

4423 **3** *1 ½* **Suedois (FR)**[14] 4389 8-9-1 109 AdamKirby 2 112
(David O'Meara) *hld up in last pair: prog jst over 2f out: drvn and tried to chal over 1f out: chsd ldng pair after and styd on same pce* **14/1**

5-3R **4** *1 ½* **Accidental Agent**[25] 3948 5-9-1 116 CharlesBishop 3 109
(Eve Johnson Houghton) *dwlt: hld up in last pair: pushed along 3f out: stl last over 1f out: styd on to take 4th ins fnl f: unable to chal* **8/1**

2201 **5** *5* **Matterhorn (IRE)**[14] 4397 4-9-1 110 JoeFanning 9 97
(Mark Johnston) *t.k.h early: trckd ldr: rdn to ld jst over 2f out: hdd jst over 1f out: wknd* **4/1**[3]

1-02 **6** *shd* **Wadilsafa**[29] 3814 4-9-1 112 JimCrowley 4 97
(Owen Burrows) *in tch in midfield: rdn and no prog over 2f out: wl btn over 1f out* **10/1**

6-12 **7** *½* **Awesometank**[42] 3342 4-8-12 106 TomMarquand 7 93
(William Haggas) *led at str pce: hdd jst over 2f out: steadily wknd* **12/1**

06-0 **8** *2 ¼* **Tip Two Win**[21] 4094 4-9-1 112 DavidProbert 6 91
(Roger Teal) *chsd ldng pair: drvn over 2f out: wknd over 1f out* **25/1**

1m 39.2s (-1.40) **Going Correction** +0.05s/f (Good) **8 Ran SP% 118.4**
Speed ratings (Par 115): **109,108,107,105,100 100,100,98**
CSF £7.96 TOTE £2.60: £1.20, £1.30, £3.60; EX 7.30 Trifecta £50.60.
Owner King Power Racing Co Ltd **Bred** A S Denniff **Trained** Kingsclere, Hants

FOCUS
Add 11 yards. A good, competitive renewal of the Group 2 feature contest. The ill-fated winner became the seventh consecutive favourite to oblige with this follow-up success. The second and third have been rated pretty much to form.

4901 WOODFORD RESERVE H'CAP 1m 3f 211y
4:35 (4:35) (Class 2) (0-105,101) 3-Y-O
£31,125 (£9,320; £4,660; £2,330; £1,165; £585) **Stalls** Low

Form RPR

26-5 **1** **Floating Artist**[92] 1737 3-9-6 **100** PatDobbs 6 108
(Richard Hannon) *trckd ldng pair: shkn up 2f out: brought to chal fnl f: rdn to ld last 120yds: styd on* **25/1**

-411 **2** *1* **Faylaq**[16] 4296 3-8-13 **93** JimCrowley 8 99+
(William Haggas) *trckd ldng trio: clsd 2f out: shkn up to ld over 1f out: rdn and hung lft ins fnl f: sn hdd and one pce* **6/4**[1]

3321 **3** *½* **Never Do Nothing (IRE)**[22] 4063 3-8-9 **89** DavidProbert 1 94
(Andrew Balding) *hld up in last trio: shkn up and no prog over 2f out: styd on fnl f to take 3rd nr fin* **14/1**

1-05 **4** *nk* **Almania (IRE)**[23] 4017 3-9-1 **95** KerrinMcEvoy 2 99
(Sir Michael Stoute) *hld up in last trio: urged along 3f out: no prog whn drvn 2f out: styd on fnl f to take 4th nr fin* **4/1**[3]

-112 **5** *nk* **Mind The Crack (IRE)**[7] 4644 3-8-12 **92** JoeFanning 4 96
(Mark Johnston) *trckd ldr: rdn to ld 2f out: hdd over 1f out: one pce and lost pls nr fin* **9/1**

2020 **6** *¾* **Htilominlo**[29] 3808 3-8-0 **80** KieranO'Neill 5 83
(Sylvester Kirk) *hld up in last: detached 1/2-way: rdn over 2f out: hanging and nvr able to threaten but kpt on* **40/1**

3344 **7** *nk* **Persian Moon (IRE)**[23] 4017 3-9-7 **101** SilvestreDeSousa 3 103
(Mark Johnston) *led at stdy pce: sent for home 3f out: drvn and hdd 2f out: steadily fdd fnl f* **7/2**[2]

2m 34.88s (2.28) **Going Correction** +0.05s/f (Good) **7 Ran SP% 115.2**
Speed ratings (Par 106): **94,93,93,92,92 92,91**
CSF £64.25 CT £582.56 TOTE £35.60: £9.10, £1.40; EX 119.30 Trifecta £955.90.
Owner Michael Pescod **Bred** Canning Bloodstock Ltd **Trained** East Everleigh, Wilts

FOCUS
Add 17 yards. A good middle-distance 3yo handicap won last year by subsequent Melbourne Cup hero Cross Counter. One of the outsiders won well, but in a modest time from just off a steady gallop. It's been rated on the positive side, with the fourth to his Royal Ascot C&D form.

4902 GL EVENTS UK H'CAP — 7f
5:10 (5:11) (Class 4) (0-85,87) 3-Y-O+

£8,345 (£2,483; £1,240; £620; £300; £300) **Stalls High**

Form — RPR

0053 **1** *nse* **Breanski**[1] 4867 5-9-6 80 .... FinleyMarsh(3) 6 90+
(Jedd O'Keeffe) *hld up in last trio: rdn and prog on nr side over 1f out: chalng whn hmpd 150yds out: rallied nr fin: jst failed: fin 2nd: awrdd the r* 11/4[1]

-442 **2** **Charles Molson**[24] 3991 8-9-12 83 .... DanielMuscutt 5 91
(Patrick Chamings) *w ldrs: led over 2f out: rdn and hung bdly lft jst over 1f out: jst hld on: fin 1st: disqualified and plcd 2nd* 7/1

5103 **3** *2* **Algaffaal (USA)**[17] 4240 4-9-3 77 .... (p) BenRobinson(3) 1 79
(Brian Ellison) *towards rr: rdn over 2f out: prog on outer over 1f out: chsd ldng pair ins fnl f: kpt on same pce* 8/1

6152 **4** *1 ½* **Mr Tyrrell (IRE)**[40] 3423 5-10-2 87 .... HollieDoyle 7 85
(Richard Hannon) *trckd ldrs: effrt over 1f out: kpt on same pce and nvr able to threaten* 10/1

31-4 **5** *¾* **Arabian Jazz (IRE)**[12] 4438 4-9-4 78 .... (h) CameronNoble(3) 10 76+
(Michael Bell) *propped s: sn chsd ldrs: drvn over 1f out: trying to chal whn hmpd jst ins fnl f: nt rcvr and one pce after* 16/1

0611 **6** *¾* **Rux Ruxx (IRE)**[12] 4438 4-9-6 77 .... SilvestreDeSousa 2 71
(Tim Easterby) *n.m.r s: hld up in last trio: prog on wd outside over 2f out: no hdwy jst over 1f out: fdd* 9/2[2]

6-00 **7** *1* **Sir Titan**[34] 3636 5-10-0 85 .... PatDobbs 9 76
(Tony Carroll) *led to over 2f out: steadily fdd over 1f out* 16/1

0211 **8** *hd* **Firmdecisions (IRE)**[11] 4492 9-9-7 85 .... IzzyClifton(7) 8 76
(Nigel Tinkler) *trckd ldr to 3f out: urged along and wknd wl over 1f out* 8/1

341 **9** *½* **Assembled**[19] 4189 3-8-12 77 .... KerrinMcEvoy 4 63
(Hugo Palmer) *towards rr: rdn over 2f out: no prog and btn over 1f out* 5/1[3]

0-30 **10** *nk* **Keeper's Choice (IRE)**[18] 4226 5-9-2 73 .... CharlesBishop 3 62
(Denis Coakley) *hld up in last trio: shkn up and no prog 2f out: wl btn over 1f out* 12/1

1m 26.78s (-0.72) **Going Correction** +0.05s/f (Good)
WFA 3 from 4yo+ 8lb — 10 Ran SP% **124.8**
Speed ratings (Par 105): **105,106,103,101,101 100,99,98,98,97**
CSF £24.37 CT £149.24 TOTE £3.30: £1.50, £2.90; EX 18.60 Trifecta £170.00.
Owner Quantum **Bred** Mrs P Good **Trained** Middleham Moor, N Yorks
■ Stewards' Enquiry : Daniel Muscutt four-day ban: interference & careless riding (Jul 28-29, Aug 2-3)

FOCUS
A tight handicap which saw the first two places reversed by the stewards. The first past the post has been rated a bit below last year's C&D form, with the third similar to his latest.
T/Plt: £117.60 to a £1 stake. Pool: £114,587.27 - 710.90 winning units T/Qpdt: £48.90 to a £1 stake. Pool: £20,681.57 - 312.74 winning units **Jonathan Neesom**

4875

CHESTER (L-H)
Saturday, July 13

OFFICIAL GOING: Good (7.0)
Wind: Light, against in straight of over 1f Weather: Overcast

4903 HASHTAG AT ROSIES EBF STALLIONS NOVICE STKS (PLUS 10 RACE) — 5f 15y
2:00 (2:01) (Class 4) 2-Y-O

£5,851 (£1,752; £876; £438; £219; £109) **Stalls Low**

Form — RPR

2 **1** **Dr Simpson (FR)**[89] 1821 2-8-13 0 .... RichardKingscote 5 88+
(Tom Dascombe) *mde all: wnt lft to inner rail over 3f out: rdn over 1f out: r.o wl to draw clr ins fnl f* 8/11[1]

2 *7* **Enjoy The Moment** 2-8-13 0 .... CallumShepherd 1 60+
(Mick Channon) *sed awkwardly: bhd and outpcd: hdwy over 2f out: kpt on to take 2nd 1f out: no ch w wnr (jockey said filly was slowly away)* 10/1[3]

0 **3** *1* **Elpheba (IRE)**[17] 4238 2-8-13 0 .... TrevorWhelan 3 56
(David Loughnane) *racd on rail w wnr: n.m.r and hmpd over 3f out: remained trcking ldrs: rdn and unable qck over 1f out: kpt on same pce ins fnl f* 25/1

00 **4** *nse* **Newsical**[10] 4516 2-9-4 0 .... DougieCostello 4 61
(Mark Walford) *prom: lft in 2nd pl over 3f out: edgd rt whn rdn and unable qck over 1f out: sn lost 2nd: kpt on same pce ins fnl f* 125/1

43 **5** *1* **Upstate New York (IRE)**[14] 4361 2-9-4 0 .... BarryMcHugh 2 57
(Richard Fahey) *in tch: clsd wl over 2f out: sn pushed along: no imp over 1f out: edgd lft whn one pce ins fnl f* 2/1[2]

44 **6** *1 ¾* **Too Hard To Hold (IRE)**[11] 4486 2-9-4 0 .... JackMitchell 6 51
(Mark Johnston) *wnt rt s and s.i.s: bhd: hung rt and nt clr run wl over 2f out: effrt on wd outer wl over 1f out: hung lft and outpcd ins fnl f: eased whn btn fnl 100yds* 10/1[3]

0 **7** *19* **Nice One Too**[12] 4433 2-8-13 0 .... LewisEdmunds 7
(David C Griffiths) *chsd ldrs: rdn and lost pl over 2f out: sn wknd: lft bhd over 1f out* 100/1

1m 3.04s (0.94) **Going Correction** +0.20s/f (Good) — 7 Ran SP% **115.0**
Speed ratings (Par 96): **100,88,87,87,85 82,52**
CSF £9.84 TOTE £1.40: £1.20, £4.00; EX 9.10 Trifecta £64.10.
Owner Russell Jones **Bred** Mme Debbiella Camacho **Trained** Malpas, Cheshire

FOCUS
The rail between the 6f and 1 1/2f point was moved in by 6 yards after racing on Friday. Add 10 yards. This lacked depth but the winner looks smart. The level is a bit fluid, but the winner has been rated in line with her debut form.

4904 HOMESERVE FILLIES' H'CAP — 6f 17y
2:35 (2:35) (Class 2) (0-100,90) 3-Y-O+

£14,940 (£4,473; £2,236; £1,118; £559; £280) **Stalls Low**

Form — RPR

3345 **1** **Pass The Gin**[5] 4736 3-8-7 80 .... WilliamCox(3) 1 86
(Andrew Balding) *chsd ldrs: forced sltly wd and rt on bnd wl over 1f out: r.o ins fnl f: str run to ld post* 7/2[1]

-000 **2** *nse* **Rock On Baileys**[24] 3994 4-9-12 90 .... (b) LewisEdmunds 4 97
(Amy Murphy) *trckd ldrs: rdn to take 2nd over 1f out: led narrowly ent fnl f: r.o for press: hdd post (jockey said filly took a false step on the run to the line)* 10/1

0050 **3** *nse* **Chapelli**[7] 4669 3-9-2 86 .... JackMitchell 2 92
(Mark Johnston) *led: rdn over 1f out: hdd narrowly ent fnl f: r.o for press: rallied towards fin* 7/2[1]

1600 **4** *1 ½* **Rose Berry**[21] 4101 5-9-6 84 .... (h) BarryMcHugh 8 86
(Charlie Wallis) *hld up: rdn and hdwy over 1f out: styd on to chse ldrs ins fnl f: nvr able to chal* 28/1

0023 **5** *¾* **Daffy Jane**[12] 4442 4-8-12 79 .... RowanScott(3) 6 79
(Nigel Tinkler) *missed break: in rr: rdn wl over 1f out: hdwy ins fnl f: r.o: nt rch ldrs* 6/1[3]

0056 **6** *1 ¼* **Come On Leicester (IRE)**[17] 4242 3-9-3 87 .... RichardKingscote 3 82
(Richard Hannon) *in tch: pushed along 4f out: outpcd over 2f out: kpt on and edgd lft ins fnl f but no imp (jockey said filly was never travelling; starter reported that the filly was the subject of a third criteria failure; trainer was informed that the filly could not run until the day after passing a stalls test)* 7/2[1]

0153 **7** *nse* **Fizzy Feet (IRE)**[12] 4458 3-8-7 77 .... AndrewMullen 7 72
(David Loughnane) *w ldr: pushed along over 2f out: rdn and lost 2nd over 1f out: sn outpcd: no ex ins fnl f* 25/1

0222 **8** *1 ¼* **Be Like Me (IRE)**[15] 4340 3-9-1 85 .... (p[1]) ColmO'Donoghue 5 76
(Marco Botti) *hld up: effrt over 1f out: one pce ins fnl f* 9/2[2]

1m 15.61s (0.11) **Going Correction** +0.20s/f (Good)
WFA 3 from 4yo+ 6lb — 8 Ran SP% **115.5**
Speed ratings (Par 96): **107,106,106,104,103 102,102,100**
CSF £39.87 CT £131.08 TOTE £4.90: £2.00, £1.70, £1.80; EX 47.50 Trifecta £206.50.
Owner Kingsclere Racing Club **Bred** Kingsclere Stud **Trained** Kingsclere, Hants

FOCUS
Add 13 yards. With the top weight 90, this wasn't the strongest of races for the level, though it looked competitive and proved just that with two noses separating the first three home. A small pb from the winner.

4905 SPORTPESA CITY PLATE STKS (LISTED RACE) — 7f 1y
3:10 (3:10) (Class 1) 3-Y-O+

£22,116 (£8,385; £4,196; £2,090; £1,049; £526) **Stalls Low**

Form — RPR

0-01 **1** **Beauty Filly**[34] 3632 4-9-0 96 .... RichardKingscote 2 105+
(William Haggas) *rrd s: racd keenly: hld up: hdwy whn nt clr run over 1f out: c through gap between horses ent fnl f: sn led: edgd rt and r.o towards fin* 5/2[1]

2236 **2** *1 ¼* **Oh This Is Us (IRE)**[14] 4397 6-9-5 110 .... ColmO'Donoghue 5 106
(Richard Hannon) *hld up: angled out and hdwy over 1f out: rn to chal ins fnl f: nt pce of wnr towards fin* 10/3[2]

5440 **3** *shd* **Salateen**[14] 4389 7-9-5 100 .... (tp) RobbieDowney 4 106
(David O'Meara) *led: rdn over 2f out whn pressed: hdd ins fnl f: styd on same pce towards fin* 16/1

4430 **4** *nk* **Marie's Diamond (IRE)**[21] 4092 3-8-11 104 .... JackMitchell 3 102
(Mark Johnston) *chsd ldrs: nt clr run over 1f out: effrt and cl up ins fnl f: kpt on towards fin: nt pce of ldrs* 5/2[1]

-552 **5** *1 ½* **Hells Babe**[12] 4442 6-9-0 87 .... LewisEdmunds 6 96
(Michael Appleby) *wnt to post early: w ldr: str chal fr 2f out: stl ev ch ins fnl f: no ex fnl 100yds* 25/1

3100 **6** *1 ¼* **Merhoob (IRE)**[15] 4331 7-9-5 101 .... BrettDoyle 1 98
(John Ryan) *in rr: pushed along whn n.m.r on inner 2f out: plld to outer over 1f out: nvr able to get involved* 20/1

-150 **7** *1 ½* **Vanbrugh (USA)**[21] 4095 4-9-5 107 .... KieranShoemark 7 94
(Charles Hills) *chsd ldrs: effrt on outer over 1f out and ev ch: stl there but nt quite pce of ldrs whn squeezed out ins fnl f: eased fnl 100yds (vet said colt lost its left fore shoe)* 4/1[3]

1m 27.67s (0.17) **Going Correction** +0.20s/f (Good)
WFA 3 from 4yo+ 8lb — 7 Ran SP% **114.7**
Speed ratings (Par 111): **107,105,105,105,103 101,100**
CSF £11.23 TOTE £2.90: £1.50, £1.70; EX 13.70 Trifecta £141.20.
Owner Sheikh Juma Dalmook Al Maktoum **Bred** Highbank Stud **Trained** Newmarket, Suffolk
■ Stewards' Enquiry : Brett Doyle three-day ban: interference & careless riding (tba)

FOCUS
Add 13 yards. A sound enough edition of this Listed feature, which was won last year by the reopposing Oh This Is Us. The third helps set the level.

4906 MBNA H'CAP — 1m 6f 87y
3:45 (3:46) (Class 3) (0-90,81) 3-Y-O £14,940 (£4,473; £2,236; £1,118) **Stalls Low**

Form — RPR

1111 **1** **Moon King (FR)**[31] 3729 3-9-7 81 .... RichardKingscote 4 93+
(Ralph Beckett) *prom: led 2f out: edgd lft over 1f out: styd on wl to draw clr ins fnl f: comf* 6/5[1]

1435 **2** *7* **Gabrial The One (IRE)**[14] 4362 3-9-7 81 .... BarryMcHugh 2 83
(Richard Fahey) *hld up in rr: effrt 2f out: chsd wnr over 1f out: no imp* 3/1[2]

4111 **3** *1 ¾* **Glutnforpunishment**[15] 4339 3-8-7 72 .... DarraghKeenan(5) 1 72
(Nick Littmoden) *led: rdn and hdd 2f out: lost 2nd over 1f out: no ex ins fnl f* 4/1[3]

2243 **4** *1 ¼* **Paradise Boy (FR)**[14] 4362 3-8-13 76 .... WilliamCox(3) 3 74
(Andrew Balding) *chsd ldrs: rdn over 2f out: sn dropped to rr: edgd rt whn outpcd over 1f out: hung lft ins fnl f whn hld (jockey said colt hung both ways under pressure)* 9/2

3m 17.16s (7.36) **Going Correction** +0.20s/f (Good) — 4 Ran SP% **108.6**
Speed ratings (Par 104): **87,83,82,81**
CSF £5.03 TOTE £1.60; EX 3.60 Trifecta £9.70.
Owner Merriebelle Irish Farm Limited **Bred** Rashit Shaykhutdinov **Trained** Kimpton, Hants

FOCUS
Add 28 yards. A small field but no doubting the strength of the form with Moon King and Glutnforpunishment having won their last seven races between them. The former completed a five-timer in tremendous fashion. The second has been rated close to form.

4907 WALKER SMITH H'CAP — 1m 2f 70y
4:20 (4:21) (Class 4) (0-80,80) 4-Y-O+

£6,339 (£1,886; £942; £471; £300; £300) **Stalls High**

Form — RPR

-560 **1** **Medalla De Oro**[29] 3816 5-9-4 77 .... (h) JackMitchell 9 85
(Tom Clover) *mde all: rdn over 2f out: hld on gamely towards fin (trainer said, regarding the improved form shown, the gelding had benefited from the reapplication of a hood)* 6/1[3]

The Form Book Flat 2019, Raceform Ltd, Newbury, RG14 5SJ

2305 **2** 1/2 **Swift Emperor (IRE)**[22] 4079 7-9-5 **78**........................ RobbieDowney 2 85
(David Barron) *midfield: pushed along and hdwy 2f out: chsd ldrs over 1f out: wnt 2nd ins fnl f: r.o u.p to press wnr: hld towards fin: lame (vet said gelding was lame on its right fore)* **9/1**

20-6 **3** 3/4 **Elhafei (USA)**[15] 4333 4-8-10 **72**........................(p) WilliamCox(3) 12 78
(Michael Appleby) *chsd wnr: rdn and lost 2nd ins fnl f: tried to angle arnd rival: kpt on: nt pce of front two towards fin* **33/1**

4221 **4** 1/2 **Bit Of A Quirke**[18] 4209 6-8-13 **72**........................(v) AndrewMullen 1 77
(Mark Walford) *chsd ldrs: rdn over 3f out: unable qck over 1f out: kpt on towards fin* **3/1**[1]

2036 **5** nk **Redgrave (IRE)**[21] 4108 5-9-4 **77**........................ KieranShoemark 8 81
(Joseph Tuite) *hld up: hdwy over 3f out: rdn 2f out: chsd ldrs ins fnl f: kpt on towards fin: nvr able to chal (jockey said gelding hung left)* **11/1**

0252 **6** 1 **Dark Devil (IRE)**[21] 4109 6-8-8 **67**........................(p) BarryMcHugh 11 69
(Richard Fahey) *missed break: in rr: rdn and sme hdwy 2f out: angled out over 1f out: styd on ins fnl f: nvr able to trble ldrs (jockey said he had failed to hear the starter shout "Blinds off" and it took two attempts to remove, after having lost his grip on the first occasion)* **9/2**[2]

1560 **7** hd **Heart Of Soul (IRE)**[14] 4362 4-9-7 **80**........................(v) RichardKingscote 3 82
(Ian Williams) *hld up: pushed along and hdwy over 1f out: styd on towards fin: nt rch ldrs* **9/2**[2]

1030 **8** nk **Citta D'Oro**[19] 4194 4-8-2 **64**........................(p) GabrieleMalune(3) 5 65
(James Unett) *midfield: rdn over 2f out: nvr able to get organised ins fnl f: no real imp* **12/1**

2-50 **9** 1 **Garden Oasis**[37] 3515 4-9-2 **80**........................ DannyRedmond(5) 10 79
(Tim Easterby) *chsd ldrs: rdn over 3f out: unable qck over 1f out: fdd fnl 100yds* **22/1**

3006 **10** 1/2 **Maghfoor**[8] 4602 5-7-13 **63**........................(p) RhiainIngram(5) 13 61
(Eric Alston) *hld up: in rr 7f out: pushed along 2f out: nt clr run over 1f out: kpt on ins fnl f: nvr a threat* **25/1**

5330 **11** 7 **Dragon Mountain**[21] 4102 4-8-11 **75**........................ DylanHogan(5) 4 59
(Keith Dalgleish) *chsd ldrs: rdn over 3f out: drvn over 2f out: wknd over 1f out* **9/1**

1-60 **12** 3 **Thaayer**[14] 4386 4-9-4 **77**........................(t) DougieCostello 7 55
(Rebecca Menzies) *in tch: rdn and wknd over 2f out* **25/1**

2m 14.72s (0.42) **Going Correction** +0.20s/f (Good) **12** Ran SP% **126.7**
Speed ratings (Par 105): **106,105,105,104,104 103,103,103,102,101 96,93**
CSF £60.52 CT £1692.32 TOTE £7.00: £2.40, £3.00, £9.30; EX 67.80 Trifecta £2334.00.
Owner The Rogues Gallery Two **Bred** Hascombe And Valiant Studs **Trained** Newmarket, Suffolk
■ Stewards' Enquiry : Jack Mitchell two-day ban: used whip above the permitted level (Jul 28-29)

FOCUS
Add 16 yards. A well contested handicap, featuring last year's winner Bit Of A Quirke, who again had the ideal draw. It's a bit muddling, but the third has been rated close to his 3yo form, and the fifth and sixth close to their recent form.

4908 SPORTPESA H'CAP 6f 17y

4:55 (4:56) (Class 4) (0-80,79) 3-Y-O

£6,080 (£1,809; £904; £452; £300; £300) **Stalls** Low

Form RPR

1203 **1** **Spirit Of May**[19] 4185 3-9-1 **73**........................ JackMitchell 1 82
(Roger Teal) *mde all: rdn over 2f out: kpt on wl fnl f* **5/2**[1]

1331 **2** 1 1/4 **Friendly Advice (IRE)**[16] 4280 3-8-13 **76**........................(p) DylanHogan(5) 6 80+
(Keith Dalgleish) *wnt to post early: s.i.s: hld up in rr: hdwy on outer 2f out: styd on wl towards fin: nt rch wnr* **6/1**

0502 **3** nk **Baby Steps**[19] 4185 3-9-3 **75**........................ TrevorWhelan 4 78
(David Loughnane) *trckd ldrs: pushed along 3f out: rdn over 1f out: styd on towards fin: nt pce of front two (vet said gelding lost its right fore shoe)* **6/1**

3210 **4** 3/4 **Abate**[14] 4368 3-9-2 **74**........................ AndrewMullen 5 74
(Adrian Nicholls) *w wnr: rdn and ev ch 2f out: unable qck over 1f out: nt pce of wnr ins fnl f: no ex fnl 75yds* **6/1**

4006 **5** 3 1/4 **Wild Edric**[14] 4359 3-9-4 **76**........................ RichardKingscote 9 65
(Tom Dascombe) *chsd ldrs: rdn over 2f out: outpcd over 1f out: one pce ins fnl f* **5/1**[3]

0005 **6** 1 **No More Regrets (IRE)**[28] 3844 3-8-11 **69**........................ BarryMcHugh 3 54
(Patrick Morris) *hld up: pushed along wl over 1f out: nvr able to get involved* **14/1**

2450 **7** 1 1/4 **Cotubanama**[13] 4420 3-9-0 **72**........................ CallumShepherd 8 53
(Mick Channon) *midfield: rdn and outpcd over 2f out: wknd fnl f* **33/1**

0603 **8** 7 **Tin Hat (IRE)**[16] 4297 3-9-0 **79**........................ GeorgiaDobie(7) 2 34
(Eve Johnson Houghton) *broke wl: lost pl after 1f: midfield: pushed along over 3f out: outpcd 2f out: wknd over 1f out (jockey said gelding stumbled going into the first bend; trainer's rep said gelding was unsuited by the track which in their opinion was too tight; vet said the gelding finished lame on its left-fore)* **9/2**[2]

0000 **9** 5 **Not So Shy**[9] 4555 3-7-9 **60** oh14........................(p) ElishaWhittington(7) 7
(Lisa Williamson) *midfield: rdn and lost pl over 2f out: lft bhd over 1f out* **66/1**

1m 16.57s (1.07) **Going Correction** +0.20s/f (Good) **9** Ran SP% **117.4**
Speed ratings (Par 102): **100,98,97,96,92 91,89,80,73**
CSF £18.32 CT £82.86 TOTE £2.60: £1.10, £1.50, £3.50; EX 15.00 Trifecta £71.50.
Owner Mrs Carol Borras **Bred** R P Phillips **Trained** Lambourn, Berks

FOCUS
Add 13 yards. Very few got involved in this fair handicap. The winner has been rated in line with his Salisbury form, and the third to his latest.

4909 CSP AUDIO VISUAL APPRENTICE H'CAP 7f 127y

5:30 (5:32) (Class 4) (0-80,86) 3-Y-O

£6,080 (£1,809; £904; £452; £300; £300) **Stalls** Low

Form RPR

3651 **1** **City Wanderer (IRE)**[18] 4225 3-8-9 **70**........................ ScottMcCullagh(5) 2 78+
(Mick Channon) *chsd ldrs: rdn over 2f out: outpcd by front two over 1f out: rallied ins fnl f: styd on to ld towards fin (vet said gelding lost its right hind shoe)* **11/4**[1]

2521 **2** 1 **Harvey Dent**[7] 4634 3-9-11 **86**........................ Pierre-LouisJamin(5) 6 91
(Archie Watson) *chsd ldrs: big effrt to take 2nd 2f out: led over 1f out: sn edgd lft: hdd and no ex towards fin* **3/1**[2]

5645 **3** 1 1/2 **Sparklealot (IRE)**[15] 4320 3-9-12 **82**........................(p) WilliamCox 5 84
(Ivan Furtado) *wnt to post early: racd keenly: led: rdn over 2f out: hdd over 1f out: kpt on same pce towards fin* **11/4**[1]

-203 **4** nk **Chatham House**[15] 4338 3-9-5 **78**........................ ThoreHammerHansen(3) 7 79+
(Richard Hannon) *hld up in rr: hdwy over 2f out: sn rdn: drifted rt ins fnl f: styd on wl towards fin* **13/2**[3]

0034 **5** 12 **Pacino**[14] 4360 3-9-9 **79**........................ ConnorMurtagh 8 52
(Richard Fahey) *chsd ldr: rdn and lost 2nd 2f out: wknd over 1f out* **8/1**

-251 **6** 1/2 **Kwela**[54] 2904 3-9-3 **78**........................ GeorgiaDobie(5) 9 50
(Eve Johnson Houghton) *midfield: outpcd over 2f out: n.d after* **10/1**

-000 **7** 3 **Andies Armies**[30] 3775 3-7-12 **61** oh16........................(p[1]) ElishaWhittington(7) 4 26
(Lisa Williamson) *hld up: pushed along and toiling over 2f out: nvr a threat* **80/1**

-000 **8** 12 **Hilbre Lake (USA)**[14] 4358 3-8-5 **61** oh16........................ RowanScott 3
(Lisa Williamson) *in rr: pushed along over 4f out: toiling over 3f out: nvr a threat* **100/1**

0-00 **9** 5 **Liberty Diva (IRE)**[8] 4606 3-7-12 **61** oh16........................ EllaMcCain(7) 1
(Alan Berry) *midfield: pushed along over 3f out: wknd over 2f out* **50/1**

1m 36.22s (0.52) **Going Correction** +0.20s/f (Good) **9** Ran SP% **116.1**
Speed ratings (Par 102): **105,104,102,102,90 89,86,74,69**
CSF £11.35 CT £24.22 TOTE £3.00: £1.10, £1.50, £1.20; EX 13.00 Trifecta £31.40.
Owner George Materna & Roger Badley **Bred** Kildaragh Stud **Trained** West Ilsley, Berks

FOCUS
Add 13 yards. A good race for the level with the two at the head of the weights rate above the ceiling mark of 80. The second has been rated in line with his recent form, with the third and fourth close to form.
T/Plt: £162.20 to a £1 stake. Pool: £62,350.83 - 280.60 winning units T/Qpdt: £51.50 to a £1 stake. Pool: £4,008.31 - 57.49 winning units **Darren Owen**

4486 HAMILTON (R-H)

Saturday, July 13

OFFICIAL GOING: Good (7.5)
Wind: Breezy, across Weather: Sunny, warm

4910 BB FOODSERVICE NOVICE AUCTION STKS (PLUS 10 RACE) (A £20,000 BB FOODSERVICE 2YO SERIES QUALIFIER) 5f 7y

5:30 (5:30) (Class 4) 2-Y-O

£5,433 (£1,617; £808; £404) **Stalls** High

Form RPR

3 **1** **Rose Bandit (IRE)**[24] 3997 2-8-11 0........................ ShaneGray 4 71
(Stef Keniry) *racd against stands' rail: mde all: rdn and hrd pressed over 1f out: kpt on gamely ins fnl f* **4/1**[3]

22 **2** 1 **Asmund (IRE)**[17] 4237 2-9-5 0........................ CliffordLee 3 75
(K R Burke) *pressed wnr: rdn and ev ch over 1f out to ins fnl f: r.o same pce towards fin* **4/5**[1]

3 1 **Never In Red (IRE)** 2-8-10 0........................ HarrisonShaw(5) 5 67
(Robyn Brisland) *trckd ldrs: effrt and rdn over 1f out: edgd rt ins fnl f: kpt on same pce* **20/1**

52 **4** 5 **Spygate**[10] 4516 2-9-5 0........................ PaddyMathers 1 53
(Richard Fahey) *in tch on outside: stdy hdwy over 2f out: rdn over 1f out: sn wknd (trainer could offer no explanation for the colt's performance)* **5/2**[2]

45 **5** 8 **Star's Daughter**[50] 3033 2-8-3 0........................ VictorSantos(7) 2 16
(Lucinda Egerton) *hld up in tch: rdn over 2f out: sn wknd* **100/1**

1m 0.67s (0.27) **Going Correction** -0.125s/f (Firm) **5** Ran SP% **109.9**
Speed ratings (Par 96): **92,90,88,80,68**
CSF £7.69 TOTE £5.90: £1.70, £1.20; EX 8.70 Trifecta £42.60.
Owner Russell Provan & James McLaughlin **Bred** M Phelan **Trained** Middleham, N Yorks

FOCUS
The going was good. GoingStick: 7.5. The loop rail was out 3yds on to fresh ground, adding approximately 8yds to the 7.05, 7.35, 8.05, 8.35 and 9.05. Stalls: 5f (2yo), 1m3f & 1m4f: stands' side; Remainder of 5f & 6f: centre; 1m: inside. Not many runners, but this juvenile novice auction looked competitive enough. The winner did it nicely. The winner has been rated as building on her C&D debut effort.

4911 DARREN HOEY MEMORIAL H'CAP 5f 7y

6:05 (6:06) (Class 5) (0-70,69) 3-Y-O+

£4,787 (£1,424; £711; £400; £400; £400) **Stalls** Centre

Form RPR

2- **1** **Art Of Unity**[20] 4151 4-9-5 **67**........................(p) HarrisonShaw(5) 9 76
(John James Feane, Ire) *racd centre: mde all: rdn over 1f out: hrd pressed fnl f: hld on wl cl home* **7/1**[3]

2636 **2** hd **Debawtry (IRE)**[7] 4632 4-9-10 **67**........................ SamJames 4 75
(Phillip Makin) *hld up in midfield centre: effrt and hdwy over 1f out: chsd wnr ins fnl f: kpt on: hld cl home* **3/1**[1]

0211 **3** 1 3/4 **Hard Solution**[12] 4434 3-9-0 **65**........................ ConorMcGovern(3) 1 65
(David O'Meara) *cl up centre: rdn along 2f out: kpt on same pce ins fnl f* **7/1**[3]

2014 **4** hd **Shepherd's Purse**[7] 4625 7-9-8 **65**........................ JamesSullivan 10 66
(Ruth Carr) *fly-jmpd s: hld up centre: effrt and swtchd to stands' side over 2f out: hung rt and kpt on fnl f: nt pce to chal* **6/1**[2]

0031 **5** 1/2 **Robot Boy (IRE)**[6] 4694 9-9-9 **69** 4ex........................ JaneElliott(3) 11 68
(Marjorie Fife) *racd alone stands' rail: rdn over 2f out: kpt on same pce ins fnl f* **7/1**[3]

4145 **6** nk **Everkyllachy (IRE)**[15] 4330 5-9-0 **64**........................(b) LauraCoughlan(7) 5 62
(Karen McLintock) *dwlt: hld up centre: rdn along over 2f out: kpt on fnl f: nrst fin* **6/1**[2]

4610 **7** 1 1/4 **Economic Crisis (IRE)**[9] 4555 10-8-10 **60**........................ HarryRussell(7) 6 54
(Alan Berry) *cl up centre: rdn over 2f out: wknd over 1f out* **28/1**

3063 **8** hd **Camanche Grey (IRE)**[10] 4500 8-8-0 **50** oh4........................ VictorSantos(7) 8 43
(Lucinda Egerton) *hld up centre: drvn along over 2f out: no imp over 1f out* **80/1**

4450 **9** 1 **Northern Society (IRE)**[7] 4632 3-9-1 **63**........................ ShaneGray 3 50
(Keith Dalgleish) *hld up bhd ldng gp in centre: effrt over 2f out: wknd fnl f* **10/1**

2205 **10** 3/4 **Honey Gg**[22] 4074 4-9-1 **65**........................ CianMacRedmond(7) 2 52
(Declan Carroll) *racd alone far side: prom tl rdn and wknd over 1f out* **11/1**

4004 **11** 6 **Our Place In Loule**[6] 4691 6-9-12 **69**........................(b) PhilDennis 7 34
(Noel Wilson) *n.m.r sn after s: hld up centre: drvn over 2f out: wknd over 1f out* **33/1**

59.42s (-0.98) **Going Correction** -0.125s/f (Firm)
WFA 3 from 4yo+ 5lb **11** Ran SP% **116.1**
Speed ratings (Par 103): **102,101,98,98,97 97,95,94,93,92 82**
CSF £27.55 CT £156.90 TOTE £7.00: £1.90, £1.80, £2.80; EX 30.00 Trifecta £172.00.
Owner D A Lynch **Bred** P Balding **Trained** Curragh, Co Kildare

The Form Book Flat 2019, Raceform Ltd, Newbury, RG14 5SJ

FOCUS
A competitive sprint handicap which produced a determined winner who led all the way. A pb from the winner, with the second rated in line with her latest effort.

4912 JFM ELECTRICAL LTD, SERVICES & FACILITIES MANAGEMENT H'CAP 6f 6y
6:35 (6:37) (Class 5) (0-70,70) 3-Y-O+

£4,787 (£1,424; £711; £400; £400; £400) **Stalls** Centre

Form | | | | RPR
64 **1** **Twentysixthstreet (IRE)**[16] 4277 3-8-13 **63** .... TadhgO'Shea 12 71
(Andrew Hughes, Ire) *bhd and pushed along on nr side of gp: effrt u.p over 1f out: led ins fnl f: kpt on wl (trainer said, regarding the improved form shown, the colt may have benefited from dropping down in trip to 6f and from running in a handicap for the first time)* **33/1**

6040 **2** 3/4 **Amazing Grazing (IRE)**[7] 4632 5-9-9 **67** .... PhilDennis 4 74
(Rebecca Bastiman) *prom on far side of gp: effrt and ev ch over 1f out to ins fnl f: edgd lft: r.o (vet said gelding lost its right hind shoe)* **5/1**[3]

5260 **3** nk **Avenue Of Stars**[15] 4335 6-9-6 **64** ....(v) ConnorBeasley 6 70
(Karen McLintock) *in tch in centre of gp: drvn over 2f out: kpt on ins fnl f: nrst fin* **8/1**

2240 **4** 1 **Tadaany (IRE)**[10] 4519 7-8-9 **53** ....(p) SamJames 10 56
(Ruth Carr) *cl up on nr side of gp: rdn to ld over 1f out: hdd ins fnl f: one pce* **20/1**

0022 **5** nk **Inexes**[20] 4149 7-9-12 **70** ....(p) JasonHart 2 72
(Ivan Furtado) *dwlt: hld up in centre of gp: effrt over 1f out: chsd ldrs ins fnl f: one pce (jockey said gelding was denied a clear run 2f out)* **11/4**[1]

-066 **6** nk **Gilmer (IRE)**[5] 4725 8-8-6 **55** .... HarrisonShaw(5) 11 56
(Stef Keniry) *bhd in centre of gp: rdn over 2f out: kpt on fnl f: nvr able to chal* **10/1**

0044 **7** 3 3/4 **Autumn Flight (IRE)**[8] 4603 3-9-1 **65** ....(p) DuranFentiman 5 53
(Tim Easterby) *cl up on far side of gp tl rdn and wknd over 1f out* **10/1**

5021 **8** 1 **Cupid's Arrow (IRE)**[23] 4037 5-8-9 **53** .... JamesSullivan 9 39
(Ruth Carr) *led on nr side of gp to over 1f out: sn wknd (trainer's rep could offer no explanation for the gelding's performance)* **9/1**

324 **9** 1 3/4 **Diamond Shower (IRE)**[14] 4367 3-9-5 **69** .... JackGarritty 1 48
(Richard Fahey) *wnt rt s: bhd on far side of gp: rdn over 2f out: hung rt and sn btn (jockey said filly hung right throughout)* **10/1**

3320 **10** nk **Ticks The Boxes (IRE)**[26] 3921 7-8-6 **57** .... KieranSchofield(7) 7 36
(Brian Ellison) *cl up in centre of gp tl rdn and wknd over 1f out* **9/2**[2]

1m 11.83s (-0.87) **Going Correction** -0.125s/f (Firm)
WFA 3 from 5yo+ 6lb **10 Ran SP% 117.6**
Speed ratings (Par 103): **100,99,98,97,96 96,91,90,87,87**
CSF £192.78 CT £1517.88 TOTE £42.10: £10.00, £1.80, £3.00; EX 349.30 Trifecta £1268.40.
Owner Thistle Bloodstock Limited **Bred** Springbank Way Stud **Trained** Kells, Co Kilkenny

■ Stewards' Enquiry : Tadhg O'Shea four-day ban: used whip above the permitted level (tba)

FOCUS
Plenty in with a chance late on, but the unexposed winner's thrust up the stands' rail proved decisive. The second and third set the level.

4913 LES HOEY MBE DREAMMAKER FOUNDATION H'CAP 1m 4f 15y
7:05 (7:05) (Class 4) (0-80,81) 3-Y-O+

£8,021 (£2,387; £1,192; £596; £400; £400) **Stalls** High

Form | | | | RPR
5433 **1** **Moll Davis (IRE)**[21] 4110 3-8-12 **75** .... ConnorBeasley 6 86+
(George Scott) *hld up: effrt whn nt clr run over 2f out to over 1f out: hdwy to ld ent fnl f: styd on wl* **7/2**[1]

0456 **2** nk **Dark Lochnagar (USA)**[6] 4689 3-9-0 **77** .... ShaneGray 10 87
(Keith Dalgleish) *chsd ldrs: rdn over 3f out: hdwy to ld over 1f out to ent fnl f: rallied: hld nr fin* **5/1**[2]

3543 **3** 3 1/2 **Euro Implosion (IRE)**[5] 4729 3-8-0 **63** oh1 .... JamesSullivan 2 67
(Keith Dalgleish) *hld up in midfield: rdn along 3f out: rallied 2f out: kpt on fnl f: nt rch first two (vet said gelding lost its right front shoe)* **11/2**[3]

-660 **4** 1 1/4 **Carbon Dating (IRE)**[16] 4274 7-9-5 **70** .... TadhgO'Shea 4 72+
(Andrew Hughes, Ire) *missed break: bhd: rdn 3f out: gd hdwy on outside over 1f out: kpt on fnl f: nrst fin* **25/1**

0045 **5** 1 **Tor**[28] 3847 5-9-9 **79** .... HarrisonShaw(5) 9 79
(Iain Jardine) *midfield on outside: drvn along 3f out: outpcd wl over 1f out: kpt on fnl f: nt pce to chal* **16/1**

1-02 **6** shd **Matewan (IRE)**[26] 3925 4-9-9 **74** ....(p) PaddyMathers 11 74
(Ian Williams) *prom: smooth hdwy to ld over 2f out: rdn and hdd over 1f out: outpcd fnl f* **11/1**

4334 **7** 1 1/4 **Sioux Frontier (IRE)**[18] 4208 4-9-5 **70** .... LewisEdmunds 8 68
(Iain Jardine) *hld up towards rr: drvn along over 3f out: no imp fnl 2f* **14/1**

0253 **8** 1/2 **Regal Mirage (IRE)**[6] 4689 5-9-4 **69** .... DuranFentiman 3 66
(Tim Easterby) *hld up: effrt and pushed along over 2f out: no further imp fr over 1f out* **10/1**

3416 **9** 3/4 **Winged Spur (IRE)**[18] 4209 4-10-2 **81** .... JasonHart 13 77
(Mark Johnston) *led to over 2f out: rallied: wknd over 1f out* **25/1**

2104 **10** 1/2 **Royal Cosmic**[25] 3973 5-9-8 **73** .... JackGarritty 7 68
(Richard Fahey) *hld up: drvn along over 3f out: nvr able to chal* **20/1**

600 **11** hd **Glan Y Gors (IRE)**[14] 4381 7-9-10 **75** ....(b) CliffordLee 14 70
(David Thompson) *cl up: rdn over 3f out: wknd over 1f out* **40/1**

/000 **12** hd **Top Notch Tonto (IRE)**[14] 4383 9-9-5 **77** .... KieranSchofield(7) 12 72
(Brian Ellison) *hld up in tch: stdy hdwy over 4f out: rdn 3f out: wknd over 1f out* **25/1**

5-02 **13** 1 1/4 **Isabella Brant (FR)**[32] 3699 3-9-0 **77** .... GrahamLee 1 71
(Ralph Beckett) *hld up towards rr: drvn along over 3f out: wknd fnl 2f (trainer's rep said filly was unsuited by the good ground which in his opinion was riding quicker than the official description and would prefer a slower surface)* **7/2**[1]

2m 34.33s (-4.27) **Going Correction** -0.125s/f (Firm)
WFA 3 from 4yo+ 12lb **13 Ran SP% 125.2**
Speed ratings (Par 105): **109,108,106,105,104 104,104,103,103,102 102,102,101**
CSF £20.14 CT £99.48 TOTE £4.30: £1.90, £2.00, £2.60; EX 24.40 Trifecta £136.30.
Owner Sonia M Rogers & Anthony Rogers **Bred** Airlie Stud & Mrs S M Rogers **Trained** Newmarket, Suffolk

FOCUS
Add 8yds. Only two in it inside the final furlong with the patiently ridden winner holding her main rival at bay. The third helps set the level.

4914 #PROUDTOBEADREAMMAKER H'CAP 1m 3f 15y
7:35 (7:36) (Class 6) (0-60,61) 3-Y-O+

£3,493 (£1,039; £519; £400; £400; £400) **Stalls** High

Form | | | | RPR
0 **1** **King And Queen (FR)**[46] 3-8-7 **52** .... JasonHart 3 72+
(Mark Johnston) *pressed ldr: led over 4f out: shkn up and qckand clr over 2f out: eased ins fnl f: readily* **7/4**[1]

-365 **2** 7 **Flood Defence (IRE)**[130] 1024 5-9-12 **60** .... LewisEdmunds 8 66
(Iain Jardine) *hld up: rdn over 3f out: hdwy to chse (clr) wnr over 1f out: kpt on: no imp* **16/1**

020 **3** nk **Frequency Code (FR)**[64] 2581 3-9-2 **61** .... CliffordLee 10 66
(Jedd O'Keeffe) *hld up towards rr: drvn along and outpcd over 3f out: rallied over 1f out: kpt on fnl f: nrst fin* **7/2**[2]

-051 **4** 1 1/2 **Steel Helmet (IRE)**[39] 3447 5-8-12 **46** oh1 .... CamHardie 12 49
(Harriet Bethell) *prom: drvn along over 3f out: rallied: kpt on same pce fr over 1f out* **25/1**

-000 **5** 1 1/4 **Zealous (IRE)**[43] 3297 6-9-11 **59** .... JackGarritty 6 60
(Alistair Whillans) *t.k.h in midfield: hdwy to dispute modest 2nd pl briefly wl over 1f out: outpcd fnl f* **20/1**

/5-4 **6** 1 **Phebes Dream (IRE)**[25] 3981 6-8-5 **46** oh1 ....(h) KieranSchofield(7) 5 45
(John C McConnell, Ire) *dwlt: hld up: effrt on outside over 3f out: rdn and no imp fnl 2f* **7/1**[3]

-350 **7** 1 1/4 **Gamesters Icon**[44] 3267 4-9-10 **58** ....(p[1]) GrahamLee 1 55
(Oliver Greenall) *t.k.h: cl up: rdn over 3f out: wknd over 1f out* **20/1**

6 **8** 3 1/2 **Hard Times (IRE)**[46] 3181 8-8-12 **46** oh1 ....(t) AndrewElliott 7 37
(Philip Kirby) *hld up: drvn along over 3f out: nvr rchd ldrs* **50/1**

6415 **9** 3 **Three Castles**[24] 4002 3-9-2 **61** .... ShaneGray 13 47
(Keith Dalgleish) *chsd ldrs: wnt 2nd over 3f out to over 1f out: sn wknd* **7/1**[3]

0005 **10** 2 1/4 **Captain Peaky**[10] 4512 6-8-7 **46** oh1 .... HarrisonShaw(5) 14 28
(Liam Bailey) *hld up: rdn over 3f out: nvr a factor* **33/1**

0145 **11** 3 **Motahassen (IRE)**[21] 4109 5-9-2 **57** ....(t) ZakWheatley(7) 2 34
(Declan Carroll) *t.k.h: led to over 4f out: rdn and wknd over 2f out* **9/1**

12 2 1/4 **Smart Lass (IRE)**[77] 2133 4-8-9 **46** oh1 ....(p[1]) ConorMcGovern(3) 9 19
(John James Feane, Ire) *hld up: drvn and outpcd over 3f out: nvr on terms* **25/1**

6630 **13** 4 **Jagerbond**[8] 4587 3-8-3 **48** ow1 ....(p) PaddyMathers 4 14
(Andrew Crook) *t.k.h in midfield: rdn over 3f out: wknd over 2f out* **40/1**

0000 **14** 39 **Judith Gardenier**[22] 4054 7-8-12 **46** oh1 ....(tp) JamesSullivan 15
(R Mike Smith) *in tch: drvn and struggling 1/2-way: lost tch and eased fr 3f out* **66/1**

2m 21.7s (-3.80) **Going Correction** -0.125s/f (Firm)
WFA 3 from 4yo+ 11lb **14 Ran SP% 125.5**
Speed ratings (Par 101): **108,102,102,101,100 99,99,96,94,92 90,88,85,57**
CSF £32.20 CT £99.10 TOTE £2.80: £1.30, £4.40, £1.50; EX 37.00 Trifecta £177.20.
Owner Jaber Abdullah **Bred** Rabbah Bloodstock Limited **Trained** Middleham Moor, N Yorks

FOCUS
Add 8yds. What looked to be quite a competitive middle-distance handicap was turned into a procession by the unexposed winner. The second has been rated to her winter best, and the fourth close to his latest.

4915 UNDER 18'S RACE FREE H'CAP (DIV I) 1m 68y
8:05 (8:07) (Class 6) (0-60,67) 3-Y-O+

£3,493 (£1,039; £519; £400; £400; £400) **Stalls** Low

Form | | | | RPR
2010 **1** **Spirit Of Sarwan (IRE)**[7] 4658 5-9-8 **61** ....(b[1]) HarrisonShaw(5) 9 68
(Stef Keniry) *missed break: hld up: hdwy on outside 3f out: sustained run fnl f to ld cl home* **15/2**

6224 **2** hd **Juniors Fantasy (IRE)**[11] 4488 3-8-13 **56** ....(t[1]) DuranFentiman 4 60
(Tim Easterby) *led 1f: cl up: regained ld over 2f out: rdn and kpt on fnl f: hdd cl home* **6/1**[3]

-603 **3** 1 1/2 **Move In Faster**[24] 4002 4-9-11 **59** ....(v[1]) ConnorBeasley 11 61
(Michael Dods) *prom: hdwy and ev ch over 1f out: hung rt and no ex ins fnl f* **6/1**[3]

220U **4** 1 3/4 **The Big House (IRE)**[11] 4488 3-8-8 **51** .... PaddyMathers 7 47
(Adrian Nicholls) *s.i.s: hld up: hdwy over 2f out: kpt on ins fnl f: nt pce to chal* **11/2**[2]

0-04 **5** 1/2 **Barney Bullet (IRE)**[10] 4512 4-8-12 **46** oh1 ....(e) PhilDennis 12 43
(Noel Wilson) *hld up: effrt whn n.m.r briefly over 2f out: rdn and r.o fnl f: no imp* **40/1**

6 1 **All About Maddy**[40] 3437 3-8-3 **46** oh1 ....(t) JamesSullivan 1 39
(Paul W Flynn, Ire) *prom: drvn along 3f out: kpt on same pce fr over 1f out (jockey said filly moved poorly in the final furlong; vet said filly was found to be coughing post-race)* **4/1**[1]

0621 **7** 1/2 **Orobas (IRE)**[11] 4473 7-9-12 **67** ....(v) VictorSantos(7) 13 60
(Lucinda Egerton) *t.k.h: hld up: effrt over 2f out: rdn and no imp over 1f out* **14/1**

3540 **8** hd **Shazzab (IRE)**[26] 3939 4-9-7 **55** ....(b[1]) CamHardie 8 48
(Richard Fahey) *t.k.h: led after 1f to over 2f out: rdn and wknd over 1f out* **10/1**

0502 **9** 1 **Temple Of Wonder (IRE)**[11] 4487 3-9-1 **58** .... JackGarritty 3 47
(Liam Bailey) *hld up on ins: effrt whn n.m.r briefly over 2f out: sn rdn and n.d (jockey said gelding was denied a clear run approaching 2f out and again 1f out)* **9/1**

0000 **10** 3/4 **Crazy Tornado (IRE)**[24] 4003 6-9-6 **54** ....(e[1]) ShaneGray 2 43
(Keith Dalgleish) *hld up on ins: drvn and outpcd over 2f out: n.d after* **12/1**

0000 **11** 2 1/2 **Eternal Destiny**[14] 4358 4-8-12 **46** oh1 ....(p) JasonHart 6 31
(Ian Williams) *in tch: rdn over 2f out: wknd wl over 1f out* **28/1**

305 **12** 3 **Clovenstone**[22] 4055 3-9-5 **62** .... GrahamLee 10 36
(Alistair Whillans) *hld up in midfield: rdn over 2f out: sn lost pl* **25/1**

0-06 **13** 7 **Kissesforeveryone**[24] 4004 4-8-12 **46** oh1 .... AndrewElliott 14 6
(Andrew Crook) *cl up: ev ch over 3f out: outpcd whn n.m.r over 2f out: sn btn* **66/1**

5 **14** 2 3/4 **Seenit Doneit Next (IRE)**[27] 3899 3-8-12 **55** .... TadhgO'Shea 5 7
(Andrew Hughes, Ire) *bhd: struggling over 4f out: sn btn (vet said filly finished lame right hind)* **25/1**

1m 47.95s (-0.45) **Going Correction** -0.125s/f (Firm)
WFA 3 from 4yo+ 9lb **14 Ran SP% 124.2**
Speed ratings (Par 101): **97,96,95,93,93 92,91,91,90,89 87,84,77,74**
CSF £51.28 CT £305.28 TOTE £9.60: £2.60, £2.60, £2.30; EX 62.00 Trifecta £532.30.
Owner Mrs Stef Keniry **Bred** John Fallon **Trained** Middleham, N Yorks

FOCUS
Add 8yds. A thrilling finish with the front two wide apart. The winner, a second on the night for 5lb claimer Harrison Shaw, did well to prevail after blowing the start. The second and third have been rated pretty much to form.

4916 UNDER 18'S RACE FREE H'CAP (DIV II) 1m 68y
8:35 (8:35) (Class 6) (0-60,62) 3-Y-O+

£3,493 (£1,039; £519; £400; £400; £400) Stalls Low

Form RPR

106/ **1** **Ocean Air (FR)**[176] 304 5-9-0 **46**................(t[1]) JackGarritty 8 54+
(John C McConnell, Ire) *hld up: hdwy on outside over 2f out: led and edgd rt ins fnl f: kpt on wl cl home* **9/4[1]**

0-06 **2** *nk* **Be Proud (IRE)**[11] 4488 3-8-8 **49**................ PhilDennis 9 54
(Jim Goldie) *hld up on ins: hdwy whn nt clr run and swtchd lft over 2f out: led over 1f out to ins fnl f: kpt on: hld cl home* **14/1**

233 **3** *2 ¼* **Ishebayorgrey (IRE)**[26] 3922 7-9-10 **61**................(h) HarrisonShaw(5) 1 63
(Iain Jardine) *cl up: effrt and ev ch over 1f out: no ex ins fnl f* **3/1[2]**

04-0 **4** *1* **Sumner Beach**[25] 3957 5-9-8 **54**................ CamHardie 7 54
(Harriet Bethell) *hld up: rdn over 2f out: hdwy over 1f out: kpt on fnl f: no imp (jockey said gelding was denied a clear run 2f out)* **11/1**

00-0 **5** *nk* **The Brora Pobbles**[45] 3224 4-9-4 **50**................ GrahamLee 11 49
(Alistair Whillans) *hld up: effrt on ins 2f out: sn rdn: keeping on but no imp whn n.m.r wl ins fnl f* **50/1**

5641 **6** *hd* **Be Bold**[10] 4512 7-9-5 **51**................(b) ConnorBeasley 5 49
(Rebecca Bastiman) *plld hrd in midfield: effrt over 2f out: kpt on same pce fr over 1f out* **8/1**

1/00 **7** *7* **Tom Dooley (IRE)**[9] 4567 8-8-13 **45**................ AndrewElliott 13 27
(Philip Kirby) *hld up: rdn over 2f out: sn n.d: btn over 1f out* **50/1**

26-6 **8** *½* **Phantasmal**[39] 3452 5-10-2 **62**................ PaddyMathers 3 43
(Stuart Coltherd) *prom tl rdn and wknd over 2f out* **9/1**

500- **9** *¾* **Jimmy Krankyar (USA)**[225] 9323 3-8-13 **54**................ SamJames 10 31
(Phillip Makin) *cl up tl rdn and wknd over 2f out* **12/1**

-004 **10** *½* **Amy Blair**[24] 4005 6-9-0 **46**................(p[1]) ShaneGray 4 24
(Stef Keniry) *led to over 2f out: wknd wl over 1f out* **13/2[3]**

1m 47.14s (-1.26) **Going Correction** -0.125s/f (Firm)
WFA 3 from 4yo+ 9lb **10** Ran SP% **116.8**
Speed ratings (Par 101): **101,100,98,97,97 96,89,89,88,88**
CSF £36.24 CT £98.88 TOTE £3.00: £1.50, £2.80, £1.10; EX 37.60 Trifecta £119.70.
Owner Rockview Racing Club **Bred** D R Tucker **Trained** Stamullen, Co Meath

FOCUS
Add 8yds. Plenty of support for the winner, who was having his first run since January. The winner has been rated to last year's form, and the second close to his 2yo turf form.

4917 RACINGTV.COM FILLIES' H'CAP 1m 68y
9:05 (9:05) (Class 5) (0-70,71) 3-Y-O+

£4,787 (£1,424; £711; £400; £400; £400) Stalls Low

Form RPR

0-66 **1** **Rosemay (FR)**[45] 3224 5-8-12 **48**................(p) JamesSullivan 4 54
(R Mike Smith) *hld up: hdwy and rdn over 1f out: led ins fnl f: kpt on wl* **4/1[2]**

0-00 **2** *1* **Iconic Code**[26] 3925 4-9-13 **63**................ ShaneGray 7 67
(Keith Dalgleish) *s.i.s: hld up: rdn and hdwy 2f out: ev ch briefly ins fnl f: hld nr fin* **9/2[3]**

5506 **3** *nse* **Set In Stone (IRE)**[16] 4278 5-10-7 **71**................ TadhgO'Shea 6 75
(Andrew Hughes, Ire) *trckd ldrs: pushed along over 2f out: effrt and swtchd lft over 1f out: ch ins fnl f: no ex nr fin* **9/1**

6-20 **4** *4 ½* **Ventura Royal (IRE)**[5] 4728 4-9-10 **63**................(h) ConorMcGovern(3) 2 57
(David O'Meara) *led: hrd pressed over 2f out: edgd lft and hdd ins fnl f: sn wknd* **9/2[3]**

6063 **5** *2 ½* **Diviner (IRE)**[16] 4285 3-9-7 **66**................ JasonHart 9 52
(Mark Johnston) *pressed ldr: ev ch over 2f out to over 1f out: wknd fnl f* **15/8[1]**

-506 **6** *nk* **Can Can Sixty Two**[31] 3718 4-9-12 **62**................(p[1]) JackGarritty 8 49
(R Mike Smith) *prom: rdn and outpcd over 2f out: n.d after* **14/1**

00B6 **7** *5* **Harperelle**[11] 4487 3-8-2 **47**................ CamHardie 5 21
(Alistair Whillans) *in tch: drvn and outpcd 3f out: btn fnl 2f* **10/1**

00-0 **8** *2* **One For Brad (IRE)**[26] 3932 4-8-4 **47** ow2................ CianMacRedmond(7) 1 18
(Alan Berry) *slowly away: bhd: struggling 1/2-way: nvr on terms* **50/1**

1m 46.77s (-1.63) **Going Correction** -0.125s/f (Firm)
WFA 3 from 4yo+ 9lb **8** Ran SP% **118.9**
Speed ratings (Par 100): **103,102,101,97,94 94,89,87**
CSF £23.37 CT £155.17 TOTE £4.50: £1.30, £1.70, £2.60; EX 20.20 Trifecta £136.40.
Owner Dal Riata - A Barclay **Bred** Alexis Chetioui **Trained** Galston, E Ayrshire

FOCUS
Add 8yds. Not the most competitive of fillies' handicaps, but that won't matter to connections of the winner, who was scoring for the first time at the 31st time of asking. The second has been rated to her best form away from soft ground.
T/Plt: £109.80 to a £1 stake. Pool: £53,483.58 - 355.50 winning units T/Qpdt: £32.00 to a £1 stake. Pool: £7,830.48 - 180.90 winning units **Richard Young**

4882 NEWMARKET (R-H)
Saturday, July 13

OFFICIAL GOING: Good to firm (watered; ovr 8.5; stands' 8.7, ctr 8.5, far 8.3)
Wind: LIGHT, ACROSS Weather: LIGHT CLOUD

4918 ROSSDALES BRITISH EBF MAIDEN FILLIES' STKS (PLUS 10 RACE) 7f
1:50 (1:51) (Class 3) 2-Y-O £7,762 (£2,310; £1,154; £577) Stalls Low

Form RPR

1 **Light Blush (IRE)** 2-9-0 0................ JamesDoyle 5 83+
(Charlie Appleby) *pressed ldng pair: effrt and rn green over 1f out: rdn to chse ldr ent fnl f: styd on to ld wl ins fnl f: pricked ears in front but r.o wl and in command towards fin* **5/2[1]**

2 *¾* **Craylands** 2-9-0 0................ OisinMurphy 3 81
(Michael Bell) *t.k.h: pressed ldr tl led 3f out: rdn over 1f out: kpt on u.p tl hdd and no ex wl ins fnl f* **14/1**

3 *¾* **Award Scheme** 2-9-0 0................ DanielTudhope 4 79
(William Haggas) *rn green and flashing tail early: t.k.h: hld up in tch: clsd and swtchd lft over 1f out: nt clr run briefly: chsd ldrs and kpt on ins fnl f* **5/1**

6 **4** *1 ¼* **Incognito (IRE)**[18] 4223 2-9-0 0................ GeraldMosse 2 76
(Mick Channon) *in tch: effrt over 1f out: swtchd lft and hdwy u.p 1f out: kpt on* **33/1**

5 *1 ¼* **Believe In Love (IRE)** 2-9-0 0................ AndreaAtzeni 7 73
(Roger Varian) *in tch in rr: effrt 2f out: hdwy over 1f out: no imp 1f out: wl hld and kpt on same pce ins fnl f* **11/1**

6 *hd* **Baaqy (IRE)** 2-9-0 0................ FrankieDettori 1 72
(John Gosden) *led tl 3f out: stl pressing ldr tl rdn and unable qck over 1f out: sn outpcd and kpt on same pce ins fnl f* **7/2[2]**

7 *nk* **Frankel's Storm** 2-9-0 0................ HarryBentley 8 71
(Mark Johnston) *in tch in midfield: niggled along over 3f out: rdn and unable qck over 1f out: wl hld and kpt on same pce ins fnl f* **4/1[3]**

0 **8** *1 ¼* **Tiritomba (IRE)**[19] 4184 2-9-0 0................ ChrisHayes 6 68
(Richard Hannon) *rn green: t.k.h: hld up wl in tch in midfield: hung lft and lost pl over 1f out: sn hung bk rt and bhd 1f out: no imp ins fnl f (jockey said filly became unbalanced and hung left-handed when travelling into the dip)* **8/1**

1m 25.23s (-0.47) **Going Correction** -0.125s/f (Firm) **8** Ran SP% **116.5**
Speed ratings (Par 95): **97,96,95,93,92 92,91,90**
CSF £40.03 TOTE £3.00: £1.40, £3.40, £1.90; EX 35.80 Trifecta £172.60.
Owner Godolphin **Bred** Mrs S M Rogers & Sir Thomas Pilkington **Trained** Newmarket, Suffolk

FOCUS
After a number of track records fell the previous day there was 3mm of water put on the track, before 0.2mm of rain overnight, and it was another warm afternoon. With the Aidan O'Brien runner taken out, not many of these seemed that well fancied and it played out like just a fair race for the track. The pace was pretty even through the middle chunk and the winner got the final 3f in 35.44 (103.04%). The action was near side. It's been rated in line with the race standard for the minor places.

4919 BET365 MILE H'CAP 1m
2:20 (2:21) (Class 2) (0-100,97) 3-Y-£18,675 (£5,592; £2,796; £1,398; £699) Stalls Low

Form RPR

1-12 **1** **Motakhayyel**[15] 4348 3-9-2 **92**................ ChrisHayes 6 101
(Richard Hannon) *racd away fr rivals towards centre: w ldr tl led 3f out: rdn and qcknd whn hung rt over 1f out: in command and styd on wl ins fnl f* **5/1**

2-65 **2** *2 ¼* **Flashcard (IRE)**[35] 3599 3-9-1 **91**................ OisinMurphy 3 95
(Andrew Balding) *t.k.h: hld up wl in tch in rr: shkn up 2f out: swtchd lft and drvn over 1f out: hdwy to chse clr wnr and edgd rt ins fnl f: kpt on but no imp* **7/2[3]**

1-32 **3** *nse* **Bayroot (IRE)**[16] 4305 3-9-7 **97**................ AndreaAtzeni 2 101
(Roger Varian) *hld up wl in tch: effrt 2f out: drvn ent fnl f: hdwy between rivals ins fnl f: kpt on but no imp fnl 100yds* **3/1[2]**

3461 **4** *½* **Victory Command (IRE)**[11] 4490 3-9-7 **97**................ RyanMoore 1 100
(Mark Johnston) *led and set stdy gallop: hdd 3f out: unable to match pce of wnr u.p over 1f out: kpt on same pce ins fnl f* **5/2[1]**

3311 **5** *½* **Akwaan (IRE)**[9] 4565 3-8-7 **83**................(p) HarryBentley 5 85
(Simon Crisford) *in tch: effrt to press ldng pair 2f out: unable qck over 1f out: sn one pce ins fnl f* **4/1**

1m 39.12s (-0.88) **Going Correction** -0.125s/f (Firm) **5** Ran SP% **112.5**
Speed ratings (Par 106): **99,96,96,96,95**
CSF £22.55 TOTE £4.70: £2.10, £1.80; EX 21.30 Trifecta £84.70.
Owner Hamdan Al Maktoum **Bred** Crossfields Bloodstock Ltd **Trained** East Everleigh, Wilts

FOCUS
A useful 3yo handicap, the pace was a steady one and the winner raced on his own for much of the race more towards the centre. The winner covered the last 3f in 34.65 (107.27%). It's been rated close to the race standard, with the fourth back close to his 2yo form.

4920 BET365 SUPERLATIVE STKS (GROUP 2) 7f
2:55 (2:55) (Class 1) 2-Y-O

£45,368 (£17,200; £8,608; £4,288; £2,152; £1,080) Stalls Low

Form RPR

1 **1** **Mystery Power (IRE)**[21] 4106 2-9-1 0................ OisinMurphy 7 111
(Richard Hannon) *pressed ldrs tl led jst over 2f out: edgd rt 2f out: styd on wl u.p ins fnl f: rdn out* **7/1**

1 **2** *1* **Juan Elcano**[36] 3551 2-9-1 0................ AndreaAtzeni 1 108
(Kevin Ryan) *dwlt: sn rcvrd and chsd ldrs: rdn and ev ch over 2f out: edgd lft over 1f out: kpt on wl but a hld ins fnl f* **6/1[3]**

10 **3** *3 ¼* **Maxi Boy**[25] 3949 2-9-1 0................ FrankieDettori 2 99
(Michael Bell) *in tch in rr: rdn over 3f out: hdwy u.p over 1f out: sn no imp and wknd ins fnl f* **7/1**

046 **4** *2* **Ropey Guest**[25] 3949 2-9-1 100................ ShaneKelly 8 94
(George Margarson) *hld up in tch: effrt over 2f out: chsd ldng trio 1f out: no imp and wl hld ins fnl f* **25/1**

1 **5** *2 ½* **Shared Belief (IRE)**[29] 3804 2-9-1 0................ DanielTudhope 3 87
(Archie Watson) *led for over 1f: styd upsides ldr: rdn over 2f out: outpcd and hung lft over 1f out: wknd ins fnl f* **16/1**

1 **6** *¾* **Wild Thunder (IRE)**[51] 3008 2-9-1 0................ SeanLevey 4 85
(Richard Hannon) *in tch in midfield: effrt over 2f out: edgd out lft over 1f out: sltly impeded 1f out: no prog and wknd ins fnl f* **9/1**

0 **7** *7* **Year Of The Tiger (IRE)**[7] 4672 2-9-1 0................ RyanMoore 6 66
(A P O'Brien, Ire) *hld up wl in tch: effrt wl over 2f out: sn edging out lft and drvn: no hdwy over 1f out: sn edgd rt and wknd ins fnl f and eased towards fin (trainer said, regards poor performance, colt returned a blood sample that had shown an incorrect blood profile)* **5/2[2]**

1 **8** *3 ¾* **King's Command**[22] 4069 2-9-1 0................ JamesDoyle 5 56+
(Charlie Appleby) *sn w ldr: led over 5f out: rdn and hdd jst over 2f out: impeded 2f out: sn lost pl and hung lft over 1f out: bhd and eased ins fnl f (trainer said colt was unsuited by the ground and would prefer an easier surface)* **9/4[1]**

1m 23.59s (-2.11) **Going Correction** -0.125s/f (Firm) **8** Ran SP% **118.4**
Speed ratings (Par 106): **107,105,102,99,97 96,88,83**
CSF £50.01 TOTE £7.20: £2.40, £1.80, £1.80; EX 41.50 Trifecta £335.30.
Owner King Power Racing Co Ltd **Bred** Ms Siobhan O'Rahilly **Trained** East Everleigh, Wilts

FOCUS
They raced near side. The first two in the betting filled the last two places, so it's hard to get that excited by this form. But the winner and runner-up had won their only previous starts and they were closely matched on a line through a horse called Subjectivist, who finished second to both of them. The winner got the final 3f in 34.51 (103.82%). The winner has been rated in line with the race standard, with the third to his Coventry figure.

4921 BET365 BUNBURY CUP (HERITAGE H'CAP) 7f
3:30 (3:31) (Class 2) 3-Y-O+

£74,700 (£22,368; £11,184; £5,592; £2,796; £1,404) Stalls Low

Form RPR

4-00 **1** **Vale Of Kent (IRE)**[14] 4385 4-9-4 **99**................ FrankieDettori 14 108
(Mark Johnston) *racd far side: overall ldr tl rdn and hdd 2f out: battled bk u.p to ld again 1f out: styd on wl: 1st of 8 in gp* **13/2[2]**

3-23 **2** ½ **Solar Gold (IRE)**[24] 3994 4-9-1 **96**........................ JamesDoyle 11 103+
(William Haggas) *racd in centre: led gp and chsd wnr tl jst over 2f out: rdn 2f out: stl chsng ldrs and kpt on wl ins fnl f: 1st of 7 in gp* **4/1**[1]

1023 **3** ½ **Admirality**[7] 4654 5-8-13 **94**........................(h) TomEaves 17 100+
(Roger Fell) *racd far side: chsd ldrs: clsd 3f out: rdn to ld 2f out: drvn and hdd 1f out: kpt on same pce ins fnl f: 2nd of 8 in gp* **12/1**

-253 **4** nk **Spanish City**[35] 3602 6-9-1 **96**........................ AndreaAtzeni 8 101
(Roger Varian) *racd in centre: midfield: effrt over 1f out: kpt on wl u.p ins fnl f: nvr quite getting to ldrs: 2nd of 7 in gp* **7/1**[3]

1200 **5** nk **Lake Volta (IRE)**[14] 4402 4-9-8 **103**........................ RyanMoore 19 107
(Mark Johnston) *racd far side: chsd ldrs: rdn 2f out: drvn over 1f out: swtchd lft and kpt on same pce ins fnl f: 3rd of 8 in gp* **14/1**

5050 **6** ½ **Ripp Orf (IRE)**[43] 3318 5-8-12 **93**........................ GeraldMosse 5 96
(David Elsworth) *racd in centre: hld up towards rr: rdn 3f out: hdwy over 1f out: kpt on ins fnl f: nvr trbld ldrs: 3rd of 7 in gp* **8/1**

3420 **7** ¾ **So Beloved**[24] 3987 9-9-10 **105**........................ DanielTudhope 9 106
(David O'Meara) *racd in centre: stdd after s: hld up in rr: swtchd lft and shkn up wl over 1f out: rdn and kpt on ins fnl f: nvr trbld ldrs: 4th of 7 in gp (starter reported that the gelding was the subject of a third criteria failure; trainer was informed that the gelding's could not run until the day after passing a stalls test)* **16/1**

4100 **8** nse **Sanaadh**[50] 3062 6-8-13 **94**........................(t) JimmyQuinn 15 95
(Michael Wigham) *racd far side: hld up in rr: rdn and hdwy over 1f out: chsng ldrs whn nt clr run and swtchd rt ins fnl f: no imp u.p fnl 100yds: 4th of 8 in gp (starter reported that the gelding was the subject of a third criteria failure; trainer was informed that the gelding's could not run until the day after passing a stalls test)* **50/1**

-000 **9** nse **Good Effort (IRE)**[142] 842 4-9-0 **95**........................ SeanLevey 20 96
(Ismail Mohammed) *racd far side: hld up in tch in midfield: swtchd rt and effrt over 1f out: drvn and clsd to chse ldrs 1f out: no ex and wknd wl ins fnl f: 5th of 8 in gp* **33/1**

0346 **10** ½ **Zap**[28] 3857 4-8-10 **91**........................(v[1]) KevinStott 18 90
(Richard Fahey) *racd far side: hld up towards rr: effrt 2f out: hdwy u.p over 1f out: no ex ins fnl f: wknd towards fin: 6th of 8 in gp* **14/1**

40-1 **11** 1½ **Ambassadorial (USA)**[24] 3991 5-9-1 **96** 6ex........................ JFEgan 13 91
(Jane Chapple-Hyam) *racd far side: chsd ldrs: unable qck u.p over 1f out: sn swtchd lft and wknd ins fnl f: 7th of 8 in gp* **11/1**

4064 **12** nk **Hajjam**[14] 4385 5-8-11 **92**........................(p[1]) ChrisHayes 16 87
(David O'Meara) *racd far side: in tch in midfield: effrt wl over 1f out: hdwy u.p over 1f out: no ex jst ins fnl f: wknd fnl 100yds: 8th of 8 in gp* **33/1**

1502 **13** 1¼ **Crossing The Line**[24] 3994 4-9-5 **100**........................ OisinMurphy 6 91
(Andrew Balding) *racd centre: rdn 3f out: unable qck u.p over 1f out: wknd ins fnl f: 5th of 7 in gp* **8/1**

1156 **14** 2¼ **Keyser Soze (IRE)**[35] 3588 5-9-7 **102**........................ StevieDonohoe 2 87
(Richard Spencer) *racd in nr side pair: hld up towards rr: swtchd lft 2f out: no imp u.p over 1f out: wknd ins fnl f: 1st of 2 in gp* **16/1**

-004 **15** 1¾ **Alemaratalyoum (IRE)**[43] 3318 5-8-13 **94**........................(t) WayneLordan 4 74
(Stuart Williams) *racd in nr side: midfield overall: rdn 2f out: sn struggling and outpcd: wknd ins fnl f: 2nd of 2 in gp* **25/1**

0406 **16** nse **Three Saints Bay (IRE)**[7] 4650 4-9-5 **100**........................ HarryBentley 10 80
(David O'Meara) *racd in centre: t.k.h: in tch in midfield: unable qck u.p and edgd lft 1f out: wknd ins fnl f: 6th of 7 in gp* **33/1**

0-60 **17** 4½ **Burnt Sugar (IRE)**[35] 3588 7-9-7 **102**........................ ShaneKelly 12 70
(Roger Fell) *racd in centre: in tch in midfield overall: rdn 2f out: sn edgd rt and outpcd: wknd ins fnl f: 7th of 7 in gp* **14/1**

1m 22.69s (-3.01) **Going Correction** -0.125s/f (Firm) 17 Ran SP% **130.5**
Speed ratings (Par 109): **112,111,110,110,110 109,108,108,108,108 106,106,104,102,100 99,94**
CSF £33.11 CT £325.70 TOTE £7.30: £2.30, £1.30, £3.70, £2.00; EX 31.10 Trifecta £529.40.
Owner Sheikh Hamdan bin Mohammed Al Maktoum **Bred** Stock Vale Ltd **Trained** Middleham Moor, N Yorks

FOCUS
A typically open edition of the race, although not for the first time this week little got involved from off the pace and the two market leaders controlled the outcome. They split into two groups and the first two home, racing far side and centre respectively, led their groups throughout. The winner covered the last 3f in 35.15sec (100.82%). The principals have been rated close to form.

4922 BEDFORD LODGE HOTEL & SPA BRITISH EBF FILLIES' H'CAP 7f
4:05 (4:07) (Class 2) (0-100,98) 3-Y-O
£15,562 (£4,660; £2,330; £1,165; £582; £292) **Stalls Low**

Form RPR

61-6 **1** **California Love**[22] 4052 3-8-10 **87**........................ StevieDonohoe 11 99
(Richard Spencer) *mde all: rdn over 2f out: drvn over 1f out: all out towards fin: a jst lasting home* **8/1**

2 hd **Salayel**[113] 1326 3-8-8 **85**........................ AndreaAtzeni 1 96
(Roger Varian) *stdd s: t.k.h: chsd ldrs: chsd wnr over 2f out: effrt over 1f out: kpt on u.p ins fnl f: clsng towards fin: nvr quite getting to wnr* **7/2**[1]

04-3 **3** 4 **Dupioni (IRE)**[22] 4072 3-8-7 **84**........................ JFEgan 3 84
(Rae Guest) *hld up in tch towards rr: nt clr run 2f out: effrt and hdwy u.p over 1f out: kpt on to chse clr ldng pair ins fnl f: no imp* **8/1**

131- **4** 1½ **Chaleur**[287] 7776 3-9-7 **98**........................ HarryBentley 6 94
(Ralph Beckett) *hld up in tch in midfield: effrt ent fnl 2f: drvn and no imp on ldng pair over 1f out: wl hld and plugged on same pce ins fnl f* **6/1**[3]

-100 **5** shd **Ice Gala**[22] 4052 3-9-4 **95**........................ JamesDoyle 8 91
(William Haggas) *taken down early: hld up in tch in midfield: effrt ent fnl 2f: edgd lft u.p and no imp over 1f out: wl hld and plugged on same pce ins fnl f* **9/2**[2]

4065 **6** 1½ **Chynna**[12] 4442 3-8-9 **86**........................ ChrisHayes 9 78
(Mick Channon) *hld up in tch in rr: nt clr run ent fnl 2f: no real hdwy u.p over 1f out: plugged to pass btn horses ins fnl f: nvr threatened ldrs* **50/1**

6-55 **7** hd **Strict Tempo**[43] 3293 3-8-3 **80**........................ JoeyHaynes 7 71
(Andrew Balding) *in tch in midfield: rdn 3f out: no imp u.p over 1f out: wknd ins fnl f* **16/1**

40 **8** 1¼ **Aim Power (IRE)**[22] 4052 3-8-11 **88**........................ OisinMurphy 10 76
(Richard Hannon) *chsd wnr tl over 2f out: unable qck and lost pl over 1f out: wknd ins fnl f* **11/1**

61-2 **9** shd **Flarepath**[35] 3603 3-8-8 **85**........................ WayneLordan 4 72
(William Haggas) *chsd ldrs: effrt over 2f out: unable qck and lost pl over 1f out: wknd ins fnl f* **9/2**[2]

2153 **10** 3 **I Am Magical**[29] 3807 3-8-2 **79**........................ JimmyQuinn 5 58
(Charlie Fellowes) *hld up in tch towards rr: effrt 2f out: sn struggling and outpcd u.p over 1f out: wknd ins fnl f* **17/2**

212- **11** hd **Red Armour**[277] 8067 3-8-4 **81** oh11 ow2........................ EoinWalsh 2 60
(Luke McJannet) *stdd s: hld up in tch: effrt over 2f out: sn struggling and outpcd over 1f out: wknd ins fnl f* **50/1**

1m 22.78s (-2.92) **Going Correction** -0.125s/f (Firm) 11 Ran SP% **123.8**
Speed ratings (Par 103): **111,110,106,104,104 102,102,101,100,97 97**
CSF £38.12 CT £244.10 TOTE £9.30: £2.80, £2.00, £2.60; EX 61.80 Trifecta £502.30.
Owner Aidan Cunningham **Bred** Ms Vivienne O'Sullivan **Trained** Newmarket, Suffolk

FOCUS
The winner (final 3f in 35.43sec/100.61%) raced up the middle and the runner-up was more near side, and they pulled clear in what looked a good fillies' handicap, although they were forwardly positioned on a day when few on this card made up significant ground. The first two have been rated towards the top end of the race averages.

4923 DARLEY JULY CUP STKS (GROUP 1) (BRITISH CHAMPIONS SERIES) 6f
4:40 (4:41) (Class 1) 3-Y-O+
£283,550 (£107,500; £53,800; £26,800; £13,450; £6,750) **Stalls Low**

Form RPR

1-54 **1** **Ten Sovereigns (IRE)**[22] 4050 3-9-0 116........................ RyanMoore 12 125
(A P O'Brien, Ire) *racd centre: led tl over 3f out: chsd ldr: rdn ent fnl 2f: led over 1f out: drvn and styd on strly ins fnl f: rdn out: 1st of 7 in gp* **9/2**[2]

2-01 **2** 2¾ **Advertise**[22] 4050 3-9-0 119........................(b) FrankieDettori 8 116
(Martyn Meade) *racd centre: in tch in midfield: effrt over 1f out: chsd wnr 1f out: styd on but no imp: 2nd of 7 in gp* **3/1**[1]

-565 **3** ¾ **Fairyland (IRE)**[25] 3950 3-8-11 112........................ SeamieHeffernan 4 111+
(A P O'Brien, Ire) *racd nr side: in tch in midfield: hdwy u.p to chse ldrs and hung lft 1f out: kpt on but no imp ins fnl f: 1st of 5 in gp* **10/1**

3-20 **4** 1 **Pretty Pollyanna**[22] 4051 3-8-11 112........................ OisinMurphy 9 107
(Michael Bell) *racd centre: chsd ldrs: rdn to press ldrs 2f out: unable to match pce of wnr ent fnl f: wl hld and kpt on same pce after: 3rd of 7 in gp* **8/1**

-310 **5** ½ **So Perfect (USA)**[21] 4092 3-8-11 107........................ WayneLordan 5 106
(A P O'Brien, Ire) *racd centre: in tch: effrt u.p over 1f out: kpt on but no threat to ldr ins fnl f: 4th of 7 in gp* **25/1**

0-0 **6** nk **Lim's Cruiser (AUS)**[21] 4094 6-9-6 114........................(b) JFEgan 7 109
(Stephen Gray, Singapore) *racd centre: swtchd lft after s: hld up in tch: effrt over 1f out: kpt on same pce and no threat to wnr ins fnl f: 5th of 7 in gp* **66/1**

-301 **7** nk **Brando**[37] 3501 7-9-6 114........................ TomEaves 11 108
(Kevin Ryan) *racd centre: hld up in rr: effrt 2f out: sme hdwy u.p over 1f out: no imp 1f out and wknd ins fnl f: 6th of 7 in gp* **18/1**

-022 **8** nse **Glorious Journey**[14] 4389 4-9-6 108........................ JamesDoyle 2 108
(Charlie Appleby) *racd nr side: dwlt: hdwy to ld gp and chsd ldrs after 2f: overall ldr over 3f out tl over 1f out: wknd ins fnl f: 2nd of 5 in gp* **20/1**

2323 **9** ½ **Major Jumbo**[41] 3388 5-9-6 109........................ KevinStott 6 106
(Kevin Ryan) *racd nr side: led gp and chsd wnr for 2f: rdn to press ldrs 2f out: sn outpcd and wknd ins fnl f: 3rd of 5 in gp* **66/1**

-112 **10** shd **Dream Of Dreams (IRE)**[21] 4094 5-9-6 119........................ DanielTudhope 1 106
(Sir Michael Stoute) *racd nr side: stdd after s: hld up in rr: effrt 2f out: nvr threatened to get on terms and wl hld whn nt clr run and swtchd rt ins fnl f: 4th of 5 in gp* **9/2**[2]

0-11 **11** 1 **Cape Byron**[21] 4095 5-9-6 113........................ AndreaAtzeni 10 103
(Roger Varian) *racd centre: chsd ldrs: rdn over 2f out: lost pl over 1f out: wknd ins fnl f: 7th of 7 in gp* **6/1**[3]

0-41 **12** 2½ **Limato (IRE)**[14] 4389 7-9-6 114........................ HarryBentley 3 95
(Henry Candy) *racd nr side: hld up in tch: effrt and sme hdwy 2f out: no imp over 1f out: wknd ins fnl f: 5th of 5 in gp* **8/1**

1m 9.31s (-2.79) **Going Correction** -0.125s/f (Firm)
WFA 3 from 4yo+ 6lb 12 Ran SP% **123.8**
Speed ratings (Par 117): **113,109,108,107,106 105,105,105,104,104 103,100**
CSF £18.72 CT £134.76 TOTE £5.00: £2.20, £1.60, £2.90; EX 21.10 Trifecta £154.80.
Owner Derrick Smith & Mrs John Magnier & Michael Tabor **Bred** Camas Park, Lynch Bages & Summerhill **Trained** Cashel, Co Tipperary

FOCUS
There was a suspicion coming into this that the older sprinters weren't up to much and so it proved, with the 3yos completely dominating, filling the first five places from as many runners. They raced in two groups, with those down the centre coming out on top. It's been rated at something like face value, with the second and third close to form.

4924 MARITIME CARGO H'CAP 1m 4f
5:15 (5:17) (Class 3) (0-90,91) 3-Y-O+ **£12,938** (£3,850; £1,924; £962) **Stalls Low**

Form RPR

321 **1** **Dubai Tradition (USA)**[20] 4143 3-8-11 **83**........................ HectorCrouch 3 93+
(Saeed bin Suroor) *mde all: rdn over 2f out: pressed and sustained duel w runner-up fr over 1f out: hld on v gamely: all out* **13/8**[1]

-513 **2** hd **Apparate**[17] 4256 3-8-13 **85**........................ AndreaAtzeni 6 94+
(Roger Varian) *chsd wnr: effrt over 2f out: clsd and chal over 1f out: sustained duel w wnr after: kpt on wl: jst hld towards fin* **11/4**[2]

1-03 **3** 2¼ **Power Of States (IRE)**[16] 4304 3-8-6 **78**........................ ChrisHayes 2 83
(Hugo Palmer) *hld up in tch: effrt ent fnl 2f: chsd ldrs jst ins fnl f: nvr threatened to get on terms w ldrs but kpt on ins fnl f* **20/1**

6-62 **4** nse **Doctor Cross (IRE)**[14] 4407 5-9-1 **75**........................ JamesDoyle 1 80
(Richard Fahey) *t.k.h early: hld up in tch: effrt over 2f out: no imp over 1f out tl styd on ins fnl f: no threat to ldrs* **7/1**

-164 **5** 2¼ **Hareeq**[21] 4102 4-10-0 **88**........................(p) FrankieDettori 5 89
(Richard Hughes) *stdd s: hld up in tch in rr: effrt 3f out: rdn 2f out: no imp and wknd ins fnl f* **8/1**

2110 **6** 2¾ **Babbo's Boy (IRE)**[23] 4017 3-9-5 **91**........................ RyanMoore 4 88
(Michael Bell) *chsd ldng pair: rdn ent fnl 2f: unable qck over 1f out: wknd ins fnl f* **4/1**[3]

2m 31.27s (-2.63) **Going Correction** -0.125s/f (Firm)
WFA 3 from 4yo+ 12lb 6 Ran SP% **113.1**
Speed ratings (Par 107): **103,102,101,101,99 98**
CSF £6.42 TOTE £2.10: £1.50, £1.70; EX 6.40 Trifecta £54.60.
Owner Godolphin **Bred** Godolphin **Trained** Newmarket, Suffolk

FOCUS
This only seriously concerned the first two, a couple of progressive 3yos. They all raced up the middle in the straight. The fourth has been rated close to form.
T/Jkpt: Not Won. T/Plt: £222.90 to a £1 stake. Pool: £166,656.27 - 545.62 winning units T/Qpdt: £31.20 to a £1 stake. Pool: £14,692.16 - 347.95 winning units **Steve Payne**

4252 SALISBURY (R-H)

Saturday, July 13

OFFICIAL GOING: Firm (good to firm in places; watered; 9.0)

Weather: Fine

4925 T & M GLASS LTD BRITISH EBF NOVICE STKS (PLUS 10 RACE) 6f 213y

5:50 (5:51) (Class 4) 2-Y-O **£5,175** (£1,540; £769; £384) **Stalls** Low

Form RPR

1 **Pyledriver** 2-9-5 0 MartinDwyer 7 86+
(William Muir) *hld up: rdn over 2f out: sn hung lft: hdwy over 1f out: swtchd rt ins fnl f: r.o to ld towards fin: comf* **50/1**

2 2 ¾ **Great Ambassador**[17] 4246 2-9-5 0 JosephineGordon 1 84
(Ralph Beckett) *s.i.s: sn rcvrd to ld: hdd 1/2-way: led again 3f out: rdn and hung lft fr over 2f out: hdd towards fin* **15/8**[1]

62 3 2 **Hexagon (IRE)**[17] 4252 2-9-5 0 JasonWatson 9 79
(Roger Charlton) *mid-div: hdwy over 4f out: rdn and hung lft over 1f out: chsd wnr briefly ins fnl f: styd on same pce* **5/2**[2]

4 2 ½ **Dubai Souq (IRE)** 2-9-5 0 RoystonFfrench 11 72
(Saeed bin Suroor) *chsd ldrs: rdn over 2f out: sn edgd lft: styd on same pce fnl f* **7/2**[3]

5 1 **Berlin Tango** 2-9-2 0 JoshuaBryan(3) 2 70
(Andrew Balding) *s.i.s: sn mid-div: hdwy over 4f out: unbalanced 1/2-way: rdn to chse wnr and edgd lft over 1f out: no ex ins fnl f* **14/1**

6 8 **Selecto** 2-9-5 0 AdamMcNamara 5 48
(Roger Charlton) *s.s: in rr: shkn up over 2f out: hung lft over 1f out: nt trble ldrs* **66/1**

7 1 **Caribeno** 2-9-5 0 LukeMorris 12 45
(Sir Mark Prescott Bt) *s.i.s: sn pushed along in rr: nvr nrr* **33/1**

0 8 hd **Premium Bond**[21] 4114 2-9-5 0 JohnFahy 8 45
(Richard Hannon) *prom: lost pl over 4f out: n.d after* **40/1**

9 nk **Inflamed** 2-9-5 0 LiamKeniry 10 44
(Ed Walker) *hld up: pushed along 1/2-way: n.d* **16/1**

05 10 1 ½ **Broughtons Compass**[23] 4030 2-9-5 0 KierenFox 3 40
(Mark Hoad) *chsd ldrs: rdn over 2f out: sn wknd* **150/1**

5 11 nk **Zingaro Boy (IRE)**[17] 4246 2-9-0 0 SebastianWoods(5) 14 39
(Hugo Palmer) *prom: chsd ldr over 4f out: led 1/2-way: hdd 3f out: rdn over 2f out: wknd fnl f* **8/1**

12 1 **D Day (IRE)** 2-9-5 0 FergusSweeney 13 36
(Richard Hannon) *s.s: nvr on terms* **20/1**

46 13 ½ **Mr Kodi (IRE)**[50] 3047 2-9-5 0 PJMcDonald 15 35
(David Evans) *hld up: pushed along 1/2-way: n.d* **50/1**

1m 27.92s (-0.78) **Going Correction** -0.075s/f (Good) **13 Ran SP% 125.5**
Speed ratings (Par 96): **101,100,97,95,93 84,83,83,83,81 80,79,79**
CSF £147.69 TOTE £72.70: £13.70, £1.10, £1.10; EX 344.10 Trifecta £871.10.
Owner Knox & Wells Limited And R W Devlin **Bred** Knox & Wells Limited & R Devlin **Trained** Lambourn, Berks

FOCUS
With little rain about recently, 34mm of water had been applied since Monday. The going was nevertheless firm with a reading of 9.0. An interesting novice with the favourite caught late on. It's been rated around the third to his C&D latest.

4926 EDNA MAY JOHN MEMORIAL H'CAP 6f

6:20 (6:21) (Class 5) (0-75,74) 3-Y-O+
£3,806 (£1,132; £566; £400; £400; £400) **Stalls** Low

Form RPR

4101 1 **Storm Melody**[10] 4494 6-9-12 74 (p) TomMarquand 3 81
(Ali Stronge) *trckd ldrs: swtchd lft over 1f out: sn chsng ldr: rdn and r.o to ld nr fin* **5/1**

5001 2 nk **Delagate This Lord**[10] 4495 5-9-11 73 CharlieBennett 1 79
(Michael Attwater) *led: rdn over 1f out: edgd lft: hdd nr fin* **11/4**[1]

40 3 nk **Dr Doro (IRE)**[9] 4560 6-9-7 69 (v) PJMcDonald 7 74
(Ian Williams) *s.i.s: hld up: nt clr run over 2f out: hdwy over 1f out: r.o wl* **17/2**

0300 4 ½ **Smokey Lane (IRE)**[38] 3462 5-9-8 70 JasonWatson 6 73
(David Evans) *s.i.s: hld up: hdwy 2f out: sn rdn and hung lft: r.o* **9/2**[3]

-445 5 7 **Glory**[63] 2630 3-9-3 71 MartinDwyer 2 51
(Richard Hannon) *s.i.s: outpcd: nvr nrr* **10/3**[2]

2125 6 1 ¼ **Sundiata**[86] 1894 3-9-2 70 (t[1]) LukeMorris 5 46
(Charles Hills) *trckd ldrs: plld hrd: rdn over 1f out: wknd ins fnl f* **10/1**

1055 7 3 ¼ **Bristol Missile (USA)**[26] 3937 5-9-0 65 (t[1]) JoshuaBryan(3) 8 32
(Richard Price) *w ldr tl shkn up and edgd lft over 2f out: wknd fnl f* **20/1**

-260 8 1 **Bbob Alula**[18] 4226 4-9-4 71 (t) RyanWhile(5) 9 34
(Bill Turner) *chsd ldrs: rdn over 2f out: wknd over 1f out* **11/1**

1m 13.85s (-0.65) **Going Correction** -0.075s/f (Good)
WFA 3 from 4yo+ 6lb **8 Ran SP% 117.3**
Speed ratings (Par 103): **101,100,100,99,90 88,84,82**
CSF £19.73 CT £116.50 TOTE £4.80: £1.60, £1.70, £2.70; EX 17.50 Trifecta £120.50.
Owner Shaw Racing Partnership 2 **Bred** Selwood B/S, Hoskins & Jonason **Trained** Eastbury, Berks

FOCUS
A tight-looking sprint handicap and a head-bobber between two last time winners. The second and third have been rated close to their recent form.

4927 SOVEREIGN WEALTH MANAGEMENT NOVICE STKS 6f 213y

6:50 (6:51) (Class 5) 3-Y-O+ **£4,528** (£1,347; £673; £336) **Stalls** Low

Form RPR

0-2 1 **Ghalyoon**[16] 4298 4-9-10 0 JimCrowley 5 93+
(Marcus Tregoning) *w ldr: led 6f out: j. path over 3f out: hdd and hung lft fr over 2f out: led again over 1f out: sn rdn: styd on* **8/11**[1]

6-43 2 ½ **Posted**[8] 4597 3-8-11 82 TomMarquand 1 83
(Richard Hannon) *chsd ldrs: swtchd lft over 2f out: rdn to chse wnr over 1f out: r.o* **11/4**[2]

3 6 **Zahee (IRE)** 4-9-10 0 OisinMurphy 4 74
(Saeed bin Suroor) *s.i.s: sn prom: chsd wnr over 4f out tl led over 2f out: hdd over 1f out: sn rdn: btn whn hung rt and lft ins fnl f* **4/1**[3]

00 4 2 **Soldier's Son**[38] 3463 3-8-13 0 GeorgiaCox(3) 2 66
(Henry Candy) *broke wl: sn lost pl: hdwy over 2f out: rdn over 1f out: sn wknd* **14/1**

6 5 34 **Mother Brown**[36] 3532 3-8-4 0 GeorgeRooke(7) 7
(Bill Turner) *led 1f: chsd ldr: rdn and lost pl 4f out: wknd 1/2-way* **66/1**

04 6 hd **Stepaside Boy**[42] 3353 3-9-2 0 JasonWatson 6
(David Evans) *s.i.s: hld up: hdwy 1/2-way: rdn and hung lft over 2f out: sn wknd and eased (jockey said gelding lost its action; vet said a post-race examination revealed the gelding finished lame on its left fore)* **66/1**

1m 26.98s (-1.72) **Going Correction** -0.075s/f (Good)
WFA 3 from 4yo 8lb **6 Ran SP% 114.2**
Speed ratings (Par 103): **106,105,98,96,57 57**
CSF £3.14 TOTE £1.70: £1.20, £1.40; EX 3.30 Trifecta £5.00.
Owner Hamdan Al Maktoum **Bred** Lordship Stud **Trained** Whitsbury, Hants

FOCUS
A small field but some intriguing contenders for this novice. The second has been rated in line with the best view of her reappearance form.

4928 REDBROOK CLINIC COSMETIC & BEAUTY TREATMENTS H'CAP 1m 6f 44y

7:20 (7:20) (Class 4) (0-80,77) 3-Y-O+ **£5,433** (£1,617; £808; £404) **Stalls** Far side

Form RPR

2331 1 **Berrahri (IRE)**[21] 4112 8-10-0 77 KierenFox 84
(John Best) *led: rdn and hdd over 2f out: rallied to ld over 1f out: edgd lft: styd on gamely* **7/1**[3]

1541 2 ¾ **Master Grey (IRE)**[17] 4257 4-9-9 72 OisinMurphy 78
(Rod Millman) *hld up: rdn and swtchd rt over 1f out: hdwy to chse wnr ins fnl f: sn ev ch: unable qck nr fin* **7/4**[2]

3311 3 2 ¾ **Mondain**[11] 4491 3-9-0 77 PJMcDonald 79
(Mark Johnston) *chsd ldrs: shkn up and j. path over 3f out: rdn over 1f out: styd on same pce ins fnl f* **4/5**[1]

0-24 4 6 **Moayadd (USA)**[34] 3091 7-10-0 77 (v[1]) JimCrowley 71
(Neil Mulholland) *w wnr tl settled into 2nd after 2f: jnd wnr again over 4f out: led over 2f out: rdn and hdd over 1f out: wknd ins fnl f* **20/1**

3m 7.01s (0.41) **Going Correction** -0.075s/f (Good)
WFA 3 from 4yo+ 14lb **4 Ran SP% 109.2**
Speed ratings (Par 105): **95,94,93,89**
CSF £19.40 TOTE £7.50; EX 19.90 Trifecta £21.20.
Owner White Turf Racing UK **Bred** Kilnamoragh Stud **Trained** Oad Street, Kent

FOCUS
Only four runners but three with realistic chances and more exciting than many big field handicaps. The second has been rated in line with his recent progress.

4929 T & M GLASS LTD H'CAP 1m 4f 5y

7:50 (7:50) (Class 5) (0-75,76) 3-Y-O+
£3,806 (£1,132; £566; £400; £400; £400) **Stalls** Low

Form RPR

4561 1 **Global Falcon**[7] 4656 3-9-4 76 GeraldMosse 6 85
(Charles Hills) *chsd ldrs: rdn over 4f out: styd on to ld wl ins fnl f (jockey said colt hung right-handed)* **7/2**[3]

1223 2 1 ¾ **Singing The Blues (IRE)**[17] 4231 4-9-13 73 DanielMuscutt 4 79
(Rod Millman) *led: qcknd 4f out: rdn over 1f out: hdd wl ins fnl f: styd on same pce* **2/1**[1]

043- 3 2 **Birthright**[316] 6755 4-9-10 70 TomMarquand 2 73
(Richard Hannon) *hld up: hdwy over 2f out: rdn over 1f out: styd on same pce fnl f* **8/1**

044 4 4 **Geomatrician (FR)**[31] 3724 3-8-13 71 OisinMurphy 3 67
(Andrew Balding) *chsd ldrs: rdn over 3f out: styd on same pce fr over 1f out* **9/4**[2]

3451 5 2 **El Borracho (IRE)**[13] 4425 4-9-7 74 (h) LeviWilliams(7) 5 67
(Simon Dow) *s.s: hld up: hdwy on outer over 5f out: wkng whn edgd rt fnl f* **7/1**

0-00 6 77 **Yamuna River**[38] 2279 4-8-13 59 (p) CharlesBishop 1
(Chris Gordon) *hld up: rdn and wknd over 3f out (jockey said filly stopped quickly)* **33/1**

2m 36.78s (-0.82) **Going Correction** -0.075s/f (Good)
WFA 3 from 4yo 12lb **6 Ran SP% 112.9**
Speed ratings (Par 103): **99,97,96,93,92 41**
CSF £11.08 TOTE £4.30: £2.20, £1.40; EX 9.10 Trifecta £56.10.
Owner Dr Johnny Hon **Bred** G R Bailey Ltd **Trained** Lambourn, Berks

FOCUS
A gritty improving 3yo makes use of the allowance. The second has been rated in line with his recent form.

4930 T & M GLASS LTD FILLIES' H'CAP 1m 1f 201y

8:20 (8:20) (Class 3) (0-95,94) 3-Y-O+ **£8,086** (£2,406; £1,202; £601) **Stalls** Low

Form RPR

5536 1 **Queen Of Time**[15] 4332 5-10-0 94 (p) JasonWatson 3 100
(Henry Candy) *chsd ldrs: nt clr run and hmpd over 1f out: swtchd rt: rdn to ld wl ins fnl f: styd on* **7/2**[3]

-045 2 nk **Time Change**[14] 4386 4-8-12 78 HarryBentley 4 83
(Ralph Beckett) *hld up: hdwy over 2f out: led and hung lft over 1f out: rdn: hung rt and hdd wl ins fnl f: styd on* **6/1**

0-21 3 1 ¾ **Amber Spark (IRE)**[24] 4007 3-8-7 83 PJMcDonald 2 85
(Richard Fahey) *chsd ldr: rdn and ev ch over 1f out: styd on same pce ins fnl f* **11/4**[2]

1-02 4 2 **Baba Ghanouj (IRE)**[58] 2768 3-8-7 83 DavidProbert 1 81
(Ed Walker) *led at stdy pce: qcknd over 3f out: rdn: hung lft and hdd over 1f out: no ex ins fnl f (jockey said filly hung left-handed under pressure and stopped quickly)* **1/1**[1]

2m 9.35s (-1.15) **Going Correction** -0.075s/f (Good)
WFA 3 from 4yo+ 10lb **4 Ran SP% 113.2**
Speed ratings (Par 104): **101,100,99,97**
CSF £21.07 TOTE £3.90; EX 15.30 Trifecta £27.10.
Owner First Of Many **Bred** Shortgrove Manor Stud **Trained** Kingston Warren, Oxon

FOCUS
A classy 5yo gives weight and a beating to her younger rivals. The winner has been rated to form.

4931 PAM BRUFORD MEMORIAL H'CAP 1m 1f 201y

8:50 (8:51) (Class 6) (0-60,62) 3-Y-O
£3,194 (£950; £475; £400; £400; £400) **Stalls** Low

Form RPR

50-0 1 **Hydroplane (IRE)**[45] 3226 3-9-8 61 LukeMorris 1 72+
(Sir Mark Prescott Bt) *s.i.s: sn prom: rdn over 3f out: swtchd lft and chsd ldr over 2f out: hung lft over 1f out: styd on u.p to ld nr fin (trainer said, regarding the improved form shown, that gelding had appreciated the firm ground and the yard were in better form)* **11/4**[1]

650 2 1 ¼ **Craneur**[29] 3809 3-9-9 62 JasonWatson 8 70
(Harry Dunlop) *w ldr tl led 3f out: rdn over 1f out: hdd nr fin* **4/1**[3]

The Form Book Flat 2019, Raceform Ltd, Newbury, RG14 5SJ

600- **3** *4 ½* **Estrela Star (IRE)**[280] 7983 3-9-7 **60** .... TomMarquand 3 59
(Ali Stronge) *s.i.s: hld up: hdwy over 2f out: rdn over 1f out: edgd rt and styd on same pce fnl f* **25/1**

0600 **4** *6* **Parisean Artiste (IRE)**[9] 4567 3-9-5 **58** .... CharlesBishop 11 45
(Eve Johnson Houghton) *s.i.s: hld up: rdn over 3f out: hung rt and hdwy over 1f out: nt trble ldrs* **9/1**

030 **5** *2* **Heatherdown (IRE)**[14] 4400 3-9-6 **59** .... JimCrowley 7 42
(Ian Williams) *hld up: rdn over 2f out: nvr on terms* **7/1**

0060 **6** *1 ¾* **Purbeck Hills (IRE)**[27] 3888 3-9-0 **53** .... FergusSweeney 6 33
(Richard Hannon) *prom: rdn and nt clr run 3f out: wknd fnl f* **14/1**

0062 **7** *4 ½* **My Lady Claire**[11] 4473 3-9-5 **58** .... OisinMurphy 4 29
(Ed Walker) *hld up: sme hdwy u.p over 1f out: wknd fnl f* **7/2**[2]

044 **8** *12* **Molotov (IRE)**[19] 4189 3-9-9 **62** .... NicolaCurrie 10 9
(Jamie Osborne) *dwlt: sn pushed along in rr: n.d* **10/1**

00 **9** *6* **Dandy Belle (IRE)**[40] 3418 3-8-3 **49** .... GeorgeRooke(7) 5
(Richenda Ford) *sn chsng ldrs: rdn over 2f out: sn wknd* **33/1**

6505 **10** *7* **Moon Artist (FR)**[14] 4400 3-8-7 **46** oh1 .... JosephineGordon 2
(Michael Blanshard) *sn led: rdn and hdd over 3f out: wknd 2f out* **20/1**

00-0 **11** *22* **Ocean Rouge**[23] 4029 3-8-11 **50** .... DavidProbert 9
(Tony Carroll) *prom on outer: racd keenly: rdn over 2f out: sn wknd: virtually p.u ins fnl f (jockey said gelding lost its action)* **40/1**

2m 7.95s (-2.55) **Going Correction** -0.075s/f (Good) **11 Ran SP% 121.1**
Speed ratings (Par 98): **107,106,102,97,96 94,91,81,76,71 53**
CSF £13.57 CT £233.53 TOTE £3.80: £1.70, £1.70, £4.50; EX 16.40 Trifecta £226.00.
Owner Axom LXXIII **Bred** Bloomsbury Stud **Trained** Newmarket, Suffolk

FOCUS
A well-run handicap, and the second has been rated to form.
T/Plt: £195.70 to a £1 stake. Pool: £51,678.38 - 192.70 winning units T/Qpdt: £72.50 to a £1 stake. Pool: £5,670.06 - 57.87 winning units **Colin Roberts**

4889 YORK (L-H)
Saturday, July 13

OFFICIAL GOING: Good to firm (watered; ovr 7.3; far 7.3, ctr 7.4, stands' 7.3)
Wind: Virtually nil Weather: Cloudy

4932 JOHN SMITH'S CITY WALLS STKS (LISTED RACE) 5f
2:05 (2:05) (Class 1) 3-Y-O+
£28,355 (£10,750; £5,380; £2,680; £1,345; £675) **Stalls Low**

Form RPR

1302 **1** **Copper Knight (IRE)**[15] 4331 5-9-1 **106** .... (t) DavidAllan 4 96
(Tim Easterby) *cl up: rdn to dispute ld over 1f out: led narrowly ent fnl f: drvn out* **2/1**[1]

5220 **2** *½* **Dark Shot**[16] 4313 6-9-1 **88** .... (p) BenCurtis 2 94
(Scott Dixon) *trckd ldng pair: hdwy 2f out: rdn over 1f out: ev ch: drvn and edgd rt ins fnl f: kpt on wl towards fin* **7/1**

0-04 **3** *shd* **Poetry**[7] 4665 3-8-5 **99** .... DavidEgan 9 87
(Michael Bell) *dwlt and in rr: pushed along and hdwy 2f out: rdn to chse ldrs ent fnl f: n.m.r: squeezed through and sltly hmpd ins fnl f: drvn and kpt on towards fin* **4/1**[3]

-603 **4** *nk* **Caspian Prince (IRE)**[7] 4665 10-9-1 **109** .... (t) AlistairRawlinson 1 93
(Michael Appleby) *led: jnd and rdn over 1f out: drvn and hdd ent fnl f: edgd lft and kpt on same pce (jockey said gelding hung right in the final furlong)* **7/2**[2]

0-46 **5** *hd* **Deia Glory**[21] 4101 3-8-5 **93** .... FrannyNorton 3 85
(Michael Dods) *trckd ldrs: hdwy 2f out: rdn and ch over 1f out: drvn and kpt on same pce fnl f* **16/1**

2001 **6** *2* **Yolo Again (IRE)**[16] 4294 3-8-5 **89** .... CamHardie 5 78
(Roger Fell) *chsd ldrs: rdn along 2f out: grad wknd* **25/1**

3-20 **7** *2 ½* **Emblazoned (IRE)**[21] 4094 4-9-1 **107** .... (b) RobertHavlin 10 76
(John Gosden) *towards rr: hdwy on outer 1/2-way: sn chsng ldrs: rdn wl over 1f out: sn btn* **9/2**

4223 **8** *nk* **Boundary Lane**[14] 4359 4-8-10 **83** .... (p) GrahamLee 7 70
(Julie Camacho) *chsd ldrs: rdn along over 2f out: sn wknd* **14/1**

58.16s (-0.04) **Going Correction** +0.225s/f (Good)
WFA 3 from 4yo+ 5lb **8 Ran SP% 119.2**
Speed ratings (Par 111): **109,108,108,107,107 104,100,99**
CSF £25.00 TOTE £2.70: £1.20, £2.30, £1.60; EX 23.60 Trifecta £150.10.
Owner Middleham Park, Ventura Racing 6&Partner **Bred** Wardstown Stud Ltd **Trained** Great Habton, N Yorks

FOCUS
The rails was 10m out from the innermost line around home bend from the 9f to entrance to home straight. Course officials added 3m of water the previous outing. After the opener riders agreed with the official going description. There was a messy finish to this solid Listed sprint. The second is the key to the form.

4933 JOHN SMITH'S SILVER CUP STKS (GROUP 3) 1m 5f 188y
2:40 (2:40) (Class 1) 4-Y-O+
£36,861 (£13,975; £6,994; £3,484; £1,748; £877) **Stalls Low**

Form RPR

-156 **1** **Red Verdon (USA)**[56] 2827 6-9-0 **107** .... (b) DavidAllan 7 115
(Ed Dunlop) *hld up towards rr: stdy hdwy 3f out: trckd ldrs wl over 1f out: swtchd rt and rdn to ld narrowly ent fnl f: sn drvn: hld on gamely towards fin* **20/1**

6-41 **2** *hd* **Gold Mount**[28] 3864 6-9-0 **112** .... PaulHanagan 4 114
(Ian Williams) *trckd ldrs: hdwy over 3f out: pushed along 2f out: cl up and rdn over 1f out: sn chal: drvn to dispute ld ins fnl f: ev ch tl no ex nr fin* **3/1**[2]

44-2 **3** *shd* **Raheen House (IRE)**[28] 3864 5-9-0 **109** .... JamieSpencer 3 114
(William Haggas) *stdd s and hld up in rr: hdwy 3f out: effrt on outer to chse ldrs wl over 1f out: sn rdn: drvn and ev ch ins fnl f: no ex towards fin* **15/8**[1]

0-61 **4** *2 ½* **Weekender**[65] 2554 5-9-0 **112** .... RobertHavlin 6 110
(John Gosden) *led: pushed along over 3f out: hdd wl over 2f out: cl up and sn rdn: drvn appr fnl f: kpt on same pce* **3/1**[2]

0621 **5** *2* **Kelly's Dino (FR)**[7] 4646 6-9-0 **102** .... (p) BenCurtis 2 107
(K R Burke) *trckd ldr: hdwy and cl up over 3f out: led wl over 2f out: rdn wl over 1f out: hdd and drvn ent fnl f: grad wknd* **11/1**

016 **6** *10* **Island Brave (IRE)**[7] 4646 5-9-0 **99** .... DavidEgan 5 93
(Heather Main) *chsd ldrs: rdn along over 3f out: wknd over 2f out* **20/1**

0/3- **7** *8* **Sea The Lion (IRE)**[16] 4311 8-9-0 **104** .... RonanWhelan 8 82
(Jarlath P Fahey, Ire) *chsd ldrs: rdn along 4f out: drvn 3f out: sn wknd (jockey said gelding ran flat)* **7/1**[3]

-056 **8** *34* **Maid Up**[24] 3995 4-8-11 **99** .... RobHornby 1 31
(Andrew Balding) *trckd ldrs: pushed along over 4f out: rdn over 3f out: sn outpcd and bhd (jockey said filly stopped quickly)* **40/1**

2m 58.6s (-1.60) **Going Correction** +0.225s/f (Good) **8 Ran SP% 117.6**
Speed ratings (Par 113): **113,112,112,111,110 104,99,80**
CSF £80.09 TOTE £26.20: £4.20, £1.30, £1.30; EX 138.60 Trifecta £547.40.
Owner The Hon R J Arculli **Bred** Liberty Road Stables **Trained** Newmarket, Suffolk

FOCUS
This Group 3 was run at a fair pace and the principals came clear in a driving finish. Add 32yds. The winner has been rated to his best, while the fifth helps set the level, rated to his recent handicap form.

4934 JOHN SMITH'S RACING H'CAP 7f 192y
3:15 (3:15) (Class 2) (0-105,99) 3-Y-O+
£15,562 (£4,660; £2,330; £1,165; £582; £292) **Stalls Low**

Form RPR

002 **1** **Escobar (IRE)**[7] 4666 5-10-0 **99** .... (t) JamieSpencer 2 109+
(David O'Meara) *hld up in tch: smooth hdwy over 2f out: cl up on bit appr fnl f: led last 100yds: cleverly* **11/4**[2]

6-12 **2** *¾* **Rise Hall**[15] 4342 4-9-9 **94** .... (b) RobHornby 1 102
(Martyn Meade) *trckd ldng pair: hdwy to ld 2f out: rdn over 1f out: sn jnd: drvn ent fnl f: hdd last 100yds: kpt on: no ch w wnr* **13/8**[1]

151U **3** *7* **Crownthorpe**[16] 4292 4-9-6 **94** .... SeanDavis(3) 7 86
(Richard Fahey) *dwlt: swtchd lft s and hld up in rr: hdwy wl over 2f out: rdn to chse ldrs over 1f out: sn drvn and kpt on same pce* **7/1**

4302 **4** *nk* **Masham Star (IRE)**[23] 4020 5-9-8 **93** .... FrannyNorton 3 84
(Mark Johnston) *led: c wd st to nr stands' rail: pushed along 3f out: rdn and hdd 2f out: sn drvn and grad wknd* **5/1**[3]

-036 **5** *¾* **Baraweez (IRE)**[49] 3069 9-9-5 **90** .... BenCurtis 6 79
(Brian Ellison) *trckd ldrs: pushed along 3f: rdn over 2f out: drvn wl over 1f out: kpt on same pce* **12/1**

-050 **6** *2 ¾* **Dark Jedi (IRE)**[23] 4016 3-8-12 **92** .... DavidEgan 4 73
(Charles Hills) *trckd ldr: c wd st and cl up on stands' rail whn n.m.r 3f out: sn rdn along: wknd fnl 2f (jockey said gelding hung left from 2f out)* **13/2**

1m 38.16s (0.66) **Going Correction** +0.225s/f (Good)
WFA 3 from 4yo+ 9lb **6 Ran SP% 115.0**
Speed ratings (Par 109): **105,104,97,96,96 93**
CSF £7.93 TOTE £3.40: £2.00, £1.40; EX 8.30 Trifecta £23.30.
Owner Withernsea Thoroughbred Limited **Bred** Peter Evans **Trained** Upper Helmsley, N Yorks

FOCUS
Not a strong handicap for the class and two came well clear. Add 28yds. The winner has been rated back to his best.

4935 JOHN SMITH'S DIAMOND JUBILEE CUP H'CAP 1m 2f 56y
3:50 (3:52) (Class 2) 3-Y-O+
£124,500 (£37,280; £18,640; £9,320; £4,660; £2,340) **Stalls Low**

Form RPR

6640 **1** **Pivoine (IRE)**[22] 4053 5-9-8 **104** .... (v) RobHornby 6 114
(Andrew Balding) *in tch: hdwy on inner wl over 2f out: chsd ldrs over 1f out: sn chal: rdn to ld ins fnl f: drvn out (trainer said, regarding the improved form shown, the gelding was suited by a return to York)* **14/1**

1441 **2** *1* **Setting Sail**[15] 4342 4-9-4 **100** 5ex .... JamieSpencer 23 108
(Charlie Appleby) *wnt lft s: trckd ldng pair: wd st towards stands' side: hdwy over 2f out: rdn to ld narrowly jst over 1f out: drvn and hdd ins fnl f: kpt on same pce* **9/2**[1]

-310 **3** *¾* **What's The Story**[24] 3987 5-9-4 **100** .... PaulHanagan 1 106
(Keith Dalgleish) *trckd ldrs: hdwy over 2f out: chsd ldrs and nt clr run whn swtchd rt jst over 1f out: sn rdn: kpt on u.p fnl f* **12/1**

050- **4** *2* **Another Touch**[322] 6552 6-8-13 **95** .... TonyHamilton 5 97
(Richard Fahey) *trckd ldrs: wd st towards stands' rail: pushed along and hdwy over 2f out: rdn to chse ldrs over 1f out: sn drvn and kpt on same pce* **50/1**

30-1 **5** *hd* **Afaak**[24] 3987 5-9-12 **108** 5ex .... DaneO'Neill 24 110
(Charles Hills) *in tch: wd st: hdwy towards stands' side 3f out: chsd ldrs 2f out: sn rdn: drvn and kpt on same pce fnl f* **14/1**

25 **6** *hd* **Big Kitten (USA)**[14] 4395 4-8-13 **95** .... LiamJones 15 96
(William Haggas) *led: wd st: pushed along 4f out: rdn over 3f out: hdd 2f out: sn drvn and kpt on same pce* **33/1**

-115 **7** *hd* **Mountain Angel (IRE)**[25] 3953 5-9-10 **106** .... DavidEgan 3 107
(Roger Varian) *trckd ldrs: hdwy and cl up 3f out: rdn to ld 2f out: sn hdd: drvn appr fnl f and kpt on same pce* **13/2**[3]

-133 **8** *½* **Aasheq (IRE)**[64] 2574 6-9-0 **96** .... DavidAllan 8 96
(Tim Easterby) *hld up: hdwy 3f out: rdn along 2f out: chsd ldrs over 1f out: sn drvn and no imp* **16/1**

-221 **9** *1* **Jazeel (IRE)**[8] 4613 4-8-12 **97** 5ex .... SeanDavis(3) 10 95+
(Jedd O'Keeffe) *hld up towards rr: hdwy towards inner over 3f out: rdn along 2f out: kpt on u.p fnl f* **11/1**

4234 **10** *¾* **Exec Chef (IRE)**[8] 4613 4-9-2 **98** .... PatCosgrave 2 94
(Jim Boyle) *trckd ldrs: pushed along and hdwy 3f out: rdn over 2f out: sn drvn and wknd* **14/1**

1164 **11** *nk* **Fayez (IRE)**[6] 4692 5-9-1 **97** .... CamHardie 7 93
(David O'Meara) *dwlt and towards rr: hdwy 3f out: rdn along over 2f out: n.d* **33/1**

1000 **12** *nk* **Aquarium**[7] 4646 4-9-7 **103** .... FrannyNorton 13 98
(Mark Johnston) *hld up in rr: sme hdwy over 2f out: n.d* **20/1**

-150 **13** *1* **Mordin (IRE)**[24] 3987 5-9-5 **106** .... (p) SeamusCronin(5) 20 99+
(Simon Crisford) *hmpd s: a towards rr* **20/1**

-400 **14** *3 ¾* **Restorer**[7] 4646 7-9-2 **98** .... AlistairRawlinson 14 84
(Ian Williams) *in tch: hdwy and wd towards stands' side st: rdn along to chse ldrs 3f out: wknd 2f out* **50/1**

1521 **15** *1* **Waarif (IRE)**[14] 4399 6-9-5 **101** 5ex .... DavidNolan 21 85
(David O'Meara) *blind removed late and dwlt: swtchd lft s: a towards rr (jockey said the blind took two attempts to remove)* **40/1**

11-0 **16** *½* **Francis Xavier (IRE)**[49] 3074 5-9-1 **97** .... RossaRyan 22 80
(Kevin Frost) *nvr bttr than midfield* **16/1**

4525 **17** *2 ¾* **Leroy Leroy**[15] 4342 3-8-6 **98** .... RachelRichardson 18 76
(Richard Hannon) *t.k.h: in tch: pushed along and lost pl 1/2-way: sn towards rr* **33/1**

0-54 **18** *shd* **Stylehunter**[24] 3987 4-9-2 **98** .... (b) RobertHavlin 12 75
(John Gosden) *dwlt: a in rr (jockey said gelding missed the break)* **6/1**[2]

0056 **19** *shd* **Original Choice (IRE)**[15] 4342 5-9-4 **100** .... (p) BenCurtis 17 77
(Nick Littmoden) *a in rr* **66/1**

206- **20** *½* **My Lord And Master (IRE)**[225] 9333 4-8-11 **98** .... CierenFallon(5) 4 74
(William Haggas) *dwlt: a in rr* **7/1**

23-2 **21** *hd* **Scarlet Dragon**[77] 143 6-9-8 **104**................................(h) TomQueally 16 79
(Alan King) *towards rr: hdwy and wd st: rdn along nr stands' rail to chse ldrs over 2f out: sn drvn and wknd* **16/1**

2m 10.38s (0.08) **Going Correction** +0.225s/f (Good) **21** Ran SP% **138.2**
WFA 3 from 4yo+ 10lb
Speed ratings (Par 109): **108,107,106,105,104 104,104,104,103,102 102,102,101,98,97 97,95,94,94,94 94**
CSF £76.53 CT £833.50 TOTE £23.90: £4.80, £1.80, £3.80, £10.70; EX 141.50 Trifecta £2033.50.
Owner King Power Racing Co Ltd **Bred** Ballymacoll Stud Farm Ltd **Trained** Kingsclere, Hants
■ Stewards' Enquiry : Jamie Spencer two-day ban: interference & careless riding (Jul 28-29)

FOCUS
Another fiercely competitive edition of this extremely valuable handicap. They were soon strung out yet the pace held up. Add 32yds. The third and fourth have been rated to form.

4936 JOHN SMITH'S STAYERS' H'CAP — 2m 56y
4:25 (4:25) (Class 3) (0-95,91) 4-Y-0+ **£9,703** (£2,887; £1,443; £721) **Stalls** Low

Form RPR
-420 **1** **Mancini**[25] 3952 5-9-7 **91**................................ JamieSpencer 3 99
(Jonathan Portman) *led: pushed along 3f out: rdn and hdd 2f out: drvn over 1f out: rallied and edgd lft ent fnl f: hrd drvn and kpt on gamely to ld again nr line* **11/10**[1]

1156 **2** *hd* **Makawee (IRE)**[20] 4145 4-9-5 **89**................................ DavidNolan 7 97
(David O'Meara) *trckd ldrs: hdwy over 3f out: rdn to ld 2f out: drvn ent fnl f: hdd and no ex nr line* **3/1**[2]

4120 **3** *3* **The Resdev Way**[16] 4308 6-7-11 **72** oh8................................ PaulaMuir(5) 1 76
(Philip Kirby) *dwlt: hld up in rr: hdwy 3f out: cl up over 1f out: sn rdn and ev ch ent fnl f: wknd last 150yds* **20/1**

0410 **4** *1 1/2* **Michael's Mount**[14] 4381 6-8-13 **83**................................(p) BenCurtis 6 85
(Ian Williams) *trckd ldr: hdwy and cl up over 2f out: sn rdn: drvn and ev ch over 1f out: wknd ent fnl f* **7/2**[3]

4630 **5** *5* **Flintrock (GER)**[50] 3044 4-8-11 **81**................................ RobHornby 4 77
(Andrew Balding) *s.i.s: sn trcking ldng pair: hdwy over 3f out: rdn along over 2f out: sn drvn and wknd wl over 1f out* **7/1**

3m 34.89s (0.99) **Going Correction** +0.225s/f (Good) **5** Ran SP% **112.1**
Speed ratings (Par 107): **106,105,104,103,101**
CSF £4.81 TOTE £1.90: £1.20, £1.70; EX 5.20 Trifecta £41.90.
Owner Laurence Bellman **Bred** Mrs James Wigan **Trained** Upper Lambourn, Berks

FOCUS
This good-quality staying handicap proved tactical. Add 32yds. The winner has been rated to his best.

4937 JOHN SMITH'S NOVICE MEDIAN AUCTION STKS (PLUS 10 RACE) — 6f
5:00 (5:02) (Class 3) 2-Y-0 **£9,703** (£2,887; £1,443; £721) **Stalls** Low

Form RPR
1222 **1** **Oh Purple Reign (IRE)**[7] 4637 2-9-8 98................................ RossaRyan 3 87+
(Richard Hannon) *chsd ldrs: rdn along wl over 1f out: drvn ent fnl f: styd on wl to ld last 50yds* **4/5**[1]

2 *1* **Abstemious** 2-9-2 0................................ JamieSpencer 4 78+
(Kevin Ryan) *t.k.h: cl up: led 1/2-way: rdn ent fnl f: hdd and no ex last 50yds* **7/2**[2]

34 **3** *nk* **No Mercy**[40] 3411 2-9-2 0................................ BenCurtis 2 77
(K R Burke) *slt ld: hdd 1/2-way: cl up: rdn along over 1f out: drvn ins fnl f: kpt on same pce towards fin* **6/1**[3]

4 *1/2* **Hello Baileys** 2-9-2 0................................ FrannyNorton 1 75
(Mark Johnston) *cl up: rdn along over 1f out: drvn and kpt on same pce fnl f* **15/2**

6 **5** *5* **Phoenix Approach (IRE)**[21] 4106 2-9-2 0................................ DavidAllan 8 59
(Tim Easterby) *wnt bdly rt s and bhd: pushed along 1/2-way: rdn 2f out: styd on fnl f* **20/1**

50 **6** *2 1/4* **Wots The Wifi Code**[21] 4125 2-9-2 0................................ DavidNolan 7 52
(Tony Coyle) *a towards rr* **40/1**

7 *3 1/2* **Staxton Hill** 2-9-2 0................................ PaulHanagan 6 41
(Richard Fahey) *dwlt: chsd ldrs: rdn along over 2f out: sn wknd* **10/1**

8 *6* **Mews House** 2-9-2 0................................ PaulMulrennan 5 22
(David Brown) *prom: rdn along over 2f out: sn wknd* **25/1**

1m 12.56s (0.96) **Going Correction** +0.225s/f (Good) **8** Ran SP% **124.0**
Speed ratings (Par 98): **102,100,100,99,92 89,85,77**
CSF £4.26 TOTE £1.70: £1.10, £1.40, £1.70; EX 4.50 Trifecta £13.90.
Owner Team Wallop **Bred** Tally-Ho Stud **Trained** East Everleigh, Wilts

FOCUS
This fair 2yo event saw changing fortunes inside the final furlong. The winner didn't need to be at his best, and the third is the key to the level in the short term.

4938 JOHN SMITH'S NURSERY H'CAP — 6f
5:35 (5:35) (Class 4) (0-85,83) 2-Y-0
£9,962 (£2,964; £1,481; £740; £300; £300) **Stalls** Low

Form RPR
0121 **1** **Troubador (IRE)**[26] 3919 2-9-7 **83**................................ PaulMulrennan 6 86
(Michael Dods) *cl up: rdn over 1f out: led jst ins fnl f: edgd lft and kpt on wl towards fin* **5/1**[3]

023 **2** *1/2* **Teenar**[14] 4384 2-8-11 **73**................................ PaulHanagan 5 74
(Richard Fahey) *slt ld: rdn over 1f out: hdd jst ins fnl f: sn drvn and edgd lft: kpt on* **6/1**

533 **3** *nse* **Endowed**[17] 4238 2-9-1 **77**................................ RossaRyan 1 79+
(Richard Hannon) *trckd ldrs: hdwy over 1f out: swtchd rt and effrt whn nt clr run and hmpd ins fnl f: swtchd rt again and styd on strly towards fin* **3/1**[2]

5251 **4** *1/2* **Dragon Command**[11] 4486 2-9-2 **78**................................(p) BenCurtis 4 77+
(George Scott) *trckd ldrs: pushed along over 1f out: rdn and keeping on whn n.m.r ins fnl f: kpt on towards fin* **9/4**[1]

1200 **5** *1/2* **Iva Reflection (IRE)**[7] 4647 2-9-4 **80**................................(p[1]) AlistairRawlinson 2 78
(Tom Dascombe) *cl up on inner: rdn along wl over 1f out: drvn and edgd rt jst ins fnl f: kpt on same pce* **14/1**

023 **6** *3/4* **My Kinda Day (IRE)**[29] 3810 2-8-9 **71**................................ TonyHamilton 9 66
(Richard Fahey) *dwlt: hld up in rr: rdn along wl over 1f out: kpt on fnl f* **8/1**

235 **7** *1/2* **Oso Rapido (IRE)**[28] 3866 2-9-1 **77**................................ JamieSpencer 3 71
(David O'Meara) *hmpd s: a in rr* **13/2**

255 **8** *14* **Olcan**[14] 4384 2-8-12 **74**................................(h[1]) DavidEgan 7 23
(David O'Meara) *chsd ldrs: rdn along 2f out: sn wknd* **18/1**

1m 12.45s (0.85) **Going Correction** +0.225s/f (Good) **8** Ran SP% **123.1**
Speed ratings (Par 96): **103,102,102,101,100 99,99,80**
CSF £37.75 CT £109.67 TOTE £5.90: £2.00, £2.20, £1.40; EX 17.90 Trifecta £128.30.
Owner J Sagar And S Lowthian **Bred** Worksop Manor Stud **Trained** Denton, Co Durham

FOCUS
They went just a routine pace in this fair nursery and it saw a muddling finish. The second has been rated close to form.
T/Plt: £11.80 to a £1 stake. Pool: £145,567.25 - 8,989.45 winning units T/Qpdt: £5.20 to a £1 stake. Pool: £9,412.11 - 1,325.94 winning units **Joe Rowntree**

4939 - 4946a (Foreign Racing) - See Raceform Interactive

4621
MAISONS-LAFFITTE (R-H)
Saturday, July 13

OFFICIAL GOING: Turf: good

4947a PRIX IDALIE (MAIDEN) (2YO) (TURF) — 6f
3:42 2-Y-0 **£12,162** (£4,864; £3,648; £2,432; £1,216)

RPR
1 **Marieta (FR)**[24] 2-8-13 0................................ TonyPiccone 6 98
(M Delcher Sanchez, France) **13/5**[2]

2 *8* **Queen Kahlua**[31] 2-8-13 0................................ AlexisBadel 3 72
(H-F Devin, France) **57/10**[3]

3 *nse* **La Reconquista**[24] 2-8-13 0................................ OlivierPeslier 1 72
(C Laffon-Parias, France) **31/5**

4 *hd* **Bavaria Baby (FR)**[19] 2-8-13 0................................ CristianDemuro 4 71
(F Chappet, France) **61/10**

5 *2* **Litigator (IRE)** 2-8-11 0................................ StephanePasquier 5 63
(Henry Spiller) *in tch on outer: cl 5th and bmpd whn drvn after 1/2-way: dropped away fnl f* **16/1**

6 *dist* **Telemaque (USA)** 2-8-11 0................................ MickaelBarzalona 2
(A Fabre, France) *slow to stride: outpcd in rr: began to lose tch fr 1/2-way: sn eased and t.o* **13/10**[1]

1m 12.21s (-1.19) **6** Ran SP% **120.0**
PARI-MUTUEL (all including 1 euro stake): WIN 3.60; PLACE 2.00, 2.90; SF 18.20.
Owner Cuadra Mediterraneo **Bred** Cuadra Mediterraneo **Trained** France

4948a PRIX DE RIS-ORANGIS (GROUP 3) (3YO+) (TURF) — 6f
5:27 3-Y-0+ **£36,036** (£14,414; £10,810; £7,207; £3,603)

RPR
1 **King Malpic (FR)**[44] 3289 6-9-1 0................................ OlivierPeslier 1 115+
(T Lemer, France) *disp 3rd on inner: angled out and qcknd to chal between horses 1f out: led fnl 75yds: readily* **22/5**[2]

2 *3/4* **Inns Of Court (IRE)**[41] 3388 5-9-7 0................................ MickaelBarzalona 2 118
(A Fabre, France) *led on inner: pushed along whn pressed ins fnl 2f: drvn over 1f out: hdd fnl 75yds: no ex* **2/5**[1]

3 *1 3/4* **Gold Vibe (IRE)**[41] 3388 6-9-1 0................................(b) CristianDemuro 3 107
(P Bary, France) *disp 3rd on outer: pressed ldr ins 2f out: ev ch over 1f out: one pce u.p fnl f* **10/1**

4 *1 1/4* **Comedia Eria (FR)**[24] 3994 7-8-11 0................................ MaximeGuyon 5 99
(P Monfort, France) *w.w in fnl pair on inner: prog 2f out: rdn and no further imp 1f out: kpt on at same pce* **11/1**

5 *1 3/4* **Hackney Road**[28] 6-8-11 0................................(p) Jose-LuisBorregoGarcia-Penue 6 93
(Fernando Perez-Gonzalez, Spain) *pressed ldr on outer: lost pl 2f out: no ch whn kpt on again u.p late* **34/1**

6 *3/4* **Stormbringer**[63] 2648 4-9-1 0................................(p) Pierre-CharlesBoudot 4 95
(Gavin Hernon, France) *settled in fnl pair on outer: angled out and rdn wl over 1 1/2f out: sn no imp: wl hld fnl f* **74/10**[3]

1m 11.1s (-2.30) **6** Ran SP% **122.1**
PARI-MUTUEL (all including 1 euro stake): WIN 5.40; PLACE 1.30, 1.10; SF 10.20.
Owner Mme Emilie Lafeu **Bred** Skymarc Farm **Trained** France

4949a PRIX D'ORGEVAL (CLAIMER) (2YO) (TURF) — 6f
6:30 2-Y-0 **£10,360** (£4,144; £3,108; £2,072; £1,036)

RPR
1 **Lloyd (IRE)** 2-9-1 0................................ MaximeGuyon 9 72
(Henry Spiller) *pressed ldr: drvn 1 1/2f out: led more than 1f out: hdd ins fnl f: rallied gamely u.p: got bk up post* **93/10**

2 *nse* **Silencious (FR)** 2-8-8 0................................ IoritzMendizabal 6 65
(Simone Brogi, France) **39/10**[3]

3 *nk* **Thavors (ITY)** 2-8-11 0................................ MickaelBarzalona 4 67+
(Andrea Marcialis, France) **14/5**[1]

4 *1 1/4* **Cristal Marvelous (FR)**[8] 2-8-11 0................................ MlleCoraliePacaut(4) 8 67
(M Boutin, France) **33/10**[2]

5 *nk* **All Revved Up (IRE)**[31] 2-8-10 0................................(p) TomLefranc(8) 2 69
(C Boutin, France) **15/1**

6 *3/4* **My Premier County (FR)**[74] 2263 2-9-1 0................................(b) AntoineHamelin 3 64
(Matthieu Palussiere, France) **59/10**

7 *1/2* **Tras Os Montes (FR)** 2-8-13 0................................(b) QuentinPerrette(5) 1 65
(Mlle L Kneip, France) **20/1**

8 *2 1/2* **Oudini (FR)** 2-8-11 0................................ HugoJourniac 7 50
(Simone Brogi, France) **9/1**

9 *3 1/2* **Trou Aux Biches (FR)** 2-8-8 0................................ CristianDemuro 5 36
(Y Barberot, France) **25/1**

1m 14.46s (1.06) **9** Ran SP% **119.0**
PARI-MUTUEL (all including 1 euro stake): WIN 10.30; PLACE 2.60, 1.90, 2.00; DF 26.30.
Owner Franconson Partners **Bred** Pat Beirne **Trained** Newmarket, Suffolk

SARATOGA (R-H)
Saturday, July 13

OFFICIAL GOING: Dirt: fast; turf: good

4950a DIANA STKS (GRADE 1) (3YO+ FILLIES & MARES) (INNER TURF) (TURF) — 1m 1f (T)
10:46 3-Y-0+
£216,535 (£78,740; £47,244; £23,622; £15,748; £11,811)

RPR
1 **Sistercharlie (IRE)**[252] 8844 5-8-12 0................................ JohnRVelazquez 4 118+
(Chad C Brown, U.S.A) *cl up in main gp bhd two clr ldrs: shkn up and hdwy 2f out: c wd into st: r.o to ld ins fnl 125yds: drvn clr* **19/10**[2]

2 1 3/4 **Rushing Fall (USA)**[35] 3613 4-8-12 0........................ JavierCastellano 2 115
(Chad C Brown, U.S.A) *hdd up main gp bhd two clr ldrs: prog over 2f out: ld ent last 1 1/2f: hdd ent fnl 125yds: styd on u.p* **8/5**[1]

3 *nk* **Homerique (USA)**[36] 4-8-6 0.. IradOrtizJr 6 108
(Chad C Brown, U.S.A) *w.w in rr: began to take clsr order after 1/2-way: hdwy to follow eventual wnr into st: styng on whn jinked lft ent fnl f: sn rcvrd: nt pce to chal* **29/10**[3]

4 3 **Secret Message (USA)**[48] 4-8-6 0.......................(b) TrevorMcCarthy 5 102
(H Graham Motion, U.S.A) *racd in fnl pair: hdwy over 2f out: keeping on whn sltly impeded 1 1/2f out: one pce u.p fnl f* **173/10**

5 1 3/4 **Mitchell Road (USA)**[56] 4-8-4 0.. JoseLezcano 3 96
(William Mott, U.S.A) *chsd ldr under restraint: lft isolated whn ldr wnt clr after 2f: clsd fr 3f out: abt to chal whn passed by rest of field fr 1 1/2f out: plugged on at one pce* **13/2**

6 8 **Thais (FR)**[90] 5-8-4 0...(b[1]) ManuelFranco 1 79
(Chad C Brown, U.S.A) *led: clr after 2f: pushed along ins last 3f: hdd 1 1/2f out and wknd* **39/1**

1m 47.93s **6 Ran SP% 119.9**
PARI-MUTUEL (all including 2 unit stake): WIN 5.80; PLACE (1-2) 3.20, 2.80; SHOW (1-2-3) 2.20, 2.20, 2.30; SF 12.40.
Owner Peter M Brant **Bred** Ecurie Des Monceaux **Trained** USA

4951 - 4953a (Foreign Racing) - See Raceform Interactive

3825

FAIRYHOUSE (R-H)

Sunday, July 14

OFFICIAL GOING: Good (good to firm in places)

4954a IRISH STALLION FARMS EBF BROWNSTOWN STKS (GROUP 3) (F&M) 7f

3:10 (3:10) 3-Y-O+

£39,864 (£12,837; £6,081; £2,702; £1,351; £675)

RPR

1 **Surrounding (IRE)**[16] 4353 6-9-8 106..........................(t) RonanWhelan 2 105
(M Halford, Ire) *trckd ldr in 2nd: on terms travelling wl 2f out and led over 1f out: styd on wl ins fnl f* **2/1**[1]

2 1 **Perfection**[22] 4095 4-9-8 101.....................................(p) ShaneFoley 8 102
(David O'Meara) *chsd ldrs in 3rd: pushed along 2f out: almost on terms over 1f out: nt match wnr fnl 100yds: kpt on same pce* **4/1**[2]

3 1/2 **Indian Blessing**[25] 3986 5-9-8 103................................ GeraldMosse 7 101
(Ed Walker) *hld up in 6th: pushed along and prog into 4th ent fnl f: kpt on wl into 3rd fnl 50yds: nvr nrr* **4/1**[2]

4 1/2 **I Remember You (IRE)**[16] 4353 3-9-0 85..................... MichaelHussey 4 97
(A P O'Brien, Ire) *chsd ldrs: rdn and prog over 1f out: 5th ent fnl f: styd on wl clsng stages into 4th: nvr on terms* **40/1**

5 3/4 **Heavenly Holly (IRE)**[25] 3994 4-9-8 96................................ WJLee 1 98
(Hugo Palmer) *led: strly pressed 2f out and sn hdd: wknd into 5th fnl 100yds* **11/2**[3]

6 3/4 **Fire Fly (IRE)**[22] 4092 3-9-0 101........................... DonnachaO'Brien 3 93
(A P O'Brien, Ire) *slowly away and in rr for 2f: prog on inner whn n.m.r 2f out: swtchd lft and kpt on wl ins fnl f: nvr nrr* **10/1**

7 3 1/2 **Gossamer Wings (USA)**[15] 4409 3-9-0 99.................. SeamieHeffernan 6 83
(A P O'Brien, Ire) *towards rr: dropped to rr after 2f: pushed along and no imp under 2f out: kpt on one pce fnl f* **14/1**

8 4 1/2 **Black Magic Woman (IRE)**[30] 3828 3-9-0 96................. GaryHalpin 5 71
(Jack W Davison, Ire) *pushed along early into mid-div: sn chsd ldrs in 4th on inner: pushed along 2f out: nt qckn over 1f: sn wknd* **8/1**

1m 27.72s (-2.78) **8 Ran SP% 118.0**
WFA 3 from 4yo+ 8lb
CSF £10.52 TOTE £2.40: £1.02, £1.30, £1.60; DF 7.30 Trifecta £23.60.
Owner P E I Newell **Bred** P E I Newell **Trained** Doneany, Co Kildare

FOCUS
A good performance from the winner, probably more progressive now than at any point in her career. The fifth and sixth help set the level.

4955 - 4958a (Foreign Racing) - See Raceform Interactive

LE TOUQUET (L-H)

Sunday, July 14

OFFICIAL GOING: Turf: good

4959a PRIX DU NOEUD VINCENT (CLAIMER) (3YO) (TURF) 6f 110y

11:25 3-Y-O **£5,405** (£2,162; £1,621; £1,081; £540)

RPR

1 **Elieden (IRE)**[11] 3-8-11 0......................................(p) TheoBachelot 12 59
(Mlle A-S Crombez, France) **77/10**

2 3 **Mortirolo (FR)**[44] 3-8-10 0... MlleLeaBails(9) 11 58
(Andrea Marcialis, France) **9/5**[1]

3 1 1/2 **Katoki Karwin**[11] 3-8-11 0...................................... EmmanuelEtienne 1 46
(Mlle A Wattel, France) **15/1**

4 *hd* **Dolynska (FR)**[31] 3-7-13 0............................(b) MlleEugenieLaffargue(9) 6 42
(M Boutin, France) **25/1**

5 1 1/4 **La Pergola (FR)**[11] 3-8-9 0..................................(p) QuentinPerrette(6) 7 46
(S Cerulis, France) **43/10**[2]

6 *nse* **Rum Lad**[16] 4357 3-8-11 0.. JeromeClaudic 10 42
(Jo Hughes, France) *hld up in fnl trio: last and nt totally at ease on tight fnl bnd: hdwy wl over 1f out: styd on ins fnl f: nvr in contention* **32/1**

7 1/2 **Adorian (FR)**[87] 3-9-4 0.................................... BayarsaikhanGanbat 13 47
(S Smrczek, Germany) **54/10**[3]

8 1/2 **Kingi Compton**[139] 906 3-9-0 0.............................(p) JenteMarien(5) 4 47
(Marian Falk Weissmeier, Germany) **38/1**

9 1 **Etoile Diamante (FR)**[46] 3-8-5 0......................(b) AlexandreChesneau(3) 9 33
(Andreas Suborics, Germany) **10/1**

10 1 **Grandee Daisy**[16] 4357 3-8-11 0..........................(b) MlleCoraliePacaut(4) 5 37
(Jo Hughes, France) *prom early: dropped towards rr of midfield wl bef 1/2-way: rdn and brief effrt 2f out: wknd over 1f out* **17/2**

11 6 **Flying Dandy (IRE)**[19] 4229 3-8-11 0.................................. StephenHellyn 8 16
(M Bouckaert, Belgium) **52/1**

1m 18.0s **11 Ran SP% 118.9**
PARI-MUTUEL (all including 1 euro stake): WIN 8.70; PLACE 2.60, 1.70, 3.70; DF 8.30.
Owner Andrew Barber & Gay Kelleway **Bred** E Ryan **Trained** France

4960a PRIX LEONCE DEPREZ (CLAIMER) (4YO+) (TURF) 6f 110y

12:25 4-Y-O+ **£5,405** (£2,162; £1,621; £1,081; £540)

RPR

1 **Amadeus Wolfe Tone (IRE)**[33] 3715 10-9-2 0........(b) JeromeClaudic 5 74
(Carina Fey, France) **68/10**[3]

2 2 1/2 **Chef Oui Chef (FR)**[11] 4532 9-9-6 0..........................(p) MrHugoBoutin 3 71
(M Boutin, France) **19/10**[1]

3 *hd* **Madame Bounty (IRE)**[83] 5-8-13 0.............................(p) TheoBachelot 7 63
(P Monfort, France) **5/1**[2]

4 1 1/4 **Heptathlete (IRE)**[90] 4-8-9 0.. MlleZoePfeil(4) 11 60
(Mme B Jacques, France) **16/1**

5 1 1/4 **Surewecan**[33] 3715 7-8-11 0... AlexisBadel 4 54
(Andrew Hollinshead, France) **7/1**

6 1 **Killing Joke (FR)**[315] 5-8-7 0..............................(b) MlleLeaBails(9) 6 56
(R Roels, Germany) **10/1**

7 *snk* **Race For Fame (IRE)**[225] 8-8-11 0................... BayarsaikhanGanbat 10 51
(S Smrczek, Germany) **10/1**

8 *nk* **Skydiving**[28] 4-8-8 0.. MlleFeliceJacobs(3) 1 50
(Mlle S Houben, France) **17/1**

9 3/4 **Janaya (FR)**[92] 8-8-3 0.. JenteMarien(5) 8 45
(Mme J Hendriks, Holland) **40/1**

10 6 **White Feather**[64] 2648 4-8-13 0.............................. MlleCoraliePacaut(3) 2 35
(Jo Hughes, France) *settled in midfield between horses: outpcd over 2f out: rdn and no imp 1 1/2f out: wl hld whn eased fnl f* **10/1**

11 9 **Bird On The Branch (FR)** 4-8-8 0.................................... StephenHellyn 9 1
(Mme J Hendriks, Holland) **43/1**

1m 15.7s **11 Ran SP% 119.9**
PARI-MUTUEL (all including 1 euro stake): WIN 7.80; PLACE 2.30, 1.40, 1.90; DF 12.10.
Owner Stall Allegra **Bred** Brian Williamson **Trained** France

4859

LONGCHAMP (R-H)

Sunday, July 14

OFFICIAL GOING: Turf: good to soft

4961a PRIX ROLAND DE CHAMBURE (LISTED RACE) (2YO) (NEW COURSE: 2ND POST) (TURF) 7f

5:00 2-Y-O **£27,027** (£10,810; £8,108; £5,405; £2,702)

RPR

1 **Well Of Wisdom**[26] 3949 2-9-2 0.................................. MickaelBarzalona 4 102
(Charlie Appleby) *mde all: drvn and rallied whn chal ins fnl 2f: styd on wl u.p fnl f: a holding runner-up* **11/2**

2 *nk* **Helter Skelter (FR)**[31] 2-9-2 0.............................. ChristopheSoumillon 3 102
(J-C Rouget, France) **2/1**[2]

3 5 **Saqqara King (USA)**[22] 4117 2-9-2 0.............................. JamesDoyle 1 88
(Charlie Appleby) *chsd ldr on inner: shkn up to try and chal 2f out: unable to pass ldr: dropped away fnl f* **7/5**[1]

4 1 1/4 **Mowaeva (FR)**[45] 2-9-2 0... MaximeGuyon 5 85
(G Botti, France) **76/10**

5 3 1/2 **Commander (FR)**[44] 2-9-2 0...................................(b) CristianDemuro 2 75
(F Chappet, France) **51/10**[3]

1m 21.61s (0.91) **Going Correction** +0.375s/f (Good) **5 Ran SP% 118.4**
Speed ratings: **109,108,102,101,97**
PARI-MUTUEL (all including 1 euro stake): WIN 6.50; PLACE 2.50, 2.00; SF 18.20.
Owner Godolphin **Bred** Godolphin **Trained** Newmarket, Suffolk

4962a PRIX MAURICE DE NIEUIL (GROUP 2) (4YO+) (GRANDE COURSE: 1ST POST) (TURF) 1m 6f

6:10 4-Y-O+ **£66,756** (£25,765; £12,297; £8,198; £4,099)

RPR

1 **Way To Paris**[49] 3123 6-9-0 0.. CristianDemuro 3 114
(Andrea Marcialis, France) *cl up on inner: n.m.r whn angled out and leaned on Call The Wind ins fnl 2f: led under 1 1/2f out: styd on strly u.p: hld on gamely cl home* **57/10**

2 *nse* **Marmelo**[14] 4430 6-9-0 0.. RyanMoore 4 114
(Hughie Morrison) *w.w in 4th: drvn on outer 2 1/2f out: styng on whn sltly impeded ins fnl 2f: styd on strly u.p fnl f: jst failed* **17/10**[1]

3 4 **Ligne D'Or**[34] 3678 4-8-10 0..................................... VincentCheminaud 6 104
(A Fabre, France) *settled in last: angled out and styd on fr over 1f out: tk 3rd cl home: no ch w front two* **14/1**

4 *snk* **Call The Wind**[49] 3123 5-9-0 0.. AurelienLemaitre 5 108
(F Head, France) *trckd ldr: rdn to chse ldr ins fnl 2 1/2f: styd on at same pce u.p: lost 3rd cl home* **27/10**[2]

5 2 **Holdthasigreen (FR)**[49] 3123 7-9-0 0................................... TonyPiccone 2 105
(B Audouin, France) *led: kicked for home 2 1/2f out: hdd ins fnl 1 1/2f: styd on at same pce tl fdd fnl 150yds* **18/5**[3]

6 1 1/4 **Shahnaza (FR)**[55] 3138 4-8-10 0............................. ChristopheSoumillon 1 99
(A De Royer-Dupre, France) *w.w in fnl pair: began to cl whn n.m.r over 1 1/2f out: sn rdn and no imp: plugged on at one pce* **36/5**

3m 0.29s **6 Ran SP% 119.6**
PARI-MUTUEL (all including 1 euro stake): WIN 6.70; PLACE 2.70, 1.80; SF 20.20.
Owner Paolo Ferrario **Bred** Grundy Bloodstock Srl **Trained** France

FOCUS
The second and third have been rated to form, with the winner in line with last year's best.

4963a JUDDMONTE GRAND PRIX DE PARIS (GROUP 1) (3YO COLTS & FILLIES) (GRANDE COURSE) (TURF) 1m 4f

6:45 3-Y-O **£308,864** (£123,567; £61,783; £30,864; £15,459)

RPR

1 **Japan**[23] 4049 3-9-2 0.. RyanMoore 6 113+
(A P O'Brien, Ire) *settled in 3rd on outer: shkn up 2f out to cl: led ins fnl 1 1/2f: r.o fnl f: readily* **1/2**[1]

2 1/2 **Slalom (FR)**[42] 3390 3-9-2 0.. MaximeGuyon 1 111+
(A Fabre, France) *missed break: wnt rt and collided w rail: sn settled in rr: tk clsr order on inner 3 1/2f out: n.m.r and angled out through narrow gap 1 1/2f out: r.o u.p fnl f: nvr quite on terms* **66/10**[2]

3 3/4 **Jalmoud**[14] 4431 3-9-2 0.. JamesDoyle 4 110
(Charlie Appleby) *chsd ldr: cl 2nd and ev ch ins fnl 2f: styd on u.p: no ex fnl 75yds* **7/1**[3]

4 nk **Roman Candle**[42] 3390 3-9-2 0 MickaelBarzalona 3 109
(A Fabre, France) *w.w in 5th: pushed along on outer 2f out: styd on u.p fr over 1f out: nt pce to get on terms* 66/10[2]
5 2 1/2 **Soft Light (FR)**[28] 3904 3-9-2 0 CristianDemuro 8 105
(J-C Rouget, France) *racd one fr last: last 3f out: drvn and began to cl over 1 1/2f out: kpt on fnl f: nvr nrr* 16/1
6 1 1/4 **In Favour**[29] 3-9-2 0 VincentCheminaud 2 103
(A Fabre, France) *racd in share of 3rd on inner: cl 4th and hrd rdn ins fnl 2f: outpcd over 1f out: wknd fnl 110yds* 27/1
7 nk **Kasaman (FR)**[28] 3904 3-9-2 0 (p) ChristopheSoumillon 7 103
(M Delzangles, France) *settled in fnl trio: drvn along 2f out but no imp: kpt on at same pce: nvr in contention* 26/1
8 3 **Western Australia (IRE)**[16] 4351 3-9-2 0 WayneLordan 5 98
(A P O'Brien, Ire) *led: kicked 3 l clr ins fnl 4f: rdn whn pressed 2f out: hdd ins fnl 1 1/2f: wknd fnl f* 52/1

2m 27.07s (-3.33) **Going Correction** +0.375s/f (Good) 8 Ran SP% 120.5
Speed ratings: **120,119,119,118,117 116,116,114**
PARI-MUTUEL (all including 1 euro stake): WIN 1.50; PLACE 1.10, 1.10, 1.10; DF 3.80.
Owner Derrick Smith & Mrs John Magnier & Michael Tabor **Bred** Newsells Park Stud **Trained** Cashel, Co Tipperary

FOCUS
All eight runners were seeking their first Group 1 win in this interesting renewal of this long-established contest, which is regarded as the 'real' French Derby after the distance was increased from 2000 metres to 2400 metres in 2005. The ground was officially described as good but it appeared to ride a bit faster and the pace was strong, thanks to Western Australia. The first four were separated by around two lengths, but the winner had more to give while the runner-up was compromised by a slow start. The second, third and fourth have been rated as improving.

4964a PRIX DE THIBERVILLE (LISTED RACE) (3YO FILLIES) (GRANDE COURSE) (TURF) 1m 4f
7:25 3-Y-O £24,774 (£9,909; £7,432; £4,954; £2,477)

RPR
1 **Star Terms**[31] 3762 3-9-0 0 RyanMoore 2 97
(Richard Hannon) *trckd ldr: drvn to ld wl over 2f out: styd on strly fnl f* 7/5[1]
2 1 1/4 **Ebony (FR)**[28] 3905 3-9-0 0 ChristopheSoumillon 1 95
(J-C Rouget, France) 17/10[2]
3 nse **Palomba (IRE)**[14] 3-9-0 0 MaximeGuyon 7 95
(C Laffon-Parias, France) 12/1
4 3/4 **Blissful Beauty (FR)**[23] 3-9-0 0 StephanePasquier 6 94
(Gavin Hernon, France) 17/1
5 3/4 **Psara**[42] 3391 3-9-0 0 AlexisBadel 4 92
(H-F Devin, France) 63/10[3]
6 nk **Princesse Mathilde**[40] 3-9-0 0 RonanThomas 5 92
(F-H Graffard, France) 36/5
7 10 **Dynamic Kitty (USA)**[78] 2137 3-9-0 0 FabriceVeron 3 76?
(Georgios Alimpinisis, France) 41/1

2m 34.82s (4.42) **Going Correction** +0.375s/f (Good) 7 Ran SP% 120.2
Speed ratings: **100,99,99,98,98 97,91**
PARI-MUTUEL (all including 1 euro stake): WIN 2.40; PLACE 1.30, 1.40; SF 5.50.
Owner R Barnett **Bred** W & R Barnett Ltd **Trained** East Everleigh, Wilts

FOCUS
They finished in a bit of a heap and the third and fourth limit the level.

4965 - 4975a (Foreign Racing) - See Raceform Interactive

4719
AYR (L-H)
Monday, July 15

OFFICIAL GOING: Good (good to firm in places; 8.0)
Wind: Light, across Weather: Overcast, dry

4976 LONGINES IRISH CHAMPIONS WEEKEND EBF STALLIONS NOVICE STKS (PLUS 10 RACE) 7f 50y
1:35 (1:36) (Class 4) 2-Y-O £4,463 (£1,328; £663; £331) Stalls High

Form RPR
21 1 **Walk In Marrakesh (IRE)**[20] 4206 2-9-5 0 JoeFanning 5 89+
(Mark Johnston) *mde all at ordinary gallop: shkn up and drew clr fnl 2f: unchal* 4/6[1]
2 2 5 **Alix James**[19] 4238 2-9-4 0 JasonHart 4 73
(Iain Jardine) *edgy in preliminaries and reluctant to load: t.k.h: trckd wnr 2f: cl up: effrt and regained 2nd wl over 1f out: rdn and sn one pce* 5/2[2]
05 3 1 1/2 **Road Rage (IRE)**[20] 4206 2-9-4 0 (p[1]) ConnorBeasley 1 69
(Michael Dods) *t.k.h: prom: effrt and disp 2nd pl over 1f out: sn one pce* 33/1
4 2 **The Wine Cellar (IRE)** 2-9-4 0 ShaneGray 3 64
(Keith Dalgleish) *s.i.s: rcvrd to chse wnr after 2f: rdn and outpcd wl over 1f out: sn btn* 14/1
2 5 7 **Woke (IRE)**[33] 3725 2-8-13 0 CliffordLee 2 41+
(K R Burke) *rein broke sn after s: sn bhd: shkn up and outpcd over 2f out: sn btn* 15/2[3]

1m 29.67s (-2.83) **Going Correction** -0.40s/f (Firm) 5 Ran SP% 109.9
Speed ratings (Par 96): **100,94,92,90,82**
CSF £2.54 TOTE £1.40: £1.10, £1.40; EX 2.40 Trifecta £19.20.
Owner Merriebelle Irish Farm Limited **Bred** Merriebelle Irish Farm Ltd **Trained** Middleham Moor, N Yorks

FOCUS
Rail movements added 15yds to this. Quickish ground, and a comfortable win for the favourite in a time 2.37sec outside standard. The winner has been rated in line with her Beverley win.

4977 AYRGOLDCUP.CO.UK H'CAP 6f
2:05 (2:09) (Class 5) (0-75,77) 3-Y-O+ £3,428 (£1,020; £509; £300; £300; £300) Stalls Centre

Form RPR
3051 1 **Tomily (IRE)**[14] 4449 5-10-0 77 DavidNolan 6 86+
(David O'Meara) *trckd ldrs: rdn to ld over 1f out: edgd lft ins fnl f: kpt on wl* 3/1[2]
0-60 2 1 1/4 **Kolossus**[56] 2896 3-9-0 69 ConnorBeasley 8 73
(Michael Dods) *led: rdn and hdd over 1f out: rallied: edgd lft and one pce ins fnl f* 12/1
0402 3 nk **Amazing Grazing (IRE)**[2] 4912 5-9-4 67 CliffordLee 2 71
(Rebecca Bastiman) *blindfold slow to remove but j. off on terms: prom: effrt and drvn along over 1f out: kpt on same pce ins fnl f* 9/4[1]
0-65 4 2 3/4 **Yes You (IRE)**[13] 4492 5-9-12 75 LewisEdmunds 1 70
(Iain Jardine) *hld up: rdn along over 2f out: hdwy over 1f out: kpt on fnl f: no imp* 22/1
103 5 2 1/4 **Metal Exchange**[23] 4129 3-9-0 69 KevinStott 4 56
(Kevin Ryan) *t.k.h: cl up tl rdn and wknd over 1f out* 14/1
0003 6 2 1/2 **Burmese Blazer (IRE)**[7] 4721 4-8-9 61 (h) BenRobinson[(3)] 3 41
(Jim Goldie) *slowly away: sn in tch: drvn over 2f out: edgd rt and wknd over 1f out* 6/1[3]

1m 11.06s (-2.04) **Going Correction** -0.40s/f (Firm)
WFA 3 from 4yo+ 6lb 6 Ran SP% 88.8
Speed ratings (Par 103): **97,95,94,91,88 84**
CSF £21.13 CT £38.25 TOTE £3.30: £1.90, £5.00; EX 26.80 Trifecta £50.70.
Owner Thoroughbred British Racing **Bred** D J Anderson **Trained** Upper Helmsley, N Yorks
■ Scuzeme was withdrawn, price at time of withdrawal 10/3. Rule 4 applies to all bets. Deduction of 20p in the pound.

FOCUS
Ordinary sprint handicap form. Rail movements added 15yds to this.

4978 BOOK DIRECT AT WESTERN HOUSE HOTEL H'CAP (DIV I) 7f 50y
2:40 (2:40) (Class 6) (0-60,61) 3-Y-O+ £2,781 (£827; £413; £300; £300; £300) Stalls High

Form RPR
0451 1 **Kodimoor (IRE)**[10] 4584 6-9-0 47 (p) DougieCostello 4 53
(Mark Walford) *t.k.h early: sn led: rdn and hrd pressed fr 2f out: hld on gamely cl home* 8/1
-043 2 nse **Retirement Beckons**[7] 4725 4-8-9 45 (h) BenRobinson[(3)] 6 51
(Linda Perratt) *s.i.s: hld up: hdwy on outside 2f out: rdn and edgd lft ins fnl f: kpt on wl: jst hld* 11/4[2]
3012 3 1/2 **Cliff Bay (IRE)**[12] 4513 5-9-5 52 ShaneGray 2 57
(Keith Dalgleish) *s.i.s: hld up on ins: stdy hdwy 2f out: effrt and ev ch ins fnl f: kpt on: hld cl home* 5/2[1]
1045 4 1 1/4 **Colour Contrast (IRE)**[24] 4060 6-10-0 61 (b) LewisEdmunds 1 63
(Iain Jardine) *in tch: hdwy over 2f out: rdn and ev ch ins fnl f: one pce fnl 100yds* 13/2[3]
-050 5 3 **Bareed (USA)**[7] 4725 4-8-12 45 (p[1]) KevinStott 9 39
(Linda Perratt) *early ldr: cl up: rdn and ev ch over 1f out: wknd ins fnl f (jockey said gelding hung right on the bend)* 20/1
0000 6 3/4 **Naples Bay**[7] 4726 5-9-9 56 JasonHart 7 48
(Katie Scott) *hld up: rdn over 2f out: edgd lft and hdwy over 1f out: kpt on fnl f: nt pce to chal* 10/1
2000 7 shd **Roaring Forties (IRE)**[10] 4584 6-9-12 59 (p) ConnorBeasley 8 51
(Rebecca Bastiman) *in tch: rdn and outpcd 2f out: n.d after* 17/2
4000 8 4 **Brendan (IRE)**[8] 4694 6-8-7 47 CoreyMadden[(7)] 5 28
(Jim Goldie) *plld hrd: trckd ldrs tl rdn and wknd over 1f out (jockey said gelding ran too free)* 28/1
0300 9 1 1/2 **Cosmic Chatter**[14] 4440 9-9-5 52 (p) AndrewMullen 3 29
(Ruth Carr) *hld up: rdn over 2f out: edgd lft and sn btn* 16/1
0-00 10 8 **Wearraah**[13] 4488 3-7-11 45 KieranSchofield[(7)] 10
(Alan Brown) *trckd ldrs: rdn and hung lft over 2f out: sn wknd* 50/1

1m 28.9s (-3.60) **Going Correction** -0.40s/f (Firm)
WFA 3 from 4yo+ 8lb 10 Ran SP% 115.4
Speed ratings (Par 101): **104,103,103,101,98 97,97,92,91,82**
CSF £29.38 CT £71.77 TOTE £7.70: £2.20, £1.30, £1.30; EX 31.00 Trifecta £79.40.
Owner Ursa Major Racing & Partner **Bred** Tally-Ho Stud **Trained** Sherriff Hutton, N Yorks

FOCUS
Add 15yds. This modest event appeared to be run at a good clip. It was the quicker division by 1.11sec. The third helps set the level, with the fourth rated in line with his recent form.

4979 BOOK DIRECT AT WESTERN HOUSE HOTEL H'CAP (DIV II) 7f 50y
3:10 (3:14) (Class 6) (0-60,60) 3-Y-O+ £2,781 (£827; £413; £300; £300; £300) Stalls High

Form RPR
2433 1 **Donnelly's Rainbow (IRE)**[5] 4784 6-9-9 56 ConnorBeasley 4 66
(Rebecca Bastiman) *replated bef s: hld up: smooth hdwy and poised to chal over 1f out: shkn up to ld ins fnl f: kpt on wl* 2/1[1]
553/ 2 1 1/4 **Midnitemudcrabs (IRE)**[42] 3435 6-9-12 59 JoeFanning 9 66
(John James Feane, Ire) *t.k.h: pressed ldr: led gng wl over 2f out: shkn up over 1f out: hdd ins fnl f: nt pce of wnr* 3/1[2]
2532 3 1 1/4 **Forever A Lady (IRE)**[12] 4512 6-9-5 59 HarryRussell[(7)] 1 63
(Keith Dalgleish) *trckd ldrs: effrt and rdn over 1f out: kpt on same pce ins fnl f* 3/1[2]
-000 4 3 1/4 **Gun Case**[28] 3922 7-9-5 52 (p) DougieCostello 7 47
(Alistair Whillans) *slowly away: hld up: rdn over 2f out: hdwy over 1f out: kpt on fnl f: nt pce to chal* 33/1
0042 5 1 1/4 **Let Right Be Done**[7] 4726 7-8-9 45 (b) BenRobinson[(3)] 6 37
(Linda Perratt) *t.k.h: led to over 2f out: rallied: wknd fnl f* 12/1
0-00 6 1 **Palavicini Run (IRE)**[7] 4720 6-8-12 45 AndrewMullen 5 34
(Linda Perratt) *plld hrd: hld up in tch: rdn over 2f out: wknd over 1f out* 66/1
0050 7 3 1/2 **Here's Rocco (IRE)**[34] 3709 3-9-0 55 JasonHart 8 32
(John Quinn) *t.k.h: hld up in tch: outpcd and edgd lft over 2f out: sn wknd* 15/2[3]
004 8 13 **Indiaro**[13] 4489 3-9-5 60 KevinStott 2 3
(Linda Perratt) *t.k.h: trckd ldrs: rdn wl over 2f out: sn wknd (jockey said gelding hung badly left from two furlongs out)* 25/1

1m 30.01s (-2.49) **Going Correction** -0.40s/f (Firm)
WFA 3 from 6yo+ 8lb 8 Ran SP% 111.1
Speed ratings (Par 101): **98,96,95,91,90 88,84,70**
CSF £7.58 CT £15.62 TOTE £2.60: £1.10, £1.60, £1.20; EX 8.20 Trifecta £15.20.
Owner Rebecca Bastiman Racing 1 **Bred** Airlie Stud **Trained** Cowthorpe, N Yorks

FOCUS
Add 15yds. The slower division by 1.11sec. The second has been rated close to form, with the third close to her recent effort.

4980 NSP PRODUCTIONS EVENT MANAGEMENT H'CAP 7f 50y
3:40 (3:40) (Class 4) (0-85,87) 3-Y-O+ £6,727 (£2,002; £1,000; £500; £300; £300) Stalls High

Form RPR
1354 1 **Ramesses**[11] 4552 3-8-8 73 SeanDavis[(3)] 7 79
(Richard Fahey) *led 1f: chsd ldr: shkn up and hdwy over 2f out: led over 1f out: edgd rt: kpt on wl fnl f* 9/2[2]
3202 2 3/4 **Esprit De Corps**[8] 4693 5-9-4 72 CliffordLee 1 79+
(David Barron) *hld up: pushed along over 2f out: hdwy over 1f out: kpt on to take 2nd cl home* 7/2[1]
3110 3 nk **Astrologer**[19] 4242 3-9-11 87 DavidNolan 6 90
(David O'Meara) *t.k.h: led: qcknd clr 1/2-way: rdn and hdd over 1f out: rallied: no ex and lost 2nd cl home* 7/1

-641 **4** *nk* **Inner Circle (IRE)**[12] 4523 5-9-1 **74**........................(p) BenSanderson(5) 4 79
(Roger Fell) *chsd ldng pair: pushed along over 2f out: hdwy over 1f out: r.o ins fnl f* **9/2**[2]

3154 **5** *2 1/4* **Howzer Black (IRE)**[13] 4492 3-9-4 **80**..........................(b[1]) ShaneGray 5 77
(Keith Dalgleish) *hld up: rdn over 2f out: hdwy over 1f out: r.o fnl f: nt pce to chal* **11/1**

2565 **6** *1 1/2* **Glengarry**[12] 4511 6-10-0 **82**..................................(b[1]) JoeFanning 8 78
(Keith Dalgleish) *slowly away: t.k.h: hld up in tch on outside: effrt over 2f out: hung lft: no imp over 1f out* **9/1**

5153 **7** *3 1/4* **Tommy G**[12] 4511 6-9-3 **78**.............................. CoreyMadden(7) 2 65
(Jim Goldie) *t.k.h: prom: rdn over 2f out: wknd over 1f out* **13/2**[3]

61-1 **8** *17* **Dutch Pursuit (IRE)**[194] 20 3-9-4 **80**...................... ConnorBeasley 3 20
(Michael Dods) *hld up in tch: drvn and struggling over 2f out: sn btn: eased whn no ch ins fnl f (trainers' rep said gelding would prefer a slower surface)* **7/1**

1m 28.59s (-3.91) **Going Correction** -0.40s/f (Firm)
WFA 3 from 5yo+ 8lb **8** Ran SP% **115.3**
Speed ratings (Par 105): **106,105,104,104,101 100,96,77**
CSF £20.83 CT £108.99 TOTE £5.30: £1.90, £1.60, £2.20; EX 22.00 Trifecta £232.00.
Owner Sir Robert Ogden **Bred** Sir Robert Ogden **Trained** Musley Bank, N Yorks

FOCUS
Add 15yds. A tight finish to this fair handicap, which was the quickest of the four races over the trip. A small pb from the third, with the fourth rated to his latest.

4981 WEDDINGS AT WESTERN HOUSE HOTEL H'CAP 1m

4:10 (4:10) (Class 2) (0-100,97) 3-Y-O+ **£15,562** (£4,660; £2,330; £1,165; £582) **Stalls** Low

Form RPR

5115 **1** **Club Wexford (IRE)**[19] 4240 8-9-0 **88**...................... BenSanderson(5) 1 95
(Roger Fell) *mde all: sn clr: pushed along over 2f out: dwindling advantage ins fnl f: edgd rt and kpt on wl cl home* **9/2**

4621 **2** *3/4* **Nicholas T**[8] 4692 7-9-3 **89** 4ex...................................... BenRobinson(3) 6 94+
(Jim Goldie) *stdd in last pl: effrt on outside over 1f out: kpt on fnl f to take 2nd cl home* **4/1**[3]

0260 **3** *nse* **Danielsflyer (IRE)**[23] 4127 5-9-6 **89**...........................(p) AndrewMullen 2 94
(Michael Dods) *chsd clr ldr: effrt and rdn 2f out: kpt on ins fnl f: lost 2nd cl home* **13/2**

3253 **4** *2 1/4* **Ventura Knight (IRE)**[18] 4292 4-10-0 **97**.......................... JoeFanning 3 97
(Mark Johnston) *chsd ldrs: rdn over 2f out: kpt on same pce fr over 1f out* **3/1**[2]

51-2 **5** *5* **Boston George (IRE)**[69] 2506 3-8-6 **87**.......................... SeanDavis(3) 5 73
(Keith Dalgleish) *t.k.h: in tch: rdn and struggling over 2f out: sn btn (jockey said colt ran flat)* **2/1**[1]

1m 37.71s (-5.09) **Going Correction** -0.40s/f (Firm)
WFA 3 from 4yo+ 9lb **5** Ran SP% **109.8**
Speed ratings (Par 109): **109,108,108,105,100**
CSF £21.74 TOTE £5.80: £4.20, £1.90; EX 17.50 Trifecta £50.90.
Owner C Varley **Bred** J S Bolger **Trained** Nawton, N Yorks

FOCUS
Add 15yds. Quite a valuable handicap, but not a particularly strong race for the grade. The winner set a good gallop and scored in a time only half a second outside the standard. A length pb from the winner, with the third rated close to form.

4982 FLOWER SHOW @ AYR RACECOURSE IN AUGUST H'CAP 1m

4:40 (4:40) (Class 5) (0-75,75) 3-Y-O+

£3,428 (£1,020; £509; £300; £300; £300) **Stalls** Low

Form RPR

4000 **1** **Alfa McGuire (IRE)**[16] 4383 4-9-12 **73**.......................... SamJames 9 81
(Phillip Makin) *mde all: rdn 2f out: kpt on u.p fnl f: jst lasted (trainer said, regards apparent improvement in form, gelding may have appreciated the drop back in trip and being ridden more prominently on this occasion)* **7/1**

0030 **2** *nse* **Strong Steps**[8] 4693 7-9-5 **66**..................................(p) CliffordLee 4 74
(Jim Goldie) *hld up in midfield: effrt and edgd lft over 2f out: hdwy over 1f out: kpt on wl fnl f: jst hld* **8/1**

0315 **3** *1* **Chinese Spirit (IRE)**[28] 3922 5-9-1 **65**...................... BenRobinson(3) 7 71
(Linda Perratt) *s.i.s and swtchd lft s: hld up: effrt and hdwy 2f out: angled rt and kpt on ins fnl f: nrst fin (jockey said gelding was slowly away)* **12/1**

3005 **4** *nse* **International Man**[16] 4403 4-9-12 **73**.......................... DavidNolan 6 79
(Richard Fahey) *in tch: rdn over 2f out: hung lft and chsd wnr over 1f out: no ex and lost two pls towards fin (vet said gelding lost it's right front shoe)* **4/1**[1]

5420 **5** *2 1/4* **Outside Inside (IRE)**[9] 4643 4-10-0 **75**.......................... JoeFanning 3 75
(Mark Johnston) *t.k.h: cl up: rdn over 2f out: outpcd fr over 1f out* **13/2**

2125 **6** *1 3/4* **Abushamah (IRE)**[9] 4634 8-9-4 **65**.......................... AndrewMullen 5 61
(Ruth Carr) *hld up: rdn along over 2f out: kpt on fnl f: nvr able to chal* **11/1**

1431 **7** *3/4* **Pudding Chare (IRE)**[7] 4725 5-8-10 **60**.......................(t) SeanDavis(3) 10 55
(R Mike Smith) *cl up: rdn over 2f out: wknd over 1f out* **9/2**[2]

-404 **8** *1* **Gworn**[24] 4057 9-9-2 **63**.. LewisEdmunds 8 55
(R Mike Smith) *hld up on outside: rdn and outpcd over 2f out: sn btn* **20/1**

0003 **9** *1 1/4* **Axe Axelrod (USA)**[18] 4288 3-8-12 **68**.......................... ConnorBeasley 1 55
(Michael Dods) *hld up on ins: drvn along over 2f out: sn no imp: btn over 1f out* **11/2**[3]

4630 **10** *13* **Jacob Black**[12] 4511 8-9-13 **74**..................................(v) ShaneGray 2 34
(Keith Dalgleish) *missed break: hld up: rdn over 2f out: sn n.d: btn over 1f out* **16/1**

1m 38.59s (-4.21) **Going Correction** -0.40s/f (Firm)
WFA 3 from 4yo+ 9lb **10** Ran SP% **117.2**
Speed ratings (Par 103): **105,104,103,103,101 99,99,98,96,83**
CSF £62.18 CT £681.75 TOTE £8.30: £2.90, £2.90, £2.70; EX 54.80 Trifecta £514.00.
Owner Ms Dawn Aldridge **Bred** O Costello & R Moorhead **Trained** Easingwold, N Yorks
■ Stewards' Enquiry : Sam James two-day ban; misuse of whip (July 29,Aug 2)

FOCUS
Add 15yds. Another winner from the front in this minor handicap. The first two have been rated to this year's form, with the third close to his Carlisle latest.

4983 JOCKEY CLUB RESTAURANT @WESTERNHOUSEHOTEL APPRENTICE H'CAP 1m 5f 26y

5:10 (5:10) (Class 5) (0-70,72) 3-Y-O+

£3,428 (£1,020; £509; £300; £300; £300) **Stalls** Low

Form RPR

000 **1** **Lizzie Loch**[8] 4690 3-7-9 **55** oh5.................................... IzzyClifton(5) 2 60
(Alistair Whillans) *led 2f: cl up: smooth hdwy on outside and regained ld over 2f out: sn hrd pressed: rdn and edgd lft over 1f out: kpt on wl fnl f (trainers' rep said, regards apparent improvement in form, filly may have appreciated the step up in trip)* **33/1**

5343 **2** *1/2* **Donnachies Girl (IRE)**[7] 4724 6-8-13 **58**...................... RhonaPindar(3) 1 64
(Alistair Whillans) *cl up: lft in ld 4f out: rdn and hdd over 2f out: styd w wnr: kpt on fnl f: hld cl home* **4/1**[2]

2624 **3** *3* **Four Kingdoms (IRE)**[8] 4689 5-10-0 **70**...................... KieranSchofield 5 71
(R Mike Smith) *prom: effrt and drvn along over 2f out: kpt on fnl f: nt rch first two* **9/2**[3]

2204 **4** *3/4* **Shine Baby Shine**[16] 4404 5-9-2 **65**.......................... NickBarratt-Atkin(7) 7 65
(Philip Kirby) *slowly away: hld up: stdy hdwy 3f out: sn pushed along: effrt over 1f out: kpt on same pce ins fnl f* **7/1**

0003 **5** *3/4* **Spark Of War (IRE)**[12] 4515 4-8-9 **56**...........................(v) ZakWheatley(5) 10 55
(Keith Dalgleish) *missed break: hld up: hdwy and pushed along 3f out: edgd lft over 1f out: kpt on fnl f: no imp* **12/1**

0-45 **6** *2 1/2* **Kajaki (IRE)**[60] 2326 6-9-13 **72**...........................(p) CianMacRedmond(3) 6 67
(Kevin Ryan) *in tch: drvn along 3f out: outpcd over 1f out: btn fnl f* **9/1**

-005 **7** *3/4* **Doon Star**[8] 4690 4-8-4 **51** oh1.................................... CoreyMadden(5) 8 45
(Jim Goldie) *t.k.h early in midfield: effrt and prom over 2f out: edgd lft and wknd over 1f out* **14/1**

0045 **8** *1/2* **Question Of Faith**[13] 4491 8-9-10 **69**.......................... HarryRussell(3) 3 62
(Martin Todhunter) *missed break: hld up: rdn along 3f out: hung lft and wknd over 1f out* **22/1**

0532 **P** **Arms Of The Angel (GER)**[4] 4834 3-7-12 **60**............ AidanRedpath(7) 4
(Mark Johnston) *cl up: led over 2f out tl broke down bdly and p.u 4f out (jockey said filly lost it's action)* **15/8**[1]

2m 51.88s (-2.52) **Going Correction** -0.40s/f (Firm)
WFA 3 from 4yo+ 13lb **9** Ran SP% **117.1**
Speed ratings (Par 103): **91,90,88,88,87 86,85,85,**
CSF £163.09 CT £730.93 TOTE £49.20: £9.10, £1.70, £1.40; EX 196.70 Trifecta £777.50.
Owner Mrs Elizabeth Ferguson **Bred** Juddmonte Farms Ltd **Trained** Newmill-On-Slitrig, Borders

FOCUS
Add 21yds. The only race on the card over further than 1m, this was a very modest event for apprentices. It produced a 1-2 for Alistair Whillans. The second has been rated to this year's form.
T/Plt: £35.80 to a £1 stake. Pool: £59,797.89 - 1,218.26 winning units T/Qpdt: £6.50 to a £1 stake. Pool: £7,725.87 - 872.81 winning units **Richard Young**

4727 RIPON (R-H)

Monday, July 15

OFFICIAL GOING: Good (watered; 8.1)
Wind: virtually nil Weather: cloudy

4984 RIPON MUSEUMS MAIDEN STKS 5f

2:20 (2:23) (Class 5) 2-Y-O **£3,881** (£1,155; £577; £288) **Stalls** High

Form RPR

054 **1** **Orlaith (IRE)**[14] 4433 2-9-0 0.................................... PaulMulrennan 3 78+
(Iain Jardine) *chsd ldrs: pushed along 2f out: rdn and kpt on wl fnl f: led towards fin: shade cosily* **13/2**[2]

65 **2** *1 1/4* **Balancing Act (IRE)**[27] 3968 2-9-0 0.......................... PJMcDonald 8 73
(Jedd O'Keeffe) *led narrowly: rdn over 1f out: kpt on but hdd towards fin* **3/1**[1]

4 **3** *3* **Precocity (IRE)**[40] 3477 2-9-0 0.................................... PaulHanagan 6 62
(Richard Fahey) *pressed ldr: rdn 2f out: no ex fnl 110yds* **3/1**[1]

4 **4** *3/4* **Stone Soldier**[45] 3290 2-9-5 0.................................... BarryMcHugh 9 65
(James Given) *prom: rdn and outpcd over 1f out: plugged on fnl f* **8/1**

0 **5** *1 1/2* **Shepherds Way (IRE)**[58] 2840 2-9-0 0.......................... GrahamLee 10 54
(Michael Dods) *chsd ldrs: rdn over 2f out: outpcd over 1f out: plugged on fnl f* **16/1**

00 **6** *1 3/4* **Invincible Bertie (IRE)**[31] 3810 2-9-2 0.......................... RowanScott(3) 4 53
(Nigel Tinkler) *dwlt sltly: sn midfield: pushed along 2f out: kpt on same pce* **66/1**

7 *3 1/2* **Araifjan** 2-9-5 0.. DanielTudhope 2 40
(David O'Meara) *midfield: pushed along over 2f out: wknd over 1f out* **15/2**[3]

45 **8** *hd* **Don Ramiro (IRE)**[13] 4486 2-9-5 0.................................... TomEaves 1 39
(Kevin Ryan) *hld up in midfield on outer: pushed along 3f out: nvr involved* **14/1**

9 *2 1/2* **Not On Your Nellie (IRE)** 2-8-9 0.......................... FayeMcManoman(5) 7 25
(Nigel Tinkler) *v.s.a and in rr: sme hdwy over 1f out: nvr involved* **25/1**

0 **10** *1/2* **Hi Harry (IRE)**[23] 4125 2-9-5 0.................................... NathanEvans 11 29
(Declan Carroll) *midfield: pushed along over 2f out: wknd over 1f out* **25/1**

6 **11** *3 1/2* **Light The Fuse (IRE)**[8] 4688 2-9-5 0.......................... MichaelStainton 5 16
(K R Burke) *wnt lft jst after s: a towards rr* **10/1**

58.52s (-0.88) **Going Correction** -0.20s/f (Firm) **11** Ran SP% **117.0**
Speed ratings (Par 94): **99,97,92,91,88 85,80,79,75,75 69**
CSF £25.71 TOTE £6.90: £2.60, £1.40, £1.30; EX 28.70 Trifecta £113.90.
Owner James Fyffe & Scott Fyffe **Bred** Grange Stud **Trained** Carrutherstown, D'fries & G'way
■ Luckyforsome was withdrawn, price at time of withdrawal 66/1. Rule 4 does not apply.

FOCUS
All distances as advertised. They went a solid pace in this modest 2yo maiden, which can be rated around the second. It's been rated around the second and third.

4985 NEWBY HALL & GARDENS NURSERY H'CAP 5f

2:50 (2:51) (Class 5) (0-70,72) 2-Y-O

£3,752 (£1,116; £557; £300; £300; £300) **Stalls** High

Form RPR

1002 **1** **Infinite Grace**[6] 4756 2-9-7 **70**.................................... DanielTudhope 1 79+
(David O'Meara) *trckd ldrs: pushed into ld appr fnl f: kpt on wl: comf* **15/8**[1]

4315 **2** *2 1/4* **Dandizette (IRE)**[16] 4361 2-9-1 **69**.......................... CierenFallon(5) 5 69
(Adrian Nicholls) *led narrowly: rdn and hdd appr fnl f: kpt on same pce and sn no ch w wnr* **3/1**[2]

0006 **3** ½ **Ice Skate**[26] 4006 2-8-4 **53** ..... DuranFentiman 6 51
(Tim Easterby) *dwlt: midfield: rdn to chse ldrs over 1f out: kpt on* **20/1**

306 **4** 1¾ **War Of Clans (IRE)**[62] 2706 2-8-9 **63** ..... HarrisonShaw(5) 2 55
(K R Burke) *hld up on outer: rdn along 3f out: sme hdwy over 1f out: one pce fnl f* **12/1**

450 **5** *hd* **Queens Blade**[40] 3469 2-8-10 **59** ..... RachelRichardson 8 50
(Tim Easterby) *prom: rdn 2f out: wknd ins fnl f* **16/1**

303 **6** 4 **Dancinginthesand (IRE)**[19] 4237 2-8-11 **60** .....(p[1]) GrahamLee 7 37
(Bryan Smart) *midfield: rdn 2f out: wknd fnl f* **12/1**

035 **7** ¾ **Javea Magic (IRE)**[11] 4550 2-8-11 **60** .....(p[1]) RichardKingscote 3 34
(Tom Dascombe) *a towards rr* **7/1**

52P2 **8** 3¾ **Sneaky**[14] 4448 2-9-9 **72** ..... HollieDoyle 4 33
(Archie Watson) *midfield on outer: rdn along 3f out: wknd over 1f out (jockey said filly became unbalanced on the undulations on this occasion)* **6/1**[3]

59.13s (-0.27) **Going Correction** -0.20s/f (Firm) **8** Ran SP% **112.6**
Speed ratings (Par 94): **94,90,89,86,86 80,78,72**
CSF £7.20 CT £79.06 TOTE £2.40: £1.10, £1.50, £4.80; EX 7.30 Trifecta £108.70.
Owner K Nicholson **Bred** Kevin Nicholson **Trained** Upper Helmsley, N Yorks

FOCUS
The first pair were always handy in this ordinary nursery.

4986 RIPON CATHEDRAL FILLIES' H'CAP — 5f
3:20 (3:20) (Class 4) (0-85,87) 3-Y-O+ **£5,369** (£1,597; £798; £399; £300) **Stalls** High

Form — RPR

0201 **1** **Queens Gift (IRE)**[10] 4595 4-10-0 **87** .....(p[1]) PaulMulrennan 5 96
(Michael Dods) *trckd ldr: rdn along 2f out: kpt on to ld fnl 50yds* **15/8**[1]

3654 **2** 1 **Merry Banter**[7] 4722 5-9-10 **83** ..... GrahamLee 4 88
(Paul Midgley) *led: rdn ent fnl f: hdd 50yds out: no ex* **15/8**[1]

6-02 **3** 1½ **Diamonique**[10] 4604 3-8-11 **75** ..... PaulHanagan 3 73
(Keith Dalgleish) *chsd ldr: rdn along 2f out: kpt on same pce* **6/1**[2]

3416 **4** ½ **Seen The Lyte (IRE)**[9] 4625 4-9-5 **83** .....(h) FayeMcManoman(5) 2 81
(Nigel Tinkler) *dwlt: hld up: rdn and sme hdwy over 1f out: one pce fnl f* **6/1**[2]

1060 **5** 7 **Midnight Malibu (IRE)**[23] 4101 6-9-12 **85** ..... RachelRichardson 1 58
(Tim Easterby) *hld up on outer: rdn along over 2f out: wknd over 1f out* **9/1**[3]

57.67s (-1.73) **Going Correction** -0.20s/f (Firm)
WFA 3 from 4yo+ 5lb **5** Ran SP% **108.1**
Speed ratings (Par 102): **105,103,101,100,89**
CSF £5.24 TOTE £2.60: £1.20, £1.40; EX 6.00 Trifecta £18.20.
Owner Geoff & Sandra Turnbull **Bred** Old Carhue & Graeng Bloodstock **Trained** Denton, Co Durham

FOCUS
A fair little fillies' sprint handicap. The second has been rated to her non-claiming rider best.

4987 ARMSTRONG MEMORIAL H'CAP — 6f
3:50 (3:50) (Class 3) (0-95,96) 3-Y-O+ **£9,703** (£2,887; £1,443; £721) **Stalls** High

Form — RPR

0064 **1** **Bossipop**[3] 4880 6-8-12 **80** .....(b) CamHardie 4 88
(Tim Easterby) *mde all: pushed along 2f out: drvn 1f out: kpt on wl* **15/2**

0001 **2** 1¼ **Arecibo (FR)**[7] 4722 4-10-0 **96** 5ex ..... DanielTudhope 6 100
(David O'Meara) *trckd ldrs: rdn to chse ldr jst ins fnl f: kpt on same pce* **3/1**[2]

6032 **3** ¾ **Roundhay Park**[9] 4649 4-9-1 **86** ..... RowanScott(3) 3 88
(Nigel Tinkler) *in tch on outer: rdn and hdwy appr fnl f: kpt on* **2/1**[1]

0005 **4** *shd* **Pipers Note**[12] 4521 9-9-5 **87** ..... JackGarritty 5 88
(Ruth Carr) *trckd ldrs: n.m.r on inner over 1f out tl jst ins fnl f: rdn and kpt on* **8/1**

0225 **5** 1 **Lorton**[37] 3583 3-8-13 **87** .....(p[1]) PaulMulrennan 7 84
(Julie Camacho) *hld up in tch: pushed along whn short of room over 1f out tl ins fnl f: angled rt towards outer but too much to do once clr fnl 75yds (jockey said filly was momentarily denied a clear run one furlong out)* **9/2**[3]

5030 **6** 1¾ **Gin In The Inn (IRE)**[16] 4406 6-8-11 **82** ..... ConnorMurtagh(3) 2 74
(Richard Fahey) *prom: rdn 2f out: wknd fnl 110yds* **11/1**

1-00 **7** 8 **Summer Daydream (IRE)**[8] 4692 3-9-7 **95** ..... PaulHanagan 1 61
(Keith Dalgleish) *sn cl up on outer: rdn over 2f out: wknd appr fnl f* **16/1**

1m 10.14s (-2.36) **Going Correction** -0.20s/f (Firm)
WFA 3 from 4yo+ 6lb **7** Ran SP% **113.6**
Speed ratings (Par 107): **107,105,104,104,102 100,89**
CSF £29.82 TOTE £7.80: £3.20, £2.50; EX 45.70 Trifecta £105.00.
Owner Ambrose Turnbull **Bred** Lady Whent **Trained** Great Habton, N Yorks

FOCUS
This feature sprint handicap was run at a stop-start pace. The second has been rated in line with his latest.

4988 FOUNTAINS ABBEY WORLD HERITAGE SITE H'CAP — 1m 4f 10y
4:20 (4:20) (Class 4) (0-85,85) 3-Y-O+
£5,369 (£1,597; £798; £399; £300; £300) **Stalls** Centre

Form — RPR

132 **1** **Alright Sunshine (IRE)**[24] 4055 4-9-13 **84** ..... DanielTudhope 1 91+
(Keith Dalgleish) *prom: pushed into ld over 1f out: rdn out ins fnl f* **4/7**[1]

3244 **2** ¾ **Mutamaded (IRE)**[19] 4241 6-9-13 **84** ..... JamesSullivan 4 88
(Ruth Carr) *trckd ldrs: rdn over 2f out: drvn over 1f out: wnt 2nd ins fnl f: styd on but nvr getting to wnr* **7/1**[3]

1312 **3** 1½ **Conundrum**[17] 4321 3-8-9 **78** ..... GrahamLee 3 81
(Jedd O'Keeffe) *led: rdn along and hung lft on bnd over 4f out: hdd over 1f out: no ex ins fnl f* **3/1**[2]

55-4 **4** *nk* **Final**[14] 4437 7-9-13 **84** ..... FrannyNorton 7 85
(Mark Johnston) *s.i.s: hld up: rdn along over 3f out: plugged on fnl f: nvr threatened ldrs* **16/1**

-000 **5** ½ **Mount Tahan (IRE)**[53] 3005 7-10-0 **85** .....(w) TomEaves 5 85
(Kevin Ryan) *hld up in rr: sme hdwy 3f out: rdn 2f out: sn no imp* **33/1**

40/0 **6** 8 **Percy (IRE)**[16] 4407 5-9-13 **84** ..... PaulMulrennan 2 72
(Frank Bishop) *in tch: rdn along over 3f out: wknd 2f out* **66/1**

2m 37.24s (0.94) **Going Correction** -0.20s/f (Firm)
WFA 3 from 4yo+ 12lb **6** Ran SP% **111.5**
Speed ratings (Par 105): **88,87,86,86,85 80**
CSF £5.35 TOTE £1.40: £1.20, £2.40; EX 4.80 Trifecta £7.10.
Owner Paul & Clare Rooney **Bred** Peter & Hugh McCutcheon **Trained** Carluke, S Lanarks

FOCUS
This fair handicap was run at an uneven pace, but the form is solid. The second has been rated to form.

4989 LIGHTWATER VALLEY NOVICE STKS — 1m 1f 170y
4:50 (4:52) (Class 5) 3-Y-O+ **£3,881** (£1,155; £577; £288) **Stalls** Low

Form — RPR

61 **1** **Country**[84] 1975 3-9-6 **0** ..... DanielTudhope 1 87+
(William Haggas) *trckd ldrs: swtchd lft to outer over 3f out: rdn to ld appr fnl f: pushed out ins fnl f* **30/100**[1]

4334 **2** 2½ **Noble Prospector (IRE)**[24] 4055 3-8-13 **76** ..... PaulHanagan 3 75
(Richard Fahey) *led: rdn and hdd appr fnl f: sn one pce* **11/4**[2]

3 6 **Flash Point (IRE)** 3-8-13 **0** ..... CamHardie 4 63
(Tracy Waggott) *hld up: rdn along 3f out: no imp in 3rd fnl 2f* **150/1**

5 **4** 9 **Point Taken (IRE)**[18] 4304 5-10-2 **0** ..... PJMcDonald 5 50
(Michael Appleby) *wnt lft s: sn prom: rdn along over 3f out: wknd 2f out* **8/1**[3]

2m 1.46s (-3.14) **Going Correction** -0.20s/f (Firm)
WFA 3 from 5yo 10lb **4** Ran SP% **115.4**
Speed ratings (Par 103): **104,102,97,90**
CSF £1.72 TOTE £1.10; EX 1.30 Trifecta £19.30.
Owner Sheikh Ahmed Al Maktoum **Bred** Godolphin **Trained** Newmarket, Suffolk
■ Pound Off You was withdrawn, price at time of withdrawal 100/1. Rule 4 does not apply.

FOCUS
This was predictably tactical. The 76-rated second sets the level.

4990 WELCOME TO YORKSHIRE H'CAP — 1m 4f 10y
5:20 (5:22) (Class 6) (0-60,60) 3-Y-O+
£3,105 (£924; £461; £300; £300; £300) **Stalls** Centre

Form — RPR

000 **1** **Stormin Norman**[40] 3482 4-9-10 **52** ..... FrannyNorton 15 59+
(Micky Hammond) *dwlt: midfield on outer: pushed along and hdwy 3f out: led over 1f out: drvn out ins fnl f (trainer said, regards apparent improvement in form, gelding appreciated the step up in trip on Good ground and what was a weaker race in his opinion)* **16/1**

0-00 **2** 1¼ **Magrevio (IRE)**[47] 3226 3-8-12 **55** ..... RowanScott(3) 4 60+
(Liam Bailey) *in tch on inner: pushed along to chse ldrs whn short of room on inner over 1f out: swtchd lft 1f out: rdn and styd on wl: wnt 2nd towards fin* **28/1**

0614 **3** ¾ **Myklachi (FR)**[8] 4690 3-9-6 **60** ..... DanielTudhope 2 64+
(David O'Meara) *midfield: pushed along and n.m.r over 2f out: fair bit to do once angled lft into clr over 1f out: rdn and styd on wl: wnt 3rd towards fin* **13/8**[1]

0035 **4** *nk* **Seek The Moon (USA)**[16] 4371 4-10-0 **56** .....(h) PaulHanagan 5 59
(Lawrence Mullaney) *prom: rdn over 2f out: kpt on same pce* **8/1**[3]

0443 **5** *shd* **Jan De Heem**[14] 4435 9-9-5 **50** .....(p) ConnorMurtagh(3) 6 56+
(Tina Jackson) *s.i.s: hld up in rr: bit clsr 3f out: gng wl but repeatedly short of room on inner 2f out tl ins fnl f: swtchd lft 110yds: kpt on but too much to do (jockey said gelding was denied a clear run approaching one furlong out)* **10/1**

1432 **6** ¾ **Dew Pond**[14] 4435 7-10-0 **56** .....(t[1]) DuranFentiman 13 58
(Tim Easterby) *hld up in midfield: rdn and sme hdwy over 1f out: kpt on fnl f* **10/1**

000 **7** *shd* **Midnight Warrior**[14] 4435 9-9-0 **47** .....(t) PaulaMuir(5) 10 49
(Ron Barr) *trckd ldrs: rdn over 2f out: one pce* **28/1**

0504 **8** ¾ **Point Of Honour (IRE)**[14] 4435 4-9-4 **46** ..... JamesSullivan 7 47
(Ruth Carr) *midfield: swtchd lft to outer and hdwy to ld over 8f out: rdn and hdd over 1f out: wknd ins fnl f (jockey said gelding missed the break and was unable to obtain a prominent position)* **15/2**[2]

-036 **9** 1 **Metronomic (IRE)**[27] 3959 5-9-3 **45** ..... CamHardie 8 44
(Peter Niven) *dwlt: hld up: racd keenly: pushed along over 2f out: nvr threatened (jockey said gelding ran too freely)* **25/1**

-060 **10** *shd* **Ateescomponent (IRE)**[28] 3926 3-9-5 **59** ..... TomEaves 3 58
(David Barron) *led: hdd over 8f out: trckd ldrs: rdn along over 2f out: wknd ins fnl f* **50/1**

/00- **11** ½ **My Renaissance**[15] 1409 9-9-10 **52** .....(bt) PaulMulrennan 12 50
(Sam England) *midfield: pushed along and n.m.r 2f out: rdn and no imp fnl f* **20/1**

-063 **12** 1½ **Burnage Boy (IRE)**[14] 4443 3-8-10 **50** ..... GrahamLee 9 46
(Micky Hammond) *in tch on inner: pushed along and edgd lft over 3f out: rdn over 2f out: lost pl and sn btn* **10/1**

0-00 **13** 1 **Royal Liberty**[12] 4518 4-9-4 **46** ..... PJMcDonald 1 40
(Geoffrey Harker) *hld up: nvr threatened (jockey said gelding was short of room approaching the final furlong)* **40/1**

-001 **14** *shd* **Strategic (IRE)**[12] 4515 4-9-5 **47** .....(h) RachelRichardson 14 41
(Eric Alston) *trckd ldrs on outer: rdn over 2f out: wknd over 1f out* **14/1**

0030 **15** 2¾ **Kostantina**[9] 4628 3-8-10 **50** .....(p[1]) NathanEvans 11 41
(Olly Williams) *a towards rr* **50/1**

2m 35.25s (-1.05) **Going Correction** -0.20s/f (Firm)
WFA 3 from 4yo+ 12lb **15** Ran SP% **122.7**
Speed ratings (Par 101): **95,94,93,93,93 92,92,92,91,91 91,90,89,89,87**
CSF £413.12 CT £1131.18 TOTE £22.20: £6.50, £11.80, £1.10; EX 662.40 Trifecta £2891.70.
Owner The Monday Club **Bred** Copgrove Hall Stud **Trained** Middleham, N Yorks

FOCUS
A weak handicap, run at a routine sort of pace. Muddling form.
T/Plt: £10.60 to a £1 stake. Pool: £69,713.49 - 4,785.93 winning units T/Qpdt: £5.80 to a £1 stake. Pool: £5,370.46 - 679.83 winning untis **Andrew Sheret**

4733 WINDSOR (R-H)
Monday, July 15

OFFICIAL GOING: Good to firm (watered; 7.5)
Wind: Light, against Weather: Fine, pleasant

4991 DOWNLOAD THE MARATHONBET APP APPRENTICE H'CAP — 1m 2f
5:30 (5:30) (Class 6) (0-60,61) 3-Y-O+
£2,781 (£827; £413; £300; £300; £300) **Stalls** Low

Form — RPR

-000 **1** **Bader**[37] 3593 3-8-10 **50** .....(b[1]) SeamusCronin 12 57
(Richard Hannon) *mde all: sn had field wl spced out: kicked for home 3f out and 6 l up: drvn 2f out: ld dwindled fnl f but a holding on (trainer said, regards apparent improvement in form, gelding benefitted from a change of tactics and the first-time application of blinkers)* **14/1**

30-3 **2** ¾ **It's How We Roll (IRE)**[45] 3298 5-8-12 **45**..........(p) ScottMcCullagh(3) 1 50
(John Spearing) *hld up in last: stl there as wnr drew clr 3f out: rapid prog against nr side rail over 1f out: r.o to take 2nd last strides: too late* **16/1**

-603 **3** nk **Tavus (IRE)**[32] 3780 3-9-5 **59**.......................... ThomasGreatrex 7 63
(Roger Charlton) *chsd ldng trio: rdn 3f out: chsd clr wnr fnl f: steadily clsd but lost 2nd last strides* **11/10**[1]

5140 **4** 2½ **Carvelas (IRE)**[11] 4568 10-9-5 **52**.......................... TobyEley(3) 8 51
(J R Jenkins) *chsd ldrs: rdn whn wnr wnt clr 3f out: kpt on one pce and n.d* **25/1**

4600 **5** nk **Jeremy's Jet (IRE)**[83] 2012 8-8-10 **45**..................(t) ElishaWhittington(5) 2 43
(Tony Carroll) *hld up towards rr: urged along whn wnr wnt clr 3f out: hanging lft fr 2f out: kpt on but n.d* **33/1**

0-50 **6** ½ **Classified (IRE)**[16] 4371 5-9-5 **52**......................(p[1]) WilliamCarver(3) 11 49
(Ed de Giles) *chsd wnr: rdn and outpcd 3f out: no imp 2f out: lost 2nd and wknd fnl f* **8/1**[3]

-630 **7** 1½ **King Athelstan (IRE)**[28] 3941 4-9-7 **58**.............(b[1]) RhysClutterbuck(7) 4 52
(Gary Moore) *hld up in last trio: rdn 3f out: no real prog fnl 2f and nvr any ch* **8/1**[3]

66-0 **8** 2½ **Midnight Mood**[15] 4426 6-9-8 **52**.......................... PoppyBridgwater 6 41
(Dominic Ffrench Davis) *racd on outer: nvr beyond midfield: rdn and no prog over 2f out* **7/1**[2]

9 nk **Cafe Sydney (IRE)**[46] 3280 3-8-8 **48**.......................... DarraghKeenan 9 37
(Tony Carroll) *nvr beyond midfield: rdn and no prog 3f out* **12/1**

-000 **10** 4 **We Are All Dottie**[55] 2926 3-7-12 **45**.......................... EllaBoardman(7) 13 27
(Pat Phelan) *awkward s and slowly away: rcvrd rapidly to chse ldng pair: wknd qckly over 2f out* **66/1**

0501 **P** **Altaira**[13] 4475 8-9-3 **50**..........................(p) GeorgiaDobie(3) 10
(Tony Carroll) *hld up in rr: no prog whn broke down over 2f out and p.u: fatally injured* **16/1**

2m 9.26s (0.26) **Going Correction** -0.075s/f (Good)
WFA 3 from 4yo+ 10lb **11** Ran SP% **116.7**
Speed ratings (Par 101): **96,95,95,93,92 92,91,89,89,85**
CSF £212.02 CT £450.07 TOTE £16.10: £3.90, £3.50, £1.10; EX 237.50 Trifecta £493.70.
Owner Robert Tyrrell And Partner **Bred** G R Bailey Ltd **Trained** East Everleigh, Wilts

FOCUS
The rail was out a further 3yds from the previous meeting, so 9yds out towards the outer rail on the bend and the 6f start to the intersection, and 7yds out from the intersection to the line. Add 27yds. It was a dry, warm day and the ground had been watered. Muddling form as the winner was allowed a clear, uncontested lead, and with the exception of the second horse, who raced stands' side, the runners came up the middle in the straight. The fourth has been rated to his latest.

4992 EBF NOVICE STKS 6f 12y

6:00 (6:01) (Class 5) 2-Y-O £3,428 (£1,020; £509; £254) **Stalls** Centre

Form RPR

2 **1** **Fleeting Prince (IRE)**[13] 4482 2-9-5 0.......................... KieranShoemark 2 86+
(Charles Hills) *mde virtually all: shkn up to draw clr wl over 1f out: comf* **11/10**[1]

0 **2** 2½ **Modern British Art (IRE)**[19] 4246 2-9-5 0.......................... JasonWatson 11 78
(Michael Bell) *w wnr to 2f out: rdn and outpcd over 1f out: kpt on* **16/1**

32 **3** ½ **Hubert (IRE)**[16] 4394 2-9-5 0.......................... OisinMurphy 1 76
(Sylvester Kirk) *chsd ldrs: rdn 2f out: sn outpcd: kpt on one pce after* **7/4**[2]

05 **4** 3 **King's View (IRE)**[16] 4388 2-9-5 0.......................... TomMarquand 6 66+
(Richard Hannon) *towards rr: pushed along bef 1/2-way: effrt on outer over 2f out: one pce and no ch w ldrs* **12/1**[3]

0 **5** hd **Bowling Russian (IRE)**[21] 4184 2-9-5 0.......................... CharlesBishop 4 66
(George Baker) *in tch in midfield: effrt towards outer over 2f out: wandered sltly u.p over 1f out: no ch w ldrs* **20/1**

3 **6** 4½ **Claudia Jean (IRE)**[38] 3530 2-9-0 0.......................... PatDobbs 9 46
(Richard Hannon) *dwlt: towards rr: shkn up 1/2-way: nvr on terms* **20/1**

60 **7** shd **Queenofthe clyde (IRE)**[34] 3689 2-9-0 0..........................(w) ShaneKelly 5 46
(K R Burke) *t.k.h: trckd ldrs 4f: wknd over 1f out* **50/1**

00 **8** 1½ **Camacho Man (IRE)**[7] 4734 2-9-5 0.......................... RossaRyan 10 46
(Jennie Candlish) *hld up in last pair: pushed along and limited prog fr 2f out: nvr in it* **66/1**

9 4½ **Comvida (IRE)** 2-9-5 0.......................... PatCosgrave 7 32
(Hugo Palmer) *dwlt: rn green in last and a bhd* **14/1**

0 **10** ½ **Staycee**[20] 4223 2-9-0 0.......................... DavidEgan 8 25
(Rod Millman) *spd on outer to 1/2-way: wknd qckly 2f out* **50/1**

11 1 **Awesome Gary** 2-9-5 0.......................... RobertWinston 3 27
(Tony Carroll) *s.i.s: in tch in midfield over 3f: sn wknd* **40/1**

1m 12.22s (0.12) **Going Correction** -0.075s/f (Good) **11** Ran SP% **121.6**
Speed ratings (Par 94): **96,92,92,88,87 81,81,79,73,72 71**
CSF £20.82 TOTE £1.90: £1.10, £4.00, £1.10; EX 21.60 Trifecta £51.80.
Owner Mrs Susan Roy **Bred** Edgeridge Ltd **Trained** Lambourn, Berks

FOCUS
The first three were always handy in this fair-looking novice. This time they all raced near side. The third helps set the level in line with his C&D latest.

4993 BRITISH EBF MAIDEN STKS 5f 21y

6:30 (6:30) (Class 5) 2-Y-O £3,428 (£1,020; £509; £254) **Stalls** Centre

Form RPR

5 **1** **Caspian Queen (IRE)**[34] 3689 2-9-0 0.......................... ShaneKelly 8 73
(Richard Hughes) *sn pressed ldr: rdn to chal over 1f out: drvn into narrow ld fnl 100yds: hld on wl* **9/4**[2]

203 **2** hd **Cool Sphere (USA)**[16] 4373 2-9-5 84.......................... AdamKirby 4 78
(Robert Cowell) *led: drvn over 1f out: narrowly hdd fnl 100yds: styd on but a jst hld* **1/1**[1]

66 **3** 2½ **Queen Aya**[14] 4448 2-8-11 0.......................... WilliamCox(3) 5 64
(Ed Walker) *t.k.h: cl up: rdn to chse ldng pair over 1f out: kpt on same pce fnl f* **20/1**

4 1¼ **Sand Diego (IRE)** 2-9-5 0.......................... PatDobbs 1 64+
(Peter Crate) *s.s: detached in 8th: swtchd lft 2f out and rt over 1f out: pushed along and styd on steadily after: nvr nrr* **20/1**

0 **5** ½ **Magical Force**[60] 2767 2-9-0 0.......................... OisinMurphy 10 57
(Rod Millman) *dwlt: spd to chse ldrs: rdn over 1f out: fdd fnl f* **10/1**[3]

6 2¾ **Stormy Girl (IRE)** 2-9-0 0.......................... DavidEgan 2 47
(David Loughnane) *in tch: rdn 2f out: no imp on ldrs after* **25/1**

7 nse **Instantly** 2-9-5 0.......................... HayleyTurner 6 52+
(Robert Cowell) *dwlt: rn green and hanging thrght: detached in last tl kpt on fnl f* **10/1**[3]

0 **8** 3¾ **Blue Venture**[14] 4448 2-9-0 0.......................... RobertWinston 9 34
(Tony Carroll) *t.k.h: pressed ldng pair tl wknd qckly wl over 1f out* **33/1**

0 **9** 3¾ **Quarrystreetmagic (IRE)**[16] 4394 2-9-5 0.......................... TomMarquand 3 25
(Brian Meehan) *pushed along in midfield bef 1/2-way: wknd 2f out* **33/1**

59.92s (-0.18) **Going Correction** -0.075s/f (Good) **9** Ran SP% **118.2**
Speed ratings (Par 94): **98,97,93,91,90 86,86,80,74**
CSF £4.58 TOTE £3.10: £1.10, £1.10, £4.40; EX 4.90 Trifecta £28.80.
Owner Davood Vakilgilani **Bred** Rabbah Bloodstock Limited **Trained** Upper Lambourn, Berks

FOCUS
An ordinary 2yo maiden, with the runner-up below form. The action was near side. The second has been rated closer to his debut run than his Norfolk effort.

4994 FEGIME "PREFERRED SUPPLIERS" H'CAP 1m 31y

7:00 (7:00) (Class 4) (0-80,80) 3-Y-O+

£5,207 (£1,549; £774; £387; £300; £300) **Stalls** Low

Form RPR

-156 **1** **Sash**[59] 2796 3-9-6 **80**.......................... PatDobbs 3 89+
(Amanda Perrett) *a gng wl: trckd ldrs: pushed into the ld over 1f out: qckly asserted fnl f: rdn out* **7/2**[2]

0432 **2** 2 **Tamerlane (IRE)**[12] 4506 4-9-4 **69**..........................(vt) AdamKirby 5 74
(Clive Cox) *hld up in tch: prog over 2f out: drvn over 1f out: styd on to take 2nd ins fnl f: no ch w wnr* **11/2**[3]

4022 **3** 1¾ **Kingston Kurrajong**[19] 4249 6-9-11 **76**.......................... JasonWatson 4 77
(William Knight) *hld up in midfield: rdn and prog over 2f out: forced way through over 1f out: drvn into 3rd ins fnl f: kpt on same pce* **13/2**

-610 **4** nk **Gin Palace**[40] 3471 3-9-3 **77**.......................... CharlesBishop 11 75
(Eve Johnson Houghton) *trckd ldr to over 1f out: outpcd after but kpt on* **13/2**

0040 **5** ¾ **Plunger**[12] 4506 4-10-0 **79**..........................(b) KieranShoemark 8 78
(Paul Cole) *taken down early: hld up in last trio: effrt on outer over 2f out: drvn and kpt on same pce over 1f out* **12/1**

0030 **6** ½ **Sir Plato (IRE)**[10] 4615 5-9-2 **67**.......................... OisinMurphy 2 64
(Rod Millman) *broke wl but needed plenty of early driving to maintain ld: rdn and hdd over 1f out: wknd* **10/3**[1]

0055 **7** 1¾ **God Has Given**[31] 3805 3-8-7 **67**..........................(p) SilvestreDeSousa 10 58
(Ian Williams) *trckd ldrs: lost pl and drvn over 2f out: nvr on terms after* **8/1**

0000 **8** ¾ **Capriolette (IRE)**[18] 4300 4-9-7 **72**.......................... ShaneKelly 7 64
(Ed Walker) *t.k.h v early: hld up: urged along in last bef 1/2-way: nvr a threat after: kpt on fnl f* **16/1**

1304 **9** 9 **Javelin**[19] 4243 4-9-0 **65**.......................... MartinDwyer 9 36
(William Muir) *in tch: prog to press ldng pair 3f out: wkng whn bmpd over 1f out: eased (jockey said filly hung right-handed)* **16/1**

0000 **10** 17 **Field Of Vision (IRE)**[20] 4227 6-8-12 **63**..........................(p) RobHornby 1
(John Flint) *in tch tl wknd qckly 2f out: t.o* **40/1**

1m 42.13s (-2.37) **Going Correction** -0.075s/f (Good)
WFA 3 from 4yo+ 9lb **10** Ran SP% **120.4**
Speed ratings (Par 105): **108,106,104,103,103 102,100,100,91,74**
CSF £24.10 CT £122.93 TOTE £4.70: £1.80, £1.90, £2.00; EX 23.80 Trifecta £108.00.
Owner K Abdullah **Bred** Juddmonte Farms Ltd **Trained** Pulborough, W Sussex
■ Stewards' Enquiry : Jason Watson four-day ban; careless riding (July 29,Aug 2-4)

FOCUS
Add 27yds. The winner found some improvement in this fair handicap. The action was near side. The second has been rated close to his AW best, and the third to this year's turf form.

4995 VISIT MARATHONBET.CO.UK H'CAP (MARATHONBET WINDSOR SPRINT SERIES QUALIFIER) 5f 21y

7:30 (7:31) (Class 3) (0-95,92) 3-Y-O £7,246 (£2,168; £1,084; £542; £270) **Stalls** Centre

Form RPR

0520 **1** **Royal Birth**[2] 4896 8-9-6 **86**..........................(t) OisinMurphy 3 93
(Stuart Williams) *in tch: rdn and clsd on ldrs over 1f out: hung lft ins fnl f but disp ld fnl 150yds: won on the nod* **13/2**[3]

1006 **2** shd **Daschas**[3] 4894 5-8-9 **82**..........................(t) MarcoGhiani(7) 7 89
(Stuart Williams) *in tch: rdn to cl on ldrs on outer over 1f out: drvn to dispute ld fnl 150yds: jst pipped* **7/1**

3100 **3** ½ **Moonraker**[17] 4331 7-9-2 **82**.......................... AlistairRawlinson 8 87
(Michael Appleby) *taken down early: dwlt sltly: in tch in last pair: rdn and prog on wd outside over 1f out: styd on fnl f to take 3rd last strides* **25/1**

-451 **4** hd **Jumira Bridge**[10] 4609 5-9-12 **92**.......................... SilvestreDeSousa 6 96
(Robert Cowell) *taken down early: hld up in tch: rdn and prog to chse ldr over 1f out: drvn to chal and upsides ins fnl f: no ex fnl 50yds* **5/2**[1]

6-30 **5** hd **Wiley Post**[30] 3856 6-8-9 **75**..........................(b) TomMarquand 1 79
(Tony Carroll) *chsd ldr: rdn over 1f out: hung lft after: jst outpcd in bunch fin* **13/2**[3]

2020 **6** 1 **Just Glamorous (IRE)**[18] 4313 6-9-2 **85**.......................... CameronNoble(3) 2 85
(Grace Harris) *led: 2 l ahd 1/2-way: drvn over 1f out: hdd and fdd fnl 150yds* **15/2**

0036 **7** 2 **Iconic Knight (IRE)**[19] 4236 4-8-11 **77**.......................... ShaneKelly 5 70
(Ed Walker) *chsd ldrs: rdn and sing to lose pl whn short of room jst ins fnl f: no ch after* **9/2**[2]

634 **8** 2 **Udontdodou**[37] 3582 6-9-8 **88**.......................... PhilipPrince 9 74
(Richard Guest) *taken down early: hld up in last pair: swtchd rt 2f out: rdn and no prog over 1f out* **9/1**

5-05 **9** ½ **Swiss Knight**[10] 4609 4-9-3 **83**..........................(t) JasonWatson 4 67
(Stuart Williams) *prom: rdn and nt qckn wl over 1f out: wknd* **12/1**

59.14s (-0.96) **Going Correction** -0.075s/f (Good) **9** Ran SP% **119.2**
Speed ratings (Par 107): **104,103,103,102,102 100,97,94,93**
CSF £53.00 CT £1088.14 TOTE £8.50: £2.40, £2.80, £7.40; EX 50.40 Trifecta £1092.30.
Owner The Morley Family **Bred** Old Mill Stud & S Williams & J Parry **Trained** Newmarket, Suffolk

FOCUS
A race lacking unexposed runners - there were no 3yos and only two 4yos, and it went to the oldest of the lot - but it was competitive. They initially raced near side but were spread across the track in the closing stages. It's been rated around the second, with the third to last year's turf form.

4996 MARATHONBET "BETTER ODDS MEAN BIGGER WINNINGS" H'CAP 1m 3f 99y

8:00 (8:01) (Class 4) (0-85,84) 3-Y-O £5,207 (£1,549; £774; £387) **Stalls** Low

Form RPR

-126 **1** **Mannaal (IRE)**[32] 3762 3-9-4 **84**.......................... MeganNicholls(3) 4 93
(Simon Crisford) *cl up: prog to ld jst over 2f out: rdn and in command over 1f out: readily* **6/1**

2035 **2** 3¼ **Fraser Island (IRE)**[11] 4549 3-9-2 **79**.......................... AdamKirby 3 82
(Mark Johnston) *cl up: shkn up wl over 2f out: styd on u.p over 1f out to take 2nd fnl f: no threat to wnr* **9/4**[2]

031 **3** 2¾ **Sendeed (IRE)**[18] 4277 3-9-3 **80**.......................... OisinMurphy 2 79
(Saeed bin Suroor) *trckd ldr: led briefly over 2f out: sn outpcd by wnr: wknd and eased ins fnl f* **5/4**[1]

343 **4** *shd* **Dilmun Dynasty (IRE)**[21] 4177 3-8-12 **75**............(v[1]) KieranShoemark 1 73
(Sir Michael Stoute) *led at stdy pce: asked to kick on 3f out but no rspnse and hdd over 2f out: dropped to last and wl btn over 1f out* **7/2**[3]
2m 27.69s (-2.01) **Going Correction** -0.075s/f (Good) **4** Ran SP% **111.7**
Speed ratings (Par 102): **104,101,99,99**
CSF £19.55 TOTE £6.80; EX 24.50 Trifecta £31.30.
Owner Sheikh Ahmed Al Maktoum **Bred** Godolphin **Trained** Newmarket, Suffolk

FOCUS
Add 27yds. It's hard to know the exact worth of the form, with the beaten runners not offering much, but the winner had been useful and steadily progressive until running poorly last time and did this well. They raced near side in the straight. The second has been rated to his recent form.

4997 VISIT ATTHERACES.COM H'CAP 1m 2f
8:30 (8:30) (Class 4) (0-85,85) 4-Y-0+
£5,207 (£1,549; £774; £387; £300; £300) **Stalls** Low

Form RPR
522 **1** **Mandarin (GER)**[31] 3806 5-9-3 **81**.................................. AdamKirby 7 93
(Ian Williams) *trckd ldng trio: clsd over 2f out: shkn up to ld over 1f out: clr fnl f: readily* **5/2**[2]
1225 **2** 3 **Hats Off To Larry**[10] 4613 5-9-4 **82**.................................. OisinMurphy 1 88
(Mick Channon) *trckd ldng pair: clsd to ld on inner over 2f out: rdn and hdd over 1f out: no ch w wnr fnl f: hld on for 2nd* **7/4**[1]
4630 **3** *¾* **Nonios (IRE)**[13] 4490 7-9-0 **83**..............................(h) DylanHogan(5) 4 87
(David Simcock) *hld up in last pair: rdn and no immediate prog over 2f out: stl only 5th over 1f out to take 3rd last strides* **20/1**
-035 **4** *hd* **Rotherwick (IRE)**[14] 4450 7-9-6 **84**..........................(t) RossaRyan 2 88
(Paul Cole) *hld up towards rr: pushed along over 3f out: no prog whn rdn over 2f out: styd on fnl f to press for 3rd last strides* **10/1**
5135 **5** *hd* **Geetanjali (IRE)**[17] 4318 4-9-0 **78**..........................(p) HayleyTurner 6 81
(Michael Bell) *hld up towards rr: rdn wl over 2f out: styd on over 1f out on outer to press for a pl nr fin* **16/1**
4343 **6** *1* **Michele Strogoff**[9] 4662 6-9-7 **85**.............................. AlistairRawlinson 5 86
(Michael Appleby) *led: rdn and hdd over 2f out: sn btn: lost 3 pls nr fin* **14/1**
2605 **7** *2 ¼* **Isomer (USA)**[75] 2273 5-9-1 **82**..........................(p) JoshuaBryan(3) 8 79
(Andrew Balding) *trckd ldr to over 2f out: sn rdn and wknd* **10/1**
-400 **8** *3 ½* **Showroom (FR)**[67] 2563 4-9-6 **84**.............................. SilvestreDeSousa 3 74
(Mark Johnston) *hld up in last pair: rdn 3f out: wandered u.p and no prog: wl btn over 1f out* **5/1**[3]
2m 7.47s (-1.53) **Going Correction** -0.075s/f (Good) **8** Ran SP% **117.1**
Speed ratings (Par 105): **103,100,100,99,99 98,97,94**
CSF £7.50 CT £68.06 TOTE £3.40: £1.40, £1.30, £4.70; EX 8.40 Trifecta £72.50.
Owner Sohi & Sohi **Bred** Dr K Schulte **Trained** Portway, Worcs

FOCUS
Add 27yds. The winner improved to take this fair handicap by a clear margin. Again, near side in the straight. The second has been rated close to form.
T/Plt: £149.60 to a £1 stake. Pool: £75,840.46 - 369.92 winning units T/Qpdt: £80.10 to a £1 stake. Pool: £8,355.34 - 77.18 winning units **Jonathan Neesom**

4763 WOLVERHAMPTON (A.W) (L-H)
Monday, July 15

OFFICIAL GOING: Tapeta: standard
Wind: Light against Weather: Fine

4998 MYRACING.COM FOR WOLVERHAMPTON TIPS H'CAP 1m 5f 219y (Tp)
5:40 (5:42) (Class 6) (0-60,59) 3-Y-0
£2,781 (£827; £413; £300; £300; £300) **Stalls** Low

Form RPR
-232 **1** **Spargrove**[10] 4594 3-9-7 **59**.. DaneO'Neill 7 70+
(Hughie Morrison) *s.i.s: hld up: hdwy on outer over 4f out: chsd ldr over 1f out: rdn to ld and hung lft over 1f out: styd on wl* **6/4**[1]
5503 **2** 5 **No Thanks**[17] 4345 3-9-5 **57**.................................. DavidProbert 8 61
(William Jarvis) *chsd ldrs: led 4f out: rdn and hdd over 1f out: styd on same pce ins fnl f (vet said gelding had post-race heat stress)* **15/2**[3]
3541 **3** *¾* **Robeam (IRE)**[14] 4435 3-9-2 **54**.................................. TonyHamilton 11 57
(Richard Fahey) *prom: lost pl after 1f: hdwy over 5f out: rdn over 3f out: edgd lft over 1f out: styd on* **12/1**
-000 **4** *¾* **Antidote (IRE)**[21] 4179 3-9-6 **58**.................................. HarryBentley 5 60
(Richard Hughes) *hld up: nt clr run over 2f out: hdwy over 1f out: nt rch ldrs* **40/1**
0031 **5** *2* **Trouble Shooter (IRE)**[33] 3741 3-8-10 **48**..................(v) RaulDaSilva 2 47
(Shaun Keightley) *hld up: hdwy on outer over 1f out: nvr nrr (vet said gelding lost it's right fore-shoe)* **10/1**
-030 **6** *7* **New Expo (IRE)**[17] 4345 3-8-7 **45**.................................. ShelleyBirkett 9 34
(Julia Feilden) *sn led: hdd 4f out: rdn over 2f out: wknd over 1f out* **50/1**
4034 **7** *8* **Kalaya (IRE)**[29] 3886 3-9-4 **59**.................................. JaneElliott(3) 12 37
(Archie Watson) *s.i.s: rcvrd to chse ldr after 1f: rdn and ev ch over 2f out: wknd over 1f out* **25/1**
030 **8** *1 ¾* **Lady Elysia**[29] 3889 3-9-2 **57**.................................. MitchGodwin(3) 6 33
(Harry Dunlop) *hld up in tch: nt clr run and pushed along 4f out: rdn and hung lft fr over 2f out: sn wknd* **40/1**
0-03 **9** *1 ¼* **Amber Rock (USA)**[25] 4038 3-8-7 **45**.................................. BarryMcHugh 1 19
(Les Eyre) *s.i.s: sn rcvrd into mid-div: rdn over 3f out: wknd over 2f out* **40/1**
6000 **10** *2 ½* **Matilda Bay (IRE)**[16] 4372 3-8-10 **48**.................................. NicolaCurrie 10 18
(Jamie Osborne) *s.i.s: hld up: rdn over 3f out: sn wknd* **80/1**
0-44 **11** *7* **Percy's Prince**[6] 4769 3-9-2 **54**.................................. LukeMorris 4 15
(Sir Mark Prescott Bt) *chsd ldrs: drvn along over 4f out: wknd over 2f out: eased over 1f out (trainers' rep could offer no explanation for the poor performance other than the jockey's report stating that the gelding had no more to give)* **2/1**[2]
6600 **12** *3 ¼* **Darwin Dream**[16] 4400 3-9-4 **56**..............................(p) LiamKeniry 3 12
(Sophie Leech) *s.i.s: a in rr: rdn over 3f out: sn wknd* **50/1**
3m 4.0s (3.00) **Going Correction** 0.0s/f (Stan) **12** Ran SP% **118.2**
Speed ratings (Par 98): **102,99,98,98,97 93,88,87,86,85 81,79**
CSF £13.02 CT £102.69 TOTE £2.10: £1.10, £1.90, £3.00; EX 14.40 Trifecta £70.30.
Owner Selwood Bloodstock & Mrs S Read **Bred** Selwood Bloodstock & Mrs S Read **Trained** East Ilsley, Berks
■ Stewards' Enquiry : Luke Morris caution; careless riding

FOCUS
They went a fair pace and the lightly raced favourite scored in emphatic style in this staying handicap. The winner has been rated in line with the race standard, with the second in line with his latest and the third close to his winter AW form.

4999 MYRACING.COM FREE TIPS EVERY DAY NOVICE AUCTION STKS 6f 20y (Tp)
6:10 (6:15) (Class 5) 2-Y-0 **£3,428** (£1,020; £509; £254) **Stalls** Low

Form RPR
021 **1** **Milltown Star**[19] 4254 2-9-5 78.................................. CallumShepherd 7 85
(Mick Channon) *restless in stalls: chsd ldrs: wnt 2nd over 2f out: led wl over 1f out: rdn clr fnl f* **15/8**[2]
2 *4 ½* **Lilkian** 2-8-12 0.................................. JosephineGordon 3 64
(Shaun Keightley) *s.i.s: outpcd: hdwy over 1f out: r.o to go 2nd nr fin: no ch w wnr* **100/1**
3 *shd* **Portugueseprincess (IRE)** 2-8-11 0.................................. LukeMorris 8 62
(Archie Watson) *prom: sn pushed along: rdn to chse wnr over 1f out: edgd lft and no ex ins fnl f* **8/1**
034 **4** *4 ½* **Paddy Elliott (IRE)**[16] 4384 2-9-0 71.................................. HarryBentley 6 51
(Brian Ellison) *prom: rdn over 2f out: styd on same pce fr over 1f out* **6/4**[1]
5 **5** *2 ¾* **Parker's Boy**[19] 4254 2-8-12 0.................................. TrevorWhelan 10 40
(Brian Barr) *led 1f: chsd ldr tl over 2f out: rdn and swtchd rt over 1f out: sn wknd* **200/1**
6 **6** *nse* **Naseeb (IRE)**[12] 4516 2-8-12 0.................................. TonyHamilton 2 40
(Richard Fahey) *s.i.s: outpcd* **7/1**[3]
7 *2* **Force Of Impact (IRE)** 2-8-12 0.................................. JFEgan 1 34
(Paul George) *hdwy to ld 5f out: rdn and hdd wl over 1f out: sn edgd lft: wknd ins fnl f* **25/1**
50 **8** *1* **Chateau Peapod**[25] 4018 2-8-8 1 ow1.................................. BrettDoyle 9 26
(Lydia Pearce) *s.i.s: sn pushed along in rr: effrt on outer over 2f out: wknd wl over 1f out* **125/1**
00 **9** *8* **Samsar (IRE)**[14] 4433 2-9-4 0.................................. BarryMcHugh 4 11
(Adrian Nicholls) *chsd ldrs: rdn over 2f out: sn wknd* **66/1**
04 **10** *2 ½* **Max's Thunder (IRE)**[4] 4839 2-9-4 0.................................. NicolaCurrie 5 3
(Jamie Osborne) *s.i.s: outpcd (jockey said colt was never travelling)* **10/1**
1m 15.41s (0.91) **Going Correction** 0.0s/f (Stan) **10** Ran SP% **115.1**
Speed ratings (Par 94): **93,87,86,80,77 77,74,73,62,59**
CSF £188.10 TOTE £2.80: £1.10, £12.90, £1.90; EX 156.30 Trifecta £2340.20.
Owner Hunscote Stud Limited And Partner **Bred** Hunscote Stud **Trained** West Ilsley, Berks

FOCUS
They went a strong pace and the leading form contender defied a penalty with plenty in hand.

5000 FOLLOW @MYRACINGTIPS ON TWITTER H'CAP 6f 20y (Tp)
6:40 (6:40) (Class 4) (0-80,81) 3-Y-0+
£5,207 (£1,549; £774; £387; £300; £300) **Stalls** Low

Form RPR
0065 **1** **Wild Edric**[2] 4908 3-9-2 **76**.................................. RichardKingscote 1 88
(Tom Dascombe) *mde all: qcknd 2f out: rdn clr fnl f* **2/1**[1]
2344 **2** *4* **With Caution (IRE)**[11] 4560 3-9-2 **81**.................................. CierenFallon(5) 8 80
(James Tate) *hld up in tch: rdn over 1f out: r.o to go 2nd nr fin: no ch w wnr* **11/2**[2]
3-16 **3** *hd* **Busby (IRE)**[45] 3301 4-9-5 **78**..............................(p) SebastianWoods(5) 5 78
(Conrad Allen) *prom: hmpd 4f out: rdn ins fnl f: styd on same pce* **10/1**
2135 **4** *1* **Steelriver (IRE)**[39] 3492 9-9-11 **79**.................................. PhilDennis 4 75
(Michael Herrington) *chsd ldrs: lost pl 5f out: rdn over 1f out: r.o ins fnl f* **12/1**
1-00 **5** *shd* **Kamikaze Lord (USA)**[58] 2835 3-9-3 **77**.................................. DanielMuscutt 3 72
(John Butler) *s.i.s: sn pushed along and prom: edgd lft and chsd wnr 4f out: rdn and edgd rt over 1f out: no ex ins fnl f* **10/1**
4203 **6** *2* **Zapper Cass (FR)**[16] 4364 6-9-0 **73**..........................(v) TheodoreLadd(5) 6 63
(Michael Appleby) *s.i.s: in rr: rdn over 1f out: nt trble ldrs* **16/1**
-466 **7** *shd* **Born To Finish (IRE)**[48] 3188 6-9-8 **76**..........................(p w) HarryBentley 7 65
(Ed de Giles) *s.i.s: outpcd: nvr nrr* **22/1**
342- **8** *¾* **Black Friday**[279] 8077 4-9-5 **73**.................................. DavidProbert 9 60
(Karen McLintock) *chsd wnr 2f: remained handy: rdn over 2f out: wknd fnl f* **12/1**
1234 **9** *1* **Cappananty Con**[14] 4458 5-9-7 **75**.................................. JackMitchell 10 59
(Charlie Wallis) *broke wl: sn stdd and lost pl: n.d after* **9/1**[3]
5-01 **10** *5* **Mendoza (IRE)**[12] 4507 3-9-2 **76**..............................(h) LukeMorris 2 43
(James Eustace) *prom: pushed along and hmpd 4f out: rdn over 2f out: wknd and eased over 1f out* **10/1**
1m 13.62s (-0.88) **Going Correction** 0.0s/f (Stan)
WFA 3 from 4yo+ 6lb **10** Ran SP% **111.6**
Speed ratings (Par 105): **105,99,99,98,97 95,95,94,92,86**
CSF £11.67 CT £85.65 TOTE £2.20: £1.70, £1.40, £3.00; EX 12.90 Trifecta £111.00.
Owner D R Passant **Bred** D R Passant **Trained** Malpas, Cheshire
■ Stewards' Enquiry : Daniel Muscutt caution (reduced from three-day ban on appeal): careless riding

FOCUS
A gamble was landed in great style by the all-the-way winner in this sprint handicap. A step up on his 2yo efforts from the winner, while the second could be rated a length better through the second.

5001 VISIT THE BLACK COUNTRY CLASSIFIED CLAIMING STKS 1m 4f 51y (Tp)
7:10 (7:16) (Class 6) 3-Y-0+
£2,781 (£827; £413; £300; £300; £300) **Stalls** Low

Form RPR
0-00 **1** **Genuine Approval (IRE)**[18] 4287 6-9-3 55..............(t) AaronJones(3) 11 66
(John Butler) *chsd ldr tl shkn up to ld over 2f out: edgd lft and rdn clr fnl f (trainer said, regards apparent improvement in form, mare was suited by the reapplication of a tongue tie and appreciated a return to the Tapeta surface)* **40/1**
310- **2** *4 ½* **Carraigin Aonair (IRE)**[341] 5883 7-9-3 57.................................. JosephineGordon 3 56+
(Olly Murphy) *pushed along towards rr at times: hdwy on outer over 2f out: rdn and styd on to go 2nd nr fin: no ch w wnr* **25/1**
5632 **3** *½* **Lafilia (GER)**[3] 4869 4-9-4 58..............................(b) LukeMorris 6 56
(Archie Watson) *led: rdn and hdd over 2f out: no ex ins fnl f* **3/1**[1]
600 **4** *2 ¼* **Raashdy (IRE)**[66] 2595 6-9-0 54..............................(p) DaneO'Neill 4 48
(Peter Hiatt) *hld up in tch: wnt 3rd over 4f out: rdn over 2f out: styd on same pce fr over 1f out* **10/1**
6006 **5** *1 ¼* **Captain Scott (IRE)**[9] 4633 4-9-0 57..............................(v[1]) JaneElliott(3) 2 49
(Heather Main) *s.i.s and n.m.r s: hld up: rdn and hung rt over 1f out: styd on ins fnl f: nvr nrr* **4/1**[2]
00-6 **6** *3 ½* **Splash Around**[21] 4190 5-9-1 57..............................(b) DavidProbert 7 42
(Bernard Llewellyn) *hld up: rdn over 2f out: nvr nrr* **40/1**

6050 **7** 1/2 **Doctor Wonderful**[17] 4346 4-9-6 56..........................(p) DanielMuscutt 12 46
(Kevin Frost) *s.i.s: hld up: nt clr run over 2f out: n.d (jockey said gelding was never travelling. Trainer said gelding had a breathing problem)* **8/1**[3]

5060 **8** 5 **Betancourt (IRE)**[9] 4661 9-9-1 52..........................(p) LiamKeniry 5 33
(Stef Keniry) *sn prom: pushed along over 4f out: rdn and wknd over 2f out* **12/1**

-400 **9** 6 **Maiden Navigator**[14] 4447 3-8-5 55..........................(h) NicolaCurrie 8 26
(David Simcock) *s.i.s: hld up: racd keenly: nt clr run over 2f out: n.d (jockey said filly was denied a clear run approaching two furlongs out)* **16/1**

0056 **10** 31 **Spiritual Boy (IRE)**[12] 4518 3-8-5 50.......................... ShelleyBirkett 10
(David O'Meara) *chsd ldrs: rdn over 3f out: wknd over 2f out* **25/1**

306/ **11** 99 **Steccando (IRE)**[229] 8206 6-9-10 50..........................(t[1]) GeraldMosse 1
(Rebecca Menzies) *edgd rt s: hld up: hdwy over 5f out: rdn and wknd over 4f out: eased (vet said gelding was suffering from cardiac arrhythmia)* **25/1**

2m 41.5s (0.70) **Going Correction** 0.0s/f (Stan) **11 Ran SP% 95.2**
WFA 3 from 4yo+ 12lb
Speed ratings (Par 101): **97,94,93,92,91 89,88,85,81,60**
CSF £553.31 TOTE £38.70: £8.60, £5.20, £1.30; EX 220.50 Trifecta £993.40.Lafilia was subject of a friendly claim by Mr A. M. B. Watson for £6,000. Raashdy was claimed by Mrs Samantha England for £2,000.
Owner Madeira Racing **Bred** Rossenarra Bloodstock Limited **Trained** Newmarket, Suffolk
■ Fern Owl was withdrawn, price at time of withdrawal 9/2. Rule 4 applies to all bets. Deduction of 15p in the pound.

FOCUS
The winner forged clear under a prominent ride in this claimer and the hold-up performers couldn't get involved. Fern Owl was wearing incorrect headgear and had to be withdrawn. The winner has been rated in line with last year's C&D form.

5002 MYRACING.COM FOR DAILY TIPS H'CAP 7f 36y (Tp)
7:40 (7:45) (Class 5) (0-75,77) 3-Y-O
£3,428 (£1,020; £509; £300; £300; £300) **Stalls High**

Form RPR

2240 **1** **Assimilation (IRE)**[17] 4338 3-9-7 75.......................... LiamKeniry 2 83
(Ed Walker) *chsd ldrs: shkn up over 2f out: swtchd rt over 1f out: rdn and r.o to ld wl ins fnl f (trainers' rep said, regards apparent improvement in form, gelding appreciated the return to an all-weather surface, and the yard was now in better form)* **7/2**[2]

-004 **2** 1 3/4 **Excelled (IRE)**[12] 4507 3-9-7 75.......................... DanielMuscutt 4 78
(James Fanshawe) *a.p: chsd ldr over 3f out: shkn up whn rdr dropped whip wl over 1f out: sn led and edgd rt: hdd wl ins fnl f: styng on same pce whn edgd lft nr fin* **3/1**[1]

-405 **3** hd **Self Assessment (IRE)**[58] 2825 3-9-1 74..........................(w) HarrisonShaw(5) 6 76
(K R Burke) *prom: racd keenly: rdn and ev ch ins fnl f: styd on same pce towards fin* **9/1**

0050 **4** 1 1/2 **Barbarosa (IRE)**[18] 4288 3-8-9 63.......................... PhilDennis 7 61
(Michael Herrington) *s.i.s: hld up: rdn over 1f out: r.o ins fnl f: nt rch ldrs* **28/1**

0-20 **5** nk **Red Romance**[37] 3603 3-9-4 72.......................... HectorCrouch 5 70
(Clive Cox) *led: hdd over 4f out: remained handy: rdn and ev ch 1f out: no ex wl ins fnl f* **16/1**

4-60 **6** 3 1/2 **Reconnaissance**[20] 4225 3-8-10 64..........................(t[1]) LukeMorris 9 52
(Tom Clover) *hld up: rdn over 1f out: nt trble ldrs* **14/1**

203 **7** shd **Moveonup (IRE)**[20] 4218 3-8-9 68.......................... CierenFallon(5) 10 56
(Gay Kelleway) *s.i.s: hld up: effrt over 1f out: nt trble ldrs* **9/1**

0611 **8** 1 **Global Destination (IRE)**[20] 4218 3-9-5 73.......................... GeraldMosse 8 58
(Ed Dunlop) *s.i.s: sn prom: led over 4f out: rdn: edgd rt and hdd over 1f out: wknd ins fnl f (trainers' rep could offer no explanation for the poor performance other than the gelding's previous best runs has been on turf)* **13/2**[3]

0000 **9** 5 **Liberation Day**[11] 4552 3-9-5 73..........................(b[1]) RichardKingscote 3 45
(Tom Dascombe) *hld up in tch: rdn over 2f out: wknd over 1f out* **7/1**

550 **10** 4 **Constant**[30] 3868 3-9-9 77.......................... RobbieDowney 1 38
(David O'Meara) *sn pushed along in rr: rdn 1/2-way: wknd over 2f out* **20/1**

1m 28.73s (-0.07) **Going Correction** 0.0s/f (Stan) **10 Ran SP% 113.8**
Speed ratings (Par 100): **100,98,97,96,95 91,91,90,84,80**
CSF £14.02 CT £84.73 TOTE £4.70: £1.80, £1.20, £2.50; EX 15.90 Trifecta £71.80.
Owner Exors Of The Late S F Hui **Bred** Rathbarry Stud **Trained** Upper Lambourn, Berks

FOCUS
This was a race of changing fortunes and the winner swooped late to score with some authority. The fourth has been rated to his handicap best, and the fifth close to her maiden form.

5003 MYRACING.COM FREE BETS AND TIPS H'CAP 1m 142y (Tp)
8:10 (8:12) (Class 6) (0-60,60) 3-Y-O+
£2,781 (£827; £413; £300; £300; £300) **Stalls Low**

Form RPR

4442 **1** **Allux Boy (IRE)**[14] 4460 5-9-0 57..........................(p) FayeMcManoman(5) 3 69+
(Nigel Tinkler) *chsd ldrs: shkn up to ld over 1f out: wnt readily clr ins fnl f* **15/8**[1]

1000 **2** 6 **Caledonia Laird**[11] 4567 8-9-2 54..........................(e[1]) DanielMuscutt 4 53
(Gay Kelleway) *hld up: hdwy on outer over 1f out: rdn and r.o to go 2nd post: no ch w wnr* **33/1**

20/2 **3** shd **Pushaq (IRE)**[39] 3522 6-9-4 56..........................(t) RobbieDowney 2 55
(Anthony McCann, Ire) *led: rdn and hdd over 1f out: no ex ins fnl f* **11/4**[2]

0-00 **4** 1/2 **Gavi Di Gavi (IRE)**[18] 4305 4-9-7 59.......................... TomQueally 11 56
(Alan King) *s.i.s: hdwy on outer to chse ldr over 6f out: jnd ldr over 5f out: rdn and ev ch over 1f out: no ex ins fnl f* **40/1**

0502 **5** 1/2 **Sharp Operator**[6] 4753 6-8-12 55..........................(h) TheodoreLadd(5) 10 51
(Charlie Wallis) *hld up: hdwy over 3f out: rdn over 1f out: styd on same pce fnl f* **13/2**[3]

5050 **6** 3/4 **King Of Naples**[12] 4513 6-9-6 58..........................(h) JackGarritty 7 53
(Ruth Carr) *hld up: nt clr run wl over 1f out: shkn up and carried hd high sn after: swtchd lft ins fnl f: nt trble ldrs* **14/1**

6000 **7** 1/2 **Laqab (IRE)**[11] 4567 6-9-3 55.......................... AndrewElliott 12 49
(Derek Shaw) *s.s: in rr tl styd on ins fnl f: nvr nrr (enq held into running and riding the gelding which was held up in rear throughout before staying on in the home straight under a hands and heels ride to finish seventh of thirteen beaten 8 lengths. Jockey reported that his instructions were to switch th* **33/1**

-000 **8** nk **Ebbisham (IRE)**[40] 3473 6-9-5 57..........................(v) JimmyQuinn 8 50
(John Mackie) *hld up: rdn over 1f out: nvr on terms* **11/1**

4-00 **9** 1/2 **Dark Crocodile (IRE)**[21] 4194 4-9-8 60..........................(t) NicolaCurrie 9 52
(Seamus Durack) *dwlt: rdn over 3f out: no ch whn swtchd rt over 1f out* **40/1**

5-36 **10** 1 1/4 **Top Offer**[146] 792 10-8-11 54..........................(p) CierenFallon(5) 5 43
(Patrick Morris) *chsd ldrs: nt clr run and lost pl over 2f out: rdn over 1f out: wknd ins fnl f* **33/1**

3100 **11** 1/2 **Mans Not Trot (IRE)**[5] 4787 4-9-4 56..........................(p) TrevorWhelan 1 44
(Brian Barr) *chsd ldrs: rdn over 3f out: hung lft and wknd ins fnl f (jockey said gelding was never travelling)* **16/1**

0350 **12** 1 **Spiritual Star (IRE)**[13] 4479 10-9-6 58..........................(t) JFEgan 13 44
(Paul George) *s.i.s: hld up: hdwy on outer over 2f out: rdn over 1f out: sn hung lft and wknd* **20/1**

-000 **13** 2 1/2 **Mister Freeze (IRE)**[23] 4115 5-9-3 55..........................(vt) LiamKeniry 6 35
(Patrick Chamings) *hld up in tch: rdn over 2f out: wknd fnl f* **100/1**

1m 48.93s (-1.17) **Going Correction** 0.0s/f (Stan) **13 Ran SP% 115.1**
Speed ratings (Par 101): **105,99,99,99,98 98,97,97,96,95 95,94,92**
CSF £78.54 CT £171.91 TOTE £2.80: £1.40, £10.50, £1.90; EX 69.80 Trifecta £236.60.
Owner M Webb **Bred** Victor Stud Bloodstock Ltd **Trained** Langton, N Yorks

FOCUS
The favourite trounced his rivals in this handicap. The winner has been rated close to his old form.

5004 FOLLOW AT THE RACES ON TWITTER NOVICE MEDIAN AUCTION STKS 1m 1f 104y (Tp)
8:40 (8:40) (Class 6) 3-4-Y-O
£2,781 (£827; £413; £206) **Stalls Low**

Form RPR

3640 **1** **Al Daayen (FR)**[76] 2262 3-8-11 49.......................... JackMitchell 7 61+
(Conrad Allen) *mde all: qcknd 3f out: shkn up over 1f out: styd on wl: comf* **9/2**[3]

0-4 **2** 3 1/4 **Imajorblush**[10] 4608 3-9-2 0.......................... PhilDennis 5 59
(Philip Kirby) *chsd ldrs: rdn to chse wnr over 2f out: edgd lft ins fnl f: styd on same pce (vet said gelding finished lame on it's right fore)* **7/1**

3 4 1/2 **Waterfall** 3-8-11 0..........................(h[1]) DavidProbert 2 45
(Lucy Wadham) *prom: n.m.r and lost pl over 8f out: hdwy u.p over 1f out: styd on to go 3rd post* **4/1**[2]

05 **4** shd **Mousquetaire (FR)**[44] 3353 3-8-9 0..........................(h) Pierre-LouisJamin(7) 1 50
(David Menuisier) *chsd ldrs: nt clr run over 8f out: rdn over 2f out: styd on same pce fr over 1f out* **40/1**

5 hd **Uzincso** 3-9-2 0.......................... DanielMuscutt 3 49+
(John Butler) *s.i.s: hld up: rdn on outer over 2f out: r.o ins fnl f: nvr nrr* **6/1**

6 3 1/2 **Starkers** 3-8-11 0.......................... LukeMorris 8 37
(Tom Clover) *chsd ldrs: rdn over 2f out: wknd over 1f out* **5/2**[1]

03 **7** 3 1/4 **Mirabelle Plum (IRE)**[18] 4277 3-8-6 0.......................... HarrisonShaw(5) 6 30
(Robyn Brisland) *restless in stalls: sn prom: rdn and wknd over 2f out* **12/1**

0 **8** 1 1/2 **My Footsteps**[21] 4189 4-9-12 0.......................... TrevorWhelan 9 33
(Paul D'Arcy) *s.i.s: sn hld up in tch: rdn over 2f out: wknd wl over 1f out* **50/1**

0-0 **9** 9 **Angel Dundee**[139] 913 3-8-6 0.......................... TheodoreLadd(5) 10 8
(Michael Appleby) *s.i.s: rdn over 3f out: wknd over 2f out* **40/1**

6000 **10** 5 **Two Faced**[13] 4472 3-8-11 39.......................... BrettDoyle 11
(Lydia Pearce) *s.i.s: rcvrd to chse wnr over 8f out: rdn and lost 2nd over 2f out: wknd over 1f out* **80/1**

11 47 **Keep On Laughing (IRE)** 4-9-4..........................(h[1]) AaronJones(3) 4
(John Butler) *s.s: a in rr: rdn and wknd over 3f out* **16/1**

2m 1.59s (0.79) **Going Correction** 0.0s/f (Stan) **11 Ran SP% 115.2**
WFA 3 from 4yo 10lb
Speed ratings (Par 101): **96,93,89,89,88 85,82,81,73,69 27**
CSF £34.57 TOTE £3.70: £1.30, £1.60, £2.00; EX 35.50 Trifecta £144.50.
Owner Mohammed Bin Hamad Khalifa Al Attiya **Bred** Mme Atoinette Tamagni-Bodmer Et Al **Trained** Newmarket, Suffolk

FOCUS
Not many got involved in this weak novice event and it was won by an exposed type with an official rating of 49.
T/Jkpt: £10,790.50 to a £1 stake. Pool: £26,976.44 - 2.50 winning units T/Plt: £14.80 to a £1 stake. Pool: £77,483.93 - 3,811.18 winning units T/Qpdt: £5.00 to a £1 stake. Pool: £8,991.79 - 1,316.18 winning units **Colin Roberts**

5005 - 5008a (Foreign Racing) - See Raceform Interactive

ARGENTAN (R-H)
Sunday, June 30

OFFICIAL GOING: Turf: good to soft

5009a PRIX WINGS OF EAGLE (CONDITIONS) (AMATEUR RIDERS) (4YO) (TURF) 1m 2f 110y
1:00 4-Y-O
£7,207 (£2,882; £2,162; £1,441; £720)

RPR

1 **Five Ice Cubes (FR)**[35] 4-10-7 0.......................... MlleMeganePeslier(7) 4 79
(D Smaga, France)

2 4 **Forrest Gump (FR)**[144] 4-10-6 0..........................(b) Jean-DanielManceau(4) 3 68
(J-M Lefebvre, France)

3 1/2 **Saglyacat (FR)**[44] 4-10-7 0.......................... MrThibaudMace 1 64
(Noam Chevalier, France)

4 hd **Gendarme (IRE)**[5] 4209 4-10-2 0..........................(b) MissHannahWelch(8) 5 67
(Alexandra Dunn)

5 1/2 **Tranquil Storm (IRE)**[42] 4-9-11 0.......................... MlleCamilleColletVidal(7) 6 60
(Gavin Hernon, France)

6 5 **Ooby Douby (FR)**[150] 4-10-2 0.......................... MlleTracyMenuet(4) 2 53
(N Leenders, France)

2m 15.5s **6 Ran**
PARI-MUTUEL (all including 1 euro stake): WIN 1.90; PLACE 1.10, 5.50.
Owner Alain Michel Haddad **Bred** Alain Michel Haddad **Trained** Lamorlaye, France

4771 BATH (L-H)

Tuesday, July 16

OFFICIAL GOING: Firm (9.1)

Wind: virtually nil Weather: Warm

5010 HUMAN LEAGUE LIVE AT BATH NURSERY H'CAP 5f 10y

2:00 (2:00) (Class 5) (0-70,68) 2-Y-O

£3,428 (£1,020; £509; £300; £300; £300) **Stalls** Centre

Form RPR

104 **1** **Exclusive (IRE)**[22] 4191 2-9-7 **68**........................ OisinMurphy 1 72
(Archie Watson) *mde all: kpt on wl: rdn out* **2/1**[2]

055 **2** *1 1/2* **Prissy Missy (IRE)**[17] 4373 2-8-11 **58**........................ HollieDoyle 3 57
(David Loughnane) *chsd ldrs: rdn to chse wnr over 1f out: kpt on but nt pce to mount chal* **7/2**[3]

4443 **3** *3 1/4* **Beignet (IRE)**[15] 4448 2-9-3 **64**........................ SilvestreDeSousa 5 51+
(Richard Hannon) *stmbld leaving stalls: sn chsng ldrs: rdn 2f out: wnt 3rd ent fnl f: nt pce to get on terms (jockey said filly stumbled leaving the stalls)* **13/8**[1]

600 **4** *2* **Shaun's Delight (IRE)**[17] 4373 2-8-9 **56**........................ DavidProbert 6 36
(Ronald Harris) *chsd ldrs: rdn to dispute 2nd over 1f out tl ent fnl f: one pce after* **20/1**

0564 **5** *nk* **Come On Girl**[10] 4652 2-8-3 **50**........................ LukeMorris 2 29
(Tony Carroll) *prom: rdn 2f out: sn one pce* **12/1**

4016 **6** *6* **Show Me Heaven**[19] 4282 2-9-6 **67**........................(p) ShaneKelly 4 24
(Bill Turner) *s.i.s: sn struggling in last: nvr on terms* **14/1**

1m 1.68s (-0.32) **Going Correction** -0.25s/f (Firm) **6 Ran SP% 112.8**

Speed ratings (Par 94): **92,89,84,81,80 71**

CSF £9.54 TOTE £3.20: £1.20, £2.10; EX 8.50 Trifecta £17.40.

Owner Rabbah Racing **Bred** Azienda Agricola Gennaro Stimola **Trained** Upper Lambourn, W Berks

FOCUS

A pretty modest nursery, in which all six runners were debuting in handicap company. On quick ground, the time was just over a second outside the standard. The first two have been rated as improving.

5011 EMPIRE FIGHTING CHANCE MAIDEN AUCTION FILLIES' STKS 5f 10y

2:30 (2:30) (Class 6) 2-Y-O **£2,781** (£827; £413; £206) **Stalls** Centre

Form RPR

52 **1** **Requiems Dream (IRE)**[8] 4727 2-8-9 0........................ FrannyNorton 3 75+
(Mark Johnston) *mde all: wl in command over 1f out: eased towards fin* **1/3**[1]

2 *5* **Simply Susan (IRE)** 2-8-10 0........................ CharlesBishop 5 57+
(Eve Johnson Houghton) *s.i.s: last: hdwy 3f out: chsd wnr jst over 1f out but nvr gng pce to get on terms (jockey said filly was slowly away and ran greenly)* **9/4**[2]

0 **3** *3 3/4* **Jane Victoria**[21] 4221 2-8-9 0........................ HollieDoyle 2 42
(Adam West) *chsd ldrs: rdn to chse wnr 2f out tl jst over 1f out: no ex fnl f* **25/1**

00 **4** *2 3/4* **Hot Poppy**[20] 4233 2-8-12 0........................ ShaneKelly 4 35
(John Gallagher) *pressed wnr tl rdn over 2f out: sn hung lft: wknd ent fnl f* **50/1**

0 **5** *12* **Mayflower Lady (IRE)**[38] 3573 2-8-10 0........................ DavidProbert 1
(Ronald Harris) *sn outpcd: wknd over 1f out (jockey said filly hung left and right-handed. Trainer said filly would prefer a slower surface. Vet said filly lost it's right hind shoe)* **18/1**[3]

1m 1.3s (-0.70) **Going Correction** -0.25s/f (Firm) **5 Ran SP% 116.9**

Speed ratings (Par 89): **95,87,81,76,57**

CSF £1.58 TOTE £1.30: £1.10, £1.20; EX 1.60 Trifecta £5.40.

Owner Carl Chapman & Johnston Racing **Bred** Wansdyke Farms Ltd & Oghill House Stud **Trained** Middleham Moor, N Yorks

FOCUS

There was no depth to this and it proved easy for the favourite, who won in a time 0.38sec quicker than the preceding nursery.

5012 VALUE RATER RACING CLUB H'CAP (VALUE RATER RACING CLUB BATH SUMMER STAYERS' SERIES QUALIFIER) 1m 6f

3:00 (3:00) (Class 5) (0-75,76) 3-Y-O+

£3,428 (£1,020; £509; £300; £300; £300) **Stalls** High

Form RPR

0531 **1** **Mister Chiang**[15] 4443 3-9-1 **74**........................(b) FrannyNorton 2 82+
(Mark Johnston) *led for over 1f: trckd ldng pair: shkn up to chal 2f out: tk narrow advantage jst over 1f out: styd on: rdn out* **5/2**[1]

1332 **2** *3/4* **Victoriano (IRE)**[18] 4345 3-8-7 **66**........................(b) HollieDoyle 5 72
(Archie Watson) *sltly hmpd after 1f: trckd ldr: led 3f out: sn rdn: narrowly hdd jst over 1f out: ev ch ins fnl f: no ex nring fin* **5/2**[1]

6326 **3** *1* **Hermocrates (FR)**[12] 4547 3-8-8 **67**........................(b) SilvestreDeSousa 7 72
(Richard Hannon) *rousted along to ld after 1f: rdn and hdd 3f out: kpt chsng ldng pair fr over 1f out but a being hld (jockey said gelding was denied a clear run)* **3/1**[2]

64-5 **4** *9* **Done Deal (IRE)**[48] 3222 4-10-1 **76**........................ LukeMorris 6 66
(Sir Mark Prescott Bt) *hld up in last pair: pushed along on bnd over 4f out: rdn over 2f out: nt pce to get on terms (jockey said gelding slipped on the top bend)* **4/1**[3]

3104 **5** *5* **Gendarme (IRE)**[16] 5009 4-10-0 **75**........................(b) OisinMurphy 3 58
(Alexandra Dunn) *in tch: effrt 3f out: wknd over 1f out* **12/1**

06-0 **6** *17* **Lady Natasha (IRE)**[31] 3847 6-8-9 **56** oh11........................(t) KieranO'Neill 1 16
(James Grassick) *hld up: struggling 5f out: little imp: wknd 2f out* **150/1**

2m 59.71s (-6.39) **Going Correction** -0.25s/f (Firm)

WFA 3 from 4yo+ 12lb **6 Ran SP% 110.5**

Speed ratings (Par 103): **108,107,107,101,99 89**

CSF £8.74 TOTE £3.40: £1.80, £1.90; EX 8.30 Trifecta £17.70.

Owner The Originals **Bred** Miss K Rausing **Trained** Middleham Moor, N Yorks

FOCUS

A fair staying handicap in which the first three, all 3yos, finished clear. The time beat the record for the trip by almost a second. The third has been rated close to his previous run here.

5013 BEST FREE TIPS AT VALUERATER.CO.UK H'CAP (VALUE RATER RACING CLUB BATH SUMMER SPRINT SERIES QUALI 5f 10y

3:30 (3:30) (Class 5) (0-70,66) 3-Y-O+ **£3,428** (£1,020; £509; £300; £300) **Stalls** Centre

Form RPR

6501 **1** **Top Boy**[8] 4733 9-9-5 **64**........................ DarraghKeenan(5) 5 72+
(Tony Carroll) *hld up 5th: shkn up over 2f out: hdwy wl over 1f out: led ent fnl f: r.o* **5/6**[1]

5656 **2** *3/4* **La Fortuna**[20] 4253 6-9-12 **66**........................(t) RichardKingscote 4 71
(Charlie Wallis) *chsd ldrs: rdn 2f out: ev ch ent fnl f: kpt on but nt quite pce of wnr* **8/1**

0211 **3** *2* **Thegreyvtrain**[6] 4772 3-9-4 **62** 6ex........................ KieranO'Neill 3 59
(Ronald Harris) *led: rdn 2f out: hdd ent fnl f: no ex* **4/1**[2]

3030 **4** *1 3/4* **Powerful Dream (IRE)**[13] 4495 6-9-10 **64**........................(p) DavidProbert 1 56
(Ronald Harris) *little slowly away: sn trcking ldrs: rdn over 2f out: kpt on but nt quite pce to chal* **9/2**[3]

-005 **5** *6* **Silverrica (IRE)**[17] 4374 9-9-9 **63**........................(t) FergusSweeney 6 33
(Malcolm Saunders) *prom: trckd ldr: rdn and ev ch wl over 1f out: wknd ent fnl f* **16/1**

1m 0.89s (-1.11) **Going Correction** -0.25s/f (Firm)

WFA 3 from 6yo+ 4lb **5 Ran SP% 109.7**

Speed ratings (Par 103): **98,96,93,90,81**

CSF £8.10 TOTE £1.60: £1.10, £3.60; EX 7.60 Trifecta £20.30.

Owner D Allen **Bred** Mrs C R Philipson & Mrs H G Lascelle **Trained** Cropthorne, Worcs

FOCUS

The first two came from the rear in this modest handicap. The second has been rated to her turf best.

5014 SKY SPORTS RACING VIRGIN 535 H'CAP 5f 10y

4:00 (4:02) (Class 3) (0-90,90) 3-Y-O **£7,470** (£2,236; £1,118; £559; £279) **Stalls** Centre

Form RPR

3542 **1** **Tinto**[11] 4609 3-8-13 **82**........................ JasonWatson 2 92
(Amanda Perrett) *little slowly away: outpcd in last over 3f out: hdwy 2f out: drifted lft but chal jst ins fnl f: r.o to ld cl home* **15/8**[1]

3114 **2** *shd* **Wise Words**[31] 3855 3-9-7 **90**........................ OisinMurphy 1 99
(James Tate) *prom: rdn to ld over 1f out: kpt on: hdd cl home* **7/2**[3]

6013 **3** *6* **Wedding Date**[8] 4736 3-9-7 **90**........................ SilvestreDeSousa 3 77
(Richard Hannon) *prom: led 3f out: rdn and hdd over 1f out: no ex fnl f* **9/4**[2]

050- **4** *1 1/2* **Glory Fighter**[325] 6551 3-9-6 **89**........................ GeraldMosse 4 71
(Charles Hills) *prom: rdn and ev ch 2f out: hld over 1f out: fdd ins fnl f* **5/1**

0-00 **5** *7* **Country Rose (IRE)**[17] 4374 3-8-3 **72**........................ KieranO'Neill 5 28
(Ronald Harris) *unsettled stalls but smartly away: kpt wd: led for 2f: rdn over 2f out: wknd over 1f out* **25/1**

1m 0.25s (-1.75) **Going Correction** -0.25s/f (Firm) **5 Ran SP% 108.3**

Speed ratings (Par 104): **104,103,94,91,80**

CSF £8.41 TOTE £2.30: £1.10, £1.80; EX 7.70 Trifecta £15.40.

Owner D James, S Jenkins & M Quigley **Bred** Llety Farms **Trained** Pulborough, W Sussex

FOCUS

A decent little sprint and the fastest of the four races over the trip. As in the previous C&D event, the principals came from the back, and they finished clear. The winner has been rated in line with the better view of his form.

5015 SKY SPORTS RACING SKY 415 FILLIES' H'CAP 5f 160y

4:30 (4:30) (Class 4) (0-80,82) 3-Y-O+ **£5,207** (£1,549; £774; £387) **Stalls** Centre

Form RPR

2451 **1** **Heritage**[13] 4496 3-9-5 **82**........................(p) LiamKeniry 4 91
(Clive Cox) *led after 1f: clr 2f out: sn rdn: r.o wl* **1/1**[1]

-024 **2** *2 3/4* **More Than Likely**[16] 4422 3-9-2 **79**........................ ShaneKelly 3 79
(Richard Hughes) *led for over 1f: chsd wnr tl 3f out: sn rdn: rallied bk into 2nd ent fnl f but nt pce to get bk on terms* **8/1**

203 **3** *1* **Peace Dreamer (IRE)**[13] 4495 5-8-12 **75**........................ DylanHogan(5) 2 73
(Robert Cowell) *little slowly away: trckd ldrs: wnt 2nd 3f out: sn rdn: nt pce to chal: no ex ent fnl f* **4/1**[3]

-453 **4** *3 1/2* **Restless Rose**[18] 4340 4-9-6 **78**........................ OisinMurphy 1 64
(Stuart Williams) *trckd ldrs: rdn 2f out: wknd ent fnl f* **5/2**[2]

1m 8.89s (-2.21) **Going Correction** -0.25s/f (Firm)

WFA 3 from 4yo+ 5lb **4 Ran SP% 109.7**

Speed ratings (Par 102): **104,100,99,94**

CSF £8.93 TOTE £1.60; EX 7.90 Trifecta £15.00.

Owner Cheveley Park Stud **Bred** Cheveley Park Stud Ltd **Trained** Lambourn, Berks

FOCUS

Fair fillies' form, and another time that dipped inside the standard. The second has been rated to her latest for now.

5016 FESTIVAL OF LEGENDS LIVE AT BATH H'CAP 1m

5:00 (5:01) (Class 6) (0-60,62) 3-Y-O+

£2,781 (£827; £413; £300; £300; £300) **Stalls** Low

Form RPR

1416 **1** **Imperial Act**[39] 3533 4-9-3 **59**........................ WilliamCarver(7) 5 68
(Andrew Balding) *in tch: hdwy over 2f out: led over 1f out: r.o strly fnl f: rdn out* **5/1**[3]

0520 **2** *1 1/4* **Red Gunner**[18] 4349 5-9-3 **52**........................ RichardKingscote 8 58
(Mark Loughnane) *hld up: swtchd to centre and hdwy fr over 2f out: sn rdn: kpt on to go 2nd ins fnl f but nt pce to rch wnr* **3/1**[2]

0054 **3** *1/2* **Sea Tea Dea**[45] 3352 5-8-10 **46** oh1........................ HollieDoyle 6 50
(Adrian Wintle) *in tch: hdwy over 2f out: rdn to chse wnr ent fnl f: kpt on same pce fnl 120yds* **25/1**

00-4 **4** *1 1/2* **The Game Is On**[49] 3208 3-9-3 **60**........................ LukeMorris 4 62+
(Sir Mark Prescott Bt) *led tl 3f out: sn rdn: hld over 1f out: kpt on to regain 4th cl home but nt pce to get bk involved* **5/2**[1]

0403 **5** *hd* **Bonny Blue**[13] 4496 3-8-12 **55**........................ OisinMurphy 7 54
(Rod Millman) *trckd ldr: led 3f out tl rdn over 1f out: fdd fnl 120yds: lost 4th cl home (jockey said filly hung badly left-handed)* **12/1**

6000 **6** *nse* **Ramblow**[53] 3038 6-8-3 **46** oh1........................(vt) AmeliaGlass(7) 3 46
(Alexandra Dunn) *trckd ldrs: rdn whn short for room over 1f out: kpt on same pce fnl 120yds* **50/1**

3-36 **7** *1 3/4* **Johni Boxit**[55] 2975 4-9-7 **59**........................(p) MeganNicholls(3) 9 56
(Brian Barr) *racd keenly: in tch: trckd ldrs after 3f: rdn 2f out: wknd ins fnl f* **10/1**

0126 **8** *1 3/4* **King Oswald (USA)**[18] 4349 6-9-6 **55**........................(tp) DavidProbert 2 48
(James Unett) *hld up: hdwy but nt clr run over 1f out: sn rdn: fdd ins fnl f (jockey said gelding suffered interference in running approaching the final furlong)* **5/1**[3]

0300 **9** *10* **The British Lion (IRE)**[28] 3967 4-9-13 **62**........................ LiamKeniry 10 32
(Alexandra Dunn) *a towards rr* **20/1**

1m 41.38s (-0.32) **Going Correction** -0.25s/f (Firm)

WFA 3 from 4yo+ 8lb **9 Ran SP% 114.3**

Speed ratings (Par 101): **91,89,89,87,87 87,85,84,74**

CSF £19.72 CT £338.22 TOTE £5.30: £2.00, £1.30, £4.50; EX 18.50 Trifecta £160.50.

Owner A M Balding **Bred** The Victrix Ludorum Partnership **Trained** Kingsclere, Hants

FOCUS

They went what appeared to be a steady pace in this modest handicap. It's been rated at face value for now, with the second and third to their recent form.

T/Plt: £19.40 to a £1 stake. Pool: £63,581.13 - 2,390.38 winning units T/Qpdt: £6.10 to a £1 stake. Pool: £5,698.31 - 681.06 winning units **Tim Mitchell**

4623 **BEVERLEY** (R-H)

Tuesday, July 16

OFFICIAL GOING: Good to firm (watered; 7.6)

Wind: Light against Weather: Cloudy with sunny periods

5017 RACING TV EBF NOVICE AUCTION STKS — 5f

1:45 (1:46) (Class 5) 2-Y-O — £4,140 (£1,232; £615; £307) Stalls Low

Form — RPR

05 **1** **Singe Anglais (IRE)**[13] 4516 2-9-0 0 .... FayeMcManoman(5) 3 — 59+
(Nigel Tinkler) *trckd ldng pair on inner: effrt and nt clr run over 1f out: sn swtchd lft: rdn to chse ldr ins fnl f: kpt on to ld last 100yds* **1/2**[1]

00 **2** ½ **Chocoholic**[24] 4125 2-9-3 0 .... GrahamLee 4 — 55
(Bryan Smart) *led: pushed along and clr over 1f out: rdn ent fnl f: hdd and no ex last 100yds* **16/1**

040 **3** ½ **Not Another Word**[25] 4075 2-8-10 43 .... AndrewMullen 1 — 46
(Nigel Tinkler) *pushed along and in rr: rdn along and hdwy 1/2-way: swtchd to inner and chsd ldrs ent fnl f: sn drvn and kpt on* **8/1**[3]

5 **4** ¾ **Zakher Alain**[10] 4631 2-9-3 0 .... ConnorBeasley 2 — 51
(Adrian Nicholls) *dwlt: t.k.h and sn chsng ldrs: rdn along wl over 1f out: kpt on fnl f* **18/1**

00 **5** 3 **The Works (IRE)**[13] 4516 2-9-0 0 .... PaulHanagan 6 — 37
(Declan Carroll) *trckd ldr: pushed along 2f out: rdn over 1f out: drvn and wknd fnl f* **7/1**[2]

6 10 **Blue Lyte** 2-8-7 0 .... RowanScott(3) 5
(Nigel Tinkler) *chsd ldrs: rdn along over 2f out: sn wknd* **11/1**

1m 5.3s (2.40) **Going Correction** +0.075s/f (Good) — **6 Ran SP% 109.8**
Speed ratings (Par 94): **83,82,81,80,75 59**
CSF £9.59 TOTE £1.40: £1.10, £4.40; EX 8.00 Trifecta £28.10.
Owner Geoff Maidment & John Raybould **Bred** Knocktartan House Stud **Trained** Langton, N Yorks

FOCUS
The inside rail from 3.5f out to 1.5f out was moved out, add 1yd to this race distance. The ground had been watered and it was a warm, dry day. This was a weak race, even for a novice auction.

5018 MALCOLM GREENSLADE DONCASTER LVA STALWART MEMORIAL H'CAP — 5f

2:15 (2:18) (Class 6) (0-60,60) 3-Y-O+ — £3,363 (£1,001; £500; £300; £300; £300) Stalls Low

Form — RPR

6100 **1** **Oriental Splendour (IRE)**[9] 4694 7-8-12 48 ....(b[1]) JamesSullivan 6 — 55
(Ruth Carr) *sltly hmpd s and in rr: hdwy 2f out: sn n.m.r: rdn and hdwy over 1f out: chsd ldrs ent fnl f: sn drvn and kpt on wl to ld nr fin* **20/1**

3045 **2** nse **Atyaaf**[19] 4307 4-9-2 52 .... AndrewElliott 5 — 59
(Derek Shaw) *pushed along and in tch: hdwy over 1f out: sn rdn: drvn to chal ins fnl f: led fnl 40yds: hdd nr line* **6/1**[3]

5300 **3** ¾ **Seamster**[19] 4307 12-9-3 56 ....(t) CameronNoble(3) 7 — 60
(David Loughnane) *led: rdn along wl over 1f out: drvn ent fnl f: hdd and no ex fnl 40yds* **22/1**

0025 **4** nk **Mr Greenlight**[9] 4694 4-9-8 58 .... DavidAllan 1 — 61
(Tim Easterby) *trckd ldrs: hdwy 2f out: rdn to chse ldr over 1f out: drvn and ev ch ins fnl f: kpt on same pce* **2/1**[1]

4516 **5** ¾ **Hello Girl**[8] 4720 4-9-1 54 .... RowanScott(3) 2 — 54
(Nigel Tinkler) *towards rr: rdn along on inner and n.m.r over 2f out: drvn to chse ldrs ent fnl f: kpt on* **11/4**[2]

406- **6** ½ **Tick Tock Croc (IRE)**[274] 8261 3-8-8 55 ....(h[1]) HarryRussell(7) 13 — 53
(Bryan Smart) *t.k.h: towards rr: hdwy wl over 2f out: rdn to chse ldrs and edgd rt 1 1/2f out: sn drvn and edgd lft ent fnl f: kpt on* **50/1**

430- **7** nk **Moonlit Sands (IRE)**[298] 7498 4-9-7 57 .... CamHardie 14 — 54
(Brian Ellison) *bhd: swtchd lft to outer and hdwy wl over 1f out: rdn and styng on whn sltly hmpd ent fnl f: kpt on u.p towards fin* **50/1**

0600 **8** shd **One Boy (IRE)**[24] 4132 8-9-1 51 .... KevinStott 3 — 48+
(Paul Midgley) *towards rr: hdwy over 2f out: n.m.r and swtchd lft over 1f out: sn rdn and sltly hmpd ent fnl f: kpt on* **16/1**

0006 **9** ½ **Twentysvnthlancers**[11] 4586 6-9-3 53 .... GrahamLee 4 — 48
(Paul Midgley) *hld up towards rr: hdwy 2f out: rdn and n.m.r over 1f out: no imp fnl f* **10/1**

3000 **10** 3¾ **Encoded (IRE)**[11] 4586 6-8-10 46 .... JoeFanning 11 — 28
(Lynn Siddall) *dwlt and bhd tl sme late hdwy* **66/1**

3210 **11** nk **Cuppacoco**[11] 4586 4-9-7 57 .... JackGarritty 8 — 38
(Ann Duffield) *cl up: rdn along wl over 1f out: sn drvn and wknd* **14/1**

5310 **12** 1¼ **Groundworker (IRE)**[24] 4132 8-9-3 53 .... DavidNolan 9 — 29
(Paul Midgley) *chsd ldrs: rdn along wl over 1f out: sn drvn and wknd appr fnl f* **16/1**

2520 **13** 1¼ **Pearl Noir**[11] 4586 9-9-4 54 ....(b) PJMcDonald 12 — 26
(Scott Dixon) *chsd ldrs: rdn along 2f out: sn wknd* **33/1**

06- **14** 3¼ **Savannah Beau**[348] 5660 7-8-11 52 .... TheodoreLadd(5) 10 — 12
(Scott Dixon) *midfield: effrt whn n.m.r 2f out: sn swtchd rt and rdn: sn wknd* **16/1**

1m 3.61s (0.71) **Going Correction** +0.075s/f (Good) — **14 Ran SP% 125.2**
WFA 3 from 4yo+ 4lb
Speed ratings (Par 101): **97,96,95,95,94 93,92,92,91,85 85,83,81,76**
CSF £135.02 CT £2719.23 TOTE £21.70: £4.30, £2.30, £7.30; EX 194.10 Trifecta £3776.80.
Owner J A Swinburne & Mrs Ruth A Carr **Bred** H R H Sultan Ahmad Shah **Trained** Huby, N Yorks

FOCUS
Add 1yd. The three non-runners were drawn 15-16-17, and the first five finishers were drawn 6-5-7-1-2. The second has been rated close to his AW best, and the fourth in line with his C&D run earlier this month.

5019 133RD YEAR OF THE WATT MEMORIAL H'CAP — 2m 32y

2:45 (2:45) (Class 4) (0-85,82) 3-Y-O+ — £6,474 (£1,938; £969) Stalls Low

Form — RPR

3432 **1** **Rochester House (IRE)**[18] 4327 3-9-2 82 .... JoeFanning 6 — 91
(Mark Johnston) *mde all: pushed along over 2f out: clr wl over 1f out: unchal* **30/100**[1]

4-44 **2** 8 **Snookered (IRE)**[17] 4383 5-9-7 72 ....(p) DanielTudhope 5 — 75
(Brian Ellison) *hld up: hdwy to trck wnr 3f out: pushed along 2f out: sn rdn: kpt on same pce* **4/1**[2]

5663 **3** 45 **Flower Power**[11] 4601 8-8-11 62 ....(p) JasonHart 4 — 7
(Tony Coyle) *trckd wnr: pushed along 4f out: rdn 3f out: sn outpcd and bhd* **8/1**[3]

3m 36.47s (-1.43) **Going Correction** +0.075s/f (Good) — **3 Ran SP% 108.0**
WFA 3 from 4yo+ 15lb
Speed ratings (Par 105): **106,102,79**
CSF £1.88 TOTE £1.20; EX 1.60 Trifecta £2.00.
Owner John Brown & Megan Dennis **Bred** Stall Ullmann **Trained** Middleham Moor, N Yorks

FOCUS
Add 2yds. A desperately uncompetitive race.

5020 ANN EVES BIRTHDAY H'CAP (DIV I) — 7f 96y

3:15 (3:15) (Class 5) (0-70,72) 3-Y-O+ — £4,284 (£1,282; £641; £320; £300; £300) Stalls Low

Form — RPR

4040 **1** **Twin Appeal (IRE)**[8] 4728 8-10-0 72 .... GemmaTutty(3) 8 — 81
(Karen Tutty) *bhd: hdwy over 2f out: swtchd rt to inner 2f out: rdn to chal over 1f out: kpt on to ld last 50yds* **7/2**[2]

3324 **2** ½ **Atletico (IRE)**[13] 4523 7-9-10 65 ....(v) PJMcDonald 2 — 72
(David Evans) *in tch: hdwy 2 1/2f out: n.m.r and swtchd lft wl over 1f out: rdn to chal ent fnl f: led last 100yds: sn drvn: hdd and no ex fnl 50yds* **2/1**[1]

2403 **3** 3 **Dandy Highwayman (IRE)**[13] 4523 5-9-1 63 ....(tp) HarryRussell(7) 11 — 62
(Ollie Pears) *trckd ldrs: hdwy on wd outside over 2f out: rdn to ld wl over 1f out: jnd and drvn 1f out: hdd ins fnl f: kpt on same pce fnl 100yds* **12/1**

-000 **4** 1¼ **Pickett's Charge**[18] 4329 6-10-0 69 ....(p) CamHardie 9 — 65
(Brian Ellison) *chsd ldr: rdn along 2f out: ev ch and drvn over 1f out: kpt on same pce fnl f* **20/1**

5553 **5** ¾ **Dominannie (IRE)**[11] 4584 6-8-9 50 oh4 .... AndrewMullen 7 — 44
(Ron Barr) *dwlt and hld up towards rr: hdwy over 2f out: rdn to chse ldrs over 1f out: sn drvn and no imp fnl f* **16/1**

0001 **6** 1½ **Primeiro Boy (IRE)**[15] 4454 3-9-3 65 .... PaulHanagan 1 — 52
(Richard Fahey) *in tch on inner: rdn along 2f out: ev ch over 1f out: sn drvn and kpt on same pce* **10/1**

0400 **7** ½ **Bob's Girl**[10] 4633 4-8-9 50 oh5 ....(b) JimmyQuinn 5 — 39
(Michael Mullineaux) *in rr: sme hdwy and n.m.r wl over 1f out: sn drvn and n.d (jockey said filly ran too keenly)* **50/1**

6600 **8** 1¾ **Fake News**[29] 3922 4-9-8 63 ....(b) JasonHart 10 — 47
(David Barron) *led: rdn along over 2f out: drvn and hdd over 1f out: sn wknd* **12/1**

0-44 **9** 2¾ **Golden Guest**[109] 1392 5-9-10 65 .... DanielTudhope 4 — 42
(Les Eyre) *in tch: hdwy towards outer over 2f out: rdn to chse ldrs over 1f out: sn drvn and btn* **7/1**[3]

-030 **10** 4 **Abie's Hollow**[25] 4080 3-9-0 62 .... DougieCostello 3 — 26
(Tony Coyle) *trckd ldr: cl up 1/2-way: rdn along wl over 2f out: sn wknd* **25/1**

36-0 **11** 11 **Mango Chutney**[20] 4239 6-10-2 71 ....(p) SamJames 6 — 9
(John Davies) *a in rr (vet said gelding was lame left hind)* **9/1**

1m 32.23s (-0.37) **Going Correction** +0.075s/f (Good) — **11 Ran SP% 119.0**
WFA 3 from 4yo+ 7lb
Speed ratings (Par 103): **105,104,101,99,98 97,96,94,91,86 74**
CSF £10.76 CT £77.10 TOTE £4.80: £2.20, £1.10, £3.10; EX 12.10 Trifecta £136.10.
Owner Mrs Mary Winetroube & Thoroughbred Homes **Bred** Glashare House Stud **Trained** Osmotherley, N Yorks

FOCUS
Add 1yd. The pace was contested, and fast enough for the winner to come from last. The winner has been rated close to last year's C&D win, while the second helps set the level to his recent form.

5021 ANN EVES BIRTHDAY H'CAP (DIV II) — 7f 96y

3:45 (3:45) (Class 5) (0-70,72) 3-Y-O+ — £4,284 (£1,282; £641; £320; £300; £300) Stalls Low

Form — RPR

6153 **1** **Ollivander (IRE)**[11] 4585 3-9-7 70 ....(v) DanielTudhope 10 — 74
(David O'Meara) *trckd ldr: led over 2f out: rdn along over 1f out: drvn ins fnl f: rdr dropped rein briefly: kpt on wl towards fin* **5/2**[1]

000 **2** 1 **Kodiline (IRE)**[48] 3215 5-9-8 64 .... PJMcDonald 2 — 68
(David Evans) *hld up in tch: hdwy over 2f out: rdn to chse ldrs over 1f out: squeezed through to chse wnr ins fnl f: sn drvn and kpt on* **6/1**[2]

0005 **3** nk **Parion**[11] 4584 3-8-2 51 .... RoystonFfrench 7 — 51
(Richard Fahey) *hld up towards rr: stdy hdwy 3f out: chsd ldrs on outer wl over 1f out: rdn and ev ch ent fnl f: sn drvn and kpt on* **6/1**[2]

0000 **4** 1 **Relight My Fire**[13] 4512 9-8-13 55 ....(b) DavidAllan 4 — 55
(Tim Easterby) *trckd ldrs on inner: hdwy over 2f out: rdn along wl over 1f out: kpt on u.p fnl f* **13/2**[3]

5550 **5** nk **Explain**[13] 4523 7-9-9 65 ....(b) JamesSullivan 3 — 65
(Ruth Carr) *trckd ldrs: hdwy 3f out: chsd wnr wl over 1f out: rdn and ev ch ent fnl f: sn drvn and no ex* **15/2**

0003 **6** 1¼ **Global Exceed**[35] 3704 4-9-3 62 ....(t) GemmaTutty(3) 1 — 61+
(Karen Tutty) *hld up in rr: hdwy and swtchd rt to inner 2f out: sn nt clr run and hmpd over 1f out: wknd after (jockey said gelding was denied a clear run approaching the final furlong)* **8/1**

6512 **7** ¾ **Thornaby Nash**[13] 4523 8-9-9 68 ....(b) ConorMcGovern(3) 9 — 62
(Jason Ward) *dwlt: hld up: a in rr* **7/1**

/000 **8** 4 **Echo Of Lightning**[4] 4875 9-9-11 72 ....(p) PaulaMuir(5) 6 — 55
(Roger Fell) *led: rdn along 3f out: hdd over 2f out: drvn and edgd rt 1 1/2f out: wknd* **14/1**

1m 32.38s (-0.22) **Going Correction** +0.075s/f (Good) — **8 Ran SP% 112.5**
WFA 3 from 4yo+ 7lb
Speed ratings (Par 103): **104,102,102,101,101 99,98,94**
CSF £16.92 CT £79.67 TOTE £3.30: £1.20, £1.90, £1.90; EX 19.50 Trifecta £114.00.
Owner York Thoroughbred Racing **Bred** Canice Farrell **Trained** Upper Helmsley, N Yorks

FOCUS
Add 1yd. The second leg of a modest handicap, but an unexposed winner of this one. The second has been rated to his turf best, and the third close to her recent best.

5022 IRISHBIGRACETRENDS.COM H'CAP — 1m 100y

4:15 (4:17) (Class 4) (0-80,78) 3-Y-O+ — £5,418 (£1,621; £810; £405) Stalls Low

Form — RPR

5045 **1** **How Bizarre**[8] 4728 4-9-3 68 .... DanielTudhope 2 — 74
(Liam Bailey) *led: pushed along over 2f out: rdn over 1f out: drvn ins fnl f: hdd narrowly towards fin: rallied gamely to ld on line* **5/2**[2]

5045 **2** shd **Welcoming (FR)**[9] 4693 3-9-4 77 .... JoeFanning 3 — 81
(Mark Johnston) *trckd wnr: hdwy over 2f out: rdn over 1f out: drvn to chal ins fnl f: kpt on to take narrow ld towards fin: no ex and hdd on line* **10/3**[3]

2052 **3** *2* **Ghayyar (IRE)**[10] 4634 5-9-6 **71**..............................(tp) RachelRichardson 5 72
(Tim Easterby) *trckd ldng pair: hdwy over 2f out: rdn along wl over 1f out: drvn appr fnl f: kpt on same pce* **2/1**[1]

0-00 **4** *7* **Dream Walker (FR)**[20] 4240 10-9-13 **78**..............................(p) DavidAllan 1 63
(Brian Ellison) *hld up in rr: sme hdwy on inner 3f out: rdn along 2f out: sn outpcd* **7/1**

1m 45.43s (-0.97) **Going Correction** +0.075s/f (Good)
WFA 3 from 4yo+ 8lb **4 Ran SP% 97.5**
Speed ratings (Par 105): **107,106,104,97**
CSF £8.49 TOTE £3.20; EX 7.10 Trifecta £12.10.
Owner Harswell Thoroughbred Racing, Fpr Ltd **Bred** Mrs Janis Macpherson **Trained** Middleham, N Yorks
■ Joe The Beau was withdrawn. Price at time of withdrawal 6/1. Rule 4 applies to all bets - deduction 10p in the pound

FOCUS
Add 1yd. A small-field ordinary handicap in which the running order barely changed. A small pb from the second, with the winner rated to this year's form.

5023 RACING AGAIN NEXT MONDAY EVENING H'CAP 1m 1f 207y
4:45 (4:47) (Class 6) (0-65,66) 3-Y-O
£3,234 (£962; £481; £300; £300; £300) **Stalls Low**

Form RPR

0021 **1** **Langholm (IRE)**[21] 4210 3-8-13 **57**..............................(t) PaulHanagan 1 64
(Declan Carroll) *mde all: rdn wl over 1f out: drvn ins fnl f: kpt on wl towards fin* **11/4**[2]

0334 **2** *1* **Brutalab**[14] 4487 3-8-7 **51**.............................. PhilDennis 3 56
(Tim Easterby) *trckd ldng pair on inner: hdwy 3f out: chsd wnr over 2f out: rdn wl over 1f out: drvn ent fnl f: kpt on* **6/1**[3]

0431 **3** *1 1/2* **Northern Lyte**[10] 4628 3-9-3 **66**.............................. FayeMcManoman(5) 4 68
(Nigel Tinkler) *in tch: hdwy on inner 3f out: rdn along to chse ldrs 2f out: drvn to chse ldng pair ins fnl f: no imp* **2/1**[1]

11-4 **4** *1 1/4* **Melgate Majeure**[47] 3271 3-9-1 **59**.............................. JamesSullivan 10 58+
(Michael Easterby) *hld up: hdwy over 3f out: rdn along 2f out: sn chsng ldrs: drvn and kpt on fnl f: nrst fin* **25/1**

645 **5** *1 3/4* **Cuba Ruba**[21] 4211 3-9-2 **60**.............................. DavidAllan 6 56
(Tim Easterby) *chsd ldrs: pushed along over 4f out: rdn along 3f out: kpt on same pce fnl 2f* **20/1**

4265 **6** *3/4* **Smeaton (IRE)**[10] 4664 3-9-5 **63**.............................. DanielTudhope 2 57
(Roger Fell) *trckd wnr: pushed along over 2f out: rdn wl over 1f out: sn wknd* **7/1**

4666 **7** *1/2* **George Mallory**[29] 3926 3-9-7 **65**.............................. TomEaves 8 58
(Kevin Ryan) *dwlt and towards rr: hdwy wl over 2f out: rdn wl over 1f out: plugged on: n.d* **7/1**

-000 **8** *2 1/4* **Seven For A Pound (USA)**[21] 4210 3-8-12 **56**.............................. TonyHamilton 7 45
(Richard Fahey) *midfield: rdn along over 3f out: sn drvn and n.d* **28/1**

0033 **9** *2 1/2* **Slaithwaite (IRE)**[27] 4005 3-8-3 **52**..............................(p) PaulaMuir(5) 5 36
(Roger Fell) *a towards rr* **16/1**

6000 **10** *14* **Lethal Guest**[13] 4518 3-8-11 **55**..............................(h) PaulMulrennan 9 11
(Ollie Pears) *a in rr* **50/1**

2m 4.51s (-1.19) **Going Correction** +0.075s/f (Good) **10 Ran SP% 119.2**
Speed ratings (Par 98): **107,106,105,104,102 102,101,99,97,86**
CSF £19.28 CT £40.12 TOTE £3.70: £1.60, £1.90, £1.10; EX 16.60 Trifecta £42.50.
Owner Steve Ryan & M J Tedham **Bred** Yeomanstown Stud **Trained** Malton, N Yorks

FOCUS
Add 1yd. The winner had the run of the race in front, so few got into this. Another pb from the winner, with the runner-up rated to the race standard.

5024 DOROTHY LAIRD MEMORIAL TROPHY LADY RIDERS' H'CAP (PRO-AM LADIES RACE) 1m 1f 207y
5:15 (5:15) (Class 6) (0-65,65) 4-Y-O+
£3,105 (£924; £461; £300; £300; £300) **Stalls Low**

Form RPR

5154 **1** **Thorntoun Care**[15] 4446 8-10-2 **65**..............................(p) MissAmyCollier(5) 4 74
(Karen Tutty) *hld up towards rr: hdwy over 2f out: sn swtchd lft to outer and rdn: str run appr fnl f: sn chal: styd on wl to ld nr fin* **9/2**[2]

-300 **2** *hd* **Bollin Ted**[10] 4658 5-10-0 **58**.............................. MissEmilyEasterby 7 66
(Tim Easterby) *led 1f: trckd ldng pair: swtchd rt to inner and hdwy wl over 1f out: sn rdn and led appr fnl f: jnd and drvn ins fnl f: hdd and no ex nr fin* **7/2**[1]

0206 **3** *3 1/4* **Amity Island**[27] 4005 4-8-13 **48**..............................(b) IzzyClifton(5) 6 50
(Ollie Pears) *midfield: hdwy to chse ldrs 1/2-way: pushed along over 2f out: rdn to chse ldrs over 1f out: ev ch whn n.m.r and edgd rt jst over 1f out: kpt on same pce* **14/1**

3004 **4** *1 3/4* **Quoteline Direct**[7] 4762 6-10-7 **65**..............................(h) MissBeckySmith 8 64
(Micky Hammond) *hld up in rr: hdwy and in tch over 4f out: rdn to chse ldrs and n.m.r over 1f out: swtchd rt and drvn ent fnl f: kpt on* **7/2**[1]

-003 **5** *nk* **Graceful Act**[10] 4633 11-8-11 **46**..............................(p) SophieSmith(5) 11 43
(Ron Barr) *sn trcking ldr: pushed along wl over 2f out: rdn wl over 1f out: kpt on same pce fnl f* **14/1**

0000 **6** *2 1/2* **Rock Warbler (IRE)**[4] 4875 6-9-3 **47**..........(p1) MissMichelleMullineaux 5 39
(Michael Mullineaux) *in rr: pushed along and hdwy over 2f out: rdn wl over 1f out: plugged on: n.d* **33/1**

0040 **7** *1* **John Caesar (IRE)**[10] 4633 8-9-2 **46** oh1....(p) MissSerenaBrotherton 10 36
(Rebecca Bastiman) *trckd ldrs: hdwy and cl up over 4f out: chal 3f out: rdn over 2f out: drvn whn n.m.r over 1f out: wknd* **14/1**

0003 **8** *2 1/4* **Jennies Gem**[28] 3959 6-9-2 **46** oh1.............................. FayeMcManoman 3 32
(Ollie Pears) *in tch: pushed along over 3f out: rdn over 2f out: n.d* **10/1**

0060 **9** *1 1/4* **Pumaflor (IRE)**[10] 4633 7-9-10 **54**..............................(p) PaulaMuir 9 37
(Philip Kirby) *chsd ldng pair: led after 1f: jnd 4f out: rdn along 3f out: drvn over 2f out: hdd 1 1/2f out: sn wknd* **33/1**

-025 **10** *nk* **Sherzy Boy**[19] 4293 4-9-12 **56**..............................(tp) MissJoannaMason 1 39
(Michael Easterby) *in tch: rdn along over 3f out: wknd wl over 1f out* **5/1**[3]

-040 **11** *1 1/2* **Dutch Artist (IRE)**[10] 4658 7-9-5 **54** ow1.......... MissBelindaJohnson(5) 2 34
(Nigel Tinkler) *dwlt: a in rr* **25/1**

2m 6.1s (0.40) **Going Correction** +0.075s/f (Good) **11 Ran SP% 118.1**
Speed ratings (Par 101): **101,100,98,96,96 94,93,92,91,90 89**
CSF £20.33 CT £202.82 TOTE £5.50: £1.70, £1.70, £3.70; EX 25.30 Trifecta £402.50.
Owner Irvine Lynch & Thoroughbred Homes Ltd **Bred** W M Johnstone **Trained** Osmotherley, N Yorks

FOCUS
Add 1yd. A moderate race that set up for the closers. The winner has been rated back to last year's best, and the second close to last year's C&D form.
T/Plt: £66.30 to a £1 stake. Pool: £61,293.50 - 674.40 winning units T/Qpdt: £9.80 to a £1 stake. Pool: £5,750.74 - 434.12 winning units **Joe Rowntree**

4658 NOTTINGHAM (L-H)
Tuesday, July 16

OFFICIAL GOING: Good (good to firm in places; watered)
Wind: Almost nil Weather: Sunny spells

5025 MANSIONBET TRAINING SERIES APPRENTICE H'CAP (RACING EXCELLENCE TRAINING SERIES) 1m 2f 50y
5:40 (5:40) (Class 6) (0-65,65) 4-Y-O+
£3,234 (£962; £481; £300; £300; £300) **Stalls Low**

Form RPR

5002 **1** **Destinys Rock**[17] 4371 4-9-9 **60**..............................(p) CierenFallon 7 67+
(Mark Loughnane) *hld up: hdwy on outer to ld over 2f out: sn edgd lft: rdn over 1f out: styd on* **6/1**[2]

0253 **2** *1/2* **Apache Blaze**[29] 3939 4-9-11 **62**.............................. TylerSaunders 13 68
(Robyn Brisland) *a.p: chsd ldr over 5f out: ev ch over 2f out: rdn and lost 2nd over 1f out: rallied to chse wnr again ins fnl f: r.o* **6/1**[2]

1513 **3** *1/2* **Tigerfish (IRE)**[21] 4215 5-9-7 **63**..............................(p) MarcoGhiani(5) 5 69
(William Stone) *w ldr over 2f: racd in 2nd tl over 5f out: rdn over 2f out: swtchd rt ins fnl f: r.o* **6/1**[2]

6260 **4** *2* **Optima Petamus**[19] 4293 7-8-11 **48**..............................(v) ScottMcCullagh 11 49
(Liam Bailey) *s.i.s: hld up: hdwy on outer over 2f out: rdn to chse wnr over 1f out tl no ex ins fnl f* **33/1**

0060 **5** *7* **Maghfoor**[3] 4907 5-9-12 **63**..............................(p) KieranSchofield 4 50
(Eric Alston) *pushed along early in rr: slipped bnd over 5f out: hdwy over 2f out: nt trble ldrs* **5/1**[1]

2005 **6** *1 1/2* **Ronni Layne**[33] 3774 5-8-4 **46** oh1..............................(p) GeorgeRooke(5) 10 30
(Louise Allan) *hld up in tch: lost pl over 7f out: hdwy on outer over 2f out: rdn and wknd over 1f out* **40/1**

-556 **7** *hd* **Tajdeed (IRE)**[11] 4615 4-9-11 **62**.............................. Pierre-LouisJamin 9 46
(Michael Appleby) *hdwy 8f out: rdn over 2f out: hung lft and wknd over 1f out* **5/1**[1]

3400 **8** *1/2* **Telekinetic**[18] 4346 4-8-9 **46** oh1.............................. SeanKirrane 3 29
(Julia Feilden) *chsd ldrs: lost pl over 5f out: nt clr run and hmpd over 2f out: n.d after* **8/1**[3]

0005 **9** *4* **Angelical Eve (IRE)**[10] 4658 5-8-9 **46** oh1.............................. AledBeech 6 21
(Dai Williams) *hld up in tch: tk clsr order over 3f out: rdn over 2f out: swtchd rt and wknd over 1f out* **50/1**

5062 **10** *nk* **Contingency Fee**[11] 4686 4-9-4 **60**..............................(p) GraceMcEntee(5) 1 34
(Phil McEntee) *pushed along to chse ldrs: lost pl 8f out: rdn and wknd over 2f out* **16/1**

3132 **11** *1/2* **Celtic Artisan (IRE)**[15] 4446 8-9-11 **65**..............................(bt) EllaMcCain(3) 8 38
(Rebecca Menzies) *led: rdn and hdd over 2f out: wknd over 1f out (jockey said gelding hung left on the bend)* **6/1**[2]

0000 **12** *4* **Rebel Cause (IRE)**[14] 4475 6-8-13 **50**.............................. TobyEley 2 15
(John Holt) *hld up in tch: racd keenly: rdn and wknd over 2f out (jockey said gelding ran too free)* **12/1**

0-00 **13** *13* **Wedding Breakfast (IRE)**[28] 3959 5-8-8 **48**..... CianMacRedmond(3) 12
(Stella Barclay) *s.s: a bhd (jockey said mare was slowly away and hung left)* **50/1**

2m 11.75s (-1.65) **Going Correction** -0.075s/f (Good) **13 Ran SP% 124.5**
Speed ratings (Par 101): **103,102,102,100,95 93,93,93,90,89 89,86,75**
CSF £42.98 CT £232.12 TOTE £7.50: £2.30, £2.50, £1.50; EX 51.90 Trifecta £355.20.
Owner Ladies Of Rock **Bred** Willoxton Farm Stud **Trained** Rock, Worcs

FOCUS
Outer track in use. The rail was out 4yds throughout. Add 12yds. The watered ground (they were making a print) was given as good, good to firm in places (Going Stick 7.4). A modest affair. Straightforward form rated around the second and third.

5026 MANSIONBET NOVICE AUCTION STKS 5f 8y
6:10 (6:11) (Class 5) 2-Y-O **£3,881** (£1,155; £577; £288) **Stalls High**

Form RPR

1 **Mr Duepearl** 2-9-0 **0**.............................. SeamusCronin(5) 1 71
(Robyn Brisland) *s.i.s: rcvrd to ld 4f out: shkn up and hung lft fr over 1f out: rdn out* **10/1**[3]

524 **2** *1/2* **Microscopic (IRE)**[15] 4448 2-9-0 **64**.............................. NicolaCurrie 3 64
(David Simcock) *led 1f: chsd wnr: shkn up and hung lft fr over 1f out: r.o* **2/1**[2]

332 **3** *2 1/4* **She Looks Like Fun**[10] 4624 2-9-0 **69**.............................. CliffordLee 2 56
(K R Burke) *w ldr 1f: chsd ldrs: rdn over 1f out: styd on same pce ins fnl f* **1/2**[1]

00 **4** *14* **Aiden's Reward (IRE)**[20] 4237 2-9-5 **0**.............................. AndrewMullen 4 11
(Ben Haslam) *s.i.s: a in rr: outpcd fr 1/2-way* **33/1**

1m 0.6s (0.40) **Going Correction** -0.075s/f (Good) **4 Ran SP% 112.0**
Speed ratings (Par 94): **93,92,88,66**
CSF £30.07 TOTE £11.50; EX 32.80 Trifecta £27.70.
Owner Mr And Mrs J Sumsion **Bred** W H R John And Partners **Trained** Danethorpe, Notts

FOCUS
A bit of a surprise here, with the newcomer proving good enough to turn over the big two in the market. The second has been rated to form.

5027 MANSIONBET BEATEN BY A HEAD H'CAP 5f 8y
6:40 (6:41) (Class 5) (0-75,76) 3-Y-O+
£3,881 (£1,155; £577; £300; £300; £300) **Stalls High**

Form RPR

-150 **1** **Grandfather Tom**[19] 4301 4-9-4 **71**.............................. CierenFallon(5) 4 83
(Robert Cowell) *mde all: shkn up over 1f out: rdn and edgd rt ins fnl f: r.o* **11/2**[3]

0654 **2** *2* **Move In Time**[19] 4279 11-10-0 **76**.............................. DougieCostello 3 81
(Paul Midgley) *chsd wnr: rdn over 1f out: styd on same pce wl ins fnl f* **3/1**[2]

0640 **3** *3 1/2* **Sheepscar Lad (IRE)**[17] 4406 5-9-6 **71**.............................. RowanScott(3) 5 63
(Nigel Tinkler) *s.i.s and hmpd s: sn prom: rdn over 1f out: styd on same pce ins fnl f: eased towards fin* **1/1**[1]

0-00 **4** *2* **Choosey (IRE)**[10] 4625 4-9-3 **72**.............................. JoshQuinn(7) 1 57
(Michael Easterby) *chsd ldrs: rdn over 1f out: wknd ins fnl f* **12/1**

2060 **5** *1 1/2* **Dragon Beat (IRE)**[5] 4829 3-9-2 **68**.............................. TomMarquand 2 46
(Michael Appleby) *s.i.s: sn pushed along in rr: nvr on terms (vet said filly was lame behind)* **9/1**

6060 **6** ½ **Arzaak (IRE)**[17] 4374 5-9-10 **72**......................(b) LewisEdmunds 6 50
(Charlie Wallis) *wnt lft s: chsd ldrs: rdn and lost pl whn hung lft and rt fr 1/2-way: nt run on* **16/1**

59.29s (-0.91) **Going Correction** -0.075s/f (Good) **6** Ran SP% **114.0**
WFA 3 from 4yo+ 4lb
Speed ratings (Par 103): **104,100,95,92,89 88**
CSF £22.72 TOTE £4.80: £2.00, £1.70; EX 21.00 Trifecta £57.10.
Owner J Sargeant **Bred** J Sargeant **Trained** Six Mile Bottom, Cambs

FOCUS
Few got into this, the winner controlling things from the start. The winner has been rated to his best.

5028 DOWNLOAD THE MANSIONBET APP H'CAP 1m 6f
7:10 (7:10) (Class 5) (0-70,66) 3-Y-O
£3,881 (£1,155; £577; £300; £300; £300) **Stalls** Low

Form RPR

2111 **1** **Champagne Marengo (IRE)**[4] 4862 3-9-9 **66** 6ex.....(p) AndreaAtzeni 4 76+
(Ian Williams) *s.i.s: hdwy 12f out: chsd ldr over 8f out: rdn to ld over 2f out: styd on wl* **4/5**[1]

5331 **2** 1¼ **Well Funded (IRE)**[30] 3886 3-9-0 **60**.................. JaneElliott(3) 3 67
(James Bethell) *hld up: racd keenly: hdwy over 3f out: rdn to chse wnr over 1f out: styd on* **6/1**[3]

06-0 **3** 2 **Road To Paris (IRE)**[49] 3195 3-8-13 **56**.................. RyanTate 2 60
(Sir Mark Prescott Bt) *hld up: pushed along over 3f out: hdwy over 1f out: r.o to go 3rd nr fin: nt rch ldrs* **11/2**[2]

6213 **4** 1 **Fantastic Ms Fox**[30] 3886 3-9-7 **64**.................. TonyHamilton 7 67
(Richard Fahey) *led: rdn and hdd over 2f out: no ex ins fnl f* **6/1**[3]

1030 **5** hd **Lincoln Tale (IRE)**[28] 3955 3-9-7 **64**.................. DavidNolan 8 67
(David O'Meara) *prom: chsd ldr 12f out tl over 8f out: remained handy: rdn over 2f out: styd on same pce fnl f* **10/1**

-600 **6** 3¼ **Dinah Washington (IRE)**[47] 3275 3-8-9 **52**.................. HayleyTurner 1 50
(Michael Bell) *s.i.s: hld up: rdn over 3f out: nt trble ldrs* **16/1**

0630 **7** nk **Yellow Label (USA)**[30] 3888 3-9-2 **62**.................. JoshuaBryan(3) 5 60
(Andrew Balding) *prom: rdn over 3f out: outpcd fr over 2f out* **18/1**

5000 **8** 11 **Gloryella**[21] 4210 3-8-2 **45**.................. JamesSullivan 6 27
(Ruth Carr) *w ldr 2f: remained handy: rdn over 3f out: wknd over 2f out* **100/1**

3m 9.4s (3.00) **Going Correction** -0.075s/f (Good) **8** Ran SP% **120.7**
Speed ratings (Par 100): **88,87,86,85,85 83,83,77**
CSF £6.82 CT £18.64 TOTE £1.90: £1.10, £1.80, £1.30; EX 5.70 Trifecta £25.90.
Owner Champagne Charlies Club **Bred** Helen Lyons **Trained** Portway, Worcs

FOCUS
Add 24yds. A straightforward opportunity for the odds-on favourite, but it still required the right ride, and he got just that. A small pb from the second.

5029 MANSIONBET'S BEST ODDS GUARANTEED H'CAP 1m 6f
7:40 (7:40) (Class 6) (0-60,61) 4-Y-O+
£3,234 (£962; £481; £300; £300; £300) **Stalls** Low

Form RPR

2266 **1** **Make Good (IRE)**[50] 2279 4-9-2 **60**.................(bt) CierenFallon(5) 1 70
(David Dennis) *a.p: chsd ldr 6f out: led over 3f out: rdn out* **10/1**

-030 **2** 2¾ **The Fiddler**[20] 4251 4-8-11 **50**.................. GeorgeWood 5 56
(Chris Wall) *hld up in tch: lost pl over 7f out: hdwy over 2f out: rdn to go 2nd ins fnl f: nt trble wnr* **5/1**[1]

-025 **3** 1½ **Artic Nel**[15] 4435 5-8-7 **46** oh1.................. MartinDwyer 2 50
(Ian Williams) *hld up: hdwy over 3f out: rdn to chse wnr over 1f out tl ins fnl f: styd on same pce* **5/1**[1]

0060 **4** nk **Lazarus (IRE)**[56] 1548 5-8-11 **50**.................(t) DavidEgan 7 53
(Amy Murphy) *hld up: rdn over 3f out: hdwy over 1f out: nt rch ldrs* **16/1**

6-05 **5** 3 **Sir Fred (IRE)**[34] 3740 4-8-2 **46** oh1.................. SophieRalston(5) 13 45
(Julia Feilden) *chsd ldrs: pushed along over 4f out: styd on same pce fr over 1f out* **10/1**

0306 **6** hd **Airplane (IRE)**[11] 4601 4-9-7 **60**.................. RachelRichardson 11 59
(Tim Easterby) *led: hdd over 12f out: led again over 11f out: rdn and hdd over 3f out: wknd ins fnl f* **7/1**[2]

0046 **7** 1¼ **Affair**[42] 3444 5-8-13 **52**.................. CharlieBennett 8 49
(Hughie Morrison) *hld up: hdwy over 7f out: rdn over 2f out: wknd fnl f* **8/1**[3]

3365 **8** shd **Seventii**[21] 4216 5-8-0 **46** oh1.................. AledBeech(7) 12 43
(Robert Eddery) *hld up: sme hdwy over 1f out: nt trble ldrs* **14/1**

0-00 **9** ¾ **Everlasting Sea**[64] 2695 5-8-4 **46** oh1.................. WilliamCox(3) 14 42
(Stuart Kittow) *hld up: rdn over 2f out: n.d* **50/1**

0056 **10** nk **Ezanak (IRE)**[15] 4446 6-9-8 **61**.................(v) AlistairRawlinson 3 57
(Michael Appleby) *chsd ldrs: pushed along and lost pl over 3f out: n.d after* **10/1**

0200 **11** ½ **Seaborough (IRE)**[18] 4333 4-9-0 **60**.................(p) RhonaPindar(7) 16 55
(David Thompson) *s.i.s: hld up: rdn over 3f out: n.d* **20/1**

-000 **12** 1 **Bogardus (IRE)**[13] 4510 8-9-4 **57**.................. DavidNolan 6 51
(Liam Bailey) *hld up: rdn over 2f out: n.d* **9/1**

5043 **13** 13 **Normandy Blue**[19] 4287 4-8-13 **52**.................. JimmyQuinn 10 27
(Louise Allan) *hld up: hdwy over 6f out: rdn and wknd 3f out* **14/1**

4610 **14** 26 **Banta Bay**[10] 4661 5-8-12 **51**.................. JosephineGordon 9
(John Best) *hld up: hdwy over 8f out: rdn and wknd over 2f out: eased (jockey said gelding hung left on the bend entering the home straight)* **12/1**

-000 **15** 3¾ **Roser Moter (IRE)**[19] 4287 4-8-4 **48**.................(p[1]) TheodoreLadd(5) 15
(Michael Appleby) *sn chsng ldr: led over 12f out tl over 11f out: chsd ldr again tl 6f out: rdn and wknd over 2f out: eased* **40/1**

3m 5.54s (-0.86) **Going Correction** -0.075s/f (Good) **15** Ran SP% **130.3**
Speed ratings (Par 101): **99,97,96,96,94 94,93,93,93,93 92,92,84,70,67**
CSF £62.90 CT £295.16 TOTE £9.90: £3.40, £3.00, £1.50; EX 89.20 Trifecta £620.70.
Owner Clan McNeil **Bred** Ivan And Mrs Eileen Heanen **Trained** Hanley Swan, Worcestershire

FOCUS
Add 24yds. This was a well-run race but the winner was never far off the pace. He gave Cieren Fallon a treble on the card. The second and third have been rated close to form.

5030 MANSIONBET FILLIES' H'CAP 1m 75y
8:10 (8:11) (Class 4) (0-80,82) 3-Y-O+
£6,469 (£1,925; £962; £481; £300; £300) **Stalls** Centre

Form RPR

4241 **1** **Al Messila**[19] 4285 3-9-5 **77**.................. PatDobbs 9 86
(Richard Hannon) *hld up: hdwy over 2f out: rdn to ld ins fnl f: r.o* **5/1**[2]

-122 **2** nk **Polyphony (IRE)**[20] 4243 4-9-7 **71**.................(h) JasonHart 6 81
(John Mackie) *hld up: hdwy over 3f out: rdn and ev ch ins fnl f: r.o* **7/2**[1]

2012 **3** 3¼ **Arletta Star**[5] 4831 3-8-7 **65**.................. JamesSullivan 7 66
(Tim Easterby) *prom: racd keenly: lost pl over 5f out: hdwy over 3f out: led 2f out: rdn: hdd and no ex ins fnl f* **8/1**

-055 **4** 3 **Ladies First**[19] 4278 5-9-12 **76**.................. NathanEvans 1 72
(Michael Easterby) *chsd ldrs: rdn over 2f out: hung rt over 1f out: styd on same pce (jockey said mare was denied a clear run approx two furlongs out)* **7/1**[3]

22-5 **5** 4½ **Lady Lizzy**[56] 2935 3-9-3 **75**.................(w) CliffordLee 4 59
(K R Burke) *chsd ldr tl led over 2f out: sn rdn: edgd lft and hdd: wknd fnl f* **8/1**

-200 **6** 1 **Kimblewick (IRE)**[25] 4052 3-9-10 **82**.................. KieranO'Neill 5 63
(John Gosden) *s.i.s: in rr: shkn up over 3f out: nvr nrr (jockey said filly was slowly into stride and denied a clear run approx two furlongs out)* **7/1**[3]

4305 **7** 4½ **Prairie Spy (IRE)**[29] 3923 3-9-7 **79**.................. JoeFanning 10 50
(Mark Johnston) *s.i.s: hld up: effrt on outer over 2f out: wknd over 1f out* **20/1**

0412 **8** 2 **Eponina (IRE)**[15] 4438 5-8-10 **65**.................. TheodoreLadd(5) 2 34
(Michael Appleby) *led: clr over 5f out tl over 3f out: rdn and hdd over 2f out: wknd over 1f out* **10/1**

123 **9** 4 **Moongazer**[105] 1495 3-9-3 **75**.................. KieranShoemark 3 32
(Charles Hills) *s.i.s: hld up: rdn over 2f out: sn wknd* **20/1**

0-54 **10** 3 **Heavenly Bliss**[19] 4285 3-8-8 **66**.................. DavidEgan 8 16
(Sir Michael Stoute) *chsd ldrs: rdn over 4f out: wknd over 2f out* **7/1**[3]

4-00 **11** 4½ **Flora Tristan**[26] 4028 4-8-10 **63**.................(h) GabrieleMalune(3) 11 5
(Ivan Furtado) *hld up: plld hrd: hdwy on outer over 5f out: wknd over 2f out* **50/1**

1m 44.31s (-2.39) **Going Correction** -0.075s/f (Good) **11** Ran SP% **119.2**
WFA 3 from 4yo+ 8lb
Speed ratings (Par 102): **106,105,102,99,94 93,89,87,83,80 75**
CSF £22.62 CT £140.75 TOTE £4.00: £2.10, £1.50, £2.90; EX 22.40 Trifecta £234.00.
Owner Al Shaqab Racing **Bred** Lofts Hall Stud & B Sangster **Trained** East Everleigh, Wilts

FOCUS
Add 12yds. A fair fillies' handicap. The third has been rated close to form.

5031 MANSIONBET H'CAP 1m 75y
8:40 (8:41) (Class 6) (0-65,66) 3-Y-O
£3,234 (£962; £481; £300; £300; £300) **Stalls** Centre

Form RPR

5606 **1** **Shifting Gold (IRE)**[15] 4453 3-8-13 **57**.................. DavidEgan 10 63
(William Knight) *hld up: hdwy over 1f out: rdn and r.o to ld post* **10/1**

1003 **2** hd **Jazz Hands (IRE)**[14] 4487 3-8-7 **51**.................. RoystonFfrench 8 56
(Richard Fahey) *hld up: hdwy over 1f out: rdn to ld wl ins fnl f: hdd post* **13/2**

-356 **3** ¾ **Beautiful Gesture**[35] 3683 3-9-2 **65**.................. HarrisonShaw(5) 1 68+
(K R Burke) *hld up: swtchd rt over 3f out: hdwy over 2f out: led over 1f out: rdn: edgd lft and hdd wl ins fnl f* **4/1**[1]

3651 **4** 4 **Lethal Laura**[10] 4642 3-8-8 **52**.................(p) BarryMcHugh 7 46
(James Given) *hld up: hdwy over 2f out: rdn to chse wnr over 1f out tl edgd lft and no ex ins fnl f* **7/1**

000 **5** 4 **Fountain Of Life**[24] 4121 3-8-13 **57**.................. JasonHart 11 42
(Philip McBride) *s.i.s: in rr: nt clr run and swtchd rt over 1f out: r.o ins fnl f: nvr nrr (jockey said gelding was denied a clear run approaching the final furlong)* **16/1**

6250 **6** ½ **Orliko (IRE)**[10] 4642 3-9-4 **62**.................(bt) RossaRyan 5 46
(Richard Hannon) *led early: chsd ldrs: rdn over 2f out: hung lft and wknd fnl f* **9/1**

4000 **7** ½ **Grey Berry (IRE)**[19] 4278 3-9-1 **59**.................(b[1]) DuranFentiman 9 42
(Tim Easterby) *plld hrd and prom: chsd ldr over 4f out: led over 2f out: rdn and hdd over 1f out: wknd fnl f* **25/1**

0050 **8** shd **Furyan**[8] 4731 3-8-5 **52**.................(p[1]) RowanScott(3) 3 34
(Nigel Tinkler) *s.i.s: pushed along in rr: hdwy u.p over 2f out: wknd over 1f out* **8/1**

-052 **9** 2¾ **Colonel Slade (IRE)**[6] 4774 3-9-5 **63**.................(t) TomMarquand 12 39
(Brian Meehan) *sn prom: rdn over 2f out: wknd fnl f* **5/1**[3]

02-4 **10** 4½ **Clem A**[64] 2689 3-9-3 **66**.................(v) CierenFallon(5) 2 32
(Alan Bailey) *trckd ldrs: racd keenly: rdn over 2f out: wknd over 1f out (jockey said gelding ran too free)* **9/2**[2]

00-0 **11** 12 **Queen Of Bradgate**[47] 3256 3-8-2 **49** oh1 ow3....... GabrieleMalune(3) 4
(Ivan Furtado) *racd keenly: sn led: rdn and hdd over 2f out: wknd over 1f out* **33/1**

1m 46.86s (0.16) **Going Correction** -0.075s/f (Good) **11** Ran SP% **123.6**
Speed ratings (Par 98): **94,93,93,89,85 84,84,83,81,76 64**
CSF £77.47 CT £317.63 TOTE £11.60: £4.50, £2.60, £2.20; EX 119.80 Trifecta £506.10.
Owner Mrs Joanna Farrant & Partner **Bred** Airlie Stud **Trained** Angmering, W Sussex

FOCUS
Add 12yds. The principals came from off the pace, the winner from the back of the field. It's been rated around the second.
T/Jkpt: Not won. T/Plt: £551.50 to a £1 stake. Pool: £59,789.20 - 79.13 winning units T/Qpdt: £11.40 to a £1 stake. Pool: £8,954.46 - 581.03 winning units **Colin Roberts**

5032 - 5034a (Foreign Racing) - See Raceform Interactive

5008

VICHY
Tuesday, July 16

OFFICIAL GOING: Turf: good to soft

5035a PRIX HUBERT DE CATHEU (H'CAP) (4YO+) (TURF) 1m 7f
12:50 4-Y-O+
£23,423 (£8,900; £6,558; £3,747; £1,873; £1,405)

RPR

1 **Badia (FR)**[24] 5-8-10 **0**.................(p) MickaelForest 11 72
(Edouard Monfort, France) **33/10**[1]

2 nse **Culmination**[8] 4748 7-9-4 **0**.................. AntoineHamelin 12 80
(Jo Hughes, France) *sn trcking pce: pushed along over 2f out: rdn and gd hdwy over 1f out: drvn to chal ins fnl f: ev ch fnl 100yds: jst failed* **40/1**

3 1¼ **Incampo (FR)**[100] 5-9-2 **0**.................. MaximeGuyon 6 76
(J-P Gauvin, France) **89/10**

4 1¼ **Palmerino (FR)**[24] 8-9-4 **0**.................. AlexisBadel 7 77
(E Leenders, France) **7/1**[3]

5 1½ **Desert Warrior (IRE)**[369] 6-8-11 **0**.................(p) NicolasPerret 10 68
(F Foresi, France) **15/1**

6 ½ **Stonebridge (FR)**[26] 4-9-3 **0**.................. Roberto-CarlosMontenegro 5 74
(C Alonso Pena, Spain) **12/1**

The Form Book Flat 2019, Raceform Ltd, Newbury, RG14 5SJ

7 2 **Rannan (FR)**[44] 4-9-6 0..(p) FranckBlondel 9 74
(R Martens, France) **23/1**
8 nk **Show The Way (IRE)**[99] 5-8-9 0................................ AnthonyCrastus 3 63
(F Foresi, France) **30/1**
9 snk **Menuetto**[24] 4-9-2 0.. MickaelBarzalona 4 70
(H-A Pantall, France) *settled in midfield: dropped to rr 4f out: urged along and swtchd lft over 2f out: rdn and hdwy over 1f out: kpt on one pce fnl f* **57/10**[2]
10 1 ½ **Gonzalo**[24] 6-8-9 0.. ValentinSeguy 8 61
(N Bellanger, France) **17/1**
11 snk **Top By Cocooning (FR)**[24] 6-9-0 0........................ GabrieleCongiu 13 66
(J-P Gauvin, France) **18/1**
12 11 **Just A Formality (FR)**[50] 5-9-3 0...................(b) ChristopheSoumillon 15 55
(C Escuder, France) **14/1**
13 1 ¼ **Le Pin (FR)**[8] 4748 6-9-5 0..(b) FabriceVeron 1 56
(B Legros, France) **23/1**
14 4 **Rosny (FR)**[93] 8-9-3 0.. IoritzMendizabal 16 49
(M Planard, France) **29/1**
15 12 **Go Fast (IRE)**[24] 5-8-11 0.. EddyHardouin 2 29
(N Caullery, France) **22/1**
16 5 ½ **Souvigne (FR)**[93] 5-8-10 0.. TonyPiccone 14 21
(J-P Gauvin, France) **16/1**
3m 15.5s **16** Ran SP% **119.8**
PARI-MUTUEL (all including 1 euro stake): WIN 4.30; PLACE 1.90, 9.70, 3.30; DF 74.60.
Owner F Rohaut **Bred** F Rohaut **Trained** France

5036 - (Foreign Racing) - See Raceform Interactive

4778 CATTERICK (L-H)
Wednesday, July 17

OFFICIAL GOING: Good to firm (good in places; watered; 8.3)
Wind: fresh variable Weather: cloudy but warm

5037 EBF FILLIES' NOVICE AUCTION STKS (PLUS 10 RACE) 5f
2:00 (2:00) (Class 5) 2-Y-O £4,140 (£1,232; £615; £307) Stalls Low

Form RPR
521 1 **Requiems Dream (IRE)**[1] 5011 2-9-4 0................................ JoeFanning 2 68+
(Mark Johnston) *pressed ldr: led 3f out: rdn and hung lft over 1f out: strly pressed 1f out: continued to hang lft: all out (jockey said filly hung left; vet said a post-race examination during routine testing of the filly found her to be lame right fore)* **4/9**[1]
31 2 nk **Rose Bandit (IRE)**[4] 4910 2-9-4 0................................ LiamKeniry 5 65
(Stef Keniry) *chsd ldrs: rdn 2f out: chal strly 1f out: kpt on* **15/8**[2]
00 3 shd **She's Easyontheeye (IRE)**[83] 2051 2-9-0 0........................ JasonHart 1 61
(John Quinn) *led narrowly: hdd 3f out but remained cl up: rdn along whn hmpd on rail over 1f out: sn dropped to 3rd: drvn and kpt on wl fnl f* **28/1**[3]
4 3 ¾ **Sweet Embrace (IRE)** 2-9-0 0................................ TomEaves 3 47
(John Wainwright) *dwlt: sn outpcd in rr: sme hdwy 1f out: edgd lft and eased fnl 75yds* **150/1**
1m 0.76s (0.26) **Going Correction** -0.15s/f (Firm) **4** Ran SP% **108.1**
Speed ratings (Par 91): **91,90,90,84**
CSF £1.52 TOTE £1.40; EX 1.50 Trifecta £2.10.
Owner Carl Chapman & Johnston Racing **Bred** Wansdyke Farms Ltd & Oghill House Stud **Trained** Middleham Moor, N Yorks
■ Stewards' Enquiry : Joe Fanning two-day ban: interference & careless riding (Aug 2-3)

FOCUS
The going was good to firm, good in places. GoingStick: 8.3. The rail on the bend turning into the home straight was dolled out 2yds adding 6yds to the 2.30, 3.0, 3.30, 4.0 and 5.0. Stalls - All races: inside. Only four runners, but this novice auction was not without incident. The winner had little to spare at the finish after looking set to score comfortably. The second has been rated to her latest.

5038 RACINGTV.COM (S) STKS 5f 212y
2:30 (2:31) (Class 6) 3-Y-O+
£3,105 (£924; £461; £300; £300; £300) Stalls Low

Form RPR
/005 1 **Betsey Trotter (IRE)**[16] 4438 4-9-2 70........................(p) DanielTudhope 6 74
(David O'Meara) *trckd ldrs: pushed into ld over 1f out: sn rdn clr: comf* **5/2**[2]
0000 2 5 **Bahuta Acha**[13] 4552 4-9-2 70..(b) JasonHart 7 58
(David Loughnane) *trckd ldrs: led over 4f out: rdn and hdd over 1f out: sn outpcd and no ch w wnr* **9/4**[1]
0024 3 ½ **Extrasolar**[11] 4630 9-9-11 59..(t) SamJames 9 66
(Geoffrey Harker) *midfield: rdn and sme hdwy over 1f out: kpt on same pce fnl f* **10/1**[3]
-000 4 1 ½ **Mightaswellsmile**[12] 4586 5-8-6 42................................ PaulaMuir(5) 11 47
(Ron Barr) *dwlt: hld up: rdn along on outside 2f out: kpt on ins fnl f: nvr trbld ldrs (jockey said mare hung left home straight)* **100/1**
0000 5 1 ½ **Naadirr (IRE)**[34] 3770 8-9-2 82................................(v) GrahamLee 10 47+
(Kevin Ryan) *slowly away: hld up: pushed along and n.m.r 2f out: swtchd rt appr fnl f: rdn and no imp* **5/2**[2]
16-0 6 1 **Majdool (IRE)**[50] 3177 6-9-7 55................................(e) DavidNolan 1 49
(Noel Wilson) *midfield: rdn along 2f out: no ex fnl f* **33/1**
00-5 7 nk **Adam's Ale**[16] 4434 10-8-13 82........................(p) ConnorMurtagh(3) 12 43
(Marjorie Fife) *sn in tch on outer: rdn over 2f out: wknd ins fnl f* **16/1**
2050 8 3 ¼ **Pea Shooter**[18] 4406 10-9-8 74................................ BenRobinson(3) 8 42
(Brian Ellison) *chsd ldrs: rdn over 2f out: wknd fnl f* **14/1**
0060 9 2 ¼ **Tavener**[6] 4833 7-9-7 56..(p) DavidAllan 2 30
(David C Griffiths) *hld up: nvr threatened* **14/1**
50 10 3 ¼ **De Latour**[6] 4823 3-8-11 56.. TomEaves 4 14
(Jason Ward) *chsd ldrs: rdn over 2f out: sn wknd (jockey said gelding finished with a wound and was lame left fore)* **50/1**
40-0 11 13 **Cotton Socks (IRE)**[26] 4078 4-9-2 42................................ JoeFanning 3
(Ann Duffield) *led: rn wd on bnd and hdd over 4f out: wknd over 2f out: eased (jockey said gelding hung left throughout)* **66/1**
1m 12.09s (-1.51) **Going Correction** -0.15s/f (Firm)
WFA 3 from 4yo+ 5lb **11** Ran SP% **123.6**
Speed ratings (Par 101): **104,97,96,94,92 91,90,86,83,79 61**
CSF £9.01 TOTE £2.70: £1.10, £1.40, £2.00; EX 10.80 Trifecta £70.90.The winner was bought in for £11,000.
Owner F Gillespie **Bred** James Hughes **Trained** Upper Helmsley, N Yorks

FOCUS
Add 6yds. Moderate fare, but the winner blew away her rivals and may be capable of winning again in better company. The third and fourth set the level.

5039 JOIN RACING TV NOW FILLIES' H'CAP (CATTERICK TWELVE FURLONG SERIES QUALIFIER) 1m 4f 13y
3:00 (3:01) (Class 5) (0-75,76) 3-Y-O+ £4,075 (£1,212; £606; £303) Stalls Low

Form RPR
0-33 1 **Quintada**[53] 3099 3-9-5 76.. JasonHart 2 84
(Mark Johnston) *led: hdd 8f out: trckd ldr: pushed along over 2f out: rdn to ld over 1f out: styd on wl* **10/11**[1]
5015 2 1 **Bollin Joan**[11] 4627 4-9-8 68..(p) DavidAllan 1 73
(Tim Easterby) *hld up in tch: trckd ldrs over 2f out: bit short of room on inner over 1f out and swtchd rt: sn chsd ldr: styd on wl but a hld* **6/1**
34-1 3 7 **Joie De Vivre (IRE)**[36] 3708 4-9-10 70................................ PaulHanagan 3 64
(Martin Todhunter) *trckd ldr: led 8f out: rdn and hdd over 1f out: wknd ins fnl f* **4/1**[3]
1-66 4 33 **Shagalla**[65] 2685 3-9-2 73..(b) DavidEgan 4 15
(Roger Varian) *dwlt: hld up in tch: rdn 4f out: sn outpcd: wknd over 2f out: eased (trainer's rep could offer no explanation for the filly's performance)* **7/2**[2]
2m 38.0s (-2.60) **Going Correction** -0.15s/f (Firm)
WFA 3 from 4yo 11lb **4** Ran SP% **108.9**
Speed ratings (Par 100): **102,101,96,74**
CSF £6.60 TOTE £1.70; EX 6.20 Trifecta £9.90.
Owner Miss K Rausing **Bred** R Cantoni **Trained** Middleham Moor, N Yorks

FOCUS
Add 6yds. A poor turn-out numerically, but the winner did enough to suggest she can prosper now she has proven her stamina over a longer trip. A small pb from the winner, with the second rated to her best.

5040 5TH REGIMENT ROYAL ARTILLERY H'CAP 5f 212y
3:30 (3:30) (Class 4) (0-85,79) 3-Y-O+
£6,080 (£1,809; £904; £452; £300; £300) Stalls Low

Form RPR
0252 1 **Zumurud (IRE)**[20] 4303 4-9-12 79................................ DanielTudhope 2 88
(Rebecca Bastiman) *trckd ldrs: pushed along to chse ldr over 1f out: swtchd rt appr fnl f: led 110yds out: pushed out* **13/8**[1]
0066 2 1 **Rose Marmara**[12] 4595 6-8-9 65........................(tp) ConnorMurtagh(3) 3 71
(Brian Rothwell) *pressed ldr: led over 2f out: rdn 2 l clr over 1f out: drvn and reduced advantage fnl f: hdd 110yds out: one pce* **16/1**
6043 3 1 ¾ **Highland Acclaim (IRE)**[6] 4835 8-9-9 76................................(h) DavidNolan 6 76
(David O'Meara) *chsd ldrs: rdn over 2f out: kpt on same pce* **8/1**
0450 4 1 ¼ **Consequences (IRE)**[18] 4406 4-9-10 77................................(t) DavidEgan 4 73
(Ian Williams) *hld up in tch: rdn along 2f out: kpt on ins fnl f: nvr trbld ldrs* **12/1**
-404 5 1 ¼ **Dizzy G (IRE)**[16] 4442 4-9-10 77................................ CliffordLee 1 69
(K R Burke) *led narrowly: hdd over 2f out: sn rdn: wknd ins fnl f (jockey said filly ran flat)* **10/3**[2]
2060 6 nk **Buccaneers Vault (IRE)**[11] 4649 7-9-8 75................................ KevinStott 5 66
(Paul Midgley) *dwlt: hld up in tch: rdn over 2f out: no imp* **8/1**
0125 7 3 ½ **Spirit Of Wedza (IRE)**[6] 4821 7-9-8 75................................ PaulHanagan 7 55
(Julie Camacho) *a in rr (trainer said gelding was slowly away)* **6/1**[3]
1m 12.34s (-1.26) **Going Correction** -0.15s/f (Firm) **7** Ran SP% **111.3**
Speed ratings (Par 105): **102,100,98,96,95 94,89**
CSF £27.77 TOTE £2.60: £1.60, £4.50; EX 33.30 Trifecta £105.30.
Owner Ms M Austerfield **Bred** Miss Sinead Looney **Trained** Cowthorpe, N Yorks

FOCUS
Add 6yds. Quite a competitive sprint handicap and a winning favourite. A small pb from the winner, in line with his recent form.

5041 WATCH RACING TV NOW MEDIAN AUCTION MAIDEN STKS 7f 6y
4:00 (4:02) (Class 6) 3-5-Y-O £3,105 (£924; £461; £230) Stalls Low

Form RPR
3/00 1 **Strawberryandcream**[149] 784 4-9-7 55................................ PaulHanagan 8 65
(James Bethell) *slowly away: outpcd in rr tl hdwy appr fnl f: rdn and r.o wl fnl f: led towards fin* **20/1**
2 ½ **Sorbonne** 3-9-5 0.. DavidAllan 4 66+
(David Barron) *trckd ldrs: pushed along 4f out: rdn to chse ldr over 1f out: kpt on ins fnl f* **11/8**[1]
3 hd **Mid Atlantic Storm (IRE)**[10] 4699 3-9-5 0................................ LiamKeniry 7 65
(Gavin Cromwell, Ire) *pressed ldr: pushed into narrow ld over 2f out: rdn over 1f out: drvn ins fnl f: one pce fnl 110yds: hdd towards fin: lost 2nd post* **15/8**[2]
64 4 4 ½ **Oblate**[22] 4211 3-9-0 0.. TomEaves 6 48
(Robyn Brisland) *trckd ldrs: rdn to chal over 2f out: wknd ins fnl f* **15/2**
-660 5 3 ¾ **Nutopia**[152] 738 4-9-7 44.. CamHardie 2 41
(Antony Brittain) *hld up: rdn over 2f out: nvr involved* **20/1**
-000 6 1 ¼ **Itsupforgrabsnow (IRE)**[26] 4078 4-9-7 41........................(h) JasonHart 3 37
(Susan Corbett) *slowly away: hld up: nvr threatened (jockey said filly jumped awkwardly from the stalls; vet said filly lost left hind shoe)* **50/1**
4306 7 5 **Raksha (IRE)**[14] 4508 3-9-0 58................................ DanielTudhope 5 21
(David O'Meara) *led narrowly: rdn and hdd over 2f out: wknd over 1f out* **11/2**[3]
0-6 8 14 **Mithayel Style (FR)**[81] 2123 3-8-7 0........................(p[1]) RhonaPindar(7) 1
(David Thompson) *trckd ldrs: racd keenly: rdn over 2f out: wknd* **66/1**
1m 26.78s (-0.62) **Going Correction** -0.15s/f (Firm)
WFA 3 from 4yo 7lb **8** Ran SP% **117.0**
Speed ratings (Par 101): **97,96,96,91,86 85,79,63**
CSF £48.26 TOTE £21.10: £3.90, £1.30, £1.20; EX 71.10 Trifecta £269.80.
Owner Mrs James Bethell **Bred** Mrs James Bethell **Trained** Middleham Moor, N Yorks

FOCUS
Add 6yds. An ordinary maiden, but it produced a dramatic finish. The level is fluid, but the winner has been rated back to her early 2yo form for now.

5042 EVERY RACE LIVE ON RACING TV H'CAP 5f
4:30 (4:31) (Class 5) (0-75,77) 3-Y-O+
£4,075 (£1,212; £606; £303; £300; £300) Stalls Low

Form RPR
0006 1 **Little Legs**[20] 4294 3-9-9 77................................ BenRobinson(3) 5 87
(Brian Ellison) *chsd ldrs: rdn to ld appr fnl f: kpt on wl* **16/1**
5063 2 2 ¼ **Something Lucky (IRE)**[12] 4593 7-9-5 66............(v) AlistairRawlinson 2 69
(Michael Appleby) *dwlt sltly: hld up: sn pushed along: r.o wl fnl f: wnt 2nd towards fin* **8/1**

-000 **3** ½ **Computable**[11] 4625 5-9-2 **63**....................(p) RachelRichardson 8 64
(Tim Easterby) *hld up: racd keenly: angled lft and hdwy over 1f out: kpt on ins fnl f* **16/1**

0305 **4** *nk* **Landing Night (IRE)**[46] 3360 7-9-7 **68**....................(vt[1]) CliffordLee 1 68
(Rebecca Menzies) *dwlt: midfield: rdn over 2f out: kpt on fnl f* **5/1**[3]

0423 **5** *hd* **Indian Pursuit (IRE)**[12] 4586 6-9-4 **65**....................(v) JasonHart 9 64
(John Quinn) *chsd ldrs: rdn along over 2f out: one pce* **7/2**[2]

0555 **6** ½ **Billy Dylan (IRE)**[14] 4514 4-9-13 **77**....................(v[1]) ConorMcGovern(3) 3 75
(David O'Meara) *led: rdn and hdd appr fnl f: sn no ex* **20/1**

5066 **7** ¾ **Qaaraat**[16] 4458 4-9-6 **67**.................... CamHardie 6 62
(Antony Brittain) *dwlt: hld up: rdn 2f out: minor late hdwy: nvr involved (jockey said gelding stumbled leaving the stalls)* **7/1**

112 **8** *nk* **The Defiant**[16] 4436 3-9-6 **71**.................... KevinStott 4 64
(Paul Midgley) *prom: rdn appr fnl f: wknd fnl 110yds* **11/4**[1]

0002 **9** 1¼ **Longroom**[14] 4514 7-9-9 **70**....................(p[1]) GrahamLee 10 59
(Noel Wilson) *dwlt: midfield on outer: rdn over 2f out: wknd ins fnl f* **12/1**

-000 **10** 5 **Guardia Svizzera (IRE)**[105] 1521 5-9-1 **67**..........(h) BenSanderson(5) 7 38
(Roger Fell) *dwlt: sn midfield: outpcd and lost pl 3f out: wknd over 1f out* **14/1**

58.91s (-1.59) **Going Correction** -0.15s/f (Firm)
WFA 3 from 4yo+ 4lb **10** Ran **SP% 120.1**
Speed ratings (Par 103): **106,102,101,101,100 100,98,98,96,88**
CSF £141.83 CT £2143.11 TOTE £15.00: £3.30, £2.90, £6.20; EX 188.00 Trifecta £2980.70.
Owner Brian Ellison Racing Club **Bred** Mrs Claire L Ellison **Trained** Norton, N Yorks

FOCUS
A sprint handicap run at a good clip. The winner scored with authority. The winner has been rated back to her early 2yo form.

5043 AJA "NOVICE" FLAT AMATEUR RIDERS' H'CAP 1m 4f 13y
5:00 (5:00) (Class 6) (0-65,67) 4-Y-0+
£2,994 (£928; £464; £300; £300; £300) **Stalls** Low

Form RPR

0313 **1** **Be Perfect (USA)**[13] 4543 10-12-0 **67**.................... MrMatthewEnnis 6 74
(Ruth Carr) *hld up: stdy hdwy fr 4f out: swtchd rt 2f out: sn chsd ldrs: rdn and styd on wl to ld 110yds out* **1/1**[1]

6-50 **2** 3 **Sheila's Empire (IRE)**[3] 4958 4-10-6 **50**.................... MrJDunne(5) 5 52
(Gavin Cromwell, Ire) *midfield: hdwy and chsd ldrs 4f out: rdn to ld narrowly 1f out: hdd 110yds out: one pce* **5/2**[2]

6210 **3** 2 **Orobas (IRE)**[4] 4915 7-11-9 **67**....................(v) MrJoshuaScott(5) 4 66
(Lucinda Egerton) *trckd ldrs: led over 3f out: rdn over 2f out: hdd 1f out: no ex* **9/2**[3]

0-00 **4** 20 **Wynfaul The Wizard (USA)**[55] 3006 4-10-6 **45**..(v[1]) MissAntoniaPeck 8 12
(Laura Morgan) *led after 3f: hdd over 3f out: sn rdn: wknd 2f out* **33/1**

-000 **5** 8 **Late For The Sky**[29] 3960 5-10-6 **45**.................... SophieSmith 3
(Stella Barclay) *trckd ldrs: outpcd and lost pl over 7f out: sn struggling in rr* **33/1**

40-0 **6** 7 **Rockliffe**[16] 4435 6-10-6 **45**....................(v[1]) AidanMacdonald 9
(Micky Hammond) *midfield: rdn over 4f out: wknd* **7/1**

000- **7** 18 **Monzino (USA)**[150] 9035 11-10-1 **45**.................... MrHakanSensoy(5) 2
(Michael Chapman) *slowly away: a in rr* **250/1**

50/0 **8** 23 **Jackman**[76] 2335 5-10-1 **45**....................(t) MrEireannCagney(5) 1
(Lee James) *led for 3f: trckd ldrs: lost pl 5f out: wknd and sn bhd* **40/1**

2m 39.15s (-1.45) **Going Correction** -0.15s/f (Firm) **8** Ran **SP% 118.0**
Speed ratings (Par 101): **98,96,94,81,76 71,59,44**
CSF £3.81 CT £7.41 TOTE £1.70: £1.10, £1.60, £1.10; EX 4.10 Trifecta £8.90.
Owner The Beer Stalkers & Ruth Carr **Bred** Joseph Allen **Trained** Huby, N Yorks

FOCUS
Add 6yds. A weak amateur riders' handicap, but it provided a popular winner. The winner has been rated in line with the better view of his recent form.
T/Plt: £92.00 to a £1 stake. Pool: £46,396.24 - 367.95 winning units T/Qpdt: £54.50 to a £1 stake. Pool: £3,256.71 - 44.16 winning units **Andrew Sheret**

4794 LINGFIELD (L-H)
Wednesday, July 17

OFFICIAL GOING: Turf course - good to firm (watered; 9.1); all-weather course - polytrack: standard

5044 FOLLOW AT THE RACES ON TWITTER H'CAP 6f 1y(P)
2:10 (2:10) (Class 6) (0-60,67) 3-Y-0
£2,781 (£827; £413; £300; £300; £300) **Stalls** Low

Form RPR

6521 **1** **Alicia Darcy (IRE)**[8] 4755 3-10-1 **67** 6ex..............(b) AdamMcNamara 6 77+
(Archie Watson) *sluggish s and hld up in rr: tk clsr order on inner at 1/2-way: shkn up 2f out and angled out: rdn over 1f out: led 150yds out: in control and pushed out cl home* **13/8**[1]

0500 **2** 2¾ **True Belief (IRE)**[29] 3961 3-9-7 **59**....................(h) RossaRyan 8 61
(Brett Johnson) *in rr: trckd wnr at 1/2-way: rdn 2f out: styd on to take 2nd 100yds out but n.d to wnr* **10/1**

4400 **3** 1¾ **Moneta**[29] 3964 3-9-7 **59**....................(t) JFEgan 4 55
(Jonathan Portman) *sn cl up in 3rd on outer: rdn wl over 1f out: led ent fnl f: hdd 150yds out: no ex and lost 2nd sn after* **7/1**

35-0 **4** 1 **Molly Blake**[79] 2204 3-9-10 **62**.................... AdamKirby 3 55
(Clive Cox) *led 1f: sn trckd ldr and t.k.h: pressed ldr at 1/2-way: led 2f out and rdn: hdd ent fnl f: plugged on* **3/1**[2]

4 **5** *shd* **Betty's Heart (IRE)**[47] 3319 3-8-9 **47**.................... KierenFox 1 39
(John Best) *t.k.h bhd ldrs on inner: effrt 2f out: one pce fnl f (jockey said filly ran too free)* **9/2**[3]

0430 **6** 4½ **Awake In Asia**[13] 4563 3-9-6 **58**....................(p) JackMitchell 5 36
(Charlie Wallis) *bhd ldrs on outer: shkn up at 1/2-way: rdn over 2f out: no imp in st* **18/1**

0004 **7** ½ **Yfenni (IRE)**[32] 3839 3-8-7 **45**.................... KieranO'Neill 2 21
(Milton Bradley) *a towards rr: rdn over 2f out: no imp in st* **18/1**

000- **8** 4½ **Illegitimate Gains**[210] 9613 3-8-9 **47**....................(p[1]) CharlieBennett 7 9
(Adam West) *pushed along to ld after 1f: effrt over 2f out: hdd 2f out: wknd qckly over 1f out* **25/1**

-000 **9** 19 **Spring Holly (IRE)**[79] 2211 3-8-7 **45**....................(w) NicolaCurrie 10
(Milton Bradley) *wnt rt s: in rr-div and racd freely: dropped to rr and rdn to hold pl at 1/2-way: no ex wl over 2f out: pushed out over 1f out: t.o (jockey said filly ran too free)* **33/1**

1m 11.32s (-0.58) **Going Correction** -0.125s/f (Stan) **9** Ran **SP% 120.2**
Speed ratings (Par 98): **98,94,92,90,90 84,83,77,52**
CSF £20.82 CT £96.52 TOTE £2.40: £1.10, £3.10, £2.60; EX 19.40 Trifecta £103.00.
Owner Boadicea Bloodstock **Bred** Tally-Ho Stud **Trained** Upper Lambourn, W Berks

FOCUS
A dry run up to a low-key meeting staged on both Polytrack and turf. Not too much to dwell on in a very ordinary handicap in which the one in-form runner won with plenty in hand. The gallop was reasonable and the first five pulled clear in the straight. The winner has been rated back close to her 2yo form.

5045 SKY SPORTS RACING ON VIRGIN 535 / EBF FILLIES' NOVICE STKS (PLUS 10 RACE) 6f 1y(P)
2:40 (2:42) (Class 5) 2-Y-0
£3,428 (£1,020; £509; £254) **Stalls** Low

Form RPR

2 **1** **Dark Lady**[13] 4557 2-9-0 0.................... RyanMoore 5 87+
(Richard Hannon) *trckd ldr: shkn up to ld over 1f out: effrt and wnt clr fnl f: easily* **11/10**[1]

5 **2** 5 **Onassis (IRE)**[22] 4223 2-9-0 0.................... TomMarquand 11 69+
(Charlie Fellowes) *mid-div: rdn 2f out: kpt on on outer fr over 1f out to take 2nd cl home: no ch w wnr* **7/2**[3]

5 **3** ½ **Diva Rock**[21] 4233 2-9-0 0.................... NicolaCurrie 9 67
(George Baker) *in last pair: rdn over 2f out: kpt on wl on inner over 1f out: tk 2nd 150yds out: lost 2nd cl home* **66/1**

4 1¼ **Carmena (IRE)** 2-9-0 0.................... SeanLevey 2 63
(Charlie Fellowes) *trckd ldrs: pushed along wl over 1f out: hmpd over 1f out: pushed out fnl f* **14/1**

30 **5** ¾ **Multiply By Eight (FR)**[28] 3983 2-9-0 0.............. SilvestreDeSousa 10 61+
(Tom Dascombe) *racd in mid-div: tk clsr order bhd front pair 2f out: rdn wl over 1f out: received slt bump sn after: pushed out fnl f* **11/4**[2]

0014 **6** *nk* **Shani**[18] 4373 2-9-0 **63**.................... KieranO'Neill 4 60
(John Bridger) *led: niggled along at 1/2-way: hdd over 1f out and sn hmpd rival: wknd fnl f* **40/1**

7 1¼ **Depose** 2-9-0 0....................(h[1]) PatCosgrave 7 56
(Hugo Palmer) *sluggish s and in last: shkn up on outer to make prog over 2f out: no imp fr over 1f out* **10/1**

4 **8** 8 **Penny Diamond**[53] 3076 2-9-0 0.................... KieranShoemark 8 30
(Amanda Perrett) *sluggish s and in last trio: rdn over 2f out: no ex over 1f out* **33/1**

0 **9** 12 **Casi Casi**[58] 2918 2-8-9 0.................... TheodoreLadd(5) 1
(Charlie Wallis) *racd in mid-div: rdn to hold pl at 1/2-way: sn struggling: wl hld over 1f out* **100/1**

1m 11.67s (-0.23) **Going Correction** -0.125s/f (Stan) **9** Ran **SP% 120.1**
Speed ratings (Par 91): **96,89,88,87,86 85,83,73,57**
CSF £5.52 TOTE £1.80: £1.10, £1.50, £11.60; EX 7.10 Trifecta £183.60.
Owner Cheveley Park Stud **Bred** Cheveley Park Stud Ltd **Trained** East Everleigh, Wilts

FOCUS
Not much in the way of strength in depth and a race in which the second favourite disappointed but a useful performance from the winner, who won with plenty in hand and should hold her own in better company. The gallop was fair. The sixth helps set the level.

5046 TU FUND MANAGERS H'CAP 5f 6y(P)
3:10 (3:11) (Class 6) (0-60,60) 3-Y-0+
£2,781 (£827; £413; £300; £300; £300) **Stalls** High

Form RPR

0000 **1** **Come On Dave (IRE)**[27] 4027 10-9-4 **58**..............(b) DarraghKeenan(5) 3 67
(John Butler) *mid-div on outer: shkn up and smooth prog 2f out: rdn over 1f out: str run on outer ent fnl f to ld 110yds out* **3/1**[1]

6405 **2** 1¼ **Terri Rules (IRE)**[7] 4772 4-9-4 **53**.................... TomMarquand 7 58
(Lee Carter) *in rr: shkn up to take clsr order 2f out: sn rdn: styd wl ent fnl f to take 2nd cl home: nrst fin (jockey said filly hung left-handed under pressure)* **13/2**[3]

1246 **3** 1½ **Hurricane Alert**[27] 4027 7-8-6 **48**.................... AledBeech(7) 1 47
(Mark Hoad) *trckd ldrs on inner: effrt 2f out and angled out ent st: nt qckn over 1f out: styd on and briefly tk 2nd 100yds out: lost 3rd sn after* **4/1**[2]

0400 **4** ¾ **Starchant**[23] 4183 3-9-0 **53**.................... KieranO'Neill 4 48
(John Bridger) *bhd ldrs: effrt over 2f out: styd on one pce fr over 1f out* **8/1**

1000 **5** *nk* **Sandfrankskipsgo**[85] 2010 10-9-7 **56**.................... TomQueally 6 51
(Peter Crate) *disp ld tl 1/2-way whn trckd ldr: rdn on inner wl over 1f out: chal ldr ent fnl f: one pce fnl 110yds* **12/1**

0210 **6** *nk* **Brogans Bay (IRE)**[14] 4501 4-9-7 **56**.................... JFEgan 10 50
(Simon Dow) *disp ldr tl clr ldr at 1/2-way: rdn wl over 1f out: strly pressed ent fnl f: hdd 110yds out and lost numerous pls sn after* **4/1**[2]

0044 **7** 1½ **Firenze Rosa (IRE)**[13] 4556 4-8-5 **47**.................... Pierre-LouisJamin(7) 2 36
(John Bridger) *in rr-div on inner: rdn over 2f out: one pce fnl f* **10/1**

0-06 **8** 1¼ **Jonnysimpson (IRE)**[14] 4501 4-9-1 **50**....................(t[1]) KierenFox 5 34
(Lee Carter) *in last pair and outpcd: niggled at times: rdn wl over 2f out: no imp fr 2f out (jockey said filly was never travelling)* **16/1**

F000 **9** 1¼ **Mercers**[27] 4025 5-9-0 **54**....................(b) SeamusCronin(5) 9 34
(Paddy Butler) *towards rr racing too wd and niggled along at times to go pce: effrt 2f out: no imp* **9/1**

58.8s **Going Correction** -0.125s/f (Stan)
WFA 3 from 4yo+ 4lb **9** Ran **SP% 122.1**
Speed ratings (Par 101): **95,93,90,89,88 88,86,84,82**
CSF £24.54 CT £82.07 TOTE £3.80: £1.60, £2.10, £1.50; EX 27.30 Trifecta £110.50.
Owner Royale Racing Syndicate **Bred** Mrs Eithne Hamilton **Trained** Newmarket, Suffolk

FOCUS
The last of the three AW races and a moderate event featuring exposed sorts. The gallop was strong and the two early leaders didn't get home. The winner has been rated in line with his winter form, and the second to her AW best.

5047 JOHN HOWE RETIREMENT H'CAP 2m 4f 44y
3:40 (3:40) (Class 5) (0-75,75) 4-Y-0+
£3,040 (£904; £452; £226) **Stalls** Centre

Form RPR

5-06 **1** **Early Summer (IRE)**[15] 4483 4-9-5 **73**.................... OisinMurphy 6 82
(Hughie Morrison) *trckd ldrs: effrt 3f out: kpt on wl and led 2f out: asserted fnl f* **4/1**[3]

5016 **2** 2¾ **Atomic Jack**[7] 4791 4-9-1 **69**.................... NicolaCurrie 1 75
(George Baker) *led: rdn 3f out: pressed over 2f out: narrowly hdd 2f out: kpt chalng tl one pce fnl f* **3/1**[2]

-466 **3** 2¾ **Graceful Lady**[18] 4404 6-9-2 **75**.................... DarraghKeenan(5) 7 78
(Robert Eddery) *sluggish s: mid-div: rdn 3f out and racd wd in st: fnd stride over 1f out: styd on wl fnl f to take 3rd cl home (jockey said mare lost left hind shoe)* **6/1**

3551 **4** ¾ **Fitzwilly**[7] 4796 9-8-10 **64** 4ex.................... SilvestreDeSousa 5 67
(Mick Channon) *hld up in rr: tk clsr order over 4f out: rdn on inner 3f out: tk 3rd 1f out: lost 3rd cl home* **9/4**[1]

-005 **5** 3¾ **Arty Campbell (IRE)**[15] 4483 9-8-13 **70**....................(p) JoshuaBryan(3) 2 69
(Bernard Llewellyn) *in last: effrt 3f out: no imp 2f out: plugged on fr over 1f out* **16/1**

0-54 **6** 2 **Templier (IRE)**[48] 3252 6-8-4 **58** oh3 ow2..............(b) JoeyHaynes 8 55
(Gary Moore) *trckd ldr: clsr and pressed ldr 7f out: rdn 3f out and stdy on tl wknd over 1f out* **20/1**

2-00 **7** 8 **Ardamir (FR)**[7] 4791 7-8-12 **66**.............................. LiamJones 4 55
(Laura Mongan) *t.k.h early: sn hld up in rr: rdn 3f out: kpt on one pce 2f out: wknd qckly over 1f out* **33/1**

5-50 **R** **Wind Place And Sho**[11] 4661 7-8-13 **67**..........................(p) RyanTate 3
(James Eustace) *ref to r: stood stl in stalls* **7/1**

4m 24.73s **8** Ran SP% **116.1**
CSF £16.74 CT £70.97 TOTE £4.90: £1.80, £1.10, £2.00; EX 16.20 Trifecta £80.30.
Owner Wardley Bloodstock **Bred** Lakin Bloodstock/Wardley Bloodstock **Trained** East Ilsley, Berks

FOCUS
The inaugural running of a race that is the fourth longest in the Flat calendar. An ordinary gallop picked up off the home turn and this wasn't a severe test of stamina. Race distance increased by 4yds. The second has been rated to form.

5048 CW SURFACING MAIDEN FILLIES' STKS 1m 3f 133y
4:10 (4:13) (Class 5) 3-Y-O+ £3,428 (£1,020; £509; £254) Stalls High

Form RPR

5-3 **1** **Maktabba**[72] 2481 3-9-1 0.............................. DaneO'Neill 7 69+
(William Haggas) *sn trckd ldr: shkn up 3f out: narrowly led wl over 1f out: cajoled along fr 1f out to maintain narrow advantage ins fnl f: snugly* **11/4**[2]

22 **2** ½ **The Very Moon**[19] 4326 3-9-1 0.............................. RyanMoore 4 68+
(Sir Michael Stoute) *led: wl over 2f out: narrowly hdd wl over 1f out: kpt on but nt get past wnr* **1/4**[1]

60 **3** 4½ **Constraint**[63] 2731 3-9-1 0.............................. RobHornby 3 61
(Andrew Balding) *a in 3rd: shuffled along fr over 2f out to maintain position: nvr involved* **40/1**

00 **4** 2 **Astral Girl**[27] 4022 3-9-1 0.............................. CharlieBennett 6 57
(Hughie Morrison) *hld up in last: effrt on outer wl over 2f out: plugged on fr over 1f out under mostly hands and heels* **66/1**

06 **5** ½ **Giving Back**[14] 4503 5-9-12 0.............................. TomMarquand 2 56
(Alan King) *racd in 5th: pushed along fr over 2f out: sme prog fnl f: nvr involved* **20/1**[3]

00 **6** 2¼ **Sharqi (IRE)**[8] 4768 3-9-1 0..........................(t) TomQueally 5 53?
(Jean-Rene Auvray) *racd in 4th on outer: shkn up 4f out and nt handle bnd over 3f out: unbalanced coming into st: no imp fr wl over 1f out* **100/1**

2m 29.41s (-4.59) **Going Correction** -0.425s/f (Firm)
WFA 3 from 5yo 11lb **6** Ran SP% **116.4**
Speed ratings (Par 100): **98,97,94,93,93 91**
CSF £4.05 TOTE £4.90: £1.50, £1.02; EX 5.70 Trifecta £20.80.
Owner Hamdan Al Maktoum **Bred** Shadwell Estate Company Limited **Trained** Newmarket, Suffolk

FOCUS
An uncompetitive event in which the two market leaders had the race to themselves in the home straight. An ordinary gallop picked up on the approach to the home turn and the bare form may not be entirely reliable. Race distance increased by 4yds.

5049 XPERTHR PRESENTS...THE MANE EVENT H'CAP 1m 2f
4:40 (4:41) (Class 6) (0-55,55) 3-Y-O+ £2,781 (£827; £413; £300; £300; £300) Stalls Low

Form RPR

-043 **1** **Whimsical Dream**[14] 4499 3-8-6 **46**.............................. KieranO'Neill 1 52
(Michael Bell) *bhd ldr on inner: swtchd out and effrt wl over 2f out: led over 2f out where sltly edgd rt and bmpd rival: styd on wl ins fnl f* **7/1**

0004 **2** 1 **All Right**[15] 4485 3-8-11 **51**.............................. DaneO'Neill 6 55
(Henry Candy) *mid-div on outer: shkn up 3f out and smooth prog over 2f out: rdn 2f out on inner: styd on wl fr over 1f out to pressed wnr fnl 110yds: no ex cl home* **9/2**[1]

3342 **3** hd **Red Archangel (IRE)**[19] 4346 3-9-1 **55**...............(p) KieranShoemark 8 59
(Richard Spencer) *mid-div on inner: sltly ct on heels over 3f out and shuffled bk to last trio: shkn up and prog over 2f out: swtchd out 2f out: fin wl fr over 1f out to grab 3rd cl home and almost snatched 2nd post: can do bttr* **6/1**[3]

0002 **4** 1¼ **Iballisticvin**[25] 4111 6-9-10 **55**..........................(v¹) HectorCrouch 9 56
(Gary Moore) *w ldr on outer: effrt 3f out: chalng whn carried sltly rt by wnr over 2f out: stuck on fr over 1f out: lost 3rd cl home* **6/1**[3]

-000 **5** nk **Fanny Chenal**[21] 4244 3-8-8 **48**.............................. NicolaCurrie 11 49
(Jim Boyle) *in rr and t.k.h: rdn in last 3f out w plenty to do: no immediate imp 2f out: fnd stride and fin wl fr over 1f* **16/1**

0006 **6** 1¼ **Rocksette**[15] 4475 5-9-3 **48**..........................(p) TomQueally 4 45
(Gary Moore) *racd in rr-div and t.k.h: prog on bnd into st: effrt over 2f out: plugged on fr over 1f out* **14/1**

0400 **7** 2 **Solveig's Song**[8] 4753 7-9-8 **53**..........................(b) TomMarquand 7 46
(Steve Woodman) *in rr and outpcd early on: rdn 3f out: plugged on fr 2f out* **50/1**

0362 **8** 2 **Clive Clifton (IRE)**[15] 4475 6-9-2 **47**.............................. OisinMurphy 10 36
(Kevin Frost) *trckd ldrs: rdn over 2f out and plugged on: no imp over 1f out and tenderly handled ins fnl f* **5/1**[2]

-004 **9** 3½ **Riverina**[39] 3593 3-8-8 **51**..........................(p¹) MitchGodwin(3) 3 34
(Harry Dunlop) *hld up in rr on inner: rdn 3f out: kpt on one pce* **12/1**

6040 **10** ½ **Rainbow Jazz (IRE)**[13] 4547 4-9-9 **54**..........................(be) CharlieBennett 2 35
(Adam West) *led: effrt wl over 2f out: hdd 2f out: wknd over 1f out* **7/1**

3003 **11** 13 **With Approval (IRE)**[15] 4475 7-9-9 **54**..........................(p) LiamJones 5 9
(Laura Mongan) *mid-div on inner and niggled along at 1/2-way: nt handle bnd over 3f out: pushed along and wknd over 1f out* **25/1**

-003 **R** **Sari Mareis**[15] 4485 3-8-11 **51**.............................. CharlesBishop 12
(Denis Coakley) *ref to r: stood stl in stalls* **12/1**

2m 6.53s (-5.67) **Going Correction** -0.425s/f (Firm)
WFA 3 from 4yo+ 9lb **12** Ran SP% **122.2**
Speed ratings (Par 101): **105,104,104,103,102 101,100,98,95,95 85,**
CSF £39.75 CT £206.88 TOTE £6.30: £2.50, £2.20, £2.40; EX 42.30 Trifecta £324.10.
Owner Bartisan Racing Ltd **Bred** Bartisan Racing Ltd **Trained** Newmarket, Suffolk

FOCUS
A low-grade handicap in which the gallop was fair and this form should prove reliable. Race distance increased by 4yds.

5050 WITHEFORD EQUINE BARRIER TRIALS AT LINGFIELD PARK H'CAP 6f
5:10 (5:11) (Class 5) (0-70,70) 3-Y-O+ £3,428 (£1,020; £509; £300; £300; £300) Stalls Centre

Form RPR

4-24 **1** **Rewaayat**[79] 2183 4-9-6 **64**.............................. DaneO'Neill 1 80+
(Charles Hills) *trckd ldrs: shkn up to take clsr order over 2f out: rdn to chal 2f out: carried hd high over 1f out and sn led: asserted ins fnl f: comf at fin* **5/2**[1]

6-00 **2** 3 **Crackin Dream (IRE)**[81] 2098 3-9-2 **65**.............................. AdamKirby 4 67
(Clive Cox) *trckd ldrs: effrt over 2f out: kpt on wl fr over 1f out to take 2nd last strides: no ch w wnr* **5/1**[3]

0550 **3** ½ **Englishman**[11] 4649 9-9-5 **63**.............................. RobertWinston 5 64
(Milton Bradley) *in rr-div on outer: effrt over 2f out: styd on wl on outer over 1f out: no ex last 110yds and lost 2nd last strides* **16/1**

520 **4** ½ **Alliseeisnibras (IRE)**[25] 4116 3-9-7 **70**.............................. SeanLevey 3 69
(Ismail Mohammed) *wl away and led on rail: pressed after 2f: rdn over 2f out: hdd ent fnl f: one pce after* **8/1**

6000 **5** ¾ **Porto Ferro (IRE)**[22] 4227 5-9-1 **59**..........................(t¹) KieranO'Neill 6 56
(John Bridger) *mid-div on outer: effrt over 2f out: styd on wl tl no ex fnl 150yds* **20/1**

2455 **6** 3½ **Cent Flying**[9] 4733 4-9-4 **62**..........................(t) MartinDwyer 8 48
(William Muir) *in rr-div on inner: rdn over 2f out: one pce fr over 1f out* **9/2**[2]

0004 **7** 2¼ **Mont Kiara (FR)**[50] 3188 6-9-7 **65**.............................. TomMarquand 7 44
(Simon Dow) *in rr: effrt wl over 2f out: one pce fr over 1f out* **15/2**

0055 **8** nk **Human Nature (IRE)**[36] 3701 6-9-5 **70**..........................(vt¹) MarcoGhiani(7) 2 48
(Stuart Williams) *bhd ldr: impr to press ldr 2f: outpcd over 2f out: wknd over 1f out* **11/2**

0002 **9** 1½ **Gold Club**[18] 4376 8-8-7 **51** oh1.............................. NicolaCurrie 9 24
(Lee Carter) *a in rr: outpcd and rdn 1/2-way: no imp (jockey said gelding was never travelling)* **14/1**

1m 8.48s (-3.02) **Going Correction** -0.425s/f (Firm)
WFA 3 from 4yo+ 5lb **9** Ran SP% **119.0**
Speed ratings (Par 103): **103,99,98,97,96 92,89,88,86**
CSF £15.57 CT £168.69 TOTE £3.20: £1.60, £2.20, £4.80; EX 15.00 Trifecta £308.40.
Owner Hamdan Al Maktoum **Bred** Shadwell Estate Company Limited **Trained** Lambourn, Berks

FOCUS
A modest event in which the gallop was sound, The field bunched against the stands' rail. The second has been rated close to form, with the fourth to her maiden form.
T/Plt: £19.40 to a £1 stake. Pool: £63,240.38 winning units T/Qpdt: £5.70 to a £1 stake. Pool: £6,175.37 - 788.51 winning units **Cathal Gahan**

4998 WOLVERHAMPTON (A.W) (L-H)
Wednesday, July 17

OFFICIAL GOING: Tapeta: standard
Wind: Fresh behind Weather: Overcast, with the odd light shower

5051 HELLERMANNTYTON / EDMUNDSON ELECTRICAL H'CAP 7f 36y (Tp)
5:50 (5:53) (Class 6) (0-60,60) 3-Y-O+ £2,781 (£827; £413; £300; £300; £300) Stalls High

Form RPR

5002 **1** **Sfumato**[7] 4785 5-9-9 **59**.............................. ConnorBeasley 10 67
(Adrian Nicholls) *s.i.s: hld up: hdwy over 1f out: r.o u.p to ld towards fin* **3/1**[2]

2100 **2** shd **Blessed To Empress (IRE)**[15] 4472 4-9-9 **59**..........(v¹) JasonWatson 2 66
(Amy Murphy) *s.i.s: sn pushed along to chse ldrs: lost pl over 5f out: hdwy over 2f out: rdn and swtchd rt over 1f out: ev ch towards fin: r.o* **6/1**[3]

0000 **3** ¾ **Viola Park**[8] 4767 5-9-6 **56**..........................(p) DavidProbert 3 61
(Ronald Harris) *sn led: hdd over 5f out: chsd ldr tl led again over 2f out: rdn clr over 1f out: hdd towards fin* **10/1**

5600 **4** 2 **Peachey Carnehan**[8] 4763 5-9-8 **58**..........................(v) JamesSullivan 8 58
(Michael Mullineaux) *s.i.s: in rr: hdwy over 1f out: r.o to go 4th nr fin* **14/1**

1200 **5** nk **La Cumparsita (IRE)**[9] 4725 5-9-2 **52**.............................. LukeMorris 12 51
(Tristan Davidson) *chsd ldrs: rdn and edgd rt over 1f out: edger lft ins fnl f: styd on same pce* **11/1**

00 **6** shd **Hidden Dream (FR)**[25] 4116 4-9-2 **55**.............................. AaronJones(3) 4 53
(John Butler) *hld up in tch: lost pl over 5f out: rdn 1/2-way: r.o ins fnl f* **50/1**

5240 **7** 1¾ **Hi Ho Silver**[19] 4349 5-9-2 **52**..........................(p) RichardKingscote 5 46
(Chris Wall) *sn chsng ldrs: led over 5f out: hdd over 2f out: no ex ins fnl f* **11/4**[1]

6055 **8** 1 **Elusif (IRE)**[14] 4501 4-9-6 **56**.............................. RaulDaSilva 9 47
(Shaun Keightley) *s.i.s: hld up: rdn over 2f out: nt trble ldrs* **14/1**

6350 **9** 1½ **Sooqaan**[23] 4195 8-9-4 **57**..........................(p) WilliamCox(3) 6 44
(Antony Brittain) *s.i.s: hdwy over 5f out: rdn and wknd over 1f out (jockey said gelding hung right under pressure)* **16/1**

2500 **10** ¾ **Gonzaga**[23] 4194 4-9-5 **60**.............................. RachealKneller(5) 7 45
(James Bennett) *hld up: rdn over 2f out: n.d* **28/1**

064 **11** 6 **Midnight Guest (IRE)**[7] 4772 4-9-9 **59**..........................(v) HarryBentley 1 40
(David Evans) *chsd ldrs: rdn over 2f out: wknd over 1f out* **25/1**

0-00 **12** 16 **Dutiful Son (IRE)**[14] 4501 9-9-10 **60**..........................(p) EoinWalsh 11
(Emma Owen) *sn pushed along and prom: rdn 1/2-way: wknd over 2f out* **100/1**

1m 28.74s (-0.06) **Going Correction** -0.05s/f (Stan) **12** Ran SP% **112.8**
Speed ratings (Par 101): **98,97,97,94,94 94,92,91,89,88 81,63**
CSF £19.59 CT £158.56 TOTE £2.70: £1.30, £1.80, £2.70; EX 19.80 Trifecta £157.90.
Owner J A Rattigan **Bred** Juddmonte Farms Ltd **Trained** Sessay, N Yorks

FOCUS
An ordinary handicap in which the first two and fourth came from off the pace. Straightforward form rated around the second.

5052 SEE MADNESS LIVE - 30TH AUGUST MEDIAN AUCTION MAIDEN STKS 7f 36y (Tp)
6:25 (6:26) (Class 5) 2-Y-O £3,428 (£1,020; £509; £254) Stalls High

Form RPR

1 **Hariboux** 2-9-5 0..........................(h¹) JackMitchell 2 81+
(Hugo Palmer) *chsd ldrs: shkn up to ld ins fnl f: r.o: comf* **14/1**

3 **2** *3* **Lord Of The Alps (IRE)**[29] 3954 2-9-5 0 JoeFanning 10 73
(Mark Johnston) *chsd ldr tl led 1/2-way: rdn and hung lft over 1f out: hdd ins fnl f: styd on same pce* **3/1**[1]

3 *2 ½* **Charles Street** 2-9-5 0 HarryBentley 11 66
(George Scott) *s.i.s: hdwy over 5f out: rdn 1/2-way: styd on* **20/1**

43 **4** *shd* **Lady Red Moon**[18] 4366 2-8-11 0 GabrieleMalune(3) 5 61
(Marco Botti) *s.i.s: hld up: plld hrd: rdn: hung lft and r.o ins fnl f: nt trble ldrs (jockey said filly ran too free)* **5/1**[3]

5 *nk* **Escape Proof** 2-9-0 0 JasonWatson 7 60+
(Roger Charlton) *s.i.s: hld up: r.o ins fnl f: nt rch ldrs* **3/1**[1]

6 *½* **Ten Chants** 2-9-5 0 DanielMuscutt 6 64
(Ed Dunlop) *prom: rdn and edgd lft over 1f out: no ex fnl f* **25/1**

4 **7** *2* **Precision Storm**[19] 4317 2-9-5 0 PJMcDonald 9 58
(Mark Loughnane) *hld up: forced wd 5f out: hdwy sn after: rdn and hung lft over 1f out: wknd wl ins fnl f* **14/1**

36 **8** *4* **Port Winston (IRE)**[57] 2931 2-9-5 0 DavidProbert 1 48
(Alan King) *restless in stalls: led to 1/2-way: rdn and ev ch 2f out: wknd ins fnl f (jockey said gelding was restless in stalls)* **9/2**[2]

9 *½* **Early Morning Mist (IRE)** 2-9-0 0 GeorgeWood 4 41
(Amy Murphy) *s.i.s: hld up: rdn over 1f out: styd on: nt trble ldrs* **28/1**

10 *1 ¼* **Sophar Sogood (IRE)** 2-9-5 0 (p[1]) LukeMorris 3 43
(Paul D'Arcy) *s.i.s: sn pushed along: rdn and wknd over 2f out* **50/1**

0 **11** *1* **Party Potential (USA)**[15] 4480 2-9-5 0 CallumShepherd 12 40
(Alan King) *s.i.s: a in rr* **66/1**

6 **12** *2* **The Mystery Wizard**[93] 1812 2-9-5 0 DuranFentiman 8 35
(Tim Easterby) *hld up: pushed along 1/2-way: a in rr* **80/1**

1m 30.21s (1.41) **Going Correction** -0.05s/f (Stan) **12 Ran SP% 114.9**
Speed ratings (Par 94): **89,85,82,82,82 81,79,74,74,72 71,69**
CSF £51.30 TOTE £12.50: £2.70, £2.20, £5.10; EX 53.70 Trifecta £1036.70.
Owner Kremlin Cottage Ix **Bred** Lady Gillian Brunton **Trained** Newmarket, Suffolk

FOCUS
They went a steady early gallop and it didn't pay to be too far off the pace.

5053 HELLERMANNTYTON / STARRETT H'CAP 2m 120y (Tp)
6:55 (6:56) (Class 6) (0-60,62) 3-Y-O+
£2,781 (£827; £413; £300; £300; £300) **Stalls** Low

Form RPR

5152 **1** **Bird For Life**[21] 4251 5-9-9 61 (p) EllieMacKenzie(7) 7 70
(Mark Usher) *s.i.s: hld up: hdwy 1/2-way: led over 4f out: rdn clr fr over 1f out* **9/1**[3]

0055 **2** *6* **Guaracha**[41] 3497 8-8-9 45 (b) CierenFallon(5) 12 47
(Alexandra Dunn) *chsd ldrs: led over 14f out: hdd over 4f out: rdn over 1f out: no ex fnl f* **40/1**

4033 **3** *½* **Yasir (USA)**[65] 2695 11-9-9 54 DavidProbert 5 55
(Sophie Leech) *s.i.s: hld up: hdwy on outer over 1f out: styd on to go 3rd post: nt rch ldrs* **20/1**

00-5 **4** *hd* **Mon Frere (IRE)**[43] 3446 3-9-2 62 LukeMorris 1 64
(Sir Mark Prescott Bt) *hld up: pushed along and hdwy over 3f out: rdn over 1f out: styd on same pce* **1/2**[1]

5600 **5** *1* **Uncle Bernie (IRE)**[23] 4190 9-10-0 59 (p) JamesSullivan 10 59
(Sarah Hollinshead) *s.i.s: hld up: hdwy on outer over 2f out: no ex ins fnl f* **66/1**

5-56 **6** *½* **Kitty's Cove**[14] 4510 4-9-0 45 (bt[1]) DuranFentiman 4 44
(Tim Easterby) *s.i.s: hld up: rdn and hung rt over 1f out: r.o ins fnl f: nvr nrr* **16/1**

4264 **7** *½* **Knight Commander**[15] 4483 6-9-12 57 (t) RaulDaSilva 6 56
(Steve Flook) *led 1f: chsd ldrs: lost pl over 6f out: rdn: nt clr run and swtchd rt over 1f out: n.d after* **6/1**[2]

0066 **8** *3* **Mood For Mischief**[7] 4796 4-9-1 51 (p) RachealKneller(5) 3 46
(James Bennett) *hld up in tch: rdn over 2f out: wknd over 1f out* **33/1**

10-6 **9** *10* **Pepper Street (IRE)**[25] 4112 4-10-3 62 (p) GeorgeWood 8 45
(Amy Murphy) *led after 1f: hdd over 14f out: chsd ldr tl over 11f out: remained handy tl rdn over 2f out: sn wknd* **25/1**

0400 **10** *1 ¼* **Omotesando**[30] 3940 9-9-9 57 MeganNicholls(3) 13 39
(Oliver Greenall) *sn prom: chsd ldr over 11f out tl led 8f out: hdd over 4f out: wknd wl over 1f out (jockey said gelding ran too free early)* **20/1**

00-0 **11** *17* **Just Another Idea (IRE)**[65] 2698 4-9-0 48 (v[1]) WilliamCox(3) 2 9
(Mandy Rowland) *chsd ldrs: rdn over 3f out: sn wknd (jockey said gelding ran too free early)* **150/1**

3m 41.13s (1.83) **Going Correction** -0.05s/f (Stan)
WFA 3 from 4yo+ 15lb **11 Ran SP% 117.7**
Speed ratings (Par 101): **93,90,89,89,89 89,88,87,82,82 74**
CSF £309.00 CT £6805.30 TOTE £8.80: £1.80, £9.80, £3.20; EX 403.70 Trifecta £1118.00.
Owner The Mark Usher Racing Club **Bred** Mrs Robert Langton **Trained** Upper Lambourn, Berks

FOCUS
The in-form winner took this with ease, while the odds-on favourite disappointed. A pb from the winner.

5054 SKY SPORTS RACING ON VIRGIN 535 H'CAP 1m 1f 104y (Tp)
7:25 (7:28) (Class 6) (0-60,67) 3-Y-O
£2,781 (£827; £413; £300; £300; £300) **Stalls** Low

Form RPR

0-01 **1** **Hydroplane (IRE)**[4] 4931 3-10-1 67 6ex LukeMorris 7 80+
(Sir Mark Prescott Bt) *mde all: set stdy pce tl shkn up: qcknd and hung rt fr over 2f out tl rdn over 1f out: styd on: comf* **6/5**[1]

0506 **2** *3 ½* **Chakrii (IRE)**[15] 4485 3-8-11 49 (p) DavidProbert 6 53
(Henry Spiller) *chsd ldrs: rdn to chse wnr over 1f out: styd on same pce fnl f* **18/1**

-034 **3** *1* **Hooflepuff (IRE)**[96] 1725 3-9-2 54 GeorgeWood 9 56
(James Fanshawe) *s.i.s: pushed along early in rr: hdwy over 1f out: styd on to go 3rd ins fnl f: nt trble ldrs* **11/4**[2]

000 **4** *2* **Arcadienne**[23] 4177 3-9-7 59 HarryBentley 10 57
(Ralph Beckett) *chsd ldrs: rdn over 2f out: sn outpcd: kpt on ins fnl f* **12/1**

000 **5** *1* **Broughtons Bear (IRE)**[71] 2506 3-8-13 51 RichardKingscote 5 47
(Stuart Williams) *edgd lft s: chsd ldrs: edgd lft over 8f out: wnt 2nd over 2f out tl rdn and edgd lft over 1f out: no ex ins fnl f* **7/1**[3]

0035 **6** *½* **Mi Laddo (IRE)**[15] 4485 3-8-9 47 (tp) NathanEvans 3 42
(Oliver Greenall) *s.i.s: and hmpd s: hld up: rdn over 1f out: nvr nrr* **20/1**

0P00 **7** *1 ½* **Gonbutnotforgotten (FR)**[21] 4244 3-8-12 50 DannyBrock 2 42
(Philip McBride) *edgd rt s: prom: nt clr run over 8f out: rdn over 1f out: wknd ins fnl f* **28/1**

-000 **8** *nse* **Milistorm**[39] 3593 3-8-7 45 EoinWalsh 4 36
(Michael Blanshard) *s.i.s and hmpd s: hld up: effrt on outer over 2f out: sn hung rt and wknd* **100/1**

0000 **9** *2* **Rock Up In Style**[26] 4070 3-9-3 62 TobyEley(7) 1 49
(Clare Ellam) *pushed along and prom: hmpd and lost pl over 8f out: n.d after (jockey said gelding suffered interference in running)* **50/1**

00-0 **10** *19* **Don Diego Vega**[64] 2715 3-8-7 45 (b[1]) JamesSullivan 8
(Daniel Kubler) *s.i.s: hdwy to chse wnr over 7f out: rdn over 3f out: lost 2nd over 2f out: wknd wl over 1f out* **40/1**

2m 1.4s (0.60) **Going Correction** -0.05s/f (Stan) **10 Ran SP% 111.2**
Speed ratings (Par 98): **95,91,91,89,88 87,86,86,84,67**
CSF £23.06 CT £49.28 TOTE £2.10: £1.10, £2.30, £1.10; EX 17.30 Trifecta £46.50.
Owner Axom LXXIII **Bred** Bloomsbury Stud **Trained** Newmarket, Suffolk
■ Stewards' Enquiry : Richard Kingscote two-day ban: interference & careless riding (Jul 24, Aug 2)

FOCUS
This was steadily run and the winner dominated throughout, even allowing for a bit of a detour off the home turn. The second and third help set the level.

5055 HELLERMANNTYTON / ELECTRIC CENTER H'CAP 1m 4f 51y (Tp)
7:55 (7:55) (Class 4) (0-85,86) 3-Y-O+
£5,207 (£1,549; £774; £387; £300; £300) **Stalls** Low

Form RPR

002- **1** **Distant Chimes (GER)**[327] 6474 4-9-2 68 LukeMorris 4 80+
(Sir Mark Prescott Bt) *a.p: racd keenly: shkn up to chse ldr over 2f out: led wl over 1f out: rdn and edgd lft ins fnl f: styd on* **7/4**[1]

-104 **2** *1 ¼* **Charlie D (USA)**[18] 4363 4-9-12 78 (tp) RichardKingscote 10 87
(Tom Dascombe) *pushed along on outer to ld after 1f: sn hdd: chsd ldr tl led again 3f out: rdn and hdd wl over 1f out: edgd rt ins fnl f: styd on same pce* **6/1**

-100 **3** *4 ½* **Robert L'Echelle (IRE)**[26] 4068 3-8-12 75 PJMcDonald 9 77
(Hughie Morrison) *s.i.s: hld up: hdwy over 1f out: styd on to go 3rd ins fnl f: nt trble ldrs* **11/2**[3]

1122 **4** *1 ¼* **Grand Inquisitor**[14] 4522 7-10-3 86 (v) GabrieleMalune(3) 1 86
(Conor Dore) *chsd ldrs: swtchd rt over 2f out: rdn and edgd lft over 1f out: wknd ins fnl f* **40/1**

141- **5** *1 ½* **Desert Friend (IRE)**[275] 8256 3-9-6 83 JamieSpencer 6 80
(David Simcock) *s.i.s: hld up: rdn over 1f out: styd on ins fnl f: nvr nrr* **7/2**[2]

0341 **6** *3 ¼* **Super Kid**[32] 3847 7-9-12 78 (tp) DavidAllan 8 70
(Tim Easterby) *hld up: hdwy over 2f out: rdn over 1f out: sn wknd* **9/1**

3-40 **7** *7* **Kaser (IRE)**[161] 617 4-9-11 77 (w) TrevorWhelan 3 58
(David Loughnane) *led 1f: remained handy: rdn over 2f out: wknd over 1f out (jockey said gelding stopped quickly; vet said a post-race examination of the gelding, revealed that it was showing signs of a prolonged recovery)* **40/1**

2-65 **8** *25* **Ticklish (FR)**[34] 3773 3-8-10 73 JoeFanning 5 14
(Mark Johnston) *led over 10f out: hdd 3f out: nt clr run and wknd over 2f out* **12/1**

40-5 **9** *15* **Throckley**[22] 2126 8-9-10 76 (t) DavidProbert 7
(Katy Price) *prom: rdn over 4f out: wknd over 3f out (jockey said gelding stopped quickly)* **100/1**

2m 36.83s (-3.97) **Going Correction** -0.05s/f (Stan)
WFA 3 from 4yo+ 11lb **9 Ran SP% 111.8**
Speed ratings (Par 105): **107,106,103,102,101 99,94,77,67**
CSF £12.06 CT £45.96 TOTE £2.70: £1.30, £1.80, £2.40; EX 14.20 Trifecta £68.60.
Owner Phil Fry - Osborne House **Bred** Gestut Wiesengrund **Trained** Newmarket, Suffolk

FOCUS
A fair heat, and they finished well strung out. The winner looks nicely ahead of his mark. The third has been rated to form.

5056 GRAND THEATRE WOLVERHAMPTON H'CAP 6f 20y (Tp)
8:25 (8:25) (Class 5) (0-70,71) 3-Y-O
£3,428 (£1,020; £509; £300; £300; £300) **Stalls** Low

Form RPR

5002 **1** **Golden Parade**[12] 4606 3-8-12 61 (p) DavidAllan 6 74
(Tim Easterby) *mde all: rdn over 1f out: styd on* **3/1**[2]

4-00 **2** *1 ¾* **Great Shout (IRE)**[22] 4207 3-9-4 67 (t) GeorgeWood 3 74
(Amy Murphy) *s.i.s: hld up: hdwy over 1f out: r.o to go 2nd post: nt rch wnr (jockey said filly fly leapt upon leaving the stalls)* **25/1**

4002 **3** *nse* **Across The Sea**[6] 4844 3-9-8 71 (b[1]) PJMcDonald 2 78
(James Tate) *s.i.s: hld up: hdwy over 1f out: rdn to chse wnr ins fnl f: styd on same pce (jockey said filly hung left throughout)* **5/2**[1]

6142 **4** *2 ¾* **Di Matteo**[14] 4507 3-9-7 70 (p[1]) DanielMuscutt 1 68
(Marco Botti) *s.i.s: sn chsng ldrs: rdn to chse wnr over 1f out tl no ex ins fnl f* **11/2**

0133 **5** *¾* **Stallone (IRE)**[14] 4507 3-9-6 69 (v) HarryBentley 7 65
(Richard Spencer) *s.i.s: hld up: pushed along over 2f out: rdn over 1f out: nt trble ldrs* **7/2**[3]

2413 **6** *nk* **Eye Of The Water (IRE)**[22] 4227 3-9-6 69 DavidProbert 8 64
(Ronald Harris) *chsd wnr tl rdn over 1f out: no ex fnl f (vet said to have found the gelding to be lame on it's left fore)* **12/1**

5-00 **7** *hd* **Requited (IRE)**[23] 4185 3-9-8 71 JasonWatson 5 65
(Hughie Morrison) *chsd ldrs: rdn over 1f out: edgd rt and styd on same pce* **16/1**

0166 **8** *24* **Klopp**[19] 4330 3-9-3 66 (h) CamHardie 9
(Antony Brittain) *hld up in tch on outer: shkn up over 2f out: wknd over 1f out* **16/1**

1m 12.85s (-1.65) **Going Correction** -0.05s/f (Stan) **8 Ran SP% 114.5**
Speed ratings (Par 100): **103,100,100,96,95 95,95,63**
CSF £70.26 CT £212.69 TOTE £4.50: £1.30, £7.00, £1.40; EX 55.80 Trifecta £246.70.
Owner David Scott & Partner **Bred** Cheveley Park Stud Ltd **Trained** Great Habton, N Yorks

FOCUS
A decent front-running performance from the winner, who clocked a time 0.41sec faster than the 5l winner of the subsequent 3yo+ novice. The second has been rated to her maiden form.

5057 WOLVERHAMPTON HOLIDAY INN NOVICE STKS 6f 20y (Tp)
8:55 (9:01) (Class 5) 3-Y-O+ **£3,428** (£1,020; £509; £254) **Stalls** Low

Form RPR

4 **1** **Aljari**[55] 3019 3-9-2 0 LukeMorris 9 82
(Marco Botti) *led early: chsd ldrs: shkn up to ld over 1f out: hung rt and rdn ins fnl f: r.o wl* **14/1**

12- **2** *5* **Promote (IRE)**[300] 7471 3-9-4 0 PJMcDonald 8 68
(James Tate) *hld up in tch: nt clr run over 1f out: rdn to chse wnr ins fnl f: styd on same pce* **11/10**[1]

34 **3** *1 ¾* **Ghaith**[96] 1728 4-9-7 0 (h) JackMitchell 13 61
(Hugo Palmer) *chsd ldrs: rdn over 1f out: edgd rt and no ex ins fnl f* **11/4**[2]

32 **4** *nse* **Springwood Drive**[16] 4439 3-8-11 0 DavidAllan 12 55+
(Tim Easterby) *chsd ldrs: sn lost pl: hdwy over 1f out: styd on* **18/1**

6 **5** *3* **Friday Fizz (IRE)**[18] 4367 3-8-11 0 RichardKingscote 11 46
(Mark Loughnane) *s.i.s: sn pushed along in rr: styd on fr over 1f out: nt trble ldrs (jockey said filly was slowly away)* **50/1**

15 **6** *3/4* **Elzaam's Dream (IRE)**[18] 4377 3-8-11 0 (h) EoinWalsh 6 49+
(Ronald Harris) *prom: racd keenly: pushed along over 3f out: hmpd over 1f out: wknd fnl f (jockey said filly hung right)* **40/1**

7 *nk* **Itmakesyouthink** 5-9-7 0 (h[1]) JohnFahy 10 48
(Mark Loughnane) *broke wl enough: sn stdd and lost pl: hld up: racd keenly: swtchd rt over 1f out: r.o ins fnl f (jockey said gelding hung right)* **100/1**

62 **8** *hd* **Great Suspense**[18] 4396 3-9-2 0 JasonWatson 5 47
(William Jarvis) *restless in stalls: s.i.s: hdwy to chse ldr over 5f out: led over 2f out: rdn and hdd over 1f out: wknd ins fnl f* **7/1**[3]

31 **9** *9* **Mendamay**[44] 3416 3-9-4 0 DuranFentiman 2 20
(Tim Easterby) *sn led: hdd over 2f out: wknd fnl f* **25/1**

0 **10** *8* **Be Together**[96] 1740 3-8-11 0 JoeFanning 7
(Charles Hills) *s.i.s: outpcd* **18/1**

11 *1/2* **Barossa Bal (IRE)** 3-8-11 0 DavidProbert 1
(Henry Spiller) *s.s: outpcd* **66/1**

12 *1 1/2* **Over The River** 3-8-11 0 CamHardie 3
(Alexandra Dunn) *s.s: outpcd* **200/1**

13 *67* **Auld Boy (USA)** 3-9-2 0 TrevorWhelan 4
(J S Moore) *s.s: outpcd (vet said gelding bled from the nose)* **100/1**

1m 13.26s (-1.24) **Going Correction** -0.05s/f (Stan)
WFA 3 from 4yo+ 5lb **13** Ran SP% **116.2**
Speed ratings (Par 103): **100,93,91,90,86 85,85,85,73,62 61,59,**
CSF £28.59 TOTE £21.50: £3.50, £1.10, £1.40; EX 49.40 Trifecta £83.50.
Owner Raed El Youssef **Bred** Newsells Park Stud **Trained** Newmarket, Suffolk

FOCUS
The winner finished clear of the rest, but the time was 0.41sec slower than the previous 0-70 handicap for 3yos. The fourth has been rated in line with her previous runs.
T/Plt: £120.70 to a £1 stake. Pool: £71,697.04 - 433.57 winning units T/Qpdt: £41.20 to a £1 stake. Pool: £8,631.32 - 154.86 winning units **Colin Roberts**

4801 YARMOUTH (L-H)

Wednesday, July 17

OFFICIAL GOING: Good to firm (watered; 7.3)
Wind: light to medium, half against Weather: dry, warm

5058 SILK SERIES LADY RIDERS' H'CAP (PRO-AM LADY RIDERS' RACE) 6f 3y

5:30 (5:30) (Class 4) (0-85,84) 3-Y-O+
£6,727 (£2,002; £1,000; £500; £300; £300) **Stalls Centre**

Form RPR

0602 **1** **Hart Stopper**[7] 4805 5-10-5 **81** (t) HayleyTurner 5 88
(Stuart Williams) *stdd after s: hld up in tch in rr: edgd out lft and clsd ent fnl 2f: effrt over 1f out: drvn to chal ins fnl f: r.o to ld cl home* **9/4**[1]

2114 **2** *nse* **Inspired Thought (IRE)**[18] 4375 3-10-3 **84** HollieDoyle 4 90
(Archie Watson) *hld up wl in tch: effrt and hdwy over 1f out: drvn to ld 1f out: hdd cl home: rdr dropped rein last strides and jst hld* **4/1**[3]

3022 **3** *1/2* **James Watt (IRE)**[30] 3935 3-9-10 **84** SaraDelFabbro[(7)] 1 88
(Michael Bell) *taken down early: led: pushed along over 1f out: hdd 1f out: stl ev ch and kpt on wl ins fnl f: no ex towards fin* **7/2**[2]

3431 **4** *1* **Athollblair Boy (IRE)**[18] 4365 6-10-2 **83** FayeMcManoman[(5)] 6 85
(Nigel Tinkler) *hood off sltly late and dwlt: t.k.h: hld up wl in tch in midfield: effrt over 1f out: drvn 1f out: swtchd rt ins fnl f: styd on wl towards fin* **4/1**[3]

403 **5** *1/2* **Dr Doro (IRE)**[4] 4926 6-9-7 **69** (v) JosephineGordon 2 70
(Ian Williams) *squeezed for room leaving stalls: trckd ldrs: effrt to press ldrs and rdn 2f out: no ex u.p ins fnl f: wknd towards fin* **15/2**

0103 **6** *3* **Red Alert**[21] 4236 5-9-11 **80** (p) ElishaWhittington[(7)] 3 71
(Tony Carroll) *chsd ldr tl ent fnl 2f: sn u.p and lost pl over 1f out: wknd ins fnl f* **12/1**

1m 13.51s (0.91) **Going Correction** +0.15s/f (Good)
WFA 3 from 5yo+ 5lb **6** Ran SP% **112.4**
Speed ratings (Par 105): **99,98,98,96,96 92**
CSF £11.55 TOTE £2.70: £1.60, £1.90; EX 13.30 Trifecta £48.50.
Owner T W Morley **Bred** Manor Farm Stud (Rutland) **Trained** Newmarket, Suffolk

FOCUS
A decent lady riders' sprint handicap. They went a modest gallop into a reported headwind and the winning time was nearly four seconds above standard. The third has been rated to form.

5059 BAZUKA / EBF NOVICE STKS (PLUS 10 RACE) 7f 3y

6:05 (6:07) (Class 4) 2-Y-O **£4,463** (£1,328; £663; £331) **Stalls Centre**

Form RPR

1 **Verboten (IRE)** 2-9-5 0 NickyMackay 5 88+
(John Gosden) *hld up in rr: clsd and shkn up over 2f out: rdn to chse clr ldr jst over 1f out: rn green and hung lft u.p 1f out: r.o ins fnl f to ld towards fin: sn in command and eased cl home* **11/2**

2 **2** *3/4* **Spreadsheet (IRE)**[20] 4290 2-9-5 0 AndreaAtzeni 6 86+
(Roger Varian) *taken down early: racd freely: sn led and j. path over 5f out: rdn 2f out: clr whn hung lft over 1f out: sn hung bk rt: hdd and no ex towards fin* **2/1**[1]

32 **3** *4* **Al Namir (IRE)**[26] 4069 2-9-5 0 JimCrowley 2 75
(Richard Hannon) *midfield: rdn 1/2-way: chsd clr wnr but no imp u.p over 1f out: carried lft 1f out: 3rd and wknd ins fnl f* **9/4**[2]

6 **4** *3 3/4* **Imperial Empire**[19] 4324 2-9-5 0 JamesDoyle 4 65
(Charlie Appleby) *led: sn hdd: chsd ldr: effrt over 2f out: lost 2nd and outpcd over 1f out: wknd ins fnl f* **5/2**[3]

5 **5** *4 1/2* **Kassab**[13] 4564 2-9-5 0 ShaneKelly 1 53
(Peter Chapple-Hyam) *chsd ldrs: effrt over 2f out: outpcd and btn over 1f out: wknd fnl f (vet said colt lost its left fore shoe)* **20/1**

00 **6** *19* **Star Of St Louis (FR)**[13] 4564 2-8-12 0 CameronIles[(7)] 3 2
(Denis Quinn) *in tch in last pair: shkn up over 2f out: sn struggling: wl bhd ins fnl f* **200/1**

1m 26.7s (1.60) **Going Correction** +0.15s/f (Good) **6** Ran SP% **113.3**
Speed ratings (Par 96): **96,95,90,86,81 59**
CSF £17.26 TOTE £7.00: £2.60, £1.40; EX 18.80 Trifecta £40.40.
Owner Godolphin **Bred** B Minde **Trained** Newmarket, Suffolk

FOCUS
A decent juvenile novice contest. The wayward favourite had to give best to a promising newcomer in the closing stages. The third has been rated close to his debut form over the C&D, with the fourth similar to his debut.

5060 FREEDERM H'CAP 1m 2f 23y

6:40 (6:40) (Class 5) (0-70,72) 3-Y-O+
£3,428 (£1,020; £509; £300; £300; £300) **Stalls Low**

Form RPR

005 **1** **The Corporal (IRE)**[20] 4296 3-9-4 **68** HollieDoyle 5 75
(Chris Wall) *led: sn hdd and chsd ldr tl over 3f out: nt clr run and swtchd lft over 2f out: ev ch u.p 1f out: kpt on to ld wl ins fnl f: sn in command (trainer said, regarding the apparent improvement in form, that gelding may have appreciated the drop in class and the drop back in trip to 1m 2f on this occasion after finishing unplaced over 1m 4f at Newmarket last time out)* **11/2**

0-23 **2** *1 1/4* **Rock The Cradle (IRE)**[26] 4071 3-9-6 **70** ShaneKelly 2 74+
(Ed Vaughan) *t.k.h: hld up in tch in midfield: clsd to join ldr over 3f out: urged along and led ent fnl f: drvn and fnd little ins fnl f: hdd wl ins fnl f: sn btn (trainer said gelding failed to stay the 1m 2f trip and will be dropped back to 1m in the future)* **9/4**[2]

4453 **3** *1 1/2* **The Night King**[30] 3937 4-10-0 **69** PatCosgrave 6 69
(Mick Quinn) *hld up in tch in last pair: clsd to chse ldrs 3f out: sn rdn: drvn and kpt on same pce ins fnl f* **7/1**

054 **4** *1* **Earth And Sky (USA)**[26] 4073 3-9-7 **71** (h) JamesDoyle 4 70
(George Scott) *led: jnd over 3f out: sn rdn: hdd ent fnl f: sn outpcd and wknd wl ins fnl f* **15/8**[1]

0060 **5** *6* **Conqueress (IRE)**[35] 3740 5-8-2 **50** oh5 MorganCole[(7)] 1 36
(Lydia Pearce) *chsd ldrs: outpcd over 2f out: wknd fnl f* **50/1**

1211 **6** *1/2* **Edgar Allan Poe (IRE)**[8] 4762 5-10-3 **72** PhilDennis 3 57
(Rebecca Bastiman) *hld up in tch in last pair: clsd to chse ldrs and rdn over 2f out: sn struggling and outpcd wl over 1f out: wknd fnl f (jockey said gelding ran flat; trainer's rep said after several runs within quick succession, believed the gelding may be in need of a break)* **9/2**[3]

2m 8.22s (-0.58) **Going Correction** +0.15s/f (Good)
WFA 3 from 4yo+ 9lb **6** Ran SP% **113.6**
Speed ratings (Par 103): **108,107,105,105,100 99**
CSF £18.66 TOTE £7.60: £2.90, £1.80; EX 19.60 Trifecta £93.80.
Owner Bringloe & Clarke **Bred** Ideal Syndicate **Trained** Newmarket, Suffolk

FOCUS
Add 10 yards. An ordinary handicap. They went an even tempo and the winner got on top a shade cosily late on up the far rail. The winner has been rated back to his 2yo form, and the third to his previous best fast ground form.

5061 DIOMED H'CAP 1m 3y

7:10 (7:11) (Class 3) (0-90,86) 3-Y-O+ **£7,439** (£2,213; £1,106; £553) **Stalls Centre**

Form RPR

4162 **1** **Smile A Mile (IRE)**[10] 4692 3-9-5 **85** JamesDoyle 5 88+
(Mark Johnston) *mde all: rdn and pressed over 1f out: asserted u.p ins fnl f: r.o wl* **8/15**[1]

0325 **2** *1 3/4* **Ultimate Avenue (IRE)**[19] 4348 5-9-9 **86** (h) DylanHogan[(5)] 4 87
(David Simcock) *v.s.a: sn rcvrd and t.k.h in rr: effrt over 1f out: drvn ent fnl f: kpt on to snatch 2nd last strides (jockey said gelding was slowly away)* **2/1**[2]

0-50 **3** *nk* **Bint Dandy (IRE)**[17] 4424 8-9-1 **73** (b) LewisEdmunds 2 73
(Charlie Wallis) *chsd wnr: effrt to press wnr over 1f out: drvn 1f out: no ex and outpcd ins fnl f: kpt on same pce and lost 2nd last strides* **12/1**[3]

6660 **4** *1* **Noble Peace**[68] 2584 6-9-1 **73** (b) PatCosgrave 1 71
(Lydia Pearce) *t.k.h: chsd ldrs: effrt ent fnl 2f: unable qck over 1f out: hld and kpt on same pce ins fnl f* **12/1**[3]

1m 39.56s (1.36) **Going Correction** +0.15s/f (Good)
WFA 3 from 5yo+ 8lb **4** Ran SP% **113.9**
Speed ratings (Par 107): **99,97,96,95**
CSF £2.06 TOTE £1.30; EX 2.00 Trifecta £4.00.
Owner Sheikh Hamdan bin Mohammed Al Maktoum **Bred** Godolphin **Trained** Middleham Moor, N Yorks

FOCUS
The feature race was a decent little handicap. The odds-on favourite controlled this contest at a gradually increasing tempo from the front. The winner has been rated in line with his recent form.

5062 4HEAD MEDIAN AUCTION MAIDEN FILLIES' STKS 7f 3y

7:40 (7:43) (Class 6) 3-4-Y-O **£2,781** (£827; £413; £206) **Stalls Centre**

Form RPR

2 **1** **Five Diamonds**[22] 4211 3-8-11 0 JimCrowley 8 74+
(William Haggas) *dwlt and wnt rt leaving stalls: hld up in tch: clsd to trck ldrs 1/2-way: effrt over 2f out: led over 1f out: drvn and kpt on ins fnl f* **1/2**[1]

3- **2** *nk* **Burning Topic (GER)**[244] 9065 3-8-11 0 ShaneKelly 6 73+
(David Lanigan) *t.k.h early: hld up in tch in midfield: clsd to trck ldrs and swtchd rt over 1f out: effrt to chal 1f out: drvn and one pce wl ins fnl f* **15/8**[2]

0605 **3** *3* **Raha**[26] 4070 3-8-11 64 ShelleyBirkett 7 64
(Julia Feilden) *chsd ldrs: wnt 2nd over 4f out tl led over 2f out: sn shkn up: rdn and hdd over 1f out: wknd ins fnl f* **12/1**[3]

0- **4** *4 1/2* **Dreamingofdiamonds (IRE)**[238] 9172 3-8-11 0 JosephineGordon 4 52
(David Lanigan) *hld up in tch: clsd to chse ldrs and rdn over 1f out: sn outpcd and wknd ins fnl f* **25/1**

0-0 **5** *8* **Forthwith**[25] 4116 3-8-11 0 HayleyTurner 1 30
(Tony Carroll) *taken down early: prom tl led over 5f out: hdd over 2f out: sn lost pl: wknd over 1f out* **33/1**

6 *12* **Phoebe Agnes** 3-8-11 0 (w) LewisEdmunds 2
(Shaun Harris) *sn outpcd in rr: lost tch 2f out* **100/1**

0-6 **7** *3* **Diamond Cara**[18] 4396 3-8-11 0 RossaRyan 3
(Stuart Williams) *t.k.h: led tl over 5f out: chsd ldr tl over 4f out: lost pl over 2f out: bhd fnl f* **66/1**

1m 26.49s (1.39) **Going Correction** +0.15s/f (Good) **7** Ran SP% **118.4**
Speed ratings (Par 98): **98,97,94,89,79 66,62**
CSF £1.78 TOTE £1.30: £1.10, £1.30; EX 2.00 Trifecta £3.40.
Owner Khalil Al Sayegh **Bred** Shadwell Estate Company Limited **Trained** Newmarket, Suffolk

FOCUS
An ordinary, effectively 3yo, fillies' maiden. The right two horses came clear up the near rail in the final furlong and the odds-on favourite pulled out more close home. The third has been rated back to her Newmarket run.

5063 AEROPAK H'CAP — 6f 3y
8:10 (8:14) (Class 6) (0-55,56) 3-Y-O+

£2,781 (£827; £413; £300; £300; £300) **Stalls** Centre

Form			RPR
6400 **1**		**Classy Cailin (IRE)**[18] 4376 4-9-1 **48**.........................(v[1]) ShaneKelly 7	55

(Pam Sly) *sn led and mde rest: rdn over 1f out: pressed and drvn ins fnl f: kpt on (trainer said, regarding the improved form shown, the mare appreciated being ridden more prominently on this occasion and is a quirky type)* **14/1**

032 **2** ½ **Sweet Forgetme Not (IRE)**[14] 4500 3-8-10 **48**...(bt) JosephineGordon 8 52
(Samuel Farrell, Ire) *hld up in tch: effrt ent fnl 2f: hdwy to chse wnr and rdn over 1f out: pressing wnr 1f out: ev ch and drvn ins fnl f: kpt on but hld towards fin* **5/1**[2]

2200 **3** ¾ **Fiery Breath**[15] 4472 4-9-7 **54**...............................(h) RossaRyan 6 57
(Robert Eddery) *dwlt: in tch in rr of main gp: swtchd and clsd whn nt clr run ent fnl 2f: swtchd lft and effrt to chse ldrs over 1f out: kpt on same pce ins fnl f* **5/1**[2]

-400 **4** 4 ½ **Praxedis**[35] 3738 4-9-6 **53**................................(p[1]) HayleyTurner 2 41
(Robert Cowell) *hld up in tch in rr of main gp: swtchd lft and hdwy jst over 1f out: no imp u.p over 1f out: wknd ins fnl f* **8/1**[3]

0031 **5** ½ **Tilsworth Rose**[13] 4563 5-9-3 **50**.........................(b) NickyMackay 4 37
(J R Jenkins) *broke wl: stdd and t.k.h early: chsd ldrs: chsd wnr jst over 2f out tl unable qck u.p over 1f out: wknd ins fnl f* **17/2**

0500 **6** *hd* **Opera Kiss (IRE)**[48] 3270 3-8-2 **45**..................(w) FayeMcManoman(5) 9 30
(Lawrence Mullaney) *hld up in tch in midfield: nt clr run over 2f out: swtchd rt wl over 1f out: no ch but kpt on ins fnl f* **66/1**

0323 **7** 1 ¾ **Josiebond**[9] 4731 3-9-2 **54**.................................... PhilDennis 10 33
(Rebecca Bastiman) *wl in tch in midfield: effrt over 2f out: unable qck and lost pl wl over 1f out: wknd ins fnl f* **5/1**[2]

006 **8** 2 ¾ **Exning Queen (IRE)**[20] 4298 3-8-8 **46**........................ ShelleyBirkett 3 17
(Julia Feilden) *s.i.s: a towards rr (jockey said filly was slowly away)* **16/1**

-356 **9** 1 ¾ **Alyx Vance**[8] 4754 3-9-3 **55**.................................. PatCosgrave 11 20
(Lydia Pearce) *in tch in midfield: effrt over 2f out: unable qck and btn over 1f out: sn wknd* **20/1**

5-00 **10** 5 **Sandkissed (IRE)**[18] 4376 4-8-12 **45**..................(b[1]) SilvestreDeSousa 1
(Amy Murphy) *t.k.h: in tch in midfield: effrt over 2f out: sn drvn and btn over 1f out: bhd and eased ins fnl f (trainer could offer no explanation for the filly's performance)* **11/4**[1]

06-0 **11** 4 ½ **Miss President**[58] 2908 3-9-4 **56**.............................. HollieDoyle 5
(Robert Cowell) *t.k.h: led: sn hdd and chsd wnr tl over 2f out: lost pl and bhd fnl f* **20/1**

1m 13.15s (0.55) **Going Correction** +0.15s/f (Good)
WFA 3 from 4yo+ 5lb **11** Ran SP% **121.9**
Speed ratings (Par 101): **102,101,100,94,93 93,91,87,85,78 72**
CSF £83.96 CT £412.03 TOTE £14.80: £3.40, £1.60, £2.30; EX 90.60 Trifecta £549.90.

Owner Peter J Moran **Bred** C M Farrell **Trained** Thorney, Cambs

FOCUS
A moderate sprint handicap. The winner made most towards the stands' rail in gutsy fashion. She's been rated to this year's AW form.

5064 IBULEVE H'CAP — 5f 42y
8:40 (8:41) (Class 5) (0-70,70) 3-Y-O

£3,428 (£1,020; £509; £300; £300; £300) **Stalls** Centre

Form RPR

-105 **1** **Tone The Barone**[20] 4297 3-8-12 **61**.........................(t[1]) JimCrowley 1 72+
(Stuart Williams) *in tch in last pair: clsd to chse ldrs 2f out: rdn to ld over 1f out: r.o wl: rdn out* **2/1**[1]

2030 **2** 1 ½ **Simba Samba**[28] 3989 3-8-4 **53**................................ HollieDoyle 4 58
(Philip McBride) *hld up in rr: clsd ent fnl 2f: swtchd rt and effrt over 1f out: chsd wnr and edgd lft 1f out: kpt on same pce ins fnl f* **7/2**[3]

-564 **3** 1 ½ **Invincible Larne (IRE)**[19] 4343 3-9-2 **65**..................(v[1]) PatCosgrave 5 65
(Mick Quinn) *awkward leaving stalls: in tch in midfield: clsd to chse ldrs 1/2-way: rdn to chse ldr 2f out tl over 1f out: one pce ins fnl f* **11/2**

3500 **4** 3 **Phoenix Star (IRE)**[23] 4185 3-9-7 **70**..................... SilvestreDeSousa 7 59
(Nick Littmoden) *w ldr tl led after 1f: rdn ent fnl 2f: drvn and hdd over 1f out: wknd ins fnl f* **11/4**[2]

-500 **5** 2 ¼ **Gifted Zebedee (IRE)**[20] 4301 3-8-12 **68**.............. StefanoCherchi(7) 3 49
(Anthony Carson) *in tch: nt clr run and swtchd rt over 1f out: hung lft and no imp jst ins fnl f* **33/1**

0005 **6** 1 **Sandridge Lad (IRE)**[19] 4343 3-9-6 **69**........................ BrettDoyle 8 46
(John Ryan) *chsd ldrs: unable qck u.p over 1f out: wknd ins fnl f (jockey said gelding hung left-handed)* **12/1**

0-00 **7** 2 ¼ **The Last Party**[11] 4651 3-9-2 **65**................................ LewisEdmunds 2 34
(James Given) *chsd ldrs: unable qck and lost pl over 1f out: wknd ins fnl f* **25/1**

-035 **8** 4 ½ **Awarded**[23] 4192 3-8-4 **53**...................................... HayleyTurner 6 6
(Robert Cowell) *led for 1f: chsd ldr tl over 2f out: lost pl and bhd ins fnl f* **16/1**

1m 2.01s (0.11) **Going Correction** +0.15s/f (Good) **8** Ran SP% **118.0**
Speed ratings (Par 100): **105,102,100,95,91 90,86,79**
CSF £9.67 CT £33.59 TOTE £3.10: £1.10, £1.40, £1.70; EX 11.00 Trifecta £43.10.

Owner B Piper And Partner **Bred** Ors Bloodstock & Stanley House Stud **Trained** Newmarket, Suffolk

FOCUS
An ordinary 3yo sprint handicap. The decisive winning favourite raced central to far side and produced easily the best comparative winning time on the card. The second and third have been rated close to their latest form.

T/Plt: £72.40 to a £1 stake. Pool: 59,738.95 - 601.65 winning units T/Qpdt: £11.70 to a £1 stake. Pool: £5,794.37 - 366.12 winning units **Steve Payne**

5065a-5074a (Foreign Racing) - See Raceform Interactive

5032 KILLARNEY (L-H)
Wednesday, July 17

OFFICIAL GOING: Good (good to yielding in places) changing to good after race 4 (7.30)

5075a IRISH STALLION FARMS EBF CAIRN ROUGE STKS (LISTED RACE) (F&M) — 1m 30y
7:30 (7:30) 3-Y-O+

£29,234 (£9,414; £4,459; £1,981; £990; £495)

RPR

1 **Viadera**[21] 4242 3-9-1 101.. ColinKeane 6 100+
(G M Lyons, Ire) *mid-div: prog to go 5th 1/2-way: pushed along over 2f out and prog to go 2nd under 2f out: styd on strly u.p to ld on line* **5/2**[1]

2 *shd* **Lady Wannabe (IRE)**[18] 4411 3-9-1 101..................... FrankieDettori 7 99
(J A Stack, Ire) *prom: sn led: stl gng wl 2f out: sn pushed along and kpt on wl u.p: no ex cl home and hdd on line* **6/1**[3]

3 1 ¼ **Simply Beautiful (IRE)**[6] 4856 3-9-1 91............................ PBBeggy 12 96+
(A P O'Brien, Ire) *bit slowly away: towards rr: pushed along 3f out and hdwy on outer to go 3rd 1f out: kpt on wl u.p but hld by front pair cl home* **8/1**

4 1 ¼ **Snapraeceps (IRE)**[26] 4084 3-9-1 87..................... DeclanMcDonogh 3 93+
(Joseph Patrick O'Brien, Ire) *towards rr: rdn over 2f out and sme prog: short of room between horses over 1f out and swtchd to outer: kpt on wl to go 4th cl home* **8/1**

5 ½ **Secret Thoughts (USA)**[70] 2521 3-9-1 98.................... WayneLordan 9 92
(A P O'Brien, Ire) *in rr of mid-div: 8th 1/2-way: rdn over 2f out and prog to go 3rd under 2f out: flashed tail u.p and no ex fr 1f out: dropped to 5th cl home* **13/2**

6 ½ **Cnoc An Oir (IRE)**[18] 4410 3-9-1 86..............................(h) GaryHalpin 11 91+
(Joseph Patrick O'Brien, Ire) *slowly away: in rr: rdn over 2f out and swtchd rt under 2f out: sme late prog but nvr nr to chal* **20/1**

7 ½ **Annie Fior (IRE)**[41] 3521 5-9-9 87.............................. DarraghO'Keeffe 4 92
(B A Murphy, Ire) *prom: 4th 1/2-way: prog to go 2nd 3f out: sn pushed along: no ex u.p fr 2f out and wknd* **20/1**

8 *nk* **Morpho Blue (IRE)**[10] 4697 3-9-1 89.............................(p[1]) TomMadden 5 89
(Mrs John Harrington, Ire) *chsd ldrs: 6th 1/2-way: rdn bhd horses over 2f out: no ex u.p fr over 1f out and one pce* **13/2**

9 2 **Thiswaycadeaux (IRE)**[19] 4353 5-9-9 83.............................(v) WJLee 1 86
(W McCreery, Ire) *sn mid-div: 7th 1/2-way: pushed along over 2f out and short of room bhd horses: sn swtchd lft to inner: kpt on but sn no ex* **40/1**

10 *shd* **Wisdom Mind (IRE)**[8] 4758 4-9-9 0..........................(t) DonnachaO'Brien 2 86
(Joseph Patrick O'Brien, Ire) *prom: 3rd 1/2-way: rdn over 2f out but sn no ex u.p and wknd* **5/1**[2]

11 6 ½ **Mona Lisa's Smile (USA)**[11] 4677 3-9-1 75............... MichaelHussey 8 69
(A P O'Brien, Ire) *chsd ldrs: prog to go 2nd bef 1/2-way: pushed along in 3rd over 2f out but sn no ex and wknd* **50/1**

1m 41.26s
WFA 3 from 4yo+ 8lb **11** Ran SP% **122.3**
CSF £17.64 TOTE £2.90: £1.50, £1.40, £2.60; DF 12.80 Trifecta £117.60.
Owner K Abdullah **Bred** Juddmonte Farms Ltd **Trained** Dunsany, Co Meath

FOCUS
The winner has a terrific attitude and pulled this out of the fire. Colin Keane was at his brilliant best again. The seventh has been rated to her best.

5076 - 5078a (Foreign Racing) - See Raceform Interactive

5035 VICHY
Wednesday, July 17

OFFICIAL GOING: Turf: good

5079a GRAND PRIX DE VICHY (GROUP 3) (3YO+) (TURF) — 1m 2f
8:45 3-Y-O+ **£36,036** (£14,414; £9,009; £9,009; £3,603)

RPR

1 **Diamond Vendome (FR)**[25] 4-9-3 0...............(p) ChristopheSoumillon 7 108+
(C Escuder, France) *mde all: asked to qckn on nr side 2f out: drvn whn chal 1f out: kpt on strly u.p ins fnl f: a doing enough* **26/5**[3]

2 1 ¾ **Soleil Marin (IRE)**[37] 3678 5-9-5 0.......................... MickaelBarzalona 3 106
(A Fabre, France) *hld up in fnl pair: pushed along and prog fr over 2f out: rdn to chal over 1f out: kpt on ins fnl f: nt match pce of wnr* **6/5**[1]

3 ½ **Royal Julius (IRE)**[37] 3678 6-9-3 0.................................. MaximeGuyon 4 103
(J Reynier, France) *w.w in rr: gained a pl after 4f: pushed along over 2f out: no immediate rspnse and rdn 1 1/2f out: responded for press ins fnl f: r.o wl to dead-heat for 3rd cl home* **13/2**

3 *dht* **Talk Or Listen (IRE)**[52] 3120 3-8-8 0.............................. FranckBlondel 1 104
(F Rossi, France) *settled in 4th on inner: pushed along to chse ldr 2f out: rdn over 1 1/2f out: unable qck ins fnl f: kpt on same pce to dead-heat for 3rd cl home* **17/1**

5 2 ½ **Subway Dancer (IRE)**[25] 4140 7-9-3 0.............................. RadekKoplik 2 98
(Z Koplik, Czech Republic) *trckd ldr on inner: pushed along and effrt in centre 2f out: sn rdn: unable to go w ldrs over 1f out: one pce ins fnl f* **32/1**

6 5 ½ **Potemkin (GER)**[24] 4157 8-9-5 0.............................. EduardoPedroza 5 89
(A Wohler, Germany) *cl up: asked for effrt over 2f out: limited rspnse and sn rdn: no imp and grad wknd fr 1f out* **6/1**

7 2 ½ **Golden Legend (FR)**[58] 3138 5-9-0 0.............................. AlexisBadel 6 79
(H-F Devin, France) *racd in 5th on outer: struggling to pce and dropped to last jst under 2f out: nt given hrd time whn wl btn over 1f out: eased clsng stages* **37/10**[2]

2m 5.29s (-3.31)
WFA 3 from 4yo+ 9lb **7** Ran SP% **119.1**
PARI-MUTUEL (all including 1 euro stake): WIN 6.20; PLACE 2.30, 1.30; SF 18.30.
Owner Mme Laurence Samoun & Georges Duca **Bred** Guy Pariente Holding **Trained** France

[4868]CHEPSTOW (L-H)

Thursday, July 18

OFFICIAL GOING: Good to firm (good in places; watered; 6.5)

Wind: Moderate across Weather: Sunny spells

5080 COUNTY MARQUEES H'CAP — 1m 14y

2:00 (2:00) (Class 5) (0-70,72) 3-Y-O+

£3,428 (£1,020; £509; £300; £300; £300) **Stalls Centre**

Form — RPR

6-54 **1** **Dargel (IRE)**[81] 2140 3-9-6 **67**........................(w) OisinMurphy 7 72+
(Clive Cox) *a.p: rdn to ld over 1f out: hrd pressed fnl f: hld on wl (vet said colt lost its right hind shoe)* **13/8**[1]

2110 **2** *3/4* **Amor Fati (IRE)**[56] 3002 4-9-8 **61**........................ NicolaCurrie 3 67+
(David Evans) *s.s: in rr: rdn 3f out: hdwy 2f out: nt clr run over 1f out and again early ins fnl f whn stl in 5th: r.o wl: tk 2nd cl home (jockey said gelding was slowly into stride and was denied a clear run)* **12/1**

2202 **3** *hd* **Loose Chippings (IRE)**[15] 4518 5-8-13 **52**.........(p) TomMarquand 5 57
(Ivan Furtado) *led tl rdn and hdd over 2f out: remained cl up and kpt on u.p: lost 2nd cl home* **7/2**[3]

0123 **4** *1* **Bond Angel**[78] 2297 4-9-9 **67**........................ KatherineBegley(5) 1 70
(David Evans) *prom: led narrowly over 2f out: rdn and sn hdd: unable qck fnl f* **16/1**

6015 **5** *1 1/2* **Swissal (IRE)**[30] 3967 4-9-11 **64**........................(p) LukeMorris 2 63
(David Dennis) *chsd ldrs: rdn and clsd 3f out: ev ch 2f out tl wknd ins fnl f* **14/1**

4050 **6** *2 1/4* **Sir Victor (IRE)**[14] 4552 3-9-11 **72**................(p[1]) RichardKingscote 9 64
(Tom Dascombe) *dwlt: detached in last: rdn over 2f out: sme hdwy over 1f out: no imp fnl f (jockey said gelding slowly away)* **11/4**[2]

-663 **7** *1/2* **Tally's Son**[17] 4453 5-8-12 **51**........................(b) RobHornby 8 44
(Grace Harris) *wnt to post early: chsd ldrs: rdn 3f out: wknd wl over 1f out* **14/1**

-000 **8** *7* **Masai Spirit**[20] 4336 3-8-9 **56**........................ DannyBrock 4 31
(Philip McBride) *hld up: rdn over 3f out: wknd over 2f out* **80/1**

1m 35.31s (-0.69) **Going Correction** -0.20s/f (Firm)
WFA 3 from 4yo+ 8lb **8 Ran SP% 115.1**
Speed ratings (Par 103): **95,94,94,93,91 89,88,81**
CSF £23.51 CT £61.88 TOTE £2.40: £1.30, £2.10, £1.40; EX 23.50 Trifecta £75.00.
Owner Trevor Fox **Bred** Yeomanstown Stud **Trained** Lambourn, Berks

FOCUS
Just 2mm of rain overnight and the going was given as good to firm, good in places (GoingStick 6.5). A modest affair won by the least exposed runner in the line-up. The first two have been rated in line with their improved spring AW form.

5081 TOTAL HOME UK LTD H'CAP — 7f 16y

2:30 (2:33) (Class 6) (0-55,56) 4-Y-O+

£2,781 (£827; £413; £300; £300; £300) **Stalls Centre**

Form — RPR

00/0 **1** **Miss Icon**[19] 4378 5-9-6 **53**........................ LiamKeniry 11 62
(Patrick Chamings) *midfield: rdn and hdwy over 2f out: r.o to ld wl ins fnl f* **8/1**

2060 **2** *1/2* **Little Miss Kodi (IRE)**[56] 3007 6-9-2 **49**.........(t) RichardKingscote 14 57
(Mark Loughnane) *trckd ldrs: rdn to ld over 1f out: kpt on: hdd wl ins fnl f* **6/1**

00-5 **3** *1 1/2* **Captain Sedgwick (IRE)**[19] 4378 5-8-10 **46**........ JaneElliott(3) 15 50
(John Spearing) *hld up: rdn and hdwy over 3f out: sn chsng ldrs: unable qck fnl f* **7/2**[1]

6633 **4** *4* **Pike Corner Cross (IRE)**[17] 4460 7-9-7 **54**........ OisinMurphy 2 47
(David Evans) *led narrowly tl rdn and hdd over 1f out: edgd rt over 1f out: wknd ins fnl f* **5/1**[3]

0060 **5** *1 1/2* **Mahna Mahna (IRE)**[23] 4216 5-8-5 **45**........ EllieMacKenzie(7) 5 35
(David W Drinkwater) *w ldr 4f: sn rdn: kpt on: outpcd by ldrs over 1f out (trainer said gelding was unsuited by the undulating track)* **33/1**

-050 **6** *1/2* **Gulland Rock**[27] 4067 8-8-9 **45**........................ WilliamCox(3) 10 33
(Anthony Carson) *prom: rdn over 2f out: wknd over 1f out* **20/1**

2005 **7** *2 1/2* **Spirit Of Ishy**[8] 4776 4-8-12 **45**........................ HollieDoyle 7 27
(Stuart Kittow) *wnt to post early: in rr: rdn over 2f out: hdwy over 1f out: no imp fnl f* **33/1**

0-05 **8** *2* **Longville Lilly**[14] 4554 4-8-7 **45**........................ RachealKneller(5) 1 22
(Trevor Wall) *in rr: rdn over 3f out: sme hdwy fnl f (trainer said filly was unsuited by the undulating track; vet said filly lost both its left and right fore shoes)* **100/1**

-021 **9** *1/2* **Papa Delta**[28] 4025 5-9-9 **56**........................ GeorgeDowning 4 31
(Tony Carroll) *plld hrd: trckd ldrs: rdn over 2f out: grad wknd (jockey said gelding ran too freely)* **4/1**[2]

000U **10** *1/2* **Indian Affair**[6] 4873 9-8-12 **45**........................(bt) RossaRyan 6 19
(Milton Bradley) *prom 3f: midfield after: rdn 3f out: wknd 2f out (jockey said horse was never travelling)* **14/1**

0-00 **11** *1 1/4* **Innstigator**[15] 4498 5-8-12 **45**........................ DavidProbert 3 16
(Sue Gardner) *wnt to post early: chsd ldrs: rdn 3f out: sn wknd* **22/1**

5000 **12** *1/2* **Burauq**[15] 4494 7-8-12 **45**........................(p) LukeMorris 13 14
(Milton Bradley) *t.k.h in midfield: rdn 3f out: wknd 2f out* **50/1**

5000 **13** *2 1/2* **Herringswell (FR)**[48] 3298 4-8-12 **45**........................ JFEgan 9 8
(Henry Spiller) *prom: rdn 2f out: wknd and eased fnl f* **12/1**

054 **14** *4 1/2* **Kafeel (USA)**[8] 4797 8-9-4 **56**........................(bt) CierenFallon(5) 8 7
(Alexandra Dunn) *rdn over 3f out: a in rr* **10/1**

1m 22.05s (-1.85) **Going Correction** -0.20s/f (Firm) **14 Ran SP% 125.7**
Speed ratings (Par 101): **102,101,99,95,93 92,90,87,87,86 85,84,81,76**
CSF £54.44 CT £181.05 TOTE £8.10: £2.60, £2.70, £2.20; EX 61.60 Trifecta £196.20.
Owner Shirley Symonds Fred Camis P Chamings **Bred** Wheelers Land Stud **Trained** Baughurst, Hants

FOCUS
The three who came in for support beforehand (all drawn high) drew clear in the closing stages. The second and third help set the level.

5082 MARKETING STOP NOVICE MEDIAN AUCTION STKS — 6f 16y

3:00 (3:02) (Class 6) 2-Y-O **£2,781** (£827; £413; £206) **Stalls Centre**

Form — RPR

6 **1** **Don't Stop Dancing (IRE)**[16] 4480 2-9-2 0........................ DavidProbert 5 78
(Ronald Harris) *mde all: got over to stands' rail after 1f: rdn and qcknd over 2f out: r.o to go 2 l up ins fnl f: pushed out towards fin and a holding runner-up* **40/1**

1 **2** *nk* **Above (FR)**[42] 3491 2-9-9 0........................ OisinMurphy 3 84
(Archie Watson) *in 2nd thrght: rdn over 2f out: 2 l down ins fnl f: r.o towards fin but a being hld by wnr* **8/11**[1]

3 *3 1/2* **Sir Boris (IRE)** 2-9-2 0........................ RichardKingscote 7 67+
(Tom Dascombe) *s.i.s: hld up: pushed along and hdwy over 2f out: shkn up to go 3rd ins fnl f: no ch w ldng pair (jockey said colt ran greenly)* **14/1**

64 **4** *3/4* **Broken Rifle**[21] 4295 2-9-2 0........................ SeanLevey 2 64
(Ivan Furtado) *t.k.h towards rr: shkn up over 2f out: sme prog over 1f out: kpt on steadily fnl f* **5/1**[3]

33 **5** *3/4* **Swinley Forest (IRE)**[16] 4482 2-9-2 0........................ MartinDwyer 4 62
(Brian Meehan) *chsd ldrs: rdn over 2f out: outpcd by ldng pair over 1f out: hung rt: wknd and lost 2 pls ins fnl f (jockey said colt hung right-handed)* **3/1**[2]

06 **6** *2* **New Jack Swing (IRE)**[8] 4798 2-9-2 0........................ TomMarquand 6 56+
(Richard Hannon) *hld up: shkn up and outpcd 2f out: kpt on fnl f: nvr a threat* **16/1**

5 **7** *1 1/4* **Poetic Lilly**[21] 4302 2-8-11 0........................ HollieDoyle 8 47
(David Menuisier) *chsd ldrs: rdn over 2f out: wknd appr fnl f* **14/1**

8 *9* **Najm** 2-9-2 0........................ LukeMorris 1 25
(Sir Mark Prescott Bt) *wnt bdly lft leaving stalls: sn in tch on outer: rdn over 3f out: wknd over 1f out* **20/1**

1m 10.61s (-0.89) **Going Correction** -0.20s/f (Firm) **8 Ran SP% 126.0**
Speed ratings (Par 92): **97,96,91,90,89 87,85,73**
CSF £77.88 TOTE £39.20: £6.00, £1.10, £3.70; EX 162.40 Trifecta £1649.60.
Owner John McCoy **Bred** Mrs Eleanor Commins **Trained** Earlswood, Monmouths

FOCUS
They went steady early and then quickened, and the front two dominated throughout.

5083 CAVENDISH MAINE H'CAP — 6f 16y

3:30 (3:33) (Class 6) (0-60,58) 3-Y-O+

£2,781 (£827; £413; £300; £300; £300) **Stalls Centre**

Form — RPR

3306 **1** **Secondo (FR)**[6] 4873 9-9-10 **58**........................(v) RichardKingscote 6 66
(Robert Stephens) *midfield: rdn 2f out and sn clsd: led ins fnl f: r.o* **7/2**[2]

4543 **2** *2* **Jaganory (IRE)**[8] 4776 7-9-6 **54**........................(v) TomMarquand 11 56
(Christopher Mason) *chsd ldrs: rdn 2f out: r.o to go 2nd towards fin: no threat to wnr* **11/2**

000- **3** *1/2* **Tawaafoq**[211] 9606 5-9-10 **58**........................(h) HollieDoyle 13 59
(Adrian Wintle) *led: rdn 2f out: hdd ins fnl f: no ex and lost 2nd towards fin* **20/1**

0-53 **4** *1 1/4* **Mad Endeavour**[41] 3543 8-9-4 **52**........................(b) FergusSweeney 4 49
(Stuart Kittow) *trckd ldr: rdn and ev ch 2f out: lost 2nd over 1f out: kpt on same pce* **12/1**

0-01 **5** *hd* **Castlerea Tess**[16] 4481 6-9-5 **53**........................(p) RobHornby 7 49
(Sarah Hollinshead) *midfield: rdn over 2f out: edgd rt and chsd ldrs over 1f out: unable qck fnl f* **3/1**[1]

3034 **6** *1* **Cool Strutter (IRE)**[15] 4500 7-9-1 **49**........................(p) RyanTate 2 42
(John Spearing) *racd far side and alone after 1f: chsd ldrs overall: rdn over 2f out: kpt on but no imp* **11/1**

00- **7** *nk* **Gilt Edge**[300] 7485 3-9-4 **57**........................ CallumShepherd 10 48
(Christopher Mason) *hld up: rdn over 2f out: hdwy over 1f out: no imp fnl f* **14/1**

0063 **8** *1/2* **Jupiter**[16] 4481 4-9-3 **51**........................(b) RossaRyan 5 42
(Alexandra Dunn) *prom: rdn over 2f out: outpcd by ldrs and no threat over 1f out* **9/2**[3]

40 **9** *1 1/2* **Shesadabber**[16] 4481 3-8-6 **45**........................ JFEgan 1 30
(Brian Baugh) *s.i.s: racd w one other on far side bef tacking over to join rest of field after 1f: towards rr: rdn and sme hdwy over 2f out: wknd fnl f* **16/1**

00-0 **10** *2* **Hold Your Breath**[10] 4733 4-8-11 **45**........................ GeorgeDowning 3 25
(Tony Carroll) *s.i.s: hld up: rdn over 2f out: no prog* **40/1**

0 **11** *9* **Hide Your Heart (IRE)**[19] 4358 3-8-9 **48**........................(p) DavidProbert 8
(David Loughnane) *prom: rdn wl over 2f out: wknd over 1f out* **16/1**

0050 **12** *9* **Little Anxious**[24] 4180 3-8-6 **45**........................(p[1]) MartinDwyer 12
(Grace Harris) *s.s: a bhd* **33/1**

1m 10.12s (-1.38) **Going Correction** -0.20s/f (Firm)
WFA 3 from 4yo+ 5lb **12 Ran SP% 125.4**
Speed ratings (Par 101): **101,98,97,96,95 94,94,93,91,88 76,64**
CSF £24.29 CT £359.57 TOTE £4.40: £1.60, £2.20, £8.20; EX 24.00 Trifecta £454.50.
Owner Robert Stephens Racing Club **Bred** John Deer **Trained** Penhow, Newport

FOCUS
An ordinary handicap.

5084 CALL STAR SPORTS ON 08000 521321 H'CAP — 5f 16y

4:00 (4:03) (Class 6) (0-55,56) 3-Y-O+

£2,781 (£827; £413; £300; £300; £300) **Stalls Centre**

Form — RPR

0241 **1** **Aquadabra (IRE)**[9] 4765 4-9-6 **51** 5ex........................ CallumShepherd 12 59
(Christopher Mason) *chsd ldrs: nt clr run and swtchd lft over 1f out: r.o u.p to ld last strides* **9/4**[1]

0603 **2** *shd* **Spot Lite**[8] 4772 4-9-7 **52**........................(p) RobHornby 11 60
(Rod Millman) *a.p: led narrowly 2f out: sn rdn: kpt on: hdd last strides* **4/1**[3]

6300 **3** *3 1/2* **Storm Lightning**[58] 2924 10-9-0 **45**........................ RossaRyan 10 40
(Kevin Frost) *cl up: rdn 2f out: ev ch tl no ex fnl 110yds* **20/1**

0013 **4** *1 3/4* **Maid From The Mist**[34] 3801 3-9-5 **54**........................ RichardKingscote 6 42
(John Gallagher) *midfield: rdn and clsd 2f out: outpcd by ldrs fnl f* **7/2**[2]

3003 **5** *3/4* **Seamster**[2] 5018 12-9-8 **56**........................(t) CameronNoble(3) 1 42
(David Loughnane) *hld up: hdwy 1/2-way: sn rdn: outpcd by ldrs fnl f* **4/1**[3]

0000 **6** *1/2* **Swendab (IRE)**[15] 4500 11-8-7 **45**........................(b) KateLeahy(7) 7 29
(John O'Shea) *led 3f: sn rdn: fdd fnl f* **33/1**

0-46 **7** *hd* **Devil Or Angel**[9] 4749 4-9-0 **52**........................ WilliamCarver(7) 2 36
(Bill Turner) *midfield: rdn and cl enough 2f out: wknd fnl f* **14/1**

0603 **8** *4* **North Korea (IRE)**[45] 3417 3-8-13 **48**........................(p) JFEgan 5 16
(Brian Baugh) *chsd ldrs: rdn over 2f out: wknd wl over 1f out* **14/1**

0005 **9** *1 3/4* **Kiowa**[9] 4755 3-8-10 **45**........................ DannyBrock 4 7
(Philip McBride) *sn drvn and outpcd* **20/1**

0-06 **10** *4* **Willa's Wish (IRE)**[9] 4755 3-8-3 **45**........................ ElishaWhittington(7) 3
(Tony Carroll) *s.i.s: a bhd* **33/1**

58.5s (-0.90) **Going Correction** -0.20s/f (Firm)
WFA 3 from 4yo+ 4lb **10 Ran SP% 121.7**
Speed ratings (Par 101): **99,98,93,90,89 88,88,81,78,72**
CSF £11.39 CT £138.90 TOTE £3.00: £3.30, £1.60, £4.30; EX 12.90 Trifecta £139.60.
Owner Brian Hicks **Bred** Rathasker Stud **Trained** Caewent, Monmouthshire
■ Willett was withdrawn. Price at time of withdrawal 50/1. Rule 4 does not apply.

FOCUS
A moderate sprint in which the first three raced on the stands' side. The second has been rated back to form.

5085 TTS NETWORKS 20TH ANNIVERSARY H'CAP 1m 2f
4:30 (4:31) (Class 5) (0-70,71) 3-Y-O
£3,428 (£1,020; £509; £300; £300; £300) **Stalls** Low

Form RPR
-444 **1** **Trelinney (IRE)**[14] 4562 3-9-6 **61** MartinDwyer 1 67+
(Marcus Tregoning) *t.k.h: shkn up to ld 2f out: pushed out fnl f: comf* **7/4**[1]
5062 **2** 1 **Bug Boy (IRE)**[31] 3947 3-9-4 **62** (p) MeganNicholls(3) 6 65
(Paul George) *s.i.s: hld up in tch: rdn and nt clr run wl over 2f out: disputing 4th ent fnl f: styd on wl: wnt 2nd nr fin (Jockey said gelding was slowly into stride)* **7/2**[3]
60-0 **3** ¾ **Garrison Law**[37] 3696 3-9-0 **60** DylanHogan(5) 2 62
(David Simcock) *hld up: rdn and hdwy over 3f out: hung lft over 2f out: kpt on u.p: unable qck fnl f* **10/1**
5503 **4** shd **Four Mile Bridge (IRE)**[16] 4476 3-9-3 **58** FergusSweeney 3 59
(Mark Usher) *led tl rdn and hdd 2f out: kpt on tl no ex and lost 2 pls towards fin* **12/1**
0504 **5** 1 ½ **Flying Dragon (FR)**[13] 4585 3-10-2 **71** SeanLevey 4 69
(Richard Hannon) *hld up in tch: rdn over 2f out: styd on same pce* **2/1**[2]
00-0 **6** 17 **Powerage (IRE)**[37] 3697 3-8-13 **54** (p[1]) RyanTate 5 18
(Malcolm Saunders) *trckd ldng pair tl lost 3rd 3f out: rdn and wkng whn hmpd sn after: qckly lost tch: t.o* **33/1**

2m 8.22s (-4.58) **Going Correction** -0.20s/f (Firm) **6** Ran SP% **111.6**
Speed ratings (Par 100): **107,106,105,105,104 90**
CSF £8.19 TOTE £2.70: £1.50, £2.00; EX 8.80 Trifecta £45.10.
Owner M P N Tregoning **Bred** Tom & Cathy Burns **Trained** Whitsbury, Hants

FOCUS
This was a bit of a tactical affair, the leader slowing things down and then the race developing into a test of speed. They finished in a heap. Muddling form.

5086 FIRST CAFES LTD APPRENTICE H'CAP 1m 2f
5:05 (5:05) (Class 5) (0-70,71) 4-Y-O+
£3,428 (£1,020; £509; £300; £300; £300) **Stalls** Low

Form RPR
1212 **1** **Seaborn (IRE)**[23] 4215 5-8-13 **67** WilliamCarver(5) 1 74+
(Patrick Chamings) *disp ld 2f: mde rest and set modest pce: rdn and increased tempo over 2f out: styd on wl* **11/8**[1]
2100 **2** 1 ½ **Simbirsk**[37] 3700 4-9-1 **71** (p[1]) KateLeahy(7) 7 75
(John O'Shea) *trckd ldrs: rdn 2f out: wnt 2nd over 1f out: kpt on but unable to chal wnr* **7/1**
0564 **3** nk **Brittanic (IRE)**[14] 4569 5-9-4 **70** DylanHogan(3) 3 73
(David Simcock) *hld up: clsd over 3f out: rdn over 2f out: styd on fnl f to press for 2nd: hld by wnr* **9/1**
3220 **4** nk **Il Sicario (IRE)**[14] 4547 5-9-2 **65** CameronNoble 5 67
(Bill Turner) *disp ld 2f: trckd wnr after: rdn 2f out: sn lost 2nd: kpt on same pce* **10/1**
3100 **5** ¾ **Bayston Hill**[22] 4235 5-9-6 **69** (p) GaryMahon 6 70
(Mark Usher) *hld up: effrt on outer over 2f out: styd on fnl f: nvr able to chal* **16/1**
6-04 **6** ½ **Paddy The Chef (IRE)**[21] 4296 4-9-0 **66** (p) ThomasGreatrex(3) 2 66
(Ian Williams) *s.i.s and rousted along early: sn trcking ldrs: rdn and nt clr run on ins 2f out: one pce and hld after (jockey said gelding was denied a clear run)* **11/2**[3]
4445 **7** hd **High Acclaim (USA)**[14] 4561 5-9-2 **70** ScottMcCullagh(5) 4 70
(Roger Teal) *hld up: rdn 2f out: kpt on but nvr able to chal* **9/2**[2]
433- **8** 5 **Saxo Jack (FR)**[387] 3811 9-9-7 **70** (t) WilliamCox 8 60
(Sophie Leech) *hld up: tk clsr order after 2f: rdn over 2f out: sn outpcd: wknd fnl f* **25/1**

2m 11.0s (-1.80) **Going Correction** -0.20s/f (Firm) **8** Ran SP% **117.0**
Speed ratings (Par 103): **102,100,100,100,99 99,99,95**
CSF £12.10 CT £64.84 TOTE £2.10: £1.10, £2.20, £2.40; EX 12.50 Trifecta £92.20.
Owner Ian Beach **Bred** Michael Fennessy **Trained** Baughurst, Hants
■ Stewards' Enquiry : Gary Mahon two-day ban: using his whip without giving his mount time to respond (July 21, Aug 2)
Dylan Hogan two-day ban: using his whip above the permitted level (Aug 2-3)

FOCUS
This was steadily run and the time was 2.78sec slower than the 0-70 handicap for 3yos that preceded it. The second has been rated close to form, and the third to his latest.
T/Jkpt: Not won. T/Plt: £52.80 to a £1 stake. Pool: £73,103.03 - 1,008.98 winning units. T/Qpdt: £11.60 to a £1 stake. Pool: £6,604.21 - 419.29 winning units. **Richard Lowther**

4832 EPSOM (L-H)
Thursday, July 18

OFFICIAL GOING: Good (good to firm in places; watered; 7.3)
Wind: Light, against Weather: Fine but cloudy

5087 FOLLOW @RACINGTV ON TWITTER APPRENTICE H'CAP 1m 113y
6:00 (6:02) (Class 5) (0-70,72) 4-Y-O+
£4,528 (£1,347; £673; £336; £300; £300) **Stalls** Low

Form RPR
4006 **1** **The Lords Walk**[14] 4561 6-9-1 **60** (v[1]) ThoreHammerHansen(3) 9 69
(Bill Turner) *s.s: hld up: 8th st: shkn up and gd prog on outer 2f out: chsd ldr fnl f: styd on strly to ld fnl 50yds (jockey said gelding hung left-handed under pressure)* **7/2**[1]
1022 **2** 1 **Amaretto**[35] 3766 4-9-2 **58** (v) PaddyBradley 3 65
(Jim Boyle) *led: shkn up to go for home over 2f out: at least 2 l ahd and drvn over 1f out: worn down fnl 50yds* **7/2**[1]
4620 **3** 2 ¼ **Lunar Deity**[13] 4615 10-8-11 **60** MarcoGhiani(7) 4 62
(Stuart Williams) *chsd ldrs: 4th st: shkn up over 2f out: prog to dispute 2nd jst over 1f out: kpt on same pce fnl f* **8/1**
0300 **4** 1 ½ **Duke Of North (IRE)**[30] 3966 7-8-10 **59** IsobelFrancis(7) 6 57
(Jim Boyle) *trckd ldng pair: rdn and nt qckn over 2f out: disp 2nd briefly over 1f out: fdd fnl f (jockey said gelding hung left-handed in the straight)* **10/1**
0546 **5** ½ **Narjes**[14] 4548 5-9-8 **67** (h) RhiainIngram(3) 7 64
(Laura Mongan) *rel to r and lft 15 l: ct up by 1/2-way: no prog over 2f out: styd on last 100yds: nvr nrr (jockey said mare was very slowly away)* **16/1**
-130 **6** hd **Gainsay**[92] 1850 4-9-7 **68** TylerSaunders(5) 1 65
(Jonathan Portman) *wl in tch: 6th st: rdn and edgd lft over 2f out: no imp on ldrs after* **7/1**[3]
4021 **7** 1 **Ascot Week (USA)**[10] 4728 5-9-13 **72** 5ex (v) CierenFallon(3) 5 66
(John Quinn) *trckd ldrs: 5th st: rdn and no prog over 2f out: wl hld over 1f out* **4/1**[2]
413- **8** ½ **Settle Petal**[218] 9510 5-9-4 **67** EllaBoardman(7) 2 60
(Pat Phelan) *taken down early: trckd ldr: urged along and nt qckn over 2f out: lost 2nd and wknd over 1f out* **25/1**
0-03 **9** 2 ½ **Gerry The Glover (IRE)**[13] 4615 7-9-1 **62** (h) GeorgiaDobie(5) 8 50
(Lee Carter) *dwlt: hld up: 7th st: urged along and no prog 3f out: nvr a factor after* **9/1**

1m 47.76s (1.36) **Going Correction** +0.175s/f (Good) **9** Ran SP% **116.9**
Speed ratings (Par 103): **101,100,98,96,96 96,95,94,92**
CSF £15.96 CT £91.98 TOTE £4.40: £1.40, £1.40, £2.60; EX 16.50 Trifecta £135.30.
Owner Mrs J V Wilkinson **Bred** Aston House Stud **Trained** Sigwells, Somerset

FOCUS
Add 25yds. This featured both the first and second from last year but many of these weren't in any form. A small pb from the second, with the winner rated close to his Irish form.

5088 EPSOM & EWELL PHAB EBF MAIDEN STKS (PLUS 10 RACE) 7f 3y
6:35 (6:35) (Class 4) 2-Y-O **£4,787** (£1,424; £711; £355) **Stalls** Low

Form RPR
1 **Alpinista** 2-9-0 0 LukeMorris 4 79+
(Sir Mark Prescott Bt) *dwlt: in tch in 5th: sltly green whn asked for effrt over 2f out: sn clsd to ld over 1f out: pushed clr: unchal after* **9/4**[2]
0 **2** 2 ½ **Bermuda Schwartz**[14] 4558 2-9-5 0 PatDobbs 6 77+
(Richard Hughes) *dwlt: hld up in last: pushed along and prog 2f out: shkn up briefly to take 2nd last 120yds: styd on wl but too late to threaten wnr* **10/1**
542 **3** 3 ½ **Goodwood Rebel (IRE)**[37] 3694 2-9-5 **77** HarryBentley 3 68
(Ralph Beckett) *w ldr: led over 2f out to over 1f out: sn lft bhd: lost 2nd last 120yds* **7/2**[3]
0 **4** 7 **Buy Nice Not Twice (IRE)**[14] 4544 2-9-0 0 TomMarquand 1 45
(Richard Hannon) *hld up in 4th: impeded over 2f out: dropped to last and sn bhd: passed two rivals fnl f but no ch to rcvr* **11/1**
5 3 ¾ **Flashing Approach (IRE)** 2-9-5 0 SilvestreDeSousa 5 40+
(Mark Johnston) *coltish preliminaries: led but pressed: rdn and hdd over 2f out: wknd wl over 1f out* **7/4**[1]
0 **6** 6 **Pearl Beach**[23] 4223 2-9-0 0 JasonWatson 2 19+
(William Knight) *trckd ldng pair: hanging v bdly lft fr over 2f out: sn wknd (jockey said filly hung badly left-handed, which in his opinion, was unrideable)* **16/1**

1m 24.64s (1.24) **Going Correction** +0.175s/f (Good) **6** Ran SP% **112.7**
Speed ratings (Par 96): **99,96,92,84,79 73**
CSF £23.79 TOTE £2.70: £2.10, £5.30; EX 19.00 Trifecta £96.10.
Owner Miss K Rausing **Bred** Miss K Rausing **Trained** Newmarket, Suffolk

FOCUS
Add 15yds. Two newcomers headed the market for this informative maiden. Mark Johnston, who saddled the favourite, was bidding for a fourth win in the race since 2013.

5089 JOIN RACING TV NOW H'CAP 1m 2f 17y
7:10 (7:10) (Class 4) (0-80,82) 3-Y-O+
£7,115 (£2,117; £1,058; £529; £300; £300) **Stalls** Low

Form RPR
-616 **1** **Multamis (IRE)**[33] 3859 3-9-10 **82** JimCrowley 1 90
(Owen Burrows) *trckd ldng trio: effrt on outer over 2f out: clsd over 1f out: drvn to chal ins fnl f: led last stride* **9/2**[3]
2302 **2** shd **Allegiant (USA)**[14] 4548 4-9-9 **72** OisinMurphy 5 80
(Stuart Williams) *trckd ldr after 2f: rdn over 2f out: clsd over 1f out: led fnl f but sn hrd pressed: hdd last stride* **13/8**[1]
2124 **3** 2 ¼ **Agent Basterfield (IRE)**[14] 4559 3-9-5 **77** DavidProbert 4 81
(Andrew Balding) *led: 3 l ahd st: same ld against rail and stl gng strly 2f out: drvn over 1f out: hdd and no ex fnl f* **4/1**[2]
-315 **4** 2 **Miss M (IRE)**[17] 4447 5-9-2 **65** JFEgan 7 65
(William Muir) *hld up in 5th: rdn 3f out: tk 4th over 1f out: kpt on but nvr pce to threaten* **10/1**
-564 **5** 4 ½ **Kheros**[17] 4445 3-9-9 **81** HollieDoyle 3 72
(Archie Watson) *trckd ldr 2f: 3rd st: rdn wl over 2f out: wknd over 1f out (jockey said gelding ran flat)* **11/2**
2331 **6** 4 ½ **Stormingin (IRE)**[21] 4283 6-10-0 **77** (b) TomQueally 2 59
(Gary Moore) *a in 6th: shkn up and no rspnse 3f out: sn btn* **12/1**
-045 **7** 8 **Hatsaway (IRE)**[35] 3778 8-8-13 **62** JosephineGordon 6 28
(Pat Phelan) *a last: detached and struggling st: bhd after* **20/1**

2m 9.92s (-0.08) **Going Correction** +0.175s/f (Good) **7** Ran SP% **113.2**
WFA 3 from 4yo+ 9lb
Speed ratings (Par 105): **107,106,105,103,99 96,89**
CSF £12.00 TOTE £5.00: £2.40, £1.10; EX 17.60 Trifecta £66.90.
Owner Hamdan Al Maktoum **Bred** Rathasker Stud **Trained** Lambourn, Berks

FOCUS
Add 25yds. This handicap revolved around Allegiant, who had looked unlucky not to win over this C&D a fortnight earlier. The first two pulled clear and fought out a bobbing finish. The second has been rated to form, and the third and fourth close to form.

5090 PREMIER COMPANIES H'CAP 7f 3y
7:40 (7:40) (Class 4) (0-85,87) 3-Y-O+
£7,115 (£2,117; £1,058; £529; £300; £300) **Stalls** Low

Form RPR
0001 **1** **Big Storm Coming**[7] 4833 9-9-1 **77** 4ex CierenFallon(5) 4 86
(John Quinn) *hld up in 4th: shkn up over 2f out: clsd on outer over 1f out: rdn to ld last 150yds: styd on wl* **11/4**[2]
3130 **2** 1 ½ **Mamillius**[30] 3963 6-9-8 **79** PatCosgrave 5 84
(George Baker) *trckd ldr: rdn to ld over 1f out: hdd and one pce last 150yds* **10/1**
0124 **3** 2 **Key Player**[13] 4598 4-9-12 **83** CharlesBishop 6 83
(Eve Johnson Houghton) *led: rdn and hdd over 1f out: fdd but hld on for 3rd* **7/1**[3]
1125 **4** ¾ **Chica De La Noche**[26] 4113 5-9-3 **74** (p) TomMarquand 3 72
(Simon Dow) *chsd ldng pair: rdn and no imp over 2f out: one pce after* **14/1**
5412 **5** 1 ¼ **Sir Busker (IRE)**[14] 4546 3-9-9 **87** (v) OisinMurphy 2 81
(William Knight) *hld up in 5th: pushed along over 2f out: keeping on one pce and no ch whn nt clr run ins fnl f: nvr in it (jockey said gelding was unsuited by the pace of the race, which in his opinion, was slow)* **11/10**[1]

-062 **6** *7* **Cool Reflection (IRE)**15 4495 3-9-4 **82**.........................(b1) LukeMorris 7 54
(Paul Cole) *a in last: struggling 3f out: sn bhd* **8/1**
1m 24.27s (0.87) **Going Correction** +0.175s/f (Good)
WFA 3 from 4yo+ 7lb **6** Ran SP% **113.7**
Speed ratings (Par 105): **102,100,98,97,95 87**
CSF £28.93 TOTE £3.30: £1.80, £3.70; EX 33.90 Trifecta £159.40.
Owner Fishlake Commercial Motors Ltd **Bred** Bearstone Stud Ltd **Trained** Settrington, N Yorks
FOCUS
Add 15yds. The market got this badly wrong with the heavily punted favourite managing only fifth behind the morning paper favourite. The second has been rated to last year's C&D form.

5091 GOOD LUCK LUCIE H'CAP 1m 4f 6y
8:15 (8:16) (Class 5) (0-75,74) 4-Y-0+ **£4,528** (£1,347; £673; £336; £300) **Stalls** Centre

Form RPR
1513 **1** **Ashazuri**14 4548 5-8-12 **72**...(h) TylerSaunders(7) 5 78
(Jonathan Portman) *trckd ldr: pushed along over 3f out: rdn to cl 2f out: kpt on wl to ld narrowly 75yds out* **11/4**2
4-06 **2** *nk* **Jawshan (USA)**21 4308 4-8-11 **64** ow1................................ JimCrowley 1 69
(Ian Williams) *led at mod pce: kicked on 4f out: drvn and edgd rt over 1f out: narrowly hdd last 75yds* **12/1**
5441 **3** *3/4* **Peace Prevails**14 4547 4-8-6 **59**.....................................(p) CharlieBennett 3 63
(Jim Boyle) *trckd ldng pair: pushed along over 3f out: grad clsd fr 2f out: ch fnl f: nt qckn* **11/10**1
-040 **4** *3* **Jumping Jack (IRE)**18 4426 5-9-0 **67**.................................(p) CharlesBishop 2 66
(Chris Gordon) *dwlt: hld up in 4th: pushed along whn pce lifted over 3f out: rdn and hung lft 2f out: one pce and nvr able to threaten* **9/1**
4515 **5** *3* **El Borracho (IRE)**5 4929 4-9-7 **74**.................................(h) TomMarquand 4 68
(Simon Dow) *dwlt: hld up in last: pushed along whn pce lifted over 3f out: no imp on ldrs after (jockey said filly ran flat, having run 5 days previously)* **4/1**3
2m 45.21s (4.41) **Going Correction** +0.175s/f (Good) **5** Ran SP% **112.0**
Speed ratings (Par 103): **92,91,91,89,87**
CSF £30.14 TOTE £3.40: £1.70, £4.00; EX 34.10 Trifecta £62.60.
Owner RWH Partnership **Bred** G Wickens And J Homan **Trained** Upper Lambourn, Berks
FOCUS
Add 25yds. They went no pace here and that failed to suit the well fancied market leader. The winning time was over 10sec slower than the standard. Muddling form, but the winner has been rated to his best, the second to his turf best and the third to his lower-grade latest for the time being.

5092 EVERY RACE LIVE ON RACING TV H'CAP 7f 3y
8:45 (8:49) (Class 6) (0-65,65) 3-Y-O
£3,881 (£1,155; £577; £300; £300; £300) **Stalls** Low

Form RPR
0-02 **1** **Lady Morpheus**22 4244 3-8-4 **48**.. HollieDoyle 4 56+
(Gary Moore) *dwlt: hld up in last: stdy prog 2f out: clsd on ldrs fnl f: shkn up and r.o wl to ld nr fin* **16/1**
3000 **2** *1/2* **Poet's Magic**23 4227 3-9-2 **60**... NicolaCurrie 6 65
(Jonathan Portman) *trckd ldrs: 5th st: clsd 2f out: pushed into ld over 1f out: styd on but hdd nr fin* **12/1**
5-00 **3** *1/2* **Fancy Flyer**24 4183 3-8-13 **62**................................. SophieRalston(5) 9 66
(Dean Ivory) *t.k.h: trckd ldng pair: 3rd st: led 2f out to over 1f out: stl pressing ldr ins fnl f: no ex nr fin* **8/1**
-000 **4** *2 1/2* **Max Guevara (IRE)**8 4789 3-9-7 **65**.............................. OisinMurphy 8 62
(William Muir) *racd wd: chsd ldrs: 4th st: shkn up over 2f out: nt qckn over 1f out but nt qckn: one pce after* **14/1**
1324 **5** *2 1/4* **Your Mothers' Eyes**19 4378 3-9-0 **63**......................(p) CierenFallon(5) 2 54
(Alan Bailey) *hld up in tch: 6th st: shkn up over 2f out: one pce and no imp on ldrs over 1f out (jockey said colt ran flat)* **11/8**1
05-0 **6** *hd* **Crimson Kiss (IRE)**166 556 3-9-0 **58**......................... CharlieBennett 7 49
(Pat Phelan) *hld up: 9th st: shkn up and no prog over 2f out: n.d after: kpt on ins fnl f* **33/1**
0063 **7** *3 3/4* **Shaleela's Dream**14 4567 3-9-3 **61**.. JFEgan 11 42
(Jane Chapple-Hyam) *s.i.s: racd wd: hld up: 8th st: no real prog over 2f out: no ch over 1f out (jockey said gelding was unsuited by the undulating track)* **9/2**2
6-60 **8** *hd* **Miss Pollyanna (IRE)**21 4306 3-8-6 **55**...................... RhiainIngram(5) 3 36
(Roger Ingram) *t.k.h: led to 2f out: wknd* **25/1**
5130 **9** *4 1/2* **Rajman**113 1358 3-9-4 **62**..(t1) LukeMorris 1 31
(Tom Clover) *plld hrd: hld up bhd ldrs: 7th st: no prog over 2f out: sn wknd* **16/1**
6460 **10** *1 3/4* **Princess Palliser (IRE)**17 4440 3-9-4 **62**..................... TomMarquand 10 26
(John Quinn) *t.k.h: trckd ldr to 3f out: sn wknd* **6/1**3
0540 **U** **Quarto Cavallo**12 4657 3-8-2 **46**..................................... JimmyQuinn 5
(Adam West) *rrd bdly and uns rdr s* **16/1**
1m 24.63s (1.23) **Going Correction** +0.175s/f (Good) **11** Ran SP% **124.5**
Speed ratings (Par 98): **100,99,98,96,93 93,88,88,83,81**
CSF £205.09 CT £1694.45 TOTE £19.00: £3.60, £2.80, £2.80; EX 131.00 Trifecta £1453.80.
Owner P B Moorhead **Bred** D R Botterill **Trained** Lower Beeding, W Sussex
FOCUS
Add 15yds. A very ordinary race. The winner overcame a slow start and a troubled passage. It's been rated around the second and third.
T/Plt: £819.20 to a £1 stake. Pool: £67,120.87 - 59.81 winning units T/Qpdt: £96.30 to a £1 stake. Pool: £7,417.34 - 56.95 winning units **Jonathan Neesom**

4910 HAMILTON (R-H)
Thursday, July 18

OFFICIAL GOING: Good (good to firm in places; watered; 7.9) changing to good after race 2 (2.10)
Wind: Fresh, half behind in sprints and in over 4f of home straight in races on the round course Weather: Overcast, showers

5093 BRITISH STALLION STUDS EBF NOVICE STKS (PLUS 10 RACE) (A £20,000 BB FOODSERVICE 2YO SERIES QUAL') 5f 7y
1:40 (1:40) (Class 4) 2-Y-O **£5,433** (£1,617; £808; £404) **Stalls** High

Form RPR
04 **1** **One Bite (IRE)**22 4238 2-9-4 0.. TomEaves 1 74
(Keith Dalgleish) *w ldrs: led 1/2-way: rdn and edgd lft over 1f out: hld on wl fnl f* **8/1**
51 **2** *shd* **Mia Diva**17 4433 2-9-5 0.. JasonHart 4 75
(John Quinn) *t.k.h: slt ld to 1/2-way: w ldrs: rdn over 1f out: kpt on wl fnl f: jst hld* **3/1**2
4 **3** *3 1/2* **Feel Good Factor**21 4275 2-8-10 0...................................... SeanDavis(3) 3 56
(Richard Fahey) *in tch: rdn and outpcd over 2f out: rallied fnl f to take 3rd towards fin: no ch w first two* **14/1**
3 **4** *1* **Ma Boy Harris (IRE)**12 4631 2-9-4 0.................................. SamJames 2 57
(Phillip Makin) *wnt sltly rt s: disp ld to over 1f out: sn rdn and no ex* **6/1**3
3 **5** *hd* **Point Of Order**12 4624 2-9-4 0.................................... DanielTudhope 5 57
(Archie Watson) *prom: effrt and angled rt 2f out: no ex fnl f* **1/1**1
1m 1.1s (0.70) **Going Correction** +0.025s/f (Good) **5** Ran SP% **107.1**
Speed ratings (Par 96): **95,94,89,87,87**
CSF £29.69 TOTE £5.60: £2.60, £2.30; EX 20.10 Trifecta £74.60.
Owner Thats My Boys **Bred** Tally-Ho Stud **Trained** Carluke, S Lanarks
FOCUS
Loop rail out 3yds, adding approximately 8yds to races 3 onwards. Morning rain totalling 3mm changed the going to good, good to firm in places from good to firm after race 2. An interesting opener and a minor surprise. The front two finished clear. A small step forward from the second.

5094 EVERY RACE LIVE ON RACING TV H'CAP 5f 7y
2:10 (2:11) (Class 6) (0-65,64) 3-Y-O+
£3,493 (£1,039; £519; £300; £300; £300) **Stalls** High

Form RPR
2100 **1** **Super Julius**27 4059 5-9-11 **63**.. BenCurtis 3 70+
(S Donohoe, Ire) *cl up centre: rdn to ld over 1f out: r.o wl fnl f* **4/1**1
3U50 **2** *1 3/4* **Popping Corks (IRE)**10 4720 3-8-8 **53** ow1..........(p1) BenRobinson(3) 7 53
(Linda Perratt) *towards rr in centre: rdn 1/2-way: hdwy and hung rt over 1f out: chsd wnr ins fnl f: r.o* **8/1**
0005 **3** *nk* **Classic Pursuit**13 4586 8-9-12 **64**..................................(v) SamJames 10 64
(Marjorie Fife) *prom stands' side: drvn along over 2f out: kpt on wl fnl f: nrst fin* **17/2**
0330 **4** *3/4* **Jacob's Pillow**31 3921 8-9-4 **56**...............................(p) DanielTudhope 4 53
(Rebecca Bastiman) *cl up centre: drvn and outpcd 2f out: rallied 1f out: one pce last 100yds* **5/1**3
6502 **5** *1/2* **Bronze Beau**14 4563 12-9-7 **59**......................................(tp) ShaneGray 9 54
(Linda Stubbs) *led against stands' rail to over 1f out: no ex ins fnl f* **10/1**
0060 **6** *1* **Trulove**16 4489 6-8-2 **45**..(p) PaulaMuir(5) 5 37
(John David Riches) *cl up in centre: edgd rt and ev ch over 1f out: no ex ins fnl f* **66/1**
4500 **7** *1 1/4* **Super Florence (IRE)**8 4785 4-9-8 **60**..................(h) LewisEdmunds 13 47
(Iain Jardine) *towards rr stands' side: drvn along 1/2-way: hdwy fnl f: kpt on: nvr able to chal* **15/2**
0630 **8** *1 1/2* **Camanche Grey (IRE)**5 4911 8-8-1 **46**..................(e1) VictorSantos(7) 2 28
(Lucinda Egerton) *in tch: sn drvn along: wknd over 1f out (vet said gelding lost its left fore shoe)* **9/1**
60-0 **9** *1/2* **Gleaming Arch**13 4586 5-9-3 **58**...................................... SeanDavis(3) 12 38
(Fred Watson) *bhd centre: drvn and outpcd 1/2-way: nvr rchd ldrs (jockey said gelding moved poorly throughout)* **25/1**
6-02 **10** *2 3/4* **Arnold**44 3452 5-9-11 **63**..(p) JoeFanning 8 33
(Ann Duffield) *dwlt: sn in tch stands' side: rdn over 2f out: wknd over 1f out* **9/2**2
64-0 **11** *10* **Jordan's Chris (IRE)**16 4489 3-8-3 **45**.......................(h) JamesSullivan 1
(Linda Perratt) *missed break: sn swtchd lft: a detached (jockey said filly was slowly away)* **66/1**
0/00 **12** *1/2* **Ya Boy Sir (IRE)**11 4694 12-8-7 **45**.............................(p) AndrewMullen 6
(Alistair Whillans) *towards rr centre: struggling 1/2-way: nvr on terms* **80/1**
1m 0.35s (-0.05) **Going Correction** +0.025s/f (Good)
WFA 3 from 4yo+ 4lb **12** Ran SP% **115.4**
Speed ratings (Par 101): **101,98,97,96,95 94,92,89,88,84 68,67**
CSF £34.58 CT £261.21 TOTE £4.80: £2.30, £4.00, £2.70; EX 37.90 Trifecta £285.70.
Owner S Donohoe **Bred** T R G Vestey **Trained** Cootehill Road, Co. Cavan
FOCUS
A moderate event but a clear-cut winner who came down the centre of the track.

5095 WELCOME TO RACING TV CLUB MEMBERS H'CAP 1m 1f 35y
2:40 (2:42) (Class 4) (0-85,87) 3-Y-O+
£8,021 (£2,387; £1,192; £596; £300; £300) **Stalls** Low

Form RPR
5212 **1** **Harvey Dent**5 4909 3-9-10 **86**..................................... PaulMulrennan 4 94
(Archie Watson) *mde all: clr and pushed along whn edgd lft over 1f out: hung lft and idled ins fnl f: kpt on* **11/4**2
2050 **2** *1/2* **Loch Ness Monster (IRE)**8 4792 3-9-11 **87**........... AlistairRawlinson 3 93
(Michael Appleby) *prom: effrt on outside over 2f out: chsd wnr over 1f out: clsd ins fnl f: hld cl home* **9/4**1
0105 **3** *3* **Ghalib (IRE)**17 4445 7-9-13 **80**..................................... LewisEdmunds 2 80
(Rebecca Bastiman) *trckd ldrs: effrt and disp 2nd pl over 2f out to over 1f out: kpt on same pce ins fnl f* **8/1**
523- **4** *nk* **Kalagia (IRE)**298 7583 4-9-12 **79**.. JoeFanning 1 78
(Mark Johnston) *chsd wnr: rdn over 2f out: kpt on same pce fr over 1f out* **5/1**3
3543 **5** *1 1/2* **Kuwait Station (IRE)**14 4565 3-9-2 **78**.......................... DanielTudhope 7 73
(David O'Meara) *hld up: stdy hdwy over 2f out: sn rdn: no imp fr over 1f out* **8/1**
2050 **6** *4* **Tough Remedy (IRE)**22 4240 4-10-0 **81**.......................... PJMcDonald 6 68
(Keith Dalgleish) *hld up: drvn and outpcd and hung rt over 2f out: sn n.d: btn over 1f out* **6/1**
0010 **7** *2 1/2* **Restive (IRE)**11 4689 6-8-10 **66**................................... BenRobinson(3) 5 47
(Jim Goldie) *hld up in tch: rdn over 2f out: sn wknd* **25/1**
1m 57.47s (-1.53) **Going Correction** +0.025s/f (Good)
WFA 3 from 4yo+ 9lb **7** Ran SP% **114.5**
Speed ratings (Par 105): **107,106,103,103,102 98,96**
CSF £9.41 TOTE £3.20: £1.70, £1.90; EX 10.70 Trifecta £51.70.
Owner Saxon Thoroughbreds **Bred** Mrs D O Joly **Trained** Upper Lambourn, W Berks
FOCUS
Add 8yds. A fair handicap that went to a 3yo for the eighth time in the last ten years. The second has been rated in line with the better view of his form.

5096 RACINGTV.COM H'CAP 1m 1f 35y
3:10 (3:11) (Class 6) (0-60,62) 3-Y-O+
£3,493 (£1,039; £519; £300; £300; £300) **Stalls** Low

Form RPR
0011 **1** **Dutch Coed**12 4633 7-9-9 **58**.. RowanScott(3) 9 66
(Nigel Tinkler) *s.i.s: hld up: hdwy on outside over 2f out: hung rt and led over 1f out: rdn out fnl f* **3/1**2
0010 **2** *1 3/4* **Glaceon (IRE)**10 4728 4-9-8 **54**.. NathanEvans 8 58
(Tina Jackson) *in tch: effrt over 2f out: edgd rt over 1f out: chsd wnr ins fnl f: kpt on* **9/1**

-041 **3** *nse* **Remember Rocky**[27] 4054 10-9-13 **62**..............(b) ConnorMurtagh(3) 10 66
(Lucy Normile) *cl up: effrt and rdn over 2f out: sltly outpcd and edgd rt over 1f out: r.o ins fnl f* **22/1**

02 **4** *2 1/4* **Bellepower (IRE)**[12] 4678 3-8-13 **54**..............(p) DanielTudhope 6 52
(John James Feane, Ire) *dwlt: sn cl up: led over 2f out: hdd over 1f out: sn edgd lft: no ex ins fnl f: eased nr fin* **6/4**[1]

6350 **5** *2 1/2* **Royal Countess**[16] 4488 3-7-13 **45**.............. PaulaMuir(5) 3 38
(Lucy Normile) *dwlt: hld up: rdn along over 2f out: no imp fr over 1f out* **12/1**

0250 **6** *4 1/2* **Bahkit (IRE)**[20] 4333 5-10-2 **62**.............. BenCurtis 5 47
(Philip Kirby) *led to over 2f out: rdn and wknd over 1f out* **7/2**[3]

0040 **7** *8* **Half Full**[48] 3299 3-8-5 **46**.............. AndrewMullen 1 14
(Stuart Coltherd) *t.k.h: trckd ldrs: rdn over 3f out: wknd over 2f out* **33/1**

1m 59.49s (0.49) **Going Correction** +0.025s/f (Good)
WFA 3 from 4yo+ 9lb **7** Ran SP% **112.2**
Speed ratings (Par 101): **98,96,96,94,92 88,81**
CSF £28.18 CT £491.10 TOTE £5.20: £2.90, £3.10; EX 23.60 Trifecta £155.80.
Owner Ms Sara Hattersley **Bred** Sara Hattersley **Trained** Langton, N Yorks

FOCUS
Add 8yds. A moderate handicap but won by a hugely in-form horse from a hugely in-form stable. The winner has been rated back to his best, the second near her best, with the third fitting.

5097 FOLLOW @RACINGTV ON TWITTER H'CAP 1m 5f 16y
3:40 (3:40) (Class 4) (0-85,86) 3-Y-0+ **£8,021** (£2,387; £1,192; £596) **Stalls** Low

Form RPR
-111 **1** **Lever Du Soleil (FR)**[8] 4782 4-9-0 **68** 10ex.............. CliffordLee 4 75+
(Gavin Cromwell, Ire) *cl up: led over 2f out: pushed along and hrd pressed over 1f out: hdd briefly ins fnl f: kpt on gamely cl home* **4/11**[1]

5352 **2** *nk* **Jabbaar**[38] 3655 6-10-4 **86**.............. LewisEdmunds 3 92
(Iain Jardine) *missed break: sn in tch: stdy hdwy over 2f out: led briefly ins fnl f: edgd rt and no ex cl home* **5/1**[2]

0065 **3** *3* **Diodorus (IRE)**[7] 4817 5-9-5 **73**.............. ConnorBeasley 1 74
(Karen McLintock) *cl up: drvn and outpcd over 2f out: rallied over 1f out: no ex ins fnl f* **10/1**[3]

3340 **4** *nk* **Desert Point (FR)**[19] 4381 7-10-0 **82**.............. TomEaves 2 83
(Keith Dalgleish) *led at stdy pce: rdn and hdd over 2f out: rallied: no ex fr over 1f out* **10/1**[3]

2m 53.71s (-0.99) **Going Correction** +0.025s/f (Good) **4** Ran SP% **108.2**
Speed ratings (Par 105): **104,103,101,101**
CSF £2.55 TOTE £1.10; EX 2.60 Trifecta £5.20.
Owner Sunrise Partnership **Bred** S C E A Haras De La Perelle **Trained** Navan, Co. Meath

FOCUS
Add 8yds. Light on numbers but no lack of interest here and it was the two form horses who came to the fore. The time was modest. The second and third have been rated to form.

5098 RACING TV HD ON SKY 426 NOVICE AUCTION STKS 1m 68y
4:10 (4:11) (Class 5) 3-Y-0+ **£4,140** (£1,232; £615; £307) **Stalls** Low

Form RPR
2 **1** **New Arrangement**[42] 3517 3-8-13 0.............. PJMcDonald 2 78+
(James Tate) *cl up: led over 3f out: hrd pressed fnl 2f: hld on wl* **1/4**[1]

22 **2** *nk* **December Second (IRE)**[13] 4600 5-9-0 0.............. NickBarratt-Atkin(7) 6 80+
(Philip Kirby) *hld up in tch: stdy hdwy over 4f out: effrt and pressed wnr over 2f out: sn ev ch: kpt on fnl f: hld nr fin* **5/2**[2]

3 *8* **Blistering Barney (IRE)** 3-8-13 0..............(t[1]) AndrewElliott 1 59?
(Christopher Kellett) *restless in stalls: t.k.h: led to over 3f out: rallied: outpcd fnl 2f* **25/1**[3]

0-00 **4** *14* **Newspeak (IRE)**[15] 4513 7-9-4 36..............(p) SeanDavis(3) 3 29
(Fred Watson) *hld up in tch: lost pl over 4f out: sn struggling: n.d after* **100/1**

4-00 **5** *1/2* **Show The World**[59] 2908 3-8-6 48..............(e[1]) VictorSantos(7) 4 26
(Lucinda Egerton) *t.k.h: chsd ldrs: hdwy over 3f out: hung rt and wknd over 2f out* **80/1**

1m 47.29s (-1.11) **Going Correction** +0.025s/f (Good)
WFA 3 from 5yo+ 8lb **5** Ran SP% **114.6**
Speed ratings (Par 103): **106,105,97,83,83**
CSF £1.32 TOTE £1.10: £1.02, £1.20; EX 1.20 Trifecta £2.40.
Owner Saeed Manana **Bred** Rabbah Bloodstock Limited **Trained** Newmarket, Suffolk

FOCUS
Add 8yds. No strength in depth to this novice event and although the market suggested a one-sided contest, the favourite would have had backers sweating. The third will prove the true worth of the form in time.

5099 RACING TV PROFITS RETURNED TO RACING H'CAP (DIV I) 1m 68y
4:40 (4:40) (Class 6) (0-55,55) 3-Y-0+
£3,493 (£1,039; £519; £300; £300; £300) **Stalls** Low

Form RPR
0432 **1** **Retirement Beckons**[3] 4978 4-8-9 **46** oh1..............(h) BenRobinson(3) 11 52
(Linda Perratt) *s.i.s: hld up: hdwy over 2f out: rdn to ld ins fnl f: kpt on wl* **4/1**[1]

-000 **2** *3/4* **French Flyer (IRE)**[15] 4518 4-9-0 **48**.............. LewisEdmunds 7 52
(Rebecca Bastiman) *led: rdn over 2f out: hdd ins fnl f: rallied: hld nr fin* **22/1**

0-56 **3** *shd* **Mr Cool Cash**[13] 4584 7-8-12 **46** oh1..............(t) SamJames 1 50
(John Davies) *hld up in midfield: hdwy and prom over 1f out: rdn and kpt on ins fnl f* **20/1**

0-30 **4** *hd* **Millie The Minx (IRE)**[12] 4633 5-8-13 **47**..............(p) JamesSullivan 2 51
(Dianne Sayer) *prom: effrt whn n.m.r briefly and outpcd over 2f out: rallied over 1f out: kpt on fnl f* **8/1**[3]

03 **5** *2* **Blue Whisper**[36] 3720 4-9-2 **50**..............(tp) BenCurtis 12 49
(S Donohoe, Ire) *s.i.s: hld up: stdy hdwy whn n.m.r briefly over 2f out: rdn over 1f out: kpt on fnl f: nrst fin* **5/1**[2]

6 *1/2* **Finsceal Rose (IRE)**[5] 4945 3-8-7 **49**.............. CliffordLee 10 45
(Gavin Cromwell, Ire) *hld up: hdwy on outside to chse ldr over 2f out: hung rt over 1f out: no ex fnl f* **8/1**[3]

0530 **7** *3/4* **Rebel State (IRE)**[15] 4512 6-9-0 **55**.............. OwenPayton(7) 13 52
(Jedd O'Keeffe) *stdd s: hld up: stdy hdwy on outside over 2f out: rdn over 1f out: no imp fnl f* **10/1**

0002 **8** *2 3/4* **Rosy Ryan (IRE)**[13] 4584 9-9-0 **48**.............. CamHardie 14 38
(Tina Jackson) *hld up towards rr: drvn along over 2f out: no imp fr over 1f out* **12/1**

6/4- **9** *3 3/4* **Phoenix Lightning (IRE)**[50] 3235 4-8-9 **46** oh1.............. SeanDavis(3) 8 28
(John James Feane, Ire) *hld up: rdn and hdwy over 2f out: wknd over 1f out* **5/1**[2]

3066 **10** *nse* **Corked (IRE)**[15] 4512 6-9-2 **53**..............(p) RowanScott(3) 5 35
(Alistair Whillans) *hld up towards rr: rdn and outpcd over 2f out: sn btn* **12/1**

46-0 **11** *4 1/2* **Palazzo**[42] 3513 3-8-8 **50**..............(p[1]) TomEaves 4 20
(Bryan Smart) *in tch: outpcd whn n.m.r over 2f out: sn struggling* **40/1**

0-04 **12** *2 3/4* **Just A Rumour (IRE)**[17] 4439 3-8-4 **46** oh1.............. PhilDennis 3 10
(Noel Wilson) *t.k.h: cl up tl rdn: edgd lft and wknd wl over 1f out* **50/1**

4304 **13** *2* **Muqarred (USA)**[48] 3297 7-9-1 **52**..............(b) GemmaTutty(3) 9 14
(Karen Tutty) *sn trcking ldr: lost pl over 2f out: sn struggling* **16/1**

1m 47.93s (-0.47) **Going Correction** +0.025s/f (Good)
WFA 3 from 4yo+ 8lb **13** Ran SP% **119.4**
Speed ratings (Par 101): **103,102,102,101,99 99,98,95,92,92 87,84,82**
CSF £99.87 CT £1639.35 TOTE £5.00: £2.30, £6.20, £5.30; EX 105.00 Trifecta £2087.10.
Owner Nil Sine Labore Partnership **Bred** Miss L A Perratt **Trained** East Kilbride, S Lanarks

FOCUS
Add 8yds. A moderate contest but a deserving winner who was second on Monday and went one better here. It's been rated as straightforward ordinary form.

5100 RACING TV PROFITS RETURNED TO RACING H'CAP (DIV II) 1m 68y
5:15 (5:15) (Class 6) (0-55,54) 3-Y-0+
£3,493 (£1,039; £519; £300; £300; £300) **Stalls** Low

Form RPR
3060 **1** **My Valentino (IRE)**[15] 4513 6-8-12 **45**..............(b) JamesSullivan 2 52
(Dianne Sayer) *s.i.s: hld up: hdwy on outside over 2f out: led and hung lft over 1f out: kpt on fnl f* **11/2**[3]

6416 **2** *nk* **Be Bold**[5] 4916 7-9-4 **51**..............(b) DavidAllan 6 58
(Rebecca Bastiman) *t.k.h in midfield: effrt whn nt clr run over 2f out: hdwy to chse ldrs whn nt clr run over 1f out: chsd wnr ins fnl f: r.o* **4/1**[2]

030 **3** *1* **Clary (IRE)**[44] 3448 9-8-12 **45**..............(h) CamHardie 7 49
(Alistair Whillans) *s.i.s: hld up: hdwy and rdn 2f out: kpt on fnl f: nrst fin* **18/1**

0002 **4** *1 1/4* **Poyle George Two**[36] 3721 4-8-13 **49**.............. RowanScott(3) 5 50
(John Hodge) *hld up on ins: pushed along over 2f out: hdwy and angled lft over 1f out: kpt on fnl f: no imp* **3/1**[1]

5540 **5** *1/2* **Kafoo**[13] 4589 6-9-0 **47**..............(b) AlistairRawlinson 11 47
(Michael Appleby) *in tch: hdwy and ev ch over 2f out to over 1f out: no ex ins fnl f* **14/1**

-045 **6** *1/2* **Barney Bullet (IRE)**[5] 4915 4-8-12 **45**..............(e) PhilDennis 10 44
(Noel Wilson) *t.k.h: prom: hdwy to ld over 2f out to over 1f out: no ex fnl f* **10/1**

445- **7** *1/2* **Carlow Boy (IRE)**[336] 6179 3-8-9 **50**.............. AndrewElliott 1 47
(Christopher Kellett) *cl up: effrt whn n.m.r over 2f out: rdn over 1f out: kpt on fnl f: no imp (jockey said gelding was denied a clear run approaching 2f out and again in the final 1 1/2f)* **66/1**

0000 **8** *1 3/4* **Dasheen**[27] 4078 6-9-3 **53**.............. GemmaTutty(3) 3 47
(Karen Tutty) *hld up: rdn whn checked 2f out: kpt on fnl f: nvr able to chal* **17/2**

0000 **9** *1 1/4* **Crazy Tornado (IRE)**[5] 4915 6-9-7 **54**..............(e) ConnorBeasley 8 45
(Keith Dalgleish) *t.k.h: led to over 2f out: rallied: wknd fnl f* **15/2**

-000 **10** *1* **Dark Crystal**[10] 4726 8-8-12 **48**.............. BenRobinson(3) 4 37
(Linda Perratt) *t.k.h: hld up: effrt on ins over 2f out: rdn and no imp over 1f out* **33/1**

0500 **11** *8* **Haymarket**[11] 4690 10-9-1 **48**.............. PJMcDonald 12 20
(R Mike Smith) *cl up tl lost pl over 2f out: sn btn* **10/1**

00/0 **12** *4 1/2* **Peach Pavlova (IRE)**[45] 3414 5-9-0 **47**.............. JoeFanning 13 9
(Ann Duffield) *missed break: hld up on outside: pushed along over 2f out: sn struggling* **40/1**

1m 49.17s (0.77) **Going Correction** +0.025s/f (Good)
WFA 3 from 4yo+ 8lb **12** Ran SP% **119.7**
Speed ratings (Par 101): **97,96,95,94,93 93,92,91,89,88 80,76**
CSF £27.76 CT £384.92 TOTE £6.00: £1.60, £1.30, £5.80; EX 29.40 Trifecta £407.30.
Owner Dennis J Coppola & Mrs Dianne Sayer **Bred** Lynch Bages Ltd & Camas Park Stud **Trained** Hackthorpe, Cumbria

FOCUS
Add 8yds. The slower of the two divisions and not form to get overly excited about. It's been rated as straightforward ordinary form.
T/Plt: £65.30 to a £1 stake. Pool: £42,435.32 - 473.76 winning units. T/Qpdt: £5.60 to a £1 stake. Pool: £3,209.16 - 421.30 winning units. **Richard Young**

4651 LEICESTER (R-H)
Thursday, July 18

OFFICIAL GOING: Good to firm (good on the bends; watered; 8.3)
Wind: Nil Weather: Cloudy

5101 COLD OVERTON NURSERY H'CAP 7f
2:20 (2:20) (Class 5) (0-75,74) 2-Y-O
£3,428 (£1,020; £509; £300; £300; £300) **Stalls** High

Form RPR
453 **1** **Making History (IRE)**[45] 3419 2-9-7 **74**.............. HectorCrouch 8 86+
(Saeed bin Suroor) *mde all: rdn clr over 1f out: comf* **5/4**[1]

335 **2** *3 3/4* **Danny Ocean (IRE)**[57] 2957 2-8-7 **65**.............. HarrisonShaw(5) 2 67
(K R Burke) *prom: racd keenly: stdd and lost pl over 5f out: pushed along and hdwy over 2f out: rdn to chse wnr over 1f out: no imp ins fnl f* **15/2**

434 **3** *3 3/4* **Fantom Force (IRE)**[22] 4254 2-9-1 **73**.............. SeamusCronin(5) 6 65
(Richard Hannon) *chsd wnr: rdn over 2f out: lost 2nd over 1f out: no ex fnl f* **9/2**[2]

030 **4** *1 1/2* **Richard R H B (IRE)**[65] 2706 2-9-6 **73**.............. TrevorWhelan 4 62
(David Loughnane) *s.i.s: hdwy 1/2-way: outpcd over 2f out: n.d after* **33/1**

505 **5** *1* **International Lion**[19] 4401 2-8-12 **65**..............(p[1]) TonyHamilton 3 51
(Richard Fahey) *s.i.s: hdwy over 5f out: hung rt and outpcd 1/2-way: rallied over 1f out: wknd fnl f* **12/1**

006 **6** *2* **Sparkling Diamond**[29] 3990 2-8-8 **61**.............. AndreaAtzeni 7 42
(Philip McBride) *hld up in tch: rdn over 2f out: wknd over 1f out* **12/1**

4321 **7** *10* **Miss Matterhorn**[26] 4114 2-9-4 **71**.............. CharlesBishop 5 27
(Eve Johnson Houghton) *chsd ldrs: rdn 1/2-way: wknd over 1f out (trainer could offer no explanation for the filly's performance)* **11/2**[3]

6550 **8** *13* **Swiss Bond**[41] 3562 2-8-4 **64**..............(b[1]) LauraCoughlan(7) 1
(J S Moore) *prom: lost pl after 1f: rdn 1/2-way: sn wknd (jockey said filly was never travelling; vet reported that the filly lost its lost left fore shoe)* **25/1**

1m 24.31s (-1.39) **Going Correction** -0.125s/f (Firm) **8** Ran SP% **111.9**
Speed ratings (Par 94): **102,97,93,91,90 88,76,62**
CSF £10.80 CT £31.78 TOTE £1.60: £1.10, £1.30, £1.90; EX 8.10 Trifecta £26.40.
Owner Godolphin **Bred** Godolphin **Trained** Newmarket, Suffolk

FOCUS
A fair nursery. The favourite outclassed this field towards the centre from the front on watered, slightly loose-topped ground officially good to firm, good in places.

5102 GAULBY (S) STKS 7f
2:50 (2:51) (Class 5) 3-Y-O

£3,428 (£1,020; £509; £300; £300; £300) **Stalls** High

Form RPR
-100 **1** **Forseti**[19] 4360 3-9-7 79..........(h) JoshuaBryan(3) 6 72+
(Andrew Balding) *stdd s: hld up: hdwy and hung rt fr over 1f out: shkn up to ld ins fnl f: r.o: comf* **8/11**[1]

0036 **2** *1 ½* **Luna Princess**[28] 4029 3-8-10 51..........(p) HayleyTurner 4 54
(Michael Appleby) *disp ld tl rdn to go on over 1f out: hdd ins fnl f: styd on same pce* **10/1**[3]

64-5 **3** *3 ¾* **Meraki**[22] 4244 3-8-10 49..........(b) TheodoreLadd(5) 2 49
(Tim Pinfield) *prom: racd keenly: rdn over 1f out: styd on same pce* **28/1**

0000 **4** *hd* **Tigerinmytank**[38] 3645 3-8-10 45.......... RoystonFfrench 3 44
(John Holt) *disp ld tl rdn over 1f out: wknd wl ins fnl f* **100/1**

4442 **5** *3 ¼* **Ventura Bay (IRE)**[29] 4005 3-9-1 65.......... TonyHamilton 5 40
(Richard Fahey) *chsd ldrs: rdn over 2f out: wknd over 1f out* **7/4**[2]

0000 **6** *18* **Little Tipple**[9] 4749 3-8-10 42.......... BrettDoyle 1
(John Ryan) *prom: rdn 1/2-way: wknd over 2f out* **66/1**

1m 24.52s (-1.18) **Going Correction** -0.125s/f (Firm) **6 Ran SP% 109.3**
Speed ratings (Par 100): **101,99,95,94,91 70**
CSF £8.52 TOTE £1.60: £1.40, £2.90; EX 7.20 Trifecta £39.00.The winner was bought in for £17,500.
Owner Mick and Janice Mariscotti **Bred** Deerfield Farm **Trained** Kingsclere, Hants

FOCUS
A fair 3yo seller. The odds-on favourite's winning time was marginally slower than the previous C&D nursery.

5103 BRITISH STALLION STUDS EBF NOVICE STKS 1m 2f
3:20 (3:20) (Class 5) 3-Y-O+ £4,948 (£1,472; £735; £367) **Stalls** Low

Form RPR
6-42 **1** **Dramatic Device**[19] 4392 4-9-9 82.......... JamesDoyle 4 81
(Chris Wall) *mde all: rdn over 1f out: hung lft ins fnl f: styd on* **10/11**[1]

2 *¾* **Final Orders** 3-9-0 0.......... RyanPowell 7 79
(Simon Crisford) *prom: racd keenly: rdn and swtchd lft 2f out: r.o to go 2nd nr fin* **14/1**

5 **3** *½* **Look Closely**[27] 4073 3-9-0 0.......... AndreaAtzeni 8 78
(Roger Varian) *s.i.s: racd wd 1f: sn prom: chsd wnr over 8f out: rdn and hung lft fr over 1f out: styd on same pce wl ins fnl f* **9/4**[2]

0 **4** *9* **Red Secret (CAN)**[40] 3584 3-9-0 0.......... HayleyTurner 1 60
(Ed Dunlop) *s.i.s: hld up: hdwy over 3f out: rdn over 2f out: sn outpcd* **20/1**

5 *5* **Magic Act (IRE)** 3-9-0 0.......... CYHo 3 50
(Mark Johnston) *chsd ldrs: pushed along 5f out: rdn and wknd over 2f out* **7/1**[3]

50 **6** *16* **Soldier Of War (USA)**[17] 4452 4-9-9 0.......... AdamKirby 6 18
(Ben Pauling) *broke wl: sn lost pl: bhd fnl 4f* **125/1**

5 **7** *53* **Sleepdancer (IRE)**[58] 2932 3-9-0 0.......... BrettDoyle 5
(John Ryan) *hld up: hung lft over 6f out: rdn over 4f out: sn wknd* **66/1**

2m 7.35s (-1.85) **Going Correction** -0.125s/f (Firm)
WFA 3 from 4yo+ 9lb **7 Ran SP% 109.4**
Speed ratings (Par 103): **102,101,101,93,89 77,34**
CSF £13.90 TOTE £1.60: £1.10, £3.60; EX 11.90 Trifecta £31.00.
Owner The Clodhoppers **Bred** Godolphin **Trained** Newmarket, Suffolk

FOCUS
A decent novice contest. The odds-on favourite toughed it out in the closing stages after a relatively easy time of things on the lead until the second half of the straight. The winner has been rated in line with his handicap latest.

5104 RACINGDIRECTORY.CO.UK H'CAP 1m 53y
3:50 (3:50) (Class 4) (0-85,87) 3-Y-O+ £4,690 (£1,395; £697; £348) **Stalls** Low

Form RPR
-223 **1** **Lyndon B (IRE)**[21] 4298 3-9-4 82..........(v[1]) JamesDoyle 2 94+
(George Scott) *s.i.s: hdwy over 6f out: swtchd lft over 2f out: nt clr run over 1f out: shkn up and qcknd to ld ins fnl f: r.o wl: comf* **8/1**

0214 **2** *2* **Silkstone (IRE)**[19] 4392 3-9-0 78.......... ShaneKelly 1 83
(Pam Sly) *chsd ldr tl led over 2f out: rdn over 1f out: hdd and unable qck ins fnl f* **7/2**[2]

1-24 **3** *2 ¾* **Hold Still (IRE)**[15] 4497 3-9-2 80.......... JamieSpencer 5 79
(William Muir) *s.i.s: hld up: hmpd over 2f out: swtchd lft over 1f out: r.o to go 3rd nr fin: nt trble ldrs* **5/1**

0301 **4** *nk* **Reggae Runner (FR)**[15] 4497 3-9-7 85.......... AndreaAtzeni 6 83
(Mark Johnston) *chsd ldrs: rdn over 3f out: no ex fnl f* **9/4**[1]

1524 **5** *¾* **Mr Tyrrell (IRE)**[5] 4902 5-9-12 87.......... SeamusCronin(5) 3 88
(Richard Hannon) *chsd ldrs: lost pl over 6f out: hdwy over 2f out: rdn whn hung rt and stmbld 1f out: no ex wl ins fnl f (jockey said that his saddle slipped)* **9/2**[3]

0550 **6** *1 ½* **God Has Given**[3] 4994 3-8-3 67..........(b[1]) DavidEgan 4 60
(Ian Williams) *led at stdy pce: qcknd 3f out: rdn: carried hd high and hdd over 2f out: wknd ins fnl f* **17/2**

1m 45.1s (-1.20) **Going Correction** -0.125s/f (Firm)
WFA 3 from 5yo 8lb **6 Ran SP% 109.5**
Speed ratings (Par 105): **101,99,96,95,95 93**
CSF £33.86 TOTE £7.70: £4.20, £2.70; EX 29.90 Trifecta £104.10.
Owner W J and T C O Gredley **Bred** Yeomanstown Stud **Trained** Newmarket, Suffolk

FOCUS
A decent handicap. In a tight market, one of the longer-priced 3yos won readily up the far rail from off a modest gallop. A pb from the second.

5105 TOM CRIBB FILLIES' H'CAP 7f
4:20 (4:20) (Class 4) (0-80,80) 3-Y-O+

£5,530 (£1,645; £822; £411; £300; £300) **Stalls** High

Form RPR
0353 **1** **Gentlewoman (IRE)**[13] 4592 3-9-0 75..........(h) NickyMackay 5 82
(John Gosden) *trckd ldrs: rdn to ld over 1f out: r.o* **4/1**[3]

31-4 **2** *1* **Eula Varner**[40] 3575 5-9-7 75.......... CharlesBishop 2 82
(Henry Candy) *chsd ldrs: shkn up over 2f out: r.o* **3/1**[2]

6323 **3** *nk* **Dashed**[32] 3892 3-8-12 73..........(b[1]) AndreaAtzeni 4 76
(Roger Varian) *s.i.s: hld up: hdwy u.p over 1f out: styd on: hung lft towards fin* **9/4**[1]

0-66 **4** *1* **Silca Mistress**[62] 2809 4-9-12 80.......... AdamKirby 6 83
(Clive Cox) *racd keenly: in 2nd tl shkn up over 2f out: rdn over 1f out: styd on same pce wl ins fnl f* **6/1**

-036 **5** *1* **Porcelain Girl (IRE)**[28] 4023 3-9-1 76.......... JamieSpencer 1 74
(Michael Bell) *stdd s: hld up: hdwy over 1f out: sn rdn: no ex wl ins fnl f* **15/2**

-030 **6** *½* **Rosamour (IRE)**[14] 4562 3-8-7 68.......... DavidEgan 3 64
(Richard Hughes) *led at stdy pce tl qcknd 1/2-way: rdn: hung lft and hdd over 1f out: no ex ins fnl f (jockey said filly hung left)* **10/1**

1m 24.08s (-1.62) **Going Correction** -0.125s/f (Firm)
WFA 3 from 4yo+ 7lb **6 Ran SP% 110.9**
Speed ratings (Par 102): **104,102,102,101,100 99**
CSF £15.91 TOTE £4.80: £2.30, £1.40; EX 16.10 Trifecta £30.70.
Owner HH Sheikha Al Jalila Racing **Bred** Godolphin **Trained** Newmarket, Suffolk

FOCUS
The feature contest was a fairly decent fillies' handicap. The winning 3yo toughed out this victory in a good comparative time. It's been rated as ordinary form, with the second to last year's Salisbury win. The third has been rated to form.

5106 KUBE EXHIBITION CENTRE H'CAP 1m 3f 179y
4:50 (4:52) (Class 6) (0-60,61) 4-Y-O+

£3,169 (£943; £471; £300; £300; £300) **Stalls** Low

Form RPR
4001 **1** **Affluence (IRE)**[14] 4568 4-9-8 61..........(p) EoinWalsh 5 71+
(Martin Smith) *hld up: hdwy over 2f out: chsd ldr over 1f out: rdn to ld ins fnl f: styd on wl* **6/1**[2]

2223 **2** *2 ¾* **Mistress Nellie**[26] 4111 4-8-9 48.......... ShaneKelly 11 54
(William Stone) *a.p: chsd ldr over 3f out: led over 2f out: rdn over 1f out: hdd ins fnl f: styd on same pce* **6/1**[2]

0041 **3** *3* **Becky Sharp**[21] 4287 4-8-12 51..........(b) CharlieBennett 9 52
(Jim Boyle) *chsd ldr tl led over 9f out: rdn and hdd over 2f out: styd on same pce fnl f* **5/1**[1]

0053 **4** *¾* **Esspeegee**[14] 4547 6-9-2 60..........(p) DarraghKeenan(5) 1 60
(Alan Bailey) *sn pushed along in mid-div: rdn over 4f out: styd on ins fnl f: nt trble ldrs* **11/1**

5304 **5** *¾* **Sauchiehall Street (IRE)**[8] 4796 4-9-6 59..........(p[1]) AdamKirby 2 58
(Noel Williams) *chsd ldrs: wnt 2nd over 5f out tl rdn over 3f out: no ex fnl f: hung lft towards fin* **13/2**[3]

6-05 **6** *½* **Jetstream (IRE)**[19] 4370 4-9-0 58.......... HarrisonShaw(5) 8 56
(D J Jeffreys) *mid-div: hdwy over 4f out: rdn over 2f out: no ex fnl f* **6/1**[2]

4R-0 **7** *1* **Threediamondrings**[44] 3444 6-8-8 47 oh1 ow1.......... NickyMackay 3 43
(Mark Usher) *s.s: bhd: swtchd lft over 2f out: n.d (jockey said gelding was reluctant to race and slowly away, losing several lengths as a result)* **40/1**

0504 **8** *5* **Little Choosey**[12] 4657 9-8-7 46..........(tp) JohnFahy 7 34
(Roy Bowring) *hld up: rdn over 2f out: n.d* **33/1**

0-52 **9** *1 ½* **Melabi (IRE)**[15] 4515 6-8-0 46.......... KieranSchofield(7) 4 32
(Stella Barclay) *s.i.s: pushed along early in rr: hdwy over 4f out: rdn over 2f out: wknd over 1f out* **14/1**

2230 **10** *1* **Albert Boy (IRE)**[13] 4601 6-9-1 59..........(p) TheodoreLadd(5) 10 43
(Scott Dixon) *led: hdd over 9f out: chsd ldr tl over 5f out: rdn and wknd over 2f out* **7/1**

05-0 **11** *23* **Kennerton Green (IRE)**[16] 4475 4-8-9 48.......... DavidEgan 6
(Lydia Pearce) *s.i.s: hld up: rdn over 3f out: wknd over 2f out* **40/1**

-003 **R** **Principia**[12] 4653 4-9-5 58..........(be[1]) RoystonFfrench 12
(Adam West) *ref to r* **20/1**

2m 33.14s (-1.86) **Going Correction** -0.125s/f (Firm) **12 Ran SP% 112.9**
Speed ratings (Par 101): **101,99,97,96,96 95,95,91,90,90 74,**
CSF £38.14 CT £190.94 TOTE £6.50: £1.90, £1.90, £2.10; EX 21.70 Trifecta £105.40.
Owner The Affluence Partnership **Bred** Mrs Michelle Smith **Trained** Newmarket, Suffolk

FOCUS
A modest middle-distance handicap. Straightforward low-grade form.

5107 MOLYNEUX APPRENTICE H'CAP 6f
5:25 (5:25) (Class 6) (0-65,66) 3-Y-O+

£3,169 (£943; £471; £300; £300; £300) **Stalls** High

Form RPR
3334 **1** **Evening Attire**[21] 4281 8-9-6 62.......... RhonaPindar(3) 8 71
(William Stone) *chsd ldr tl rdn to ld over 1f out: styd on* **11/8**[1]

4-60 **2** *nk* **Lilbourne Star (IRE)**[23] 4227 4-9-9 65.......... AmeliaGlass(3) 7 73
(Clive Cox) *stdd s: hld up: hdwy over 2f out: rdn to chse wnr ins fnl f: ev ch whn eased wl ins fnl f: shkn up nr fin: r.o* **17/2**

0-00 **3** *6* **Chez Vegas**[51] 3208 6-8-10 52.......... CianMacRedmond(3) 4 42
(Scott Dixon) *chsd ldrs: rdn 1/2-way: no ex fnl f* **7/1**[3]

0-00 **4** *3 ½* **Tilsworth Prisca**[48] 3304 4-8-7 46 oh1..........(h) TobyEley 5 26
(J R Jenkins) *s.s: in rr: rdn over 1f out: nt trble ldrs (jockey said filly anticipated the start and missed the break as a result)* **66/1**

000 **5** *½* **Case Key**[21] 4303 6-9-11 64.......... KieranSchofield 9 42
(Michael Appleby) *chsd ldrs: rdn and lost pl over 3f out: n.d after* **7/1**[3]

6-45 **6** *nk* **Kath's Lustre**[14] 4556 4-9-8 66..........(b) GeorgeRooke(5) 6 43
(Richard Hughes) *s.i.s: sn prom: rdn over 1f out: wknd fnl f* **8/1**

2350 **7** *2 ¼* **First Excel**[43] 3476 7-8-13 52..........(b) AledBeech 3 22
(Roy Bowring) *led over 4f: wknd ins fnl f (jockey said gelding stopped quickly)* **6/1**[2]

6310 **8** *1 ½* **Princess Florence (IRE)**[9] 4754 3-8-3 52..........(p) LauraPearson(5) 1 17
(John Ryan) *dwlt: outpcd* **14/1**

0660 **9** *5* **Thedevilinneville**[16] 4477 3-7-11 46 oh1..........(b[1]) KeelanBaker(5) 10
(Adam West) *s.i.s: hld up: rdn and wknd 1/2-way (jockey said gelding was never travelling)* **40/1**

1m 11.93s (-0.17) **Going Correction** -0.125s/f (Firm)
WFA 3 from 4yo+ 5lb **9 Ran SP% 113.6**
Speed ratings (Par 101): **96,95,87,82,82 81,78,76,70**
CSF £13.68 CT £61.22 TOTE £2.40: £1.20, £1.80, £2.60; EX 15.20 Trifecta £94.10.
Owner Miss Caroline Scott **Bred** Howard Barton Stud **Trained** West Wickham, Cambs
■ Stewards' Enquiry : Amelia Glass ten-day ban; failing to ride out approaching the finish (Aug 1-10)

FOCUS
A modest apprentice riders' handicap. The favourite held on well, but the jockey on board the narrow runner-up had stopped riding a shade earlier thinking she had reached the finish. It's been rated around the balance of the first two.
T/Plt: £62.10 to a £1 stake. Pool: £42,802.95 - 502.51 winning units. T/Qpdt: £29.60 to a £1 stake. Pool: £3,894.43 - 97.09 winning units. **Colin Roberts**

5108 - 5111a (Foreign Racing) - See Raceform Interactive

4852 LEOPARDSTOWN (L-H)
Thursday, July 18

OFFICIAL GOING: Good (good to firm in places; watered)

5112a MELD STKS (GROUP 3) 1m 1f
7:50 (7:50) 3-Y-O+

£31,891 (£10,270; £4,864; £2,162; £1,081; £540)

RPR

1 **Mohawk (IRE)**46 3390 3-9-5 109 DonnachaO'Brien 2 114+
(A P O'Brien, Ire) *settled in 5th: clsr 2f out: qckd wl to ld over 1f out: pushed clr ins fnl f: kpt on wl* 9/4[1]

2 2 **Up Helly Aa (IRE)**45 3439 3-9-0 0 WJLee 1 104+
(W McCreery, Ire) *racd towards rr: rdn in 6th 2f out: kpt on wl on outer ent fnl f into 2nd fnl 100yds: nt trble wnr* 7/2[3]

3 1 1/2 **Ancient Spirit (GER)**124 4-10-0 112 (p[1]) KevinManning 6 107
(J S Bolger, Ire) *ponied to s: led: 3 l advantage at 1/2-way: rdn over 1f out and sn hdd: kpt on same pce and dropped to 3rd fnl 100yds* 14/1

4 2 1/2 **Zihba (IRE)**19 4411 4-9-9 104 (t) ChrisHayes 3 97
(J A Stack, Ire) *chsd ldrs on inner in 4th: wnt 3rd over 2f out: rdn and nt qckn appr fnl f: kpt on same pce* 16/1

5 2 1/4 **Pincheck (IRE)**19 4410 5-9-12 110 ShaneFoley 5 95
(Mrs John Harrington, Ire) *chsd ldrs in 3rd: pushed along in 4th under 3f out: nt qckn over 1f out: sn one pce* 3/1[2]

6 1 **Tinandali (IRE)**40 3612 3-9-0 104 OisinOrr 7 89
(D K Weld, Ire) *sn chsd ldr in 2nd: rdn over 2f out: nt qckn over 1f out: sn no ex* 4/1

7 12 **Zabriskie (IRE)**19 4411 4-9-9 95 (t) WayneLordan 8 65
(Luke Comer, Ire) *in rr thrght: detached under 3f out: nvr a factor* 66/1

1m 54.98s (-2.82) **Going Correction** +0.25s/f (Good)
WFA 3 from 4yo+ 9lb 7 Ran SP% 112.0
Speed ratings: **112,110,108,106,104 103,93**
CSF £9.98 TOTE £2.80: £1.70, £2.00; DF 9.00 Trifecta £71.70.
Owner Derrick Smith & Mrs John Magnier & Michael Tabor **Bred** Whisperview Trading Ltd **Trained** Cashel, Co Tipperary

FOCUS
The winner was dropping in class having contested Classics on his last two starts, this certainly looks more his level. A fair step forward from the winner, with the third and fourth rated in line with their recent figures.

5113 - 5114a (Foreign Racing) - See Raceform Interactive

4961 LONGCHAMP (R-H)
Thursday, July 18

OFFICIAL GOING: Turf: good

5115a PRIX DE L'UNIVERSITE (CLAIMER) (4YO+) (AMATEUR RIDERS) (GRANDE COURSE) (TURF) 1m 7f
4:20 4-Y-O+ £7,207 (£2,882; £2,162; £1,441; £720)

RPR

1 **Classic Joy (FR)**42 4-10-11 0 (p) MrFlorentGuy 7 68
(Andrea Marcialis, France) 9/5[1]

2 snk **Tres Solid (FR)**76 8-10-8 0 (p) MrHugoBoutin 8 64
(M Boutin, France) 31/10[3]

3 nk **Panatos (FR)**37 3686 4-10-2 0 MissHannahWelch(8) 4 66
(Alexandra Dunn) *urged along early to ld: rowed along 2f out to hold advantage: rdn and hdd over 1f out: kpt on ins fnl f* 14/1

4 2 **Kenny (GER)**51 4-10-4 0 (b) FrauBeritWeber(4) 1 62
(Waldemar Hickst, Germany) 27/10[2]

5 nk **Sky Bolt (FR)**40 6-10-2 0 (b) MmePaulineMenges(8) 3 63
(Pauline Menges, France) 11/1

6 1 1/4 **Etalondes (FR)**146 9-10-4 0 (p) MlleCamilleColletVidal(8) 6 64
(F Vermeulen, France) 17/2

7 3 1/2 **Rye House (IRE)**85 10-10-0 0 MissJulieHenderson(3) 5 51
(Patrick Dejaeger, Belgium) 12/1

3m 22.38s (6.38) 7 Ran SP% 120.4
PARI-MUTUEL (all including 1 euro stake): WIN 2.80; PLACE 1.40, 1.60, 2.60; DF 4.00.
Owner Moreno Poggioni **Bred** Ecurie Skymarc Farm **Trained** France

5079 VICHY
Thursday, July 18

OFFICIAL GOING: Turf: good to soft

5116a PRIX DU HARAS DE BOUQUETOT-JACQUES BOUCHARA (LISTED RACE) (2YO) (TURF) 5f
1:25 2-Y-O £27,027 (£10,810; £8,108; £5,405; £2,702)

RPR

1 **Lady Galore (IRE)**16 2-8-10 0 JulienAuge 6 95
(C Ferland, France) 115/10

2 1/2 **Wheels On Fire (FR)**29 3988 2-9-0 ClementLecoeuvre 11 97
(Matthieu Palussiere, France) 12/1

3 shd **Has D'Emra (FR)**24 2-9-0 0 (b) MaximeGuyon 9 96
(F Rossi, France) 41/10[1]

4 shd **Brand New Day (IRE)**29 3983 2-8-10 0 (b[1]) AntoineHamelin 10 92
(Matthieu Palussiere, France) 51/10

5 3/4 **Augustine (FR)**18 2-8-10 0 AlexandreRoussel 7 89
(Louis Baudron, France) 27/1

6 3/4 **Emblematique (FR)**21 2-8-10 0 FranckBlondel 5 87
(F Rossi, France) 19/1

7 1/2 **Xaaros (FR)**40 2-9-0 0 AnthonyCrastus 2 89
(P Sogorb, France) 59/10

8 nk **Companion**19 4387 2-8-10 0 IoritzMendizabal 1 84
(Mark Johnston) *chsd ldrs: rowed along over 2f out: rdn and no imp over 1f out: kpt on same pce fnl f* 43/10[3]

9 shd **Vinyl Track (IRE)**18 2-9-0 0 PierreBazire 3 87
(G Botti, France) 46/1

10 4 **Alkaid (FR)**64 2757 2-9-0 0 TheoBachelot 12 73
(Gianluca Bietolini, France) 25/1

11 10 **Ask Me Not (IRE)**60 2-9-0 0 (p) ChristopheSoumillon 4 37
(F Vermeulen, France) 42/10[2]

11 Ran SP% 118.8
PARI-MUTUEL (all including 1 euro stake): WIN 12.50; PLACE 3.40, 3.50, 2.20; DF 45.70.
Owner Prime Equestrian S.A.R.L. **Bred** Haras Du Mont Dit Mont **Trained** France

FOCUS
They finished in a heap and the race has been rated negatively.

5093 HAMILTON (R-H)
Friday, July 19

OFFICIAL GOING: Good to soft changing to soft after race 2 (6.35)
Wind: Nil Weather: Overcast, raining

5117 HEINEKEN UK APPRENTICE H'CAP 1m 68y
6:00 (6:00) (Class 5) (0-70,71) 4-Y-O+

£4,140 (£1,232; £615; £400; £400; £400) Stalls Low

Form RPR

5063 1 **Set In Stone (IRE)**6 4917 5-9-11 71 RowanScott 1 80
(Andrew Hughes, Ire) *cl up: led and hrd pressed over 2f out: edgd lft ins fnl f: kpt on wl* 7/2[1]

0302 2 1 1/4 **Strong Steps**4 4982 7-9-6 66 (p) BenRobinson 7 72
(Jim Goldie) *prom: hdwy over 2f out: ev ch and hung rt over 1f out: kpt on same pce ins fnl f* 5/1

2246 3 3/4 **Zoravan (USA)**7 4879 6-9-8 68 (b) ConorMcGovern 2 72
(Keith Dalgleish) *t.k.h: led to over 2f out: rallied and ev ch whn faltered over 1f out: kpt on same pce ins fnl f (jockey said gelding shied at the rail 2f out and became unbalanced)* 8/1

-002 4 1 3/4 **Iconic Code**6 4917 4-9-3 63 BenSanderson 4 63
(Keith Dalgleish) *hld up in tch: effrt over 2f out: kpt on same pce ins fnl f* 9/2[3]

1354 5 nk **Equidae**31 3970 4-8-13 66 (t) IzzyClifton(7) 5 66
(Iain Jardine) *hld up on ins: pushed along 3f out: hdwy over 1f out: no further imp fnl f* 4/1[2]

5402 6 4 **Dubai Acclaim (IRE)**33 3880 4-9-6 69 SeanDavis(3) 8 59
(Richard Fahey) *s.i.s: t.k.h in last pl: effrt and rdn over 2f out: wknd over 1f out* 5/1

6000 7 7 **Jo's Girl (IRE)**52 3199 4-9-2 62 DylanHogan 9 36
(Micky Hammond) *cl up tl rdn and wknd over 2f out* 18/1

0406 8 1 3/4 **Alexandrakollontai (IRE)**51 3223 9-9-2 62 (b) ConnorMurtagh 6 32
(Alistair Whillans) *hld up: drvn along over 2f out: sn wknd* 33/1

1m 48.89s (0.49) **Going Correction** +0.25s/f (Good) 8 Ran SP% 113.1
Speed ratings (Par 103): **107,105,105,103,102 98,91,90**
CSF £20.71 CT £128.85 TOTE £4.50: £1.60, £1.50, £2.50; EX 20.50 Trifecta £130.70.
Owner Thistle Bloodstock Limited **Bred** Thistle Bloodstock Limited **Trained** Kells, Co Kilkenny

FOCUS
All distances as advertised. A modest apprentice riders' handicap in which the market rightly favoured the winner following consistent rain turning the ground officially good to soft. The third has been rated to form, and the second close to his latest.

5118 BB FOODSERVICE EBF MAIDEN STKS (PLUS 10 RACE) (A £20,000 BB FOODSERVICE 2YO SERIES QUALIFIER) 6f 6y
6:35 (6:36) (Class 4) 2-Y-O £5,757 (£1,713; £856; £428) Stalls High

Form RPR

2 1 **Byline**27 4098 2-9-5 0 TomEaves 1 82+
(Kevin Ryan) *pressed ldr: led after 2f: pushed along over 1f out: drew clr ins fnl f: readily* 8/13[1]

2 3 1/2 **Dark Regard** 2-9-0 0 PJMcDonald 2 67
(Mark Johnston) *prom: effrt and pressed wnr over 1f out: kpt on same pce ins fnl f* 7/2[2]

3 2 **Magic Timing** 2-9-5 0 ShaneGray 5 66+
(Keith Dalgleish) *dwlt: rn green in rr: effrt and swtchd rt 2f out: sn prom: outpcd fnl f* 12/1

3 4 2 1/4 **Lexington Warfare (IRE)**61 2869 2-9-2 0 SeanDavis(3) 6 60
(Richard Fahey) *prom: effrt whn nt clr run wl over 1f out: sn rdn and outpcd: n.d after* 7/1[3]

5 3 1/4 **My Dandy Doc (IRE)** 2-9-0 0 JasonHart 4 44
(John Quinn) *dwlt: hld up: rdn and carried rt 2f out: sn wknd* 16/1

5 6 5 **Romininthegloamin (IRE)**22 4275 2-9-0 0 TadhgO'Shea 3 29
(Andrew Hughes, Ire) *t.k.h: led 2f: w wnr to over 2f out: wknd over 1f out* 40/1

1m 15.06s (2.36) **Going Correction** +0.25s/f (Good) 6 Ran SP% 112.7
Speed ratings (Par 96): **94,89,86,83,79 72**
CSF £3.08 TOTE £1.40: £1.10, £2.00; EX 3.40 Trifecta £15.00.
Owner Highclere Thoroughbred Racing-Ls Lowry 1 **Bred** Toby Barker **Trained** Hambleton, N Yorks

FOCUS
A fair juvenile maiden. It was hard work for these young horses in worsening conditions, but the odds-on favourite won pretty decisively. The going was officially changed to soft after this race.

5119 HEINEKEN UK H'CAP 5f 7y
7:05 (7:05) (Class 4) (0-85,86) 3-Y-O+ £8,021 (£2,387; £1,192; £596) Stalls Centre

Form RPR

-400 1 **Orion's Bow**43 3509 8-9-1 74 (p) DavidAllan 3 80
(Tim Easterby) *chsd clr ldr: hdwy over 2f out: rdn to ld ins fnl f: jst lasted* 7/2[2]

-100 2 nse **Zig Zag Zyggy (IRE)**22 4279 4-9-8 81 TadhgO'Shea 5 87
(Andrew Hughes, Ire) *chsd ldrs: effrt and rdn over 1f out: kpt on wl fnl f: jst hld* 7/1[3]

1060 3 2 1/4 **Poyle Vinnie**20 4406 9-9-13 86 (b) JamesSullivan 6 84
(Ruth Carr) *t.k.h: led and sn clr: rdn over 1f out: hdd and no ex ins fnl f* 7/2[2]

-004 4 2 1/4 **Holmeswood**7 4894 5-9-11 84 PaulMulrennan 4 74
(Julie Camacho) *stdd in tch: effrt and rdn over 2f out: wknd over 1f out (trainer rep said gelding was unsuited by the Soft ground on this occasion and would prefer a sounder surface)* 10/11[1]

1m 0.83s (0.43) **Going Correction** +0.25s/f (Good)
WFA 3 from 4yo+ 4lb 4 Ran SP% 109.3
Speed ratings (Par 105): **106,105,102,98**
CSF £22.37 TOTE £4.10; EX 20.00 Trifecta £31.10.
Owner T J Swiers **Bred** Cheveley Park Stud Ltd **Trained** Great Habton, N Yorks

FOCUS
A decent little sprint handicap. The second has been rated to his best.

5120 HEINEKEN UK SCOTTISH STEWARDS' CUP H'CAP 6f 6y
7:40 (7:41) (Class 2) (0-105,105) 3-Y-0+
£21,165 (£6,337; £3,168; £1,584; £792; £397) **Stalls** Centre

Form RPR
0110 **1** **Air Raid**[20] 4379 4-9-2 **95**.......... JackGarritty 8 106
(Jedd O'Keeffe) *cl up: led over 2f out: rdn over 1f out: edgd rt ins fnl f: kpt on wl* **6/1**
2005 **2** 1 ¼ **Lake Volta (IRE)**[6] 4921 4-9-7 **100**.......... PJMcDonald 2 107
(Mark Johnston) *in tch: effrt and rdn 2f out: chsd wnr ins fnl f: kpt on* **5/1**[2]
0001 **3** 1 ¼ **Staxton**[20] 4379 4-9-7 **100**..........(p) DavidAllan 7 103
(Tim Easterby) *chsd ldrs: rdn over 2f out: effrt over 1f out: kpt on same pce ins fnl f* **7/1**
0233 **4** 1 **Admirality**[6] 4921 5-9-1 **94**..........(h) PaulMulrennan 12 94
(Roger Fell) *hld up in tch: stdy hdwy gng wl over 2f out: effrt and pushed along over 1f out: kpt on same pce ins fnl f* **9/2**[1]
-205 **5** 4 **Yousini**[34] 3865 3-8-9 **93**.......... TomEaves 15 79
(Kevin Ryan) *hld up towards rr: pushed along over 2f out: kpt on fnl f: nt pce to chal* **11/1**
4060 **6** ½ **Aeolus**[41] 3589 8-8-10 **89**.......... JamesSullivan 10 74
(Ruth Carr) *towards rr: drvn along 1/2-way: kpt on fnl f: nvr rchd ldrs* **33/1**
5100 **7** shd **Dark Defender**[16] 4521 6-8-5 **87**..........(b) RowanScott(3) 9 72
(Rebecca Bastiman) *chsd ldrs: rdn over 2f out: edgd rt over 1f out: wknd fnl f* **33/1**
0053 **8** hd **Golden Apollo**[20] 4402 5-8-12 **91**.......... JasonHart 3 75
(Tim Easterby) *towards rr: rdn along over 2f out: sme late hdwy: nvr rchd ldrs* **11/2**[3]
2060 **9** shd **George Bowen (IRE)**[20] 4402 7-9-6 **102**..........(v) SeanDavis(3) 14 86
(Richard Fahey) *dwlt: bhd and sn pushed along: drvn over 2f out: kpt on fnl f: no imp* **20/1**
2-40 **10** 1 **Lomu (IRE)**[20] 4406 5-8-8 **87**.......... ShaneGray 13 68
(Keith Dalgleish) *racd alone against stands' rail: overall ldr to over 2f out: wknd over 1f out* **18/1**
-432 **11** ¾ **Laugh A Minute**[20] 4380 4-9-12 **105**.......... DavidEgan 11 84
(Roger Varian) *hld up towards rr: drvn along over 2f out: edgd rt: btn over 1f out* **8/1**
0310 **12** nse **Dalton**[20] 4379 5-8-7 **86**..........(b[1]) CliffordLee 5 64
(Julie Camacho) *bhd and outpcd: shortlived effrt 2f out: sn btn* **14/1**
6100 **13** 2 ¾ **Teruntum Star (FR)**[41] 3602 7-8-12 **96**..........(v) DylanHogan(5) 4 66
(Kevin Ryan) *cl up: ev ch over 2f out to over 1f out: wknd qckly fnl f* **33/1**

1m 12.24s (-0.46) **Going Correction** +0.25s/f (Good)
WFA 3 from 4yo+ 5lb **13 Ran SP% 122.0**
Speed ratings (Par 109): **113,111,109,108,103 102,102,101,101,100 99,99,95**
CSF £35.42 CT £215.93 TOTE £7.70: £2.60, £2.70, £2.80; EX 43.50 Trifecta £416.60.
Owner Caron & Paul Chapman **Bred** Meon Valley Stud **Trained** Middleham Moor, N Yorks

FOCUS
A good quality sprint handicap. Two horses with winning soft-ground form filled the first two places. The fourth-favourite won a shade cosily centrally. The second has been rated to his Bunbury Cup run, and the third close to his AW latest.

5121 BRITISH STALLION STUDS EBF GLASGOW STKS (LISTED RACE) 1m 3f 15y
8:10 (8:10) (Class 1) 3-Y-0
£24,385 (£9,245; £4,626; £2,304; £1,156; £580) **Stalls** Low

Form RPR
3201 **1** **Sameem (IRE)**[11] 4730 3-9-5 90.......... DavidAllan 7 102
(James Tate) *t.k.h early: mde all at modest gallop: shkn up and qcknd clr over 2f out: rdn and r.o wl fnl f: unchal* **7/2**[2]
3440 **2** 3 **Persian Moon (IRE)**[6] 4901 3-9-5 101.......... PJMcDonald 5 97
(Mark Johnston) *prom: niggled along after 3f: hdwy to chse (clr) wnr over 2f out: kpt on fnl f: nt pce to chal* **11/10**[1]
533 **3** 4 **Aspire Tower (IRE)**[28] 4063 3-9-5 83.......... ShaneGray 6 90
(Steve Gollings) *chsd ldrs: wnt 2nd 1/2-way to over 2f out: sn rdn and outpcd: kpt on ins fnl f to take 3rd cl home* **25/1**
5250 **4** shd **Leroy Leroy**[6] 4935 3-9-5 98..........(p[1]) CliffordLee 4 90
(Richard Hannon) *chsd wnr to 1/2-way: cl up: effrt and angled lft over 2f out: one pce fnl f: lost 3rd cl home* **8/1**
112 **5** ½ **Southern Rock (IRE)**[15] 4553 3-9-5 83.......... DavidNolan 1 89
(David O'Meara) *hld up in last pl: drvn along 3f out: no imp fr 2f out* **10/1**
1402 **6** 1 ¼ **Mackaar (IRE)**[24] 4224 3-9-5 94.......... DavidEgan 2 87
(Roger Varian) *t.k.h: hld up in tch: drvn and outpcd over 2f out: sn btn (trainer's rep could offer no explanation for the colt's performance)* **9/2**[3]

2m 25.92s (0.42) **Going Correction** +0.25s/f (Good) **6 Ran SP% 112.1**
Speed ratings (Par 108): **108,105,102,102,102 101**
CSF £7.75 TOTE £5.00: £1.80, £1.10; EX 12.10 Trifecta £114.10.
Owner Sultan Ali **Bred** Rabbah Bloodstock Limited **Trained** Newmarket, Suffolk

FOCUS
The feature race was a good quality Listed 3yo contest won in 2017 by this year's Group 1 Coronation Cup and Group 2 Hardwicke Stakes winner Defoe. The second-favourite won unchallenged from the front and did not need to improve. The third looks the key to the form, with the fifth also finishing close enough.

5122 CLYDE SCAFFOLDING LTD, PREMIER SCAFFOLDING SERVICES H'CAP 1m 3f 15y
8:45 (8:45) (Class 5) (0-70,72) 3-Y-0+
£4,140 (£1,232; £615; £400; £400; £400) **Stalls** Low

Form RPR
01 **1** **King And Queen (FR)**[6] 4914 3-8-6 **58** 6ex.......... PJMcDonald 9 71+
(Mark Johnston) *led: stdd pce 1/2-way: hdd over 3f out: sn pushed along: rdn and regained ld over 1f out: drew clr fnl f* **1/5**[1]
6604 **2** 4 **Carbon Dating (IRE)**[6] 4913 7-10-0 **70**.......... TadhgO'Shea 5 75
(Andrew Hughes, Ire) *t.k.h: hld up: hdwy on outside to ld over 3f out: swtchd to far rail over 2f out: rdn and hdd over 1f out: kpt on same pce* **8/1**[2]
0000 **3** ¾ **Ad Libitum**[11] 4724 4-9-6 **67**..........(p) BenSanderson(5) 1 71
(Roger Fell) *stdd s: hld up: hdwy and prom 2f out: sn rdn and edgd rt: kpt on same pce ins fnl f* **22/1**
0625 **4** ¾ **Trinity Star (IRE)**[10] 4762 8-9-13 **69**..........(v) JasonHart 6 71
(Karen McLintock) *hld up in tch: rdn over 2f out: no imp over 1f out* **14/1**[3]
5664 **5** 2 ½ **Pammi**[11] 4724 4-8-7 **52**..........(p) SeanDavis(3) 10 50
(Jim Goldie) *cl up: drvn and outpcd over 2f out: n.d after* **16/1**
66-0 **6** 5 **Mercer's Troop (IRE)**[20] 4404 4-10-0 **70**..........(p) PaulMulrennan 8 60
(Alistair Whillans) *t.k.h: cl up tl rdn and wknd over 2f out* **50/1**
1500 **7** 1 ¼ **Star Ascending (IRE)**[14] 4601 7-9-5 **61**..........(p) DavidNolan 7 49
(Jennie Candlish) *dwlt: sn prom: drvn and outpcd over 2f out: sn btn* **33/1**

2m 30.93s (5.43) **Going Correction** +0.25s/f (Good)
WFA 3 from 4yo+ 10lb **7 Ran SP% 116.2**
Speed ratings (Par 103): **90,87,86,86,84 80,79**
CSF £2.66 CT £13.19 TOTE £1.10: £1.10, £2.50; EX 3.40 Trifecta £14.70.
Owner Jaber Abdullah **Bred** Rabbah Bloodstock Limited **Trained** Middleham Moor, N Yorks

FOCUS
An ordinary middle-distance handicap. The long odds-on favourite was the only 3yo in the line up, but became the fifth consecutive winner in this race from that age-group. The winning time was five seconds slower than the previous C&D Listed contest in a slowly-run affair. The second has been rated in line with this year's form.

5123 EXTERNAL SYSTEMS LTD H'CAP 6f 6y
9:15 (9:16) (Class 5) (0-70,69) 3-Y-0+
£4,140 (£1,232; £615; £400; £400; £400) **Stalls** Centre

Form RPR
0415 **1** **Dancing Rave**[29] 4033 3-9-4 **69**.......... DavidNolan 1 79
(David O'Meara) *wnt rt s: prom: effrt over 1f out: led ins fnl f: drifted lft: pushed out* **15/2**
0404 **2** 1 ¾ **Chookie Dunedin**[11] 4721 4-9-8 **68**.......... TomEaves 2 74
(Keith Dalgleish) *led: rdn over 1f out: hdd ins fnl f: one pce whn hmpd towards fin* **6/1**[3]
0414 **3** 1 ¼ **Poet's Pride**[10] 4767 4-9-7 **67**.......... RobbieDowney 4 68
(David Barron) *pressed ldr to over 1f out: drvn and one pce ins fnl f* **11/4**[1]
3124 **4** 1 ¼ **Fairy Stories**[21] 4335 3-8-13 **67**.......... SeanDavis(3) 3 63
(Richard Fahey) *hld up in tch: effrt and angled lft wl over 1f out: no imp fnl f* **11/4**[1]
641 **5** 2 ¼ **Twentysixthstreet (IRE)**[6] 4912 3-9-4 **69** 6ex.......... TadhgO'Shea 7 58
(Andrew Hughes, Ire) *prom: rdn over 2f out: edgd rt and wknd over 1f out (jockey said colt ran flat)* **9/2**[2]
4660 **6** ½ **Born To Finish (IRE)**[4] 5000 6-9-7 **67**..........(p) DavidEgan 5 55
(Ed de Giles) *hld up bhd ldng gp: drvn and outpcd over 2f out: n.d after* **6/1**[3]

1m 13.84s (1.14) **Going Correction** +0.25s/f (Good)
WFA 3 from 4yo+ 5lb **6 Ran SP% 111.9**
Speed ratings (Par 103): **102,99,98,96,93 92**
CSF £49.25 TOTE £6.40: £2.90, £3.00; EX 56.70 Trifecta £145.50.
Owner David Lumley & Partner **Bred** Frazer Hood **Trained** Upper Helmsley, N Yorks
■ Stewards' Enquiry : David Nolan three-day ban; careless riding (Aug 2-4)

FOCUS
A modest sprint handicap. The third has been rated to his turf best.
T/Plt: £148.60 to a £1 stake. Pool: £57,815.95 - 283.88 winning units T/Qpdt: £20.50 to a £1 stake. Pool: £5,321.79 - 191.77 winning units **Richard Young**

4644 HAYDOCK (L-H)
Friday, July 19

OFFICIAL GOING: Good (watered; 8.2) changing to good to soft after race 1 (2.10)
Wind: Light, half against in straight of over 4f Weather: Cloudy with rain

5124 RACINGTV.COM H'CAP 1m 2f 42y
2:10 (2:11) (Class 5) (0-75,76) 3-Y-0
£4,851 (£1,443; £721; £360; £300; £300) **Stalls** Centre

Form RPR
6-12 **1** **Dreamweaver (IRE)**[13] 4671 3-9-1 **69**.......... LiamKeniry 3 81+
(Ed Walker) *hld up: impr to midfield 6f out: rdn and nt clr run over 2f out: swtchd rt under 2f out: hdwy over 1f out: led ins fnl f: styd on strly to draw clr fnl 100yds* **5/4**[1]
5405 **2** 4 **Lola's Theme**[15] 4553 3-9-4 **72**..........(p) RichardKingscote 2 75
(Tom Dascombe) *chsd ldrs: rdn over 2f out: unable qck over 1f out: rallied wl ins fnl f: styd on to take 2nd nr fin: no ch w wnr* **8/1**
3400 **3** nk **Guildhall**[21] 4321 3-9-8 **76**.......... BenCurtis 7 78
(Ralph Beckett) *prom: chsd ldrs after 2f: rdn over 2f out: chalng 1f out: styd on same pce and unable to go w wnr fnl 100yds: lost 2nd nr fin* **9/1**
3-43 **4** 1 ¼ **Global Express**[79] 2289 3-9-6 **74**.......... DavidAllan 1 74
(Ed Dunlop) *hld up in rr: sltly checked 7f out: rdn over 3f out: hdwy u.p ins fnl f: styd on: nvr able to chal* **10/1**
0162 **5** nk **Creek Island (IRE)**[9] 4773 3-9-5 **73**.......... JoeFanning 4 72
(Mark Johnston) *led: rdn whn pressed over 2f out: hdd ins fnl f: no ex fnl 150yds* **5/1**[2]
1 **6** 2 ¾ **Balgees Time (FR)**[57] 3-9-7 **75**.......... DanielTudhope 8 68
(Kevin Ryan) *chsd ldr after 2f: rdn and ev ch over 2f out: stl there 1f out: lost pl ins fnl f: fdd fnl 100yds: eased towards fin* **25/1**
2606 **7** 8 **Deebee**[28] 4068 3-9-2 **70**..........(t[1]) KevinStott 5 47
(Declan Carroll) *hld up: n.m.r and shuffled bk 7f out: rdn over 3f out: no imp: bhd and toiling ins fnl f* **7/1**[3]
0-04 **8** 4 ½ **Ride The Monkey (IRE)**[28] 4077 3-9-6 **74**..........(p[1]) ConnorBeasley 6 42
(Michael Dods) *racd keenly: midfield: drvn and lost pl 4f out: lft bhd over 1f out* **18/1**

2m 12.2s (1.40) **Going Correction** -0.15s/f (Firm) **8 Ran SP% 112.9**
Speed ratings (Par 100): **88,84,84,83,83 81,74,71**
CSF £11.66 CT £62.38 TOTE £2.00: £1.10, £2.10, £2.30; EX 12.90 Trifecta £83.50.
Owner Mrs Olivia Hoare **Bred** Mrs Olivia Hoare **Trained** Upper Lambourn, Berks

FOCUS
Rain meant the going description was changed to good to soft after this race, having been good to firm in the morning. The inner home straight was used, and this opener was run over 28yds further than advertised. After riding in the first, Liam Keniry called the ground good to soft, while Richard Kingscote described it as on the slow side. They stayed on the inside in this ordinary handicap. The second has been rated to this year's form.

5125 BRITISH STALLION STUDS EBF NOVICE STKS (PLUS 10 RACE) 6f
2:40 (2:40) (Class 4) 2-Y-0
£6,469 (£1,925; £962; £481) **Stalls** Centre

Form RPR
3 **1** **Treble Treble (IRE)**[20] 4401 2-9-5 0.......... KevinStott 5 88+
(Kevin Ryan) *dwlt: midfield: hdwy 3f out: led over 1f out: r.o ins fnl f* **4/1**[2]
2 1 ¾ **Cobra Eye** 2-9-5 0.......... JasonHart 3 83+
(John Quinn) *dwlt: hld up: rdn over 2f out: angled rt and hdwy 2f out: chsd wnr 1f out but nvr able to chal* **11/1**
220 **3** 2 ¼ **Jm Jackson (IRE)**[28] 4048 2-9-0 89.......... JoeFanning 6 71
(Mark Johnston) *led: rdn and hdd over 1f out: styd on same pce ins fnl f* **7/4**[1]

4 ½ **Three Fans (FR)** 2-9-5 0 RichardKingscote 4 75
(Tom Dascombe) *chsd ldrs: rdn over 2f out: unable qck over 1f out: kpt on ins fnl f wout threatening* **10/1**[3]

5 ¾ **Good Job Power (IRE)** 2-9-5 0 SilvestreDeSousa 10 72
(Richard Hannon) *in tch: effrt to chse ldrs over 2f out: one pce ins fnl f* **4/1**[2]

0 6 1 **Asstech (IRE)**[50] 3265 2-9-5 0 JackGarritty 9 69
(Richard Fahey) *missed break: hld up: pushed along over 1f out: kpt on ins fnl f: nvr able to trble ldrs* **25/1**

7 3 **Glorious Zoff (IRE)** 2-9-5 0 DanielTudhope 7 60
(Charles Hills) *prom: rdn over 2f out: wknd 1f out* **14/1**

56 8 ¾ **Foad**[90] 1953 2-9-5 0 DavidAllan 1 58
(Ed Dunlop) *in tch: effrt over 2f out: wknd 1f out* **33/1**

9 4 **Dogged** 2-9-5 0 SeanLevey 2 46
(David Elsworth) *dwlt: towards rr: pushed along 3f out: lft bhd over 2f out (jockey said colt was never travelling)* **12/1**

10 2¼ **Pull Harder Con** 2-9-5 0 GrahamLee 11 39
(Robyn Brisland) *missed break: pushed along thrght: a bhd* **100/1**

1m 12.04s (-1.86) **Going Correction** -0.15s/f (Firm) 10 Ran SP% **115.9**
Speed ratings (Par 96): **106,103,100,100,99 97,93,92,87,84**
CSF £46.19 TOTE £4.80: £1.50, £2.90, £1.30; EX 45.70 Trifecta £120.10.
Owner B T McDonald **Bred** G H S Bloodstock & J C Bloodstock **Trained** Hambleton, N Yorks

FOCUS
This interesting novice event went to one of those with experience. The 2016 winner South Seas was Group 1-placed later that season.

5126 JOIN RACINGTV NOW H'CAP 6f
3:15 (3:17) (Class 4) (0-85,85) 3-Y-O
£7,115 (£2,117; £1,058; £529; £300; £300) **Stalls** Centre

Form RPR
2U02 1 **Dominus (IRE)**[19] 4420 3-9-7 **85** BenCurtis 3 93
(Brian Meehan) *a.p: led wl over 2f out: sn rdn and pressed: r.o gamely and kpt finding towards fin* **7/2**[3]

-152 2 ¾ **Pendleton**[14] 4603 3-9-4 **82** GrahamLee 5 87
(Michael Dods) *chsd ldrs: effrt over 2f out: chalng ins fnl f: nt quite pce of wnr towards fin* **5/2**[1]

1144 3 hd **Mark's Choice (IRE)**[20] 4368 3-9-4 **82** JackGarritty 7 86
(Ruth Carr) *hld up: hdwy over 2f out: chalng fr over 1f out: kpt on ins fnl f: nt quite pce of wnr towards fin* **14/1**

2061 4 2 **The Night Watch**[22] 4297 3-9-7 **85** DanielTudhope 1 83
(William Haggas) *missed break: hld up in tch: effrt over 2f out: ch over 1f out: no ex fnl 100yds* **3/1**[2]

5331 5 nse **Tenax (IRE)**[14] 4603 3-9-2 **85** FayeMcManoman(5) 4 82
(Nigel Tinkler) *trckd ldrs: lost pl and outpcd wl over 2f out: edgd rt over 1f out: kpt on ins fnl f wout troubling ldrs* **3/1**[2]

404- 6 26 **Sabai Sabai (IRE)**[303] 7417 3-8-9 **73** (w) SilvestreDeSousa 2
(K R Burke) *led: pushed along and hdd wl over 2f out: wknd qckly: eased whn wl btn over 1f out (vet said filly had been struck into behind; vet said filly had lost its left hind-shoe)* **25/1**

1m 11.9s (-2.00) **Going Correction** -0.15s/f (Firm) 6 Ran SP% **111.3**
Speed ratings (Par 102): **107,106,105,103,103 68**
CSF £12.44 TOTE £4.40: £2.40, £1.20; EX 12.60 Trifecta £75.10.
Owner G P M Morland & J W Edgedale **Bred** Morgan Cahalan **Trained** Manton, Wilts

FOCUS
Just a small field, but a decent sprint handicap. The third, rated to his Ripon form, helps set the level.

5127 LIKE RACINGTV ON FACEBOOK H'CAP 1m 6f
3:50 (3:50) (Class 4) (0-85,83) 3-Y-O
£10,350 (£3,080; £1,539; £769; £300; £300) **Stalls** Low

Form RPR
-041 1 **Calculation**[21] 4327 3-9-2 **78** (v) RichardKingscote 2 89+
(Sir Michael Stoute) *in tch: effrt 2f out: sn chsd wnr: chalng ins fnl f: styd on to ld towards fin* **11/10**[1]

3113 2 ½ **Mondain**[6] 4928 3-9-1 **77** JoeFanning 5 87
(Mark Johnston) *broke wl: chsd ldr: led 3f out: rdn over 2f out: pressed ins fnl f: hdd and hld towards fin* **11/2**[3]

-216 3 5 **Buriram (IRE)**[23] 4256 3-9-7 **83** SilvestreDeSousa 3 86
(Ralph Beckett) *hld up: rdn over 2f out: kpt on to take 3rd ins fnl f: no imp on front two* **7/2**[2]

3320 4 1¾ **Tidal Point (IRE)**[13] 4644 3-8-11 **73** (p) RoystonFfrench 4 74
(Steph Hollinshead) *trckd ldrs: wnt 2nd wl over 2f out: lost 2nd jst ins fnl 2f: one pce u.p fr over 1f out* **12/1**

6-54 5 ½ **Billy No Mates (IRE)**[34] 3862 3-9-7 **83** ConnorBeasley 6 83
(Michael Dods) *stdd s: hld up: hdwy 3f out: wl there u.p 2f out: no imp on front two over 1f out: no ex ins fnl f* **6/1**

-350 6 7 **Fox Fearless**[44] 3474 3-8-11 **73** (v[1]) BenCurtis 1 63
(K R Burke) *bustled along s: led: rdn and hdd 3f out: wknd over 2f out (vet said filly lost its right fore-shoe)* **33/1**

3m 7.93s (3.33) **Going Correction** -0.15s/f (Firm) 6 Ran SP% **110.1**
Speed ratings (Par 102): **84,83,80,79,79 75**
CSF £7.31 TOTE £1.80: £1.10, £2.60; EX 5.40 Trifecta £16.40.
Owner The Queen **Bred** The Queen **Trained** Newmarket, Suffolk

FOCUS
Add 52yds. This was run in a heavy downpour. In contrast to the earlier race on the round course, they came over to the stands' side in the home straight. The first two are both sons of Dubawi. The third and fourth have been rated close to form.

5128 INTRODUCING RACINGTV NOVICE STKS 6f 212y
4:20 (4:21) (Class 5) 3-Y-O+ **£4,851** (£1,443; £721; £360) **Stalls** Low

Form RPR
4-1 1 **Mubtasimah**[20] 4405 3-9-4 0 DanielTudhope 3 88+
(William Haggas) *hld up: clsd over 2f out: rdn over 1f out: led fnl 100yds: pushed out and r.o towards fin* **10/11**[1]

66 2 1 **Mogsy (IRE)**[25] 4196 3-8-13 0 JaneElliott(3) 1 83
(Tom Dascombe) *chsd ldr: led 3f out: rdn over 2f out: hung rt u.p over 1f out: hdd fnl 100yds: kpt on but hld towards fin* **40/1**

3-22 3 ¾ **Enough Already**[13] 4635 3-9-2 85 KevinStott 6 81
(Kevin Ryan) *hld up: effrt 2f out: chsd ldrs ins fnl f: kpt on* **5/1**[3]

11 4 2¾ **Vitralite (IRE)**[14] 4608 3-10-2 94 BenCurtis 7 88
(K R Burke) *racd keenly: chsd ldrs: rdn and ev ch over 2f out: unable qck over 1f out: no ex fnl 100yds* **7/4**[2]

03 5 5 **Little Miss Muffin**[18] 4439 3-8-11 0 NathanEvans 5 56?
(Sam England) *led: hdd 3f out: sn rdn: stl there chsng ldrs 2f out: wknd over 1f out* **100/1**

4 6 4½ **Red Derek**[20] 4358 3-8-9 0 ElishaWhittington(7) 2 49
(Lisa Williamson) *hld up: pushed along 3f out: lft bhd over 1f out* **100/1**

7 18 **Yestaahel** 3-9-2 0 LiamKeniry 4 2
(Kevin Frost) *dwlt: hld up: rdn over 3f out: lft bhd over 2f out* **100/1**

1m 26.56s (-2.74) **Going Correction** -0.15s/f (Firm) 7 Ran SP% **110.8**
Speed ratings (Par 103): **109,107,107,103,98 93,72**
CSF £32.02 TOTE £1.50: £1.30, £10.00; EX 38.30 Trifecta £143.40.
Owner Sheikh Juma Dalmook Al Maktoum **Bred** Panda Bloodstock **Trained** Newmarket, Suffolk

FOCUS
Add 6yds. The time was decent for the conditions race and this looks good novice stakes form, although the proximity of the runner-up does lead to doubts. This time they raced on the stands' side in the straight, although a couple stayed on the far side at first. The fifth and sixth likely limit the level, and the third has been rated near his reappearance C&D form for now.

5129 MARLEN ROBERTS CONDITIONS STKS 6f 212y
4:50 (4:50) (Class 3) 3-Y-O+ **£10,673** (£3,176; £1,587; £793) **Stalls** Low

Form RPR
4304 1 **Marie's Diamond (IRE)**[6] 4905 3-8-12 104 JoeFanning 5 104
(Mark Johnston) *chsd ldr: led 3f out: rdn over 1f out: kpt on wl towards fin* **6/4**[1]

-250 2 ½ **Hey Jonesy (IRE)**[27] 4095 4-9-5 105 KevinStott 1 106
(Kevin Ryan) *chsd ldrs: effrt over 2f out: ev ch ins fnl f: kpt on but a hld* **6/4**[1]

4403 3 1¼ **Salateen**[6] 4905 7-9-9 100 (tp) ConnorBeasley 3 106
(David O'Meara) *led: hdd 3f out: remained prom: rdn 2f out: styd on same pce fnl 100yds* **4/1**[2]

1/4P 4 nk **Remarkable**[69] 2609 6-9-5 107 (b) LiamKeniry 2 102
(David O'Meara) *in rr: u.p fr over 2f out: kpt on towards fin: nvr able to chal* **9/1**[3]

1m 26.56s (-2.74) **Going Correction** -0.15s/f (Firm)
WFA 3 from 4yo+ 7lb 4 Ran SP% **110.0**
Speed ratings (Par 107): **109,108,107,106**
CSF £4.06 TOTE £2.00; EX 4.20 Trifecta £7.90.
Owner Middleham Park Racing LXXXVI **Bred** Tony Ashley **Trained** Middleham Moor, N Yorks

FOCUS
Add 6yds. A good conditions event, which was run in an identical time to the earlier novice stakes. It was another race where they tacked over in the straight. It's been rated a bit cautiously, with the third to his latest.

5130 HAYDOCK PARK TRAINING SERIES APPRENTICE H'CAP (PART OF THE RACING EXCELLENCE INITIATIVE) 7f 212y
5:25 (5:25) (Class 5) (0-75,81) 4-Y-O+
£4,851 (£1,443; £721; £360; £300; £300) **Stalls** Low

Form RPR
6631 1 **Scofflaw**[49] 3322 5-9-7 **72** (v) JessicaCooley(3) 1 79
(David Evans) *stdd after nrly 1f: hld up: rdn and hdwy whn swtchd lft 2f out: edgd lft ins fnl f: r.o to ld fnl 110yds: in command after* **16/1**

0564 2 1¼ **Moxy Mares**[24] 4209 4-9-12 **74** (p[1]) SeanKirrane 4 78
(Mark Loughnane) *prom: upsides 4f out: rdn over 2f out: led ins fnl f: sn hdd: hld towards fin* **6/1**[3]

3000 3 ½ **Calder Prince (IRE)**[14] 4607 6-9-8 **77** PoppyFielding(7) 7 80
(Tom Dascombe) *led: jnd 4f out: rdn over 1f out: hdd ins fnl f: styd on same pce towards fin* **8/1**

5054 4 1½ **Indomeneo**[13] 4627 4-9-8 **73** CianMacRedmond(3) 6 72
(Richard Fahey) *in tch: rdn to chse ldrs over 2f out: kpt on same pce fnl 100yds* **4/1**[2]

2-51 5 2 **Grey Spirit (IRE)**[8] 4837 4-10-5 **81** 5ex WilliamCarver 5 76
(Sir Mark Prescott Bt) *dwlt: hld up in rr: hdwy 3f out: rdn over 2f out: no imp on ldrs over 1f out: one pce fnl f* **8/11**[1]

0002 6 14 **Isabella Ruby**[20] 4358 4-8-4 **55** oh10 (h) ElishaWhittington(3) 2 18
(Lisa Williamson) *wnt to post early: racd keenly: trckd ldrs: pushed along and lost pl over 3f out: bhd over 2f out* **50/1**

0000 7 1 **Sayesse**[15] 4552 5-8-12 **60** (p) TobyEley 3 20
(Lisa Williamson) *dwlt: trckd ldrs after 2f: rdn and wknd over 2f out* **80/1**

1m 40.87s (-1.83) **Going Correction** -0.15s/f (Firm) 7 Ran SP% **112.4**
Speed ratings (Par 103): **103,101,101,99,97 83,82**
CSF £102.59 TOTE £12.20: £4.00, £2.00; EX 52.10 Trifecta £252.30.
Owner John Abbey & Emma Evans **Bred** Mrs M E Slade **Trained** Pandy, Monmouths

FOCUS
Add 6yds. Modest handicap form. They came over to the stands' side once in line for home. The second and third have both been rated below this year's best.
T/Plt: £19.80 to a £1 stake. Pool: £53,814.84 - 1982.10 winning units T/Qpdt: £10.50 to a £1 stake. Pool: £4,121.29 - 290.32 winning unit **Darren Owen**

4838 NEWBURY (L-H)
Friday, July 19

OFFICIAL GOING: Good to soft (good in places; watered; 7.3) changing to good to soft after race 2 (2.30)
Wind: quite strong across at times Weather: light rain

5131 SPINAL INJURIES ASSOCIATION EBF NOVICE STKS (PLUS 10 RACE) 7f (S)
2:00 (2:02) (Class 4) 2-Y-O **£6,404** (£1,905; £952; £476) **Stalls** Centre

Form RPR
2 1 **Encipher**[15] 4551 2-9-5 0 OisinMurphy 10 87
(John Gosden) *a.p: led 2f out: drifted rt but kpt on wl fnl f: comf* **6/5**[1]

2 2¼ **Native Tribe** 2-9-5 0 JamesDoyle 8 81
(Charlie Appleby) *led tl 2f out: sn rdn: kpt pressing wnr tl no ex fnl 120yds* **7/2**[2]

3 2½ **Maori Knight (IRE)** 2-9-5 0 ShaneKelly 2 75+
(Richard Hughes) *jinked lft s and slowly away: towards rr: prog over 1f out: kpt on nicely fnl f: wnt 3rd towards fin: improve* **25/1**

0 4 ½ **Desert Palms**[42] 3542 2-9-5 0 AndreaAtzeni 13 73
(Richard Hannon) *trckd ldrs: rdn over 2f out: kpt on same pce fnl f* **25/1**

4 5 hd **Bealach (IRE)**[36] 3760 2-9-5 0 CharlesBishop 11 73
(Eve Johnson Houghton) *in tch: rdn to chse ldrs 2f out: kpt on same pce fnl f* **18/1**

6 2¾ **Oslo** 2-9-5 0 RyanMoore 5 66+
(Sir Michael Stoute) *trckd ldrs: rdn over 2f out: sn one pce* **12/1**

6 7 nse **What An Angel**[14] 4611 2-9-5 0 TomMarquand 3 66
(Richard Hannon) *mid-div: rdn and hdwy 2f out: wnt 3rd ent fnl f: no ex fnl 100yds* **22/1**

8 *hd* **Slavonic Dance (IRE)** 2-9-0 0 .... HarryBentley 14 60
(Ralph Beckett) *s.i.s: sn mid-div: rdn over 2f out: little imp* **50/1**

6 9 *½* **Game Over (IRE)**[27] 4117 2-9-5 0 .... PatDobbs 7 64
(Richard Hannon) *nvr bttr than mid-div* **50/1**

10 *2¼* **Protagonist (FR)** 2-9-5 0 .... JamieSpencer 4 58
(Jamie Osborne) *hld up towards rr: sme minor late prog: nvr trbld ldrs* **50/1**

11 *1* **Ascension** 2-9-5 0 .... JimCrowley 1 55+
(Roger Varian) *trckd ldrs: rdn 2f out: wknd ent fnl f* **9/2[3]**

12 *5* **Sky Flyer** 2-9-5 0 .... RobHornby 6 42
(Ralph Beckett) *s.i.s: nvr travelling: a towards rr* **50/1**

13 *2¼* **Clandestine Affair (IRE)** 2-9-5 0 .... NicolaCurrie 12 36
(Jamie Osborne) *a towards rr* **66/1**

14 *4* **Fighting Don (FR)** 2-9-5 0 .... KieranShoemark 9 26
(Harry Dunlop) *trckd ldrs: rdn over 2f out: sn wknd* **100/1**

1m 29.33s (2.33) **Going Correction** +0.425s/f (Yiel) 14 Ran SP% **121.2**
Speed ratings (Par 96): **103,100,97,97,96 93,93,93,92,90 89,83,80,76**
CSF £4.70 TOTE £2.00: £1.10, £1.70, £10.10; EX 5.80 Trifecta £84.40.

Owner Godolphin **Bred** Montcastle Bloodstock Ltd **Trained** Newmarket, Suffolk

FOCUS
The far bends were railed out from the innermost position and added distance to races 3 & 5, which started in the back straight. There was a fair amount of rain around before racing and the ground was changed to good to soft prior from good, good to firm in places. Plenty of runners but there were only a handful with serious claims.

5132 BET365 EBF FILLIES' NOVICE STKS (PLUS 10 RACE) 6f
2:30 (2:38) (Class 4) 2-Y-O £6,404 (£1,905; £952; £476) **Stalls** Centre

Form RPR

2 1 **Nasaiym (USA)**[62] 2840 2-9-0 0 .... RyanMoore 7 86
(James Tate) *trckd ldrs: chal 2f out: sn rdn: kpt on ins fnl f: led fnl 100yds: rdn out* **6/4[1]**

2 *nk* **Nina Bailarina** 2-9-0 0 .... ShaneKelly 5 85+
(Ed Walker) *led: rdn whn hdd and stmbld fnl 100yds: kpt on* **20/1**

3 *2* **Run Wild (GER)** 2-9-0 0 .... (h[1]) OisinMurphy 2 79+
(John Gosden) *s.i.s: in last pair: hdwy over 1f out: drifting lft but wnt 3rd ins fnl f: kpt on wl towards fin (jockey said filly was slowly away)* **5/1[2]**

4 *1¾* **Dirty Dancer (FR)** 2-9-0 0 .... HarryBentley 9 74
(Ralph Beckett) *mid-div: rdn and stdy prog fr 2f out: kpt on ins fnl f but nt pce to threaten* **8/1[3]**

5 *nk* **Time To Strike (IRE)** 2-9-0 0 .... JamieSpencer 4 73+
(David Simcock) *s.i.s: towards rr: hdwy over 2f out: hung lft over 1f out: chal for hld 3rd ent fnl f: kpt on same pce* **12/1**

3 6 *1¼* **Elegant Erin (IRE)**[8] 4840 2-9-0 0 .... FergusSweeney 12 69
(Richard Hannon) *mid-div: rdn and hdwy over 1f out: kpt on same pce fnl f* **12/1**

7 *2¼* **Sorteo (IRE)** 2-9-0 0 .... RobHornby 10 63+
(Andrew Balding) *mid-div: hdwy wl over 1f out: rdn and hld whn short of room ent fnl f: one pce after* **16/1**

8 *2½* **Spurofthemoment** 2-9-0 0 .... KieranShoemark 3 55
(Charles Hills) *unsettled stalls: trckd ldrs: rdn in cl 3rd 2f out: wknd ent fnl f (jockey said filly was restless in the stalls)* **25/1**

9 *1¾* **Gently Spoken (IRE)** 2-9-0 0 .... TomMarquand 13 50
(Martyn Meade) *sn trcking ldrs: effrt over 2f out: wknd jst over 1f out* **20/1**

10 *2¾* **Dutch Painting** 2-9-0 0 .... AndreaAtzeni 6 41
(Michael Bell) *mid-div: pushed along over 3f out: rdn 2f out: sn wknd* **14/1**

11 *1½* **Golden Cygnet** 2-9-0 0 .... JamesDoyle 1 37
(Ralph Beckett) *mid-div: hdwy over 2f out: sn rdn to chse ldrs: wknd over 1f out* **20/1**

12 *nk* **Acquire** 2-9-0 0 .... PatDobbs 8 36
(Richard Hannon) *trckd ldr: rdn over 2f out: wknd over 1f out* **40/1**

13 *1¼* **Greater Love** 2-9-0 0 .... NicolaCurrie 11 32
(Jonathan Portman) *dwlt: a bhd (jockey said filly was slowly away)* **100/1**

1m 15.96s (2.76) **Going Correction** +0.425s/f (Yiel) 13 Ran SP% **117.3**
Speed ratings (Par 93): **98,97,94,92,92 90,87,84,81,78 76,75,74**
CSF £41.70 TOTE £1.80: £1.10, £6.30, £2.10; EX 40.60 Trifecta £198.40.

Owner Sheikh Juma Dalmook Al Maktoum **Bred** Nicole Gunther **Trained** Newmarket, Suffolk

FOCUS
This fillies' only event appeared to revolve around the once-raced favourite, who holds several big-race entries.

5133 ROSS BROOKE CHARTERED ACCOUNTANTS FILLIES' H'CAP 1m 5f 61y
3:05 (3:07) (Class 2) (0-100,96) 3-Y-O+ **£25,876** (£7,700; £3,848; £1,924) **Stalls** Low

Form RPR

-165 1 **Jedhi**[30] 3995 4-9-7 **85** .... RyanMoore 3 90
(Hughie Morrison) *hld up bhd ldrs: hdwy 3f out: chal over 1f out: sn drvn: carried rt fnl 100yds: styd on wl: led fnl stride* **8/1[3]**

-105 2 *nse* **Point In Time (IRE)**[16] 4504 4-8-12 **76** .... HollieDoyle 2 81
(Mark Usher) *trckd ldrs: tk narrow advantage jst over 1f out but sn hanging rt: bmpd chalr fnl 120yds and again nring fin: hdd fnl stride (jockey said filly hung badly right-handed)* **33/1**

451 3 *nk* **Sea Of Faith (IRE)**[33] 3882 3-9-6 **95** .... JamesDoyle 6 100
(William Haggas) *slowly away: hld up last but wl in tch: hdwy 3f out: rdn 2f out: cl 4th ent fnl f: carried sltly rt fnl 100yds: styd on* **4/5[1]**

-450 4 *nk* **Lorelina**[37] 3726 6-10-0 **92** .... OisinMurphy 5 96
(Andrew Balding) *trckd ldr: led over 2f out: rdn and hdd over 1f out: sn edgd rt: stl ev ch whn bmpd fnl 100yds: battling on but probably hld whn short of room cl home* **12/1**

012 5 *10* **Motivate Me (FR)**[42] 3553 3-8-7 **82** .... AndreaAtzeni 4 73
(Roger Varian) *trckd ldrs: pushed along over 4f out: rdn over 2f out: wknd over 1f out* **3/1[2]**

-636 6 *1¼* **I'll Have Another (IRE)**[65] 2745 3-9-7 **96** .... JimCrowley 1 85
(Mark Johnston) *led: rdn and hdd over 2f out: wknd over 1f out* **14/1**

2m 58.24s (3.84) **Going Correction** +0.425s/f (Yiel)
WFA 3 from 4yo+ 11lb 6 Ran SP% **109.0**
Speed ratings (Par 96): **105,104,104,104,98 97**
CSF £162.05 TOTE £7.70: £2.20, £9.20; EX 193.80 Trifecta £837.30.

Owner Pickford, Malcolm, Morrison & De Zoete **Bred** Selwood Bloodstock & Mrs S Read **Trained** East Ilsley, Berks

FOCUS
Add 26 yards. Only a small field but his proved highly competitive with the first four home involved in a blanket finish. The deterioration in the ground likely played more to the strengths of the older horses. The fourth has been rated to this year's form.

5134 IRISH THOROUGHBRED MARKETING ROSE BOWL STKS (LISTED RACE) 6f
3:40 (3:41) (Class 1) 2-Y-O
£14,461 (£5,482; £2,743; £1,366; £685; £344) **Stalls** Centre

Form RPR

10 1 **Shadn (IRE)**[30] 3983 2-8-9 0 .... OisinMurphy 4 97
(Andrew Balding) *trckd ldr: rdn over 1f out: kpt on wl ins fnl f: led towards fin* **10/1**

3130 2 *¾* **Misty Grey (IRE)**[29] 4012 2-9-0 94 .... RyanMoore 5 100
(Mark Johnston) *led: rdn over 1f out: kpt on but no ex whn hdd towards fin* **7/1[3]**

11 3 *1¾* **Al Aakif (IRE)**[20] 4401 2-9-0 0 .... JimCrowley 1 95
(William Haggas) *trckd ldr: rdn 2f out: kpt on but nt pce to chal* **15/8[2]**

1 4 *nse* **Repartee (IRE)**[64] 2780 2-9-0 0 .... AndreaAtzeni 6 95
(Kevin Ryan) *trckd ldr: rdn over 1f out: edgd lft jst ins fnl f: kpt on same pce* **6/4[1]**

1 5 *2¾* **Old News**[11] 4734 2-9-0 0 .... ShaneKelly 3 86
(Richard Hughes) *hld up bhd ldrs: rdn 2f out: kpt on but nt pce to threaten* **25/1**

10 6 *¾* **Lord Of The Lodge (IRE)**[31] 3949 2-9-0 0 .... TomMarquand 2 84
(K R Burke) *hld up bhd ldrs: rdn 2f out: kpt on but nt pce to threaten* **10/1**

1m 15.55s (2.35) **Going Correction** +0.425s/f (Yiel) 6 Ran SP% **109.3**
Speed ratings (Par 102): **101,100,97,97,93 92**
CSF £69.77 TOTE £9.90: £2.80, £2.20; EX 56.80 Trifecta £240.10.

Owner Alrabban Racing **Bred** Barronstown Stud **Trained** Kingsclere, Hants

FOCUS
The going was changed to good to soft after the 3.05. A good looking edition of this Listed feature, which was won back in 2014 by the high-class Limato. Victory went the way of the only filly in the race. The form is probably just par for the grade.

5135 REGUS H'CAP 1m 4f
4:10 (4:11) (Class 3) (0-90,86) 3-Y-O+ **£7,762** (£2,310; £1,154; £577) **Stalls** Low

Form RPR

-554 1 **Skymax (GER)**[21] 4327 3-8-13 **81** .... (b[1]) HarryBentley 4 94
(Ralph Beckett) *mde all: styd on wl to draw clr fnl f: pushed out* **10/3[2]**

3-43 2 *7* **Prejudice**[21] 4342 3-9-4 **86** .... JamieSpencer 5 88
(David Simcock) *hld up bhd ldrs: hdwy to chse wnr over 2f out: sn drvn: wandered u.p: nt pce to get on terms but kpt on for clr 2nd* **8/11[1]**

2-05 3 *8* **Past Master**[39] 3663 6-9-9 **80** .... NicolaCurrie 6 68
(Henry Candy) *racd keenly: trckd ldrs: rdn 3f out: one pce fnl 2f* **11/2[3]**

/1-5 4 *10* **Noble Behest**[20] 4363 5-9-3 **74** .... KieranShoemark 2 46
(Ian Williams) *hld up bhd ldrs: trckd ldrs 5f out: rdn over 2f out: wknd over 1f out* **20/1**

0621 5 *1¼* **Lexington Law (IRE)**[16] 4522 6-10-0 **85** .... (v) TomMarquand 3 55
(Alan King) *trckd ldr: rdn over 2f out: wknd over 1f out* **16/1**

2m 41.03s (3.03) **Going Correction** +0.425s/f (Yiel)
WFA 3 from 5yo+ 11lb 5 Ran SP% **107.0**
Speed ratings (Par 107): **106,101,96,89,88**
CSF £5.84 TOTE £3.90: £2.00, £1.10; EX 6.60 Trifecta £12.70.

Owner Bermuda Thoroughbred Racing Limited **Bred** Niarchos Family **Trained** Kimpton, Hants

FOCUS
Add 26 yards. This proved hard work in the conditions and they came home at intervals more associated with 3m chasers. The second has been rated similar to his reappearance figure here.

5136 RACING TV H'CAP 1m (S)
4:40 (4:42) (Class 5) (0-75,76) 4-Y-O+ **£3,428** (£1,020; £509; £300; £300) **Stalls** Centre

Form RPR

0001 1 **Fortune And Glory (USA)**[9] 4787 6-8-10 **69** 5ex .... ScottMcCullagh(5) 7 79
(Joseph Tuite) *trckd ldrs: shkn up to ld ins fnl f: readily* **7/2[2]**

002 2 *2* **First Response**[52] 3199 4-9-6 **74** .... ShaneKelly 4 79
(Linda Stubbs) *trckd ldrs: rdn over 1f out: kpt on to go 2nd fnl 100yds: nt pce of wnr* **5/1**

2-22 3 *3¼* **Lucky Louie**[20] 4365 6-9-8 **76** .... (p) KieranShoemark 1 76
(Roger Teal) *led: rdn and hdd ins fnl f: sn no ex* **15/8[1]**

0012 4 *½* **Sir Jamie**[21] 4349 6-8-2 **56** oh3 .... (b) HollieDoyle 2 52
(Tony Carroll) *last pair: struggling over 2f out: kpt on ins fnl f but nvr any threat* **8/1**

-210 5 *12* **Delicate Kiss**[18] 4453 5-9-3 **71** .... (b) LiamJones 3 40
(John Bridger) *trckd ldrs: rdn over 2f out: wknd over 1f out* **10/1**

0551 P **Biotic**[14] 4615 8-9-7 **75** .... OisinMurphy 8
(Rod Millman) *s.i.s: nvr really travelling but in tch: p.u over 2f out (b.b.v) (vet said gelding had bled from the nose and had an irregular heartbeat)* **9/2[3]**

1m 42.6s (2.70) **Going Correction** +0.425s/f (Yiel) 6 Ran SP% **112.1**
Speed ratings (Par 103): **103,101,97,97,85**
CSF £20.77 CT £40.63 TOTE £3.80: £1.80, £2.20; EX 20.10 Trifecta £46.30.

Owner Richard J Gurr **Bred** Dromoland Farm **Trained** Lambourn, Berks

FOCUS
Stamina was again at a premium in testing conditions. The second has been rated to his latest.

5137 OAKLEY COACHBUILDERS APPRENTICE H'CAP 7f (S)
5:15 (5:17) (Class 5) (0-75,79) 3-Y-O+ **£3,428** (£1,020; £509; £300; £300) **Stalls** Centre

Form RPR

0066 1 **Misu Pete**[18] 4460 7-8-6 **56** .... (p) IsobelFrancis(5) 3 68
(Mark Usher) *chsd ldrs: led over 2f out: sn pushed clr: drifted lft: comf* **7/1**

2026 2 *6* **Stay Forever (FR)**[20] 4378 3-8-7 **64** .... KayleighStephens(5) 1 57
(Andrew Balding) *awkwardly away: bhd: hdwy over 3f out: chsd wnr 2f out: nt pce to get on terms: fdd ins fnl f* **11/4[2]**

0321 3 *7* **Crystal Casque**[23] 4248 4-9-6 **70** .... OliverSearle(5) 6 48
(Rod Millman) *racd keenly: disp ld after 1f: hdd 3f out: sn rdn: wknd over 1f out* **5/2[1]**

4-5 4 *2½* **Rock Boy Grey (IRE)**[36] 3768 4-9-6 **70** .... StefanoCherchi(5) 2 42
(Mark Loughnane) *chsd ldrs: rdn over 2f out: wknd over 1f out (jockey said gelding hung left-handed)* **6/1[3]**

1011 **5** *8* **Jungle Juice (IRE)**[7] 4874 3-9-8 **79** 6ex.......................... GeorgeBass[(5)] 5 27
(Mick Channon) *set str pce: jnd after 1f: rdn and hdd 3f out: sn wknd (trainer said filly was unsuited by the going)* **11/4**[2]

1m 30.39s (3.39) **Going Correction** +0.425s/f (Yiel) **5 Ran SP% 108.7**
WFA 3 from 4yo+ 7lb
Speed ratings (Par 103): **97,90,82,79,70**
CSF £25.38 TOTE £8.10: £3.10, £2.80; EX 24.10 Trifecta £80.90.
Owner The Mark Usher Racing Club **Bred** A C M Spalding **Trained** Upper Lambourn, Berks

FOCUS
A fair race on paper but the form amounts to little with the majority of these failing to give their true running in the soft ground. The winner has been rated back to something like his best.
T/Jkpt: £28,833.10 to a £1 stake. Pool: £40,610.11 - 1 winning unit T/Plt: £582.30 to a £1 stake. Pool: £64,524.75 - 80.89 winning units T/Qpdt: £240.80 to a £1 stake. Pool: £5,110.43 - 15.70 winning units **Tim Mitchell**

4918 NEWMARKET (R-H)

Friday, July 19

OFFICIAL GOING: Good to firm (watered; 8.1)
Wind: light to medium, behind Weather: showers

5138 32RED FILLIES' H'CAP (JOCKEY CLUB GRASSROOTS MIDDLE DISTANCE SERIES QUALIFIER) 1m 2f

5:45 (5:47) (Class 5) (0-75,77) 3-Y-O+
£4,528 (£1,347; £673; £400; £400; £400) **Stalls** Centre

Form RPR

2-24 **1** **Bint Soghaan**[14] 4597 3-9-7 **75**.......................... JimCrowley 1 86
(Richard Hannon) *stdd s: hld up in rr: swtchd lft and effrt over 2f out: edgd rt and clsd over 1f out: drvn to chse ldrs 1f out: str chal ins fnl f: styd on wl to ld nr fin* **7/2**[2]

4111 **2** *nk* **Sigrid Nansen**[7] 4868 4-8-8 **58**.......................... (p) CierenFallon[(5)] 3 68
(Alexandra Dunn) *hld up in midfield: effrt over 2f out: chsd ldr 2f out: kpt on and drvn to ld over 1f out: hrd pressed ins fnl f: kpt on wl tl hdd and no ex nr fin* **6/1**[3]

1411 **3** *3* **Junoesque**[19] 4426 5-9-6 **65**.......................... (p) JamesDoyle 5 69
(John Gallagher) *chsd ldr for over 1f out: styd chsng ldrs: rdn over 2f out: unable qck u.p over 1f out: kpt on same pce ins fnl f* **7/1**

-533 **4** *2* **Eesha's Smile (IRE)**[13] 4628 3-9-0 **68**.......................... (p[1]) SilvestreDeSousa 2 68
(Ivan Furtado) *led: rdn 3f out: drvn and hdd over 1f out: wknd ins fnl f* **8/1**

3-31 **5** *7* **Fearlessly (IRE)**[9] 4804 3-9-9 **77** 6ex.......................... AndreaAtzeni 7 63
(Roger Varian) *chsd ldr over 8f out tl unable qck and lost 2nd 2f out: sn edgd lft and outpcd: hung lft and wknd ins fnl f (jockey said filly hung left-handed)* **5/4**[1]

0635 **6** *3* **Trulee Scrumptious**[21] 4336 10-8-4 **56**.......................... (v) AledBeech[(7)] 4 36
(Peter Charalambous) *restrained after s: t.k.h: hld up in last pair: effrt wl over 2f out: sn struggling: wl btn over 1f out* **16/1**

30-0 **7** *6* **Give Me Breath**[27] 4110 3-9-1 **69**.......................... RyanMoore 6 37
(Sir Michael Stoute) *midfield: lost pl and rdn 3f out: sn wl btn and bhd* **18/1**

2m 6.52s (-0.58) **Going Correction** +0.075s/f (Good) **7 Ran SP% 115.7**
WFA 3 from 4yo+ 9lb
Speed ratings (Par 100): **105,104,102,100,95 92,87**
CSF £25.11 TOTE £4.40: £2.20, £2.90; EX 30.80 Trifecta £148.00.
Owner Hamdan Al Maktoum **Bred** Shadwell Estate Company Limited **Trained** East Everleigh, Wilts

FOCUS
Far side course used. Stalls: far side, except 1m2f: centre. Add 21yds. This looked pretty open despite the presence of a relatively short-priced favourite. She proved disappointing but the lightly-raced winner looks firmly on the improve now and, with the second and third both bang in-form, this rates solid enough form for the grade. The second has been rated to her Chepstow win, with the third close to her latest.

5139 32RED FILLIES' NOVICE STKS (PLUS 10 RACE) 7f

6:15 (6:15) (Class 4) 2-Y-O
£5,175 (£1,540; £769; £384) **Stalls** High

Form RPR

2 **1** **Wasaayef (IRE)**[16] 4502 2-9-0 0.......................... JimCrowley 6 88
(John Gosden) *w ldrs tl led 5f out: rdn 2f out: forged ahd 1f out: styd on wl ins fnl f* **7/4**[2]

2 *1* **Alpen Rose (IRE)** 2-9-0 0.......................... BrettDoyle 4 85+
(Charlie Appleby) *dwlt: rn green and in tch midfield: swtchd rt and effrt to chse ldrs wl over 1f out: kpt on wl u.p ins fnl f: wet 2nd wl ins fnl f* **11/2**[3]

3 *3/4* **National Treasure (IRE)** 2-9-0 0.......................... JamesDoyle 5 83+
(Charlie Appleby) *led for 1f: styd prom: rdn and ev ch 2f out tl nt quite match pce of wnr 1f out: kpt on same pce and lost 2nd wl ins fnl f* **6/4**[1]

4 *9* **Itmusthavebeenlove (IRE)** 2-9-0 0.......................... JamieSpencer 2 60
(Michael Bell) *in tch in last pair: effrt 2f out: unable qck and outpcd over 1f out: wl hld 4th ins fnl f* **20/1**

5 *3* **Sea Of Marmoon** 2-9-0 0.......................... RyanMoore 3 52
(Mark Johnston) *sn prom: led 6f out tl 5f out: rdn ent fnl 2f: sn outpcd: wl btn fnl f* **8/1**

6 *1 1/2* **Egotistic** 2-9-0 0.......................... AndreaAtzeni 1 48
(David Simcock) *t.k.h: hld up in tch: rdn 2f out: sn outpcd and btn: bhd ins fnl f* **33/1**

1m 25.72s (0.02) **Going Correction** +0.075s/f (Good) **6 Ran SP% 110.6**
Speed ratings (Par 93): **102,100,100,89,86 84**
CSF £11.33 TOTE £2.50: £1.50, £2.30; EX 9.70 Trifecta £13.70.
Owner Ms Hissa Hamdan Al Maktoum **Bred** Mrs T Mahon **Trained** Newmarket, Suffolk

FOCUS
This looked a warm heat despite the small field, with some smart pedigrees on show, and the first three could all turn out to be above average. The opening level is fluid.

5140 UNIBET H'CAP 1m

6:45 (6:47) (Class 4) (0-85,86) 3-Y-O **£6,469** (£1,925; £962; £481; £400) **Stalls** High

Form RPR

-361 **1** **Alfred Boucher**[20] 4377 3-9-3 **80**.......................... RyanMoore 3 85
(Henry Candy) *mde virtually all: rdn 2f out: drvn over 1f out: styd on wl u.p ins fnl f* **11/8**[1]

-036 **2** *3/4* **James Park Woods (IRE)**[20] 4362 3-8-13 **76**.......................... RobHornby 4 79
(Ralph Beckett) *chsd wnr: ev ch and rdn 2f out: drvn and str chal over 1f out: nt quite match pce of wnr ins fnl f: kpt on* **7/1**[3]

1-64 **3** *3/4* **House Of Kings (IRE)**[21] 4325 3-9-7 **84**.......................... AdamKirby 1 85
(Clive Cox) *stdd and dropped in after s: hld up in tch: clsd to chse ldrs and nt clr run over 2f out: effrt wl over 1f out: drvn and kpt on same pce ins fnl f* **7/2**[2]

-056 **4** *1/2* **Athmad (IRE)**[13] 4669 3-9-9 **86**.......................... MartinDwyer 5 86
(Brian Meehan) *taken down early: t.k.h: hld up in tch: clsd to press ldrs 3f out: unable qck u.p over 1f out: kpt on same pce ins fnl f* **7/1**[3]

3321 **5** *2 1/2* **Saikung (IRE)**[15] 4554 3-8-9 **72**.......................... SilvestreDeSousa 6 66
(Charles Hills) *stdd s: t.k.h: hld up in rr: clsd 3f out: effrt ent fnl 2f: no imp over 1f out: wl hld and eased towards fin* **7/2**[2]

1m 40.35s (0.35) **Going Correction** +0.075s/f (Good) **5 Ran SP% 111.5**
Speed ratings (Par 102): **101,100,99,99,96**
CSF £11.59 TOTE £2.00: £1.40, £2.80; EX 10.30 Trifecta £28.00.
Owner Robert Allcock **Bred** Robert Allcock **Trained** Kingston Warren, Oxon

FOCUS
No more than ordinary form for the grade, with the front two filling those places throughout, despite the fact they got racing a fair way out. The second and third have been rated to form.

5141 UNIBET FILLIES' NOVICE STKS 1m

7:20 (7:20) (Class 4) 3-Y-O+ **£5,563** (£1,655; £827; £413) **Stalls** High

Form RPR

2 **1** **Whispering Beauty (USA)**[21] 4341 3-8-11 0.......................... JFEgan 5 84
(William Haggas) *led for 2f: styd w ldr tl led again 3f out: pushed along wl over 1f out: drvn and pressed ins fnl f: kpt on and a lasting home* **11/8**[1]

2 *nk* **Loving Glance** 3-8-11 0.......................... RyanMoore 7 83
(Martyn Meade) *hld up in tch: nt clr run over 2f out: swtchd rt and chsd wnr wl over 1f out: clsd u.p and pressing wnr ins fnl f: kpt on wl and clsng towards fin: nvr quite getting to wnr* **9/1**

1- **3** *1 1/2* **Ardiente**[238] 9224 3-9-4 0.......................... (w) JamesDoyle 2 87+
(Ed Vaughan) *hld up in rr: clsd and nt clr run over 2f out: swtchd rt and effrt 2f out: rdn and hdwy to chse ldng pair jst over 1f out: styd on but nvr getting on terms: eased nr fin* **5/2**[2]

4 *8* **Happy Face (IRE)** 3-8-11 0.......................... (t[1]) JackMitchell 4 62
(Hugo Palmer) *chsd ldrs early: stdd bk and keen towards rr: clsd 3f out: unable qck u.p over 1f out: wknd ins fnl f* **12/1**

5 *2* **Lenya** 3-8-11 0.......................... FrankieDettori 6 57
(John Gosden) *stdd s: in tch: clsd to chse ldrs over 5f out: chsd wnr jst over 2f out tl wl over 1f out: sn outpcd and wknd ins fnl f* **7/2**[3]

0 **6** *6* **Annakonda (IRE)**[14] 4592 3-8-11 0.......................... BrettDoyle 8 43
(Peter Chapple-Hyam) *broke wl: t.k.h: restrained and hld up in tch: rdn ent fnl 2f: sn struggling and outpcd: bhd ins fnl f* **50/1**

0 **7** *8* **Your Thoughts (FR)**[27] 4121 3-8-11 0.......................... MartinDwyer 1 25
(Paul Webber) *stdd s: t.k.h: hdwy to ld after 2f: hdd 3f out: sn lost pl: bhd ins fnl f* **40/1**

1m 40.33s (0.33) **Going Correction** +0.075s/f (Good) **7 Ran SP% 115.0**
Speed ratings (Par 102): **101,100,99,91,89 83,75**
CSF £15.43 TOTE £2.40: £1.50, £3.10; EX 15.40 Trifecta £30.30.
Owner Ms A Gigliola Da Silva **Bred** Fred W Hertrich III **Trained** Newmarket, Suffolk

FOCUS
A decent fillies' event on paper and the front three came clear, suggesting they might be above average.

5142 BRITISH EBF UNIBET CONDITIONS STKS 5f

7:50 (7:53) (Class 3) 3-Y-O+ **£9,703** (£2,887) **Stalls** High

Form RPR

5-00 **1** **Judicial (IRE)**[31] 3950 7-9-5 105.......................... (h w) DougieCostello 2 98
(Julie Camacho) *taken down early and led to s: chsd rival: clsd and upsides 1/2-way: pushed into narrow ld jst over 1f out: drvn ins fnl f: kpt on: jst prevailed* **8/15**[1]

6030 **2** *shd* **Encore D'Or**[21] 4331 7-9-9 101.......................... RyanMoore 3 101
(Robert Cowell) *led: jnd 1/2-way: hdd narrowly and rdn over 1f out: kpt on wl ins fnl f: jst hld* **6/4**[2]

59.01s (0.31) **Going Correction** +0.075s/f (Good) **2 Ran SP% 105.2**
WFA 3 from 6yo+ 4lb
Speed ratings (Par 107): **100,99**
TOTE £1.30.
Owner Elite Racing Club **Bred** Elite Racing Club **Trained** Norton, N Yorks

FOCUS
Just a match but Judicial was well in here on the numbers and he got the job done, although his supporters were made to sweat close home. It's been rated a bit cautiously.

5143 BRITISH STALLION STUDS EBF FILLIES' H'CAP 6f

8:25 (8:25) (Class 3) (0-95,95) 3-Y-O+ **£12,938** (£3,850; £1,924; £962) **Stalls** High

Form RPR

0460 **1** **Sunday Star**[23] 4242 3-9-9 **95**.......................... AndreaAtzeni 10 105
(Ed Walker) *racd far side: midfield: clsd to chse ldrs and swtchd rt over 1f out: drvn to chal ins fnl f: styd on wl to ld towards fin: 1st of 7 in gp* **7/1**

61 **2** *3/4* **Emily Goldfinch**[21] 4340 6-9-8 **89**.......................... (p) SilvestreDeSousa 2 97
(Phil McEntee) *racd in centre: led gp and chsd overall ldr: rdn and led overall 2f out: drvn and kpt on wl u.p tl hdd and no ex towards fin: 1st of 3 in gp* **9/1**

-310 **3** *nk* **Belated Breath**[30] 3994 4-9-7 **88**.......................... JamesDoyle 1 95
(Hughie Morrison) *racd in centre: midfield: effrt 2f out: edging lft but clsng ins fnl f: styd on wl fnl 100yds to go 3rd towards fin: 2nd of 3 in gp* **5/1**[1]

6-12 **4** *3/4* **Furious**[29] 4023 3-9-4 **90**.......................... OisinMurphy 6 94
(David Simcock) *racd far side: chsd ldrs: ev ch u.p over 1f out: no ex wl ins fnl f: wknd towards fin: 2nd of 7 in gp* **6/1**[2]

2031 **5** *1 1/2* **Cale Lane**[18] 4442 4-8-9 **76** oh3.......................... KieranO'Neill 3 76
(Julie Camacho) *racd in centre: midfield: effrt 2f out: clsd and edgd lft over 1f out: no imp ins fnl f: wknd towards fin: 3rd of 3 in gp* **10/1**

2320 **6** *1 1/4* **Goodnight Girl (IRE)**[30] 3994 4-9-4 **92**.......................... (p) TylerSaunders[(7)] 8 88
(Jonathan Portman) *dwlt and impeded leaving stalls: hld up towards rr: effrt over 2f out: kpt on ins fnl f: nvr trbld ldrs: 3rd of 7 in gp* **13/2**[3]

0333 **7** *1/2* **Lady Dancealot (IRE)**[15] 4560 4-9-3 **84**.......................... RyanMoore 5 78
(David Elsworth) *racd far side: stdd s: hld up in midfield: effrt over 1f out: kpt on same pce and no imp ins fnl f: 4th of 7 in gp* **5/1**[1]

1661 **8** *2 1/4* **Shorter Skirt**[15] 4560 3-8-10 **82**.......................... CharlesBishop 7 68
(Eve Johnson Houghton) *racd far side: dwlt: hld up in rr: swtchd rt and effrt 2f out: no imp and one pce fnl f: 5th of 7 in gp (trainer's rep said that the filly was unsuited by the step up in class and also the Good to Firm ground on this occasion, which in her opinion had become loose on top due to the recent rainfall throughout the evening and would therefore prefer an easier* **7/1**

0115 **9** *1 1/2* **Bungee Jump (IRE)**[21] 4353 4-9-8 **89**.......................... RossaRyan 9 71
(Grace Harris) *racd far side: wnt rt leaving stalls: sn led: hdd 2f out: sn outpcd and wknd ins fnl f: 6th of 7 in gp* **12/1**

3400 **10** 1 ¾ **Indian Tygress**[29] 4023 4-9-3 **84** .... GeorgeWood 4 61
(James Fanshawe) *taken down early: racd far side: hld up towards rr: effrt over 1f out: no imp and bhd ins fnl f: 7th of 7 in gp* **14/1**

1m 11.85s (-0.25) **Going Correction** +0.075s/f (Good)
WFA 3 from 4yo+ 5lb **10** Ran SP% **119.4**
Speed ratings (Par 104): **104,103,102,101,99 97,97,94,92,89**
CSF £70.07 CT £356.69 TOTE £8.50: £3.40, £2.40, £2.70; EX 95.90 Trifecta £339.00.
Owner D Ward **Bred** D Ward **Trained** Upper Lambourn, Berks

FOCUS
A strongly run sprint in which they were spread across the track. Sunday Star got the perfect tow into it up the far side and could have been called the winner a fair way out. The second has been rated as confirming the merit of her previous win, while the third helps set the level.

5144 32RED H'CAP 7f
8:55 (8:56) (Class 5) (0-70,71) 4-Y-O+
£4,528 (£1,347; £673; £400; £400; £400) **Stalls** High

Form RPR

0551 **1** **Fighting Temeraire (IRE)**[27] 4115 6-9-5 **68** .... MartinDwyer 3 81+
(Dean Ivory) *restless in stalls: stdd s: hld up in rr: clsd and wl in tch 3f out: rdn to ld over 1f out: clr and r.o strly ins fnl f* **9/4**[2]

0506 **2** 2 ¼ **Full Intention**[13] 4643 5-9-5 **68** ....(p) JackMitchell 12 74
(Lydia Pearce) *chsd ldrs: edgd rt u.p over 1f out: nt match pce of wnr 1f out: kpt on to go 2nd wl ins fnl f* **14/1**

4163 **3** *hd* **Coverham (IRE)**[21] 4336 5-9-8 **71** .... RyanTate 2 76
(James Eustace) *racd in last trio: rdn and clsd 3f out: kpt on press to chse ldrs and edgd lft over 1f out: no threat to wnr but kpt on to go 3rd wl ins fnl f* **6/1**[3]

5331 **4** 1 **Angel's Whisper (IRE)**[21] 4336 4-9-8 **71** .... SilvestreDeSousa 4 73
(Amy Murphy) *midfield: clsd to press ldrs and rdn over 2f out: led 2f out: drvn and hdd over 1f out: no ex 1f out: kpt on same pce and lost 2 pls ins fnl f* **15/8**[1]

0426 **5** 1 ¼ **Pearl Spectre (USA)**[17] 4472 8-8-9 **58** ....(v) OisinMurphy 6 57
(Phil McEntee) *chsd ldrs: ev ch 3f out: unable qck u.p over 1f out: kpt on same pce ins fnl f* **12/1**

0-00 **6** 2 ¾ **Ocean Temptress**[31] 3967 5-8-2 **51** oh2........(p) JimmyQuinn 11 43
(Louise Allan) *dwlt: in tch in midfield: effrt ent fnl 2f: kpt on same pce and no imp ins fnl f* **40/1**

6300 **7** 11 **Exchequer (IRE)**[26] 4149 8-9-2 **65** ....(p) PhilipPrince 8 27
(Richard Guest) *pressed ldr tl led over 2f out: sn rdn and hdd: lost pl over 1f out: fdd ins fnl f* **16/1**

060 **8** 1 ¼ **Marilyn**[13] 4643 5-9-7 **70** ....(v) AdamKirby 9 28
(Shaun Keightley) *led tl over 2f out: sn struggling and btn over 1f out: fdd ins fnl f* **16/1**

-300 **9** 6 **Garth Rockett**[58] 2971 5-8-9 **63** ....(tp) CierenFallon(5) 7 5
(Mike Murphy) *midfield: effrt to press ldrs 3f out: lost pl and btn over 1f out: fdd fnl f* **16/1**

2205 **10** 2 **Holy Tiber (IRE)**[9] 4807 4-8-10 **59** ....(bt) JoeyHaynes 10
(Paul Howling) *mounted on crse: t.k.h: chsd ldrs: rdn over 2f out: sn dropped out: bhd fnl f* **25/1**

3F00 **11** 9 **Spanish Mane (IRE)**[21] 4349 4-8-3 **52** ....(h[1]) ShelleyBirkett 1
(Julia Feilden) *a in rr: lost tch over 2f out: t.o (jockey said filly was never travelling)* **25/1**

1m 25.99s (0.29) **Going Correction** +0.075s/f (Good) **11** Ran SP% **122.0**
Speed ratings (Par 103): **101,98,98,97,95 92,79,78,71,69 59**
CSF £35.03 CT £179.50 TOTE £3.00: £1.40, £3.20, £1.80; EX 37.70 Trifecta £220.40.
Owner Michael & Heather Yarrow **Bred** Hot Ticket Partnership **Trained** Radlett, Herts

FOCUS
As in the last race, they spread across the track and went a good gallop. The winner is thriving. The third has been rated to his turf best.
T/Plt: £65.10 to a £1 stake. Pool: £50,768.40 - 568.79 winning units T/Qpdt: £3.80 to a £1 stake. Pool: £4,582.74 - 884.49 winning units **Steve Payne**

5025 NOTTINGHAM (L-H)
Friday, July 19

OFFICIAL GOING: Good (watered bends; 8.0) changing to good (good to soft in places) after race 1 (1.45)
Wind: Light against Weather: Showers

5145 MANSIONBET EBF MAIDEN STKS 6f 18y
1:45 (1:46) (Class 5) 2-Y-O **£3,881** (£1,155; £577; £288) **Stalls** Centre

Form RPR

23 **1** **Visible Charm (IRE)**[35] 3804 2-9-5 0........ AdamKirby 8 78
(Charlie Appleby) *chsd ldrs: shkn up over 2f out: rdn to ld and edgd lft ins fnl f: styd on* **11/8**[1]

2 1 ¼ **Ventura Bounty (FR)** 2-9-5 0........ RossaRyan 5 74+
(Richard Hannon) *s.i.s: hdwy over 3f out: edgd lft fr over 1f out: ev ch ins fnl f: styd on same pce towards fin* **5/2**[2]

60 **3** ½ **Little Brown Trout**[15] 4564 2-9-0 0........ TheodoreLadd(5) 3 73
(William Stone) *chsd ldr: rdn over 1f out: ev ch ins fnl f: styd on same pce towards fin* **16/1**

03 **4** ½ **Dark Silver (IRE)**[15] 4558 2-9-5 0........ HectorCrouch 11 71
(Ed Walker) *s.i.s: hld up: hdwy over 2f out: shkn up over 1f out: styd on* **4/1**[3]

0 **5** 3 ¾ **Just Norman**[15] 4564 2-9-5 0........ TomQueally 2 60
(Paul D'Arcy) *s.i.s: hld up: hdwy over 1f out: nt trble ldrs* **66/1**

45 **6** 1 ½ **Coast Ofalfujairah (IRE)**[50] 3245 2-9-5 0........ FrannyNorton 7 56
(Kevin Ryan) *led: rdn over 1f out: hdd & wknd ins fnl f* **7/1**

0 **7** 6 **William Alexander**[29] 4032 2-9-5 0........ LewisEdmunds 4 38
(Les Eyre) *s.i.s: sn prom: rdn and wknd over 1f out* **100/1**

05U **8** 9 **Champagne Victory (IRE)**[50] 3244 2-9-0 0........ CamHardie 1 6
(Brian Ellison) *sn pushed along in rr: wknd over 2f out* **50/1**

9 6 **Courtney Rose** 2-8-11 0........ GabrieleMalune(3) 9
(Ivan Furtado) *s.s: outpcd (jockey said filly was never travelling)* **40/1**

1m 15.26s (1.46) **Going Correction** +0.15s/f (Good) **9** Ran SP% **115.9**
Speed ratings (Par 94): **96,94,93,93,88 86,78,66,58**
CSF £4.93 TOTE £1.50: £1.10, £1.20, £3.90; EX 5.60 Trifecta £29.60.
Owner Godolphin **Bred** Niarchos Family **Trained** Newmarket, Suffolk

FOCUS
Outer track. With the rail out 6yds on the home bend, races on the round course were extended by 18yds. Rain had already eased the ground before the card started and the official going was given as 'good', quickly changing to 'good, good to soft in places' after the evidence of the opening race. \n \n\x\x An ordinary maiden.

5146 MANSIONBET NURSERY H'CAP (JOCKEY CLUB GRASSROOTS NURSERY SERIES QUALIFIER) 6f 18y
2:20 (2:21) (Class 6) (0-65,67) 2-Y-O
£3,234 (£962; £481; £300; £300; £300) **Stalls** Centre

Form RPR

056 **1** **Ebony Adams**[20] 4394 2-9-5 **62**........ JasonWatson 6 65
(Brian Meehan) *prom: pushed along over 3f out: rdn over 1f out: edgd lft and styd on to ld towards fin* **13/2**[3]

005 **2** ½ **Winnetka (IRE)**[15] 4544 2-9-10 **67**........ JohnFahy 1 69
(Richard Hannon) *hld up in tch: rdn over 1f out: led wl ins fnl f: hdd towards fin* **7/1**

4501 **3** *nk* **Ambyfaeirvine (IRE)**[10] 4756 2-9-6 **66** 6ex........ GabrieleMalune(3) 2 67
(Ivan Furtado) *chsd ldr to 1/2-way: wnt 2nd again over 1f out: rdn: hung lft and ev ch ins fnl f: styd on* **3/1**[1]

000 **4** *nk* **Mr Gus (IRE)**[38] 3679 2-8-10 **53**........ PaulHanagan 4 53
(Richard Fahey) *sn pushed along in rr: hdwy over 1f out: rdn and edgd lft ins fnl f: r.o* **8/1**

052 **5** 3 ¼ **Navajo Dawn (IRE)**[22] 4275 2-9-7 **64**........ AndrewMullen 9 54
(Robyn Brisland) *led: rdn over 1f out: hdd and no ex wl ins fnl f* **15/2**

355 **6** 6 **Champagne Supanova (IRE)**[80] 2257 2-9-10 **67**........ StevieDonohoe 10 39
(Richard Spencer) *wnt rt s: hdwy over 4f out: chsd ldr 1/2-way tl rdn over 1f out: wknd fnl f* **16/1**

040 **7** 2 ¾ **Geepower (IRE)**[55] 3098 2-9-7 **64**........ CamHardie 7 28
(Brian Ellison) *sn pushed along in rr: effrt over 2f out: wknd over 1f out* **33/1**

6054 **8** 2 ¼ **Lexington Quest (IRE)**[10] 4756 2-9-4 **66**........ SeamusCronin(5) 8 23
(Richard Hannon) *s.i.s: outpcd* **7/2**[2]

005 **9** 6 **Walton Thorns (IRE)**[47] 3371 2-9-4 **61**........ RobertWinston 3
(Charles Hills) *s.s: hdwy over 2f out: wknd over 1f out (jockey said gelding was slowly away and ran too free thereafter)* **9/1**

1m 15.79s (1.99) **Going Correction** +0.15s/f (Good) **9** Ran SP% **114.8**
Speed ratings (Par 92): **92,91,90,90,86 78,74,71,63**
CSF £50.90 CT £165.00 TOTE £9.30: £3.00, £3.10, £1.60; EX 47.20 Trifecta £181.90.
Owner Bearstone Stud Limited **Bred** Bearstone Stud **Trained** Manton, Wilts

FOCUS
Just one previous winner in this low-grade nursery and there was something of a slow-motion, bunched finish. The second has been rated to his latest.

5147 MANSIONBET BEATEN BY A HEAD H'CAP 6f 18y
2:50 (2:53) (Class 6) (0-60,62) 3-Y-O+
£3,234 (£962; £481; £300; £300; £300) **Stalls** Centre

Form RPR

6-00 **1** **Amelia R (IRE)**[38] 3684 3-8-13 **52**........ JimmyQuinn 12 67
(Ray Craggs) *chsd ldr: led over 1f out: rdn clr (trainer said, regarding the improved form shown, the filly appreciated the drop in trip to 6f from 7f)* **25/1**

0456 **2** 6 **Dubai Elegance**[37] 3738 5-8-12 **46**........(p) PaddyMathers 2 44
(Derek Shaw) *s.i.s: hld up: hdwy over 1f out: r.o to go 2nd nr fin: no ch w wnr* **14/1**

2006 **3** ¾ **Champagne Mondays**[36] 3775 3-8-9 **48**........(b[1]) KieranO'Neill 5 43
(Scott Dixon) *led: rdn and hdd over 1f out: no ex ins fnl f* **20/1**

2221 **4** *shd* **Queen Of Kalahari**[37] 3716 4-9-1 **49**........ LewisEdmunds 6 44
(Les Eyre) *chsd ldrs: rdn over 2f out: styd on same pce ins fnl f* **9/2**[2]

-130 **5** 2 ¾ **Aghast**[28] 4080 3-9-9 **62**........ FrannyNorton 14 48
(Kevin Ryan) *s.i.s: hld up: hdwy and hung lft over 1f out: no ex fnl f* **7/2**[1]

6-00 **6** 2 **Vicky Cristina (IRE)**[13] 4657 4-8-11 **45**........ BarryMcHugh 9 26
(John Holt) *mid-div: rdn over 2f out: wknd fnl f* **16/1**

0525 **7** 1 ¾ **Red Tycoon (IRE)**[10] 4749 7-9-7 **58**........ FinleyMarsh(3) 3 34
(Ken Cunningham-Brown) *chsd ldrs: rdn over 1f out: wknd fnl f* **12/1**

4664 **8** ½ **Always Amazing**[10] 4765 5-9-6 **54**........ TomQueally 7 28
(Derek Shaw) *hld up: sme hdwy and hung lft over 1f out: wknd fnl f* **18/1**

00-0 **9** ½ **Congress Place (IRE)**[39] 3651 3-9-6 **59**........ AlistairRawlinson 10 31
(Michael Appleby) *chsd ldrs: pushed along and lost pl over 3f out: n.d after* **14/1**

040 **10** ¾ **Bold Show**[43] 3510 3-9-8 **61**........(p) PaulHanagan 4 31
(Richard Fahey) *s.i.s: sn pushed along in rr: rdn over 2f out: hung lft and wknd over 1f out* **7/1**[3]

-630 **11** 1 ¼ **Grandstand (IRE)**[22] 4286 3-9-6 **59**........ DaneO'Neill 8 25
(Richard Price) *hld up: bhd fr 1/2-way* **25/1**

0506 **12** *nk* **Coastal Drive**[18] 4434 4-9-2 **50**........ DougieCostello 11 16
(Paul Midgley) *chsd ldrs: pushed along 1/2-way: wknd wl over 1f out* **11/1**

0-00 **13** 5 **Whigwham**[27] 4132 5-8-11 **45**........ CamHardie 1
(Gary Sanderson) *mid-div: rdn over 2f out: wknd over 1f out* **50/1**

4465 **14** 7 **Coastal Cyclone**[44] 3476 5-8-10 **47** ow1........(b) MitchGodwin(3) 13
(Harry Dunlop) *hld up: sme hdwy over 2f out: wkng whn hung lft over 1f out (jockey said gelding was never travelling; trainer said gelding was unsuited by the going and would prefer a quicker surface)* **9/1**

1m 14.08s (0.28) **Going Correction** +0.15s/f (Good)
WFA 3 from 4yo+ 5lb **14** Ran SP% **117.8**
Speed ratings (Par 101): **104,96,95,94,91 88,86,85,84,83 82,81,75,65**
CSF £323.79 CT £7137.08 TOTE £26.90: £6.10, £4.30, £7.50; EX 362.60 Trifecta £4398.20.
Owner Ray Craggs **Bred** M J Rozenbroek **Trained** Sedgefield, Co Durham

FOCUS
Heavy rain preceded the third race on the card. This was an uncompetitive, moderate sprint.

5148 BRITISH STALLION STUDS EBF MANSIONBET FILLIES' NOVICE STKS 1m 2f 50y
3:25 (3:25) (Class 5) 3-Y-O+ **£3,881** (£1,155; £577; £288) **Stalls** Low

Form RPR

35 **1** **Ojooba**[21] 4341 3-8-12 0........ DaneO'Neill 2 85
(Owen Burrows) *mde all: qcknd over 3f out: shkn up over 1f out: styd on wl* **4/1**[2]

1 **2** 2 ¾ **Sweet Promise**[21] 4326 3-9-5 0........ GeorgeWood 1 87
(James Fanshawe) *trckd ldrs: chsd wnr over 2f out: rdn and edgd lft over 1f out: styd on same pce ins fnl f* **6/4**[1]

3 1 ¾ **Midnights' Gift** 3-8-12 0........ DavidProbert 3 76
(Alan King) *hld up: hdwy over 6f out: rdn over 1f out: styd on same pce ins fnl f* **33/1**

4- **4** ½ **Alemagna**[275] 8329 3-8-12 0........ StevieDonohoe 6 75+
(David Simcock) *broke wl: stdd and lost pl after 1f: shkn up and hdwy over 1f out: nt rch ldrs* **8/1**

5 3 **Expressionism (IRE)** 3-8-12 0........ JackMitchell 8 69
(Charlie Appleby) *s.i.s: rcvrd to chse wnr after 1f: shkn up over 3f out: lost 2nd over 2f out: sn hung lft: wknd fnl f* **9/2**[3]

The Form Book Flat 2019, Raceform Ltd, Newbury, RG14 5SJ

5 **6** 2 1/4 **Hazaranda**[64] 2770 3-8-12 0 JasonWatson 5 65
(Sir Michael Stoute) *prom: lost pl over 6f out: shkn up over 3f out: sn outpcd* 9/2[3]

0-0 **7** 3/4 **I Think So (IRE)**[14] 4600 4-9-0 0 LauraCoughlan(7) 4 62?
(David Loughnane) *w wnr 1f: remained handy: rdn over 2f out: wknd over 1f out* 200/1

0-1 **8** 16 **Break The Rules**[133] 1077 3-9-3 0 EoinWalsh 7 36
(Martin Smith) *s.i.s: a in rr: wknd over 3f out (trainer said filly was unsuited by the undulating track)* 40/1

2m 14.79s (1.39) **Going Correction** +0.15s/f (Good) 8 Ran SP% 113.4
WFA 3 from 4yo 9lb
Speed ratings (Par 100): **100,97,96,96,93 91,91,78**
CSF £10.22 TOTE £4.00: £1.30, £1.30, £6.60; EX 10.90 Trifecta £160.10.
Owner Hamdan Al Maktoum **Bred** Shadwell Estate Company Limited **Trained** Lambourn, Berks

FOCUS
Probably an okay fillies' novice. Add 18yds. The fourth has been rated close to her debut run.

5149 DOWNLOAD THE MANSIONBET APP H'CAP 1m 2f 50y
4:00 (4:01) (Class 3) (0-90,90) 3-Y-O+ **£9,703** (£2,887; £1,443; £721) **Stalls** Low

Form RPR

6314 **1** **Great Example**[23] 4256 3-9-6 **90** JasonWatson 1 105+
(Saeed bin Suroor) *sn chsng ldr: hung lft fr over 3f out: shkn up to ld over 2f out: rdn clr over 1f out: eased nr fin (jockey said colt hung badly left)* 11/8[1]

0235 **2** 2 1/4 **Ayutthaya (IRE)**[26] 4144 4-9-12 **87** DougieCostello 2 93
(Kevin Ryan) *led: rdn and hdd over 2f out: nt clr run and swtchd rt over 1f out: styd on same pce fnl f* 8/1

044 **3** 1 1/2 **Sod's Law**[36] 3763 4-9-7 **82** DaneO'Neill 5 85
(Hughie Morrison) *hld up: rdn and edgd lft fr over 2f out: styd on to go 3rd post: nt trble ldrs* 8/1

-213 **4** nse **Asian Angel (IRE)**[25] 4187 3-9-2 **86** FrannyNorton 3 89
(Mark Johnston) *s.i.s: hdwy over 8f out: rdn over 2f out: styd on same pce* 11/4[2]

152 **5** 2 1/2 **Kripke (IRE)**[27] 4108 4-9-9 **84** PaulHanagan 4 82
(David Barron) *prom: lost pl over 8f out: n.d after* 13/2[3]

-416 **6** 9 **My Boy Sepoy**[20] 4407 4-9-4 **79** RossaRyan 6 59
(Stuart Williams) *chsd ldrs: rdn over 2f out: wknd over 1f out* 14/1

2m 12.52s (-0.88) **Going Correction** +0.15s/f (Good) 6 Ran SP% 111.0
WFA 3 from 4yo 9lb
Speed ratings (Par 107): **109,107,106,105,103 96**
CSF £12.77 TOTE £1.80: £1.30, £3.70; EX 10.50 Trifecta £54.40.
Owner Godolphin **Bred** Usk Valley Stud **Trained** Newmarket, Suffolk

FOCUS
This looked like a fair event and the winner did it well. Add 18yds. The second has been rated close to form.

5150 MANSIONBET BEST ODDS GUARANTEED H'CAP 1m 75y
4:30 (4:30) (Class 3) (0-95,96) 3-Y-O+ **£9,703** (£2,887; £1,443; £721) **Stalls** Centre

Form RPR

005- **1** **Silver Line (IRE)**[293] 7777 5-9-12 **95** JosephineGordon 7 106
(Saeed bin Suroor) *broke wl: racd keenly: sn stdd and lost pl: hdwy to ld over 2f out: shkn up over 1f out: qcknd clr fnl f* 7/2[2]

0316 **2** 6 **Oasis Prince**[7] 4882 3-9-5 **96** FrannyNorton 5 91
(Mark Johnston) *s.i.s: rcvrd to chse ldr after 1f: rdn over 2f out: outpcd fnl f (jockey said colt slipped in the stalls and lost its back end upon leaving the stalls)* 5/4[1]

0030 **3** 3/4 **Jackpot Royale**[7] 4867 4-9-2 **85** (p[1]) AlistairRawlinson 4 80
(Michael Appleby) *hld up: shkn up over 2f out: styd on fr over 1f out: nt trble ldrs* 18/1

1055 **4** 1 **Name The Wind**[20] 4385 3-9-5 **96** JasonWatson 6 87
(James Tate) *led: racd keenly: rdn and hdd over 2f out: wknd ins fnl f* 6/1[3]

1-30 **5** 6 **Tahreek**[29] 4020 4-9-2 **85** DaneO'Neill 3 69
(Sir Michael Stoute) *trckd ldrs: plld hrd: rdn over 2f out: wknd over 1f out: eased* 7/2[2]

1m 47.24s (0.54) **Going Correction** +0.15s/f (Good) 5 Ran SP% 108.4
WFA 3 from 4yo+ 8lb
Speed ratings (Par 107): **103,97,96,95,89**
CSF £8.09 TOTE £4.30: £2.20, £1.10; EX 9.10 Trifecta £35.90.
Owner Godolphin **Bred** Ringfort Stud **Trained** Newmarket, Suffolk

FOCUS
A small field but the form makes sense and it was another convincing Godolphin winner on the card. Add 18yds.

5151 MANSIONBET H'CAP 1m 75y
5:00 (5:00) (Class 6) (0-65,67) 3-Y-O+
£3,234 (£962; £481; £300; £300; £300) **Stalls** Centre

Form RPR

4001 **1** **Salam Zayed**[7] 4875 3-9-8 **65** 6ex PaulHanagan 9 73+
(Richard Fahey) *chsd ldr: led over 2f out: drvn out* 2/1[1]

0651 **2** hd **Mr Strutter (IRE)**[9] 4785 5-10-4 **67** 5ex AndrewElliott 3 77+
(Ronald Thompson) *chsd ldrs: nt clr run and swtchd rt over 1f out: r.o* 9/1

5001 **3** 2 3/4 **Duchess Of Avon**[31] 3966 4-9-13 **62** HectorCrouch 2 66
(Gary Moore) *prom: racd keenly: rdn over 2f out: styd on* 4/1[3]

2204 **4** 3 **Baashiq (IRE)**[14] 4615 5-10-0 **63** (p) DaneO'Neill 5 60
(Peter Hiatt) *s.s: hdwy over 5f out: rdn over 2f out: wknd ins fnl f* 7/2[2]

0002 **5** 2 3/4 **Vincenzo Coccotti (USA)**[9] 4797 7-8-13 **51** (p) FinleyMarsh(3) 4 42
(Ken Cunningham-Brown) *hld up in tch: lost pl over 5f out: rdn over 2f out: hung lft over 1f out: wknd fnl f* 14/1

4553 **6** 3 **Foxy Rebel**[16] 4512 5-8-10 **45** AndrewMullen 10 29
(Ruth Carr) *led: rdn and hdd over 2f out: wknd fnl f* 11/1

0- **7** 1/2 **Admodum (USA)**[107] 1530 6-9-8 **62** DarraghKeenan(5) 6 45
(John Butler) *s.i.s: a in rr* 7/1

0-00 **8** 2 1/2 **Kings Academy**[10] 4767 5-9-8 **57** (v) JimmyQuinn 7 35
(John Mackie) *s.i.s: hld up: effrt on inner over 2f out: wknd over 1f out* 28/1

1m 48.32s (1.62) **Going Correction** +0.15s/f (Good) 8 Ran SP% 116.5
WFA 3 from 4yo+ 8lb
Speed ratings (Par 101): **97,96,94,91,88 85,84,82**
CSF £21.82 CT £67.79 TOTE £3.00: £1.20, £2.80, £2.50; EX 18.90 Trifecta £58.10.
Owner Dr Marwan Koukash **Bred** Newsells Park Stud **Trained** Musley Bank, N Yorks

FOCUS
Just a modest race but the majority arrived in form, including three last-time-out winners. Add 18yds.
T/Plt: £106.40 to a £1 stake. Pool: £50,935.11 - 349.43 winning units T/Qpdt: £61.70 to a £1 stake. Pool: £4,845.72 - 58.11 winning units **Colin Roberts**

[4756] PONTEFRACT (L-H)
Friday, July 19

OFFICIAL GOING: Good changing to good to soft after race 3 (7.30)
Wind: Virtually nil Weather: Persistent Rain

5152 LUCY STEVENS 30TH BIRTHDAY CELEBRATIONS EBF NOVICE AUCTION STKS (PLUS 10 RACE) 6f
6:25 (6:27) (Class 4) 2-Y-O **£4,528** (£1,347; £673; £336) **Stalls** Low

Form RPR

31 **1** **Tomfre**[22] 4295 2-9-4 0 RichardKingscote 6 80
(Ralph Beckett) *cl up: niggled along over 2f out: pushed along to ld wl over 1f out: sn rdn: drvn ins fnl f: kpt on wl towards fin* 5/4[1]

2 2 **Pop Dancer (IRE)** 2-9-2 0 TonyHamilton 1 72
(Richard Fahey) *trckd ldng pair: hdwy on inner 2f out: effrt over 1f out: chsd wnr: green and stmbld sltly jst ins fnl f: sn rdn and kpt on* 7/4[2]

3 1/2 **Spiritofthenorth (FR)** 2-9-0 0 SamJames 4 69
(Kevin Ryan) *t.k.h: sn slt ld: rdn along 2f out: sn hdd: drvn and kpt on same pce fnl f* 16/1

22 **4** nk **Sword Beach (IRE)**[23] 4254 2-9-5 0 DavidProbert 3 73
(Eve Johnson Houghton) *trckd ldrs: pushed along and hdwy wl over 1f out: rdn ent fnl f: kpt on same pce* 5/1[3]

5 3 **Hooroo (IRE)** 2-8-11 0 HarrisonShaw(5) 7 61
(K R Burke) *dwlt and in rr: hdwy over 2f out: sn rdn and kpt on fnl f* 20/1

6 **6** 9 **Honnold**[23] 4238 2-8-12 0 GrahamLee 2 30
(Donald McCain) *a in rr* 40/1

7 3 1/2 **Bertie's Princess (IRE)** 2-8-4 0 FayeMcManoman(5) 5 16
(Nigel Tinkler) *chsd ldrs on outer: rdn along over 2f out: sn outpcd* 50/1

1m 20.29s (3.19) **Going Correction** +0.55s/f (Yiel) 7 Ran SP% 112.5
Speed ratings (Par 96): **100,97,96,96,92 80,75**
CSF £3.49 TOTE £2.10: £1.40, £1.50; EX 5.00 Trifecta £21.10.
Owner Mrs Philip Snow & Partners **Bred** Mrs P Snow & Partners **Trained** Kimpton, Hants

FOCUS
An overcast evening and 7.5mm of rain during the day had eased the ground. Add 8yds to the distance of this interesting juvenile novice auction event. The pace was solid enough and the market spoke correctly.

5153 CELEBRATING 25 YEARS OF RED SHIRT NIGHT NOVICE STKS (PLUS 10 RACE) 1m 4f 5y
6:55 (6:55) (Class 4) 3-Y-O **£6,469** (£1,925; £962) **Stalls** Low

Form RPR

61 **1** **Tribal Craft**[33] 3889 3-9-4 0 DavidProbert 1 89+
(Andrew Balding) *mde most: pushed clr over 3f out: kpt on strly unchal* 5/6[1]

1 **2** 20 **Mankayan (IRE)**[38] 3699 3-9-9 0 StevieDonohoe 4 69
(Charlie Fellowes) *awkward and pushed first 100yds: trckd ldng pair: pushed along over 4f out: sn shkn up and hung sharply rt: rdn along to chse wnr wl over 2f out: drvn fr wl over 1f out: plodded on: no ch w wnr* 11/10[2]

00 **3** 39 **Jukebox Blues (FR)**[9] 4779 3-9-2 0 FrannyNorton 2
(Mark Johnston) *trckd wnr: pushed along over 4f out: rdn over 3f out: sn outpcd and wl bhd fnl 2f* 20/1[3]

2m 46.79s (5.69) **Going Correction** +0.55s/f (Yiel) 3 Ran SP% 106.9
Speed ratings (Par 102): **103,89,63**
CSF £2.06 TOTE £1.80; EX 1.80 Trifecta £2.20.
Owner J C Smith **Bred** Littleton Stud **Trained** Kingsclere, Hants

FOCUS
Add 8yds to the distance of this desperately uncompetitive race for the money on offer. They finished well strung out.

5154 BETFRED SUPPORTS JACK BERRY HOUSE H'CAP 5f 3y
7:30 (7:30) (Class 3) (0-95,97) 3-Y-O **£9,337** (£2,796; £1,398; £699; £349) **Stalls** Low

Form RPR

0310 **1** **Corinthia Knight (IRE)**[27] 4095 4-10-4 **97** DanielTudhope 2 106
(Archie Watson) *wnt rt s: trckd ldrs: hdwy wl mover 1f out: swtchd lft to inner and chal 1f out: rdn to ld ins fnl f: pushed out* 9/2[3]

0115 **2** 1 1/2 **Angel Alexander (IRE)**[20] 4359 3-9-8 **91** RichardKingscote 3 94+
(Tom Dascombe) *sltly hmpd s: t.k.h: cl up: led jst over 2f out: rdn over 1f out: drvn and hdd ins fnl f: kpt on same pce* 7/4[1]

4320 **3** 1 3/4 **Excessable**[7] 4894 6-9-1 **80** RachelRichardson 6 78
(Tim Easterby) *sn led on outer: pushed along and hdd over 2f out: rdn wl over 1f out: drvn and kpt on same pce fnl f* 8/1

1205 **4** 3/4 **Fendale**[20] 4406 7-9-7 **86** GrahamLee 5 81
(Bryan Smart) *hmpd s and bhd: pushed along bef 1/2-way: rdn 2f out: styd on fnl f* 7/1

1111 **5** 9 **Dapper Man (IRE)**[14] 4593 5-9-10 **89** (b) BenCurtis 1 52
(Roger Fell) *cl up on inner: rdn along 2f out: wknd over 1f out: sn bhd and eased (jockey said that the gelding jumped awkwardly from the stalls; trainer said that the gelding was unsuited by the rain softened Good ground on this occasion, which was changed to Good to Soft after this race)* 2/1[2]

1m 5.67s (1.77) **Going Correction** +0.55s/f (Yiel) 5 Ran SP% 111.5
WFA 3 from 4yo+ 4lb
Speed ratings (Par 107): **107,104,101,100,86**
CSF £13.02 TOTE £5.60: £2.00, £1.20; EX 13.50 Trifecta £46.30.
Owner Ontoawinner & Partner **Bred** Tally-Ho Stud **Trained** Upper Lambourn, W Berks

FOCUS
Add 8yds to the distance of this decent sprint handicap. The gallop was fair for the conditions, which were changed to good to soft after the race, and the winner came from off the pace. A turf pb from the winner and not far below this year's AW form.

5155 VW VOLKSWAGEN VAN CENTRE (LEEDS) LTD OPTIONAL CLAIMING H'CAP 1m 6y
8:00 (8:02) (Class 2) 4-Y-O+ **£19,407** (£5,775; £2,886; £1,443) **Stalls** Low

Form RPR

0412 **1** **Star Of Southwold (FR)**[23] 4240 4-8-13 **88** TheodoreLadd(5) 5 98
(Michael Appleby) *trckd ldrs: hdwy 2f out: sn chsng ldr: rdn over 1f out: led ins fnl f: styd on* 7/2[2]

6436 **2** 1 **Calvados Spirit**[11] 4723 6-8-2 **72** PaddyMathers 3 79+
(Richard Fahey) *dwlt and in rr: hdwy 3f out: rdn along wl over 1f out: drvn to chse ldrs ent fnl f: fin strly* 7/1[3]

1455 **3** *1* **Enigmatic (IRE)**[8] 4851 5-9-0 **89** .... DarraghKeenan(5) 6 94
(Alan Bailey) *cl up: led 2f out: rdn over 1f out: drvn and hdd ins fnl f: kpt on same pce* **7/1**[3]

1032 **4** *4* **Tadaawol**[11] 4723 6-8-11 **81** ....(p) BenCurtis 9 77
(Roger Fell) *in tch: hdwy 3f out: rdn to chse ldrs wl over 1f out: sn drvn and no imp fnl f* **16/1**

6104 **5** *1 1/4* **Brother McGonagall**[17] 4490 5-8-12 **82** .... DuranFentiman 2 75
(Tim Easterby) *sn slt ld: rdn along and hdd 2f out: sn drvn and grad wknd* **16/1**

6444 **6** *3* **Juanito Chico (IRE)**[13] 4662 5-8-4 **74** ....(h) FrannyNorton 4 60
(Stuart Williams) *trckd ldrs on inner: pushed along 3f out: rdn over 2f out: sn btn* **11/1**

-145 **7** *2* **Wind In My Sails**[20] 4365 7-8-9 **79** .... BarryMcHugh 8 60
(Ed de Giles) *a towards rr* **33/1**

/005 **8** *2 3/4* **Max Zorin (IRE)**[44] 3472 5-9-7 **91** .... DavidProbert 1 66
(Andrew Balding) *chsd ldrs: rdn along 3f out: sn wknd* **14/1**

5210 **9** *13* **Waarif (IRE)**[6] 4935 6-10-0 **98** .... DanielTudhope 7 43
(David O'Meara) *trckd ldrs on outer: pushed along 3f out: rdn over 2f out: sn wknd (jockey said gelding ran flat)* **5/2**[1]

3024 **10** *4* **Masham Star (IRE)**[6] 4934 5-9-9 **93** .... JoeFanning 10 29
(Mark Johnston) *hld up on outer: a towards rr* **9/1**

1m 48.57s (2.67) **Going Correction** +0.55s/f (Yiel) **10** Ran SP% **115.5**
Speed ratings (Par 109): **108,107,106,102,100 97,95,93,80,76**
CSF £28.06 CT £162.58 TOTE £4.00: £1.60, £2.90, £2.40; EX 26.80 Trifecta £187.00.
Owner Middleham Park Racing XXXIII **Bred** S C Snig Elevage **Trained** Oakham, Rutland

FOCUS
Rail re-alignment added 8yds to the distance and the official going was changed to good to soft ahead of this competitive handicap. The winner was always near the decent pace and came widest of all. The winner has been rated similar to his latest, with the third to form.

5156 SUNFLOWER FOUNDATION MAIDEN H'CAP 1m 2f 5y
8:35 (8:36) (Class 5) (0-70,70) 3-Y-O+
£3,881 (£1,155; £577; £400; £400; £400) Stalls Low

Form RPR

0206 **1** **Kwanza**[20] 4371 4-9-4 **58** .... JoeFanning 8 69
(Mark Johnston) *trckd ldr: cl up 4f out: led wl over 1f out: sn rdn and edgd lft: kpt on wl fnl f* **8/1**

5-02 **2** *1 3/4* **Lady Scatterley (FR)**[13] 4628 3-9-4 **67** .... CamHardie 6 73
(Tim Easterby) *trckd ldrs: hdwy over 3f out: rdn wl over 1f out: chsd wnr and drvn ins fnl f: kpt on* **5/1**

4-20 **3** *4* **No Dress Rehearsal**[37] 3729 3-9-7 **70** .... NathanEvans 1 68
(Michael Easterby) *sn led: pushed along 3f out: rdn over 2f out: hdd wl over 1f out: n.m.r and swtchd rt 1f out: sn drvn and kpt on one pce* **7/2**[2]

60-0 **4** *4 1/2* **Calevade (IRE)**[60] 2912 3-8-6 **55** .... AndrewMullen 4 44+
(Ben Haslam) *hld up in rr: pushed along and hdwy on inner 2f out: rdn over 1f out: drvn and styd on fnl f (jockey said gelding hung left throughout)* **14/1**

64-3 **5** *4 1/2* **Alfa Dawn (IRE)**[10] 4761 3-9-7 **70** .... SamJames 10 50
(Phillip Makin) *hld up: hdwy 3f out: effrt to chse ldrs wl over 1f out: sn rdn: drvn and wknd fnl f* **4/1**[3]

6060 **6** *3/4* **Shakiah (IRE)**[53] 3162 4-8-9 **49** oh4 .... PaddyMathers 7 27
(Sharon Watt) *chsd ldrs: pushed along 3f out: rdn over 2f out: sn wknd* **40/1**

402- **7** *hd* **Knightly Spirit**[249] 9032 4-9-13 **67** .... BenCurtis 9 44
(Iain Jardine) *in tch: hdwy to trck ldrs over 4f out: rdn along 3f out: drvn over 2f out: sn wknd* **20/1**

2/34 **8** *10* **Flying Raconteur**[11] 4728 5-9-9 **68** ....(t) FayeMcManoman(5) 3 25
(Nigel Tinkler) *chsd ldrs: rdn along 3f out: sn wknd (jockey said gelding stopped quickly)* **11/4**[1]

0/05 **9** *23* **Howbaar (USA)**[28] 4076 4-9-6 **60** ....(t[1]) DanielTudhope 5
(James Bethell) *a in rr* **12/1**

2m 19.52s (4.52) **Going Correction** +0.55s/f (Yiel)
WFA 3 from 4yo+ 9lb **9** Ran SP% **118.2**
Speed ratings (Par 103): **103,101,98,94,91 90,90,82,64**
CSF £48.88 CT £168.34 TOTE £9.60: £2.90, £1.30, £1.80; EX 47.90 Trifecta £221.20.
Owner Miss K Rausing **Bred** Miss K Rausing **Trained** Middleham Moor, N Yorks

FOCUS
Add 8yds to the distance. It paid to be near the ordinary pace and few got into it. The third has been rated close to her C&D form two starts back.

5157 JOHN NIXON SUPPORTS JACK BERRY HOUSE H'CAP 6f
9:05 (9:05) (Class 5) (0-75,83) 3-Y-O+
£3,881 (£1,155; £577; £400; £400; £400) Stalls Low

Form RPR

3600 **1** **Mr Orange (IRE)**[18] 4440 6-9-10 **71** ....(p) GrahamLee 3 80
(Paul Midgley) *towards rr: pushed along over 2f out: hdwy on outer wl over 1f out: sn rdn: styd on to ld ins fnl f* **5/1**[3]

0660 **2** *1/2* **Requinto Dawn (IRE)**[13] 4625 4-9-5 **66** ....(p) TonyHamilton 2 73
(Richard Fahey) *trckd ldrs: pushed along 2f out: rdn: n.m.r and swtchd lft ent fnl f: sn drvn and kpt on* **14/1**

0041 **3** *1 3/4* **Musharrif**[10] 4759 7-9-9 **77** 4ex ....(t) ZakWheatley(7) 8 78
(Declan Carroll) *trckd ldng pair: hdwy 2f out: rdn to chal over 1f out: ev ch ent fnl f: kpt on same pce towards fin* **11/2**

2211 **4** *3/4* **Beryl The Petal (IRE)**[9] 4781 3-10-3 **83** 6ex ....(v) DanielTudhope 4 81
(David O'Meara) *led: rdn along wl over 1f out: drvn ent fnl f: sn hdd & wknd* **2/1**[1]

005 **5** *4 1/2* **Round The Island**[18] 4440 6-8-9 **56** .... LewisEdmunds 5 41
(Richard Whitaker) *dwlt and in rr: rdn along and hanging lft fnl 2f: nvr a factor* **9/4**[2]

0265 **6** *12* **Rickyroadboy**[32] 3936 4-9-2 **63** ....(p[1]) AndrewMullen 1 9
(Mark Walford) *cl up on inner: rdn along 2f out: sn wknd* **8/1**

1m 20.98s (3.88) **Going Correction** +0.55s/f (Yiel)
WFA 3 from 4yo+ 5lb **6** Ran SP% **113.9**
Speed ratings (Par 103): **96,95,93,92,86 70**
CSF £64.61 CT £396.55 TOTE £5.10: £2.20, £5.10; EX 88.20 Trifecta £99.60.
Owner J Blackburn & A Turton **Bred** Rathbarry Stud **Trained** Westow, N Yorks

FOCUS
Add 8yds to the distance of this modest sprint handicap. The first two came from off the pace, which collapsed, and the race has been rated around them.
T/Plt: £537.10 to a £1 stake. Pool: £46,669.08 - 63.42 winning units T/Qpdt: £181.10 to a £1 stake. Pool: £4,940.57 - 20.11 winning units **Joe Rowntree**

5158 - 5164a (Foreign Racing) - See Raceform Interactive

5116 VICHY
Friday, July 19

OFFICIAL GOING: Turf: soft

5165a PRIX DE PARAY LE FRESIL (CLAIMER) (3YO) (TURF) 5f
12:50 3-Y-O £7,207 (£2,882; £2,162; £1,441; £720)

RPR

1 **Bonarda (FR)**[11] 3-9-2 0 ow1 .... MaximeGuyon 6 71
(M Boutin, France) **2/1**[1]

2 *nk* **Hit The Track Jack**[24] 4229 3-8-5 0 ow1 .... JeremieMonteiro(7) 3 66
(N Caullery, France) **61/10**

3 *4* **Velvet Vixen (IRE)**[24] 4229 3-9-2 0 ow1 .... MickaelBarzalona 11 56
(Jo Hughes, France) *Well into stride: disp ld early: urged along and hdd over 2f out: rdn to chse ldr over 1f out: drvn and kpt on ins fnl f* **43/5**

4 *1* **Love To Excel (IRE)**[230] 9363 3-8-8 0 ow1 ....(b) MlleSarahLeger(9) 5 53
(F Foresi, France) **28/1**

5 *3/4* **Voltereta (IRE)**[17] 3-8-2 0 ow2 .... Joseph-MathieuMighty(8) 4 44
(M Delcher Sanchez, France) **48/1**

6 *3/4* **Carolingien (FR)**[30] 3-9-10 0 ow2 ....(p) ChristopheSoumillon 8 55
(F Vermeulen, France) **19/5**[2]

7 *1/2* **Amethyst (FR)**[43] 3526 3-8-4 0 ow1 ....(p) MlleMarieWaldhauser(8) 10 41
(C Escuder, France) **23/5**[3]

8 *1 1/4* **Shanghaizhengchang**[36] 3-8-13 0 ow2 ....(b) VincentCheminaud 2 38
(M Delzangles, France) **11/1**

9 *1 1/4* **Van Mayor (FR)**[100] 3-9-5 0 ow1 .... NicolasPerret 9 39
(J Reynier, France) **15/1**

10 *2* **Deluree (FR)**[24] 4229 3-8-9 0 ow1 ....(b) SylvainRuis 7 22
(N Caullery, France) **48/1**

11 *nse* **Georgia Du Rabutin (FR)**[19] 3-8-9 0 ow1 .... LudovicBoisseau 1 22
(N Bellanger, France) **89/1**

59.4s **11** Ran SP% **119.2**
PARI-MUTUEL (all including 1 euro stake): WIN 3.00; PLACE 1.40, 1.80, 2.30; DF 7.60.
Owner Diego Fernandez-Ortega **Bred** S.C.E.A. Des Prairies, B Jeffroy & T Jeffroy **Trained** France

5166a PRIX DE SAINT-FELIX (CLAIMER) (2YO FILLIES) (TURF) 7f
1:20 2-Y-O £7,207 (£2,882; £2,162; £1,441; £720)

RPR

1 **Joa De Gibraltar (IRE)** 2-9-0 0 ow1 .... AntonioOrani(5) 11 78+
(J Reynier, France) **57/10**[3]

2 *2 1/2* **Diva Du Dancing (FR)**[24] 4228 2-9-0 0 ow1 .... MlleMarieVelon(6) 7 72
(P Decouz, France) **9/1**

3 *nk* **La Fripouille (FR)** 2-8-13 0 ow2 .... EddyHardouin 5 64
(K Borgel, France) **24/1**

4 *3 1/2* **Tea Time Desert (ITY)** 2-8-13 0 ow2 ....(p) IoritzMendizabal 6 55
(Simone Brogi, France) **18/5**[2]

5 *1* **Kelydor (FR)** 2-9-5 0 ow1 .... FranckForesi 3 59
(F Foresi, France) **27/10**[1]

6 *nk* **Villa Anabaa (FR)** 2-9-3 0 ow1 .... FranckBlondel 8 56
(Charley Rossi, France) **12/1**

7 *1* **Kepou (FR)** 2-9-2 0 ow1 ....(p) MaximeGuyon 1 52
(C Escuder, France) **14/1**

8 *nk* **Can't Hold Us (FR)**[42] 3562 2-8-13 0 ow2 .... MlleAlisonMassin(4) 12 52
(D Allard, France) **24/1**

9 *2 1/2* **Via Con Me (FR)** 2-8-6 0 ow1 .... MlleMarieWaldhauser(6) 10 41
(M Pimbonnet, France) **58/10**

10 *nk* **Kiss Me Forever (FR)** 2-9-2 0 ow1 .... TonyPiccone 2 44
(K Borgel, France) **15/1**

11 *dist* **Storm Wings (IRE)**[79] 2275 2-8-13 0 ow2 .... AntoineHamelin 4
(Jo Hughes, France) *in rr early: urged along after 1f: sn adrift: nvr a factor and eased over 1f out* **38/1**

1m 29.85s **11** Ran SP% **119.6**
PARI-MUTUEL (all including 1 euro stake): WIN 6.70; PLACE 2.40, 3.60, 6.10; DF 18.50.
Owner Jean-Claude Seroul **Bred** J-C Seroul **Trained** France

5167a (Foreign Racing) - See Raceform Interactive

5168a PRIX JACQUES DE BREMOND (LISTED RACE) (4YO+) (TURF) 1m
3:05 4-Y-O+ £23,423 (£9,369; £7,027; £4,684; £2,342)

RPR

1 **Skalleti (FR)**[27] 4-9-1 0 ow1 .... MaximeGuyon 4 101
(J Reynier, France) **9/10**[1]

2 *1/2* **Wagram (FR)**[27] 4-9-1 0 ow1 .... RadekKoplik 10 100
(Z Koplik, Czech Republic) **55/1**

3 *3/4* **Palavas (FR)**[33] 4-9-1 0 ow1 ....(p) MarvinGrandin 6 98
(Cedric Rossi, France) **24/1**

4 *1/2* **Kayenne (FR)**[43] 7-8-11 0 ow1 .... MickaelBarzalona 8 93
(C Escuder, France) **13/1**

5 *nk* **Volfango (IRE)**[26] 4157 5-9-5 0 ow1 .... ChristopheSoumillon 7 100
(F Vermeulen, France) **68/10**[3]

6 *nk* **Wireless (FR)**[47] 8-9-1 0 ow1 .... TheoBachelot 2 96
(Vaclav Luka Jr, Czech Republic) **16/1**

7 *2 1/2* **Yanling (FR)**[13] 4680 5-8-11 0 ow1 .... AntoineHamelin 3 86
(Matthieu Palussiere, France) **11/1**

8 *3/4* **Cherisy (FR)**[19] 4432 4-9-2 0 ow1 .... IoritzMendizabal 5 89
(Cedric Rossi, France) **33/1**

9 *4 1/2* **Hopeless (FR)**[13] 4680 6-9-1 0 ow1 .... FranckBlondel 1 78
(Mme C Barande-Barbe, France) **24/1**

P **New Graduate (IRE)**[20] 4397 4-9-1 0 ow1 .... TonyPiccone 9
(James Tate) *trckd ldrs: lost action and p.u over 2f out* **18/5**[2]

1m 40.68s **10** Ran SP% **121.3**
PARI-MUTUEL (all including 1 euro stake): WIN 1.90; PLACE 1.50, 8.90, 4.90; DF 63.60.
Owner Jean-Claude Seroul **Bred** Guy Pariente Holding **Trained** France

4825 **DONCASTER** (L-H)
Saturday, July 20

OFFICIAL GOING: Good (good to soft in places; watered; 7.8)
Wind: Strong against Weather: Sunny and breezy

5169 CHILDREN'S AIR AMBULANCE APPRENTICE H'CAP 5f 3y
5:40 (5:40) (Class 5) (0-70,72) 3-Y-O+
£3,428 (£1,020; £509; £400; £400; £400) **Stalls** Centre

Form RPR
3005 1 **Point Of Woods**30 4037 6-8-9 **56**...(t[1]) EllaMcCain(3) 8 64
(Tina Jackson) *trckd ldr: hdwy 2f out: rdn to ld ent fnl f: kpt on wl towards fin* **8/1**
3646 2 3/4 **Valentino Sunrise**26 4183 3-8-4 **57**... GeorgeBass(5) 4 61
(Mick Channon) *led: rdn along 2f out: hdd and drvn ent fnl f: kpt on wl u.p towards fin* **7/1**
6362 3 1 1/4 **Debawtry (IRE)**7 4911 4-9-7 **70**... ZakWheatley(5) 2 71
(Phillip Makin) *trckd ldr: hdwy 2f out: sn chal: rdn and ev ch ent fnl f: sn drvn: edgd lft and kpt on same pce* **5/2**2
5003 4 nk **Bashiba (IRE)**9 4829 8-9-3 **66**...(t) IzzyClifton(5) 9 66
(Nigel Tinkler) *hld up in tch: hdwy to trck ldrs 2f out: effrt and n.m.r over 1f out: sn rdn and kpt on same pce* **2/1**1
-400 5 1 1/4 **Burtonwood**17 4519 7-8-12 **59**...(p) HarryRussell(3) 3 54
(Julie Camacho) *prom: rdn along 2f out: wknd over 1f out* **12/1**
060- 6 2 1/4 **Lets Go Flo (IRE)**361 5319 3-8-3 **51** oh1... KieranSchofield 6 37
(Brian Ellison) *chsd ldrs: rdn along over 2f out: sn wknd* **16/1**
-354 7 1/2 **Normal Equilibrium**21 4369 9-9-2 **63**... RhonaPindar(3) 5 48
(Ivan Furtado) *t.k.h in rr: swtchd rt and hdwy on outer 3f out: sn chsng ldrs: rdn along 2f out: sn wknd (jockey said the saddle slipped when leaving the stalls)* **13/2**3
0315 R **Robot Boy (IRE)**7 4911 9-10-0 **72**... GeorgiaDobie 1
(Marjorie Fife) *ref to r (jockey said gelding anticipated the start, causing to hit its head on the starting stalls and subsequently refusing to race; vet said the gelding had a bleed to its left nostril as a likely result from hitting its head on the starting stalls)* **10/1**

1m 1.78s (2.18) **Going Correction** +0.175s/f (Good)
WFA 3 from 4yo+ 4lb 8 Ran SP% **121.5**
Speed ratings (Par 103): **89,87,85,85,83 79,78,**
CSF £66.13 CT £185.32 TOTE £9.50: £2.50, £2.00, £1.20; EX 69.60 Trifecta £530.10.
Owner H L Thompson **Bred** Bearstone Stud Ltd **Trained** Liverton, Cleveland

FOCUS
Exposed sorts in this 5f apprentice handicap. The going was officially just on the easy side of good but the time here was 3.88 seconds slower than standard. The pace was ordinary. Straightforward form, with the first two rated to this year's form.

5170 #THECREW CHILDREN'S CLUB EBF MAIDEN FILLIES' STKS (PLUS 10 RACE) 7f 6y
6:15 (6:17) (Class 5) 2-Y-O
£3,428 (£1,020; £509; £254) **Stalls** Centre

Form RPR
1 **Dalanijujo (IRE)** 2-9-0 0... CharlesBishop 9 80+
(Mick Channon) *racd towards stands' side: trckd ldrs: swtchd lft and hdwy to ld 2f out: rdn over 1f out: jnd and drvn ent fnl f: edgd lft: hld on gamely towards fin* **6/1**
2 shd **Tadreej** 2-9-0 0... GeorgeWood 8 80+
(Saeed bin Suroor) *racd towards stands' side: in tch: swtchd lft and hdwy 2f out: rdn over 1f out: chal ent fnl f: sn drvn and ev ch: carried lft and kpt on* **4/1**2
35 3 2 3/4 **Topkapi Star**24 4245 2-9-0 0... DavidEgan 10 73
(Roger Varian) *racd towards stands' side: prom: cl up 1/2-way: rdn along 2f out: drvn and edgd lft over 1f out: kpt on same pce* **6/1**
4 nk **Virgin Snow** 2-9-0 0... TomQueally 6 72
(Ed Dunlop) *trckd ldrs centre: hdwy and prom 2f out: sn rdn: wknd over 1f out* **16/1**
2 5 1 1/4 **Fraternity (IRE)**15 4605 2-9-0 0... TonyHamilton 3 69
(Richard Fahey) *trckd ldrs centre: pushed along and hdwy 2f out: sn rdn and hung lft over 1f out: wknd* **3/1**1
P 6 3 1/2 **Love Powerful (IRE)**24 4245 2-9-0 0... TomMarquand 2 60
(Richard Hannon) *racd centre: led: rdn along and hdd 2f out: sn drvn and wknd* **6/1**
7 nk **Expensive Dirham** 2-9-0 0... JoeFanning 1 59
(Mark Johnston) *trckd ldrs centre: rdn along 2f out: hld whn sltly hmpd and swtchd rt over 1f out: wknd after* **9/2**3
8 3/4 **Divine Summer (USA)** 2-9-0 0... PJMcDonald 4 57
(Ed Walker) *prom centre: rdn along wl over 2f out: sn wknd* **16/1**
9 1/2 **Carriage Clock** 2-8-7 0... TobyEley(7) 7 56
(Steph Hollinshead) *dwlt and a towards rr (jockey said filly ran green)* **66/1**
10 6 **Rainbow Jet (IRE)** 2-9-0 0... TomEaves 5 40
(John Mackie) *a towards rr* **25/1**

1m 29.25s (2.85) **Going Correction** +0.175s/f (Good) 10 Ran SP% **123.1**
Speed ratings (Par 91): **90,89,86,86,84 80,80,79,79,72**
CSF £32.11 TOTE £7.30: £2.70, £1.50, £2.10; EX 38.30 Trifecta £200.80.
Owner C R Hirst **Bred** Limetree Stud **Trained** West Ilsley, Berks

FOCUS
Although there were some well-bred sorts in the line-up it's hard to gauge the value of the form as only three of the ten had been out before and one of them failed to complete the course. To complicate matters further they initially split into two distinct groups and the first three were the three that raced stands' side, though they edged left in the closing stages and the groups merged. The opening level is fluid.

5171 VISIT THEAIRAMBULANCESERVICE.ORG.UK TO FIND OUT MORE FILLIES' NURSERY H'CAP 6f 2y
6:45 (6:45) (Class 4) (0-85,81) 2-Y-O
£4,463 (£1,328; £663; £400; £400; £400) **Stalls** Centre

Form RPR
11 1 **Oti Ma Boati**23 4290 2-9-5 **79**... TonyHamilton 2 82
(Richard Fahey) *t.k.h: hld up in rr: hdwy 2f out: effrt ent fnl f: sn rdn to chal: kpt on wl to ld nr line* **9/4**1
414 2 hd **Rosadora (IRE)**21 4387 2-9-7 **81**... BenCurtis 1 83
(Ralph Beckett) *trckd ldng pair: hdwy 2f out: rdn to take slt ld over 1f out: drvn ins fnl f: hdd and no ex nr line* **5/2**2
633 3 nk **Pentewan**15 4583 2-9-0 **74**... DanielTudhope 5 76
(Phillip Makin) *trckd ldng pair: hdwy on outer 2f out: rdn to chal and edgd lft 1f out: sn drvn and ev ch whn edgd lft ins fnl f: kpt on towards fin* **9/2**
5122 4 shd **Insania**53 3196 2-9-2 **76**... PJMcDonald 6 77
(K R Burke) *led: rdn along 2f out: hdd over 1f out: sn drvn: cl up and ev ch whn sltly hmpd ins fnl f: kpt on towards fin* **7/2**3
2234 5 5 **Inyamazane (IRE)**21 4398 2-9-2 **76**... CharlesBishop 3 62
(Mick Channon) *t.k.h: hld up in rr: pushed along 2f out: sn rdn and outpcd* **10/1**
3010 6 5 **Amnaa**21 4387 2-8-12 **72**... ConnorBeasley 4 43
(Adrian Nicholls) *cl up: rdn along over 2f out: sn wknd (jockey said filly hung left-handed in the closing stages)* **12/1**

1m 14.27s (1.57) **Going Correction** +0.175s/f (Good) 6 Ran SP% **116.5**
Speed ratings (Par 93): **96,95,95,95,88 81**
CSF £8.66 TOTE £2.70: £1.60, £1.90; EX 8.60 Trifecta £34.80.
Owner R A Fahey **Bred** Bearstone Stud **Trained** Musley Bank, N Yorks

FOCUS
A 0-80 fillies nursery with all six making their handicap debuts. The pace was moderate and the first four finished in a heap which suggests the form is nothing out of the ordinary.

5172 KEEPING HOPE ALIVE NOVICE STKS (PLUS 10 RACE) 6f 2y
7:15 (7:17) (Class 4) 2-Y-O
£4,463 (£1,328; £663; £331) **Stalls** Centre

Form RPR
44 1 **Stone Circle (IRE)**18 4482 2-9-2 0... DanielTudhope 9 79+
(Michael Bell) *trckd ldr: hdwy to chal over 1f out: rdn to ld ins fnl f: kpt on wl* **11/2**3
6 2 1/2 **Atheeb**29 4069 2-9-2 0... LouisSteward 7 77
(Sir Michael Stoute) *trckd ldrs: hdwy 2f out: rdn over 1f out: drvn and styd on to chse wnr wl ins fnl f: sn edgd lft and kpt on* **6/1**
3 1/2 **Embolden (IRE)** 2-8-13 0... SeanDavis(3) 5 76+
(Richard Fahey) *trckd ldrs: rdn along and sltly outpcd wl over 1f out: styng on wl whn n.m.r and hmpd wl ins fnl f: kpt on towards fin* **14/1**
21 4 hd **One Hart (IRE)**23 4275 2-9-8 0... JoeFanning 1 80
(Mark Johnston) *led: rdn along and jnd over 1f out: drvn and hdd ins fnl f: edgd rt and no ex wl ins fnl f (vet said colt lost its right-hind shoe)* **7/4**1
4 5 hd **Qaaddim (IRE)**24 4246 2-9-2 0... DavidEgan 2 74
(Roger Varian) *trckd ldng pair: hdwy 2f out: rdn along over 1f out: drvn ins fnl f: kpt on same pce* **5/2**2
6 6 3 1/2 **Kuwait Shield**28 4098 2-9-2 0... TonyHamilton 6 63
(Richard Fahey) *in tch: pushed along and hdwy 2f out: sn rdn and no imp* **20/1**
7 1 **Proclaimer** 2-9-2 0... KevinStott 3 60
(Julie Camacho) *a towards rr* **14/1**
8 nk **Maurice Dancer** 2-9-2 0... PaulMulrennan 4 59
(Julie Camacho) *chsd ldrs: rdn along wl over 2f out: sn wknd* **25/1**
9 12 **Glorious Rio (IRE)** 2-9-2 0... KieranShoemark 8 23
(Charles Hills) *dwlt: a in rr (jockey said colt was slowly away)* **16/1**

1m 15.01s (2.31) **Going Correction** +0.175s/f (Good) 9 Ran SP% **122.4**
Speed ratings (Par 96): **91,90,89,89,89 84,83,82,66**
CSF £40.92 TOTE £6.20: £1.90, £2.20, £4.20; EX 36.90 Trifecta £365.50.
Owner The Fitzrovians 3 **Bred** Stephen Curran **Trained** Newmarket, Suffolk

FOCUS
A 6f juvenile novice in which the four with experience were at the head of the market. The first five finished in a bit of a heap which suggests the form is nothing special.

5173 SPECIALIST AVIATION SERVICES H'CAP 7f 6y
7:45 (7:49) (Class 3) (0-95,94) 3-Y-O+
£7,762 (£2,310; £1,154; £577) **Stalls** Centre

Form RPR
3100 1 **Kaeso**21 4403 5-9-12 **92**... HollieDoyle 9 106
(Nigel Tinkler) *trckd ldrs on outer: smooth hdwy over 2f out: led wl over 1f out: jnd and rdn ent fnl f: kpt on strly (trainer said, regarding the improved form shown, the gelding was unsuited by being drawn wide on the round course at York and was better suited by the straight course here today)* **5/1**1
1002 2 2 **Ventura Ocean (IRE)**11 4759 3-9-0 **90**... SeanDavis(3) 10 96
(Richard Fahey) *hld up towards rr: hdwy over 2f out: chal jst over 1f out: sn rdn and edgd lft: ev ch tl drvn and kpt on same pce last 100yds* **22/1**
3-50 3 1 3/4 **Breath Of Air**66 2746 3-9-4 **91**... KieranShoemark 7 92
(Charles Hills) *hld up in tch: hdwy over 2f out: chal over 1f out: sn rdn and ev ch: drvn and kpt on same pce fnl f* **12/1**
3315 4 1/2 **Tukhoom (IRE)**16 4552 6-8-11 **77**...(b) DavidEgan 6 80
(David O'Meara) *led: rdn along and hdd wl over 1f out: sn drvn: grad wknd* **7/1**
3000 5 1 1/4 **Presidential (IRE)**23 4299 5-9-6 **86**... BenCurtis 11 85
(Roger Fell) *awkward: rrd and dwlt s: bhd and swtchd lft after 2f: hdwy over 2f out: sn rdn and chsd ldrs over 1f out: sn no imp* **11/2**2
-012 6 2 1/4 **Came From The Dark (IRE)**32 3971 3-8-11 **84**... LiamKeniry 3 74
(Ed Walker) *hld up towards rr: hdwy over 2f out: rdn along over 1f out: sn no imp* **11/2**2
420- 7 2 **Piece Of History (IRE)**256 8899 4-10-0 **94**... CallumShepherd 2 82
(Saeed bin Suroor) *chsd ldrs: rdn along 2f out: wknd over 1f out* **7/1**
-024 8 4 **Byron's Choice**28 4127 4-9-12 **92**... PaulMulrennan 5 69
(Michael Dods) *chsd ldrs: rdn along 2f out: sn wknd (jockey said gelding ran too freely)* **6/1**3
3040 9 4 **Queen's Sargent (FR)**22 4320 4-9-0 **80**...(p) KevinStott 8 46
(Kevin Ryan) *prom: cl up 1/2-way: rdn along over 2f out: sn wknd* **10/1**
034 10 3 3/4 **Givinitsum (SAF)**22 4348 3-9-7 **87**... CharlesBishop 4 43
(Eve Johnson Houghton) *trckd ldr: pushed along 3f out: sn rdn and wknd* **14/1**
1-04 11 1/2 **Mutafani**45 3472 4-9-12 **92**...(t[1]) PJMcDonald 1 47
(Simon Crisford) *chsd ldrs: rdn along 3f out: sn wknd (trainer said colt did not face the application of a first time tongue tie)* **9/1**

1m 26.37s (-0.03) **Going Correction** +0.175s/f (Good)
WFA 3 from 4yo+ 7lb 11 Ran SP% **124.5**
Speed ratings (Par 107): **107,104,102,102,100 98,95,91,86,82 81**
CSF £121.51 CT £1283.69 TOTE £5.70: £2.30, £6.20, £3.80; EX 135.60 Trifecta £1146.20.
Owner M Webb **Bred** Sir Eric Parker **Trained** Langton, N Yorks

FOCUS
Mainly exposed sorts in this 7f handicap which was run at no more than a fair gallop. The second and third have been rated close to form.

5174 ARLO H'CAP — 1m 2f 43y
8:15 (8:16) (Class 4) (0-85,87) 4-Y-0+
£5,207 (£1,549; £774; £400; £400; £400) **Stalls** High

Form				RPR
0304	1		**Benadalid**[12] 4730 4-9-0 **78** JoeFanning 8	85
			(Chris Fairhurst) *hld up: hdwy 4f out: cl up 3f out: rdn to take slt ld wl over 1f out: drvn ins fnl f: hld on gamely towards fin* **13/2**	
-454	2	nk	**Autumn War (IRE)**[24] 4250 4-9-7 **85** KieranShoemark 6	91
			(Charles Hills) *hld up in rr: pushed along and hdwy over 2f out: rdn wl over 1f out: styd on strly fnl f: jst hld* **5/2**[2]	
133	3	nk	**Freerolling**[23] 4305 4-9-7 **85** TomMarquand 9	90
			(Charlie Fellowes) *sn led: pushed along 3f out: rdn over 2f out: hdd wl over 1f out: cl up and drvn ent fnl f: ev ch tl no ex towards fin* **2/1**[1]	
-020	4	nk	**Sputnik Planum (USA)**[36] 3811 5-9-6 **84** (t) AlistairRawlinson 2	89
			(Michael Appleby) *trckd ldng pair: hdwy and cl up 3f out: chal wl over 1f out: sn rdn: drvn ent fnl f: ev ch tl no ex towards fin* **6/1**[3]	
233-	5	3	**Fannie By Gaslight**[276] 8332 4-9-0 **78** CharlesBishop 1	77
			(Mick Channon) *trckd ldrs: hdwy on inner 3f out: rdn along to chse ldrs 2f out: drvn over 1f out: sn one pce* **7/1**	
1100	6	21	**Harbour Breeze (IRE)**[15] 4613 4-9-9 **87** (t) PaulMulrennan 4	44
			(Lucy Wadham) *trckd ldr: rdn along 3f out: wknd 2f out: sn bhd and eased (jockey said colt ran too freely)* **13/2**	

2m 11.79s (-0.51) **Going Correction** +0.175s/f (Good) **6** Ran SP% **115.4**
Speed ratings (Par 105): **109,108,108,108,105 89**
CSF £23.91 CT £44.34 TOTE £6.50: £3.30, £1.80; EX 20.30 Trifecta £63.90.
Owner Mrs Shirley France **Bred** P Balding **Trained** Middleham, N Yorks

FOCUS
Add 18 yards due to rail movements. This was a fair 1m2f 66-85 handicap but the pace wasn't strong and it produced a bunched finish.

5175 DONATE £5 TEXT FLY5 TO 70800 H'CAP — 1m 3f 197y
8:45 (8:46) (Class 5) (0-70,75) 3-Y-0
£3,428 (£1,020; £509; £400; £400; £400) **Stalls** Low

Form				RPR
6021	1		**Funny Man**[22] 4345 3-9-0 **63** (b) DanielTudhope 4	74+
			(David O'Meara) *hld up in rr: swtchd rt to outer and smooth hdwy 3f out: chsd ldrs 2f out: rdn to ld over 1f out: sn clr: readily* **11/4**[1]	
0054	2	1¼	**Menin Gate (IRE)**[19] 4443 3-8-10 **59** (p[1]) TonyHamilton 6	65
			(Richard Fahey) *hld up towards rr: hdwy 3f out: chsd ldrs 2f out: sn rdn: kpt on fnl f: no ch w wnr* **16/1**	
-642	3	3	**Bullion Boss (IRE)**[34] 3882 3-9-9 **72** (p) PaulMulrennan 3	73
			(Michael Dods) *trckd ldr: hdwy and cl up 3f out: rdn to take slt ld 2f out: drvn and hdd over 1f out: kpt on same pce* **7/1**	
0-06	4	hd	**Philonikia**[45] 3482 3-9-4 **67** KevinStott 8	68
			(Ralph Beckett) *trckd ldng pair: hdwy on inner 4f out: cl up 3f out: rdn and ev ch 2f out: sn drvn and kpt on same pce* **9/1**	
0032	5	3¾	**Born Leader (FR)**[21] 4372 3-8-5 **54** DavidEgan 5	49
			(Hughie Morrison) *in tch: hdwy over 3f out: rdn along over 2f out: sn drvn and kpt on one pce* **4/1**[2]	
0203	6	2¼	**Frequency Code (FR)**[7] 4914 3-8-12 **61** PJMcDonald 9	52
			(Jedd O'Keeffe) *chsd ldrs: rdn along over 3f out: sn drvn and wknd* **5/1**[3]	
362	7	2¾	**Cormier (IRE)**[42] 3585 3-9-7 **70** LiamKeniry 10	57
			(Stef Keniry) *hld up: hdwy and in tch 5f out: rdn along over 3f out: sn wknd* **7/1**	
-P05	8	2½	**Tribal Commander**[14] 4671 3-9-4 **67** KieranShoemark 11	50
			(Ian Williams) *in tch on outer: hdwy 4f out: rdn along to chse ldrs 3f out: sn drvn and wknd* **12/1**	
2165	9	2¼	**Cuban Sun**[30] 4034 3-9-9 **72** TomEaves 2	51
			(James Given) *led: rdn along 3f out: drvn and hdd 2f out: sn wknd* **25/1**	
0-00	10	38	**Tigerskin**[75] 2485 3-8-13 **62** BenCurtis 7	
			(Ralph Beckett) *a towards rr: rdn along over 4f out: sn outpcd and bhd (trainer's rep said gelding had a breathing problem)* **12/1**	

2m 35.49s (-1.11) **Going Correction** +0.175s/f (Good) **10** Ran SP% **123.4**
Speed ratings (Par 100): **110,109,107,107,104 103,101,99,98,72**
CSF £53.61 CT £294.07 TOTE £3.50: £1.60, £4.00, £2.40; EX 61.00 Trifecta £838.40.
Owner Apple Tree Stud **Bred** Apple Tree Stud **Trained** Upper Helmsley, N Yorks

FOCUS
Due to rail movements this 3yo handicap was run over 18 yards further than advertised. The pace was decent and the winner came from last to first. Sound form, with the third and fourth rated close to form.
T/Plt: £674.80 to a £1 stake. Pool: £76,711.26 - 82.98 winning units T/Qpdt: £101.70 to a £1 stake. Pool: £10,097.44 - 73.44 winning units **Joe Rowntree**

5124 HAYDOCK (L-H)
Saturday, July 20

OFFICIAL GOING: Good to soft (watered; 6.8)
Wind: light breeze Weather: sunny intervals, warm and pleasant

5176 RACINGTV.COM H'CAP — 7f 212y
6:00 (6:00) (Class 5) (0-75,77) 3-Y-0
£4,851 (£1,443; £721; £400; £400; £400) **Stalls** Low

Form				RPR
1131	1		**Mayfair Spirit (IRE)**[28] 4107 3-10-0 **77** (t) StevieDonohoe 9	84+
			(Charlie Fellowes) *trckd ldrs: pushed along to chal 2f out: sn drvn into ld: rdn in narrow ld 1f out: drifted lft but r.o wl fnl f* **9/4**[1]	
4-00	2	1	**Mutasaamy (IRE)**[50] 3306 3-9-6 **69** JackMitchell 2	73
			(Roger Varian) *mid-div: pushed along and hdwy 2f out: rdn in cl 2nd 1f out: carried lft fnl f: kpt on wl but a hld* **3/1**[2]	
0033	3	hd	**Power Player**[12] 4732 3-9-0 **68** HarrisonShaw(5) 5	72
			(K R Burke) *hld up: effrt and rdn 2f out: wnt 3rd 1f out: r.o fnl f* **14/1**	
023	4	2¼	**Military Tactic (IRE)**[26] 4196 3-10-0 **77** (p) HectorCrouch 10	76
			(Saeed bin Suroor) *chsd ldr: rdn and lost pl 2f out: 6th 1f out: kpt on into 4th fnl f* **10/3**[3]	
1540	5	¾	**Plumette**[22] 4316 3-9-6 **69** (t[1]) TrevorWhelan 7	66
			(David Loughnane) *slowly away: sn rcvrd to r in mid-div: drvn 2f out: sn rdn: one pce (jockey said filly was slowly away)* **25/1**	
20-0	6	nk	**Ugo Gregory**[29] 4080 3-8-12 **61** RachelRichardson 8	57
			(Tim Easterby) *led: pushed along in narrow ld 2f out: sn drvn and hdd: rdn and wknd over 1f out* **25/1**	
6	7	2	**Vivacious Spirit**[15] 4585 3-8-10 **62** ConorMcGovern(3) 6	54
			(Phillip Makin) *hld up: pushed along 3f out: rdn 2f out: no imp* **9/1**	
0000	8	6	**Andies Armies**[7] 4909 3-7-9 **51** oh6 (p) ElishaWhittington(7) 3	29
			(Lisa Williamson) *chsd ldr: drvn and lost pl over 2f out: sn rdn and wknd* **40/1**	
0305	9	10	**My Boy Lewis (IRE)**[11] 4761 3-9-2 **70** BenSanderson(5) 4	25
			(Roger Fell) *bhd: drvn and lost tch over 2f out* **6/1**	

1m 42.37s (-0.33) **Going Correction** +0.10s/f (Good) **9** Ran SP% **119.9**
Speed ratings (Par 100): **105,104,103,101,100 100,98,92,82**
CSF £9.36 CT £77.76 TOTE £3.40: £1.40, £1.50, £3.20; EX 12.90 Trifecta £80.90.
Owner J Soiza **Bred** Ringfort Stud Ltd **Trained** Newmarket, Suffolk

FOCUS
There was 3mm of rain after racing the previous evening, and the going was given as good to soft (GoingStick 6.8). Inner straight in use. Add 6yds. A fair handicap in which they came towards the stands' side rail in the straight, although the first two, who battled it out inside the final 2f, drifted away from it in the closing stages. A small pb from the second, with the third and fourth rated close to form.

5177 BRITISH STALLION STUDS EBF NOVICE STKS (PLUS 10 RACE) — 6f 212y
6:30 (6:32) (Class 4) 2-Y-O
£6,469 (£1,925; £962; £481) **Stalls** Low

Form				RPR
01	1		**Fred**[23] 4282 2-9-8 0 FrannyNorton 11	80
			(Mark Johnston) *mde all: rousted along fr wd draw to ld: 4 l ld 3f out: hld together in much reduced ld 2f out: rdn in narrow ld 1f out: r.o bravely u.p fnl f: jst hld on* **2/1**[1]	
	2	hd	**He's A Keeper (IRE)** 2-9-2 0 JackMitchell 9	73+
			(Tom Dascombe) *hld up in rr: pushed along 3f out: drvn and hdwy 2f out: rdn over 1f out: swtchd to stands' rail ent fnl f: r.o strly: tk 2nd last stride: jst failed to catch wnr* **14/1**	
0	3	nk	**Always Fearless (IRE)**[22] 4324 2-9-2 0 StevieDonohoe 5	73
			(Richard Hannon) *chsd ldr: drvn to chal 2f out: rdn in cl 2nd 1f out: kpt on fnl f: lost 2nd last stride* **20/1**	
	4	nk	**Tritonic** 2-8-13 0 FinleyMarsh(3) 1	72+
			(Alan King) *hld up: drvn 3f out: hdwy 2f out: rn green over 1f out: r.o wl fnl f: nvr nrr (jockey said colt took a false step inside the final furlong)* **50/1**	
	5	nk	**Tell Me All** 2-9-2 0 LukeMorris 4	72+
			(Sir Mark Prescott Bt) *chsd ldrs: shkn up in 4th 2f out: drvn and reminder over 1f out: kpt on fnl f* **4/1**[3]	
3	6	¾	**You're My Rock**[23] 4289 2-9-2 0 DavidNolan 3	69
			(Richard Fahey) *chsd ldrs: pushed along in cl 4th 2f out: rdn over 1f out: no ex fnl f* **5/1**	
0	7	¾	**Genever Dragon (IRE)**[71] 2594 2-8-13 0 JaneElliott(3) 8	68
			(Tom Dascombe) *mid-div: rdn over 2f out: r.o fnl f: hld whn nt clr run nr fin* **3/1**[2]	
	8	shd	**Mambo Nights (IRE)** 2-9-2 0 RossaRyan 10	67
			(Richard Hannon) *hld up: drvn 3f out: hdwy 2f out: reminder ent fnl f: kpt on* **12/1**	
	9	4½	**Two Sox** 2-9-2 0 RachelRichardson 6	55
			(Tim Easterby) *hld up: drvn and wknd over 2f out* **50/1**	
404	10	2½	**We Owen A Dragon**[28] 4106 2-8-11 0 CierenFallon(5) 2	48
			(Tom Dascombe) *mid-div: drvn and wknd 3f out* **20/1**	
5	11	1	**Danking**[19] 4456 2-9-2 0 HectorCrouch 7	45+
			(Alan King) *hld up: drvn 3f out: no imp whn hmpd 2f out (jockey said colt suffered interference in running)* **33/1**	

1m 28.77s (-0.53) **Going Correction** +0.10s/f (Good) **11** Ran SP% **125.7**
Speed ratings (Par 96): **107,106,106,106,105 104,104,103,98,95 94**
CSF £33.57 TOTE £2.20: £1.20, £3.80, £6.40; EX 25.20 Trifecta £356.70.
Owner The Burke Family **Bred** Normandie Stud Ltd **Trained** Middleham Moor, N Yorks

FOCUS
Add 6yds. They all finished in a bit of a heap as the field closed in on the long-time leader and those who had gone after him first.

5178 STEVE YARBOROUGH MEMORIAL H'CAP — 1m 2f 42y
7:00 (7:00) (Class 5) (0-75,77) 4-Y-0+
£4,851 (£1,443; £721; £400; £400; £400) **Stalls** Centre

Form				RPR
0544	1		**Indomeneo**[1] 5130 4-9-2 **73** ConnorMurtagh(3) 16	81
			(Richard Fahey) *trckd ldrs: chal and shkn up 2f out: rdn into ld over 1f out: 1 l ld ent fnl f: r.o: a holding runner-up* **5/1**[2]	
3-54	2	nk	**Statuario**[16] 4548 4-9-9 **77** LukeMorris 15	84
			(Richard Spencer) *trckd across fr wd draw to ld: drvn in narrow ld 2f out: hdd and rdn over 1f out: rallied u.p fnl f: a jst hld* **11/2**[3]	
6046	3	¾	**Remmy D (IRE)**[13] 4690 4-8-2 **56** (b) CamHardie 8	61
			(Jim Goldie) *mid-div: drvn 2f out: hdwy into 3rd over 1f out: rdn fnl f: r.o* **16/1**	
2530	4	hd	**Regal Mirage (IRE)**[7] 4913 5-9-2 **70** RachelRichardson 5	75+
			(Tim Easterby) *hld up: pushed along 2f out: rdn and hdwy over 1f out: swtchd and r.o wl fnl f: nvr nrr* **6/1**	
0360	5	1½	**Lucy's Law (IRE)**[30] 4036 5-8-1 **60** PaulaMuir(5) 7	62
			(Tom Tate) *mid-div: hdwy to trck ldrs 4f out: drvn 2f out: rdn in 4th 1f out: no ex fnl f (jockey said mare was slowly away)* **14/1**	
4500	6	2½	**Harbour Vision**[24] 4249 4-9-4 **72** FrannyNorton 3	69
			(Derek Shaw) *hld up: rdn in last 2f out: r.o fnl f but nvr a threat* **10/1**	
-001	7	½	**Gloweth**[43] 3541 4-8-6 **63** WilliamCox(3) 1	59
			(Stuart Kittow) *mid-div: rdn 2f out: no imp* **5/1**[2]	
0501	8	1	**Prevent**[16] 4561 4-9-8 **76** (p) JackMitchell 9	70
			(Ian Williams) *rrd and lost several l at s: sn rcvrd to go prom: cl 2nd 3f out: drvn 2f out: sn rdn and wknd (jockey said gelding reared as the stalls opened and was slowly away)* **4/1**[1]	
3020	9	2¼	**Elixsoft (IRE)**[22] 4333 4-8-8 **67** (p) BenSanderson(5) 13	56
			(Roger Fell) *hld up: hdwy 3f out: wknd fr 2f out* **16/1**	
0560	10	4	**Critical Thinking (IRE)**[11] 4767 5-9-0 **68** (tp) StevieDonohoe 11	49
			(David Loughnane) *mid-div: drvn and wknd 2f out* **14/1**	
610	11	6	**Tum Tum**[45] 3462 4-9-7 **75** (h) PhilDennis 2	44
			(Michael Herrington) *trckd ldr: lost pl 3f out: sn drvn and wknd* **10/1**	

2m 13.39s (2.59) **Going Correction** +0.10s/f (Good) **11** Ran SP% **126.3**
Speed ratings (Par 103): **93,92,92,92,90 88,88,87,85,82 77**
CSF £35.41 CT £428.62 TOTE £5.80: £2.30, £2.30, £5.10; EX 30.80 Trifecta £567.20.
Owner Middleham Park Racing LX **Bred** Hungerford Park Stud **Trained** Musley Bank, N Yorks

FOCUS
Add 28yds. A pretty open handicap. Straightforward form, with the third helping to set the level.

5179 DAVID FARRELL 40TH BIRTHDAY H'CAP (JOCKEY CLUB GRASSROOTS STAYERS' SERIES QUALIFIER) 1m 6f
7:30 (7:30) (Class 4) (0-80,82) 4-Y-0+

£7,115 (£2,117; £1,058; £529; £400; £400) Stalls Low

Form RPR
-516 1 **Follow Intello (IRE)**[32] [3973] 4-9-0 73 JackMitchell 11 80+
(Chris Wall) *hld up: hdwy 3f out: drvn into ld over 1f out: 1 l ld 1f out: rdn fnl f: r.o wl* 4/1[2]
-602 2 1 **Contrebasse**[21] [4370] 4-8-5 64 RachelRichardson 9 69
(Tim Easterby) *hld up: pushed along and hdwy 2f out: looking for room 1f out: rdn and r.o wl fnl f: hld nr fin* 14/1
-040 3 3/4 **Polish**[16] [4543] 4-9-7 80 HectorCrouch 3 84
(John Gallagher) *prom: led 1/2-way: drvn in narrow ld 3f out: rdn and hdd over 1f out: kpt on fnl f* 9/1
-335 4 2 3/4 **Archippos**[22] [4333] 6-9-0 73 PhilDennis 8 73
(Michael Herrington) *mid-div: pushed along 3f out: rdn 2f out: wnt 4th ent fnl f: sn no ex* 8/1
0-06 5 3/4 **Sarvi**[12] [4724] 4-8-9 68 CamHardie 12 67
(Jim Goldie) *hld up: drvn 3f out: nt clr run over 1f out: rdn fnl f: one pce* 33/1
31-6 6 nk **Beer With The Boys**[15] [4614] 4-8-12 71 FrannyNorton 7 70
(Mick Channon) *mid-div: rdn on stands' rail 2f out: wknd over 1f out* 5/1[3]
0-55 7 shd **Steaming (IRE)**[54] [3145] 5-8-5 69 CierenFallon(5) 5 68
(Ralph Beckett) *trckd ldrs: cl up and drvn 3f out: rdn 2f out: wknd over 1f out* 7/1
-101 8 1/2 **Buckland Boy (IRE)**[32] [3973] 4-8-13 72 StevieDonohoe 6 70+
(Charlie Fellowes) *dwlt losing several l: latched on to pack 1/2-way: pushed along and hdwy 3f out: drvn over 2f out: rdn over 1f out: wknd and eased fnl f (jockey said gelding dwelt in the stalls and was slowly away)* 7/4[1]
6-00 9 1/2 **Bill Cody (IRE)**[36] [3816] 4-8-5 67 (w) ConorMcGovern(3) 1 64
(Julie Camacho) *t.k.h: led: hdd 1/2-way: 2nd 4f out: drvn 3f out: sn rdn: wknd over 1f out* 20/1

3m 9.4s (4.80) **Going Correction** +0.10s/f (Good) 9 Ran SP% 121.0
Speed ratings (Par 105): **90,89,89,87,87 86,86,86,86**
CSF £60.94 CT £487.08 TOTE £4.90: £1.80, £3.20, £2.70; EX 44.90 Trifecta £383.20.
Owner Ms Aida Fustoq **Bred** Deerfield Farm **Trained** Newmarket, Suffolk

FOCUS
Add 52yds. Plenty were close enough 2f out but the winner always looked to have things in hand. Muddling form, but the winner has been rated as running a small pb, with the second rated close to his best.

5180 INTRODUCING RACINGTV H'CAP 5f
8:00 (8:01) (Class 4) (0-80,81) 3-Y-0+

£7,115 (£2,117; £1,058; £529; £400; £400) Stalls Centre

Form RPR
6000 1 **Spirit Power**[47] [3413] 4-8-7 61 oh2 PhilDennis 8 69
(Eric Alston) *prom: rdn to ld over 1f out: rdn clr fnl f: pushed out nr fin* 14/1
1031 2 1 1/4 **Somewhere Secret**[26] [4181] 5-8-10 64 (p) NathanEvans 5 68
(Michael Mullineaux) *slowly away: bhd and rdn 2f out: n.m.r over 1f out: in clr fnl f where str late run: tk 2nd last stride* 3/1[1]
10-0 3 shd **Louis Treize (IRE)**[77] [2412] 3-9-0 81 LukeMorris 4 83
(Richard Spencer) *hld up: drvn 2f out: hdwy over 1f out: rdn into 2nd fnl f: no ex nr fin: lost 2nd last stride* 7/2[2]
0000 4 nk **Brandy Station (IRE)**[16] [4555] 4-8-0 61 ElishaWhittington(7) 7 63
(Lisa Williamson) *chsd ldrs: drvn over 1f out: sn rdn: kpt on fnl f* 25/1
3363 5 1 1/2 **Red Stripes (USA)**[8] [4880] 7-8-7 61 oh6 (b) AndrewMullen 6 58
(Lisa Williamson) *led: drvn 2f out: rdn and hdd over 1f out: wknd fnl f* 12/1
0-05 6 hd **Arcavallo (IRE)**[14] [4625] 4-9-12 80 (p) DavidNolan 2 76
(Michael Dods) *mid-div: drvn 2f out: rdn over 1f out: no imp* 8/1
0003 7 2 **Quench Dolly**[28] [4105] 5-9-11 79 (b) HectorCrouch 10 68
(John Gallagher) *prom: drvn 2f out: rdn and wknd over 1f out* 9/2
3001 8 3/4 **Show Palace**[23] [4307] 6-9-6 74 (p) RossaRyan 9 60
(Jennie Candlish) *mid-div: pushed along 2f out: sn drvn: rdn and wknd fnl f (jockey said gelding ran flat)* 4/1[3]
0000 9 8 **Cox Bazar (FR)**[14] [4654] 5-9-10 78 (e) TrevorWhelan 3 35
(Ivan Furtado) *awkward leaving stalls and slowly away: a bhd (jockey said gelding took a false step)* 16/1

1m 0.24s (-0.16) **Going Correction** +0.10s/f (Good)
WFA 3 from 4yo+ 4lb 9 Ran SP% 120.6
Speed ratings (Par 105): **105,103,102,102,99 99,96,95,82**
CSF £58.48 CT £188.90 TOTE £19.00: £4.70, £1.60, £1.50; EX 84.80 Trifecta £482.10.
Owner The Selebians **Bred** Lordship Stud **Trained** Longton, Lancs

FOCUS
A fair sprint handicap. The second has been rated in line with his recent form.

5181 JOIN RACINGTV NOW FILLIES' H'CAP 5f
8:30 (8:33) (Class 5) (0-70,71) 3-Y-0+

£4,851 (£1,443; £721; £400; £400; £400) Stalls Centre

Form RPR
0401 1 **Aperitif**[36] [3801] 3-8-11 62 CameronNoble(3) 3 72+
(Michael Bell) *slowly away: bhd: pushed along and hdwy 2f out: rdn to ld over 1f out: rdn clr fnl f: pushed out nr fin* 9/4[1]
/63- 2 1 **Dandyman Port (IRE)**[16] [4571] 5-9-6 71 (b) PaddyHarnett(7) 11 77
(Des Donovan, Ire) *dwlt: bhd: pushed along and hdwy 1 1/2f out: rdn over 1f out where jockey lost whip: kpt on into 2nd fnl f* 10/1
0U00 3 3/4 **Red Allure**[26] [4182] 4-8-7 51 oh6 NathanEvans 8 54
(Michael Mullineaux) *unruly s and reluctant to enter stalls: prom: pushed along 2f out: cl up and rdn 1f out: kpt on fnl f* 16/1
3056 4 1/2 **Mininggold**[53] [3206] 6-9-7 70 (p) PaulaMuir(5) 5 71
(Michael Dods) *mid-div: hdwy 2f out: sn ev ch: rdn over 1f out: one pce* 8/1
-440 5 3/4 **Kodiac Dancer (IRE)**[12] [4731] 3-8-4 52 CamHardie 10 50
(Julie Camacho) *chsd ldrs: cl up and pushed along 2f out: rdn over 1f out: no ex fnl f* 14/1
0-06 6 1 **Marietta Robusti (IRE)**[80] [2296] 4-9-8 69 FinleyMarsh(3) 9 64
(Stella Barclay) *mid-div: rdn over 1f out: no imp* 25/1
0205 7 1 1/4 **Celerity (IRE)**[8] [4880] 5-8-5 52 (p) NoelGarbutt(3) 13 42
(Lisa Williamson) *hld up: hdwy 2f out: drvn and lost pl over 1f out: no ex* 20/1
504 8 nk **Mayfair Madame**[26] [4183] 3-8-6 57 WilliamCox(3) 12 45
(Stuart Kittow) *hld up: rdn 2f out: no imp (jockey said filly stumbled leaving the stalls)* 9/1
0044 9 3 1/4 **Lydiate Lady**[28] [4105] 7-9-2 60 RachelRichardson 7 38
(Eric Alston) *led: drvn and hdd over 1f out: wknd* 9/2[2]
3203 10 1 1/4 **David's Beauty (IRE)**[14] [4632] 6-9-1 59 (b) LukeMorris 4 32
(Brian Baugh) *prom: drvn and wknd 2f out* 13/2[3]
0000 11 1/2 **Lambrini Lullaby**[16] [4555] 4-8-5 52 oh6 ow1 (p[1]) ConorMcGovern(3) 1 23
(Lisa Williamson) *hld up: drvn 2f out: dropped away fnl f* 50/1
0062 12 2 **Teepee Time**[13] [4694] 6-8-7 51 oh4 (b) AndrewMullen 6 15
(Michael Mullineaux) *chsd ldrs: drvn and lost pl 2f out: dropped to last over 1f out: eased fnl f* 8/1

1m 0.28s (-0.12) **Going Correction** +0.10s/f (Good)
WFA 3 from 4yo+ 4lb 12 Ran SP% 126.7
Speed ratings (Par 100): **104,102,101,100,99 97,95,95,89,87 87,83**
CSF £27.93 CT £318.84 TOTE £3.00: £1.60, £3.60, £5.10; EX 33.70 Trifecta £475.50.
Owner Lordship Stud **Bred** Lordship Stud **Trained** Newmarket, Suffolk

FOCUS
Just an ordinary fillies' sprint, but the time was similar to the 0-80 that preceded it, and the winner is lightly raced and progressing.
T/Plt: £138.10 to a £1 stake. Pool: £70,714.85 - 373.79 winning units T/Qpdt: £45.20 to a £1 stake. Pool: £8,322.17 - 136.05 winning units **Keith McHugh**

5131 NEWBURY (L-H)
Saturday, July 20

OFFICIAL GOING: Soft (watered; 6.0) changing to good to soft after race 1 (1.50)
Wind: light across Weather: warm

5182 BET365 STKS (LISTED RACE) (REGISTERED AS THE STEVENTON STAKES) 1m 2f
1:50 (1:50) (Class 1) 3-Y-0+

£20,982 (£7,955; £3,981; £1,983; £995) Stalls Low

Form RPR
132 1 **Fox Chairman (IRE)**[30] [4013] 3-8-11 107 SilvestreDeSousa 1 113
(Andrew Balding) *hld up 4th: hdwy to chal over 2f out: led wl over 1f out: drifted lft ins fnl f: kpt on wl: rdn out (vet said colt lost its left fore shoe)* 8/13[1]
4116 2 1 **Pondus**[29] [4049] 3-8-11 98 OisinMurphy 4 111
(James Fanshawe) *trckd ldrs: rdn over 2f out: chsd wnr over 1f out: swtchd rt ins fnl f: styd on towards fin but a being hld* 7/2[2]
3503 3 3 1/2 **First Nation**[15] [4612] 5-9-6 106 JamesDoyle 6 104
(Charlie Appleby) *hld up 5th: rdn and stdy prog 2f out: styd into 3rd jst ins fnl f but nt gng pce of front pair* 6/1[3]
1-00 4 1 1/2 **Dolphin Vista (IRE)**[32] [3953] 6-9-6 108 RichardKingscote 2 101
(Ralph Beckett) *led: rdn and hdd wl over 1f out: kpt on same pce fnl f* 14/1
-204 5 10 **What About Carlo (FR)**[40] [3646] 8-9-6 96 TomMarquand 5 81
(Eve Johnson Houghton) *trckd ldr: rdn over 3f out: wknd 2f out* 25/1

2m 10.08s (0.38) **Going Correction** +0.575s/f (Yiel)
WFA 3 from 5yo+ 9lb 5 Ran SP% 108.9
Speed ratings (Par 111): **107,106,103,102,94**
CSF £2.95 TOTE £1.40: £1.20, £1.90; EX 2.80 Trifecta £5.30.
Owner King Power Racing Co Ltd **Bred** Manister House Stud **Trained** Kingsclere, Hants

FOCUS
Following 8mm of overnight rain on top of the 9mm which had fallen on Friday, the official going was described as soft. Going Stick 6.0 on Sat 8:00am. Add 7 yards. Older horses had the best recent record in this Listed contest but this looked an excellent opportunity for 3yo Fox Chairman to avenge his luckless Royal Ascot defeat. They were running into a headwind in the straight and the winner may have been in front plenty soon enough. The winning time was over 8sec slower than standard. The second, who has been credited with a pb, is possibly the key to the form, with the third rated close to his latest.

5183 MARSH CUP (H'CAP) 2m 110y
2:25 (2:27) (Class 2) 3-Y-0+

£62,250 (£18,640; £9,320; £4,660; £2,330; £1,170) Stalls Low

Form RPR
/10- 1 **Withhold**[269] [8566] 6-9-10 107 (p w) JasonWatson 12 116
(Roger Charlton) *mde all: shkn up over 1f out: pushed out and in command fnl f: styd on wl* 17/2[3]
65 2 1 3/4 **Billy Ray**[42] [3600] 4-8-6 89 DavidProbert 4 96
(Mick Channon) *mid-div: hdwy over 3f out: rdn to chse ldrs over 2f out: chsd wnr jst ins fnl f: styd on but a being hld* 14/1
2153 3 3 **Coeur De Lion**[21] [4381] 6-8-5 93 (p) ThoreHammerHansen(5) 6 96
(Alan King) *trckd wnr: chal 3f out: ev ch whn rdn 2f out: styd on same pce fnl f* 10/1
-321 4 shd **Who Dares Wins (IRE)**[21] [4382] 7-9-7 104 (p) TomMarquand 10 107
(Alan King) *hld up towards rr: pushed along for stdy prog fr 3f out: rdn over 2f out: styd on ins fnl f: wnt 4th cl home* 7/1[2]
3102 5 1/2 **Rare Groove (IRE)**[21] [4381] 4-8-13 96 PJMcDonald 3 99
(Jedd O'Keeffe) *trckd ldrs: rdn over 3f out: styd on same pce fnl 2f* 12/1
6033 6 1 1/2 **Proschema (IRE)**[21] [4382] 4-9-7 104 RichardKingscote 8 105
(Tom Dascombe) *mid-div: hdwy over 4f out: chal 3f out: sn rdn: ev ch 2f out: hld ent fnl f: no ex* 5/1[1]
1-01 7 nk **The Grand Visir**[32] [3952] 5-9-8 105 (t[1]) JamesDoyle 13 106
(Ian Williams) *mid-div: hdwy over 3f out: effrt over 2f out: nvr quite on terms: kpt on same pce fnl f* 7/1[2]
0-30 8 1 **Reshoun (FR)**[64] [2801] 5-8-12 95 (w) JimCrowley 7 94
(Ian Williams) *rdn over 2f out: a mid-div* 12/1
9 hd **Litterale Ci (FR)**[24] [3005] 6-8-6 89 JosephineGordon 9 88
(Harry Fry) *rdn over 2f out: nvr bttr than mid-div* 33/1
04 10 1 **Hermoso Mundo (SAF)**[14] [4670] 6-9-3 100 OisinMurphy 16 98
(Hughie Morrison) *racd keenly: hld up towards rr: hanging lft and little imp whn rdn over 1f out: nt pce to get involved* 33/1
60-0 11 2 1/4 **Temple Church (IRE)**[29] [4053] 5-8-13 96 AndreaAtzeni 15 91
(Hughie Morrison) *hld up towards rr: hdwy over 2f out: sn rdn: nvr threatened: wknd fnl f* 33/1
0306 12 1/2 **Jukebox Jive (FR)**[28] [4096] 5-8-8 91 (t) NicolaCurrie 2 86
(Jamie Osborne) *trckd ldrs: rdn over 2f out: wknd jst over 1f out* 50/1
2014 13 10 **Lucky Deal**[28] [4096] 4-9-6 103 FrannyNorton 14 86
(Mark Johnston) *a towards rr* 25/1
1460 14 18 **Making Miracles**[21] [4382] 4-9-10 107 SilvestreDeSousa 11 68
(Mark Johnston) *s.i.s: a towards rr* 10/1

The Form Book Flat 2019, Raceform Ltd, Newbury, RG14 5SJ

2111 **15** *13* **Carnwennan (IRE)**[21] 4381 4-8-11 **94**.......................... StevieDonohoe 5 39
(Charlie Fellowes) *mid-div: effrt over 2f out: sn wknd: eased whn btn (trainer said gelding was unsuited by the going which, in his opinion, was riding tacky having dried from soft earlier in the day)* **5/1**[1]

1002 **16** *1 3/4* **Al Kout**[17] 4505 5-8-3 **86**.......................... LukeMorris 1 29
(Heather Main) *racd keenly: trckd ldrs: rdn over 3f out: sn wknd (jockey said gelding stopped quickly)* **33/1**

3m 44.24s (-2.06) **Going Correction** +0.575s/f (Yiel) **16** Ran SP% **126.7**
Speed ratings (Par 109): **113,112,110,110,110 109,109,109,109,108 107,107,102,94,88 87**
CSF £118.95 CT £1234.45 TOTE £9.80: £2.70, £3.30, £2.40, £1.50; EX 247.90 Trifecta £1998.20.

Owner Tony Bloom **Bred** Millsec Limited **Trained** Beckhampton, Wilts

■ Stewards' Enquiry : Thore Hammer Hansen four-day ban: used whip above the permitted level (Aug 3-6)

FOCUS

The going was changed to good to soft after the opener. Add 7 yards. An ultra competitive and strong edition of this valuable staying handicap, which featured the last two winners the Northumberland Plate and this season's Northumberland Vase and Ascot Stakes scorers. They went a steady pace and Withhold ground them into submission from the front, providing his owner with back-to-back wins in the race. The form looks sound rated around the second, third and fourth.

5184 BET365 HACKWOOD STKS (GROUP 3) 6f

3:00 (3:03) (Class 1) 3-Y-O+

£34,026 (£12,900; £6,456; £3,216; £1,614; £810) **Stalls** Centre

Form RPR

5-21 **1** **Waldpfad (GER)**[17] 4534 5-9-10 106.......................... AndreaAtzeni 3 116
(D Moser, Germany) *hld up: hdwy over 2f out: led over 1f out: drifted rt fnl f: r.o wl: rdn out* **33/1**

1-10 **2** *1 3/4* **Khaadem (IRE)**[29] 4050 3-9-2 107.......................... JimCrowley 10 106+
(Charles Hills) *hld up: nt clr run wl over 1f out: hdwy ent fnl f: wnt 2nd fnl 100yds: r.o wl wout threatening to rch wnr* **13/2**[3]

1010 **3** *nk* **Keystroke**[28] 4094 7-9-10 109.......................... (t) PJMcDonald 6 109+
(Stuart Williams) *hld up: hdwy whn nt clr run jst over 1f out: chal for hld 2nd fnl 120yds: r.o* **33/1**

1-62 **4** *1* **Donjuan Triumphant (IRE)**[44] 3501 6-9-7 111....... SilvestreDeSousa 4 103
(Andrew Balding) *led: rdn and hdd over 1f out: kpt on same pce fnl f* **13/2**[3]

4005 **5** *1/2* **Barbill (IRE)**[9] 4847 3-9-2 98.......................... FrannyNorton 2 100
(Mick Channon) *trckd ldrs: effrt over 2f out: kpt on same pce fnl f* **16/1**

5-12 **6** *1 3/4* **Oxted**[63] 2826 3-9-2 105.......................... DavidProbert 7 95
(Roger Teal) *trckd ldrs: rdn and ev ch over 1f out tl ent fnl f: fdd fnl 100yds* **11/1**

0-36 **7** *hd* **The Tin Man**[28] 4094 7-9-7 116.......................... OisinMurphy 8 95
(James Fanshawe) *hld up: hdwy 3f out: rdn over 1f out: fdd fnl f* **6/4**[1]

6-00 **8** *nk* **Projection**[28] 4094 6-9-7 109.......................... (t[1]) JasonWatson 9 94
(Roger Charlton) *mid-div: rdn over 2f out: nvr any imp* **16/1**

1-31 **9** *1 1/2* **Snazzy Jazzy (IRE)**[34] 3891 4-9-7 110.......................... AdamKirby 5 89
(Clive Cox) *trckd ldrs: rdn over 2f out: wknd ent fnl f* **5/1**[2]

4201 **10** *19* **Recon Mission (IRE)**[35] 3865 3-9-2 104.......................... RobertWinston 1 27
(Tony Carroll) *prom: rdn over 2f out: wknd over 1f out: eased fnl f* **14/1**

1m 15.83s (2.63) **Going Correction** +0.575s/f (Yiel)
WFA 3 from 4yo+ 5lb **10** Ran SP% **116.0**
Speed ratings (Par 113): **105,102,102,100,100 97,97,97,95,69**
CSF £233.68 TOTE £35.90: £5.80, £2.30, £7.90; EX 225.40 Trifecta £6017.70.

Owner Gestut Brummerhof **Bred** Gestut Brummerhof **Trained** Germany

FOCUS

Triple Group 1 winner The Tin Man, a former winner of this race, topped the market for a strong renewal of this Group 3 sprint. However, victory went to the rank outsider of the party and improving German raider, Waldpfad. The likes of the fifth help set the level.

5185 WEATHERBYS SUPER SPRINT STKS 5f 34y

3:40 (3:41) (Class 2) 2-Y-O

£122,925 (£52,275; £24,600; £14,750; £9,825; £7,375) **Stalls** Centre

Form RPR

2211 **1** **Bettys Hope**[14] 4637 2-8-4 79.......................... SilvestreDeSousa 25 88
(Rod Millman) *hld up towards rr: rdn and stdy prog fr 2f out: r.o wl fnl f: led fnl stride* **14/1**

152 **2** *hd* **Show Me Show Me**[57] 3055 2-8-10 84.......................... PaddyMathers 21 93
(Richard Fahey) *mid-div: hdwy over 2f out: rdn to ld over 1f out: kpt on: hdd fnl stride* **33/1**

2262 **3** *1 1/4* **Mighty Spirit (IRE)**[15] 4583 2-8-9 92.......................... PJMcDonald 6 88
(Richard Fahey) *trckd ldrs: rdn and ev ch jst over 1f out: kpt on but hld ins fnl f* **6/1**[3]

112 **4** *1/2* **Ventura Rebel**[30] 4012 2-9-0 107.......................... PaulHanagan 7 91+
(Richard Fahey) *mid-div: rdn whn nt clr run briefly 2f out: hdwy over 1f out: kpt on ins fnl f: wnt 4th fnl 100yds* **5/4**[1]

6313 **5** *3/4* **Ocasio Cortez (IRE)**[25] 4221 2-8-4 74.......................... FrannyNorton 23 78
(Richard Hannon) *mid-div: hdwy over 2f out: rdn w ch over 1f out: sn drifted lft: kpt on same pce ins fnl f* **50/1**

6102 **6** *1/2* **Separate**[21] 4398 2-8-6 83.......................... AndreaAtzeni 24 78
(Richard Hannon) *trckd ldrs: rdn over 1f out: sn drifted lft: kpt on same pce fnl f* **14/1**

1640 **7** *3/4* **Electric Ladyland (IRE)**[31] 3988 2-8-6 87.......................... (p[1]) LukeMorris 4 76
(Archie Watson) *prom: overall ldr 2f out: sn rdn and drifted rt: hdd over 1f out: no ex fnl f* **20/1**

1 **8** *shd* **Never In Paris (IRE)**[14] 4659 2-8-8 0.......................... BenCurtis 14 77
(K R Burke) *trckd ldrs: rdn in cl 4th over 1f out: kpt on same pce fnl f* **5/1**[2]

1 **9** *3/4* **Odyssey Girl (IRE)**[9] 4840 2-8-2 0.......................... LiamJones 15 72
(Richard Spencer) *trckd ldrs: rdn whn tight for room and snatched up over 1f out: kpt on fnl f but no ch after* **33/1**

3343 **10** *1 3/4* **Audio**[10] 4798 2-8-10 75.......................... (t[1]) PatDobbs 9 70
(Richard Hannon) *hld up towards rr: hdwy over 1f out: kpt on fnl f but nt gng pce to get on terms* **33/1**

5 **11** *nk* **Dearly Beloved (IRE)**[15] 4583 2-8-7 0.......................... RowanScott 17 66
(Keith Dalgleish) *hld up towards rr: rdn and hdwy over 1f out: kpt on ins fnl f but nvr any threat* **100/1**

220 **12** *1/2* **Clay Regazzoni**[28] 4091 2-8-12 82.......................... JimCrowley 8 70
(Keith Dalgleish) *hld up towards rr: nt clr run and snatched up wl over 1f out: kpt on ins fnl f but nvr any threat* **33/1**

0434 **13** *1 1/4* **Bacchalot (IRE)**[31] 3990 2-8-4 64 ow2.......................... JohnFahy 16 57+
(Richard Hannon) *mid-div: nt best of runs over 1f out: kpt on whn in the clr fnl f but no ch* **150/1**

15 **14** *nk* **Emten (IRE)**[30] 4012 2-8-8 0.......................... NicolaCurrie 18 60+
(Jamie Osborne) *mid-div whn tight for room and lost pl after 1f: nvr bk on terms (jockey said filly suffered interference in running in the early stages)* **16/1**

2210 **15** *3/4* **Taxiwala (IRE)**[31] 3988 2-9-1 89.......................... (b) OisinMurphy 10 64
(Archie Watson) *in tch: rdn over 2f out: wknd fnl f* **20/1**

1303 **16** *4 1/2* **Manolith**[8] 4893 2-8-9 75.......................... JasonWatson 13 42
(David O'Meara) *racd keenly in mid-div: rdn 2f out: wknd jst over 1f out (jockey said colt ran too freely and hung left-handed)* **100/1**

310 **17** *1/2* **Charlemaine (IRE)**[31] 3988 2-8-6 0.......................... (p[1]) JosephineGordon 19 37
(Paul Cole) *disp ld tl rdn and hdd wl over 1f out: sn wknd* **80/1**

1042 **18** *3/4* **Baileys In Bloom (FR)**[10] 4780 2-8-3 73.......................... RoystonFfrench 20 32
(Richard Fahey) *disp ld tl rdn over 2f out: sn wknd (jockey said filly was restless in the stalls)* **33/1**

1055 **19** *1* **Great Dame (IRE)**[21] 4417 2-8-9 87.......................... DavidProbert 22 34
(David O'Meara) *chsd ldrs: rdn over 2f out: wknd over 1f out* **50/1**

435 **20** *1 1/4* **Dynamighty**[10] 4802 2-8-5 69.......................... SeanKirrane 1 25
(Richard Spencer) *rrd leaving stalls: sn mid-div: effrt 2f out: wknd fnl f (jockey said filly was slowly away)* **100/1**

33 **21** *shd* **Maybellene (IRE)**[86] 2052 2-8-2 0.......................... JimmyQuinn 5 22
(George Scott) *mid-div: rdn over 2f out: wknd ent fnl f* **66/1**

00 **22** *4* **Kyllwind**[9] 4826 2-9-0 0.......................... JamesDoyle 26 20
(Martyn Meade) *a towards rr* **80/1**

306 **23** *3 1/4* **River Of Kings (IRE)**[44] 3498 2-8-9 68.......................... FergusSweeney 3
(Keith Dalgleish) *mid-div tl wknd over 2f out* **150/1**

2133 **24** *21* **Daddies Diva**[35] 3835 2-8-0 74.......................... RaulDaSilva 2
(Rod Millman) *chsd ldr tl wknd over 2f out* **20/1**

1m 5.32s (3.82) **Going Correction** +0.575s/f (Yiel) **24** Ran SP% **135.8**
Speed ratings (Par 100): **92,91,89,88,87 86,85,85,84,81 81,80,78,77,76 69,68,67,65,63 63,57,52,18**
CSF £438.18 TOTE £17.70: £4.20, £8.90, £2.40; EX 588.70 Trifecta £6645.20.

Owner Mrs Louise Millman **Bred** Llety Farms **Trained** Kentisbeare, Devon

FOCUS

The market was dominated by last month's Norfolk Stakes second, but he failed to replicate that form and could finish only fourth in a competitive but not vintage renewal. They raced in two groups, the group towards the stands' side doing marginally best with horses drawn in stalls 25 and 21 leading home a pair of Fahey-trained runners from 6 and 7.

5186 BET365 EBF NOVICE STKS (PLUS 10 RACE) (C&G) 6f

4:10 (4:15) (Class 4) 2-Y-O **£4,625** (£1,376; £687; £343) **Stalls** Centre

Form RPR

43 **1** **Owney Madden**[24] 4252 2-9-0 0.......................... JasonWatson 5 83
(Martyn Meade) *little slowly away: sn mid-div: rdn and hdwy over 1f out: swtchd lft jst bef fnl f: r.o wl: led fnl 50yds (jockey said colt hung left and right-handed)* **17/2**

3 **2** *shd* **Written Broadcast (IRE)**[15] 4596 2-9-0 0.......................... AndreaAtzeni 12 83
(Richard Hannon) *trckd ldrs: rdn wl over 1f out: led ent fnl f: kpt on but no ex whn hdd fnl 50yds* **6/1**

3 *1/2* **Fox Duty Free (IRE)** 2-9-0 0.......................... SilvestreDeSousa 2 81+
(Andrew Balding) *bdly hmpd s: towards rr: swtchd out 2f out: hdwy over 1f out: r.o wl ins fnl f: wnt 3rd fnl 100yds: clsng on front pair at fin* **5/2**[1]

4 **4** *4* **Hello Baileys**[7] 4937 2-9-0 0.......................... OisinMurphy 9 69
(Mark Johnston) *trckd ldr: rdn and ev ch over 1f out: bmpd jst ins fnl f: no ex* **5/1**[3]

332 **5** *shd* **Good Earth (IRE)**[12] 4734 2-9-0 78.......................... NicolaCurrie 11 69
(Jamie Osborne) *led: rdn and hdd ent fnl f: sn no ex* **10/1**

6 *1 1/4* **Fantasy Believer (IRE)** 2-9-0 0.......................... PaulHanagan 3 65
(Charles Hills) *wnt bdly lft s: towards rr: rdn 2f out: no ch but kpt on fnl f* **20/1**

7 *1/2* **Station To Station** 2-9-0 0.......................... JamesDoyle 13 66
(Clive Cox) *in tch: gng wl enough in 4th 2f out but sn hanging bdly lft: unable to ride out fnl f (jockey said colt hung badly left-handed under pressure)* **16/1**

6 **8** *3* **Sir Oliver (IRE)**[64] 2792 2-9-0 0.......................... ShaneKelly 4 55
(Richard Hughes) *trckd ldrs: rdn over 2f out: wknd fnl f* **9/2**[2]

9 *3/4* **Optio** 2-9-0 0.......................... JimCrowley 6 52
(Brian Meehan) *mid-div: struggling 1/2-way: sn lost pl* **22/1**

10 *1/2* **Giuseppe Cassioli** 2-9-0 0.......................... RobertWinston 1 51+
(Charles Hills) *hmpd s: a towards rr* **20/1**

0 **11** *hd* **Timon (IRE)**[12] 4734 2-8-9 0.......................... ScottMcCullagh(5) 7 50
(Mick Channon) *mid-div: rdn over 2f out: wknd ent fnl f* **40/1**

65 **12** *37* **Dandy Dancer**[8] 4871 2-9-0 0.......................... FergusSweeney 14
(Richard Hughes) *racd keenly: mid-div: struggling over 2f out: wknd qckly* **33/1**

1m 17.1s (3.90) **Going Correction** +0.575s/f (Yiel) **12** Ran SP% **122.5**
Speed ratings (Par 96): **97,96,96,90,90 89,88,84,83,82 82,33**
CSF £56.52 TOTE £9.40: £2.90, £2.10, £1.60; EX 57.40 Trifecta £331.60.

Owner Chelsea Thoroughbreds - Owney Madden 1 **Bred** Simon W Clarke **Trained** Manton, Wilts

FOCUS

An informative race, the first two home showing the benefit of previous experience, ahead of a big eyecatcher in third. The form looks sound rated around the fourth and fifth.

5187 BRITISH EBF PREMIER FILLIES' H'CAP 1m (S)

4:45 (4:47) (Class 2) (0-100,99) 3-Y-O+

£18,675 (£5,592; £2,796; £1,398; £699; £351) **Stalls** Centre

Form RPR

4612 **1** **Sufficient**[9] 4828 3-8-4 **83**.......................... (h) JimmyQuinn 3 89
(Rod Millman) *hld up: pushed along and hdwy fr 2f out: sltly hmpd over 1f out: str chal ent fnl f: led narrowly fnl 75yds: hld on* **8/1**

-240 **2** *nse* **Pure Shores**[13] 4706 5-8-9 **80** oh1.......................... AndreaAtzeni 8 88
(Ian Williams) *trckd ldrs: led over 1f out: strly chal ent fnl f: kpt on w ev ch whn hdd fnl 75yds: jst hld* **5/1**[3]

6000 **3** *4* **Pattie**[11] 4758 5-9-7 **92**.......................... DavidProbert 7 94+
(Mick Channon) *in tch: making hdwy whn bdly hmpd over 1f out: kpt on into 3rd ins fnl f but no ch after* **10/1**

310 **4** *nk* **Bubble And Squeak**[42] 3581 4-9-6 **91**.......................... JasonWatson 9 89
(Sylvester Kirk) *hld up: hdwy 2f out: sn rdn: wnt 3rd briefly jst ins fnl f: kpt on same pce (jockey said filly hung right-handed)* **6/1**

6330 **5** *4 1/2* **Red Starlight**[31] 3987 4-10-0 **99**.......................... PatDobbs 2 87+
(Richard Hannon) *trckd ldrs: attempting to mount chal whn bdly hmpd over 1f out: nt pce to get bk on terms* **2/1**[1]

-104 **6** *3/4* **Divinity**[38] 3728 3-8-11 **90**.......................... CliffordLee 4 74
(K R Burke) *led: drifted bdly rt and hmpd over 1f out: sn hdd: fdd fnl f* **13/2**

1601 **7** ¾ **Daddies Girl (IRE)**[28] 4113 4-8-13 91 .... OliverSearle(7) 1 75
(Rod Millman) *trckd ldr tl rdn over 2f out: wknd jst over 1f out (jockey said filly hung right-handed)* **9/2**[2]

1m 43.62s (3.72) **Going Correction** +0.575s/f (Yiel)
WFA 3 from 4yo+ 8lb **7** Ran SP% **116.0**
Speed ratings (Par 96): **104,103,99,99,95 94,93**
CSF £48.34 CT £407.83 TOTE £7.60: £3.30, £2.40; EX 50.00 Trifecta £250.60.
Owner Whitsbury Manor Stud And Mrs M E Slade **Bred** Whitsbury Manor Stud And Mrs M E Slade **Trained** Kentisbeare, Devon
■ Stewards' Enquiry : Clifford Lee four-day ban: interference & careless riding (Aug 3-6)

FOCUS
The first two pulled clear as those in behind got in each other's way. The winner has been rated as improving in line with her Doncaster latest, with the third running as well as ever on turf.

5188 GRUNDON RECYCLING H'CAP 7f (S)
5:20 (5:20) (Class 2) (0-110,100) 3-Y-O+ **£12,938** (£3,850; £1,924; £962) **Stalls** Centre

Form RPR

0-50 **1** **Makzeem**[23] 4299 6-9-4 **98** ....(t) JasonWatson 8 108
(Roger Charlton) *hld up: gd hdwy to ld over 1f out: qckmd clr fnl f: comf* **6/1**[2]

00-5 **2** 4 **George William**[23] 4299 6-9-2 **96** .... AndreaAtzeni 5 95
(Ed Walker) *trckd ldrs: rdn to chse wnr over 1f out: kpt on but nt pce to get on terms* **3/1**[1]

4303 **3** 1 ½ **Cliffs Of Capri**[30] 4020 5-9-2 **96** ....(p) DougieCostello 6 91
(Jamie Osborne) *trckd ldrs: rdn 2f out: kpt on but nt pce to chal* **15/2**

0013 **4** 1 **Raydiance**[21] 4385 4-9-2 **96** .... CliffordLee 1 88
(K R Burke) *prom: rdn and ev ch 2f out tl over 1f out: kpt on same pce fnl f* **3/1**[1]

5/0- **5** shd **Yattwee (USA)**[555] 172 6-9-6 **100** .... AdamKirby 2 92
(Saeed bin Suroor) *prom: rdn to ld briefly 2f out: kpt on same pce ins fnl f* **6/1**[2]

5105 **6** ½ **War Glory (IRE)**[21] 4399 6-9-4 **98** .... PatDobbs 4 89
(Richard Hannon) *cl up: rdn wl over 1f out: sn one pce* **7/1**[3]

3000 **7** 3 ¼ **Glendevon (USA)**[23] 4292 4-9-2 **96** ....(h) ShaneKelly 3 78
(Richard Hughes) *hld up: rdn 2f out: no imp* **16/1**

-650 **8** 1 ½ **Fighting Irish (IRE)**[28] 4095 4-9-2 **96** .... JimCrowley 9 74
(Harry Dunlop) *led tl rdn 2f out: wknd ent fnl f* **10/1**

1m 29.48s (2.48) **Going Correction** +0.575s/f (Yiel) **8** Ran SP% **117.8**
Speed ratings (Par 109): **108,103,101,100,100 99,96,94**
CSF £25.18 CT £139.33 TOTE £7.10: £2.30, £1.50, £2.00; EX 20.70 Trifecta £247.80.
Owner D J Deer **Bred** D J And Mrs Deer **Trained** Beckhampton, Wilts

FOCUS
A weak race for the lofty grade, though it was a dominant performance from the winner, who was ending a lengthy losing run off a fair mark. The winner has been rated to last year' form.
T/Jkpt: Not Won. T/Plt: £1,574.20 to a £1 stake. Pool: £137,824.00 - 63.91 winning units T/Qpdt: £424.30 to a £1 stake. Pool: £10,271.18 - 17.91 winning units **Tim Mitchell**

5138 NEWMARKET (R-H)
Saturday, July 20

OFFICIAL GOING: Good (7.4)
Wind: medium, behind Weather: fine

5189 LETTERGOLD FILLIES' NOVICE AUCTION STKS (PLUS 10 RACE) 7f
2:05 (2:08) (Class 4) 2-Y-O **£5,175** (£1,540; £769; £384) **Stalls** High

Form RPR

3 **1** **Ananya**[23] 4295 2-8-7 0 .... BrettDoyle 8 84+
(Peter Chapple-Hyam) *hld up in tch towards rr: swtchd rt and effrt ent fnl 2f: hdwy u.p to chse ldr 1f out: led ins fnl f: sn clr and r.o v strly* **8/1**

64 **2** 4 ½ **Incognito (IRE)**[7] 4918 2-8-12 0 .... CallumShepherd 11 77
(Mick Channon) *chsd ldrs: nt clr run over 2f out: rdn and hdwy over 1f out: chsd ldrs 1f out: wnt 2nd wl ins fnl f: no ch w wnr* **13/2**[3]

2 **3** 1 ½ **Fromnowon (IRE)**[9] 4840 2-8-12 0 .... SeanLevey 10 74
(Richard Hannon) *in tch in midfield: clsd and nt clrest of runs ent fnl 2f: rdn and hdwy to ld over 1f out: hdd ins fnl f: sn outpcd: lost 2nd and wknd wl ins fnl f* **4/1**[2]

5 **4** 2 ½ **Wallaby (IRE)**[28] 4114 2-8-6 0 .... HayleyTurner 9 61
(Jonathan Portman) *t.k.h to post: in tch in midfield: struggling to qckn whn swtchd rt over 1f out: no ch w wnr but kpt on ins fnl f* **25/1**

5 ¾ **Gonna Dancealot (IRE)** 2-8-9 0 .... JFEgan 6 62
(Jane Chapple-Hyam) *w ldrs: pressing ldr and rdn 2f out: unable qck and outpcd ent fnl f: wknd ins fnl f* **16/1**

522 **6** ¾ **Blausee (IRE)**[21] 4366 2-8-7 71 .... PhilDennis 5 58
(Philip McBride) *w ldr tl led 3f out: rdn ent fnl 2f: hdd over 1f out: no ex and wknd ins fnl f* **7/1**

26 **7** 1 ½ **Mrs Dukesbury (FR)**[16] 4544 2-8-8 0 .... HollieDoyle 4 55
(Archie Watson) *in tch in midfield: effrt and hdwy to chse ldrs and drvn 2f out: unable qck ent fnl f: wknd ins fnl f* **10/1**

5134 **8** 4 **Brazen Safa**[39] 3689 2-9-0 76 .... CameronNoble(3) 12 54
(Michael Bell) *led tl 3f out: sn rdn and outpcd 2f out: lost pl and btn over 1f out: wknd ins fnl f* **7/1**

33 **9** ½ **Atmospheric**[24] 4254 2-8-13 0 .... HectorCrouch 7 48
(Clive Cox) *in tch in midfield: clsd and effrt 2f out: chsng ldrs but unable qck u.p over 1f out: sn btn and wknd ins fnl f (trainer's rep said filly became unbalanced when entering the dip)* **7/2**[1]

10 1 ½ **Magnificia (IRE)** 2-8-9 0 .... GeorgeWood 2 41
(Ed Dunlop) *wnt bdly rt leaving stalls: in tch in rr: rdn over 2f out: sn struggling and wl btn over 1f out* **50/1**

11 3 **Junvieve (FR)** 2-8-5 0 .... SeamusCronin(5) 3 34
(Richard Hannon) *towards rr: effrt and hdwy 3f out: no ex and lost pl over 1f out: fdd ins fnl f* **25/1**

1m 24.85s (-0.85) **Going Correction** -0.075s/f (Good) **11** Ran SP% **116.3**
Speed ratings (Par 93): **101,95,94,91,90 89,87,83,82,81 77**
CSF £57.43 TOTE £10.80: £3.10, £2.10, £1.80; EX 92.40 Trifecta £478.00.
Owner W Prosser **Bred** Moyns Park Estate And Stud Ltd **Trained** Newmarket, Suffolk
■ Tinuviel was withdrawn. Price at time of withdrawal 25/1. Rule 4 does not apply

FOCUS
Far side course used. Stalls: far side, except 1m2f & 1m4f: centre. There was a blustery tailwind, and after the opener winning jockey Brett Doyle said that the ground was on the fast side of good. A wide-margin winner of what was probably an ordinary race, in a time 1.85sec outside standard. The 2017 winner, Capla Temptress, went on to win a Grade 1 in Canada. The second and third have been rated near their pre-race marks.

5190 RIC AND MARY HAMBRO APHRODITE FILLIES' STKS (LISTED RACE) 1m 4f
2:40 (2:43) (Class 1) 3-Y-O+
£22,684 (£8,600; £4,304; £2,144; £1,076; £540) **Stalls** Centre

Form RPR

1-2 **1** **Dame Malliot**[44] 3495 3-8-5 0 .... HollieDoyle 2 111+
(Ed Vaughan) *stdd after s: hld up in last pair: swtchd rt and clsd 2f out: rdn to ld 1f out: styd on v strly and sn clr* **11/2**[3]

0-14 **2** 5 **Spirit Of Appin**[27] 4145 4-9-2 95 .... MartinDwyer 12 103
(Brian Meehan) *hld up in tch in midfield: clsd to join ldr 3f out: rdn to ld jst over 2f out: hdd 1f out: nt match pce of wnr and kpt on same pce ins fnl f* **20/1**

-103 **3** ¾ **Sparkle Roll (FR)**[30] 4014 3-8-5 106 .... KieranO'Neill 5 102
(John Gosden) *dwlt: t.k.h: sn rcvrd and wl in tch in midfield: effrt whn impeded 3f out: n.m.r over 2f out: hdwy and rdn to chse ldrs over 1f out: nt match pce of wnr and one pce ins fnl f* **7/4**[1]

1035 **4** 1 ¾ **Love So Deep (JPN)**[30] 4014 3-8-5 101 .... JFEgan 8 99
(Jane Chapple-Hyam) *in tch in midfield: clsd to chse ldr 3f out: rdn to chse ldr 2f out tl no ex 1f out: wknd ins fnl f* **12/1**

1-50 **5** 8 **Blue Gardenia (IRE)**[50] 3316 3-8-5 96 .... ShaneGray 9 89
(David O'Meara) *midfield: rdn 4f out: keeping on same pce whn squeezed for room and hmpd over 1f out: wl hld fnl f* **10/1**

-664 **6** shd **Magnolia Springs (IRE)**[42] 3586 4-9-2 96 .... CharlesBishop 1 86
(Eve Johnson Houghton) *hld up in tch: effrt 3f out: no imp u.p whn edgd lft over 1f out: wl hld fnl f* **20/1**

431 **7** 4 **Happy Hiker (IRE)**[63] 2838 3-8-5 86 .... HayleyTurner 11 80
(Michael Bell) *chsd ldrs tl clsd to press ldr 6f out: rdn 3f out: sn outpcd and struggling: edgd rt and btn over 1f out: wknd fnl f* **33/1**

-152 **8** hd **Dance Legend**[27] 4145 4-9-2 95 .... SeanLevey 4 79
(Rae Guest) *chsd ldrs: pressed ldr 6f out: rdn 3f out: sn struggling and lost pl 2f out: wknd fnl f* **10/1**

1 **9** ¾ **Kesia (IRE)**[71] 2566 3-8-5 0 .... NickyMackay 6 78
(John Gosden) *chsd ldr tl led over 6f out: rdn and hrd pressed 3f out: hdd jst over 2f out: hung rt and lost pl over 1f out: sn wknd (jockey said filly hung right-handed)* **5/1**[2]

21-6 **10** shd **Alexana**[56] 3096 4-9-2 86 .... DanielMuscutt 7 78
(William Haggas) *in tch: rdn 3f out: sn struggling and outpcd: wl btn over 1f out: wknd* **16/1**

21-4 **11** 10 **Skill Set (IRE)**[59] 2961 4-9-2 84 .... DaneO'Neill 10 62
(Henry Candy) *led tl over 6f: midfield and rdn 3f out: lost pl and bhd 1f out: wknd* **40/1**

30-5 **12** 66 **Four White Socks**[36] 3820 4-9-2 95 .... JamieSpencer 3
(Harry Fry) *stdd s: hld up in rr: eased over 1f out: virtually p.u ins fnl f: t.o (jockey said filly was never travelling)* **14/1**

2m 27.52s (-6.38) **Going Correction** -0.075s/f (Good) course record
WFA 3 from 4yo 11lb **12** Ran SP% **121.7**
Speed ratings (Par 108): **118,114,114,113,107 107,104,104,104,104 97,53**
CSF £117.09 TOTE £5.90: £2.30, £7.40, £1.10; EX 149.80 Trifecta £502.30.
Owner A E Oppenheimer **Bred** Hascombe And Valiant Studs **Trained** Newmarket, Suffolk

FOCUS
Add 21yds. This looked a competitive edition of this Listed event, but it produced a dominant winner. The first four finished clear and the winning time beat the record for the remeasured distance by just over a second, helped by the tailwind. The second has been rated in line with her Goodwood win, with the third below her Ribblesdale form.

5191 LYNN CUMMINGS H'CAP (JOCKEY CLUB GRASSROOTS SPRINT SERIES QUALIFIER) 6f
3:15 (3:16) (Class 4) (0-80,80) 3-Y-O+
£6,469 (£1,925; £962; £481; £300; £300) **Stalls** High

Form RPR

0012 **1** **Gold At Midnight**[14] 4651 3-9-3 **74** .... HollieDoyle 4 80
(William Stone) *sn led and mde rest: rdn over 1f out: drvn and forged ahd ins fnl f: styd on wl* **7/1**

4041 **2** ¾ **Suzi's Connoisseur**[28] 4123 8-9-10 **76** ....(v) JFEgan 1 81
(Jane Chapple-Hyam) *hld up in tch in last pair: effrt and hdwy over 1f out: drvn and kpt on ins fnl f: wnt 2nd towards fin* **5/1**[2]

3222 **3** ½ **Lethal Angel**[16] 4560 4-9-4 **70** ....(p[1]) MartinDwyer 6 73
(Stuart Williams) *broke wl: restrained and pressed wnr: rdn and ev ch over 1f out: no ex ins fnl f: kpt on same pce and lost 2nd towards fin* **6/1**[3]

1202 **4** 1 ¾ **Queen Of Burgundy**[14] 4660 3-9-6 **77** .... JoeyHaynes 5 74
(Christine Dunnett) *t.k.h: pressed ldng pair: effrt u.p over 1f out: no ex ins fnl f: wknd towards fin* **7/1**

6001 **5** ½ **Cartmell Cleave**[21] 4369 7-10-0 **80** .... TomEaves 3 76
(Ruth Carr) *stdd s: hld up in tch in last pair: swtchd lft over 2f out: effrt over 1f out: no imp and kpt on same pce ins fnl f: fin lame (vet said a post-race examination found the gelding to be lame on its left fore)* **13/8**[1]

1260 **6** 2 ¼ **Obee Jo (IRE)**[28] 4099 3-9-2 **73** .... RobHornby 2 61
(Tim Easterby) *wl in tch in midfield: unable qck u.p over 1f out: wknd ins fnl f* **5/1**[2]

1m 11.92s (-0.18) **Going Correction** -0.075s/f (Good) **6** Ran SP% **110.7**
WFA 3 from 4yo+ 5lb
Speed ratings (Par 105): **98,97,96,94,93 90**
CSF £39.42 TOTE £6.80: £2.90, £2.30; EX 46.40 Trifecta £90.70.
Owner Mrs Denis Haynes **Bred** Wretham Stud **Trained** West Wickham, Cambs

FOCUS
Just a fair sprint handicap. The second and third have been rated close to form.

5192 AFH WEALTH MANAGEMENT H'CAP 1m
3:50 (3:51) (Class 2) (0-105,100) 3-Y-O+ **£19,407** (£5,775; £2,886; £1,443) **Stalls** High

Form RPR

21 **1** **Indeed**[31] 3992 4-10-0 **100** .... LiamKeniry 4 112
(Dominic Ffrench Davis) *chsd ldrs tl shkn up to ld 2f out: rdn over 1f out: pressed ins fnl f: fnd ex and asserted towards fin: quite comf* **3/1**[1]

-420 **2** 1 ¼ **Thrave**[35] 3857 4-9-6 **92** .... DaneO'Neill 11 101
(Henry Candy) *chsd ldrs: effrt u.p ent fnl 2f: chsd wnr out: kpt on and pressing wnr ins fnl f: no ex and brushed aside towards fin* **9/2**[2]

The Form Book Flat 2019, Raceform Ltd, Newbury, RG14 5SJ

-003 **3** 4½ **Alternative Fact**[35] 3857 4-9-4 **90**........ JamieSpencer 7 89
(Ed Dunlop) *hld up in tch in last trio: effrt over 1f out: kpt on to go 3rd ins fnl f: no threat to ldng pair* **8/1**

-060 **4** 1 **Kuwait Currency (USA)**[30] 4017 3-9-0 **94**........ SeanLevey 1 88
(Richard Hannon) *racd away fr rivals: prom: ev ch 3f out tl unable to match pce of wnr wl over 1f out: wknd ins fnl f* **20/1**

4614 **5** 1 **Victory Command (IRE)**[7] 4919 3-9-3 **97**........ CYHo 8 89
(Mark Johnston) *in tch: effrt 3f out: outpcd wl over 1f out: no threat to ldrs but plugged on ins fnl f* **7/1**

0016 **6** hd **Via Serendipity**[14] 4666 5-9-10 **96**........(t) HayleyTurner 6 90
(Stuart Williams) *w ldr tl led ent fnl 3f: hdd 2f out and sn outpcd u.p: wknd ins fnl f* **10/1**

4103 **7** 2 **Apex King (IRE)**[23] 4299 5-9-4 **90**........ HollieDoyle 9 79
(David Loughnane) *sn led: hdd ent fnl 3f: outpcd u.p and btn over 1f out: wknd ins fnl f* **6/1[3]**

2111 **8** 4½ **Global Gift (FR)**[22] 4325 3-8-11 **91**........(h) GeraldMosse 2 68
(Ed Dunlop) *stdd s: hld up in last pair: effrt over 2f out: nvr threatened to get on terms: wknd ins fnl f (trainer said gelding was unsuited by the going and would prefer an easier surface)* **9/2[2]**

0010 **9** 1 **Circus Couture (IRE)**[31] 3987 7-9-11 **97**........(v) JFEgan 3 73
(Jane Chapple-Hyam) *hld up in tch in last trio: effrt over 2f out: nvr threatened to get on terms: wknd ins fnl f* **33/1**

1m 36.94s (-3.06) **Going Correction** -0.075s/f (Good)
WFA 3 from 4yo+ 8lb **9** Ran SP% **116.1**
Speed ratings (Par 109): **112,110,106,105,104 104,102,97,96**
CSF £16.48 CT £98.16 TOTE £3.70: £1.60, £2.00, £2.60; EX 18.70 Trifecta £124.10.
Owner Marchwood Aggregates **Bred** Juddmonte Farms Ltd **Trained** Lambourn, Berks

FOCUS
Two finished nicely clear in this warm handicap. The level is a bit fluid.

5193 EUNISURE NOVICE STKS 7f
4:25 (4:25) (Class 4) 3-Y-0+ **£5,563** (£1,655; £827; £413) **Stalls** High

Form RPR

03 **1** **Torochica**[56] 3067 3-9-0 0........ KierenFox 7 84
(John Best) *mde all: rdn 2f out: drvn and forged 2 l clr 1f out: pressed wl ins fnl f: a jst doing enough towards fin* **7/1[3]**

03 **2** hd **Alnaseem**[21] 4405 3-9-0 0........(h[1]) EoinWalsh 10 83
(Luke McJannet) *stdd s: hld up off the pce in rr: clsd 3f out: chsd ldng pair and rdn over 1f out: kpt on to go 2nd ins fnl f: kpt on and clsd but nvr quite getting to wnr (jockey said filly ran green)* **25/1**

2201 **3** 2¾ **King Ademar (USA)**[12] 4738 3-9-5 95........ RobHornby 6 81
(Martyn Meade) *chsd wnr: effrt 2f out: drvn and little rspnse over 1f out: sn hung lft and btn: lost 2nd ins fnl f and eased towards fin* **4/11[1]**

00 **4** 11 **Eventura**[12] 4738 3-9-0 0........ BrettDoyle 11 46
(Tony Carroll) *midfield: effrt whn bmpd and pushed lft over 2f out: no threat to ldrs after: plugged on u.p to go modest 4th ins fnl f (jockey said filly suffered interference)* **100/1**

5 **5** 5 **Lope Scholar (IRE)**[15] 4592 3-9-0 0........ SeanLevey 8 33
(Ralph Beckett) *chsd ldrs: rdn 3f out: dropped away and btn over 1f out: fdd ins fnl f: burst blood vessel (vet said filly had bled from the nose)* **3/1[2]**

00 **6** 2¼ **Cinzento (IRE)**[19] 4452 3-9-5 0........ CallumShepherd 5 32
(Stuart Williams) *s.i.s: bhd: rdn and struggling 4f out: n.d after: plugged on to pass btn horses fnl f* **40/1**

00 **7** 1¼ **Interrogator (IRE)**[15] 4590 3-9-5 0........ JoeyHaynes 9 28
(Alan Bailey) *midfield: rdn and jst getting outpcd whn hmpd over 2f out: wknd over 1f out (jockey said gelding suffered interference)* **100/1**

8 1 **Knightfall** 3-9-5 0........ DanielMuscutt 1 26
(David Lanigan) *rn green and sn wl bhd: plugged on to pass btn horses ins fnl f: nvr involved (jockey said colt ran green early on)* **7/1[3]**

9 9 **Goldfox Grey** 3-9-0 0........ SeamusCronin(5) 4
(Robyn Brisland) *wnt rt s: midfield: 4th and outpcd 3f out: wnt bdly lft u.p over 2f out: no ch after: eased ins fnl f* **50/1**

50 **10** 2¼ **Sleepdancer (IRE)**[2] 5103 3-9-0 0........ DarraghKeenan(5) 2
(John Ryan) *midfield: struggling u.p 3f out: sn outpcd: wl bhd ins fnl f* **28/1**

0 **11** 10 **Maryellen**[15] 4590 3-9-0 0........ JFEgan 3
(Alan Bailey) *bmpd and hmpd s: sn rcvrd and in tch in midfield: rdn 3f out: sn struggling and steadily lost pl: wl bhd ins fnl f: t.o* **66/1**

1m 24.63s (-1.07) **Going Correction** -0.075s/f (Good) **11** Ran SP% **138.5**
Speed ratings (Par 105): **103,102,99,87,81 78,77,76,65,63 51**
CSF £166.49 TOTE £13.70: £2.10, £6.10, £1.10; EX 225.80 Trifecta £890.80.
Owner A Graham - Bankruptcy Trustee M Stanley **Bred** Petches Farm Ltd **Trained** Oad Street, Kent

FOCUS
A pretty weak event, especially with the favourite not giving his running. The level is a bit fluid.

5194 AFH COMMERCIAL & GENERAL H'CAP 1m 2f
5:00 (5:03) (Class 3) (0-90,92) 3-Y-0 **£9,056** (£2,695; £1,346; £673) **Stalls** Centre

Form RPR

3521 **1** **Ironclad**[32] 3958 3-9-2 **81**........ PatCosgrave 4 92+
(Hugo Palmer) *chsd ldr: effrt 2f out: upsides and u.p over 1f out: led 1f out: styd on wl: rdn out* **9/2**

2-21 **2** ¾ **Durrell**[42] 3584 3-9-5 **84**........ DanielMuscutt 2 93+
(James Fanshawe) *t.k.h: led: rdn 2f out: hdd 1f out: kpt on but a hld ins fnl f* **5/2[2]**

1121 **3** 3¾ **Cardano (USA)**[21] 4392 3-9-4 **83**........(p) JamieSpencer 5 84
(Ian Williams) *hld up in tch in rr: swtchd lft and effrt u.p over 1f out: chsd ldrs and no imp u.p over 1f out: wl hld and kpt on same pce ins fnl f* **4/1[3]**

354 **4** 2¾ **Target Zone**[63] 2833 3-9-13 **92**........ GeraldMosse 6 88
(David Elsworth) *chsd ldng pair and styd wd early: effrt 3f out: edgd lft u.p and unable qck over 1f out: lost 3rd and wknd ins fnl f* **12/1**

2-31 **5** 39 **Qarasu (IRE)**[40] 3664 3-9-6 **85**........ AdamMcNamara 3 80+
(Roger Charlton) *hld up in tch in last pair: effrt 3f out: cl enough but struggling to qckn whn nudged lft over 1f out: btn whn rdr looked down jst over 1f out: sn heavily eased and virtually p.u fnl f (trainer said colt was unsuited by the going and would prefer more cut in the ground)* **7/4[1]**

2m 6.25s (-0.85) **Going Correction** -0.075s/f (Good) **5** Ran SP% **110.8**
Speed ratings (Par 104): **100,99,96,94,63**
CSF £16.09 TOTE £4.40: £1.80, £1.90; EX 14.40 Trifecta £34.50.
Owner K Abdullah **Bred** Juddmonte Farms Ltd **Trained** Newmarket, Suffolk

FOCUS
Add 21yds. A good little handicap featuring some progressive 3yos. The third has been rated a little below his recent C&D win.

5195 SAMANTHA COPPER H'CAP 7f
5:35 (5:35) (Class 3) (0-90,89) 3-Y-0+ **£9,056** (£2,695; £1,346; £673) **Stalls** High

Form RPR

3221 **1** **Qutob (IRE)**[15] 4590 3-9-2 **84**........ DaneO'Neill 7 90
(Charles Hills) *mde all: rdn over 1f out: all out towards fin: jst lasted home* **11/4[2]**

4006 **2** shd **Deep Intrigue**[14] 4654 3-9-7 **89**........ JFEgan 6 94
(Mark Johnston) *chsd ldrs: wnt 2nd after 2f: drvn over 1f out: edgd lft ent fnl f and lost 2nd jst ins fnl f: swtchd rt and rallied to chse wnr again wl ins fnl f: styd on wl: jst hld (jockey said colt hung left-handed down the hill)* **6/1**

1114 **3** ½ **Glenn Coco**[14] 4654 5-9-10 **85**........(t) SeanLevey 4 91
(Stuart Williams) *chsd ldrs: effrt 2f out: drvn over 1f out: chsd wnr jst ins fnl f: kpt on but lost 2nd wl ins fnl f* **5/1[3]**

-041 **4** 2¼ **Daddy's Daughter (CAN)**[34] 3892 4-9-8 **83**........(h) RobHornby 8 89+
(Dean Ivory) *chsd wnr for 2f: wl in tch in midfield after: effrt 2f out: 4th and keeping on same pce whn squeezed for room and hmpd 1f out: no imp after (jockey said filly suffered interference)* **9/4[1]**

1254 **5** ½ **Right Action**[36] 3813 5-9-8 **83**........ HayleyTurner 3 82
(Richard Fahey) *racd away fr rivals: chsd ldrs early: in tch in midfield and rdn 3f out: edgd lft and no imp over 1f out: kpt on same pce ins fnl f* **11/2**

0500 **6** 1½ **Haddaf (IRE)**[61] 2910 4-9-4 **84**........(t[1]) JamieSpencer 5 79
(Stuart Williams) *stdd s: hld up in tch in last pair: effrt 2f out: no imp over 1f out: kpt on same pce ins fnl f* **14/1**

5130 **7** ½ **Central City (IRE)**[84] 2095 4-9-1 **83**........(p) RPWalsh(7) 2 77
(Ian Williams) *stdd s: hld up in tch in last pair: effrt 2f out: drifted rt and no hdwy u.p over 1f out: wl hld and one pce fnl f* **25/1**

1m 24.55s (-1.15) **Going Correction** -0.075s/f (Good)
WFA 3 from 4yo+ 7lb **7** Ran SP% **114.3**
Speed ratings (Par 107): **103,102,102,99,87 97,96**
CSF £19.47 CT £77.46 TOTE £3.30: £2.00, £2.60; EX 15.60 Trifecta £83.40.
Owner Hamdan Al Maktoum **Bred** Max Morris **Trained** Lambourn, Berks

FOCUS
Decent handicap form. A small pb from the winner, with the second running his best turf race and the third helping to set the level.
T/Plt: £54.20 to a £1 stake. Pool: £87,038.25 - 1,171.48 winning units T/Qpdt: £15.90 to a £1 stake. Pool: £5,482.06 - 255.0 winning units **Steve Payne**

4984 RIPON (R-H)
Saturday, July 20

OFFICIAL GOING: Good (watered; 8.0)
Wind: fresh variable Weather: cloudy

5196 DOBSONS GASKETS (S) STKS 6f
1:45 (1:46) (Class 6) 2-Y-0
£3,105 (£924; £461; £300; £300; £300) **Stalls** High

Form RPR

5366 **1** **Isobar Wind (IRE)**[41] 3634 2-9-0 68........(v[1]) DanielTudhope 6 69+
(David Evans) *mde all: pushed clr over 1f out: kpt on wl* **13/2[3]**

1361 **2** 6 **Calippo (IRE)**[14] 4652 2-8-7 76........(p) Pierre-LouisJamin(7) 10 51
(Archie Watson) *hld up in midfield: swtchd rt to outside over 2f out: rdn and hdwy over 1f out: wnt 2nd ins fnl f: kpt on but no ch w wnr* **8/11[1]**

0000 **3** 1 **Beautrix**[11] 4756 2-8-9 50........ ConnorBeasley 3 43
(Michael Dods) *pressed ldr: rdn and outpcd over 1f out: one pce in 3rd ins fnl f* **20/1**

6402 **4** ¾ **Classy Lady**[29] 4075 2-8-7 62 ow1........ BenRobinson(3) 1 42
(Ollie Pears) *prom on outer: rdn over 2f out: outpcd over 1f out* **5/1[2]**

4250 **5** ½ **Gin Gembre (FR)**[14] 4647 2-8-9 69........(v[1]) HarrisonShaw(5) 2 44
(K R Burke) *dwlt: sn trckd ldrs: rdn and edgd lft over 1f out: sn outpcd* **10/1**

0 **6** ½ **Now I'm A Believer**[11] 4750 2-8-9 0........ DavidEgan 9 38
(Mick Channon) *hld up: rdn along 2f out: kpt on ins fnl f: nvr threatened* **16/1**

00 **7** 3¾ **Fulbeck Rose**[29] 4075 2-8-9 0........(t) LewisEdmunds 5 27
(Nigel Tinkler) *s.i.s: hld up: nvr threatened* **50/1**

0604 **8** 3¼ **Comeatchoo (IRE)**[10] 4778 2-9-0 59........ DuranFentiman 4 22
(Tim Easterby) *trckd ldrs: rdn over 2f out: wknd over 1f out* **33/1**

0365 **9** 2¼ **Bob's Oss (IRE)**[14] 4652 2-8-11 63........(v[1]) SeanDavis(3) 8 15
(John Quinn) *midfield: rdn over 2f out: wknd over 1f out* **20/1**

1m 12.15s (-0.35) **Going Correction** -0.10s/f (Good) **9** Ran SP% **117.3**
Speed ratings (Par 92): **98,90,88,87,87 86,81,77,74**
CSF £11.40 TOTE £7.00: £1.80, £1.10, £5.60; EX 14.30 Trifecta £150.10.There was no bid for the winner.
Owner E R Griffiths **Bred** Eric Griffiths **Trained** Pandy, Monmouths

FOCUS
All distances as advertised. A fair seller. Three of the runners sported first-time headgear, and the race developed down the stands' side with the winner pulling clear.

5197 BRITISH STALLION STUDS EBF MAIDEN STKS (PLUS 10 RACE) 5f
2:20 (2:20) (Class 4) 2-Y-0 **£5,175** (£1,540; £769; £384) **Stalls** High

Form RPR

4 **1** **Cloudea (IRE)**[27] 4142 2-9-0 0........ TonyHamilton 7 76+
(Richard Fahey) *mde all: pushed along over 1f out: kpt on wl to draw clr fnl f* **7/2[2]**

2 **2** 4½ **Enjoy The Moment**[7] 4903 2-9-0 0........ DavidEgan 4 60
(Mick Channon) *chsd ldrs: rdn 2f out: kpt on same pce: no ch w wnr fnl f* **7/1**

05 **3** nk **With Virtue**[22] 4337 2-9-0 0........ KieranShoemark 2 59
(James Tate) *bmpd sltly s: in tch on outer: pushed along over 1f out: kpt on ins fnl f* **12/1**

423 **4** nk **Mecca's Hot Steps**[54] 3156 2-9-0 71........ PaulMulrennan 5 58
(Michael Dods) *chsd ldrs: rdn 2f out: one pce fnl f* **13/8[1]**

5 1½ **Augustus Caesar (USA)** 2-9-5 0........ DanielTudhope 1 57
(David O'Meara) *dwlt sltly and carried rt s: sn on wd outside: swtchd lft after 1f: hld up: pushed along 2f out: kpt on ins fnl f* **4/1[3]**

55 **6** nk **Interrupted Dream**[23] 4290 2-9-5 0........ JoeFanning 6 56
(Mark Johnston) *pressed ldr: rdn 2f out: no ex ins fnl f* **6/1**

7 15 **Petite Steps (IRE)** 2-8-9 0 .... DMSimmonson(5) 3
(Miss Katy Brown, Ire) *s.i.s: hld up: rdn over 2f out: sn wknd* 25/1
59.01s (-0.39) **Going Correction** -0.10s/f (Good) 7 Ran SP% 118.6
Speed ratings (Par 96): **99,91,91,90,88 87,63**
CSF £29.25 TOTE £4.20: £2.30, £2.00; EX 21.60 Trifecta £171.60.
Owner Richard Fahey Ebor Racing Club Ltd **Bred** Mrs Jacqueline Norris **Trained** Musley Bank, N Yorks

FOCUS
A moderate juvenile maiden for sprinters, and as in the opener the action developed down the stands' side with the winner pulling away from the best draw.

5198 SKY BET GO-RACING-IN-YORKSHIRE SUMMER FESTIVAL H'CAP 1m 1f 170y
2:55 (2:55) (Class 4) (0-80,81) 3-Y-O+
£6,016 (£1,790; £894; £447; £300; £300) Stalls Low

Form RPR
045 1 **Cockalorum (IRE)**[13] 4689 4-9-11 **78** .... DavidEgan 1 89+
(Roger Fell) *trckd ldrs: pushed along 3f out: n.m.r on inner tl swtchd lft appr fnl f: rdn to ld 110yds out: styd on wl to draw clr* 11/4[1]
241 2 2 ¼ **Billy Roberts (IRE)**[14] 4627 6-9-3 **70** .... ConnorBeasley 6 75
(Richard Whitaker) *trckd ldrs: rdn to chal 2f out: drvn to ld appr fnl f: hdd 110yds out: one pce* 9/2[2]
2-01 3 nk **Stagehand**[12] 4732 3-9-2 **78** .... KieranShoemark 3 82
(Charles Hills) *led: rdn and pressed 2f out: hdd appr fnl f: one pce* 11/4[1]
4133 4 9 **Amadeus Grey (IRE)**[12] 4723 3-9-5 **81** ....(t) DuranFentiman 4 67
(Tim Easterby) *prom: rdn 3f out: wknd over 1f out* 13/2[3]
0013 5 4 ½ **Dutch Uncle**[30] 4035 7-9-8 **78** ....(p) SeanDavis(3) 8 55
(Tom Clover) *hld up: rdn 3f out: sn btn* 20/1
5405 6 nk **Delph Crescent (IRE)**[16] 4548 4-9-8 **75** ....(p) TonyHamilton 7 51
(Richard Fahey) *midfield: rdn over 3f out: wknd 2f out* 12/1
0-10 7 3 ½ **Briardale (IRE)**[29] 4057 7-9-6 **73** .... DanielTudhope 2 42
(James Bethell) *hld up: pushed along over 3f out: rdn over 2f out: wknd (jockey said gelding stopped quickly)* 7/1
22-3 8 4 ½ **Snowdon**[46] 3449 4-9-8 **75** ....(p[1]) AndrewMullen 5 35
(Michael Dods) *midfield: rdn over 3f out: sn wknd (vet said a post-race examination revealed the filly to be in season)* 10/1
2m 1.97s (-2.63) **Going Correction** -0.10s/f (Good) 8 Ran SP% 118.9
WFA 3 from 4yo+ 9lb
Speed ratings (Par 105): **106,104,103,96,93 92,90,86**
CSF £16.07 CT £37.36 TOTE £3.50: £1.30, £2.10, £1.20; EX 18.40 Trifecta £95.80.
Owner H Dean & R Fell **Bred** Jim Bradley **Trained** Nawton, N Yorks

FOCUS
Three-year-olds had won four of the last six runnings of this interesting handicap, but it was a 4yo who came out on top this time around. The first three pulled clear and the form looks solid. The second has been rated to his best over the past year.

5199 RIPON BELL-RINGER H'CAP 1m 4f 10y
3:30 (3:30) (Class 2) (0-100,97) 3-Y-O+
£15,562 (£4,660; £2,330; £1,165; £582; £292) Stalls Centre

Form RPR
2050 1 **Everything For You (IRE)**[14] 4646 5-9-7 **90** ....(p) KevinStott 7 98
(Kevin Ryan) *trckd ldrs: rdn over 2f out: styd on fnl f: led towards fin* 7/1
0030 2 nk **My Reward**[28] 4102 7-9-4 **87** .... ConnorBeasley 4 94
(Tim Easterby) *led narrowly: drvn 2f out: styd on but hdd towards fin* 9/1
1640 3 ¾ **Fayez (IRE)**[7] 4935 5-9-12 **95** .... DanielTudhope 2 101+
(David O'Meara) *stdd s: hld up: hdwy gng wl whn short of room 2f out: swtchd lft ent fnl f: kpt on: wnt 3rd towards fin (jockey said gelding was denied a clear run inside 2f out)* 3/1[1]
1150 4 shd **Charles Kingsley**[14] 4646 4-10-0 **97** .... JoeFanning 9 103+
(Mark Johnston) *prom: rdn over 2f out: drvn over 1f out: keeping on in 3rd whn n.m.r towards fin: lost 3rd post* 5/1[2]
2442 5 ¾ **Mutamaded (IRE)**[5] 4988 6-9-1 **84** .... JamesSullivan 1 91+
(Ruth Carr) *trckd ldrs: pushed along over 2f out: persistently short of room on inner fnl 2f (jockey said gelding was denied a clear run approaching the final furlong)* 11/2[3]
3522 6 ¾ **Jabbaar**[2] 5097 6-9-3 **86** .... LewisEdmunds 3 89
(Iain Jardine) *dwlt: sn midfield: pushed along and nt much 2f out: rdn appr fnl f: kpt on* 7/1
-320 7 2 ¼ **Koeman**[14] 4646 5-9-13 **96** .... DavidEgan 8 95
(Mick Channon) *midfield: pushed along over 3f out: rdn over 2f out: no imp* 5/1[2]
0-00 8 5 **Daawy (IRE)**[38] 3726 5-8-12 **86** ....(p) PaulaMuir(5) 5 77
(Roger Fell) *hld up in midfield: rdn over 2f out: wknd over 1f out* 22/1
/450 9 17 **Cohesion**[21] 4382 6-9-11 **94** .... KieranShoemark 6 58
(David Bridgwater) *a in rr (jockey said gelding lost its action)* 33/1
2m 34.51s (-1.79) **Going Correction** -0.10s/f (Good) 9 Ran SP% 116.0
Speed ratings (Par 109): **101,100,100,100,99 99,97,94,83**
CSF £68.20 CT £229.96 TOTE £6.80: £2.20, £2.30, £1.80; EX 66.50 Trifecta £447.50.
Owner T A Rahman **Bred** Highbank Stud Llp **Trained** Hambleton, N Yorks

FOCUS
Two of the last runnings went to an improving 3yo, but there weren't any present this time around and it was slowly-run, the runner-up almost making all. There were a few hard-luck stories.

5200 RAMSDENS CURRENCY - BEST RATES GUARANTEED H'CAP 1m
4:05 (4:05) (Class 4) (0-85,92) 3-Y-O+
£6,339 (£1,886; £942; £471; £300; £300) Stalls Low

Form RPR
11-0 1 **Alfred Richardson**[109] 1502 5-10-0 **85** .... KevinStott 4 92
(John Davies) *trckd ldrs: rdn 2f out: drvn to chal 1f out: styd on to ld 75yds out* 16/1
1124 2 nk **Saisons D'Or (IRE)**[24] 4240 4-9-2 **80** .... OwenPayton(7) 5 86
(Jedd O'Keeffe) *led: rdn over 2f out: drvn and hdd 75yds out: one pce* 4/1[2]
0400 3 1 **Vive La Difference (IRE)**[35] 3867 5-9-2 **73** .... DuranFentiman 7 77+
(Tim Easterby) *s.i.s: hld up: rdn along 2f out: kpt on fnl f to go 3rd fnl 50yds* 16/1
1621 4 1 ¼ **Smile A Mile (IRE)**[3] 5061 3-9-13 **92** 6ex.......................... JoeFanning 6 91
(Mark Johnston) *prom: rdn over 2f out: no ex ins fnl f* 7/4[1]
0010 5 ¾ **Storm Ahead (IRE)**[24] 4239 6-9-6 **77** ....(b) JamesSullivan 1 76
(Tim Easterby) *midfield: rdn along 2f out: one pce and nvr threatened* 5/1
1022 6 ¾ **Zip**[38] 3728 3-8-6 **74** .... SeanDavis(3) 8 70
(Richard Fahey) *hld up: rdn over 2f out: nvr threatened* 9/2[3]

5060 7 3 ¼ **Gallipoli (IRE)**[21] 4385 6-10-0 **85** ....(v) TonyHamilton 3 75
(Richard Fahey) *in tch: rdn 2f out: already lost pl whn sltly hmpd 1f out: wknd* 10/1
1m 38.82s (-2.18) **Going Correction** -0.10s/f (Good) 7 Ran SP% 112.1
WFA 3 from 4yo+ 8lb
Speed ratings (Par 105): **106,105,104,103,102 101,98**
CSF £75.14 CT £1048.51 TOTE £19.60: £5.30, £2.40; EX 88.10 Trifecta £424.10.
Owner K Kirkup & J Davies **Bred** J J Davies & K Kirkup **Trained** Piercebridge, Durham

FOCUS
Several improvers in the line-up for this average handicap, though they didn't go flat out and remained bunched at the finish. The winner has been rated close to his AW win off this mark, and the second as running as well as ever.

5201 INN AT SOUTH STAINLEY H'CAP 1m 4f 10y
4:40 (4:43) (Class 4) (0-80,82) 3-Y-O+
£5,369 (£1,597; £798; £399; £300; £300) Stalls Centre

Form RPR
4124 1 **Battle Of Wills (IRE)**[16] 4549 3-9-5 **82** ....(p[1]) DanielTudhope 3 96
(James Tate) *mde all: pushed clr over 1f out: rdn out ins fnl f* 13/8[1]
-214 2 1 ½ **Rowland Ward**[51] 3260 3-9-4 **81** .... KevinStott 1 92
(Ralph Beckett) *s.i.s: sn midfield: rdn along 3f out: swtchd lft to outer over 2f out: edgd rt but sn hdwy: rdn to go 2nd ins fnl f: styd on wl but nvr getting to wnr* 5/2[2]
4415 3 6 **Appointed**[24] 4241 5-9-12 **78** ....(t) DuranFentiman 9 78
(Tim Easterby) *trckd ldrs: rdn to chal 2f out: wknd ins fnl f* 15/2
10-0 4 1 ½ **Moving Forward (IRE)**[66] 2748 4-9-8 **77** .... SeanDavis(3) 4 75
(Tony Coyle) *hld up: rdn along over 3f out: one pce and nvr threatened* 33/1
0402 5 2 **Ideological (IRE)**[12] 4729 3-9-3 **80** .... JoeFanning 10 75
(Mark Johnston) *midfield: rdn over 2f out: wknd fnl f* 5/1[3]
0000 6 1 ¾ **Multellie**[24] 4241 7-9-9 **80** .... DannyRedmond(5) 6 72
(Tim Easterby) *pressed ldr: rdn along 3f out: wknd over 1f out* 14/1
3000 7 7 **Desert Ruler**[24] 4241 6-9-13 **79** .... PaulMulrennan 5 59
(Jedd O'Keeffe) *hld up: rdn along 3f out: nvr threatened (jockey said gelding was never travelling)* 12/1
260- 8 19 **Crimson Skies (IRE)**[113] 8113 4-9-2 **68** .... ConnorBeasley 2 18
(John Davies) *prom: rdn over 3f out: sn wknd (jockey said filly was never travelling)* 33/1
2m 34.42s (-1.88) **Going Correction** -0.10s/f (Good) 8 Ran SP% 115.3
WFA 3 from 4yo+ 11lb
Speed ratings (Par 105): **102,101,97,96,94 93,88,76**
CSF £5.84 CT £21.00 TOTE £2.60: £1.20, £1.30, £1.90; EX 6.80 Trifecta £26.50.
Owner Saeed Manana **Bred** Fermoir Ltd **Trained** Newmarket, Suffolk

FOCUS
A tight handicap but the favourite won easily having made all.

5202 ENTER ITV7 ON SUNDAY FOR FREE MAIDEN H'CAP 6f
5:15 (5:19) (Class 5) (0-70,72) 3-Y-O+
£3,752 (£1,116; £557; £300; £300; £300) Stalls High

Form RPR
0422 1 **Montalvan (IRE)**[12] 4731 3-9-7 **62** ....(p) DanielTudhope 6 72
(Roger Fell) *mde all: pushed along and in command over 1f out: rdn out ins fnl f* 9/4[1]
4203 2 1 ½ **Perfect Swiss**[12] 4720 3-8-13 **54** .... DuranFentiman 7 59+
(Tim Easterby) *hld up: rdn over 2f out: hdwy on outer over 1f out: kpt on to go 2nd fnl 50yds: nvr getting to wnr* 15/2
05 3 1 **War Ensign (IRE)**[28] 4132 4-8-10 **46** .... LewisEdmunds 4 49
(Tim Easterby) *chsd ldrs: rdn over 2f out: kpt on same pce fnl f* 10/1
005 4 2 **Torque Of The Town (IRE)**[54] 3157 3-8-11 **55** .....(p[1]) BenRobinson(3) 3 51
(Noel Wilson) *prom: rdn 2f out: no ex ins fnl f* 25/1
4500 5 1 **Saltie Girl**[12] 4725 3-9-0 **55** .... AndrewMullen 1 47
(David Barron) *midfield: pushed along over 3f out: rdn over 2f out: kpt on same pce (vet said filly lost its right fore shoe)* 16/1
0522 6 4 **Dancingwithwolves (IRE)**[8] 4874 3-10-3 **72** .... KieranShoemark 8 52
(Ed Dunlop) *midfield: rdn over 2f out: wknd over 1f out* 3/1[2]
5005 7 2 **Alqaab**[9] 4829 4-9-10 **60** ....(h) JamesSullivan 2 34
(Ruth Carr) *dwlt: hld up: nvr threatened* 10/1
40-0 8 7 **Jean Valjean**[85] 2078 3-10-2 **71** ....(h) PaulMulrennan 11 22
(Richard Spencer) *dwlt: hld up: pushed along over 2f out: swtchd rt over 1f out: nvr threatened* 6/1[3]
3000 9 5 **Sophia Maria**[29] 4080 3-9-7 **62** ....(b[1]) AndrewElliott 10
(James Bethell) *midfield: rdn over 2f out: wknd over 1f out* 20/1
-302 P **Jungle Secret (IRE)**[17] 4508 3-8-13 **57** ....(h) SeanDavis(3) 9
(Richard Fahey) *chsd ldrs: bit short of room on rail 4f out: lost pl and sn bhd: eased and p.u over 1f out (vet said filly was struck into on its left fore)* 16/1
1m 11.58s (-0.92) **Going Correction** -0.10s/f (Good) 10 Ran SP% 120.4
WFA 3 from 4yo 5lb
Speed ratings (Par 103): **102,100,98,96,94 89,86,77,70,**
CSF £20.71 CT £146.20 TOTE £3.20: £1.70, £1.90, £3.20; EX 17.60 Trifecta £141.60.
Owner High Hopes 2017 **Bred** Nesco II Ltd & Kathryn Nikfel **Trained** Nawton, N Yorks

FOCUS
A warm sprint handicap for the grade, and four of the last five winners triumphed again during their next two outings. It was the third sprint on the card won by the horse closest to the stands' rail. The second has been rated to his latest.
T/Plt: £124.20 to a £1 stake. Pool: £70,627.14 - 415.06 winning units T/Qpdt: £41.60 to a £1 stake. Pool: £5,111.77 - 90.73 winning units **Andrew Sheret**

5203a-5204a (Foreign Racing) - See Raceform Interactive

4408 CURRAGH (R-H)
Saturday, July 20

OFFICIAL GOING: Good (good to firm in places on round course)

5205a TOTE SCURRY H'CAP (PREMIER HANDICAP) 6f 63y
3:25 (3:27) 3-Y-O+
£66,441 (£21,396; £10,135; £4,504; £2,252; £1,126) Stalls Centre

RPR
1 **Verhoyen**[3] 5070 4-8-4 **82** oh2..........................(b) RoryCleary 8 93
(M C Grassick, Ire) *trckd ldr towards far side and sn led: styd on wl ins fnl f to maintain advantage* 14/1
2 ¾ **Buffer Zone**[21] 4408 4-9-2 **94** .... ColinKeane 4 103
(G M Lyons, Ire) *chsd ldrs far side: wnt 4th under 2f out: styd on wl into 2nd fnl 150yds: kpt on wl clsng stages wout matching wnr in clr 2nd* 6/1[2]

3 2 3/4 **Ice Cold In Alex (IRE)**[22] 4355 5-8-5 **83**....................(t) NGMcCullagh 16 83+
(K J Condon, Ire) *racd in mid-div of stands' side gp: gd prog to ld stands' side gp 1f out: kpt on strly clsng stages into overall 3rd: nrst fin* **13/2**[3]

4 hd **Intisaab**[21] 4402 8-9-9 **101**....................(p) FrankieDettori 7 101
(David O'Meara) *racd in mid-div on far side: clsr under 2f out: wnt 4th ent fnl f: kpt on same pce into 3rd cl home: dropped to 4th on line* **7/1**

5 1/2 **Texas Rock (IRE)**[44] 3521 8-9-2 **94**....................(p) WJLee 6 92
(M C Grassick, Ire) *broke wl and led far side: sn hdd and trckd ldr in 2nd tl ins fnl f: wknd into 5th cl home* **25/1**

6 hd **Blairmayne (IRE)**[21] 4408 6-8-4 **82** oh3.................... WayneLordan 20 79+
(Miss Natalia Lupini, Ire) *chsd ldr of stands' side gp in 2nd: led stands' side gp over 1f out tl ins fnl f: kpt on wl in overall 6th clsng stages* **20/1**

7 1 1/4 **Ardhoomey (IRE)**[23] 4313 7-9-7 **102**....................(t) DonaghO'Connor(3) 1 95
(G M Lyons, Ire) *chsd ldrs far side: 3rd at 1/2-way: nt qckn fnl 150yds: kpt on same pce* **16/1**

8 nk **Eclipse Storm**[30] 4016 3-8-10 **96**....................(b[1]) ConorMaxwell(3) 5 87
(J A Stack, Ire) *racd in mid-div on far side: overall 8th 1f out: kpt on same pce* **25/1**

9 1 1/4 **Medicine Jack**[21] 4408 5-8-11 **89**....................(b) ChrisHayes 3 77
(G M Lyons, Ire) *racd in rr of far side gp: pushed along over 2f out: no imp ent fnl f: kpt on same pce* **25/1**

10 nk **Gustavus Weston (IRE)**[62] 2882 3-9-3 **100**.................... GaryCarroll 15 86
(Joseph G Murphy, Ire) *racd in mid-div stands' side: prog in centre of trck appr fnl f: kpt on wl: nvr nrr* **16/1**

11 nk **Smash Williams (IRE)**[23] 4313 6-9-5 **104**....................(t) GavinRyan(7) 14 90
(J S Bolger, Ire) *racd towards rr of stands' side gp: prog over 1f out: kpt on wl ins fnl f: nvr on terms* **11/2**[1]

12 3/4 **True Blue Moon (IRE)**[16] 4571 4-8-10 **88**....................(t) DeclanMcDonogh 9 72
(Joseph Patrick O'Brien, Ire) *racd in rr of mid-div of stands' side gp: pushed along 2f out: kpt on in centre of trck ins fnl f: nvr on terms* **20/1**

13 hd **On A Session (USA)**[28] 4092 3-8-5 **93**....................(p) AndrewSlattery(5) 18 75
(Aidan F Fogarty, Ire) *chsd ldrs on stands' side: rdn and no imp over 1f out: kpt on one pce* **16/1**

14 nk **Manshood (IRE)**[23] 4313 6-8-7 **85**....................(v) KillianLeonard 13 67
(Paul Midgley) *chsd ldr of stands' side gp in 3rd: rdn and nt qckn 1f out: no ex* **16/1**

15 1/2 **Freescape**[34] 3896 4-9-1 **93**....................(b) ColmO'Donoghue 10 74
(David Marnane, Ire) *racd in rr of stands' side gp: pushed along over 2f out: kpt on late ins fnl f: nvr a factor* **33/1**

16 1/2 **Chessman (IRE)**[21] 4409 5-9-9 **101**.................... OisinOrr 11 80
(Richard John O'Brien, Ire) *racd in rr of mid-div of stands' side gp: pushed along over 2f out: no imp appr fnl f* **8/1**

17 4 1/4 **Gabrial The Saint (IRE)**[7] 4896 4-8-13 **91**.................... GaryHalpin 12 57
(Richard Fahey) *chsd ldrs stands' side in 4th: wknd appr fnl f* **20/1**

18 1 1/2 **Mr Scarlet**[260] 8816 5-9-1 **93**....................(t) RobbieColgan 2 54
(Ms Sheila Lavery, Ire) *racd in mid-div on far side: rdn and no imp over 1f out: wknd* **50/1**

19 19 **Brick By Brick (IRE)**[46] 3457 4-9-2 **94**.................... ShaneFoley 19
(Mrs John Harrington, Ire) *led stands' side gp to 2f out: wknd qckly and eased fnl f (jockey said gelding never let himself down on the ground)* **20/1**

1m 14.37s (-3.33) **Going Correction** 0.0s/f (Good)
WFA 3 from 4yo+ 5lb **19** Ran SP% **132.3**
Speed ratings: **110,109,105,105,104 104,102,102,100,100 99,98,98,97,97 96,90,88,63**
CSF £88.15 CT £641.24 TOTE £18.50: £3.50, £2.10, £1.60, £1.70; DF 137.80 Trifecta £698.30.
Owner Paul Cullen & Joseph E Keeling & E J Dwyer & Patri **Bred** Miss K Rausing **Trained** Curragh, Co. Kildare

■ Stewards' Enquiry : Frankie Dettori caution: excessive use of whip

FOCUS
Typically competitive. They split into two groups and those drawn low were favoured. Ice Cold In Alex did best of those who raced towards the stands' side rail. The first two have been credited with personal bests.

5206a JEBEL ALI RACECOURSE AND STABLES ANGLESEY STKS (GROUP 3) 6f 63y
4:00 (4:01) 2-Y-O

£34,549 (£11,126; £5,270; £2,342; £1,171; £585) **Stalls Centre**

RPR

1 **Roman Turbo (IRE)**[22] 4350 2-9-3 92.................... RonanWhelan 6 102
(M Halford, Ire) *chsd ldrs in 3rd: pushed along under 2f out: clsr and almost on terms fnl 150yds: styd on wl to ld ins fnl 50yds* **6/1**

2 3/4 **Lil Grey (IRE)**[29] 4048 2-9-0 91.................... RobbieColgan 5 97
(Ms Sheila Lavery, Ire) *trckd ldr in 2nd: travelled wl to ld over 1f out: sn strly pressed: kpt on wl: hdd ins fnl 50yds* **4/1**[2]

3 hd **Soul Search (IRE)**[9] 4852 2-9-0 0.................... ColinKeane 4 96
(G M Lyons, Ire) *settled off ldrs in 5th: traveled wl 2f out: rdn appr fnl f in rr: styd on strly on outer fnl 100yds into 3rd cl home: nrst fin* **5/1**[3]

4 nk **Between Hills (IRE)**[48] 3378 2-9-0 0.................... ShaneFoley 2 95
(Mrs John Harrington, Ire) *settled off ldrs in 4th: swtchd rt under 2f out and clsr: rdn to press ldr in 2nd ent fnl f: dropped to 3rd fnl 100yds: kpt on same pce and ct cl home for 3rd* **14/1**

5 nk **Mount Fuji (IRE)**[30] 4012 2-9-3 0.................... DonnachaO'Brien 7 97
(A P O'Brien, Ire) *sn led: 2 l advantage at 1/2-way: pushed along under 2f out: hdd over 1f out and dropped to 5th ent fnl f: kpt on again fnl 100yds* **4/1**[2]

6 1 1/4 **Pistoletto (USA)**[62] 2878 2-9-3 0.................... RyanMoore 3 94
(A P O'Brien, Ire) *racd towards rr: keen early: pushed along and briefly clsr appr fnl f: no imp ins fnl 150yds: kpt on same pce* **9/4**[1]

7 3/4 **Real Appeal (GER)**[30] 4012 2-9-3 0....................(p[1]) KevinManning 1 92
(J S Bolger, Ire) *t.k.h early and sn restrained in rr: swtchd rt to far side 2f out travelling wl: pushed along to press ldrs in 3rd ent fnl f: no ex fnl 100yds and dropped to rr* **11/1**

1m 16.79s (-0.91) **Going Correction** 0.0s/f (Good) **7** Ran SP% **116.7**
Speed ratings: **103,102,101,101,100 99,98**
CSF £31.09 TOTE £7.00: £2.90, £2.50; DF 30.00 Trifecta £141.40.
Owner Sammy Hon Kit Ma **Bred** Swish Syndicate **Trained** Doneany, Co Kildare

FOCUS
Less than two lengths separated the first five home. The winner was officially rated 92 coming here, while the second had a mark of 91, so it probably was not a vintage renewal.

5207a PADDY POWER MINSTREL STKS (GROUP 2) 7f
4:35 (4:36) 3-Y-O+

£63,783 (£20,540; £9,729; £4,324; £2,162; £1,081)

RPR

1 **Romanised (IRE)**[32] 3948 4-9-8 115....................(t) WJLee 6 119
(K J Condon, Ire) *bit slowly away: sn mid-div: 6th at 1/2-way: gd hdwy in 3rd over 1f out: pressed ldr in 2nd ent fnl f: qcknd to ld fnl 150yds: pushed out clsng stages* **2/1**[2]

2 1 **Hey Gaman**[51] 3289 4-9-8 113.................... FrankieDettori 4 116
(James Tate) *trckd ldr in clr 2nd tl led gng wl under 2f out: strly pressed ent fnl f: hdd fnl 150yds and nt qckn w wnr: kpt on same pce in 2nd: lost rt front shoe (vet said colt was found to have lost a right front shoe in running)* **7/4**[1]

3 1/2 **Safe Voyage (IRE)**[42] 3588 6-9-8 113.................... JasonHart 1 115+
(John Quinn) *racd in mid-div: chsd ldrs in 4th at 1/2-way: wnt 3rd over 1f out: nt qckn w principals ent fnl f: kpt on wl clsng stages* **5/1**[3]

4 2 3/4 **Gordon Lord Byron (IRE)**[21] 4409 11-9-8 104.................... ChrisHayes 10 107
(T Hogan, Ire) *racd in mid-div: pushed along in 5th at 1/2-way: kpt on same pce in 4th ins fnl f: nvr nrr* **25/1**

5 1 1/4 **Flight Risk (IRE)**[21] 4410 8-9-8 110.................... KevinManning 8 104
(J S Bolger, Ire) *racd towards rr: pushed along in mid-div 2f out: kpt on same pce into 5th fnl 100yds: nvr nrr* **8/1**

6 1/2 **Mr Lupton (IRE)**[21] 4380 6-9-8 111.................... GaryHalpin 9 103+
(Richard Fahey) *hld up in rr: prog over 1f out: kpt on fnl f: nvr on terms* **16/1**

7 1/2 **Dunkirk Harbour (USA)**[4] 5032 3-9-1 99....................(b) RyanMoore 7 98
(A P O'Brien, Ire) *chsd ldrs in 3rd: rdn and nt qckn 2f out: sn one pce* **14/1**

8 4 1/2 **All The King's Men (IRE)**[13] 4697 3-9-1 92.................... SeamieHeffernan 5 86
(A P O'Brien, Ire) *sn led: hdd under 2f out: wknd fnl f* **50/1**

9 1 3/4 **North Wind (IRE)**[91] 1962 3-9-1 90....................(t[1]) ColinKeane 3 81
(Damian Joseph English, Ire) *chsd early ldrs on inner: mid-div at 1/2-way: rdn and no imp over 2f out: kpt on one pce* **66/1**

10 1 **San Andreas (IRE)**[83] 2156 3-9-1 94.................... DonnachaO'Brien 2 79
(A P O'Brien, Ire) *a towards rr: pushed along and nt qckn under 2f out: sn one pce* **33/1**

1m 22.07s (-2.93) **Going Correction** 0.0s/f (Good)
WFA 3 from 4yo+ 7lb **10** Ran SP% **120.3**
Speed ratings: **116,114,114,111,109 109,108,103,101,100**
CSF £5.96 TOTE £2.90: £1.02, £1.20, £1.50; DF 6.00 Trifecta £16.80.
Owner Robert Ng **Bred** Mrs Monica Aherne **Trained** Rathbride, Co Kildare

FOCUS
The winner was scoring for the first time since last year's Irish 2000 Guineas, and was decisive in doing so. He's been rated close to that level.

5208a KERRYGOLD IRISH OAKS (GROUP 1) (FILLIES) 1m 4f
5:10 (5:12) 3-Y-O

£205,405 (£68,468; £32,432; £14,414; £7,207; £3,603)

RPR

1 **Star Catcher**[30] 4014 3-9-0 110.................... FrankieDettori 3 115
(John Gosden) *mde all: qcknd to extend advantage 2f out: ld reduced clsng stages: kpt on wl* **7/2**[2]

2 1/2 **Fleeting (IRE)**[30] 4014 3-9-0 110.................... DonnachaO'Brien 8 115+
(A P O'Brien, Ire) *racd in mid-div: prog 2f out: rdn to chse clr ldr in 2nd appr fnl f: styd on wl to reduce deficit fnl 100yds: hld cl home* **9/2**

3 4 1/2 **Pink Dogwood (IRE)**[22] 4354 3-9-0 112.................... RyanMoore 4 107
(A P O'Brien, Ire) *bit slowly away and racd in rr: prog under 2f out: kpt on wl into 3rd ent fnl f: no imp fnl 100yds* **5/2**[1]

4 3/4 **Search For A Song (IRE)**[24] 4263 3-9-0 0.................... ChrisHayes 5 106+
(D K Weld, Ire) *racd in mid-div: keen early: pushed along over 2f out: hung lft over 1f out: kpt on wl into 4th clsng stages: nvr on terms* **14/1**

5 1 1/2 **Manuela De Vega (IRE)**[50] 3316 3-9-0 108.................... HarryBentley 2 103
(Ralph Beckett) *trckd ldrs on inner in 3rd: rdn along in 4th over 2f out: no imp in 5th ent fnl f: kpt on same pce* **7/1**

6 2 1/2 **Peach Tree (IRE)**[9] 4856 3-9-0 100.................... SeamieHeffernan 6 99
(A P O'Brien, Ire) *trckd ldr in 2nd: rdn and nt qckn w ldr under 2f out: wknd fnl f* **20/1**

7 2 **Iridessa (IRE)**[22] 4354 3-9-0 113.................... WayneLordan 10 96
(Joseph Patrick O'Brien, Ire) *a in rr: pushed along 2f out: edgd rt ent fnl f: kpt on one pce: nvr on terms* **4/1**[3]

8 2 3/4 **Trethias**[24] 4263 3-9-0 105.................... ShaneFoley 7 92
(Mrs John Harrington, Ire) *chsd ldrs in 4th: pushed along in 3rd over 2f out: nt qckn and dropped to rr ent fnl f: no ex* **12/1**

2m 34.49s (-4.21) **Going Correction** 0.0s/f (Good) **8** Ran SP% **120.6**
Speed ratings: **114,113,110,110,109 107,106,104**
CSF £20.93 CT £46.98 TOTE £3.40: £1.50, £1.90, £1.20; DF 21.00 Trifecta £63.50.
Owner A E Oppenheimer **Bred** Hascombe And Valiant Studs **Trained** Newmarket, Suffolk

FOCUS
The winner benefited from a vintage front-running ride from Dettori, one could see what was going to happen from pretty early in this race, his rivals were powerless to do anything about it.

5209 - 5211a (Foreign Racing) - See Raceform Interactive

4125 REDCAR (L-H)
Sunday, July 21

OFFICIAL GOING: Good to firm (good in places; 8.7)
Wind: fresh largely behind Weather: sunny, cloudy after 3rd

5212 SKYBET BRITAINS MOST POPULAR ONLINE BOOKMAKER EBF NOVICE STKS 7f
2:20 (2:21) (Class 5) 2-Y-O **£3,881** (£1,155; £577; £288) **Stalls Centre**

Form RPR

1 1 **Thunderous (IRE)**[23] 4324 2-9-9 0.................... JoeFanning 3 90+
(Mark Johnston) *dwlt: sn trckd ldr: pushed into ld over 1f out: rdn and edgd lft ins fnl f: kpt on wl* **4/9**[1]

32 2 2 **Saint Of Katowice (IRE)**[13] 4719 2-9-2 0.................... TonyHamilton 1 77
(Richard Fahey) *t.k.h trcking ldrs early: sn settled in tch: pushed along to chse ldrs over 2f out: rdn to go 2nd appr fnl f: kpt on but a hld* **9/2**[2]

04 **3** 7 **Arthur's Court (IRE)**[29] 4117 2-9-2 0 BenCurtis 8 58
(Hugo Palmer) *in tch: rdn over 2f out: sn outpcd: swtchd lft appr fnl f: plugged on in modest 3rd fnl f (jockey said colt hung right-handed throughout)* **6/1**[3]

0 **4** 4 **Yorkshire Grey (IRE)**[19] 4486 2-9-2 0 GrahamLee 4 47
(Ann Duffield) *led: rdn and hdd over 1f out: edgd rt appr fnl f: sn wknd* **66/1**

5 nk **Bodyline (IRE)** 2-9-2 0 LukeMorris 6 46
(Sir Mark Prescott Bt) *dwlt: sn chsd ldrs: rdn along over 3f out: sn outpcd and btn* **20/1**

6 1 **America First (IRE)** 2-9-2 0 PaulMulrennan 9 44
(Michael Dods) *s.i.s: hld up: rdn along 3f out: nvr threatened* **33/1**

6 **7** 6 **Grimbold**[24] 4275 2-8-11 0 (p[1]) HarrisonShaw(5) 2 28
(K R Burke) *chsd ldrs: rdn over 3f out: sn wknd* **80/1**

1m 23.41s (-1.99) **Going Correction** -0.20s/f (Firm) 7 Ran SP% **112.1**
Speed ratings (Par 94): **103,100,92,88,87 86,79**
CSF £2.59 TOTE £1.30: £1.10, £1.20; EX 2.90 Trifecta £4.20.
Owner Highclere T'Bred Racing - George Stubbs **Bred** Rabbah Bloodstock Limited **Trained** Middleham Moor, N Yorks

FOCUS
All distances as advertised. Hard to believe this was anything more than a fair maiden unless the winner keeps progressing. The second has been rated as improving a bit.

5213 CELEBRATE THE LIFE OF PETER CHAPMAN H'CAP (DIV I) 1m 1f
2:55 (2:58) (Class 6) (0-65,67) 3-Y-O+ £3,234 (£962; £481; £240) Stalls Low

Form RPR

640 **1** **Whatwouldyouknow (IRE)**[27] 4194 4-9-11 **62** GrahamLee 8 72
(Richard Guest) *in tch: chsd ldrs over 2f out: rdn into narrow ld appr fnl f: drvn and edgd lft ins fnl f: hld on wl* **8/1**

0-40 **2** nk **Mina Vagante**[23] 4341 3-9-7 **67** BenCurtis 6 74
(Hugo Palmer) *prom: rdn along over 2f out: drvn to chal strly over 1f out: kpt on wl but a jst hld* **5/1**[2]

5446 **3** 4 1/2 **First Dance (IRE)**[9] 4892 5-10-0 **65** TomEaves 1 65
(Tom Tate) *dwlt: hld up: hdwy 3f out: rdn 2f out: kpt on to go 3rd towards fin* **9/4**[1]

0220 **4** 1/2 **Tom's Anna (IRE)**[11] 4785 9-8-6 **46** JaneElliott(3) 7 45
(Sean Regan) *led: rdn and strly pressed over 1f out: hdd appr fnl f: wknd ins fnl f* **25/1**

-024 **5** 1/2 **Farhh Away**[29] 4130 4-10-2 **67** (p) ConnorBeasley 5 65
(Michael Dods) *hld up: rdn over 2f out: plugged on fnl f: nvr trbld ldrs* **5/1**[2]

0000 **6** hd **Intense Pleasure (IRE)**[11] 4785 4-8-11 **48** (h) JamesSullivan 4 46
(Ruth Carr) *midfield: rdn over 2f out: one pce and nvr threatened* **16/1**

0404 **7** 1 1/4 **Im Dapper Too**[24] 4293 8-9-1 **52** ShaneGray 9 48
(John Davies) *trckd ldrs: rdn over 3f out: sn outpcd and btn* **14/1**

0000 **8** nk **Lord Rob**[29] 4131 8-8-9 **46** oh1 PaddyMathers 2 41
(David Thompson) *dwlt: sn midfield: outpcd and dropped towards rr 3f out: no threat after* **40/1**

/005 **9** 3 **Eldelbar (SPA)**[11] 4784 5-9-7 **58** (h) KevinStott 10 47
(Geoffrey Harker) *hld up in rr: sme hdwy on outer over 3f out: rdn over 2f out: wknd ins fnl f* **15/2**[3]

0-40 **10** 1 3/4 **Donnago (IRE)**[19] 4487 3-8-4 **50** CamHardie 3 34
(Brian Ellison) *in tch: rdn over 3f out: sn wknd* **11/1**

1m 52.68s (-1.82) **Going Correction** -0.20s/f (Firm) 10 Ran SP% **114.1**
WFA 3 from 4yo+ 9lb
Speed ratings (Par 101): **100,99,95,95,94 94,93,93,90,89**
CSF £46.71 CT £123.03 TOTE £10.00: £2.60, £1.80, £1.10; EX 59.40 Trifecta £280.30.
Owner Dearing Plastics Ltd & Partner **Bred** Holamo Partnership **Trained** Ingmanthorpe, W Yorks

FOCUS
The first division of a modest handicap, in which previous winning form was hard to find. A minor pb from the winner, but the likes of the fourth suggest the form can't be much better than rated.

5214 CELEBRATE THE LIFE OF PETER CHAPMAN H'CAP (DIV II) 1m 1f
3:30 (3:32) (Class 6) (0-65,67) 3-Y-O+ £3,234 (£962; £481; £240) Stalls Low

Form RPR

4-0 **1** **Effernock Fizz (IRE)**[16] 1900 4-8-5 **47** DMSimmonson(5) 9 54
(Miss Katy Brown, Ire) *mde all: rdn over 2f out: drvn over 1f out: styd on wl* **8/1**

-02 **2** 1 **Greengage (IRE)**[14] 4690 4-9-3 **54** (h) LukeMorris 8 59
(Tristan Davidson) *hld up: rdn and hdwy on outer 3f out: drvn to chse ldr over 1f out: edgd lft and styd on ins fnl f* **9/4**[1]

4422 **3** 1/2 **One To Go**[12] 4761 3-9-4 **64** (b) DuranFentiman 7 67
(Tim Easterby) *midfield: hdwy 3f out: drvn to chse ldr over 1f out: kpt on same pce* **3/1**[2]

0556 **4** 3 1/4 **Canoodling**[15] 4628 3-9-7 **67** BenCurtis 10 64
(Ian Williams) *trckd ldrs: chal over 2f out: sn rdn: wknd fnl f* **16/1**

0035 **5** nse **Graceful Act**[5] 5024 11-8-6 **46** (p) RowanScott(3) 4 43
(Ron Barr) *in tch: rdn and outpcd over 2f out: plugged on fnl f* **20/1**

606- **6** 2 1/4 **Mr Sundowner (USA)**[275] 8391 7-9-11 **62** PhilDennis 3 55
(Michael Herrington) *midfield: pushed along over 2f out: no imp* **8/1**

-000 **7** 1 **Hitman**[18] 4523 6-9-12 **63** LewisEdmunds 6 54
(Rebecca Bastiman) *hld up: rdn over 2f out: nvr threatened* **25/1**

2404 **8** hd **Lukoutoldmakezebak**[15] 4633 6-8-9 **46** oh1 (p) PaddyMathers 2 37
(David Thompson) *trckd ldr: rdn along 3f out: sn outpcd and btn* **14/1**

2353 **9** 3/4 **Straight Ash (IRE)**[15] 4657 4-9-11 **65** BenRobinson(3) 5 54
(Ollie Pears) *hld up: rdn over 2f out: nvr threatened* **13/2**[3]

5000 **10** 1 1/4 **Happy Hannah (IRE)**[16] 4584 3-8-3 **49** oh1 ow3 RoystonFfrench 1 35
(John Davies) *in tch: rdn 3f out: wknd over 1f out* **25/1**

1m 51.52s (-2.98) **Going Correction** -0.20s/f (Firm) 10 Ran SP% **116.3**
WFA 3 from 4yo+ 9lb
Speed ratings (Par 101): **105,104,103,100,100 98,97,97,97,95**
CSF £25.60 CT £66.17 TOTE £6.40: £2.80, £1.10, £1.60; EX 30.90 Trifecta £71.90.
Owner T B Sheridan **Bred** T B Sheridan **Trained** Rathangan, Co Kildare

FOCUS
The second division of a modest contest. The first three home hadn't won a Flat race between them previously. The third has been rated near his recent best.

5215 JACKS COACHES H'CAP 7f
4:05 (4:07) (Class 5) (0-70,69) 3-Y-O £3,881 (£1,155; £577; £288) Stalls Centre

Form RPR

0204 **1** **Firsteen**[13] 4725 3-8-6 **54** PaulHanagan 1 62
(Alistair Whillans) *hld up: hdwy fr over 2f out: pushed along over 1f out: rdn to ld 110yds out: kpt on* **7/1**[3]

5650 **2** 1/2 **Muhallab (IRE)**[16] 4586 3-8-2 **50** oh1 AndrewMullen 4 56
(Adrian Nicholls) *in tch: keen early: rdn to chse ldr over 1f out: kpt on* **22/1**

-602 **3** 3/4 **Kolossus**[6] 4977 3-9-7 **69** ConnorBeasley 2 73
(Michael Dods) *led: drvn and edgd rt over 1f out: hdd 110yds out: no ex* **7/2**[1]

0066 **4** 1 1/2 **Gylo (IRE)**[46] 3478 3-9-2 **64** (v[1]) DavidNolan 12 64
(David O'Meara) *hld up: rdn along over 3f out: hdwy over 1f out: kpt on ins fnl f* **12/1**

2663 **5** 1/2 **Kind Review**[15] 4635 3-9-5 **67** CamHardie 7 66
(Tracy Waggott) *trckd ldrs: pushed along 3f out: sn hung lft: drvn over 1f out: one pce (jockey said gelding hung left-handed throughout)* **8/1**

0500 **6** 1/2 **Furyan**[5] 5031 3-8-2 **50** oh1 (v) JamesSullivan 11 47
(Nigel Tinkler) *hld up: rdn along over 3f out: plugged on fnl f: nvr threatened ldrs* **20/1**

0662 **7** 1 1/4 **Ghathanfar (IRE)**[33] 3970 3-8-10 **58** RoystonFfrench 3 52
(Tracy Waggott) *sn prom: rdn over 2f out: wknd ins fnl f* **12/1**

06-0 **8** 3/4 **Charlie's Boy (IRE)**[18] 4519 3-8-11 **59** PaulMulrennan 9 51
(Michael Dods) *hld up: pushed along and hmpd over 1f out: nvr threatened* **14/1**

-236 **9** 3/4 **Mac Ailey**[13] 4728 3-9-0 **62** RachelRichardson 5 52
(Tim Easterby) *chsd ldrs: rdn over 2f out: wknd fnl f* **5/1**[2]

40 **10** nk **Rangefield Express (IRE)**[13] 4731 3-8-9 **57** KevinStott 8 46
(Geoffrey Harker) *midfield: rdn along over 2f out: no imp* **25/1**

3003 **11** 3/4 **Fume (IRE)**[13] 4728 3-9-7 **69** PJMcDonald 6 56
(James Bethell) *midfield: rdn over 2f out: hung lft over 1f out: wknd ins fnl f (jockey said gelding was never travelling; vet said gelding had lost its left fore shoe)* **5/1**[2]

4663 **12** 1 1/4 **Gunnison**[13] 4726 3-8-4 **55** SeanDavis(3) 10 39
(Richard Fahey) *midfield: rdn over 2f out: hung lft over 1f out and wknd* **20/1**

1m 22.88s (-2.52) **Going Correction** -0.20s/f (Firm) 12 Ran SP% **118.9**
Speed ratings (Par 100): **106,105,104,102,102 101,100,99,98,98 97,95**
CSF £156.47 CT £509.59 TOTE £8.90: £3.00, £8.30, £1.20; EX 186.50 Trifecta £1127.70.
Owner Star Racing **Bred** Star Racing **Trained** Newmill-On-Slitrig, Borders

FOCUS
A weak event, unlikely to produce too many winners in the short term. A length pb from the winner, with the third rated to his latest.

5216 HELP FOR HEROES & ROYAL BRITISH LEGION CLASSIFIED CLAIMING STKS 1m 2f 1y
4:40 (4:43) (Class 6) 3-Y-O+ £3,234 (£962; £481; £240) Stalls Low

Form RPR

3230 **1** **Anif (IRE)**[10] 4838 5-9-1 72 PJMcDonald 3 65+
(David Evans) *mde all: rdn and strly pressed over 1f out: drvn fnl f: hld on wl* **4/6**[1]

-0R3 **2** hd **First Flight (IRE)**[23] 4333 8-9-0 73 BenRobinson(3) 1 67+
(Brian Ellison) *trckd ldrs: drvn to chal strly over 1f out: kpt on but a jst hld* **7/4**[2]

-000 **3** 7 **Royal Liberty**[6] 4990 4-8-13 46 KevinStott 4 49
(Geoffrey Harker) *dwlt: hld up in tch: rdn along over 2f out: sn outpcd: wnt poor 3rd ins fnl f* **40/1**

0330 **4** 1 **Slaithwaite (IRE)**[5] 5023 3-8-2 52 (p) PaulaMuir(5) 2 51
(Roger Fell) *prom: rdn over 2f out: wknd over 1f out* **14/1**[3]

5200 **5** 12 **Highwayman**[15] 4633 6-9-2 45 (h) CamHardie 5 28
(David Thompson) *hld up in tch: rdn along over 2f out: sn wknd* **66/1**

2m 8.58s (1.68) **Going Correction** -0.20s/f (Firm) 5 Ran SP% **106.9**
WFA 3 from 4yo+ 9lb
Speed ratings (Par 101): **85,84,79,78,68**
CSF £1.88 TOTE £1.50: £1.02, £1.60; EX 2.00 Trifecta £7.90.Anif was claimed by M. Herrington for £5,000
Owner Dave & Emma Evans **Bred** Shadwell Estate Company Limited **Trained** Pandy, Monmouths
■ Stewards' Enquiry : Ben Robinson six-day ban: used whip above the permitted level (Aug 4-9)

FOCUS
Only two of these made appeal to punters and they pulled away in the final stages.

5217 SKY BET GO-RACING-IN-YORKSHIRE SUMMER FESTIVAL H'CAP 5f 217y
5:15 (5:15) (Class 3) (0-90,91) 3-Y-O+ £8,086 (£2,406; £1,202; £601) Stalls Centre

Form RPR

4610 **1** **Royal Prospect (IRE)**[18] 4521 4-9-7 **85** GrahamLee 5 93
(Julie Camacho) *hld up in tch: sltly hmpd and swtchd lft over 2f out: sme hdwy ent fnl f: drvn and kpt on wl: led 75yds out* **13/2**

1024 **2** 1/2 **Muscika**[11] 4805 5-9-13 **91** (v) DavidNolan 10 97
(David O'Meara) *sn led: rdn 2f out: hdd 75yds out: one pce* **8/1**

0010 **3** nk **Citron Major**[29] 4127 4-9-8 **89** (t[1]) RowanScott(3) 2 94
(Nigel Tinkler) *dwlt: hld up: pushed along over 2f out: rdn and hdwy towards far side appr fnl f: kpt on* **11/4**[1]

1044 **4** hd **The Armed Man**[18] 4521 6-9-0 **83** PaulaMuir(5) 6 87
(Chris Fairhurst) *prom: rdn 2f out: edgd lft and one pce ins fnl f* **5/1**[3]

6-06 **5** nse **Lahore (USA)**[45] 3501 5-9-12 **90** PaulMulrennan 4 94
(Phillip Makin) *hld up: hmpd over 2f out and swtchd rt: pushed along and hdwy appr fnl f: kpt on* **16/1**

0315 **6** 1 3/4 **Galloway Hills**[22] 4369 4-9-2 **83** (p) SeanDavis(3) 3 82
(Phillip Makin) *trckd ldrs: rdn along over 2f out: sn edgd lft: one pce whn hmpd 100yds out* **4/1**[2]

0054 **7** 1/2 **Pipers Note**[6] 4987 9-9-9 **87** JackGarritty 7 84
(Ruth Carr) *trckd ldrs: rdn along 2f out: no ex ins fnl f* **7/1**

2003 **8** 4 1/2 **East Street Revue**[15] 4625 6-8-10 **74** DuranFentiman 9 57
(Tim Easterby) *midfield: rdn over 2f out: wknd over 1f out* **16/1**

40-5 **P** **Prince Ahwahnee**[14] 4691 4-9-4 **82** BenCurtis 8
(Phillip Makin) *prom: wnt wrong over 2f out: p.u dismntd* **40/1**

1m 9.92s (-1.88) **Going Correction** -0.20s/f (Firm) 9 Ran SP% **114.5**
Speed ratings (Par 107): **108,107,106,106,106 104,103,97,**
CSF £56.74 CT £176.94 TOTE £7.10: £2.30, £1.80, £1.40; EX 71.90 Trifecta £213.00.
Owner Geoff & Sandra Turnbull **Bred** Highpark Bloodstock Ltd **Trained** Norton, N Yorks

FOCUS
This was a decent sprint handicap and it produced a tight finish. The second has been rated to form.

5218 REDCAR CRICKET CLUB FILLIES' H'CAP 7f 219y
5:45 (5:46) (Class 4) (0-85,83) 3-Y-O+ £5,822 (£1,732; £865; £432) Stalls Centre

Form RPR

4121 **1** **Warning Fire**[10] 4831 3-9-4 **81** JoeFanning 1 86+
(Mark Johnston) *trckd ldr: racd quite keenly: led 4f out: pushed along over 2f out: rdn and pressed ins fnl f: kpt on wl* **10/11**[1]

2130 **2** nk **Never Be Enough**[12] 4758 4-9-7 **83** HarryRussell(7) 4 89
(Keith Dalgleish) *dwlt: hld up in 4th: hdwy and trckd ldr over 2f out: rdn over 1f out: drvn to chal ins fnl f: kpt on* **3/1**[2]

2160 **3** *1 ½* **Verdigris (IRE)**[23] 4322 4-8-13 **68**.................................. TomEaves 3 71
(Ruth Carr) *in tch in 3rd: rdn 2f out: kpt on same pce* **7/1**
5324 **4** *2 ¾* **Queen Penn**[24] 4278 4-9-5 **74**...................................... PaulHanagan 2 70
(Richard Fahey) *led: hdd 4f out: chsd ldr: rdn over 2f out: edgd lft and wknd ins fnl f* **4/1**[3]

1m 37.43s (0.83) **Going Correction** -0.20s/f (Firm)
WFA 3 from 4yo 8lb **4 Ran SP% 109.9**
Speed ratings (Par 102): **87,86,85,82**
CSF £3.98 TOTE £1.90; EX 3.10 Trifecta £12.00.
Owner Sheikh Hamdan bin Mohammed Al Maktoum **Bred** Godolphin **Trained** Middleham Moor, N Yorks

FOCUS
This form probably won't prove to be overly strong but the winner is a tough sort. Straightforward form rated around the second and third to their handicap form.

5219 GO RACING IN YORKSHIRE FUTURE STARS APPRENTICE H'CAP 1m 5f 218y
6:15 (6:16) (Class 5) (0-70,73) 4-Y-0+ **£3,557** (£1,058; £529; £264) **Stalls** Low

Form RPR
3432 **1** **Donnachies Girl (IRE)**[6] 4983 6-8-12 **56**.................... KieranSchofield 1 64
(Alistair Whillans) *led: jnd over 7f out: hdd 4f out: remained chalng: rdn along 3f out: drvn 2f out: styd on to ld again towards fin* **13/8**[1]
4435 **2** *½* **Jan De Heem**[6] 4990 9-8-4 **51** oh1...........................(p) EllaMcCain(3) 5 58
(Tina Jackson) *dwlt: sn trckd ldrs: n.m.r and swtchd lft over 2f out: pushed into narrow ld wl over 1f out: sn rdn along: drvn ins fnl f: hdd towards fin* **9/2**
001 **3** *3 ½* **Nearly There**[29] 4126 6-8-9 **56**..(t) RhonaPindar(3) 3 58
(Wilf Storey) *in tch: hdwy and jnd ldr over 7f out: led narrowly 4f out: rdn and hdd wl over 1f out: wknd ins fnl f* **7/2**[3]
-310 **4** *½* **Oi The Clubb Oi's**[36] 3861 4-9-12 **70**......................... ScottMcCullagh 7 71
(Ian Williams) *prom: trckd ldrs over 7f out: rdn along 3f out: outpcd and btn over 1f out* **5/2**[2]
2000 **5** *1* **Seaborough (IRE)**[5] 5029 4-9-2 **60**............................ TobyEley 6 60
(David Thompson) *hld up: rdn over 3f out: no imp* **12/1**

3m 2.04s (-4.96) **Going Correction** -0.20s/f (Firm) **5 Ran SP% 114.8**
Speed ratings (Par 103): **106,105,103,103,102**
CSF £9.79 TOTE £2.60: £1.40, £2.20; EX 8.20 Trifecta £15.50.
Owner Mrs Karen Spark **Bred** Darley **Trained** Newmill-On-Slitrig, Borders
■ Sweet Marmalade was withdrawn. Price at of withdrawal 20-1. Rule 4 \n\x\x does not apply

FOCUS
A moderate staying event. Muddling form. The winner has been rated to her latest.
T/Jkpt: Not Won. T/Plt: £14.30 to a £1 stake. Pool: £72,292.04 - 3687.49 winning units. T/Qpdt: £8.20 to a £1 stake. Pool: £5,376.08 - 482.17 winning units. **Andrew Sheret**

5220 - 5221a (Foreign Racing) - See Raceform Interactive

5203
CURRAGH (R-H)
Sunday, July 21

OFFICIAL GOING: Straight course - good (good to firm in places); round course - good to firm

5222a FRIARSTOWN STUD SAPPHIRE STKS (GROUP 2) 5f
3:10 (3:11) 3-Y-0+
£63,873 (£20,630; £9,819; £4,414; £2,252; £1,171) **Stalls** Centre

RPR
1 **Soffia**[44] 3557 4-9-4 **104**...................................... DeclanMcDonogh 9 118+
(Edward Lynam, Ire) *chsd ldrs in 4th: clsr appr fnl f into 2nd: qcknd wl to ld fnl 150yds and sn clr* **6/1**
2 *3 ½* **El Astronaute (IRE)**[24] 4313 6-9-7 **111**........................ JasonHart 8 109
(John Quinn) *trckd ldrs in 3rd in centre of trck: rdn in 3rd ent fnl f: kpt on same pce into 2nd fnl 50yds: nt trble wnr* **4/1**[3]
3 *½* **Garrus (IRE)**[15] 4665 3-9-3 **109**................................ KieranShoemark 4 106
(Charles Hills) *slowly away and detached in rr early: prog 1/2-way: gd hdwy ent fnl f in 6th: styd on wl into 3rd cl home: nrst fin* **7/1**
4 *¾* **Soldier's Call**[33] 3950 3-9-3 **114**.............................. DanielTudhope 10 103
(Archie Watson) *smartly away and trckd ldr in centre of trck in 2nd: pushed along under 2f out: nt qckn in 4th ent fnl f: kpt on same pce: lost shoe (jockey said colt pulled a shoe in running)* **2/1**[1]
5 *hd* **Caspian Prince (IRE)**[8] 4932 10-9-7 **106**...............(t) AlistairRawlinson 3 104
(Michael Appleby) *sn led towards far side: hdd fnl 150yds: wknd into 5th cl home* **20/1**
6 *2* **Equilateral**[33] 3950 4-9-7 **109**..................................... ColinKeane 5 96
(Charles Hills) *chsd ldrs far side in 5th: no imp ent fnl f: kpt on same pce* **10/3**[2]
7 *2 ¾* **Fantasy (IRE)**[37] 3818 3-9-0 **89**.................................. RyanMoore 7 82
(A P O'Brien, Ire) *racd in mid-div to 1/2-way: pushed along and dropped to rr 2f out: kpt on again ins fnl f: nvr on terms* **25/1**
8 *2 ¾* **Lethal Promise (IRE)**[44] 3557 3-9-0 **101**.......................(h) WJLee 2 73
(W McCreery, Ire) *slowly away and a towards rr: no imp under 2f out: kpt on same pce* **20/1**
9 *½* **Rapid Reaction (IRE)**[24] 4313 4-9-4 **90**........................ AndrewSlattery 1 72
(J F Grogan, Ire) *chsd ldrs far side tl nt qckn over 1f out: sn no ex* **50/1**

58.51s (-1.89) **Going Correction** +0.125s/f (Good)
WFA 3 from 4yo+ 4lb **9 Ran SP% 118.5**
Speed ratings: **120,114,113,112,112 108,104,100,99**
CSF £29.53 TOTE £6.40: £2.00, £1.60, £2.30; DF 27.20 Trifecta £201.60.
Owner Lady O'Reilly **Bred** Newsells Park Stud **Trained** Dunshaughlin, Co Meath

FOCUS
The winner surprised everybody with the performance she put up here and she is now a leading sprinter. A pb from the winner, with the placed horses setting the level.

5223a KILBOY ESTATE STKS (GROUP 2) (F&M) 1m 1f
3:45 (3:45) 3-Y-0+ **£61,126** (£19,684; £9,324; £4,144; £2,072)

RPR
1 **Red Tea**[32] 3986 6-9-9 **107**..................................... DonnachaO'Brien 1 102+
(Joseph Patrick O'Brien, Ire) *mde all: rdn to extend advantage ent fnl f: styd on strly* **11/10**[1]
2 *2* **Goddess (USA)**[25] 4263 3-9-0 **91**................................ RyanMoore 4 96
(A P O'Brien, Ire) *bmpd leaving stalls: chsd ldrs in 3rd: pushed along into 2nd ent fnl f: kpt on same pce wout troubling wnr* **7/2**[2]
3 *hd* **Annie Fior (IRE)**[4] 5075 5-9-9 **89**................................ PBBeggy 3 97
(B A Murphy, Ire) *rrd up leaving stalls and bmpd rival: trckd ldr in 2nd tl nt qckn in 3rd ent fnl f: kpt on same pce* **25/1**
4 *3 ½* **Chablis (IRE)**[25] 4263 3-9-0 **97**.................................. WayneLordan 5 89
(A P O'Brien, Ire) *bmpd leaving stalls: hld up in 4th: pushed along and no imp ent fnl f: sn one pce* **9/2**
5 *3 ¼* **Coral Beach (IRE)**[15] 4681 3-9-0 **100**.......................(t) SeamieHeffernan 8 82
(A P O'Brien, Ire) *in rr thrght: pushed along and detached under 2f out: nvr a factor* **4/1**[3]

1m 55.31s (-0.29) **Going Correction** +0.125s/f (Good)
WFA 3 from 4yo+ 9lb **5 Ran SP% 111.9**
Speed ratings: **106,104,104,100,98**
CSF £5.40 TOTE £1.80: £1.20, £2.30; DF 5.60 Trifecta £51.70.
Owner Capel Street Syndicate **Bred** Sheikh Hamdan Bin Maktoum Al Maktoum **Trained** Owning Hill, Co Kilkenny

FOCUS
One of the most poorly contested races at this level one is likely to see, not helped by the probable odds-on favourite being withdrawn.

5224 - 5226a (Foreign Racing) - See Raceform Interactive

4747
DEAUVILLE (R-H)
Sunday, July 21

OFFICIAL GOING: Turf: good to soft

5227a PRIX DE BAGATELLE (LISTED RACE) (3YO FILLIES) (STRAIGHT COURSE) (TURF) 1m (R)
1:35 3-Y-0 **£24,774** (£9,909; £7,432; £4,954; £2,477)

RPR
1 **Twist 'N' Shake**[30] 4051 3-8-11 **0**.................................. FrankieDettori 4 109+
(John Gosden) *settled in 3rd s: smooth hdwy to ld centre: shkn up to go clr 1 1/2f out: r.o: comfortable* **1/2**[1]
2 *3 ½* **Fount**[56] 3121 3-8-11 **0**.. Pierre-CharlesBoudot 3 100
(A Fabre, France) **27/10**[2]
3 *2* **Simplicity (FR)**[16] 4621 3-8-11 **0**..............................(b) CristianDemuro 5 96
(F Chappet, France) **11/1**[3]
4 *4* **So Unique (FR)**[41] 3677 3-8-11 **0**.............................. StephanePasquier 7 86
(N Clement, France) **15/1**
5 *hd* **Hermiona (USA)**[41] 3677 3-8-11 **0**............................ MickaelBarzalona 2 86
(F Chappet, France) **23/1**
6 *8* **Nayala**[28] 3-8-11 **0**...(p) EddyHardouin 6 68
(A Wohler, Germany) **18/1**
7 *6* **Pietra Della Luna (IRE)**[22] 4416 3-8-11 **0**.................. AntoineHamelin 1 54
(M Figge, Germany) **42/1**

1m 37.12s (-3.68) **7 Ran SP% 120.0**
PARI-MUTUEL (all including 1 euro stake): WIN 1.50; PLACE 1.10, 1.10; SF 2.30.
Owner Helena Springfield Ltd **Bred** Meon Valley Stud **Trained** Newmarket, Suffolk

5228a DARLEY PRIX ROBERT PAPIN (GROUP 2) (2YO COLTS & FILLIES) (STRAIGHT COURSE) (TURF) 5f 110y
2:50 2-Y-0 **£66,756** (£25,765; £12,297; £8,198; £4,099)

RPR
1 **A'Ali (IRE)**[31] 4012 2-9-2 **0**.. FrankieDettori 6 112+
(Simon Crisford) *settled towards rr: moved into midfield by 1/2-way: hdwy on outer 1 1/2f out: shkn up appr fnl f: sustained run to reel in ldr: led fnl 75yds: wl on top at fin* **3/5**[1]
2 *¾* **My Love's Passion (FR)**[51] 3333 2-8-13 **0**................. TheoBachelot 1 106
(Y Barberot, France) *broke wl fr ins draw: qckly tacked over and led in centre of crse: drvn wl over 1f out: hdd fnl 75yds: no match for wnr* **26/1**
3 *1 ¾* **Jolie (FR)**[22] 4417 2-8-13 **0**.. MaximeGuyon 2 100
(Andrea Marcialis, France) *settled towards rr: rowed along over 2f out: styd on ins fnl 1 1/2f: tk 3rd cl home: nvr trbld front two* **61/10**[2]
4 *¾* **Fan Club Rules (IRE)**[22] 4417 2-9-2 **0**...................... AntoineHamelin 9 101
(Matthieu Palussiere, France) *racd keenly early: chsd ldrs: 3rd and shkn up over 1 1/2f out: sn rdn and styd on at same pce fnl f* **51/1**
5 *shd* **Istanbul (IRE)**[15] 4624 2-9-2 **0**.......................... Pierre-CharlesBoudot 10 100
(Richard Fahey) *chsd ldr: rdn but unable qck appr fnl f: dropped away last 150yds* **14/1**
6 *1 ½* **Classy Moon (USA)**[10] 4846 2-9-2 **0**.................................. CliffordLee 4 95
(K R Burke) *prom: outpcd and pushed along 2f out: styd on at same pce fnl f* **20/1**
7 *hd* **Rayong**[16] 4610 2-9-2 **0**.. SilvestreDeSousa 3 95
(K R Burke) *midfield towards inner: outpcd and rdn 2f out: kpt on ins fnl f: nvr in contention* **14/1**
8 *hd* **Fantastic Diamond (FR)**[32] 2-8-13 **0**......................... VincentCheminaud 5 91
(H-A Pantall, France) *midfield on outer: 5th but no imp whn rdn 1 1/2f out: dropped away ins fnl f* **9/1**[3]
9 *¾* **Salar Island (ITY)**[29] 2-9-2 **0**.. CristianDemuro 8 91
(Andrea Marcialis, France) *racd in fnl pair: unable qck whn asked ins fnl 2f: nvr in contention* **11/1**
10 *1 ½* **Dutch Chop (FR)**[32] 2-9-2 **0**.. HugoJourniac 7 87
(Jane Soubagne, France) *missed break: in rr: a bhd* **43/1**

1m 4.38s **10 Ran SP% 120.9**
PARI-MUTUEL (all including 1 euro stake): WIN 1.60; PLACE 1.10, 2.00, 1.30; DF 19.70.
Owner Shaikh Duaij Al Khalifa **Bred** Tally-Ho Stud **Trained** Newmarket, Suffolk

FOCUS
The straightforward level is governed by the third, rated to her recent level, together with the sixth and seventh rated close to their pre-race levels.

5229a PRIX DE LA PEPINIERE - FONDS EUROPEEN DE L'ELEVAGE (LISTED) (4YO+ FILLIES & MARES) (ROUND) (TURF) 1m 2f
3:25 4-Y-0+ **£21,621** (£8,648; £6,486; £4,324; £2,162)

RPR
1 **Spirit Of Nelson (IRE)**[32] 4011 4-8-13 **0**.................. MaximeGuyon 10 104+
(J Reynier, France) **91/10**
2 *½* **Musis Amica (IRE)**[29] 4140 4-8-13 **0**......................... MickaelBarzalona 5 103
(A Fabre, France) *midfield outside rival: shkn up 2f out: hdwy 1 1/2f out: led w 1f to run: hdd last 50yds: no ex* **7/10**[1]
3 *2* **Watayouna (FR)**[52] 4-8-13 **0**................................ Pierre-CharlesBoudot 3 99
(F-H Graffard, France) **9/2**[2]
4 *1* **Fira (FR)**[49] 4-8-13 **0**.. CristianDemuro 9 97
(S Dehez, France) **21/1**
5 *nk* **Palmyre (FR)**[32] 4011 4-8-13 **0**...................................... AlexisBadel 1 96
(H-F Devin, France) **9/1**[3]
6 *1 ¼* **Bella Bolide (FR)**[19] 5-8-13 **0**.................................. AnthonyCrastus 4 94
(M Brasme, France) **33/1**

7 4 **Strong And Stable (FR)**32 4011 4-8-13 0................ GregoryBenoist 2 86
(Mme Pia Brandt, France) **32/1**
8 2 1/2 **Msaikah (IRE)**45 4-8-13 0................................ TonyPiccone 6 81
(H-F Devin, France) **31/1**
9 8 **Fierte D'Amour (FR)**32 4011 4-8-13 0...................... TheoBachelot 7 65
(L Gadbin, France) **60/1**
10 10 **Dancing Brave Bear (USA)**23 4332 4-8-13 0..............(p) FrankieDettori 8 45
(Ed Vaughan) *moved up on outer to ld after 1f: sn 3 l clr: c bk to field 3f out: drvn and hdd ins fnl 2f: wknd qckly and heavily eased* **11/1**

2m 3.46s (-6.74) **10** Ran SP% **120.5**
PARI-MUTUEL (all including 1 euro stake): WIN 10.10; PLACE 1.40, 1.10, 1.30; DF 6.20.
Owner Jean-Claude Seroul **Bred** Jean-Claude Seroul **Trained** France

3877 DUSSELDORF (R-H)
Sunday, July 21

OFFICIAL GOING: Turf: good

5230a RACEBETS.DE - MEILEN TROPHY (GROUP 2) (3YO+) (TURF) 1m
3:55 3-Y-O+ £36,036 (£13,963; £7,207; £3,603; £2,252)

RPR
1 **Robin Of Navan (FR)**32 3987 6-9-2 0..................(p) AlexanderPietsch 5 110+
(Harry Dunlop) *mde virtually all: led bef end of 1f: kicked clr 1 1/2f out: styd on strly* **154/10**
2 2 **Indian Blessing**7 4954 5-8-13 0.............................. GeraldMosse 8 102+
(Ed Walker) *racd keenly: hld up towards rr: tk clsr order fnl bnd: hdwy on outer 1 1/2f out: styd on to go 2nd fnl 100yds: no ch w wnr* **13/5**2
3 1 **Nica (GER)**52 3288 4-8-13 0.............................. RenePiechulek 3 100
(Dr A Bolte, Germany) *racd keenly: hld up bhd ldrs: 3rd and scrubbed along 2 1/2f out: outpcd ins fnl 2f: styd on gamely u.p fnl f to regain 3rd* **96/10**
4 nk **Wonnemond (GER)**63 6-9-2 0.................... BayarsaikhanGanbat 9 102
(S Smrczek, Germany) *cl up on outer: 4th and pushed along 2 1/2f out: unable qck 1 1/2f out whn ldr wnt clr: kpt on u.p fnl f* **89/10**
5 1 3/4 **Broderie**35 3907 4-8-13 0.............................. SoufianeSaadi 7 95
(H-A Pantall, France) *racd in fnl pair: drvn and sed to cl over 2f out: kpt on u.p fnl f: nt pce to get involved* **77/10**3
6 hd **Shalona (FR)**20 4461 3-8-5 0.............................. MaximPecheur 1 93
(Henk Grewe, Germany) *towards rr on inner: tk clsr order 1/2-way: wknd u.p fnl f* **17/10**1
7 hd **Degas (GER)**28 4157 6-9-2 0.............................. AdriedeVries 4 97
(Markus Klug, Germany) *in rr: sme prog 1 1/2f out: kpt on same pce fnl f: nvr in contention* **29/1**
8 1 **Palace Prince (GER)**28 4157 7-9-2 0....................(p) FilipMinarik 6 95
(Jean-Pierre Carvalho, Germany) *pressed ldr: outpcd whn ldr kicked for home 1 1/2f out: wknd fnl f* **144/10**
9 6 1/2 **Kronprinz (GER)**8 4-9-2 0.............................. EduardoPedroza 2 80
(P Schiergen, Germany) *hld up in midfield: rdn and no imp: sn wknd* **136/10**

1m 35.6s (-5.56) **9** Ran SP% **118.6**
WFA 3 from 4yo+ 8lb
PARI-MUTUEL (all including 1 euro stake): WIN 16.40 PLACE: 4.20, 1.60, 3.40; SF: 38.00.
Owner Haven't A Pot & Richard Foden **Bred** Mme Monique Lepeudry **Trained** Lambourn, Berks

5231 - (Foreign Racing) - See Raceform Interactive

4684 LES LANDES
Sunday, July 21

OFFICIAL GOING: Turf: firm

5232 DERBY DAY DASH H'CAP SPRINT (TURF) 5f 100y
3:05 (3:05) 3-Y-O+ £1,780 (£640; £380)

Form RPR
43-4 1 **Chapeau Bleu (IRE)**42 7-9-0 0.................... MissSerenaBrotherton 47
(Mrs C Gilbert, Jersey) *trckd ldrs: 4th into st: led wl ins fnl f: drvn out* **10/1**
0-12 2 1 1/4 **Relaxed Boy (FR)**16 4685 6-10-12 0..................(t) MrFrederickTett 69
(Mrs A Malzard, Jersey) *trckd ldr in cl 2nd : ev ch wl ins fnl f: no ex* **13/8**2
3163 3 1 3/4 **Fruit Salad**16 4685 6-9-13 0.............................. MarkQuinlan 50
(K Kukk, Jersey) *s.s: sn trckd ldrs: 5th intro st: rdr lost whip over 1f out: kpt on one pce to go 3rd cl home* **11/2**3
2230 4 1/2 **Country Blue (FR)**16 4685 10-9-8 0....................(p) VictoriaMalzard 43
(Mrs A Malzard, Jersey) *led: hdd wl ins fnl f: wknd* **9/1**
6550 5 6 **Limelite (IRE)**16 4685 5-9-3 0..........................(p) GeorgeRooke 19
(K Kukk, Jersey) *trckd ldrs: 3rd into st: hung lft u.p & wknd fr over 1f out* **9/1**
1121 6 nk **Man Of The Sea (IRE)**16 4685 3-10-2 0..................(tp) MattieBatchelor 34
(Neil Mulholland) *outpcd: sn bhd: nvr a factor* **4/5**1

Owner Saltire Racing **Bred** Woodleigh Stables **Trained** Jersey

5233 ANIMAL HEALTH TRUST H'CAP (TURF) 1m 1f
4:15 (4:15) 3-Y-O+ £1,780 (£640; £380)

Form RPR
1S11 1 **Molliana**30 4175 4-9-6 0.............................. MattieBatchelor 29
(Neil Mulholland) *led in: trckd ldr: wnt on over 4f out: rdn out* **1/1**1
00 2 1 3/4 **Snejinska (FR)**16 4684 5-8-10 0..........................(h) GeorgeRooke 15
(Mrs C Gilbert, Jersey) *hld up: t.k.h: tk clsr order 5f out: wnt 2nd 3f out: kpt on one pce* **14/1**
5-26 3 1 1/4 **Hard To Handel**16 4686 7-10-6 0.................... MissSerenaBrotherton 36
(Mrs A Malzard, Jersey) *hld up: out pced fr 3f out: kpt on one pce* **4/1**3
1510 4 1/2 **Honcho (IRE)**16 4685 7-10-8 0.............................. VictoriaMalzard 37
(Mrs A Malzard, Jersey) *led to over 4f out: btn fr 3f out* **4/1**3
36-3 5 1 3/4 **Ice Royal (IRE)**16 4686 6-10-12 0..................(t) MrFrederickTett 38
(Mrs A Malzard, Jersey) *hld up: out pced fr 3f out: n.d* **2/1**2
U553 6 4 **Brown Velvet**16 4684 7-8-12 0 ow1.............................. DarraghKeogh
(Mrs C Gilbert, Jersey) *hld up: bhd fr 3f out: nvr a factor* **6/1**

Owner Dajam Ltd **Bred** Norman Court Stud **Trained** Limpley Stoke, Wilts

4976 AYR (L-H)
Monday, July 22

OFFICIAL GOING: Good to soft (7.2)
Wind: Fairly strong, half against in sprints and in over 3f of home straight in races on the round course Weather: Cloudy, bright

5234 AYRGOLDCUP.CO.UK NOVICE STKS 6f
1:30 (1:31) (Class 5) 2-Y-O £3,428 (£1,020; £509; £254) Stalls High

Form RPR
4 1 **Dick Datchery (IRE)**15 4688 2-9-5 0..........................(t1) DavidNolan 8 78+
(David O'Meara) *reluctant to enter stalls: trckd ldrs: shkn up and wnt 2nd over 2f out: led ent fnl f: edgd rt: pushed out: comf* **11/2**3
2 1 1/4 **Master McGrath (IRE)** 2-9-5 0.............................. KevinStott 7 74+
(Kevin Ryan) *green in preliminaries: led against stands' rail: rdn over 1f out: hdd ent fnl f: kpt on: bttr for r* **11/10**1
35 3 3/4 **Leapers Wood**49 3411 2-9-5 0.............................. PaulMulrennan 1 74
(Michael Dods) *hld up: effrt and shkn up whn hmpd over 1f out: hdwy fnl f: clsng at fin* **13/2**
4 1 **Custodian (IRE)** 2-9-5 0.............................. PaulHanagan 5 69+
(Richard Fahey) *dwlt: t.k.h: hld up in tch: effrt whn hung lft over 1f out: kpt on same pce ins fnl f (jockey said colt hung left in the final furlong)* **5/1**2
02 5 1/2 **Maysong**39 3767 2-9-5 0.............................. TomQueally 6 68
(Ed Dunlop) *noisy in paddock: prom on outside: effrt and rdn over 1f out: carried lft ins fnl f: one pce* **8/1**
6 3 3/4 **Shadow Leader** 2-9-5 0.............................. ConnorBeasley 4 56
(Michael Dods) *t.k.h: hld up in tch: rdn and outpcd whn edgd rt over 1f out: sn btn* **22/1**
7 1/2 **Panist (IRE)** 2-9-5 0.............................. PJMcDonald 3 55
(Mark Johnston) *trckd ldr to over 2f out: rdn and wknd over 1f out* **14/1**
8 4 1/2 **Burrows Seeside (FR)** 2-9-5 0.............................. TomEaves 2 41
(Philip Kirby) *dwlt: rn green in rr: struggling over 2f out: sn btn: fin lame (vet said colt finished lame right fore)* **66/1**

1m 15.86s (2.76) **Going Correction** +0.05s/f (Good) **8** Ran SP% **116.6**
Speed ratings (Par 94): **83,81,80,79,78 73,72,66**
CSF £12.22 TOTE £7.00: £1.80, £1.10, £1.70; EX 15.50 Trifecta £64.40.
Owner F Gillespie **Bred** Ballylinch Stud **Trained** Upper Helmsley, N Yorks

FOCUS
Races 4, 5, 6 and 7 increased by 18yds, race 8 increased by 30yds. A fair novice event in which the gallop was reasonable. The form's rated around the third and fifth.

5235 SCOTTISH SUN LADIES NIGHT H'CAP 6f
2:00 (2:02) (Class 6) (0-65,66) 3-Y-O+ £2,781 (£827; £413; £300; £300; £300) Stalls High

Form RPR
04-1 1 **Tai Sing Yeh (IRE)**16 4674 5-9-5 **61**..................(t) DonaghO'Connor(3) 2 68
(J F Levins, Ire) *trckd far side ldrs: rdn to ld over 1f out: drvn out fnl f: 1st of 4 in gp* **10/3**1
3304 2 1 **Jacob's Pillow**4 5094 8-9-3 **56**..........................(p) ConnorBeasley 10 60
(Rebecca Bastiman) *led stands' side gp: drvn along 2f out: kpt on fnl f: nt rch far side wnr: 1st of 13 in gp* **16/1**
4452 3 nse **Kodicat (IRE)**14 4720 5-9-5 **58**..........................(p) KevinStott 8 62
(Kevin Ryan) *cl up stands' side gp: drvn along 2f out: kpt on fnl f: 2nd of 13 in gp* **11/2**2
0000 4 1/2 **Jessie Allan (IRE)**14 4720 8-8-1 **47**.............................. CoreyMadden(7) 11 49
(Jim Goldie) *hld up on outside of stands' side gp: hdwy over 2f out: rdn over 1f out: kpt on fnl f: 3rd of 13 in gp* **28/1**
6000 5 3/4 **Star Cracker (IRE)**14 4720 7-8-7 **46** oh1..........................(p) PhilDennis 12 46
(Jim Goldie) *prom: rdn along 2f out: kpt on ins fnl f: 4th of 13th* **33/1**
-060 6 shd **Beechwood Izzy (IRE)**16 4632 3-9-8 **66**.............................. ShaneGray 4 65
(Keith Dalgleish) *cl up far side: effrt and ev ch that gp over 1f out: kpt on same pce ins fnl f: 2nd of 4 in gp* **25/1**
0040 7 3/4 **Indiaro**7 4979 3-8-11 **60**.............................. HarrisonShaw(5) 17 57
(Linda Perratt) *hld up stands' side: n.m.r briefly over 2f out: hdwy over 1f out: kpt on fnl f: nt pce to chal: 5th of 13 in gp* **66/1**
0210 8 hd **Cupid's Arrow (IRE)**9 4912 5-9-0 **53**.............................. TomEaves 3 50
(Ruth Carr) *led far side to over 1f out: rdn and one pce ins fnl f: 3rd of 4 in gp* **10/1**
-065 9 shd **Patrick (IRE)**65 2847 7-9-3 **56**.............................. DavidNolan 15 53
(Paul Midgley) *hld up stands' side: nt clr run over 2f out: hdwy over 1f out: kpt on: nvr able to chal: 6th of 13 in gp* **14/1**
0046 10 1/2 **Thorntoun Lady (USA)**14 4726 9-8-7 **46** oh1..........................(p) PJMcDonald 1 41
(Jim Goldie) *in tch far side: rdn along over 2f out: kpt on same pce ins fnl f: last of 4 in gp* **33/1**
2404 11 1 1/4 **Tadaany (IRE)**9 4912 7-8-13 **52**..........................(p) PaulHanagan 7 43
(Ruth Carr) *prom stands' side: rdn along over 2f out: no ex fr over 1f out: 7th of 13 in gp* **10/1**
0000 12 3/4 **Brendan (IRE)**7 4978 6-8-7 **46**.............................. PaddyMathers 5 35
(Jim Goldie) *t.k.h: hld up on outside of stands' side gp: rdn along 2f out: sn no imp: btn fnl f: 8th of 13 in gp* **33/1**
50/0 13 1 1/4 **Night Law**14 4720 5-8-2 **46** oh1..........................(p) AndrewBreslin(5) 16 31
(Katie Scott) *dwlt and blkd s: bhd stands' side: rdn and effrt over 1f out: sn no imp: 9th of 13 in gp* **33/1**
0222 14 3/4 **Ventura Secret (IRE)**16 4630 5-9-3 **56**..........................(tp) PaulMulrennan 14 39
(Michael Dods) *in tch: rdn over 2f out: n.m.r briefly over 1f out: sn btn: 10th of 13 in gp (jockey said gelding ran flat)* **11/2**2
0611 15 2 **Tarnhelm**11 4824 4-8-9 **55**.............................. RhonaPindar(7) 6 32
(Wilf Storey) *missed break: bhd on outside of stands' side gp: short-lived effrt 2f out: sn btn: 11th of 13 in gp (jockey said filly missed the break)* **13/2**3
20-0 16 2 3/4 **Dixieland (IRE)**11 4820 3-9-4 **65**.............................. BenRobinson(3) 13 33
(Marjorie Fife) *bhd stands' side: drvn and struggling over 2f out: sn btn: 12th of 13 in gp* **66/1**
660 17 1 3/4 **Night Fury**50 3372 3-7-12 **49** ow3.............................. VictorSantos(7) 9 12
(Lucinda Egerton) *bhd: struggling over 2f out: sn wknd: last of 13 in gp* **80/1**

1m 13.53s (0.43) **Going Correction** +0.05s/f (Good) **17** Ran SP% **121.2**
WFA 3 from 4yo+ 5lb
Speed ratings (Par 101): **99,97,97,96,95 95,94,94,94,93 92,91,89,88,85 82,79**
CSF £54.71 CT £304.21 TOTE £4.20: £1.40, £3.10, £1.50, £4.70; EX 56.50 Trifecta £209.10.
Owner Hugh P Ward **Bred** Rabbah Bloodstock Limited **Trained** The Curragh, Co Kildare

FOCUS
A moderate handicap in which the field split into two groups with the winner emerging from the smaller far side bunch. The gallop was sound and the second and third help pin a straightforward level of the form.

5236 WEDDINGS AT WESTERN HOUSE HOTEL H'CAP 5f
2:30 (2:32) (Class 6) (0-65,67) 3-Y-O

£2,781 (£827; £413; £300; £300; £300) **Stalls** High

Form RPR
33 **1** **Compton's Finale**[65] 2852 3-8-12 **60**.........(t) CierenFallon(5) 8 68
(Adrian Paul Keatley, Ire) *missed break: hld up: swtchd lft and gd hdwy to ld over 1f out: pushed clr ins fnl f: comf (trainer said, regarding the improved form shown, the gelding may have benefited from a 65 day break)* **6/1**[3]
0-05 **2** 2 **Kaafy (IRE)**[34] 3964 3-9-6 **63**......... KevinStott 4 64
(Grant Tuer) *hld up: rdn and hdwy over 1f out: chsd wnr ins fnl f: kpt on: nt pce to chal* **6/1**[3]
2113 **3** nk **Hard Solution**[9] 4911 3-9-7 **64**......... DavidNolan 10 68
(David O'Meara) *hld up: effrt whn no room fr over 2f out to ins fnl f: kpt on last 100yds: nrst fin* **7/2**[1]
3150 **4** 1 1/2 **Frosted Lass**[24] 4328 3-9-0 **57**......... PaulMulrennan 11 51
(David Barron) *prom: nt clr run over 2f out and over 1f out: rdn and r.o fnl f: nvr able to chal* **14/1**
U502 **5** nk **Popping Corks (IRE)**[4] 5094 3-8-6 **52**.........(p) BenRobinson(3) 3 45
(Linda Perratt) *prom: effrt and ev ch briefly over 1f out: chsd wnr to ins fnl f: sn no ex (jockey said filly hung right throughout)* **9/2**[2]
4500 **6** 1 1/4 **Northern Society (IRE)**[9] 4911 3-9-4 **61**.........(b[1]) ShaneGray 6 50
(Keith Dalgleish) *led to over 1f out: rdn and wknd ins fnl f: lost hind shoe (vet said filly lost its left hind shoe)* **17/2**
-000 **7** 2 1/4 **Pritty Livvy**[23] 4358 3-7-11 **45**.........(p) AndrewBreslin(5) 1 26
(Noel Wilson) *cl up: rdn over 2f out: wknd ins fnl f* **100/1**
6-20 **8** 1 3/4 **Swinging Eddie**[25] 4286 3-9-10 **67**......... TomEaves 5 41
(Kevin Ryan) *hld up in midfield: rdn and short-lived effrt over 1f out: sn wknd* **9/1**
5614 **9** 2 **Dream House**[17] 4604 3-9-5 **62**......... DuranFentiman 9 29
(Tim Easterby) *prom: rdn over 2f out: outpcd whn checked ins fnl f: sn btn* **9/2**[2]
6-05 **10** 4 1/2 **Little Thornton**[16] 4629 3-7-12 **45** ow3......... VictorSantos(7) 2
(Stella Barclay) *in tch on outside: drvn along over 2f out: sn wknd* **100/1**
1m 1.09s (1.09) **Going Correction** +0.05s/f (Good) **10** Ran SP% **116.3**
Speed ratings (Par 98): **93,89,89,86,86 84,80,78,74,67**
CSF £41.79 CT £148.41 TOTE £7.60: £2.20, £2.40, £1.10; EX 43.80 Trifecta £276.10.
Owner Ontoawinner Syndicate **Bred** Crossfields Bloodstock Ltd **Trained** Rossmore Cottage, Co Kildare

FOCUS
A modest handicap in which the gallop was sound throughout. The third was unlucky not to finish a fair bit closer and the form's rated around the runner-up.

5237 BOOK DIRECT AT WESTERN HOUSE HOTEL H'CAP (DIV I) 7f 50y
3:05 (3:06) (Class 6) (0-65,65) 3-Y-O+ **£2,781** (£827; £413; £300; £300) **Stalls** High

Form RPR
0000 **1** **Roaring Forties (IRE)**[7] 4978 6-9-8 **59**.........(p) LewisEdmunds 1 67
(Rebecca Bastiman) *prom: drvn and hdwy over 1f out: led wl ins fnl f: r.o* **12/1**
-661 **2** nk **Royal Duchess**[14] 4726 9-9-10 **61**......... PhilDennis 2 68
(Lucy Normile) *trckd ldr: rdn and led over 1f out: hdd and no ex wl ins fnl f* **5/1**[2]
554 **3** 1 3/4 **Annexation (FR)**[22] 4421 3-9-6 **64**......... TomQueally 5 66+
(Ed Dunlop) *hld up: effrt whn nt clr run over 2f out: swtchd lft and hdwy over 1f out: kpt on fnl f: nt rch ldrs (jockey said colt was outpaced in the early stage)* **11/4**[1]
6300 **4** shd **Cardaw Lily (IRE)**[11] 4824 4-8-9 **46** oh1......... TomEaves 11 49
(Ruth Carr) *led: rdn and hdd over 1f out: no ex ins fnl f* **28/1**
2665 **5** 2 1/4 **Cameo Star (IRE)**[16] 4630 4-10-0 **65**......... PaulHanagan 9 62
(Richard Fahey) *s.i.s: hld up: rdn and hdwy over 1f out: edgd lft: kpt on fnl f: nt pce to chal* **5/1**[2]
0000 **5** dht **Dark Crystal**[4] 5100 8-8-6 **46**......... BenRobinson(3) 6 43
(Linda Perratt) *hld up towards rr: rdn along over 2f out: sn no imp: kpt on fnl f: nvr able to chal* **20/1**
-006 **7** shd **Palavicini Run (IRE)**[7] 4979 6-8-4 **46** oh1......... PaulaMuir(5) 3 43
(Linda Perratt) *plld hrd in tch: effrt and rdn 2f out: wknd ins fnl f* **50/1**
0-06 **8** 1/2 **Epaulini**[11] 4823 3-8-13 **57**......... ConnorBeasley 8 50
(Michael Dods) *s.i.s: hld up: rdn along over 2f out: sme late hdwy: nvr on terms* **14/1**
-002 **9** 2 1/2 **Prince Of Time**[11] 4824 7-8-13 **50**......... PaulMulrennan 4 39
(Stella Barclay) *t.k.h: cl up: ev ch over 2f out to over 1f out: wknd fnl f: lost front shoe (vet said gelding lost its left front shoe)* **16/1**
0666 **10** 3/4 **Gilmer (IRE)**[9] 4912 8-8-11 **53**......... HarrisonShaw(5) 10 40
(Stef Keniry) *hld up on outside: hdwy and prom over 2f out: wknd over 1f out* **13/2**
4640 **11** 21 **Epona**[24] 4330 3-9-6 **64**......... ShaneGray 7
(Keith Dalgleish) *in tch tl rdn and wknd 2f out: eased whn btn fnl f (jockey said filly stopped quickly)* **6/1**[3]
1m 32.31s (-0.19) **Going Correction** +0.05s/f (Good)
WFA 3 from 4yo+ 7lb **11** Ran SP% **118.0**
Speed ratings (Par 101): **103,102,100,100,97 97,97,97,94,93 69**
CSF £69.98 CT £216.85 TOTE £12.90: £3.10, £1.90, £1.40; EX 68.10 Trifecta £320.00.
Owner Mrs K Hall & Partner **Bred** Agricola Del Parco **Trained** Cowthorpe, N Yorks

FOCUS
Add 18 yds. A run of the mill handicap in which the pace was no more than fair and those held up were at a bit of a disadvantage. The fourth and Dark Crystal limit the form.

5238 BOOK DIRECT AT WESTERN HOUSE HOTEL H'CAP (DIV II) 7f 50y
3:35 (3:36) (Class 6) (0-65,65) 3-Y-O+

£2,781 (£827; £413; £300; £300; £300) **Stalls** High

Form RPR
0/4- **1** **Eleuthera**[281] 8240 7-9-2 **56**.........(t[1]) DonaghO'Connor(3) 2 63
(J F Levins, Ire) *trckd ldrs: smooth hdwy to ld appr fnl f: sn rdn: hld on wl cl home* **13/2**
3551 **2** nk **Macs Blessings (IRE)**[12] 4784 3-8-7 **56**.........(v) HarrisonShaw(5) 6 59
(Stef Keniry) *hld up towards rr: effrt on outside wl over 1f out: rdn and kpt on wl fnl f to take 2nd cl home* **11/2**[3]
4321 **3** 1/2 **Retirement Beckons**[4] 5099 4-8-10 **50** 5ex.........(h) BenRobinson(3) 8 55
(Linda Perratt) *s.i.s: hld up towards rr: hdwy and prom 2f out: rdn and r.o ins fnl f* **3/1**[1]
4603 **4** hd **Leeshaan (IRE)**[11] 4823 4-8-9 **46** oh1......... PhilDennis 10 51
(Rebecca Bastiman) *s.i.s: hld up: nt clr run over 2f out: swtchd rt and hdwy over 1f out: r.o fnl f: nrst fin* **25/1**
5323 **5** 1/2 **Forever A Lady (IRE)**[7] 4979 6-9-8 **59**......... CYHo 3 62
(Keith Dalgleish) *w ldr: led over 2f out tl hdd appr fnl f: rallied: no ex last 75yds* **8/1**
466 **6** 1 1/4 **Valley Of Fire**[18] 4552 7-9-13 **64**......... LewisEdmunds 5 64
(Les Eyre) *hld up in midfield on ins: effrt and pushed along 2f out: no further imp fnl f* **5/1**[2]
53 **7** 2 3/4 **Duhallow Noelie (IRE)**[16] 4678 3-8-11 **60**.........(t) CierenFallon(5) 7 50
(Adrian Paul Keatley, Ire) *hld up in midfield: effrt and wandered over 2f out: outpcd whn hmpd ent fnl f (jockey said gelding suffered interference 1f out)* **5/1**[2]
0505 **8** 3 **Bareed (USA)**[7] 4978 4-8-9 **46** oh1.........(p) TomEaves 1 32
(Linda Perratt) *t.k.h: led to over 2f out: rallied: wknd fnl f* **33/1**
0434 **9** 2 3/4 **Olivia R (IRE)**[11] 4820 3-9-6 **64**.........(h) DavidNolan 11 40
(David Barron) *hld up: drvn along over 2f out: nvr on terms* **10/1**
330 **10** 3 1/4 **Battle Of Yarmouk (IRE)**[46] 3517 3-9-7 **65**.........(w) KevinStott 4 33
(Kevin Ryan) *prom: rdn along over 2f out: wknd over 1f out* **12/1**
-005 **11** 7 **Show The World**[4] 5098 3-7-12 **49** ow1.........(be[1]) VictorSantos(7) 9
(Lucinda Egerton) *slowly away: bhd: struggling over 2f out: sn btn* **100/1**
1m 32.09s (-0.41) **Going Correction** +0.05s/f (Good)
WFA 3 from 4yo+ 7lb **11** Ran SP% **122.7**
Speed ratings (Par 101): **104,103,103,102,102 100,97,94,91,87 79**
CSF £43.63 CT £135.73 TOTE £6.80: £2.50, £3.10, £1.40; EX 44.20 Trifecta £150.20.
Owner J M O'Riordan **Bred** G Reed **Trained** The Curragh, Co Kildare
■ Stewards' Enquiry : C Y Ho two-day ban: used whip above the permitted level (Aug 5-6)
Harrison Shaw two-day ban: used whip above the permitted level (Aug 5-6)

FOCUS
Add 18yds. Division two of a very ordinary handicap and a race in which the gallop was a reasonable one. The form's rated around the principals.

5239 AYRSHIRE CANCER SUPPORT H'CAP 1m
4:10 (4:12) (Class 6) (0-65,65) 4-Y-O+

£2,781 (£827; £413; £300; £300; £300) **Stalls** Low

Form RPR
-661 **1** **Rosemay (FR)**[9] 4917 5-8-6 **50**.........(p) PaulHanagan 8 56
(R Mike Smith) *trckd ldrs: effrt and rdn 2f out: led ins fnl f: drvn out* **13/2**[3]
2112 **2** nk **Betty Grable (IRE)**[16] 4633 5-8-3 **54**......... RhonaPindar(7) 2 59
(Wilf Storey) *prom: hdwy to ld over 2f out: hdd ins fnl f: rallied: hld cl home* **3/1**[1]
3153 **3** 1/2 **Chinese Spirit (IRE)**[7] 4982 5-9-4 **65**......... BenRobinson(3) 3 69
(Linda Perratt) *prom: effrt on outside over 2f out: kpt on ins fnl f* **4/1**[2]
0050 **4** 1 3/4 **Doon Star**[7] 4983 4-8-4 **48**......... PaddyMathers 11 48
(Jim Goldie) *t.k.h: hld up towards rr: rdn over 2f out: hdwy over 1f out: r.o fnl f* **20/1**
6033 **5** nse **Move In Faster**[9] 4915 4-9-1 **59**.........(v) ConnorBeasley 10 60
(Michael Dods) *led: rdn and hdd over 1f out: rallied: one pce whn hmpd ins fnl f* **13/2**[3]
4040 **6** 3/4 **Gworn**[7] 4982 9-9-5 **63**......... PJMcDonald 12 62+
(R Mike Smith) *hld up: rdn along over 2f out: hdwy over 1f out: r.o ins fnl f: nt pce to chal* **12/1**
2103 **7** 1 3/4 **Orobas (IRE)**[5] 5043 7-9-0 **65**.........(v) VictorSantos(7) 5 60
(Lucinda Egerton) *hld up: hdwy on outside over 2f out: hung lft: wknd over 1f out* **14/1**
6000 **8** 6 **Fake News**[6] 5020 4-9-5 **63**......... KevinStott 7 45
(David Barron) *t.k.h: hld up: rdn and outpcd over 2f out: sn btn* **14/1**
3000 **9** hd **Squire**[85] 2145 8-8-13 **57**.........(tp) PaulMulrennan 13 38
(Marjorie Fife) *pressed ldr to over 2f out: rdn and wknd over 1f out* **40/1**
3040 **10** 3/4 **Scots Sonnet**[41] 3704 5-9-7 **65**.........(h) PhilDennis 9 44
(Jim Goldie) *hld up in midfield on ins: rdn over 2f out: wknd over 1f out* **20/1**
6615 **11** 1 1/2 **Home Before Dusk**[16] 4633 4-9-6 **64**.........(v) ShaneGray 1 40
(Keith Dalgleish) *s.i.s: hld up: rdn and struggling over 2f out: sn btn (jockey said gelding boiled over in the preliminaries)* **8/1**
1m 42.6s (-0.20) **Going Correction** +0.05s/f (Good) **11** Ran SP% **115.8**
Speed ratings (Par 101): **103,102,102,100,100 99,97,91,91,90 89**
CSF £25.16 CT £88.75 TOTE £5.90: £2.00, £1.40, £1.60; EX 25.90 Trifecta £64.40.
Owner Dal Riata - A Barclay **Bred** Alexis Chetioui **Trained** Galston, E Ayrshire
■ Stewards' Enquiry : Rhona Pindar three-day ban: interference & careless riding (Aug 5-7)
Paul Hanagan two-day ban: used whip above the permitted level (Aug 5-6)

FOCUS
Add 18yds. Mainly exposed sorts in an ordinary handicap. The gallop was only fair and those up with the pace held the edge. The form could be rated a length better.

5240 FLOWER SHOW @ AYR RACECOURSE IN AUGUST H'CAP 1m 2f
4:45 (4:45) (Class 4) (0-85,86) 3-Y-O+

£6,727 (£2,002; £1,000; £500; £300; £300) **Stalls** Low

Form RPR
6212 **1** **Nicholas T**[7] 4981 7-9-11 **85**......... BenRobinson(3) 4 95
(Jim Goldie) *hld up in tch: hdwy on outside to ld over 1f out: sn rdn and edgd lft kpt on wl fnl f* **9/4**[1]
2134 **2** 2 3/4 **Asian Angel (IRE)**[3] 5149 3-9-6 **86**......... CYHo 3 90
(Mark Johnston) *led: rdn and hdd over 1f out: rallied and chsd wnr ins fnl f: no imp* **5/2**[2]
-456 **3** nk **Royal Regent**[31] 4057 7-8-8 **70**......... PaulaMuir(5) 2 73
(Lucy Normile) *cl up: ev ch over 2f out to over 1f out: lost 2nd ins fnl f: one pce* **10/1**
6-35 **4** 1 **Glasses Up (USA)**[15] 4692 4-9-10 **81**......... PaddyMathers 1 82
(R Mike Smith) *prom: effrt and drvn along 2f out: kpt on same pce fnl f* **7/1**[3]
5066 **5** 3/4 **Can Can Sixty Two**[9] 4917 4-8-2 **66** oh7......... KieranSchofield(7) 8 66
(R Mike Smith) *pressed ldr: ev ch over 2f out: outpcd and hung lft over 1f out: no imp fnl f* **40/1**
0650 **6** 1/2 **Mapped (USA)**[14] 4724 4-8-11 **68**......... PaulMulrennan 9 67
(Iain Jardine) *bhd: hdwy into midfield after 2f: rdn over 2f out: no imp fr over 1f out* **12/1**
0634 **7** 3 3/4 **Windsor Cross (IRE)**[23] 4386 4-9-3 **74**......... PaulHanagan 7 65
(Richard Fahey) *hld up: pushed along over 2f out: sn outpcd: n.d after* **8/1**
/005 **8** 3/4 **Shrewd**[31] 4057 9-9-11 **82**......... TomEaves 6 72
(Iain Jardine) *hld up in last pl: shkn up and outpcd over 2f out: nvr on terms* **33/1**

3000 **9** *1 ½* **Employer (IRE)**[14] 4723 4-9-6 **77** .... LewisEdmunds 5 64
(Jim Goldie) *hld up towards rr: pushed along over 2f out: hung lft and wknd over 1f out* **14/1**

2m 11.86s (-0.54) **Going Correction** +0.05s/f (Good) **9** Ran SP% **111.8**
WFA 3 from 4yo+ 9lb
Speed ratings (Par 105): **104,101,101,100,100 99,96,96,94**
CSF £7.58 CT £42.29 TOTE £3.00: £1.20, £1.10, £2.60; EX 7.60 Trifecta £64.60.
Owner James Callow & J S Goldie **Bred** W M Johnstone **Trained** Uplawmoor, E Renfrews

FOCUS
Add 18yds. A reasonable handicap in which the gallop was an ordinary one. The winner rates pretty much back to his best.

5241 WESTERN HOUSE HOTEL APPRENTICE H'CAP 2m 1f 105y
5:15 (5:15) (Class 5) (0-75,69) 4-Y-O+ **£3,428** (£1,020; £509; £300; £300) **Stalls** Low

Form RPR

40-3 **1** **Burn Some Dust (IRE)**[38] 3816 4-9-12 **69** .... KieranSchofield 1 75
(Brian Ellison) *trckd ldrs: hdwy 3f out: rdn and edgd lft 2f out: rallied and led ins fnl f: kpt on wl* **11/8**[1]

5304 **2** *½* **Hugoigo**[11] 4825 5-8-2 **50** oh3 .... CoreyMadden(5) 5 55
(Jim Goldie) *stdd in last pl: smooth hdwy on outside over 2f out: rdn over 1f out: pressed wnr ins fnl f: kpt on: hld cl home* **5/1**[3]

4/31 **3** *shd* **Tawseef (IRE)**[25] 4308 11-9-5 **65** ....(p) EllaMcCain(3) 2 70
(Donald McCain) *led 2f: chsd ldr: regained ld 6f out: rdn 2f out: hdd ins fnl f: one pce towards fin (jockey said gelding hung right throughout)* **9/4**[2]

0450 **4** *7* **Question Of Faith**[7] 4983 8-9-7 **69** .... ZakWheatley(5) 3 66
(Martin Todhunter) *missed break: hld up in tch: rdn over 2f out: edgd lft and outpcd fr wl over 1f out* **8/1**

-000 **5** *6* **Golden Jeffrey (SWI)**[31] 4056 6-9-3 **65** ....(p) IzzyClifton(5) 4 56
(Iain Jardine) *t.k.h: led after 2f to 6f out: pressed ldr to over 2f out: drvn and wknd wl over 1f out* **10/1**

3m 58.06s (-3.44) **Going Correction** +0.05s/f (Good) **5** Ran SP% **109.7**
Speed ratings (Par 103): **110,109,109,106,103**
CSF £8.54 TOTE £2.30: £1.30, £2.60; EX 7.40 Trifecta £21.30.
Owner Dan Gilbert **Bred** Dan Gilbert **Trained** Norton, N Yorks

FOCUS
Add 30yds. A modest handicap run at a fair gallop and a race in which the first three pulled clear in the closing stages. The winner is rated only to form.
T/Jkpt: Not won. T/Plt: £13.40 to a £1 stake. £46,675.49 - 2,537.39 winning units T/Qpdt: £5.80 to a £1 stake. Pool: £7,825.76 - 996.74 winning units **Richard Young**

5017 BEVERLEY (R-H)
Monday, July 22

OFFICIAL GOING: Good to firm (8.2)
Wind: Light across Weather: Warm & sunny

5242 ITV7 STARTS NOW MAIDEN H'CAP 2m 32y
5:55 (5:56) (Class 6) (0-65,67) 3-Y-O
£3,105 (£924; £461; £300; £300; £300) **Stalls** Low

Form RPR

462 **1** **Platform Nineteen (IRE)**[35] 3931 3-9-7 **63** ....(p) CliffordLee 6 77+
(Michael Bell) *hld up in rr: swtchd lft to outer and smooth hdwy 3f out: led over 1f out: sn rdn clr: easily* **11/8**[1]

5462 **2** *8* **Kensington Art**[17] 4587 3-9-4 **60** ....(p) TonyHamilton 1 64
(Richard Fahey) *set stdy pce: pushed along and qcknd 3f out: rdn over 2f out: hdd and drvn over 1f out: kpt on: no ch w wnr* **10/1**

-004 **3** *8* **Barb's Prince (IRE)**[20] 4484 3-8-10 **52** ....(p) BenCurtis 4 46
(Ian Williams) *in tch: rdn along and sltly outpcd over 2f out: kpt on one pce u.p appr fnl f* **20/1**

0544 **4** *½* **Spring Run**[24] 4345 3-9-0 **56** .... DavidAllan 8 50
(Jonathan Portman) *hld up towards rr: hdwy wl over 2f out: rdn wl over 1f out: sn drvn and plugged on one pce (jockey said filly was denied a clear run two furlongs out)* **9/2**[2]

4365 **5** *2 ¼* **Tucson**[46] 3505 3-9-11 **67** .... DanielTudhope 10 58
(James Bethell) *hld up towards rr: pushed along and outpcd 3f out: sme hdwy on inner over 2f out: sn rdn: n.d (jockey said colt hung left in the home straight)* **13/2**

050- **6** *1* **Volcanique (IRE)**[240] 9254 3-8-10 **52** .... RyanTate 5 42
(Sir Mark Prescott Bt) *trckd ldng pair: pushed along on outer 4f out: rdn 3f out: sn drvn and wknd* **12/1**

0000 **7** *3 ½* **Feebi**[35] 3931 3-8-3 **45** .... JoeFanning 3 31
(Chris Fairhurst) *trckd ldng pair on inner: rdn along over 3f out: wknd over 2f out* **14/1**

000 **8** *41* **Whims Of Desire**[129] 1217 3-8-13 **55** .... LukeMorris 2
(Sir Mark Prescott Bt) *trckd ldr: pushed along over 4f out: rdn along 3f out: drvn over 2f out: sn lost pl: bhd and eased over 1f out (jockey said filly stopped quickly)* **6/1**[3]

3m 37.67s (-0.23) **Going Correction** -0.075s/f (Good) **8** Ran SP% **116.1**
Speed ratings (Par 98): **97,93,89,88,87 87,85,64**
CSF £17.00 CT £195.40 TOTE £2.10: £1.10, £1.80, £4.20; EX 14.80 Trifecta £140.40.
Owner The Royal Ascot Racing Club **Bred** Watership Down Stud **Trained** Newmarket, Suffolk

FOCUS
Distance increased by 1yd. A very warm and breezy evening. A fair pace for this weak 3yo stayers' handicap and the winner scored with plenty to spare.

5243 RACING TV EBF FILLIES' NOVICE STKS (PLUS 10 RACE) 5f
6:25 (6:27) (Class 5) 2-Y-O **£4,032** (£1,207; £603; £302; £150) **Stalls** Low

Form RPR

1 **Seize The Time (IRE)** 2-9-0 0 .... CliffordLee 1 75+
(K R Burke) *trckd ldrs: swtchd rt to inner at cut off over 2f out: sn chsng ldr: rdn over 1f out: led ent fnl f: kpt on wl* **2/1**[1]

10 **2** *1* **Three Coins**[44] 3564 2-9-4 0 .... TonyHamilton 7 75
(Richard Fahey) *trckd ldr: pushed along 2f out: rdn over 1f out: kpt on ins fnl f* **12/1**

3312 **3** *shd* **Dream Kart (IRE)**[12] 4799 2-9-4 **84** .... JoeFanning 10 75
(Mark Johnston) *sn led: pushed along 2f out: rdn and edgd bdly lft over 1f out: hdd ent fnl f: sn drvn and kpt on same pce* **9/4**[2]

4 *hd* **Reviette** 2-9-0 0 .... DougieCostello 6 70
(Kevin Ryan) *chsd ldrs: hdwy on inner 2f out: rdn over 1f out: kpt on fnl f* **33/1**

335 **5** *1* **Stars In The Night (IRE)**[53] 3244 2-9-0 **77** .... GrahamLee 9 67
(Kevin Ryan) *trckd ldng pair: cl up on outer 2f out: sn rdn and kpt on same pce fnl f* **7/1**

6 *2 ¼* **Spring Campaign (IRE)** 2-9-0 0 .... DanielTudhope 2 59
(Michael Bell) *green and hld up towards rr: hdwy wl over 1f out: kpt on fnl f* **4/1**[3]

5 **7** *1 ½* **Imperial Eagle (IRE)**[19] 4517 2-9-0 0 .... DavidAllan 5 53
(Lawrence Mullaney) *chsd ldrs: rdn along 2f out: sn drvn and grad wknd (jockey said filly hung left)* **16/1**

8 *¾* **Bay Filly Rolla** 2-9-0 0 .... AndrewMullen 4 50
(Michael Dods) *dwlt: a in rr* **20/1**

5 **9** *7* **Sombra De Mollys**[16] 4624 2-9-0 0 .... CamHardie 12 25
(Brian Ellison) *dwlt and wnt lft s: towards rr: sme hdwy on outer and in tch 1/2-way: sn rdn and wknd* **50/1**

10 *10* **Gelsmoor Bay** 2-9-0 0 .... AndrewElliott 8
(Derek Shaw) *a in rr: outpcd and bhd fnl 2f* **125/1**

1m 3.71s (0.81) **Going Correction** -0.075s/f (Good) **10** Ran SP% **120.6**
Speed ratings (Par 91): **90,88,88,87,86 82,80,79,67,51**
CSF £27.70 TOTE £3.30: £1.80, £2.60, £1.10; EX 34.80 Trifecta £99.80.
Owner Phoenix Thoroughbred Limited **Bred** Dr T K Chah **Trained** Middleham Moor, N Yorks

FOCUS
Distance increased by 1yd. The first four home in this fairly decent fillies' novice sprint enjoyed the benefit of racing near the cutaway on the far rail and there was not much between them.

5244 JAIMIE KERR MEMORIAL H'CAP 5f
7:00 (7:04) (Class 5) (0-75,73) 3-Y-O+
£4,284 (£1,282; £641; £320; £300; £300) **Stalls** Low

Form RPR

1311 **1** **Ginger Jam**[17] 4586 4-9-6 **72** .... FayeMcManoman(5) 8 86+
(Nigel Tinkler) *hld up in rr: swtchd to outer and hdwy over 1f out: str run ent fnl f: led last 60yds: sn clr* **6/4**[1]

400- **2** *1 ¼* **Four Wheel Drive**[217] 9589 3-8-13 **64** .... GrahamLee 11 68
(David Brown) *led: rdn along over 1f out: drvn and edgd lft ins fnl f: hdd last 60yds* **50/1**

0034 **3** *hd* **Suwaan (IRE)**[16] 4632 5-9-6 **67** ....(h) JamesSullivan 1 71
(Ruth Carr) *t.k.h: hld up in tch: effrt and nt clr run over 1f out: sn swtchd lft and rdn: carried hd high but styd on wl fnl f* **5/1**[2]

2003 **4** *½* **Red Pike (IRE)**[11] 4821 8-9-3 **71** .... HarryRussell(7) 4 73
(Bryan Smart) *prom: rdn to chse ldr over 1f out: drvn ent fnl f: kpt on same pce last 100yds* **11/2**[3]

0322 **5** *½* **Afandem (IRE)**[11] 4821 5-9-5 **71** ....(p) DannyRedmond(5) 3 72
(Tim Easterby) *chsd ldrs on inner: rdn along wl over 1f out: drvn and kpt on same pce fnl f* **11/2**[3]

4005 **6** *½* **Burtonwood**[2] 5169 7-8-9 **59** .... ConorMcGovern(3) 7 58
(Julie Camacho) *t.k.h: hld up towards rr: hdwy and nt clr run over 1f out: kpt on same pce after (jockey said gelding was denied a clear run inside the final furlong)* **12/1**

5013 **7** *½* **Decision Maker (IRE)**[24] 4335 5-8-13 **60** .... JimmyQuinn 2 57
(Roy Bowring) *dwlt: t.k.h towards rr: rdn along wl over 1f out: kpt on fnl f (jockey said gelding was restless in the stalls)* **10/1**

2011 **8** *½* **Gamesome (FR)**[16] 4632 8-9-6 **70** .... ConnorMurtagh(3) 12 65
(Paul Midgley) *t.k.h: in tch on outer: hdwy to chse ldrs 2f out: sn rdn and one pce (jockey said gelding ran too freely)* **14/1**

30-0 **9** *3 ¼* **Moonlit Sands (IRE)**[6] 5018 4-8-10 **57** .... CamHardie 5 41
(Brian Ellison) *chsd ldrs: rdn along 2f out: wknd over 1f out* **16/1**

3010 **10** *2 ¾* **Desert Ace (IRE)**[10] 4880 8-9-12 **73** .... LukeMorris 10 47
(Paul Midgley) *t.k.h: chsd ldr: rdn along over 1f out: sn wknd* **33/1**

1m 3.01s (0.11) **Going Correction** -0.075s/f (Good)
WFA 3 from 4yo+ 4lb **10** Ran SP% **121.7**
Speed ratings (Par 103): **96,94,93,92,92 91,90,89,84,80**
CSF £103.22 CT £341.94 TOTE £2.40: £1.10, £14.30, £2.20; EX 106.60 Trifecta £689.80.
Owner Walter Veti **Bred** Bearstone Stud Ltd **Trained** Langton, N Yorks
■ Gorgeous General was withdrawn. Price at time of withdrawal 11-1. Rule 4 applies to all bets struck prior to withdrawal, but not to SP bets. Deduction - 5p in the pound. New market formed.

FOCUS
Distance increased by 1yd. A lack of pace and the winner came from last to first, so can be marked up a bit. The runner-up rates to his early 2yo form.

5245 GEORGE KILBURN MEMORIAL H'CAP 1m 1f 207y
7:30 (7:31) (Class 5) (0-75,76) 3-Y-O+
£4,284 (£1,282; £641; £320; £300; £300) **Stalls** Low

Form RPR

3002 **1** **Bollin Ted**[6] 5024 5-8-13 **58** .... DavidAllan 10 67
(Tim Easterby) *trckd ldrs: hdwy over 2f out: rdn to chal over 1f out: led jst ins fnl f: drvn out* **7/2**[1]

2040 **2** *1 ¼* **Ideal Candy (IRE)**[23] 4371 4-9-8 **70** ....(h) GemmaTutty(3) 5 76
(Karen Tutty) *trckd ldr: led after 2f: rdn along 2f out: drvn over 1f out: hdd jst ins fnl f: kpt on same pce* **5/1**

-000 **3** *nk* **Detachment**[37] 3867 6-10-3 **76** .... BenCurtis 1 81
(Roger Fell) *hld up in rr: hdwy over 2f out: chsd ldrs over 1f out: rdn and kpt on fnl f* **9/2**[3]

01 **4** *¾* **Miss Sheridan (IRE)**[59] 3053 5-10-0 **73** .... NathanEvans 9 77
(Michael Easterby) *led 2f: trckd ldr: pushed along on inner 2f out: rdn over 1f out: drvn and kpt on same pce fnl f* **25/1**

6151 **5** *1* **Zihaam**[11] 4817 5-9-3 **67** ....(p) BenSanderson(5) 3 69
(Roger Fell) *hld up: pushed along and hdwy wl over 2f out: rdn wl over 1f out: drvn and no imp fnl f* **10/1**

4421 **6** *1 ¼* **Allux Boy (IRE)**[7] 5003 5-8-12 **62** 5ex .... FayeMcManoman(5) 8 61
(Nigel Tinkler) *trckd ldrs: hdwy to chse ldr 1/2-way: rdn along over 2f out: drvn and wknd over 1f out (jockey said gelding ran too free)* **9/2**[3]

-304 **7** *2 ¼* **Kingson (IRE)**[16] 4663 3-9-1 **72** .... SeanDavis(3) 7 68
(Richard Fahey) *in tch: pushed along over 4f out: rdn along 3f out: grad wknd* **12/1**

53-0 **8** *6* **Dyagilev**[16] 4639 4-9-8 **67** ....(p[1]) AndrewElliott 2 50
(Lydia Pearce) *a towards rr (jockey said gelding hung left throughout)* **50/1**

4431 **9** *18* **Maqaadeer**[16] 4664 3-9-5 **73** .... DaneO'Neill 6 21
(Ed Dunlop) *dwlt: sn in tch: hdwy to trck ldrs 1/2-way: rdn along over 3f out: wknd and eased fnl 2f (trainers' rep could offer no explanation for the poor performance)* **4/1**[2]

2m 3.87s (-1.83) **Going Correction** -0.075s/f (Good)
WFA 3 from 4yo+ 9lb **9** Ran SP% **117.8**
Speed ratings (Par 103): **104,103,102,102,101 100,98,93,79**
CSF £21.77 CT £80.71 TOTE £4.20: £1.60, £2.10, £1.40; EX 21.00 Trifecta £137.40.
Owner Neil Arton & Partner **Bred** Habton Farms **Trained** Great Habton, N Yorks

FOCUS
Distance increased by 1yd. An ordinary handicap run at a generous clip. The winner came from off the pace and found a bit on his latest form.

5246 RICHARD AND CAROL HUDSON H'CAP 7f 96y
8:00 (8:00) (Class 4) (0-85,87) 3-Y-O+
£6,553 (£1,961; £980; £490; £300; £300) **Stalls Low**

Form RPR

5533 **1** **Luis Vaz De Torres (IRE)**[18] 4546 7-9-1 **78**........................ SeanDavis(3) 3 85
(Richard Fahey) *hld up in rr: hdwy over 2f out: chsd ldrs over 1f out: rdn to chal ins fnl f: drvn and kpt on wl to ld last 50yds* **10/1**

-310 **2** *nk* **Helovaplan (IRE)**[105] 1644 5-9-11 **85**........................ GrahamLee 1 91
(Bryan Smart) *prom: hdwy 3f out: chsd ldr wl over 1f out: sn rdn and led ent fnl f: sn drvn: hdd and no ex last 50yds* **20/1**

6410 **3** *½* **Lamloom (IRE)**[26] 4240 5-9-13 **87**........................ DanielTudhope 7 92
(David O'Meara) *led: pushed along 2f out: rdn and edgd lft over 1f out: sn drvn and hdd: kpt on same pce fnl f* **7/1**

6210 **4** *1* **I Am A Dreamer**[10] 4887 3-9-2 **83**........................ JoeFanning 2 82
(Mark Johnston) *chsd ldrs: rdn along over 2f out: drvn over 1f out: kpt on same pce* **6/1**[3]

0436 **5** *hd* **King's Pavilion (IRE)**[14] 4730 6-9-9 **86**........................ ConorMcGovern(3) 4 88
(Jason Ward) *hld up towards rr: hdwy on outer 3f out: chsd ldrs 2f out: rdn over 1f out: drvn and kpt on same pce fnl f* **14/1**

5500 **6** *hd* **Al Erayg (IRE)**[16] 4654 6-9-3 **77**........................ DavidAllan 6 78
(Tim Easterby) *hld up: effrt on inner wl over 2f out and sn pushed along: rdn wl over 1f out: drvn and kpt on same pce fnl f* **11/4**[1]

1134 **7** *1* **Kylie Rules**[16] 4626 4-9-8 **82**........................ JamesSullivan 5 80
(Ruth Carr) *t.k.h: hld up towards rr: hdwy on wd outside wl over 2f out: rdn wl over 1f out: sn btn* **7/1**

1242 **8** *1¾* **Saisons D'Or (IRE)**[2] 5200 4-9-6 **80**........................ JackGarritty 9 74
(Jedd O'Keeffe) *trckd ldr: pushed along over 2f out: rdn wl over 1f out: sn drvn and wknd appr fnl f (jockey said gelding ran flat)* **7/2**[2]

5220 **9** *2¼* **Proud Archi (IRE)**[10] 4879 5-9-8 **82**........................ AndrewMullen 8 70
(Michael Dods) *in tch on outer: pushed along 3f out: rdn over 2f out: sn wknd (jockey said gelding stopped quickly)* **9/1**

1m 30.71s (-1.89) **Going Correction** -0.075s/f (Good)
WFA 3 from 4yo+ 7lb **9** Ran SP% **118.7**
Speed ratings (Par 105): **107,106,106,104,104 104,103,101,98**
CSF £190.14 CT £1506.43 TOTE £11.80: £3.20, £6.60, £1.60; EX 160.90 Trifecta £2140.00.
Owner Lets Go Racing 1 **Bred** Peter Molony **Trained** Musley Bank, N Yorks

FOCUS
Distance increased by 1yd. The gallop was decent for this fair handicap and the winner took the shortest route, coming from off the pace. The winner is rated in line with this year's form.

5247 SKY BET GO-RACING-IN-YORKSHIRE SUMMER FESTIVAL H'CAP 7f 96y
8:30 (8:31) (Class 6) (0-60,59) 3-Y-O+
£3,105 (£924; £461; £300; £300; £300) **Stalls Low**

Form RPR

2620 **1** **Red Seeker**[16] 4633 4-9-10 **57**........................(t) DavidAllan 2 64
(Tim Easterby) *chsd clr ldr: hdwy 3f out: led 2f out: sn rdn: drvn ins fnl f: hld on wl towards fin* **15/8**[1]

0600 **2** *hd* **Etikaal**[42] 3657 5-9-8 **55**........................ JackGarritty 9 62
(Grant Tuer) *t.k.h early: hld up in tch: hdwy wl over 2f out: chsd wnr over 1f out: sn rdn: drvn and styd on wl to chal ins fnl f: ev ch tl no ex nr fin* **16/1**

0020 **3** *2¾* **Rosy Ryan (IRE)**[4] 5099 9-8-12 **48**........................ ConnorMurtagh(3) 14 48
(Tina Jackson) *hld up: hdwy 3f out: rdn along wl over 1f out: styd on fnl f: nrst fin* **9/1**

0130 **4** *hd* **Fitzy**[20] 4487 3-9-2 **56**........................(p) CamHardie 7 52
(David Brown) *hld up towards rr: hdwy 2f out: sn rdn: styd on wl fnl f: nrst fin* **12/1**

0006 **5** *nk* **Wensley**[12] 4785 4-9-6 **53**........................ DanielTudhope 4 52
(Rebecca Bastiman) *trckd ldrs: hdwy on inner 2f out: rdn over 1f out: kpt on same pce fnl f* **9/1**

-40R **6** *½* **Erastus**[11] 4823 4-8-13 **46**........................ NathanEvans 12 44
(Ruth Carr) *t.k.h: swtchd rt s and hld up in rr: hdwy on inner 2f out: rdn and nt clr run jst over 1f out: swtchd lft and drvn ent fnl f: kpt on wl towards fin (jockey said gelding was denied a clear run on several occasions in the final two furlongs)* **50/1**

4042 **7** *1¼* **Fard**[11] 4820 4-9-6 **58**........................ BenSanderson(5) 10 52
(Roger Fell) *hld up: hdwy over 2f out: rdn over 1f out: drvn and styd on wl fnl f* **6/1**[2]

0-13 **8** *½* **Quick Monet (IRE)**[33] 3996 6-9-2 **49**........................ GrahamLee 8 42
(Shaun Harris) *midfield: hdwy on inner wl over 1f out: sn rdn to chse ldrs: drvn and kpt on same pce fnl f* **25/1**

5300 **9** *1¼* **Rebel State (IRE)**[4] 5099 6-9-1 **55**........................ OwenPayton(7) 11 45
(Jedd O'Keeffe) *hld up towards rr: hdwy on wd outside wl over 2f out: sn rdn and no imp* **13/2**[3]

0-05 **10** *hd* **Shamaheart (IRE)**[19] 4523 9-9-12 **59**........................(tp) AndrewMullen 15 48
(Geoffrey Harker) *stdd and swtchd rt s: hld up: a in rr* **25/1**

3040 **11** *1¾* **Muqarred (USA)**[4] 5099 7-9-2 **52**........................ GemmaTutty(3) 5 38
(Karen Tutty) *chsd ldrs: rdn along over 2f out: hld whn n.m.r over 1f out: wknd* **16/1**

5000 **12** *2* **Quduraat**[18] 4567 3-8-11 **54**........................ SeanDavis(3) 1 31
(Michael Appleby) *chsd ldrs: hdwy 3f out: rdn along 2f out: sn drvn and wknd* **66/1**

0004 **13** *½* **Relight My Fire**[6] 5021 9-9-3 **55**........................(b) DannyRedmond(5) 6 34
(Tim Easterby) *midfield: effrt and hdwy 3f out: rdn over 2f out: sn btn* **8/1**

0460 **14** *½* **Adventureman**[14] 4728 7-9-2 **49**........................ JamesSullivan 13 27
(Ruth Carr) *chsd ldng pair: rdn along 3f out: sn drvn and wknd 2f out* **28/1**

2400 **15** *17* **Elikapeka (FR)**[25] 4284 3-9-5 **59**........................(v[1]) DougieCostello 3
(Kevin Ryan) *led and sn clr: pushed along 3f out: rdn over 2f out: sn wknd* **20/1**

1m 31.61s (-0.99) **Going Correction** -0.075s/f (Good)
WFA 3 from 4yo+ 7lb **15** Ran SP% **132.3**
Speed ratings (Par 101): **102,101,98,98,98 97,96,95,94,93 91,89,88,88,68**
CSF £37.96 CT £254.10 TOTE £2.50: £1.30, £6.00, £3.40; EX 34.90 Trifecta £282.40.
Owner Brian Valentine **Bred** Aunty Ifl **Trained** Great Habton, N Yorks
■ Stewards' Enquiry : David Allan two-day ban; misuse of whip (Aug 5-6)

FOCUS
Distance increased by 1yd. A modest handicap and not many got into it. The first two drew a little way clear of the remainder and the form's fairly straightforward.

5248 RACING AGAIN NEXT TUESDAY H'CAP 1m 1f 207y
9:00 (9:04) (Class 6) (0-55,55) 3-Y-O+
£3,363 (£1,001; £500; £300; £300; £300) **Stalls Low**

Form RPR

4000 **1** **Bob's Girl**[6] 5020 4-9-1 **46** oh1........................(b) JimmyQuinn 3 52
(Michael Mullineaux) *prom: chsd clr ldr after 2f: hdwy to take clsr order over 2f out: rdn to ld over 1f out: drvn ins fnl f: kpt on wl towards fin* **25/1**

0400 **2** *½* **John Caesar (IRE)**[6] 5024 8-9-1 **46** oh1........................(p) DanielTudhope 5 51
(Rebecca Bastiman) *towards rr: pushed along and hdwy wl over 2f out: rdn wl over 1f out: drvn and styd on strly fnl f: jst failed* **6/1**[3]

0356 **3** *nk* **Mi Laddo (IRE)**[5] 5054 3-8-5 **48** ow1........................(tp) ConorMcGovern(3) 2 53
(Oliver Greenall) *towards rr: hdwy and in tch over 3f out: rdn to chse ldrs whn hung rt 2f out: drvn over 1f out: kpt on wl fnl f* **14/1**

5401 **4** *hd* **Blyton Lass**[19] 4518 4-9-4 **49**........................ LukeMorris 12 53
(James Given) *midfield: hdwy and in tch over 3f out: chsd ldrs 2f out: sn rdn: drvn and kpt on fnl f* **12/1**

00-0 **5** *2½* **Jimmy Krankyar (USA)**[9] 4916 3-8-12 **52**........................ BenCurtis 8 52
(Phillip Makin) *bhd: rdn along over 3f out: hdwy wl over 1f out: styd on strly fnl f: nrst fin* **25/1**

-002 **6** *nk* **Bigbadboy (IRE)**[34] 3959 6-9-1 **46**........................ AndrewMullen 4 45
(Clive Mulhall) *chsd ldrs: rdn along over 2f out: drvn over 1f out: kpt on same pce* **4/1**[2]

0000 **7** *nk* **Laqab (IRE)**[7] 5003 6-9-10 **55**........................ AndrewElliott 16 53
(Derek Shaw) *dwlt and bhd: hdwy over 3f out: effrt on inner and rdn wl over 1f out: styd on fnl f: nrst fin* **20/1**

3342 **8** *½* **Brutalab**[6] 5023 3-8-11 **51**........................ RachelRichardson 17 49
(Tim Easterby) *qckly away: led and sn clr: pushed along 3f out: rdn over 2f out: sn hdd: drvn and wknd over 1f out* **5/2**[1]

3144 **9** *2½* **Majestic Stone (IRE)**[17] 4601 5-9-4 **49**........................ GrahamLee 15 42
(Julie Camacho) *dwlt and towards rr: hdwy into midfield 1/2-way: effrt over 3f out: rdn to chse ldrs 2f out: sn drvn and grad wknd* **8/1**

000- **10** *2* **Bigdabog**[287] 8055 4-9-1 **46**........................ CamHardie 10 35
(Stella Barclay) *dwlt: a towards rr* **40/1**

0655 **11** *nk* **Call Him Al (IRE)**[12] 4785 3-8-12 **55**........................ ConnorMurtagh(3) 11 44
(Richard Fahey) *nvr bttr than midfield* **16/1**

0050 **12** *4½* **Inflexiball**[23] 4371 7-9-2 **47**........................ JoeFanning 1 27
(John Mackie) *chsd ldrs on inner: pushed along to chse ldng pair 1/2-way: rdn along 3f out: drvn 2f out: sn wknd* **12/1**

-442 **13** *2¼* **Don't Be Surprised**[33] 4002 4-9-7 **55**........................ SeanDavis(3) 13 33
(Seb Spencer) *chsd ldrs: rdn along 3f out: drvn whn bdly hmpd 2f out: wknd after* **12/1**

004 **14** *14* **Thornton Le Clay**[36] 3882 3-8-8 **48**........................ NathanEvans 9
(Michael Easterby) *a towards rr: outpcd and bhd fnl 3f* **20/1**

2m 5.13s (-0.57) **Going Correction** -0.075s/f (Good)
WFA 3 from 4yo+ 9lb **14** Ran SP% **129.2**
Speed ratings (Par 101): **99,98,98,98,96 95,95,95,93,91 91,87,86,74**
CSF £171.19 CT £2250.41 TOTE £24.80: £8.00, £2.00, £5.10; EX 241.80 Trifecta £2142.50.
Owner S A Pritchard **Bred** Aston Mullins Stud **Trained** Alpraham, Cheshire

FOCUS
Distance increased by 1yd. A poor handicap and a muddling affair. The winner was never too far off a strong early gallop set by the keen-going favourite, who folded. Not form to dwell on.
T/Plt: £92.10 to a £1 stake. Pool: £67,371.59 - 533.64 winning units T/Qpdt: £48.60 to a £1 stake. £7,665.34 - 116.67 winning units **Joe Rowntree**

4991 WINDSOR (R-H)
Monday, July 22

OFFICIAL GOING: Good to firm (good in places; 7.0)
Wind: light, behind Weather: Fine, hot

5249 JEWEL RUNAWAY BAY H'CAP 1m 3f 99y
5:45 (5:46) (Class 6) (0-65,65) 3-Y-O
£2,781 (£827; £413; £300; £300; £300) **Stalls Low**

Form RPR

032 **1** **Mukha Magic**[35] 3938 3-9-3 **61**........................(v) TomMarquand 10 73+
(Gay Kelleway) *in tch in midfield: shkn up 4f out: making prog whn hmpd over 2f out: sn rdn to cl on ldrs: led jst over 1f out: styd on wl and drew clr* **7/1**[3]

-004 **2** *7* **Goodwood Sonnet (IRE)**[34] 3965 3-8-7 **51**........................(v[1]) DavidEgan 16 52
(William Knight) *restrained into midfield: prog over 4f out: led 2f out to over 1f out: qckly lft bhd by wnr* **9/1**

0-54 **3** *1¾* **Closer Than Close**[22] 4423 3-9-7 **65**........................(h) RobHornby 5 63
(Jonathan Portman) *racd in last of main gp and sme way off the pce: urged along 4f out: racd awkwardly but prog over 2f out: styd on to take 3rd nr fin* **10/1**

00-1 **4** *½* **Whistler Bowl**[23] 4372 3-9-6 **64**........................ HectorCrouch 15 61+
(Gary Moore) *trckd ldr: rdn to ld briefly jst over 2f out: sn btn: wknd fnl f* **11/4**[1]

0-04 **5** *½* **Ocean Reach**[28] 4177 3-8-3 **50**........................ JaneElliott(3) 4 47
(Richard Price) *hld up wl in rr: pushed along and stdy prog on outer 3f out: nvr rchd ldrs* **50/1**

4526 **6** *2* **Sea Art**[20] 4484 3-9-6 **64**........................(v) SilvestreDeSousa 2 57
(William Knight) *chsd ldrs: rdn over 3f out: outpcd over 2f out: n.d after* **17/2**

0220 **7** *11* **Junior Rip (IRE)**[39] 3777 3-9-5 **63**........................(bt) JasonWatson 11 39
(Roger Charlton) *led at str pce: drvn 3f out: hdd jst over 2f out: wknd qckly* **5/1**[2]

0-04 **8** *½* **Sephton**[16] 4664 3-8-13 **57**........................ DavidProbert 9 32
(Alan King) *a towards rr: urged along over 4f out: no prog and btn 3f out* **16/1**

0400 **9** *1¼* **Another Approach (FR)**[49] 3418 3-8-9 **53**........................ HayleyTurner 13 26
(Amanda Perrett) *nvr beyond midfield: rdn and struggling 4f out: no ch fr 3f out* **20/1**

0000 **10** *9* **Break Of Day**[16] 4642 3-8-6 **50**........................(b) LiamJones 1 9
(William Haggas) *t.k.h: prom tl wknd over 3f out: t.o* **14/1**

-504 **11** *23* **Spice Of Life**[21] 4447 3-8-11 **55**........................(b[1]) HarryBentley 3
(Ralph Beckett) *chsd ldr: u.p fr 1/2-way: wknd 4f out: sn wl t.o* **8/1**

3-00 **12** *¾* **Midoura**[41] 3697 3-8-10 **54**........................ CharlieBennett 12
(Laura Mongan) *a towards rr: wknd over 4f out: sn wl t.o* **100/1**

6060 **13** *15* **Blue Beirut (IRE)**[13] 4769 3-8-9 **53**..............................(p[1]) NicolaCurrie 7
(William Muir) *immediately detached in last: wl t.o by 1/2-way (jockey said colt was never travelling)* **50/1**

0014 **U** **Twpsyn (IRE)**[44] 3594 3-9-1 **59**..............................(b) JFEgan 14 61+
(David Evans) *hld up in midfield: prog 4f out: cl 4th and looked to be gng best whn stmbld and uns rdr over 2f out* **33/1**

2m 26.78s (-2.92) **Going Correction** -0.15s/f (Firm) **14** Ran SP% **121.7**
Speed ratings (Par 98): **104,98,97,97,96 95,87,87,86,79 62,62,51,**
CSF £66.92 CT £641.81 TOTE £7.20: £2.30, £2.80, £4.00; EX 70.30 Trifecta £867.20.
Owner P Crook, J Moynihan, R Mortlock **Bred** Alvediston Stud **Trained** Exning, Suffolk

FOCUS
Distance increased by 27yds. Lowly 3yo form, the race fell apart after the overly strong pace collapsed. The winner built on his recent level.

5250 JAMAICA ONE LOVE EBF FILLIES' NOVICE AUCTION STKS (PLUS 10 RACE) 6f 12y
6:15 (6:18) (Class 4) 2-Y-O **£4,463** (£1,328; £663; £331) **Stalls** Centre

Form RPR

4 **1** **Mitty's Smile (IRE)**[11] 4840 2-8-13 0.............................. OisinMurphy 13 70
(Archie Watson) *w ldr: led over 2f out: drvn over 1f out: kpt on wl* **15/8**[1]

2 **2** *1 1/4* **Mild Illusion (IRE)**[27] 4221 2-8-11 0.............................. RobHornby 1 64
(Jonathan Portman) *hld up wl in rr: prog over 2f out: rdn over 1f out: styd on to take 2nd last strides* **5/2**[2]

40 **3** *shd* **The Blue Bower (IRE)**[27] 4222 2-8-12 0.............................. JasonWatson 5 65
(Suzy Smith) *hld up wl in rr: prog 1/2-way: rdn to chse wnr over 1f out: kpt on but a hld: lost 2nd last strides* **16/1**

4 *2 1/4* **Queen Salamah (IRE)** 2-9-0 0.............................. JamieSpencer 12 60
(Richard Spencer) *trckd ldrs: rdn to dispute 2nd briefly wl over 1f out: fdd* **9/2**[3]

54 **5** *2 1/4* **Santorini Sal**[44] 3595 2-8-11 0.............................. KieranO'Neill 8 50
(John Bridger) *w ldng pair early: pushed along 1/2-way: nt qckn whn drvn over 1f out: outpcd* **25/1**

6 *nk* **Disarming (IRE)** 2-8-13 0.............................. KierenFox 4 52
(Dr Jon Scargill) *towards rr: pushed along and sme prog 2f out: no hdwy over 1f out* **50/1**

7 *1/2* **You Don't Own Me (IRE)** 2-8-11 0.............................. CharlesBishop 11 48+
(Joseph Tuite) *s.s: rn green and wl in rr: struggling 2f out: kpt on fnl f* **7/2**[2]

44 **8** *3/4* **Tilly Tamworth**[10] 4871 2-8-12 0.............................. DavidEgan 9 47
(Rod Millman) *led to jst over 2f out: wknd over 1f out* **16/1**

9 *1* **Lethal Blast** 2-8-8 0..............................(h[1]) MeganNicholls(3) 2 43
(Paul George) *rn green and wl in rr: stl green and hanging over 1f out: kpt on nr fin* **20/1**

10 *hd* **Joanna Vassa** 2-8-6 0.............................. RhiainIngram(5) 6 42
(Roger Ingram) *trckd ldrs 4f: pushed along and wknd* **100/1**

11 *11* **Power Packed** 2-8-12 0.............................. DavidProbert 3 10
(Henry Candy) *chsd ldrs to 1/2-way: wknd over 2f out: t.o* **10/1**

12 *6* **Woodsmokehill** 2-9-0 0.............................. CharlieBennett 10
(Rod Millman) *s.i.s: rcvrd to chse ldrs after 2f: hung bdly lft 1/2-way and sn dropped to rr again: t.o (jockey said filly hung badly left-handed)* **33/1**

1m 12.15s (0.05) **Going Correction** -0.15s/f (Firm) **12** Ran SP% **119.8**
Speed ratings (Par 93): **93,91,91,88,85 84,84,83,81,81 66,58**
CSF £6.10 TOTE £2.50: £1.30, £1.30, £5.20; EX 7.20 Trifecta £67.60.
Owner M Aziz **Bred** Summerseat Stables Ltd **Trained** Upper Lambourn, W Berks

FOCUS
Modest juvenile form and a straightforward win for the favourite.

5251 DOWNLOAD THE MARATHONBET APP FILLIES' H'CAP 6f 12y
6:50 (6:51) (Class 4) (0-85,84) 3-Y-O+
£5,207 (£1,549; £774; £387; £300; £300) **Stalls** Centre

Form RPR

1155 **1** **Always A Drama (IRE)**[18] 4560 4-9-4 **74**.............................. KieranShoemark 1 82
(Charles Hills) *t.k.h: hld up in last pair: prog over 2f out: rdn to ld over 1f out: sn hrd pressed: drvn out and styd on wl* **7/1**

-005 **2** *1* **Zain Hana**[24] 4340 4-9-7 **84**..............................(h[1]) AledBeech(7) 4 89
(John Butler) *trckd ldng trio: clsd 2f out: rdn to chal over 1f out: pressed wnr tl nt qckn last 100yds* **10/1**

40-6 **3** *2 1/2* **Sweet Pursuit**[18] 4560 5-9-6 **76**.............................. OisinMurphy 5 74
(Rod Millman) *trckd ldng pair: rdn 2f out: sltly impeded over 1f out: one pce after (jockey said mare suffered interference two furlongs out)* **11/2**[3]

0242 **4** *nse* **More Than Likely**[6] 5015 3-9-4 **79**.............................. ShaneKelly 6 75
(Richard Hughes) *led 2f: pressed ldr: led again 2f out against rail: hung lft and hdd over 1f out (jockey said filly hung left-handed)* **7/2**[2]

1130 **5** *1/2* **Philipine Cobra**[11] 4847 3-9-8 **83**..............................(h[1]) JosephineGordon 2 77
(Phil McEntee) *hld up in 5th: effrt on outer over 2f out: nt qckn over 1f out: one pce after (jockey said filly was never travelling)* **6/4**[1]

4-60 **6** *1 3/4* **Elizabeth Bennet (IRE)**[49] 3427 4-9-7 **77**..............................(p[1]) TomMarquand 7 66
(Robert Cowell) *w ldr: led after 2f to 2f out: hanging lft and wknd (jockey said filly hung left-handed)* **25/1**

20-0 **7** *6* **Daphinia**[66] 2810 3-9-0 **75**.............................. SilvestreDeSousa 3 44
(Dean Ivory) *t.k.h: hld up in last: taken wd and pushed along over 2f out: no prog and rdn over 1f out: eased ins fnl f (jockey said filly had no more to give)* **7/1**

1m 10.86s (-1.24) **Going Correction** -0.15s/f (Firm)
WFA 3 from 4yo+ 5lb **7** Ran SP% **115.5**
Speed ratings (Par 102): **102,100,97,97,96 94,86**
CSF £72.67 TOTE £8.10: £3.60, £4.30; EX 77.80 Trifecta £293.50.
Owner B W Neill **Bred** Patrick Kelly **Trained** Lambourn, Berks

FOCUS
Ordinary sprinting form, they raced away from the rail in the straight with the action unfolding more down the centre. The winner is rated to her AW form.

5252 MARATHONBET "BETTER ODDS MEAN BIGGER WINNINGS" H'CAP (MARATHONBET SPRINT SERIES QUALIFIER) 5f 21y
7:20 (7:20) (Class 3) (0-90,88) 3-Y-O **£7,246** (£2,168; £1,084; £542; £270) **Stalls** Centre

Form RPR

0062 **1** **Daschas**[7] 4995 5-8-11 **81**..............................(t) MarcoGhiani(7) 7 88
(Stuart Williams) *trckd clr ldng pair gng wl: shkn up over 1f out: chal fnl f: rdn and r.o to ld last strides* **4/1**[2]

1600 **2** *nk* **The Daley Express (IRE)**[26] 4236 5-9-8 **85**.............................. DavidProbert 6 91
(Ronald Harris) *hld up in rr: prog on outer 2f out: drvn to ld jst ins fnl f: kpt on but hdd last strides (jockey said gelding hung left-handed)* **16/1**

3033 **3** *nk* **Shamshon (IRE)**[10] 4888 8-9-3 **80**.............................. OisinMurphy 3 85
(Stuart Williams) *hld up in rr: shkn up wl over 1f out: no prog tl fnl f: edgd lft but r.o to take 3rd and clsng at fin* **8/1**

1003 **4** *1 1/2* **Moonraker**[7] 4995 7-9-5 **82**.............................. AlistairRawlinson 4 82
(Michael Appleby) *taken down early: w ldr and 3 l ahd of rest: drvn over 1f out: edgd lft after: fdd last 100yds* **13/2**

0043 **5** *1 1/4* **Leo Minor (USA)**[17] 4609 5-8-11 **74**..............................(p) TomMarquand 8 69
(Robert Cowell) *s.i.s: mostly in last pair: shkn up over 1f out: kpt on same pce fnl f: n.d* **7/1**

6434 **6** *nse* **Our Oystercatcher**[26] 4230 5-8-8 **71**.............................. SilvestreDeSousa 1 66
(Mark Pattinson) *led and clr w one rival: hrd rdn and hung lft over 1f out: hdd & wknd jst ins fnl f (trainer said gelding was unsuited by the ground and would prefer a softer surface)* **9/4**[1]

4435 **7** *nk* **Pettochside**[11] 4844 10-8-7 **70**.............................. KieranO'Neill 5 64
(John Bridger) *hld up towards rr: rdn and no rspnse over 1f out: no ch after: kpt on nr fin* **14/1**

1230 **8** *3/4* **Joegogo (IRE)**[10] 4872 4-9-2 **79**.............................. JFEgan 9 70
(David Evans) *pushed along to chse ldrs fr s: nvr able to chal: fdd fnl f* **33/1**

13-5 **9** *3 1/2* **Dancing Warrior**[87] 2086 3-9-7 **88**.............................. JasonWatson 2 65
(William Knight) *slowly away: a in last pair: shkn up and no prog over 1f out (jockey said filly missed the break)* **6/1**[3]

58.39s (-1.71) **Going Correction** -0.15s/f (Firm)
WFA 3 from 4yo+ 4lb **9** Ran SP% **117.5**
Speed ratings (Par 107): **107,106,106,103,101 101,101,99,94**
CSF £66.13 CT £495.85 TOTE £4.60: £1.50, £4.30, £2.30; EX 68.40 Trifecta £319.20.
Owner T W Morley **Bred** Juddmonte Farms Ltd **Trained** Newmarket, Suffolk

FOCUS
As in the previous race the runners drifted away from the rail in the straight with the action unfolding centre-field. The winner was one of three in the race for his owner. Straightforward form.

5253 BRITISH EBF FILLIES' H'CAP 1m 2f
7:50 (7:50) (Class 4) (0-85,86) 3-Y-O+
£6,727 (£1,501; £500; £300; £300) **Stalls** Low

Form RPR

-221 **1** **Birdcage Walk**[39] 3773 3-9-2 **80**..............................(h) JamesDoyle 4 87+
(Hugo Palmer) *led at mod pce to over 6f out: trckd ldr tl led again 2f out and drvn for home: inclined to idle but styd on and nvr in serious danger after* **3/1**[2]

342 **2** *1* **Gallic**[23] 4393 3-9-7 **85**.............................. ShaneKelly 5 89
(Ed Walker) *hld up in rr: outpcd and rdn over 3f out: no prog tl over 1f out: styd on fnl f: nrst fin (jockey said filly hung right-handed)* **4/1**[3]

1-60 **2** *dht* **Spanish Aria**[31] 4052 3-9-4 **82**.............................. NickyMackay 3 86
(John Gosden) *trckd ldrs: rdn over 2f out: nt qckn wl over 1f out: styd on to chse wnr ins fnl f: no imp* **5/1**

-046 **4** *1 1/2* **Elegant Love**[18] 4562 3-8-2 **66**.............................. DavidEgan 6 67
(David Evans) *hld up tl swift move to ld over 6f out: kicked on over 3f out: hdd 2f out: one pce after* **20/1**

-160 **5** *3/4* **Flighty Almighty**[31] 4052 3-9-7 **85**.............................. RichardKingscote 9 85
(Tom Dascombe) *hld up in last: lft bhd whn pce lifted over 3f out: shkn up over 2f out: nvr in it but kpt on steadily over 1f out* **14/1**

4-14 **6** *1* **Geizy Teizy (IRE)**[46] 3495 3-8-13 **77**.............................. SilvestreDeSousa 8 75
(Marco Botti) *trckd ldr 3f: styd prom: rdn over 2f out: chsd wnr over 1f out tl ins fnl f: wknd qckly last 100yds* **11/4**[1]

6616 **7** *6* **Cape Islay (FR)**[10] 4864 3-9-8 **86**.............................. OisinMurphy 1 72
(Mark Johnston) *t.k.h: hld up in tch: rdn wl over 2f out: sn wknd* **6/1**

2m 8.11s (-0.89) **Going Correction** -0.15s/f (Firm)
WFA 3 from 4yo 9lb **7** Ran SP% **114.0**
Speed ratings (Par 102): **97,96,96,95,94 93,88**
WIN: BW 2.50 PL: G 1.10, SA 1.20, BW 1.80; EX: BW/SA 9.60, BW/G 6.30 CSF: BW/SA 7.67, BW/G 9.11; TF: BW/G/SA 29.40, BW/SA/G 32.70; TC: BW/G/SA 28.36, BW/SA/G 29.73 TOTE £2.50: £1.80, £1.20, £1.10.
Owner G Schoeningh **Bred** G Schoeningh **Trained** Newmarket, Suffolk

FOCUS
Add 27yds. Little gallop on here and the winner very much enjoyed the run of the race. The form's rated around the fourth.

5254 COOL RUNNING MAIDEN STKS 1m 2f
8:20 (8:24) (Class 5) 3-4-Y-O **£3,428** (£1,020; £509; £254) **Stalls** Low

Form RPR

2 **1** **Dubai Future**[17] 4608 3-9-5 0.............................. OisinMurphy 13 85
(Saeed bin Suroor) *dwlt but sn trckd ldr: chal and upsides over 2f out: gd battle after: gained upper hand ins fnl f* **3/1**[1]

3 **2** *1/2* **Two Bids**[37] 3860 3-9-5 0.............................. JamesDoyle 12 84
(William Haggas) *led: stretched on over 3f out: jnd over 2f out: gd battle after tl hdd and jst hld ins fnl f* **3/1**[1]

3 *2 1/2* **Invictus Spirit** 3-9-5 0.............................. PatDobbs 2 79
(Sir Michael Stoute) *t.k.h early: mostly chsd ldng pair: shkn up and no imp over 2f out: styd on same pce* **7/1**[2]

3 **4** *1 3/4* **Fly The Flag**[16] 4641 3-9-0 0.............................. KieranO'Neill 3 70
(John Gosden) *wl in tch: pushed along sn after 1/2-way: racd awkwardly fr 3f out and no imp on ldrs: kpt on to take 4th fnl f* **7/1**[2]

0 **5** *1 3/4* **Hermosura**[13] 4768 3-9-0 0.............................. HarryBentley 4 67
(Ralph Beckett) *in tch in ldng gp: urged along fr 1/2-way: stl in w ch of a pl over 1f out: no ex* **50/1**

5 **6** *3/4* **Vibrance**[24] 4326 3-9-0 0.............................. GeorgeWood 15 65
(James Fanshawe) *in tch in ldng gp: outpcd 3f out: shkn up and styd on same pce fnl 2f: nt disgracd* **33/1**

05 **7** *6* **Mr Nice Guy (IRE)**[26] 4234 3-9-5 0.............................. JasonWatson 8 58
(Sylvester Kirk) *wl bhd in last pair early: clsd up over 4f out: lft bhd again over 3f out: pushed along and kpt on steadily fnl 2f* **100/1**

8 *1/2* **Zest Of Zambia (USA)** 3-9-0 0.............................. CharlieBennett 6 52
(Dai Burchell) *wl bhd in last pair early: clsd up over 4f out: lft bhd again over 3f out: shkn up over 2f out: n.d but kpt on steadily* **100/1**

04- **9** *4 1/2* **Into The Zone**[214] 9637 3-9-5 0..............................(t w) JackMitchell 14 48
(Simon Crisford) *in tch in ldng gp to 4f out: shkn up and wknd 3f out* **25/1**[3]

5 **10** *8* **Mr Carpenter (IRE)**[67] 2764 3-9-5 0.............................. DanielMuscutt 10 32
(David Lanigan) *disp 3rd pl tl wknd qckly jst over 2f out (jockey said gelding hung right-handed under pressure)* **25/1**[3]

6 **11** *1/2* **Eighteenhundred (IRE)**[35] 3946 3-9-2 0.............................. MeganNicholls(3) 5 31
(Paul Nicholls) *a in last quartet: shkn up and outpcd over 3f out: sn bhd* **80/1**

00 **12** *3 3/4* **My Footsteps**[7] 5004 4-10-0 0.............................. TrevorWhelan 9 23
(Paul D'Arcy) *a in last quartet: wknd 3f out (jockey said colt hung left-handed)* **100/1**

2m 7.39s (-1.61) **Going Correction** -0.15s/f (Firm)
WFA 3 from 4yo 9lb **12** Ran SP% **91.8**
Speed ratings (Par 103): **100,99,97,96,94 94,89,89,85,79 78,75**
CSF £5.85 TOTE £2.80: £1.50, £1.10, £1.60; EX 6.80 Trifecta £33.70.

Owner Godolphin **Bred** Godolphin **Trained** Newmarket, Suffolk
■ Allocated (100-1) and No 2 Reaction Time (9-4F) were withdrawn not under orders. Rule 4 applies to all bets. Deduct 30p in the pound.
FOCUS
Add 27yds. Just a steady gallop on here and it paid to race prominently. Decent form, the race rated to the top end of the averages.

5255 VISIT JAMAICA SUMMER H'CAP 1m 31y
8:50 (8:50) (Class 5) (0-75,77) 3-Y-O+
£3,428 (£1,020; £509; £300; £300; £300) **Stalls** Low

Form RPR
41-5 1 **Seductive Moment (GER)**[195] 126 3-9-8 **77**........ SilvestreDeSousa 5 88
(Mark Johnston) *uns rdr bef ent stalls: trckd ldr: shkn up to ld wl over 1f out: sn drvn clr* **13/2**
5003 2 2 ¼ **Data Protection**[11] 4837 4-9-11 **72**........(t) NicolaCurrie 1 79
(William Muir) *trckd ldng pair: rdn and nt qckn 2f out: styd on fnl f to take 2nd last 100yds: no threat* **3/1**[3]
0230 3 2 **Casement (IRE)**[21] 4445 5-10-0 **75**........ AlistairRawlinson 4 77
(Michael Appleby) *led: rdn and hdd wl over 1f out: fdd fnl f* **10/1**
3004 4 1 ¼ **Duke Of North (IRE)**[4] 5087 7-8-5 **59**........ IsobelFrancis(7) 2 59
(Jim Boyle) *hld up in last: detached after 3f: pushed along and no prog over 2f out: shkn up and kpt on to take 4th last strides: nvr in it* **10/1**
3123 5 nse **Leo Davinci (USA)**[18] 4566 3-9-8 **77**........(t[1]) HarryBentley 6 74
(George Scott) *chsd ldrs: drvn over 2f out: disp 3rd over 1f out: fdd ins fnl f* **2/1**[1]
0-35 6 ¾ **I'lletyougonow**[22] 4424 3-9-3 **72**........ OisinMurphy 3 68
(Mick Channon) *hld up in last pair: pushed along over 2f out: no prog whn reminder over 1f out: kpt on nr fin but nvr in it* **11/4**[2]

1m 42.19s (-2.31) **Going Correction** -0.15s/f (Firm)
WFA 3 from 4yo+ 8lb **6 Ran SP% 116.5**
Speed ratings (Par 103): **105,102,100,99,99 98**
CSF £27.33 CT £195.96 TOTE £6.70: £2.70, £1.80; EX 40.70 Trifecta £122.80.
Owner Kingsley Park 10 **Bred** Gestut Hof Ittlingen **Trained** Middleham Moor, N Yorks
FOCUS
Add 27yds. Ordinary handicap form, with the two market leaders disappointing, but an unexposed and progressive winner. The form's rated around the runner-up.
T/Plt: £219.20 to a £1 stake. Pool: £100,167.72 - 333.56 winning units T/Qpdt: £31.10 to a £1 stake. Pool: £10,991.14 - 261.10 winning units **Jonathan Neesom**

5256a-5262a (Foreign Racing) - See Raceform Interactive

3710 DIEPPE (R-H)
Monday, July 22

OFFICIAL GOING: Turf: soft

5263a PRIX DES MOTEURS HYBRID (CLAIMER) (2YO) (TURF) 5f 110y
4:20 2-Y-O £7,207 (£2,882; £2,162; £1,441; £720)

RPR
1 **Paper Star**[12] 4799 2-9-1 0........ TheoBachelot 1 69
(George Baker) *wl into stride: led: shkn up over 2f out: rdn and chal over 1f out: drvn and kpt on strly ins fnl f* **2/1**[2]
2 nk **Jayadeeva (FR)**[37] 2-9-2 0........ MaximeGuyon 7 69
(A Giorgi, Italy) **16/5**[3]
3 1 ¼ **Coply (FR)**[27] 4228 2-8-7 0 ow1........(p) TomLefranc(5) 4 61
(Matthieu Palussiere, France) **27/1**
4 2 ½ **Vereny Ka (FR)**[27] 4228 2-8-3 0........ ThomasTrullier(5) 6 49
(C Lerner, France) **81/10**
5 1 **Skip The Queue (IRE)**[17] 2-9-4 0........(b) AntoineHamelin 8 55
(Matthieu Palussiere, France) **19/10**[1]
6 3 ½ **Lost In France (IRE)**[27] 4228 2-8-11 0........ DelphineSantiago(4) 2 41
(R Le Gal, France) **63/10**

1m 6.33s **6 Ran SP% 119.9**
PARI-MUTUEL (all including 1 euro stake): WIN 3.00; PLACE 1.20, 1.30, 2.90; DF 5.50.
Owner Edward J Ware **Bred** Mrs D J James **Trained** Chiddingfold, Surrey

4637 CHELMSFORD (A.W) (L-H)
Tuesday, July 23

OFFICIAL GOING: Polytrack: standard
Wind: light, half behind Weather: hot and sunny

5264 HILLS PROSPECT SIMPLY THE BEST APPRENTICE H'CAP 6f (P)
5:20 (5:23) (Class 6) (0-55,54) 3-Y-O+
£3,105 (£924; £461; £300; £300; £300) **Stalls** Centre

Form RPR
4422 1 **Tarseekh**[18] 4589 6-9-1 **51**........(b) WilliamCarver(3) 12 57
(Charlie Wallis) *sn prom fr wd draw: led over 4f out: mde rest: 4 l clr 2f out: edgd lft ins fnl f: a jst lasting home* **9/2**[2]
-023 2 ½ **Prince Rock (IRE)**[18] 4589 4-8-5 **45**........(h) LeviWilliams(7) 5 50
(Simon Dow) *hld up in midfield: effrt and hdwy over 1f out: nt clrest of runs and swtchd rt ent fnl f: styd on wl to go 2nd cl home: nvr quite getting to wnr* **9/2**[2]
0504 3 ½ **Quick Recovery**[13] 4776 4-9-6 **53**........(b) CierenFallon 4 56
(Jim Boyle) *taken down early: chsd ldrs: bumping w rival wl over 1f out: sn chsng wnr and drvn: clsd: nt clrest of runs and swtchd rt ins fnl f: styd on but nvr quite getting to wnr: lost 2nd cl home* **3/1**[1]
-060 4 1 ¼ **Red Skye Delight (IRE)**[111] 1514 3-9-1 **53**........ ThoreHammerHansen 1 51
(Luke McJannet) *taken down early: chsd ldrs: nt clr run and swtchd rt wl over 1f out: kpt on same pce u.p ins fnl f* **14/1**
3053 5 nk **Le Manege Enchante (IRE)**[14] 4765 6-8-10 **46**........(v) AledBeech(3) 8 44
(Derek Shaw) *in tch in midfield: effrt u.p over 1f out: kpt on u.p but nvr enough pce to get on terms* **10/1**
3300 6 shd **Catapult**[20] 4501 4-8-13 **49**........(p) JessicaCooley(3) 3 47
(Shaun Keightley) *hld up in rr of main gp: swtchd lft and hdwy over 1f out: swtchd ent fnl f: kpt on but nvr enough pce to get on terms* **6/1**[3]
0342 7 5 **Red Snapper**[14] 4749 4-8-5 **45**........(p) MarcoGhiani(7) 2 28
(William Stone) *led for over 1f out: chsd wnr: edging out rt and bumping w rival wl over 1f out: sn 2nd and wknd ins fnl f* **8/1**
00 8 2 **Alaskan Bay (IRE)**[32] 4074 4-8-10 **50**........ StefanoCherchi(7) 7 27
(Rae Guest) *hld up in rr of main gp: effrt on inner over 1f out: nvr threatened ldrs* **25/1**
6500 9 2 ¾ **Dandy Lad (IRE)**[14] 4765 3-8-13 **51**........ ThomasGreatrex 9 19
(Natalie Lloyd-Beavis) *taken down early: chsd ldrs tl lost pl and hung rt over 1f out: bhd ins fnl f (jockey said gelding hung badly right-handed)* **50/1**
50-4 10 3 ¼ **Farol**[171] 550 3-8-13 **51**........ BenSanderson 11 9
(James Given) *a towards rr: wl bhd fnl f* **14/1**
3035 11 2 ½ **Wild Flower (IRE)**[21] 4481 7-9-2 **49**........(b) RhiainIngram 6
(Jimmy Fox) *restless in stalls: sat bk as stalls opened and v.s.a: nvr rcvrd (jockey said mare anticipated the start and accelerated the gate at the same moment as the race had been started)* **14/1**

1m 13.03s (-0.67) **Going Correction** -0.10s/f (Stan)
WFA 3 from 4yo+ 5lb **11 Ran SP% 121.7**
Speed ratings (Par 101): **97,96,95,94,93 93,86,84,80,76 72**
CSF £26.09 CT £73.26 TOTE £5.80: £2.10, £1.90, £1.60; EX 23.80 Trifecta £87.70.
Owner P E Axon **Bred** Cheveley Park Stud Ltd **Trained** Ardleigh, Essex
FOCUS
A low-grade opener, the winner always on the sharp end and little got into contention from the rear. Straightforward, limited form.

5265 HILLS PROSPECT CHAMPAGNE & PROSECCO NOVICE STKS (PLUS 10 RACE) 6f (P)
5:50 (5:52) (Class 4) 2-Y-O £5,822 (£1,732; £865; £432) **Stalls** Centre

Form RPR
3 1 **Hector Loza**[27] 4246 2-9-5 0........ NickyMackay 4 80
(Simon Dow) *chsd ldrs: wnt clr in ldng trio 1/2-way: effrt to press ldrs 2f out: sustained chal u.p: drvn ahd towards fin* **11/8**[1]
3552 2 hd **Return To Senders (IRE)**[11] 4861 2-9-5 77........(b) NicolaCurrie 10 79
(Jamie Osborne) *t.k.h: chsd ldrs tl hdwy to ld 4f out: drvn and hrd pressed over 1f out: kpt on wl u.p: hdd and no ex towards fin* **3/1**[3]
3 2 **Vasari (USA)** 2-9-5 0........ RyanMoore 12 73
(Sir Michael Stoute) *broke fast fr wd draw and sn led: hdd 4f out: chsd ldr and clr in ldng trio: ev ch 2f out: sn rdn: no ex 100yds out: wknd towards fin* **5/2**[2]
0 4 10 **Najm**[5] 5082 2-9-5 0........ RyanTate 6 43
(Sir Mark Prescott Bt) *midfield: outpcd by ldng trio over 3f out: nvr a threat to ldrs after: modest 4th and no imp fnl f* **25/1**
03 5 3 ½ **Rochford (IRE)**[18] 4588 2-9-5 0........ JFEgan 2 33
(Henry Spiller) *off the pce in last trio: sme prog but nvr on terms w ldrs 2f out: modest 5th and no imp fnl f* **33/1**
6 2 **Positive Light (IRE)** 2-9-0 0........ LukeMorris 1 22
(Sir Mark Prescott Bt) *midfield: outpcd by ldng trio over 3f out: nvr a threat to ldrs after: wl btn whn rn green u.p 1f out* **10/1**
0 7 ¾ **Comvida (IRE)**[8] 4992 2-9-5 0........(p[1]) PatCosgrave 7 25
(Hugo Palmer) *led early but rousted along: sn hdd: 4th and outpcd over 3f out: wknd over 1f out* **20/1**
00 8 6 **Prosecutor (IRE)**[85] 2191 2-9-0 0........ DougieCostello 9
(Mark H Tompkins) *sn rousted along: midfield but nvr on terms: wl btn fr 3f out* **100/1**
00 9 5 **Jochi Khan (USA)**[15] 4734 2-9-0 0........(h[1]) CierenFallon(5) 11
(Robert Cowell) *rn green and hung rt: a towards rr: wl bhd fnl 3f: eased towards fin* **33/1**
00 10 13 **Casi Casi**[6] 5045 2-9-0 0........ CallumShepherd 3
(Charlie Wallis) *sn outpcd: t.o* **100/1**

1m 12.98s (-0.72) **Going Correction** -0.10s/f (Stan) **10 Ran SP% 121.2**
Speed ratings (Par 96): **97,96,94,80,76 73,72,64,57,40**
CSF £5.72 TOTE £1.90: £1.10, £1.30, £1.20; EX 6.50 Trifecta £19.30.
Owner Robert Moss **Bred** Saleh Al Homaizi & Imad Al Sagar **Trained** Epsom, Surrey
FOCUS
Little strength in depth to this novice event and the three market leaders pulled well clear of the remainder. The 1-2 are rated around their pre-race form.

5266 HILLS PROSPECT NUMBER ONE DRINKS DISTRIBUTOR H'CAP 6f (P)
6:20 (6:21) (Class 2) (0-100,97) 3-Y-O+ £12,938 (£3,850; £1,924; £962) **Stalls** Centre

Form RPR
3131 1 **Alkaraama (USA)**[17] 4638 3-8-12 **88**........ JimCrowley 3 97+
(Sir Michael Stoute) *wl in tch in midfield: effrt over 1f out: hdwy u.p to chal ins fnl f: drvn to ld 100yds out: r.o wl and gng away at fin (vet said colt lost its right fore shoe)* **11/8**[1]
1633 2 1 **Intuitive (IRE)**[17] 4638 3-8-8 **84**........ SilvestreDeSousa 1 90+
(James Tate) *trckd ldrs on inner: effrt whn hung rt and swtchd lft over 1f out: drvn and ev ch ins fnl f: nt match pce of wnr towards fin (jockey said colt hung right-handed under pressure)* **7/4**[2]
1100 3 1 **Watchable**[10] 4896 9-9-12 **97**........(p) AdamKirby 6 101
(David O'Meara) *sn pushed into ld: drvn over 1f out: hdd 100yds out: no ex* **12/1**
6103 4 2 ¼ **Katheefa (USA)**[24] 4379 5-8-8 **84**........ HarrisonShaw(5) 2 81
(Ruth Carr) *hld up in tch in last trio: effrt and chsd ldrs whn nt clr run and swtchd rt 1f out: kpt on but no threat to ldrs ins fnl f* **10/1**
1305 5 1 ¼ **Walk On Walter (IRE)**[22] 4451 4-9-9 **94**........(h) RobHornby 7 87
(Jonathan Portman) *sn chsng ldr tl unable qck and lost 2nd over 1f out: hung lft and btn jst ins fnl f: wknd fnl 100yds* **8/1**[3]
3/60 6 2 ½ **Unabated (IRE)**[13] 4805 5-9-7 **95**........(e) PaddyBradley(3) 5 80
(Jane Chapple-Hyam) *hld up in rr: effrt over 1f out: sn no imp and wl hld ins fnl f* **40/1**
51-5 7 ¾ **Power Link (USA)**[151] 875 3-8-8 **84**........ PJMcDonald 8 65
(James Tate) *hld up in last trio: nt clr run over 1f out: wl hld and one pce fnl f* **16/1**
0641 8 7 **Bossipop**[8] 4987 6-8-9 **80** 5ex........(b) LukeMorris 9 40
(Tim Easterby) *chsd ldrs: rdn ent fnl 2f: lost pl over 1f out: wknd fnl f* **25/1**

1m 11.2s (-2.50) **Going Correction** -0.10s/f (Stan)
WFA 3 from 4yo+ 5lb **8 Ran SP% 118.5**
Speed ratings (Par 109): **109,107,106,103,101 98,97,88**
CSF £4.16 CT £18.66 TOTE £2.10: £1.10, £1.10, £2.00; EX 4.60 Trifecta £26.30.
Owner Hamdan Al Maktoum **Bred** Frank Hutchinson **Trained** Newmarket, Suffolk
FOCUS
A good quality sprint handicap and with two unexposed 3yos fighting out the finish, this looks a solid piece of form. The first two both have some upside.

5267 HARROGATE SPA WATER H'CAP 1m (P)
6:50 (6:54) (Class 4) (0-80,82) 3-Y-O+
£5,692 (£1,694; £846; £423; £300; £300) **Stalls** Low

Form RPR
2306 1 **Attainment**[25] 4338 3-9-6 **81**........ PJMcDonald 2 88
(James Tate) *sn led and mde rest: rdn 2f out: drvn ins fnl f: all out towards fin: a jst holding on* **7/2**[1]

3065 **2** *nk* **Philamundo (IRE)**[17] 4643 4-9-10 **77**.....................(b) AdamKirby 1 85
(Richard Spencer) *in rr: clsd and in tch 3f out: swtchd rt and effrt over 1f out: str run u.p ins fnl f: wnt 2nd wl ins fnl f: nt quite rch wnr* **8/1**

2033 **3** *½* **Lawmaking**[24] 4386 6-10-1 **82**.....................(p[1]) RobHornby 10 90+
(Michael Scudamore) *pushed along early: dropped in after 1f and racd in last pair: clsd and in tch 3f out: nt clr run 1f out: swtchd rt 1f out: hdwy ins fnl f: r.o strly fnl 100yds: nt quite rch ldrs (jockey said gelding was denied a clear run)* **14/1**

2-55 **4** *½* **Monaadhil (IRE)**[26] 4300 5-9-13 **80**.....................(p[1]) JimCrowley 8 86
(Marcus Tregoning) *hld up in tch: effrt over 1f out: drvn and edgd lft 1f out: kpt on ins fnl f* **5/1**[2]

1-03 **5** *shd* **Cantiniere (USA)**[17] 4640 4-10-0 **81**..................... HayleyTurner 7 86
(Saeed bin Suroor) *wl in tch in midfield: effrt over 1f out: hdwy and edgd lft 1f out: chsd wnr briefly ins fnl f: one pce and lost 3 pls wl ins fnl f* **6/1**[3]

2040 **6** *2* **Glory Awaits (IRE)**[19] 4566 9-9-2 **74**.....................(b) DylanHogan[(5)] 6 75
(David Simcock) *rousted along leaving stalls: chsd wnr ent fnl 6f: unable qck u.p over 1f out: lost 2nd ins fnl f: wknd fnl 100yds* **25/1**

1-26 **7** *2¼* **Millions Memories**[48] 3471 3-9-5 **80**..................... StevieDonohoe 3 74
(David Lanigan) *chsd ldrs: effrt but unable qck u.p over 1f out: wknd ins fnl f* **8/1**

3150 **8** *hd* **Lothario**[25] 4322 5-9-4 **71**..................... RobertWinston 4 66
(Dean Ivory) *chsd wnr tl ent fnl 6f: swtchd rt over 2f out: unable qck u.p 1f out: wknd ins fnl f (jockey said gelding lugged left-handed)* **6/1**[3]

-420 **9** *6* **Jabalaly (IRE)**[53] 3307 3-9-2 **77**..................... RyanMoore 5 64
(Ed Dunlop) *midfield: rdn after 2f: no imp over 1f out: btn and eased ins fnl f (trainer's rep could offer no explanation for the gelding's performance)* **5/1**[2]

1m 38.05s (-1.85) **Going Correction** -0.10s/f (Stan)
WFA 3 from 4yo+ 8lb **9 Ran SP% 116.9**
Speed ratings (Par 105): **105,104,104,103,103 101,99,99,93**
CSF £32.55 CT £352.98 TOTE £2.80: £1.30, £2.80, £4.20; EX 33.20 Trifecta £403.40.
Owner Saeed Manana **Bred** Rabbah Bloodstock Limited **Trained** Newmarket, Suffolk

FOCUS
A competitive enough race for the grade and the winner landed some good support under a well-judged front-running ride. He's rated to his best.

5268 BUDWEISER BREWING GROUP NOVICE STKS (DIV I) 1m (P)
7:20 (7:25) (Class 4) 3-Y-0+ **£5,530** (£1,645; £822; £411) **Stalls** Low

Form RPR

1-2 **1** **Lady Lawyer (USA)**[18] 4597 3-9-4 0..................... FrankieDettori 9 85
(John Gosden) *mounted in the chute and taken down early: nt that wl away: hdwy to ld after 1f: mde rest: rdn over 1f out: edgd rt and hrd pressed ins fnl f: kpt on: jst prevailed* **11/4**[3]

-05 **2** *nse* **Ghaly**[43] 3648 3-9-2 0..................... PatCosgrave 3 82
(Saeed bin Suroor) *led for 1f: chsd wnr tl 6f out: styd chsng ldrs: effrt over 1f out: chsd wnr and swtchd lft ins fnl f: str chal wl ins fnl f: jst hld* **8/1**

5 **3** *3¾* **Rapture (FR)**[18] 4597 3-8-11 0..................... HollieDoyle 10 68
(Archie Watson) *chsd wnr 6f out: ev ch 2f out: sn u.p and unable qck 1f out: wknd ins fnl f* **20/1**

3 **4** *5* **Fiery Mission (USA)**[23] 4423 3-9-2 0..................... RyanMoore 4 62+
(Sir Michael Stoute) *midfield: effrt but ldng trio gng clr whn lft 4th and bdly hmpd wl over 1f out: no threat to ldrs and kpt on same pce fnl f* **15/8**[1]

5 **5** *¾* **Sea Wings**[31] 4121 3-9-2 0.....................(b[1]) JamesDoyle 2 60+
(William Haggas) *rousted along leaving stalls: racd in last quartet: effrt but ldrs gng clr whn hmpd wl over 1f out: no imp and plugged on same pce after* **2/1**[2]

50 **6** *nk* **Lope Athena**[45] 3603 3-8-11 0..................... SilvestreDeSousa 5 54
(Stuart Williams) *chsd ldrs: u.p and outpcd whn rn wd off bnd 2f out: sn btn and wknd over 1f out* **50/1**

0 **7** *4* **Rifft (IRE)**[136] 1094 4-9-10 0..................... CallumShepherd 7 52
(Lydia Richards) *midfield: outpcd u.p whn nudged wl over 1f out: sn wknd* **100/1**

5 **8** *4½* **Black Kalanisi (IRE)**[32] 4066 6-9-10 0..................... RobHornby 6 42
(Joseph Tuite) *rousted along early: a towards rr: rdn over 2f out: sn outpcd and wl btn over 1f out* **40/1**

04 **9** *3½* **Bricklebrit**[42] 3690 3-8-11 0..................... JFEgan 8 26
(Rae Guest) *a towards rr: bhd over 1f out* **100/1**

10 *9* **Blue Laurel** 3-9-2 0..................... ShaneKelly 11 11
(Richard Hughes) *s.i.s: a bhd: lost tch over 1f out* **50/1**

0 **P** **Shining Sea (IRE)**[14] 4768 3-8-11 0..................... LukeMorris 1
(Sir Mark Prescott Bt) *midfield: effrt in 4th whn lost action 2f out: eased and p.u: dismntd* **25/1**

1m 38.88s (-1.02) **Going Correction** -0.10s/f (Stan)
WFA 3 from 4yo+ 8lb **11 Ran SP% 122.8**
Speed ratings (Par 105): **101,100,97,92,91 91,87,82,79,70**
CSF £24.78 TOTE £3.30: £1.30, £1.60, £4.30; EX 32.10 Trifecta £275.00.
Owner Sheikh Juma Dalmook Al Maktoum **Bred** Claiborne Farm **Trained** Newmarket, Suffolk

FOCUS
This looked an interesting contest beforehand but with two of the market principals underperforming, and nothing getting into it from behind, it may not be form to be overly positive about. It was the slower division by 0.8sec.

5269 BUDWEISER BREWING GROUP NOVICE STKS (DIV II) 1m (P)
7:50 (7:56) (Class 4) 3-Y-0+ **£5,530** (£1,645; £822; £411) **Stalls** Low

Form RPR

0-1 **1** **Ghaziyah**[20] 4520 3-9-4 0..................... JamesDoyle 5 85+
(William Haggas) *chsd ldrs: wnt 2nd 6f out tl led wl over 1f out: hung lft over 1f out: styd on wl and a doing enough ins fnl f* **10/11**[1]

3- **2** *1¼* **Maximum Effect**[216] 9603 3-8-11 0..................... FrankieDettori 1 75+
(John Gosden) *trckd ldrs: swtchd rt and effrt 2f out: chsd wnr jst over 1f out: kpt on but a hld ins fnl f* **6/4**[2]

3 *3¾* **Knockacullion (USA)** 3-9-2 0..................... ShaneKelly 8 71
(Richard Hughes) *chsd ldrs but stuck on outer: effrt over 2f out: 4th and unable to match pce of ldng pair over 1f out: wnt 3rd and kpt on same pce ins fnl f* **20/1**

4 *3* **Harbour City (USA)** 3-8-11 0..................... PJMcDonald 2 59
(James Tate) *led tl wl over 1f out: unable qck and outpcd in 3rd 1f out: wknd ins fnl f* **8/1**[3]

60 **5** *1* **Ecstasea (IRE)**[31] 4121 3-8-11 0..................... JFEgan 3 57
(Rae Guest) *chsd ldr for 2f: styd chsng ldrs: effrt over 2f out: outpcd and btn over 1f out: kpt on same pce ins fnl f* **50/1**

65 **6** *nk* **Rudy Lewis (IRE)**[35] 3972 3-9-2 0..................... StevieDonohoe 10 61+
(Charlie Fellowes) *hld up towards rr: short of room wl over 3f out: effrt and hung lft over 1f out: n.d but kpt on ins fnl f* **12/1**

06 **7** *½* **Petite Malle (USA)**[22] 4452 3-8-11 0..................... GeorgeWood 6 55+
(James Fanshawe) *in tch in midfield: effrt over 2f out: outpcd and btn over 1f out: wl hld and kpt on same pce ins fnl f* **33/1**

00 **8** *½* **Yvette**[181] 370 3-8-11 0..................... LukeMorris 9 54+
(Sir Mark Prescott Bt) *towards rr: rdn over 3f out: struggling and outpcd over 2f out: wl hld and kpt on same pce ins fnl f* **40/1**

0-0 **9** *3¼* **Logan's Choice**[49] 3445 4-9-5 0..................... ThomasGreatrex[(5)] 7 54
(Roger Charlton) *hld up towards rr: effrt on inner over 1f out: no prog: wknd ins fnl f* **50/1**

005 **10** *3½* **Bambys Boy**[36] 3946 8-9-10 0..................... AdamKirby 4 46
(Neil Mulholland) *hld up in rr: struggling and rdn over 2f out: sn bhd and hung lft (jockey said hung left-handed from 3f out)* **40/1**

1m 38.08s (-1.82) **Going Correction** -0.10s/f (Stan)
WFA 3 from 4yo+ 8lb **10 Ran SP% 127.7**
Speed ratings (Par 105): **105,103,100,97,96 95,95,94,91,87**
CSF £2.65 TOTE £1.70: £1.10, £1.10, £4.40; EX 3.00 Trifecta £26.40.
Owner Sheikh Juma Dalmook Al Maktoum **Bred** Denford Stud Ltd **Trained** Newmarket, Suffolk

FOCUS
The market suggested this was a match and so it proved in the race itself, the winner creating a positive impression in overcoming her penalty. Once again nothing held up got into the race. It was the faster division by 0.8sec, but a race lacking depth.

5270 GENTLEMEN'S DAY 3RD AUGUST H'CAP 7f (P)
8:20 (8:25) (Class 4) (0-80,78) 3-Y-O
£5,692 (£1,694; £846; £423; £300; £300) **Stalls** Low

Form RPR

4005 **1** **Battle Of Waterloo (IRE)**[19] 4565 3-8-12 **74**..................... CierenFallon[(5)] 4 81
(John Ryan) *hld up in tch: clsd to trck ldrs 2f out: effrt to chal 1f out: edgd lft but rdn to ld ins fnl f: styd on wl* **8/1**

4-21 **2** *¾* **Shawaaheq (IRE)**[45] 3565 3-9-5 **76**..................... JimCrowley 3 81
(Ed Dunlop) *hld up in tch: swtchd rt and effrt over 1f out: hdwy u.p ins fnl f: styd on wl to snatch 2nd last stride* **7/2**[2]

2034 **3** *shd* **Chatham House**[10] 4909 3-9-7 **78**..................... RyanMoore 7 82
(Richard Hannon) *led: rdn over 1f out: drvn and hdd ins fnl f: kpt on same pce fnl 100yds: lost 2nd last stride* **3/1**[1]

4053 **4** *1* **Self Assessment (IRE)**[8] 5002 3-8-12 **74**..................... HarrisonShaw[(5)] 5 76
(K R Burke) *broke wl: restrained and chsd ldrs: effrt over 1f out: drvn and kpt on same pce ins fnl f* **7/1**[3]

0060 **5** *1* **Indian Sounds (IRE)**[15] 4723 3-9-2 **73**..................... SilvestreDeSousa 8 72
(Mark Johnston) *sn chsng ldr: effrt and ev ch over 1f out: hrd drvn and unable qck 1f out: wknd ins fnl f* **7/2**[2]

1000 **6** *½* **Love Your Work (IRE)**[20] 4506 3-9-4 **75**.....................(b) CharlieBennett 2 73
(Adam West) *stdd and bmpd leaving stalls: hld up in tch: swtchd rt and effrt wl over 1f out: styd on wl u.p 1f out: nt rch ldrs* **25/1**

6405 **7** *1* **Bullington Boy (FR)**[13] 4788 3-9-1 **72**..................... JFEgan 1 67
(Jane Chapple-Hyam) *chsd ldrs early: lost pl and last trio over 6f out: effrt over 1f out: no imp and one pce ins fnl f* **8/1**

03-2 **8** *¾* **Characteristic (IRE)**[104] 1677 3-9-6 **77**..................... LukeMorris 6 70
(Tom Clover) *awkward leaving stalls: in tch in midfield: rdn over 2f out: unable qck over 1f out: wknd ins fnl f* **8/1**

1m 25.77s (-1.43) **Going Correction** -0.10s/f (Stan) **8 Ran SP% 119.1**
Speed ratings (Par 102): **104,103,103,101,100 100,99,98**
CSF £37.74 CT £106.31 TOTE £9.10: £2.60, £1.50, £1.30; EX 43.10 Trifecta £176.60.
Owner Gerry McGladery **Bred** Anything & Everything Associates **Trained** Newmarket, Suffolk

FOCUS
This looked competitive beforehand and there were several in contention as the field swung for home. Ordinary-looking form.

5271 CELEBRATE JULY'S HERO GAYNOR WAREHAM H'CAP 1m 6f (P)
8:50 (8:52) (Class 6) (0-65,65) 4-Y-0+
£3,105 (£924; £461; £300; £300; £300) **Stalls** Low

Form RPR

0604 **1** **Beau Knight**[18] 4594 7-8-3 **47**.....................(p[1]) HollieDoyle 13 53
(Alexandra Dunn) *t.k.h: sn w ldr: led over 2f out: rdn and sustained duel fr over 1f out: kpt on wl: jst prevailed* **20/1**

0514 **2** *shd* **Steel Helmet (IRE)**[10] 4914 5-8-3 **47**..................... JosephineGordon 7 53
(Harriet Bethell) *sn prom: effrt to chse ldr over 2f out: ev ch and sustained duel w wnr fr over 1f out: kpt on wl: jst hld* **20/1**

1135 **3** *¾* **Croeso Cymraeg**[18] 4594 5-9-1 **59**..................... RaulDaSilva 5 64+
(James Evans) *taken down early: stdd after s: t.k.h: hld up in last trio: hdwy on outer 3f out: pressed ldrs 2f out: ev ch u.p ent fnl f: no ex and jst outpcd fnl 100yds* **7/2**[2]

6425 **4** *½* **Barca (USA)**[28] 4220 5-8-13 **57**..................... JimCrowley 10 61
(Marcus Tregoning) *hld up in tch in midfield: effrt over 1f out: kpt on u.p ins fnl f: nt rch ldrs* **5/2**[1]

3133 **5** *2½* **Murhib (IRE)**[42] 3700 7-8-13 **57**.....................(h) LukeMorris 1 58
(Lydia Richards) *t.k.h: trckd ldrs: rdn over 3f out: lost pl over 2f out: rallied and kpt on ins fnl f: no threat to ldrs* **12/1**

0610 **6** *hd* **Sacred Sprite**[54] 3272 4-9-2 **60**..................... JFEgan 2 62
(John Berry) *hld up in tch in midfield: nt clr run and shuffled bk towards rr over 2f out: swtchd rt and effrt over 1f out: styd on wl ins fnl f: nt rch ldrs* **7/1**

0203 **7** *1½* **Ness Of Brodgar**[18] 4594 4-8-8 **52**.....................(t) GeorgeWood 4 51
(Mark H Tompkins) *prom early: in tch in midfield after: hdwy to chse ldrs 4f out: outpcd u.p over 1f out: kpt on same pce ins fnl f* **10/1**

1051 **8** *nk* **Thresholdofadream (IRE)**[27] 4251 4-9-0 **58**..................... PatDobbs 11 56
(Amanda Perrett) *hld up towards rr: swtchd rt and effrt 2f out: kpt on but nvr threatened ldrs* **8/1**

3-34 **9** *shd* **Joycetick (FR)**[49] 3444 5-9-6 **64**.....................(t) SilvestreDeSousa 6 62
(Nick Littmoden) *hld up in tch in midfield: nt clr run over 2f out: swtchd rt and effrt wl over 1f out: kpt on ins fnl f: nvr trbld ldrs* **6/1**[3]

3660 **10** *1¼* **Velvet Vision**[24] 4371 4-9-5 **63**..................... DougieCostello 9 60
(Mark H Tompkins) *s.i.s: sn swtchd lft and hld up in rr: nt clr run ent fnl 2f: kpt on ins fnl f: nvr trbld ldrs* **12/1**

-000 **11** *1* **Tyrsal (IRE)**[41] 3740 8-8-2 **46** oh1.....................(p) KieranO'Neill 8 41
(Shaun Keightley) *t.k.h: effrt over 3f out: unable qck and btn over 1f out: wknd ins fnl f* **50/1**

0642 **12** *2* **Princess Harley (IRE)**[40] 3778 4-9-5 **63**..................... PatCosgrave 12 56
(Mick Quinn) *t.k.h: hld up in tch in midfield: hdwy to chse ldrs 4f out: lost pl u.p and btn over 1f out: wknd ins fnl f* **14/1**

223/ **13** *34* **Jupiter Custos (FR)**[793] 6804 7-9-2 **65**..................... CierenFallon[(5)] 3 14
(Michael Scudamore) *led tl over 2f out: sn dropped out: bhd and virtually p.u ins fnl f: t.o* **25/1**

3m 1.89s (-1.31) **Going Correction** -0.10s/f (Stan) **13 Ran SP% 135.2**
Speed ratings (Par 101): **99,98,98,98,96 96,95,95,95,94 94,93,73**
CSF £397.11 CT £1763.45 TOTE £27.90: £7.20, £6.10, £1.80; EX 384.10 Trifecta £2468.10.

Owner West Buckland Bloodstock Ltd **Bred** Mr & Mrs A E Pakenham **Trained** West Buckland, Somerset
FOCUS
A low-grade staying event with a tight finish, the third emerging with plenty of credit in the circumstances.
T/Plt: £9.60 to a £1 stake. Pool: £41,634.15 - 4,327.83 winning units T/Qpdt: £6.40 to a £1 stake. Pool: £5,572.97 - 866.04 winning units **Steve Payne**

4508 MUSSELBURGH (R-H)
Tuesday, July 23

OFFICIAL GOING: Good (good to firm in places; 8.2)
Wind: Fresh, across Weather: Sunny, very warm

5272 LIKE RACING TV ON FACEBOOK H'CAP 1m 2y
2:00 (2:01) (Class 6) (0-65,65) 3-Y-O
£3,105 (£924; £461; £300; £300; £300) **Stalls** Low

Form RPR
30-5 1 **My Ukulele (IRE)**[15] 4725 3-9-0 **58** JasonHart 11 65+
(John Quinn) *stdd and swtchd rt s: hld up: pushed along and hung rt over 2f out: hdwy on outside over 1f out: sustained run to ld ins fnl f: r.o* **15/2**
0635 2 ¾ **Diviner (IRE)**[10] 4917 3-9-7 **65** JoeFanning 2 70
(Mark Johnston) *led at ordinary gallop: rdn 2f out: hdd ins fnl f: no ex nr fin* **9/2**[2]
2242 3 2 **Juniors Fantasy (IRE)**[10] 4915 3-9-1 **59**(t) DuranFentiman 1 60
(Tim Easterby) *s.i.s: sn prom: effrt and disp 2nd pl over 1f out: kpt on same pce ins fnl f* **4/1**[1]
1044 4 nk **Molly Mai**[22] 4454 3-9-7 **65** PhilDennis 7 65
(Philip McBride) *hld up: hdwy over 2f out: chsd ldr over 1f out to ins fnl f: one pce* **9/2**[2]
0563 5 1¾ **Arriba De Toda (IRE)**[20] 4518 3-7-10 **47** KieranSchofield(7) 5 44
(Brian Ellison) *missed break: hld up: effrt whn nt clr run briefly 2f out: sn rdn: kpt on fnl f: no imp* **7/1**[3]
636 6 1¾ **God Of Dreams**[12] 4820 3-9-1 **59** PaulMulrennan 6 51
(Iain Jardine) *t.k.h: prom: effrt whn n.m.r briefly over 2f out: wknd over 1f out* **11/1**
5020 7 ¾ **Temple Of Wonder (IRE)**[10] 4915 3-9-0 **58** DanielTudhope 8 48
(Liam Bailey) *chsd ldrs: rdn over 2f out: wknd over 1f out* **10/1**
46-5 8 2¼ **Darwina**[15] 4726 3-8-10 **57**(h) RowanScott(3) 9 42
(Alistair Whillans) *hld up on outside: rdn and effrt over 2f out: wknd over 1f out* **25/1**
530 9 1 **Duhallow Noelie (IRE)**[1] 5238 3-8-13 **60**(t) SeanDavis(3) 4 43
(Adrian Paul Keatley, Ire) *chsd ldr: rdn over 2f out: wknd over 1f out* **7/1**[3]
1m 41.15s (1.15) **Going Correction** +0.10s/f (Good) **9 Ran SP% 114.4**
Speed ratings (Par 98): **98,97,95,94,93 91,90,88,87**
CSF £40.79 CT £155.67 TOTE £8.20: £2.40, £1.50, £1.60; EX 47.20 Trifecta £309.20.
Owner Andrew W Robson **Bred** Andrew W Robson **Trained** Settrington, N Yorks
FOCUS
The ground was good, good to firm in places. GoingStick: 8.2. Race distances were as advertised and there was a cutaway on the stands' side at the 1.5f point. Stalls - 5f and 2m: stands' side. Remainder: inside. Plenty in with a chance up the home straight with the winner collaring the long-time leader deep inside the final furlong. Straightforward form, rated around the runner-up.

5273 IRISH STALLION FARMS EBF MAIDEN AUCTION STKS (PLUS 10 RACE) 7f 33y
2:30 (2:32) (Class 4) 2-Y-O **£4,463** (£1,328; £663; £331) **Stalls** Low

Form RPR
5 1 **Anniemation (IRE)**[25] 4317 2-9-1 0 JackGarritty 4 74
(Stella Barclay) *t.k.h early: trckd ldrs: effrt and edgd lft 2f out: led ins fnl f: edgd lft: kpt on wl* **33/1**
25 2 1¾ **Northern Hope**[26] 4289 2-9-1 0 DanielTudhope 7 69
(David O'Meara) *pressed ldr: led over 2f out: hdd ins fnl f: kpt on same pce* **11/10**[1]
0 3 2¾ **Harswell Approach (IRE)**[17] 4623 2-8-13 0 PaulMulrennan 5 60
(Liam Bailey) *hld up: hdwy over 2f out: chsd ldng pair over 1f out: kpt on fnl f: no imp* **50/1**
4 1½ **Magna Moralia (IRE)** 2-9-3 0 JasonHart 1 60+
(John Quinn) *missed break: hld up on ins: rdn and outpcd over 2f out: rallied over 1f out: kpt on fnl f: nt pce to chal* **8/1**
5 5 hd **Bye Bye Euro (IRE)**[12] 4819 2-8-8 0 GrahamLee 9 50+
(Keith Dalgleish) *prom on outside: rdn over 2f out: outpcd fr over 1f out* **6/1**[3]
6 2¾ **Jack Ryan (IRE)** 2-8-12 0 DavidAllan 2 47
(John Ryan) *sn trcking ldrs: effrt over 2f out: wknd fnl f* **14/1**
36 7 1 **Breck's Selection (FR)**[14] 4766 2-9-1 0 JoeFanning 3 48
(Mark Johnston) *led to over 2f out: rdn and wknd over 1f out* **9/2**[2]
45 8 3¾ **Time Force (IRE)**[20] 4509 2-8-9 0 RhonaPindar(7) 8 39
(K R Burke) *t.k.h: hld up: rdn and hung rt 2f out: sn wknd (jockey said colt ran too free)* **25/1**
43 9 nk **Typsy Toad**[17] 4623 2-8-10 0 SeanDavis(3) 6 35
(Richard Fahey) *early to post: plld hrd in rr: struggling whn hung lft over 2f out: sn btn (jockey said colt ran too free)* **10/1**
1m 30.72s (1.72) **Going Correction** +0.10s/f (Good) **9 Ran SP% 115.7**
Speed ratings (Par 96): **94,92,88,87,86 83,82,78,78**
CSF £69.65 TOTE £34.00: £8.20, £1.10, £10.60; EX 99.00 Trifecta £4338.60.
Owner W Buckley **Bred** Ballyphilip Stud **Trained** Garstang, Lancs
FOCUS
A fair maiden auction and a winner who promises to go on to better things.

5274 FOLLOW @RACINGTV ON TWITTER H'CAP 7f 33y
3:00 (3:07) (Class 5) (0-75,74) 3-Y-O+
£3,752 (£1,116; £557; £300; £300; £300) **Stalls** Low

Form RPR
-232 1 **Northernpowerhouse**[22] 4444 3-9-6 **73**(p[1]) GrahamLee 7 79+
(Bryan Smart) *chsd ldrs: led and hung lft 2f out: hung rt ins fnl f: drvn out* **11/2**[3]
0451 2 ½ **How Bizarre**[7] 5022 4-9-5 **72** 5ex JonathanFisher(7) 1 79
(Liam Bailey) *led: rdn and hdd 2f out: rallied: kpt on same pce towards fin* **7/1**
4331 3 hd **Donnelly's Rainbow (IRE)**[8] 4979 6-9-1 **61** 5ex ConnorBeasley 9 67
(Rebecca Bastiman) *s.i.s: hld up: rdn over 2f out: hdwy over 1f out: kpt on fnl f to take 3rd cl home* **11/2**[3]
5-15 4 ¾ **Gometra Ginty (IRE)**[25] 4334 3-9-2 **69** ShaneGray 6 70
(Keith Dalgleish) *in tch: rdn over 2f out: kpt on same pce fnl f* **16/1**
0345 5 1 **Lucky Violet (IRE)**[15] 4723 7-9-3 **63**(h) KevinStott 3 68
(Linda Perratt) *s.i.s: hld up in midfield: effrt and rdn over 1f out: keeping on whn hmpd last 75yds: one pce (jockey said mare suffered interference in the final half furlong)* **13/2**
1332 6 1½ **Mujassam**[12] 4833 7-10-0 **74**(b) DanielTudhope 2 72
(David O'Meara) *trckd ldrs: effrt and rdn over 1f out: no ex ins fnl f* **7/2**[1]
1030 7 nk **Orobas (IRE)**[1] 5239 7-8-12 **65**(v) VictorSantos(7) 5 62
(Lucinda Egerton) *hld up: drvn and effrt on outside over 2f out: hung rt and wknd over 1f out* **33/1**
1331 8 8 **Gabrial The Tiger (IRE)**[11] 4879 7-9-10 **73** SeanDavis(3) 8 48
(Richard Fahey) *t.k.h: w ldr: hung lft bnd 4f out: rdn and wknd over 1f out (trainer said gelding was unsuited by the ground and would prefer a slower surface)* **5/1**[2]
5022 9 ½ **Spirit Of Lund (IRE)**[45] 3565 3-9-6 **73**(p[1]) PaulMulrennan 10 44
(Iain Jardine) *hld up: drvn and struggling over 2f out: sn btn* **16/1**
0640 10 3¾ **Intense Style (IRE)**[26] 4207 7-9-3 **70**(p) IzzyClifton(7) 4 34
(Les Eyre) *s.i.s: hld up: rdn and outpcd over 2f out: sn btn* **20/1**
1m 28.17s (-0.83) **Going Correction** +0.10s/f (Good)
WFA 3 from 4yo+ 7lb **10 Ran SP% 115.0**
Speed ratings (Par 103): **108,107,107,106,105 103,103,94,93,89**
CSF £43.11 CT £225.60 TOTE £5.70: £1.90, £2.20, £2.60; EX 47.90 Trifecta £270.20.
Owner Michael Moses & Terry Moses **Bred** Bearstone Stud Ltd **Trained** Hambleton, N Yorks
FOCUS
A competitive handicap. The winner saw it out well on his first try at 7f. He didn't need to find much improvement.

5275 JOIN RACING TV NOW NURSERY H'CAP 5f 1y
3:30 (3:35) (Class 4) (0-85,85) 2-Y-O
£6,986 (£2,079; £1,038; £519; £300; £300) **Stalls** High

Form RPR
3152 1 **Dandizette (IRE)**[8] 4985 2-8-2 **69** SeanDavis(3) 5 74
(Adrian Nicholls) *mde all: rdn along 2f out: kpt on wl fnl f* **5/1**[3]
1010 2 ¾ **Bill Neigh**[18] 4610 2-9-7 **85** PaulMulrennan 4 88
(John Ryan) *sn bhd: hdwy and swtchd lft over 1f out: chsd wnr ins fnl f: r.o* **11/4**[1]
0105 3 1 **Harswell (IRE)**[11] 4893 2-8-9 **73** PhilDennis 7 72
(Liam Bailey) *chsd ldrs: rdn and angled lft over 1f out: kpt on ins fnl f* **18/1**
1202 4 nk **Exclusively**[17] 4659 2-9-6 **84** AdamMcNamara 1 82
(Archie Watson) *prom: effrt and drvn along over 1f out: kpt on same pce ins fnl f* **11/2**
313 5 ½ **Tom Tulliver**[22] 4433 2-9-2 **80** TomEaves 3 76
(Declan Carroll) *prom: rdn along over 1f out: no ex ins fnl f* **13/2**
3226 6 ½ **Birkenhead**[34] 3997 2-8-10 **74**(v) DavidAllan 8 68
(Les Eyre) *pressed wnr: drvn along over 1f out: outpcd ins fnl f (jockey said colt hung right)* **8/1**
440 7 nse **Il Maestro (IRE)**[67] 2783 2-8-2 **66**(v[1]) AndrewMullen 6 60
(John Quinn) *dwlt: bhd and sn pushed along: no imp fr over 1f out* **25/1**
5410 8 2¾ **Dazzling Des (IRE)**[18] 4610 2-9-3 **81** DanielTudhope 2 69+
(David O'Meara) *hld up on outside: hdwy over 2f out: rdn and wknd over 1f out* **7/2**[2]
1m 1.35s (1.65) **Going Correction** +0.10s/f (Good) **8 Ran SP% 114.5**
Speed ratings (Par 96): **90,88,87,86,85 85,85,80**
CSF £19.20 CT £226.85 TOTE £5.30: £1.70, £1.30, £4.80; EX 20.40 Trifecta £194.70.
Owner Ne-Chance **Bred** L Lynch & R Sherrard **Trained** Sessay, N Yorks
FOCUS
Plenty of depth to this quite valuable nursery handicap. The winner is pacy and likeable. The third and fourth fit in with the form.

5276 RACINGTV.COM H'CAP 5f 1y
4:00 (4:06) (Class 6) (0-65,66) 3-Y-O+
£3,105 (£924; £461; £300; £300; £300) **Stalls** High

Form RPR
1046 1 **Boudica Bay (IRE)**[19] 4555 4-9-3 **55** DavidAllan 12 64
(Eric Alston) *trckd ldrs: effrt and rdn over 1f out: led ins fnl f: kpt on wl* **2/1**[1]
5363 2 1¼ **Amazing Alba**[20] 4508 3-9-3 **59**(h) KevinStott 3 63
(Alistair Whillans) *prom: rdn 1/2-way: hdwy over 1f out: chsd wnr ins fnl f: r.o* **16/1**
6R42 3 nk **Piazon**[31] 4132 8-9-5 **57**(be) NathanEvans 1 60
(Julia Brooke) *cl up: led over 1f out to ins fnl f: kpt on same pce towards fin* **16/1**
331 4 ½ **Compton's Finale**[1] 5236 3-9-10 **66** 6ex(t) JoeFanning 6 67+
(Adrian Paul Keatley, Ire) *dwlt: hld up: hdwy on wd outside over 1f out: kpt on fnl f: nvr able to chal* **4/1**[2]
6100 5 ½ **Economic Crisis (IRE)**[10] 4911 10-9-4 **59** ConnorMurtagh(3) 9 59
(Alan Berry) *hld up: hdwy over 1f out: rdn and r.o fnl f: nt pce to chal* **33/1**
5024 6 ½ **Picks Pinta**[12] 4823 8-8-7 **52** ow3(p) HarryRussell(7) 8 50+
(John David Riches) *dwlt: bhd: rdn 2f out: kpt on wl fnl f: nrst fin* **33/1**
0036 7 ½ **Burmese Blazer (IRE)**[8] 4977 4-9-6 **61**(v[1]) SeanDavis(3) 13 57
(Jim Goldie) *led to over 1f out: wknd ins fnl f* **12/1**
4663 8 1 **Jeffrey Harris**[16] 4694 4-9-2 **54** PhilDennis 4 47
(Jim Goldie) *towards rr: hdwy 1/2-way: drvn and outpcd fnl f* **10/1**
0053 9 2¼ **Classic Pursuit**[5] 5094 8-9-12 **64**(v) DanielTudhope 5 49
(Marjorie Fife) *midfield on outside: rdn over 2f out: wknd over 1f out* **7/1**[3]
0003 10 hd **Computable**[6] 5042 5-9-11 **63**(p) RachelRichardson 11 47
(Tim Easterby) *blkd s: towards rr: drvn along 2f out: nvr on terms* **8/1**
3100 11 1¼ **Groundworker (IRE)**[7] 5018 8-9-1 **53** PaulMulrennan 7 32
(Paul Midgley) *midfield: rdn over 2f out: wknd over 1f out* **25/1**
59.94s (0.24) **Going Correction** +0.10s/f (Good)
WFA 3 from 4yo+ 4lb **11 Ran SP% 115.2**
Speed ratings (Par 101): **102,100,99,98,97 97,96,94,91,90 88**
CSF £34.75 CT £355.55 TOTE £2.50: £1.50, £3.80, £2.90; EX 29.60 Trifecta £291.90.
Owner The Grumpy Old Geezers **Bred** Abbey Farm Stud **Trained** Longton, Lancs
FOCUS
Good support for the winner, who scored in clear-cut fashion. Straightforward form.

5277 WATCH RACING TV NOW H'CAP 1m 5f 216y
4:30 (4:33) (Class 6) (0-60,62) 4-Y-O+
£3,105 (£924; £461; £300; £300; £300) **Stalls** Low

Form RPR
350- 1 **True Romance (IRE)**[31] 8422 5-8-12 **51** GrahamLee 7 61+
(Julia Brooke) *hld up in midfield: nt clr run briefly over 2f out: hdwy over 1f out: rdn to ld ins fnl f: kpt on wl* **5/1**[3]

-566 **2** *nk* **Kitty's Cove**[6] 5053 4-8-7 **46** oh1 (bt) DuranFentiman 9 54
(Tim Easterby) *slowly away and sn pushed along in rr: hdwy on outside over 2f out: ev ch over 1f out to ins fnl f: kpt on: hld cl home* **16/1**

0000 **3** *nk* **Kaizer**[9] 4515 4-8-6 **52** IzzyClifton(7) 11 60
(Alistair Whillans) *pressed ldr: led 2f out: hdd ins fnl f: one pce cl home* **10/1**

0124 **4** *9* **Sosian**[20] 4515 4-8-7 **49** (b) SeanDavis(3) 8 45
(Richard Fahey) *prom: drvn along over 3f out: outpcd by first three fr over 1f out* **12/1**

-034 **5** *3 ½* **Iolani (GER)**[25] 4036 7-9-9 **62** PaulMulrennan 12 54
(Dianne Sayer) *in tch: lost pl 1/2-way: rallied over 2f out: hung rt: kpt on fr over 1f out: no imp* **9/2**[2]

0035 **6** *2 ½* **Spark Of War (IRE)**[8] 4983 4-9-3 **56** (v) ShaneGray 2 45
(Keith Dalgleish) *hld up in tch: rdn over 2f out: wknd over 1f out* **6/1**

40-0 **7** *½* **Princess Nearco (IRE)**[24] 4370 5-9-1 **54** DanielTudhope 4 42
(Liam Bailey) *missed break: bhd: rdn 3f out: sme late hdwy: nvr rchd ldrs (jockey said mare was slowly away)* **25/1**

3315 **8** *1 ¼* **Percy Prosecco**[12] 4825 4-9-7 **60** AdamMcNamara 5 46
(Archie Watson) *led: rdn and hdd 2f out: wknd appr fnl f (jockey said gelding stopped quickly)* **11/4**[1]

0304 **9** *hd* **Elite Icon**[20] 4510 5-8-9 **48** (v) PhilDennis 6 34
(Jim Goldie) *hld up in tch: drvn along over 3f out: wknd over 1f out* **9/1**

0302 **10** *½* **Highway Robber**[36] 3929 6-8-4 **48** (t) PaulaMuir(5) 3 33
(Wilf Storey) *midfield: drvn along over 2f out: sn outpcd: btn over 1f out* **16/1**

-250 **11** *2* **Frame Rate**[31] 3705 4-9-0 **53** (p) DavidAllan 1 36
(Iain Jardine) *prom: rdn along over 3f out: wknd fnl 2f* **14/1**

-500 **12** *1 ¾* **Dizoard**[54] 3272 9-8-7 **46** oh1 AndrewMullen 10 26
(Iain Jardine) *hld up: rdn over 3f out: sn n.d: btn fnl 2f* **80/1**

00/6 **13** *54* **Abouttimeyoutoldme**[17] 4636 5-8-7 **46** oh1 JoeFanning 13
(Alistair Whillans) *slowly away: bhd: lost tch 3f out: t.o* **33/1**

3m 2.33s (-1.57) **Going Correction** +0.10s/f (Good) **13 Ran SP% 123.8**
Speed ratings (Par 101): **108,107,107,102,100 99,98,98,97,97 96,95,64**
CSF £84.60 CT £791.31 TOTE £5.30: £2.20, £4.50, £3.20; EX 117.30 Trifecta £769.50.
Owner K S Ward **Bred** Tower Place Bloodstock **Trained** Middleham, N Yorks

FOCUS
Plenty of runners in this staying handicap, but the first three pulled well clear and the winner landed a gamble. The second and third set a fairly ordinary level.

5278 EVERY RACE LIVE ON RACING TV CLASSIFIED STKS 5f 1y
5:00 (5:05) (Class 6) 3-Y-O+
£3,105 (£924; £461; £300; £300; £300) **Stalls High**

Form RPR

20-2 **1** **Your Pal Tal**[78] 2495 9-9-1 50 (v) SeanDavis(3) 5 57
(J F Levins, Ire) *bhd: hdwy on outside 2f out: rdn and led ins fnl f: kpt on wl* **7/1**[2]

053 **2** *nk* **War Ensign (IRE)**[3] 5202 4-9-4 46 DavidAllan 12 56
(Tim Easterby) *in tch: effrt and swtchd rt over 1f out: led briefly ins fnl f: kpt on: hld nr fin* **5/4**[1]

60-6 **3** *2 ½* **Lets Go Flo (IRE)**[3] 5169 3-9-0 50 DanielTudhope 11 46
(Brian Ellison) *s.i.s: bhd and outpcd: hdwy over 1f out: chsd clr ldng pair ins fnl f: kpt on: nt pce to chal* **7/1**[2]

6300 **4** *1 ½* **Camanche Grey (IRE)**[5] 5094 8-8-11 46 VictorSantos(7) 9 42
(Lucinda Egerton) *sn pushed along towards rr: hdwy over 1f out: kpt on fnl f: nvr able to chal (vet said gelding finished moving unlevel infront)* **25/1**

500- **5** *shd* **Your Just Desserts (IRE)**[285] 8131 4-9-4 43 ShaneGray 14 41
(Paul Collins) *dwlt: bhd: rdn and hdwy over 1f out: kpt on fnl f: nvr able to chal* **50/1**

0656 **6** *hd* **Sir Walter (IRE)**[73] 2633 4-9-4 43 RachelRichardson 13 40
(Eric Alston) *chsd ldrs: effrt over 1f out: no ex ins fnl f* **25/1**

5430 **7** *½* **I'll Be Good**[21] 4493 10-9-1 48 ConnorMurtagh(3) 8 39
(Alan Berry) *cl up: effrt and ev ch over 1f out: outpcd ins fnl f* **20/1**

0004 **8** *¾* **Jessie Allan (IRE)**[1] 5235 8-8-11 47 CoreyMadden(7) 3 36
(Jim Goldie) *dwlt: bhd: hdwy over 1f out: kpt on fnl f: no imp* **16/1**

5226 **9** *nse* **Angel Eyes**[14] 4765 4-8-11 48 HarryRussell(7) 6 36
(John David Riches) *led: rdn over 1f out: hdd ins fnl f: sn btn* **8/1**[3]

4-60 **10** *1 ¼* **Thornaby Princess**[71] 2678 8-9-1 40 (p) ConorMcGovern(3) 4 31
(Jason Ward) *prom: rdn along 2f out: wknd fnl f* **25/1**

-051 **11** *1 ¼* **Alisia R (IRE)**[20] 4508 3-8-7 50 IzzyClifton(7) 7 26+
(Les Eyre) *sddle sn slipped forward: t.k.h: trckd ldrs tl hung rt and wknd over 1f out* **9/1**

0000 **12** *8* **Gunnabedun (IRE)**[21] 4493 3-9-0 50 (b) JoeFanning 2
(Iain Jardine) *midfield on outside: rdn over 2f out: wknd over 1f out* **20/1**

0000 **13** *12* **Encoded (IRE)**[7] 5018 6-9-1 46 RowanScott(3) 1 +
(Lynn Siddall) *s.v.s: t.o thrght (jockey said mare was slowly away)* **50/1**

1m 0.36s (0.66) **Going Correction** +0.10s/f (Good)
WFA 3 from 4yo+ 4lb **13 Ran SP% 121.4**
Speed ratings (Par 101): **98,97,93,91,90 90,89,88,88,86 84,71,52**
CSF £14.97 CT £69.54 TOTE £7.50: £2.00, £1.40, £2.50; EX 22.00 Trifecta £163.50.
Owner Jason McGannon **Bred** Manor Farm Stud (Rutland) **Trained** The Curragh, Co Kildare

FOCUS
A modest sprint handicap. The winner was well in on the best of this year's Irish form and foiled a gamble on the runner-up.
T/Jkpt: Not won. T/Plt: £270.30 to a £1 stake. Pool: £70,611.61 - 190.65 winning units T/Qpdt: £118.72 to a £1 stake. Pool: £6,942.73 - 63.88 winning units **Richard Young**

5051 WOLVERHAMPTON (A.W) (L-H)
Tuesday, July 23

OFFICIAL GOING: Tapeta: standard
Wind: Light behind Weather: Fine

5279 JESS GLYNNE LIVE AT LADIES DAY NURSERY H'CAP 5f 21y (Tp)
2:15 (2:15) (Class 6) (0-65,65) 2-Y-O
£2,781 (£827; £413; £300; £300; £300) **Stalls Low**

Form RPR

5301 **1** **Blitzle**[13] 4778 2-9-4 **65** BenRobinson(3) 1 70
(Ollie Pears) *mde all: shkn up over 1f out: rdn and edgd rt ins fnl f: styd on* **2/1**[1]

4433 **2** *2 ¼* **Beignet (IRE)**[7] 5010 2-9-6 **64** SeanLevey 4 61
(Richard Hannon) *chsd ldrs: chse wnr 2f out: sn rdn: styd on same pce ins fnl f* **4/1**[3]

063 **3** *nk* **Two Hearts**[13] 4778 2-8-1 **45** JamesSullivan 5 41
(Grant Tuer) *prom: chsd wnr over 3f out tl 2f out: sn rdn: styd on same pce ins fnl f* **9/1**

0206 **4** *hd* **Hollaback Girl**[49] 3441 2-8-12 **63** SeanKirrane(7) 3 58+
(Richard Spencer) *s.i.s: hdwy 1/2-way: rdn and swtchd lft over 1f out: styd on same pce ins fnl f (jockey said filly missed the break)* **16/1**

426 **5** *4* **Forced**[61] 2996 2-9-2 **60** (p[1]) ShaneKelly 7 41
(Richard Hughes) *s.i.s: drvn along over 3f out: hdwy 1/2-way: wknd fnl f* **7/1**

4505 **6** *1* **Queens Blade**[8] 4985 2-9-1 **59** (b[1]) CamHardie 9 36
(Tim Easterby) *s.i.s: sn pushed along in rr: nvr on terms* **14/1**

0552 **7** *1 ½* **Prissy Missy (IRE)**[7] 5010 2-9-0 **58** OisinMurphy 8 30
(David Loughnane) *s.i.s: sn prom: edgd lft and lost pl over 3f out: n.d after* **11/4**[2]

006 **8** *6* **Tiltilys Rock (IRE)**[22] 4433 2-8-3 **47** AndrewElliott 6
(Andrew Crook) *chsd wnr tl over 3f out: rdn 1/2-way: wknd 2f out* **33/1**

1m 2.23s (0.33) **Going Correction** +0.025s/f (Slow) **8 Ran SP% 118.0**
Speed ratings (Par 92): **98,94,93,93,87 85,83,73**
CSF £10.76 CT £58.97 TOTE £2.50: £1.10, £2.00, £2.30; EX 10.50 Trifecta £63.00.
Owner Np Racing Syndicate & Ollie Pears **Bred** John Jackson **Trained** Norton, N Yorks

FOCUS
Few got into this, the winner dominating throughout. Weakish form, rated with feet on the ground.

5280 STAY AT THE WOLVERHAMPTON HOLIDAY INN NOVICE STKS 5f 21y (Tp)
2:45 (2:46) (Class 5) 2-Y-O
£3,428 (£1,020; £509; £254) **Stalls Low**

Form RPR

22 **1** **X Force (IRE)**[11] 4871 2-9-5 0 OisinMurphy 3 79+
(Archie Watson) *chsd ldr 4f out: shkn up to ld over 1f out: rdn out* **8/11**[1]

4 **2** *1* **Dana Forever (IRE)**[17] 4659 2-9-0 0 RichardKingscote 9 70+
(Tom Dascombe) *hld up: swtchd lft sn after s: hdwy over 1f out: r.o to go 2nd wl ins fnl f: no ch w wnr* **2/1**[2]

03 **3** *2 ¼* **Elpheba (IRE)**[10] 4903 2-9-0 0 TrevorWhelan 4 62
(David Loughnane) *edgd lft s: led: rdn: edgd rt and hdd over 1f out: styd on same pce ins fnl f (jockey said filly jumped left at the start and hung right under pressure)* **11/1**[3]

4 *nk* **Hot Heels** 2-9-2 0 JaneElliott(3) 1 66
(Tom Dascombe) *racd keenly: hdwy over 3f out: shkn up and edgd rt fr over 1f out: styd on same pce ins fnl f* **14/1**

0 **5** *5* **Last Date**[27] 4246 2-9-2 0 GabrieleMalune(3) 2 48
(Ivan Furtado) *chsd ldrs: rdn over 1f out: wknd fnl f* **50/1**

40 **6** *1 ½* **Dorchester Dom (IRE)**[17] 4652 2-9-5 0 (t[1]) LiamKeniry 10 43
(David Evans) *s.i.s: hld up: plld hrd: rdn and hung lft fr over 1f out: n.d* **25/1**

7 *2 ¾* **La Chica Lobo** 2-9-0 0 CamHardie 5 28
(Lisa Williamson) *s.i.s: sn rcvrd to chse ldr: lost 2nd 4f out: hung rt 3f out: rdn 1/2-way: wknd wl over 1f out* **200/1**

0 **8** *1 ¼* **Northern Grace**[95] 1923 2-8-11 0 BenRobinson(3) 7 23
(Brian Ellison) *prom: lost pl 4f out: wknd 1/2-way* **50/1**

40 **9** *hd* **Flowing Magic (IRE)**[24] 4384 2-9-5 0 HarryBentley 8 28
(George Scott) *s.i.s: swtchd lft and pushed along sn after s: a in rr* **14/1**

46 **10** *3 ¼* **Call Me Cheers**[64] 2903 2-9-5 0 KieranO'Neill 6 16
(David Evans) *chsd ldrs: hung rt and lost pl over 3f out: wknd 1/2-way* **25/1**

1m 2.39s (0.49) **Going Correction** +0.025s/f (Slow) **10 Ran SP% 125.0**
Speed ratings (Par 94): **97,95,91,91,83 80,76,74,74,69**
CSF £2.48 TOTE £1.40: £1.10, £1.10, £2.20; EX 3.20 Trifecta £13.40.
Owner Qatar Racing Limited & David Redvers **Bred** Maurice Burns **Trained** Upper Lambourn, W Berks

FOCUS
A modest novice with the third a feasible anchor to the form.

5281 BLACK COUNTRY H'CAP 6f 20y (Tp)
3:15 (3:16) (Class 5) (0-75,80) 3-Y-O+
£3,428 (£1,020; £509; £300; £300; £300) **Stalls Low**

Form RPR

5023 **1** **Baby Steps**[10] 4908 3-9-7 **75** RichardKingscote 7 83
(David Loughnane) *led early: led again 5f out: hrd rdn fr rdn over 1f out: edgd rt towards fin: all out* **5/1**[3]

0651 **2** *hd* **Wild Edric**[8] 5000 3-9-9 **80** 6ex JaneElliott(3) 9 87
(Tom Dascombe) *s.i.s: rcvrd to join wnr over 4f out: rdn and ev ch whn edgd rt over 1f out: styd on (vet said gelding lost it's right fore shoe)* **11/8**[1]

4-05 **3** *hd* **Laubali**[183] 347 4-9-10 **73** (p) DavidNolan 4 80
(David O'Meara) *chsd ldrs: rdn over 1f out: r.o (vet said gelding lost it's right fore shoe)* **16/1**

0025 **4** *¾* **Lucky Lodge**[14] 4764 9-9-7 **70** (b) CamHardie 2 74
(Antony Brittain) *pushed along leaving stalls: racd keenly and sn hld up in tch: rdn over 1f out: running on whn nt clr run towards fin (jockey said gelding was denied a clear run on the run to the line)* **16/1**

505 **5** *1 ¼* **Poeta Brasileiro (IRE)**[56] 3207 4-9-0 **63** RaulDaSilva 5 63
(David Brown) *sn led: hdd 5f out: chsd ldrs: rdn over 1f out: no ex towards fin* **5/1**[3]

2-30 **6** *nse* **Painted Dream**[85] 2204 3-9-0 **68** TomQueally 3 67+
(George Margarson) *chsd ldrs: n.m.r and lost pl after 1f: rdn: edgd lft and r.o ins fnl f* **33/1**

313 **7** *1 ½* **Creek Harbour (IRE)**[14] 4764 4-9-5 **68** JackMitchell 8 63
(Milton Bradley) *s.i.s: hld up: shkn up and hung lft fr over 2f out: styd on ins fnl f: n.d (jockey said gelding hung right)* **25/1**

4552 **8** *nk* **Take Fright**[14] 4767 3-9-0 **68** (p) OisinMurphy 1 61
(Hugo Palmer) *s.i.s: hld up: rdn over 1f out: nvr on terms* **4/1**[2]

1055 **9** *4* **Secret Potion**[27] 4230 5-8-13 **62** DavidProbert 11 44
(Ronald Harris) *prom: rdn over 2f out: sn wknd* **25/1**

0-00 **10** *4* **Our Lord**[20] 4495 7-9-6 **69** CharlieBennett 6 38
(Michael Attwater) *s.i.s: sn rcvrd into mid-div: rdn over 2f out: wknd over 1f out* **66/1**

1m 14.81s (0.31) **Going Correction** +0.025s/f (Slow)
WFA 3 from 4yo+ 5lb **10 Ran SP% 119.3**
Speed ratings (Par 103): **98,97,97,96,94 94,92,92,87,81**
CSF £12.20 CT £107.90 TOTE £7.00: £2.30, £2.00, £3.30; EX 14.80 Trifecta £111.50.
Owner David Lowe **Bred** The Lowe Family **Trained** Tern Hill, Shropshire

FOCUS
A fair handicap and another race in which the pace held up. The winner's rated in line with his early 2yo best.

5282 FOLLOW AT THE RACES ON TWITTER H'CAP — 7f 36y (Tp)
3:45 (3:46) (Class 6) (0-65,65) 4-Y-0+

£2,781 (£827; £413; £300; £300; £300) **Stalls** High

Form				RPR
1144	1		**Fantastic Flyer**[27] 4247 4-9-2 **60**...(p[1]) JoeyHaynes 12 (Dean Ivory) *s.i.s and bmpd s: sn rcvrd to ld: pushed clr fr over 2f out: comf* 14/1	73
5021	2	5	**Sonnet Rose (IRE)**[13] 4807 5-9-0 **63**...(bt) SebastianWoods(5) 10 (Conrad Allen) *chsd ldrs: rdn over 2f out: wnt 2nd over 1f out: styd on same pce fnl f* 13/2[3]	64
-004	3	3/4	**Gavi Di Gavi (IRE)**[8] 5003 4-9-1 **59**... TomQueally 3 (Alan King) *hld up in tch: swtchd rt 3f out: rdn over 1f out: styd on same pce fnl f* 12/1	58+
0003	4	1 1/4	**Art Echo**[22] 4455 6-8-11 **62**...(vt) TobyEley(7) 7 (John Mackie) *pushed along early in rr: hdwy over 1f out: r.o to go 4th nr fin (jockey said gelding did not face the kick back)* 10/1	58+
002	5	1/2	**Kodiline (IRE)**[7] 5021 5-9-6 **64**... OisinMurphy 4 (David Evans) *sn pushed along in mid-div: rdn over 2f out: styd on same pce fr over 1f out* 5/2[1]	59
0020	6	3/4	**Shortbackandsides (IRE)**[33] 4037 4-9-1 **64**... DannyRedmond(5) 8 (Tim Easterby) *prom: rdn over 2f out: styd on same pce fr over 1f out* 33/1	57
6-06	7	2 1/2	**Majdool (IRE)**[6] 5038 6-9-3 **61**...(e) DavidNolan 9 (Noel Wilson) *hld up on outer: styd on fr over 1f out: nvr trble ldrs* 14/1	48+
101-	8	1/2	**Deleyll**[410] 3539 5-9-2 **65**... DarraghKeenan(5) 11 (John Butler) *s.i.s: r.o ins fnl f: nvr nrr (jockey said gelding was never travelling)* 33/1	50+
0500	9	1 1/2	**Gunmaker (IRE)**[13] 4784 5-9-1 **59**... JamesSullivan 5 (Ruth Carr) *in rr: nt clr run over 2f out: nvr on terms (jockey said gelding was denied a clear run)* 10/1	41+
3025	10	1 3/4	**Ghazan (IRE)**[17] 4657 4-9-7 **65**...(b[1]) RossaRyan 1 (Kevin Frost) *sn chsng wnr: rdn over 2f out: lost 2nd over 1f out: sn wknd* 11/2[2]	42
4063	11	11	**Grey Destiny**[14] 4767 9-9-4 **62**...(p) CamHardie 2 (Antony Brittain) *hld up: racd keenly: rdn over 2f out: wknd over 1f out* 12/1	13+
-100	12	11	**Weloof (FR)**[61] 3002 5-9-7 **65**... SeanLevey 6 (John Butler) *s.i.s: a in rr* 14/1	

1m 27.95s (-0.85) **Going Correction** +0.025s/f (Slow) 12 Ran SP% **116.7**
Speed ratings (Par 101): **105,99,98,97,96 95,92,92,90,88 75,63**
CSF £100.77 CT £1142.79 TOTE £14.20: £4.50, £2.80, £3.50; EX 91.90 Trifecta £1324.30.
Owner Mrs L A Ivory **Bred** Gracelands Stud **Trained** Radlett, Herts

FOCUS
A positive ride on the winner, and once again it proved hard to make up ground from off the pace.

5283 SKY SPORTS RACING ON SKY 415 H'CAP — 7f 36y (Tp)
4:15 (4:18) (Class 4) (0-80,79) 3-Y-0+

£5,207 (£1,549; £774; £387; £300; £300) **Stalls** High

Form				RPR
2111	1		**Street Poet (IRE)**[14] 4767 6-9-0 **71**... DannyRedmond(5) 12 (Michael Herrington) *edgd lft s: sn chsng ldrs: wnt 2nd over 5f out: led 2f out: rdn ins fnl f: hung rt towards fin: jst hld on* 10/1	79
0405	2	hd	**Blame Culture (USA)**[62] 2978 4-9-13 **79**... DavidProbert 10 (George Margarson) *s.i.s and hmpd s: hld up: hdwy over 1f out: rdn and r.o to go 2nd towards fin: nt rch wnr (jockey said gelding suffered interference leaving the stalls and on the run to the line. Vet said gelding lost it's right hind shoe)* 8/1[3]	86+
3-20	3	3/4	**Be Kool (IRE)**[38] 3867 6-9-8 **77**...(p[1]) BenRobinson(3) 11 (Brian Ellison) *hmpd s: sn prom: rdn over 1f out: styng on whn hmpd towards fin* 20/1	82
1-02	4	1/2	**Engrossed (IRE)**[109] 1567 3-9-2 **75**... OisinMurphy 8 (Martyn Meade) *hmpd s: hdwy over 5f out: rdn over 1f out: styng on whn hmpd towards fin* 4/1[2]	77
000-	5	1 3/4	**Siege Of Boston (IRE)**[258] 8924 6-9-3 **69**... KieranO'Neill 4 (John Butler) *hld up: hdwy 1/2-way: shkn up over 1f out: styd on same pce ins fnl f* 25/1	68
3242	6	3/4	**Atletico (IRE)**[7] 5020 7-9-13 **79**...(b[1]) HarryBentley 2 (David Evans) *pushed along leaving stalls: sn mid-div: hdwy over 2f out: rdn over 1f out: styd on same pce ins fnl f* 7/2[1]	76
2011	7	1/2	**Soar Above**[13] 4786 4-9-5 **76**...(p) DarraghKeenan(5) 5 (John Butler) *chsd ldr: led over 5f out: hdd 2f out: no ex ins fnl f* 8/1[3]	72
-061	8	2 1/4	**Delilah Park**[27] 4247 5-9-10 **76**... JackMitchell 3 (Chris Wall) *sn led: racd keenly: hdd over 5f out: chsd ldrs: rdn and nt clr run over 1f out: wknd ins fnl f* 7/2[1]	65
0106	9	shd	**Nezar (IRE)**[28] 4226 8-9-4 **75**... SophieRalston(5) 9 (Dean Ivory) *s.i.s and hmpd s: nvr nrr* 16/1	64
22-3	10	1 1/4	**So Macho (IRE)**[64] 2895 4-9-3 **69**... JamesSullivan 1 (Grant Tuer) *s.i.s: sn pushed along and prom: lost pl over 3f out: hdwy whn nt clr run over 1f out: nt rcvr* 14/1	55
000-	11	14	**Sinfonietta (FR)**[320] 6989 7-9-9 **75**... LiamKeniry 7 (Sophie Leech) *hmpd sn after s: in rr: wknd over 2f out* 66/1	23
2000	12	4	**Inaam (IRE)**[62] 2966 6-9-6 **72**... SeanLevey 6 (John Butler) *s.i.s and hmpd sn after s: a in rr: wknd over 2f out* 25/1	9

1m 28.46s (-0.34) **Going Correction** +0.025s/f (Slow)
WFA 3 from 4yo+ 7lb 12 Ran SP% **122.3**
Speed ratings (Par 105): **102,101,100,100,98 97,96,94,94,92 76,72**
CSF £86.78 CT £1069.00 TOTE £9.90: £3.30, £1.90, £5.40; EX 109.80 Trifecta £2417.10.
Owner Mrs H Lloyd-Herrington **Bred** Mrs C Regalado-Gonzalez **Trained** Cold Kirby, N Yorks
■ Stewards' Enquiry : Danny Redmond two-day ban; careless riding (tba)

FOCUS
The winner remains in great heart but one or two in behind looked unlucky. The winner was close to his early best.

5284 GRAND THEATRE WOLVERHAMPTON MAIDEN H'CAP — 1m 142y (Tp)
4:45 (4:48) (Class 6) (0-65,65) 3-Y-0+ £2,781 (£827; £413; £300; £300) **Stalls** Low

Form				RPR
0023	1		**Toro Dorado**[12] 4836 3-9-4 **62**... OisinMurphy 3 (Ed Dunlop) *chsd ldrs: lost pl after 1f: hdwy over 2f out: shkn up to ld ins fnl f: edgd rt: pushed out* 6/5[1]	68+
660	2	nk	**Stormbomber (CAN)**[40] 3764 3-9-6 **64**... LiamKeniry 11 (Ed Walker) *broke wl enough: sn stdd and lost pl: swtchd rt and hdwy over 1f out: rdn ins fnl f: r.o wl* 7/1[3]	69
0544	3	2 1/4	**Canasta**[26] 4284 3-9-4 **62**... DanielMuscutt 5 (James Fanshawe) *chsd ldrs: rdn and ev ch ins fnl f: styd on same pce* 6/1[2]	63
26-0	4	nk	**Is It Off (IRE)**[21] 3429 4-9-8 **62**...(p) DarraghKeenan(5) 4 (Sean Curran) *pushed along to ld: rdn over 1f out: hdd and edgd rt ins fnl f: styd on same pce* 25/1	63
6655	5	1/2	**Charlie Arthur (IRE)**[22] 4454 3-9-1 **62**... FinleyMarsh(3) 10 (Richard Hughes) *s.i.s: hld up: nt clr run over 2f out: hdwy and swtchd lft ins fnl f: sn rdn: styd on same pce towards fin* 12/1	61+
5420	5	dht	**Picture Poet (IRE)**[33] 4038 3-9-1 **59**... RobbieDowney 6 (Henry Spiller) *pushed along to chse ldrs: rdn over 1f out: styd on same pce ins fnl f* 28/1	58
500	7	nk	**Warning Light**[69] 2737 4-9-0 **49**... JosephineGordon 8 (Shaun Keightley) *wnt rt s: sn prom: rdn over 3f out: hung lft fr over 1f out: kpt on* 25/1	48
2203	8	1 1/4	**Lonicera**[17] 4642 3-9-2 **60**... DavidProbert 13 (Henry Candy) *racd keenly: hdwy to go 2nd over 7f out: rdn over 1f out: no ex ins fnl f* 8/1	56
0225	9	3/4	**Joyful Dream (IRE)**[14] 4753 5-8-9 **47**...(b) MeganNicholls(3) 9 (John Butler) *s.i.s and hmpd s: hld up: edgd lft and styd on ins fnl f: nt trble ldrs (jockey said mare suffered interference leaving the stalls)* 20/1	42
4604	10	1/2	**Gates Pass**[27] 4235 4-10-0 **63**...(t) TrevorWhelan 12 (Brian Barr) *s.s: hld up: hdwy over 1f out: rdn: edgd lft and no ex wl ins fnl f (jockey said gelding reared as the stalls opened)* 20/1	57
4650	11	1 1/2	**Lethal Lover**[28] 4225 3-9-0 **58**...(t[1]) HectorCrouch 1 (Clive Cox) *hld up in tch: rdn and nt clr run over 1f out: wknd ins fnl f* 20/1	48
0304	12	nk	**Solfeggio (IRE)**[13] 4788 3-9-7 **65**...(h) GeorgeWood 7 (Chris Wall) *hld up: rdn over 2f out: nt clr run over 1f out: n.d* 8/1	54
0030	13	nk	**Muraadef**[18] 4584 4-9-0 **49**... JamesSullivan 2 (Ruth Carr) *hld up: rdn on outer over 2f out: nvr on terms* 33/1	39

1m 49.92s (-0.18) **Going Correction** +0.025s/f (Slow)
WFA 3 from 4yo+ 9lb 13 Ran SP% **130.5**
Speed ratings (Par 101): **101,100,98,98,98 98,97,96,95,95 94,93,93**
WIN: 2.20 Toro Dorado; PL: 3.10 Stormbomber 1.90 Canasta 1.20 Toro Dorado; EX: 15.20; CSF: 9.80; TC: 45.81; TF: 86.90 CSF £9.80 CT £45.81 TOTE £2.20: £1.20, £3.10, £1.90; EX 15.20 Trifecta £86.90.
Owner R Foden, M Mitchell & Plows **Bred** Brook Stud Bloodstock Ltd **Trained** Newmarket, Suffolk

FOCUS
A modest affair. The third's a better guide than most.

5285 VISIT ATTHERACES.COM H'CAP — 1m 4f 51y (Tp)
5:15 (5:16) (Class 6) (0-55,60) 4-Y-0+

£2,781 (£827; £413; £300; £300; £300) **Stalls** Low

Form				RPR
0042	1		**Fern Owl**[29] 4190 7-9-6 **54**...(e[1]) JoeyHaynes 12 (John Butler) *s.i.s: racd wd and sn prom: led over 2f out: rdn clr fnl f* 8/1[3]	63
-001	2	2 1/4	**Genuine Approval (IRE)**[8] 5001 6-9-7 **60** 5ex...(t) DarraghKeenan(5) 7 (John Butler) *led: hdd over 10f out: chsd ldrs: rdn over 1f out: styd on* 7/2[2]	66
2262	3	1 1/2	**Givepeaceachance**[38] 3834 4-9-7 **55**... OisinMurphy 1 (Denis Coakley) *hld up: hmpd after 1f: nt clr run and lost pl over 2f out: swtchd rt and hdwy over 1f out: r.o to go 3rd nr fin* 9/4[1]	58
5110	4	1	**Greenview Paradise (IRE)**[27] 4251 5-9-5 **53**... KieranO'Neill 11 (Jeremy Scott) *chsd ldrs: wnt 2nd over 6f out tl led over 3f out: hdd over 2f out: no ex ins fnl f* 8/1[3]	54
1133	5	1	**Majeste**[35] 3960 5-9-5 **53**... LewisEdmunds 2 (Rebecca Bastiman) *chsd ldrs: lost pl over 7f out: hdwy over 1f out: styd on* 11/1	53
0333	6	3 1/2	**Yasir (USA)**[6] 5053 11-9-6 **54**... DavidProbert 10 (Sophie Leech) *s.s: hld up: r.o ins fnl f: nvr nrr (jockey said gelding was denied a clear run)* 12/1	48
1434	7	1	**Perceived**[40] 3774 7-9-5 **53**...(p) CamHardie 6 (Antony Brittain) *led over 10f out: hdd 8f out: chsd ldrs: rdn over 1f out: wknd fnl f (jockey said mare hung right in the final two furlongs)* 22/1	46
600	8	nk	**Incredible Dream (IRE)**[26] 4287 6-9-0 **53**...(t[1]) SebastianWoods(5) 8 (Conrad Allen) *s.s: hdwy over 8f out: reminder over 6f out: rdn over 3f out: wknd over 1f out* 12/1	45
140	9	12	**Muraaqeb**[19] 4547 5-9-4 **52**...(p) JackMitchell 4 (Milton Bradley) *hld up: nvr on terms* 11/1	25
-060	10	1 1/4	**Island Flame (IRE)**[61] 3006 6-9-2 **50**... RossaRyan 9 (Jennie Candlish) *prom: rdn over 3f out: wknd over 2f out (jockey said mare was never travelling)* 14/1	21
-000	11	nk	**Let's Be Happy (IRE)**[97] 1858 5-9-4 **55**...(b) WilliamCox(3) 5 (Mandy Rowland) *s.s: rdn over 2f out: a in rr (jockey said mare was slowly away)* 50/1	25
-000	12	16	**Mythological (IRE)**[18] 4594 4-9-4 **52**...(v) JosephineGordon 3 (Louise Allan) *hdwy to ld 8f out: hdd over 3f out: wknd over 2f out: eased over 1f out* 100/1	

2m 41.6s (0.80) **Going Correction** +0.025s/f (Slow) 12 Ran SP% **121.2**
Speed ratings (Par 101): **98,96,95,94,94 91,91,90,82,82 81,71**
CSF £36.58 CT £86.67 TOTE £11.50: £3.00, £1.80, £1.80; EX 53.10 Trifecta £212.60.
Owner J Butler **Bred** Sir Thomas Pilkington **Trained** Newmarket, Suffolk

FOCUS
A bit of a tactical affair. The winner was fully entitled to win in this grade on the best of this year's form.
T/Plt: £46.50 to a £1 stake. Pool: £77,065.37 - 1207.93 winning units T/Qpdt: £28.60 to a £1 stake. Pool: £7,457.18 - 192.87 winning units **Colin Roberts**

4770 COMPIEGNE (L-H)
Tuesday, July 23

OFFICIAL GOING: Turf: good to soft

5286a PRIX DE DRESLINCOURT (CLAIMER) (2YO) (TURF) — 7f
12:10 2-Y-0 £12,162 (£4,864; £3,648; £2,432; £1,216)

			RPR
1		**Glory Maker (FR)**[19] 4551 2-9-2 0 ow1... TonyPiccone 5 (K R Burke) *wl into stride: led: hdd after 1f: remained cl up: rdn to chal 1 1/2f out: drvn into ld 1f out: kpt on strly ins fnl f* 54/10[3]	76
2	1 1/4	**Miss Tiche (IRE)**[17] 2-8-7 0 ow1... ThomasTrullier(5) 8 (S Wattel, France) 3/1[1]	69

3 2 **Big Boss Man (FR)** 2-9-5 0 ow1......................(b) ChristopheSoumillon 3 71
(Cedric Rossi, France) **9/2**[2]
4 snk **Soliers (FR)**[17] 4679 2-9-1 0 ow1........................(b) AlexandreChesneau(5) 9 71
(G Botti, France) **63/10**
5 hd **Get Set (IRE)**[34] 2-9-5 0 ow1..................................(p) AntoineHamelin 7 70
(Matthieu Palussiere, France) **7/1**
6 snk **Pic Cel (FR)**[17] 4679 2-8-13 0 ow2..........................(b[1]) HugoJourniac 10 64
(J-C Rouget, France) **66/10**
7 5 **Moontide (IRE)**[17] 4679 2-8-13 0 ow2.................. MickaelBarzalona 6 51
(J S Moore) *settled in 3rd: rowed along 2f out: rdn w limited rspnse over 1f out: wknd fnl f* **67/10**
8 shd **The Nile Song (FR)**[17] 4679 2-8-5 0 ow1.............. ClementGuitraud(7) 2 49
(Y Barberot, France) **15/1**
9 15 **Xquisite (IRE)**[64] 2915 2-8-4 0 ow1............................ AlexisPouchin(5) 4 7
(J S Moore) *hld up towards rr: rdn along over 2f out: fnd little: eased fnl f* **52/1**

1m 26.46s **9 Ran SP% 119.3**
PARI-MUTUEL (all including 1 euro stake): WIN 6.40; PLACE 1.80, 1.40, 1.70; DF 9.20.
Owner Ahmad Al Shaikh **Bred** Mme Genevieve Neveux & Mr Hubert Delpech **Trained** Middleham Moor, N Yorks

5010 BATH (L-H)
Wednesday, July 24

OFFICIAL GOING: Good to firm (firm in places; 8.5)
Wind: Quite a strong headwind Weather: Fine and warm

5287 BRISTOL AIRPORT AMAZING JOURNEYS START HERE H'CAP 1m 2f 37y
2:00 (2:01) (Class 6) (0-60,60) 3-Y-O
£2,781 (£827; £413; £300; £300; £300) **Stalls** Low

Form RPR
0-44 **1** **The Game Is On**[8] 5016 3-9-7 **60**.......................... RyanTate 6 68+
(Sir Mark Prescott Bt) *s.i.s: sn led and mde rest: drvn over 1f out: styd on wl* **1/1**[1]
045 **2** 2 **Uncertain Smile (IRE)**[24] 4423 3-9-7 **60**.................. HollieDoyle 1 62+
(Clive Cox) *s.i.s: hld up in last: pushed along 4f out: drvn 2f out: stl 5th ent fnl f: r.o wl: wnt 2nd cl home* **13/2**[3]
0042 **3** ½ **Melo Pearl**[22] 4477 3-8-7 **46**..........................(v) RoystonFfrench 8 47
(Mrs Ilka Gansera-Leveque) *chsd ldrs: rdn and wnt 2nd over 2f out: no imp fnl f: lost 2nd cl home* **12/1**
0050 **4** ¾ **Sibylline**[22] 4476 3-9-0 **53**.................................. CallumShepherd 7 53
(David Simcock) *hld up: rdn and hdwy over 2f out: hung lft over 1f out: kpt on same pce* **12/1**
0305 **5** 1 **Colonelle (USA)**[14] 4804 3-9-5 **58**............................. StevieDonohoe 4 56
(Ed Vaughan) *led early: sn trcking wnr: rdn and lost 2nd over 2f out: wknd ins fnl f* **11/2**[2]
606 **6** 2 ¾ **Iris's Spirit**[22] 4476 3-8-7 **46** oh1................................ KieranO'Neill 5 38
(Tony Carroll) *hld up in tch: rdn 3f out: kpt on same pce tl wknd fnl f* **25/1**
305 **7** 3 ¾ **Heatherdown (IRE)**[11] 4931 3-9-4 **57**.....................(p) TomMarquand 3 42
(Ian Williams) *prom: rdn over 3f out: wknd 2f out* **7/1**
003R **R** **Sari Mareis**[7] 5049 3-8-12 **51**.. RobHornby 2
(Denis Coakley) *reluctant to go to post: ref to r* **10/1**

2m 9.14s (-1.96) **Going Correction** -0.125s/f (Firm) **8 Ran SP% 119.5**
Speed ratings (Par 98): **102,100,100,99,98 96,93,**
CSF £8.67 CT £53.33 TOTE £2.20: £1.40, £1.90, £1.90; EX 9.90 Trifecta £47.20.
Owner Timothy J Rooney **Bred** Mrs Ann Greenwood **Trained** Newmarket, Suffolk

FOCUS
Add 6yds to this low-grade handicap in which the favourite set a strong gallop. He can improve again.

5288 HUNTER ACCOUNTANTS/EBF NOVICE MEDIAN AUCTION STKS (PLUS 10 RACE) 5f 10y
2:30 (2:30) (Class 4) 2-Y-O **£4,463** (£1,328; £663; £331) **Stalls** Centre

Form RPR
1 **Streamline** 2-9-5 0..(h[1]) HectorCrouch 2 78+
(Clive Cox) *s.i.s: hld up in tch and racd keenly: rdn over 2f out: clsd over 1f out: r.o u.p between horses to ld wl ins fnl f* **6/1**[2]
2 **2** ½ **Fanzone (IRE)**[12] 4889 2-9-5 0.................................. HollieDoyle 5 77
(Archie Watson) *chsd ldng pair: rdn and wnt 2nd wl over 1f out: r.o and ev ch ins fnl f: jst hld towards fin* **30/100**[1]
446 **3** 1 **Too Hard To Hold (IRE)**[11] 4903 2-9-5 62.................... JasonWatson 1 73
(Mark Johnston) *led: drvn 2f out: hdd and lost 2nd too wl ins fnl f* **11/1**
66 **4** 9 **Dreamy Rascal (IRE)**[14] 4802 2-9-0 0.......................... TomMarquand 3 36
(Richard Hannon) *chsd ldr: jst losing pl whn faltered over 1f out: hanging lft after: eased fnl f (jockey said filly hung left)* **7/1**[3]
0 **5** 6 **Born For Fun (IRE)**[13] 4839 2-9-5 0................................ RobHornby 4 19
(Ali Stronge) *s.i.s: rdn over 3f out: a in rr* **50/1**

1m 2.49s (0.49) **Going Correction** -0.125s/f (Firm) **5 Ran SP% 114.0**
Speed ratings (Par 96): **91,90,88,74,64**
CSF £8.75 TOTE £8.50: £2.90, £1.02; EX 7.60 Trifecta £34.70.
Owner Mainline Racing **Bred** Whitsbury Manor Stud **Trained** Lambourn, Berks

FOCUS
There was an upset in this novice event run at a good tempo. The facourite failed to quite back up her York promise turned out quickly.

5289 RAINBOW CASINO BRISTOL H'CAP (VALUE RATER RACING CLUB BATH SUMMER SPRINT SERIES QUALIFIER) 5f 160y
3:00 (3:00) (Class 5) (0-70,71) 3-Y-O+
£3,428 (£1,020; £509; £300; £300; £300) **Stalls** Centre

Form RPR
060- **1** **Bay Watch (IRE)**[263] 8830 5-8-7 **50** oh5.............................. JohnFahy 3 61
(Tracey Barfoot-Saunt) *hld up in last: stl plenty to do whn swtchd rt over 1f out: rdn to chse ldr ins fnl f: r.o wl to ld cl home: comf* **40/1**
4004 **2** 1 ¼ **George Dryden (IRE)**[64] 2940 7-10-0 **71**...................... JackMitchell 2 78
(George Boughey) *led: 3 l clr 1/2-way: rdn over 1f out: edgd rt ins fnl f: hdd cl home* **10/3**[2]
1303 **3** 2 **Devils Roc**[20] 4556 3-9-7 **69**.. RobHornby 7 68
(Jonathan Portman) *prom: rdn over 2f out: chsd ldr over 1f out: no imp and lost 2nd ins fnl f* **6/1**
2201 **4** ¾ **Holdenhurst**[14] 4776 4-9-0 **62**.................................. CierenFallon(5) 4 60
(Bill Turner) *chsd ldr: rdn over 2f out: lost 2nd over 1f out: no ex (jockey said gelding hung left)* **9/4**[1]
6100 **5** 1 **Miracle Garden**[12] 4879 7-9-0 **62**.........................(v) PoppyBridgwater(5) 8 57
(Ian Williams) *chsd ldrs: rdn 2f out: unable qck* **6/1**
0200 **6** 1 **Coronation Cottage**[28] 4230 5-9-10 **67**.............................. PatDobbs 6 58
(Malcolm Saunders) *hld up: rdn 2f out: no imp fnl f* **5/1**[3]
1325 **7** 1 ¾ **Essaka (IRE)**[22] 4478 7-9-5 **67**................................ SophieRalston(5) 5 52
(Tony Carroll) *t.k.h: hld up: rdn on outer 2f out: wknd 1f out* **10/1**
0622 **8** nk **Upavon**[23] 4449 9-9-7 **64**... RobertWinston 1 48
(Tony Carroll) *hld up in tch: rdn 3f out: wknd appr fnl f* **12/1**

1m 9.73s (-1.37) **Going Correction** -0.125s/f (Firm)
WFA 3 from 4yo+ 5lb **8 Ran SP% 118.3**
Speed ratings (Par 103): **100,98,95,94,93 92,89,89**
CSF £175.10 CT £960.26 TOTE £44.60: £10.90, £1.20, £2.10; EX 513.80 Trifecta £2372.30.
Owner P Ponting **Bred** D J & Mrs Brown **Trained** Charfield, Gloucs

FOCUS
A modest handicap with plenty of course specialists on show but won by a longshot who was 0-8. He's rated back to his early form.

5290 BRISTOL RAINBOW CASINO H'CAP (VALUE RATER RACING CLUB BATH SUMMER STAYERS' SERIES QUALIFIER) 1m 6f
3:30 (3:32) (Class 5) (0-70,69) 4-Y-O+
£3,428 (£1,020; £509; £300; £300; £300) **Stalls** High

Form RPR
466 **1** **Horatio Star**[13] 4841 4-9-6 **68**.............................(p) JasonWatson 6 73
(Brian Meehan) *trckd ldr tl led 1/2-way: hdd and drvn 2f out: led again ins fnl f: sn hung rt: qckly stened and styd on* **7/4**[1]
0352 **2** ¾ **Filament Of Gold (USA)**[14] 4777 8-8-3 **51**..............(b) KieranO'Neill 8 54
(Roy Brotherton) *hld up: rdn over 3f out: hdwy on outer over 2f out: chalng ldr whn carried rt ins fnl f: rallied to go 2nd last strides* **11/1**
600- **3** hd **Cotton Club (IRE)**[116] 9723 8-9-6 **68**............................. JackMitchell 3 71
(George Boughey) *s.i.s: sn in midfield: tk clsr order 1/2-way: rdn to ld 2f out: hung rt and hdd ins fnl f: lost 2nd last strides* **9/1**
-641 **4** nk **Rosie Royale (IRE)**[12] 4869 7-9-0 **62**.......................... RobertWinston 4 64
(Roger Teal) *hld up: rdn 3f out: swtchd rt 2f out and sn chsng ldrs: styd on fnl f* **3/1**[2]
0-01 **5** 6 **Street Jester**[14] 4777 5-8-2 **50**............................ JosephineGordon 1 44
(Robert Stephens) *uns rdr and rn loose bef s: led 1f: chsd ldrs: rdn over 3f out: grad wknd fnl 2f* **7/1**[3]
0334 **6** nk **Butterfield (IRE)**[14] 4777 6-7-11 **50**....................(v[1]) SophieRalston(5) 7 43
(Tony Carroll) *t.k.h: led after 1f tl hdd 1/2-way: remained in 2nd tl over 2f out: wknd over 1f out* **7/1**[3]
6-04 **7** nse **Kay Sera**[21] 4498 11-8-2 **50** oh4.............................. RoystonFfrench 2 43
(Tony Newcombe) *hld up: rdn over 3f out: wknd wl over 1f out* **25/1**
125- **8** ¾ **Compatriot (IRE)**[17] 1734 5-9-2 **69**.......................... CierenFallon(5) 5 61
(Olly Murphy) *midfield: rdn 3f out: sn wknd* **12/1**

3m 2.35s (-3.75) **Going Correction** -0.125s/f (Firm) **8 Ran SP% 116.2**
Speed ratings (Par 103): **105,104,104,104,100 100,100,100**
CSF £23.13 CT £139.50 TOTE £2.10: £1.30, £2.50, £3.00; EX 23.40 Trifecta £241.80.
Owner J H Widdows **Bred** J H Widdows **Trained** Manton, Wilts
■ Stewards' Enquiry : Jack Mitchell two-day ban: careless riding (7-8 Aug)

FOCUS
Add 6yds for this competitive staying contest for the grade. The winner's rated to his early form.

5291 RAINBOW CASINO BIRMINGHAM H'CAP 5f 160y
4:00 (4:01) (Class 3) (0-90,89) 3-Y-O+ **£7,698** (£2,290; £1,144; £572) **Stalls** Centre

Form RPR
10-0 **1** **Miss Celestial (IRE)**[54] 3317 3-9-7 **89**...........................(p) RyanTate 2 102
(Sir Mark Prescott Bt) *mde all: drvn 2f out: r.o wl fnl f* **5/1**[3]
4511 **2** 2 ¼ **Heritage**[8] 5015 3-9-6 **88** 6ex...............................(p) LiamKeniry 5 94
(Clive Cox) *chsd ldng pair: impr into 2nd over 1f out: sn drvn: kpt on fnl f but no imp on wnr* **10/11**[1]
6004 **3** 3 ¼ **Rose Berry**[11] 4904 5-9-6 **83**..................................(h) JasonWatson 1 79
(Charlie Wallis) *hld up in 4th: rdn and outpcd 3f out: r.o down outside to go 3rd last strides: nvr able to threaten ldrs* **7/1**
5050 **4** hd **Boom The Groom (IRE)**[25] 4406 8-9-6 **83**................... RobertWinston 3 79
(Tony Carroll) *chsd wnr: drvn 2f out: lost 2nd over 1f out: wknd fnl f: lost 3rd last strides* **12/1**
1011 **5** 6 **Storm Melody**[11] 4926 6-8-9 **77**..............................(p) CierenFallon(5) 4 53
(Ali Stronge) *s.i.s: rdn 3f out: a in rr (jockey said gelding was slowly away)* **7/2**[2]

1m 8.37s (-2.73) **Going Correction** -0.125s/f (Firm)
WFA 3 from 5yo+ 5lb **5 Ran SP% 111.5**
Speed ratings (Par 107): **109,106,101,101,93**
CSF £10.28 TOTE £4.60: £1.90, £1.50; EX 10.20 Trifecta £31.00.
Owner John Pearce Racing Ltd **Bred** Ballymacoll Stud Farm Ltd **Trained** Newmarket, Suffolk

FOCUS
A good sprint race with two improving types coming to the fore. The time was decent.

5292 RAINBOW CASINO CARDIFF H'CAP 1m
4:30 (4:30) (Class 4) (0-80,79) 3-Y-O+ **£5,207** (£1,549; £774; £387; £300) **Stalls** Low

Form RPR
1450 **1** **Wind In My Sails**[5] 5155 7-9-9 **79**......................... SeamusCronin(5) 5 87
(Ed de Giles) *hld up: hdwy 3f out: led wl over 1f out: rdn out* **4/1**[3]
-361 **2** 2 ½ **Conspiritor**[14] 4773 3-8-13 **72**.................................. KieranShoemark 6 72
(Charles Hills) *hld up: rdn and hdwy on outer 2f out: wnt 2nd over 1f out: no imp on wnr fnl f* **11/2**
0452 **3** ½ **Welcoming (FR)**[8] 5022 3-9-2 **75**.............................. RoystonFfrench 3 74
(Mark Johnston) *trckd ldr: rdn 3f out: lost 2nd over 1f out: kpt on* **5/2**[2]
3451 **4** 6 **Canal Rocks**[20] 4562 3-9-5 **78**.................................. JasonWatson 2 63+
(Henry Candy) *trckd ldrs: losing pl whn bec unbalanced on inner 2f out: sn hmpd: no ch after (jockey said gelding was unbalanced in home straight)* **11/8**[1]
0-23 **5** 16 **Shake Me Handy**[145] 963 4-9-6 **71**............................. RobertWinston 1 22
(Roger Teal) *wnt to post early: led: rdn 3f out: hdd wl over 1f out: wknd qckly (jockey said gelding hung both ways; vet said gelding bled from nose)* **12/1**

1m 40.54s (-1.16) **Going Correction** -0.125s/f (Firm)
WFA 3 from 4yo+ 8lb **5 Ran SP% 113.8**
Speed ratings (Par 105): **100,97,97,91,75**
CSF £25.18 TOTE £5.40: £2.60, £2.20; EX 23.70 Trifecta £74.30.
Owner John Manser **Bred** Meon Valley Stud **Trained** Ledbury, H'fords

FOCUS
Add 6yds. A ordinary race for the grade, run at a muddling gallop, and there are doubts over the form.

5293 RAINBOW CASINO BRISTOL CLASSIFIED STKS 1m
5:00 (5:00) (Class 6) 3-Y-O+

£2,781 (£827; £413; £300; £300; £300) Stalls Low

Form RPR
-000 1 **Guardiola (USA)**[28] 4232 4-9-5 44..........................(t[1]) JoshuaBryan[(3)] 10 50
(Bernard Llewellyn) *hld up towards rr: hdwy 4f out: rdn and swtchd rt over 1f out: sn chsng wnr: carried rt ins fnl f: led last strides* **16/1**
0543 2 *hd* **Sea Tea Dea**[8] 5016 5-9-5 44.............................. FinleyMarsh[(3)] 1 50
(Adrian Wintle) *chsd ldrs: hdwy over 2f out: drifted rt and led over 1f out: drvn and edgd rt fnl f: hdd last strides* **10/1**
5400 3 3 ¾ **Parknacilla (IRE)**[22] 4485 3-8-9 48..................(p[1]) PoppyBridgwater[(5)] 4 40
(Henry Spiller) *s.i.s: hld up: nt clr run on inner over 3f out: sn rdn: hung rt and hdwy over 1f out: r.o fnl f: wnt 3rd towards fin* **8/1[3]**
0/00 4 ½ **Lovely Acclamation (IRE)**[43] 3687 5-9-3 45......(p) RachealKneller[(5)] 11 40
(Matthew Salaman) *chsd ldrs: rdn whn hmpd and pushed rt over 1f out: kpt on same pce* **50/1**
0303 5 *hd* **Spirit Of Lucerne (IRE)**[15] 4754 3-8-7 48................ GraceMcEntee[(7)] 2 37
(Phil McEntee) *midfield: lost pl 4f out: rdn 3f out: hung rt and hdwy over 1f out: r.o fnl f* **16/1**
0001 6 *hd* **Bader**[9] 4991 3-8-9 50...(b) SeamusCronin[(5)] 9 37
(Richard Hannon) *trckd ldr tl lost 2nd over 4f out: rdn and carried rt over 1f out: hung lft after: unable qck fnl f: lost 3rd towards fin* **11/10[1]**
3035 7 2 ¼ **Three C's (IRE)**[25] 4376 5-9-3 49.................................(b[1]) CierenFallon[(5)] 5 34
(George Boughey) *s.i.s: sn in midfield: rdn 3f out: edgd rt over 1f out: no real imp* **5/2[2]**
0600 8 1 ¼ **Society Sweetheart (IRE)**[22] 4485 3-9-0 49..............(p[1]) KieranO'Neill 7 29
(J S Moore) *prom: rdn whn nt clr run over 2f out: wknd over 1f out* **20/1**
00-0 9 ¾ **Harbour Sunrise**[63] 969 4-9-8 42.............................(h[1]) MartinDwyer 8 29
(Shaun Harris) *towards rr: rdn 3f out: hung lft 2f out: modest late hdwy* **50/1**
0000 10 5 **Tsarmina (IRE)**[64] 2943 3-9-0 48.............................. RobertWinston 13 16
(David Evans) *s.i.s: a towards rr* **14/1**
0005 11 ½ **Yet Another (IRE)**[14] 4774 4-9-1 35.............................. KeelanBaker[(7)] 14 16
(Grace Harris) *led: drvn and hdd over 2f out: wknd over 1f out* **40/1**
-000 12 8 **Rock N Roll Queen**[30] 4193 3-9-0 50...........................(p) StevieDonohoe 3
(John Mackie) *t.k.h: prom: wnt 2nd over 4f out: led narrowly over 2f out tl hdd over 1f out: wknd qckly* **33/1**
0-00 13 52 **Davina**[15] 4753 4-9-5 36...(v[1]) MitchGodwin[(3)] 12
(Bill Turner) *prom tl wnt wd and lost pl bnd over 4f out: rdn and no rspnse: wknd rapidly: t.o fnl 3f (jockey said filly was unsuited by the good to firm ground and would prefer easier going)* **50/1**

1m 40.69s (-1.01) **Going Correction** -0.125s/f (Firm)
WFA 3 from 4yo+ 8lb **13 Ran SP% 130.8**
Speed ratings (Par 101): **100,99,96,95,95 95,92,91,90,85 85,77,25**
CSF £172.56 TOTE £21.20: £2.30, £2.70, £3.40; EX 231.80 Trifecta £793.70.
Owner Gethyn Mills & B J Llewellyn **Bred** Godolphin **Trained** Fochriw, Caerphilly
■ Stewards' Enquiry : Finley Marsh two-day ban: careless riding (7-8 Aug)

FOCUS
6yds was added after rail movements. A weak contest run at a sound gallop, meaning plenty of those help up came to the fore. The first two were clear but it's not form to be positive about.
T/Plt: £73.90 to a £1 stake. Pool: £56,646.19. 559.20 winning units. T/Qpdt: £46.90 to a £1 stake. Pool: £4,478.41. 70.56 winning units. **Richard Lowther**

5037 CATTERICK (L-H)
Wednesday, July 24

OFFICIAL GOING: Good to soft (good in places; 7.6)
Wind: light, largely across Weather: hot and sunny

5294 ITV7 STARTS NOW EBF MAIDEN STKS 5f 212y
2:10 (2:10) (Class 5) 2-Y-O £4,140 (£1,232; £615; £307) Stalls Low

Form RPR
42 1 **Incinerator**[20] 4564 2-9-5 0.......................................(t) BenCurtis 1 75+
(Hugo Palmer) *chsd ldr: rdn along over 2f out: 2 1/2 l down 1f out: drvn and kpt on: led post* **10/11[1]**
03 2 *hd* **Kendred Soul (IRE)**[16] 4727 2-9-0 0.............................. JackGarritty 11 69
(Jedd O'Keeffe) *across fr wd draw and sn led: rdn over 1f out: 2 1/2 l up 1f out: drvn and one pce ins fnl f: hdd post* **12/1**
06 3 3 ¼ **Schumli**[21] 4517 2-9-0 0.. DanielTudhope 4 59
(David O'Meara) *chsd ldrs: rdn 2f out: one pce* **25/1**
4 1 **Frost At Midnight (USA)** 2-9-0 0.................................. JoeFanning 3 55
(Mark Johnston) *midfield pushed along over 2f out: kpt on same pce* **13/2[3]**
60 5 *nk* **Light The Fuse (IRE)**[9] 4984 2-8-12 0.............................. RhonaPindar[(7)] 8 59+
(K R Burke) *hld up: pushed along 2f out: hung lft but kpt on fr over 1f out (jockey said colt hung left home straight)* **25/1**
5 6 1 ¼ **A Go Go**[53] 3350 2-9-0 0.. DavidAllan 9 50
(David Evans) *in tch: rdn along over 2f out: no ex ins fnl f* **40/1**
7 ½ **Max's Voice (IRE)** 2-9-5 0.. PhilDennis 7 54+
(David Loughnane) *midfield: rdn along 2f out: no imp* **50/1**
8 ¾ **Bal Mal (FR)** 2-9-5 0... JasonHart 10 51
(John Quinn) *midfield: rdn along 2f out: wknd ins fnl f* **5/1[2]**
4 9 ½ **Lady Celia**[21] 4509 2-8-11 0.. SeanDavis[(3)] 6 45
(Richard Fahey) *hld up: nvr threatened* **8/1**
60 10 1 ¾ **Jazz Style (IRE)**[28] 4238 2-9-5 0.............................. PaulMulrennan 2 44
(David Brown) *hld up: pushed along and sme hdwy over 1f out: wknd ins fnl f* **50/1**
40 11 ½ **Noddy Shuffle**[40] 3810 2-9-5 0.............................. NathanEvans 5 43
(Michael Easterby) *a towards rr: hung lft 2f out (jockey said gelding hung left under pressure)* **33/1**

1m 16.32s (2.72) **Going Correction** +0.175s/f (Good) **11 Ran SP% 118.2**
Speed ratings (Par 94): **88,87,83,82,81 80,79,78,77,75 74**
CSF £12.50 TOTE £1.60: £1.10, £2.50, £6.80; EX 11.60 Trifecta £143.40.
Owner V I Araci **Bred** V I Araci **Trained** Newmarket, Suffolk

FOCUS
The going was given as good to soft, good in places (Going Stick 7.6). The rail on the bend turning into the home straight was dolled out 4yds. Add 12yds. A modest maiden in which the favourite never looked like winning until the final few yards. Pace held up.

5295 GO RACING IN YORKSHIRE SUMMER FESTIVAL (S) STKS 7f 6y
2:40 (2:41) (Class 6) 2-Y-O

£3,105 (£924; £461; £300; £300; £300) Stalls Low

Form RPR
0 1 **Laughter Lounge (IRE)**[61] 3049 2-8-10 0.............................. BenCurtis 3 57
(David Evans) *hld up: pushed along in rr over 3f out: drvn 2f out: stl only 8th appr fnl f: r.o strly: led towards fin* **25/1**
365 2 ¾ **It's Not My Fault (IRE)**[12] 4876 2-8-7 62.............................. JaneElliott[(3)] 9 55
(Tom Dascombe) *sn prom: drvn into narrow ld 1f out: kpt on but hdd towards fin* **9/1**
06 3 1 ½ **Susie Javea**[33] 4075 2-8-10 0.............................. CamHardie 6 51
(Ollie Pears) *midfield: rdn over 2f out: kpt on ins fnl f* **66/1**
151 4 *hd* **Gold Venture (IRE)**[43] 3694 2-9-2 70.............................. DanielTudhope 5 56
(Archie Watson) *trckd ldrs: rdn and ev ch appr fnl f: no ex ins fnl f* **1/2[1]**
4024 5 ¾ **Classy Lady**[4] 5196 2-8-7 61.............................. (p[1]) BenRobinson[(3)] 8 48
(Ollie Pears) *led after 1f: rdn over 2f out: hdd 1f out: wknd ins fnl f* **5/1[2]**
00 6 *shd* **Cersei Lannister (IRE)**[13] 4819 2-8-10 0................(v[1]) ConnorBeasley 4 48
(Adrian Nicholls) *slowly away: hld up: rdn and sme hdwy over 1f out: kpt on ins fnl f* **33/1**
030 7 1 ½ **Our Dave**[18] 4623 2-9-1 57.............................. JasonHart 1 50
(John Quinn) *hld up in midfield: pushed along over 2f out: rdn and sme hdwy over 1f out: no ex ins fnl f* **13/2[3]**
00 8 3 ¼ **Miss Chilli**[75] 2594 2-8-10 0.............................. NathanEvans 7 35
(Michael Easterby) *hld up in midfield: rdn along over 2f out: wknd over 1f out* **22/1**
000 9 9 **Jakodobro**[21] 4517 2-9-1 28.............................. GrahamLee 2 16
(Bryan Smart) *led for 1f: chsd ldrs: rdn along 3f out: wknd over 1f out* **66/1**

1m 30.82s (3.42) **Going Correction** +0.175s/f (Good) **9 Ran SP% 120.8**
Speed ratings (Par 92): **87,86,84,84,83 83,81,77,67**
CSF £225.81 TOTE £35.40: £6.20, £2.10, £11.20; EX 312.10 Trifecta £3258.10.The winner was sold to Mr Claes Bjorling for £11,000. Gold Venture was claimed by Mr P. Kirby for £7,000. It's Not My Fault was claimed by Mr P. T. Midgley for £7,000.
Owner Mrs I M Folkes **Bred** Aidan Sexton **Trained** Pandy, Monmouths

FOCUS
Add 12yds. A bit of a turn up here, especially in play, with the winner hitting the maximum price. There are lots of question marks over this form.

5296 JOCK BENNETT/KENNY WILLIAMS LIFETIME IN RACING NURSERY H'CAP 7f 6y
3:10 (3:11) (Class 5) (0-70,70) 2-Y-O

£4,075 (£909; £303; £300; £300) Stalls Low

Form RPR
0060 1 **Bankawi**[37] 3927 2-8-0 **49** oh1.............................. JamesSullivan 9 53
(Michael Easterby) *prom: led appr fnl f: sn rdn 2 l clr: drvn out* **40/1**
0332 2 1 ¼ **Breguet Man (IRE)**[12] 4878 2-9-6 **69**.............................. ShaneGray 13 70
(Keith Dalgleish) *midfield: rdn over 2f out: sme hdwy over 1f out: kpt on fnl f* **9/2[3]**
006 2 *dht* **Percy Green (IRE)**[57] 3190 2-8-9 **58**.............................. BenCurtis 8 59+
(K R Burke) *hld up: pushed along and hdwy 2f out: angled rt to outer over 1f out: rdn and kpt on wl* **12/1**
5013 4 ¾ **Ambyfaeirvine (IRE)**[5] 5146 2-9-5 **68**.............................. DavidAllan 11 68
(Ivan Furtado) *chsd ldrs: rdn over 2f out: kpt on same pce fnl f* **3/1[1]**
3554 5 2 ¼ **Knightcap**[16] 4727 2-9-4 **67**.............................. RachelRichardson 7 60
(Tim Easterby) *led: rdn over 2f out: hdd appr fnl f: wknd fnl 110yds* **25/1**
0463 6 ¾ **Rusalka (IRE)**[14] 4780 2-8-9 **58**.............................. DuranFentiman 14 49
(Tim Easterby) *s.i.s: hld up: pushed along over 2f out: kpt on ins fnl f: nvr trbld ldrs (jockey said filly jumped right and missed the break)* **16/1**
334 7 2 **What A Business (IRE)**[21] 4517 2-9-4 **67**.............................. DanielTudhope 10 52
(Roger Fell) *midfield: rdn and hdwy to chse ldrs over 2f out: wknd fnl f* **7/2[2]**
060 8 *nk* **Never Said Nothing (IRE)**[55] 3245 2-8-8 **60**.............................. BenRobinson[(3)] 3 45+
(Brian Ellison) *hld up: nvr threatened* **18/1**
0001 9 1 ¼ **Rain Cap**[33] 4075 2-9-3 **66**.............................. JasonHart 5 47
(Mick Channon) *in tch: rdn over 2f out: wknd over 1f out* **14/1**
0654 10 3 **Sparkling Breeze**[40] 3812 2-9-2 **70**.............................. PaulaMuir[(5)] 4 43
(Michael Dods) *hld up in midfield: rdn along over 2f out: wknd over 1f out* **20/1**
004 11 1 ¾ **Lady Erimus**[36] 3954 2-8-11 **60**.............................. KevinStott 6 28
(Kevin Ryan) *hld up in midfield: rdn over 2f out: wknd over 1f out* **20/1**
605 12 *nse* **The Trendy Man (IRE)**[33] 4075 2-8-7 **56**.............................. (p) CamHardie 12 24
(David O'Meara) *hld up: rdn over 3f out: wknd over 1f out* **33/1**
6400 13 9 **Pearlwood (IRE)**[15] 4756 2-8-4 **56**.............................. SeanDavis[(3)] 1
(Richard Fahey) *a towards rr* **33/1**
0556 14 1 **Stormy Bay**[15] 4756 2-8-4 **53**.............................. (p) AndrewMullen 2
(Keith Dalgleish) *chsd ldrs: rdn over 3f out: wknd over 2f out* **12/1**

1m 28.84s (1.44) **Going Correction** +0.175s/f (Good) **14 Ran SP% 120.3**
Speed ratings (Par 94): **98,96,96,95,93 92,90,89,88,84 82,82,72,71**
WIN: £65.70; PL: B £13.20, BM £1.80, PG £5.30; EX: B/BM £317.70, B/PG £785.50; CSF: B/BM £99.99, B/PG £217.47; TC: B/BM/PG £1,176.98, B/PG/BM £1,299.37; TF: B/BM/PG £1,186.50, B/PG/BM £1,186.50.
Owner South Bank Racing **Bred** M W Easterby **Trained** Sheriff Hutton, N Yorks

FOCUS
Add 12yds. A modest nursery, very competitive but lacking obvious types to progress.

5297 MILLBRY HILL CLAIMING STKS 7f 6y
3:40 (3:43) (Class 6) 3-4-Y-O

£3,105 (£924; £461; £300; £300; £300) Stalls Low

Form RPR
1531 1 **Ollivander (IRE)**[8] 5021 3-9-3 70..............................(v) DanielTudhope 7 77
(David O'Meara) *pressed ldr: led 5f out: rdn and in command over 2f out: drvn out fr over 1f out* **4/6[1]**
3523 2 1 ½ **Bedtime Bella (IRE)**[21] 4519 3-8-6 64.............................. SeanDavis[(3)] 9 65
(Michael Appleby) *sn chsd ldrs on outer: rdn to chse ldr over 2f out: drvn over 1f out: kpt on but a hld* **7/2[3]**
4023 3 2 ¼ **Sarasota (IRE)**[15] 4749 4-8-6 60.............................. AndrewBreslin[(5)] 2 57
(Alexandra Dunn) *trckd ldrs: lost pl 4f out: sn pushed along and towards rr: kpt on fr over 1f out: wnt 3rd fnl 50yds* **3/1[2]**

-060 **4** 2 1/4 **Our Secret (IRE)**[33] 4078 3-8-0 45......................(p[1]) JamesSullivan 3 44
(Liam Bailey) *chsd ldrs: rdn over 3f out: wknd ins fnl f: lost 3rd fnl 50yds* **10/1**

-000 **5** 1 1/2 **Se Green**[43] 3684 3-8-4 43.............................. DuranFentiman 8 44
(Tim Easterby) *midfield: rdn over 2f out: no imp* **20/1**

-506 **6** 2 3/4 **Mandarin Princess**[24] 3929 4-8-10 41.................... AndrewMullen 1 39
(Kenny Johnson) *a towards rr* **125/1**

-000 **7** 3 **Liberty Diva (IRE)**[11] 4909 3-7-11 40 ow2..................(p[1]) PaulaMuir(5) 6 26
(Alan Berry) *hld up: rdn and brief hdwy over 2f out: wknd over 1f out* **50/1**

0-0 **8** 36 **Last Glance (IRE)**[203] 18 4-8-12 40.......................... KevinStott 5
(Tracy Waggott) *led: hdd 5f out: rdn over 3f out: sn wknd: eased over 1f out* **50/1**

1m 28.58s (1.18) **Going Correction** +0.175s/f (Good)
WFA 3 from 4yo 7lb **8** Ran SP% **125.8**
Speed ratings (Par 101): **100,98,95,93,91 88,84,43**
CSF £3.98 TOTE £1.50: £1.10, £1.30, £1.30; EX 4.30 Trifecta £7.40.
Owner York Thoroughbred Racing **Bred** Canice Farrell **Trained** Upper Helmsley, N Yorks

FOCUS
Add 12yds. At the weights this was a three-horse race really, and they filled the first three positions, the favourite making most. Straightforward form.

5298 SKY BET GO-RACING-IN-YORKSHIRE SUMMER FESTIVAL H'CAP 5f
4:10 (4:10) (Class 4) (0-85,82) 3-Y-O+
£6,080 (£1,809; £904; £452; £300; £300) Stalls Low

Form RPR

0511 **1** **Tomily (IRE)**[9] 4977 5-9-12 82 5ex.......................... DanielTudhope 6 93+
(David O'Meara) *squeezed out sltly s: hld up: swtchd lft over 1f out: rdn and sn hdwy: led ins fnl f: kpt on pushed out: cosily* **11/4[2]**

0000 **2** 1 1/2 **Alsvinder**[12] 4880 6-9-6 76.......................... KevinStott 3 82
(Philip Kirby) *chsd ldrs: rdn over 2f out: drvn to ld appr fnl f: hdd ins fnl f: kpt on* **33/1**

1521 **3** 2 1/2 **Timetodock**[23] 4436 3-8-12 72..............................(b) DavidAllan 4 68
(Tim Easterby) *pressed ldr: rdn 2f out: no ex ins fnl f* **9/4[1]**

3054 **4** 1 1/2 **Landing Night (IRE)**[7] 5042 7-8-12 68....................(bt[1]) CliffordLee 1 60
(Rebecca Menzies) *chsd ldrs: rdn 2f out: no ex ins fnl f (jockey said gelding hung left)* **13/2**

0632 **5** 1 **Something Lucky (IRE)**[7] 5042 7-8-7 66....................(v) SeanDavis(3) 7 54
(Michael Appleby) *hld up: rdn along over 2f out: nvr threatened* **14/1**

6542 **6** nse **Merry Banter**[9] 4986 5-9-12 82.......................... PaulMulrennan 8 70
(Paul Midgley) *sn led on outer: rdn 2f out: hdd appr fnl f: wknd ins fnl f* **4/1[3]**

3325 **7** 5 **Hawaam (IRE)**[27] 4301 4-9-7 77..............................(p) LewisEdmunds 5 47
(Roger Fell) *prom: rdn over 2f out: wknd appr fnl f (trainer could offer no explanation for the gelding's performance)* **7/1**

59.22s (-1.28) **Going Correction** +0.175s/f (Good)
WFA 3 from 4yo+ 4lb **7** Ran SP% **112.9**
Speed ratings (Par 105): **105,102,98,96,94 94,86**
CSF £73.25 CT £233.32 TOTE £3.90: £1.90, £12.10; EX 88.60 Trifecta £344.70.
Owner Thoroughbred British Racing **Bred** D J Anderson **Trained** Upper Helmsley, N Yorks

FOCUS
The winner confirmed himself firmly on the way back for his new stable, edging closer to his old form.

5299 NEVER MISS A RACE ON RACING TV H'CAP (DIV I) 5f 212y
4:40 (4:40) (Class 6) (0-60,59) 3-Y-O+
£3,105 (£924; £461; £300; £300; £300) Stalls Low

Form RPR

0500 **1** **Someone Exciting**[23] 4434 6-8-8 48.......................... HarrisonShaw(5) 9 58
(David Thompson) *midfield: rdn and hdwy appr fnl f: led ins fnl f: kpt on wl* **14/1**

1354 **2** 1 3/4 **Steelriver (IRE)**[9] 5000 9-9-10 59.......................... PhilDennis 8 63
(Michael Herrington) *chsd ldrs: rdn into narrow ld appr fnl f: hdd ins fnl f: edgd lft and one pce* **13/2**

0464 **3** 1 **Spirit Of Zebedee (IRE)**[16] 4720 6-9-1 50....................(v) JasonHart 7 51
(John Quinn) *prom: rdn to chal strly appr fnl f: edgd lft and no ex fnl 110yds* **3/1[1]**

-000 **4** 1 1/2 **Ingleby Molly (IRE)**[49] 3476 4-8-7 45....................(h) ConorMcGovern(3) 3 41
(Jason Ward) *hld up: rdn over 2f out: kpt on to go modest 4th towards fin: nvr involved* **33/1**

3453 **5** 3/4 **B Fifty Two (IRE)**[13] 4824 10-9-6 58....................(tp) JaneElliott(3) 2 52
(Marjorie Fife) *in tch: rdn over 2f out: no ex ins fnl f* **15/2**

0420 **6** 1 1/2 **Fard**[2] 5247 4-9-4 58.......................... BenSanderson(5) 4 47
(Roger Fell) *dwlt: hld up: rdn along over 2f out: nvr threatened* **6/1[3]**

0063 **7** 1 1/2 **Champagne Mondays**[5] 5147 3-8-8 48....................(b) JamesSullivan 10 31
(Scott Dixon) *sn led: rdn over 2f out: hdd appr fnl f: wknd* **8/1**

0-06 **8** 1 1/4 **Dragons Will Rise (IRE)**[55] 3270 3-8-12 52.................. MichaelStainton 1 31
(Micky Hammond) *dwlt: a towards rr* **14/1**

6000 **9** 3/4 **Chickenfortea (IRE)**[14] 4785 5-9-5 54.......................... DavidAllan 5 32
(Eric Alston) *midfield: rdn over 2f out: wknd over 1f out (jockey said gelding got upset in the stalls and missed the break)* **7/2[2]**

1m 14.32s (0.72) **Going Correction** +0.175s/f (Good)
WFA 3 from 4yo+ 5lb **9** Ran SP% **114.0**
Speed ratings (Par 101): **102,99,98,96,95 93,91,89,88**
CSF £100.37 CT £348.93 TOTE £16.40: £4.10, £2.60, £1.10; EX 132.30 Trifecta £904.70.
Owner Jordan Souster **Bred** Trebles Holford Farm Thoroughbreds **Trained** Bolam, Co Durham

FOCUS
Add 12yds. An ordinary sprint handicap but the quicker of the two divisions by 0.35sec. Straightforward form in behind the winner.

5300 NEVER MISS A RACE ON RACING TV H'CAP (DIV II) 5f 212y
5:10 (5:10) (Class 6) (0-60,59) 3-Y-O+
£3,105 (£924; £461; £300; £300; £300) Stalls Low

Form RPR

0254 **1** **Mr Greenlight**[8] 5018 4-9-8 57.......................... DavidAllan 9 64
(Tim Easterby) *prom: pushed into ld over 1f out: drvn ins fnl f: hld on towards fin* **6/1[3]**

0004 **2** nk **Mightaswellsmile**[7] 5038 5-8-5 45.......................... PaulaMuir(5) 11 51
(Ron Barr) *hld up in midfield: pushed along over 2f out: rdn and hdwy appr fnl f: kpt on wl* **16/1**

5512 **3** hd **Macs Blessings (IRE)**[2] 5238 3-8-11 56....................(v) HarrisonShaw(5) 10 60
(Stef Keniry) *midfield: rdn over 2f out: hdwy appr fnl f: kpt on wl* **9/4[1]**

0450 **4** 1 **Vallarta (IRE)**[16] 4720 9-8-13 48.......................... JamesSullivan 7 50
(Ruth Carr) *chsd ldrs: rdn over 2f out: kpt on same pce fnl f* **10/1**

0000 **5** nk **Lexington Palm (IRE)**[16] 4720 3-8-7 50.......................... SeanDavis(3) 6 50
(Keith Dalgleish) *in tch: rdn over 2f out: kpt on same pce fnl f: bit short of room towards fin* **16/1**

6400 **6** 1 1/4 **Crosse Fire**[37] 3928 7-8-13 55..............................(p) KieranSchofield(7) 4 52
(Scott Dixon) *hld up: rdn over 2f out: sme hdwy over 1f out: one pce ins fnl f (jockey said gelding missed break)* **16/1**

050 **7** 3/4 **The Retriever (IRE)**[48] 3517 4-9-3 52.......................... GrahamLee 12 47
(Micky Hammond) *hld up in rr: rdn over 2f out: kpt on ins fnl f: nvr threatened* **25/1**

5000 **8** 2 **Super Florence (IRE)**[6] 5094 4-9-2 58....................(h) HarryRussell(7) 1 46
(Iain Jardine) *led: rdn over 2f out: hdd appr fnl f: wknd* **12/1**

0243 **9** 3 1/4 **Extrasolar**[7] 5038 9-9-10 59..............................(t) KevinStott 2 37
(Geoffrey Harker) *midfield: rdn over 2f out: wknd ins fnl f and eased* **5/1[2]**

2400 **10** 8 **Ascot Dreamer**[21] 4519 3-9-0 54..............................(t) PaulMulrennan 5 5
(David Brown) *chsd ldrs: rdn over 2f out: wknd over 1f out* **9/1**

0006 **11** 1/2 **Itsupforgrabsnow (IRE)**[7] 5041 4-8-10 45....................(h) PhilDennis 3
(Susan Corbett) *dwlt: a towards rr* **25/1**

0665 **12** 1 1/2 **Supreme Dream**[16] 4731 3-8-6 46..............................(p[1]) RachelRichardson 8
(Ollie Pears) *a outpcd in rr* **28/1**

1m 14.67s (1.07) **Going Correction** +0.175s/f (Good)
WFA 3 from 4yo+ 5lb **12** Ran SP% **117.3**
Speed ratings (Par 101): **99,98,98,97,96 94,93,91,86,76 75,73**
CSF £94.18 CT £257.05 TOTE £6.30: £1.80, £5.00, £1.70; EX 102.60 Trifecta £398.70.
Owner Richard Taylor & Philip Hebdon **Bred** Usk Valley Stud **Trained** Great Habton, N Yorks
■ Stewards' Enquiry : Paula Muir four-day ban: used whip with excessive frequency (Aug 7-10)

FOCUS
Add 12yds. A bunched finish and the slower of the two legs by 0.35sec. The winner has better back form and could improve on this in the short term.

5301 CATTERICKBRIDGE.CO.UK APPRENTICE TRAINING SERIES H'CAP (RACING EXCELLENCE TRAINING SERIES) 1m 4f 13y
5:45 (5:46) (Class 6) (0-65,66) 4-Y-O+
£3,105 (£924; £461; £300; £300; £300) Stalls Low

Form RPR

0360 **1** **Metronomic (IRE)**[9] 4990 5-8-3 45.......................... ZakWheatley(5) 4 50
(Peter Niven) *rrd s: sn midfield: pushed along to chse ldrs 2f out: rdn to ld appr fnl f: styd on* **14/1**

6323 **2** nk **Lafilia (GER)**[9] 5001 4-9-9 60..............................(b) Pierre-LouisJamin 10 65
(Archie Watson) *prom: rdn along over 2f out: styd on ins fnl f* **8/1**

0030 **3** hd **Fillydelphia (IRE)**[21] 4515 8-8-5 45..............................(p) RhonaPindar(3) 9 49
(Liam Bailey) *hld up in rr: rdn and hdwy on outer 2f out: styd on fnl f* **40/1**

5545 **4** 1/2 **Corton Lad**[16] 4724 9-10-1 66..............................(bt) ScottMcCullagh 3 69
(Keith Dalgleish) *hld up in midfield: pushed along and hdwy 2f out: rdn and kpt on fnl f* **9/1**

3066 **5** hd **Airplane (IRE)**[8] 5029 4-9-9 60.......................... EllaMcCain 12 63
(Tim Easterby) *led: rdn over 1f out: hdd appr fnl f: no ex towards fin* **11/2[3]**

4222 **6** 3 **Mr Carbonator**[18] 4627 4-9-2 60.......................... NickBarratt-Atkin(7) 8 58
(Philip Kirby) *trckd ldrs towards outer: racd quite keenly: rdn over 2f out: wknd ins fnl f* **4/1[2]**

20-2 **7** 1 3/4 **Calliope**[27] 4274 6-9-7 61..............................(t) HarryRussell(3) 11 56
(Dianne Sayer) *hld up in midfield: rdn along over 3f out: wknd ins fnl f* **7/2[1]**

000 **8** 3 **Midnight Warrior**[9] 4990 9-8-5 47..............................(t) IzzyClifton(5) 6 38
(Ron Barr) *trckd ldrs: rdn along over 2f out: wknd over 1f out* **16/1**

-423 **9** 2 3/4 **Rose Crown**[12] 4869 5-9-6 62.......................... GeorgeBass(5) 2 48
(Mick Channon) *hld up: rdn over 2f out: sn btn* **13/2**

6010 **10** 13 **Oborne Lady (IRE)**[35] 2593 6-9-1 52.......................... WilliamCarver 1 17
(Seamus Mullins) *midfield: rdn 3f out: sn wknd (jockey said mare was never travelling)* **10/1**

2m 42.1s (1.50) **Going Correction** +0.175s/f (Good) **10** Ran SP% **116.1**
Speed ratings (Par 101): **102,101,101,101,101 99,98,96,94,85**
CSF £120.66 CT £4326.88 TOTE £12.40: £3.10, £2.30, £5.90; EX 179.70 Trifecta £2019.20.
Owner Keep The Faith Partnership **Bred** Pier House Stud **Trained** Barton-le-Street, N Yorks

FOCUS
Add 12yds. An ordinary race and a tight finish. Very limited form.
T/Plt: £869.70 to a £1 stake. Pool: £47,540.11. 39.90 winning units. T/Qpdt: £27.60 to a £1 stake. Pool: £6,596.28. 176.62 winning units. **Andrew Sheret**

5101 LEICESTER (R-H)
Wednesday, July 24

OFFICIAL GOING: Good to firm (good in places; 7.9)
Wind: Almost nil Weather: Fine

5302 A.J.A NOVICE AMATEUR RIDERS' H'CAP 7f
5:40 (5:41) (Class 6) (0-60,62) 4-Y-O+
£3,057 (£948; £473; £300; £300; £300) Stalls High

Form RPR

6306 **1** **Winklemann (IRE)**[27] 4281 7-11-4 59....................(p) MissImogenMathias(3) 1 68
(John Flint) *s.i.s: sn pushed along in rr: hdwy over 1f out: edgd rt and r.o to ld wl ins fnl f* **7/2[1]**

5005 **2** 1 **Chetan**[19] 4615 7-11-7 59.......................... MissSarahBowen 7 66
(Tony Carroll) *prom: pushed along and outpcd 1/2-way: rallied over 1f out: led ins fnl f: hdd and unable qck wl ins fnl f* **4/1[2]**

3112 **3** 2 1/2 **Confrerie (IRE)**[22] 4472 4-11-7 62.......................... MrNathanMcCann(3) 15 62
(George Baker) *s.i.s: in rr: hdwy over 2f out: rdn and edgd rt ins fnl f: no ex towards fin* **4/1[2]**

0056 **4** 2 1/2 **Ronni Layne**[8] 5025 5-10-7 45..............................(v) MrAlexChadwick 5 39
(Louise Allan) *hld up: hdwy u.p over 1f out: wknd wl ins fnl f* **25/1**

1000 **5** 3 **Limerick Lord (IRE)**[23] 4460 7-10-10 51....................(p) MrSamFeilden(3) 12 38+
(Julia Feilden) *chsd ldrs: pushed along 1/2-way: led and edgd rt over 1f out: hdd ins fnl f: sn wknd* **16/1**

0506 **6** 1/2 **Gulland Rock**[6] 5081 8-10-4 45....................(p) MissKerryanneAlexander(3) 11 30+
(Anthony Carson) *w ldr to 1/2-way: edgd rt over 1f out: wknd ins fnl f* **22/1**

0400 **7** 1/2 **Dutch Artist (IRE)**[8] 5024 7-10-12 53....................(p) MissBelindaJohnson(3) 14 37
(Nigel Tinkler) *s.s: outpcd: r.o ins fnl f: nvr nrr* **25/1**

0502 **8** hd **Just An Idea (IRE)**[72] 2693 5-11-2 57....................(b) MissCamillaSwift(3) 8 41+
(Roger Ingram) *prom: hung rt fr over 2f out: wknd ins fnl f* **20/1**

0006 **9** 2 3/4 **Rock Warbler (IRE)**[8] 5024 6-10-6 47....................(p) MrPatrickBarlow(3) 3 24
(Michael Mullineaux) *hld up: hdwy 2f out: wknd over 1f out* **12/1**

6500 **10** 3/4 **Silvington**[12] 4873 4-10-7 45..............................(b) MrMatthewEnnis 10 20
(Mark Loughnane) *s.i.s: ld up: hdwy u.p and hung rt fr over 2f out: wknd over 1f out* **50/1**

3100 **11** *shd* **Rock In Society (IRE)**[29] 4217 4-11-1 **53**..............(p) MrGeorgeEddery 4 28+
(John Butler) *prom: hmpd over 2f out: rdn and wknd over 1f out* **6/1**[3]

-040 **12** *5* **Ad Valorem Queen (IRE)**[19] 4615 4-10-10 **48**............... SophieSmith 9 10
(J R Jenkins) *hld up: n.m.r 1/2-way: sn rdn: n.d* **25/1**

500- **13** *2 1/2* **L'Es Fremantle (FR)**[33] 8745 8-10-4 **45**.............. MrHakanSensoy(3) 13 1+
(Michael Chapman) *prom: hung rt over 4f out: wknd 1/2-way* **200/1**

4650 **14** *nk* **Coastal Cyclone**[5] 5147 5-10-5 **46**..............(p) MissRachelDavies(3) 16 1+
(Harry Dunlop) *led: clr 2f out: edgd rt and hdd over 1f out: wknd ins fnl f: b.b.v (vet said gelding bled from the nose)* **16/1**

60 **15** *7* **Plucky Dip**[19] 4589 8-10-4 **45**..............................(p) MrThomasMiles(3) 2
(John Ryan) *hld up: nvr on terms: eased over 1f out* **33/1**

1m 24.63s (-1.07) **Going Correction** -0.10s/f (Good) **15** Ran SP% **122.0**
Speed ratings (Par 101): **102,100,98,95,91 91,90,90,87,86 86,80,77,77,69**
CSF £15.45 CT £61.34 TOTE £3.70: £1.50, £1.90, £1.50; EX 18.20 Trifecta £86.30.
Owner Mel Mathias **Bred** Allevamento La Nuova Sbarra **Trained** Kenfig Hill, Bridgend

FOCUS
The going was good to firm, good in places (GoingStick 7.9). The opener was a modest amateurs' event confined to riders who hadn't ridden more than three winners under any Rules of Racing before April 1st. A race of changing fortunes with the leaders going off far too quick and setting it up for the closers. The winner featured on a good mark.

5303 SUTTON H'CAP 7f
6:10 (6:10) (Class 4) (0-80,77) 3-Y-0+

£5,207 (£1,549; £774; £387; £300; £300) **Stalls** High

Form RPR

1-65 **1** **Golden Force**[24] 4420 3-9-2 **76**.................................... AdamKirby 1 81
(Clive Cox) *w ldr: led 4f out: rdn and hung lft fr over 1f out: styd on u.p (vet said gelding lost its right hind shoe)* **9/1**

3154 **2** *shd* **Tukhoom (IRE)**[4] 5173 6-9-10 **77**..............................(b) RobbieDowney 4 84
(David O'Meara) *racd alone stands' side: led 3f: remained w wnr: rdn over 2f out: r.o* **9/2**[3]

2022 **3** *2 1/4* **Esprit De Corps**[9] 4980 5-9-7 **74**.................................. DavidEgan 3 76
(David Barron) *hld up: hdwy over 2f out: rdn over 1f out: styd on same pce ins fnl f* **9/2**[3]

6421 **4** *1 1/4* **Global Spirit**[17] 4693 4-9-9 **76**.................................. BenCurtis 5 75
(Roger Fell) *trckd ldrs: rdn over 2f out: edgd lft over 1f out: no ex ins fnl f* **11/4**[1]

4-11 **5** *1 1/2* **Keepup Kevin**[29] 4207 5-9-9 **76**.................................. CallumShepherd 2 71
(Pam Sly) *chsd ldr: rdn over 2f out: edgd lft over 1f out: wknd wl ins fnl f* **11/2**

5022 **6** *3 1/2* **Real Smooth (IRE)**[32] 4116 3-9-3 **77**............................ TomMarquand 6 61
(Richard Hannon) *sn pushed along in rr: rdn and edgd lft fr over 2f out: no rspnse (jockey said colt was never travelling; vet said colt finished lame on its right fore)* **10/3**[2]

1m 22.76s (-2.94) **Going Correction** -0.10s/f (Good)
WFA 3 from 4yo+ 7lb **6** Ran SP% **111.5**
Speed ratings (Par 105): **112,111,109,107,106 102**
CSF £47.21 TOTE £7.40: £4.00, £2.00; EX 46.10 Trifecta £180.30.
Owner Racegoers Club Owners Group **Bred** Mrs Tina Cox **Trained** Lambourn, Berks

FOCUS
A fair handicap which had gone to a 3yo in the last five runnings and did so again. The first two dominated throughout, but took different paths. The winner is rated back to his best.

5304 MEDBOURNE (S) STKS 1m 53y
6:40 (6:41) (Class 5) 3-Y-0

£3,752 (£1,116; £557; £300; £300; £300) **Stalls** Low

Form RPR

3203 **1** **Lippy Lady (IRE)**[14] 4797 3-8-2 54..........................(h) RhiainIngram(5) 6 58
(Paul George) *s.v.s: wl bhd: hdwy over 1f out: styd on to ld post* **5/1**

0520 **2** *hd* **Colonel Slade (IRE)**[8] 5031 3-8-12 63..........................(t) BenCurtis 3 63
(Brian Meehan) *a.p: chsd ldr over 6f out: rdn to ld and edgd lft fr over 1f out: hdd post* **15/8**[1]

5550 **3** *1 1/4* **Klipperty Klopp**[55] 3271 3-8-12 55.................................. CamHardie 1 60
(Antony Brittain) *s.i.s: hld up in tch: plld hrd: nt clr run over 5f out: shkn up over 3f out: rdn to chse ldr and edgd lft fr over 1f out: styng on same pce whn nt clr run nr fin* **16/1**

0006 **4** *4 1/2* **Little Tipple**[6] 5102 3-8-0 42..............................(p) LauraPearson(7) 5 44
(John Ryan) *led: racd wd: hdd over 1f out: styd on same pce* **80/1**

1152 **5** *nk* **Izvestia (IRE)**[16] 4735 3-9-5 74..............................(b) HollieDoyle 4 56
(Archie Watson) *pushed along and prom: rdn over 2f out: nt run on (jockey said filly was never travelling)* **9/4**[2]

0004 **6** *3/4* **Max Guevara (IRE)**[6] 5092 3-9-2 62..............................(p) DavidEgan 2 51
(William Muir) *chsd ldr tl over 6f out: remained handy: rdn and ev ch wl over 1f out: wknd ins fnl f* **7/2**[3]

1m 45.29s (-1.01) **Going Correction** -0.10s/f (Good) **6** Ran SP% **111.6**
Speed ratings (Par 100): **101,100,99,95,94 94**
CSF £14.66 TOTE £6.80: £2.80, £2.10; EX 18.20 Trifecta £115.30.There was no bid for the winner. Colonel Slade was claimed by P. J. Makin for £7,000.
Owner Miss Karen George **Bred** McCracken Farms **Trained** Crediton, Devon

FOCUS
A poor race, but a remarkable performance from the winner. The form is rated at face value.

5305 BURTON H'CAP 1m 3f 179y
7:15 (7:17) (Class 4) (0-85,84) 4-Y-0+

£5,207 (£1,549; £774; £387; £300; £300) **Stalls** Low

Form RPR

2-43 **1** **Volcanic Sky**[28] 4241 4-9-7 **84**.................................. CallumShepherd 8 93
(Saeed bin Suroor) *mde all: set stdy pce tl qcknd over 2f out: rdn and edgd lft over 1f out: r.o wl* **7/4**[1]

6650 **2** *2 3/4* **Escape The City**[13] 4841 4-8-9 **72**.................................. HollieDoyle 7 77
(Hughie Morrison) *prom: hmpd and chsd wnr 10f out: rdn over 1f out: styd on same pce ins fnl f* **5/1**[3]

2252 **3** *3/4* **C'Est No Mour (GER)**[24] 4425 6-9-2 **79**......................(p) TomMarquand 4 83
(Peter Hedger) *s.i.s: hld up: racd keenly: rdn over 1f out: r.o to go 3rd post: nvr nrr* **7/1**

-246 **4** *shd* **Chingachgook**[28] 4241 4-8-11 **74**..............................(bt) BenCurtis 6 78
(Tristan Davidson) *hld up in tch: racd keenly: rdn over 1f out: styd on same pce ins fnl f* **5/1**[3]

4160 **5** *2 3/4* **Winged Spur (IRE)**[11] 4913 4-9-3 **80**.............................. DanielTudhope 5 79
(Mark Johnston) *chsd wnr 2f: remained handy: rdn over 2f out: no ex fnl f* **9/1**

4-34 **6** *4 1/2* **Quicksand (IRE)**[55] 3269 4-9-4 **81**.................................. AdamKirby 1 73
(Hughie Morrison) *trckd ldrs: racd keenly: lost pl over 9f out: shkn up over 2f out: wknd fnl f* **4/1**[2]

2m 38.73s (3.73) **Going Correction** -0.10s/f (Good) **6** Ran SP% **112.2**
Speed ratings (Par 105): **83,81,80,80,78 75**
CSF £10.81 CT £47.04 TOTE £2.80: £1.70, £3.70; EX 9.80 Trifecta £43.90.
Owner Godolphin **Bred** Godolphin **Trained** Newmarket, Suffolk

FOCUS
A fair handicap, but the favourite had things all his own way and made no mistake under a finely judged ride. The winner gave the fourth a bigger beating than last time.

5306 BRITISH STALLION STUDS EBF NOVICE STKS 5f
7:45 (7:46) (Class 5) 3-Y-O+ **£5,433** (£1,617; £808; £404) **Stalls** High

Form RPR

06- **1** **Swiss Chill**[389] 4404 4-9-6 0.. AdamKirby 2 64
(Clive Cox) *wnt rt s: mde all: shkn up 1/2-way: hrd rdn fr over 1f out: edgd lft ins fnl f: all out (vet said gelding lost both front shoes)* **6/1**[3]

-466 **2** *shd* **Ricochet (IRE)**[18] 4655 3-9-2 72.................................. DanielTudhope 5 62
(Jamie Osborne) *hld up: hrd rdn fr over 1f out: r.o wl ins fnl f: jst failed* **1/2**[1]

3 *2* **Oh So Nice** 3-8-11 0.. TomMarquand 6 50
(Tony Carroll) *s.i.s: sn chsng wnr: rdn and ev ch over 1f out: no ex wl ins fnl f* **16/1**

0004 **4** *nk* **Zaula**[15] 4755 3-8-11 48.. DavidEgan 3 49
(Mick Channon) *chsd ldrs: rdn over 1f out: styd on same pce fnl f (vet said filly lost left hind shoe)* **14/1**

60 **5** *2* **Rebecke (IRE)**[43] 3696 3-8-11 0.. LiamKeniry 1 42
(Clive Cox) *s.i.s: racd keenly: hdwy over 3f out: shkn up over 1f out: no ex fnl f* **11/2**[2]

1m 0.7s (-1.10) **Going Correction** -0.10s/f (Good)
WFA 3 from 4yo 4lb **5** Ran SP% **108.9**
Speed ratings (Par 103): **104,103,100,100,96**
CSF £9.43 TOTE £8.80: £2.90, £1.10; EX 12.30 Trifecta £49.40.
Owner Mrs Olive Shaw **Bred** Tobias B P Coles **Trained** Lambourn, Berks

■ Stewards' Enquiry : Daniel Tudhope two-day ban: used whip above permitted level (Aug 7-8)

FOCUS
A weak novice, especially for the money, and not a race to live long in the memory. The fourth limits the form.

5307 OSBASTON FILLIES' H'CAP 1m 2f
8:20 (8:22) (Class 5) (0-70,71) 3-Y-O+

£3,752 (£1,116; £557; £300; £300; £300) **Stalls** Low

Form RPR

0234 **1** **Beguiling Charm (IRE)**[26] 4336 3-9-5 **68**.......................... LiamKeniry 3 75
(Ed Walker) *hld up: hdwy and hung rt fr over 1f out: sn rdn: styd on to ld wl ins fnl f* **11/2**[3]

4313 **2** *1* **Northern Lyte**[8] 5023 3-8-12 **66**..........................(t[1]) FayeMcManoman(5) 1 71
(Nigel Tinkler) *s.i.s: nt clr run 8f out: hdwy over 2f out: led over 1f out: rdn and hdd wl ins fnl f* **7/2**[1]

0000 **3** *2 3/4* **Takiah**[22] 4475 4-8-9 **49** oh4..........................(p[1]) PaddyMathers 5 49
(Peter Hiatt) *hld up in tch: racd keenly: rdn over 1f out: hmpd ins fnl f: kpt on* **50/1**

6021 **4** *1 1/4* **Perfect Grace**[14] 4771 3-9-5 **68**.................................. HollieDoyle 4 65+
(Archie Watson) *s.i.s: sn rcvrd to ld: hdd over 8f out: nt clr run and lost pl over 2f out: rallied over 1f out: styd on same pce ins fnl f* **7/2**[1]

5033 **5** *shd* **Fragrant Belle**[18] 4656 3-9-7 **70**.................................. BenCurtis 8 67
(Ralph Beckett) *s.i.s: racd keenly: hdwy over 8f out: chsd ldr over 7f out: led over 2f out: rdn and hdd over 1f out: no ex ins fnl f (jockey said filly ran too free)* **4/1**[2]

5-25 **6** *1* **Aubretia (IRE)**[13] 4828 3-9-8 **71**.................................. TomMarquand 2 66
(Richard Hannon) *prom: nt clr run and lost pl 8f out: rdn over 2f out: nt clr run 1f out: no ex* **11/2**[3]

2461 **7** *4 1/2* **Dear Miriam (IRE)**[14] 4794 3-9-0 **63**.......................... CallumShepherd 7 49
(Mick Channon) *led at stdy pce over 8f out: rdn: hung lft and hdd over 2f out: wknd ins fnl f* **12/1**

1-03 **8** *1* **Minnelli**[14] 4804 3-9-3 **66**.. DanielTudhope 6 50
(Philip McBride) *sn prom: rdn over 2f out: wknd over 1f out* **11/1**

2m 7.8s (-1.40) **Going Correction** -0.10s/f (Good)
WFA 3 from 4yo 9lb **8** Ran SP% **113.2**
Speed ratings (Par 100): **101,100,98,97,96 96,92,91**
CSF £24.54 CT £858.06 TOTE £6.30: £2.40, £1.30, £8.80; EX 24.80 Trifecta £666.00.
Owner Matthew Cottis **Bred** Bernard Cooke **Trained** Upper Lambourn, Berks

FOCUS
A modest fillies' handicap and despite the pace not being strong, the first two came from the back. Ordinary form.

5308 MERCIA H'CAP 6f
8:50 (8:50) (Class 5) (0-70,71) 3-Y-O **£3,752** (£1,116; £557; £300; £300) **Stalls** High

Form RPR

5211 **1** **Alicia Darcy (IRE)**[7] 5044 3-9-9 **71** 6ex..................(b) AdamMcNamara 6 76
(Archie Watson) *s.i.s: sn chsng ldrs: rdn to ld over 1f out: styd on* **7/2**[2]

4500 **2** *3/4* **Cotubanama**[11] 4908 3-9-2 **69**.................................. ScottMcCullagh(5) 1 71
(Mick Channon) *stdd sn after s: hld up: hdwy to chse wnr over 1f out: sn rdn: styd on* **12/1**[3]

0505 **3** *1/2* **One One Seven (IRE)**[23] 4436 3-8-3 **51**.......................... CamHardie 7 51
(Antony Brittain) *stdd s: hld up: pushed along 1/2-way: rdn over 1f out: r.o ins fnl f: nt rch ldrs* **14/1**

4221 **4** *1 3/4* **Montalvan (IRE)**[4] 5202 3-9-6 **68** 6ex..........................(p) DanielTudhope 2 62
(Roger Fell) *led: rdn and hdd over 1f out: edgd lft and styd on same pce ins fnl f* **8/15**[1]

-031 **5** *nk* **Awa Bomba**[116] 1430 3-9-4 **66**.................................. JoeyHaynes 3 59
(Tony Carroll) *chsd ldr tl rdn over 1f out: styd on same pce fnl f (jockey said gelding ran too free)* **16/1**

1m 12.19s (0.09) **Going Correction** -0.10s/f (Good) **5** Ran SP% **107.7**
Speed ratings (Par 100): **95,94,93,91,90**
CSF £35.27 TOTE £3.60: £2.00, £3.00; EX 43.30 Trifecta £120.00.
Owner Boadicea Bloodstock **Bred** Tally-Ho Stud **Trained** Upper Lambourn, W Berks

FOCUS
A modest 3yo sprint handicap in which the market got it wrong. The form doesn't look solid.
T/Plt: £87.10 to a £1 stake. Pool: £43,252.25. 362.40 winning units. T/Qpdt: £18.00 to a £1 stake. Pool: £5,037.31. 205.96 winning units. **Colin Roberts**

The Form Book Flat 2019, Raceform Ltd, Newbury, RG14 5SJ

5044 LINGFIELD (L-H)
Wednesday, July 24

OFFICIAL GOING: Turf course - good to firm (good in places; 8.8); aw course - polytrack: standard
Wind: light, behind Weather: sunny and hot

5309 MAC AND ANNE GOLDEN WEDDING ANNIVERSARY H'CAP 1m 1y(P)
2:20 (2:22) (Class 6) (0-65,65) 4-Y-0+
£2,781 (£827; £413; £300; £300; £300) Stalls High

Form RPR
0-12 1 **Kendergarten Kop (IRE)**[12] 4873 4-9-7 **65**..............(p[1]) DavidProbert 11 75
(David Flood) *chsd ldrs: clsd to join ldr over 2f out and sn kicked clr: sustained duel w ldr fr over 1f out: forged ahd towards fin* **8/1**
3010 2 *nk* **Classic Charm**[14] 4787 4-9-2 **60**.................. JoeyHaynes 4 69
(Dean Ivory) *sn led: hdd over 6f out: chse ldr tl led again over 2f out and sn kicked clr w wnr: sustained duel fr over 1f out: hdd and no ex towards fin* **11/1**
0000 3 3 1/4 **Mochalov**[14] 4807 4-8-8 **57**..................(e) DarraghKeenan(5) 3 59+
(Jane Chapple-Hyam) *midfield: effrt and outpcd ent fnl 2f: nvr a threat to ldng pair after: kpt on to go 3rd last strides* **33/1**
4420 4 *hd* **Takeonefortheteam**[18] 4657 4-9-5 **63**.............. OisinMurphy 1 64+
(Mark Loughnane) *in tch in midfield: outpcd and swtchd rt ent fnl 2f: no threat to ldng pair after: kpt on to go and battling for 3rd towards fin* **5/1[2]**
1526 5 *hd* **Mullarkey**[24] 4426 5-9-1 **59**..................(t) KierenFox 2 60
(John Best) *broke wl: chsd ldrs: 3rd and outpcd u.p ent fnl 2f: no threat to ldng pair after and kpt on same pce: lost 2 pls towards fin* **7/1[3]**
052 6 3 1/2 **Savitar (IRE)**[47] 3543 4-9-3 **61**..................(h) PatCosgrave 10 56+
(Jim Boyle) *dwlt: towards rr: nt clrest of runs jst over 2f out: sme hdwy u.p over 1f out: kpt on ins fnl f: nvr trbld ldrs* **7/2[1]**
5455 7 *nk* **Arlecchino's Leap**[30] 4194 7-8-12 **63**..............(p) EllieMacKenzie(7) 5 55
(Mark Usher) *midfield on outer: outpcd and rdn ent fnl 2f: no ch and kpt on same pce fr over 1f out* **9/1**
-340 8 1 3/4 **Barrsbrook**[47] 3537 5-9-6 **64**..................(vt) HarryBentley 13 52+
(Gary Moore) *dwlt: midfield: rdn over 2f out: sn struggling: wl hld and plugged on same pce fr over 1f out* **15/2**
6005 9 2 1/4 **The Warrior (IRE)**[13] 4837 7-9-2 **63**..............(p) PaddyBradley(3) 8 46+
(Lee Carter) *dwlt: hld up in rr: outpcd over 2f out: no ch after* **20/1**
05-0 10 3 1/4 **Dependable (GER)**[55] 3264 4-9-3 **61**.................. JimCrowley 9 37
(Charles Hills) *midfield: outpcd ent fnl 2f: swtchd rt over 1f out: sn wknd* **16/1**
3020 11 2 1/2 **Monsieur Fox**[23] 4453 4-8-12 **56**.................. LukeMorris 6 26
(Lydia Richards) *midfield: rdn 4f out: losing pl over 2f out: wl btn over 1f out* **25/1**
0000 12 *hd* **Mrs Benson (IRE)**[32] 4115 4-8-13 **57**.................. CharlesBishop 7 26+
(Michael Blanshard) *s.i.s: a towards rr: outpcd over 2f out: n.d after (jockey said filly was slowly away)* **18/1**
53-2 13 4 **Your Choice**[145] 963 4-9-5 **63**..................(p) LiamJones 14 23
(Laura Mongan) *led over 6f out tl over 2f out: sn outpcd and lost pl 2f out: bhd ins fnl f* **20/1**
1m 37.5s (-0.70) **Going Correction** -0.05s/f (Stan) 13 Ran SP% **120.1**
Speed ratings (Par 101): **101,100,97,97,97 93,93,91,89,86 83,83,79**
CSF £88.42 CT £2830.85 TOTE £6.60: £2.20, £3.80, £9.90; EX 111.10 Trifecta £1173.30.
Owner Mrs Anne Cowley **Bred** Kildaragh Stud **Trained** Chiseldon, Wiltshire

FOCUS
Little got into this moderate handicap, the front two staying clear having kicked for home a fair way out. A minor pb from the winner.

5310 VISIT ATTHERACES.COM (S) H'CAP 1m 2f (P)
2:50 (2:55) (Class 6) (0-60,60) 4-Y-0+
£2,781 (£827; £413; £300; £300; £300) Stalls Low

Form RPR
0066 1 **Rocksette**[7] 5049 5-8-7 **45** oh1..................(p) HarryBentley 3 58
(Gary Moore) *wl in tch in midfield: clsd to trck ldrs over 2f out: effrt to chse ldr 2f out: rdn to ld ent fnl f: hung rt but r.o strly ins fnl f: drew wl clr* **7/2[1]**
5025 2 9 **Sharp Operator**[9] 5003 6-9-4 **57**..................(h) OisinMurphy 7 52
(Charlie Wallis) *t.k.h: hld up wl in tch in midfield: clsd to chse ldrs 5f out tl led over 2f out: hdd jst over 1f out: wknd ins fnl f* **4/1[2]**
0533 3 *nk* **Prerogative (IRE)**[14] 4771 5-8-0 **45** oh1.......... ElishaWhittington(7) 11 40
(Tony Carroll) *hld up in last quintet: effrt and hdwy towards inner over 1f out: styd on ins fnl f: no ch w wnr* **8/1**
3400 4 1/2 **Natch**[16] 4737 4-9-2 **55**..................(p) CharlieBennett 6 48
(Michael Attwater) *chsd ldrs tl led 8f out: hdd and rdn over 2f out: sn struggling: wl hld and plugged on same pce ins fnl f* **8/1**
0-13 5 1/2 **Hi There Silver (IRE)**[84] 2283 5-8-7 **45** oh1.............. GeorgeWood 5 38
(Michael Madgwick) *hld up in tch in midfield: effrt over 2f out: sn outpcd: no ch w wnr and plugged on same pce ins fnl f* **10/1**
65-0 6 2 1/4 **Pivello**[88] 2112 4-8-10 **49**.................. LukeMorris 1 37
(Tom Clover) *in tch in midfield: rdn over 4f out: outpcd and struggling over 2f out: wl hld over 1f out (jockey said gelding hung left-handed throughout)* **7/1**
000- 7 1/2 **Brilliant Riposte**[322] 6945 4-8-6 **52**.................. MichaelPitt(7) 12 39
(Denis Coakley) *hld up in last quintet: edgd lft 3f out: edgd rt bnd 2f out: sme prog wl over 1f out: no imp after: nvr involved: fin lame (vet said gelding was lame right hind leg)* **50/1**
0333 8 1 1/4 **Captain Marmalade (IRE)**[46] 3592 7-8-7 **45** oh1.......... HayleyTurner 8 31
(Jimmy Fox) *t.k.h: hld up in last quintet: hmpd 3f out: effrt whn nt clr run on inner ent fnl 2f: no ch after* **11/2[3]**
6-00 9 1 1/2 **Premium Pink (IRE)**[181] 379 4-8-8 **47**.................. EoinWalsh 4 29
(Luke McJannet) *led: restrained and sn hdd: in tch in midfield: effrt over 2f out: sn outpcd: wknd over 1f out* **50/1**
-R00 10 3/4 **Duhr (IRE)**[22] 4475 5-8-8 **46** oh1 ow1.................. KierenFox 9 28
(Ralph J Smith) *sn rdn in rr: effrt on outer over 2f out: no imp and bumping w rival bnd 2f out: wl btn after (jockey said gelding was never travelling)* **66/1**
0020 11 2 **Don't Cry About It (IRE)**[47] 3533 4-9-0 **53**..........(bt) CharlesBishop 13 30
(Ali Stronge) *sn chsng ldrs on outer: chsd ldr tl over 2f out: sn outpcd and sltly impeded: swtchd rt and wknd over 1f out* **16/1**
6-00 12 10 **Bay Dude**[32] 4111 4-8-11 **50**..................(p[1]) RossaRyan 14 8
(Brett Johnson) *stdd s: a towards rr: no imp and bumping w rival bnd 2f out: sn bhd (jockey said gelding suffered interference round bnd)* **20/1**
40-0 13 7 **Full Suit**[23] 4447 5-9-1 **54**.................. DavidProbert 2
(Ralph J Smith) *taken down early: broke fast: sn restained and hld up in tch: lost pl and in rr whn hmpd 3f out: eased over 1f out* **28/1**
2m 5.94s (-0.66) **Going Correction** -0.05s/f (Stan) 13 Ran SP% **120.9**
Speed ratings (Par 101): **100,92,92,92,91 89,89,88,87,86 85,77,71**
CSF £16.65 CT £107.54 TOTE £4.80: £1.80, £2.00, £2.20; EX 17.90 Trifecta £98.40.There was no bid for the winner. Natch was claimed by John McConnell for £6,400.
Owner Hide & Seekers **Bred** Brook Stud Bloodstock Ltd **Trained** Lower Beeding, W Sussex
■ Stewards' Enquiry : Michael Pitt four-day ban: careless riding (Aug 7-10)

FOCUS
One-way traffic in this lowly handicap, the favourite bolting up. She's rated back to her best.

5311 FLEETWEATHER - OCEAN ROUTING SERVICES H'CAP 1m 4f (P)
3:20 (3:24) (Class 5) (0-75,76) 3-Y-0+
£3,428 (£1,020; £509; £300; £300; £300) Stalls Low

Form RPR
02-1 1 **Distant Chimes (GER)**[7] 5055 4-9-12 **73** 5ex.................. LukeMorris 11 86+
(Sir Mark Prescott Bt) *wl in tch in midfield: chsd ldr over 2f out: rdn to ld 2f out: wnt lft u.p 1f out: kpt on ins fnl f* **1/1[1]**
3-30 2 *nk* **Ambling (IRE)**[13] 4841 3-9-4 **76**..................(h) NickyMackay 5 86
(John Gosden) *mounted in chute and taken down early: hld up in tch in midfield: clsd to trck ldrs over 2f out: chsd ldng pair over 1f out: kpt on u.p ins fnl f: wnt 2nd towards fin* **8/1**
1-36 3 1/2 **Zuba**[41] 3765 3-9-3 **75**.................. JimCrowley 9 84
(Amanda Perrett) *hld up in tch in midfield: clsd to trck ldrs over 2f out: chsd wnr 2f out: keeping on same pce whn nt clr run and swtchd rt jst ins fnl f: lost 2nd towards fin* **5/1[3]**
5-50 4 12 **Island Jungle (IRE)**[91] 2035 3-8-12 **70**..................(p[1]) FergusSweeney 13 60
(Mark Usher) *hld up in tch in midfield: effrt over 2f out: sn outpcd and wl hld over 1f out: wnt modest 4th ins fnl f* **66/1**
0216 5 3 3/4 **Tangramm**[25] 4392 7-9-10 **71**..................(p) JoeyHaynes 3 54
(Dean Ivory) *rn in snatches towards rr: swtchd rt and sme prog u.p: plugged on but nvr nr ldrs* **16/1**
600- 6 1 1/2 **Wojood**[313] 7257 3-8-10 **68**..................(bt[1]) OisinMurphy 1 49
(Hugo Palmer) *led: rdn and hdd 2f out: sn outpcd: wknd over 1f out* **16/1**
3542 7 5 **Sawasdee (IRE)**[14] 4795 3-8-8 **66**..................(p) SilvestreDeSousa 8 39
(Andrew Balding) *chsd ldr for 2f: styd chsng ldrs: unable qck u.p over 2f out: sn hung rt and struggling: wknd over 1f out (jockey said colt hung right-handed)* **4/1[2]**
-000 8 8 **Accessor (IRE)**[14] 4792 4-9-1 **62**.................. JFEgan 2 22
(Michael Wigham) *awkward leaving stalls: hld up in rr: effrt on outer over 2f out: nvr getting on terms: wknd over 1f out* **100/1**
6-54 9 3/4 **Ace Cheetah (USA)**[147] 921 5-8-10 **64**.................. TobyEley(7) 6 22
(J R Jenkins) *hld up in last quartet: hung lft and no hdwy u.p over 2f out: wknd over 1f out (jockey said gelding was never travelling and hung left-handed throughout)* **100/1**
1660 10 7 **Eye Of The Storm (IRE)**[14] 4792 9-9-10 **71**.................. HayleyTurner 7 18
(Conor Dore) *stdd s: hld up in midfield: lost pl and struggling u.p 3f out: wl bhd fnl 2f: t.o* **40/1**
-060 11 16 **Stormwave (IRE)**[46] 3604 3-9-3 **75**..................(b) HarryBentley 12
(Ralph Beckett) *chsd ldr 10f out tl over 2f out: sn dropped out: t.o ins fnl f* **12/1**
2220 12 1 1/4 **Hackbridge**[20] 4548 4-9-11 **75**..................(b[1]) PaddyBradley(3) 4
(Pat Phelan) *chsd ldrs tl drvn and lost pl over 2f out: eased ins fnl f: t.o (jockey said gelding stopped quickly)* **33/1**
5240 13 35 **Stormy Blues**[91] 1329 5-9-9 **70**..................(tp w) RossaRyan 10
(Nigel Hawke) *rousted along leaving stalls: a towards rr: lost tch over 3f out: eased: t.o (jockey said gelding stopped quickly)* **33/1**
2m 30.56s (-2.44) **Going Correction** -0.05s/f (Stan) 13 Ran SP% **129.0**
WFA 3 from 4yo+ 11lb
Speed ratings (Par 103): **106,105,105,97,94 93,90,85,84,80 69,68,45**
CSF £11.10 CT £34.40 TOTE £1.80: £1.10, £2.20, £1.60; EX 12.00 Trifecta £41.40.
Owner Phil Fry - Osborne House **Bred** Gestut Wiesengrund **Trained** Newmarket, Suffolk

FOCUS
No great gallop on in what was an ordinary handicap but three managed to pull some 12l clear. There's more to come from the winner.

5312 STRATUM5 - DIGITALISING THE SHIPPING INDUSTRY CLASSIFIED STKS 7f 135y
3:50 (3:53) (Class 3) 3-Y-0+
£7,246 (£2,168; £1,084; £542; £270) Stalls Centre

Form RPR
3110 1 **Mutaraffa (IRE)**[18] 4650 3-9-0 **90**..................(h) JimCrowley 5 96
(Charles Hills) *mde all: rdn 2f out: kpt on wl u.p ins fnl f* **2/1[1]**
2213 2 1/2 **Spirit Warning**[25] 4399 3-9-0 **88**.................. OisinMurphy 4 94
(Andrew Balding) *pressed wnr: rdn and ev ch over 1f out: kpt on u.p but a jst hld ins fnl f* **5/2[3]**
0640 3 1 3/4 **Hajjam**[11] 4921 5-9-8 **88**..................(p) DavidNolan 1 92
(David O'Meara) *hld up in tch in last pair: clsd and effrt to chse ldr 2f out: kpt on same pce ins fnl f* **7/1**
0001 4 5 **Aces (IRE)**[26] 4319 7-9-8 **90**.................. SilvestreDeSousa 2 88
(Ian Williams) *hld up in tch in last pair: clsd and effrt to chse ldrs jst over 2f out: no ex and lost action 1f out: eased ins fnl f (trainer said, regarding why he was running gelding on going described as Good To Firm, having declared gelding on same official description at Newmarket on 13th July, that in his opinion the ground was quicker than described at Newmarket so were happy f* **9/4[2]**
063P 5 22 **You Never Can Tell (IRE)**[96] 1920 3-9-0 **90**..................(b) LukeMorris 6 63
(Richard Spencer) *rousted along leaving stalls: chsd ldrs: rdn 1/2-way: lost pl and bhd 2f out: eased ins fnl f* **16/1**
1m 28.24s (-3.46) **Going Correction** -0.40s/f (Firm) 5 Ran SP% **111.1**
WFA 3 from 4yo+ 8lb
Speed ratings (Par 107): **101,100,98,93,71**
CSF £7.42 TOTE £2.90: £1.30, £2.20; EX 7.50 Trifecta £20.50.
Owner Hamdan Al Maktoum **Bred** Messrs Mark Hanly & James Hanly **Trained** Lambourn, Berks

FOCUS
They raced stands' side in what was a useful little handicap. The 1-2 both progressed a bit further.

5313 SKY SPORTS RACING ON VIRGIN 535 NURSERY H'CAP 7f
4:20 (4:26) (Class 6) (0-65,67) 2-Y-0
£2,781 (£827; £413; £300; £300; £300) Stalls Centre

Form RPR
003 1 **Sir Arthur Dayne (IRE)**[13] 4832 2-9-9 **67**..........(p[1]) SilvestreDeSousa 2 81
(Mick Channon) *hld up in tch: clsd 1/2-way: rdn to ld and edgd rt 2f out: sn drew clr: r.o strly: v readily* **5/2[2]**

The Form Book Flat 2019, Raceform Ltd, Newbury, RG14 5SJ

000 **2** 9 **Victochop (FR)**[37] 3943 2-8-6 **50** LukeMorris 4 40
(George Baker) *in tch in midfield: clsd to chse ldr briefly over 2f out: sn outpcd: no ch w wnr: plugged on to go modest 2nd wl ins fnl f* **13/2**[3]

500 **3** ¾ **Ask Siri (IRE)**[14] 4798 2-8-4 **48** ow3 LiamJones 3 36
(John Bridger) *loose bef s: t.k.h: chsd ldrs tl led over 3f out: hdd 2f out and sn outpcd: wl btn fnl f: lost 2nd wl ins fnl f* **40/1**

0540 **4** hd **Lexington Quest (IRE)**[5] 5146 2-9-8 **66** (p[1]) RossaRyan 7 53
(Richard Hannon) *led tl over 3f out: u.p and outpcd over 2f out: wl btn and plugged on same pce ins fnl f* **9/1**

0343 **5** nse **Fashion Free**[15] 4756 2-9-8 **66** OisinMurphy 6 53+
(Archie Watson) *t.k.h: hld up in tch in midfield: stmbld path over 5f out: outpcd and hung lft ent fnl 2f: wl btn and kpt on same pce ins fnl f* **2/1**[1]

440 **6** 6 **Leave Em Alone (IRE)**[65] 2907 2-9-4 **62** JFEgan 8 33
(David Evans) *chsd ldrs: j. path over 5f out: lost pl and hung lft over 2f out: sn bhd* **11/1**

000 **7** 6 **Aust Ferry**[20] 4557 2-8-11 **55** CharlesBishop 10 10
(Eve Johnson Houghton) *midfield: outpcd and dropping out whn carried lft over 2f out: wl bhd over 1f out (jockey said filly never travelling)* **13/2**[3]

640 **8** ½ **Capp It All (IRE)**[13] 4819 2-8-10 **54** (p[1]) DavidProbert 9 8
(David Loughnane) *a struggling to go pce in last pair: lost tch 2f out (jockey said filly never travelling)* **14/1**

000 **9** ½ **Sir Chancealot (IRE)**[43] 3694 2-8-1 **45** (b[1]) JimmyQuinn 5
(Amanda Perrett) *s.i.s: a towards rr: hung lft over 2f out: sn lost tch (jockey said gelding never travelling and slowly away)* **25/1**

1m 21.22s (-3.08) **Going Correction** -0.40s/f (Firm) 2y crse rec **9 Ran SP% 119.9**
Speed ratings (Par 92): **101,90,89,89,89 82,75,75,74**
CSF £20.25 CT £458.74 TOTE £3.50: £1.40, £2.00, £9.50; EX 24.10 Trifecta £929.90.
Owner M Channon **Bred** Tally-Ho Stud **Trained** West Ilsley, Berks
■ Stewards' Enquiry : J F Egan four-day ban: improper conduct towards other jockey (Aug 7-10)

FOCUS
A modest nursery that was turned into an absolute rout by the top weight. The form's rated negatively overall.

5314 FOLLOW AT THE RACES ON TWITTER NOVICE AUCTION STKS 7f
4:50 (4:56) (Class 6) 2-Y-O £2,781 (£827; £413; £206) **Stalls Centre**

Form RPR

23 **1** **Space Ace (FR)**[37] 3919 2-8-12 0 (p) AdamMcNamara 16 77
(Archie Watson) *chsd ldr: rdn to ld and hung lft over 1f out: styd on but stl edging lft ins fnl f* **14/1**

61 **2** 1¾ **Little Bird (IRE)**[25] 4366 2-9-3 0 SeanLevey 9 77
(Richard Hannon) *wl in tch in midfield: clsd to press ldrs over 2f out: rdn to chse wnr over 1f out: kpt on same pce ins fnl f* **9/2**[2]

5 **3** hd **The City's Phantom**[33] 4069 2-9-1 0 JamieSpencer 6 75+
(Richard Spencer) *hld up towards rr: clsd and nt clr run over 3f out: hdwy over 1f out: chsd ldrs and swtchd rt ins fnl f: kpt on but nvr threatening wnr* **5/2**[1]

3 **4** 7 **Sweet Sixteen (GER)**[32] 4114 2-8-12 0 OisinMurphy 18 53
(Amy Murphy) *flashed tail leaving stalls: led: rdn and hdd over 1f out: sn outpcd: wknd ins fnl f* **6/1**[3]

5 1 **Lucander (IRE)** 2-9-5 0 HarryBentley 13 57
(Ralph Beckett) *midfield: effrt ent fnl 3f: shifting lft over 1f out: no ch w ldrs but kpt on steadily ins fnl f* **12/1**

6 **6** 1½ **Aldrich Bay (IRE)**[25] 4388 2-9-1 0 DavidProbert 14 49
(William Knight) *towards rr: rdn over 3f out: sme hdwy over 1f out: no threat to ldrs but kpt on steadily ins fnl f* **20/1**

26 **7** ¾ **Wightman (IRE)**[28] 4252 2-9-3 0 SilvestreDeSousa 15 49
(Mick Channon) *wl in tch in midfield: effrt over 2f out: no imp and wl hld over 1f out: wknd ins fnl f* **5/2**[1]

60 **8** 2½ **Souter Johnnie (IRE)**[14] 4798 2-9-5 0 FergusSweeney 4 44
(Richard Hughes) *s.i.s: towards rr: hdwy into midfield 1/2-way: pushed along: rn green and outpcd over 2f out: wknd over 1f out* **33/1**

00 **9** hd **Premium Bond**[11] 4925 2-9-1 0 RossaRyan 10 39
(Richard Hannon) *chsd ldrs tl lost pl u.p over 2f out: wknd over 1f out* **33/1**

00 **10** 3½ **Lightning Bug (IRE)**[29] 4221 2-8-10 0 JimmyQuinn 8 25
(Suzy Smith) *s.i.s: nt clrest of runs and wnt lft over 2f out: wl btn over 1f out* **100/1**

11 ¾ **Herre Dittery** 2-9-1 0 CharlieBennett 11 28
(Pat Phelan) *s.i.s: bhd: j. path over 5f out: nvr involved* **50/1**

12 1 **Stopnsearch** 2-9-1 0 TomQueally 12 25
(Brett Johnson) *t.k.h: chsd ldrs tl 1/2-way: lost pl and bhd 2f out: wknd* **40/1**

13 10 **Diligent Lass** 2-8-5 0 DarraghKeenan(5) 17
(Michael Blanshard) *midfield: struggling and dropped to rr 3f out: wl bhd ins fnl f* **100/1**

14 1 **Rajguru** 2-9-3 0 LukeMorris 5
(Tom Clover) *midfield: rdn 3f out: sn struggling and dropped to rr 2f out: wl bhd ins fnl f* **25/1**

15 2¾ **Abenakian (IRE)** 2-9-3 0 JFEgan 7
(Jane Chapple-Hyam) *wl in tch in midfield: lost pl over 3f out: wl bhd ins fnl f (jockey said gelding had no more to give)* **40/1**

1m 21.89s (-2.41) **Going Correction** -0.40s/f (Firm) **15 Ran SP% 127.3**
Speed ratings (Par 92): **97,95,94,86,85 83,83,80,79,75 75,73,62,61,58**
CSF £74.68 TOTE £14.10: £3.20, £1.90, £1.40; EX 74.70 Trifecta £579.90.
Owner Ontoawinner & Partner **Bred** Sam Sangster Bloodstock **Trained** Upper Lambourn, W Berks

FOCUS
Three pulled clear in what was a modest novice. The winner left her previous form behind.

5315 WITHEFORD EQUINE BARRIER TRIALS HERE 30TH JULY FILLIES' H'CAP 6f
5:20 (5:26) (Class 5) (0-70,75) 3-Y-O+ £3,428 (£1,020; £509; £300; £300) **Stalls Centre**

Form RPR

0051 **1** **Betsey Trotter (IRE)**[7] 5038 4-10-3 **75** 5ex (p) DavidNolan 1 82
(David O'Meara) *mde all: rdn over 1f out: r.o wl ins fnl f* **6/4**[1]

4052 **2** 1¼ **Terri Rules (IRE)**[7] 5046 4-8-10 **54** RossaRyan 4 57
(Lee Carter) *hld up in tch in rr: swtchd lft and effrt over 1f out: kpt on u.p to go 2nd towards fin* **12/1**

0355 **3** ½ **Mrs Worthington (IRE)**[30] 4183 3-9-0 **63** (p[1]) JamieSpencer 6 63
(Jonathan Portman) *hld up in tch: swtchd lft and effrt 2f out: drvn to chse wnr and edgd rt ent fnl f: flashed tail u.p and one pce fnl f: lost 2nd towards fin* **3/1**[2]

-503 **4** 2½ **Molly's Game**[27] 4286 3-9-4 **67** HayleyTurner 2 59
(David Elsworth) *chsd wnr after 1f: unable qck u.p and lost 2nd ent fnl f: wknd ins fnl f* **6/1**

4355 **5** ¾ **Miss Elsa**[18] 4651 3-8-9 **65** (p[1]) GeorgiaDobie(7) 3 55
(Eve Johnson Houghton) *chsd wnr for 1f: chsd ldrs: swtchd lft and unable qck over 1f out: wl hld ins fnl f (jockey said filly ran to free in early stages)* **5/1**[3]

1m 10.03s (-1.47) **Going Correction** -0.40s/f (Firm)
WFA 3 from 4yo+ 5lb **5 Ran SP% 103.6**
Speed ratings (Par 100): **93,91,90,87,86**
CSF £16.15 TOTE £2.10: £1.30, £3.00; EX 8.80 Trifecta £33.50.
Owner F Gillespie **Bred** James Hughes **Trained** Upper Helmsley, N Yorks
■ Porto Ferro was withdrawn. Price at time of withdrawal 8-1. Rule 4 applies to all bets - deduction 10p in the pound.

FOCUS
A moderate sprint won, as the market predicted, by the penalised top weight. The third is a fair guide.
T/Jkpt: Part won. £21,564.30 to a £1 stake. Pool: £30,564.30. 0.50 winning units. T/Plt: £91.20 to a £1 stake. Pool: £68,053.02. 544.29 winning units. T/Qpdt: £12.20 to a £1 stake. Pool: £7,418.44. 449.24 winning units. **Steve Payne**

4665 SANDOWN (R-H)
Wednesday, July 24

OFFICIAL GOING: Good (good to firm in places on round course; 7.3)
Wind: Light, against Weather: Sunny, hot

5316 RACINGTV.COM APPRENTICE H'CAP (JOCKEY CLUB GRASSROOTS FLAT MIDDLE DISTANCE SERIES QUALIFIER) 1m 1f 209y
6:00 (6:00) (Class 5) (0-70,71) 4-Y-O+
£4,528 (£1,347; £673; £336; £300; £300) **Stalls Low**

Form RPR

6-00 **1** **Geranium**[43] 3700 4-9-2 **60** WilliamCox 6 70
(Hughie Morrison) *led 1f: chsd clr ldr: clsd to chal 2f out: chsd new ldr after: rallied to ld narrowly last 150yds: kpt on wl* **6/1**[2]

2143 **2** nk **Broad Appeal**[22] 4426 5-9-6 **64** TylerSaunders 8 73
(Jonathan Portman) *hld up towards rr: prog on outer 3f out: led and edgd rt 2f out: sn pressed: hdd and nt qckn last 150yds: styd on* **7/2**[1]

4052 **3** 3¾ **Grange Walk (IRE)**[16] 4737 4-9-6 **64** PaddyBradley 3 66
(Pat Phelan) *hld up in rr: rdn and prog over 2f out: kpt on to take 3rd fnl f: nt pce to chal* **6/1**[2]

010 **4** 1¼ **Neff (GER)**[51] 3429 4-9-0 **63** RhysClutterbuck(5) 7 62
(Gary Moore) *trckd clr ldng pair: clsd to chal jst over 2f out: chsd ldng pair over 1f out but nt qckn: lost 3rd fnl f* **8/1**[3]

324- **5** 2¼ **Hope Is High**[244] 9215 6-9-10 **68** MeganNicholls 1 63
(John Berry) *trckd clr ldrs: rdn to cl over 2f out: outpcd and btn over 1f out* **14/1**

1200 **6** 1 **Perfect Refuge**[24] 4426 4-9-13 **71** ThomasGreatrex 2 67
(Clive Cox) *hld up in midfield: rdn and trying to chal whn hmpd 2f out: snatched up and nt rcvr* **9/1**

6203 **7** 1 **Lunar Deity**[6] 5087 10-8-11 **60** MarcoGhiani(5) 5 53
(Stuart Williams) *looked wl: dwlt: hld up in last: sme prog on inner whn hmpd wl over 1f out: no hdwy after* **6/1**[2]

1015 **8** 1¼ **Couldn't Could She**[21] 4499 4-9-9 **67** TobyEley 4 55
(Adam West) *towards rr: rdn over 2f out: no prog over 1f out: wknd* **8/1**[3]

-040 **9** 8 **Nordic Flight**[20] 4561 4-8-13 **62** (b[1]) LukeCatton(5) 9 34
(James Eustace) *racd freely: led after 1f and sn clr: hdd and carried rt 2f out: wknd qckly* **6/1**[2]

2m 8.75s (-1.45) **Going Correction** +0.025s/f (Good) **9 Ran SP% 118.3**
Speed ratings (Par 103): **106,105,102,101,99 99,98,97,90**
CSF £28.02 CT £133.95 TOTE £6.00: £2.80, £1.70, £2.20; EX 26.20 Trifecta £72.80.
Owner Trenchard, Morrison & Margadale **Bred** Viscountess Trenchard **Trained** East Ilsley, Berks
■ Stewards' Enquiry : Tyler Saunders two-day ban: careless riding (Aug 7, 8)

FOCUS
A hot day resulted in the ground drying out to Good, good to firm in places. Rail movements added 16yds to the race distance. This was a modest but quite competitive apprentice handicap, and two came clear. The winner was on a good mark compared with her AW form.

5317 BRITISH STALLION STUDS EBF MAIDEN FILLIES' STKS (PLUS 10 RACE) 5f 10y
6:30 (6:34) (Class 4) 2-Y-O £4,787 (£1,424; £711; £355) **Stalls Low**

Form RPR

6 **1** **Jouska**[20] 4557 2-9-0 0 DaneO'Neill 5 87+
(Henry Candy) *quite str: looked wl: towards rr: gd prog 2f out: rdn to ld jst ins fnl f: edgd rt but styd on strly: quite impressive* **12/1**

3 **2** 2½ **Poets Dance**[49] 3469 2-9-0 0 DavidProbert 7 78
(Rae Guest) *compact: dwlt: t.k.h and sn in midfield: prog 2f out: brought to chal 1f out: styd on but readily outpcd by wnr fnl f* **15/8**[1]

42 **3** 2¾ **Allez Sophia (IRE)**[28] 4233 2-9-0 0 CharlesBishop 6 68
(Eve Johnson Houghton) *athletic: sltly on toes: led: rdn and hdd jst ins fnl f: sn outpcd in 3rd: short of room briefly 100yds out* **4/1**[2]

4 1 **Liscahann** 2-9-0 0 RobHornby 8 65
(Seamus Mullins) *workmanlike: sltly on toes: dwlt: wl in rr: sltly impeded 1/2-way: pushed along and kpt on over 1f out to take 4th ins fnl f* **50/1**

30 **5** 2¾ **Airbrush (IRE)**[14] 4790 2-9-0 0 OisinMurphy 10 55
(Richard Hannon) *quite tall: w ldr to over 1f out: fdd* **10/1**

6 2½ **Hot Affair** 2-9-0 0 JackMitchell 2 46
(Tom Dascombe) *leggy: on toes: chsd ldng pair to over 1f out: wknd* **5/1**[3]

7 1 **Up To Speed** 2-9-0 0 PJMcDonald 4 42
(James Tate) *compact: chsd ldng pair to over 1f out: wknd* **14/1**

8 1½ **Reassure** 2-9-0 0 JamesDoyle 1 37
(William Haggas) *athletic: bit bkward: dwlt: outpcd in last: effrt on wd outside 1/2-way: sn no prog (jockey said filly was slowly away and hung left-handed)* **5/1**[3]

40 **9** hd **Krishmaya (IRE)**[14] 4798 2-9-0 0 CharlieBennett 9 36
(Adam West) *leggy: sweating: on toes: chsd ldrs 2f: sn lost pl and struggling* **80/1**

0 **10** 5 **Red Hottie**[27] 4302 2-9-0 0 AlistairRawlinson 3 18+
(Michael Appleby) *leggy: chsd ldrs: 5th whn stmbld wl over 2f out: dropped to rr and nt rcvr (jockey said filly stumbled 3f out)* **25/1**

1m 1.11s (-0.19) **Going Correction** +0.025s/f (Good) **10 Ran SP% 118.6**
Speed ratings (Par 93): **102,98,93,92,87 83,82,79,79,71**
CSF £35.23 TOTE £13.40: £3.10, £1.50, £1.70; EX 48.70 Trifecta £164.80.
Owner A Davis **Bred** Equity Growth Partners Ltd **Trained** Kingston Warren, Oxon

FOCUS
This juvenile fillies' maiden is usually won by a horse with previous experience and that was the case again. The first two look decent types and the form is rated at face value.

5318 WATCH RACING TV NOW H'CAP — 5f 10y
7:05 (7:07) (Class 4) (0-80,81) 3-Y-O+

£6,145 (£1,828; £913; £456; £300; £300) **Stalls Low**

Form				RPR
/453 **1** **Indian Raj**[14] 4805 5-9-6 72 ....(t) OisinMurphy 2 82+
(Stuart Williams) *trckd ldr: shkn up 2f out: drvn to ld jst ins fnl f: hrd pressed after but kpt on wl* **13/8**[1]

-002 **2** 1/2 **Han Solo Berger (IRE)**[13] 4829 4-9-6 72 ....(p) GeorgeWood 3 80
(Chris Wall) *trckd ldrs: gng strly 2f out: clsd to chal fnl f: ev ch but nt qckn last 100yds* **9/2**[2]

2162 **3** nk **Big Time Maybe (IRE)**[19] 4593 4-8-8 60 .... NicolaCurrie 8 67
(Michael Attwater) *carried lft s: in tch: rdn over 1f out: limited prog tl styd on wl to take 3rd last 75yds: gaining at fin* **14/1**

0012 **4** 1 **Delagate This Lord**[11] 4926 5-9-9 75 .... CharlieBennett 1 78
(Michael Attwater) *led: shkn up 2f out: hdd u.p jst ins fnl f: wknd last 100yds* **6/1**[3]

0130 **5** 1 1/4 **Waseem Faris (IRE)**[28] 4253 10-10-1 81 .... JimCrowley 7 80
(Ken Cunningham-Brown) *sltly impeded s: hld up in tch: rdn and no rspnse over 1f out: no imp on ldrs after* **14/1**

0554 **6** 3/4 **Pink Iceburg (IRE)**[16] 4736 3-9-0 70 .... KierenFox 4 65
(Peter Crate) *in tch: drvn and no imp on ldrs over 1f out* **16/1**

5641 **7** 1/2 **Whataguy**[29] 4213 3-9-8 81 ....(p) MeganNicholls(3) 6 74
(Paul Nicholls) *broke wl but then swvd bdly lft: chsd ldrs on outer: lost pl over 1f out: n.d fnl f (jockey said gelding jumped left-handed from stalls and hung left-handed throughout)* **7/1**

5312 **8** 21 **A Sure Welcome**[29] 4213 5-9-12 78 ....(b) LukeMorris 5
(John Spearing) *slowly away: a last: jockey looking down after 2f: eased over 1f out (jockey said gelding reared as stalls open and bit slipped through geldings mouth)* **13/2**

1m 1.29s (-0.01) **Going Correction** +0.025s/f (Good)
WFA 3 from 4yo+ 4lb — **8 Ran SP% 115.6**
Speed ratings (Par 105): **101,100,99,98,96 94,94,60**
CSF £9.07 CT £75.05 TOTE £2.20: £1.10, £1.70, £3.60; EX 8.20 Trifecta £118.40.
Owner J W Parry & Partner **Bred** Old Mill Stud & S Williams & J Parry **Trained** Newmarket, Suffolk

FOCUS
This fair sprint handicap was surprisingly run 0.18secs slower than the preceding juvenile maiden and produced a close finish. The winner can rate higher.

5319 EVERY RACE LIVE ON RACING TV H'CAP — 7f
7:35 (7:36) (Class 3) (0-90,89) 3-Y-O+

£9,337 (£2,796; £1,398; £699; £349; £175) **Stalls Low**

Form

2140 **1** **Moraawed**[39] 3865 3-9-3 87 .... JimCrowley 4 92+
(Roger Varian) *looked wl: uns rdr on way to s: hld up in last pair: pushed along and prog 2f out: rdn to take narrow ldr jst ins fnl f: styd on wl and asserted nr fin* **6/4**[1]

0034 **2** 3/4 **Qaysar (FR)**[34] 4020 4-9-12 89 .... SeanLevey 6 95
(Richard Hannon) *trckd ldr: chal 2f out: shkn up to ld 1f out and edgd lft briefly: sn hdd: styd on but hld nr fin* **11/4**[2]

3312 **3** 3/4 **Call Out Loud**[26] 4319 7-9-4 81 ....(vt) AlistairRawlinson 7 85
(Michael Appleby) *led: rdn and pressed 2f out: hdd 1f out: styd on same pce* **7/1**

600 **4** 1 **Shady McCoy (USA)**[12] 4887 9-9-12 89 .... JamesDoyle 1 90
(Ian Williams) *hld up: pushed along in last pair 2f out: no prog tl styd on fnl f to take 4th last strides: nvr a threat* **13/2**[3]

6122 **5** 1/2 **Quick Breath**[14] 4786 4-8-13 83 .... TylerSaunders(7) 5 83
(Jonathan Portman) *t.k.h: disp 2nd pl to 1/2-way: shkn up 2f out: nt qckn over 1f out: one pce after (jockey said, regarding appearing to stop riding shortly before winning post, that he had taken a precautionary check off the heels of a weakening Call Out Loud in order to avoid clipping heels)* **8/1**

1402 **6** 1 **Buckingham (IRE)**[18] 4643 3-9-0 84 .... CharlesBishop 2 78
(Eve Johnson Houghton) *dwlt: hld up in last: pushed along 2f out: one pce and nvr able to threaten* **9/1**

1m 30.82s (1.52) **Going Correction** +0.025s/f (Good)
WFA 3 from 4yo+ 7lb — **6 Ran SP% 113.6**
Speed ratings (Par 107): **92,91,90,89,88 87**
CSF £5.94 TOTE £2.40: £1.50, £1.90; EX 6.30 Trifecta £29.40.
Owner Hamdan Al Maktoum **Bred** Whitsbury Manor Stud **Trained** Newmarket, Suffolk

FOCUS
Rail movements added 16yds to the race distance. The feature race and a decent competitive handicap, but they went steady early, as the time testifies. Ordinary form for the grade.

5320 PURE STORAGE H'CAP — 1m
8:10 (8:10) (Class 4) (0-85,84) 3-Y-O+

£6,469 (£1,925; £962; £481; £300; £300) **Stalls Low**

Form | | | | RPR

3-31 **1** **Motawaj**[14] 4788 3-9-4 82 .... AndreaAtzeni 6 96
(Roger Varian) *looked wl: trckd ldng trio: pushed along over 2f out: prog on outer to ld over 1f out: rdn fnl f: styd on strly and drew rt away* **1/1**[1]

62-6 **2** 6 **Cheer The Title (IRE)**[55] 3268 4-9-10 80 .... LukeMorris 3 82
(Tom Clover) *sweating: hld up in last pair: effrt whn nt clr run wl over 1f out: prog to take 2nd jst over 1f out: drvn and sn lft bhd by wnr* **20/1**

0050 **3** 1 **Dragons Tail (IRE)**[26] 4320 4-9-12 82 ....(p) AlistairRawlinson 7 82
(Tom Dascombe) *looked wl: hld up in tch: rdn over 2f out: styd on over 1f out to take 3rd last strides: no ch w wnr* **20/1**

21-5 **4** nk **Let Rip (IRE)**[28] 4249 5-9-9 79 .... KieranShoemark 1 78
(Henry Candy) *sweating: led but pressed: rdn and hdd over 1f out: wknd fnl f (jockey said gelding hung left-handed)* **5/2**[2]

1602 **5** 1 3/4 **Masked Identity**[12] 4867 4-9-5 80 .... SebastianWoods(5) 2 75
(Shaun Keightley) *trckd ldng pair: rdn over 2f out: cl enough on inner over 1f out: sn btn* **11/2**[3]

0300 **6** 1 1/2 **Pactolus (IRE)**[19] 4613 8-10-0 84 ....(t) OisinMurphy 4 76
(Stuart Williams) *w ldr: stl upsides over 2f out: lost 2nd and wknd wl over 1f out* **12/1**

0/0- **7** 4 **Sea Sovereign (IRE)**[462] 1893 6-8-6 69 ....(h) RPWalsh(7) 5 51
(Ian Williams) *sltly awkward s: a in last: pushed along and detached 3f out: no prog* **25/1**

1m 42.04s (-1.26) **Going Correction** +0.025s/f (Good)
WFA 3 from 4yo+ 8lb — **7 Ran SP% 115.0**
Speed ratings (Par 105): **107,101,100,99,97 96,92**
CSF £26.57 TOTE £1.80: £1.10, £6.90; EX 20.60 Trifecta £211.50.
Owner Sheikh Ahmed Al Maktoum **Bred** Godolphin **Trained** Newmarket, Suffolk

FOCUS
Rail movements added 16yds to the race distance. Another close-knit handicap on paper, but the favourite routed his rivals and is on the up. The race did lack some depth.

5321 DEVINE HOMES H'CAP — 1m 6f
8:40 (8:40) (Class 4) (0-85,86) 4-Y-O+

£6,469 (£1,925; £962; £481; £300; £300) **Stalls Low**

Form | | | | RPR

4024 **1** **Emenem**[19] 4614 5-9-1 79 .... OisinMurphy 2 87
(Simon Dow) *wl in tch: plld out and prog over 2f out: rdn to ld over 1f out: sn hrd pressed: styd on wl to assert last 100yds* **7/2**[1]

6505 **2** 1 1/4 **Archimento**[20] 4543 6-9-2 80 .... JasonWatson 1 86
(William Knight) *prom: rdn over 2f out: chsd wnr jst over 1f out and sn chalng: nt qckn last 100yds* **9/1**

-402 **3** nk **Machine Learner**[19] 4614 6-9-8 86 .... SeanLevey 4 92
(Joseph Tuite) *looked wl: hld up in rr: prog over 2f out: rdn to cl on ldrs whn squeezed out over 1f out: rallied to take 3rd ins fnl f: styd on wl nr fin* **4/1**[2]

0230 **4** 2 **Petrastar**[28] 4250 4-9-1 79 ....(h[1]) DavidProbert 7 82
(Clive Cox) *t.k.h: prog to trck ldr after 4f: rdn to ld 2f out: wandered and hdd over 1f out: hanging and fdd (jockey said gelding ran too freely in early stages and hung left and right-handed in home str)* **12/1**

46-0 **5** 3/4 **Darksideoftarnside (IRE)**[32] 4118 5-9-4 82 ....(p) JimCrowley 10 84
(Ian Williams) *in tch: rdn and no prog over 2f out: kpt on same pce after* **16/1**

-060 **6** hd **Guns Of Leros (USA)**[45] 3635 6-9-3 81 ....(v) HectorCrouch 3 82
(Gary Moore) *s.i.s: hld up in last trio: rdn wl over 2f out: kpt on one pce and n.d (jockey said gelding was slowly away)* **6/1**[3]

0-45 **7** 4 **Trouble And Strife (IRE)**[14] 4782 4-9-2 80 ....(p) LukeMorris 6 76
(Sir Mark Prescott Bt) *trckd ldr 4f: styd prom: drvn wl over 2f out: steadily wknd* **7/1**

222 **8** 4 **Dono Di Dio**[28] 4257 4-9-4 82 .... GeorgeWood 8 72
(Michael Madgwick) *taken down early and rather on edge: s.i.s: hld up in last trio: rdn and no prog wl over 2f out (jockey said filly was never travelling)* **6/1**[3]

-230 **9** 2 1/4 **Mandalayan (IRE)**[21] 4505 4-9-7 85 .... RobHornby 5 72
(Jonathan Portman) *led to 2f out: wknd qckly over 1f out* **9/1**

60-0 **10** 28 **Seaport**[29] 4224 8-8-13 77 ....(t) TomQueally 9 25
(Seamus Durack) *hld up in rr: brief effrt over 2f out: sn wknd: eased over 1f out: t.o* **25/1**

3m 3.97s (-2.03) **Going Correction** +0.025s/f (Good) — **10 Ran SP% 120.7**
Speed ratings (Par 105): **106,105,105,103,103 103,101,98,97,81**
CSF £37.07 CT £134.52 TOTE £4.20: £1.70, £2.80, £1.70; EX 31.00 Trifecta £214.00.
Owner Robert Moss **Bred** D R Tucker **Trained** Epsom, Surrey

FOCUS
Rail movements added 16yds to the race distance. This staying handicap was run at an even gallop and the winner came from off the pace. He reversed form with the third.
T/Plt: £7.10 to a £1 stake. Pool: £70,327.25. 7,155.75 winning units. T/Qpdt: £4.20 to a £1 stake. Pool: £6,681.10. 1,154.93 winning units. **Jonathan Neesom**

5322 - 5324a (Foreign Racing) - See Raceform Interactive

4672 NAAS (L-H)
Wednesday, July 24

OFFICIAL GOING: Good (good to firm in places)

5325a YEOMANSTOWN STUD IRISH EBF STKS (LISTED RACE) (F&M) — 6f
7:25 (7:28) 3-Y-O+

£31,891 (£10,270; £4,864; £2,162; £1,081; £540)

RPR

1 **Servalan (IRE)**[75] 2605 3-9-0 97 .... ShaneFoley 2 100
(Mrs John Harrington, Ire) *chsd ldrs far side: rdn and prog whn briefly short of room 1f out: 4th ent fnl 100yds: kpt on strly to ld cl home* **11/2**[1]

2 shd **Woody Creek**[25] 4409 3-9-0 98 .... ChrisHayes 8 100
(J A Stack, Ire) *chsd ldrs: pushed along 2f out: 6th ent fnl f: kpt on strly to dispute fnl 50yds: hdd cl home* **11/2**[1]

3 1/2 **Gold Filigree (IRE)**[32] 4101 4-9-5 96 .... ShaneKelly 16 99
(Richard Hughes) *sn chsd ldrs: trckd ldrs in 4th at 1/2-way: disp appr fnl f tl led fnl 100yds: hdd ins fnl 50yds where dropped to 3rd* **25/1**

4 1/2 **Cava (IRE)**[28] 4242 3-9-0 96 ....(p[1]) DonnachaO'Brien 17 96
(Joseph Patrick O'Brien, Ire) *hld up towards rr: rdn and plenty to do ent fnl f: wnt 6th fnl 100yds: styd on strly into 4th cl home: nrst fin* **8/1**[2]

5 1/2 **Madam Seamstress (IRE)**[73] 2661 3-9-0 91 .... KevinManning 11 95+
(J S Bolger, Ire) *sn outpcd in rr: stl last over 1f out: styd on strly on outer fnl f into 5th cl home: nrst fin* **33/1**

6 1/2 **Heavenly Holly (IRE)**[10] 4954 4-9-5 96 .... RonanWhelan 1 94
(Hugo Palmer) *disp for 1f: trckd ldr in 2nd tl disp over 1f out: hdd fnl 100yds: wknd fnl 50yds* **11/2**[1]

7 1/2 **Gossamer Wings (USA)**[10] 4954 3-9-0 97 ....(b) WayneLordan 13 92+
(A P O'Brien, Ire) *trckd ldrs tl led on outer after 2f tl hdd over 1f out: wknd ins fnl 100yds* **16/1**

8 nk **Mid Winster**[10] 4952 3-9-0 90 .... BenCoen 9 91
(Andrew Slattery, Ire) *racd in mid-div: pushed along 1/2-way: no imp appr fnl f: kpt on same pce fnl f* **20/1**

9 2 **Probability (IRE)**[34] 4023 3-9-0 89 .... GaryCarroll 10 84
(Archie Watson) *trckd early ldrs tl led after 1f: trckd ldrs tl ent fnl f: wknd* **20/1**

10 1 3/4 **Nevereversaynever (IRE)**[264] 8810 3-9-0 0 .... LeighRoche 6 79
(J A Stack, Ire) *racd in mid-div: t.k.h: briefly clsr appr fnl f: sn one pce* **20/1**

11 1/2 **Nitro Boost (IRE)**[27] 4313 3-9-0 99 .... NathanCrosse 5 77
(W McCreery, Ire) *racd in mid-div far side: keen early: rdn whn sltly bmpd over 1f out: sn no ex* **16/1**

12 nk **Rapid Reaction (IRE)**[3] 5222 4-9-5 90 .... AndrewSlattery 14 77
(J F Grogan, Ire) *t.k.h early in rr of mid-div: pushed along and no imp over 1f out* **33/1**

13 1 3/4 **Mona Lisa's Smile (USA)**[7] 5075 3-9-0 74 ....(b[1]) SeamieHeffernan 7 71
(A P O'Brien, Ire) *a towards rr: rdn along 2f out: sn no ex* **50/1**

14 1/2 **Shimmering Dawn (IRE)**[34] 4023 3-9-0 90 .... TomEaves 15 69
(James Tate) *slowly away: a towards rr: nvr a factor* **10/1**[3]

15 2 1/2 **Lethal Promise (IRE)**[3] 5222 3-9-3 100 ....(p[1]) WJLee 12 64
(W McCreery, Ire) *sn chsd ldrs: pushed along 2f out: nt qckn appr fnl f: sn no ex* **10/1**[3]

16 3 **Bailly**[18] 4675 3-9-0 85 ColinKeane 4 51
(G M Lyons, Ire) *disp for 1f: trckd ldrs to 2f out: wknd qckly over 1f out: eased ins fnl f* **16/1**
17 2 1/2 **Fantasy (IRE)**[3] 5222 3-9-0 89 PBBeggy 3 43
(A P O'Brien, Ire) *chsd ldrs to 2f out: wknd qckly ent fnl f: eased* **14/1**
1m 11.98s (-1.22)
WFA 3 from 4yo 5lb **17 Ran SP% 125.7**
CSF £30.68 TOTE £6.20: £2.20, £2.10, £7.80; DF 27.60 Trifecta £595.90.
Owner Vimal Khosla **Bred** Mrs Noeleen McCreevy **Trained** Moone, Co Kildare
FOCUS
A thrilling finish to proceedings, with the winner just getting out in time to record a deserved success. They finished in a heap and the fifth may limit the form.

5326 - 5328a (Foreign Racing) - See Raceform Interactive

5165 VICHY
Wednesday, July 24

OFFICIAL GOING: Turf: very soft

5329a PRIX VICHY SPA HOTEL LES CELESTINS (MAIDEN) (3YO FILLIES) (TURF) 1m
10:25 3-Y-O **£9,009** (£3,603; £2,702; £1,801; £900)

RPR
1 **Ridaa (IRE)**[32] 3-9-0 0 ow1 TristanBaron(3) 5 64
(J E Hammond, France) *led: mde all: urged along 2f out: rdn to hold advantage over 1f out: kpt on strly ins fnl f* **19/10**[2]
2 3 1/2 **Nefyn Beach (IRE)**[70] 2759 3-9-3 0 ow1 AurelienLemaitre 8 56
(Jo Hughes, France) *trckd ldr: pushed along 2f out: rdn to chse ldr over 1f out: styd on ins fnl f but a being hld* **13/1**
3 1 1/4 **Nicky Style (FR)** 3-8-13 0 ow2 MaximeGuyon 7 49
(G Botti, France) **6/4**[1]
4 hd **Dosila** 3-8-11 0 ow1 ThomasTrullier(6) 3 53
(C Laffon-Parias, France) **76/10**[3]
5 nk **History Wotton (FR)** 3-8-13 0 ow2 ChristopheBillardello 6 48
(R Martens, France) **42/1**
6 5 1/2 **Money Back (FR)**[21] 3-9-3 0 ow1 FabriceVeron 1 39
(F Vermeulen, France) **17/1**
7 4 1/2 **Devolution (FR)** 3-8-13 0 ow2 MickaelForest 2 25
(F Vermeulen, France) **43/5**
8 nk **Soltanaa (FR)** 3-9-3 0 ow1 AntoineHamelin 4 28
(F Vermeulen, France) **11/1**
1m 45.13s **8 Ran SP% 119.9**
PARI-MUTUEL (all including 1 euro stake): WIN 2.90; PLACE 1.20, 2.70, 1.20; DF 17.60.
Owner Hamdan Al Maktoum **Bred** Shadwell Estate Co Ltd **Trained** France

5169 DONCASTER (L-H)
Thursday, July 25

OFFICIAL GOING: Good to firm (watered; 8.2)
Wind: Moderate against Weather: Sunny and very warm

5330 ITV7 STARTS NOW H'CAP 6f 2y
5:45 (5:45) (Class 5) (0-70,72) 4-Y-O+
£3,428 (£1,020; £509; £300; £300; £300) **Stalls High**

Form RPR
-462 1 **Atalanta's Boy**[63] 3014 4-9-2 70 (h) ThomasGreatrex(5) 6 81+
(David Menuisier) *towards rr: hdwy 1/2-way: pushed along to trck ldrs over 2f out: sn swtchd lft and chsd ldrs: rdn to chal ent fnl f: kpt on wl to ld fnl 100yds* **9/4**[1]
0121 2 1 1/4 **Ninjago**[14] 4823 9-9-1 64 (v) DanielTudhope 8 71
(Paul Midgley) *trckd ldrs: smooth hdwy 2f out: slt ld jst over 1f out: sn jnd and rdn: drvn and hdd fnl 100yds* **4/1**[2]
1533 3 2 **Lucky Beggar (IRE)**[38] 3928 9-9-7 70 DavidAllan 9 71
(David C Griffiths) *in tch: hdwy on outer to chse ldrs over 2f out: rdn wl over 1f out: drvn and kpt on same pce fnl f* **10/1**
2420 4 nse **Mutabaahy (IRE)**[27] 4335 4-9-5 68 CamHardie 11 68
(Antony Brittain) *trckd ldrs: hdwy over 2f out: rdn wl over 1f out: drvn and kpt on same pce fnl f (jockey said gelding fly leapt leaving the stalls; vet said gelding was treated for post-race heat stress)* **7/1**[3]
4023 5 1/2 **Amazing Grazing (IRE)**[10] 4977 5-9-5 68 PhilDennis 10 67
(Rebecca Bastiman) *in tch: hdwy over 2f out: rdn along and sltly outpcd wl over 1f out: sn n.m.r and swtchd lft ent fnl f: kpt on towards fin* **7/1**[3]
0002 6 3/4 **Duke Cosimo**[16] 4764 9-8-12 61 JasonHart 2 57
(Michael Herrington) *sn outpcd and bhd: pushed along 1/2-way: rdn over 2f out: hdwy over 1f out: n.m.r ins fnl f: kpt on* **14/1**
0-00 7 hd **Militia**[13] 4894 4-9-9 72 PaulHanagan 5 68
(Richard Fahey) *cl up: rdn to take slt ld 2f out: drvn and hdd appr fnl f: sn wknd* **17/2**
1- 8 6 **Mambila (FR)**[310] 7394 5-9-7 70 (w) KevinStott 7 47
(Geoffrey Harker) *led: rdn along and hdd 2f out: sn drvn and wknd* **12/1**
0000 9 1/2 **Guardia Svizzera (IRE)**[8] 5042 5-9-4 67 (h) BenCurtis 1 42
(Roger Fell) *chsd ldrs: rdn along wl over 2f out: sn wknd* **33/1**
50-0 10 3 3/4 **Bobby's Charm (USA)**[58] 3207 4-9-1 64 (p) JamesSullivan 3 27
(Scott Dixon) *a towards rr* **40/1**
1m 10.64s (-2.06) **Going Correction** -0.175s/f (Firm) **10 Ran SP% 115.1**
Speed ratings (Par 103): **106,104,101,101,100 99,99,91,91,86**
CSF £10.67 CT £73.20 TOTE £3.10: £1.20, £1.70, £2.40; EX 13.70 Trifecta £54.70.
Owner Mrs Monica Josefina Borton & Partner **Bred** Monica Martinez-Trumm **Trained** Pulborough, W Sussex
FOCUS
Modest sprinting form, they raced centre-field. The winner can do better still.

5331 TRENT REFRACTORIES NOVICE STKS (PLUS 10 RACE) 7f 6y
6:15 (6:16) (Class 4) 2-Y-O **£4,463** (£1,328; £663; £331) **Stalls High**

Form RPR
3 1 **Valdermoro (USA)**[33] 4106 2-9-5 0 TonyHamilton 8 87+
(Richard Fahey) *trckd ldr: smooth hdwy 2f out: led over 1f out: shkn up jst ins fnl f: sn qcknd clr: readily* **5/4**[1]
2 3 1/4 **Global Storm (IRE)** 2-9-5 0 DanielTudhope 3 77+
(Charlie Appleby) *trckd ldrs: hdwy 2f out: sn rdn and sltly outpcd over 1f out: kpt on fnl f* **11/8**[2]
3 1 **Maqtal (USA)** 2-9-5 0 DaneO'Neill 6 74
(Roger Varian) *dwlt and sltly hmpd s: towards rr: hdwy 2f out: rdn over 1f out: styd on wl fnl f* **6/1**[3]
0 4 1/2 **Shevchenko Park (IRE)**[77] 2561 2-9-2 0 JaneElliott(3) 9 73
(Tom Dascombe) *led: pushed along wl over 2f out: rdn and hdd over 1f out: grad wknd* **14/1**
5 1 1/4 **Sky Vega (IRE)** 2-9-5 0 RossaRyan 5 70
(Richard Hannon) *towards rr: hdwy on outer over 3f out: rdn along to chse ldrs 2f out: kpt on same pce fnl f* **8/1**
6 1 3/4 **Into Faith (FR)** 2-9-5 0 KevinStott 1 65
(David Menuisier) *hld up: pushed along 3f out: hdwy over 2f out: rdn wl over 1f out: kpt on same pce* **33/1**
0 7 7 **Grand Pianola**[29] 4238 2-9-5 0 RachelRichardson 4 47
(Tim Easterby) *t.k.h: chsd ldrs: rdn along 3f out: sn wknd* **80/1**
0 8 nk **Ontheradar (IRE)**[22] 4516 2-9-5 0 AndrewElliott 7 46
(Ronald Thompson) *prom: pushed along 3f out: rdn wl over 2f out: sn wknd* **100/1**
1m 24.9s (-1.50) **Going Correction** -0.175s/f (Firm) **8 Ran SP% 123.8**
Speed ratings (Par 96): **101,97,96,95,94 92,84,83**
CSF £3.63 TOTE £2.10: £1.10, £1.10, £1.80; EX 3.90 Trifecta £10.20.
Owner M J Macleod **Bred** Cesa Farm & Laberinto Farm & Racing Corp **Trained** Musley Bank, N Yorks
FOCUS
A fair novice won in good style by a potentially useful sort. They again raced centre-field.

5332 SKY BET GO-RACING IN YORKSHIRE SUMMER FESTIVAL FILLIES' H'CAP 1m 3f 197y
6:50 (6:50) (Class 4) (0-85,85) 3-Y-O+ **£5,207** (£1,549; £774; £387) **Stalls High**

Form RPR
0152 1 **Bollin Joan**[8] 5039 4-9-1 68 (p) DavidAllan 4 72+
(Tim Easterby) *trckd ldng pair: hdwy over 2f out: rdn to chal over 1f out: led ent fnl f: kpt on* **3/1**[2]
1105 2 3/4 **Katiesheidinlisa**[41] 3800 3-9-4 85 JaneElliott(3) 2 86
(Tom Dascombe) *trckd ldr: hdwy on inner to ld 2f out: sn rdn: hdd and drvn ent fnl f: kpt on* **4/1**[3]
0311 3 1/2 **Arctic Ocean (IRE)**[20] 4599 3-9-3 81 JimmyQuinn 1 81
(Sir Michael Stoute) *set stdy pce: qcknd over 4f out: pushed along 3f out: rdn and hdd 2f out: cl up: drvn appr fnl f: kpt on* **1/1**[1]
2104 4 3 1/2 **Voi**[51] 3449 5-9-0 74 (t) WilliamCarver(7) 3 69
(Conrad Allen) *hld up in rr: hdwy over 3f out: pushed along over 2f out: sn rdn and no imp* **6/1**
2m 34.26s (-2.34) **Going Correction** -0.175s/f (Firm)
WFA 3 from 4yo+ 11lb **4 Ran SP% 109.3**
Speed ratings (Par 102): **100,99,99,96**
CSF £13.99 TOTE £3.30; EX 9.20 Trifecta £16.90.
Owner Richard Taylor & Philip Hebdon **Bred** Habton Farms **Trained** Great Habton, N Yorks
FOCUS
Add 18yds. No great gallop on here and any one of three still held a chance racing into the final furlong. They stayed on the far rail in the straight. The winner probably only had to run to form.

5333 BRITISH EBF PREMIER FILLIES' H'CAP 7f 6y
7:20 (7:21) (Class 4) (0-85,78) 3-Y-O+ **£7,374** (£2,194; £1,096; £548) **Stalls High**

Form RPR
31-0 1 **Inhale**[27] 4341 3-9-7 78 GrahamLee 1 87+
(Amanda Perrett) *hld up in rr: hdwy wl over 1f out: sn rdn: styd on wl fnl f to ld fnl 100yds* **7/2**[3]
2114 2 1 **Caustic Love (IRE)**[14] 4822 3-9-6 77 ShaneGray 6 83
(Keith Dalgleish) *led: jnd and pushed along 3f out: rdn and hdd narrowly wl over 1f out: drvn and ev ch ins fnl f: kpt on* **6/4**[1]
6116 3 1/2 **Rux Ruxx (IRE)**[12] 4902 4-9-13 77 SilvestreDeSousa 5 84
(Tim Easterby) *sn trcking ldng pair: hdwy and cl up 1/2-way: rdn to chal 2f out: slt ld over 1f out: drvn and wandered ins fnl f: hdd fnl 100yds* **7/4**[2]
2616 4 5 **Penny Pot Lane**[24] 4440 6-9-2 66 LewisEdmunds 3 60
(Richard Whitaker) *trckd ldr: pushed along 3f out: rdn wl over 2f out: sn wknd* **17/2**
1m 25.08s (-1.32) **Going Correction** -0.175s/f (Firm)
WFA 3 from 4yo+ 7lb **4 Ran SP% 109.1**
Speed ratings (Par 102): **100,98,98,92**
CSF £9.21 TOTE £3.70; EX 10.30 Trifecta £16.00.
Owner K Abdullah **Bred** Juddmonte Farms Ltd **Trained** Pulborough, W Sussex
FOCUS
Just the four of them, they headed down the middle and the pace was just ordinary. The two 3yos came to the fore and the form makes sense at face value.

5334 OWLERTON GREYHOUND STADIUM SHEFFIELD H'CAP 1m 2f 43y
7:55 (7:55) (Class 5) (0-70,68) 3-Y-O **£3,428** (£1,020; £509; £300) **Stalls High**

Form RPR
5065 1 **Debbonair (IRE)**[38] 3947 3-9-2 63 (b) BenCurtis 6 69
(Hugo Palmer) *trckd ldng pair: hdwy over 2f out: rdn to ld over 1f out: drvn ins fnl f: kpt on wl towards fin* **5/1**[3]
-022 2 1/2 **Lady Scatterley (FR)**[6] 5156 3-9-6 67 DavidAllan 2 72
(Tim Easterby) *trckd ldr: hdwy 3f out: slt ld 2f out and sn rdn: hdd over 1f out: drvn and rallied to have ev ch ins fnl f: kpt on same pce towards fin* **11/10**[1]
005 3 1 1/4 **Lucky Number**[38] 3932 3-9-3 64 DanielTudhope 5 67
(William Haggas) *hld up in rr: hdwy wl over 2f out: rdn and ev ch ent fnl f: sn drvn and kpt on same pce* **15/8**[2]
4405 4 3/4 **Osmosis**[19] 4628 3-8-13 63 ConorMcGovern(3) 3 64
(Jason Ward) *led: pushed along 3f out: rdn and hdd 2f out: sn drvn: kpt on same pce fnl f* **8/1**
2m 10.7s (-1.60) **Going Correction** -0.175s/f (Firm) **4 Ran SP% 110.2**
Speed ratings (Par 100): **99,98,97,97**
CSF £11.27 TOTE £4.70; EX 9.40 Trifecta £17.80.
Owner Commission Air Limited **Bred** P Delaney **Trained** Newmarket, Suffolk
FOCUS
Add 18yds. Another small field, there was near enough four in a row passing the 2f marker and the form isn't worth a great deal. It does make some sense around the 1-2.

5335 ARTEX H'CAP 6f 2y
8:25 (8:29) (Class 4) (0-80,82) 3-Y-O
£5,272 (£1,568; £784; £392; £300; £300) **Stalls High**

Form RPR
0021 1 **Golden Parade**[8] 5056 3-8-9 67 6ex (p) DavidAllan 4 78+
(Tim Easterby) *mde most: rdn over 1f out: drvn ent fnl f: kpt on strly* **5/2**[1]

0643 **2** *2* **Coolagh Magic**[26] 4368 3-9-3 **75**.........................(p) PaulHanagan 8 79
(Richard Fahey) *wnt bdly lft s: trckd ldrs: hdwy over 2f out: rdn over 1f out: drvn ent fnl f: kpt on* **5/1**[3]

1443 **3** *nk* **Mark's Choice (IRE)**[6] 5126 3-9-10 **82**......................... JackGarritty 1 85
(Ruth Carr) *trckd ldrs: hdwy 2f out and sn chal: rdn and ev ch ent fnl f: sn drvn and kpt on same pce* **11/4**[2]

2034 **4** *4* **Stronsay (IRE)**[15] 4781 3-8-13 **71**.........................(p) GrahamLee 10 61
(Bryan Smart) *towards rr: hdwy over 2f out: rdn along wl over 1f out: kpt on: nvr nr ldrs* **7/1**

0030 **5** *1 1/2* **House Deposit**[34] 4070 3-8-6 **64**......................... CamHardie 6 49
(Roger Fell) *hmpd s: towards rr: sme late hdwy* **9/1**

4000 **6** *7* **Fares Kodiac (IRE)**[25] 4420 3-9-10 **82**.........................(t) GeraldMosse 5 45
(Marco Botti) *hmpd s: a towards rr* **9/1**

0-00 **7** *4* **Lovin (USA)**[89] 2121 3-9-5 **77**.........................(vt[1] w) DanielTudhope 2 27
(David O'Meara) *trckd ldrs: effrt over 2f out: sn rdn and wknd wl over 1f out* **20/1**

0050 **8** *8* **Oberyn Martell**[25] 4420 3-9-7 **79**......................... SilvestreDeSousa 7 4
(Eve Johnson Houghton) *hmpd s: sn cl up: disp ld 1/2-way: rdn over 2f out: sn wknd (jockey said gelding moved poorly)* **16/1**

1m 10.87s (-1.83) **Going Correction** -0.175s/f (Firm) 8 Ran SP% **115.0**
Speed ratings (Par 102): **105,102,101,96,94 85,79,69**
CSF £15.54 CT £36.11 TOTE £3.00: £1.30, £3.20, £1.10; EX 13.90 Trifecta £40.10.
Owner David Scott & Partner **Bred** Cheveley Park Stud Ltd **Trained** Great Habton, N Yorks

FOCUS
Three pulled clear in this ordinary sprint. The winner is progressing. The action took place down the centre of the track.

5336 JOHNSONS HOTEL, RESTAURANT AND CATERING DIVISION NOVICE STKS 7f 6y
8:55 (8:59) (Class 5) 3-Y-O+ **£3,428** (£1,020; £509; £254) **Stalls** High

Form RPR

022 **1** **Siglo Six**[22] 4520 3-9-2 80.........................(h) BenCurtis 3 86+
(Hugo Palmer) *trckd ldrs: pushed along and hdwy over 2f out: rdn to chse ldng pair wl over 1f out: drvn to chal jst ins fnl f: styd on to ld fnl 100yds* **4/5**[1]

5-23 **2** *1/2* **Aluqair (IRE)**[20] 4590 3-9-2 83.........................(h) GeraldMosse 6 84
(Simon Crisford) *trckd ldr: hdwy to ld wl over 2f out: clr and rdn over 1f out: jnd and drvn ins fnl f: hdd fnl 100yds: no ex* **5/4**[2]

0 **3** *7* **Blank Canvas**[14] 4827 3-8-11 0......................... ShaneGray 7 60
(Keith Dalgleish) *led: rdn along and hdd wl over 1f out: sn one pce* **25/1**

66 **4** *6* **Teemlucky**[17] 4738 3-8-11 0......................... JasonHart 1 44
(Ian Williams) *hld up towards rr: sme hdwy fnl 2f: nvr a factor* **14/1**[3]

6- **5** *2 3/4* **Sephira Park**[341] 6281 4-8-13 0......................... SebastianWoods(5) 8 39
(Chris Wall) *chsd ldng pair: rdn along 3f out: wknd over 2f out* **25/1**

6 *2* **Thornaby Spirit (IRE)** 4-9-9 0......................... GrahamLee 9 39
(Jason Ward) *s.i.s: a bhd* **14/1**[3]

00 **7** *22* **Lady Sebastian**[22] 4520 3-8-8 0......................... ConorMcGovern(3) 5
(Jason Ward) *t.k.h: chsd ldrs: pushed along 3f out: sn outpcd and bhd fnl 2f* **100/1**

1m 25.17s (-1.23) **Going Correction** -0.175s/f (Firm)
WFA 3 from 4yo 7lb 7 Ran SP% **122.0**
Speed ratings (Par 103): **100,99,91,84,81 79,54**
CSF £2.26 TOTE £1.50: £1.10, £1.40; EX 2.20 Trifecta £12.60.
Owner John Livock **Bred** W Hennessey **Trained** Newmarket, Suffolk
■ Sally Hope was withdrawn, price at time of withdrawal 25/1. Rule 4 does not apply.

FOCUS
Only two mattered in this novice and they duly dominated. They again raced centre-field. The winner can do better again.
T/Plt: £187.60 to a £1 stake. Pool: £66,222.23 - 257.56 winning units T/Qpdt: £125.20 to a £1 stake. £5,428.29 - 32.08 winning units **Joe Rowntree**

5182 NEWBURY (L-H)
Thursday, July 25

OFFICIAL GOING: Good to firm (good in places; watered; 6.6)
Wind: Light, across Weather: Hot

5337 RACING TV AMATEUR RIDERS' H'CAP (DIV I) 1m 2f
4:55 (4:56) (Class 5) (0-70,72) 3-Y-O+ **£3,306** (£1,025; £512; £300; £300; £300) **Stalls** Low

Form RPR

663 **1** **The Throstles**[20] 4602 4-10-9 **70**......................... MrMAGalligan(5) 3 79
(Kevin Frost) *t.k.h: chsd ldr tl led over 3f out: rdn 2f out: drvn fnl f: kpt on u.p and a holding on* **7/2**[1]

2255 **2** *nk* **Light Of Air (FR)**[14] 4838 6-9-11 **60**.........................(b) MissKatyBrooks(7) 6 68
(Gary Moore) *stdd s: hld up in tch in last pair: hdwy over 3f out: effrt to chse ldrs 2f out: rdn and kpt on to chse wnr ins fnl f: steadily clsd but nvr quite getting to wnr* **9/2**[3]

426 **3** *1 3/4* **Banksy's Art**[21] 4569 4-9-12 **61**......................... MissDanielleSmith(7) 9 65
(Amanda Perrett) *stdd and swtchd lft after s: hld up in tch in last pair: hdwy on inner over 3f out: effrt and cl up in 4th 2f out: rdn over 1f out: kpt on same pce and wnt 3rd wl ins fnl f* **8/1**

5445 **4** *1* **Edge (IRE)**[15] 4797 8-9-9 **56**.........................(b) MissJessicaLlewellyn(5) 2 58
(Bernard Llewellyn) *t.k.h: pressed wnr over 3f out: rdn 2f out: drvn over 1f out: kpt on same pce and lost 2 pls ins fnl f* **14/1**

4450 **5** *9* **Grandscape**[24] 4446 4-10-8 **69**.........................(p[1]) SophieSmith(5) 7 53
(Ed Dunlop) *dwlt: sn rcvrd and wl in tch in midfield: effrt 3f out: 5th and outpcd 2f out: wknd fnl f* **12/1**

0214 **6** *8* **Elsie Violet (IRE)**[21] 4568 3-9-6 **62**.........................(p) MrGeorgeEddery(5) 8 31
(Robert Eddery) *trckd ldrs: rdn over 3f out: outpcd and btn 2f out: sn wknd* **5/1**

0-55 **7** *3/4* **Harlow**[159] 754 5-10-6 **67**......................... MrNathanSeery(5) 5 34
(Ian Williams) *hld up wl in tch in midfield: effrt 3f out: sn outpcd: wl btn over 1f out* **10/1**

2163 **8** *26* **Greyzee (IRE)**[71] 2734 3-9-9 **60**......................... MrPatrickMillman 1
(Rod Millman) *t.k.h: led: hdd over 3f out: sn dropped out: t.o fnl 2f: sddle slipped (jockey said the saddle slipped)* **4/1**[2]

2m 12.09s (2.39) **Going Correction** +0.075s/f (Good)
WFA 3 from 4yo+ 9lb 8 Ran SP% **111.6**
Speed ratings (Par 103): **93,92,91,90,83 76,76,55**
CSF £18.37 CT £112.68 TOTE £5.10: £1.30, £2.10, £1.90; EX 18.10 Trifecta £124.80.
Owner Kevin Frost Racing Club & Trisha Keane **Bred** Aislabie Bloodstock Ltd **Trained** Newcastle-under-Lyme, Staffs

FOCUS
No horses returned to the winner's enclosure due to the heat, with all horses dismounted on the track under veterinary supervision. The rails on the far bends were 2 metres out from the innermost line, meaning the addition of 7yds to races 1,2,5, and 8. A modest handicap and not much pace on. The first four finished clear. A turf pb from the winner.

5338 RACING TV AMATEUR RIDERS' H'CAP (DIV II) 1m 2f
5:30 (5:30) (Class 5) (0-70,71) 3-Y-O+ **£3,306** (£1,025; £512; £300; £300; £300) **Stalls** Low

Form RPR

021 **1** **Blue Medici**[19] 4658 5-10-13 **68**......................... MissBeckySmith 1 78
(Mark Loughnane) *led: hdd narrowly 4f out: rdn and ev ch over 1f out: led again ins fnl f: styd on wl* **11/10**[1]

0364 **2** *1 1/4* **Gravity Wave (IRE)**[21] 4543 5-10-0 **62**.........(p) MissImogenMathias(7) 6 69
(John Flint) *t.k.h: chsd wnr tl led narrowly 4f out: rdn 2f out: hdd and one pce ins fnl f* **6/1**[3]

13 **3** *1 1/4* **Magic Shuffle (IRE)**[17] 4737 3-10-2 **66**......................... MissLillyPinchin 2 71
(Barry Brennan) *racd wd thrght: chsd ldrs: effrt over 2f out: kpt on same pce u.p ins fnl f* **8/1**

0113 **4** *1/2* **Lucky's Dream**[28] 4283 4-11-0 **69**......................... MrSimonWalker 8 73
(Ian Williams) *chsd ldrs: effrt over 1f out: unable qck and kpt on same pce ins fnl f* **3/1**[2]

-666 **5** *6* **William Hunter**[14] 4838 7-10-9 **71**.........................(t) MrJamieNeild(7) 4 63
(Nigel Twiston-Davies) *hld up in tch in last trio: effrt over 2f out: no imp and btn over 1f out: wknd ins fnl f* **12/1**

-000 **6** *3/4* **Imminent Approach**[23] 4475 4-9-11 **52**......................... MrPatrickMillman 5 42
(Tony Newcombe) *hld up in last trio: effrt over 2f out: no imp and sn outpcd: wknd fnl f* **50/1**

4000 **7** *2 3/4* **Kismat**[20] 4615 4-9-8 **56**.........................(p) MissGeorgiaKing(7) 9 41
(Alan King) *wl in tch in midfield: effrt 2f out: sn outpcd and btn: wknd fnl f* **25/1**

3050 **8** *6* **Double Legend (IRE)**[29] 4251 4-9-12 **60**.........................(b) MrGuyMitchell(7) 7 33
(Amanda Perrett) *hld up in detached last: nvr involved* **20/1**

2m 11.56s (1.86) **Going Correction** +0.075s/f (Good)
WFA 3 from 4yo+ 9lb 8 Ran SP% **116.3**
Speed ratings (Par 103): **95,94,93,92,87 87,85,80**
CSF £8.34 CT £36.53 TOTE £1.90: £1.10, £1.80, £2.00; EX 7.20 Trifecta £41.70.
Owner Laurence Bellman **Bred** Kirtlington Stud Ltd **Trained** Rock, Worcs

FOCUS
Add 7yds. A no-nonsense ride on the market leader who won a shade cosily. The winning time was quicker than the first division, but not by much, and again the gallop wasn't strong. The first four were clear and the second and third help the standard.

5339 HORATIO'S GARDEN EBF NOVICE STKS (PLUS 10 RACE) 6f
6:00 (6:00) (Class 4) 2-Y-O **£4,463** (£1,328; £663; £331) **Stalls** Centre

Form RPR

1 **1** **Knight Shield (IRE)**[31] 4184 2-9-8 0......................... JamesDoyle 1 87+
(William Haggas) *trckd ldrs tl clsd to go upsides ldr ent fnl 2f: pushed ahd jst ins fnl f: asserting and rdn 100yds out: r.o wl* **1/2**[1]

0 **2** *1 1/2* **Cotai Again (IRE)**[33] 4098 2-9-2 0......................... KieranShoemark 2 76
(Charles Hills) *led: shkn up ent fnl 2f: drvn ent fnl f: hdd and one pce jst ins fnl f* **9/1**[3]

6 **3** *3 1/4* **Striding Edge (IRE)**[29] 4246 2-9-2 0......................... RichardKingscote 3 66
(Mark Johnston) *chsd ldr tl jst over 2f out: sn rdn and unable to match ldrs: chsd clr ldng pair ins fnl f: no imp* **3/1**[2]

06 **4** *3 1/4* **Boy George**[17] 4734 2-9-2 0......................... LiamKeniry 7 56
(Dominic Ffrench Davis) *stdd s: hld up in rr of main gp: effrt and reminders 2f out: sn outpcd: no threat to ldrs but kpt on ins fnl f* **40/1**

5 *3/4* **Island Warrior (IRE)** 2-9-2 0......................... DavidEgan 4 54+
(Heather Main) *wnt rt leaving stalls: t.k.h: chsd ldrs: wnt 3rd 2f out: rn green and edgd lft over 1f out: wknd ins fnl f* **18/1**

6 *14* **Wrath Of Hector** 2-9-2 0......................... CallumShepherd 6 12
(Tony Newcombe) *s.i.s: in tch in rr of main gp: rdn over 2f out: sn outpcd: wl bhd fnl f* **250/1**

7 *2 1/2* **Tigerten** 2-9-2 0......................... RobHornby 5
(Joseph Tuite) *rn green and sn outpcd: nvr on terms* **40/1**

1m 14.71s (1.51) **Going Correction** +0.075s/f (Good) 7 Ran SP% **112.2**
Speed ratings (Par 96): **92,90,85,81,80 61,58**
CSF £5.91 TOTE £1.30: £1.10, £2.80; EX 4.40 Trifecta £8.80.
Owner M M Stables **Bred** M P & R J Coleman **Trained** Newmarket, Suffolk

FOCUS
Not much strength in depth here. The market suggested it would be one-sided and it ultimately was. The pace was modest.

5340 SOUTH DOWNS WATER NURSERY H'CAP 6f
6:30 (6:31) (Class 5) (0-75,74) 2-Y-O **£3,816** (£1,135; £567; £300; £300; £300) **Stalls** Centre

Form RPR

4343 **1** **Fantom Force (IRE)**[7] 5101 2-9-6 **73**......................... TomMarquand 9 76
(Richard Hannon) *chsd ldrs tl rdn to ld over 1f out: hung rt: hdd and bmpd ins fnl f: stl edging lft but kpt on to ld again last strides* **4/1**[3]

0104 **2** *hd* **Seraphinite (IRE)**[19] 4637 2-9-7 **74**......................... NicolaCurrie 4 76
(Jamie Osborne) *stdd s: t.k.h: hld up in tch: clsd to trck ldrs and swtchd lft 2f out: shifted lft 1f out: hung rt but rdn to ld ins fnl f: hung lft u.p towards fin: hdd last strides* **7/2**[2]

4434 **3** *1* **Bartat**[15] 4799 2-8-9 **62**......................... DavidProbert 5 61
(Mick Channon) *stdd s: clsd and swtchd lft 2f out: effrt to chse ldrs whn pushed lft 1f out: kpt on u.p ins fnl f* **20/1**

502 **4** *nk* **Chromium**[30] 4222 2-8-12 **65**.........................(p[1]) HayleyTurner 8 64
(Mark Usher) *chsd ldrs: rdn and pressing ldrs over 1f out: kpt on same pce ins fnl f* **10/1**

460 **5** *1 3/4* **Champagne Highlife (GER)**[47] 3595 2-9-2 **69**......................... CharlesBishop 2 62
(Eve Johnson Houghton) *sn prom: led after 1f: rdn and hdd over 1f out: no ex and wknd wl ins fnl f* **14/1**

6050 **6** *nk* **Birkie Queen (IRE)**[34] 4075 2-8-5 **58**......................... JFEgan 7 50
(J S Moore) *hld up in tch in midfield: effrt over 1f out: kpt on same pce u.p ins fnl f* **50/1**

204 **7** *4 1/2* **Red Sun (IRE)**[21] 4558 2-9-5 **72**......................... KieranShoemark 6 51
(Charles Hills) *hld up in tch: effrt 2f out: unable qck over 1f out: wknd ins fnl f* **9/2**

336 **8** *5* **Don't Joke**[67] 2869 2-9-3 **70**......................... JamesDoyle 3 34
(Mark Johnston) *led for 1f: chsd ldr tl unable qck and lost pl over 1f out: wknd ins fnl f (trainer's rep could offer no explanation for the colt's performance)* **3/1**[1]

5500 **9** *4* **Swiss Bond**[7] 5101 2-8-4 **64**.................... LauraCoughlan(7) 10 16
(J S Moore) *hld up in tch: effrt 2f out: sn u.p and outpcd: wknd fnl f* **50/1**

055 **10** *28* **Good Times Too**[61] 3088 2-8-5 **58**.................... DavidEgan 1
(Mick Channon) *t.k.h to post: chsd ldrs tl over 2f out: sn bhd: t.o (jockey said colt ran freely to post)* **14/1**

1m 15.61s (2.41) **Going Correction** +0.075s/f (Good) **10** Ran SP% **116.5**
Speed ratings (Par 94): **86,85,84,84,81 81,75,68,63,25**
CSF £18.11 CT £251.56 TOTE £5.60: £2.40, £1.50, £4.90; EX 20.70 Trifecta £296.20.
Owner Excel Racing **Bred** Pier House Stud **Trained** East Everleigh, Wilts

FOCUS
Not the strongest of nurseries but an exciting finish and fortunes changed inside the final furlong.

5341 RELYON CLEANING NEWBURY H'CAP 1m 2f

7:05 (7:06) (Class 4) (0-85,84) 3-Y-O £6,404 (£1,905; £952; £476; £300) Stalls Low

Form RPR

-333 **1** **Just The Man (FR)**[45] 3647 3-9-3 **80**.................... OisinMurphy 4 87
(Clive Cox) *t.k.h: hld up wl in tch: nt clr run 3f out tl effrt and hdwy 1f out: led 100yds out: r.o strly* **15/8**[1]

521 **2** *1* **Incredulous**[16] 4768 3-9-3 **80**.................... JamesDoyle 3 85
(William Haggas) *chsd ldr: ev ch and rdn ent fnl 2f: kpt on wl: nt quite match pce of wnr fnl 100yds* **5/2**[2]

-320 **3** *nse* **Rhythmic Intent (IRE)**[14] 4841 3-9-4 **81**.................... RichardKingscote 5 85
(Stuart Williams) *chsd ldrs on outer: effrt over 1f out: kpt on u.p ins fnl f: nt quite match pce of wnr fnl 100yds* **7/2**[3]

-512 **4** *shd* **Sophosc (IRE)**[14] 4830 3-9-7 **84**.................... RobHornby 1 88
(Joseph Tuite) *led: rdn ent fnl 2f: kpt on u.p tl hdd and nt quite match pce of wnr fnl 100yds* **6/1**

3-10 **5** *8* **Madame Tantzy**[103] 1751 3-9-1 **78**.................... CharlesBishop 2 66
(Eve Johnson Houghton) *trckd ldrs on inner: nt clr run 3f out: swtchd lft 2f out: outpcd u.p over 1f out: wknd ins fnl f* **10/1**

2m 7.48s (-2.22) **Going Correction** +0.075s/f (Good) **5** Ran SP% **109.0**
Speed ratings (Par 102): **111,110,110,110,103**
CSF £6.66 TOTE £2.50: £1.30, £1.80; EX 7.20 Trifecta £15.40.
Owner Paul & Clare Rooney **Bred** Compagnia Generale Srl **Trained** Lambourn, Berks

FOCUS
Add 7yds. A useful handicap and a good winner who came home strongly. A bunch finish but the form is taken at face value around the fourth.

5342 PEPPER PINK GIN EBF MAIDEN FILLIES' STKS (PLUS 10 RACE) 7f (S)

7:35 (7:38) (Class 4) 2-Y-O £4,463 (£1,328; £663; £331) Stalls Centre

Form RPR

4 **1** **Boomer**[21] 4551 2-9-0 0.................... RichardKingscote 3 88+
(Tom Dascombe) *racd keenly: pressed ldrs tl led 2f out: rn green and hung rt over 1f out: reminders and r.o v strly ins fnl f: readily* **7/2**[3]

2 *3 1/2* **Deep Snow** 2-9-0 0.................... OisinMurphy 7 78
(Saeed bin Suroor) *hld up in tch: clsd and shkn up ent fnl 2f: chsd wnr and edgd lft ent fnl f: kpt on but outpcd by wnr fnl 150yds* **3/1**[2]

3 *1/2* **Stylistique** 2-9-0 0.................... AndreaAtzeni 10 77
(Roger Varian) *stdd s: hld up in tch in last trio: shkn up and hdwy 2f out: chsd ldng pair 1f out: rn green: hung lft and one pce ins fnl f* **5/2**[1]

0 **4** *1 3/4* **Fast And Free**[14] 4849 2-9-0 0.................... JamesDoyle 5 72
(William Haggas) *pressed ldr tl 2f out: chsd wnr and rdn over 1f out: lost 2nd and unable qck ent fnl f: wl hld and one pce after* **6/1**

5 *3 1/2* **Kalsara** 2-9-0 0.................... RobHornby 8 63
(Andrew Balding) *hld up in tch in midfield: effrt 2f out: rn green: hung lft and outpcd over 1f out: wknd ins fnl f* **12/1**

6 **6** *1 3/4* **Divine Connection**[22] 4502 2-9-0 0.................... TrevorWhelan 1 58
(Jonathan Portman) *hld up in tch in last trio: effrt ent fnl 2f: sn outpcd and hung rt over 1f out: wknd fnl f* **50/1**

7 *2 1/2* **Hiconic** 2-9-0 0.................... DavidProbert 2 52
(Mick Channon) *hld up in tch in midfield: effrt ent fnl 2f: outpcd and btn over 1f out: wknd fnl f* **25/1**

8 *8* **New Tune** 2-9-0 0.................... HarryBentley 6 31
(Ralph Beckett) *jostled and dropped to rr sn after s: nvr travelling wl: lost tch 2f out* **10/1**

9 *1 1/2* **Hot News (IRE)** 2-8-11 0.................... GaryMahon(3) 4 27
(Sylvester Kirk) *taken down early and led to post: led tl 2f out: sn hung lft and wknd: eased ins fnl f* **25/1**

1m 26.79s (-0.21) **Going Correction** +0.075s/f (Good) **9** Ran SP% **116.5**
Speed ratings (Par 93): **104,100,99,97,93 91,88,79,77**
CSF £14.32 TOTE £4.40: £1.70, £1.40, £1.70; EX 11.70 Trifecta £37.40.
Owner Chasemore Farm **Bred** Chasemore Farm **Trained** Malpas, Cheshire

FOCUS
This could be a useful maiden. It was won last year by Star Terms, who was 14-1 to win the 1,000 Guineas in May - and this winner looked useful.

5343 MATTHEW FEDRICK FARRIERY H'CAP 7f (S)

8:10 (8:12) (Class 5) (0-75,77) 3-Y-O+
£3,428 (£1,020; £509; £300; £300; £300) Stalls Centre

Form RPR

3120 **1** **Marshal Dan (IRE)**[19] 4634 4-9-4 **75**.................... StefanoCherchi(7) 6 86
(Heather Main) *awkward leaving stalls: chsd ldr tl led 2f out: sn rdn: r.o wl and a doing enough ins fnl f* **4/1**[3]

4234 **2** *1 1/4* **Majestic Mac**[21] 4546 3-9-6 **77**.................... CharlieBennett 5 82
(Hughie Morrison) *hld up in tch: clsd over 2f out: rdn to chse wnr jst over 1f out: kpt on u.p but a hld ins fnl f* **7/2**[2]

215 **3** *4 1/2* **In The Cove (IRE)**[15] 4789 3-9-2 **73**.................... SeanLevey 3 66
(Richard Hannon) *led tl rdn and hdd 2f out: outpcd and lost 2nd jst over 1f out: wl hld and kpt on same pce ins fnl f* **13/2**

2261 **4** *3/4* **Ragstone View (IRE)**[14] 4838 4-9-11 **75**.................... (h) OisinMurphy 7 69
(Rod Millman) *t.k.h: hld up in tch: effrt ent fnl 2f: outpcd and hung lft over 1f out: no threat to ldrs and kpt on same pce ins fnl f* **5/2**[1]

0301 **5** *hd* **Gambon (GER)**[19] 4655 3-9-6 **77**.................... CharlesBishop 1 67
(Eve Johnson Houghton) *chsd ldrs: effrt ent fnl 2f: unable qck over 1f out: wl hld and kpt on same pce ins fnl f* **5/1**

6560 **6** *6* **Jellmood**[29] 4249 4-9-9 **73**.................... (t) DavidProbert 4 50
(Chris Gordon) *hld up in tch in rr: wnt lft and racd away fr rivals 4f out: unable qck and btn over 1f out: wknd ins fnl f (jockey said gelding hung badly left-handed)* **10/1**

006 **7** *6* **Fly The Nest (IRE)**[52] 3422 3-9-2 **73**.................... TomMarquand 2 31
(Tony Carroll) *rring in stalls: in tch: dropped to rr over 2f out: sn struggling and wl bhd ins fnl f* **33/1**

1m 26.76s (-0.24) **Going Correction** +0.075s/f (Good)
WFA 3 from 4yo 7lb **7** Ran SP% **112.8**
Speed ratings (Par 103): **104,102,97,96,96 89,82**
CSF £17.85 TOTE £4.00: £2.00, £1.70; EX 14.40 Trifecta £81.30.
Owner Coxwell Partnership **Bred** Deerpark Stud **Trained** Kingston Lisle, Oxon

FOCUS
An open-looking race but the finish only concerned the front two as they were some way clear of the rest. The winner rates to a personal best with the jockey's claim.

5344 AJC PREMIER FILLIES' H'CAP 1m 4f

8:40 (8:40) (Class 5) (0-70,71) 3-Y-O+
£3,428 (£1,020; £509; £300; £300; £300) Stalls Low

Form RPR

-353 **1** **Lightening Dance**[24] 4447 5-10-2 **71**.................... (b) JimCrowley 6 78
(Amanda Perrett) *hld up in midfield: clsd and wl in tch 5f out: smooth hdwy to chse ldrs over 2f out: pushed into ld over 1f out: asserted u.p and edgd lft 1f out: kpt on and in command fnl 100yds* **4/1**[3]

0-30 **2** *1 1/4* **Shufoog**[21] 4561 6-9-3 **65**.................... EllieMacKenzie(7) 11 70
(Mark Usher) *stdd s: hld up in rr: clsd and in tch 5f out: nt clrest of runs over 2f out: hdwy and edgd lft 1f out: chsd wnr wl ins fnl f: kpt on but nvr getting to wnr* **20/1**

3154 **3** *1 1/2* **Miss M (IRE)**[7] 5089 5-9-10 **65**.................... JFEgan 2 68
(William Muir) *hld up in midfield: clsd and wl in tch 5f out: smooth hdwy to trck ldr over 2f out: rdn and ev ch over 1f out: unable qck and sltly impeded 1f out: kpt on same pce and lost 2nd wl ins fnl f* **7/2**[2]

434 **4** *1 1/4* **J Gaye (IRE)**[27] 4326 3-9-2 **68**.................... DavidProbert 10 69
(Richard Phillips) *hld up in last trio: clsd and in tch 5f out: effrt on inner over 2f out: swtchd rt 1f out: kpt on same pce u.p ins fnl f* **6/1**

U3/0 **5** *3/4* **Tobougaloo**[33] 4112 8-9-5 **63**.................... WilliamCox(3) 9 62
(Stuart Kittow) *mounted in chute and taken down early: dwlt: hld up in last pair: clsd and in tch 5f out: rdn over 3f out: styd on and edgd lft over 1f out: kpt on same pce ins fnl f (jockey said mare was slowly away)* **14/1**

6-00 **6** *2 1/4* **Midnight Mood**[10] 4991 6-8-11 **52**.................... CallumShepherd 1 48
(Dominic Ffrench Davis) *chsd clr ldng trio: clsd and wl in tch 5f out: nt clr run over 2f out: no imp over 1f out: kpt on same pce ins fnl f* **14/1**

4-63 **7** *nk* **Harmonise**[69] 2793 5-9-10 **65**.................... HectorCrouch 3 60
(Sheena West) *led: rdn over 2f out: hdd over 1f out: no ex and wknd ins fnl f* **3/1**[1]

2215 **8** *13* **Top Rock Talula (IRE)**[50] 2974 4-9-6 **61**.................... (p[1]) OisinMurphy 5 36
(Warren Greatrex) *dwlt: rcvrd and hdwy to chse ldr after over 1f out: lost pl over 2f out: bhd ins fnl f* **7/1**

-250 **9** *1* **Cwynar**[22] 4499 4-9-2 **57**.................... (t) RobHornby 4 30
(Rebecca Curtis) *chsd ldr for over 1f out: styd chsng ldrs tl lost pl over 2f out: bhd and eased ins fnl f* **25/1**

2m 36.22s (-1.78) **Going Correction** +0.075s/f (Good)
WFA 3 from 4yo+ 11lb **9** Ran SP% **115.9**
Speed ratings (Par 100): **108,107,106,105,104 103,103,94,93**
CSF £78.81 CT £307.17 TOTE £3.90: £1.60, £4.50, £1.70; EX 98.30 Trifecta £694.90.
Owner Mrs Alexandra J Chandris **Bred** Mrs J Chandris **Trained** Pulborough, W Sussex

FOCUS
Add 7yds. A modest handicap to end with but a clear-cut winner who's rated back to her best.
T/Jkpt: £938.60 to a £1 stake. Pool: £50,235.52 - 38.00 winning units T/Plt: £14.10 to a £1 stake. Pool: £49,841.16 - 2,574.95 winning units T/Qpdt: £4.50 to a £1 stake. Pool: £5,400.64 - 875.57 winning units **Steve Payne**

5316 SANDOWN (R-H)

Thursday, July 25

OFFICIAL GOING: Good (good to firm in places; watered; 7.3) changing to good to firm (good in places) after race 4 (3.20)
Wind: Moderate, across Weather: 36 degrees

5345 MARTIN DENSHAM MEMORIAL EBF MAIDEN STKS (PLUS 10 RACE) 7f

1:45 (1:46) (Class 4) 2-Y-O £6,792 (£2,021; £1,010; £505) Stalls Low

Form RPR

1 **Kameko (USA)** 2-9-5 0.................... OisinMurphy 7 81+
(Andrew Balding) *quite tall: scope: looked wl: trckd ldng trio: pushed along and prog jst over 2f out: shkn up to ld jst over 1f out: r.o and in command though ld dwindled nr fin* **15/2**

2 *1/2* **It's Good To Laugh (IRE)** 2-9-5 0.................... AdamKirby 2 80+
(Clive Cox) *str: looked wl: dwlt: sn in 5th: pushed along over 2f out: prog on wd outside over 1f out: tk 2nd fnl 100yds: r.o and clsd on wnr but nvr quite got there* **7/1**

3 *3 3/4* **No Show (IRE)** 2-9-5 0.................... AndreaAtzeni 8 70
(Richard Hannon) *compact: trckd ldr: led jst over 2f out and sent for home: hdd and one pce jst over 1f out* **5/1**[3]

4 *4* **Mephisto (IRE)** 2-9-5 0.................... HarryBentley 6 60
(Ralph Beckett) *quite ly: coltish: slow to get gng: mostly in last pair: shkn up and no prog over 2f out: passed rivals to take modest 4th nr fin* **12/1**

5 *1/2* **Star Of Wells (IRE)** 2-9-5 0.................... JamesDoyle 3 58+
(William Haggas) *quite str: sn in last pair: effrt on outer over 2f out: no prog over 1f out: sn lft wl bhd* **13/8**[1]

6 *nse* **Jack Ruby (IRE)** 2-9-5 0.................... SeanLevey 4 58
(Richard Hannon) *compact: nvr beyond midfield: hanging and green whn shkn up over 2f out: lft bhd over 1f out* **14/1**

0 **7** *nk* **Kentucky Hardboot (IRE)**[12] 4897 2-9-5 0.................... CallumShepherd 1 57
(Mick Channon) *workmanlike: bit on the leg: chsd ldng pair: shkn up over 2f out: wknd over 1f out* **16/1**

8 *8* **Unresolved** 2-9-5 0.................... SilvestreDeSousa 5 37
(Mark Johnston) *quite str: led to jst over 2f out: wknd rapidly over 1f out* **9/2**[2]

1m 30.2s (0.90) **Going Correction** -0.075s/f (Good) **8** Ran SP% **117.4**
Speed ratings (Par 96): **91,90,86,81,81 80,80,71**
CSF £60.04 TOTE £7.40: £1.80, £2.50, £1.90; EX 68.70 Trifecta £866.00.
Owner Qatar Racing Limited **Bred** Calumet Farm **Trained** Kingsclere, Hants

The Form Book Flat 2019, Raceform Ltd, Newbury, RG14 5SJ

FOCUS
2.5mm of irrigation was applied to the back and home straight overnight. A scorching day at the Esher venue, with 16yds added to this maiden for rail movements. Some well-bred horses on show and this looks sure to be informative going forward. The front two pulled clear of the remainder.

5346 BRITISH STALLION STUDS EBF STAR STKS (LISTED RACE) (FILLIES) 7f
2:15 (2:20) (Class 1) 2-Y-O

£17,013 (£6,450; £3,228; £1,608; £807; £405) **Stalls** Low

Form RPR

211 **1** **Walk In Marrakesh (IRE)**[10] 4976 2-9-0 0 FrankieDettori 6 99
(Mark Johnston) *athletic: mde all: stretched 2 l clr 2f out: drvn fnl f as pack clsd: clung on nr fin* **2/1**[2]

1 **2** ½ **Light Blush (IRE)**[12] 4918 2-9-0 0 JamesDoyle 4 98
(Charlie Appleby) *athletic: trckd ldng pair: shkn up to take 2nd 2f out: clsd w others fnl f: jst hld* **15/8**[1]

1 **3** *hd* **Rhea**[62] 3049 2-9-0 0 AndreaAtzeni 2 97+
(Kevin Ryan) *quite tall: s.i.s: mostly in last pair: pushed along over 2f out: no prog over 1f out and struggling: styd on wl fnl 100yds: gaining at fin* **9/1**

31 **4** ¾ **Romsey**[47] 3578 2-9-0 0 OisinMurphy 1 95
(Hughie Morrison) *ly: cl up: pushed along over 2f out: clsd w others on wnr fnl f: keeping on but hld whn short of room nr fin* **7/1**[3]

1 **5** ½ **West End Girl**[20] 4605 2-9-0 0 SilvestreDeSousa 5 97
(Mark Johnston) *str: t.k.h: trckd wnr to 2f out: clsd w others fnl f: stl disputing 2nd and keeping on whn nt clr run and then hmpd fnl 75yds* **9/1**

12 **6** ½ **Ursulina (IRE)**[26] 4387 2-9-0 0 RichardKingscote 3 93
(Tom Dascombe) *leggy: sltly on toes: sweating: a in last pair: pushed along 3f out: detached in last jst over 1f out: styd on wl nr fin* **7/1**[3]

1m 29.53s (0.23) **Going Correction** -0.075s/f (Good) **6** Ran SP% **113.1**
Speed ratings (Par 99): **95,94,94,93,92 92**
CSF £6.27 TOTE £2.60: £1.60, £1.80; EX 7.10 Trifecta £24.70.
Owner Merriebelle Irish Farm Limited **Bred** Merriebelle Irish Farm Ltd **Trained** Middleham Moor, N Yorks

FOCUS
Add 16yds for this competitive renewal of the Listed fillies' event in which they went a decent gallop. The winner made the most of poaching a healthy lead at the 2f pole but was hanging on at the end. Billesdon Brook was third in this before winning the 1000 Guineas so it could pay to follow the form of this.

5347 YOUNG STAYERS H'CAP 1m 6f
2:50 (2:55) (Class 3) (0-95,93) 3-Y-O

£18,675 (£5,592; £2,796; £1,398; £699; £351) **Stalls** Low

Form RPR

6431 **1** **Just Hubert (IRE)**[17] 4729 3-8-9 81 TomMarquand 3 90
(William Muir) *looked wl: hld up in 5th: rdn 3f out as ldrs wnt for home: prog 2f out to ld over 1f out: hrd pressed ins fnl f: abt a nk up whn swvd bdly lft 50yds out* **10/1**

01-6 **2** ½ **Buckman Tavern (FR)**[54] 3337 3-8-5 77 NicolaCurrie 6 85+
(Sir Mark Prescott Bt) *stdd s: hld up in last: rdn over 3f out as ldrs wnt for home: prog 2f out: plld out and drvn to chse ldr ins fnl f: clsng and abt a nk down whn hmpd 50yds out* **8/1**

441 **3** 3 **Space Walk**[33] 4104 3-8-8 80 (t) OisinMurphy 2 84+
(William Haggas) *sweating: won fierce early battle for ld: stdd pce after 4f but hdd 1/2-way: trckd ldr tl led over 2f out: hdd over 1f out: fdd* **11/8**[1]

-051 **4** 4 **State Of Affair (USA)**[21] 4549 3-8-6 78 AndreaAtzeni 5 76+
(Ed Walker) *sweating: hld up in 4th: swift move to ld 1/2-way: rdn and hdd over 2f out: wknd over 1f out* **6/1**[3]

0352 **5** ½ **Fraser Island (IRE)**[10] 4996 3-8-7 79 SilvestreDeSousa 1 77
(Mark Johnston) *looked wl: tried to ld but unable to: chsd ldng pair to 1/2-way: rdn wl over 2f out: wknd over 1f out* **7/1**

1304 **6** 140 **Summer Moon**[19] 4644 3-9-7 93 FrankieDettori 4
(Mark Johnston) *tried to ld but unable to do so: chsd ldr to 1/2-way: wknd over 4f out: virtually p.u fnl 3f (jockey said colt stopped quickly; post-race examination failed to reveal any abnormalities)* **3/1**[2]

3m 1.08s (-4.92) **Going Correction** -0.075s/f (Good) course record **6** Ran SP% **114.1**
Speed ratings (Par 104): **111,110,109,106,106**
CSF £82.78 TOTE £9.60: £3.10, £3.90; EX 77.10 Trifecta £247.40.
Owner Foursome Thoroughbreds **Bred** Ringfort Stud **Trained** Lambourn, Berks

FOCUS
Add 16yds. A decent staying handicap for 3yos. A strong gallop was evident throughout and the winner had to survive a stewards' enquiry. There was a new course record of 3mins 1.08secs. It's usually a good race and has been rated in line with that despite the market 1-2 not being at their best.

5348 HAMPTON COURT H'CAP 1m 1f 209y
3:20 (3:29) (Class 4) (0-85,85) 3-Y-O+

£6,469 (£1,925; £962; £481; £300; £300) **Stalls** Low

Form RPR

135 **1** **Victory Chime (IRE)**[15] 4792 4-9-10 81 (v[1]) HarryBentley 5 91
(Ralph Beckett) *sn led: rdn and hdd wl over 1f out: pressed ldr after: n.m.r against rail but drvn ahd again ins fnl f: kpt on stoutly* **12/1**[3]

1-31 **2** ½ **Marronnier (IRE)**[19] 4671 3-9-1 81 (t) OisinMurphy 4 90
(Stuart Williams) *rrd sltly s: sn prom: trckd wnr after 2f: shkn up to ld wl over 1f out: pressed after and sed hanging rt: hdd and outbattled ins fnl f (jockey said gelding hung right-handed)* **5/6**[1]

0/11 **3** 6 **Match Maker (IRE)**[14] 4841 4-10-0 85 (t) JamesDoyle 6 82
(Simon Crisford) *looked wl: hld up in detached last: rdn over 2f out: mod prog to take 3rd jst over 1f out but ldng pair clr: no imp after* **2/1**[2]

2134 **4** 3 **Water's Edge (IRE)**[119] 1386 3-8-10 76 NicolaCurrie 1 67
(George Baker) *trckd ldr 2f: styd cl up: rdn over 2f out: wknd over 1f out* **25/1**

1-30 **5** 2 ¾ **Mainsail Atlantic (USA)**[29] 4250 4-9-10 81 (p[1]) AdamKirby 3 67
(James Fanshawe) *w ldrs 1f but sn settled in 4th: rdn over 2f out: outpcd by ldng pair wl over 1f out: wknd* **14/1**

6345 **6** 7 **Wimpole Hall**[29] 4250 6-9-7 78 (b) SilvestreDeSousa 2 58
(William Jarvis) *hld up in 5th: dropped to last over 2f out: nt clr run briefly sn after and again wl over 1f out: no ch after and eased (jockey said gelding ran flat)* **12/1**[3]

2m 7.08s (-3.12) **Going Correction** -0.075s/f (Good)
WFA 3 from 4yo+ 9lb **6** Ran SP% **113.8**
Speed ratings (Par 105): **109,108,103,101,99 93**
CSF £23.34 TOTE £13.70: £4.70, £1.10; EX 31.20 Trifecta £76.50.
Owner A Nevin **Bred** M Downey & Kildaragh Stud **Trained** Kimpton, Hants

FOCUS
Add 16yds for this competitive middle-distance handicap. The front two had it between them from some way out and the winner's rated in line with his Leicester form.

5349 TWICKENHAM FILLIES' H'CAP 1m 1f 209y
3:55 (4:01) (Class 5) (0-75,73) 3-Y-O

£4,528 (£1,347; £673; £336; £300; £300) **Stalls** Low

Form RPR

0512 **1** **Confils (FR)**[22] 4498 3-8-4 61 CierenFallon(5) 6 70
(George Baker) *hld up in last: pushed along over 2f out: stdy prog wl over 1f out: rdn and produced between rivals to ld fnl 150yds: styd on wl* **11/2**

4-34 **2** 1 ¾ **Alandalos**[28] 4305 3-9-7 73 JimCrowley 3 78
(Charles Hills) *looked wl: led 3f: pressed ldr: shkn up to ld jst over 2f out: drvn and pressed over 1f out: kpt on but hdd and outpcd fnl 150yds* **3/1**[2]

4542 **3** 1 ¾ **Lady Mascara**[19] 4664 3-9-4 70 OisinMurphy 1 72
(James Fanshawe) *trckd ldrs: shkn up over 2f out: clsd to chal over 1f out: nt qckn and outpcd in 3rd fnl f (jockey said filly hung left-handed under pressure)* **5/2**[1]

0163 **4** 3 ¼ **Amorously (IRE)**[25] 4424 3-9-7 73 SeanLevey 4 68
(Richard Hannon) *t.k.h: hld up in tch: rdn on outer over 2f out: no imp jst over 1f out: wknd fnl f* **8/1**

-530 **5** *hd* **Tronada**[19] 4663 3-9-6 72 TomMarquand 7 67
(Alan King) *trckd ldng pair: rdn to chal over 2f out to over 1f out: wknd fnl f (jockey said filly hung left-handed throughout)* **14/1**

4-36 **6** 1 ¼ **Innocent (IRE)**[33] 4110 3-9-7 73 HarryBentley 2 65
(Ralph Beckett) *led after 3f to jst over 2f out: wknd over 1f out* **6/1**

004 **7** ½ **Daryana**[27] 4341 3-9-7 73 CharlesBishop 5 64
(Eve Johnson Houghton) *compact: sn hld up in last pair: dropped to last 4f out: detached and struggling 3f out: no prog after* **5/1**[3]

2m 8.82s (-1.38) **Going Correction** -0.075s/f (Good) **7** Ran SP% **117.7**
Speed ratings (Par 97): **102,100,99,96,96 95,95**
CSF £23.36 TOTE £6.30: £2.80, £2.20; EX 29.70 Trifecta £60.00.
Owner Confidence Partnership **Bred** E A R L Haras De Mandore **Trained** Chiddingfold, Surrey

FOCUS
Add 16yds. Just a modest fillies' handicap and the bottom weight proved best under a good ride.

5350 CHRISTMAS PARTIES AT SANDOWN PARK H'CAP 1m
4:25 (4:30) (Class 5) (0-75,76) 3-Y-O

£4,528 (£1,347; £673; £336; £300; £300) **Stalls** Low

Form RPR

-342 **1** **Eligible (IRE)**[15] 4788 3-9-10 76 AdamKirby 3 84
(Clive Cox) *trckd ldng pair: plld out and shkn up 2f out: led over 1f out: drvn and styd on wl fnl f* **7/4**[1]

33-2 **2** 2 **Quarry Beach**[21] 4562 3-9-5 71 DavidProbert 8 74
(Henry Candy) *hld up in 6th: effrt on outer 2f out: drvn and prog over 1f out: styd on to take 2nd nr fin but wnr beyond recall* **5/2**[2]

-203 **3** *nk* **Kings Royal Hussar (FR)**[19] 4664 3-9-2 68 TomMarquand 7 71
(Alan King) *sweating: stdd s: hld up in last: rdn 2f out: prog over 1f out: r.o to take 3rd last strides: too late to threaten* **15/2**

5045 **4** *nk* **Flying Dragon (FR)**[7] 5085 3-9-5 71 SeanLevey 4 73
(Richard Hannon) *trckd ldr: led 2f out: rdn and hdd over 1f out: one pce fnl f and lost 2 pls nr fin* **5/1**[3]

0551 **5** 2 ½ **Black Medick**[24] 4453 3-9-7 73 LiamJones 6 69
(Laura Mongan) *stdd s: hld up in 5th: pushed along 2f out: no prog and no ch whn rdn fnl f* **25/1**

465- **6** 1 **Lolita Pulido (IRE)**[363] 5429 3-9-4 70 CharlesBishop 5 64
(Eve Johnson Houghton) *trckd ldng trio: pushed along over 2f out: steadily fdd over 1f out* **20/1**

0330 **7** 2 ¾ **Sassoon**[46] 3638 3-9-6 72 (p) JimCrowley 1 60
(Paul Cole) *led at mod pce: shkn up and hdd 2f out: wknd jst over 1f out* **7/1**

1m 44.46s (1.16) **Going Correction** -0.075s/f (Good) **7** Ran SP% **114.5**
Speed ratings (Par 100): **91,89,88,88,85 84,82**
CSF £6.32 CT £24.16 TOTE £2.40: £1.30, £2.10; EX 6.30 Trifecta £29.40.
Owner A D Spence **Bred** Nick Bradley Bloodstock **Trained** Lambourn, Berks

FOCUS
Add 16yds. A fair mile handicap and the winner finished with something in hand. The first two are improving.

5351 MOLSON COORS H'CAP 7f
5:00 (5:05) (Class 5) (0-75,75) 3-Y-O+

£4,528 (£1,347; £673; £336; £300; £300) **Stalls** Low

Form RPR

6-21 **1** **Bring Us Paradise**[37] 3964 3-8-6 65 CierenFallon(5) 4 72+
(Tony Carroll) *hld up in 6th: shkn up and prog 2f out: hanging lft but led 1f out: hung lft but styd on wl and in command after (jockey said gelding hung left-handed)* **9/4**[1]

2105 **2** 1 ½ **Delicate Kiss**[6] 5136 5-9-10 71 (b) LiamJones 7 76
(John Bridger) *hld up in last trio: prog on outer jst over 2f out: tried to chal jst over 1f out: nt pce of wnr but kpt on wl to take 2nd last strides* **20/1**

5136 **3** ½ **Perfect Symphony (IRE)**[14] 4833 5-8-8 62 IsobelFrancis(7) 9 66
(Mark Pattinson) *racd on outer: trckd ldng pair: wd bnd 4f out: chal over 1f out: upsides sn after: outpcd fnl f: lost 2nd last strides* **25/1**

4005 **4** *nse* **Oloroso (IRE)**[27] 4316 3-9-4 75 JoshuaBryan(3) 1 76
(Andrew Balding) *t.k.h: led: kpt on whn pressed 2f out: hdd 1f out: veered lft briefly ins fnl f: kpt on* **11/4**[2]

0341 **5** 5 **Chikoko Trail**[15] 4797 4-9-6 67 HectorCrouch 8 59
(Gary Moore) *awkward s: chsd ldr: chal 2f out: lost 2nd and wknd over 1f out* **11/2**[3]

-633 **6** 1 **Roller**[27] 4319 6-9-10 74 (p) GeorgiaCox(3) 2 64
(Mark Loughnane) *t.k.h: hld up in last pair: struggling on inner and dropped to last 2f out: nvr on terms after* **7/1**

-000 **7** ½ **Another Boy**[30] 4226 6-8-10 57 (p) HarryBentley 6 46
(Ralph Beckett) *chsd ldrs in 5th: rdn and no prog 2f out: wknd over 1f out* **8/1**

21-5 **8** 3 ¼ **Wild Dancer**[29] 4247 6-9-4 65 JoeyHaynes 5 46
(Patrick Chamings) *hld up in last: drvn and no prog 2f out: wknd over 1f out* **10/1**

1005 **9** 4 **Chevallier**[14] 4833 7-9-13 74 (p) AdamKirby 3 46
(Michael Attwater) *trckd ldng pair to over 2f out: wknd qckly* **16/1**

1m 28.09s (-1.21) **Going Correction** -0.075s/f (Good)
WFA 3 from 4yo+ 7lb **9** Ran SP% **120.0**
Speed ratings (Par 103): **103,101,100,100,94 93,93,89,84**
CSF £51.80 CT £931.80 TOTE £3.20: £1.50, £4.50, £6.70; EX 54.10 Trifecta £1124.40.
Owner D Boocock **Bred** Boocock Trading Ltd **Trained** Cropthorne, Worcs
■ Stewards' Enquiry : Isobel Francis caution: careless riding

FOCUS
Add 16yds for this moderate handicap, won by a 3yo receiving a weight-for-age allowance. Ordinary form for the track.
T/Plt: £197.50 to a £1 stake. Pool: £54,552.25 - 201.62 winning units T/Qpdt: £43.10 to a £1 stake. Pool: £5,479.86 - 94.04 winning units **Jonathan Neesom**

5058 YARMOUTH (L-H)
Thursday, July 25

OFFICIAL GOING: Good to firm (watered; 7.4)
Wind: Light across Weather: Fine

5352 HAVEN SEASHORE HOLIDAY PARK H'CAP — 6f 3y
2:05 (2:12) (Class 6) (0-65,67) 3-Y-O+
£2,781 (£827; £413; £300; £300; £300) **Stalls** Centre

Form — RPR
0322 **1** **Sweet Forgetme Not (IRE)**[8] 5063 3-8-4 **48**.....(vt[1]) JosephineGordon 6 — 53
(Phil McEntee) *prom: shkn up over 2f out: chsd ldr over 1f out: rdn to ld and hung rt wl ins fnl f: styd on* **6/1**[3]
005 **2** *nk* **Case Key**[7] 5107 6-9-4 **64**.....(b[1]) KieranSchofield[(7)] 4 — 69
(Michael Appleby) *w ldr: led 5f out: rdn over 1f out: hung rt and hdd wl ins fnl f: styd on* **16/1**
465 **3** *2* **Tulloona**[28] 4286 3-9-7 **65**..... JackMitchell 9 — 63
(Tom Clover) *s.i.s: sn prom: rdn over 1f out: styd on* **13/2**
3210 **4** *1 1/4* **Princess Keira (IRE)**[17] 4733 4-9-11 **64**..... PatCosgrave 5 — 59
(Mick Quinn) *hld up: hdwy over 1f out: sn rdn: styd on same pce wl ins fnl f* **4/1**[2]
0-10 **5** *1/2* **Desert Fox**[59] 3147 5-10-0 **67**..... RossaRyan 2 — 61
(Mike Murphy) *hmpd s: hld up: hdwy over 1f out: rdn and no ex wl ins fnl f* **8/1**
0300 **6** *1 1/4* **Kraka (IRE)**[28] 4307 4-9-12 **65**.....(p) KieranO'Neill 3 — 55
(Christine Dunnett) *edgd lft s: led 1f: chsd ldr: rdn over 2f out: lost 2nd over 1f out: no ex ins fnl f* **12/1**
-602 **7** *6* **Lilbourne Star (IRE)**[7] 5107 4-9-5 **65**..... AmeliaGlass[(7)] 1 — 37
(Clive Cox) *hld up: racd keenly: hdwy over 4f out: wknd fnl f (jockey said gelding hung right-handed. trainer rep said gelding was unsuited by Good to Firm ground on this occasion and would prefer a slower surface)* **6/4**[1]
4000 **8** *3* **Budaiya Fort (IRE)**[42] 3775 3-8-1 **48**.....(p) SeanDavis[(3)] 8 — 10
(Phil McEntee) *in rr and pushed along over 3f out: wknd over 2f out* **40/1**
1304 **9** *1 1/2* **Time To Reason (IRE)**[35] 4027 6-9-6 **64**.....(p) DylanHogan[(5)] 7 — 23
(Charlie Wallis) *hld up: wknd over 2f out* **33/1**

1m 11.93s (-0.67) **Going Correction** +0.025s/f (Good)
WFA 3 from 4yo+ 5lb — **9** Ran SP% **117.7**
Speed ratings (Par 101): **105,104,101,100,99 97,89,85,83**
CSF £97.01 CT £651.73 TOTE £4.70: £1.70, £3.10, £2.10; EX 63.00 Trifecta £463.20.
Owner Miss Robin Blaze McEntee **Bred** M Morrissey **Trained** Newmarket, Suffolk

FOCUS
Nothing more than moderate sprinting form. Horses wearing first-time headgear dominated the finish.

5353 INJURED JOCKEYS FUND NOVICE AUCTION STKS (PLUS 10 RACE) — 6f 3y
2:35 (2:41) (Class 4) 2-Y-O — **£4,463** (£1,328; £663; £331) **Stalls** Centre

Form — RPR
2 **1** **Nirodha (IRE)**[16] 4766 2-8-7 0..... SeanDavis[(3)] 1 — 72
(Amy Murphy) *chsd ldr: rdn to ld over 1f out: styd on* **3/1**[2]
2 *nk* **River Cam** 2-9-0 0..... PJMcDonald 4 — 75+
(James Tate) *s.i.s: sn prom: swtchd rt over 3f out: chsd wnr ins fnl f: r.o* **4/7**[1]
0640 **3** *3 3/4* **Craigburn**[19] 4647 2-8-12 66..... JackMitchell 3 — 62
(Tom Clover) *led: rdn and hdd over 1f out: no ex ins fnl f* **6/1**[3]
4 *hd* **Robert Frost (USA)** 2-8-12 0..... CameronNoble[(3)] 5 — 64+
(Jane Chapple-Hyam) *s.i.s: sn chsng ldrs: shkn up over 1f out: styd on same pce fnl f* **12/1**
00 **5** *8* **Conker**[15] 4802 2-9-0 0..... DylanHogan[(5)] 2 — 44
(Charlie Wallis) *rrd s: hld up: rdn and wknd over 1f out* **80/1**

1m 14.58s (1.98) **Going Correction** +0.025s/f (Good) — **5** Ran SP% **111.9**
Speed ratings (Par 96): **87,86,81,81,70**
CSF £5.24 TOTE £3.90: £2.20, £1.10; EX 6.50 Trifecta £10.30.
Owner Daniel Macauliffe & Anoj Don **Bred** Leaf Stud **Trained** Newmarket, Suffolk

FOCUS
A weak novice auction event, in which two came slightly away from the remainder.

5354 WELL BALANCED LEDGER H'CAP — 1m 2f 23y
3:10 (3:10) (Class 6) (0-65,67) 3-Y-O+
£2,781 (£827; £413; £300; £300; £300) **Stalls** Low

Form — RPR
3-60 **1** **Go Fox**[30] 4220 4-10-1 **66**..... JackMitchell 2 — 72
(Tom Clover) *chsd ldrs: lost grnd on front pair over 7f out: tk clsr order and swtchd to r alone far side over 3f out: rdn to chse ldr over 1f out: styd on to ld wl ins fnl f (trainer said, regarding apparent improvement in form, that gelding had benefitted from the return to good to firm ground having finished unplaced on good to soft ground last time out)* **4/1**[3]
3002 **2** *1 3/4* **Hidden Dream (IRE)**[21] 4568 4-8-9 **46**.....(p) KieranO'Neill 3 — 49
(Christine Dunnett) *chsd ldrs: lost grnd on front pair over 7f out: tk clsr order over 4f out: led over 2f out: rdn and hdd ins fnl f (vet said filly lost left hind shoe)* **8/1**
0425 **3** *1 1/2* **Percy Toplis**[15] 4801 5-8-9 **46** oh1.....(b) EoinWalsh 1 — 46
(Christine Dunnett) *s.s: hld up: rdn over 3f out: hdwy over 1f out: styd on to go 3rd post: nt rch ldrs* **50/1**
0620 **4** *hd* **Contingency Fee**[9] 5025 4-9-2 **60**.....(p) GraceMcEntee[(7)] 6 — 59
(Phil McEntee) *sn pushed along to ld: wnt clr w one rival over 7f out tl over 4f out: rdn and hdd over 2f out: styd on same pce fnl f* **22/1**
3004 **5** *4 1/2* **Homesick Boy (IRE)**[27] 4346 3-8-11 **57**..... JamieSpencer 9 — 49
(Ed Dunlop) *s.i.s: hld up: rdn over 1f out: nvr nrr* **4/1**[3]
0636 **6** *1/2* **Cedar**[14] 4836 3-7-13 **50** ow2.....(t) DarraghKeenan[(5)] 7 — 41
(Mohamed Moubarak) *sn w ldr: wnt clr w ldr over 7f out tl over 4f out: ev ch over 2f out: sn edgd rt: wknd over 1f out* **16/1**
062 **7** *1* **Winterkoenigin**[15] 4801 3-9-7 **67**.....(p) DanielMuscutt 8 — 56
(David Lanigan) *stdd s: hld up: rdn over 1f out: n.d* **5/2**[1]
6-00 **8** *1 1/4* **Right About Now (IRE)**[43] 3744 5-9-9 **65**..... DylanHogan[(5)] 5 — 51
(Charlie Wallis) *hld up: rdn over 3f out: n.d (vet said gelding lost left hind shoe)* **33/1**
1412 **9** *49* **Act Of Magic (IRE)**[54] 3348 3-9-1 **64**..... SeanDavis[(3)] 4
(Mohamed Moubarak) *s.i.s: sn pushed along in rr: wknd and eased over 1f out (jockey said gelding moved poorly throughout the race and lost action when turning into home str; post-race examination failed to reveal any abnormalities)* **3/1**[2]

2m 8.54s (-0.26) **Going Correction** +0.025s/f (Good)
WFA 3 from 4yo+ 9lb — **9** Ran SP% **119.8**
Speed ratings (Par 101): **102,100,99,99,95 95,94,93,54**
CSF £36.50 CT £1406.83 TOTE £4.80: £1.50, £2.20, £12.80; EX 36.10 Trifecta £2058.20.
Owner R & S Marchant, C Holmes & G Jarvis **Bred** Whitsbury Manor Stud And Mrs M E Slade **Trained** Newmarket, Suffolk

FOCUS
Add 10yds, making the official distance 1m2f 33yds. If you were held up in this, behind what looked a good pace, you had no chance.

5355 JOHN KEMP 4 X 4 CENTRE OF NORWICH MAIDEN H'CAP — 1m 3f 104y
3:40 (3:41) (Class 5) (0-75,75) 3-Y-O+
£3,428 (£1,020; £509; £300; £300; £300) **Stalls** Low

Form — RPR
5222 **1** **Starczewski (USA)**[21] 4549 3-9-4 **72**..... JamieSpencer 4 — 78+
(David Simcock) *stdd s: hld up: hdwy over 2f out: rdn to ld and hung lft wl ins fnl f: styd on (vet said gelding lost right-hind shoe)* **11/8**[1]
0352 **2** *1 1/4* **Starfighter**[14] 4841 3-9-7 **75**..... PJMcDonald 3 — 79
(Ed Walker) *hld up: hdwy over 2f out: led wl over 1f out: sn rdn and hung rt: hdd and unable qck wl ins fnl f* **2/1**[2]
-343 **3** *1/2* **Fragrant Dawn**[19] 4663 3-9-5 **73**..... DanielMuscutt 7 — 76
(Charles Hills) *led 10f out: hung rt almost thrght: rdn and hdd wl over 1f out: ev ch whn hmpd and rdr dropped whip ins fnl f: styd on same pce (jockey said filly hung badly right-handed)* **9/1**
0023 **4** *7* **Monsieur Lambrays**[27] 4339 3-9-6 **74**.....(b[1]) JackMitchell 1 — 66
(Tom Clover) *hld up: effrt over 2f out: nt clr run sn after: sn btn* **4/1**[3]
4-00 **5** *1/2* **Guroor**[33] 4110 3-8-9 **70**.....(h) StefanoCherchi[(7)] 6 — 61
(Marco Botti) *chsd ldr: rdn over 2f out: wknd fnl f* **25/1**
5560 **6** *1* **Tajdeed (IRE)**[9] 5025 4-9-1 **62**..... SeanDavis[(3)] 5 — 50
(Michael Appleby) *led: hdd 10f out: chsd ldrs: rdn over 2f out: wknd fnl f* **33/1**

2m 25.8s (-2.00) **Going Correction** +0.025s/f (Good)
WFA 3 from 4yo 10lb — **6** Ran SP% **112.2**
Speed ratings (Par 103): **108,107,106,101,101 100**
CSF £4.36 TOTE £2.20: £1.20, £1.40; EX 4.30 Trifecta £12.40.
Owner Jos & Mrs Jane Rodosthenous **Bred** Nesco II Limited **Trained** Newmarket, Suffolk

FOCUS
Add 10yds, making the official distance 1m3f 114yds. This was a fair handicap but it remains to be seen whether many of those beaten secure a win anytime soon. The form's rated around the second and third.

5356 MARTIN FOULGER MEMORIAL H'CAP — 5f 42y
4:15 (4:15) (Class 4) (0-80,81) 3-Y-O
£5,207 (£1,549; £774; £387; £300; £300) **Stalls** Centre

Form — RPR
6230 **1** **Thegreatestshowman**[26] 4368 3-9-6 **78**..... JackMitchell 4 — 86
(Amy Murphy) *hld up in tch: plld hrd: led over 1f out: drvn out: edgd lft towards fin* **10/3**[2]
1051 **2** *1* **Tone The Barone**[8] 5064 3-8-9 **67** 6ex.....(t) PJMcDonald 2 — 71
(Stuart Williams) *hld up in tch: rdn and ev ch ins fnl f: no ex towards fin* **11/8**[1]
2431 **3** *1/2* **Enchanted Linda**[15] 4783 3-9-4 **79**..... SeanDavis[(3)] 3 — 81
(Michael Herrington) *w ldrs: led wl over 1f out: sn rdn and hdd: styd on same pce wl ins fnl f* **9/1**
2623 **4** *1* **Mr Buttons (IRE)**[20] 4604 3-9-3 **75**..... ShaneKelly 5 — 74
(Linda Stubbs) *led: hdd over 4f out: remained w ldr: rdn over 1f out: styd on same pce ins fnl f* **15/2**
6201 **5** *shd* **Major Blue**[16] 4757 3-9-2 **74**.....(b) RyanTate 7 — 75+
(James Eustace) *s.i.s: plld hrd and sn prom: nt clr run fr over 1f out tl swtchd lft ins fnl f: nt trble ldrs (jockey said gelding ran too freely in early stages and was denied a clear run)* **7/1**
225 **6** *2 3/4* **True Hero**[20] 4604 3-9-4 **81**..... FayeMcManoman[(5)] 6 — 69
(Nigel Tinkler) *plld hrd: led over 4f out: hdd wl over 1f out: wknd ins fnl f (jockey said gelding ran too freely)* **6/1**[3]

1m 1.44s (-0.46) **Going Correction** +0.025s/f (Good) — **6** Ran SP% **113.7**
Speed ratings (Par 102): **104,102,101,100,99 95**
CSF £8.55 TOTE £3.30: £1.40, £1.80; EX 9.60 Trifecta £59.40.
Owner Amy Murphy **Bred** Biddestone Stud Ltd **Trained** Newmarket, Suffolk

FOCUS
The three that stayed more towards the middle of the track seemed to have an advantage over the other three. The winner bounced back from a lesser effort.

5357 GROSVENOR CASINO OF GREAT YARMOUTH FILLIES' NOVICE STKS — 6f 3y
4:45 (4:46) (Class 5) 3-4-Y-O — **£3,428** (£1,020; £509; £254) **Stalls** Centre

Form — RPR
-542 **1** **Mrs Discombe**[28] 4297 3-8-11 72..... PatCosgrave 5 — 72
(Mick Quinn) *mde all: rdn over 1f out: r.o wl* **7/2**[1]
31 **2** *2* **Fashionesque (IRE)**[33] 4129 3-9-2 0..... ConnorBeasley 6 — 71
(Rae Guest) *prom: chsd wnr over 3f out: rdn over 1f out: styd on same pce wl ins fnl f* **9/2**[2]
3 *nk* **Sloane Garden** 3-8-11 0..... PJMcDonald 3 — 65
(James Tate) *s.i.s: hld up: shkn up and hdwy over 1f out: edgd lft and styd on same pce wl ins fnl f* **7/2**[1]
60- **4** *3/4* **Geneva Spur (USA)**[227] 9484 3-8-11 0..... JackMitchell 1 — 62+
(Roger Varian) *chsd wnr tl over 3f out: rdn over 1f out: no ex wl ins fnl f* **8/1**[3]
6- **5** *14* **Danzena**[279] 8390 4-9-2 0..... AlistairRawlinson 2 — 18
(Michael Appleby) *hld up: plld hrd: rdn and wknd over 1f out* **25/1**

1m 12.77s (0.17) **Going Correction** +0.025s/f (Good)
WFA 3 from 4yo 5lb — **5** Ran SP% **77.6**
Speed ratings (Par 100): **99,96,95,94,76**
CSF £8.89 TOTE £2.90: £1.40, £1.30; EX 7.10 Trifecta £16.10.
Owner Kenny Bruce **Bred** Dalwhinnie Bloodstock **Trained** Newmarket, Suffolk

■ Lady Bowthorpe was withdrawn, price at time of withdrawal 7/4f. Rule 4 applies to all bets. Deduction of 35p in the pound.

FOCUS
An ordinary race of its type and there was drama at the start when market leader Lady Bowthorpe unshipped Jamie Spencer, meaning they didn't take part. Straightforward form.

5358 BBC RADIO NORFOLK MAIDEN H'CAP 7f 3y
5:20 (5:20) (Class 5) (0-70,65) 3-Y-O+
£3,428 (£1,020; £509; £300; £300; £300) Stalls Centre

Form RPR

04-0 1 **Rita's Folly**[42] [3780] 3-8-7 **56**........................ DarraghKeenan(5) 5 60
(Anthony Carson) *chsd ldrs: rdn and edgd lft ins fnl f: r.o to ld nr fin (trainer rep said, regarding improvement in form, filly appreciated the return to Good to Firm going on this occasion, having previously finished unplaced on Soft last time out. he further added, filly appreciated drop in trip from 1m to 7f and the yard* **9/1**

-000 2 *shd* **Secret Treaties**[27] [4328] 3-8-8 **52**........................ KieranO'Neill 1 55
(Christine Dunnett) *edgd rt s: led 1f: chsd ldr tl led again over 2f out: rdn over 1f out: hdd nr fin* **22/1**

-002 3 *½* **Crackin Dream (IRE)**[8] [5050] 3-9-7 **65**........................ PatCosgrave 2 67
(Clive Cox) *hmpd s: hld up in tch: rdn and ev ch fr over 1f out: unable qck nr fin* **10/11**[1]

45-0 4 *1 ½* **Reddiac (IRE)**[51] [3440] 3-9-5 **63**........................ PJMcDonald 6 61
(Ed Dunlop) *hld up: rdn over 1f out: r.o ins fnl f: nt rch ldrs* **7/2**[2]

00-5 5 *¾* **Ample Plenty**[180] [437] 3-8-10 **59**........................ DylanHogan(5) 4 55
(David Simcock) *hld up: hdwy over 2f out: rdn over 1f out: styd on same pce ins fnl f* **7/1**[3]

0-00 6 *8* **Mallons Spirit (IRE)**[52] [3421] 3-7-9 **46**........................ KieranSchofield(7) 3 20
(Michael Appleby) *trckd ldrs: racd keenly: abt to be rdn whn rdr dropped whip over 1f out: wknd ins fnl f* **10/1**

0-00 7 *70* **Exousia**[86] [2240] 3-8-2 **46** oh1........................(b[1]) JosephineGordon 7
(Henry Spiller) *s.i.s and wnt rt s: rcvrd to ld 6f out: rdn and hdd over 2f out: sn wknd: virtually p.u ins fnl f* **25/1**

1m 25.4s (0.30) **Going Correction** +0.025s/f (Good) **7** Ran SP% **114.4**
Speed ratings (Par 103): **99,98,98,96,95 86,6**
CSF £164.57 CT £350.15 TOTE £10.50: £4.20, £8.40; EX 169.80 Trifecta £376.20.
Owner Rita's Racing **Bred** Minster Stud **Trained** Newmarket, Suffolk

FOCUS
This looks to be weak form. The winner's rated back to her debut level.
T/Plt: £48.80 to a £1 stake. Pool: £57,840.67 - 864.60 winning units T/Qpdt: £12.60 to a £1 stake. Pool: £6,925.70 - 405.27 winning units **Colin Roberts**

5359 - 5360a (Foreign Racing) - See Raceform Interactive

5108
LEOPARDSTOWN (L-H)
Thursday, July 25
OFFICIAL GOING: Good (good to firm in places; watered)

5361a JOCKEY CLUB OF TURKEY SILVER FLASH STKS (GROUP 3) (FILLIES) 7f 20y
6:55 (6:56) 2-Y-O
£31,891 (£10,270; £4,864; £2,162; £1,081; £540)

RPR

1 **Love (IRE)**[14] [4852] 2-9-0 0........................ SeamieHeffernan 6 105+
(A P O'Brien, Ire) *mde all: 1 l clr 3f out: drvn and extended advantage under 2f out: rdn out and styd on wl ins fnl f where in command: easily* **8/1**

2 *3 ¼* **Unforgetable (IRE)**[11] [4951] 2-9-0 0........................ DonnachaO'Brien 1 97
(Joseph Patrick O'Brien, Ire) *wnt sltly rt s: settled bhd ldr early: 3rd 1/2-way: impr into 2nd under 2f out: sn rdn and no imp on easy wnr ins fnl f: kpt on wl* **7/1**

3 *1* **So Wonderful (USA)**[11] [4951] 2-9-0 87........................ WayneLordan 2 94
(A P O'Brien, Ire) *chsd ldrs: 5th 1/2-way: sme hdwy far side under 2f out and sn swtchd lft: rdn in 3rd 1f out where n.m.r on inner briefly and no imp on easy wnr: kpt on same pce* **14/1**

4 *½* **Precious Moments (IRE)**[27] [4352] 2-9-0 0........................ RyanMoore 8 93+
(A P O'Brien, Ire) *w.w: 6th 1/2-way: sme hdwy nr side fr over 1f out: no imp on easy wnr in 4th wl ins fnl f: kpt on same pce* **2/1**[1]

5 *2* **One Last Look (IRE)**[35] [4040] 2-9-0 0........................ ColinKeane 3 87
(G M Lyons, Ire) *sweated up befhand: cl up: 2nd 1/2-way: rdn under 2f out and sn no imp on easy wnr in 3rd: wknd ins fnl f* **11/2**[3]

6 *1 ¾* **Schroders Mistake (IRE)**[7] [5108] 2-9-0 0........................ WJLee 4 83
(K J Condon, Ire) *chsd ldrs: 4th 1/2-way: rdn under 2f out and sn no ex: one pce in 6th ins fnl f* **25/1**

7 *1 ½* **Isabeau (IRE)**[21] [4580] 2-9-0 92........................ LeighRoche 7 79
(M D O'Callaghan, Ire) *hld up towards rr: pushed along in 7th fr bef 1/2-way: rdn and no imp 2f out: one pce after: nvr a factor* **14/1**

8 *2* **Windracer (IRE)**[28] [4309] 2-9-0 0........................ ShaneFoley 5 74
(Mrs John Harrington, Ire) *slowly away and edgd sltly rt s: in rr thrght: pushed along and struggling bef 1/2-way: rdn and no imp under 2f out: nvr a factor (jockey said filly was slowly away and never travellled)* **11/4**[2]

1m 30.84s (-0.76) **Going Correction** +0.15s/f (Good) **8** Ran SP% **116.2**
Speed ratings: **110,106,105,104,102 100,98,96**
CSF £63.19 TOTE £8.50: £2.40, £1.60, £3.30; DF 65.00 Trifecta £248.50.
Owner Michael Tabor & Derrick Smith & Mrs John Magnier **Bred** Coolmore **Trained** Cashel, Co Tipperary

FOCUS
A taking front-running display from Love, a progressive filly who looks to have a bright future. She's been rated in line with the better winners of this.

5362a JAPAN RACING ASSOCIATION TYROS STKS (GROUP 3) 7f 20y
7:30 (7:30) 2-Y-O £31,891 (£10,270; £4,864; £2,162)

RPR

1 **Armory (IRE)**[28] [4310] 2-9-3 0........................ RyanMoore 5 108+
(A P O'Brien, Ire) *prom tl sn settled bhd ldr in 2nd: impr to ld gng best over 1f out: rdn briefly and qcknd clr to assert wl ins fnl f: easily* **2/5**[1]

2 *5* **Toronto (IRE)**[35] [4043] 2-9-3 0........................ DonnachaO'Brien 2 94
(A P O'Brien, Ire) *got upset in stalls: sn led: 1 l clr at 1/2-way: pushed along under 2f out: rdn and hdd over 1f out: sn no ch w easy wnr: kpt on same pce* **7/1**[3]

3 *2 ½* **Zarzyni (IRE)**[39] [3894] 2-9-3 0........................ RonanWhelan 4 88
(M Halford, Ire) *dwlt sltly and pushed along briefly in rr early where racd keenly: last at 1/2-way: sme hdwy on outer 3f out to chal under 2f out: sn rdn in 3rd and no imp on easy wnr: kpt on same pce* **7/2**[2]

4 *3 ¾* **Innervisions (IRE)**[28] [4309] 2-9-0 0........................ WJLee 3 75
(W McCreery, Ire) *prom tl sn settled bhd ldrs in 3rd: pushed along bhd ldrs fr 2f out and sn no ex u.p in rr: one pce fnl f* **14/1**

1m 32.39s (0.79) **Going Correction** +0.15s/f (Good) **4** Ran SP% **112.8**
Speed ratings: **101,95,92,88**
CSF £4.18 TOTE £1.30; DF 2.70 Trifecta £4.10.
Owner Mrs John Magnier & Michael Tabor & Derrick Smith **Bred** Coolmore **Trained** Cashel, Co Tipperary

FOCUS
A sixth straight win in this race for Aidan O'Brien, who's won this Group 3 with future Classic winners Anthony Van Dyck, Churchill and Gleneagles in recent seasons. This didn't look a strong renewal on paper and Armory probably faced a straightforward enough task but the style in which he stretched clear was impressive.

5363a (Foreign Racing) - See Raceform Interactive

5364a KINGDOM OF BAHRAIN VINNIE ROE STKS (LISTED RACE) 1m 6f
8:30 (8:30) 3-Y-O
£26,576 (£8,558; £4,054; £1,801; £900; £450)

RPR

1 **South Sea Pearl (IRE)**[14] [4856] 3-9-0 98........................ RyanMoore 2 103+
(A P O'Brien, Ire) *hld up in tch: 5th 1/2-way: tk clsr order bhd ldrs into st: sn swtchd lft to chal on terms 1 1/2f out: rdn to ld over 1f out and styd on wl to assert nr fin: comf* **11/8**[1]

2 *3* **Simply Beautiful (IRE)**[8] [5075] 3-9-0 95........................ DonnachaO'Brien 6 99
(A P O'Brien, Ire) *chsd ldrs: disp 3rd at 1/2-way: impr to chal on terms briefly 1 1/2f out: sn rdn and hdd: no imp on wnr in 2nd ins fnl f: kpt on same pce* **3/1**[2]

3 *2* **Masaff (IRE)**[17] [4745] 3-9-5 105........................ ChrisHayes 4 101
(D K Weld, Ire) *w.w in rr: last at 1/2-way: hdwy nr side 2f out to chal briefly 1 1/2f out: sn rdn and no imp on wnr u.p in 3rd ins fnl f: kpt on same pce* **6/1**

4 *2 ¾* **Flowering Peach (IRE)**[10] [5007] 3-9-0 88........................ SeamieHeffernan 3 92
(A P O'Brien, Ire) *led briefly tl sn jnd and hdd after 1f: settled in 2nd: disp ld fr bef 1/2-way and led narrowly into st: sn rdn and hdd 1 1/2f out: sn dropped to 4th and no ex ins fnl f* **12/1**

5 *4 ¾* **Chesapeake Shores (IRE)**[10] [5005] 3-9-0 72........................(p) LeighRoche 1 86
(J A Stack, Ire) *cl up and disp ld briefly early tl settled in 3rd after 1f: disp 3rd at 1/2-way: drvn bhd ldrs under 3f out and dropped to rr fr 2f out: no imp after: kpt on one pce into mod 5th cl home* **33/1**

6 *hd* **Nate The Great**[14] [4845] 3-9-5 100........................ HollieDoyle 5 90
(Archie Watson) *cl up tl sn disp and led after 1f: jnd and disp ld fr bef 1/2-way: drvn over 3f out and hdd u.p into st: wknd 1 1/2f out* **7/2**[3]

3m 5.82s (2.62) **Going Correction** +0.15s/f (Good) **6** Ran SP% **114.2**
Speed ratings: **98,96,95,93,90 90**
CSF £5.94 TOTE £2.20: £1.20, £2.10; DF 5.70 Trifecta £22.10.
Owner Derrick Smith & Mrs John Magnier & Michael Tabor **Bred** Barronstown Stud **Trained** Cashel, Co Tipperary

FOCUS
Quite a straightforward success from an improving stayer. The second, third and fourth have been rated to form.

5365a (Foreign Racing) - See Raceform Interactive

4896
ASCOT (R-H)
Friday, July 26
OFFICIAL GOING: Good to firm (good in places on round course; stands' 8.5, ctr 8.9, far 8.5, rnd 7.8)
Wind: Almost nil Weather: Fine, warm

5366 JOHN GUEST RACING BRITISH EBF FILLIES' NOVICE STKS (PLUS 10 RACE) 7f
1:50 (1:51) (Class 4) 2-Y-O £6,727 (£2,002; £1,000; £500) Stalls Centre

Form RPR

1 **Cloak Of Spirits (IRE)** 2-9-0 0........................ AndreaAtzeni 4 94+
(Richard Hannon) *str: looked wl: awkward s and rdr briefly lost an iron: sn trckd ldr in centre: led 2f out: shkn up and clr over 1f out: styd on wl: taking debut* **3/1**[2]

2 *3 ½* **Queen Daenerys (IRE)** 2-9-0 0........................ RyanMoore 9 83+
(Roger Varian) *quite str: dwlt: hld up in last of nr side gp: prog wl over 1f out: styd on to take 2nd last 100yds: no ch w wnr* **6/1**

2 3 *1 ½* **Game And Set**[28] [4337] 2-9-0 0........................ DavidProbert 7 79
(Andrew Balding) *athletic: sweating: led gp towards nr side: chsd clr wnr in other gp over 1f out: no imp: lost 2nd last 100yds* **10/1**

4 *4* **Reehaam** 2-9-0 0........................ KieranO'Neill 6 69
(John Gosden) *compact: plld hrd: trckd ldrs towards nr side: shkn up and ch of a pl over 1f out: steadily wknd* **12/1**

5 *2 ¾* **Stars In The Sky** 2-9-0 0........................ OisinMurphy 2 61
(William Haggas) *compact: in tch in centre gp: outpcd 2f out: steadily wknd* **4/1**[3]

6 *5* **Walkonby** 2-9-0 0........................ PatDobbs 1 48
(Mick Channon) *leggy: chsd ldrs in centre: shkn up over 2f out: wknd over 1f out* **50/1**

04 7 *1 ¼* **Buy Nice Not Twice (IRE)**[8] [5088] 2-9-0 0........................ TomMarquand 3 45
(Richard Hannon) *workmanlike: c out of stall slowly: last of centre gp: shkn up and no prog over 2f out* **50/1**

4 8 *shd* **Dubai Paradise (IRE)**[15] [4849] 2-9-0 0........................ JamesDoyle 5 45+
(Charlie Appleby) *athletic: overall ldr in centre to 2f out: wknd qckly: eased fnl f* **11/4**[1]

9 *1* **Veleta** 2-9-0 0........................ HectorCrouch 8 42
(Clive Cox) *quite str: trckd ldr towards nr side tl wknd qckly wl over 1f out* **10/1**

1m 28.67s (1.17) **Going Correction** +0.25s/f (Good) **9** Ran SP% **115.7**
Speed ratings (Par 93): **103,99,97,92,89 83,82,82,81**
CSF £21.53 TOTE £3.80: £1.80, £1.80, £2.50; EX 23.30 Trifecta £160.10.
Owner Sheikh Mohammed Obaid Al Maktoum **Bred** Sheikh Mohammed Obaid Al Maktoum **Trained** East Everleigh, Wilts

FOCUS
Just 1mm of rain overnight and the going was given as good to firm on the Straight course (GoingStick 8.6; stands' side 8.5, centre 8.9, far side 8.5) and good to firm, good in places on the Round course (GoingStick 7.8). The course was at its widest configuration and all distances were as advertised. They split into two groups here, racing slightly apart, but it's hard to say there was a track bias, the field finishing well strung out behind a winner who looks well worth her place in Pattern company.

5367 ANDERS FOUNDATION BRITISH EBF CROCKER BULTEEL MAIDEN STKS (PLUS 10 RACE) (NOT RUN MORE THAN ONCE) 6f
2:25 (2:26) (Class 2) 2-Y-O
£12,450 (£3,728; £1,864; £932; £466; £234) **Stalls** Centre

Form RPR
1 **Mums Tipple (IRE)** 2-9-0 0 OisinMurphy 3 82
(Richard Hannon) *quite str: mde all: 2 l clr and gng best wl over 1f out: hung lft fnl f: hld on (jockey said colt hung left-handed under pressure)* 5/1[2]

2 nk **Molatham** 2-9-0 0 JimCrowley 4 81
(Roger Varian) *str: looked wl: mostly trckd wnr: shkn up and no imp 2f out: styd on fnl f: gaining steadily at fin but jst hld* 14/1

3 nk **Man Of Promise (USA)** 2-9-0 0 JamesDoyle 7 80
(Charlie Appleby) *leggy: athletic: hld up: shkn up over 2f out: prog on nr side of gp over 1f out: rdn and trying to cl on wnr whn impeded ins fnl f: kpt on nr fin (jockey suffered interference inside the final half furlong)* 10/11[1]

4 nk **Mr Kiki (IRE)** 2-9-0 0 CallumShepherd 2 79
(Michael Bell) *quite str: awkward bef gng into stall: swvd rt s: sn prom: rdn over 2f out: disp 2nd but no imp on wnr over 1f out: kpt on wl fnl f (jockey said colt jumped awkwardly from the stalls)* 10/1

5 2 3/4 **Surf Dancer (IRE)** 2-9-0 0 RyanMoore 1 73+
(William Haggas) *quite str: looked wl: dwlt: hld up in last pair: shkn up over 2f out: prog over 1f out: keeping on but hld whn short of room ins fnl f* 13/2[3]

4 6 8 **Shoot To Kill (IRE)**[15] 4826 2-9-0 TomMarquand 6 47
(George Scott) *unfurnished: prom: rdn over 2f out: wknd qckly over 1f out* 10/1

7 nse **My Thought (IRE)** 2-9-0 KieranO'Neill 5 47
(John Gosden) *compact: t.k.h: hld up: wknd over 2f out: sn bhd* 12/1

1m 15.63s (1.93) **Going Correction** +0.25s/f (Good) 7 Ran SP% 114.9
Speed ratings (Par 100): **97,96,96,95,92 92,81**
CSF £68.18 TOTE £5.10: £2.20, £6.70; EX 50.40 Trifecta £180.60.
Owner Marian Lyons & Patricia Zanelli **Bred** Abbey Bloodstock Limited **Trained** East Everleigh, Wilts

FOCUS
Once again they initially split into two groups but they merged around halfway. They finished in a heap and time will tell how the form works out. The level is very fluid.

5368 JOHN GUEST RACING BROWN JACK H'CAP 1m 7f 209y
3:00 (3:00) (Class 3) (0-95,93) 3-Y-O+
£18,675 (£5,592; £2,796; £1,398; £699; £351) **Stalls** Low

Form RPR
0205 1 **Themaxwecan (IRE)**[20] 4644 3-8-13 93 JamesDoyle 7 102+
(Mark Johnston) *trckd ldr: led over 2f out: drvn over 1f out: styd on and a holding chalrs fnl f* 2/1[1]

-230 2 1 1/4 **Sleeping Lion (USA)**[34] 4102 4-9-11 90 OisinMurphy 3 97
(James Fanshawe) *looked wl: hld up in last tl sme prog on outer 5f out: rdn and hdwy over 2f out: chsd wnr over 1f out: styd on but nvr able to chal* 5/1[3]

-250 3 nse **Blue Laureate**[46] 3655 4-9-7 86 JimCrowley 1 93
(Ian Williams) *t.k.h early: hld up: dropped to last 5f out: drvn and prog on outer over 2f out: styd on to press for 2nd nr fin: a hld* 8/1

50-5 4 2 3/4 **Quloob**[89] 2143 5-9-12 91 HectorCrouch 8 95
(Gary Moore) *trckd ldng trio: rdn to chse wnr 2f out to over 1f out: fdd ins fnl f* 20/1

655 5 1 1/2 **October Storm**[27] 4404 6-8-11 76 AndreaAtzeni 5 78
(Mick Channon) *racd in 6th: reminders 5f out: no prog u.p over 2f out: kpt on to chse ldrs over 1f out: fdd ins fnl f* 11/1

2201 6 4 1/2 **Knight Crusader**[21] 4614 7-9-5 84 LiamJones 2 81
(John O'Shea) *chsd ldng quartet: rdn and no prog over 2f out: wknd over 1f out* 16/1

610- 7 11 **Piedita (IRE)**[359] 5605 5-9-5 84 LukeMorris 6 67
(Sir Mark Prescott Bt) *t.k.h early: trckd ldng pair to over 2f out: wknd qckly over 1f out* 16/1

-103 8 6 **Crystal King**[34] 4102 4-10-0 93 RyanMoore 4 69
(Sir Michael Stoute) *led: rdn and hdd over 2f out: sn wknd qckly: eased (trainer's rep could offer no explanation for the gelding's performance)* 5/2[2]

3m 35.53s (2.23) **Going Correction** +0.25s/f (Good)
WFA 3 from 4yo+ 15lb 8 Ran SP% 114.5
Speed ratings (Par 107): **104,103,103,101,101 98,93,90**
CSF £12.50 CT £64.71 TOTE £2.40: £1.20, £1.70, £2.70; EX 10.70 Trifecta £52.60.
Owner Douglas Livingston **Bred** Niarchos Family **Trained** Middleham Moor, N Yorks

FOCUS
A race that had been good to the 3yos over the previous decade (4 winners, 3 runners-up, 2 of whom chased home another 3yo, and 3 who failed to make the places). The only 3yo in this line-up improved that record further. The second and third set the level.

5369 ACORN INSURANCE BRITISH EBF VALIANT STKS (LISTED RACE) (F&M) 7f 213y(R)
3:35 (3:35) (Class 1) 3-Y-O+
£34,026 (£12,900; £6,456; £3,216; £1,614; £810) **Stalls** Low

Form RPR
-431 1 **Duneflower (IRE)**[15] 4828 3-8-9 92 KieranO'Neill 8 107+
(John Gosden) *looked wl: hld up in last: brought to outer and rdn 2f out: prog over 1f out: styd on wl to ld last 100yds* 11/1

0-40 2 3/4 **Look Around**[82] 2443 3-8-9 99 OisinMurphy 3 105
(Andrew Balding) *chsd ldng pair: rdn to cl on outer 2f out: led jst over 1f out but pressed: hdd and one pce last 100yds* 11/1

4-12 3 1 **Magnetic Charm**[35] 4052 3-8-9 109 RyanMoore 1 103
(William Haggas) *trckd ldng pair: pushed along to cl over 2f out: rdn to chal over 1f out: w ldr jst ins fnl f: one pce last 120yds* 8/11[1]

5-20 4 2 1/4 **Preening**[37] 3986 4-9-3 99 PatDobbs 7 100
(James Fanshawe) *hld up in last trio: rdn to cl on ldrs over 1f out: nt pce to chal but kpt on to take 4th ins fnl f* 12/1

0216 5 1/2 **Anna Nerium**[37] 3986 4-9-6 107 TomMarquand 4 102
(Richard Hannon) *looked wl: trapped wd in midfield: rdn over 2f out: dropped to last over 1f out: kpt on nr fin but no ch* 5/1[2]

0-41 6 1 **Jadeerah**[21] 4592 3-8-9 86 (h) JimCrowley 2 95
(John Gosden) *led: rdn 2f out: hdd & wknd jst over 1f out* 10/1[3]

-010 7 1 1/4 **Main Edition (IRE)**[35] 4051 3-9-0 107 AndreaAtzeni 5 97
(Mark Johnston) *chsd ldr to over 1f out: wknd* 10/1[3]

0 8 1 1/4 **Morpho Blue (IRE)**[9] 5075 3-8-9 89 (p) MartinDwyer 6 89
(Mrs John Harrington, Ire) *dwlt: hld up in last trio: effrt and clsd briefly on ldrs wl over 1f out: fdd fnl f* 25/1

1m 41.56s (0.96) **Going Correction** +0.25s/f (Good)
WFA 3 from 4yo 8lb 8 Ran SP% 121.0
Speed ratings (Par 111): **105,104,103,101,100 99,98,97**
CSF £128.66 TOTE £8.80: £1.90, £2.60, £1.10; EX 98.70 Trifecta £323.20.
Owner HRH Princess Haya Of Jordan **Bred** Godolphin **Trained** Newmarket, Suffolk

FOCUS
Something of a surprise, with the favourite a bit below form, and the winner coming from last to first to land this Listed race. It's been rated around the fourth to her form in this race last year.

5370 JOHN GUEST RACING H'CAP 1m 3f 211y
4:10 (4:11) (Class 2) (0-105,100) 3-Y-O+
£18,675 (£5,592; £2,796; £1,398; £699; £351) **Stalls** Low

Form RPR
-141 1 **Sextant**[27] 4395 4-9-12 98 RyanMoore 7 108
(Sir Michael Stoute) *mde all: shkn up and drew 2 l clr wl over 1f out: drvn out fnl f and styd on wl* 5/4[1]

1210 2 1 1/4 **Almost Midnight**[37] 3984 3-8-12 95 PatDobbs 4 103
(David Simcock) *looked wl: hld up in 5th: rdn and prog 2f out: tk 2nd jst ins fnl f and briefly threatened to cl on wnr: no imp last 75yds* 3/1[2]

1323 3 1 3/4 **Hyanna**[21] 4613 4-8-11 90 GeorgiaDobie(7) 3 95
(Eve Johnson Houghton) *trckd ldng pair on outer: rdn over 2f out: chsd wnr over 1f out but no imp: lost 2nd jst ins fnl f: one pce* 11/2

6310 4 6 **Gossip Column (IRE)**[14] 4877 4-9-0 86 MartinDwyer 5 81
(Ian Williams) *looked wl: hld up in last: detached and shoved along 4f out: no prog tl passed two wkng rivals fnl f* 14/1

10-0 5 3 **Protected Guest**[99] 1889 4-9-5 91 TomQueally 2 82
(George Margarson) *hld up in 4th: rdn over 2f out: fnd nil and sn btn* 25/1

211 6 4 **Anythingtoday (IRE)**[14] 4890 5-9-11 97 (p) JimCrowley 1 81
(David O'Meara) *chsd wnr: tried to chal over 2f out: lost 2nd and wknd qckly over 1f out (trainer's rep said, although the gelding had won on good to firm ground on its previous run at York, it may have been unsuited by the good to firm ground on this occasion and, in her opinion, she would be seen to better effect on an easier surface)* 5/1[3]

2m 36.16s (3.56) **Going Correction** +0.25s/f (Good)
WFA 3 from 4yo+ 11lb 6 Ran SP% 112.0
Speed ratings (Par 109): **98,97,96,92,90 87**
CSF £5.17 TOTE £1.90: £1.20, £1.80; EX 5.50 Trifecta £15.60.
Owner The Queen **Bred** The Queen **Trained** Newmarket, Suffolk

FOCUS
A bit of a tactical affair, the winner dominating from the front. The third has been rated close to form.

5371 NEPTUNE INVESTMENT MANAGEMENT SUPPORTS CHILD BEREAVEMENT UK H'CAP 5f
4:45 (4:45) (Class 2) 3-Y-O+
£28,012 (£8,388; £4,194; £2,097; £1,048; £526) **Stalls** Centre

Form RPR
4311 1 **Only Spoofing (IRE)**[15] 4821 5-8-1 80 KieranO'Neill 12 92
(Jedd O'Keeffe) *pressed ldr in main gp: rdn to ld over 1f out: jnd fnl f: fnd ex last 75yds* 5/1[1]

0012 2 1/2 **Arecibo (FR)**[11] 4987 4-9-0 93 RobertWinston 7 103
(David O'Meara) *looked wl: dwlt: hld up in rr: prog 1/2-way: tk 2nd 1f out and sn chalng: upsides wnr 100yds out: styd on but jst outpcd nr fin* 7/1[2]

0133 3 2 3/4 **Wedding Date**[10] 5014 3-8-2 90 ThoreHammerHansen(5) 10 89
(Richard Hannon) *hld up in last: detached and urged along sn after 1/2-way: rapid prog fnl f: snatched 3rd last strides* 20/1

0621 4 nk **Daschas**[4] 5252 5-8-7 86 5ex (t) MartinDwyer 4 85
(Stuart Williams) *prom: rdn over 1f out: nt pce to chal but pressed for 3rd nr fin* 7/1[2]

0001 5 hd **Mountain Peak**[14] 4888 4-8-10 89 LiamKeniry 5 87
(Ed Walker) *in tch: rdn over 1f out: kpt on to press for 3rd nr fin but nvr pce to threaten* 7/1[2]

5011 6 nse **Ornate**[38] 3956 6-9-10 103 PhilDennis 3 101
(David C Griffiths) *led main gp: overall ldr 1f and again 2f out: hdd over 1f out: fdd fnl f* 12/1

0-50 7 1/2 **Koditime (IRE)**[13] 4896 4-8-12 91 PatDobbs 11 87
(Clive Cox) *trckd ldrs: stl gng wl 2f out: shkn up and no rspnse over 1f out* 14/1

6123 8 1 **Harome (IRE)**[13] 4896 5-8-12 91 NicolaCurrie 13 84
(Roger Fell) *a towards rr: rdn and no real prog wl over 1f out (jockey said gelding was never travelling)* 9/1

6025 9 nse **The Cruising Lord**[20] 4665 3-9-4 101 JFEgan 15 92
(Michael Attwater) *nvr beyond midfield and pushed along bef 1/2-way: no prog* 12/1

3-30 10 1/2 **Kick On Kick On**[83] 2403 4-9-0 93 HectorCrouch 9 84
(Clive Cox) *nvr beyond midfield: rdn and no prog wl over 1f out* 9/1

0302 11 3/4 **Encore D'Or**[7] 5142 7-9-8 101 RyanMoore 8 89
(Robert Cowell) *stdd s: hld up: struggling in last pair 2f out: v modest late prog (vet said gelding had lost his left-fore shoe)* 14/1

-200 12 1 1/4 **Vibrant Chords**[48] 3602 6-9-4 97 GeraldMosse 14 80
(Henry Candy) *nvr beyond midfield: rdn 2f out: wknd over 1f out* 16/1

1115 13 1/2 **Dapper Man (IRE)**[7] 5154 5-8-3 89 (b) AngusVilliers(7) 1 71
(Roger Fell) *racd along towards far side: led after 1f to 2f out: wknd (vet said gelding had lost his left-fore shoe)* 20/1

4514 14 3 3/4 **Jumira Bridge**[11] 4995 5-8-13 92 JimCrowley 2 60
(Robert Cowell) *chsd ldrs: rdn 2f out: sn wknd* 17/2[3]

1m 0.27s (-0.43) **Going Correction** +0.25s/f (Good)
WFA 3 from 4yo+ 4lb 14 Ran SP% 128.8
Speed ratings (Par 109): **113,112,107,107,107 106,106,104,104,103 102,100,99,93**
CSF £41.27 CT £665.42 TOTE £5.30: £2.10, £2.80, £5.90; EX 42.80 Trifecta £678.30.
Owner Mrs H Mannion, B Carter & F Durbin **Bred** Limestone And Tara Studs **Trained** Middleham Moor, N Yorks

FOCUS
The first two are progressive types and finished nicely clear. The second has been rated as running a pb, but in line with his French form, with the third to her latest.

5372 SARAH CHANDLER OCTOBER CLUB SUPPORTING SIA FILLIES' H'CAP 5f
5:15 (5:15) (Class 4) (0-85,85) 3-Y-O+

£6,727 (£2,002; £1,000; £500; £300; £300) **Stalls Centre**

Form RPR
421 **1** **Texting**[28] 4343 3-8-11 **74** .... GeraldMosse 4 83+
(Mohamed Moubarak) *dwlt: sn trckd ldrs: led wl over 1f out: rdn and pressed fnl f: styd on wl* **13/8**[1]
1251 **2** 1 **Pink Flamingo**[24] 4478 3-9-4 **81** .... JimCrowley 1 86
(Michael Attwater) *looked wl: hld up in last: prog to chse ldng pair over 1f out: tried to chal fnl f but nt qckn: tk 2nd last stride* **15/2**
4363 **3** shd **Three Little Birds**[15] 4844 4-8-8 **67** .... JFEgan 5 73
(Sylvester Kirk) *hld up bhd ldrs: prog to chse wnr over 1f out and sn chalng: drvn and nt qckn fnl f: lost 2nd last stride* **8/1**
4164 **4** 2 **Seen The Lyte (IRE)**[11] 4986 4-9-7 **83** ....(h) RowanScott(3) 3 82
(Nigel Tinkler) *led to wl over 1f out: fdd* **9/1**
-164 **5** ½ **Lorna Cole (IRE)**[21] 4595 3-8-9 **72** .... MartinDwyer 6 68
(William Muir) *pressed ldr to 2f out: fdd over 1f out* **10/1**
1151 **6** 4½ **Peggie Sue**[27] 4375 4-9-12 **85** .... NicolaCurrie 2 66
(Adam West) *chsd ldrs: urged along sn after 1/2-way: wknd over 1f out* **5/1**[3]
115 **7** 25 **Chitra**[37] 4008 3-9-3 **80** .... RobertWinston 7
(Daniel Kubler) *chsd ldrs to 1/2-way: wknd qckly over 1f out and virtually p.u fnl f* **9/2**[2]

1m 0.76s (0.06) **Going Correction** +0.25s/f (Good)
WFA 3 from 4yo 4lb **7 Ran SP% 114.9**
Speed ratings (Par 102): **109,107,107,104,103 96,56**
CSF £14.81 TOTE £2.50: £1.70, £2.70; EX 18.40 Trifecta £78.80.
Owner M Moubarak **Bred** Laundry Cottage Stud Farm **Trained** Newmarket, Suffolk

FOCUS
A fairly competitive fillies' sprint handicap. The winner has been rated in line with her previous win, and the third to this year's form.
T/Jkpt: Part won. £10,000.00 to a £1 stake. Pool: £14,084.51 - 0.50 winning units. T/Plt: £113.20 to a £1 stake. Pool: £104,955.65 - 676.37 winning units T/Qpdt: £8.00 to a £1 stake. Pool: £11,625.93 - 1,066.04 winning units **Jonathan Neesom**

5080 CHEPSTOW (L-H)
Friday, July 26

OFFICIAL GOING: Good to firm (6.6)
Wind: Quite a strong breeze, across Weather: Cloudy

5373 HOT TUBS SPLASH AND DASH H'CAP 1m 14y
5:45 (5:49) (Class 5) (0-70,72) 3-Y-O+

£3,428 (£1,020; £509; £400; £400; £400) **Stalls Centre**

Form RPR
1102 **1** **Amor Fati (IRE)**[8] 5080 4-9-5 **61** .... RossaRyan 14 76
(David Evans) *trckd ldrs: rdn over 2f out: led ent fnl f: r.o strly and sn clr* **4/1**[2]
6330 **2** 5 **Balata Bay**[22] 4562 3-9-3 **72** ....(b[1]) KatherineBegley(5) 4 73
(Richard Hannon) *t.k.h: cl up: led after 2f: rdn over 1f out: hdd ent fnl f: qckly outpcd by wnr: wkng towards fin but hld on to 2nd* **9/1**
23-0 **3** ½ **Glorious Jem**[29] 4283 4-10-0 **70** ....(p[1]) ShaneKelly 10 72
(David Lanigan) *led 2f: remained prom: rdn over 2f out: sltly outpcd by ldrs over 1f out: styd on fnl f* **7/1**[3]
02U1 **4** shd **Gold Hunter (IRE)**[14] 4873 9-10-0 **70** ....(tp) RaulDaSilva 15 72
(Steve Flook) *hld up: clsd 1/2-way: rdn over 2f out: kpt on fnl f to press for 3rd* **10/1**
5363 **5** 1¾ **Mister Musicmaster**[14] 4873 10-9-1 **60** .... NoelGarbutt(3) 13 58
(Ron Hodges) *in rr: pushed along after 3f: rdn over 2f out: hdwy over 1f out: kpt on same pce fnl f* **14/1**
0316 **6** 1¾ **Khaan**[44] 3744 4-8-12 **54** .... AlistairRawlinson 5 48
(Michael Appleby) *s.i.s: sn chsng ldrs: swtchd lft over 2f out: sn rdn: wknd fnl f* **14/1**
3-10 **7** ½ **Freckles**[30] 4235 4-9-3 **66** .... WilliamCarver(7) 8 58
(Marcus Tregoning) *wnt to post early: s.i.s: in rr: rdn 3f out: hung lft and hdwy 2f out: sn edgd rt: no imp fnl f* **9/1**
0-06 **8** 2¾ **Powerage (IRE)**[8] 5085 3-8-4 **54** .... JimmyQuinn 3 38
(Malcolm Saunders) *midfield on outer: rdn over 2f out: fdd fnl f* **50/1**
0110 **9** ¾ **Fitzrovia**[22] 4552 4-9-12 **68** .... PatCosgrave 12 52
(Ed de Giles) *t.k.h in midfield: rdn 3f out: outpcd by ldrs 2f out: no ch after (trainer said gelding was unsuited by the undulating track)* **7/1**[3]
2225 **10** 1¼ **Dashing Poet**[26] 4426 5-9-9 **65** .... KieranShoemark 16 46
(Heather Main) *dwlt: in rr: pushed along over 2f out: no real imp (jockey said mare was slowly away)* **10/3**[1]
15 **11** 1 **He's Our Star (IRE)**[66] 2927 4-10-2 **72** .... CharlesBishop 7 51
(Ali Stronge) *prom: rdn 3f out: wknd wl over 1f out* **16/1**

1m 33.26s (-2.74) **Going Correction** -0.30s/f (Firm)
WFA 3 from 4yo+ 8lb **11 Ran SP% 118.3**
Speed ratings (Par 103): **101,96,95,95,93 91,91,88,87,86 85**
CSF £40.35 CT £252.31 TOTE £4.30: £1.70, £4.30, £2.30; EX 44.20 Trifecta £517.30.
Owner Mrs I M Folkes **Bred** Tony O'Meara **Trained** Pandy, Monmouths

FOCUS
This ordinary handicap had a competitive look to it, but it was won with a huge amount of authority by Amor Fati. The second and third have been rated close to form.

5374 COMPAREBETTINGSITES.COM BEST BETTING SITES NOVICE AUCTION STKS 6f 16y
6:15 (6:16) (Class 5) 2-Y-O

£3,428 (£1,020; £509; £254) **Stalls Centre**

Form RPR
1 **Malvern** 2-9-2 0 .... RossaRyan 9 76
(Richard Hannon) *s.i.s and wnt sltly rt leaving stalls: led one other on stands' side and cl up overall: led over 2f out: sn rdn: r.o wl fnl f* **3/1**[2]
2 2¼ **Cosmic Power (IRE)** 2-9-2 0 .... CharlesBishop 4 69
(Eve Johnson Houghton) *trckd ldrs: rdn over 2f out: styd on fnl f: nvr able to chal* **4/1**[3]
0 **3** ¾ **Lin Chong**[15] 4839 2-9-2 0 .... KieranShoemark 11 67
(Paul Cole) *wnt rt leaving stalls: trckd one other on stands' side and chsd ldrs overall: rdn 2f out: disp hld 2nd fnl f tl fdd nr fin* **6/1**
4 hd **Passing Fashion (IRE)** 2-9-2 0 .... DavidProbert 3 66+
(Ralph Beckett) *towards rr: niggled along 3f out: rdn and swtchd lft ins fnl f: r.o wl (jockey said gelding ran green)* **9/2**
0 **5** hd **Twittering (IRE)**[13] 4897 2-9-2 0 .... CallumShepherd 7 66
(Jamie Osborne) *led main body of field in centre: rdn and hdd over 2f out: stl disputing hld 2nd towards fin* **14/1**
02 **6** 1¾ **Bermuda Schwartz**[8] 5088 2-9-2 0 .... ShaneKelly 8 61
(Richard Hughes) *t.k.h: prom: rdn 2f out: sn unable qck: wknd ins fnl f* **9/4**[1]
06 **7** 5 **Ohnotanotherone**[30] 4233 2-8-11 0 .... FergusSweeney 6 41
(Stuart Kittow) *t.k.h in midfield: swtchd rt over 2f out: sn rdn: wknd fnl f* **100/1**
8 9 **Royal Bassett (FR)** 2-9-2 0 .... GeorgeDowning 5 19
(Robin Dickin) *s.s: in rr: pushed along over 3f out: bhd fnl 2f* **66/1**

1m 11.36s (-0.14) **Going Correction** -0.30s/f (Firm) **8 Ran SP% 117.4**
Speed ratings (Par 94): **88,85,84,83,83 81,74,62**
CSF £15.99 TOTE £3.60: £1.40, £2.00, £1.90; EX 13.90 Trifecta £79.30.
Owner Owners Group 042 **Bred** R J Vines **Trained** East Everleigh, Wilts

FOCUS
There wasn't a great deal of depth to this but there were a couple of performances of note, particularly from the ready winner. The stands' side proved the place to be, as it had in the opener. The level is fluid.

5375 COMPAREBETTINGSITES.COM ONLINE BETTING H'CAP 5f 16y
6:45 (6:46) (Class 5) (0-70,72) 3-Y-O+

£3,428 (£1,020; £509; £400; £400; £400) **Stalls Centre**

Form RPR
2-00 **1** **Compton Poppy**[23] 4494 5-8-12 **56** ....(b[1]) GeorgeDowning 5 65
(Tony Carroll) *trckd ldrs: rdn over 1f out: led wl ins fnl f* **10/1**[3]
0451 **2** ½ **Broadhaven Dream (IRE)**[32] 4182 3-9-0 **62** .... DavidProbert 7 68
(Ronald Harris) *disp ld tl def advantage 1/2-way: hrd pressed: rdn and hung lft fr 2f out: hdd wl ins fnl f (jockey said gelding hung badly left-handed)* **6/5**[1]
1462 **3** ½ **Show Me The Bubbly**[16] 4783 3-9-8 **70** ....(p[1]) LiamJones 4 74
(John O'Shea) *squeezed out sltly s: hld up: rdn after 2f: hdwy over 1f out: r.o fnl f: unable qck towards fin* **4/1**[2]
0234 **4** ¾ **Union Rose**[48] 3576 7-9-7 **72** ....(p) WilliamCarver(7) 3 74
(Ronald Harris) *wnt rt leaving stalls: chsd ldrs: rdn 2f out: sn sltly outpcd: kpt on towards fin* **4/1**[2]
-040 **5** 1 **Glamorous Rocket (IRE)**[48] 3576 4-9-12 **70** .... CallumShepherd 1 69
(Christopher Mason) *sn prom: rdn to chal 2f out: ev ch tl wknd fnl 100yds (jockey said filly was denied a clear run)* **12/1**
0055 **6** 1¼ **Silverrica (IRE)**[10] 5013 9-9-5 **63** .... JimmyQuinn 2 57
(Malcolm Saunders) *slipped leaving stalls: hld up: rdn 2f out: hld whn n.m.r ins fnl f (jockey said mare slipped leaving stalls)* **25/1**
-000 **7** 16 **Quantum Dot (IRE)**[14] 4880 8-9-8 **66** ....(b) PatCosgrave 6 3
(Ed de Giles) *disp ld tl rdn and hdd 1/2-way: losing pl whn n.m.r wl over 1f out: sn eased (jockey said gelding hung badly left-handed)* **11/1**

58.85s (-0.55) **Going Correction** -0.30s/f (Firm)
WFA 3 from 4yo+ 4lb **7 Ran SP% 114.4**
Speed ratings (Par 103): **92,91,90,89,87 85,60**
CSF £22.63 TOTE £11.10: £3.80, £1.40; EX 27.60 Trifecta £82.90.
Owner Paul Downing **Bred** Llety Farms **Trained** Cropthorne, Worcs

FOCUS
Ordinary sprinting form. The second has been rated in line with his previous C&D win.

5376 COMPAREBETTINGSITES.COM FREE BETS FILLIES' H'CAP 7f 16y
7:15 (7:17) (Class 5) (0-75,75) 3-Y-O+ **£3,428** (£1,020; £509; £400) **Stalls Centre**

Form RPR
1154 **1** **Dream World (IRE)**[51] 3470 4-9-11 **72** .... AlistairRawlinson 6 78
(Michael Appleby) *mde all: shkn up over 1f out: rdn out fnl f* **6/5**[1]
4064 **2** 1¼ **Roman Spinner**[16] 4786 4-9-11 **72** ....(t) DavidProbert 1 75
(Rae Guest) *hld up in last: impr a pl wl over 2f out: sn rdn: clsd on ldng pair fnl f: tk 2nd nr fin* **9/2**[3]
0040 **3** hd **Zoraya (FR)**[26] 4424 4-9-9 **70** .... RossaRyan 2 72
(Paul Cole) *trckd ldng pair: wnt 2nd 1/2-way: drvn 2f out: unable qck fnl f: lost 2nd nr fin* **11/8**[2]
0050 **4** 13 **Angelical Eve (IRE)**[10] 5025 5-8-6 **45** oh11 .... NoelGarbutt(3) 7 23
(Dai Williams) *trckd wnr to 1/2-way: sn rdn and outpcd in last: lost tch over 1f out* **33/1**

1m 21.63s (-2.27) **Going Correction** -0.30s/f (Firm)
WFA 3 from 4yo+ 7lb **4 Ran SP% 108.7**
Speed ratings (Par 100): **100,98,98,83**
CSF £6.74 TOTE £1.90; EX 4.60 Trifecta £6.70.
Owner Rod In Pickle Partnership **Bred** Miss L Cronin & Mrs U Lawler **Trained** Oakham, Rutland

FOCUS
This fillies' handicap was decimated by non-runners on account of the lively conditions. The winner has been rated as building slightly on her previous form this year.

5377 COMPAREBETTINGSITES.COM BETTING H'CAP 7f 16y
7:45 (7:46) (Class 6) (0-60,62) 3-Y-O

£2,781 (£827; £413; £400; £400; £400) **Stalls Centre**

Form RPR
0064 **1** **Seafaring Girl (IRE)**[23] 4518 3-8-2 **47** ow2 ....(p[1]) SeanKirrane(7) 12 54
(Mark Loughnane) *mde all: rdn 2f out: rdn out fnl f* **6/1**[2]
0-00 **2** 2 **Harbour Times (IRE)**[31] 4217 3-8-1 **46** .... WilliamCarver(7) 6 48+
(Patrick Chamings) *midfield on outer: rdn and hdwy over 2f out: styd on fnl f: wnt 2nd nr fin* **8/1**[3]
0-0 **3** nk **Gilt Edge**[8] 5083 3-9-5 **57** .... CallumShepherd 9 58
(Christopher Mason) *a.p: rdn over 2f out: chsd wnr over 1f out: unable qck fnl f: lost 2nd nr fin* **10/1**
2313 **4** 2¼ **Glamorous Crescent**[14] 4874 3-9-7 **59** .... JimmyQuinn 8 54
(Grace Harris) *s.i.s: sn in midfield: hdwy 1/2-way: rdn over 2f out: outpcd by ldrs fnl f* **5/2**[1]
0040 **5** 1¼ **Yfenni (IRE)**[9] 5044 3-8-7 **45** .... RaulDaSilva 11 37
(Milton Bradley) *prom: chsd wnr 1/2-way: sn rdn: lost 2nd over 1f out: fdd ins fnl f* **33/1**
6065 **6** ½ **Aquarius (IRE)**[17] 4754 3-9-5 **57** ....(v) LiamJones 15 48
(Michael Appleby) *midfield: rdn to chse ldrs over 2f out: styd on same pce fnl f* **8/1**[3]
0050 **7** 1¾ **Grey Hare**[17] 4754 3-8-4 **45** ....(t) WilliamCox(3) 10 31
(Tony Carroll) *s.i.s: sn in midfield: rdn 3f out: sn outpcd by ldrs: kpt on again ins fnl f but no threat* **12/1**
-020 **8** shd **Global Goddess (IRE)**[66] 2926 3-9-1 **58** ....(p) ScottMcCullagh(5) 14 44
(Gay Kelleway) *hld up: rdn over 2f out: hdwy over 1f out: no imp fnl f* **20/1**

The Form Book Flat 2019, Raceform Ltd, Newbury, RG14 5SJ

-000 **9** 3/4 **Tasman Sea**[56] 3310 3-9-10 **62** CharlesBishop 7 46
(Eve Johnson Houghton) *chsd ldrs: rdn over 2f out: outpcd over 1f out: wknd ins fnl f* **12/1**

1630 **10** 2 1/2 **Sepahi**[25] 4457 3-9-9 **61** (p) DavidProbert 4 38
(Henry Spiller) *swtchd rt leaving stalls: hld up: rdn over 2f out: no real imp* **16/1**

00-0 **11** 3/4 **Swiper (IRE)**[14] 4874 3-9-10 **62** RossaRyan 3 37
(John O'Shea) *towards rr: rdn over 2f out: wknd over 1f out* **20/1**

-000 **12** 3 1/2 **Illywhacker (IRE)**[46] 3665 3-9-6 **58** ShaneKelly 13 24
(Gary Moore) *towards rr: drvn over 3f out: wknd 2f out* **11/1**

3100 **13** 4 1/2 **Princess Florence (IRE)**[8] 5107 3-9-0 **52** KieranShoemark 5 7
(John Ryan) *prom: rdn over 2f out: wknd wl over 1f out (jockey said filly lost action)* **16/1**

1m 22.22s (-1.68) **Going Correction** -0.30s/f (Firm) **13** Ran SP% **122.1**
Speed ratings (Par 98): **97,94,94,91,90 89,87,87,86,83 83,79,73**
CSF £53.29 CT £501.16 TOTE £6.60: £2.60, £3.40, £3.80; EX 65.20 Trifecta £994.90.
Owner Greens & Blues Syndicate **Bred** Mrs Eleanor Commins **Trained** Rock, Worcs

FOCUS
A big field but few got involved. It's been rated a shade negatively.

5378 COMPAREBETTINGSITES.COM BETTING SITES H'CAP 1m 4f
8:15 (8:18) (Class 6) (0-60,59) 3-Y-O+

£2,781 (£827; £413; £400; £400; £400) **Stalls** Low

Form RPR

-013 **1** **Kaylen's Mischief**[39] 3941 6-9-0 **50** ScottMcCullagh(5) 2 57
(D J Jeffreys) *mde all: rdn 2f out: hung rt over 1f out: styd on wl (jockey said gelding hung right-handed in the straight)* **7/1**[2]

6-03 **2** 1 **Road To Paris (IRE)**[10] 5028 3-9-0 **56** RyanTate 8 62+
(Sir Mark Prescott Bt) *chsd ldrs: rdn over 2f out: sn swtchd lft: styd on fnl f: chsd wnr 100yds out: clsng nr fin* **10/11**[1]

5-05 **3** 1 **Purple Jazz (IRE)**[14] 4868 4-9-8 **53** (t) ShaneKelly 7 57
(Jeremy Scott) *chsd ldrs: rdn and clsd 2f out: styd on to dispute 2nd ins fnl f: hld towards fin* **28/1**

000- **4** 1/2 **Aussie Breeze**[239] 9308 3-8-6 **48** RoystonFfrench 1 52
(Tom George) *chsd wnr to 4f out: rdn and wnt 2nd again 3f out: one pce fnl f: lost 2nd and no ex fnl 100yds* **28/1**

3 **5** 6 **Born To Frolic (IRE)**[73] 2720 4-9-4 **56** GeorgiaDobie(7) 12 49+
(Matthew Salaman) *in rr: rdn over 3f out: styd on fr 2f out: no imp fnl f* **10/1**

005 **6** 1 **Dancing Lilly**[32] 4177 4-9-2 **52** RachealKneller(5) 9 44
(Matthew Salaman) *towards rr: rdn 2f out: sn swtchd rt: r.o fnl f: nvr trbld ldrs* **25/1**

400 **7** 1 **Muraaqeb**[3] 5285 5-9-0 **52** (p) WilliamCarver(7) 10 42
(Milton Bradley) *midfield: rdn over 3f out: sn outpcd: styd on fnl f but no threat* **33/1**

0430 **8** 3 **General Brook (IRE)**[48] 3571 9-10-0 **59** (p) RossaRyan 13 44
(John O'Shea) *prom: chsd wnr 4f out to 3f out: sn drvn: wknd over 1f out* **16/1**

0-03 **9** 1 **Carnage**[14] 4868 4-9-7 **52** CharlesBishop 3 36
(Nikki Evans) *chsd ldrs: rdn 4f out: wknd 2f out* **12/1**

060 **10** 1/2 **Miss Harriett**[40] 3889 3-8-10 **55** WilliamCox(3) 14 39
(Stuart Kittow) *towards rr: rdn and sme hdwy 3f out: no ch fnl 2f* **50/1**

0503 **11** hd **Dimmesdale**[23] 4498 4-9-9 **54** LiamJones 5 37
(John O'Shea) *a towards rr* **14/1**

-302 **12** nk **Das Kapital**[14] 4868 4-9-4 **49** (p) JFEgan 11 31
(John Berry) *s.i.s: in rr: hdwy into midfield after 4f: chsng ldrs and rdn over 3f out: wknd over 1f out* **9/1**[3]

626- **13** 6 **Good Impression**[130] 9448 4-9-11 **56** CharlieBennett 17 29
(Dai Burchell) *hld up: sme hdwy 7f out: rdn 3f out: wknd 2f out* **50/1**

05-2 **14** 1 1/4 **Frantical**[30] 4232 7-9-4 **49** PatCosgrave 16 20
(Tony Carroll) *hld up: rdn over 3f out: no prog* **14/1**

006- **15** 99 **Endean**[324] 6953 4-9-9 **54** CallumShepherd 4
(William Muir) *midfield: rdn over 4f out: wknd qckly: t.o fnl 3f (jockey said gelding moved poorly)* **50/1**

2m 34.02s (-6.28) **Going Correction** -0.30s/f (Firm)
WFA 3 from 4yo+ 11lb **15** Ran SP% **130.4**
Speed ratings (Par 101): **96,95,94,94,90 89,89,87,86,86 85,85,81,80,14**
CSF £13.94 CT £194.36 TOTE £7.70: £2.10, £1.40, £9.60; EX 17.90 Trifecta £295.80.
Owner Mark E Smith **Bred** Trickledown Stud Limited **Trained** Stow-On-The-Wold, Gloucs

FOCUS
Low-grade stuff. The winner's recent Windsor form could be rated this high.

5379 COMPAREBETTINGSITES.COM H'CAP 2m
8:45 (8:46) (Class 6) (0-65,67) 4-Y-O+

£2,781 (£827; £413; £400; £400; £400) **Stalls** Low

Form RPR

6414 **1** **So Near So Farhh**[14] 4881 4-9-9 **67** CallumShepherd 1 74
(Mick Channon) *hld up: rdn and hdwy 4f out: chsd ldng pair over 2f out: styd on to ld nr fin* **11/4**[2]

00-3 **2** 3/4 **Danglydontask**[16] 4796 8-8-3 **47** (b) RaulDaSilva 3 53
(Mike Murphy) *led 1f: chsd ldr: rdn and chal 3f out: led jst over 1f out: edgd rt wl ins fnl f: hdd nr fin* **10/1**

1253 **3** nk **Panatos (FR)**[8] 5115 4-9-2 **60** RossaRyan 11 66
(Alexandra Dunn) *rousted along to ld after 1f: rdn and pressed 3f out: hdd jst over 1f out: keeping on but jst hld in cl 3rd whn sltly hmpd wl ins fnl f* **2/1**[1]

6050 **4** 4 1/2 **Demophon**[16] 4777 5-8-3 **46** oh1 ow1 RoystonFfrench 8 47
(Steve Flook) *chsd ldng pair: lost 3rd 5f out: rdn over 3f out: styd on fnl 2f* **25/1**

0-20 **5** 3/4 **General Allenby**[12] 3653 5-8-1 **52** WilliamCarver(7) 12 51
(Peter Bowen) *chsd ldrs: drvn over 2f out: styd on same pce* **6/1**

3-62 **6** 5 **Royal Hall (FR)**[16] 4796 7-8-0 **47** WilliamCox(3) 6 40
(Gary Moore) *chsd ldrs: lost pl 6f out: rdn over 3f out: styd on same pce and no threat* **5/1**[3]

366- **7** nk **Bumble Bay**[17] 5426 9-8-2 **46** oh1 (tp) JimmyQuinn 4 39
(Robert Stephens) *hld up: drvn over 3f out: outpcd and no imp* **20/1**

-060 **8** 12 **Perfect Summer (IRE)**[14] 4881 9-9-7 **65** (v) KieranShoemark 7 44
(Ian Williams) *s.i.s: in rr: rdn 5f out: wknd 3f out* **16/1**

5040 **9** 2 1/4 **Sellingallthetime (IRE)**[23] 4498 8-7-9 **46** (p) IsobelFrancis(7) 9 22
(Mark Usher) *midfield: hdwy 4f out: drvn and hung lft over 3f out: wknd 2f out (jockey said gelding hung left-handed in the home straight)* **20/1**

00/- **10** 99 **Caviar Royale**[75] 8870 4-9-0 **58** (h) JohnFahy 10
(Nikki Evans) *a in rr: lost tch 7f out: t.o* **66/1**

3m 30.35s (-11.75) **Going Correction** -0.30s/f (Firm) **10** Ran SP% **120.8**
Speed ratings (Par 101): **105,104,104,102,101 99,99,93,92,42**
CSF £29.90 CT £67.87 TOTE £3.70: £1.40, £2.00, £1.30; EX 46.40 Trifecta £208.80.
Owner Mrs Nicola Murray **Bred** Whitwell Bloodstock **Trained** West Ilsley, Berks

FOCUS
Three pulled clear in this moderate staying contest. The winner and third have been rated near their recent marks.
T/Plt: £67.60 to a £1 stake. Pool: £56,507.76 - 609.32 winning units T/Qpdt: £16.30 to a £1 stake. Pool: £6,010.22 - 271.96 winning units **Richard Lowther**

5189 NEWMARKET (R-H)
Friday, July 26

OFFICIAL GOING: Good to firm (firm in places; watered; 7.7)
Wind: virtually nil Weather: light cloud, warm

5380 32RED FILLIES' H'CAP (LONDON MILE SERIES QUALIFIER) 1m
5:35 (5:41) (Class 5) (0-70,72) 3-Y-O+

£4,528 (£1,347; £673; £400; £400; £400) **Stalls** High

Form RPR

6356 **1** **Trulee Scrumptious**[7] 5138 10-8-7 **56** (v) AledBeech(7) 4 64
(Peter Charalambous) *mde all and sn clr: rdn ent fnl 2f: 3 l clr 1f out: kpt on gamely and a doing enough: rdn out (regarding the apparent improvement in form, trainer said the mare appreciated the drop back in trip from 1 mile and 2 furlongs to 1 mile on this occasion and appreciated the front running tactics today after having been dropped in last time out)* **9/2**[3]

0013 **2** 1 **Duchess Of Avon**[7] 5151 4-9-6 **62** JasonWatson 1 68
(Gary Moore) *hld up off the pce in midfield: clsd to chse clr wnr 3f out: rdn ent fnl 2f: 3 l down 1f out: kpt on and grad clsd but nvr quite getting to wnr* **7/2**[2]

0201 **3** 2 3/4 **Cape Cyclone (IRE)**[20] 4657 4-8-6 **55** MarcoGhiani(7) 3 55
(Stuart Williams) *chsd clr wnr tl 3f out: rdn over 2f out: 3rd and kpt on steadily ins fnl f: nvr threatened wnr* **11/2**

0102 **4** 2 **Song Of The Isles (IRE)**[14] 4870 3-8-11 **66** CierenFallon(5) 8 59
(Heather Main) *hld up off the pce in rr of main gp: effrt over 2f out: 4th and kpt on ins fnl f: nvr getting on terms w wnr and eased cl home (jockey said filly was never travelling)* **11/4**[1]

6060 **5** 3 1/4 **Margaret J**[16] 4801 3-7-10 **51** oh6 (p) SophieRalston(5) 9 37
(Phil McEntee) *chsd ldng pair tl 3f out: sn lost pl u.p: nvr a threat and wl btn over 1f out* **33/1**

0224 **6** 1 1/4 **Universal Effect**[34] 4109 3-9-4 **68** StevieDonohoe 6 51
(David Lanigan) *stdd s: t.k.h: hld up off the pce in midfield: effrt jst over 2f out: no imp over 1f out: nvr a threat* **6/1**

301 **7** 6 **Kachumba**[17] 4751 4-10-2 **72** AdamKirby 7 43
(Rae Guest) *off the pce in midfield: effrt 3f out: no imp and wl btn over 1f out: wknd fnl f* **13/2**

5000 **8** 17 **Plissken**[27] 4372 3-8-8 **58** (h) GeorgeWood 2
(Tom Clover) *s.i.s: nvr travelling and sn detached in last: t.o 1/2-way (jockey said filly was slowly away)* **25/1**

1m 37.87s (-2.13) **Going Correction** -0.175s/f (Firm)
WFA 3 from 4yo+ 8lb **8** Ran SP% **116.9**
Speed ratings (Par 100): **103,102,99,97,94 92,86,69**
CSF £21.16 CT £88.85 TOTE £4.90: £1.50, £1.80, £1.80; EX 22.20 Trifecta £146.80.
Owner pcracing.co.uk **Bred** Dxb Bloodstock Ltd **Trained** Newmarket, Suffolk
■ Fleeting Freedom was withdrawn. Price at time of withdrawal 12/1. Rule 4 applies to all bets struck prior to withdrawal, but not SP bets. Deduct 5p in the £. New market formed.

FOCUS
Stands'-side course used. Stalls Far Side except 1m4f: Centre. Not a vintage contest for the track but the winner, who opened up a big lead early, was gaining her third success in the race. The second helps set the level to her recent form.

5381 32RED NOVICE MEDIAN AUCTION STKS (PLUS 10 RACE) 6f
6:10 (6:12) (Class 4) 2-Y-O **£5,175** (£1,540; £769; £384) **Stalls** High

Form RPR

5 **1** **Hamish Macbeth**[71] 2761 2-9-5 0 JamesDoyle 7 83
(Hugo Palmer) *stdd s: hld up in tch in midfield: nt clr run over 2f out: clsd to chse ldrs and swtchd rt over 1f out: r.o wl under hands and heels riding to ld wl ins fnl f: eased cl home: comf* **7/4**[1]

2 **2** 1/2 **Laikaparty (IRE)**[16] 4798 2-9-5 0 HollieDoyle 5 81
(Archie Watson) *chsd ldr tl effrt to chal over 1f out: sn rdn to ld: hdd and nt match pce of wnr wl ins fnl f* **5/2**[2]

3 2 1/2 **Follia** 2-9-0 0 JasonWatson 1 69+
(Marco Botti) *wnt rt leaving stalls: hld up in tch: effrt 2f out: nt clrest of runs and swtchd rt over 1f out: styd on wl ins fnl f: no threat to ldrs (jockey said filly was denied a clear run)* **20/1**

6 **4** 2 **Angel Grey (IRE)**[15] 4840 2-9-0 0 RobHornby 8 63
(Andrew Balding) *led: rdn and hrd pressed over 1f out: sn hdd & wknd ins fnl f* **11/4**[3]

00 **5** 2 1/2 **Speed Merchant (IRE)**[13] 4897 2-9-5 0 DaneO'Neill 6 60+
(Brian Meehan) *t.k.h: hld up in tch in midfield: pushed along and nt clrest of runs over 1f out: kpt on same pce and no imp ins fnl f* **28/1**

6 nk **Big Impact** 2-9-5 0 EoinWalsh 4 59
(Luke McJannet) *wnt rt leaving stalls: sn rcvrd and chsd ldrs: effrt ent fnl 2f: unable qck u.p over 1f out: wknd ins fnl f* **33/1**

5 **7** 1 **Burniston Rocks**[16] 4798 2-9-5 0 StevieDonohoe 2 56
(Ed Vaughan) *wnt rt leaving stalls and s.i.s: hld up in tch in rr: effrt 2f out: no imp u.p over 1f out: wknd ins fnl f* **14/1**

8 2 1/4 **Kayat** 2-9-5 0 AdamKirby 9 49
(David Simcock) *chsd ldrs: unable qck and edgd rt over 1f out: wknd ins fnl f* **20/1**

05 **9** 3/4 **Leg It Lenny (IRE)**[29] 4282 2-9-0 0 CierenFallon(5) 3 47
(Robert Cowell) *hld up in tch towards rr: effrt wl over 2f out: unable qck and outpcd over 1f out: wknd ins fnl f* **25/1**

1m 11.69s (-0.41) **Going Correction** -0.175s/f (Firm) **9** Ran SP% **118.0**
Speed ratings (Par 96): **95,94,91,88,85 84,83,80,79**
CSF £5.93 TOTE £2.50: £1.10, £1.20, £4.50; EX 6.10 Trifecta £53.50.
Owner Hunscote Stud Ltd & Mrs Lynne Maclennan **Bred** Whitsbury Manor Stud & R J Cornelius **Trained** Newmarket, Suffolk

FOCUS
A good pace on in this maiden auction event and the winner was produced late under a confident ride. The second has been rated to his debut form.

5382 UNIBET NURSERY H'CAP (JOCKEY CLUB GRASSROOTS NURSERY SERIES QUALIFIER) 7f
6:40 (6:40) (Class 4) (0-85,87) 2-Y-O £6,469 (£1,925; £962; £481) Stalls High

Form RPR
321 1 **Path Of Thunder (IRE)**[22] 4551 2-9-7 **84**..................(p[1]) JamesDoyle 3 92
(Charlie Appleby) *mde all: rdn 2f out: wnt lft u.p and hit rail jst ins fnl f: styd on and a doing enough after and in command whn edgd rt towards fin* **11/8**[1]

210 2 ¾ **Light Angel**[38] 3949 2-9-5 **87**.................................. CierenFallon[(5)] 4 93
(John Gosden) *t.k.h: trckd wnr: wnt 2nd and swtchd rt 2f out: kpt on u.p but a hld ins fnl f: carried rt towards fin* **7/2**[3]

4531 3 13 **Making History (IRE)**[8] 5101 2-8-12 **80** 6ex.......... ThomasGreatrex[(5)] 1 51
(Saeed bin Suroor) *t.k.h: chsd wnr for 1f: effrt and chsd wnr again over 2f out tl 2f out: outpcd and btn over 1f out: wknd ins fnl f* **7/4**[2]

304 4 4 **Dorset Blue (IRE)**[17] 4750 2-8-6 **69**.............................. HollieDoyle 2 29
(Richard Hannon) *t.k.h: chsd wnr after 1f tl over 2f out: outpcd u.p and btn over 1f out: wknd ins fnl f* **11/1**

1m 24.19s (-1.51) **Going Correction** -0.175s/f (Firm) **4** Ran SP% **109.0**
Speed ratings (Par 96): **101,100,85,80**
CSF £6.42 TOTE £2.10; EX 6.00 Trifecta £8.80.
Owner Godolphin **Bred** Rabbah Bloodstock Limited **Trained** Newmarket, Suffolk

FOCUS
A small field for the nursery but still an interesting contest and the front two came home well clear.

5383 UNIBET H'CAP 1m
7:10 (7:10) (Class 3) (0-90,88) 3-Y-O+ £9,056 (£2,695; £1,346; £673) Stalls High

Form RPR
6042 1 **Arigato**[15] 4837 4-9-6 **79**..................(p) JosephineGordon 5 86
(William Jarvis) *trckd ldr: rdn to ld over 1f out: edgd lft jst ins fnl f: hld on wl u.p fnl 100yds* **11/2**

3304 2 ½ **Al Jellaby**[25] 4450 4-10-0 **87**.................................. AdamKirby 4 93
(Clive Cox) *led: drvn and hdd over 1f out: kpt on u.p and ev ch after: unable qck and hld fnl 100yds* **5/2**[2]

-024 3 hd **Baba Ghanouj (IRE)**[13] 4930 3-9-2 **83**.......................... AndreaAtzeni 3 86
(Ed Walker) *hld up in tch in last trio: nt clr run and swtchd rt 2f out: hdwy u.p to press ldng pair 1f out: kpt on wl* **7/2**[3]

-420 4 2¼ **Almashriq (USA)**[14] 4882 3-9-7 **88**..................(v[1]) DaneO'Neill 1 86
(John Gosden) *styd away fr rivals early: chsd ldrs: effrt to press ldng pair 2f out: unable qck u.p 1f out: wknd ins fnl f* **15/8**[1]

-120 5 nk **Balgair**[15] 4851 5-9-12 **85**.................................(h) LukeMorris 2 85
(Tom Clover) *hld up in tch in rr: effrt over 2f out: no imp and hung lft jst ins fnl f: wl hld and plugged on same pce after (jockey said gelding lugged left-handed)* **8/1**

1m 37.69s (-2.31) **Going Correction** -0.175s/f (Firm) **5** Ran SP% **112.1**
WFA 3 from 4yo+ 8lb
Speed ratings (Par 107): **104,103,103,101,100**
CSF £19.75 TOTE £6.90: £2.40, £1.70; EX 21.20 Trifecta £38.70.
Owner Ms E L Banks **Bred** Mrs Susan Field **Trained** Newmarket, Suffolk

FOCUS
A disappointing turnout for this 0-90 handicap and probably not form to get carried away with, the time just 0.18 seconds faster than the 0-70 fillies' handicap that opened the card. It's been rated around the first two.

5384 UNIBET NOVICE STKS 1m 4f
7:40 (7:40) (Class 3) 3-4-Y-O £9,703 (£2,887; £1,443; £721) Stalls Centre

Form RPR
21 1 **Away He Goes (IRE)**[15] 4842 3-9-8 0.............................. SeanLevey 7 98
(Ismail Mohammed) *trckd ldr: effrt and ev ch over 2f out: edgd rt u.p and bmpd rival 1f out: led ins fnl f: kpt on wl: drvn out* **11/8**[1]

2 ½ **Adonijah** 3-9-2 0.. JasonWatson 1 91
(Henry Candy) *wnt lft leaving stalls: trckd ldng pair: effrt over 2f out: sn rdn: swtchd lft over 1f out: kpt on wl u.p ins fnl f: wnt 2nd towards fin* **7/2**[3]

2 3 ½ **Passion And Glory (IRE)**[15] 4842 3-9-2 0........................ TomQueally 5 90
(Saeed bin Suroor) *led: rdn and hrd pressed over 2f out: drvn over 1f out: bmpd 1f out: sn hdd: kpt on same pce u.p: lost 2nd towards fin* **15/8**[2]

04 4 25 **Persepone**[23] 4503 3-8-11 0.. AndreaAtzeni 6 45
(Hugo Palmer) *stdd after s: hld up in tch in rr: swtchd lft over 3f out: sn rdn and struggling: wl btn 2f out: wknd* **8/1**

5 10 **Seventeenpointfour** 3-9-2 0...................................... GeorgeWood 3 34
(Amy Murphy) *pushed lft leaving stalls: hld up in tch in last pair: rdn and hung lft over 3f out: sn outpcd and wl btn 2f out: wknd* **20/1**

2m 32.14s (-1.76) **Going Correction** -0.175s/f (Firm) **5** Ran SP% **115.0**
Speed ratings (Par 107): **98,97,97,80,74**
CSF £7.01 TOTE £2.20: £1.30, £1.80; EX 6.80 Trifecta £9.90.
Owner Khalifa Saeed Sulaiman **Bred** Rabbah Bloodstock Limited **Trained** Newmarket, Suffolk

FOCUS
Another small field on the night but this looked a good contest and the first three home should all have bright futures ahead of them. Muddling form. The third has been rated to his debut form for now.

5385 32RED H'CAP 1m 4f
8:10 (8:11) (Class 5) (0-75,73) 3-Y-O £4,528 (£1,347; £673) Stalls Centre

Form RPR
-011 1 **Hydroplane (IRE)**[9] 5054 3-9-7 **73** 6ex..................(p[1]) LukeMorris 3 80+
(Sir Mark Prescott Bt) *hld up in tch in 3rd: effrt to chal ent fnl 2f: drvn to ld 1f out: styd on and asserted ins fnl f: eased towards fin* **8/13**[1]

024 2 2 **Artistic Language**[48] 3604 3-9-7 **73**..........................(v) JasonWatson 2 76
(Brian Meehan) *led: sn hdd and chsd ldr tl led over 2f out: sn rdn and wnt lft u.p 2f out: hung rt and btn ins fnl f* **2/1**[2]

326 3 16 **Frankadore (IRE)**[22] 4549 3-8-12 **67**..................(p) JaneElliott[(3)] 1 44
(Tom Dascombe) *t.k.h: sn led: hdd and rdn over 2f out: outpcd 2f out and wknd fnl f* **7/1**[3]

2m 29.86s (-4.04) **Going Correction** -0.175s/f (Firm) **3** Ran SP% **107.8**
Speed ratings (Par 100): **106,104,94**
CSF £2.14 TOTE £1.50; EX 2.40 Trifecta £1.60.
Owner Axom LXXIII **Bred** Bloomsbury Stud **Trained** Newmarket, Suffolk

FOCUS
An uneventful handicap with the hot favourite completing his hat-trick despite still looking to be learning on the job.

5386 32RED CASINO H'CAP 7f
8:40 (8:40) (Class 4) (0-85,87) 3-Y-O+ £6,469 (£1,925; £962; £481; £400; £400) Stalls High

Form RPR
3052 1 **Graphite Storm**[20] 4654 5-9-13 **83**.................................. AdamKirby 3 92
(Clive Cox) *hld up in last pair: swtchd rt and effrt 2f out: hdwy u.p 1f out: str chal ins fnl f: kpt on wl to ld towards fin* **15/8**[1]

3/13 2 hd **That Is The Spirit**[37] 3991 8-9-9 **84**.......................... CierenFallon[(5)] 2 92
(Michael Appleby) *led: sn hdd but styd pressing ldr: rdn ent fnl 2f: led again ent fnl f: kpt on wl u.p: hdd and no ex towards fin* **7/1**

2432 3 2¾ **Chloellie**[30] 4247 4-8-8 **71**.. TobyEley[(7)] 5 72
(J R Jenkins) *s.i.s: hld up in rr: clsd and nt clr run over 1f out: rdn to chse ldrs 1f out: sn no imp and outpcd wl ins fnl f* **20/1**

0064 4 1 **Maksab (IRE)**[14] 4887 4-10-0 **84**................................ AndreaAtzeni 4 82
(Mick Channon) *in tch in midfield: effrt over 2f out: drvn over 1f out: no ex and wknd ins fnl f* **10/3**[3]

5401 5 3¼ **Swift Approval (IRE)**[31] 4226 7-9-9 **79**........................ JasonWatson 1 69
(Stuart Williams) *sn led: rdn ent 2f out: edgd rt and hdd ent fnl f: no ex and wknd ins fnl f* **13/2**

-026 6 5 **Turn 'n Twirl (USA)**[20] 4639 3-9-10 **87**..................(h[1]) JamesDoyle 6 60
(Simon Crisford) *chsd ldrs: effrt wl over 1f out: sn rdn and unable qck: lost pl and bhd whn eased ins fnl f (jockey said filly stopped quickly)* **3/1**[2]

1m 23.78s (-1.92) **Going Correction** -0.175s/f (Firm) **6** Ran SP% **113.5**
WFA 3 from 4yo+ 7lb
Speed ratings (Par 105): **103,102,99,98,94 89**
CSF £15.87 TOTE £2.50: £1.60, £2.80; EX 19.20 Trifecta £334.20.
Owner Mrs Olive Shaw **Bred** Mrs O A Shaw **Trained** Lambourn, Berks

FOCUS
A strongly run finale and a cracking finish, the well-backed favourite coming through late to beat a game runner-up. The winner has been rated similar to his Leicester second.
T/Plt: £41.70 to a £1 stake. Pool: £48,915.70 - 855.10 winning units T/Qpdt: £15.50 to a £1 stake. Pool: £3,883.06 - 184.41 winning units **Steve Payne**

4516 THIRSK (L-H)
Friday, July 26

OFFICIAL GOING: Good (good to firm in places) changing to good after race 4 (3.55)
Wind: virtually nil Weather: overcast but warm, heavy showers after 2nd

5387 UNLIMITED FREE RACE REPLAYS AT SPORTINGLIFE.COM EBF FILLIES' NOVICE STKS (PLUS 10 RACE) 7f
2:10 (2:11) (Class 4) 2-Y-O £5,175 (£1,540; £769; £384) Stalls Low

Form RPR
4 1 **Diamond Sparkles (USA)**[15] 4819 2-8-11 0........................ SeanDavis[(3)] 10 77
(Richard Fahey) *hld up in midfield: pushed along and hdwy 2f out: chal appr fnl f: rdn to ld 110yds out: kpt on wl* **10/1**

0 2 ¾ **Frankel's Storm**[13] 4918 2-9-0 0.................................. JoeFanning 6 75+
(Mark Johnston) *led: rdn along and hdd over 1f out: styd on ins fnl f* **7/2**[3]

42 3 hd **Imperial Gloriana (IRE)**[21] 4596 2-9-0 0.................. DanielTudhope 11 74
(David O'Meara) *hld up in midfield: pushed along and hdwy on outer over 2f out: led over 1f out: sn drvn: hdd 110yds out: no ex towards fin* **9/4**[2]

40 4 4 **Galadriel**[35] 4048 2-9-0 0.. KevinStott 8 64
(Kevin Ryan) *trckd ldrs: rdn along 2f out: wknd ins fnl f* **7/4**[1]

6 5 ½ **Sun Crystal (IRE)**[41] 3866 2-9-0 0.............................. TonyHamilton 1 62
(Richard Fahey) *midfield: rdn along 2f out: bit outpcd over 1f out: plugged on ins fnl f* **33/1**

6 6 1¼ **Secret Passion**[15] 4819 2-9-0 0.................................. AdamMcNamara 9 59
(Archie Watson) *prom: rdn over 2f out: wknd ins fnl f* **40/1**

7 shd **Sweet Serenade** 2-9-0 0.. PJMcDonald 4 59
(James Tate) *s.i.s: hld up in midfield: pushed along over 2f out: nvr involved* **16/1**

06 8 1¼ **Carriesmatic**[20] 4623 2-9-0 0...................................... AndrewMullen 12 55
(David Barron) *s.i.s: hld up: nvr threatened* **100/1**

4 9 ¾ **Impression**[31] 4206 2-9-0 0.................................. SilvestreDeSousa 2 53
(Amy Murphy) *trckd ldrs: rdn along over 2f out: wknd fnl f* **28/1**

25 10 1¾ **Woke (IRE)**[11] 4976 2-9-0 0.. CliffordLee 3 49
(K R Burke) *midfield: rdn 2f out: wknd fnl f* **40/1**

11 6 **Boulevard Beauty (IRE)** 2-9-0 0.................................. DavidAllan 5 32
(Tim Easterby) *slowly away: a in rr (jockey said filly was slowly away)* **50/1**

1m 26.75s (-0.85) **Going Correction** -0.075s/f (Good) **11** Ran SP% **118.5**
Speed ratings (Par 93): **101,100,99,95,94 93,93,91,90,88 82**
CSF £43.63 TOTE £6.70: £1.50, £1.70, £1.40; EX 39.90 Trifecta £169.20.
Owner Mrs Richard Henry **Bred** Premier Bloodstock **Trained** Musley Bank, N Yorks

FOCUS
Add 10 yards. A fairly decent juvenile fillies' novice contest. The fourth-favourite won a shade cosily towards the centre from midfield.

5388 SKY BET GO-RACING-IN-YORKSHIRE SUMMER FESTIVAL EBF NOVICE STKS 5f
2:45 (2:46) (Class 5) 2-Y-O £3,881 (£1,155; £577; £288) Stalls Centre

Form RPR
1 **Ventura Lightning (FR)** 2-9-5 0.................................. TonyHamilton 2 74+
(Richard Fahey) *trckd ldrs: pushed along over 1f out: kpt on wl fnl 150yds: led towards fin* **13/2**[3]

3 2 nk **Baltic State (IRE)**[18] 4719 2-9-5 0.................................. KevinStott 4 73
(Kevin Ryan) *led: rdn along over 1f out: drvn and edgd lft ins fnl f: kpt on but hdd towards fin* **11/10**[1]

5 3 nse **Hostelry**[15] 4826 2-9-0 0.. ConnorBeasley 1 68
(Michael Dods) *prom: rdn 2f out: kpt on* **5/1**[2]

4 ¾ **Sam's Call** 2-9-5 0.. NathanEvans 6 70
(Michael Easterby) *prom: pushed along 2f out: rdn ins fnl f: one pce towards fin* **25/1**

05 5 ¾ **Shepherds Way (IRE)**[11] 4984 2-9-0 0.............................. GrahamLee 9 62
(Michael Dods) *prom: rdn over 1f out: one pce fnl f* **25/1**

0 6 shd **Not On Your Nellie (IRE)**[11] 4984 2-8-9 0.......... FayeMcManoman[(5)] 5 62+
(Nigel Tinkler) *dwlt: sn trckd ldrs: pushed along 2f out: kpt on ins fnl f* **50/1**

The Form Book Flat 2019, Raceform Ltd, Newbury, RG14 5SJ

4 **7** *4* **Rapid Russo**[20] 4624 2-9-5 0 TomEaves 7 53
(Michael Dods) *dwlt: hld up in rr: pushed along and sme hdwy over 1f out: nvr trbld ldrs* 7/1

05 **8** *2 3/4* **Street Life**[30] 4238 2-9-5 0 PaulHanagan 3 43
(Richard Fahey) *hld up: nvr threatened* 14/1

00 **9** *nk* **Rebel Redemption**[15] 4826 2-9-5 0 JasonHart 10 42
(John Quinn) *hld up: pushed along 3f out: sn btn* 12/1

59.52s (0.12) **Going Correction** -0.075s/f (Good) **9** Ran SP% **114.1**
Speed ratings (Par 94): **96,95,95,94,93 92,86,82,81**
CSF £13.64 TOTE £6.60: £1.90, £1.40, £1.40; EX 16.60 Trifecta £57.60.
Owner Middleham Park Racing LXXXI & Partner **Bred** Snowdrop Stud Corporation Limited **Trained** Musley Bank, N Yorks

FOCUS
A fair juvenile novice sprint contest. The third-favourite won well on debut. The level will take time to settle.

5389 PROJECT MANAGEMENT SCOTLAND (S) H'CAP 7f 218y
3:20 (3:21) (Class 6) (0-60,59) 3-Y-O
£3,058 (£910; £454; £300; £300; £300) **Stalls** Centre

Form RPR

20U4 **1** **The Big House (IRE)**[13] 4915 3-8-12 **50** AndrewMullen 8 61+
(Adrian Nicholls) *prom: rdn to ld over 1f out: kpt on wl to draw clr ins fnl f* 4/1[2]

0050 **2** *4* **Smashing Lass (IRE)**[23] 4518 3-8-9 **47** (p) PaddyMathers 9 49
(Ollie Pears) *dwlt: hld up in midfield: rdn and hdwy over 1f out: kpt on ins fnl f: wnt 2nd towards fin* 28/1

5635 **3** *nk* **Arriba De Toda (IRE)**[3] 5272 3-8-6 **47** BenRobinson(3) 13 48
(Brian Ellison) *hld up in midfield: hdwy and n.m.r over 1f out: swtchd rt ent fnl f: kpt on wl* 5/1[3]

0000 **4** *hd* **Grey Berry (IRE)**[10] 5031 3-9-7 **59** (b) DavidAllan 12 60
(Tim Easterby) *led: rdn and hdd over 1f out: no ex and lost 2 pls towards fin* 14/1

4344 **5** *1/2* **Tails I Win (CAN)**[20] 4653 3-9-4 **56** (h) BenCurtis 11 56
(Roger Fell) *midfield: rdn over 2f out: sme hdwy over 1f out: one pce ins fnl f* 7/2[1]

2040 **6** *1/2* **Lady Lavinia**[16] 4785 3-8-13 **51** NathanEvans 16 50
(Michael Easterby) *hld up in rr: rdn over 2f out: swtchd rt to outer 2f out: styd on fnl f* 16/1

6514 **7** *5* **Lethal Laura**[10] 5031 3-9-0 **52** (p) PJMcDonald 5 39
(James Given) *trckd ldrs: rdn over 2f out: wknd fnl f* 11/2

0053 **8** *1/2* **Parion**[10] 5021 3-8-10 **51** SeanDavis(3) 1 37
(Richard Fahey) *midfield: rdn over 2f out: wknd over 1f out* 8/1

-006 **9** *3* **George's Law**[21] 4582 3-8-10 **48** DuranFentiman 6 27
(Tim Easterby) *midfield: rdn over 2f out: wknd over 1f out* 25/1

0305 **10** *3 1/2* **Um Shama (IRE)**[18] 4735 3-9-5 **57** JasonHart 14 28
(David Loughnane) *hld up: nvr threatened* 22/1

04-0 **11** *shd* **Lady Rouda (IRE)**[24] 4487 3-8-7 **45** SilvestreDeSousa 3 16
(Philip Kirby) *prom: rdn over 2f out: wknd over 1f out* 14/1

3000 **12** *2 1/2* **Lexikon**[23] 4518 3-8-13 **51** JamieGormley 2 16
(Ollie Pears) *trckd ldrs: rdn over 2f out: wknd over 1f out* 20/1

60-0 **13** *1 1/2* **Stainforth Swagger**[28] 4328 3-8-12 **50** AndrewElliott 7 12
(Ronald Thompson) *a towards rr (vet said gelding lost both front shoes)* 50/1

1m 40.89s (-0.81) **Going Correction** -0.075s/f (Good) **13** Ran SP% **123.0**
Speed ratings (Par 98): **101,97,96,96,96 95,90,90,87,83 83,80,79**
CSF £123.45 CT £588.14 TOTE £5.20: £2.10, £8.50, £1.70; EX 137.90 Trifecta £691.50.There was no bid for the winner.
Owner Dave Stone **Bred** Peter Molony **Trained** Sessay, N Yorks

FOCUS
Add 10 yards. A modest 3yo selling handicap. There was a sharp thunderstorm ahead of this contest and the decisive winner's time suggested any potential sting in the ground had been negated. The second helps set the straightforward level.

5390 ANDERSON BARROWCLIFF CHARTERED ACCOUNTANTS NURSERY H'CAP 6f
3:55 (3:55) (Class 3) (0-95,86) 2-Y-O **£9,703** (£2,887; £1,443; £721) **Stalls** Centre

Form RPR

1211 **1** **Troubador (IRE)**[13] 4938 2-9-7 **86** PaulMulrennan 4 91
(Michael Dods) *mde all: pushed along over 1f out: rdn ins fnl f: kpt on wl* 7/2[1]

343 **2** *1 1/2* **No Mercy**[13] 4937 2-8-12 **77** BenCurtis 5 77
(K R Burke) *prom: rdn 2f out: drvn fnl f: kpt on but a hld* 4/1[2]

123 **3** *hd* **Coastal Mist (IRE)**[24] 4486 2-8-10 **75** JasonHart 3 74
(John Quinn) *dwlt: sn in tch: rdn along 2f out: edgd lft and kpt on fnl f* 11/2[3]

631 **4** *3/4* **Aberama Gold**[20] 4631 2-8-13 **78** ShaneGray 7 75
(Keith Dalgleish) *prom: pushed along over 2f out: rdn and bit outpcd over 1f out: plugged on fnl f* 6/1

1120 **5** *1* **Rose Of Kildare (IRE)**[34] 4091 2-9-4 **83** JoeFanning 9 77
(Mark Johnston) *s.i.s: hld up: sn swtchd lft towards far side: hdwy and trckd ldrs over 2f out: rdn over 1f out: edgd lft and no ex fnl f* 4/1[2]

624 **6** *2 1/4* **Star Of St James (GER)**[29] 4302 2-8-9 **74** PaulHanagan 6 61
(Richard Fahey) *hld up in tch: rdn along over 2f out: nvr threatened* 10/1

315 **7** *hd* **Bushtucker Trial (IRE)**[25] 4433 2-8-10 **75** HayleyTurner 2 62
(Michael Bell) *trckd ldrs: rdn 2f out: wknd ins fnl f* 14/1

0243 **8** *7* **Corndavon Lad (IRE)**[20] 4647 2-8-6 **74** (p[1]) SeanDavis(3) 8 40
(Richard Fahey) *a in rr* 22/1

1m 12.8s **Going Correction** -0.075s/f (Good) **8** Ran SP% **112.0**
Speed ratings (Par 98): **97,95,94,93,92 89,89,79**
CSF £16.82 CT £73.02 TOTE £4.00: £1.70, £1.60, £1.70; EX 19.10 Trifecta £112.50.
Owner J Sagar And S Lowthian **Bred** Worksop Manor Stud **Trained** Denton, Co Durham

FOCUS
The feature contest was a decent nursery. The favourite made all in a good comparative time considering the official going was eased to good after the race. It's been rated as straightforward form rated around the second and third.

5391 TOMRODS STEEL STOCKHOLDER AND SERVICE CENTRE H'CAP 2m 13y
4:30 (4:30) (Class 4) (0-80,80) 3-Y-O+
£6,016 (£1,790; £894; £447; £300; £300) **Stalls** Centre

Form RPR

1132 **1** **Mondain**[7] 5127 3-8-10 **77** JoeFanning 2 92+
(Mark Johnston) *prom: pushed into ld over 2f out: sn clr: eased towards fin* 1/2[1]

4623 **2** *10* **Remember The Days (IRE)**[15] 4817 5-9-8 **74** GrahamLee 5 74
(Jedd O'Keeffe) *led: rdn and hdd over 2f out: outpcd and sn no ch w wnr* 9/1[3]

2504 **3** *1/2* **Royal Flag**[23] 4522 9-8-8 **63** BenRobinson(3) 7 62
(Brian Ellison) *midfield: rdn along over 3f out: plugged on* 20/1

2-34 **4** *1/2* **Final Rock**[14] 4890 4-10-0 **80** PaulMulrennan 6 79
(Sir Mark Prescott Bt) *hld up in rr: racd alone towards far rail in st and pushed along briefly over 3f out: rdn over 1f out: plugged on fnl f* 8/1[2]

3416 **5** *12* **Super Kid**[9] 5055 7-9-12 **78** (tp) DavidAllan 1 62
(Tim Easterby) *hld up: rdn over 3f out: sn wknd* 8/1[2]

1406 **6** *17* **Valkenburg**[20] 4661 4-8-11 **66** (b) SeanDavis(3) 4 30
(Harriet Bethell) *midfield: wnt in snatches: rdn over 5f out: wknd and bhd fnl 3f* 14/1

3m 32.76s (-0.84) **Going Correction** -0.075s/f (Good)
WFA 3 from 4yo+ 15lb **6** Ran SP% **110.3**
Speed ratings (Par 105): **99,94,93,93,87 79**
CSF £5.55 CT £36.33 TOTE £1.30: £1.20, £2.30; EX 5.70 Trifecta £31.30.
Owner Sheikh Hamdan bin Mohammed Al Maktoum **Bred** Godolphin **Trained** Middleham Moor, N Yorks

FOCUS
Add 27 yards. A fair staying handicap. There was further evidence that the ground had eased on the round course, but that didn't stop the odds-on favourite routing his opposition in the second half of the straight. The second has been rated to his recent form.

5392 JW 4X4 NORTHALLERTON FILLIES' H'CAP 6f
5:05 (5:06) (Class 5) (0-70,72) 3-Y-O+
£4,722 (£1,405; £702; £351; £300; £300) **Stalls** Centre

Form RPR

0004 **1** **Fumbo Jumbo (IRE)**[23] 4519 6-9-2 **60** JamieGormley 9 70
(Rebecca Bastiman) *slowly away: hld up: rdn and gd hdwy appr fnl f: kpt on wl: led towards fin* 9/1

002 **2** *nk* **Fox Hill**[15] 4823 3-8-1 **55** PaulaMuir(5) 7 63
(Eric Alston) *led: rdn 2 l clr whn jinked rt over 1f out: edgd lft ins fnl f: flashed tail 75yds out: hdd towards fin* 11/2[3]

2250 **3** *2 3/4* **Supaulette (IRE)**[15] 4822 4-9-9 **67** (bt) PaulMulrennan 4 67
(Tim Easterby) *trckd ldrs: rdn over 2f out: kpt on same pce fnl f* 10/1

3-13 **4** *1* **Local History**[30] 4248 3-9-7 **70** PJMcDonald 8 66
(James Tate) *prom: rdn over 2f out: no ex ins fnl f* 9/4[1]

-406 **5** *1 1/2* **Elysee Star**[34] 4130 4-8-7 **51** oh4 (b[1]) AndrewMullen 11 43
(Ben Haslam) *midfield: rdn over 2f out: outpcd over 1f out: plugged on fnl f* 22/1

5203 **6** *1 1/2* **Santafiora**[17] 4763 5-8-11 **55** GrahamLee 5 42
(Julie Camacho) *slowly away: hld up: minor late hdwy: nvr threatened* 15/2

1-56 **7** *1/2* **Essenza (IRE)**[15] 4822 3-9-2 **65** TonyHamilton 6 50
(Richard Fahey) *midfield: rdn over 2f out: wknd fnl f* 20/1

335 **8** *3* **Sapphire Jubilee**[56] 3291 3-8-8 **60** BenRobinson(3) 3 35
(Ollie Pears) *trckd ldrs: racd keenly: rdn over 2f out: wknd over 1f out* 25/1

4615 **9** *3 1/4* **Raspberry**[25] 4444 3-9-4 **70** ConnorMurtagh(3) 1 35
(Olly Williams) *prom: lost pl over 3f out: rdn over 2f out: sn wknd* 33/1

5541 **10** *4 1/2* **Stewardess (IRE)**[20] 4660 4-10-0 **72** DavidNolan 2 23
(Richard Fahey) *midfield: rdn over 2f out: edgd lft and wknd over 1f out (trainer's rep could offer no explanation for the filly's performance)* 7/2[2]

1m 12.14s (-0.66) **Going Correction** -0.075s/f (Good)
WFA 3 from 4yo+ 5lb **10** Ran SP% **115.1**
Speed ratings (Par 100): **101,100,96,95,93 91,90,86,82,76**
CSF £53.99 CT £518.42 TOTE £12.70: £4.40, £1.80, £2.70; EX 68.40 Trifecta £427.00.
Owner Let's Be Lucky Racing 21 & Partner **Bred** Tally-Ho Stud **Trained** Cowthorpe, N Yorks

FOCUS
An ordinary fillies' handicap. An in-form mare got up late in a good comparative time despite a modest beginning. The second has been rated as backing up her Carlisle latest.

5393 SCOUTING FOR GIRLS - LIVE @THIRSKRACES 16TH AUGUST APPRENTICE H'CAP (REX HANDS AND HEELS SERIES) 5f
5:40 (5:43) (Class 6) (0-60,62) 3-Y-O+
£3,058 (£910; £454; £300; £300; £300) **Stalls** Centre

Form RPR

2463 **1** **Monarch Maid**[142] 1038 8-8-10 **46** ElishaWhittington 10 60
(Peter Hiatt) *prom: pushed along 2f out: led 1f out: kpt on wl* 33/1

4300 **2** *4* **Dancing Mountain (IRE)**[18] 4720 3-8-12 **52** (b[1]) RhonaPindar 6 51
(Roger Fell) *sn led: pushed along 2f out: hdd 1f out: one pce and sn no ch w wnr* 18/1

2100 **3** *1/2* **Cuppacoco**[10] 5018 4-9-7 **57** GavinAshton 7 55
(Ann Duffield) *in tch: pushed along over 2f out: kpt on ins fnl f* 14/1

0300 **4** *shd* **Racquet**[39] 3933 6-8-10 **45** oh1 (b) RussellHarris 1 44
(Ruth Carr) *prom: pushed along over 2f out: one pce fnl f* 25/1

5165 **5** *1/2* **Hello Girl**[10] 5018 4-9-1 **54** IzzyClifton(3) 5 50
(Nigel Tinkler) *chsd ldrs: pushed along over 2f out: plugged on* 5/2[1]

0003 **6** *2 1/2* **Suitcase 'N' Taxi**[20] 4630 5-9-10 **60** AidenBlakemore 2 47
(Tim Easterby) *dwlt: hld up: pushed along and sme hdwy 2f out: nvr threatened* 5/1

0004 **7** *1/2* **Shall We Begin (IRE)**[25] 4436 3-8-6 **49** ZakWheatley(3) 9 33
(Michael Easterby) *s.i.s: outpcd in rr tl minor late hdwy* 9/2[3]

0051 **8** *3/4* **Point Of Woods**[6] 5169 6-9-11 **61** 5ex (t) EllaMcCain 4 44
(Tina Jackson) *dwlt: hld up: nvr threatened (jockey said gelding was never travelling)* 4/1[2]

6032 **9** *1* **Spot Lite**[8] 5084 4-8-11 **50** (p) OliverSearle(3) 3 29+
(Rod Millman) *hld up: sddle slipped sn after s: rdr wout irons over 2f out: nvr threatened (jockey said his saddle slipped shortly after leaving the stalls)* 6/1

0-00 **10** *3 1/2* **Legal Tender (IRE)**[25] 4436 3-9-8 **62** (h) HarryRussell 8 27
(Bryan Smart) *hld up in tch: pushed along over 2f out: wknd over 1f out* 50/1

59.57s (0.17) **Going Correction** -0.075s/f (Good)
WFA 3 from 4yo+ 4lb **10** Ran SP% **118.4**
Speed ratings (Par 101): **95,88,87,87,86 82,82,80,79,73**
CSF £525.21 CT £8411.53 TOTE £25.00: £5.00, £3.30, £3.40; EX 265.10 Trifecta £2234.30.
Owner P W Hiatt **Bred** Oakhill Stud **Trained** Hook Norton, Oxon

FOCUS
A modest apprentice riders' sprint handicap. It's been rated a shade conservatively.
T/Plt: £72.60 to a £1 stake. Pool: £54,049.24 - 542.89 winning units T/Qpdt: £28.60 to a £1 stake. Pool: £5,124.66 - 132.46 winning units **Andrew Sheret**

4932 YORK (L-H)

Friday, July 26

OFFICIAL GOING: Good (ovr 7.1, far 7.2, ctr 7.2, stands' 7.0)

Wind: Virtually nil Weather: Heavy cloud and showers

5394 EVENTMASTERS.CO.UK SILK SERIES LADY RIDERS' H'CAP (PRO-AM LADY RIDERS' RACE) 1m 177y

6:00 (6:01) (Class 4) (0-80,82) 3-Y-O

£8,983 (£2,673; £1,335; £667; £400; £400) **Stalls** Low

Form RPR

-211 **1** **Chance**[20] 4662 3-10-8 **82** MeganNicholls(3) 3 94+
(Simon Crisford) *hld up towards rr: smooth hdwy over 3f out: led 2f out: rdn clr ent fnl f: kpt on strly* 9/4[1]

3300 **2** 2 ¾ **Balladeer**[46] 3647 3-10-7 **78** (v[1]) HayleyTurner 7 82
(Michael Bell) *trckd ldrs: pushed along 3f out: rdn 2f out: kpt on u.p fnl f* 12/1

2132 **3** ½ **Highwaygrey**[35] 4077 3-9-12 **69** RachelRichardson 4 72
(Tim Easterby) *trckd ldr: hdwy and cl up 3f out: rdn along 2f out: ev ch tl drvn appr fnl f and kpt on same pce* 12/1

2-32 **4** nk **Brandy Spirit**[67] 2895 3-10-0 **76** (h) MissJoannaMason(5) 2 78
(Michael Easterby) *awkward s: t.k.h: hld up in rr: hdwy 3f out: swtchd lft towards inner and rdn 2f out: styd on fnl f: nrst fin* 14/1

4011 **5** ¾ **Potenza (IRE)**[29] 4284 3-9-3 **67** LauraCoughlan(7) 5 68
(Stef Keniry) *in tch on inner: effrt 3f out and sn pushed along: rdn and sltly outpcd 2f out: kpt on u.p fnl f* 8/1

1125 **6** ½ **Antico Lady (IRE)**[28] 4329 3-9-9 **71** MissBeckySmith(5) 10 71
(Brian Ellison) *trckd ldng pair: effrt over 3f out: rdn along to ld briefly wl over 2f out: hdd and drvn 2f out: grad wknd* 7/1

6464 **7** 1 **Noble Account**[15] 4838 3-9-9 **66** (h) ShelleyBirkett 8 63
(Julia Feilden) *dwlt and a towards rr* 16/1

-506 **8** ½ **Sootability (IRE)**[20] 4626 3-9-7 **69** MissEmmaTodd(5) 1 65
(Richard Fahey) *hld up towards rr: hdwy 3f out: chsd ldrs 2f out: sn rdn and wknd over 1f out* 25/1

1334 **9** 5 **Amadeus Grey (IRE)**[6] 5198 3-10-3 **81** (t) MissEmilyEasterby(7) 9 66
(Tim Easterby) *chsd ldrs: rdn along on outer 3f out: sn wknd* 13/2[3]

353 **10** 9 **Moftris**[25] 4452 3-10-1 **75** (p[1]) GeorgiaCox(3) 6 40
(William Haggas) *led: pushed along 3f out: rdn and hdd wl over 2f out: sn wknd (jockey said gelding ran too free)* 11/2[2]

1m 50.71s (0.31) **Going Correction** +0.125s/f (Good) **10 Ran SP% 114.9**
Speed ratings (Par 102): **103,100,100,99,99 98,97,97,92,84**
CSF £30.95 CT £267.25 TOTE £3.20: £1.90, £3.40, £2.40; EX 36.10 Trifecta £278.00.
Owner Khalifa Saeed Sulaiman **Bred** Haras D'Etreham & Eric De Chambure **Trained** Newmarket, Suffolk

FOCUS
Race distances as advertised. The going was good, good to firm in places with a going stick reading of 7.1 taken at 14:30. There had been 4mm in sharp showers this afternoon. A strong field for this lady riders' handicap and a second successive win for Megan Nicholls. It's been rated at face value around the second and third, which fits the race standard.

5395 IRISH THOROUGHBRED MARKETING H'CAP 6f

6:30 (6:33) (Class 4) (0-80,81) 4-Y-O+

£9,962 (£2,964; £1,481; £740; £400; £400) **Stalls** High

Form RPR

1212 **1** **Tricky Dicky**[25] 4440 6-9-6 **79** BenCurtis 10 89
(Roger Fell) *mde all: rdn wl over 1f out: drvn ins fnl f: kpt on wl towards fin* 4/1[1]

0360 **2** 1 ¼ **Iconic Knight (IRE)**[11] 4995 4-9-4 **77** PaulHanagan 7 83
(Ed Walker) *trckd ldrs: hdwy 2f out: rdn to chal over 1f out: drvn and kpt on same pce fnl f* 10/1

-654 **3** 1 **Yes You (IRE)**[11] 4977 5-8-11 **75** HarrisonShaw(5) 9 78+
(Iain Jardine) *in rr: hdwy over 2f out: rdn wl over 1f out: kpt on wl fnl f: nrst fin* 25/1

0235 **4** ½ **Daffy Jane**[13] 4904 4-9-1 **79** FayeMcManoman(5) 4 80
(Nigel Tinkler) *trckd ldrs: hdwy over 2f out: rdn to chse ldng pair over 1f out: kpt on same pce fnl f (vet said filly lost left fore shoe)* 14/1

1214 **5** nse **Equiano Springs**[20] 4649 5-9-8 **81** JamesSullivan 16 82
(Tom Tate) *towards rr: pushed along on outer and hdwy over 2f out: rdn wl over 1f out: kpt on fnl f: nrst fin* 7/1[2]

-053 **6** 2 ¾ **Our Little Pony**[41] 3868 4-9-1 **74** DanielTudhope 5 66
(Lawrence Mullaney) *in tch: hdwy to chse ldrs 2f out: sn rdn and no imp* 15/2[3]

0-61 **7** 1 ½ **Cool Spirit**[70] 2788 4-9-7 **80** BarryMcHugh 13 67
(Richard Fahey) *chsd ldrs: effrt wl over 2f out: sn rdn and no imp (jockey said gelding was briefly denied a clear run 2f out)* 8/1

4103 **8** 1 ¼ **John Kirkup**[14] 4879 4-9-4 **77** (p) ConnorBeasley 6 60
(Michael Dods) *trckd ldrs: hdwy over 2f out: rdn wl over 1f out: kpt on same pce* 10/1

4005 **9** 1 ½ **Russian Realm**[38] 3971 9-8-11 **70** KevinStott 12 49
(Paul Midgley) *towards rr tl styd on fr over 1f out: n.d* 33/1

1041 **10** 2 ½ **Rasheeq (IRE)**[31] 4227 6-8-12 **76** (p) SeamusCronin(5) 2 47
(Mohamed Moubarak) *towards rr: hdwy and in tch 2f out: sn rdn and btn* 11/1

1000 **11** 1 **Gullane One (IRE)**[15] 4829 4-8-9 **68** (t) JasonHart 18 35
(Tim Easterby) *cl up: rdn to chal over 2f out: drvn wl over 1f out: grad wknd* 33/1

1640 **12** ½ **Nick Vedder**[20] 4649 5-9-7 **80** (b) CamHardie 14 46
(Michael Wigham) *a in rr* 20/1

0660 **13** nse **Qaaraat**[9] 5042 4-8-3 **67** KieranSchofield(5) 11 33
(Antony Brittain) *prom: rdn along 2f out: sn wknd* 33/1

000 **14** 6 **Double Up**[20] 4649 8-9-6 **79** (vt) SilvestreDeSousa 19 25
(Ian Williams) *chsd ldrs: rdn along over 2f out: sn drvn and wknd (jockey said gelding ran flat)* 16/1

4001 **15** 4 ½ **Spring Romance (IRE)**[29] 4303 4-9-2 **75** JoeyHaynes 8 7
(Dean Ivory) *in tch: rdn along wl over 2f out: sn wknd (jockey said gelding was never travelling)* 12/1

4001 **16** 9 **Orion's Bow**[7] 5119 8-9-5 **78** 4ex (p) DavidAllan 3
(Tim Easterby) *in tch on inner: rdn along over 2f out: sn wknd (jockey said gelding lost its action)* 14/1

1m 11.43s (-0.17) **Going Correction** +0.125s/f (Good) **16 Ran SP% 126.2**
Speed ratings (Par 105): **106,104,103,102,102 98,96,94,92,89 88,87,87,79,73 61**
CSF £42.29 CT £900.58 TOTE £4.40: £1.50, £2.90, £7.90, £3.20; EX 56.90 Trifecta £2977.20.
Owner Eight Gents and a Lady **Bred** Onslow, Stratton & Parry **Trained** Nawton, N Yorks
■ Followthesteps was withdrawn. Price at time of withdrawal 20/1. Rule 4 does not apply.

FOCUS
A cracking 6f handicap was won from the front by the in-form Tricky Dicky. The winner has been rated pretty much to his old AW best, and the second to this year's form.

5396 PREMIER DESIGN AND PRINT NOVICE MEDIAN AUCTION STKS (PLUS 10 RACE) 7f

7:00 (7:04) (Class 3) 2-Y-O

£9,703 (£2,887; £1,443; £721) **Stalls** Low

Form RPR

1 **1** **Boosala (IRE)**[39] 3943 2-9-8 0 DanielTudhope 6 91+
(William Haggas) *prom: trckd ldr after 2f: cl up over 2f out: shkn up to ld 1 1/2f out: sn clr: easily* 1/6[1]

2 3 ½ **Yoshimi (IRE)** 2-9-2 0 PaulHanagan 7 71+
(Richard Fahey) *dwlt and in rr: pushed along over 2f out: swtchd lft: rdn and hdwy over 1f out: styd on wl fnl f* 8/1[2]

3 ½ **Viceregent** 2-9-2 0 TonyHamilton 2 69
(Richard Fahey) *t.k.h: trckd ldrs: hdwy 3f out: rdn along over 2f out: n.m.r and kpt on same pce fnl f* 14/1[3]

4 1 ½ **Stroxx (IRE)** 2-9-2 0 DuranFentiman 5 65
(Tim Easterby) *hld up in tch: hdwy 3f out: rdn to chse ldrs 2f out: drvn and kpt on same pce fnl f* 20/1

0 **5** 2 ¼ **Idoapologise**[41] 3866 2-9-2 0 PJMcDonald 3 59
(James Bethell) *sn led: jnd over 2f out and sn pushed along: rdn and hdd 1 1/2f out: sn drvn and wknd* 25/1

65 **6** 1 ¾ **Phoenix Approach (IRE)**[13] 4937 2-9-2 0 DavidAllan 4 54
(Tim Easterby) *prom: rdn along 3f out: sn wknd* 14/1[3]

00 **7** 7 **My Havana**[45] 3703 2-8-11 0 FayeMcManoman(5) 1 35
(Nigel Tinkler) *dwlt: a in rr: outpcd and bhd fr 1/2-way* 40/1

1m 27.38s (2.78) **Going Correction** +0.125s/f (Good) **7 Ran SP% 121.2**
Speed ratings (Par 98): **89,85,84,82,80 78,70**
CSF £2.77 TOTE £1.10: £1.10, £2.50; EX 2.60 Trifecta £7.40.
Owner Sheikh Ahmed Al Maktoum **Bred** Godolphin **Trained** Newmarket, Suffolk

FOCUS
A straightforward win for the odds-on favourite. The level is fluid in behind the winner.

5397 BRITISH STALLION STUDS EBF LYRIC FILLIES' STKS (LISTED RACE) 1m 2f 56y

7:30 (7:30) (Class 1) 3-Y-O+

£28,355 (£10,750; £5,380; £2,680; £1,345; £675) **Stalls** Low

Form RPR

-130 **1** **Fanny Logan (IRE)**[36] 4014 3-8-9 **94** (h[1]) PJMcDonald 7 108
(John Gosden) *t.k.h early: trckd ldrs: hdwy over 2f out: rdn to chal over 1f out: led ent fnl f: sn drvn and kpt on strly (regarding the apparent improvement in form, trainer's rep said filly benefited from a drop in trip from 1m 4f to 1m 2f, a drop in class and the first time application of a hood as she filly ran quite freely last time)* 6/1

-335 **2** 2 ¼ **Glance**[28] 4332 3-8-9 **100** HarryBentley 2 103
(Ralph Beckett) *hld up in tch on inner: hdwy 3f out: cl up 2f out: sn rdn and ev ch tl drvn ins fnl f and kpt on same pce* 10/1

-266 **3** 2 ¼ **Frankellina**[36] 4014 3-8-9 **105** TomMarquand 4 99
(William Haggas) *t.k.h early: trckd ldrs: hdwy 3f out: sn cl up: rdn to ld 1 1/2f out: drvn and hdd ent fnl f: kpt on same pce* 7/4[1]

0564 **4** 2 **Rasima**[28] 4332 4-9-4 **98** (p) DavidEgan 5 94
(Roger Varian) *sn led: pushed along over 2f out: rdn and hdd 1 1/2f out: sn drvn and grad wknd* 33/1

11 **5** 1 ¼ **Kirstenbosch**[36] 4022 3-8-9 **98** DanielMuscutt 3 92
(James Fanshawe) *hld up in rr: effrt and sme hdwy 3f out: rdn along over 2f out: n.d (jockey said filly lost right fore shoe)* 3/1[2]

22 **6** 2 ½ **Encapsulation (IRE)**[20] 4667 3-8-9 **102** OisinMurphy 8 87
(Andrew Balding) *sn trcking ldr: hdwy and cl up 4f out: rdn along wl over 2f out: sn drvn and wknd* 7/2[3]

2m 9.75s (-0.55) **Going Correction** +0.125s/f (Good) **6 Ran SP% 109.9**
WFA 3 from 4yo 9lb
Speed ratings (Par 108): **107,105,103,101,100 98**
CSF £56.35 TOTE £5.20: £1.90, £3.50; EX 58.00 Trifecta £128.90.
Owner HH Sheikha Al Jalila Racing **Bred** Godolphin **Trained** Newmarket, Suffolk

FOCUS
The feature event and an intriguing affair with the pace looking uneven and a bit of a turn-up. The third has been rated close to her Musidora form, and the fourth close to form.

5398 SBFM COMMERCIAL CLEANING SERVICES H'CAP 7f 192y

8:00 (8:00) (Class 3) (0-95,97) 3-Y-O+

£9,703 (£2,887; £1,443; £721) **Stalls** Low

Form RPR

5021 **1** **Irv (IRE)**[27] 4403 3-8-4 **78** JamesSullivan 3 87+
(Micky Hammond) *hld up: hdwy over 3f out: chsd ldrs over 2f out: rdn to take slt ld 1 1/2f out: drvn ins fnl f: kpt on wl towards fin* 10/3[1]

-220 **2** 1 ¾ **Baltic Baron (IRE)**[29] 4292 4-10-3 **97** DanielTudhope 2 104
(David O'Meara) *hld up in rr: stdy hdwy wl over 2f out: chsd ldrs and n.m.r over 1f out: swtchd lft and rdn to chal jst ins fnl f: sn drvn and ev ch: kpt on same pce towards fin* 7/2[2]

620 **3** 2 ¼ **Just Hiss**[34] 4097 6-9-9 **89** (p) RachelRichardson 1 91
(Tim Easterby) *led: pushed along 3f out: rdn 2f out: hdd narrowly 2f out: sn drvn: grad wknd ent fnl f* 5/1[3]

1104 **4** ¾ **Universal Gleam**[34] 4097 4-9-9 **89** JoeFanning 8 89
(Keith Dalgleish) *in tch: hdwy on inner to trck ldrs over 3f out: rdn to chal 2f out: ev ch tl drvn and wknd appr fnl f* 13/2

-500 **5** 1 ¾ **Garden Oasis**[13] 4907 4-8-11 **77** DavidAllan 4 73
(Tim Easterby) *chsd ldrs: rdn along 3f out: drvn and kpt on same pce fnl 2f (jockey said gelding was denied a clear run approaching 1 1/2f out and again approx 1f out)* 10/1

51U3 **6** ¾ **Crownthorpe**[13] 4934 4-9-11 **94** SeanDavis(3) 10 88
(Richard Fahey) *hld up in rr: hdwy on outer 3f out: rdn along 2f out: sn wknd* 9/1

0054 **7** 2 **International Man**[11] 4982 4-8-6 **75** oh2 ConnorMurtagh(3) 9 65
(Richard Fahey) *trckd ldrs: effrt and cl up over 3f out: rdn along wl over 2f out: sn wknd* 9/1

0324 **8** 3 **Tadaawol**[7] 5155 6-8-11 **82** (p) BenSanderson(5) 5 65
(Roger Fell) *trckd ldng pair: hdwy over 3f out: cl up and rdn along over 2f: sn wknd* 16/1

504- **9** 4 **Destroyer**[240] 9285 6-8-9 **75** oh1 TomEaves 7 49
(Tom Tate) *trckd ldr: rdn along 3f out: sn wknd* 20/1

1m 36.73s (-0.77) **Going Correction** +0.125s/f (Good) **9 Ran SP% 115.0**
WFA 3 from 4yo+ 8lb
Speed ratings (Par 107): **108,106,104,103,101 100,98,95,91**
CSF £15.10 CT £56.69 TOTE £3.80: £1.50, £1.80, £1.70; EX 14.80 Trifecta £60.30.
Owner Irvine Lynch **Bred** Mrs Marion Emerson **Trained** Middleham, N Yorks

FOCUS
A solid race with the finish contested by the two market principals. The third has been rated in line with this year's form.

5399 SKY BET SUPPORTING PJA 50TH ANNIVERSARY H'CAP 5f 89y
8:30 (8:31) (Class 4) (0-85,85) 3-Y-O
£9,962 (£2,964; £1,481; £740; £400; £400) Stalls High

Form				RPR
-034	1		**Que Amoro (IRE)**[29] 4294 3-9-2 80.....................(p) PaulMulrennan 2 (Michael Dods) *qckly away: mde all: rdn clr wl over 1f out: unchal* 8/1	99
0335	2	7	**Lady Calcaria**[15] 4822 3-8-11 75.............................. DuranFentiman 6 (Tim Easterby) *prom: pushed along and sltly outpcd 2f out: sn rdn: styd on fnl f: no ch w wnr* 10/1	69
3315	3	1 1/2	**Tenax (IRE)**[7] 5126 3-9-7 85.............................. SilvestreDeSousa 3 (Nigel Tinkler) *hld up: hdwy 1/2-way: chsd wnr 1 1/2f out: sn rdn: drvn and kpt on one pce fnl f* 10/11[1]	73
0050	4	nk	**Nicki's Angel (IRE)**[14] 4894 3-8-13 80.............. SeanDavis(3) 7 (Richard Fahey) *towards rr: hdwy 2f out: sn rdn: drvn and no imp over 1f out* 20/1	67
2216	5	5	**Magical Spirit (IRE)**[21] 4603 3-9-0 78.............. KevinStott 8 (Kevin Ryan) *prom on outer: rdn along 2f out: sn drvn and wknd* 6/1[3]	47
0061	6	1 1/2	**Little Legs**[9] 5042 3-9-2 83 6ex.............................. BenRobinson(3) 4 (Brian Ellison) *chsd ldng pair: stmbld after 1f: rdn along over 2f out: sn wknd (jockey said filly stumbled shortly after start)* 4/1[2]	47

1m 2.99s (-0.61) **Going Correction** +0.125s/f (Good) 6 Ran SP% 111.6
Speed ratings (Par 102): **109,97,95,94,86 84**
CSF £76.33 CT £137.98 TOTE £9.40: £3.50, £4.00; EX 80.50 Trifecta £113.90.
Owner P Appleton & Mrs Anne Elliott **Bred** Rathasker Stud **Trained** Denton, Co Durham

FOCUS
A modest sprint handicap but a very impressive winner.
T/Plt: £1,971.60 to a £1 stake. Pool: £76,680.02 - 28.39 winning units T/Qpdt: £234.30 to a £1 stake. Pool: £7,174.07 - 22.65 winning units **Joe Rowntree**

5400 - 5403a (Foreign Racing) - See Raceform Interactive

4133 DOWN ROYAL (R-H)
Friday, July 26

OFFICIAL GOING: Good (good to firm in places on straight course)

5404a HER MAJESTY'S PLATE (LISTED RACE) 1m 6f
7:35 (7:35) 4-Y-O+
£26,576 (£8,558; £4,054; £1,801; £900; £450)

			RPR
1		**Downdraft (IRE)**[18] 4745 4-9-8 98.....................(t) DonnachaO'Brien 2 (Joseph Patrick O'Brien, Ire) *wnt sltly rt s and sltly bmpd rival: chsd ldrs: mod 4th bef 1/2-way: clsr 4th after 1/2-way: drvn to chal over 1f out where swtchd rt in 2nd: led gng best ins fnl f and wnt clr: eased cl home* 11/4[2]	104+
2	3	**The King (IRE)**[28] 4351 4-9-5 110.............................. ShaneFoley 1 (Mrs John Harrington, Ire) *sltly bmpd s: prom tl sn settled bhd ldrs: mod 3rd bef 1/2-way: clsr 3rd after 1/2-way: drvn to ld under 2f out: hdd u.p ins fnl f where hung sltly lft: no ex* 11/8[1]	95+
3	5	**Giuseppe Garibaldi (IRE)**[113] 4-9-5 105.............(t) ColmO'Donoghue 3 (John M Oxx, Ire) *hld up in rr: mod 7th bef 1/2-way: swtchd in rr 2f out and hdwy nr side: rdn into 3rd ins fnl f where no imp on ldrs: kpt on one pce* 4/1[3]	89+
4	1 1/4	**Noble Expression**[4] 5261 4-9-5 76.....................(b) KillianLeonard 6 (R K Watson, Ire) *sn chsd ldr in 2nd: clsr 2nd after 1/2-way: pushed along bhd ldr 3f out and no ex between horses in 3rd 2f out: sn wknd* 66/1	87
5	1/2	**Tritonix**[22] 4572 4-9-0 77.............................. RoryCleary 5 (Gavin Cromwell, Ire) *chsd ldrs: mod 5th bef 1/2-way: clsr 5th after 1/2-way: rdn in cl 4th 2f out and sn wknd* 12/1	81
6	1/2	**Altra Vita**[62] 3096 4-9-0 90.....................(v[1]) ColinKeane 4 (Sir Mark Prescott Bt) *sn led: 4 l clr bef 1/2-way: reduced ld after 1/2-way: drvn and strly pressed over 2f out: hdd under 2f out and sn wknd u.p* 6/1	81
7	1/2	**Utah (IRE)**[48] 3609 5-9-5 82.............................. WJLee 7 (J J Lambe, Ire) *swtchd rt after s and settled in rr: mod 6th bef 1/2-way: tk clsr order after 1/2-way: pushed along in clsr 6th over 2f out: no imp u.p in rr over 1f out: short of room briefly ins fnl f* 25/1	85

2m 58.14s (-11.46) 7 Ran SP% 116.1
CSF £7.15 TOTE £2.90: £1.80, £1.40; DF 6.10 Trifecta £29.10.
Owner O T I Racing **Bred** Airlie Stud **Trained** Owning Hill, Co Kilkenny

FOCUS
A stylish success for Downdraft. He faced a stiff enough task off these terms but proved himself a class apart. The fourth and fifth limit the level of the form.

5405 - 5406a (Foreign Racing) - See Raceform Interactive

5227 DEAUVILLE (R-H)
Friday, July 26

OFFICIAL GOING: Polytrack: standard; turf: good to soft

5407a PRIX DE CLICHY (CLAIMER) (3YO COLTS & GELDINGS) (ALL-WEATHER TRACK) (POLYTRACK) 1m 1f 110y(P)
12:07 (12:07) 3-Y-O £10,360 (£4,144; £3,108; £2,072; £1,036)

			RPR
1		**Sparkle In His Eye**[28] 4321 3-9-4 0.................... ChristopheSoumillon 2 (William Haggas) *sn led: hdd after 3f: remained cl up: urged along to a short ld 2f out: rdn over 1f out: drvn to hold advantage ins fnl f: kpt on strly* 8/5[1]	82
2	1	**Hodeng (IRE)**[27] 3-9-2 0.....................................(b[1]) CristianDemuro 7 (J-C Rouget, France) 9/5[2]	78
3	2	**Jukov (FR)**[26] 3-8-7 0.............................. ClementGuitraud(8) 3 (Y Barberot, France) 17/1	73
4	3/4	**Chief Mambo (FR)** 3-8-11 0.............................. AlexisBadel 8 (H-F Devin, France) 78/10	68
5	snk	**Gold Bere (FR)**[22] 3-8-11 0.....................(p) AurelienLemaitre 4 (M Rolland, France) 9/1	67
6	1/2	**Strike Bomber (FR)**[29] 3-8-13 0.............................. QuentinPerrette(5) 6 (Andrea Marcialis, France) 59/10[3]	73
7	8	**Pinaclouddown (IRE)**[62] 1741 3-8-8 0.............. AlexandreChesneau(3) 1 (J-Y Artu, France) 49/1	51
8	hd	**Confetti (FR)**[41] 3878 3-8-8 0.............................. MlleAlisonMassin(3) 5 (Yannick Fouin, France) 75/1	50

1m 59.42s 8 Ran SP% 118.9
PARI-MUTUEL (all including 1 euro stake): WIN 2.60; PLACE 1.20, 1.30, 2.30 DF 3.10.Sparkle In His Eye was claimed by Pia Brandt for 32001 euros
Owner A E Oppenheimer **Bred** Hascombe And Valiant Studs **Trained** Newmarket, Suffolk

5408a PRIX DE FRENEUSE (CLAIMER) (3YO) (APPRENTICE & YOUNG JOCKEYS) (ALL-WEATHER TRACK) (POLYTRACK) 6f 110y(P)
1:20 3-Y-O £8,558 (£3,423; £2,567; £1,711; £855)

			RPR
1		**Capla Gilda**[41] 3878 3-8-10 0.............................. MlleLeaBails(9) 7 (Andrea Marcialis, France) 1/1[1]	75
2	snk	**Mudeer (IRE)**[48] 3-8-3 0.............................. AnnaelleDidon-Yahlali(8) 5 (G Botti, France) 20/1	67
3	1 3/4	**Hurricane Gold (FR)**[170] 3-8-8 0.....................(b) MlleMarieVelon(7) 8 (Matthieu Palussiere, France) 29/1	66
4	1 3/4	**La Pergola (FR)**[12] 4959 3-8-3 0.............................. QuentinPerrette(5) 3 (S Cerulis, France) 78/10	54
5	1 1/4	**Baylagan (FR)**[31] 4229 3-9-1 0.....................(b) AlexandreChesneau(3) 2 (Mme G Rarick, France) 9/2[2]	60
6	snk	**Katoki Karwin**[12] 4959 3-8-6 0.....................(p) ThomasTrullier(5) 6 (Mlle A Wattel, France) 67/10[3]	53
7	3/4	**Champion Brogie (IRE)**[30] 4236 3-8-13 0.............. AlexisPouchin(5) 1 (J S Moore) *trckd ldrs: pushed along over 2f out: rdn w limited rspnse over 1f out: wknd fnl f* 15/1	58
8	9	**Storm Katy (FR)**[5] 3-8-7 0.............................. MlleEugenieLaffargue(9) 4 (M Boutin, France) 10/1	31
9	nk	**Baileys Coquette (FR)**[32] 3-8-10 0.....................(b[1]) ClementGuitraud(6) 9 (J-V Toux, France) 21/1	30

1m 17.4s 9 Ran SP% 120.5
PARI-MUTUEL (all including 1 euro stake): WIN 2.00; PLACE 1.40, 4.10, 5.40; DF 15.80.
Owner Montgomery Motto **Bred** Alvediston Stud **Trained** France

5409a (Foreign Racing) - See Raceform Interactive

5410a PRIX DE MERICOURT (CLAIMER) (4YO+) (ALL-WEATHER TRACK) (POLYTRACK) 2m 1f
4:50 4-Y-O+ £8,558 (£3,423; £2,567; £1,711; £855)

			RPR
1		**Culmination**[10] 5035 7-9-8 0.............................. AntoineHamelin 3 (Jo Hughes, France) *settled in 3rd: rowed along over 3f out: rdn over 2f out: drvn into ld 2f out: kpt on u.str.p ins fnl f: all out* 53/10[3]	80
2	1/2	**Vienna Woods (FR)**[18] 4748 5-8-8 0.............................. ClementGuitraud(8) 8 (Y Barberot, France) 67/10	73
3	hd	**Cosmic City**[44] 7-9-0 0.............................. MlleMarieVelon(8) 4 (J-P Gauvin, France) 17/10[1]	79
4	3	**Vaudou Des Ongrais (FR)**[18] 4748 10-8-11 0.....(b) MorganDelalande 2 (P Chemin & C Herpin, France) 20/1	64
5	1	**Foxboro (GER)**[18] 4748 4-8-11 0.............................. TheoBachelot 6 (P Schiergen, Germany) 10/1	63
6	5	**Tres Solid (FR)**[8] 5115 8-9-2 0.....................(p) MrHugoBoutin 9 (M Boutin, France) 10/1	62
7	1	**Mo Green (FR)**[994] 9-8-6 0.............................. ThomasTrullier(5) 1 (W Gulcher, Germany) 33/1	56
8	3/4	**Le Pin (FR)**[10] 5035 6-8-10 0.....................(p) JeremieMonteiro(6) 7 (B Legros, France) 36/5	60
9	dist	**Gipsy Song (FR)**[80] 4-9-5 0.............................. VincentCheminaud 5 (M Delzangles, France) 5/1[2]	

3m 37.44s 9 Ran SP% 120.6
PARI-MUTUEL (all including 1 euro stake): WIN 6.30; PLACE 1.90, 1.90, 1.30; DF 19.90.
Owner Tim & Miranda Johnson **Bred** Juddmonte Farms Ltd **Trained** France

FOCUS
The race has been rated around the balance of the first two.

5366 ASCOT (R-H)
Saturday, July 27

OFFICIAL GOING: Good to soft
Wind: Almost nil Weather: Overcast but dry

5411 PRINCESS MARGARET KEENELAND STKS (GROUP 3) (FILLIES) 6f
1:50 (1:51) (Class 1) 2-Y-O
£28,355 (£10,750; £5,380; £2,680; £1,345; £675) Stalls Centre

Form				RPR
1	1		**Under The Stars (IRE)**[19] 4727 2-9-0 0.............................. PJMcDonald 12 (James Tate) *stdd s: hld up in last: gd prog over 1f out: clsd to ld 100yds out: r.o wl* 25/1	104
4243	2	1/2	**Aroha (IRE)**[36] 4048 2-9-0 100.............................. OisinMurphy 2 (Brian Meehan) *trckd ldr: led wl over 1f out: drvn and pressed fnl f: hdd last 100yds: styd on* 16/1	102
31	3	hd	**Living In The Past (IRE)**[22] 4583 2-9-0 0.............................. FrankieDettori 4 (K R Burke) *wl in tch: prog 2f out: chsd ldr 1f out and sn chalng: styd on but outpcd last 100yds* 12/1	101
21	4	1 3/4	**Dark Lady**[10] 5045 2-9-0 0.............................. RyanMoore 6 (Richard Hannon) *trckd ldrs: pushed along over 2f out: nt clr run briefly sn after: rdn and kpt on one pce over 1f out: nvr able to threaten* 8/1[2]	96
211	5	1	**Good Vibes**[71] 2805 2-9-0 96.............................. JimCrowley 1 (David Evans) *led: rdn and hdd wl over 1f out: lost 2nd and fdd fnl f* 9/1[3]	93
11	6	nk	**Summer Romance (IRE)**[28] 4387 2-9-0 105.............................. JamesDoyle 7 (Charlie Appleby) *hld up in rr: pushed along over 2f out: making no prog whn nt clr run briefly over 1f out: kpt on last 150yds (trainer could offer no explanation for the poor performance other than the vet reporting that the filly finished lame on it's right hind)* 4/5[1]	92+
1	7	hd	**So Sharp**[23] 4557 2-9-0 0.............................. HollieDoyle 9 (Archie Watson) *t.k.h: wl in tch: rdn wl over 1f out: one pce and no prog (vet said filly lost it's right hind shoe)* 8/1[2]	92+
10	8	4	**Flaming Princess (IRE)**[38] 3983 2-9-0 0.............................. BarryMcHugh 8 (Richard Fahey) *t.k.h: trckd ldrs: rdn 2f out: losing pl and btn whn hmpd 1f out* 14/1	82
10	9	3 1/4	**Diligent Deb (IRE)**[36] 4048 2-9-0 0.............................. JasonWatson 3 (William Muir) *taken down early: dwlt: in tch 4f: wknd qckly* 50/1	70

1m 17.04s (3.34) **Going Correction** +0.55s/f (Yiel) 9 Ran SP% 113.8
Speed ratings (Par 101): **99,98,98,95,94 94,93,88,84**
CSF £340.40 TOTE £31.60: £6.10, £3.80, £2.10; EX 410.80 Trifecta £2409.60.

Owner Saeed Manana **Bred** Rabbah Bloodstock Limited **Trained** Newmarket, Suffolk
■ Punita Arora was withdrawn. Price at time of withdrawal 14-1. Rule 4 applies to all bets - deduction 5p in the pound.

FOCUS
All race distances as advertised. Conditions had eased considerably following 9mm of overnight rain and further morning showers, the official going description changed to good to soft from good to firm prior to the first race. There have been very few upsets in this Group 3 contest in recent years but there was something of a boil over here as things went badly wrong for the odds-on favourite. It's been rated as a weaker renewal.

5412 PORSCHE H'CAP — 1m (S)
2:25 (2:25) (Class 2) 3-Y-O
£28,012 (£8,388; £4,194; £2,097; £1,048; £526) **Stalls** Centre

Form — RPR

-652 **1** **Flashcard (IRE)**[14] 4919 3-8-11 **91** .... OisinMurphy 5 107+
(Andrew Balding) *stdd s: t.k.h: hld up in 5th: smooth prog to ld wl over 1f out: clr whn shkn up fnl f: impressive* **3/1**[1]

513 **2** *4* **Prince Of Harts**[15] 4865 3-8-3 **83** .... HollieDoyle 8 89
(Rod Millman) *slowly away: hld up in last pair: rdn 2f out: prog over 1f out: styd on to take 2nd ins fnl f: no ch w wnr* **4/1**[3]

1-61 **3** *1 ½* **Rectory Road**[190] 289 3-8-4 **87** .... WilliamCox(3) 1 90
(Andrew Balding) *stdd s: t.k.h: hld up in last pair: rdn and prog towards far side over 2f out: chsd clr wnr jst over 1f out tl ins fnl f: kpt on same pce* **12/1**

1561 **4** *2 ½* **Sash**[12] 4994 3-8-7 **87** .... HayleyTurner 3 84
(Amanda Perrett) *t.k.h: hld up in tch: rdn and outpcd 2f out: kpt on one pce after* **15/2**

0604 **5** *1 ¼* **Kuwait Currency (USA)**[7] 5192 3-8-13 **93** .... SeanLevey 6 87
(Richard Hannon) *led to wl over 1f out: sn wknd* **9/1**

-121 **6** *6* **Motakhayyel**[14] 4919 3-9-4 **98** .... JimCrowley 4 78
(Richard Hannon) *t.k.h: prom: pushed along 3f out: rdn and outpcd 2f out: sn wknd (trainer said colt was unsuited by the ground on this occasion and would prefer a faster surface)* **4/1**[3]

-121 **7** *8* **Wings Of Time**[16] 4851 3-9-2 **96** .... JamesDoyle 2 58
(Charlie Appleby) *trckd ldr: pushed along over 3f out: lost pl and wknd qckly jst over 2f out (trainer said gelding was unsuited by the ground on this occasion and would prefer a faster surface)* **7/2**[2]

1m 42.52s (1.12) **Going Correction** +0.55s/f (Yiel) — **7 Ran SP% 116.7**
Speed ratings (Par 106): **116,112,110,108,106 100,92**
CSF £15.85 CT £125.45 TOTE £4.10: £2.00, £2.70; EX 16.10 Trifecta £159.90.
Owner Kennet Valley Thoroughbreds II **Bred** Coole House Farm **Trained** Kingsclere, Hants

FOCUS
A useful 3yo handicap that was dominated by the favourite. The raced centre-field. The second has been rated in line with his C&D latest, and the third in line with his latest AW win.

5413 MOET & CHANDON INTERNATIONAL STKS (HERITAGE H'CAP) — 7f
3:00 (3:02) (Class 2) 3-Y-O+
£93,375 (£27,960; £13,980; £6,990; £3,495; £1,755) **Stalls** Centre

Form — RPR

6-43 **1** **Raising Sand**[38] 3987 7-9-7 **103** .... NicolaCurrie 21 114
(Jamie Osborne) *dwlt: sn chsd ldrs nr side: rdn 2f out: prog over 1f out: chsd ldr ins fnl f: styd on wl to ld nr fin: 1st of 14 in gp* **7/1**[2]

1001 **2** *hd* **Kaeso**[7] 5173 5-8-13 **95** 3ex .... HollieDoyle 23 106
(Nigel Tinkler) *prom nr side: overall ldr over 1f out: drvn fnl f: styd on but hdd nr fin: 2nd of 14 in gp* **11/2**[1]

4-60 **3** *2 ½* **Blue Mist**[35] 4097 4-9-0 **96** .... (t[1]) PatDobbs 27 100
(Roger Charlton) *trckd ldrs nr side: rdn and prog to chse ldr over 1f out to ins fnl f: styd on same pce: 3rd of 14 in gp* **11/1**

0506 **4** *½* **Ripp Orf (IRE)**[14] 4921 5-8-11 **93** .... (t[1]) HayleyTurner 26 96
(David Elsworth) *hld up in last of nr side gp: gd prog wl over 1f out: chsd ldrs fnl f: styd on same pce last 100yds: 4th of 14 in gp* **10/1**

2334 **5** *2* **Admirality**[8] 5120 5-8-12 **94** .... (h) OisinMurphy 1 92
(Roger Fell) *hld up in rr far side: stdy prog 2f out: rdn and styd on to ld gp nr fin: nt on terms w nr side ldrs: 1st of 9 in gp (jockey said gelding hung left-handed under pressure)* **16/1**

0201 **6** *hd* **Firmament**[42] 3863 7-9-3 **99** .... (p) ShaneFoley 19 96
(David O'Meara) *trckd nr side ldrs: rdn 2f out: racd awkwardly and one pce after: 5th of 14 in gp* **22/1**

-204 **7** *1* **Larchmont Lad (IRE)**[28] 4389 5-9-5 **106** .... ScottMcCullagh(5) 2 100
(Joseph Tuite) *trckd ldrs far side: led gp over 1f out but nt on terms w nr side ldrs: styd on but lost ld nr fin: 2nd of 9 in gp* **33/1**

5600 **8** *hd* **Another Batt (IRE)**[78] 2572 4-9-5 **101** .... ShaneKelly 5 95
(Richard Hughes) *hld up far side: gng strly 2f out: prog over 1f out: styd on fnl f: nrst fin: 3rd of 9 in gp* **33/1**

0052 **9** *shd* **Lake Volta (IRE)**[8] 5120 4-9-4 **100** .... RyanMoore 17 94
(Mark Johnston) *overall ldr nr side to over 1f out: fdd: 6th of 14 in gp* **14/1**

0062 **10** *nse* **Kimifive (IRE)**[21] 4650 4-8-7 **92** .... WilliamCox(3) 24 85
(Joseph Tuite) *hld up towards rr nr side: rdn 2f out: kpt on fnl f: nvr on terms: 7th of 14 in gp* **33/1**

5644 **11** *¾* **Arbalet (IRE)**[28] 4397 4-9-5 **101** .... (t) JamesDoyle 15 93
(Hugo Palmer) *prom nr side: rdn 2f out: wknd over 1f out: 8th of 14 in gp* **14/1**

2502 **12** *1* **Hey Jonesy (IRE)**[8] 5129 4-9-9 **105** .... SeamieHeffernan 28 94
(Kevin Ryan) *pressed ldr nr side: lost pl 2f out: fdd: 9th of 14 in gp* **25/1**

-001 **13** *1 ¼* **Vale Of Kent (IRE)**[14] 4921 4-9-5 **101** 3ex .... FrankieDettori 8 87
(Mark Johnston) *led far side gp and on terms to 2f out: hdd & wknd over 1f out: 4th of 9 in gp* **8/1**[3]

-516 **14** *hd* **Diocles Of Rome (IRE)**[28] 4385 4-8-5 **87** .... RaulDaSilva 6 72
(Ralph Beckett) *hld up in rr far side: effrt 2f out: modest late prog: nvr a factor: 5th of 9 in gp* **25/1**

-600 **15** *3* **Burnt Sugar (IRE)**[14] 4921 7-9-6 **102** .... PJMcDonald 18 79
(Roger Fell) *hld up on nr side: rdn and no prog 2f out: n.d after: 10th of 14 in gp* **25/1**

0000 **16** *¾* **Good Effort (IRE)**[14] 4921 4-8-13 **95** .... SeanLevey 13 70
(Ismail Mohammed) *pressed ldr far side: chal gng strly jst over 2f out: wknd qckly over 1f out: 6th of 9 in gp (vet said colt lost it's left fore shoe)* **33/1**

1043 **17** *nk* **Fanaar (IRE)**[37] 4016 3-8-11 **100** .... (b) TomMarquand 29 72
(William Haggas) *taken down early: dwlt: hld up towards rr nr side: rdn and no prog 2f out: 11th of 14 in gp* **8/1**[3]

0040 **18** *3 ¼* **Alemaratalyoum (IRE)**[14] 4921 5-8-12 **94** .... (t) WayneLordan 25 60
(Stuart Williams) *hld up in last trio nr side: gng wl enough over 2f out: sn rdn and no rspnse: 12th of 14 in gp* **50/1**

-156 **19** *3 ¾* **Documenting**[99] 1922 6-9-2 **98** .... RossaRyan 9 54
(Kevin Frost) *chsd far side ldrs tl wknd qckly wl over 1f out: 7th of 9 in gp* **50/1**

5044 **20** *¾* **Intisaab**[7] 5205 8-9-5 **101** .... (p) KieranShoemark 4 55
(David O'Meara) *chsd far side ldrs 5f: wknd: 8th of 9 in gp* **50/1**

4424 **21** *1* **Reputation (IRE)**[22] 4607 6-9-1 **97** .... JamesSullivan 16 49
(Ruth Carr) *rrd bdly s: a in rr nr side: nvr a factor: 13th of 14 in gp* **40/1**

-501 **22** *19* **Makzeem**[7] 5188 6-9-5 **101** 3ex .... (t) JasonWatson 3 3
(Roger Charlton) *dwlt: hld up in last far side: wknd 2f out: t.o: last of 9 in gp (trainer said gelding became unsettled in the stalls)* **9/1**

-121 **23** *13* **Mubhij (IRE)**[28] 4385 4-9-2 **98** .... JimCrowley 12
(Roger Varian) *hld up towards rr nr side: wknd qckly over 2f out: t.o: last of 14 in gp (trainers' rep said gelding was unsuited by the ground on this occasion and would prefer a faster surface)* **14/1**

1m 28.78s (1.28) **Going Correction** +0.55s/f (Yiel)
WFA 3 from 4yo+ 7lb — **23 Ran SP% 139.4**
Speed ratings (Par 109): **114,113,110,110,108 107,106,106,106,106 105,104,102,102,99 98,98,94,90,89 88,66,51**
CSF £43.54 CT £448.82 TOTE £7.90: £2.20, £2.40, £3.80, £2.60; EX 46.00 Trifecta £772.10.
Owner Nick Bradley Racing 22 & Partner **Bred** Meon Valley Stud **Trained** Upper Lambourn, Berks

FOCUS
There were some notable withdrawals on account of the deteriorating ground, but this was still an ultra competitive edition of this Heritage Handicap. They raced in two groups towards the centre of the track, the first four home coming from those that raced nearside. The two at the top of the betting fought out a close finish and previous C&D form proved invaluable, the first five home all having contested the Victoria Cup earlier in the year. A pb from the winner, with the second backing up his improved Doncaster latest.

5414 KING GEORGE VI AND QUEEN ELIZABETH QIPCO STKS (GROUP 1) (BRITISH CHAMPIONS SERIES) — 1m 3f 211y
3:40 (3:40) (Class 1) 3-Y-O+
£708,875 (£268,750; £134,500; £67,000; £33,625; £16,875) **Stalls** Low

Form — RPR

11-1 **1** **Enable**[21] 4668 5-9-4 125 .... FrankieDettori 11 127
(John Gosden) *trapped out wd 1st 4f: hld up in last quartet: prog over 4f out: clsd qckly fr 3f out to ld 2f out: shkn up and pressed by runner-up after: narrow but decisive ld last 100yds and mostly pushed out nr fin* **8/15**[1]

-111 **2** *nk* **Crystal Ocean**[38] 3985 5-9-7 127 .... JamesDoyle 9 129
(Sir Michael Stoute) *trckd clr ldrs: prog to go 2nd 3f out: led over 2f out but sn pounced on by wnr and narrowly hdd: fought on bravely and stl upsides ins fnl f: narrowly but clrly hld last 100yds* **7/2**[2]

5-13 **3** *1 ¾* **Waldgeist**[38] 3985 5-9-7 122 .... Pierre-CharlesBoudot 4 126
(A Fabre, France) *hld up in midfield: hdwy over 3f out: 5th over 2f out: sn prog u.p to chse ldng pair: nvr able to chal and but styd on wl and edgd clsr nr fin* **12/1**

-130 **4** *7* **Salouen (IRE)**[35] 4093 5-9-7 115 .... JimCrowley 5 115
(Sylvester Kirk) *stdd s: hld up in last pair: sme prog 4f out: rdn 3f out: kpt on u.p fnl 2f to take modest 4th last strides* **80/1**

4446 **5** *nk* **Hunting Horn (IRE)**[21] 4668 4-9-7 115 .... (p[1]) SeamieHeffernan 10 114
(A P O'Brien, Ire) *prog to chse ldng pair after 2f: rdn to dispute 2nd briefly 3f out: wknd over 2f out: lost modest 4th last strides* **66/1**

/4-2 **6** *3 ½* **Cheval Grand (JPN)**[119] 1446 7-9-7 119 .... OisinMurphy 6 109
(Yasuo Tomomichi, Japan) *hld up in last quartet: sme prog over 3f out but u.p: nvr a threat but plugged on fnl 2f* **33/1**

2003 **7** *7* **Norway (IRE)**[28] 4414 3-8-10 104 .... (p) WayneLordan 8 99
(A P O'Brien, Ire) *led at blistering pce: hdd & wknd qckly over 2f out* **66/1**

-104 **8** *14* **Morando (FR)**[35] 4093 6-9-7 115 .... PJMcDonald 2 75
(Andrew Balding) *a in rr: toiling in last pl sn after 1/2-way: t.o* **66/1**

4211 **9** *nk* **Defoe (IRE)**[35] 4093 5-9-7 119 .... AndreaAtzeni 3 75
(Roger Varian) *a in rr: nt gng wl fr 5f out: wknd over 3f out: t.o (jockey said gelding had no more to give. Trainers' rep said gelding was unsuited by the ground on this occasion and would prefer a faster surface)* **10/1**

-112 **10** *5* **Anthony Van Dyck (IRE)**[28] 4414 3-8-10 118 .... (p[1]) RyanMoore 7 68
(A P O'Brien, Ire) *chsd ldng trio: rdn 5f out: wknd 4f out: t.o (trainers' rep said colt was unsuited by the ground on this occasion and would prefer a faster surface)* **7/1**[3]

5322 **11** *11* **Magic Wand (IRE)**[29] 4354 4-9-4 109 .... (p[1]) DonnachaO'Brien 1 46
(A P O'Brien, Ire) *chsd ldr at str pce to 3f out: wknd rapidly: t.o* **28/1**

2m 32.42s (-0.18) **Going Correction** +0.55s/f (Yiel)
WFA 3 from 4yo+ 11lb — **11 Ran SP% 128.8**
Speed ratings (Par 117): **122,121,120,115,115 113,108,99,99,95 88**
CSF £3.04 CT £14.23 TOTE £1.40: £1.10, £1.40, £3.10; EX 3.30 Trifecta £16.00.
Owner K Abdullah **Bred** Juddmonte Farms Ltd **Trained** Newmarket, Suffolk

FOCUS
A cracking edition of the race with three top-notch older performers dominating, pulling some 7l clear of the rest. The big duel everyone had hoped for very much developed, with last year's runner-up Crystal Ocean and the brilliant Enable locking horns from around 2f out. Although a few of the participants failed to give their running, being beaten before the straight, there's little doubt it was the race of the season, just as it had promised to be. The pace was brisk through the early stages, controlled by the Ballydoyle runners, and only increased, resulting in a proper test at the distance. The second has been rated to his best, and the third as confirming the level he showed in the Ganay.

5415 WOOLDRIDGE GROUP PAT EDDERY STKS (LISTED RACE) (FORMERLY THE WINKFIELD STAKES) — 7f
4:15 (4:18) (Class 1) 2-Y-O
£17,013 (£6,450; £3,228; £1,608; £807; £405) **Stalls** Centre

Form — RPR

1 **1** **Al Dabaran**[28] 4388 2-9-3 0 .... JamesDoyle 3 103+
(Charlie Appleby) *t.k.h: trckd ldrs: rdn to chse ldr 2f out: no imp over 1f out: styd on fnl f to ld last strides* **11/4**[2]

514 **2** *nk* **Sun Power (FR)**[35] 4091 2-9-3 93 .... OisinMurphy 7 102+
(Richard Hannon) *t.k.h: trckd ldr: led 4f out: rdn and more than a l ahd over 1f out: wilted ins fnl f: hdd last strides* **9/2**

0464 **3** *2 ½* **Ropey Guest**[14] 4920 2-9-3 98 .... ShaneKelly 2 96
(George Margarson) *t.k.h: hld up in rr: rdn and no prog jst over 2f out: kpt on fnl f to take 3rd last 75yds* **10/1**

2221 **4** *1* **Oh Purple Reign (IRE)**[14] 4937 2-9-3 98 .... RossaRyan 1 93
(Richard Hannon) *hld up in tch: rdn to dispute 2nd wl over 1f out: nt qckn after: fdd ins fnl f* **7/2**[3]

21 **5** *2 ¾* **Buhturi (IRE)**[23] 4550 2-9-3 0 .... JimCrowley 4 86
(Charles Hills) *stdd s: t.k.h: hld up in last: effrt over 2f out: rdn and no prog over 1f out: wknd (jockey said colt ran too freely)* **9/1**

221 **6** *1 ¾* **Subjectivist**[22] 4588 2-9-3 **91** RyanMoore 5 82+
(Mark Johnston) *led at mod pce for 3f: rdn over 2f out: sn lost pl and wknd (trainer said, regards poor performance, colt was the lowest rated horse and had not shown the necessary improvement required in order to be competitive)* **5/2**[1]

1m 31.27s (3.77) **Going Correction** +0.55s/f (Yiel) **6** Ran SP% **114.7**
Speed ratings (Par 102): **100,99,96,95,92 90**
CSF £15.85 TOTE £3.10: £2.00, £2.20; EX 15.70 Trifecta £91.60.
Owner Godolphin **Bred** Godolphin **Trained** Newmarket, Suffolk

FOCUS
Experience has often proved key in this Listed event, only the top-class pair Raven's Pass (2007) and Toronado (2012) having bucked that trend by winning it on their second start, so this was a good effort from Al Dabaran. It's been rated as a fairly good renewal.

5416 LONGINES H'CAP (FOR LADY AMATEUR RIDERS) 7f
4:50 (4:50) (Class 3) (0-90,89) 3-Y-O+ **£8,110** (£2,515; £1,257; £629) **Stalls** Centre

Form RPR

1152 **1** **Redarna**[15] 4875 5-9-13 **78** (p) MissEmmaSayer 1 89
(Dianne Sayer) *racd apart fr main gp w one other: on terms: overall ldr 3f out: clr whn hung bdly lft fnl f: styd on (jockey said gelding hung left-handed under pressure)* **5/1**[3]

004 **2** *2 ½* **Shady McCoy (USA)**[3] 5319 9-10-10 **89** MissSerenaBrotherton 4 94
(Ian Williams) *restrained s: t.k.h: hld up in last pair: urged along 2f out: no prog tl styd on fnl f to take 2nd nr fin* **2/1**[1]

-141 **3** *¾* **Fieldsman (USA)**[30] 4281 7-9-0 **70** MissSarahBowen(5) 9 73
(Tony Carroll) *sn led main gp and overall ldr to 3f out: chsd wnr after but outpcd: lost 2nd nr fin* **13/2**

0400 **4** *1 ¼* **Frankelio (FR)**[26] 4445 4-9-11 **76** (p) MissBeckySmith 8 75
(Micky Hammond) *hld up in tch: clsd on ldrs gng wl 2f out: shkn up and nt qckn over 1f out: one pce after* **8/1**

-006 **5** *nk* **Ower Fly**[18] 4759 6-9-12 **82** MissEmilyBullock(5) 2 81
(Ruth Carr) *racd w wnr apart fr rest: wl on terms: rdn 2f out: outpcd over 1f out: n.d after* **16/1**

0011 **6** *1 ¼* **Big Storm Coming**[9] 5090 9-10-3 **82** MrsCarolBartley 7 77
(John Quinn) *hld up in tch: pushed along over 2f out: no prog and btn over 1f out* **7/1**

5033 **7** *nk* **Normandy Barriere (IRE)**[15] 4866 7-10-8 **87** MissJoannaMason 5 81
(Nigel Tinkler) *trckd ldr in main gp: pushed along 2f out: nt qckn over 1f out: fdd (trainer could offer no explanation for the poor performance)* **4/1**[2]

3210 **8** *2 ½* **Mister Music**[15] 4867 10-9-7 **77** MissSophieColl(5) 3 65
(Tony Carroll) *stdd s: hld up in last pair: no prog over 2f out: bhd over 1f out* **16/1**

1m 31.41s (3.91) **Going Correction** +0.55s/f (Yiel)
WFA 3 from 4yo+ 7lb **8** Ran SP% **118.7**
Speed ratings (Par 107): **99,96,95,93,93 92,91,88**
CSF £16.10 CT £67.94 TOTE £5.50: £1.70, £1.30, £2.60; EX 16.80 Trifecta £100.80.
Owner Graham Lund And Dianne Sayer **Bred** A H Bennett **Trained** Hackthorpe, Cumbria

FOCUS
A smaller field than usual for this amateur lady riders' handicap, they raced centre field with the winner and one other racing a little apart from the rest for much of the contest. Average form. The second has been rated to this year's form, and the third close to his recent.

5417 PLYMOUTH FRUIT CUP H'CAP 1m 3f 211y
5:20 (5:20) (Class 3) (0-90,91) 3-Y-O+ **£9,703** (£2,887; £1,443; £721) **Stalls** Low

Form RPR

-534 **1** **Western Duke (IRE)**[27] 4425 5-9-11 **83** PJMcDonald 8 93
(Ian Williams) *hld up in last pair: stl only 7th 3f out: gd prog on outer 2f out to chse ldr over 1f out: sustained effrt to ld last 150yds: styd on wl* **14/1**

0253 **2** *1* **Vivid Diamond (IRE)**[15] 4877 3-9-8 **91** RyanMoore 7 99
(Mark Johnston) *led and kpt wd tl swtchd to inner 3f out: drvn over 1f out: kpt on but hdd and one pce last 150yds* **7/2**[3]

6212 **3** *1 ¾* **Kiefer**[31] 4256 3-9-5 **88** CharlesBishop 5 94+
(Eve Johnson Houghton) *hld up in last trio: prog into 4th 4f out: rdn and no hdwy over 2f out: styd on again fnl f to take 3rd last 75yds: gng on at fin* **15/8**[1]

2222 **4** *1 ¾* **Lariat**[42] 3842 3-9-7 **90** OisinMurphy 2 93
(Andrew Balding) *trckd ldr: rdn over 2f out: briefly tried to cl over 1f out: sn no imp and lost 2nd: fdd ins fnl f* **9/4**[2]

5514 **5** *4 ½* **Production**[21] 4671 3-8-6 **80** ThoreHammerHansen(5) 3 76
(Richard Hannon) *trckd ldng pair: racd wd fr 1/2-way: drvn over 2f out: wknd over 1f out* **11/1**

5424 **6** *hd* **Ravenous**[13] 4257 8-8-12 **75** PoppyBridgwater(5) 1 70
(Luke Dace) *trckd ldng trio: lost pl 4f out: rdn whn n.m.r briefly 2f out: no ch over 1f out* **20/1**

4425 **7** *5* **Mutamaded (IRE)**[7] 5199 6-9-13 **85** JamesSullivan 6 72
(Ruth Carr) *hld up in 5th: rdn over 2f out: n.m.r briefly sn after: wknd over 1f out* **12/1**

3100 **8** *1 ¼* **Tralee Hills**[31] 4250 5-9-5 **77** (p) NicolaCurrie 4 62
(Peter Hedger) *a in last and nvr gng wl: no prog over 2f out (jockey said gelding was never travelling)* **33/1**

2m 38.05s (5.45) **Going Correction** +0.55s/f (Yiel)
WFA 3 from 5yo+ 11lb **8** Ran SP% **118.2**
Speed ratings (Par 107): **103,102,101,100,97 96,93,92**
CSF £64.71 CT £138.30 TOTE £16.20: £3.30, £1.50, £1.20; EX 89.40 Trifecta £166.60.
Owner London City Bloodstock **Bred** Epona Bloodstock Ltd **Trained** Portway, Worcs

FOCUS
An informative renewal of this middle-distance handicap, in which St Leger entry Kiefer headed the market. The winner has been rated close to his old turf best, which came over this C&D, the second as running a small pb, and the third in line with his Salisbury form.
T/Jkpt: Not Won. T/Plt: £412.70 to a £1 stake. Pool: 202,620.19 - 358.38 winning units T/Qpdt: £7.50 to a £1 stake. Pool: £23,814.12 - 2,347.13 winning units **Jonathan Neesom**

4903 CHESTER (L-H)
Saturday, July 27

OFFICIAL GOING: Good to soft changing to soft after race 2 (2.35)
Wind: light across Weather: steady rain

5418 STELLA ARTOIS NOVICE MEDIAN AUCTION STKS (PLUS 10 RACE) 5f 15y
2:00 (2:01) (Class 4) 2-Y-O **£5,851** (£1,752; £876; £438; £219) **Stalls** Low

Form RPR

3135 **1** **Ocasio Cortez (IRE)**[7] 5185 2-9-0 **80** SeamusCronin(5) 1 81+
(Richard Hannon) *mde all: narrow ld tl pushed clr over 1f out: rdn out ins fnl f* **6/4**[1]

4 **2** *1 ¾* **Hot Heels**[4] 5280 2-9-4 0 AlistairRawlinson 2 74
(Tom Dascombe) *chsd ldrs: rdn to go 2nd over 1f out: kpt on but nvr getting to wnr* **6/1**

202 **3** *4* **Ventura Flame (IRE)**[24] 4509 2-8-10 **79** SeanDavis(3) 3 54
(Keith Dalgleish) *dwlt: rcvrd to sn chse ldrs: rdn and outpcd over 1f out: plugged on ins fnl f* **4/1**[3]

42 **4** *4 ½* **Spanish Angel (IRE)**[64] 3039 2-9-4 0 DavidProbert 4 43
(Andrew Balding) *pressed ldr: rdn 2f out: wknd over 1f out* **7/4**[2]

5 *12* **Unauthorised Act (IRE)** 2-8-8 0 HarrisonShaw(5) 6
(Alan Berry) *a outpcd in rr* **100/1**

1m 3.39s (1.29) **Going Correction** +0.625s/f (Yiel) **5** Ran SP% **111.6**
Speed ratings (Par 96): **105,102,95,88,69**
CSF £10.95 TOTE £2.40: £1.10, £3.00; EX 10.50 Trifecta £27.00.
Owner K Sohi **Bred** Paul McEnery **Trained** East Everleigh, Wilts

FOCUS
Quite a decent contest but the winner was much the best. Prior to the first race the going was changed from good, good to soft in places, to good to soft. The second is the key to the form.

5419 MBNA FILLIES' H'CAP 7f 127y
2:35 (2:36) (Class 4) (0-85,83) 3-Y-O+
£6,080 (£1,809; £904; £452; £300; £300) **Stalls** Low

Form RPR

123 **1** **Arletta Star**[11] 5030 3-8-3 **65** JamieGormley 3 75
(Tim Easterby) *trckd ldr: rdn to ld appr fnl f: kpt on wl to draw clr* **9/4**[2]

0315 **2** *4* **Cale Lane**[8] 5143 4-9-5 **73** GrahamLee 9 75+
(Julie Camacho) *s.i.s and sn swtchd lft to inner: hld up: pushed along and sme hdwy over 2f out: swtchd rt to outer over 1f out: rdn and kpt on wl: wnt 2nd towards fin: no ch w wnr* **10/1**

-450 **3** *nk* **Conga**[43] 3815 3-9-2 **78** TomEaves 5 77
(Kevin Ryan) *led: rdn and hdd appr fnl f: wknd fnl 110yds: lost 2nd nr fin* **14/1**

0656 **4** *1 ¾* **Chynna**[14] 4922 3-9-7 **83** AdamMcNamara 2 78
(Mick Channon) *hld up: pushed along and hdwy over 2f out: rdn over 1f out: swtchd lft 1f out: kpt on same pce* **9/1**

33-1 **5** *1 ½* **Kitcarina (FR)**[52] 3468 4-9-7 **75** DavidProbert 6 68
(Andrew Balding) *trckd ldrs: rdn along 2f out: sn outpcd and no threat after* **2/1**[1]

4120 **6** *1 ½* **Eponina (IRE)**[11] 5030 5-8-11 **65** AlistairRawlinson 7 54
(Michael Appleby) *prom: rdn 2f out: wknd appr fnl f* **8/1**[3]

0056 **7** *2 ¼* **No More Regrets (IRE)**[14] 4908 3-8-4 **66** ShaneGray 4 48
(Patrick Morris) *midfield: rdn over 2f out: wknd appr fnl f* **22/1**

2333 **8** *10* **Bell Heather (IRE)**[15] 4875 6-8-9 **66** (p) SeanDavis(3) 8 25
(Patrick Morris) *chsd ldrs: sn pushed along: lost pl over 3f out: wknd over 1f out (jockey said mare ran flat)* **8/1**[3]

-636 **9** *6* **Poetic Era**[17] 4804 3-8-3 **65** JimmyQuinn 1 7
(David Simcock) *s.i.s: a in rr* **16/1**

1m 36.85s (1.15) **Going Correction** +0.625s/f (Yiel)
WFA 3 from 4yo+ 8lb **9** Ran SP% **122.3**
Speed ratings (Par 102): **106,102,101,99,98 96,94,84,78**
CSF £27.19 CT £271.82 TOTE £2.90: £1.30, £2.70, £4.40; EX 30.30 Trifecta £274.70.
Owner M J Macleod **Bred** Max Weston **Trained** Great Habton, N Yorks
■ Stewards' Enquiry : Graham Lee four-day ban; misuse of whip (Aug 10-13)

FOCUS
A good handicap for fillies and mares but racing prominently proved to be beneficial. A pb from the winner, with the third rated to form.

5420 MAGNERS H'CAP 5f 15y
3:10 (3:11) (Class 3) (0-95,96) 3-Y-O+
£11,827 (£3,541; £1,770; £885; £442; £222) **Stalls** Low

Form RPR

1152 **1** **Angel Alexander (IRE)**[8] 5154 3-9-7 **91** AlistairRawlinson 1 108
(Tom Dascombe) *mde all: pushed clr over 1f out: rdn and kpt on wl: easily* **2/1**[1]

4100 **2** *6* **Gabrial The Saint (IRE)**[7] 5205 4-9-10 **90** ShaneGray 3 86
(Richard Fahey) *chsd ldrs: rdn 2f out: wnt 2nd 1f out: kpt on but no ch w wnr* **4/1**[2]

0621 **3** *nk* **Gabrial The Devil (IRE)**[21] 4649 4-9-3 **86** SeanDavis(3) 6 81
(Richard Fahey) *in tch: briefly short of room appr fnl f: rdn 1f out: kpt on to chal for 2nd towards fin* **7/1**

2203 **4** *2* **Acclaim The Nation (IRE)**[15] 4894 6-9-5 **85** (p) TomEaves 7 73
(Eric Alston) *prom: rdn and outplcd by wnr over 1f out: edgd rt and no ex ins fnl f* **11/1**

3415 **5** *nse* **Canford Bay (IRE)**[15] 4894 5-8-12 **83** KieranSchofield(5) 5 71
(Antony Brittain) *midfield: rdn over 2f out: swtchd rt to outside ins fnl f: kpt on* **9/1**

0045 **6** *nk* **Orvar (IRE)**[15] 4888 6-9-9 **89** GrahamLee 2 76
(Paul Midgley) *hld up: pushed along and hdwy whn n.m.r over 1f out: kpt on ins fnl f* **6/1**[3]

0662 **7** *2 ¾* **Bellevarde (IRE)**[15] 4880 5-8-10 **76** NickyMackay 4 53
(Richard Price) *midfield: rdn over 2f out: no imp* **16/1**

0021 **8** *½* **Powerallied (IRE)**[15] 4880 6-8-12 **85** RussellHarris(7) 13 60
(Richard Fahey) *dwlt: hld up: nvr threatened (vet said gelding lost it's left fore shoe)* **16/1**

1003 **9** *1 ½* **Venturous (IRE)**[19] 4722 6-9-7 **87** DavidProbert 14 57
(David Barron) *rrd s and s.i.s: sn swtchd lft to inner: hld up: nvr threatened (jockey said gelding reared in the stalls)* **20/1**

0062 **10** *hd* **Abel Handy (IRE)**[28] 4359 4-9-10 **90** AdamMcNamara 11 59
(Declan Carroll) *chsd ldrs: rdn over 2f out: wknd over 1f out (trainers' rep said gelding was unsuited by the Soft ground and would prefer a faster surface)* **14/1**

3250 **11** *4 ½* **Hawaam (IRE)**[3] 5298 4-8-4 77...............................(b[1]) WilliamCarver(7) 9 30
(Roger Fell) *midfield: rdn over 2f out: wknd over 1f out* **20/1**
1m 2.31s (0.21) **Going Correction** +0.625s/f (Yiel)
WFA 3 from 4yo+ 4lb **11** Ran SP% **126.4**
Speed ratings (Par 107): **109,99,98,95,95 95,90,89,87,87 80**
CSF £10.46 CT £49.68 TOTE £2.40: £1.30, £1.80, £2.40; EX 11.60 Trifecta £53.40.
Owner Birbeck Mound Trowbridge & Owen **Bred** Mountarmstrong Stud **Trained** Malpas, Cheshire

FOCUS
Prior to this race the going was changed from good to soft to soft. All very simple again in a sprint round this track. The winner was drawn one, made all, and has been rated as taking a big step forward.

5421 CORONA FILLIES' NOVICE STKS 1m 4f 63y
3:50 (3:52) (Class 3) 3-Y-0+

£9,337 (£2,796; £1,398; £699; £349; £175) **Stalls** Low

Form RPR
1 **1** **Litigious**[48] 3637 3-9-3 0.. NickyMackay 9 96+
(John Gosden) *prom: quite keen early: pushed into ld over 2f out: in command over 1f out: kpt on nudged out ins fnl f: comf* **4/6**[1]
5235 **2** *2 ¾* **Inclyne**[46] 3699 3-8-11 78....................................... DavidProbert 4 84
(Andrew Balding) *sn trckd ldrs: chal over 2f out: sn rdn: styd on but hld in 2nd fr over 1f out* **2/1**[2]
50 **3** *7* **Dubious Affair (IRE)**[50] 3553 3-8-11 0.......................... JimmyQuinn 3 73
(Sir Michael Stoute) *midfield: rdn along over 2f out: plugged on to go 3rd towards fin: no threat to ldng pair* **5/1**[3]
-020 **4** *¾* **Say Nothing**[41] 3886 3-8-8 73.. SeanDavis(3) 7 72
(Hughie Morrison) *led at stdy pce: rdn along and hdd over 2f out: sn outpcd in 3rd: wknd ins fnl f and lost 3rd towards fin* **8/1**
5 **5** *9* **Pensee**[24] 4503 3-8-11 0... AdamMcNamara 8 57
(Roger Charlton) *hld up: rdn along over 2f out: sn wknd* **16/1**
-446 **6** *10* **Misty Breese (IRE)**[21] 4658 4-9-5 41............................ NoelGarbutt(3) 6 40
(Sarah Hollinshead) *dwlt: hld up: wknd over 2f out (jockey said filly was slowly away)* **50/1**
0660 **7** *1* **Just Heather (IRE)**[20] 4690 5-9-3 38...........................(p) HarrisonShaw(5) 1 39
(John Wainwright) *trckd ldrs: rdn wl over 3f out: wknd over 2f out (jockey said mare hung right)* **100/1**
3- **8** *4 ½* **Leannes Lady (IRE)**[5] 5465 7-9-8 0.............................. GrahamLee 2 31
(Alan Berry) *midfield tl wknd over 2f out* **100/1**
0050 **9** *29* **Lots Ov (IRE)**[39] 3955 5-9-8 33................................... TomEaves 5
(John Wainwright) *hld up: wknd and bhd fnl 4f* **100/1**
2m 52.05s (9.85) **Going Correction** +0.625s/f (Yiel)
WFA 3 from 4yo+ 11lb **9** Ran SP% **131.9**
Speed ratings (Par 104): **92,90,85,85,79 72,71,68,49**
CSF £2.83 TOTE £1.40: £1.10, £1.10, £1.50; EX 2.40 Trifecta £5.80.
Owner Cheveley Park Stud **Bred** Cheveley Park Stud Ltd **Trained** Newmarket, Suffolk

FOCUS
Despite being drawn wide everything fell right for the favourite. The form makes sense down the field.

5422 BUD LIGHT APPRENTICE H'CAP 7f 127y
4:25 (4:29) (Class 3) (0-90,90) 3-Y-O

£11,827 (£3,541; £1,770; £885; £442; £222) **Stalls** Low

Form RPR
-216 **1** **Be More**[14] 4898 3-8-13 **82**.. WilliamCarver(3) 3 90+
(Andrew Balding) *dwlt: hld up in rr: pushed along 4f out: stl last whn swtchd rt to outer over 1f out: r.o strly fnl f: led towards fin* **2/1**[1]
163 **2** *¾* **Lincoln Park**[21] 4650 3-9-3 **90**.. LukeCatton(7) 7 96
(Michael Appleby) *led: qcknd 4 l clr 2f out: drvn ins fnl f: reduced advantage fnl 110yds: wknd and hdd towards fin* **3/1**[2]
0011 **3** *hd* **Salam Zayed**[8] 5151 3-8-5 **71** oh2............................... HarrisonShaw 8 76
(Richard Fahey) *in tch: dropped bk towards rr after 2f: rdn and hdwy over 1f out: styd on ins fnl f* **5/1**[3]
-060 **4** *2 ½* **Daafr (IRE)**[15] 4895 3-8-12 **81**...................................(p) KieranSchofield(3) 1 80
(Antony Brittain) *trckd ldrs: rdn to chse ldr 3f out: outpcd in 2nd 2f out: one pce ins fnl f: lost 2 pls fnl 75yds* **25/1**
3312 **5** *3 ¾* **Friendly Advice (IRE)**[14] 4908 3-8-12 **77** ow1..............(p) DylanHogan 2 67
(Keith Dalgleish) *dwlt: sn midfield: rdn along 3f out: wknd ins fnl f* **5/1**[3]
0345 **6** *8* **Pacino**[14] 4909 3-8-7 **78**.. RussellHarris(5) 4 47
(Richard Fahey) *sn midfield: rdn 3f out: wknd over 1f out* **12/1**
-452 **7** *2 ¼* **Felix The Poet**[21] 4639 3-9-5 **88**...........................(b) Pierre-LouisJamin(3) 5 52
(Archie Watson) *prom: rdn along over 3f out: sn lost pl: wknd and bhd over 1f out* **6/1**
1m 40.87s (5.17) **Going Correction** +0.625s/f (Yiel) **7** Ran SP% **117.5**
Speed ratings (Par 104): **99,98,98,95,91 83,81**
CSF £8.60 CT £25.97 TOTE £2.40: £1.80, £1.60; EX 9.60 Trifecta £41.20.
Owner George Strawbridge **Bred** George Strawbridge **Trained** Kingsclere, Hants

FOCUS
A well-run race in testing conditions, which saw the winner come from off the gallop.

5423 GOOSE ISLAND H'CAP 1m 5f 84y
5:00 (5:02) (Class 4) (0-80,82) 4-Y-O+

£6,080 (£1,809; £904; £452; £300; £300) **Stalls** Low

Form RPR
2-62 **1** **Overhaugh Street**[28] 4362 6-8-7 **65**.................................. ShaneGray 4 76
(Ed de Giles) *mde all: rdn over 1f out: hld on wl towards fin* **7/1**
4602 **2** *¾* **Diocletian (IRE)**[42] 3861 4-9-10 **82**............................. DavidProbert 7 92+
(Andrew Balding) *hld up: prog in midfield 3f out: pushed along and hdwy to chse ldr over 1f out: styd on wl* **3/1**[1]
3121 **3** *7* **Angel Gabrial (IRE)**[28] 4363 10-8-2 **65**.........(p) KieranSchofield(5) 13 65
(Patrick Morris) *prom rdn along 3f out: wknd ins fnl f* **8/1**
0455 **4** *½* **Tor**[14] 4913 5-9-0 **77**... HarrisonShaw(5) 2 76
(Iain Jardine) *midfield: rdn and hdwy to briefly chse ldrs wl over 1f out: no ex ins fnl f* **9/2**[2]
6243 **5** *1* **Four Kingdoms (IRE)**[12] 4983 5-8-4 **69**........................ SeanKirrane(7) 6 66
(R Mike Smith) *in tch on inner: bit short of room 3f out tl over 2f out: rdn over 1f out: no imp* **14/1**
3311 **6** *14* **Berrahri (IRE)**[14] 4928 8-9-7 **79**.................................... KierenFox 12 55
(John Best) *trckd ldrs: rdn over 3f out: wknd 2f out (jockey said gelding was never travelling)* **5/1**[3]
5600 **7** *20* **Heart Of Soul (IRE)**[14] 4907 4-9-4 **79**...........................(v) SeanDavis(3) 5 25
(Ian Williams) *prom: reminder 4f out: rdn and hung rt over 2f out: wknd qckly and eased* **11/1**
5206 **8** *5* **Ebqaa (IRE)**[28] 4363 5-8-7 **65**...(p) JimmyQuinn 1
(James Unett) *dwlt: sn midfield: wknd 3f out and eased* **12/1**
062 **9** *6* **Marengo**[42] 3847 8-8-12 **70**...(b) GeorgeWood 10
(Bernard Llewellyn) *wnt lft s: hld up: wnt in snatches: wknd and bhd fnl 3f* **9/1**
0002 **10** *1* **Miss Ranger (IRE)**[15] 4881 7-8-2 **60** oh3.....................(b) JamieGormley 3
(Roger Fell) *dwlt: hld up in midfield towards outer: lost pl and dropped to rr over 5f out: wknd 3f out (trainers' rep said mare was unsuited by the Soft ground and would prefer a quicker surface)* **20/1**
3300 **11** *27* **Dragon Mountain**[14] 4907 4-9-1 **73**................................... GrahamLee 11
(Keith Dalgleish) *midfield: rdn and over 4f out: wknd and eased* **25/1**
04-0 **12** *¾* **Liva (IRE)**[28] 4404 4-8-12 **70**...(p) TomEaves 8
(Stef Keniry) *dwlt and sltly hmpd s: a in rr* **25/1**
3m 8.32s (11.72) **Going Correction** +0.625s/f (Yiel) **12** Ran SP% **128.6**
Speed ratings (Par 105): **88,87,83,82,82 73,61,58,54,54 37,36**
CSF £30.06 CT £181.13 TOTE £8.20: £2.40, £1.80, £2.20; EX 44.70 Trifecta £301.90.
Owner Sharron & Robert Colvin **Bred** World Racing Network **Trained** Ledbury, H'fords

FOCUS
This took plenty of getting in what were demanding conditions, but the winner was somehow allowed an untroubled time at the head of affairs and duly took full advantage.

5424 INTILERY H'CAP 1m 2f 70y
5:35 (5:35) (Class 4) (0-80,81) 3-Y-0

£6,080 (£1,809; £904; £452; £300; £300) **Stalls** High

Form RPR
4562 **1** **Dark Lochnagar (USA)**[14] 4913 3-9-8 **81**.............................. ShaneGray 2 91
(Keith Dalgleish) *mde all: rdn over 2f out: drvn and pressed over 1f out: styd on wl to draw clr fnl 110yds* **2/1**[1]
4352 **2** *3 ½* **Gabrial The One (IRE)**[14] 4906 3-9-4 **80**....................... SeanDavis(3) 4 83
(Richard Fahey) *prom: drvn to chal over 1f out: one pce and hld in 2nd fnl 110yds* **3/1**[2]
432 **3** *9* **Better Than Ever (IRE)**[46] 3690 3-9-0 **73**....................... GrahamLee 1 58
(Marco Botti) *trckd ldrs: rdn over 2f out: wknd over 1f out* **7/1**
2434 **4** *nk* **Paradise Boy (FR)**[14] 4906 3-9-1 **74**............................... DavidProbert 8 58
(Andrew Balding) *dwlt: hld up in tch: hdwy and trckd ldrs 3f out: rdn 2f out: sn wknd* **4/1**
4052 **5** *6* **Lola's Theme**[8] 5124 3-9-0 **73**..............................(p) AlistairRawlinson 3 45
(Tom Dascombe) *hld up in tch: wnt in snatches: rdn 4f out: wknd over 2f out (jockey said filly was never travelling)* **10/3**[3]
0000 **6** *23* **Caramel Curves**[29] 4316 3-7-13 **61** oh11........................ NoelGarbutt(3) 6
(Lisa Williamson) *trckd ldrs: rdn over 4f out: wknd and bhd over 2f out* **50/1**
2m 24.92s (10.62) **Going Correction** +0.625s/f (Yiel) **6** Ran SP% **115.9**
Speed ratings (Par 102): **82,79,72,71,66 48**
CSF £8.72 CT £33.95 TOTE £3.10: £2.00, £2.80; EX 8.60 Trifecta £39.20.
Owner Weldspec Glasgow Limited **Bred** Chelston & Orpendale **Trained** Carluke, S Lanarks

FOCUS
Another race on the card where the winner made every yard of the running.
T/Plt: £35.40 to a £1 stake. Pool: £66,540.23 - 1,368.79 winning units T/Qpdt: £5.20 to a £1 stake. Pool: £6,037.53 - 848.57 winning units **Andrew Sheret**

5309 LINGFIELD (L-H)
Saturday, July 27

OFFICIAL GOING: Soft (7.6)
Wind: moderate head wind in straight Weather: overcast

5425 WESSEX GARAGE DOORS 30TH ANNIVERSARY H'CAP 1m 3f 133y
5:30 (5:31) (Class 6) (0-65,67) 3-Y-O+

£2,781 (£827; £413; £400; £400; £400) **Stalls** High

Form RPR
00-0 **1** **Celtic Classic (IRE)**[24] 4498 3-8-0 **48** oh3....................(b[1]) HollieDoyle 4 57
(Paul Cole) *hld up in rr: drvn into midfield over 2f out: gd hdwy u.p over 1f out: hung lft 1f out: drvn and styd on strly to ld wl ins fnl f* **14/1**
6143 **2** *1* **Myklachi (FR)**[12] 4990 3-8-12 **60**.................................... JasonWatson 1 67
(David O'Meara) *racd in midfield: effrt to cl on ldrs over 2f out: rdn and gd hdwy to ld over 1f out: drvn and kpt on wl but hdd by wnr wl ins fnl f* **3/1**[2]
5114 **3** *1 ½* **Kingfast (IRE)**[30] 4287 4-9-6 **62**..............................(p) CierenFallon(5) 5 66
(David Dennis) *hld up in rr of midfield: pushed along to cl on ldrs over 2f out: sn rdn and ev ch 1f out: kpt on fnl f* **9/4**[1]
5243 **4** *2* **Agent Gibbs**[28] 4370 7-9-5 **63**...(p) KateLeahy(7) 9 64
(John O'Shea) *trckd ldr tl led 5f out: rdn along and pressed 2f out: hdd over 1f out: kpt on one pce fnl f* **6/1**[3]
6-00 **5** *4* **Gordalan**[60] 3200 3-8-11 **59**... JoeyHaynes 2 54
(Philip Kirby) *racd in midfield: rdn along to go 3rd 3f out: sn drvn and kpt on one pce fr 1f out* **33/1**
003R **6** *½* **Principia**[9] 5106 4-9-7 **58**... AndrewElliott 6 52
(Adam West) *dwlt and racd in last: rdn in rr over 2f out: sme late hdwy (jockey said filly was never travelling)* **20/1**
2-03 **7** *1 ¼* **Ban Shoof**[17] 4795 6-10-0 **65**..(b) HectorCrouch 7 57
(Gary Moore) *racd in midfield: rdn along and no imp over 2f out: kpt on one pce fnl f* **7/1**
1-00 **8** *2 ¼* **Lyrica's Lion (IRE)**[48] 3633 5-9-11 **67**........................ RobJFitzpatrick(5) 3 55
(Sheena West) *trckd ldr: pushed along over 2f out: sn rdn and no imp over 1f out: wknd fnl f* **13/2**
6504 **9** *7* **Lawyersgunsn'money**[32] 4220 4-9-9 **60**............................. RyanTate 10 37
(Roger Teal) *trckd ldr: pushed along and upsides ldr 3f out: rdn and unable qck 2f out: wknd fnl f* **12/1**
4624 **10** *33* **Passing Clouds**[60] 3186 4-8-9 **46** oh1.................................. LiamJones 8
(Michael Attwater) *led: rdn along and qckly lost pl 5f out: sn bhd* **28/1**
2m 35.8s (1.80) **Going Correction** +0.275s/f (Good)
WFA 3 from 4yo+ 11lb **10** Ran SP% **121.4**
Speed ratings (Par 101): **105,104,103,102,99 99,98,96,92,70**
CSF £57.19 CT £136.16 TOTE £16.30: £3.40, £1.50, £1.50; EX 97.80 Trifecta £138.10.
Owner P F I Cole Ltd **Bred** Gerard Corry & Cristian Healy **Trained** Whatcombe, Oxon

FOCUS
Add 3yds to the distance of the opener. After significant rain over the previous 24 hours, ground conditions were officially described as soft going into this seven-race card. The time of this modest opening handicap, 10sec slower than standard, indicated that description was fairly accurate. They didn't look to go particularly hard at any stage, understandably in the conditions, but the finish was still dominated by horses coming from off the pace. The third has been rated back to form.

5426 STRONG RECRUITMENT GROUP H'CAP — 1m 6f
6:00 (6:00) (Class 5) (0-70,72) 3-Y-O — **£3,428** (£1,020; £509; £400) **Stalls** Centre

Form — RPR

0211 **1** **Funny Man**[7] 5175 3-9-5 **70**.....................(b) DavidNolan 3 79+
(David O'Meara) *hld up in last: bmpd along over 6f out: wnt 3rd over 3f out: rdn to chse ldr over 2f out: sn drvn and styd on wl to ld wl ins fnl f* **6/5**[1]

3055 **2** 2 ¼ **Arthur Pendragon (IRE)**[15] 4862 3-9-7 **72**.....................(b) JasonWatson 2 76
(Brian Meehan) *trckd ldr: led gng wl 5f out: rdn along w short ld 2f out: drvn fnl f: hdd by wnr wl ins fnl f: no ex* **11/2**

3263 **3** ½ **Hermocrates (FR)**[11] 5012 3-9-2 **67**.....................(b) RossaRyan 4 70
(Richard Hannon) *racd in 3rd: wnt 2nd 5f out: rdn along to chse ldr and hung lft 2f out: sn drvn over 1f out: kpt on but nt match wnr fnl f (jockey said gelding hung left-handed from 3f out)* **7/2**[3]

5201 **4** 25 **Narina (IRE)**[25] 4484 3-9-5 **70**.....................(p[1]) LiamJones 1 38
(William Haggas) *pushed along fr stalls to ld: rdn along and hdd 5f out: sn bhd (trainer's rep said filly was unsuited by the ground and would prefer a quicker surface)* **11/4**[2]

3m 11.37s (0.17) **Going Correction** +0.275s/f (Good) **4 Ran SP% 109.7**
Speed ratings (Par 100): **110,108,108,94**
CSF £7.91 TOTE £1.80; EX 8.90 Trifecta £25.00.
Owner Apple Tree Stud **Bred** Apple Tree Stud **Trained** Upper Helmsley, N Yorks

FOCUS
Add 3yds. A small field but they appeared to go a reasonable gallop and it was won by one of the two last-time out winners, although he had to work very hard to do so.

5427 INDEPENDENT CATERING NOVICE STKS — 4f 217y
6:30 (6:31) (Class 5) 2-Y-O — **£3,428** (£1,020; £509; £254) **Stalls** Centre

Form — RPR

1 **Maystar (IRE)** 2-9-5 0..................... HollieDoyle 8 77+
(Archie Watson) *broke wl and mde all: pushed along and drifted lft off rail 2f out: sn rdn and drew clr despite greenness over 1f out: pushed out fnl f* **2/1**[2]

0 **2** 4 **Instantly**[12] 4993 2-9-5 0..................... JasonWatson 4 61
(Robert Cowell) *in tch on outer: pushed along whn bmpd by rival and stmbld 2f out: sn rdn and rcvrd wl: kpt on fnl f (jockey said colt hung right-handed)* **14/1**[3]

03 **3** ½ **Jane Victoria**[11] 5011 2-9-0 0..................... AndrewElliott 1 53+
(Adam West) *hld up: pushed along and outpcd over 2f out: rdn 1f out and kpt on wl ins fnl f: should improve* **50/1**

00 **4** nk **Oribi**[17] 4790 2-8-11 0..................... GeorgiaCox(3) 6 52
(William Haggas) *trckd ldr: jinked lft and bmpd rival whn pushed along 2f out: sn rdn and one pce fnl f* **14/1**[3]

36 **5** ½ **Claudia Jean (IRE)**[12] 4992 2-9-0 0..................... KieranO'Neill 7 50
(Richard Hannon) *hld up: rdn along and rn green 2f out: kpt on ins fnl f* **20/1**

220 **6** nse **Partridge (IRE)**[38] 3983 2-9-0 79..................... RossaRyan 5 50
(Richard Hannon) *racd in midfield: rdn along to chse wnr 2f out: drvn and no ex 1f out: one pce after (trainers' rep said, regards poor performance, filly ran too free in the early stages and would prefer a quicker surface. Vet said filly lost her right-hind shoe and had a small laceration on her left-fore leg)* **4/7**[1]

7 12 **Billesdon** 2-9-5 0..................... LiamKeniry 2 12
(Michael Madgwick) *dwlt and racd in rr: nvr on terms* **40/1**

1m 0.93s (2.23) **Going Correction** +0.275s/f (Good) **7 Ran SP% 119.5**
Speed ratings (Par 94): **93,86,85,85,84 84,65**
CSF £28.97 TOTE £2.90: £1.20, £5.60; EX 36.00 Trifecta £247.50.
Owner Hambleton Racing Ltd XXXVI **Bred** Ballinvana House Stud **Trained** Upper Lambourn, W Berks

FOCUS
The poor effort from 81-rated Partridge holds the form back to an extent but this still threw up a most impressive winner who could easily be well above average.

5428 EDUCATER LTD NOVICE MEDIAN AUCTION STKS — 7f
7:00 (7:04) (Class 6) 3-5-Y-O — **£2,781** (£827; £413; £206) **Stalls** Centre

Form — RPR

-532 **1** **Quirky Gertie (IRE)**[35] 4129 3-8-9 64..................... NicolaCurrie 10 72+
(Mick Channon) *settled in 4th: hdwy gng wl 2f out: led on bit over 1f out: readily drew clr under hands and heels 1f out: pushed out: comf* **11/4**[3]

2222 **2** 4 **Voltaic**[17] 4800 3-9-0 74.....................(t) JasonWatson 9 67
(Paul Cole) *racd in midfield: hdwy amongst rivals 2f out: rdn to chse wnr over 1f out: kpt on fnl f but no match for wnr* **2/1**[2]

0-4 **3** 4 **Dreamingofdiamonds (IRE)**[10] 5062 3-8-9 0..................... KieranO'Neill 7 52
(David Lanigan) *trckd ldr tl led 3f out: rdn along and hdd by wnr over 1f out: kpt on one pce fnl f* **16/1**

4 1 ½ **Brambledown** 3-9-0 0..................... HectorCrouch 6 53
(Gary Moore) *led: rdn along and hdd 3f out: drvn and no imp over 1f out: kpt on one pce fnl f* **16/1**

0 **5** ¾ **Vipin (FR)**[147] 979 4-9-4 0..................... GeorgiaCox(3) 3 54
(William Muir) *racd keenly in midfield: rdn along and no imp 2f out: kpt on one pce fnl f* **25/1**

0 **6** shd **Tilsworth Diamond**[66] 2967 4-9-2 0..................... RaulDaSilva 4 49
(Mike Murphy) *hld up: pushed along in rr over 2f out: sn rdn and no imp: n.d* **50/1**

0 **7** 2 ½ **Misread**[16] 4842 3-8-9 0..................... RyanTate 1 40
(Geoffrey Deacon) *trckd ldr: pushed along and lost pl 3f out: wknd fr 2f out* **100/1**

8 hd **Reigning Ice** 3-8-9 0..................... HollieDoyle 2 39
(Clive Cox) *hld up: pushed along and green over 2f out: a bhd (jockey said filly ran green)* **6/4**[1]

1m 26.95s (2.65) **Going Correction** +0.275s/f (Good)
WFA 3 from 4yo 7lb **8 Ran SP% 118.6**
Speed ratings (Par 101): **95,90,85,84,83 83,80,80**
CSF £9.01 TOTE £3.90: £1.10, £1.20, £2.50; EX 8.40 Trifecta £47.60.
Owner The Endless Folly Partnership **Bred** Acorn Stud **Trained** West Ilsley, Berks

FOCUS
Nothing special in here but the winner took advantage to open her account in taking style.

5429 DALE STREET BIRTHDAY & ANNIVERSARY CELEBRATIONS FILLIES' H'CAP — 7f
7:30 (7:32) (Class 5) (0-70,70) 3-Y-O — **£3,428** (£1,020; £509; £400; £400) **Stalls** Centre

Form — RPR

-205 **1** **Red Romance**[12] 5002 3-9-8 **70**..................... HectorCrouch 4 75
(Clive Cox) *trckd ldr: effrt to chse ldr 2f out: sn rdn and styd on wl to ld fnl 100yds: a doing enough* **5/4**[1]

3503 **2** hd **Caen Na Coille (USA)**[15] 4870 3-9-7 **69**..................... JasonWatson 5 73
(Ed Dunlop) *trckd ldr and travelled wl thrght: led gng best over 1f out: sn rdn and kpt on wl but hdd by wnr fnl 100yds* **11/4**[3]

660- **3** 3 **Abuja (IRE)**[278] 8470 3-8-7 **55**.....................(h[1]) NicolaCurrie 6 51
(Michael Madgwick) *led: rdn along and hdd over 1f out: kpt on one pce fnl f* **25/1**

3064 **4** 2 **So Claire**[18] 4754 3-8-4 **52**..................... HollieDoyle 1 43
(William Muir) *hld up: rdn and outpcd over 2f out: n.d* **5/2**[2]

0230 **5** 86 **Gabriela Laura**[75] 2689 3-9-0 **67**..................... CierenFallon(5) 3
(Alexandra Dunn) *j. awkwardly and rdr lost irons leaving stalls: sn bhd and heavily eased 2f out (jockey said he lost his irons leaving the stalls and was unable to regain them)* **10/1**

1m 26.66s (2.36) **Going Correction** +0.275s/f (Good) **5 Ran SP% 112.6**
Speed ratings (Par 97): **97,96,93,91,**
CSF £5.18 TOTE £1.70: £1.10, £2.00; EX 4.80 Trifecta £37.70.
Owner Clipper Logistics **Bred** Highclere Stud & Jake Warren Ltd **Trained** Lambourn, Berks

FOCUS
Not a particularly strong fillies' handicap but the front two came clear and look on the up at lowly level.

5430 INDEPENDENT CATERING H'CAP — 7f
8:00 (8:02) (Class 6) (0-55,57) 3-Y-O+
£2,781 (£827; £413; £400; £400; £400) **Stalls** Centre

Form — RPR

4511 **1** **Kodimoor (IRE)**[12] 4978 6-9-6 **50**.....................(p) DougieCostello 17 56
(Mark Walford) *trckd ldr: pushed along to ld over 2f out: rdn over 1f out: kpt on gamely ins fnl f* **5/2**[1]

0-50 **2** nk **Master Poet**[57] 3298 4-9-7 **51**..................... HectorCrouch 2 56
(Gary Moore) *trckd ldr: pushed along to chse wnr 2f out: sn rdn and str chal 1f out: kpt on wl but unable to rch wnr* **5/1**[3]

0630 **3** 1 ¼ **Jupiter**[9] 5083 4-9-2 **51**.....................(b) CierenFallon(5) 1 53
(Alexandra Dunn) *midfield on outer: rdn along to chse wnr 2f out: kpt on wl fnl f: no match for front pair* **7/2**[2]

-603 **4** ½ **Flying Sakhee**[28] 4378 6-9-3 **47**.....................(v) KieranO'Neill 13 48
(John Bridger) *in rr of midfield: hdwy u.p over 2f out: rdn over 1f out: kpt on* **6/1**

6000 **5** 7 **Golconda Prince (IRE)**[22] 4615 5-9-3 **50**.....................(vt) FinleyMarsh(3) 18 32
(Mark Pattinson) *in rr of midfield: drvn along and no imp 2f out: one pce fnl f* **14/1**

0000 **6** 2 **Lisnamoyle Lady (IRE)**[52] 3476 4-8-8 **45**.....................(bt) JacobClark(7) 7 22
(Martin Smith) *hld up in last: rdn along 3f out: minor late hdwy* **25/1**

0-R0 **7** 2 **Free Talkin**[32] 4219 4-9-1 **45**..................... NicolaCurrie 5 17
(Michael Attwater) *hld up: rdn along and no imp over 2f out: kpt on passed btn horses fnl f (jockey said filly was slowly away)* **25/1**

0-05 **8** 7 **Lewis Slack**[25] 4477 3-9-3 **57**.....................(t) JoshuaBryan(3) 6 8
(Richard J Bandey) *racd in midfield: rdn and no hdwy 2f out: nvr on terms* **20/1**

-005 **9** 1 ½ **Such Promise**[53] 3442 3-9-4 **55**.....................(b[1]) RossaRyan 16 2
(Mike Murphy) *led: rdn along and hdd over 2f out: wknd fnl f (jockey said gelding ran too free)* **7/1**

4-00 **10** 3 ½ **Uponastar (IRE)**[171] 614 3-9-1 **52**..................... JasonWatson 14
(Amy Murphy) *trckd ldr: rdn along 3f out: lost pl 2f out: wknd fnl f* **12/1**

00-6 **11** 2 ¼ **Gladden (IRE)**[178] 474 4-8-10 **45**..................... SophieRalston(5) 4
(Lee Carter) *hld up: rdn and outpcd over 2f out: a in rr* **20/1**

1m 26.31s (2.01) **Going Correction** +0.275s/f (Good)
WFA 3 from 4yo+ 7lb **11 Ran SP% 125.8**
Speed ratings (Par 101): **99,98,97,96,88 86,84,76,74,70 67**
CSF £15.48 CT £46.12 TOTE £3.40: £2.20, £1.40, £2.40; EX 18.70 Trifecta £82.50.
Owner Ursa Major Racing & Partner **Bred** Tally-Ho Stud **Trained** Sherriff Hutton, N Yorks

FOCUS
Not many got into this weak handicap and it was won by the only in-form contender. Straightforward form rated around the principals.

5431 EDUCATER LTD H'CAP — 7f 135y
8:30 (8:33) (Class 6) (0-65,64) 3-Y-O
£2,781 (£827; £413; £400; £400; £400) **Stalls** Centre

Form — RPR

0000 **1** **Sussex Solo**[56] 3354 3-8-4 **47**..................... KieranO'Neill 9 56
(Luke Dace) *mde all: pushed along to extend ld to 3 l over 1f out: sn in command and pushed out fnl f (trainers' rep said, regards apparent improvement in form, gelding benefitted from a break and being treated for a back issue)* **16/1**

5630 **2** 2 **Hey Ho Let's Go**[33] 4181 3-9-6 **63**.....................(h[1]) HectorCrouch 5 67
(Clive Cox) *racd in midfield: pushed along to chse wnr 2f out: kpt on fnl f but no match for wnr* **5/1**[2]

5543 **3** ½ **Annexation (FR)**[5] 5237 3-9-7 **64**..................... LiamKeniry 4 67
(Ed Dunlop) *racd in midfield: effrt to chse wnr over 2f out: rdn and wnt 3rd 1f out: kpt on fnl f* **11/10**[1]

2260 **4** 2 **Redemptive**[36] 4071 3-9-2 **64**.....................(t[1]) CierenFallon(5) 7 62
(John Butler) *racd in midfield: clsd gng wl 2f out: sn rdn and unable qck over 1f out: one pce fnl f* **13/2**[3]

0-00 **5** 1 **Savoy Brown**[67] 2926 3-9-0 **57**..................... JasonWatson 14 53
(Michael Attwater) *in rr of midfield: rdn along and outpcd over 2f out: kpt on fnl f* **16/1**

-000 **6** 2 ¾ **Sittin Handy (IRE)**[58] 3246 3-7-11 **45**.....................(p) SophieRalston(5) 10 34
(Dean Ivory) *trckd wnr: rdn along and no imp over 2f out: wknd fnl f* **25/1**

540U **7** 3 ½ **Quarto Cavallo**[9] 5092 3-8-3 **46**.....................(h[1]) RaulDaSilva 6 27
(Adam West) *in tch in 4th: rdn along and outpcd 2f out: wknd fnl f* **14/1**

000 **8** 5 **Dandy Belle (IRE)**[14] 4931 3-7-12 **46**..................... RhiainIngram(5) 8 15
(Richenda Ford) *chsd wnr: drvn along and lost pl 2f out: no ex fnl f* **33/1**

2506 **9** 5 **Orliko (IRE)**[11] 5031 3-9-4 **61**.....................(bt) RossaRyan 3 18
(Richard Hannon) *hld up: rdn in rr 3f out: nvr on terms (jockey said gelding was never travelling)* **7/1**

4000 **10** hd **Confab (USA)**[17] 4787 3-9-4 **61**..................... PatCosgrave 1 17
(George Baker) *hld up: rdn and outpcd 3f out: nvr on terms* **14/1**

000 **11** *10* **Red Moon Lady**[19] 4738 3-8-4 **47** ow2 JoeyHaynes 11
(Dean Ivory) *racd in midfield: drvn along 3f out: sn lost pl over 2f out* **50/1**
1m 34.17s (2.47) **Going Correction** +0.275s/f (Good) **11 Ran SP% 124.0**
Speed ratings (Par 98): **98,96,95,93,92 89,86,81,76,76 66**
CSF £98.01 CT £169.57 TOTE £23.20: £4.60, £1.80, £1.20; EX 194.80 Trifecta £666.20.
Owner Richard L Page **Bred** Copped Hall Farm & Stud **Trained** Pulborough, W Sussex

FOCUS
A desperately weak affair won by a horse who came here so badly out of form that he couldn't seriously be considered. The second has been rated in line with his previous 7f form at Leicester.
T/Plt: £35.00 to a £1 stake. Pool: £60,403.35 - 1,257.52 winning units T/Qpdt: £9.90 to a £1 stake. Pool: £7,086.02 - 527.95 winning units **Mark Grantham**

4379 NEWCASTLE (A.W) (L-H)
Saturday, July 27

OFFICIAL GOING: Tapeta: standard
Wind: Almost nil Weather: Overcast

5432 COLLINGWOOD TAXI INSURANCE FILLIES' H'CAP 5f (Tp)
1:40 (1:40) (Class 4) (0-80,77) 4-Y-O+ **£5,272** (£1,568; £784; £392) **Stalls** Centre

Form RPR
0515 **1** **Dandy's Beano (IRE)**[22] 4593 4-9-7 **77** (h) KevinStott 1 91
(Kevin Ryan) *mde all: shkn up and qcknd over 1f out: edgd rt: pushed out fnl f: comf* **5/4**[1]
5545 **2** *3 1/4* **Oriental Lilly**[19] 4722 5-9-4 **74** PhilDennis 3 76
(Jim Goldie) *dwlt: prom: effrt and chsd wnr 2f out: kpt on same pce fnl f* **2/1**[2]
-066 **3** *1 3/4* **Marietta Robusti (IRE)**[7] 5181 4-8-10 **66** CamHardie 2 62
(Stella Barclay) *t.k.h: pressed wnr to 2f out: rallied: outpcd fnl f* **20/1**
1456 **4** *2 1/2* **Everkyllachy (IRE)**[14] 4911 5-8-0 **63** (b) LauraCoughlan(7) 4 50
(Karen McLintock) *chsd ldrs: drvn and outpcd 1/2-way: btn over 1f out* **3/1**[3]
59.92s (0.42) **Going Correction** +0.20s/f (Slow) 4 Ran SP% **107.5**
Speed ratings (Par 102): **104,98,96,92**
CSF £4.00 TOTE £1.90; EX 3.00 Trifecta £12.90.
Owner Hambleton Racing Ltd XLVII **Bred** Ruskerne Ltd **Trained** Hambleton, N Yorks

FOCUS
A fair little fillies' sprint handicap. The strong favourite made all convincingly from off her own increasing tempo.

5433 COLLINGWOOD INSURANCE COMPANY EBF NOVICE AUCTION STKS (PLUS 10 RACE) 7f 14y (Tp)
2:10 (2:12) (Class 4) 2-Y-O **£7,374** (£2,194; £1,096; £548) **Stalls** Centre

Form RPR
5 **1** **Morisco (IRE)**[22] 4611 2-9-2 0 JaneElliott(3) 5 77+
(Tom Dascombe) *dwlt: plld hrd in rr in centre of gp: drvn and outpcd over 2f out: hdwy nr side: hung lft and gd hdwy to ld ins fnl f: edgd rt: r.o wl: comf* **6/1**[3]
2 *1 1/4* **Flylikeaneagle (IRE)** 2-9-5 0 FrannyNorton 6 74+
(Mark Johnston) *led in centre of gp: rdn and hdd 2f out: rallied and ev ch briefly ins fnl f: sn chsng wnr: kpt on* **3/1**[2]
3 *1 3/4* **Flames Of York** 2-8-12 0 JonathanFisher(7) 2 70
(K R Burke) *prom on far side of gp: stdy hdwy over 2f out: rdn and sltly outpcd over 1f out: r.o ins fnl f* **16/1**
2 **4** *3/4* **Reclaim Victory (IRE)**[30] 4289 2-8-11 0 BenRobinson(3) 7 63
(Brian Ellison) *cl up in centre of gp: rdn and ev ch over 1f out: no ex ins fnl f* **5/2**[1]
5 *1* **Lyricist Voice** 2-9-5 0 GeraldMosse 8 65
(Marco Botti) *dwlt: hld up on nr side of gp: gd hdwy to ld 2f out: hdd ins fnl f: edgd lft and sn btn* **11/1**
6 *1/2* **Abbotside** 2-9-5 0 TomQueally 10 64
(James Bethell) *dwlt: hld up in midfield on nr side of gp: hdwy and cl up 2f out: sn outpcd: no ex fnl f* **33/1**
6 **6** *dht* **Ten Chants**[10] 5052 2-9-5 0 LouisSteward 1 64
(Ed Dunlop) *prom on far side of gp: rdn and outpcd 2f out: no imp fnl f* **20/1**
5 **8** *1 1/2* **Hooroo (IRE)**[8] 5152 2-9-5 0 CliffordLee 3 60
(K R Burke) *cl up in centre of gp: rdn and outpcd 2f out: sn btn* **8/1**
0 **9** *nk* **Trevie Fountain**[16] 4826 2-9-5 0 PaulHanagan 9 60
(Richard Fahey) *hld up in centre of gp: pushed along whn checked wl over 1f out: sn n.d* **16/1**
10 *nse* **Ten Thousand Stars** 2-9-0 0 KevinStott 4 54
(Adrian Nicholls) *dwlt: bhd on far side of gp: struggling over 2f out: sn btn* **28/1**
11 *6* **Sunshine Fantasy (IRE)** 2-9-0 0 AndrewMullen 11 39+
(Archie Watson) *cl up on nr side of gp: rdn and outpcd whn hmpd over 1f out: sn btn* **15/2**
1m 29.09s (2.89) **Going Correction** +0.20s/f (Slow) **11 Ran SP% 122.0**
Speed ratings (Par 96): **91,89,87,86,85 85,85,83,82,82 76**
WIN: 7.10 Morisco; PL: 3.90 Flames Of York 1.60 Flylikeaneagle 2.70 Morisco; EX: 32.60; CSF: 24.76; TF: 398.40 CSF £24.76 TOTE £7.10: £2.70, £1.60, £3.90; EX 32.60 Trifecta £398.40.
Owner Mrs Caroline Ingram **Bred** Kildaragh Stud **Trained** Malpas, Cheshire

FOCUS
An ordinary juvenile novice contest. The third-favourite defied his clear inexperience to get well on top late from off a steady gallop. The opening level is fluid.

5434 COLLINGWOOD LEARNER DRIVER INSURANCE "BEESWING" H'CAP 7f 14y (Tp)
2:45 (2:45) (Class 3) (0-95,92) 3-Y-O+ **£16,172** (£4,812; £2,405; £1,202) **Stalls** Centre

Form RPR
3502 **1** **Barristan The Bold**[28] 4360 3-9-4 **89** FrannyNorton 9 98
(Tom Dascombe) *prom: rdn over 2f out: rallied and led over 1f out: kpt on strly fnl f* **5/1**[2]
1-1 **2** *1 1/2* **Honest Albert**[30] 4305 3-9-5 **90** JosephineGordon 10 95
(John Gosden) *trckd ldr: rdn over 2f out: led briefly over 1f out: kpt on fnl f: nt pce of wnr* **11/8**[1]
1000 **3** *hd* **Portledge (IRE)**[15] 4887 5-9-5 **83** (b) StevieDonohoe 6 90
(James Bethell) *hld up: hdwy and prom over 1f out: rdn and kpt on ins fnl f* **33/1**
5656 **4** *1 3/4* **Glengarry**[12] 4980 6-8-11 **80** (b) BenSanderson(5) 12 83
(Keith Dalgleish) *dwlt: sn prom: rdn over 2f out: edgd lft over 1f out: no ex ins fnl f* **18/1**
3611 **5** *1 1/4* **Defence Treaty (IRE)**[30] 4288 3-8-10 **81** (p) PaulHanagan 5 77
(Richard Fahey) *hld up: rdn and outpcd over 2f out: sme late hdwy: nvr rchd ldrs* **9/1**[3]
0532 **6** *nk* **Breanski**[14] 4902 5-9-6 **84** JackGarritty 4 83
(Jedd O'Keeffe) *hld up in rr: rdn over 2f out: kpt on fnl f: nvr able to chal (jockey said gelding ran flat)* **5/1**[2]
4115 **7** *1/2* **Gentle Look**[51] 3493 3-9-4 **89** TomQueally 1 83
(Saeed bin Suroor) *hld up in tch: rdn over 2f out: hdwy over 1f out: wknd ins fnl f* **9/1**[3]
0060 **8** *1* **Commander Han (FR)**[28] 4403 4-9-5 **83** (p) KevinStott 11 77
(Kevin Ryan) *led tl rdn and hdd over 1f out: sn wknd* **11/1**
2605 **9** *1 3/4* **Areen Heart (FR)**[38] 3991 5-10-0 **92** CamHardie 2 82
(David O'Meara) *hld up: drvn along over 2f out: sn no imp: btn fnl f* **33/1**
2600 **10** *3* **Showboating (IRE)**[40] 3922 11-9-2 **80** (p) LewisEdmunds 7 62
(John Balding) *cl up: drvn and outpcd over 2f out: sn btn* **66/1**
02-0 **11** *6* **Monsieur Jimmy**[29] 4329 7-8-8 **75** BenRobinson(3) 8 40
(Brian Ellison) *hld up: rdn and struggling wl over 2f out: sn btn* **40/1**
1m 26.1s (-0.10) **Going Correction** +0.20s/f (Slow)
WFA 3 from 4yo+ 7lb **11 Ran SP% 118.8**
Speed ratings (Par 107): **108,106,106,104,102 102,101,100,98,95 88**
CSF £12.10 CT £210.44 TOTE £5.80: £1.80, £1.10, £7.40; EX 15.50 Trifecta £249.50.
Owner Chasemore Farm & Kevin Costello **Bred** Chasemore Farm **Trained** Malpas, Cheshire

FOCUS
The feature contest was a fairly good handicap. One of the four 3yos in the field got well on top towards the centre in a good comparative time.

5435 COLLINGWOOD CONVICTED DRIVER INSURANCE H'CAP 2m 56y (Tp)
3:20 (3:20) (Class 6) (0-60,59) 4-Y-O+
£2,781 (£827; £413; £300; £300; £300) **Stalls** Low

Form RPR
5142 **1** **Steel Helmet (IRE)**[4] 5271 5-8-9 **47** JosephineGordon 3 53
(Harriet Bethell) *hld up on ins: stdy hdwy over 2f out: chsng ldrs and rdn over 1f out: led ins fnl f: r.o wl* **7/2**[3]
25/3 **2** *1/2* **My Mo (FR)**[53] 3447 7-8-12 **50** KevinStott 2 55+
(Tristan Davidson) *t.k.h early: led 3f: cl up: regained ld gng wl over 2f out: rdn over 1f out: hdd ins fnl f: kpt on* **11/4**[1]
0000 **3** *1 3/4* **Sweetest Smile (IRE)**[46] 3686 4-8-5 **46** (b[1]) JaneElliott(3) 12 49
(Ed de Giles) *s.i.s: sn prom: effrt and rdn over 2f out: edgd lft: kpt on same pce ins fnl f (jockey said filly hung left in the final two furlongs)* **20/1**
-350 **4** *1 3/4* **Misscarlett (IRE)**[46] 3686 5-8-7 **45** CamHardie 6 46
(Philip Kirby) *midfield: hdwy to ld after 3f: rdn and hdd over 2f out: rallied: one pce fnl f* **14/1**
2050 **5** *1 1/4* **Basildon**[53] 3448 4-9-0 **55** (b) BenRobinson(3) 5 55
(Brian Ellison) *hld up in midfield: drvn along and outpcd over 2f out: rallied over 1f out: no imp fnl f* **10/3**[2]
6645 **6** *nk* **Pammi**[8] 5122 4-8-12 **50** (p) PhilDennis 4 49
(Jim Goldie) *dwlt: hld up: stdy hdwy on outside 1/2-way: rdn along and effrt over 2f out: no imp fr over 1f out* **20/1**
0402 **7** *1* **St Andrews (IRE)**[16] 4825 6-9-4 **59** MeganNicholls(3) 1 57
(Gillian Boanas) *hld up: rdn 3f out: hdwy 2f out: no imp fnl f* **7/1**
0410 **8** *8* **Rock N'Stones (IRE)**[24] 4510 8-8-10 **48** FrannyNorton 10 37
(Gillian Boanas) *cl up tl rdn and wknd fr 2f out* **20/1**
0253 **9** *2 1/2* **Artic Nel**[11] 5029 5-8-7 **45** PaulHanagan 13 31
(Ian Williams) *t.k.h: hld up: rdn over 2f out: sn no imp: btn over 1f out* **9/1**
4023 **10** *6* **Foxrush Take Time (FR)**[46] 3705 4-8-7 **45** (e) PhilipPrince 14 23
(Richard Guest) *dwlt and sn swtchd lft s: hld up: rdn along 3f out: sn btn* **18/1**
20/0 **11** *19* **Byronegetonefree**[10] 3447 8-8-7 **45** (b) AndrewMullen 11 1
(Stuart Coltherd) *hld up in tch: drvn over 3f out: wknd over 2f out: t.o* **50/1**
3m 38.55s (3.55) **Going Correction** +0.20s/f (Slow) **11 Ran SP% 122.6**
Speed ratings (Par 101): **99,98,97,97,96 96,95,91,90,87 77**
CSF £13.47 CT £174.39 TOTE £4.60: £1.60, £1.30, £5.10; EX 17.80 Trifecta £256.70.
Owner W A Bethell **Bred** Rabbah Bloodstock Limited **Trained** Arnold, E Yorks

FOCUS
A modest staying handicap. They went a start-stop, muddling gallop and the winning third-favourite was the only one to make up significant ground to prevail up the far rail. The form could be rated a pound or two higher.

5436 COLLINGWOOD YOUNG DRIVER INSURANCE SILK SERIES LADY RIDERS' H'CAP (PRO-AM LADY RIDERS' RACE) 1m 2f 42y (Tp)
3:55 (3:56) (Class 4) (0-85,86) 3-Y-O+ **£5,433** (£1,617; £808; £404; £300; £300) **Stalls** High

5202 **1** **Furzig**[15] 4892 4-10-1 **80** MeganNicholls(3) 4 93
(Richard Fahey) *hld up bhd ldng gp: stdy hdwy over 2f out: chsd ldr and effrt over 1f out: led ins fnl f: r.o wl* **7/2**[3]
6421 **2** *1 1/4* **Teodora De Vega (IRE)**[16] 4836 3-9-0 **71** JosephineGordon 3 82
(Ralph Beckett) *hld up in tch: shkn up briefly after 3f: hdwy to ld over 2f out: rdn over 1f out: hdd ins fnl f: one pce towards fin* **3/1**[2]
5306 **3** *8* **Zabeel Star (IRE)**[28] 4383 7-9-9 **78** (p) LauraCoughlan(7) 10 72
(Karen McLintock) *s.i.s: hld up: hdwy on outside over 2f out: effrt and prom over 1f out: outpcd by first two fnl f* **18/1**
5310 **4** *3 1/4* **Autretot (FR)**[20] 4689 4-10-2 **83** MissEmmaTodd(5) 11 71
(David O'Meara) *t.k.h: cl up: disp ld over 2f out to wl over 1f out: wknd fnl f* **5/1**
5125 **5** *1/2* **Global Art**[32] 4209 4-9-13 **82** SophieSmith(7) 1 69
(Ed Dunlop) *hld up bhd ldng gp: effrt over 2f out: wknd over 1f out* **14/1**
2111 **6** *1 1/2* **Gas Monkey**[22] 4601 4-10-3 **79** (h) ShelleyBirkett 2 63
(Julia Feilden) *prom: effrt over 2f out: wknd over 1f out (jockey said gelding ran flat)* **11/4**[1]
3005 **7** *2 1/4* **Dance King**[15] 4890 9-9-9 **78** (tp) MissEmilyEasterby(7) 8 57
(Tim Easterby) *s.i.s: bhd: stdy hdwy over 2f out: sn no imp (jockey said gelding was denied a clear run two furlongs out)* **25/1**
0002 **8** *8* **Paparazzi**[29] 4329 4-10-2 **78** LucyAlexander 6 41
(Tracy Waggott) *s.i.s: t.k.h in rr: pushed along and outpcd over 2f out: sn btn* **20/1**
1224 **9** *8* **Grand Inquisitor**[10] 5055 7-10-5 **86** (v) KatherineBegley(5) 5 33
(Conor Dore) *in tch: effrt on outside over 2f out: sn wknd* **40/1**
32-0 **10** *3 3/4* **True North (IRE)**[17] 4791 4-9-3 **68** (b) JaneElliott(3) 7
(Sir Mark Prescott Bt) *cl up: led over 4f out to over 2f out: sn rdn and wknd (jockey said gelding hung left in the home straight)* **12/1**
660 **11** *84* **Elenora Delight**[40] 3930 4-9-1 **70** RhonaPindar(7) 9
(Ron Barr) *led to over 4f out: wknd qckly over 3f out: t.o* **66/1**
2m 9.91s (-0.49) **Going Correction** +0.20s/f (Slow)
WFA 3 from 4yo+ 9lb **11 Ran SP% 122.7**
Speed ratings (Par 105): **109,108,101,99,98 97,95,89,82,79 12**
CSF £14.64 CT £172.19 TOTE £4.40: £1.60, £1.60, £4.70; EX 20.60 Trifecta £263.50.
Owner Mr & Mrs P Ashton **Bred** Mr & Mrs P Ashton **Trained** Musley Bank, N Yorks
■ Stewards' Enquiry : Miss Emma Todd two-day ban; misuse of whip (tba)

FOCUS
A decent lady riders' handicap. Quite a strong pace took its toll on the prominent runners and the next wave took over in the second half of the straight.

5437 COLLINGWOOD VAN INSURANCE H'CAP 1m 4f 98y (Tp)
4:30 (4:31) (Class 3) (0-95,96) 3-Y-O+ **£7,762** (£2,310; £1,154; £577) **Stalls** High

Form RPR
-141 1 **Derevo**[34] 4144 3-8-13 **91** LouisSteward 5 100+
(Sir Michael Stoute) *trckd ldr: led gng wl over 2f out: shkn up and edgd lft over 1f out: r.o wl fnl f* **5/6**[1]
1365 2 ¾ **Claire Underwood (IRE)**[28] 4407 4-9-4 **85** PaulHanagan 7 92
(Richard Fahey) *prom: hdwy to press wnr over 2f out: sn rdn: kpt on ins fnl f* **15/2**[3]
-102 3 1½ **Lexington Empire**[37] 4021 4-9-9 **90** (b) StevieDonohoe 6 94
(David Lanigan) *hld up: hdwy to chse ldng pair 2f out: sn rdn: kpt on fnl f: nt pce to chal* **11/2**[2]
5-44 4 10 **Final**[12] 4988 7-9-1 **82** FrannyNorton 2 70
(Mark Johnston) *bhd and sn pushed along: rdn over 3f out: plugged on fnl 2f: nvr able to chal* **14/1**
5503 5 10 **Al Hamdany (IRE)**[24] 4504 5-9-12 **93** GeraldMosse 4 65
(Marco Botti) *trckd ldrs tl rdn and wknd 2f out* **11/2**[2]
4305 6 2¼ **Cosmelli (ITY)**[28] 4382 6-9-8 **96** (b) HarryRussell(7) 3 65
(Gay Kelleway) *hld up in tch on ins: drvn and outpcd over 3f out: struggling fnl 2f* **12/1**
6010 7 1¾ **Finniston Farm**[29] 4342 4-9-11 **95** (p) JaneElliott(3) 1 61
(Tom Dascombe) *t.k.h: led at ordinary gallop: rdn and hdd over 2f out: sn wknd (jockey said gelding ran too free)* **25/1**

2m 39.71s (-1.39) **Going Correction** +0.20s/f (Slow)
WFA 3 from 4yo+ 11lb **7 Ran SP% 115.3**
Speed ratings (Par 107): **112,111,110,103,97 95,94**
CSF £8.12 TOTE £1.70: £1.20, £3.20; EX 9.30 Trifecta £35.80.
Owner K Abdullah **Bred** Juddmonte Farms Ltd **Trained** Newmarket, Suffolk

FOCUS
A good middle-distance handicap. The odds-on favourite made full use of his hefty weight-for-age allowance to turn away the runner-up from over 1f out in a fair time.

5438 COLLINGWOOD OVER 50'S INSURANCE H'CAP 1m 5y (Tp)
5:05 (5:09) (Class 6) (0-60,59) 4-Y-O+
£2,781 (£827; £413; £300; £300; £300) **Stalls** Centre

Form RPR
4430 1 **Beverley Bullet**[15] 4892 6-9-7 **59** (p) PhilDennis 12 65
(Lawrence Mullaney) *cl up: led over 2f out: rdn and hrd pressed fr over 1f out: hld on wl cl home* **4/1**[1]
4040 2 *nse* **Im Dapper Too**[6] 5213 8-9-0 **52** (b[1]) SamJames 14 58
(John Davies) *prom: effrt and drvn along over 2f out: disp ld ins fnl f: kpt on: jst hld* **9/1**
3200 3 1¼ **Traveller (FR)**[53] 3448 5-9-5 **57** (tp) CamHardie 11 60
(Antony Brittain) *cl up: rdn over 2f out: effrt over 1f out: no ex ins fnl f* **16/1**
-360 4 *nk* **Top Offer**[12] 5003 10-8-11 **52** (p) MeganNicholls(3) 11 54
(Patrick Morris) *hld up in tch: rdn over 2f out: hdwy over 1f out: r.o ins fnl f* **22/1**
0354 5 ½ **Seek The Moon (USA)**[12] 4990 4-9-3 **55** (h) LewisEdmunds 7 56
(Lawrence Mullaney) *t.k.h: hld up in tch: rdn along and effrt 2f out: kpt on same pce fnl f* **8/1**
0000 6 1¼ **Proceeding**[32] 4207 4-9-0 **52** KevinStott 5 51
(Tracy Waggott) *hld up in rr: rdn and outpcd over 2f out: hdwy fnl f: r.o: nrst fin* **20/1**
0660 7 *nk* **Corked (IRE)**[9] 5099 6-9-3 **55** (p) TomQueally 6 53
(Alistair Whillans) *in tch on outside: effrt and ch over 1f out: wknd ins fnl f* **33/1**
5400 8 1¾ **Shazzab (IRE)**[14] 4915 4-9-1 **53** (b) PaulHanagan 9 47
(Richard Fahey) *hld up: rdn and outpcd over 2f out: n.d after* **7/1**[3]
4-04 9 1½ **Sumner Beach**[14] 4916 5-9-1 **53** JosephineGordon 2 44
(Harriet Bethell) *hld up on outside: drvn and outpcd over 2f out: sn btn* **10/1**
002 10 *nk* **Billy Wedge**[39] 3969 4-9-2 **54** JackGarritty 1 48
(Tracy Waggott) *t.k.h: overall ldr on outside to over 2f out: rallied: wkng whn hmpd ins fnl f* **9/2**[2]
1035 11 1 **Midnight Vixen**[59] 3223 5-9-3 **55** (p) AndrewMullen 4 43
(Ben Haslam) *dwlt: hld up: rdn along 3f out: sn struggling* **11/1**
621- 12 2¼ **Troop**[422] 3268 4-9-0 **52** FrannyNorton 8 35
(Ann Duffield) *hld up bhd ldng gp: drvn and struggling over 2f out: sn btn* **16/1**
0-00 13 3 **Sunstorm**[35] 4131 4-8-10 **51** (v[1]) AaronJones(3) 3 27
(Stef Keniry) *dwlt: hld up: rdn and struggling 3f out: sn wknd* **15/2**

1m 40.79s (2.19) **Going Correction** +0.20s/f (Slow) **13 Ran SP% 124.8**
Speed ratings (Par 101): **97,96,95,95,94 93,93,91,90,89 88,86,83**
CSF £41.11 CT £415.66 TOTE £4.10: £2.00, £3.10, £5.30; EX 41.70 Trifecta £916.40.
Owner Mrs Jean Stapleton & Rob Wilson **Bred** Keith Trowbridge **Trained** Great Habton, N Yorks
■ Stewards' Enquiry : Tom Queally three-day ban; careless riding (Aug 10-12)

FOCUS
A modest handicap and a contest dominated by those draw high, racing towards the near rail. The favourite prevailed on the bob of the heads in a tight photo-finish. Straightforward, limited form.
T/Plt: £32.90 to a £1 stake. Pool: £50,224.37 - 1,112.87 winning units T/Qpdt: £6.00 to a £1 stake. Pool: £5,419.61 - 657.80 winning units **Richard Young**

5380 NEWMARKET (R-H)
Saturday, July 27

OFFICIAL GOING: Good (8.4)
Wind: light to medium, half behind Weather: overcast, after morning rain

5439 HEATH COURT HOTEL BRITISH EBF MAIDEN STKS (PLUS 10 RACE) 7f
2:15 (2:15) (Class 4) 2-Y-O **£5,175** (£1,540; £769; £384) **Stalls** High

Form RPR
1 **Military March** 2-9-5 0 HectorCrouch 1 85+
(Saeed bin Suroor) *wnt rt leaving stalls: sn chsng ldr: effrt 2f out: sn drvn and ev ch: led jst ins fnl f: styd on wl: rdn out* **5/1**[3]
2 1¼ **Jacksonian** 2-9-5 0 HarryBentley 2 82
(Ralph Beckett) *chsd ldng trio: effrt 2f out: clsd u.p to press ldng pair 1f out: kpt on same pce ins fnl f: wnt 2nd towards fin* **4/1**[2]
2 3 ¾ **Ursa Minor (IRE)**[28] 4388 2-9-5 0 KieranO'Neill 6 80
(John Gosden) *chsd ldng pair: swtchd rt and effrt 2f out: struggling to qckn u.p whn swtchd rt again 1f out: kpt on fnl 100yds: wnt 3rd last strides (jockey said colt ran green)* **4/5**[1]
4 *hd* **Johan** 2-9-5 0 LiamJones 3 79
(William Haggas) *led: rdn 2f out: hrd pressed and edgd rt ent fnl f: hdd jst ins fnl f: no ex and one pce fnl 100yds: lost 2 pls towards fin* **16/1**
5 9 **Visibility (IRE)** 2-9-5 0 RobHornby 8 56
(Martyn Meade) *in tch in midfield: effrt ent fnl 2f: sn struggling and outpcd over 1f out: wknd ins fnl f* **9/1**
0 6 3¼ **Hermano Bello (FR)**[14] 4897 2-9-5 0 JohnFahy 4 48
(Richard Hannon) *midfield: effrt over 2f out: sn struggling and outpcd: wl btn over 1f out: wknd ins fnl f* **40/1**
7 3¼ **Great Fengshui (IRE)** 2-9-5 0 FergusSweeney 5 39
(Richard Hannon) *hld up in last pair: shkn up over 2f out: sn outpcd and wl btn over 1f out: wknd ins fnl f* **33/1**
8 1 **Master Rocco (IRE)** 2-9-5 0 AdamKirby 7 37
(Jane Chapple-Hyam) *s.i.s and bustled along leaving stalls: in rr: effrt over 2f out: sn struggling and wl btn whn hung lft over 1f out: wknd ins fnl f* **33/1**
9 19 **Honore Daumier (IRE)** 2-9-5 0 PatCosgrave 9
(Henry Candy) *sn niggled along and nvr travelling wl: a towards rr: rdn 4f out: lost tch over 1f out: t.o* **40/1**

1m 24.29s (-1.41) **Going Correction** -0.175s/f (Firm) **9 Ran SP% 118.9**
Speed ratings (Par 96): **101,99,98,98,88 84,80,79,57**
CSF £25.38 TOTE £5.60: £1.50, £1.60, £1.10; EX 20.30 Trifecta £34.80.
Owner Godolphin **Bred** Godolphin **Trained** Newmarket, Suffolk

FOCUS
The going was good. Going Stick: 8.4. Stands' side track; Stalls 1m2f and 1m6f: centre. Remainder: far side. Some nicely-bred debutants, but the once-raced favourite was all the rage with punters. The same owners' newcomer took the honours and looks a nice prospect.

5440 HEATH COURT HOTEL "BE OUR GUEST" H'CAP 1m 2f
2:50 (2:51) (Class 3) (0-95,96) 3-Y-O+ **£9,056** (£2,695; £1,346; £673) **Stalls** Centre

Form RPR
-122 1 **Rise Hall**[14] 4934 4-10-0 **96** (b) RobHornby 8 105
(Martyn Meade) *chsd ldr tl led over 8f out: rdn 2f out: edgd lft u.p 1f out: styd on wl ins fnl f* **7/2**[2]
13-5 2 1¼ **Herculean**[43] 3806 4-9-8 **90** HarryBentley 5 96
(Roger Charlton) *stdd s and t.k.h early: hld up in tch in midfield: swtchd lft and effrt over 1f out: chsd wnr 1f out: kpt on u.p but a hld ins fnl f* **13/8**[1]
5302 3 ½ **Dark Red (IRE)**[15] 4877 7-9-8 **90** (b) AdamKirby 4 95
(Ed Dunlop) *dwlt and rousted along early: clsd and effrt 2f out: rdn: edgd lft and bmpd jst ins fnl f: stl edging lft but kpt on u.p ins fnl f* **14/1**
2-51 4 *nk* **Caradoc (IRE)**[49] 3605 4-9-7 **89** LiamKeniry 6 93
(Ed Walker) *chsd ldrs: effrt 2f out: hung rt over 1f out: bumping w rival jst ins fnl f: kpt on u.p fnl 150yds* **10/3**[2]
5200 5 2½ **Society Red**[21] 4646 5-9-8 **90** JoeFanning 2 89
(Richard Fahey) *chsd ldr tl chsd ldr over 2f out: sn rdn: unable qck and lost 2nd 1f out: wknd ins fnl f (jockey said gelding hung left-handed)* **9/1**
/565 6 35 **Shargiah (IRE)**[15] 4892 6-9-2 **84** LukeMorris 1 13
(Michael Appleby) *led tl over 8f out: chsd ldr tl over 2f out: sn rdn: lost pl over 1f out: sn eased and virtually p.u ins fnl f: t.o: fin lame (jockey said gelding stopped quickly. Vet said gelding was lame on it's right fore)* **20/1**
0003 7 40 **Maifalki (FR)**[15] 4890 6-9-9 **91** DavidEgan 3
(Jason Ward) *t.k.h: hld up in tch in midfield: effrt 3f out: sn struggling: bhd and eased over 1f out: t.o (jockey said gelding stopped quickly)* **28/1**
/40- 8 3 **Great Order (USA)**[288] 8162 6-9-13 **95** HectorCrouch 7
(Saeed bin Suroor) *hld up in last pair: rdn over 3f out: sn struggling: bhd and eased over 1f out: t.o (jockey said gelding was never travelling)* **10/1**

2m 1.7s (-5.40) **Going Correction** -0.175s/f (Firm) **8 Ran SP% 117.4**
Speed ratings (Par 107): **114,113,112,112,110 82,50,47**
CSF £9.89 CT £69.80 TOTE £4.70: £1.80, £1.10, £2.00; EX 11.50 Trifecta £85.80.
Owner R C Bond **Bred** Bond Thoroughbred Corporation **Trained** Manton, Wilts

FOCUS
A competitive handicap on paper, but the winner dictated matters and always looked to be holding the upper hand.

5441 PARK REGIS KRIS KIN HOTEL DUBAI FILLIES' H'CAP 7f
3:25 (3:25) (Class 2) (0-100,90) 3-Y-O+ **£12,938** (£3,850; £1,924; £962) **Stalls** High

Form RPR
-310 1 **Breathtaking Look**[15] 4887 4-9-12 **88** AdamKirby 3 98
(Stuart Williams) *mde all: rdn 2f out: styd on wl ins fnl f: rdn out* **7/4**[2]
15 2 ½ **Fabulist**[14] 4898 3-8-13 **82** HarryBentley 5 88
(John Gosden) *trckd wnr: rdn 2f out: drvn over 1f out: kpt on ins fnl f but a hld* **6/4**[1]
4-33 3 2 **Dupioni (IRE)**[14] 4922 3-9-0 **83** JFEgan 2 83
(Rae Guest) *chsd ldng pair: effrt 2f out: drvn over 1f out: kpt on same pce and no imp ins fnl f* **4/1**[3]
0240 4 ¾ **Impulsion (IRE)**[15] 4891 3-9-7 **90** (p) DavidEgan 4 88
(Roger Varian) *hld up in tch in 4th: effrt 2f out: unable qck over 1f out: kpt on same pce and no imp ins fnl f* **8/1**
412- 5 7 **Melodies**[371] 5216 4-9-12 **88** RobHornby 1 70
(Ed Dunlop) *dropped in bhd sn after s: hld up in tch in rr: shkn up over 1f out: sn pushed along and outpcd: wknd ins fnl f* **16/1**

1m 24.1s (-1.60) **Going Correction** -0.175s/f (Firm)
WFA 3 from 4yo 7lb **5 Ran SP% 113.4**
Speed ratings (Par 96): **102,101,99,98,90**
CSF £4.96 TOTE £2.40: £1.30, £1.20; EX 5.50 Trifecta £11.60.
Owner J W Parry **Bred** Ellis Stud And Bellow Hill Stud **Trained** Newmarket, Suffolk

FOCUS
Decent prize money up for grabs and the winner snatched the lion's share of it under a skilful ride from the front, quickening things up after setting only a steady early gallop.

5442 HEATH COURT HOTEL H'CAP 6f
4:00 (4:00) (Class 2) (0-105,98) 3-Y-O
£28,012 (£8,388; £4,194; £2,097; £1,048; £526) **Stalls** High

Form RPR
3030 1 **Kinks**[16] 4847 3-8-11 **88** JoeFanning 5 96
(Mick Channon) *hld up in tch in midfield: swtchd rt and hdwy over 1f out: chsd ldrs and swtchd rt again 1f out: styd on strly u.p ins fnl f: led last strides* **12/1**
011 2 *nk* **Pass The Vino (IRE)**[16] 4847 3-8-13 **90** LukeMorris 10 97
(Paul D'Arcy) *chsd ldrs: rdn 2f out: drvn and clsd to chal 1f out: led jst ins fnl f: kpt on u.p: hdd last strides* **11/2**[3]

1153 **3** *1 3/4* **Cristal Breeze (IRE)**[21] 4669 3-8-6 **83**................................ JFEgan 1 84
(William Haggas) chsd ldr: rdn 2f out: drvn over 1f out: lost 2nd and no ex jst ins fnl f: outpcd fnl 100yds **18/1**

-300 **4** *hd* **Konchek**[36] 4050 3-9-7 **98**................................(tp) AdamKirby 9 99
(Clive Cox) led: rdn 2f out: drvn over 1f out: hdd jst ins fnl f: no ex and sn lost 2nd: outpcd wl ins fnl f **11/1**

23-1 **5** *shd* **Swindler**[15] 4866 3-8-13 **90**................................ LiamKeniry 2 90
(Ed Walker) bmpd and stdd leaving stalls: sn dropped in and hld up in last trio: clsd 2f out: drvn and no imp ent fnl f: styd on towards fin: nvr trbld ldrs **5/2**[1]

5414 **6** *1 1/4* **Princess Power (IRE)**[16] 4847 3-8-10 **87**................(v) RoystonFfrench 8 83
(Nigel Tinkler) chsd ldrs early: sn in tch in midfield: effrt over 2f out: unable qck and n.m.r over 1f out: kpt on same pce ins fnl f **8/1**

U021 **7** *shd* **Dominus (IRE)**[8] 5126 3-8-12 **89**................................ HarryBentley 7 85
(Brian Meehan) t.k.h: chsd ldrs: u.p 2f out: unable qck u.p: outpcd and btn whn nt clrest of runs ins fnl f **4/1**[2]

2255 **8** *1/2* **Lorton**[12] 4987 3-8-9 **86**................................(p) KieranO'Neill 6 81
(Julie Camacho) taken down early: in tch in rr: effrt over 2f out: drvn over 1f out: nt clr run and swtchd rt ins fnl f: kpt on towards fin: nvr trbld ldrs **16/1**

0223 **9** *1 1/2* **James Watt (IRE)**[10] 5058 3-8-2 **84**................................ AndrewBreslin(5) 3 74
(Michael Bell) wnt rt s: in tch in midfield: unable qck and no prog u.p over 1f out: wknd ins fnl f **25/1**

4214 **10** *1 1/2* **Revolutionise (IRE)**[17] 4793 3-8-1 **78**................................ DavidEgan 4 63
(Roger Varian) wnt rt leaving stalls: in tch in rr: no hdwy u.p over 1f out: nvr involved and bhd ins fnl f **6/1**

1m 9.54s (-2.56) **Going Correction** -0.175s/f (Firm) **10** Ran SP% **120.4**
Speed ratings (Par 106): **110,109,107,107,106 105,105,104,102,100**
CSF £79.18 CT £1229.71 TOTE £19.30: £4.30, £2.10, £3.70; EX 153.50 Trifecta £3100.50.
Owner David Hudd, Chris Wright & Ann Black **Bred** Mike Channon Bloodstock Ltd **Trained** West Ilsley, Berks

FOCUS
A competitive sprint with one or two improving sorts high in the betting, but it was a more exposed handicapper who prevailed.

5443 HEATH COURT DINING CLUB H'CAP 1m 6f
4:35 (4:37) (Class 3) (0-95,97) 4-Y-O+ **£9,703** (£2,887; £1,443; £721) **Stalls** Centre

Form RPR

1504 **1** **Charles Kingsley**[7] 5199 4-9-12 **97**................................ JoeFanning 8 104
(Mark Johnston) wl in tch in midfield: clsd and pressed ldr jst over 2f out: rdn to ld over 1f out: in command and styd on wl ins fnl f: comf **2/1**[1]

50-4 **2** *1 1/2* **Sovereign Duke (GER)**[63] 3078 4-9-5 **90**................................ HarryBentley 7 95
(Henry Candy) hld up in tch in last pair: effrt ent fnl 3f: clsd u.p to chse ldrs over 1f out: chsd wnr ins fnl f: no imp but kpt on **9/2**[3]

6-41 **3** *nse* **Infrastructure**[15] 4877 4-9-7 **92**................................ RobHornby 4 97
(Martyn Meade) in tch in midfield: clsd to chse ldrs 3f out: rdn and swtchd rt over 1f out: edging lft but kpt on ins fnl f (vet said gelding lost it's right fore shoe) **11/4**[2]

2-10 **4** *1 1/4* **Imperial Court (IRE)**[30] 4308 4-8-2 **73** oh3................ RoystonFfrench 6 76
(David Simcock) t.k.h: hld up in tch in last pair: effrt jst over 2f out: rdn over 1f out: no threat to wnr but kpt on steadily ins fnl f **20/1**

213- **5** *1 1/2* **African Jazz (IRE)**[295] 7952 4-9-7 **92**................................(tp) AdamKirby 1 93
(Charlie Appleby) led: rdn 3f out: hdd over 1f out: no ex and lost 2nd ins fnl f: sn wknd **5/1**

6060 **6** *2 1/4* **Manjaam (IRE)**[15] 4884 6-8-13 **84**................................(p) RobertWinston 3 82
(Ian Williams) chsd ldr: rdn ent fnl 2f: styd pressing ldrs tl unable qck and lost pl over 1f out: wknd ins fnl f: eased towards fin **8/1**

-P00 **7** *30* **Shabeeb (USA)**[14] 4899 6-9-7 **92**................................(p) DavidEgan 5 48
(Ian Williams) dwlt: t.k.h: chsd ldrs tl 4f out: sn rdn and lost pl 3f out: wl btn and eased ins fnl f **20/1**

2m 57.39s (-2.51) **Going Correction** -0.175s/f (Firm) **7** Ran SP% **115.5**
Speed ratings (Par 107): **100,99,99,98,97 96,79**
CSF £11.71 CT £23.47 TOTE £2.60: £1.60, £2.70; EX 11.90 Trifecta £39.60.
Owner Sheikh Hamdan bin Mohammed Al Maktoum **Bred** Godolphin **Trained** Middleham Moor, N Yorks

FOCUS
A decent staying contest won by a typically-tough Mark Johnston handicapper.

5444 PARK REGIS KRIS KIN HOTEL DUBAI H'CAP 5f
5:10 (5:10) (Class 4) (0-85,86) 3-Y-O+ **£6,469** (£1,925; £962; £481; £300) **Stalls** High

Form RPR

0333 **1** **Shamshon (IRE)**[5] 5252 8-9-0 **80**................................ MarcoGhiani(7) 2 87
(Stuart Williams) dropped in after s: hld up in tch in rr: clsd to trck ldrs over 1f out: gap opened and qcknd to ld between rivals 100yds out: r.o strly **13/8**[1]

0000 **2** *1 1/4* **Captain Colby (USA)**[28] 4406 7-9-12 **85**................................ PatCosgrave 6 88
(Paul Midgley) led fr 1f: styd upsides ldr: rdn 2f out: drvn over 1f out: maintained chal tl unable to match pce of wnr fnl 100yds **9/2**[3]

4114 **3** *1/2* **Jack The Truth (IRE)**[16] 4821 5-9-10 **83**................................ HarryBentley 5 84
(George Scott) chsd ldrs: clsd to press ldrs 2f out: sn rdn and led jst over 1f out: hdd and unable to match pce of wnr fnl 100yds **2/1**[2]

1250 **4** *1* **Spirit Of Wedza (IRE)**[10] 5040 7-8-7 **73**................................ VictorSantos(7) 1 70
(Julie Camacho) trckd ldrs: effrt 2f out: kpt on same pce ins fnl f **7/1**

111- **5** *1 1/4* **Laith Alareen**[353] 5885 4-9-13 **86**................................(t) DougieCostello 3 79
(Ivan Furtado) t.k.h: w ldr tl led after 1f: rdn and hdd jst over 1f out: wknd ins fnl f **9/1**

57.75s (-0.95) **Going Correction** -0.175s/f (Firm) **5** Ran SP% **112.1**
Speed ratings (Par 105): **100,98,97,95,93**
CSF £9.46 TOTE £2.20: £1.30, £2.10; EX 9.00 Trifecta £15.10.
Owner T W Morley & Regents Racing **Bred** Stonethorn Stud Farms Ltd **Trained** Newmarket, Suffolk

FOCUS
Only five runners, but an interesting sprint handicap which saw the winner repeat last year's success.

5445 HEATH COURT HOTEL BESTWESTERN.CO.UK H'CAP 1m
5:40 (5:40) (Class 5) (0-75,83) 3-Y-O+
£4,528 (£1,347; £673; £336; £300; £300) **Stalls** High

Form RPR

1-51 **1** **Seductive Moment (GER)**[5] 5255 3-9-12 **83** 6ex................ JoeFanning 6 96+
(Mark Johnston) s.i.s: in rr: smooth hdwy to press ldrs 3f out: sn led: hung lft but sn clr: in n.d fr over 1f out: eased towards fin: v easily **2/1**[1]

-130 **2** *3 3/4* **Pinnata (IRE)**[140] 1101 5-10-0 **77**................................(t) AdamKirby 1 81
(Stuart Williams) led: rdn and hdd over 2f out: sn outpcd by wnr: wl hld but battled on to hold 2nd ins fnl f **6/1**[3]

3410 **3** *shd* **Assembled**[14] 4902 3-9-5 **76**................................ PatCosgrave 7 78
(Hugo Palmer) hld up wl in tch in midfield: effrt 3f out: no ch w wnr but kpt on u.p and battling for 2nd 1f out: plugged on **15/2**

0543 **4** *2 1/4* **Crimewave (IRE)**[16] 4838 3-9-4 **75**................................(b[1]) DavidEgan 3 72
(Tom Clover) pressed ldr: rdn 2f out: no ch w easy wnr over 1f out: one pce in 4th ins fnl f **11/4**[2]

3325 **5** *3 1/4* **Society Guest (IRE)**[21] 4655 3-9-2 **73**................................ RobHornby 8 62
(Mick Channon) chsd ldr for over 1f out: styd chsng ldrs: rdn over 2f out: sn struggling and lost pl: wl btn over 1f out: wknd fnl f **12/1**

4205 **6** *nse* **Greek Kodiac (IRE)**[29] 4338 3-9-4 **75**................................ RobertWinston 2 64
(Mick Quinn) chsd ldrs: clsd to press ldrs and rdn 3f out: sn outpcd by wnr: wl btn 5th over 1f out: wknd ins fnl f **14/1**

1033 **7** *2 1/4* **Algaffaal (USA)**[14] 4902 4-9-7 **77**................................(p) StefanoCherchi(7) 5 63
(Brian Ellison) in tch in midfield: effrt 3f out: sn struggling and outpcd: wl btn over 1f out: wknd fnl f **7/1**

-210 **8** *1 1/4* **My Dear Friend**[16] 4841 3-9-5 **76**................................ HarryBentley 9 57
(Ralph Beckett) a in last pair: rdn 1/2-way: no prog and wl btn over 1f out **16/1**

1m 37.91s (-2.09) **Going Correction** -0.175s/f (Firm)
WFA 3 from 4yo+ 8lb **8** Ran SP% **118.8**
Speed ratings (Par 103): **103,99,99,96,93 93,91,90**
CSF £15.35 CT £77.70 TOTE £2.90: £1.80, £2.10, £2.30; EX 15.10 Trifecta £75.90.
Owner Kingsley Park 10 **Bred** Gestut Hof Ittlingen **Trained** Middleham Moor, N Yorks

FOCUS
A handicap which was torn to pieces by the easy winner who will surely go on to better things.
T/Plt: £24.70 to a £1 stake. Pool: £63,056.24 - 1,856.51 winning units T/Qpdt: £18.70 to a £1 stake. Pool: £3,643.14 - 143.95 winning units **Steve Payne**

4925 SALISBURY (R-H)
Saturday, July 27

OFFICIAL GOING: Good to firm (good in places; watered; 8.2)
Wind: Light across Weather: Sunny spells with a heavy shower after race 4

5446 AJN HENSTRIDGE "CARNARVON" H'CAP (FOR GENTLEMAN AMATEUR RIDERS) 1m
5:15 (5:17) (Class 5) (0-70,72) 3-Y-O+ **£3,606** (£1,118; £558; £400; £400) **Stalls** Low

Form RPR

3663 **1** **Greeley (IRE)**[17] 4773 3-10-12 **66**................................(p) MrPatrickMillman 2 72
(Rod Millman) disp ld tl wnt on 3f out: rdn and edgd lft over 1f out: styd on: idled nr fin **10/11**[1]

0550 **2** *1 1/4* **Bounty Pursuit**[26] 4453 7-11-4 **64**................................ MrJamesKing 1 69
(Michael Blake) s.i.s: hld up: hdwy: nt clr run and swtchd lft over 2f out: sn chsng wnr: rdn and hung lft over 1f out: styd on **9/2**[3]

-004 **3** *4 1/2* **Wynfaul The Wizard (USA)**[10] 5043 4-9-11 **48** oh3(v) MrAlexChadwick(5) 4 43
(Laura Morgan) hld up: outpcd over 2f out: styd on ins fnl f **25/1**

0-00 **4** *3* **Bakht A Rawan (IRE)**[27] 4426 7-11-0 **67**................................ MrKaiLenihan(7) 3 55
(Roger Teal) chsd ldrs: rdn whn carried lft over 2f out: wknd fnl f **12/1**

1234 **5** *3 1/4* **Bond Angel**[9] 5080 4-10-13 **66**................................ MrPhilipThomas(7) 5 51
(David Evans) disp ld tl pushed along 3f out: carried lft over 2f out: wknd and eased fnl f **5/2**[2]

1m 46.67s (3.17) **Going Correction** +0.125s/f (Good)
WFA 3 from 4yo+ 8lb **5** Ran SP% **110.7**
Speed ratings (Par 103): **89,87,83,80,77**
CSF £5.52 TOTE £1.70: £1.10, £2.00; EX 5.90 Trifecta £35.80.
Owner The Greeley Syndicate **Bred** Tally-Ho Stud **Trained** Kentisbeare, Devon

FOCUS
A modest amateur riders' handicap and a small field for a race of its type. The form looks far from strong.

5447 AJN STEELSTOCK EBF MAIDEN STKS (PLUS 10 RACE) 6f
5:45 (5:46) (Class 4) 2-Y-O **£4,851** (£1,443; £721; £360) **Stalls** Low

Form RPR

2 **1** **Ethic**[23] 4558 2-9-5 0................................ TomMarquand 1 80+
(William Haggas) chsd ldrs: swtchd lft over 2f out: sn chsng ldr: shkn up to ld over 1f out: rdn out **4/6**[1]

2 *3/4* **Stoweman** 2-9-2 0................................ WilliamCox(3) 4 78
(Clive Cox) broke wl: sn stdd but hld up in tch: rdn and ev ch fr over 1f out: styd on **12/1**

3 *6* **We're Reunited (IRE)** 2-9-5 0................................ EoinWalsh 5 60
(Ronald Harris) dwlt: plld hrd and hdwy over 4f out: sn hung rt: nt clr run and outpcd wl over 3f out: hdwy over 2f out: styd on same pce fnl f (jockey said colt ran too free and also ran green) **33/1**

4 **4** *4* **Miss Paxman**[23] 4557 2-9-0 0................................ FergusSweeney 6 43
(Martyn Meade) sn led: hdd over 4f out: chsd ldr: rdn over 2f out: sn hung lft: wknd fnl f **5/2**[2]

5 *2 3/4* **Castel Angelo (IRE)** 2-9-5 0................................ KieranShoemark 7 40+
(Henry Candy) plld hrd: sn w ldr: led over 4f out: hdd over 1f out: wknd fnl f (jockey said colt ran too free) **8/1**[3]

00 **6** *1/2* **Timon (IRE)**[7] 5186 2-9-0 0................................ ScottMcCullagh(5) 2 38+
(Mick Channon) in tch whn hmpd and lost pl wl over 3f out: n.d after **25/1**

1m 15.1s (0.60) **Going Correction** +0.125s/f (Good) **6** Ran SP% **114.2**
Speed ratings (Par 96): **101,100,92,86,83 82**
CSF £10.90 TOTE £1.50: £1.10, £3.40; EX 8.40 Trifecta £49.60.
Owner Miss Yvonne Jacques **Bred** Carisbrooke Stud **Trained** Newmarket, Suffolk

FOCUS
In recent years those with previous experience have a slight edge over newcomers in this juvenile maiden and that proved the case this time, with the first two, who both look decent, coming clear. The opening level is a bit fluid.

5448 AJN SUPPORTS RIDBA NOVICE STKS 6f
6:15 (6:17) (Class 5) 3-Y-O+ **£4,528** (£1,347; £673; £336) **Stalls** Low

Form RPR

2-45 **1** **Monsieur Noir**[21] 4654 3-9-3 **84**................................ AndreaAtzeni 4 79
(Roger Varian) sn led: rdn over 1f out: drvn out **4/11**[1]

61- **2** *1 1/4* **Angel Mead**[372] 5170 3-9-5 0................................(w) FergusSweeney 3 77
(Joseph Tuite) s.i.s and n.m.r s: racd keenly and sn prom: swtchd lft and chsd wnr over 2f out: styd on **5/1**[2]

00- **3** *3 1/4* **Tell William**[285] 8280 3-9-3 0................................(p[1] w) KieranShoemark 6 65
(Marcus Tregoning) s.i.s and hmpd s: hmpd over 4f out: hdwy on outer over 2f out: sn rdn: styd on same pce fnl f (jockey said gelding suffered interference approaching the four furlong marker) **7/1**[3]

0 **4** *8* **Disey's Edge**[27] 4421 3-8-9 0........................ WilliamCox(3) 2 34
(Christopher Mason) *wnt lft s: led early: lost pl over 5f out: hung lft fr over 4f out: sn lost pl: styd on to go 4th wl ins fnl f (jockey said filly hung left throughout)* **100/1**

6 **5** *1 ¼* **Strathspey Stretto (IRE)**[27] 4421 4-9-3 0........................ TomMarquand 1 31
(Marcus Tregoning) *s.i.s: hmpd over 4f out: hdwy over 2f out: wknd over 1f out (vet said filly was lame on it's left fore)* **20/1**

6 *16* **Del's Edge** 3-8-9 0........................ MitchGodwin(3) 5
(Christopher Mason) *wnt lft s: racd keenly and sn chsng wnr: rdn and lost 2nd over 2f out: wknd wl over 1f out* **33/1**

1m 15.3s (0.80) **Going Correction** +0.125s/f (Good)
WFA 3 from 4yo 5lb
Speed ratings (Par 103): **99,97,93,82,80 59** **6** Ran SP% **111.2**
CSF £2.48 TOTE £1.20: £1.10, £1.80; EX 2.50 Trifecta £5.10.
Owner Sheikh Mohammed Obaid Al Maktoum **Bred** Highclere Stud And Floors Farming **Trained** Newmarket, Suffolk

FOCUS
This novice stakes was basically a match on paper. The time was a fifth of a second slower than the preceding juvenile contest, so the form needs treating with caution.

5449 AJN STEELSTOCK DALEY GOREHAM H'CAP 5f
6:45 (6:45) (Class 6) (0-65,63) 3-Y-O+
£3,058 (£910; £454; £400; £400; £400) **Stalls** Low

Form RPR

60-1 **1** **Bay Watch (IRE)**[3] 5289 5-8-13 **50** 5ex........................ JohnFahy 2 67+
(Tracey Barfoot-Saunt) *hld up: hdwy and nt clr run over 1f out: shkn up to ld ins fnl f: qcknd clr: comf* **5/4**[1]

5220 **2** *3 ¼* **Ghepardo**[31] 4230 4-9-12 **63**........................ TomMarquand 7 66
(Patrick Chamings) *chsd ldrs: rdn and ev ch ins fnl f: styd on same pce* **9/1**

2411 **3** *1 ½* **Aquadabra (IRE)**[9] 5084 4-9-4 **55**........................ CallumShepherd 6 53
(Christopher Mason) *slipped s: sn chsng ldr: rdn to ld over 1f out: edgd lft and hdd ins fnl f: no ex* **7/2**[2]

5603 **4** *1* **Pharoh Jake**[28] 4376 11-8-7 **47**........................ MitchGodwin(3) 5 41
(John Bridger) *chsd ldrs: rdn over 1f out: styd on same pce fnl f* **33/1**

2406 **5** *1* **Cobweb Catcher**[55] 3376 3-9-2 **57**........................ SeanLevey 4 47
(Rod Millman) *hld up: swtchd lft 2f out: rdn over 1f out: nt trble ldrs* **7/1**

0304 **6** *2 ¼* **Powerful Dream (IRE)**[11] 5013 6-9-10 **61**........................(p) KieranShoemark 3 44
(Ronald Harris) *s.i.s: hld up: shkn up and edgd lft over 1f out: nt trble ldrs (jockey said mare was slowly away)* **6/1**[3]

2113 **7** *3 ½* **Thegreyvtrain**[11] 5013 3-9-7 **62**........................ EoinWalsh 1 31
(Ronald Harris) *led: racd keenly: rdn and hdd over 1f out: wknd ins fnl f (jockey said filly stopped quickly)* **11/1**

1m 1.33s (0.83) **Going Correction** +0.125s/f (Good)
WFA 3 from 4yo+ 4lb
Speed ratings (Par 101): **98,92,90,88,87 83,78** **7** Ran SP% **114.7**
CSF £13.95 TOTE £2.10: £1.60, £4.60; EX 14.50 Trifecta £61.40.
Owner P Ponting **Bred** D J & Mrs Brown **Trained** Charfield, Gloucs

FOCUS
A low-grade sprint handicap but a winner who is on a roll. It's been rated as straightforward form in behind him.

5450 JEAN BOYDEN H'CAP 6f 213y
7:15 (7:16) (Class 4) (0-80,79) 3-Y-O
£5,433 (£1,617; £808; £404; £400; £400) **Stalls** Low

Form RPR

-432 **1** **Posted**[14] 4927 3-9-7 **79**........................ TomMarquand 5 94
(Richard Hannon) *s.i.s: hld up: hdwy and edgd lft over 2f out: rdn to ld over 1f out: edgd rt wl ins fnl f: r.o* **2/1**[1]

-550 **2** *1 ½* **Strict Tempo**[14] 4922 3-9-5 **77**........................ OisinMurphy 2 88
(Andrew Balding) *hld up: hdwy over 2f out: led wl over 1f out: sn rdn: edgd rt and hdd: no ex nr fin* **9/4**[2]

2-00 **3** *9* **Steeve**[41] 3885 3-9-0 **72**........................(p[1]) SeanLevey 4 59
(Rod Millman) *chsd ldrs: hung rt wl over 3f out: rdn over 2f out: wknd ins fnl f* **8/1**

6054 **4** *3 ½* **Sheila's Showcase**[21] 4669 3-9-5 **77**........................ CharlesBishop 3 54
(Denis Coakley) *prom: rdn over 2f out: wkng whn hung rt over 1f out* **5/1**[3]

0115 **5** *½* **Jungle Juice (IRE)**[8] 5137 3-9-2 **79**........................ ScottMcCullagh(5) 1 55
(Mick Channon) *led 1f: remained w ldr: led again 3f out: rdn and hdd wl over 1f out: edgd lft and wknd ins fnl f* **10/1**

5-30 **6** *6* **Phosphor (IRE)**[49] 3590 3-9-5 **77**........................ FergusSweeney 6 37
(Martyn Meade) *led 6f out: hdd 3f out: rdn and ev ch 2f out: wknd over 1f out* **13/2**

2516 **7** *2 ½* **Kwela**[14] 4909 3-8-13 **78**........................ GeorgiaDobie(7) 7 31
(Eve Johnson Houghton) *chsd ldrs on outer: rdn and hung lft over 2f out: sn wknd* **25/1**

1m 28.56s (-0.14) **Going Correction** +0.125s/f (Good)
Speed ratings (Par 102): **105,103,93,89,88 81,78** **7** Ran SP% **118.2**
CSF £7.17 CT £28.81 TOTE £2.90: £2.20, £1.70; EX 9.20 Trifecta £40.60.
Owner R Barnett **Bred** W & R Barnett Ltd **Trained** East Everleigh, Wilts

FOCUS
The feature race and a fair 3yo handicap in which the market leaders came away from the rest.

5451 AJN KENTFORD NOVICE STKS 1m 1f 201y
7:45 (7:47) (Class 5) 3-Y-O+
£4,528 (£1,347; £673; £336) **Stalls** Low

Form RPR

2 **1** **Global Hunter (IRE)**[19] 4738 3-9-8 0........................ OisinMurphy 8 90+
(Saeed bin Suroor) *racd keenly: hld up in tch on outer: shkn up to ld over 2f out: rdn and hung lft ins fnl f: r.o* **4/6**[1]

04 **2** *2 ½* **Hazm (IRE)**[22] 4600 4-9-10 0........................ TomMarquand 11 77
(Tim Vaughan) *edgd lft s: prom: stdd and lost pl after 1f: hdwy 3f out: rdn to chse wnr over 1f out: styd on same pce ins fnl f* **50/1**

2364 **3** *3 ¼* **Ritchie Valens (IRE)**[43] 3808 3-9-1 77........................ SeanLevey 6 71
(Richard Hannon) *prom: racd keenly: rdn and ev ch over 2f out: no ex fnl f* **11/4**[2]

50 **4** *hd* **Black Kalanisi (IRE)**[4] 5268 6-9-10 0........................ CharlesBishop 2 70
(Joseph Tuite) *s.i.s: hld up: shkn up over 2f out: r.o ins fnl f: nvr nrr* **40/1**

0- **5** *nk* **Sandyman**[245] 9255 3-8-12 0........................(w) MitchGodwin(3) 1 70
(Paul Cole) *chsd ldrs: rdn and hung lft over 2f out: styd on same pce fr over 1f out* **50/1**

0-3 **6** *1 ¼* **Aladaala (IRE)**[22] 4592 3-8-10 0........................ JimCrowley 4 63
(William Haggas) *led 1f: chsd ldr: ev ch over 2f out: rdn over 1f out: wknd ins fnl f* **3/1**[3]

21 **7** *3 ¼* **Zephyrina (IRE)**[49] 3574 3-9-1 0........................ KieranShoemark 3 61
(Daniel Kubler) *led after 1f: rdn and hdd over 2f out: wknd over 1f out* **20/1**

00 **8** *1 ¾* **Mini Milk**[16] 4842 3-8-6 3 ow3........................ TylerSaunders(7) 7 56
(Jonathan Portman) *hld up: rdn over 3f out: btn over 2f out* **100/1**

9 *5* **Binmar's Sexy Lexy (CAN)** 3-8-7 0........................ WilliamCox(3) 9 43
(Stuart Kittow) *s.i.s: hld up: rdn and hung lft over 2f out: n.d (jockey said filly ran green)* **100/1**

2m 11.17s (0.67) **Going Correction** +0.125s/f (Good)
WFA 3 from 4yo+ 9lb
Speed ratings (Par 103): **102,100,97,97,97 96,93,92,88** **9** Ran SP% **124.8**
CSF £59.97 TOTE £1.50: £1.10, £8.80, £1.10; EX 44.40 Trifecta £104.80.
Owner Godolphin **Bred** Mrs Clodagh McStay **Trained** Newmarket, Suffolk

FOCUS
A fair novice stakes but uncompetitive with only three considered in the market. It didn't work out quite that way as they went steady and it developed into a bit of a sprint.

5452 JOHN BOYDEN H'CAP 1m 6f 44y
8:15 (8:15) (Class 5) (0-75,77) 3-Y-O+
£3,737 (£1,112; £555; £400; £400; £400) **Stalls** Far side

Form RPR

-041 **1** **Oydis**[40] 3947 3-9-4 **77**........................ SeanLevey 96
(Ralph Beckett) *mde all: rdn clr whn hung lft over 1f out: styd on strly: edgd rt towards fin* **10/1**

00-1 **2** *8* **Blame It On Sally (IRE)**[16] 4834 3-8-4 **63**........................ LukeMorris 71
(Sir Mark Prescott Bt) *chsd wnr: shkn up 10f out: rdn over 3f out: hung lft over 1f out: styd on same pce* **5/2**[1]

5425 **3** *2 ¾* **Johnny Kidd**[19] 4739 3-9-0 **73**........................ OisinMurphy 77
(Andrew Balding) *hld up: hdwy over 4f out: rdn over 2f out: no ex fr over 1f out* **8/1**

0252 **4** *¾* **Australis (IRE)**[17] 4803 3-9-2 **75**........................ AndreaAtzeni 78
(Roger Varian) *prom: pushed along 8f out: rdn over 2f out: no ex fr over 1f out* **11/4**[2]

-023 **5** *1 ½* **War Brigade (FR)**[40] 3940 5-9-8 **69**........................(p) JimCrowley 68
(Ian Williams) *hld up: swtchd lft over 3f out: rdn over 2f out: nt trble ldrs* **17/2**

5412 **6** *1 ¾* **Master Grey (IRE)**[14] 4928 4-9-12 **73**........................ TomMarquand 69
(Rod Millman) *hld up: rdn over 2f out: nt trble ldrs* **11/1**

-321 **7** *2 ¾* **Goscote**[21] 4661 4-9-11 **72**........................ CharlesBishop 65
(Henry Candy) *prom: hmpd over 4f out: sn lost pl: n.d after* **6/1**[3]

-261 **8** *4 ½* **Sufi**[31] 4231 5-9-11 **72**........................ PatDobbs 58
(Ken Cunningham-Brown) *prom: rdn over 3f out: wknd 2f out* **14/1**

0-06 **9** *4 ½* **Universal Command**[31] 4257 4-9-11 **72**........................(h) KieranShoemark 52
(Jack R Barber) *chsd ldrs: rdn over 4f out: wknd over 2f out* **66/1**

-244 **10** *88* **Moayadd (USA)**[14] 4928 7-10-0 **75**........................(v) FergusSweeney
(Neil Mulholland) *hld up: rdn and over wknd over 2f out: eased (jockey said gelding had no more to give)* **66/1**

3m 5.68s (-0.92) **Going Correction** +0.125s/f (Good)
WFA 3 from 4yo+ 12lb
Speed ratings (Par 103): **107,102,100,100,99 98,97,94,91,41** **10** Ran SP% **118.2**
CSF £35.76 CT £216.28 TOTE £12.70: £3.40, £1.50, £2.10; EX 55.20 Trifecta £346.20.
Owner J C Smith **Bred** Littleton Stud **Trained** Kimpton, Hants

FOCUS
An interesting staying handicap, but dominated by the winner and a clean sweep for the 3yos.
T/Plt: £6.20 to a £1 stake. Pool: £42,576.23 - 4,991.98 winning units T/Qpdt: £3.20 to a £1 stake. Pool: £5,690.05 - 1,296.06 winning units **Colin Roberts**

5394 YORK (L-H)
Saturday, July 27

OFFICIAL GOING: Soft (good to soft in places; 6.0) changing to soft after race 4 (3.45)
Wind: Moderate half against Weather: Heavy cloud and rain

5453 SKY BET "GET KNOTTED" H'CAP 7f
2:05 (2:06) (Class 3) (0-95,97) 4-Y-O+
£12,450 (£3,728; £1,864; £932; £466; £234) **Stalls** Low

Form RPR

6625 **1** **Bedouin's Story**[30] 4292 4-9-3 **94**........................(p[1]) GabrieleMalune(3) 6 105
(Saeed bin Suroor) *hld up towards rr: swtchd rt to outer and hdwy over 2f out: str run fr over 1f out: rdn to ld ent fnl f: kpt on strly* **11/2**[3]

0-04 **2** *2 ¼* **Medahim (IRE)**[30] 4299 5-9-7 **95**........................ DanielTudhope 4 99
(Ivan Furtado) *trckd ldrs: hdwy over 2f out: effrt to ld wl over 1f out: sn rdn: hdd ent fnl f: sn drvn and kpt on same pce* **11/2**[3]

-500 **3** *4* **Get Knotted (IRE)**[42] 3863 7-9-2 **90**........................(p) PaulMulrennan 7 83
(Michael Dods) *trckd ldrs: smooth hdwy over 2f out: rdn wl over 1f out: kpt on same pce* **7/2**[1]

0245 **4** *1 ¼* **Tommy Taylor (USA)**[15] 4887 5-8-13 **87**........................ JamieSpencer 8 77
(Kevin Ryan) *hld up in rr: hdwy over 2f out: n.m.r over 1f out: rdn and kpt on fnl f* **5/1**[2]

-060 **5** *1 ½* **Maggies Angel (IRE)**[29] 4320 4-8-3 **77**........................ PaddyMathers 9 63
(Richard Fahey) *chsd ldr: rdn along over 2f out: drvn over 1f out: kpt on one pce* **14/1**

0006 **6** *shd* **Parys Mountain (IRE)**[24] 4511 5-8-8 **82**........................(t) DavidAllan 5 67
(Tim Easterby) *led: pushed along over 2f out: rdn and hdd wl over 1f out: sn wknd* **14/1**

2053 **7** *½* **Whinmoor**[22] 4598 4-8-8 **85**........................ RowanScott(3) 2 69
(Nigel Tinkler) *in tch: pushed along wl over 2f out: rdn wl over 1f out: sn one pce* **12/1**

1005 **8** *2* **Love Dreams (IRE)**[21] 4650 5-9-9 **97**........................(v) SilvestreDeSousa 3 76
(Mark Johnston) *blind removed late and dwlt: towards rr: sme hdwy on inner 3f out: sn rdn and n.d (jockey was slow to remove blindfold, explaining that it became stuck in the bridle and took two attempts to remove it)* **7/1**

0200 **9** *½* **Starlight Romance (IRE)**[36] 4072 5-8-10 **87**........................ ConnorMurtagh(3) 1 64
(Richard Fahey) *trckd ldrs: pushed along 3f out: rdn 2f out: sn drvn and wknd* **8/1**

5641 **10** *15* **Penwortham (IRE)**[29] 4320 6-8-11 **85**........................ TonyHamilton 11 22
(Richard Fahey) *t.k.h: in tch on outer: pushed along over 3f out: sn lost pl and bhd fnl 2f* **25/1**

1m 26.29s (1.69) **Going Correction** +0.675s/f (Yiel)
Speed ratings (Par 107): **117,114,109,108,106 106,106,103,103,86** **10** Ran SP% **118.1**
CSF £36.37 CT £122.25 TOTE £6.40: £2.20, £2.20, £1.40; EX 35.60 Trifecta £110.10.
Owner Godolphin **Bred** Dukes Stud & Overbury Stallions Ltd **Trained** Newmarket, Suffolk

FOCUS
With rain continuing to fall since Friday, the ground was easing all the time. They came down the centre in this decent handicap, which appeared to be run at a reasonable gallop. The time was 4.29sec outside the standard.

5454 SKY BET DASH H'CAP 6f
2:40 (2:42) (Class 2) (0-105,104) 3-Y-O+
£31,125 (£9,320; £4,660; £2,330; £1,165; £585) **Stalls** Low

Form RPR
00-5 **1** **Dakota Gold**[29] 4331 5-9-2 **96** ConnorBeasley 9 105
(Michael Dods) *racd centre: led: rdn along wl over 1f out: hdd narrowly and drvn ins fnl f: rallied gamely to ld again last 50yds* **10/1**

0242 **2** ½ **Muscika**[6] 5217 5-8-8 **91** (v) ConnorMcGovern(3) 4 98
(David O'Meara) *in tch on inner: hdwy 2f out: rdn to chal over 1f out: drvn and ev ch ins fnl f: kpt on* **20/1**

3200 **3** *shd* **Jawwaal**[28] 4402 4-8-8 **88** BenCurtis 13 95
(Michael Dods) *t.k.h early in centre: trckd ldrs: hdwy 2f out: sn cl up: rdn to chal over 1f out: drvn to take slt ld ins fnl tk f: hdd and no ex last 50yds* **11/1**

0530 **4** 1 ¼ **Golden Apollo**[8] 5120 5-8-10 **90** (p) JasonHart 14 93
(Tim Easterby) *sltly hmpd s and towards rr: pushed along 1/2-way: sn rdn: styd on wl u.p appr fnl f: nrst fin* **8/1**[3]

0040 **5** 1 **Flying Pursuit**[28] 4402 6-8-12 **92** (p) RachelRichardson 16 91
(Tim Easterby) *racd towards stands' side: in tch: rdn along over 2f out: hdwy and drvn over 1f out: kpt on fnl f* **6/1**[1]

-531 **6** 1 **Camacho Chief (IRE)**[41] 3883 4-9-6 **100** PaulMulrennan 8 96
(Michael Dods) *t.k.h: in tch centre: hdwy 1/2-way: rdn along wl over 1f out: kpt on same pce appr fnl f* **9/1**

4520 **7** *shd* **Growl**[14] 4896 7-8-9 **92** ConnorMurtagh(3) 5 88
(Richard Fahey) *awkward s and in rr: hdwy 2f out: sn rdn: kpt on u.p fnl f: nrst fin* **10/1**

303 **8** *nse* **Paddy Power (IRE)**[25] 4492 6-8-2 **82** PaddyMathers 1 78
(Richard Fahey) *dwlt and wnt lft s: in rr: rdn along and hdwy wl over 1f out: kpt on u.p fnl f* **22/1**

2100 **9** ½ **Hyperfocus (IRE)**[28] 4402 5-8-11 **91** DavidAllan 18 85
(Tim Easterby) *racd towards stands' rail: in tch: hdwy 1/2-way: rdn along 2f out: sn drvn and no imp* **20/1**

5111 **10** 3 ¼ **Tomily (IRE)**[3] 5298 5-8-7 **87** 5ex SilvestreDeSousa 3 71
(David O'Meara) *prom on inner: rdn along 2f out: sn drvn and grad wknd* **6/1**[1]

1020 **11** *nk* **Duke Of Firenze**[30] 4313 10-8-10 **90** RichardKingscote 15 73
(David C Griffiths) *dwlt and in rr towards stands' side: pushed along and hdwy whn n.m.r wl over 1f out: one pce after* **33/1**

1655 **12** 2 **Brian The Snail (IRE)**[14] 4896 5-8-9 **89** TonyHamilton 11 65
(Richard Fahey) *in tch: rdn along 1/2-way: sn wknd* **20/1**

4002 **13** 1 ¾ **Savalas (IRE)**[15] 4888 4-8-10 **90** ow1 (p) JamieSpencer 17 61
(Kevin Ryan) *in tch towards stands' side: pushed along over 2f out: sn rdn and wknd wl over 1f out* **20/1**

0013 **14** 3 ¾ **Staxton**[8] 5120 4-9-6 **100** (p) DuranFentiman 6 59
(Tim Easterby) *cl up centre: rdn along over 2f out: sn wknd (jockey said gelding lost it's action approaching the final furlong)* **10/1**

0341 **15** 7 **Gulliver**[28] 4402 5-9-6 **100** (tp) DanielTudhope 7 36
(David O'Meara) *prom centre: cl up 1/2-way: rdn along 2f out: sn wknd (jockey said gelding stopped quickly)* **7/1**[2]

1m 14.1s (2.50) **Going Correction** +0.675s/f (Yiel) **15** Ran SP% **124.1**
Speed ratings (Par 109): **110,109,109,107,106 104,104,104,104,99 99,96,94,89,79**
CSF £204.77 CT £2303.33 TOTE £11.00: £3.40, £8.90, £4.90; EX 232.00 Trifecta £4147.80.
Owner Doug Graham & Ian Davison **Bred** Redgate Bstock & Peter Bottowley Bstock **Trained** Denton, Co Durham

FOCUS
Michael Dods had the winner and third in this competitive and valuable sprint. The pace was centre to far side, and the first three had it between them heading down to the final furlong.

5455 SKY BET YORK STKS (GROUP 2) 1m 2f 56y
3:15 (3:15) (Class 1) 3-Y-O+
£68,052 (£25,800; £12,912; £6,432; £3,228; £1,620) **Stalls** Low

Form RPR
4131 **1** **Elarqam**[22] 4612 4-9-6 111 DaneO'Neill 3 122
(Mark Johnston) *sn trcking ldr: hdwy 3f out: led 2f out: rdn clr wl over 1f out: styd on strly* **7/1**

3-41 **2** 3 ¼ **Addeybb (IRE)**[39] 3953 5-9-6 114 (p) DanielTudhope 5 115
(William Haggas) *trckd ldrs: hdwy 3f out: effrt and n.m.r 2f out: sn rdn: chsd wnr appr fnl f: sn drvn and no imp* **11/8**[1]

0-20 **3** 1 ½ **Knight To Behold (IRE)**[62] 3122 4-9-6 114 (b[1]) BenCurtis 2 112
(Harry Dunlop) *led: pushed along 3f out: sn rdn and hdd 2f out: drvn over 1f out: kpt on same pce* **12/1**

-313 **4** ½ **Regal Reality**[21] 4668 4-9-6 120 RichardKingscote 4 111
(Sir Michael Stoute) *hld up: hdwy 3f out: chsd wnr wl over 1f out: sn rdn and edgd rt: drvn over 1f out and kpt on same pce* **11/4**[2]

1102 **5** 3 ¾ **Bangkok (IRE)**[36] 4049 3-8-11 109 SilvestreDeSousa 6 105
(Andrew Balding) *hld up in rr: hdwy 3f out: n.m.r and swtchd lft over 2f out: sn rdn and n.m.r again wl over 1f out: sn drvn and btn* **9/2**[3]

-021 **6** 2 ¾ **Forest Ranger (IRE)**[78] 2573 5-9-9 112 TonyHamilton 1 101
(Richard Fahey) *t.k.h: prom: pushed along 3f out: rdn 2f out: sn wknd (vet said gelding lost both front shoes)* **16/1**

2m 12.47s (2.17) **Going Correction** +0.675s/f (Yiel)
WFA 3 from 4yo+ 9lb **6** Ran SP% **113.0**
Speed ratings (Par 115): **118,115,114,113,110 108**
CSF £17.45 TOTE £7.80: £3.00, £1.50; EX 20.70 Trifecta £107.00.
Owner Hamdan Al Maktoum **Bred** Floors Farming **Trained** Middleham Moor, N Yorks

FOCUS
Add 11yds. A decent renewal of this Group 2 contest, but a bit of a messy race after the field had come over to the stands' side in the straight.

5456 SKYBET BRITAIN'S MOST POPULAR ONLINE BOOKMAKER NOVICE MEDIAN AUCTION STKS (PLUS 10 RACE) 6f
3:45 (3:45) (Class 3) 2-Y-O **£9,703** (£2,887; £1,443; £721) **Stalls** Low

Form RPR
2 **1** **Abstemious**[14] 4937 2-9-5 0 JamieSpencer 3 90+
(Kevin Ryan) *mde all: clr over 2f out: unchal* **11/8**[1]

0 **2** 5 **Abbey Wharf (IRE)**[35] 4125 2-8-11 0 RowanScott(3) 5 67
(Nigel Tinkler) *chsd ldrs: hdwy over 2f out: rdn wl over 1f out: kpt on u.p fnl f: tk 2nd nr fin* **16/1**

2 **3** ½ **Mr Jones And Me**[16] 4826 2-9-5 0 RichardKingscote 4 70
(Tom Dascombe) *sn chsng wnr: rdn along 2f out: drvn over 1f out: kpt on same pce: lost 2nd nr fin* **5/2**[2]

4 *shd* **Creativity** 2-9-0 0 TonyHamilton 6 65
(Richard Fahey) *dwlt and wnt bdly rt s: green and in rr whn j. path after 150yds: hdwy to chse ldrs 1/2-way: rdn along wl over 1f out: kpt on same pce* **5/1**[3]

5 5 **Internationaltiger** 2-9-5 0 PaddyMathers 1 55
(Richard Fahey) *dwlt and a towards rr* **9/1**

53 **6** 6 **Outtake**[15] 4871 2-9-5 0 DaneO'Neill 2 37
(Richard Hannon) *prom: pushed along over 3f out: rdn wl over 2f out: sn wknd* **15/2**

1m 16.57s (4.97) **Going Correction** +0.675s/f (Yiel) **6** Ran SP% **115.0**
Speed ratings (Par 98): **93,86,85,85,78 70**
CSF £24.98 TOTE £2.00: £1.50, £5.70; EX 33.80 Trifecta £93.10.
Owner Guy Reed Racing 1 **Bred** Copgrove Hall Stud **Trained** Hambleton, N Yorks

FOCUS
Run in teeming rain, this produced a very easy winner indeed, who was value for considerably further. The opening level is fluid.

5457 SKY BET BEST ODDS GUARANTEED H'CAP 2m 56y
4:20 (4:23) (Class 3) (0-90,92) 4-Y-O+ **£9,703** (£2,887; £1,443; £721) **Stalls** Low

Form RPR
-320 **1** **Always Resolute**[28] 4381 8-7-13 **75** (p) AngusVilliers(7) 9 85
(Ian Williams) *trckd ldr: cl up 1/2-way: led 6f out: jnd and rdn over 2f out: hdd over 1f out: rallied gamely u.p ins fnl f: led again last 100yds* **10/1**

1562 **2** ¾ **Makawee (IRE)**[14] 4936 4-9-7 **90** DanielTudhope 8 99+
(David O'Meara) *hld up: smooth hdwy 4f out: cl up over 2f out: shkn up to ld over 1f out: rdn jst ins fnl f: sn drvn: hdd and no ex last 100yds* **5/2**[1]

4505 **3** 5 **Grandee (IRE)**[15] 4884 5-9-6 **89** SilvestreDeSousa 5 92
(Roger Fell) *hld up: hdwy 4f out: chsd ldrs 3f out: rdn along 2f out: sn drvn and kpt on one pce* **5/2**[1]

1225 **4** 12 **Orin Swift (IRE)**[35] 4118 5-9-2 **85** RichardKingscote 7 74
(Jonathan Portman) *trckd ldrs: hdwy to chse wnr 4f out: rdn along 3f out: drvn over 2f out: sn wknd* **7/2**[2]

-340 **5** 22 **Yabass (IRE)**[39] 3952 4-9-7 **90** (t[1]) BenCurtis 1 52
(Archie Watson) *led: pushed along and hdd 6f out: rdn over 4f out: sn wknd* **8/1**[3]

-41P **6** 83 **Mixboy (FR)**[39] 3952 9-9-9 **92** JamieSpencer 3
(Keith Dalgleish) *trckd ldrs: pushed along over 4f out: rdn wl over 3f out: sn wknd and bhd: eased fnl 2f (trainers' rep said gelding was unsuited by the Soft ground)* **8/1**[3]

01- **P** **Le Maitre Chat (USA)**[321] 7100 8-8-13 **82** (p) PaulMulrennan 6
(Micky Hammond) *hld up: in tch whn lost action and p.u over 5f out (vet said gelding was lame on it's right fore)* **20/1**

3m 43.16s (9.26) **Going Correction** +0.675s/f (Yiel) **7** Ran SP% **115.4**
Speed ratings (Par 107): **103,102,100,94,83 41,**
CSF £35.97 CT £83.62 TOTE £11.50: £3.90, £1.90; EX 45.20 Trifecta £126.50.
Owner Ne-Chance **Bred** Jarvis Associates **Trained** Portway, Worcs

FOCUS
Add 11yds. This proved quite a test in the deteriorating conditions, with the official going now changed to soft, and the form isn't solid. The pace was fairly steady, and they raced up the centre of the straight.

5458 SKY BET SUPPORTING NEW BEGINNINGS BRITISH EBF FILLIES' H'CAP 1m 2f 56y
4:55 (4:57) (Class 3) (0-90,89) 3-Y-O+
£15,562 (£4,660; £2,330; £1,165; £582; £292) **Stalls** Low

Form RPR
0554 **1** **Ladies First**[11] 5030 5-9-0 **75** NathanEvans 1 84
(Michael Easterby) *trckd ldng pair: hdwy 3f out: led 2f out: sn rdn: drvn ins fnl f: kpt on wl towards fin* **10/1**

-504 **2** ¾ **Red Hot (FR)**[29] 4318 3-9-1 **85** DanielTudhope 7 93
(Richard Fahey) *hld up in rr: stdy hdwy 3f out: chsd wnr over 1f out: rdn and ev ch ins fnl f: drvn and no ex last 100yds* **7/1**

4153 **3** 3 ¼ **Appointed**[7] 5201 5-9-2 **77** (t) DavidAllan 8 78
(Tim Easterby) *hld up in rr: hdwy wl over 2f out: rdn wl over 1f out: chsd ldng pair ent fnl f: kpt on same pce* **11/2**[3]

0-00 **4** 6 **Empress Ali (IRE)**[43] 3811 8-9-6 **81** JasonHart 10 70
(Tom Tate) *led: rdn along 3f out: hdd 2f out: sn drvn and grad wknd (vet said mare had small wounds on both hind legs)* **25/1**

-221 **5** 1 ¼ **Audarya (FR)**[36] 4076 3-9-3 **87** DanielMuscutt 2 74+
(James Fanshawe) *trckd ldrs on outer: smooth hdwy and cl up 3f out: rdn 2f out: sn drvn and btn* **10/3**[2]

-213 **6** ½ **Amber Spark (IRE)**[14] 4930 3-8-13 **83** TonyHamilton 9 69
(Richard Fahey) *sn cl up: rdn along 3f out: drvn over 2f out: sn wknd* **9/1**

0204 **7** 7 **Double Reflection**[58] 3255 4-9-6 **81** BenCurtis 4 52
(K R Burke) *hld up in tch: effrt and sme hdwy 4f out: rdn along 3f out: wknd over 2f out* **33/1**

-631 **8** 21 **Nette Rousse (GER)**[42] 3860 3-8-10 **80** RichardKingscote 3 10+
(Ralph Beckett) *hld up: effrt and hdwy over 3f out: rdn along over 2f out: sn btn and eased (trainers' rep said filly was unsuited by the Soft ground)* **6/4**[1]

2m 16.26s (5.96) **Going Correction** +0.675s/f (Yiel)
WFA 3 from 4yo+ 9lb **8** Ran SP% **116.8**
Speed ratings (Par 104): **103,102,99,95,94 93,88,71**
CSF £78.87 CT £429.28 TOTE £9.30: £2.20, £2.10, £2.00; EX 92.90 Trifecta £371.50.
Owner Casino Royale Racing **Bred** Bond Thoroughbred Corporation **Trained** Sheriff Hutton, N Yorks

FOCUS
Add 11yds. This time they raced on the stands' side once in line for home.

5459 SPORTING LIFE FAST RESULTS H'CAP 7f
5:25 (5:27) (Class 4) (0-85,87) 3-Y-O
£9,962 (£2,964; £1,481; £740; £300; £300) **Stalls** Low

Form RPR
231 **1** **Triple Distilled**[15] 4895 3-9-2 **83** RowanScott(3) 6 92+
(Nigel Tinkler) *hld up in tch: hdwy and swtchd rt to stands' rail 3f out: nt clr run 2f out: swtchd lft and rdn wl over 1f out: styd on to chse clr ldr ins fnl f: sn drvn and kpt on wl to ld nr fin* **11/4**[1]

3103 **2** *nk* **Kapono**[22] 4603 3-8-5 **74** (p) BenSanderson(5) 1 82
(Roger Fell) *hld up in rr: gd hdwy on inner over 2f out: rdn to ld 1 1/2f out: sn clr: drvn ins fnl f: wknd and hdd nr fin* **20/1**

4-43 **3** 2 3/4 **Praxidice**[40] 3923 3-8-10 74 ....(w) BenCurtis 3 75
(K R Burke) *prom: cl up 3f out: rdn to dispute ld 2f out: drvn over 1f out: kpt on same pce* **5/1**[3]

6453 **4** 1/2 **Sparklealot (IRE)**[14] 4909 3-9-4 82 ....(p) TrevorWhelan 9 82
(Ivan Furtado) *led: rdn along and wd st towards stands' side: jnd over 2f out: sn hdd and drvn: grad wknd* **7/1**

3541 **5** 3 1/4 **Ramesses**[12] 4980 3-8-12 76 .... PaddyMathers 5 67
(Richard Fahey) *hld up in tch: hdwy 3f out: chsd ldrs over 2f out: sn rdn and btn* **6/1**

1103 **6** 4 **Astrologer**[12] 4980 3-9-9 87 ....(h) DanielTudhope 8 68
(David O'Meara) *trckd ldrs: wd st to stands' rail: cl up over 3f out: rdn along wl over 2f out: sn drvn and btn* **9/2**[2]

1446 **7** 4 **Socru (IRE)**[17] 4781 3-8-8 72 .... NathanEvans 2 43
(Michael Easterby) *rrd and lost several l s: a in rr (jockey said gelding reared at the stalls opened and missed the break)* **20/1**

0566 **8** 5 **Come On Leicester (IRE)**[14] 4904 3-9-7 85 .... SilvestreDeSousa 4 43
(Richard Hannon) *t.k.h: hld up: a towards rr* **10/1**

2104 **9** nse **I Am A Dreamer**[5] 5246 3-9-5 83 .... JasonHart 7 40
(Mark Johnston) *prom: rdn along wl over 2f out: sn wknd* **17/2**

1m 28.81s (4.21) **Going Correction** +0.675s/f (Yiel) **9 Ran SP% 117.4**
Speed ratings (Par 102): **102,101,98,97,94 89,85,79,79**
CSF £63.12 CT £261.71 TOTE £3.60: £1.50, £5.30, £2.00; EX 64.30 Trifecta £270.50.
Owner John R Saville **Bred** Copgrove Hall Stud **Trained** Langton, N Yorks

FOCUS
Another race in which they migrated to the stands' side. Fairly useful handicap form.
T/Plt: £1,129.40 to a £1 stake. Pool: £136,217.03 - 88.04 winning units T/Qpdt: £46.30 to a £1 stake. Pool: £9,350.55 - 149.21 winning units **Joe Rowntree**

5460a-5467a (Foreign Racing) - See Raceform Interactive

5407 DEAUVILLE (R-H)
Saturday, July 27

OFFICIAL GOING: Polytrack: standard; turf: very soft

5468a ARQANA PRIX DE TANCARVILLE (MAIDEN) (UNRACED 2YO COLTS & GELDINGS) (STRAIGHT COURSE) (TURF) 6f
1:17 2-Y-O £12,162 (£4,864; £3,648; £2,432; £1,216)

RPR

1 **Devil (IRE)** 2-9-2 0 .... MaximeGuyon 5 81
(F Head, France) **58/10**

2 1 1/2 **Juliusjuliusson (USA)** 2-9-2 0 .... StephanePasquier 6 77
(P Bary, France) **26/5**

3 snk **Golden Boy (FR)** 2-9-2 0 .... TheoBachelot 8 76
(S Wattel, France) **31/10**[2]

4 1 3/4 **Ganbaru (IRE)** 2-9-2 0 .... MickaelBarzalona 7 71
(A Fabre, France) *broke wl: cl up on outer: outpcd and scrubbed along ins fnl 2f: kpt on again over 1f out: run flattened out fnl 150yds* **39/10**[3]

5 1 3/4 **Zabarqan (IRE)** 2-9-2 0 .... ChristopheSoumillon 4 66
(J-C Rouget, France) *racd keenly: chsd ldrs: smooth prog to chal 2f out: sn rdn and nt qckn: wknd fnl f* **5/2**[1]

6 5 **Mr Shady (IRE)** 2-9-2 0 .... TonyPiccone 3 51
(J S Moore) *hld up towards rr: rdn and no imp fr 2 1/2f out* **17/1**

7 snk **On Your Marks** 2-9-2 0 .... CristianDemuro 2 50
(Andrea Marcialis, France) **13/1**

8 3 1/2 **Superior Badolat (IRE)** 2-9-2 0 .... PierantonioConvertino 1 40
(Andrea Marcialis, France) **33/1**

1m 15.05s (4.05) **8 Ran SP% 119.8**
PARI-MUTUEL (all including 1 euro stake): WIN 6.80; PLACE 1.90, 1.90, 1.70; DF 15.80.
Owner Wertheimer & Frere **Bred** Wertheimer & Frere **Trained** France

5469a PRIX SIX PERFECTIONS SKY SPORTS RACING (GROUP 3) (2YO FILLIES) (ROUND COURSE) (TURF) 7f
1:52 2-Y-O £36,036 (£14,414; £10,810; £7,207; £3,603)

RPR

1 **Tropbeau**[21] 2-8-11 0 .... MickaelBarzalona 5 102+
(A Fabre, France) *broke wl: racd keenly: led early: hdd end of 1f: chsd ldr: shkn up to regain ld ins fnl 2f: rdn and styd on strly fnl f: wl on top fin* **7/5**[1]

2 2 1/2 **Alocasia**[27] 2-8-11 0 .... AlexisBadel 7 95
(H-F Devin, France) *chsd ldrs on outer: 4th and pushed along 2 1/2f out: styd on u.p fnl f: nt pce to trble wnr* **32/5**

3 snk **Kenlova (FR)**[28] 4417 2-8-11 0 .... ChristopheSoumillon 8 95
(P Bary, France) *towards rr on outer: tk clsr order 2f out: styd on ins fnl f: nvr nrr* **54/10**[3]

4 nk **Sesame Birah (IRE)**[29] 4317 2-8-11 0 .... MaximeGuyon 4 94
(Richard Hannon) *led after 1f: drvn along over 2f out: hdd ins fnl 2f: one pce u.p* **63/10**

5 2 1/2 **Alabama Whitman**[16] 4819 2-8-11 0 .... MartinDwyer 1 88
(Richard Spencer) *towards rr on inner: 5th and pushed along 2 1/2f out: rdn and kpt on over 1f out: effrt flattened out fnl 150yds: nvr trbld ldrs* **4/1**[2]

6 3/4 **Eversweet (FR)**[46] 2-8-11 0 .... TristanBaron 2 86
(J E Hammond, France) *chsd ldrs on inner: rdn over 1 1/2f out: plugged on at one pce: nvr in contention* **19/1**

7 1/2 **Famiglia (FR)**[34] 2-8-11 0 .... PierantonioConvertino 6 85
(Charley Rossi, France) *racd in fnl pair: outpcd and drvn ins fnl 2f: kpt on ins fnl f: n.d* **12/1**

8 12 **Butterfly Pose (IRE)**[87] 2282 2-8-11 0 .... TonyPiccone 3 55
(J S Moore) *a last: lost tch fr 2f out* **43/1**

1m 29.43s (1.13) **8 Ran SP% 119.5**
PARI-MUTUEL (all including 1 euro stake): WIN 2.40; PLACE 1.30, 1.60, 1.60; DF 5.80.
Owner Lady Bamford **Bred** Lord Margadale **Trained** Chantilly, France

FOCUS
This is often a weak Group 3.

5470a PRIX DE PSYCHE (GROUP 3) (3YO FILLIES) (ROUND COURSE) (TURF) 1m 2f
2:32 3-Y-O £36,036 (£14,414; £10,810; £7,207; £3,603)

RPR

1 **Villa Marina**[16] 3-8-11 0 .... OlivierPeslier 3 107+
(C Laffon-Parias, France) *a.p on inner: qcknd to chal over 1 1/2f out: led ent fnl f: styd on strly u.p despite edging lft: readily* **43/5**

2 1 3/4 **Edisa (USA)**[27] 4429 3-8-11 0 .... ChristopheSoumillon 8 104
(A De Royer-Dupre, France) *hld up in rr: clsd on outer fr 2 1/2f out: str run to chal 1 1/2f out: styd on fnl f: no match for wnr last half f* **19/10**[1]

3 nk **Romanciere (IRE)**[28] 4416 3-8-11 0 .... MaximeGuyon 5 103
(A Fabre, France) *led: hdd after 1 1/2f: remained cl up: drvn to regain ld over 2f out: hrd pressed over 1 1/2f out: hdd ent fnl f: styd on same pce u.p* **3/1**[2]

4 1 **Alzire (FR)**[47] 3677 3-8-11 0 .... MickaelBarzalona 2 103
(J-C Rouget, France) *dwlt: racd keenly: hld up towards rr: clsd to chse ldrs but nt clr run 2f out: sn in open and styd on u.p: no ex fnl 75yds* **14/1**

5 1 1/2 **All Grace (FR)**[49] 3-8-11 0 .... VincentCheminaud 1 99
(A Fabre, France) *w.w in fnl pair: last and pushed along 2 1/2f out: effrt u.p 1 1/2f out: dropped away ins fnl f* **12/1**

6 3/4 **Paramount (FR)**[41] 3905 3-8-11 0 .... JulienAuge 4 97
(C Ferland, France) *chsd ldrs on outer: cl up and drvn over 1 1/2f out: wknd ins fnl f* **14/1**

7 2 1/2 **Cartiem (FR)**[41] 3905 3-9-2 0 .... CristianDemuro 6 98
(J-C Rouget, France) *pressed ldr on outer: led after 1 1/2f: hdd over 2f out: wknd fnl f* **43/10**[3]

8 hd **Preciosa (GER)**[56] 3-8-11 0 .... CyrilleStefan 7 92
(R Dzubasz, Germany) *wnt lft s: midfield on outer: rdn 2f out but sn outpcd: kpt on again late but nvr in contention* **9/1**

2m 9.59s (-0.61) **8 Ran SP% 119.8**
PARI-MUTUEL (all including 1 euro stake): WIN 9.60; PLACE 1.60, 1.30, 1.40; DF 9.80.
Owner Sarl Darpat France **Bred** Sarl Darpat France **Trained** Chantilly, France

FOCUS
The winner has been rated as a major improver, but it looked no fluke, and the second has been rated near her mark.

5471a PRIX DU CERCLE - SAUTERNES'S CUP (LISTED RACE) (3YO+) (STRAIGHT COURSE) (TURF) 5f
3:10 3-Y-O+ £23,423 (£9,369; £7,027; £4,684; £2,342)

RPR

1 **Ken Colt (IRE)**[33] 4205 4-9-2 0 .... StephanePasquier 6 108
(F Chappet, France) **18/5**[2]

2 2 **Pocket Dynamo (USA)**[21] 4665 3-8-11 0 .... ChristopheSoumillon 9 99
(Robert Cowell) *fly j. as stalls opened: last of five in gp towards centre: angled out and smooth hdwy more than 1 1/2f out: sn rdn and chsd clr ldr appr fnl f: kpt on but no imp fnl 150yds* **26/5**[3]

3 nk **Gold Vibe (IRE)**[14] 4948 6-9-2 0 ....(b) CristianDemuro 2 100
(P Bary, France) **13/5**[1]

4 3 **Coco City (FR)**[42] 5-9-2 0 .... OlivierPeslier 7 89
(M Delcher Sanchez, France) **16/1**

5 1/2 **Red Torch (FR)**[39] 4-9-2 0 .... VincentCheminaud 8 87
(H-A Pantall, France) **54/10**

6 shd **Deia Glory**[14] 4932 3-8-8 0 .... MickaelBarzalona 1 82
(Michael Dods) *cl up in gp of four towards stands' rail: dropped towards rr overall bef 1/2-way: kpt on ins fnl 1 1/2f: nvr in contention* **16/1**

7 1 **Antonella**[42] 5-8-13 0 .... BorjaFayosMartin 4 80
(T J Martins Novais, Spain) **66/10**

8 3 1/2 **Qayes**[12] 4-9-2 0 ....(b) AlexisBadel 5 71
(P Ventena Alves, France) **16/1**

9 1/2 **Little Kim**[15] 4891 3-8-8 0 .... TonyPiccone 3 64
(K R Burke) *cl up in gp of four towards stands' rail: outpcd and drvn over 2f out: wl hld whn eased fnl f* **13/1**

58.25s (0.75)
WFA 3 from 4yo+ 4lb **9 Ran SP% 119.2**
PARI-MUTUEL (all including 1 euro stake): WIN 4.60; PLACE 1.50, 2.00, 1.40; DF 14.40.
Owner Roy Racing Ltd **Bred** Stratford Place Stud **Trained** France

5152 PONTEFRACT (L-H)
Sunday, July 28

OFFICIAL GOING: Good (7.4)
Wind: Moderate against Weather: Heavy cloud

5472 BRITISH STALLION STUDS EBF MAIDEN STKS (PLUS 10 RACE) 5f 3y
2:20 (2:20) (Class 4) 2-Y-O £6,469 (£1,925; £962; £481) Stalls Low

Form RPR

2 **1** **Pop Dancer (IRE)**[9] 5152 2-9-5 0 .... TonyHamilton 3 90
(Richard Fahey) *cl up: led after 1f: pushed along and qcknd clr 2f out: rdn ins fnl f: kpt on wl towards fin* **6/5**[1]

2 3/4 **Queen's Order** 2-9-0 0 .... DanielTudhope 2 82+
(Kevin Ryan) *slt ld 1f: trckd wnr: hdwy over 1f out: chal ins fnl f: sn rdn and ev ch: kpt on same pce towards fin* **11/4**[2]

5 **3** 7 **Augustus Caesar (USA)**[8] 5197 2-9-5 0 .... DavidNolan 6 62
(David O'Meara) *trckd ldng pair: hdwy on inner 2f out: rdn along wl over 1f out: kpt on same pce* **8/1**

34 **4** 5 **Ma Boy Harris (IRE)**[10] 5093 2-9-5 0 .... BenCurtis 5 44
(Phillip Makin) *in tch: rdn along over 2f out: kpt on one pce* **16/1**

002 **5** 1 3/4 **Ellenor Gray (IRE)**[27] 4433 2-9-0 70 .... PaulHanagan 7 33
(Richard Fahey) *chsd ldng pair: rdn along over 2f out: grad wknd (jockey said filly hung left-handed)* **7/1**[3]

54 **6** 2 1/4 **Zakher Alain**[12] 5017 2-9-5 0 .... DavidAllan 1 30
(Adrian Nicholls) *dwlt and bhd: rdn along over 2f out: kpt on fr over 1f out* **33/1**

7 1 1/4 **Slaidburn** 2-9-5 0 .... GrahamLee 8 25
(Tim Easterby) *green and a towards rr* **14/1**

1m 3.64s (-0.26) **Going Correction** +0.275s/f (Good) **7 Ran SP% 111.2**
Speed ratings (Par 96): **113,111,100,92,89 86,84**
CSF £4.27 TOTE £1.90: £1.10, £1.60; EX 5.40 Trifecta £16.60.
Owner Richard Fahey Ebor Racing Club Ltd **Bred** Marston Stud **Trained** Musley Bank, N Yorks

FOCUS
The front pair pulled clear in this ordinary juvenile maiden.

5473 ITV7 STARTS NOW H'CAP 1m 4f 5y
2:50 (2:50) (Class 5) (0-70,71) 3-Y-O+
£3,881 (£1,155; £577; £400; £400; £400) Stalls Low

Form RPR

-406 **1** **Breathable**[41] 3925 4-9-11 64 .... DavidAllan 3 76
(Tim Easterby) *trckd ldr: cl up 4f out: led over 2f out: sn rdn clr: kpt on wl fnl f* **15/2**[3]

505 **2** 4 1/2 **Vintage Rose**[46] 3724 3-8-13 63 .... KevinStott 2 68
(Mark Walford) *trckd ldrs: hdwy over 2f out: rdn wl over 1f out: drvn and chsd wnr fnl f: no imp* **25/1**

0054 **3** *2 3/4* **Sempre Presto (IRE)**[17] 4817 4-9-13 **66**........................ PaulHanagan 1 66
(Richard Fahey) *dwlt and hld up in rr: hdwy 3f out: rdn along to chse ldrs wl over 1f out: kpt on fnl f* **11/2**[2]

011 **4** *1 3/4* **King And Queen (FR)**[9] 5122 3-9-2 **66**........................ JasonHart 5 64
(Mark Johnston) *led: jnd and pushed along over 3f out: rdn and hdd wl over 2f out: sn drvn and wknd wl over 1f out* **1/2**[1]

0626 **5** *5* **Low Profile**[33] 4208 4-10-0 **67**........................(p) DanielTudhope 8 57
(Rebecca Bastiman) *hld up in rr: sme hdwy 3f out: rdn along and wd st: nvr nr ldrs* **12/1**

-050 **6** *6* **Correggio**[27] 4446 9-8-9 **48** oh1........................ AndrewMullen 4 28
(Micky Hammond) *a towards rr* **33/1**

000 **7** *5* **Mousebird (IRE)**[49] 3637 3-9-0 **64**........................ SilvestreDeSousa 7 36
(Hughie Morrison) *trckd ldng pair: rdn along 3f out: sn wknd (trainers' rep said filly would prefer a quicker surface)* **8/1**

6106 **8** *hd* **Champagne Rules**[19] 4762 8-10-4 **71**........................ PhilDennis 6 43
(Sharon Watt) *chsd ldrs: rdn along over 3f out: sn wknd (jockey said gelding ran flat)* **16/1**

2m 44.0s (2.90) **Going Correction** +0.275s/f (Good) **8 Ran SP% 125.3**
WFA 3 from 4yo+ 11lb
Speed ratings (Par 103): **101,98,96,95,91 87,84,84**
CSF £176.54 CT £1133.34 TOTE £9.20: £2.10, £5.20, £1.50; EX 214.90 Trifecta £886.80.
Owner B Guerin J Westoll & Habton Farms **Bred** Mr & Mrs A E Pakenham **Trained** Great Habton, N Yorks

FOCUS
One-way traffic in this modest handicap.

5474 IN THE ZONE FAMILY DAY ON 18TH AUGUST H'CAP — 1m 2f 5y
3:20 (3:22) (Class 4) (0-80,81) 3-Y-O+
£6,469 (£1,925; £962; £481; £400; £400) **Stalls Low**

Form RPR

5304 **1** **Regal Mirage (IRE)**[8] 5178 5-9-6 **70**........................ DavidAllan 6 79
(Tim Easterby) *hld up in tch: hdwy over 3f out: chsd ldrs wl over 1f out: rdn over 1f out: led ins fnl f: drvn out* **6/1**[3]

4001 **2** *1* **Firewater**[41] 3938 3-8-5 **64**........................(p) PaddyMathers 4 71
(Richard Fahey) *trckd ldrs: hdwy 3f out: chsd ldr over 1f out: sn rdn: drvn and ev ch ins fnl f: no ex towards fin* **10/1**

612 **3** *1 1/4* **Railport Dolly**[22] 4653 4-9-11 **75**........................(h) LiamKeniry 3 79
(David Barron) *trckd ldr: cl up 1/2-way: led over 2f out: rdn clr over 1f out: drvn ins fnl f: sn hdd and grad wknd* **14/1**

4463 **4** *6* **First Dance (IRE)**[7] 5213 5-9-1 **65**........................ JamesSullivan 7 57
(Tom Tate) *hld up in rr: hdwy 3f out: rdn along wl over 1f out: kpt on: nvr nr ldrs* **12/1**

412 **5** *5* **Billy Roberts (IRE)**[8] 5198 6-9-6 **70**........................ JasonHart 1 52
(Richard Whitaker) *led: pushed along over 3f out: rdn and hdd over 2f out: sn drvn and wknd wl over 1f out* **15/8**[1]

443 **6** *2 3/4* **Sod's Law**[9] 5149 4-10-3 **81**........................ DanielTudhope 8 58
(Hughie Morrison) *hld up in rr: effrt 3f out: sn rdn along and n.d* **5/2**[2]

-455 **7** *1 3/4* **Frankster (FR)**[47] 3704 6-8-10 **60**........................(tp) PaulHanagan 5 33
(Micky Hammond) *hld up: sme hdwy over 3f out: rdn along over 2f out: sn btn* **25/1**

11/0 **8** *1/2* **Pete So High (GER)**[21] 4689 5-10-0 **78**........................ GrahamLee 2 50
(Julia Brooke) *in tch: rdn along 3f out: sn wknd* **20/1**

2214 **9** *60* **Bit Of A Quirke**[15] 4907 6-9-8 **72**........................(v) AndrewMullen 9
(Mark Walford) *chsd ldng pair on outer: rdn along 4f out: wknd 3f out: bhd and eased 2f out* **16/1**

2m 15.57s (0.57) **Going Correction** +0.275s/f (Good) **9 Ran SP% 115.6**
WFA 3 from 4yo+ 9lb
Speed ratings (Par 105): **108,107,106,101,97 95,93,93,45**
CSF £64.01 CT £804.73 TOTE £6.70: £2.00, £2.20, £3.10; EX 58.00 Trifecta £427.40.
Owner Ryedale Partners No 7 **Bred** Norelands, Lofts Hall & A Gold **Trained** Great Habton, N Yorks

FOCUS
Modest enough form, with the first three pulling clear.

5475 SKY BET GO-RACING-IN-YORKSHIRE SUMMER FESTIVAL POMFRET STKS (LISTED RACE) — 1m 6y
3:55 (3:57) (Class 1) 3-Y-O+
£28,010 (£10,665; £5,340; £2,665; £1,335; £670) **Stalls Low**

Form RPR

3041 **1** **Marie's Diamond (IRE)**[9] 5129 3-8-11 **103**........................ SilvestreDeSousa 4 107
(Mark Johnston) *mde all: jnd and rdn over 2f out: hrd pressed and drvn ins fnl f: styd on gamely towards fin* **3/1**[2]

-053 **2** *3/4* **Di Fede (IRE)**[21] 4706 4-9-0 **102**........................ HarryBentley 5 102
(Ralph Beckett) *trckd ldng pair: hdwy 3f out: cl up 2f out: chal and rdn over 1f out: drvn and ev ch ins fnl f: kpt on same pce towards fin* **4/1**[3]

03-3 **3** *1/2* **Khafoo Shememi (IRE)**[29] 4397 5-9-5 **105**........................ DanielTudhope 1 106
(Sir Michael Stoute) *trckd wnr: effrt 2f out: rdn over 1f out: drvn ins fnl f: kpt on same pce* **6/4**[1]

0241 **4** *1* **Exhort**[19] 4758 4-9-3 **97**........................ PaulHanagan 3 102
(Richard Fahey) *hld up in tch: hdwy on inner wl over 1f out: sn rdn: drvn and kpt on same pce fnl f* **11/2**

2362 **5** *3/4* **Oh This Is Us (IRE)**[15] 4905 6-9-5 **108**........................ TomMarquand 6 102
(Richard Hannon) *hld up in tch: hdwy on outer over 1f out: rdn ins fnl f: kpt on towards fin* **12/1**

2402 **6** *4 1/2* **Pure Shores**[8] 5187 5-9-0 **83**........................ BenCurtis 8 87
(Ian Williams) *dwlt: sn trcking ldrs: pushed along over 3f out: rdn over 2f out: sn drvn and wknd wl over 1f out* **33/1**

1m 45.97s (0.07) **Going Correction** +0.275s/f (Good) **6 Ran SP% 111.0**
WFA 3 from 4yo+ 8lb
Speed ratings (Par 111): **110,109,108,107,107 102**
CSF £14.89 TOTE £2.50: £1.50, £2.30; EX 13.60 Trifecta £29.30.
Owner Middleham Park Racing LXXXVI **Bred** Tony Ashley **Trained** Middleham Moor, N Yorks

FOCUS
A fair Listed race won in dogged fashion by a progressive 3yo.

5476 TIESPLANET.COM - TIES FOR EVERY OCCASION H'CAP — 6f
4:30 (4:31) (Class 3) (0-90,89) 3-Y-O+
£9,337 (£2,796; £1,398; £699; £349; £175) **Stalls Low**

Form RPR

002 **1** **Highly Sprung (IRE)**[35] 4148 6-8-4 **72**........................ HarrisonShaw(5) 6 80
(Les Eyre) *awkward and sltly hmpd s: sn pushed along to chse ldrs: rdn along over 2f out: gd hdwy over 1f out: rdn to ld ent fnl f: kpt on strly* **6/1**[3]

0413 **2** *1* **Musharrif**[9] 5157 7-8-9 **79**........................(t) ZakWheatley(7) 4 84
(Declan Carroll) *trckd ldrs: hdwy 2f out: rdn to chal over 1f out: disp ld and ev ch ent fnl f: sn drvn: kpt on* **8/1**

4201 **3** *1/2* **Magical Effect (IRE)**[27] 4440 7-9-0 **77**........................ JamesSullivan 1 80
(Ruth Carr) *hld up in rr: effrt on inner whn nt clr run and hmpd bnd 2f out: hdwy over 1f out: nt clr run and swtchd rt ent fnl f: sn rdn and kpt on* **11/4**[1]

10-0 **4** *nk* **Big Les (IRE)**[150] 952 4-9-6 **83**........................ JasonHart 3 85
(Karen McLintock) *in tch: hdwy 2f out: chsd ldrs whn n.m.r over 1f out: sn rdn and kpt on fnl f* **8/1**

4405 **5** *2 1/2* **Society Queen (IRE)**[23] 4595 3-8-9 **77**........................ PaulHanagan 2 70
(Richard Fahey) *dwlt and in rr: hdwy 2f out: rdn over 1f out: chsd ldrs ent fnl f: kpt on (vet said filly lost her right fore shoe)* **11/2**[2]

1000 **6** *3 1/2* **Dark Defender**[9] 5120 6-9-8 **85**........................(b) DanielTudhope 7 68
(Rebecca Bastiman) *wnt lft s: cl up: led wl over 1f out: sn rdn: hdd ent fnl f: sn wknd* **7/1**

2540 **7** *6* **Diamond Dougal (IRE)**[41] 3945 4-9-7 **89**........................ ScottMcCullagh(5) 9 53
(Mick Channon) *hld up towards rr: hdwy on wd outside 2f out: rdn wl over 1f out: sn drvn and wknd* **11/2**[2]

0433 **8** *9* **Highland Acclaim (IRE)**[11] 5040 8-8-13 **76**........................(h) LiamKeniry 10 11
(David O'Meara) *cl up on outer: rdn along over 2f out: sn wknd* **20/1**

-056 **9** *1 1/4* **Arcavallo (IRE)**[8] 5180 4-9-0 **77**........................(p) TomEaves 5 8
(Michael Dods) *led: rdn along 2f out: sn hdd & wknd* **16/1**

1m 18.39s (1.29) **Going Correction** +0.275s/f (Good) **9 Ran SP% 117.1**
WFA 3 from 4yo+ 5lb
Speed ratings (Par 107): **102,100,100,99,96 91,83,71,69**
CSF £53.79 CT £163.10 TOTE £4.10: £1.60, £3.10, £1.20; EX 32.30 Trifecta £91.70.
Owner A Turton & Dr V Webb **Bred** Patrick J Moloney **Trained** Catwick, N Yorks

FOCUS
Modest enough sprint form.

5477 HAPPY 70TH BIRTHDAY JACKIE BARBER MAIDEN STKS — 1m 6y
5:05 (5:06) (Class 5) 3-4-Y-O
£3,881 (£1,155; £577; £288) **Stalls Low**

Form RPR

43 **1** **Joyful Mission (USA)**[23] 4608 3-9-5 0........................(h[1]) DanielTudhope 2 92+
(Sir Michael Stoute) *mde all: rdn clr wl over 1f out: readily* **4/5**[1]

4 **2** *5* **Baladio (IRE)**[22] 4636 3-9-0 0........................ TonyHamilton 7 73
(Richard Fahey) *trckd ldrs: hdwy over 2f out: rdn along on inner wl over 1f out: kpt on to chse wnr ins fnl f: sn no imp (vet said filly lost her right fore shoe)* **16/1**

2233 **3** *6* **Al Mureib (IRE)**[17] 4830 3-9-5 85........................(v[1]) CallumShepherd 9 64
(Saeed bin Suroor) *trckd wnr: cl up 1/2-way: pushed along 3f out: rdn 2f out: sn drvn and kpt on one pce* **2/1**[2]

6 **4** *1 1/2* **Olympic Conqueror (IRE)**[31] 4305 3-9-5 0........................ GeorgeWood 8 61
(James Fanshawe) *midfield: hdwy over 2f out: sn rdn along: kpt on fnl f: nrst fin* **33/1**

2 **5** *2 1/4* **Gazton**[19] 4760 3-9-5 0........................(h) PaulHanagan 6 56
(Ivan Furtado) *t.k.h: chsd ldrs: rdn along 3f out: sn one pce* **7/1**[3]

6-0 **6** *10* **Arabian King**[36] 4120 3-9-5 0........................ SilvestreDeSousa 11 33
(David Elsworth) *t.k.h: hld up in rr and rn wd bnd after 1f: sme hdwy on outer 2f out: sn rdn and plugged on: n.d* **12/1**

6300 **7** *1 1/2* **Jagerbond**[15] 4914 3-9-5 46........................(p) PaddyMathers 1 29
(Andrew Crook) *chsd ldrs: rdn along over 3f out: sn outpcd* **100/1**

8 *7* **Detonation** 3-8-13 0 ow1........................ AidenBlakemore(7) 3 14
(Shaun Harris) *a towards rr* **150/1**

0 **9** *nk* **Spotton (IRE)**[200] 133 3-9-5 0........................ LewisEdmunds 12 12
(Rebecca Bastiman) *stdd and swtchd lft s: a bhd* **66/1**

66 **10** *3* **High Fort (IRE)**[41] 3932 4-9-13 0........................ JasonHart 10 7
(Karen McLintock) *a in rr* **100/1**

06 **11** *3 1/2* **Juniors Dream (IRE)**[23] 4608 3-9-2 0........................ GabrieleMalune(3) 5
(Ivan Furtado) *a towards rr (jockey said gelding stopped quickly)* **66/1**

12 *28* **Alkhadra** 3-9-5 0........................ GrahamLee 4
(Paul Midgley) *in tch: rdn along over 3f out: sn lost pl and bhd* **50/1**

1m 47.18s (1.28) **Going Correction** +0.275s/f (Good) **12 Ran SP% 125.5**
WFA 3 from 4yo 8lb
Speed ratings (Par 103): **104,99,93,91,89 79,77,70,70,67 63,35**
CSF £19.75 TOTE £1.70: £1.10, £3.20, £1.10; EX 25.10 Trifecta £36.90.
Owner K Abdullah **Bred** Juddmonte Farms Inc **Trained** Newmarket, Suffolk

FOCUS
All about the favourite in this maiden, with them coming home at intervals.

5478 FLY HIGH FAYE NICKELS H'CAP — 5f 3y
5:40 (5:41) (Class 5) (0-70,70) 3-Y-O+
£3,881 (£1,155; £577; £400; £400; £400) **Stalls Low**

Form RPR

4002 **1** **Johnny Cavagin**[31] 4307 10-9-12 **70**........................ GrahamLee 8 79
(Paul Midgley) *hld up: hdwy 2f out: rdn over 1f out: styd on to chse ldr ins fnl f: drvn and fin wl to ld nr line* **3/1**[2]

1001 **2** *hd* **Super Julius**[10] 5094 5-9-11 **69**........................ BenCurtis 2 77
(S Donohoe, Ire) *slt ld: rdn clr wl over 1f out: drvn ins fnl f: hdd and no ex nr line* **11/4**[1]

1-43 **3** *4* **Tobeeornottobee**[164] 720 3-8-10 **65**........................ JessicaAnderson(7) 4 58
(Declan Carroll) *hld up in tch: hdwy on inner 2f out: rdn over 1f out: kpt on fnl f* **16/1**

403 **4** *1/2* **Astrophysics**[33] 4212 7-8-13 **57**........................ PaulMulrennan 6 49
(Lynn Siddall) *trckd ldrs on inner: hdwy 2f out: rdn to chse ldr over 1f out: drvn ins fnl f: kpt on same pce* **14/1**

0-04 **5** *3 3/4* **Young Tiger**[17] 4829 6-8-7 **51**........................ PaulHanagan 7 30
(Tom Tate) *a towards rr* **8/1**

2050 **6** *1* **Celerity (IRE)**[8] 5181 5-8-7 **51** oh1........................(p) PaddyMathers 5 26
(Lisa Williamson) *a towards rr* **40/1**

0144 **7** *1* **Shepherd's Purse**[15] 4911 7-9-6 **64**........................ JamesSullivan 9 35
(Ruth Carr) *chsd ldrs on outer: rdn along over 2f out: sn wknd* **4/1**[3]

6065 **8** *1* **Paco Escostar**[17] 4824 4-8-8 **52**........................(v) CamHardie 3 20
(Julie Camacho) *cl up: rdn along 2f out: sn drvn and wknd* **6/1**

-100 **9** *7* **Highly Focussed (IRE)**[22] 4632 5-9-4 **65**........................ SeanDavis(3) 1 8
(Ann Duffield) *dwlt: a bhd* **20/1**

1m 5.06s (1.16) **Going Correction** +0.275s/f (Good) **9 Ran SP% 116.8**
WFA 3 from 4yo+ 4lb
Speed ratings (Par 103): **101,100,94,93,87 85,84,82,71**
CSF £11.87 CT £112.02 TOTE £3.60: £1.30, £1.60, £3.00; EX 12.60 Trifecta £262.50.
Owner A Bell **Bred** A Bell **Trained** Westow, N Yorks

FOCUS
Modest sprinting form.

T/Jkpt: £6,598.40 to a £1 stake. Pool: £27,880.60 - 3 winning units T/Plt: £141.90 to a £1 stake. Pool: £163,889.10 - 843.08 winning units T/Qpdt: £14.20 to a £1 stake. Pool: £20,102.88 - 1,043.70 winning units **Joe Rowntree**

The Form Book Flat 2019, Raceform Ltd, Newbury, RG14 5SJ

[5468]DEAUVILLE (R-H)

Sunday, July 28

OFFICIAL GOING: Polytrack: standard; turf: good to soft

5479a PRIX ROTHSCHILD (GROUP 1) (3YO+ FILLIES & MARES) (STRAIGHT COURSE) (TURF) 1m (R)

2:50 3-Y-O+ **£154,432** (£61,783; £30,891; £15,432; £7,729)

RPR

1 **Laurens (FR)**[40] 3948 4-9-3 0.......................... PJMcDonald 6 116
(K R Burke) *led gp of six in centre of trck: tk overall ld appr 1/2-way: had nrly all rivals off the bridle over 3f out: drvn 1 1/2f out: kpt on gamely ins fnl f to hold on* **9/5**[1]

2 1/2 **With You**[63] 3122 4-9-3 0..........................(b[1]) AurelienLemaitre 2 115
(F Head, France) *w.w last of three in single-file trio nr stands' side: outpcd and pushed along 1/2-way: in last and drvn over 2 1/2f out: plenty to do appr fnl 1 1/2f: r.o u.p fnl f: nt quite rch wnr* **57/10**

3 1 1/2 **Obligate**[56] 3387 3-8-10 0 ow1.......... Pierre-CharlesBoudot 3 111
(P Bary, France) *racd keenly: trckd ldr in stands' side trio: sltly outpcd and pushed along over 2 1/2f out: 8th overall and rdn appr fnl 1 1/2f: styd on fnl f: nt pce to chal* **23/5**[3]

4 3 **Joplin (GER)**[21] 4706 5-9-3 0.......................... UmbertoRispoli 8 105
(D Fechner, Germany) *towards rr of centre gp: clsd fr 1/2-way and stl travelling wl enough 2 1/2f out: 3rd whn drvn over 1 1/2f out: wnt 3 l 2nd ent fnl f but sing to labour: dropped two pls fnl 100yds* **16/1**

5 2 **East**[63] 3115 3-8-9 0.......................... RyanMoore 7 99
(Kevin Ryan) *chsd ldr in gp in centre of trck: drvn to hold pl more than 3f out: struggling wl over 1f out: grad dropped away fnl f* **41/5**

6 3/4 **Move Swiftly**[39] 3986 4-9-3 0.......................... JamesDoyle 9 99
(William Haggas) *settled in fnl pair in centre gp: tried to cl 1/2-way: kpt on at same pce: nvr a threat* **41/10**[2]

7 snk **Qabala (USA)**[16] 4885 3-8-9 0..........................(b[1]) AndreaAtzeni 5 97
(Roger Varian) *chsd ldr in centre gp: outpcd and drvn 3f out: sn lost pl: kpt on ins fnl f but wl hld at the time* **15/1**

8 3 **Magical Dreamer (IRE)**[22] 4680 5-9-3 0..........................(p) PierreBazire 1 92
(E J O'Neill, France) *settled in fnl pair in centre gp: rdn over 3f out but no imp: wl hld fnl 1 1/2f: nvr in contention* **44/1**

9 dist **Beshaayir**[16] 4885 4-9-3 0.......................... ChristopheSoumillon 4
(William Haggas) *broke wl: led single-file trio towards stands' side and overall ldr: hdd appr 1/2-way: sn in trble: wknd qckly: eased and t.o fr 2f out* **14/1**

1m 36.71s (-4.09)
WFA 3 from 4yo+ 8lb **9 Ran SP% 120.0**
PARI-MUTUEL (all including 1 euro stake): WIN 2.80; PLACE 1.30, 1.80, 1.60; DF 8.80.
Owner John Dance **Bred** Bloodstock Agency Ltd **Trained** Middleham Moor, N Yorks

FOCUS
This wasn't an overly strong race for the level, and the market leader was more than entitled to take it. The ground appeared to be riding pretty testing considering lots of the horses were finishing really tired in the final stages. It's been rated around the winner to her level, with the second back to last year's best.

5480a PRIX DE TOURGEVILLE (LISTED RACE) (3YO COLTS & GELDINGS) (ROUND COURSE) (TURF) 1m (R)

4:00 3-Y-O **£24,774** (£9,909; £7,432; £4,954; £2,477)

RPR

1 **Delaware**[45] 3-8-13 0.......................... VincentCheminaud 4 108+
(A Fabre, France) **68/10**

2 3 **Dan**[26] 3-8-13 0.......................... ChristopheSoumillon 2 101
(J-C Rouget, France) **13/5**[1]

3 1/2 **Dave (FR)**[66] 3029 3-8-13 0.......................... MaximeGuyon 1 100
(Mme Pia Brandt, France) **5/1**

4 3/4 **Influencer**[31] 3-8-13 0.......................... MickaelBarzalona 6 98
(A Fabre, France) *led after 1f: drvn along and hdd under 2f out: rdn along and kpt on fnl f: rdn out* **63/10**

5 1 3/4 **Go To Hollywood (FR)**[59] 3287 3-8-13 0.......................... JeromeCabre 3 94
(Y Barberot, France) **14/1**

6 snk **Tantpispoureux (IRE)**[28] 4428 3-8-13 0.......... Pierre-CharlesBoudot 5 95
(F-H Graffard, France) **17/5**[2]

7 nk **Set Piece**[85] 2411 3-8-13 0..........................(b[1]) JamesDoyle 7 93
(Hugo Palmer) *little s.i.s: sn in midfield: drvn along 2f out: no imp and rdn 1f out: hung rt and lost position: wl hld fnl 1/2f: drvn out* **43/10**[3]

1m 41.9s (1.10) **7 Ran SP% 119.2**
PARI-MUTUEL (all including 1 euro stake): WIN 7.80; PLACE 3.20, 2.00; SF 21.60.
Owner K Abdullah **Bred** Juddmonte Farms **Trained** Chantilly, France

5481a DARLEY PRIX DE CABOURG (GROUP 3) (2YO) (STRAIGHT COURSE) (TURF) 6f

4:35 2-Y-O **£36,036** (£14,414; £10,810; £7,207; £3,603)

RPR

1 **Earthlight (IRE)**[26] 2-9-0 0.......................... MickaelBarzalona 2 110+
(A Fabre, France) *racd keenly: hld up next to last: shkn up and qcknd to ld appr fnl f: drvn clr: readily* **13/10**[1]

2 4 **Well Of Wisdom**[14] 4961 2-9-0 0.......................... JamesDoyle 3 98
(Charlie Appleby) *chsd ldr: shkn up to dispute ld 1/2-way: drvn and nt qckn 1 1/2f out and hdd narrowly: styd on fnl f: no ch w wnr* **49/10**

3 1/2 **Dubai Station**[38] 4012 2-9-0 0.......................... RyanMoore 1 97
(K R Burke) *w.w in rr: hdwy 1f out: styd on u.p fnl f: nvr on terms* **2/1**[2]

4 3/4 **Jolie (FR)**[7] 5228 2-8-10 0.......................... MaximeGuyon 4 90
(Andrea Marcialis, France) *settled in 3rd: rdn and short-lived effrt over 1f out: kpt on at one pce fnl f* **47/10**[3]

5 1 1/4 **Mowaeva (FR)**[14] 4961 2-9-0 0.......................... ChristopheSoumillon 5 91
(G Botti, France) *led: jnd at 1/2-way: hdd appr fnl f: grad dropped away* **12/1**

1m 10.3s (-0.70) **5 Ran SP% 119.0**
PARI-MUTUEL (all including 1 euro stake): WIN 2.30; PLACE 1.70, 2.20; SF 8.50.
Owner Godolphin SNC **Bred** Godolphin **Trained** Chantilly, France

5482 - (Foreign Racing) - See Raceform Interactive

[2310]MUNICH (L-H)

Sunday, July 28

OFFICIAL GOING: Turf: good

5483a GROSSER DALLMAYR-PREIS - BAYERISCHES ZUCHTRENNEN (GROUP 1) (3YO+) (TURF) 1m 2f

3:40 3-Y-O+ **£90,090** (£27,027; £13,513; £6,306; £2,702)

RPR

1 **Danceteria (FR)**[22] 4668 4-9-6 0.......................... JamieSpencer 5 115+
(David Menuisier) *hld up towards rr: tk clsr order on outer 3f out: chsd ldr 1 1/2f out: rdn to chal ent fnl f: led last 150yds: styd on wl* **11/5**[2]

2 1 1/4 **Wai Key Star (GER)**[56] 3386 6-9-6 0..........................(b) GeraldMosse 7 113
(Frau S Steinberg, Germany) *towards rr: hdwy 2f out: chsd ldng pair appr fnl f: styd on u.p: nt pce to match wnr* **184/10**

3 2 **Quest The Moon (GER)**[21] 4707 3-8-11 0.......................... OisinMurphy 8 110
(Frau S Steinberg, Germany) *a cl up: trckd ldng pair 2 1/2f out: tk over 2f out and drvn 2 l clr: wandered u.p ent fnl f: hdd last 150yds: no ex* **21/10**[1]

4 4 **Alounak (FR)**[28] 4427 4-9-6 0.......................... ClementLecoeuvre 6 101
(Waldemar Hickst, Germany) *w.w in midfield: drvn to chse ldrs 2f out: sn rdn and no further imp: dropped away ins fnl f* **239/10**

5 13 **Sword Peinture (GER)**[21] 4-9-3 0.......................... FilipMinarik 2 74
(Andreas Suborics, Germany) *in rr: sme late prog past btn horses: nvr in contention* **205/10**

6 8 **Stormy Antarctic**[40] 3948 6-9-6 0.......................... AlexanderPietsch 4 61
(Ed Walker) *chsd ldrs: outpcd and scrubbed along ins fnl 3f: bhd fnl 1 1/2f* **19/5**[3]

7 8 **Matterhorn (IRE)**[15] 4900 4-9-6 0.......................... JoeFanning 1 46
(Mark Johnston) *led: hdd briefly after 1f but led again gng into first bnd: pressed thrght: sing to labour and hdd 2f out: sn wknd* **23/5**

8 1 **Runnymede**[56] 3385 3-8-11 0.......................... RenePiechulek 9 45
(Frau S Steinberg, Germany) *a little slow to stride: rushed up to ld briefly after 1f: hdd first bnd: pressed ldr on outer: hrd rdn and nt qckn wl over 2f out: sn wknd* **32/1**

2m 14.96s (5.99)
WFA 3 from 4yo+ 9lb **8 Ran SP% 119.1**
PARI-MUTUEL (all including 1 euro stake): WIN 3.20 PLACE: 1.50, 2.70, 1.40; SF: 43.30.
Owner Australian Bloodstock & Clive Washbourn **Bred** Berend Van Dalfsen **Trained** Pulborough, W Sussex

FOCUS
The third has been rated to this year's best.

WOODBINE (L-H)

Sunday, July 28

OFFICIAL GOING: Turf: firm

5484a NIJINSKY STKS (GRADE 2) (3YO+) (TURF) 1m 4f (T)

9:51 3-Y-O+

£72,413 (£20,114; £11,063; £5,028; £2,614; £1,005)

RPR

1 **Tiz A Slam (CAN)**[36] 5-8-9 0.......................... StevenRonaldBahen 5 111
(Roger L Attfield, Canada) **21/20**[1]

2 4 1/4 **Sir Sahib (USA)**[36] 4-8-5 0.......................... LuisContreras 3 100
(Kevin Attard, Canada) **51/10**[2]

3 1 1/4 **Pumpkin Rumble (USA)**[28] 8-8-7 0.......................... EuricoRosaDaSilva 1 100
(Kevin Attard, Canada) **11/2**[3]

4 1 1/4 **Dark Templar (USA)**[24] 4-8-5 0.......................... Emma-JayneWilson 6 96
(Kelsey Danner, U.S.A) **174/10**

5 nk **Avie's Mesa (CAN)**[36] 5-8-5 0..........................(b) DJMoran 7 96
(Josie Carroll, Canada) **198/10**

6 nk **Arthur Kitt**[38] 4013 3-8-0 0.......................... RafaelManuelHernandez 2 102
(Tom Dascombe) *in tch in midfield on inner: drvn and effrt ins fnl 2f: run flattened out fnl f: n.d* **29/4**

7 2 **Bourbon Resolution (USA)**[42] 4-8-9 0.......................... ChrisLanderos 4 96
(Ian R Wilkes, U.S.A) **57/10**

2m 24.45s (-5.15)
WFA 3 from 4yo+ 11lb **7 Ran SP% 117.8**
.
Owner Chiefswood Stable **Bred** Chiefswood Stables Limited **Trained** Canada

[5234]AYR (L-H)

Monday, July 29

OFFICIAL GOING: Soft (good to soft in places; 7.0)

Wind: Light, half against in sprints and in over 3f of home straight in races on the round course Weather: Overcast

5485 JOIN RACING TV NOW EBF NOVICE STKS 5f 110y

2:00 (2:01) (Class 5) 2-Y-O **£3,428** (£1,020; £509; £254) **Stalls** Centre

Form RPR

2100 1 **Makyon (IRE)**[24] 4610 2-9-6 95.......................... JoeFanning 4 86
(Mark Johnston) *t.k.h early: trckd ldrs: led and shkn up 2f out: pushed clr fnl f: readily* **11/8**[1]

34 2 3 3/4 **Kilham**[45] 3810 2-9-2 0.......................... PaulHanagan 1 71
(Declan Carroll) *t.k.h: prom: effrt and chsd wnr over 1f out: no imp fnl f* **16/1**

3 1 1/2 **Solemn Pledge** 2-8-11 0.......................... BenCurtis 7 60+
(K R Burke) *pressed ldr: pushed along: edgd rt and outpcd over 1f out: kpt on same pce fnl f* **9/2**[3]

06 4 1/2 **Pearl Stream**[48] 3679 2-8-11 0.......................... PaulMulrennan 3 58
(Michael Dods) *chsd ldng gp: pushed along and outpcd over 2f out: rallied ins fnl f: r.o* **33/1**

2200 5 2 **Clay Regazzoni**[9] 5185 2-9-2 80.......................... DanielTudhope 6 57
(Keith Dalgleish) *led to 2f out: rdn and sn wknd* **13/8**[2]

6 6 **Garnock Valley** 2-8-11 0.......................... PaddyMathers 2 32
(R Mike Smith) *missed break: bhd and green: struggling 1/2-way: nvr on terms* **150/1**

7 4 1/2 **Summer Heights** 2-8-11 0 ... CamHardie 5 17
(Jim Goldie) *missed break: rn green in rr: nvr on terms (jockey said filly ran green)* **100/1**

1m 7.96s (1.46) **Going Correction** +0.30s/f (Good) **7 Ran SP% 108.9**
Speed ratings (Par 94): **102,97,95,94,91 83,77**
CSF £20.90 TOTE £1.90: £1.10, £5.40; EX 15.80 Trifecta £44.90.

Owner The Makyowners **Bred** Ballylinch Stud **Trained** Middleham Moor, N Yorks

FOCUS
The ground had eased slightly to soft, good to soft in places (from good to soft, soft in places). GoingStick: 7.0. The home bend was out 7yds and the stable bend out 2yds, with the stands' rail out 4yds and the far rail on its innermost line. An uncompetitive novice, featuring a couple back down in class after tackling much stronger company. They raced up the centre and the winning time was 4.46sec outside standard, confirming the ground had plenty of cut in it. The fourth looks the key to the form.

5486 WATCH ON RACING TV H'CAP — 6f
2:30 (2:31) (Class 6) (0-65,64) 3-Y-0+

£2,781 (£827; £413; £300; £300; £300) **Stalls Centre**

Form — RPR

3235 **1** **Forever A Lady (IRE)**[7] 5238 6-9-7 **59** ... CYHo 10 65
(Keith Dalgleish) *midfield: hdwy against stands' rail to ld over 1f out: edgd lft ins fnl f: hld on wl cl home* **5/1**[3]

3004 **2** nk **Cardaw Lily (IRE)**[7] 5237 4-8-7 **45** ... JamesSullivan 3 50
(Ruth Carr) *cl up: effrt and ev ch over 1f out to ins fnl f: kpt on: hld nr fin* **9/2**[2]

0040 **3** 1/2 **Jessie Allan (IRE)**[6] 5278 8-8-2 **47** ... CoreyMadden(7) 1 51
(Jim Goldie) *dwlt: racd wd of main gp: stdy hdwy over 2f out: effrt and ch ins fnl f: kpt on: hld cl home* **10/1**

0005 **4** 3/4 **Star Cracker (IRE)**[7] 5235 7-8-7 **45** ... (p) PhilDennis 6 46
(Jim Goldie) *in tch: drvn along over 2f out: rallied over 1f out: r.o ins fnl f* **12/1**

0305 **5** 1 1/2 **House Deposit**[4] 5335 3-9-7 **64** ... BenCurtis 4 60
(Roger Fell) *racd wd in midfield: effrt over 2f out: kpt on fnl f: nt pce to chal* **11/4**[1]

0-00 **6** 1/2 **Arogo**[36] 4149 3-9-3 **60** ... TomEaves 8 54
(Kevin Ryan) *led to over 1f out: rdn and wknd ins fnl f (jockey said gelding hung right)* **12/1**

0040 **7** 3/4 **Jacksonfire**[27] 4481 7-8-7 **45** ... (p) NathanEvans 2 38
(Michael Mullineaux) *racd wd of main gp: prom: effrt over 2f out: wknd fnl f* **20/1**

-650 **8** hd **Milabella**[21] 4726 3-7-12 **46** ow1 ... PaulaMuir(5) 9 38
(R Mike Smith) *dwlt: bhd: drvn along over 2f out: n.d after* **50/1**

040- **9** 1 3/4 **Sienna Dream**[265] 8902 4-8-12 **50** ... GrahamLee 5 37
(Alistair Whillans) *hld up: rdn over 2f out: wknd over 1f out* **18/1**

0060 **10** 6 **Palavicini Run (IRE)**[7] 5237 6-8-7 **45** ... CamHardie 7 14
(Linda Perratt) *dwlt: bhd: struggling over 2f out: sn btn (jockey said mare stopped quickly)* **40/1**

436- **11** 2 **It's Never Enough**[123] 7448 5-9-9 **61** ... (t) JackGarritty 11 24
(James Ewart) *prom: rdn and outpcd over 2f out: wknd over 1f out (jockey said gelding hung right)* **9/1**

0400 **12** nk **Indiaro**[7] 5235 3-8-11 **57** ... BenRobinson(3) 12 18
(Linda Perratt) *bhd: drvn and struggling over 2f out: sn btn (jockey said gelding hung right)* **20/1**

1m 14.96s (1.86) **Going Correction** +0.30s/f (Good) **12 Ran SP% 115.2**
WFA 3 from 4yo+ 5lb
Speed ratings (Par 101): **99,98,97,96,94 94,93,93,90,82 80,79**
CSF £25.64 CT £218.83 TOTE £6.50: £1.90, £2.00, £3.10; EX 32.70 Trifecta £232.20.

Owner Ken McGarrity **Bred** Mick McGinn **Trained** Carluke, S Lanarks

FOCUS
A moderate sprint handicap with several of these hard to win with. The main action unfolded closer to the nearside rail. The form is limited, but straightforward rated around the principals.

5487 WEDDINGS AT WESTERN HOUSE HOTEL H'CAP — 2m 1f 105y
3:00 (3:00) (Class 4) (0-80,82) 3-Y-0+

£6,727 (£2,002; £1,000; £500; £300; £300) **Stalls Low**

Form — RPR

0-41 **1** **Land Of Oz**[19] 4803 3-8-7 **64** ... LukeMorris 9 76+
(Sir Mark Prescott Bt) *plld hrd early: prom: effrt on outside over 2f out: hung lft and led over 1f out: sn rdn clr: eased towards fin* **4/5**[1]

3042 **2** 2 1/4 **Hugoigo**[7] 5241 5-8-2 **51** oh4 ... (p) CoreyMadden(7) 1 57
(Jim Goldie) *hld up on ins: hdwy over 2f out: angled rt and chsd (clr) wnr appr fnl f: nt pce to chal* **10/1**

45/0 **3** 4 **Wynford (IRE)**[52] 3294 6-9-7 **70** ... (w) VictorSantos(7) 5 72
(Lucinda Egerton) *led 5f: cl up: regained ld over 2f out to over 1f out: outpcd fnl f* **100/1**

0305 **4** 6 **Attention Seaker**[43] 3886 9-9-11 **67** ... (t) DavidAllan 8 62
(Tim Easterby) *pressed ldr: rdn and outpcd over 2f out: no imp fr over 1f out* **10/1**

4504 **5** 1 3/4 **Question Of Faith**[7] 5241 8-9-10 **66** ... PaulHanagan 3 59
(Martin Todhunter) *slowly away: hld up: pushed along over 3f out: no imp fr over 2f out* **18/1**

00-2 **6** 1 1/2 **Forewarning**[36] 4146 5-9-11 **67** ... GrahamLee 2 58
(Julia Brooke) *missed break: hld up: niggled along 1/2-way: effrt over 3f out: wknd fr 2f out* **5/1**[2]

5530 **7** 11 **Buyer Beware (IRE)**[18] 4825 7-9-7 **63** ... (p) DanielTudhope 4 42
(Liam Bailey) *prom: drvn and outpcd over 3f out: struggling fnl 2f* **12/1**

5152 **8** 8 **Lord Lamington**[19] 4782 3-9-11 **82** ... JoeFanning 7 56
(Mark Johnston) *cl up: led after 5f to over 2f out: sn wknd: lost hind shoe (vet said gelding had lost its right hind shoe)* **13/2**[3]

4m 1.11s (-0.39) **Going Correction** +0.30s/f (Good) **8 Ran SP% 117.7**
WFA 3 from 5yo+ 15lb
Speed ratings (Par 105): **107,105,104,101,100 99,94,90**
CSF £10.75 CT £475.20 TOTE £1.50: £1.10, £2.30, £19.40; EX 10.40 Trifecta £388.60.

Owner John Brown & Megan Dennis **Bred** Stetchworth & Middle Park Studs Ltd **Trained** Newmarket, Suffolk

FOCUS
Actual race distance 2m1f 138y. A fair staying handicap and they went a sensible pace in the conditions, but still finished well spread out. They came up the centre on reaching the straight. The winner is progressive.

5488 EVERY RACE LIVE ON RACING TV H'CAP — 7f 50y
3:30 (3:30) (Class 4) (0-85,87) 3-Y-0+

£5,207 (£1,549; £774; £387; £300; £300) **Stalls High**

Form — RPR

0000 **1** **Start Time (IRE)**[17] 4879 6-9-0 **70** ... KevinStott 9 79
(Paul Midgley) *mde all: qcknd clr over 1f out: hld on wl fnl f (trainer said regarding apparent improvement in form that the gelding may have appreciated being able to dominate on this occasion)* **15/2**

0005 **2** 3/4 **Presidential (IRE)**[9] 5173 5-10-0 **84** ... BenCurtis 7 91+
(Roger Fell) *slowly away: hld up: effrt on outside 2f out: chsd (clr) wnr ins fnl f: kpt on fin (jockey said gelding jumped awkwardly and was slowly away)* **4/1**[2]

1-25 **3** 1/2 **Boston George (IRE)**[14] 4981 3-9-10 **87** ... PaulHanagan 8 90
(Keith Dalgleish) *hld up: hdwy on outside to chse (clr) wnr over 1f out to ins fnl f: kpt on same pce* **15/2**

2004 **4** 1 1/2 **Knowing Glance (IRE)**[30] 4365 4-8-10 **69** ... SeanDavis(3) 1 71
(Richard Fahey) *hld up in midfield: effrt over 2f out: hung lft: kpt on fnl f: nt pce to chal* **14/1**

5006 **5** 3/4 **Al Erayg (IRE)**[7] 5246 6-9-7 **77** ... DavidAllan 2 77
(Tim Easterby) *hld up: pushed along and outpcd over 2f out: rallied and nt clr run briefly over 1f out: kpt on fnl f: nvr able to chal* **11/4**[1]

4642 **6** 1 **Zylan (IRE)**[42] 3930 7-8-11 **72** ... (p) BenSanderson(5) 5 69
(Roger Fell) *t.k.h: trckd ldrs: drvn and outpcd over 1f out: btn fnl f* **16/1**

5424 **7** 3/4 **Logi (IRE)**[17] 4879 5-8-11 **67** ... (b) JamieGormley 6 62
(Rebecca Bastiman) *hld up in tch on outside: rdn and outpcd over 2f out: n.d after* **9/1**

0606 **8** 3/4 **Aeolus**[10] 5120 8-10-3 **87** ... (p) JamesSullivan 3 80
(Ruth Carr) *t.k.h: prom: rdn over 2f out: wknd over 1f out* **20/1**

6214 **9** 1 1/2 **Luzum (IRE)**[31] 4320 4-8-13 **69** ... NathanEvans 4 58
(Michael Easterby) *chsd wnr: drvn over 2f out: wknd fr over 1f out* **5/1**[3]

1m 33.66s (1.16) **Going Correction** +0.30s/f (Good)
WFA 3 from 4yo+ 7lb **9 Ran SP% 114.2**
Speed ratings (Par 105): **105,104,103,101,101 99,99,98,96**
CSF £37.13 CT £199.81 TOTE £9.00: £3.40, £1.60, £2.10; EX 40.50 Trifecta £225.70.

Owner The Howarting's Partnership **Bred** Darley **Trained** Westow, N Yorks

FOCUS
Actual race distance 7f 71y. Another fair handicap and a well-judged front-running ride on the winner, who had dropped to a good mark. They stuck to the inside rail this time.

5489 AYRSHIRE CANCER SUPPORT H'CAP — 1m 2f
4:00 (4:01) (Class 3) (0-95,95) 3-Y-0+ **£9,380** (£2,791; £1,394; £697) **Stalls Low**

Form — RPR

2121 **1** **Nicholas T**[7] 5240 7-9-9 **93** 4ex ... BenRobinson(3) 6 100
(Jim Goldie) *hld up in midfield on ins: effrt and pushed along over 2f out: angled rt over 1f out: sustained run fnl f to ld towards fin* **11/1**

0451 **2** nk **Cockalorum (IRE)**[9] 5198 4-9-4 **85** ... BenCurtis 1 91
(Roger Fell) *chsd ldrs: drvn along over 2f out: kpt on wl fnl f to take 2nd towards fin: jst hld* **6/1**[3]

6505 **3** 3/4 **Hortzadar**[17] 4863 4-9-10 **91** ... DanielTudhope 3 96
(David O'Meara) *led 1f: cl up: regained ld over 2f out: rdn fnl f: hdd and no ex towards fin* **12/1**

-354 **4** 3/4 **Glasses Up (USA)**[7] 5240 4-9-0 **81** ... PaddyMathers 4 84
(R Mike Smith) *s.i.s: hld up: rdn over 2f out: hdwy and edgd lft over 1f out: kpt on fnl f: nvr able to chal* **18/1**

6011 **5** 1 **Jackamundo (FR)**[52] 3548 3-8-5 **81** ... PaulHanagan 5 83
(Declan Carroll) *trckd ldrs: drvn along over 2f out: kpt on same pce fnl f* **9/4**[1]

0305 **6** hd **Rashdan (FR)**[30] 4383 4-8-9 **76** oh3 ... JamieGormley 2 77
(Iain Jardine) *hld up: rdn over 2f out: kpt on fnl f: nvr able to chal* **50/1**

2352 **7** 1 **Ayutthaya (IRE)**[10] 5149 4-9-6 **87** ... TomEaves 8 86
(Kevin Ryan) *led after 1f: rdn and hdd over 2f out: wknd over 1f out* **17/2**

3401 **8** 4 **Borodin (IRE)**[39] 4035 4-9-11 **95** ... (p) SeanDavis(3) 7 86
(Richard Fahey) *t.k.h: sn stdd in tch: rdn and edgd lft over 2f out: wknd over 1f out* **7/1**

516- **9** nk **Shoot For Gold**[275] 8663 3-9-4 **94** ... KevinStott 9 85
(Saeed bin Suroor) *s.i.s: hld up: rdn on outside over 2f out: wknd wl over 1f out (trainer could offer no explanation for the colt's performance)* **7/2**[2]

2m 14.99s (2.59) **Going Correction** +0.30s/f (Good)
WFA 3 from 4yo+ 9lb **9 Ran SP% 113.6**
Speed ratings (Par 107): **101,100,100,99,98 98,97,94,94**
CSF £74.05 CT £807.58 TOTE £11.20: £2.70, £2.40, £2.40; EX 65.70 Trifecta £515.50.

Owner James Callow & J S Goldie **Bred** W M Johnstone **Trained** Uplawmoor, E Renfrews

FOCUS
Actual race distance 1m2f 21y. The feature race of the day, but they didn't go a great pace until just before halfway. All bar one were taken away from the inside rail in the straight. The first two have been rated as better than ever, with the third and fourth helping to set the standard.

5490 GET DAILY TIPS AT RACINGTV.COM H'CAP — 1m
4:30 (4:31) (Class 5) (0-75,75) 3-Y-0+

£3,428 (£1,020; £509; £300; £300; £300) **Stalls Low**

Form — RPR

3022 **1** **Strong Steps**[10] 5117 7-9-7 **68** ... (p) CliffordLee 13 75
(Jim Goldie) *cl up in chsng gp: hdwy to ld over 1f out: rdn and r.o wl fnl f* **9/1**

1533 **2** nk **Chinese Spirit (IRE)**[7] 5239 5-9-1 **65** ... BenRobinson(3) 4 71
(Linda Perratt) *in tch: effrt over 2f out: ev ch over 1f out to ins fnl f: kpt on: hld cl home (jockey said gelding hung right)* **7/2**[1]

3545 **3** nse **Equidae**[10] 5117 4-9-4 **65** ... (t) JoeFanning 1 71
(Iain Jardine) *t.k.h: chsd clr ldr: effrt and ev ch over 1f out: kpt on fnl f: hld towards fin* **8/1**

-000 **4** 2 1/4 **Theodorico (IRE)**[49] 3649 6-9-7 **75** ... VictorSantos(7) 9 76
(Lucinda Egerton) *led and sn clr: rdn over 2f out: hdd over 1f out: wknd ins fnl f* **50/1**

6000 **5** 1 **Royal Shaheen (FR)**[42] 3922 6-9-7 **68** ... (v) GrahamLee 12 67
(Alistair Whillans) *hld up in midfield: pushed along over 2f out: kpt on fr over 1f out: no imp* **12/1**

4003 **6** 1 **Vive La Difference (IRE)**[9] 5200 5-9-12 **73** ... DavidAllan 14 69
(Tim Easterby) *s.i.s: hld up: rdn over 2f out: kpt on fnl f: nvr rchd ldrs* **9/2**[2]

4630 **7** ½ **Najashee (IRE)**[17] 4892 5-9-3 **69** BenSanderson(5) 8 64
(Roger Fell) *s.i.s: hld up: rdn over 2f out: sme late hdwy: nvr a factor: lost hind shoe (vet said gelding lost its right hind shoe)* **10/1**

0-65 **8** 1½ **Mustaqbal (IRE)**[31] 4322 7-9-12 **73** PaulMulrennan 10 65
(Michael Dods) *t.k.h: in tch: rdn over 2f out: wknd over 1f out* **13/2**[3]

4310 **9** *hd* **Pudding Chare (IRE)**[14] 4982 5-9-1 **65** (t) SeanDavis(3) 5 56
(R Mike Smith) *t.k.h early: in tch: drvn and outpcd over 2f out: btn over 1f out* **20/1**

2010 **10** 1 **Zodiakos (IRE)**[38] 4067 6-9-11 **72** (p) BenCurtis 7 61
(Roger Fell) *s.i.s: sn pushed along in rr: struggling over 2f out: sn btn* **7/1**

0000 **11** 18 **My Amigo**[17] 4875 6-9-9 **70** (p) LukeMorris 11 18
(Marjorie Fife) *s.i.s: hld up: drvn and hung lft over 2f out: sn wknd: lost tch and eased fnl f* **28/1**

1m 45.55s (2.75) **Going Correction** +0.30s/f (Good) **11 Ran SP% 114.3**
Speed ratings (Par 103): **98,97,97,95,94 93,92,91,91,90 72**
CSF £38.58 CT £269.45 TOTE £7.60: £2.70, £1.20, £3.10; EX 24.30 Trifecta £293.50.
Owner Mrs M Craig & G Adams **Bred** Exors Of The Late J Ellis **Trained** Uplawmoor, E Renfrews
■ Stewards' Enquiry : Clifford Lee four-day ban; misuse of whip (Aug 12-15)

FOCUS
Actual race distance 1m 21y. An ordinary handicap featuring the last two winners of the race. It favoured those racing handily with the first four holding those positions throughout, albeit not in the order they finished.

5491 BOOK FOR SCOTTISH SUN LADIES NIGHT H'CAP 5f
5:05 (5:07) (Class 6) (0-55,57) 3-Y-O+
£2,781 (£827; £413; £300; £300; £300) **Stalls** Centre

Form RPR

R423 **1** **Piazon**[6] 5276 8-9-9 **57** (be) NathanEvans 6 64
(Julia Brooke) *mde all: rdn and clr over 1f out: kpt on wl fnl f* **7/2**[2]

6000 **2** 1¾ **One Boy (IRE)**[13] 5018 8-9-1 **49** KevinStott 5 50
(Paul Midgley) *hld up in tch: effrt and rdn over 1f out: chsd wnr ins fnl f: kpt on: nt pce to chal* **6/1**[3]

3042 **3** *nk* **Jacob's Pillow**[7] 5235 8-9-7 **55** (p) DanielTudhope 9 55
(Rebecca Bastiman) *chsd wnr: rdn 2f out: lost 2nd ins fnl f: one pce* **13/8**[1]

6630 **4** ¾ **Jeffrey Harris**[6] 5276 4-9-6 **54** CamHardie 2 51
(Jim Goldie) *hld up in tch: effrt and pushed along 2f out: no imp fnl f* **6/1**[3]

5025 **5** ¾ **Popping Corks (IRE)**[7] 5236 3-8-12 **53** (p) BenRobinson(3) 3 46
(Linda Perratt) *bhd: pushed along over 2f out: hdwy over 1f out: kpt on: nvr able to chal* **7/1**

0000 **6** 1½ **Corton Lass**[27] 4493 4-8-12 **46** oh1 JoeFanning 11 35
(Keith Dalgleish) *hld up: rdn and effrt over 2f out: no imp fr over 1f out* **25/1**

0000 **7** 1¾ **Brendan (IRE)**[7] 5235 6-8-12 **46** PaddyMathers 4 29
(Jim Goldie) *dwlt: t.k.h in rr: pushed along 2f out: sn n.d* **12/1**

0-40 **8** *nse* **Raise A Billion**[22] 4694 8-8-12 **46** oh1 GrahamLee 10 28
(Alan Berry) *bhd: rdn along 1/2-way: nvr able to chal* **66/1**

0005 **9** 2½ **Lady Joanna Vassa (IRE)**[24] 4685 6-8-12 **46** oh1 (v) PhilipPrince 1 19
(Richard Guest) *in tch: rdn over 1f out: wknd fnl f* **25/1**

-000 **10** 2½ **Minty Jones**[47] 3723 10-8-12 **46** oh1 (v) TomEaves 8 10
(Michael Mullineaux) *prom tl rdn and wknd qckly fnl f* **66/1**

-000 **11** 2¼ **Zizum**[22] 4694 4-8-9 **46** oh1 (b) ConnorMurtagh(3) 12 2
(Alan Berry) *dwlt: bhd and outpcd: no ch fr 1/2-way* **100/1**

1m 1.2s (1.20) **Going Correction** +0.30s/f (Good)
WFA 3 from 4yo+ 4lb **11 Ran SP% 120.7**
Speed ratings (Par 101): **102,99,98,97,96 93,91,91,87,83 79**
CSF £24.73 CT £47.07 TOTE £3.90: £1.80, £2.20, £1.10; EX 25.60 Trifecta £56.00.
Owner The Body Warmers **Bred** Peter Baldwin **Trained** Middleham, N Yorks

FOCUS
A moderate sprint handicap to end with nearly half the field effectively out of the weights. Those at the top of the handicap dominated. Straightforward, limited form.
T/Plt: £95.50 to a £1 stake. Pool: £73,653.17 - 562.21 winning units T/Qpdt: £28.40 to a £1 stake. Pool: £8,106.20 - 210.93 winning units **Richard Young**

FFOS LAS (L-H)
Monday, July 29
OFFICIAL GOING: Good to firm (watered; 8.5)
Wind: Light across Weather: Overcast with showers

5492 UNIVERSAL HARDWARE SUPPLIES MAIDEN H'CAP 5f
5:10 (5:10) (Class 5) (0-75,72) 3-Y-O+ **£3,428** (£1,020; £509; £300) **Stalls** High

Form RPR

646 **1** **Perfect Charm**[27] 4489 3-8-9 **60** (b1) OisinMurphy 1 68+
(Archie Watson) *mde all: rdn over 1f out: r.o* **7/2**[3]

-322 **2** 1½ **Delachance (FR)**[27] 4489 3-9-7 **72** StevieDonohoe 4 74
(David Simcock) *chsd ldng pair: wnt 2nd wl over 1f out: sn drvn: r.o ins fnl f: a being hld* **1/1**[1]

3 3¾ **Jarrocho (IRE)**[22] 4696 3-8-6 **57** KieranO'Neill 2 46
(David Marnane, Ire) *dwlt: in rr: rdn 2f out: wnt 3rd early ins fnl f: no threat to ldrs* **7/4**[2]

4-06 **4** 1¼ **Layla's Dream**[19] 4772 3-8-5 **56** MartinDwyer 3 40
(Tony Carroll) *plld hrd: trckd wnr: drvn 2f out: sn lost 2nd: wknd fnl f* **12/1**

56.8s (-2.20) **Going Correction** -0.375s/f (Firm) **4 Ran SP% 116.3**
Speed ratings (Par 103): **102,99,93,91**
CSF £8.13 TOTE £3.70; EX 8.10 Trifecta £12.80.
Owner Mildmay Racing & D H Caslon **Bred** Theakston Stud **Trained** Upper Lambourn, W Berks

FOCUS
A weak maiden handicap, with the two market leaders turned over.

5493 DOOR DECOR & MORE NOVICE STKS (PLUS 10 RACE) 7f 80y(R)
5:45 (5:47) (Class 4) 2-Y-O **£4,463** (£1,328; £663; £331) **Stalls** Low

Form RPR

5 **1** **Berlin Tango**[16] 4925 2-9-5 0 OisinMurphy 4 80+
(Andrew Balding) *mde all: shkn up over 1f out: r.o strly fnl f* **1/1**[1]

4 **2** 4½ **Itkaann (IRE)**[32] 4282 2-9-5 0 DaneO'Neill 3 69+
(Owen Burrows) *a.p: wnt clr 2nd over 1f out: kpt on: outpcd by wnr fnl f* **5/2**[2]

3 2¾ **Arabian Moon** 2-9-5 0 RobHornby 2 62
(Ralph Beckett) *t.k.h early: prom: disp 2nd 4f out tl edgd lft u.p over 1f out: no ex fnl f* **5/1**[3]

0 **4** ¾ **Clandestine Affair (IRE)**[10] 5131 2-9-5 0 DougieCostello 1 60+
(Jamie Osborne) *t.k.h early: chsd ldrs: rdn over 1f out: sn outpcd* **33/1**

0 **5** ½ **Son Of Prancealot (IRE)**[63] 3165 2-9-5 0 (t1) RossaRyan 5 59
(David Evans) *a similarly plcd: rdn over 2f out: kpt on same pce* **25/1**

0 **6** 3½ **Inflamed**[16] 4925 2-9-5 0 StevieDonohoe 6 51
(Ed Walker) *a similarly plcd: rdn 2f out: no imp* **8/1**

7 ¾ **Kings Creek (IRE)** 2-9-5 0 TomMarquand 7 49
(Alan King) *a in last pair: rdn 3f out: no imp* **9/1**

8 6 **Puzzlebook** 2-9-0 0 JFEgan 8 29
(David Evans) *s.i.s: a in rr: rdn over 2f out: wknd over 1f out* **20/1**

1m 31.69s (-1.41) **Going Correction** -0.375s/f (Firm) **8 Ran SP% 127.9**
Speed ratings (Par 96): **93,87,84,83,83 79,78,71**
CSF £4.24 TOTE £2.20: £1.10, £1.10, £1.90; EX 4.50 Trifecta £12.70.
Owner George Strawbridge **Bred** George Strawbridge **Trained** Kingsclere, Hants

FOCUS
One-way traffic in this novice, with the market leaders dominating, headed by the impressive favourite.

5494 EUROPEAN BREEDERS FUND MAIDEN STKS 7f 80y(R)
6:15 (6:20) (Class 5) 3-Y-O+ **£4,204** (£1,251; £625; £312) **Stalls** Low

Form RPR

1 **Jered Maddox**[13] 5033 3-9-2 62 DonaghO'Connor(3) 4 70
(David Marnane, Ire) *hld up: rdn over 2f out: hdwy to chse ldrs over 1f out: led on outer fnl 150yds: pushed out* **7/2**[3]

6 **2** ¾ **Midas Girl (FR)**[24] 4592 3-9-0 0 OisinMurphy 7 63
(Ed Walker) *s.i.s: hld up: hdwy over 3f out: rdn over 2f out: ev ch ins fnl f: unable qck towards fin* **10/1**

-455 **3** ½ **My Style (IRE)**[35] 4196 3-9-5 75 CharlesBishop 5 67
(Eve Johnson Houghton) *a.p: rdn to chal 2f out: ev ch tl unable qck fnl 150yds* **3/1**[2]

-032 **4** ¾ **Desert Land (IRE)**[23] 4655 3-9-5 75 StevieDonohoe 6 65
(David Simcock) *chsd ldr tl led 3f out: drvn and pressed 2f out: hdd fnl 150yds: no ex* **1/1**[1]

5 2¾ **Young General (IRE)** 3-9-5 0 TomMarquand 2 58
(Richard Hannon) *chsd ldrs: rdn 3f out: outpcd over 1f out: styd on ins fnl f* **7/1**

5 **6** 13 **Peggotty**[29] 4421 3-9-0 0 DaneO'Neill 1 19
(Tony Carroll) *t.k.h: hld up: drvn 2f out: wknd over 1f out* **50/1**

00 **7** 2 **Jazzameer**[89] 2280 4-9-2 0 RachealKneller(5) 3 17
(Matthew Salaman) *led to 3f out: sn drvn: wknd 2f out: hung lft over 1f out (jockey said filly stopped quickly)* **100/1**

1m 29.82s (-3.28) **Going Correction** -0.375s/f (Firm)
WFA 3 from 4yo 7lb **7 Ran SP% 121.8**
Speed ratings (Par 103): **103,102,101,100,97 82,80**
CSF £40.06 TOTE £4.80: £2.20, £4.70; EX 45.50 Trifecta £151.70.
Owner City Equine II Syndicate **Bred** Times Of Wigan Ltd **Trained** Bansha, Co Tipperary

FOCUS
Modest maiden form, they stayed clear of the far rail in the straight. They didn't appear to go that fast early, yet the pace didn't hold up. The winner rates an improver on recent turf form.

5495 UNIVERSAL HARDWARE SUPPLIES H'CAP 6f
6:50 (6:54) (Class 5) (0-75,76) 3-Y-O+
£3,428 (£1,020; £509; £300; £300; £300) **Stalls** High

Form RPR

3150 **1** **Handytalk (IRE)**[25] 4545 6-10-2 **76** (v1) OisinMurphy 4 84
(Rod Millman) *led: rdn over 1f out: narrowly hdd ent fnl f: rallied to ld again fnl 100yds* **5/2**[2]

-1 **2** ¾ **Nigg Bay (IRE)**[21] 4721 5-9-9 **72** (v) DonaghO'Connor(3) 5 78
(J F Levins, Ire) *trckd ldng pair: wnt 2nd over 4f out: rdn 2f out: led narrowly ent fnl f: sn edgd lft: hdd fnl 100yds* **2/1**[1]

3004 **3** 1¼ **Smokey Lane (IRE)**[16] 4926 5-9-10 **70** (v1) JFEgan 7 72
(David Evans) *chsd wnr over 1f: remained handy: drvn 2f out: swtchd lft over 1f out: kpt on ins fnl f* **4/1**[3]

3061 **4** 2 **Secondo (FR)**[11] 5083 9-9-3 **63** (v) TomMarquand 1 59
(Robert Stephens) *chsd ldrs: drvn 2f out: wknd fnl f* **9/2**

0425 **5** 1¼ **Blaine**[26] 4495 9-10-2 **76** TrevorWhelan 6 68
(Brian Barr) *awkward s: a in last pair: rdn 2f out: no imp* **9/1**

5503 **6** 2½ **Englishman**[12] 5050 9-8-9 **62** WilliamCarver(7) 2 46
(Milton Bradley) *a in last pair: rdn and hung lft 2f out: wknd fnl f* **8/1**

1m 7.46s (-3.44) **Going Correction** -0.375s/f (Firm) course record **6 Ran SP% 121.2**
Speed ratings (Par 103): **107,106,104,101,100 96**
CSF £8.80 TOTE £4.00: £2.40, £1.40; EX 9.90 Trifecta £36.40.
Owner Cantay Racing **Bred** Edmond Kinane & Donal Sweeney **Trained** Kentisbeare, Devon

FOCUS
They raced stands' side in this ordinary sprint, and the winner made nearly all the running.

5496 DOOR DECOR & MORE H'CAP 2m (R)
7:25 (7:25) (Class 4) (0-85,87) 4-Y-O+ **£5,207** (£1,549; £774; £387) **Stalls** Low

Form RPR

10-0 **1** **Toshima (IRE)**[11] 4614 4-9-7 **80** (t1) OisinMurphy 1 86
(Robert Stephens) *hld up in cl 3rd: rdn 4f out and sn dropped to last: wnt 3rd again over 1f out: styd on wl to ld fnl 110yds* **11/4**[3]

0055 **2** 1 **Arty Campbell (IRE)**[12] 5047 9-8-8 **67** (b1) JFEgan 3 72
(Bernard Llewellyn) *hld up in cl 4th: impr a pl over 3f out: drvn to ld over 2f out: edgd lft ins fnl f: hdd and one pce fnl 110yds* **6/1**

3060 **3** 2¼ **Jukebox Jive (FR)**[9] 5183 5-10-0 **87** (t) DougieCostello 2 89
(Jamie Osborne) *led 1f: trckd ldr: rdn over 2f out: sn ev ch: carried lft and lost 2nd ins fnl f: no ex* **5/4**[1]

/15- **4** 8 **Dell' Arca (IRE)**[86] 6525 10-9-7 **80** (b w) TomMarquand 5 73
(David Pipe) *cl up tl led after 1f: rdn and hdd over 2f out: wknd wl over 1f out* **5/2**[2]

3m 28.05s (-8.65) **Going Correction** -0.375s/f (Firm) **4 Ran SP% 114.0**
Speed ratings (Par 105): **106,105,104,100**
CSF £17.14 TOTE £3.80; EX 14.50 Trifecta £29.50.
Owner Threes Company **Bred** New England Stud, Myriad & Lord Derby **Trained** Penhow, Newport

FOCUS
Ordinary staying form, they headed centre-field in the straight. The winner has been rated back to the level of his standout Newcastle win for his previous trainer.

5497 BLACK DRAGON HARDWARE H'CAP 1m 2f (R)
8:00 (8:00) (Class 6) (0-65,66) 3-Y-O+
£2,781 (£827; £413; £300; £300; £300) **Stalls** Low

Form RPR

-054 **1** **Renardeau**[35] 4176 3-9-8 **66** (p w) TomMarquand 6 73
(Ali Stronge) *reluctant to leave paddock: hld up in midfield: rdn and nt clr run over 2f out: hdwy over 1f out: r.o to ld fnl 110yds: drvn out* **8/1**

The Form Book Flat 2019, Raceform Ltd, Newbury, RG14 5SJ

014U **2** ½ **Twpsyn (IRE)**[7] 5249 3-9-1 **59**.....................(b) JFEgan 4 65
(David Evans) *chsd ldrs: rdn over 2f out: led wl over 1f out tl hdd fnl 110yds: kpt on* **9/2**[3]

3332 **3** 2¼ **Queen's Soldier (GER)**[25] 4547 3-9-4 **62**..................... OisinMurphy 10 64
(Andrew Balding) *prom: led after 2f tl over 6f out: trckd ldrs tl rdn to ld again 2f out: sn hdd: styd on same pce* **11/8**[1]

6502 **4** 5 **Craneur**[16] 4931 3-9-7 **65**..................... CharlesBishop 3 57
(Harry Dunlop) *cl up: led over 6f out tl drvn and hdd 2f out: wknd fnl f (vet said gelding lost his right fore shoe)* **2/1**[2]

6306 **5** 1¼ **Espresso Freddo (IRE)**[27] 4479 5-9-12 **61**..................... DaneO'Neill 11 50
(Robert Stephens) *dropped in and hld up: hdwy over 2f out: rdn over 1f out: sn hld by ldrs* **12/1**

6630 **6** 1¼ **Tally's Son**[11] 5080 5-9-1 **50**.....................(b) RobHornby 2 37
(Grace Harris) *prom: rdn over 2f out: wknd over 1f out* **28/1**

1506 **7** 1¾ **Arrowzone**[104] 1836 8-9-5 **54**..................... StevieDonohoe 8 37
(Katy Price) *hld up: last and rdn 3f out: sn btn* **25/1**

056 **8** 6 **Mystical Jadeite**[35] 4179 3-9-0 **58**..................... RossaRyan 7 31
(Grace Harris) *hld up in tch: rdn over 2f out: wknd over 1f out* **33/1**

6-15 **9** 8 **Sea Of Marengo (IRE)**[83] 2517 3-8-13 **64**..................... KeelanBaker(7) 9 22
(Grace Harris) *t.k.h: led 2f: remained cl up: drvn 3f out: wknd 2f out (jockey said gelding hung both ways under pressure)* **16/1**

2m 5.38s (-7.32) **Going Correction** -0.375s/f (Firm)
WFA 3 from 5yo+ 9lb **9 Ran SP% 128.5**
Speed ratings (Par 101): **105,104,102,98,97 96,95,90,84**
CSF £48.15 CT £82.91 TOTE £6.80: £1.60, £1.40, £1.20; EX 55.10 Trifecta £176.40.
Owner Laurence Bellman **Bred** Litex Commerce **Trained** Eastbury, Berks

FOCUS
They avoided the rail once again and those challenging right down the centre came out on top. A minor pb from the winner.

5498 WALTERS GROUP H'CAP 7f 80y(R)
8:30 (8:32) (Class 6) (0-60,62) 3-Y-O+
£2,781 (£827; £413; £300; £300; £300) **Stalls** Low

Form RPR

1030 **1** **Incentive**[32] 4281 5-10-0 **62**.....................(p) RobHornby 4 68
(Stuart Kittow) *hld up in midfield: rdn 2f out: nt clr run and swtchd rt over 1f out: stl only 5th 1f out: r.o to ld fnl 75yds* **6/1**

000 **2** hd **Mabo**[35] 4181 4-9-2 **50**.....................(b) JFEgan 11 56
(Grace Harris) *s.i.s: sn chsng ldrs: rdn 2f out: edgd lft: bmpd and stmbld sltly jst over 1f out: ev ch ins fnl f: r.o* **33/1**

0006 **3** ½ **Cooperess**[17] 4870 6-8-12 **46** oh1..................... RossaRyan 8 50
(Adrian Wintle) *t.k.h: led 1f: remained prom: rdn 2f out: ev ch whn bmpd jst over 1f out: led briefly 100yds out: jst hld towards fin* **11/1**

4050 **4** ½ **Cuttin' Edge (IRE)**[112] 1655 5-9-10 **58**.....................(w) MartinDwyer 9 61
(William Muir) *cl up: led after 1f: drvn and hrd pressed 2f out: hdd 100yds out: no ex* **11/2**

-400 **5** ½ **Gold Flash**[17] 4873 7-7-7 **55**.....................(v) OisinMurphy 2 57
(Rod Millman) *hld up: nt clr run over 2f out: rdn wl over 1f out: sn edgd rt: r.o fnl f: nt rch ldrs* **9/2**[3]

6 1 **Tynamite (IRE)**[22] 4700 5-8-12 **46** oh1..................... KieranO'Neill 7 45
(David Marnane, Ire) *hld up: rdn over 2f out: carried sltly rt over 1f out: styd on: nvr able to threaten ldrs* **11/4**[1]

5432 **7** nk **Jaganory (IRE)**[11] 5083 7-9-6 **54**.....................(p) CallumShepherd 10 53
(Christopher Mason) *prom: drvn 2f out: ev ch whn n.m.r and bmpd appr fnl f: wknd fnl 100yds* **10/1**

2314 **8** shd **Hedging (IRE)**[20] 4753 5-10-0 **62**.....................(b) CharlesBishop 5 60
(Eve Johnson Houghton) *racd keenly: chsd ldrs: rdn over 2f out: grad wknd fnl f* **3/1**[2]

0-00 **9** 1 **Paco Dawn**[56] 3410 5-8-9 **46** oh1..................... MeganNicholls(3) 1 42
(Tony Carroll) *s.i.s: hld up: rdn over 2f out: no real imp* **50/1**

-540 **10** 1¼ **Boorowa**[35] 4180 3-8-13 **54**..................... TomMarquand 6 44
(Ali Stronge) *s.i.s: hld up in midfield: rdn 3f out: wknd over 1f out* **8/1**

1m 31.34s (-1.76) **Going Correction** -0.375s/f (Firm)
WFA 3 from 4yo+ 7lb **10 Ran SP% 133.0**
Speed ratings (Par 101): **95,94,94,93,93 91,91,91,90,88**
CSF £201.16 CT £2240.69 TOTE £8.40: £2.90, £12.90, £3.90; EX 439.30 Trifecta £1168.40.
Owner Stuart Kittow **Bred** The Hon Mrs R Pease **Trained** Blackborough, Devon

FOCUS
Moderate form, they stayed on the far rail initially in the straight but several drifted more centre-field and that's where the first two came from. The winner has been rated to her best.
T/Plt: £466.80 to a £1 stake. Pool: £50,268.24 - 78.60 winning units T/Qpdt: £72.60 to a £1 stake. Pool: £6,300.60 - 64.21 winning units **Richard Lowther**

5249 WINDSOR (R-H)
Monday, July 29

OFFICIAL GOING: Good (good to firm in places, 6.9) changing to good to firm after race 1 (5.00)
Wind: Almost nil Weather: Fine, warm

5499 MARATHONBET "BETTER ODDS MEAN BIGGER WINNINGS" H'CAP 1m 3f 99y
5:00 (5:03) (Class 6) (0-55,53) 4-Y-O+
£2,781 (£827; £413; £300; £300; £300) **Stalls** Low

Form RPR

0-32 **1** **It's How We Roll (IRE)**[14] 4991 5-8-10 **47**.....................(p) ScottMcCullagh(5) 2 57+
(John Spearing) *hld up wl in rr: smooth prog over 3f out: nt clr run wl over 2f out to over 1f out: clsd swiftly on ldr after: rdn to ld 100yds out: styd on* **6/1**[2]

0-63 **2** ¾ **Aria Rose**[32] 4308 4-9-2 **53**..................... CierenFallon(5) 13 60
(Harry Whittington) *a in ldng trio: led 3f out and sent for home over 2f out: drvn over 1f out: hdd and hld last 100yds: styd on* **1/1**[1]

0/00 **3** 4½ **Bird To Love**[26] 4503 5-9-4 **50**..................... DavidProbert 5 49
(Mark Usher) *trckd ldrs: impeded and stmbld 3f out: rdn and prog 3f out: chsd ldr 2f out to jst over 1f out: one pce* **40/1**

0500 **4** 2½ **Tobacco Road (IRE)**[24] 4615 9-9-3 **52**.....................(t) JoshuaBryan(3) 15 47
(Mark Pattinson) *hld up: swift prog to trck ldrs 7f out: rdn 3f out: one pce and outpcd fr 2f out (jockey said gelding was slowly into stride)* **9/1**

6-50 **5** 1¼ **Turnbury**[54] 3473 8-8-13 **45**.....................(p) NicolaCurrie 7 38
(Nikki Evans) *t.k.h: swift move fr midfield to join ldr 7f out: led 4f out to 3f out: wknd 2f out* **50/1**

1404 **6** 4 **Carvelas (IRE)**[14] 4991 10-8-11 **50**..................... TobyEley(7) 9 37
(J R Jenkins) *wl in tch: rdn and prog to chal 3f out: sn btn: wknd wl over 1f out* **12/1**

-135 **7** 3¼ **Hi There Silver (IRE)**[5] 5310 5-8-13 **45**..................... GeorgeWood 11 26
(Michael Madgwick) *hld up: rdn and sme prog 3f out: no hdwy on outer wl over 1f out: sn wknd* **16/1**

0000 **8** ½ **Roser Moter (IRE)**[13] 5029 4-9-2 **48**.....................(p) AlistairRawlinson 8 28
(Michael Appleby) *t.k.h: hld up in tch: rdn and no prog 3f out: wknd 2f out* **50/1**

0004 **9** 3½ **Windsorlot (IRE)**[23] 4658 6-9-2 **48**.....................(t) GeorgeDowning 6 23
(Tony Carroll) *a towards rr: rdn and no prog wl over 3f out* **20/1**

0010 **10** ½ **Shovel It On (IRE)**[24] 4594 4-9-4 **50**.....................(bt) RaulDaSilva 16 24
(Steve Flook) *trckd ldr to 7f out: rdn on outer 3f out: sn wknd* **16/1**

000 **11** 8 **Quiet Shy (FR)**[31] 4326 4-8-13 **45**..................... DavidEgan 10 6
(Michael Scudamore) *a wl in rr: no ch over 2f out* **12/1**

0500 **12** 20 **Doctor Wonderful**[14] 5001 4-9-7 **53**.....................(t[1]) PJMcDonald 12
(Kevin Frost) *s.i.s: nvr gng wl and a in rr: heavily eased whn no ch fnl f (jockey said gelding was never travelling; trainers' rep said the gelding did not face the application of a first time tongue tie)* **7/1**[3]

00 **13** 13 **Dragon Girl (IRE)**[23] 4657 4-9-6 **52**.....................(p) LiamKeniry 4
(Roy Brotherton) *led to 4f out: wknd qckly: sn t.o* **50/1**

2m 27.57s (-2.13) **Going Correction** -0.125s/f (Firm) **13 Ran SP% 127.0**
Speed ratings (Par 101): **102,101,98,96,95 92,90,89,87,86 81,66,57**
CSF £12.68 CT £242.24 TOTE £5.30: £1.80, £1.30, £9.80; EX 16.60 Trifecta £304.00.
Owner Kinnersley Partnership **Bred** Smythson **Trained** Kinnersley, Worcs

FOCUS
A bright, sunny evening. Following drying conditions throughout the day, with temperatures around 24C, the ground had firmed up. All distances as advertised. A modest handicap to start, and the pace was decent.

5500 VISIT MARATHONBET.CO.UK EBF MAIDEN STKS 5f 21y
5:35 (5:38) (Class 5) 2-Y-O
£3,428 (£1,020; £509; £254) **Stalls** Centre

Form RPR

6 **1** **Golden Dragon (IRE)**[25] 4564 2-9-5 **0**..................... JamesDoyle 3 79+
(Stuart Williams) *trckd ldr: led 2f out: shkn up and styd on wl fnl f: readily* **7/2**[2]

P6 **2** 1¼ **Love Powerful (IRE)**[9] 5170 2-9-0 **0**..................... SilvestreDeSousa 5 70
(Richard Hannon) *chsd ldng trio: prog on outer to chse wnr over 1f out: rdn and styd on but nvr able to chal* **4/1**[3]

0 **3** 3¼ **Colonel Whitehead (IRE)**[18] 4839 2-9-5 **0**..................... DavidEgan 8 63
(Heather Main) *off the pce in midfield: pushed along 1/2-way: styd on over 1f out to take 3rd last 100yds* **25/1**

425 **4** 2 **Swinley (IRE)**[42] 3943 2-9-5 **77**..................... ShaneKelly 4 56
(Richard Hughes) *chsd ldng pair and racd against rail: rdn and outpcd over 1f out: n.d after: lost 3rd last 100yds* **3/1**[1]

44 **5** 2½ **Royal Ambition (IRE)**[70] 2903 2-9-5 **0**..................... LiamKeniry 10 47+
(Clive Cox) *dwlt: racd in 7th and off the pce: nvr on terms but kpt on over 1f out (jockey said colt reared when leaving the stalls)* **6/1**

6 **6** 1¼ **Treaty Of Dingle**[66] 3039 2-9-0 **0**..................... CharlieBennett 1 37
(Hughie Morrison) *off the pce in midfield: shkn up 2f out: no prog* **9/1**

7 1½ **Bright Red (IRE)** 2-9-5 **0**..................... SeanLevey 7 37
(Richard Hannon) *dwlt: rn green in last trio and pushed along: nvr on terms* **14/1**

63 **8** 1¾ **Saras Hope**[32] 4302 2-9-5 **0**..................... PJMcDonald 2 30
(John Gallagher) *led to 2f out: wknd qckly over 1f out* **7/1**

60 **9** 4½ **Jungle Boogaloo (IRE)**[44] 3835 2-9-0 **0**..................... HollieDoyle 6 9
(Ali Stronge) *bolted to post then uns rdr: a in last trio: nvr a factor* **25/1**

10 10 **Pure Purfection (IRE)** 2-9-0 **0**..................... PatCosgrave 9
(Jim Boyle) *dwlt: a in last trio: t.o* **25/1**

59.8s (-0.30) **Going Correction** -0.125s/f (Firm) **10 Ran SP% 122.2**
Speed ratings (Par 94): **97,95,89,86,82 80,78,75,68,52**
CSF £18.53 TOTE £4.50: £1.80, £1.90, £7.50; EX 20.80 Trifecta £271.50.
Owner Happy Valley Racing & Breeding Limited **Bred** Ms Morna McDowall **Trained** Newmarket, Suffolk

FOCUS
A solid pace for a race that lacked depth. The level is fluid.

5501 DOWNLOAD THE MARATHONBET APP EBF NOVICE STKS (PLUS 10 RACE) 6f 12y
6:05 (6:05) (Class 4) 2-Y-O
£4,657 (£1,386; £692; £346) **Stalls** Centre

Form RPR

5333 **1** **Endowed**[16] 4938 2-9-5 **80**..................... SilvestreDeSousa 6 87+
(Richard Hannon) *led or disp thrght: shkn up to take def advantage over 2f out: wl in command over 1f out: pushed out* **11/10**[1]

3 **2** 2½ **Smokey Bear (IRE)**[21] 4734 2-9-5 **0**..................... AdamMcNamara 7 80
(Roger Charlton) *chsd ldng pair: rdn to take 2nd 2f out: kpt on after but nvr able to threaten wnr* **11/2**

6 **3** 1¼ **Powertrain (IRE)**[18] 4826 2-9-5 **0**..................... JamesDoyle 4 76
(Hugo Palmer) *in tch: rdn and prog to chse ldng pair over 1f out: kpt on same pce after* **7/2**[2]

5 **4** ¾ **Can't Stop Now (IRE)**[89] 2267 2-9-5 **0**..................... HectorCrouch 3 74+
(Clive Cox) *chsd ldrs in 5th: nvr gng pce to cl but kpt on fr over 1f out* **9/2**[3]

5 **5** 5 **Utopian Lad (IRE)**[81] 2561 2-9-5 **0**..................... FrannyNorton 9 59+
(Tom Dascombe) *dwlt and carried lft s: racd in last but gng wl enough: swtchd lft 2f out: styd on steadily after: signs of promise* **16/1**

6 3 **Owhatanight** 2-9-5 **0**..................... RobertHavlin 8 50
(Ed Dunlop) *wnt lft s: rn green in rr: nvr a factor: kpt on ins fnl f* **20/1**

00 **7** ¾ **Comvida (IRE)**[6] 5265 2-9-5 **0**.....................(p) PatCosgrave 1 47
(Hugo Palmer) *w wnr to over 2f out: sn wknd qckly* **50/1**

40 **8** 9 **Penny Diamond**[12] 5045 2-9-0 **0**.....................(b[1]) KieranShoemark 5 15
(Amanda Perrett) *a wl in rr: shkn up and no prog 2f out: wknd qckly* **50/1**

00 **9** 2 **Quarrystreetmagic (IRE)**[14] 4993 2-9-5 **0**..................... PJMcDonald 2 14
(Brian Meehan) *chsd ldrs over 3f: wknd qckly* **66/1**

1m 11.35s (-0.75) **Going Correction** -0.125s/f (Firm) **9 Ran SP% 119.5**
Speed ratings (Par 96): **100,96,95,94,87 83,82,70,67**
CSF £7.97 TOTE £2.00: £1.10, £1.50, £1.40; EX 7.20 Trifecta £24.40.
Owner Ben CM Wong **Bred** Aislabie Bloodstock Ltd **Trained** East Everleigh, Wilts

FOCUS
A fair novice with a few who looked in need of the experience, although some of these should be able to rate higher.

5502 MARATHONBET LIVE CASINO H'CAP — 1m 3f 99y
6:40 (6:41) (Class 4) (0-85,87) 3-Y-0+

£5,207 (£1,549; £774; £387; £300; £300) **Stalls** Low

Form					RPR
5-62	**1**		**Zoffee**[35] 4187 3-8-11 **77** ... SilvestreDeSousa 3 *(Tom Dascombe) t.k.h: trckd ldr: narrow ld 3f out: rdn to assert 2f out: styd on wl* **5/2**[2]		89
-043	**2**	1 ¾	**Oh It's Saucepot**[33] 4250 5-9-7 **77** ... JackMitchell 1 *(Chris Wall) trckd ldng trio: shkn up 3f out: kpt on to take 2nd fnl f: unable to chal* **7/1**		85
514	**3**	¾	**Gold Stick (IRE)**[60] 3263 3-9-7 **87** ... RobertHavlin 8 *(John Gosden) led: tried to stretch on over 3f out but sn hdd: pressed wnr to 2f out: nt qckn and wl hld after: lost 2nd fnl f* **11/4**[3]		94
321	**4**	2 ¼	**Mukha Magic**[7] 5249 3-8-1 **67** 6ex ... (v) HollieDoyle 2 *(Gay Kelleway) mostly in last pair and nvr gng that wl: urged along over 3f out: tk 4th over 1f out but nvr any threat* **6/4**[1]		69
2010	**5**	8	**Lost History (IRE)**[52] 3545 6-9-0 **73** ... JaneElliott(3) 6 *(John Spearing) t.k.h: trckd ldng pair tl wknd qckly 2f out* **25/1**		59
1-54	**6**	3 ¾	**Noble Behest**[10] 5135 5-9-2 **72** ... (p) PJMcDonald 7 *(Ian Williams) in tch in rr to over 3f out: sn bhd* **28/1**		51

2m 26.31s (-3.39) **Going Correction** -0.125s/f (Firm)
WFA 3 from 4yo+ 10lb — 6 Ran SP% **115.0**
Speed ratings (Par 105): **107,105,105,103,97 95**
CSF £20.40 CT £50.74 TOTE £3.70: £2.40, £2.10; EX 20.00 Trifecta £63.40.
Owner Alan Peterson **Bred** The Pocock Family **Trained** Malpas, Cheshire

FOCUS
Modest for the grade and the pace was ordinary, but the winner is progressive.

5503 SILK SERIES LADY RIDERS' H'CAP (PRO-AM LADY RIDERS' RACE) — 6f 12y
7:15 (7:16) (Class 4) (0-80,81) 3-Y-0+

£5,692 (£1,694; £846; £423; £300; £300) **Stalls** Centre

Form					RPR
6043	**1**		**Oeil De Tigre (FR)**[17] 4872 8-9-10 **76** ... ElishaWhittington(7) 1 *(Tony Carroll) mde all: shkn up over 1f out: in command fnl f: pushed out* **7/1**		86
45-4	**2**	1 ½	**Typhoon Ten (IRE)**[110] 1691 3-10-2 **80** ... HollieDoyle 3 *(Richard Hannon) chsd ldrs: prog 2f out: rdn over 1f out: tk 2nd ins fnl f: kpt on but nt pce to chal* **5/1**[3]		85
6030	**3**	½	**Tin Hat (IRE)**[16] 4908 3-9-8 **79** ... (p) GeorgiaDobie(7) 5 *(Eve Johnson Houghton) pressed wnr: rdn and nt qckn 2f out: one pce after and lost 2nd ins fnl f* **20/1**		82
0-45	**4**	2 ¾	**Clear Spring (IRE)**[18] 4835 11-9-12 **74** ... JaneElliott(3) 9 *(John Spearing) in tch: shkn up and nt qckn 2f out: one pce and n.d after* **20/1**		69
2644	**5**	shd	**Young John (IRE)**[49] 3649 6-10-3 **76** ... JosephineGordon 10 *(Mike Murphy) prom on outer: rdn 2f out: fdd over 1f out* **7/1**		71
0460	**6**	nk	**Vegas Boy (IRE)**[17] 4866 4-10-7 **80** ... (t) NicolaCurrie 7 *(Jamie Osborne) v.s.a and lost several l: mostly in last: sme prog jst over 1f out but no ch to be involved (jockey said gelding was slowly away)* **7/2**[2]		74
2122	**7**	½	**Big Lachie**[19] 4775 5-9-13 **75** ... GeorgiaCox(3) 11 *(Mark Loughnane) s.s: racd in last pair: prog over 2f out: chsd ldrs over 1f out: fdd fnl f* **8/1**		67
1005	**8**	1 ¾	**Miracle Garden**[5] 5289 7-8-12 **62** ... (v) PoppyBridgwater(5) 4 *(Ian Williams) towards rr and sn pushed along: nvr pce to be a factor* **14/1**		49
6-35	**9**	hd	**Excellent George**[177] 551 7-10-1 **81** ... (t) MissJuliaEngstrom(7) 6 *(Stuart Williams) prom on outer 4f: wknd* **28/1**		67
3442	**10**	4	**With Caution (IRE)**[14] 5000 3-10-2 **80** ... HayleyTurner 2 *(James Tate) trckd ldrs: rdn 2f out and no rspnse: sn wknd (trainers' rep could offer no explanation for the poor performance)* **10/3**[1]		52
0040	**11**	½	**Mont Kiara (FR)**[12] 5050 6-8-12 **62** ... SophieRalston(5) 8 *(Simon Dow) dwlt: a towards rr: struggling in last pair 2f out (vet said gelding bled from the nose)* **20/1**		34

1m 11.41s (-0.69) **Going Correction** -0.125s/f (Firm)
WFA 3 from 4yo+ 5lb — 11 Ran SP% **122.5**
Speed ratings (Par 105): **99,97,96,92,92 92,91,89,88,83 82**
CSF £41.29 CT £687.48 TOTE £7.40: £2.50, £2.00, £4.80; EX 59.40 Trifecta £1232.20.
Owner A W Carroll **Bred** Jedburgh Stud & Madame Clody Norton **Trained** Cropthorne, Worcs

FOCUS
The looks pretty ordinary form.

5504 MARATHONBET SPORTSBOOK WINDSOR SPRINT SERIES FINALE H'CAP (SERIES FINAL) — 6f 12y
7:50 (7:53) (Class 2) 3-Y-0+

£46,192 (£13,905; £6,952; £3,465; £1,740; £877) **Stalls** Centre

Form					RPR
-445	**1**		**Show Stealer**[19] 4805 6-8-11 **84** ... (p) SilvestreDeSousa 5 *(Rae Guest) wl in rr early: prog on wd outside of main gp bef 1/2-way: clsd to chal over 1f out: drvn ahd ins fnl f: hld on (jockey said mare hung left-handed)* **20/1**		93
0012	**2**	hd	**Open Wide (USA)**[16] 4896 5-9-8 **95** ... (b) PatDobbs 7 *(Amanda Perrett) hld up towards rr: prog over 2f out: drvn and styd on wl fnl f: tk 2nd last stride: jst hld* **8/1**		103
3103	**3**	nse	**Belated Breath**[10] 5143 4-9-2 **89** ... JamesDoyle 13 *(Hughie Morrison) led and racd towards outer of main gp: drvn and briefly hdd jst over 1f out: kpt on wl u.p but hdd ins fnl f: lost 2nd last stride* **6/1**[2]		97
2151	**4**	½	**Second Collection**[29] 4420 3-8-5 **83** ... (h) DavidEgan 4 *(Tony Carroll) hld up in last: taken away fr nr side rail over 2f out: gd prog wl over 1f out: clsd on ldrs fnl f: n.m.r nr fin but styd on* **11/1**		88+
5314	**5**	nk	**Embour (IRE)**[16] 4896 4-9-8 **95** ... SeanLevey 11 *(Richard Hannon) pressed ldr and racd towards outer: drvn to ld briefly jst over 1f out: no ex last 100yds* **7/1**[3]		100
0122	**6**	1 ¾	**Equitation**[28] 4451 5-9-0 **87** ... (t) PJMcDonald 14 *(Stuart Williams) racd in trio on far side: led gp 2f out: clr of other pair after but nvr quite on terms w ldrs of main gp* **9/1**		87
3400	**7**	¾	**Blue De Vega (GER)**[16] 4896 6-8-11 **89** ... (p) CierenFallon(5) 12 *(Robert Cowell) cl up: drvn to chal on outer 2f out: fdd fnl f* **16/1**		86
1142	**8**	2 ¾	**Dark Shadow (IRE)**[21] 4736 3-8-9 **87** ... HectorCrouch 6 *(Clive Cox) towards rr: rdn and sme prog in centre over 2f out: nt on terms and no hdwy over 1f out* **20/1**		74
-211	**9**	shd	**Molls Memory**[42] 3945 4-8-10 **83** ... LiamKeniry 1 *(Ed Walker) wl plcd to 1/2-way: lost pl over 2f out: struggling over 1f out: one pce after (trainer said filly was unsuited by the ground and would prefer a slower surface)* **2/1**[1]		71
3331	**10**	1 ½	**Shamshon (IRE)**[2] 5444 8-8-4 **84** 4ex ... MarcoGhiani(7) 3 *(Stuart Williams) wl in rr: rdn and no prog 2f out: nvr on terms* **33/1**		67
1061	**11**	1	**Free Love**[21] 4736 3-8-12 **90** ... AlistairRawlinson 10 *(Michael Appleby) chsd ldrs over 3f: sn lft bhd* **33/1**		69
6022	**12**	hd	**Sunsprite (IRE)**[17] 4866 3-9-3 **95** ... (p) ShaneKelly 8 *(Richard Hughes) wl in rr: rdn and no real prog over 2f out* **11/1**		74
0034	**13**	3	**Moonraker**[7] 5252 7-8-9 **82** ... DavidProbert 2 *(Michael Appleby) taken down early: stdd s: hld up wl in rr: rdn and no prog over 2f out* **33/1**		52
5201	**14**	2 ½	**Royal Birth**[14] 4995 8-9-1 **88** ... (t) KieranShoemark 16 *(Stuart Williams) racd in far side trio: in tch to 1/2-way: wknd 2f out: eased* **25/1**		50
1020	**15**	2	**Street Parade**[18] 4847 3-9-9 **101** ... (t) JackMitchell 15 *(Stuart Williams) led trio on far side to 2f out: sn wknd and bhd: eased* **40/1**		56
0263	**16**	12	**Ice Age (IRE)**[28] 4451 6-9-3 **97** ... GeorgiaDobie(7) 9 *(Eve Johnson Houghton) prom to 1/2-way: wknd rapidly: t.o (trainer could offer no explanation for the poor form shown)* **20/1**		14

1m 10.8s (-1.30) **Going Correction** -0.125s/f (Firm)
WFA 3 from 4yo+ 5lb — 16 Ran SP% **133.2**
Speed ratings (Par 109): **103,102,102,102,101 99,98,94,94,92 91,90,86,83,80 64**
CSF £172.68 CT £1156.32 TOTE £18.70: £3.30, £2.30, £2.20, £2.80; EX 225.70 Trifecta £1412.10.
Owner Colin Joseph **Bred** Max Weston **Trained** Newmarket, Suffolk

FOCUS
A seriously competitive handicap for a decent pot. A trio raced far side, the remainder towards the stands' side and middle, and a tight finish ensued. This rates sound form, with the winner close to last year's best.

5505 MARATHONBET OFFICIAL GLOBAL PARTNER OF MANCHESTER CITY H'CAP — 1m 31y
8:20 (8:21) (Class 5) (0-75,77) 3-Y-O

£3,428 (£1,020; £509; £300; £300; £300) **Stalls** Low

Form					RPR
6104	**1**		**Gin Palace**[14] 4994 3-9-1 **76** ... GeorgiaDobie(7) 4 *(Eve Johnson Houghton) trckd ldr: led 2f out: rdn and kpt on steadily over 1f out: a fending off rivals* **7/2**[2]		83
3406	**2**	1 ¼	**Noble Fox**[32] 4306 3-9-1 **69** ... HectorCrouch 3 *(Clive Cox) racd in last trio: pushed along 3f out: prog wl over 1f out: drvn and kpt on fnl f to take 2nd nr fin* **8/1**		73
-552	**3**	½	**Mums Hope**[16] 4898 3-9-9 **77** ... JamesDoyle 6 *(Hughie Morrison) pckd s and s.i.s: rcvrd to dispute 3rd pl after 2f: rdn over 2f out: tk 2nd briefly ins fnl f but unable to threaten wnr (jockey said filly stumbled leaving the stalls)* **10/11**[1]		80
0503	**4**	½	**Cromwell**[19] 4794 3-7-11 **56** ... SophieRalston(5) 2 *(Luke Dace) t.k.h to 1/2-way: cl up: stl gng strly over 2f out: chal between rivals over 1f out: fnd little* **6/1**[3]		58
-005	**5**	4 ½	**Hackle Setter (USA)**[19] 4793 3-9-7 **75** ... DavidEgan 8 *(Sylvester Kirk) a in last trio: urged along and no prog wl over 2f out* **8/1**		66
4060	**6**	3	**Thunderoad**[19] 4789 3-8-12 **66** ... ShaneKelly 1 *(Tony Carroll) led to 2f out: wknd qckly* **33/1**		50
420-	**7**	5	**Hieronymus**[317] 7294 3-9-8 **76** ... TomQueally 7 *(Seamus Durack) sn in last: v awkward and hanging bnd after 2f: nvr any prog (jockey said gelding did not handle the bend)* **20/1**		49

1m 43.21s (-1.29) **Going Correction** -0.125s/f (Firm) — 7 Ran SP% **118.8**
Speed ratings (Par 100): **101,99,99,98,94 91,86**
CSF £32.61 CT £45.22 TOTE £4.10: £2.00, £4.00; EX 32.00 Trifecta £77.00.
Owner Mrs Zara Campbell-Harris **Bred** Mrs Z C Campbell-Harris **Trained** Blewbury, Oxon
■ Corrida De Toros was withdrawn (11-2). Rule 4 applies to bets struck prior to withdrawal, but not to SP bets. Deduction - 15p in the pound. New market formed

FOCUS
This rates a length pb from the winner.
T/Jkpt: Not won. T/Plt: £199.00 to a £1 stake. Pool: £93,081.96 - 341.33 winning units T/Qpdt: £30.90 to a £1 stake. Pool: £13,128.26 - 314.11 winning units **Jonathan Neesom**

5506a-50507a (Foreign Racing) - See Raceform Interactive

GALWAY (R-H)
Monday, July 29

OFFICIAL GOING: Good (yielding in places on flat course)

5508a CONNACHT HOTEL (Q.R.) H'CAP (PREMIER HANDICAP) — 2m 179y
7:40 (7:41) (70-100,98) 4-Y-O+

£63,783 (£20,540; £9,729; £4,324; £2,162; £1,081)

				RPR
1		**Great White Shark (FR)**[59] 3330 5-10-3 **80** ... MissJTownend(7) 13 *(W P Mullins, Ire) w.w towards rr: prog on outer fr over 2f out gng wl: rdn 1 1/2f out and r.o wl nr side to ld wl ins fnl f: comf (trainer said, regards apparent improvement in form, mare disappointed the last day and was given a break to freshen up)* **8/1**[2]		90+
2	1 ¾	**Dalton Highway (IRE)**[64] 3117 6-10-1 **78** ... (p[1]) MrMJMO'Sullivan(7) 21 *(D K Weld, Ire) mid-div: prog over 2f out: rdn in 4th into st and ev ch almost on terms nr side ins fnl f: kpt on wl in 2nd nr fin* **20/1**		84
3	¾	**Litterale Ci (FR)**[9] 5183 6-10-12 **89** ... MissABO'Connor(7) 6 *(Harry Fry) in rr of mid-div: hdwy over 2f out: n.m.r into st and sn swtchd lft: r.o between horses into 3rd ins fnl f: nt trble wnr* **20/1**		94
4	¾	**Mr Adjudicator**[25] 4576 5-10-6 **81** ... MrRDeegan(5) 12 *(W P Mullins, Ire) mid-div: tk clsr order bhd ldrs in 8th bef st where n.m.r bhd horses: nt clr run in 5th into st: r.o ins fnl f where swtchd rt: nt trble wnr* **9/4**[1]		85+
5	¾	**Neverushacon (IRE)**[287] 8292 8-10-1 **78** ow2.(tp) MrLJMcGuinness(7) 8 *(Mrs John Harrington, Ire) chsd ldrs: 5th over 5f out: disp ld over 2f out and led narrowly over 1f out: hdd wl ins fnl f and wknd nr fin* **14/1**		81
6	¾	**Baba Boom (IRE)**[364] 5572 4-11-4 **88** ... MrDerekO'Connor 16 *(J P Murtagh, Ire) mid-div: drvn over 2f out and no imp on ldrs u.p over 1f out where short of room briefly: r.o clsng stages: nvr trbld ldrs* **10/1**[3]		90

7 *nk* **Royal Illusion (IRE)**[9] 5209 7-10-9 **82**.................................. MrMJO'Hare(3) 14 84
(W P Mullins, Ire) *chsd ldrs early: racd keenly: 10th over 5f out: sltly bmpd rival over 3f out: tk clsr order on outer over 2f out: drvn into st and no imp on ldrs: kpt on one pce ins fnl f* **8/1**[2]

8 *2 1/2* **Great Trango (IRE)**[17] 5634 6-11-1 **85**.................................(b) MrJJCodd 19 84
(David Harry Kelly, Ire) *hld up: last at 1/2-way: swtchd lft over 2f out and hdwy on outer into st: r.o wl nr side ins fnl f where edgd sltly lft and sltly bmpd rival: nrst fin* **12/1**

9 *hd* **Act Of God**[24] 3788 4-10-8 **78**.................................(h) MsLO'Neill 3 77
(E J O'Grady, Ire) *chsd ldrs: rdn and no ex over 2f out: sn wknd: bmpd ins fnl f* **20/1**

10 *nk* **Shakespear'sgalley (IRE)**[8] 5226 4-10-11 **86**.........(t) MrTHamilton(5) 4 84
(Joseph Patrick O'Brien, Ire) *cl up: 3rd over 5f out: disp ld over 2f out: hdd into st and sn wknd* **11/1**

11 *1/2* **Brawler (IRE)**[11] 4-10-1 **78**.................................(t[1]) MrJHogan(7) 1 76
(Denis Gerard Hogan, Ire) *dwlt: sn chsd ldrs: 4th over 5f out: rdn over 2f out and sn wknd* **50/1**

12 *nk* **Prospectus**[51] 3609 6-10-4 **79**.................................(p) MrHDDunne(5) 2 76
(Gavin Cromwell, Ire) *sn led: rdn and jnd over 2f out: hdd u.p over 1f out and wknd* **40/1**

13 *1 1/4* **Mr Everest (IRE)**[99] 8860 6-11-0 **87**.................................(t) MrDGLavery(3) 17 83
(A J Martin, Ire) *mid-div: tk clsr order over 2f out: n.m.r into st and over 1f out where swtchd rt: one pce after* **10/1**[3]

14 *nk* **Rovetta (FR)**[163] 7406 5-11-1 **88**................................. MrFinianMaguire(3) 20 84
(Mrs John Harrington, Ire) *hld up towards rr: disp 18th at 1/2-way: hdwy on outer over 5f out to chse ldrs: rdn and wknd fr over 2f out: sltly bmpd rival ins fnl f* **25/1**

15 *1 1/4* **Legal Spin (IRE)**[30] 4415 4-11-3 **87**................................. MrPWMullins 7 81+
(W P Mullins, Ire) *mid-div: drvn over 2f out where n.m.r and sn hmpd: no imp after and short of room over 1f out: one pce after* **8/1**[2]

16 *1 3/4* **Newcross (IRE)**[57] 3384 6-11-1 **90**.................................(t) MrROHarding(5) 18 82
(A J Martin, Ire) *mid-div: pushed along towards rr 2f out where sltly hmpd and no imp into st: kpt on one pce ins fnl f* **14/1**

17 *3 1/4* **Brazos (USA)**[8] 5226 5-12-0 **98**.................................(p) MrBO'Neill 9 86
(John Joseph Murphy, Ire) *cl up: drvn almost on terms over 2f out and sn no ex: wknd into st* **50/1**

18 *17* **Arctic Fire (GER)**[41] 3952 10-11-5 **94**.................................(h) MrJCBarry(5) 15 62+
(Denis W Cullen, Ire) *s.i.s and sltly awkward s: towards rr: sme hdwy over 2f out where sn short of room and bdly hmpd: almost uns rdr and no imp after: eased (jockey said gelding clipped a heel and stumbled badly on the approach to the straight)* **25/1**

19 *23* **Chess Grand Master**[30] 4415 6-10-5 **82**.............(t[1]) MrNBashford(7) 23 22+
(Joseph Patrick O'Brien, Ire) *slowly away and w.w in rr: disp 18th at 1/2-way: no imp towards rr whn bdly hmpd and almost uns rdr 2f out: rdr lost irons: eased* **33/1**

20 *14* **Lustrous Light (IRE)**[10] 5164 6-10-9 **86**...............(tp) MrEPO'Brien(7) 22 9
(J Motherway, Ire) *mid-div: bmpd on outer over 3f out: sn rdn and wknd to rr over 2f out* **66/1**

3m 44.43s **20** Ran SP% **144.4**
CSF £176.80 CT £3196.44 TOTE £10.20: £2.50, £4.00, £6.00, £1.40; DF 215.70 Trifecta £4262.40.
Owner Malcolm C Denmark **Bred** Mme Anne-Marie D'Estainville Gedik **Trained** Muine Bheag, Co Carlow

FOCUS
A terribly messy race, which is par for the course in this contest, but Jody Townend kept wide and avoided all trouble, emulating Willie Mullins' previous two winners who were ridden the same way. It was a career highlight for Townend, not long back from injury, and one which illustrates her talents on a major stage as a good 7lb claimer who can do light.

5509 - (Foreign Racing) - See Raceform Interactive

4679 CLAIREFONTAINE (R-H)
Monday, July 29

OFFICIAL GOING: Turf: good to firm

5510a PRIX CASINO TRANCHANT DE VILLERS-SUR-MER (LISTED RACE) (4YO+ FILLIES & MARES) (TURF) 1m 4f
2:00 4-Y-O+ **£21,621** (£8,648; £6,486; £4,324; £2,162)

RPR

1 **Birch Grove (IRE)**[17] 4864 4-9-0 0................................. MickaelBarzalona 9 102
(David Simcock) *midfield: impr to take clsr order 2 1/2f out: rdn to ld 2f out: drvn over 1f out: kpt on strly ins fnl f* **17/1**

2 *3/4* **Hermaphrodite (FR)**[40] 4011 4-9-0 0................ ChristopheSoumillon 8 101
(F-H Graffard, France) **56/10**[2]

3 *1* **Listen In (IRE)**[57] 3389 5-9-4 0................................. MaximeGuyon 7 103
(F Head, France) **9/10**[1]

4 *snk* **River On The Hills (FR)**[40] 4011 5-9-0 0................... GregoryBenoist 3 99
(Mme Pia Brandt, France) **35/1**

5 *3 1/2* **Dance Legend**[9] 5190 4-9-0 0................................. IoritzMendizabal 4 93
(Rae Guest) *trckd ldr: shkn up over 2f out: rdn to chse ldr over 1f out: kpt on same pce fnl f* **17/1**

6 *2 1/2* **Enchanting Skies (IRE)**[47] 4-9-0 0.................. Pierre-CharlesBoudot 10 89
(A Fabre, France) **6/1**[3]

7 *2 1/2* **Duchess Of Danzig (GER)**[37] 4140 4-9-0 0......................... AlexisBadel 1 85
(H-F Devin, France) **29/1**

8 *3 1/2* **Waheebah (IRE)**[47] 4-9-0 0................................. TheoBachelot 5 80
(Rod Collet, France) **9/1**

9 *4* **Alacovia (FR)**[49] 5-9-0 0.................................(p) StephanePasquier 6 73
(S Cerulis, France) **16/1**

10 *nk* **Yellow Storm (FR)**[39] 5-9-0 0................................. MarcNobili 11 73
(Stephane Chevalier, France) **64/1**

11 *12* **Cheshmeh (FR)**[60] 4-9-0 0.................................(b[1]) AntoineHamelin 2 54
(Henk Grewe, Germany) **20/1**

2m 28.7s (-9.20) **11** Ran SP% **121.5**
PARI-MUTUEL (all including 1 euro stake): WIN 18.00; PLACE 3.10, 1.90, 1.20; DF 42.60.
Owner Rathordan Partnership **Bred** Glenvale Stud **Trained** Newmarket, Suffolk

511a (Foreign Racing) - See Raceform Interactive

5242 BEVERLEY (R-H)
Tuesday, July 30

OFFICIAL GOING: Good (6.8)
Wind: Moderate half behind Weather: Fine & dry

5512 VIRGINIA BURKE CARNIVAL EBF MAIDEN STKS 7f 96y
2:05 (2:06) (Class 5) 2-Y-O **£4,140** (£1,232; £615; £307) **Stalls** Low

Form RPR

5 **1** **Tell Me All**[10] 5177 2-9-5 0................................. LukeMorris 6 82+
(Sir Mark Prescott Bt) *mde all: pushed along and qcknd over 2f out: rdn clr wl over 1f out: kpt on strly* **5/4**[1]

4 **2** *2 1/4* **Cloud Drift**[28] 4480 2-9-5 0................................. CliffordLee 5 77
(Michael Bell) *trckd ldrs: effrt and nt clr run on inner 2f out: swtchd lft wl over 1f out and sn rdn: styd on to chse wnr ins fnl f: no imp towards fin* **5/2**[3]

32 **3** *2 1/4* **Lord Of The Alps (IRE)**[13] 5052 2-9-5 0......................... JoeFanning 2 71
(Mark Johnston) *trckd ldng pair on inner: pushed along over 2f out: rdn wl over 1f out: sn drvn and kpt on same pce* **9/4**[2]

5 **4** *8* **King's Charisma (IRE)**[24] 4623 2-9-5 0......................... DavidNolan 8 51
(David O'Meara) *trckd wnr: pushed along 3f out: sn rdn: wknd wl over 1f out* **33/1**

5 *9* **Fast Deal** 2-9-5 0................................. RachelRichardson 4 29
(Tim Easterby) *trckd ldrs: pushed along 3f out: rdn over 2f out: sn outpcd* **80/1**

6 *2* **Noble Bertie (USA)** 2-9-5 0................................. DuranFentiman 3 24
(Tim Easterby) *dwlt: a in rr* **50/1**

7 *3 3/4* **Genesius (IRE)** 2-9-5 0................................. PaulHanagan 1 15
(Julie Camacho) *dwlt: a in rr* **20/1**

1m 32.3s (-0.30) **Going Correction** -0.075s/f (Good) **7** Ran SP% **114.7**
Speed ratings (Par 94): **98,95,92,83,73 71,66**
CSF £4.67 TOTE £1.80: £1.10, £1.50; EX 4.60 Trifecta £8.10.
Owner Cheveley Park Stud **Bred** Cheveley Park Stud Ltd **Trained** Newmarket, Suffolk

FOCUS
Add 1yd. A fair juvenile maiden. The favourite gamely made all in about two seconds outside of the standard time. The third and fourth have been rated roughly near their pre-race marks.

5513 HOLDERNESS PONY CLUB (S) H'CAP (BEVERLEY MIDDLE DISTANCE SERIES) 1m 4f 23y
2:40 (2:40) (Class 6) (0-65,64) 3-Y-O+ **£3,105** (£924; £461; £300; £300; £300) **Stalls** Low

Form RPR

3233 **1** **Siyahamba (IRE)**[27] 4510 5-8-9 **45**.................................(p) GrahamLee 5 52
(Bryan Smart) *trckd ldng pair: pushed along 3f out: rdn to chal wl over 1f out: slt ld appr fnl f: sn drvn and hld on gamely towards fin* **7/2**[2]

5043 **2** *hd* **Royal Flag**[4] 5391 9-9-10 **63**................................. BenRobinson(3) 3 70
(Brian Ellison) *trckd ldng pair: pushed along 3f out: rdn 2f out: drvn to chal ent fnl f: ev ch: no ex nr fin* **7/2**[2]

3232 **3** *2* **Lafilia (GER)**[6] 5301 4-9-10 **60**.................................(b) AdamMcNamara 4 63
(Archie Watson) *trckd ldr: hdwy to ld 3f out: rdn along 2f out: drvn and hdd appr fnl f: kpt on same pce* **3/1**[1]

50-0 **4** *3/4* **Chant (IRE)**[36] 4190 9-10-0 **64**................................. PaulHanagan 6 66
(Ann Duffield) *hld up in rr: hdwy on outer wl over 2f out: chsd ldrs over 1f out: rdn to chal ent fnl f: sn drvn and kpt on same pce* **25/1**

3650 **5** *1 3/4* **Seventii**[14] 5029 5-8-2 **45**................................. AledBeech(7) 2 44
(Robert Eddery) *hld up in tch: pushed along and hdwy over 3f out: rdn and outpcd 2f out: plugged on u.p fnl f* **9/1**[3]

0665 **6** *1 1/2* **Airplane (IRE)**[6] 5301 4-9-8 **58**................................. RachelRichardson 1 55
(Tim Easterby) *led: pushed along over 3f out: sn hdd and drvn: wknd 2f out* **3/1**[1]

0030 **7** *1* **Jennies Gem**[14] 5024 6-8-9 **45**................................. JamieGormley 7 40
(Ollie Pears) *hld up in tch: smooth hdwy on outer 3f out: cl up over 2f out: sn chal and ev ch tl rdn and wknd over 1f out* **20/1**

2m 36.5s (-2.30) **Going Correction** -0.075s/f (Good) **7** Ran SP% **113.1**
Speed ratings (Par 101): **104,103,102,102,100 99,99**
CSF £15.76 TOTE £4.10: £1.70, £2.00; EX 13.10 Trifecta £50.00.There was no bid for the winner. Lafilia was claimed by Mr G. Fierro for £6000.
Owner B Smart **Bred** Noel Carter **Trained** Hambleton, N Yorks

FOCUS
Add 1yd. A modest middle-distance selling handicap. In a busy finish, two of the more fancied runners fought out an engaging tussle in the final 150 yards.

5514 ROBERTA MARSHALL MEMORIAL NOVICE AUCTION STKS 5f
3:15 (3:16) (Class 5) 2-Y-O **£4,140** (£1,232; £615; £307) **Stalls** Low

Form RPR

21 **1** **Harry Love (IRE)**[27] 4516 2-9-2 0................................. BenRobinson(3) 9 82+
(Ollie Pears) *cl up: led 2f out: rdn clr over 1f out: edgd rt fnl f: readily* **2/1**[2]

0 **2** *3 1/2* **Vintage Times**[73] 2840 2-8-7 0................................. DuranFentiman 10 57
(Tim Easterby) *trckd ldrs: hdwy 2f out: rdn and hung bdly lft over 1f out: kpt on u.p fnl f (jockey said filly hung left-handed)* **10/1**

0 **3** *1/2* **Bertie's Princess (IRE)**[11] 5152 2-8-11 0......................... RowanScott(3) 7 63
(Nigel Tinkler) *dwlt and bhd: hdwy 2f out: rdn over 1f out: kpt on wl fnl f: nrst fin* **66/1**

5 **4** *1 1/4* **Carmel**[35] 4221 2-8-10 0................................. BenCurtis 1 54
(Archie Watson) *cl up on inner: slt ld 3f out: hdd 2f out and sn rdn along: drvn over 1f out: kpt on same pce* **6/4**[1]

0403 **5** *1/2* **Not Another Word**[14] 5017 2-8-7 **47**......................... AndrewMullen 6 49
(Nigel Tinkler) *towards rr: pushed along 1/2-way: rdn 2f out: styd on u.p fnl f* **40/1**

6 *1 1/4* **Wade's Magic** 2-9-1 0................................. RachelRichardson 2 53
(Tim Easterby) *in rr: green and rdn along over 2f out: kpt on fnl f* **25/1**

3 **7** *2 3/4* **Never In Red (IRE)**[17] 4910 2-8-12 0......................... LukeMorris 4 40
(Robyn Brisland) *towards rr: rdn along and sme hdwy over 2f out: n.d* **9/2**[3]

003 **8** *nk* **She's Easyontheeye (IRE)**[13] 5037 2-9-0 **70**............ RobbieDowney 11 41
(John Quinn) *slt ld 2f: cl up: rdn along 2f out: sn wknd* **16/1**

4 **9** *9* **Sweet Embrace (IRE)**[13] 5037 2-8-10 0......................... TomEaves 3
(John Wainwright) *chsd ldrs: rdn along 1/2-way: sn outpcd and bhd* **50/1**

10 *3 1/4* **Violette Szabo (IRE)** 2-8-10 0................................. RoystonFfrench 5
(Nigel Tinkler) *dwlt and wnt bdly lft s: green and a bhd (jockey said filly missed the break)* **33/1**

1m 2.55s (-0.35) **Going Correction** -0.075s/f (Good) **10** Ran SP% **119.2**
Speed ratings (Par 94): **99,93,92,90,89 87,83,82,68,63**
CSF £21.72 TOTE £3.00: £1.10, £2.80, £13.50; EX 22.70 Trifecta £1295.70.

Owner Ownaracehorse Ltd & Ollie Pears **Bred** Kenneth Purcell & Lawman Syndicate **Trained** Norton, N Yorks
FOCUS
Add 1yd. Not much substance to this form.

5515 MCCLARRON INSURANCE SUPPORTS ANTIBIOTIC RESEARCH UK H'CAP 5f
3:50 (3:51) (Class 5) (0-75,77) 3-Y-O+

£4,284 (£1,282; £641; £320; £300; £300) **Stalls** Low

Form				RPR
3111	1		**Ginger Jam**[8] 5244 4-9-9 77 5ex....................... FayeMcManoman(5) 10 (Nigel Tinkler) *chsd ldrs: hdwy on wd outside over 1f out: rdn and str run ent fnl f: led towards fin* **5/4**[1]	87+
0056	2	3/4	**Burtonwood**[8] 5244 7-8-8 57....................... GrahamLee 4 (Julie Camacho) *chsd ldrs: hdwy over 1f out: swtchd lft and rdn ent fnl f: sn drvn and kpt on wl towards fin* **8/1**	64
5556	3	nk	**Billy Dylan (IRE)**[13] 5042 4-9-9 75....................(v) ConorMcGovern(3) 8 (David O'Meara) *led: qcknd clr 1/2-way: rdn over 1f out: drvn ins fnl f: hdd and no ex towards fin* **22/1**	81
020	4	3/4	**Arnold**[12] 5094 5-8-13 62....................(p) JoeFanning 1 (Ann Duffield) *trckd ldrs on inner: hdwy 2f out: rdn to chse ldr jst over 1f out: drvn ins fnl f: kpt on same pce* **12/1**	65
4534	5	nk	**Restless Rose**[14] 5015 4-9-12 75....................(t[1]) BenCurtis 3 (Stuart Williams) *towards rr: rdn along over 2f out: styd on fnl f: nrst fin* **11/2**[2]	77
6600	6	1/2	**Qaaraat**[4] 5395 4-9-2 65....................... CamHardie 2 (Antony Brittain) *chsd ldr: rdn along 2f out: drvn over 1f out: kpt on same pce fnl f* **13/2**[3]	65
0606	7	2	**Buccaneers Vault (IRE)**[13] 5040 7-9-9 72....................... KevinStott 6 (Paul Midgley) *a towards rr* **12/1**	65
3623	8	5	**Debawtry (IRE)**[10] 5169 4-9-1 69....................(p[1]) DannyRedmond(5) 7 (Phillip Makin) *chsd ldr: rdn along wl over 1f out: sn wknd (trainer could offer no explanation for the poor performance)* **9/1**	44
3-00	9	6	**Rosina**[19] 4821 6-9-10 73....................(p) ShaneGray 9 (Ann Duffield) *a in rr* **40/1**	27

1m 1.55s (-1.35) **Going Correction** -0.075s/f (Good)
WFA 3 from 4yo+ 4lb **9** Ran SP% **116.4**
Speed ratings (Par 103): **107,105,105,104,103 102,99,91,82**
CSF £12.17 CT £151.18 TOTE £1.90: £1.10, £1.70, £6.00; EX 11.80 Trifecta £171.90.
Owner Walter Veti **Bred** Bearstone Stud Ltd **Trained** Langton, N Yorks
■ Packington Lane was withdrawn. Price at time of withdrawal 25/1. Rule 4 does not apply.
FOCUS
Add 1yd. A fair sprint handicap.

5516 WILFORD WATTS MEMORIAL H'CAP 1m 100y
4:20 (4:22) (Class 4) (0-85,89) 3-Y-O+

£6,553 (£1,961; £980; £490; £300; £300) **Stalls** Low

Form				RPR
4365	1		**King's Pavilion (IRE)**[8] 5246 6-10-1 86................. ConorMcGovern(3) 5 (Jason Ward) *trckd ldrs on inner: pushed along 3f out: swtchd rt to inner at cut-off wl over 1f out: sn rdn: styd on to ld ins fnl f: drvn out* **14/1**	94
3025	2	1	**Candelisa (IRE)**[18] 4879 6-9-12 80....................(t) TrevorWhelan 8 (David Loughnane) *trckd ldng pair: hdwy 3f out: rdn to ld wl over 1f out: drvn and hdd ins fnl f: kpt on same pce* **25/1**	86
0003	3	1 1/2	**Detachment**[8] 5245 6-9-8 76....................... BenCurtis 4 (Roger Fell) *hld up in rr: hdwy over 3f out: effrt wl over 1f out: chsd ldrs ent fnl f: sn rdn and kpt on same pce* **4/1**[1]	79
0105	4	nk	**Storm Ahead (IRE)**[10] 5200 6-9-8 76....................(b) CamHardie 3 (Tim Easterby) *hld up: hdwy 3f out: chsd ldrs wl over 1f out: sn rdn: drvn and ev ch ent fnl f: kpt on same pce* **20/1**	78
4512	5	3 1/2	**How Bizarre**[7] 5274 4-8-10 71....................... JonathanFisher(7) 2 (Liam Bailey) *chsd clr ldr: hdwy 3f out: cl up and rdn along 2f out: drvn and wknd over 1f out* **9/2**[2]	65
2320	6	7	**Markazi (FR)**[18] 4867 5-10-5 87....................(v[1]) DavidNolan 6 (David O'Meara) *led and sn wl clr: pushed along over 2f out: jnd and rdn wl over 1f out: sn hdd and drvn: wknd appr fnl f (jockey said gelding ran too free)* **13/2**[3]	66
5645	7	31	**Kheros**[12] 5089 3-9-2 78....................(p[1]) AdamMcNamara 1 (Archie Watson) *towards rr: rdn along over 3f out: sn outpcd and bhd (jockey said gelding lost it's action)* **12/1**	

1m 45.5s (-0.90) **Going Correction** -0.075s/f (Good)
WFA 3 from 4yo+ 8lb **7** Ran SP% **74.5**
Speed ratings (Par 105): **101,100,98,98,94 87,56**
CSF £114.72 CT £394.07 TOTE £11.60: £4.00, £7.30; EX 108.60 Trifecta £752.90.
Owner Peter Ward **Bred** Darley **Trained** Sessay, N Yorks
■ Seductive Moment was withdrawn. Price at time of withdrawal 11/8F. Rule 4 applies to all bets - deduction 40p in the £.
FOCUS
Add 1yd. The feature contest was a decent handicap, but the short-priced favourite refused to enter the stalls, the other 3yo was quickly beaten after a poor start and the fourth-favourite did too much too soon on the lead.

5517 RACING TV H'CAP 7f 96y
4:55 (4:56) (Class 5) (0-70,67) 3-Y-O+

£4,284 (£1,282; £641; £320; £300; £300) **Stalls** Low

Form				RPR
6201	1		**Red Seeker**[8] 5247 4-9-4 62 5ex....................(t) DannyRedmond(5) 9 (Tim Easterby) *stdd and swtchd rt s: hld up towards rr: hdwy on inner wl over 1f out: effrt and nt clr run jst over 1f out: sn swtchd lft and rdn: fin strly to ld nr line* **9/2**[2]	73+
0004	2	hd	**Pickett's Charge**[14] 5020 6-10-0 67....................(p) BenCurtis 1 (Brian Ellison) *trckd ldrs: hdwy over 2f out: cl up and shifted rt over 1f out: sn rdn and led ins fnl f: sn drvn: hdd and no ex nr line* **4/1**[1]	75
-642	3	2	**Dreamseller (IRE)**[22] 4725 3-8-8 54....................... DuranFentiman 13 (Tim Easterby) *trckd ldrs: hdwy over 2f out: sn cl up: rdn to ld jst over 1f out: drvn and hdd ins fnl f: kpt on same pce* **15/2**	54
3553	4	3/4	**Puchita (IRE)**[91] 2241 4-8-9 48 oh3....................(p) CamHardie 10 (Antony Brittain) *hld up towards rr: hdwy over 2f out: rdn over 1f out: styd on wl fnl f: nrst fin (jockey said filly hung right-handed throughout)* **33/1**	49
1056	5	nse	**Kentuckyconnection (USA)**[27] 4523 6-9-7 67....................... HarryRussell(7) 8 (Bryan Smart) *in rr: rdn along over 3f out: hdwy wl over 1f out: drvn and styd on strly fnl f: nrst fin* **8/1**	68
6341	6	1 1/2	**Muatadel**[25] 4582 6-9-13 66....................... PaulMulrennan 7 (John Wainwright) *in tch: pushed along over 2f out: rdn wl over 1f out: kpt on u.p fnl f* **25/1**	63
0504	7	3/4	**Barbarosa (IRE)**[15] 5002 3-9-2 62....................... PhilDennis 14 (Michael Herrington) *in rr: hdwy on wd outside 2f out: rdn wl over 1f out: kpt on fnl f* **12/1**	54
2214	8	nk	**Queen Of Kalahari**[11] 5147 4-8-5 49....................(p) FayeMcManoman(5) 15 (Les Eyre) *towards rr: hdwy on inner over 2f out: sn rdn: kpt on fnl f (jockey said filly was denied a clear run two furlongs out)* **22/1**	43+
0065	9	1/2	**Wensley**[8] 5247 4-9-0 53....................(p) ConnorBeasley 2 (Rebecca Bastiman) *sn led: rdn along over 2f out: drvn and hdd wl over 1f out: grad wknd* **12/1**	46
0005	10	hd	**Chaplin Bay (IRE)**[21] 4767 7-8-13 52....................... JackGarritty 5 (Ruth Carr) *midfield: effrt over 2f out: sn rdn along and n.d* **15/2**	44
050	11	1	**Make On Madam (IRE)**[25] 4584 7-8-13 52....................... LewisEdmunds 6 (Les Eyre) *chsd ldrs on inner: rdn along 2f out: sn drvn and wknd* **16/1**	42
3566	12	1/2	**Christmas Night**[36] 4195 4-8-13 55....................(p[1]) BenRobinson(3) 11 (Ollie Pears) *cl up: rdn to take slt ld wl over 1f out: sn hdd appr fnl f: sn wknd* **16/1**	43
0003	13	nk	**Prince Consort (IRE)**[25] 4582 4-8-6 48 oh2....(p) ConorMcGovern(3) 4 (John Wainwright) *in tch: rdn along over 2f out: sn drvn and wknd* **80/1**	36
032	14	2 1/2	**Bibbidibobbidiboo (IRE)**[20] 4784 4-9-10 63....................... JoeFanning 3 (Ann Duffield) *a in rr (jockey said gelding was slowly away and never travelling)* **7/1**[3]	44
0-00	15	7	**Destination Aim**[25] 4584 12-8-9 48 oh2....................... ShaneGray 12 (Fred Watson) *cl up: rdn along over 2f out: sn drvn and wknd* **66/1**	11

1m 32.59s (-0.01) **Going Correction** -0.075s/f (Good)
WFA 3 from 4yo+ 7lb **15** Ran SP% **126.3**
Speed ratings (Par 103): **97,96,94,93,93 91,91,90,90,89 88,88,87,84,76**
CSF £22.85 CT £142.36 TOTE £6.60: £2.80, £2.50, £2.30; EX 26.90 Trifecta £247.60.
Owner Brian Valentine **Bred** Aunty Ifl **Trained** Great Habton, N Yorks
FOCUS
Add 1yd. A modest handicap but a progressive winner.

5518 LADY JANE BETHELL MEMORIAL H'CAP (FOR LADY AMATEUR RIDERS) 1m 1f 207y
5:30 (5:37) (Class 6) (0-65,67) 3-Y-O+

£3,244 (£1,006; £502; £300; £300; £300) **Stalls** Low

Form				RPR
0355	1		**Graceful Act**[9] 5214 11-8-12 46....................(p) MissAntoniaPeck(5) 10 (Ron Barr) *cl up: led 1/2-way: rdn along 2f out: kpt on wl fnl f* **25/1**	52
5014	2	1 3/4	**Colony Queen**[38] 4110 3-10-1 67....................... MissJoannaMason 4 (Steve Gollings) *trckd ldrs: hdwy over 2f out: rdn over 1f out: drvn ins fnl f: kpt on wl towards fin* **9/2**[2]	71
0-00	3	hd	**Maldonado (FR)**[24] 4633 5-9-10 58....................... MissAmyCollier(5) 8 (Michael Easterby) *prom: cl up whn hung lft bnd over 4f out: rdn along 2f out: drvn over 1f out: chsd wnr ent fnl f: kpt on same pce* **25/1**	60
0021	4	nk	**Bollin Ted**[8] 5245 5-10-9 66 5ex....................(p[1]) MissEmilyEasterby 7 (Tim Easterby) *led: hdd 1/2-way: trckd ldrs on inner: effrt and hdwy to chse wnr 2f out: rdn over 1f out: kpt on same pce fnl f* **2/1**[1]	68
4002	5	nk	**John Caesar (IRE)**[8] 5248 8-9-2 45....................(p) MissSerenaBrotherton 6 (Rebecca Bastiman) *hld up in tch: hdwy 3f out: rdn along wl over 1f out: drvn and kpt on fnl f* **6/1**[3]	46
2604	6	3/4	**Optima Petamus**[14] 5025 7-8-12 46....................(v) MissSarahBowen(5) 3 (Liam Bailey) *towards rr: hdwy over 2f out: chsd ldrs and rdn over 1f out: kpt on fnl f* **8/1**	46
2063	7	nk	**Amity Island**[14] 5024 4-9-4 47....................(b) MissAmieWaugh 5 (Ollie Pears) *hld up in rr: hdwy on wd outside 3f out: chsd ldrs 2f out: rdn and edgd rt over 1f out: sn btn* **12/1**	46
0-00	8	12	**Paddy's Rock (IRE)**[54] 3511 8-9-7 50....................(p) MissEmmaTodd 9 (Lynn Siddall) *a in rr (vet said gelding was lame right fore)* **40/1**	26
0300	9	4 3/4	**Anchises**[38] 4130 4-10-7 64....................(t[1]) MissBeckySmith 11 (Rebecca Menzies) *chsd ldrs: rdn along over 3f out: sn lost pl and bhd fnl 2f (jockey said gelding stopped quickly; vet said gelding was lame left hind)* **25/1**	31

2m 7.23s (1.53) **Going Correction** -0.075s/f (Good)
WFA 3 from 4yo+ 9lb **9** Ran SP% **98.6**
Speed ratings (Par 101): **90,88,88,88,87 87,87,77,73**
CSF £100.38 CT £1879.12 TOTE £20.40: £4.30, £1.70, £4.80; EX 97.00 Trifecta £1233.10.
Owner D Thomson & Mrs R E Barr **Bred** Mayden Stud, J A And D S Dewhurst **Trained** Seamer, N Yorks
■ King Of Naples 14/1, Outlaw Torn 50/1 & Seek The Moon 100/30 were withdrawn. Rule 4 applies to all bets - deduct 25p in the £
FOCUS
Add 1yd. A modest handicap for lady amateur riders. The second, third and fourth help confirm a straightforward level.
T/Plt: £864.50 to a £1 stake. Pool: £48,945.74 - 41.33 winning units. T/Qpdt: £251.20 to a £1 stake. Pool: £4,239.92 - 12.49 winning units. **Joe Rowntree**

4061 GOODWOOD (R-H)
Tuesday, July 30

OFFICIAL GOING: Good (good to firm in places; 7.8) changing to good after race 1 (1.50)
Wind: strong, half against Weather: windy, showers

5519 UNIBET H'CAP 1m 1f 197y
1:50 (1:56) (Class 2) 4-Y-O+

£46,687 (£13,980; £6,990; £3,495; £1,747; £877) **Stalls** Low

Form				RPR
6403	1		**Fayez (IRE)**[10] 5199 5-8-12 95....................... DanielTudhope 11 (David O'Meara) *stdd after s: hld up in last trio: stl plenty to do and swtchd rt over 1f out: qcknd and gd hdwy and wnt between rivals ins fnl f to ld towards fin: quite comf* **25/1**	106+
2210	2	1/2	**Jazeel (IRE)**[17] 4935 4-8-11 94....................... JamieSpencer 13 (Jedd O'Keeffe) *broke wl: restrained and hld up in tch in midfield: hdwy and edging rt over 1f out: styd on wl ins fnl f: wnt 2nd last strides* **8/1**	103
4412	3	nk	**Setting Sail**[17] 4935 4-9-7 104....................... JamesDoyle 7 (Charlie Appleby) *looked wl; sn pressing ldr tl led jst over 2f out: drvn over 1f out: battled on wl u.p ins fnl f: hdd and lost 2 pls towards fin* **5/1**[1]	112
2534	4	1 1/2	**Ventura Knight (IRE)**[15] 4981 4-8-13 96....................... RyanMoore 3 (Mark Johnston) *wl in tch in midfield: clsd to chse ldrs: nt clr run and swtchd lft over 1f out: ev ch u.p 1f out: no ex and wknd towards fin* **16/1**	101
1502	5	nk	**Beringer**[25] 4613 4-9-2 99....................(p) AndreaAtzeni 8 (Alan King) *in tch in midfield: clsd to chse ldr and nt clr run wl over 1f out: rdn and effrt ent fnl 2f: keeping on whn nt clr run again and no imp wl ins fnl f (jockey said gelding was denied a clear run)* **10/1**	103

0 **6** $^{3}/_{4}$ **Johnny Drama (IRE)**^{39} 4053 4-9-0 **97** SilvestreDeSousa 1 100+
(Andrew Balding) *looked wl; s.i.s: sn rcvrd and t.k.h in midfield: nt clr run and swtchd lft over 1f out: styd on wl ins fnl f: nt rch ldrs* 13/2^{2}

2340 **7** *hd* **Exec Chef (IRE)**^{17} 4935 4-8-13 **96** PatCosgrave 6 99
(Jim Boyle) *broke wl and led briefly: chsd ldrs: effrt ent fnl 2f: drvn over 1f out: kpt on same pce ins fnl f* 16/1

1100 **8** *nk* **Mountain Hunter (USA)**^{42} 3953 5-9-5 **107** CierenFallon$^{(5)}$ 12 109
(Saeed bin Suroor) *wl in tch in midfield: effrt 2f out: hung lft: sltly impeded and outpcd over 1f out: rallied u.p ins fnl f: styd on wl: nt rch ldrs* 15/2^{3}

5112 **9** *hd* **Soto Sizzler**^{27} 4504 4-8-10 **93** OisinMurphy 10 95
(William Knight) *in tch in midfield: nt clr run 2f out: effrt jst over 1f out: sn rdn: kpt on same pce ins fnl f* 5/1^{1}

0000 **10** *hd* **Aquarium**^{17} 4935 4-9-4 **101** FrannyNorton 14 102+
(Mark Johnston) *stdd and dropped in bhd after s: hld up in last pair: clsd and nt clr run over 1f out: sn swtchd rt and sme hdwy: continually denied a run and no imp ins fnl f (jockey said colt was denied a clear run)* 16/1

-500 **11** 1 $^{3}/_{4}$ **Plutonian (IRE)**^{41} 3992 5-8-13 **96** PJMcDonald 4 94
(Charles Hills) *sn led: hdd over 2f out: no ex u.p ent fnl f: wknd ins fnl f* 20/1

-042 **12** 4 **Bless Him (IRE)**^{31} 4399 5-8-10 **93** (h) StevieDonohoe 17 83
(David Simcock) *stdd after s: hld up in rr: no hdwy over 1f out: nvr involved* 16/1

0033 **13** $^{3}/_{4}$ **Lunar Jet**^{18} 4877 5-8-11 **94** JimmyQuinn 5 82
(John Mackie) *dwlt and rousted along early: midfield: effrt over 2f out: no imp and wknd ins fnl f* 28/1

-004 **14** 3 **First Sitting**^{32} 4342 8-9-0 **97** GeraldMosse 16 79
(Chris Wall) *chsd ldrs after over 1f out: rdn ent fnl 2f: hung rt and btn over 1f out: wknd ins fnl f (jockey said gelding hung right-handed; vet said gelding spread a plate)* 14/1

-032 **15** 3 $^{1}/_{4}$ **Nicklaus**^{34} 4255 4-8-10 **93** (t^{1}) TomMarquand 18 69
(William Haggas) *stdd after s: t.k.h: hld up in last quartet: no hdwy u.p over 1f out: wknd fnl f* 25/1

6300 **16** 1 $^{1}/_{4}$ **Master The World (IRE)**^{42} 3953 8-9-6 **103** (p) SeanLevey 9 76
(David Elsworth) *midfield: lost pl and bhd 2f out: wknd fnl f* 50/1

2m 9.26s (0.36) **Going Correction** +0.30s/f (Good) **16 Ran SP% 126.7**
Speed ratings (Par 109): **110,109,109,108,107 107,107,106,106,106 105,102,101,99,96 95**
CSF £211.70 CT £1193.84 TOTE £35.80: £5.30, £2.50, £1.60, £3.10; EX 329.00 Trifecta £3773.40.
Owner Northern Lads & Nawton Racing **Bred** Miss Siobhan Ryan **Trained** Upper Helmsley, N Yorks

FOCUS
The going was given as good, good to firm in places (GoingStick 7.8), but it was a windy, showery day and after the first the going was changed to good all round. The rail was dolled out on the top and bottom bends and the full length of the straight. Add 5yds. The first three rate on the upgrade, with the fourth helping to set the standard.

5520 QATAR VINTAGE STKS (GROUP 2) 7f
2:25 (2:33) (Class 1) 2-Y-O

£113,420 (£43,000; £21,520; £10,720; £5,380; £2,700) **Stalls Low**

Form RPR

111 **1** **Pinatubo (IRE)**^{38} 4091 2-9-1 110 JamesDoyle 5 121+
(Charlie Appleby) *in tch in midfield: clsd to chse ldr over 2f out: led 2f out: sn rdn and readily qcknd clr: r.o v strly: impressive* 6/4^{1}

1 **2** 5 **Positive**^{34} 4252 2-9-1 0 AdamKirby 4 109+
(Clive Cox) *ly; dwlt: hld up in tch in last pair: effrt 2f out: hdwy to chse clr wnr over 1f out: kpt on but no imp* 12/1

2 **3** 5 **Lope Y Fernandez (IRE)**^{38} 4091 2-9-1 0 RyanMoore 7 96
(A P O'Brien, Ire) *looked wl; s.i.s: hld up in rr: swtchd lft ent fnl 2f: hdwy u.p to chse clr ldng pair jst over 1f out: no imp and wknd ins fnl f* 9/2^{3}

13 **4** 3 $^{1}/_{2}$ **Visinari (FR)**^{19} 4846 2-9-1 0 FrankieDettori 1 87
(Mark Johnston) *tall: ly; led: rdn over 2f out: hdd 2f and outpcd by wnr over 1f out: wknd fnl f* 7/2^{2}

2122 **5** $^{3}/_{4}$ **Platinum Star (IRE)**^{19} 4846 2-9-1 107 OisinMurphy 6 85
(Saeed bin Suroor) *in tch in last trio: effrt and clsd jst over 2f out: no imp u.p and outpcd over 1f out: wknd fnl f* 16/1

11 **6** 1 **Mystery Power (IRE)**^{17} 4920 2-9-4 112 SilvestreDeSousa 3 86
(Richard Hannon) *str: looked wl; trckd ldrs: nt clr run jst over 2f out: effrt u.p over 1f out: sn no imp and wknd fnl f (jockey said colt was never travelling; trainer said colt was unsuited by the good ground in this higher class of race and that quicker ground would be preferable)* 6/1

0211 **7** 10 **Milltown Star**^{15} 4999 2-9-1 87 FrannyNorton 2 58
(Mick Channon) *str; unruly on way to s and led part of the way: t.k.h: chsd ldr tl over 2f out: sn dropped out and bhd* 100/1

1m 27.03s (0.33) **Going Correction** +0.30s/f (Good) **7 Ran SP% 109.3**
Speed ratings (Par 106): **110,104,98,94,93 92,81**
CSF £19.28 TOTE £2.00: £1.20, £4.20; EX 15.40 Trifecta £81.70.
Owner Godolphin **Bred** Godolphin **Trained** Newmarket, Suffolk

FOCUS
Add 10yds. The winner was seriously impressive in a fast time and has been rated to a level normally associated with a Group 1 horse.

5521 QATAR LENNOX STKS (GROUP 2) 7f
3:00 (3:05) (Class 1) 3-Y-O+

£176,935 (£67,080; £33,571; £16,723; £8,392; £4,212) **Stalls Low**

Form RPR

0-04 **1** **Sir Dancealot (IRE)**^{46} 3814 5-9-3 111 GeraldMosse 2 119
(David Elsworth) *stdd s: hld up in tch: clsd and swtchd lft over 1f out: rdn and hdwy to press ldrs 1f out: led ins fnl f: r.o wl* 6/1^{3}

-112 **2** 1 **Hey Gaman**^{10} 5207 4-9-3 113 FrankieDettori 5 116
(James Tate) *led: sn hdd and chsd ldr tl rdn to ld over 1f out: edgd lft u.p 1f out: hdd and one pce ins fnl f* 5/2^{1}

4233 **3** 1 **Suedois (FR)**^{17} 4900 8-9-3 109 (p^{1}) AdamKirby 7 113
(David O'Meara) *stdd after s: hld up in tch in rr: effrt 2f out: clsd: nt clr run and hmpd 1f out: swtchd lft and kpt on wl ins fnl f: nt rch ldrs* 8/1

0-24 **4** *nk* **Speak In Colours**^{31} 4409 4-9-3 111 (t) WayneLordan 3 113+
(Joseph Patrick O'Brien, Ire) *hld up in tch in last quartet: clsd on inner whn nt clr run over 1f out: swtchd lft and kpt on wl ins fnl f: nt rch ldrs* 8/1

501- **5** $^{1}/_{2}$ **Flaming Spear (IRE)**^{251} 9173 7-9-3 109 JoeyHaynes 6 111
(Dean Ivory) *looked wl; t.k.h: chsd ldrs: effrt to chal and hung lft 1f out: no ex and one pce ins fnl f* 16/1

2301 **6** 1 **Space Traveller**^{38} 4092 3-8-10 113 DanielTudhope 8 105
(Richard Fahey) *in tch in midfield: unable qck u.p and no imp over 1f out: kpt on ins fnl f* 7/1

-112 **7** $^{1}/_{2}$ **Zaaki**^{17} 4900 4-9-3 112 RyanMoore 10 107
(Sir Michael Stoute) *hld up in tch in last quartet: effrt over 1f out: sn drvn: kpt on ins fnl f: nvr trbld ldrs* 10/3^{2}

-624 **8** $^{1}/_{2}$ **Donjuan Triumphant (IRE)**^{10} 5184 6-9-3 108 SilvestreDeSousa 9 106
(Andrew Balding) *sn led and t.k.h: hdd and rdn over 1f out: stl pressing ldr but jst getting outpcd whn bdly hmpd 1f out: nt rcvr and one pce after (jockey said horse ran too free)* 20/1

-305 **9** $^{1}/_{2}$ **Breton Rock (IRE)**^{31} 4389 9-9-3 104 AndreaAtzeni 1 104
(David Simcock) *hld up in tch in midfield: unable qck u.p and lost pl over 1f out: bhd ins fnl f (vet said gelding lost it's right-fore shoe)* 33/1

1m 28.1s (1.40) **Going Correction** +0.30s/f (Good)
WFA 3 from 4yo+ 7lb **9 Ran SP% 114.2**
Speed ratings (Par 115): **104,102,101,101,100 99,99,98,97**
CSF £21.12 CT £121.34 TOTE £6.70: £2.00, £1.20, £2.30; EX 20.30 Trifecta £122.60.
Owner C Benham/ D Whitford/ L Quinn/ K Quinn **Bred** Vincent Duignan **Trained** Newmarket, Suffolk

■ Stewards' Enquiry : Frankie Dettori four-day ban; careless riding (Aug 13-16)

FOCUS
Add 10yds. This was run at a good gallop and set up well for those closing from behind. The winner has been rated back to his best.

5522 QATAR GOODWOOD CUP STKS (GROUP 1) (BRITISH CHAMPIONS SERIES) 2m
3:35 (3:36) (Class 1) 3-Y-O+

£283,550 (£107,500; £53,800; £26,800; £13,450; £6,750) **Stalls Low**

Form RPR

1-11 **1** **Stradivarius (IRE)**^{40} 4015 5-9-9 120 FrankieDettori 2 123+
(John Gosden) *hld up in midfield: steadily clsd 5f out: swtchd lft and effrt ent fnl 2f: rdn and hdwy to ld ent fnl f: r.o wl: in command and rdr celebrating towards fin* 4/5^{1}

-112 **2** *nk* **Dee Ex Bee**^{40} 4015 4-9-9 118 SilvestreDeSousa 6 121
(Mark Johnston) *looked wl; t.k.h early: racd in 3rd bhd clr ldr: grad clsd 6f out: effrt to ld 2f out: drvn and hdd over 1f out: kpt on and chsd wnr 100yds out: a hld but clsd nr fin as winning rdr celebrated* 11/2^{3}

1-14 **3** 1 $^{3}/_{4}$ **Cross Counter**^{40} 4015 4-9-9 118 JamesDoyle 3 119
(Charlie Appleby) *hld up in midfield: grad clsd 6f out: rdn to chse ldrs 2f out: led over 1f out: sn hdd: no ex u.p 100yds out: wknd towards fin* 3/1^{2}

3264 **4** 7 **Southern France (IRE)**^{32} 4351 4-9-9 113 RyanMoore 8 111
(A P O'Brien, Ire) *looked wl; hld up in last trio: grad clsd 6f out: effrt ent fnl 2f: drvn: edgd rt and no imp over 1f out: wl hld but plugged on ins fnl f to go 4th last strides* 16/1

2314 **5** *nk* **Dashing Willoughby**^{19} 4848 3-8-8 113 OisinMurphy 7 111
(Andrew Balding) *t.k.h early: chsd clr ldr: grad clsd 6f out tl led over 2f out: sn hdd and outpcd u.p over 1f out: wknd ins fnl f* 14/1

1 **6** *nk* **South Pacific**^{40} 4017 3-8-8 101 WayneLordan 9 110
(A P O'Brien, Ire) *hld up in last trio: grad clsd 6f out: effrt and edging rt over 1f out: no imp: wl hld and plugged on same pce ins fnl f* 16/1

6 **7** 20 **Harpo Marx (IRE)**^{41} 3984 3-8-8 97 (b) AndreaAtzeni 4 88
(A P O'Brien, Ire) *s.i.s: hld up in rr: grad clsd 6f out: reminders and rdn 4f out: wl btn over 1f out: eased ins fnl f* 50/1

14-1 **8** 6 **Wells Farhh Go (IRE)**^{31} 4390 4-9-9 112 DavidAllan 1 79
(Tim Easterby) *looked wl; t.k.h: led and sn wl clr: grad reduced ld fr 6f out: hdd over 2f out: sn rdn and btn: bhd and eased ins fnl f (jockey said colt ran too free)* 16/1

3m 29.11s (-1.79) **Going Correction** +0.30s/f (Good)
WFA 3 from 4yo+ 15lb **8 Ran SP% 122.2**
Speed ratings (Par 117): **116,115,114,111,111 111,101,98**
CSF £6.54 CT £10.71 TOTE £1.50: £1.10, £1.60, £1.30; EX 6.40 Trifecta £10.00.
Owner B E Nielsen **Bred** Bjorn Nielsen **Trained** Newmarket, Suffolk

FOCUS
Add 13yds. The three who mattered from the Ascot Gold Cup were here once again and they finished in the same order, pulling 7l clear of the rest with the brilliant stayer Stradivarius doing what he does best - winning - and for the third consecutive time in the race no less, equalling Double Trigger's record. The early stages of the race were frantic, with Wells Farhh Go bolting into a clear lead, and although he was largely ignored, it was still a thorough test at the trip. The first two have been rated as improving slightly.

5523 EUROPEAN BREEDERS FUND EBF MAIDEN STKS (PLUS 10 RACE) (C&G) 6f
4:10 (4:12) (Class 2) 2-Y-O **£15,752** (£4,715; £2,357; £1,180; £587) **Stalls High**

Form RPR

2 **1** **Cobra Eye**^{11} 5125 2-9-0 0 FrankieDettori 1 84
(John Quinn) *compact; hld up in rr of main gp: clsd to chse ldrs over 2f out: effrt and rdn to chal over 1f out: sustained chal to ld towards fin: kpt on wl* 15/8^{1}

2 *shd* **Fuwayrit (IRE)** 2-9-0 0 RyanMoore 5 84
(Mark Johnston) *str; chsd ldrs tl wnt 2nd ent fnl 2f: rdn and ev ch over 1f out: sustained effrt and drvn to ld ins fnl f: hdd towards fin: kpt on wl: jst hld* 8/1

2 **3** 1 $^{1}/_{2}$ **Lost In Time**^{25} 4588 2-9-0 0 OisinMurphy 9 79
(Saeed bin Suroor) *looked wl; travelled strly: chsd ldr tl led ent fnl 2f: rdn and wandered whn hrd pressed ent fnl f: hdd ins fnl f: no ex and wknd towards fin* 9/2^{3}

4 1 $^{1}/_{4}$ **Impressor (IRE)** 2-9-0 0 MartinDwyer 6 77+
(Marcus Tregoning) *leggy; athletic; wnt lft leaving stalls: sn rcvrd to chse ldrs: squeezed for room and jostled 2f out: rallied to chse ldrs ins fnl f: kpt on wl but nvr able to chal* 20/1

05 **5** 1 $^{3}/_{4}$ **Bowling Russian (IRE)**^{15} 4992 2-9-0 0 PatCosgrave 4 70
(George Baker) *compact; hld up in tch in rr of main gp: clsd whn nt clr run and edgd lft 2f out: kpt on ins fnl wout threatening ldrs (jockey said colt hung left-handed)* 33/1

5 **6** $^{1}/_{2}$ **Good Job Power (IRE)**^{11} 5125 2-9-0 0 SilvestreDeSousa 11 69
(Richard Hannon) *str; led tl hdd and rdn jst over 1f out: 4th and no ex 1f out: wknd ins fnl f* 12/1

7 2 $^{3}/_{4}$ **Wadi Al Sail (IRE)** 2-9-0 0 TomMarquand 10 60+
(Gay Kelleway) *leggy; in tch in midfield: nt clr run and swtchd rt ent fnl 2f: sn pushed lft: nt rcvr and wl hld fnl f* 66/1

0 **8** *hd* **Cheat (IRE)**^{19} 4826 2-9-0 0 PatDobbs 8 60
(Richard Hannon) *athletic; dwlt: hld up in tch in rr of main gp: clsd whn squeezed for room: jostled and pushed lft 2f out: nt rcvr and wl hld fnl f* 33/1

32 **9** *2 3/4* **Written Broadcast (IRE)**[10] 5186 2-9-0 0 AndreaAtzeni 2 52
(Richard Hannon) *leggy; athletic; chsd ldrs: effrt and pressing ldrs ent 2f out: unable qck and btn over 1f out: wknd fnl f (trainer said colt would prefer a quicker surface and was unsuited by being drawn on the wide outside)* **5/2**[2]

10 *2 3/4* **Mr Wilton (IRE)** 2-9-0 0 PJMcDonald 7 43+
(Charles Hills) *tall; looked wl; v.s.i.s: detached in last: clsd and in tch over 2f out: sn pushed along and btn wl over 1f out: wknd (jockey said colt was slowly away)* **33/1**

1m 13.63s (1.53) **Going Correction** +0.30s/f (Good) 10 Ran SP% **115.4**
Speed ratings (Par 100): **101,100,98,97,94 94,90,90,86,82**
CSF £16.47 TOTE £2.50: £1.20, £2.40, £1.50; EX 18.90 Trifecta £62.00.
Owner Phoenix Thoroughbred Limited **Bred** Zalim Bifov **Trained** Settrington, N Yorks

FOCUS
Usually a decent maiden. The winner had already run to a useful level on his debut and there were some promising performances in behind.

5524 CHELSEA BARRACKS H'CAP 5f
4:45 (4:46) (Class 2) (0-105,102) 4-Y-0+ £18,903 (£5,658; £2,829; £1,416; £705) Stalls High

Form				RPR
3005	**1**		**Green Power**[36] 4186 4-8-13 **94** PJMcDonald 14	102
			(John Gallagher) *in tch in rr: clsd and nt clr run over 1f out: swtchd rt and hdwy 1f out: r.o strly ins fnl f to ld last strides* **16/1**	
0603	**2**	*hd*	**Poyle Vinnie**[11] 5119 9-8-4 **85** (b) JamesSullivan 13	92
			(Ruth Carr) *looked wl; taken down early and led to post: t.k.h: trckd ldrs: nt clr run 2f out: swtchd rt and rdn to ld 1f out: r.o u.p ins fnl f: hdd last strides* **33/1**	
-241	**3**	*hd*	**Maygold**[44] 3893 4-8-4 **85** SilvestreDeSousa 9	91
			(Ed Walker) *stdd s: hld up in tch towards rr: rdn and hdwy over 1f out: pressing ldr ins fnl f: ev ch kpt on u.p towards fin* **7/2**[1]	
0200	**4**	*nk*	**Duke Of Firenze**[3] 5454 10-8-10 **91** ow1 DavidAllan 12	96
			(David C Griffiths) *in tch in rr: clsd over 1f out: squeezed through to chse ldrs ins fnl f: kpt on wl towards fin* **12/1**	
1456	**5**	*1*	**Lord Riddiford (IRE)**[18] 4888 4-8-11 **92** JasonHart 11	94
			(John Quinn) *led: rdn wl over 1f out: hdd 1f out: no ex and outpcd ins fnl f* **8/1**	
0504	**6**	*1 1/4*	**Boom The Groom (IRE)**[6] 5291 8-8-2 **83** (bt[1]) DavidEgan 7	80
			(Tony Carroll) *pressed ldr: ev ch and rdn over 1f out: no ex jst ins fnl f: wknd fnl 100yds* **16/1**	
0630	**7**	*1/2*	**Line Of Reason (IRE)**[17] 4896 9-8-7 **88** HarryBentley 1	83
			(Paul Midgley) *stdd s: in tch towards rr: clsd 1/2-way: effrt over 1f out: no imp u.p jst ins fnl f: wknd towards fin* **9/1**	
-500	**8**	*1*	**Koditime (IRE)**[4] 5371 4-8-10 **91** HectorCrouch 3	83
			(Clive Cox) *in tch in midfield: swtchd rt and effrt over 1f out: no imp and one pce ins fnl f* **7/1**	
0300	**9**	*hd*	**A Momentofmadness**[52] 3582 6-9-3 **98** (h) KieranShoemark 10	89
			(Charles Hills) *chsd ldrs: rdn over 1f out: unable qck u.p and wknd ins fnl f* **20/1**	
1004	**10**	*nk*	**Saaheq**[18] 4888 5-8-3 **89** CierenFallon(5) 5	79
			(Michael Appleby) *looked wl; in tch in midfield: effrt to chse ldrs over 1f out: squeezed out and snatched up ins fnl f: nt rcvr* **6/1**[2]	
0601	**11**	*2*	**Count Otto (IRE)**[26] 4545 4-8-9 **90** (b) PatDobbs 4	73
			(Amanda Perrett) *in tch in midfield: effrt over 1f out: sn outpcd and btn 1f out: wknd ins fnl f* **14/1**	
2202	**12**	*1/2*	**Dark Shot**[17] 4932 6-8-9 **90** (p) OisinMurphy 2	71
			(Scott Dixon) *chsd ldrs: unable qck u.p over 1f out: wknd ins fnl f* **13/2**[3]	
2526	**13**	*5*	**Harry Hurricane**[27] 4495 7-8-2 **83** oh3 (p) JosephineGordon 6	46
			(George Baker) *hood removed after leaving stall: in tch: effrt over 1f out: squeezed for room and hmpd 1f out: nt rcvr and bhd ins fnl f (jockey was slow to remove the blindfold explaining that she was unable to remove it on the first attempt due to the gelding putting it's head forward)* **16/1**	

58.72s (0.62) **Going Correction** +0.30s/f (Good) 13 Ran SP% **123.2**
Speed ratings (Par 109): **107,106,106,105,104 102,101,99,99,99 95,95,87**
CSF £468.39 CT £2275.24 TOTE £20.80: £4.90, £11.20, £1.80; EX 594.70 Trifecta £4553.80.
Owner Nino's Partnership **Bred** Crossfields Bloodstock Ltd **Trained** Chastleton, Oxon

FOCUS
A useful sprint in which they raced centre to stands' side, and it was those more down the middle who came out on top. The winner has been rated to his best.

5525 UNIBET FILLIES' H'CAP 1m
5:15 (5:18) (Class 3) (0-95,97) 3-Y-0+ £15,752 (£4,715; £2,357; £1,180; £587) Stalls Low

Form				RPR
0413	**1**		**Maid For Life**[20] 4793 3-8-6 **81** (h) PJMcDonald 7	88
			(Charlie Fellowes) *hld up in tch: effrt and hdwy on inner over 1f out: chsd ldr 1f out: switching lft and then swtchd bk rt ins fnl f: r.o wl to ld towards fin* **12/1**	
1211	**2**	*1/2*	**Warning Fire**[9] 5218 3-8-12 **87** 6ex FrannyNorton 4	93
			(Mark Johnston) *looked wl; led and clr after 2f: rdn wl over 1f out: hung lft ins fnl f: hdd towards fin* **8/1**	
31-4	**3**	*1/2*	**Chaleur**[17] 4922 3-9-8 **97** HarryBentley 8	102
			(Ralph Beckett) *in tch in last trio: effrt and 2f out: swtchd lft jst over 1f out: r.o strly ins fnl f: nt quite rch ldrs* **8/1**	
2313	**4**	*3/4*	**Infanta Isabella**[38] 4113 5-9-6 **92** (t) CierenFallon(5) 12	97
			(George Baker) *hung lft thrght: in tch in midfield on outer: lost pl over 3f out: hdwy u.p over 1f out: styd on wl ins fnl f: nt rch ldrs (jockey said mare hung left-handed)* **15/2**[3]	
3220	**5**	*1*	**Hateya (IRE)**[45] 3857 4-10-0 **95** PatCosgrave 1	98
			(Jim Boyle) *t.k.h: chsd ldrs tl chsd ldr after 2f: rdn and lost 2nd over 1f out: kpt on same pce ins fnl f* **9/1**	
-201	**6**	*1/2*	**Clara Peeters**[31] 4393 3-8-10 **85** SilvestreDeSousa 3	85
			(Gary Moore) *wl in tch in midfield: effrt 2f out: hdwy u.p to chse ldr over 1f out tl 1f out: kpt on same pce ins fnl f* **7/2**[1]	
2411	**7**	*nk*	**Al Messila**[14] 5030 3-8-7 **82** DavidEgan 13	81
			(Richard Hannon) *looked wl; swtchd rt after s: hld up in tch rr: effrt on inner over 1f out: kpt on u.p: nvr threatened ldrs* **7/1**[2]	
0003	**8**	*1 1/4*	**Pattie**[10] 5187 5-9-11 **92** GeraldMosse 9	90
			(Mick Channon) *propped forward as stalls opened: stdd and hld up in tch in midfield: nt clr run 2f out: effrt over 1f out: kpt on same pce ins fnl f* **16/1**	
56-0	**9**	*1 1/4*	**Dance Diva**[21] 4758 4-9-13 **94** DanielTudhope 2	89
			(Richard Fahey) *chsd ldrs: swtchd rt 2f out: effrt over 1f out: jst getting outpcd and sltly impeded 1f out: sn wknd* **20/1**	
-010	**10**	*1 1/4*	**Layaleena (IRE)**[39] 4052 3-9-2 **91** JimCrowley 10	81
			(Sir Michael Stoute) *stdd s: hld up in last pair: nt clr run over 2f out: effrt over 1f out: no imp: wknd ins fnl f* **9/1**	
4-65	**11**	*5*	**Savaanah (IRE)**[58] 3374 4-9-12 **93** FrankieDettori 5	74
			(Roger Charlton) *chsd ldrs: effrt 2f out: jst getting outpcd whn squeezed for room jst over 1f out: wknd ins fnl f (trainers' rep said filly was unsuited by the ground and would prefer a quicker surface)* **7/1**[2]	

1m 40.92s (1.72) **Going Correction** +0.30s/f (Good)
WFA 3 from 4yo+ 8lb 11 Ran SP% **119.5**
Speed ratings (Par 104): **103,102,102,101,100 99,99,98,96,95 90**
CSF £106.36 CT £827.20 TOTE £13.00: £3.40, £2.50, £3.10; EX 115.70 Trifecta £1318.80.
Owner Normandie Stud Ltd **Bred** Normandie Stud Ltd **Trained** Newmarket, Suffolk
■ Stewards' Enquiry : David Egan two-day ban; misuse of whip (Aug 13-14)

FOCUS
Add 10yds. This looked pretty competitive beforehand, and they finished in a bit of a heap. The first four have been rated as improving.
T/Jkpt: Not won. T/Plt: £19.20 to a £1 stake. Pool: £272,118.93 - 10,334.41 winning units. T/Qpdt: £6.60 to a £1 stake. Pool: £22,828.35 - 2,558.62 winning units. **Steve Payne**

[5352] YARMOUTH (L-H)
Tuesday, July 30

OFFICIAL GOING: Good to firm (watered; 7.2)
Wind: Fresh half-against Weather: Fine

5526 RACING WELFARE H'CAP 7f 3y
1:40 (1:40) (Class 6) (0-60,61) 3-Y-0+
£2,781 (£827; £413; £300; £300; £300) Stalls Centre

Form				RPR
6002	**1**		**Etikaal**[8] 5247 5-9-7 **55** JackMitchell 9	63
			(Grant Tuer) *hld up in tch: led over 1f out: edgd rt ins fnl f: rdn out* **15/8**[1]	
3053	**2**	*1 1/4*	**Global Hope (IRE)**[22] 4733 4-9-5 **60** (t) TobyEley(7) 10	65
			(Gay Kelleway) *plld hrd and prom: rdn over 1f out: hung lft ins fnl f: styd on (jockey said gelding hung left in the final furlong)* **9/2**[2]	
0034	**3**	*nk*	**Global Acclamation**[26] 4567 3-9-0 **55** (p) RobertHavlin 11	56
			(Ed Dunlop) *s.i.s: hld up: hdwy over 2f out: rdn over 1f out: styd on* **7/1**[3]	
0042	**4**	*1 3/4*	**Miss Liberty Belle (AUS)**[21] 4755 2-9-2 **57** (p[1]) DavidProbert 5	53
			(William Jarvis) *s.i.s: hld up: hdwy over 2f out: sn rdn: styd on same pce wl ins fnl f* **7/1**[3]	
0630	**5**	*1 3/4*	**Shaleela's Dream**[12] 5092 3-9-4 **59** JFEgan 4	51
			(Jane Chapple-Hyam) *hld up: hdwy on outer over 2f out: sn rdn: styd on same pce fnl f* **15/2**	
0036	**6**	*hd*	**Penarth Pier (IRE)**[26] 4567 3-9-3 **61** GabrieleMalune(3) 2	52
			(Christine Dunnett) *s.i.s: hld up: hdwy u.p over 1f out: nt trble ldrs* **16/1**	
3000	**7**	*1 1/4*	**Garth Rockett**[11] 5144 5-9-12 **60** (tp) HayleyTurner 7	51
			(Mike Murphy) *led 1f: chsd ldr tl led again over 2f out: rdn and hdd over 1f out: wknd ins fnl f* **16/1**	
6550	**8**	*3/4*	**Steal The Scene (IRE)**[112] 1660 7-9-12 **60** RossaRyan 1	49
			(Kevin Frost) *s.i.s: hld up: swtchd rt over 2f out: hdwy u.p over 1f out: nt trble ldrs* **16/1**	
0-12	**9**	*5*	**Kennocha (IRE)**[21] 4763 3-9-2 **60** (t) SeanDavis(3) 12	33
			(Amy Murphy) *chsd ldrs: rdn over 2f out: wknd over 1f out* **16/1**	
6004	**10**	*6*	**Miss Communicate**[36] 4179 3-8-12 **53** BrettDoyle 6	11
			(Lydia Pearce) *mid-div: rdn over 2f out: wknd over 1f out (vet said filly lost its right hind shoe)* **33/1**	
-004	**11**	*8*	**Tilsworth Prisca**[12] 5107 4-8-12 **46** oh1 (b[1]) NickyMackay 8	
			(J R Jenkins) *hood removed late: s.i.s: racd keenly and rcvrd to ld 6f out: shkn up and hdd over 2f out: wknd over 1f out* **66/1**	
0-60	**P**		**Until Midnight (IRE)**[146] 1036 9-9-4 **52** (b) NicolaCurrie 3	
			(Eugene Stanford) *prom: rdn over 2f out: sn wknd: p.u and dismntd ins fnl f (jockey said gelding stopped quickly)* **50/1**	

1m 28.24s (3.14) **Going Correction** +0.35s/f (Good)
WFA 2 from 3yo 35lb 3 from 4yo+ 7lb 12 Ran SP% **119.7**
Speed ratings (Par 101): **96,94,94,92,90 90,88,87,82,75 66,**
CSF £9.68 CT £50.00 TOTE £2.70: £1.30, £2.50, £2.10; EX 11.70 Trifecta £61.00.
Owner Moment of Madness **Bred** Shadwell Estate Company Limited **Trained** Birkby, N Yorks

FOCUS
Bottom bend dolled out, adding 10yds to races 3 and 4. The pace was true and one that was officially well-in was chased home by an in-form pair, so the form looks reasonable for the grade. The field came down the centre, gradually edging towards the stands side.

5527 PALM COURT HOTEL OF GREAT YARMOUTH NOVICE AUCTION STKS 7f 3y
2:15 (2:19) (Class 6) 2-Y-O £2,781 (£827; £413; £206) Stalls Centre

Form				RPR
	1		**Ikigai** 2-8-8 1 ow1 BrettDoyle 7	85
			(Mrs Ilka Gansera-Leveque) *s.i.s: hld up: hdwy over 2f out: led wl over 1f out: wnt clr fnl f* **66/1**	
0	**2**	*6*	**Magnificia (IRE)**[10] 5189 2-8-11 0 RobertHavlin 9	72
			(Ed Dunlop) *wnt rt s: racd keenly and sn prom: swtchd to chse ldr stands' side 5f out: rdn over 1f out: styd on same pce fnl f* **20/1**	
1	**3**	*2 1/2*	**Hariboux**[13] 5052 2-9-7 0 (h) JackMitchell 2	76
			(Hugo Palmer) *chsd ldrs: rdn and ev ch wl over 1f out: wknd ins fnl f* **4/6**[1]	
2	**4**	*6*	**Lilkian**[15] 4999 2-8-12 0 HayleyTurner 6	53
			(Shaun Keightley) *plld hrd: trckd ldrs: shkn up and nt clr run over 2f out: rdn over 1f out: wknd fnl f* **7/2**[2]	
0	**5**	*5*	**Grace Note**[21] 4766 2-8-7 0 HollieDoyle 3	33
			(Archie Watson) *chsd ldrs tl rdn and wknd over 1f out (starter reported that the filly was reluctant to enter the stalls; trainer was informed that the filly could not run until the day after passing a stalls test)* **4/1**[3]	
	6	*shd*	**Koovers (IRE)** 2-8-12 0 DanielMuscutt 4	38
			(Gay Kelleway) *hld up in tch: rdn and wknd over 1f out* **14/1**	
0	**7**	*4*	**Hot Date**[75] 2761 2-8-4 0 JaneElliott(3) 8	23
			(George Margarson) *sn led: j. path over 5f out: sn swtchd to stands' rail: rdn and edgd lft over 2f out: hdd wl over 1f out: sn wknd (jockey said filly ran green; vet said filly lost its left hind shoe)* **12/1**	
	8	*18*	**Paisley's Promise (IRE)** 2-8-10 1 ow1 RossaRyan 5	
			(Mike Murphy) *s.i.s: a in rr: rdn and wknd over 2f out* **50/1**	

1m 28.43s (3.33) **Going Correction** +0.35s/f (Good) 8 Ran SP% **124.8**
Speed ratings (Par 92): **95,88,85,78,72 72,68,47**
CSF £975.36 TOTE £74.80: £8.50, £4.40, £1.10; EX 1341.70 Trifecta £3749.20.
Owner Mrs I Gansera-Leveque **Bred** Saleh Al Homaizi & Imad Al Sagar **Trained** Newmarket, Suffolk

The Form Book Flat 2019, Raceform Ltd, Newbury, RG14 5SJ

FOCUS
A shock result suggests this is a race to view with caution, acknowledging the way the winner kicked clear was rather impressive. The pace was steady to start with and it was perhaps an advantage to have cover from the wind.

5528 SEADELL SHOPS & HOLIDAY HEMSBY CHALETS H'CAP — 1m 3f 104y
2:50 (2:51) (Class 6) (0-65,65) 4-Y-0+

£2,781 (£827; £413; £300; £300; £300) Stalls Low

Form — RPR

5133 **1** **Tigerfish (IRE)**[14] 5025 5-9-5 63.....................................(p) HollieDoyle 15 69
(William Stone) *chsd ldrs: rdn over 3f out: swtchd lft over 2f out: styd on to ld wl ins fnl f* 5/1[2]

3150 **2** ¾ **Percy Prosecco**[7] 5277 4-8-9 60.. KateLeahy(7) 3 65
(Archie Watson) *hld up: hdwy over 3f out: led over 1f out: rdn: hung lft and hdd wl ins fnl f* 5/1[2]

-046 **3** ½ **Paddy The Chef (IRE)**[12] 5086 4-9-7 65.......................(p) DavidProbert 14 69+
(Ian Williams) *hld up: hdwy 2f out: r.o to go 3rd towards fin* 10/1

6000 **4** ¾ **Incredible Dream (IRE)**[7] 5285 6-8-3 53 ow1.....(tp) WilliamCarver(7) 12 57
(Conrad Allen) *s.i.s: hdwy over 9f out: led over 2f out: sn rdn and edgd lft: hdd over 1f out: styd on same pce whn nt clr run towards fin* 16/1

-320 **5** 2 ¼ **Maroon Bells (IRE)**[33] 4287 4-9-2 60............................ JasonWatson 13 59+
(David Menuisier) *hld up: hdwy over 1f out: sn rdn: nt rch ldrs* 9/2[1]

6530 **6** 5 **Roy Rocket (FR)**[20] 4796 9-8-6 57 ow1.................... GeorgiaDobie(7) 10 48
(John Berry) *hld up: effrt on outer over 2f out: nt trble ldrs* 33/1

1545 **7** nk **Sir Gnet (IRE)**[78] 2696 5-9-4 62.................................... DanielMuscutt 1 52
(Ed Dunlop) *hld up: hdwy over 2f out: sn rdn: wknd fnl f* 14/1

-055 **8** nk **Sir Fred (IRE)**[14] 5029 4-7-11 46 oh1..................... SophieRalston(5) 6 36
(Julia Feilden) *hld up: pushed along and hdwy over 2f out: sn rdn: wknd fnl f* 14/1

3-10 **9** hd **Kirtling**[94] 2111 8-9-0 58...(t) JackMitchell 4 47
(Andi Brown) *dwlt: hld up: hdwy over 1f out: wknd ins fnl f* 20/1

0300 **10** 1 **Citta D'Oro**[17] 4907 4-9-5 63.......................................(p) RobHornby 9 51
(James Unett) *hld up in tch: lost pl over 7f out: hdwy over 2f out: rdn over 1f out: wknd fnl f* 12/1

0506 **11** 1 ½ **Belabour**[19] 4825 6-9-1 59.. EoinWalsh 7 44
(Kevin Frost) *in rr and pushed along: rdn over 3f out: n.d* 33/1

6204 **12** 1 ¾ **Contingency Fee**[5] 5354 4-8-8 59.........................(p) GraceMcEntee(7) 8 41
(Phil McEntee) *chsd ldr: led 10f out: clr over 5f out tl over 3f out: rdn and hdd over 2f out: wknd over 1f out* 10/1

3052 **13** 3 ½ **Mobham (IRE)**[25] 4601 4-9-4 62.................................(p) RobertHavlin 2 39
(J R Jenkins) *hld up: rdn over 2f out: wknd over 1f out* 8/1[3]

00-0 **14** ¾ **Sexy Secret**[32] 4346 8-8-0 51.............................(p) MorganCole(7) 11 26
(Lydia Pearce) *led: hdd 10f out: chsd ldrs: rdn over 3f out: wknd over 2f out* 33/1

00/0 **15** 3 ¾ **Lady Carduros (IRE)**[25] 4589 5-7-13 46 oh1............... JaneElliott(3) 16 15
(Michael Appleby) *prom: chsd ldr over 8f out: rdn and ev ch over 2f out: wknd over 1f out* 66/1

6-05 **16** 6 **Peggy McKay**[22] 4737 4-9-2 63...................................... JoshuaBryan(3) 5 22
(Andrew Balding) *prom tl wknd over 2f out (jockey said filly was never travelling)* 12/1

2m 28.48s (0.68) **Going Correction** +0.35s/f (Good) **16** Ran SP% **130.5**
Speed ratings (Par 101): **109,108,108,107,105 102,102,101,101,100 99,98,96,95,92 88**
CSF £30.93 CT £256.89 TOTE £4.50: £1.20, £1.60, £2.40, £5.20; EX 35.60 Trifecta £158.70.
Owner Miss Caroline Scott **Bred** Swordlestown Little **Trained** West Wickham, Cambs

FOCUS
Add 10yds. This was well run and the market principals came to the fore, determination the difference between the first two in the closing stages.

5529 MOMENTS RESTAURANT OF SCRATBY H'CAP — 1m 2f 23y
3:25 (3:25) (Class 5) (0-75,76) 3-Y-0+

£3,428 (£1,020; £509; £300; £300; £300) Stalls Low

Form — RPR

-032 **1** **Knowing**[43] 3946 3-9-2 72... GeorgeWood 6 80+
(James Fanshawe) *chsd ldrs who wnt clr 8f out: tk clsr order over 4f out: rdn to ld wl ins fnl f: styd on* 2/1[1]

-324 **2** ¾ **Infuse (IRE)**[33] 4304 3-9-6 76..................................... JasonWatson 4 82
(Roger Charlton) *led 7f: sn rdn: styd on to go 2nd towards fin* 5/1[3]

0-63 **3** ½ **Elhafei (USA)**[17] 4907 4-9-11 72.............................. AlistairRawlinson 5 77
(Michael Appleby) *chsd ldr tl led 3f out: rdn over 1f out: hdd and unable qck wl ins fnl f* 8/1

-354 **4** ¾ **Sudona**[26] 4561 4-9-12 73..(p[1]) JackMitchell 1 77
(Hugo Palmer) *hld up: hdwy over 4f out: nt clr run fr over 2f out: swtchd rt 1f out: styd on but nvr able to chal* 7/2[2]

1044 **5** 3 **Voi**[5] 5332 5-9-6 74...(t) WilliamCarver(7) 2 72
(Conrad Allen) *s.i.s: hld up: hdwy over 2f out: rdn over 1f out: hung lft and no ex ins fnl f* 15/2

545 **6** ¾ **San Sebastian (IRE)**[38] 4120 3-9-6 76............................ RobertHavlin 3 73
(Ed Dunlop) *hld up: hdwy over 2f out: rdn over 1f out: styd on same pce* 5/1[3]

2m 9.06s (0.26) **Going Correction** +0.35s/f (Good)
WFA 3 from 4yo+ 9lb **6** Ran SP% **111.8**
Speed ratings (Par 103): **110,109,109,108,106 105**
CSF £12.19 TOTE £2.40: £1.40, £2.60; EX 10.60 Trifecta £47.20.
Owner Gary Marney **Bred** Mr & Mrs G Marney **Trained** Newmarket, Suffolk

FOCUS
Add 10yds. The early fractions were strong, leaving the pair ridden positively vulnerable in the last 2f, but the winner is still full value. It's form to be positive about on the whole.

5530 SHIRLEY GILL MEMORIAL H'CAP — 6f 3y
4:00 (4:01) (Class 3) (0-95,90) 3-Y-0+ £7,439 (£2,213; £1,106; £553) Stalls Centre

Form — RPR

632U **1** **Royal Residence**[47] 3770 4-9-9 87................................ CallumShepherd 3 96
(James Tate) *chsd ldrs: shkn up to ld and edgd lft ins fnl f: r.o* 5/2[2]

501 **2** hd **Majaalis (FR)**[19] 4827 3-9-0 83.. DaneO'Neill 4 90
(William Haggas) *s.i.s: hld up: hdwy over 1f out: rdn and ev ch ins fnl f: r.o* 5/4[1]

3400 **3** 1 ¾ **Mokaatil**[31] 4379 4-9-1 86.. AngusVilliers(7) 6 89
(Ian Williams) *led: rdn over 1f out: sn edgd lft: hdd ins fnl f: styd on same pce* 7/1[3]

-230 **4** 3 **Rocket Action**[73] 2835 3-9-4 87...........................(t[1] w) DavidProbert 2 79
(Robert Cowell) *chsd ldrs: rdn over 1f out: nt clr run sn after: no ex ins fnl f* 15/2

660 **5** ¾ **Polybius**[18] 4866 8-9-12 90... HayleyTurner 5 81
(David Simcock) *stdd s: hld up: hdwy 2f out: rdn over 1f out: no ex ins fnl f* 8/1

-400 **6** 5 **Victory Angel (IRE)**[29] 4451 5-9-9 87.............................. RobertHavlin 1 62
(Robert Cowell) *chsd ldrs: rdn whn hmpd 1f out: sn wknd* 14/1

1m 14.51s (1.91) **Going Correction** +0.35s/f (Good)
WFA 3 from 4yo+ 5lb **6** Ran SP% **115.1**
Speed ratings (Par 107): **101,100,98,94,93 86**
CSF £6.26 TOTE £3.30: £1.60, £1.30; EX 7.20 Trifecta £40.90.
Owner Saeed Manana **Bred** Genesis Green Stud & Mr P Scott **Trained** Newmarket, Suffolk

FOCUS
The first two are going the right way and came nicely clear after the third had set a steady pace in sprinting terms.

5531 SKY SPORTS RACING ON VIRGIN 535 H'CAP — 1m 3y
4:30 (4:31) (Class 6) (0-65,66) 3-Y-0+

£2,781 (£827; £413; £300; £300; £300) Stalls Centre

Form — RPR

0041 **1** **Mitigator**[40] 4029 3-9-1 58.......................................(b) BrettDoyle 8 67
(Lydia Pearce) *sn prom: led 2f out: shkn up over 1f out: rdn out* 6/1[3]

-606 **2** 4 **Reconnaissance**[15] 5002 3-9-4 61..............................(bt[1]) JackMitchell 4 61
(Tom Clover) *s.i.s: hld up: hdwy over 1f out: sn rdn: styd on same pce ins fnl f* 3/1[1]

4604 **3** ¾ **Agent Of Fortune**[20] 4807 4-9-6 58......................(p) GabrieleMalune(3) 7 58
(Christine Dunnett) *hld up: hdwy over 1f out: rdn ins fnl f: styd on same pce* 15/2

1260 **4** 1 **King Oswald (USA)**[14] 5016 6-9-5 54.............................(tp) RobHornby 1 52
(James Unett) *s.i.s: hld up: swtchd lft and hdwy 2f out: rdn over 1f out: hung lft and no ex ins fnl f (jockey said gelding hung left in the final furlong)* 7/2[2]

2-40 **5** 2 ¾ **Clem A**[14] 5031 3-9-2 64.. DarraghKeenan(5) 9 53
(Alan Bailey) *chsd ldrs: led 3f out: hdd 2f out: sn rdn: wknd fnl f (vet said gelding lost its right hind shoe)* 10/1

0252 **6** 6 **Sharp Operator**[6] 5310 6-9-1 57...........................(h) WilliamCarver(7) 5 35
(Charlie Wallis) *chsd ldrs: rdn over 2f out: wknd over 1f out* 7/2[2]

0000 **7** 5 **Reformed Character (IRE)**[41] 3996 3-8-6 49............ AdrianMcCarthy 6 13
(Lydia Pearce) *hld up: hdwy u.p over 2f out: wknd over 1f out* 33/1

-005 **8** 9 **Summer Angel (IRE)**[21] 4751 4-8-10 45.........................(p) LiamJones 2
(Michael Appleby) *chsd ldrs: rdn over 2f out: wknd over 1f out* 40/1

2-45 **9** 32 **Just Later**[18] 4874 3-9-6 66......................................(b[1]) SeanDavis(3) 3
(Amy Murphy) *led 5f: sn rdn and wknd: eased over 1f out* 12/1

1m 41.33s (3.13) **Going Correction** +0.35s/f (Good)
WFA 3 from 4yo+ 8lb **9** Ran SP% **117.7**
Speed ratings (Par 101): **98,94,93,92,89 83,78,69,37**
CSF £24.86 CT £140.21 TOTE £5.70: £2.00, £1.60, £2.10; EX 29.80 Trifecta £222.30.
Owner W Prosser **Bred** Adweb Ltd & Mrs R J Gallagher **Trained** Newmarket, Suffolk

FOCUS
A moderate handicap dominated by one that is in a rich vein of form. The pace was even and they raced down the centre again.

5532 JOHN KEMP 4 X 4 CENTRE OF NORWICH H'CAP — 5f 42y
5:05 (5:08) (Class 5) (0-70,72) 3-Y-0+

£3,428 (£1,020; £509; £300; £300; £300) Stalls Centre

Form — RPR

4035 **1** **Dr Doro (IRE)**[13] 5058 6-9-12 70...................................(v) DavidProbert 8 78
(Ian Williams) *wnt rt s: sn chsng ldr: shkn up to ld and edgd lft over 1f out: sn rdn: jst hld on* 8/1[3]

0022 **2** hd **Han Solo Berger (IRE)**[6] 5318 4-10-0 72.....................(p) GeorgeWood 7 80
(Chris Wall) *hmpd s: hld up: racd keenly: nt clr run over 1f out: swtchd rt and r.o ins fnl f: nt quite get there* 6/4[1]

-326 **3** 2 **Lalania**[137] 1209 4-9-9 67.. RossaRyan 4 67
(Stuart Williams) *hld up: swtchd rt over 4f out: hdwy and nt clr run over 1f out: sn rdn: styd on same pce ins fnl f* 8/1[3]

1014 **4** 3 ¾ **King Crimson**[24] 4660 7-9-8 71...............................(t) DarraghKeenan(5) 2 58
(John Butler) *stall opened early: led: edgd rt over 3f out: rdn and hdd over 1f out: wknd wl ins fnl f* 11/1

0315 **5** nse **Tilsworth Rose**[13] 5063 5-8-7 51 oh1.............................(b) NickyMackay 5 37
(J R Jenkins) *hld up: rdn over 1f out: wknd ins fnl f* 16/1

5005 **6** 1 ¾ **Gifted Zebedee (IRE)**[13] 5064 3-8-9 64.................... StefanoCherchi(7) 3 43
(Anthony Carson) *chsd ldrs: rdn 1/2-way: wknd ins fnl f* 33/1

0042 **7** ¾ **George Dryden (IRE)**[6] 5289 7-9-13 71............................ JackMitchell 1 48
(George Boughey) *hld up: plld hrd: hdwy 1/2-way: rdn over 1f out: wknd ins fnl f* 2/1[2]

0606 **U** **Arzaak (IRE)**[14] 5027 5-9-11 69...................................(b) NicolaCurrie 6
(Charlie Wallis) *wnt rt s: chsd ldrs: nt clr run and losing pl whn hmpd and uns rdr over 1f out* 33/1

1m 4.23s (2.33) **Going Correction** +0.35s/f (Good)
WFA 3 from 4yo+ 4lb **8** Ran SP% **115.7**
Speed ratings (Par 103): **95,94,91,85,85 82,81,**
CSF £20.73 CT £100.20 TOTE £8.70: £2.30, £1.10, £1.90; EX 24.60 Trifecta £117.90.
Owner Allwins Stables **Bred** S Rudolf **Trained** Portway, Worcs

FOCUS
They didn't go quick and the field congregated in a bunch towards the stands' side this time, resulting in some interference to the runner-up and causing Arzaak to clip heels and unseat Nicola Currie.
T/Plt: £13.90 to a £1 stake. Pool: £51,447.14 - 2,683.36 winning units. T/Qpdt: £5.70 to a £1 stake. Pool: £4,441.77 - 568.78 winning units. **Colin Roberts**

5533 - 5534a (Foreign Racing) - See Raceform Interactive

5506 GALWAY (R-H)
Tuesday, July 30

OFFICIAL GOING: Good (good to yielding in places on flat course; chase course watered)

5535a COLM QUINN BMW MILE H'CAP (PREMIER HANDICAP) — 1m 123y
7:40 (7:40) 3-Y-0+

£63,783 (£20,540; £9,729; £4,324; £2,162; £1,081)

RPR

1 **Saltonstall**[31] 4412 5-8-12 89.......................................(tp) ColinKeane 14 96+
(Adrian McGuinness, Ire) *hld up in rr of mid-div: tk clsr order gng wl over 2f out: pushed along and prog nr side into st: rdn ins fnl f and r.o wl to ld nr fin: readily* 9/1[3]

2 ½ **Innamorare (IRE)**[19] 4855 4-8-5 **82**....(v) LeighRoche 12 88+
(Gavin Cromwell, Ire) *mid-div: tk clsr order and disp 5th over 2f out: rdn to chal over 1f out and led narrowly briefly ins fnl f tl sn hdd: hld by wnr cl home: jst hld 2nd* **12/1**

3 hd **Quizical (IRE)**[45] 3875 4-8-7 **91**.... GavinRyan(7) 3 96
(Ms Sheila Lavery, Ire) *chsd ldrs: rdn in 4th 2f out and outpcd into st: n.m.r 1f out and sn swtchd lft in 6th: r.o nr fin: jst failed for 2nd* **16/1**

4 1 ½ **Rufus King**[22] 4730 4-8-12 **89**.... WJLee 10 91
(Mark Johnston) *chsd ldrs: rdn in 3rd 2f out and no imp on wnr u.p in 4th wl ins fnl f: kpt on same pce* **10/1**

5 nse **Marshall Jennings (IRE)**[11] 5160 7-9-6 **100**.... TomMadden(3) 5 102
(Mrs John Harrington, Ire) *chsd ldrs: drvn disputing 5th over 2f out and clsd u.p to dispute ld briefly ins fnl f tl sn hdd: no ex and one pce nr fin* **25/1**

6 ¾ **Numerian (IRE)**[40] 4016 3-8-13 **98**.... DonnachaO'Brien 4 99+
(Joseph Patrick O'Brien, Ire) *mid-div: pushed along in 11th over 2f out and sme late hdwy u.p ins fnl f: nrst fin* **9/2**[1]

7 nse **Magnetic North (IRE)**[19] 4855 4-8-11 **88**.... RobbieColgan 6 88
(Ms Sheila Lavery, Ire) *cl up tl sn settled bhd ldrs: rdn in 4th 2f out and no ex 1f out where n.m.r briefly: one pce ins fnl f* **9/1**[3]

8 1 ¼ **Onlyhuman (IRE)**[45] 3875 6-9-5 **96**.... ShaneFoley 7 94+
(Mrs John Harrington, Ire) *sltly awkward s and short of room briefly sn after: towards rr: swtchd lft under 2f out and bmpd rival: rdn and hdwy ins fnl f: nvr nrr (jockey said gelding hit the gates of the starting stalls before they opened)* **9/2**[1]

9 ¾ **Trading Point (FR)**[65] 3116 5-8-10 **87**.... RoryCleary 16 83
(Damian Joseph English, Ire) *sn led briefly tl hdd after 1f and settled bhd ldr: drvn to ld over 2f out: strly pressed u.p ent fnl f and sn hdd: wknd clsng stages* **25/1**

10 1 **Aussie Valentine (IRE)**[19] 4855 8-8-11 **88**....(tp) ConorHoban 17 82
(Adrian McGuinness, Ire) *cl up tl led after 1f: pushed along under 3f out and hdd over 2f out: no ex u.p in 2nd into st: wknd 1f out* **33/1**

11 ½ **Jassaar**[31] 4412 4-8-9 **91**.... BenCoen(5) 11 84
(D K Weld, Ire) *mid-div: 8th after 2f: drvn and no imp over 2f out* **5/1**[2]

12 1 **Zabriskie (IRE)**[12] 5112 4-9-1 **92**....(bt[1]) RossCoakley 1 83
(Luke Comer, Ire) *in rr of mid-div best: drvn and no imp towards rr over 2f out: kpt on one pce ins fnl f* **50/1**

13 hd **Hamley (FR)**[19] 4855 6-9-0 **91**....(b[1]) RonanWhelan 13 81
(Peter Fahey, Ire) *towards rr and niggled along early: pushed along over 3f out and sme hdwy on outer 2f out: no ex over 1f out and one pce after* **14/1**

14 ¾ **Insignia Of Rank (IRE)**[19] 4855 4-9-12 **103**....(b) GaryCarroll 2 92
(Joseph G Murphy, Ire) *in rr of mid-div best: short of room briefly on inner bef st: rdn and kpt on one pce ins fnl f: nvr a factor* **25/1**

15 5 ½ **Baraweez (IRE)**[17] 4934 9-8-11 **88**.... ChrisHayes 9 65
(Brian Ellison) *mid-div: rdn over 2f out where swtchd lft and no imp into st where hmpd sltly: wknd* **16/1**

16 4 **Wee Jim (IRE)**[31] 4410 3-8-4 **89**.... KillianLeonard 8 57
(Luke Comer, Ire) *hooded to load: in rr of mid-div best: rdn and no imp in rr over 2f out* **66/1**

17 1 **Allegio (IRE)**[11] 5160 6-9-3 **101**.... JMSheridan(7) 15 67
(Denis Gerard Hogan, Ire) *chsd ldrs: drvn disputing 5th over 2f out and sn wknd* **50/1**

18 3 ¾ **Turnberry Isle (IRE)**[8] 5259 3-9-1 **100**.... SeamieHeffernan 18 58
(A P O'Brien, Ire) *sweated up befhand: in rr early: rdn in 15th over 2f out and hmpd bef st where dropped to rr: no imp after* **12/1**

1m 47.44s
WFA 3 from 4yo+ 9lb **18** Ran SP% **135.8**
CSF £117.69 CT £1812.52 TOTE £11.60: £2.50, £2.60, £3.60, £2.70; DF 165.60 Trifecta £3933.00.
Owner Dooleys & O'Sullivan Partnership **Bred** Cheveley Park Stud Ltd **Trained** Lusk, Co Dublin

FOCUS
The in-form winner has been rated close to his best, with a small pb from the second.

5536a (Foreign Racing) - See Raceform Interactive

5537a CAULFIELDINDUSTRIAL.COM H'CAP 7f
8:40 (8:41) (60-80,80) 4-Y-O+ **£9,051** (£2,925; £1,393; £627; £321; £168)

RPR

1 **Make A Challenge (IRE)**[46] 3829 4-9-7 **73**....(p) JoeDoyle 7 83
(Denis Gerard Hogan, Ire) *mid-div: hdwy in 9th on outer fr 2f out: rdn to ld wl ins fnl f where edgd rt: all out cl home where strly pressed: jst hld on* **10/1**

2 nse **Beckwith Place (IRE)**[27] 4526 4-9-12 **78**....(t) RonanWhelan 6 90+
(Tracey Collins, Ire) *rrd leaving stalls and sddle shifted briefly: settled towards rr: last over 4f out: stl gng wl into st where sn swtchd rt and hdwy: nt clr run and swtchd lft in 6th wl ins fnl f: r.o wl: jst failed* **2/1**[1]

3 1 ¼ **Moxy Mares**[11] 5130 4-9-9 **75**....(p) SeamieHeffernan 9 82+
(Mark Loughnane) *chsd ldrs early: drvn in 7th 2f out and nt clr run into st: rdn in 9th 1f out and r.o wl into nvr threatening 3rd fnl strides* **14/1**

4 nk **War Hero (IRE)**[13] 5070 4-8-12 **71**....(vt) GavinRyan(7) 19 77
(Adrian McGuinness, Ire) *chsd ldrs: rdn in 3rd 2f out and clsd u.p to dispute ld briefly ins fnl f tl sn hdd: hmpd in 2nd wl ins fnl f: dropped to 4th fnl strides* **25/1**

5 ½ **Atlas (IRE)**[11] 4412 6-9-10 **76**....(b) KillianLeonard 17 81
(Denis Gerard Hogan, Ire) *towards rr: drvn over 2f out and sme late hdwy nr side fr over 1f out: r.o: nrst fin* **12/1**

6 ½ **Tintoretto (IRE)**[14] 5034 4-10-0 **80**.... NGMcCullagh 1 83
(John Joseph Murphy, Ire) *led briefly early tl sn hdd and settled bhd ldrs: rdn in 5th 2f out and clsd u.p to chal in 3rd 1f out: no ex wl ins fnl f and wknd nr fin where short of room and checked sltly* **9/1**

7 nse **Elegant Drama (IRE)**[16] 4952 4-9-6 **72**....(p) GaryHalpin 3 75
(Jane M Foley, Ire) *mid-div: pushed along on inner in 8th 2f out: sme hdwy fr over 1f out where n.m.r on inner: kpt on nr fin* **12/1**

8 1 **Lincoln (IRE)**[26] 4571 8-9-13 **79**.... RoryCleary 12 80
(Denis Gerard Hogan, Ire) *sn led: hdd fr 4f out tl regained ld fr 2f out: rdn into st and hdd u.p ins fnl f: wknd clsng stages* **14/1**

9 2 **Highly Approved (IRE)**[12] 5110 4-9-5 **71**.... ShaneFoley 14 67
(Adrian McGuinness, Ire) *chsd ldrs: rdn in 6th 2f out and no ex ins fnl f ins fnl f where sltly impeded: wknd and eased nr fin* **10/1**

10 ½ **Eastern Racer (IRE)**[8] 5256 7-9-0 **73**....(p) JMSheridan(7) 15 67
(Denis Gerard Hogan, Ire) *sn trckd ldr: 4th 3f out: drvn bhd ldrs 2f out and wknd over 1f out* **25/1**

11 1 ¼ **Red Striker (IRE)**[14] 5034 4-9-13 **79**....(p) ColinKeane 10 70
(G M Lyons, Ire) *in rr of mid-div best: pushed along towards rr 2f out and no imp wd into st: rdn briefly ins fnl f and kpt on nr fin* **7/1**[3]

12 1 **Have A Nice Day**[32] 4355 9-9-12 **78**....(v) RobbieColgan 5 67
(T G McCourt, Ire) *mid-div: drvn 2f out and no imp 1f out where short of room: one pce fnl f* **33/1**

13 nk **Sagittarius Rising (IRE)**[45] 3870 4-9-11 **77**....(t) GaryCarroll 18 65
(John C McConnell, Ire) *mid-div: drvn over 2f out and sn wknd* **20/1**

14 1 ½ **Shifted Strategy (IRE)**[54] 3522 4-9-4 **75**....(p) ShaneCrosse(5) 8 59
(J A Stack, Ire) *hld up towards rr: rdn and no imp 2f out* **16/1**

15 1 **Sors (IRE)**[31] 4408 7-9-2 **73**....(v) BenCoen(5) 2 54+
(Andrew Slattery, Ire) *hooded to load: settled in mid-div: rdn over 2f out and sn no ex: wknd ins fnl f where hmpd: eased nr fin* **16/1**

16 2 ¼ **Sky Moon (IRE)**[45] 3874 4-9-7 **73**.... OisinOrr 11 49+
(Peter Fahey, Ire) *hld up towards rr: rn freely and rapid hdwy over 4f out to sn ld: rdn over 2f out and sn hdd: wknd into st: eased ins fnl f (vet said colt was be blowing hard post race)* **6/1**[2]

1m 29.0s (-2.60) **Going Correction** -0.20s/f (Firm) **16** Ran SP% **144.2**
Speed ratings: **106,105,104,104,103 103,102,101,99,98 97,96,96,94,93 90**
Pick Six: Dividend: 23,064.90 - Pool: 46,129.92. Tote Aggregates: 2019: 556,721, 2018: 751,012 CSF £34.34 CT £326.81 TOTE £11.80: £2.80, £1.30, £2.10, £7.10; DF 51.40 Trifecta £1025.80.
Owner M G Hogan & Walter O'Connor & James Joseph Reilly **Bred** Godolphin **Trained** Cloughjordan, Co Tipperary

FOCUS
An agonising defeat for Beckwith Place, who flew home when getting daylight.
T/Jkpt: @4,530.30. Pool: @17,474.37 T/Plt: @173.90. Pool: @62,687.47 **Brian Fleming**

5536 - 5537a (Foreign Racing) - See Raceform Interactive

5479 DEAUVILLE (R-H)
Tuesday, July 30

OFFICIAL GOING: Polytrack: standard; turf: good

5538a PRIX DE BONNEBOSQ (CLAIMER) (3YO) (ALL-WEATHER TRACK) (POLYTRACK) 6f 110y(P)
2:20 3-Y-O **£12,162** (£4,864; £3,648; £2,432; £1,216)

RPR

1 **Rocquemont (FR)**[101] 3-8-6 0.... ThomasTrullier(5) 4 77
(F Rohaut, France) **13/5**[2]

2 1 ½ **Tosen Shauna (IRE)**[33] 3-9-2 0.... MaximeGuyon 6 78
(F Rossi, France) **19/10**[1]

3 2 ½ **Power Best (IRE)**[8] 3-9-5 0....(b) CristianDemuro 5 74
(G Botti, France) **58/10**

4 snk **She's Still Mine**[16] 3-8-8 0....(b) ClementLecoeuvre 3 62
(Matthieu Palussiere, France) **23/1**

5 1 ¼ **I'm Freezing (IRE)**[38] 3-8-11 0....(p) EddyHardouin 7 62
(P Monfort, France) **76/1**

6 hd **El Junco (FR)**[22] 3-8-11 0.... ChristopheSoumillon 1 61
(M Boutin, France) **37/10**[3]

7 2 **Tolosa (FR)**[40] 4047 3-8-11 0.... MickaelBarzalona 9 56
(D Guillemin, France) **83/10**

8 nk **Montfiquet (FR)**[27] 3-8-10 0.... JeremieMonteiro(8) 2 62
(N Caullery, France) **55/1**

9 dist **Wishbone (IRE)**[277] 8606 3-8-11 0.... TonyPiccone 8
(J S Moore) *hld up in rr: adrift and pushed along 3f out: eased once ch had gone* **47/1**

1m 17.59s **9** Ran SP% **118.3**
PARI-MUTUEL (all including 1 euro stake): WIN 3.60; PLACE 1.40, 1.30, 1.70; DF 4.00.
Owner Gerard Augustin-Normand **Bred** Sonia Thomas & Clement Thomas **Trained** Sauvagnon, France

5539a (Foreign Racing) - See Raceform Interactive

5519 GOODWOOD (R-H)
Wednesday, July 31

OFFICIAL GOING: Good (7.7)
Wind: medium, half against Weather: fine

5540 UNIBET GOODWOOD H'CAP 2m 4f 134y
1:50 (1:51) (Class 2) (0-105,105) 3-Y-O+
£31,125 (£9,320; £4,660; £2,330; £1,165; £585) **Stalls** Far side

Form RPR

111- 1 **Timoshenko**[355] 5963 4-8-0 **81**....(p) LukeMorris 89+
(Sir Mark Prescott Bt) *t.k.h: chsd ldrs: effrt 4f out: swtchd lft over 2f out: kpt on and stl chsng ldrs whn swtchd rt ent fnl f: styd on wl to ld towards fin* **9/1**

6316 2 nk **Seinesational**[28] 4505 4-8-0 **81**....(v) KieranO'Neill 88
(William Knight) *t.k.h: chsd ldrs: effrt and swtchd lft over 2f out: drvn and clsd to chse ldr despite v awkward high hd carriage: led jst ins fnl f: hdd and no ex towards fin* **22/1**

2121 3 ¾ **True Destiny**[32] 4404 4-8-1 **82**.... DavidEgan 88+
(Roger Charlton) *looked wl; midfield: effrt 4f out: clsd u.p over 1f out: styd on wl to go 3rd ins fnl f: gng on fin but nvr quite getting to ldrs* **11/2**[3]

3/40 4 2 **The Cashel Man (IRE)**[19] 2781 7-8-9 **90**....(b) PJMcDonald 94
(Nicky Henderson) *hld up in midfield: clsd and shifting rt over 2f out: kpt on and clsd over 1f out: swtchd and styd on ins fnl f: nvr quite getting on terms w ldrs* **16/1**

5 nk **Party Playboy (GER)**[28] 4527 5-8-0 **81** oh1....(p) HayleyTurner 85
(Anthony Mullins, Ire) *t.k.h: led after 2f: hdd 3f out: rdn to ld again over 1f out: hdd and no ex u.p jst ins fnl f: wknd towards fin* **12/1**

2/1- 6 2 **Lil Rockerfeller (USA)**[140] 5605 8-9-4 **99**....(b) SilvestreDeSousa 101
(Neil King) *sed off towards rr and t.k.h: hdwy to chse ldrs 13f out: chsd ldr over 5f out tl led 3f out: sn drvn: hdd over 1f out: no ex and wknd ins fnl f* **4/1**[1]

4201 7 2 ½ **Mancini**[18] 4936 5-8-12 **93**.... JamieSpencer 93
(Jonathan Portman) *looked wl; led for 2f: chsd ldr tl over 5f out: 4th and struggling to qckn u.p 2f out: no ex and wknd ins fnl f* **14/1**

3423 8 nk **Bailarico (IRE)**[52] 3635 6-8-0 **81** oh8....(b) JimmyQuinn 80
(Warren Greatrex) *hld up in tch in midfield: hdwy to chse ldrs 5f out: unable qck u.p and lost pl over 2f out: no threat to ldrs and kpt on same pce fnl 2f* **33/1**

0403 9 1 ¾ **Polish**[11] 5179 4-8-1 **82** oh1 ow1.... PaddyMathers 79
(John Gallagher) *in tch in midfield: effrt 4f out: drvn and no imp over 2f out: kpt on same pce after* **25/1**

0/15 **10** *2* **Paddys Motorbike (IRE)**[39] 4096 7-8-11 **92**...................... LiamKeniry 87
(Nigel Twiston-Davies) *t.k.h: chsd ldrs: effrt and hung rt over 3f out: rdn 3f out: no imp and btn and stl shifting rt over 1f out: wknd ins fnl f* **16/1**

42-2 **11** *nse* **Dubawi Fifty**[32] 4382 6-9-7 **102**...............................(p) DanielTudhope 97
(Karen McLintock) *hld up towards rr: sme prog 7f out: swtchd lft and effrt wl over 2f out: nvr threatened to get on terms and nvr involved* **5/1[2]**

0-54 **12** *1* **Fun Mac (GER)**[43] 3952 8-8-9 **90**...............................(t) AndreaAtzeni 84
(Hughie Morrison) *midfield: effrt over 3f out: no imp u.p and wl hld over 1f out* **17/2**

0-34 **13** *1 1/2* **Zubayr (IRE)**[38] 349 7-8-4 **85**.. MartinDwyer 78
(Ian Williams) *t.k.h: hld up in midfield: short of room and hmpd over 2f out: swtchd lft and no imp u.p over 1f out: wknd ins fnl f* **16/1**

-633 **14** *2 1/2* **Miss Latin (IRE)**[19] 4881 4-8-0 **84** oh7 ow3........................ SeanDavis(3) 74
(David Simcock) *hld up towards rr: effrt 3f out: no prog and wl bhd 2f out* **66/1**

/51- **15** *3 1/4* **Dounyapour (FR)**[57] 8990 6-8-9 **90**...............................(w) DavidProbert 77
(Dr Richard Newland) *midfield tl dropped towards rr 12f out: effrt 3f out: no imp and wl btn over 1f out: wknd* **33/1**

2432 **16** *3/4* **Cristal Spirit**[44] 3940 4-8-3 **84** oh10 ow3............................(p) RaulDaSilva 70
(George Baker) *t.k.h: hld up in rr: effrt over 3f out: swtchd lft wl over 2f out: no prog and nvr involved* **50/1**

-061 **17** *3 1/2* **Early Summer (IRE)**[14] 5047 4-8-0 **81** oh4........................ HollieDoyle 64
(Hughie Morrison) *midfield tl lost pl and rr 10f out: effrt and pushed lft 3f out: no prog and wl btn 2f out (jockey said filly hung badly left-handed throughout)* **16/1**

0606 **18** *3 3/4* **Guns Of Leros (USA)**[7] 5321 6-8-0 **81**.......................(v) JosephineGordon 60
(Gary Moore) *in rr: prog into midfield 12f out: rdn and struggling over 4f out: bhd 2f out: wknd (jockey said gelding hung left-handed in the final furlong)* **50/1**

-213 **19** *19* **Age Of Wisdom (IRE)**[50] 3693 6-7-9 **81** oh10..........(p) AndrewBreslin(5) 41
(Gary Moore) *t.k.h: hld up in midfield: sltly impeded 14f out: effrt over 4f out: lost pl and bhd over 2f out: wknd* **50/1**

4m 33.0s (1.20) **Going Correction** +0.225s/f (Good) **19** Ran SP% **131.9**
Speed ratings (Par 109): **106,105,105,104,104 103,103,102,102,101 101,101,100,99,98 98,96,95,88**
CSF £209.71 CT £1223.70 TOTE £10.50: £2.60, £4.90, £2.00, £3.60; EX 286.10 Trifecta £2312.10.
Owner Middleham Park Racing XXXVI **Bred** Miss K Rausing **Trained** Newmarket, Suffolk
■ Stewards' Enquiry : Kieran O'Neill 15-day ban: misuse of the whip (Aug 16-23, Aug 26-27 & Oct 8-12)

FOCUS
Following 2.2mm of rain on the opening day and 0.2mm overnight, the ground for the second day of the meeting was officially 'good'. The rails were again slightly out from the inner line extending distances in races using the bends. Add 15yds. The first three rate on the upgrade.

5541 UNIBET H'CAP — 1m 3f 218y
2:25 (2:27) (Class 2) (0-105,101) 3-Y-O
£46,687 (£13,980; £6,990; £3,495; £1,747; £877) **Stalls** High

Form RPR

1101 **1** **Sir Ron Priestley**[25] 4644 3-9-4 **98**................................ FrannyNorton 12 110
(Mark Johnston) *looked wl; trckd ldrs: chal wl over 2f out: rdn to ld over 1f out: strly chal thrght fnl f: kpt on gamely: holding on wl at fin: all out* **6/1[2]**

-411 **2** *nk* **Durston**[46] 3842 3-8-8 **88**.. SilvestreDeSousa 10 99
(David Simcock) *hld up towards rr: nt clr run briefly whn making gd hdwy over 2f out: drvn for str chal thrght fnl f: kpt on wl but hld nring fin* **13/2[3]**

-3 **3** *3 1/4* **Eminence (IRE)**[14] 5071 3-9-1 **95**...................................... RyanMoore 2 100
(A P O'Brien, Ire) *mid-div: hdwy 3f out: nt clrest of runs but steadily swtchd off rails fr over 2f out: rdn over 1f out: kpt on fnl f but nt pce of ldng pair* **8/1**

3-11 **4** *2 3/4* **Le Don De Vie**[60] 3341 3-9-2 **96**.................................. OisinMurphy 13 97
(Hughie Morrison) *looked wl; prom: rdn to ld over 2f out: hdd over 1f out: kpt on same pce fnl f* **9/1**

1125 **5** *3/4* **Mind The Crack (IRE)**[18] 4901 3-8-12 **92**........................ JoeFanning 8 92
(Mark Johnston) *trckd ldrs tl 6f out: in tch: tk clsr order again 3f out: rdn and ev ch 2f out: sn hung rt and hld: kpt on same pce fnl f* **12/1**

4402 **6** *1/2* **Persian Moon (IRE)**[12] 5121 3-9-6 **100**........................ PJMcDonald 14 99
(Mark Johnston) *led: rdn and hdd over 2f out: sn hld: one pce fnl f* **16/1**

611 **7** *1 1/4* **Tribal Craft**[12] 5153 3-8-9 **89**.. DavidProbert 9 86
(Andrew Balding) *tall: looked wl; hmpd s: towards rr: hdwy over 3f out: nt clr run over 2f out: sn rdn: nt pce to threaten* **14/1**

4131 **8** *1* **Desert Icon (FR)**[35] 4256 3-8-12 **92**........................ JamesDoyle 11 87+
(William Haggas) *looked wl; hld up towards rr: swtchd to centre over 3f out: nt best of runs over 2f out: sn rdn: little imp* **11/2[1]**

1060 **9** *1* **Severance**[20] 4845 3-8-13 **93**...............................(h) CallumShepherd 4 87
(Mick Channon) *taken down early: hld up towards rr: rdn 3f out: nt pce to get involved* **25/1**

3113 **10** *nse* **Future Investment**[39] 4136 3-8-9 **89**........................ HarryBentley 7 83
(Ralph Beckett) *looked wl; mid-div: rdn 3f out: slt bump over 2f out: nvr any imp* **10/1**

22-0 **11** *2 1/2* **Three Comets (GER)**[81] 2619 3-9-1 **95**........................ AndreaAtzeni 6 85
(Roger Varian) *mid-div: effrt over 2f out: wknd ent fnl f* **25/1**

61-5 **12** *4 1/2* **Kosciuszko (IRE)**[20] 4842 3-8-11 **91**........................ FrankieDettori 1 74
(John Gosden) *looked wl; trckd ldrs: rdn 3f out: losing pl whn tight for room over 2f out: wknd over 1f out* **7/1**

3211 **13** *22* **Dubai Tradition (USA)**[18] 4924 3-8-8 **88**........................ HectorCrouch 5 35
(Saeed bin Suroor) *mid-div: effrt in centre over 2f out: little imp: wknd over 1f out: eased* **14/1**

2m 37.17s (-2.43) **Going Correction** +0.225s/f (Good) **13** Ran SP% **120.3**
Speed ratings (Par 106): **117,116,114,112,112 111,111,110,109,109 108,105,90**
CSF £45.14 CT £315.84 TOTE £6.60: £2.40, £2.10, £2.30; EX 44.80 Trifecta £518.30.
Owner Paul Dean **Bred** Mascalls Stud **Trained** Middleham Moor, N Yorks

FOCUS
Distance increased by 5yds. Strong 3yo form, the right horses came to the fore with two pulling clear inside the last furlong. The first three rate on the upgrade.

5542 MARKEL INSURANCE MOLECOMB STKS (GROUP 3) — 5f
3:00 (3:02) (Class 1) 2-Y-O
£42,532 (£16,125; £8,070; £4,020; £2,017; £1,012) **Stalls** High

Form RPR

1141 **1** **Liberty Beach**[26] 4610 2-8-12 **102**.................................. JasonHart 12 105+
(John Quinn) *t.k.h: hld up in tch in midfield: swtchd lft and nt clr run over 1f out: gap opened and hdwy u.p jst ins fnl f: qckndl to ld 100yds out: r.o strly* **11/8[1]**

2 **2** *1* **Alligator Alley**[18] 4940 2-9-1 0.................................. DonnachaO'Brien 6 104+
(Joseph Patrick O'Brien, Ire) *str: looked wl; hld up in tch towards rr: clsd whn nt clr run 2f out: squeezed for room and hdwy hmpd ent fnl f: pushed through and hdwy ins fnl f: r.o wl to go 2nd towards fin* **8/1[3]**

1522 **3** *1* **Show Me Show Me**[11] 5185 2-9-1 94........................ PaddyMathers 11 100
(Richard Fahey) *compact; s.i.s: outpcd in rr and sn rdn: hdwy 1f out: styd on wl to pass btn horses ins fnl f: snatched 3rd on post (vet reported colt lost its left fore shoe)* **25/1**

044 **4** *nse* **Fan Club Rules (IRE)**[10] 5228 2-9-1 101........................ LukeMorris 2 100
(Matthieu Palussiere, France) *athletic: looked wl; stmbld leaving stalls: in tch in midfield: swtchd rt and effrt ent fnl 2f: drvn and ev ch jst over 1f out: wnt lft u.p 1f out: no ex and outpcd fnl 100yds (vet reported colt lost its right-fore shoe)* **33/1**

02 **5** *shd* **Wheels On Fire (FR)**[13] 5116 2-9-1 96........................ DanielTudhope 13 99
(Matthieu Palussiere, France) *wl in tch in midfield: rdn and hdwy to ld over 1f out: hdd 100yds out: no ex and outpcd towards fin* **20/1**

321 **6** *1 1/2* **Raahy**[32] 4373 2-9-1 92.. HarryBentley 8 94
(George Scott) *compact; dwlt and short of room leaving stalls: in tch towards rr: effrt ent fnl 2f: swtchd lft and drvn over 1f out: no imp and wknd ins fnl f* **14/1**

02 **7** *1/2* **Air Force Jet**[27] 4580 2-9-1 99.................................. OisinMurphy 4 92
(Joseph Patrick O'Brien, Ire) *in tch in midfield: effrt and clsd to chse ldrs over 1f out: no ex u.p 1f out: sn pushed rt and wknd ins fnl f* **9/1**

21 **8** *3/4* **Dr Simpson (FR)**[18] 4903 2-8-12 0........................ RichardKingscote 10 86
(Tom Dascombe) *broke wl: restrained and chsd ldrs: effrt over 1f out: sn struggling to qckn: wknd ins fnl f* **14/1**

1 **9** *hd* **Hand On My Heart**[32] 4398 2-8-12 0........................ RyanMoore 5 86
(Clive Cox) *athletic: looked wl; chsd ldrs: u.p over 1f out: stl cl enough but struggling to qckn whn pushed rt jst ins fnl f: sn wknd* **11/1**

1 **10** *1 1/2* **Maven (USA)**[32] 4417 2-9-4 0..................................(bt) FrankieDettori 7 86
(Wesley A Ward, U.S.A) *str; wnt lft leaving stalls: sn led: hdd 3f out: tongue lolling out and hung rt 2f out: stl hanging and btn 1f out: wknd ins fnl f* **9/2[2]**

032 **11** *1 3/4* **Cool Sphere (USA)**[16] 4993 2-9-1 81..................(v[1]) SilvestreDeSousa 3 79
(Robert Cowell) *pressed ldr tl led 3f out: hdd and hung rt jst over 1f out: nt clr run and impeded jst ins fnl f: sn wknd* **50/1**

1146 **12** *2 1/4* **Zulu Zander (IRE)**[25] 4637 2-9-1 81........................ PJMcDonald 1 69
(David Evans) *leggy; in tch towards rr: effrt over 1f out: no prog: wknd ins fnl f* **66/1**

16 **P** **Aussie Showstopper (FR)**[26] 4610 2-9-1 0........................ ShaneKelly 9
(Richard Hughes) *hld up in tch towards rr: lost action and p.u over 1f out: fatally injured* **25/1**

58.88s (0.78) **Going Correction** +0.225s/f (Good) **13** Ran SP% **121.9**
Speed ratings (Par 104): **102,100,98,98,98 96,95,94,93,91 88,85,**
CSF £11.99 TOTE £2.20: £1.10, £2.50, £6.60; EX 13.70 Trifecta £203.50.
Owner Philip Wilkins **Bred** Phillip Wilkins **Trained** Settrington, N Yorks

FOCUS
This is a well-established juvenile sprint, but it rarely produces a top-notcher. This rates a straightforward renewal.

5543 QATAR SUSSEX STKS (GROUP 1) (BRITISH CHAMPIONS SERIES) — 1m
3:35 (3:39) (Class 1) 3-Y-O+
£593,391 (£225,938; £113,127; £56,458; £28,281; £14,193) **Stalls** Low

Form RPR

2231 **1** **Too Darn Hot**[24] 4705 3-9-0 121.................................. FrankieDettori 3 121+
(John Gosden) *travelled strly: trckd ldng pair: nt clr run over 2f out: swtchd lft 2f out: effrt to chal over 1f out: rdn to ld and edgd rt 1f out: r.o wl and in command fnl 75yds* **1/1[1]**

-161 **2** *1/2* **Circus Maximus (IRE)**[43] 3951 3-9-0 117........................(b) RyanMoore 6 119
(A P O'Brien, Ire) *sweating; chsd ldr tl rdn and clsd to ld over 2f out: drvn and hrd pressed over 1f out: hdd 1f out: battled on wl u.p but hld fnl 75yds* **9/2[2]**

6233 **3** *1 1/4* **I Can Fly**[19] 4885 4-9-5 110.................................. DonnachaO'Brien 5 115
(A P O'Brien, Ire) *looked wl; dwlt: hld up in tch in last trio: effrt ent fnl 2f: hdwy u.p over 1f out: chsd clr ldng pair ins fnl f: kpt on but nvr getting on terms* **14/1**

1310 **4** *shd* **Happy Power (IRE)**[39] 4092 3-9-0 110........................ SilvestreDeSousa 2 116
(Andrew Balding) *t.k.h: hld up in tch in midfield: effrt 2f out: hung rt over 1f out: squeezed through ins fnl f: kpt on u.p: no threat to ldng pair (jockey said colt hung right-handed under pressure. vet reported colt lost its left hind shoe)* **33/1**

-301 **5** *1 1/4* **Lord Glitters (FR)**[43] 3948 6-9-8 117........................ DanielTudhope 7 115+
(David O'Meara) *stdd after s: hld up in last pair: effrt 2 out: u.p and no imp over 1f out: swtchd rt ins fnl f: kpt on: nvr trbld ldrs* **6/1**

2-16 **6** *1 1/4* **Phoenix Of Spain (IRE)**[43] 3951 3-9-0 120........................ JamieSpencer 4 110
(Charles Hills) *led: hdd and rdn over 2f out: edgd lft u.p and unable qck over 1f out: wknd ins fnl f* **11/2[3]**

1100 **7** *3/4* **Zabeel Prince (IRE)**[25] 4668 6-9-8 117........................ AndreaAtzeni 8 110
(Roger Varian) *looked wl; chsd ldng trio: effrt 2f out: chsd ldrs u.p over 1f out: no ex 1f out: wknd ins fnl f* **20/1**

-3R4 **8** *nk* **Accidental Agent**[18] 4900 5-9-8 115..........................(p[1]) CharlesBishop 1 109
(Eve Johnson Houghton) *edgy; dwlt: hld up in tch in last pair: effrt and no imp over 1f out: swtchd lft 1f out: kpt on but nvr involved* **33/1**

1m 38.57s (-0.63) **Going Correction** +0.225s/f (Good)
WFA 3 from 4yo+ 8lb **8** Ran SP% **115.2**
Speed ratings (Par 117): **112,111,110,110,108 107,106,106**
CSF £5.63 CT £35.90 TOTE £1.80: £1.10, £1.60, £3.50; EX 5.60 Trifecta £40.10.
Owner Lord Lloyd-Webber **Bred** Watership Down Stud **Trained** Newmarket, Suffolk

FOCUS
Distance increased by 10yds. Hardly vintage Group 1 form, with a couple of notable disappointments, and it was the 3yos who came to the fore. They didn't go particularly fast and it paid to race prominently. The winner didn't need to match his best.

5544 EUROPEAN BREEDERS FUND ALICE KEPPEL EBF FILLIES' CONDITIONS STKS (PLUS 10 RACE) — 5f
4:10 (4:10) (Class 2) 2-Y-O
£31,125 (£9,320; £4,660; £2,330; £1,165; £585) **Stalls** High

Form RPR

6211 **1** **Mrs Bouquet**[19] 4893 2-9-0 89.................................. JoeFanning 6 97
(Mark Johnston) *athletic: looked wl; mde virtually all: rdn over 1f out: sustained duel w runner-up: hung rt but forged ahd ins fnl f: styd on wl (jockey said filly hung right handed under pressure)* **3/1[2]**

2623 **2** 1 **Mighty Spirit (IRE)**[11] 5185 2-9-0 91 PJMcDonald 3 93
(Richard Fahey) *sn w wnr: ev ch and rdn over 1f out: sustained duel w wnr after: hung rt 1f out: no ex and jst outpcd wl ins fnl f (jockey said filly hung right-handed under pressure)* **15/8**[1]

3110 **3** ½ **Flippa The Strippa (IRE)**[42] 3983 2-9-3 93 SilvestreDeSousa 7 95
(Charles Hills) *wnt lft leaving stalls: s.i.s: in tch: hdwy u.p to chse ldng pair 1f out: kpt on wl ins fnl f: nt quite rch ldrs* **3/1**[2]

0541 **4** ¾ **Orlaith (IRE)**[16] 4984 2-9-0 78 PaulMulrennan 1 89
(Iain Jardine) *leggy; pushed along early: in tch towards rr: hdwy over 2f out: rdn over 1f out: kpt on ins fnl f: nvr quite enough pce to threaten ldrs* **20/1**

0 **5** 1 ¾ **Daughter In Law (IRE)**[42] 3983 2-9-0 88 (b) JasonWatson 4 83
(Roger Charlton) *in tch towards rr: swtchd rt over 2f out: clsd u.p 2f out: no ex and edgd rt 1f out: wknd ins fnl f* **13/2**[3]

061 **6** ½ **Glamorous Anna**[19] 4871 2-9-0 80 MitchGodwin 2 81
(Christopher Mason) *str; chsd ldrs: effrt ent fnl 2f: edgd rt and no ex u.p over 1f out: wknd ins fnl f* **20/1**

6400 **7** 6 **Electric Ladyland (IRE)**[11] 5185 2-9-0 87 (p) LukeMorris 5 59
(Archie Watson) *looked wl; broke wl and pressed wnr briefly: sn in tch in midfield: lost pl u.p over 2f out: bhd ins fnl f* **14/1**

58.96s (0.86) **Going Correction** +0.225s/f (Good) **7 Ran SP% 114.3**
Speed ratings (Par 97): **102,100,99,98,95 94,85**
CSF £9.06 TOTE £3.30: £1.70, £2.30; EX 10.00 Trifecta £24.00.
Owner Garrett J Freyne **Bred** Hatford Enterprises **Trained** Middleham Moor, N Yorks

FOCUS
A 5f conditions stakes for 2yo fillies, this was a new race for Glorious Goodwood and the three top-rated filled the places. The winner is progressing quickly.

5545 BRITISH EBF PREMIER FILLIES' H'CAP — 1m 1f 197y
4:45 (4:46) (Class 2) (0-105,92) 3-Y-O+ £10,903 (£5,658; £2,829; £1,416; £705) Stalls Low

Form RPR

1261 **1** **Mannaal (IRE)**[16] 4996 3-8-13 89 MeganNicholls(3) 8 99
(Simon Crisford) *hld up wl in tch towards rr: hdwy u.p to ld over 1f out: edgd rt but kpt on wl ins fnl f* **12/1**

3114 **2** ¾ **Vivionn**[25] 4640 3-9-4 91 RyanMoore 4 102+
(Sir Michael Stoute) *chsd ldrs: swtchd rt and hung rt over 1f out: nt clr run and hmpd sn after: rallied ins fnl f: chsd wnr wl ins fnl and clsng towards fin (jockey said filly was denied a clear run)* **9/2**[3]

16-1 **3** 1 **Naqaawa (IRE)**[25] 4640 4-10-0 92 JamesDoyle 10 98
(William Haggas) *looked wl; broke wl: sn restrained and in tch on outer: clsd and edgd rt u.p over 1f out: chsd wnr 1f out: kpt on same pce and lost 2nd wl ins fnl f* **6/1**

151 **4** ¾ **Moment Of Hope (IRE)**[30] 4459 3-8-0 76 SeanDavis(3) 9 81
(David Simcock) *stdd s: hld up wl in tch in rr: swtchd lft 2f out: hdwy on outer over 1f out to chse ldrs 1f out: kpt on same pce ins fnl f* **25/1**

4331 **5** 1 **Moll Davis (IRE)**[18] 4913 3-8-7 80 HayleyTurner 7 83+
(George Scott) *looked wl; stdd s: hld up in tch in last pair: clsd on inner 4f out: nt clr run and swtchd lft over 2f out: continually denied a run: bdly hmpd ent fnl f: swtchd lft: pushed along and r.o strly fnl 100yds (jockey said filly was denied a clear run for a sustained period behind the weakening Itizzit)* **4/1**[2]

6131 **6** hd **Ocala**[33] 4318 4-9-6 84 DavidProbert 1 86
(Andrew Balding) *looked wl; nt that wl away: sn w ldr tl led on inner 7f out: rdn 2f out: hdd over 1f out: no ex and outpcd ins fnl f* **6/1**

104 **7** ½ **Bubble And Squeak**[11] 5187 4-9-12 90 JasonWatson 6 92+
(Sylvester Kirk) *hld up wl in tch: nt clr run and shuffled bk 2f out: hdwy u.p over 1f out: kpt on same pce ins fnl f* **25/1**

125- **8** 1 **Thimbleweed**[299] 7951 4-9-9 87 (w) HarryBentley 3 86
(Ralph Beckett) *tall; ly; chsd ldrs on inner: effrt ent fnl 2f: struggling to qckn and bmpd over 1f out: wknd ins fnl f* **12/1**

-122 **9** 6 **Nearooz**[33] 4318 3-9-0 87 AndreaAtzeni 5 74
(Roger Varian) *looked wl; broke wl: sn restrained and chsd ldrs: struggling to qckn u.p and squeezed for room over 1f out: wknd ins fnl f* **7/2**[1]

3210 **10** 3 **Itizzit**[20] 4838 3-8-8 81 PJMcDonald 2 62
(Hughie Morrison) *led: hdd 7f out but styd upsides ldr: rdn ent fnl 2f: outpcd and btn ent fnl f: wknd ins fnl f* **25/1**

2m 8.72s (-0.18) **Going Correction** +0.225s/f (Good)
WFA 3 from 4yo 9lb **10 Ran SP% 115.9**
Speed ratings (Par 96): **109,108,107,107,106 106,105,104,100,97**
CSF £63.43 CT £357.98 TOTE £14.40: £3.70, £2.00, £2.20; EX 98.00 Trifecta £662.40.
Owner Sheikh Ahmed Al Maktoum **Bred** Godolphin **Trained** Newmarket, Suffolk

FOCUS
Distance increased by 5yds. A useful fillies' handicap, although a couple of the market leaders disappointed and there were a couple of hard-luck stories in behind the winner, so messy form.

5546 NEW & LINGWOOD H'CAP — 7f
5:55 (5:56) (Class 3) (0-95,95) 3-Y-O+ £16,752 (£4,715; £2,357; £1,180; £587) Stalls Low

Form RPR

3523 **1** **Dirty Rascal (IRE)**[19] 4887 3-8-11 87 (b) TomMarquand 1 95
(Richard Hannon) *chsd ldrs: nt clr run on inner over 1f out: gap opened and hdwy u.p ins fnl f: r.o wl to ld cl home* **7/1**[2]

1200 **2** nk **Salute The Soldier (GER)**[25] 4666 4-9-12 95 AdamKirby 6 105
(Clive Cox) *chsd ldr for 2f: effrt over 1f out: drvn to ld jst ins fnl f: edgd rt and hdd cl home* **12/1**

2231 **3** ¾ **Lyndon B (IRE)**[13] 5104 3-8-13 89 (v) FrankieDettori 4 94+
(George Scott) *t.k.h: hld up towards rr: short of room over 4f out: swtchd lft over 2f out: hdwy over 1f out: r.o strly fnl 100yds: nt quite rch ldrs* **7/1**[2]

3033 **4** ¾ **Cliffs Of Capri**[11] 5188 5-9-11 94 (p) DougieCostello 2 100
(Jamie Osborne) *niggled along early: midfield: clsd on inner over 1f out: nvr much room ins fnl f: kpt on towards fin* **20/1**

3460 **5** hd **Zap**[18] 4921 4-9-6 89 (v) TonyHamilton 10 94
(Richard Fahey) *chsd ldrs: effrt 2f out: kpt on u.p ins fnl f: nvr quite enough pce to rch ldrs* **25/1**

-456 **6** nk **Whitefountainfairy (IRE)**[88] 2402 4-9-2 85 SilvestreDeSousa 9 90+
(Andrew Balding) *awkward and hit side of stall s: s.i.s: hld up in rr: swtchd rt and clsd over 1f out: hdwy and hung rt 1f out: sn swtchd lft: r.o wl fnl 100yds: n.m.r towards fin: nt rch ldrs* **12/1**

6201 **7** nk **Blackheath**[25] 4654 4-9-6 89 LiamKeniry 3 93
(Ed Walker) *hld up in midfield: hmpd over 5f out: nt clr run and switching lft over 1f out: kpt on u.p ins fnl f: no threat to ldrs* **11/1**

4421 **8** ½ **Charles Molson**[18] 4902 8-9-3 86 DanielMuscutt 5 88
(Patrick Chamings) *wl in tch in midfield: effrt over 1f out: kpt on same pce u.p ins fnl f* **20/1**

5245 **9** 1 ½ **Mr Tyrrell (IRE)**[13] 5104 5-9-3 86 RyanMoore 8 84
(Richard Hannon) *hld up in tch in midfield: nt clr run over 1f out: effrt u.p ent fnl f: kpt on but nvr a threat* **33/1**

2-30 **10** shd **Aljady (FR)**[46] 3863 4-9-8 94 SeanDavis(3) 7 92
(Richard Fahey) *in tch in midfield: effrt over 1f out: kpt on same pce ins fnl f: nvr threatened ldrs* **10/1**

0503 **11** 1 **Chapelli**[18] 4904 3-8-11 87 JoeFanning 17 79
(Mark Johnston) *led: rdn 2f out: hdd over 1f out: jst getting outpcd whn short of room ins fnl f: sn wknd* **25/1**

0102 **12** ¾ **La Maquina**[19] 4887 4-9-2 85 (t) JimCrowley 16 78
(George Baker) *awkward leaving stalls: hld up in rr: effrt and hdwy over 1f out: pushed lft jst ins fnl f: nt rcvr* **9/1**[3]

1030 **13** nk **Apex King (IRE)**[11] 5192 5-9-7 90 DanielTudhope 20 83
(David Loughnane) *in tch in midfield: effrt u.p over 1f out: nvr getting on terms and one pce ins fnl f* **18/1**

0600 **14** nk **Gallipoli (IRE)**[11] 5200 6-8-10 82 (v) MeganNicholls(3) 18 74
(Richard Fahey) *stdd s: hld up towards rr: effrt 2f out: kpt on but nvr threatened to get on terms* **40/1**

5241 **15** shd **Revich (IRE)**[27] 4546 3-8-12 88 LukeMorris 11 77
(Richard Spencer) *midfield: effrt 2f out: no imp and edgd lft 1f out: wknd ins fnl f* **25/1**

3-31 **16** ½ **Light And Dark**[19] 4887 3-9-3 93 CallumShepherd 12 80
(Saeed bin Suroor) *chsd ldrs: wnt 2nd 5f out: rdn to ld over 1f out: hdd jst ins fnl f: losing pl and bmpd ins fnl f: sn wknd* **3/1**[1]

0-10 **17** 1 ¾ **Ambassadorial (USA)**[18] 4921 5-9-10 93 DavidEgan 13 78
(Jane Chapple-Hyam) *midfield: lost pl u.p ent fnl 2f: swtchd rt over 1f out: bhd fnl f* **25/1**

0000 **18** 1 ¾ **Glendevon (USA)**[11] 5188 4-9-8 91 (h) ShaneKelly 14 72
(Richard Hughes) *hld up in rr: hmpd over 2f out: no hdwy over 1f out: bhd ins fnl f* **80/1**

1m 27.38s (0.68) **Going Correction** +0.225s/f (Good)
WFA 3 from 4yo+ 7lb **18 Ran SP% 129.6**
Speed ratings (Par 107): **105,104,103,102,102 102,102,101,99,99 98,97,97,96,96 96,94,92**
CSF £81.38 CT £449.54 TOTE £7.70: £1.90, £3.30, £2.00, £4.50; EX 100.90 Trifecta £1570.40.
Owner Charlie Rosier & Mrs Julia Rosier **Bred** Rosetown Bloodstock & E McEvoy **Trained** East Everleigh, Wilts

■ Stewards' Enquiry : Silvestre De Sousa two-day ban: careless riding (Aug 16-17)
Frankie Dettori two-day ban: careless riding (Aug 12,17)

FOCUS
Add 10yds. This is always competitive; this year was no different and there was plenty of trouble in running. The first four home were drawn 1-6-4-2. The winner has been rated close to his 2yo best, rated around the runner-up.
T/Jkpt: £8,131.20 to a £1 stake. Pool: £17,178.62 - 1.50 winning units T/Plt: £66.30 to a £1 stake. Pool: £299,420.67 - 3294.27 winning units T/Qpdt: £10.00 to a £1 stake. Pool: £24,165.45 - 1773.34 winning units **Steve Payne & Tim Mitchell**

5302 LEICESTER (R-H)
Wednesday, July 31

OFFICIAL GOING: Heavy (5.3)
Wind: Light across Weather: Overcast

5547 LONGINES IRISH CHAMPIONS WEEKEND EBF MEDIAN AUCTION MAIDEN FILLIES' STKS (PLUS 10 RACE) — 6f
5:45 (5:47) (Class 4) 2-Y-O £4,787 (£1,424; £711; £355) Stalls High

Form RPR

1 **Entrancing** 2-9-0 0 BarryMcHugh 11 79+
(Richard Fahey) *s.s: in rr and pushed along 4f out: hdwy to chse ldr over 1f out: shkn up to ld and edgd rt ins fnl f: r.o (jockey said filly ran green)* **11/4**[2]

03 **2** 1 ½ **Barbarella (IRE)**[43] 3968 2-9-0 0 TomEaves 9 74
(Kevin Ryan) *sn led: edgd rt fr over 3f out: rdn over 1f out: hdd and unable qck ins fnl f* **6/4**[1]

3 3 ¾ **Autumn Trail** 2-9-0 0 NickyMackay 2 63
(Rae Guest) *s.i.s: swtchd rt over 4f out: hdwy to chse ldr over 3f out tl rdn and hung rt over 1f out: no ex fnl f* **15/2**

20 **4** nse **Doncaster Rosa**[74] 2820 2-8-11 0 GabrieleMalune(3) 5 63
(Ivan Furtado) *hmpd s: sn chsng ldrs: rdn over 3f out: sn outpcd: styd on ins fnl f (stewards held an enquriy to whether the jockey had appeared to ride the final furlong under tender handling. jockey said that he continued to ride to the line, albeit not as aggressively due to the filly becoming unbalanced on just her third run)* **12/1**

22 **5** 3 ½ **Enjoy The Moment**[11] 5197 2-9-0 0 GeraldMosse 13 52
(Mick Channon) *w ldr 1f: remained handy: rdn and hung rt fr over 2f out: wknd over 1f out* **7/1**[3]

6 5 **Pettinger** 2-9-0 0 RobertWinston 3 37+
(Charles Hills) *s.s: outpcd: sme hdwy over 2f out: sn wknd* **7/1**[3]

42 **7** 15 **Fumbleintheforest**[47] 3803 2-9-0 0 AndrewMullen 6
(Robyn Brisland) *wnt rt s: sn chsng ldrs: rdn 1/2-way: hung rt fr over 2f out: sn wknd (jockey said filly hung both ways)* **25/1**

0 **8** 8 **Courtney Rose**[12] 5145 2-9-0 0 TrevorWhelan 7
(Ivan Furtado) *s.s: outpcd (jockey said filly ran green)* **66/1**

1m 15.73s (3.63) **Going Correction** +0.60s/f (Yiel) **8 Ran SP% 116.5**
Speed ratings (Par 93): **99,97,92,91,87 80,60,49**
CSF £7.42 TOTE £3.20: £1.50, £1.20, £1.80; EX 8.30 Trifecta £57.40.
Owner Cheveley Park Stud **Bred** Cheveley Park Stud Ltd **Trained** Musley Bank, N Yorks

FOCUS
Plenty of rain had hit the course (29mm overnight, 80mm in total over the previous four days) and the going was given as heavy (GoingStick 5.3). Just an ordinary maiden, and a bit of a test in the conditions.

5548 LUTTERWORTH (S) STKS — 1m 2f
6:20 (6:20) (Class 5) 3-Y-O
£3,752 (£1,116; £557; £300; £300; £300) Stalls Low

Form RPR

-506 **1** **Crystal Tiara**[20] 4834 3-8-11 48 GeraldMosse 7 55
(Mick Channon) *led over 8f out: rdn clr fnl f: eased nr fin* **7/4**[1]

0050 **2** 4 ½ **Risk Mitigation (USA)**[21] 4794 3-9-2 53 (v) AndrewMullen 2 51
(David Evans) *chsd ldrs: rdn over 2f out: chsd wnr fnl f: no imp* **16/1**

0064 **3** ¾ **Little Tipple**[7] 5304 3-8-11 40 NickyMackay 3 45
(John Ryan) *sn led: hdd over 8f out: chsd wnr: rdn over 2f out: styng on same pce whn lost 2nd 1f out* **33/1**

1525 4 8 **Izvestia (IRE)**[7] 5304 3-9-7 74..........(p) HollieDoyle 8 40
(Archie Watson) *s.i.s: pushed along in rr at various stages: rdn over 2f out: no rspnse (jockey said filly was never travelling)* **5/2**[2]

4000 5 1 3/4 **Maiden Navigator**[16] 5001 3-8-11 52..........(h) TomEaves 9 27
(David Simcock) *s.i.s: hld up: hdwy over 2f out: rdn and wknd over 1f out* **8/1**

00-0 6 2 1/2 **Leebellinsummerbee (IRE)**[84] 2531 3-8-4 46.......... EllaMcCain(7) 6 23
(Donald McCain) *prom: rdn over 2f out: hung rt and wknd over 1f out* **33/1**

03 7 1 **Beechwood James (FR)**[23] 4735 3-8-11 0(p1) ThoreHammerHansen(5) 4 26
(Richard Hannon) *s.i.s and hmpd s: hld up: rdn and wknd over 2f out (jockey said colt suffered slight interference when leaving the stalls)* **5/1**[3]

1455 8 16 **Warrior Display (IRE)**[10] 2341 3-9-6 59..........(p) StevieDonohoe 1
(Bernard Llewellyn) *prom: lost pl over 7f out: rdn over 3f out: wknd over 2f out* **10/1**

2m 15.29s (6.09) **Going Correction** +0.60s/f (Yiel) 8 Ran SP% **113.6**
Speed ratings (Par 100): **99,95,94,88,87 85,84,71**
CSF £31.47 TOTE £2.60: £1.10, £3.40, £6.60; EX 31.80 Trifecta £728.80.The winner was bought in for £12,000.
Owner The Sweet Partnership **Bred** Mike Channon Bloodstock Ltd **Trained** West Ilsley, Berks

FOCUS
A weak race but notable for a decent punt being landed.

5549 BOSWORTH FIELD FILLIES' H'CAP 1m 2f
6:55 (6:55) (Class 5) (0-75,72) 3-Y-O+
£3,428 (£1,020; £509; £300; £300; £300) Stalls Low

Form RPR

4212 1 **Teodora De Vega (IRE)**[4] 5436 3-9-6 71.......... RobHornby 4 82
(Ralph Beckett) *s.i.s and pushed along early in rr: hdwy over 3f out: shkn up over 2f out: rdn to chse ldr over 1f out: led wl ins fnl f: r.o: comf* **4/9**[1]

00-1 2 1 1/4 **Seascape (IRE)**[90] 2341 3-9-0 65.......... JosephineGordon 2 73
(Henry Candy) *led at stdy pce tl qcknd 3f out: rdn over 1f out: hdd wl ins fnl f: styd on same pce* **7/1**[2]

0036 3 8 **Forbidden Dance**[21] 4788 3-9-7 72.......... HollieDoyle 3 64
(Hughie Morrison) *hld up: outpcd 3f: r.o to go 3rd nr fin* **7/1**[2]

023 4 1 1/2 **Elena**[36] 4211 3-9-3 68.......... KieranShoemark 6 57
(Charles Hills) *chsd ldr: chal over 2f out tl rdn over 1f out: sn hung rt: wknd ins fnl f* **11/1**[3]

0003 5 1 3/4 **Takiah**[7] 5307 4-8-9 51 oh6..........(p) AndrewMullen 1 36
(Peter Hiatt) *broke wl: stdd to trck ldrs: ev ch fr over 2f out tl rdn over 1f out: wknd fnl f* **20/1**

0-00 6 4 **I Think So (IRE)**[12] 5148 4-9-2 65.......... LauraCoughlan(7) 5 42
(David Loughnane) *s.i.s: sn chsng ldrs: rdn over 3f out: wknd over 2f out* **50/1**

2m 15.54s (6.34) **Going Correction** +0.60s/f (Yiel)
WFA 3 from 4yo 9lb 6 Ran SP% **109.3**
Speed ratings (Par 100): **98,97,90,89,88 84**
CSF £3.83 TOTE £1.20: £1.10, £2.60; EX 4.30 Trifecta £13.60.
Owner Waverley Racing **Bred** Norelands Stud & Lofts Hall Stud **Trained** Kimpton, Hants

FOCUS
This was steadily run early on but they got racing for home plenty soon enough in the straight. The winner has been rated to her last-time-out Newcastle second.

5550 BRITISH STALLION STUDS EBF NOVICE STKS (PLUS 10 RACE) 6f
7:30 (7:30) (Class 4) 2-Y-O £4,787 (£1,424; £711; £355) Stalls High

Form RPR

1 **Yorkshire Gold** 2-9-2 0.......... KevinStott 2 82+
(Kevin Ryan) *dwlt: sn pushed along and rn green in rr: swtchd rt over 2f out: hdwy on outer over 1f out: shkn up to ld ins fnl f: comf* **7/2**[3]

2 1 3/4 **Bright Valentine** 2-8-11 0.......... RobHornby 5 71
(Richard Spencer) *s.i.s: sn prom: led over 1f out: rdn and hdd ins fnl f: styd on same pce (vet reported filly lost its right hind shoe)* **12/1**

51 3 2 1/2 **Silver Mission (IRE)**[41] 4032 2-9-8 0.......... JackGarritty 6 74
(Richard Fahey) *chsd ldrs: rdn over 3f out: swtchd rt over 2f out: styd on same pce fnl f* **9/4**[1]

03 4 1/2 **Always Fearless (IRE)**[11] 5177 2-9-2 0.......... RossaRyan 7 67
(Richard Hannon) *led: rdn and hdd over 1f out: no ex ins fnl f* **7/2**[3]

2 5 nk **Dark Regard**[12] 5118 2-8-11 0.......... JasonHart 1 61
(Mark Johnston) *chsd ldr: chal over 2f out tl rdn over 1f out: no ex ins fnl f* **5/2**[2]

1m 16.54s (4.44) **Going Correction** +0.60s/f (Yiel) 5 Ran SP% **111.5**
Speed ratings (Par 96): **94,91,88,87,87**
CSF £37.19 TOTE £4.50: £2.00, £6.60; EX 47.00 Trifecta £294.10.
Owner Sheikh Mohammed Obaid Al Maktoum **Bred** Rabbah Bloodstock Limited **Trained** Hambleton, N Yorks

FOCUS
A nice performance from the winner, who overcame greenness to win comfortably.

5551 QUORN H'CAP 6f
8:05 (8:06) (Class 5) (0-70,72) 3-Y-O+
£3,752 (£1,116; £557; £300; £300; £300) Stalls High

Form RPR

0225 1 **Inexes**[18] 4912 7-9-12 69..........(p) JasonHart 5 76
(Ivan Furtado) *s.i.s: hdwy over 2f out: led over 1f out: rdn out* **10/3**[3]

0002 2 3/4 **Bahuta Acha**[14] 5038 4-9-8 65..........(b) RossaRyan 9 69
(David Loughnane) *chsd ldrs: rdn over 2f out: edgd rt ins fnl f: r.o (jockey said gelding hung left handed travelling from 3f out)* **14/1**

0400 3 1 1/4 **Jacksonfire**[2] 5486 7-8-0 50 oh5..........(p) LauraCoughlan(7) 4 50
(Michael Mullineaux) *broke wl enough: sn lost pl: hdwy over 1f out: styd on to go 3rd post* **12/1**

3341 4 shd **Evening Attire**[13] 5107 8-9-9 66.......... HollieDoyle 1 66
(William Stone) *led 1f: chsd ldrs: rdn over 2f out: ev ch over 1f out: no ex wl ins fnl f* **5/2**[2]

-241 5 3/4 **Rewaayat**[14] 5050 4-10-1 72.......... KieranShoemark 3 70
(Charles Hills) *plld hrd and prom: led 5f out: rdn and hdd over 1f out: no ex ins fnl f* **7/4**[1]

0000 6 1 3/4 **Minty Jones**[2] 5491 10-8-4 50 oh5..........(v) JaneElliott(3) 8 42
(Michael Mullineaux) *chsd ldrs: sn pushed along and lost pl: n.d after* **66/1**

4503 7 8 **Fair Alibi**[45] 3884 3-9-4 66.......... TomEaves 6 31
(Tom Tate) *w ldrs 2f: shkn up over 2f out: wknd over 1f out* **10/1**

1m 15.12s (3.02) **Going Correction** +0.60s/f (Yiel)
WFA 3 from 4yo+ 5lb 7 Ran SP% **113.0**
Speed ratings (Par 103): **103,102,100,100,99 96,86**
CSF £45.13 CT £494.39 TOTE £4.20: £2.00, £6.90; EX 56.30 Trifecta £383.20.
Owner 21st Century Racing **Bred** Meon Valley Stud **Trained** Wiseton, Nottinghamshire

FOCUS
Modest sprint handicap form and there's a fair chance the winner didn't need to improve on this year's level.

5552 SHANGTON H'CAP 1m 53y
8:40 (8:40) (Class 6) (0-60,61) 3-Y-O
£3,169 (£943; £471; £300; £300; £300) Stalls Low

Form RPR

0163 1 **Kermouster**[50] 3685 3-9-8 61.......... SamJames 5 71
(Grant Tuer) *hld up: hdwy over 2f out: led over 1f out: r.o* **11/2**[3]

2656 2 2 1/4 **Smeaton (IRE)**[15] 5023 3-9-7 60.......... JasonHart 7 65
(Roger Fell) *trckd ldrs: racd keenly: led wl over 1f out: sn hdd: edgd rt and styd on same pce ins fnl f* **7/2**[2]

1256 3 4 **Dolly Dupree**[25] 4664 3-8-11 50.......... HollieDoyle 1 46
(Paul D'Arcy) *hld up: hdwy and hung rt fr over 1f out: styd on to go 3rd ins fnl f: nt trble ldrs* **14/1**

0000 4 2 3/4 **Invincible One (IRE)**[21] 4794 3-9-1 54.......... RobHornby 14 44
(Sylvester Kirk) *chsd ldrs on outer: ev ch 2f out: wknd ins fnl f* **20/1**

046 5 3 1/2 **Heart In Havana**[36] 4211 3-9-4 57..........(t1) NathanEvans 8 40
(Michael Easterby) *led: rdn and hdd wl over 1f out: wknd fnl f* **16/1**

0-50 6 1/2 **Cambeleza (IRE)**[23] 4726 3-9-0 53.......... KevinStott 9 34
(Kevin Ryan) *hld up: rdn and hung rt over 1f out: nt trble ldrs* **8/1**

0032 7 3/4 **Jazz Hands (IRE)**[15] 5031 3-9-0 53.......... JackGarritty 3 33
(Richard Fahey) *hld up: rdn over 2f out: swtchd lft over 1f out: n.d (trainer's rep said, the gelding was unsuited by the heavy going on this occasion)* **5/2**[1]

0650 8 nse **Forty Four Sunsets (FR)**[22] 4754 3-8-8 52(b) ThoreHammerHansen(5) 6 32
(Richard Hannon) *s.i.s: nvr on terms (jockey said filly was never travelling)* **11/1**

0-05 9 1 3/4 **Asensio**[21] 4806 3-9-8 61.......... GeraldMosse 2 37
(Mohamed Moubarak) *sn chsng ldrs: rdn over 3f out: wknd over 1f out* **9/1**

000- 10 16 **My Boy Monty**[228] 9556 3-8-0 46 oh1.......... AledBeech(7) 11
(Gary Sanderson) *hld up in tch on outer: rdn over 2f out: sn wknd (jockey said colt stopped quickly)* **66/1**

-000 11 11 **Sherella**[71] 2943 3-8-7 46.......... NickyMackay 12
(J R Jenkins) *chsd ldr tl rdn over 3f out: wknd over 2f out (jockey said filly stopped quickly)* **28/1**

1m 51.08s (4.78) **Going Correction** +0.60s/f (Yiel) 11 Ran SP% **117.9**
Speed ratings (Par 98): **100,97,93,91,87 87,86,86,84,68 57**
CSF £24.65 CT £264.26 TOTE £5.20: £1.60, £1.60, £3.50; EX 26.20 Trifecta £275.90.
Owner D R Tucker **Bred** D R Tucker **Trained** Birkby, N Yorks

FOCUS
A modest affair, but the first two pulled nicely clear.
T/Plt: £585.40 to a £1 stake. Pool: £44,270.07 - 55.20 winning units T/Qpdt: £60.30 to a £1 stake. Pool: £5,742.79 - 70.39 winning units **Colin Roberts**

5212 REDCAR (L-H)
Wednesday, July 31

OFFICIAL GOING: Good (good to firm in places; 8.2)
Wind: fresh largely against Weather: overcast, odd shower

5553 BEST FLAT RACES LIVE ON RACING TV BRITISH EBF NOVICE STKS (PLUS 10 RACE) 5f 217y
2:10 (2:13) (Class 4) 2-Y-O £6,145 (£1,828; £913; £456) Stalls Centre

Form RPR

1 1 **Macho Time (IRE)**[24] 4688 2-9-8 0.......... CliffordLee 12 83
(K R Burke) *mde all: narrow ld: rdn and edgd lft over 1f out: drvn appr fnl f: kpt on wl* **9/4**[1]

44 2 1 1/2 **Dutch Decoy**[67] 3098 2-9-2 0.......... PaulHanagan 5 72
(Richard Fahey) *pressed ldr: rdn 2f out: one pce towards fin* **11/4**[2]

322 3 2 **Cruising**[25] 4631 2-9-2 76..........(e1) DavidNolan 14 66
(David Brown) *trckd ldrs: pushed along to chal over 1f out: sn drvn: one pce ins fnl f* **5/1**[3]

5 4 nk **My Dandy Doc (IRE)**[12] 5118 2-8-11 0.......... RobbieDowney 13 60
(John Quinn) *hld up: swtchd rt and hdwy over 1f out: sn rdn: kpt on ins fnl f* **50/1**

5 nse **Cold Light Of Day** 2-8-11 0.......... CamHardie 11 60+
(Michael Dods) *dwlt: hld up: pushed along over 2f out: kpt on wl fnl f: nrst fin* **25/1**

0 6 1/2 **Proclaimer**[11] 5172 2-9-2 0.......... KevinStott 2 63
(Julie Camacho) *dwlt but sn prom: rdn 2f out: no ex ins fnl f* **8/1**

7 1/2 **Lasting Legacy** 2-8-11 0.......... MichaelStainton 10 57
(Chris Fairhurst) *outpcd in rr tl kpt on fnl f* **25/1**

5 8 1 3/4 **Sushi Power (IRE)**[33] 4323 2-8-11 0.......... DavidAllan 3 51
(Tim Easterby) *trckd ldrs: rdn 2f out: wknd ins fnl f* **10/1**

0 9 nk **Redzone**[20] 4826 2-9-2 0.......... GrahamLee 4 55
(Bryan Smart) *dwlt: hld up: nvr threatened* **12/1**

00 10 3/4 **Inductive**[28] 4517 2-9-2 0.......... ConnorBeasley 1 53
(Michael Dods) *hld up: rdn along over 3f out: nvr threatened* **20/1**

00 11 nk **William Alexander**[12] 5145 2-9-2 0.......... LewisEdmunds 6 52
(Les Eyre) *midfield: rdn 2f out: wknd ins fnl f* **150/1**

60 12 4 **The Mystery Wizard**[14] 5052 2-9-2 0.......... DuranFentiman 9 39
(Tim Easterby) *trckd ldrs: rdn over 2f out: wknd over 1f out* **200/1**

00 13 nk **Teasel's Rock (IRE)**[25] 4623 2-8-11 0.......... RachelRichardson 8 33
(Tim Easterby) *prom tl wknd 2f out* **50/1**

1m 13.29s (1.49) **Going Correction** +0.20s/f (Good) 13 Ran SP% **119.5**
Speed ratings (Par 96): **102,100,97,96,96 96,95,93,92,91 91,86,85**
CSF £7.85 TOTE £2.80: £1.10, £1.30, £2.40; EX 10.50 Trifecta £24.90.
Owner J C Fretwell **Bred** Denis McDonnell **Trained** Middleham Moor, N Yorks

FOCUS
Ground that was officially good, good to firm in places, but they were leaving a print. The market leaders came to the fore in this novice event. It was a race where those drawn high appeared to hold an advantage.

5554 WATCH RACING TV IN STUNNING HD NOVICE STKS 7f
2:45 (2:47) (Class 5) 3-Y-O+ £4,528 (£1,347; £673; £336) Stalls Centre

Form RPR

-0 1 **Farzeen**[196] 251 3-8-12 0.......... JackMitchell 11 82+
(Roger Varian) *in tch: hdwy over 2f out: led gng wl appr fnl f: pushed along and edgd lft: kpt on wl to draw clr fnl 110yds: readily* **7/4**[1]

5-33 **2** 3¼ **Shaqwar**[43] 3974 3-8-12 70........................(p[1]) GrahamLee 10 71
(Kevin Ryan) *led: rdn along over 2f out: hdd appr fnl f: kpt on same pce and no ch w wnr ins fnl f* **8/1**

0 **3** 2½ **Narak**[48] 3761 3-8-12 0........................ ConnorBeasley 1 64
(George Scott) *wnt lft s: sn in tch: rdn over 2f out: kpt on fnl f* **20/1**

2 **4** ¾ **Sorbonne**[14] 5041 3-9-3 0........................ BenCurtis 2 67
(David Barron) *prom: rdn over 2f out: outpcd appr fnl f: kpt on fnl 110yds* **5/1[3]**

6245 **5** 4 **Royal Welcome**[28] 4520 3-8-12 75........................ DavidAllan 12 51
(James Tate) *trckd ldrs: rdn over 2f out: wknd fnl f* **5/2[2]**

5 **6** 1 **Gleniffer**[20] 4827 3-9-3 0........................ EoinWalsh 9 54
(Jim Goldie) *midfield: rdn along over 2f out and rn green: kpt on ins fnl f* **33/1**

-000 **7** 6 **Wearraah**[16] 4978 3-9-3 38........................(b[1]) DavidNolan 6 38
(Alan Brown) *trckd ldrs: rdn along 3f out: wknd over 1f out* **200/1**

050 **8** 1 **Guarded Secret**[44] 3920 3-8-9 45........................(b[1]) BenRobinson(3) 3 30
(Michael Dods) *dwlt: sn in tch: rdn and lost pl over 2f out: wknd over 1f out* **100/1**

9 nk **High Gloss** 3-8-12 0........................ KevinStott 5 29
(James Fanshawe) *dwlt: hld up in midfield: pushed along over 2f out: wknd over 1f out (vet reported filly lost its right fore shoe)* **7/1**

0-60 **10** 3 **Allsfineandandy (IRE)**[23] 4731 3-9-0 49........................ ConorMcGovern(3) 4 26
(Lynn Siddall) *a towards rr* **200/1**

40- **11** 1¼ **New Rhythm**[490] 1427 4-9-2 0........................ RowanScott(3) 7 21
(Alistair Whillans) *a in rr* **200/1**

0 **12** 9 **Graciarose**[50] 3707 3-8-12 0........................ RoystonFfrench 8
(Tracy Waggott) *slowly away: a in rr* **200/1**

1m 25.19s (-0.21) **Going Correction** +0.20s/f (Good)
WFA 3 from 4yo 7lb **12 Ran SP% 115.9**
Speed ratings (Par 103): **109,105,102,101,97 95,89,87,87,84 82,72**
CSF £16.36 TOTE £2.30: £1.30, £1.80, £4.90; EX 16.90 Trifecta £200.20.
Owner Helena Springfield Ltd **Bred** Meon Valley Stud **Trained** Newmarket, Suffolk

FOCUS
An ordinary novice event which was dominated by fillies. The first two were both drawn high.

5555 JOIN RACING TV NOW (S) STKS 1m 2f 1y

3:20 (3:21) (Class 5) 3-Y-O+

£3,500 (£1,041; £520; £300; £300; £300) **Stalls Low**

Form RPR

0R32 **1** **First Flight (IRE)**[10] 5216 8-9-3 73........................ BenRobinson(3) 2 64+
(Brian Ellison) *prom: pushed into ld over 1f out: kpt on wl and clr appr fnl f* **1/1[1]**

0550 **2** 6 **Silk Mill Blue**[23] 4728 5-9-6 48........................ PhilDennis 6 50
(Richard Whitaker) *stdd s: midfield: pushed along and hdwy to chse ldr wl over 1f out: sn rdn: kpt on same pce and sn no ch w wnr* **25/1**

5056 **3** shd **Biz Markee (IRE)**[26] 4587 3-8-11 52........................(b) BenCurtis 7 51
(Roger Fell) *dwlt: sn trckd ldrs: rdn over 2f out: bit outpcd over 1f out: kpt on ins fnl f* **13/2[3]**

4535 **4** 2 **Hayward Field (IRE)**[28] 4515 6-9-6 45........................(e) ConnorBeasley 10 46
(Noel Wilson) *hld up in rr: hdwy 2f out: rdn over 1f out: kpt on ins fnl f* **18/1**

6000 **5** nse **Carry On Deryck**[23] 4730 7-9-6 87........................ CamHardie 12 46
(Ollie Pears) *t.k.h early: sn stdd in tch: rdn along 2f out: bmpd sltly over 1f out: one pce* **9/4[2]**

0100 **6** ¾ **Restive (IRE)**[13] 5095 6-9-11 65........................(t[1]) EoinWalsh 9 49
(Jim Goldie) *hld up in midfield: rdn along over 2f out: hung lft over 1f out: one pce and nvr threatened* **9/1**

5066 **7** ½ **Mandarin Princess**[7] 5297 4-8-12 41........................ RowanScott(3) 4 39
(Kenny Johnson) *trckd ldrs: rdn over 2f out: wknd ins fnl f* **200/1**

0003 **8** 3 **Royal Liberty**[10] 5216 4-9-6 44........................ SamJames 8 38
(Geoffrey Harker) *hld up: nvr threatened* **33/1**

0000 **9** 1½ **Lord Rob**[10] 5213 8-9-1 43........................ HarrisonShaw(5) 1 35
(David Thompson) *led: rdn and hdd over 2f out: wknd over 1f out* **50/1**

10 8 **Fast And Friendly (IRE)**[38] 5-9-6 0........................ DavidNolan 11 20
(Barry Murtagh) *a towards rr* **200/1**

11 15 **Canneyhill Bob**[15] 4-9-6 0........................ GrahamLee 5
(Kenny Johnson) *s.i.s: hld up: tk str hold: plld way into midfield 7f out: swtchd rt to outside 5f out: wknd 3f out: sn bhd* **100/1**

2m 8.45s (1.55) **Going Correction** +0.20s/f (Good)
WFA 3 from 4yo+ 9lb **11 Ran SP% 120.1**
Speed ratings (Par 103): **101,96,96,94,94 93,93,91,89,83 71**
CSF £37.67 TOTE £1.70: £1.10, £5.50, £1.90; EX 32.80 Trifecta £200.50.There was no bid for the winner. Restive was claimed by Mick Appleby for £6,000.
Owner Kristian Strangeway **Bred** Darley **Trained** Norton, N Yorks

FOCUS
Not much depth to this seller.

5556 EVERY RACE LIVE ON RACING TV H'CAP 1m 2f 1y

3:55 (3:56) (Class 5) (0-70,70) 3-Y-O+

£3,737 (£1,112; £555; £300; £300; £300) **Stalls Low**

Form RPR

2110 **1** **Mr Coco Bean (USA)**[19] 4892 5-10-0 70........................ GrahamLee 3 86+
(David Barron) *hld up: smooth hdwy fr 3f out: jnd ldr on bit appr fnl f: led ins fnl f: pushed clr fnl 110yds: easily* **5/1[3]**

-402 **2** 1¾ **Mina Vagante**[10] 5213 3-9-2 67........................ PatCosgrave 6 74
(Hugo Palmer) *dwlt: sn midfield: pushed along and hdwy 3f out: led wl over 1f out: rdn and jnd appr fnl f: hdd ins fnl f: kpt on but no ch w wnr* **4/1[1]**

0463 **3** 2 **Placebo Effect (IRE)**[25] 4627 4-9-9 68........................ BenRobinson(3) 4 71
(Ollie Pears) *midfield: pushed along whn sltly hmpd 3f out: rdn and hdwy to chse ldrs over 1f out: kpt on* **9/2[2]**

0003 **4** 1½ **Ad Libitum**[12] 5122 4-9-10 66........................(p) BenCurtis 7 66
(Roger Fell) *hld up in midfield: rdn and sme hdwy on outer 2f out: kpt on fnl f* **12/1**

0605 **5** nse **Maghfoor**[15] 5025 5-8-13 60........................ HarrisonShaw(5) 13 60
(Eric Alston) *dwlt: hld up: pushed along and hdwy 3f out: rdn 2f out: kpt on same pce* **12/1**

0005 **6** ¾ **Seaborough (IRE)**[10] 5219 4-8-9 58........................(p) RhonaPindar(7) 10 56
(David Thompson) *hld up: rdn along and sme hdwy on inner over 2f out: styd on ins fnl f* **33/1**

/340 **7** 2¾ **Flying Raconteur**[12] 5156 5-9-8 67........................(t) RowanScott(3) 8 60
(Nigel Tinkler) *hld up in midfield: rdn and sme hdwy on outside over 2f out: wknd ins fnl f* **12/1**

4054 **8** 1½ **Osmosis**[6] 5334 3-8-9 63........................(p[1]) ConorMcGovern(3) 12 53
(Jason Ward) *led at gd pce: rdn and hdd over 2f out: wknd over 1f out* **20/1**

4-35 **9** ¾ **Alfa Dawn (IRE)**[12] 5156 3-9-4 69........................ SamJames 9 57
(Phillip Makin) *trckd ldrs: rdn 3f out: wknd over 1f out* **16/1**

0102 **10** ½ **Glaceon (IRE)**[13] 5096 4-8-12 54........................ NathanEvans 14 41
(Tina Jackson) *trckd ldrs: rdn 3f out: wknd over 1f out (vet reported filly had a wound to her right fore leg)* **20/1**

3221 **11** 1 **Neileta**[24] 4690 3-8-10 61........................(p) DuranFentiman 2 46
(Tim Easterby) *in tch: rdn over 2f out: wknd over 1f out (jockey said gelding ran flat)* **5/1[3]**

0463 **12** hd **Remmy D (IRE)**[11] 5178 4-9-0 56........................(b) EoinWalsh 15 41
(Jim Goldie) *sn prom: rdn to ld over 2f out: hdd wl over 1f out: wknd (jockey said gelding stopped quickly)* **28/1**

/000 **13** 13 **Ennjaaz (IRE)**[24] 4689 5-9-11 67........................(p) DavidNolan 5 26
(Marjorie Fife) *trckd ldrs: rdn over 3f out: wknd 2f out* **50/1**

0006 **14** 1½ **Intense Pleasure (IRE)**[10] 5213 4-8-9 51 oh3........................(h) JamesSullivan 1 7
(Ruth Carr) *in tch: rdn over 3f out: wknd over 1f out* **40/1**

1304 **15** 4 **Fitzy**[9] 5247 3-8-5 56........................(p) CamHardie 11 5
(David Brown) *dwlt: a in rr (jockey said gelding hung left-handed throughout)* **20/1**

2m 6.95s (0.05) **Going Correction** +0.20s/f (Good)
WFA 3 from 4yo+ 9lb **15 Ran SP% 125.5**
Speed ratings (Par 103): **107,105,104,102,102 102,99,98,98,97 96,96,86,85,82**
CSF £23.93 CT £101.27 TOTE £6.80: £1.50, £1.90, £2.40; EX 26.50 Trifecta £182.60.
Owner S Raines **Bred** Stewart Larkin Armstrong **Trained** Maunby, N Yorks

FOCUS
An easy winner of this handicap, which was run at what seemed a decent gallop and in a time 1.5sec quicker than the preceding seller.

5557 RACINGTV.COM STRAIGHT-MILE SERIES H'CAP (QUALIFIER FOR THE RACING UK STRAIGHT MILE SERIES FINAL) 7f 219y

4:30 (4:32) (Class 4) (0-85,83) 3-Y-O

£6,339 (£1,886; £942; £471; £300; £300) **Stalls Centre**

Form RPR

3051 **1** **Edaraat**[21] 4789 3-9-7 83........................ JackMitchell 2 91+
(Roger Varian) *midfield: racd quite keenly: trckd ldrs gng wl 2f out: swtchd rt over 1f out: pushed into narrow ld 150yds out: sn edgd lft: rdn out fnl 75yds* **5/2[1]**

4223 **2** ½ **One To Go**[10] 5214 3-8-2 64........................(b) CamHardie 5 71
(Tim Easterby) *dwlt: hld up: pushed along and hdwy 2f out: drvn to chal appr fnl f: led ins fnl f: sn hdd: kpt on wl but a jst hld* **8/1**

1625 **3** 3¼ **Creek Island (IRE)**[12] 5124 3-8-10 72........................ CYHo 4 72
(Mark Johnston) *prom: rdn to ld over 1f out: sn drvn: hdd ins fnl f: sn no ex* **16/1**

5435 **4** 1¼ **Kuwait Station (IRE)**[13] 5095 3-9-0 76........................(v[1]) DavidNolan 1 73
(David O'Meara) *led: rdn and hdd over 1f out: no ex fnl f* **11/1**

0226 **5** nk **Zip**[11] 5200 3-8-11 73........................ GrahamLee 3 69
(Richard Fahey) *midfield: rdn 2f out: no imp (vet reported gelding had lost its right hind and right fore shoes)* **5/1[3]**

0113 **6** 3 **Salam Zayed**[4] 5422 3-8-7 69........................ PaulHanagan 7 58
(Richard Fahey) *midfield: racd quite keenly: rdn 2f out: wknd ins fnl f* **4/1[2]**

424 **7** nk **Double Honour**[33] 4334 3-9-2 78........................ CliffordLee 8 66
(James Bethell) *dwlt: hld up: rdn along over 2f out: edgd lft and wknd 1f out* **13/2**

8 2 **Jupiter Road**[28] 4528 3-9-2 83........................ FayeMcManoman(5) 6 67
(Nigel Tinkler) *trckd ldrs: rdn 2f out: wknd fnl f* **11/1**

1m 39.99s (3.39) **Going Correction** +0.20s/f (Good) **8 Ran SP% 112.2**
Speed ratings (Par 102): **91,90,87,86,85 82,82,80**
CSF £22.25 CT £257.81 TOTE £2.70: £1.30, £2.10, £4.20; EX 23.10 Trifecta £216.10.
Owner Hamdan Al Maktoum **Bred** Shadwell Estate Company Limited **Trained** Newmarket, Suffolk

FOCUS
Two pulled clear in this fair handicap.

5558 GET SO MUCH MORE WITH RACING TV H'CAP (DIV I) 5f 217y

5:00 (5:03) (Class 6) (0-55,57) 3-Y-O+

£3,500 (£1,041; £520; £300; £300; £300) **Stalls Centre**

Form RPR

0-00 **1** **Grimsdyke**[20] 4823 3-8-7 46 oh1........................ DuranFentiman 10 52
(Tim Easterby) *prom: drvn to chal strly appr fnl f: kpt on: led post* **25/1**

2032 **2** nse **Perfect Swiss**[11] 5202 3-9-1 54........................ DavidAllan 18 60
(Tim Easterby) *midfield: gd hdwy 2f out: rdn into narrow ld appr fnl f: drvn ins fnl f: kpt on but hdd post* **15/8[1]**

5100 **3** ½ **Mansfield**[25] 4630 6-9-4 57........................ BenSanderson(5) 20 62
(Stella Barclay) *dwlt: hld up: hdwy 2f out: rdn to chse ldrs: kpt on* **11/1**

4562 **4** 1½ **Dubai Elegance**[12] 5147 5-8-12 46........................(p) AndrewElliott 16 46
(Derek Shaw) *hld up in midfield: hdwy and n.m.r bhd ldrs appr fnl f: angled rt ins fnl f: rdn and kpt on wl fnl 110yds* **12/1**

0-00 **5** ½ **Nifty Niece (IRE)**[34] 4276 5-8-12 46 oh1........................ GrahamLee 12 45
(Ann Duffield) *dwlt: hld up: rdn and hdwy towards far side over 1f out: kpt on fnl f* **50/1**

05 **6** ½ **Searanger (USA)**[44] 3924 6-9-5 53........................ CliffordLee 1 50
(Rebecca Menzies) *chsd ldrs: rdn over 2f out: one pce* **11/2[3]**

4643 **7** hd **Spirit Of Zebedee (IRE)**[7] 5299 6-9-2 50........................(v) RobbieDowney 13 47
(John Quinn) *chsd ldrs: rdn to chal over 1f out: no ex fnl 50yds* **9/2[2]**

6650 **8** ¾ **Supreme Dream**[7] 5300 3-8-7 46........................ CamHardie 6 39
(Ollie Pears) *chsd ldrs: rdn 2f out: one pce* **16/1**

-000 **9** 2½ **Princess Apollo**[23] 4726 5-8-9 46 oh1........................(b[1]) RowanScott(3) 7 32
(Donald Whillans) *pressed ldr: led over 3f out: rdn over 2f out: hdd appr fnl f: wknd ins fnl f* **40/1**

-040 **10** 2 **Just A Rumour (IRE)**[13] 5099 3-8-7 46 oh1........................ JamesSullivan 4 25
(Noel Wilson) *dwlt: hld up: hung lft to far rail over 3f out: rdn over 1f out: nvr threatened* **33/1**

034 **11** 2¼ **Joey Boy (IRE)**[23] 4731 3-9-3 56........................(p) ShaneGray 3 28
(Kevin Ryan) *prom: rdn over 2f out: wknd fnl f* **15/2**

2260 **12** 2½ **Angel Eyes**[8] 5278 4-8-7 48........................(h) HarryRussell(7) 11 13
(John David Riches) *midfield: rdn over 2f out: wknd over 1f out* **25/1**

5500 **13** ½ **The Gingerbreadman**[26] 4602 4-8-7 46 oh1........................ PaulaMuir(5) 17 9
(Chris Fairhurst) *a towards rr* **33/1**

0000 **14** 2 **Khitaamy (IRE)**[21] 4784 5-8-12 46 oh1........................(vt) NathanEvans 19 3
(Tina Jackson) *hld up: rdn over 2f out: sn btn* **50/1**

0-60 **15** 3½ **Mithayel Style (FR)**[14] 5041 3-8-6 52........................(p) RhonaPindar(7) 2
(David Thompson) *a towards rr: edgd lft to far rail over 3f out* **50/1**

/00- **16** *24* **Go Bananas**[303] 7839 4-8-9 **48**.................................. HarrisonShaw(5) 9
(Ron Barr) *led narrowly: hdd over 3f out: wknd qckly: eased* **40/1**

1m 13.0s (1.20) **Going Correction** +0.20s/f (Good)
WFA 3 from 4yo+ 5lb **16** Ran SP% **126.4**
Speed ratings (Par 101): **104,103,103,101,100 99,99,98,95,92 89,86,85,83,78 46**
CSF £70.54 CT £612.92 TOTE £26.60: £5.70, £1.30, £2.30, £1.70; EX 91.90 Trifecta £1861.10.
Owner James Bowers **Bred** J Bowers **Trained** Great Habton, N Yorks
■ Stewards' Enquiry : David Allan four-day ban: misuse of the whip (Aug 14-17)

FOCUS
It had started raining by this stage. A 1-2 with 3yos for the Tim Easterby stable, an outsider pipping the well supported favourite. High numbers came out on top.

5559 GET SO MUCH MORE WITH RACING TV H'CAP (DIV II) 5f 217y

5:30 (5:34) (Class 6) (0-55,57) 3-Y-0+

£3,500 (£1,041; £520; £300; £300; £300) **Stalls** Centre

Form RPR

0022 **1** **Fox Hill**[5] 5392 3-8-12 **55**.................................. HarrisonShaw(5) 9 62
(Eric Alston) *slowly away: bhd: pushed along and hdwy 2f out: drvn over 1f out: rdn fnl f: str run last 150yds: drvn to ld last few strides* **11/4**[1]

00-5 **2** *nk* **Radjash**[65] 3158 5-8-12 **52**.................................(t[1]) ZakWheatley(7) 5 59
(Declan Carroll) *chsd ldrs: pushed along and hdwy 2f out: reminder over 1f out: drvn to ld ent fnl f: sn rdn and r.o: hdd last few strides* **5/1**[3]

0-50 **3** *1 ¼* **Ad Vitam (IRE)**[58] 3413 11-8-7 **45**.......................(bt) FayeMcManoman(5) 7 48
(Suzzanne France) *hld up: drvn and hdwy 2f out: sn rdn: chal 1f out: kpt on into 3rd fnl f* **50/1**

6300 **4** *½* **Roaring Rory**[20] 4823 6-8-13 **49**.................................. ConorMcGovern(3) 4 50
(Ollie Pears) *mid-div: pushed along 2f out: hdwy and drvn to chal 1f out: rdn fnl f: kpt on* **20/1**

532 **5** *1 ½* **War Ensign (IRE)**[8] 5278 4-8-12 **45**.................................(p[1]) DavidAllan 15 42+
(Tim Easterby) *hld up: pushed along and hdwy 2f out: rdn and cl up over 1f out: no ex fnl f* **10/3**[2]

0004 **6** *½* **Tigerinmytank**[13] 5102 3-8-7 **45**.................................. RoystonFfrench 6 39
(John Holt) *led: rdn over 1f out: hdd ent fnl f: no ex* **40/1**

3002 **7** *2 ¼* **Dancing Mountain (IRE)**[5] 5393 3-9-0 **52**.......................(b) BenCurtis 10 39+
(Roger Fell) *trckd ldrs: rdn over 1f out: one pce fnl f* **16/1**

0042 **8** *¾* **Mightaswellsmile**[7] 5300 5-8-7 **45**.................................. PaulaMuir(5) 8 30
(Ron Barr) *trckd ldrs: pushed along over 1f out: rdn fnl f: no imp (trainer said the mare was unsuited by the straight 6f and in his opinion would prefer racing around a bend)* **14/1**

0246 **9** *1 ¼* **Picks Pinta**[8] 5276 8-9-2 **49**.................................(p) LewisEdmunds 12 30+
(John David Riches) *slowly away: bhd: drvn and effrt 2f out: rdn over 1f out: no imp (vet reported gelding was lame on its right fore)* **50/1**

0/00 **10** *½* **Peach Pavlova (IRE)**[13] 5100 5-8-12 **45**.................................. GrahamLee 1 25
(Ann Duffield) *hld up: drvn 2f out: mod hdwy fnl f* **40/1**

-000 **11** *½* **Whigwham**[12] 5147 5-8-12 **45**.................................. CamHardie 11 23+
(Gary Sanderson) *mid-div: drvn 2f out: wknd over 1f out* **66/1**

4504 **12** *1 ½* **Vallarta (IRE)**[7] 5300 9-9-1 **48**.................................(p[1]) JamesSullivan 2 21
(Ruth Carr) *prom: drvn 2f out: sn rdn and wknd* **12/1**

5001 **13** *¾* **Someone Exciting**[7] 5299 6-9-6 **53** 5ex.................................. JamieGormley 19 24+
(David Thompson) *hld up: pushed along and hdwy 2f out: rdn over 1f out: wknd fnl f* **14/1**

3542 **14** *nk* **Steelriver (IRE)**[7] 5299 9-9-5 **57**.................................. DannyRedmond(5) 17 27+
(Michael Herrington) *mid-div: trckd ldrs 2f out: rdn and wknd over 1f out* **15/2**

4314 **15** *4 ½* **Billyoakes (IRE)**[41] 4025 7-9-4 **54**.................................(p) BenRobinson(3) 20 10+
(Ollie Pears) *prom: drvn 2f out: sn wknd* **33/1**

06-6 **16** *¾* **Tick Tock Croc (IRE)**[15] 5018 3-8-8 **53**.......................(h) HarryRussell(7) 14 5
(Bryan Smart) *hld up: drvn 2f out: rdn over 1f out: no imp* **33/1**

-000 **17** *3 ¾* **Dothraki (IRE)**[30] 4434 3-8-8 **46**.................................. EoinWalsh 16
(Ronald Thompson) *bhd: drvn 1/2-way: rdn 2f out: no rspnse* **100/1**

3060 **18** *1* **Raksha (IRE)**[14] 5041 3-9-3 **55**.................................(h[1]) DavidNolan 13
(David O'Meara) *t.k.h: chsd ldrs: drvn and lost pl 2f out: sn dropped away and eased (vet reported filly had a wound on its left hind leg)* **33/1**

00-5 **19** *nk* **Your Just Desserts (IRE)**[8] 5278 4-8-12 **45**.................................. ShaneGray 18
(Paul Collins) *hld up: drvn 2f out: fdd over 1f out: eased fnl f* **66/1**

-050 **20** *10* **Little Thornton**[9] 5236 3-8-7 **45**.................................(p[1]) DuranFentiman 3
(Stella Barclay) *prom on far side: drvn and wknd 2f out: heavily eased whn btn* **100/1**

1m 13.35s (1.55) **Going Correction** +0.20s/f (Good)
WFA 3 from 4yo+ 5lb **20** Ran SP% **132.4**
Speed ratings (Par 101): **101,100,98,98,96 95,92,91,89,89 88,86,85,85,79 78,73,71,71,58**
CSF £15.90 CT £611.53 TOTE £3.60: £1.30, £2.20, £10.50, £4.60; EX 23.30 Trifecta £2110.50.
Owner Whitehills Racing Syndicate **Bred** Itchen Valley Stud **Trained** Longton, Lancs

FOCUS
The slower division by 0.35sec. The pace was down the centre in this big-field sprint.

5560 AJA NOVICE FLAT AMATEUR RIDERS' H'CAP 7f 219y

6:00 (6:01) (Class 5) (0-70,71) 4-Y-0+

£3,606 (£1,118; £558; £300; £300; £300) **Stalls** Centre

Form RPR

0000 **1** **Insurplus (IRE)**[23] 4725 6-10-3 **55**.................................. MissShannonWatts(3) 4 64
(Jim Goldie) *trckd ldrs: dropped bk to midfield 5f out: swtchd lft 2f out: sn hdwy: rdn to chal 1f out: led 110yds out: kpt on* **10/1**

5120 **2** *1* **Thornaby Nash**[15] 5021 8-11-5 **68**.......................(b) MissAmyCollier 13 75
(Jason Ward) *midfield: hdwy and chsd ldrs over 2f out: rdn into narrow ld 1f out: hdd 110yds out: edgd rt and one pce* **12/1**

0210 **3** *3 ¾* **Ascot Week (USA)**[13] 5087 5-11-8 **71**.......................(v) MrThomasGreenwood 5 69
(John Quinn) *dwlt: hld up: hdwy over 2f out: rdn to chal over 1f out: sn edgd lft to far rail: no ex fnl 110yds* **8/1**[3]

0040 **4** *½* **Relight My Fire**[9] 5247 9-10-4 **53**.......................(b) MissJessicaGillam 6 50
(Tim Easterby) *midfield: pushed along over 1f out: rdn and styd on fnl f* **25/1**

1413 **5** *¾* **Fieldsman (USA)**[4] 5416 7-11-7 **70**.................................. MissSarahBowen 8 65
(Tony Carroll) *led: rdn 2f out: hdd 1f out: wknd ins fnl f* **2/1**[1]

1256 **6** *1 ½* **Abushamah (IRE)**[16] 4982 8-11-1 **64**.................................. MrMatthewEnnis 12 56
(Ruth Carr) *prom: rdn over 2f out: wknd ins fnl f* **9/1**

4000 **7** *nk* **Dutch Artist (IRE)**[7] 5302 7-10-1 **53**.......................(p) MissBelindaJohnson(3) 7 44
(Nigel Tinkler) *slowly away: hld up: rdn and sme hdwy over 1f out: nvr threatened* **33/1**

050- **8** *¾* **Dose**[278] 8597 6-10-8 **60**.................................. MrEireannCagney(3) 10 49
(Richard Fahey) *hld up: rdn along 3f out: nvr threatened* **33/1**

606 **9** *¾* **Irish Minister (USA)**[25] 4634 4-10-10 **62**.................................. MrHenryNewcombe(3) 14 50
(David Thompson) *slowly away and in rr: sme late hdwy: nvr involved* **25/1**

0000 **10** *3 ¾* **Rebel Cause (IRE)**[15] 5025 6-10-2 **51** oh5.......................(p) MrPhilipArmson 3 30
(John Holt) *hld up: rdn and edgd lft towards far rail over 3f out: nvr threatened* **20/1**

1-03 **11** *3* **Firby (IRE)**[40] 4054 4-11-4 **70**.................................. MissRachelTaylor(3) 1 42
(Michael Dods) *wnt sltly lft s: sn chsd ldrs: rdn along 2f out: edgd lft and wknd 1f out* **9/2**[2]

6600 **12** *2 ½* **Rosin Box (IRE)**[30] 4460 6-10-1 **53**.......................(t) MissSallyDavison(3) 11 19
(Tristan Davidson) *chsd ldrs: lost pl over 2f out: sn wknd* **12/1**

5106 **13** *¾* **Mama Africa (IRE)**[19] 4872 5-11-1 **64**.......................(p) MissImogenMathias 9 29
(John Flint) *chsd ldrs: wknd 2f out* **25/1**

0-05 **14** *3 ¾* **The Brora Pobbles**[18] 4916 4-9-13 **51** oh2.................................. MrConnorWood(3) 2 7
(Alistair Whillans) *chsd ldrs: lost pl 5f out: rdn and sn struggling towards rr* **20/1**

1m 40.69s (4.09) **Going Correction** +0.20s/f (Good) **14** Ran SP% **124.0**
Speed ratings (Par 103): **87,86,82,81,81 79,79,78,77,73 70,68,67,63**
CSF £115.71 CT £1047.80 TOTE £14.40: £3.10, £3.00, £1.90; EX 142.60 Trifecta £1651.20.
Owner D Renton & J Goldie **Bred** Patrick J Monahan **Trained** Uplawmoor, E Renfrews

FOCUS
Inexperienced riders, and modest form.
T/Plt: £12.30 to a £1 stake. Pool: £50,194.91 - 2963.30 winning units T/Qpdt: £6.30 to a £1 stake. Pool: £4,284.01 - 500.85 winning units **Andrew Sheret & Keith McHugh**

5345 SANDOWN (R-H)
Wednesday, July 31

OFFICIAL GOING: Good (good to soft in places; 6.7)
Wind: light breeze Weather: fine

5561 EVERY RACE LIVE ON RACING TV APPRENTICE H'CAP 1m

5:35 (5:38) (Class 5) (0-70,70) 3-Y-O

£4,528 (£1,347; £673; £336; £300; £300) **Stalls** Low

Form RPR

0262 **1** **Stay Forever (FR)**[12] 5137 3-8-13 **64**.................................. MariePerrault(7) 5 68
(Andrew Balding) *hld up off the pce in last pair: stl in last whn effrt over 2f out on outer: gd prog over 1f out: kpt on wl fnl f and pushed out to ld last strides* **12/1**

-045 **2** *nk* **Classic Star**[25] 4642 3-8-9 **60**.................................. LukeBacon(7) 9 63
(Dean Ivory) *trckd ldrs and wd early: clsr at 1/2-way: effrt over 2f out: led 1f out: kpt on one pce fnl f: hdd last strides* **15/2**

0454 **3** *½* **Flying Dragon (FR)**[6] 5350 3-9-5 **70**.................................. LukeCatton(7) 4 72
(Richard Hannon) *in last pair off the pce: effrt over 2f out: gd prog over 1f out: ev ch fnl f: no ex cl home (vet reported gelding lost its left fore shoe)* **9/2**[2]

623 **4** *½* **Grab And Run (IRE)**[33] 4334 3-9-10 **68**.................................. ConnorMurtagh 1 69
(Richard Fahey) *trckd clr ldrs: effrt wl over 2f out: led 2f out: hdd 1f out: one pce fnl f* **6/1**

0004 **5** *¾* **Toybox**[31] 4424 3-9-3 **66**.................................. TylerSaunders(5) 3 65
(Jonathan Portman) *racd in mid-div: effrt over 2f out: kpt on one pce fr over 1f out* **7/1**

232 **6** *1 ¼* **Image Of The Moon**[36] 4225 3-9-5 **70**.................................(p[1]) GavinAshton(7) 6 66
(Shaun Keightley) *racd in mid-div: effrt over 2f out: kpt on one pce fr over 1f out* **3/1**[1]

54-6 **7** *4* **The Dancing Poet**[140] 1171 3-9-9 **70**.................................. CierenFallon(3) 7 57
(Ed Vaughan) *hld up in rr-div: effrt over 2f out: no imp over 1f out* **11/2**[3]

6352 **8** *shd* **Diviner (IRE)**[8] 5272 3-9-4 **65**.................................. AndrewBreslin(3) 8 52
(Mark Johnston) *sn led and set str pce: increased advantage over 3f out: effrt 3f out: hdd 2f out: sn wknd* **9/1**

5-06 **9** *15* **Crimson Kiss (IRE)**[13] 5092 3-8-8 **55**.................................. DarraghKeenan(3) 2 7
(Pat Phelan) *loaded wout jockey and reluctant: early pce but sn chsd ldrs: cajoled along at 1/2-way: no ex 2f out* **33/1**

1m 44.72s (1.42) **Going Correction** +0.225s/f (Good) **9** Ran SP% **117.8**
Speed ratings (Par 100): **101,100,100,99,98 97,93,93,78**
CSF £100.23 CT £476.69 TOTE £13.00: £3.20, £2.50, £2.00; EX 127.50 Trifecta £701.50.
Owner Kingsclere Racing Club **Bred** E A R L Qatar Bloodstock Ltd **Trained** Kingsclere, Hants

FOCUS
Add 12yds. A modest handicap and one run at a strong pace. The winner came from a long way back to provide her rider with a winner on her first ride. The first two have been rated to this year's form.

5562 PROVIDEO NURSERY H'CAP (JOCKEY CLUB GRASSROOTS NURSERY QUALIFIER) 5f 10y

6:05 (6:06) (Class 5) (0-75,77) 2-Y-O

£4,528 (£1,347; £673; £336; £300; £300) **Stalls** Low

Form RPR

3100 **1** **Charlemaine (IRE)**[11] 5185 2-9-7 **74**.................................(b[1]) SeanLevey 3 77
(Paul Cole) *t.k.h in rr: gng wl on heels over 2f out: rdn over 1f out: qckned 1f out between horses: sn led: kpt on wl* **5/1**[3]

350 **2** *1 ¼* **Royal Council (IRE)**[43] 3954 2-9-2 **69**.................................. RobertHavlin 6 68
(James Tate) *hld up: rdn 2f out: angled to outer over 1f out: ev ch 1f out: kpt on wl and tk 2nd 100yds out: no ex cl home* **9/2**[2]

2P20 **3** *1 ½* **Sneaky**[16] 4985 2-9-2 **69**.................................(h[1]) OisinMurphy 1 62
(Archie Watson) *led: rdn wl over 1f out: hdd jst ins fnl f and lost 2nd sn after* **15/2**

5522 **4** *1* **Return To Senders (IRE)**[8] 5265 2-9-10 **77**.......................(b) DaneO'Neill 7 67
(Jamie Osborne) *cl up on outer: effrt over 1f out: outpcd whn sltly hmpd jst ins fnl f: no ex cl home* **2/1**[1]

1041 **5** *2 ¾* **Exclusive (IRE)**[15] 5010 2-9-7 **74**.................................. AdamMcNamara 4 54
(Archie Watson) *trckd ldr: rdn over 2f out: nt qckn and wknd ent fnl f* **8/1**

4332 **6** *6* **Beignet (IRE)**[8] 5279 2-8-10 **63**.................................. JohnFahy 2 21
(Richard Hannon) *trckd ldrs on inner: rdn over 2f out: no ex over 1f out* **10/1**

556 **7** *5* **Interrupted Dream**[11] 5197 2-8-9 **62**.................................. FrannyNorton 5
(Mark Johnston) *trckd ldr on outer: rdn 2f out: no ex over 1f out* **9/2**[2]

1m 4.57s (3.27) **Going Correction** +0.225s/f (Good) **7** Ran SP% **118.3**
Speed ratings (Par 94): **82,80,77,76,71 62,54**
CSF £28.94 TOTE £6.30: £2.60, £2.60; EX 23.80 Trifecta £257.20.
Owner P F I Cole Ltd **Bred** Haras Du Mont Dit Mont **Trained** Whatcombe, Oxon

FOCUS
A modest nursery run at what looked a reasonable gallop. The first two home came from off the pace. This rates straightforward form around and the winner, second and fourth, with a pb from the winner.

5563 BRITISH STALLION STUDS EBF NOVICE STKS (PLUS 10 RACE) 7f
6:35 (6:35) (Class 4) 2-Y-O **£4,787** (£1,424; £711; £355) **Stalls** Low

Form RPR
0 **1** **Tammani**[19] 4886 2-9-2 0 .... JamesDoyle 3 91
(William Haggas) *trckd ldr in 3rd: shkn up jst over 2f out: rdn between horses over 1f out: strly pressed ldr fr 1f out tl led 100yds out: asserted cl home* **9/2**[2]
22 **2** *nk* **Riot (IRE)**[26] 4611 2-9-2 0 .... OisinMurphy 5 90
(John Gosden) *sn led: shkn up over 2f out: rdn 2f out: effrt over 1f out: strly pressed by wnr fr 1f out: no ex 100yds out and fdd cl home* **8/15**[1]
4 **3** *7* **Dubai Souq (IRE)**[18] 4925 2-9-2 0 .... GeorgeWood 7 72
(Saeed bin Suroor) *w ldr and sltly keen early: shkn up over 2f out: rdn 2f out: lft bhd by front pair ent fnl f: pushed out fnl f* **9/2**[2]
4 *2 ½* **Berkshire Savvy** 2-9-2 0 .... DavidProbert 6 65
(Andrew Balding) *trckd ldrs in 4th: effrt over 2f out and carried hd high: plugged on fr over 1f out* **28/1**
5 *nse* **Tinnahalla (IRE)** 2-9-2 0 .... DaneO'Neill 4 65
(Jamie Osborne) *squeezed up s: settled in last pair: effrt over 2f out: sn hld* **18/1**[3]
6 *8* **Ocho Grande (IRE)** 2-9-2 0 .... CharlesBishop 1 44
(Eve Johnson Houghton) *racd in last pair: effrt over 2f out: nt qckn and plugged on fr over 1f out* **33/1**
1m 30.3s (1.00) **Going Correction** +0.225s/f (Good) **6** Ran SP% **113.2**
Speed ratings (Par 96): **103,102,94,91,91 82**
CSF £7.45 TOTE £5.00: £2.00, £1.10; EX 7.20 Trifecta £13.20.
Owner Prince A A Faisal **Bred** Nawara Stud Company Ltd S A **Trained** Newmarket, Suffolk

FOCUS
Add 12yds. A decent little contest with the odds-on favourite setting a good standard. He succumbed again, but only to a horse with Group 1 entries, and the front two finished a long way clear of the rest.

5564 JOIN RACING TV NOW H'CAP 1m
7:10 (7:11) (Class 3) (0-95,91) 3-Y-O+
£9,337 (£2,796; £1,398; £699; £349; £175) **Stalls** Low

Form RPR
2210 **1** **Maamora (IRE)**[40] 4052 3-9-2 **88** .... OisinMurphy 5 101
(Simon Crisford) *hld up in rr-div on inner: tk clsr order on inner over 3f out: pushed along and angled out wl over 1f out: sn upsides runner-up and rdn: disp tl nosed into ld 150yds out: asserted cl home* **4/1**[3]
-100 **2** *½* **Solid Stone (IRE)**[19] 4882 3-9-2 **88** .... JamesDoyle 3 100
(Sir Michael Stoute) *trckd ldr: led wl over 2f out: rdn over 1f out: sn pressed by wnr: marginally hdd fnl 150yds: stuck on wl but no ex cl home* **7/2**[2]
3436 **3** *5* **Michele Strogoff**[16] 4997 6-9-6 **84** .... AlistairRawlinson 6 86
(Michael Appleby) *led and set decent pce: hdd wl over 2f out and sn rdn: plugged on fr over 1f out* **25/1**
0033 **4** *½* **Alternative Fact**[11] 5192 4-9-11 **89** .... RobertHavlin 7 90
(Ed Dunlop) *hld up in rr: rdn over 2f out: sme prog over 1f out: flattened out fnl f* **8/1**
1-16 **5** *4 ½* **Pesto**[19] 4865 3-9-5 **91** .... SeanLevey 4 80
(Richard Hannon) *in rr and niggled along early to go pce: travelled bttr at 1/2-way: effrt wl over 2f out: shuffled along after* **7/2**[2]
6214 **6** *3 ¾* **Smile A Mile (IRE)**[11] 5200 3-9-3 **89** .... FrannyNorton 8 69
(Mark Johnston) *in last trio on outer: effrt wl over 3f out: no ex over 1f out* **14/1**
-363 **7** *¾* **Rogue**[20] 4860 4-9-2 **85** .... CierenFallon(5) 2 65
(Alexandra Dunn) *hld up in rr-div: rdn wl over 2f out: sn one pce* **12/1**
-132 **8** *3 ¾* **Muraad (IRE)**[19] 4865 3-9-5 **91** .... DaneO'Neill 1 61
(Owen Burrows) *trckd ldng pair: effrt wl over 2f out: no imp over 1f out and wknd (trainer could offer no explanation for the gelding's performance. jockey said gelding ran flat)* **3/1**[1]
1m 42.33s (-0.97) **Going Correction** +0.225s/f (Good)
WFA 3 from 4yo+ 8lb **8** Ran SP% **118.8**
Speed ratings (Par 107): **113,112,107,107,102 98,98,94**
CSF £19.25 CT £313.17 TOTE £4.80: £1.70, £1.50, £6.60; EX 19.30 Trifecta £286.80.
Owner Sheikh Ahmed Al Maktoum **Bred** Godolphin **Trained** Newmarket, Suffolk

FOCUS
Add 12yds. The first two have been rated as improving, with the third to his latest.

5565 FOLLOW @RACINGTV ON TWITTER FILLIES' H'CAP 1m 1f
7:45 (7:45) (Class 5) (0-75,77) 3-Y-O+
£4,528 (£1,347; £673; £336; £300; £300) **Stalls** Low

Form RPR
525 **1** **Norma**[52] 3637 3-9-9 **77** .... GeorgeWood 6 89+
(James Fanshawe) *covered up in mid-div: shkn up over 2f out: smooth prog to trck ldr over 1f out: sn rdn: led jst ins fnl f: edgd rt cl home: pushed out: easily* **6/1**
2531 **2** *1 ¾* **New Jazz (USA)**[21] 4806 3-9-8 **76** .... RobertHavlin 9 84
(John Gosden) *prom: led after 2f: rdn wl over 1f out: hdd jst ins fnl f: no ex whn wnr edgd across fnl 55yds: eased and pushed out cl home* **7/4**[1]
04-3 **3** *3 ¾* **Miss Blondell**[20] 4841 6-9-3 **67** .... WilliamCarver(5) 7 68
(Marcus Tregoning) *in rr-div on outer: tk clsr order 2f out and sn rdn: ev ch over 1f out: sn lft bhd* **9/2**[2]
4563 **4** *nk* **Mrs Meader**[44] 3947 3-8-8 **62** .... (h) LukeMorris 5 61
(Seamus Mullins) *awkward s and in rr: t.k.h: shkn up 3f out: attempted to angle between horses wl over 2f out but squeezed out: sn rdn and kpt on again fr 1f out* **9/1**
4224 **5** *2* **Nooshin**[20] 4828 3-9-7 **75** .... JamesDoyle 1 70
(Charles Hills) *led 2f: sn trckd ldr: rdn over 2f out: plugged on (jockey said filly lost its action)* **5/1**[3]
0600 **6** *2 ¾* **First Link (USA)**[20] 4838 4-9-1 **63** .... (h[1]) SeanDavis(3) 8 53
(Jean-Rene Auvray) *in last and t.k.h early: shkn up wl over 3f out: effrt over 2f out: plugged on* **33/1**
3050 **7** *4* **Prairie Spy (IRE)**[15] 5030 3-9-8 **76** .... FrannyNorton 2 56
(Mark Johnston) *racd in mid-div: pushed along wl over 3f out: no imp 2f out* **20/1**
33P3 **8** *7* **Cabarita**[41] 4022 3-9-6 **74** .... HarryBentley 4 38
(Ralph Beckett) *trckd ldng pair: rdn over 3f out: outpcd over 2f out: no ex over 1f out* **7/1**
3000 **9** *8* **Woggle (IRE)**[53] 3571 4-8-6 **54** oh9 .... (p) GeorgiaCox(3) 3
(Geoffrey Deacon) *sluggish s and hld up towards rr on inner: pushed along wl over 3f out: hld and wknd sn after* **33/1**
1m 58.65s (2.35) **Going Correction** +0.225s/f (Good)
WFA 3 from 4yo+ 9lb **9** Ran SP% **118.6**
Speed ratings (Par 100): **98,96,93,92,91 88,85,78,71**
CSF £17.10 CT £52.17 TOTE £7.00: £2.10, £1.20, £1.60; EX 20.10 Trifecta £61.50.
Owner Normandie Stud Ltd **Bred** Normandie Stud Ltd **Trained** Newmarket, Suffolk
■ Stewards' Enquiry : George Wood caution: careless riding

FOCUS
Add 12yds. Not bad form for the grade, with the winner making her handicap debut and the front two coming clear, both rated as improvers.

5566 CHRISTMAS PARTIES AT SANDOWN PARK H'CAP 1m 6f
8:20 (8:20) (Class 4) (0-80,86) 3-Y-O **£9,337** (£2,796; £1,398; £699; £349) **Stalls** Low

Form RPR
-636 **1** **Young Merlin (IRE)**[21] 4803 3-8-11 **70** .... (p[1]) JasonWatson 6 79
(Roger Charlton) *racd in 3rd: prog at 1/2-way to press ldr: rdn to chse ldr over 2f out: kpt on and led over 1f out: pressed by runner-up fr 1f out: edgd lft sn after: fought on and jst prevailed* **12/1**
1-62 **2** *shd* **Buckman Tavern (FR)**[6] 5347 3-9-4 **77** .... LukeMorris 5 86
(Sir Mark Prescott Bt) *hld up in last and t.k.h: effrt over 2f out: ev ch 1f out whn almost upsides wnr: received bump jst ins fnl f and rdr dropped whip sn after: fought on but nt get past* **6/4**[1]
-041 **3** *4* **Wannie Mae (IRE)**[40] 4064 3-8-12 **71** .... JamesDoyle 1 74
(William Haggas) *racd in 4th: effrt over 2f out: plugged on fr over 1f out* **11/4**[3]
2134 **4** *4 ½* **Fantastic Ms Fox**[15] 5028 3-8-2 **64** .... SeanDavis(3) 4 61
(Richard Fahey) *sn led: pushed along 3f out: hdd over 2f out: no ex sn after* **16/1**
1321 **5** *nk* **Mondain**[5] 5391 3-9-13 **86** 6ex .... JoeFanning 2 82
(Mark Johnston) *early ldr: sn 2nd and t.k.h: 3rd at 1/2-way: shkn up over 3f out and quick move to ld over 2f out: sn rdn: fnd little and hdd over 1f out: no ex fnl f* **9/4**[2]
3m 9.33s (3.33) **Going Correction** +0.225s/f (Good) **5** Ran SP% **111.0**
Speed ratings (Par 102): **99,98,96,94,93**
CSF £30.96 TOTE £12.00: £3.20, £1.30; EX 34.40 Trifecta £111.00.
Owner Daniel Macauliffe & Anoj Don **Bred** M Ryan **Trained** Beckhampton, Wilts
■ Stewards' Enquiry : Jason Watson two-day ban: misuse of the whip (Aug 14-15)

FOCUS
Add 12yds. A decent little contest in which the front two, both of which still have plenty of upside, came clear. They came together in the closing stages but Young Merlin survived a stewards inquiry to open his account.
T/Plt: £55.80 to a £1 stake. Pool: £61,743.49 - 807.14 winning units T/Qpdt: £4.70 to a £1 stake. Pool: 9,701.35 - 1511.41 winning units **Cathal Gahan**

5567 - 5569a (Foreign Racing) - See Raceform Interactive

5087
EPSOM (L-H)
Thursday, August 1

OFFICIAL GOING: Good (good to firm in places; 6.8)
Wind: Almost nil Weather: Fine becoming cloudy, sharp shower before race 5 (8.00)

5570 STEVE DONOGHUE APPRENTICE H'CAP 1m 2f 17y
5:45 (5:46) (Class 5) (0-70,72) 4-Y-O+
£4,528 (£1,347; £673; £336; £300; £300) **Stalls** Low

Form RPR
1045 **1** **Gendarme (IRE)**[16] 5012 4-9-12 **72** .... (b) CierenFallon(3) 9 80
(Alexandra Dunn) *trckd ldr: cajoled along to ld over 1f out: jnd ins fnl f: kpt on gamely nr fin (trainer could offer no explanation for the apparent improvement in form)* **10/1**
0061 **2** *hd* **The Lords Walk**[14] 5087 6-9-4 **64** .... (v) ThoreHammerHansen(3) 5 71
(Bill Turner) *hld up: 7th st: prog on outer over 2f out: chsd wnr fnl f: drew upsides 100yds out and looked sure to win: hung lft after and out-fought nr fin* **2/1**[1]
1005 **3** *2 ¾* **Bayston Hill**[14] 5086 5-9-6 **68** .... (p) ScottMcCullagh(5) 3 69
(Mark Usher) *hld up in last pair: nt clr run over 2f out to wl over 1f out: prog after: styd on to take 3rd nr fin: no ch to chal* **14/1**
2552 **4** *1* **Light Of Air (FR)**[7] 5337 6-8-10 **60** .... (b) LouisGaroghan(7) 4 59+
(Gary Moore) *hld up in last pair: nt clr run over 2f out tl swtchd rt over 1f out: styd on wl to take 4th last strides: too late* **4/1**[3]
0222 **5** *¾* **Amaretto**[14] 5087 4-8-13 **59** .... (v) SebastianWoods(3) 7 57
(Jim Boyle) *led: rdn and hdd over 1f out: lost 2nd and wknd fnl f* **3/1**[2]
13-0 **6** *hd* **Settle Petal**[14] 5087 5-9-10 **67** .... PaddyBradley 1 64
(Pat Phelan) *hld up: prog and 5th st: chsd ldng pair jst over 2f out: wknd fnl f* **25/1**
6330 **7** *5* **Dream Magic (IRE)**[38] 4190 5-9-4 **66** .... (p) SeanKirrane(5) 10 53
(Mark Loughnane) *chsd ldng pair to jst over 2f out: wknd qckly* **25/1**
0400 **8** *2 ¾* **Rainbow Jazz (IRE)**[15] 5049 4-8-10 **52** ow1 .... (b) FinleyMarsh 6 35
(Adam West) *chsd ldrs: 6th and sing to struggling st: wknd 2f out (jockey said gelding stopped quickly)* **14/1**
0420 **9** *2* **Subliminal**[38] 4194 4-9-2 **66** .... LeviWilliams(7) 8 44
(Simon Dow) *chsd ldng trio: pushed along 3f out: sn lost pl and btn* **10/1**
2m 8.51s (-1.49) **Going Correction** -0.05s/f (Good) **9** Ran SP% **117.5**
Speed ratings (Par 103): **103,102,100,99,99 99,95,92,91**
CSF £30.94 CT £285.22 TOTE £12.70: £3.20, £1.30, £4.10; EX 37.00 Trifecta £307.10.
Owner Helium Racing Ltd **Bred** Gillian, Lady Howard De Walden **Trained** West Buckland, Somerset

FOCUS
Rail on inner (Derby) line with all distances as advertised. They didn't hang about in this ordinary handicap for apprentice riders and this rates a small pb from the winner.

5571 FOCUS RIGGING H'CAP 1m 4f 6y
6:20 (6:25) (Class 5) (0-75,76) 4-Y-O+
£5,175 (£1,540; £769; £384; £300; £300) **Stalls** Centre

Form RPR
4413 **1** **Peace Prevails**[14] 5091 4-7-12 **59** .... (p) IsobelFrancis(7) 4 67
(Jim Boyle) *t.k.h: hld up in last: brought v wd in st and stdy prog fr 3f out: shkn up and clsd on ldng pair over 1f out: led fnl 100yds: won gng away* **6/1**
3022 **2** *1 ½* **Allegiant (USA)**[14] 5089 4-9-7 **75** .... HectorCrouch 7 81
(Stuart Williams) *hld up: 7th st: prog to chse ldr wl over 1f out: clsd and upsides whn wnr wnt past 100yds out: outpcd* **4/1**[2]

1112 **3** 3/4 **Sigrid Nansen**[13] 5138 4-8-5 **64**..............................(p) CierenFallon(5) 10 69
(Alexandra Dunn) *trckd ldrs: 5th st: prog to ld jst over 2f out: rdn over 1f out: hdd and no ex fnl 100yds* **7/1**

34-0 **4** 5 **Amanto (GER)**[53] 3633 9-8-13 **67**..............................(tp w) RobertHavlin 9 64
(Ali Stronge) *hld up: 8th st: rdn and sme prog 3f out: chsd clr ldng trio over 1f out: no imp* **20/1**

5524 **5** 1 1/4 **Carp Kid (IRE)**[21] 4841 4-9-3 **74**..............................(p) FinleyMarsh(3) 1 69
(John Flint) *hld up in midfield: 6th st: rdn and no prog over 2f out: nvr on terms after* **8/1**

-062 **6** 2 1/4 **Jawshan (USA)**[14] 5091 4-8-7 **66**..............(p[1]) ThoreHammerHansen(5) 5 57
(Ian Williams) *led after 2f to jst over 2f out: sn wknd* **14/1**

33-5 **7** 3/4 **Fannie By Gaslight**[12] 5174 4-9-3 **76**.................... ScottMcCullagh(5) 3 66
(Mick Channon) *hld up: 9th st: rdn and no real prog over 2f out: mod late hdwy* **8/1**

2232 **8** hd **Singing The Blues (IRE)**[19] 4929 4-9-5 **73**.................... RobHornby 6 63
(Rod Millman) *led 2f: settled bhd ldrs: 4th st: rdn over 2f out: sn outpcd: wl btn over 1f out (trainer could offer no explanation for the poor performance)* **7/2**[1]

5131 **9** nk **Ashazuri**[14] 5091 5-9-0 **75**..............................(h) TylerSaunders(7) 8 64
(Jonathan Portman) *prom: trckd ldr after 4f: rdn and lost pl over 2f out: wknd* **5/1**[3]

0560 **10** 19 **Ezanak (IRE)**[16] 5029 6-8-4 **58**..............................(vt) LiamJones 2 17
(Michael Appleby) *pushed up to go prom after 3f: 3rd st: sn wknd: t.o* **33/1**

2m 36.97s (-3.83) **Going Correction** -0.05s/f (Good) **10** Ran SP% **122.3**
Speed ratings (Par 103): **108,107,106,103,102 100,100,100,100,87**
CSF £31.86 CT £177.82 TOTE £7.90: £2.60, £1.40, £2.30; EX 40.20 Trifecta £237.10.
Owner Epsom Equine Spa Partnership **Bred** W A Tinkler **Trained** Epsom, Surrey

FOCUS
The principals forged clear in this modest handicap.

5572 BRITISH STALLION STUDS EBF NOVICE STKS (PLUS 10 RACE) 7f 3y
6:55 (6:57) (Class 4) 2-Y-O **£4,787** (£1,424; £711; £355) **Stalls** Low

Form RPR

5 **1** **Bodyline (IRE)**[11] 5212 2-9-5 0.............................. RyanTate 4 75
(Sir Mark Prescott Bt) *s.i.s: racd in last tl clsd and 5th st: stl green and nt handling trck but prog to chse ldr fnl f: styd on to ld nr fin* **16/1**

3 **2** 1/2 **Magic Twist (USA)**[25] 4688 2-9-0 0.............................. FrannyNorton 5 69
(Mark Johnston) *t.k.h: led and stdd pce after 2f: kicked on again over 2f out: kpt on but hdd and outpcd nr fin* **5/2**[2]

3 3/4 **Inca Man (FR)** 2-9-5 0.............................. HectorCrouch 2 72+
(Paul Cole) *rn green in rr: last after 3f: stl last and shoved along jst over 1f out: styd on fnl 100yds to take 3rd post* **12/1**

0 **4** nse **Glorious Zoff (IRE)**[13] 5125 2-9-5 0.............................. KieranShoemark 3 72
(Charles Hills) *trckd ldng pair: shkn up to dispute 2nd over 1f out: kpt on same pce fnl f: nvr able to chal* **12/1**

0 **5** 3/4 **Wild Hero (IRE)**[20] 4886 2-9-5 0.............................. RobHornby 1 70
(Andrew Balding) *chsd ldng pair: shkn up on outer over 2f out: tried to cl over 1f out: one pce after* **11/4**[3]

520 **6** 3/4 **Mass Media**[20] 4886 2-9-5 80..............................(p[1]) RobertHavlin 6 69
(John Gosden) *trckd ldr: shkn up and no rspnse wl over 1f out: lost 2nd and fdd sn after* **7/4**[1]

1m 24.28s (0.88) **Going Correction** -0.05s/f (Good) **6** Ran SP% **112.9**
Speed ratings (Par 96): **93,92,91,91,90 89**
CSF £56.40 TOTE £19.60: £6.30, £2.30; EX 82.60 Trifecta £303.80.
Owner Tim Bunting - Osborne House Iv **Bred** Razza Del Velino **Trained** Newmarket, Suffolk

FOCUS
This fair little novice event was run at a messy pace and they finished in a heap.

5573 BRITISH EBF FIFINELLA FILLIES' H'CAP 7f 3y
7:30 (7:30) (Class 4) (0-80,81) 3-Y-O+
£9,337 (£2,796; £1,398; £699; £349; £300) **Stalls** Low

Form RPR

1254 **1** **Chica De La Noche**[14] 5090 5-9-7 **73**..............................(p) SilvestreDeSousa 1 81
(Simon Dow) *mde all: urged along over 2f out: holding rivals over 1f out: drvn out fnl f* **4/1**[2]

0403 **2** 1/2 **Zoraya (FR)**[6] 5376 4-9-4 **70**.............................. DavidProbert 3 77
(Paul Cole) *hld up in 5th: shkn up over 2f out: no prog tl styd on strly ins fnl f: tk 2nd fnl 50yds and clsd on wnr fin* **9/2**[3]

624 **3** 1 **Material Girl**[46] 3892 3-8-9 **74**..............................(v[1]) SeanKirrane(7) 2 76
(Richard Spencer) *trckd ldng pair: rdn to chse wnr 2f out: nt qckn and hld over 1f out: lost 2nd fnl 50yds* **4/1**[2]

6336 **4** 2 **Hunni**[21] 4828 4-9-6 **75**.............................. CameronNoble(3) 5 74
(Tom Clover) *trckd ldng trio: rdn over 2f out: one pce and no prog over 1f out (trainer said filly was unsuited by the undulating track)* **5/1**

1155 **5** 3 1/2 **Jungle Juice (IRE)**[5] 5450 3-9-2 **79**.............................. ScottMcCullagh(5) 4 66
(Mick Channon) *chsd wnr to 2f out: sn wknd* **9/1**

2416 **6** 1 **Comeonfeeltheforce (IRE)**[26] 4642 3-8-2 **67**.........(t) GeorgiaDobie(7) 6 52
(Lee Carter) *stdd s: hld up in last pair: shkn up over 2f out: no prog (jockey said filly was slowly away)* **11/1**

3-14 **7** 3 **Ascended (IRE)**[40] 4119 3-9-4 **81**.............................. CierenFallon(5) 7 58
(William Haggas) *taken down early: dwlt: hld up in last pair: pushed along over 2f out: no prog and nvr in it (trainer said filly was unsuited by the undulating track and would prefer a slower surface)* **3/1**[1]

1m 22.57s (-0.83) **Going Correction** -0.05s/f (Good)
WFA 3 from 4yo+ 6lb **7** Ran SP% **118.2**
Speed ratings (Par 102): **102,101,100,98,94 92,89**
CSF £23.35 TOTE £3.90: £1.40, £3.20; EX 18.00 Trifecta £88.40.
Owner Robert Moss **Bred** Horizon Bloodstock Limited **Trained** Epsom, Surrey

FOCUS
A tight-looking fillies' handicap, run at a fair pace, and a small pb from the winner.

5574 JEM ROBINSON H'CAP 1m 113y
8:00 (8:03) (Class 4) (0-80,75) 3-Y-O+
£6,469 (£1,925; £962; £481; £300; £300) **Stalls** Low

Form RPR

0032 **1** **Data Protection**[10] 5255 4-9-11 **72**..............................(t) DanielTudhope 2 81
(William Muir) *led at mod pce: stretched on 1/2-way: rdn and narrowly hdd over 1f out: rallied to ld again fnl 100yds: on top at fin* **3/1**[2]

0560 **2** nk **Rampant Lion (IRE)**[20] 4887 4-9-12 **73**..............................(p) DavidProbert 1 81
(William Jarvis) *sltly awkward s: trckd ldng trio: wnt 2nd 3f out: pushed into narrow ld on inner over 1f out: drvn fnl f: hdd and nt qckn fnl 100yds (jockey was slow to remove the blindfold explaining that it got caught on the brow band and took two attempts to remove it)* **5/1**[3]

5465 **3** 3 3/4 **Narjes**[14] 5087 5-9-6 **67**..............................(h) HectorCrouch 6 67
(Laura Mongan) *s.s: t.k.h in last pair: pushed along and prog to chse ldng pair over 1f out: nvr any inroads after* **16/1**

6511 **4** 3 1/2 **City Wanderer (IRE)**[19] 4909 3-9-6 **75**.............................. SilvestreDeSousa 4 67
(Mick Channon) *stmbld bdly s: sn chsd wnr: drvn and lost 2nd 3f out: sn btn (jockey said gelding stumbled leaving the stalls)* **5/6**[1]

0044 **5** 3 **Duke Of North (IRE)**[10] 5255 7-8-3 **57**.............................. IsobelFrancis(7) 3 42
(Jim Boyle) *dwlt: t.k.h: hld up in last pair: rdn and no prog over 2f out (jockey said gelding hung left-handed in the home straight)* **12/1**

06-0 **6** 22 **Albishr (IRE)**[169] 699 4-9-7 **75**..............................(b) LeviWilliams(7) 5 9
(Simon Dow) *chsd ldng pair to 3f out: wknd qckly: t.o* **33/1**

1m 45.22s (-1.18) **Going Correction** -0.05s/f (Good)
WFA 3 from 4yo+ 8lb **6** Ran SP% **112.7**
Speed ratings (Par 105): **103,102,99,96,93 74**
CSF £18.19 TOTE £4.00: £2.30, £2.40; EX 16.60 Trifecta £75.10.
Owner Muir Racing Partnership - Santa Anita **Bred** Mr & Mrs J Laws **Trained** Lambourn, Berks

FOCUS
It paid to be handy in this modest little handicap.

5575 FRANK BUCKLE H'CAP 7f 3y
8:30 (8:32) (Class 6) (0-65,70) 3-Y-O
£3,557 (£1,058; £529; £300; £300; £300) **Stalls** Low

Form RPR

53-0 **1** **Alotabottle**[37] 4212 3-9-4 **62**.............................. DanielTudhope 2 72+
(Kevin Ryan) *hld up: 4th st: effrt over 2f out: drvn to chse ldr fnl f: clsd suddenly to ld fnl 75yds: gng away* **5/2**[1]

5321 **2** 1 1/4 **Quirky Gertie (IRE)**[5] 5428 3-9-7 **70** 6ex.............................. ScottMcCullagh(5) 8 77
(Mick Channon) *trckd ldr after 2f: led 2f out: drvn fnl f: hdd and outpcd fnl 75yds* **3/1**[2]

4030 **3** 2 **Ifton**[21] 4820 3-9-3 **61**.............................. JamesSullivan 4 63
(Ruth Carr) *t.k.h: hld up in 6th: effrt over 2f out: rdn and nt qckn wl over 1f out: kpt on to take 3rd last strides* **6/1**[3]

0002 **4** hd **Poet's Magic**[14] 5092 3-8-13 **62**.............................. CierenFallon(5) 1 63
(Jonathan Portman) *in tch: 5th st: clsd on ldrs 2f out: nt handling trck too wl over 1f out: kpt on fnl f to press for 3rd nr fin* **3/1**[2]

0306 **5** 1 **Rosamour (IRE)**[14] 5105 3-9-7 **65**..............................(p[1]) ShaneKelly 9 63
(Richard Hughes) *won early battle for ld: hdd 2f out: lost 2nd and fdd fnl f* **10/1**

00-0 **6** 8 **Illegitimate Gains**[15] 5044 3-8-2 **46** oh1..............................(t[1]) JimmyQuinn 3 24
(Adam West) *stdd s: t.k.h: hld up in last and detached: pushed along and no prog over 2f out: nvr in it* **20/1**

030 **7** 1 1/2 **Laxmi (IRE)**[90] 2355 3-9-8 **66**..............................(p[1]) DavidProbert 7 40
(Brian Meehan) *trckd ldr 2f: 3rd st: wknd 2f out: bhd fnl f (jockey said filly stopped quickly)* **11/1**

1m 23.23s (-0.17) **Going Correction** -0.05s/f (Good) **7** Ran SP% **115.0**
Speed ratings (Par 98): **98,96,94,94,92 83,82**
CSF £10.40 CT £39.36 TOTE £3.40: £2.10, £2.70; EX 14.20 Trifecta £57.60.
Owner Gordon Bulloch & Steve Ryan **Bred** Saxtead Livestock Ltd **Trained** Hambleton, N Yorks

FOCUS
They went a brisk early pace in this moderate 3yo handicap.
T/Plt: £133.80 to a £1 stake. Pool: £66,510.96 - 362.70 winning units T/Qpdt: £18.40 to a £1 stake. Pool: £8,142.20 - 326.36 winning units **Jonathan Neesom**

5492 FFOS LAS (L-H)
Thursday, August 1

OFFICIAL GOING: Good to firm (good in places; watered; 8.0) changing to good to firm on straight course after race 2 (6.10)
Wind: Light breeze, partially against Weather: Fine

5576 TIP TOP TOILETS NURSERY H'CAP 6f
5:35 (5:35) (Class 6) (0-65,73) 2-Y-O
£2,781 (£827; £413; £300; £300; £300) **Stalls** High

Form RPR

3435 **1** **Fashion Free**[8] 5313 2-9-8 **66**.............................. HollieDoyle 9 71
(Archie Watson) *rousted along early: chsd ldr tl led 2f out: sn rdn: briefly edgd rt ins fnl f: kpt on (jockey said filly hung left and right-handed)* **9/2**[2]

0031 **2** nk **Sir Arthur Dayne (IRE)**[8] 5313 2-10-1 **73** 6ex...........(p) CharlesBishop 6 77+
(Mick Channon) *chsd ldrs: rdn wl over 2f out: ev ch over 1f out: r.o fnl f: jst hld* **8/11**[1]

5645 **3** nk **Come On Girl**[16] 5010 2-8-4 **48**.............................. RaulDaSilva 5 51
(Tony Carroll) *s.i.s: hld up: hdwy over 2f out: rdn over 1f out: disputing 2nd whn briefly carried rt ins fnl f: r.o* **33/1**

5024 **4** 1 1/4 **Chromium**[7] 5340 2-9-0 **65**..............................(p) EllieMacKenzie(7) 3 64
(Mark Usher) *hld up: hdwy and nt clr run over 2f out: sn rdn: swtchd lft over 1f out: styd on fnl f: nt rch ldrs* **8/1**[3]

066 **5** nk **New Jack Swing (IRE)**[14] 5082 2-9-1 **59**.............................. FergusSweeney 2 57
(Richard Hannon) *hld up: rdn and hdwy over 2f out: no imp over 1f out: styd on fnl f* **14/1**

4340 **6** 1/2 **Bacchalot (IRE)**[12] 5185 2-9-6 **64**.............................. RossaRyan 4 61
(Richard Hannon) *t.k.h towards rr: rdn over 2f out: hdwy over 1f out: styd on fnl f* **8/1**[3]

000 **7** 2 **Port Noir**[30] 4480 2-8-6 **50**.............................. LukeMorris 1 40
(Grace Harris) *chsd ldrs on outer: drvn 1/2-way: ev ch over 1f out: wknd ins fnl f* **33/1**

030 **8** 1 3/4 **Luscifer**[23] 4766 2-8-3 **54**.............................. AngusVilliers(7) 8 39
(Richard Hughes) *prom: rdn over 2f out: outpcd over 1f out: grad wknd* **16/1**

006 **9** 3/4 **Red Cinderella**[54] 3573 2-8-6 **50**.............................. JFEgan 10 33
(David Evans) *led: j. patch on trck wl over 2f out: rdn and hdd 2f out: sn outpcd: wknd ins fnl f* **33/1**

060 **10** 19 **Es Que Pearl (IRE)**[51] 3695 2-8-7 **51**.............................. CharlieBennett 7
(Rod Millman) *hld up in midfield: rdn 1/2-way: sn hung lft and wknd qckly: t.o (jockey said filly stopped quickly)* **25/1**

1m 10.61s (-0.29) **Going Correction** -0.30s/f (Firm) **10** Ran SP% **123.5**
Speed ratings (Par 92): **89,88,88,86,86 85,82,80,79,54**
CSF £8.37 CT £96.46 TOTE £7.00: £2.40, £1.02, £9.90; EX 12.50 Trifecta £290.60.
Owner Andrew Rosen And Partner **Bred** Aston Mullins Stud & S Barrow Esq **Trained** Upper Lambourn, W Berks

FOCUS
This modest nursery lacked depth and they finished in a heap, but a minor pb from the winner.

5577 PLAN A CONSULTING NOVICE STKS — 6f
6:10 (6:11) (Class 5) 2-Y-O £3,428 (£1,020; £509; £254) Stalls High

Form RPR
323 1 **Hubert (IRE)**[17] 4992 2-9-5 78 LukeMorris 4 78
(Sylvester Kirk) *trckd ldr: drvn 2f out: kpt on u.p to ld nr fin* **3/1[2]**
35 2 nk **Point Of Order**[14] 5093 2-9-5 0 HollieDoyle 7 77
(Archie Watson) *led nr stands' rail: rdn over 1f out: edgd sltly lft ins fnl f: hdd nr fin* **13/2**
23 3 1 ½ **Forbidden Land (IRE)**[46] 3890 2-9-5 0 RossaRyan 3 72
(Richard Hannon) *wnt lft and bmpd leaving stalls: chsd ldrs: drvn 2f out: unable qck: styd on fnl f* **10/11[1]**
4 ¾ **Lexington Rebel (FR)** 2-9-5 0 KieranO'Neill 6 70+
(Richard Hannon) *s.i.s: towards rr: rdn and hdwy over 2f out: nt clr run over 1f out: kpt on same pce and disp 3rd fnl f* **11/2[3]**
0 5 2 ½ **Lets Go Lucky**[30] 4480 2-9-0 0 (h[1]) JFEgan 1 57
(David Evans) *wnt lft leaving stalls: hld up in tch: rdn over 2f out: outpcd by ldrs over 1f out* **33/1**
06 6 6 **Now I'm A Believer**[12] 5196 2-9-0 0 CharlesBishop 2 38
(Mick Channon) *wnt rt and bmpd leaving stalls: a in rr* **33/1**
56 7 4 ½ **A Go Go**[8] 5294 2-9-0 0 JasonWatson 5 23
(David Evans) *prom: rdn over 2f out and sn lost pl: wknd fnl f* **33/1**

1m 9.73s (-1.17) **Going Correction** -0.30s/f (Firm) 7 Ran SP% 114.9
Speed ratings (Par 94): **95,94,92,91,88 80,74**
CSF £22.15 TOTE £3.10: £1.10, £3.10; EX 17.60 Trifecta £41.40.
Owner Neil Simpson **Bred** M Fahy **Trained** Upper Lambourn, Berks

FOCUS
A fair little novice and the pace was genuine. The winner has been rated to his mark.

5578 KP TYRES & EXHAUSTS MAIDEN STKS — 1m 3f 209y(R)
6:40 (6:40) (Class 5) 3-Y-O+ £3,428 (£1,020; £509; £254) Stalls Low

Form RPR
32 1 **Paths Of Glory**[40] 4104 4-10-0 0 (t) JackMitchell 7 77+
(Hugo Palmer) *midfield: hdwy after 3f and sn trcking ldr: led 3f out: shkn up 2f out: styd on: 2 l up whn reminder ins fnl f: ld being reduced cl home but a holding runner-up* **1/6[1]**
2 nk **All Yours (FR)**[12] 8-10-0 0 LiamKeniry 1 74
(Sean Curran) *midfield: impr into 2nd over 2f out gng wl: rdn 2f out: 2 l down ins fnl f: styd on towards fin but a being hld* **12/1**
0 3 8 **Cochise**[21] 4842 3-9-4 0 JasonWatson 9 62
(Roger Charlton) *hld up: hdwy over 2f out: swtchd lft and chsd ldrs over 1f out: sn outpcd by ldng pair: styd on* **4/1[2]**
06 4 2 ½ **Voice Of Salsabil**[53] 3637 3-8-13 0 JFEgan 11 53
(David Evans) *t.k.h: hld up: rdn and hdwy on outer 2f out: styd on same pce after (trainer said filly was unsuited by the ground and would prefer a slower surface)* **33/1**
00 5 ½ **Zaydanides (FR)**[38] 4177 7-9-9 0 WilliamCarver[(5)] 10 56
(Tim Pinfield) *hld up in midfield: shkn up over 2f out: n.m.r wl over 1f out: one pce after and no imp on ldrs* **80/1**
0 6 2 **Zest Of Zambia (USA)**[10] 5254 3-8-13 0 CharlieBennett 8 49
(Dai Burchell) *hld up in last: rdn and sme prog 3f out: styd on same pce and no ch fnl 2f* **40/1**
4 7 nk **Lady Of Mercia**[22] 4774 3-8-13 0 KieranO'Neill 3 49
(John Flint) *chsd ldr 4f: remained prom: rdn 3f out: losing pl whn hmpd over 2f out: sn wknd* **50/1**
06 8 hd **Champ Ayr**[27] 4600 3-8-11 0 Pierre-LouisJamin[(7)] 5 53
(David Menuisier) *prom: rdn over 3f out: wknd over 1f out* **14/1**
04 9 22 **Sherwood Forrester**[45] 3946 3-9-4 0 LukeMorris 6 18
(Paul George) *led tl rdn and hdd 3f out: wknd 2f out: t.o (jockey said gelding stopped quickly)* **9/1[3]**

2m 34.45s (-5.75) **Going Correction** -0.30s/f (Firm)
WFA 3 from 4yo+ 10lb 9 Ran SP% 138.6
Speed ratings (Par 103): **107,106,101,99,99 98,97,97,83**
CSF £6.77 TOTE £1.10: £1.02, £4.50, £1.10; EX 9.20 Trifecta £20.90.
Owner China Horse Club International Limited **Bred** Dayton Investments Ltd **Trained** Newmarket, Suffolk

FOCUS
A weak maiden which the long odds-on favourite took with relative ease. The first two drew well clear.

5579 PURE VAPE WALES H'CAP — 7f 80y(R)
7:15 (7:17) (Class 5) (0-75,75) 3-Y-O+ £3,428 (£1,020; £509; £300; £300) Stalls Low

Form RPR
-223 1 **Lucky Louie**[13] 5136 6-9-12 75 (p) RossaRyan 6 83
(Roger Teal) *hld up: swtchd lft over 2f out: sn rdn: stl 4th ent fnl f: r.o u.p to ld last strides* **15/8[2]**
343 2 nk **Ghaith**[15] 5057 4-9-9 72 (h) JackMitchell 1 79
(Hugo Palmer) *chsd ldng pair: rdn to ld over 1f out: drvn and nt run on ins fnl f: hdd last strides* **11/4[3]**
3005 3 1 ¾ **Air Of York (IRE)**[30] 4479 7-9-1 64 (p) KieranO'Neill 5 66
(John Flint) *hld up: sltly outpcd and rdn after 3f: swtchd rt 2f out: stl last 1f out: r.o: no imp towards fin* **16/1**
4322 4 1 ½ **Sir Roderic (IRE)**[37] 4226 6-9-12 75 JasonWatson 4 74
(Rod Millman) *trckd ldr: drvn to ld narrowly 2f out: hdd over 1f out: no ex ins fnl f* **7/4[1]**
0054 5 ¾ **Harry Beau**[24] 4733 5-9-0 63 (vt) JFEgan 3 60
(David Evans) *led: drvn 3f out: hdd 2f out: wkng whn sltly hmpd ins fnl f* **8/1**

1m 31.06s (-2.04) **Going Correction** -0.30s/f (Firm) 5 Ran SP% 114.8
Speed ratings (Par 103): **99,98,96,94,94**
CSF £7.83 TOTE £4.10: £1.40, £1.80; EX 10.70 Trifecta £51.30.
Owner Great Shefford Racing **Bred** Whatton Manor Stud **Trained** Lambourn, Berks

FOCUS
Not a deep handicap for the grade. The winner came from off the decent pace.

5580 WEST WALES PROPERTIES H'CAP — 1m 2f (R)
7:45 (7:47) (Class 6) (0-65,67) 3-Y-O
£2,781 (£827; £413; £300; £300; £300) Stalls Low

Form RPR
0622 1 **Bug Boy (IRE)**[14] 5085 3-9-0 63 (p) RhiainIngram[(5)] 6 69
(Paul George) *s.i.s: hld up: rdn and hdwy on outer 2f out: led 1f out: r.o* **13/2[3]**
000 2 1 ¼ **Verify**[60] 3372 3-9-5 63 LiamKeniry 9 67
(Ed Walker) *t.k.h: hld up: nt clr run over 2f out: rdn and sn clsd: chal ent fnl f: unable qck towards fin* **9/2[2]**
-455 3 ½ **Chinese Alphabet**[48] 3797 3-9-7 65 (p[1]) JasonWatson 7 68
(William Knight) *prom: rdn to ld 2f out: drvn and hdd 1f out: kpt on* **13/2[3]**
0464 4 nk **Elegant Love**[10] 5253 3-9-8 66 JFEgan 5 68
(David Evans) *chsd ldrs: rdn and nt clr run over 2f out: outpcd by ldrs over 1f out: styd on wl towards fin* **11/1**
-441 5 2 ¼ **The Game Is On**[8] 5287 3-9-6 64 6ex LukeMorris 10 62+
(Sir Mark Prescott Bt) *sed awkwardly: sn trcking ldr: led briefly jst over 2f out: sn drvn: outpcd by ldrs appr fnl f* **10/11[1]**
00-0 6 9 **Big Ian**[65] 3204 3-8-5 54 WilliamCarver[(5)] 1 35
(Alan Jones) *led: rdn 3f out: hdd jst over 2f out: wknd over 1f out* **20/1**
1630 7 12 **Greyzee (IRE)**[7] 5337 3-9-2 60 CharlieBennett 2 18
(Rod Millman) *prom: lost pl and drvn 3f out: sn in rr: eased fnl f (jockey said gelding stopped quickly)* **25/1**

2m 7.91s (-4.79) **Going Correction** -0.30s/f (Firm) 7 Ran SP% 114.2
Speed ratings (Par 98): **107,106,105,105,103 96,86**
CSF £35.34 CT £197.68 TOTE £6.90: £3.10, £1.50; EX 35.00 Trifecta £99.40.
Owner A Coutts And K George **Bred** Windflower Overseas **Trained** Crediton, Devon

FOCUS
Fairly competitive low-grade stuff and the first two came from off the pace, which was modest early on. The winner has been rated to his mark, and a step forward from the second.

5581 AE ROOFING SERVICES H'CAP — 6f
8:15 (8:16) (Class 4) (0-85,85) 3-Y-O £5,207 (£1,549; £774; £387) Stalls High

Form RPR
1142 1 **Inspired Thought (IRE)**[15] 5058 3-9-7 85 (p[1]) HollieDoyle 1 94+
(Archie Watson) *carried lft sn after leaving stalls: hld up in tch in last: clsd 2f out: rdn over 1f out: led ent fnl f: r.o* **5/4[2]**
2041 2 1 ¾ **Swiss Pride (IRE)**[38] 4193 3-8-3 74 AngusVilliers[(7)] 4 77
(Richard Hughes) *wnt lft sn after leaving stalls: plld hrd and prom: rdn wl over 1f out: ch ent fnl f: kpt on but outpcd by wnr* **11/2[3]**
2031 3 ½ **Spirit Of May**[19] 4908 3-9-0 78 JackMitchell 2 79
(Roger Teal) *t.k.h: trckd ldr tl led after 2f: rdn 2f out: hdd ent fnl f: unable qck* **6/5[1]**
-006 4 4 **Autumn Splendour (IRE)**[52] 3659 3-8-9 73 RaulDaSilva 5 62
(Milton Bradley) *racd alone on stands' rail: led 2f: drvn 2f out: sn outpcd: fdd fnl f* **20/1**

1m 9.36s (-1.54) **Going Correction** -0.30s/f (Firm) 4 Ran SP% 110.0
Speed ratings (Par 102): **98,95,95,89**
CSF £8.01 TOTE £1.70; EX 5.80 Trifecta £8.80.
Owner Clipper Logistics **Bred** L Wright **Trained** Upper Lambourn, W Berks

FOCUS
Weak for the grade, although the pace was genuine. The first three came up the centre of the track. A length pb from the winner, rated around the second.

5582 MINTBET H'CAP — 5f
8:45 (8:46) (Class 6) (0-60,66) 3-Y-O+
£2,781 (£827; £413; £300; £300; £300) Stalls High

Form RPR
6461 1 **Perfect Charm**[3] 5492 3-9-10 66 6ex (b) HollieDoyle 8 72
(Archie Watson) *s.i.s: racd on stands' rail: sn chsng ldrs: rdn to ld over 1f out: r.o: in command whn edgd lft cl home* **6/5[1]**
0320 2 ½ **Spot Lite**[6] 5393 4-9-2 55 (p) JasonWatson 2 60
(Rod Millman) *s.i.s: in tch: rdn and hdwy on outer 1/2-way: ev ch 2f out: sn edgd rt: stened up ins fnl f: kpt on* **5/1[3]**
0004 3 ¾ **Brandy Station (IRE)**[12] 5180 4-9-0 60 ElishaWhittington[(7)] 7 63
(Lisa Williamson) *a.p: rdn over 1f out: kpt on* **6/1**
2416 4 ½ **Toolatetodelegate**[22] 4776 5-8-7 53 (tp) AngusVilliers[(7)] 3 54
(Brian Barr) *in rr: rdn 1/2-way: hdwy on outer 2f out: r.o ins fnl f: unable to chal* **12/1**
6222 5 2 ½ **Edged Out**[22] 4772 9-8-13 55 MitchGodwin[(3)] 6 47
(Christopher Mason) *led tl rdn and hdd over 1f out: wknd ins fnl f* **7/2[2]**
0330 6 2 **Chop Chop (IRE)**[34] 4328 3-8-13 55 (t[1]) TrevorWhelan 5 39
(Brian Barr) *dwlt: in rr: rdn 1/2-way: sme hdwy over 1f out: no further imp (jockey said filly was slowly away)* **12/1**
0000 7 12 **Not So Shy**[19] 4908 3-7-13 46 (b[1]) RhiainIngram[(5)] 4
(Lisa Williamson) *cl up: rdn 1/2-way: wknd and eased over 1f out* **66/1**
0000 8 ¾ **Spring Holly (IRE)**[15] 5044 3-8-4 46 oh1 (p) RaulDaSilva 1
(Milton Bradley) *prom: rdn 1/2-way: wknd over 1f out* **66/1**

57.11s (-1.89) **Going Correction** -0.30s/f (Firm)
WFA 3 from 4yo+ 3lb 8 Ran SP% 117.0
Speed ratings (Par 101): **103,102,101,100,96 93,73,72**
CSF £7.94 CT £26.09 TOTE £2.80: £2.10, £1.10, £1.70; EX 7.60 Trifecta £36.60.
Owner Mildmay Racing & D H Caslon **Bred** Theakston Stud **Trained** Upper Lambourn, W Berks

FOCUS
A modest sprint and the winner made virtually all, bringing up a treble on the night for Hollie Doyle and Archie Watson.
T/Plt: £58.00 to a £1 stake. Pool: £52,935.15 - 665.72 winning units T/Qpdt: £18.70 to a £1 stake. Pool: £5,888.72 - 232.11 winning units **Richard Lowther**

5540 GOODWOOD (R-H)
Thursday, August 1

OFFICIAL GOING: Good (7.9)
Wind: Fine Weather: Light, against

5583 UNIBET H'CAP — 1m 1f 197y
1:50 (1:51) (Class 2) 3-Y-O
£46,687 (£13,980; £6,990; £3,495; £1,747; £877) Stalls Low

Form RPR
1214 1 **Forest Of Dean**[75] 2828 3-8-4 93 HarryBentley 5 105
(John Gosden) *looked wl; pushed along leaving stalls: in tch in midfield: nt clr run 2f out: hdwy to chal 1f out: sn led and lft: r.o strly and drew clr fnl 100yds: readily* **4/1[1]**
-110 2 2 ½ **Fox Premier (IRE)**[42] 4017 3-8-6 95 SilvestreDeSousa 3 102
(Andrew Balding) *in tch in midfield: effrt ent fnl 2f: hdwy u.p to ld over 1f out: hdd jst ins fnl f: nt match pce of wnr fnl 100yds* **11/2[2]**
2120 3 nk **Sinjaari (IRE)**[42] 4017 3-8-7 96 PJMcDonald 7 102
(William Haggas) *looked wl; in tch in last trio: swtchd lft and effrt over 2f out: keeping on u.p whn rdr dropped reins over 1f out: styd on wl ins fnl f: no threat to wnr* **4/1[1]**

6145 **4** *hd* **Victory Command (IRE)**[12] 5192 3-8-7 **96**.................. FrannyNorton 10 101
(Mark Johnston) *in tch in midfield: effrt jst over 2f out: clsd u.p and pressing ldrs ent fnl f: kpt on same pce ins fnl f* **25/1**

-054 **5** *3/4* **Almania (IRE)**[19] 4901 3-8-6 **95**.................. AndreaAtzeni 8 99
(Sir Michael Stoute) *sweating; hld up in rr: effrt on outer over 2f out: styd on ins fnl f: no threat to wnr* **15/2[3]**

0312 **6** *nk* **Korcho**[20] 4882 3-8-4 **93**.................. DavidEgan 1 96
(Hughie Morrison) *broke wl: settled bk and in tch in midfield: clsd and ev ch ent fnl 2f: jst getting outpcd whn pushed lft jst ins fnl f: wknd wl ins fnl f* **10/1**

2251 **7** *2 3/4* **Walkinthesand (IRE)**[20] 4882 3-9-7 **110**.................. RyanMoore 4 108
(Richard Hannon) *pressed ldr for 2f: styd chsng ldrs: n.m.r over 2f out: unable qck u.p over 1f out: wknd ins fnl f* **11/2[2]**

-531 **8** *3/4* **Dalaalaat (IRE)**[26] 4639 3-8-0 **89**.................. HayleyTurner 9 88
(William Haggas) *looked wl; chsd ldrs tl jnd ldr after 2f: led over 2f out: hdd and no ex u.p over 1f out: wknd ins fnl f* **10/1**

3116 **9** *1 3/4* **Coolagh Forest (IRE)**[30] 4490 3-8-2 **94**.................. SeanDavis(3) 6 87
(Richard Fahey) *stmbld leaving stalls: rousted along leaving stalls: racd awkwardly bnd 5f out: swtchd rt 3f out: no imp over 1f out: wknd ins fnl f (jockey said colt stumbled leaving the stalls and hung left-handed on the bend)* **50/1**

0-46 **10** *12* **Wargrave (IRE)**[46] 3901 3-8-12 **101**.................. JamieSpencer 11 70
(J A Stack, Ire) *tall; midfield: hdwy to chse ldrs after 2f: rdn over 2f out: lost pl and btn over 1f out: wknd ins fnl f* **25/1**

2520 **11** *2 1/4* **The Trader (IRE)**[20] 4882 3-8-3 **92**.................. JoeFanning 2 56
(Mark Johnston) *led tl over 2f out: lost pl over 1f out: wknd ins fnl f* **12/1**

2m 3.79s (-5.11) **Going Correction** -0.075s/f (Good) **11 Ran SP% 118.1**
Speed ratings (Par 106): **114,112,111,111,111 110,108,107,106,96 95**
CSF £25.29 CT £94.49 TOTE £4.80: £1.90, £2.40, £1.60; EX 32.30 Trifecta £136.40.
Owner HRH Princess Haya Of Jordan **Bred** Car Colston Hall Stud **Trained** Newmarket, Suffolk
■ Stewards' Enquiry : Harry Bentley caution; careless riding

FOCUS
Just 0.2mm of rain overnight and the going was good (GoingStick 7.9). The rail at the top and bottom bends was dolled out and fresh ground was provided in the straight. Add 5yds. A typically strong race and the winner improved again.

5584 QATAR RICHMOND STKS (GROUP 2) (C&G) 6f
2:25 (2:29) (Class 1) 2-Y-O
£113,420 (£43,000; £21,520; £10,720; £5,380; £2,700) **Stalls High**

Form RPR

415 **1** **Golden Horde (IRE)**[44] 3949 2-9-0 103.................. AdamKirby 5 111
(Clive Cox) *looked wl; chsd ldr: effrt ent 2f out: drvn to ld over 1f out: sustained duel w runner-up after: styd on wl and asserted wl ins fnl f* **15/2[3]**

12 **2** *3/4* **Threat (IRE)**[44] 3949 2-9-0 0.................. TomMarquand 1 109
(Richard Hannon) *wnt rt leaving stalls: sn rcvrd and chsd ldrs: pressed ldrs 2f out: rdn and str chal over 1f out: sustained duel w wnr after: no ex and outpcd wl ins fnl f* **11/8[1]**

3 *3* **Royal Dornoch (IRE)**[15] 5066 2-9-0 0.................. WayneLordan 7 100
(A P O'Brien, Ire) *str; hld up in last trio: swtchd rt over 2f out: hdwy on outer over 1f out: styd on to go 3rd wl ins fnl f: no threat to ldng pair* **25/1**

1 **4** *1/2* **Volatile Analyst (USA)**[24] 4719 2-9-0 0.................. DanielTudhope 2 99
(Keith Dalgleish) *leggy; hld up in tch in midfield: clsd to chse ldrs 2f out: effrt u.p over 1f out: nt match pce of ldng pair 1f out: kpt on same pce ins fnl f* **28/1**

14 **5** *shd* **Symbolize (IRE)**[43] 3988 2-9-0 0.................. DavidProbert 3 98
(Andrew Balding) *looked wl; in tch in midfield: effrt wl over 1f out: sn drvn: kpt on same pce and no threat to ldng pair ins fnl f* **15/2[3]**

1302 **6** *1/2* **Misty Grey (IRE)**[13] 5134 2-9-0 98.................. JoeFanning 8 97
(Mark Johnston) *led: rdn and hdd over 1f out: 3rd and outpcd 1f out: lost 3 pls ins fnl f (vet said colt lost it's right-hind shoe)* **16/1**

132 **7** *1 3/4* **Dream Shot (IRE)**[27] 4610 2-9-0 96.................. JamieSpencer 4 91
(James Tate) *coltish; chsd ldrs: effrt and hdwy into midfield whn wnt sharply lft over 1f out: sn rdn and no hdwy: wknd ins fnl f (vet said colt lost it's left-hind shoe)* **25/1**

41 **8** *1/2* **Royal Commando (IRE)**[27] 4596 2-9-0 0.................. KieranShoemark 10 90
(Charles Hills) *athletic; looked wl; restless in stalls: wnt rt leaving stalls: hld up in tch: effrt whn short of room: pushed lft and hmpd over 1f out: nt rcvr and wl hld ins fnl f* **14/1**

103 **9** *nk* **Maxi Boy**[19] 4920 2-9-0 101.................. FrankieDettori 13 89
(Michael Bell) *in tch in midfield: effrt u.p but no imp over 1f out: wknd ins fnl f* **10/1**

265 **10** *1/2* **King Neptune (USA)**[21] 4846 2-9-0 99.................. RyanMoore 11 89
(A P O'Brien, Ire) *hld up in tch towards rr: effrt nr stands' rail 2f out: no hdwy u.p over 1f out: nvr involved* **25/1**

61 **11** *1* **Don't Stop Dancing (IRE)**[14] 5082 2-9-0 0.................. PJMcDonald 6 85
(Ronald Harris) *leggy; restless in stalls: t.k.h: chsd ldrs tl lost pl u.p over 1f out: wknd ins fnl f* **80/1**

134 **12** *3/4* **Guildsman (FR)**[21] 4846 2-9-0 106.................. OisinMurphy 9 88+
(Archie Watson) *rrd as stalls opened: s.i.s and bmpd leaving stalls: a towards rr: short-lived effrt 2f out: no prog and nvr involved* **7/1[2]**

21 **13** *9* **Fleeting Prince (IRE)**[17] 4992 2-9-0 0.................. JamesDoyle 12 73+
(Charles Hills) *leggy; athletic; t.k.h: chsd ldrs early: in tch in midfield: squeezed for room: snatch up and dropped to rr over 1f out: sn eased* **33/1**

1m 11.01s (-1.09) **Going Correction** -0.075s/f (Good) **13 Ran SP% 118.9**
Speed ratings (Par 106): **104,103,99,98,98 97,95,94,94,93 92,91,79**
CSF £16.74 CT £265.60 TOTE £9.10: £2.70, £1.20, £8.00; EX 24.40 Trifecta £452.50.
Owner AlMohamediya Racing **Bred** Cn Farm Ltd **Trained** Lambourn, Berks

FOCUS
Just an average edition, but the first two finished nicely clear of the rest. They didn't go that quick early on and it paid to be handy. The winner rates an improver, with the second to his Ascot level.

5585 QATAR GORDON STKS (GROUP 3) 1m 3f 218y
3:00 (3:05) (Class 1) 3-Y-O
£99,242 (£37,625; £18,830; £9,380; £4,707; £2,362) **Stalls High**

Form RPR

6532 **1** **Nayef Road (IRE)**[21] 4845 3-9-1 104.................. SilvestreDeSousa 6 111
(Mark Johnston) *chsd ldrs: wnt 2nd after 1f tl 8f out: clsd and upsides ldrs over 3f out: rdn to ld jst over 2f out: sustained duel w runner-up: outbattled him and gamely forged ahd wl ins fnl f: all out* **9/1**

3-12 **2** *nk* **Constantinople (IRE)**[42] 4017 3-9-4 110.................. RyanMoore 7 113
(A P O'Brien, Ire) *sweating; in last pair early: hdwy into midfield after 2f: jnd ldr 8f out: ev ch and rdn 2f out: sustained duel w wnr after but hung rt: hung into rail 1f out: wnt bk lft ins fnl f: outbattled towards fin* **2/1[1]**

-521 **3** *hd* **Spanish Mission (USA)**[21] 4845 3-9-4 110.................. JamieSpencer 2 113+
(David Simcock) *sweating; stdd and dropped in after s: hld up in tch: hdwy into midfield 7f out: chsd ldrs 6f out: effrt whn nt clr run over 1f out: swtchd lft ins fnl f: styd on strly u.p towards fin* **11/2[3]**

6-51 **4** *1* **Floating Artist**[19] 4901 3-9-1 103.................. PatDobbs 8 108
(Richard Hannon) *hld up in tch in last pair: clsd over 2f out: chsd ldrs u.p over 1f out: keeping on same pce whn sltly impeded and wnt lft ins fnl f* **25/1**

1-11 **5** *2 1/4* **Dal Horrisgle**[28] 4553 3-9-1 98.................. DanielTudhope 3 104+
(William Haggas) *str; hld up in tch: effrt over 2f out: swtchd lft over 1f out: kpt on ins fnl f: no threat to ldrs* **8/1**

1251 **6** *2 1/2* **Technician (IRE)**[49] 3789 3-9-1 103.................. OisinMurphy 9 100
(Martyn Meade) *hld up in tch: hdwy to chse ldrs over 3f out: no ex u.p and outpcd over 1f out: wknd ins fnl f* **16/1**

1023 **7** *nk* **Jalmoud**[18] 4963 3-9-1 110..................(h) JamesDoyle 4 100
(Charlie Appleby) *looked wl; led: rdn and hdd ent fnl 2f: outpcd u.p and btn over 1f out: wknd ins fnl f* **4/1[2]**

8 *1 1/4* **Leo De Fury (IRE)**[19] 4939 3-9-1 0.................. ShaneFoley 5 98
(Mrs John Harrington, Ire) *leggy; t.k.h: hld up in tch: squeezed through and hdwy 4f out: sn chsng ldrs: no ex u.p and btn over 1f out: wknd ins fnl f* **8/1**

-240 **9** *29* **Cap Francais**[42] 4013 3-9-1 103.................. AndreaAtzeni 1 52
(Ed Walker) *chsd ldr for over 1f: chsd ldrs tl rdn and lost pl bnd 5f out: wnt lft over 4f out: bhd over 1f out: eased ins fnl f: t.o (jockey said colt stopped quickly)* **14/1**

2m 35.67s (-3.93) **Going Correction** -0.075s/f (Good) **9 Ran SP% 117.3**
Speed ratings (Par 110): **110,109,109,109,107 105,105,104,85**
CSF £27.84 TOTE £10.10: £2.90, £1.20, £1.70; EX 35.30 Trifecta £176.00.
Owner Mohamed Obaida **Bred** B V Sangster **Trained** Middleham Moor, N Yorks

FOCUS
Distance increased by 5yds. A messy race but the winner rates an improver.

5586 QATAR NASSAU STKS (GROUP 1) (BRITISH CHAMPIONS SERIES) (F&M) 1m 1f 197y
3:35 (3:44) (Class 1) 3-Y-O+
£340,260 (£129,000; £64,560; £32,160; £16,140; £8,100) **Stalls Low**

Form RPR

2-46 **1** **Deirdre (JPN)**[43] 3985 5-9-7 113.................. OisinMurphy 4 118
(Mitsuru Hashida, Japan) *sweating; hld up in last trio: clsd and nt clr run 3f out: hdwy on inner over 1f out: chsd ldr jst ins fnl f: r.o wl to ld wl ins fnl f: sn in command* **20/1**

1101 **2** *1 1/4* **Mehdaayih**[32] 4429 3-8-13 108.................. FrankieDettori 3 116+
(John Gosden) *nt that wl away and pushed along leaving stalls: sn w ldr and racd keenly: led over 8f out: rdn ent fnl 2f: clr and hung lft 1f out: hdd and no ex wl ins fnl f* **3/1[2]**

-322 **3** *1 1/4* **Rawdaa**[43] 3986 4-9-7 111.................. DanielTudhope 9 113
(Sir Michael Stoute) *stdd and dropped in after s: hld up in rr: swtchd lft and effrt over 2f out: styd on over 1f out: chsd ldng pair ins fnl f: gng on fin but nt getting to ldrs* **6/1[3]**

-311 **4** *2 1/2* **Sun Maiden**[34] 4332 4-9-7 106.................. JamesDoyle 1 108
(Sir Michael Stoute) *looked wl; chsd ldrs tl wnt 2nd over 3f out: rdn wl over 2f out: no imp u.p over 1f out: lost 2nd and wknd jst ins fnl f* **14/1**

-600 **5** *3/4* **Just Wonderful (USA)**[26] 4681 3-8-13 110.................. WayneLordan 7 107
(A P O'Brien, Ire) *awkward leaving stalls: hld up in last trio: clsd and nt clr run over 2f out: effrt u.p and shifting rt over 1f out: no imp and one pce ins fnl f* **20/1**

0024 **6** *1 1/2* **Nyaleti (IRE)**[26] 4645 4-9-7 105.................. JoeFanning 6 104
(Mark Johnston) *sweating; chsd ldrs: effrt over 2f out: drvn and no imp over 1f out: wknd ins fnl f* **50/1**

1 **7** *1/2* **Channel (IRE)**[46] 3905 3-8-13 112.................. Pierre-CharlesBoudot 8 103
(F-H Graffard, France) *str; looked wl; hld up in midfield: clsd over 3f out: unable qck and no imp over 1f out: wknd ins fnl f* **11/1**

-110 **8** *2 3/4* **Maqsad (FR)**[62] 3316 3-8-13 109.................. JimCrowley 2 97
(William Haggas) *hld up in midfield: effrt jst over 2f out: no imp u.p over 1f out: wknd ins fnl f (jockey said filly ran flat)* **15/2**

-112 **9** *38* **Hermosa (IRE)**[41] 4051 3-8-13 116.................. RyanMoore 5 21
(A P O'Brien, Ire) *led for over 1f: chsd ldr: rdn over 3f out: sn lost pl and btn: bhd over 1f out: eased fnl f: t.o (trainer could offer no explanation for the poor performance)* **13/8[1]**

2m 2.93s (-5.97) **Going Correction** -0.075s/f (Good)
WFA 3 from 4yo+ 8lb **9 Ran SP% 115.6**
Speed ratings (Par 117): **118,117,116,114,113 112,111,109,79**
CSF £78.17 CT £418.05 TOTE £19.30: £3.40, £1.60, £1.90; EX 110.50 Trifecta £795.20.
Owner Toji Morita **Bred** Northern Farm **Trained** Japan

FOCUS
Add 5yds. This looked a competitive Nassau on paper, and with the big two in the market both wanting the early lead, the pace was good from the off. It was set up for a closer to swoop and the winner rates an improver.

5587 TELEGRAPH NURSERY H'CAP 7f
4:10 (4:24) (Class 2) 2-Y-O
£15,752 (£4,715; £2,357; £1,180; £587) **Stalls Low**

Form RPR

511 **1** **Governor Of Punjab (IRE)**[23] 4750 2-9-0 **83**.................. RyanMoore 5 92+
(Mark Johnston) *tall; str; scope; looked wl; short of room and hmpd sn after s: midfield: rdn and hdwy over 1f out: swtchd lft ent fnl f: r.o strly to ld wl ins fnl f: sn in command* **9/2[1]**

224 **2** *1* **Sword Beach (IRE)**[13] 5152 2-8-10 **79**.................. TomMarquand 13 85+
(Eve Johnson Houghton) *hld up in rr: nt clr run over 2f out: rdn and hdwy between rivals jst over 1f out: r.o strly ins fnl f: snatched 2nd last stride* **33/1**

512 **3** *shd* **Toro Strike (USA)**[31] 4441 2-9-2 **85**.................. TonyHamilton 1 91
(Richard Fahey) *ly; looked wl; sn led: rdn 2f out: kpt on wl u.p tl hdd and no ex wl ins fnl f: lost 2nd last stride* **10/1**

441 **4** *1/2* **Stone Circle (IRE)**[12] 5172 2-8-11 **80**.................. DanielTudhope 9 85+
(Michael Bell) *compact; in tch in midfield: nt clr run 2f out: effrt u.p and edging rt over 1f out: styd on wl ins fnl f* **12/1**

0231 **5** *1 3/4* **Indian Creak (IRE)**[28] 4544 2-8-11 **80**.................. DavidProbert 6 82
(Mick Channon) *wnt rt sn after s: wl in tch in midfield: clsd to chse ldrs and nt clrest of runs ent fnl 2f: edgd out lft and drvn jst over 1f out: no ex and outpcd wl ins fnl f* **16/1**

011 **6** *1* **Fred**[12] 5177 2-9-4 **87**.................. FrannyNorton 7 85
(Mark Johnston) *athletic; chsd ldr: rdn 2f out: drvn and stl pressing ldr over 1f out: no ex and wknd ins fnl f* **5/1[2]**

461 **7** *1 1/2* **Picture Frame**[37] 4223 2-9-1 **84**.................. OisinMurphy 16 78
(Saeed bin Suroor) *str; hld up towards rr: effrt ent fnl 2f: swtchd lft and hdwy over 1f out: kpt on to pass btn horses ins fnl f: nvr trbld ldrs* **10/1**

631 **8** 3/4 **Full Verse (IRE)**[61] 3335 2-9-7 **90**.................. JamesDoyle 10 82
(Charlie Appleby) *hld up in rr: effrt and hdwy on inner over 1f out: no imp ins fnl f and wl hld whn wnt lft towards fin* **6/1**[3]

046 **9** 2 **Pitcher**[28] 4558 2-8-1 **70**.................. JimmyQuinn 17 57
(Richard Hannon) *swtchd rt after s: hld up in rr: effrt and reminder 2f out: rdn over 1f out: kpt on ins fnl f: nvr involved* **80/1**

024 **10** nk **Willa**[29] 4502 2-8-5 **74**.................. MartinDwyer 3 60
(Richard Hannon) *compact; scrimmaging w rivals sn after s: chsd ldrs: awkward and stmbld bnd 5f out: lost pl u.p and btn over 1f out: wknd ins fnl f* **25/1**

1224 **11** 1 **Insania**[12] 5171 2-8-7 **76**..................(p[1]) PJMcDonald 4 59
(K R Burke) *workmanlike; scrimmaging w rivals sn after s: wl in tch in midfield: unable qck u.p over 1f out: wknd ins fnl f* **25/1**

242 **12** 1 **When Comes Here (IRE)**[44] 3962 2-8-11 **80**.................. JimCrowley 11 61
(Andrew Balding) *hld up towards rr: effrt 3f out: sme prog but nvr threatened to get on terms: swtchd rt 1f out: no imp fnl f* **10/1**

2514 **13** 2 3/4 **Dragon Command**[19] 4938 2-8-9 **78**..................(v[1]) SilvestreDeSousa 2 53+
(George Scott) *scrimmaging w rivals sn after s: chsd ldrs: swtchd lft 3f out: outpcd u.p over 1f out and btn whn bmpd ent fnl f: bhd and eased ins fnl f* **5/1**[2]

1243 **14** 3 **Xcelente**[26] 4637 2-9-1 **84**.................. JoeFanning 8 50
(Mark Johnston) *compact; t.k.h: racd wd in midfield: lost pl and bhd whn hung rt over 1f out: wknd fnl f* **16/1**

1m 26.39s (-0.31) **Going Correction** -0.075s/f (Good) **14** Ran SP% **124.4**
Speed ratings (Par 100): **98,96,96,96,94 93,91,90,88,87 86,85,82,78**
CSF £167.62 CT £1484.22 TOTE £5.60: £2.00, £11.60, £3.20; EX 244.50 Trifecta £1916.70.
Owner Rob Ferguson **Bred** Mrs Joan Murphy **Trained** Middleham Moor, N Yorks
■ London Calling was withdrawn, price at time of withdrawal 25/1. Rule 4 does not apply.
FOCUS
Add 10yds. This is usually a deep race and the winner is progressive. It's been rated a shade positively.

5588 MARKEL INSURANCE BRITISH EBF MAIDEN FILLIES' STKS (PLUS 10 RACE) 7f
4:45 (4:58) (Class 2) 2-Y-O **£15,752** (£4,715; £2,357; £1,180; £587) **Stalls** Low

Form RPR
3 **1** **Vividly**[28] 4557 2-9-0 0.................. KieranShoemark 16 81
(Charles Hills) *unfurnished: looked wl; mde all and styd wd early: rdn 2f out: drvn fnl f: all out cl home: jst hld on* **16/1**

2 **2** shd **Craylands**[19] 4918 2-9-0 0.................. FrankieDettori 12 81
(Michael Bell) *str; t.k.h: chsd ldrs: clsd to chse wnr wnt rt 2f out: effrt over 1f out: 1 l down 1f out: grad clsd u.p ins fnl f: jst hld* **11/4**[1]

2 **3** 1 1/2 **Tulip Fields**[21] 4819 2-9-0 0.................. PJMcDonald 1 77
(Mark Johnston) *leggy: athletic: looked wl; t.k.h: chsd ldrs: effrt ent fnl 2f: chsd clr ldng pair 1f out: kpt on but nvr getting on terms* **11/4**[1]

4 2 1/2 **African Swift (USA)** 2-9-0 0.................. FrannyNorton 7 70+
(Mark Johnston) *tall: str; chsd ldr tl 5f out: outpcd 2f out: sn rdn: kpt on same pce fr over 1f out* **14/1**

642 **5** nk **Incognito (IRE)**[12] 5189 2-9-0 76.................. AndreaAtzeni 9 70
(Mick Channon) *workmanlike; t.k.h: hld up wl in tch in midfield: effrt ent fnl 2f: chsd clr ldng pair over 1f out: no imp: kpt on same pce ins fnl f* **12/1**

6 2 1/2 **Salsa (IRE)** 2-9-0 0.................. RyanMoore 3 63+
(A P O'Brien, Ire) *str: bit bkward; midfield and rn green early: pushed along 3f out: no imp: rdn over 1f out: no threat to ldrs but kpt on steadily ins fnl f* **5/1**[2]

7 hd **Hold Fast (IRE)** 2-9-0 0.................. DavidProbert 6 63+
(Andrew Balding) *unfurnished: scope; hld up in midfield: effrt ent 2f out: no imp and swtchd lft over 1f out: kpt on same pce ins fnl f* **25/1**

53 **8** 3/4 **Diva Rock**[15] 5045 2-9-0 0.................. ShaneKelly 15 61+
(George Baker) *workmanlike; t.k.h: in tch in midfield on outer: outpcd 2f out: no threat to ldrs after and kpt on same pce ins fnl f* **50/1**

9 3/4 **Lady Pendragon** 2-9-0 0.................. EoinWalsh 2 59
(Martin Smith) *str; s.i.s: sn rcvrd and in midfield: effrt ent fnl 2f: no imp: edgd lft and wl hld over 1f out* **66/1**

10 1/2 **Isayalittleprayer** 2-9-0 0.................. GeraldMosse 14 57+
(Gary Moore) *compact; t.k.h: hld up in rr: modest late hdwy: nvr involved* **50/1**

11 1 **Good Reason** 2-9-0 0.................. OisinMurphy 13 55+
(Saeed bin Suroor) *leggy; s.i.s: racd in last trio: reminder 2f out: edging rt and no imp over 1f out: nvr involved* **20/1**

12 hd **Phantom Bride (IRE)** 2-9-0 0.................. JamesDoyle 8 54
(K R Burke) *workmanlike; midfield tl dropped towards rr 5f out: n.d after* **33/1**

13 1/2 **Ruby Power (IRE)** 2-9-0 0.................. SilvestreDeSousa 10 53
(Richard Hannon) *compact; t.k.h: chsd ldrs: wnt 2nd 5f out tl 2f out: sn outpcd and wknd fnl f* **16/1**

14 2 **Al Dawodiya (IRE)** 2-9-0 0.................. SeanLevey 11 48
(Richard Hannon) *athletic; t.k.h: hld up in midfield: effrt 2f out: outpcd and btn over 1f out: wknd ins fnl f* **11/1**[3]

15 18 **Moondance** 2-9-0 0.................. JimCrowley 5 1
(Gary Moore) *workmanlike; edgd lft leaving stalls: a bhd* **33/1**

1m 27.59s (0.89) **Going Correction** -0.075s/f (Good) **15** Ran SP% **124.4**
Speed ratings (Par 97): **91,90,89,86,85 83,82,82,81,80 79,79,78,76,55**
CSF £58.14 TOTE £17.60: £3.80, £1.80, £1.60; EX 61.90 Trifecta £293.60.
Owner K Abdullah **Bred** Juddmonte Farms Ltd **Trained** Lambourn, Berks
FOCUS
Add 10yds. This looked a good fillies' maiden and it should throw up a number of winners.

5589 TATLER H'CAP 5f
5:20 (5:29) (Class 3) (0-95,91) 3-Y**£15,752** (£4,715; £2,357; £1,180; £587) **Stalls** High

Form RPR
1211 **1** **Celsius (IRE)**[21] 4829 3-8-9 **79**..................(t) PJMcDonald 9 89+
(Tom Clover) *stdd and bmpd leaving stalls: hld up in rr: nt clr run 2f out: hdwy over 1f out: str chal ins fnl f: r.o wl to ld nr fin* **11/2**[3]

0223 **2** shd **Mercenary Rose (IRE)**[22] 4783 3-8-5 **75**..................(t) DavidEgan 16 84
(Paul Cole) *chsd ldrs: led over 1f out: kpt on wl u.p ins fnl f: hdd and no ex nr fin* **25/1**

1042 **3** 1 1/2 **Lufricia**[27] 4595 3-9-3 **87**.................. AndreaAtzeni 10 90
(Roger Varian) *chsd ldrs: effrt and ev ch over 1f out: no ex and outpcd fnl 100yds* **13/2**

5421 **4** 3/4 **Tinto**[16] 5014 3-9-3 **87**.................. PatDobbs 12 88+
(Amanda Perrett) *in rr: nt clr run 2f out: swtchd rt 1f out: r.o strly ins fnl f: nt rch ldrs* **14/1**

0506 **5** nk **Concierge (IRE)**[20] 4866 3-9-7 **91**..................(b[1]) HarryBentley 6 90
(George Scott) *midfield: swtchd rt and hdwy between horses over 1f out: kpt on u.p ins fnl f* **22/1**

1520 **6** 1/2 **Top Breeze (IRE)**[21] 4847 3-9-7 **91**.................. ShaneKelly 8 89
(Richard Hughes) *wl in tch in midfield: clsd to chse ldrs and rdn over 1f out: kpt on same pce u.p ins fnl f* **8/1**

-400 **7** 2 1/4 **Blame Roberta (USA)**[40] 4101 3-9-3 **87**..................(p[1]) JoeFanning 14 77
(Robert Cowell) *rousted along leaving stalls: short of room sn after and hld up in tch in midfield: nt clr run and edgd lft over 1f out: squeezed through and kpt on ins fnl f: no threat to ldrs (vet said filly lost it's left-fore shoe)* **33/1**

6410 **8** 1/2 **Whataguy**[8] 5318 3-8-8 **81**..................(p) MeganNicholls[(3)] 11 69
(Paul Nicholls) *in tch in midfield: effrt over 1f out: kpt on same pce ins fnl f* **28/1**

20- **9** 1/2 **Jungle Speed (FR)**[103] 3-9-6 **90**..................(t[1]) Pierre-CharlesBoudot 7 76
(F Chappet, France) *led: edgd lft 3f out: rdn and hdd over 1f out: wknd ins fnl f (vet said colt lost it's left-fore shoe)* **16/1**

3-50 **10** 1/2 **Dancing Warrior**[10] 5252 3-9-4 **88**.................. JimCrowley 15 72
(William Knight) *chsd ldr tl 2f out: lost pl over 1f out: wknd ins fnl f* **33/1**

3451 **11** 1/2 **Pass The Gin**[19] 4904 3-8-9 **82**.................. WilliamCox[(3)] 4 64
(Andrew Balding) *wnt rt leaving stalls: hld up towards rr: swtchd rt and hdwy 2f out: no imp 1f out: wknd ins fnl f* **14/1**

511 **12** 1 1/4 **Amplify (IRE)**[32] 4422 3-9-0 **84**.................. OisinMurphy 17 62
(Brian Meehan) *hld up in tch in midfield: nt clr run and shuffled bk to rr 2f out: swtchd rt ins fnl f: no ch (trainers' rep said colt was unsuited by the undulations of the track and would prefer a flatter track)* **9/2**[1]

5025 **12** dht **Good Luck Fox (IRE)**[20] 4872 3-8-10 **80**..................(b[1]) SilvestreDeSousa 2 58
(Richard Hannon) *pushed rt leaving stalls: racd in centre: midfield: hdwy to chse ldrs and rdn 2f out: no ex over 1f out: wknd ins fnl f* **12/1**

0440 **14** 1/2 **Alfie Solomons (IRE)**[21] 4847 3-8-13 **83**..................(t[1]) SeanLevey 1 59
(Richard Spencer) *pushed rt s: racd in centre: midfield: effrt to chse ldrs 2f out: no ex u.p over 1f out: wknd ins fnl f* **5/1**[2]

50-4 **15** 1 1/4 **Glory Fighter**[16] 5014 3-9-2 **86**.................. GeraldMosse 3 58
(Charles Hills) *pushed rt leaving stalls: midfield: effrt u.p over 1f out: unable qck and wknd ins fnl f* **25/1**

06-1 **16** nk **Get The Rhythm**[40] 4128 3-8-9 **82**.................. SeanDavis[(3)] 5 52
(Richard Fahey) *midfield: effrt ent fnl 2f: nudged rt and impeded over 1f out: no prog whn nt clr run and hmpd ins fnl f* **14/1**

57.24s (-0.86) **Going Correction** -0.075s/f (Good) **16** Ran SP% **129.6**
Speed ratings (Par 104): **103,102,100,99,98 97,94,93,92,91 91,89,89,88,86 85**
CSF £152.08 CT £940.35 TOTE £6.50: £1.90, £6.80, £2.00, £3.40; EX 234.20 Trifecta £1487.80.
Owner J Collins, C Fahy & S Piper **Bred** Owenstown Stud **Trained** Newmarket, Suffolk
FOCUS
A wide-open 3yo sprint, the high-drawn runners nearer to the stands' side were seen to best effect. The first two rate as improvers.
T/Jkpt: Not Won. T/Plt: £39.20 to a £1 stake. Pool: £294,746.90 - 5,488.68 winning units T/Qpdt: £16.90 to a £1 stake. Pool: £20,718.19 - 904.33 winning units **Steve Payne**

5145 NOTTINGHAM (L-H)
Thursday, August 1
OFFICIAL GOING: Soft (heavy in places; 5.5)
Wind: Light across Weather: Sunny spells

5590 MANSIONBET EBF FILLIES' NOVICE STKS (PLUS 10 RACE) 5f 8y
1:40 (1:43) (Class 5) 2-Y-O **£3,881** (£1,155; £577; £288) **Stalls** High

Form RPR
1 **Ishvara** 2-9-0 0.................. RichardKingscote 3 80
(Robert Cowell) *w ldr: rdn over 1f out: styd on to ld wl ins fnl f* **8/1**[3]

32 **2** 3/4 **Poets Dance**[8] 5317 2-9-0 0.................. DaneO'Neill 4 77
(Rae Guest) *led: rdn: hung lft and hdd wl ins fnl f: styd on same pce* **1/3**[1]

3 8 **Baracca Rocks** 2-9-0 0.................. BenCurtis 1 48
(K R Burke) *edgd lft s: sn prom: rdn over 1f out: wknd fnl f* **5/1**[2]

0 **4** hd **Champagne Angel (IRE)**[44] 3968 2-9-0 0.................. DuranFentiman 2 47
(Tim Easterby) *chsd ldrs: edgd lft 4f out: rdn 1/2-way: wknd fnl f* **66/1**

5 16 **Light Lily** 2-9-0 0.................. DanielMuscutt 5
(Paul D'Arcy) *s.i.s: sn in tch: shkn up 1/2-way: wknd wl over 1f out* **33/1**

6 nk **Prisma (IRE)** 2-9-0 0.................. JasonHart 6
(Ivan Furtado) *in tch: shkn up and edgd lft 1/2-way: wknd wl over 1f out* **25/1**

1m 3.49s (3.29) **Going Correction** +0.45s/f (Yiel) **6** Ran SP% **111.1**
Speed ratings (Par 91): **91,89,77,76,51 50**
CSF £11.21 TOTE £8.70: £2.60, £1.02; EX 14.10 Trifecta £42.00.
Owner Manor Farm Stud & John Rose **Bred** Manor Farm Stud (Rutland) **Trained** Six Mile Bottom, Cambs
FOCUS
Plenty of rain hit the course through the week (notably 25mm on Tuesday and overnight) and the going was given as soft, heavy in places (GoingStick 5.5). The outer track is in use, with all distances as advertised. Not a strong fillies' novice, most of the field either inexperienced or short of ability, and it was a better attitude that proved the difference between the front two in the end. The time was 5.49 seconds slower than standard, underlining that conditions were rather testing.

5591 MANSIONBET EBF MAIDEN STKS 6f 18y
2:15 (2:16) (Class 5) 2-Y-O **£3,881** (£1,155; £577; £288) **Stalls** High

Form RPR
3 **1** **Sir Boris (IRE)**[14] 5082 2-9-5 0.................. RichardKingscote 6 90+
(Tom Dascombe) *mde all: rdn clr fnl f: edgd lft towards fin* **9/1**

6 **2** 6 **Plymouth Rock (IRE)**[33] 4401 2-9-5 0.................. JasonHart 5 72
(John Quinn) *s.i.s: sn trcking ldrs: swtchd lft to chse wnr over 1f out: sn rdn and edgd lft: styd on same pce fnl f* **11/10**[1]

35 **3** 2 1/2 **Jump The Gun (IRE)**[58] 3451 2-9-5 0.................. CallumShepherd 2 65
(Jamie Osborne) *s.i.s: hld up: hdwy over 2f out: wknd fnl f (jockey said colt lost left hind shoe)* **11/2**

3 **4** 2 1/4 **Spiritofthenorth (FR)**[13] 5152 2-9-5 0.................. TomEaves 4 58
(Kevin Ryan) *chsd wnr: shkn up over 2f out: hmpd and lost 2nd wl over 1f out: sn wknd* **4/1**[2]

5 4 **Bryn Du** 2-9-5 0.................. BenCurtis 3 46
(William Haggas) *s.i.s: sn pushed along in rr: outpcd fr 4f out* **5/1**[3]

6 13 **Live In The Moment (IRE)** 2-9-5 0.................. AndrewElliott 1 7
(Adam West) *chsd ldrs on outer tl shkn up and edgd lft over 2f out: sn wknd* **66/1**

1m 17.02s (3.22) **Going Correction** +0.45s/f (Yiel) **6** Ran SP% **111.2**
Speed ratings (Par 94): **96,88,84,81,76 59**
CSF £19.20 TOTE £8.20: £2.80, £1.10; EX 28.10 Trifecta £94.90.
Owner Mr & Mrs R Scott **Bred** Parks Farm Stud **Trained** Malpas, Cheshire

FOCUS
Just a fair 2yo maiden with the exception of the winner, who dictated an even pace and was in control from a good way out.

5592 MANSIONBET NOVICE MEDIAN AUCTION STKS 1m 75y
2:50 (2:54) (Class 6) 3-5-Y-0 **£3,234** (£962; £481; £240) **Stalls** Centre

Form RPR
1 **Miss O Connor (IRE)**[85] 2537 4-9-6 0 GeorgiaCox(3) 7 91+
(William Haggas) *mde virtually all: rdn clr over 1f out: easily* **2/5**[1]
6 2 11 **Al Moataz (IRE)**[127] 1352 3-9-0 0 DanielMuscutt 14 64
(Marco Botti) *racd keenly in 2nd: rdn over 1f out: sn outpcd* **12/1**
3-36 3 2 3/4 **Pamper**[51] 3707 3-8-9 72 GeorgeWood 6 53
(James Fanshawe) *chsd ldrs: shkn up over 2f out: no ex fr over 1f out* **9/2**[2]
4 2 3/4 **Sally Hope** 3-8-9 0 JoeyHaynes 3 47
(John Gallagher) *chsd ldrs: rdn over 2f out: no ex fr over 1f out* **33/1**
0 5 2 1/2 **Storm Eleanor**[90] 2354 3-8-9 0 JosephineGordon 10 41+
(Hughie Morrison) *hld up: racd keenly: swtchd rt over 3f out: nvr trbld ldrs* **16/1**
6 1 1/4 **Riverfront (FR)** 3-8-11 0 JoshuaBryan(3) 4 43+
(Andrew Balding) *s.i.s: hld up: shkn up over 2f out: nvr on terms* **8/1**[3]
00 7 1 1/2 **Ximena**[77] 2762 3-8-10 1 ow1 (h[1]) CallumShepherd 15 36+
(William Jarvis) *hld up: shkn up on outer over 3f out: n.d* **50/1**
0 8 hd **Goldfox Grey**[12] 5193 3-9-0 0 AndrewMullen 2 40+
(Robyn Brisland) *hld up in tch: rdn over 2f out: wknd over 1f out* **100/1**
04 9 4 **Sharp Talk (IRE)**[22] 4800 3-9-0 0 CYHo 11 31+
(Shaun Keightley) *hld up: in tch: shkn up over 3f out: wknd wl over 1f out* **66/1**
00 10 4 **Capricorn Prince**[31] 4452 3-9-0 0 TomQueally 12 22+
(Gary Moore) *hld up: shkn up and wknd over 3f out* **100/1**
11 4 **Inteldream** 3-8-11 0 AaronJones(3) 13 13+
(Marco Botti) *s.i.s: hld up: shkn up and wknd over 3f out* **25/1**
12 6 **Winalotwithalittle (IRE)** 3-8-9 0 NickyMackay 8
(J R Jenkins) *s.i.s: a in rr: wknd over 3f out* **66/1**

1m 48.47s (1.77) **Going Correction** +0.45s/f (Yiel)
WFA 3 from 4yo 7lb **12** Ran SP% **128.0**
Speed ratings (Par 101): **107,96,93,90,88 86,85,85,81,77 73,67**
CSF £8.10 TOTE £1.30: £1.10, £2.70, £1.60; EX 7.50 Trifecta £23.90.
Owner Lael Stable **Bred** Kilnamoragh Stud **Trained** Newmarket, Suffolk

FOCUS
A stern pace in testing ground exposed the lack of depth in this novice, the bulk of them finishing tired while the favourite powered clear in good style. There weren't many eye-catchers in behind.

5593 MANSIONBET BEATEN BY A HEAD H'CAP 1m 75y
3:25 (3:26) (Class 5) (0-70,70) 3-Y-O+
£3,881 (£1,155; £577; £300; £300; £300) **Stalls** Centre

Form RPR
0102 1 **Classic Charm**[8] 5309 4-9-4 60 JoeyHaynes 1 77
(Dean Ivory) *sn prom: chsd ldr over 6f out: led over 3f out: rdn clr fr over 1f out: easily* **2/1**[1]
50-4 2 7 **Bruyere (FR)**[37] 4225 3-9-3 66 (h) RobertWinston 10 66
(Dean Ivory) *s.i.s: hld up: hdwy 3f out: rdn to chse wnr over 1f out: no imp fnl f* **13/2**[3]
-003 3 2 **Carey Street (IRE)**[48] 3805 3-9-5 68 JasonHart 4 63
(John Quinn) *hld up in tch: outpcd over 2f out: styd on to go 3rd wl ins fnl f* **14/1**
6000 4 3/4 **Showboating (IRE)**[5] 5434 11-9-11 67 (p) CamHardie 5 62
(John Balding) *hld up: rdn over 2f out: r.o ins fnl f: nvr nrr* **20/1**
6512 5 1/2 **Mr Strutter (IRE)**[13] 5151 5-10-0 70 AndrewElliott 8 63
(Ronald Thompson) *led 1f: remained handy: chsd wnr over 2f out tl rdn and edgd lft over 1f out: wknd ins fnl f* **7/1**
0000 6 1 1/4 **Hitman**[11] 5214 6-9-7 63 LewisEdmunds 13 54
(Rebecca Bastiman) *hld up: hdwy over 2f out: rdn over 1f out: wknd fnl f* **33/1**
0-00 7 1/2 **Dawn Breaking**[27] 4584 4-8-9 51 oh2 PhilDennis 9 40
(Richard Whitaker) *s.i.s: hdwy over 6f out: rdn over 2f out: wknd over 1f out* **12/1**
0550 8 3 3/4 **Bristol Missile (USA)**[19] 4926 5-9-0 63 JonathanFisher(7) 3 44
(Richard Price) *s.i.s: hld up: hdwy over 2f out: rdn and wknd over 1f out* **22/1**
6455 9 8 **Tarbeyah (IRE)**[20] 4870 4-9-9 65 TomEaves 11 27
(Kevin Frost) *hld up: pushed along 1/2-way: wknd over 2f out* **14/1**
2023 10 4 1/2 **Loose Chippings (IRE)**[14] 5080 5-8-10 52 (p) BenCurtis 6 4
(Ivan Furtado) *led 7f out: hdd over 3f out: wknd over 2f out (trainer said gelding was unsuited by the soft, heavy in places going, and would prefer a quicker surface)* **9/2**[2]
200 11 17 **Vixen (IRE)**[37] 4226 5-10-0 70 JosephineGordon 12
(Emma Lavelle) *s.i.s: plld hrd and sn prom: stdd and lost pl over 6f out: wknd 3f out (jockey said mare ran too free)* **10/1**

1m 48.07s (1.37) **Going Correction** +0.45s/f (Yiel)
WFA 3 from 4yo+ 7lb **11** Ran SP% **119.5**
Speed ratings (Par 103): **109,102,100,99,98 97,97,93,85,80 63**
CSF £14.86 CT £150.98 TOTE £3.00: £1.40, £2.40, £3.80; EX 17.80 Trifecta £359.10.
Owner Solario Racing (tring) **Bred** Gracelands Stud **Trained** Radlett, Herts

FOCUS
This was strongly run but it didn't have any great effect on the result, with few making significant inroads from the back. The front pair will be of interest again.

5594 DOWNLOAD THE MANSIONBET APP H'CAP 1m 2f 50y
4:00 (4:02) (Class 4) (0-85,83) 3-Y-O+
£6,469 (£1,925; £962; £481; £300; £300) **Stalls** Low

Form RPR
2252 1 **Hats Off To Larry**[17] 4997 5-9-13 82 CallumShepherd 8 90
(Mick Channon) *a.p: chsd ldr 6f out tl led over 2f out: rdn over 1f out: r.o* **10/3**[1]
-462 2 1 3/4 **Zzoro (IRE)**[22] 4792 6-9-9 78 RoystonFfrench 1 83
(Amanda Perrett) *chsd ldr after 1f tl 6f out: remained handy: rdn over 1f out: chsd wnr ins fnl f: styd on same pce towards fin* **8/1**[3]
0-62 3 1/2 **Junderstand**[35] 4283 4-9-7 76 PaulHanagan 12 80
(Alan King) *chsd ldrs: rdn and ev ch over 1f out: edgd lft: styd on same pce wl ins fnl f* **12/1**
6-63 4 hd **Memphis Bleek**[41] 4055 3-8-13 76 (p) JasonHart 7 80
(Ivan Furtado) *hld up: hdwy over 2f out: rdn over 1f out: swtchd lft ins fnl f: styd on (vet said gelding lost left hind shoe)* **11/1**
0365 5 2 1/2 **Redgrave (IRE)**[19] 4907 5-9-7 76 TomQueally 9 74
(Joseph Tuite) *hld up: hdwy on outer over 1f out: sn rdn and hung lft: styd on same pce ins fnl f* **10/1**
1613 6 1/2 **Music Seeker (IRE)**[20] 4892 5-9-7 83 (t) ZakWheatley(7) 3 80
(Declan Carroll) *chsd ldrs: nt clr run and swtchd lft over 3f out: rdn over 1f out: styd on same pce* **4/1**[2]
1053 7 2 **Ghalib (IRE)**[14] 5095 7-9-10 79 LewisEdmunds 13 72
(Rebecca Bastiman) *led over 7f: wknd ins fnl f* **16/1**
1-00 8 1 1/4 **War Eagle (IRE)**[18] 2796 3-8-10 73 BenCurtis 4 65
(Ian Williams) *s.i.s: hld up: rdn over 2f out: nvr on terms* **22/1**
4512 9 4 **El Picador (IRE)**[26] 4663 3-8-13 76 (v) RichardKingscote 5 60
(Sir Michael Stoute) *hld up: effrt over 2f out: wknd over 1f out* **10/3**[1]
0005 10 18 **Mount Tahan (IRE)**[17] 4988 7-9-13 82 TomEaves 6 29
(Kevin Ryan) *s.i.s: a in rr: rdn and wknd over 2f out* **28/1**
11 21 **Sauron's Eye**[117] 1599 3-8-4 67 (h[1] w) JoeyHaynes 10
(Ivan Furtado) *s.i.s: a in rr: shkn up over 3f out: sn wknd* **40/1**

2m 17.56s (4.16) **Going Correction** +0.45s/f (Yiel)
WFA 3 from 4yo+ 8lb **11** Ran SP% **118.5**
Speed ratings (Par 105): **101,99,99,99,97 96,95,94,90,76 59**
CSF £30.23 CT £290.15 TOTE £5.20: £2.40, £2.90, £2.50; EX 32.10 Trifecta £190.60.
Owner T Radford & Partner **Bred** W A Harrison-Allan **Trained** West Ilsley, Berks

FOCUS
The first six home all arrived in good form, so this is a race to be positive about on the whole. The pace was fair given the conditions but it still proved hard to make up ground from the rear. The winner has been rated in line with a better view of his recent form, with the second and third to form.

5595 MANSIONBET BEST ODDS GUARANTEED H'CAP 5f 8y
4:35 (4:39) (Class 5) (0-75,77) 3-Y-O+ **£3,881** (£1,155; £577; £300) **Stalls** High

Form RPR
0010 1 **Show Palace**[12] 5180 6-9-8 73 (p) GrahamLee 5 82
(Jennie Candlish) *led: hdd over 3f out: led again over 1f out: rdn out: edgd lft nr fin* **13/8**[1]
-030 2 1/2 **Gnaad (IRE)**[82] 2625 5-9-4 74 DarraghKeenan(5) 1 81
(Alan Bailey) *wnt lft s: sn chsng ldrs: rdn over 1f out: styd on* **9/4**[2]
-000 3 5 **Requited (IRE)**[15] 5056 3-8-6 67 (p[1]) JosephLyons(7) 2 55
(Hughie Morrison) *s.i.s: hdwy to ld over 3f out: hdd over 1f out: wknd fnl f* **9/2**
-004 4 3 1/2 **Choosey (IRE)**[16] 5027 4-9-4 69 NathanEvans 6 46
(Michael Easterby) *chsd ldrs: lost pl after 1f: sn pushed along: edgd lft 1/2-way: wknd over 1f out* **4/1**[3]

1m 2.48s (2.28) **Going Correction** +0.45s/f (Yiel)
WFA 3 from 4yo+ 3lb **4** Ran SP% **107.0**
Speed ratings (Par 103): **99,98,90,84**
CSF £5.43 TOTE £2.20; EX 5.40 Trifecta £12.10.
Owner P and Mrs G A Clarke **Bred** M C Humby **Trained** Basford Green, Staffs

■ Kodiac Express was withdrawn, price at time of withdrawal 15/2. Rule 4 applies to board prices prior to withdrawal, but not to SP bets. Deduction of 10p in the pound. New market formed.

FOCUS
A well-run sprint despite the small field and the only pair to give their running came comfortably clear. The winner has been rated in line with his C&D win from two starts ago.

5596 MANSIONBET H'CAP 2m
5:10 (5:12) (Class 6) (0-65,69) 3-Y-O+
£3,234 (£962; £481; £300; £300; £300) **Stalls** Low

Form RPR
4621 1 **Platform Nineteen (IRE)**[10] 5242 3-9-5 69 6ex CliffordLee 3 78
(Michael Bell) *hld up: pushed along over 4f out: hdwy over 2f out: rdn to ld ins fnl f: styd on wl* **4/5**[1]
3312 2 3 1/4 **Well Funded (IRE)**[16] 5028 3-8-12 62 PaulHanagan 6 67
(James Bethell) *chsd ldrs: led over 1f out: sn rdn and hung lft: hdd ins fnl f: styd on same pce* **5/1**[2]
5662 3 1 1/2 **Kitty's Cove**[9] 5277 4-8-9 46 oh1 DuranFentiman 15 47
(Tim Easterby) *s.s and rel to r: hdwy over 2f out: rdn and hung lft fr over 1f out: styd on u.p: nt rch ldrs (jockey said filly was slowly away)* **12/1**
603 4 hd **Constraint**[15] 5048 3-8-11 64 JoshuaBryan(3) 5 67
(Andrew Balding) *sn led: hdd after 1f: remained handy: rdn over 2f out: edgd lft and no ex wl ins fnl f* **25/1**
3322 5 1 3/4 **Victoriano (IRE)**[16] 5012 3-9-3 67 AdamMcNamara 7 68
(Archie Watson) *led after 1f: sn hdd: chsd ldr who wnt clr 12f out: tk clsr order over 3f out: rdn over 2f out: no ex ins fnl f* **6/1**[3]
0003 6 1 1/4 **Sweetest Smile (IRE)**[5] 5435 4-8-9 46 RoystonFfrench 13 43
(Ed de Giles) *led over 14f out: clr 12f out: c bk to the field over 3f out: rdn and hdd over 1f out: wknd ins fnl f* **40/1**
2530 7 5 **Artic Nel**[5] 5435 5-8-2 46 oh1 RPWalsh(7) 8 37
(Ian Williams) *hld up: hdwy over 3f out: rdn and wknd over 1f out* **20/1**
6040 8 3/4 **Final Choice**[20] 2239 6-10-0 65 AndrewElliott 14 56
(Adam West) *s.i.s: in rr: rdn over 3f out: nvr nrr* **33/1**
0063 9 10 **Harry The Norseman**[46] 3888 3-8-7 57 JasonHart 11 38
(Jonjo O'Neill) *s.i.s: hld up: rdn over 3f out: sn wknd* **10/1**
0000 10 1 1/2 **Tilsworth Sammy**[27] 4594 4-8-9 46 oh1 AndrewMullen 12 23
(J R Jenkins) *hld up: a in rr: wknd over 3f out* **50/1**
0006 11 8 **Interrogation (FR)**[20] 4868 4-8-9 46 oh1 JoeyHaynes 1 13
(Alan Bailey) *s.i.s: hld up: hdwy over 5f out: rdn and wknd over 3f out* **100/1**
600 12 21 **Triple Genius (IRE)**[47] 3860 3-8-3 53 JosephineGordon 4
(Ed Dunlop) *hld up: rdn over 5f out: wknd over 4f out* **22/1**
36-0 13 33 **Duration (IRE)**[141] 160 4-9-3 54 GrahamLee 10
(J R Jenkins) *hld up: hdwy on outer over 6f out: rdn and wknd over 4f out* **80/1**

3m 44.83s (10.33) **Going Correction** +0.45s/f (Yiel)
WFA 3 from 4yo+ 13lb **13** Ran SP% **125.8**
Speed ratings (Par 101): **92,90,89,89,88 88,85,85,80,79 75,64,48**
CSF £4.77 CT £33.39 TOTE £1.80: £1.10, £1.60, £2.30; EX 6.40 Trifecta £37.10.
Owner The Royal Ascot Racing Club **Bred** Watership Down Stud **Trained** Newmarket, Suffolk

FOCUS
Form to view quite positively with lightly raced 3yos filling three of the first four positions. Sweetest Smile raced in a clear lead but the remainder went a reasonable pace.
T/Plt: £13.70 to a £1 stake. Pool: £39,187.39 - 2,077.4 winning units T/Qpdt: £5.00 to a £1 stake. Pool: £3,726.16 - 550.54 winning units **Colin Roberts**

5567 GALWAY (R-H)

Thursday, August 1

OFFICIAL GOING: Good (good to yielding in places on flat course; watered)

5597a **ROCKSHORE H'CAP** **1m 98y**
3:10 (3:10) 4-Y-O+ **£10,648** (£3,441; £1,639; £738; £378; £198)

RPR

1 **Waitingfortheday (IRE)**[12] 5204 4-10-0 **90**...........(p) DonnachaO'Brien 4 100+
(Joseph Patrick O'Brien, Ire) *dwlt sltly: sn chsd ldrs: gng wl in 3rd 2f out: impr to chal into st and led ent fnl f: sn rdn and strly pressed nr fin: hld on wl* **7/1**[2]

2 ½ **Emphatic (IRE)**[2] 5536 4-8-4 **66**..(t) RoryCleary 8 75
(J Larkin, Ire) *cl up: 2nd at 1/2-way: drvn in 2nd over 2f out and led narrowly into st tl hdd ent fnl f: kpt on wl u.p and strly pressed wnr nr fin: hld* **7/1**[2]

3 ¾ **Yuften**[13] 5160 8-9-4 **87**.. JMSheridan(7) 20 94+
(Denis Gerard Hogan, Ire) *on toes befhand: slowly away and detached in rr early: hdwy in 17th fr 2f out: swtchd lft into st and r.o strly nr side ins fnl f into 3rd fnl strides: nrst fin* **20/1**

4 nk **Koybig (IRE)**[16] 5034 7-8-11 **76**.............................. DonaghO'Connor(3) 6 83
(David Marnane, Ire) *sweated up befhand: hld up in tch: 7th 1/2-way: tk clsr order bhd ldrs 2f out where n.m.r on inner: swtchd into st and sn rdn in 4th: no imp on ldrs in 3rd ins fnl f: denied 3rd fnl strides* **5/1**[1]

5 1 **Ciao (IRE)**[17] 5007 4-9-2 **78**..(v[1]) ChrisHayes 7 82
(Gavin Cromwell, Ire) *hld up in rr of mid-div: drvn into 8th 2f out and clsd u.p into 5th over 1f out: no imp on ldrs ins fnl f: kpt on one pce* **7/1**[2]

6 nk **Stormy Belle (IRE)**[96] 2129 5-9-0 **83**..........................(t) GavinRyan(7) 10 87
(P A Fahy, Ire) *slowly away and pushed along towards rr early: prog fr over 2f out: rdn into st and r.o far side ins fnl f to dispute 4th briefly: no ex nr fin* **20/1**

7 2½ **Stringybark Creek**[35] 4283 5-9-1 **82**........................ ShaneCrosse(5) 11 80
(David Loughnane) *chsd ldrs: rdn disputing 5th over 2f out and no imp on ldrs u.p over 1f out: one pce fnl f* **20/1**

8 nk **Honor Oak (IRE)**[25] 4697 7-9-9 **85**.. WJLee 3 82
(T Hogan, Ire) *led: narrow advantage at 1/2-way: rdn into st and hdd: sn no ex bhd ldrs and wknd ins fnl f* **8/1**[3]

9 hd **Star Quality**[28] 4574 5-8-10 **75**.................................... TomMadden(3) 16 72
(Mrs John Harrington, Ire) *mid-div: tk clsr order and disp 5th briefly between horses over 2f out: no ex into st where sltly impeded: one pce fnl f* **16/1**

10 ½ **Spiorad Saoirse**[15] 5074 4-9-5 **81**...............................(b[1]) KillianLeonard 21 77
(Andrew Slattery, Ire) *mid-div: rdn over 2f out and no imp into st: one pce fnl f* **16/1**

11 1 **Sirjack Thomas (IRE)**[13] 5160 4-9-8 **84**.................................... OisinOrr 19 77
(Adrian McGuinness, Ire) *in rr of mid-div: stl gng wl over 2f out where n.m.r briefly: sn pushed along and no imp towards rr into st where rdn: swtchd rt 1f out and kpt on one pce* **16/1**

12 1 **Have A Nice Day**[2] 5537 9-9-2 **78**................................(v) NGMcCullagh 12 69
(T G McCourt, Ire) *chsd ldrs: rdn in 4th 2f out and no ex over 1f out where wknd: eased ins fnl f* **33/1**

13 1¼ **Wentwood**[13] 5160 4-9-2 **83**...(p) BenCoen(5) 5 71
(D K Weld, Ire) *hld up: rdn over 2f out: disputing 5th and sn no ex: wknd into st* **8/1**[3]

14 1 **Master Speaker (IRE)**[13] 5160 9-9-13 **89**.................... RonanWhelan 15 75
(Adrian McGuinness, Ire) *hld up towards rr: drvn over 2f out and sme hdwy 1f out: kpt on one pce: nvr a factor* **12/1**

15 2 **Brendan Brackan (IRE)**[15] 5071 10-9-8 **84**.................... ColinKeane 1 65
(G M Lyons, Ire) *towards rr: short of room bef st where dropped to rr: kpt on one pce under hands and heels ins fnl f: nvr a factor* **20/1**

16 4½ **Parabellum (IRE)**[13] 5-9-13 **99**................................(p) AlanGlynn(10) 2 70
(Denis Gerard Hogan, Ire) *mid-div: drvn and wknd fr over 2f out* **50/1**

17 ¾ **Tintoretto (IRE)**[2] 5537 4-9-4 **80**.................................. RobbieColgan 13 49
(John Joseph Murphy, Ire) *rrd bef s: mid-div: drvn in 10th under 2f out and wknd into st* **10/1**

18 23 **Shifted Strategy (IRE)**[2] 5537 4-8-13 **75**..................(p) LeighRoche 14
(J A Stack, Ire) *slowly away and pushed along briefly towards rr early: tk clsr order in rr of mid-div after 2f: pushed along on outer after 1/2-way and no ex in 11th over 2f out: wknd into st and eased* **33/1**

1m 45.48s (-4.72) **18** Ran SP% **137.7**
CSF £56.74 CT £1020.27 TOTE £6.80: £1.80, £2.10, £4.20, £1.60; DF 64.50 Trifecta £1336.50.
Owner J Dollard **Bred** James Fennelly **Trained** Owning Hill, Co Kilkenny

FOCUS
Another good performance from the winner, a filly who keeps improving and could make her presence felt at stakes level.

5598a (Foreign Racing) - See Raceform Interactive

5599a **OPEN GATE PURE BREW H'CAP** **1m 4f**
5:30 (5:31) (55-70,72) 3-Y-O+ **£9,051** (£2,925; £1,393; £627; £321; £168)

RPR

1 **One Cool Poet (IRE)**[2] 5536 7-10-2 **72** 6ex..................(bt) WJLee 18 77+
(Matthew J Smith, Ire) *hld up towards rr: stl gng wl 3f out: gd hdwy 2f out and sn swtchd lft to chse ldrs ent fnl f: rdn in 3rd ins fnl f and r.o strly to ld nr fin: comf* **4/1**[2]

2 1½ **Fayetta**[23] 4769 3-9-3 **69**..(b) ChrisHayes 1 72
(David Loughnane) *prom tl sn settled bhd ldr: disp 2nd at times: rdn in 3rd over 2f out and impr into 2nd u.p over 1f out: dropped to 3rd briefly wl ins fnl f: kpt on: nt trble wnr* **20/1**

3 1¼ **Lusis Naturea**[6] 5405 8-9-9 **72** 6ex.............................. AdamFarragher(7) 3 72+
(Paul Traynor, Ire) *hld up in rr of mid-div: prog fr over 2f out where n.m.r and bmpd rival: rdn over 1f out and r.o u.p ins fnl f to snatch 3rd on line: nrst fin* **3/1**[1]

4 nse **Shamad (IRE)**[5] 5466 5-9-8 **69** 6ex.................................. BenCoen(5) 19 69
(Peter Fahey, Ire) *mid-div: hdwy after 1/2-way: rdn into 4th fr 2f out: short of room briefly and swtchd lft ins fnl f: kpt on same pce: nt trble wnr* **14/1**

5 shd **Champagne Terri (IRE)**[14] 5114 3-9-4 **70**..................(p) LeighRoche 14 71
(Adrian Paul Keatley, Ire) *cl up bhd ldr and disp 2nd at times: impr to load into st: sn rdn and reduced advantage wl ins fnl f where hdd: denied 3rd fnl stride where dropped to 5th* **8/1**[3]

6 1¾ **Chaparral Dream (IRE)**[9] 1406 4-9-9 **65**.......................... ColinKeane 10 62
(Adrian McGuinness, Ire) *mid-div: prog between horses into 7th 2f out: sn swtchd lft and no imp on ldrs u.p over 1f out: short of room briefly ins fnl f and kpt on one pce clsng stages* **4/1**[2]

7 ¾ **Storm Steps (IRE)**[24] 4746 4-9-5 **66**........................... ShaneCrosse(5) 16 62
(Timothy Doyle, Ire) *dwlt and towards rr: stl clsr order over 2f out where short of room briefly: sn pushed along and sme hdwy u.p over 1f out: kpt on ins fnl f: nvr nrr* **33/1**

8 ½ **Marine One**[67] 3117 5-9-6 **69**... JMSheridan(7) 9 64
(Denis Gerard Hogan, Ire) *hld up towards rr: pushed along and sme hdwy on outer 2f out: rdn over 1f out and sn swtchd lft: kpt on nr fin: nvr nrr* **11/1**

9 ¾ **Bar Room Bore (IRE)**[15] 5065 3-9-2 **68**........................ RossCoakley 6 63
(Fergal Birrane, Ire) *chsd ldrs: 5th 1/2-way: rdn bhd ldrs over 2f out and sn no ex: wknd* **28/1**

10 2¼ **Dancing Doll (IRE)**[10] 5259 6-9-3 **66**........................(t) AlanPersse(7) 12 56
(M Flannery, Ire) *sn led: 2 l clr at 1/2-way: rdn and strly pressed 2f out: hdd into st and wknd fr over 1f out* **33/1**

11 1¾ **Lleyton (IRE)**[18] 4702 7-9-7 **63**...................................... RobbieColgan 20 50
(J R Finn, Ire) *dwlt: hld up towards rr: pushed along in rr over 2f out where n.m.r briefly: rdn into st and kpt on ins fnl f: nvr nrr* **33/1**

12 1 **Nasee**[49] 3778 4-9-11 **67**...(p) RoryCleary 21 53
(John Joseph Hanlon, Ire) *hld up: gng wl in rr of mid-div 3f out: bmpd over 2f out and pushed along: sn rdn and no imp into st where n.m.r briefly: one pce fnl f* **20/1**

13 shd **Happy Company (IRE)**[15] 5078 5-9-8 **64**.............................. GaryHalpin 4 50
(P J Hassett, Ire) *hld up in tch: drvn in 5th over 2f out and sn wknd* **8/1**[3]

14 8½ **Tashman (IRE)**[7] 7790 4-9-2 **65**.. GavinRyan(7) 7 37
(Gavin Cromwell, Ire) *hld up in tch: pushed along in mid-div over 3f out: sn forced lft and bmpd rival: wknd* **33/1**

15 nk **Royal Admiral (IRE)**[15] 5078 5-9-9 **68**...................(v) TomMadden(3) 15 40
(Adrian McGuinness, Ire) *in rr of mid-div: pushed along and sme hdwy on outer 3f out: no ex into st and wknd* **14/1**

16 2¼ **Commander**[10] 5256 5-9-11 **67**......................................(b) KillianLeonard 2 35
(Denis Gerard Hogan, Ire) *hld up in tch: 4th 1/2-way: rdn and wknd over 2f out where short of room on inner and checked* **20/1**

17 38 **Uluru Park (IRE)**[96] 1622 4-9-7 **63**................................(p) RonanWhelan 8
(Brendan W Duke, Ire) *chsd ldrs: rdn in 6th over 3f out and no ex u.p over 2f out: sn wknd qckly: eased into st* **25/1**

2m 36.78s (-6.32) **Going Correction** -0.225s/f (Firm)
WFA 3 from 4yo+ 10lb **17** Ran SP% **142.2**
Speed ratings: **112,111,110,110,110 108,108,108,107,106 104,104,104,98,98 96,71**
CSF £95.91 CT £290.41 TOTE £4.50: £1.40, £4.20, £1.40, £3.90; DF 103.00 Trifecta £413.50.
Owner DRFG Partnership **Bred** Caroline Brazil **Trained** Kilmessan, Co. Meath

FOCUS
The winner became the first horse to double up over the course of the week under another terrific ride from Billy Lee. This rates a small pb.

5510 CLAIREFONTAINE (R-H)

Thursday, August 1

OFFICIAL GOING: Turf: good to firm

5600a **PRIX BISCUITERIE JEANNETTE ET CITRONNADE MIMOUNA (CLAIMER) (2YO) (TURF)** **7f**
4:20 2-Y-O **£8,558** (£3,423; £2,567; £1,711; £855)

RPR

1 **Get Set (IRE)**[9] 5286 2-9-4 0.......................................(b) AntoineHamelin 6 77
(Matthieu Palussiere, France) **31/10**[2]

2 6 **Hunter Valley (FR)** 2-9-1 0.. CristianDemuro 8 58
(Cedric Rossi, France) **14/5**[1]

3 ½ **Aban (IRE)**[37] 4228 2-9-1 0...................................(p) ClementLecoeuvre 10 57
(Henk Grewe, Germany) **33/10**[3]

4 1¼ **Lalacelle (FR)**[37] 4228 2-9-1 0.............................. ChristopheSoumillon 4 54
(S Cerulis, France) **42/10**

5 ¾ **Trou Aux Biches (FR)**[19] 4949 2-8-5 0............(p) MlleAlisonMassin(3) 1 45
(Y Barberot, France) **32/1**

6 2 **Carmague (IRE)**[26] 4679 2-9-1 0.................................... GregoryBenoist 3 47
(J S Moore) *settled midfield: rowed along over 2f out: rdn to chse ldrs over 1f out: no ex ins fnl f* **13/1**

7 3 **Kikana (FR)**[38] 2-8-11 0......................................(b) StephanePasquier 2 36
(L Rovisse, France) **23/1**

8 4 **Secret Wedding** 2-9-1 0...(p) TheoBachelot 9 32
(P Monfort, France) **17/1**

9 15 **Lovely Melody (FR)** 2-8-8 0................................ MlleCoraliePacaut(3) 5
(R Rohne, Germany) **27/1**

10 2½ **Devilla (FR)** 2-8-11 0.. IoritzMendizabal 7
(J Bertran De Balanda, France) **46/1**

1m 24.6s **10** Ran SP% **118.8**
PARI-MUTUEL (all including 1 euro stake): WIN 4.10; PLACE 1.50, 1.30, 1.60; DF 6.30.
Owner Mrs Theresa Marnane **Bred** C Marnane **Trained** France

5287 BATH (L-H)

Friday, August 2

OFFICIAL GOING: Firm (good to firm in places: 8.8)
Wind: light across Weather: sunny periods

5601 **NOVIA HIGH FLYER H'CAP** **1m 3f 137y**
5:05 (5:08) (Class 6) (0-65,62) 3-Y-O
£2,781 (£827; £413; £400; £400; £400) **Stalls Low**

Form RPR

5032 1 **No Thanks**[18] 4998 3-9-2 **57**..................................... CallumShepherd 4 64
(William Jarvis) *trckd ldr: tk narrow advantage over 2f out: rdn clr over 1f out: kpt on wl* **10/3**[2]

-411 2 1 **Sadlers Beach (IRE)**[30] 4499 3-9-7 **62**........................(h) HayleyTurner 3 67
(Marcus Tregoning) *trckd ldrs: rdn over 2f out: kpt on to go 2nd ins fnl f but nt pce to threaten wnr* **13/8**[1]

0501 3 ¾ **Hammy End (IRE)**[31] 4485 3-9-0 **58**........................(h) MitchGodwin(3) 6 62
(William Muir) *trckd ldrs: rdn over 2f out: kpt on ins fnl f but nt pce to chal* **11/1**

6040 **4** *shd* **Ideal Grace**[29] 4547 3-8-5 **53**....................(p[1]) GeorgiaDobie(7) 1 57
(Eve Johnson Houghton) *led: rdn and hdd over 1f out: hld whn edgd rt over 1f out: kpt on same pce fnl f (b.b.v) (vet said filly had bled from the nose)* **8/1**

50-6 **5** *1 1/4* **Volcanique (IRE)**[11] 5242 3-8-11 **52**....................(p[1]) RyanTate 5 54
(Sir Mark Prescott Bt) *hld up bhd ldrs: rdn over 2f out: kpt on but nt quite pce to threaten (jockey said filly was denied a clear run)* **15/2**

14U2 **6** *1 1/4* **Twpsyn (IRE)**[4] 5497 3-9-4 **59**....................(b) HectorCrouch 7 59
(David Evans) *hld up bhd ldrs: hdwy 2f out: edgd lft u.p whn hld ent fnl f: fdd fnl 120yds* **7/2**[3]

2m 29.35s (-1.45) **Going Correction** -0.15s/f (Firm) **6 Ran SP% 114.6**
Speed ratings (Par 98): **98,97,96,96,95 95**
CSF £9.50 TOTE £4.40: £2.00, £1.70; EX 12.20 Trifecta £78.10.
Owner P C J Dalby & R D Schuster **Bred** Mr & Mrs Sandy Orr **Trained** Newmarket, Suffolk
■ Stewards' Enquiry : Mitch Godwin six-day ban; excessive use of whip (Aug 16-21)

FOCUS
The ground continued to dry out and was now firm, good to firm in places (from good to firm, firm in places). GoingStick 8.8. Exit of the bottom bend railed out to 2yds off the inner and returned at the 3f point in the straight. Add 6yds to races on the round course, making the opener 1m3f 143yds. This was a modest 3yo handicap in which they went an even pace before the tempo quickened inside the last 3f. Callum Shepherd described the ground as "Bath firm."

5602 SDS MAIDEN AUCTION STKS — 5f 160y
5:40 (5:40) (Class 5) 2-Y-O — £3,428 (£1,020; £509; £254) **Stalls** Centre

Form — RPR

3430 **1** **Audio**[13] 5185 2-9-0 75....................(t) ThoreHammerHansen(5) 3 77
(Richard Hannon) *sn prom: disp led gng best over 2f out: led over 1f out: kpt on: rdn out* **6/4**[1]

2 **2** *2 1/2* **Simply Susan (IRE)**[17] 5011 2-8-0 0.................... GeorgiaDobie(7) 6 57
(Eve Johnson Houghton) *hld up in cl 5th: hdwy over 2f out: sn rdn and hung lft: chsd wnr ent fnl f: kpt on but nt pce to get on terms* **2/1**[2]

330 **3** *hd* **Maybellene (IRE)**[13] 5185 2-8-9 70.................... HayleyTurner 5 58
(George Scott) *trckd ldrs: rdn 2f out: kpt on to chal for 2nd ins fnl f but nt pce to get on terms w wnr* **9/2**[3]

66 **4** *2 1/2* **Hollywood Waltz**[38] 4221 2-8-7 0.................... RaulDaSilva 1 47
(Mick Channon) *led: rdn whn jnd over 2f out: hdd over 1f out: sn hld: no ex ins fnl f* **11/2**

0 **5** *4 1/2* **Halfacrown (IRE)**[41] 4114 2-8-12 0.................... CallumShepherd 2 37
(Jamie Osborne) *trckd ldrs: rdn over 2f out: wknd ent fnl f* **12/1**

1m 11.25s (0.15) **Going Correction** -0.15s/f (Firm) **5 Ran SP% 114.6**
Speed ratings (Par 94): **93,89,89,86,80**
CSF £5.07 TOTE £1.80: £1.50, £1.10; EX 5.70 Trifecta £17.40.
Owner Highclere T'Bred Racing-Hilton-Barber 1 **Bred** D A Bloodstock **Trained** East Everleigh, Wilts

FOCUS
Not a deep race.

5603 VISIT VALUERATER.CO.UK FOR BEST FREE TIPS H'CAP (VALUE RATER RACING CLUB SUMMER SPRINT QUAL) — 5f 10y
6:10 (6:10) (Class 5) (0-70,62) 3-Y-O — £3,428 (£1,020; £509; £400) **Stalls** Centre

Form — RPR

4512 **1** **Broadhaven Dream (IRE)**[7] 5375 3-9-7 **62**.................... KieranO'Neill 3 68
(Ronald Harris) *led: rdn and hdd over 1f out: rallied wl to regain ld ins fnl f: r.o wl* **5/6**[1]

1130 **2** *3/4* **Thegreyvtrain**[6] 5449 3-9-7 **62**.................... DavidProbert 5 65
(Ronald Harris) *prom: rdn to ld over 1f out: hdd ins fnl f: kpt on but no ex* **10/3**[2]

4-40 **3** *1/2* **Society Star**[39] 4192 3-9-6 **61**.................... RaulDaSilva 4 62
(Robert Cowell) *trckd ldrs: chal 2f out: sn rdn: kpt on same pce ins fnl f* **9/2**[3]

1200 **4** *nk* **Tomahawk Ridge (IRE)**[28] 4586 3-9-7 **62**.................... HectorCrouch 1 62
(John Gallagher) *trckd ldrs: sltly outpcd in 4th over 2f out: kpt on again ins fnl f* **9/2**[3]

1m 1.19s (-0.81) **Going Correction** -0.15s/f (Firm) **4 Ran SP% 114.0**
Speed ratings (Par 100): **100,98,98,97**
CSF £4.25 TOTE £1.60; EX 3.10 Trifecta £8.40.
Owner M Doocey, S Doocey & P J Doocey **Bred** Ms Sinead Maher **Trained** Earlswood, Monmouths

FOCUS
An ordinary 3yo sprint handicap. Ron Harris saddled two of the four remaining runners and they finished 1-2. There wasn't much covering the four runners at the line. It's been rated around the first two.

5604 PLAY "FOUR FROM THE TOP" AT VALUERATER.CO.UK H'CAP (VALUE RATER RACING CLUB SUMMER STAYERS' QUAL) — 2m 1f 24y
6:45 (6:45) (Class 5) (0-75,75) 4-Y-O+ £3,428 (£1,020; £509; £400; £400) **Stalls** Centre

Form — RPR

1042 **1** **Charlie D (USA)**[16] 5055 4-9-4 **75**....................(tp) JaneElliott(3) 3 85
(Tom Dascombe) *trckd ldrs: led over 2f out: styd on wl at assert fnl 120yds: rdn out* **9/4**[2]

4661 **2** *1 1/2* **Horatio Star**[9] 5290 4-9-5 **73** 5ex....................(p) TomMarquand 6 81
(Brian Meehan) *w ldr for 2f: trckd clr ldr: led briefly over 2f out: sn rdn: kpt pressing wnr tl no ex fnl 100yds* **6/4**[1]

4-56 **3** *6* **Gemini**[95] 2214 4-8-13 **67**.................... RobbieDowney 1 68
(John Quinn) *trckd ldrs: rdn wl over 2f out: styd on into 3rd ent fnl f: nvr gng pce to trble front pair* **13/2**

1-66 **4** *1 1/2* **Beer With The Boys**[13] 5179 4-9-0 **68**.................... CallumShepherd 5 68
(Mick Channon) *led for 2f: trckd clr ldr: led over 3f out: rdn and hdd over 2f out: kpt chsng ldng pair tl wknd ent fnl f* **4/1**[3]

640 **5** *33* **Knight Commander**[16] 5053 6-8-3 **57** oh1 ow1............(bt) RaulDaSilva 4 20
(Steve Flook) *led after 2f and sn 8 l clr: 12 l clr 7f out: reduced advantage 5f out: hdd over 3f out: wknd over 2f out: t.o* **10/1**

3m 43.86s (-7.54) **Going Correction** -0.15s/f (Firm) **5 Ran SP% 113.2**
Speed ratings (Par 103): **111,110,107,106,91**
CSF £6.27 TOTE £2.70: £1.50, £1.10; EX 7.00 Trifecta £31.60.
Owner D R Passant & T Dascombe **Bred** Rabbah Bloodstock Ltd **Trained** Malpas, Cheshire

FOCUS
Actual race distance 2m1f 30yds. A routine staying handicap especially with Le Torrent a late non-runner. This was a decent test, though, with Knight Commander going off like a scalded cat. A pb from the second.

5605 SDS INTELLISTORM H'CAP — 1m 2f 37y
7:20 (7:21) (Class 4) (0-85,86) 3-Y-O — £5,207 (£1,549; £774; £400) **Stalls** Low

Form — RPR

2-13 **1** **Universal Order**[42] 4068 3-9-8 **86**.................... StevieDonohoe 1 92
(David Simcock) *trckd ldrs: rdn over 2f out: str run ins fnl f: led towards fin* **2/1**[1]

1-24 **2** *1* **Alnadir (USA)**[25] 4739 3-9-7 **85**....................(h) DavidProbert 3 89
(Simon Crisford) *led: rdn and hdd jst over 2f out: rallied to regain ld jst ins fnl f: styd on: hdd towards fin* **4/1**

401- **3** *hd* **Albanita**[356] 6001 3-8-12 **76**.................... RyanTate 4 80
(Sir Mark Prescott Bt) *trckd ldr: led jst over 2f out: rdn over 1f out: hdd jst ins fnl f: styd on* **5/2**[3]

-241 **4** *3 1/2* **Bint Soghaan**[14] 5138 3-9-3 **81**.................... TomMarquand 2 78
(Richard Hannon) *trckd ldrs: rdn over 2f out: nt pce to chal: fdd fnl f* **9/4**[2]

2m 9.09s (-2.01) **Going Correction** -0.15s/f (Firm) **4 Ran SP% 112.7**
Speed ratings (Par 102): **102,101,101,98**
CSF £10.12 TOTE £3.00; EX 9.30 Trifecta £18.90.
Owner Abdulla Al Mansoori **Bred** Rabbah Bloodstock Limited **Trained** Newmarket, Suffolk

FOCUS
Actual race distance 1m2f 43yds. A tight 3yo handicap despite just the four runners and the market got it right. It's been rated around the second to the better view of his form.

5606 SDS GEOLIGHT H'CAP — 5f 10y
7:50 (7:51) (Class 4) (0-85,85) 4-Y-O+
£5,207 (£1,549; £774; £400; £400; £400) **Stalls** Centre

Form — RPR

0121 **1** **Rose Hip**[23] 4775 4-8-10 **74**.................... TomMarquand 4 83+
(Tony Carroll) *sltly hmpd s: trckd ldrs: led wl over 1f out: sn rdn: hdd briefly ent fnl f: hld on: all out* **13/8**[1]

1006 **2** *hd* **Miracle Works**[71] 3021 4-8-11 **75**.................... CallumShepherd 6 83
(Robert Cowell) *hld up: hdwy over 2f out: led briefly ent fnl f: ev ch and kpt on wl fnl 120yds: jst hld* **14/1**

015 **3** *1 1/4* **Foxy Forever (IRE)**[37] 4253 9-9-4 **82**....................(bt) HectorCrouch 7 87+
(Michael Wigham) *outpcd in last 3f out: hdwy over 1f out: wnt cl 3rd but nt clr run ins fnl f: swtchd rt fnl 100yds but no ch* **6/1**

3120 **4** *1/2* **A Sure Welcome**[9] 5318 5-9-0 **78**....................(p) RyanTate 5 79
(John Spearing) *stmbld leaving stalls: chsd ldrs: rdn over 1f out: kpt on ins fnl f but nt pce to trble ldrs* **6/1**

0206 **5** *2* **Just Glamorous (IRE)**[18] 4995 6-8-12 **83**....................(p[1]) AngusVilliers(7) 3 77
(Grace Harris) *hmpd s: led after 1f: rdn and hdd wl over 1f out: fdd ins fnl f* **4/1**[3]

0651 **6** *nk* **Harrogate (IRE)**[22] 4835 4-9-1 **79**....................(b) CharlieBennett 2 72
(Jim Boyle) *led for 1f: prom: rdn over 2f out: hld over 1f out: fdd ins fnl f* **3/1**[2]

1m 0.29s (-1.71) **Going Correction** -0.15s/f (Firm) **6 Ran SP% 118.3**
Speed ratings (Par 105): **107,106,104,103,100 100**
CSF £26.76 TOTE £2.70: £1.70, £7.20; EX 19.70 Trifecta £70.40.
Owner Lady Whent **Bred** Lady Whent **Trained** Cropthorne, Worcs

FOCUS
A fair sprint handicap and a thrilling finish. The second has been rated to his AW best.

5607 SKY SPORTS RACING 415 H'CAP — 5f 160y
8:20 (8:21) (Class 5) (0-70,72) 3-Y-O+
£3,428 (£1,020; £509; £400; £400; £400) **Stalls** Centre

Form — RPR

5250 **1** **Red Tycoon (IRE)**[14] 5147 7-9-5 **56**....................(b) HectorCrouch 2 63
(Ken Cunningham-Brown) *trckd ldrs: swtchd rt wl over 1f out: sn rdn: str run ins fnl f: led cl home* **9/2**

4320 **2** *hd* **Jaganory (IRE)**[4] 5498 7-9-3 **54**....................(v) CallumShepherd 8 60
(Christopher Mason) *trckd ldrs: chal over 2f out: rdn over 1f out: narrow advantage ins fnl f: kpt on: hdd cl home* **4/1**[3]

2344 **3** *1/2* **Union Rose**[7] 5375 7-10-2 **72**....................(p) WilliamCarver(5) 7 76
(Ronald Harris) *trckd ldrs: tk narrow advantage over 2f out: sn rdn: edgd lft over 1f out: narrowly hdd ins fnl f: kpt on w ev ch: no ex cl home* **10/3**[2]

0600 **4** *1 1/2* **Knockabout Queen**[27] 4651 3-9-0 **55**.................... CharlieBennett 1 53
(Tony Carroll) *hld up: hdwy 2f out: sltly hmpd whn chalng over 1f out: ev ch ent fnl f: no ex fnl 100yds* **8/1**

0550 **5** *1* **Secret Potion**[10] 5281 5-9-11 **62**.................... DavidProbert 5 58
(Ronald Harris) *led tl rdn over 2f out: sn one pce* **3/1**[1]

0134 **6** *2 1/2* **Maid From The Mist**[15] 5084 3-8-9 **53**.................... JaneElliott(3) 6 40
(John Gallagher) *prom: rdn over 2f out: edgd lft over 1f out: hld whn tight for room sn after (jockey said filly was denied a clear run)* **15/2**

0556 **7** *3* **Silverrica (IRE)**[7] 5375 9-9-9 **60**.................... TomMarquand 3 38
(Malcolm Saunders) *trckd ldrs: mounting chal whn bdly squeezed out jst over 1f out: no ch after (jockey said mare was denied a clear run)* **8/1**

1m 10.49s (-0.61) **Going Correction** -0.15s/f (Firm)
WFA 3 from 4yo+ 4lb **7 Ran SP% 120.2**
Speed ratings (Par 103): **98,97,97,95,93 90,86**
CSF £24.36 CT £69.02 TOTE £5.20: £2.80, £2.10; EX 32.70 Trifecta £140.10.
Owner David Henery **Bred** Redpender Stud Ltd **Trained** Danebury, Hants

FOCUS
A lesser sprint handicap than the previous race, but quite a thriller and a rough race to boot. The winner has been rated to this year's form, and the second close to this year's C&D best.
T/Plt: £13.00 to a £1 stake. Pool: £39,651.27 - 2,224.56 winning units T/Qpdt: £8.30 to a £1 stake. Pool: £4,693.46 - 416.96 winning units **Tim Mitchell**

5583 GOODWOOD (R-H)
Friday, August 2

OFFICIAL GOING: Good (good to firm in places) changing to good to firm (good in places) after race 1 (1.50)
Wind: light, across Weather: sunny and warm

5608 THEO FENNELL OAK TREE STKS (GROUP 3) (F&M) — 7f
1:50 (1:52) (Class 1) 3-Y-O+
£45,368 (£17,200; £8,608; £4,288; £2,152; £1,080) **Stalls** Low

Form — RPR

3012 **1** **Billesdon Brook**[24] 4758 4-9-3 104.................... SeanLevey 10 107
(Richard Hannon) *hld up towards rr: effrt 2f out: hdwy over 1f out: str run u.p ins fnl f to ld last strides* **12/1**

2002 **2** *nk* **Perfection**[19] 4954 4-9-3 101....................(p) SilvestreDeSousa 4 106
(David O'Meara) *rousted along leaving stalls: wl in tch in midfield: effrt 3f out: hdwy u.p and pressing ldrs over 1f out: drvn to ld ins fnl f: edgd lft but kpt on wl: hdd last strides (jockey said filly hung left-handed)* **14/1**

-113 **3** *3/4* **Jubiloso**[42] 4051 3-8-11 110.................... RyanMoore 6 102+
(Sir Michael Stoute) *midfield: pushed lft bnd over 4f out: nt clr run ent fnl 2f: forced to switch lft and in the clr over 1f out: hdwy 1f out: styd on strly u.p ins fnl f: nt rch ldrs* **1/1**[1]

-500 **4** ¾ **Rocques (FR)**[61] 3387 3-8-11 100 JimCrowley 8 100
(F Chappet, France) *in tch in midfield: clsd ent fnl 2f: drvn and chsd ldrs over 1f out: kpt on same pce and much room briefly ins fnl f* **25/1**

4351 **5** *shd* **Royal Intervention (IRE)**[21] 4891 3-9-0 106 FrankieDettori 14 103+
(Ed Walker) *styd wd early: chsd ldrs tl led and crossed to inner 5f out: rdn wl over 1f out: drvn and hdd ins fnl f: no ex towards fin* **10/1**[3]

6400 **6** ½ **Foxtrot Lady**[21] 4891 4-9-3 96 DavidProbert 9 100
(Andrew Balding) *chsd ldrs tl chsd ldr over 4f out: effrt 2f out: lost 2nd and struggling to qckn u.p ent fnl f: jst outpcd fnl 150yds* **33/1**

41-0 **7** ½ **Blizzard**[48] 3863 4-9-3 98 HarryBentley 2 99
(Ralph Beckett) *wl in tch in midfield: effrt 2f out: u.p over 1f out: kpt on ins fnl f: nvr quite enough pce to threaten ldrs* **100/1**

-206 **8** *shd* **Mot Juste (USA)**[21] 4885 3-8-11 103 AndreaAtzeni 17 97+
(Roger Varian) *hld up in rr: swtchd lft 2f out: effrt u.p over 1f out: hdwy and styd on strly ins fnl f: nt rch ldrs* **33/1**

3443 **9** 1 **Angel's Hideaway (IRE)**[41] 4092 3-8-11 108 RobertHavlin 1 94
(John Gosden) *chsd ldrs on inner: effrt and unable qck over 1f out: kpt on same pce and no imp ins fnl f* **7/1**[2]

5-1 **10** *nse* **Lyzbeth (FR)**[28] 4597 3-8-11 0 RobHornby 5 94
(Martyn Meade) *hld up in midfield: short of room and wnt lft bnd over 4f out: effrt over 1f out: rdn and sme hdwy 1f out: kpt on ins fnl f: no threat to ldrs* **25/1**

1-10 **11** *nse* **Pretty Baby (IRE)**[44] 3986 4-9-6 106 JamieSpencer 16 99+
(William Haggas) *midfield tl dropped in and towards rr after 2f: effrt on outer 2f out: hdwy 1f out: styd on wl ins fnl f: nvr trbld ldrs* **12/1**

60-4 **12** *shd* **Beyond Reason (IRE)**[27] 4667 3-8-11 102 JamesDoyle 3 93
(Charlie Appleby) *led for 2f: chsd ldr tl over 4f out: no ex u.p over 1f out: wknd ins fnl f* **28/1**

-232 **13** *nk* **Solar Gold (IRE)**[20] 4921 4-9-3 98 TomMarquand 18 95+
(William Haggas) *hld up in rr: effrt wl over 2f out: hdwy u.p 1f out: kpt on ins fnl f: nvr trbld ldrs* **16/1**

6530 **14** ½ **Island Of Life (USA)**[21] 4891 5-9-3 92 (tp) PatDobbs 11 93
(William Haggas) *hld up towards rr: effrt on inner 2f out: sme hdwy over 1f out: no imp and kpt on same pce ins fnl f* **66/1**

0302 **15** 1 **Gypsy Spirit**[28] 4621 3-8-11 95 BenCurtis 15 89
(Tom Clover) *hld up towards rr: no real imp u.p over 1f out: nvr trbld ldrs* **100/1**

4305 **16** 1 **Devant (FR)**[28] 4621 3-8-11 99 PJMcDonald 13 86
(H-A Pantall, France) *hld up towards rr: effrt over 1f out: no imp and nvr involved* **25/1**

031- **17** 7 **Stage Play (IRE)**[271] 8863 3-8-11 98 DanielTudhope 7 67
(Michael Bell) *chsd ldrs tl lost pl u.p over 1f out: wknd fnl f* **66/1**

1m 23.75s (-2.95) **Going Correction** -0.15s/f (Firm) course record
WFA 3 from 4yo+ 6lb **17** Ran SP% **125.4**
Speed ratings (Par 113): **110,109,108,107,107 107,106,106,105,105 105,105,104,104,103 102,94**
CSF £160.07 TOTE £14.50: £3.00, £3.80, £1.20; EX 179.60 Trifecta £502.20.

Owner Pall Mall Partners & Mrs R J McCreery **Bred** Stowell Hill Partners **Trained** East Everleigh, Wilts

FOCUS
Day four of the Glorious meeting and fresh ground was provided on the top and bottom bends. All distances as advertised. Tom Marquand said: 'It's beautiful ground, a touch quicker than yesterday,' while winning rider Sean Levey added: 'It's good to firm.' It was changed to good to firm, good in places following this race. There was a mixed bag of fillies in this Group 3. Predictably they went hard early on and the course record was lowered. The likes of the second, sixth and seventh help set the level.

5609 BONHAMS THOROUGHBRED STKS (GROUP 3) 1m
2:25 (2:27) (Class 1) 3-Y-O
£56,710 (£21,500; £10,760; £5,360; £2,690; £1,350) **Stalls** Low

Form RPR

5051 **1** **Duke Of Hazzard (FR)**[22] 4850 3-9-1 111 (b) PJMcDonald 6 114+
(Paul Cole) *t.k.h: hld up in tch: clsd and nt clr run 2f out: chsng ldrs: stl nt clr run and swtchd lft ent fnl f: qcknd u.p ins fnl f: r.o to ld towards fin* **3/1**[1]

11-1 **2** ½ **Turjomaan (USA)**[35] 4334 3-9-1 93 (b[1]) JimCrowley 9 112
(Roger Varian) *stdd s: t.k.h: hld up in rr: effrt and clsd jst over 2f out: rdn and ev ch whn leaned on rival 1f out: drvn to ld ins fnl f: hdd and no ex towards fin* **15/2**

2062 **3** 2 **Momkin (IRE)**[22] 4850 3-9-1 108 (b) OisinMurphy 10 107
(Roger Charlton) *hld up in tch: clsd to chse ldrs 2f out: rdn to press ldr and edgd rt over 1f out: led ent fnl f: edgd lft and bumping w rival 1f out: hdd ins fnl f: outpcd fnl 100yds* **6/1**

3-00 **4** 1½ **Old Glory (IRE)**[34] 4410 3-9-1 102 RyanMoore 3 103+
(A P O'Brien, Ire) *trckd ldrs on inner: nt clr run and shuffled bk over 2f out: forced to switch lft over 1f out: rallied and styd on ins fnl f: no threat to ldrs* **8/1**

4135 **5** *nk* **Fifth Position (IRE)**[28] 4612 3-9-1 100 AndreaAtzeni 2 103
(Roger Varian) *chsd ldr tl led 3f out: drvn and hrd pressed whn edgd lft over 1f out: sn hdd: wknd ins fnl f* **10/1**

1-11 **6** 3 **I Could Do Better (IRE)**[32] 4439 3-9-1 95 (t[1]) SilvestreDeSousa 4 96
(Ian Williams) *t.k.h: hld up wl in tch in midfield: effrt ent fnl 2f: drvn and unable qck over 1f out: wknd ins fnl f* **12/1**

2-11 **7** 8 **Art Du Val**[33] 4428 3-9-1 104 JamesDoyle 11 93+
(Charlie Appleby) *restless in stalls: chsd ldrs: effrt to chse ldr 2f out tl lost 2nd: squeezed for room and bdly hmpd over 1f out: no rcvr and wl btn fnl f (vet said colt had sustained a laceration to its gum)* **7/2**[2]

1121 **8** 8 **Biometric**[43] 4016 3-9-1 101 HarryBentley 5 59
(Ralph Beckett) *pushed along leaving stalls: in tch towards rr: u.p over 2f out: sn outpcd: wl btn 1f out* **5/1**[3]

423 **9** 1 **Irish Trilogy (IRE)**[19] 3-9-1 96 DanielTudhope 1 57
(Nina Lensvik, Sweden) *led tl 3f out: outpcd 2f out: sn lost pl and bhd ins fnl f* **66/1**

1m 35.7s (-3.50) **Going Correction** -0.15s/f (Firm) **9** Ran SP% **119.3**
Speed ratings (Par 110): **111,110,108,107,106 103,95,87,86**
CSF £27.17 CT £130.11 TOTE £3.60: £1.40, £2.70, £2.00; EX 28.90 Trifecta £124.70.

Owner Mrs Fitri Hay **Bred** Runnymede Farm Inc & Catesby W Clay **Trained** Whatcombe, Oxon

FOCUS
This looked an ordinary Group 3; nothing amazing but competitive. The winner and third have been rated similar to their Newmarket latest.

5610 UNIBET GOLDEN MILE H'CAP 1m
3:00 (3:03) (Class 2) 3-Y-O+
£93,375 (£27,960; £13,980; £6,990; £3,495; £1,755) **Stalls** Low

Form RPR

0411 **1** **Beat Le Bon (FR)**[27] 4650 3-8-13 **104** 3ex PatDobbs 3 113+
(Richard Hannon) *mid-div: qcknd up wl whn gap appeared against far rail over 1f out: led fnl 120yds: drifted lft: readily* **17/2**

0010 **2** 1 **Vale Of Kent (IRE)**[6] 5413 4-9-3 **101** 3ex FrannyNorton 17 109
(Mark Johnston) *a.p: led jst over 2f out: sn rdn: hdd fnl 120yds: kpt on but nt pce of wnr* **25/1**

021 **3** 1 **Escobar (IRE)**[20] 4934 5-9-3 **101** 3ex (t) JamieSpencer 12 107
(David O'Meara) *towards rr of mid-div: hdwy over 1f out but nt clrest of runs wout getting stopped: rdn whn clr ent fnl f: edgd rt: r.o wl (starter reported that the gelding was the subject of a third criteria failure; trainer was informed that the gelding could not run until the day after passing a stalls test)* **10/1**

4024 **4** ½ **Seniority**[36] 4292 5-9-3 **101** RyanMoore 11 107+
(William Haggas) *towards rr of mid-div: hdwy 2f out: running on whn bdly hmpd over 1f out: kpt on ins fnl f but no ch after* **10/1**

2202 **5** ¾ **Baltic Baron (IRE)**[7] 5398 4-8-13 **97** (v[1]) DanielTudhope 6 100+
(David O'Meara) *towards rr of midfield: hdwy whn nt clr run over 1f out: kpt on ins fnl f but no ch* **16/1**

10/1 **6** *hd* **Mojito (IRE)**[27] 4666 5-9-6 **104** 3ex FrankieDettori 9 106
(William Haggas) *trckd ldrs: disputing 2nd whn rdn over 1f out: no ex fnl 120yds* **10/3**[1]

0111 **7** ½ **Gossiping**[63] 3313 7-8-13 **97** ShaneKelly 21 98
(Gary Moore) *in tch: effrt 2f out: kpt on ins fnl f but nt pce to threaten* **25/1**

0560 **8** *shd* **Original Choice (IRE)**[20] 4935 5-9-1 **99** SilvestreDeSousa 8 100
(Nick Littmoden) *in tch: tk clsr order 3f out: sn rdn: chsd ldr over 1f out tl jst ins fnl f: hld whn leaned on by 3rd fnl 75yds* **40/1**

4123 **9** 1¾ **Game Player (IRE)**[41] 4097 4-8-11 **95** AndreaAtzeni 1 98+
(Roger Varian) *in tch: effrt over 2f out: keeping on at same pce and hld whn bdly hmpd over 1f out* **15/2**[3]

1056 **10** ¾ **War Glory (IRE)**[13] 5188 6-9-0 **98** SeanLevey 4 93
(Richard Hannon) *mid-div: hdwy over 2f out: nt clr run over 1f out: sn swtchd rt: nt pce to get on terms: fdd fnl 120yds* **66/1**

3103 **11** ½ **What's The Story**[20] 4935 5-9-2 **100** (p) TomMarquand 2 94
(Keith Dalgleish) *mid-div: rdn over 2f out: little imp whn hmpd sn after: nvr threatened (jockey said gelding was denied a clear run)* **12/1**

0-15 **12** ¾ **Afaak**[20] 4935 5-9-10 **108** JimCrowley 14 100
(Charles Hills) *mid-div: rdn over 2f out: no imp whn jinked lft ins fnl f* **16/1**

0004 **13** *shd* **Key Victory (IRE)**[27] 4666 4-9-5 **103** (p) JamesDoyle 20 95
(Charlie Appleby) *s.i.s: in last pair: pushed along 2f out: keeping on but no ch whn carried lft ins fnl f* **33/1**

3010 **14** *nk* **History Writer (IRE)**[27] 4666 4-8-13 **97** (t) PJMcDonald 13 88
(David Menuisier) *hld up towards rr: nt clr run fr over 1f out: nvr able to land a blow (jockey said gelding was denied a clear run)* **33/1**

0404 **15** 1¼ **Dark Vision (IRE)**[21] 4882 3-8-12 **103** (b[1]) OisinMurphy 19 91
(Mark Johnston) *mid-div on outer: effrt over 2f out: nt pce to get involved: carried lft ins fnl f* **8/1**

4200 **16** *shd* **So Beloved**[20] 4921 9-9-6 **104** (h) GeraldMosse 10 92
(David O'Meara) *dwlt bdly: bhd: nvr any threat but making sme prog whn nt clr run jst over 1f out (jockey said gelding was slowly away and denied a clear run)* **33/1**

3050 **17** 2¼ **Zhui Feng (IRE)**[27] 4666 6-9-3 **101** (p) MartinDwyer 7 84
(Amanda Perrett) *led tl jst over 2f out: sn rdn and hung lft: corrected rt over 1f out and bmpd: sn wknd* **33/1**

1025 **18** 1 **Clon Coulis (IRE)**[24] 4758 5-9-5 **103** (h) BenCurtis 18 84
(David Barron) *a towards rr on outer (vet said mare lost both front shoes)* **33/1**

211 **19** *nse* **Indeed**[13] 5192 4-9-5 **103** 3ex LiamKeniry 16 84
(Dominic Ffrench Davis) *sn trcking ldrs: rdn over 2f out: sltly hmpd sn after: wknd over 1f out (b.b.v) (vet said gelding had bled from the nose)* **7/1**[2]

60 **20** 2½ **Lush Life (IRE)**[27] 4666 4-8-10 **94** (b[1]) HarryBentley 15 69
(Jamie Osborne) *nt best of runs over 1f out: a towards rr* **50/1**

1m 35.28s (-3.92) **Going Correction** -0.15s/f (Firm) course record
WFA 3 from 4yo+ 7lb **20** Ran SP% **134.9**
Speed ratings (Par 109): **113,112,111,110,109 109,109,108,107,106 105,105,105,104,103 103,101,100,100,97**
CSF £222.78 CT £2252.41 TOTE £11.50: £2.90, £5.40, £2.00, £3.00; EX 282.60 Trifecta £5280.20.

Owner Sullivan B'Stock/ Merriebelle Irish Farm **Bred** Gestut Zur Kuste Ag **Trained** East Everleigh, Wilts

■ Stewards' Enquiry : Pat Dobbs two-day ban: used whip in an incorrect place on the run to the line (tba)

FOCUS
Another quality edition of this highly valuable handicap. As ever a double-figure stall was a huge disadvantage and the winner came up the far rail. It was another course record broken. The third has been rated close to form, with the fourth and fifth helping to set the level.

5611 KING GEORGE QATAR STKS (GROUP 2) 5f
3:35 (3:35) (Class 1) 3-Y-O+
£176,935 (£67,080; £33,571; £16,723; £8,392; £4,212) **Stalls** High

Form RPR

4-12 **1** **Battaash (IRE)**[45] 3950 5-9-5 123 JimCrowley 5 122
(Charles Hills) *mounted in chute: travelled strly: chsd ldr tl led ent fnl 2f: rdn over 1f out: kpt up to work and a in command ins fnl f* **1/4**[1]

6-0 **2** ¾ **Houtzen (AUS)**[45] 3950 5-8-13 108 (b) RyanMoore 4 113
(Martyn Meade) *taken down early: hld up in tch: clsd and nt clr run over 1f out: hdwy u.p to chse wnr 150yds out: r.o wl but nvr seriously threatening wnr* **16/1**

0116 **3** 2½ **Ornate**[7] 5371 6-9-2 103 PhilDennis 8 107
(David C Griffiths) *led tl hdd and rdn ent fnl 2f: unable to match pce of wnr over 1f out: 3rd and kpt on same pce fnl 150yds* **33/1**

3-00 **4** 1 **Rumble Inthejungle (IRE)**[27] 4665 3-8-13 105 FrankieDettori 6 102
(Richard Spencer) *stdd after s: hld up in rr: clsd and effrt over 1f out: no imp and kpt on same pce ins fnl f* **10/1**[3]

0112 **5** 1 **El Astronaute (IRE)**[12] 5222 6-9-2 111 JasonHart 3 100
(John Quinn) *chsd ldrs: rdn ent fnl 2f: unable to match pce of wnr and btn over 1f out: wknd ins fnl f* **7/1**[2]

-001 **6** 1 1/4 **Judicial (IRE)**[14] 5142 7-9-2 104......................(h) PJMcDonald 7 95
(Julie Camacho) *taken down early and led to post: in tch in midfield: rdn and unable to match pce of wnr over 1f out: wknd ins fnl f* **28/1**

3021 **7** nk **Copper Knight (IRE)**[20] 4932 5-9-2 106......................(t) DavidAllan 10 94
(Tim Easterby) *chsd ldrs: rdn ent fnl 2f: sn struggling and outpcd over 1f out: wknd ins fnl f* **14/1**

01 **8** 1 **Big Brothers Pride (FR)**[111] 1780 3-8-10 110.................. OisinMurphy 9 87
(F Rohaut, France) *hld up in tch: effrt over 1f out: unable qck and sn btn: wknd ins fnl f* **7/1**[2]

16-1 **9** 4 **Rebecca Rocks**[41] 4101 5-8-13 96.................................. HarryBentley 11 73
(Henry Candy) *taken down early and led to post: racd alone nr stands' rail and hung rt: chsd ldrs tl 1/2-way: bhd ins fnl f* **25/1**

56.2s (-1.90) **Going Correction** -0.15s/f (Firm) course record
WFA 3 from 5yo+ 3lb **9** Ran SP% **136.9**
Speed ratings (Par 115): **109,107,103,102,100 98,98,96,90**
CSF £10.28 CT £112.38 TOTE £1.20: £1.10, £4.00, £7.20; EX 9.80 Trifecta £132.60.
Owner Hamdan Al Maktoum **Bred** Ballyphilip Stud **Trained** Lambourn, Berks

FOCUS
They all raced a bit off the near rail, except last-placed Rebecca Rocks who hugged the fence but was hanging. The third helps set the level.

5612 UNIBET NURSERY H'CAP — 6f
4:10 (4:11) (Class 2) 2-Y-O £15,752 (£4,715; £2,357; £1,180; £587) **Stalls** High

Form RPR

421 **1** **Homespin (USA)**[34] 4394 2-9-3 83.................................. JamesDoyle 9 91
(Mark Johnston) *sn led: hdd over 3f out: styd prom: ev ch u.p over 1f out: led 1f out: styd on wl and asserted ins fnl f* **7/1**[2]

2102 **2** 1 1/4 **Dylan De Vega**[21] 4893 2-9-6 86.................................. TonyHamilton 15 90
(Richard Fahey) *restless in stalls: hld up wl in tch in rr: clsd over 2f out: rdn and ev ch over 1f out: no ex and nt match pce of wnr ins fnl f* **14/1**

432 **3** 1 1/2 **Born To Destroy**[35] 4344 2-8-11 77.................................. HarryBentley 2 77
(Richard Spencer) *chsd ldrs: drvn and pressing ldrs over 1f out: no ex and wknd ins fnl f* **16/1**

2311 **4** nk **Praxeology (IRE)**[47] 3890 2-9-7 87.................................. RyanMoore 7 86
(Mark Johnston) *t.k.h: sn prom: led over 3f out: rdn over 1f out: hdd 1f out: no ex and wknd ins fnl f* **3/1**[1]

511 **5** 3/4 **Hard Nut (IRE)**[22] 4839 2-9-6 86.................................. OisinMurphy 11 83+
(Richard Hannon) *stdd s: t.k.h: hld up wl in tch in rr: swtchd lft 2f out: kpt on u.p but edging rt ins fnl f: nvr trbld ldrs* **10/1**

034 **6** 1/2 **Dark Silver (IRE)**[14] 5145 2-8-9 75.................................. SilvestreDeSousa 3 70
(Ed Walker) *in tch in midfield: effrt and hdwy u.p over 1f out: no imp 1f out and kpt on same pce ins fnl f* **8/1**[3]

222 **7** 3/4 **Asmund (IRE)**[20] 4910 2-8-13 79..................................(v[1]) BenCurtis 1 72
(K R Burke) *in tch in midfield: effrt u.p and edgd lft over 1f out: no imp 1f out and wknd ins fnl f* **25/1**

1026 **8** 1 3/4 **Separate**[13] 5185 2-9-3 83.................................. SeanLevey 8 71
(Richard Hannon) *s.i.s: hld up in tch in rr: effrt over 1f out: kpt on ins fnl f: nvr trbld ldrs* **10/1**

1233 **9** 1/2 **Coastal Mist (IRE)**[7] 5390 2-8-9 75.................................. JasonHart 16 61
(John Quinn) *broke wl and led: sn hdd: chsd ldrs tl lost pl u.p over 1f out: wknd ins fnl f* **16/1**

0232 **10** 1/2 **Teenar**[20] 4938 2-8-8 74.................................. PaddyMathers 10 59
(Richard Fahey) *hld up in tch in midfield: no hdwy u.p over 1f out: wknd ins fnl f* **14/1**

431 **11** 1/2 **Owney Madden**[13] 5186 2-9-1 81.................................. RobHornby 5 64
(Martyn Meade) *hld up wl in tch towards rr: effrt 2f out: no imp u.p and btn over 1f out: nvr involved* **9/1**

510 **12** 3/4 **Wentworth Amigo (IRE)**[28] 4610 2-8-13 79.................................. PatDobbs 6 60
(Jamie Osborne) *in tch in midfield: effrt 2f out: sn u.p and no imp: wknd ins fnl f* **33/1**

2040 **13** 1/2 **Red Sun (IRE)**[8] 5340 2-8-6 72.................................. MartinDwyer 13 51
(Charles Hills) *in tch in midfield: effrt over 2f out: lost pl u.p and bhd over 1f out* **66/1**

0311 **14** 13 **Eton College (IRE)**[21] 4861 2-9-7 87.................................. PJMcDonald 4 27
(Mark Johnston) *awkward leaving stalls and dwlt: hdwy to chse ldrs over 3f out: rdn ent fnl 2f: lost pl qckly over 1f out: wl bhd ins fnl f (jockey said colt got upset in the preliminaries)* **7/1**[2]

1m 11.17s (-0.93) **Going Correction** -0.15s/f (Firm) **14** Ran SP% **122.7**
Speed ratings (Par 100): **100,98,96,95,94 94,93,90,90,89 88,87,87,69**
CSF £101.89 CT £1577.64 TOTE £7.40: £2.60, £4.30, £5.90; EX 121.20 Trifecta £2163.10.
Owner Sheikh Hamdan bin Mohammed Al Maktoum **Bred** Godolphin **Trained** Middleham Moor, N Yorks

FOCUS
This fair nursery was run at a sound pace and the main action developed nearer the stands' side, although they didn't want to know about the rail. The second has been rated as taking a small step forward.

5613 L'ORMARINS QUEEN'S PLATE GLORIOUS STKS (GROUP 3) — 1m 3f 218y
4:40 (4:40) (Class 1) 4-Y-O+ £56,710 (£21,500; £10,760; £5,360; £2,690) **Stalls** High

Form RPR

3003 **1** **Desert Encounter (IRE)**[22] 4848 7-9-1 114..................(h) JamieSpencer 3 116
(David Simcock) *stdd s: hld up in tch: clsd and trcking rivals 3f out: swtchd lft and effrt 1f out: qcknd and pounced to ld ins fnl f: sn in command* **15/2**[3]

-132 **2** 2 1/4 **Mirage Dancer**[22] 4848 5-9-1 116.................................. RyanMoore 4 112
(Sir Michael Stoute) *trckd ldrs: effrt over 2f out: clsd and drvn to ld ent fnl f: hdd and nt match pce of wnr ins fnl f* **4/6**[1]

3115 **3** 1 1/2 **Baghdad (FR)**[22] 4848 4-9-1 109.................................. FrankieDettori 1 110
(Mark Johnston) *mounted in chute: led: rdn wl over 2f out: hdd ent fnl f: no ex and outpcd ins fnl f* **5/2**[2]

0000 **4** 1/2 **Aquarium**[3] 5519 4-9-1 101.................................. FrannyNorton 2 109
(Mark Johnston) *s.i.s: in tch: clsd to trck ldrs 1/2-way: effrt over 2f out: jst getting outpcd whn n.m.r ent fnl f: swtchd lft and kpt on same pce ins fnl f* **20/1**

0-40 **5** 10 **Prince Of Arran**[125] 1441 6-9-1 110.................................. JamesDoyle 5 93
(Charlie Fellowes) *chsd ldr: rdn and ev ch over 2f out tl no ex and lost pl over 1f out: wknd ins fnl f* **16/1**

2m 34.75s (-4.85) **Going Correction** -0.15s/f (Firm) **5** Ran SP% **111.0**
Speed ratings (Par 113): **110,108,107,107,100**
CSF £13.40 TOTE £7.90: £2.30, £1.10; EX 13.70 Trifecta £23.90.
Owner Abdulla Al Mansoori **Bred** Tally-Ho Stud **Trained** Newmarket, Suffolk

FOCUS
Just exposed types for this 4yo+ contest but another smart performance from the likeable winner. The fourth, rated to his best, limits the level.

5614 TDN AUSTRALIA H'CAP — 1m 3f 44y
5:15 (5:15) (Class 3) (0-90,89) 3-Y-£15,752 (£4,715; £2,357; £1,180; £587) **Stalls** High

Form RPR

342 **1** **Aktau**[64] 3263 3-9-2 84.................................. AndreaAtzeni 11 97+
(Roger Varian) *hld up in last quintet: hdwy and sltly impeded jst over 2f out: rdn and clsd to ld and wnt rt ent fnl f: r.o wl* **5/2**[1]

2213 **2** 1 3/4 **Sapa Inca (IRE)**[42] 4064 3-9-1 83.................................. FrannyNorton 7 92
(Mark Johnston) *chsd ldrs: nt clr run over 2f out: effrt and hdwy between horses to press ldrs over 1f out: kpt on same pce ins fnl f: wnt 2nd towards fin* **14/1**

221 **3** 1/2 **Harrovian**[24] 4760 3-9-7 89..................................(p[1]) FrankieDettori 3 97+
(John Gosden) *wl in tch in midfield: nt clr run over 2f out: edgd out lft and effrt 2f out: rdn and hdwy to ld over 1f out: sn hdd and pushed rt: kpt on same pce ins fnl f: lost 2nd towards fin* **4/1**[3]

5006 **4** 1 3/4 **Mordred (IRE)**[22] 4851 3-9-4 86.................................. SeanLevey 8 91
(Richard Hannon) *stdd s: hld up in last pair: clsd and nt clrest of runs over 2f out: chsd ldrs and effrt over 1f out: drvn and kpt on same pce fnl f* **33/1**

-253 **5** 1 **High Commissioner (IRE)**[22] 4842 3-9-3 85.................................. PJMcDonald 9 88
(Paul Cole) *chsd ldrs: rdn to ld 2f out: hdd over 1f out: stl pressing ldrs but struggling to qckn whn squeezed for room and hmpd jst ins fnl f: one pce after* **10/1**

0-31 **6** 1/2 **Fox Vardy (USA)**[39] 4187 3-9-1 83.................................. SilvestreDeSousa 5 85+
(Martyn Meade) *bustled along early: in tch in midfield: edgd out lft and effrt over 2f out: keeping on same pce whn impeded ent fnl f: no imp and one pce fnl f (trainer's rep said colt was unsuited by the ground and would appreciate an easier surface)* **7/2**[2]

2-22 **7** 1/2 **Deal A Dollar**[91] 2375 3-9-3 85..................................(t[1]) RyanMoore 6 87
(Sir Michael Stoute) *hld up in last quintet: effrt 3f out: no imp tl kpt on ins fnl f: nvr trbld ldrs* **8/1**

8 hd **Grey D'Ars (FR)**[64] 3-8-11 79.................................. BenCurtis 2 80
(Nick Littmoden) *t.k.h: hld up in midfield: swtchd rt clsd and nt clr run on inner 2f out: swtchd lft over 1f out: kpt on but no ch w ldrs (jockey said colt ran too free in the early stages and was denied a clear run)* **50/1**

1 **9** nk **Yellow Tiger (FR)**[27] 4636 3-9-1 83..................................(p[1]) JamieSpencer 14 84
(Ian Williams) *stdd s: hld up in last pair: effrt on outer ent fnl 2f: no imp over 1f out: nvr trbld ldrs* **25/1**

1342 **10** 1 1/2 **Asian Angel (IRE)**[11] 5240 3-8-12 85.................................. AndrewBreslin(5) 1 83
(Mark Johnston) *s.i.s: a towards rr: rdn over 2f out: nvr getting on terms: hung rt over 1f out* **12/1**

-331 **11** 7 **Quintada**[16] 5039 3-8-12 80.................................. JasonHart 4 66
(Mark Johnston) *led tl rdn and hdd 2f out: lost pl over 1f out: wknd fnl f* **16/1**

5-24 **12** 7 **Top Power (FR)**[161] 858 3-9-0 82.................................. RobHornby 10 56
(Andrew Balding) *chsd ldr: ev ch and rdn ent fnl 2f: outpcd and btn over 1f out: wknd ins fnl f* **50/1**

-401 **13** dist **Jersey Wonder (IRE)**[25] 4739 3-9-6 88.................................. PatDobbs 12
(Jamie Osborne) *midfield: pushed along over 3f out: lost pl: bhd and eased over 2f out: t.o (jockey said gelding stopped quickly; vet said a post-race examination of the gelding found him to be suffering from an irregular heartbeat)* **33/1**

2m 23.4s (-4.90) **Going Correction** -0.15s/f (Firm) **13** Ran SP% **124.9**
Speed ratings (Par 104): **111,109,109,108,107 107,106,106,106,105 100,95,**
CSF £41.01 CT £143.66 TOTE £3.60: £1.70, £3.80, £1.70; EX 43.80 Trifecta £303.60.
Owner Nurlan Bizakov, Keith Allen, Gerald Moss **Bred** Hesmonds Stud Ltd **Trained** Newmarket, Suffolk

FOCUS
Subsequent dual Group 1 winner Poet's Word won this off 88 in 2016. This looks good form.
T/Jkpt: Not Won T/Plt: £58.50 to a £1 stake. Pool: £296,568.68 - 3,695.92 winning units T/Qpdt: £25.40 to a £1 stake. Pool: £19,662.56 - 571.88 winning units **Steve Payne & Tim Mitchell**

5272 MUSSELBURGH (R-H)
Friday, August 2

OFFICIAL GOING: Good (7.0)
Wind: Light, across Weather: Overcast

5615 IRISH STALLIONS FARMS EBF NOVICE MEDIAN AUCTION STKS — 7f 33y
5:30 (5:31) (Class 5) 2-Y-O £3,881 (£1,155; £577; £288) **Stalls** Low

Form RPR

12 **1** **Above (FR)**[15] 5082 2-9-6 0.................................. AdamMcNamara 5 82+
(Archie Watson) *trckd ldrs: stdy hdwy over 2f out: led wl over 1f out: edgd rt ins fnl f: kpt on wl cl home* **11/8**[1]

322 **2** 1/2 **Saint Of Katowice (IRE)**[12] 5212 2-8-13 0.................................. SeanDavis(3) 2 77
(Richard Fahey) *trckd ldr: chal wl over 1f out: carried rt ins fnl f: kpt on: hld nr fin* **9/4**[2]

3 **3** 4 **Magic Timing**[14] 5118 2-9-2 0.................................. ShaneGray 1 66
(Keith Dalgleish) *led at modest gallop: rdn over 2f out: hdd wl over 1f out: sn outpcd* **10/1**

03 **4** hd **Harswell Approach (IRE)**[10] 5273 2-9-2 0.................................. PaulMulrennan 4 66
(Liam Bailey) *trckd ldrs: outpcd and edgd lft 2f out: no imp fnl f* **33/1**

5 3/4 **Um Elnadim (FR)** 2-8-11 0.................................. CYHo 3 59+
(Mark Johnston) *slowly away: hld up in tch: effrt over 2f out: rn green and outpcd fr over 1f out* **3/1**[3]

1m 31.6s (2.60) **Going Correction** +0.075s/f (Good) **5** Ran SP% **109.9**
Speed ratings (Par 94): **88,87,82,82,81**
CSF £4.73 TOTE £2.40: £1.10, £1.60; EX 4.90 Trifecta £11.90.
Owner Qatar Racing Limited **Bred** J Kilpatrick & Mme D Ades Hazan **Trained** Upper Lambourn, W Berks

The Form Book Flat 2019, Raceform Ltd, Newbury, RG14 5SJ

FOCUS
Add 7yds. A juvenile novice run at a modest gallop, though the pace increased appreciably when the leaders straightened for home. The first two, who were the first two in the market, were clear of the other three. Straightforward form, with the second and third rated roughly to their pre-race marks.

5616 BERNARD HUNTER MOBILE CRANES H'CAP 7f 33y
6:00 (6:02) (Class 5) (0-75,75) 4-Y-0+

£3,752 (£1,116; £557; £400; £400; £400) **Stalls** Low

Form RPR
3313 **1** **Donnelly's Rainbow (IRE)**[10] 5274 6-8-5 **59**............... NathanEvans 11 68
(Rebecca Bastiman) *stdd fr wd draw: hld up: hdwy and pushed along whn nt clr run briefly over 1f out: sn swtchd rt: edgd lft and effrt ins fnl f: kpt on wl to ld cl home* **7/1**

0100 **2** *nk* **Smugglers Creek (IRE)**[26] 4693 5-8-12 **66**............(p) PaulMulrennan 12 74
(Iain Jardine) *led: rdn over 2f out: kpt on fnl f: hdd and no ex cl home* **50/1**

42-0 **3** *2 ¼* **Black Friday**[18] 5000 4-9-0 **71**...............................(p) SeanDavis(3) 4 73
(Karen McLintock) *hld up: effrt over 2f out: hdwy whn nt clr run briefly over 1f out: kpt on fnl f: nt rch first two* **20/1**

1542 **4** *1 ¼* **Tukhoom (IRE)**[9] 5303 6-9-4 **75**........................(b) ConorMcGovern(3) 8 74
(David O'Meara) *t.k.h: cl up: effrt and ev ch over 2f out to over 1f out: one pce whn blkd ins fnl f* **10/3**[1]

0454 **5** *½* **Colour Contrast (IRE)**[18] 4978 6-8-6 **60**..................(b) JamieGormley 3 57
(Iain Jardine) *hld up: effrt over 2f out: hdwy and prom over 1f out: one pce fnl f* **11/1**

5-13 **6** *1 ½* **Aliento**[23] 4785 4-8-10 **64**.. GrahamLee 1 57
(Michael Dods) *in tch: rdn over 2f out: nt clr run and outpcd over 1f out: n.d after* **5/1**[2]

5505 **7** *¾* **Explain**[17] 5021 7-8-9 **63**.......................................(b) JamesSullivan 2 54
(Ruth Carr) *t.k.h: trckd ldrs: rdn and edgd lft wl over 1f out: outpcd fnl f* **20/1**

455 **8** *2* **Lucky Violet (IRE)**[10] 5274 7-8-9 **63**...............................(h) KevinStott 7 49
(Linda Perratt) *hld up: rdn over 2f out: no imp whn hmpd over 1f out: nvr able to chal* **8/1**

0004 **9** *½* **Theodorico (IRE)**[4] 5490 6-9-0 **75**................................ VictorSantos(7) 6 59
(Lucinda Egerton) *cl up: drvn along over 2f out: wknd over 1f out* **14/1**

3500 **10** *2 ¼* **Make Me**[41] 4108 4-9-0 **68**..................................... RachelRichardson 5 46
(Tim Easterby) *midfield: rdn along and outpcd over 2f out: btn over 1f out* **11/1**

6300 **11** *1 ¼* **Jacob Black**[18] 4982 8-9-4 **72**.. ShaneGray 9 47
(Keith Dalgleish) *in tch: rdn over 2f out: edgd rt and wknd over 1f out* **20/1**

0021 **12** *4 ½* **Etikaal**[3] 5526 5-8-6 **60** 5ex.. DuranFentiman 10 23
(Grant Tuer) *s.i.s: hld up: rdn and struggling over 2f out: sn btn (jockey said gelding became upset in the stalls and missed the break)* **13/2**[3]

1m 28.17s (-0.83) **Going Correction** +0.075s/f (Good) **12** Ran SP% **116.3**
Speed ratings (Par 103): **107,106,104,102,102 100,99,97,96,94 92,87**
CSF £325.10 CT £6586.23 TOTE £7.10: £2.00, £14.10, £5.30; EX 254.60 Trifecta £2189.40.
Owner Rebecca Bastiman Racing 1 **Bred** Airlie Stud **Trained** Cowthorpe, N Yorks

FOCUS
Add 7yds. Mainly exposed sorts here but quite a few have been running well so the form should be fair. The pace was decent, with the winner coming from last to first but the second only just failing to make all. The second has been rated pretty much to his best.

5617 GEOGHEGANS CENTENARY H'CAP 5f 1y
6:35 (6:38) (Class 3) (0-90,90) 3-Y-0+

£8,092 (£2,423; £1,211; £605; £302; £152) **Stalls** High

Form RPR
3122 **1** **Jabbarockie**[21] 4894 6-9-2 **87**.................................... HarrisonShaw(5) 9 101
(Eric Alston) *mde all: shkn up and edgd rt over 1f out: drew clr fnl f: readily* **10/11**[1]

662 **2** *4 ½* **War Whisper (IRE)**[27] 4625 6-9-2 **82**............................ PaulMulrennan 5 80
(Paul Midgley) *prom: effrt and rdn 2f out: chsd (clr) wnr ins fnl f: no imp* **9/2**[2]

-023 **3** *nk* **Diamonique**[18] 4986 3-8-6 **75**... ShaneGray 7 71
(Keith Dalgleish) *in tch: rdn over 2f out: kpt on fnl f: nvr able to chal* **14/1**

4000 **4** *nk* **Royal Brave (IRE)**[58] 3480 8-9-2 **85**.............................. RowanScott(3) 6 81
(Rebecca Bastiman) *dwlt: bhd and sn pushed along: kpt on fnl f: nrst fin* **8/1**

-010 **5** *nk* **Machree (IRE)**[20] 4896 4-8-13 **86**................................... ZakWheatley(7) 8 81
(Declan Carroll) *w wnr to over 1f out: no ex ins fnl f (vet said filly bled from the nose)* **10/1**

203 **6** *2 ¼* **Excessable**[14] 5154 6-8-12 **78**...............................(t) RachelRichardson 2 64
(Tim Easterby) *chsd ldrs on outside: rdn over 2f out: wknd fnl f* **13/2**[3]

0040 **7** *2 ½* **Shining Armor**[105] 1920 3-8-9 **83**................................ DarraghKeenan(5) 10 59
(John Ryan) *bhd and sn rdn along: struggling 1/2-way: nvr on terms* **20/1**

58.86s (-0.84) **Going Correction** +0.075s/f (Good)
WFA 3 from 4yo+ 3lb **7** Ran SP% **115.5**
Speed ratings (Par 107): **109,101,101,100,100 96,92**
CSF £5.44 CT £33.50 TOTE £1.60: £1.40, £1.70; EX 6.10 Trifecta £37.50.
Owner M Balmer, K Sheedy, P Copple, C Dingwall **Bred** Paul Green **Trained** Longton, Lancs

FOCUS
This wasn't the strongest of 5f handicaps and it was won in fine style by the well-backed favourite. The winner has been rated to form.

5618 LIKE RACING TV ON FACEBOOK NURSERY H'CAP 5f 1y
7:10 (7:11) (Class 6) (0-65,65) 2-Y-0

£3,105 (£924; £461; £400; £400; £400) **Stalls** High

Form RPR
4463 **1** **Too Hard To Hold (IRE)**[9] 5288 2-9-4 **62**................................. CYHo 4 73+
(Mark Johnston) *chsd ldrs: rdn 1/2-way: led over 1f out: kpt on wl fnl f* **4/1**[2]

0633 **2** *1 ½* **Two Hearts**[10] 5279 2-8-4 **48** ow3....................................... NathanEvans 7 54
(Grant Tuer) *in tch: nt clr run and angled rt over 1f out: chsd wnr ins fnl f: kpt on: hld nr fin* **7/1**

0002 **3** *3* **Flight Of Thunder (IRE)**[23] 4778 2-8-13 **57**......................... KevinStott 9 52
(Kevin Ryan) *w ldrs: rdn over 2f out: outpcd by first two ins fnl f* **7/2**[1]

536 **4** *hd* **Lara Silvia**[76] 2840 2-9-7 **65**.. JamieGormley 5 59
(Iain Jardine) *w ldrs to over 1f out: kpt on same pce ins fnl f* **11/2**[3]

006 **5** *hd* **Invincible Bertie (IRE)**[18] 4984 2-8-9 **56**...................... RowanScott(3) 6 51
(Nigel Tinkler) *dwlt: hld up in tch: nt clr run over 2f out to ins fnl f: kpt on: nt pce to chal (jockey said gelding was denied a clear run 1½f out)* **8/1**

6040 **6** *1* **Comeatchoo (IRE)**[13] 5196 2-8-12 **56**............................ DuranFentiman 2 46
(Tim Easterby) *hld up: rdn and effrt 2f out: no imp fnl f* **33/1**

5056 **7** *3* **Queens Blade**[10] 5279 2-8-13 **57**..............................(p[1]) JamesSullivan 3 36
(Tim Easterby) *hld up: hdwy on outside over 2f out: rdn and wknd fnl f* **16/1**

002 **8** *½* **Chocoholic**[17] 5017 2-8-12 **56**.. GrahamLee 1 33
(Bryan Smart) *wnt rt s: bhd and detached: nvr on terms (jockey said gelding was slowly away and hung badly right throughout)* **14/1**

0525 **9** *1 ¼* **Navajo Dawn (IRE)**[14] 5146 2-9-5 **63**.............................. AndrewMullen 8 36
(Robyn Brisland) *mde most to over 1f out: sn wknd* **4/1**[2]

1m 0.91s (1.21) **Going Correction** +0.075s/f (Good) **9** Ran SP% **116.7**
Speed ratings (Par 92): **93,90,85,85,85 83,78,77,75**
CSF £32.50 CT £108.31 TOTE £5.30: £1.80, £2.30, £1.90; EX 34.50 Trifecta £176.10.
Owner Garrett J Freyne **Bred** A M F Persse & F Persse **Trained** Middleham Moor, N Yorks

FOCUS
Probably an ordinary nursery. It's been rated a shade negatively.

5619 ATHOLL DUNCAN AND FRIENDS H'CAP 7f 33y
7:40 (7:41) (Class 5) (0-75,80) 3-Y-0

£3,752 (£1,116; £557; £400; £400; £400) **Stalls** Low

Form RPR
-154 **1** **Gometra Ginty (IRE)**[10] 5274 3-9-1 **69**.............................. ShaneGray 2 76
(Keith Dalgleish) *pressed ldr: led over 2f out: rdn fnl f: hld on wl cl home* **5/2**[1]

0051 **2** *1 ¼* **Battle Of Waterloo (IRE)**[10] 5270 3-9-7 **80** 6ex...... DarraghKeenan(5) 3 84
(John Ryan) *t.k.h: hld up on ins: stdy hdwy over 2f out: effrt and pressed wnr over 1f out: ch ins fnl f: kpt on: hld nr fin* **7/2**[2]

0062 **3** *8* **Woodside Wonder**[23] 4781 3-9-4 **75**...........................(p) SeanDavis(3) 1 57
(Keith Dalgleish) *trckd ldrs tl rdn: edgd lft and outpcd fr over 1f out* **4/1**[3]

0013 **4** *2 ½* **Bumbledom**[23] 4781 3-8-13 **67**..................................(p) AndrewMullen 6 43
(Michael Dods) *led to over 2f out: wknd over 1f out (jockey said gelding stumbled leaving the stalls)* **7/1**

0440 **5** *nk* **Autumn Flight (IRE)**[20] 4912 3-8-9 **63**.........................(p) GrahamLee 4 38
(Tim Easterby) *t.k.h: hld up in tch: drvn and struggling over 2f out: sn btn* **14/1**

3520 **6** *15* **Diviner (IRE)**[2] 5561 3-8-11 **65**.. CYHo 5 22
(Mark Johnston) *in tch on outside: drvn and outpcd over 2f out: btn and eased fr over 1f out* **7/2**[2]

1m 28.4s (-0.60) **Going Correction** +0.075s/f (Good) **6** Ran SP% **112.2**
Speed ratings (Par 100): **106,104,95,92,92 75**
CSF £11.46 TOTE £3.50: £2.20, £1.60; EX 12.20 Trifecta £43.70.
Owner Ken McGarrity & Partner **Bred** Tally-Ho Stud **Trained** Carluke, S Lanarks

FOCUS
Add 7yds. Although this appeared to be a tight handicap for three-year-olds they finished strung out with the first two, both of whom would have been better in future handicaps, were well clear of the rest. The pace was fair. Personal bests from the first two.

5620 JOIN RACING TV NOW H'CAP 5f 1y
8:10 (8:11) (Class 6) (0-65,64) 3-Y-0+

£3,105 (£924; £461; £400; £400; £400) **Stalls** High

Form RPR
0461 **1** **Boudica Bay (IRE)**[10] 5276 4-9-6 **60** 5ex........................... GrahamLee 1 66+
(Eric Alston) *cl up on outside: shkn up: edgd lft and led over 1f out: rdn out fnl f* **5/2**[1]

-052 **2** *nk* **Kaafy (IRE)**[11] 5236 3-9-6 **63**.. SamJames 4 67
(Grant Tuer) *bhd and sn pushed along: hdwy on outside over 1f out: chsd wnr ins fnl f: r.o* **11/2**

3-00 **3** *¾* **The Grey Zebedee**[74] 2908 3-8-11 **54**.......................(b) DuranFentiman 9 55
(Tim Easterby) *led to over 1f out: rallied: kpt on fnl f: hld nr fin* **25/1**

1005 **4** *shd* **Economic Crisis (IRE)**[10] 5276 10-9-0 **59**............... HarrisonShaw(5) 5 61
(Alan Berry) *prom: effrt and drvn along 2f out: kpt on fnl f: keeping on but hld whn n.m.r cl home (jockey said mare was caught on heels approaching the line, causing him to sit up briefly and possibly lose third place)* **14/1**

5006 **5** *½* **Northern Society (IRE)**[11] 5236 3-9-1 **61**...............(b) SeanDavis(3) 3 60+
(Keith Dalgleish) *hld up bhd ldng gp: effrt and rdn wl over 1f out: checked ins fnl f: kpt on same pce* **18/1**

6304 **6** *nk* **Jeffrey Harris**[4] 5491 4-8-7 **54**................................ CoreyMadden(7) 11 53
(Jim Goldie) *dwlt: bhd: effrt whn nt clr run fr over 1f out to ins fnl f: kpt on fin (jockey said gelding was continually denied a clear run from 2f out)* **11/4**[2]

4044 **7** *3 ¼* **Tease Maid**[24] 4763 3-9-3 **60**...................................... PaulMulrennan 8 46
(John Quinn) *chsd ldrs: drvn along 2f out: wknd ins fnl f* **10/1**

1133 **8** *1 ¼* **Hard Solution**[11] 5236 3-9-4 **64**............................ ConorMcGovern(3) 10 46
(David O'Meara) *cl up tl rdn and wknd over 1f out* **4/1**[3]

3004 **9** *hd* **Camanche Grey (IRE)**[10] 5278 8-8-1 **48** ow3............ VictorSantos(7) 6 30
(Lucinda Egerton) *in tch: lost pl 1/2-way: sn struggling: n.d after* **33/1**

1m 0.27s (0.57) **Going Correction** +0.075s/f (Good)
WFA 3 from 4yo+ 3lb **9** Ran SP% **118.4**
Speed ratings (Par 101): **98,97,96,96,95 94,89,87,87**
CSF £17.32 CT £282.72 TOTE £3.20: £1.10, £2.70, £7.40; EX 20.70 Trifecta £442.90.
Owner The Grumpy Old Geezers **Bred** Abbey Farm Stud **Trained** Longton, Lancs
■ Stewards' Enquiry : Sam James two-day ban; careless riding (Aug 16-17)

FOCUS
A 5f handicap run at a sound gallop but there was quite a bunch finish so the form is unlikely to be anything special. The likes of the fourth help set the straightforward, modest level.

5621 EVERY RACE LIVE ON RACING TV AMATEUR RIDERS' H'CAP 1m 5f
8:40 (8:40) (Class 5) (0-70,72) 4-Y-0+

£3,618 (£1,122; £560; £400; £400; £400) **Stalls** Low

Form RPR
5454 **1** **Corton Lad**[9] 5301 9-10-10 **66**.................................(tp) MrsCarolBartley 6 73
(Keith Dalgleish) *cl up: jnd ldr after 2f and sn clr of rest: led 3f out: hrd pressed fr over 1f out: hld on gamely fnl f* **11/1**

1541 **2** *nk* **Thorntoun Care**[17] 5024 8-10-8 **69**........................ MissAmyCollier(5) 2 75
(Karen Tutty) *hld up: hdwy 3f out: effrt and disp ld over 1f out: kpt on fnl f: hld nr fin* **9/1**

504F **3** *nk* **Native Fighter (IRE)**[13] 2636 5-11-2 **72**................... MissBeckySmith 7 77
(Jedd O'Keeffe) *hld up: stdy hdwy over 3f out: effrt and rdn over 1f out: edgd lft ins fnl f: kpt on: hld nr fin* **2/1**[1]

0466 **4** *3 ¾* **Tapis Libre**[29] 4543 11-11-1 **71**................................ MissJoannaMason 3 70
(Jacqueline Coward) *prom chsng gp: effrt and pushed along 3f out: kpt on same pce fnl 2f* **7/1**[3]

3131 **5** *¾* **Be Perfect (USA)**[16] 5043 10-10-9 **70**.................. MissEmilyBullock(5) 1 68
(Ruth Carr) *hld up: pushed along and hdwy over 3f out: no imp fr 2f out* **4/1**[2]

0633 **6** *9* **Duke Of Yorkshire**[22] 4825 9-10-2 **58**..................(p) MissEmilyEasterby 4 43
(Tim Easterby) *chsd clr ldng pair: rdn over 3f out: edgd lft and wknd wl over 1f out* **10/1**

-065 **7** *1* **Sarvi**[13] 5179 4-10-10 **66**................................ MrJamesHarding 8 49
(Jim Goldie) *hld up: stdy hdwy over 5f out: effrt over 3f out: wknd over 2f out* **16/1**

5/03 **8** *½* **Wynford (IRE)**[4] 5487 6-11-0 **70**................................ MrSimonWalker 9 53
(Lucinda Egerton) *led: jnd after 2f and pair sn clr of rest: hdd 3f out: edgd lft and wknd 2f out* **4/1**[2]

5000 **9** *½* **Dizoard**[10] 5277 9-9-2 **51** oh6.................................. MrEireannCagney(7) 5 33
(Iain Jardine) *hld up in midfield: lost grnd over 5f out: rdn and struggling fnl 3f* **50/1**

2m 52.83s (1.13) **Going Correction** +0.075s/f (Good) **9** Ran SP% **121.1**
Speed ratings (Par 103): **99,98,98,96,95 90,89,89,89**
CSF £110.04 CT £284.20 TOTE £13.40: £2.70, £3.00, £1.40; EX 101.80 Trifecta £357.80.
Owner J Hutton **Bred** Frank Brady And Brian Scanlon **Trained** Carluke, S Lanarks

FOCUS
Add 7yds. A strongly-run handicap for amateur riders' in which two, one of them the winner, raced well clear of the others for most of the way. The second has been rated to his best since his 3yo days, and the third to this year's form.
T/Plt: £43.00 to a £1 stake. Pool: £45,443.88 - 770.53 winning units T/Qpdt: £4.50 to a £1 stake. Pool: £5,077.71 - 832.15 winning units **Richard Young**

5439 NEWMARKET (R-H)

Friday, August 2

OFFICIAL GOING: Good to firm (good in places)
Wind: nil Weather: very hot and sunny; 26 degrees

5622 UNIBET H'CAP — 6f
5:20 (5:21) (Class 5) (0-70,71) 3-Y-0
£4,528 (£1,347; £673; £400; £400; £400) **Stalls High**

Form RPR

66-0 **1** **Lordsbridge Boy**[50] 3764 3-8-4 **58**........................ SophieRalston(5) 11 67
(Dean Ivory) *mde all: pushed along 2f out: styd on wl ins fnl f (trainer said regarding apparent improvement in form that the gelding appreciated the drop back down in trip from 7f to 6f and was suited by the Good to Firm, Good in Places ground on this occasion, having ran on soft ground in its previous race)* **16/1**

4042 **2** *½* **Gregorian Girl**[37] 4248 3-8-7 **61**........................ CierenFallon(5) 3 68
(Dean Ivory) *chsd ldrs: rdn 2f out: hdwy and hung rt fnl f: wnt 2nd 100yds out: nt rch wnr* **5/1**[2]

0656 **3** *1¼* **Aquarius (IRE)**[7] 5377 3-8-8 **57**........................ LiamJones 5 60
(Michael Appleby) *taken down early: towards rr: drvn and outpcd 3f out tl rallied and hdwy over 1f out: kpt on wl ins fnl f: unable to chal* **8/1**

-100 **4** *nk* **Lady Monica**[47] 3884 3-9-0 **63**........................ RoystonFfrench 2 65
(John Holt) *plld hrd in midfield: drvn and effrt over 1f out: styng on fnl 100yds* **20/1**

1424 **5** *1* **Di Matteo**[16] 5056 3-9-4 **70**........................ GabrieleMalune(3) 10 69
(Marco Botti) *chsd ldrs: rdn 2f out: hung rt fnl f: no imp fnl 100yds* **7/2**[1]

2530 **6** *¾* **Sirius Slew**[27] 4655 3-9-5 **71**........................(p) JoshuaBryan(3) 7 67
(Alan Bailey) *prom: rdn 2f out: nt qckn ins fnl f* **9/1**

1335 **7** *¾* **Stallone (IRE)**[16] 5056 3-9-5 **68**........................(b[1]) AdamKirby 13 62
(Richard Spencer) *cl up: drvn 2f out: wknd wl ins fnl f* **7/2**[1]

0250 **8** *hd* **Molaaheth**[30] 4507 3-9-6 **69**........................(bt[1]) DaneO'Neill 8 62
(Richard Hannon) *midfield: rdn 2f out: hld whn hung rt fnl f* **7/1**[3]

-306 **9** *5* **Painted Dream**[10] 5281 3-9-5 **68**........................ TomQueally 4 45
(George Margarson) *t.k.h on outer: drvn and btn over 2f out* **12/1**

0-60 **10** *¾* **Diamond Cara**[16] 5062 3-8-2 **51** oh6........................ DavidEgan 12 26
(Stuart Williams) *pressed wnr: drvn 2f out: lost pl over 1f out* **33/1**

0000 **11** *11* **Budaiya Fort (IRE)**[8] 5352 3-7-13 **51** oh3........................(p) NoelGarbutt(3) 9
(Phil McEntee) *awkward leaving stalls: rdn and reluctant in rr: t.o fnl 2f* **50/1**

506- **12** *2* **The Great Phoenix**[350] 6238 3-9-6 **69**........................(h[1]) KieranShoemark 1
(Gay Kelleway) *racd on outside: struggling 1/2-way: eased and t.o fnl f* **16/1**

1m 11.27s (-0.83) **Going Correction** -0.05s/f (Good) **12** Ran SP% **123.8**
Speed ratings (Par 100): **103,102,100,100,98 97,96,96,90,89 74,71**
CSF £96.89 CT £721.47 TOTE £20.20: £5.20, £1.90, £2.60; EX 164.70 Trifecta £1960.30.
Owner Roger S Beadle **Bred** Mrs I L Sneath **Trained** Radlett, Herts

FOCUS
Far side course used. Stalls: far side, except 1m4f: centre. The warm weather caused the ground to be changed to Good to firm, good in places. A modest 3yo sprint handicap affected by the late withdrawal of the forecast favourite. The form looks moderate. The second has been rated in line with her recent form.

5623 UNIBET FILLIES' H'CAP — 1m 4f
5:50 (5:53) (Class 5) (0-75,76) 3-Y-0+
£4,528 (£1,347; £673; £400; £400; £400) **Stalls Centre**

Form RPR

-014 **1** **Cambric**[27] 4656 3-9-0 **68**........................ OisinMurphy 9 77
(Roger Charlton) *2nd tl led 1f out: sn drvn clr: in command whn wandered lft clsng stages* **7/2**[2]

-351 **2** *2* **Chicago Doll**[27] 4653 3-9-7 **75**........................ TomQueally 5 81
(Alan King) *chsd ldrs: drvn and outpcd 3f out: rallied on outer 1f out: wnt 2nd fnl 100yds: nt rch wnr* **10/1**

-433 **3** *½* **Swansdown**[24] 4769 3-8-8 **67**........................(p) CierenFallon(5) 2 72
(William Haggas) *t.k.h to s: settled in 3rd: rdn and outpcd briefly 2f out: kpt on ins fnl f: hld last 100yds (jockey said filly ran too freely when travelling to post and throughout the race)* **15/8**[1]

-623 **4** *1¼* **Potters Lady Jane**[29] 4569 7-9-13 **71**........................(p) JackMitchell 4 75
(Lucy Wadham) *taken down early: stdd s: hdwy 3f out: pressed ldrs over 1f out: rdn and no ex ins fnl f* **5/1**[3]

0-10 **5** *¾* **Break The Rules**[14] 5148 3-9-2 **70**........................ EoinWalsh 8 72
(Martin Smith) *stdd s: keen in last pl: drvn over 3f out: nvr looked like getting involved after (jockey said filly was denied a clear run for a couple of strides approximately 2½f)* **50/1**

2614 **6** *nk* **Francophilia**[24] 4752 4-10-4 **76**........................ AdamKirby 1 78
(Mark Johnston) *chsd ldrs and keen on inner: rdn and racing awkwardly 2f out: wl hld after* **5/1**[3]

1205 **7** *½* **Vin D'Honneur (IRE)**[34] 4372 3-8-4 **58**........................(p) DavidEgan 7 59
(Stuart Williams) *led: rdn and tried to qckn clr 3f out: hdd 1f out: lost pl rapidly* **20/1**

6140 **8** *1½* **Navigate By Stars (IRE)**[27] 4671 3-9-5 **73**........................(p) AlistairRawlinson 6 71
(Tom Dascombe) *t.k.h trcking ldrs: rdn and no ex 2f out* **10/1**

2m 33.9s **Going Correction** -0.05s/f (Good)
WFA 3 from 4yo+ 10lb **8** Ran SP% **115.2**
Speed ratings (Par 100): **98,96,96,95,95 94,94,93**
CSF £38.12 CT £83.64 TOTE £4.80: £1.60, £2.10, £1.30; EX 36.40 Trifecta £115.80.
Owner D J Deer **Bred** D J And Mrs Deer **Trained** Beckhampton, Wilts

FOCUS
Add 20yds. A fair fillies' handicap in which the younger generation dominated the finish.

5624 UNIBET BRITISH EBF NOVICE STKS (PLUS 10 RACE) — 6f
6:25 (6:27) (Class 4) 2-Y-0
£5,175 (£1,540; £769; £384) **Stalls High**

Form RPR

1 **Lazuli (IRE)** 2-9-2 0........................ WilliamBuick 1 86+
(Charlie Appleby) *chsd ldrs gng wl: pushed up to chal over 1f out: sn led and clr: readily* **11/10**[1]

44 **2** *2½* **Hello Baileys**[13] 5186 2-9-2 0........................ AdamKirby 9 75
(Mark Johnston) *led: bmpd along and hdd 1f out: sn outpcd by wnr but holding rest* **5/1**[3]

0 **3** *½* **Ziggle Pops**[77] 2792 2-9-2 0........................ RossaRyan 11 74
(Richard Hannon) *cl up: rdn 1/2-way: chsd ldng pair vainly ins fnl f* **15/2**

44 **4** *½* **Mellad**[56] 3551 2-9-2 0........................ LukeMorris 5 72
(Peter Chapple-Hyam) *veered bdly rt s: sn chsng ldrs: drvn over 2f out: no imp ins fnl f (jockey said colt jumped right-handed when leaving the stalls)* **25/1**

5 *½* **Skontonovski** 2-9-2 0........................ OisinMurphy 2 71+
(Richard Spencer) *impeded s: towards rr: pushed along 2f out: kpt on steadily ins fnl f: capable of bttr* **7/2**[2]

0 **6** *1½* **Winning Streak**[34] 4394 2-9-2 0........................ KieranShoemark 3 66
(Stuart Williams) *sltly impeded s: racd freely: chsd ldrs: rdn and no ex over 1f out (jockey said colt ran green)* **66/1**

45 **7** *1* **Qaaddim (IRE)**[13] 5172 2-9-2 0........................ DavidEgan 10 63
(Roger Varian) *t.k.h: chsd ldrs: rdn 1/2-way: no ex over 1f out* **10/1**

021 **8** *1½* **Lincoln Blue**[34] 4361 2-9-8 **80**........................ JFEgan 8 65
(Jane Chapple-Hyam) *edgd rt s: pressed ldr: drvn 2f out: wknd 1f out* **14/1**

6 **9** *½* **Aysar (IRE)**[34] 4384 2-9-2 0........................ DaneO'Neill 7 57
(Ed Dunlop) *impeded s: chsd ldrs tl rdn and wknd 2f out* **33/1**

05 **10** *4½* **Just Norman**[14] 5145 2-9-2 0........................ TomQueally 6 44
(Paul D'Arcy) *sn outpcd* **66/1**

0 **11** *½* **Wizardry (FR)**[36] 4295 2-8-9 0........................ JessicaCooley(7) 4 42
(George Scott) *hmpd and carried rt s: a bhd* **66/1**

1m 12.4s (0.30) **Going Correction** -0.05s/f (Good) **11** Ran SP% **125.3**
Speed ratings (Par 96): **96,92,92,91,90 88,87,85,84,78 78**
CSF £7.43 TOTE £1.80: £1.10, £1.60, £2.20; EX 8.30 Trifecta £42.90.
Owner Godolphin **Bred** Godolphin **Trained** Newmarket, Suffolk

FOCUS
Several interesting types in this juvenile novice, which was run 1.13sec slower than the earlier 3yo handicap. Nevertheless, some promising types on show. The level is a bit fluid.

5625 32RED H'CAP — 1m 4f
7:00 (7:02) (Class 4) (0-85,86) 4-Y-0+
£6,469 (£1,925; £962; £481; £400; £400) **Stalls Centre**

Form RPR

221 **1** **Mandarin (GER)**[18] 4997 5-9-8 **86**........................ AdamKirby 8 97+
(Ian Williams) *settled towards rr and gng wl: effrt and taken lft 2f out: led 1f out: sn in command* **4/5**[1]

-053 **2** *2½* **Past Master**[14] 5135 6-9-0 **78**........................ DaneO'Neill 9 84
(Henry Candy) *t.k.h: settled in 2nd or 3rd: rdn to ld 2f out: hdd 1f out: chsd wnr vainly after* **4/1**[2]

5000 **3** *2* **Galactic Spirit**[38] 4224 4-8-5 **72**........................ GabrieleMalune(3) 1 75
(James Evans) *plld hrd and racd w awkward hd carriage in rr: rdn and effrt 2f out: swtchd lft to go 3rd ins fnl f but nvr got in a blow* **25/1**

0452 **4** *½* **Battle Of Marathon (USA)**[29] 4569 7-8-4 **73**........................ CierenFallon(5) 12 75
(John Ryan) *a abt same pl: rdn 2f out: edgd rt and wknd 1f out (jockey said gelding hung right-handed throughout)* **8/1**

10 **5** *4½* **Unit Of Assessment (IRE)**[28] 4614 5-9-3 **81**........................(vt) DavidEgan 5 76
(William Knight) *prom: rdn over 2f out: wknd over 1f out: eased cl home* **8/1**

0263 **6** *3* **Thaqaffa (IRE)**[24] 3091 6-9-1 **79**........................(h) GeorgeWood 11 69
(Amy Murphy) *taken down early: t.k.h in rr: drvn 3f out: sn struggling* **25/1**

4-54 **7** *nk* **Done Deal (IRE)**[17] 5012 4-8-11 **75**........................ LukeMorris 7 65
(Sir Mark Prescott Bt) *led at stdy pce: rdn and hdd 2f out: wknd rapidly* **7/1**[3]

2m 33.6s (-0.30) **Going Correction** -0.05s/f (Good) **7** Ran SP% **118.0**
Speed ratings (Par 105): **99,97,96,95,92 90,90**
CSF £4.61 CT £40.58 TOTE £1.70: £1.40, £2.30; EX 4.50 Trifecta £44.60.
Owner Sohi & Sohi **Bred** Dr K Schulte **Trained** Portway, Worcs

FOCUS
Add 20yds. The field for this decent handicap was reduced by nearly half due to withdrawals. They went a steady early pace but the time was 0.3sec faster than the earlier fillies' handicap. The second has been rated close to form.

5626 UNIBET.CO.UK H'CAP — 7f
7:30 (7:33) (Class 4) (0-85,86) 4-Y-0+
£6,469 (£1,925; £962; £481; £400; £400) **Stalls High**

Form RPR

0300 **1** **Rum Runner**[21] 4887 4-9-4 **82**........................ OisinMurphy 6 93
(Richard Hannon) *travelled wl towards rr: smooth prog 2f out: led 1f out: sn drvn clr (trainer's rep could offer no explanation for the colt's apparent improvement in form other than the colt is inconsistent)* **7/1**[3]

1225 **2** *2* **Quick Breath**[9] 5319 4-8-12 **83**........................ TylerSaunders(7) 5 89
(Jonathan Portman) *sn pushed along towards rr: hdwy over 2f out: wnt 2nd 1f out: kpt on ins fnl f but no match for wnr* **16/1**

5511 **3** *1¼* **Fighting Temeraire (IRE)**[14] 5144 6-8-11 **75**........................ JoeyHaynes 2 77
(Dean Ivory) *stdd s: keen in rr: rdn and effrt 2f out: wnt 3rd but no imp fnl f* **9/4**[1]

-000 **4** *1* **Sir Titan**[20] 4902 5-9-4 **82**........................ RossaRyan 9 82
(Tony Carroll) *prom: rdn 2f out: ev ch 1f out: sn btn* **16/1**

5006 **5** *1¼* **Haddaf (IRE)**[13] 5195 4-8-11 **82**........................(t) MarcoGhiani(7) 7 78
(Stuart Williams) *chsd ldrs: rdn 2f out: no ex over 1f out* **33/1**

3123 **6** *2¾* **Call Out Loud**[9] 5319 7-9-3 **81**........................(vt) AlistairRawlinson 1 70
(Michael Appleby) *led: drvn and tried to get clr 1/2-way: put hd in air and hdd 1f out: lost pl rapidly* **12/1**

2110 **7** 2 1/4 **Firmdecisions (IRE)**[20] 4902 9-9-7 **85** SilvestreDeSousa 8 68
(Nigel Tinkler) *midfield: shkn up and no rspnse 1/2-way: sn btn* **11/1**

1242 **8** hd **Jalaad (IRE)**[28] 4598 4-9-8 **86** AdamKirby 3 68
(Saeed bin Suroor) *prom tl rdn 2f out: wknd over 1f out* **7/2**[2]

012 **9** 5 **Club Tropicana**[28] 4615 4-8-8 **72** (t[1]) LukeMorris 12 41
(Richard Spencer) *stdd s: towards rr: rdn 1/2-way: no rspnse and sn btn: t.o* **14/1**

-632 **10** 5 **Zeyzoun (FR)**[21] 4879 5-9-0 **78** (h) GeraldMosse 11 33
(Chris Wall) *pressed ldrs tl rdn and lost pl rapidly 2f out: t.o (stewards considered performance of gelding; trainer said gelding ran too freely having had insufficient cover and was unsuited by the good to firm, good in places ground on this occasion and would prefer a slower surface which was noted)* **7/2**[2]

1m 23.97s (-1.73) **Going Correction** -0.05s/f (Good) **10** Ran SP% **125.1**
Speed ratings (Par 105): **107,104,103,102,100 97,95,94,89,83**
CSF £120.04 CT £338.95 TOTE £8.20: £2.50, £4.90, £1.50; EX 144.60 Trifecta £517.10.
Owner Michael Geoghegan **Bred** Biddestone Stud **Trained** East Everleigh, Wilts

FOCUS
Quite a competitive handicap on paper, but they came to the stands' rail, went a good pace and those drawn low had the best of things. The winner ran a pb to win over the C&D last year and has been rated back to that level.

5627 32RED NOVICE STKS 1m
8:00 (8:03) (Class 4) 3-Y-O+ **£5,563** (£1,655; £827; £413) **Stalls** High

Form RPR

1 **Subaana (IRE)** 3-8-11 0 AndreaAtzeni 6 88+
(Roger Varian) *cl up and gng wl: led 2f out: pushed along and kpt on stoutly fnl f: decisively* **10/1**

2 **2** 1 1/4 **Loving Glance**[14] 5141 3-8-11 0 RobHornby 8 85
(Martyn Meade) *chsd ldrs: rdn over 1f out: kpt on to go 2nd wl ins fnl f: sustained effrt but a hld* **7/2**[2]

63 **3** 1/2 **Magical Rhythms (USA)**[35] 4341 3-8-11 0 RobertHavlin 9 84
(John Gosden) *prom: rdn 2f out: nt qckn ins fnl f: lost 2nd cl home* **8/1**

1- **4** 2 **Art Song (USA)**[280] 8600 3-9-9 0 WilliamBuick 10 91
(Charlie Appleby) *led: rdn and hdd 2f out: racd awkwardly whn hld ins fnl f* **1/1**[1]

3- **5** 1 1/4 **Dubai Discovery (USA)**[321] 7283 3-8-11 0 (w) OisinMurphy 2 76
(Saeed bin Suroor) *prom tl rdn and wl hld over 1f out* **15/2**[3]

33 **6** 3 3/4 **Abr Al Hudood (JPN)**[24] 4768 3-8-11 0 JackMitchell 3 67
(Hugo Palmer) *midfield: rdn and btn wl over 1f out* **16/1**

0-3 **7** 2 **Social Network (IRE)**[206] 128 3-8-11 0 KieranShoemark 4 62
(James Tate) *chsd ldrs: rdn 2f out: sn btn* **25/1**

0 **8** 3 3/4 **Elena Osorio (IRE)**[58] 3464 3-8-11 0 GeraldMosse 1 53
(David Elsworth) *t.k.h towards rr: effrt 1/2-way: drvn and wknd 2f out* **33/1**

9 1 1/4 **Adashelby (IRE)** 3-8-4 0 LauraPearson(7) 7 50
(John Ryan) *slowly away: a bhd: lost tch 1/2-way* **100/1**

10 17 **Cheerful** 3-8-11 0 SilvestreDeSousa 5 9
(Philip McBride) *slowly away: a bhd: lost tch 1/2-way: eased and t.o* **14/1**

1m 37.85s (-2.15) **Going Correction** -0.05s/f (Good) **10** Ran SP% **124.5**
Speed ratings (Par 105): **108,106,106,104,103 99,97,93,92,75**
CSF £47.73 TOTE £11.60: £3.00, £1.10, £2.00; EX 67.40 Trifecta £327.90.
Owner Sheikh Mohammed Obaid Al Maktoum **Bred** Sheikh Mohammed Obaid Al Maktoum **Trained** Newmarket, Suffolk

FOCUS
All fillies bar one colt in this interesting 3yo novice contest. The colt was favourite but the fillies prevailed and could be useful.

5628 32RED CASINO H'CAP 6f
8:30 (8:32) (Class 3) (0-90,91) 3-Y-O+ **£9,056** (£2,695; £1,346; £673) **Stalls** High

Form RPR

-050 **1** **Colonel Frank**[36] 4300 5-8-11 **75** JackMitchell 6 81
(Mick Quinn) *cl up: n.m.r on ins 2f out tl drifted rt over 1f out: sn rdn: grad wore down ldr to get up fnl stride (trainer said regarding apparent improvement in from that the gelding settled in the race better today over 6f having run too freely over a mile last time out)* **8/1**

612 **2** nse **Emily Goldfinch**[14] 5143 6-9-13 **91** (p) SilvestreDeSousa 2 97
(Phil McEntee) *led: rdn 1/2-way: kpt fending off chalr tl pipped on post (mare anticipated the start and accelerated the gate at the same moment as the race had been started)* **15/8**[1]

3330 **3** 1/2 **Lady Dancealot (IRE)**[14] 5143 4-9-4 **82** GeraldMosse 8 88+
(David Elsworth) *t.k.h on ins: towards rr: swtchd rt over 1f out: fin strly on outside under urgings: too much to do* **11/4**[2]

0412 **4** 2 1/2 **Suzi's Connoisseur**[13] 5191 8-8-13 **77** (v) JFEgan 5 73
(Jane Chapple-Hyam) *drvn along thrght: wnt 2nd 2f out tl 1f out: wknd ins fnl f to lose 3rd* **5/1**[3]

0-24 **5** 6 **Miracle Of Medinah**[28] 4609 8-9-12 **90** FergusSweeney 3 67
(Mark Usher) *missed break: sn handy: rdn and btn over 1f out* **8/1**

061 **6** 1 **Tawny Port**[53] 3662 5-9-9 **87** (t) OisinMurphy 1 61
(Stuart Williams) *racd freely: pressed ldr for 4f: rdn and btn after being hmpd over 1f out* **5/1**[3]

1m 11.14s (-0.96) **Going Correction** -0.05s/f (Good)
WFA 3 from 4yo+ 4lb **6** Ran SP% **117.0**
Speed ratings (Par 107): **104,103,103,99,91 90**
CSF £24.71 CT £53.37 TOTE £9.80: £3.90, £1.70; EX 26.80 Trifecta £100.50.
Owner Kenny Bruce **Bred** Eliza Park International Pty Ltd **Trained** Newmarket, Suffolk
■ Stewards' Enquiry : Jack Mitchell two-day ban; careless riding (Aug 16-17)

FOCUS
The feature race and a good sprint handicap that was run only fractionally faster than the quicker of the two earlier races over the trip on the night. Only six runners but quite a rough race and a very close finish. It's been rated around the second to her recent form.
T/Plt: £51.80 to a £1 stake. Pool: £64,879.70 - 914.27 winning units T/Qpdt: £9.70 to a £1 stake. Pool: £8,091.89 - 616.71 winning units **Iain Mackenzie**

5279 WOLVERHAMPTON (A.W) (L-H)
Friday, August 2

OFFICIAL GOING: Tapeta: standard
Wind: Almost nil Weather: Sunny spells

5629 VISIT EQUINOX-RACING.CO.UK TO JOIN TODAY H'CAP 6f 20y (Tp)
1:30 (1:31) (Class 6) (0-60,59) 3-Y-O+
£2,781 (£827; £413; £300; £300; £300) **Stalls** Low

Form RPR

2223 **1** **Daring Guest (IRE)**[43] 4025 5-9-7 **56** (t) LukeMorris 13 65
(Tom Clover) *broke wl: sn stdd and lost pl: hdwy over 1f out: shkn up to ld ins fnl f: r.o: comf* **15/2**

0020 **2** 2 1/4 **Pearl Of Qatar**[73] 2940 3-9-5 **58** ConnorBeasley 6 59
(Tristan Davidson) *chsd ldr 5f out: led over 1f out: rdn and hdd ins fnl f: styd on same pce* **9/2**[2]

0-00 **3** 1/2 **Kingsley Klarion (IRE)**[43] 4025 6-9-6 **55** TomEaves 4 56
(John Butler) *dwlt: hld up: swtchd lft and hdwy over 1f out: r.o to go 3rd wl ins fnl f* **9/4**[1]

000R **4** 1/2 **Dandilion (IRE)**[34] 4376 6-9-1 **50** HollieDoyle 11 49
(Alex Hales) *s.i.s: hld up: swtchd rt over 1f out: r.o ins fnl f: nt rch ldrs* **28/1**

0020 **5** 1/2 **Prince Of Time**[11] 5237 7-8-10 **50** BenSanderson(5) 2 48
(Stella Barclay) *s.i.s: sn prom: rdn and hung lft fr over 1f out: styd on same pce ins fnl f* **20/1**

6000 **6** 1 1/2 **Trust Me (IRE)**[39] 4185 3-9-5 **58** JoeyHaynes 9 50
(Dean Ivory) *hld up: hdwy over 1f out: styd on same pce ins fnl f* **20/1**

0004 **7** 1/2 **Ingleby Molly (IRE)**[9] 5299 4-8-12 **50** BenRobinson(3) 10 42
(Jason Ward) *prom: pushed along and lost pl over 4f out: hdwy over 1f out: styd on same pce ins fnl f (jockey said filly hung right throughout)* **20/1**

0404 **8** 3/4 **Jill Rose**[23] 4783 3-9-3 **56** (p) CamHardie 3 45
(Richard Whitaker) *chsd ldrs: rdn and nt clr run over 1f out: edgd lft and no ex fnl f* **14/1**

466 **9** 3/4 **Spenny's Lass**[24] 4763 4-9-3 **52** (p) BrettDoyle 7 39
(John Ryan) *prom: sn pushed along and lost pl: n.d after: eased nr fin* **13/2**[3]

0452 **10** 2 1/4 **Atyaaf**[17] 5018 4-9-5 **54** AndrewElliott 12 35
(Derek Shaw) *s.i.s: hld up: nvr on terms* **14/1**

4500 **11** 3 1/4 **Just For The Craic (IRE)**[46] 3936 4-9-7 **56** StevieDonohoe 5 27
(Neil Mulholland) *led over 5f out: rdn and hdd over 1f out: wknd ins fnl f* **50/1**

004- **12** 3 1/2 **Madame Ritz (IRE)**[350] 6262 4-9-7 **59** JaneElliott(3) 1 19
(Richard Phillips) *s.i.s: sn prom: rdn and wknd over 1f out* **33/1**

640 **13** 2 3/4 **Midnight Guest (IRE)**[16] 5051 4-9-6 **55** RossaRyan 8 7
(David Evans) *led early: chsd ldrs: hung rt and wknd over 1f out (jockey said filly hung right throughout)* **28/1**

1m 14.49s (-0.01) **Going Correction** +0.075s/f (Slow)
WFA 3 from 4yo+ 4lb **13** Ran SP% **113.5**
Speed ratings (Par 101): **103,100,99,98,98 96,95,94,93,90 86,81,77**
CSF £35.03 CT £103.79 TOTE £4.80: £1.80, £2.00, £1.50; EX 41.20 Trifecta £250.20.
Owner Mrs Gay Jarvis **Bred** Ringfort Stud **Trained** Newmarket, Suffolk

FOCUS
A low-grade sprint handicap, run in a time 2.69 outside the standard. It's been rated as straightforward, limited form.

5630 GOLDEN EQUINOX RACING BREEDING FUTURE STARS FILLIES' (S) STKS 6f 20y (Tp)
2:00 (2:01) (Class 6) 2-Y-O
£2,781 (£827; £413; £300; £300; £300) **Stalls** Low

Form RPR

4235 **1** **My Motivate Girl (IRE)**[25] 4727 2-9-0 68 (b[1]) HollieDoyle 1 59
(Archie Watson) *s.i.s: hld up: swtchd rt and hdwy wl over 1f out: rdn to ld and hung lft 1f out: hung rt and lft ins fnl f: styd on* **10/11**[1]

0 **2** 2 1/4 **Hiconic**[8] 5342 2-9-0 0 GeorgeDowning 6 52
(Mick Channon) *hld up: racd keenly: hdwy on outer over 1f out: styd on to go 2nd nr fin* **16/1**

0106 **3** nk **Amnaa**[13] 5171 2-9-5 70 ConnorBeasley 5 56
(Adrian Nicholls) *sn pushed along and prom: rdn over 1f out: hmpd sn after: styd on same pce ins fnl f (vet said filly lost its right fore shoe)* **11/4**[2]

0003 **4** 1 1/4 **Beautrix**[13] 5196 2-9-0 49 TomEaves 2 47
(Michael Dods) *sn led: hdd over 2f out: no ex ins fnl f* **16/1**

0 **5** 1 **Petite Steps (IRE)**[13] 5197 2-8-9 0 DMSimmonson(5) 8 44
(Miss Katy Brown, Ire) *chsd ldr tl led over 2f out: rdn and hdd 1f out: no ex ins fnl f* **66/1**

4406 **6** 1 3/4 **Leave Em Alone (IRE)**[9] 5313 2-9-0 62 (v[1]) RossaRyan 3 38
(David Evans) *chsd ldrs: rdn over 1f out: hung lft and no ex fnl f* **11/2**[3]

0506 **7** 10 **Birkie Queen (IRE)**[8] 5340 2-9-0 58 LukeMorris 7 6
(J S Moore) *hld up: rdn and wknd over 2f out (jockey said filly was never travelling)* **18/1**

00 **8** 27 **Helluvasunset**[23] 4798 2-9-0 0 (p[1]) StevieDonohoe 4
(Mark Usher) *s.i.s: stmbld sn after s: outpcd (jockey said filly stumbled badly shortly after the start)* **80/1**

1m 16.22s (1.72) **Going Correction** +0.075s/f (Slow) **8** Ran SP% **114.2**
Speed ratings (Par 89): **91,88,87,85,84 82,68,32**
CSF £19.11 TOTE £1.60: £1.02, £4.20, £1.10; EX 11.40 Trifecta £43.20.There was no bid for the winner.
Owner L Dickinson **Bred** Mrs Andrea Ryan **Trained** Upper Lambourn, W Berks

FOCUS
Comfortable enough for the market leader in this seller confined to fillies. The winner has been rated near her recent level.

5631 GOLDEN EQUINOX RACING ARE ALWAYS TOURING H'CAP 1m 5f 219y (Tp)
2:35 (2:36) (Class 5) (0-75,80) 4-Y-O+
£3,428 (£1,020; £509; £300; £300; £300) **Stalls** Low

Form RPR

2-11 **1** **Distant Chimes (GER)**[9] 5311 4-9-12 **80** 5ex (p[1]) LukeMorris 3 91+
(Sir Mark Prescott Bt) *plld hrd and prom: wnt 2nd over 11f out: led over 3f out: drvn along over 1f out: hung lft ins fnl f: styd on* **8/15**[1]

4103 **2** 2 1/4 **Houlton**[34] 4383 4-9-1 **76** (tp) StefanoCherchi(7) 5 81
(Marco Botti) *prom: lost pl over 12f out: hdwy over 6f out: chse wnr 2f out: no imp ins fnl f* **9/1**[3]

1521 **3** 2 1/4 **Bird For Life**[16] 5053 5-8-7 **68**....................(p) EllieMacKenzie(7) 11 70+
(Mark Usher) *hld up: hdwy over 2f out: styd on to go 3rd nr fin: nt rch ldrs (vet said mare lost its left fore shoe)* **14/1**

63/2 **4** nk **The Blues Master (IRE)**[34] 4383 5-8-13 **67**.................... PatCosgrave 1 68
(Alan King) *s.i.s: sn prom: chsd ldr after 1f tl over 11f out: remained handy: pushed along to chse wnr over 3f out tl 2f out: styd on same pce fnl f* **8/1**[2]

0020 **5** 3 **Enmeshing**[71] 2998 6-8-7 **61**.................... CamHardie 7 58
(Alexandra Dunn) *hld up: hdwy over 3f out: rdn over 1f out: no ex* **25/1**

-1P4 **6** 5 **Raven's Raft (IRE)**[34] 4362 4-8-8 **62**.................... HollieDoyle 2 52
(David Loughnane) *chsd ldr 1f: remained handy: pushed along over 4f out: wknd over 2f out* **20/1**

60 **7** 34 **Rail Dancer**[23] 4792 7-8-6 **67**....................(v) GavinAshton(7) 8 10
(Shaun Keightley) *hld up: a in rr: wknd over 2f out* **33/1**

0421 **8** 2 1/4 **Fern Owl**[10] 5285 7-8-4 **58** 4ex....................(e) JoeyHaynes 10
(John Butler) *s.i.s: hdwy over 12f out: reminders over 7f out: wknd and eased over 3f out (jockey said gelding was never travelling)* **14/1**

0405 **9** 13 **Taurean Dancer (IRE)**[22] 4843 4-8-5 **62**....................(b[1]) JaneElliott(3) 6
(Roger Teal) *led: racd keenly: clr 7f out tl over 4f out: rdn and hdd over 3f out: wknd over 2f out (jockey said gelding ran too free)* **50/1**

144- **10** 46 **Willyegolassiego**[40] 1196 6-9-4 **72**....................(vt[1]) StevieDonohoe 9
(Neil Mulholland) *hld up: rdn and lost tch over 6f out* **100/1**

000P **11** 3/4 **More Harry**[63] 3298 4-7-9 **56** oh11.................... IsobelFrancis(7) 4
(Clare Ellam) *s.i.s: sn in mid-div: lost pl over 6f out: wknd over 5f out (jockey said gelding hung right and was never travelling; vet said gelding was lame on its left fore)* **250/1**

3m 2.82s (1.82) **Going Correction** +0.075s/f (Slow) 11 Ran SP% **114.6**
Speed ratings (Par 103): **97,95,94,94,92 89,70,68,61,35 34**
CSF £5.06 CT £34.02 TOTE £1.40: £1.10, £2.40, £2.20; EX 6.20 Trifecta £35.50.
Owner Phil Fry - Osborne House **Bred** Gestut Wiesengrund **Trained** Newmarket, Suffolk

FOCUS
They finished strung out in this staying handicap. The second has been rated to his best.

5632 GOLDEN EQUINOX RACING THANKS ALAN WOODS H'CAP 7f 36y (Tp)
3:10 (3:10) (Class 6) (0-65,65) 3-Y-O+
£2,781 (£827; £413; £300; £300; £300) **Stalls High**

Form RPR

1441 **1** **Fantastic Flyer**[10] 5282 4-9-12 **65** 5ex....................(p) JoeyHaynes 1 74
(Dean Ivory) *mde all: rdn over 1f out: styd on* **2/1**[1]

5110 **2** 1/2 **Fly True**[46] 3939 6-9-5 **58**.................... NickyMackay 5 66
(Ivan Furtado) *chsd wnr: ev ch over 2f out: rdn over 1f out: r.o* **25/1**

0021 **3** nk **Sfumato**[16] 5051 5-9-9 **62**.................... ConnorBeasley 9 69
(Adrian Nicholls) *hld up in tch: racd keenly: rdn over 2f out: r.o to go 3rd nr fin: nt rch ldrs* **3/1**[3]

0016 **4** 3/4 **Primeiro Boy (IRE)**[17] 5020 3-9-2 **64**.................... ConnorMurtagh(3) 4 67
(Richard Fahey) *chsd ldrs: rdn over 1f out: styd on same pce wl ins fnl f* **14/1**

0411 **5** 1 **Mitigator**[3] 5531 3-9-5 **64** 6ex....................(b) BrettDoyle 6 65
(Lydia Pearce) *pushed along to chse ldrs: rdn over 1f out: styd on same pce ins fnl f* **11/4**[2]

4500 **6** 3 **Smoki Smoka (IRE)**[19] 4602 3-8-10 **62**....................(p) EllaMcCain(7) 7 55
(Donald McCain) *prom: racd keenly: rdn over 2f out: no ex fnl f* **40/1**

1352 **7** 1/2 **Brockey Rise (IRE)**[60] 3413 4-9-4 **62**....................(b) KatherineBegley(5) 12 56
(David Evans) *hld up: hdwy u.p over 1f out: nt trble ldrs* **33/1**

1- **8** 15 **Descendant**[89] 2453 4-9-0 **58**.................... DMSimmonson(5) 10 15
(Miss Katy Brown, Ire) *s.i.s: hld up: rdn and wknd over 2f out: eased over 1f out (jockey said gelding moved poorly in the home straight; vet said gelding lost its right fore shoe)* **8/1**

1000 **9** 3/4 **Weloof (FR)**[10] 5282 5-9-9 **65**.................... GeorgiaCox(3) 2 26
(John Butler) *s.i.s: a in rr: wknd over 2f out* **100/1**

-200 **10** 10 **Pushkin Museum (IRE)**[24] 4767 8-9-9 **62**.................... LewisEdmunds 11
(John Butler) *hld up: wknd over 2f out* **150/1**

1m 30.39s (1.59) **Going Correction** +0.075s/f (Slow)
WFA 3 from 4yo+ 6lb 10 Ran SP% **113.7**
Speed ratings (Par 101): **93,92,92,91,90 86,86,68,68,56**
CSF £57.43 CT £152.09 TOTE £2.60: £1.20, £3.30, £1.20; EX 31.20 Trifecta £88.10.
Owner Mrs L A Ivory **Bred** Gracelands Stud **Trained** Radlett, Herts

FOCUS
The pace held up in this modest handicap. The winner has been rated in line with her latest.

5633 GOLDEN EQUINOX RACING £24.99 MONTHLY MEMBERSHIP H'CAP 1m 142y (Tp)
3:45 (3:46) (Class 6) (0-55,55) 3-Y-O+
£2,781 (£827; £413; £300; £300; £300) **Stalls Low**

Form RPR

03 **1** **Enzo (IRE)**[35] 4349 4-9-7 **55**.................... JoeyHaynes 3 67
(John Butler) *hmpd s: sn prom: chsd ldr over 2f out: led over 1f out: sn rdn and hung lft: styd on* **4/1**[1]

661 **2** shd **Misu Pete**[14] 5137 7-9-0 **55**....................(p) EllieMacKenzie(7) 7 67
(Mark Usher) *led early: chsd ldr tl led over 5f out: rdn and hdd over 1f out: ev ch ins fnl f: styd on* **8/1**

6334 **3** 6 **Pike Corner Cross (IRE)**[15] 5081 7-9-5 **53**.................... StevieDonohoe 1 52
(David Evans) *chsd ldrs: rdn over 1f out: styd on same pce* **6/1**[3]

4005 **4** 3 1/4 **Gold Flash**[4] 5498 7-9-7 **55**....................(v) HollieDoyle 2 48
(Rod Millman) *prom: sn lost pl: nt clr run over 2f out: swtchd rt over 1f out: styd on: nt trble ldrs* **5/1**[2]

0002 **5** 1/2 **Caledonia Laird**[18] 5003 8-9-6 **54**....................(e) ConnorBeasley 9 46
(Gay Kelleway) *hld up: hdwy on outer over 1f out: nt trble ldrs* **16/1**

5405 **6** 2 3/4 **Kafoo**[15] 5100 6-9-3 **51**....................(be[1]) LewisEdmunds 4 37
(Michael Appleby) *s.s: hdwy over 5f out: rdn and wknd over 1f out (jockey said gelding missed the break)* **16/1**

0-02 **7** 2 **Sir Magnum**[32] 4453 4-9-5 **53**.................... BrettDoyle 12 35
(Tony Carroll) *chsd ldrs: rdn over 2f out: wknd over 1f out* **16/1**

1000 **8** 1 1/2 **Mans Not Trot (IRE)**[18] 5003 4-9-6 **54**....................(vt[1]) TrevorWhelan 5 32
(Brian Barr) *unruly in stalls: wnt lft s: rcvrd to ld 8f out: hdd over 5f out: rdn over 2f out: wknd over 1f out (jockey said gelding was restless in the stalls)* **33/1**

006 **9** hd **Hidden Dream (FR)**[16] 5051 4-9-5 **53**.................... JosephineGordon 6 31
(John Butler) *stdd s: hld up: shkn up over 2f out: nvr nr to chal* **12/1**

4-01 **10** hd **Effernock Fizz (IRE)**[12] 5214 4-8-13 **52** 5ex.......... DMSimmonson(5) 13 30
(Miss Katy Brown, Ire) *s.i.s: hld up: rdn on outer over 3f out: n.d (jockey said filly was never travelling)* **5/1**[2]

0640 **11** hd **Perfect Soldier (IRE)**[55] 3592 5-8-9 **50**.................... GavinAshton(7) 10 27
(Shaun Keightley) *hld up: effrt over 2f out: wknd over 1f out* **14/1**

0000 **12** 1/2 **Stoneyford Lane (IRE)**[39] 4182 5-9-2 **50**....................(b[1]) TomEaves 11 26
(Steph Hollinshead) *s.i.s: hld up: rdn on outer over 2f out: n.d* **50/1**

0-00 **13** 24 **Symbolic Star (IRE)**[36] 4293 7-8-13 **50**..........(p w) ConnorMurtagh(3) 8
(Barry Murtagh) *s.i.s: sn pushed along and a in rr: wknd over 2f out (jockey said gelding was slowly away)* **100/1**

1m 50.25s (0.15) **Going Correction** +0.075s/f (Slow) **13** Ran SP% **116.6**
Speed ratings (Par 101): **102,101,96,93,93 90,89,87,87,87 87,86,65**
CSF £34.71 CT £197.03 TOTE £5.50: £2.30, £3.40, £2.80; EX 30.20 Trifecta £195.40.
Owner J Butler **Bred** Rabbah Bloodstock Limited **Trained** Newmarket, Suffolk

FOCUS
The first two, who were both prominent throughout, finished clear.

5634 GOLDEN EQUINOX RACING SUPPORTS JE3 FOUNDATION NOVICE STKS 1m 4f 51y (Tp)
4:20 (4:20) (Class 5) 3-Y-O+
£3,428 (£1,020; £509; £254) **Stalls Low**

Form RPR

6- **1** **Trueshan (FR)**[289] 8327 3-9-2 0.................... HollieDoyle 6 85
(Alan King) *s.i.s: hld up: hdwy on outer over 2f out: chsd ldr over 1f out: rdn and r.o to ld post* **33/1**

24 **2** shd **Caravan Of Hope (IRE)**[42] 4066 3-9-2 0.................... PatCosgrave 2 84
(Hugo Palmer) *chsd ldr tl led over 8f out: shkn up and qcknd over 2f out: rdn over 1f out: hdd post* **11/4**[3]

0-1 **3** 4 **Baltic Song (IRE)**[161] 858 3-9-9 0.................... NickyMackay 1 85
(John Gosden) *led: stmbld sn after s: hdd over 8f out: chsd ldr: rdn over 2f out: lost 2nd over 1f out: no ex fnl f* **2/1**[2]

3 **4** 2 1/4 **Invictus Spirit**[11] 5254 3-9-2 0.................... LouisSteward 5 74
(Sir Michael Stoute) *chsd ldrs: rdn over 2f out: edgd lft and no ex over 1f out* **7/4**[1]

5 9 **Desert Secret** 3-9-2 0.................... JosephineGordon 3 60
(Saeed bin Suroor) *s.s: pushed along and rn green in rr: hdwy over 5f out: wknd over 2f out* **8/1**

2m 40.7s (-0.10) **Going Correction** +0.075s/f (Slow)
WFA 3 from 5yo 10lb **5** Ran SP% **110.4**
Speed ratings (Par 103): **103,102,100,98,92**
CSF £118.95 TOTE £24.10: £10.30, £1.50; EX 54.40 Trifecta £354.20.
Owner Barbury Lions 5 **Bred** Didier Blot **Trained** Barbury Castle, Wilts

FOCUS
An interesting novice event in which two finished clear. The second has been rated in line with his previous runs.

5635 GOLDEN EQUINOX RACING AUTISM AWARENESS NOVICE STKS 5f 21y (Tp)
4:50 (4:50) (Class 5) 2-Y-O
£3,428 (£1,020; £509; £254) **Stalls Low**

Form RPR

1 **He's A Laddie (IRE)** 2-9-5 0.................... HollieDoyle 1 79+
(Archie Watson) *disp ld tl wnt on over 3f out: rdn clr ins fnl f* **9/4**[2]

2 3 1/4 **On Tick (IRE)**[35] 4350 2-9-0 0.................... DMSimmonson(5) 3 67
(Miss Katy Brown, Ire) *disp ld tl over 3f out: chsd wnr: rdn over 1f out: styd on same pce ins fnl f* **4/1**[3]

43 **3** 1 1/4 **Feel Good Factor**[15] 5093 2-9-0 0.................... BarryMcHugh 6 58
(Richard Fahey) *s.i.s: sn prom: outpcd over 3f out: r.o ins fnl f* **15/2**

3325 **4** 3/4 **Good Earth (IRE)**[13] 5186 2-9-5 **78**.................... DougieCostello 5 60
(Jamie Osborne) *chsd ldrs: pushed along 1/2-way: rdn and swtchd rt over 1f out: no ex ins fnl f* **11/8**[1]

0 **5** 3 1/2 **La Chica Lobo**[10] 5280 2-9-0 0.................... CamHardie 7 42
(Lisa Williamson) *hld up: outpcd fr over 3f out* **150/1**

05 **6** 13 **Twittering (IRE)**[7] 5374 2-9-2 0.................... GeorgiaCox(3) 4
(Jamie Osborne) *s.i.s: outpcd* **16/1**

1m 2.41s (0.51) **Going Correction** +0.075s/f (Slow) **6** Ran SP% **111.2**
Speed ratings (Par 94): **98,92,90,89,84 63**
CSF £11.38 TOTE £3.50: £1.50, £2.70; EX 11.70 Trifecta £37.30.
Owner Arjun Waney **Bred** Kildaragh Stud **Trained** Upper Lambourn, W Berks

FOCUS
Just fairly useful juvenile form. It's been rated with feet on the ground.
T/Plt: £13.30 to a £1 stake. Pool: £48,959.21 - 2,669.70 winning units T/Qpdt: £6.00 to a £1 stake. Pool: £4,362.31 - 532.24 winning units **Colin Roberts**

5636a-5640a (Foreign Racing) - See Raceform Interactive

5538 DEAUVILLE (R-H)
Friday, August 2

OFFICIAL GOING: Polytrack: standard; turf: good

5641a PRIX DE BRETONCELLES (CLAIMER) (3YO) (ALL-WEATHER TRACK) (POLYTRACK) 1m 4f 110y(P)
12:50 3-Y-O
£10,360 (£4,144; £3,108; £2,072; £1,036)

RPR

1 **Gimme Joy (FR)** 3-8-8 0.................... ClementGuitraud 6 60
(Y Barberot, France) **7/5**[1]

2 1 3/4 **Alter Poseidon (GER)**[25] 3-8-11 0.................... HugoBesnier 5 60
(Andrea Marcialis, France) **23/5**[3]

3 1 3/4 **Holbox (FR)**[101] 3-8-11 0....................(b) MarcNobili 9 57
(F Vermeulen, France) **31/10**[2]

4 3/4 **Joe Blining (FR)**[7] 3-8-11 0.................... MlleFriedaValleSkar(4) 7 60
(C Lerner, France) **8/1**

5 3/4 **Delta Bravo (IRE)**[32] 4447 3-8-8 0.................... MlleAlisonMassin(3) 3 55
(J S Moore) *settled in midfield: pushed along over 2f out: rdn w limited rspnse over 1f out: no ex ins fnl f* **33/1**

6 1 1/4 **Swingy (FR)**[35] 3-9-1 0....................(b) GlenBraem 8 57
(D Smaga, France) **17/1**

7 3 1/2 **Flag Of St George (FR)**[63] 3-8-8 0.................... AnnaelleDidon-Yahlali(3) 1 47
(G Botti, France) **69/10**

8 9 **Wat Arun (FR)** 3-8-11 0.................... AntoineCoutier 2 33
(C Lotoux, France) **57/1**

9 12 **Colourful Sky (FR)**[32] 4452 3-8-8 0.................... EmmanuelEtienne 4 10
(J S Moore) *disp ld early: settled to trck ldrs: urged along over 2f out: wknd qckly and eased ins fnl f* **51/1**

2m 43.11s **9** Ran SP% **119.8**
PARI-MUTUEL (all including 1 euro stake): WIN 2.40; PLACE 1.10, 1.40, 1.30; DF 4.90.
Owner Jean Justin Fournier **Bred** T De La Heronniere & Sarl Jedburgh Stud **Trained** France

The Form Book Flat 2019, Raceform Ltd, Newbury, RG14 5SJ

5642a PRIX D'ETREHAM (MAIDEN) (2YO COLTS & GELDINGS) (ROUND COURSE) (TURF) 7f 110y

1:20 2-Y-0 £12,162 (£4,864; £3,648; £2,432; £1,216)

RPR

1 **Troilus (FR)**[30] 2-9-2 0 .... TheoBachelot 11 76
(S Wattel, France) **179/10**

2 ¾ **Bolero Dei Grif (ITY)** 2-9-2 0 .... CristianDemuro 3 74
(G Botti, France) **61/10**

3 *snk* **Le Bayou (FR)**[27] 2-9-2 0 ....(b) AurelienLemaitre 5 74
(Christopher Head, France) **10/1**

4 ¾ **Lionel (FR)**[30] 2-9-2 0 ....(p) FabriceVeron 10 72
(C Lerner, France) **20/1**

5 ½ **Wally (IRE)**[30] 2-9-2 0 .... ChristopheSoumillon 2 71
(J-C Rouget, France) **17/5**[2]

6 *1* **Barakatle**[27] 2-9-2 0 .... StephanePasquier 4 68
(P Bary, France) **77/10**

7 *nse* **Aarhus (FR)**[15] 2-9-2 0 .... VincentCheminaud 6 68
(J-P Dubois, France) **34/1**

8 *snk* **Monte Cinto (IRE)**[30] 2-9-2 0 .... MickaelBarzalona 1 68
(Louis Baudron, France) **26/5**[3]

9 *4* **Baratin (FR)** 2-8-6 0 .... AugustinMadamet(5) 8 53
(T Castanheira, France) **51/1**

10 *nse* **Veritas (IRE)**[30] 2-9-2 0 .... MaximeGuyon 7 58
(A Fabre, France) **12/5**[1]

11 *1¼* **Mr Shady (IRE)**[6] 5468 2-9-2 0 .... TonyPiccone 9 55
(J S Moore) *dwlt: in rr and adrift early: nvr in contention and eased wl ins fnl f* **72/1**

1m 34.67s (6.27) **11 Ran SP% 119.1**
PARI-MUTUEL (all including 1 euro stake): WIN 18.90; PLACE 5.00, 2.70, 3.50; DF 84.10.
Owner P H Betts **Bred** Ecurie Skymarc Farm **Trained** France

5643a PRIX DE BEUZEVILLE (CLAIMER) (4YO+) (ALL-WEATHER TRACK) (POLYTRACK) 7f 110y(P)

4:55 4-Y-0+ £10,360 (£4,144; £3,108; £2,072; £1,036)

RPR

1 **Plunger**[18] 4994 4-9-4 0 ....(b) TonyPiccone 2 80
(Paul Cole) *wl into stride: led: mde all: rowed along over 2f out: rdn to hold advantage over 1f out: drvn and kpt on ins fnl f: all out* **139/10**

2 *hd* **Ziveri (FR)**[26] 4704 4-9-1 0 ....(b) StephanePasquier 10 77
(F Rossi, France) **49/10**[2]

3 *1* **Pedro The First (FR)**[30] 4-8-6 0 ....(p) MlleAmbreMolins(9) 6 74
(F Rossi, France) **14/1**

4 *1* **Zanzibar (FR)**[31] 5-9-4 0 .... TheoBachelot 5 75
(Cedric Rossi, France) **57/10**[3]

5 ½ **My Mate (IRE)**[42] 4090 7-9-2 0 .... AlexisBadel 7 71
(L W J Van Der Meulen, Holland) **19/1**

6 *2½* **My Buddy (FR)**[150] 4-8-11 0 .... AlexandreRoussel 9 60
(E Libaud, France) **12/1**

7 *nk* **Zock (FR)**[127] 5-8-11 0 .... EddyHardouin 12 59
(Vaclav Luka Jr, Czech Republic) **29/1**

8 *snk* **Irish Emperor (IRE)**[30] 4-8-11 0 .... MaximeGuyon 8 59
(Mme Pia Brandt, France) **9/1**

9 *3* **Dylan Dancing (IRE)**[27] 4680 6-8-11 0 .... DelphineSantiago(4) 3 55
(C Le Veel, France) **21/1**

10 *1¼* **Ascot Angel (FR)**[22] 4860 5-9-2 0 .... MickaelBarzalona 13 53
(Jane Soubagne, France) **17/5**[1]

11 *1¼* **Motajaasid (IRE)**[32] 4455 4-9-1 0 .... FabriceVeron 4 49
(P Monfort, France) **24/1**

12 *1* **Daring Match (GER)**[73] 2955 8-8-11 0 ....(b[1]) AntoineHamelin 1 43
(J Hirschberger, Germany) **28/1**

13 *1½* **Il Pittore (FR)**[8] 8-8-11 0 ....(p) MlleAlisonMassin(4) 14 43
(C Escuder, France) **12/1**

14 *4* **Black Cat (FR)**[153] 992 4-8-6 0 .... QuentinPerrette(5) 11 29
(Mlle A Wattel, France) **17/1**

1m 27.09s **14 Ran SP% 119.2**
PARI-MUTUEL (all including 1 euro stake): WIN 14.90; PLACE 4.40, 2.30, 3.90; DF 45.90.
Owner A H Robinson **Bred** A H And C E Robinson Partnership **Trained** Whatcombe, Oxon

5644a PRIX DE LEAUPARTIE (CONDITIONS) (3YO) (STRAIGHT COURSE) (TURF) 6f

5:28 3-Y-0 £12,612 (£4,792; £3,531; £2,018; £1,009; £756)

RPR

1 **Zazen**[44] 3-8-10 0 .... MaximeGuyon 1 76
(A Fabre, France) **14/5**[1]

2 *snk* **Pardon My French (IRE)**[25] 3-9-3 0 .... MickaelBarzalona 9 83
(Vaclav Luka Jr, Czech Republic) **4/1**[2]

3 *snk* **Kerka (FR)**[29] 3-8-7 0 .... MlleCoraliePacaut(3) 5 76
(J-C Rouget, France) **16/1**

4 *2* **Champion Brogie (IRE)**[7] 5408 3-8-8 0 .... AlexisPouchin(6) 8 73
(J S Moore) *trckd ldr down centre of crse: rdn along 2f out: drvn to chse ldrs over 1f out: kpt on one pce fnl f* **65/1**

5 ½ **Affogato (FR)**[41] 3-9-3 0 .... CristianDemuro 7 75
(J-C Rouget, France) **7/1**[3]

6 *1½* **Sosume (FR)**[44] 3-9-3 0 .... Pierre-CharlesBoudot 4 70
(Gavin Hernon, France) **84/10**

7 *shd* **Dream With You (FR)**[9] 3-9-0 0 .... AlexisBadel 6 66
(N Caullery, France) **12/1**

8 *5½* **Hold True**[44] 3-9-0 0 .... StephanePasquier 2 49
(D Smaga, France) **10/1**

9 *2½* **Takuendo (IRE)**[29] 3-9-3 0 .... AurelienLemaitre 3 44
(F Head, France) **14/5**[1]

1m 10.21s (-0.79) **9 Ran SP% 120.0**
PARI-MUTUEL (all including 1 euro stake): WIN 3.80; PLACE 1.70, 2.00, 3.40; DF 9.30.
Owner Wertheimer & Frere **Bred** Wertheimer & Frere **Trained** Chantilly, France

5231 SARATOGA (R-H)

Friday, August 2

OFFICIAL GOING: Turf: firm

5645a SARATOGA OAKS INVITATIONAL STKS (BLACK TYPE CONDITIONS) (3YO FILLIES) (INNER TURF) (TURF) 1m 1f 110y

10:51 3-Y-0 £314,960 (£110,236; £59,055; £39,370; £23,622; £17,716)

RPR

1 **Concrete Rose (USA)**[27] 4681 3-8-9 0 .... JulienRLeparoux 5 112+
(George R Arnold II, U.S.A) **30/100**[1]

2 *4¾* **Happen (USA)**[42] 4051 3-8-9 0 ....(t) WayneLordan 2 102+
(A P O'Brien, Ire) *s.i.s: trckd ldng trio on ins: swtchd rt and rdn ent st: r.o: no ch w wnr* **6/1**[3]

3 *nse* **Kelsey's Cross (USA)**[27] 3-8-9 0 ....(b) FlorentGeroux 4 102
(Patrick L Biancone, U.S.A) **215/10**

4 *hd* **Coral Beach (IRE)**[12] 5223 3-8-9 0 ....(t) JohnRVelazquez 3 101
(A P O'Brien, Ire) *trckd ldr: rdn over 2f out: kpt on same pce* **157/10**

5 ¾ **Olendon (FR)**[27] 4681 3-8-9 0 ....(b[1]) IradOrtizJr 1 100
(Chad C Brown, U.S.A) **23/5**[2]

1m 55.34s **5 Ran SP% 119.5**
Owner Ashbrook Farm & BBN Racing LLC **Bred** Ron Patterson **Trained** USA

5264 CHELMSFORD (A.W) (L-H)

Saturday, August 3

OFFICIAL GOING: Polytrack: standard
Wind: Almost nil Weather: Sunny spells

5646 BET TOTEPLACEPOT AT TOTESPORT.COM FILLIES' NOVICE STKS (PLUS 10 RACE) 6f (P)

1:40 (1:42) (Class 4) 2-Y-0 £6,469 (£1,925; £962; £481) Stalls Centre

Form RPR

1 **Dear Power (IRE)** 2-9-0 0 .... JackMitchell 7 83+
(Roger Varian) *chsd ldrs: shkn up to ld ins fnl f: r.o wl* **6/1**[3]

2203 2 *2¼* **Jm Jackson (IRE)**[15] 5125 2-9-0 87 .... FrannyNorton 3 76
(Mark Johnston) *led: edgd rt over 4f out: rdn and hdd ins fnl f: styd on same pce* **2/1**[2]

3 *1¼* **Jovial** 2-9-0 0 .... LouisSteward 8 72+
(Sir Michael Stoute) *trckd ldrs: stdd and lost pl over 4f out: racd wd: hdwy on outer over 2f out: shkn up and hung lft fr over 1f out: r.o (jockey said filly hung left-handed and ran green)* **10/11**[1]

5 4 *1¼* **Masaakin**[58] 3506 2-9-0 0 .... HollieDoyle 9 69
(Richard Hannon) *edgd rt s: chsd ldr 5f out: rdn and hung lft over 1f out: no ex ins fnl f (jockey said filly hung left-handed in the home straight)* **8/1**

6 5 *9* **Egotistic**[15] 5139 2-9-0 0 .... HayleyTurner 2 42
(David Simcock) *s.i.s: racd keenly and sn prom: lost pl over 4f out: shkn up and wknd over 1f out* **14/1**

6 6 *1¾* **Positive Light (IRE)**[11] 5265 2-9-0 0 .... LukeMorris 5 36
(Sir Mark Prescott Bt) *s.i.s: a in rr: shkn up over 2f out: wknd over 1f out* **33/1**

7 ½ **Wonderful Effort (IRE)** 2-9-0 0 .... FergusSweeney 6 35
(Ed Vaughan) *s.i.s: hld up: shkn up over 2f out: wknd over 1f out* **20/1**

0 8 *9* **Gelsmoor Bay**[12] 5243 2-9-0 0 .... KierenFox 1 8
(Derek Shaw) *sn chsng ldrs: rdn 1/2-way: wknd over 2f out* **200/1**

1m 12.81s (-0.89) **Going Correction** -0.15s/f (Stan) **8 Ran SP% 126.0**
Speed ratings (Par 93): **99,96,94,92,80 78,77,65**
CSF £20.34 TOTE £8.40: £2.10, £1.20, £1.10; EX 24.20 Trifecta £67.30.
Owner King Power Racing Co Ltd **Bred** Kildaragh Stud **Trained** Newmarket, Suffolk

FOCUS
An informative affair with newcomers finishing first and third.

5647 BET TOTEEXACTA AT TOTESPORT.COM H'CAP 6f (P)

2:10 (2:13) (Class 4) (0-80,83) 3-Y-0+
£7,148 (£2,127; £1,063; £531; £300; £300) Stalls Centre

Form RPR

2301 1 **Thegreatestshowman**[9] 5356 3-9-11 83 .... JackMitchell 1 90+
(Amy Murphy) *s.i.s: hld up: swtchd wd and hdwy over 1f out: rdn to ld ins fnl f: r.o* **5/2**[1]

0412 2 *nk* **Swiss Pride (IRE)**[2] 5581 3-8-13 74 .... FinleyMarsh(3) 6 78
(Richard Hughes) *hld up in tch: rdn and ev ch ins fnl f: r.o* **11/4**[2]

2024 3 *1* **Queen Of Burgundy**[14] 5191 3-9-4 76 .... LiamKeniry 2 77
(Christine Dunnett) *s.i.s: sn chsng ldrs: wnt 2nd over 3f out: rdn and ev ch ins fnl f: edgd lft: styd on same pce towards fin* **7/1**[3]

6325 4 ¾ **Something Lucky (IRE)**[10] 5298 7-9-2 70 ....(v) AlistairRawlinson 3 69
(Michael Appleby) *led early: plld hrd: sn stdd to trck ldrs: shkn up over 1f out: styd on* **10/1**

0-05 5 *nk* **Michaels Choice**[29] 4603 3-9-3 75 .... RyanTate 10 72
(William Jarvis) *s.i.s: rcvrd to ld over 5f out: rdn over 1f out: hdd ins fnl f: styd on same pce* **25/1**

-005 6 ½ **Kamikaze Lord (USA)**[19] 5000 3-9-3 75 ....(t[1]) LukeMorris 8 71
(John Butler) *edgd rt s: hld up: styd on u.p fr over 1f out: nt rch ldrs* **10/1**

0435 7 *1* **Leo Minor (USA)**[12] 5252 5-8-13 72 ....(p) DylanHogan(5) 5 66
(Robert Cowell) *hld up: hdwy u.p over 1f out: no ex wl ins fnl f* **12/1**

0006 8 *6* **Fares Kodiac (IRE)**[9] 5335 3-9-1 80 ....(t) StefanoCherchi(7) 7 53
(Marco Botti) *chsd ldr over 5f out tl over 3f out: rdn over 1f out: wknd fnl f* **14/1**

1m 12.42s (-1.28) **Going Correction** -0.15s/f (Stan)
WFA 3 from 4yo+ 4lb **8 Ran SP% 104.1**
Speed ratings (Par 105): **102,101,100,99,98 98,96,88**
CSF £7.84 CT £28.77 TOTE £2.70: £1.20, £1.20, £1.90; EX 7.00 Trifecta £21.30.
Owner Amy Murphy **Bred** Biddestone Stud Ltd **Trained** Newmarket, Suffolk
■ Cappananty Con and Consequences were withdrawn. Prices at time of withdrawal 16/1 & 8/1. Rule 4 applies to all bets - deduction 10p in the pound

The Form Book Flat 2019, Raceform Ltd, Newbury, RG14 5SJ

FOCUS
The market proved a good guide to this sprint handicap, which was run minus Consequences and Cappananty Con, who got upset in the stalls. It's been rated around the second and third.

5648 FULL WORKS FACILITIES MANAGEMENT H'CAP 1m 6f (P)
2:45 (2:46) (Class 6) (0-60,62) 3-Y-O

£3,428 (£1,020; £509; £300; £300; £300) **Stalls** Low

Form RPR

0-54 **1** **Mon Frere (IRE)**[17] 5053 3-9-12 **62**..........................(p[1]) LukeMorris 2 70+
(Sir Mark Prescott Bt) *a.p: swtchd rt over 8f out: chsd ldr over 6f out: led over 2f out: rdn over 1f out: styd on* **5/2**[1]

0315 **2** *1 ¾* **Trouble Shooter (IRE)**[19] 4998 3-8-12 **48**..................(v) RaulDaSilva 11 54
(Shaun Keightley) *s.i.s: hld up: hdwy over 2f out: rdn over 1f out: r.o to go 2nd wl ins fnl f: nt rch wnr* **6/1**

0004 **3** *2 ¾* **Antidote (IRE)**[19] 4998 3-9-3 **56**..........................(p[1]) FinleyMarsh(3) 5 58
(Richard Hughes) *led 1f: chsd ldr tl over 6f out: remained handy: rdn to chse wnr over 1f out: hung lft and styd on same pce ins fnl f* **8/1**

0-01 **4** *2 ½* **Celtic Classic (IRE)**[7] 5425 3-9-2 **52**..........................(b) JackMitchell 6 51
(Paul Cole) *hld up: pushed along and hdwy on outer over 7f out: led over 6f out: hdd over 2f out: wknd ins fnl f* **9/2**[2]

5645 **5** *4 ½* **Ignatius (IRE)**[23] 4834 3-9-4 **54**.................................. KierenFox 8 47
(John Best) *hld up: swtchd rt and hdwy over 1f out: nvr nrr* **5/1**[3]

3153 **6** *1* **Highway Robbery**[23] 4834 3-8-7 **48**..................(p) SophieRalston(5) 12 40
(Julia Feilden) *hld up on outer: racd keenly: outpcd over 6f out: hdwy over 2f out: rdn: hung lft and wknd over 1f out (vet reported gelding lost its left hind shoe)* **8/1**

0300 **7** *1 ½* **Spirit Of Nicobar**[29] 4594 3-9-2 **55**.......................... JoshuaBryan(3) 7 45
(Andrew Balding) *hld up: hdwy over 3f out: rdn: hung lft and wknd over 1f out* **20/1**

0340 **8** *12* **Kalaya (IRE)**[19] 4998 3-9-7 **57**.................................. HollieDoyle 9 31
(Archie Watson) *chsd ldrs: pushed along over 5f out: wknd wl over 1f out (jockey said filly was never travelling)* **16/1**

0300 **9** *4 ½* **Kostantina**[19] 4990 3-8-11 **47**.................................. RyanTate 4 15
(Olly Williams) *s.i.s: hdwy over 11f out: rdn and wknd over 2f out* **33/1**

-000 **10** *½* **Loving Pearl**[23] 4834 3-9-6 **56**.................................. FrannyNorton 10 24
(John Berry) *hld up: bhd fnl 6f* **25/1**

6006 **11** *shd* **Dinah Washington (IRE)**[18] 5028 3-8-13 **49**............(v[1]) HayleyTurner 1 17
(Michael Bell) *s.i.s: hld up: pushed along over 4f out: wknd over 3f out* **12/1**

006 **12** *8* **Cala Sveva (IRE)**[26] 4735 3-8-2 **45**..........................(p[1]) IsobelFrancis(7) 3
(Mark Usher) *led at stdy pce after 1f: hdd over 6f out: rdn and wknd over 2f out* **66/1**

-000 **13** *60* **Supreme Chance**[64] 3299 3-8-9 **45**..........................(p[1]) CharlieBennett 13
(Michael Blanshard) *hld up: bhd fnl 7f (trainer said gelding had a breathing problem)* **66/1**

3m 0.02s (-3.18) **Going Correction** -0.15s/f (Stan) 13 Ran SP% **128.0**
Speed ratings (Par 98): **103,102,100,99,96 95,95,88,85,85 85,80,46**
CSF £18.20 CT £112.85 TOTE £2.60: £1.40, £2.10, £2.50; EX 20.30 Trifecta £201.50.
Owner Elite Racing Club **Bred** Elite Racing Club **Trained** Newmarket, Suffolk

FOCUS
This was moderate and revolved around a potential improver from Sir Mark Prescott's yard. They went steadily early but things quickly developed when Celtic Classic went to the front early on the final circuit. A minor pb from the second, with the third among those helping to set the opening level.

5649 BET TOTEQUADPOT AT TOTESPORT.COM H'CAP 5f (P)
3:20 (3:23) (Class 3) (0-95,87) 3-Y-O+ £9,703 (£2,887; £1,443; £721) **Stalls** Low

Form RPR

3140 **1** **Zac Brown (IRE)**[22] 4880 8-8-12 **78**..........................(t) JoshuaBryan(3) 7 86
(Charlie Wallis) *led: wnt lft sn after s: rdn and hdd 1f out: rallied to ld post* **8/1**

-003 **2** *shd* **Prince Of Rome (IRE)**[37] 4294 3-9-3 **86**..............(t[1] w) FinleyMarsh(3) 1 93
(Richard Hughes) *chsd wnr tl over 3f out: remained handy: rdn to ld 1f out: edgd rt ins fnl f: hdd post* **6/4**[1]

0221 **3** *1 ¾* **Green Door (IRE)**[44] 4026 8-9-5 **82**..........................(v) LukeMorris 4 84
(Robert Cowell) *hmpd s: sn trcking ldrs: rdn and hung lft over 1f out: r.o* **10/1**

2-30 **4** *1 ¾* **Airshow**[77] 2824 4-9-10 **87**.................................. AlistairRawlinson 3 82
(Michael Appleby) *wnt rt s: hmpd sn after s: prom: chsd wnr over 3f out tl rdn and hung rt over 1f out: no ex ins fnl f* **11/4**[2]

1164 **5** *1 ¾* **Global Tango (IRE)**[78] 2791 4-9-10 **87**..........................(b) RyanTate 6 76
(Sir Mark Todd) *hmpd s: hld up: rdn 1/2-way: nt trble ldrs* **7/2**[3]

00- **6** *¾* **Isle Of Innisfree (USA)**[313] 7632 3-9-7 **87**.......................... JackMitchell 5 72
(Paul D'Arcy) *hmpd s: in rr and pushed along 1/2-way: n.d* **20/1**

59.26s (-0.94) **Going Correction** -0.15s/f (Stan)
WFA 3 from 4yo+ 3lb 6 Ran SP% **113.9**
Speed ratings (Par 107): **101,100,98,95,92 91**
CSF £21.05 TOTE £8.20: £3.50, £1.30; EX 24.30 Trifecta £91.40.
Owner Porterhouse Ltd J Goddard **Bred** Tally-Ho Stud **Trained** Ardleigh, Essex
■ Stewards' Enquiry : Joshua Bryan one-day ban: failed to ride to draw (Aug 17)
Finley Marsh two-day ban: misuse of the whip (Aug 17-18)

FOCUS
This lacked the depth you'd generally expect in sprint races at this level. The winner has been rated in line with his winter best.

5650 BET TOTETRIFECTA AT TOTESPORT.COM NOVICE STKS 7f (P)
3:55 (3:58) (Class 4) 3-Y-O+ £6,469 (£1,925; £962; £481) **Stalls** Low

Form RPR

21 **1** **Mutamaasik**[40] 4196 3-9-8 0.................................. JackMitchell 12 94+
(Roger Varian) *s.i.s and hmpd s: sn prom: jnd ldr over 5f out: rdn to ld over 1f out: styd on* **8/13**[1]

50 **2** *½* **Visionara**[36] 4341 3-8-11 0.................................. HollieDoyle 1 81
(Simon Crisford) *pushed along to ld: rdn and hdd over 1f out: styd on* **10/1**

4 **3** *½* **Motfael (IRE)**[59] 3463 3-9-2 0.................................. LukeMorris 9 85
(Owen Burrows) *chsd ldrs: rdn over 1f out: r.o* **7/1**[3]

4 *nk* **Reine De Vitesse (FR)**[233] 3-8-11 0.................................. HayleyTurner 5 79
(Jane Chapple-Hyam) *hld up: hdwy over 2f out: shkn up over 1f out: r.o u.p* **12/1**

4- **5** *¾* **Lady Bowthorpe**[317] 7471 3-8-11 0.................................. RyanTate 8 77+
(William Jarvis) *s.i.s: pushed along into mid-div: over 5f out: hung rt fr over 4f out: hdwy on outer over 2f out: styd on (jockey said filly hung right-handed)* **20/1**

6 *hd* **Mayne (IRE)** 3-8-13 0.................................. JoshuaBryan(3) 6 82
(Andrew Balding) *hld up in tch: rdn and swtchd rt over 1f out: styd on* **20/1**

3 **7** *1 ¼* **Zahee (IRE)**[21] 4927 4-9-8 0.................................. HectorCrouch 4 80
(Saeed bin Suroor) *chsd ldrs: rdn over 1f out: no ex ins fnl f (vet reported colt lost its left fore shoe)* **5/1**[2]

0 **8** *6* **Knightfall**[14] 5193 3-9-2 0.................................. FrannyNorton 13 62
(David Lanigan) *wnt lft s: sn prom: rdn and wknd over 1f out* **50/1**

9 *¾* **Breath Of Spring (IRE)** 3-8-13 0.................................. GabrieleMalune(3) 11 60
(Marco Botti) *hld up: rdn over 2f out: nvr on terms (jockey said gelding was never travelling)* **50/1**

10 *8* **Maqboola (USA)** 3-8-8 0.................................. FinleyMarsh(3) 7 33
(Richard Hughes) *s.s: outpcd (jockey said filly was slowly away)* **66/1**

11 *1 ¼* **Can I Kick It (IRE)** 3-8-11 0.................................. FergusSweeney 14 30
(Stuart Williams) *s.s: sn pushed along and a in rr* **100/1**

00 **12** *21* **Mazmerize**[102] 2023 3-9-2 0..........................(t[1]) LiamKeniry 2
(Christine Dunnett) *s.i.s: outpcd* **125/1**

1m 25.61s (-1.59) **Going Correction** -0.15s/f (Stan)
WFA 3 from 4yo 6lb 12 Ran SP% **124.6**
Speed ratings (Par 105): **103,102,101,101,100 100,99,92,91,82 80,56**
CSF £8.36 TOTE £1.30: £1.10, £2.90, £1.50; EX 10.60 Trifecta £52.30.
Owner Hamdan Al Maktoum **Bred** Shadwell Estate Company Limited **Trained** Newmarket, Suffolk

FOCUS
This looked a good opportunity for the favourite, despite his penalty. He got the job done but it was really hard work. It's been rated a bit positively for now.

5651 BET TOTESWINGER AT TOTESPORT.COM H'CAP 1m (P)
4:30 (4:34) (Class 5) (0-75,78) 3-Y-O+

£5,433 (£1,617; £808; £404; £300; £300) **Stalls** Low

Form RPR

4-56 **1** **Alma Linda**[25] 4768 3-9-0 **67**..........................(p[1]) LukeMorris 4 76+
(Sir Mark Prescott Bt) *sn pushed along to chse ldrs: rdn and hung lft fr over 1f out: styd on to ld wl ins fnl f* **7/4**[1]

1300 **2** *1 ¼* **Filles De Fleur**[24] 4789 3-9-4 **71**.................................. HollieDoyle 7 76
(George Scott) *hld up: hdwy on outer over 1f out: r.o to go 2nd towards fin: nt rch wnr (jockey said filly was outpaced in the early stages)* **33/1**

0406 **3** *½* **Glory Awaits (IRE)**[11] 5267 9-9-7 **72**..........................(b) DylanHogan(5) 10 77
(David Simcock) *hld up: hdwy u.p over 1f out: styd on to go 3rd nr fin* **20/1**

/003 **4** *½* **Lady Of Aran (IRE)**[30] 4552 4-9-12 **72**.................................. HayleyTurner 5 76
(Charlie Fellowes) *trckd ldrs: racd keenly: rdn to ld and hung lft ins fnl f: sn hdd: styd on same pce* **4/1**[2]

0652 **5** *1 ¾* **Philamundo (IRE)**[11] 5267 4-10-4 **78**..........................(b) LiamKeniry 8 78
(Richard Spencer) *stdd s: hld up: hdwy on outer over 1f out: sn rdn: edgd lft and no ex wl ins fnl f* **7/1**[3]

2-20 **6** *1 ¼* **Al Reeh (IRE)**[43] 4067 5-9-10 **73**..........................(p) GabrieleMalune(3) 6 70
(Marco Botti) *led: rdn and hdd over 1f out: no ex ins fnl f (jockey said gelding stopped quickly)* **7/1**[3]

0605 **7** *1 ¼* **Indian Sounds (IRE)**[11] 5270 3-9-3 **70**..........................(b[1]) FrannyNorton 12 63
(Mark Johnston) *sn chsng ldr: rdn to ld over 1f out: hdd & wknd ins fnl f* **12/1**

0006 **8** *1 ¼* **Love Your Work (IRE)**[11] 5270 3-9-7 **74**..........................(b) CharlieBennett 2 64
(Adam West) *s.s: outpcd: r.o ins fnl f: nvr nrr* **33/1**

5515 **9** *1* **Black Medick**[9] 5350 3-9-5 **72**.................................. LiamJones 3 60
(Laura Mongan) *s.i.s: sn pushed along: hdwy u.p over 1f out: hung lft and wknd ins fnl f (jockey said filly hung left handed)* **33/1**

2-45 **10** *1 ¼* **Camelot Rakti (IRE)**[45] 4007 3-9-10 **77**.................................. LouisSteward 1 62
(James Tate) *chsd ldrs: rdn over 2f out: wknd fnl f* **8/1**

153 **11** *1* **In The Cove (IRE)**[9] 5343 3-9-6 **73**.................................. FergusSweeney 9 56
(Richard Hannon) *mid-div: rdn over 2f out: wknd ins fnl f* **16/1**

1m 38.24s (-1.66) **Going Correction** -0.15s/f (Stan)
WFA 3 from 4yo+ 7lb 11 Ran SP% **119.6**
Speed ratings (Par 103): **102,100,100,99,98 96,95,94,93,92 91**
CSF £81.32 CT £886.93 TOTE £2.70: £1.20, £10.30, £5.40; EX 77.10 Trifecta £665.20.
Owner Miss K Rausing **Bred** Miss K Rausing **Trained** Newmarket, Suffolk

FOCUS
This ordinary handicap was won with some authority by a Sir Mark Prescott handicap debutante. The second has been rated in line with her Wolverhampton run.

5652 CHANDLER PAVING EXPERTS H'CAP (DIV I) 1m 2f (P)
5:05 (5:08) (Class 6) (0-55,57) 3-Y-O+

£3,428 (£1,020; £509; £300; £300; £300) **Stalls** Low

Form RPR

5000 **1** **Warning Light**[11] 5284 4-9-0 **46**..........................(t[1]) JosephineGordon 1 52
(Shaun Keightley) *mde all: rdn and hung rt fr over 1f out: styd on (jockey said filly hung right handed in the home straight)* **4/1**[2]

054 **2** *½* **Zappiness (USA)**[44] 4022 3-9-2 **56**.................................. JackMitchell 6 62
(Peter Chapple-Hyam) *chsd ldrs: rdn over 1f out: chsd wnr and edgd rt ins fnl f: styd on* **5/1**[3]

4253 **3** *shd* **Percy Toplis**[9] 5354 5-8-13 **45**..........................(b) LiamKeniry 5 50
(Christine Dunnett) *s.i.s: hld up: hdwy over 1f out: r.o wl* **10/1**

3530 **4** *2* **Be Thankful**[37] 4287 4-9-6 **57**.................................. PoppyBridgwater(5) 12 58
(Martin Keighley) *s.i.s: racd keenly and sn prom chsd wnr over 6f out: ev ch whn carried rt wl over 1f out: styd on same pce ins fnl f* **6/1**

-000 **5** *1 ¾* **London Pride**[24] 4794 3-9-1 **55**.................................. LukeMorris 8 54
(Jonathan Portman) *chsd wnr tl over 6f out: remained handy: rdn over 1f out: no ex ins fnl f* **16/1**

3600 **6** *¾* **Outlaw Torn (IRE)**[95] 2234 10-8-13 **45**..........................(e) PhilipPrince 9 41
(Richard Guest) *hld up: plld hrd: hdwy on outer over 5f out: rdn over 1f out: styd on same pce* **25/1**

0350 **7** *½* **Luxford**[25] 4753 5-9-2 **48**.................................. TomQueally 4 43
(Gary Moore) *hld up: hdwy over 1f out: sn rdn: no imp ins fnl f* **6/1**

0000 **8** *¾* **Hooriya**[45] 3989 3-8-10 **53**..........................(b) GabrieleMalune(3) 7 48
(Marco Botti) *hld up: rdn and nt clr run over 1f out: edgd lft ins fnl f: nt trble ldrs* **25/1**

4000 **9** *¾* **Irish Times**[33] 4460 4-9-2 **53**..........................(t[1]) DylanHogan(5) 2 46
(Henry Spiller) *trckd ldrs: rdn over 1f out: wknd fnl f* **10/1**

53 **10** *¾* **Bidding War**[23] 4831 4-9-3 **52**.................................. JoshuaBryan(3) 3 43
(Michael Appleby) *hld up: rdn over 1f out: wknd ins fnl f* **5/2**[1]

2m 7.81s (-0.79) **Going Correction** -0.15s/f (Stan)
WFA 3 from 4yo+ 8lb 10 Ran SP% **125.6**
Speed ratings (Par 101): **97,96,96,94,93 92,92,91,91,90**
CSF £26.58 CT £192.56 TOTE £4.60: £1.50, £2.00, £3.30; EX 28.70 Trifecta £245.20.
Owner Simon Lockyer & Tim Clarke **Bred** Mr & Mrs J Davis & P Mitchell B'Stock **Trained** Newmarket, Suffolk
■ Stewards' Enquiry : Poppy Bridgwater two-day ban: misuse of the whip (Aug 17-18)

FOCUS
The first division of this low grade handicap was dominated by Warning Light in his first-time cheekpieces.

5653 CHANDLER PAVING EXPERTS H'CAP (DIV II) 1m 2f (P)
5:40 (5:42) (Class 6) (0-55,56) 3-Y-O+
£3,428 (£1,020; £509; £300; £300; £300) Stalls Low

Form RPR

000 1 **Muraaqeb**[8] 5378 5-9-2 **50**.....(p) JoshuaBryan[(3)] 4 55
(Milton Bradley) *hld up: hdwy over 2f out: swtchd rt over 1f out: rdn to ld 1f out: all out* **10/1**

5062 2 *hd* **Chakrii (IRE)**[17] 5054 3-8-10 **49**.....(p) HayleyTurner 1 55
(Henry Spiller) *chsd ldrs: rdn and ev ch fnl f: styd on* **7/2**[1]

0016 3 *1 ¼* **Bader**[10] 5293 3-9-2 **55**.....(b) FergusSweeney 5 58
(Richard Hannon) *prom: rdn and hung lft over 2f out: swtchd rt ins fnl f: styd on* **10/1**

4000 4 *½* **Rainbow Jazz (IRE)**[2] 5570 4-9-7 **52**.....(b) CharlieBennett 6 53
(Adam West) *led: rdn and hdd 1f out: styd on same pce* **10/1**

0022 5 *2 ¼* **Hidden Dream (IRE)**[9] 5354 4-9-2 **47**.....(p) LiamKeniry 8 44
(Christine Dunnett) *hld up: hdwy u.p over 1f out: nt trble ldrs* **8/1**

0005 6 *1* **Fountain Of Life**[18] 5031 3-8-11 **55**..... DylanHogan[(5)] 10 51
(Philip McBride) *s.i.s: hdwy into mid-div: over 7f out: rdn over 2f out: hung lft over 1f out: styd on same pce fnl f* **8/1**

0526 7 *1* **Tilsworth Lukey**[42] 4111 6-9-3 **48**..... FrannyNorton 3 41
(J R Jenkins) *hld up: styd on fr over 1f out: nt trble ldrs* **9/2**[2]

0000 8 *shd* **Out Of The Ashes**[29] 4589 6-9-0 **45**.....(t) RyanTate 9 38
(Mohamed Moubarak) *hld up: effrt on outer over 1f out: n.d* **25/1**

3423 9 *3* **Red Archangel (IRE)**[17] 5049 3-9-3 **56**.....(p) JosephineGordon 11 44
(Richard Spencer) *s.i.s: hld up: shkn up on outer and edgd lft over 1f out: nvr on terms (jockey said filly ran too free)* **6/1**[3]

0230 10 *2 ¾* **Foxrush Take Time (FR)**[7] 5435 4-9-0 **45**.....(e) PhilipPrince 12 27
(Richard Guest) *sn prom: rdn over 2f out: wknd over 1f out* **8/1**

0000 11 *3 ½* **Squire**[12] 5239 8-9-7 **55**.....(tp) JaneElliott[(3)] 7 30
(Marjorie Fife) *chsd ldr after 1f tl rdn over 1f out: wknd fnl f* **25/1**

00-6 12 *4 ½* **Woofie (IRE)**[94] 2283 7-9-0 **45**..... LiamJones 2 12
(Laura Mongan) *s.i.s: pushed along into mid-div: over 7f out: rdn over 3f out: wknd over 2f out* **20/1**

2m 6.17s (-2.43) **Going Correction** -0.15s/f (Stan)
WFA 3 from 4yo+ 8lb 12 Ran SP% **127.8**
Speed ratings (Par 101): **103,102,101,101,99 98,98,97,95,93 90,86**
CSF £47.43 CT £376.45 TOTE £10.90: £3.40, £1.80, £3.20; EX 136.90 Trifecta £1364.30.
Owner E A Hayward **Bred** Peter Winkworth **Trained** Sedbury, Gloucs

FOCUS
This looked marginally the stronger of the two divisions and the winning time was 1.64sec quicker. Ordinary, straightforward form rated around the first three, with the winner to his recent best.
T/Plt: £7.80 to a £1 stake. Pool: £25,424.33 - 3,230.88 winning units T/Qpdt: £8.80 to a £1 stake. Pool: £1,978.77 - 222.93 winning units **Colin Roberts**

5330 DONCASTER (L-H)
Saturday, August 3

OFFICIAL GOING: Soft (good to soft in places; 6.9) changing to good to soft after race 2 (2.55)
Wind: light breeze, across Weather: warm and sunny, gradually clouding over

5654 ERIC ROBERTS MEMORIAL H'CAP 1m 3f 197y
2:20 (2:20) (Class 4) (0-80,80) 3-Y-O
£5,207 (£1,549; £774; £387; £300; £300) Stalls High

Form RPR

-061 1 **Baasem (USA)**[24] 4795 3-9-7 **80**..... DaneO'Neill 6 98
(Owen Burrows) *chsd ldrs: hdwy into 6 l 2nd 3f out: eased into ld over 2f out: sn clr: drvn in 8 l ld 1f out: plld further clr fnl f: eased nr fin: easily* **11/4**[1]

2142 2 *14* **Withoutdestination**[44] 4024 3-9-2 **78**.....(b) AaronJones[(3)] 1 74
(Marco Botti) *hld up in rr: rdn 4f out: hdwy into 3rd over 1f out: styd on into 2nd fnl f* **14/1**

542 3 *1 ¾* **Skerryvore**[37] 4304 3-9-1 **74**..... DanielMuscutt 5 67
(James Fanshawe) *hld up: pushed along and effrt over 3f out: rdn over 2f out: wnt into 8 l 2nd 1 1/2f out: no ex and lost 2nd ins fnl f* **11/4**[1]

0211 4 *3 ¾* **Langholm (IRE)**[18] 5023 3-8-4 **63**.....(t) NathanEvans 4 50
(Declan Carroll) *led: 12 l clr 1/2-way: 6 l ld 3f out: sn drvn: hdd over 2f out: wknd (jockey said gelding ran too freely)* **11/2**[3]

6423 5 *3 ¼* **Bullion Boss (IRE)**[14] 5175 3-8-13 **72**.....(p) KevinStott 3 54
(Michael Dods) *chsd clr ldr: 12 l 2nd 1/2-way: pushed along 4f out: drvn and dropped to 3rd 3f out: sn rdn and wknd (trainer could offer no explanation for the gelding's performance)* **3/1**[2]

6043 6 *23* **Star Talent (IRE)**[24] 4779 3-8-8 **67**..... KieranO'Neill 2 12
(Gay Kelleway) *t.k.h: hld up: pushed along 5f out: rdn and dropped to last over 3f out: sn lost tch* **8/1**

2m 36.57s (-0.03) **Going Correction** +0.225s/f (Good) 6 Ran SP% **111.5**
Speed ratings (Par 102): **109,99,98,96,93 78**
CSF £37.23 TOTE £3.20: £1.60, £4.30; EX 34.80 Trifecta £119.50.
Owner Hamdan Al Maktoum **Bred** Shadwell Farm LLC **Trained** Lambourn, Berks
■ Stewards' Enquiry : Dane O'Neill two-day ban: misuse of the whip (Aug 17-18)

FOCUS
Add 18yds. Drying ground but still very much on the slow side. Sensibly, the main body of runners ignored the tearaway leader who went off too hard in the conditions and was already on the retreat early in the straight. Baasem was the only one on the bridle three out and he cruised clear to win as he liked. It's hard to pin down the level.

5655 THOMPSONS ACTING FOR UNISON (EBF) MAIDEN AUCTION STKS (PLUS 10 RACE) 7f 6y
2:55 (2:56) (Class 4) 2-Y-O £4,463 (£1,328; £663; £331) Stalls High

Form RPR

1 **Wyclif** 2-9-2 0..... AdamKirby 9 81+
(Ralph Beckett) *slowly away: sn rcvrd to r in mid-div: hdwy over 2f out: led 2f out: drvn in 2 l ld 1f out: pushed out fnl f: comf* **7/4**[1]

2 *3 ¼* **Sea Trout Reach (IRE)** 2-9-5 0..... DanielMuscutt 2 76
(William Haggas) *mid-div: drvn and hdwy 2f out: wnt into 2 l 2nd 1f out: kpt on fnl f* **11/4**[2]

00 3 *2* **Genever Dragon (IRE)**[14] 5177 2-9-5 0..... DavidProbert 10 71
(Tom Dascombe) *prom: pushed along and ev ch 2f out: rdn in 3rd over 1f out: no ex fnl f* **13/2**[3]

4 *2 ¼* **Philosophical** 2-9-0 0..... KevinStott 6 60+
(Jedd O'Keeffe) *hld up: drvn 2f out: hdwy over 1f out: r.o into 4th ins fnl f* **16/1**

53 5 *¾* **Speed Dating (FR)**[50] 3812 2-9-2 0..... AndrewElliott 3 61
(Derek Shaw) *led: drvn and hdd 2f out: sn rdn and wknd* **12/1**

6 *nk* **Glen Esk** 2-8-12 0..... GeorgeWood 7 56
(Chris Wall) *mid-div: pushed along over 2f out: rdn over 1f out: one pce fnl f* **40/1**

0 7 *2* **Two Sox**[14] 5177 2-8-12 0..... DuranFentiman 4 51
(Tim Easterby) *chsd ldrs: drvn 2f out: no ex fr over 1f out* **16/1**

8 *1* **Vitellius** 2-8-12 0..... NickyMackay 1 48
(Stuart Williams) *prom: drvn 2f out: wknd over 1f out* **28/1**

60 9 *½* **Grimbold**[13] 5212 2-8-12 0.....(b[1]) RhonaPindar[(7)] 8 54
(K R Burke) *chsd ldr: drvn and lost pl 3f out: wknd* **50/1**

5 10 *1* **Thunder King (FR)**[42] 4106 2-9-5 0..... DaneO'Neill 5 52
(Amy Murphy) *mid-div: drvn and lost pl over 2f out: sn rdn and wknd* **17/2**

11 *2* **Duke Of Condicote** 2-9-2 0..... CameronNoble[(3)] 12 47
(Alan King) *bhd: drvn 3f out: no imp* **12/1**

0 12 *8* **Full Strength**[37] 4289 2-9-2 0..... KieranO'Neill 11 24
(Ivan Furtado) *mid-div: drvn over 3f out: sn rdn and dropped away* **40/1**

50 13 *19* **Saoirse's Gift (IRE)**[36] 4317 2-9-0 0..... RobertWinston 13
(Tim Easterby) *a bhd: lost tch over 2f out: sn eased* **50/1**

1m 28.81s (2.41) **Going Correction** +0.225s/f (Good) 13 Ran SP% **126.3**
Speed ratings (Par 96): **95,91,89,86,85 85,82,81,81,80 77,68,46**
CSF £6.49 TOTE £2.40: £1.40, £1.50, £2.30; EX 8.50 Trifecta £33.40.
Owner Quantum Leap Racing Ix **Bred** Miss K Rausing & Bba 2010 Ltd **Trained** Kimpton, Hants
■ Stewards' Enquiry : Kevin Stott caution: careless riding

FOCUS
The market warned that a big run was in the offing from newcomer Wyclif and that's exactly how it transpired. He powered clear of a horse who holds a Derby entry and this could be quite useful form. The runners with previous experience suggest this is a sensible opening level.

5656 UNISON SUPPORTING YOUR COMMUNITY NOVICE STKS 1m 2f 43y
3:30 (3:31) (Class 5) 3-Y-O+ £3,428 (£1,020; £509; £254) Stalls High

Form RPR

21 1 **First In Line**[60] 3445 3-9-7 0..... KieranO'Neill 1 97+
(John Gosden) *mde all: drvn 2f out: 2 l ld 1f out: drew clr fnl f: comf* **8/11**[1]

032- 2 *6* **Wise Ruler**[282] 8576 3-8-11 80..... CameronNoble[(3)] 7 78
(Simon Crisford) *trckd ldrs: drvn in 3rd 2f out: rdn into 2nd over 1f out: kpt on fnl f: no ch w wnr* **7/2**[3]

22 3 *3 ½* **Jomrok**[28] 4641 3-8-9 0.....(h[1]) DaneO'Neill 11 68
(Owen Burrows) *prom: drvn in 2nd 2f out: rdn and dropped to 3rd over 1f out: no ex fnl f* **3/1**[2]

4 *1* **Gabrials Boy** 3-8-11 0..... ConnorMurtagh[(3)] 13 69
(Richard Fahey) *chsd ldrs: pushed along 2f out: drvn into 4th over 1f out: kpt on fnl f* **25/1**

0-4 5 *2 ¼* **Dreams And Visions (IRE)**[190] 405 3-8-8 ow1..... JoshQuinn[(7)] 4 66
(Michael Easterby) *chsd ldrs: drvn 2f out: no ex fr over 1f out* **40/1**

46 6 *½* **Red Derek**[15] 5128 3-9-0 0..... AndrewElliott 10 64
(Lisa Williamson) *hld up: pushed along 4f out: drvn and mod hdwy over 2f out: rdn over 1f out: kpt on fnl f* **100/1**

05 7 *2* **Hermosura**[12] 5254 3-8-9 0..... DavidProbert 3 55
(Ralph Beckett) *hld up: drvn 2f out: rdn over 1f out: no imp* **18/1**

8 *1 ½* **Capla Huntress** 3-8-9 0..... GeorgeWood 2 52
(Chris Wall) *mid-div: drvn over 2f out: sn wknd* **66/1**

9 *1 ¾* **Double Esprit** 3-9-0 0..... KevinStott 6 53
(Donald McCain) *bhd: drvn 3f out: rdn over 1f out: no imp* **33/1**

04 10 *2 ¾* **Red Secret (CAN)**[16] 5103 3-9-0 0..... DanielMuscutt 12 48
(Ed Dunlop) *hld up: pushed along 3f out: sn drvn and wknd* **25/1**

5/5 11 *10* **Ningaloo (GER)**[26] 4732 5-9-8 0..... RobbieDowney 5 27
(Rebecca Bastiman) *hld up: pushed along 3f out: wknd and dropped away over 2f out* **80/1**

12 *3 ¾* **Honey Lane (IRE)** 3-8-9 0..... AdrianMcCarthy 8 15
(William Jarvis) *hld up: drvn and lost tch 2f out* **33/1**

05 13 *17* **Ezzrah**[28] 4636 3-9-0 0..... RobertWinston 9
(Mark Walford) *a bhd: rdn and lost tch over 2f out* **66/1**

2m 13.3s (1.00) **Going Correction** +0.225s/f (Good)
WFA 3 from 5yo 8lb 13 Ran SP% **131.6**
Speed ratings (Par 103): **105,100,97,96,94 94,92,91,90,88 80,77,63**
CSF £3.89 TOTE £1.50: £1.10, £1.50, £1.20; EX 4.80 Trifecta £7.10.
Owner A E Oppenheimer **Bred** Hascombe And Valiant Studs **Trained** Newmarket, Suffolk

FOCUS
Add 18yds. An impressive performance from the penalised First In Line who handed out a thrashing to two rivals that had shown pretty useful form. A clear pb from the winner, with the second rated to form and the fifth rated in line with his AW form in January.

5657 UNISON CAMPAIGNING FOR PUBLIC SERVICES H'CAP 1m 2f 43y
4:05 (4:06) (Class 2) (0-105,104) 3-Y-O+
£12,450 (£3,728; £1,864; £932; £466; £234) Stalls High

Form RPR

22-0 1 **Spanish Archer (FR)**[44] 4021 4-9-4 **94**.....(h) DanielMuscutt 10 103
(James Fanshawe) *chsd ldrs: drvn to chal 2f out: rdn over 1f out: r.o wl fnl f: led last few strides* **10/1**

0501 2 *hd* **Everything For You (IRE)**[14] 5199 5-9-2 **92**.....(p) KevinStott 6 100
(Kevin Ryan) *prom: pushed along and cl up over 2f out: sn rdn: led ent fnl f: hdd last few strides* **7/1**

1500 3 *2* **Mordin (IRE)**[21] 4935 5-10-0 **104**.....(p) DavidProbert 4 108
(Simon Crisford) *mid-div: hdwy over 2f out: rdn in cl 4th over 1f out: kpt on into 3rd fnl f but nt pce of first two* **5/1**[3]

2342 4 *1* **Desert Fire (IRE)**[45] 3992 4-9-12 **102**.....(v) AdamKirby 1 104
(Saeed bin Suroor) *chsd ldrs: pushed into ld over 2f out: rdn over 1f out: hdd ent fnl f: no ex* **2/1**[1]

1-00 5 *1 ½* **Francis Xavier (IRE)**[21] 4935 5-9-5 **95**..... RobertWinston 7 94
(Kevin Frost) *hld up: drvn and hdwy over 2f out: sn rdn: one pce fnl f* **10/1**

2-03 6 *4* **Buzz (FR)**[49] 3864 5-9-8 **98**..... DaneO'Neill 8 90
(Hughie Morrison) *hld up: pushed along in bhd ldrs 2f out: rdn and wknd over 1f out* **3/1**[2]

40/5 7 *1* **Tamleek (USA)**[125] 1460 5-9-6 **96**..... RobbieDowney 9 85
(David O'Meara) *hld up: drvn 2f out: mod late hdwy* **33/1**

3-05 8 *nk* **Awake My Soul (IRE)**[52] 3726 10-9-3 **93** ow1..... KieranO'Neill 3 81
(Tom Tate) *t.k.h: led: drvn and hdd over 2f out: sn wknd (jockey said gelding ran too freely)* **20/1**

4110 9 *1 ½* **Mulligatawny (IRE)**[44] 4035 6-8-5 **88**.....(p) RhonaPindar[(7)] 2 73
(Roger Fell) *mid-div: tk clsr order 4f out: pushed along 3f out: sn drvn and wknd* **25/1**

011/ **10** *11* **Muraabit**[1051] 6549 7-9-2 **92**.. DuranFentiman 5 55
(Tim Easterby) *hld up: drvn and wknd 3f out* **33/1**

4500 **11** *16* **Cohesion**[14] 5199 6-8-13 **89**.. NickyMackay 13 20
(David Bridgwater) *in rr: pushed along 4f out: sn lost tch* **50/1**

P000 **P** **Shabeeb (USA)**[7] 5443 6-8-8 **87**.. CameronNoble(3) 11
(Ian Williams) *slowly away: bhd: drvn and lost tch 3f out: t.o whn p.u over 2f out: bled fr nose (vet reported gelding bled from the nose)* **50/1**

2m 12.56s (0.26) **Going Correction** +0.225s/f (Good) 12 Ran SP% **124.1**
Speed ratings (Par 109): **108,107,106,105,104 101,100,100,98,90 77,**
CSF £76.20 CT £401.63 TOTE £10.90: £2.90, £2.10, £2.00; EX 70.20 Trifecta £234.70.
Owner Fred Archer Racing - Iroquois **Bred** Marquise Soledad De Moratalla **Trained** Newmarket, Suffolk

FOCUS
Add 18yds. A big field handicap but the gallop looked steady and the first four home all raced near the pace. The winner was one of the least exposed runners in the field and it was some effort from him to tough this out from some gnarled handicappers. The second is the key to the form as he's been rated as running a small pb for now. The third has been rated close to form, with the fourth a bit below his latest.

5658 UNISON DEFENDING YOUR NHS CONDITIONS STKS 6f 2y
4:40 (4:40) (Class 3) 3-Y-O+ **£9,337** (£2,796; £1,398; £699) **Stalls** High

Form RPR

101- **1** **Tabdeed**[302] 7950 4-9-7 103.. DaneO'Neill 2 109+
(Owen Burrows) *t.k.h: trckd ldr: pushed along and hdwy to ld over 1f out: sn clr: pushed out fnl f: comf* **1/1**[1]

01-6 **2** *2 1/2* **Bernardo O'Reilly**[56] 3589 5-9-2 90.. AdamKirby 4 96
(Richard Spencer) *hld up in last: pushed along 2f out: drvn into 2nd ent fnl f: kpt on but no imp on wnr* **15/2**[3]

-012 **3** *4 1/2* **Heath Charnock**[28] 4638 3-8-12 86.. KieranO'Neill 1 81
(Michael Dods) *led: drvn 2f out: rdn and hdd over 1f out: wknd fnl f* **12/1**

-126 **4** *5* **Oxted**[14] 5184 3-8-12 105.. DavidProbert 3 73
(Roger Teal) *prom: drvn and lost pl 1 1/2f out: wkng whn hmpd over 1f out: sn eased* **6/4**[2]

1m 14.43s (1.73) **Going Correction** +0.225s/f (Good)
WFA 3 from 4yo+ 4lb 4 Ran SP% **109.5**
Speed ratings (Par 107): **97,93,87,81**
CSF £8.42 TOTE £1.70; EX 8.10 Trifecta £14.30.
Owner Hamdan Al Maktoum **Bred** Red House Stud & Ketton Ashwell Ltd **Trained** Lambourn, Berks
■ Stewards' Enquiry : Dane O'Neill three-day ban: careless riding (Aug 19,20,24)

FOCUS
A taking performance from Tabdeed who took this field apart despite having his first run of the season but the disappointing effort from market rival Oxted gives the form a shakey look. The winner didn't need to run to his best, while the second has been rated to form.

5659 UNISON AND LV LIVERPOOL VICTORIA CAR INSURANCE FILLIES' H'CAP 6f 2y
5:15 (5:15) (Class 5) (0-70,70) 3-Y-O+
£3,428 (£1,020; £509; £300; £300; £300) **Stalls** High

Form RPR

5624 **1** **Dubai Elegance**[3] 5558 5-8-4 **51** oh5..(p) NoelGarbutt(3) 7 58
(Derek Shaw) *hld up: pushed along and hdwy over 1f out: rdn fnl f: r.o wl to ld 100yds out: sn clr* **20/1**

324 **2** *1 1/2* **Springwood Drive**[17] 5057 3-9-0 **62**.. DuranFentiman 4 63
(Tim Easterby) *chsd ldrs: drvn 2f out: cl up and rdn over 1f out: kpt on fnl f: tk 2nd nr fin* **16/1**

-335 **3** *nk* **Maid Of Spirit (IRE)**[59] 3470 4-9-12 **70**.. AdamKirby 2 71
(Clive Cox) *led: rdn in narrow ld over 1f out: hdd 100yds out: no ex and lost 2nd nr fin* **9/2**[2]

5-21 **4** *3/4* **Orange Blossom**[145] 1139 3-9-8 **70**.. BarryMcHugh 1 68
(Richard Fahey) *prom: rdn in cl 2nd over 1f out: wknd fnl f* **17/2**[3]

0041 **5** *hd* **Fumbo Jumbo (IRE)**[8] 5392 6-9-6 **64**.. DavidProbert 9 62
(Rebecca Bastiman) *hld up: pushed along 2f out: rdn over 1f out: kpt on fnl f* **10/1**

2036 **6** *1* **Santafiora**[8] 5392 5-8-11 **55**.. KieranO'Neill 10 50
(Julie Camacho) *slowly away: bhd: pushed along and hdwy 2f out: rdn over 1f out: one pce fnl f* **14/1**

-001 **7** *1/2* **Amelia R (IRE)**[15] 5147 3-8-13 **61**.. DaneO'Neill 8 53
(Ray Craggs) *prom: drvn 2f out: rdn and wknd over 1f out* **9/2**[2]

4304 **8** *nk* **Senorita Grande (IRE)**[36] 4328 3-8-9 **57**..(v) KevinStott 3 48
(John Quinn) *chsd ldrs: drvn and lost pl 2f out: rdn and wknd 1f out* **10/1**

4011 **9** *3 3/4* **Aperitif**[14] 5181 3-9-3 **68**.. CameronNoble(3) 5 47
(Michael Bell) *hld up: drvn over 2f out: sn rdn and wknd (trainer's rep could offer no explanation for the performance shown)* **2/1**[1]

4340 **10** *3 3/4* **Olivia R (IRE)**[12] 5238 3-9-0 **62**.. DanielMuscutt 6 29
(David Barron) *hld up: drvn and dropped to last 2f out: sn lost tch* **12/1**

1m 13.68s (0.98) **Going Correction** +0.225s/f (Good)
WFA 3 from 4yo+ 4lb 10 Ran SP% **123.4**
Speed ratings (Par 100): **102,100,99,98,98 97,96,95,90,85**
CSF £317.34 CT £1755.78 TOTE £27.90: £5.90, £3.60, £2.00; EX 366.20 Trifecta £1463.50.
Owner Million Dreams Racing 1 **Bred** Glebe Stud & J F Dean **Trained** Sproxton, Leics

FOCUS
A few lightly-raced 3yos in here but the winner was an exposed mare racing from 5lb out of the handicap, suggesting the form isn't up to much. It's been rated a bit cautiously, with the second in line with the better view of her form and the third to her latest.

5660 CLIFF WILLIAMS MEMORIAL H'CAP 5f 3y
5:45 (5:46) (Class 5) (0-75,72) 3-Y-O
£3,428 (£1,020; £509; £300; £300; £300) **Stalls** High

Form RPR

154 **1** **Melrose Way**[42] 4129 3-9-1 **66**.. KieranO'Neill 1 72
(Paul Midgley) *chsd ldr: rdn into cl 2nd 1f out: persistent chal fnl f: r.o wl to ld last two strides* **7/1**

0426 **2** *nk* **Vee Man Ten**[29] 4604 3-9-7 **72**..(p[1]) AdamKirby 2 77
(Ivan Furtado) *led: rdn in narrow ld 1f out: strly pressed fnl f: kpt on wl: hdd last two strides* **5/2**[2]

1244 **3** *1/2* **Fairy Stories**[15] 5123 3-8-11 **65**.. ConnorMurtagh(3) 4 68
(Richard Fahey) *dwlt: bhd: hdwy 2f out: drvn in 3rd 1f out: rdn fnl f: kpt on (jockey said filly hung right)* **9/4**[1]

2020 **4** *1* **Scale Force**[36] 4343 3-9-4 **69**..(v) GeorgeWood 5 69
(Gay Kelleway) *hld up: drvn 2f out: rdn and hdwy 1f out: r.o wl fnl f: nvr nrr* **12/1**

51 **5** *2 1/4* **Good Answer**[49] 3836 3-9-7 **72**.. DaneO'Neill 6 65
(Robert Cowell) *hld up: drvn 2f out: sn rdn and wknd* **7/1**

1504 **6** *2 1/2* **Frosted Lass**[12] 5236 3-8-5 **56**.. NickyMackay 3 41
(David Barron) *chsd ldr: drvn and lost pl 2f out: sn rdn and wknd* **8/1**

5213 **7** *6* **Timetodock**[10] 5298 3-9-7 **72**..(b) DuranFentiman 7 38
(Tim Easterby) *hld up: rdn 2f out: sn wknd and dropped away* **6/1**[3]

1m 0.65s (1.05) **Going Correction** +0.225s/f (Good) 7 Ran SP% **117.4**
Speed ratings (Par 100): **100,99,98,97,93 89,79**
CSF £25.94 TOTE £8.00: £3.70, £2.10; EX 36.30 Trifecta £89.70.
Owner David W Armstrong **Bred** Highfield Farm Llp **Trained** Westow, N Yorks

FOCUS
Just an ordinary little contest with nothing rated above 72, but the winner was making her handicap debut. The second has been rated to form, and the third to her best.
T/Plt: £165.10 to a £1 stake. Pool: £55,950.58 - 247.25 winning units T/Qpdt: £46.00 to a £1 stake. Pool: £4,126.47 - 66.26 winning units **Keith McHugh**

5608 GOODWOOD (R-H)
Saturday, August 3

OFFICIAL GOING: Good to firm (good in places; watered; 8.2)
Wind: light, half behind Weather: fine and warm

5661 QATAR STEWARDS' SPRINT H'CAP (CONSOLATION RACE FOR THE STEWARDS' CUP) 6f
1:50 (1:52) (Class 2) 3-Y-O+
£46,687 (£13,980; £6,990; £3,495; £1,747; £877) **Stalls** High

Form RPR

6032 **1** **Poyle Vinnie**[4] 5524 9-9-5 **86**..(p) JamesSullivan 1 97
(Ruth Carr) *racd far side: hld up: hdwy over 2f out: qckned up wl whn asked ent fnl f: drifting lft but led fnl 100yds: r.o* **20/1**

0030 **2** *nk* **Venturous (IRE)**[7] 5420 6-9-5 **86**.. HarryBentley 4 96
(David Barron) *racd far side: travelled wl in midfield: smooth hdwy over 2f out: rdn to ld ins fnl f: hdd fnl 100yds: kpt on: hld cl home* **16/1**

1530 **3** *1 3/4* **Tommy G**[19] 4980 6-8-11 **78**.. SilvestreDeSousa 20 82
(Jim Goldie) *racd stands' side: trckd ldrs: rdn to ld over 1f out: drifting rt whn hdd ins fnl f: kpt on but no ex* **8/1**[2]

6253 **4** *3/4* **Primo's Comet**[27] 4691 4-8-8 **75**.. DavidEgan 24 77
(Jim Goldie) *mid-div on stands' side: rdn and hdwy over 1f out: drifting rt fnl f: wnt 4th fnl 140yds: kpt on but nt pce to threaten* **50/1**

3030 **5** *1/2* **Paddy Power (IRE)**[7] 5454 6-9-1 **82**.. JoeFanning 22 82
(Richard Fahey) *racd stands' side: hld up: hdwy over 1f out: swtchd rt ent fnl f: r.o but nt pce to get on terms* **25/1**

6010 **6** *2* **Count Otto (IRE)**[4] 5524 4-9-9 **90** 6ex..(h) PatDobbs 11 84
(Amanda Perrett) *racd stands' side: hld up: hdwy whn swtchd to centre over 2f out: nt clrest of runs jst over 1f out: kpt on same pce fnl f* **20/1**

041 **7** *hd* **Secretinthepark**[22] 4894 9-8-12 **79** 6ex..(b) RichardKingscote 21 72
(Michael Mullineaux) *prom on stands' side: led over 2f out: rdn and hdd over 1f out: kpt on same pce fnl f* **50/1**

0021 **8** *2* **Boy In The Bar**[42] 4103 8-9-2 **83**..(v) RyanMoore 23 70
(Ian Williams) *racd stands' side: trckd ldrs: rdn and hld whn hmpd over 1f out: kpt on ins fnl f* **12/1**

6465 **9** *nse* **Lightning Charlie**[22] 4866 7-8-11 **78**.. JasonWatson 7 64
(Amanda Perrett) *racd stands' side: mid-div: effrt over 1f out: kpt on same pce fnl f* **25/1**

0210 **10** *hd* **Powerallied (IRE)**[7] 5420 6-9-6 **87** 6ex.. JackGarritty 3 73
(Richard Fahey) *racd far side: trckd ldr: rdn and ev ch 2f out: one pce fnl f* **66/1**

122 **11** *hd* **Puds**[57] 3544 4-9-9 **90**.. ShaneKelly 6 75
(Richard Hughes) *racd keenly in mid-div on stands' side: hdwy 2f out: sn rdn: nt quite pce to chal: no ex fnl 120yds* **7/1**[1]

6-10 **12** *nk* **Get The Rhythm**[2] 5589 3-8-11 **82**.. PJMcDonald 5 65
(Richard Fahey) *prom on far side: rdn and ev ch over 1f out: wknd fnl f* **16/1**

4003 **13** *3/4* **Mokaatil**[4] 5530 4-8-12 **86**.. AngusVilliers(7) 12 68
(Ian Williams) *racd stands' side: mid-div: struggling to hold pce 3f out: no threat but kpt on fnl f wout having the best of runs* **25/1**

2020 **14** *hd* **Dark Shot**[4] 5524 6-9-7 **88**..(p) BenCurtis 2 69
(Scott Dixon) *mid-div on far side: hdwy over 2f out: sn rdn to chse ldrs: wknd fnl f* **14/1**

6550 **15** *1/2* **Brian The Snail (IRE)**[7] 5454 5-9-9 **90**.. TonyHamilton 16 70+
(Richard Fahey) *racd stands' side: mid-div: rdn over 2f out: nt clr run over 1f out: kpt on but nt pce to get involved* **20/1**

5624 **16** *1 1/4* **King Robert**[35] 4364 6-8-5 **77**.. WilliamCarver(5) 10 53
(Charlie Wallis) *trckd ldrs on stands' side: rdn over 2f out: wknd fnl f* **25/1**

4000 **17** *nse* **Blue De Vega (GER)**[5] 5504 6-9-4 **90**..(tp) CierenFallon(5) 13 65+
(Robert Cowell) *hld up on stands' side: pushed along and stl towards rr whn nt clr run over 1f out: nvr able to get involved (jockey said gelding was denied a clear run)* **12/1**

2004 **18** *2 3/4* **Duke Of Firenze**[4] 5524 10-9-9 **90**.. PhilDennis 14 57
(David C Griffiths) *mid-div: effrt 2f out: nvr threatened: wknd fnl f* **25/1**

6213 **19** *hd* **Gabrial The Devil (IRE)**[7] 5420 4-9-7 **88** 6ex.. FrankieDettori 9 54
(Richard Fahey) *racd stands' side: mid-div: hdwy 2f out: effrt over 1f out: wknd ent fnl f (trainer said gelding was unsuited by the track and would prefer a flatter surface)* **7/1**[1]

1002 **20** *1 1/2* **Gabrial The Saint (IRE)**[7] 5420 4-9-5 **91**.. ScottMcCullagh(5) 18 52
(Richard Fahey) *trckd ldr on stands' side: rdn over 2f out: wknd over 1f out* **25/1**

1622 **21** *shd* **Ballyquin (IRE)**[42] 4123 4-9-1 **82**.. JamesDoyle 19 43
(Andrew Balding) *racd stands' side: overall ldr tl rdn over 2f out: wknd over 1f out (jockey said he took a precautionary check when colt was weakening, as he was concerned that the field was closing on him from both sides)* **8/1**[2]

4214 **22** *1/2* **Tinto**[2] 5589 3-9-2 **87** 6ex.. JimCrowley 15 45
(Amanda Perrett) *mid-div on stands' side: rdn over 2f out: sn btn (trainer's rep said the gelding was unsuited by the ground in which his opinion was riding loose on top)* **11/1**[3]

0312 **23** *3* **Somewhere Secret**[14] 5180 5-7-10 **70** oh3 ow3..(p) LauraCoughlan(7) 8 20
(Michael Mullineaux) *racd stands' side: mid-div tl wknd over 2f out* **33/1**

1m 10.65s (-1.45) **Going Correction** -0.075s/f (Good)
WFA 3 from 4yo+ 4lb 23 Ran SP% **135.1**
Speed ratings (Par 109): **106,105,103,102,101 98,98,96,95,95 95,95,94,93,93 91,91,87,87,85 85,84,80**
CSF £289.67 CT £2842.91 TOTE £24.20: £5.70, £4.50, £2.10, £17.20; EX 383.30 Trifecta £3515.20.
Owner Formulated Polymer Products Ltd **Bred** Cecil And Miss Alison Wiggins **Trained** Huby, N Yorks

FOCUS
There was 4mm of water applied to the straight and bends after racing the previous day, and the weather was again dry and warm for this final card of the meeting. All distances as advertised. There were two groups early on in this Stewards' Cup consolation race, the majority middle to stands' side, but a bunch of five runners, more far side but still some way off the fence, produced the first two home. Mainly exposed runners. The winner has been rated as running his best race for two years, and the second as running his best race since his 3yo days.

5662 QATAR SUMMER H'CAP 1m 6f
2:25 (2:25) (Class 2) 3-Y-O+

£62,250 (£18,640; £9,320; £4,660; £2,330; £1,170) **Stalls** Low

Form | RPR

1161 **1** **King's Advice**[22] 4884 5-9-10 **108**........................ JoeFanning 14 118
(Mark Johnston) *chsd ldrs: effrt and ev ch jst over 2f out: nt quite match pce of ldr over 1f out but sustained effrt and battled on wl to ld 75yds out: v game* **7/2**[1]

11-6 **2** *nk* **Outbox**[22] 4884 4-9-4 **102**........................ AndreaAtzeni 12 111
(Simon Crisford) *in tch in midfield: effrt and hdwy to ld ent fnl 2f: sn rdn and forged ahd over 1f out: drvn 1f out: hdd 75yds out: kpt on but hld after* **5/1**[3]

6215 **3** *1 ½* **Shailene (IRE)**[28] 4645 4-9-0 **98**........................ SilvestreDeSousa 4 104
(Andrew Balding) *hld up in last trio: plenty to do and effrt 3f out: clsd u.p ent fnl 2f: drvn to chse ldrs and edgd rt 1f out: kpt on but no imp ins fnl f* **25/1**

3-20 **4** *1 ½* **Scarlet Dragon**[21] 4935 6-9-3 **101**........................(h) TomMarquand 3 105
(Alan King) *t.k.h: hld up in tch in midfield: edgd out lft and effrt to chse ldrs 2f out: drvn and unable qck over 1f out: kpt on same pce ins fnl f* **25/1**

5041 **5** *hd* **Charles Kingsley**[7] 5443 4-9-2 **100**........................ FrankieDettori 11 104
(Mark Johnston) *chsd ldrs: effrt to press ldrs ent fnl 2f: unable qck u.p over 1f out: kpt on same pce ins fnl f* **9/2**[2]

040 **6** *2 ¼* **Hermoso Mundo (SAF)**[14] 5183 7-8-13 **97**........................ PJMcDonald 13 98
(Hughie Morrison) *led for over 1f: chsd ldr tl led again 3f out: sn rdn and hdd 2f out: no ex u.p over 1f out: wknd ins fnl f* **66/1**

5503 **7** *hd* **Desert Skyline (IRE)**[22] 4884 5-9-10 **108**........................(p) GeraldMosse 2 109
(David Elsworth) *in tch in midfield: rdn 4f out: drvn and edging lft over 2f out: kpt on ins fnl f: nvr trbld ldrs* **10/1**

0240 **8** *1 ¾* **What A Welcome**[22] 4884 5-9-1 **99**........................ JoeyHaynes 6 97
(Patrick Chamings) *hld up in last trio: effrt ent fnl 2f: nvr threatened to get on terms and no imp over 1f out: plugged on same pce* **20/1**

0336 **9** *4 ½* **Proschema (IRE)**[14] 5183 4-9-6 **104**........................ RichardKingscote 1 96
(Tom Dascombe) *rousted along leaving stalls: hdwy to ld after over 1f out: hdd and rdn 3f out: outpcd 2f out: wknd over 1f out* **8/1**

-214 **10** *1* **Bartholomeu Dias**[35] 4382 4-9-0 **98**........................ KieranShoemark 9 89
(Charles Hills) *in tch in midfield: effrt and hdwy over 2f out: no ex u.p and btn over 1f out: wknd ins fnl f* **16/1**

166 **11** *1* **Island Brave (IRE)**[21] 4933 5-9-1 **99**........................ BenCurtis 8 88
(Heather Main) *stdd s: hld up in rr: struggling and losing tch over 3f out: no ch after* **20/1**

0-50 **12** *40* **Top Tug (IRE)**[43] 4053 8-9-1 **99**........................ RyanMoore 7 32
(Alan King) *in tch in midfield: effrt over 2f out: sn struggling and wl btn over 1f out: virtually p.u fnl f: t.o (jockey said gelding had no more to give)* **12/1**

6-34 **13** *86* **Corgi**[43] 4053 4-9-1 **99**........................ JimCrowley 10
(Hughie Morrison) *hld up towards rr: lost tch over 4f out: t.o and eased fnl 2f (vet reported gelding had lost its right-fore show and had an irregular heartbeat)* **6/1**

2m 59.58s (-4.12) **Going Correction** -0.075s/f (Good) **13** Ran SP% **123.8**
Speed ratings (Par 109): **108,107,106,106,106 104,104,103,101,100 99,77,27**
CSF £19.88 CT £394.51 TOTE £4.10: £1.60, £2.30, £8.50; EX 27.90 Trifecta £511.70.
Owner Saeed Jaber **Bred** Rabbah Bloodstock Limited **Trained** Middleham Moor, N Yorks

FOCUS
They were soon strung out in this classy staying handicap. Rock-solid form. The fifth has been rated to his latest, and the sixth to his handicap latest.

5663 QATAR LILLIE LANGTRY STKS (GROUP 2) (F&M) 1m 6f
3:00 (3:00) (Class 1) 3-Y-O+

£176,935 (£67,080; £33,571; £16,723; £8,392; £4,212) **Stalls** Low

Form | RPR

-121 **1** **Enbihaar (IRE)**[28] 4645 4-9-9 108........................ JimCrowley 4 118
(John Gosden) *hld up in last pair: clsd and travelling strly 3f out: pushed into ld 2f out and sn qckning clr: r.o strly and in n.d after: v readily: impressive* **7/2**[1]

-245 **2** *5* **Manuela De Vega (IRE)**[14] 5208 3-8-9 108........................ HarryBentley 2 108
(Ralph Beckett) *in tch in midfield: edging rt and short of room 3f out: swtchd lft over 2f out: rallied and hdwy to chse clr wnr whn hung rt over 1f out: kpt on but no imp* **7/2**[1]

41 **3** *1 ¾* **South Sea Pearl (IRE)**[9] 5364 3-8-9 99........................ RyanMoore 3 105+
(A P O'Brien, Ire) *hld up in tch in last pair: effrt but jst getting outpcd whn nt clr run and swtchd lft ent fnl 2f: kpt on 1f out and wnt 3rd ins fnl f: no ch w wnr* **7/2**[1]

64 **4** *½* **Flowering Peach (IRE)**[9] 5364 3-8-9 88........................ SeanLevey 6 104
(A P O'Brien, Ire) *w ldr tl led after over 1f: rdn 3f out: hdd 2f out and immediately outpcd by wnr: wl hld and plugged on same pce fnl f* **33/1**

-343 **5** *nk* **Pilaster**[56] 3586 4-9-6 102........................ DavidEgan 5 103
(Roger Varian) *led for over 1f out: effrt and ev ch 3f out: nt match pce of wnr wl over 1f out: wl hld and plugged on same pce fnl f* **6/1**[3]

2016 **6** *14* **Peach Tree (IRE)**[14] 5208 3-8-9 100........................ AndreaAtzeni 1 82
(A P O'Brien, Ire) *wl in tch in midfield: rdn over 2f out: sn outpcd and wl btn over 1f out: wknd fnl f* **9/1**

-012 **7** *26* **Dramatic Queen (USA)**[28] 4645 4-9-6 107........................ JamesDoyle 7 39
(William Haggas) *chsd ldrs: rdn and outpcd over 2f out: wl btn over 1f out: bhd and virtually p.u ins fnl f (jockey said filly stopped quickly; trainer's rep said filly was unsuited by the undulations of the track; vet reported filly was displaying signs of a slow recovery)* **4/1**[2]

2m 58.69s (-5.01) **Going Correction** -0.075s/f (Good)
WFA 3 from 4yo 11lb **7** Ran SP% **113.9**
Speed ratings (Par 115): **111,108,107,106,106 98,83**
CSF £15.83 TOTE £4.20: £2.20, £2.30; EX 16.80 Trifecta £61.30.
Owner Hamdan Al Maktoum **Bred** Haras Du Mezeray **Trained** Newmarket, Suffolk

FOCUS
This tight-looking fillies' Group 2 was run at a routine sort of pace pace. The second has been rated to her Oaks form.

5664 UNIBET STEWARDS' CUP (HERITAGE H'CAP) 6f
3:40 (3:42) (Class 2) 3-Y-O+

£155,625 (£46,600; £23,300; £11,650; £5,825; £2,925) **Stalls** High

Form | RPR

-102 **1** **Khaadem (IRE)**[14] 5184 3-9-6 **107**........................ JimCrowley 3 119
(Charles Hills) *racd far side tl gps merged over 2f out: hld up in midfield: swtchd rt: pushed along and hdwy against far rail over 1f out: rdn to ld 100yds out: hung lft but qcknd clr: easily* **4/1**[1]

0122 **2** *2 ¾* **Open Wide (USA)**[5] 5504 5-8-12 **95**........................(b) PatDobbs 8 99+
(Amanda Perrett) *racd far side tl gps merged over 2f out: stdd after s: bhd: clsd and nt clr run 2f out: swtchd rt and hdwy ent fnl f: r.o strly to go 2nd cl home: no ch w wnr* **14/1**

2641 **3** *¾* **Raucous**[24] 4805 6-9-4 **106** 6ex........................(tp) CierenFallon(5) 18 108+
(Robert Cowell) *racd stands' side: midfield: effrt and hdwy over 1f out: drvn to chse overall ldr 1f out: clsd to ld ins fnl f: sn hdd and outpcd by wnr: lost 2nd cl home* **28/1**

253 **4** *nk* **Summerghand (IRE)**[28] 4648 5-9-3 **100**........................ RyanMoore 6 101
(David O'Meara) *racd far side tl gps merged over 2f out: midfield: nt clr run and swtchd lft over 1f out: hdwy and swtchd rt ins fnl f: styd on fnl 100yds: no ch w wnr* **12/1**

0-00 **5** *nk* **Justanotherbottle (IRE)**[35] 4402 5-9-0 **97**........................ JamesDoyle 9 97
(Declan Carroll) *racd far side tl gps merged over 2f out: led gp and chsd clr overall ldr: rdn over 1f out: drvn and kpt on same pce ins fnl f* **7/1**[2]

3410 **6** *½* **Gulliver**[7] 5454 5-9-3 **100**........................(tp) GeraldMosse 5 98
(David O'Meara) *racd far side tl gps merged over 2f out: towards rr: effrt and hdwy whn bmpd over 1f out: styd on wl ins fnl f: no ch w wnr* **33/1**

0520 **7** *nk* **Lake Volta (IRE)**[7] 5413 4-9-3 **100**........................ JoeFanning 1 97
(Mark Johnston) *racd far side tl gps merged over 2f out: prom in chsng gp: effrt u.p over 1f out: unable qck and kpt on same pce ins fnl f* **15/2**[3]

0006 **8** *nk* **Stone Of Destiny**[21] 4896 4-9-3 **100**........................ SilvestreDeSousa 27 96
(Andrew Balding) *racd stands' side tl gps merged over 2f out: midfield: effrt 2f out: clsd u.p and chsd ldrs 1f out: no ex and no imp ins fnl f* **33/1**

5200 **9** *½* **Growl**[7] 5454 7-8-9 **92**........................ CallumShepherd 4 87
(Richard Fahey) *racd far side tl gps merged over 2f out: midfield: edgd out lft and effrt 2f out: hdwy to chse ldrs u.p over 1f out: no ex ins fnl f: wknd towards fin* **16/1**

0620 **10** *1 ¼* **Kimifive (IRE)**[7] 5413 4-8-9 **92**........................ ShaneKelly 26 83+
(Joseph Tuite) *racd stands' side tl gps merged over 2f out: stdd s: hld up in rr: clsd but nt clr run over 1f out: swtchd rt ins fnl f: styd on: nvr trbld ldrs* **25/1**

3145 **11** *shd* **Embour (IRE)**[5] 5504 4-9-1 **98** 6ex........................ SeanLevey 17 88
(Richard Hannon) *racd in centre tl gps merged over 2f out: midfield: effrt over 1f out: edging out rt: rdn and kpt on ins fnl f: nvr trbld ldrs* **40/1**

2433 **12** *nk* **El Hombre**[36] 4331 5-8-4 **92**........................ AndrewBreslin(5) 7 81
(Keith Dalgleish) *racd far side tl gps merged over 2f out: s.i.s: hdwy to go prom in chsng gp after 2f: unable qck u.p over 1f out: wknd ins fnl f* **50/1**

0122 **13** *nk* **Arecibo (FR)**[8] 5371 4-9-0 **97** 6ex........................ FrankieDettori 21 86
(David O'Meara) *racd stands' side tl gps merged over 2f out: midfield: effrt over 1f out: kpt on but no real imp ins fnl f: nvr trbld ldrs* **12/1**

-242 **14** *nk* **Cosmic Law (IRE)**[35] 4379 3-8-11 **98**........................ PJMcDonald 22 85
(Richard Fahey) *racd stands' side tl gps merged over 2f out: midfield tl outpcd and dropped to rr over 2f out: swtchd lft 1f out: styd on u.p ins fnl f: nvr trbld ldrs* **25/1**

-546 **15** *½* **Gunmetal (IRE)**[42] 4095 6-9-6 **103**........................ HarryBentley 24 89
(David Barron) *racd stands' side tl gps merged over 2f out: hld up in midfield: swtchd lft and effrt 2f out: hung rt no imp over 1f out: nvr trbld ldrs* **14/1**

0100 **16** *hd* **Soldier's Minute**[35] 4402 4-8-10 **98**........................ ScottMcCullagh(5) 20 83
(Keith Dalgleish) *racd stands' side tl gps merged over 2f out: prom in chsng gp: unable qck u.p over 1f out: wknd ins fnl f (vet reported gelding lost its left-fore shoe)* **50/1**

0421 **17** *shd* **Buridan (FR)**[56] 3597 4-8-8 **91**........................ TomMarquand 19 76
(Richard Hannon) *racd stands' side tl gps merged over 2f out: midfield: effrt u.p over 1f out: no imp and wl hld ins fnl f* **40/1**

1163 **18** *nse* **Ornate**[1] 5611 6-9-6 **103**........................ PhilDennis 15 88
(David C Griffiths) *racd in centre: led and sn clr: pushed along over 2f out: rdn over 1f out: hdd over 100yds out: sn btn and fdd towards fin* **33/1**

2534 **19** *1 ¼* **Spanish City**[21] 4921 6-8-13 **96**........................(b[1]) DavidEgan 13 77
(Roger Varian) *racd centre tl gps merged over 2f out: drvn and no imp whn swtchd rt 1f out: wknd ins fnl f* **16/1**

106 **20** *¾* **Sir Maximilian (IRE)**[35] 4402 10-8-4 **94**........................(v) AngusVilliers(7) 23 72
(Ian Williams) *racd stands' side tl gps merged over 2f out: s.i.s: nvr travelling and sn rdn towards rr: swtchd rt 2f out: no prog and wl hld whn nt clr run jst ins fnl f* **66/1**

0600 **21** *¾* **George Bowen (IRE)**[15] 5120 7-9-5 **102**........................(v) TonyHamilton 25 78
(Richard Fahey) *awkward leaving stalls and s.i.s: racd stands' side tl gps merged over 1f out: towards rr: effrt over 1f out: no prog and nt clr run jst ins fnl f: nvr involved* **33/1**

1101 **22** *shd* **Air Raid**[15] 5120 4-9-4 **101** 6ex........................ JackGarritty 12 77
(Jedd O'Keeffe) *racd in centre tl gps merged over 2f out: prom in chsng gp: rdn and lost pl over 1f out: wknd and short of room ins fnl f* **18/1**

1500 **23** *hd* **Vanbrugh (USA)**[21] 4905 4-9-10 **107**........................ KieranShoemark 16 82
(Charles Hills) *racd stands' side tl gps merged over 2f out: prom in chsng gp: rdn and unable qck over 1f out: btn whn pushed rt ins fnl f* **25/1**

1000 **24** *¾* **Hyperfocus (IRE)**[7] 5454 5-8-8 **91**........................(p[1]) JamesSullivan 2 64
(Tim Easterby) *racd far side tl gps merged over 2f out: prom in chsng gp: rdn 2f out: unable qck and lost pl over 1f out: wknd ins fnl f* **66/1**

0-44 **25** *1 ¼* **True Mason**[70] 3083 3-8-13 **100**........................(w) BenCurtis 14 68
(K R Burke) *racd in centre tl gps merged over 1f out: hld up in midfield: swtchd lft and effrt over 1f out: wkng whn nt clr run jst ins fnl f* **40/1**

-560 **26** *1 ¼* **Baron Bolt**[42] 4095 6-9-5 **102**........................(b[1]) RossaRyan 10 67
(Paul Cole) *racd in centre tl gps merged over 2f out: midfield: drvn and no hdwy over 1f out: wknd ins fnl f* **25/1**

-131 **27** *½* **Flavius Titus**[56] 3602 4-9-2 **99**........................ AndreaAtzeni 11 62
(Roger Varian) *racd in centre tl gps merged over 2f out: prom in chsng gp: rdn and unable qck over 1f out: sn btn and eased ins fnl f (jockey said gelding stopped quickly)* **9/1**

1m 9.79s (-2.31) **Going Correction** -0.075s/f (Good)
WFA 3 from 4yo+ 4lb **27** Ran SP% **144.8**
Speed ratings (Par 109): **112,108,107,106,106 105,105,105,104,102 102,102,101,101,100 100,100,100,98,97 96,96,96,95,93**
CSF £58.05 CT £1520.74 TOTE £4.80: £2.00, £4.40, £7.00, £4.00; EX 86.10 Trifecta £3627.00.
Owner Hamdan Al Maktoum **Bred** Yeomanstown Stud **Trained** Lambourn, Berks

FOCUS
There were three groups early, then two, before the field were spread all over the place in the closing stages. But six of the first seven finishers came from a nine-horse group on the far side. The time was 0.86sec quicker than the consolation race. The winner looks every bit a Group horse, while the second has been rated a bit below his latest.

5665 QATAR EBF STALLIONS MAIDEN STKS (PLUS 10 RACE) (C&G) 7f
4:15 (4:17) (Class 2) 2-Y-O £18,903 (£5,658; £2,829; £1,416; £705) Stalls Low

Form RPR

1 **Persuasion (IRE)** 2-9-0 0 JamesDoyle 8 87+
(Charles Hills) *travelled wl in mid-div: nt best of runs over 2f out: qcknd up smartly whn clr over 1f out: r.o wl: led towards fin: comf* 16/1

0 2 ½ **Celtic Art (FR)**[22] 4886 2-9-0 0 PJMcDonald 5 86
(Paul Cole) *hld up: shkn up and hdwy over 1f out: r.o strly fnl f: snatched 2nd cl home* 14/1

22 3 nk **Great Ambassador**[21] 4925 2-9-0 0 HarryBentley 11 85
(Ralph Beckett) *awkwardly away: sn prom: led wl over 1f out: sn rdn: kpt on but no ex whn hdd towards fin* 8/1

4 4 ¾ **Berkshire Rocco (FR)**[21] 4897 2-9-0 0 JimCrowley 1 83+
(Andrew Balding) *in tch: rdn in 4th over 1f out: kpt on but nt pce to chal ins fnl f* 11/2[3]

5 5 ½ **Dyami (FR)**[38] 4252 2-9-0 0 BenCurtis 4 82
(George Baker) *trckd ldrs: rdn 2f out: disputing 2nd ent fnl f: kpt on same pce* 33/1

0 6 4½ **Mambo Nights (IRE)**[14] 5177 2-9-0 0 AndreaAtzeni 10 70
(Richard Hannon) *mid-div: rdn over 2f out: sn edgd rt: little imp* 20/1

2 7 ¾ **Smuggler**[43] 4062 2-9-0 0 MartinDwyer 9 68
(Marcus Tregoning) *hld up: rdn and sme prog over 1f out: nvr gng pce to get involved* 8/1

0 8 nk **King Of Athens (USA)**[46] 3949 2-9-0 0 RyanMoore 2 67+
(A P O'Brien, Ire) *mid-div: pushed along over 3f out: drvn 2f out: nvr any imp* 6/4[1]

9 1¾ **Junkanoo** 2-9-0 0 KieranShoemark 3 63
(Gary Moore) *hld up: hdwy over 2f out: sn rdn: nvr threatened to get on terms: wknd fnl f (jockey said colt hung left-handed)* 50/1

03 10 3 **Gold Souk (IRE)**[35] 4388 2-9-0 0 SilvestreDeSousa 6 55
(Mark Johnston) *led: rdn and hdd wl over 1f out: wknd fnl f (jockey said colt took a false step approximately 5f out and was never travelling thereafter)* 4/1[2]

3 11 9 **Lawaa (FR)**[30] 4544 2-9-0 0 TonyHamilton 7 31
(Richard Fahey) *cl up: rdn over 2f out: wknd over 1f out* 33/1

1m 26.01s (-0.69) **Going Correction** -0.075s/f (Good) 11 Ran SP% 122.8
Speed ratings (Par 100): **100,99,99,98,97 92,91,91,89,85 75**
CSF £219.11 TOTE £22.10: £4.40, £4.00, £2.20; EX 288.70 Trifecta £2117.40.
Owner Mrs Susan Roy **Bred** Norelands Bloodstock **Trained** Lambourn, Berks

FOCUS
Usually a decent 2yo maiden. It was run at a solid pace and ought to produce numerous future winners.

5666 QATAR H'CAP 7f
4:50 (4:52) (Class 2) (0-105,100) 3-Y£18,903 (£5,658; £2,829; £1,416; £705) Stalls Low

Form RPR

2511 1 **Land Of Legends (IRE)**[37] 4299 3-9-3 96 CallumShepherd 4 107+
(Saeed bin Suroor) *s.i.s: towards rr: swtchd to centre and gd hdwy over 1f out: drifted rt ent fnl f: sn led: comf* 9/2[2]

2600 2 1¾ **Jack's Point**[23] 4847 3-8-13 92 MartinDwyer 1 98
(William Muir) *trckd ldrs: rdn 2f out: kpt on ins fnl f: wnt 2nd towards fin: no ch w wnr* 16/1

2112 3 nk **Warning Fire**[4] 5525 3-8-5 84 JoeFanning 6 89
(Mark Johnston) *led: rdn over 1f out: hdd jst ins fnl f: kpt on but nt pce of wnr: no ex whn losing 2nd towards fin* 9/2[2]

12-1 4 1 **Marhaba Milliar (IRE)**[36] 4348 3-9-2 95 FrankieDettori 5 97
(John Gosden) *in tch: rdn over 2f out: nt pce to get on terms but kpt on into 4th ins fnl f* 11/4[1]

-503 5 hd **Breath Of Air**[14] 5173 3-8-10 89 KieranShoemark 8 92+
(Charles Hills) *hld up: pushed along and stdy prog fr over 2f out: swtchd rt jst ins fnl f: keeping on but no ch whn nt clr run towards fin (jockey said colt was denied a clear run in the final furlong)* 20/1

5060 6 ¾ **Fintas**[28] 4669 3-8-9 88 (t) BenCurtis 7 88
(David O'Meara) *trckd ldr: rdn and ev ch 2f out jst over 1f out: no ex* 33/1

-323 7 ¾ **Bayroot (IRE)**[21] 4919 3-9-4 97 AndreaAtzeni 3 95
(Roger Varian) *s.i.s: sn midfield: rdn wl over 2f out: sn one pce* 6/1[3]

4124 8 nk **Adelante (FR)**[29] 4621 3-8-9 93 CierenFallon(5) 10 90
(George Baker) *mid-div: rdn over 2f out: kpt on but no ch fnl f* 40/1

6100 9 hd **Pogo (IRE)**[44] 4016 3-9-7 100 JamesDoyle 9 101+
(Charles Hills) *hld up: stl last trio 2f out: sn shkn up: nt clr run and swtchd rt over 1f out: running on but no ch whn nt clr run fnl 100yds* 10/1

1160 10 nk **Artistic Rifles (IRE)**[23] 4851 3-8-7 86 DavidEgan 2 82
(Charles Hills) *chsd ldrs: rdn wl over 2f out: fdd fnl f* 16/1

2000 11 ½ **Blown By Wind**[23] 4847 3-9-7 100 RyanMoore 11 94
(Mark Johnston) *last pair: struggling 3f out: no ch but kpt on ins fnl f* 14/1

4316 12 16 **Fox Leicester (IRE)**[36] 4325 3-8-9 88 SilvestreDeSousa 13 39
(Andrew Balding) *last pair: struggling 3f out: wknd over 1f out* 18/1

1m 25.29s (-1.41) **Going Correction** -0.075s/f (Good) 12 Ran SP% 120.2
Speed ratings (Par 106): **105,103,102,101,101 100,99,99,99,98 98,79**
CSF £73.84 CT £354.06 TOTE £5.20: £1.60, £4.50, £1.90; EX 92.50 Trifecta £532.00.
Owner Godolphin **Bred** Godolphin **Trained** Newmarket, Suffolk
■ Stewards' Enquiry : Callum Shepherd two-day ban: misuse of the whip (Aug 17-18)

FOCUS
A good handicap and a taking winner. The winner looks a Group horse in the making, with the second rated to his best.

5667 QATAR APPRENTICE H'CAP 1m 1f 11y
5:25 (5:26) (Class 3) (0-95,96) 3-Y£06,752 (£4,715; £2,357; £1,180; £587) Stalls Low

Form RPR

22-1 1 **Gifts Of Gold (IRE)**[38] 4258 4-9-9 90 CierenFallon(3) 5 103+
(Saeed bin Suroor) *hld up in midfield: effrt over 2f out: hdwy and rdn to ld 1f out: hung rt but styd on wl ins fnl f* 9/4[1]

-362 2 1¾ **You're Hired**[25] 4752 6-9-2 83 (p[1]) ScottMcCullagh(3) 4 92
(Amanda Perrett) *chsd ldrs: effrt and clsd over 2f out: ev ch u.p over 1f out: chsd wnr and kpt on same pce ins fnl f* 8/1

0354 3 ½ **Rotherwick (IRE)**[19] 4997 7-9-0 83 (b) WilliamCarver(5) 8 91
(Paul Cole) *s.i.s and pushed along early: bhd: swtchd lft and effrt over 2f out: hdwy u.p over 1f out: styd on wl ins fnl f: nt rch ldrs (jockey said gelding was slowly away)* 10/1

0-20 4 3 **Poet's Prince**[93] 2320 4-9-11 92 AndrewBreslin(3) 10 93
(Mark Johnston) *chsd ldrs: effrt 3f out: keeping on whn swtchd lft over 1f out: one pce and no imp ins fnl f* 16/1

2324 5 3 **Storting**[48] 3885 3-8-0 79 GeorgeBass(7) 14 74+
(Mick Channon) *t.k.h: midfield: hdwy to join ldrs 7f out: led over 5f out: hung lft in st: racing against stands' rail u.p over 1f out: hdd 1f out: sn wknd (jockey said gelding hung badly left-handed)* 15/2[3]

0223 6 ¾ **Kingston Kurrajong**[19] 4994 6-8-6 75 Pierre-LouisJamin(5) 2 68
(William Knight) *midfield: effrt over 2f out: keeping on but nt threatening to get on terms whn wnt lft over 1f out: no prog and wl hld fnl f* 25/1

2301 7 nk **Mr Scaramanga**[30] 4548 5-9-0 85 LeviWilliams(7) 15 77
(Simon Dow) *chsd ldr tl 7f out: clr in ldng trio over 4f out: rdn and ev ch 2f out: lost pl and btn over 1f out: wknd ins fnl f* 22/1

4250 8 1¼ **Aiya (IRE)**[49] 3845 4-9-2 80 (h) WilliamCox 9 70
(Tim Easterby) *midfield: effrt jst over 2f out: drvn 2f out: nvr threatened to get on terms and wknd ins fnl f* 40/1

2-50 9 ¾ **Thechildren'strust (IRE)**[197] 294 4-8-4 75 LouisGaroghan(7) 17 63
(Gary Moore) *taken down early: t.k.h: led tl over 5f out: clr in ldng trio over 4f out tl outpcd 2f out: wl btn over 1f out: wknd fnl f* 50/1

4041 10 nk **Harbour Spirit (FR)**[31] 4506 3-8-6 85 AngusVilliers(7) 1 72
(Richard Hughes) *mounted in chute and taken down early: hld up in rr: effrt 3f out: nvr threatened to get on terms: wl hld whn swtchd lft ent fnl f* 14/1

5344 11 ½ **Ventura Knight (IRE)**[4] 5519 4-10-4 96 PhilDennis 3 82
(Mark Johnston) *midfield tl short of room and dropped towards rr after 2f: effrt 3f out: no prog u.p over 1f out: nvr involved* 10/3[2]

4501 12 4½ **Wind In My Sails**[10] 5292 7-9-0 83 TobyEley(5) 11 59
(Ed de Giles) *taken down early: hld up in midfield: effrt over 2f out: sn struggling and btn over 1f out: wknd fnl f* 25/1

3014 13 4½ **Reggae Runner (FR)**[16] 5104 3-8-10 85 ThomasGreatrex(3) 12 51
(Mark Johnston) *midfield: rdn 4f out: struggling u.p 3f out: sn btn: wknd over 1f out (jockey said colt was never travelling)* 16/1

5363 14 nse **C Note (IRE)**[34] 4425 6-8-11 82 StefanoCherchi(7) 13 48
(Heather Main) *stmbld leaving stalls: hld up towards rr: effrt 3f out: no prog and wl btn over 1f out* 22/1

0011 15 5 **Fortune And Glory (USA)**[15] 5136 6-8-7 74 DarraghKeenan(3) 16 29
(Joseph Tuite) *midfield: lost pl u.p over 2f out: wl btn over 1f out* 10/1

0 16 10 **Perfect City (IRE)**[40] 2742 4-9-12 90 MitchGodwin 7 23
(Jonjo O'Neill) *sn dropped towards rr: rdn over 3f out: sn wl btn and wl bhd over 1f out: t.o (jockey said gelding lost its action)* 50/1

1231 17 2 **In The Red (IRE)**[127] 1392 6-8-8 79 (p) JacobClark(7) 6 8
(Martin Smith) *t.k.h early: hld up in midfield: lost pl and bhd 4f out: sn rdn and btn: wl bhd over 1f out: t.o* 25/1

1m 53.26s (-4.14) **Going Correction** -0.075s/f (Good) 17 Ran SP% 139.9
WFA 3 from 4yo+ 8lb
Speed ratings (Par 107): **115,113,113,110,107 107,106,105,104,104 104,100,96,96,91 82,81**
CSF £22.12 CT £173.98 TOTE £2.80: £1.30, £2.50, £2.60, £4.90; EX 34.70 Trifecta £298.20.
Owner Godolphin **Bred** Paul Hyland **Trained** Newmarket, Suffolk
■ Stewards' Enquiry : Jacob Clark five-day ban: misuse of the whip (Aug 17-21)

FOCUS
This was a decent handicap of its type, but it proved messy and few got involved. The second has been rated back to last year's form, and the third as running his best race this year.
T/Jkpt: Not Won. T/Plt: £809.00 to a £1 stake. Pool: £295,075.33 - 266.24 winning units T/Qpdt: £46.60 to a £1 stake. Pool: £23,400.95 - 370.82 winning units **Steve Payne & Tim Mitchell**

5117 HAMILTON (R-H)
Saturday, August 3

OFFICIAL GOING: Good to soft (6.7) (racing abandoned after race 3 (6.50) - waterlogged)
Wind: Light, across Weather: Overcast, warm, heavy rain before race 3 (6.50)

5668 BB FOODSERVICE NURSERY H'CAP (A £20,000 BB FOODSERVICE 2YO SERIES QUALIFIER) 6f 6y
5:50 (5:51) (Class 4) (0-80,77) 2-Y-O
£5,433 (£1,617; £808; £404; £400; £400) Stalls High

Form RPR

034 1 **Good Night Mr Tom (IRE)**[35] 4401 2-9-7 77 CYHo 7 83
(Mark Johnston) *mde all: rdn over 1f out: styd on strly fnl f* 9/2[2]

6333 2 2 **Pentewan**[14] 5171 2-9-4 74 (b[1]) SamJames 5 74
(Phillip Makin) *bhd: pushed along over 2f out: hdwy and hung rt over 1f out: chsd wnr ins fnl f: kpt on: nt pce to chal* 9/2[2]

426 3 2 **Yarrow Gate**[56] 3564 2-9-1 71 GrahamLee 2 65
(Michael Dods) *chsd ldng gp: effrt and pushed along 2f out: wnt 3rd ins fnl f: kpt on: nt pce to chal* 9/2[2]

6314 4 ¾ **Aberama Gold**[8] 5390 2-9-7 77 ShaneGray 6 69
(Keith Dalgleish) *pressed wnr: effrt and rdn over 1f out: no ex ins fnl f* 11/4[1]

041 5 ¾ **One Bite (IRE)**[16] 5093 2-9-7 77 TomEaves 3 67
(Keith Dalgleish) *prom on outside: rdn over 2f out: outpcd fr over 1f out* 5/1[3]

312 6 ¾ **Rose Bandit (IRE)**[17] 5037 2-8-13 74 HarrisonShaw(5) 4 61
(Stef Keniry) *cl up: rdn along over 2f out: outpcd over 1f out: sn btn* 17/2

234 7 2¼ **Mr Fudge**[66] 3220 2-9-0 73 SeanDavis(3) 1 54
(Richard Fahey) *sn pushed along in rr: drvn over 2f out: sn wknd* 14/1

1m 12.54s (-0.16) **Going Correction** +0.075s/f (Good) 7 Ran SP% 115.1
Speed ratings (Par 96): **104,101,98,97,96 95,92**
CSF £25.19 TOTE £3.90: £2.60, £2.70; EX 21.50 Trifecta £205.70.
Owner Paul & Clare Rooney **Bred** Peter Molony **Trained** Middleham Moor, N Yorks

FOCUS
The ground was officially good to soft having dried during the preceding 48 hours. This was a competitive nursery in which all seven could be given a chance.

5669 BOE VIOLET GIN NOVICE STKS 6f 6y
6:20 (6:23) (Class 5) 3-Y-O+ £4,787 (£1,424; £711; £355) Stalls Centre

Form RPR

5232 1 **Bedtime Bella (IRE)**[10] 5297 3-8-11 64 (v) SeanDavis(3) 3 67
(Michael Appleby) *chsd ldr: rdn over 2f out: hdwy to ld over 1f out: kpt on strly fnl f* 5/4[1]

03 2 1½ **Blank Canvas**[9] 5336 3-9-0 0 ShaneGray 6 62
(Keith Dalgleish) *t.k.h: led against stands' rail: rdn and hdd over 1f out: kpt on same pce ins fnl f* 10/3[2]

-200 **3** *3* **Swinging Eddie**[12] 5236 3-9-5 66 .... TomEaves 7 58
(Kevin Ryan) *hld up: hdwy and hung rt over 2f out: no imp fr over 1f out (vet reported gelding lost its right fore shoe)* **7/2**[3]

0 **4** *5* **Lyons Lane**[110] 1816 3-9-0 0 .... GrahamLee 4 37
(Michael Dods) *prom: rdn along over 2f out: wknd over 1f out* **6/1**

5 *16* **Look Who It Isnae (IRE)** 3-8-9 0 .... HarrisonShaw(5) 5
(Alan Berry) *prom: drvn along over 2f out: wknd wl over 1f out: t.o* **66/1**

6 *23* **Its Toytown** 3-9-5 0 .... DougieCostello 1
(R Mike Smith) *s.v.s: t.o thrght (jockey said gelding was slowly away and ran green)* **20/1**

1m 12.69s (-0.01) **Going Correction** +0.075s/f (Good) **6** Ran SP% **110.3**
Speed ratings (Par 103): **103,101,97,90,69 38**
CSF £5.44 TOTE £1.80: £1.10, £2.50; EX 5.30 Trifecta £8.80.
Owner Rod In Pickle Partnership **Bred** Gce Farm Ltd **Trained** Oakham, Rutland

FOCUS
A low-grade novice event in which the winner was a seven-race maiden rated just 64. The winner has been rated to form.

5670 GAS CALL SERVICES SILK SERIES LADY RIDERS' H'CAP (PRO-AM LADY RIDERS' RACE) 6f 6y
6:50 (6:55) (Class 4) (0-80,81) 3-Y-O+
£8,021 (£2,387; £894; £400; £400) **Stalls** Centre

Form RPR

3152 **1** **Cale Lane**[7] 5419 4-9-9 73 .... PaulaMuir(5) 5 83
(Julie Camacho) *hld up: hdwy on outside 2f out: led ins fnl f: edgd lft: rdn out* **7/2**[2]

4151 **2** *1 ¼* **Dancing Rave**[15] 5123 3-9-11 74 .... ShelleyBirkett 1 79
(David O'Meara) *in tch: effrt and rdn over 1f out: chsd wnr ins fnl f: r.o* **13/2**[3]

6543 **3** *½* **Yes You (IRE)**[8] 5395 5-10-0 73 .... LucyAlexander 7 77
(Iain Jardine) *towards rr: pushed along over 2f out: gd hdwy fnl f: r.o wl* **15/2**

0360 **3** *dht* **Lucky Lucky Man (IRE)**[35] 4369 4-10-2 78 .... MissEmmaSayer(3) 6 82
(Richard Fahey) *towards rr: rdn and hdwy over 1f out: kpt on fnl f: nvr able to chal* **8/1**

-610 **5** *2 ¾* **Cool Spirit**[8] 5395 4-10-4 80 .... MeganNicholls(3) 3 76
(Richard Fahey) *chsd clr ldng pair to over 1f out: sn rdn and outpcd* **11/4**[1]

2126 **6** *½* **Jordan Electrics**[26] 4721 3-9-2 68 .... (h) GemmaTutty(3) 9 61
(Linda Perratt) *led against stands' rail: rdn over 1f out: hdd ins fnl f: sn btn* **10/1**

021- **7** *3 ¾* **Airglow (IRE)**[277] 8719 4-10-3 81 .... (h) MissJoannaMason(5) 4 63
(Michael Easterby) *dwlt: towards rr: pushed along over 2f out: no imp over 1f out* **9/1**

254 **8** *1 ¼* **Scuzeme**[33] 4440 5-9-7 71 .... FayeMcManoman(5) 8 49
(Phillip Makin) *pressed ldr and sn clr of rest: rdn over 2f out: wknd over 1f out* **13/2**[3]

0000 **9** *3 ½* **Zizum**[5] 5491 4-8-9 61 oh16 .... MissShannonWatts(7) 2 28
(Alan Berry) *dwlt: bhd and outpcd: struggling fr 1/2-way* **100/1**

1m 15.1s (2.40) **Going Correction** +0.075s/f (Good)
WFA 3 from 4yo+ 4lb **9** Ran SP% **118.5**
Speed ratings (Par 105): **87,85,84,84,81 80,75,73,69**
WIN: 3.80 Cale Lane; PL: 1.50 Yes You, 1.40 Cale Lane, 1.60 Dancing Rave, Lucky Lucky Man; EX: 27.90; CSF: 27.39; TC: CL/DR/LLM 86.85, CL/DR/YY 82.02; TF: CL/DR/LLM 130.10, CL/DR/YY 115.20;.
Owner David W Armstrong **Bred** Highfield Farm Llp **Trained** Norton, N Yorks
■ Stewards' Enquiry : Paula Muir two-day ban: misuse of the whip (Aug 17-18)

FOCUS
This was a sprint for pro-am women riders run in driving rain. The pace was overly strong and it collapsed in the final furlong with the closers fighting out the finish. With less than two lengths separating the first four home the form is unlikely to prove anything special. The second helps set the level, with the third to this year's form. As a result of waterlogging following the heavy rainfall, the rest of the card was abandoned.

5671 BRITISH STALLION STUDS EBF SOBA CONDITIONS STKS 5f 7y
(7:20) (Class 3) 3-Y-O+
£

5672 TOP CAT WINDOW BLINDS H'CAP 1m 3f 15y
(7:50) (Class 5) (0-75,) 3-Y-O+
£

5673 MARGARET SMITH MEMORIAL H'CAP 1m 1f 35y
(8:20) (Class 6) (0-60,) 3-Y-O+
£

5674 MACGREGOR FLOORING CO LTD H'CAP 1m 68y
(8:50) (Class 5) (0-75,) 3-Y-O+
£

T/Plt: £6.20 to a £1 stake. Pool: £54,505.30 - 6,334.36 winning units T/Qpdt: £1.20 to a £1 stake. Pool: £7,411.66 - 4,544.63 winning units **Richard Young**

5425 LINGFIELD (L-H)
Saturday, August 3

OFFICIAL GOING: Good to firm (8.6)
Wind: Virtually nil Weather: Warm, overcast

5675 WITHEFORD EQUINE BARRIER TRIALS AT LINGFIELD PARK APPRENTICE H'CAP 7f 135y
4:55 (5:05) (Class 6) (0-60,62) 4-Y-O+
£2,781 (£827; £413; £400; £400; £400) **Stalls** Centre

Form RPR

6303 **1** **Jupiter**[7] 5430 4-8-12 51 .... (v[1]) LukeCatton(5) 1 60
(Alexandra Dunn) *trckd ldrs: hdwy to ld on bit 2f out: rdn and qcknd up wl to assert wl ins fnl f* **9/2**[2]

-53 **2** *1 ¼* **Captain Sedgwick (IRE)**[16] 5081 5-8-7 46 .... SaraDelFabbro(5) 6 52
(John Spearing) *wnt to post early: racd in midfield: smooth hdwy to chse wnr 2f out: rdn almost upsides wnr and ev ch 1f out: kpt on but no match for wnr* **2/1**[1]

0330 **3** *2 ¾* **Accomplice**[22] 4870 5-9-8 56 .... JessicaCooley 15 57
(Michael Blanshard) *settled in midfield: hdwy u.p 2f out: rdn and kpt on fnl f: no match for front pair (jockey said mare was outpaced in the early stages)* **8/1**

-030 **4** *2 ¼* **Gerry The Glover (IRE)**[16] 5087 7-9-10 58 .... (v[1]) GeorgiaDobie 2 52
(Lee Carter) *hld up: drvn along over 2f out: mde sme late hdwy fnl f* **6/1**[3]

0-00 **5** *¾* **Alexandria**[24] 4787 4-9-3 54 .... (v[1]) AledBeech(3) 8 46
(Charlie Fellowes) *j. awkwardly and racd in rr: rdn along and minor hdwy 2f out: kpt on wl fnl f* **10/1**

3000 **6** *1 ¼* **Star Attraction (FR)**[61] 3410 4-8-9 46 oh1 .... (t[1]) GavinAshton(3) 12 35
(Tony Carroll) *racd in rr of midfield: rdn and no imp 2f out: one pce fnl f* **50/1**

0205 **7** *1* **Lord Murphy (IRE)**[56] 3592 6-8-10 54 .... (tp) MolliePhillips(10) 7 41
(Mark Loughnane) *hld up: stl gng wl but short of room 2f out: sn rdn and minor hdwy fnl f* **14/1**

0-00 **8** *1 ½* **Aegean Legend**[42] 4116 4-8-9 48 .... (p) GeorgeRooke(5) 4 31
(John Bridger) *in rr of midfield: rdn along wl over 1f out: drvn and no imp 1f out: one pce after* **25/1**

0240 **9** *1 ¼* **Soaring Spirits (IRE)**[46] 3966 9-9-1 59 .... (b) LukeBacon(10) 9 39
(Dean Ivory) *led: rdn along and hdd by wnr 2f out: wknd fr 1f out* **11/1**

0005 **10** *4* **Golconda Prince (IRE)**[7] 5430 5-8-8 47 .... (vt) IsobelFrancis(5) 14 18
(Mark Pattinson) *racd in rr of midfield: rdn and outpcd 3f out: nvr on terms (jockey said gelding was denied a clear run)* **25/1**

365- **11** *2 ¾* **Tallulah's Quest (IRE)**[375] 5324 5-9-5 53 .... SeanKirrane 13 17
(Julia Feilden) *chsd ldr: rdn along and outpcd 2f out: wknd fr over 1f out* **12/1**

0-00 **12** *4* **Hold Your Breath**[16] 5083 4-8-6 46 oh1 .... (h[1]) ElishaWhittington(6) 11
(Tony Carroll) *chsd ldr: rdn along and lost pl qckly 2f out (jockey said filly ran too freely and the saddle slipped)* **28/1**

-000 **13** *5* **Premium Pink (IRE)**[10] 5310 4-8-7 46 oh1 .... GraceMcEntee(5) 10
(Luke McJannet) *prom: rdn along and lost pl over 2f out: sn bhd* **40/1**

1m 29.63s (-2.07) **Going Correction** -0.375s/f (Firm) **13** Ran SP% **124.2**
Speed ratings (Par 101): **95,93,91,88,88 86,85,84,83,79 76,72,67**
CSF £13.71 CT £76.29 TOTE £5.00: £1.80, £1.50, £2.80; EX 13.30 Trifecta £63.30.
Owner Team Dunn & W B B **Bred** D Curran **Trained** West Buckland, Somerset

FOCUS
The going was given as good to firm (Going Stick 8.6). A moderate affair in which the first two drew clear.

5676 PHOENIX CARPET COMPANY 30TH ANNIVERSARY NOVICE MEDIAN AUCTION STKS 7f 135y
5:30 (5:37) (Class 6) 2-Y-O
£2,781 (£827; £413; £206) **Stalls** Centre

Form RPR

4 **1** **Passing Fashion (IRE)**[8] 5374 2-9-3 0 .... RichardKingscote 8 80+
(Ralph Beckett) *wnt rt s: hdd to stands' rail and mde all: pushed along: green and hung bdly lft over to far rail wl over 1f out: rdn and a doing enough fnl f w rail to help (jockey said gelding hung violenty left handed)* **3/1**[2]

1 **2** *1* **Wren**[38] 4245 2-9-5 0 .... JasonWatson 3 80
(Roger Charlton) *trckd wnr: rdn to chse wnr over 1f out: kpt on wl fnl f but unable to match wnr* **4/6**[1]

3 *5* **Wailea Nights (IRE)** 2-8-12 0 .... ShaneKelly 1 61+
(Marco Botti) *racd in midfield: hdwy on outer 2f out: sn rdn and kpt on for remote 3rd fnl f* **25/1**

4 *2 ¼* **Costello** 2-9-3 0 .... RossaRyan 2 61
(Mike Murphy) *in tch in 4th: rdn and outpcd over 1f out: kpt on one pce fnl f* **40/1**

5 *1 ½* **Webuyanyhorse** 2-9-3 0 .... TrevorWhelan 7 57
(Jamie Osborne) *racd in midfield: rdn along and no imp 2f out: kpt on one pce fnl f* **33/1**

42 **6** *½* **Commit No Nuisance (IRE)**[23] 4839 2-9-3 0 .... TomMarquand 11 56
(William Knight) *chsd wnr on rail: rdn and outpcd over 1f out: one pce fnl f* **9/2**[3]

7 *3 ¼* **Margaretha (IRE)** 2-8-5 0 .... SeanKirrane(7) 10 43
(Amy Murphy) *hld up: rdn along 2f out: nvr on terms* **66/1**

04 **8** *nk* **Forus**[25] 4766 2-8-12 0 .... ThoreHammerHansen(5) 5 47
(Jamie Osborne) *racd in midfield: pushed along 3f out: sn rdn and no imp 2f out: wknd fnl f* **20/1**

9 *½* **Bad Attitude** 2-9-3 0 .... EoinWalsh 9 46
(Luke McJannet) *hld up: rdn and outpcd over 2f out: a in rr* **25/1**

10 *3* **Dazzling Darren (IRE)** 2-9-3 0 .... BrettDoyle 4 39
(Adam West) *hld up: rdn and outpcd over 2f out: nvr on terms* **33/1**

1m 29.74s (-1.96) **Going Correction** -0.375s/f (Firm) **10** Ran SP% **125.4**
Speed ratings (Par 92): **94,93,88,85,84 83,80,80,79,76**
CSF £5.46 TOTE £3.80: £1.30, £1.02, £6.40; EX 6.40 Trifecta £60.00.
Owner P D Savill **Bred** Oak Hill Stud **Trained** Kimpton, Hants

FOCUS
The first two finished clear and the winner was value for an easier success.

5677 WATCH SKY SPORTS RACING IN HD H'CAP 7f
6:05 (6:07) (Class 5) (0-70,72) 3-Y-O+
£3,428 (£1,020; £509; £400; £400; £400) **Stalls** Centre

Form RPR

2114 **1** **Magical Ride**[24] 4801 4-9-4 68 .... SeanKirrane(7) 10 88
(Richard Spencer) *trckd ldr: hdwy to ld gng wl 2f out: sn rdn and readily asserted over 1f out: pushed out fnl f: easily* **13/8**[1]

-400 **2** *9* **Arctic Flower (IRE)**[39] 4227 6-8-0 50 oh5 .... GeorgeRooke(7) 7 46
(John Bridger) *led: rdn along and hdd by wnr 2f out: kpt on for remote 2nd fnl f* **20/1**

2600 **3** *1 ¼* **Bbob Alula**[21] 4926 4-9-6 68 .... (t[1]) ThoreHammerHansen(5) 9 61
(Bill Turner) *racd in midfield: rdn along and making hdwy whn briefly short of room 1f out: kpt on fnl f* **22/1**

4023 **4** *1* **Grey Galleon (USA)**[24] 4786 5-10-0 71 .... (p) HectorCrouch 12 61
(Clive Cox) *hld up: pushed along and no hdwy over 2f out: rdn and minor hdwy into midfield over 1f out: kpt on for remote 4th fnl f* **5/1**[2]

4265 **5** *1 ¼* **Pearl Spectre (USA)**[15] 5144 8-8-7 57 .... (v) GraceMcEntee(7) 5 44
(Phil McEntee) *chsd ldr on outer: rdn along and outpcd 2f out: wknd fnl f* **20/1**

3320 **6** *nse* **Choral Music**[34] 4424 4-9-8 72 .... EllieMacKenzie(7) 1 58
(John E Long) *racd in midfield: rdn and no imp on outer over 2f out: one pce after* **7/1**

0051 **7** *hd* **Kyllachys Tale (IRE)**[22] 4870 5-9-5 62 .... JasonWatson 11 48
(Roger Teal) *racd in midfield: short of room against rail after 1f: rdn and no imp 2f out: one pce fnl f* **11/2**[3]

4000 **8** *2 1/4* **Ardimento (IRE)**[47] 3947 3-8-12 **61**........................ RichardKingscote 8 39
(Rod Millman) *racd in midfield: rdn along and outpcd 3f out: wknd fnl f* **8/1**

004 **9** *1 3/4* **Eventura**[14] 5193 3-8-4 **53**........................ RaulDaSilva 6 26
(Tony Carroll) *hld up: rdn along on outer over 2f out: nvr on terms* **20/1**

2305 **10** *3/4* **Gabriela Laura**[7] 5429 3-9-4 **67**........................(h[1]) RossaRyan 4 38
(Alexandra Dunn) *hld up: a in rr* **50/1**

0000 **11** *3* **The Right Choice (IRE)**[41] 4148 4-9-9 **66**........................ ShaneKelly 2 31
(Jamie Osborne) *racd in tch: rdn along and lost pl 2f out: sn bhd* **12/1**

1m 20.46s (-3.84) **Going Correction** -0.375s/f (Firm) course record
WFA 3 from 4yo+ 6lb **11** Ran SP% **122.0**
Speed ratings (Par 103): **106,95,94,93,91 91,91,88,86,86 82**
CSF £45.68 CT £564.67 TOTE £2.20: £1.20, £3.90, £6.00; EX 39.60 Trifecta £684.20.
Owner The Magic Horse Syndicate **Bred** Highclere Stud **Trained** Newmarket, Suffolk
■ Stewards' Enquiry : George Rooke two-day ban: careless riding (Aug 17-18)

FOCUS
This modest handicap was taken apart by the favourite, who is clearly still well ahead of his mark. The level is hard to pin down.

5678 MAX YULL 18TH BIRTHDAY CELEBRATIONS H'CAP 6f
6:35 (6:38) (Class 6) (0-65,67) 3-Y-0+
£2,781 (£827; £413; £400; £400; £400) **Stalls** Centre

Form RPR
0-11 **1** **Bay Watch (IRE)**[7] 5449 5-9-7 **60**........................ JohnFahy 5 73+
(Tracey Barfoot-Saunt) *restrained and swtchd rt out of stalls: hdwy u.p 2f out: rdn and qcknd up wl to ld ins fnl f: cosily* **6/5**[1]

5253 **2** *1 1/4* **Urban Highway (IRE)**[25] 4755 3-9-4 **61**........................ TomMarquand 16 65
(Tony Carroll) *racd in midfield against stands' rail: effrt to cl over 2f out: led on rail over 1f out: sn rdn and hdd by wnr ins fnl f: no ex* **13/2**[3]

0-43 **3** *3/4* **Threefeetfromgold (IRE)**[24] 4800 3-9-8 **65**........................(h) EoinWalsh 6 67
(Martin Smith) *racd in midfield: rdn along over 1f out: sn drvn and kpt on wl ins fnl f* **8/1**

3415 **4** *1/2* **Chikoko Trail**[9] 5351 4-9-12 **65**........................(vt) HectorCrouch 11 66
(Gary Moore) *racd in midfield: hdwy u.p over 2f out: rdn along and ev ch over 1f out: one pce fnl f* **7/2**[2]

3006 **5** *1/2* **Catapult**[11] 5264 4-8-2 **48**........................(p) GavinAshton(7) 8 48
(Shaun Keightley) *chsd ldr: rdn along to ld on outer 2f out: hung lft and hdd over 1f out: one pce fnl f (jockey said gelding hung left-handed in the final furlong)* **12/1**

0-00 **6** *nk* **Crimson Princess**[35] 4376 4-8-7 **46** oh1........................ BrettDoyle 12 45
(Nikki Evans) *led and racd keenly: rdn along and hdd 2f out: one pce fnl f* **66/1**

140- **7** *4 1/2* **Wotadoll**[218] 9733 5-9-10 **63**........................ RossaRyan 7 48
(Mike Murphy) *racd in midfield: rdn along and no rspnse over 1f out: no ex* **8/1**

0020 **8** *7* **Sir Ottoman (FR)**[42] 4103 6-10-0 **67**........................(p) TrevorWhelan 9 31
(Ivan Furtado) *chsd ldr: rdn along and fnd little 2f out: wknd fnl f (jockey said gelding hung left-handed and stopped quickly)* **16/1**

00-0 **9** *31* **And Yet She Moves (IRE)**[35] 4377 3-7-12 **46** oh1........ RhiainIngram(5) 2
(Adam West) *hld up: rdn along and detached 1/2-way (jockey said filly was outpaced)* **40/1**

1m 9.9s (-1.60) **Going Correction** -0.375s/f (Firm)
WFA 3 from 4yo+ 4lb **9** Ran SP% **120.7**
Speed ratings (Par 101): **95,93,92,91,91 90,84,75,33**
CSF £10.39 CT £47.66 TOTE £2.20: £1.10, £2.80, £1.80; EX 11.80 Trifecta £50.60.
Owner P Ponting **Bred** D J & Mrs Brown **Trained** Charfield, Gloucs

FOCUS
An ordinary sprint but won by a very much in-form gelding. Limited form in behind the winner.

5679 KEN & MARGARET GOLDEN WEDDING ANNIVERSARY H'CAP 1m 3f 133y
7:05 (7:08) (Class 6) (0-60,60) 3-Y-0+
£2,781 (£827; £413; £400; £400; £400) **Stalls** High

Form RPR
2040 **1** **Contingency Fee**[4] 5528 4-9-5 **58**........................(p) GraceMcEntee(7) 5 64
(Phil McEntee) *mde virtually all: rdn along w 1 l ld 2f out: drvn and hld on gamely ins fnl f (trainer's rep said, regarding the apparent improved form shown, the gelding appreciated the smaller field on this occasion which allowed him to settle better and dictate the pace)* **8/1**

160- **2** *1 1/4* **Lily Ash (IRE)**[261] 9067 6-9-10 **56**........................ RossaRyan 6 60
(Mike Murphy) *racd in midfield: effrt to chse wnr over 2f out: sn rdn to chse wnr over 1f out: kpt on fnl f* **9/1**

0001 **3** *1* **Sir Canford (IRE)**[63] 3348 3-9-4 **60**........................(p) TomMarquand 8 63
(Ali Stronge) *hld up: hdwy u.p on outer 2f out: rdn and hung sltly lft 1f out: kpt on fnl f: nt rch front pair (jockey said gelding hung left-handed under pressure)* **2/1**[1]

2506 **4** *1* **Mr Fox**[35] 4400 3-9-3 **59**........................ CallumShepherd 2 61
(Michael Attwater) *hld up: pushed along in rr 3f out: rdn and no imp 2f out: kpt on fnl f (jockey said gelding clipped heels coming down the hill)* **16/1**

540- **5** *nk* **Milldean Felix (IRE)**[20] 8575 3-8-13 **55**........................(b) TrevorWhelan 10 56
(Suzi Best) *racd in midfield: drvn to chse wnr 2f out: kpt on one pce fnl f* **50/1**

0450 **6** *1 3/4* **Hatsaway (IRE)**[16] 5089 8-9-11 **60**........................ PaddyBradley(3) 3 57
(Pat Phelan) *hld up: rdn along and no imp 2f out: one pce after* **7/1**[2]

-242 **7** *1 1/4* **Zamperini (IRE)**[69] 1498 7-9-13 **59**........................ HectorCrouch 7 54
(Gary Moore) *hld up: rdn and outpcd over 2f out: nvr on terms* **2/1**[1]

6401 **8** *2 1/2* **Al Daayen (FR)**[19] 5004 3-9-4 **60**........................ JackMitchell 4 52
(Conrad Allen) *chsd ldr and racd keenly: rdn along and ev ch over 1f out: wknd qckly fnl f* **15/2**[3]

2m 29.65s (-4.35) **Going Correction** -0.375s/f (Firm)
WFA 3 from 4yo+ 10lb **8** Ran SP% **119.9**
Speed ratings (Par 101): **99,98,97,96,96 95,94,92**
CSF £79.99 CT £201.70 TOTE £10.10: £2.60, £1.70, £1.10; EX 77.40 Trifecta £270.60.
Owner M Hall **Bred** Whitwell Bloodstock **Trained** Newmarket, Suffolk

FOCUS
Those who were held up were edging closer as the line approached but the winner just about made every yard. The winner has been rated in line with the best of this year's turf form.

5680 SKY SPORTS RACING ON VIRGIN 535 H'CAP 1m 2f
7:35 (7:37) (Class 6) (0-60,60) 3-Y-0+
£2,781 (£827; £413; £400; £400; £400) **Stalls** Low

Form RPR
0 **1** **Cafe Sydney (IRE)**[19] 4991 3-8-7 **48**........................ BrettDoyle 11 60+
(Tony Carroll) *racd in midfield: smooth hdwy to chse ldr 2f out: rdn and readily asserted over 1f out: comf* **10/1**

6061 **2** *3 1/4* **Shifting Gold (IRE)**[18] 5031 3-9-5 **60**........................ DavidEgan 10 66
(William Knight) *hld up: effrt on outer to chse ldr 2f out: sn rdn and hung lft 1f out: kpt on to take 2nd clsng stages* **10/3**[3]

0431 **3** *1 1/2* **Whimsical Dream**[17] 5049 3-8-8 **49**........................ LukeMorris 7 52
(Michael Bell) *settled in 4th: smooth hdwy to ld 2f out: sn rdn and hdd by wnr over 1f out: lost 2nd clsng stages* **6/4**[1]

00-3 **4** *2 1/2* **Estrela Star (IRE)**[21] 4931 3-9-3 **58**........................ TomMarquand 4 56
(Ali Stronge) *racd in midfield: rdn and outpcd 2f out: kpt on one pce fnl f* **3/1**[2]

/0-0 **5** *3* **Skylark Lady (IRE)**[22] 4870 6-8-7 **45**........................(p) SophieRalston(5) 1 37
(Nikki Evans) *hld up: rdn along in rr over 2f out: nvr on terms* **50/1**

0-04 **6** *1* **Buzz Lightyere**[24] 4771 6-9-12 **59**........................(v) CharlieBennett 13 49
(Patrick Chamings) *dwlt but sn rcvrd to chse ldr: rdn along and lost pl over 1f out: wknd fnl f* **7/1**

400 **7** *1/2* **Valentine Mist (IRE)**[49] 3843 7-8-12 **45**........................ JohnFahy 6 34
(James Grassick) *led: rdn along and hdd 2f out: wknd fnl f* **66/1**

0000 **8** *4* **Inspirational (IRE)**[39] 4217 3-8-7 **48**........................ HollieDoyle 5 30
(Ed Dunlop) *chsd ldr early: rdn along and lost pl over 2f out: sn bhd* **16/1**

2m 6.78s (-5.42) **Going Correction** -0.375s/f (Firm)
WFA 3 from 4yo+ 8lb **8** Ran SP% **119.0**
Speed ratings (Par 101): **106,103,102,100,97 97,96,93**
CSF £45.22 CT £80.30 TOTE £12.10: £2.20, £1.50, £1.10; EX 55.70 Trifecta £117.30.
Owner Contubernium Racing **Bred** John Walsh **Trained** Cropthorne, Worcs

FOCUS
A moderate handicap. It's been rated at face value.

5681 VISIT ATTHERACES.COM EBF NOVICE STKS 4f 217y
8:05 (8:05) (Class 5) 2-Y-O
£3,428 (£1,020) **Stalls** Centre

Form RPR
254 **1** **Al Raya**[29] 4610 2-9-0 **94**........................ AndreaAtzeni 1 87+
(Simon Crisford) *mde all: nudged along w short ld over 1f out: rdn and asserted fnl f* **1/16**[1]

2 *3 1/2* **Band Practice (IRE)** 2-9-0 **0**........................ HollieDoyle 2 74+
(Archie Watson) *chsd wnr and racd keenly: v green at times: pushed upsides wnr over 1f out: rdn and no match for wnr fnl f* **6/1**[2]

57.71s (-0.99) **Going Correction** -0.375s/f (Firm) **2** Ran SP% **108.4**
Speed ratings (Par 94): **92,86**
TOTE £1.10.
Owner H H SH Nasser Bin Hamad Al Khalifa **Bred** Ed's Stud Ltd **Trained** Newmarket, Suffolk

FOCUS
The long odds-on favourite was found a nice opening, but the runner-up shaped with plenty of promise as well.
T/Plt: £10.00 to a £1 stake. Pool: £47,228.81 - 3,417.50 winning units T/Qpdt: £7.40 to a £1 stake. Pool: £6,450.92 - 638.80 winning units **Mark Grantham**

5622 NEWMARKET (R-H)
Saturday, August 3

OFFICIAL GOING: Good to firm (good in places; watered; 7.5)
Wind: nil Weather: very warm and sunny; 23 degrees

5682 BRITISH STALLION STUDS EBF CHALICE STKS (LISTED RACE) (F&M) 1m 4f
2:05 (2:07) (Class 1) 3-Y-O+
£22,684 (£8,600; £4,304; £2,144; £1,076; £540) **Stalls** Centre

Form RPR
0354 **1** **Love So Deep (JPN)**[14] 5190 3-8-9 **100**........................ JFEgan 2 104
(Jane Chapple-Hyam) *midfield: effrt 3f out: rdn to ld 2f out: a doing enough fnl f* **6/1**

1111 **2** *2* **Bella Vita**[22] 4864 3-8-9 **91**........................ CharlesBishop 3 101
(Eve Johnson Houghton) *taken steadily towards rr: effrt on outer fr 4f out: rdn and chsd wnr wl over 1f out: kpt on gamely but no imp* **5/2**[2]

-220 **3** *1* **Shambolic (IRE)**[44] 4014 3-8-9 **98**........................ RobertHavlin 6 99
(John Gosden) *disp 3rd tl led 3f out: rdn and hdd 2f out: a hld by ldng pair after* **7/2**[3]

-142 **4** *1/2* **Spirit Of Appin**[14] 5190 4-9-5 **97**........................ OisinMurphy 5 97
(Brian Meehan) *cl up: rdn 2f out: nt qckn fnl f* **9/4**[1]

-505 **5** *nk* **Blue Gardenia (IRE)**[14] 5190 3-8-9 **95**........................(p[1]) JamieSpencer 4 98
(David O'Meara) *settled in rr: effrt 3f out: drvn and chsd ldrs over 1f out: sn no imp* **8/1**

1423 **6** *26* **Vampish**[42] 4118 4-9-5 **74**........................ RobHornby 8 55
(Philip McBride) *pressed ldr tl 3f out: completely t.o fnl 2f: eased* **66/1**

0-50 **7** *6* **Crystal Moonlight**[41] 4145 4-9-5 **88**........................ ColmO'Donoghue 1 46
(Sir Michael Stoute) *plld too hrd: pressed ldrs tl over 3f out: completely t.o and eased fnl 2f* **20/1**

5212 **8** *hd* **Incredulous**[9] 5341 3-8-9 **80**........................ LiamJones 7 46
(William Haggas) *taken down early: led: rdn and hdd 3f out: fdd rapidly: completely t.o and eased fnl f* **25/1**

2m 31.76s (-2.14) **Going Correction** +0.075s/f (Good)
WFA 3 from 4yo 10lb **8** Ran SP% **117.1**
Speed ratings (Par 111): **110,108,108,107,107 90,86,86**
CSF £21.60 TOTE £7.80: £1.80, £1.30, £1.50; EX 25.60 Trifecta £110.70.
Owner Love So Deep Syndicate **Bred** Daylesford Stud **Trained** Dalham, Suffolk

FOCUS
Far side course used. Stalls: far side, except 1m2f & 1m4f: centre. Add 20yds. Not a strong Listed race, but it went to the highest-rated filly. The pace was ordinary and they headed more central in the straight. The third has been rated close to form.

5683 EUROPEAN BLOODSTOCK NEWS BRITISH EBF FILLIES' NURSERY H'CAP 6f
2:40 (2:41) (Class 2) 2-Y-O
£16,178; £3,728; £1,864; £932; £468 **Stalls** Low

Form RPR
1205 **1** **Rose Of Kildare (IRE)**[8] 5390 2-9-1 **81**........................ WilliamBuick 12 89
(Mark Johnston) *uns rdr in paddock: prom: led after 3f: rdn over 1f out: kpt on wl tl jnd on line* **4/1**[1]

104 **1** **Graceful Magic**[24] 4790 2-8-10 **76**........................ CharlesBishop 8 86+
(Eve Johnson Houghton) *t.k.h: chsd ldrs: n.m.r and swtchd rt over 1f out: drvn and styd on wl fnl f to force a dead-heat* **12/1**

216 **3** *1 3/4* **Bredenbury (IRE)**[22] 4883 2-9-5 **85**........................ JamieSpencer 9 88
(David Simcock) *stdd s: t.k.h towards rr: rdn to cl over 1f out: no imp fnl 100yds* **4/1**[1]

4142 **4** *3/4* **Rosadora (IRE)**[14] 5171 2-9-2 **82**........................ OisinMurphy 13 83
(Ralph Beckett) *prom: drvn and ev ch 200yds out: nt qckn after* **4/1**[1]

The Form Book Flat 2019, Raceform Ltd, Newbury, RG14 5SJ

2116 **5** *2* **Go Well Spicy (IRE)**[28] 4647 2-8-10 **76**.................. RobHornby 5 71
(Mick Channon) *chsd ldrs: n.m.r 2f out and rdn: rallied and r.o wl to pass two rivals cl home (jockey said filly was denied a clear run)* **20/1**

1042 **6** *3/4* **Seraphinite (IRE)**[9] 5340 2-8-11 **77**.................. RobertHavlin 7 69
(Jamie Osborne) *dwlt: plld hrd: n.m.r 2f out: hdwy over 1f out: kpt on wout threatening fnl f (jockey said filly was denied a clear run)* **16/1**

0021 **7** *1* **Infinite Grace**[19] 4985 2-9-0 **80**.................. ColmO'Donoghue 6 69
(David O'Meara) *midfield: rdn and kpt on ins fnl f: nt rch ldrs* **14/1**

4154 **8** *hd* **Bella Brazil (IRE)**[24] 4780 2-8-5 **71**.................. JFEgan 2 60
(David Barron) *t.k.h: effrt 1/2-way: rdn and no ex over 1f out* **25/1**

4131 **9** *2* **Know No Limits (IRE)**[22] 4878 2-9-4 **87**.................. JaneElliott(3) 11 70
(Tom Dascombe) *led 3f: rdn and btn 2f out* **7/1**[3]

102 **10** *3/4* **Three Coins**[12] 5243 2-8-9 **75**.................. PaddyMathers 1 55
(Richard Fahey) *n.m.r 2f out: struggling u.p in rr after (jockey said filly was denied a clear run)* **20/1**

465 **11** *nk* **Falconidae (IRE)**[23] 4849 2-8-5 **71**.................. JohnFahy 4 51
(Richard Hannon) *cl up for over 4f* **20/1**

512 **12** *hd* **Mia Diva**[16] 5093 2-8-11 **77**.................. JasonHart 3 56
(John Quinn) *t.k.h: nvr bttr than midfield: short of room over 1f out* **13/2**[2]

1514 **13** *3/4* **Gold Venture (IRE)**[10] 5295 2-8-1 **67**.................. JimmyQuinn 10 44
(Philip Kirby) *cl up tl drvn and wknd wl over 1f out* **66/1**

1m 12.37s (0.27) **Going Correction** +0.075s/f (Good) **13** Ran SP% **125.7**
Speed ratings (Par 97): **101,101,98,97,95 94,92,92,89,88 88,88,87**WIN: 2.50 Rose Of Kildare, 7.90 Graceful Magic; PL: 1.60 Bredenbury, 2.20 Rose Of Kildare, 3.90 Graceful Magic; EX: ROK/GM 30.20, GM/ROK 47.90; CSF: ROK/GB 27.19, GM/ROK 29.30; TC: ROK/GM/B 106.45, GM/ROK/B 118.84; TF: ROK/GM/B 212.80, GM/ROK/B 732.60; TOTE £27: £Owner, £Kingsley Park 14, £Bred, £Wansdyke Farms LtdTrained Middleham Moor, N Yorks.
Owner The Kimber Family **Bred** Dr Scott Kimber **Trained** Blewbury, Oxon

FOCUS
A fair nursery and the first two proved inseparable. Solid form.

5684 NEWMARKET EQUINE HOSPITAL BRITISH EBF FILLIES' NOVICE STKS (PLUS 10 RACE) 7f

3:15 (3:16) (Class 4) 2-Y-O **£5,175** (£1,540; £769; £384) **Stalls** Low

Form RPR

4 **1** **Angel Of Delight (IRE)**[60] 3441 2-9-0 0.................. JosephineGordon 7 79
(Hugo Palmer) *slowly away: sn cl up: shkn up 3f out: rdn to ld fnl 120yds: kpt on steadily* **12/1**

4 **2** *1 1/4* **Dirty Dancer (FR)**[15] 5132 2-9-0 0.................. RobHornby 6 76
(Ralph Beckett) *led: rdn over 1f out: hdd fnl 120yds: a hld after* **7/4**[1]

3 *3/4* **Amber Island (IRE)** 2-9-0 0.................. WilliamBuick 2 74+
(Charlie Appleby) *prom: rdn over 2f out: sn outpcd: rallied wl to go 3rd fnl 50yds* **2/1**[2]

4 *1/2* **Festive Star** 2-9-0 0.................. OisinMurphy 3 73
(Simon Crisford) *pressed ldrs: rdn and wnt 2nd 2f out: one pce fnl f: lost 3rd cl home* **7/1**

5 *1* **A La Voile** 2-9-0 0.................. ColmO'Donoghue 1 70
(Sir Michael Stoute) *towards rr: rdn and hung lft over 1f out: no imp fnl 100yds* **16/1**

6 *1/2* **Mira Star (IRE)** 2-9-0 0.................. JamieSpencer 8 69+
(Ed Vaughan) *towards rr: pushed along 1/2-way: kpt on wout threatening ins fnl f* **13/2**[3]

7 *hd* **Parikarma (IRE)** 2-9-0 0.................. TomQueally 4 68
(Ed Dunlop) *racd keenly towards rr: rdn 2f out: nt trble ldrs after* **40/1**

8 *16* **Lovers' Gait (IRE)** 2-9-0 0.................. RobertHavlin 5 27
(Ed Dunlop) *awkward leaving stalls: wl bhd 2f out: completely t.o* **25/1**

9 *4 1/2* **Exotic Escape** 2-9-0 0.................. JFEgan 9 15
(David Lanigan) *bhd: remote 2f out: completely t.o* **33/1**

1m 26.76s (1.06) **Going Correction** +0.075s/f (Good) **9** Ran SP% **118.3**
Speed ratings (Par 93): **96,94,93,93,92 91,91,72,67**
CSF £33.88 TOTE £13.70: £2.30, £1.10, £1.10; EX 57.30 Trifecta £170.30.
Owner Dr Ali Ridha **Bred** Roundhill Stud & J S Investments **Trained** Newmarket, Suffolk

FOCUS
Not a particularly strong novice for the track and those racing more down the centre were see to best effect. It's been rated as ordinary form.

5685 FEDERATION OF BLOODSTOCK AGENTS H'CAP 7f

3:50 (3:51) (Class 3) (0-90,91) 3-Y-O **£9,056** (£2,695; £1,346; £673) **Stalls** Low

Form RPR

0022 **1** **Ventura Ocean (IRE)**[14] 5173 3-9-8 **91**.................. PaddyMathers 3 99
(Richard Fahey) *pressed ldrs: rdn to ld 2f out: got first run on fnl chalr and hung on gamely* **7/2**[3]

4324 **2** *nse* **Fastman (IRE)**[22] 4895 3-9-5 **88**.................. JamieSpencer 1 95
(David O'Meara) *racd in last pair: drvn and effrt wl over 1f out: sustained chal fnl 100yds: jst too much to do* **9/4**[1]

3210 **3** *1 1/2* **Jaleel**[22] 4887 3-9-0 **83**..................(b[1]) OisinMurphy 4 86
(Roger Varian) *t.k.h: racd in last pair: rdn and effrt over 1f out: ev ch ins fnl f: wknd cl home* **3/1**[2]

-355 **4** *2* **Motagally**[42] 4123 3-8-10 **79**.................. ColmO'Donoghue 7 77
(Charles Hills) *stdd s: plld hrd in rr: effrt 2f out: pressing ldrs 1f out: wknd fnl 100yds* **12/1**

5234 **5** *1/2* **Reeves**[43] 4065 3-9-3 **86**.................. JimmyQuinn 2 82
(Robert Cowell) *t.k.h: pressed ldr: rdn 2f out: no rspnse and edgd lft: btn over 1f out* **11/2**

-003 **6** *1* **Blonde Warrior (IRE)**[36] 4348 3-9-7 **90**..................(p) RobertHavlin 6 84
(Hugo Palmer) *led: drvn and hdd 2f out: sn lost pl* **13/2**

1m 25.7s **Going Correction** +0.075s/f (Good) **6** Ran SP% **114.4**
Speed ratings (Par 104): **103,102,101,98,98 97**
CSF £12.16 CT £25.30 TOTE £4.10: £2.10, £1.50; EX 12.10 Trifecta £28.60.
Owner Middleham Park Racing Xix & Partner **Bred** Mrs Renata Coleman **Trained** Musley Bank, N Yorks

FOCUS
Not overly strong form for the grade. They again headed down the middle. The second has been rated as improving in line with his profile, and the third close to his June C&D win.

5686 CROWN AT STOWUPLAND H'CAP 1m 4f

4:25 (4:25) (Class 3) (0-95,88) 3-Y-O+ **£9,703** (£2,887; £1,443; £721) **Stalls** Centre

Form RPR

3000 **1** **Stamford Raffles**[35] 4381 6-9-7 **84**.................. TimClark(3) 2 90
(Jane Chapple-Hyam) *settled in 3rd pl: effrt to ld 2f out: rdn and hanging lft after: kpt on same pce but a had enough in reserve (trainer's rep could offer no explanation for the improved form shown)* **11/1**

0020 **2** *2* **Fairy Tale (IRE)**[21] 4899 4-9-11 **85**.................. JimmyQuinn 5 88
(Gay Kelleway) *settled in last pl: rdn and outpcd 3f out: wandering arnd in clsng stages but plodded into 2nd cl home* **11/2**[3]

6502 **3** *1* **Escape The City**[10] 5305 4-8-12 **72**.................. OisinMurphy 3 73
(Hughie Morrison) *pressed ldr: rdn 2f out: sn outpcd by wnr: lost 2nd fnl 50yds* **1/1**[1]

5126 **4** *20* **Oasis Fantasy (IRE)**[22] 4890 8-10-0 **88**.................. JamieSpencer 4 76
(David Simcock) *led tl rdn and hdd 2f out: nt keen and sn btn: t.o and eased fnl f (trainer's rep could offer no explanation for the performance shown)* **7/4**[2]

2m 34.13s (0.23) **Going Correction** +0.075s/f (Good) **4** Ran SP% **110.1**
Speed ratings (Par 107): **102,100,100,86**
CSF £56.91 TOTE £12.30; EX 45.90 Trifecta £89.70.
Owner Mrs Jane Chapple-Hyam **Bred** C A Cyzer **Trained** Dalham, Suffolk

FOCUS
Add 20yds. A bit of a turn-up here and not form to take much notice of moving forward. The winner has been rated back to his old turf form.

5687 BRITISH EBF MARITIME CARGO FILLIES' H'CAP 1m 2f

5:00 (5:01) (Class 3) (0-90,88) 3-Y-O+ **£9,703** (£2,887; £1,443; £721) **Stalls** Centre

Form RPR

424 **1** **Clarion**[32] 4474 3-8-11 **78**.................. ColmO'Donoghue 8 87+
(Sir Michael Stoute) *trckd ldrs: rdn and outpcd 2f out: rallied to ld ins fnl f: pushed clr: comf* **7/1**

313 **2** *1 3/4* **Tabassor (IRE)**[35] 4377 3-8-12 **79**.................. WilliamBuick 7 83
(Charles Hills) *led: rdn 3f out: hdd over 1f out: kpt on to regain 2nd ins fnl f: no ch w wnr* **13/2**

-012 **3** *1/2* **Manorah (IRE)**[35] 4391 3-8-13 **80**.................. OisinMurphy 5 83
(Roger Varian) *prom: rdn to chal for ld over 1f out: ev ch 200yds out: no ex* **15/8**[1]

1455 **4** *hd* **Elisheba (IRE)**[43] 4068 3-9-0 **81**..................(p[1]) RobertHavlin 6 83
(John Gosden) *pressed ldr: rdn to dispute ld over 1f out: hdd and nt qckn fnl 200yds* **6/1**

2405 **5** *3 1/4* **Star Of War (USA)**[23] 4841 3-9-1 **82**.................. JamieSpencer 3 78
(Richard Hannon) *racd in last pair: rdn 2f out: btn and hanging lft fnl f* **4/1**[2]

1116 **6** *7* **Arctic Fox**[28] 4644 3-9-7 **88**.................. PaddyMathers 2 70
(Richard Fahey) *t.k.h: racd in last pair: rdn over 2f out: sn btn: eased ins fnl f (jockey said filly had no more to give)* **9/2**[3]

2m 8.06s (0.96) **Going Correction** +0.075s/f (Good) **6** Ran SP% **113.1**
Speed ratings (Par 104): **99,97,97,97,94 88**
CSF £49.97 CT £118.34 TOTE £5.80: £2.30, £3.20; EX 28.60 Trifecta £77.80.
Owner The Queen **Bred** The Queen **Trained** Newmarket, Suffolk

FOCUS
Add 20yds. A fair 3yo handicap run at a steady gallop. Muddling form, with the fourth rated to her recent handicap form for now.

5688 ST ANDREWS BUREAU H'CAP 1m

5:35 (5:39) (Class 4) (0-85,82) 3-Y-O+
£6,469 (£1,925; £962; £481; £300; £300) **Stalls** Low

Form RPR

032 **1** **Alnaseem**[14] 5193 3-9-3 **78**..................(h) OisinMurphy 5 85+
(Luke McJannet) *settled trcking ldrs: shkn up over 1f out: led ins fnl f: edgd lft briefly but a looked like holding on* **4/1**[3]

5006 **2** *1* **Harbour Vision**[14] 5178 4-9-2 **70**..................(v[1]) PaddyMathers 2 76
(Derek Shaw) *last early: r.o u.p fr over 1f out: wnt 2nd cl home: nt looking v enthusiastic and a hld* **11/1**

1-42 **3** *1/2* **Eula Varner**[16] 5105 5-9-8 **76**.................. CharlesBishop 6 81
(Henry Candy) *t.k.h and pressed ldr: u.p 2f out: nt qckn ins fnl f: lost 2nd cl home* **5/2**[2]

0362 **4** *1 1/4* **James Park Woods (IRE)**[15] 5140 3-9-1 **76**.................. RobHornby 3 77
(Ralph Beckett) *led: rdn 2f out: hdd 200yds out: fading fnl 100yds* **2/1**[1]

3415 **5** *2 3/4* **Liliofthelamplight (IRE)**[28] 4626 3-9-2 **77**.................. WilliamBuick 1 72
(Mark Johnston) *t.k.h: prom: rdn 2f out: wknd over 1f out* **15/2**

2005 **6** *2 3/4* **Top Mission**[22] 4867 5-9-7 **82**.................. MarcoGhiani(7) 4 71
(Marco Botti) *towards rr: rdn to lost tch 2f out: wandering arnd fnl f* **15/2**

1m 39.45s (-0.55) **Going Correction** +0.075s/f (Good)
WFA 3 from 4yo+ 7lb **6** Ran SP% **113.8**
Speed ratings (Par 105): **105,104,103,102,99 96**
CSF £43.95 TOTE £4.50: £2.30, £3.90; EX 52.10 Trifecta £177.10.
Owner Miss Rebecca Dennis **Bred** Shadwell Estate Company Limited **Trained** Newmarket, Suffolk

FOCUS
An ordinary handicap and no surprise to see one of the 3yos come to the fore. It's been rated around the second to his turf best.
T/Plt: £6,513.50 to a £1 stake. Pool: £76,735.41 - 8.60 winning units T/Qpdt: £384.60 to a £1 stake. Pool: £4,641.99 - 8.93 winning units **Iain Mackenzie**

5387 THIRSK (L-H)

Saturday, August 3

OFFICIAL GOING: Good to soft (soft in places)
Wind: virtually nil Weather: sunshine and cloud

5689 BRITISH EBF NOVICE STKS (PLUS 10 RACE) 5f

1:45 (1:49) (Class 4) 2-Y-O **£5,822** (£1,732; £865; £432) **Stalls** Centre

Form RPR

1 **Wonderwork (IRE)** 2-9-5 0.................. CliffordLee 8 85+
(K R Burke) *dwlt but sn led: mde rest: pushed along 2f out: edgd rt over 1f out but sn clr: kpt on wl: comf* **6/4**[1]

02 **2** *3 3/4* **Instantly**[7] 5427 2-9-5 0.................. CamHardie 5 69
(Robert Cowell) *prom: rdn and outpcd by wnr over 1f out: kpt on same pce ins fnl f (vet reported colt lost its left fore shoe)* **7/1**[3]

06 **3** *nse* **Not On Your Nellie (IRE)**[8] 5388 2-8-9 0.................. FayeMcManoman(5) 10 64
(Nigel Tinkler) *dwlt: hld up: racd keenly: rdn and along and hdwy over 1f out: kpt on ins fnl f (jockey said filly hung left in the closing stages)* **9/1**

6 **4** *1 3/4* **Shadow Leader**[12] 5234 2-9-5 0.................. ConnorBeasley 2 63
(Michael Dods) *chsd ldrs: rdn 2f out: no ex ins fnl f* **18/1**

0 **5** *1/2* **Maurice Dancer**[14] 5172 2-9-5 0.................. PaulHanagan 9 61
(Julie Camacho) *midfield: pushed along 2f out: kpt on ins fnl f: nvr threatened* **11/1**

50 **6** *3/4* **Sombra De Mollys**[12] 5243 2-9-0 0.................. BenRobinson 7 53
(Brian Ellison) *chsd ldrs: rdn over 2f out: no ex fnl f* **33/1**

7 *1 1/2* **Romantic Vision (IRE)** 2-9-5 0.................. DanielTudhope 6 53
(Kevin Ryan) *hld up: gng wl but short of room 2f out: pushed along appr fnl f: nvr threatened* **11/4**[2]

00 **8** *nse* **Northern Grace**[11] 5280 2-8-7 0.................. HarryRussell(7) 3 47
(Brian Ellison) *midfield: rdn 2f out: wknd ins fnl f* **66/1**

0 **9** *nk* **Tenbobmillionaire**[28] 4624 2-9-5 0............ RachelRichardson 1 51
(Tim Easterby) *wnt lft s but sn in tch on outer: pushed along over 2f out: wknd over 1f out* **50/1**

10 *5* **Norton Lad** 2-9-5 0............ DavidAllan 4 33
(Tim Easterby) *hld up: rdn along 2f out: wknd ins fnl f* **12/1**

1m 1.31s (1.91) **Going Correction** +0.05s/f (Good) **10** Ran SP% **116.8**
Speed ratings (Par 96): **86,80,79,77,76 75,72,72,72,64**
CSF £12.75 TOTE £2.20: £1.30, £1.90, £2.10; EX 10.20 Trifecta £47.20.
Owner H Strecker & Mrs E Burke **Bred** Drumlin Bloodstock **Trained** Middleham Moor, N Yorks

FOCUS
A total of 6mm of rain had fallen in the preceding 24 hours, turning the ground Good to Soft, (Soft in Places). A dry afternoon, with temperatures around 22C. A weak novices' sprint and the pace was ordinary, but the winner did it well.

5690 LAURA BARRY MEMORIAL EBF NOVICE STKS 7f 218y
2:15 (2:16) (Class 4) 3-Y-0+ **£6,469** (£1,925; £962; £481) **Stalls** Low

Form RPR

3 **1** **Eva Maria**[31] 4520 3-8-11 0............ PaulHanagan 5 86+
(Richard Fahey) *trckd ldrs: pushed into ld 2f out: sn edgd lft: rdn over 1f out: styd on wl to draw clr ins fnl f* **2/1**[1]

52 **2** *4* **Critical Time**[24] 4806 3-8-11 0............ DanielTudhope 4 77
(William Haggas) *dwlt: sn in tch: pushed along and hdwy over 2f out: drvn to chse ldr over 1f out: styd on but no ch w wnr* **7/2**[3]

4 **3** *2 ½* **Happy Face (IRE)**[15] 5141 3-8-11 0............(t) CliffordLee 9 71
(Hugo Palmer) *prom: rdn along and outpcd 2f out: kpt on same pce in 3rd fnl f* **14/1**

16 **4** *2 ¼* **Trinity Lake**[84] 2634 3-9-9 0............ DavidNolan 6 78
(Declan Carroll) *midfield: rdn over 2f out: styd on fnl f* **13/2**

22 **5** *1 ¼* **Beauty Of Deira (IRE)**[29] 4592 3-8-11 0............ PatCosgrave 2 63
(Hugo Palmer) *trckd ldrs: rdn over 2f out: wknd ins fnl f* **11/4**[2]

04 **6** *4 ½* **Nataleena (IRE)**[43] 4076 3-8-11 0............ AndrewMullen 1 53
(Ben Haslam) *midfield: rdn over 2f out: wknd over 1f out* **100/1**

332 **7** *shd* **Morning Duel (IRE)**[26] 4732 3-9-2 77............(t) CamHardie 3 58
(David O'Meara) *led: rdn and hdd 2f out: wknd over 1f out* **10/1**

8 *2 ½* **Rent's Dew (IRE)** 3-9-2 0............ DavidAllan 10 52
(Tim Easterby) *dwlt: a towards rr* **20/1**

5 **9** *1 ¼* **Laulloir (IRE)**[158] 913 3-8-11 0............ PaulMulrennan 7 44
(Kevin Ryan) *hld up: rdn along and minor hdwy over 1f out: wknd ins fnl f* **50/1**

0 **10** *¾* **Hunters Step**[28] 4636 3-9-2 0............ LewisEdmunds 8 47
(Noel Wilson) *dwlt: hld up: nvr threatened* **100/1**

1m 40.72s (-0.98) **Going Correction** +0.05s/f (Good) **10** Ran SP% **120.0**
Speed ratings (Par 105): **106,102,99,97,96 91,91,88,87,86**
CSF £9.42 TOTE £2.70: £1.10, £1.60, £2.50; EX 11.60 Trifecta £89.60.
Owner W J and T C O Gredley **Bred** Stetchworth & Middle Park Studs Ltd **Trained** Musley Bank, N Yorks

FOCUS
Not a deep race and the early gallop was modest, but a couple of nice types should go on to rate higher. They finished well strung out. The fourth has been rated in line with his debut win and helps set the level.

5691 EVERY RACE LIVE ON RACING TV H'CAP 5f
2:50 (2:51) (Class 4) (0-85,86) 3-Y-0+
£7,309 (£2,175; £1,087; £543; £300; £300) **Stalls** Centre

Form RPR

2500 **1** **Hawaam (IRE)**[7] 5420 4-9-0 74............(p) DanielTudhope 10 86
(Roger Fell) *swtchd rt after s to r against stands' rail: mde all: pushed clr over 1f out: rdn out ins fnl f: unchal (trainer said, regarding the apparent improvement in form, that gelding appreciated the uncontested lead on this occasion)* **9/1**

0536 **2** *3 ½* **Our Little Pony**[8] 5395 4-8-8 73............ FayeMcManoman(5) 4 72+
(Lawrence Mullaney) *hld up towards centre: pushed along and hdwy over 1f out: kpt on wl fnl f: wnt 2nd towards fin: no ch w wnr* **7/1**[3]

0444 **3** *1 ½* **The Armed Man**[13] 5217 6-9-4 83............ PaulaMuir(5) 5 77
(Chris Fairhurst) *chsd ldrs towards centre: rdn along 2f out: kpt on same pce ins fnl f* **6/1**[2]

0323 **4** *½* **Roundhay Park**[19] 4987 4-9-9 86............(p[1]) RowanScott(3) 11 78
(Nigel Tinkler) *racd towards stands' side: chsd ldr: rdn over 2f out: edgd lft appr fnl f: kpt on same pce* **11/4**[1]

2020 **5** *1 ¾* **Bowson Fred**[22] 4880 7-9-3 77............(h[1]) DavidAllan 6 63
(Michael Easterby) *prom centre: rdn over 2f out: wknd ins fnl f* **7/1**[3]

0620 **6** *2* **Manshood (IRE)**[14] 5205 6-9-10 84............(v) PaulMulrennan 12 63
(Paul Midgley) *dwlt: racd stands' side and sn chsd ldr: rdn over 2f out: wknd fnl f* **15/2**

2-50 **7** *shd* **Almurr (IRE)**[28] 4649 3-9-1 78............ PaulHanagan 1 55
(Phillip Makin) *hld up in centre: rdn along and sme hdwy over out: nvr threatened* **25/1**

4155 **8** *1* **Canford Bay (IRE)**[7] 5420 5-9-8 82............ CamHardie 7 57
(Antony Brittain) *prom in centre: rdn over 2f out: wknd fnl f* **8/1**

0040 **9** *1 ¾* **Confessional**[35] 4359 12-9-8 82............(e) JamieGormley 2 50
(Tim Easterby) *hld up: nvr threatened* **16/1**

4006 **10** *2 ¼* **Henley**[23] 4821 7-9-1 75............ BarryMcHugh 8 35
(Tracy Waggott) *midfield in centre: rdn over 2f out: wknd over 1f out* **20/1**

0002 **11** *3 ¼* **Alsvinder**[10] 5298 6-9-2 76............ DavidNolan 3 25
(Philip Kirby) *midfield in centre: rdn over 2f out: wknd over 1f out* **14/1**

59.05s (-0.35) **Going Correction** +0.05s/f (Good)
WFA 3 from 4yo+ 3lb **11** Ran SP% **120.0**
Speed ratings (Par 105): **104,98,96,95,92 89,89,87,84,81 75**
CSF £72.19 CT £423.87 TOTE £11.40: £3.20, £2.50, £2.10; EX 98.50 Trifecta £580.90.
Owner Arcane Racing Partnership **Bred** Knocklong House Stud **Trained** Nawton, N Yorks

FOCUS
Fair for the grade. The draw can prove critical in sprints at this track and the winner made all from a decent berth. The winner has been rated to his best.

5692 TOMAHAWK H'CAP 7f
3:25 (3:26) (Class 3) (0-90,91) 3-Y-0+ **£12,938** (£3,850; £1,924; £962) **Stalls** Low

Form RPR

221 **1** **Shawaamekh**[50] 3813 5-9-6 83............(t) DavidNolan 6 94+
(Declan Carroll) *trckd ldrs: pushed along 2f out: led appr fnl f: rdn and kpt on wl* **3/1**[1]

0400 **2** *2* **Queen's Sargent (FR)**[14] 5173 4-9-0 77............ PatCosgrave 15 82
(Kevin Ryan) *sn prom: pushed into ld 2f out: rdn and hdd appr fnl f: kpt on* **12/1**

004 **3** *1 ¼* **Gymkhana**[36] 4319 6-9-8 85............(v) CamHardie 10 87
(David O'Meara) *midfield: rdn and hdwy over 1f out: kpt on: wnt 3rd towards fin* **33/1**

1030 **4** *shd* **John Kirkup**[8] 5395 4-8-13 76............(p) ConnorBeasley 13 77
(Michael Dods) *trckd ldrs: racd quite keenly: rdn over 1f out: one pce ins fnl f: lost 3rd towards fin* **20/1**

0223 **5** *½* **Esprit De Corps**[10] 5303 5-8-10 73............ BenRobinson 8 73
(David Barron) *midfield: pushed along and sme hdwy appr fnl f: drvn and kpt on same pce (vet reported gelding lost its left hind shoe)* **14/1**

4460 **6** *nk* **Socru (IRE)**[7] 5459 3-8-2 71............(h[1]) JamieGormley 12 68+
(Michael Easterby) *slowly away: hld up in rr: rdn and stl lot to do on wd outside over 1f out: kpt on (jockey said gelding reared as the stalls opened and missed the break)* **25/1**

2545 **7** *1 ½* **Right Action**[14] 5195 5-9-5 82............ PaulHanagan 2 77
(Richard Fahey) *trckd ldrs: rdn 2f out: wknd ins fnl f (vet reported gelding lost its right fore shoe)* **12/1**

0060 **8** *nse* **Von Blucher (IRE)**[25] 4759 6-9-2 79............(p) CliffordLee 7 74
(Rebecca Menzies) *hld up: rdn over 2f out: kpt on ins fnl f: nvr threatened* **25/1**

6403 **9** *1 ¼* **Hajjam**[10] 5312 5-9-10 87............(p) DanielTudhope 5 79
(David O'Meara) *hld up: rdn along 2f out: sme late hdwy: nvr threatened* **7/2**[2]

2603 **10** *nk* **Danielsflyer (IRE)**[19] 4981 5-9-12 89............(p) AndrewMullen 1 80
(Michael Dods) *in tch: rdn over 2f out: wknd ins fnl f* **10/1**[3]

2200 **11** *¾* **Proud Archi (IRE)**[12] 5246 5-9-3 80............ PaulMulrennan 11 69
(Michael Dods) *hld up in midfield: rdn over 2f out: nvr threatened* **12/1**

6-00 **12** *nk* **Fuente**[35] 4379 3-8-13 87............ BenSanderson(5) 9 73
(Keith Dalgleish) *dwlt: hld up: nvr threatened* **33/1**

1404 **13** *3 ¾* **Stoney Lane**[37] 4303 4-8-12 75............ LewisEdmunds 3 53
(Richard Whitaker) *in tch: rdn along and lost pl over 2f out: wknd over 1f out* **12/1**

0066 **14** *½* **Parys Mountain (IRE)**[7] 5453 5-9-3 80............(t) DavidAllan 14 57
(Tim Easterby) *led: rdn and hdd 2f out: wknd* **16/1**

0405 **15** *2* **Flying Pursuit**[7] 5454 6-10-0 91............(p) RachelRichardson 4 62
(Tim Easterby) *hld up: rdn over 2f out: wknd over 1f out* **11/1**

1m 26.8s (-0.80) **Going Correction** +0.05s/f (Good)
WFA 3 from 4yo+ 6lb **15** Ran SP% **126.3**
Speed ratings (Par 107): **106,103,102,102,101 101,99,99,98,97 96,96,92,91,89**
CSF £38.96 CT £1052.07 TOTE £3.30: £1.60, £4.40, £8.90; EX 44.90 Trifecta £1327.20.
Owner Highgreen Partnership **Bred** Lady Lonsdale & Richard Kent **Trained** Malton, N Yorks

FOCUS
Well contested, although not overly competitive, with only five runners within 7lb of the ceiling. The pace was fair for the conditions and the sole last-time-out winner in the field followed up. The second has been rated to his recent form.

5693 WILLIAM HILL THIRSK SUMMER CUP H'CAP 7f 218y
4:00 (4:01) (Class 3) (0-90,90) 3-Y-0+ **£19,407** (£5,775; £2,886; £1,443) **Stalls** Low

Form RPR

1340 **1** **Kylie Rules**[12] 5246 4-9-1 81............ NathanEvans 7 91
(Ruth Carr) *stdd s: hld up in rr: swtchd rt to outer over 3f out: sn gd hdwy: rdn to chse ldrs appr fnl f: led 75yds out: kpt on wl* **20/1**

46-1 **2** *1 ¾* **Lord Of The Rock (IRE)**[98] 2104 7-9-4 84............ PatCosgrave 16 90
(Lawrence Mullaney) *dwlt: sn prom on outer: led narrowly 6f out: drvn and hdd over 1f out: remained chalng: kpt on ins fnl f* **20/1**

5052 **3** *nse* **Mikmak**[26] 4730 6-9-2 82............(p) DavidAllan 14 88
(Tim Easterby) *prom: pushed into narrow ld 2f out: drvn appr fnl f: hdd 75yds out: kpt on: lost 2nd post* **9/2**[2]

1-01 **4** *nk* **Alfred Richardson**[14] 5200 5-9-9 89............ ConnorBeasley 4 94
(John Davies) *midfield: pushed along over 2f out: swtchd lft to ins over 1f out: rdn and kpt on wl fnl f* **20/1**

3121 **5** *½* **Star Shield**[22] 4867 4-9-2 82............ DanielTudhope 12 86
(David O'Meara) *hld up on outer: prog into midfield over 3f out: hdwy and chsd ldrs over 1f out: rdn and sn edgd lft: kpt on same pce ins fnl f* **4/1**[1]

1045 **6** *nk* **Brother McGonagall**[15] 5155 5-8-11 80............ ConorMcGovern(3) 8 83
(Tim Easterby) *in tch: rdn over 2f out: drvn over 1f out: kpt on same pce fnl f* **25/1**

5260 **7** *2 ½* **Fennaan (IRE)**[44] 4021 4-9-7 87............ CamHardie 6 85
(Phillip Makin) *hld up: pushed along and bit short of room 2f out: rdn over 1f out: kpt on ins fnl f: nvr trbld ldrs* **25/1**

1513 **8** *½* **Irreverent**[22] 4895 3-9-1 88............ PaulHanagan 10 83
(Richard Fahey) *midfield: rdn over 2f out: no imp* **7/1**[3]

525 **9** *1 ¾* **Kripke (IRE)**[15] 5149 4-9-3 83............ BenRobinson 3 75
(David Barron) *midfield: rdn over 2f out: wknd fnl f* **16/1**

1044 **10** *¾* **Universal Gleam**[8] 5398 4-9-8 88............ CliffordLee 2 79
(Keith Dalgleish) *hld up: rdn over 2f out: nvr threatened* **16/1**

0000 **11** *½* **Give It Some Teddy**[35] 4403 5-8-12 78............ RachelRichardson 15 68
(Tim Easterby) *in tch on outer: rdn over 2f out: wknd over 1f out* **25/1**

4362 **12** *¾* **Calvados Spirit**[15] 5155 6-8-11 77............ AndrewMullen 9 65
(Richard Fahey) *in tch: rdn to chse ldrs over 2f out: wknd over 1f out* **12/1**

3200 **13** *14* **Tulfarris**[22] 4882 3-9-3 90............ StevieDonohoe 11 45
(Charlie Fellowes) *hld up: nvr travelling: rdn over 2f out: sn btn: eased ins fnl f (vet reported colt was lame on its right fore)* **4/1**[1]

133 **14** *1 ¾* **Alexander James (IRE)**[58] 3499 3-9-2 89............ PaulMulrennan 5 40
(Iain Jardine) *led: hdd 6f out: remained prom: rdn over 2f out: sn wknd* **16/1**

1300 **15** *1 ¼* **Hayadh**[35] 4403 6-9-10 90............ LewisEdmunds 1 39
(Rebecca Bastiman) *trckd ldrs: rdn along and lost pl over 3f out: wknd and bhd over 1f out* **16/1**

1m 40.63s (-1.07) **Going Correction** +0.05s/f (Good)
WFA 3 from 4yo+ 7lb **15** Ran SP% **127.7**
Speed ratings (Par 107): **107,105,105,104,104 104,101,101,99,98 98,97,83,81,80**
CSF £362.43 CT £2162.19 TOTE £24.80: £6.50, £5.80, £2.00; EX 775.80.
Owner J A Knox and Mrs M A Knox **Bred** J A Knox **Trained** Huby, N Yorks

FOCUS
With plenty in form, this valuable handicap proved a competitive renewal and the pace was fair for the conditions. The sole filly in the race came from last to first to gain a fifth win in eight starts this season. A clear pb from the winner, with the second, third and fourth helping to set the level.

5694 JW 4X4 NORTHALLERTON H'CAP 1m 4f 8y
4:35 (4:35) (Class 4) (0-80,82) 3-Y-0+
£7,309 (£2,175; £1,087; £543; £300; £300) **Stalls** High

Form RPR

6254 **1** **Trinity Star (IRE)**[15] 5122 8-9-2 68............(v) CliffordLee 9 77
(Karen McClintock) *hld up: rdn along and hdwy over 2f out: led over 1f out: sn hung bdly lft: styd on wl to draw clr ins fnl f* **20/1**

150 **2** *3* **Kashagan**[42] 4136 3-9-2 78............(b[1]) PaulMulrennan 5 82
(Archie Watson) *trckd ldrs: wnt prom 6f out: rdn along to ld 2f out: hdd over 1f out: sn carried lft by wnr: drvn and styd on same pce ins fnl f* **16/1**

-033 **3** *nk* **Power Of States (IRE)**[21] 4924 3-9-2 **78**........................ PatCosgrave 3 81
(Hugo Palmer) *trckd ldrs: rdn over 2f out: drvn over 1f out: hung lft ins fnl f: styd on same pce* **5/1**[3]

0050 **4** *nk* **Dance King**[7] 5436 9-9-6 **77**..................................(t) DannyRedmond(5) 6 80
(Tim Easterby) *s.i.s: hld up in rr: rdn over 2f out: drvn over 1f out: styd on wl fnl f: nrst fin* **16/1**

0000 **5** *nse* **Top Notch Tonto (IRE)**[21] 4913 9-9-8 **74**.................... BenRobinson 10 77
(Brian Ellison) *midfield: rdn along whn sltly hmpd and lost pl 2f out: drvn over 1f out: styd on ins fnl f (jockey said gelding was briefly denied a clear run approaching 2f out)* **12/1**

3041 **6** *2 ¼* **Benadalid**[14] 5174 4-10-0 **80**.. RoystonFfrench 7 79
(Chris Fairhurst) *prom: rdn over 2f out: wknd ins fnl f* **8/1**

0006 **7** *1 ½* **Multellie**[14] 5201 7-9-12 **78**.. DavidAllan 2 75
(Tim Easterby) *led: rdn along and hdd 2f out: wknd appr fnl f* **14/1**

4131 **8** *¾* **Where's Jeff**[38] 4241 4-10-1 **81**...................................... NathanEvans 8 77
(Michael Easterby) *midfield: prog and trckd ldrs over 6f out: rdn along 3f out: wknd over 1f out* **4/1**[2]

2163 **9** *1 ½* **Buriram (IRE)**[15] 5127 3-9-6 **82**.................................... DanielTudhope 4 75
(Ralph Beckett) *dwlt: hld up: rdn along over 2f out: sn no hdwy and btn (trainer's rep could offer no explanation for the performance shown)* **7/4**[1]

60-0 **10** *10* **Crimson Skies (IRE)**[14] 5201 4-8-13 **65**........................ ConnorBeasley 1 42
(John Davies) *midfield: rdn along 4f out: wknd over 2f out* **66/1**

2m 38.56s (-1.44) **Going Correction** +0.05s/f (Good)
WFA 3 from 4yo+ 10lb **10** Ran SP% **116.5**
Speed ratings (Par 105): **106,104,103,103,103 102,101,100,99,92**
CSF £301.65 CT £1851.37 TOTE £24.10: £4.20, £4.30, £1.90; EX 203.60 Trifecta £1266.60.
Owner Trinity Racing **Bred** Ms Natalie Cleary **Trained** Ingoe, Northumberland

FOCUS
Competitive for the class although the margin of victory flattered the winner, who tightened up a couple of rivals 1f out. The winner has been rated back to last year's form, and the third to his latest.

5695 SCOUTING FOR GIRLS LIVE @THIRSKRACES FRIDAY 16TH AUGUST H'CAP 7f 218y
5:10 (5:11) (Class 5) (0-70,72) 3-Y-O
£4,528 (£1,347; £673; £336; £300; £300) **Stalls** Low

Form RPR

0-51 **1** **My Ukulele (IRE)**[11] 5272 3-9-1 **61**.................................. BenRobinson 11 70+
(John Quinn) *hld up: rdn and hdwy on outer over 2f out: chsd ldr appr fnl f: styd on wl: led 75yds out* **7/1**

0U41 **2** *1 ½* **The Big House (IRE)**[8] 5389 3-8-4 **57**.......................... EllaMcCain(7) 6 63
(Adrian Nicholls) *prom: led over 4f out: rdn 4 l clr 2f out: reduced advantage ins fnl f: hdd 75yds out: no ex* **13/2**[3]

0300 **3** *nk* **Abie's Hollow**[18] 5020 3-9-0 **60**...................................... PaulHanagan 8 65
(Tony Coyle) *trckd ldrs: rdn 2f out: kpt on* **33/1**

2232 **4** *2 ¼* **One To Go**[3] 5557 3-9-4 **64**...(b) DavidAllan 14 64
(Tim Easterby) *midfield towards outer: rdn and hdwy over 2f out: drvn to chse ldr over 1f out: no ex ins fnl f* **7/4**[1]

0664 **5** *¾* **Gylo (IRE)**[13] 5215 3-8-13 **62**..................................(v) ConorMcGovern(3) 13 60
(David O'Meara) *hld up in midfield: rdn and hdwy over 2f out: edgd lft over 1f out: no ex fnl f* **16/1**

16 **6** *5* **Balgees Time (FR)**[15] 5124 3-9-12 **72**............................. PatCosgrave 1 59
(Kevin Ryan) *dwlt: hld up: rdn along over 2f out: minor hdwy over 1f out: nvr trbld ldrs* **25/1**

-060 **7** *5* **Epaulini**[12] 5237 3-8-8 **54**.. ConnorBeasley 7 29
(Michael Dods) *in tch: racd quite keenly: rdn over 2f out: wknd over 1f out* **25/1**

060 **8** *1 ½* **Ripon Spa**[46] 3972 3-9-5 **65**... PaulMulrennan 12 37
(Jedd O'Keeffe) *dwlt: hld up: rdn along 3f out: nvr threatened* **20/1**

6562 **9** *2 ½* **Smeaton (IRE)**[3] 5552 3-9-0 **60**..................................... LewisEdmunds 5 26
(Roger Fell) *trckd ldrs: chsd ldr 3f out: sn rdn: wknd over 1f out* **6/1**[2]

441 **10** *1 ½* **Amber Star (IRE)**[23] 4818 3-9-7 **67**............................... DanielTudhope 3 29
(David O'Meara) *midfield: rdn along 3f out: sn wknd (trainer's rep could offer no explanation for the performance shown)* **6/1**[2]

5006 **11** *¾* **Furyan**[13] 5215 3-8-4 **50** oh1 ow2..............................(v) RoystonFfrench 2 11
(Nigel Tinkler) *sn rdn along and a towards rr* **33/1**

6620 **12** *1 ¼* **Ghathanfar (IRE)**[13] 5215 3-8-11 **57**............................ CamHardie 4 15
(Tracy Waggott) *trckd ldrs: rdn 3f out: sn wknd (jockey said gelding lost its action entering the bend and hung left in the home straight)* **28/1**

-005 **13** *17* **Musical Sky**[23] 4820 3-8-11 **57**....................................... CliffordLee 9
(Michael Dods) *led: hdd over 4f out: sn rdn along: wknd over 2f out* **33/1**

4000 **14** *66* **Second Sight**[25] 4769 3-9-0 **60**..............................(v) StevieDonohoe 10
(Charlie Fellowes) *sn rdn along in rr: eased and t.o fnl 3f (jockey said colt stumbled entering the home straight, so he felt it prudent to ease down)* **33/1**

1m 41.26s (-0.44) **Going Correction** +0.05s/f (Good) **14** Ran SP% **124.3**
Speed ratings (Par 100): **104,102,102,99,99 94,89,87,85,83 82,81,64,**
CSF £48.26 CT £1403.70 TOTE £8.80: £2.10, £2.20, £10.70; EX 51.40 Trifecta £1178.20.
Owner Andrew W Robson **Bred** Andrew W Robson **Trained** Settrington, N Yorks

FOCUS
Competitive, if weak for the grade and the pace was solid. The first two have been rated as backing up their latest wins. The third helps set the level, rated to this year's form.
T/Plt: £611.90 to a £1 stake. Pool: £55,696.94 - 66.44 winning units T/Qpdt: £201.10 to a £1 stake. Pool: £4,005.92 - 14.74 winning units **Andrew Sheret**

5696 - 5702a (Foreign Racing) - See Raceform Interactive

5418 CHESTER (L-H)
Sunday, August 4

OFFICIAL GOING: Good to soft (6.6)
Wind: light against Weather: Overcast but warm

5703 BRITVIC NURSERY H'CAP 5f 15y
2:00 (2:01) (Class 4) (0-85,83) 2-Y-O
£6,080 (£1,809; £904; £452; £400; £400) **Stalls** Low

Form RPR

3123 **1** **Dream Kart (IRE)**[13] 5243 2-9-7 **83**................................. FrannyNorton 3 88
(Mark Johnston) *trckd ldrs: pushed along 2f out: rdn to ld jst ins fnl f: kpt on wl* **9/2**[3]

322 **2** *2 ¼* **Sermon (IRE)**[36] 4361 2-9-4 **80**................................... RichardKingscote 2 77
(Tom Dascombe) *prom: rdn 2f out: carried sltly rt by ldr over 1f out: kpt on same pce fnl f* **10/11**[1]

0166 **3** *1 ¾* **Shammah (IRE)**[23] 4893 2-9-2 **78**.................................... SeanLevey 1 69
(Richard Hannon) *led: rdn and edgd rt over 1f out: hdd jst ins fnl f: no ex towards fin* **11/4**[2]

3650 **4** *¾* **Bob's Oss (IRE)**[15] 5196 2-8-0 **62** oh3.............................. CamHardie 6 50
(Alan Berry) *hld up in tch: rdn along 2f out: kpt on ins fnl f: nvr trbld ldrs* **66/1**

0342 **5** *2 ½* **Lexi The One (IRE)**[29] 4647 2-8-1 **66**.......................... SeanDavis(3) 9 45
(Richard Fahey) *s.i.s: sn pushed along in rr: kpt on ins fnl f: nvr involved* **16/1**

0236 **6** *½* **Bezzas Lad (IRE)**[29] 4624 2-8-10 **72**..............................(b[1]) SamJames 7 49
(Phillip Makin) *hld up: rdn over 2f out: nvr threatened* **16/1**

004 **7** *1 ¾* **Newsical**[22] 4903 2-8-4 **66**... AndrewMullen 5 37
(Mark Walford) *chsd ldrs: sn pushed along: rdn over 2f out: wknd fnl f* **20/1**

1m 2.92s (0.82) **Going Correction** +0.225s/f (Good) **7** Ran SP% **115.3**
Speed ratings (Par 96): **102,98,95,94,90 89,86**
CSF £9.15 CT £12.86 TOTE £5.90: £1.70, £1.10; EX 10.20 Trifecta £17.50.
Owner John O'Connor & Partner **Bred** John O'Connor **Trained** Middleham Moor, N Yorks
■ Stewards' Enquiry : Sean Davis £290 fine: using mobile phone outside the zone

FOCUS
Add 20yds. A clean sweep for the bottom three stalls, who were in the leading trio throughout. A step up from the winner, with the second rated close to his mark.

5704 THYME PEOPLE EBF NOVICE STKS (PLUS 10 RACE) 7f 1y
2:35 (2:35) (Class 4) 2-Y-O
£5,851 (£1,752; £876; £438; £219; £109) **Stalls** Low

Form

3 **1** **Breathalyze (FR)**[37] 4324 2-9-2 0................................. RichardKingscote 2 82+
(Tom Dascombe) *led for 1f: cl up on outer: rdn to ld again 2f out: styd on wl to draw clr ins fnl f* **13/8**[2]

6213 **2** *4* **The New Marwan**[23] 4878 2-9-5 81................................. SeanDavis(3) 5 78
(Richard Fahey) *sltly awkward s but sn chsd ldrs: rdn along 3f out: kpt on ins fnl f to go 2nd towards fin: no ch w wnr* **5/2**[3]

3 *1 ¼* **Cognac (IRE)** 2-9-2 0... FrannyNorton 1 68
(Mark Johnston) *led narrowly after 1f: rdn along and hdd 2f out: no ex ins fnl f and lost 2nd towards fin* **6/4**[1]

0 **4** *17* **Thomas Hawk**[38] 4289 2-9-2 0.. AndrewMullen 3 24
(Alan Brown) *dwlt: hld up: rdn along 3f out: wknd and bhd 2f out* **40/1**

66 **5** *nk* **Contract Kid (IRE)**[38] 4302 2-9-2 0.................................... ShaneKelly 4 23
(Mark Loughnane) *in tch: rdn along over 4f out: wknd over 2f out (vet reported colt lost his right fore shoe)* **33/1**

6 *2* **Mrs Tiffen** 2-8-11 0... CamHardie 6 13
(Lisa Williamson) *hld up: rdn along 3f out: wknd and bhd 2f out* **50/1**

1m 29.41s (1.91) **Going Correction** +0.225s/f (Good) **6** Ran SP% **114.0**
Speed ratings (Par 96): **98,93,92,72,72 69**
CSF £6.21 TOTE £2.50: £1.90, £1.10; EX 5.90 Trifecta £7.90.
Owner More Turf Racing **Bred** Bloodstock Agency Ltd **Trained** Malpas, Cheshire

FOCUS
Add 24yds. A fair novice and only three of them mattered.

5705 MBNA QUEENSFERRY STKS (LISTED RACE) 6f 17y
3:10 (3:10) (Class 1) 3-Y-O+
£20,982 (£7,955; £3,981; £1,983; £995; £499) **Stalls** Low

Form RPR

3230 **1** **Major Jumbo**[22] 4923 5-9-1 107................................... KevinStott 3 113
(Kevin Ryan) *mde all: pushed along and qcknd clr wl over 1f out: rdn appr fnl f: kpt on wl* **6/4**[1]

0002 **2** *3 ½* **Rock On Baileys**[22] 4904 4-8-10 91...........................(b) LewisEdmunds 5 97
(Amy Murphy) *midfield: rdn and hdwy over 1f out: wnt 2nd 110yds out: kpt on but no ch w wnr* **20/1**

0-01 **3** *1* **Miss Celestial (IRE)**[11] 5291 3-8-6 97..............................(p) LukeMorris 4 92
(Sir Mark Prescott Bt) *chsd ldr: rdn and outpcd in 2nd over 1f out: lost 2nd 110yds out: one pce* **6/1**[3]

1003 **4** *nk* **Gold Filigree (IRE)**[11] 5325 4-8-10 96................................ ShaneKelly 2 92
(Richard Hughes) *pressed ldr for 1f: chsd ldr: rdn over 2f out: kpt on same pce* **9/1**

0450 **5** *1* **Vintage Brut**[57] 3621 3-8-11 105..(p) DavidAllan 1 93
(Tim Easterby) *midfield: rdn 2f out: kpt on ins fnl f: nvr trbld ldrs* **9/1**

0016 **6** *shd* **Yolo Again (IRE)**[22] 4932 3-8-6 89...................................... CamHardie 7 88
(Roger Fell) *hld up: rdn and sme hdwy over 1f out: kpt on ins fnl f: nvr trbld ldrs* **50/1**

-005 **7** *1 ¾* **Stay Classy (IRE)**[23] 4891 3-8-6 94..................................... HarryBentley 8 82
(Richard Spencer) *dwlt: hld up: rdn along and bit short of room appr fnl f: nvr threatened* **12/1**

1521 **8** *nk* **Angel Alexander (IRE)**[8] 5420 3-8-11 101.............. RichardKingscote 9 86
(Tom Dascombe) *midfield on outer: lost pl over 2f out: pushed along over 1f out: sn btn* **10/3**[2]

1006 **9** *¾* **Merhoob (IRE)**[22] 4905 7-9-1 101...................................... LiamKeniry 10 85
(John Ryan) *s.i.s: hld up: nvr threatened* **25/1**

4003 **10** *17* **Reflektor (IRE)**[26] 4759 6-9-1 89...................................... PaulHanagan 6 30
(Tom Dascombe) *chsd ldr on outer: rdn and lost pl over 2f out: wknd over 1f out* **33/1**

1m 14.91s (-0.59) **Going Correction** +0.225s/f (Good)
WFA 3 from 4yo+ 4lb **10** Ran SP% **118.6**
Speed ratings (Par 111): **112,107,106,105,104 104,101,101,100,77**
CSF £40.25 TOTE £1.90: £1.30, £5.50, £1.60; EX 40.20 Trifecta £216.30.
Owner T A Rahman **Bred** D R Botterill **Trained** Hambleton, N Yorks

FOCUS
Add 24yds. The favourite dominated this ordinary Listed sprint. The second has been rated to her C&D handicap latest.

5706 PARADE WITH AIDEN BYRNE H'CAP 1m 4f 63y
3:40 (3:41) (Class 4) (0-85,87) 3-Y-O+
£6,080 (£1,809; £904; £452; £400; £400) **Stalls** Low

Form RPR

613 **1** **Hereby (IRE)**[32] 4503 3-8-6 **72**.................................... HarryBentley 5 80+
(Ralph Beckett) *trckd ldrs: effrt and angled rt bnd over 1f out: led and hrd pressed ins fnl f: hld on wl cl home* **9/4**[1]

3104 **2** *hd* **Gossip Column (IRE)**[9] 5370 4-10-1 **85**................... RichardKingscote 3 92
(Ian Williams) *s.i.s: hld up bhd ldng gp: pushed along and hdwy 2f out: ev ch ins fnl f: kpt on: hld cl home* **4/1**[3]

5621 **3** *1 ¼* **Dark Lochnagar (USA)**[8] 5424 3-9-7 **87**............................ ShaneGray 8 92
(Keith Dalgleish) *led at ordinary gallop: rdn 2f out: hdd ins fnl f: kpt on same pce* **5/2**[2]

0000 **4** *3 ¼* **Ice Canyon**[65] 3321 5-8-10 **66**... PaulHanagan 6 66
(Kevin Frost) *hld up: effrt and rdn wl over 1f out: kpt on fnl f: nvr able to chal* **25/1**

3522 **5** *shd* **Gabrial The One (IRE)**[8] 5424 3-8-11 **80**.............................. SeanDavis(3) 7 80
(Richard Fahey) *prom: rdn over 2f out: hung lft and no imp fr over 1f out*
5/1

6160 **6** *1 1/4* **Cape Islay (FR)**[13] 5253 3-9-5 **85**.............................. FrannyNorton 9 83
(Mark Johnston) *pressed ldr: rdn whn checked bnd over 1f out: wknd ins fnl f*
11/1

1P46 **7** *2 1/4* **Raven's Raft (IRE)**[2] 5631 4-8-9 **65** oh3.............................. LukeMorris 4 59
(David Loughnane) *in tch: drvn along and outpcd 2f out: n.d after*
33/1

4165 **8** *1 1/2* **Super Kid**[9] 5391 7-9-7 **77**.............................. (tp) JasonHart 2 69
(Tim Easterby) *hld up: rdn along 2f out: sn btn*
14/1

0/06 **9** *14* **Percy (IRE)**[20] 4988 5-9-10 **80**.............................. PaulMulrennan 1 49
(Frank Bishop) *slowly away: bhd: struggling 3f out: sn btn*
33/1

2m 44.17s (1.97) **Going Correction** +0.225s/f (Good) **9** Ran SP% **120.7**
WFA 3 from 4yo+ 10lb
Speed ratings (Par 105): **102,101,101,98,98 97,96,95,86**
CSF £12.11 CT £23.91 TOTE £2.90: £1.10, £1.20, £1.70; EX 13.30 Trifecta £41.00.
Owner J H Richmond-Watson **Bred** Lawn Stud **Trained** Kimpton, Hants
■ Stewards' Enquiry : Shane Gray two day ban: careless riding (Aug 18-19)

FOCUS
Add 40yds. A decent handicap and no surprise to see it fall to one of the 3yos. The pace was a steady one. The second helps set the level, rated to this year's form, with the third similar to his 1m2f latest here.

5707 WHITE HORSE EBF STALLIONS CONDITIONS STKS (PLUS 10 RACE) (C&G) 6f 17y
4:15 (4:16) (Class 2) 2-Y-O **£11,827** (£3,541; £1,770; £885; £442) **Stalls** Low

Form RPR

2214 **1** **Oh Purple Reign (IRE)**[8] 5415 2-9-2 **97**.............................. SeanLevey 2 95
(Richard Hannon) *trckd ldrs: plld out and shkn up to ld over 1f out: r.o strly fnl f*
10/11[1]

0102 **2** *2* **Bill Neigh**[12] 5275 2-9-4 **87**.............................. PaulMulrennan 3 91
(John Ryan) *pressed ldr: effrt and disp ld over 1f out: kpt on same pce ins fnl f*
8/1

2103 **3** *hd* **Monoski (USA)**[34] 4441 2-9-4 **95**.............................. FrannyNorton 1 90
(Mark Johnston) *t.k.h: hld up in tch: effrt and rdn over 1f out: kpt on ins fnl f: nt pce to chal*
5/2[2]

23 **4** *2* **Mr Jones And Me**[8] 5456 2-8-12 0.............................. RichardKingscote 5 78
(Tom Dascombe) *prom: effrt and c wd bnd over 1f out: sn drvn and no ex*
14/1

2110 **5** *2* **Hurstwood**[24] 4846 2-9-8 **90**.............................. DavidAllan 4 82
(Tim Easterby) *led to over 1f out: rdn and wknd ins fnl f*
15/2[3]

1m 17.22s (1.72) **Going Correction** +0.225s/f (Good) **5** Ran SP% **110.5**
Speed ratings (Par 100): **97,94,94,91,88**
CSF £8.92 TOTE £1.50: £1.10, £3.10; EX 9.40 Trifecta £20.30.
Owner Team Wallop **Bred** Tally-Ho Stud **Trained** East Everleigh, Wilts

FOCUS
Add 24yds. A useful juvenile conditions race won by the highest-rated.

5708 COMMONHALL STREET SOCIAL H'CAP 7f 127y
4:50 (4:56) (Class 3) (0-95,96) 3-Y-O+
£7,470 (£2,236; £1,118; £559; £279; £140) **Stalls** Low

Form RPR

2605 **1** **Humble Gratitude**[23] 4875 4-9-0 **78**.............................. (p) PaulMulrennan 9 87
(Ian Williams) *replated bef s: hld up: hdwy and angled to outside ent st: led wl ins fnl f: r.o wl*
12/1

1151 **2** *nk* **Club Wexford (IRE)**[20] 4981 8-9-7 **90**.............................. BenSanderson(5) 6 98+
(Roger Fell) *hld up in tch on outside: hdwy to ld over 1f out: hdd wl ins fnl f: kpt on: jst hld*
7/1

-005 **3** *4 1/2* **Akvavera**[36] 4393 4-9-11 **89**.............................. HarryBentley 4 87
(Ralph Beckett) *in tch: n.m.r over 2f out: effrt and chsd clr ldng pair ins fnl f: r.o*
9/1

6410 **4** *nk* **Penwortham (IRE)**[8] 5453 6-9-7 **85**.............................. TonyHamilton 7 82
(Richard Fahey) *stdd s: t.k.h in rr: effrt on outside over 1f out: kpt on fnl f: nt pce to chal*
14/1

0050 **5** *1* **Love Dreams (IRE)**[8] 5453 5-10-4 **96**.............................. (p[1]) FrannyNorton 8 91
(Mark Johnston) *t.k.h: cl up: led over 2f out to over 1f out: wknd ins fnl f*
9/1

0503 **6** *1 3/4* **Dragons Tail (IRE)**[11] 5320 4-9-3 **81**.............................. (p) RichardKingscote 2 72
(Tom Dascombe) *trckd ldrs: n.m.r briefly over 2f out: rdn over 1f out: hung lft and wknd ins fnl f (jockey said gelding was denied a clear run)*
9/2[2]

0050 **7** *1 1/2* **Max Zorin (IRE)**[16] 5155 5-9-9 **87**.............................. RobHornby 10 74
(Andrew Balding) *prom on outside: effrt and ch briefly ent st: wknd ins fnl f*
20/1

3456 **8** *4* **Pacino**[8] 5422 3-8-3 **77**.............................. SeanDavis(3) 3 54
(Richard Fahey) *hld up in midfield on ins: rdn and outpcd over 2f out: btn over 1f out*
22/1

3310 **9** *nse* **Gabrial The Tiger (IRE)**[12] 5274 7-8-9 **73**.............................. PaulHanagan 5 51
(Richard Fahey) *led tl rdn and hdd over 2f out: wknd over 1f out*
5/1[3]

0155 **10** *3/4* **Sha La La La Lee**[43] 4097 4-9-11 **92**.............................. (p[1]) JaneElliott(3) 1 68
(Tom Dascombe) *dwlt: bhd: struggling over 2f out: sn btn (jockey said gelding was slowly away)*
9/4[1]

1m 35.77s (0.07) **Going Correction** +0.225s/f (Good) **10** Ran SP% **121.6**
WFA 3 from 4yo+ 7lb
Speed ratings (Par 107): **108,107,103,102,101 100,98,94,94,93**
CSF £97.36 CT £827.87 TOTE £17.70: £5.80, £1.20, £2.80; EX 140.50 Trifecta £1530.00.
Owner Dr Marwan Koukash **Bred** Whitsbury Manor Stud **Trained** Portway, Worcs
■ Stewards' Enquiry : Sean Davis two-day ban: careless riding (Aug 18-19)

FOCUS
Add 24yds. The front two pulled clear in this decent handicap. The winner has been rated in line with his 1m2f run here in May.

5709 1539 H'CAP 1m 2f 70y
5:20 (5:23) (Class 4) (0-80,78) 3-Y-O+
£6,080 (£1,809; £904; £452; £400; £400) **Stalls** High

Form RPR

6311 **1** **Scofflaw**[16] 5130 5-9-12 **76**.............................. (v) HarryBentley 8 84
(David Evans) *hld up: rdn and hdwy over 3f out: led over 1f out: kpt on strly fnl f*
6/1[3]

6000 **2** *2 1/4* **Heart Of Soul (IRE)**[8] 5423 4-10-0 **78**.............................. (p) RichardKingscote 7 81
(Ian Williams) *in tch: rdn and outpcd over 3f out: rallied 2f out: kpt on fnl f to take 2nd cl home: no ch w wnr*
7/1

2526 **3** *nse* **Dark Devil (IRE)**[22] 4907 6-9-2 **66**.............................. (p) PaulHanagan 2 69
(Richard Fahey) *hld up: pushed along and hdwy over 2f out: chsd (clr) wnr briefly wl ins fnl f: kpt on*
7/2[2]

2040 **4** *3/4* **Confrontational (IRE)**[43] 4108 5-9-13 **77**.............................. AndrewMullen 11 79
(Jennie Candlish) *chsd clr ldng pair: rdn over 3f out: wnt 2nd over 2f out: effrt and ch over 1f out: no ex ins fnl f*
12/1

3330 **5** *nk* **Bell Heather (IRE)**[8] 5419 6-8-13 **66**.............................. (p) SeanDavis(3) 4 67
(Patrick Morris) *t.k.h: pressed ldr: led and maintained decent gallop 4f out: hdd over 1f out: no ex ins fnl f*
12/1

-100 **6** *8* **Nightingale Valley**[38] 4283 6-9-12 **76**.............................. RobHornby 10 61
(Stuart Kittow) *hld up: rdn over 3f out: no imp fr 2f out*
20/1

013- **7** *3* **Parole (IRE)**[408] 4068 7-9-5 **69**.............................. (t) DavidAllan 3 48
(Tim Easterby) *dwlt: hld up: pushed along and hdwy over 2f out: wknd over 1f out*
10/1

0506 **8** *5* **Tough Remedy (IRE)**[17] 5095 4-9-9 **78**.............................. (b[1]) AndrewBreslin(5) 9 47
(Keith Dalgleish) *dwlt: bhd and sn pushed along: drvn and outpcd 1/2-way: nvr on terms*
16/1

3655 **9** *9* **Redgrave (IRE)**[3] 5594 5-9-7 **76**.............................. ScottMcCullagh(5) 1 27
(Joseph Tuite) *led at decent gallop: hdd 4f out: chsd ldr to over 2f out: sn wknd (jockey said gelding ran flat)*
3/1[1]

0553 **10** *21* **Manfadh (IRE)**[43] 4109 4-9-0 **64**.............................. FrannyNorton 6
(Kevin Frost) *in tch: drvn and struggling over 3f out: sn wknd: t.o*
7/1

054- **11** *23* **Bold Statement (IRE)**[29] 4677 4-8-9 **59** oh2.............................. CamHardie 5
(Alan Berry) *midfield: struggling sn after 1/2-way: btn fnl 4f: t.o*
50/1

2m 14.97s (0.67) **Going Correction** +0.225s/f (Good) **11** Ran SP% **123.6**
Speed ratings (Par 105): **106,104,104,103,103 96,94,90,83,66 48**
CSF £50.34 CT £174.45 TOTE £5.90: £1.70, £2.50, £1.30; EX 63.10 Trifecta £522.30.
Owner John Abbey & Emma Evans **Bred** Mrs M E Slade **Trained** Pandy, Monmouths

FOCUS
Add 28yds. They were strung out a long way from the finish in this modest handicap, with the leaders going fast enough, and the closers came to the fore. The second has been rated to this year's form.
T/Plt: £12.30 to a £1 stake. Pool: £104,719.50 - 6,186.65 winning units T/Qpdt: £9.40 to a £1 stake. Pool: £9,145.84 - 715.92 winning units **Richard Young & Andrew Sheret**

5696 GALWAY (R-H)
Sunday, August 4

OFFICIAL GOING: Jumps - good (good to yielding in places); flat - good to yielding changing to yielding after race 3 (3.20) changing to soft on both courses after race 4 (3.55)

5710a FORAN EQUINE IRISH EBF AUCTION MAIDEN (PLUS 10 RACE) 7f
3:20 (3:20) 2-Y-O
£13,288 (£4,279; £2,027; £900; £450; £225)

RPR

1 **Raven's Cry (IRE)**[32] 4524 2-9-0 0.............................. WJLee 14 86
(P Twomey, Ire) *sn chsd ldrs: disp 3rd at 1/2-way: pushed along in 3rd over 2f out and tk clsr order on outer into st: led fr 1f out and rdn: kpt on wl to assert nr fin*
7/2[2]

2 *1 3/4* **Natural Power (IRE)**[17] 5108 2-8-13 0.............................. RobbieColgan 3 80
(Mrs D A Love, Ire) *pushed along to ld: drvn over 2f out and hdd u.p fr 1f out: kpt on wl wout matching wnr*
10/1

3 *1 1/4* **Helvic Dream (IRE)**[43] 4133 2-8-11 0.............................. ColinKeane 7 75
(Noel Meade, Ire) *w.w: 8th after 2f: pushed along over 2f out and hdwy into st: rdn into 4th ent fnl f and r.o into nvr threatening 3rd*
16/1

4 *3* **Gunmetal Jack (IRE)**[11] 5323 2-8-13 **70**.............................. LeighRoche 5 69
(M D O'Callaghan, Ire) *sn trckd ldr: cl 2nd at 1/2-way: drvn in 2nd over 2f out and no ex u.p over 1f out where dropped to 3rd: one pce ins fnl f where dropped to 4th*
50/1

5 *1* **The Truant (IRE)**[15] 5203 2-8-11 0.............................. ShaneFoley 12 65
(Mrs John Harrington, Ire) *bmpd rival s: settled in mid-div: disp 6th after 2f: rdn in 5th over 2f out and no imp on ldrs u.p into st: kpt on one pce ins fnl f*
7/1

6 *1/2* **Majeski Man (IRE)** 2-8-11 0.............................. RoryCleary 11 64
(Mrs Denise Foster, Ire) *dwlt and sltly hmpd s: in rr: last after 3f: pushed along and hdwy over 2f out: rdn into 8th ins fnl f and r.o nr fin: nvr trbld ldrs*
50/1

7 *2* **Potala Palace**[27] 4740 2-9-1 **84**.............................. DonnachaO'Brien 9 62
(Joseph Patrick O'Brien, Ire) *wnt lft s and sltly bmpd rival: settled in mid-div: disp 6th after 3f: pushed along and short of room briefly between horses over 2f out where bmpd sltly: rdn into 4th briefly and no ex over 1f out: sn wknd*
11/4[1]

8 *1 3/4* **At War (IRE)**[18] 5072 2-9-2 **76**.............................. (p[1]) BenCoen(5) 1 64
(Thomas Cooper, Ire) *chsd ldrs and t.k.h early: disp 3rd at 1/2-way: rdn in 4th over 2f out and sn no ex: wknd u.p over 1f out*
20/1

9 *1/2* **Borelli (IRE)**[30] 4616 2-8-13 0.............................. NGMcCullagh 10 54
(J P Murtagh, Ire) *wnt lft s and bmpd rival: hld up: 11th after 3f: rdn and disp 8th briefly 2f out: no ex into st and one pce fnl f*
17/2

10 *hd* **Spiritual Son (IRE)** 2-8-11 0.............................. RonanWhelan 4 52
(Jarlath P Fahey, Ire) *dismntd bef s for tack adjstment: dwlt sltly: towards rr: 12th after 3f: rdn over 2f out: no imp in 9th ins fnl f: one pce clsng stages*
25/1

11 *1/2* **Troop Commander (IRE)**[17] 5109 2-9-1 0.............................. GaryHalpin 6 55
(Kevin Prendergast, Ire) *dwlt: in rr and pushed along briefly early: 13th after 3f: pushed along over 2f out and no imp into st: kpt on one pce ins fnl f*
33/1

12 *8 1/2* **Jm Barrie**[28] 4695 2-9-1 0.............................. OisinOrr 2 33
(David Marnane, Ire) *chsd ldrs and racd keenly early: 5th bef 1/2-way: lost pl after 1/2-way and swtchd lft over 2f out where bmpd sltly: sn rdn in 7th and no ex bef st: wknd under 2f out*
14/1

13 *5 1/2* **Bigz Belief (IRE)**[17] 5108 2-8-11 0.............................. ChrisHayes 8 14+
(Matthew J Smith, Ire) *hld up towards rr: t.k.h: n.m.r briefly over 2f out: eased into st: nvr a factor (jockey said colt ran free during the race)* **16/1**

14 *1 1/2* **Mensen Ernst (IRE)**[26] 4750 2-9-7 0.............................. BenCurtis 13 20+
(Richard Hannon) *dwlt sltly and pushed along towards rr after s: disp 9th bef 1/2-way: rdn over 2f out where hung lft in 10th: rn off bnd into st and eased nr side fr over 1f out: bit slipped through mouth (jockey said the bit went through his horses mouth and he hung left thereafter)*
5/1[3]

1m 29.6s (-2.00) **14** Ran SP% **131.6**
CSF £40.70 TOTE £4.10: £1.70, £3.40, £3.40; DF 37.30 Trifecta £704.10.
Owner Mrs Emma Kennedy **Bred** Tullpark Limited **Trained** Cashel, Co Tipperary

The Form Book Flat 2019, Raceform Ltd, Newbury, RG14 5SJ

FOCUS
A lot of dead wood in this contest but a well contested race among those that had shown some form and the winner looks a nice filly. The second has been rated as improving slightly.

5711a IRISH STALLION FARMS EBF "AHONOORA" H'CAP (PREMIER HANDICAP) 7f

3:55 (3:56) 3-Y-O+

£63,783 (£20,540; £9,729; £4,324; £2,162; £1,081)

RPR

1 **Laughifuwant (IRE)**[50] [3875] 4-8-11 **88**.................... SeamieHeffernan 16 99
(Gerard Keane, Ire) *broke wl fr wd draw and sn led: rdn to extend advantage over 1f out and clr ins fnl f: kpt on wl* **20/1**

2 *¾* **On A Session (USA)**[15] [5205] 3-8-9 **92**.............................. LeighRoche 6 100+
(Aidan F Fogarty, Ire) *chsd early ldrs: mid-div at 1/2-way: wnt 6th 1f out: styd on wl fnl f into clr 2nd: nt rch wnr* **14/1**

3 *3 ½* **Magnetic North (IRE)**[5] [5535] 4-8-1 **88**.................... PaddyHarnett(10) 14 88+
(Ms Sheila Lavery, Ire) *chsd ldrs: rdn under 3f out in 5th: no imp appr fnl f: styd on again into 3rd cl home* **14/1**

4 *nk* **Turnberry Isle (IRE)**[5] [5535] 3-9-3 **100**..................... DonnachaO'Brien 3 97
(A P O'Brien, Ire) *racd in mid-div: clsr on inner to chse ldrs home turn: wnt 3rd ent fnl f: kpt on same pce and dropped to 4th cl home* **8/1[3]**

5 *¾* **Katiymann (IRE)**[11] [5327] 7-8-12 **89**.....................(t) RonanWhelan 2 86
(M Halford, Ire) *racd in rr: prog towards inner over 1f out: kpt on wl fnl f into 5th fnl 100yds: nvr nrr* **14/1**

6 *½* **Quizical (IRE)**[5] [5535] 4-9-0 **91**.............................. RobbieColgan 15 86+
(Ms Sheila Lavery, Ire) *racd in mid-div: pushed along on outer home turn: kpt on wl fnl f into 6th clsng stages: nvr nrr* **8/1[3]**

7 *1* **Hit The Silk (IRE)**[50] [3870] 6-8-6 **90** ow2.....................(h) GavinRyan(7) 18 83
(P J F Murphy, Ire) *racd towards rr: rdn and sme prog over 1f out: kpt on wl: nvr on terms* **20/1**

8 *½* **Saltonstall**[5] [5535] 5-9-5 **96** 7ex...................................(tp) ColinKeane 7 87
(Adrian McGuinness, Ire) *a mid-div: wd into st: kpt on ins fnl f: nvr on terms* **3/1[1]**

9 *nk* **Rufus King**[5] [5535] 4-8-12 **89**.. WJLee 4 80
(Mark Johnston) *trckd ldrs on inner in 3rd tl 1/2-way: pushed along over 2f into 2nd: no imp on wnr ent fnl f: sn wknd* **5/1[2]**

10 *shd* **Magical Wish (IRE)**[24] [4847] 3-9-0 **97**.................................... BenCurtis 8 85
(Richard Hannon) *trckd ldr in 2nd tl over 2f out: sn rdn and wknd home turn* **12/1**

11 *4 ¼* **Master Speaker (IRE)**[3] [5597] 9-8-7 **89**........................... BenCoen(5) 5 68
(Adrian McGuinness, Ire) *a in rr of mid-div: rdn along 2f out: no imp home turn* **16/1**

12 *½* **Certain Lad**[30] [4607] 3-9-2 **99**... ShaneFoley 13 74
(Mick Channon) *t.k.h early and chsd ldrs in 4th: disp 2nd 3f out: rdn and wknd fnl f: eased* **14/1**

13 *3 ½* **Insignia Of Rank (IRE)**[5] [5535] 4-9-12 **103**..................(b) GaryCarroll 10 71
(Joseph G Murphy, Ire) *racd in rr of mid-div: rdn over 2f out: no imp on outer home turn* **25/1**

14 *nk* **Madam Seamstress (IRE)**[11] [5325] 3-8-8 **91**..................... KevinManning 9 56
(J S Bolger, Ire) *a towards rr: rdn and no imp home turn over 1f out* **12/1**

15 *3 ¾* **Apex King (IRE)**[4] [5546] 5-8-13 **90**............................... ChrisHayes 12 47
(David Loughnane) *t.k.h early in mid-div: clsr to chse ldrs at 1/2-way on outer: rdn and nt qckn appr home turn where unbalanced and sltly hmpd: sn no ex: nt hrd rdn* **16/1**

16 *3* **Above The Rest (IRE)**[36] [4380] 8-9-4 **100**..............(h) ShaneCrosse(5) 11 49
(David Barron) *racd in rr of mid-div: dropped to rr 3f out: sn rdn and no imp* **20/1**

1m 27.92s (-3.68)
WFA 3 from 4yo+ 6lb **16** Ran SP% **135.8**
CSF £292.56 CT £4212.17 TOTE £39.40: £6.90, £2.50, £3.60, £1.90; DF 859.40.
Owner Mrs E Keane & Mrs F Cumiskey **Bred** Gerry Cumiskey **Trained** Trim, Co Meath

FOCUS
It was not a surprise to the winning trainer, as he was very grateful to see the rain for his charge. The level is set around the third, fourth and fifth.

5712a JPK FENCING H'CAP 1m 5f 186y

5:30 (5:30) (50-75,75) 3-Y-O+

£9,051 (£2,925; £1,393; £627; £321; £168)

RPR

1 **Linger (IRE)**[6] [3458] 6-9-4 **65**.................................... DonnachaO'Brien 17 83+
(Joseph Patrick O'Brien, Ire) *racd towards rr: prog on outer 3f out travelling wl: wnt 3rd 2f out: led gng wl over 1f out and sn rdn clr* **7/2[2]**

2 *6 ½* **Eight And Bob**[4] [5569] 6-9-7 **68**.. ColinKeane 5 76+
(W P Mullins, Ire) *racd in mid-div: rdn over 3f out: sltly short of room 2f out: sn rdn and no imp in 5th off home turn: styd on wl fnl f into 2nd cl home: nt trble wnr* **9/4[1]**

3 *½* **Sbraase**[27] [4724] 8-9-7 **68**.. OisinOrr 9 75
(Noel C Kelly, Ire) *racd in mid-div: gd hdwy to chse ldrs 3f out: rdn into 2nd 2f out: briefly on terms home turn: sn hdd and nt match wnr: kpt on same pce: ct for 2nd cl home* **12/1**

4 *3* **King Christophe (IRE)**[10] [5365] 7-8-11 **58**..................(b) RonanWhelan 8 61
(Peter Fahey, Ire) *led tl hdd over 1f out: sn no ex in 3rd: one pce and dropped to 4th fnl 100yds* **28/1**

5 *¾* **Dinard Rose (IRE)**[10] [5365] 3-8-6 **68**.....................(b) NathanCrosse(5) 21 73
(Noel Meade, Ire) *chsd ldrs: 5th at 1/2-way: rdn in 4th 2f out: swtchd to inner home turn: no imp ent fnl f: kpt on same pce* **12/1**

6 *5 ½* **Snookered (IRE)**[19] [5019] 5-9-9 **70**..............................(p) BenCurtis 15 64
(Brian Ellison) *racd in mid-div: rdn along 3f out: no imp 2f out: kpt on one pce* **25/1**

7 *½* **Elusive Exclusive (IRE)**[12] [3673] 6-8-11 **58**...................... RoryCleary 12 52
(P J Rothwell, Ire) *bit slowly away and racd in rr for most: kpt on fr over 1f out: nvr nrr* **25/1**

8 *1 ½* **Itsalonglongroad**[13] [5262] 5-10-0 **75**............................(t) RossCoakley 14 67
(John C McConnell, Ire) *chsd ldrs in 3rd: clsr in 2nd at 1/2-way: rdn in 5th 2f out: sn no ex: wknd* **33/1**

9 *6 ½* **Fayetta**[3] [5599] 3-8-12 **69**.......................................(b) ChrisHayes 10 54
(David Loughnane) *trckd ldr in 2nd: 3rd at 1/2-way: rdn 3f out: wknd under 2f out* **12/1**

10 *4 ¾* **Upgraded (IRE)**[4] [5569] 5-9-3 **71** 6ex.......................(t) GavinRyan(7) 19 47
(A J Martin, Ire) *nvr bttr than mid-div: pushed along towards rr over 3f out: no imp fnl 2f* **9/2[3]**

11 *3 ½* **Ilikehim (IRE)**[361] [5893] 5-8-8 **58**........................... TomMadden(3) 7 29
(William Durkan, Ire) *racd in mid-div: rdn along on inner 2f out: sn no ex* **40/1**

12 *2 ¼* **Tracker Saga (IRE)**[17] [5114] 3-8-13 **70**............................ KevinManning 1 41
(J S Bolger, Ire) *chsd ldrs: 6th at 1/2-way: travelled wl 3f out: rdn and nt qckn under 2f out: sn no ex: eased fnl f* **20/1**

13 *3* **Grove Hill (IRE)**[4] [5567] 6-9-4 **65**.................................(t) GaryCarroll 20 29
(Michael Mulvany, Ire) *a in rr of mid-div: rdn and no imp under 2f out* **50/1**

14 *1 ¼* **Macquarie (IRE)**[38] [4315] 3-9-4 **75**......................(b) SeamieHeffernan 2 40
(A P O'Brien, Ire) *chsd ldrs: 4th at 1/2-way: rdn and nt qckn over 2f out: sn wknd* **9/1**

15 *27* **Military Hill (IRE)**[13] [5260] 6-8-11 **58**...........................(v) ShaneFoley 18
(Paul Stafford, Ire) *a towards rr: pushed along and no imp over 2f out: eased fr home turn* **20/1**

16 *17* **Acclamatio (IRE)**[104] [8588] 5-9-12 **73**.........................(t) RobbieColgan 11
(A J Martin, Ire) *racd in rr of mid-div: pushed along and no imp under 3f out: eased under 2f out* **25/1**

S **Eadbhard (IRE)**[1] [5700] 4-9-5 **71**.....................................(h) BenCoen(5) 3
(Peter Fahey, Ire) *racd in mid-div: clipped heels and slipped up after 2f* **14/1**

3m 10.7s (2.70)
WFA 3 from 4yo+ 11lb **17** Ran SP% **142.8**
CSF £12.34 CT £100.91 TOTE £4.40: £1.50, £1.10, £5.00, £3.80; DF 11.10 Trifecta £266.10.
Owner Rugby & Racing Syndicate **Bred** Newtown Stud And T J Pabst **Trained** Owning Hill, Co Kilkenny

FOCUS
This was competitive. Linger and Upgraded had won here earlier on in the week and were back for more. The third, fourth and fifth dictate the level, rated to their latest efforts.

5641 DEAUVILLE (R-H)

Sunday, August 4

OFFICIAL GOING: Polytrack: standard; turf: good

5713a PRIX HIPODROMO DE SAN ISIDRO (H'CAP) (2YO) (STRAIGHT COURSE) (TURF) 6f

1:00 2-Y-O **£11,261** (£4,504; £3,378; £2,252; £1,126)

RPR

1 **Aggression (ITY)**[76] 2-8-0 0.............................. MlleMickaelleMichel(4) 3 68
(G Botti, France) **15/2[3]**

2 *shd* **Coply (FR)**[13] [5263] 2-8-6 0...............................(p) EddyHardouin 11 70
(Matthieu Palussiere, France) **22/1**

3 *1* **Galloon (FR)**[127] [1448] 2-8-6 0...................................... CristianDemuro 9 67
(Y Barberot, France) **83/10**

4 *1* **Atlantica (FR)**[58] [3562] 2-8-10 0..................................(b) AnthonyCrastus 8 68
(Stephane Chevalier, France) **13/1**

5 *shd* **Vereny Ka (FR)**[13] [5263] 2-7-12 0........................... MlleAlisonMassin(4) 4 60
(C Lerner, France) **24/1**

6 *½* **Best Evening (FR)**[35] 2-8-9 0......................................(p) UmbertoRispoli 6 65
(Andreas Suborics, Germany) **23/1**

7 *hd* **Jayadeeva (FR)**[13] [5263] 2-8-13 0...................... Pierre-CharlesBoudot 13 69
(A Giorgi, Italy) **76/10**

8 *¾* **Kongastet (FR)**[29] [4679] 2-9-4 0.....................................(b) TheoBachelot 10 71
(S Wattel, France) **26/5[2]**

9 *nk* **My Premier County (FR)**[22] [4949] 2-8-11 0........(b) ClementLecoeuvre 2 64
(Matthieu Palussiere, France) **27/1**

10 *1 ¼* **All Revved Up (IRE)**[22] [4949] 2-8-8 0.......................... StephanePasquier 14 57
(C Boutin, France) **22/1**

11 *2* **Pink Princess**[53] 2-8-9 0...(p) MickaelBarzalona 5 52
(P Monfort, France) **47/10[1]**

12 *1 ¼* **Fact Or Fable (IRE)**[29] [4679] 2-8-8 0...........................(b) HugoJourniac 1 47
(J S Moore) *midfield on inner: jnd ldrs 1/2-way: rdn and nt qckn 2f out: wknd fnl f* **13/1**

13 *snk* **Zo Lane (FR)**[29] [4679] 2-8-9 0..(p) MaximeGuyon 7 48
(F Rossi, France) **77/10**

14 *2 ½* **Mehanydream (FR)**[14] 2-8-11 0.. TomLefranc(6) 12 48
(C Boutin, France) **18/1**

1m 12.04s (1.04) **Going Correction** +0.15s/f (Good) **14** Ran SP% **119.3**
Speed ratings: **99,98,97,96,96 95,95,94,93,92 89,87,87,84**
PARI-MUTUEL (all including 1 euro stake): WIN 8.50; PLACE 3.00, 6.90, 3.10; DF 108.6.00.
Owner Scuderia Magenta & G Botti **Bred** Razza Del Velino Srl **Trained** France

5714a PRIX CLUB HIPICO SANTIAGO - PRIX MOONLIGHT CLOUD (LISTED RACE) (3YO) (STRAIGHT COURSE) (TURF) 6f

1:35 3-Y-O **£24,774** (£9,909; £7,432; £4,954; £2,477)

RPR

1 **Glass Slippers**[23] [4891] 3-8-8 0.. TomEaves 8 105
(Kevin Ryan) *a.p on outer: clsd smoothly to join ldr bef 1/2-way: shkn up to ld over 1 1/2f out: styd on wl u.p fnl f despite being carried rt by runner-up last 100yds* **10/1**

2 *shd* **Bravo Sierra**[79] 3-8-8 0...................................... VincentCheminaud 2 97+
(A Fabre, France) *qckly into stride: cl up: pushed along 2f out: rdn to chse eventual wnr over 1f out: kpt on wl ins fnl f: jst hld* **18/1**

3 *2 ½* **Kenbaio (FR)**[9] 3-8-11 0...................................... StephanePasquier 6 100
(P Bary, France) **41/5**

4 *¾* **Sunday Star**[16] [5143] 3-8-8 0.. AndreaAtzeni 5 95
(Ed Walker) *racd in fnl pair but wl in tch: moved to outside 1/2-way: clsd 2f fr home: rdn to chal for pls over 1f out: wnt 3rd ins fnl f: no ex and dropped to 4th cl home* **51/10**

5 *¾* **Tertius (FR)**[143] [1200] 3-9-1 0.. HugoJourniac 3 99
(M Nigge, France) **17/5[2]**

6 *hd* **Epic Hero (FR)**[28] [4703] 3-8-11 0............................... MickaelBarzalona 1 95
(A Fabre, France) *dwlt sltly: racd keenly: hld up towards rr on inner: pushed along wl over 1 1/2f out but no imp: rdn over 1f out: kpt on fnl 150yds: nvr in contention* **32/5**

7 *1 ¾* **Pretty Boy (IRE)**[28] [4705] 3-8-11 0...................................... MaximeGuyon 7 89
(Mme Pia Brandt, France) **5/1[3]**

8 *2* **We Go (FR)**[28] [4703] 3-8-11 0.................................. Pierre-CharlesBoudot 4 83
(H-A Pantall, France) **31/10[1]**

1m 9.05s (-1.95) **Going Correction** +0.15s/f (Good) **8** Ran SP% **118.9**
Speed ratings: **115,114,111,110,109 109,106,104**
PARI-MUTUEL (all including 1 euro stake): WIN 11.00; PLACE 3.30, 5.40, 2.60; DF 75.70.
Owner Bearstone Stud Limited **Bred** Bearstone Stud Ltd **Trained** Hambleton, N Yorks

5715a PRIX HIPODROMO DE CHILE (H'CAP) (5YO+) (ALL-WEATHER TRACK) (POLYTRACK) 6f 110y(P)

2:15 5-Y-O+ £23,423 (£8,900; £6,558; £3,747; £1,873; £1,405)

RPR

1 **Shere Calm (FR)**[224] 6-8-11 0 AurelienLemaitre 11 82
(G Doleuze, France) **174/10**

2 1 1/2 **Rayon Vert (FR)**[28] 4704 5-10-1 0 ChristopheSoumillon 6 96
(Laurent Loisel, France) **9/2**[1]

3 1/2 **Cry Baby (IRE)**[29] 4680 5-9-10 0 TheoBachelot 9 90
(Y Barberot, France) **9/1**

4 hd **Komodo (FR)**[172] 6-9-4 0 StephanePasquier 10 83
(R Chotard, France) **10/1**

5 snk **Verti Chop (FR)**[59] 6-8-2 0 AnthonyCrastus 2 67
(C Boutin, France) **13/1**

6 1/2 **Hanabaal Tun (FR)**[59] 5-8-4 0 (b) AlexisBadel 4 67
(R Le Dren Doleuze, France) **6/1**[2]

7 3/4 **Lightoller (IRE)**[75] 2956 5-8-5 0 (b) MaximeGuyon 12 66
(P Monfort, France) **32/5**[3]

8 nse **Vedeux (IRE)**[75] 8-9-4 0 (p) CristianDemuro 8 79
(C Lerner, France) **81/10**

9 1/2 **Lefortovo (FR)**[88] 2675 6-8-7 0 MickaelBarzalona 1 66
(Jo Hughes, France) *midfield on inner: dropped towards rr bef 1/2-way: sme prog on rail fnl bnd: rdn and kpt on over 1f out: effrt petered out ins fnl f* **14/1**

10 nse **Art Collection (FR)**[27] 6-9-5 0 TomEaves 13 78
(Andrew Hollinshead, France) **17/1**

11 3/4 **Imperial Tango (FR)**[32] 5-9-6 0 PierreBazire 14 77
(G Botti, France) **16/1**

12 1 **Ultimate Fight (FR)**[18] 5-9-3 0 RadekKoplik 16 71
(Z Koplik, Czech Republic) **25/1**

13 1 **Calaf (FR)**[27] 4747 7-8-2 0 (p) ThomasTrullier 15 53
(H Fortineau, France) **22/1**

14 4 **Wikita (FR)**[145] 8-8-4 0 MlleJessicaMarcialis 3 44
(Charley Rossi, France) **17/1**

1m 16.27s 14 Ran SP% **120.5**
PARI-MUTUEL (all including 1 euro stake): WIN 18.40; PLACE 5.10, 2.60, 3.50; DF 63.40.
Owner Mlle Claire Stephenson **Bred** Ecurie Peregrine SAS **Trained** France

5716a LARC PRIX MAURICE DE GHEEST (GROUP 1) (3YO+) (STRAIGHT COURSE) (TURF) 6f 110y(S)

2:47 3-Y-O+ £195,614 (£78,259; £39,129; £19,547; £9,790)

RPR

1 **Advertise**[22] 4923 3-8-13 0 (b) FrankieDettori 10 119
(Martyn Meade) *in tch on far side: rdn and hdwy fr 2f out: led 1 1/2f out: edgd lft ins fnl f: sn strly pressed and drvn: kpt on wl* **11/5**[1]

2 nk **Brando**[22] 4923 7-9-3 0 TomEaves 7 118
(Kevin Ryan) *hld up towards rr of midfield in centre: rdn and hdwy fr over 2f out: briefly short of room 2f out: gd hdwy to press ldr strly ins fnl f: kpt on wl: jst hld* **48/1**

3 3/4 **Space Blues (IRE)**[28] 4705 3-8-13 0 WilliamBuick 3 116
(Charlie Appleby) *midfield on nr side: rdn and crossed towards centre 2f out: styd on fr 1 1/2f out: nt able to chal* **58/10**[3]

4 hd **Spinning Memories (IRE)**[31] 4581 4-9-0 0 ChristopheSoumillon 13 112
(P Bary, France) *towards rr on far side: smooth hdwy fr over 2f out: rdn and kpt on fnl f: nt able to chal* **33/1**

5 1/2 **One Master**[23] 4885 5-9-0 0 Pierre-CharlesBoudot 2 111
(William Haggas) *towards rr of midfield in centre: rdn and swtchd towards nr side 2f out: styd on fr over 1f out* **87/10**

6 1/2 **Pretty Pollyanna**[22] 4923 3-8-9 0 OisinMurphy 14 109
(Michael Bell) *prom on far side: rdn over 2f out: wknd steadily fnl f* **11/1**

7 1 1/4 **Polydream (IRE)**[31] 4581 4-9-0 0 MaximeGuyon 1 106
(F Head, France) *hld up in rr in centre: swtchd to nr side 1/2-way: rdn and hdwy fr over 2f out: no further imp fnl f* **57/10**[2]

8 nse **So Perfect (USA)**[22] 4923 3-8-9 0 AndreaAtzeni 6 105
(A P O'Brien, Ire) *trckd ldrs in centre: rdn over 2f out: drvn and wknd steadily fnl f* **47/1**

9 3/4 **Fox Champion (IRE)**[28] 4705 3-8-13 0 SilvestreDeSousa 8 107
(Richard Hannon) *led in centre: rdn 2f out: hdd 1 1/2f out: wknd fnl f* **33/1**

10 3/4 **Mr Lupton (IRE)**[15] 5207 6-9-3 0 CristianDemuro 11 104
(Richard Fahey) *towards rr on far side: rdn over 2f out: drvn and one pce fr 1 1/2f out* **71/1**

11 1 1/2 **Le Brivido (FR)**[43] 4094 5-9-3 0 RyanMoore 12 100
(A P O'Brien, Ire) *towards rr of midfield on far side: rdn and effrt over 2f out: wknd over 1f out* **15/1**

12 1 1/2 **King Malpic (FR)**[22] 4948 6-9-3 0 OlivierPeslier 5 96
(T Lemer, France) *prom on nr side: rdn 2f out: wknd 1 1/2f out* **11/1**

13 1 1/4 **Invincible Army (IRE)**[36] 4380 4-9-3 0 PJMcDonald 4 92
(James Tate) *midfield in centre: rdn 2f out: wknd 1 1/2f out* **10/1**

14 1 1/2 **Munitions (USA)**[28] 4705 3-8-13 0 (p) MickaelBarzalona 9 88
(A Fabre, France) *trckd ldrs in centre: rdn 2 1/2f out: wknd under 2f out* **25/1**

15 1 1/4 **Namos (GER)**[28] 4705 3-8-13 0 WladimirPanov 15 84
(D Moser, Germany) *towards rr of midfield on far side: rdn and outpcd 2 1/2f out: sn wl btn: eased fnl f* **58/1**

1m 15.35s (-1.85) **Going Correction** +0.15s/f (Good)
WFA 3 from 4yo+ 4lb 15 Ran SP% **120.1**
Speed ratings: **116,115,114,114,114 113,112,111,111,110 108,106,105,103,102**
PARI-MUTUEL (all including 1 euro stake): WIN 3.20; PLACE 1.50, 6.90, 2.30; DF 55.10.
Owner Phoenix Thoroughbred Limited 1 **Bred** Cheveley Park Stud Ltd **Trained** Manton, Wilts

FOCUS
Eight of the fifteen runners were trained in the UK and a further two in Ireland while the second, fourth, fifth and seventh from the July Cup were all re-opposing in this Group 1 over nearly half a furlong further. The main action unfolded in the middle of the track and two of the first three home were 3yos, with the 7yo Brando, a previous winner, sandwiching them. It's been rated around the balance of the first three.

5717a PRIX CLUB HIPICO CONCEPCION - PRIX MICHEL HOUYVET (LISTED RACE) (3YO) (ROUND COURSE) (TURF) 1m 6f

3:32 3-Y-O £24,774 (£9,909; £7,432; £4,954; £2,477)

RPR

1 **San Huberto (IRE)**[49] 3904 3-9-0 0 TonyPiccone 8 102+
(F Chappet, France) **112/10**

2 3/4 **Verimli (FR)**[29] 3-9-0 0 ChristopheSoumillon 4 100+
(A De Royer-Dupre, France) **13/5**[1]

3 snk **In Favour**[21] 4963 3-9-0 0 VincentCheminaud 6 100
(A Fabre, France) **31/5**

4 snk **Battle Of Toro (IRE)**[26] 4770 3-9-0 0 MickaelBarzalona 2 100
(A Fabre, France) *chsd ldrs: 3rd and drvn 3f out: angled out and chal between horses 2f out: styd on u.p: led narrowly 1f out: hdd last 110yds: no ex* **37/10**[3]

5 2 1/2 **Mister Nino (FR)**[41] 3-9-0 0 MaximeGuyon 7 97
(J-M Beguigne, France) **57/10**

6 1 1/2 **Campront (FR)**[53] 3-9-0 0 CristianDemuro 1 94
(Mme Pia Brandt, France) **20/1**

7 5 **Thematic (USA)**[41] 3-9-0 0 Pierre-CharlesBoudot 5 87
(P Bary, France) **21/1**

8 2 **Nate The Great**[10] 5364 3-9-0 0 JamesDoyle 3 85
(Archie Watson) *sn settled in midfield: clsd to chse ldrs sn after 1/2-way: drvn but nt qckn 3f out: wknd over 1f out* **16/5**[2]

3m 2.76s 8 Ran SP% **119.2**
PARI-MUTUEL (all including 1 euro stake): WIN 12.20; PLACE 2.90, 1.80, 2.30; DF 16.10.
Owner Maurice Lagasse **Bred** Gestut Zur Kuste Ag **Trained** France

5718a PRIX VALPARAISO SPORTING CLUB - PRIX DE REUX (GROUP 3) (3YO+) (ROUND COURSE) (TURF) 1m 4f 110y

4:40 3-Y-O+ £36,036 (£14,414; £10,810; £7,207; £3,603)

RPR

1 **Ashrun (FR)**[42] 3-8-9 0 StephanePasquier 5 109+
(A Wohler, Germany) *in tch in midfield: rdn over 2f out: styd on fr 1 1/2f out: led narrowly under 1f out: kpt on wl and grad asserted* **128/10**

2 snk **Walton Street**[36] 4390 5-9-5 0 (p) WilliamBuick 2 107
(Charlie Appleby) *led: rdn over 2f out: drvn 1 1/2f out: hdd narrowly under 1f out: kpt on wl but wnr grad asserted* **9/5**[1]

3 2 **First Nation**[15] 5182 5-9-5 0 JamesDoyle 1 105
(Charlie Appleby) *midfield on inner: rdn over 2f out: hdwy appr fnl f: drvn ins fnl f: no ex fnl 75yds* **59/10**[3]

4 1/2 **Master's Spirit (IRE)**[19] 5036 8-9-5 0 IoritzMendizabal 8 103
(J Reynier, France) *towards rr of midfield: rdn over 2f out: kpt on fnl f* **15/2**

5 hd **Gyllen (USA)**[63] 3389 4-9-5 0 MickaelBarzalona 4 103
(A Fabre, France) *trckd ldrs: rdn to chse ldr over 2f out: no ex fnl f* **59/10**[3]

6 3 **Ferblue (FR)**[33] 3-8-9 0 CristianDemuro 3 100
(J-C Rouget, France) *towards rr: rdn over 2f out: kpt on ins fnl f: n.d* **18/5**[2]

7 2 **Replenish (FR)**[32] 6-9-5 0 VincentCheminaud 6 95
(S Cerulis, France) *chsd ldr: rdn and dropped to 3rd over 2f out: wknd over 1f out* **22/1**

8 4 **Bartaba (FR)**[70] 3123 4-9-2 0 MaximeGuyon 7 85
(A Fabre, France) *a in rr* **9/1**

2m 42.69s (-3.71) **Going Correction** +0.15s/f (Good)
WFA 3 from 4yo+ 10lb 8 Ran SP% **119.8**
Speed ratings: **106,105,104,104,104 102,101,98**
PARI-MUTUEL (all including 1 euro stake): WIN 13.80; PLACE 3.10, 1.50, 2.50; DF 21.20.
Owner Stall Turffighter **Bred** H Wirth **Trained** Germany

5230 **DUSSELDORF** (R-H)
Sunday, August 4

OFFICIAL GOING: Turf: good

5719a FRITZ HENKEL STIFTUNG-RENNEN (GROUP 3) (3YO+) (TURF) 1m 4f

2:10 3-Y-O+ £28,828 (£10,810; £5,405; £2,702; £1,801)

RPR

1 **Bristano**[26] 4770 3-8-4 0 FilipMinarik 3 106
(M G Mintchev, Germany) *trckd ldrs: rdn to chal 2 1/2f out: drvn and led 1 1/2f out: kpt on wl fnl f* **119/10**

2 1/2 **Accon (GER)**[28] 4707 3-8-8 0 JiriPalik 2 109
(Markus Klug, Germany) *hld up: rdn and hdwy on outside fr under 3f out: ev ch fnl f: kpt on wl: jst hld* **7/5**[1]

3 hd **Oriental Eagle (GER)**[35] 4427 5-9-0 0 JackMitchell 1 104
(J Hirschberger, Germany) *led: rdn over 3f out: hdd over 1f 1/2f out: kpt on fnl f* **69/10**

4 1 1/2 **Colomano**[35] 4427 5-9-2 0 MaximPecheur 4 103
(Markus Klug, Germany) *hld up: rdn and hdwy on inner 2f out: ev ch 1f out: no ex fnl 100yds* **16/5**[2]

5 nk **Amorella (IRE)**[30] 4622 4-8-13 0 AdriedeVries 5 100
(Markus Klug, Germany) *racd keenly: in tch: rdn and effrt 2f out: drvn over 1f out: no ex fnl f* **6/1**

6 4 **Nikkei (GER)**[30] 4622 4-9-2 0 AndraschStarke 6 96
(P Schiergen, Germany) *chsd ldr: rdn 2f out: wknd fr 1 1/2f out* **41/10**[3]

2m 25.82s (-3.72)
WFA 3 from 4yo+ 10lb 6 Ran SP% **119.8**
PARI-MUTUEL (all including 1 euro stake): WIN 12.90 PLACE: 3.80, 1.70; SF: 19.80.
Owner Litex Commerce Ad **Bred** Litex Commerce **Trained** Germany

5720a 161ST HENKEL-PREIS DER DIANA - GERMAN OAKS (GROUP 1) (3YO FILLIES) (TURF) 1m 3f

4:00 3-Y-O

£270,270 (£90,090; £45,045; £24,324; £11,711; £9,009)

RPR

1 **Diamanta (GER)**[21] 3-9-2 0 MaximPecheur 1 103
(Markus Klug, Germany) *trckd ldrs: rdn 2 1/2f out: drvn under 2f out: chal 1f out: led 150yds out: sn clr: kpt on wl* **235/10**

2 1 3/4 **Naida (GER)**[21] 3-9-2 0 BauyrzhanMurzabayev 2 100
(Yasmin Almenrader, Germany) *midfield: rdn and stdy hdwy fr 2 1/2f out: styd on strly fnl 100yds: snatched 2nd last stride* **173/10**

3 shd **Durance (GER)**[29] 4683 3-9-2 0 (p) AndraschStarke 10 100
(P Schiergen, Germany) *racd keenly: in tch: forward move to ld 4f out: rdn 2f out: chal 1f out: hdd 150yds out: sn no ex: lost 2nd last stride* **29/10**[1]

4 nse **Satomi (GER)**[56] 3639 3-9-2 0 RenePiechulek 11 100
(Markus Klug, Germany) *hld up towards rr: stdy hdwy on outside fr over 3f out: rdn under 3f out: v wd into st: j. path 2f out: styd on strly fnl f: nrst fin* **179/10**

5 1 1/4 **Akribie (GER)**[56] 3639 3-9-2 0 AdriedeVries 7 98
(Markus Klug, Germany) *chsd ldr: dropped to 4th 3 1/2f out: rdn and effrt over 2f out: drvn under 2f out: no ex ins fnl f* **57/10**[3]

6 shd **Donjah (GER)**[273] 8869 3-9-2 0 AntoineHamelin 6 97
(Henk Grewe, Germany) *in tch: wd into st: rdn and kpt on same pce fr over 2f out* **37/10**[2]

7 1/2 **Skyful Sea (FR)**[35] 4427 3-9-2 0 MartinDwyer 4 97
(P Schiergen, Germany) *racd keenly: towards rr: rdn and kpt on steadily fr 2 1/2f out: nvr gng pce to threaten* **113/10**

8 1 **Shining Pass (GER)**[29] 4683 3-9-2 0 EduardoPedroza 3 95
(A Wohler, Germany) *midfield: rdn and effrt on inner 2f out: wknd steadily fnl f* **147/10**

9 nk **Mythica (IRE)**[50] 3877 3-9-2 0 GeraldMosse 12 94
(Jean-Pierre Carvalho, Germany) *led: hdd 4f out: pushed wd into st by loose horse: rdn over 2f out: wknd 1 1/2f out* **179/10**

10 nk **Apadanah (GER)**[42] 4171 3-9-2 0 JackMitchell 13 94
(Waldemar Hickst, Germany) *sn bhd and pushed along: rdn 2 1/2f out: kpt on steadily fr over 1f out: nvr in contention* **192/10**

11 1/2 **Freedom Rising (GER)**[28] 3-9-2 0 MlleAnnaVanDenTroost 9 93
(Yasmin Almenrader, Germany) *a towards rr* **41/1**

12 3/4 **Liberty London (GER)**[29] 4683 3-9-2 0 MarcoCasamento 5 91
(H-J Groschel, Germany) *a towards rr* **29/1**

U **Ismene (GER)**[21] 3-9-2 0 FilipMinarik 8
(Jean-Pierre Carvalho, Germany) *stmbld and uns rdr leaving stalls* **78/10**

2m 15.78s **13 Ran SP% 118.5**
PARI-MUTUEL (all including 1 euro stake): WIN 24.50 PLACE: 3.90, 3.10, 1.50, 3.20; SF: 533.60.
Owner Gestut Brummerhof **Bred** Gestut Brummerhof **Trained** Germany

5721 - (Foreign Racing) - See Raceform Interactive

4817 CARLISLE (R-H)

Monday, August 5

OFFICIAL GOING: Good to soft (good in places; 6.7)
Wind: Breezy, half against in over 2f of home straight Weather: Cloudy

5722 GLO & GO TANNING LOUNGE H'CAP (PRO-AM LADY RIDERS' RACE) 5f

5:45 (5:47) (Class 6) (0-65,64) 4-Y-O+

£3,493 (£1,039; £519; £300; £300; £300) Stalls Low

Form RPR

0-00 1 **Moonlit Sands (IRE)**[14] 5244 4-9-11 **54** (t[1]) MeganNicholls 9 61
(Brian Ellison) *dwlt: bhd in centre of gp: hdwy over 1f out: led ins fnl f: r.o wl (trainer's rep could offer no explanation for the improved form shown)* **9/1**

434 2 nk **Gorgeous General**[31] 4586 4-10-0 **57** FayeMcManoman 3 63
(Lawrence Mullaney) *midfield on far side of gp: hdwy to ld over 1f out: hdd ins fnl f: kpt on: hld nr fin* **5/1**[2]

0000 3 1 3/4 **Guardia Svizzera (IRE)**[11] 5330 5-10-7 **64** (h) PaulaMuir 2 64
(Roger Fell) *bdly hmpd s: bhd on far side of gp: hdwy and prom over 1f out: kpt on same pce ins fnl f* **14/1**

0036 4 1 1/2 **Suitcase 'N' Taxi**[10] 5393 5-10-1 **58** RachelRichardson 7 52
(Tim Easterby) *w ldr in centre of gp: rdn 2f out: kpt on same pce ins fnl f* **9/2**[1]

0054 5 nk **Star Cracker (IRE)**[7] 5486 7-9-2 **45** (p) MrsCarolBartley 6 38
(Jim Goldie) *towards rr in centre of gp: pushed along and hdwy over 1f out: edgd rt: one pce ins fnl f* **8/1**[3]

1001 6 3/4 **Oriental Splendour (IRE)**[20] 5018 7-9-3 **51** (b) MissEmilyBullock(5) 14 41
(Ruth Carr) *dwlt: hld up on nr side of gp: effrt over 1f out: edgd rt: no imp fnl f* **17/2**

0403 7 nk **Jessie Allan (IRE)**[7] 5486 8-8-12 **46** MissShannonWatts(5) 13 35+
(Jim Goldie) *bhd on nr side of gp: hdwy against stands' rail over 1f out: no imp fnl f* **8/1**[3]

4535 8 1/2 **B Fifty Two (IRE)**[12] 5299 10-10-0 **57** (vt) JaneElliott 12 45
(Marjorie Fife) *led on nr side of gp: rdn and hdd over 1f out: wknd ins fnl f* **10/1**

0620 9 hd **Teepee Time**[16] 5181 6-9-4 **47** (b) MissMichelleMullineaux 10 34
(Michael Mullineaux) *cl up in centre of gp tl rdn and wknd over 1f out* **33/1**

60-0 10 3/4 **Red Forever**[29] 4694 8-9-2 **45** (p) MissHelenCuthbert 11 29
(Helen Cuthbert) *midfield on nr side of gp: pushed along over 2f out: wknd over 1f out* **66/1**

034 11 1/2 **Astrophysics**[8] 5478 7-10-0 **57** MissEmmaTodd 4 39
(Lynn Siddall) *prom on far side of gp: rdn over 1f out: wknd fnl f* **12/1**

0530 12 nk **Classic Pursuit**[13] 5276 8-10-5 **62** (v) MissBeckySmith 1 43
(Marjorie Fife) *wnt lft s: bhd on far side of gp: rdn and shortlived effrt 2f out: btn fnl f* **20/1**

-000 13 1 1/2 **Whispering Soul (IRE)**[60] 3518 6-9-2 **45** (v) LauraCoughlan 5 21
(Brian Baugh) *in tch in centre of gp: rdn and wknd over 1f out* **80/1**

0040 14 8 **Astraea**[98] 2215 4-9-10 **53** MissJoannaMason 8 +
(Michael Easterby) *s.v.s: t.o thrght (jockey said filly froze when the gates opened and was slowly away, losing many lengths)* **12/1**

1m 2.66s (0.56) **Going Correction** +0.025s/f (Good) **14 Ran SP% 119.2**
Speed ratings (Par 101): **96,95,92,90,89 88,88,87,87,85 85,84,82,69**
CSF £51.63 CT £656.40 TOTE £11.00: £3.40, £2.10, £4.00; EX 63.50 Trifecta £755.50.
Owner Keith Brown **Bred** Grange Stud **Trained** Norton, N Yorks

FOCUS
Ground as the official, namely good to soft, good in places.\n\x\x An open contest to start lady riders night, with the field spread across the width of the track as they turned into the straight. Professional riders were on board the first four home. Straightforward form that won't be far out.

5723 GLO & GO PREMIUM QUALITY TANNING H'CAP (PRO-AM LADY RIDERS' RACE) (JC GRASSROOTS SPRINT SERIES) 5f 193y

6:15 (6:16) (Class 5) (0-75,77) 4-Y-O+

£4,204 (£1,251; £625; £312; £300; £300) Stalls Low

Form RPR

0306 1 **Redrosezorro**[24] 4880 5-9-11 **65** (h) ShelleyBirkett 5 76+
(Eric Alston) *trckd ldrs in centre of gp: shkn up to ld over 1f out: clr ins fnl f: r.o wl* **7/2**[2]

6360 2 1 1/4 **Madrinho (IRE)**[24] 4880 6-9-13 **72** MissSarahBowen(5) 6 77
(Tony Carroll) *hld up in centre of gp: rdn over 2f out: gd hdwy over 1f out: chsd wnr wl ins fnl f: kpt on fin* **6/1**

0000 3 3/4 **Gullane One (IRE)**[10] 5395 4-9-13 **67** (t) RachelRichardson 13 70
(Tim Easterby) *led in centre of gp: rdn and hdd over 1f out: edgd rt: no ex and lost 2nd pl wl ins fnl f* **11/1**

6110 4 1/2 **Tarnhelm**[14] 5235 4-9-2 **56** oh2 RhonaPindar 12 57
(Wilf Storey) *s.i.s: hld up on nr side of gp: pushed along 2f out: hdwy fnl f: kpt on: nrst fin* **11/1**

1360 5 1 **Gottardo (IRE)**[39] 4281 4-9-9 **68** SophieSmith(5) 3 66
(Ed Dunlop) *s.i.s: hld up in midfield on far side of gp: effrt 2f out: kpt on fnl f: no imp* **11/1**

315R 6 2 **Robot Boy (IRE)**[16] 5169 9-10-4 **72** JaneElliott 9 63
(Marjorie Fife) *prom on nr side of gp: effrt and edgd lft wl over 1f out: wknd ins fnl f* **33/1**

2220 7 3/4 **Ventura Secret (IRE)**[14] 5235 5-8-11 **56** oh1 (tp) MissChloeDods(5) 7 45
(Michael Dods) *hld up in midfield in centre of gp: shkn up and effrt over 1f out: edgd rt: sn no imp* **5/1**[3]

0034 8 1/2 **Kenny The Captain (IRE)**[60] 3503 8-9-10 **64** (p) MissEmilyEasterby 4 51
(Tim Easterby) *in tch on far side of gp: pushed along over 2f out: wknd over 1f out* **3/1**[1]

3200 9 1 1/2 **Dodgy Bob**[54] 3716 6-9-2 **56** oh8 (v) MrsCarolBartley 10 39
(Michael Mullineaux) *hld up on nr side of gp: effrt over 2f out: hung rt and outpcd over 1f out* **40/1**

0-50 10 2 1/2 **Adam's Ale**[19] 5038 10-10-7 **75** (p) MissBeckySmith 1 50
(Marjorie Fife) *cl up on far side of gp: rdn over 2f out: wknd wl over 1f out* **18/1**

0060 11 8 **Rock Warbler (IRE)**[12] 5302 6-9-2 **56** oh11 (e) MissMichelleMullineaux 11 5
(Michael Mullineaux) *bhd towards nr side of gp: drvn and struggling over 2f out: sn btn* **66/1**

1m 14.2s (-0.40) **Going Correction** +0.025s/f (Good) **11 Ran SP% 115.3**
Speed ratings (Par 103): **103,101,100,99,98 95,94,94,92,88 78**
CSF £24.07 CT £212.18 TOTE £3.10: £1.70, £2.10, £3.00; EX 30.80 Trifecta £167.20.
Owner Red Rose Partnership **Bred** Whitsbury Manor Stud & Jointsense Ltd **Trained** Longton, Lancs

FOCUS
The winner built on his latest form and is rated back to his best.

5724 MEGASUN LOUNGE @ GLO & GO H'CAP (PROFESSIONAL LADY RIDERS' RACE) 5f 193y

6:45 (6:46) (Class 4) (0-85,84) 3-Y-O

£8,086 (£2,406; £1,202; £601; £300; £300) Stalls Low

Form RPR

3301 1 **Gale Force Maya**[25] 4822 3-8-6 **74** PaulaMuir(5) 5 82
(Michael Dods) *trckd ldrs: effrt over 1f out: led and edgd lft ins fnl f: kpt on wl* **7/4**[1]

3153 2 1/2 **Tenax (IRE)**[10] 5399 3-9-2 **84** FayeMcManoman(5) 6 90
(Nigel Tinkler) *hld up: stdy hdwy 2f out: effrt and cl 2nd whn edgd rt and blkd ins fnl f: sn pressing wnr: r.o* **3/1**[2]

6023 3 1 1/2 **Kolossus**[15] 5215 3-8-4 **70** MeganNicholls(3) 2 71
(Michael Dods) *led: rdn over 1f out: hdd whn carried sltly lft and blkd ins fnl f: one pce* **9/2**[3]

1333 4 1 1/4 **Nubough (IRE)**[74] 2997 3-9-4 **84** (h) JaneElliott(3) 4 81
(Iain Jardine) *cl up: rdn along 2f out: edgd rt and outpcd ins fnl f* **7/1**

6053 5 4 1/2 **Raha**[19] 5062 3-7-11 **65** oh1 SophieRalston(5) 1 48
(Julia Feilden) *hld up: outpcd and detached 1/2-way: sme late hdwy: nvr on terms (jockey said filly was never travelling)* **16/1**

2114 6 1 1/2 **Beryl The Petal (IRE)**[17] 5157 3-9-6 **83** (v) ShelleyBirkett 3 61
(David O'Meara) *hld up in tch: rdn over 2f out: wknd over 1f out* **11/1**

1360 7 1 3/4 **Look Out Louis**[25] 4847 3-9-7 **84** RachelRichardson 7 56
(Tim Easterby) *t.k.h: prom tl rdn and wknd over 1f out* **10/1**

1m 13.53s (-1.07) **Going Correction** +0.025s/f (Good) **7 Ran SP% 115.4**
Speed ratings (Par 102): **106,105,103,101,95 93,91**
CSF £7.28 TOTE £2.50: £1.50, £2.90; EX 7.30 Trifecta £25.10.
Owner Frank Lowe **Bred** Mrs J Imray **Trained** Denton, Co Durham
■ Stewards' Enquiry : Paula Muir caution: careless riding

FOCUS
The winner progressed again, with her stablemate in third close to recent form.

5725 GLO LIKE A WINNER H'CAP (PRO-AM LADY RIDERS' RACE) 1m 1f

7:15 (7:15) (Class 5) (0-75,77) 4-Y-O+

£4,204 (£1,251; £625; £312; £300; £300) Stalls Low

Form RPR

0005 1 **Zealous (IRE)**[23] 4914 6-9-6 **57** (p[1]) ShelleyBirkett 6 68+
(Alistair Whillans) *midfield: gd hdwy to ld over 2f out: clr over 1f out: edgd rt ins fnl f: kpt on wl (trainer's rep said, regarding the improved form shown, the gelding benefited from the application of cheekpieces for the first time)* **18/1**

514 2 2 1/2 **Granite City Doc**[38] 4333 6-10-1 **66** PaulaMuir 3 71
(Lucy Normile) *hld up: hdwy over 2f out: chsd (clr) wnr ins fnl f: kpt on: nt pce to chal* **12/1**

0352 3 1 3/4 **Kannapolis (IRE)**[28] 4728 4-10-7 **72** MissJoannaMason 8 73
(Michael Easterby) *prom chsng gp: hdwy to ld briefly over 2f out: chsd wnr to ins fnl f: one pce* **5/1**[2]

0523 4 1/2 **Ghayyar (IRE)**[20] 5022 5-10-5 **70** (tp) RachelRichardson 2 70
(Tim Easterby) *hld up: hdwy over 2f out: effrt and hung rt over 1f out: no imp fnl f* **13/2**[3]

2116 5 nse **Edgar Allan Poe (IRE)**[19] 5060 5-10-12 **77** MissSerenaBrotherton 5 77
(Rebecca Bastiman) *hld up: hdwy 2f out: rdn and no further imp fnl f* **7/1**

5441 **6** *1* **Indomeneo**[16] 5178 4-10-11 **76**.. MeganNicholls 1 74
(Richard Fahey) *hld up in midfield: effrt whn n.m.r briefly over 2f out: effrt over 1f out: nvr able to chal* **5/1**[2]

2301 **7** *hd* **Anif (IRE)**[15] 5216 5-10-7 **72**.. MissBeckySmith 7 69
(Michael Herrington) *dwlt: hld up: effrt on outside over 2f out: no imp over 1f out* **4/1**[1]

0214 **8** *1 3/4* **Bollin Ted**[6] 5518 5-9-10 **61**.. MissEmilyEasterby 9 54
(Tim Easterby) *chsd clr ldng pair: rdn over 2f out: wknd over 1f out* **10/1**

0402 **9** *5* **Ideal Candy (IRE)**[14] 5245 4-10-5 **70**..(h) GemmaTutty 11 52
(Karen Tutty) *racd wd fr draw early: led to over 2f out: sn wknd* **8/1**

2602 **10** *2 3/4* **The Navigator**[25] 4817 4-10-11 **76**.. MissEmmaSayer 10 52
(Dianne Sayer) *dwlt: hld up: rdn and effrt on wd outside over 2f out: wknd over 1f out* **10/1**

0001 **11** *11* **Bob's Girl**[14] 5248 4-9-2 **53** oh4..(b) JaneElliott 4 5
(Michael Mullineaux) *chsd ldr and sn clr of rest: drvn and outpcd 3f out: wknd 2f out* **25/1**

1m 58.3s (-0.70) **Going Correction** +0.025s/f (Good) 11 Ran SP% **125.3**
Speed ratings (Par 103): **104,101,100,99,99 98,98,97,92,90 80**
CSF £230.69 CT £1286.46 TOTE £18.80: £5.50, £4.00, £2.10; EX 182.00 Trifecta £1576.60.
Owner W J E Scott & Mrs M A Scott **Bred** Knocklong House Stud **Trained** Newmill-On-Slitrig, Borders

FOCUS
Add 8yds.\n\x\x An overly strong pace for this 1m1f handicap and the winner, who was providing Shelley Birkett with a double on the card, benefited from being perfectly placed throughout. He's rated close to last year's non-claim best.

5726 ON YOUR MARKS GET SET GLO H'CAP (PRO-AM LADY RIDERS' RACE) 7f 173y

7:45 (7:46) (Class 4) (0-85,84) 4-Y-O+

£8,086 (£2,406; £1,202; £601; £300; £300) **Stalls** Low

Form RPR

1521 **1** **Redarna**[9] 5416 5-10-7 **84**..(p) MissEmmaSayer 10 94
(Dianne Sayer) *led 2f: pressed ldr: brought to stands' rail and regained ld over 1f out: rdn and r.o wl fnl f* **3/1**[1]

50 **2** *3/4* **Donncha (IRE)**[45] 4079 8-10-7 **84**.. PaulaMuir 9 92
(Seb Spencer) *hld up: hdwy to press wnr over 1f out: kpt on fnl f: hld nr fin* **16/1**

0042 **3** *2 1/4* **Pickett's Charge**[6] 5517 6-9-4 **67**..(p) MeganNicholls 3 70
(Brian Ellison) *t.k.h: in tch: rdn and outpcd 2f out: rallied to chse clr ldng pair ins fnl f: r.o* **4/1**[2]

0005 **4** *1/2* **Royal Shaheen (FR)**[7] 5490 6-9-5 **68**..(v) JaneElliott 8 70
(Alistair Whillans) *pressed ldr: led after 2f: rdn over 2f out: hdd over 1f out: one pce fnl f* **9/1**

4301 **5** *3/4* **Beverley Bullet**[9] 5438 6-9-3 **66**..(p) FayeMcManoman 1 66
(Lawrence Mullaney) *hld up on ins: effrt and rdn 2f out: kpt on fnl f: nt pce to chal* **6/1**[3]

1216 **6** *1/2* **Oud Metha Bridge (IRE)**[32] 4566 5-9-10 **73**.................. ShelleyBirkett 2 72
(Julia Feilden) *chsd ldrs: rdn and edgd rt over 1f out: wknd ins fnl f* **8/1**

2463 **7** *1 1/4* **Zoravan (USA)**[17] 5117 6-9-4 **67**..(b) MrsCarolBartley 5 63
(Keith Dalgleish) *t.k.h: hld up: effrt over 1f out: no imp fnl f* **9/1**

0036 **8** *3/4* **Vive La Difference (IRE)**[7] 5490 5-9-10 **73**........... RachelRichardson 4 67
(Tim Easterby) *s.i.s: hld up: rdn wl over 1f out: nvr rchd ldrs* **10/1**

-650 **9** *8* **Mustaqbal (IRE)**[7] 5490 7-9-5 **73**..(p) MissSophieDods(5) 7 49
(Michael Dods) *hld up: pushed along wl over 1f out: sn wknd* **20/1**

0600 **10** *5* **New Look (FR)**[40] 4240 4-9-12 **75**..(b[1]) MissEmilyEasterby 6 40
(Tim Easterby) *prom tl rdn and wknd fr 2f out* **12/1**

1m 40.49s (0.49) **Going Correction** +0.025s/f (Good) 10 Ran SP% **117.8**
Speed ratings (Par 105): **98,97,95,94,93 93,92,91,83,78**
CSF £54.09 CT £201.51 TOTE £3.30: £2.80, £3.70, £1.40; EX 46.80 Trifecta £150.40.
Owner Graham Lund And Dianne Sayer **Bred** A H Bennett **Trained** Hackthorpe, Cumbria
■ Stewards' Enquiry : Paula Muir four-day ban: misuse of the whip (Aug 19,20,24,25)

FOCUS
Not a strong race for the grade but the winner, who was switched to the stands' rail in the straight, continued his fine run of form this year. This was another pb from him. Add 8yds.

5727 GOLDEN GLO @ GLO & GO H'CAP (PRO-AM LADY RIDERS' RACE) 2m 1f 47y

8:15 (8:15) (Class 5) (0-70,72) 4-Y-O+

£4,204 (£1,251; £625; £312; £300; £300) **Stalls** Low

Form RPR

0001 **1** **Stormin Norman**[21] 4990 4-9-9 **55**.. MissBeckySmith 14 69+
(Micky Hammond) *in tch: smooth hdwy to ld over 2f out: sn clr: pushed out: readily* **9/2**[2]

0432 **2** *6* **Royal Flag**[6] 5513 9-10-1 **61**.. MeganNicholls 11 68
(Brian Ellison) *hld up on outside: hdwy and prom over 3f out: chsd (clr) wnr over 1f out: no imp* **5/1**[3]

313 **3** *4* **Tawseef (IRE)**[14] 5241 11-10-6 **66**..(p) EllaMcCain 3 69
(Donald McCain) *hld up in midfield: hdwy and prom over 3f out: rdn and one pce fnl 2f* **11/2**

3040 **4** *2 1/4* **Elite Icon**[13] 5277 5-9-2 **48**..(v) JaneElliott 2 49
(Jim Goldie) *hld up: rdn and outpcd 4f out: rallied 2f out: kpt on: nvr able to chal (jockey said gelding was never travelling)* **12/1**

5045 **5** *2 1/2* **Question Of Faith**[7] 5487 8-10-6 **66**..(p[1]) LucyAlexander 8 64
(Martin Todhunter) *missed break: hld up: pushed along 4f out: hdwy 2f out: sn no imp* **25/1**

4020 **6** *3/4* **St Andrews (IRE)**[9] 5435 6-9-9 **55**.. MissEmmaTodd 5 52
(Gillian Boanas) *hld up: rdn over 3f out: no imp fr 2f out* **9/1**

0-00 **7** *1 1/2* **Excalibur (POL)**[60] 3500 6-9-2 **48** oh3...........(p) MissSerenaBrotherton 7 43
(Micky Hammond) *hld up on ins: hdwy and prom over 3f out: rdn and wknd over 1f out* **33/1**

4664 **8** *nse* **Tapis Libre**[3] 5621 11-10-11 **71**..(p) MissJoannaMason 6 66
(Jacqueline Coward) *cl up: hdwy to ld over 3f out: hdd over 2f out: chsd wnr tl wknd over 1f out* **11/1**

0-20 **9** *2 1/4* **Calliope**[12] 5301 6-10-0 **60**..(t) MissEmmaSayer 9 53
(Dianne Sayer) *dwlt: hld up: pushed along and shortlived effrt over 2f out: sn btn* **10/1**

4-11 **10** *8* **Perla Blanca (USA)**[25] 4825 5-10-6 **71**.. SophieSmith(5) 10 55
(Ed Dunlop) *hld up: rdn and outpcd over 3f out: sn wknd (jockey said mare jumped the road crossing and was never travelling thereafter. vet reported mare was lame left fore)* **10/3**[1]

0020 **11** *24* **Miss Ranger (IRE)**[9] 5423 7-9-11 **57**..(b) PaulaMuir 1 15
(Roger Fell) *t.k.h: cl up: led after 6f: sn clr: hdd over 3f out: sn wknd: t.o (jockey said mare ran too free)* **33/1**

4100 **12** *24* **Rock N'Stones (IRE)**[9] 5435 8-9-2 **48**.. ShelleyBirkett 12
(Gillian Boanas) *led 6f: chsd clr ldr to over 4f out: wknd over 3f out: t.o (trainer said gelding was unsuited by the going and would prefer a faster surface)* **40/1**

3m 53.1s (-1.20) **Going Correction** +0.025s/f (Good) 12 Ran SP% **120.6**
Speed ratings (Par 103): **103,100,98,97,96 95,95,94,93,90 78,67**
CSF £26.87 CT £129.46 TOTE £5.20: £1.60, £1.80, £2.10; EX 23.80 Trifecta £103.70.
Owner The Monday Club **Bred** Copgrove Hall Stud **Trained** Middleham, N Yorks

FOCUS
A modest staying event but run at a good pace and the winner made it 2-2 in handicaps with an authoritative performance. Add 8yds.

5728 TRACY GANNON INSPIRATIONAL LADY GLO & GO H'CAP (PRO-AM LADY RIDERS' RACE) 1m 3f 39y

8:45 (8:45) (Class 5) (0-70,70) 4-Y-O+

£4,204 (£1,251; £625; £312; £300; £300) **Stalls** High

Form RPR

4061 **1** **Breathable**[8] 5473 4-10-6 **69** 5ex.. MissEmilyEasterby 6 79
(Tim Easterby) *hld up: hdwy and swtchd rt 2f out: shkn up to ld ins fnl f: edgd lft and sn clr: comf* **4/1**[2]

1335 **2** *2 1/2* **Majeste**[13] 5285 5-10-2 **65**.. MissSerenaBrotherton 8 71
(Rebecca Bastiman) *hld up in tch: hdwy to chse ldr 3f out: led over 1f out: edgd rt and hdd ins fnl f: one pce* **7/1**

5412 **3** *3/4* **Thorntoun Care**[3] 5621 8-10-1 **69**..(p) MissAmyCollier(5) 9 74
(Karen Tutty) *hld up: hdwy and prom over 1f out: effrt and ev ch ins fnl f: one pce towards fin* **7/2**[1]

0345 **4** *1/2* **Iolani (GER)**[13] 5277 7-9-12 **61**..(tp) MissEmmaSayer 4 65
(Dianne Sayer) *hld up in midfield on ins: hdwy and prom over 1f out: rdn and one pce ins fnl f (jockey said gelding was denied a clear run approaching the final 2f)* **7/1**

2532 **5** *2* **Apache Blaze**[20] 5025 4-10-0 **63**.. MeganNicholls 5 63
(Robyn Brisland) *hld up: pushed along over 4f out: hdwy over 1f out: kpt on fnl f: no imp* **6/1**[3]

5000 **6** *1* **Star Ascending (IRE)**[17] 5122 7-9-9 **58**..(p) JaneElliott 16 57
(Jennie Candlish) *t.k.h: prom: effrt over 2f out: hung rt and outpcd fr over 1f out* **33/1**

1515 **7** *3/4* **Zihaam**[14] 5245 5-10-4 **67**..(p) PaulaMuir 1 65
(Roger Fell) *trckd ldrs: effrt and rdn over 1f out: wknd fnl f* **9/1**

4505 **8** *3/4* **Grandscape**[11] 5337 4-9-12 **66**.. SophieSmith(5) 15 62
(Ed Dunlop) *midfield: pushed along and effrt 2f out: no imp appr fnl f* **16/1**

4-13 **9** *1/2* **Joie De Vivre (IRE)**[19] 5039 4-10-7 **70**..(h[1]) LucyAlexander 7 65
(Martin Todhunter) *hld up: rdn on wd outside over 3f out: nvr rchd ldrs* **12/1**

255- **10** *3/4* **Our Kylie (IRE)**[38] 4908 7-9-13 **62**.. EllaMcCain 14 56
(Donald McCain) *midfield on outside: pushed along after 3f: drvn over 4f out: outpcd fnl 2f* **33/1**

-030 **11** *3/4* **Firby (IRE)**[5] 5560 4-10-2 **70**.. MissRachelTaylor(5) 10 63
(Michael Dods) *t.k.h: hld up: gd hdwy on outside to ld over 3f out: rdn and hdd over 1f out: wknd fnl f* **25/1**

34-4 **12** *1 1/2* **Card High (IRE)**[47] 4009 9-10-3 **66**..(t) RhonaPindar 12 56
(Wilf Storey) *t.k.h in midfield: effrt and shkn up over 1f out: sn wknd* **16/1**

305 **13** *4* **Sweet Marmalade (IRE)**[26] 4779 4-9-13 **62**.......... FayeMcManoman 13 45
(Lawrence Mullaney) *hld up towards rr: pushed along over 2f out: sn wknd* **33/1**

6-06 **14** *3 1/4* **Mercer's Troop (IRE)**[17] 5122 4-10-4 **67**..(p) RachelRichardson 2 45
(Alistair Whillans) *led to over 3f out: wknd over 2f out* **33/1**

11-0 **15** *1 1/4* **Itlaaq**[52] 3816 13-10-1 **69**..(t) MissMaisieSharp(5) 17 45
(Michael Easterby) *hld up in tch on outside: rdn and wknd 2f out* **40/1**

0- **16** *28* **Carta Blanca (IRE)**[400] 618 6-9-2 **51** oh6.. ShelleyBirkett 3
(David Thompson) *chsd ldr to over 3f out: wknd over 2f out: t.o* **50/1**

2m 28.08s (-1.62) **Going Correction** +0.025s/f (Good) 16 Ran SP% **131.0**
Speed ratings (Par 103): **104,102,101,101,99 99,98,98,97,97 96,95,92,90,89 68**
CSF £32.87 CT £114.62 TOTE £4.10: £1.20, £2.20, £1.90, £2.40; EX 35.90 Trifecta £122.30.
Owner B Guerin J Westoll & Habton Farms **Bred** Mr & Mrs A E Pakenham **Trained** Great Habton, N Yorks
■ Stewards' Enquiry : Ella McCain four-day ban: misuse of the whip (Aug 19,20,24,25)

FOCUS
Add 8yds. The winner was better than ever, with the second rated to his recent best.
T/Jkpt: Not Won. T/Plt: £237.20 to a £1 stake. Pool: £75,432.46 - 232.09 winning units T/Qpdt: £22.00 to a £1 stake. Pool: £9,434.41 - 316.69 winning units **Richard Young**

4786 KEMPTON (A.W) (R-H)

Monday, August 5

OFFICIAL GOING: Polytrack: standard to slow (watered)
Wind: light, across Weather: fine

5729 MATCHBOOK BETTING EXCHANGE NOVICE AUCTION STKS 5f (P)

1:45 (1:45) (Class 5) 2-Y-O **£3,881** (£1,155; £577; £288) **Stalls** Low

Form RPR

1 **1** **Streamline**[12] 5288 2-9-7 0..(h) AdamKirby 6 80+
(Clive Cox) *in tch: effrt and rdn over 1f out: hdwy to ld ins fnl f: sn clr and r.o strly* **4/5**[1]

0 **2** *3 3/4* **Force Of Impact (IRE)**[21] 4999 2-8-13 0.. LukeMorris 1 59
(Paul George) *pushed along leaving stalls: sn led: rdn wl over 1f out: drvn and hdd ins fnl f: immediately outpcd: kpt on to hold 2nd* **16/1**

3 *1* **Simply Silca (IRE)** 2-8-11 0.. ShaneKelly 4 53+
(Richard Hughes) *s.i.s: in tch in rr: effrt wl over 1f out: reminder and swtchd lft 1f out: styd on to go 3rd towards fin: no ch w wnr* **14/1**[3]

103 **4** *1/2* **Better The Devil (USA)**[26] 4802 2-9-7 **80**.. HollieDoyle 3 61+
(Archie Watson) *rousted along leaving stalls: sn chsd ldr: effrt ent fnl 2f: unable qck u.p over 1f out: no ch w wnr and kpt on same pce ins fnl f* **15/8**[2]

66 **5** *1/2* **Treaty Of Dingle**[7] 5500 2-8-8 0.. CharlieBennett 2 46
(Hughie Morrison) *chsd ldrs: effrt on inner over 1f out: unable qck: no ch w wnr and kpt on same pce ins fnl f* **16/1**

1m 1.21s (0.71) **Going Correction** +0.10s/f (Slow) 5 Ran SP% **108.8**
Speed ratings (Par 94): **98,92,90,89,88**
CSF £13.91 TOTE £1.50: £1.10, £8.50; EX 15.50 Trifecta £71.90.
Owner Mainline Racing **Bred** Whitsbury Manor Stud **Trained** Lambourn, Berks

FOCUS
The track was ameliorated to a depth of 110mm and the Polytrack was described as standard to slow. This novice auction looked a straight fight between the two previous winners beforehand, but one disappointed leaving it at the mercy of the other. The winning time was 2.41sec outside, though this was the only race using the inner track.

5730 GET SWITCHED ON WITH MATCHBOOK H'CAP (DIV I) 1m (P)
2:15 (2:17) (Class 5) (0-70,70) 3-Y-O

£3,752 (£1,116; £557; £300; £300; £300) **Stalls** Low

Form RPR

-002 **1** **Mutasaamy (IRE)**[16] 5176 3-9-7 **70** JimCrowley 2 84
(Roger Varian) *broke wl: sn restrained and hld up in midfield: effrt and clsd on inner jst over 2f out: pushed along to chal ent fnl f: led ins fnl f: r.o wl* **6/4**[1]

602 **2** *2 ¾* **Stormbomber (CAN)**[13] 5284 3-9-4 **67** LiamKeniry 4 75
(Ed Walker) *led for over 1f out: trckd ldrs 5f out: swtchd lft and effrt ent fnl 2f: rdn to ld over 1f out: hdd ins fnl f: one pce* **2/1**[2]

1130 **3** *5* **Sir Ox (USA)**[119] 1656 3-9-5 **68** (p) LukeMorris 8 65
(Robert Cowell) *hdwy to ld after over 1f out: rdn 2f out: drvn and hdd over 1f out: wknd ins fnl f* **20/1**

0605 **4** *½* **Maisie Moo**[55] 3697 3-8-5 **54** HollieDoyle 3 49
(Shaun Keightley) *midfield: unable qck u.p and no imp over 1f out: plugged on same pce ins fnl f* **10/1**[3]

4054 **5** *5* **Huddle**[24] 4870 3-8-12 **61** JasonWatson 9 45
(William Knight) *in tch: hdwy to join ldr 5f out: outpcd and btn over 1f out: sn wknd* **12/1**

404 **6** *1 ¾* **Undercolours (IRE)**[31] 4590 3-9-7 **70** DanielMuscutt 6 50
(Marco Botti) *chsd ldr early: effrt wl over 2f out: sn struggling and wl btn over 1f out* **33/1**

030 **7** *10* **Moveonup (IRE)**[21] 5002 3-8-12 **66** (e[1]) CierenFallon(5) 7 23
(Gay Kelleway) *last trio and struggling u.p over 3f out: wl bhd fnl 2f* **20/1**

0-10 **8** *22* **Pushmi Pullyu (IRE)**[45] 4071 3-9-2 **68** TimClark(3) 1
(Jane Chapple-Hyam) *stdd s: t.k.h: hld up in rr: struggling over 3f out: wl bhd virtually p.u ins fnl f: t.o (jockey said filly stopped quickly)* **10/1**[3]

6-00 **9** *3 ¼* **Seeing Red (IRE)**[74] 3013 3-8-13 **62** (p[1]) KieranShoemark 5
(Amanda Perrett) *last trio and struggling u.p over 3f out: wl bhd fnl 2f: t.o (vet reported filly lost its left fore shoe)* **20/1**

1m 39.8s **Going Correction** +0.10s/f (Slow) **9** Ran SP% **116.4**
Speed ratings (Par 100): **104,101,96,95,90 89,79,57,53**
CSF £4.30 CT £38.50 TOTE £2.10: £1.10, £1.10, £2.40; EX 5.50 Trifecta £34.60.
Owner Hamdan Al Maktoum **Bred** Shadwell Estate Company Limited **Trained** Newmarket, Suffolk

FOCUS
The first division of an ordinary 3yo handicap and not that many got into it. They finished well spread out and the time was 1.14sec quicker than division two.

5731 GET SWITCHED ON WITH MATCHBOOK H'CAP (DIV II) 1m (P)
2:45 (2:47) (Class 5) (0-70,70) 3-Y-O

£3,752 (£1,116; £557; £300; £300; £300) **Stalls** Low

Form RPR

-541 **1** **Dargel (IRE)**[18] 5080 3-9-7 **70** AdamKirby 5 81+
(Clive Cox) *hld up in tch: effrt ent fnl 2f: qcknd to ld over 1f out: sn clr and r.o strly: easily (jockey said colt hung right-handed under pressure)* **11/4**[2]

335 **2** *4 ½* **Corinthian Girl (IRE)**[27] 4768 3-9-4 **67** StevieDonohoe 3 68+
(David Lanigan) *dwlt: midfield: effrt over 2f out: no ch w wnr and kpt on same pce fnl f: wnt 2nd on post* **9/2**[3]

4455 **3** *nse* **Glory**[23] 4926 3-9-6 **69** TomMarquand 4 70
(Richard Hannon) *chsd ldrs: effrt 3f out: no ch w wnr but kpt on to go 2nd ins fnl f: lost 2nd on post* **8/1**

5064 **4** *½* **Padura Brave**[26] 4789 3-8-13 **62** (p) DavidProbert 1 62
(Mark Usher) *chsd ldrs: effrt over 2f out: no ch w wnr and kpt on same pce ins fnl f (jockey said filly hung left-handed)* **8/1**

0300 **5** *½* **Vino Rosso (IRE)**[38] 4328 3-8-5 **54** CharlieBennett 9 53
(Michael Blanshard) *sn dropped to last pair: effrt ent fnl f: no ch w wnr but kpt on ins fnl f* **100/1**

-406 **6** *shd* **Fares Alpha (USA)**[46] 4031 3-9-4 **67** (b[1]) AndreaAtzeni 8 65
(Marco Botti) *sn w ldr tl outpcd u.p over 1f out: no ch w wnr and kpt on same pce ins fnl f* **16/1**

-602 **7** *¾* **Recuerdame (USA)**[26] 4787 3-9-2 **65** HarryBentley 2 62
(Simon Dow) *led tl hdd and outpcd over 1f out: lost 2nd and wknd ins fnl f* **2/1**[1]

4430 **8** *1* **Fiction Writer (USA)**[47] 4000 3-9-5 **68** FrannyNorton 6 62
(Mark Johnston) *sn dropped to rr and nvr travelling wl: effrt over 2f out: nt clr run and swtchd lft ins fnl f: nvr involved* **14/1**

1m 40.94s (1.14) **Going Correction** +0.10s/f (Slow) **8** Ran SP% **113.9**
Speed ratings (Par 100): **98,93,93,92,92 92,91,90**
CSF £15.49 CT £86.20 TOTE £3.10: £1.10, £1.80, £2.10; EX 14.00 Trifecta £60.40.
Owner Trevor Fox **Bred** Yeomanstown Stud **Trained** Lambourn, Berks

FOCUS
The winner of this division was even more impressive than the winner of the first, though the winning time was over a second slower. The winner improved significantly again.

5732 MATCHBOOK/BRITISH STALLION STUDS EBF MAIDEN FILLIES' STKS (PLUS 10 RACE) 1m (P)
3:15 (3:17) (Class 4) 2-Y-O **£5,822** (£1,732; £865; £432) **Stalls** Low

Form RPR

1 **Miss Yoda (GER)** 2-9-0 0 RobertHavlin 2 78+
(John Gosden) *mounted in chute: hld up in tch in rr: swtchd lft and effrt wl over 1f out: hdwy 1f out: styd on wl to ld ins fnl f: sn in command: gng away at fin* **11/4**[2]

2 *2* **Zagrah** 2-9-0 0 JimCrowley 1 72
(Owen Burrows) *in tch in midfield: effrt 2f out: flashed tail but kpt on ins fnl f: wnt 2nd last strides* **4/1**[3]

0 **3** *nk* **Expensive Dirham**[16] 5170 2-9-0 0 FrannyNorton 8 71
(Mark Johnston) *hdwy to ld after over 1f: rdn and hdd over 1f out: stl ev ch u.p tl outpcd towards fin* **16/1**

6 **4** *hd* **Gloryana**[31] 4605 2-9-0 0 HollieDoyle 7 71
(Archie Watson) *led for over 1f: styd trckd ldrs: effrt to ld again over 1f out: hdd and no ex ins fnl f: one pce towards fin* **16/1**

5 *1 ½* **South Coast (USA)** 2-9-0 0 OisinMurphy 9 67+
(Saeed bin Suroor) *s.i.s: steadily rcvrd on outer: hdwy to join ldr 5f out tl outpcd over 1f out: kpt on same pce ins fnl f* **11/8**[1]

6 *nk* **Eltham Palace** 2-9-0 0 JamieSpencer 5 66+
(David Simcock) *mostly chsd ldr tl 5f out: styd handy tl unable qck over 1f out: wknd ins fnl f* **10/1**

0 **7** *2 ¼* **Prestigious (IRE)**[73] 3049 2-9-0 0 AdamMcNamara 3 61
(Archie Watson) *in tch in midfield: effrt over 2f out: outpcd and btn over 1f out: wknd ins fnl f* **33/1**

6 **8** *4* **Walkonby**[10] 5366 2-9-0 0 CallumShepherd 6 52
(Mick Channon) *t.k.h: stdd after s: hld up in tch: outpcd over 1f out: wknd ins fnl f* **50/1**

0 **9** *¾* **Loretta Lass**[44] 4106 2-9-0 0 DavidProbert 4 50
(Adam West) *dwlt and bustled along early: in tch in last trio: effrt over 2f out: sn struggling: wknd fnl f* **100/1**

1m 43.74s (3.94) **Going Correction** +0.10s/f (Slow) **9** Ran SP% **115.5**
Speed ratings (Par 93): **84,82,81,81,80 79,77,73,72**
CSF £14.15 TOTE £4.20: £1.60, £1.60, £2.40; EX 15.60 Trifecta £134.50.
Owner Westerberg **Bred** Gestut Etzean **Trained** Newmarket, Suffolk

FOCUS
An interesting fillies' maiden featuring some expensive purchases from big yards. The pace was modest, but one of the newcomers made quite an impression. She can rate considerably higher than this bare form.

5733 MATCHBOOK/BRITISH STALLION STUDS EBF FILLIES' NOVICE STKS (PLUS 10 RACE) 7f (P)
3:45 (3:49) (Class 4) 2-Y-O **£5,822** (£1,732; £865; £432) **Stalls** Low

Form RPR

1 **Melnikova** 2-9-0 0 JamesDoyle 9 81+
(Sir Michael Stoute) *styd wd early: chsd ldrs: effrt and pressed ldrs 2f out: kpt on wl u.p to ld cl home* **8/1**

3 **2** *nk* **Stylistique**[11] 5342 2-9-0 0 AndreaAtzeni 1 80
(Roger Varian) *mde most: rdn ent fnl 2f: drvn ent fnl f: hdd ins fnl f: kpt on wl cl home* **11/8**[1]

3 *hd* **Tanita** 2-9-0 0 RyanMoore 6 79+
(Sir Michael Stoute) *in tch in midfield: effrt on inner ent fnl 2f: str chal ent fnl f: led ins fnl f: hdd and lost 2 pls last strides* **9/2**[3]

3 **4** *2* **Run Wild (GER)**[17] 5132 2-9-0 0 (h) OisinMurphy 8 74
(John Gosden) *sn w ldr: unable qck u.p ent fnl f: wknd fnl 100yds* **2/1**[2]

5 *2 ¾* **Alqifaar (USA)** 2-9-0 0 JimCrowley 4 67
(Owen Burrows) *chsd ldrs: effrt 2f out: pushed along and unable qck over 1f out: wl hld and one pce ins fnl f* **16/1**

0 **6** *nse* **Junvieve (FR)**[16] 5189 2-9-0 0 PatDobbs 13 67
(Richard Hannon) *midfield: effrt over 2f out: kpt on ins fnl f: nvr trbld ldrs* **50/1**

7 *1 ¼* **Angels Tread** 2-9-0 0 JamieSpencer 3 64
(David Simcock) *chsd ldrs: effrt and unable qck over 1f out: wknd ins fnl f* **40/1**

66 **8** *3 ¼* **Secret Passion**[10] 5387 2-9-0 0 HollieDoyle 7 55
(Archie Watson) *a towards rr of main gp: rdn over 2f out: sn wl btn* **50/1**

9 *½* **Liberty Filly** 2-9-0 0 JasonWatson 10 54
(Roger Charlton) *off the pce in midfield: rdn over 2f out: sn outpcd and wl btn* **66/1**

10 *4 ½* **Kalfu** 2-9-0 0 HectorCrouch 5 42
(Clive Cox) *off the pce in midfield: rdn over 2f out: sn btn: bhd fnl f* **40/1**

11 *7* **Kitos** 2-9-0 0 LukeMorris 11 24
(Sir Mark Prescott Bt) *s.i.s: a outpcd and detached in rr (jockey said filly ran green)* **66/1**

12 *½* **Showing** 2-9-0 0 DavidProbert 2 23
(Michael Blanshard) *s.i.s: a in rr of main gp: n.d* **100/1**

1m 27.54s (1.54) **Going Correction** +0.10s/f (Slow) **12** Ran SP% **123.4**
Speed ratings (Par 93): **95,94,94,92,89 88,87,83,83,78 70,69**
CSF £19.99 TOTE £11.00: £3.00, £1.10, £1.90; EX 28.80 Trifecta £101.60.
Owner Cheveley Park Stud **Bred** Cheveley Park Stud Ltd **Trained** Newmarket, Suffolk

FOCUS
Another interesting fillies' contest with several top stables represented.

5734 MATCHBOOK BETTING PODCAST H'CAP 1m 3f 219y(P)
4:15 (4:20) (Class 4) (0-85,86) 3-Y-O

£6,469 (£1,925; £962; £481; £300; £300) **Stalls** Low

Form RPR

-363 **1** **Zuba**[12] 5311 3-8-13 **77** JimCrowley 3 85
(Amanda Perrett) *led: sn hdd and wl in tch in midfield: effrt to chal ent fnl 2f: led 1f out: kpt on wl* **7/2**[2]

-124 **2** *nk* **Laafy (USA)**[45] 4063 3-9-7 **85** RyanMoore 5 92
(Sir Michael Stoute) *dwlt: hdwy to press ldr after 2f: rdn to ld over 2f out: hdd 1f out: kpt on wl but a jst hld fnl f* **7/2**[2]

223 **3** *1* **Selino**[52] 3802 3-9-1 **79** DanielMuscutt 1 84
(James Fanshawe) *hld up in tch in last pair: effrt ent fnl 2f: hung rt 1f out: kpt on ins fnl f (jockey said gelding hung right-handed under pressure)* **7/1**[3]

5211 **4** *½* **Ironclad**[16] 5194 3-9-8 **86** JamesDoyle 2 91
(Hugo Palmer) *chsd ldrs: effrt over 2f out: drvn over 1f out: kpt on same pce ins fnl f* **5/4**[1]

3433 **5** *8* **Fragrant Dawn**[11] 5355 3-8-8 **72** SilvestreDeSousa 4 64
(Charles Hills) *hdwy to ld after 1f: rdn and hdd over 2f out: sn outpcd and wl btn over 1f out* **16/1**

41-5 **6** *9* **Desert Friend (IRE)**[19] 5055 3-9-4 **82** JamieSpencer 6 59
(David Simcock) *hld up in last pair: pushed along 3f out: sn struggling and lost tch 2f out* **16/1**

2m 33.35s (-1.15) **Going Correction** +0.10s/f (Slow) **6** Ran SP% **113.2**
Speed ratings (Par 102): **107,106,106,105,100 94**
CSF £16.28 TOTE £4.10: £1.70, £2.90; EX 16.10 Trifecta £60.10.
Owner John Connolly & Odile Griffith **Bred** Qatar Bloodstock & Newsells Park Stud **Trained** Pulborough, W Sussex

FOCUS
A fair little 3yo handicap, but the pace was ordinary and didn't pick up until entering the last half-mile. The form's rated around the runner-up.

5735 MATCHBOOK CASINO FILLIES' H'CAP 1m 3f 219y(P)
4:45 (4:48) (Class 3) (0-95,95) 3-Y-O+

£9,337 (£2,796; £1,398; £699; £349; £175) **Stalls** Low

Form RPR

-104 **1** **Hameem**[24] 4864 4-10-0 **93** JimCrowley 2 106+
(John Gosden) *chsd ldr tl led 2f out: sn rdn clr and in command 1f out: easily* **11/10**[1]

-020 **2** *5* **Isabella Brant (FR)**[23] 4913 3-8-2 **77** JosephineGordon 4 81
(Ralph Beckett) *hld up in last pair: reminder 5f out: rdn over 3f out: no ch w wnr: kpt on to go 2nd wl ins fnl f* **8/1**

6366 **3** ½ **I'll Have Another (IRE)**[17] 5133 3-9-6 **95**............................ FrannyNorton 5 98
(Mark Johnston) wl in tch in midfield: effrt wl over 2f out: no ch w wnr but wnt 2nd ins fnl 1f: no imp and lost 2nd wl ins fnl f **10/1**

4445 **4** 3 **White Chocolate (IRE)**[24] 4864 5-9-5 **84**..................(b[1]) JamieSpencer 3 82
(David Simcock) s.i.s: rcvrd and chsd ldrs after 2f: effrt over 2f out: no ch w wnr and n.m.r over 1f out: wknd ins fnl f **5/1**[3]

1065 **5** 1 **Plait**[75] 2961 4-9-9 **88**.. JamesDoyle 6 85
(Michael Bell) led: rdn and hdd 2f out: sn outpcd: wknd ins fnl f **7/1**

1052 **6** 7 **Point In Time (IRE)**[17] 5133 4-8-11 **76**.......................... DavidProbert 1 62
(Mark Usher) a in rr: effrt over 2f out: sn struggling and wl btn over 1f out (jockey said filly stopped quickly) **4/1**[2]

2m 34.2s (-0.30) **Going Correction** +0.10s/f (Slow) **6 Ran SP% 113.6**
WFA 3 from 4yo+ 10lb
Speed ratings (Par 104): **105,101,101,99,98 94**
CSF £11.04 TOTE £1.70: £1.30, £2.90; EX 10.30 Trifecta £59.60.
Owner Ms Hissa Hamdan Al Maktoum **Bred** Haras De Chevotel **Trained** Newmarket, Suffolk

FOCUS
Quite a valuable fillies' handicap, but it wasn't a strong race for the grade and there was only one horse in it late on. The time was 0.85sec slower than the 3yos in the preceding race.

5736 MATCHBOOK 2% NET WIN FILLIES' H'CAP — 6f (P)
5:15 (5:15) (Class 4) (0-85,85) 3-Y-O+
£6,469 (£1,925; £962; £481; £300; £300) **Stalls** Low

Form — RPR

0-31 **1** **Lapidary**[44] 4116 3-8-12 **75**.. LukeMorris 1 83
(Heather Main) mde virtually all: rdn 2f out: hrd pressed ins fnl f: hld on wl towards fin: gamely **11/4**[1]

2220 **2** shd **Be Like Me (IRE)**[23] 4904 3-9-7 **84**.............................. AndreaAtzeni 7 91
(Marco Botti) restless in stalls: awkward leaving stalls: hld up in tch: clsd and effrt wl over 1f out: drvn to press wnr ins fnl f: ev ch fnl 100yds: kpt on but jst hld **11/2**[2]

0043 **3** 2½ **Rose Berry**[12] 5291 5-9-8 **81**..........................(h) SilvestreDeSousa 3 81
(Charlie Wallis) taken down early: t.k.h: hld up in tch in last pair: effrt 2f out: kpt on u.p to go 3rd towards fin: nvr getting to ldrs **11/4**[1]

1645 **4** ½ **Lorna Cole (IRE)**[10] 5372 3-8-6 **69**.............................. MartinDwyer 6 66
(William Muir) wnt lft leaving stalls: t.k.h: sn w ldr: rdn 2f out: unable qck 1f out: wknd ins fnl f **13/2**[3]

1516 **5** ½ **Peggie Sue**[10] 5372 4-9-12 **85**.................................... DavidProbert 2 82
(Adam West) in tch in midfield: effrt over 1f out: no imp u.p ins fnl f **14/1**

0-63 **6** ½ **Sweet Pursuit**[14] 5251 5-9-2 **75**.................................. OisinMurphy 4 70
(Rod Millman) pressed ldrs early: sn settled into midfield: effrt 2f out: unable qck over 1f out: wknd ins fnl f **13/2**[3]

11- **7** 4 **Irene May (IRE)**[324] 7276 3-9-1 **78**.............................. JasonWatson 5 59
(Sylvester Kirk) t.k.h early: chsd ldrs: drvn ent fnl 2f: lost pl and btn 1f out: wknd ins fnl f **9/1**

1m 14.37s (1.27) **Going Correction** +0.10s/f (Slow) **7 Ran SP% 112.1**
WFA 3 from 4yo+ 4lb
Speed ratings (Par 102): **95,94,91,90,90 89,84**
CSF £17.44 TOTE £3.80: £2.00, £3.10; EX 17.90 Trifecta £70.70.
Owner Andrew Knott & Wetumpka Racing **Bred** Trebles Holford Farm Thoroughbreds **Trained** Kingston Lisle, Oxon

FOCUS
A fair fillies' sprint handicap and a fair pace with a disputed lead. The winner progressed again.
T/Plt: £34.70 to a £1 stake. Pool: £56,096.49 - 1,178.92 winning units T/Qpdt: £10.50 to a £1 stake. Pool: £5,094.45 - 358.30 winning units **Steve Payne**

5196
RIPON (R-H)
Monday, August 5

OFFICIAL GOING: Good to soft (7.1)
Wind: fresh largely behind Weather: sunny

5737 LONGINES IRISH CHAMPIONS WEEKEND EBF FILLIES' NOVICE STKS (PLUS 10 RACE) — 6f
2:00 (2:00) (Class 4) 2-Y-O
£5,175 (£1,540; £769; £384) **Stalls** High

Form — RPR

1 **Final Option** 2-9-0 0.. PJMcDonald 7 87+
(William Muir) dwlt sltly: hld up in tch: hdwy and trckd ldrs whn bit short of room 3f out: swtchd rt 2f out: rdn to ld 1f out: kpt on wl to draw clr **14/1**

24 **2** 4½ **Feelinlikeasomeone**[24] 4876 2-9-0 0.............................. JoeFanning 2 73
(Mark Johnston) pressed ldr: rdn over 2f out: kpt on same pce ins fnl f: no ch w wnr **3/1**[2]

42 **3** 1¼ **Heavens Open**[43] 4142 2-9-0 0.................................. TonyHamilton 3 69
(Richard Fahey) led narrowly: rdn 2f out: hdd 1f out: hung rt and wknd fnl 110yds (vet reported filly was lame on its right fore) **9/2**

2023 **4** 3 **Ventura Flame (IRE)**[9] 5418 2-8-11 76...................... SeanDavis(3) 6 60
(Keith Dalgleish) trckd ldrs: rdn along over 2f out: outpcd and btn over 1f out **13/2**

6 **5** ½ **Led Astray**[25] 4849 2-9-0 0.................................... DanielTudhope 5 59
(Michael Bell) hld up in tch: pushed along and hdwy on outer over 2f out: rdn to chal 2f out: wknd fnl f **4/1**[3]

0 **6** 4 **Cindy Bear (IRE)**[61] 3461 2-9-0 0.............................. DavidEgan 1 47
(Roger Varian) cl up on outer: rdn over 2f out: wknd over 1f out **11/4**[1]

0 **7** 1¼ **Azure World**[33] 4517 2-9-0 0..................................... TomEaves 4 43
(Kevin Ryan) hld up: rdn over 2f out: wknd over 1f out **40/1**

1m 14.99s (2.49) **Going Correction** +0.225s/f (Good) **7 Ran SP% 112.3**
Speed ratings (Par 93): **92,86,84,80,79 74,72**
CSF £53.74 TOTE £17.80: £8.00, £2.10; EX 84.90 Trifecta £451.80.
Owner Foursome Thoroughbreds **Bred** Foursome Thoroughbreds **Trained** Lambourn, Berks

FOCUS
The rail on the bend from back straight to home straight dolled out by 2yds adding about 4yds to races on the round course. The stands' side was unsurprisingly favoured in this modest 2yo fillies' event. A winning time 4.49sec slower than standard advertised the cut underfoot. The winner posted a decent level for a race here.

5738 FUN FOR LEGO FANS (S) H'CAP — 5f
2:30 (2:30) (Class 6) (0-65,64) 3-Y-O
£3,105 (£924; £461; £300; £300; £300) **Stalls** High

Form — RPR

00-2 **1** **Four Wheel Drive**[14] 5244 3-9-7 **64**..........................(p) GrahamLee 4 72
(David Brown) chsd ldr: rdn 2f out: drvn to ld ins fnl f: kpt on **2/1**[2]

2220 **2** 2¾ **Fairy Fast (IRE)**[28] 4731 3-9-7 **64**........................(b) PJMcDonald 2 62
(George Boughey) dwlt sltly: led after 1f: rdn 2f out: drvn appr fnl f: hdd ins fnl f: one pce **9/2**

605 **3** 2 **Skeetah**[45] 4081 3-9-5 **62**.. JasonHart 1 53
(John Quinn) chsd ldr on outer: rdn 2f out: one pce in 3rd ins fnl f **15/8**[1]

0630 **4** 2½ **Champagne Mondays**[12] 5299 3-8-3 **46**..................(b) PaddyMathers 5 28
(Scott Dixon) led for 1f: chsd ldr: rdn over 2f out: no ex ins fnl f **4/1**[3]

500 **5** 1½ **De Latour**[19] 5038 3-8-2 **48**.................................. SeanDavis(3) 6 25
(Jason Ward) hld up in tch: pushed along over 3f out: nvr trbld ldrs **14/1**

0000 **6** 5 **Pritty Livvy**[14] 5236 3-7-11 **45**....................(t[1]) AndrewBreslin(5) 3 4
(Noel Wilson) hld up: rdn over 2f out: wknd over 1f out **50/1**

0000 **7** 16 **Swiss Chime**[31] 4604 3-8-0 **48**................................ PaulaMuir(5) 7
(Alan Berry) dwlt: a in rr **50/1**

1m 0.53s (1.13) **Going Correction** +0.225s/f (Good) **7 Ran SP% 116.9**
Speed ratings (Par 98): **100,95,92,88,86 78,52**
CSF £12.04 TOTE £2.50: £1.30, £2.30; EX 11.40 Trifecta £24.70.There was no bid for the winner.
Owner Bratwa **Bred** A C M Spalding **Trained** Averham Park, Notts

FOCUS
A typically weak 3yo selling handicap but the winner looks improved.

5739 WEATHERBYS TBA H'CAP — 1m 6f
3:00 (3:00) (Class 4) (0-85,80) 4-Y-O+
£5,369 (£1,597; £798; £399; £300; £300) **Stalls** High

Form — RPR

0404 **1** **Stormin Tom (IRE)**[26] 4782 7-8-8 **67**........................ DuranFentiman 6 73
(Tim Easterby) led: slipped 4 l clr over 5f out: rdn and reduced advantage over 2f out: drvn and jnd 2f out: hdd narrowly appr fnl f: styd on gamely to ld again post **13/2**

0235 **2** nse **War Brigade (FR)**[9] 5452 5-8-10 **69**........................(p) PJMcDonald 4 75
(Ian Williams) chsd ldr: rdn along 3f out: chal strly 2f out: drvn into narrow ld appr fnl f: styd on: hdd post **11/10**[1]

-444 **3** 1¼ **Final**[9] 5437 7-9-7 **80**.. JoeFanning 2 84
(Mark Johnston) dwlt: hld up: rdn along and hdwy on outer over 3f out: chal strly 2f out: one pce towards fin **7/2**[2]

321- **4** 1¾ **Chebsey Beau**[191] 7033 9-9-0 **73**.................................. JasonHart 5 75
(John Quinn) midfield: rdn along over 4f out: outpcd over 3f out: styd on ins fnl f **12/1**

20-0 **5** ¾ **Orsino (IRE)**[37] 4383 5-9-0 **73**.................................. TomEaves 1 74?
(Seb Spencer) hld up: rdn along 2f out: no imp **40/1**

-210 **6** ¾ **Auxiliary**[37] 4404 6-8-13 **72**.............................(p) DanielTudhope 3 71
(Liam Bailey) in tch: rdn over 3f out: wknd ins fnl f **4/1**[3]

3m 8.42s (6.02) **Going Correction** +0.225s/f (Good) **6 Ran SP% 113.3**
Speed ratings (Par 105): **91,90,90,89,88 88**
CSF £14.47 TOTE £6.30: £2.80, £1.10; EX 16.50 Trifecta £72.10.
Owner Three Jolly Farmers **Bred** Mill House, Donald, Fowlston & McStay **Trained** Great Habton, N Yorks

■ Stewards' Enquiry : Duran Fentiman two-day ban: misuse of the whip (Aug 19-20)
P J McDonald two-day ban: misuse of the whip (Aug 19-20)

FOCUS
There was no hanging around in this modest staying handicap and it saw a cracking finish. Muddling form, however. Add 4yds.

5740 DAVID CHAPMAN MEMORIAL H'CAP — 6f
3:30 (3:30) (Class 3) (0-95,97) 3-Y-O+
£9,337 (£2,796; £1,398; £699; £349; £175) **Stalls** High

Form — RPR

065 **1** **Lahore (USA)**[15] 5217 5-9-8 **90**............................... PaulMulrennan 3 99
(Phillip Makin) dwlt sltly: hld up in tch: pushed along and hdwy on outer over 2f out: led appr fnl f: rdn out ins fnl f **6/1**[3]

2422 **2** 1 **Muscika**[9] 5454 5-9-10 **92**..............................(v) DanielTudhope 6 98
(David O'Meara) led narrowly: rdn 2f out: hdd appr fnl f: sn drvn: kpt on same pce **13/8**[1]

3100 **3** nk **Dalton**[17] 5120 5-9-3 **85**.. GrahamLee 4 90
(Julie Camacho) hld up: rdn and outplcd in rr over 3f out: hdwy on outer appr fnl f: kpt on wl **6/1**[3]

0200 **4** 4 **Upstaging**[24] 4879 7-8-9 **77**...............................(p) BarryMcHugh 9 69
(Noel Wilson) hld up: rdn over 3f out: kpt on ins fnl f **22/1**

0540 **5** 3¼ **Pipers Note**[15] 5217 9-9-3 **85**................................. JackGarritty 1 67
(Ruth Carr) trckd ldrs: rdn to chal over 1f out: wknd ins fnl f **11/2**[2]

0306 **6** 1¾ **Gin In The Inn (IRE)**[21] 4987 6-8-9 **80**........................ SeanDavis(3) 8 56
(Richard Fahey) chsd ldrs: rdn and lost pl 2f out: short of room on rail over 1f out and dropped to rr: plugged on ins fnl f **10/1**

1000 **7** nk **Teruntum Star (FR)**[17] 5120 7-9-12 **94**.......................(v) KevinStott 7 69
(Kevin Ryan) chsd ldrs: rdn over 2f out: wknd over 1f out **9/1**

6410 **8** 4 **Bossipop**[13] 5266 6-9-3 **85**......................................(b) CamHardie 5 47
(Tim Easterby) pressed ldr tl wknd over 1f out **9/1**

1m 13.35s (0.85) **Going Correction** +0.225s/f (Good) **8 Ran SP% 115.5**
Speed ratings (Par 107): **103,101,101,95,91 89,88,83**
CSF £16.37 CT £61.58 TOTE £7.10: £1.90, £1.10, £2.20; EX 15.80 Trifecta £64.00.
Owner Mrs Wendy Burdett **Bred** Nawara Stud Company Ltd **Trained** Easingwold, N Yorks

FOCUS
Once again the stands' side was the place to be in this feature. The principals came clear and the form's rated around the runner-up.

5741 BANK HOLIDAY FAMILY DAY 26TH AUGUST H'CAP — 1m 1f 170y
4:00 (4:02) (Class 4) (0-85,85) 3-Y-O+
£5,369 (£1,597; £798; £399; £300; £300) **Stalls** Low

Form — RPR

1125 **1** **Southern Rock (IRE)**[17] 5121 3-9-6 **85**...................... DanielTudhope 10 94
(David O'Meara) trckd ldrs towards outer: rdn over 2f out: led over 1f out: drvn out fnl f **3/1**[2]

-004 **2** 1 **Empress Ali (IRE)**[9] 5458 8-9-6 **77**.......................... JamesSullivan 6 84
(Tom Tate) hld up in midfield: pushed along early: rdn 4f out: sme hdwy over 1f out: edgd lft to outer 1f out: styd on: wnt 2nd nr fin **16/1**

4512 **3** hd **Cockalorum (IRE)**[7] 5489 4-10-0 **85**........................(p) BenCurtis 9 92
(Roger Fell) midfield: pushed along over 3f out: rdn over 2f out: swtchd rt and hdwy over 1f out: chal ins fnl f: kpt on same pce **13/8**[1]

4056 **4** 2¼ **Delph Crescent (IRE)**[16] 5198 4-8-12 **72**................(v[1]) SeanDavis(3) 2 74
(Richard Fahey) prom: rdn to ld over 2f out: hdd over 1f out: no ex ins fnl f **14/1**

3050 **5** 2 **Sands Chorus**[51] 3867 7-9-2 **73**............................(p) BarryMcHugh 1 71
(Scott Dixon) led: rdn and hdd over 2f out: wknd ins fnl f **10/1**

0-12 **6** 1¼ **Livvys Dream (IRE)**[66] 3300 4-9-9 **80**.......................(h) PJMcDonald 7 76
(Charles Hills) hld up in midfield: pushed along over 4f out: rdn over 2f out: plugged on ins fnl f: nvr threatened **8/1**[3]

5-03 **7** 2¼ **Scottish Summit (IRE)**[72] 3087 6-9-12 **83**....................... KevinStott 4 76
(Geoffrey Harker) trckd ldrs: rdn to chal 2f out: drvn over 1f out: wknd fnl 110yds and eased **16/1**

1136 **8** 1 3/4 **Hammer Gun (USA)**[38] 4322 6-8-13 **70**....................(v) PaddyMathers 8 58
(Derek Shaw) *s.i.s: hld up: nvr threatened* **50/1**
-324 **9** 1/2 **Brandy Spirit**[10] 5394 3-8-11 **76**....................(h) NathanEvans 3 64
(Michael Easterby) *dwlt: hld up in midfield: rdn 4f out: sn btn* **9/1**
4025 **10** 52 **Ideological (IRE)**[16] 5201 3-9-1 **80**.................... JoeFanning 5
(Mark Johnston) *hld up: rdn 4f out: sn wknd: eased and t.o* **16/1**
2m 5.68s (1.08) **Going Correction** +0.225s/f (Good)
WFA 3 from 4yo+ 8lb **10** Ran SP% **119.6**
Speed ratings (Par 105): **104,103,103,101,99 98,96,95,95,53**
CSF £51.79 CT £104.69 TOTE £5.20: £1.70, £4.10, £1.10; EX 51.20 Trifecta £176.00.
Owner O T I Racing & Middleham Park Racing Vi **Bred** Godolphin **Trained** Upper Helmsley, N Yorks
FOCUS
This competitive handicap was run at a routine pace. The third helps with the standard. Add 4yds.

5742 VISIT RIPON-RACES.CO.UK NOVICE STKS 1m 4f 10y
4:30 (4:34) (Class 5) 3-Y-O+ **£3,881** (£1,155; £577; £288) **Stalls** Centre

Form RPR
35 **1** **Beyond The Clouds**[27] 4760 6-9-10 0.................... TomEaves 10 86+
(Kevin Ryan) *led: hdd over 6f out: remained prom: led again over 2f out: rdn over 1f out: kpt on wl (trainer said, regarding the improved form shown, the gelding was suited by the step up in trip and benefited from the easier ground)* **22/1**
3-2 **2** 1 1/4 **Navajo Pass**[54] 3724 3-9-0 0.................... GrahamLee 9 83
(Donald McCain) *trckd ldrs: rdn along 3f out: drvn 2f out: styd on fnl f: wnt 2nd towards fin* **4/1**[3]
32 **3** 1 1/4 **Two Bids**[14] 5254 3-9-0 0.................... DanielTudhope 11 81
(William Haggas) *prom: racd keenly: led over 6f out: hdd over 2f out: sn rdn along: no ex and lost 2nd towards fin (jockey said colt ran too freely)* **5/6**[1]
2 **4** 22 **Final Orders**[18] 5103 3-9-0 0.................... RyanPowell 7 46
(Simon Crisford) *trckd ldrs: rdn on outer over 3f out: wknd 2f out* **2/1**[2]
3 **5** 4 1/2 **Flash Point (IRE)**[21] 4989 3-9-0 0.................... CamHardie 5 39
(Tracy Waggott) *hld up in midfield: pushed along over 5f out: sn outpcd and btn: plugged on fnl 2f* **66/1**
6 15 **Pound Off You** 3-8-9 0.................... PhilDennis 4 10
(Gillian Boanas) *in tch: rdn along over 4f out: sn wknd (jockey said filly hung left throughout)* **125/1**
7 3 3/4 **Portofino (IRE)** 3-9-0 0.................... DavidNolan 6 9
(David O'Meara) *dwlt: sn midfield: rdn along 5f out: wknd over 3f out* **14/1**
00- **8** 7 **Archie's Sister**[256] 9205 3-8-9 0....................(t[1] w) AndrewElliott 3
(Philip Kirby) *v.s.a: a towards rr (jockey said filly was slowly away)* **50/1**
5 **9** 19 **Magic Act (IRE)**[18] 5103 3-9-0 0.................... JoeFanning 1
(Mark Johnston) *dwlt: hld up in midfield: rdn along 4f out: sn wknd* **18/1**
10 10 **Profile Prince** 3-9-0 0.................... PaulMulrennan 2
(Micky Hammond) *s.i.s: hld up: wknd and bhd fnl 3f* **80/1**
2m 37.11s (0.81) **Going Correction** +0.225s/f (Good)
WFA 3 from 6yo 10lb **10** Ran SP% **129.6**
Speed ratings (Par 103): **106,105,104,89,86 76,74,69,56,50**
CSF £118.27 TOTE £26.70: £4.90, £1.70, £1.10; EX 97.80 Trifecta £454.70.
Owner Guy Reed Racing **Bred** Exors Of The Late G Reed **Trained** Hambleton, N Yorks
FOCUS
Add 4yds. A good effort by the winner giving at least 10lb to all of his rivals. The first four finished well clear and the form's a bit shaky.

5743 FOLLOW @RIPONRACES ON TWITTER H'CAP 1m 4f 10y
5:00 (5:00) (Class 5) (0-75,76) 4-Y-O+
£3,752 (£1,116; £557; £300; £300; £300) **Stalls** Centre

Form RPR
-026 **1** **Matewan (IRE)**[23] 4913 4-9-5 **73**.................... PJMcDonald 2 82
(Ian Williams) *hld up: pushed along over 3f out: hdwy 2f out: led appr fnl f: styd on pushed out* **9/4**[1]
5404 **2** 1 **Deinonychus**[49] 3937 8-8-2 **59**....................(p[1]) SeanDavis[(3)] 4 66
(Michael Appleby) *led: rdn over 2f out: hdd appr fnl f: kpt on* **33/1**
6133 **3** 1 1/2 **Ingleby Hollow**[16] 4437 7-9-8 **76**....................(t) DanielTudhope 5 81
(David O'Meara) *stdd s: hld up in rr: hdwy on inner over 3f out: chsd ldr whn short of room over 1f out: swtchd lft 1f out: rdn and kpt on (jockey said gelding was denied a clear run 1 1/2f out)* **9/4**[1]
-624 **4** 3 **Doctor Cross (IRE)**[23] 4924 5-9-4 **75**.................... ConnorMurtagh[(3)] 7 75
(Richard Fahey) *in tch: rdn 2f out: hung rt over 1f out: no ex fnl f* **9/2**[3]
4326 **5** nk **Dew Pond**[21] 4990 7-8-2 **56**....................(bt) DuranFentiman 6 55
(Tim Easterby) *trckd ldrs: rdn 2f out: no ex ins fnl f* **16/1**
4554 **6** 2 1/2 **Tor**[9] 5423 5-9-6 **74**.................... JoeFanning 3 69
(Iain Jardine) *midfield: n.m.r over 2f out: sn rdn: outpcd and btn over 1f out* **4/1**[2]
2300 **7** 13 **Albert Boy (IRE)**[18] 5106 6-8-3 **57**.................... PaddyMathers 1 32
(Scott Dixon) *dwlt: sn prom: rdn 3f out: wknd 2f out* **16/1**
2m 37.45s (1.15) **Going Correction** +0.225s/f (Good) **7** Ran SP% **114.4**
Speed ratings (Par 103): **105,104,103,101,101 99,90**
CSF £73.79 TOTE £3.60: £2.20, £9.50; EX 73.10 Trifecta £431.30.
Owner Michael Watt And Billy Slater (Aus) **Bred** Ringfort Stud **Trained** Portway, Worcs
FOCUS
This modest handicap was run at something of an uneven pace. A length pb from the winner. Add 5yds.
T/Plt: £26.50 to a £1 stake. Pool: £72,400.31 - 1,988.82 winning units T/Qpdt: £4.40 to a £1 stake. Pool: £7,995.99 - 1,339.07 winning units **Andrew Sheret**

5499 WINDSOR (R-H)
Monday, August 5
OFFICIAL GOING: Good to firm (watered; 7.3)
Wind: Moderate, behind Weather: Fine but cloudy

5744 GALLIARD HOMES H'CAP 1m 3f 99y
5:30 (5:31) (Class 6) (0-65,67) 3-Y-O+
£2,781 (£827; £413; £300; £300; £300) **Stalls** Low

Form RPR
-630 **1** **Harmonise**[11] 5344 5-9-12 **63**.................... HectorCrouch 8 71
(Sheena West) *chsd ldng pair: clsd over 3f out: rdn to ld wl over 1f out: hrd pressed fnl f and hung lft briefly: hld on wl* **4/1**
0011 **2** 1/2 **Affluence (IRE)**[18] 5106 4-10-0 **65**....................(p) EoinWalsh 1 72
(Martin Smith) *hld up in midfield: prog over 3f out: rdn over 2f out: chsd wnr jst over 1f out and sn chalng: carried lft briefly ins fnl f: nt qckn nr fin* **5/2**[1]
3040 **3** 1 **Cogital**[32] 4561 4-10-0 **65**....................(h) PatDobbs 7 71
(Amanda Perrett) *hld up in last trio: prog over 2f out: drvn whn nt clr run over 1f out: chsd ldng pair ins fnl f: kpt on but no imp nr fin* **3/1**[2]
0413 **4** 1/2 **Becky Sharp**[18] 5106 4-9-0 **51**....................(b) CharlieBennett 4 56
(Jim Boyle) *led at decent pce: rdn and hdd over 2f out: kpt on one pce over 1f out* **7/1**
6240 **5** 2 1/2 **Passing Clouds**[9] 5425 4-8-9 **46** oh1.................... KierenFox 3 47
(Michael Attwater) *chsd ldr: rdn over 3f out: led over 2f out to wl over 1f out: wknd fnl f* **50/1**
060 **6** 5 **Eagle Queen**[30] 4641 3-9-3 **63**.................... RobHornby 6 57
(Andrew Balding) *sn in midfield: reminder wl over 3f out: no prog whn rdn over 2f out: wknd over 1f out* **7/2**[3]
0520 **7** 4 1/2 **Mobham (IRE)**[6] 5528 4-9-11 **62**....................(p) AlistairRawlinson 2 48
(J R Jenkins) *s.i.s: mostly in last trio: urged along 4f out: no prog over 2f out: wknd (jockey said gelding was never travelling)* **16/1**
40/- **8** 9 **Linguine (FR)**[15] 6889 9-10-2 **67**....................(p) TrevorWhelan 5 38
(Dai Williams) *urged along early but unable to take prom pl: dropped to last and rdn over 4f out: sn bhd (jockey said gelding was never travelling)* **40/1**
2m 26.59s (-3.11) **Going Correction** -0.25s/f (Firm)
WFA 3 from 4yo+ 9lb **8** Ran SP% **118.6**
Speed ratings (Par 101): **101,100,99,99,97 94,90,84**
CSF £15.07 CT £34.35 TOTE £4.90: £1.50, £2.00, £1.40; EX 15.10 Trifecta £50.20.
Owner Ian Poysden **Bred** J Repard & S Dibb **Trained** Falmer, E Sussex
FOCUS
A moderate handicap, they got racing a fair way out, with the pace a decent one, and the main action took place away from the rail late on. Straightforward form.

5745 ECL CIVIL ENGINEERING MAIDEN AUCTION FILLIES' STKS (PLUS 10 RACE) 6f 12y
6:00 (6:02) (Class 5) 2-Y-O **£3,428** (£1,020; £509; £254) **Stalls** Centre

Form RPR
22 **1** **Mild Illusion (IRE)**[14] 5250 2-8-10 0.................... RobHornby 1 73+
(Jonathan Portman) *taken steadily to post: mde all: pushed along 2f out: sn in command: comf* **8/11**[1]
5 **2** 1 1/2 **Epsom Faithfull**[58] 3595 2-8-10 0.................... CharlieBennett 2 65
(Pat Phelan) *pressed wnr: hanging lft fr 1/2-way: rdn 2f out: wl hld after but kpt on and clr of rest* **25/1**
545 **3** 2 3/4 **Santorini Sal**[14] 5250 2-8-7 54.................... MitchGodwin[(3)] 3 57
(John Bridger) *mostly chsd ldng pair: rdn 2f out: one pce over 1f out* **18/1**
0 **4** nk **You Don't Own Me (IRE)**[14] 5250 2-8-10 0.................... RossaRyan 7 56
(Joseph Tuite) *chsd ldrs: shkn up 2f out: kpt on same pce fnl f* **6/1**[3]
6 **5** 7 **Where Next Jo**[77] 2915 2-8-13 0.................... LiamKeniry 6 38
(David Evans) *sn off the pce in last trio: nvr a factor but passed wkng rivals ins fnl f* **16/1**
00 **6** 3 1/2 **Hot Date**[6] 5527 2-8-11 0.................... ShaneKelly 8 26
(George Margarson) *chsd ldrs to 1/2-way: sn outpcd and shkn up: no ch fnl 2f* **40/1**
7 1/2 **Annie Quickstep (IRE)** 2-8-7 0.................... WilliamCox[(3)] 4 23
(Jonathan Portman) *slowly away: rn green in last pair: a bhd (jockey said filly ran green)* **33/1**
8 nk **Sahhab (USA)** 2-8-12 0.................... TrevorWhelan 5 24
(Geoffrey Deacon) *slowly away: mostly in last pair and outpcd: no prog over 1f out (jockey said filly was slowly away and ran green)* **40/1**
9 hd **Chisana** 2-8-12 0.................... GeorgeWood 9 24
(Chris Wall) *chsd ldrs to 1/2-way: sn outpcd and rdn: wknd over 1f out* **20/1**
4 **10** 1/2 **Queen Salamah (IRE)**[14] 5250 2-8-13 0.................... JamieSpencer 10 50+
(Richard Spencer) *trckd ldrs: shkn up to dispute 3rd and wl in tch 2f out: wknd rapidly jst over 1f out: heavily eased (jockey said filly lost its action)* **7/2**[2]
1m 11.59s (-0.51) **Going Correction** -0.25s/f (Firm) **10** Ran SP% **122.0**
Speed ratings (Par 91): **93,91,87,86,77 72,72,71,71,70**
CSF £32.63 TOTE £1.50: £1.10, £6.30, £3.90; EX 21.50 Trifecta £104.00.
Owner Old Stoic Racing Club **Bred** Marston Stud **Trained** Upper Lambourn, Berks
FOCUS
Lowly juvenile form, the favourite made all.

5746 BUXTED BOUNTY H'CAP 6f 12y
6:30 (6:30) (Class 3) (0-95,94) 3-Y-O- **£7,246** (£2,168; £1,084; £542; £270) **Stalls** Centre

Form RPR
0103 **1** **Citron Major**[15] 5217 4-9-4 **89**....................(t) RowanScott[(3)] 2 95
(Nigel Tinkler) *s.i.s: hld up in last: rdn over 1f out: stl in last pair jst ins fnl f: swtchd lft and str burst to ld last 60yds* **3/1**[2]
0030 **2** hd **Mokaatil**[2] 5661 4-8-11 **86**.................... AngusVilliers[(7)] 1 91
(Ian Williams) *hld up bhd ldrs: rdn over 1f out: squeezed through wl ins fnl f: r.o but jst outpcd* **7/1**
3206 **3** shd **Goodnight Girl (IRE)**[17] 5143 4-9-8 **90**.................... RobHornby 7 95
(Jonathan Portman) *nt that wl away but sn pressed ldr: rdn 2f out: stl upsides wl ins fnl f: jst outpcd nr fin* **11/4**[1]
4152 **4** nk **Little Boy Blue**[32] 4545 4-9-7 **92**....................(h) CameronNoble[(3)] 6 96
(Bill Turner) *prom: pressed ldr over 2f out: narrow ld 1f out but nt finding much u.p: hdd last 60yds* **9/2**[3]
1150 **5** nk **Bungee Jump (IRE)**[17] 5143 4-9-5 **87**.................... RossaRyan 3 90
(Grace Harris) *led: drvn 2f out: narrowly hdd 1f out: stl upsides ins fnl f: fdd last 75yds* **8/1**
0060 **6** hd **Doc Sportello (IRE)**[24] 4866 7-8-7 **75** oh2....................(p) FrannyNorton 5 77
(Tony Carroll) *hld up in tch: clsd on ldrs on outer over 1f out: drvn to chal ins fnl f: nt qckn last 75yds (jockey said gelding hung left-handed)* **16/1**
2000 **7** 4 **Vibrant Chords**[10] 5371 6-9-12 **94**.................... AdamKirby 4 84
(Henry Candy) *chsd ldrs: lost pl 1/2-way: struggling in last over 1f out* **6/1**
1m 10.32s (-1.78) **Going Correction** -0.25s/f (Firm) **7** Ran SP% **113.6**
Speed ratings (Par 107): **101,100,100,100,99 99,94**
CSF £23.62 TOTE £4.20: £2.40, £3.10; EX 26.90 Trifecta £81.70.
Owner Walter Veti & Sara Hattersley **Bred** Bearstone Stud Ltd **Trained** Langton, N Yorks

FOCUS
A remarkably tight finish given there was only seven runners, with all bar one of them in with a chance entering the last furlong. The winner's rated basically in line with his best form.

5747 ROBERT DALES BUILDING SERVICES H'CAP 1m 2f
7:00 (7:01) (Class 5) (0-70,72) 3-Y-O+
£3,428 (£1,020; £509; £300; £300; £300) **Stalls** Low

Form RPR
4450 **1** **High Acclaim (USA)**18 5086 5-9-12 **69** SilvestreDeSousa 8 78
(Roger Teal) *trckd ldng trio: clsd to take 2nd over 2f out: rdn to ld wl over 1f out: drvn clr fnl f* **11/4**2
2006 **2** 2 3/4 **Perfect Refuge**12 5316 4-9-13 **70** AdamKirby 4 73
(Clive Cox) *hld up in 5th: clsd on ldrs fr 2f out: plld out and drvn over 1f out: styd on to take 2nd nr fin but no ch w wnr* **9/4**1
0233 **3** *nk* **Sarasota (IRE)**12 5297 4-8-13 **59** WilliamCox(3) 3 61
(Mark Gillard) *hld up in 6th: prog on outer wl over 2f out: chsd wnr over 1f out and tried to chal: nt qckn and wl hld fnl f: lost 2nd nr fin* **20/1**
2204 **4** 3 1/4 **Il Sicario (IRE)**18 5086 5-9-4 **64** (p) CameronNoble(3) 1 60
(Bill Turner) *trckd ldng pair: rdn over 2f out: hanging lft after and nt qckn over 1f out: wknd* **15/2**
0-63 **5** 2 1/2 **Essenaitch (IRE)**58 3572 6-9-0 **62** KatherineBegley(5) 5 53
(David Evans) *pushed up to ld and then t.k.h: hdd & wknd wl over 1f out (trainer's rep said the gelding was unsuited by the going and would prefer a slower surface)* **4/1**3
-006 **6** 2 1/2 **Dawn Treader (IRE)**24 4874 3-9-2 **67** RossaRyan 7 54
(Richard Hannon) *trckd ldr: hanging lft 3f out: lost 2nd and wknd over 2f out* **15/2**
60 **7** *3* **Rakematiz**35 4453 5-10-1 **72** TomQueally 2 52
(Brett Johnson) *hld up: a last: no ch whn shkn up over 1f out: nvr in it* **10/1**

2m 5.98s (-3.02) **Going Correction** -0.25s/f (Firm) **7** Ran SP% **114.8**
WFA 3 from 4yo+ 8lb
Speed ratings (Par 103): **102,99,99,96,94 92,90**
CSF £9.48 CT £98.18 TOTE £4.30: £2.70, £1.80; EX 10.20 Trifecta £113.10.
Owner Excel Racing **Bred** Regis Farms Lp **Trained** Lambourn, Berks

FOCUS
A modest handicap run at a steady gallop. The winner was close to his winter form on the AW.

5748 EPS REAL ESTATE FILLIES' NOVICE STKS 1m 2f
7:30 (7:32) (Class 5) 3-4-Y-O
£3,428 (£1,020; £509; £254) **Stalls** Low

Form RPR
21 **1** **Whispering Beauty (USA)**17 5141 3-9-4 0 JFEgan 8 89
(William Haggas) *trckd ldr: led 4f out and sent for home: shkn up over 1f out: styd on wl* **5/6**1
2 1 1/4 **Strelka** 3-8-11 0 HarryBentley 2 80+
(Ralph Beckett) *t.k.h: hld up in 4th: clsd to take 2nd 3f out but hanging lft and green: continued to hang lft but styd on steadily fnl 2f wout being able to chal (jockey said filly hung left-handed)* **7/4**2
64 **3** *4* **Gallatin**30 4641 3-8-11 0 OisinMurphy 4 72
(Andrew Balding) *led to 4f out: lost 2nd 3f out: steadily outpcd by ldng pair but kpt on* **3/1**3
4 *6* **Ruby Wine** 3-8-11 0 KieranO'Neill 10 60
(Jeremy Scott) *pushed along in midfield 1/2-way: outpcd over 3f out but tk 4th sn after: nvr able to cl but kpt on* **33/1**
5 *11* **Gibraltarian (IRE)** 3-8-11 0 CharlieBennett 1 38
(Jim Boyle) *s.s: urged along in last bef 1/2-way: wl bhd over 3f out: kpt on fnl 2f to take remote 5th nr fin* **20/1**
60 **6** 1 3/4 **Necoleta**131 1352 3-8-11 0 LiamKeniry 9 34
(Sylvester Kirk) *in tch tl outpcd and pushed along over 3f out: wknd 2f out* **100/1**
7 *3* **Urban Scene** 3-8-11 0 CallumShepherd 7 28
(Linda Jewell) *dwlt: a towards rr: outpcd and pushed along over 3f out: wknd 2f out* **100/1**
0 **8** *22* **Winalotwithalittle (IRE)**4 5592 3-8-11 0 NickyMackay 6
(J R Jenkins) *pressed ldng pair to 4f out: wknd rapidly: t.o* **100/1**
00 **9** *18* **Dee Dee Dottie**58 3574 3-8-11 0 TrevorWhelan 3
(Geoffrey Deacon) *s.s: a in rr: wknd 4f out: t.o* **66/1**

2m 6.14s (-2.86) **Going Correction** -0.25s/f (Firm) **9** Ran SP% **128.1**
Speed ratings (Par 100): **101,100,96,92,83 81,79,61,47**
CSF £2.99 TOTE £1.70: £1.10, £1.10, £1.10; EX 3.50 Trifecta £4.40.
Owner Ms A Gigliola Da Silva **Bred** Fred W Hertrich III **Trained** Newmarket, Suffolk

FOCUS
A fair fillies' novice dominated by the market leaders. The winner progressed again.

5749 ROB KENDAL DERBY H'CAP 1m 31y
8:00 (8:00) (Class 4) (0-85,84) 3-Y-O
£5,207 (£1,549; £774; £387; £300; £300) **Stalls** Low

Form RPR
-356 **1** **I'lletyougonow**14 5255 3-8-7 **70** (p1) SilvestreDeSousa 5 77
(Mick Channon) *mde all and set gd pce: drvn 2f out: kpt on u.p and hld on wl* **8/1**
-243 **2** *1* **Hold Still (IRE)**18 5104 3-9-2 **79** JasonWatson 1 83+
(William Muir) *stdd s: hld up in last: prog on outer over 2f out: drvn and cl up over 1f out: styd on fnl f to take 2nd last stride* **7/2**3
-643 **3** *hd* **House Of Kings (IRE)**17 5140 3-9-6 **83** AdamKirby 3 86
(Clive Cox) *t.k.h: trckd ldng pair: rdn to chse wnr over 1f out and tried to chal: nt qckn and lost 2nd nr fin* **11/4**1
1031 **4** 1 1/2 **Wild Hope**28 4723 3-9-5 **82** FrannyNorton 7 82
(Kevin Ryan) *trckd wnr: rdn over 2f out: lost 2nd and one pce over 1f out* **3/1**2
34-4 **5** *3/4* **Aussie View (IRE)**93 2399 3-9-7 **84** TomQueally 8 82
(George Margarson) *sltly anticipated s: chsd ldng trio: shkn up 3f out: stl wl in tch over 1f out: fdd ins fnl f* **33/1**
-105 **6** *1/2* **Madame Tantzy**11 5341 3-8-13 **76** CharlesBishop 2 73
(Eve Johnson Houghton) *s.i.s: hld up in 6th: no prog whn rdn over 1f out* **16/1**
1345 **7** 1 3/4 **Absolutio (FR)**31 4607 3-9-5 **82** ShaneKelly 4 75
(K R Burke) *plld hrd: hld up in 5th: shkn up over 2f out: sn dropped to last: n.d after* **7/2**3

1m 41.1s (-3.40) **Going Correction** -0.25s/f (Firm) **7** Ran SP% **116.0**
Speed ratings (Par 102): **107,106,105,104,103 103,101**
CSF £37.01 CT £97.86 TOTE £10.10: £3.60, £2.00; EX 46.50 Trifecta £184.40.
Owner Mrs J P E Cunningham & G M Cunningham **Bred** Whatton Manor Stud **Trained** West Ilsley, Berks

FOCUS
An open handicap run at a good gallop and the pace held out. A small pb from the winner.

5750 OWEN CONTRACTORS H'CAP 5f 21y
8:30 (8:31) (Class 5) (0-70,70) 3-Y-O+
£3,428 (£1,020; £509; £300; £300; £300) **Stalls** Centre

Form RPR
0300 **1** **Look Surprised**33 4494 6-8-13 **62** WilliamCox(3) 8 74
(Roger Teal) *w ldng pair gng strly: led wl over 1f out: shkn up and sn clr: comf* **11/2**3
2223 **2** 2 1/4 **Lethal Angel**16 5191 4-9-3 **70** (p) MarcoGhiani(7) 9 73
(Stuart Williams) *dwlt and sltly impeded s: towards rr: effrt on outer 2f out: drvn and styd on to take 2nd last 100yds: fin wl but no ch w wnr* **11/8**1
1605 **3** 2 1/4 **Toni's A Star**32 4555 7-8-7 **60** ElishaWhittington(7) 10 55
(Tony Carroll) *disp ld to wl over 1f out: outpcd after and lost 2nd last 100yds (jockey said mare ran too keenly in the early stages)* **10/1**
0034 **4** *1* **Bashiba (IRE)**16 5169 8-9-2 **65** (t) RowanScott(3) 6 56
(Nigel Tinkler) *chsd ldrs: rdn wl over 1f out: racd awkwardly and sn outpcd (vet reported gelding lost its right hind shoe)* **5/2**2
0440 **5** 1 1/2 **Firenze Rosa (IRE)**19 5046 4-8-5 **51** oh6 KieranO'Neill 3 37
(John Bridger) *disp ld to wl over 1f out: wknd* **16/1**
5044 **6** *1* **Deer Song**46 4026 6-8-5 **51** oh6 (b) LiamJones 1 33
(John Bridger) *chsd ldrs: outpcd 1/2-way: struggling after* **50/1**
0510 **7** *1/2* **Alisia R (IRE)**13 5278 3-8-2 **51** oh1 JimmyQuinn 4 31
(Les Eyre) *dwlt: a in rr: nvr a factor* **12/1**
060 **8** *3* **Fly The Nest (IRE)**11 5343 3-9-5 **68** (h1) GeorgeDowning 2 37
(Tony Carroll) *a towards rr: pushed along bef 1/2-way: sn struggling* **20/1**

58.66s (-1.44) **Going Correction** -0.25s/f (Firm)
WFA 3 from 4yo+ 3lb **8** Ran SP% **115.4**
Speed ratings (Par 103): **101,97,93,92,89 88,87,82**
CSF £13.63 CT £73.88 TOTE £6.60: £1.70, £1.40, £2.60; EX 14.70 Trifecta £76.30.
Owner Starting Gate Racing **Bred** Withyslade **Trained** Lambourn, Berks

FOCUS
Moderate sprint form. The winner is rated back to her best.
T/Plt: £86.40 to a £1 stake. Pool: £84,139.42 - 710.42 winning units T/Qpdt: £30.90 to a £1 stake. Pool: £8,715.32 - 208.29 winning units **Jonathan Neesom**

5751 - 5758a (Foreign Racing) - See Raceform Interactive

5600 CLAIREFONTAINE (R-H)
Monday, August 5

OFFICIAL GOING: Turf: good

5759a PRIX NORMANDIE GRANDS EVENEMENTS (CLAIMER) (2YO) (TURF) 7f
1:25 2-Y-O
£10,360 (£4,144; £3,108; £2,072; £1,036)

RPR
1 **Assier**36 2-9-1 0 MaximeGuyon 4 76+
(A Fabre, France) **78/10**
2 2 1/2 **Big Boss Man (FR)**13 5286 2-9-4 0 (b) ChristopheSoumillon 1 72
(Cedric Rossi, France) **37/10**2
3 1 1/4 **Norohna (FR)** 2-8-10 0 ThomasTrullier(6) 6 67
(F Rossi, France) **29/10**1
4 *3/4* **Thavors (ITY)**23 4949 2-9-4 0 CristianDemuro 7 67
(Andrea Marcialis, France) **9/2**3
5 *1* **Pic Cel (FR)**13 5286 2-8-11 0 (b) HugoJourniac 10 57
(J-C Rouget, France) **9/1**
6 *shd* **Get The Look (IRE)**45 4048 2-8-8 0 IoritzMendizabal 12 54
(J S Moore) *led after 1f: asked to qckn whn pressed 2 1/2f out: hdd 2f out: grad wknd u.p fr over 1f out: no ex* **20/1**
7 *shd* **Moontide (IRE)**13 5286 2-8-11 0 MickaelBarzalona 5 57
(J S Moore) *trckd ldr on inner: pushed along over 2 1/2f out: nt qckn w eventual wnr: rdn ent fnl f: kpt on same pce* **89/10**
8 *3* **Forever Coco (FR)** 2-8-8 0 MlleZoePfeil(3) 2 49+
(Andrea Marcialis, France) **29/1**
9 *4* **Ciachope (FR)** 2-8-8 0 StephanePasquier 3 35
(L Rovisse, France) **12/1**
10 4 1/2 **The Nile Song (FR)**13 5286 2-8-7 0 (b) ClementGuitraud(8) 9 30
(Y Barberot, France) **17/1**
11 *9* **Brainwave (FR)**80 2-8-11 0 (p) YanisAouabed 8
(J-M Baudrelle, France) **92/1**

1m 27.1s **11** Ran SP% **119.0**
PARI-MUTUEL (all including 1 euro stake): WIN 8.80; PLACE 2.40, 1.80, 1.60; DF 20.30.
Owner Prince A A Faisal **Bred** Nawara Stud Co Ltd **Trained** Chantilly, France

LES SABLES-D'OLONNE (L-H)
Monday, August 5

OFFICIAL GOING: Turf: good

5760a PRIX PORT BOURGENAY (CLAIMER) (4YO+) (TURF) 1m 1f 165y
3:30 4-Y-O+
£5,405 (£2,162; £1,621; £1,081; £540)

RPR
1 **Savile Row (FR)**25 5-9-1 0 (p) AntoineCoutier 5 72
(Carina Fey, France)
2 1 1/4 **Canford's Joy (IRE)**59 3540 4-9-4 0 AdrienFouassier 6 72
(Alexandra Dunn) *settled in 4th: drvn to cl on outer 2f out: angled rnd rival ent fnl f: chsd wnr to the line but a hld*
3 3 1/2 **Fantastic Bere (FR)**50 4-8-11 0 ChristopherGrosbois 4 58
(E Leenders, France)
4 *1* **Waqt (IRE)**32 4566 5-8-13 0 (p) HugoBesnier(5) 7 63
(Alexandra Dunn) *led: hdd and dropped to 3rd wl over 1f: kpt on same pce u.p: lost 3rd cl home*
5 *2* **War Asset (ITY)**25 6-9-8 0 AlexandreRoussel 1 63
(Gianluca Bietolini, France)
6 *4* **Engaging Smile**125 7-8-8 0 MathieuAndrouin 3 41
(W Delalande, France)

Owner Dietmar Hilgert **Bred** Capricorn Stud Sa **Trained** France

The Form Book Flat 2019, Raceform Ltd, Newbury, RG14 5SJ

5761a PRIX JACQUES DE HILLERIN (H'CAP) (5YO+) (TURF) 1m 1f 165y

4:00 5-Y-0+ **£7,657** (£3,063; £2,297; £1,531; £765)

RPR

1 **Early Enough (FR)**^{696} 6-9-8 0 .... MlleLucieOger(7) 9 68
(T Mercier, France)

2 *nk* **Secret Pearl (FR)**^{81} 5-9-3 0 ....(b) AlexandreRoussel 5 55
(P Monfort, France)

3 *hd* **Goldy Baby (FR)**^{63} 9-9-2 0 ....(p) WilliamsSaraiva 3 54
(N Paysan, France)

4 *1* **Usain Best (FR)**^{11} 7-9-3 0 .... MathieuAndrouin 6 53
(B Legros, France)

5 *1 1/4* **Full Court Press (IRE)**^{81} 6-8-11 0 .... MlleFeliceJacobs(4) 8 48
(P Leblanc, France)

6 *1 1/4* **Martalouna (FR)**^{25} 6-9-4 0 ....(b) MlleAnaisDumont(7) 4 56
(N Paysan, France)

7 *9* **Chiavari (IRE)**^{25} 4859 5-9-11 0 .... HugoBesnier(3) 1 41
(Alexandra Dunn) *broke wl: led: sn hdd but remained prom: rdn and nt qckn ins fnl 2f: wknd appr fnl f*

8 *2* **Speak Softly (FR)**^{344} 10-8-4 0 .... ChristopherGrosbois 7 13
(T Poche, France)

Owner Thierry Mercier **Bred** Scuderia Sant'Ambroeus S.R.L. **Trained** France

5762a PRIX CHARLES DU BREIL (CONDITIONS) (AMATEUR RIDERS) (4YO) (TURF) 1m 5f 110y

6:00 4-Y-0 **£5,405** (£2,162; £1,621; £1,081; £540)

RPR

1 **American Saint (FR)**^{234} 4-10-8 0 ....(p) MrGonzagueCottreau 6 68
(N Paysan, France) **14/5**^{1}

2 *2* **Rebel Queen (FR)**^{64} 4-10-9 0 ....(b) MrThibaudMace 3 66
(P Monfort, France)

3 *9 1/2* **Janajka (FR)** 4-9-12 0 .... LucasZuliani(4) 1 45
(J-L Guillochon, France)

4 *1 1/2* **Trio Gagnant (FR)** 4-10-3 0 .... MrAdrienFoucher(5) 5 49
(F Foucher, France)

5 *4* **Farah Di Belle (FR)** 4-9-11 0 .... MlleMarieDeAsisTrem(7) 7 39
(Alain Couetil, France)

6 *6 1/2* **European Blue (FR)** 4-10-0 0 .... MlleAstridPeltier(8) 8 33
(P Peltier, France)

7 *2* **Sigrid Nansen**^{4} 5571 4-10-3 0 ....(p) MissHannahWelch(8) 4 33
(Alexandra Dunn) *chsd ldrs: rdn to chal on inner 2f out: dropped away ins fnl 1 1/2f: sddle slipped*

8 *5 1/2* **Lakeside (FR)**^{50} 4-10-1 0 .... MlleJustineMercier(3) 2 18
(T Mercier, France)

Owner Gerald Meyer, Nicolas Paysan & Pierre-Henri Rebill **Bred** Stall Radiant Sea **Trained** France

5329 VICHY

Monday, August 5

OFFICIAL GOING: Turf: good to soft

5763a PRIX DE BILLOM (CLAIMER) (2YO COLTS & GELDINGS) (TURF) 7f

5:12 2-Y-0 **£6,756** (£2,702; £2,027; £1,351; £675)

RPR

1 **Victochop (FR)**^{12} 5313 2-9-2 0 ow1 .... AnthonyCrastus 7 60
(George Baker) *qckly into stride: disp tl trckd ldr after 1f: pushed along on nr side 3f out: rdn to chse ldr 1 1/2f out: kpt on wl for press ins fnl f: led fnl 50yds* **26/5**

2 *nk* **Another Planet (FR)**^{30} 4679 2-9-1 0 ow1 ....(b) TomLefranc(5) 4 63
(Matthieu Palussiere, France) **32/5**

3 *1 1/2* **Morgenstern (FR)**^{70} 3171 2-8-13 0 ow2 .... MlleMarieVelon(7) 9 59
(C Escuder, France) **27/10**^{1}

4 *1* **Skip The Queue (IRE)**^{14} 5263 2-8-13 0 ow2 ....(b) ClementLecoeuvre 2 50
(Matthieu Palussiere, France) **29/10**^{2}

5 *7 1/2* **Go Canada (IRE)**^{54} 2-8-13 0 ow2 .... FabriceVeron 8 30
(A Giorgi, Italy) **22/5**^{3}

6 *1 1/4* **Hudson Hornet (FR)** 2-9-5 0 ow1 .... JiriChaloupka 5 33
(Jiri Chaloupka, Czech Republic) **41/1**

7 *4 1/2* **Two Penny'S (FR)** 2-9-2 0 ow1 ....(b^{1}) SylvainRuis 1 18
(J-V Toux, France) **21/1**

8 *1 1/2* **Thurstan (FR)** 2-8-7 0 ow1 .... MlleAmbreMolins(9) 10 14
(J Parize, France) **57/1**

9 *1* **Storm Wave (FR)** 2-8-13 0 ow2 .... FranckBlondel 3 9
(J-V Toux, France) **15/1**

10 *7 1/2* **Giorgio (FR)** 2-9-2 0 ow1 ....(p) GuillaumeTrolleyDePrevaux(3) 6
(C Scandella, France) **26/1**

1m 29.33s **10 Ran SP% 119.4**
PARI-MUTUEL (all including 1 euro stake): WIN 6.20; PLACE 2.30, 2.00, 1.40; DF 19.20.
Owner P Bowden **Bred** Alain Chopard **Trained** Chiddingfold, Surrey

5294 CATTERICK (L-H)

Tuesday, August 6

OFFICIAL GOING: Good to soft (7.2)

Wind: Fresh, half behind in 5f race and in over 2f of home straight in races on the round course Weather: Overcast

5764 BRITISH STALLION STUDS EBF MAIDEN STKS 7f 6y

2:00 (2:00) (Class 5) 2-Y-0 **£4,140** (£1,232; £615; £307) **Stalls** Low

Form RPR

30 1 **Mischief Star**^{38} 4401 2-9-5 0 .... DanielTudhope 12 71
(David O'Meara) *t.k.h: trckd ldrs on outside: rdn to ld over 1f out: kpt on wl towards fin* **10/3**^{2}

5 2 *1* **Fast Deal**^{7} 5512 2-9-5 0 .... DavidAllan 4 67
(Tim Easterby) *prom: effrt and pushed along 2f out: rdn and chsd wnr ins fnl f: kpt on fin* **66/1**

3 *nse* **Oh Mary Oh Mary** 2-9-0 0 .... NathanEvans 6 62+
(Michael Easterby) *missed break: last and green: plenty to do bnd ent st: shkn up and gd hdwy over 1f out: reminders ins fnl f: kpt on wl: improve (jockey said filly was slowly away)* **40/1**

44 4 *hd* **Zuckerberg (IRE)**^{45} 4125 2-9-5 0 .... PJMcDonald 1 67
(Ivan Furtado) *trckd ldrs: effrt and pushed along 2f out: edgd lft: hdwy and disp 2nd pl ins fnl f: no ex cl home* **7/4**^{1}

66 5 *3/4* **Kuwait Shield**^{17} 5172 2-9-5 0 .... TonyHamilton 10 65
(Richard Fahey) *led: jnd over 2f out: hdd over 1f out: chsd wnr to ins fnl f: sn outpcd* **16/1**

43 6 *1 1/4* **Woven Quality (IRE)**^{25} 4876 2-9-5 0 .... AndrewMullen 11 62
(Donald McCain) *t.k.h: pressed ldr: ev ch over 2f out to over 1f out: rdn and no ex ins fnl f* **6/1**^{3}

4 7 *nk* **Magna Moralia (IRE)**^{14} 5273 2-9-5 0 .... JasonHart 8 61
(John Quinn) *sn pushed along towards rr: effrt and edgd lft wl over 1f out: no imp fnl f* **13/2**

34 8 *hd* **Lexington Warfare (IRE)**^{18} 5118 2-9-2 0 .... SeanDavis(3) 9 60+
(Richard Fahey) *midfield: pushed along over 2f out: outpcd fr over 1f out* **11/1**

0060 9 *6* **Tiltilys Rock (IRE)**^{14} 5279 2-9-5 45 .... AndrewElliott 5 45
(Andrew Crook) *t.k.h: hld up: pushed along 2f out: sn wknd* **250/1**

10 *nk* **Topflighttoafrica** 2-9-0 0 .... ShaneGray 7 39
(David O'Meara) *s.i.s: bhd: struggling over 2f out: sn btn (vet reported filly was lame right fore)* **33/1**

00 11 *7* **Ontheradar (IRE)**^{12} 5331 2-9-5 0 .... GrahamLee 2 26
(Ronald Thompson) *midfield: rdn over 2f out: wknd wl over 1f out* **250/1**

12 *shd* **Fast Track Flyer (IRE)** 2-9-0 0 .... CamHardie 3 20
(Brian Ellison) *s.i.s: bhd: struggling over 2f out: sn btn* **28/1**

1m 28.83s (1.43) **Going Correction** -0.025s/f (Good) **12 Ran SP% 112.4**
Speed ratings (Par 94): **90,88,88,88,87 86,85,85,78,78 70,70**
CSF £218.48 TOTE £3.80: £1.50, £10.90, £8.00; EX 223.50.
Owner Three Men And A Trainer **Bred** The Red Mischief Partnership **Trained** Upper Helmsley, N Yorks

FOCUS
Bend into home straight dolled out 4yds. The leaders went pretty hard in this modest 2yo maiden. The winner didn't need to progress. Add 12yds.

5765 FORCES' FAMILY DAY H'CAP 5f

2:30 (2:32) (Class 6) (0-55,54) 3-Y-0+

£3,105 (£924; £461; £300; £300; £300) **Stalls** Low

Form RPR

0020 1 **Dancing Mountain (IRE)**^{6} 5559 3-9-3 **52** ....(b) BenCurtis 14 59
(Roger Fell) *bhd on outside: rdn and hdwy over 1f out: led wl ins fnl f: eased cl home* **11/2**^{1}

-003 2 *3/4* **The Grey Zebedee**^{4} 5620 3-9-5 **54** ....(b) DuranFentiman 7 58
(Tim Easterby) *led against far rail: rdn and hrd pressed over 1f out: hdd wl ins fnl f: kpt on* **6/1**^{2}

00-0 3 *1/2* **Sambucca Spirit**^{92} 2477 3-8-10 **45** .... KevinStott 2 47
(Paul Midgley) *early to post: trckd ldrs: wnt 2nd 1/2-way: effrt and ev ch over 1f out: one pce wl ins fnl f* **16/1**

4040 4 *shd* **Tadaany (IRE)**^{15} 5235 7-9-5 **51** ....(p) JackGarritty 15 54
(Ruth Carr) *early to post: restless in stalls: sn prom on outside: effrt and edgd lft over 1f out: kpt on same pce ins fnl f (jockey said gelding became upset in the stalls)* **11/2**^{1}

0460 5 *2* **Rockley Point**^{39} 4335 6-9-5 **51** ....(b) PhilDennis 1 47
(Katie Scott) *sn pushed along in midfield against stands' rail: effrt and rdn 2f out: outpcd ins fnl f* **7/1**^{3}

4100 6 *1* **Optimickstickhill**^{42} 4212 4-9-3 **49** ....(b) KieranO'Neill 4 41
(Scott Dixon) *prom: sn pushed along: drvn along 1/2-way: fdd over 1f out* **6/1**^{2}

0020 7 *1 1/2* **Bluella**^{43} 4182 4-8-13 **45** ....(v) PJMcDonald 10 32
(Robyn Brisland) *pressed ldr to 1/2-way: cl up tl wknd over 1f out* **10/1**

3530 8 *1 1/4* **Glyder**^{45} 4132 5-8-13 **45** ....(p) RoystonFfrench 6 27
(John Holt) *dwlt: bhd and outpcd: sme late hdwy: nvr rchd ldrs (jockey said mare was restless in the stalls and missed the break)* **14/1**

0506 9 *1/2* **Celerity (IRE)**^{9} 5478 5-8-11 **50** ....(p) GavinAshton(7) 9 30
(Lisa Williamson) *bhd: struggling 1/2-way: nvr on terms* **33/1**

3004 10 *nk* **Racquet**^{11} 5393 6-8-13 **45** ....(b) JamesSullivan 3 24
(Ruth Carr) *towards rr: rdn 2f out: sn btn (jockey said gelding slipped and stumbled leaving stalls)* **8/1**

0000 11 *2 1/4* **Furni Factors**^{28} 4765 4-9-4 **50** ....(v) JasonHart 8 21
(Ronald Thompson) *towards rr: pushed along whn stmbld over 2f out: sn btn (jockey said gelding stumbled 2 1/2f out)* **16/1**

2334 12 *6* **Sing Bertie (IRE)**^{88} 2592 3-8-7 **45** .... RowanScott(3) 12
(Derek Shaw) *dwlt: hld up: shortlived effrt 1/2-way: rdn and wknd wl over 1f out* **25/1**

59.43s (-1.07) **Going Correction** -0.025s/f (Good)
WFA 3 from 4yo+ 3lb **12 Ran SP% 117.3**
Speed ratings (Par 101): **107,105,105,104,101 100,97,95,94,94 90,81**
CSF £37.32 CT £507.05 TOTE £6.00: £2.40, £1.70, £6.20; EX 44.80 Trifecta £2439.80.
Owner Arthington Barn Racing & D Swales **Bred** Tally-Ho Stud **Trained** Nawton, N Yorks

FOCUS
A weak sprint handicap. The winner finally clicked for Roger Fell.

5766 BOOK NOW FOR 21ST SEPTEMBER H'CAP 1m 4f 13y

3:05 (3:06) (Class 6) (0-55,55) 3-Y-0+

£3,105 (£924; £461; £300; £300; £300) **Stalls** Low

Form RPR

50-1 1 **True Romance (IRE)**^{14} 5277 5-9-10 **55** .... GrahamLee 8 71+
(Julia Brooke) *hld up in midfield: smooth hdwy over 2f out: led on bit over 1f out: shkn up and sn clr: readily* **11/4**^{1}

0356 2 *3 3/4* **Spark Of War (IRE)**^{14} 5277 4-9-8 **53** ....(b^{1}) ShaneGray 7 60
(Keith Dalgleish) *t.k.h: prom: hdwy to ld over 2f out: drvn and hdd over 1f out: no ch w wnr* **14/1**

3601 3 *1 3/4* **Metronomic (IRE)**^{13} 5301 5-8-8 **46** .... ZakWheatley(7) 11 50
(Peter Niven) *dwlt: hld up: hdwy over 2f out: effrt and swtchd rt over 1f out: kpt on fnl f: nt pce to chal* **9/1**

304 4 *3 3/4* **Millie The Minx (IRE)**^{17} 5099 5-9-2 **47** ....(p) JamesSullivan 4 45+
(Dianne Sayer) *hld up on ins: outpcd over 4f out: gd hdwy on outside fnl f: kpt on wl cl home* **4/1**^{2}

4352 **5** 1 ¼ **Jan De Heem**[16] 5219 9-9-5 **53**............(p) ConnorMurtagh(3) 1 49
(Tina Jackson) *hld up in midfield on ins: stdy hdwy over 2f out: rdn over 1f out: sn one pce* **8/1**[3]

0-06 **6** 1 ¾ **Rockliffe**[20] 5043 6-9-1 **46** oh1............ PJMcDonald 13 39
(Micky Hammond) *hld up towards rr: pushed along and outpcd over 3f out: hdwy over 1f out: kpt on: no imp (jockey said gelding lost its left fore shoe)* **33/1**

0303 **7** 1 ½ **Fillydelphia (IRE)**[13] 5301 8-9-1 **46** oh1............(p) DanielTudhope 15 37
(Liam Bailey) *dwlt: hld up: pushed along over 3f out: hdwy over 1f out: n.d* **22/1**

0000 **8** ½ **Richard Strauss (IRE)**[15] 4435 5-9-6 **51**............(p) KevinStott 14 41
(Philip Kirby) *in tch on outside: rdn over 2f out: wknd over 1f out* **16/1**

6024 **9** 2 ½ **Watch And Learn**[26] 4834 3-8-7 **55**............ EllaMcCain(7) 6 42
(Donald McCain) *hld up towards rr: rdn and outpcd over 3f out: n.d after* **10/1**

0-05 **10** nk **Jimmy Krankyar (USA)**[15] 5248 3-8-7 **48**............(p1) BenCurtis 3 35
(Phillip Makin) *prom tl rdn and wknd fr 2f out* **8/1**[3]

0000 **11** hd **Lord Rob**[6] 5555 8-9-1 **46** oh1............ PaddyMathers 10 31
(David Thompson) *blkd s: t.k.h in midfield: rdn over 2f out: wknd over 1f out* **100/1**

0000 **12** 3 ¾ **Crazy Tornado (IRE)**[19] 5100 6-9-6 **51**............(h) JoeFanning 2 30
(Keith Dalgleish) *t.k.h: led: clr after 4f tl hdd over 2f out: sn wknd* **20/1**

13 hd **Machine Head (USA)**[587] 8933 5-9-5 **50**............ SamJames 5 29
(Geoffrey Harker) *hld up: drvn and struggling 3f out: sn btn* **66/1**

0400 **14** 7 **Half Full**[19] 5096 3-8-5 **46** oh1............ LukeMorris 9 15
(Stuart Coltherd) *chsd clr ldr to over 2f out: sn wknd* **100/1**

2m 39.1s (-1.50) **Going Correction** -0.025s/f (Good)
WFA 3 from 4yo+ 10lb **14** Ran SP% **116.1**
Speed ratings (Par 101): **104,101,100,97,97 95,94,94,92,92 92,90,89,85**
CSF £39.23 CT £306.61 TOTE £3.20: £1.40, £3.60, £3.50; EX 39.50 Trifecta £302.80.
Owner K S Ward **Bred** Tower Place Bloodstock **Trained** Middleham, N Yorks

FOCUS
A steady gallop really picked up after a couple of furlongs in this moderate handicap. Fair form for the class. The winner transferred his hurdles progress back. Add 12yds.

5767 ABF THE SOLDIERS' CHARITY H'CAP (DIV I) 5f 212y
3:35 (3:35) (Class 6) (0-60,60) 3-Y-O+ **£3,105** (£924; £461; £300; £300) **Stalls** Low

Form RPR

0/00 **1** **Night Law**[15] 5235 5-8-10 **46** oh1............(b1) PhilDennis 7 54
(Katie Scott) *cl up: led over 2f out: rdn out fnl f (trainer said, regarding the improved form shown, the mare appreciated the application of blinkers for the first time today)* **25/1**

5000 **2** 1 ¾ **Deeds Not Words (IRE)**[39] 4335 8-9-7 **57**............(p) BenCurtis 8 59
(Tracy Waggott) *prom: effrt and rdn 2f out: edgd lft: kpt on fnl f to take 2nd cl home: nt rch wnr (vet reported gelding lost its right hind shoe)* **16/1**

4523 **3** hd **Kodicat (IRE)**[15] 5235 5-9-8 **58**............(p) KevinStott 3 60
(Kevin Ryan) *trckd ldrs: effrt and wnt 2nd over 1f out: kpt on fnl f tl no ex and lost 2nd cl home* **9/4**[1]

3000 **4** ¾ **Cosmic Chatter**[22] 4978 9-9-0 **50**............(p) JackGarritty 6 49+
(Ruth Carr) *bhd and sn outpcd: rdn and hdwy fnl f: kpt on: nt pce to chal (jockey said gelding was slowly away)* **7/1**[3]

0000 **5** ¾ **Sophia Maria**[17] 5202 3-9-3 **57**............(p1) PJMcDonald 2 53
(James Bethell) *in tch: effrt and angled rt wl over 1f out: r.o fnl f: nrst fin* **16/1**

0000 **5** dht **Chickenfortea (IRE)**[13] 5299 5-8-11 **52**............ HarrisonShaw(5) 12 49+
(Eric Alston) *stmbld bdly leaving stalls: rcvrd and led after 1f: sn crossed to ins rail: rdn and hdd over 2f out: wknd ins fnl f (jockey said gelding slipped leaving the stalls)* **9/1**

4600 **7** shd **Princess Palliser (IRE)**[19] 5092 3-9-5 **59**............(p1) JasonHart 9 55
(John Quinn) *dwlt: bhd: rdn over 2f out: kpt on fnl f: no imp* **9/1**

0042 **8** 1 ½ **Cardaw Lily (IRE)**[8] 5486 4-8-10 **46** oh1............ JamesSullivan 10 38
(Ruth Carr) *prom: effrt and rdn 2f out: wknd ins fnl f* **9/2**[2]

0060 **9** 2 **Mitchum**[50] 3933 10-8-5 **46** oh1............ PaulaMuir(5) 5 31
(Ron Barr) *towards rr: rdn along over 2f out: nvr rchd ldrs (trainer said gelding was struck into and had lost a shoe)* **40/1**

0003 **10** 1 ¾ **Major Crispies**[62] 3476 8-8-10 **46** oh1............(b) AndrewElliott 11 26
(Ronald Thompson) *hld up: rdn and outpcd over 2f out: swtchd lft over 1f out: sn wknd* **22/1**

1260 **11** 10 **Viking Way (IRE)**[34] 4519 4-9-1 **51**............(b) RachelRichardson 1
(Olly Williams) *dwlt: bhd: struggling over 2f out: sn btn (vet reported gelding finished lame left fore)* **15/2**

1m 13.95s (0.35) **Going Correction** -0.025s/f (Good)
WFA 3 from 4yo+ 4lb **11** Ran SP% **115.6**
Speed ratings (Par 101): **96,93,93,92,91 91,91,89,86,84 70**
CSF £364.08 CT £1265.81 TOTE £37.90: £8.80, £4.50, £1.40; EX 433.00 Trifecta £3393.70.
Owner B T McDonald **Bred** George Strawbridge **Trained** Galasheils, Scottish Borders

FOCUS
A poor race in which the frantic pace took most of these out of their comfort zone. The winner was well in last year's Irish form. Add 12yds.

5768 ABF THE SOLDIERS' CHARITY H'CAP (DIV II) 5f 212y
4:10 (4:10) (Class 6) (0-60,59) 3-Y-O+
£3,105 (£924; £461; £300; £300; £300) **Stalls** Low

Form RPR

5350 **1** **B Fifty Two (IRE)**[1] 5722 10-9-5 **57**............(tp) JaneElliott(3) 6 63
(Marjorie Fife) *trckd ldrs: rdn to ld over 1f out: r.o wl fnl f* **10/1**

0420 **2** 1 ¼ **Mightaswellsmile**[6] 5559 5-8-6 **46**............ PaulaMuir(5) 10 48
(Ron Barr) *in tch on outside: hdwy 2f out: chsd wnr ins fnl f: r.o* **15/2**

0010 **3** hd **Someone Exciting**[6] 5559 6-8-13 **53**............ HarrisonShaw(5) 9 54
(David Thompson) *dwlt: hld up: rdn and hdwy over 1f out: kpt on fnl f: nrst fin* **13/2**[3]

0000 **4** ¾ **Caledonian Gold**[25] 4880 6-8-3 **45**............ GavinAshton(7) 12 44
(Lisa Williamson) *chsd ldr to over 2f out: effrt and rdn over 1f out: one pce fnl f* **80/1**

2100 **5** hd **Cupid's Arrow (IRE)**[15] 5235 5-9-3 **52**............ JamieGormley 7 50
(Ruth Carr) *led to over 1f out: drvn and no ex ins fnl f (jockey said gelding had anticipated the start and hit its head on the gate)* **9/2**[2]

4006 **6** 3 **Crosse Fire**[13] 5300 7-9-4 **53**............(p) LukeMorris 11 42
(Scott Dixon) *hld up: rdn over 2f out: kpt on fnl f: nvr able to chal* **20/1**

610 **7** ½ **Sovereign State**[28] 4763 4-9-6 **55**............ EoinWalsh 8 42
(Tony Newcombe) *sn midfield: rdn and outpcd over 2f out: n.d after* **25/1**

0005 **8** 2 **Lexington Palm (IRE)**[13] 5300 3-8-7 **49**............(b1) SeanDavis(3) 4 29
(Keith Dalgleish) *prom: rdn over 2f out: hung lft and wknd over 1f out (jockey said filly became unbalanced on the bend turning into the straight)* **10/1**

0-63 **9** hd **Lets Go Flo (IRE)**[14] 5278 3-8-9 **48**............ BenCurtis 5 27
(Brian Ellison) *hld up on ins: rdn and outpcd over 2f out: sn btn* **9/1**

0500 **10** ¾ **The Retriever (IRE)**[13] 5300 4-9-1 **50**............ GrahamLee 2 28
(Micky Hammond) *dwlt: hld up: drvn and struggling 2f out: sn wknd* **16/1**

2541 **11** 4 **Mr Greenlight**[13] 5300 4-9-10 **59**............ DavidAllan 3 40
(Tim Easterby) *t.k.h: in tch: rdn over 2f out: sn wknd (trainer could offer no explanation for the performance shown)* **5/2**[1]

1m 14.05s (0.45) **Going Correction** -0.025s/f (Good)
WFA 3 from 4yo+ 4lb **11** Ran SP% **115.8**
Speed ratings (Par 101): **96,94,94,93,92 88,88,85,85,84 78**
CSF £80.01 CT £528.62 TOTE £9.10: £2.70, £2.60, £1.30; EX 89.80 Trifecta £543.70.
Owner Fat Badger Racing **Bred** Mull Enterprises Ltd **Trained** Stillington, N Yorks

FOCUS
This second division of the ordinary 6f handicap was only marginally slower than the first. Weak form. Add 12yds.

5769 RACING TV PROFITS RETURNED TO RACING H'CAP 1m 7f 189y
4:40 (4:40) (Class 4) (0-85,87) 3-Y-O+ **£6,162** (£1,845; £922; £461) **Stalls** Low

Form RPR

4321 **1** **Rochester House (IRE)**[21] 5019 3-9-5 **87**............ JoeFanning 1 98+
(Mark Johnston) *chsd ldr: shkn up to ld over 2f out: clr whn edgd lft over 1f out: eased last 75yds* **1/3**[1]

10-0 **2** 7 **Piedita (IRE)**[11] 5368 5-10-0 **83**............ LukeMorris 4 84
(Sir Mark Prescott Bt) *t.k.h: chsd ldng pair: effrt over 2f out: chsd (clr) wnr over 1f out: edgd lft and sn no imp: eased whn hld last 50yds* **8/1**[3]

3405 **3** 4 ½ **Yabass (IRE)**[10] 5457 4-10-4 **87**............(b1) DanielTudhope 2 83
(Archie Watson) *led to over 2f out: rdn and wknd over 1f out* **13/2**[2]

203 **4** 1 ¾ **The Resdev Way**[24] 4936 6-8-10 **70**............ PaulaMuir(5) 3 64
(Philip Kirby) *slowly away: hld up in last pl: struggling over 3f out: drifted rt and no imp fnl 2f* **14/1**

3m 32.62s (-3.38) **Going Correction** -0.025s/f (Good)
WFA 3 from 4yo+ 13lb **4** Ran SP% **106.1**
Speed ratings (Par 105): **107,103,101,100**
CSF £3.32 TOTE £1.10; EX 3.40 Trifecta £4.80.
Owner John Brown & Megan Dennis **Bred** Stall Ullmann **Trained** Middleham Moor, N Yorks

FOCUS
Not surprisingly the feature proved a tactical affair. The winner improved for 2m, but it was a weak race for the grade. Add 24yds.

5770 SUBSCRIBE TO RACING TV ON YOUTUBE H'CAP 7f 6y
5:10 (5:11) (Class 5) (0-75,75) 4-Y-O+
£4,140 (£1,232; £615; £307; £300; £300) **Stalls** Low

Form RPR

0540 **1** **International Man**[11] 5398 4-9-1 **72**............(b1) SeanDavis(3) 11 81
(Richard Fahey) *hld up in tch: hdwy over 2f out: rdn to ld over 1f out: edgd lft ins fnl f: r.o* **8/1**

3326 **2** ¾ **Mujassam**[14] 5274 7-9-6 **74**............(b) DanielTudhope 10 81
(David O'Meara) *prom: hdwy to ld over 2f out: sn rdn: hdd over 1f out: rallied ins fnl f: hld nr fin* **9/2**[1]

0401 **3** 1 ½ **Twin Appeal (IRE)**[21] 5020 8-9-4 **75**............ GemmaTutty(3) 15 78
(Karen Tutty) *hld up on outside: effrt and pushed along 2f out: hdwy to chse ldng pair ins fnl f: kpt on* **9/1**

4-04 **4** 4 **Bea Ryan (IRE)**[56] 3707 4-8-8 **62**............ CamHardie 3 54
(Declan Carroll) *prom: rdn and outpcd 3f out: rallied fnl f: kpt on fin (jockey said filly hung right-handed throughout)* **7/1**[3]

0050 **5** nse **Eldelbar (SPA)**[16] 5213 5-8-2 **56** oh1............(h) PaddyMathers 1 48
(Geoffrey Harker) *slowly away: sn midfield: effrt and rdn over 2f out: outpcd ins fnl f (jockey said he was slow to remove the blindfold resulting in the gelding being slowly away)* **33/1**

-600 **6** ½ **Barton Mills**[38] 4369 4-9-1 **69**............ GrahamLee 12 60
(Michael Easterby) *hld up in midfield on outside: hdwy and prom over 2f out: sn rdn: no ex fnl f* **50/1**

0300 **7** shd **Magic City (IRE)**[52] 3867 10-8-12 **66**............ NathanEvans 5 56
(Michael Easterby) *hld up on ins: rdn over 2f out: hdwy over 1f out: sn no imp* **20/1**

4042 **8** ½ **Chookie Dunedin**[18] 5123 4-9-1 **69**............ TomEaves 9 58
(Keith Dalgleish) *cl up on outside: led after 1f: rdn and hdd over 2f out: no ex fr over 1f out* **12/1**

0345 **9** 1 ½ **The Stalking Moon (IRE)**[49] 3969 5-8-8 **62**............ AndrewMullen 13 47
(Adrian Nicholls) *slowly away: bhd and outpcd: sme late hdwy: nvr on terms (jockey said mare missed the break and jumped the road crossing)* **7/1**[3]

6-00 **10** hd **Mango Chutney**[21] 5020 6-9-2 **70**............(b1) SamJames 8 54
(John Davies) *s.i.s: bhd: struggling over 2f out: sn btn* **22/1**

-000 **11** 1 ¼ **Watheer**[29] 4728 4-8-13 **67**............(b) BenCurtis 4 48
(Roger Fell) *t.k.h: disp ld after 1f to over 2f out: sn rdn and wknd* **25/1**

5050 **12** 7 **Explain**[4] 5616 7-8-9 **63**............(b) JamesSullivan 7 25
(Ruth Carr) *hld up: rdn and struggling over 2f out: sn wknd (trainer said gelding had a breathing problem)* **6/1**[2]

5100 **13** 7 **Sword Exceed (GER)**[31] 4643 5-9-6 **74**............ JasonHart 6 17
(Ivan Furtado) *t.k.h: led: 1f: cl up tl rdn and wknd over 2f out* **6/1**[2]

1m 26.47s (-0.93) **Going Correction** -0.025s/f (Good) **13** Ran SP% **118.4**
Speed ratings (Par 103): **104,103,101,96,96 96,96,95,93,93 92,84,76**
CSF £40.61 CT £270.12 TOTE £9.30: £2.80, £1.80, £3.00; EX 49.30 Trifecta £204.50.
Owner P D Smith Holdings Ltd **Bred** Bearstone Stud Ltd **Trained** Musley Bank, N Yorks

FOCUS
This wide-open handicap proved a lively betting heat. Helped by his rider's claim, the winner is rated to this year's form. Add 12yds.

5771 28TH AUGUST IS LADIES' DAY H'CAP 7f 6y
5:45 (5:46) (Class 6) (0-65,68) 3-Y-O
£3,105 (£924; £461; £300; £300; £300) **Stalls** Low

Form RPR

3-01 **1** **Alotabottle**[5] 5575 3-9-10 **68** 6ex............ SeanDavis(3) 7 81+
(Kevin Ryan) *prom: effrt and chsd ldr over 1f out: led ent fnl f: kpt on strly to draw clr* **11/4**[2]

5123 **2** 3 ½ **Macs Blessings (IRE)**[13] 5300 3-8-11 **57**............(v) HarrisonShaw(5) 6 61
(Stef Keniry) *hld up in midfield on outside: effrt 2f out: chsd (clr) wnr ins fnl f: kpt on: nt pce to chal (jockey said his saddle slipped)* **9/2**[3]

U412 **3** hd **The Big House (IRE)**[3] 5695 3-9-2 **57**............ AndrewMullen 9 60
(Adrian Nicholls) *led: rdn along 2f out: hdd ent fnl f: sn lost 2nd and one pce* **5/4**[1]

0500 **4** ¾ **Uncle Norman (FR)**[29] 4731 3-8-10 **51**............(b) DuranFentiman 8 53
(Tim Easterby) *s.i.s: hld up: rdn over 2f out: hdwy and edgd lft over 1f out: kpt on: no imp* **20/1**

6-50 **5** 5 **Darwina**[14] 5272 3-8-11 **55**......(h) RowanScott(3) 11 44
(Alistair Whillans) *s.i.s: hld up on outside: pushed along over 2f out: sme late hdwy: nvr rchd ldrs (starter reported that the filly was the subject of a third criteria failure; trainer was informed that the filly could not run until the day after passing a stalls test)* **33/1**

2545 **6** *hd* **Ey Up Its Mick**[46] 4080 3-9-2 **57**......(v) DougieCostello 2 45
(Tony Coyle) *hld up: rdn and outpcd 3f out: rallied fnl f: nvr rchd ldrs* **16/1**

005 **7** *1¼* **Cheam Avenue (IRE)**[50] 3920 3-8-12 **53**...... GrahamLee 4 38
(Paul Midgley) *trckd ldrs: effrt over 2f out: wknd over 1f out* **25/1**

035 **8** *2¾* **Little Miss Muffin**[18] 5128 3-9-5 **60**...... CamHardie 5 38
(Sam England) *midfield: drvn and outpcd over 2f out: wknd over 1f out* **33/1**

604 **9** *1¼* **Our Secret (IRE)**[13] 5297 3-7-13 **45**......(p) AndrewBreslin(5) 3 19
(Liam Bailey) *in tch on ins: drvn and outpcd 3f out: btn fnl 2f (jockey said filly hung left-handed throughout)* **40/1**

400 **10** *3* **Rangefield Express (IRE)**[16] 5215 3-8-13 **54**......(v[1]) SamJames 10 21
(Geoffrey Harker) *cl up tl rdn and wknd 2f out* **20/1**

040- **11** *3* **Crystal Carole**[273] 8896 3-8-4 **45**...... PaddyMathers 1 4
(John Quinn) *s.i.s: bhd: struggling over 3f out: sn btn* **40/1**

1m 27.2s (-0.20) **Going Correction** -0.025s/f (Good) **11 Ran SP% 119.3**
Speed ratings (Par 98): **100,96,95,94,89 88,87,84,82,79 76**
CSF £14.34 CT £22.07 TOTE £2.60: £1.20, £1.30, £1.30; EX 13.70 Trifecta £25.90.
Owner Gordon Bulloch & Steve Ryan **Bred** Saxtead Livestock Ltd **Trained** Hambleton, N Yorks

FOCUS
This wasn't a bad 3yo handicap for the grade and it was run at a solid pace. The winner was value for a bit extra. Add 12yds.
T/Plt: £505.50 to a £1 stake. Pool: £62,080.06 - 89.64 winning units T/Qpdt: £44.10 to a £1 stake. Pool: £7,181.51 - 120.44 winning units **Richard Young**

5337 NEWBURY (L-H)
Tuesday, August 6

OFFICIAL GOING: Good (good to firm in places; watered; 7.2)
Wind: strong at times, half against Weather: sunny periods with light showers from 5.15pm

5772 JOHN DREW MEMORIAL MAIDEN FILLIES' STKS (PLUS 10 RACE) 6f
2:15 (2:19) (Class 4) 2-Y-O **£4,463** (£1,328; £663; £331) **Stalls** High

Form RPR

1 **Wejdan (FR)** 2-9-0 0...... JamesDoyle 13 83+
(William Haggas) *s.i.s: towards rr: gd hdwy over 1f out: led fnl 100yds: r.o wl: readily* **13/2[3]**

4 **2** *½* **Predictable Tully (IRE)**[27] 4790 2-9-0 0...... HectorCrouch 2 80
(Clive Cox) *led: rdn over 1f out: edgd lft ins fnl f: hdd fnl 100yds: kpt on* **4/1[1]**

3 *2* **Lady Lynetta (IRE)** 2-9-0 0...... ShaneKelly 9 74
(Richard Hughes) *trckd ldrs: rdn to chse ldr over 1f out: kpt on but nt pce of front pair ins fnl f* **50/1**

4 *2¼* **Populaire (FR)** 2-9-0 0...... PatDobbs 6 67+
(Amanda Perrett) *mid-div: pushed along and hdwy over 1f out: kpt on nicely fnl f wout threatening to get involved: improve* **40/1**

5 *shd* **Charming Spirit (IRE)** 2-9-0 0...... AndreaAtzeni 1 66+
(Roger Varian) *little slowly away: towards rr: hdwy over 1f out: kpt on nicely fnl f but nt gng pce to get on terms: improve* **11/1**

4 **6** *2¼* **Gypsy Whisper**[27] 4798 2-8-9 0...... CierenFallon(5) 7 60
(David Menuisier) *mid-div: rdn over 2f out: kpt on ins fnl f but nt pce to get on terms* **16/1**

0 **7** *1¾* **Sorteo (IRE)**[18] 5132 2-9-0 0...... OisinMurphy 10 54
(Andrew Balding) *trckd ldr tl rdn over 1f out: wknd fnl 120yds* **7/1**

8 *1½* **Catechism** 2-9-0 0...... KieranShoemark 18 50+
(Richard Spencer) *trckd ldrs: rdn 2f out: wknd fnl f* **16/1**

305 **9** *hd* **Multiply By Eight (FR)**[20] 5045 2-9-0 83...... SilvestreDeSousa 3 49
(Tom Dascombe) *towards rr: sme late prog: nvr on terms* **11/2[2]**

0 **10** *2¼* **Farewell Kiss (IRE)**[26] 4849 2-9-0 0...... SeanLevey 14 43
(Michael Bell) *in tch: rdn over 1f out: wknd fnl f* **40/1**

11 *½* **Gleeds Girl** 2-9-0 0...... CallumShepherd 16 41
(Mick Channon) *hmpd s: towards rr: sme prog 2f out: nvr threatened: wknd fnl f* **20/1**

0 **12** *¾* **Bockos Amber (IRE)**[36] 4448 2-9-0 0...... DavidProbert 11 40
(Roger Teal) *mid-div: rdn over 2f out: wknd over 1f out* **66/1**

13 *½* **Arabian Dream** 2-9-0 0...... HarryBentley 15 37
(Ralph Beckett) *wnt rt s and s.i.s: sn mid-div: effrt 2f out: sn wknd* **14/1**

40 **14** *hd* **Cece Ceylon**[49] 3968 2-9-0 0...... RobHornby 17 37
(Ralph Beckett) *in tch: rdn over 2f out: wknd over 1f out* **50/1**

15 *5* **Queen Of Clubs** 2-9-0 0......(t[1]) JasonWatson 8 22
(Roger Charlton) *s.i.s: a towards rr* **20/1**

1m 14.27s (1.07) **Going Correction** -0.025s/f (Good) **15 Ran SP% 107.8**
Speed ratings (Par 93): **91,90,87,84,84 81,79,77,76,73 73,72,71,71,64**
CSF £23.26 TOTE £5.30: £2.20, £1.40, £13.80; EX 27.40 Trifecta £1564.10.
Owner Mohamed Saeed Al Shahi **Bred** Ecurie Normandie Pur Sang **Trained** Newmarket, Suffolk
■ Areehaa was withdrawn. Price at time of withdrawal 5/1. Rule 4 applies to all bets - deduction 15p in the pound

FOCUS
The watered ground was given as good, good to firm in places (GoingStick 7.2). The rails at the 7f and 5f bends were out 5 metres from the inside line, increasing distances of the 1m2f+ races by 18yds. Just a fair maiden, but the winner did well to catch the placed horses and can rate higher.

5773 DONNINGTON GROVE VETERINARY SURGERY H'CAP 7f (S)
2:45 (2:49) (Class 4) (0-85,85) 3-Y-O
£5,207 (£1,549; £774; £387; £300; £300) **Stalls** High

Form RPR

0343 **1** **Chatham House**[14] 5270 3-9-0 **78**...... SeanLevey 1 90
(Richard Hannon) *hld up in last pair: hdwy 2f out: led jst over 1f out: kpt on wl: pushed out* **6/1**

5502 **2** *1¼* **Strict Tempo**[10] 5450 3-9-1 **79**...... OisinMurphy 7 88
(Andrew Balding) *cl up: lost pl over 2f out: hdwy whn swtchd rt ent fnl f: sn chsng wnr: kpt on but a being hld* **2/1[1]**

6610 **3** *4½* **Shorter Skirt**[18] 5143 3-9-3 **81**...... CharlesBishop 3 78
(Eve Johnson Houghton) *s.i.s: in last pair: hdwy ent fnl f: wnt 3rd fnl 120yds: kpt on but nt pce to get on terms w front pair* **12/1**

2332 **4** *2½* **Nefarious (IRE)**[27] 4793 3-9-4 **82**...... DavidProbert 5 72
(Henry Candy) *trckd ldrs: led jst ins 2f out: sn rdn: hdd jst over 1f out: no ex* **7/2[3]**

3210 **5** *6* **After John**[59] 3599 3-9-6 **84**...... CallumShepherd 2 58
(Mick Channon) *trckd ldrs: rdn and ev ch over 1f out: fdd ins fnl f* **3/1[2]**

20-0 **6** *nk* **Hieronymus**[8] 5505 3-8-12 **76**......(v[1]) ShaneKelly 9 49
(Seamus Durack) *led: 3 l clr after 3f: rdn and hdd wl over 1f out: wknd fnl f* **50/1**

2401 **7** *7* **Assimilation (IRE)**[22] 5002 3-9-3 **81**...... LiamKeniry 6 35
(Ed Walker) *trckd ldr: rdn over 2f out: wknd over 1f out (trainer said gelding was unsuited by the going and would prefer a slower surface)* **11/1**

1m 26.46s (-0.54) **Going Correction** -0.025s/f (Good) **7 Ran SP% 112.8**
Speed ratings (Par 102): **102,100,95,92,85 85,77**
CSF £17.95 CT £137.75 TOTE £6.10: £2.60, £1.80; EX 20.40 Trifecta £115.60.
Owner Denford Stud **Bred** Denford Stud Ltd **Trained** East Everleigh, Wilts

FOCUS
The early gallop didn't appear that strong, but those who were held up came through to take the first three places. The first pair were clear, with the runner-up rated to her latest form.

5774 MILDMAY FARM AND STUD NOVICE MEDIAN AUCTION STKS (DIV I) 7f (S)
3:20 (3:22) (Class 5) 2-Y-O **£3,428** (£1,020; £509; £254) **Stalls** High

Form RPR

214 **1** **Sesame Birah (IRE)**[10] 5469 2-9-5 0...... SilvestreDeSousa 1 82
(Richard Hannon) *trckd ldr: chal over 2f out: led over 1f out: sn drifted rt: kpt on: rdn out* **1/1[1]**

2 *½* **Mr Poy** 2-9-4 0...... CharlieBennett 7 80+
(Hughie Morrison) *hmpd s: in last trio: hdwy over 1f out: rdn to press wnr jst ins fnl f: kpt on: hld nring fin* **20/1**

6 **3** *2½* **Fantasy Believer (IRE)**[17] 5186 2-9-4 0...... KieranShoemark 8 73
(Charles Hills) *wnt lft s: t.k.h: in tch: kpt on to go 3rd ins fnl f but nt pce to get on terms* **7/1[3]**

6 **4** *¾* **Selecto**[24] 4925 2-9-4 0...... JasonWatson 6 71
(Roger Charlton) *trckd ldrs: swtchd lft for effrt 2f out: sn rdn: kpt on same pce fnl f* **10/1**

5 **5** *nk* **Punchbowl Flyer (IRE)**[35] 4480 2-9-4 0...... CharlesBishop 3 70+
(Eve Johnson Houghton) *prom: led over 2f out: rdn and hdd over 1f out: kpt on same pce fnl f* **14/1**

6 *2¾* **Afraid Of Nothing** 2-8-13 0...... OisinMurphy 5 58
(Ralph Beckett) *cl up: effrt 2f out: nt quite pce to chal: fdd ins fnl f* **4/1[2]**

7 *3* **Machios** 2-9-4 0...... DavidProbert 2 56+
(Andrew Balding) *in last pair: rdn over 2f out: little imp: wknd ins fnl f* **14/1**

8 *3¼* **Burning (IRE)** 2-9-4 0...... StevieDonohoe 9 47
(Charlie Fellowes) *in tch: rdn over 2f out: wknd over 1f out* **50/1**

9 *2¾* **Grimsthorpe Castle** 2-9-4 0...... LiamKeniry 4 40
(Ed Walker) *in last trio: effrt 2f out: wknd over 1f out* **25/1**

0 **10** *10* **Union Spirit**[25] 4886 2-9-4 0...... JackMitchell 10 14
(Peter Chapple-Hyam) *led tl over 2f out: sn wknd* **33/1**

1m 28.12s (1.12) **Going Correction** -0.025s/f (Good) **10 Ran SP% 118.4**
Speed ratings (Par 94): **92,91,88,87,87 84,80,77,73,62**
CSF £29.78 TOTE £1.70: £1.10, £6.50, £2.60; EX 26.00 Trifecta £219.80.
Owner Middleham Park Racing XXIV **Bred** Rathasker Stud **Trained** East Everleigh, Wilts

FOCUS
The quicker of the two divisions by 0.22sec, and the winner's previous experience, including in Group company, saw her home ahead of a promising newcomer.

5775 MILDMAY FARM AND STUD NOVICE MEDIAN AUCTION STKS (DIV II) 7f (S)
3:50 (3:52) (Class 5) 2-Y-O **£3,428** (£1,020; £509; £254) **Stalls** High

Form RPR

0 **1** **D Day (IRE)**[24] 4925 2-9-5 0...... JamesDoyle 2 83+
(Richard Hannon) *mde all in centre: kpt on wl to draw clr fnl f: rdn out* **11/2**

2 *3¼* **Lost Empire (IRE)** 2-9-5 0......(b[1]) SeanLevey 4 75
(Harry Dunlop) *prom in centre: rdn w ch over 1f out: sn drifted rt: kpt on but nt pce of wnr fnl 140yds* **20/1**

44 **3** *2½* **Chairlift Chat (IRE)**[33] 4544 2-9-5 0...... CharlesBishop 3 68
(Eve Johnson Houghton) *racd centre: trckd ldng pair: rdn 2f out: sn wandered u.p: nt pce to chal* **11/4[1]**

4 *1¾* **Perfect Outing** 2-9-0 0...... HectorCrouch 1 59
(Clive Cox) *racd centre: wnt lft s: sn trcking ldrs: rdn 2f out: sn one pce* **7/2[2]**

0 **5** *½* **Optio**[17] 5186 2-9-5 0...... OisinMurphy 9 62+
(Brian Meehan) *led stands' side trio: rdn over 2f out: sn one pce* **9/2[3]**

00 **6** *2¼* **Party Potential (USA)**[20] 5052 2-9-5 0...... DavidProbert 8 56+
(Alan King) *trckd ldr on stands' side: hung lft whn rdn 2f out: wknd ins fnl f* **66/1**

7 *nse* **Luigi Vampa (FR)** 2-9-5 0...... JimCrowley 5 56
(David Menuisier) *racd centre: hld up: rdn 2f out: little imp: wknd fnl f* **16/1**

05 **8** *2½* **Son Of Prancealot (IRE)**[8] 5493 2-9-0 0...... KatherineBegley(5) 6 50
(David Evans) *racd centre: hld up: rdn 2f out: nvr threatened: wknd fnl f* **25/1**

9 *11* **Serious Jockin** 2-9-5 0...... CallumShepherd 7 21+
(Mick Channon) *chsd ldr on stands' side: rdn over 2f out: sn wknd (jockey said colt stopped quickly)* **9/2[3]**

1m 28.34s (1.34) **Going Correction** -0.025s/f (Good) **9 Ran SP% 116.6**
Speed ratings (Par 94): **91,87,84,82,81 79,79,76,63**
CSF £106.37 TOTE £6.20: £1.70, £6.00, £1.20; EX 104.70 Trifecta £374.10.
Owner Mrs J Wood **Bred** Exors Of The Late Mrs I L Sneath **Trained** East Everleigh, Wilts

FOCUS
They split into three small groups this time, the two racing more towards the centre of the track merging after 2f or so. They finished well strung out, in a time 0.22sec slower than the first leg, and the three on the stands' finished fifth, sixth and last.

5776 MELBOURNE 10 "ONLY 36 DAYS TO LAYTOWN RACES" H'CAP 1m (S)
4:25 (4:27) (Class 3) (0-90,90) 3-Y-O+ **£7,439** (£2,213; £1,106; £553) **Stalls** High

Form RPR

0342 **1** **Qaysar (FR)**[13] 5319 4-10-0 **90**...... JamesDoyle 5 105
(Richard Hannon) *hld up in last pair: hdwy over 2f out: led over 1f out: sn edgd rt: kpt on strly: comf (jockey said gelding hung right-handed)* **6/1[3]**

4-02 **2** *4½* **Wafy (IRE)**[25] 4863 4-10-0 **90**...... JimCrowley 3 97+
(Charles Hills) *hld up in tch: hdwy over 1f out: sn rdn: wnt 2nd fnl 120yds: nt pce to get on terms w wnr (jockey said gelding was denied a clear run)* **4/1[2]**

5513 **3** *1½* **Mr Top Hat**[61] 3515 4-10-0 **90**...... HarryBentley 7 91
(David Evans) *led: rdn whn jnd over 2f out: hdd over 1f out: sn hld: no ex whn lost 2nd fnl 120yds (jockey said gelding hung right-handed)* **11/1**

-634 **4** *3* **Baryshnikov**[25] 4865 3-8-8 **77**....................(p[1]) AndreaAtzeni 4 70
(Ed Walker) *s.i.s: in last pair: rdn over 2f out: kpt on ins fnl f: wnt 4th towards fin: nvr threatened to get on terms (jockey said gelding jumped poorly and was never travelling)* **9/4**[1]

1P06 **5** *nk* **He's Amazing (IRE)**[25] 4863 4-9-6 **82**.................... HectorCrouch 8 76
(Ed Walker) *trckd ldr: disp ld u.p over 2f out tl over 1f out: sn short of room: no ex ins fnl f* **16/1**

0564 **6** *3/4* **Athmad (IRE)**[18] 5140 3-9-1 **84**....................(p[1]) DavidProbert 2 75
(Brian Meehan) *trckd ldrs: trckd ldrs: rdn over 2f out: wknd ins fnl f* **14/1**

5023 **7** *2 3/4* **Dawaaleeb (USA)**[46] 4079 5-9-13 **89**....................(v) LewisEdmunds 6 75
(Les Eyre) *trckd ldr: rdn over 2f out: wknd fnl f* **12/1**

2614 **8** *1 1/4* **Ragstone View (IRE)**[12] 5343 4-8-13 **75**....................(h) OisinMurphy 9 58
(Rod Millman) *trckd ldrs: rdn over 2f out: fdd ent fnl f* **14/1**

06-0 **9** *7* **Surrey Hope (USA)**[31] 4639 5-9-10 **86**.................... JasonWatson 10 53
(Hughie Morrison) *trckd ldrs: rdn over 2f out: wknd over 1f out* **16/1**

4224 **10** *11* **Salt Whistle Bay (IRE)**[46] 4061 5-9-2 **78**.................... SilvestreDeSousa 1 19
(Rae Guest) *hld up in tch: effrt over 2f out: wknd over 1f out (jockey said gelding had no more to give)* **9/1**

1m 38.82s (-1.08) **Going Correction** -0.025s/f (Good)
WFA 3 from 4yo+ 7lb **10** Ran SP% **116.2**
Speed ratings (Par 107): **104,99,98,95,94 93,91,89,82,71**
CSF £30.12 CT £259.40 TOTE £4.50: £1.90, £1.90, £4.50; EX 27.10 Trifecta £123.70.
Owner Al Shaqab Racing **Bred** S N C Scuderia Waldeck **Trained** East Everleigh, Wilts

FOCUS
A good handicap, and it paid to be held up off the pace. The winner was back to his previous best, which also came at Newbury.

5777 ARCHIE WATSON RACING NURSERY H'CAP 7f (S)

4:55 (4:58) (Class 5) (0-75,76) 2-Y-O

£3,428 (£1,020; £509; £300; £300; £300) **Stalls** High

Form RPR

246 **1** **Miss Villanelle**[24] 4897 2-9-7 **72**.................... KieranShoemark 1 76
(Charles Hills) *mde all: edgd rt wl over 1f out: kpt on gamely fnl f: rdn out (trainer could offer no explanation for the improved form shown)* **14/1**

220 **2** *1 1/4* **Nat Love (IRE)**[50] 3943 2-9-1 **71**.................... ScottMcCullagh(5) 5 72
(Mick Channon) *hld up: hdwy 2f out: sn swtchd lft and rdn: kpt on wl fnl f: snatched 2nd towards fin* **20/1**

652 **3** *1/2* **Divine Covey**[39] 4323 2-9-2 **67**.................... PatDobbs 11 67
(Richard Hannon) *hld up: hdwy over 1f out but nt best of runs briefly: chsd wnr fnl 150yds: sn rdn: nt pce to chal: no ex cl home* **9/1**

445 **4** *1* **Hashtagmetoo (USA)**[26] 4840 2-9-5 **70**.................... OisinMurphy 10 68
(Jamie Osborne) *wnt rt s: hld up in tch: nt clr run 2f out: hdwy ent fnl f: sn rdn: kpt on but nt pce to threaten* **8/1**

053 **5** *1 1/4* **London Calling (IRE)**[35] 4480 2-9-6 **71**....................(h[1]) HarryBentley 8 65
(Richard Spencer) *trckd ldrs: rdn to dispute 2nd wl over 1f out: edgd lft and no ex fnl 130yds* **3/1**[2]

3352 **6** *3/4* **Danny Ocean (IRE)**[19] 5101 2-9-3 **68**.................... JamesDoyle 3 60
(K R Burke) *in tch: hdwy over 2f out: rdn to dispute 2nd over 1f out: no ex fnl 130yds* **5/2**[1]

231 **7** *3 3/4* **Space Ace (FR)**[13] 5314 2-9-11 **76**....................(p) AdamMcNamara 6 58
(Archie Watson) *in tch: rdn in cl 4th over 1f out: fdd ins fnl f* **11/2**[3]

2125 **8** *4* **Lili Wen Fach (IRE)**[31] 4647 2-9-6 **71**.................... JasonWatson 2 43
(David Evans) *trckd ldrs: rdn to dispute 2nd 2f out: wknd jst over 1f out* **12/1**

3210 **9** *11* **Miss Matterhorn**[19] 5101 2-9-3 **68**.................... CharlesBishop 9 11
(Eve Johnson Houghton) *prom: rdn over 2f out: wknd over 1f out (jockey said filly stopped quickly)* **20/1**

1m 28.0s (1.00) **Going Correction** -0.025s/f (Good) **9** Ran SP% **113.9**
Speed ratings (Par 94): **93,91,91,89,88 87,83,78,66**
CSF £251.05 CT £2646.76 TOTE £16.90: £3.80, £5.70, £2.00; EX 305.70 Trifecta £5494.70.
Owner J H Widdows & Partners **Bred** Mrs J Imray **Trained** Lambourn, Berks

FOCUS
This was a bit of a messy race, the hold-up horses getting held up in traffic and the winner holding them off after kicking from the front. The winner's rated back to her debut form.

5778 COVERMARQUE.COM FOR BLOODSTOCK INSURANCE H'CAP 1m 4f

5:30 (5:30) (Class 5) (0-70,72) 3-Y-O

£3,428 (£1,020; £509; £300; £300; £300) **Stalls** High

Form RPR

6033 **1** **Tavus (IRE)**[22] 4991 3-8-11 **60**.................... JasonWatson 5 69+
(Roger Charlton) *trckd ldrs: rdn to ld jst over 2f out: styd on wl and a doing enough fnl f: rdn out* **11/8**[1]

030 **2** *1* **Ned Pepper (IRE)**[26] 4842 3-9-4 **67**.................... TomQueally 10 74+
(Alan King) *hld up in last pair: rdn over 3f out: hdwy over 2f out: chsd wnr ent fnl f: styd on but a being hld fnl 120yds* **25/1**

0234 **3** *1 1/4* **Monsieur Lambrays**[12] 5355 3-9-9 **72**....................(b) OisinMurphy 7 77
(Tom Clover) *hld up in last trio: hdwy 2f out: sn rdn: wnt 3rd fnl 120yds: styd on* **8/1**[3]

6335 **4** *3/4* **Vindolanda**[49] 3955 3-9-5 **68**.................... KieranShoemark 4 72
(Charles Hills) *mid-div: hdwy 3f out: sn rdn: chsd wnr 2f out: ch jst over 1f out: styd on same pce fnl 120yds* **8/1**[3]

1114 **5** *1 3/4* **Cherry Cola**[27] 4795 3-9-7 **70**.................... HectorCrouch 2 71
(Sheena West) *mid-div: hdwy 3f out: sn drvn: disputing cl 3rd ent fnl f: no ex fnl 120yds* **10/1**

2633 **6** *1/2* **Hermocrates (FR)**[10] 5426 3-9-4 **67**....................(b) PatDobbs 9 67
(Richard Hannon) *trckd ldr: rdn over 2f out: sn one pce (jockey said gelding hung left-handed)* **11/1**

1113 **7** *1/2* **Glutnforpunishment**[24] 4906 3-9-9 **72**.................... SilvestreDeSousa 1 71
(Nick Littmoden) *trckd ldrs: lost pl whn outpcd over 2f out: no threat but styd on again fnl f* **13/2**[2]

4204 **8** *6* **L'Un Deux Trois (IRE)**[27] 4803 3-9-6 **69**....................(p[1]) HayleyTurner 6 59
(Michael Bell) *sn led: rdn and hdd 2f out: sn wknd* **8/1**[3]

050 **9** *11* **Mr Nice Guy (IRE)**[15] 5254 3-8-11 **60**.................... RobHornby 3 32
(Sylvester Kirk) *in tch tl wknd 3f out* **22/1**

2m 34.35s (-3.65) **Going Correction** -0.025s/f (Good) **9** Ran SP% **114.4**
Speed ratings (Par 100): **109,108,107,107,105 105,105,101,93**
CSF £41.75 CT £209.99 TOTE £2.00: £1.20, £6.00, £2.20; EX 34.30 Trifecta £453.10.
Owner Tony Bloom **Bred** Gillian, Lady Howard De Walden **Trained** Beckhampton, Wilts

FOCUS
Add 18yds. A modest handicap and they finished in a bit of a heap. This rates a clear pb from the winner.

5779 SEVENTEEN GROUP RACES WON BY OAKGROVE GRADUATES H'CAP 1m 2f

6:05 (6:06) (Class 5) (0-75,77) 3-Y-O

£3,428 (£1,020; £509; £300; £300; £300) **Stalls** High

Form RPR

3643 **1** **Ritchie Valens (IRE)**[10] 5451 3-9-9 **76**.................... OisinMurphy 12 85
(Richard Hannon) *hld up: hdwy 2f out: sn rdn: str chal ent fnl f: tk narrow advantage fnl 100yds: hld on: all out* **6/1**[1]

03-6 **2** *nk* **Fantastic Blue**[65] 3373 3-9-4 **71**.................... SeanLevey 7 79
(Ismail Mohammed) *mid-div: rdn and stdy prog fr 2f out: styd on wl ins fnl f: snatched 2nd fnl stride* **10/1**

-523 **3** *nse* **Tammooz**[40] 4291 3-9-9 **76**.................... AndreaAtzeni 2 84
(Roger Varian) *in tch: rdn 3f out: led over 1f out: narrowly hdd fnl 100yds: styd on: lost 2nd fnl stride* **6/1**[1]

-342 **4** *6* **Alandalos**[12] 5349 3-9-9 **76**.................... JimCrowley 11 72+
(Charles Hills) *trckd ldr: rdn over 2f out: cl 3rd ent fnl f: styd on same pce* **13/2**[2]

-323 **5** *1 1/2* **Jack D'Or**[27] 4789 3-9-7 **74**.................... LiamKeniry 6 67
(Ed Walker) *mid-div: hdwy over 2f out: sn rdn: styd on but nt pce to get on terms* **10/1**

-210 **6** *3/4* **Edmond Dantes (IRE)**[46] 4068 3-9-5 **72**.................... KieranShoemark 10 64
(David Menuisier) *hld up towards rr: rdn wl over 2f out: styd on fnl f: nvr gng pce to get involved (vet said gelding lost its right hind shoe)* **12/1**

366 **7** *1/2* **Stone Mason (IRE)**[52] 3860 3-9-1 **68**.................... JasonWatson 1 59
(Roger Charlton) *hld up towards rr: rdn and stdy prog fr over 2f out: disp hld 5th ent fnl f: styd on same pce fnl 120yds* **8/1**[3]

2221 **8** *2* **Sashenka (GER)**[59] 3598 3-9-7 **77**.................... GaryMahon(3) 13 64
(Sylvester Kirk) *sn led: 6 l clr 4f out: rdn and hdd over 1f out: sn wknd* **14/1**

0631 **9** *3/4* **Mandocello (FR)**[85] 2689 3-9-4 **71**.................... CharlieBennett 3 56
(Rod Millman) *trckd ldr: rdn over 2f out: wknd over 1f out* **11/1**

0040 **10** *1* **Daryana**[12] 5349 3-9-5 **72**.................... CharlesBishop 9 55
(Eve Johnson Houghton) *hld up towards rr of midfield: rdn and sme prog over 2f out: nvr threatened to get involved* **25/1**

3363 **11** *shd* **Isolate (FR)**[40] 4296 3-9-7 **74**.................... RobHornby 8 57
(Martyn Meade) *in tch: rdn over 3f out: wknd over 1f out* **6/1**[1]

4-00 **12** *5* **Extreme Force (IRE)**[26] 4838 3-9-2 **69**.................... DavidProbert 4 42
(Jonjo O'Neill) *towards rr of midfield: rdn over 3f out: wknd wl over 2f out* **100/1**

-256 **13** *3/4* **Aubretia (IRE)**[13] 5307 3-9-2 **69**.................... PatDobbs 5 41
(Richard Hannon) *in tch: rdn 3f out: wknd 2f out* **16/1**

2m 8.07s (-1.63) **Going Correction** -0.025s/f (Good) **13** Ran SP% **118.9**
Speed ratings (Par 100): **105,104,104,99,98 98,97,96,95,94 94,90,90**
CSF £64.94 CT £380.41 TOTE £7.20: £2.50, £3.60, £2.30; EX 71.40 Trifecta £377.90.
Owner Chelsea Thoroughbreds - La Bamba **Bred** Denis Noonan **Trained** East Everleigh, Wilts

FOCUS
Add 18yds. This was run at a good gallop and suited those ridden with a bit of patience. The first three finished clear and the winner completed a five-timer on the card for trainer Richard Hannon.
T/Jkpt: Not Won. T/Plt: £85.30 to a £1 stake. Pool: £87,186.14 - 745.43 winning units T/Qpdt: £24.00 to a £1 stake. Pool: £7,985.86 - 245.77 winning units **Tim Mitchell**

5590 NOTTINGHAM (L-H)

Tuesday, August 6

OFFICIAL GOING: Soft (good to soft in places; 5.9)
Wind: Fresh against Weather: Sunny spells

5780 MYRACING.COM FOR NOTTINGHAM TIPS BRITISH EBF NOVICE MEDIAN AUCTION STKS 6f 18y

5:25 (5:25) (Class 5) 2-Y-O **£3,881** (£1,155; £577; £288) **Stalls** Low

Form RPR

31 **1** **Sir Boris (IRE)**[5] 5591 2-9-9 0.................... RichardKingscote 8 90+
(Tom Dascombe) *mde all: rdn over 1f out: wnt readily clr ins fnl f* **5/6**[1]

04 **2** *4 1/2* **Order Of St John**[33] 4564 2-9-2 0.................... PaulMulrennan 6 70+
(John Ryan) *hmpd s: hld up: hdwy over 2f out: styd on to go 2nd nr fin: no ch w wnr (jockey said colt hung right inside the final furlong)* **12/1**[3]

44 **3** *1/2* **Stone Soldier**[22] 4984 2-9-2 0.................... BarryMcHugh 12 66
(James Given) *chsd ldrs: rdn over 2f out: styd on same pce fnl f* **20/1**

22 **4** *2* **Fanzone (IRE)**[13] 5288 2-9-2 0.................... HollieDoyle 9 60
(Archie Watson) *chsd ldrs: pushed along 1/2-way: rdn over 1f out: no ex ins fnl f* **4/1**[2]

5 *nse* **Fedora Fits** 2-8-8 0.................... MeganNicholls(3) 11 55+
(Mark Loughnane) *s.i.s: styd on ins fnl f: nvr nrr* **33/1**

36 **6** *1 1/4* **You're My Rock**[17] 5177 2-9-2 0.................... PaulHanagan 3 56
(Richard Fahey) *prom on outer: rdn over 2f out: wknd fnl f* **4/1**[2]

66 **7** *1* **Ten Chants**[10] 5433 2-9-2 0.................... LouisSteward 7 53
(Ed Dunlop) *hld up: swtchd lft and hdwy over 2f out: hung lft and nt clr run over 1f out: wknd ins fnl f* **25/1**

0 **8** *3/4* **Pull Harder Con**[18] 5125 2-9-2 0.................... DavidNolan 14 51
(Robyn Brisland) *s.i.s: sn pushed along in rr: n.d* **150/1**

9 *1/2* **Hootenanny (IRE)** 2-9-2 0.................... RaulDaSilva 2 49
(Adam West) *s.i.s: sn chsng ldrs on outer: rdn over 2f out: wknd fnl f* **66/1**

00 **10** *2 1/4* **Gypsy Rocker (IRE)**[64] 3419 2-9-2 0....................(h[1]) TomMarquand 4 43
(Brian Meehan) *chsd ldrs: rdn 1/2-way: wknd over 1f out* **40/1**

0 **11** *6* **Moonshine Mo**[66] 3335 2-9-2 0.................... RossaRyan 10 25
(Kevin Frost) *prom: rdn and lost pl over 3f out: wknd over 1f out* **50/1**

0 **12** *6* **Khalaty**[26] 4826 2-8-11 0.................... DavidEgan 13 2
(James Given) *s.i.s: sn pushed along in rr: wknd 1/2-way* **150/1**

13 *1 1/2* **American Dreamer** 2-9-2 0.................... ShaneKelly 5 2
(Jamie Osborne) *s.i.s and wnt rt s: a in rr (vet said colt lost his right hind shoe)* **50/1**

P **Honeysuckle Moon** 2-8-8 0.................... ConorMcGovern(3) 1
(Tim Easterby) *s.i.s: a bhd: eased fnl fr over 4f out: p.u over 2f out (jockey said filly lost her action around 4 1/2f out)* **50/1**

1m 17.55s (3.75) **Going Correction** +0.25s/f (Good) **14** Ran SP% **123.0**
Speed ratings (Par 94): **85,79,78,75,75 73,72,71,70,67 59,51,49,**
CSF £13.17 TOTE £1.60: £1.10, £2.80, £4.80; EX 11.60 Trifecta £125.50.
Owner Mr & Mrs R Scott **Bred** Parks Farm Stud **Trained** Malpas, Cheshire

FOCUS
An overcast evening and dry since 25mm of rain fell two days prior to this evening meeting. The official description was Soft (Good to Soft in Places) with a GoingStick reading of 5.9. A novice auction sprint lacking in depth. They came stands' side and the winner did it easily. He'll be up in grade from here.

5781 MYRACING.COM FREE TIPS EVERY DAY NURSERY H'CAP (JOCKEY CLUB GRASSROOTS NURSERY QUALIFIER) 1m 75y
6:00 (6:01) (Class 5) (0-75,77) 2-Y-O
£3,881 (£1,155; £577; £300; £300; £300) **Stalls** Centre

Form RPR

331 **1** **Gallaside (FR)**[40] 4289 2-9-10 **77** .... HollieDoyle 8 87+
(Archie Watson) *sn led: shkn up over 2f out: rdn over 1f out: sn edgd rt: stdy on* **4/5**[1]

6535 **2** ¾ **G For Gabrial (IRE)**[25] 4878 2-8-9 **62** .... PaulHanagan 5 68
(Richard Fahey) *chsd ldrs: rdn to chse wnr over 1f out: stdy on* **6/1**[2]

5055 **3** 2 **International Lion**[19] 5101 2-8-8 **61** ....(p) BarryMcHugh 3 63
(Richard Fahey) *s.i.s: hld up: hdwy over 2f out: rdn over 1f out: styd on same pce ins fnl f* **9/1**[3]

4040 **4** 1¾ **We Owen A Dragon**[17] 5177 2-8-12 **65** .... RichardKingscote 6 63
(Tom Dascombe) *led early: chsd wnr: wnt upsides 1/2-way tl rdn over 2f out: lost 2nd over 1f out: no ex fnl f* **16/1**

0010 **5** 2 **Rain Cap**[13] 5296 2-8-9 **62** .... FrannyNorton 4 55
(Mick Channon) *plld hrd and prom: lost pl over 5f out: rdn over 2f out: styd on same pce fr over 1f out* **9/1**[3]

3044 **6** 2 **Dorset Blue (IRE)**[11] 5382 2-9-0 **67** .... FergusSweeney 7 56
(Richard Hannon) *hld up: rdn over 3f out: nt trble ldrs* **16/1**

054 **7** 1¼ **King's View (IRE)**[22] 4992 2-9-2 **69** .... TomMarquand 1 55
(Richard Hannon) *sn pushed along and prom: rdn over 3f out: wknd over 1f out* **12/1**

1m 49.82s (3.12) **Going Correction** +0.25s/f (Good) **7 Ran SP% 109.3**
Speed ratings (Par 94): **94,93,91,89,87 85,84**
CSF £5.27 CT £20.79 TOTE £1.30: £1.10, £2.60; EX 6.00 Trifecta £26.00.
Owner Apple Tree Stud **Bred** Safsaf Canarias Srl & Mme Felix Miranda-Suarez **Trained** Upper Lambourn, W Berks

FOCUS
Add 6yds to the distance. Modest for the grade and all were up in trip. The pace was ordinary for the conditions.

5782 MYRACING SUPPORTS GORACINGGREEN H'CAP 1m 75y
6:30 (6:30) (Class 5) (0-75,76) 3-Y-O+
£3,881 (£1,155; £577; £300; £300; £300) **Stalls** Centre

Form RPR

3215 **1** **Saikung (IRE)**[18] 5140 3-9-5 **72** .... GeraldMosse 6 83
(Charles Hills) *s.s: hld up: nt clr run: swtchd rt and hdwy over 2f out: led over 1f out: rdn and hung lft ins fnl f: r.o wl* **7/1**[3]

4026 **2** 3½ **Dubai Acclaim (IRE)**[18] 5117 4-9-8 **68** .... PaulHanagan 1 72
(Richard Fahey) *chsd ldrs: led over 1f out: sn rdn and hdd: styd on same pce ins fnl f* **15/2**

2165 **3** 1¾ **Tangramm**[13] 5311 7-9-10 **70** ....(p) RyanTate 5 70
(Dean Ivory) *pushed along thrght: sn chsng ldrs: rdn and hung lft over 1f out: no ex ins fnl f* **11/1**

664 **4** 2¾ **Recondite (IRE)**[43] 4178 3-9-6 **73** .... RichardKingscote 4 66
(Ralph Beckett) *chsd ldrs: rdn and ev ch wl over 1f out: wknd ins fnl f* **3/1**[1]

0030 **5** *hd* **Madeleine Bond**[36] 4450 5-9-6 **73** .... GeorgiaDobie(7) 7 66
(Henry Candy) *led: hdd over 6f out: chsd ldr tl led again over 3f out: rdn and hdd over 1f out: wknd ins fnl f* **4/1**[2]

1100 **6** 1½ **Fitzrovia**[11] 5373 4-9-8 **68** .... PatCosgrave 2 58
(Ed de Giles) *hld up: hdwy over 2f out: rdn and looked hld whn hmpd 1f out: sn wknd* **4/1**[2]

0300 **7** ¾ **Orobas (IRE)**[14] 5274 7-8-10 **63** ....(v) VictorSantos(7) 9 51
(Lucinda Egerton) *pushed along and prom: led over 6f out: hdd over 3f out: rdn and wknd over 1f out* **33/1**

241 **8** 11 **Desert Lion**[27] 4774 3-9-9 **76** .... TrevorWhelan 8 38
(David Simcock) *restless in stalls: s.i.s: hld up: hdwy over 3f out: wknd 2f out* **7/1**[3]

1m 46.91s (0.21) **Going Correction** +0.25s/f (Good)
WFA 3 from 4yo+ 7lb **8 Ran SP% 113.0**
Speed ratings (Par 103): **108,104,102,100,99 98,97,86**
CSF £56.43 CT £572.07 TOTE £8.80: £2.40, £2.50, £3.20; EX 58.10 Trifecta £922.60.
Owner Kangyu International Racing (HK) Limited **Bred** M Fahy **Trained** Lambourn, Berks
■ Stewards' Enquiry : Ryan Tate two-day ban: interference & careless riding (Aug 20, 24)

FOCUS
Rail re-alignment added 6yds. Ordinary for the grade although the pace was decent for the conditions and the winner came from off it to score decisively. The form is taken at face value.

5783 FOLLOW @MYRACINGTIPS ON TWITTER NOVICE STKS 1m 2f 50y
7:00 (7:00) (Class 5) 3-Y-O+ **£3,881** (£1,155; £577; £288) **Stalls** Low

Form RPR

1 **1** **Last Look (IRE)**[31] 4641 3-8-13 0 .... GabrieleMalune(3) 8 95
(Saeed bin Suroor) *racd keenly in disp 2nd tl wnt clr 2nd over 4f out: led 2f out: rdn over 1f out: r.o: comf* **4/7**[1]

632- **2** 2 **Narynkol**[425] 3522 4-9-8 84 .... DavidEgan 1 89
(Roger Varian) *sn led: shkn up and hdd 2f out: styd on same pce wl ins fnl f* **9/4**[2]

06- **3** 13 **Omnivega (FR)**[297] 8186 3-9-0 0 .... StevieDonohoe 7 67
(David Simcock) *broke wl: plld hrd and led early: sn stdd to trck ldrs: shkn up over 2f out: wknd over 1f out* **6/1**[3]

4 4½ **Viking Prince (IRE)** 3-9-0 0 .... RichardKingscote 9 54
(Ian Williams) *s.i.s: hld up: hung lft and wknd over 2f out* **40/1**

5 1½ **Paintball Wizard (IRE)** 3-9-0 0 .... ShelleyBirkett 4 51
(Julia Feilden) *hld up: hung rt and wknd over 2f out* **100/1**

6 ½ **Welsh Rarebit**[113] 6-9-1 0 .... VictorSantos(7) 2 50
(Lucinda Egerton) *disp 2nd tl over 4f out: sn rdn: wknd over 2f out* **100/1**

2m 14.65s (1.25) **Going Correction** +0.25s/f (Good)
WFA 3 from 4yo+ 8lb **6 Ran SP% 113.1**
Speed ratings (Par 103): **105,103,93,89,88 87**
CSF £2.17 TOTE £1.40: £1.10, £1.60; EX 2.00 Trifecta £2.90.
Owner Godolphin **Bred** Godolphin **Trained** Newmarket, Suffolk

FOCUS
Add 6yds to the distance. Not a deep novice and they went no great pace. The market spoke correctly with the top two drawing well clear and the form looks strong, rated around the 1-2.

5784 MYRACING.COM FOR DAILY TIPS H'CAP 1m 2f 50y
7:30 (7:31) (Class 6) (0-60,62) 3-Y-O
£3,234 (£962; £481; £300; £300; £300) **Stalls** Low

Form RPR

5061 **1** **Crystal Tiara**[6] 5548 3-9-1 **54** 6ex .... GeraldMosse 4 60+
(Mick Channon) *sn led: qcknd over 3f out: rdn over 1f out: styd on: eased nr fin* **10/3**[1]

0452 **2** 1¼ **Uncertain Smile (IRE)**[13] 5287 3-9-8 **61** ....(h[1]) HollieDoyle 6 65
(Clive Cox) *hld up in tch: on outer: racd keenly: wnt 2nd over 6f out: rdn over 2f out: styd on same pce ins fnl f* **8/1**

-004 **3** *shd* **Ragstone Cowboy (IRE)**[27] 4794 3-9-4 **57** .... ShaneKelly 3 61
(Gary Moore) *sn prom: racd keenly: rdn over 3f out: r.o* **10/1**

0002 **4** 2½ **Tattenhams**[27] 4794 3-8-10 **49** .... FrannyNorton 2 48
(Adam West) *sn chsng ldr: lost 2nd over 6f out: remained handy: rdn over 2f out: hung lft and no ex ins fnl f* **12/1**

-620 **5** 7 **Purgatory**[40] 4284 3-9-6 **59** .... GeorgeWood 7 45
(Chris Wall) *s.i.s and pushed along early in rr: rdn over 3f out: styd on appr fnl f: nvr on terms (jockey said gelding was slowly away)* **11/1**

045 **6** 2¾ **Ocean Reach**[15] 5249 3-8-6 **48** .... JaneElliott(3) 9 30
(Richard Price) *led early: chsd ldrs: rdn over 2f out: wknd over 1f out (vet said filly lost her left hind shoe)* **12/1**

006 **7** 1¼ **Cinzento (IRE)**[17] 5193 3-8-13 **52** .... RichardKingscote 5 31
(Stuart Williams) *s.i.s: hld up: rdn over 3f out: nvr on terms* **5/1**[2]

0-40 **8** ¾ **Pinkie Pie (IRE)**[23] 4210 3-8-7 **46** oh1 .... KieranO'Neill 1 24
(Andrew Crook) *hld up: hdwy over 3f out: rdn and wknd over 1f out* **66/1**

0-03 **9** 2½ **Garrison Law**[19] 5085 3-9-7 **60** .... StevieDonohoe 11 33
(David Simcock) *s.i.s: hld up: racd keenly: rdn over 3f out: n.d* **13/2**

440 **10** 16 **Molotov (IRE)**[24] 4931 3-9-6 **59** .... TomMarquand 8 4
(Jamie Osborne) *s.i.s: in rr and drvn along 1/2-way: wknd over 3f out* **33/1**

-550 **11** 12 **Beaufort (IRE)**[50] 3926 3-9-9 **62** ....(v[1]) PaulMulrennan 10
(Michael Dods) *hld up: rdn and wknd over 3f out* **6/1**[3]

2m 14.52s (1.12) **Going Correction** +0.25s/f (Good) **11 Ran SP% 115.7**
Speed ratings (Par 98): **105,104,103,101,96 94,93,92,90,77 68**
CSF £29.72 CT £241.76 TOTE £4.30: £2.90, £2.20, £2.60; EX 30.70 Trifecta £217.30.
Owner The Sweet Partnership **Bred** Mike Channon Bloodstock Ltd **Trained** West Ilsley, Berks

FOCUS
Add 6yds to the distance. Few got into this very modest handicap. The winner built on her plating win.

5785 MYRACING.COM FREE BETS AND TIPS FILLIES' H'CAP 1m 2f 50y
8:00 (8:01) (Class 4) (0-80,82) 3-Y-O+
£6,469 (£1,925; £962; £481; £300; £300) **Stalls** Low

Form RPR

0000 **1** **Capriolette (IRE)**[22] 4994 4-9-5 **68** .... TomMarquand 6 74
(Ed Walker) *sn chsng ldr: rdn and edgd lft fr over 2f out: led over 1f out: styd on* **7/1**[3]

1650 **2** ¾ **Cuban Sun**[17] 5175 3-8-13 **70** .... BarryMcHugh 5 74
(James Given) *sn led at stdy pce: qcknd over 2f out: rdn and hdd over 1f out: styd on same pce towards fin* **9/1**

3255 **3** ¾ **Society Guest (IRE)**[10] 5445 3-8-13 **70** .... GeraldMosse 4 73
(Mick Channon) *hld up: effrt and nt clr run over 1f out: r.o: nt rch ldrs* **8/1**

-602 **4** *nk* **Spanish Aria**[15] 5253 3-9-11 **82** .... RobertHavlin 1 84
(John Gosden) *trckd ldrs: nt clr run and swtchd rt over 1f out: r.o* **1/1**[1]

0222 **5** *hd* **Lady Scatterley (FR)**[12] 5334 3-8-12 **69** .... PaulHanagan 2 71
(Tim Easterby) *plld hrd and prom: rdn over 2f out: r.o* **9/2**[2]

0052 **6** ½ **Overtrumped**[50] 3937 4-8-11 **60** ....(v[1]) RossaRyan 7 61
(Mike Murphy) *broke wl: sn stdd and lost pl: rdn over 2f out: r.o ins fnl f: nt rch ldrs* **9/1**

2m 16.79s (3.39) **Going Correction** +0.25s/f (Good)
WFA 3 from 4yo 8lb **6 Ran SP% 111.8**
Speed ratings (Par 102): **96,95,94,94,94 94**
CSF £62.34 TOTE £11.70: £3.80, £4.30; EX 56.80 Trifecta £304.40.
Owner Mr & Mrs Andrew Blaxland **Bred** Tom Wallace **Trained** Upper Lambourn, Berks
■ Stewards' Enquiry : Robert Havlin two-day ban: interference & careless riding (Aug 20, 24)

FOCUS
Add 6yds to the distance. A weak fillies' handicap for the grade, which was not run at a genuine gallop. The first two were always to the fore and they finished in a heap. The form is open to question and has been rated on the cautious side.

5786 MYRACING SUPPORTS MENTAL HEALTH AWARENESS H'CAP 6f 18y
8:30 (8:32) (Class 5) (0-75,74) 3-Y-O
£3,881 (£1,155; £577; £300; £300; £300) **Stalls** Low

Form RPR

0-06 **1** **Ugo Gregory**[17] 5176 3-8-5 **58** .... NathanEvans 6 69
(Tim Easterby) *chsd ldrs: shkn up to ld wl over 1f out: r.o: comf* **8/1**[3]

0422 **2** 2½ **Gregorian Girl**[4] 5622 3-8-8 **61** ....(p[1]) JoeyHaynes 8 64
(Dean Ivory) *chsd ldrs: led over 2f out: rdn and hdd wl over 1f out: styd on same pce ins fnl f* **7/4**[1]

004 **3** 1¼ **Soldier's Son**[24] 4927 3-8-7 **67** .... EmmaTaff(7) 4 66
(Henry Candy) *led: hdd over 2f out: no ex wl ins fnl f* **14/1**

3540 **4** ½ **Edgewood**[40] 4288 3-9-6 **73** .... KieranO'Neill 5 70
(Paul Midgley) *hld up: hdwy over 2f out: sn ev ch: rdn over 1f out: styd on same pce fnl f* **5/2**[2]

1-00 **5** *nk* **Absolute Dream (IRE)**[25] 4895 3-9-6 **73** .... PaulHanagan 2 69
(Richard Fahey) *pushed along early in rr: rdn and hung lft over 1f out: nt trble ldrs* **8/1**[3]

5500 **6** 3¼ **Constant**[22] 5002 3-9-7 **74** ....(p[1]) DavidNolan 1 60
(David O'Meara) *prom: rdn over 2f out: wknd fnl f* **16/1**

0606 **7** 7 **Beechwood Izzy (IRE)**[15] 5235 3-8-11 **64** .... TomMarquand 7 28
(Keith Dalgleish) *racd keenly: w ldr tl rdn over 2f out: wknd over 1f out* **8/1**[3]

1m 15.64s (1.84) **Going Correction** +0.25s/f (Good) **7 Ran SP% 110.8**
Speed ratings (Par 100): **97,93,92,91,90 86,77**
CSF £21.09 CT £184.85 TOTE £10.20: £4.70, £1.30; EX 31.50 Trifecta £484.40.
Owner F Gillespie **Bred** Brook Stud Bloodstock Ltd **Trained** Great Habton, N Yorks

FOCUS
An ordinary sprint handicap and they came up the centre of the track. Not the most solid form.
T/Plt: £304.50 to a £1 stake. Pool: £51,772.29 - 124.11 winning units T/Qpdt: £97.20 to a £1 stake. Pool: £5,855.75 - 44.58 winning units **Colin Roberts**

5737 RIPON (R-H)

Tuesday, August 6

OFFICIAL GOING: Good to soft (7.3)

Wind: light behind Weather: Sunshine and Could

5787 JOIN OVER 8,000 ROA MEMBERS APPRENTICE H'CAP 1m

5:50 (5:50) (Class 6) (0-60,58) 4-Y-0+

£3,105 (£924; £461; £300; £300; £300) **Stalls** Low

Form RPR

4040 1 **Lukoutoldmakezebak**[16] 5214 6-8-13 **45**......................(p) AledBeech 4 52
(David Thompson) *trckd ldrs: rdn over 2f out: led ins fnl f: kpt on* **16/1**

1122 2 1 1/4 **Betty Grable (IRE)**[15] 5239 5-9-6 **55**...................... ElishaWhittington(3) 7 59+
(Wilf Storey) *trckd ldrs: rdn over 2f out: kpt on to go 2nd fnl 50yds* **3/1**[1]

21-0 3 1/2 **Troop**[10] 5438 4-9-2 **51**...................... GavinAshton(3) 1 54
(Ann Duffield) *in tch: swtchd lft 2f out: sn hdwy: kpt on ins fnl f: wnt 3rd nr fin (vet said gelding lost its right hind shoe)* **20/1**

2204 4 nk **Tom's Anna (IRE)**[16] 5213 9-8-8 **45**...................... IsobelFrancis(5) 2 47
(Sean Regan) *prom: rdn to ld over 2f out: hdd ins fnl f: no ex and lost 2 more pls fnl 50yds* **12/1**

3000 5 1 1/4 **Rebel State (IRE)**[15] 5247 6-8-11 **53**......................(p) OwenPayton(10) 9 52
(Jedd O'Keeffe) *hld up in rr: rdn and hdwy on inner over 1f out: kpt on ins fnl f* **9/1**

0203 6 1 **Rosy Ryan (IRE)**[15] 5247 9-9-2 **48**...................... EllaMcCain 10 45
(Tina Jackson) *hld up in midfield: rdn along 3f out: swtchd lft over 1f out: kpt on: nvr threatened ldrs* **8/1**[3]

3240 7 1 **Snooker Jim**[36] 4460 4-9-3 **52**......................(t) TobyEley(3) 14 47
(Steph Hollinshead) *dwlt and swtchd rt to ins rail: hld up in midfield: hmpd over 6f out: rdn over 2f out: plugged on* **11/1**

0043 8 4 1/2 **Wynfaul The Wizard (USA)**[10] 5446 4-8-8 **45**......................(b[1]) GeorgeBass(5) 3 29
(Laura Morgan) *s.i.s: hld up nvr threatened* **33/1**

00-0 9 1 1/2 **Jessinamillion**[40] 4293 5-8-9 **51**......................(p) VictoriaSanchez(10) 12 32
(James Bethell) *hld up: nudged along and sme hdwy over 1f out: eased towards fin* **20/1**

0456 10 1/2 **Barney Bullet (IRE)**[19] 5100 4-8-6 **45**......................(e) NickBarratt-Atkin(7) 18 25
(Noel Wilson) *dwlt: hld up in midfield: rdn along over 2f out: nvr involved* **33/1**

0026 11 1 1/4 **Bigbadboy (IRE)**[15] 5248 6-9-0 **46**...................... JoshQuinn 11 23
(Clive Mulhall) *midfield: rdn along 3f out: wknd over 1f out* **10/1**

4600 12 nse **Adventureman**[15] 5247 7-9-2 **48**......................(b) JessicaCooley 6 25
(Ruth Carr) *dwlt but sn led: rdn and hdd over 2f out: wknd over 1f out* **25/1**

2-00 13 nk **Monsieur Jimmy**[10] 5434 7-9-7 **58**...................... ZakWheatley(5) 13 34
(Brian Ellison) *hld up: pushed along and sme hdwy on outside 4f out: wknd 2f out* **12/1**

0002 14 2 1/2 **French Flyer (IRE)**[19] 5099 4-8-13 **48**...................... HarryRussell(3) 5 18
(Rebecca Bastiman) *prom: rdn 3f out: wknd 2f out* **9/2**[2]

0040 15 13 **Amy Blair**[24] 4916 6-8-11 **46** ow1......................(h) AidenBlakemore(3) 17
(Stef Keniry) *in tch on outside: rdn 4f out: wknd qckly and t.o* **25/1**

-050 16 1/2 **Magic Ship (IRE)**[29] 4728 4-8-10 **45**...................... RussellHarris(3) 8
(John Norton) *midfield: wknd 3f out and bhd* **50/1**

1m 41.9s (0.90) **Going Correction** +0.025s/f (Good) **16 Ran SP% 128.0**

Speed ratings (Par 101): **96,94,94,93,92 91,90,86,84,84 82,82,82,80,67 66**

CSF £61.62 CT £1028.89 TOTE £27.70: £5.70, £1.50, £1.30, £3.00; EX 128.00 Trifecta £604.30.

Owner NE1 Racing Club **Bred** Peter J McMahon **Trained** Bolam, Co Durham

FOCUS

Add 4 yards. A modest apprentice riders' handicap. Three of the first four horses home were drawn low and raced relatively prominently. Sound but limited form.

5788 ROA: A VOICE FOR RACEHORSE OWNERS EBF FILLIES' NOVICE MEDIAN AUCTION STKS (PLUS 10 RACE) 5f

6:20 (6:22) (Class 5) 2-Y-O

£3,881 (£1,155; £577; £288) **Stalls** High

Form RPR

02 1 **Vintage Times**[7] 5514 2-8-12 0...................... DavidAllan 6 73
(Tim Easterby) *mde all: pushed along over 1f out: rdn out ins fnl f* **13/8**[2]

6 2 3/4 **Hot Affair**[13] 5317 2-8-12 0...................... DanielTudhope 2 71+
(Tom Dascombe) *wnt rt s: trckd ldr: rdn to chse ldr appr fnl f: drvn and kpt on* **6/1**[3]

220 3 3 3/4 **Ruby Wonder**[81] 2805 2-8-12 71...................... RobbieDowney 7 57
(David O'Meara) *prom: rdn 2f out: no ex in 3rd ins fnl f* **6/1**[3]

41 4 nk **Cloudea (IRE)**[17] 5197 2-9-4 0...................... TonyHamilton 1 62+
(Richard Fahey) *dwlt and carried rt s: sn chsd ldrs: rdn along 2f out: edgd rt and outpcd appr fnl f: kpt on same pce (jockey said filly jumped right handed leaving the stalls)* **6/4**[1]

40 5 1 3/4 **Lady Celia**[13] 5294 2-8-9 0...................... ConnorMurtagh(3) 3 50
(Richard Fahey) *hld up: sn pushed along and outpcd: kpt on ins fnl f: nvr involved* **40/1**

5 6 9 **Midnight Mimosa (IRE)**[41] 4237 2-8-12 0...................... RachelRichardson 4 17
(Tim Easterby) *wnt lft s: a outplcd in rr* **33/1**

59.74s (0.34) **Going Correction** +0.025s/f (Good) **6 Ran SP% 112.0**

Speed ratings (Par 91): **98,96,90,90,87 73**

CSF £11.70 TOTE £3.30: £1.80, £2.10; EX 10.20 Trifecta £37.50.

Owner Ontoawinner 10 & Partner **Bred** Mrs D O'Brien **Trained** Great Habton, N Yorks

FOCUS

A fair juvenile fillies' novice sprint contest. The favourite was carried right from an unfavourable draw leaving the gates and the well-backed second-favourite made all up the near rail. The ratings will prove fluid.

5789 ROA OWNERS JACKPOT NURSERY H'CAP 6f

6:50 (6:51) (Class 5) (0-70,70) 2-Y-O

£3,752 (£1,116; £557; £300; £300; £300) **Stalls** High

Form RPR

051 1 hd **Singe Anglais (IRE)**[21] 5017 2-8-9 **63**...................... FayeMcManoman(5) 5 66+
(Nigel Tinkler) *rrd s and slowly away: hld up far side: hdwy and chsd ldr over 1f out: checked by ldr ins fnl f: swtchd lft and 1 1/2 l down: kpt on wl fnl 110yds: gaining at fin: fin 2nd: plcd 1st (jockey said gelding reared leaving the stalls)* **11/1**

3064 2 **War Of Clans (IRE)**[22] 4985 2-8-7 **61**...................... HarrisonShaw(5) 2 65
(K R Burke) *led quartet far side: rdn and overall ldr over 1f out: wandered appr fnl f: edgd rt and impeded rival ins fnl f: drvn all out: fin 1st: plcd 2nd* **12/1**

050 3 3/4 **Little Ted**[31] 4623 2-8-12 **61**...................... JamesSullivan 3 62
(Tim Easterby) *in tch far side: rdn and hdwy to chse ldr over 1f out: kpt on: 3rd of 4 in gp* **25/1**

340 4 nk **What A Business (IRE)**[13] 5296 2-9-2 **65**...................... BenCurtis 4 65+
(Roger Fell) *swtchd lft s to r stands' side: sn prom: rdn over 2f out: led gp appr fnl f: kpt on: 1st of 11 in gp* **5/1**[2]

5545 5 3/4 **Knightcap**[13] 5296 2-9-1 **64**...................... DavidAllan 12 62+
(Tim Easterby) *led stands' side gp and overall ldr tl over 1f out: rdn and hdd in gp appr fnl f: kpt on: 2nd of 11 in gp* **11/2**[3]

3661 6 1/2 **Isobar Wind (IRE)**[17] 5196 2-9-7 **70**......................(v) DanielTudhope 8 66+
(David Evans) *dwlt: hld up on stands' side: rdn and hdwy over 1f out: kpt on ins fnl f: 3rd of 11 in gp (jockey said gelding missed the break)* **10/3**[1]

0063 7 hd **Ice Skate**[22] 4985 2-8-3 **52**...................... DuranFentiman 13 48+
(Tim Easterby) *in tch stands' side: rdn and hdwy to for ld in gp over 1f out: one pce ins fnl f: 4th of 11 in gp* **16/1**

0004 8 3 3/4 **Mr Gus (IRE)**[18] 5146 2-8-5 **54**...................... PaddyMathers 11 38
(Richard Fahey) *dwlt: hld up stands' side: outpcd tl kpt on fr over 1f out: 5th of 11 in gp (jockey said colt missed the break)* **8/1**

666 9 1 **Secret Identity**[32] 4583 2-9-1 **64**...................... JackGarritty 14 45
(Jedd O'Keeffe) *chsd ldrs stands' side: rdn over 2f out: wknd over 1f out: 6th of 11 in gp* **9/1**

055 10 3 1/4 **Shepherds Way (IRE)**[11] 5388 2-9-1 **64**...................... GrahamLee 15 36
(Michael Dods) *in tch stands' side: rdn over 2f out: wknd over 1f out: 7th of 11 in gp* **16/1**

3060 11 3/4 **River Of Kings (IRE)**[17] 5185 2-9-3 **66**...................... JoeFanning 6 35
(Keith Dalgleish) *swtchd lft after s to r stands' side: a towards rr: 8th of 11 in gp* **25/1**

4400 12 1/2 **Il Maestro (IRE)**[14] 5275 2-9-0 **63**......................(v) JasonHart 7 31
(John Quinn) *midfield on outer of stands' side gp: rdn over 2f out: wknd over 1f out: 9th of 11 in gp* **20/1**

063 13 shd **Schumli**[13] 5294 2-8-12 **61**...................... RobbieDowney 10 28
(David O'Meara) *midfield: rdn along 2f out: outpcd and btn whn hmpd appr fnl f: 10th of 11 in gp* **33/1**

000 14 hd **Fulbeck Rose**[17] 5196 2-8-2 **47** oh4 ow2...................... AndrewMullen 9 18
(Nigel Tinkler) *wnt lft s: a in rr stands' side: last of 11 in gp* **100/1**

430 15 1 **Typsy Toad**[14] 5273 2-8-6 **58**...................... SeanDavis(3) 1 22
(Richard Fahey) *chsd ldr far side: rdn along 3f out: wknd 2f out* **28/1**

1m 13.09s (0.59) **Going Correction** +0.025s/f (Good) **15 Ran SP% 123.9**

Speed ratings (Par 94): **96,97,95,95,94 93,93,88,87,82 81,81,80,80,79**

CSF £128.98 CT £1938.77 TOTE £13.90: £4.90, £3.30, £5.90; EX 137.90 Trifecta £1269.10.

Owner Geoff Maidment & John Raybould **Bred** Knocktartan House Stud **Trained** Langton, N Yorks

■ Stewards' Enquiry : Harrison Shaw two-day ban: interference & careless riding (Aug 20, 24)

FOCUS

An ordinary nursery. Three of the four horses who raced far side finished notably ahead of four horses who came slightly clear up the near rail. The first past the post hampered the fast-finishing runner-up in the final furlong and the stewards felt the interference was enough to reverse the placings.

5790 ROA REWARDS MEMBERS H'CAP 1m

7:20 (7:20) (Class 3) (0-95,96) 3-Y-O

£9,451 (£2,829; £1,414; £708) **Stalls** Low

Form RPR

1142 1 **Caustic Love (IRE)**[12] 5333 3-8-9 **77**...................... ShaneGray 2 86
(Keith Dalgleish) *trckd ldr: pushed along over 2f out: drvn to chal appr fnl f: led 110yds out: kpt on* **9/4**[2]

1046 2 1 3/4 **Divinity**[17] 5187 3-9-7 **89**...................... BenCurtis 1 93
(K R Burke) *led: rdn along over 2f out: pressed appr fnl f: sn drvn: hdd 110yds out: one pce* **7/2**[3]

3162 3 1 3/4 **Oasis Prince**[18] 5150 3-10-0 **96**...................... JoeFanning 3 96
(Mark Johnston) *trckd ldr: rdn along 3f out: outpcd and hld over 1f out* **13/8**[1]

132 4 hd **Sandret (IRE)**[25] 4895 3-8-12 **80**...................... AndrewMullen 4 80
(Ben Haslam) *hld up: pushed along over 3f out: bit clsr 2f out: drvn and no further imp* **4/1**

1m 39.91s (-1.09) **Going Correction** +0.025s/f (Good) **4 Ran SP% 111.1**

Speed ratings (Par 104): **106,104,102,102**

CSF £10.11 TOTE £4.00; EX 9.90 Trifecta £18.40.

Owner Weldspec Glasgow Limited **Bred** Mrs C Holohan **Trained** Carluke, S Lanarks

FOCUS

Add 4 yards. The feature contest was a good little 3yo handicap. The second-favourite came through to win a shade cosily from off a decent gallop. The form's rated around the runner-up.

5791 REWARDING OWNERSHIP WITH THE ROA H'CAP 5f

7:50 (7:51) (Class 4) (0-85,83) 3-Y-O

£5,369 (£1,597; £798; £399; £300; £300) **Stalls** High

Form RPR

60- 1 **Count D'orsay (IRE)**[41] 4261 3-9-0 **76**...................... DavidAllan 5 84
(Tim Easterby) *chsd ldrs: rdn into narrow ld ins fnl f: drvn and kpt on* **7/2**[3]

2230 2 3/4 **James Watt (IRE)**[10] 5442 3-9-7 **83**...................... DanielTudhope 4 90+
(Michael Bell) *hld up in tch: gng wl but short of room appr fnl f: swtchd rt to outer jst ins fnl f: rdn and r.o wl (jockey said gelding was denied a clear run approximately 1 1/2f out)* **9/4**[1]

4215 3 1/2 **Ginvincible**[27] 4783 3-8-3 **65**...................... JamesSullivan 3 68
(James Given) *dwlt sltly: hld up: pushed along and hdwy on outer over 1f out: rdn to chal ins fnl f: one pce towards fin* **9/1**

2256 4 1 1/2 **True Hero**[12] 5356 3-9-1 **80**...................... RowanScott(3) 2 78
(Nigel Tinkler) *in tch: pushed along to chse ldrs over 1f out: rdn and one pce ins fnl f* **14/1**

2310 5 nse **Exalted Angel (FR)**[32] 4609 3-9-4 **80**...................... BenCurtis 1 78
(K R Burke) *cl up on outer: rdn 2f out: drvn into narrow ld 1f out: sn hdd: no ex fnl 50yds* **13/2**

2104 6 2 1/4 **Abate**[24] 4908 3-8-11 **73**...................... AndrewMullen 7 63
(Adrian Nicholls) *pressed ldr: rdn into narrow ld 2f out: hdd 1f out: sn wknd* **11/4**[2]

051 7 hd **Hawk In The Sky**[31] 4629 3-8-9 **71**...................... ConnorBeasley 6 60
(Richard Whitaker) *led narrowly: rdn and hdd 2f out: wknd fnl f* **20/1**

59.42s (0.02) **Going Correction** +0.025s/f (Good) **7 Ran SP% 114.4**

Speed ratings (Par 102): **100,98,98,95,95 91,91**

CSF £11.85 TOTE £3.70: £2.80, £1.40; EX 12.90 Trifecta £79.40.

Owner Ambrose Turnbull & John Cruces **Bred** Corrin Stud **Trained** Great Habton, N Yorks

The Form Book Flat 2019, Raceform Ltd, Newbury, RG14 5SJ

FOCUS
A decent 3yo sprint handicap. The third-favourite's winning time was marginally quicker than the earlier C&D juvenile fillies' novice contest. The winner improved on his latest breakthrough win.

5792 BENEFITS FOR ROA MEMBERS AT ROA.CO.UK H'CAP 1m 4f 10y
8:20 (8:20) (Class 5) (0-70,70) 3-Y-O
£3,752 (£1,116; £557; £300; £300; £300) **Stalls** Centre

Form RPR
3416 1 **Theatro (IRE)**[40] 4291 3-9-7 **70**............ GrahamLee 7 82+
(Jedd O'Keeffe) *trckd ldrs: rdn over 2f out: drvn to chal strly appr fnl f: led 75yds out: styd on wl* **3/1**[3]
5433 2 1 ¾ **Euro Implosion (IRE)**[24] 4913 3-8-13 **62**............ JoeFanning 5 72
(Keith Dalgleish) *prom: rdn to ld 3f out: drvn and strly pressed appr fnl f: hdd 75yds out: no ex* **5/2**[1]
0542 3 6 **Menin Gate (IRE)**[17] 5175 3-8-12 **61**............(p) TonyHamilton 2 61
(Richard Fahey) *in tch: rdn over 2f out: outpcd in dispute of 3rd appr fnl f: plugged on ins fnl f* **6/1**
2210 4 1 **Neileta**[6] 5556 3-8-12 **61**............(p) DavidAllan 8 59
(Tim Easterby) *trckd ldrs: drvn over 2f out: outpcd in dispute of 3rd appr fnl f: no ex ins fnl f* **6/1**
1421 5 1 ¼ **Gold Arch**[28] 4769 3-9-3 **66**............(b) DanielMuscutt 3 62
(David Lanigan) *dwlt: hld up in tch: rdn and hdwy on outer 3f out: drvn and outpcd in dispute of 3rd appr fnl f: wknd ins fnl f (jockey said gelding became unbalanced on the undulations on this occasion)* **11/4**[2]
4660 6 1 ¼ **Alpasu (IRE)**[50] 3931 3-9-5 **68**............(p) ConnorBeasley 4 62
(Adrian Nicholls) *led: rdn and hdd 3f out: outpcd and btn over 1f out* **33/1**
2-40 7 32 **Coup De Gold (IRE)**[34] 4520 3-9-7 **70**............(h) BenCurtis 1 13
(David Thompson) *dwlt: hld up in rr: wknd and bhd over 3f out* **33/1**

2m 37.19s (0.89) **Going Correction** +0.025s/f (Good) **7 Ran SP% 114.7**
Speed ratings (Par 100): **98,96,92,92,91 90,69**
CSF £11.04 CT £39.71 TOTE £3.30: £2.00, £1.60; EX 14.90 Trifecta £53.60.
Owner Geoff & Sandra Turnbull **Bred** Elwick Stud **Trained** Middleham Moor, N Yorks

FOCUS
Add 4 yards. An ordinary middle-distance 3yo handicap. The right two horses came clear of their opponents and the third-favourite won readily. The form looks sound.
T/Plt: £934.60 to a £1 stake. Pool: £70,441.12 - 55.02 winning units T/Qpdt: £123.40 to a £1 stake. Pool: £7,962.82 - 47.74 winning units **Andrew Sheret**

5601 BATH (L-H)
Wednesday, August 7

OFFICIAL GOING: Good to firm (8.0)
Wind: Light against Weather: Sunny periods

5793 BEST FREE TIPS AT VALUERATER.CO.UK H'CAP (BATH SUMMER SPRINT SERIES QUALIFIER) 5f 10y
2:10 (2:10) (Class 6) (0-65,67) 3-Y-O+
£2,781 (£827; £413; £300; £300; £300) **Stalls** Centre

Form RPR
3633 1 **Three Little Birds**[12] 5372 4-9-11 **67**............ WilliamCarver(5) 7 75
(Sylvester Kirk) *hld up bhd ldrs: hdwy 2f out: shkn up to ld jst over 1f out: edgd lft: r.o: readily* **13/8**[1]
1623 2 1 ¾ **Big Time Maybe (IRE)**[14] 5318 4-9-9 **60**............(p) HarryBentley 3 62
(Michael Attwater) *trckd ldrs: rdn and ev ch jst over 1f out: kpt on but nt pce of wnr fnl f* **3/1**[2]
2225 3 4 **Edged Out**[6] 5582 9-8-13 **55**............ PoppyBridgwater(5) 4 42
(Christopher Mason) *led: rdn and hdd jst over 1f out: kpt on same pce* **5/1**[3]
06-1 4 1 **Swiss Chill**[14] 5306 4-9-10 **61**............ HollieDoyle 5 45
(Clive Cox) *trckd ldr: rdn 2f out: short of room briefly jst over 1f out: kpt on same pce fnl f (jockey said gelding suffered interference inside the final furlong)* **6/1**
1136 5 5 **Ever Rock (IRE)**[27] 4844 3-9-0 **61**............ LauraCoughlan(7) 6 26
(J S Moore) *s.i.s: sn outpcd in detached last: sme minor late prog: nvr on terms (jockey said filly was slowly away)* **11/1**
2006 6 ¾ **Coronation Cottage**[14] 5289 5-10-1 **66**............ TomQueally 1 29
(Malcolm Saunders) *trckd ldrs: rdn 2f out: wknd ent fnl f* **12/1**
-064 7 9 **Layla's Dream**[9] 5492 3-9-2 **56**............(h[1]) DaneO'Neill 2
(Tony Carroll) *in last pair: rdn wl over 2f out: nvr any imp: wknd over 1f out (jockey said filly moved poorly)* **40/1**

1m 1.42s (-0.58) **Going Correction** -0.05s/f (Good)
WFA 3 from 4yo+ 3lb **7 Ran SP% 112.5**
Speed ratings (Par 101): **102,99,92,91,83 82,67**
CSF £6.37 TOTE £2.00: £1.30, £2.90; EX 8.80 Trifecta £20.70.
Owner Miss Amanda Rawding **Bred** T J Cooper **Trained** Upper Lambourn, Berks

FOCUS
A well-run modest sprint handicap in which two finished clear.

5794 EBF MAIDEN STKS 5f 160y
2:40 (2:40) (Class 5) 2-Y-O **£3,428** (£1,020; £509; £254) **Stalls** Centre

Form RPR
02 1 **Modern British Art (IRE)**[23] 4992 2-9-5 0............ JasonWatson 6 80+
(Michael Bell) *mde all: kpt on wl: unchal* **5/4**[1]
44 2 1 ½ **Aryaaf (IRE)**[33] 4583 2-9-0 0............ DaneO'Neill 5 70
(Simon Crisford) *trckd ldrs: rdn to chse wnr over 2f out: sn hung lft: nt pce to chal* **4/1**[3]
3 4 **Just May** 2-9-0 0............ HollieDoyle 1 60+
(Clive Cox) *s.i.s: sn pushed along in last: hdwy to chse ldng pair over 2f out: nt pce to get on terms (jockey said filly was slowly away and ran green)* **6/4**[2]
50 4 3 ¼ **Butterfly Pose (IRE)**[11] 5469 2-9-0 0............ TrevorWhelan 3 46
(J S Moore) *trckd ldrs: rdn over 2f out: wknd fnl f (sddle slipped) (jockey said the saddle slipped)* **40/1**
05 5 3 ½ **Born For Fun (IRE)**[14] 5288 2-9-5 0............ LukeMorris 2 40
(Ali Stronge) *racd keenly: trckd ldr tl rdn over 2f out: wknd ent fnl f* **100/1**
6 nk **Calbuco** 2-9-5 0............(w) HarryBentley 4 39
(Rod Millman) *trckd ldrs: rdn over 2f out: wknd ent fnl f* **20/1**

1m 12.11s (1.01) **Going Correction** -0.05s/f (Good) **6 Ran SP% 112.6**
Speed ratings (Par 94): **91,89,83,79,74 74**
CSF £6.71 TOTE £1.60: £1.10, £1.70; EX 5.80 Trifecta £8.40.
Owner R A Green **Bred** E Phelan **Trained** Newmarket, Suffolk

FOCUS
The market leader got away smartly and managed to make all the running. The first two were nicely in front of the remainder, with the runner-up rated as improving.

5795 SKY SPORTS RACING SKY 415 FILLIES' H'CAP 1m 2f 37y
3:10 (3:12) (Class 5) (0-66,68) 3-Y-O+
£3,428 (£1,020; £509; £300; £300; £300) **Stalls** Low

Form RPR
-212 1 **Princess Way (IRE)**[32] 4657 5-9-7 **63**............(v) RhiainIngram(5) 8 72
(Paul George) *trckd ldr: led over 5f out: kicked clr 3f out: styd on wl and a holding on fnl f: pushed out* **10/1**
0214 2 1 **Perfect Grace**[14] 5307 3-9-9 **68**............ HollieDoyle 1 75
(Archie Watson) *trckd ldrs: rdn over 2f out: chsd wnr over 1f out: styd on fnl f but a being hld* **3/1**[2]
0-05 3 4 **Ramatuelle**[28] 4771 3-8-3 **48**............ LukeMorris 6 47
(Sir Mark Prescott Bt) *rousted along leaving stalls: chsd ldrs: rdn over 3f out: sn hung lft: nt pce to chal but styd on into 3rd ins fnl f* **7/2**[3]
0150 4 1 **Couldn't Could She**[14] 5316 4-10-0 **65**............ JimmyQuinn 5 62
(Adam West) *hld up: hdwy over 3f out: sn rdn: chsd ldng pair over 1f out: nt pce to chal: no ex fnl 120yds* **18/1**
4441 5 1 **Trelinney (IRE)**[20] 5085 3-9-6 **65**............ MartinDwyer 4 60
(Marcus Tregoning) *s.i.s: mid-div: hdwy over 3f out: rdn to chse wnr over 2f out tl over 1f out: no ex fnl f (trainer could offer no explanation for the filly's performance)* **11/8**[1]
0545 6 1 **Delirium (IRE)**[26] 4869 5-8-12 **49**............(p) AdamMcNamara 9 42
(Ed de Giles) *hld up: rdn and stdy prog fr over 2f out: drifted lft ent fnl f: nvr gng pce to get involved (jockey said mare was never travelling)* **14/1**
132/ 7 2 **Kiruna Peak (IRE)**[17] 5275 5-9-5 **63**............ KateLeahy(7) 3 52
(Fergal O'Brien) *mid-div tl outpcd 3f out: no threat after* **25/1**
1006 8 2 ½ **Brockagh Cailin**[35] 4499 4-9-6 **57**............(p[1]) TrevorWhelan 2 41
(J S Moore) *s.i.s: a towards rr (vet said filly lost both hind shoes)* **33/1**
000 9 30 **Valentine Mist (IRE)**[4] 5680 7-8-9 **46** oh1............ JohnFahy 7
(James Grassick) *led tl over 5f out: wknd over 2f out: t.o* **100/1**

2m 9.36s (-1.74) **Going Correction** -0.05s/f (Good)
WFA 3 from 4yo+ 8lb **9 Ran SP% 118.1**
Speed ratings (Par 100): **104,103,100,99,98 97,96,94,70**
CSF £40.72 CT £129.96 TOTE £8.00: £2.60, £1.10, £1.40; EX 28.40 Trifecta £245.30.
Owner David Renfree And Paul George **Bred** Tally-Ho Stud **Trained** Crediton, Devon

FOCUS
Add 6yds, making the official distance 1m2f 43yds. A competitive race for the level, run at a solid pace. The winner is progressing.

5796 BATH & WEST WEALTH MANAGEMENT H'CAP 1m 2f 37y
3:40 (3:42) (Class 3) (0-90,90) 3-Y-O **£7,561** (£2,263; £1,131; £566; £282) **Stalls** Low

Form RPR
0452 1 **Time Change**[25] 4930 4-9-4 **80**............ HarryBentley 3 88+
(Ralph Beckett) *trckd ldrs: shkn up over 2f out: led jst over 1f out: styd on wl: comf* **4/1**[2]
5-0 2 2 ½ **Mutaabeq (IRE)**[33] 4613 4-10-0 **90**............(h[1]) DaneO'Neill 6 93
(Marcus Tregoning) *trckd ldrs: rdn over 2f out: sn hanging lft: chal over 1f out: styd on but nt pce of wnr fnl f (jockey said gelding hung left)* **8/1**
6303 3 hd **Nonios (IRE)**[23] 4997 7-9-1 **82**............(h) DylanHogan(5) 7 85
(David Simcock) *hld up in last pair: hdwy over 2f out: sn rdn: ev ch jst over 1f out: sn hld by wnr: styd on same pce* **10/1**
150/ 4 nse **Banish (USA)**[286] 8188 6-9-1 **77**............(t) HayleyTurner 1 80?
(Tom George) *trckd ldrs: nt clrest of runs but nvr stopped whn switching rt over 1f out: rdn ent fnl f: fin wl but no ch w wnr* **66/1**
4363 5 1 **Michele Strogoff**[7] 5564 6-9-8 **84**............ LukeMorris 5 85
(Michael Appleby) *led: rdn whn strly chal over 2f out: hld onto narrow advantage tl hdd jst over 1f out: no ex fnl 120yds* **7/1**[3]
1360 6 2 **Uther Pendragon (IRE)**[31] 4704 4-9-0 **76**............(p) TrevorWhelan 2 73
(J S Moore) *hld up in last pair: rdn over 2f out: kpt on but nt pce to get involved* **20/1**
1-33 7 12 **Mubariz**[34] 4553 3-9-4 **88**............(p) JasonWatson 4 89+
(Roger Charlton) *trckd ldrs: rdn for str chal over 2f out: stl ev ch whn bdly squeezed out jst over 1f out: eased whn no ch after (jockey said gelding lost his action after suffering interference)* **10/11**[1]

2m 9.39s (-1.71) **Going Correction** -0.05s/f (Good)
WFA 3 from 4yo+ 8lb **7 Ran SP% 111.3**
Speed ratings (Par 107): **104,102,101,101,101 99,89**
CSF £33.08 TOTE £6.10: £3.10, £3.30; EX 39.80 Trifecta £140.60.
Owner R Barnett **Bred** W & R Barnett Ltd **Trained** Kimpton, Hants

FOCUS
Add 6yds, making the official distance 1m2f 43yds. A useful event, if ordinary for the grade, won nicely by the only filly in the field.

5797 SKY SPORTS RACING VIRGIN 535 H'CAP 1m
4:10 (4:14) (Class 6) (0-65,67) 3-Y-O
£2,781 (£827; £413; £300; £300; £300) **Stalls** Low

Form RPR
0053 1 **Lucky Number**[13] 5334 3-9-3 **64**............ GeorgiaCox(3) 6 71+
(William Haggas) *trckd ldrs: rdn to ld over 2f out: sn in command: styd on wl: comf (jockey said gelding suffered interference upon leaving the stalls)* **5/1**[3]
4003 2 1 ¾ **Parknacilla (IRE)**[14] 5293 3-8-1 **48**............(p) GabrieleMalune(3) 8 50
(Henry Spiller) *mid-div: hdwy over 2f out: sn rdn: drifted lft whn chsng wnr over 1f out: styd on but a being comf hld (jockey said filly hung left under pressure)* **9/1**
0-00 3 2 ¼ **Clipsham Tiger (IRE)**[34] 4563 3-7-9 **46** oh1............ GeorgeRooke(7) 9 43
(Michael Appleby) *mid-div: rdn and hdwy 2f out: nt clr run ent fnl f: sn chsng ldng pair: styd on but nt pce to get on terms* **40/1**
0-05 4 1 **Forthwith**[21] 5062 3-8-2 **46** oh1............(h[1]) HayleyTurner 2 41
(Tony Carroll) *led: rdn and hdd over 2f out: styd on same pce* **16/1**
-150 5 ½ **Sea Of Marengo (IRE)**[9] 5497 3-9-6 **64**............ TrevorWhelan 3 57
(Grace Harris) *mid-div: rdn and hdwy over 1f out: styd on same pce fnl f (vet said gelding lost his right fore shoe)* **33/1**
0-00 6 ¾ **Duke Of Yorkie (IRE)**[32] 4642 3-8-2 **46**............ JimmyQuinn 7 38
(Adam West) *s.i.s: bhd: rdn over 2f out: styd on fnl f: nvr any threat (jockey said gelding was slowly away)* **40/1**
620 7 ¾ **Winterkoenigin**[13] 5354 3-9-9 **67**............(p) DaneO'Neill 11 57
(David Lanigan) *hld up towards rr: rdn over 1f out: styd on ins fnl f but nvr any threat* **5/1**[3]
5000 8 nse **Dance To Freedom**[28] 4794 3-8-5 **49**............ MartinDwyer 12 39
(Stuart Williams) *trckd ldr: rdn over 2f out: sn edgd lft: one pce fnl f* **16/1**

6000 **9** *1* **Society Sweetheart (IRE)**[14] 5293 3-7-9 **46**.........(b[1]) IsobelFrancis(7) 1 33
(J S Moore) *rdn over 2f out: hung rt and fdd ins fnl f (jockey said filly hung right inside the final furlong)* **33/1**

6-05 **10** *1* **Denis The Diva**[60] 3574 3-9-7 **65**.......... LukeMorris 4 50
(Rae Guest) *trckd ldrs: rdn over 2f out: wknd ent fnl f* **10/1**

0456 **11** *1* **Corrida De Toros (IRE)**[29] 4767 3-9-9 **67**.........(p[1]) AdamMcNamara 10 50
(Ed de Giles) *mid-div: rdn over 2f out: wkng whn tight for room over 1f out (jockey said colt stopped quickly; vet said colt lost his left hind shoe)* **3/1**[1]

0231 **12** *nk* **Toro Dorado**[15] 5284 3-9-8 **66**.......... TomQueally 13 48
(Ed Dunlop) *hld up towards rr: hdwy over 2f out: sn rdn: nvr threatened ldrs: wknd ent fnl f* **4/1**[2]

1m 41.56s (-0.14) **Going Correction** -0.05s/f (Good) **12 Ran SP% 119.9**
Speed ratings (Par 98): **98,96,94,93,92 91,91,90,89,88 87,87**
CSF £48.69 CT £1620.33 TOTE £4.50: £1.30, £3.00, £10.30; EX 39.00 Trifecta £1955.10.
Owner Somerville Lodge Limited **Bred** Saleh Al Homaizi & Imad Al Sagar **Trained** Newmarket, Suffolk

FOCUS
Add 6yds, making it 1m 6yds. Plenty of the field seemed keen to get on with things, so the early pace was decent. The bare form is modest.

5798 PLAY "FOUR FROM THE TOP" AT VALUERATER.CO.UK H'CAP (BATH SUMMER STAYERS' SERIES QUALIFIER) 1m 6f
4:40 (4:40) (Class 6) (0-65,67) 3-Y-O **£2,781** (£827; £413; £300) **Stalls** High

Form RPR

3225 **1** **Victoriano (IRE)**[6] 5596 3-9-9 **67**.........(b) AdamMcNamara 4 75
(Archie Watson) *pressed ldr: led over 2f out: rdn clr and sn in command: comf* **3/1**[2]

-623 **2** *4 ½* **Sinndarella (IRE)**[36] 4484 3-8-2 **49**.......... JaneElliott(3) 5 51
(Sarah Hollinshead) *racd keenly: trckd ldrs: rdn to chse wnr over 2f out: styd on but nt pce to chal* **13/2**[3]

0-12 **3** *¾* **Blame It On Sally (IRE)**[11] 5452 3-9-7 **65**.........(p) LukeMorris 1 66
(Sir Mark Prescott Bt) *led: bmpd along fr over 4f out: rdn and hdd over 2f out: styd on to chal for 2nd ent fnl f but no ch w wnr* **4/7**[1]

1054 **4** *10* **Twenty Years On**[27] 4843 3-9-7 **65**.........(b[1]) DaneO'Neill 3 56
(Richard Hughes) *trckd ldrs: effrt over 2f out: wknd over 1f out: eased ins fnl f* **12/1**

3m 4.06s (-2.04) **Going Correction** -0.05s/f (Good) **4 Ran SP% 109.7**
Speed ratings (Par 98): **103,100,100,94**
CSF £18.75 TOTE £3.10; EX 14.50 Trifecta £20.20.
Owner Ebury Racing 3 **Bred** Godolphin **Trained** Upper Lambourn, W Berks

FOCUS
Add 6yds, making the official distance 1m6f 6yds. A modest staying event, with the favourite below par.

5799 SKY SPORTS RACING SKY 415 APPRENTICE H'CAP 5f 160y
5:10 (5:11) (Class 5) (0-70,70) 3-Y-O+
£3,428 (£1,020; £509; £300; £300; £300) **Stalls** Centre

Form RPR

0-03 **1** **Gilt Edge**[12] 5377 3-8-8 **56**.......... RhiainIngram 8 66
(Christopher Mason) *s.i.s: sn pushed along in last: hdwy over 2f out: edgd lft 2f out: tk narrow advantage over 1f out: kpt on wl: asserting cl home* **10/1**

3443 **2** *½* **Union Rose**[5] 5607 7-9-9 **70**.........(p) WilliamCarver(3) 7 79
(Ronald Harris) *trckd ldrs: edgd rt 2f out whn ldng: sn narrowly hdd: ev ch ins fnl f: no ex cl home* **4/1**[2]

0052 **3** *2 ½* **Case Key**[13] 5352 6-9-1 **66**.........(b) LukeCatton(5) 5 67
(Michael Appleby) *trckd ldrs: rdn over 2f out: kpt on to chse ldng pair over 1f out but nt pce to chal* **5/1**[3]

0002 **4** *6* **Swanton Blue (IRE)**[30] 4733 6-8-13 **64**.......... AngusVilliers(7) 4 45
(Ed de Giles) *led tl 3f out: rdn whn tight for room 2f out: one pce after* **4/1**[2]

1363 **5** *5* **Perfect Symphony (IRE)**[13] 5351 5-8-11 **62**.........(p) IsobelFrancis(7) 2 26
(Mark Pattinson) *prom: led 3f out tl 2f out sn tight for room: wknd fnl f* **3/1**[1]

3-00 **6** *2 ¾* **Atty's Edge**[26] 4874 3-8-8 **56**.......... PoppyBridgwater 1 10
(Christopher Mason) *s.i.s: sn trcking ldrs: rdn over 2f out: wknd over 1f out* **16/1**

345 **7** *3* **Es Que Magic (IRE)**[49] 3996 3-7-13 **54**.......... GeorgeRooke(7) 3
(Alex Hales) *in tch: rdn over 2f out: wknd over 1f out* **6/1**

1m 10.64s (-0.46) **Going Correction** -0.05s/f (Good)
WFA 3 from 4yo+ 4lb **7 Ran SP% 110.9**
Speed ratings (Par 103): **101,100,97,89,82 78,74**
CSF £46.43 CT £216.98 TOTE £8.80: £5.00, £2.20; EX 37.70 Trifecta £121.70.
Owner S Bishop And C Mason **Bred** Christopher & Annabelle Mason **Trained** Caewent, Monmouthshire

FOCUS
The leaders seemed to go off too quickly, as the first and third got behind early on. Therefore, credit goes to the runner-up. The form is unconvincing.
T/Plt: £101.80 to a £1 stake. Pool: £58,790.82 - 421.5 winning units T/Qpdt: £54.10 to a £1 stake. Pool: £4,267.12 - 58.28 winning units **Tim Mitchell**

4749 BRIGHTON (L-H)
Wednesday, August 7

OFFICIAL GOING: Good to firm (watered; 8.3)
Wind: Strong, against Weather: Fine

5800 VISIT MARATHONBET.CO.UK NURSERY H'CAP 5f 60y
2:00 (2:00) (Class 6) (0-65,67) 2-Y-O **£2,781** (£827; £413; £300; £300) **Stalls** Low

Form RPR

4343 **1** **Bartat**[13] 5340 2-8-12 **62**.......... ScottMcCullagh(5) 4 65
(Mick Channon) *t.k.h: in tch: effrt to chse ldrs 2f out: kpt on u.p and chsd ldr ins fnl f: styd on wl to ld towards fin* **10/3**[2]

305 **2** *½* **Airbrush (IRE)**[14] 5317 2-9-7 **66**.......... OisinMurphy 3 67
(Richard Hannon) *led: pushed over 1f out: rdn ins fnl f: kpt on same pce u.p: hdd and no ex towards fin* **6/4**[1]

4605 **3** *2* **Champagne Highlife (GER)**[13] 5340 2-9-8 **67**.......... CharlesBishop 5 61
(Eve Johnson Houghton) *chsd ldr: unable qck u.p over 1f out: kpt on same pce and lost 2nd ins fnl f* **5/1**

0400 **4** *1 ½* **Geepower (IRE)**[19] 5146 2-9-2 **61**.........(b[1]) RobHornby 1 50
(Brian Ellison) *chsd ldrs: effrt 2f out: unable qck and kpt on same pce fnl f* **10/1**

2064 **5** *½* **Hollaback Girl**[15] 5279 2-8-10 **62**.........(p[1]) SeanKirrane(7) 2 49
(Richard Spencer) *s.i.s: hld up in tch in rr: swtchd rt and effrt over 2f out: no imp: kpt on same pce ins fnl f* **4/1**[3]

1m 3.46s (0.46) **Going Correction** -0.10s/f (Good) **5 Ran SP% 108.8**
Speed ratings (Par 92): **92,91,88,85,84**
CSF £8.58 TOTE £3.30: £1.50, £1.20; EX 6.90 Trifecta £19.00.
Owner The Wentworth Amigos **Bred** Mike Channon Bloodstock Limited **Trained** West Ilsley, Berks

FOCUS
This ordinary nursery was run at an uneven pace, but the form is straightforward.

5801 DOWNLOAD THE MARATHONBET APP EBF NOVICE STKS 6f 210y
2:30 (2:30) (Class 5) 2-Y-O **£3,428** (£1,020; £509; £254) **Stalls** Centre

Form RPR

13 **1** **Hariboux**[8] 5527 2-9-6 0.........(h) JackMitchell 4 81
(Hugo Palmer) *stdd s: t.k.h: chsd ldng pair: effrt on inner 2f out: drvn jst over 1f out: led ins fnl f: styd on* **7/2**[2]

4 **2** *1* **Frost At Midnight (USA)**[14] 5294 2-8-11 0.......... FrannyNorton 2 69
(Mark Johnston) *led: edgd rt over 2f out: rdn ent fnl 2f: hdd ins fnl f: kpt on same pce fnl 100yds* **8/1**[3]

5 **3** *hd* **Sky Vega (IRE)**[13] 5331 2-9-2 0.......... TomMarquand 3 74
(Richard Hannon) *chsd ldr: hung rt over 3f out: effrt ent fnl 2f: edgd lft u.p and stl ev ch over 1f out: kpt on same pce ins fnl f* **4/7**[1]

0 **4** *4 ½* **Slavonic Dance (IRE)**[19] 5131 2-8-11 0.......... RobHornby 5 57
(Ralph Beckett) *a same pce but on terms w ldrs: effrt ent fnl 2f: edgd lft and no prog over 1f out: wl hld fnl f* **10/1**

00 **5** *2 ½* **Kentucky Hardboot (IRE)**[13] 5345 2-8-11 0.......... ScottMcCullagh(5) 6 55
(Mick Channon) *stdd and dropped in bhd after s: nvr involved (jockey said gelding was slow into stride)* **25/1**

1m 24.35s (0.55) **Going Correction** -0.10s/f (Good) **5 Ran SP% 109.9**
Speed ratings (Par 94): **92,90,90,85,82**
CSF £27.85 TOTE £3.10: £1.60, £2.80; EX 14.90 Trifecta £23.60.
Owner Kremlin Cottage Ix **Bred** Lady Gillian Brunton **Trained** Newmarket, Suffolk

FOCUS
This interesting novice event was run at a sound pace. The winner is rated in line with his Wolverhampton win.

5802 ROGER ADDEMS (S) H'CAP 1m 3f 198y
3:00 (3:01) (Class 6) (0-60,58) 4-Y-O+
£2,781 (£827; £413; £300; £300; £300) **Stalls** High

Form RPR

4442 **1** **Born To Reason (IRE)**[57] 3682 5-8-4 **46**.........(p[1]) CierenFallon(5) 9 52
(Alexandra Dunn) *chsd ldrs tl wnt 2nd over 7f out: swtchd rt and effrt ent fnl 3f: rdn to ld over 2f out: clr over 1f out: kpt on and a holding on wl ins fnl f* **11/4**[1]

3346 **2** *½* **Butterfield (IRE)**[14] 5290 6-8-13 **50**.......... EoinWalsh 6 55
(Tony Carroll) *in tch in midfield: effrt 3f out: chsd wnr over 1f out: kpt on u.p and steadily clsd ins fnl f: nvr quite getting to wnr* **13/2**

2005 **3** *¾* **Sussex Girl**[36] 4475 5-8-11 **48**.......... TomMarquand 5 52
(John Berry) *hld up in last trio: effrt over 2f out: rdn and hdwy over 1f out: drvn and chsd ldng pair 1f out: kpt on but nvr quite getting to wnr* **6/1**

0400 **4** *2 ½* **Sellingallthetime (IRE)**[12] 5379 8-8-5 **45**.........(p) WilliamCox(3) 7 45
(Mark Usher) *chsd ldrs: effrt over 2f out: chsd wnr ent fnl 2f: no imp and lost 2nd over 1f out: kpt on same pce ins fnl f* **25/1**

5333 **5** *nk* **Prerogative (IRE)**[14] 5310 5-8-1 **45**.......... ElishaWhittington(7) 3 45
(Tony Carroll) *in rr and rn in snatches: reminder 5f out: hdwy over 1f out: kpt on ins fnl f: nvr trbld ldrs (jockey said gelding was never travelling)* **11/2**[3]

0600 **6** *4 ½* **Mouchee (IRE)**[42] 4231 4-9-4 **58**.........(p) MitchGodwin(3) 1 50
(Michael Blake) *midfield: no imp u.p and hung lft over 1f out: wl hld fnl f* **22/1**

0100 **7** *4 ½* **Shovel It On (IRE)**[9] 5499 4-8-13 **50**.........(bt) RaulDaSilva 11 35
(Steve Flook) *midfield: effrt 4f out: nvr threatened to get on terms w ldrs: wl hld and wnt lft over 1f out* **14/1**

340/ **8** *4 ½* **Swift Blade (IRE)**[1178] 8159 11-9-6 **57**.......... RossaRyan 2 35
(Gary Moore) *hld up in midfield: clsd over 3f out: effrt and chsd ldrs over 2f out: sn struggling and btn over 1f out: wknd fnl f* **16/1**

0400 **9** *3 ¼* **Hidden Stash**[29] 4753 5-8-3 **45**.........(p) DarraghKeenan(5) 8 18
(William Stone) *chsd ldr tl over 7f out: steadily lost pl: bhd 2f out: wknd* **11/1**

60-0 **10** *21* **Awesome Rock (IRE)**[33] 4594 10-8-8 **45**.......... FrannyNorton 4
(Roger Ingram) *hld up in rr: bhd 2f out: wknd* **66/1**

-546 **11** *5* **Templier (IRE)**[21] 5047 6-9-2 **53**.........(b) HectorCrouch 10
(Gary Moore) *led tl over 2f out: sn lost pl: bhd ins fnl f* **9/2**[2]

2m 33.91s (-2.09) **Going Correction** -0.10s/f (Good) **11 Ran SP% 118.4**
Speed ratings (Par 101): **102,101,101,99,99 96,93,90,88,74 70**
CSF £20.53 CT £100.98 TOTE £2.80: £1.20, £2.10, £2.30; EX 19.80 Trifecta £124.80.There was no bid for the winner.
Owner West Buckland Bloodstock Ltd **Bred** Christopher Glynn **Trained** West Buckland, Somerset

FOCUS
A typically weak selling handicap.

5803 MARATHONBET LIVE CASINO H'CAP 1m 1f 207y
3:30 (3:33) (Class 6) (0-55,56) 3-Y-O+
£2,781 (£827; £413; £300; £300; £300) **Stalls** High

Form RPR

2046 **1** **Creative Talent (IRE)**[55] 3766 7-9-7 **55**.......... GeorgeDowning 10 63
(Tony Carroll) *hld up towards rr: hdwy over 2f out: rdn to ld over 1f out: clr and hung lft fnl f: a doing enough: kpt on (trainer said, regarding the improved form shown, the gelding had appreciated the drop in grade; jockey said gelding hung left-handed under pressure)* **12/1**

0064 **2** *¾* **Sandy Steve**[47] 4070 3-8-12 **54**.......... OisinMurphy 14 62+
(Stuart Williams) *hld up in tch in midfield: hdwy over 1f out: chsd clr wnr ins fnl f: styd on strly fnl 100yds: nvr quite getting to wnr* **7/2**[2]

6235 **3** *4 ½* **Fair Power (IRE)**[40] 4346 5-9-2 **55**.......... DarraghKeenan(5) 5 53
(John Butler) *midfield: clsd to chse ldrs over 3f out: effrt over 2f out: wl hld 3rd and kpt on same pce ins fnl f* **10/3**[1]

0163 **4** *3 ¼* **Bader**[4] 5653 3-8-13 **55**.........(b) FergusSweeney 11 48
(Richard Hannon) *led for over 1f: chsd ldr tl rdn to ld again ent fnl 2f: hdd over 1f out: no ex and wknd ins fnl f* **11/2**

0030 **5** *2 ¼* **With Approval (IRE)**[21] 5049 7-9-5 **53**.........(p) HectorCrouch 4 41
(Laura Mongan) *in rr: effrt 3f out: carried lft and sme prog 1f out: kpt on to pass btn horses ins fnl f: nvr trbld ldrs* **18/1**

0006 **6** *nk* **Ramblow**[22] 5016 6-8-7 **46** oh1 ....(vt) CierenFallon(5) 9 33
(Alexandra Dunn) *t.k.h: hld up in tch in midfield: effrt over 2f out: no imp and wl hld whn hung lft 1f out (jockey said mare ran too free in the early stages)* **33/1**

4000 **7** *1* **Solveig's Song**[21] 5049 7-9-0 **48** .... JackMitchell 6 33
(Steve Woodman) *hld up in rr: swtchd rt and effrt 3f out: no imp u.p over 1f out: wknd fnl f* **14/1**

03R6 **8** *¾* **Principia**[11] 5425 4-9-7 **55** ....(p[1]) CharlieBennett 12 39
(Adam West) *dwlt: towards rr: hdwy into midfield 1/2-way: rdn 4f out: lost pl and btn 2f out: wknd fnl f* **20/1**

506 **9** *1¼* **Soldier Of War (USA)**[20] 5103 4-8-9 **46** oh1 .... WilliamCox(3) 8 27
(Ben Pauling) *chsd ldrs: rdn and unable qck over 2f out: lost pl and btn over 1f out: wknd* **40/1**

-056 **10** *½* **Jetstream (IRE)**[20] 5106 4-9-3 **56** ....(t[1]) ScottMcCullagh(5) 2 36
(D J Jeffreys) *chsd ldrs tl led over 8f out: rdn and hdd over 2f out: lost pl and wl btn over 1f out: wknd* **9/2**[3]

0643 **11** *7* **Little Tipple**[7] 5548 3-8-4 **46** oh1 .... AdrianMcCarthy 1 14
(John Ryan) *midfield: effrt over 2f out: no prog and wl btn over 1f out: wknd* **25/1**

-600 **12** *4½* **Miss Pollyanna (IRE)**[20] 5092 3-8-8 **50** .... EoinWalsh 13 10
(Roger Ingram) *stdd s: t.k.h: hld up in rr: hdwy on outer 3f out: sn u.p and outpcd: wl bhd fnl f (jockey said filly ran too free)* **50/1**

003 **13** *38* **Jukebox Blues (FR)**[19] 5153 3-8-4 **46** oh1 .... FrannyNorton 3
(Mark Johnston) *chsd ldrs for tl 1/2-way: lost pl and bhd over 3f out: lost tch and eased: t.o: fin lame (vet said colt was lame on its right-fore leg)* **14/1**

2m 3.66s (-1.34) **Going Correction** -0.10s/f (Good)
WFA 3 from 4yo+ 8lb **13** Ran SP% **121.1**
Speed ratings (Par 101): **101,100,96,94,92 92,91,90,89,89 83,80,49**
CSF £51.82 CT £178.65 TOTE £14.60: £3.80, £1.50, £1.40; EX 92.10 Trifecta £380.60.
Owner The Rebelle Boys **Bred** Pitrizzia Partnership **Trained** Cropthorne, Worcs

FOCUS
They went a solid pace in this moderate handicap. Form that seems sound for the grade.

5804 BOMBARDIER BRIGHTON MILE CHALLENGE TROPHY H'CAP (FOR THE BRIGHTON MILE CHALLENGE TROPHY) 7f 211y

4:00 (4:00) (Class 4) (0-80,82) 3-Y-0+

£13,196 (£3,927; £1,962; £981; £300; £300) **Stalls** Centre

Form RPR

-114 **1** **De Vegas Kid (IRE)**[40] 4322 5-9-9 **79** .... DarraghKeenan(5) 12 89
(Tony Carroll) *stdd after s: hld up in last trio: effrt in centre over 2f out: hdwy and edging lft over 1f out: led ins fnl f: r.o wl: comf* **9/1**

3346 **2** *2* **Medieval (IRE)**[26] 4887 5-9-12 **77** ....(b) RossaRyan 6 82
(Paul Cole) *chsd clr ldr: clsd and effrt over 2f out: drvn to ld and hung lft wl over 1f out: hdd and one pce ins fnl f (jockey said gelding hung left-handed from three out)* **9/4**[1]

0164 **3** *1¼* **Poetic Force (IRE)**[26] 4867 5-10-0 **79** ....(t) GeorgeDowning 9 82
(Tony Carroll) *hld up in midfield: effrt over 2f out: clsd and shifting lft over 1f out: kpt on to go 3rd wl ins fnl f (jockey said gelding hung left-handed in the final furlong)* **16/1**

2-00 **4** *¾* **Baltic Prince (IRE)**[26] 4875 9-9-11 **76** .... RobertWinston 11 77
(Tony Carroll) *sn led and clsd: reduced ld and rdn over 2f out: hdd wl over 1f out: no ex ins fnl f: wknd fnl 75yds* **66/1**

6336 **5** *1* **Roller**[13] 5351 6-9-7 **72** ....(p) FrannyNorton 10 71
(Mark Loughnane) *midfield: effrt over 2f out: pushed lft over 1f out: no threat to ldrs but kpt on ins fnl f: eased towards fin* **14/1**

1243 **6** *1¼* **Key Player**[20] 5090 4-10-3 **82** ....(p) CharlesBishop 8 78
(Eve Johnson Houghton) *prom in chsng gp: clsd over 2f out: chsd ldrs over 1f out: edgd lft and no ex u.p jst ins fnl f: wknd fnl 100yds* **16/1**

0132 **7** *½* **Duchess Of Avon**[12] 5380 4-8-11 **62** .... HectorCrouch 5 56
(Gary Moore) *prom in chsng gp: effrt over 2f out: struggling to qckn and no imp whn pushed lft over 1f out: wknd ins fnl f* **7/1**[3]

1-53 **8** *1* **Water Diviner (IRE)**[32] 4643 3-9-6 **78** .... TomMarquand 4 69
(Richard Hannon) *prom in chsng gp: swtchd rt and effrt over 2f out: no ex over 1f out: wknd ins fnl f* **10/1**

0350 **9** *¾* **Pour La Victoire (IRE)**[26] 4867 9-9-2 **72** .... CierenFallon(5) 3 65
(Tony Carroll) *hld up in last trio: effrt and swtchd lft 2f out: nt clr run and hmpd jst over 1f out: nt rcvr and no hdwy ins fnl f (jockey said gelding was denied a clear run)* **16/1**

2342 **10** *nk* **Majestic Mac**[13] 5343 3-9-6 **78** .... CharlieBennett 2 67
(Hughie Morrison) *midfield: effrt on inner over 2f out: no imp and wnt lft over 1f out: wknd ins fnl f* **5/1**[2]

3140 **11** *nse* **Hedging (IRE)**[9] 5498 5-8-4 **62** ....(b) GeorgiaDobie(7) 1 52
(Eve Johnson Houghton) *a towards rr: no hdwy u.p: nvr involved* **20/1**

1001 **12** *11* **Forseti**[20] 5102 3-9-4 **79** .... JoshuaBryan(3) 7 42
(Andrew Balding) *stdd s: t.k.h: hld up in midfield: effrt over 2f out: sn struggling and btn over 1f out: bhd and eased ins fnl f (jockey said gelding ran too free)* **15/2**

1m 34.85s (-2.05) **Going Correction** -0.10s/f (Good)
WFA 3 from 4yo+ 7lb **12** Ran SP% **121.4**
Speed ratings (Par 105): **106,104,102,102,101 99,99,98,97,97 97,86**
CSF £30.13 CT £341.86 TOTE £9.60: £2.60, £1.40, £4.30; EX 37.30 Trifecta £747.70.
Owner The Rebelle Boys **Bred** Miriam O'Donnell & Kevin F O'Donnell **Trained** Cropthorne, Worcs

FOCUS
There was no hanging about in this feature handicap. The winner rates better than ever.

5805 MARATHONBET "BIGGER ODDS MEAN BIGGER WINNINGS" EBF FILLIES' H'CAP 6f 210y

4:30 (4:30) (Class 4) (0-85,87) 3-Y-0+ **£5,207** (£1,549; £774) **Stalls** Centre

Form RPR

010 **1** **Kachumba**[12] 5380 4-8-8 **72** .... StefanoCherchi(7) 3 81
(Rae Guest) *stdd s: in tch: clsd to trck ldrs 3f out: pressed ldr and shkn up ent fnl 2f: rdn to ld over 1f out: in command and r.o wl ins fnl f* **11/2**[2]

1123 **2** *2½* **Warning Fire**[4] 5666 3-9-7 **84** .... FrannyNorton 1 84
(Mark Johnston) *led: pushed along and hdd over 1f out: nt match pce and wnr and one pce fnl f* **2/7**[1]

4600 **3** *12* **Concello (IRE)**[42] 4242 3-9-10 **87** ....(p) TomMarquand 4 55
(Archie Watson) *chsd ldr: rdn over 3f out: lost 2nd over 2f out: wl btn and wnt lft over 1f out: wknd fnl f* **7/1**[3]

1m 22.73s (-1.07) **Going Correction** -0.10s/f (Good)
WFA 3 from 4yo 6lb **3** Ran SP% **105.6**
Speed ratings (Par 102): **102,99,85**
CSF £7.92 TOTE £4.40; EX 5.70 Trifecta £7.00.
Owner The Bucket List Racing Syndicate **Bred** Brook Stud Bloodstock Ltd **Trained** Newmarket, Suffolk

FOCUS
After two defections this was predictably tactical and there was a turn-up. The form isn't entirely convincing.

5806 SUMMERTIMELIVE.CO.UK CLASSIC IBIZA 7 SEPTEMBER H'CAP 6f 210y

5:00 (5:01) (Class 6) (0-52,52) 3-Y-0+

£2,781 (£827; £413; £300; £300; £300) **Stalls** Centre

Form RPR

2250 **1** **Joyful Dream (IRE)**[15] 5284 5-8-12 **46** ....(b) JoshuaBryan(3) 3 55
(John Butler) *in tch in midfield: effrt over 2f out: rdn to ld and hung lft over 1f out: clr and styd on wl ins fnl f* **5/1**[3]

-021 **2** *3¼* **Lady Morpheus**[20] 5092 3-9-1 **52** .... HectorCrouch 10 50+
(Gary Moore) *s.i.s: bhd: c wd and effrt over 2f out: hdwy u.p and edging lft 1f out: styd on to snatch 2nd last strides: no ch w wnr* **3/1**[1]

3600 **3** *nse* **Kellington Kitty (USA)**[65] 3410 4-9-1 **46** oh1 ....(p) RossaRyan 6 47
(Mike Murphy) *hld up in last quartet: hdwy: jostling w rival and squeezing through over 1f out: chsd ldrs and kpt on ins fnl f: no ch w wnr (jockey said filly was also denied a clear run)* **25/1**

6036 **4** *nk* **Imbucato**[50] 3966 5-9-5 **50** .... RobertWinston 5 50
(Tony Carroll) *pressed ldrs: ev ch and rdn ent fnl 2f: led wl over 1f out: sn hdd and getting outpcd whn sltly impeded jst ins fnl f: lost 2 pls last strides* **9/2**[2]

0000 **5** *2¼* **Malaysian Boleh**[28] 4797 9-8-8 **46** oh1 ....(p) GraceMcEntee(7) 11 39
(Phil McEntee) *hld up in tch in midfield: edgd out rt and effrt wl over 1f out: jostling w rival and hdwy over 1f out: no imp and one pce ins fnl f* **50/1**

0205 **6** *1¾* **Brother In Arms (IRE)**[36] 4473 5-8-12 **46** oh1 .... MitchGodwin(3) 9 34
(Tony Carroll) *dwlt: in rr: effrt wl over 2f out: swtchd lft 1f out: styd on to pass btn horses ins fnl f* **16/1**

0005 **7** *½* **Limerick Lord (IRE)**[14] 5302 7-9-5 **50** ....(p) CharlieBennett 7 37
(Julia Feilden) *chsd ldrs: unable qck u.p over 1f out: wl hld fnl f* **20/1**

3054 **8** *½* **Bayards Cove**[26] 4873 4-9-1 **46** oh1 .... RobHornby 4 32
(Stuart Kittow) *in tch in midfield: no hdwy u.p over 1f out: wl hld and plugged on same pce fnl f* **33/1**

0641 **9** *¾* **Seafaring Girl (IRE)**[12] 5377 3-8-8 **52** ....(p) SeanKirrane(7) 2 34
(Mark Loughnane) *sn led: rdn over 2f out: hdd wl over 1f out: no ex and btn 1f out: wknd fnl f* **12/1**

1000 **10** *1¼* **Princess Florence (IRE)**[12] 5377 3-8-9 **51** .... CierenFallon(5) 16 29
(John Ryan) *hld up towards rr: no hdwy u.p over 1f out: nvr involved* **33/1**

0050 **11** *hd* **Spirit Of Ishy**[20] 5081 4-9-1 **46** oh1 ....(t[1]) FergusSweeney 12 26+
(Stuart Kittow) *taken down early: hld up towards rr: effrt on inner 2f out: swtchd rt and nt clr run over 1f out: nvr trbld ldrs* **50/1**

0341 **12** *2¾* **Harlequin Rose (IRE)**[29] 4753 5-9-4 **49** ....(v) CharlesBishop 1 31+
(Patrick Chamings) *dwlt: sn rcvrd and chsd ldrs: effrt 2f out: nt clr run and hmpd over 1f out: nt rcvr and eased ins fnl f (jockey said mare was denied a clear run)* **9/2**[2]

40U0 **13** *2* **Quarto Cavallo**[11] 5431 3-8-9 **46** oh1 ....(p[1]) RaulDaSilva 15 11
(Adam West) *midfield: rdn over 2f out: lost pl and btn 2f out: wknd fnl f* **50/1**

0002 **14** *4* **Sugar Plum Fairy**[28] 4776 4-9-1 **46** oh1 .... BrettDoyle 14 2
(Tony Carroll) *midfield: effrt 2f out: sn u.p and lost pl over 1f out: wknd fnl f* **14/1**

1000 **15** *1½* **Rock In Society (IRE)**[14] 5302 4-9-2 **52** ....(b) DarraghKeenan(5) 8 4
(John Butler) *w ldr tl ent fnl 2f: lost pl over 1f out: bhd ins fnl f* **14/1**

1m 22.72s (-1.08) **Going Correction** -0.10s/f (Good)
WFA 3 from 4yo+ 6lb **15** Ran SP% **125.3**
Speed ratings (Par 101): **102,98,98,97,95 93,92,92,91,89 89,86,84,79,77**
CSF £19.72 CT £360.49 TOTE £5.30: £1.70, £1.40, £6.00; EX 33.00 Trifecta £620.50.
Owner Gerry Dolan **Bred** Malih Al Basti **Trained** Newmarket, Suffolk

FOCUS
What had looked a competitive handicap was won dominant fashion by one of the market leaders. Those coming from off the pace were seen to best effect in what was a bit of a messy race.
T/Plt: £230.80 to a £1 stake. Pool: £68,831.72 - 217.63 winning units T/Qpdt: £62.90 to a £1 stake. Pool: £6,810.91 - 80.02 winning units **Steve Payne**

5729 KEMPTON (A.W) (R-H)

Wednesday, August 7

OFFICIAL GOING: Polytrack: standard to slow (watered)
Wind: Virtually nil Weather: Cloudy, warm, shower before racing

5807 BET AT RACINGTV.COM H'CAP 1m (P)

5:30 (5:30) (Class 6) (0-65,65) 3-Y-0+

£3,105 (£924; £461; £300; £300; £300) **Stalls** Low

Form RPR

2044 **1** **Baashiq (IRE)**[19] 5151 5-9-10 **61** ....(p) AdamKirby 3 71
(Peter Hiatt) *early pce: sn trckd ldr: pushed along 2f out: rdn over 1f out: led ent fnl f: in control fnl 110yds and rdn out* **9/4**[1]

0003 **2** *1¾* **Mochalov**[14] 5309 4-9-2 **56** .... PaddyBradley(3) 4 62+
(Jane Chapple-Hyam) *hld up in rr-div: prog between horses over 2f out: rdn 2f out: kpt on fr over 1f out: no ch w wnr cl home* **8/1**

-006 **3** *1¾* **Bhodi (IRE)**[44] 4194 4-9-11 **62** .... GeorgeWood 14 64
(Kevin Frost) *wnt to post early: slow s and hld up in rr: pushed along over 2f out: swtchd to inner 2f out: kpt on wl fr over 1f out (jockey said gelding was slowly away because blindfold became caught on the bridle and required two attempts to be removed)* **33/1**

3230 **4** *1* **Seraphim**[28] 4807 3-9-6 **64** ....(t) AndreaAtzeni 2 63
(Marco Botti) *bhd ldrs: rdn 2f out: ev ch over 1f out: no ex and kpt on one pce fnl f* **4/1**[2]

5404 **5** *3½* **Cashel (IRE)**[28] 4787 4-9-13 **64** .... AlistairRawlinson 10 56
(Michael Appleby) *racd in mid-div: ct wd on bnd 4f out and niggled along: clsr over 2f out where rdn: stuck on fr over 1f out (jockey said gelding hung left-handed round bnd)* **6/1**[3]

-405 **6** *1* **Salmon Fishing (IRE)**[34] 4567 3-9-1 **59** ....(t) GeraldMosse 9 47
(Mohamed Moubarak) *in rr-div on outer: pushed along at 1/2-way: effrt over 2f out: plugged on fr over 1f out* **12/1**

-300 **7** *¾* **Bigshotte**[33] 4594 4-9-8 **59** .... RobertHavlin 13 47
(Luke Dace) *sn led fr wd draw: rdn over 2f out: kpt on tl hdd ent fnl f: wknd qckly fnl 110yds* **40/1**

631- **8** *1½* **Declamation (IRE)**[238] 9507 9-9-11 **62** .... SeanLevey 6 46
(John Butler) *hld up in rr: shkn up over 2f out and prog: rdn 2f out: one pce fr over 1f out* **16/1**

4550 **9** 3/4 **Arlecchino's Leap**[14] 5309 7-9-11 **62**..............................(p) PatDobbs 11 44
(Mark Usher) *racd in last: stl in last w plenty to do over 1f out: sme hdwy fnl f being shuffled along: nvr involved* **16/1**

040 **10** 3/4 **Wall Of Sapphire (IRE)**[54] 3797 3-9-7 **65**.............................. ShaneKelly 5 45
(Mark Loughnane) *mid-div on inner: effrt over 2f out: no imp over 1f out* **20/1**

006 **11** 1 1/4 **Deadly Accurate**[89] 2596 4-9-9 **60**.............................. LiamKeniry 7 38
(Roy Brotherton) *bhd ldrs: pushed along fr 1/2-way to hold position: rdn over 2f out: no ex over 1f out* **33/1**

4063 **12** 2 1/4 **Sweet Nature (IRE)**[28] 4787 4-9-8 **59**..............................(p) JimCrowley 12 32
(Laura Mongan) *trckd ldrs: effrt over 2f out: no ex over 1f out and wknd fnl f* **16/1**

1m 40.45s (0.65) **Going Correction** +0.125s/f (Slow)
WFA 3 from 4yo+ 7lb **12** Ran SP% **114.6**
Speed ratings (Par 101): **101,99,97,96,93 92,91,89,89,88 87,84**
CSF £18.84 CT £466.79 TOTE £2.80: £1.30, £1.60, £7.80; EX 16.70 Trifecta £370.90.
Owner Phil Kelly **Bred** Shadwell Estate Company Limited **Trained** Hook Norton, Oxon

FOCUS
A modest affair. The winner is rated to this year's best.

5808 MATCHBOOK BETTING EXCHANGE NOVICE STKS 1m (P)
6:00 (6:03) (Class 4) 3-Y-O+ £6,469 (£1,925; £962; £481) Stalls Low

Form RPR

1- **1** **Dubai Warrior**[272] 8954 3-9-8 0.............................. RobertHavlin 6 99+
(John Gosden) *trckd ldr on outer: shkn up and led 2f out: effrt over 1f out: galloped clr ent fnl f: easily* **4/11**[1]

31 **2** 4 1/2 **Muhaarar's Nephew**[43] 4211 3-9-5 0.............................. JimCrowley 7 82
(Owen Burrows) *bhd ldrs: rdn over 2f out: kpt on fr over 1f out: tk 2nd 1f out: no ch w wnr* **7/1**[2]

3 2 **Khabeerah** 3-8-11 0.............................. AndreaAtzeni 12 69+
(Roger Varian) *cl up in mid-div: rn green at times: rdn over 2f out: no immediate imp tl kpt on wl fr over 1f out* **10/1**[3]

4 4 **Qatar Queen (IRE)** 3-8-11 0..............................(h[1]) OisinMurphy 5 60+
(James Fanshawe) *cl up in mid-div: effrt over 2f out: stuck on fr over 1f out: keeping on fnl f* **10/1**[3]

53 **5** 2 1/2 **Rapture (FR)**[15] 5268 3-8-11 0.............................. HollieDoyle 4 54
(Archie Watson) *led: rdn over 2f out: hdd 2f out: stuck on over 1f out tl no ex and lost 2nd 1f out: wknd qckly sn after* **11/1**

6 nk **Pentimento** 3-9-2 0.............................. KierenFox 2 59
(John Best) *bhd ldr on inner: rdn over 2f out: plugged on* **80/1**

5 **7** 1 **Young General (IRE)**[9] 5494 3-9-2 0.............................. SeanLevey 14 56
(Richard Hannon) *racd in mid-div: rdn over 2f out: no imp over 1f out* **50/1**

6 **8** 3 1/2 **Chamomile**[61] 3546 3-8-11 0.............................. KieranShoemark 11 43
(Daniel Kubler) *in rr-div: rdn over 2f out: kpt on one pce* **66/1**

55 **9** 1 3/4 **Sea Wings**[15] 5268 3-9-2 0..............................(b) AdamKirby 13 44
(William Haggas) *s.s and in rr: shuffled along over 2f out: plugged on fr over 1f out* **20/1**

10 nk **Melburnian** 3-8-13 0.............................. PaddyBradley(3) 1 44
(Jane Chapple-Hyam) *hld up in rr: effrt over 2f out: no imp (jockey said gelding ran green)* **66/1**

06 **11** 3 3/4 **Kasuku**[60] 3574 3-8-11 0.............................. JackMitchell 3 30
(Ralph Beckett) *hld up in rr-div: effrt over 2f out: no imp* **66/1**

12 3 **Aspiring Diva** 3-8-11 0..............................(h[1]) GeraldMosse 8 23
(Mohamed Moubarak) *s.s: in last: rn green thrght: nvr involved* **50/1**

65 **13** 10 **So Strictly**[30] 4738 3-9-2 0.............................. LiamKeniry 10
(Paul Cole) *bhd ldrs on outer and racd keenly at times: pushed along over 3f out: wknd over 2f out* **66/1**

1m 38.75s (-1.05) **Going Correction** +0.125s/f (Slow) **13** Ran SP% **128.2**
Speed ratings (Par 105): **110,105,103,99,97 96,95,92,90,90 86,83,73**
CSF £3.88 TOTE £1.20: £1.02, £1.80, £2.90; EX 4.10 Trifecta £16.80.
Owner Sheikh Mohammed Bin Khalifa Al Maktoum **Bred** Essafinaat Ltd **Trained** Newmarket, Suffolk

FOCUS
The odds-on favourite made a successful return to the track, and it'll be interesting to see which way connections go with him now. He'll be a Group horse, at least on the AW.

5809 MATCHBOOK/BRITISH STALLION STUDS EBF NOVICE STKS (PLUS 10 RACE) 7f (P)
6:30 (6:31) (Class 4) 2-Y-O £5,822 (£1,732; £865; £432) Stalls Low

Form RPR

0 **1** **Eshaasy**[26] 4886 2-9-5 0.............................. JimCrowley 9 79+
(John Gosden) *bhd ldrs: shkn up over 2f out: rdn 2f out: kpt on wl on outer to ld jst ins fnl f: in control and cajoled along cl home to fend off runner-up* **13/8**[1]

2 nk **Harrison Point (FR)** 2-9-5 0.............................. HollieDoyle 8 78+
(Archie Watson) *briefly led 1f: sn bhd ldr: rdn 2f out on inner: ev ch over 1f out: briefly led ent fnl f: styd on wl but nt get past wnr* **25/1**

0 **3** 1 1/4 **Protagonist (FR)**[19] 5131 2-9-5 0.............................. TomMarquand 5 76+
(Jamie Osborne) *hld up in rr: rn green and pushed along over 3f out: fnd stride 2f out on inner and gd prog: ev ch but sltly outpcd over 1f out: no ch w front pair fnl 150yds: shuffled along and kpt on encouragingly in 3rd cl home* **33/1**

50 **4** 2 1/4 **Zingaro Boy (IRE)**[25] 4925 2-9-5 0.............................. OisinMurphy 6 69+
(Hugo Palmer) *reluctant early ldr: sn taken bk to mid-div: rdn over 2f out: outpcd over 1f out: kpt on wl fnl f: shuffled along fnl 110yds* **25/1**

5 nk **Impatient** 2-9-5 0.............................. HarryBentley 11 68+
(Ralph Beckett) *tk awkward step leaving stalls: impr to sit in mid-div 1/2-way: rdn over 2f out: kpt on one pce over 1f out: styd on again wl ins fnl f* **7/1**

6 **6** hd **Oslo**[19] 5131 2-9-5 0.............................. JasonWatson 12 68+
(Sir Michael Stoute) *pushed along fr wd draw and disp ld on inner after 2f: rdn over 2f out: stuck on disputing over 1f out: no ex ent fnl f: plugged on after* **14/1**

7 1/2 **Spirit Of Light (IRE)** 2-9-5 0..............................(h[1]) WilliamBuick 13 67
(Charlie Appleby) *early spd fr wd draw to dispute ld on outer after 2f: rdn 2f out: kpt on disputing for ld over 1f out: hdd ent fnl f: wandered sltly lft sn after and wknd (jockey said gelding hung right-handed in str)* **6/1**[3]

8 1 1/2 **Perfected** 2-9-5 0.............................. AndreaAtzeni 3 63
(Roger Varian) *racd in mid-div on inner: rdn over 2f out: outpcd and no imp* **9/2**[2]

0 **9** 1 1/4 **Dogged**[19] 5125 2-9-5 0.............................. GeraldMosse 7 59
(David Elsworth) *hld up in rr-div: rdn over 2f out: one pce* **40/1**

10 hd **Huwaiteb** 2-9-5 0..............................(h[1]) KieranShoemark 4 59
(Owen Burrows) *tk fierce hold between horses in mid-div: pushed along over 2f out: no imp fr 2f out (jockey said colt ran free)* **25/1**

60 **11** 12 **Game Over (IRE)**[19] 5131 2-9-5 0.............................. SeanLevey 10 28
(Richard Hannon) *racd in mid-div on outer and t.k.h at times: rdn wl over 3f out: wknd 2f out: t.o (jockey said colt did not handle bnd)* **66/1**

12 8 **General Joe (IRE)** 2-9-5 0.............................. AdamKirby 2 7
(Clive Cox) *a in last and rn green thrght: no ex over 2f out: t.o (jockey said colt ran very green)* **10/1**

1m 27.42s (1.42) **Going Correction** +0.125s/f (Slow) **12** Ran SP% **117.2**
Speed ratings (Par 96): **96,95,94,91,91 91,90,88,87,87 73,64**
CSF £56.18 TOTE £2.40: £1.10, £4.90, £11.20; EX 42.60 Trifecta £728.90.
Owner Hamdan Al Maktoum **Bred** Pantile Stud **Trained** Newmarket, Suffolk

FOCUS
The early pace wasn't that strong and they finished in a bit of a heap. The bare form can't really be rated much higher.

5810 GET SWITCHED ON WITH MATCHBOOK FILLIES' NOVICE STKS 1m 3f 219y(P)
7:00 (7:02) (Class 3) 3-Y-O+ £9,337 (£2,796; £1,398; £699; £349; £175) Stalls Low

Form RPR

5 **1** **Expressionism (IRE)**[19] 5148 3-8-11 0.............................. WilliamBuick 8 85+
(Charlie Appleby) *mid-div on outer: rn green: kidded and cajoled thrght: rdn 3f out: clsng on clr ldrs over 1f out: stuck on wl fnl f and led cl home: snug at fin* **7/1**[2]

21 **2** 1 1/4 **Illumined (IRE)**[35] 4503 3-9-3 0.............................. RobertHavlin 3 92+
(John Gosden) *bhd clr ldr w gap to pack: smooth prog to cl on ldr 3f out and led over 2f out: effrt 2f out and kicked three l clr ent fnl f: stride shortening fnl 150yds: ct cl home* **5/6**[1]

4-4 **3** 1 1/4 **Alemagna**[19] 5148 3-8-11 0.............................. AndreaAtzeni 4 81
(David Simcock) *racd in 3rd and ldng pack: rdn wl over 2f out: chsd ldr fr 2f out: lost 2nd 110yds out: no ex* **15/2**[3]

56 **4** 7 **Vibrance**[16] 5254 3-8-11 0.............................. HarryBentley 7 70+
(James Fanshawe) *racd in rr-div: pushed along wl over 4f out and smooth prog: shuffled along fr over 2f out: no imp on ldrs fr over 1f out: nvr involved* **16/1**

5 3 **Baaqiah** 3-8-11 0.............................. JimCrowley 9 65+
(Roger Varian) *hld up in rr: effrt over 3f out w plenty to do: stuck on one pce* **7/1**[2]

0-3 **6** 9 **Royal Family (FR)**[189] 474 3-8-11 0.............................. JackMitchell 5 51
(Amy Murphy) *hld up in rr: shuffled along w plenty to do fr over 3f out: nvr involved* **33/1**

05 **7** 14 **Albanderi**[33] 4600 3-8-11 0..............................(v[1]) JasonWatson 1 28
(Sir Michael Stoute) *clr ldr: ld reduced over 4f out: sn rdn: hdd over 2f out: no ex (jockey said filly stopped quickly; post-race examination failed to reveal any abnormalities)* **25/1**

40 **8** 2 1/4 **Walk It Talk It**[40] 4326 3-8-11 0.............................. GeorgeWood 10 25
(Chris Wall) *restless in stalls: darted to inner and t.k.h in rr: hrd rdn wl over 4f out: no imp in st* **50/1**

3 **9** 1 1/2 **Waterfall**[23] 5004 3-8-11 0.............................. HayleyTurner 2 22
(Lucy Wadham) *racd in mid-div on inner: rdn to hold pl wl over 4f out: no ex 2f out and eased* **100/1**

02 **10** 44 **Rewrite The Stars (IRE)**[35] 4503 3-8-11 0.............................. OisinMurphy 6
(James Tate) *bhd ldrs in main gp: dropped to rr over 3f out: eased sn after and t.o (jockey said filly stopped quickly. vet said filly bled from nse)* **10/1**

2m 33.63s (-0.87) **Going Correction** +0.125s/f (Slow) **10** Ran SP% **116.0**
Speed ratings (Par 104): **107,106,105,100,98 92,83,81,80,51**
CSF £12.90 TOTE £6.50: £2.50, £1.10, £2.40; EX 12.40 Trifecta £76.20.
Owner Godolphin **Bred** M Gittins & Eadling Farm Ltd **Trained** Newmarket, Suffolk

FOCUS
Plenty of pace on here and the winner swooped late. The form's rated slightly positively.

5811 MATCHBOOK BETTING PODCAST H'CAP 1m 3f 219y(P)
7:30 (7:34) (Class 4) (0-85,87) 4-Y-O+ £6,469 (£1,925; £962; £481; £300; £300) Stalls Low

Form RPR

114- **1** **Garbanzo (IRE)**[207] 7768 5-9-6 **84**.............................. LiamKeniry 1 94
(Ed Walker) *hld up in rr-div: angled to outer wl over 2f out: rdn 2f out: qcknd up over 1f out and led ent fnl f: sltly hung rt sn after: strly pressed fnl f: hld on wl* **13/2**[3]

-301 **2** nk **The Pinto Kid (FR)**[42] 4250 4-9-3 **81**..............................(t) GeorgeWood 2 90
(James Fanshawe) *sn settled in rr-div: clsr over 2f out: rdn 2f out and swtchd to inner: led briefly over 1f out: styd pressing wnr fnl f: no ex cl home* **11/8**[1]

5643 **3** 6 **Brittanic (IRE)**[20] 5086 5-8-5 **69**.............................. HollieDoyle 8 68
(David Simcock) *hld up in rr: rdn on inner over 2f out: kpt on wl over 1f out tl lft bhd by front pair ent fnl f: plugged on* **20/1**

5404 **4** 1 1/4 **Noble Gift**[28] 4792 9-9-2 **80**.............................. KierenFox 4 77
(William Knight) *rousted along leaving stalls to ld after 2f: slowed tempo at 1/2-way: shkn up wl over 3f out and injected sme pce: rdn 3f out: kicked over 2f out: hdd over 1f out: one pce after* **12/1**

3355 **5** 1 1/4 **Running Cloud (IRE)**[42] 4257 4-8-13 **77**..............................(v) TomMarquand 6 72
(Alan King) *s.s and hld up in rr: rdn and outpcd fr wl over 1f out (jockey said gelding was slowly away)* **7/1**

0105 **6** nk **Lost History (IRE)**[9] 5502 6-8-9 **73**.............................. JackMitchell 5 68
(John Spearing) *hld up in rr-div: rdn over 2f out: plugged on* **20/1**

-000 **7** 3 3/4 **Torcello (IRE)**[28] 4792 5-8-7 **78**.............................. ElishaWhittington(7) 3 67
(Shaun Lycett) *early pce and led for 2f: sn trckd ldr: rdn over 2f out: outpcd wl over 1f out* **100/1**

-541 **8** 21 **Frontispiece**[43] 4224 5-9-7 **85**.............................. KieranShoemark 9 40
(Amanda Perrett) *trckd ldrs on inner: rdn over 2f out: plugged on (jockey said gelding lost action around bnd; post-race examination failed to reveal any abnormalities)* **5/1**[2]

1645 **9** 50 **Hareeq**[25] 4924 4-9-9 **87**..............................(b[1]) ShaneKelly 7
(Richard Hughes) *bhd ldr: rdn over 3f out and wknd qckly: eased over 1f out: t.o (jockey said colt stopped quickly. vet said colt had cardiac arrhythmia)* **8/1**

2m 34.15s (-0.35) **Going Correction** +0.125s/f (Slow) **9** Ran SP% **113.9**
Speed ratings (Par 105): **106,105,101,100,100 99,97,83,50**
CSF £15.31 CT £169.48 TOTE £7.80: £2.50, £1.10, £5.00; EX 18.40 Trifecta £234.60.
Owner Chris Stedman **Bred** Herbertstown House Stud **Trained** Upper Lambourn, Berks

FOCUS
The first two drew well clear and had a good scrap. Both improved but there was no great depth to this.

5812 MATCHBOOK CASINO H'CAP (JOCKEY CLUB GRASSROOTS STAYERS' SERIES QUALIFIER) 1m 7f 218y(P)
8:00 (8:03) (Class 4) (0-85,82) 3-Y-O+
£6,469 (£1,925; £962; £481; £300; £300) **Stalls** Low

Form RPR
-411 1 **Land Of Oz**[9] 5487 3-8-3 **70** 6ex........ LukeMorris 7 88+
(Sir Mark Prescott Bt) *hld up in last: shkn up over 2f out and cruised past rivals over 1f out: breezed upsides ldr ent fnl f: shkn up to ld and wnt clr sn after: canter* **4/6**[1]
1002 2 3 ¾ **Le Torrent**[28] 4791 7-9-6 **74**........ TomMarquand 5 80
(Emma Lavelle) *t.k.h early in rr: rdn over 2f out: plugged on fr over 1f out to take 2nd cl home: no ch w v easy wnr* **8/1**[3]
2304 3 nk **Petrastar**[14] 5321 4-9-11 **79**........(h) AdamKirby 2 84
(Clive Cox) *sn led: rdn 2f out: kpt on wl tl wnr breezed upsides over 1f out: lft bhd sn after: stuck on and lost 2nd cl home* **10/1**
000- 4 1 ½ **Author's Dream**[436] 3152 6-10-0 **82**........(v) JasonWatson 6 85
(William Knight) *t.k.h early bhd ldrs: rdn over 2f out: plugged on fr over 1f out* **66/1**
0533 5 3 ¾ **Gavlar**[28] 4791 8-9-5 **73**........(v) CallumShepherd 1 72
(William Knight) *bhd ldrs: rdn over 2f out: plugged on* **16/1**
6513 6 6 **Jumping Cats**[28] 4782 4-9-10 **78**........(p) JackMitchell 4 70
(Chris Wall) *trckd ldr: rdn 4f out: no ex 2f out and wknd (trainer could offer no explanation for gelding's performance)* **7/2**[2]
-060 7 6 **Sunblazer (IRE)**[46] 4118 9-9-1 **69**........(tp) JimCrowley 3 53
(Kim Bailey) *mid-div: effrt 2f out on inner and ev ch: nt qckn and wknd fnl f* **33/1**
3m 33.25s (3.15) **Going Correction** +0.125s/f (Slow)
WFA 3 from 4yo+ 13lb **7 Ran SP% 112.7**
Speed ratings (Par 105): **97,95,94,94,92 89,86**
CSF £6.78 TOTE £1.50: £1.10, £3.10; EX 7.00 Trifecta £29.70.
Owner John Brown & Megan Dennis **Bred** Stetchworth & Middle Park Studs Ltd **Trained** Newmarket, Suffolk

FOCUS
This proved pretty uncompetitive, the winner confirming he's well ahead of his current mark. The second and third are rated to form.

5813 MATCHBOOK 2% NET WIN H'CAP 7f (P)
8:30 (8:30) (Class 5) (0-75,75) 3-Y-O
£3,752 (£1,116; £557; £300; £300; £300) **Stalls** Low

Form RPR
2-02 1 **Dubrava**[33] 4590 3-9-3 **73**........ AndreaAtzeni 8 82
(Roger Varian) *settled bhd ldrs: rdn 2f out: sltly outpcd over 1f out in centre: fnd stride ent fnl f and styd on wl to ld last strides* **4/1**[2]
-000 2 hd **Indian Viceroy**[41] 4300 3-9-3 **73**........(p[1]) OisinMurphy 9 81
(Hughie Morrison) *sn led fr wd draw: rdn 2f out: kpt on wl fr over 1f out tl hdd last strides* **11/1**
1634 3 1 **Amorously (IRE)**[13] 5349 3-9-2 **72**........ SeanLevey 1 77
(Richard Hannon) *racd in mid-div on inner: effrt over 2f out: styd on fnl f* **10/1**
1-25 4 1 ¼ **Carnival Rose**[69] 3278 3-9-5 **75**........ GeorgeWood 3 77
(James Fanshawe) *early pce: sn cl up in mid-div: rdn 2f out: kpt on one pce fnl f* **3/1**[1]
3302 5 ¾ **Balata Bay**[12] 5373 3-9-5 **75**........(b) PatDobbs 2 75
(Richard Hannon) *racd in rr: pushed along fr 2f out: nvr nrr* **5/1**[3]
43-5 6 hd **Deference**[95] 2405 3-9-3 **73**........ RobertHavlin 7 72
(Amanda Perrett) *hld up in rr-div: effrt 2f out: outpcd and shuffled along fr over 1f out* **12/1**
2111 7 ¾ **Alicia Darcy (IRE)**[14] 5308 3-9-4 **74**........(b) AdamMcNamara 4 71
(Archie Watson) *bhd ldrs and a shade keen: rdn 2f out: outpcd and plugged on fr over 1f out (jockey said filly ran too free)* **9/1**
1-60 8 1 **Airwaves**[92] 2510 3-9-4 **74**........ RobHornby 5 68
(Martyn Meade) *early pce: sn bhd ldr on inner: rdn 2f out: ev ch over 1f out: nt qckn fnl f and plugged on* **10/1**
4020 9 ½ **John Betjeman**[34] 4562 3-9-2 **72**........ TomMarquand 6 65
(Mark Gillard) *hld up in rr-div and t.k.h early: rdn over 2f out: no imp* **20/1**
-064 10 nk **Spencers Son (IRE)**[54] 3805 3-9-4 **74**........(p) AdamKirby 10 66
(Richard Spencer) *a in last: effrt over 2f out: no imp* **12/1**
1m 27.65s (1.65) **Going Correction** +0.125s/f (Slow) **10 Ran SP% 118.3**
Speed ratings (Par 100): **95,94,93,92,91 91,90,89,88,88**
CSF £48.30 CT £424.22 TOTE £4.00: £2.10, £4.30, £3.50; EX 45.40 Trifecta £722.60.
Owner Unknown **Bred** Sheikh Mohammed Obaid Al Maktoum **Trained** Newmarket, Suffolk
■ Stewards' Enquiry : Andrea Atzeni two-day ban: excessive use of whip (Aug 24-25)

FOCUS
It didn't pay to be too far off the lead here, with the runner-up controlling the pace. The third helps with the standard.
T/Plt: £5.70 to a £1 stake. Pool: £63,626.08 - 8,033.19 winning units T/Qpdt: £3.00 to a £1 stake. Pool: £7,159.42 - 1,720.04 winning units **Cathal Gahan**

5472 PONTEFRACT (L-H)
Wednesday, August 7

OFFICIAL GOING: Good (good to soft in places; 7.4)
Wind: fairly strong, largely across Weather: Fine, shower during race 4

5814 SOLUTIONS4CLEANING MAIDEN H'CAP (FOR GENTLEMAN AMATEUR RIDERS) 1m 2f 5y
2:20 (2:20) (Class 5) (0-70,70) 3-Y-O+
£3,743 (£1,161; £580; £300; £300; £300) **Stalls** Low

Form RPR
6506 1 **The Rutland Rebel (IRE)**[29] 4761 3-10-13 **62**........ MrPatrickMillman 4 67
(Micky Hammond) *prom: led narrowly over 4f out: rdn over 2f out: asserted 1f out: drvn out (trainer said, regarding the apparent improvement in form, that gelding was suited by a step up in trip to 1m 2f and benefitted from what was, in his opinion, a weaker race here)* **10/1**
6645 2 1 ¼ **Gylo (IRE)**[4] 5695 3-10-8 **62**........(v) MrMatthewEnnis[(5)] 6 64
(David O'Meara) *led for 1f: trckd ldrs: rdn 2f out: wnt 2nd 1f out: styd on but a hld* **3/1**[2]
3420 3 4 ½ **Brutalab**[16] 5248 3-10-5 **54**........ MrWilliamEasterby 3 47
(Tim Easterby) *trckd ldrs: lost pl sltly over 4f out: rdn 2f out: hung lft and sn one pce in 4th: wnt modest 3rd post* **5/4**[1]
0630 4 hd **Burnage Boy (IRE)**[23] 4990 3-9-8 **48**........ AidanMacdonald[(5)] 2 41
(Micky Hammond) *dwlt: hld up in tch: hdwy and trckd ldrs over 6f out: pressed ldr over 4f out: rdn over 2f out: lost 2nd 1f out: sn no ex: lost 3rd post* **9/2**[3]
400- 5 10 **Fading Icon**[21] 6719 4-10-2 **50**........ MrHenryNewcombe[(7)] 7 22
(Philip Kirby) *hld up: rdn over 2f out: sn wknd* **40/1**
5-03 6 17 **Uh Oh Chongo**[187] 524 3-10-5 **61**........ MrEireannCagney[(7)] 1
(Michael Easterby) *led after 1f: hdd over 4f out: sn wknd* **8/1**
2m 17.33s (2.33) **Going Correction** +0.05s/f (Good)
WFA 3 from 4yo 8lb **6 Ran SP% 110.3**
Speed ratings (Par 103): **92,91,87,87,79 65**
CSF £38.37 TOTE £12.50: £3.70, £1.80; EX 44.20 Trifecta £156.70.
Owner Stephen Sugden And Ryder Sugden **Bred** Kildaragh Stud **Trained** Middleham, N Yorks

FOCUS
A moderate handicap run at a steady gallop and it paid to race prominently. The form's rated around the runner-up.

5815 JAYNE - ON COURSE LADY BOOKMAKER EBF NOVICE STKS (PLUS 10 RACE) 6f
2:50 (2:56) (Class 4) 2-Y-O
£5,175 (£1,540; £769; £384) **Stalls** Low

Form RPR
4 1 **Custodian (IRE)**[16] 5234 2-9-5 0........ PaulHanagan 5 81+
(Richard Fahey) *trckd ldrs: pushed along to chal over 1f out: led 1f out: rdn and kpt on wl to draw clr fnl 110yds* **7/2**[2]
4 2 3 **Ainsdale**[30] 4719 2-9-5 0........ BenCurtis 8 72
(K R Burke) *pressed ldr: racd quite keenly: pushed into ld over 2f out: drvn and hdd 1f out: one pce fnl 110yds* **4/1**[3]
4 3 2 **Three Fans (FR)**[19] 5125 2-9-5 0........ RichardKingscote 1 66
(Tom Dascombe) *trckd ldr: rdn along 2f out: drvn over 1f out: kpt on same pce in 3rd fnl f* **11/10**[1]
4 2 ¼ **Jackate** 2-9-5 0........ CamHardie 4 59
(Ollie Pears) *hld up in tch: pushed along 2f out: kpt on same pce fnl f* **33/1**
04 5 1 ½ **Yorkshire Grey (IRE)**[17] 5212 2-9-5 0........(h) GrahamLee 9 55
(Ann Duffield) *dwlt: hld up in tch: pushed along and outpcd 2f out: nvr threatened* **25/1**
62 6 shd **Streaker**[31] 4688 2-9-5 0........ TomEaves 6 54
(Kevin Ryan) *led narrowly: rdn along and hdd over 2f out: wknd fnl f* **4/1**[3]
000 7 1 ¼ **My Havana**[12] 5396 2-9-2 0........ RowanScott[(3)] 3 51
(Nigel Tinkler) *s.i.s: hld up: sn rdn along: nvr threatened* **50/1**
8 11 **The Saddle Rock (IRE)** 2-9-0 0........ JamesSullivan 7 13
(John Wainwright) *slowly away: a towards rr* **50/1**
1m 19.02s (1.92) **Going Correction** +0.05s/f (Good) **8 Ran SP% 120.6**
Speed ratings (Par 96): **89,85,82,79,77 77,75,60**
CSF £18.37 TOTE £4.10: £1.20, £1.70, £1.10; EX 21.00 Trifecta £51.20.
Owner Cheveley Park Stud **Bred** Newstead Breeding **Trained** Musley Bank, N Yorks

FOCUS
Ordinary juvenile form, but a nice effort from the winner.

5816 BET WITH JAYNE - YOUR LOCAL BOOKMAKER H'CAP (DIV I) 1m 6y
3:20 (3:24) (Class 5) (0-70,68) 3-Y-O+
£3,881 (£1,155; £577; £300; £300; £300) **Stalls** Low

Form RPR
-040 1 **Sumner Beach**[11] 5438 5-8-11 **51**........ CamHardie 6 59
(Harriet Bethell) *hld up in rr: swtchd rt to outer over 1f out: qcknd up wl to ld ins fnl f: drvn out* **10/1**
4162 2 1 **Be Bold**[20] 5100 7-8-9 **52**........(b) RowanScott[(3)] 4 58
(Rebecca Bastiman) *trckd ldrs: chal over 2f out: rdn to ld wl over 1f out: hdd ins fnl f: kpt on same pce* **7/1**
6-00 3 nse **Charlie's Boy (IRE)**[17] 5215 3-8-8 **55**........ AndrewMullen 3 60
(Michael Dods) *trckd ldrs: rdn over 2f out: drvn and kpt on fnl f* **6/1**[3]
4550 4 1 ½ **Frankster (FR)**[10] 5474 6-9-6 **60**........(tp) GrahamLee 8 63
(Micky Hammond) *midfield: pushed along and hdwy to chse ldrs over 2f out: rdn over 2f out: one pce* **9/1**
/001 5 2 ½ **Strawberryandcream**[21] 5041 4-9-10 **64**........ PaulHanagan 1 61
(James Bethell) *dwlt: hld up: rdn and sme hdwy over 1f out: one pce ins fnl f* **5/1**[2]
2360 6 hd **Mac Ailey**[17] 5215 3-8-13 **60**........ DavidAllan 10 55
(Tim Easterby) *prom: rdn into narrow ld over 2f out: hdd wl over 1f out: sn drvn: wknd ins fnl f* **7/2**[1]
5600 7 nse **Critical Thinking (IRE)**[18] 5178 5-9-12 **66**........(tp) BenCurtis 2 62
(David Loughnane) *midfield: pushed along over 1f out: rdn and one pce fnl f* **7/2**[1]
6400 8 4 **Intense Style (IRE)**[15] 5274 7-9-8 **67**........ FayeMcManoman[(5)] 7 54
(Les Eyre) *dwlt: hld up: rdn 2f out: wknd ins fnl f* **16/1**
3-00 9 7 **Dyagilev**[16] 5245 4-9-9 **63**........(b[1]) RoystonFfrench 5 34
(Lydia Pearce) *led: rdn and hdd over 2f out: wknd over 1f out* **40/1**
1m 45.35s (-0.55) **Going Correction** +0.05s/f (Good)
WFA 3 from 4yo+ 7lb **9 Ran SP% 115.3**
Speed ratings (Par 103): **104,103,102,101,98 98,98,94,87**
CSF £77.71 CT £460.34 TOTE £12.40: £3.10, £1.90, £2.10; EX 78.70 Trifecta £773.30.
Owner Keith Brown **Bred** Hellwood Stud Farm **Trained** Arnold, E Yorks

FOCUS
Moderate handicap form, but a useful effort from the winner to came from last place. The form's rated around the runner-up and fourth.

5817 BET WITH JAYNE - YOUR LOCAL BOOKMAKER H'CAP (DIV II) 1m 6y
3:50 (3:54) (Class 5) (0-70,71) 3-Y-O+
£3,881 (£1,155; £577; £300; £300; £300) **Stalls** Low

Form RPR
-000 1 **Dawn Breaking**[6] 5593 4-8-9 **49**........(b[1]) PhilDennis 4 60
(Richard Whitaker) *mde all: slipped 4 l clr over 2f out: rdn over 1f out: unchal* **7/1**[3]
2446 2 3 **Newmarket Warrior (IRE)**[40] 4329 8-10-0 **68**........(p) DavidAllan 1 73
(Iain Jardine) *hld up in midfield: pushed along and hdwy over 1f out: wnt 2nd 1f out: kpt on but no ch w wnr* **5/1**[2]
5650 3 1 **Star Of Valour (IRE)**[72] 3163 4-9-1 **55**........(w) PaulMulrennan 5 57
(Lynn Siddall) *slowly away: hld up: rdn over 1f out: kpt on fnl f: wnt 3rd fnl 75yds* **8/1**
0044 4 2 ¼ **Quoteline Direct**[22] 5024 6-9-9 **63**........(h) GrahamLee 2 60
(Micky Hammond) *trckd ldrs: rdn over 2f out: drvn to chse clr ldr over 1f out: wknd ins fnl f* **5/1**[2]

0000 5 3/4 **Laqab (IRE)**[16] 5248 6-8-13 **53**........................ PaddyMathers 6 48
(Derek Shaw) *v.s.a: hld up in rr: sme late hdwy: nvr threatened (jockey said gelding missed the break)* **11/1**

2-30 6 1/2 **So Macho (IRE)**[15] 5283 4-9-12 **66**........................ SamJames 7 60
(Grant Tuer) *trckd ldrs: rdn along and lost pl whn bit short of room over 2f out: wknd ins fnl f* **5/1**[2]

0506 7 1 1/4 **Sir Victor (IRE)**[20] 5080 3-9-10 **71**..................(p) RichardKingscote 8 61
(Tom Dascombe) *prom: rdn along over 3f out: outpcd over 2f out: wknd ins fnl f (vet said gelding lost its left hind shoe)* **7/1**[3]

2423 8 2 1/2 **Juniors Fantasy (IRE)**[15] 5272 3-8-11 **58**..................(t) DuranFentiman 3 42
(Tim Easterby) *midfield: rdn and sme hdwy on outside over 1f out: wknd ins fnl f (trainer's rep could offer no explanation for the gelding's performance)* **4/1**[1]

4400 9 10 **Tagur (IRE)**[30] 4728 5-9-13 **67**..................(p) TomEaves 9 29
(Kevin Ryan) *rdn along leaving stalls: midfield: hdwy and chsd ldrs on outer over 4f out: rdn along 3f out: wknd over 1f out* **33/1**

1m 45.46s (-0.44) **Going Correction** +0.05s/f (Good)
WFA 3 from 4yo+ 7lb 9 Ran SP% **117.4**
Speed ratings (Par 103): **104,101,100,97,97 96,95,92,82**
CSF £42.61 CT £291.12 TOTE £8.30: £2.50, £2.20, £2.30; EX 38.70 Trifecta £358.50.
Owner D Gration, G Sutcliffe, N Farman, Jeaton **Bred** Mrs M J Blackburn **Trained** Scarcroft, W Yorks

FOCUS
The second leg of a lowly handicap and, in contrast to division one, where the winner came from last place, the winner made every yard. The runner-up looks the best guide.

5818 TIESPLANET.COM - LADIES LOVE GUYS IN TIES H'CAP 1m 4f 5y
4:20 (4:20) (Class 3) (0-90,90) 3-Y-O+

£9,337 (£2,796; £1,398; £699; £349; £175) **Stalls** Low

Form RPR

6322 1 **Qawamees (IRE)**[36] 4491 4-8-13 **75**..................(bt) KieranO'Neill 7 82
(Michael Easterby) *hld up in rr: pushed along over 3f out: hdwy on outer 2f out: drvn to chse ldrs over 1f out: led 110yds out: styd on wl* **20/1**

1232 2 1 1/2 **Speed Company (IRE)**[26] 4890 6-9-13 **89**........................ BenCurtis 6 94
(Ian Williams) *in tch: pushed along 2f out: drvn over 1f out: styd on fnl f: wnt 2nd post* **5/1**[3]

-431 3 shd **Volcanic Sky**[14] 5305 4-9-12 **88**........................ CallumShepherd 3 93
(Saeed bin Suroor) *dwlt: hld up: hdwy to trck ldrs over 3f out: rdn to ld appr fnl f: hdd 100yds out: one pce: lost 2nd post* **6/4**[1]

13-0 4 2 3/4 **Archi's Affaire**[53] 3862 5-10-0 **90**........................ PaulMulrennan 5 90
(Michael Dods) *prom: rdn to ld over 1f out: hdd appr fnl f: wknd ins fnl f* **9/1**

4250 5 nk **Mutamaded (IRE)**[11] 5417 6-9-8 **84**........................ JamesSullivan 2 84
(Ruth Carr) *trckd ldrs: rdn along 2f out: wknd ins fnl f* **9/1**

610- 6 1 1/4 **Elysian Flame**[265] 9083 3-8-6 **78**........................ NathanEvans 1 80+
(Michael Easterby) *hld up in tch: pushed along and hdwy whn short of room on inner 1f out: no ch after: short of room again fnl 110yds (jockey said gelding was continually denied a clear run in the final furlong)* **6/1**

302 7 3 1/4 **My Reward**[18] 5199 7-9-12 **88**........................ DavidAllan 4 81
(Tim Easterby) *led: rdn and hdd over 1f out: sn wknd (trainer's rep could offer no explanation for the poor form shown)* **9/2**[2]

2m 39.83s (-1.27) **Going Correction** +0.05s/f (Good)
WFA 3 from 4yo+ 10lb 7 Ran SP% **113.9**
Speed ratings (Par 107): **106,105,104,103,102 102,99**
CSF £113.92 TOTE £21.60: £7.40, £2.70; EX 104.40 Trifecta £328.80.
Owner The Irrational Group & J Blackburn **Bred** Shadwell Estate Company Limited **Trained** Sheriff Hutton, N Yorks
■ Stewards' Enquiry : Kieran O'Neill two-day ban: interference & careless riding (Aug 24-25)

FOCUS
The early gallop was fairly steady, but increased a fair way out and the winner came from off the pace. Solid form rated around the runner-up.

5819 CHAPLINS CLUB H'CAP 5f 3y
4:50 (4:51) (Class 5) (0-75,75) 3-Y-O+

£3,881 (£1,155; £577; £300; £300; £300) **Stalls** Low

Form RPR

6542 1 **Move In Time**[22] 5027 11-9-7 **75**........................ HarrisonShaw(5) 3 88
(Paul Midgley) *prom: rdn and hdwy to ld over 1f out: sn clr: comf* **11/4**[2]

0343 2 3 1/2 **Suwaan (IRE)**[16] 5244 5-9-4 **67**..................(h) JamesSullivan 4 67
(Ruth Carr) *stdd in last pl: pushed along and effrt wl over 1f out: chsd (clr) wnr ins fnl f: kpt on: nt pce to chal* **5/1**

3635 3 1 1/2 **Red Stripes (USA)**[18] 5180 7-8-0 **56** oh1..................(b) GavinAshton(7) 5 51
(Lisa Williamson) *chsd ldng pair: rdn along 2f out: kpt on same pce ins fnl f* **20/1**

0021 4 nk **Johnny Cavagin**[10] 5478 10-9-11 **74** 4ex........................ GrahamLee 6 68
(Paul Midgley) *in tch: rdn and outpcd 2f out: rallied ins fnl f: kpt on: no imp* **5/2**[1]

-000 5 3/4 **Militia**[13] 5330 4-9-4 **70**........................ SeanDavis(3) 9 61
(Richard Fahey) *slt ld to over 1f out: rdn and wknd ins fnl f* **12/1**

0060 6 1 1/4 **Henley**[4] 5691 7-9-12 **75**........................ BenCurtis 8 62
(Tracy Waggott) *hld up: effrt on outside 2f out: sn no imp* **16/1**

5563 7 1/2 **Billy Dylan (IRE)**[8] 5515 4-9-9 **75**..................(v) ConorMcGovern(3) 7 60
(David O'Meara) *disp ld to 2f out: rdn and wknd fnl f* **12/1**

1530 8 4 1/2 **Fizzy Feet (IRE)**[25] 4904 3-9-8 **74**........................ RichardKingscote 2 42
(David Loughnane) *hld up on ins: rdn and struggling 2f out: sn btn* **4/1**[3]

1m 2.62s (-1.28) **Going Correction** +0.05s/f (Good)
WFA 3 from 4yo+ 3lb 8 Ran SP% **117.9**
Speed ratings (Par 103): **112,106,104,103,102 100,99,92**
CSF £17.65 CT £231.12 TOTE £3.50: £1.10, £1.90, £4.40; EX 17.70 Trifecta £179.80.
Owner A Turton, J Blackburn & R Bond **Bred** Bond Thoroughbred Corporation **Trained** Westow, N Yorks

FOCUS
Veteran sprinters headed up the market for this contest and the formerly high-class winner proved much the best. With his jockey's claim, he's rated in line with this year's form.

5820 RIU HOTELS AND RESORTS LADIES DAY VETERANS' H'CAP 1m 6y
5:20 (5:20) (Class 4) (0-80,79) 6-Y-O+

£5,207 (£1,549; £774; £387; £300; £300) **Stalls** Low

Form RPR

5424 1 **Tukhoom (IRE)**[5] 5616 6-9-7 **79**..................(p) DavidNolan 8 85
(David O'Meara) *pressed ldr: led over 2f out: rdn clr over 1f out: dwindling advantage ins fnl f: hld on wl cl home* **4/1**[2]

1054 2 hd **Storm Ahead (IRE)**[8] 5516 6-9-4 **76**..................(b) DavidAllan 7 81
(Tim Easterby) *hld up: shkn up and hdwy to chse (wnr) over 1f out: sn rdn: edgd lft and kpt on wl fnl 100yds: jst hld* **4/1**[2]

-124 3 3/4 **Bollihope**[174] 722 7-8-8 **66**........................ JasonHart 2 69
(Shaun Keightley) *dwlt: hld up in last pl: effrt on outside over 1f out: edgd lft and kpt on fnl f: nrst fin* **7/1**[3]

-004 4 3 1/4 **Dream Walker (FR)**[22] 5022 10-9-2 **74**..................(t[1]) BenCurtis 3 70
(Brian Ellison) *hld up on ins: effrt and angled rt over 1f out: kpt on fnl f: nt rch first three* **8/1**

6604 5 1 **Noble Peace**[21] 5061 6-8-12 **70**........................ PJMcDonald 5 64
(Lydia Pearce) *prom: effrt and pushed along over 2f out: fdd fnl f* **12/1**

0003 6 2 **Calder Prince (IRE)**[19] 5130 6-9-5 **77**........................ RichardKingscote 6 66
(Tom Dascombe) *stmbld leaving stalls: sn cl up: rdn over 2f out: wknd fnl f (jockey said gelding stumbled at the start and missed the break and was subsequently denied getting a prominent position)* **3/1**[1]

-000 7 1 3/4 **Capton**[26] 4875 6-9-5 **77**........................ NathanEvans 1 62
(Michael Easterby) *prom: lost pl 2f out: rdn and no imp whn nt clr run ins fnl f (jockey said gelding was denied a clear run just inside the final furlong)* **7/1**[3]

0000 8 3 **Echo Of Lightning**[22] 5021 9-8-0 **65**..................(p) IzzyClifton(7) 4 43
(Roger Fell) *led to over 2f out: rdn and wknd over 1f out* **18/1**

1m 44.28s (-1.62) **Going Correction** +0.05s/f (Good) 8 Ran SP% **114.1**
Speed ratings: **110,109,109,105,104 102,101,98**
CSF £20.28 CT £107.61 TOTE £4.50: £1.80, £1.50, £2.40; EX 16.70 Trifecta £96.80.
Owner R Bremer **Bred** Kabansk Ltd & Rathbarry Stud **Trained** Upper Helmsley, N Yorks

FOCUS
Ordinary form, rated a bit cautiously around the runner-up.

5821 KEITH HAMMILL MEMORIAL H'CAP 6f
5:50 (5:51) (Class 4) (0-80,82) 3-Y-O+

£5,207 (£1,549; £774; £387; £300; £300) **Stalls** Low

Form RPR

6001 1 **Mr Orange (IRE)**[19] 5157 6-9-7 **75**..................(p) GrahamLee 2 84
(Paul Midgley) *prom: pushed along 1/2-way: hdwy to ld 1f out: drvn and kpt on wl fnl f* **8/1**

0231 2 1 **Baby Steps**[15] 5281 3-9-6 **78**........................ RichardKingscote 6 83
(David Loughnane) *pressed ldr: effrt and ev ch 1f out: kpt on: hld nr fin* **13/2**[2]

2013 3 shd **Magical Effect (IRE)**[10] 5476 7-9-9 **77**........................ JamieGormley 11 83+
(Ruth Carr) *hld up on outside: hdwy 2f out: pressed ldrs ins fnl f: kpt on* **11/2**[1]

6164 4 1 1/4 **Penny Pot Lane**[13] 5333 6-8-11 **65**..................(p) LewisEdmunds 12 67+
(Richard Whitaker) *hld up: rdn over 2f out: kpt on wl fnl f: nrst fin* **25/1**

5062 5 nk **Full Intention**[19] 5144 5-9-1 **69**..................(p) RoystonFfrench 8 70
(Lydia Pearce) *hld up: rdn along over 2f out: r.o fnl f: nt pce to chal* **20/1**

021 6 nk **Highly Sprung (IRE)**[10] 5476 6-9-4 **77** 5ex........................ HarrisonShaw(5) 7 77
(Les Eyre) *prom: drvn and outpcd over 2f out: rallied over 1f out: one pce wl ins fnl f* **11/2**[1]

003 7 1 **Private Matter**[39] 4365 5-9-9 **77**..................(b) BenCurtis 4 74
(Amy Murphy) *hld up: rdn 2f out: hdd 1f out: sn wknd* **9/1**

2603 8 1/2 **Avenue Of Stars**[25] 4912 6-8-10 **64**..................(v) JasonHart 3 59
(Karen McLintock) *hld up on ins: drvn along over 2f out: effrt over 1f out: no imp fnl f* **12/1**

3156 9 hd **Galloway Hills**[17] 5217 4-9-11 **82**..................(p) ConorMcGovern(3) 5 76
(Phillip Makin) *hld up towards rr: drvn along over 2f out: no imp fr over 1f out* **7/1**[3]

0065 10 2 1/2 **Ower Fly**[11] 5416 6-9-12 **80**........................ PJMcDonald 9 66
(Ruth Carr) *dwlt: hld up: drvn along over 2f out: nvr a factor* **8/1**

0-40 11 nk **Wasntexpectingthat**[117] 1736 3-9-5 **80**..................(w) SeanDavis(3) 1 64
(Richard Fahey) *trckd ldrs: smooth hdwy over 2f out: rdn and wknd over 1f out* **12/1**

2140 12 1 3/4 **Luzum (IRE)**[9] 5488 4-9-0 **68**........................ KieranO'Neill 10 48
(Michael Easterby) *hld up: drvn along over 2f out: wknd wl over 1f out* **14/1**

1m 16.43s (-0.67) **Going Correction** +0.05s/f (Good)
WFA 3 from 4yo+ 4lb 12 Ran SP% **119.5**
Speed ratings (Par 105): **106,104,104,102,102 102,100,100,99,96 96,93**
CSF £59.76 CT £320.73 TOTE £7.20: £2.40, £2.70, £2.00; EX 74.70 Trifecta £737.40.
Owner J Blackburn & A Turton **Bred** Rathbarry Stud **Trained** Westow, N Yorks

FOCUS
An open sprint in which the winner was close to his old best.
T/Jkpt: Not Won. T/Plt: £391.10 to a £1 stake. Pool: £62,421.42 - 116.5 winning units T/Qpdt: £55.50 to a £1 stake. Pool: £6,374.67 - 84.88 winning units **Andrew Sheret**

5526 YARMOUTH (L-H)
Wednesday, August 7

OFFICIAL GOING: Good to firm (watered; 7.5)
Wind: Breezy Weather: Very warm and sunny spells; 25 degrees

5822 JOHN KEMP 4 X 4 CENTRE OF NORWICH H'CAP 5f 42y
5:15 (5:15) (Class 6) (0-60,71) 3-Y-O+

£2,781 (£827; £413; £300; £300; £300) **Stalls** Centre

Form RPR

-005 1 **Haveoneyerself (IRE)**[34] 4563 4-9-5 **56**..................(p) DavidEgan 6 67
(John Butler) *led stands' side quartet: led overall fr 1/2-way: rdn and in command fnl f* **7/1**

5025 2 2 1/4 **Bronze Beau**[20] 5094 12-9-4 **58**..................(tp) CameronNoble(3) 2 61
(Linda Stubbs) *taken down early: led centre quartet: chsd wnr fr 1/2-way: drvn over 1f out: edgd rt and a hld* **6/1**[3]

4-50 3 1 **Swell Song**[34] 4563 3-8-10 **50**..................(p[1]) JosephineGordon 1 48
(Robert Cowell) *chsd ldrs in centre: rdn to go 3rd over 1f out: no imp after* **16/1**

125- 4 1 **Broughton Excels**[264] 9098 4-9-2 **53**........................ StevieDonohoe 3 49
(Stuart Williams) *chsd centre quartet ldr: drvn 2f out: btn over 1f out (vet said gelding lost right-hind shoe)* **10/3**[2]

-050 5 nk **Raise A Little Joy**[39] 4378 4-8-5 **45**..................(v[1]) NoelGarbutt(3) 8 40
(J R Jenkins) *last on stands' side: drvn and outpcd 1/2-way: passed faders ins fnl f: no ch* **50/1**

30-0 6 3 1/2 **Mysusy (IRE)**[65] 3425 3-8-11 **51**..................(v[1]) DavidProbert 5 32
(Robert Cowell) *chsd ldrs stands' side: rdn 1/2-way: fnd nil and btn wl over 1f out* **14/1**

4611 7 1/2 **Perfect Charm**[6] 5582 3-9-10 **71** 12ex..................(b) Pierre-LouisJamin(7) 7 50
(Archie Watson) *bhd on stands' side: rdn and struggling 1/2-way (jockey said filly was never travelling)* **11/8**[1]

4330 **8** 1 1/4 **Tina Teaspoon**[28] 4776 5-8-8 **45**......(h) JoeyHaynes 4 21+
(Derek Shaw) *stdd and lost 6 l s: plld hrd in last pl in centre: drvn and floundering 1/2-way* **11/1**

1m 1.41s (-0.49) **Going Correction** +0.025s/f (Good)
WFA 3 from 4yo+ 3lb **8** Ran SP% **114.8**
Speed ratings (Par 101): **104,100,98,97,96 91,90,88**
CSF £48.45 CT £651.51 TOTE £8.20: £4.10, £3.10, £7.10; EX 54.40 Trifecta £324.40.
Owner J Butler **Bred** Michael M Byrne **Trained** Newmarket, Suffolk

FOCUS
A modest sprint handicap. The ground had officially dried out to good to firm, firm in places, but heavy watering was in evidence with a loose-topped surface in places. The field split in two, racing centrally and near side. The winner readily made virtually all up the near rail, and is rated back to last year's best which came over C&D.

5823 MATCHBOOK EBF FUTURE STAYERS NOVICE STKS (PLUS 10 RACE) (SIRE AND DAM RESTRICTED RACE) 7f 3y

5:45 (5:45) (Class 4) 2-Y-O **£9,056** (£2,695; £1,346; £673) **Stalls** Centre

Form RPR
1 **With Promise** 2-9-5 0...... DanielMuscutt 2 76+
(David Lanigan) *trckd ldrs in slowly run r: rdn 2f out: led over 1f out: styd on wl* **14/1**

2 3/4 **Zafeer (JPN)** 2-9-5 0...... DavidEgan 3 74+
(Marco Botti) *lost 6 l at s: sn in tch but green thrght: t.k.h tl shkn up 3f out: wnt 2nd fnl 100yds but wl hld* **13/2**[2]

3 nk **Collette (IRE)** 2-9-0 0...... PatCosgrave 1 68+
(Hugo Palmer) *lost 6 l at s: plld hrd and sn in tch: rdn and styd on to go 3rd 75yds out: rn green and decent effrt* **8/1**[3]

4 1 1/4 **Sun Cuisine (USA)** 2-9-5 0...... JamesDoyle 4 70
(Charlie Appleby) *pressed ldr: led over 2f out: sn pushed along and nt really extending himself: hdd over 1f out: lost two pls in fnl 100yds* **30/100**[1]

0 **5** 15 **Abenakian (IRE)**[14] 5314 2-9-2 0...... TimClark(3) 5 29
(Jane Chapple-Hyam) *racd freely and led at modest pce tl rdn and hdd over 2f out: dropped out rapidly: t.o (jockey said gelding stopped quickly)* **66/1**

1m 27.42s (2.32) **Going Correction** +0.025s/f (Good) **5** Ran SP% **109.5**
Speed ratings (Par 96): **87,86,85,84,67**
CSF £89.46 TOTE £12.50: £4.00, £2.20; EX 48.10 Trifecta £109.40.
Owner Abdulla Al Mansoori **Bred** Rabbah Bloodstock Limited **Trained** Newmarket, Suffolk

FOCUS
The feature race was a juvenile novice contest with very little form on offer beforehand, restricted to the progeny of winners over at least 1m2f. They went a slow gallop and the long odds-on favourite finished held on debut. The time was ordinary.

5824 LOWESTOFT HYDRAULICS H'CAP 1m 2f 23y

6:15 (6:15) (Class 6) (0-65,66) 4-Y-O+
£2,781 (£827; £413; £300; £300; £300) **Stalls** Low

Form RPR
1 **Mauricio (IRE)**[9] 3677 5-9-8 **66**...... PatCosgrave 4 72+
(Dr Richard Newland) *midfield: rdn fr 1/2-way: effrt over 1f out: vigorously drvn to ld between rivals 100yds out: sn clr: gd ride* **13/2**[3]

4000 **2** 1 1/4 **Telekinetic**[22] 5025 4-8-2 **46** oh1...... ShelleyBirkett 2 50
(Julia Feilden) *led 1f: chsd ldrs: lost pl briefly 4f out: rdn and rallied on outer to go 2nd wl over 1f out: led 1f out tl overwhelmed by wnr fnl 100yds* **14/1**

25-3 **3** 3/4 **Konigin**[216] 38 4-9-5 **63**......(t) StevieDonohoe 9 65
(John Berry) *stdd s: last tl 4f out: rdn and hdwy on outer over 1f out: fin wl to go 3rd cl home: too much to do* **9/1**

3506 **4** 1 3/4 **Makambe (IRE)**[41] 4296 4-9-7 **65**...... JoeyHaynes 3 64
(Chelsea Banham) *settled towards rr: shkn up to improve 3f out: led 2f out tl rdn and hdd 1f out: plodded on: lost 2nd 100yds out and lost 3rd fnl 75yds* **7/1**

0004 **5** 5 **Incredible Dream (IRE)**[8] 5528 6-8-6 **50**......(tp) NickyMackay 1 39
(Conrad Allen) *reluctant to leave paddock: drvn to begin: sn prom: led 1/2-way: rdn and hdd 2f out: fnd nil and sn btn* **9/2**[2]

2030 **6** 3/4 **Lunar Deity**[14] 5316 10-8-7 **58**...... MarcoGhiani(7) 6 46
(Stuart Williams) *racd freely: led after 1f: hdd 1/2-way: rdn and lost pl tamely over 2f out* **13/2**[3]

30-4 **7** nse **Visor**[39] 4370 4-9-5 **63**......(h) DanielMuscutt 8 51
(James Fanshawe) *cl up tl drvn and no rspnse 3f out: sn toiling (trainer rep could offer no explanation for gelding's poor performance other than he may prefer a softer surface than Good To Firm)* **6/4**[1]

2m 7.32s (-1.48) **Going Correction** +0.025s/f (Good) **7** Ran SP% **114.0**
Speed ratings (Par 101): **106,105,104,103,99 98,98**
CSF £85.93 CT £816.37 TOTE £3.90: £2.60, £6.10; EX 148.30 Trifecta £992.80.
Owner J A Provan & Partner **Bred** T Jones **Trained** Claines, Worcs

FOCUS
Add 10 yards. A modest handicap. The tempo increased notably after a couple of furlongs and it produced a decisive winner.

5825 NORWICH OFFICE FURNITURE H'CAP 1m 6f 17y

6:45 (6:46) (Class 5) (0-75,74) 3-Y-O+ **£3,428** (£1,020; £509; £300) **Stalls** High

Form RPR
-032 **1** **Road To Paris (IRE)**[12] 5378 3-8-3 **58**...... DavidEgan 3 71+
(Sir Mark Prescott Bt) *mde all: racd enthusiastically: rdn over 3f out: kpt finding and in command whn edging rt fr 1f out: pushed out* **8/11**[1]

0014 **2** 4 **Manton Warrior (IRE)**[30] 4729 3-8-13 **68**...... StevieDonohoe 4 72
(Charlie Fellowes) *settled in 3rd: rdn over 3f out: chsd wnr 1f out: nvr making any imp on wnr* **7/1**[3]

4-01 **3** 1 1/2 **Highland Sky (IRE)**[27] 4843 4-9-11 **69**......(h) JamesDoyle 5 71
(David Simcock) *settled in last pl: 8 l bhd home turn: rdn 3f out: wnt 2nd ins fnl f but nvr looked like chalng* **9/1**

2301 **4** 6 **Trailboss (IRE)**[39] 4370 4-10-0 **72**......(b) PatCosgrave 2 69
(Ed Vaughan) *chsd wnr: drvn over 2f out: flattered briefly: wknd after and lost two pls fr 1f out: eased (trainer rep said, regarding poor performance, gelding failed to stay 1m6f trip)* **5/2**[2]

3m 6.71s (2.01) **Going Correction** +0.025s/f (Good)
WFA 3 from 4yo+ 11lb **4** Ran SP% **109.0**
Speed ratings (Par 103): **95,92,91,88**
CSF £6.23 TOTE £1.60; EX 5.70 Trifecta £11.80.
Owner Jones, Julian, Lee, Royle & Wicks **Bred** Rabbah Bloodstock Limited **Trained** Newmarket, Suffolk

FOCUS
Add 10 yards. A fair staying handicap. The odds-on favourite readily dictated his own modest to even gallop.

5826 MOULTON NURSERIES OF ACLE H'CAP 5f 42y

7:15 (7:15) (Class 5) (0-75,74) 3-Y-O **£3,428** (£1,020; £509; £300) **Stalls** Centre

Form RPR
5643 **1** **Invincible Larne (IRE)**[21] 5064 3-8-10 **63**......(v) PatCosgrave 2 70
(Mick Quinn) *sn led: drvn clr over 1f out: easily* **15/8**[2]

5004 **2** 3 3/4 **Phoenix Star (IRE)**[21] 5064 3-9-0 **67**...... JosephineGordon 3 61
(Nick Littmoden) *t.k.h: stdd in last pl: rdn 2f out: wnt 2nd wl ins fnl f: no ch w wnr* **9/2**[3]

6234 **3** 1/2 **Mr Buttons (IRE)**[13] 5356 3-9-4 **74**...... CameronNoble(3) 4 66
(Linda Stubbs) *rdn and pressed wnr over 2f out: readily outpcd over 1f out: lost 2nd fnl 50yds (jockey said gelding was never travelling)* **11/10**[1]

640- **4** 3 1/4 **Disruptor (FR)**[352] 6348 3-9-3 **70**...... DavidEgan 1 50
(Charlie Wallis) *pressed wnr tl rdn over 2f out: wknd and racd awkwardly fr over 1f out* **10/1**

1m 1.22s (-0.68) **Going Correction** +0.025s/f (Good) **4** Ran SP% **109.7**
Speed ratings (Par 100): **106,100,99,94**
CSF £9.92 TOTE £2.40; EX 9.40 Trifecta £17.60.
Owner Kenny Bruce **Bred** Hall Of Fame Stud Ltd **Trained** Newmarket, Suffolk

FOCUS
A fair 3yo sprint handicap. The second-favourite made virtually all in clear-cut fashion centrally in a good comparative time.

5827 MICHAEL FOULGER FILLIES' H'CAP 1m 3y

7:45 (7:45) (Class 4) (0-85,81) 3-Y-O+ **£5,207** (£1,549; £774; £387; £300) **Stalls** Centre

Form RPR
4-32 **1** **Scentasia**[42] 4258 3-9-3 **79**...... NickyMackay 2 90+
(John Gosden) *taken down early: mde all: readily drew clr under hands and heels fnl f* **10/11**[1]

-333 **2** 2 1/2 **Dupioni (IRE)**[11] 5441 3-9-5 **81**...... DavidProbert 4 86
(Rae Guest) *settled trcking ldrs: rdn to go 2nd over 1f out: chal briefly: sn outpcd* **7/2**[2]

-636 **3** 5 **Romola**[40] 4318 3-9-5 **81**...... JamesDoyle 1 75
(Sir Michael Stoute) *3rd tl rdn to go 2nd over 2f out tl over 1f out: sn fdd* **9/2**[3]

-503 **4** 2 3/4 **Bint Dandy (IRE)**[21] 5061 8-9-3 **72**......(b) DavidEgan 3 60
(Charlie Wallis) *pressed ldr tl rdn and dropped out rapidly over 2f out* **25/1**

1041 **5** 1 1/2 **Coastline (IRE)**[34] 4566 3-9-2 **78**...... LouisSteward 5 62
(James Tate) *towards rr: rdn and labouring over 2f out: sn wl bhd (trainer rep could offer no explanation for filly's performance)* **6/1**

1m 37.3s (-0.90) **Going Correction** +0.025s/f (Good)
WFA 3 from 8yo 7lb **5** Ran SP% **110.9**
Speed ratings (Par 102): **105,102,97,94,93**
CSF £4.45 TOTE £1.60: £1.10, £2.30; EX 4.10 Trifecta £10.60.
Owner Sheikh Juma Dalmook Al Maktoum **Bred** Godolphin **Trained** Newmarket, Suffolk

FOCUS
A fairly decent fillies' handicap. The odds-on favourite quickened up well to win going away off her own gradually increasing tempo.

5828 GROSVENOR CASINO OF GREAT YARMOUTH FILLIES' H'CAP 7f 3y

8:15 (8:16) (Class 5) (0-70,71) 3-Y-O+
£3,428 (£1,020; £509; £300; £300; £300) **Stalls** Centre

Form RPR
F000 **1** **Spanish Mane (IRE)**[19] 5144 4-8-7 **51** oh2...... ShelleyBirkett 4 57
(Julia Feilden) *t.k.h: led after 3f: pushed along and edgd lft ins fnl f: jnd fnl 100yds: won on nod: gamely (trainer said, regarding improvement in form, filly benefited from making running today and may have appreciated the removal of hood)* **33/1**

0642 **2** hd **Roman Spinner**[12] 5376 4-9-13 **71**......(t) DavidProbert 7 76
(Rae Guest) *dwlt: rdn and hdwy 2f out: str chal ins fnl f: upsides wnr fnl 100yds: jst pipped* **7/1**

4323 **3** nse **Chloellie**[12] 5386 4-9-5 **70**...... TobyEley(7) 6 75
(J R Jenkins) *towards rr: rdn and str run ins fnl f: edgd lft: too much to do and jst failed (jockey said filly hung left under pressure)* **12/1**

0212 **4** 1 3/4 **Sonnet Rose (IRE)**[15] 5282 5-9-0 **63**......(bt) SebastianWoods(5) 2 63
(Conrad Allen) *led 3f: pressed wnr: drvn 1f out: no ex fnl 100yds* **7/2**[2]

6241 **5** 3/4 **Dubai Elegance**[4] 5659 5-8-4 **51** 5ex......(p) NoelGarbutt(3) 3 52
(Derek Shaw) *t.k.h: pressed ldrs: rdn over 2f out: wnt rt and btn over 1f out* **9/2**[3]

5032 **6** 2 1/2 **Caen Na Coille (USA)**[11] 5429 3-9-7 **71**...... JamesDoyle 8 68
(Ed Dunlop) *dwlt: cl up after 3f: rdn over 2f out: nt much luck in running and btn whn bmpd and snatched up ins fnl f* **9/2**[3]

53-4 **7** 1 1/4 **Backstreet Girl (IRE)**[32] 4651 3-9-1 **65**...... DavidEgan 5 51
(Roger Varian) *towards rr: rdn and btn over 1f out (trainer rep said filly didn't stay the 7f trip on this occasion)* **9/4**[1]

1m 25.46s (0.36) **Going Correction** +0.025s/f (Good)
WFA 3 from 4yo+ 6lb **7** Ran SP% **112.5**
Speed ratings (Par 100): **98,97,97,95,94 92,90**
CSF £232.61 CT £2931.94 TOTE £28.40: £8.90, £3.80; EX 251.00 Trifecta £729.70.
Owner Stowstowquickquickstow Partnership **Bred** Ringfort Stud **Trained** Exning, Suffolk

FOCUS
An ordinary fillies' handicap. One of the outsiders raced keenly into the lead, gradually came over to the possibly favoured near rail and showed guts to fend off challengers on either side close home.
T/Plt: £3,991.30 to a £1 stake. Pool: £50,301.72 - 9.2 winning units T/Qpdt: £57.70 to a £1 stake. Pool: £7,833.91 - 100.32 winning units **Iain Mackenzie**

5829 - 5836a (Foreign Racing) - See Raceform Interactive

5800 BRIGHTON (L-H)

Thursday, August 8

OFFICIAL GOING: Good to firm (8.6)
Wind: light, half against Weather: fine

5837 GOLDEN LION GROUP (S) H'CAP 6f 210y

2:10 (2:10) (Class 6) (0-60,60) 3-Y-O+
£2,781 (£827; £413; £300; £300; £300) **Stalls** Centre

Form RPR
0364 **1** **Imbucato**[1] 5806 5-9-0 **50**......(p1) TomMarquand 6 56
(Tony Carroll) *midfield: effrt and chsd ldng pair ent fnl 2f: clsd u.p over 1f out: hung lft but led ins fnl f: styd on (jockey said gelding hung left-handed)* **11/8**[1]

0000 **2** ¾ **Rock In Society (IRE)**[1] 5806 4-8-11 **52**..............(b) DarraghKeenan(5) 8 56
(John Butler) *sn chsng clr ldr: pushed along ent fnl 2f: rdn and clsd over 1f out: ev ch 1f out: chsd wnr and kpt on same pce ins fnl f* **9/1**

0422 **3** 3¼ **Tarrzan (IRE)**[30] 4754 3-8-11 **53**.............................. HectorCrouch 3 46
(John Gallagher) *taken down early: midfield: effrt wl over 2f out: kpt on u.p ins fnl f: nvr trbld ldrs* **4/1**[2]

0200 **4** ¾ **Don't Cry About It (IRE)**[15] 5310 4-9-1 **51**..............(bt) CharlesBishop 4 44
(Ali Stronge) *midfield: effrt over 2f out: sme hdwy u.p over 1f out: kpt on ins fnl f: nvr trbld ldrs* **9/1**

0-66 **5** ¾ **Hellovaqueen**[45] 4181 4-9-3 **60**..............(b) GeorgeRooke(7) 2 51+
(Richard Hughes) *led and sn clr: rdn over 1f out: hdd ins fnl f: sn btn and wknd fnl 100yds* **7/1**[3]

5400 **6** 2 **Seaforth (IRE)**[27] 4873 7-8-13 **49**..............(p) HollieDoyle 7 35
(Adrian Wintle) *taken down early: chsd ldr early: chsd ldng pair after: rdn over 2f out: sn struggling and lost pl 2f out: wl hld fnl f* **8/1**

0005 **7** 5 **Malaysian Boleh**[1] 5806 9-8-10 **46** oh1..............(v) JasonWatson 5 18
(Phil McEntee) *s.i.s: sn rdn and nvr travelling wl in rr: nvr involved (jockey said gelding was never travelling)* **14/1**

0340 **8** nk **The Special One (IRE)**[30] 4749 6-8-10 **46**..............(t) RossaRyan 1 17
(Phil McEntee) *a in rr of main gp: rdn and no hdwy over 2f out: nvr involved* **16/1**

1m 21.5s (-2.30) **Going Correction** -0.325s/f (Firm)
WFA 3 from 4yo+ 6lb **8 Ran SP% 118.3**
Speed ratings (Par 101): **100,99,95,94,93 91,85,85**
CSF £15.75 CT £42.97 TOTE £2.10: £1.10, £3.00, £1.60; EX 14.60 Trifecta £65.50.There was no bid for the winner.
Owner D Allen **Bred** Razza Del Sole Societa Agricola Srl **Trained** Cropthorne, Worcs

FOCUS
Add 3 yards. A modest selling handicap. The strong favourite was reined back off a fast pace after breaking well and outstayed his rivals from over 1f out. Straightforward, limited form.

5838 IMF INDEPENDENT MOTOR FACTORS MAIDEN AUCTION STKS 6f 210y
2:40 (2:40) (Class 5) 2-Y-O £3,428 (£1,020; £509; £254) **Stalls Centre**

Form RPR

1 **Anna Of Sussex (IRE)** 2-8-10 0.............................. TomMarquand 4 64
(Sylvester Kirk) *chsd ldr for 1f: chsd ldng pair after tl effrt to chse ldr again jst over 2f out: clsd u.p over 1f out: led ins fnl f: styd on wl* **7/1**

2 1 **Cottonopolis** 2-9-1 0.............................. FrannyNorton 2 67
(Mark Johnston) *s.i.s: bhd: effrt over 2f out: hdwy u.p over 1f out: chsd wnr ins fnl f: kpt on but hld fnl 50yds* **11/8**[1]

3 ¾ **Moorland Spirit (IRE)** 2-9-0 0..............(b[1]) HollieDoyle 7 64
(Archie Watson) *s.i.s: pushed along in last pair: effrt over 2f out: clsd u.p over 1f out: kpt on ins fnl f: nvr getting to ldrs* **10/3**[3]

66 **4** 2½ **Positive Light (IRE)**[5] 5646 2-9-0 0.............................. RyanTate 8 57
(Sir Mark Prescott Bt) *chsd ldr after 1f: rdn to ld over 2f out: rn green u.p ent fnl f: hdd ins fnl f and wknd fnl 100yds* **20/1**

403 **5** 5 **The Blue Bower (IRE)**[17] 5250 2-8-9 68.............................. JasonWatson 5 39
(Suzy Smith) *stdd after s: midfield: effrt over 2f out: sme hdwy u.p over 1f out: no imp 1f out: wknd ins fnl f* **3/1**[2]

6 **6** 22 **Koovers (IRE)**[9] 5527 2-8-13 0.............................. DanielMuscutt 1
(Gay Kelleway) *led tl over 2f out: hung lft: dropped to rr and btn over 1f out: eased ins fnl f (jockey said gelding hung left-handed)* **16/1**

1m 23.26s (-0.54) **Going Correction** -0.325s/f (Firm) **6 Ran SP% 113.3**
Speed ratings (Par 94): **90,88,88,85,79 54**
CSF £17.50 TOTE £7.00: £3.30, £1.20; EX 21.90 Trifecta £52.70.
Owner Timothy Pearson & Sylvester Kirk **Bred** Amrath Business Management Ltd **Trained** Upper Lambourn, Berks

FOCUS
Add 3 yards. An ordinary juvenile maiden. It's hard tp in down the form and a cautious view has been taken. The winner's time was nearly two seconds slower than the previous C&D selling handicap for older horses.

5839 SILK SERIES LADY RIDERS' H'CAP (PRO-AM LADY RIDERS' RACE) 6f 210y
3:10 (3:12) (Class 4) (0-80,84) 3-Y-O+
£5,433 (£1,617; £808; £404; £300; £300) **Stalls Centre**

Form RPR

0423 **1** **Pickett's Charge**[3] 5726 6-9-5 **67**..............(t[1]) MeganNicholls(3) 9 73
(Brian Ellison) *midfield: wd and effrt over 2f out: styd on strly u.p ins fnl f to ld last strides* **3/1**[1]

1204 **2** nk **De Little Engine (IRE)**[37] 4479 5-9-4 **66**..............(p) JaneElliott(3) 4 71
(Alexandra Dunn) *dwlt: in tch in midfield: effrt on outer over 2f out: chsd ldrs 1f out: clsd u.p ins fnl f and ev ch towards fin: kpt on* **10/1**

0431 **3** nse **Oeil De Tigre (FR)**[10] 5503 8-10-0 **80** 4ex.............. MissSophieColl(7) 10 85
(Tony Carroll) *t.k.h: chsd ldrs: wnt 2nd over 4f out tl over 1f out: edgd lft u.p but chsd ldr again 1f out: kpt on to ld towards fin: hdd and lost 2 pls last strides* **7/1**[3]

-004 **4** ¾ **Baltic Prince (IRE)**[1] 5804 9-9-10 **76**.............. MissSarahBowen(7) 7 79
(Tony Carroll) *led: rdn over 1f out: kpt on u.p tl hdd and no ex towards fin* **9/1**

1302 **5** 1½ **Mamillius**[21] 5090 6-10-7 **80**.............................. HayleyTurner 2 79
(George Baker) *s.i.s: t.k.h: hdwy into midfield after 2f: chsd ldrs 4f out: effrt 2f out: sn drvn: no ex and outpcd fnl 100yds* **10/3**[2]

4045 **6** 1¼ **Dizzy G (IRE)**[22] 5040 4-9-9 **75**.............................. RhonaPindar(7) 3 70
(K R Burke) *taken down early: t.k.h: hld up in tch in midfield: clsd to press ldr ent fnl 2f: rdn over 1f out: no ex and wknd ins fnl f* **8/1**

1400 **7** nk **Strawberry Jack**[27] 4872 3-9-5 **77**..............(bt[1]) JessicaCooley(7) 6 70
(George Scott) *s.i.s: hld up in tch in rr: swtchd lft 2f out: effrt u.p on inner over 1f out: kpt on same pce ins fnl f* **10/1**

5631 **8** 1 **Wilson (IRE)**[51] 3967 4-9-1 **65**..............(p) KatherineBegley(5) 5 57
(Julia Feilden) *dwlt: pushed along and in tch in rr: u.p over 1f out: no imp ins fnl f* **12/1**

2U14 **9** hd **Gold Hunter (IRE)**[13] 5373 9-9-11 **70**..............(tp) HollieDoyle 8 61
(Steve Flook) *chsd ldr tl over 4f out: styd chsng ldrs tl unable qck u.p over 1f out: wknd ins fnl f* **8/1**

1m 20.7s (-3.10) **Going Correction** -0.325s/f (Firm)
WFA 3 from 4yo+ 6lb **9 Ran SP% 118.7**
Speed ratings (Par 105): **104,103,103,102,101 99,99,98,97**
CSF £34.71 CT £198.64 TOTE £3.60: £1.60, £2.90, £2.60; EX 31.10 Trifecta £363.00.
Owner Brian Ellison Racing Club **Bred** Stratford Place Stud **Trained** Norton, N Yorks

FOCUS
Add 3 yards. A fair lady riders' handicap. The favourite came with a withering late run centre to stands' side from off the pace to narrowly get up in the closing stages in a good comparative time. The form's rated around the first three.

5840 MARATHONBET "BETTER ODDS MEAN BIGGER WINNINGS" H'CAP (FOR THE BRIGHTON CHALLENGE CUP) 1m 3f 198y
3:40 (3:40) (Class 4) (0-80,78) 3-Y-O+
£12,854 (£3,847; £1,923; £962; £479; £300) **Stalls High**

Form RPR

504 **1** shd **Black Kalanisi (IRE)**[12] 5451 6-9-10 **74**.............................. CharlesBishop 8 82
(Joseph Tuite) *hld up in tch in midfield: clsd over 2f out: effrt to chal 1f out: sustained chal but bmpd ins fnl f: kpt on wl to ld last strides: hdd last stride: fin 2nd: awrdd r* **8/1**

0206 **2** **Htilominlo**[26] 4901 3-9-4 **78**.............................. JasonWatson 2 86
(Sylvester Kirk) *hld up in rr: hdwy on outer over 1f out: chal and hung lft 1f out: sustained chal but leaning lft and bumping ins fnl f: kpt on to ld last stride: disqualified and plcd 2nd* **7/1**[3]

1243 **3** nk **Agent Basterfield (IRE)**[21] 5089 3-9-2 **76**.............................. DavidProbert 4 83
(Andrew Balding) *chsd ldr trio: clsd to press ldrs and travelling wl whn lft in ld 2f out: rdn over 1f out: hrd pressed 1f out: drvn and kpt on ins fnl f: hdd last strides* **4/1**[2]

3525 **4** 3 **Fraser Island (IRE)**[14] 5347 3-9-4 **78**.............................. JimCrowley 5 81
(Mark Johnston) *midfield: effrt ent fnl 2f: kpt on same pce ins fnl f* **5/1**[2]

5311 **5** ¾ **Mister Chiang**[23] 5012 3-9-2 **76**..............(b) FrannyNorton 3 77
(Mark Johnston) *chsd ldr tl over 8f out: styd chsng ldrs: swtchd rt and effrt to press ldr whn bmpd and hmpd 2f out: kpt on same pce fnl f* **4/1**[1]

2523 **6** ¾ **C'Est No Mour (GER)**[15] 5305 6-10-0 **78**..............(p) TomMarquand 9 78
(Peter Hedger) *dwlt: hld up in last trio: hdwy into midfield 7f out: effrt over 2f out: no imp over 1f out: kpt on same pce ins fnl f* **10/1**

-343 **7** 4 **Fields Of Fortune**[33] 4661 5-9-2 **66**..............(p[1]) HollieDoyle 10 60
(Alan King) *towards rr and niggled along at times: effrt over 2f out: no imp and wl hld whn hung lft 1f out* **9/1**

-621 **8** 11 **Overhaugh Street**[12] 5423 6-9-6 **70**.............................. PatCosgrave 11 46
(Ed de Giles) *led: hrd pressed whn bmpd and hdd 2f out: nt rcvr and wl btn after* **14/1**

-344 **9** 3¼ **Final Rock**[13] 5391 4-10-0 **78**..............(b[1]) RyanTate 1 49
(Sir Mark Prescott Bt) *t.k.h: chsd ldrs tl wnt 2nd over 8f out: ev ch whn wnt lft and cannoned into rival 2f: wl btn after* **12/1**

4246 **10** 38 **Ravenous**[12] 5417 8-9-4 **73**.............................. PoppyBridgwater(5) 7
(Luke Dace) *s.i.s: hld up in rr: swtchd rt and effrt 3f out: no hdwy: t.o and eased ins fnl f* **10/1**

2m 28.8s (-7.20) **Going Correction** -0.325s/f (Firm)
WFA 3 from 4yo+ 10lb **10 Ran SP% 122.8**
Speed ratings (Par 105): **110,111,110,108,108 107,105,97,95,70**
CSF £66.44 CT £264.21 TOTE £12.10: £2.70, £3.30, £1.60; EX 94.50 Trifecta £803.70.
Owner The Harefield Racing Club **Bred** Mrs J O Onions **Trained** Lambourn, Berks

FOCUS
Add 3 yards. The feature contest was a fair middle-distance handicap. It produced an exciting three-way go in the final furlong and the stewards rightly reversed the photo-finish verdict.

5841 DOWNLOAD THE MARATHONBET APP H'CAP 1m 1f 207y
4:10 (4:11) (Class 4) (0-85,86) 3-Y-O+ £5,207 (£1,549; £774; £387; £300) **Stalls High**

Form RPR

13-6 **1** **Long Call**[202] 292 6-8-12 **68**.............................. TomMarquand 4 74
(Tony Carroll) *stdd s: hld up in rr: effrt over 2f out: clsd u.p to chse ldrs 1f out: styd on wl u.p to ld wl ins fnl f* **17/2**

-242 **2** 1 **Alnadir (USA)**[6] 5605 3-9-7 **85**..............(h) DavidProbert 1 89
(Simon Crisford) *led tl 4f out: chsd ldr and effrt over 2f out: rdn to ld again over 1f out: hdd and one pce fnl 75yds* **2/1**[2]

4640 **3** ¾ **Noble Account**[13] 5394 3-8-1 **65** oh1.............................. HollieDoyle 5 68
(Julia Feilden) *broke wl: restrained to chse ldrs and t.k.h: effrt over 2f out: clsd u.p to press ldrs 1f out: kpt on same pce ins fnl f* **4/1**[3]

2040 **4** 1¼ **Double Reflection**[12] 5458 4-9-0 **77**.............................. RhonaPindar(7) 6 77
(K R Burke) *t.k.h: stdd s: chsd ldrs tl hdwy to join ldr over 6f out: led 4f out: rdn and hdd over 1f out: no ex and wknd wl ins fnl f* **10/1**

6161 **5** 3¾ **Multamis (IRE)**[21] 5089 3-9-8 **86**.............................. JimCrowley 2 79
(Owen Burrows) *t.k.h: chsd ldr tl over 6f out: effrt u.p over 1f out: unable qck and wknd ins fnl f (trainer's rep could offer no explanation for the performance shown)* **11/8**[1]

2m 0.02s (-4.98) **Going Correction** -0.325s/f (Firm)
WFA 3 from 4yo+ 8lb **5 Ran SP% 115.1**
Speed ratings (Par 105): **106,105,104,103,100**
CSF £26.96 TOTE £8.80: £3.70, £1.20; EX 40.30 Trifecta £84.70.
Owner A A Byrne **Bred** Rabbah Bloodstock Limited **Trained** Cropthorne, Worcs

FOCUS
Add 3 yards. A decent handicap. Tom Marquand produced his 6yo mount to perfection to win a shade cosily from well off the pace in a good comparative time. The form's rated around the runner-up.

5842 FRP ADVISORY H'CAP 7f 211y
4:40 (4:40) (Class 6) (0-60,62) 3-Y-O+
£2,781 (£827; £413; £300; £300; £300) **Stalls Centre**

Form RPR

0536 **1** **Cristal Pallas Cat (IRE)**[50] 3989 4-8-7 **46**.............................. RhiainIngram(5) 10 54
(Roger Ingram) *led for over 1f: clsd and lft in ld again 2f out: hld on wl u.p ins fnl f: all out* **20/1**

6353 **2** nk **Arriba De Toda (IRE)**[13] 5389 3-8-2 **46**.............................. MeganNicholls(3) 3 52
(Brian Ellison) *s.i.s: sn rcvrd and in tch in midfield: hdwy press wnr 1f out: sustained chal u.p but hld towards fin (jockey said gelding was slowly away)* **5/1**[2]

0066 **3** 3¼ **Ramblow**[1] 5803 6-8-7 **46** oh1..............(vt) AndrewBreslin(5) 8 46
(Alexandra Dunn) *dwlt: hld up in rr: hdwy u.p over 1f out: chsd clr ldng pair ins fnl f: no imp* **20/1**

5050 **4** ¾ **Moon Artist (FR)**[26] 4931 3-8-5 **46** oh1.............................. HollieDoyle 5 43
(Michael Blanshard) *t.k.h: chsd ldrs: drvn over 1f out: unable qck and plugged on same pce ins fnl f* **25/1**

0423 **5** ½ **Melo Pearl**[15] 5287 3-8-5 **46**..............(v) AntonioFresu 11 42
(Mrs Ilka Gansera-Leveque) *midfield: effrt over 2f out: edgd lft and no imp u.p 1f out: plugged on same pce ins fnl f* **11/2**[3]

0-0 **6** hd **Admodum (USA)**[20] 5151 6-9-7 **60**.............................. DarraghKeenan(5) 6 57
(John Butler) *dwlt: hld up in last pair: effrt over 1f out: kpt on ins fnl f: nvr trbld ldrs* **7/1**

1123 7 ½ **Confrerie (IRE)**[15] 5302 4-10-0 **62** PatCosgrave 1 57
(George Baker) *hld up towards rr: effrt ent fnl 2f: swtchd lft and drvn over 1f out: no imp and wknd ins fnl f* **15/8**[1]

000 8 2 **My Footsteps**[17] 5254 4-8-12 **46** oh1 (bt[1]) TomMarquand 7 37
(Paul D'Arcy) *midfield: effrt ent fnl 2f: no imp and btn whn nt clr run 1f out: wknd ins fnl f* **20/1**

066 9 2 ¼ **Iris's Spirit**[15] 5287 3-8-5 **46** oh1 HayleyTurner 4 31
(Tony Carroll) *hld up in last pair: effrt 2f out: nt clr run and hmpd jst over 1f out: nvr trbld ldrs* **20/1**

5034 P **Cromwell**[10] 5505 3-9-1 **56** (b[1]) FergusSweeney 9 +
(Luke Dace) *t.k.h: chsd ldr tl led over 6f out and sn clr: eased over 2f out: hdd 2f out and sn t.o: p.u and dismntd ins fnl f: rein broke (jockey said his rein snapped)* **11/2**[3]

1m 34.26s (-2.64) **Going Correction** -0.325s/f (Firm)
WFA 3 from 4yo+ 7lb **10** Ran SP% **117.6**
Speed ratings (Par 101): **100,99,96,95,95 95,94,92,90,**
CSF £109.56 CT £2098.18 TOTE £21.90: £5.50, £1.60, £6.40; EX 150.80 Trifecta £1378.30.
Owner Keith Tollick **Bred** Joseph Broderick **Trained** Epsom, Surrey

FOCUS
Add 3 yards. A modest handicap. One of the outsiders won bravely from an always prominent pitch. He has the scope to do a bit better than this.

5843 VISIT ATTHERACES.COM H'CAP 5f 60y
5:10 (5:10) (Class 5) (0-75,75) 4-Y-O+ **£3,428** (£1,020; £509; £300; £300) **Stalls** Low

Form RPR

0266 1 **Enthaar**[40] 4374 4-9-2 **70** (tp) JasonWatson 4 77
(Stuart Williams) *chsd ldng pair: effrt jst over 2f out: chsd ldr and clsd u.p over 1f out: styd on wl to ld towards fin* **7/2**[2]

0144 2 ½ **King Crimson**[9] 5532 7-8-12 **71** (t) DarraghKeenan(5) 1 76
(John Butler) *led and sn clr: rdn over 1f out: drvn ins fnl f: hdd and one pce towards fin* **5/1**[3]

-305 3 ¾ **Wiley Post**[24] 4995 6-9-7 **75** (b) TomMarquand 5 78
(Tony Carroll) *dwlt: racd in 4th: effrt over 2f out: drvn over 1f out: kpt on ins fnl f: nvr quite getting to ldrs* **10/11**[1]

3250 4 ½ **Essaka (IRE)**[15] 5289 7-8-12 **66** HayleyTurner 2 67
(Tony Carroll) *stdd s: hld up in rr: effrt ent fnl 2f: edgd lft over 1f out: kpt on u.p ins fnl f: nvr quite getting to ldrs* **7/1**

030 5 ¾ **Kodiac Express (IRE)**[54] 3856 4-9-2 **73** GabrieleMalune(3) 3 71
(Mike Murphy) *chsd ldr tl over 1f out: kpt on same pce ins fnl f* **10/1**

1m 0.72s (-2.28) **Going Correction** -0.325s/f (Firm) **5** Ran SP% **112.9**
Speed ratings (Par 103): **105,104,103,102,101**
CSF £20.63 TOTE £4.30: £1.70, £2.30; EX 14.90 Trifecta £35.30.
Owner B Piper & D Cobill **Bred** Abbey Farm Stud **Trained** Newmarket, Suffolk

FOCUS
Add 3 yards. A fair sprint handicap. The second-favourite won well in marginally the quickest comparative time on the card. The winner's rated in line with this year's turf form.
T/Plt: £308.60 to a £1 stake. Pool: £66,900.90. 158.23 winning units. T/Qpdt: £79.30 to a £1 stake. Pool: £5,068.43. 47.24 winning units. **Steve Payne**

5176 HAYDOCK (L-H)
Thursday, August 8

OFFICIAL GOING: Good to firm (good in places; 7.9)
Wind: faint breeze Weather: sunny and warm, clouding over later

5844 MANCHESTER ACADEMY OF GYMNASTICS FILLIES' H'CAP 7f 212y
2:00 (2:01) (Class 5) (0-75,74) 3-Y-O+
£4,851 (£1,443; £721; £360; £300; £300) **Stalls** Low

Form RPR

2003 1 **This Girl**[35] 4554 4-10-0 **74** RichardKingscote 8 82
(Tom Dascombe) *prom: led over 2f out: sn drvn: rdn in 1 l ld 1f out: reduced ld and strly pressed ins fnl f: kpt on wl* **7/1**

0024 2 nk **Iconic Code**[20] 5117 4-9-2 **62** JoeFanning 3 69
(Keith Dalgleish) *hld up on inner: swtchd to outer and hdwy 2f out: drvn to chal over 1f out: clsd on wnr and ev ch ins fnl f: rdn and no ex nr fin* **5/1**[3]

5060 3 2 ¼ **Sootability (IRE)**[13] 5394 3-8-12 **65** TonyHamilton 2 66+
(Richard Fahey) *mid-div: n.m.r on inner 2f out: swtchd over 1f out: sn rdn: r.o wl fnl f: tk 3rd nr fin* **9/1**

231 4 nk **Arletta Star**[12] 5419 3-9-5 **72** DavidAllan 4 72
(Tim Easterby) *mid-div: pushed along in bhd ldrs over 2f out: drvn over 1f out: rdn fnl f: one pce* **2/1**[1]

2-55 5 nk **Lady Lizzy**[23] 5030 3-9-6 **73** BenCurtis 5 72
(K R Burke) *hld up: hdwy gng wl on outer over 2f out: drvn to chal 1 1/2f out: rdn over 1f out: wknd fnl f (jockey said filly hung left handed under pressure)* **7/2**[2]

-415 6 3 ¼ **Hunterwali**[34] 4585 3-9-7 **74** PhilDennis 11 66
(Michael Dods) *prom on outer: drvn and lost pl over 2f out: sn rdn and wknd* **20/1**

014 7 1 ½ **Miss Sheridan (IRE)**[17] 5245 5-9-12 **72** NathanEvans 7 62
(Michael Easterby) *led: pushed along in narrow ld 3f out: drvn and hdd over 2f out: sn rdn and wknd* **9/1**

060 8 5 **Alexandrakollontai (IRE)**[20] 5117 9-8-10 **59** (b) ConnorMurtagh(3) 10 37
(Alistair Whillans) *slowly away: bhd: rdn over 2f out: no imp (jockey said mare jumped awkwardly from the stalls and was never travelling thereafter)* **25/1**

1m 39.78s (-2.92) **Going Correction** -0.425s/f (Firm)
WFA 3 from 4yo+ 7lb **8** Ran SP% **113.3**
Speed ratings (Par 100): **97,96,94,94,93 90,89,84**
CSF £40.94 CT £319.43 TOTE £8.60: £2.40, £1.70, £2.40; EX 44.80 Trifecta £282.40.
Owner David Lowe **Bred** Liam Sheridan **Trained** Malpas, Cheshire

FOCUS
Inner Home Straight in use. The going was given as good to firm, good in places (GoingStick 7.9). Add 11yds. Just a fair fillies' handicap, but it was sound run and the first two are rated close to their bests.

5845 BRITISH STALLION STUDS EBF NOVICE STKS (PLUS 10 RACE) 6f
2:30 (2:31) (Class 4) 2-Y-O **£6,469** (£1,925; £962; £481) **Stalls** Centre

Form RPR

106 1 **Lord Of The Lodge (IRE)**[20] 5134 2-9-3 **91** HarrisonShaw(5) 2 100+
(K R Burke) *mde all: pushed 2 l clr 2f out: drvn and qcknd into 4 l ld 1f out: kpt up to work and extended ld fnl f: easily* **3/1**[2]

0 2 5 **Black Caspian (IRE)**[54] 3866 2-9-2 0 TomEaves 9 79
(Kevin Ryan) *chsd ldrs: drvn in 3rd 2f out: rdn into 4 l 2nd 1f out: kpt on fnl f: no ch w wnr* **20/1**

3 3 ½ **Embolden (IRE)**[19] 5172 2-9-2 0 TonyHamilton 7 77
(Richard Fahey) *trckd ldrs: pushed along 2f out: rdn over 1f out: kpt on into 3rd fnl f* **15/2**

4 shd **Gifted Ruler** 2-9-2 0 RichardKingscote 6 77+
(Tom Dascombe) *slowly away: bhd: drvn 1/2-way: reminders over 2f and 1f out: kpt on into 4th fnl f* **4/1**[3]

3 5 3 ½ **No Show (IRE)**[14] 5345 2-9-2 0 AndreaAtzeni 3 66
(Richard Hannon) *prom: drvn in 2nd 2f out: rdn over 1f out: wknd fnl f* **2/1**[1]

43 6 3 ½ **Centurion Song (IRE)**[28] 4839 2-9-2 0 OisinMurphy 8 56
(Brian Meehan) *hld up: pushed along in 5th 2f out: drvn 1f out: wknd fnl f* **6/1**

7 4 **Captain Corelli (IRE)** 2-9-2 0 GrahamLee 5 44
(Julie Camacho) *slowly away: bhd: pushed along in rr 1/2-way: reminder over 1f out: no imp* **100/1**

8 3 **Temper Trap** 2-9-2 0 DavidAllan 4 35
(Tim Easterby) *slowly away: bhd: pushed along 1/2-way: drvn over 2f out: sn dropped to last* **33/1**

1m 11.73s (-2.17) **Going Correction** -0.425s/f (Firm) **8** Ran SP% **113.1**
Speed ratings (Par 96): **95,88,87,87,82 78,72,68**
CSF £56.98 TOTE £4.10: £1.30, £4.90, £2.20; EX 67.50 Trifecta £312.30.
Owner Mrs Elaine M Burke **Bred** Mountarmstrong Stud **Trained** Middleham Moor, N Yorks

FOCUS
A comfortable success for the class-dropping winner. The form is taken at face value.

5846 ROSCOE ROOFING FILLIES' H'CAP 6f
3:00 (3:00) (Class 3) (0-95,95) 3-Y-O+
£9,337 (£2,796; £1,398; £699; £349; £175) **Stalls** Centre

Form RPR

2-06 1 **Princes Des Sables**[38] 4442 3-8-11 **84** TomEaves 2 101
(Kevin Ryan) *mde all: 2 l ld 1/2-way: qcknd and pushed into 5 l ld 1f out: reminder and readily plld further clr fnl f: easily (trainer said, regarding the improved form shown, he could offer no explanation other than the filly had been more relaxed in the preliminaries on this occasion)* **12/1**

2354 2 8 **Daffy Jane**[13] 5395 4-8-4 **78** FayeMcManoman(5) 8 70
(Nigel Tinkler) *chsd ldrs: pushed along 2f out: drvn 1f out: rdn into 2nd fnl f: nvr nr wnr* **4/1**[2]

1644 3 nk **Seen The Lyte (IRE)**[13] 5372 4-8-10 **82** (h) RowanScott(3) 5 73
(Nigel Tinkler) *slowly away: bhd: pushed along in 5th 1/2-way: drvn 2f out: rdn and kpt on to secure 3rd fnl f* **8/1**

1230 4 4 **Isaan Queen (IRE)**[27] 4891 3-9-8 **95** AdamMcNamara 1 73
(Archie Watson) *chsd ldr: pushed along 1/2-way: rdn 2f out: wknd fnl f* **6/1**[3]

-000 5 1 ½ **Summer Daydream (IRE)**[24] 4987 3-9-3 **90** JoeFanning 7 63
(Keith Dalgleish) *bhd: drvn and detached fr rest 1/2-way: one pce into 5th fnl f* **8/1**

2063 6 3 ¾ **Goodnight Girl (IRE)**[3] 5746 4-9-7 **90** PJMcDonald 3 52
(Jonathan Portman) *prom: drvn and lost pl over 2f out: sn rdn and wknd: dropped to last fnl f (jockey said the filly run flat having run 3 days ago)* **11/10**[1]

1m 9.04s (-4.86) **Going Correction** -0.425s/f (Firm) course record
WFA 3 from 4yo 4lb **6** Ran SP% **111.8**
Speed ratings (Par 104): **109,98,97,92,90 85**
CSF £57.72 CT £407.26 TOTE £10.80: £5.10, £2.00; EX 58.10 Trifecta £467.00.
Owner J C G Chua & C K Ong **Bred** Jcg Chua & Ck Ong **Trained** Hambleton, N Yorks

FOCUS
A one-horse race, the winner bouncing back to form in style and making every yard. The time was quick and this was a smart effort.

5847 JOIN RACING TV NOW H'CAP 6f 212y
3:30 (3:31) (Class 5) (0-70,72) 3-Y-O
£4,851 (£1,443; £721; £360; £300; £300) **Stalls** Low

Form RPR

0400 1 **Jack Randall**[42] 4286 3-8-3 **52** DuranFentiman 3 60
(Tim Easterby) *trckd ldrs on inner: pushed along and hdwy on rail to ld 1 1/2f out: rdn clr fnl f* **5/1**

0400 2 2 ¾ **Bold Show**[20] 5147 3-8-9 **58** (v[1]) TonyHamilton 11 58
(Richard Fahey) *prom: shkn up and ev ch 2f out: rdn in 3rd 1f out: r.o into 2nd fnl f: no threat to wnr* **12/1**

20-0 3 nk **Flint Said No**[80] 2897 3-9-7 **70** GrahamLee 9 69
(Bryan Smart) *t.k.h: chsd ldrs on outer: tk clsr order 3f out: pushed along and ev ch 2f out: rdn in 2nd 1f out: no ex and lost 2nd fnl f* **6/1**

4406 4 2 ¾ **Jack Berry House**[42] 4288 3-9-8 **71** (t) StevieDonohoe 6 63
(Charlie Fellowes) *hld up: last 3f out: pushed along 2f out: rdn over 1f out: r.o fnl f: tk 4th nr fin* **4/1**[3]

6110 5 hd **Global Destination (IRE)**[24] 5002 3-9-4 **72** CierenFallon(5) 5 63
(Ed Dunlop) *hld up: pushed along to chse ldrs 2f out: rdn over 1f out: one pce fnl f* **9/4**[1]

0134 6 5 **Bumbledom**[6] 5619 3-9-4 **67** (p) TomEaves 7 45
(Michael Dods) *led: rdn in narrow ld 2f out: hdd & wknd 1 1/2f out* **7/2**[2]

0000 7 ½ **Andies Armies**[19] 5176 3-8-2 **51** oh6 (p) NathanEvans 1 27
(Lisa Williamson) *t.k.h: hld up: pushed along 3f out: drvn 2f out: sn rdn and dropped away* **100/1**

0000 8 2 ½ **Not So Shy**[7] 5582 3-7-10 **52** oh5 ow1 IzzyClifton(7) 8 22
(Lisa Williamson) *t.k.h: mid-div: pushed along and swtchd to outer 3f out: sn rdn and wknd* **66/1**

1m 26.28s (-3.02) **Going Correction** -0.425s/f (Firm) **8** Ran SP% **114.1**
Speed ratings (Par 100): **100,96,96,93,93 87,86,84**
CSF £61.40 CT £370.02 TOTE £5.60: £1.40, £2.80, £2.00; EX 57.50 Trifecta £282.50.
Owner Mrs Janis Macpherson **Bred** Whitsbury Manor Stud **Trained** Great Habton, N Yorks

FOCUS
Add 11yds. A fairly open handicap but the market 1-2 were below form. The early pace wasn't too strong and it paid to be fairly handy.

5848 BRITISH EBF NOVICE STKS (PLUS 10 RACE) 6f 212y
4:00 (4:00) (Class 4) 2-Y-O **£6,469** (£1,925; £962; £481) **Stalls** Low

Form RPR

62 1 **Atheeb**[19] 5172 2-9-5 0 DaneO'Neill 2 80
(Sir Michael Stoute) *trckd ldrs: pushed along in 4th 2f out: sn drvn: rdn and hdwy fnl f: led 1/2f out: drvn out nr fin* **13/8**[1]

2 nk **End Zone** 2-9-5 0 OisinMurphy 10 79+
(David Simcock) *hld up: hdwy on outer 2f out: drvn over 1f out: chal and almost upsides wnr 1/2f out: rdn and r.o wl: jst hld* **12/1**

3 1 **Throne Hall** 2-9-5 0 AndreaAtzeni 8 77+
(Kevin Ryan) *chsd ldr: pushed along in 2nd over 2f out: rdn over 1f out: one pce and dropped to 3rd fnl f* 11/4[2]

5 4 2 3/4 **Flashing Approach (IRE)**[21] 5088 2-9-5 0 JoeFanning 1 69
(Mark Johnston) *led: pushed along in 1 l ld 2f out: rdn in 1 1/2 l ld 1f out: clsd down ins fnl f: hdd 1/2f out: no ex (vet reported colt was lame on its right fore)* 10/1

5 1 1/2 **King Carney** 2-9-5 0 StevieDonohoe 4 66+
(Charlie Fellowes) *mid-div: drvn 2f out: kpt on fnl f* 12/1

40 6 2 1/4 **Precision Storm**[22] 5052 2-9-0 0 CierenFallon(5) 6 60
(Mark Loughnane) *hld up: n.m.r over 2f out: sn pushed along and in clr: reminder over 1f out: one pce fnl f* 50/1

6 7 hd **America First (IRE)**[18] 5212 2-9-5 0 GrahamLee 5 59
(Michael Dods) *chsd ldrs: pushed along 2f out: reminder over 1f out: wknd fnl f* 50/1

8 3 3/4 **Make Me Laugh (IRE)** 2-9-5 0 TonyHamilton 3 49
(Richard Fahey) *mid-div: drvn and lost pl 3f out: reminders over 1f out: wknd* 16/1

04 9 1/2 **Shevchenko Park (IRE)**[14] 5331 2-9-5 0 RichardKingscote 11 48
(Tom Dascombe) *hld up: pushed along 2f out: drvn over 1f out: no imp* 6/1[3]

10 5 **Clever Trick** 2-9-5 0 TomEaves 9 35
(Kevin Ryan) *uns rdr on way to post: slowly away: bhd: effrt on outer over 2f out: sn drvn and wknd* 33/1

1m 27.4s (-1.90) **Going Correction** -0.425s/f (Firm) **10** Ran SP% **116.3**
Speed ratings (Par 96): **93,92,91,88,86 84,83,79,79,73**
CSF £23.03 TOTE £2.30: £1.10, £3.30, £1.30; EX 18.50 Trifecta £61.70.
Owner Hamdan Al Maktoum **Bred** Newsells Park Stud **Trained** Newmarket, Suffolk

FOCUS
Add 11yds. Just a fair novice, but several made good impressions.

5849 SWIFT DEBT HELP H'CAP 1m 3f 140y
4:30 (4:31) (Class 4) (0-80,82) 4-Y-O+
£7,115 (£2,117; £1,058; £529; £300; £300) Stalls Centre

Form RPR

222 1 **December Second (IRE)**[21] 5098 5-9-9 82 AndrewElliott 13 97+
(Philip Kirby) *chsd ldrs: pushed into 3rd 3f out: led 2f out: 2 l ld 1f out: drvn clr fnl f: eased nr fin: easily* 3/1[2]

0513 2 5 **Celestial Force (IRE)**[26] 4899 4-9-6 79 (v) PJMcDonald 12 84
(Tom Dascombe) *chsd ldr: disp ld 3f out: drvn and hdd 2f out: sn rdn and outpcd by wnr: kpt on fnl f* 11/4[1]

3544 3 1/2 **Glasses Up (USA)**[10] 5489 4-9-6 79 PaddyMathers 3 83
(R Mike Smith) *hld up: drvn and hdwy on outer 3f out: rdn 2f out: one pce in 3rd fnl f* 11/2[3]

54 4 1 1/4 **Point Taken (IRE)**[24] 4989 5-8-9 73 (p) CierenFallon(5) 11 75
(Michael Appleby) *hld up: rdn in 7th over 2f out: kpt on fr 2f out: tk 4th ins fnl f* 25/1

1521 5 1 **Bollin Joan**[14] 5332 4-8-13 72 (p) DavidAllan 10 73
(Tim Easterby) *mid-div: pushed along to trck ldrs over 2f out: rdn over 1f out: wknd fnl f* 8/1

5601 6 2 3/4 **Medalla De Oro**[26] 4907 5-9-7 80 (h) RichardKingscote 8 76
(Tom Clover) *led: drvn and jnd 3f out: sn rdn: hdd 2f out: wknd over 1f out* 3/1[2]

0050 7 1 3/4 **Shrewd**[17] 5240 9-9-5 78 TomEaves 4 71
(Iain Jardine) *hld up: plenty to do and pushed along over 2f out: reminder 2f out: no imp* 28/1

0/ 8 12 **Lady Camelot (IRE)**[112] 8711 4-9-2 82 NickBarratt-Atkin(7) 9 56
(Philip Kirby) *hld up: rdn in last over 2f out: no imp* 40/1

0-04 9 1 **Moving Forward (IRE)**[19] 5201 4-9-2 75 DougieCostello 1 48
(Tony Coyle) *chsd ldrs: rdn and lost pl over 3f out: sn dropped away: eased fnl f* 33/1

2m 25.52s (-7.78) **Going Correction** -0.425s/f (Firm) course record **9** Ran SP% **115.8**
Speed ratings (Par 105): **108,104,104,103,102 101,99,91,91**
CSF £11.29 CT £42.35 TOTE £4.00: £1.40, £1.50, £1.50; EX 13.10 Trifecta £38.70.
Owner David Platt **Bred** Hadi Al-Tajir **Trained** East Appleton, N Yorks

FOCUS
Add 17yds. This was strongly run. The winner is a very useful bumper horse and showed himself well treated off a mark of 82 on his handicap debut.

5850 RACING TV HAYDOCK APPRENTICE TRAINING SERIES H'CAP (RACING EXCELLENCE) (JC GRASSROOTS QUALIFIER) 1m 2f 42y
5:00 (5:00) (Class 5) (0-70,72) 4-Y-O+
£4,851 (£1,443; £721; £360; £300; £300) Stalls High

Form RPR

2435 1 **Four Kingdoms (IRE)**[12] 5423 5-9-2 67 GianlucaSanna(7) 10 79+
(R Mike Smith) *hld up: hdwy on inner 4f out: pushed into ld 2f out: sn clr: 4 l ld 1f out: pushed out fnl f: eased nr fin: easily* 5/1

211 2 4 **Blue Medici**[14] 5338 5-10-0 72 CierenFallon 2 75
(Mark Loughnane) *hld up: hdwy on outer 4f out: drvn 3f out: rdn in share of 2nd 1f out: kpt on to secure 2nd fnl f* 6/4[1]

1002 3 1/2 **Simbirsk**[21] 5086 4-9-8 71 (p) KateLeahy(5) 8 73
(John O'Shea) *chsd ldrs on outer: pushed along and hdwy 3f out: rdn in share of 2nd 1f out: one pce and dropped to 3rd fnl f* 7/1

0111 4 4 **Dutch Coed**[21] 5096 7-9-1 62 AidenBlakemore(3) 4 56
(Nigel Tinkler) *led: narrow ld 3f out: hdd and rdn 2f out: no ex fnl f* 4/1[2]

0021 5 3 **Destinys Rock**[23] 5025 4-9-6 64 (p) GeorgiaDobie 3 52
(Mark Loughnane) *slowly away: bhd but in tch: hdwy on outer 3f out: rdn and wknd over 2f out (jockey said filly hung slightly right-handed off the home bend)* 9/2[3]

0000 6 5 **Aljunood (IRE)**[41] 4349 5-8-7 51 oh6 TylerSaunders 5 29
(John Norton) *t.k.h: chsd ldr: drvn and lost pl 3f out: dropped to last and rdn over 2f out: sn lost tch* 40/1

2m 11.2s (0.40) **Going Correction** -0.425s/f (Firm) **6** Ran SP% **109.8**
Speed ratings (Par 103): **81,77,77,74,71 67**
CSF £12.40 CT £46.38 TOTE £4.80: £2.10, £1.50; EX 13.90 Trifecta £55.00.
Owner Smith And Stewart **Bred** Camogue Stud Ltd **Trained** Galston, E Ayrshire

FOCUS
Add 33yds. A modest affair but a good winner, rated to a best view of his form.
T/Jkpt: £45,491.50 to a £1 stake. Pool: £86,4980.70. 13.5 winning units. T/Plt: £339.60 to a £1 stake. Pool: £7,1862.18. 154.47 winning units. T/Qpdt: £33.40 to a £1 stake. Pool: £7,032.11. 155.35 winning units. **Keith McHugh**

5432 NEWCASTLE (A.W) (L-H)
Thursday, August 8

OFFICIAL GOING: Tapeta: standard
Wind: Breezy, half against in races on the straight course and in over 3f of home straight in races on the Weather: Fine, dry

5851 SPORTS BETTING AT BETUK.COM APPRENTICE H'CAP 1m 2f 42y (Tp)
5:30 (5:30) (Class 6) (0-60,58) 3-Y-O+
£2,781 (£827; £413; £300; £300; £300) Stalls High

Form RPR

1-44 1 **Melgate Majeure**[23] 5023 3-9-5 58 Pierre-LouisJamin 12 67
(Michael Easterby) *trckd ldrs: shkn up over 2f out: led over 1f out: rdn and r.o wl fnl f* 2/1[1]

4050 2 1 1/2 **Sulafaat (IRE)**[36] 4518 4-8-13 47 (p) RussellHarris(3) 6 52
(Rebecca Menzies) *hld up in midfield: hdwy over 2f out: chsd wnr ins fnl f: kpt on same pce towards fin* 25/1

00-0 3 nk **My Renaissance**[17] 4990 9-9-4 54 (tp) SaraDelFabbro(5) 1 58
(Sam England) *chsd ldr and sn clr of rest: led over 2f out to over 1f out: lost 2nd and one pce ins fnl f* 80/1

6046 4 1 1/4 **Optima Petamus**[9] 5518 7-8-8 46 (b) OwenPayton(7) 9 48
(Liam Bailey) *missed break: bhd: pushed along over 2f out: gd hdwy fnl f: nrst fin (jockey said, regarding running and riding, his instructions were to keep the gelding on the bridle for as long as possible before making an effort in the home straight. he added that he was slapping his mount down the neck approximately 2 1/2f out and t* 25/1

000 5 nk **Yvette**[16] 5269 3-9-2 58 GavinAshton(3) 8 61
(Sir Mark Prescott Bt) *prom: effrt over 2f out: edgd lft over 1f out: sn one pce* 7/2[2]

3604 6 1 1/4 **Top Offer**[12] 5438 10-9-5 50 (p) AledBeech 4 49
(Patrick Morris) *hld up towards rr: hdwy and in tch over 1f out: rdn and no ex ins fnl f* 18/1

-022 7 nse **Greengage (IRE)**[18] 5214 4-9-10 55 (h) JoshQuinn 3 54
(Tristan Davidson) *hld up: stdy hdwy over 2f out: effrt and rdn over 1f out: kpt on same pce ins fnl f* 4/1[3]

006- 8 1/2 **Bromance**[289] 8505 6-9-1 46 EllaMcCain 10 44
(Peter Niven) *hld up in midfield: rdn and effrt over 2f out: edgd rt and outpcd over 1f out* 25/1

3563 9 3/4 **Mi Laddo (IRE)**[17] 5248 3-8-4 48 (tp) KeelanBaker(5) 5 46
(Oliver Greenall) *hld up: shkn up and shortlived effrt on outside over 2f out: sn n.d (jockey said gelding was never travelling)* 16/1

3300 10 2 1/4 **Splash Of Verve (IRE)**[33] 4633 7-8-12 48 IsobelFrancis(5) 7 41
(David Thompson) *s.i.s: hld up: effrt on wd outside over 2f out: nvr able to chal (jockey said gelding was slowly away)* 16/1

0B60 11 1/2 **Harperelle**[26] 4917 3-8-1 45 (p[1]) CoreyMadden(5) 11 38
(Alistair Whillans) *in tch: rdn over 2f out: wknd over 1f out* 50/1

0000 12 1/2 **Amourie**[49] 4039 3-8-6 45 LauraCoughlan 13 37
(Ray Craggs) *hld up in midfield: rdn over 2f out: wknd over 1f out* 100/1

0506 13 2 1/2 **King Of Naples**[24] 5003 6-9-9 57 (h) HarryRussell(3) 14 44
(Ruth Carr) *hld up: pushed along over 2f out: hung lft and wknd wl over 1f out* 22/1

1250 14 3 3/4 **Kodi Koh (IRE)**[36] 4515 4-8-11 47 GeorgeBass(5) 2 27+
(Simon West) *led at decent gallop: rdn and hdd over 2f out: wknd over 1f out* 10/1

2m 13.35s (2.95) **Going Correction** +0.15s/f (Slow) **14** Ran SP% **121.7**
WFA 3 from 4yo+ 8lb
Speed ratings (Par 101): **94,92,92,91,91 90,90,89,89,87 87,86,84,81**
CSF £65.98 CT £3145.24 TOTE £2.80: £1.50, £6.60, £8.50; EX 65.90 Trifecta £2071.60.
Owner Bernard Hoggarth Racing **Bred** Whitwell Bloodstock **Trained** Sheriff Hutton, N Yorks

FOCUS
They were soon well strung out in this weak handicap, confined to apprentice riders. Limited form.

5852 BET £10 GET £10 AT BETUK.COM H'CAP 7f 14y (Tp)
6:00 (6:02) (Class 6) (0-65,65) 3-Y-O+
£2,781 (£827; £413; £300; £300; £300) Stalls Centre

Form RPR

3-60 1 **Castle Quarter (IRE)**[50] 4000 3-9-3 62 (p[1]) DavidNolan 10 68
(Seb Spencer) *in tch in centre of gp: effrt and edgd lft over 1f out: led ins fnl f: drvn out* 33/1

2041 2 nk **Firsteen**[18] 5215 3-8-13 58 PaulHanagan 1 63
(Alistair Whillans) *hld up on far side of gp: effrt and hdwy over 1f out: chsd wnr ins fnl f: kpt on: hld cl home* 8/1[3]

6655 3 3/4 **Cameo Star (IRE)**[17] 5237 4-9-7 63 (p) SeanDavis(3) 8 68
(Richard Fahey) *cl up in centre of gp: rdn to ld over 1f out: hdd ins fnl f: sn one pce* 18/1

-020 4 3/4 **Mywayistheonlyway (IRE)**[71] 3214 6-9-8 61 SamJames 12 66+
(Grant Tuer) *hld up on nr side of gp: hdwy whn nt clr run briefly over 1f out: rdn and r.o fnl f: nrst fin (jockey said gelding was denied a clear run 1 1/2f out)* 9/1

0601 5 nse **Sharrabang**[28] 4820 3-8-10 55 CamHardie 11 56
(Stella Barclay) *led towards centre of gp: rdn and hdd over 1f out: rallied: one pce ins fnl f* 20/1

5000 6 nk **Gunmaker (IRE)**[16] 5282 5-8-11 57 HarryRussell(7) 9 60
(Ruth Carr) *hld up in centre of gp: rdn along and hdwy over 1f out: edgd lft: one pce ins fnl f* 14/1

130 7 1 3/4 **Blazing Dreams (IRE)**[61] 3570 3-9-2 61 (p) AndrewMullen 6 57
(Ben Haslam) *slowly away and swtchd to nr side sn after s: hld up: effrt over 2f out: rdn and no imp fr over 1f out (jockey said gelding reared as the stalls opened resulting in the gelding being slowly away)* 8/1[3]

20-6 8 1 **Global Humor (USA)**[192] 463 4-9-11 64 (w) ConnorBeasley 13 60
(Tristan Davidson) *in tch on nr side of gp: effrt and drvn along 2f out: wknd ins fnl f* 7/2[1]

0506 9 1 1/4 **Rich Approach (IRE)**[34] 4606 3-9-6 65 (p[1]) DanielTudhope 2 56
(James Bethell) *prom on far side of gp: rdn over 2f out: wknd over 1f out* 7/1[2]

5125 10 1/2 **Mr Strutter (IRE)**[7] 5593 5-9-7 65 BenSanderson(5) 5 56
(Ronald Thompson) *prom in centre of gp: rdn over 2f out: wknd over 1f out* 7/1[2]

0400 11 1/2 **Muqarred (USA)**[17] 5247 7-9-6 62 GemmaTutty(3) 3 52
(Karen Tutty) *prom on far side of gp: drvn and outpcd over 2f out: n.d after* 66/1

2005 12 3/4 **La Cumparsita (IRE)**[22] 5051 5-8-11 50 LukeMorris 14 38
(Tristan Davidson) *prom on nr side of gp tl rdn and wknd over 1f out* 11/1

0060 **13** 1 ½ **Robben Rainbow**[29] 4784 5-9-1 **54**........................ PhilDennis 4 39
(Katie Scott) *midfield towards far side of gp: drvn and outpcd over 2f out: n.d after* **40/1**

6-60 **14** 2 **Phantasmal**[26] 4916 5-9-5 **58**........................ JasonHart 7 38
(Stuart Coltherd) *hld up in centre of gp: drvn and outpcd over 2f out: sn btn (vet reported gelding bled from the nose)* **16/1**

1m 26.64s (0.44) **Going Correction** +0.15s/f (Slow)
WFA 3 from 4yo+ 6lb **14** Ran SP% **117.2**
Speed ratings (Par 101): **103,102,101,100,100 100,98,97,95,95 94,93,92,89**
CSF £267.17 CT £4990.88 TOTE £36.70: £8.80, £3.00, £5.20; EX 347.90 Trifecta £1687.90.
Owner R Postlethwaite **Bred** Mrs T Brudenell **Trained** Malton, N Yorks
■ Stewards' Enquiry : David Nolan two day ban: misuse of the whip (Aug 24-25)

FOCUS
They went a routine pace in this moderate handicap and there was a bunched finish. The winner is rated within 3lb of last year's best.

5853 PLAY SLOTS AT BETUK.COM NURSERY H'CAP 7f 14y (Tp)
6:30 (6:30) (Class 4) (0-85,78) 2-Y-O **£4,463** (£1,328; £663) **Stalls** Centre

Form RPR

635 **1** **Bravo Faisal (IRE)**[68] 3335 2-9-5 **76**........................ PaulHanagan 3 77
(Richard Fahey) *trckd ldr: effrt and disp ld fr over 1f out: kpt on wl towards fin: jst prevailed on nod* **9/2**[2]

531 **2** *nse* **St Ives**[28] 4826 2-9-7 **78**........................ DanielTudhope 2 79
(William Haggas) *trckd ldng pair: smooth hdwy to dispute ld over 1f out: rdn and kpt on wl fnl f: jst lost out on nod* **4/11**[1]

3322 **3** 2 ½ **Breguet Man (IRE)**[15] 5296 2-9-1 **72**........................ ShaneGray 1 66
(Keith Dalgleish) *led at ordinary gallop to over 1f out: sn rdn and outpcd* **5/1**[3]

1m 30.12s (3.92) **Going Correction** +0.15s/f (Slow) **3** Ran SP% **108.2**
Speed ratings (Par 96): **83,82,80**
CSF £6.99 TOTE £3.70; EX 4.50 Trifecta £11.20.
Owner Sheikh Abdullah Almalek Alsabah **Bred** Lynn Lodge Stud **Trained** Musley Bank, N Yorks

FOCUS
This fair little nursery was a tactical affair. It's hard to rate the form much higher.

5854 PLAY ROULETTE AT BETUK.COM FILLIES' H'CAP 5f (Tp)
7:05 (7:05) (Class 5) (0-75,74) 3-Y-O
£3,428 (£1,020; £509; £300; £300; £300) **Stalls** Centre

Form RPR

350 **1** **Sapphire Jubilee**[13] 5392 3-8-4 **57**........................ CamHardie 5 62
(Ollie Pears) *mde all: rdn over 1f out: hld on wl fnl f* **5/1**[3]

6150 **2** ¾ **Raspberry**[13] 5392 3-8-11 **67**........................ ConnorMurtagh(3) 1 69
(Olly Williams) *trckd ldrs: effrt and wnt 2nd appr fnl f: kpt on: hld towards fin* **16/1**

0233 **3** ½ **Diamonique**[6] 5617 3-9-7 **74**........................ ShaneGray 3 74
(Keith Dalgleish) *in tch: stdy hdwy over 2f out: rdn and sltly outpcd over 1f out: r.o ins fnl f* **9/4**[2]

000 **4** ¾ **Lovin (USA)**[14] 5335 3-9-7 **74**........................(vt) DanielTudhope 6 72
(David O'Meara) *trckd ldrs: effrt and rdn over 1f out: kpt on same pce ins fnl f* **8/1**

650 **5** ½ **Gorgeous Gobolina**[28] 4827 3-8-6 **59**........................ PhilDennis 4 55
(Susan Corbett) *pressed wnr to appr fnl f: sn drvn and no ex* **16/1**

2301 **6** 4 **Pinarella (FR)**[31] 4731 3-8-12 **65**........................ AndrewMullen 7 46
(Ben Haslam) *hld up in tch: rdn over 2f out: wknd over 1f out (trainer said filly was unsuited by being unable to dominate over 5f)* **2/1**[1]

-620 **7** ½ **Willow Brook**[101] 2197 3-7-12 **58** oh1 ow3........................(h) VictorSantos(7) 2 38
(Julie Camacho) *slowly away and swtchd rt s: hld up: effrt over 2f out: edgd lft and wknd over 1f out* **10/1**

59.97s (0.47) **Going Correction** +0.15s/f (Slow) **7** Ran SP% **112.7**
Speed ratings (Par 97): **102,100,100,98,98 91,90**
CSF £72.89 TOTE £5.60: £3.00, £2.60; EX 69.60 Trifecta £187.90.
Owner Mrs S D Pearson **Bred** J A Knox And Mrs M A Knox **Trained** Norton, N Yorks

FOCUS
A modest 3yo fillies' sprint handicap. It's been rated a bit negatively.

5855 BETUK.COM FILLIES' H'CAP 1m 4f 98y (Tp)
7:35 (7:35) (Class 5) (0-70,71) 3-Y-O+
£3,428 (£1,020; £509; £300; £300; £300) **Stalls** High

Form RPR

0020 **1** **Soloist (IRE)**[29] 4803 3-9-5 **68**........................(b[1]) DanielTudhope 1 76
(William Haggas) *cl up: shkn up to ld wl over 1f out: kpt on wl fnl f* **10/3**[2]

36-0 **2** 1 ¾ **Scheme**[30] 4768 3-9-7 **70**........................ LukeMorris 2 75
(Sir Mark Prescott Bt) *prom: rn green and outpcd over 3f out: rallied 2f out: chsd wnr ins fnl f: styd on* **2/1**[1]

000- **3** ½ **Lady Shanawell (IRE)**[48] 8541 3-8-1 **50**........................ AndrewMullen 6 54
(Ben Haslam) *hld up: pushed along over 2f out: hdwy and hung lft over 1f out: kpt on same pce ins fnl f* **16/1**

3502 **4** 2 ¼ **Scenesetter (IRE)**[38] 4447 3-9-2 **65**........................(p) GrahamLee 5 65
(Marco Botti) *led at ordinary gallop: rdn and hdd wl over 1f out: outpcd ins fnl f* **7/1**

4321 **5** 5 **Donnachies Girl (IRE)**[18] 5219 6-9-3 **59**........................ RowanScott(3) 4 51
(Alistair Williams) *pressed ldr: drvn along over 2f out: wknd over 1f out (jockey said mare wan flat)* **7/2**[3]

0544 **6** *nse* **Earth And Sky (USA)**[22] 5060 3-9-8 **71**........................ BenCurtis 3 63
(George Scott) *dwlt: hld up in tch: shkn up and effrt wl over 1f out: wknd fnl f* **5/1**

2m 43.73s (2.63) **Going Correction** +0.15s/f (Slow)
WFA 3 from 6yo 10lb **6** Ran SP% **113.7**
Speed ratings (Par 100): **97,95,95,94,90 90**
CSF £10.68 TOTE £4.30: £2.50, £1.40; EX 14.40 Trifecta £130.70.
Owner Highclere Thoroughbred Racing - Houghton **Bred** Grenane House Stud **Trained** Newmarket, Suffolk

FOCUS
Not a bad fillies' handicap for the class, but rather muddling form.

5856 HIT THE TARGET AT BETUK.COM/ IRISH STALLION FARMS EBF NOVICE MEDIAN AUCTION STKS (PLUS 10 RACE) 6f (Tp)
8:05 (8:11) (Class 4) 2-Y-O **£4,787** (£1,424; £711; £355) **Stalls** Centre

Form RPR

1 **Huraiz (IRE)** 2-9-5 0........................ JasonHart 1 81+
(Mark Johnston) *cl up on far side of gp: edgd lft and hdwy to join ldr over 1f out: led ins fnl f: drvn out* **13/2**[2]

2 **2** 2 ½ **River Cam**[14] 5353 2-9-0 0........................ PJMcDonald 9 69
(James Tate) *led on nr side of gp: pushed along and hrd pressed over 1f out: hdd ins fnl f: kpt on same pce* **7/4**[1]

04 **3** ¾ **Najm**[16] 5265 2-9-5 0........................ LukeMorris 2 71
(Sir Mark Prescott Bt) *cl up on far side of gp: rdn over 2f out: edgd lft ent fnl f: kpt on same pce* **25/1**

33 **4** *nk* **Kayewhykelly (IRE)**[36] 4516 2-9-0 0........................ GrahamLee 6 65+
(Julie Camacho) *hld up in centre of gp: pushed along and hdwy over 1f out: kpt on ins fnl f: nt pce to chal* **8/1**

0 **5** 1 ¾ **Kayat**[13] 5381 2-9-5 0........................ ShaneGray 10 65
(David Simcock) *trckd ldrs on nr side of gp tl rdn and outpcd fr over 1f out* **33/1**

6 **6** *hd* **Abbotside**[12] 5433 2-9-5 0........................ DanielTudhope 4 64
(James Bethell) *in tch towards far side of gp: rdn and outpcd over 2f out: rallied over 1f out: no imp ins fnl f* **7/1**[3]

7 2 **Spantik** 2-9-5 0........................ BenCurtis 11 58
(Archie Watson) *hld up on nr side of gp: rdn and outpcd over 2f out: n.d after* **13/2**[2]

06 **8** 1 ½ **Asstech (IRE)**[20] 5125 2-9-5 0........................ PaulHanagan 3 54
(Richard Fahey) *hld up and sn swtchd to centre of gp: rdn and outpcd over 2f out: sn btn* **14/1**

0 **9** 1 ½ **Rushcutters Bay**[29] 4798 2-9-5 0........................ CliffordLee 7 49
(Hugo Palmer) *cl up in centre of gp tl rdn and wknd appr fnl f* **12/1**

0 **10** 3 **Staxton Hill**[26] 4937 2-9-2 0........................ SeanDavis(3) 13 40
(Richard Fahey) *midfield on nr side of gp: rdn and struggling over 2f out: sn btn* **25/1**

11 *nk* **Jamaal Danehill** 2-9-0 0........................ PaulMulrennan 5 34
(Kevin Ryan) *bhd and green in centre of gp: struggling bef 1/2-way: nvr on terms* **14/1**

12 29 **Top Attraction** 2-9-5 0........................ MichaelStainton 8
(Chris Fairhurst) *bhd and sn struggling: t.o fr 1/2-way* **100/1**

1m 12.87s (0.37) **Going Correction** +0.15s/f (Slow) **12** Ran SP% **119.3**
Speed ratings (Par 96): **103,99,98,98,95 95,93,91,89,85 84,45**
CSF £17.75 TOTE £6.10: £2.30, £1.20, £7.00; EX 24.00 Trifecta £371.80.
Owner Hamdan Al Maktoum **Bred** Shadwell Estate Company Limited **Trained** Middleham Moor, N Yorks

FOCUS
Quite a taking effort from the winner.

5857 BETUK.COM YOUR HOME FOR ONLINE BETTING H'CAP 6f (Tp)
8:35 (8:41) (Class 6) (0-55,56) 3-Y-O+
£2,781 (£827; £413; £300; £300; £300) **Stalls** Centre

Form RPR

0040 **1** **Ingleby Molly (IRE)**[6] 5629 4-8-12 **49**........................(h) ConorMcGovern(3) 6 55
(Jason Ward) *cl up in centre of gp: led over 2f out: sn hrd pressed: hld on gamely fnl f* **12/1**

0650 **2** *shd* **Patrick (IRE)**[17] 5235 7-9-6 **54**........................ DavidNolan 3 60
(Paul Midgley) *cl up on far side of gp: effrt and ev ch fr over 1f out: kpt on wl fnl f: jst hld* **8/1**

3200 **3** 1 ¼ **Ticks The Boxes (IRE)**[26] 4912 7-9-8 **56**........................ BenCurtis 13 58
(Brian Ellison) *trckd ldrs on nr side of gp: effrt and ev ch over 1f out: kpt on same pce ins fnl f* **3/1**[1]

6324 **4** *nk* **The Bull (IRE)**[28] 4824 4-9-6 **54**........................(p) AndrewMullen 12 55
(Ben Haslam) *in tch on nr side of gp: effrt and rdn over 1f out: kpt on same pce ins fnl f* **11/2**[3]

0205 **5** *nk* **Prince Of Time**[6] 5629 7-9-1 **49**........................ CamHardie 14 49
(Stella Barclay) *hld up on nr side of gp: rdn and hdwy over 1f out: edgd lft and kpt on ins fnl f (jockey said gelding was denied a clear run inside the final 1 1/2f)* **18/1**

3004 **6** 1 ¼ **Roaring Rory**[8] 5559 6-9-2 **55**........................ HarrisonShaw(5) 11 51
(Ollie Pears) *s.i.s: hld up on nr side of gp: effrt and hdwy over 1f out: one pce ins fnl f (jockey said gelding was slowly away)* **4/1**[2]

4000 **7** ½ **Ascot Dreamer**[15] 5300 3-9-1 **53**........................ PaulMulrennan 1 47
(David Brown) *in tch on far side of gp: rdn over 2f out: no ex fr over 1f out* **20/1**

0400 **8** ¾ **Astraea**[3] 5722 4-9-5 **53**........................(b) NathanEvans 2 46
(Michael Easterby) *racd away fr main gp: cl up: rdn over 2f out: wknd fnl f* **18/1**

1104 **9** 2 **Tarnhelm**[3] 5723 4-8-13 **54**........................ IsobelFrancis(7) 10 41
(Wilf Storey) *s.s: bhd and outpcd away fr main gp: sme late hdwy: nvr on terms (jockey said filly was slowly away and never travelling)* **13/2**

0000 **10** ¾ **Princess Apollo**[8] 5558 5-8-12 **46** oh1........................(v[1]) JasonHart 8 30
(Donald Whillans) *led on nr side of gp: rdn and hdd over 2f out: wknd over 1f out* **40/1**

-600 **11** 1 ½ **Thornaby Princess**[16] 5278 8-8-9 **46** oh1........................(p) ConnorMurtagh(3) 9 26
(Jason Ward) *t.k.h: prom in centre of gp tl wknd over 1f out* **100/1**

00 **12** 1 ¼ **Breathoffreshair**[40] 4376 5-9-2 **50**........................(tp) PhilipPrince 4 26
(Richard Guest) *bhd on far side of gp: struggling over 2f out: sn btn* **20/1**

5006 **13** 1 ¾ **Opera Kiss (IRE)**[22] 5063 3-8-8 **46** oh1........................ ShaneGray 7 16
(Lawrence Mullaney) *bhd in centre of gp: drvn and struggling over 2f out: wknd* **50/1**

600 **14** 25 **Killer Queen**[147] 1195 4-8-12 **46** oh1........................(p[1]) PhilDennis 5
(David C Griffiths) *t.k.h: in tch in centre of gp: struggling over 2f out: lost tch and eased fnl f* **66/1**

1m 13.03s (0.53) **Going Correction** +0.15s/f (Slow)
WFA 3 from 4yo+ 4lb **14** Ran SP% **119.5**
Speed ratings (Par 101): **102,101,100,99,99 97,97,96,93,92 90,88,86,53**
CSF £98.13 CT £376.11 TOTE £12.00: £3.70, £2.80, £1.80; EX 142.20 Trifecta £935.20.
Owner Ingleby Bloodstock Limited **Bred** Ingleby Bloodstock Ltd **Trained** Sessay, N Yorks

FOCUS
An ordinary sprint handicap in which it paid to be handy.
T/Plt: £5,715.60 to a £1 stake. Pool: £47,526.16. 6.07 winning units. T/Qpdt: £220.00 to a £1 stake. Pool: £5,326.82. 17.91 winning units. **Richard Young**

5561 SANDOWN (R-H)
Thursday, August 8

OFFICIAL GOING: Good (good to firm in places; rnd 7.0, str 7.2)
Wind: Almost nil Weather: Fine but cloudy, warm

5858 SLUG AND LETTUCE 2-4-1 COCKTAILS AMATEUR RIDERS' H'CAP 1m 1f 209y
5:40 (5:42) (Class 4) (0-80,82) 3-Y-O+
£6,239 (£1,935; £967; £484; £300; £300) **Stalls** Low

Form RPR

4166 **1** **My Boy Sepoy**[20] 5149 4-10-13 **78**........................ MissSerenaBrotheron 6 86
(Stuart Williams) *hld up towards rr: prog over 2f out: rdn to ld over 1f out: edgd rt fnl f: in command whn lft clr nr fin* **6/1**[3]

-003 **2** *1 ½* **Steeve**[12] 5450 3-9-10 **69**..(p) MrPatrickMillman 1 77+
(Rod Millman) *pressed ldr: led 3f out: rdn 2f out: hdd over 1f out: kpt on to press wnr after: stl cl up but hld whn impeded 50yds and dramatically snatched up fnl strides* **9/1**

6050 **3** *2* **Isomer (USA)**[24] 4997 5-10-7 **79**.................... MissClaudiaMetaireau(7) 2 80
(Andrew Balding) *trckd ldrs: shkn up to chal 2f out: outpcd by ldng pair over 1f out: one pce after* **6/1[3]**

0135 **4** *¾* **Dutch Uncle**[19] 5198 7-10-5 **75**............................ MrCharlesClover(5) 9 75
(Tom Clover) *trckd ldrs: rdn 2f out: nt qckn and outpcd over 1f out: kpt on fnl f* **7/1**

1302 **5** *3 ¾* **French Mix (USA)**[35] 4543 5-10-10 **78**............... MissHannahWelch(3) 7 70
(Alexandra Dunn) *led but pressed: hdd 3f out: wknd u.p 2f out* **3/1[1]**

1300 **6** *2* **Central City (IRE)**[19] 5195 4-10-12 **82**..................(p) MrNathanSeery(5) 4 70
(Ian Williams) *hld up in last: impeded over 8f out: shkn up and no prog over 2f out* **10/1**

0632 **7** *4* **War Of Succession**[29] 4771 5-9-4 **60** oh2.................... SophieSmith(5) 8 40
(Tony Newcombe) *racd wd: prog to join ldrs after 2f: lost pl 4f out: last 3f out: no ch after* **17/2**

5051 **8** *3 ¼* **Arctic Sea**[31] 4737 5-10-7 **72**.. MrSimonWalker 3 46
(Paul Cole) *t.k.h: hld up in tch: stmbld over 8f out and dropped to last pair: shkn up and no prog over 2f out (jockey said gelding clipped heels approximately 1 furlong after the start)* **4/1[2]**

2m 10.11s (-0.09) **Going Correction** +0.025s/f (Good)
WFA 3 from 4yo+ 8lb **8** Ran SP% **115.7**
Speed ratings (Par 105): **101,99,98,97,94 93,89,87**
CSF £58.57 CT £338.89 TOTE £5.40: £1.50, £2.60, £2.00; EX 56.90 Trifecta £531.30.
Owner Mr & Mrs George Bhatti **Bred** Old Mill Stud Ltd **Trained** Newmarket, Suffolk
■ Stewards' Enquiry : Miss Serena Brotherton three day ban: careless riding (Aug 24-26)

FOCUS
All distances as advertised. There was little gallop on in this amateur riders' handicap and the form is just average. There was a stewards' enquiry but rightly the result was left alone.

5859 SLUG AND LETTUCE CHRISTMAS PARTY EBF MAIDEN STKS (PLUS 10 RACE) 5f 10y
6:10 (6:13) (Class 4) 2-Y-O **£4,787** (£1,424; £711; £355) **Stalls** Low

Form RPR
2 **1** **Master McGrath (IRE)**[17] 5234 2-9-5 **0**.. KevinStott 5 77
(Kevin Ryan) *fast away: mde virtually all: rdn 2f out: hanging rt fnl f but styd on wl nr fin* **13/8[1]**

4 **2** *½* **Sand Diego (IRE)**[24] 4993 2-9-5 **0**.. PatDobbs 9 75+
(Peter Crate) *dwlt: sn in midfield gng strly: prog 2f out: rdn and r.o to take 2nd last 100yds: clsd on wnr but a jst hld* **14/1**

03 **3** *1 ½* **Colonel Whitehead (IRE)**[10] 5500 2-9-2 **0**..................... JaneElliott(3) 8 70
(Heather Main) *racd wd: chsd ldrs: rdn 2f out: styd on u.p fnl f to take 3rd nr fin* **25/1**

4 *½* **Phuket Power (IRE)** 2-9-5 **0**............................... SilvestreDeSousa 10 68+
(Tom Dascombe) *dwlt and wnt lft s: mostly in last pair: rdn 2f out: stl in last pair 1f out: drvn and r.o wl last 150yds: gaining at fin* **7/1[3]**

3 **5** *nk* **Vasari (USA)**[16] 5265 2-9-5 **0**.. RyanMoore 1 67
(Sir Michael Stoute) *racd against rail: pressed wnr: chal and upsides fr 2f out to 150yds out: wknd nr fin* **2/1[2]**

6 *hd* **Qinwan** 2-9-5 **0**... OisinMurphy 6 66
(Andrew Balding) *dwlt: towards rr: pushed along 2f out: kpt on steadily fnl f: nt disgracd* **14/1**

4 **7** *1* **Liscahann**[15] 5317 2-9-0 **0**.. RobHornby 2 58
(Seamus Mullins) *chsd ldrs: rdn 2f out: fdd ins fnl f* **16/1**

0 **8** *¾* **Spurofthemoment**[20] 5132 2-9-0 **0**......................... KieranShoemark 3 55
(Charles Hills) *chsd ldng pair to over 1f out: wknd fnl f* **10/1**

5 **9** *1 ¼* **Castel Angelo (IRE)**[12] 5447 2-9-5 **0**.......................... CharlesBishop 7 55
(Henry Candy) *stdd s: hld up in last pair: pushed along over 1f out: no prog and nvr in it: possible improver* **20/1**

0 **10** *4 ½* **Surrajah (IRE)**[42] 4295 2-9-5 **0**.................................. DavidProbert 4 39
(Tom Clover) *chsd ldrs tl wknd qckly 2f out* **50/1**

1m 1.42s (0.12) **Going Correction** +0.025s/f (Good) **10** Ran SP% **122.8**
Speed ratings (Par 96): **100,99,96,96,95 95,93,92,90,83**
CSF £27.81 TOTE £2.50: £1.10, £3.90, £5.40; EX 29.80 Trifecta £281.70.
Owner The Masters **Bred** Highpark Bloodstock Ltd **Trained** Hambleton, N Yorks

FOCUS
Not a particularly strong sprint maiden, but it went to the market leader. The winner is the type to do better again.

5860 SLUG AND LETTUCE 2-4-1 TANQUERAY THURSDAYS EBF MAIDEN STKS (PLUS 10 RACE) 1m
6:45 (6:45) (Class 4) 2-Y-O **£4,787** (£1,424; £711; £355) **Stalls** Low

Form RPR
2 **1** **Native Tribe**[20] 5131 2-9-5 **0**.. WilliamBuick 2 85+
(Charlie Appleby) *led at mod pce: tried to kick on over 2f out but move nt decisive: rdn and hdd over 1f out: carried sltly rt but drvn to ld again ins fnl f: barging match w rival last 50yds: jst hld on (jockey said colt ran green)* **8/15[1]**

2 *nse* **Dubai Mirage (IRE)** 2-9-5 **0**....................................... OisinMurphy 4 85+
(Saeed bin Suroor) *hld up in 4th: prog to trck ldr over 2f out: pushed into ld over 1f out: edgd rt and hdd ins fnl f: rallied wl and barging match w rival last 50yds: jst failed* **5/1[3]**

6 **3** *5* **Herman Hesse**[70] 3274 2-9-5 **0**.. RobertHavlin 3 73
(John Gosden) *trckd ldr: pushed along 1/2-way: lost 2nd over 2f out and nt clr run shortly after: sn outpcd and dropped to 4th: kpt on ins fnl f* **4/1[2]**

4 *2 ¼* **Jean Baptiste (IRE)** 2-9-5 **0**.. RyanMoore 1 68
(Sir Michael Stoute) *trckd ldng pair: pushed along and effrt on inner over 2f out: outpcd over 1f out: wknd ins fnl f* **14/1**

5 *4 ½* **Tiger Zone (IRE)** 2-9-5 **0**.. AdamKirby 5 57
(Clive Cox) *a in last: outpcd over 2f out: sn no ch* **20/1**

1m 45.71s (2.41) **Going Correction** +0.025s/f (Good) **5** Ran SP% **113.3**
Speed ratings (Par 96): **88,87,82,80,76**
CSF £3.92 TOTE £1.30: £1.10, £2.70; EX 3.30 Trifecta £5.80.
Owner Godolphin **Bred** Chippenham Lodge Stud **Trained** Newmarket, Suffolk

FOCUS
The Godolphin pair dominated this useful maiden, indeed they fought out a cracking finish and were separated by just a nose. They did make contact and there was a Stewards' enquiry, but the result was unchanged.

5861 FIZZ FRIDAYS AT SLUG AND LETTUCE H'CAP 1m 1f 209y
7:15 (7:17) (Class 3) (0-90,88) 3-Y-O **£9,337** (£2,796; £1,398; £699; £349; £175) **Stalls** Low

Form RPR
2100 **1** **Migration (IRE)**[27] 4882 3-9-7 **88**............................... SilvestreDeSousa 8 103+
(David Menuisier) *stdd s: hld up and last to 1/2-way: prog on outer over 2f out: rdn to ld over 1f out: edgd rt after: clr ins fnl f: styd on* **7/2[2]**

3331 **2** *1 ½* **Just The Man (FR)**[14] 5341 3-9-2 **83**.................................... AdamKirby 2 94+
(Clive Cox) *hld up in tch: waiting for a gap briefly over 2f out: rdn and prog over 1f out: chsd wnr and impeded jst ins fnl f: styd on but no real threat after* **13/2**

-212 **3** *2 ¼* **Durrell**[19] 5194 3-9-6 **87**.. DanielMuscutt 1 92
(James Fanshawe) *t.k.h: trckd ldrs: rdn and lost pl 2f out and sn outpcd: kpt on again fnl f to take 3rd nr fin* **9/2[3]**

-121 **4** *1* **Dreamweaver (IRE)**[20] 5124 3-8-10 **77**.............................. OisinMurphy 5 80
(Ed Walker) *led after 1f: increased pce after 4f: shkn up and hdd 2f out: steadily fdd fnl f* **5/2[1]**

-312 **5** *nk* **Marronnier (IRE)**[14] 5348 3-9-6 **87**..................................(t) SeanLevey 4 89+
(Stuart Williams) *prom: trckd ldr after 4f: rdn to ld 2f out: hdd over 1f out: sing to wknd whn briefly short of room sn after* **6/1**

-311 **6** *2 ¼* **Mokammal**[41] 4321 3-9-7 **88**... JimCrowley 3 86+
(Sir Michael Stoute) *led 1f: styd prom: rdn and lost pl whn squeezed for room over 1f out: no ch after* **6/1**

1605 **7** *1 ¼* **Flighty Almighty**[17] 5253 3-9-2 **83**.................................. DavidProbert 6 78
(Tom Dascombe) *hld up: last fr 1/2-way: rdn and no prog over 2f out* **25/1**

2m 8.39s (-1.81) **Going Correction** +0.025s/f (Good) **7** Ran SP% **114.7**
Speed ratings (Par 104): **108,106,105,104,103 102,101**
CSF £26.28 CT £103.25 TOTE £4.30: £2.10, £2.90; EX 27.60 Trifecta £74.50.
Owner Gail Brown Racing (IX) **Bred** Ms C Peddie **Trained** Pulborough, W Sussex
■ Stewards' Enquiry : Silvestre De Sousa four-day ban: careless riding (Aug 11,25,26,27)

FOCUS
Another race run at a pretty steady gallop, the winner did mightily well considering he was slow to start and raced in rear. Decent form, with most of these looking capable of better.

5862 SLUG AND LETTUCE COCKTAIL MASTERANDICAP 7f
7:45 (7:48) (Class 4) 3-Y-O+ **£6,469** (£1,925; £962; £481; £300; £300) **Stalls** Low

Form RPR
4015 **1** **Swift Approval (IRE)**[13] 5386 7-9-6 **78**.............................. JimCrowley 2 86
(Stuart Williams) *hld up in last as ldrs set scorching pce: rdn over 2f out: prog over 1f out: styd on wl fnl f to ld last 50yds* **6/1**

6016 **2** *½* **Mountain Rescue (IRE)**[27] 4867 7-9-11 **83**.................(p) DavidProbert 6 89+
(Michael Attwater) *w ldr at breaknk pce: led 3f out and 3 l ahd 2f out: drvn over 1f out: clung on really wl but hdd last 50yds* **10/1**

1040 **3** *¾* **I Am A Dreamer**[12] 5459 3-9-4 **82**........................(v[1]) SilvestreDeSousa 7 84
(Mark Johnston) *trckd clr ldng pair: rdn over 2f out: chsd ldr wl over 1f out: grad clsd fnl f but no ex and dropped to 3rd nr fin* **5/1[3]**

0340 **4** *3* **Givinitsum (SAF)**[19] 5173 4-9-12 **84**.............................. CharlesBishop 5 80
(Eve Johnson Houghton) *hld up: rdn and briefly disp 2nd 2f out: no hdwy over 1f out: fdd* **11/1**

3330 **5** *hd* **Martineo**[28] 4851 4-9-8 **80**.. AdamKirby 3 75
(John Butler) *hld up: shkn up and dropped to last over 2f out: wandering and no prog after: swtchd lft fnl f and styd on last 100yds* **5/2[2]**

-651 **6** *1* **Golden Force**[15] 5303 3-9-1 **79**... OisinMurphy 1 70+
(Clive Cox) *led at breaknk pce but jnd: wd bnd over 4f out: hdd 3f out: sn cracked: wknd over 1f out (jockey said gelding ran too free)* **7/4[1]**

1m 27.94s (-1.36) **Going Correction** +0.025s/f (Good)
WFA 3 from 4yo+ 6lb **6** Ran SP% **113.3**
Speed ratings (Par 105): **108,107,106,103,102 101**
CSF £59.62 TOTE £6.80: £2.80, £5.00; EX 64.70 Trifecta £238.20.
Owner JLM Racing **Bred** Mrs Jean Brennan **Trained** Newmarket, Suffolk

FOCUS
No hanging around in this useful handicap, with the runner-up and disappointing favourite setting a really strong gallop. The winner came from last.

5863 SLUG AND LETTUCE AFTERNOON TEA H'CAP 1m
8:15 (8:16) (Class 5) (0-75,75) 3-Y-O+ **£4,528** (£1,347; £673; £336; £300; £300) **Stalls** Low

Form RPR
-232 **1** **Rock The Cradle (IRE)**[22] 5060 3-9-3 **73**.......................... OisinMurphy 6 84+
(Ed Vaughan) *hld up in last pair: rdn and prog 2f out: clsd to ld narrowly 150yds out: drvn out and a fending off rival* **5/2[1]**

2303 **2** *nk* **Casement (IRE)**[17] 5255 5-9-10 **73**.........................(p) AlistairRawlinson 3 84
(Michael Appleby) *taken down early: trckd ldr: rdn to ld wl over 1f out: drvn and narrowly hdd 150yds out: fought on wl but jst hld* **8/1**

4446 **3** *4* **Juanito Chico (IRE)**[20] 5155 5-9-9 **72**............................(p) JimCrowley 5 74
(Stuart Williams) *trckd ldrs: rdn and tried to cl 2f out: readily lft bhd by ldng pair fnl f* **5/1**

5602 **4** *1 ½* **Rampant Lion (IRE)**[7] 5574 4-9-10 **73**..........................(p) DavidProbert 4 71
(William Jarvis) *hld up in last: rdn and nt qckn 2f out: n.d after: kpt on fnl f (jockey said gelding ran flat)* **11/4[2]**

3-22 **5** *¾* **Quarry Beach**[14] 5350 3-9-2 **72**....................................... CharlesBishop 2 68
(Henry Candy) *taken down early: led and racd freely: shkn up and hdd wl over 1f out: sn wknd* **3/1[3]**

-154 **6** *6* **City Tour**[80] 2897 3-9-5 **75**... RobertHavlin 1 57
(Lydia Richards) *chsd ldng pair to jst over 2f out: wknd qckly* **20/1**

1m 43.1s (-0.20) **Going Correction** +0.025s/f (Good)
WFA 3 from 4yo+ 7lb **6** Ran SP% **112.8**
Speed ratings (Par 103): **102,101,97,96,95 89**
CSF £22.46 TOTE £2.70: £1.70, £4.20; EX 22.30 Trifecta £78.00.
Owner Moroney, Singh & Partner **Bred** D Bourke **Trained** Newmarket, Suffolk

FOCUS
Just a fair handicap, the pace was an ordinary one but two still managed to pull clear late on. The form's rated around the runner-up.
T/Plt: £505.40 to a £1 stake. Pool: £60,775.25. 87.77 winning units. T/Qpdt: £59.90 to a £1 stake. Pool: £7,062.80. 87.20 winning units. **Jonathan Neesom**

5822YARMOUTH (L-H)
Thursday, August 8

OFFICIAL GOING: Good to firm (firm in places; 7.7)
Wind: breezy Weather: hot and sunny; 25 degrees

5864 BEST ODDS GUARANTEED MAIDEN H'CAP — 6f 3y
2:20 (2:23) (Class 6) (0-65,65) 3-Y-0+
£2,781 (£827; £413; £300; £300; £300) **Stalls** Centre

Form — RPR

0532 **1** **Global Hope (IRE)**[9] 5526 4-9-0 **60**..........(tp) TobyEley(7) 1 — 68
(Gay Kelleway) *cl up and travelled wl: shkn up to ld 1 1/2f out: clr 1f out: easily* **4/6**[1]

0000 **2** 4 ½ **Quduraat**[17] 5247 3-8-8 **51**.......... DavidEgan 6 — 45
(Michael Appleby) *wore a nosenet: towards rr: rdn over 2f out: sn racing awkwardly: kpt on to go v wl hld 2nd fnl 75yds* **14/1**

00-0 **3** ¾ **Remission**[99] 2300 3-8-1 **47**.......... NoelGarbutt(3) 4 — 38
(Derek Shaw) *plld hrd: cl 2nd tl wnr drew clr over 1f out: no ex and lost 2nd clsng stages* **66/1**

0060 **4** ½ **Exning Queen (IRE)**[22] 5063 3-8-3 **46**..........(t[1]) ShelleyBirkett 5 — 36
(Julia Feilden) *lost 8 l s: effrt to chse ldrs 1/2-way: nt qckn over 1f out (jockey said filly was slowly away)* **14/1**

4004 **5** 1 ¼ **Praxedis**[22] 5063 4-8-5 **51**..........(p) AngusVilliers(7) 7 — 38
(Robert Cowell) *t.k.h towards rr: rdn over 2f out: sn btn: hanging bdly lft ins fnl f* **5/1**[3]

4600 **6** 4 **Azets**[29] 4788 3-8-12 **55**..........(p[1]) MartinDwyer 2 — 29
(Amanda Perrett) *led tl rdn and hdd 1 1/2f out: dropped out rapidly: eased clsng stages* **4/1**[2]

1m 13.07s (0.47) **Going Correction** +0.10s/f (Good)
WFA 3 from 4yo 4lb — **6** Ran SP% **111.5**
Speed ratings (Par 101): **100,94,93,92,90 85**
CSF £11.69 TOTE £1.40: £1.10, £4.80; EX 8.60 Trifecta £99.40.
Owner M Walker, N Scandrett, G Kelleway **Bred** Airlie Stud & Mrs S M Rogers **Trained** Exning, Suffolk

FOCUS
Bottom bend dolled out 3m adding in 10yds to all round races. This was uncompetitive and the market leader won as he was entitled to do. The form's rated cautiously.

5865 BRITISH STALLION STUDS EBF NOVICE STKS (PLUS 10 RACE) — 6f 3y
2:50 (2:54) (Class 4) 2-Y-0 — **£4,851** (£1,443; £721; £360) **Stalls** Centre

Form — RPR

4 **1** **Mr Kiki (IRE)**[13] 5367 2-9-5 0.......... CallumShepherd 6 — 77+
(Michael Bell) *pressed ldr: pushed ahd 2f out: a holding chalrs fnl f* **4/6**[1]

2 ¾ **Double Or Bubble (IRE)** 2-9-0 0.......... GeraldMosse 2 — 70+
(Chris Wall) *prom and t.k.h: rdn 2f out: chsd wnr ins fnl f: no imp but kpt on pleasingly* **18/1**

3 ¾ **Tyler Durden (IRE)** 2-9-5 0..........(h[1]) MartinDwyer 7 — 73+
(Richard Spencer) *racd in last pl: hdwy over 1f out: drvn and tried to chal ins fnl f: wnt 3rd 100yds out: kpt on but hld after* **25/1**

4 ¾ **Robert Guiscard (IRE)** 2-9-5 0.......... HarryBentley 9 — 70+
(Mark Johnston) *towards rr: rdn and effrt 2f out: sn pressing wnr: no ex ins fnl f and lost 3rd 100yds out* **8/1**[3]

64 **5** 4 ½ **Red Jasper**[34] 4588 2-9-5 0.......... LiamJones 1 — 57
(Michael Appleby) *t.k.h: chsd ldrs: shkn up 1/2-way: wl btn whn wandered rt and lft ins fnl f* **100/1**

6 5 **Al Muthanna (IRE)** 2-9-5 0.......... JamesDoyle 3 — 42
(William Haggas) *led tl hdd 2f out: dropped out rapidly: eased fnl f* **9/4**[2]

7 1 ¼ **Order Of Merritt (IRE)** 2-9-5 0.......... JimmyQuinn 8 — 38
(Sir Mark Prescott Bt) *t.k.h: chsd ldrs to 1/2-way: sn outpcd* **33/1**

1m 14.17s (1.57) **Going Correction** +0.10s/f (Good) — **7** Ran SP% **114.9**
Speed ratings (Par 96): **93,92,91,90,84 77,75**
CSF £15.90 TOTE £1.40: £1.10, £3.60; EX 15.40 Trifecta £105.40.
Owner Amo Racing Limited **Bred** Canice Farrell Jnr **Trained** Newmarket, Suffolk

FOCUS
This was an interesting maiden with several well-bred newcomers involved. Experience won out.

5866 BEATEN BY A HEAD H'CAP — 1m 2f 23y
3:20 (3:20) (Class 6) (0-65,65) 3-Y-0
£2,781 (£827; £413; £300; £300; £300) **Stalls** Low

Form — RPR

4-35 **1** **Dame Freya Stark**[138] 1288 3-9-7 **65**.......... DavidEgan 4 — 72+
(Mark Johnston) *mde all: upped tempo 3f out: drvn clr over 1f out and kpt on v stoutly* **9/4**[1]

3363 **2** 2 ¼ **Catch My Breath**[29] 4801 3-9-5 **63**.......... JosephineGordon 9 — 66
(John Ryan) *midfield: rdn to chse wnr wl over 2f out: nvr got in a blow but a holding rest* **9/4**[1]

4444 **3** 1 ¾ **Winter Snowdrop (IRE)**[28] 4836 3-7-11 **46** oh1.......... SophieRalston(5) 2 — 46
(Julia Feilden) *pressed ldr tl 4f out: pushed along wl over 1f out: 3rd and no imp fnl f* **5/1**[3]

5-04 **4** 3 **Reddiac (IRE)**[14] 5358 3-9-3 **61**.......... JamesDoyle 3 — 55
(Ed Dunlop) *midfield: rdn 3f out: plugged on at same pce fnl 2f* **4/1**[2]

45-0 **5** 2 ¼ **Carlow Boy (IRE)**[21] 5100 3-8-4 **48**.......... KieranO'Neill 5 — 38
(Christopher Kellett) *3rd tl wnt 2nd 4f out: sn rdn: lost pl wl over 2f out (trainer said gelding was unsuited by the going and would prefer an easier surface)* **14/1**

-000 **6** 1 ¼ **Lynchpin (IRE)**[29] 4787 3-9-3 **61**.......... BrettDoyle 6 — 48
(Lydia Pearce) *t.k.h towards rr: effrt and pushed along on outer over 3f out: fdd 2f out* **14/1**

0200 **7** 19 **Global Goddess (IRE)**[13] 5377 3-8-6 **57**.......... TobyEley(7) 7 — 8
(Gay Kelleway) *a last: u.p over 4f out: fnd nil: t.o 2f out: eased (jockey said filly was never travelling. trainer said the filly was in season and was also unsuited by the going, and would prefer an easier surface)* **28/1**

2m 7.57s (-1.23) **Going Correction** +0.10s/f (Good) — **7** Ran SP% **115.0**
Speed ratings (Par 98): **108,106,104,102,100 99,84**
CSF £7.42 CT £21.57 TOTE £2.90: £1.80, £1.90; EX 8.60 Trifecta £30.50.
Owner Miss K Rausing **Bred** Miss K Rausing **Trained** Middleham Moor, N Yorks

FOCUS
Add 10yds. Only a moderate handicap but it is still early days for the winner who does have scope to improve. The next two dictate a modest level.

5867 BRITISH RACING H'CAP — 1m 1f 21y
3:50 (3:50) (Class 6) (0-55,57) 3-Y-0+
£2,781 (£827; £413; £300; £300; £300) **Stalls** Low

Form — RPR

0042 **1** **All Right**[22] 5049 3-8-11 **52**.......... HarryBentley 7 — 59+
(Henry Candy) *trckd ldrs: effrt 3f out: led wl over 1f out: rdn and clr 1f out: styd on steadily* **11/8**[1]

2533 **2** 1 ¾ **Percy Toplis**[5] 5652 5-8-12 **45**..........(b) EoinWalsh 1 — 48
(Christine Dunnett) *towards rr: rdn and squeezed for room over 3f out: 5th and plenty to do 1f out: str late run to pass three rivals cl home and snatch wl hld 2nd* **7/1**[3]

0035 **3** *nk* **Takiah**[8] 5549 4-8-13 **46**..........(p) KieranO'Neill 12 — 48
(Peter Hiatt) *towards rr: hdwy 3f out: 4th and rdn 2f out: disp wl hld 2nd ins fnl f* **12/1**

0253 **4** *hd* **Approve The Dream (IRE)**[37] 4477 3-9-0 **55**.......... ShelleyBirkett 13 — 57
(Julia Feilden) *t.k.h and prom on outer: led briefly 2f out: pushed along and outpcd by wnr 1f out: ev ch of 2nd tl fnl strides (jockey said gelding ran too free)* **8/1**

4454 **5** *nk* **Edge (IRE)**[14] 5337 8-9-4 **54**..........(b) JoshuaBryan(3) 10 — 55
(Bernard Llewellyn) *settled in rr: effrt 4f out: looking for room 3f out tl drvn over 1f out: chal for 2nd ins fnl f: nt rch wnr and no ex cl home* **6/1**[2]

3035 **6** 3 **Spirit Of Lucerne (IRE)**[15] 5293 3-8-6 **47**.......... JimmyQuinn 4 — 42
(Phil McEntee) *drvn thrght: chsd ldrs but nvr travelling: btn wl over 1f out (jockey said filly was never travelling)* **20/1**

0001 **7** *nk* **Guardiola (USA)**[15] 5293 4-8-11 **47**..........(tp) MitchGodwin(3) 9 — 42
(Bernard Llewellyn) *midfield: rdn over 3f out: btn 2f out* **12/1**

000 **8** 6 **Set Point Charlie (IRE)**[31] 4738 3-9-2 **57**.......... TomQueally 14 — 40
(Seamus Durack) *chsd ldrs tl rdn and wknd 3f out* **28/1**

0605 **9** 1 ¼ **Conqueress (IRE)**[22] 5060 5-8-12 **45**..........(p) RoystonFfrench 3 — 25
(Lydia Pearce) *led narrowly tl rdn and fdd 3f out* **33/1**

0006 **10** *hd* **Sittin Handy (IRE)**[12] 5431 3-7-13 **45**..........(p) SophieRalston(5) 8 — 25
(Dean Ivory) *w ldr: led narrowly 3f out tl rdn and hdd 2f out: sn dropped out* **25/1**

005- **11** 16 **General Patton**[292] 8424 5-8-12 **45**.......... AdrianMcCarthy 6
(Lydia Pearce) *nvr bttr than midfield: struggling over 3f out: t.o and eased* **66/1**

0240 **12** 1 **Coachella (IRE)**[29] 4771 5-9-5 **52**..........(b) DavidEgan 2
(Ed de Giles) *last early: nvr gng wl: struggling 4f out: t.o and eased* **10/1**

1m 54.74s (0.24) **Going Correction** +0.10s/f (Good)
WFA 3 from 4yo+ 8lb — **12** Ran SP% **121.0**
Speed ratings (Par 101): **102,100,100,100,99 97,96,91,90,90 75,75**
CSF £10.61 CT £88.32 TOTE £2.00: £1.10, £2.00, £4.20; EX 11.00 Trifecta £113.90.
Owner Major M G Wyatt **Bred** Dunchurch Lodge Stud Company **Trained** Kingston Warren, Oxon

FOCUS
Add 10yds. A modest affair but won in clear-cut style by an unexposed filly.

5868 CASINO APP H'CAP — 6f 3y
4:20 (4:20) (Class 4) (0-85,84) 3-Y-0+ — **£5,207** (£1,549; £774; £387) **Stalls** Centre

Form — RPR

4001 **1** **Yimou (IRE)**[28] 4844 4-9-3 **75**.......... MartinDwyer 3 — 83+
(Dean Ivory) *led: jnd and drvn wl over 1f out: plld out ex to edge clr fnl 100yds and r.o gamely* **5/6**[1]

12-2 **2** 1 **Promote (IRE)**[22] 5057 3-9-3 **79**.......... DavidEgan 1 — 83
(James Tate) *plld hrd: 2nd tl rdn to join wnr wl over 1f out: ev ch tl outpcd fnl 100yds* **7/2**[2]

6400 **3** 8 **Nick Vedder**[13] 5395 5-9-5 **77**..........(b) GeraldMosse 2 — 56
(Michael Wigham) *chsd ldng pair: drvn and fnd nil wl over 2f out: struggling after* **15/2**[3]

6021 **4** 11 **Hart Stopper**[22] 5058 5-9-4 **83**..........(t) MarcoGhiani(7) 7 — 27+
(Stuart Williams) *sddle slipped and plunging early and rdr forced to take a pull: continued t.o (jockey said his saddle slipped leaving the stalls, causing the gelding to bronc for several strides)* **7/2**[2]

1m 12.41s (-0.19) **Going Correction** +0.10s/f (Good)
WFA 3 from 4yo+ 4lb — **4** Ran SP% **110.8**
Speed ratings (Par 105): **105,103,93,78**
CSF £4.19 TOTE £1.90; EX 4.70 Trifecta £12.00.
Owner Andrew L Cohen **Bred** Alexander Bloodstock **Trained** Radlett, Herts

FOCUS
A useful little sprint although it was robbed of some interest after an incident just after the gates opened involving Hart Stopper where his saddle slipped.

5869 MANSIONBET BEST ODDS GUARANTEED H'CAP — 7f 3y
4:50 (4:50) (Class 6) (0-60,62) 3-Y-0
£2,781 (£827; £413; £300; £300; £300) **Stalls** Centre

Form — RPR

000 **1** **Dutch Story**[47] 4116 3-8-7 **46** oh1..........(p[1]) MartinDwyer 7 — 56+
(Amanda Perrett) *sn led: rdn 2f out: racing idly but a doing enough w decisive advantage fnl f (trainer's rep said, regarding the improved form shown, the yard appeared to be coming back into firm and that the gelding benefitted from the first-time application of cheekpieces)* **11/1**

6300 **2** 1 ¾ **Sepahi**[13] 5377 3-9-2 **60**..........(p) SebastianWoods(5) 8 — 65
(Henry Spiller) *taken down early: bhd: rdn and hdwy 3f out: chsd wnr 2f out: a hld fnl f* **20/1**

5454 **3** 6 **Deconso**[27] 4874 3-8-12 **51**.......... CallumShepherd 10 — 40
(Christopher Kellett) *t.k.h: prom: rdn 3f out: little rspnse and btn 1f out* **8/1**

0000 **4** ¾ **Impressionable**[30] 4763 3-9-2 **55**..........(h[1]) HarryBentley 6 — 42
(Marco Botti) *taken down early: bhd: rdn 3f out: kpt on ins fnl f but n.d* **7/1**

3245 **5** ½ **Your Mothers' Eyes**[21] 5092 3-9-6 **62**..........(p) JoshuaBryan(3) 4 — 47
(Alan Bailey) *prom: rdn 2f out: fdd tamely* **7/4**[1]

605 **6** 2 ¾ **Ecstasea (IRE)**[16] 5269 3-9-7 **60**.......... JosephineGordon 2 — 38
(Rae Guest) *midfield: rdn and wkng whn squeezed out 2f out (jockey said filly was denied a clear run)* **5/1**[3]

4-01 **7** 1 ¾ **Rita's Folly**[14] 5358 3-9-5 **58**..........(b[1]) GeraldMosse 1 — 31
(Anthony Carson) *bmpd after s: bhd early: effrt and rdn and edging rt 2f out: wknd 1f out: eased (trainer could offer no explanation for the filly's performance)* **7/2**[2]

-006 **8** 4 ½ **Mallons Spirit (IRE)**[14] 5358 3-8-7 **46** oh1..........(v[1]) LiamJones 3 — 7
(Michael Appleby) *t.k.h but racing awkwardly: prom tl veered violently lft over 2f out and nt rcvr (jockey said filly hung badly left)* **25/1**

1m 26.23s (1.13) **Going Correction** +0.10s/f (Good) — **8** Ran SP% **115.8**
Speed ratings (Par 98): **97,95,88,87,86 83,81,76**
CSF £198.44 CT £1281.19 TOTE £12.00: £3.50, £5.80, £1.70; EX 175.40 Trifecta £1129.70.

Owner Mr & Mrs R Scott & & Mrs D Bevan **Bred** Mr & Mrs R & P Scott **Trained** Pulborough, W Sussex

FOCUS

Modest stuff here, but the front two did pull a long way clear of the rest. Improvement from the winner.

5870 RACING WELFARE APPRENTICE H'CAP — 7f 3y

5:20 (5:20) (Class 5) (0-75,75) 4-Y-O+

£3,428 (£1,020; £509; £300; £300; £300) Stalls Centre

Form				RPR
4-26	1		**Envisaging (IRE)**[40] 4365 5-9-4 **74**....(t) LorenzoAtzori(7) 4 *(James Fanshawe) t.k.h in last pl: swtchd rt and str run on stands' side to ld over 1f out: sn pushed clr* **4/1**[3]	87
3024	2	6	**Seprani**[28] 4833 5-9-5 **71**.... StefanoCherchi(3) 5 *(Amy Murphy) prom: led gng wl 3f out: pushed along and hdd over 1f out: immediately outpcd by wnr* **6/1**	68
3561	3	7	**Trulee Scrumptious**[13] 5380 10-8-9 **58**....(v) GraceMcEntee 2 *(Peter Charalambous) rdn into clr ld and swtchd to far side: hdd 3f out: outpcd over 1f out: edgding rt but wnt remote 3rd ins fnl f* **10/1**	36
1633	4	1	**Coverham (IRE)**[20] 5144 5-9-5 **71**....(p) MarcoGhiani(3) 3 *(James Eustace) cl up: pushed along 2f out: btn over 1f out: lost 3rd ins fnl f* **11/4**[2]	46
1541	5	1 1/2	**Dream World (IRE)**[13] 5376 4-9-8 **74**.... LukeCatton(3) 7 *(Michael Appleby) prom: rdn 2f out: wknd over 1f out (trainer said filly was unsuited by the fast pace on this occasion)* **7/4**[1]	45
6166	6	5	**Bond Street Beau**[73] 3144 4-8-3 **59**.... AliceBond(7) 1 *(Philip McBride) lost 3 l s: cl up by 1/2-way: pushed along and fdd over 1f out* **16/1**	17

1m 24.66s (-0.44) **Going Correction** +0.10s/f (Good) 6 Ran SP% **112.3**

Speed ratings (Par 103): **106,99,91,90,88 82**

CSF £27.19 TOTE £4.70: £2.60, £2.10; EX 29.10 Trifecta £175.90.

Owner Fred Archer Racing - Ormonde **Bred** David McGuinness **Trained** Newmarket, Suffolk

FOCUS

Not a bad handicap featuring some in-form horses but it produced the easiest winner of the day, and a first win for his young jockey. Tricky form to assess.

T/Plt: £166.20 to a £1 stake. Pool: £55,422.58. 243.36 winning units. T/Qpdt: £93.30 to a £1 stake. Pool: £4,074.75. 32.30 winning units. **Iain Mackenzie**

5871 - 5873a (Foreign Racing) - See Raceform Interactive

5359 LEOPARDSTOWN (L-H)

Thursday, August 8

OFFICIAL GOING: Good to firm (good in places)

5874a GRENKE FINANCE BALLYROAN STKS (GROUP 3) — 1m 4f

6:55 (6:56) 3-Y-O+

£33,486 (£10,783; £5,108; £2,270; £1,135; £567)

				RPR
	1		**Latrobe (IRE)**[41] 4351 4-9-8 112.... DonnachaO'Brien 3 *(Joseph Patrick O'Brien, Ire) trckd ldr: cl 2nd at 1/2-way: gng wl into st and disp ld under 2f out: led over 1f out and rdn: kpt on wl ins fnl f where pressed: a in command* **9/10**[1]	110+
	2	3/4	**Guaranteed (IRE)**[40] 4414 3-8-12 107....(t) KevinManning 2 *(J S Bolger, Ire) dismntd bef s for tack adjstment: chsd ldrs: racd keenly: 3rd bef 1/2-way: lost pl over 3f out: impr into 3rd under 2f out: rdn into 2nd ins fnl f and pressed wnr: kpt on wl clsng stages: a hld* **9/2**[3]	109
	3	1 3/4	**Broad Street**[53] 3901 4-9-8 0.... OisinOrr 5 *(D K Weld, Ire) w.w towards rr: 5th 1/2-way: n.m.r between horses into st where swtchd rt and sltly bmpd rival: rdn in 5th 1 1/2f out and r.o wl ins fnl f into nvr threatening 3rd cl home* **7/2**[2]	106+
	4	1/2	**Blenheim Palace (IRE)**[33] 4682 3-8-12 106.... SeamieHeffernan 1 *(A P O'Brien, Ire) broke wl to ld: narrow advantage at 1/2-way: pushed along into st and jnd under 2f out where hdd: hdd over 1f out and sn no imp on wnr u.p in 3rd: dropped to 4th cl home* **8/1**	105
	5	4 1/2	**Massif Central (IRE)**[31] 4745 5-9-8 97.... RonanWhelan 4 *(M Halford, Ire) chsd ldrs: 4th bef 1/2-way: clsr in 3rd over 3f out: drvn 2f out and sn no imp on ldrs in 4th: wknd into 5th fr 1f out* **22/1**	97
	6	7 1/2	**Giuseppe Garibaldi (IRE)**[13] 5404 4-9-8 101....(t) ColmO'Donoghue 6 *(John M Oxx, Ire) settled in rr: last at 1/2-way: pushed along and tk clsr order on outer briefly 3f out: bmpd sltly into st and sn no ex in rr: eased wl ins fnl f* **20/1**	85

2m 35.53s (-2.77) **Going Correction** +0.10s/f (Good)

WFA 3 from 4yo+ 10lb 6 Ran SP% **113.3**

Speed ratings: **113,112,111,111,108 103**

CSF £5.50 TOTE £1.70: £1.10, £1.90; DF 4.90 Trifecta £14.80.

Owner Lloyd J Williams **Bred** Sweetmans Bloodstock **Trained** Owning Hill, Co Kilkenny

FOCUS

A workmanlike performance from the winner, his first success since last year's Irish Derby. The second and fourth limit the level.

5875 - 5877a (Foreign Racing) - See Raceform Interactive

5837 BRIGHTON (L-H)

Friday, August 9

OFFICIAL GOING: Good to firm (8.3)

Wind: medium to strong, against Weather: fine, breezy

5878 PH BECK BUILDERS CELEBRATING 50 YEARS H'CAP — 5f 215y

2:00 (2:00) (Class 6) (0-65,61) 3-Y-O £2,781 (£827; £413; £300) Stalls Low

Form				RPR
051	1		**Nervous Nerys (IRE)**[45] 4219 3-8-7 **47**.... HollieDoyle 1 *(Alex Hales) in tch: effrt to chse ldr 2f out: clsd u.p to ld ins fnl f: hld on cl home* **5/2**[2]	53
2532	2	hd	**Urban Highway (IRE)**[6] 5678 3-9-7 **61**.... TomMarquand 3 *(Tony Carroll) stdd s: t.k.h: hld up in tch: effrt ent fnl 2f: drvn over 1f out: clsd u.p and pressing wnr wl ins fnl f: kpt on but nvr quite getting to wnr (jockey said gelding ran too free in the early stages)* **4/7**[1]	66
0044	3	1 1/2	**Zaula**[16] 5306 3-8-8 **48**.... DavidEgan 2 *(Mick Channon) chsd ldr tl led wl over 2f out: rdn over 1f out: hdd ins fnl f: no ex and wknd towards fin (vet said filly had lost her left-fore shoe)* **7/1**[3]	48
0000	4	17	**Dandy Belle (IRE)**[13] 5431 3-8-0 **45**....(v) RhiainIngram(5) 4 *(Richenda Ford) rousted along leaving stalls: sn led: hdd wl over 2f out: dropped to rr 2f out: sn wknd (jockey said filly took a false step coming down the hill; trainer said that the filly was unsuited by coming down the hill at Brighton and would prefer a flatter track)* **20/1**	

1m 11.22s (0.12) **Going Correction** -0.10s/f (Good) 4 Ran SP% **109.5**

Speed ratings (Par 98): **95,94,92,70**

CSF £4.45 TOTE £3.10; EX 4.80 Trifecta £6.80.

Owner Golden Equinox Racing **Bred** Mrs B Gardiner **Trained** Edgcote, Northamptonshire

FOCUS

Add 6 yards. A modest little 3yo sprint handicap. They went a modest gallop and the odds-on favourite couldn't quite get past a resolute filly in receipt of plenty of weight. Straightforward form, rated around the second and third. It's been rated as straightforward form around the second and third.

5879 DOWNLOAD THE MARATHONBET APP EBF NOVICE STKS — 5f 215y

2:30 (2:31) (Class 5) 2-Y-O £3,428 (£1,020; £509; £254) Stalls Low

Form				RPR
1	1		**Malvern**[14] 5374 2-9-6 0.... RossaRyan 1 *(Richard Hannon) mde all: rdn over 1f out: rn green and hung rt 1f out: stl hanging but in command ins fnl f: styd on (jockey said colt hung right-handed from 2f out)* **4/7**[1]	79
02	2	1	**Cotai Again (IRE)**[15] 5339 2-9-2 0.... KieranShoemark 4 *(Charles Hills) hld up in tch: clsd over 2f out: rdn to chse wnr 2f out: swtchd rt ins fnl f: kpt on but a hld* **2/1**[2]	72
	3	2 1/2	**Global Agreement** 2-9-2 0.... HollieDoyle 2 *(Milton Harris) in tch in rr: effrt and clsd to chse wnr briefly ent fnl 2f: 3rd and unable qck whn edgd lft u.p over 1f out: kpt on same pce fnl f* **33/1**	64
0	4	5	**Miarka (FR)**[30] 4790 2-8-11 0.... TomMarquand 3 *(Harry Dunlop) broke wl: restrained and chsd ldrs: rdn ent fnl 2f: sn outpcd and wl hld over 1f out: wknd fnl f* **8/1**[3]	43
0	5	14	**Billesdon**[13] 5427 2-9-2 0.... LiamKeniry 5 *(Michael Madgwick) chsd wnr tl ent fnl 2f: sn lost pl: wl bhd ins fnl f* **66/1**	

1m 11.0s (-0.10) **Going Correction** -0.10s/f (Good) 5 Ran SP% **112.5**

Speed ratings (Par 94): **96,94,91,84,66**

CSF £2.04 TOTE £1.40: £1.10, £1.10; EX 2.10 Trifecta £9.40.

Owner Owners Group 042 **Bred** R J Vines **Trained** East Everleigh, Wilts

FOCUS

Add 6 yards. A fair juvenile novice contest. They went a muddling gallop but the odds-on favourite won quite comfortably from the front despite hanging right-handed up the camber. He's only rated to his debut form. The winner has been rated to his debut form.

5880 ON SIDE HOSPITALITY H'CAP — 1m 3f 198y

3:00 (3:00) (Class 6) (0-65,65) 3-Y-O £2,781 (£827; £413; £300; £300) Stalls High

Form				RPR
01	1		**Cafe Sydney (IRE)**[6] 5680 3-8-10 **54** 6ex.... BrettDoyle 4 *(Tony Carroll) hld up in tch: clsd to press ldrs wl over 2f out: pushed into ld and hung lft over 1f out: racing awkwardly but in command ins fnl f: eased cl home* **10/11**[1]	62
0306	2	2 1/2	**New Expo (IRE)**[25] 4998 3-8-2 **46** oh1.... HollieDoyle 5 *(Julia Feilden) led: sn hdd and chsd ldr: pushed along over 3f out: rdn to ld jst over 2f out: hdd over 1f out: a hld and one pce ins fnl f: eased cl home* **4/1**[3]	49
133	3	6	**Magic Shuffle (IRE)**[15] 5338 3-9-7 **65**.... TomMarquand 2 *(Barry Brennan) chsd ldng pair: rdn 4f out: outpcd u.p 2f out: no ch w ldng pair but plugged on ins fnl f: snatched 3rd last strides* **3/1**[2]	58
6430	4	nk	**Little Tipple**[2] 5803 3-8-2 **46** oh1.... AdrianMcCarthy 3 *(John Ryan) t.k.h and sn led: rdn and hdd jst over 2f out: sn outpcd and wl hld 1f out: wknd ins fnl f (jockey said filly ran too free)* **33/1**	39
0-60	5	2	**Hidden Pearl**[30] 4803 3-9-5 **63**.... LiamKeniry 1 *(John Berry) stdd s: hld up in rr: effrt over 2f out: no imp u.p 2f out: wl hld after* **13/2**	52

2m 34.7s (-1.30) **Going Correction** -0.10s/f (Good) 5 Ran SP% **113.7**

Speed ratings (Par 98): **100,98,94,94,92**

CSF £5.24 TOTE £1.80: £1.10, £2.10; EX 5.10 Trifecta £12.90.

Owner Contubernium Racing **Bred** John Walsh **Trained** Cropthorne, Worcs

FOCUS

Add 6 yards. A modest 3yo middle-distance handicap, and the bare form can't be rated any higher. The odds-on favourite proved she stays 1m4f in no uncertain manner. The balance of the second and fourth suggest the form can't be rated much higher than this.

5881 MARATHONBET "BETTER ODDS MEAN BIGGER WINNINGS" H'CAP — 1m 1f 207y

3:30 (3:30) (Class 4) (0-80,78) 3-Y-O+ £5,207 (£1,549; £774) Stalls High

Form				RPR
4113	1		**Junoesque**[21] 5138 5-9-1 **65**....(p) HectorCrouch 4 *(John Gallagher) mde all and dictated stdy gallop: rdn over 2f out: kpt on wl u.p ins fnl f* **11/8**[1]	71
1021	2	3/4	**Amor Fati (IRE)**[14] 5373 4-9-3 **72**.... DarraghKeenan(5) 2 *(David Evans) trckd rivals: clsd to press rivals 3f out: effrt over 1f out: ev ch and drvn fnl f: a hld* **5/2**[3]	76
0451	3	7	**Gendarme (IRE)**[8] 5570 4-9-3 **72**....(b) CierenFallon(5) 1 *(Alexandra Dunn) trckd wnr: rdn over 2f out: outpcd u.p over 1f out: wl btn ins fnl f: eased towards fin (trainer could offer no explanation for the gelding's performance)* **13/8**[2]	64

2m 3.42s (-1.58) **Going Correction** -0.10s/f (Good) 3 Ran SP% **108.8**

Speed ratings (Par 105): **102,101,95**

CSF £4.80 TOTE £2.20; EX 3.90 Trifecta £5.00.

Owner The Juniper Racing Club Ltd **Bred** Adweb Ltd **Trained** Chastleton, Oxon

FOCUS

Add 6 yards. A fair handicap. The favourite dictated a muddling gallop and outstayed the runner-up from over 2f out. The winner has been rated in line with her Windsor June win.

5882 HARRY BLOOM MEMORIAL "BRIGHTON BULLET" H'CAP — 5f 215y

4:00 (4:03) (Class 4) (0-80,81) 3-Y-O+

£8,021 (£2,387; £1,192; £596; £300; £300) Stalls Low

Form				RPR
0303	1		**Tin Hat (IRE)**[11] 5503 3-9-0 **79**....(p) GeorgiaDobie(7) 10 *(Eve Johnson Houghton) chsd ldrs: effrt ent fnl 2f: drvn to ld over 1f out: hld on wl towards fin* **12/1**	88
1036	2	nk	**Red Alert**[23] 5058 5-9-11 **79**....(p) TomMarquand 9 *(Tony Carroll) in tch in rr: effrt jst over 2f out: hdwy u.p 1f out: wnt 2nd and chalng 100yds out: kpt on but hld towards fin* **12/1**	88

3500 **3** 2 **Pour La Victoire (IRE)**[2] 5804 9-9-4 72....................(p) GeorgeDowning 6 75
(Tony Carroll) *reluctant to go to s and led most of the way down: hld up in tch: effrt over 1f out: swtchd lft 1f out and chsd wnr briefly ins fnl f: lost 2nd and outpcd fnl 100yds* **5/1**[3]
1220 **4** 1 1/4 **Big Lachie**[11] 5503 5-9-0 75.. SeanKirrane(7) 8 74
(Mark Loughnane) *dwlt: hld up in tch: hdwy ent fnl 2f: drvn to press ldrs over 1f out: no ex and wknd ins fnl f* **6/1**
0121 **5** 1 **Gold At Midnight**[20] 5191 3-9-6 78.. HollieDoyle 5 72
(William Stone) *wl in tch in midfield: effrt ent fnl 2f: lost pl and bhd over 1f out: kpt on ins fnl f: no threat to ldrs (vet said filly had lost its right-fore shoe)* **11/4**[1]
-055 **6** hd **Michaels Choice**[6] 5647 3-9-3 75.. RyanTate 7 69
(William Jarvis) *chsd ldr: effrt ent fnl 2f: chsd wnr and drvn over 1f out: no ex and wknd ins fnl f* **16/1**
0033 **7** nse **Dream Catching (IRE)**[29] 4833 4-9-8 76....................(v) DavidProbert 1 71
(Andrew Balding) *dwlt: swtchd rt sn after s: hld up in tch: effrt 2f out: nt clr run 1f out: kpt on same pce and no imp fnl f* **7/2**[2]
1501 **8** 1 1/4 **Handytalk (IRE)**[11] 5495 6-9-8 81 5ex..........................(b) CierenFallon(5) 3 72
(Rod Millman) *led: drvn and hdd over 1f out: wknd ins fnl f* **6/1**
6220 **9** 1/2 **Upavon**[16] 5289 9-8-9 63... EoinWalsh 2 52
(Tony Carroll) *pushed along leaving stalls: in tch: effrt over 2f out: no imp 1f out: nt clrest of runs and wknd ins fnl f (jockey said gelding was denied a clear run inside the final furlong)* **33/1**

1m 9.95s (-1.15) **Going Correction** -0.10s/f (Good)
WFA 3 from 4yo+ 4lb **9** Ran SP% **118.3**
Speed ratings (Par 105): **103,102,99,98,96 96,96,94,94**
CSF £148.34 CT £827.56 TOTE £12.60: £3.60, £3.00, £2.10; EX 127.40 Trifecta £538.30.
Owner Eden Racing IV **Bred** M Phelan **Trained** Blewbury, Oxon
■ Stewards' Enquiry : Ryan Tate one-day ban; failing to take all reasonable and permissible measures to obtain the best possible placing (Aug 24)

FOCUS
Add 6 yards. The feature contest was a fair sprint handicap. One of the three 3yos won well in a notably good comparative time, and the form seems sound. The winner has been rated to his best, with the second helping to set the level.

5883 MARK LLOYD POWELL 40TH BIRTHDAY H'CAP 5f 215y
4:30 (4:30) (Class 6) (0-60,62) 4-Y-O+
£2,781 (£827; £413; £300; £300; £300) **Stalls** Low

Form RPR
4556 **1** **Cent Flying**[23] 5050 4-9-7 60.......................................(t w) MartinDwyer 4 77
(William Muir) *sn trcking ldrs: effrt on inner over 2f out: rdn to ld over 1f out: r.o wl and drew clr fnl f: easily* **7/4**[1]
00-3 **2** 7 **Tawaafoq**[22] 5083 5-9-4 57..(h) RossaRyan 2 55
(Adrian Wintle) *led: rdn over 2f out: hdd and drvn over 1f out: no ch w wnr but hld on for 2nd ins fnl f* **4/1**[3]
5150 **3** nk **Napping**[36] 4567 6-8-13 59.. SeanKirrane(7) 9 56
(Amy Murphy) *dwlt: in tch: effrt 2f out: unable qck ent fnl f: no ch w wnr but plugged on ins fnl f* **4/1**[3]
4061 **4** 1 3/4 **Knockout Blow**[31] 4749 4-9-4 57..............................(p) HectorCrouch 7 48
(John E Long) *chsd ldr tl over 1f out: sn outpcd u.p: no ch w wnr fnl f: wknd and nt clrest of runs towards fin* **7/2**[2]
0350 **5** 3/4 **Wild Flower (IRE)**[17] 5264 7-8-10 49..............................(p) EoinWalsh 6 38
(Luke McJannet) *in tch: outpcd u.p and wl hld over 1f out: plugged on ins fnl f* **8/1**
045U **6** 6 **Noble Deed**[67] 3406 9-8-7 46 oh1.................................(p) KierenFox 8 16
(Michael Attwater) *in tch: dropped to rr 4f out: no hdwy and hung lft 2f out: wl btn fnl f* **33/1**

1m 10.05s (-1.05) **Going Correction** -0.10s/f (Good) **6** Ran SP% **112.6**
Speed ratings (Par 101): **103,93,93,90,89 81**
CSF £9.16 CT £23.26 TOTE £2.50: £1.40, £2.10; EX 11.10 Trifecta £28.90.
Owner Clarke, Edginton, Niven **Bred** Frank Brady **Trained** Lambourn, Berks

FOCUS
Add 6 yards. A modest sprint handicap. The favourite turned this race into a procession in a good comparative time for the grade.

5884 VISIT ATTHERACES.COM H'CAP 5f 60y
5:00 (5:01) (Class 6) (0-55,55) 3-Y-O+
£2,781 (£827; £413; £300; £300; £300) **Stalls** Low

Form RPR
-460 **1** **Devil Or Angel**[22] 5084 4-8-12 49...................(p[1]) ThoreHammerHansen(5) 9 58
(Bill Turner) *in tch in midfield: hdwy u.p over 1f out: led ins fnl f: r.o wl: readily* **12/1**
4631 **2** 2 1/2 **Monarch Maid**[14] 5393 8-9-0 53.................................... ElishaWhittington(7) 8 53+
(Peter Hiatt) *dwlt: hld up in tch in last trio: effrt 2f out: nt clr run and edging lft ent fnl f: swtchd lft ins fnl f: r.o wl fnl 100yds to snatch 2nd last strides: no ch w wnr (jockey said filly was slowly away)* **9/2**[2]
0046 **3** hd **Tigerinmytank**[9] 5559 3-8-7 45.................................... WilliamCox(3) 2 43
(John Holt) *in tch in midfield: effrt on inner ent fnl 2f: hdwy u.p to chse ldrs 1f out: kpt on but nt match pce of wnr ins fnl f* **13/2**
6050 **4** nk **Ask The Guru**[50] 4027 9-9-0 46......................................(p) KierenFox 4 44
(Michael Attwater) *led: rdn over 1f out: drvn 1f out: hdd ins fnl f: sn outpcd by wnr: lost 2 pls last strides* **16/1**
00R4 **5** 1 1/2 **Dandilion (IRE)**[7] 5629 6-9-4 50.. LiamKeniry 3 43+
(Alex Hales) *hld up in tch in last pair: clsd over 1f out: nt clr run 1f out: swtchd rt and then bk lft ins fnl f: no ch w wnr but r.o towards fin (jockey said mare was denied a clear run)* **6/1**
6034 **6** nk **Pharoh Jake**[13] 5449 11-8-9 46.................................... DarraghKeenan(5) 5 38
(John Bridger) *chsd ldrs: effrt over 1f out: unable qck u.p and wknd ins fnl f* **14/1**
0000 **7** shd **Flowing Clarets**[36] 4556 6-9-2 51................................ MitchGodwin(3) 10 42
(John Bridger) *taken down early and mounted on crse: chsd ldr: effrt 2f out: no ex u.p and lost 2nd ent fnl f: wknd ins fnl f* **14/1**
4164 **8** shd **Toolatetodelegate**[8] 5582 5-9-0 53...........................(tp) AngusVilliers(7) 1 44
(Brian Barr) *hld up in tch in last pair: effrt on inner over 1f out: nt clrest of runs and no imp ins fnl f (trainer's rep said mare was unsuited by the hill at Brighton and would prefer a flatter track)* **4/1**[1]
2463 **9** 1 1/2 **Hurricane Alert**[23] 5046 7-9-1 47................................... DavidProbert 6 33
(Mark Hoad) *taken down early: t.k.h: chsd ldrs: lost pl u.p and btn over 1f out: wknd ins fnl f* **7/1**
6004 **R** **Knockabout Queen**[7] 5607 3-9-6 55..............................(p[1]) EoinWalsh 7
(Tony Carroll) *ref to r* **5/1**[3]

1m 2.38s (-0.62) **Going Correction** -0.10s/f (Good)
WFA 3 from 4yo+ 3lb **10** Ran SP% **121.9**
Speed ratings (Par 101): **100,96,95,95,92 92,92,92,89,**
CSF £68.35 CT £402.74 TOTE £15.50: £3.60, £1.40, £2.70; EX 90.40 Trifecta £798.20.
Owner Mrs Tracy Turner **Bred** Lady Whent **Trained** Sigwells, Somerset

FOCUS
Add 6 yards. A moderate sprint handicap. The first three home came through from off a strong gallop. Straightforward, limited form, with the third and fourth helping to pin the level.
T/Plt: £90.40 to a £1 stake. Pool: £59,890.72. - 483.25 winning units. T/Qpdt: £20.80 to a £1 stake. Pool: £5,484.19. - 194.74 winning units. **Steve Payne**

5646 CHELMSFORD (A.W) (L-H)
Friday, August 9

OFFICIAL GOING: Polytrack: standard
Wind: Blustery Weather: Sunny spells

5885 BET AT TOTESPORT.COM NURSERY H'CAP 7f (P)
5:50 (5:51) (Class 6) (0-65,67) 2-Y-O **£3,428** (£1,020; £509; £400) **Stalls** Low

Form RPR
434 **1** **Lady Red Moon**[23] 5052 2-8-13 67.................................. StefanoCherchi(7) 1 70+
(Marco Botti) *s.i.s and n.m.r after s: sn chsng ldrs: nt clr run over 1f out: sn rdn and hung lft: swtchd rt ins fnl f: r.o to ld towards fin* **11/8**[1]
061 **2** nk **Constanzia**[62] 3579 2-9-4 65.. ShaneKelly 3 67
(Jamie Osborne) *chsd ldr: rdn over 2f out: led over 1f out: hdd towards fin* **9/2**[3]
050 **3** 3 1/4 **Leg It Lenny (IRE)**[14] 5381 2-9-6 67.............................. CharlesBishop 2 60
(Robert Cowell) *led at stdy pce: qcknd over 2f out: rdn and hdd over 1f out: no ex ins fnl f* **15/8**[2]
6403 **4** 13 **Craigburn**[15] 5353 2-9-2 63.. LukeMorris 4 21
(Tom Clover) *hld up: rdn over 2f out: sn swtchd rt: wknd over 1f out* **7/1**

1m 28.33s (1.13) **Going Correction** -0.10s/f (Stan) **4** Ran SP% **107.6**
Speed ratings (Par 92): **89,88,84,70**
CSF £7.47 TOTE £2.00; EX 6.50 Trifecta £12.30.
Owner Giulio Spozio & Partner **Bred** Mrs C E Cone **Trained** Newmarket, Suffolk

FOCUS
The track had been lightly decompacted and gallop master finished to 2 inches for raceday. A moderate nursery to begin with, and a finish which concerned two of three making their first forays into this sphere. Stalls on inner. The runner-up is rated to her C&D form.

5886 TOTEPOOL CASHBACK CLUB AT TOTESPORT.COM NURSERY H'CAP 1m (P)
6:25 (6:26) (Class 6) (0-60,62) 2-Y-O
£3,428 (£1,020; £509; £400; £400; £400) **Stalls** Low

Form RPR
000 **1** **Mac McCarthy (IRE)**[51] 3990 2-9-4 59.............................. FinleyMarsh(3) 6 63
(Richard Hughes) *led 1f: chsd ldrs: shkn up over 1f out: rdn and r.o to ld towards fin* **11/1**
500 **2** nk **Luna Wish**[42] 4337 2-8-7 45.. JimmyQuinn 7 49
(George Margarson) *led 7f out: rdn and edgd rt over 1f out: hdd towards fin* **16/1**
600 **3** 2 **Souter Johnnie (IRE)**[16] 5314 2-9-10 62........................... ShaneKelly 5 61
(Richard Hughes) *hld up in tch: shkn up over 1f out: styd on* **9/2**[3]
000 **4** 2 1/2 **Pilsdon Pen**[41] 4394 2-9-10 62....................................... CharlesBishop 4 55
(Joseph Tuite) *prom: chsd ldr over 6f out: rdn and ev ch wl over 1f out: no ex ins fnl f* **7/2**[2]
0062 **5** 1/2 **Percy Green (IRE)**[16] 5296 2-9-9 61................................ JimCrowley 2 53
(K R Burke) *trckd ldrs: plld hrd: rdn over 1f out: no ex ins fnl f* **2/1**[1]
0105 **6** 2 1/4 **Rain Cap**[3] 5781 2-9-5 62......................................(p[1]) ScottMcCullagh(5) 3 49
(Mick Channon) *s.i.s: hld up: rdn on outer over 1f out: nvr trbld ldrs* **7/2**[2]
000 **7** 2 1/2 **Lightning Bug (IRE)**[16] 5314 2-8-12 50.......................... LukeMorris 1 31
(Suzy Smith) *s.i.s: hld up: plld hrd: rdn over 1f out: eased whn btn ins fnl f* **25/1**

1m 44.14s (4.24) **Going Correction** -0.10s/f (Stan) **7** Ran SP% **114.0**
Speed ratings (Par 92): **74,73,71,69,68 66,63**
CSF £156.37 TOTE £13.00: £4.90, £6.60; EX 178.30 Trifecta £372.20.
Owner R Gander & Partner **Bred** Ballyphilip Stud **Trained** Upper Lambourn, Berks

FOCUS
As in the opening nursery, the front pair finished well clear. They've both been rated minor improvers.

5887 EXTRA PLACES AT TOTESPORT.COM NOVICE AUCTION STKS (PLUS 10 RACE) 6f (P)
7:00 (7:03) (Class 4) 2-Y-O **£6,727** (£2,001; £1,000; £500) **Stalls** Centre

Form RPR
1320 **1** **Dream Shot (IRE)**[8] 5584 2-9-6 96.................................... AdamKirby 5 80+
(James Tate) *chsd ldr: shkn up to ld and hung lft fr over 1f out: r.o: comf* **1/5**[1]
0 **2** 1 1/4 **Rajguru**[16] 5314 2-9-0 0... LukeMorris 2 71
(Tom Clover) *sn pushed along to ld: rdn and hdd over 1f out: nt clr run sn after: kpt on* **33/1**
4 **3** 2 3/4 **Robert Frost (USA)**[15] 5353 2-8-11 0.......................... CameronNoble(3) 3 62+
(Jane Chapple-Hyam) *hld up in tch: racd keenly: rdn over 1f out: styd on same pce ins fnl f* **12/1**[3]
54 **4** 3/4 **Carmel**[10] 5514 2-8-8 0.. JimmyQuinn 1 54
(Archie Watson) *chsd ldrs: rdn over 1f out: no ex ins fnl f* **6/1**[2]
5 2 **William Thomas (IRE)** 2-8-13 0.................................... KieranO'Neill 4 53+
(Robert Eddery) *s.i.s: hld up: rdn and edgd rt over 1f out: n.d* **16/1**
05 **6** 3 **Halfacrown (IRE)**[7] 5602 2-8-13 0................................. ShaneKelly 6 44
(Jamie Osborne) *s.i.s: hld up: pushed along 1/2-way: wknd over 1f out (vet said colt lost its right hind shoe)* **40/1**

1m 14.56s (0.86) **Going Correction** -0.10s/f (Stan) **6** Ran SP% **116.6**
Speed ratings (Par 96): **90,88,84,83,81 77**
CSF £12.86 TOTE £1.10: £1.10, £8.60; EX 11.80 Trifecta £45.70.
Owner Saeed Manana **Bred** Gerard & Anne Corry **Trained** Newmarket, Suffolk

FOCUS
Stalls in centre. All very straightforward for the long odds-on favourite, who didn't need to match his best.

5888 IRISH LOTTO AT TOTESPORT.COM H'CAP 5f (P)
7:30 (7:31) (Class 3) (0-90,92) 3-Y-O+ **£14,231** (£4,235; £2,116; £1,058) **Stalls** Low

Form RPR
0511 **1** **Harry's Bar**[39] 4458 4-9-9 85... GeorgeWood 1 96+
(James Fanshawe) *s.i.s: hld up: shkn up and hdwy over 1f out: rdn and r.o to ld wl ins fnl f* **11/10**[1]
0062 **2** 1 **Miracle Works**[7] 5606 4-8-9 78................................... MarcoGhiani(7) 6 85
(Robert Cowell) *chsd ldrs: led 1f out: rdn and hdd wl ins fnl f* **12/1**

3111 **3** 1 1/2 **Only Spoofing (IRE)**[14] 5371 5-9-11 **87**.......................... KieranO'Neill 4 89
(Jedd O'Keeffe) *plld hrd: w ldr: rdn and ev ch over 1f out: styd on same pce wl ins fnl f* **9/2**[2]

5140 **4** 1/2 **Jumira Bridge**[14] 5371 5-9-11 **92**.......................... CierenFallon(5) 5 92
(Robert Cowell) *s.i.s: hld up: shkn up on outer over 1f out: edgd lft and r.o ins fnl f: wnt 4th nr fin* **14/1**

1401 **5** nk **Zac Brown (IRE)**[6] 5649 8-9-3 **82** 4ex..................(t) JoshuaBryan(3) 2 81
(Charlie Wallis) *led: rdn: edgd rt and hdd 1f out: no ex wl ins fnl f* **8/1**

1110 **6** nk **Tomily (IRE)**[13] 5454 5-9-12 **88**.......................... JimCrowley 3 86
(David O'Meara) *chsd ldrs: lost pl over 3f out: hdwy and nt clr run over 1f out: styd on same pce ins fnl f* **6/1**[3]

2515 **7** 1 1/4 **You're Cool**[39] 4458 7-9-7 **83**..........................(t) LewisEdmunds 7 76
(John Balding) *chsd ldrs: lost pl 1/2-way: sn rdn: styd on same pce fnl f* **20/1**

2213 **8** 1 1/4 **Green Door (IRE)**[6] 5649 8-9-6 **82**..........................(v) LukeMorris 8 71
(Robert Cowell) *chsd ldrs on outer: rdn over 1f out: wknd ins fnl f* **16/1**

58.27s (-1.93) **Going Correction** -0.10s/f (Stan) **8** Ran SP% **116.2**
Speed ratings (Par 107): **111,109,107,106,105 105,103,101**
CSF £16.68 CT £46.85 TOTE £1.70: £1.10, £2.40, £1.90; EX 12.30 Trifecta £54.50.

Owner Jan and Peter Hopper **Bred** Jan & Peter Hopper **Trained** Newmarket, Suffolk

FOCUS
Stalls on inner. A good smattering of in-form opponents in this sprint feature, and the thriving favourite completed the hat-trick despite an early scare.

5889 BET IN PLAY AT TOTESPORT.COM H'CAP 6f (P)
8:05 (8:05) (Class 5) (0-70,71) 4-Y-0+

£5,175 (£1,540; £769; £400; £400; £400) **Stalls** Centre

Form RPR

3130 **1** **Creek Harbour (IRE)**[17] 5281 4-8-13 **67**.......................... WilliamCarver(5) 5 74
(Milton Bradley) *chsd ldrs: rdn over 1f out: r.o to ld nr fin* **16/1**

-105 **2** 1/2 **Desert Fox**[15] 5352 5-9-3 **66**.......................... RossaRyan 8 71+
(Mike Murphy) *s.i.s: hld up: hdwy on outer over 1f out: r.o to go 2nd nr fin* **9/2**[1]

5055 **3** nk **Poeta Brasileiro (IRE)**[17] 5281 4-8-13 **62**..................(b[1]) RaulDaSilva 2 66
(David Brown) *led 1f: chsd ldrs: led again over 1f out: rdn and edgd rt ins fnl f: hdd nr fin* **5/1**[2]

0210 **4** 1/2 **Papa Delta**[22] 5081 5-8-11 **60**.......................... GeorgeDowning 4 63
(Tony Carroll) *chsd ldrs: lost pl over 3f out: rdn and n.m.r over 1f out: r.o* **9/2**[1]

4346 **5** 3/4 **Our Oystercatcher**[18] 5252 5-9-4 **70**.......................... FinleyMarsh(3) 6 70
(Mark Pattinson) *plld hrd: led 5f out: rdn and hdd over 1f out: styng on same pce whn nt clr run towards fin* **6/1**[3]

5050 **6** 1/2 **Mystical Moon (IRE)**[39] 4440 4-8-4 **53**.......................... JimmyQuinn 1 52
(David C Griffiths) *prom: nt clr run and lost pl over 5f out: sn pushed along: r.o ins fnl f: eased nr fin* **12/1**

2036 **7** nk **Zapper Cass (FR)**[25] 5000 6-9-8 **71**..................(v) AlistairRawlinson 3 69
(Michael Appleby) *s.i.s: sn pushed along and hmpd over 5f out: hld up: racd keenly: hdwy on outer over 2f out: rdn over 1f out: styd on* **6/1**[3]

2231 **8** 1 **Daring Guest (IRE)**[7] 5629 5-8-12 **61** 5ex..................(t) LukeMorris 7 56
(Tom Clover) *prom: sn lost pl: n.d after (jockey said gelding moved poorly)* **5/1**[2]

-000 **9** 3 **Dark Side Dream**[39] 4455 7-9-2 **70**..................(p w) CierenFallon(5) 10 55
(Charlie Wallis) *s.i.s: sn prom: chsd ldr over 3f out: rdn and ev ch over 1f out: wknd ins fnl f* **25/1**

6002 **P** **Sir Hector (IRE)**[50] 4026 4-8-12 **61**..................(h) LewisEdmunds 9
(Charlie Wallis) *rrd s: bhd: p.u over 3f out (jockey said gelding lost its action)* **25/1**

1m 12.13s (-1.57) **Going Correction** -0.10s/f (Stan) **10** Ran SP% **119.5**
Speed ratings (Par 103): **106,105,104,104,103 102,102,100,96,**
CSF £88.85 CT £429.67 TOTE £29.70: £7.00, £1.50, £2.00; EX 139.90 Trifecta £1186.40.

Owner Carl Price **Bred** Keatingstown Bloodstock **Trained** Sedbury, Gloucs

FOCUS
Stalls in centre. Fairly competitive for the grade, and plenty still held some sort of a chance halfway up the straight. The winner refound his form.

5890 DOUBLE DELIGHT HAT-TRICK HEAVEN H'CAP 6f (P)
8:40 (8:41) (Class 6) (0-55,57) 3-Y-0

£3,428 (£1,020; £509; £400; £400; £400) **Stalls** Centre

Form RPR

6563 **1** **Aquarius (IRE)**[7] 5622 3-9-7 **55**.......................... LiamJones 6 61
(Michael Appleby) *chsd ldr over 5f out: led wl over 1f out: sn rdn: jst hld on* **4/1**[3]

4040 **2** nse **Maid Millie**[60] 3651 3-9-1 **54**..........................(v) CierenFallon(5) 2 60
(Robert Cowell) *hld up in tch: nt clr run over 1f out: rdn to chse wnr ins fnl f: r.o wl* **7/2**[2]

066- **3** 3 **Catheadans Fiyah**[258] 9246 3-9-9 **57**.......................... LukeMorris 1 54
(Martin Bosley) *racd keenly: trckd ldrs: nt clr run turning for home: rdn to chse wnr over 1f out tl ins fnl f: styd on same pce* **25/1**

000 **4** 1 **Twilighting**[60] 3661 3-9-1 **49**.......................... CharlesBishop 3 43+
(Henry Candy) *s.i.s: hld up: nt clr run over 1f out: r.o ins fnl f: nt trble ldrs* **11/8**[1]

063 **5** 2 1/2 **Miss Gargar**[39] 4457 3-9-6 **54**..........................(v) GeorgeWood 4 40
(Harry Dunlop) *chsd ldrs: rdn and nt clr run over 1f out: no ex fnl f* **8/1**

030 **6** 1/2 **Obsession For Gold (IRE)**[122] 1665 3-9-7 **55**.............(t) AntonioFresu 7 40+
(Mrs Ilka Gansera-Leveque) *rrd s: hld up: nt clr run and hdwy over 1f out: no ex ins fnl f* **7/1**

0-00 **7** 6 **Queen Of Bradgate**[24] 5031 3-8-12 **46** oh1..................(p[1]) KieranO'Neill 8 13
(Ivan Furtado) *sn led: rdn and hdd wl over 1f out: hmpd sn after: sn edgd rt: wknd fnl f* **33/1**

-000 **8** 7 **Uponastar (IRE)**[13] 5430 3-9-0 **48**..........................(vt[1]) TomMarquand 5
(Amy Murphy) *awkward s: hld up: rdn over 2f out: sn wknd* **33/1**

1m 12.49s (-1.21) **Going Correction** -0.10s/f (Stan) **8** Ran SP% **117.7**
Speed ratings (Par 98): **104,103,99,98,95 94,86,77**
CSF £18.66 CT £306.54 TOTE £4.30: £1.10, £1.30, £3.90; EX 17.40 Trifecta £272.60.

Owner C L Bacon **Bred** Michael Downey & Roalso Ltd **Trained** Oakham, Rutland

FOCUS
Stalls in centre. Not too many were able to get seriously involved in this weak affair, contested by an octet with a combined record of 1-51 beforehand. The winner is rated up a fraction on her recent sound form.

5891 BOOK TICKETS AT CHELMSFORDCITYRACECOURSE.COM H'CAP 2m (P)
9:10 (9:11) (Class 6) (0-65,66) 4-Y-0+

£3,428 (£1,020; £509; £400; £400; £400) **Stalls** Low

Form RPR

4254 **1** **Barca (USA)**[17] 5271 5-8-13 **57**.......................... JimCrowley 2 65+
(Marcus Tregoning) *trckd ldrs: nt clr run over 1f out: rdn to ld 1f out: styd on* **11/8**[1]

6106 **2** 1 **Sacred Sprite**[17] 5271 4-8-10 **59**.......................... DylanHogan(5) 5 64
(John Berry) *hld up: swtchd rt over 4f out: hdwy on outer over 3f out: rdn and ev ch 1f out: kpt on* **6/1**[3]

1216 **3** 3/4 **Heron (USA)**[53] 3940 5-9-8 **66**..........................(p) DanielMuscutt 6 70
(Brett Johnson) *hld up: hdwy and nt clr run over 1f out: styd on: nt rch ldrs* **7/1**

0504 **4** 1 1/2 **Demophon**[14] 5379 5-8-2 **46** oh1.......................... RaulDaSilva 3 48
(Steve Flook) *chsd ldr: rdn and ev ch over 1f out: no ex ins fnl f* **20/1**

0604 **5** hd **Lazarus (IRE)**[24] 5029 5-8-5 **49**..........................(t) GeorgeWood 8 51
(Amy Murphy) *hld up: rdn and nt clr run over 1f out: swtchd lft and styd on ins fnl f: nt trble ldrs* **20/1**

6041 **6** 3 1/4 **Beau Knight**[17] 5271 7-8-6 **50**..........................(p) HollieDoyle 1 48
(Alexandra Dunn) *led: rdn: edgd rt and hdd 1f out: wknd wl ins fnl f* **5/1**[2]

065 **7** 1/2 **Giving Back**[23] 5048 5-9-2 **60**.......................... TomMarquand 10 58
(Alan King) *prom: rdn and ev ch over 1f out: no ex ins fnl f* **7/1**

00 **8** 5 **Sea Of Mystery (IRE)**[30] 4791 6-9-7 **65**..................(v[1]) AlistairRawlinson 4 57
(Michael Appleby) *hld up: rdn over 3f out: n.d* **25/1**

5514 **9** 25 **Fitzwilly**[23] 5047 9-9-1 **64**..........................(p) ScottMcCullagh(5) 9 26
(Mick Channon) *s.i.s: hdwy over 14f out: rdn over 3f out: wknd over 2f out (jockey said gelding stopped quickly)* **16/1**

456 **10** 33 **Nineteenrbo'Malley**[31] 4760 7-8-1 **52**.......................... SeanKirrane(7) 7
(Robyn Brisland) *s.i.s: rdn over 5f out: sn edgd rt: wknd over 3f out* **66/1**

3m 27.66s (-2.34) **Going Correction** -0.10s/f (Stan) **10** Ran SP% **118.8**
Speed ratings (Par 101): **101,100,100,99,99 97,97,94,82,65**
CSF £9.58 CT £45.10 TOTE £2.00: £1.20, £1.80, £2.30; EX 11.20 Trifecta £57.90.

Owner The Barca Partnership **Bred** Barronstown Stud **Trained** Whitsbury, Hants
■ Stewards' Enquiry : Raul Da Silva four-day ban; misuse of whip (Aug 24-27)

FOCUS
Stalls on inner. A moderate but keenly contested marathon handicap.
T/Plt: £837.70 to a £1 stake. Pool: £32,581.26. - 38.89 winning units. T/Qpdt: £6.80 to a £1 stake. Pool: £4,663.75. - 681.32 winning units. **Colin Roberts**

5844 HAYDOCK (L-H)
Friday, August 9

OFFICIAL GOING: Soft (6.7)
Wind: breezy, behind home straight Weather: overcast with early shower, brighter later

5892 WATCH RACING TV NOW H'CAP (FOR LADY AMATEUR RIDERS) 5f
5:05 (5:06) (Class 5) (0-70,72) 4-Y-0+

£4,679 (£1,451; £725; £400; £400; £400) **Stalls** Centre

Form RPR

0663 **1** **Marietta Robusti (IRE)**[13] 5432 4-10-0 **63**.......................... MissJoannaMason 8 70
(Stella Barclay) *hld up: hdwy to trck ldrs 2f out: pushed into ld and reminder 1f out: reminder and pushed clr fnl f: comf* **11/2**[3]

6200 **2** 1 3/4 **Teepee Time**[4] 5722 6-9-2 **51** oh4..........(b) MissMichelleMullineaux 5 52
(Michael Mullineaux) *prom: drvn 2f out: rdn and led over 1f out: sn hdd: kpt on fnl f* **15/2**

15R6 **3** 1 **Robot Boy (IRE)**[4] 5723 9-10-9 **72**.......................... MissBeckySmith 1 69
(Marjorie Fife) *racd alone on far side: prom: pushed along 2f out: rdn fnl f: one pce* **3/1**[2]

4235 **4** 1 1/2 **Indian Pursuit (IRE)**[23] 5042 6-10-1 **64**..................(v) MrsCarolBartley 6 56
(John Quinn) *chsd ldrs: one pce on stands' side fr 2f out (trainer's rep said gelding was unsuited by the soft going which in their opinion was riding tacky)* **5/2**[1]

4300 **5** nk **I'll Be Good**[17] 5278 10-8-11 **51** oh4.......................... SophieSmith(5) 4 42
(Alan Berry) *led: drvn in narrow ld 2f out: reminders and hdd over 1f out: wknd fnl f* **6/1**

0535 **6** 1 **Le Manege Enchante (IRE)**[17] 5264 6-9-2 **51** oh5(v) MissSerenaBrotherton 2 38
(Derek Shaw) *bhd: pushed along over 2f out: rdn over 1f out: no imp (jockey said gelding was slowly away)* **6/1**

-000 **7** 14 **The Lacemaker**[43] 4281 5-9-6 **62**..........................(p) MrsDawnScott(7) 7
(Milton Harris) *dwlt bdly losing at least 15 l: a wl bhd (jockey said mare was very slowly away)* **28/1**

1m 0.72s (0.32) **Going Correction** +0.125s/f (Good) **7** Ran SP% **112.7**
Speed ratings (Par 103): **102,99,97,95,94 93,70**
CSF £43.71 CT £144.82 TOTE £6.80: £3.40, £4.10; EX 45.70 Trifecta £171.80.

Owner Messrs Chrimes, Winn & Wilson **Bred** Rathasker Stud **Trained** Garstang, Lancs

FOCUS
There was plenty of rain throughout the day and the going was changed to soft. All races were run on the inner home straight. Races three, four and five were run over 11 yards further than advertised, with 24 yards added to race six, and the final race distance was increased by 33 yards. \n\x\x A minor handicap in which the winner produced a strong finishing effort to improve her strike-rate to 4-16. The time was 2.52 seconds slower than standard.

5893 RACINGTV.COM FILLIES' H'CAP (JOCKEY CLUB GRASSROOTS SPRINT SERIES QUALIFIER) 5f
5:35 (5:35) (Class 5) (0-70,67) 3-Y-0+

£5,175 (£1,540; £769; £400; £400; £400) **Stalls** Centre

Form RPR

3242 **1** **Springwood Drive**[6] 5659 3-9-2 **62**.......................... JamesSullivan 6 73+
(Tim Easterby) *mid-div: pushed along and hdwy 2f out: drvn into ld over 1f out: rdn clr fnl f: comf* **11/10**[1]

5060 **2** 2 1/4 **Celerity (IRE)**[3] 5765 5-8-4 **50**..........................(v) NoelGarbutt(3) 1 54
(Lisa Williamson) *led: 1 l ld 2f out: drvn and hdd over 1f out: one pce fnl f* **33/1**

U003 **3** 1 **Red Allure**[20] 5181 4-8-0 **50**.......................... GeorgeRooke(7) 5 50
(Michael Mullineaux) *hld up: pushed along over 2f out: rdn and effrt over 1f out: wnt 3rd ent fnl f: kpt on* **9/2**[3]

3240 **4** 1/2 **Diamond Shower (IRE)**[27] 4912 3-9-7 **67**........................ PaulHanagan 2 65
(Richard Fahey) *hld up: drvn over 1f out: rdn and kpt on into 4th fnl f* **7/1**

4240 **5** 3/4 **Sarasota Bay**[34] 4651 3-9-6 **66**........................ JasonHart 3 61
(John Quinn) *chsd ldr: drvn in 2nd 2f out: lost pl and rdn over 1f out: wknd fnl f* **5/2[2]**

0000 **6** 21 **Swiss Chime**[4] 5738 3-7-11 **50** oh2........................(b[1]) IzzyClifton(7) 4
(Alan Berry) *slowly away: sn rcvrd to chse ldr: rdn and wknd 2f out: sn lost tch: eased* **50/1**

1m 1.24s (0.84) **Going Correction** +0.125s/f (Good)
WFA 3 from 4yo+ 3lb **6** Ran SP% **111.8**
Speed ratings (Par 100): **98,94,92,92,90 57**
CSF £36.76 TOTE £1.60: £1.30, £5.60; EX 23.30 Trifecta £79.30.
Owner David W Armstrong **Bred** Highfield Farm Llp **Trained** Great Habton, N Yorks

FOCUS
The pace was fair and an unexposed 3yo justified favouritism in good style under a prominent ride. The winner progressed again.

5894 RACING TV NOVICE STKS (PLUS 10 RACE) 7f 212y
6:10 (6:12) (Class 4) 2-Y-O **£6,469** (£1,925; £962; £481) **Stalls** Low

Form RPR

2 **1** **He's A Keeper (IRE)**[20] 5177 2-9-5 0........................ RichardKingscote 6 85+
(Tom Dascombe) *prom: led 2f out: drvn 4 l clr 1f out: pushed out fnl f: easily* **5/6[1]**

2 4 **On Guard** 2-9-5 0........................ RoystonFfrench 3 76+
(John Gosden) *restless in stalls: t.k.h: hld up: hdwy 3f out: reminder and drvn into 2nd 1 1/2f out: kpt on fnl f: no ch w wnr* **5/2[2]**

3 3 3/4 **Stockbridge Tap** 2-9-5 0........................ PaulHanagan 5 68
(James Bethell) *slowly away: bhd: pushed along in 5th 3f out: drvn and hdwy on outer 2f out: reminder over 1f out: one pce fnl f* **25/1**

4 7 **Trumpets Call (IRE)** 2-9-5 0........................ JasonHart 2 53
(David Loughnane) *unruly and reluctant to load: trckd ldrs: pushed along 3f out: drvn and wknd 2f out* **40/1**

0 **5** 1 3/4 **Unresolved**[15] 5345 2-9-5 0........................ FrannyNorton 4 49
(Mark Johnston) *led: pushed along over 2f out: hdd & wknd 2f out* **5/1[3]**

6 17 **Hart's Dream** 2-9-5 0........................ DougieCostello 1 11
(Kevin Ryan) *slowly away: bhd: drvn in last 4f out: wknd and lost tch 3f out* **16/1**

1m 44.01s (1.31) **Going Correction** +0.125s/f (Good) **6** Ran SP% **112.0**
Speed ratings (Par 96): **98,94,90,83,81 64**
CSF £3.10 TOTE £1.60: £1.10, £2.20; EX 3.60 Trifecta £19.50.
Owner N Canning **Bred** Tinnakill Bloodstock & Jack Cantillon **Trained** Malpas, Cheshire

FOCUS
Race distance increased by 11 yards. The favourite landed the odds in emphatic style but there was also clear promise from a newcomer in second. The form will prove fluid.

5895 SEVEN SISTERS MEDIAN AUCTION MAIDEN FILLIES' STKS (PLUS 10 RACE) 6f 212y
6:45 (6:45) (Class 4) 2-Y-O **£6,469** (£1,925; £962; £481) **Stalls** Low

Form RPR

24 **1** **Reclaim Victory (IRE)**[13] 5433 2-8-11 0........................ MeganNicholls(3) 3 72
(Brian Ellison) *slowly away: hld up: pushed along and hdwy 2f out: swtchd to outer and rdn over 1f out: led over 1/2f out: clr whn shifted rt nr fin: comf* **5/2[2]**

03 **2** 1 1/2 **I Had A Dream**[45] 4222 2-9-0 0........................ DougieCostello 4 68
(Tom Clover) *unruly s: led: rdn in 1 l ld over 2f out: 1/2 l ld 1f out: hdd over 1/2f out: no ex* **13/2**

0 **3** hd **Angels Faces (IRE)**[71] 3244 2-9-0 0........................ SamJames 10 68
(Grant Tuer) *chsd ldrs on outer: pushed into 3rd 3f out: drvn into 2nd 2f out: rdn over 1f out: dropped to 3rd ent fnl f: kpt on nr fin* **4/1[3]**

4 1 1/2 **High Flying Bird (FR)** 2-9-0 0........................ RichardKingscote 1 64
(Tom Dascombe) *trckd ldrs on inner: pushed along in 4th 3f out: looking for room 2f out: in clr and drvn over 1f out: one pce fnl f* **15/8[1]**

0 **5** 3/4 **Rainbow Jet (IRE)**[20] 5170 2-9-0 0........................ FrannyNorton 8 62
(John Mackie) *bhd: pushed along in 7th 3f out: sn drvn: kpt on fnl f* **20/1**

0 **6** 2 **Carriage Clock**[20] 5170 2-9-0 0........................ RoystonFfrench 6 57
(Steph Hollinshead) *chsd ldr: pushed along in 2nd 3f out: drvn and reminder over 2f out: wknd over 1f out* **25/1**

7 11 **She's A Unicorn** 2-8-7 0........................ PoppyFielding(7) 9 30
(Tom Dascombe) *slowly away: in rr and sn detached fr rest: styd on past wkng rivals ins fnl f (jockey said, regarding running and riding, that her instructions were to jump on the filly, get a lead and allow the filly to travel; she added that the filly was slowly into stride and felt green so she concentrated on getting the filly balanced before* **12/1**

0 **8** 1 **Boulevard Beauty (IRE)**[14] 5387 2-9-0 0........................ RachelRichardson 7 27
(Tim Easterby) *hld up: drvn over 3f out: lost tch 2f out* **40/1**

0 **9** 9 **Youarefullofchat**[43] 4302 2-9-0 0........................ JamesSullivan 5 5
(Robyn Brisland) *mid-div: pushed along 4f out: drvn and wknd 3f out: sn lost tch* **50/1**

1m 30.26s (0.96) **Going Correction** +0.125s/f (Good) **9** Ran SP% **117.4**
Speed ratings (Par 93): **99,97,97,95,94 92,79,78,68**
CSF £18.60 TOTE £3.50: £1.50, £1.30, £1.50; EX 16.00 Trifecta £46.80.
Owner Quickly Group Holdings Ltd & Partner **Bred** Denis Noonan **Trained** Norton, N Yorks

■ Stewards' Enquiry : Poppy Fielding seven-day ban; failing to take all reasonable and permissible measures to obtain the post possible placing (Aug 23-29)

FOCUS
Race distance increased by 11 yards. The leading form contender finished well to make it third time lucky. An ordinary race for the track.

5896 BRITANNIA NURSERY H'CAP (JOCKEY CLUB GRASSROOTS NURSERY QUALIFIER) 6f 212y
7:20 (7:20) (Class 4) (0-80,79) 2-Y-O **£7,115** (£2,117; £1,058; £529; £400; £400) **Stalls** Low

Form RPR

053 **1** nk **Road Rage (IRE)**[25] 4976 2-8-10 **68**........................(p) ConnorBeasley 5 74
(Michael Dods) *led: rdn in narrow ld 2f out: hdd 1f out: rallied fnl f and coming together w wnr: fighting bk whn briefly lost footing nr fin: jst hld: fin 2nd: plcd 1st* **13/2**

541 **2** **Rich Belief**[39] 4456 2-9-6 **78**........................ RobertWinston 6 85
(James Bethell) *hld up on outer: hdwy into 2nd 3f out: almost upsides ldr and pushed along 2f out: shkn up to ld narrowly 1f out: sustained duel and coming together w runner-up fnl f: gained upper hand last few strides: fin 1st: plcd 2nd (jockey said colt hung left-handed)* **13/5[2]**

4502 **3** 6 **Out Of Breath**[34] 4652 2-8-8 **66**........................ SamJames 3 57
(Grant Tuer) *hld up: pushed along 3f out: n.m.r 2f out: swtchd to outer 1 1/2f out: sn drvn: rdn and r.o into 3rd fnl f* **7/1**

6060 **4** 2 1/4 **The Ginger Bullet**[31] 4756 2-8-2 **60**........................ DuranFentiman 4 46
(Richard Fahey) *hld up: hdwy on outer 3f out: drvn and reminder 2f out: sn rdn: 3rd 1f out: no ex and lost 3rd fnl f* **14/1**

3431 **5** 5 **Fantom Force (IRE)**[15] 5340 2-9-5 **77**........................ RichardKingscote 1 50
(Richard Hannon) *in rr: pushed along over 4f out: rdn over 2f out: no imp (jockey said colt was never travelling)* **2/1[1]**

250 **6** 1/2 **Kilig**[50] 4032 2-8-6 **64**........................ JamesSullivan 7 36
(Tim Easterby) *prom: drvn and lost pl 3f out: sn rdn and wknd* **20/1**

634 **7** 3 1/2 **Welcome Surprise (IRE)**[43] 4290 2-9-7 **79**........................(p[1]) RoystonFfrench 2 42
(Saeed bin Suroor) *trckd ldr on inner: drvn and lost pl 3f out: rdn 2f out: dropped to last fnl f* **11/2[3]**

1m 29.44s (0.14) **Going Correction** +0.125s/f (Good) **7** Ran SP% **113.8**
Speed ratings (Par 96): **103,103,96,94,88 87,83**
CSF £23.52 TOTE £7.20: £3.00; EX 30.00 Trifecta £152.60.
Owner Merchants and Missionaries **Bred** Aidan Sexton **Trained** Denton, Co Durham

FOCUS
Race distance increased by 11 yards.The favourite was disappointing but the first two had a good battle and pulled well clear.

5897 JOIN RACING TV NOW H'CAP 2m 45y
7:50 (7:50) (Class 4) (0-80,81) 4-Y-O+ **£7,115** (£2,117; £1,058; £529; £400; £400) **Stalls** Low

Form RPR

6022 **1** **Contrebasse**[20] 5179 4-8-9 **66**........................ JasonHart 6 75
(Tim Easterby) *chsd ldr: 1 l 2nd 3f out: drvn to chal 2f out: sn rdn: disp ld 1f out: led ins fnl f: grad asserted: gng away at fin* **15/2[3]**

-011 **2** 1 **Nuits St Georges (IRE)**[61] 3635 4-9-7 **78**........................ DavidNolan 9 86
(David Menuisier) *led: racd wd early: trckd across to stands' rail 4f out: drvn in 1 l ld 3f out: jnd 1f out: hdd ins fnl f: kpt on* **7/4[2]**

10/1 **3** 8 **Agrapart (FR)**[91] 2571 8-9-7 **81**........................ MeganNicholls(3) 7 79
(Nick Williams) *racd in 3rd: pushed along 4f out: drvn 3f out: rdn 2f out: one pce: bled fr nose (vet said gelding had bled from the nose)* **5/4[1]**

5231 **4** 2 1/4 **Nafaayes (IRE)**[28] 4881 5-8-10 **67**........................(p) PaulHanagan 8 63
(Jean-Rene Auvray) *hld up: hdwy into 4th over 4f out: drvn over 3f out: rdn over 2f out: no imp* **12/1**

1213 **5** nk **Angel Gabrial (IRE)**[13] 5423 10-8-8 **65**........................(p) BarryMcHugh 4 60
(Patrick Morris) *hld up: 5th 4f out: pushed along 3f out: rdn 1 1/2f out: one pce* **8/1**

060/ **6** 64 **Star Of Namibia (IRE)**[506] 7775 9-8-2 **59** oh14........................ JamesSullivan 5
(Michael Mullineaux) *bhd: drvn in rr 6f out: lost tch 4f out* **66/1**

3m 37.87s (1.17) **Going Correction** +0.125s/f (Good) **6** Ran SP% **112.9**
Speed ratings (Par 105): **102,101,97,96,96 64**
CSF £21.40 CT £27.02 TOTE £5.90: £2.60, £1.50; EX 18.70 Trifecta £48.80.
Owner The Harmonious Lot & Partner **Bred** Brook Stud Bloodstock Ltd **Trained** Great Habton, N Yorks

FOCUS
Race distance increased by 24 yards. The went a decent pace in this staying handicap and the first two pulled well clear. A pb from the winner.

5898 RAINHILL H'CAP 1m 2f 42y
8:25 (8:25) (Class 5) (0-70,71) 3-Y-O **£5,175** (£1,540; £769; £400; £400; £400) **Stalls** High

Form RPR

6660 **1** **George Mallory**[24] 5023 3-9-2 **63**........................ TomEaves 8 71
(Kevin Ryan) *mde all: 1 l ld 3f out: drvn 2f out: rdn in narrow ld 1f out: r.o gamely u.p fnl f: gng away nr fin* **6/1[3]**

0012 **2** 1 **Firewater**[12] 5474 3-9-3 **64**........................(p) PaulHanagan 4 70
(Richard Fahey) *chsd ldr: pushed along in 1 l 2nd 3f out: sn drvn: rdn in cl 2nd 1f out: r.o fnl f: hld nr fin* **7/2[1]**

0115 **3** 2 1/4 **Potenza (IRE)**[14] 5394 3-9-2 **66**........................ GabrieleMalune(3) 2 68
(Stef Keniry) *mid-div: drvn 3f out: rdn 2f out: hdwy 1f out: kpt on into 3rd fnl f* **13/2**

036 **4** 3/4 **Helian (IRE)**[46] 4178 3-9-7 **68**........................ TomQueally 7 68
(Ed Dunlop) *hld up: pushed along 3f out: drvn and hdwy on stands' rail 2f out: sn rdn: kpt on fnl f* **11/1**

-406 **5** 1/2 **Flint Hill**[49] 4077 3-9-10 **71**........................(p) ConnorBeasley 5 70
(Michael Dods) *hld up: pushed along and hdwy 3f out: drvn 2f out: sn rdn: no ex fnl f* **6/1[3]**

1323 **6** 3/4 **Highwaygrey**[14] 5394 3-9-7 **68**........................ RachelRichardson 9 66
(Tim Easterby) *t.k.h: chsd ldr: pushed along and cl up over 2f out: rdn over 1f out: wknd fnl f* **13/2**

0333 **7** 1 3/4 **Power Player**[20] 5176 3-9-7 **68**........................ CliffordLee 3 62
(K R Burke) *hld up: rdn and effrt 2f out: wknd over 1f out: eased fnl f (trainer's rep said gelding ran too freely in rear and may benefit from being ridden more prominently)* **6/1[3]**

0335 **8** nk **Fragrant Belle**[16] 5307 3-9-7 **68**........................ RichardKingscote 1 61
(Ralph Beckett) *mid-div: chsd ldrs and drvn 3f out: rdn over 2f out: wknd over 1f out* **9/2[2]**

000 **9** 4 1/2 **Half Bolly**[148] 1195 3-8-8 **55**........................ JamesSullivan 6 39
(Mark Walford) *hld up: pushed along in last 4f out: drvn and lost tch 3f out* **40/1**

2m 18.3s (7.50) **Going Correction** +0.125s/f (Good) **9** Ran SP% **120.7**
Speed ratings (Par 100): **75,74,72,71,71 70,69,69,65**
CSF £28.66 CT £145.21 TOTE £7.30: £2.60, £1.70, £2.50; EX 37.40 Trifecta £182.20.
Owner F Gillespie **Bred** Ecurie Des Charmes **Trained** Hambleton, N Yorks

FOCUS
Race distance increased by 33 yards. The pace was steady and the winner made all. The runner-up helps with the standard.
T/Plt: £74.30 to a £1 stake. Pool: £49,845.84. - 489.30 winning units. T/Qpdt: £7.90 to a £1 stake. Pool: £5,443.31. - 505.23 winning units. **Keith McHugh**

5615 **MUSSELBURGH** (R-H)
Friday, August 9

OFFICIAL GOING: Soft
Wind: Breezy, half behind in sprints and in approximately 4f of home straight in races on the round course Weather: Overcast

5899 BAM CONSTRUCTION LTD H'CAP — 1m 208y
2:10 (2:10) (Class 5) (0-70,71) 3-Y-O+
£4,722 (£1,405; £702; £351; £300; £300) **Stalls** Low

Form — RPR

-365 **1** **Pioneering (IRE)**[35] 4602 5-9-7 **65**......(p) BenSanderson(5) 1 77
(Roger Fell) *sn niggled along in tch: shkn up and hdwy to ld over 2f out: pushed clr fnl f* **11/4**[2]

0000 **2** 3½ **Crazy Tornado (IRE)**[3] 5766 6-8-12 **51**......(h) ShaneGray 3 56
(Keith Dalgleish) *sn chsng ldr: effrt and led briefly over 2f out: kpt on same pce appr fnl f* **20/1**

2061 **3** 1 **Kwanza**[21] 5156 4-9-12 **65**...... JoeFanning 8 68
(Mark Johnston) *led tl rdn and hdd over 2f out: one pce over 1f out* **5/2**[1]

4350 **4** 1½ **Zeshov (IRE)**[52] 3957 8-10-0 **67**......(p) PhilDennis 9 66
(Rebecca Bastiman) *dwlt: hld up: effrt and rdn along over 2f out: no imp over 1f out* **20/1**

550 **5** 1¼ **Lucky Violet (IRE)**[7] 5616 7-9-9 **62**......(h) GrahamLee 6 59
(Linda Perratt) *t.k.h early: in tch: rdn over 2f out: outpcd fr over 1f out* **17/2**

4216 **6** 2¼ **Allux Boy (IRE)**[18] 5245 5-9-5 **63**...... FayeMcManoman(5) 10 55
(Nigel Tinkler) *slowly away: hld up: stdy hdwy over 2f out: rdn and wknd appr fnl f* **5/1**

4-30 **7** 2¾ **Ballymount**[28] 4875 4-10-0 **67**......(p) NathanEvans 2 53
(Michael Easterby) *chsd ldr early: cl up: drvn along over 2f out: wknd over 1f out* **4/1**[3]

2m 2.34s (9.24) **Going Correction** +1.00s/f (Soft) **7 Ran SP% 112.0**
Speed ratings (Par 103): **98,94,94,92,91 89,87**
CSF £49.33 CT £150.79 TOTE £3.30: £2.10, £6.90; EX 62.90 Trifecta £426.20.
Owner Ebor Racing Club Vi **Bred** Miss Joan Murphy **Trained** Nawton, N Yorks

FOCUS
There had been 6mm of rain earlier in the day, and the ground had eased to soft. The bottom bend was out from the inner by 2yds, and there was a cutaway on the stands' side at the 1.5f point. Add 7yds. This was sound run and the winner's rated back to his latter 2018 form.

5900 EBF CONDITIONS STKS (PLUS 10 RACE) — 5f 1y
2:40 (2:40) (Class 3) 2-Y-O
£8,092 (£2,423; £1,211; £605) **Stalls** High

Form — RPR

21 **1** **Pop Dancer (IRE)**[12] 5472 2-8-13 **0**...... TonyHamilton 7 90
(Richard Fahey) *mde virtually all: pushed along over 1f out: kpt on strly fnl f* **5/4**[2]

1001 **2** 1¼ **Makyon (IRE)**[11] 5485 2-8-13 **95**...... JoeFanning 5 86
(Mark Johnston) *trckd ldrs: effrt and ev ch over 1f out to ins fnl f: one pce last 100yds* **4/6**[1]

16 **3** 1¾ **Proper Beau**[78] 3023 2-8-13 **0**......(t[1] w) GrahamLee 4 79
(Bryan Smart) *w wnr: rdn along 2f out: one pce last 150yds* **10/1**[3]

0 **4** 7 **Summer Heights**[11] 5485 2-8-8 **0**...... PaddyMathers 6 49
(Jim Goldie) *dwlt: bhd and outpcd: no ch fr 1/2-way* **66/1**

1m 3.83s (4.13) **Going Correction** +1.00s/f (Soft) **4 Ran SP% 115.0**
Speed ratings (Par 98): **107,105,102,91**
CSF £2.63 TOTE £2.30; EX 3.50 Trifecta £3.90.
Owner Richard Fahey Ebor Racing Club Ltd **Bred** Marston Stud **Trained** Musley Bank, N Yorks

FOCUS
Just the four runners, but three of them had a chance a furlong out. Not form to be too confident about.

5901 WATERMANS H'CAP — 5f 1y
3:10 (3:10) (Class 4) (0-80,78) 3-Y-O+ **£5,692** (£1,694; £846; £423; £300) **Stalls** High

Form — RPR

0034 **1** **Red Pike (IRE)**[18] 5244 8-9-4 **70**...... GrahamLee 4 79
(Bryan Smart) *trckd ldrs: rdn to ld 1f out: kpt on strly* **5/2**[3]

2333 **2** 2¼ **Diamonique**[1] 5854 3-9-5 **74**...... ShaneGray 2 74
(Keith Dalgleish) *trckd ldrs: effrt and chsd wnr ent fnl f: kpt on: nt pce to chal* **2/1**[1]

0010 **3** 2¼ **Orion's Bow**[14] 5395 8-9-12 **78**......(p) DavidAllan 1 71
(Tim Easterby) *sn pushed along bhd ldrs: hdwy whn nt clr run and swtchd rt over 1f out: drvn and one pce ins fnl f* **11/4**

0020 **4** 2½ **Longroom**[23] 5042 7-9-2 **68**......(t) PhilDennis 3 52
(Noel Wilson) *disp ld to 1f out: sn rdn and wknd* **7/1**

1266 **5** 2½ **Jordan Electrics**[6] 5670 3-8-8 **68**......(h) HarrisonShaw(5) 5 42
(Linda Perratt) *led or disp ld to 1f out: sn drvn and wknd* **9/4**[2]

1m 4.25s (4.55) **Going Correction** +1.00s/f (Soft) **5 Ran SP% 131.8**
WFA 3 from 7yo+ 3lb
Speed ratings (Par 105): **103,99,95,91,87**
CSF £9.82 TOTE £3.00: £1.40, £2.80; EX 9.20 Trifecta £15.70.
Owner T Eyre & P Watson **Bred** Mrs M Marnane **Trained** Hambleton, N Yorks

FOCUS
A fair sprint handicap. The winner found a bit on this year's form.

5902 GLENRATH FARMS ARCHERFIELD CUP H'CAP — 1m 5f 216y
3:40 (3:40) (Class 3) (0-95,91) 4-Y-O+
£12,450 (£3,728; £1,864; £932; £466; £234) **Stalls** Low

Form — RPR

1321 **1** **Alright Sunshine (IRE)**[25] 4988 4-9-4 **88**...... JoeFanning 5 97+
(Keith Dalgleish) *t.k.h early: trckd ldrs: smooth hdwy to ld over 2f out: sn pushed along and drifted lft: continued to hang lft ins fnl f: kpt on strly towards fin* **11/10**[1]

5226 **2** 1¼ **Jabbaar**[20] 5199 6-9-3 **87**...... JamieGormley 7 93
(Iain Jardine) *hld up in tch: effrt over 2f out: chsd wnr ins fnl f: r.o* **7/1**[3]

3652 **3** ½ **Claire Underwood (IRE)**[13] 5437 4-9-0 **87**...... SeanDavis(3) 1 92
(Richard Fahey) *pressed ldr: led over 3f out to over 2f out: rallied: lost 2nd and one pce ins fnl f* **7/1**[3]

612 **4** 16 **Dragons Voice**[52] 3973 5-9-2 **86**...... KevinStott 2 69
(David Menuisier) *prom: drvn along over 2f out: wknd over 1f out* **11/4**[2]

5-30 **5** 12 **Needs To Be Seen (FR)**[69] 3361 4-8-4 **74**......(p) PaddyMathers 8 40
(Jim Goldie) *hld up: rdn along 3f out: wknd fr 2f out* **20/1**

22P0 **6** 22 **Ulster (IRE)**[27] 4899 4-9-7 **91**......(b[1]) AdamMcNamara 4 26
(Archie Watson) *led: rdn and hdd over 3f out: wknd qckly over 2f out: t.o* **7/1**[3]

3m 16.35s (12.45) **Going Correction** +1.00s/f (Soft) **6 Ran SP% 116.5**
Speed ratings (Par 107): **104,103,103,93,87 74**
CSF £10.29 CT £38.48 TOTE £1.90: £1.20, £2.20; EX 8.70 Trifecta £31.70.
Owner Paul & Clare Rooney **Bred** Peter & Hugh McCutcheon **Trained** Carluke, S Lanarks

FOCUS
Add 7yds. Not a strong race for the grade. The winner is improving and justified his short odds despite wandering over to the stands' rail in the straight.

5903 EDGEN MURRAY H'CAP — 7f 33y
4:10 (4:12) (Class 4) (0-80,82) 3-Y-O+
£5,692 (£1,694; £846; £423; £300; £300) **Stalls** Low

Form — RPR

1163 **1** **Rux Ruxx (IRE)**[15] 5333 4-9-10 **77**...... DavidAllan 5 84
(Tim Easterby) *dwlt: t.k.h: hld up: shkn up and hdwy 2f out: drvn and led ins fnl f: r.o* **5/1**[3]

4240 **2** ¾ **Logi (IRE)**[11] 5488 5-9-0 **67**......(b) JamieGormley 1 72
(Rebecca Bastiman) *rn wout hind shoes: t.k.h early: cl up: rdn over 2f out: led over 1f out to ins fnl f: kpt on: hld nr fin (stewards gave permission for the gelding to run without hind shoes)* **10/1**

5125 **3** hd **How Bizarre**[10] 5516 4-9-5 **72**...... KevinStott 2 76
(Liam Bailey) *led at ordinary gallop: rdn and hdd over 1f out: rallied: one pce ins fnl f* **7/1**

6414 **4** 1¼ **Inner Circle (IRE)**[25] 4980 5-9-7 **74**......(p) AdamMcNamara 10 75
(Roger Fell) *hld up: hdwy whn nt clr run over 2f out and over 1f out: rdn and one pce ins fnl f (jockey said gelding was continually denied a clear run in the final 2f)* **8/1**

2321 **5** 2¼ **Northernpowerhouse**[17] 5274 3-9-2 **75**......(p) GrahamLee 6 68
(Bryan Smart) *t.k.h early: chsd ldrs: drvn along over 2f out: wknd over 1f out* **5/2**[1]

6564 **6** 2 **Glengarry**[13] 5434 6-9-7 **79**......(b) BenSanderson(5) 4 69
(Keith Dalgleish) *s.i.s: hld up on ins: stdy hdwy over 2f out: effrt and ev ch over 1f out: wknd fnl f* **10/1**

1541 **7** 2¾ **Gometra Ginty (IRE)**[7] 5619 3-9-1 **74** 6ex...... ShaneGray 9 54
(Keith Dalgleish) *pressed ldr: drvn and outpcd over 2f out: btn over 1f out (trainer could offer no explanation for the filly's performance)* **11/4**[2]

5452 **8** 7 **Oriental Lilly**[13] 5432 5-9-6 **73**...... PaddyMathers 8 36
(Jim Goldie) *stdd s: hld up: drvn and outpcd wl over 2f out: nvr on terms* **12/1**

1m 35.27s (6.27) **Going Correction** +1.00s/f (Soft) **8 Ran SP% 121.4**
WFA 3 from 4yo+ 6lb
Speed ratings (Par 105): **104,103,102,101,98 96,93,85**
CSF £56.47 CT £358.32 TOTE £5.30: £1.90, £2.90, £2.00; EX 81.30 Trifecta £514.60.
Owner King Power Racing Co Ltd **Bred** Yeomanstown Stud **Trained** Great Habton, N Yorks

FOCUS
Add 7yds. They didn't go much of a gallop early on and there were several still in with a chance a furlong out. The runner-up helps with the standard.

5904 BOOGIE IN THE MORNING H'CAP — 5f 1y
4:40 (4:40) (Class 6) (0-60,61) 3-Y-O+
£3,105 (£924; £461; £300; £300; £300) **Stalls** High

Form — RPR

0054 **1** **Economic Crisis (IRE)**[7] 5620 10-9-1 **58**...... HarrisonShaw(5) 1 67
(Alan Berry) *mde all: rdn over 1f out: kpt on strly fnl f* **3/1**[2]

0360 **2** 2¼ **Burmese Blazer (IRE)**[17] 5276 4-9-7 **59**......(h) PhilDennis 6 60
(Jim Goldie) *trckd ldrs: effrt and wnt 2nd over 1f out: sn rdn: kpt on same pce last 100yds* **7/2**[3]

3632 **3** 3 **Amazing Alba**[17] 5276 3-9-5 **60**......(h) KevinStott 2 49
(Alistair Whillans) *w wnr to 1/2-way: outpcd and hung lft over 1f out: r.o ins fnl f: nt rch first two* **3/1**[2]

6140 **4** 1 **Dream House**[18] 5236 3-9-6 **61**...... DavidAllan 5 47
(Tim Easterby) *prom on outside: drvn along 2f out: outpcd fnl f* **5/2**[1]

0065 **5** shd **Northern Society (IRE)**[7] 5620 3-9-1 **59**......(b) SeanDavis(3) 7 44
(Keith Dalgleish) *fly-jmpd s: bhd: drvn along 2f out: sn no imp* **9/2**

0400 **6** 1¼ **Just A Rumour (IRE)**[9] 5558 3-7-13 **45**......(p[1]) AndrewBreslin(5) 4 26
(Noel Wilson) *dwlt: bhd: drvn over 2f out: sn n.d: btn over 1f out* **18/1**

1m 3.82s (4.12) **Going Correction** +1.00s/f (Soft) **6 Ran SP% 124.2**
WFA 3 from 4yo+ 3lb
Speed ratings (Par 101): **107,103,98,97,96 94**
CSF £15.69 TOTE £4.20: £1.60, £2.00; EX 12.20 Trifecta £34.00.
Owner William Burns & Alan Berry **Bred** Philip Hore Jnr **Trained** Cockerham, Lancs

FOCUS
An ordinary sprint won by a course regular. This form could be rated higher but there are reservations.

5905 MILLER HOMES LTD H'CAP — 1m 4f 104y
5:10 (5:10) (Class 6) (0-60,62) 3-Y-O+
£3,752 (£1,116; £557; £300; £300; £300) **Stalls** Low

Form — RPR

4332 **1** **Euro Implosion (IRE)**[3] 5792 3-9-4 **62**...... JoeFanning 6 76
(Keith Dalgleish) *mde all at modest gallop: shkn up over 2f out: rdn clr fnl f: unchal* **8/13**[1]

3265 **2** 4½ **Dew Pond**[4] 5743 7-9-8 **56**......(bt) DavidAllan 10 61
(Tim Easterby) *chsd wnr 4f: cl up: regained 2nd over 3f out: rdn over 2f out: one pce appr fnl f* **4/1**[2]

3652 **3** ½ **Flood Defence (IRE)**[27] 4914 5-9-12 **60**...... PhilDennis 2 65
(Iain Jardine) *t.k.h: hld up: hdwy to chse ldrs over 2f out: sn rdn: one pce fr over 1f out* **6/1**[3]

214- **4** 8 **Lyford (IRE)**[111] 7650 4-9-8 **56**...... KevinStott 11 49
(Alistair Whillans) *hld up in tch: rdn and outpcd over 2f out: wknd over 1f out* **25/1**

0000 **5** 7 **Seven For A Pound (USA)**[24] 5023 3-8-9 **53**...... TonyHamilton 3 36
(Richard Fahey) *t.k.h: in tch: drvn and outpcd over 2f out: sn btn* **16/1**

0000 **6** 31 **Bogardus (IRE)**[24] 5029 8-9-7 **55**......(b[1]) GrahamLee 7
(Liam Bailey) *dwlt: hld up: reminders bef 1/2-way: struggling over 4f out: t.o* **22/1**

000- **7** 20 **Unite The Clans (IRE)**[296] 8319 5-9-2 **50**...... NathanEvans 1
(Sandy Thomson) *dwlt: t.k.h in rr: hdwy to chse wnr after 4f: drvn and lost pl qckly over 3f out: sn btn: t.o* **20/1**

2m 56.02s (11.52) **Going Correction** +1.00s/f (Soft) **7 Ran SP% 115.0**
WFA 3 from 4yo+ 10lb
Speed ratings (Par 101): **101,98,97,92,87 67,53**
CSF £3.30 CT £7.52 TOTE £1.30: £1.10, £2.60; EX 3.60 Trifecta £8.70.
Owner J S Morrison **Bred** Aaron Boland **Trained** Carluke, S Lanarks

The Form Book Flat 2019, Raceform Ltd, Newbury, RG14 5SJ

FOCUS
Add 7yds. A steadily run affair which didn't take much winning.
T/Plt: £271.90 to a £1 stake. Pool: £53,169.98. - 142.71 winning units. T/Qpdt: £28.80 to a £1 stake. Pool: £4,995.48. - 128.11 winning units. **Richard Young**

5682 NEWMARKET (R-H)
Friday, August 9

OFFICIAL GOING: Good (watered; 7.7)
Wind: blustery Weather: very changeable; 22 degrees

5906 32RED FILLIES' NOVICE STKS (PLUS 10 RACE) 6f
5:25 (5:25) (Class 4) 2-Y-O **£5,175** (£1,540; £769; £384) **Stalls High**

Form RPR
2 **1** **Nina Bailarina**[21] 5132 2-9-0 0 OisinMurphy 4 85
(Ed Walker) *mde all: rdn clr over 1f out: unchal* **10/11**[1]
0 **2** *5* **Strawberry Hind (IRE)**[78] 2996 2-9-0 0 DavidEgan 7 70
(Mick Channon) *midfield: drvn along 1/2-way: swtchd outside 2f out: wnt 2nd ins fnl f: nvr nr wnr* **33/1**
3 *1 3/4* **Kodiellen (IRE)** 2-9-0 0 SeanLevey 1 65
(Richard Hannon) *chsd wnr: rdn and outpcd by her over 1f out: lost 2nd and nt qckn fnl 200yds* **14/1**
3 **4** *3* **East Of Eden (IRE)**[29] 4849 2-9-0 0 JamesDoyle 5 56
(Hugo Palmer) *plld too hrd in 3rd pl tl rdn and wknd over 1f out (jockey said filly raced awkwardly in the early stages)* **11/4**[2]
0 **5** *1 1/4* **Sri Sene Power (IRE)**[79] 2968 2-9-0 0 SilvestreDeSousa 3 52+
(Richard Hannon) *lost 6 l s: drvn and nvr travelling in rr* **11/1**
5 **6** *1 1/2* **Time To Strike (IRE)**[21] 5132 2-9-0 0 JamieSpencer 6 48+
(David Simcock) *lost 6 l s: swtchd rt and effrt over 2f out: wknd and hung lft ins fnl f* **4/1**[3]
0 **7** *2* **Clever Candy**[27] 4897 2-9-0 0 HayleyTurner 9 42
(Michael Bell) *chsd ldrs: rdn and btn wl over 1f out* **40/1**
6 **8** *25* **Kelinda Dice**[108] 2020 2-9-0 0 JackMitchell 2
(Mick Quinn) *sn rdn and nvr gng pce: t.o over 1f out: eased* **66/1**

1m 12.74s (0.64) **Going Correction** +0.075s/f (Good) **8 Ran SP% 120.9**
Speed ratings (Par 93): **98,91,89,85,83 81,78,45**
CSF £43.61 TOTE £1.70: £1.10, £6.80, £3.20; EX 40.70 Trifecta £248.00.
Owner Brightwalton Bloodstock Ltd **Bred** Brightwalton Bloodstock Ltd **Trained** Upper Lambourn, Berks

FOCUS
Stands' side course used. Stalls: far side, except 1m4f: centre. This looked a good opportunity for the favourite, who'd run with considerable promise when second on debut. She got the job done in impressive fashion, despite some unease in the market.

5907 UNIBET (S) STKS 7f
6:00 (6:00) (Class 4) 2-Y-O
£4,528 (£1,347; £673; £400; £400; £400) **Stalls High**

Form RPR
60 **1** **Walkonby**[4] 5732 2-8-8 0 DavidEgan 5 60
(Mick Channon) *pressed ldng pair: drvn 3f out: 3 l down and outpcd over 2f out: styd on u.p despite racing awkwardly wl ins fnl f and led between rivals 50yds out* **2/1**[1]
5404 **2** *3/4* **Lexington Quest (IRE)**[16] 5313 2-8-13 64 (p) SilvestreDeSousa 2 63
(Richard Hannon) *led: rdn over 2f out: clr ins fnl f: fnd nthing and ct cl home* **2/1**[1]
040 **3** *1* **Max's Thunder (IRE)**[25] 4999 2-8-13 68 OisinMurphy 1 60
(Jamie Osborne) *pressed ldr after 3f: rdn over 1f out: nt qckn fnl 100yds and lost 2nd sn after* **9/4**[2]
500 **4** *7* **Chateau Peapod**[25] 4999 2-8-8 54 RaulDaSilva 3 36
(Lydia Pearce) *pressed ldr tl rdn after 3f: struggling over 2f out (vet said filly lost its right hind shoe)* **10/1**[3]
00 **5** *2 3/4* **Gifted Dreamer (IRE)**[31] 4766 2-8-6 0 (p[1]) EllieMacKenzie(7) 6 34
(Mark Usher) *wnt lft s: towards rr fr 1/2-way: rdn and lost tch over 2f out* **50/1**
0 **6** *12* **Goodman Square**[29] 4840 2-8-8 0 (p[1]) HayleyTurner 4
(Mark Usher) *dwlt: keen and sn chsng ldrs: rdn and fdd wl over 2f out: t.o over 1f out: eased* **22/1**
0000 **7** *7* **Sir Chancealot (IRE)**[16] 5313 2-8-13 38 (b) RobertHavlin 7
(Amanda Perrett) *slowly away and n.m.r: drvn and reluctant in rr: t.o 2f out: eased* **20/1**

1m 26.29s (0.59) **Going Correction** +0.075s/f (Good) **7 Ran SP% 117.6**
Speed ratings (Par 96): **99,98,97,89,85 72,64**
CSF £6.51 TOTE £2.90: £1.50, £1.60; EX 7.50 Trifecta £18.40.The winner was bought in for £5,800. Max's Thunder was claimed by Mr D M I Simcock for £10,000.
Owner M Channon **Bred** Mike Channon Bloodstock Limited **Trained** West Ilsley, Berks

FOCUS
Add 20yds. The first three pulled clear in this ordinary juvenile seller. Improvement from the winner.

5908 32RED BRITISH EBF "NEWCOMERS" MAIDEN STKS (PLUS 10 RACE) 7f
6:35 (6:36) (Class 4) 2-Y-O **£5,175** (£1,540; £769; £384) **Stalls High**

Form RPR
1 **Cepheus** 2-9-5 0 OisinMurphy 9 84+
(Brian Meehan) *pressed ldrs: rdn over 1f out: sustained run on far rails ins fnl f and drvn ahd nr fin* **25/1**
2 *nk* **Volkan Star (IRE)** 2-9-5 0 WilliamBuick 2 83
(Charlie Appleby) *pressed ldrs: effrt to ld over 2f out: sn pushed along: kpt on tl hdd cl home* **4/5**[1]
3 *2 3/4* **Afro Blue (IRE)** 2-9-5 0 SeanLevey 4 76
(Richard Hannon) *dwlt: hdwy over 2f out: rdn and ev ch over 1f out: nt qckn fnl 120yds* **20/1**
4 *nse* **Red Missile (IRE)** 2-9-5 0 JamesDoyle 1 76
(William Haggas) *bhd: effrt over 2f out: nvr trbld ldrs but styng on ins fnl f and almost snatched 3rd* **10/1**
5 *1 3/4* **Baptism (IRE)** 2-9-5 0 RobertHavlin 8 71
(John Gosden) *led: rdn and hdd over 2f out: stl cl up over 1f out: no ex* **6/1**[3]
6 *shd* **Vindicate** 2-9-5 0 LouisSteward 7 71
(Sir Michael Stoute) *sn towards rr: one pce and no imp fnl 2f* **16/1**
7 *hd* **Jellystone (IRE)** 2-9-5 0 HarryBentley 3 71+
(Ralph Beckett) *pressed ldr tl rdn over 2f out: wknd fnl 200yds* **9/2**[2]
8 *4* **Many A Star (IRE)** 2-9-5 0 SilvestreDeSousa 5 60+
(James Given) *lost 6 l s: effrt 1/2-way: drvn over 2f out: ev ch over 1f out: sn wknd* **16/1**
9 *3 1/2* **Debt Of Honour** 2-9-5 0 HayleyTurner 6 51
(Michael Bell) *dwlt: a bhd* **40/1**

1m 27.35s (1.65) **Going Correction** +0.075s/f (Good) **9 Ran SP% 119.9**
Speed ratings (Par 96): **93,92,89,89,87 87,87,82,78**
CSF £46.76 TOTE £30.30: £4.80, £1.10, £4.20; EX 61.50 Trifecta £663.40.
Owner G P M Morland **Bred** Biddestone Stud Ltd **Trained** Manton, Wilts

FOCUS
An informative maiden for newcomers and plenty to like about the performances of a pair of Sea The Stars colts, who came clear in tricky windy conditions. They could be decent.

5909 UNIBET H'CAP (96PLUS RACE) 1m 4f
7:10 (7:10) (Class 2) (0-110,105) 3-Y-O+ **£16,172** (£4,812; £2,405; £1,202) **Stalls Centre**

Form RPR
6215 **1** **Kelly's Dino (FR)**[27] 4933 6-10-0 105 (p) BenCurtis 3 112
(K R Burke) *disp 3rd pl: rdn 3f out: chal 1f out: led u.p fnl 100yds: jst holding persistent rival after* **7/1**
1-20 **2** *shd* **Corelli (USA)**[48] 4096 4-9-6 97 (t) FrankieDettori 5 104
(John Gosden) *led: rdn 3f out: narrowly hdd 100yds out: kpt on wl cl home but jst hld* **4/1**[2]
1-62 **3** *2* **Outbox**[6] 5662 4-9-11 102 (p[1]) JackMitchell 2 106
(Simon Crisford) *disp 3rd pl: rdn and wnt 2nd 3f out: ev ch tl edgd lft 1f out: one pce after* **6/5**[1]
5-00 **4** *4* **Blakeney Point**[86] 2742 6-9-10 101 (bt) JasonWatson 7 98
(Roger Charlton) *racd in last pair: rdn and effrt over 2f out: nvr nr ldng trio* **20/1**
0004 **5** *3 1/2* **Aquarium**[7] 5613 4-9-10 101 WilliamBuick 1 93
(Mark Johnston) *stdd s: keen in last pair: rdn 3f out: racd awkwardly and lost tch 2f out* **7/1**
2102 **6** *30* **Almost Midnight**[14] 5370 3-8-11 98 OisinMurphy 6 43
(David Simcock) *pressed ldr tl rdn and fdd rapidly 3f out: hanging rt and t.o fnl f: virtually p.u (trainer could offer no explanation for the colt's performance)* **9/2**[3]

2m 31.27s (-2.63) **Going Correction** +0.075s/f (Good)
WFA 3 from 4yo+ 10lb **6 Ran SP% 113.4**
Speed ratings (Par 109): **111,110,109,106,104 84**
CSF £35.01 TOTE £6.40: £2.80, £2.30; EX 31.50 Trifecta £93.60.
Owner Liam Kelly & Mrs E Burke **Bred** S C E A De Maulepaire **Trained** Middleham Moor, N Yorks

FOCUS
Add 20yds. Not the biggest of fields for this feature handicap but the form looks rock solid for the grade. The race is rated around the runner-up.

5910 BRITISH EBF UNIBET FILLIES' H'CAP 1m
7:40 (7:40) (Class 3) (0-95,94) 3-Y-O+ **£9,703** (£2,887; £1,443) **Stalls High**

Form RPR
4-11 **1** **Mubtasimah**[21] 5128 3-9-5 91 JamesDoyle 4 99+
(William Haggas) *trckd rival pair: effrt gng best to ld 1f out: sn pushed clr: readily* **4/5**[1]
-106 **2** *1* **Desirous**[34] 4667 3-9-2 88 HarryBentley 3 93
(Ralph Beckett) *t.k.h: led for 3f: rdn over 2f out: ev ch 1f out: no match for wnr after* **5/2**[2]
-232 **3** *1/2* **Pennywhistle (IRE)**[47] 4147 3-9-2 88 (b[1]) FrankieDettori 1 92
(John Gosden) *led after 3f: drvn 2f out: hdd 1f out: sn wl hld* **11/4**[3]

1m 39.63s (-0.37) **Going Correction** +0.075s/f (Good) **3 Ran SP% 110.8**
Speed ratings (Par 104): **104,103,102**
CSF £3.17 TOTE £1.70; EX 2.60 Trifecta £5.00.
Owner Sheikh Juma Dalmook Al Maktoum **Bred** Panda Bloodstock **Trained** Newmarket, Suffolk

FOCUS
Another small field but it featured some progressive fillies. Mubtasimah travelled best and completed her hat-trick in cosy fashion.

5911 32RED CASINO H'CAP 6f
8:15 (8:15) (Class 3) (0-95,94) 3-Y-O+ **£9,056** (£2,695; £1,346; £673) **Stalls High**

Form RPR
0000 **1** **Good Effort (IRE)**[13] 5413 4-9-10 92 SeanLevey 5 102
(Ismail Mohammed) *cl up and travelling wl: led over 1f out: sn rdn clr* **5/2**[1]
0106 **2** *2* **Count Otto (IRE)**[6] 5661 4-9-8 90 (h) JasonWatson 4 94
(Amanda Perrett) *towards rr: drvn 1/2-way: wnt 2nd ins fnl f: no ch w wnr after* **7/2**[3]
-050 **3** *3/4* **Swiss Knight**[25] 4995 4-8-12 80 (t) OisinMurphy 1 81
(Stuart Williams) *taken down early: restrained in last pl: rdn and effrt 2f out: tk 3rd cl home but nvr got in a blow* **7/1**
0501 **4** *3/4* **Colonel Frank**[7] 5628 5-8-12 80 5ex JackMitchell 2 79
(Mick Quinn) *led and t.k.h: rdn 2f out: hdd over 1f out: sn no ex: lost 3rd cl home* **10/3**[2]
4132 **5** *hd* **Musharrif**[12] 5476 7-8-11 79 (t) StevieDonohoe 6 77
(Declan Carroll) *chsd ldrs: rdn 2f out: one pce and wl hld fnl f* **8/1**
01-4 **6** *14* **Ice Lord (IRE)**[115] 1829 7-9-12 94 JamesDoyle 3 47
(Chris Wall) *stdd s: towards rr: rdn and struggling 2f out: sn racing awkwardly and hanging rt: t.o and eased (jockey said gelding hung right and moved poorly)* **5/1**

1m 12.32s (0.22) **Going Correction** +0.075s/f (Good) **6 Ran SP% 114.2**
Speed ratings (Par 107): **101,98,97,96,96 77**
CSF £11.80 TOTE £2.90: £1.70, £2.20; EX 10.70 Trifecta £48.90.
Owner Abdulla Al Mansoori **Bred** Rabbah Bloodstock Limited **Trained** Newmarket, Suffolk

FOCUS
This lacked depth but the winner created a good impression on his first try at sprinting.
T/Plt: £40.60 to a £1 stake. Pool: £54,503.07. - 979.74 winning units. T/Qpdt: £25.00 to a £1 stake. Pool: £5,621.78. - 166.13 winning units. **Iain Mackenzie**

5689 THIRSK (L-H)

Friday, August 9

OFFICIAL GOING: Good to soft (soft in places) changing to soft after race 1 (1.50)

Wind: light across Weather: sunshine, heavy shower during race 6

5912 BRITISH STALLION STUDS EBF FILLIES' NURSERY H'CAP 7f 218y

1:50 (1:51) (Class 5) (0-70,66) 2-Y-O

£5,692 (£1,694; £846; £423; £300; £300) Stalls Low

Form RPR

0040 1 **Lady Erimus**[16] 5296 2-8-12 **57**.......................... TomEaves 4 62
(Kevin Ryan) *prom: led over 3f out: sn rdn along: edgd rt over 1f out: drvn out fnl f (trainer said regarding apparent improvement in form that the filly was suited by a step up in trip and travelled better on this occasion)* **22/1**

063 2 1 1/4 **Susie Javea**[16] 5295 2-8-3 **48**.......................... CamHardie 2 50
(Ollie Pears) *dwlt: hld up: pushed along and hdwy whn bit short of room over 1f out: sn rdn: styd on to go 2nd fnl 110yds (jockey said filly was denied a clear run 2f out)* **12/1**

260 3 1 1/2 **Mrs Dukesbury (FR)**[20] 5189 2-9-6 **65**.......................... DanielTudhope 1 64
(Archie Watson) *trckd ldrs: pushed along over 4f out: rdn 3f out: plugged on to go modest 3rd ins fnl f* **11/4**[2]

036 4 3 **Boston Girl (IRE)**[42] 4344 2-8-10 **55**.......................... PJMcDonald 5 47
(Ed Dunlop) *trckd ldrs: rdn to chse ldr 2f out: wknd ins fnl f* **11/1**

4565 5 2 1/2 **Callipygian**[31] 4756 2-9-3 **62**.......................... BarryMcHugh 6 49
(James Given) *led: hdd over 3f out: sn rdn and outpcd: wknd fnl f* **4/1**[3]

0561 6 1 3/4 **Ebony Adams**[21] 5146 2-9-7 **66**.......................... RichardKingscote 3 49
(Brian Meehan) *dwlt sltly: hld up: rdn over 3f out: drvn over 2f out: no imp: eased ins fnl f (trainer's rep said filly was unsuited by the Good to Soft, Soft in places going, which was subsequently changed to Soft, and would prefer a faster surface)* **11/8**[1]

1m 47.42s (5.72) **Going Correction** +0.325s/f (Good) **6** Ran SP% **109.1**
Speed ratings (Par 91): **84,82,81,78,75 74**
CSF £218.75 TOTE £17.30: £6.40, £3.30; EX 74.40 Trifecta £357.40.
Owner Riverside Racing Syndicate **Bred** Peter & Tony Hockenhull **Trained** Hambleton, N Yorks

FOCUS
Overnight rain eased the going to Good to soft, soft in places. A very modest fillies' nursery but the outsider scored and the form looks very ordinary.

5913 TOPSPORT EQUISAND NOVICE STKS (PLUS 10 RACE) 5f

2:20 (2:21) (Class 4) 2-Y-O

£6,469 (£1,925; £962; £481) Stalls Centre

Form RPR

652 1 **Balancing Act (IRE)**[25] 4984 2-9-0 73.......................... PJMcDonald 10 74+
(Jedd O'Keeffe) *chsd ldrs: pushed along 2f out: rdn to ld ins fnl f: kpt on* **13/8**[1]

2 3/4 **Sendacard** 2-8-11 0.......................... ConnorMurtagh(3) 3 71+
(Richard Fahey) *midfield: pushed along 2f out: rdn and kpt on fnl f: wnt 2nd towards fin* **20/1**

32 3 1 **Baltic State (IRE)**[14] 5388 2-9-5 0.......................... CliffordLee 9 73
(Kevin Ryan) *led: pushed along 2f out: drvn and edgd lft appr fnl f: hdd ins fnl f: continued to edgd lft: no ex and lost 2nd towards fin (colt ran without its right hind shoe)* **5/2**[2]

0 4 2 **Araifjan**[25] 4984 2-9-5 0.......................... DanielTudhope 11 66
(David O'Meara) *prom: pushed along and bit outpcd over 1f out: rdn and no ex ins fnl f* **16/1**

5 1 1/2 **Music Therapist (IRE)** 2-9-5 0.......................... ConnorBeasley 12 60
(George Scott) *dwlt: sn midfield: pushed along over 2f out: no imp (vet said gelding lost its right fore shoe)* **16/1**

342 6 shd **Kilham**[11] 5485 2-9-5 0.......................... DavidNolan 1 60
(Declan Carroll) *chsd ldrs: rdn along 2f out: wknd ins fnl f* **7/2**[3]

04 7 2 **Champagne Angel (IRE)**[8] 5590 2-9-0 0.......................... DuranFentiman 5 48+
(Tim Easterby) *s.i.s: hld up: nvr threatened* **66/1**

8 3 3/4 **The Grey Bay (IRE)** 2-9-5 0.......................... PaulMulrennan 8 39
(Julie Camacho) *dwlt: hld up: pushed along over 2f out: wknd over 1f out* **12/1**

1m 0.71s (1.31) **Going Correction** +0.325s/f (Good) **8** Ran SP% **114.6**
Speed ratings (Par 96): **102,100,99,96,93 93,90,84**
CSF £37.49 TOTE £2.30: £1.10, £4.60, £1.30; EX 37.70 Trifecta £131.60.
Owner John Dance **Bred** Lynn Lodge Stud **Trained** Middleham Moor, N Yorks

FOCUS
The going was changed to soft before this race. This was a fair looking juvenile novice although the field was reduced by a third due to withdrawals.

5914 PETER BELL MEMORIAL H'CAP 6f

2:50 (2:51) (Class 6) (0-60,62) 3-Y-O

£4,140 (£1,232; £615; £307; £300; £300) Stalls Centre

Form RPR

4040 1 **Jill Rose**[7] 5629 3-9-3 **56**..........................(b[1]) BarryMcHugh 14 67
(Richard Whitaker) *racd stands' side: mde all: rdn clr over 1f out: drvn out ins fnl f* **14/1**

-001 2 3 **Grimsdyke**[9] 5558 3-8-12 **51** 6ex.......................... DuranFentiman 6 53+
(Tim Easterby) *trckd ldrs centre: rdn to ld gp 1f out: r.o wl to draw clr in gp ins fnl f but no ch w wnr: 1st of 7 in gp* **4/1**[1]

6000 3 1 1/2 **Princess Palliser (IRE)**[3] 5767 3-9-6 **59**..........................(p) JasonHart 9 57
(John Quinn) *swtchd rt after 1f to r stands' side: sn chsd ldr: rdn and outplcd by wnr over 1f out: plugged on fnl f: 2nd of 8 in gp* **13/2**[3]

1166 4 3/4 **Lincoln Red**[30] 4807 3-9-4 **57**.......................... PaulMulrennan 15 52
(Olly Williams) *hld up stands' side: rdn and hdwy over 1f out: kpt on ins fnl f: 3rd of 8 in gp* **8/1**

5000 5 1/2 **The Thorny Rose**[42] 4328 3-8-13 **52**..........................(w) TomEaves 2 46+
(Michael Dods) *chsd ldr on outer of centre gp: rdn 2f out: kpt on ins fnl f: 2nd of 7 in gp* **16/1**

5005 6 2 3/4 **Saltie Girl**[20] 5202 3-8-13 **52**.......................... AndrewMullen 5 38+
(David Barron) *wnt lft ss: hld up centre: drvn and sme hdwy over 1f out: hung lft: plugged on ins fnl f: nvr threatened: 3rd of 7 in gp* **10/1**

3055 7 1 1/4 **House Deposit**[11] 5486 3-9-9 **62**.......................... JosephineGordon 16 44
(Roger Fell) *hld up stands' side: rdn 2f out: plugged on fnl f: nvr threatened: 4th of 8 in gp* **5/1**[2]

-030 8 1/2 **Highjacked**[70] 3292 3-8-10 **49**.......................... ConnorBeasley 11 29
(John Davies) *swtchd rt after 1f to r stands' side: sn in tch: rdn over 2f out: edgd lft and wknd fnl f: 5th of 8 in gp* **17/2**

3230 9 1/2 **Josiebond**[23] 5063 3-8-11 **53**.......................... RowanScott(3) 8 32+
(Rebecca Bastiman) *hld up centre: nvr threatened: 4th of 7 in gp* **8/1**

0-00 10 1/2 **Dixieland (IRE)**[18] 5235 3-9-7 **60**.......................... DanielTudhope 7 37+
(Marjorie Fife) *led centre gp: chsd ldr overall: rdn and hdd in gp over 1f out: sn wknd: 5th of 7 in gp* **33/1**

0-00 11 2 **Kyllachy Castle**[41] 4367 3-8-8 **47**.......................... CamHardie 4 18+
(Lynn Siddall) *s.i.s: a towards rr centre: 6th of 7 in gp (jockey said gelding hung left throughout)* **66/1**

4000 12 3 1/2 **Rangefield Express (IRE)**[3] 5771 3-9-1 **54**..........................(b) SamJames 12 15
(Geoffrey Harker) *swtchd rt after 1f to r stands' side: sn in tch: rdn over 2f out: wknd over 1f out: 6th of 8 in gp* **16/1**

500- 13 nk **Hey Jazzy Lady (IRE)**[317] 7666 3-9-0 **53**.......................... AndrewElliott 3 13+
(Andrew Crook) *chsd ldrs centre: rdn over 2f out: wknd over 1f out: last of 7 in gp* **66/1**

0000 14 1/2 **Wearraah**[9] 5554 3-8-5 **47** oh1 ow1..........................(b) ConnorMurtagh(3) 17 5
(Alan Brown) *chsd ldr stands' side: wknd 2f out: 7th of 8 in gp* **50/1**

063 15 2 **Dilly Dilly (IRE)**[34] 4629 3-8-6 **48** oh1 ow2.......................... ConorMcGovern(3) 10
(John Wainwright) *swtchd rt after s to r stands' side: hld up: racd keenly: wknd fnl 2f* **33/1**

1m 13.37s (0.57) **Going Correction** +0.325s/f (Good) **15** Ran SP% **121.1**
Speed ratings (Par 98): **109,105,103,102,101 97,96,95,94,94 91,86,86,85,82**
CSF £67.53 CT £420.63 TOTE £16.20: £4.60, £1.90, £2.60; EX 91.70 Trifecta £461.00.
Owner J W 's Wotafun Club **Bred** Hellwood Stud Farm & Mrs Jill Willows **Trained** Scarcroft, W Yorks

FOCUS
A low-grade but competitive looking 3yo sprint handicap in which they split into two groups and those racing stands' side had the advantage. The winner is rated back to her best.

5915 TOPSPORT EQUISAND H'CAP 1m 4f 8y

3:20 (3:21) (Class 6) (0-60,62) 3-Y-O

£4,075 (£1,212; £606; £303; £300; £300) Stalls High

Form RPR

3152 1 **Trouble Shooter (IRE)**[6] 5648 3-8-11 **48**..........................(v) JosephineGordon 1 55
(Shaun Keightley) *hld up in rr: rdn along over 4f out: hdwy on wd outside over 2f out: led ins fnl f: styd on* **4/1**[2]

5413 2 1 1/2 **Robeam (IRE)**[25] 4998 3-9-3 **54**..........................(p) DavidNolan 14 59
(Richard Fahey) *midfield: rdn along and hdwy 2f out: drvn to ld appr fnl f: sn edgd lft: hdd ins fnl f: one pce* **13/2**[3]

0005 3 1 1/4 **Somewhat Sisyphean**[38] 4487 3-8-7 **47** ow2.......................... RowanScott(3) 11 50
(Wilf Storey) *dwlt: hld up: rdn over 3f out: hdwy towards inner over 2f out: chal over 1f out: one pce fnl 110yds* **20/1**

6455 4 hd **Cuba Ruba**[24] 5023 3-9-7 **58**.......................... DuranFentiman 8 61
(Tim Easterby) *in tch: pushed along and hdwy over 2f out: rdn to chse ldrs over 1f out: styd on fnl f* **16/1**

-603 5 3/4 **Land Of Winter (FR)**[57] 3777 3-9-0 **51**.......................... ConnorBeasley 10 52+
(Rae Guest) *trckd ldrs: sltly hmpd on bnd over 8f out: rdn to ld over 2f out: edgd lft over 1f out: hdd appr fnl f: no ex fnl 75yds* **3/1**[1]

0025 6 7 **Ritchie Star (IRE)**[50] 4039 3-8-13 **57**.......................... HarryRussell(7) 2 48
(Ben Haslam) *midfield: rdn over 3f out: plugged on: nvr threatened* **25/1**

7 7 **Summer Glamour (IRE)**[26] 4958 3-8-6 **46** ow1(t[1]) ConorMcGovern(3) 13 26
(Adrian Paul Keatley, Ire) *rrd s and slowly away: hld up: rdn and sme hdwy over 2f out: wknd over 1f out* **16/1**

1432 8 5 **Myklachi (FR)**[13] 5425 3-9-11 **62**.......................... DanielTudhope 12 35
(David O'Meara) *hld up in midfield: sme hdwy on outer over 4f out: rdn 3f out: sn btn* **3/1**[1]

0-04 9 1 3/4 **Calevade (IRE)**[21] 5156 3-9-1 **52**.......................... AndrewMullen 6 22
(Ben Haslam) *hld up: dropped to rr over 4f out: sn bhd: plugged on past btn rivals fr over 1f out (jockey said gelding ran in snatches)* **20/1**

506 10 2 1/2 **Rodney After Dave (IRE)**[45] 4210 3-8-8 **45**.......................... CamHardie 7 12
(Marjorie Fife) *in tch: rdn over 3f out: wknd 2f out* **25/1**

0600 11 nk **Ateescomponent (IRE)**[25] 4990 3-9-4 **55**.......................... TomEaves 5 21
(David Barron) *led: hung rt on bnd over 8f out: rdn and hdd over 2f out: sn wknd* **33/1**

6-66 12 3/4 **Transpennine Gold**[59] 3680 3-9-6 **57**.......................... PaulMulrennan 4 22
(Michael Dods) *midfield: reminder over 6f out: rdn 4f out: sn btn* **40/1**

654 13 10 **Geyser**[50] 4039 3-8-5 **45**.......................... ConnorMurtagh(3) 3
(Barry Murtagh) *in tch: rdn over 3f out: wknd over 2f out* **40/1**

3000 14 10 **Kostantina**[6] 5648 3-8-3 **47**..........................(bt[1]) RhonaPindar(7) 9 +
(Olly Williams) *dwlt: hld up: hdwy on outer to go prom over 8f out: rdn over 3f out: sn wknd* **50/1**

2m 42.11s (2.11) **Going Correction** +0.325s/f (Good) **14** Ran SP% **122.1**
Speed ratings (Par 98): **106,105,104,104,103 98,94,90,89,88 87,87,80,74**
CSF £27.33 CT £477.76 TOTE £5.20: £1.60, £2.00, £6.20; EX 30.90 Trifecta £371.80.
Owner Simon Lockyer **Bred** Kildaragh Stud & M Downey **Trained** Newmarket, Suffolk

FOCUS
Another moderate but competitive 3yo handicap, this time over twice as far. They went a good gallop in the ground and it suited those held up.

5916 BRITISH EBF CONDITIONS STKS 7f

3:50 (3:50) (Class 3) 3-Y-O+

£9,703 (£2,887; £1,443; £721) Stalls Low

Form RPR

4060 1 **Three Saints Bay (IRE)**[27] 4921 4-9-4 98.......................... DavidNolan 2 105
(David O'Meara) *mde all: rdn 2f out: pressed briefly 1f out: sn edgd rt to stands' rail: kpt on wl* **9/1**

-220 2 1 1/4 **Dan's Dream**[51] 3986 4-8-13 103.......................... CallumShepherd 4 97
(Mick Channon) *in tch: pushed along and hdwy 2f out: rdn to chal 1f out: drvn and one pce* **5/4**[1]

0134 3 1 3/4 **Raydiance**[20] 5188 4-9-4 92.......................... CliffordLee 1 97
(K R Burke) *trckd ldr: rdn along 3f out: sn one pce* **9/2**[3]

/4P4 4 shd **Remarkable**[21] 5129 6-9-4 102..........................(b) DanielTudhope 5 97
(David O'Meara) *dwlt: hld up in tch: rdn along over 2f out: no imp: edgd lft fnl f* **2/1**[2]

0-60 5 3/4 **The Broghie Man**[56] 3818 4-9-4 96..........................(b) PaulMulrennan 3 95
(Adrian Paul Keatley, Ire) *hld up: rdn along over 2f out: no imp* **14/1**

1m 28.54s (0.94) **Going Correction** +0.325s/f (Good) **5** Ran SP% **112.6**
Speed ratings (Par 107): **107,105,103,103,102**
CSF £21.50 TOTE £9.40: £2.70, £1.40; EX 26.20 Trifecta £72.20.
Owner Gary Douglas **Bred** Epona Bloodstock Ltd **Trained** Upper Helmsley, N Yorks

FOCUS
The feature race and a race not far short of Listed standard, despite the small field. The winner made all but the form is difficult to quantify. The winner's rated pretty much to his best.

5917 WORLD OF JAMES HERRIOT NOVICE STKS 5f

4:20 (4:23) (Class 5) 3-Y-O+

£4,851 (£1,443; £721; £360)

Form RPR

-403 1 **Society Star**[7] 5603 3-8-11 61..........................(p[1]) CamHardie 5 64
(Robert Cowell) *mde all: kpt on pushed out fr over 1f out* **8/11**[1]

The Form Book Flat 2019, Raceform Ltd, Newbury, RG14 5SJ

0 **2** 1 ½ **Marvel**[162] 954 3-9-2 0.. PaulMulrennan 3 62
(Julie Camacho) *chsd ldr: rdn over 1f out: swtchd lft 1f out: kpt on same pce in 2nd fnl f* **13/2**[3]

325 **3** 4 ½ **War Ensign (IRE)**[9] 5559 4-9-5 51..........................(p) DuranFentiman 1 46
(Tim Easterby) *chsd ldr: rdn 2f out: wknd ins fnl f* **2/1**[2]

60 **4** 3 **Final Legacy**[48] 4129 3-8-4 0.. AledBeech(7) 2 30
(Derek Shaw) *s.i.s: hld up: hdwy and chsd ldr 2f out: rdn and hung lft over 1f out: wknd ins fnl f* **25/1**

00- **5** 21 **Thornton Katie**[442] 3003 3-8-8 0..........................(e1) ConnorMurtagh(3) 4
(Brian Rothwell) *hld up: wknd and bhd fnl 2f* **80/1**

1m 1.68s (2.28) **Going Correction** +0.325s/f (Good)
WFA 3 from 4yo 3lb **5** Ran SP% **109.7**
Speed ratings (Par 103): **94,91,84,79,46**
CSF £6.18 TOTE £1.50: £1.10, £2.40; EX 6.00 Trifecta £7.10.
Owner W Prosser **Bred** P Fitzsimons **Trained** Six Mile Bottom, Cambs

FOCUS
This very moderate novice was delayed by a thunderstorm and was then started by flag. The form is very ordinary, rated around the winner.

5918 GO RACING IN YORKSHIRE FUTURE STARS APPRENTICE MAIDEN H'CAP 6f
4:50 (4:55) (Class 5) (0-70,68) 4-Y-O+

£5,175 (£1,540; £769; £384; £300; £300) **Stalls** Centre

Form RPR

2003 **1** **Blindingly (GER)**[29] 4820 4-9-10 **68**..........................(p) HarryRussell(2) 7 76
(Ben Haslam) *mde all: rdn over 2f out: drvn over 1f out: strly pressed ins fnl f: hld on wl* **5/1**[2]

0-52 **2** shd **Radjash**[9] 5559 5-8-6 **52**..........................(t) ZakWheatley(4) 3 59
(Declan Carroll) *hld up: reminders over 2f out: pushed along and hdwy on outer over 1f out: chal ins fnl f: rdn 110yds out: kpt on but a jst hld* **6/5**[1]

6060 **3** 3 **Henrietta's Dream**[32] 4720 5-8-7 **49** oh4.......................... LauraCoughlan 2 46
(John Wainwright) *hld up: sn pushed along: kpt on ins fnl f: wnt 3rd fnl 50yds: no threat to ldng pair* **50/1**

0004 **4** ¾ **Caledonian Gold**[3] 5768 6-8-5 **49** oh4.......................... GavinAshton(2) 10 44
(Lisa Williamson) *chsd ldrs: rdn over 2f out: no ex ins fnl f: lost 3rd 50yds out* **11/1**

5535 **5** 3 **Dominannie (IRE)**[24] 5020 6-8-7 **49** oh3.......................... AledBeech 4 34
(Ron Barr) *dwlt: hld up: rdn over 2f out: plugged on ins fnl f: nvr threatened* **8/1**

4206 **6** 2 ¼ **Fard**[16] 5299 4-8-13 **57**.. RhonaPindar(2) 11 35
(Roger Fell) *prom: rdn over 2f out: wknd fnl f* **11/2**[3]

0050 **7** 2 **Alqaab**[20] 5202 4-9-1 **57**..........................(h) TobyEley 6 29
(Ruth Carr) *midfield: rdn over 2f out: wknd over 1f out (jockey said gelding was never travelling)* **11/1**

-000 **8** ½ **Bevsboy (IRE)**[34] 4630 5-8-7 **49** oh4.......................... Pierre-LouisJamin 5 19
(Lynn Siddall) *sn pushed along and a towards rr* **50/1**

0026 **9** 1 ¼ **Isabella Ruby**[21] 5130 4-8-3 **49** oh4..........................(h) KeelanBaker(4) 8 15
(Lisa Williamson) *chsd ldrs tl wknd 2f out* **20/1**

1m 16.42s (3.62) **Going Correction** +0.325s/f (Good) **9** Ran SP% **114.0**
Speed ratings (Par 103): **88,87,83,82,78 75,73,72,70**
CSF £11.04 CT £256.20 TOTE £5.40: £1.40, £1.20, £11.20; EX 13.30 Trifecta £441.90.
Owner Mrs C Barclay **Bred** Gestut Westerberg **Trained** Middleham Moor, N Yorks

FOCUS
A moderate apprentice maiden that was run 3.05secs slower than the earlier 3yo handicap over the distance, suggesting the rain had got into the ground. The form's rated around the runner-up.
T/Jkpt: Not Won. T/Plt: £188.50 to a £1 stake. Pool: £56,777.93. - 219.84 winning units. T/Qpdt: £11.00 to a £1 stake. Pool: £6,049.09. - 406.91 winning units. **Andrew Sheret**

5919 - 5921a (Foreign Racing) - See Raceform Interactive

5220 CURRAGH (R-H)
Friday, August 9

OFFICIAL GOING: Yielding to soft changing to soft after race 2 (5.45)

5922a KEENELAND PHOENIX STKS (GROUP 1) (ENTIRE COLTS & FILLIES) 6f
6:50 (6:53) 2-Y-O **£154,054** (£51,351; £24,324; £10,810; £5,405) **Stalls** Centre

RPR

1 **Siskin (USA)**[41] 4413 2-9-3 110.. ColinKeane 2 116
(G M Lyons, Ire) *cl up early tl sn settled bhd ldrs in 4th: swtchd rt after 1/2-way and hdwy far side gng wl 2f out: pushed along to ld over 1f out: rdn and strly pressed ins fnl f: kpt on wl to assert nr fin* **10/11**[1]

2 ¾ **Monarch Of Egypt (USA)**[41] 4413 2-9-3 0.......................... RyanMoore 5 114
(A P O'Brien, Ire) *trckd ldrs in 3rd: racd keenly: pushed along to chal nr side under 2f out: rdn and strly pressed wnr almost on terms ins fnl f: kpt on wl wout matching wnr nr fin* **6/4**[2]

3 hd **Royal Lytham (FR)**[29] 4846 2-9-3 106.......................... DonnachaO'Brien 3 113
(A P O'Brien, Ire) *led: pressed clly 2f out and pushed along: hdd over 1f out and sn dropped to 3rd: n.m.r briefly and swtchd rt wl ins fnl f and rdn: kpt on wl nr fin: rdr reported sddle slipped leaving stalls (jockey said that his saddle slipped leaving the stalls)* **9/2**[3]

4 7 **Mount Fuji (IRE)**[20] 5206 2-9-3 95.......................... SeamieHeffernan 1 92
(A P O'Brien, Ire) *uns rdr and rn loose bef s: dwlt sltly and pushed along briefly to sn trck ldr in 2nd: drvn over 2f out and sn no imp on ldrs in 4th 1 1/2f out: wknd* **25/1**

5 2 ¼ **Think Big (IRE)**[14] 5400 2-9-3 89.......................... RobbieColgan 4 85
(John Joseph Murphy, Ire) *in rr thrght: pushed along under 2f out and no imp on ldrs ins fnl f where rdn: wknd* **50/1**

1m 17.14s (2.94) **Going Correction** +0.75s/f (Yiel) **5** Ran SP% **116.4**
Speed ratings: **110,109,108,99,96**
CSF £2.78 TOTE £1.70: £1.02, £1.20; DF 2.60 Trifecta £3.70.
Owner K Abdullah **Bred** Juddmonte Farms Inc **Trained** Dunsany, Co Meath

FOCUS
A first domestic success for Ger Lyons and Colin Keane with a horse who confirmed himself the real deal with an awesome performance. He was trimmed into odds of 10-1 for next year's 2,000 Guineas and, on this evidence, he'll get further in future. The front three emerged with real credit but the winner could be something special.

5923a QATAR RACING AND EQUESTRIAN CLUB PHOENIX SPRINT STKS (GROUP 3) 6f
7:25 (7:25) 3-Y-O+

£31,891 (£10,270; £4,864; £2,162; £1,081; £540) **Stalls** Centre

RPR

1 **Gustavus Weston (IRE)**[20] 5205 3-9-3 98.......................... GaryCarroll 5 111
(Joseph G Murphy, Ire) *trckd ldrs in 3rd: tk clsr order nr side 1 1/2f out: rdn to ld over 1f out: strly pressed u.p wl ins fnl f: hld on wl* **16/1**

2 nk **Woody Creek**[16] 5325 3-9-0 98.......................... ChrisHayes 6 107+
(J A Stack, Ire) *settled in rr early: 7th 1/2-way: gng wl bhd horses under 2f out: sn pushed along and prog over 1f out: rdn in 2nd and strly pressed wnr wl ins fnl f: kpt on wl nr fin: jst hld* **7/1**[3]

3 2 ½ **Gordon Lord Byron (IRE)**[20] 5207 11-9-7 106.......................... WJLee 1 103
(T Hogan, Ire) *broke wl to ld narrowly: pushed along and jnd under 2f out: sn rdn and hdd over 1f out: dropped to dispute 4th briefly ins fnl f and no imp on ldrs tl kpt on again into 3rd nr fin* **11/1**

4 ½ **Beckford**[41] 4409 4-9-7 105.......................... DonnachaO'Brien 7 101
(Gordon Elliott, Ire) *w.w in 6th early: gng wl bhd horses over 2f out: sn pushed along and tk clsr order over 1f out where swtchd rt: rdn to dispute 3rd briefly and no imp on ldrs: kpt on same pce* **15/8**[1]

5 nk **Buffer Zone**[20] 5205 4-9-7 99.......................... ColinKeane 8 100
(G M Lyons, Ire) *hld up bhd ldrs in 5th: tk clsr order nr side over 2f out: sn pushed along and rdn 1 1/2f out: no ex ins fnl f and one pce clsng stages* **7/2**[2]

6 2 **Servalan (IRE)**[16] 5325 3-9-0 99.......................... ShaneFoley 3 90
(Mrs John Harrington, Ire) *hld up towards rr: 8th 1/2-way: pushed along over 2f out and sme hdwy far side 1 1/2f out: sltly impeded ent fnl f and sn no imp on ldrs: eased in 6th nr fin (jockey said that his mount lost its action at about half way)* **7/1**[3]

7 1 ¼ **Southern Horse (ARG)**[41] 4409 4-9-7 102..........(p1) KevinManning 4 90
(J S Bolger, Ire) *trckd ldrs in 4th: pushed along and prog far side 2f out to dispute ld briefly over 1f out tl sn hdd u.p: wknd and eased ins fnl f* **7/1**[3]

8 2 ¾ **Angelic Light (IRE)**[91] 2605 3-9-0 93..........................(tp) LeighRoche 2 77
(M D O'Callaghan, Ire) *cl up bhd ldr: cl 2nd at 1/2-way: drvn and disp ld briefly under 2f out tl hdd over 1f out: wknd qckly into 8th ins fnl f and eased* **25/1**

9 6 ½ **San Andreas (IRE)**[20] 5207 3-9-3 93..........................(b1) RyanMoore 9 59
(A P O'Brien, Ire) *hld up towards rr early: last at 1/2-way: drvn in rr over 2f out and no ex u.p 1 1/2f out: wknd and eased ins fnl f* **18/1**

1m 15.42s (1.22) **Going Correction** +0.75s/f (Yiel)
WFA 3 from 4yo+ 4lb **9** Ran SP% **117.8**
Speed ratings: **115,114,111,110,110 107,105,102,93**
CSF £125.32 TOTE £18.00: £3.80, £2.00, £2.70; DF 95.10 Trifecta £402.20.
Owner Alfred Sweetnam **Bred** M Orlandi & J Harrod **Trained** Fethard, Co Tipperary

FOCUS
A purely domestic affair dominated by a pair of 98-trained runners, a gelding and a filly, from the Classic generation. Ability to handle soft ground was crucial. The fifth helps set the level.

5924 - 5925a (Foreign Racing) - See Raceform Interactive

5759 CLAIREFONTAINE (R-H)
Friday, August 9

OFFICIAL GOING: Turf: good to soft

5926a PRIX DEFI DU GALOP - ETALON RECORDER - HARAS DE MONTFORT ET PREAUX (LISTED RACE) (4YO+) (TURF) 1m 1f
3:05 4-Y-O+ **£23,423** (£9,369; £7,027; £4,684; £2,342)

RPR

1 **Dolphin Vista (IRE)**[20] 5182 6-9-2 0.......................... ChristopheSoumillon 6 106
(Ralph Beckett) *uns rdr and rn loose gng to post: sat on ldr's quarters: pushed along to chal leaving fnl bnd: led narrowly 2f out: styd on wl: asserted last 150yds* **32/5**

2 ¾ **Stunning Spirit**[55] 3879 5-9-2 0.......................... AurelienLemaitre 7 105
(F Head, France) **17/10**[1]

3 ¾ **Rolando (IRE)**[48] 4140 5-9-4 0.......................... MaximeGuyon 3 105
(A Wohler, Germany) **12/5**[2]

4 snk **Bubble And Squeak**[9] 5545 4-8-9 0.......................... AlexisBadel 4 96
(Sylvester Kirk) *settled in fnl trio on inner: tk clsr order over 2f out: styd on u.p: nt pce to get on terms* **22/1**

5 ¾ **Apollo Flight (FR)**[26] 4-8-13 0.......................... TheoBachelot 2 98
(L Gadbin, France) **78/10**

6 ½ **Ficelle Du Houley (FR)**[12] 4-8-9 0.......................... JeromeCabre 5 93
(Y Barberot, France) **11/1**

7 3 **Aubevoye (FR)**[26] 4-8-13 0.......................... CristianDemuro 1 91
(J-C Rouget, France) **54/10**[3]

1m 50.8s **7** Ran SP% **119.6**
PARI-MUTUEL (all including 1 euro stake): WIN 7.40; PLACE 2.70, 1.50; SF 27.30.
Owner Y Nasib **Bred** Jim McDonald **Trained** Kimpton, Hants

5411 ASCOT (R-H)
Saturday, August 10

OFFICIAL GOING: Good (good to firm in places; str 8.2, rnd 7.5)
Wind: Strong, half against in home straight Weather: Fine but cloudy, showers between races 3 and 4.

5927 DUBAI DUTY FREE SHERGAR CUP DASH (H'CAP) 5f
1:05 (1:06) (Class 2) (0-105,105) 3-Y-O+

£29,508 (£10,332; £4,722; £3,684; £3,246; £2,364) **Stalls** High

Form RPR

0060 **1** **Stone Of Destiny**[7] 5664 4-9-4 **97**.......................... FilipMinarik 1 103
(Andrew Balding) *t.k.h: hld up in last pair: prog on outer 2f out: clsd on ldng pair fnl f: r.o to ld last stride* **11/2**[2]

-222 **2** *nse* **Final Venture**[53] 3956 7-9-10 **103**.......................... JamieKah 12 109
(Paul Midgley) *mounted on crse and taken down early: wl away: led and racd against nr side rail: hrd pressed fnl f: kpt on wl but hdd last strides* **7/1**[3]

-131 **3** *shd* **Danzeno**[35] 4648 8-9-12 **105**.......................... GeraldMosse 5 111
(Michael Appleby) *dwlt: sn wl in tch: prog to press ldr wl over 1f out: str chal and upsides fnl f: nt qckn last strides* **13/8**[1]

2010 **4** *nk* **Recon Mission (IRE)**[21] 5184 3-9-8 **104**.......................... TadhgO'Shea 4 108
(Tony Carroll) *chsd ldng pair to 2f out: remained cl up: rdn and styd on fnl f: jst unable to chal* **9/1**

3101 **5** *2 3/4* **Corinthia Knight (IRE)**[22] 5154 4-9-10 **103**.......................... AdriedeVries 11 98
(Archie Watson) *towards rr: rdn 2f out: kpt on to take 5th ins fnl f: no imp on ldrs* **10/1**

0-04 **6** *1* **Lancelot Du Lac (ITY)**[170] 837 9-9-6 **99**..........................(h) HayleyTurner 8 90
(Dean Ivory) *hld up towards rr: rdn over 1f out: one pce and no imp on ldrs* **18/1**

0345 **7** *3/4* **Caspian Prince (IRE)**[20] 5222 10-9-12 **105**..........................(t) YugaKawada 7 93
(Michael Appleby) *s.s: racd in last: swtchd rt and rdn over 1f out: kpt on same pce and n.d (jockey said gelding anticipated the start and missed the break)* **9/1**

3020 **8** *nk* **Foolaad**[43] 4331 8-9-3 **99**..........................(t) NanakoFujita(3) 2 86
(Roy Bowring) *taken down early: chsd ldr to wl over 1f out: steadily wknd* **14/1**

3020 **9** *2 1/4* **Encore D'Or**[15] 5371 7-9-7 **100**.......................... DanielTudhope 3 79
(Robert Cowell) *chsd ldrs to 1/2-way: sn lost pl u.p* **14/1**

0200 **10** *shd* **Street Parade**[12] 5504 3-9-4 **100**..........................(t) CYHo 6 78
(Stuart Williams) *chsd ldrs to 1/2-way: wknd u.p* **18/1**

1m 0.74s (0.04) **Going Correction** +0.225s/f (Good) **10 Ran SP% 118.9**
WFA 3 from 4yo+ 3lb
Speed ratings (Par 109): **108,107,107,107,102 101,100,99,96,95**
CSF £44.74 CT £93.55 TOTE £6.00: £1.90, £2.10, £1.20; EX 41.40 Trifecta £129.90.
Owner King Power Racing Co Ltd **Bred** Biddestone Stud **Trained** Kingsclere, Hants
■ Stewards' Enquiry : Gerald Mosse caution; careless riding
Jamie Kah two-day ban; misuse of whip (Aug 13, 25)
Tadhg O'Shea one-day ban; failure to ride from draw (Aug 19)

FOCUS
As always with this novelty event the form of the races needs treating with caution. Adrie De Vries reported the ground to be riding on the 'firm side'. Often a competitive sprint, it looked more open than the betting suggested and duly produced a cracking finish, with three of them involved in a photo and the fourth just a neck further back. They raced stands' side. Straightforward form, rated around the second and third.

5928 DUBAI DUTY FREE SHERGAR CUP STAYERS (H'CAP) 1m 7f 209y

1:40 (1:40) (Class 2) (0-100,99) 4-Y-O+
£29,508 (£10,332; £4,722; £3,684; £3,246; £2,364) **Stalls** Low

Form RPR

1350 **1** **Eddystone Rock (IRE)**[29] 4884 7-9-6 **91**.......................... HayleyTurner 6 100
(John Best) *stdd s: hld up but in tch: briefly dropped to rr 5f out: smooth prog over 2f out: shkn up to ld over 1f out: styd on stoutly* **13/2**

005 **2** *2 1/4* **Theglasgowwarrior**[42] 4381 5-9-5 **90**.......................... MarkZahra 7 96
(Jim Goldie) *sn hld up towards rr: prog over 2f out: rdn to chse wnr over 1f out: styd on but no imp fnl f* **12/1**

2400 **3** *2 3/4* **What A Welcome**[7] 5662 5-9-13 **98**.......................... FilipMinarik 8 101
(Patrick Chamings) *t.k.h: hld up in tch: plld way through to chse ldng pair 7f out: tried to chal 2f out: kpt on one pce over 1f out* **4/1**[2]

5053 **4** *1 1/2* **Grandee (IRE)**[14] 5457 5-9-4 **89**.......................... YugaKawada 4 90
(Roger Fell) *mostly trckd ldrs: cl up and waiting for a gap 2f out: rdn and kpt on same pce over 1f out* **6/1**

4600 **5** *2* **Aircraft Carrier (IRE)**[42] 4382 4-10-0 **99**..........................(v) TadhgO'Shea 5 98
(John Ryan) *hld up in tch: effrt on inner over 2f out: one pce and no ch w ldrs over 1f out* **16/1**

0020 **6** *nse* **Al Kout**[21] 5183 5-9-0 **85**..........................(h) GeraldMosse 12 83
(Heather Main) *t.k.h: trckd ldr: led wl over 2f out to over 1f out: wknd fnl f* **22/1**

4504 **7** *2 3/4* **Lorelina**[22] 5133 6-9-7 **92**.......................... JamieKah 1 87
(Andrew Balding) *prom: rdn over 2f out: steadily wknd* **12/1**

2503 **8** *1 3/4* **Blue Laureate**[15] 5368 4-9-0 **88**.......................... NanakoFujita(3) 3 81
(Ian Williams) *hld up in detached last: same pl and rdr looking down fr 3f out: shkn up and racd awkwardly over 2f out: nvr in it* **11/2**[3]

52 **9** *7* **Billy Ray**[21] 5183 4-9-7 **92**.......................... DanielTudhope 11 77
(Mick Channon) *hld up in 9th: shkn up and no prog 3f out: wknd over 1f out (trainer said colt would prefer an easier surface)* **11/4**[1]

15-4 **10** *137* **Alfredo (IRE)**[208] 238 7-9-8 **93**..........................(tp) JamieSpencer 10
(Seamus Durack) *awkward s but sn led: pushed along and hdd wl over 2f out: heavily eased 2f out: t.o (jockey said gelding moved poorly in the home straight. Trainer said gelding was unsuited by the ground and would prefer an easier surface)* **16/1**

3m 31.83s (-1.47) **Going Correction** +0.225s/f (Good) **10 Ran SP% 121.2**
Speed ratings (Par 109): **112,110,109,108,107 107,106,105,101,**
CSF £84.73 CT £358.06 TOTE £8.10: £2.30, £3.40, £1.70; EX 88.20 Trifecta £680.60.
Owner Curtis, Malt & Williams **Bred** Ballygallon Stud Limited **Trained** Oad Street, Kent

FOCUS
Distance increased by 16yds. A useful staying handicap that was run at a good gallop and it set up for the closers. The second has been rated to form.

5929 DUBAI DUTY FREE SHERGAR CUP CHALLENGE (H'CAP) 1m 3f 211y

2:15 (2:16) (Class 3) (0-95,95) 4-Y-O+
£29,508 (£10,332; £4,722; £3,684; £3,246; £2,364) **Stalls** Low

Form RPR

2604 **1** **Indianapolis (IRE)**[35] 4646 4-9-7 **95**..........................(p[1]) MarkZahra 10 102
(James Given) *hld up in last trio: rdn over 2f out: prog on outer over 1f out: styd on wl fnl f to ld last strides* **7/1**[3]

-504 **2** *1/2* **Genetics (FR)**[42] 4418 5-9-4 **92**.......................... CYHo 6 98+
(Andrew Balding) *led and clr: 6 l ahd 1/2-way: c bk to rivals over 3f out: kicked on again over 2f out: looked like holding on but collared last strides* **7/1**[3]

2211 **3** *nse* **Mandarin (GER)**[8] 5625 5-9-4 **92**.......................... FilipMinarik 11 98
(Ian Williams) *hld up in last pair: rdn over 2f out: stl only 9th over 1f out: styd on wl fnl f to take 3rd last strides* **7/2**[1]

3200 **4** *1/2* **Koeman**[21] 5199 5-9-3 **94**.......................... NanakoFujita(3) 9 99
(Mick Channon) *hld up in midfield: prog 4f out: rdn 2f out: chsd ldr 1f out: styd on but lost 2 pls nr fin* **12/1**

4000 **5** *1 1/4* **Restorer**[28] 4935 7-9-7 **95**.......................... AdriedeVries 4 98
(Ian Williams) *trckd ldrs: shkn up jst over 2f out: nt qckn over 1f out: styd on same pce fnl f* **14/1**

3233 **6** *nk* **Hyanna**[15] 5370 4-9-2 **90**.......................... TadhgO'Shea 8 93
(Eve Johnson Houghton) *hld up in 7th: effrt whn nt clr run 2f out and again over 1f out: styd on but no ch to threaten* **8/1**

256 **7** *2* **Big Kitten (USA)**[28] 4935 4-9-6 **94**.......................... YugaKawada 5 93
(William Haggas) *trckd clr ldr: rdn 2f out: lost 2nd and wknd 1f out* **6/1**[2]

-300 **8** *1 3/4* **Reshoun (FR)**[21] 5183 5-9-7 **95**..........................(p) JamieSpencer 2 92
(Ian Williams) *slow to get gng and reminder: mostly in last pair: rdn and no prog over 2f out (trainers' rep said gelding was unsuited by the ground and would prefer an easier surface)* **10/1**

-000 **9** *1 1/2* **Melting Dew**[35] 4646 5-9-6 **94**..........................(p) HayleyTurner 3 88
(Sir Michael Stoute) *trckd ldng pair: disp 2nd pl 4f out to jst over 2f out: hrd rdn and wknd* **7/1**[3]

5110 **10** *6* **Badenscoth**[36] 4613 5-9-5 **93**.......................... DanielTudhope 12 78
(Dean Ivory) *trckd ldrs: rdn over 2f out: no prog over 1f out: wknd rapidly fnl f (vet said gelding lost it's right hind shoe)* **10/1**

2m 33.4s (0.80) **Going Correction** +0.225s/f (Good) **10 Ran SP% 117.7**
Speed ratings (Par 107): **106,105,105,105,104 104,102,101,100,96**
CSF £55.82 CT £202.57 TOTE £8.10: £2.30, £2.60, £1.60; EX 77.60 Trifecta £395.60.
Owner Alex Owen **Bred** Smithfield Inc **Trained** Willoughton, Lincs
■ Stewards' Enquiry : Mark Zahra two-day ban; misuse of whip (Aug 13, 25)

FOCUS
Distance increased by 13yds. They got racing a long way out in this good-quality handicap and the first and third came from the rear. The winner has been rated to his best.

5930 DUBAI DUTY FREE SHERGAR CUP MILE (H'CAP) 7f 213y(R)

2:50 (2:53) (Class 2) (0-100,100) 4-Y-O+
£29,508 (£10,332; £4,722; £3,684; £3,246; £2,364) **Stalls** Low

Form RPR

-201 **1** **Power Of Darkness**[45] 4255 4-9-7 **94**.......................... CYHo 2 105+
(Marcus Tregoning) *hld up in last trio: prog 2f out: swtchd lft to chse ldrs over 1f out: drvn and r.o to ld last 100yds: sn in command* **11/4**[1]

0500 **2** *1* **Zhui Feng (IRE)**[8] 5610 6-9-10 **97**.......................... GeraldMosse 11 104
(Amanda Perrett) *hld up but prom in chsng gp: clsd over 2f out: drvn into narrow ld over 1f out: styd on but hdd and outpcd last 100yds* **15/2**[3]

0400 **3** *nk* **Zwayyan**[52] 3987 6-9-11 **98**..........................(b) YugaKawada 3 104
(Andrew Balding) *hld up but prom in chsng gp: clsd over 2f out: drvn to chal over 1f out: pressed ldr after tl 100yds out: kpt on* **9/1**

1211 **4** *1 1/2* **Nicholas T**[12] 5489 7-9-9 **96**.......................... JamieSpencer 8 99
(Jim Goldie) *awkward s: hld up in last: shkn up over 2f out: prog on inner over 1f out: drvn and styd on to take 4th nr fin: no ch to chal* **15/2**[3]

0560 **5** *3/4* **War Glory (IRE)**[8] 5610 6-9-9 **96**.......................... FilipMinarik 4 97
(Richard Hannon) *hld up in rr: prog 2f out: rdn and styd on same pce over 1f out* **14/1**

0166 **6** *3/4* **Via Serendipity**[21] 5192 5-9-8 **95**..........................(t) TadhgO'Shea 6 94
(Stuart Williams) *pressed ldr at str pce and clr of rest: led over 2f out: hdd over 1f out: fdd* **5/1**[2]

10 **7** *4* **Breden (IRE)**[35] 4666 9-9-13 **100**.......................... MarkZahra 7 90
(Linda Jewell) *hld up towards rr: effrt over 2f out: no prog over 1f out: wknd fnl f* **25/1**

5600 **8** *1* **Original Choice (IRE)**[8] 5610 5-9-10 **97**.......................... AdriedeVries 10 85
(Nick Littmoden) *sn in midfield: rdn and no prog whn n.m.r over 1f out: wknd* **12/1**

6000 **9** *1/2* **Another Batt (IRE)**[14] 5413 4-9-13 **100**.......................... JamieKah 1 86
(Richard Hughes) *chsd ldng pair to over 2f out: wkng whn impeded over 1f out (vet said gelding had been struck into on it's right fore)* **5/1**[2]

2100 **10** *1 1/4* **Waarif (IRE)**[22] 5155 6-9-7 **97**.......................... NanakoFujita(3) 5 81
(David O'Meara) *led at str pce: hdd over 2f out: sn btn* **12/1**

1m 42.11s (1.51) **Going Correction** +0.225s/f (Good) **10 Ran SP% 119.4**
Speed ratings (Par 109): **101,100,99,98,97 96,92,91,91,89**
CSF £24.52 CT £171.48 TOTE £3.50: £1.60, £2.70, £3.10; EX 28.80 Trifecta £206.30.
Owner R C C Villers **Bred** Mrs C R Philipson & Lofts Hall Stud **Trained** Whitsbury, Hants

FOCUS
Distance increased by 5yds. No hanging around here, with them going a right good gallop, and the pace predictably failed to hold up. The second and third set the level.

5931 DUBAI DUTY FREE SHERGAR CUP CLASSIC (H'CAP) 1m 3f 211y

3:25 (3:26) (Class 3) (0-95,95) 3-Y-O
£29,508 (£10,332; £4,722; £3,684; £3,246; £2,364) **Stalls** Low

Form RPR

2132 **1** **Sapa Inca (IRE)**[8] 5614 3-9-5 **86**.......................... HayleyTurner 9 96+
(Mark Johnston) *hld up off the pce in midfield: clsd over 3f out: rdn and prog over 2f out: chsd ldr wl over 1f out: drvn ahd 1f out: edgd rt fnl 100yds but hld on wl* **4/1**[1]

3213 **2** *3/4* **Never Do Nothing (IRE)**[28] 4901 3-9-8 **89**.......................... MarkZahra 7 97
(Andrew Balding) *reluctant to enter stall: hld up in last pair and off the pce: rdn and prog jst over 2f out: chsd wnr ins fnl f: styd on but hld whn impeded last strides* **9/2**[2]

333 **3** *1 1/2* **Aspire Tower (IRE)**[22] 5121 3-9-5 **86**.......................... CYHo 8 91
(Steve Gollings) *chsd ldrs in 5th: rdn over 2f out: kpt on u.p fnl f to take 3rd last strides* **11/1**

10 **4** *hd* **Yellow Tiger (FR)**[8] 5614 3-9-1 **82**..........................(p) JamieKah 4 87
(Ian Williams) *chsd clr ldng pair: clsd 3f out: shkn up to ld jst over 2f out: hdd 1f out: fdd last 100yds* **20/1**

3631 **5** *nk* **Zuba**[5] 5734 3-8-10 **80** 3ex.......................... NanakoFujita(3) 12 85
(Amanda Perrett) *hld up in last trio: stl there whn effrt on outer 2f out: styd on over 1f out: nvr nrr* **13/2**

3420 **6** *shd* **Asian Angel (IRE)**[8] 5614 3-9-4 **85**.......................... JamieSpencer 11 89
(Mark Johnston) *rousted to get gng and racd in last: prog 2f out: drvn and kpt on over 1f out but nvr able to threaten* **7/1**

2532 **7** *3/4* **Vivid Diamond (IRE)**[14] 5417 3-9-12 **93**.......................... TadhgO'Shea 10 96
(Mark Johnston) *chsd ldrs in 6th: rdn over 2f out: cl up over 1f out: one pce after* **6/1**[3]

-340 **8** *3 1/2* **Boerhan**[30] 4845 3-10-0 **95**.......................... DanielTudhope 3 93+
(William Haggas) *mde most at str pce: hdd jst over 2f out: wknd over 1f out* **9/2**[2]

5124 **9** *14* **Sophosc (IRE)**[16] 5341 3-9-3 **84**.......................... AdriedeVries 5 59
(Joseph Tuite) *w ldr at str pce: wknd qckly over 2f out* **16/1**

2136 **10** *10* **Amber Spark (IRE)**[14] 5458 3-9-1 **82**.......................... GeraldMosse 1 41
(Richard Fahey) *chsd ldng trio to 3f out: wknd rapidly 2f out: t.o (jockey said filly had no more to give)* **22/1**

2m 32.57s (-0.03) **Going Correction** +0.225s/f (Good) **10 Ran SP% 119.8**
Speed ratings (Par 104): **109,108,107,107,107 107,106,104,94,88**
CSF £22.61 CT £187.17 TOTE £4.40: £1.80, £1.60, £3.70; EX 14.40 Trifecta £46.90.
Owner China Horse Club International Limited **Bred** Desert Star Phoenix Jvc **Trained** Middleham Moor, N Yorks

FOCUS
Distance increased by 13yds. Another race run at a strong gallop and four of the first five home raced in the second half of the field in the early stages. It's been rated on the positive side, with the third running as well as ever and the fifth to his latest AW win.

5932 DUBAI DUTY FREE SHERGAR CUP SPRINT (H'CAP) 6f
4:00 (4:01) (Class 2) (0-100,99) 3-Y-O

£29,508 (£10,332; £4,722; £3,684; £3,246; £2,364) **Stalls** High

Form RPR
4-12 **1** **Victory Day (IRE)**[56] 3865 3-9-11 **96**........................ JamieSpencer 12 106+
(William Haggas) *hld up in last: rapid prog wl over 1f out towards nr side: drvn to ld last 150yds: styd on wl* **7/4**[1]
0112 **2** *1* **Pass The Vino (IRE)**[14] 5442 3-9-10 **95**........................ HayleyTurner 2 101
(Paul D'Arcy) *hld up bhd ldrs: rdn 2f out: clsd over 1f out: drvn to ld briefly jst ins fnl f: styd on but outpcd last 100yds* **9/2**[3]
420 **3** *1* **Woven**[30] 4847 3-9-7 **92**........................ YugaKawada 10 95
(David Simcock) *hld up in rr: shkn up and prog over 1f out: styd on fnl f to take 3rd nr fin but nt pce to chal* **25/1**
0301 **4** *nk* **Kinks**[14] 5442 3-9-9 **94**........................ AdriedeVries 1 96
(Mick Channon) *stdd s: hld up in rr: prog on outer 2f out: rdn and styd on same pce over 1f out: nvr able to chal (vet said gelding lost it's left fore shoe)* **10/1**
6002 **5** *hd* **Jack's Point**[7] 5666 3-9-9 **94**........................ GeraldMosse 11 95
(William Muir) *trckd ldr: rdn to ld jst over 1f out to jst ins fnl f: one pce after* **11/1**
0055 **6** *½* **Barbill (IRE)**[21] 5184 3-9-13 **98**........................ MarkZahra 8 98
(Mick Channon) *hld up in rr: prog on outer 2f out: rdn over 1f out: kpt on same pce fnl f* **10/1**
3200 **7** *2* **Magical Wish (IRE)**[6] 5711 3-9-12 **97**........................ CYHo 5 90
(Richard Hannon) *chsd ldrs: lost pl u.p wl over 1f out: n.d after* **12/1**
-310 **8** *1 ¾* **Hero Hero (IRE)**[51] 4016 3-9-9 **94**........................ DanielTudhope 3 82
(Andrew Balding) *chsd ldr to wl over 1f out: wknd u.p* **4/1**[2]
0-02 **9** *nk* **Junius Brutus (FR)**[41] 4422 3-9-13 **98**........................ JamieKah 4 85
(Ralph Beckett) *fast away: led: hdd & wknd jst over 1f out* **20/1**
0250 **10** *2 ¼* **The Cruising Lord**[15] 5371 3-10-0 **99**........................ FilipMinarik 7 79
(Michael Attwater) *prom tl wknd 2f out* **25/1**

1m 14.44s (0.74) **Going Correction** +0.225s/f (Good) **10 Ran SP% 121.2**
Speed ratings (Par 106): **104,102,101,100,100 100,97,95,94,91**
CSF £9.71 CT £147.67 TOTE £2.40: £1.30, £1.50, £7.70; EX 10.90 Trifecta £296.10.
Owner Clipper Logistics **Bred** J Hanly **Trained** Newmarket, Suffolk

FOCUS
Back to the straight course and, continuing the theme of the day, the hold-up horses came to the fore. Smart sprint form, with the form horses coming to the fore. The third and fourth have been rated to form.
T/Jkpt: Not won. T/Plt: £37.50 to a £1 stake. Pool: £158,861.23 - 3,085.01 winning units T/Qpdt: £7.20 to a £1 stake. Pool: £13,615.96 - 1,385.29 winning units **Jonathan Neesom**

5485 AYR (L-H)
Saturday, August 10

OFFICIAL GOING: Heavy (6.3)
Wind: Breezy, half against in sprints and in over 3f of home straight in races on the round course Weather: Cloudy, bright

5933 FUNKIN COCKTAILS LADY RIDERS' H'CAP (FOR PROFESSIONAL AND AMATEUR LADY RIDERS) 1m
5:20 (5:21) (Class 6) (0-65,65) 4-Y-O+

£2,781 (£827; £413; £400; £400; £400) **Stalls** Low

Form RPR
3213 **1** **Retirement Beckons**[19] 5238 4-9-6 **50**........................(h) RhonaPindar 5 57
(Linda Perratt) *in tch in chsng gp: hdwy over 2f out: sustained run fnl f to ld towards fin* **5/1**[3]
1622 **2** *nk* **Be Bold**[3] 5816 7-9-8 **52**........................(b) MissSerenaBrotherton 10 58
(Rebecca Bastiman) *trckd ldrs: effrt on outside and jnd ldr over 2f out: led ins fnl f: hdd and no ex towards fin* **10/3**[2]
5453 **3** *¾* **Equidae**[12] 5490 4-10-7 **65**........................(t) PaulaMuir 4 69
(Iain Jardine) *t.k.h early: led at reasonable gallop: rdn on outside and hrd pressed over 2f out: hdd ins fnl f: kpt on same pce* **3/1**[1]
0101 **4** *2 ¼* **Spirit Of Sarwan (IRE)**[28] 4915 5-10-7 **65**........................(v[1]) MeganNicholls 7 64
(Stef Keniry) *slowly away: bhd: pushed along 3f out: hdwy 2f out: kpt on fnl f: nt rch ldrs (jockey said gelding was slowly away)* **7/1**
0005 **5** *3* **Dark Crystal**[19] 5237 8-9-2 **46** oh1........................ MissAlysonDeniel 8 39
(Linda Perratt) *prom chsng gp: pushed along and outpcd over 2f out: rallied fnl f: no imp* **22/1**
035 **6** *½* **Blue Whisper**[23] 5099 4-9-6 **50**........................(tp) MrsCarolBartley 9 42
(S Donohoe, Ire) *s.i.s: hld up: rdn along over 2f out: kpt on fnl f: nrst fin* **12/1**
533/ **7** *1 ½* **Feeling Easy (IRE)**[15] 5405 7-8-13 **46** oh1........(b[1]) SiobhanRutledge(3) 2 34
(R K Watson, Ire) *t.k.h: pressed ldr to over 3f out: prom tl wknd over 1f out* **10/1**
0504 **8** *hd* **Doon Star**[19] 5239 4-9-0 **47**........................ MissShannonWatts(3) 6 35
(Jim Goldie) *prom in chsng gp: drvn and outpcd over 2f out: n.d after* **7/1**
3100 **9** *shd* **Pudding Chare (IRE)**[12] 5490 5-10-6 **64**........................(t) FayeMcManoman 3 52
(R Mike Smith) *prom in chsng gp: drvn and struggling over 2f out: sn btn (trainers' rep said gelding was unsuited by the Heavy ground and would prefer a faster surface)* **12/1**
P-00 **10** *3 ¼* **Indie Groove (IRE)**[50] 4054 4-8-13 **46** oh1........................ MorganCole(3) 1 27
(Linda Perratt) *slowly away: bhd: struggling 3f out: nvr on terms* **80/1**

1m 47.56s (4.76) **Going Correction** +0.625s/f (Yiel) **10 Ran SP% 119.8**
Speed ratings (Par 101): **101,100,99,97,94 94,92,92,92,89**
CSF £22.72 CT £61.22 TOTE £5.50: £1.70, £1.70, £1.60; EX 23.30 Trifecta £76.30.
Owner Nil Sine Labore Partnership **Bred** Miss L A Perratt **Trained** East Kilbride, S Lanarks

FOCUS
The going had eased to heavy all round. Rail movements added 12yds to the race distance. A modest lady riders' race but it produced a good finish between the market leaders.

5934 SCOTTISH SUN ON SUNDAY EBF NOVICE AUCTION STKS 6f
5:55 (5:56) (Class 5) 2-Y-O **£3,428** (£1,020; £509; £254) **Stalls** Centre

Form RPR
2 **1** **Fuwayrit (IRE)**[11] 5523 2-9-1 0........................ JoeFanning 2 70+
(Mark Johnston) *pressed ldr: shkn up to ld over 1f out: pushed out fnl f: comf* **8/11**[1]
60 **2** *¾* **Ralphy Boy Two (IRE)**[34] 4688 2-9-1 0........................ KevinStott 7 68
(Alistair Whillans) *s.i.s: hld up in tch: pushed along and hdwy over 1f out: chsd wnr ins fnl f: kpt on fin* **25/1**
00 **3** *nk* **Trevie Fountain**[14] 5433 2-9-2 0........................ PaddyMathers 4 68
(Richard Fahey) *chsd ldrs: drvn and outpcd 2f out: rallied ins fnl f: r.o* **25/1**
10 **4** *shd* **Commanche Falls**[38] 4516 2-9-6 0........................ ConnorBeasley 6 72+
(Michael Dods) *pressed ldrs: pushed along after 2f: rdn and outpcd 2f out: kpt on ins fnl f* **9/4**[2]
41 **5** *1* **Mitty's Smile (IRE)**[19] 5250 2-9-2 0........................ AdamMcNamara 3 65
(Archie Watson) *led: rdn and hdd over 1f out: chsd wnr to ins fnl f: sn no ex* **6/1**[3]

1m 17.16s (4.06) **Going Correction** +0.625s/f (Yiel) **5 Ran SP% 110.7**
Speed ratings (Par 94): **97,96,95,95,94**
CSF £19.54 TOTE £1.50: £1.10, £6.40; EX 17.00 Trifecta £86.20.
Owner H E Sherida Al-Kaabi **Bred** Charel Bloodstock **Trained** Middleham Moor, N Yorks

FOCUS
Some big yards represented in this juvenile novice auction, but they finished in a heap and the form looks worth treating with caution. The fourth has been rated tentatively in line with his debut.

5935 STAGECOACH WEST SCOTLAND H'CAP 6f
6:25 (6:28) (Class 6) (0-65,60) 3-Y-O+

£2,781 (£827; £413; £400; £400; £400) **Stalls** Centre

Form RPR
3300 **1** **Mr Shelby (IRE)**[34] 4694 5-9-6 **54**........................(p) KevinStott 8 61
(S Donohoe, Ire) *trckd ldrs: effrt and wnt 2nd over 1f out: sn rdn: led wl ins fnl f: jst hld on (trainer said, regarding apparent improvement in form, that gelding benefitted from being ridden by a professional on this occasion)* **12/1**
1232 **2** *nse* **Macs Blessings (IRE)**[4] 5771 3-9-2 **57**........................(b[1]) MeganNicholls(3) 6 63
(Stef Keniry) *sn pushed along bhd ldng gp: rdn and effrt against stands' rail over 1f out: kpt on strly ins fnl f: jst failed* **7/4**[1]
2351 **3** *1 ¼* **Forever A Lady (IRE)**[12] 5486 6-9-12 **60**........................ JoeFanning 9 63
(Keith Dalgleish) *pressed ldr: led and rdn over 1f out: hdd and no ex wl ins fnl f* **4/1**[2]
4030 **4** *5* **Jessie Allan (IRE)**[5] 5722 8-8-5 **46**........................ CoreyMadden(7) 1 34
(Jim Goldie) *sn bhd: rdn over 2f out: kpt on fnl f: nt pce to chal* **6/1**
0423 **5** *1* **Jacob's Pillow**[12] 5491 8-9-8 **56**........................(p) LewisEdmunds 4 40
(Rebecca Bastiman) *led to over 1f out: rdn and wknd ins fnl f (trainer could offer no explanation for the poor performance other than the gelding stopped quickly)* **6/1**
40-0 **6** *½* **Ancient Astronaut**[112] 1965 6-8-11 **45**........................(h) ConnorBeasley 3 29
(Karl Thornton, Ire) *hld up: rdn and outpcd over 2f out: sme late hdwy: nvr on terms* **9/2**[3]
0600 **7** *½* **Palavicini Run (IRE)**[12] 5486 6-8-8 **45**........................ ConnorMurtagh(3) 7 27
(Linda Perratt) *prom: drvn and outpcd over 2f out: btn over 1f out* **40/1**
4000 **8** *9* **Indiaro**[12] 5486 3-9-3 **55**........................ JamieGormley 5 9
(Linda Perratt) *prom: lost pl over 2f out: sn struggling (jockey said gelding hung left-handed throughout)* **28/1**

1m 16.22s (3.12) **Going Correction** +0.625s/f (Yiel)
WFA 3 from 4yo+ 4lb **8 Ran SP% 116.7**
Speed ratings (Par 101): **104,103,102,95,94 93,92,80**
CSF £34.23 CT £103.90 TOTE £11.50: £3.30, £1.20, £1.30; EX 46.40 Trifecta £228.70.
Owner S Donohoe **Bred** John Webb **Trained** Cootehill Road, Co. Cavan
■ Stewards' Enquiry : Kevin Stott four-day ban; misuse of whip (Aug 24-27)

FOCUS
This low-grade sprint handicap was run 0.94secs faster than the preceding juvenile contest. It resulted in a desperately close finish. Straightforward form, with the winner rated near his recent best.

5936 SCOTTISH SUN H'CAP 5f
6:55 (6:56) (Class 4) (0-85,83) 3-Y-O+ **£5,207** (£1,549; £774) **Stalls** Centre

Form RPR
5151 **1** **Dandy's Beano (IRE)**[14] 5432 4-9-11 **83**........................(h) KevinStott 3 87
(Kevin Ryan) *mde all: rdn and pressed over 1f out: hung lft ins fnl f: hld on wl cl home* **10/11**[1]
0012 **2** *nk* **Super Julius**[1] 5924 5-9-2 **74**........................ BenRobinson 4 77
(S Donohoe, Ire) *t.k.h: chsd wnr: effrt and ev ch over 1f out: carried lft ins fnl f: hld nr fin* **6/4**[2]
0000 **3** *2 ¼* **He'Zanarab (IRE)**[45] 4236 3-9-7 **82**........................(h) PaddyMathers 2 76
(Jim Goldie) *awkward s: chsd ldrs: drvn and outpcd wl over 1f out: rallied ins fnl f: no imp* **11/2**[3]

1m 3.27s (3.27) **Going Correction** +0.625s/f (Yiel)
WFA 3 from 4yo+ 3lb **3 Ran SP% 107.8**
Speed ratings (Par 105): **98,97,93**
CSF £2.58 TOTE £1.70; EX 1.50 Trifecta £2.40.
Owner Hambleton Racing Ltd XLVII **Bred** Ruskerne Ltd **Trained** Hambleton, N Yorks

FOCUS
The feature race but a disappointing turnout, although it produced a good race. The winner confirmed she's better than ever.

5937 FABULOUS MAGAZINE H'CAP 1m 2f
7:25 (7:25) (Class 5) (0-75,76) 3-Y-O+

£3,428 (£1,020; £509; £400; £400; £400) **Stalls** Low

Form RPR
150 **1** **Three Castles**[28] 4914 3-8-1 **60**........................ AndrewBreslin(5) 2 69+
(Keith Dalgleish) *s.i.s: hld up: rdn and hdwy 2f out: led ins fnl f: kpt on strly (trainers' rep said, regards apparent improvement in form, gelding was suited by the Heavy ground on this occasion)* **5/1**[2]
0650 **2** *nk* **Sarvi**[8] 5621 4-9-4 **64**........................(p) JamieGormley 6 71
(Jim Goldie) *hld up in last pl: hdwy and pushed along 2f out: pressed wnr ins fnl f: kpt on fin* **9/1**
4563 **3** *2* **Royal Regent**[19] 5240 7-9-6 **69**........................ ConnorMurtagh(3) 7 72
(Lucy Normile) *cl up: led after 3f: qcknd 3f out: wandered u.p and hdd ins fnl f: one pce* **3/1**[1]
4630 **4** *5* **Remmy D (IRE)**[10] 5556 4-8-10 **56**........................(v[1]) PaddyMathers 1 49
(Jim Goldie) *sn led: hdd after 3f: cl up: rdn over 2f out: outpcd fr over 1f out* **9/1**
-634 **5** *1 ¾* **Memphis Bleek**[9] 5594 3-9-8 **76**........................(p) KevinStott 5 66
(Ivan Furtado) *hld up in tch: pushed along over 2f out: no imp fr over 1f out* **3/1**[1]
6416 **6** *1 ¼* **Maulesden May (IRE)**[72] 3267 6-10-0 **74**........................ JoeFanning 9 61
(Keith Dalgleish) *s.i.s: sn prom: rdn and outpcd over 2f out: btn over 1f out* **10/1**

0406 **7** ¾ **Gworn**[19] 5239 9-9-0 **60** .... LewisEdmunds 3 46
(R Mike Smith) *in tch: drvn and outpcd over 2f out: sn btn* **9/1**

0665 **8** 2 **Can Can Sixty Two**[19] 5240 4-8-11 **62** .... (p) PaulaMuir(5) 4 44
(R Mike Smith) *early ldr: cl up tl rdn and wknd over 2f out (trainers' rep said filly ran too free)* **15/2**[3]

2m 17.04s (4.64) **Going Correction** +0.625s/f (Yiel) **8** Ran SP% **117.5**
WFA 3 from 4yo+ 8lb
Speed ratings (Par 103): **106,105,104,100,98 97,97,95**
CSF £50.03 CT £159.15 TOTE £7.20: £2.10, £2.50, £1.60; EX 66.40 Trifecta £366.90.
Owner Keith Dalgleish **Bred** W M Johnstone **Trained** Carluke, S Lanarks

FOCUS
Rail movements added 12yds to the race distance. An ordinary handicap in which the first two were the last pair turning for home. It's been rated around the third in line with his latest effort in higher grade.

5938 CALA HOMES H'CAP — 7f 50y
7:55 (7:57) (Class 5) (0-70,67) 3-Y-O+
£3,428 (£1,020; £509; £400; £400; £400) **Stalls** High

Form RPR

0050 **1** **Chaplin Bay (IRE)**[11] 5517 7-8-10 **50** .... JamieGormley 2 56
(Ruth Carr) *mde all: rdn and hrd pressed over 1f out: hld on gamely towards fin* **5/1**[3]

6234 **2** hd **Grab And Run (IRE)**[10] 5561 3-9-7 **67** .... PaddyMathers 5 71
(Richard Fahey) *prom: hdwy to chal over 1f out: rdn and kpt on fnl f: hld nr fin* **2/1**[1]

40-0 **3** 1¼ **Sienna Dream**[12] 5486 4-8-4 **49** oh2 .... AndrewBreslin(5) 7 51
(Alistair Whillans) *t.k.h: hld up: pushed along over 2f out: kpt on fnl f: nt rch first two* **25/1**

0001 **4** 1¾ **Roaring Forties (IRE)**[19] 5237 6-9-8 **62** .... (p) LewisEdmunds 6 60
(Rebecca Bastiman) *pressed wnr: rdn over 2f out: kpt on same pce fr over 1f out* **9/1**

6612 **5** nk **Royal Duchess**[19] 5237 9-9-6 **63** .... ConnorMurtagh(3) 1 60
(Lucy Normile) *trckd ldrs: rdn whn rdr dropped reins wl over 1f out: no ex ins fnl f* **6/1**

655- **6** 2 **Nakakande (IRE)**[24] 5069 3-9-3 **63** .... (b) ConnorBeasley 3 53
(Karl Thornton, Ire) *t.k.h: hld up in tch: effrt and rdn 2f out: wknd fnl f* **8/1**

5332 **7** hd **Chinese Spirit (IRE)**[12] 5490 5-9-11 **65** .... BenRobinson 8 57
(Linda Perratt) *in tch: drvn and effrt over 2f out: wknd over 1f out (jockey said gelding ran flat)* **7/2**[2]

1005 **8** 2½ **Carlovian**[30] 4823 6-9-0 **54** .... (p) DougieCostello 9 40
(Mark Walford) *hld up: drvn along over 2f out: wknd wl over 1f out* **14/1**

1m 36.31s (3.81) **Going Correction** +0.625s/f (Yiel) **8** Ran SP% **118.1**
WFA 3 from 4yo+ 6lb
Speed ratings (Par 103): **103,102,101,99,99 96,96,93**
CSF £16.02 CT £233.91 TOTE £6.10: £2.00, £1.40, £5.10; EX 22.20 Trifecta £304.30.
Owner Miss B Houlston,Mrs M Chapman,Mrs R Carr **Bred** Stonethorn Stud Farms Ltd **Trained** Huby, N Yorks

FOCUS
Rail movements added 12yds to the race distance. This moderate 7f handicap produced another close finish. It's been rated as routine form, with the third to her recent best.

5939 BOOK FOR THE AYR FLOWER SHOW H'CAP — 1m 7f
8:25 (8:26) (Class 6) (0-60,56) 4-Y-O+
£2,781 (£827; £413; £400; £400; £400) **Stalls** Low

Form RPR

-110 **1** **Clearance**[9] 1334 5-9-6 **55** .... JamieGormley 1 67+
(Iain Jardine) *trckd ldr: styd alone far side ent st: led 2f out: shkn up and qcknd clr fnl f: eased towards fin* **3/1**[1]

56-0 **2** 2¾ **Oromo (IRE)**[11] 1573 6-8-10 **45** .... (t) ConnorBeasley 8 52
(Karl Thornton, Ire) *led at v stdy gallop: rdn and c wd ent st: hdd over 2f out: hung lft over 1f out: kpt on: no ch w wnr* **15/2**

6456 **3** nk **Pammi**[14] 5435 4-8-13 **48** .... (p) PaddyMathers 4 54
(Jim Goldie) *t.k.h: trckd ldrs: drvn along 2f out: kpt on fnl f: nt pce to chal* **6/1**[3]

46/3 **4** ¾ **Black Label**[11] 3976 8-9-7 **56** .... (t) DougieCostello 7 61
(Karl Thornton, Ire) *dwlt: sn in tch: rdn and outpcd over 2f out: rallied fnl f: no imp* **7/1**

0404 **5** nk **Elite Icon**[5] 5727 5-8-10 **48** .... (v) MeganNicholls(3) 2 53
(Jim Goldie) *in tch: pushed along and outpcd 2f out: n.d after* **10/3**[2]

0422 **6** 2¼ **Hugoigo**[12] 5487 5-8-10 **52** .... (p) CoreyMadden(7) 5 54
(Jim Goldie) *hld up in last pl: drvn over 2f out: sn outpcd: n.d after (jockey said gelding was unsuited by the slow pace of the race)* **3/1**[1]

0000 **7** ½ **Morley Gunner (IRE)**[34] 4690 4-8-10 **45** .... BenRobinson 3 47
(S Donohoe, Ire) *t.k.h: hld up: rdn and outpcd over 2f out: sn no imp: btn over 1f out (jockey said gelding ran too free)* **33/1**

3m 51.78s (24.78) **Going Correction** +0.625s/f (Yiel) **7** Ran SP% **114.6**
Speed ratings (Par 101): **58,56,56,55,55 54,54**
CSF £25.82 CT £126.31 TOTE £3.80: £2.20, £3.60; EX 20.70 Trifecta £112.90.
Owner Kildonan Gold Racing 2 & Partner **Bred** Richard W Farleigh **Trained** Carrutherstown, D'fries & G'way

FOCUS
Rail movements added 33yds to the race distance. This moderate staying handicap was run very steadily for a mile and it paid to race close to the pace, as the first three held those positions throughout. The third suggests this level is a sensible starting point.
T/Plt: £14.20 to a £1 stake. Pool: £47,407.82 - 2426.59 winning units T/Qpdt: £12.50 to a £1 stake. Pool: £5,069.81 - 297.97 winning units **Richard Young**

5885 CHELMSFORD (A.W) (L-H)
Saturday, August 10

OFFICIAL GOING: Polytrack: standard
Wind: strong, behind Weather: cloudy

5940 BET TOTEPLACEPOT AT TOTESPORT.COM MAIDEN STKS — 1m (P)
1:35 (1:37) (Class 5) 2-Y-O
£4,204 (£1,251; £625; £312) **Stalls** Low

Form RPR

33 **1** **Moolhim (FR)**[36] 4611 2-9-5 0 .... JackMitchell 4 77
(Simon Crisford) *chsd ldr: effrt ent fnl 2f: rdn and upsides ldr over 1f out: led ins fnl f: styd on* **3/1**[2]

2 **2** ½ **Global Storm (IRE)**[16] 5331 2-9-5 0 .... JamesDoyle 1 76
(Charlie Appleby) *led: rdn ent fnl 2f: hrd press and u.p over 1f out: hdd ins fnl f: kpt on but a hld after* **4/9**[1]

5 **3** nk **Cipango**[43] 4324 2-9-5 0 .... LukeMorris 6 75+
(Marco Botti) *wl in tch in midfield: rdn ent fnl 3f: chsd ldng pair 1f out: styd on wl u.p fnl 100yds* **14/1**

4 4½ **Falcon Claws (USA)** 2-9-5 0 .... ShaneKelly 3 65
(Marco Botti) *in tch in last pair: effrt over 2f out: chsd clr ldng trio ins fnl f: drifted rt and no imp after* **22/1**

5 2 **Daheer (USA)** 2-9-5 0 .... JimCrowley 5 60
(Owen Burrows) *hld up in tch in last pair: effrt over 2f out: drifted rt off bnd 2f out: wl hld after* **10/1**[3]

0 **6** 1 **Master Rocco (IRE)**[14] 5439 2-9-5 .... JFEgan 2 58
(Jane Chapple-Hyam) *t.k.h: trckd ldrs: effrt over 2f out: outpcd u.p over 1f out: wknd ins fnl f* **50/1**

1m 40.54s (0.64) **Going Correction** -0.20s/f (Stan) **6** Ran SP% **116.3**
Speed ratings (Par 94): **88,87,87,82,80 79**
CSF £4.91 TOTE £4.00: £1.20, £1.10; EX 6.00 Trifecta £15.70.
Owner Sheikh Ahmed Al Maktoum **Bred** S C E A De Marancourt, L Vincent Et Al **Trained** Newmarket, Suffolk

FOCUS
The track had been lightly de-compacted with a gallop master finish to two inches. The going was standard. With the first three finishing in a heap this didn't look a great maiden and odds-on punters got their fingers burnt. The level is fluid.

5941 BET TOTEEXACTA AT TOTESPORT.COM FILLIES' H'CAP — 1m (P)
2:10 (2:11) (Class 5) (0-70,73) 3-Y-O+
£5,175 (£1,540; £769; £384; £300; £300) **Stalls** Low

Form RPR

2246 **1** **Universal Effect**[15] 5380 3-9-3 **66** .... (h) ShaneKelly 3 77
(David Lanigan) *in tch in midfield: effrt and qcknd to ld 2f out: in command and styd on wl fnl f: readily (trainer said regarding apparent improvement in form that the filly was suited by the return to the All Weather)* **11/1**

3563 **2** 3 **Beautiful Gesture**[25] 5031 3-9-3 **66** .... TomMarquand 2 70
(K R Burke) *led: sn hdd and chsd ldrs: effrt and hdwy u.p whn swtchd rt over 1f out: kpt on to go 2nd wl ins fnl f: no ch w wnr* **5/1**[3]

-561 **3** ¾ **Alma Linda**[7] 5651 3-9-10 **73** .... (p) LukeMorris 6 75+
(Sir Mark Prescott Bt) *hdwy to ld after 1f and t.k.h: rdn and hdd 2f out: drvn and unable to match pce of wnr over 1f out: kpt on same pce and lost 2nd wl ins fnl f* **4/5**[1]

-410 **4** 1¾ **Billie Beane**[43] 4349 4-8-7 **54** .... DarraghKeenan(5) 1 53
(Dr Jon Scargill) *in tch in midfield: effrt ent fnl f: unable qck u.p over 1f out: kpt on same pce and no imp ins fnl f* **14/1**

0065 **5** ¾ **Kodiac Lass (IRE)**[30] 4831 3-9-1 **67** .... (p) GabrieleMalune(3) 7 64
(Marco Botti) *t.k.h: sn pressed ldr: lost 2nd and rdn ent fnl 2f: outpcd u.p over 1f out: wknd ins fnl f (jockey said filly ran too free)* **16/1**

-444 **6** 1 **Regal Banner**[45] 4248 3-9-9 **72** .... JackMitchell 4 66
(Roger Varian) *in tch in last trio: drvn and no imp over 1f out: wl hld fnl f* **7/2**[2]

6200 **7** ½ **Winterkoenigin**[3] 5797 3-8-13 **67** .... (p) CierenFallon(5) 5 60
(David Lanigan) *stdd leaving stalls: hld up in last pair: effrt ent fnl 2f: no imp over 1f out: nvr trbld ldrs* **16/1**

0-55 **8** 5 **Ample Plenty**[16] 5358 3-8-8 **57** .... HollieDoyle 8 39
(David Simcock) *hld up in last pair: effrt ent fnl 2f: no hdwy u.p over 1f out: wl btn fnl f* **20/1**

1m 39.77s (-0.13) **Going Correction** -0.20s/f (Stan) **8** Ran SP% **126.0**
WFA 3 from 4yo 7lb
Speed ratings (Par 100): **92,89,88,86,85 84,84,79**
CSF £71.42 CT £97.58 TOTE £11.30: £3.00, £1.90, £1.10; EX 79.70 Trifecta £307.20.
Owner Saif Ali **Bred** Rabbah Bloodstock Limited **Trained** Newmarket, Suffolk

FOCUS
An ordinary 3yo fillies' handicap and another reverse for short-price favourite backers. A pb from the winner, with the second rated close to her latest.

5942 BET TOTEQUADPOT AT TOTESPORT.COM OPTIONAL CLAIMING H'CAP — 6f (P)
2:45 (2:46) (Class 2) 4-Y-O+
£19,407 (£5,775; £2,886; £1,443) **Stalls** Centre

Form RPR

/606 **1** **Unabated (IRE)**[18] 5266 5-8-7 **83** .... (t) JasonWatson 7 92+
(Jane Chapple-Hyam) *in tch in midfield on outer: effrt over 2f out: hdwy u.p over 1f out: led jst ins fnl f: styd on wl: rdn out* **14/1**

1034 **2** ½ **Katheefa (USA)**[18] 5266 5-8-3 **79** .... NathanEvans 2 86
(Ruth Carr) *hld up in tch in midfield: swtchd rt and clsd to press ldrs whn struck on nose by rivals whip over 1f out: hdwy ins fnl f: wnt 2nd towards fin: styd on* **6/1**

1003 **3** 1 **Watchable**[18] 5266 9-9-7 **97** .... (p) DavidProbert 4 101
(David O'Meara) *restless in stalls: led: nr side cheekpiece fell off after 1f: rdn over 1f out: drvn and hdd jst ins fnl f: no ex and lost 2nd towards fin* **5/1**[3]

0050 **4** ½ **Desert Doctor (IRE)**[56] 3863 4-9-4 **94** .... LukeMorris 1 96
(Ed Walker) *chsd ldrs: ev ch and rdn over 1f out: unable qck and kpt on same pce ins fnl f* **4/1**[2]

605 **5** nk **Polybius**[11] 5530 8-9-2 **92** .... ShaneKelly 6 93
(David Simcock) *hld up in tch in rr: effrt on inner over 1f out: no imp and one pce fnl 100yds* **20/1**

0210 **6** ½ **Boy In The Bar**[7] 5661 8-8-2 **83** .... (v) CierenFallon(5) 3 83
(Ian Williams) *hld up in tch in midfield: effrt whn nt clr run and swtchd rt over 1f out: swtchd bk lft 1f out: kpt on same pce ins fnl f* **7/2**[1]

163 **7** shd **Busby (IRE)**[26] 5000 4-8-1 **77** .... (p) KieranO'Neill 9 76
(Conrad Allen) *chsd ldr: rdn jst over 2f out: unable qck over 1f out: wknd ins fnl f* **8/1**

1-04 **8** 2¼ **Encrypted**[42] 4380 4-9-4 **104** .... DarraghKeenan(5) 8 96
(Hugo Palmer) *chsd ldrs: unable qck u.p over 1f out: wknd ins fnl f (jockey said gelding stopped quickly)* **5/1**[3]

2010 **9** shd **Royal Birth**[12] 5504 8-9-8 **98** .... (t) TomMarquand 5 90
(Stuart Williams) *hld up in last pair: effrt over 1f out: no imp: nvr trbld ldrs* **8/1**

1m 10.53s (-3.17) **Going Correction** -0.20s/f (Stan) **9** Ran SP% **123.5**
Speed ratings (Par 109): **113,112,111,110,109 109,109,106,106**
CSF £101.80 CT £495.76 TOTE £19.20: £4.00, £2.00, £2.30; EX 124.90 Trifecta £745.90.
Owner Mrs Jane Chapple-Hyam **Bred** Mubarak Al Naemi **Trained** Dalham, Suffolk

FOCUS
A warm sprint handicap with only the first two in to be claimed and racing off lower marks than their official ratings as a result. There was no messing about and although the field was still tightly packed starting up the straight, they dipped under standard time. It's been rated around the second, with the third close to his recent C&D run.

5943 BET TOTETRIFECTA AT TOTESPORT.COM H'CAP 1m 6f (P)
3:20 (3:20) (Class 2) 3-Y-O

£28,012 (£8,388; £4,194; £2,097; £1,048; £526) Stalls Low

Form RPR
2221 1 **Starczewski (USA)**[16] 5355 3-8-6 74........................ HollieDoyle 4 86+
(David Simcock) *stdd s: hld up in last pair: effrt and swtchd rt ent fnl 2f: rdn and hdwy to ld 1f out: clr and styd on wl fnl 100yds: comf* 9/2[3]
4413 2 2 3/4 **Space Walk**[16] 5347 3-8-7 80........................(t) CierenFallon(5) 1 87
(William Haggas) *t.k.h: chsd ldr: effrt over 2f out: wnt lft u.p over 1f out: chsd wnr 100yds out: kpt on but no imp (jockey said colt ran too free)* 15/8[1]
-622 3 1 1/2 **Buckman Tavern (FR)**[10] 5566 3-8-13 81...................(p[1]) LukeMorris 3 86
(Sir Mark Prescott Bt) *led: rdn ent fnl 2f: drvn over 1f out: hdd 1f out: no ex and one pce ins fnl f* 7/2[2]
1111 4 3/4 **Champagne Marengo (IRE)**[25] 5028 3-8-4 72..........(v[1]) KieranO'Neill 2 76
(Ian Williams) *hld up in rr: effrt and wd bnd 2f out: kpt on ins fnl f: no threat to wnr* 7/1
3215 5 3 **Mondain**[10] 5566 3-9-7 89........................ JasonWatson 6 89
(Mark Johnston) *in tch in midfield: chsd ldrs over 3f out: unable qck u.p over 1f out: wknd ins fnl f* 10/1
5611 6 4 1/2 **Global Falcon**[28] 4929 3-8-11 79........................ JimCrowley 5 72
(Charles Hills) *chsd ldrs: rdn over 2f out: lost pl and bhd over 1f out: wknd fnl f* 9/2[3]

2m 55.99s (-7.21) **Going Correction** -0.20s/f (Stan) 6 Ran SP% 115.0
Speed ratings (Par 106): **112,110,109,109,107 104**
CSF £13.87 TOTE £5.50: £2.50, £1.30; EX 17.40 Trifecta £65.90.
Owner Jos & Mrs Jane Rodosthenous **Bred** Nesco II Limited **Trained** Newmarket, Suffolk

FOCUS
A warm little staying 3yo handicap with most of these coming into the race in good form. They went an even pace. It's been rated on the positive side, with the third to form.

5944 BET TOTESWINGER AT TOTESPORT.COM FAIRWOOD FILLIES' H'CAP 7f (P)
3:55 (3:56) (Class 2) (0-105,99) 3-Y-O+

£31,125 (£9,320; £4,660; £2,330; £1,165; £585) Stalls Low

Form RPR
1-21 1 **Lady Lawyer (USA)**[18] 5268 3-8-9 90........................ FrankieDettori 1 99
(John Gosden) *mounted in chute and taken down early: mde all: wnt rt 4f out: rdn over 1f out: kpt on u.p and a holding runner-up ins fnl f* 5/2[1]
1-61 2 1/2 **California Love**[28] 4922 3-8-13 94........................ LukeMorris 2 101
(Richard Spencer) *chsd wnr: effrt over 2f out: hrd drvn over 1f out: kpt on wl u.p but a hld ins fnl f* 7/1
5020 3 1 **Crossing The Line**[28] 4921 4-9-10 99........................ DavidProbert 9 105
(Andrew Balding) *hld up in midfield: edgd out rt and effrt over 1f out: kpt on wl u.p ins fnl f: nvr quite getting to ldng pair* 6/1
-416 4 1 1/4 **Jadeerah**[15] 5369 3-8-11 92........................(h) JimCrowley 6 93
(John Gosden) *pushed lft leaving stalls: hld up in tch in midfield: effrt over 1f out: kpt on same pce and no imp ins fnl f* 3/1[2]
0030 5 shd **Pattie**[11] 5525 5-8-13 88........................ CallumShepherd 7 91
(Mick Channon) *restless in stalls: wnt sharply lft leaving stalls: chsd ldrs: effrt ent fnl 2f: unable qck u.p 1f out: kpt on same pce ins fnl f* 14/1
5300 6 1 1/4 **Island Of Life (USA)**[8] 5608 5-9-5 99..........(tp) CierenFallon(5) 8 98
(William Haggas) *hld up in midfield: effrt over 1f out: swtchd lft ins fnl f: no imp and wknd fnl 100yds* 9/2[3]
-110 7 hd **Invitational**[50] 4052 3-8-11 92........................ JackMitchell 5 89+
(Roger Varian) *short of room and hmpd leaving stalls: hld up in last pair: effrt whn swtchd lft over 1f out: kpt on but nvr trbld ldrs* 8/1
6010 8 3/4 **Daddies Girl (IRE)**[21] 5187 4-8-13 91........................ JoshuaBryan(3) 4 88
(Rod Millman) *pushed rt leaving stalls: hld up in last pair: effrt over 1f out: kpt on u.p but nvr involved* 20/1
122 9 3/4 **Emily Goldfinch**[8] 5628 6-9-3 92........................(p) JasonWatson 3 87
(Phil McEntee) *pushed rt leaving stalls: t.k.h: chsd ldrs: effrt over 1f out: sn drvn and unable qck: wknd ins fnl f* 16/1

1m 24.57s (-2.63) **Going Correction** -0.20s/f (Stan)
WFA 3 from 4yo+ 6lb 9 Ran SP% 127.0
Speed ratings (Par 96): **107,106,105,103,103 102,102,101,100**
CSF £23.34 CT £103.19 TOTE £3.40: £1.40, £1.90, £2.30; EX 16.10 Trifecta £50.70.
Owner Sheikh Juma Dalmook Al Maktoum **Bred** Claiborne Farm **Trained** Newmarket, Suffolk

FOCUS
A warm fillies' handicap, but plenty of trouble at the start and the pair who found themselves out in front after a furlong were the first two home. The second helps set the level, and the third has been rated to form.

5945 LOOKERS LANDROVER BISHOP'S STORTFORD H'CAP 7f (P)
4:30 (4:31) (Class 3) (0-90,90) 3-Y-O+ £9,703 (£2,887; £1,443; £721) Stalls Low

Form RPR
1-10 1 **Habub (USA)**[85] 2791 4-10-0 90........................ JasonWatson 4 101
(Owen Burrows) *mde all: rdn and edgd rt over 1f out: styd on strly ins fnl f (jockey said colt hung right-handed under pressure)* 9/2[2]
-650 2 1 **Karnavaal (IRE)**[56] 3858 3-8-11 79........................ JimCrowley 6 85
(Sir Michael Stoute) *hld up in tch in midfield: effrt u.p over 1f out: hdwy to chse wnr 100yds out: kpt on but a hld* 11/8[1]
-134 3 1 1/2 **San Carlos**[35] 4638 3-9-4 86........................ ShaneKelly 3 88
(Shaun Keightley) *trckd ldrs: edgd out rt and n.m.r wl over 1f out: effrt over 1f out: sn drvn and kpt on same pce ins fnl f* 9/2[2]
0644 4 nk **Maksab (IRE)**[15] 5386 4-9-6 82........................ CallumShepherd 8 85
(Mick Channon) *chsd wnr: rdn ent fnl 2f: unable qck over 1f out: kpt on same pce and lost 2 pls fnl 100yds* 12/1
6050 5 3/4 **Areen Heart (FR)**[14] 5434 5-9-9 90..........(h) CierenFallon(5) 1 91
(David O'Meara) *taken down early: stdd and n.m.r after s: t.k.h: hld up in tch: effrt on inner over 1f out: kpt on same pce and no imp fnl 100yds* 8/1[3]
-360 6 1/2 **Papa Stour (USA)**[29] 4867 4-8-11 73..........(v[1]) DavidProbert 5 73
(Andrew Balding) *hld up in tch in midfield: effrt over 1f out: kpt on same pce ins fnl f* 8/1[3]
4052 7 1 **Blame Culture (USA)**[18] 5283 4-9-5 81........................ JFEgan 7 78
(George Margarson) *t.k.h: hld up in tch in midfield on outer: effrt over 2f out: drvn and no hdwy over 1f out: wl hld and one pce ins fnl f* 8/1[3]
2426 8 nse **Atletico (IRE)**[18] 5283 7-9-2 78..........(v) JosephineGordon 2 75
(David Evans) *stdd after s: hld up in tch in rr: effrt over 1f out: swtchd lft ins fnl f: nvr trbld ldrs* 16/1

1m 24.84s (-2.36) **Going Correction** -0.20s/f (Stan)
WFA 3 from 4yo+ 6lb 8 Ran SP% 125.4
Speed ratings (Par 107): **105,103,102,101,100 100,99,99**
CSF £12.33 CT £31.89 TOTE £4.50: £1.60, £1.10, £1.70; EX 15.20 Trifecta £86.40.
Owner Hamdan Al Maktoum **Bred** Summer Wind Farm **Trained** Lambourn, Berks

FOCUS
A decent handicap and a 1-2 for owner Hamdan Al Maktoum with the winner carrying the second colours. The third has been rated to form.

5946 MINISTRY OF SOUND THE ANNUAL CLASSICAL H'CAP 1m 2f (P)
5:00 (5:01) (Class 6) (0-60,62) 3-Y-O+

£3,105 (£924; £461; £300; £300; £300) Stalls Low

Form RPR
2200 1 **Junior Rip (IRE)**[19] 5249 3-9-9 62........................ JasonWatson 8 70
(Roger Charlton) *in tch in midfield: effrt to chal 2f out: led and rn green over 1f out: styd on and drew clr ins fnl f* 2/1[1]
0001 2 2 1/4 **Muraaqeb**[7] 5653 5-9-5 53........................(p) JoshuaBryan(3) 4 56
(Milton Bradley) *hld up in tch in midfield: hdwy u.p over 1f out: pressed wnr 1f out: no ex and outpcd fnl 100yds* 9/4[2]
060 3 1 1/4 **Tronador (IRE)**[54] 3946 3-9-7 60........................ ShaneKelly 5 61
(David Lanigan) *v.s.a: green and reminder sn after s: hld up in rr: swtchd rt and effrt wd bnd 2f out: rn green and hung lft over 1f out: chsd ldrs: kpt on same pce and stl gng lft ins fnl f* 3/1[3]
-046 4 2 3/4 **Buzz Lightyere**[7] 5680 6-9-7 57........................(b[1]) CierenFallon(5) 6 52
(Patrick Chamings) *hld up in last pair: effrt and hdwy over 1f out: no imp and wl hld whn swtchd lft ins fnl f* 8/1
0000 5 2 **Tyrsal (IRE)**[18] 5271 8-9-0 45........................(v) JosephineGordon 3 36
(Shaun Keightley) *s.i.s: sn rcvrd and in tch in midfield: nt clr run and shuffled bk to rr over 1f out: kpt on ins fnl f but nt rcvr (jockey said gelding was denied a clear run)* 12/1
6006 6 shd **Outlaw Torn (IRE)**[7] 5652 10-9-0 45........................(e) JFEgan 1 36
(Richard Guest) *taken down early: led: rdn ent fnl 2f: hdd over 1f out: no ex and wknd ins fnl f* 14/1
605 7 1 1/2 **Margaret J**[15] 5380 3-8-3 45........................(p) NoelGarbutt(3) 2 34
(Phil McEntee) *chsd ldrs tl lost pl u.p over 1f out: wknd ins fnl f* 16/1
6-00 8 5 **Mr Spirit (IRE)**[31] 4787 3-9-1 61........................(b) StefanoCherchi(7) 7 41
(Marco Botti) *chsd ldr 8f out: rdn and ev ch ent fnl 2f: lost pl over 1f out: wknd ins fnl f* 20/1

2m 5.36s (-3.24) **Going Correction** -0.20s/f (Stan)
WFA 3 from 5yo+ 8lb 8 Ran SP% 125.2
Speed ratings (Par 101): **104,102,101,99,97 97,96,92**
CSF £7.62 CT £13.97 TOTE £2.50: £1.10, £1.20, £1.50; EX 8.20 Trifecta £16.10.
Owner Nick Bradley Racing 19 & Sohi **Bred** Pigeon Park Stud **Trained** Beckhampton, Wilts

FOCUS
A moderate handicap to end. The winner has been rated back to this year's best.
T/Plt: £17.50 to a £1 stake. Pool: £26,490.67 - 1511.03 winning units T/Qpdt: £17.10 to a £1 stake. Pool: £2,076.18 - 121.14 winning units **Steve Payne**

5892 HAYDOCK (L-H)
Saturday, August 10

OFFICIAL GOING: Heavy
Wind: strong, blustery, across Weather: squally showers, mild

5947 RACING TV H'CAP 1m 37y
1:25 (1:26) (Class 4) (0-85,86) 3-Y-O

£7,115 (£2,117; £1,058; £529; £300; £300) Stalls Low

Form RPR
2422 1 **Barossa Red (IRE)**[128] 1550 3-9-0 76........................ OisinMurphy 9 86
(Andrew Balding) *hld up on outer: hdwy on stands' side 2f out: drvn to ld over 1f out: rdn out fnl f* 6/1
6433 2 1 **House Of Kings (IRE)**[5] 5749 3-9-7 83........................ HectorCrouch 1 91
(Clive Cox) *hld up on inner: hdwy to trck ldrs 3f out: shkn up to chal 1 1/2f out: sn rdn: 2nd ent fnl f: r.o* 11/2
211 3 3 **Bring Us Paradise**[16] 5351 3-8-9 71........................ BenCurtis 6 72
(Tony Carroll) *prom: drvn to ld 2f out: rdn and hdd over 1f out: one pce fnl f* 9/2[2]
2225 4 4 1/2 **Ginger Fox**[29] 4865 3-9-3 79........................(p) PJMcDonald 8 70
(Ian Williams) *trckd ldrs: pushed along to chal 2f out: rdn and wknd over 1f out* 11/4[1]
6060 5 1 **Deebee**[22] 5124 3-8-6 68........................(vt[1]) JimmyQuinn 4 56
(Declan Carroll) *hld up: drvn and reminder 3f out: rdn over 1f out: no imp* 16/1
0534 6 nk **Self Assessment (IRE)**[18] 5270 3-8-11 73........................ ChrisHayes 5 61
(K R Burke) *chsd ldrs: cl up 3f out: pushed along 2f out: rdn and wknd over 1f out* 12/1
2-00 7 6 **Drogon (IRE)**[77] 3082 3-9-10 86........................ RichardKingscote 3 60
(Tom Dascombe) *led: 1 l ld 3f out: drvn and hdd 2f out: wknd* 16/1
-02 8 10 **Hawridge Storm (IRE)**[50] 4065 3-9-4 80........................ HarryBentley 7 31
(Rod Millman) *slowly away: bhd: drvn over 3f out: no imp (jockey said gelding was never travelling)* 5/1[3]
6166 9 1 **La Voix Magique**[81] 2934 3-9-6 82........................ GrahamLee 2 31
(Steph Hollinshead) *hld up: drvn 3f out: rdn 2f out: no imp* 12/1

1m 46.61s (1.71) **Going Correction** +0.425s/f (Yiel) 9 Ran SP% 118.3
Speed ratings (Par 102): **108,107,104,99,98 98,92,82,81**
CSF £39.96 CT £165.52 TOTE £7.20: £2.30, £1.90, £1.80; EX 24.60 Trifecta £93.60.
Owner Another Bottle Racing 2 **Bred** Epona Bloodstock Ltd **Trained** Kingsclere, Hants

FOCUS
Stands' side home straight in use. After 27mm of rain through Thursday night and Friday, another 8mm of rain fell in a cloudburst at 12.45pm and prompted the official going to be changed from soft to heavy. With more showers forecast later in afternoon and a maximum wind speed of 45mph, conditions were difficult at best. A competitive, if arguably substandard edition of this 3yo handicap. A clear pb from the winner, and another pb from the second, in line with the better view of his form.

5948 VULCAN VILLAGE H'CAP (LONDON MILE SERIES QUALIFIER) 1m 37y
1:55 (1:57) (Class 3) (0-90,90) 3-Y-O+ £16,172 (£4,812; £2,405; £1,202) Stalls Low

Form RPR
0523 1 **Mikmak**[7] 5693 6-9-6 82........................(p) JackGarritty 10 91
(Tim Easterby) *hld up: trckd ldrs 2f out: sn pushed along: drvn to chal 1f out: rdn fnl f: led last 75yds: r.o wl* 8/1

0065 **2** *nk* **Al Erayg (IRE)**[12] 5488 6-8-12 **74**........................(p[1]) ColmO'Donoghue 2 82
(Tim Easterby) *mid-div: drvn and hdwy 2f out: cl up and rdn 1f out: led 1/2f out: hdd last 75yds: kpt on* **12/1**

R321 **3** *2 3/4* **First Flight (IRE)**[10] 5555 8-8-11 **73**............................ BenRobinson 9 75
(Brian Ellison) *trckd ldrs on outer: cl up on stands' rail 3f out: drvn 2f out: rdn 1f out: kpt on fnl f: tk 3rd last stride* **20/1**

1512 **4** *nse* **Club Wexford (IRE)**[6] 5708 8-9-9 **90**...................... BenSanderson(5) 1 92
(Roger Fell) *trckd ldrs: drvn and hdwy to ld 2f out: sn rdn: hdd 1/2f out: wknd last 100yds: lost 3rd last stride* **10/1**

6045 **5** *hd* **Kuwait Currency (USA)**[14] 5412 3-9-7 **90**........................ RossaRyan 8 90
(Richard Hannon) *chsd ldrs: drvn to chal 2f out: rdn and ev ch over 1f out: one pce fnl f* **12/1**

1311 **6** *nk* **Mayfair Spirit (IRE)**[21] 5176 3-8-12 **81**................(t) StevieDonohoe 16 81
(Charlie Fellowes) *hld up: effrt 3f out: pushed along and hdwy over 2f out: rdn 1f out: kpt on fnl f* **6/1[2]**

05-2 **7** *1* **Young Fire (FR)**[73] 4-9-12 **88**.................................... OisinMurphy 5 87+
(David O'Meara) *hld up: pushed along and hdwy on far side 2f out: rdn fnl f: no ex* **9/2[1]**

3651 **8** *nk* **King's Pavilion (IRE)**[11] 5516 6-9-10 **89**.............. ConorMcGovern(3) 13 87
(Jason Ward) *prom: rdn and wknd 2f out* **8/1**

3111 **9** *nk* **Scofflaw**[6] 5709 5-9-5 **81** 5ex.............................(b) HarryBentley 14 78
(David Evans) *led: narrow ld 3f out: drvn and hdd 2f out: sn rdn and wknd* **9/1**

3206 **10** *3/4* **Markazi (FR)**[11] 5516 5-9-10 **86**..............................(p) ShaneGray 4 82
(David O'Meara) *bhd: drvn 2f out: mod hdwy over 1f out: no ex fnl f* **22/1**

0/44 **11** *1* **Mustarrid (IRE)**[35] 4650 5-9-7 **83**................................ PJMcDonald 12 76
(Ian Williams) *hld up: drvn 3f out: rdn over 2f out: clsd sltly over 1f out: no ex (jockey said gelding was never travelling)* **15/2[3]**

0252 **12** *12* **Candelisa (IRE)**[11] 5516 6-9-4 **80**............................(t) TrevorWhelan 7 47
(David Loughnane) *mid-div: pushed along bhd ldrs 3f out: rdn and wknd 2f out* **25/1**

331 **13** *1* **Mount Ararat (IRE)**[60] 3680 4-9-1 **77**............................ BenCurtis 6 42
(K R Burke) *mid-div: pushed along 3f out: rdn and wknd over 2f out (trainers' rep could offer no explanation for the poor performance)* **11/1**

1m 47.18s (2.28) **Going Correction** +0.425s/f (Yiel)
WFA 3 from 4yo+ 7lb **13 Ran SP% 122.2**
Speed ratings (Par 107): **105,104,101,101,101 101,100,100,99,99 98,86,85**
CSF £99.92 CT £1924.30 TOTE £8.50: £2.30, £4.80, £6.60; EX 106.50 Trifecta £2241.90.
Owner K J Racing **Bred** H & Mrs C Robinson **Trained** Great Habton, N Yorks

FOCUS
This was hotly contested, despite four absentees. The finish was fought out by a pair of Tim Easterby-trained runners. The winner has been rated as finding a bit on his recent form.

5949 BRITISH STALLION STUDS EBF DICK HERN STKS (LISTED RACE) (F&M) 1m 37y
2:30 (2:31) (Class 1) 3-Y-O+

£26,653 (£10,105; £5,057; £2,519; £1,264; £634) **Stalls** Low

Form RPR

1 **1** **Miss O Connor (IRE)**[9] 5592 4-9-2 92............................ OisinMurphy 4 108+
(William Haggas) *led after 1/2 f: mde rest: 1 l ld 3f out and 2f out: drvn into 2 l ld 1f out: drvn out fnl f* **11/10[1]**

3305 **2** *2 1/4* **Red Starlight**[21] 5187 4-9-2 98................................ RossaRyan 7 101
(Richard Hannon) *hld up: last 3f out: drvn and swtchd to far side over 2f out: rdn in 2nd 1f out: kpt on fnl f* **8/1**

11- **3** *1 1/2* **Feliciana De Vega**[237] 9570 3-8-9 0............................ HarryBentley 1 96
(Ralph Beckett) *trckd ldrs: 3rd 3f out: drven 2f out: rdn over 1f out: kpt on fnl f* **2/1[2]**

4131 **4** *nk* **Maid For Life**[11] 5525 3-8-9 85..................................(h) ChrisHayes 2 95
(Charlie Fellowes) *hld up: drvn and effrt over 2f out: sn rdn: one pce fnl f* **14/1**

0143 **5** *nk* **Muchly**[35] 4667 3-8-9 100................................ PJMcDonald 6 95
(John Gosden) *led 1/2f: remained prom whn hdd: 1 l 2nd 3f out: drvn 2f out: no ex fnl f* **7/1[3]**

0266 **6** *6* **Contrive (IRE)**[34] 4706 4-9-2 93............................ ColmO'Donoghue 9 83
(Roger Varian) *chsd ldrs on outer: tk clsr order on stands' rail 4f out: drvn 2f out: rdn and wknd over 1f out* **33/1**

-454 **7** *3 1/4* **New Day Dawn (IRE)**[32] 4758 4-9-2 92.................... RichardKingscote 5 76
(Tom Dascombe) *mid-div: pushed along 3f out: rdn and wknd 2f out: eased fnl f* **25/1**

1m 46.36s (1.46) **Going Correction** +0.425s/f (Yiel)
WFA 3 from 4yo 7lb **7 Ran SP% 118.0**
Speed ratings (Par 111): **109,106,105,104,104 98,95**
CSF £11.87 TOTE £1.90: £1.40, £3.20; EX 11.30 Trifecta £24.90.
Owner Lael Stable **Bred** Kilnamoragh Stud **Trained** Newmarket, Suffolk

FOCUS
A fascinating renewal of this Listed contest. Victory went the way of a William Haggas-trained filly for the third time in six years. The second has been rated to her recent best.

5950 ROSE OF LANCASTER STKS (GROUP 3) 1m 2f 100y
3:05 (3:05) (Class 1) 3-Y-O+

£35,727 (£13,545; £6,778; £3,376; £1,694; £850) **Stalls** Centre

Form RPR

412 **1** **Addeybb (IRE)**[14] 5455 5-9-5 114..........................(p) RichardKingscote 4 116
(William Haggas) *chsd ldrs: wnt 2nd over 4f out: cl 2nd 3f out: drvn to ld over 1f out: rdn clr fnl f* **11/10[1]**

1162 **2** *2 1/4* **Pondus**[21] 5182 3-8-11 105................................ DanielMuscutt 2 111
(James Fanshawe) *mid-div: trckd ldrs 3f out: pushed along 2f out: rdn into 2nd ent fnl f: r.o but no match for wnr* **5/1[3]**

-110 **3** *1 1/4* **Raise You (IRE)**[69] 3390 3-8-11 105............................ OisinMurphy 7 108
(Andrew Balding) *led: narrow ld 3f out: pushed along and hdd over 1f out: reminder and drvn 1f out: no ex* **2/1[2]**

-026 **4** *3* **Wadilsafa**[28] 4900 4-9-5 110.................................... ChrisHayes 5 102
(Owen Burrows) *t.k.h: chsd ldr: dropped to 3rd over 4f out: pushed along 3f out: sn drvn: rdn and no ex fr over 1f out* **11/1**

2335 **5** *nk* **Surrey Thunder (FR)**[34] 4707 3-8-11 106.................... HarryBentley 3 101
(Joseph Tuite) *hld up in rr: drvn over 2f out: rdn over 1f out: no imp* **10/1**

0330 **6** *8* **Lunar Jet**[11] 5519 5-9-5 93.................................... JimmyQuinn 6 85
(John Mackie) *hld up: drvn 2f out: rdn and lost tch over 1f out* **40/1**

2m 15.47s (-1.13) **Going Correction** +0.425s/f (Yiel)
WFA 3 from 4yo+ 8lb **6 Ran SP% 117.5**
Speed ratings (Par 113): **121,119,118,115,115 109**
CSF £7.84 TOTE £1.90: £1.20, £2.40; EX 6.10 Trifecta £14.40.
Owner Sheikh Ahmed Al Maktoum **Bred** Rabbah Bloodstock Limited **Trained** Newmarket, Suffolk

FOCUS
The morning defection of Wissahickon lessened the depth of this Group 3, though it's hard to fault the effort of convincing winner, Addeybb. Straightforward form, with the second and third rated to their marks.

5951 DUKE OF LANCASTER'S OWN YEOMANRY H'CAP 6f
3:40 (3:40) (Class 4) (0-85,85) 3-Y-O+

£7,115 (£2,117; £1,058; £529; £300; £300) **Stalls** High

Form RPR

3-11 **1** **Last Empire**[39] 4489 3-9-3 **80**.................................... SamJames 2 97+
(Kevin Ryan) *prom: cl 2nd gng wl 2f out: eased into ld 1 1/2f out: sn pushed along: kpt up to work and readily c clr fnl f: easily* **5/1**

-021 **2** *4 1/2* **Fantasy Keeper**[56] 3856 5-9-8 **81**............................ OisinMurphy 8 85
(Michael Appleby) *prom: led over 2f out: drvn and hdd 1 1/2f out: rdn over 1f out: kpt on fnl f: no ch w easy wnr: lost shoe (vet said gelding lost it's left fore shoe)* **7/2[2]**

0030 **3** *1/2* **Captain Jameson (IRE)**[42] 4369 4-9-10 **83**.................... BenCurtis 5 86
(John Quinn) *hld up: trckd ldrs 1/2-way: rdn over 1f out: r.o into 3rd fnl f* **11/2**

2130 **4** *1 1/4* **Gabrial The Devil (IRE)**[7] 5661 4-9-5 **85**.............. AngusVilliers(7) 7 84
(Richard Fahey) *slowly away: sn rcvrd to go prom: drvn 2f out: rdn over 1f out: one pce fnl f* **9/2[3]**

0043 **5** *3/4* **Gymkhana**[7] 5692 6-9-11 **84**....................................(v) ShaneGray 6 81
(David O'Meara) *hld up: drvn 2f out: no imp* **10/1**

5030 **6** *shd* **Fair Alibi**[10] 5551 3-8-0 **66** oh3............................ JaneElliott(3) 10 61
(Tom Tate) *trckd ldr on stands' side: drvn and lost pl over 2f out: wknd* **25/1**

0126 **7** *2* **Came From The Dark (IRE)**[21] 5173 3-9-6 **83**.............. PJMcDonald 9 72
(Ed Walker) *led on stands' rail: drvn and hdd over 2f out: sn wknd* **5/2[1]**

2100 **8** *nk* **Powerallied (IRE)**[7] 5661 6-9-11 **84**............................ JackGarritty 1 73
(Richard Fahey) *mid-div far side: drvn 2f out: rdn 1f out: dropped away fnl f (jockey said gelding hung left-handed)* **25/1**

1m 16.25s (2.35) **Going Correction** +0.425s/f (Yiel)
WFA 3 from 4yo+ 4lb **8 Ran SP% 117.8**
Speed ratings (Par 105): **101,95,94,92,91 91,88,88**
CSF £23.64 CT £99.30 TOTE £4.90: £1.70, £1.60, £1.90; EX 22.70 Trifecta £95.50.
Owner Clipper Logistics **Bred** Mrs G S Rees And Douglas McMahon **Trained** Hambleton, N Yorks

FOCUS
This competitive looking field was taken apart by the rapidly progressive Last Empire. The second has been rated close to his best.

5952 WATCH RACING TV NOW H'CAP 5f
4:15 (4:15) (Class 5) (0-70,74) 3-Y-O+

£4,851 (£1,443; £721; £360; £300; £300) **Stalls** High

Form RPR

3120 **1** **Somewhere Secret**[7] 5661 5-9-11 **64**........................(p) JackGarritty 3 74
(Michael Mullineaux) *mid-div: pushed along and hdwy 2f out: drvn into ld 1f out: rdn fnl f: r.o wl* **4/1[2]**

6353 **2** *2* **Red Stripes (USA)**[3] 5819 7-8-9 **55**....................(b) GavinAshton(7) 4 58
(Lisa Williamson) *prom: drvn into ld over 1f out: sn rdn: hdd 1f out: one pce fnl f* **8/1**

340 **3** *3/4* **Astrophysics**[5] 5722 7-9-3 **56**................................(p[1]) PJMcDonald 1 56
(Lynn Siddall) *bhd: pushed along in last 1/2-way: hdwy 2f out: rdn in 4th ent fnl f: kpt on into 3rd 1/2f out* **12/1**

4262 **4** *3* **Vee Man Ten**[7] 5660 3-9-11 **74**............................(p) AngusVilliers(7) 5 62
(Ivan Furtado) *led: pushed along in narrow ld 2f out: drvn and hdd over 1f out: rdn and wknd fnl f* **4/1[2]**

0043 **5** *3/4* **Brandy Station (IRE)**[9] 5582 4-9-0 **60**.............. ElishaWhittington(7) 6 47
(Lisa Williamson) *prom: pushed along 2f out: rdn and wknd 1 1/2f out (jockey said gelding hung slightly right-handed in the closing stages)* **8/1**

0022 **6** *1 1/2* **Bahuta Acha**[10] 5551 4-9-12 **65**....................(b) RichardKingscote 7 46
(David Loughnane) *hld up: rdn over 2f out: no imp (trainer said gelding was unsuited by the Heavy ground and would prefer a faster surface)* **11/4[1]**

060 **7** *1/2* **The Golden Cue**[65] 3504 4-8-13 **59**............................ TobyEley(7) 2 38
(Steph Hollinshead) *slowly away: bhd: rcvrd to chse ldrs 1/2-way: drvn and wknd over 2f out (jockey said gelding was slowly away and never travelling thereafter)* **16/1**

0001 **8** *7* **Spirit Power**[21] 5180 4-9-12 **65**................................ GrahamLee 9 19
(Eric Alston) *mid-div on stands' rail: drvn and lost pl 1/2-way: sn rdn and dropped away (trainers' rep said gelding was unsuited by the ground and would prefer a faster surface)* **5/1[3]**

1m 2.59s (2.19) **Going Correction** +0.425s/f (Yiel)
WFA 3 from 4yo+ 3lb **8 Ran SP% 119.1**
Speed ratings (Par 103): **99,95,94,89,88 86,85,74**
CSF £37.28 CT £359.14 TOTE £4.70: £1.60, £1.70, £3.10; EX 37.50 Trifecta £314.00.
Owner Mia Racing **Bred** Mia Racing **Trained** Alpraham, Cheshire

FOCUS
It paid to race towards the centre of the track in this modest sprint handicap. The winner has been rated back to his 2018 best.

5953 RACINGTV.COM H'CAP 7f 37y
4:45 (4:46) (Class 3) (0-95,94) 3-Y-O **£12,938** (£3,850; £1,924; £962) **Stalls** Low

Form RPR

0105 **1** **Finoah (IRE)**[35] 4669 3-8-13 **89**............................(v) JaneElliott(3) 3 96
(Tom Dascombe) *led: drvn in narrow ld 2f out: rdn and hdd 1 1/2f out: rallied to ld early ins fnl f: drvn out nr fin* **11/2**

4125 **2** *3/4* **Sir Busker (IRE)**[23] 5090 3-9-0 **87**............................(v) HarryBentley 4 92
(William Knight) *hld up: drvn 3f out: rdn 2f out: hdwy over 1f out: r.o wl fnl f: tk 2nd last 100yds* **7/1**

1-00 **3** *1/2* **The Great Heir (FR)**[63] 3599 3-8-12 **85**........................ ShaneGray 6 89+
(Kevin Ryan) *mid-div: hdwy 2f out: drvn into ld 1 1/2f out: sn rdn: hdd early ins fnl f: no ex and lost 2nd last 100yds* **20/1**

1032 **4** *3 3/4* **Kapono**[14] 5459 3-8-5 **78**..(p) BenCurtis 9 72
(Roger Fell) *mid-div on outer: pushed along and hdwy 2f out: rdn in 3rd over 1f out: no ex and dropped to 4th fnl f* **5/1[3]**

2345 **5** *1 3/4* **Reeves**[7] 5685 3-8-11 **84**..(p) PJMcDonald 5 74
(Robert Cowell) *prom: pushed along and lost pl 3f out: drvn and one pce fr 2f out* **6/1**

151- **6** *6* **Jonah Jones (IRE)**[301] 8196 3-9-7 **94**..............(w) RichardKingscote 2 68
(Tom Dascombe) *hld up: rdn 3f out: no imp: sn wknd (trainer could offer no explanation for the poor performance)* **4/1[2]**

433 **7** *2 1/4* **Praxidice**[14] 5459 3-8-2 **75** oh2............................ JimmyQuinn 8 43
(K R Burke) *prom on outer: cl 2nd 3f out: drvn and wknd over 2f out* **12/1**

1-31 **8** *8* **Wise Counsel**[56] 3858 3-9-4 **91**........ OisinMurphy 1 38
(Clive Cox) *mid-div: pushed along 2f out: drvn and wknd over 1f out: eased fnl f (trainers' rep could offer no explanation for the poor performance other than the jockey reported that the colt stopped quickly)* **3/1**[1]

1m 33.74s (2.34) **Going Correction** +0.425s/f (Yiel) **8** Ran SP% **116.3**
Speed ratings (Par 104): **103,102,101,97,95 88,85,76**
CSF £44.08 CT £718.17 TOTE £6.30: £1.80, £2.30, £4.10; EX 49.90 Trifecta £577.20.
Owner Alan & Sue Cronshaw & Peter Birbeck **Bred** Azienda Agricola La Rovere **Trained** Malpas, Cheshire

FOCUS
Not a bad handicap, and the winner has been rated as running a length pb. The second has been rated in line with the better view of his form, and the third to his 2yo form.
T/Plt: £232.30 to a £1 stake. Pool: £101,275.77 - 318.24 winning units T/Qpdt: £19.90 to a £1 stake. Pool: £8,561.59 - 317.73 winning units **Keith McHugh**

5675 LINGFIELD (L-H)
Saturday, August 10

OFFICIAL GOING: Good (good to firm in places; 7.0)
Wind: Very strong tail wind in straight Weather: overcast and very windy

5954 CELEBRATING 70 YEARS OF ROBIN STOREY H'CAP 1m 5f
5:10 (5:10) (Class 5) (0-75,76) 3-Y-O
£3,428 (£1,020; £509; £400; £400; £400) **Stalls** Centre

Form RPR
5115 **1** **Earl Of Harrow**[47] 4187 3-9-2 **73**........ ScottMcCullagh(5) 4 79
(Mick Channon) *hld up: gd hdwy between rivals 2f out: rdn to ld over 1f out: drvn out fnl f* **7/1**[3]

6411 **2** *nk* **Oliver Hardy**[53] 3965 3-9-5 **71**........(t) TomMarquand 2 76
(Paul Cole) *trckd ldng pair: rdn to chse ldr 2f out: ev ch 1f out: kpt on wl but unable to match wnr fnl 100yds (jockey said colt hung right-handed under pressure)* **7/2**[2]

01-3 **3** *1* **Albanita**[8] 5605 3-9-10 **76**........(p[1]) RyanTate 1 80
(Sir Mark Prescott Bt) *hld up: smooth hdwy to chse ldrs 2f out: rdn and ev ch 1f out: no ex fnl f* **1/1**[1]

4265 **4** *1 ¼* **Hummdinger (FR)**[35] 4656 3-8-10 **62**........ GeorgeWood 7 64
(Alan King) *trckd ldr: pushed along to ld on outer 2f out: sn rdn and hdd by wnr over 1f out: one pce after* **11/1**

2620 **5** *1 ¼* **Fayetta**[6] 5712 3-9-0 **71**........(b) ThomasGreatrex(5) 5 71
(David Loughnane) *led: rdn along and hdd 2f out: wkng whn hmpd 1f out: no ex* **10/1**

0444 **6** *8* **Geomatrician (FR)**[28] 4929 3-9-0 **69**........ WilliamCox(3) 6 57
(Andrew Balding) *racd in midfield: pushed along and outpcd 3f out: sn rdn and detached over 1f out* **15/2**

2m 52.02s **6** Ran SP% **113.9**
CSF £31.96 TOTE £9.30: £3.00, £1.80; EX 29.70 Trifecta £74.90.
Owner Peter Taplin & Partner **Bred** Norman Court Stud **Trained** West Ilsley, Berks

FOCUS
Ordinary staying handicap form and there were no obvious excuses for the short-priced favourite who held every chance up the inside. The fifth has been rated close to form.

5955 VISTAVIS LTD NOVICE MEDIAN AUCTION STKS 1m 2f
5:45 (5:48) (Class 6) 3-5-Y-O **£2,781** (£827; £413; £206) **Stalls** Low

Form RPR
0-5 **1** **Sandyman**[14] 5451 3-9-5 0........ LiamKeniry 2 77
(Paul Cole) *trckd ldr: decisive move on outer to ld 4f out: qckly wnt 5 l clr 3f out: rdn and in n.d over 1f out: kpt on wl* **5/1**[3]

23 **2** *2 ¼* **Aegeus (USA)**[81] 2932 3-9-5 0........ JackMitchell 9 73
(Amanda Perrett) *racd in midfield: hdwy on outer 3f out: wnt 2nd and rdn to chse wnr 2f out: drvn and clsd gap 1f out: kpt on wl* **7/2**[2]

4 **3** *3 ¼* **Voice Of Calm**[32] 4768 3-8-11 0........ MitchGodwin(3) 8 62
(Harry Dunlop) *racd in midfield: hdwy u.p over 2f out: rdn and wnt 3rd over 1f out: kpt on but no ch w wnr* **6/1**

4 **4** *2 ¼* **Brambledown**[14] 5428 3-9-5 0........ HectorCrouch 13 63
(Gary Moore) *hld up: rdn along on outer 3f out: kpt on wl enough passed btn horses ins fnl f* **22/1**

21 **5** *nk* **Five Diamonds**[24] 5062 3-9-5 0........ DaneO'Neill 4 63+
(William Haggas) *in tch in 4th: hdwy on outer whn slipped on bnd over 3f out: sn rdn and no imp 2f out: kpt on one pce (jockey said filly slipped on the bend)* **4/5**[1]

6 **6** *1 ¼* **Riverfront (FR)**[9] 5592 3-9-2 0........ WilliamCox(3) 3 60
(Andrew Balding) *racd in midfield: rdn along and no hdwy over 2f out: kpt on one pce fnl f* **14/1**

0 **7** *10* **Angels Chant**[40] 4452 3-9-0 0........(t[1]) CharlieBennett 11 37
(Jim Boyle) *dwlt and racd in rr: nvr on terms* **50/1**

6 **8** *16* **Stevie Smith**[31] 4779 3-9-0 0........ HollieDoyle 5 8
(Amy Murphy) *led: pushed along and hdd by wnr 4f out: rdn and awkward off home bnd over 3f out: sn lost pl (jockey said filly stopped quickly)* **50/1**

0 **9** *1 ½* **Little Lady Luck**[152] 1142 3-8-7 0........ EllieMacKenzie(7) 1
(Mark Usher) *trckd ldr: rdn to chse wnr 3f out: lost pl fr 2f out: sn bhd* **33/1**

2m 8.2s (-4.00) **Going Correction** -0.20s/f (Firm) **9** Ran SP% **126.6**
Speed ratings (Par 101): **108,106,103,101,101 100,92,79,78**
CSF £24.65 TOTE £7.80: £1.90, £1.50, £1.80; EX 33.60 Trifecta £147.70.
Owner The Fairy Story Partnership **Bred** Deepwood Farm Stud **Trained** Whatcombe, Oxon

FOCUS
Not much depth to this novice event but the winner is looking quite progressive now and he may well have won even if things had gone to plan for market leader Five Diamonds.

5956 QUALITY CARE INSURANCE SERVICES 10TH ANNIVERSARY EBF NOVICE STKS 7f 135y
6:15 (6:17) (Class 5) 2-Y-O **£3,428** (£1,020; £509; £254) **Stalls** Centre

Form RPR
4 **1** **Johan**[14] 5439 2-9-5 0........ TomMarquand 7 81+
(William Haggas) *dwlt sltly but rcvrd to make virtually all on rail: pushed along w short ld 2f out: rdn and drew clr fnl f* **10/11**[1]

2 *3 ½* **Rovaniemi (IRE)** 2-9-5 0........ JamieSpencer 4 73+
(David Simcock) *settled wl in midfield: hdwy to trck wnr 2f out: rdn and ev ch 1f out: nt match wnr fnl f* **13/8**[2]

034 **3** *2* **Always Fearless (IRE)**[10] 5550 2-9-5 73........ PatDobbs 6 68
(Richard Hannon) *trckd wnr on outer: pushed along to chse wnr 2f out: rdn and kpt on one pce fnl f* **6/1**[3]

4 *2 ¾* **Red For All** 2-9-5 0........ HollieDoyle 3 62+
(Ed Dunlop) *midfield: pushed along and a little green 2f out: kpt on one pce fnl f: bttr for run* **12/1**

5 *1 ¾* **Isolde (IRE)** 2-9-0 0........ GeorgeWood 9 53
(Amy Murphy) *racd in midfield: rdn and outpcd over 2f out: kpt on one pce fnl f* **40/1**

0 **6** *1* **Max's Voice (IRE)**[17] 5294 2-9-0 0........ ThomasGreatrex(5) 5 55
(David Loughnane) *chsd wnr: rdn along and outpcd over 2f out: one pce after* **33/1**

04 **7** *13* **Clandestine Affair (IRE)**[12] 5493 2-9-5 0........ KieranShoemark 10 25
(Jamie Osborne) *hld up: rdn in rr 2f out: nvr on terms (jockey said colt was slow into stride)* **50/1**

05 **8** *6* **Resplendent Rose**[57] 3798 2-9-0 0........ LiamKeniry 8 6
(Michael Madgwick) *in tch: pushed along 3f out: lost pl and bhd over 1f out* **80/1**

9 *4* **One Alc (FR)** 2-9-5 0........ JoeyHaynes 2
(Dean Ivory) *hld up: pushed along and outpcd over 2f out: nvr on terms* **33/1**

10 *1 ½* **Tamar (IRE)** 2-9-5 0........ TomQueally 1
(Alan King) *hld up: a in rr* **25/1**

1m 31.06s (-0.64) **Going Correction** -0.20s/f (Firm) **10** Ran SP% **127.8**
Speed ratings (Par 94): **95,91,89,86,85 84,71,65,61,59**
CSF £2.81 TOTE £1.70: £1.10, £1.10, £1.90; EX 2.80 Trifecta £10.00.
Owner Jon and Julia Aisbitt **Bred** Jon And Julia Aisbitt **Trained** Newmarket, Suffolk

FOCUS
Not a bad little novice event with the front two both potentially above average.

5957 TRUSTEE FIRE & SECURITY LTD H'CAP 7f 135y
6:45 (6:47) (Class 6) (0-60,61) 3-Y-O
£2,781 (£827; £413; £400; £400; £400) **Stalls** Centre

Form RPR
0000 **1** **Break Of Day**[19] 5249 3-8-8 **47**........(b) TomMarquand 8 57
(William Haggas) *hld up: hdwy between rivals 2f out: rdn to ld over 1f out: kpt on wl fnl f (trainer said, regards apparent improvement in form, filly appreciated the drop in trip)* **13/2**

0452 **2** *3* **Classic Star**[10] 5561 3-9-3 **61**........ SophieRalston(5) 12 64+
(Dean Ivory) *hld up in last: making hdwy whn nt clr run 2f out: rdn and rapid hdwy ins fnl f: too much to do (jockey said gelding was denied a clear run approaching the final two furlongs)* **2/1**[1]

0405 **3** *3 ¾* **Yfenni (IRE)**[15] 5377 3-8-7 **46** oh1........ RaulDaSilva 11 40
(Milton Bradley) *led: rdn along and hdd by wnr over 1f out: kpt on one pce fnl f* **33/1**

1032 **4** *½* **Poetic Motion**[35] 4642 3-8-11 **50**........ CharlieBennett 9 43
(Jim Boyle) *trckd ldr: pushed along to chse ldr over 2f out: rdn and no imp over 1f out: one pce after* **4/1**[2]

0004 **5** *½* **Invincible One (IRE)**[10] 5552 3-8-8 **52**........(p[1]) WilliamCarver(5) 5 44
(Sylvester Kirk) *racd in midfield: rdn and outpcd over 2f out: kpt on one pce fnl f* **7/1**

0001 **6** *1 ½* **Sussex Solo**[14] 5431 3-8-12 **51**........ TomQueally 7 40
(Luke Dace) *dwlt bdly and racd in last: rdn on outer over 2f out: sme late hdwy (jockey said gelding was slowly away)* **7/1**

156 **7** *¾* **Elzaam's Dream (IRE)**[24] 5057 3-9-1 **54**........(h) KieranO'Neill 4 41
(Ronald Harris) *racd alone in midfield on outer: rdn and unable qck 2f out: one pce fnl f* **6/1**[3]

005 **8** *5* **Savoy Brown**[14] 5431 3-9-2 **55**........ JackMitchell 6 30
(Michael Attwater) *hld up: pushed along and short of room 2f out: sn rdn and no imp: n.d* **12/1**

60-3 **9** *11* **Abuja (IRE)**[14] 5429 3-9-1 **54**........(h) LiamKeniry 10 3
(Michael Madgwick) *trckd ldr: rdn along and outpcd 2f out: wknd fnl f* **33/1**

0000 **10** *19* **Illywhacker (IRE)**[15] 5377 3-9-2 **55**........(b[1]) HectorCrouch 2
(Gary Moore) *racd in midfield: rdn along and lost pl over 2f out: sn bhd* **16/1**

0456 **P** **Sukalia**[31] 4794 3-8-12 **54**........ MitchGodwin(3) 3
(John Bridger) *hld up: pushed along 3f out: lost action and qckly p.u over 2f out* **25/1**

1m 31.27s (-0.43) **Going Correction** -0.20s/f (Firm) **11** Ran SP% **129.3**
Speed ratings (Par 98): **94,91,87,86,86 84,84,79,68,49**
CSF £21.64 CT £430.74 TOTE £8.20: £2.40, £1.40, £10.70; EX 29.30 Trifecta £549.40.
Owner The Queen **Bred** The Queen **Trained** Newmarket, Suffolk

FOCUS
A weak handicap in which market leader Classic Star had a nightmare run. However, the winner posted a much improved effort and might well have won anyway.

5958 CORE GROUP NURSERY H'CAP 6f
7:15 (7:18) (Class 6) (0-60,68) 2-Y-O
£2,781 (£827; £413; £400; £400; £400) **Stalls** Centre

Form RPR
560 **1** **Foad**[22] 5125 2-9-6 **59**........(b[1]) JimCrowley 6 65
(Ed Dunlop) *racd in tch: gd hdwy to chse ldr 2f out: rdn along to ld over 1f out: drvn and kpt on strly fnl f* **7/2**[1]

6453 **2** *hd* **Come On Girl**[9] 5576 2-8-11 **50**........ RaulDaSilva 2 55
(Tony Carroll) *midfield on outer: pushed along to chse wnr 2f out: sn rdn over 1f out: kpt on wl fnl f: nt quite rch wnr* **6/1**[3]

0665 **3** *2 ¾* **New Jack Swing (IRE)**[9] 5576 2-9-5 **58**........(p[1]) TomMarquand 11 55
(Richard Hannon) *in rr of midfield: hdwy u.p to chse wnr 2f out: sn rdn and unable to match pce of wnr 1f out: kpt on* **7/2**[1]

004 **4** *1 ¼* **Grace Plunkett**[78] 3055 2-9-2 **55**........(b[1]) KieranShoemark 8 48
(Richard Spencer) *led: rdn along and hdd by wnr over 1f out: one pce fnl f* **20/1**

460 **5** *nk* **Mr Kodi (IRE)**[28] 4925 2-9-8 **61**........ JasonWatson 9 53
(David Evans) *trckd ldr on rail: rdn along and swtchd lft over 1f out: kpt on fnl f (jockey said gelding hung left-handed under pressure)* **8/1**

3431 **6** *shd* **Bartat**[3] 5800 2-9-10 **68** 6ex........ ScottMcCullagh(5) 5 60
(Mick Channon) *in rr: hdwy u.p on outer 2f out: sn rdn and kpt on fnl f* **9/2**[2]

6004 **7** *3 ½* **Shaun's Delight (IRE)**[25] 5010 2-9-0 **53**........ LiamKeniry 3 34
(Ronald Harris) *racd in midfield: strly rdn and no imp 2f out: one pce after* **33/1**

060 **8** *2 ¾* **Thomas Lanfiere (FR)**[37] 4564 2-9-2 **60**........ DylanHogan(5) 10 33
(David Simcock) *in rr of midfield: rdn along and outpcd 2f out: plugged on* **12/1**

365 **9** *½* **Claudia Jean (IRE)**[14] 5427 2-9-1 **54**........ PatDobbs 1 26
(Richard Hannon) *wnt lft s and hld up in rr: rdn in rr 3f out: nvr on terms* **12/1**

5003 **10** 3 1/4 **Ask Siri (IRE)**[17] 5313 2-8-7 **46**........................ KieranO'Neill 4 8
(John Bridger) *chsd ldr: rdn and outpcd over 2f out: wknd fnl f* **12/1**

033 **11** 1 1/2 **Jane Victoria**[14] 5427 2-8-13 **57**........................ ThoreHammerHansen(5) 7 14
(Adam West) *in rr of midfield: stl gng wl amongst rivals over 2f out: sn rdn and fnd little over 1f out: wknd whn btn (jockey said filly was never travelling)* **12/1**

1m 11.07s (-0.43) **Going Correction** -0.20s/f (Firm) 11 Ran SP% **126.5**
Speed ratings (Par 92): **94,93,90,88,88 87,83,79,78,74 72**
CSF £26.79 CT £84.67 TOTE £4.70: £1.80, £1.60, £1.70; EX 28.00 Trifecta £108.20.
Owner Hamdan Al Maktoum **Bred** Fittocks Stud **Trained** Newmarket, Suffolk

FOCUS
A modest nursery in which the front two came away in the final furlong. The winner has potential but he was all out to see off a more exposed rival so the form probably isn't anything to get excited about.

5959 DEVINE HOMES, HAMMONDS MILL H'CAP 6f
7:45 (7:45) (Class 5) (0-75,80) 3-Y-O+
£3,428 (£1,020; £509; £400; £400; £400) **Stalls** Centre

Form RPR

1141 **1** **Magical Ride**[7] 5677 4-9-7 **80**........................ SeanKirrane(7) 2 98
(Richard Spencer) *trckd pce: shkn up to ld 2f out: rdn and readily drew clr over 1f out: eased cl home: easily* **6/5**[1]

0242 **2** 7 **Seprani**[2] 5870 5-9-2 **71**........................ GabrieleMalune(3) 3 67
(Amy Murphy) *racd in midfield: rdn along to chse wnr over 2f out: kpt on to take remote 2nd cl home* **9/2**[2]

2300 **3** 1 1/4 **Joegogo (IRE)**[19] 5252 4-9-10 **76**........................ JasonWatson 4 68
(David Evans) *led: rdn and hdd by wnr 2f out: kpt on but lost 2nd clsng stages* **11/1**

033 **4** 1 1/2 **Peace Dreamer (IRE)**[25] 5015 5-9-7 **73**........................ TomMarquand 6 60
(Robert Cowell) *hld up: rdn and outpcd 2f out: nvr on terms* **9/1**

5434 **5** 1 1/4 **Crimewave (IRE)**[14] 5445 3-9-4 **74**........................(b) JackMitchell 5 56
(Tom Clover) *hld up: rdn along and outpcd 2f out: one pce fnl f* **9/2**[2]

3340 **6** 1 1/2 **Monumental Man**[148] 1209 10-9-2 **68**........................ HollieDoyle 7 46
(Jamie Osborne) *chsd ldr: rdn and lost pl 2f out: no ex* **16/1**

/5-3 **7** 1 **Springbourne**[49] 4116 5-9-4 **75**........................ ThoreHammerHansen(5) 1 50
(Bill Turner) *hld up: rdn in rr 1/2-way: nvr on terms (jockey said gelding was never travelling)* **8/1**[3]

1m 9.51s (-1.99) **Going Correction** -0.20s/f (Firm) 7 Ran SP% **117.1**
WFA 3 from 4yo+ 4lb
Speed ratings (Par 103): **105,95,94,92,90 88,87**
CSF £7.25 TOTE £1.80: £1.40, £2.30; EX 6.60 Trifecta £43.90.
Owner The Magic Horse Syndicate **Bred** Highclere Stud **Trained** Newmarket, Suffolk

FOCUS
This ordinary handicap was dominated by the one really progressive runner in the field and he is proving a real star for connections this season.

5960 TRACY & BETHAN BIRTHDAY CELEBRATIONS MAIDEN STKS 4f 217y
8:15 (8:15) (Class 5) 3-Y-O+ **£3,428** (£1,020; £509; £254) **Stalls** Centre

Form RPR

443 **1** **Kodiak Attack (IRE)**[42] 4396 3-9-5 65........................ JasonWatson 2 62
(Sylvester Kirk) *trckd ldr: pushed along to ld narrowly 2f out: rdn over 1f out w short ld: drvn rt out fnl f: jst hld on* **8/11**[1]

4004 **2** nk **Starchant**[24] 5046 3-9-0 51........................ KieranO'Neill 6 56
(John Bridger) *led: rdn along and hdd by wnr 2f out: drvn and kpt on really wl fnl f: jst failed* **9/2**[2]

0463 **3** 6 **Tigerinmytank**[1] 5884 3-8-11 44........................ WilliamCox(3) 4 34
(John Holt) *racd in midfield: rdn along and outpcd by front pair 2f out: kpt on fnl f* **5/1**[3]

4 2 3/4 **Excelinthejungle (IRE)** 3-9-5 0........................ TomQueally 8 29
(Seamus Durack) *dwlt and racd in rr: hdwy into midfield 1/2-way: rdn 2f out and no imp: one pce fnl f* **7/1**

0500 **5** shd **More Salutes (IRE)**[42] 4378 4-9-3 43........................(p) ScottMcCullagh(5) 3 30
(Michael Attwater) *midfield: rdn and readily outpcd 2f out: one pce fnl f* **20/1**

-600 **6** 3 3/4 **Diamond Cara**[8] 5622 3-8-7 29........................ MarcoGhiani(7) 5 11
(Stuart Williams) *hld up: a in rr* **16/1**

65 **7** nse **Mother Brown**[28] 4927 3-8-9 0........................ ThoreHammerHansen(5) 1 10
(Bill Turner) *hld up: drvn along in rr 2f out: nvr on terms* **20/1**

6-00 **8** hd **Miss President**[24] 5063 3-9-0 52........................(v[1]) TomMarquand 7 10
(Robert Cowell) *broke wl and settled in midfield: sn lost pl and dropped to last 3f out: sn btn* **12/1**

57.78s (-0.92) **Going Correction** -0.20s/f (Firm) 8 Ran SP% **128.4**
WFA 3 from 4yo 3lb
Speed ratings (Par 103): **99,98,88,84,84 78,78,77**
CSF £5.39 TOTE £1.50: £1.10, £1.60, £1.50; EX 5.30 Trifecta £12.50.
Owner Mrs J Fowler **Bred** Tally-Ho Stud **Trained** Upper Lambourn, Berks

FOCUS
A weak maiden won by the standout form choice, although he was all out to hold on from a 51-rated rival close home which holds the form back somewhat. The second has been rated to this year's best.
T/Plt: £72.30 to a £1 stake. Pool: £58,641.24 - 591.61 winning units T/Qpdt: £4.50 to a £1 stake. Pool: £9,415.32 - 1538.38 winning units **Mark Grantham**

5906 NEWMARKET (R-H)
Saturday, August 10

OFFICIAL GOING: Good to firm (good in places; watered; 7.7)
Wind: very blustery Weather: overcast early then good sunny spells; 22 degrees

5961 SEA THE MOON 'NEWCOMERS' MAIDEN FILLIES' STKS (PLUS 10 RACE) 7f
2:00 (2:01) (Class 4) 2-Y-O **£5,175** (£1,540; £769; £384) **Stalls** Low

Form RPR

1 **Leafhopper (IRE)** 2-9-0 0........................ RobertHavlin 4 83+
(John Gosden) *trckd ldrs: effrt to go 2nd over 1f out: drvn to ld 75yds out: kpt on resolutely* **9/4**[2]

2 hd **Thread Of Silver** 2-9-0 0........................(h[1]) WilliamBuick 3 82+
(Charlie Appleby) *prom: led over 2f out: rdn over 1f out: hdd fnl 75yds: jst hld after* **1/1**[1]

3 3 1/4 **Call Me Katie (IRE)** 2-9-0 0........................ NickyMackay 6 73
(John Gosden) *led: rdn and hdd over 2f out: wknd 1f out* **8/1**

4 1 **Thanielle (FR)** 2-9-0 0........................ SeanLevey 7 71
(Richard Hannon) *racd freely and pressed ldrs: drvn over 2f out: edgd lft and lost tch w ldng pair 1f out (jockey said filly hung left)* **6/1**[3]

5 6 **Fair Sabra** 2-9-0 0........................ DaneO'Neill 5 54
(David Elsworth) *lost 5 l s: bhd: struggling over 2f out* **33/1**

6 2 3/4 **Princess Siyouni (IRE)** 2-9-0 0........................ PatCosgrave 8 47
(Mick Quinn) *chsd ldrs: rdn over 2f out: lost tch wl over 1f out* **25/1**

7 nk **Fluttershy** 2-9-0 0........................ AdrianMcCarthy 1 46
(John Ryan) *bhd: drvn over 2f out: sn struggling* **33/1**

1m 29.04s (3.34) **Going Correction** -0.075s/f (Good) 7 Ran SP% **115.9**
Speed ratings (Par 93): **77,76,73,71,65 61,61**
CSF £4.92 TOTE £3.20: £1.80, £1.30; EX 5.10 Trifecta £22.80.
Owner Godolphin **Bred** Grangemore Stud **Trained** Newmarket, Suffolk

FOCUS
Stands' side course used. Stalls: all races stands' side. A good fillies' maiden for debutantes won by the high-class Wuheida in 2016. They went a sensible gallop into a reportedly strong, gusting crosswind and the second-favourite's winning time was modest on officially good to firm ground.

5962 POPPY NURSERY H'CAP 7f
2:35 (2:36) (Class 3) (0-95,92) 2-Y-O **£9,056** (£2,695; £1,346; £673) **Stalls** Low

Form RPR

311 **1** **Tomfre**[22] 5152 2-9-1 **86**........................ RobHornby 2 90
(Ralph Beckett) *cl up and gng wl: rdn to ld 200yds out: pushed out and ears pricked cl home: smething in hand* **3/1**[3]

231 **2** 3/4 **Visible Charm (IRE)**[22] 5145 2-8-12 **83**........................ WilliamBuick 3 85
(Charlie Appleby) *pressed ldr: pushed along 2f out: ev ch 1f out: no imp on wnr after* **5/2**[2]

421 **3** nse **Incinerator**[17] 5294 2-8-5 **76**........................(t) JosephineGordon 1 78
(Hugo Palmer) *led and racd keenly: rdn over 2f out: hdd fnl 200yds: nt qckn after* **15/2**

0312 **4** 1 1/2 **Sir Arthur Dayne (IRE)**[9] 5576 2-8-10 **81**........................(p) CharlesBishop 4 79
(Mick Channon) *chsd ldrs: drvn over 2f out: wl hld after* **7/1**

2102 **5** 1/2 **Light Angel**[15] 5382 2-9-7 **92**........................ RobertHavlin 5 88
(John Gosden) *plld hrd and stdd in last pl: rdn 2f out: btn over 1f out* **2/1**[1]

1m 25.26s (-0.44) **Going Correction** -0.075s/f (Good) 5 Ran SP% **111.2**
Speed ratings (Par 98): **99,98,98,96,95**
CSF £10.96 TOTE £3.50: £1.80, £1.60; EX 9.90 Trifecta £40.20.
Owner Mrs Philip Snow & Partners **Bred** Mrs P Snow & Partners **Trained** Kimpton, Hants

FOCUS
A fairly good nursery. The third-favourite won a shade cosily and his winning time was nearly four seconds quicker than the opening C&D fillies' maiden.

5963 BBAG-SALES.DE H'CAP 1m
3:10 (3:12) (Class 2) (0-100,101) 3-Y-O **£12,938** (£3,850; £1,924; £962) **Stalls** Low

Form RPR

-110 **1** **Davydenko**[51] 4016 3-8-13 **90**........................ LouisSteward 3 102
(Sir Michael Stoute) *pressed ldr: drvn over 2f out: chal over 1f out: sn hanging lft: led 120yds and easily c clr* **5/1**[3]

2-16 **2** 3 1/2 **Good Fortune**[163] 956 3-9-5 **96**........................ WilliamBuick 1 100
(Charlie Appleby) *led: rdn over 1f out: edgd lft and hdd fnl 120yds: readily outpcd by wnr and wkng cl home (jockey said gelding hung left)* **11/2**

-130 **3** 1/2 **Dubai Legacy (USA)**[51] 4016 3-9-7 **98**........................(p[1]) AdamKirby 2 101
(Saeed bin Suroor) *lost 6 l at s: rdn to chse ldrs at 1/2-way: 3rd and no imp fnl f (jockey said gelding missed the break)* **4/1**[2]

5021 **4** 2 **Barristan The Bold**[14] 5434 3-9-4 **95**........................ FrannyNorton 4 93
(Tom Dascombe) *stdd s: a towards rr: drvn over 2f out: fdd over 1f out* **5/1**[3]

-410 **5** 8 **Beatboxer (USA)**[51] 4016 3-9-10 **101**........................(t) RobertHavlin 6 81
(John Gosden) *bhd: drvn and struggling bdly and racing awkwardly over 2f out* **6/1**

-311 **6** 64 **Motawaj**[17] 5320 3-9-6 **97**........................ JamesDoyle 5
(Roger Varian) *cl up tl rdn and lost action wl over 2f out: sn heavily eased (jockey said gelding was restless in the stalls and lost it's action)* **9/4**[1]

1m 37.1s (-2.90) **Going Correction** -0.075s/f (Good) 6 Ran SP% **113.8**
Speed ratings (Par 106): **111,107,107,105,97 33**
CSF £32.14 TOTE £5.70: £2.70, £2.40; EX 43.50 Trifecta £225.40.
Owner Cheveley Park Stud **Bred** Cheveley Park Stud Ltd **Trained** Newmarket, Suffolk

FOCUS
A good 3yo handicap. The winner had to come around the wayward front-running runner-up and came nicely clear in a good comparative time towards the far rail. The third's Goodwood form is solid and he helps set the level.

5964 GERMAN-THOROUGHBRED.COM SWEET SOLERA STKS (GROUP 3) (FILLIES) 7f
3:45 (3:47) (Class 1) 2-Y-O
£28,355 (£10,750; £5,380; £2,680; £1,345; £675) **Stalls** Low

Form RPR

15 **1** **West End Girl**[16] 5346 2-9-0 0........................ FrannyNorton 1 103
(Mark Johnston) *mde virtually all: rdn over 2f out: jnd 1f out: bmpd briefly: edgd lft but styd on wl cl home* **11/2**

1 **2** 1 1/4 **Soffika (IRE)**[48] 4142 2-9-0 0........................ JamesDoyle 2 99
(Sir Michael Stoute) *towards rr: rdn and outpcd 1/2-way: gd prog 2f out: kpt on ins fnl f to go wl hld 2nd fnl 50yds* **9/2**[3]

214 **3** 1/2 **Dark Lady**[14] 5411 2-9-0 95........................ PatDobbs 4 98
(Richard Hannon) *prom: wnt 2nd over 2f out: chal wnr and edgd rt 1f out: nt qckn after: lost 2nd cl home* **8/1**

314 **4** 1 **Romsey**[16] 5346 2-9-0 92........................ SeanLevey 3 95
(Hughie Morrison) *pressed wnr tl over 2f out: rdn and wknd 1f out* **14/1**

31 **5** 1/2 **Ananya**[21] 5189 2-9-0 0........................ BrettDoyle 7 94
(Peter Chapple-Hyam) *rrd s and lost 10 l: rdn 1/2-way: kpt on ins fnl f but nvr trbld ldrs (jockey said filly was slowly away)* **7/1**

1 **6** 6 **Dalanijujo (IRE)**[21] 5170 2-9-0 0........................ CharlesBishop 5 78
(Mick Channon) *lost 5 l at s: drvn 1/2-way: a bhd* **16/1**

12 **7** 1 3/4 **Light Blush (IRE)**[16] 5346 2-9-0 0........................ WilliamBuick 9 73
(Charlie Appleby) *cl up tl rdn and fdd 2f out* **4/1**[2]

1 **8** 23 **Ultra Violet**[43] 4337 2-9-0 0........................ KieranShoemark 6 11
(Ed Vaughan) *plld too hrd: sn towards rr and racing awkwardly: btn over 2f out: eased and t.o (jockey said filly ran too free)* **11/4**[1]

1m 25.32s (-0.38) **Going Correction** -0.075s/f (Good) 8 Ran SP% **116.4**
Speed ratings (Par 101): **99,97,97,95,95 88,86,60**
CSF £30.99 TOTE £6.70: £2.00, £1.40, £2.10; EX 31.80 Trifecta £260.00.
Owner A D Spence & M B Spence **Bred** Car Colston Hall Stud **Trained** Middleham Moor, N Yorks

FOCUS
The feature race was a good quality renewal of a Group 3 fillies' contest won by the high-class juvenile White Moonstone in 2010. The fourth-favourite is still learning her trade, but bravely outstayed her opponents on the climb to the line.

5965 BBAG GERMANY'S YEARLING SALES H'CAP — 7f
4:20 (4:21) (Class 2) (0-105,102) 3-Y-O+ **£12,938** (£3,850; £1,924; £962) **Stalls** Low

Form / RPR

3421 **1** **Qaysar (FR)**[4] [5776] 4-9-7 **95** 5ex................ JamesDoyle 8 — 105
(Richard Hannon) *pressed ldrs on outside: wnt 2nd 2f out: shkn up over 1f out: sn led: edging rt but holding rival cl home* **9/4**[2]

-064 **2** *nk* **Ibraz**[67] [3450] 4-9-2 **90**................ DavidEgan 3 — 99
(Roger Varian) *2nd tl led 2f out: rdn and hdd 1f out: kpt on nr fin but a hld* **9/2**[3]

1111 **3** *2 ¾* **Nahaarr (IRE)**[36] [4591] 3-8-10 **93**................ GeorgiaCox(3) 7 — 94+
(William Haggas) *stdd in last pl and racing keenly: rdn and swtchd outside to cl over 2f out: 3rd and wl hld fnl f* **11/10**[1]

4033 **4** *1 ¾* **Salateen**[22] [5129] 7-10-0 **102**................(tp) AdamKirby 1 — 101
(David O'Meara) *edgd lft s: led tl rdn and hdd 2f out: btn over 1f out* **16/1**

0400 **5** *1 ¼* **Alemaratalyoum (IRE)**[14] [5413] 5-9-4 **92**................(vt[1]) SeanLevey 5 — 88
(Stuart Williams) *t.k.h towards rr: rdn and outpcd 2f out* **14/1**

0/ **6** *8* **Duplication (IRE)**[659] [8225] 5-8-10 **84**................ FrannyNorton 4 — 61
(John Ryan) *t.k.h: sn bhd: rdn and lost tch qckly over 2f out* **33/1**

1m 25.33s (-0.37) **Going Correction** -0.075s/f (Good)
WFA 3 from 4yo+ 6lb **6** Ran SP% **112.1**
Speed ratings (Par 109): **99,98,95,93,92 82**
CSF £12.65 CT £15.34 TOTE £2.80: £1.50, £2.10; EX 8.50 Trifecta £15.90.
Owner Al Shaqab Racing **Bred** S N C Scuderia Waldeck **Trained** East Everleigh, Wilts

FOCUS
A good handicap. The second-favourite did well to defy a penalty from a wide enough track position. The winner has been rated as backing up his Newbury latest with a similar effort.

5966 ROYAL BRITISH LEGION H'CAP — 1m 2f
4:55 (4:57) (Class 2) (0-100,96) 3-Y-O+ **£12,938** (£3,850; £1,924; £962) **Stalls** Low

Form / RPR

4-56 **1** **Waldstern**[30] [4845] 3-9-6 **96**................(v[1]) RobertHavlin 5 — 109
(John Gosden) *last away: sn rcvrd to chse ldrs on outer: effrt to last of three gng clr 3f out: rdn to ld over 1f out: edgd rt but sn asserted* **11/2**

1310 **2** *2 ¼* **Desert Icon (FR)**[10] [5541] 3-9-1 **91**................ JamesDoyle 6 — 99
(William Haggas) *3rd tl wnt 2nd 1/2-way: rdn and chsd wnr over 1f out: sn outpcd by him* **9/4**[1]

1351 **3** *4 ½* **Victory Chime (IRE)**[16] [5348] 4-9-6 **88**................(v) RobHornby 9 — 87
(Ralph Beckett) *led and t.k.h: drvn over 2f out: hdd over 1f out: racd awkwardly: qckly lost tch w ldng pair* **14/1**

420- **4** *1 ¾* **Eynhallow**[414] [4064] 5-10-0 **96**................ WilliamBuick 4 — 92
(Charlie Appleby) *taken down early: midfield: rdn and outpcd 3f out: no ch after: plugged on* **7/2**[3]

3440 **5** *3 ¾* **Ventura Knight (IRE)**[7] [5667] 4-10-0 **96**................ FrannyNorton 2 — 84
(Mark Johnston) *bhd: drvn 3f out: no rspnse and qckly dropped out* **15/2**

10-2 **6** *3* **Howman (IRE)**[42] [4386] 4-8-13 **81**................ DavidEgan 3 — 63
(Roger Varian) *t.k.h in last pl: drvn and lost tch qckly 3f out (trainers' rep could offer no explanation for the poor performance)* **3/1**[2]

-056 **7** *3 ¾* **Ashington**[63] [3600] 4-9-5 **87**................(v) JasonHart 1 — 62
(John Quinn) *t.k.h pressing ldr tl rdn and lost pl qckly 1/2-way: toiling fnl 3f: t.o* **20/1**

2m 2.4s (-4.70) **Going Correction** -0.075s/f (Good)
WFA 3 from 4yo+ 8lb **7** Ran SP% **116.6**
Speed ratings (Par 109): **115,113,109,108,105 102,99**
CSF £18.96 CT £166.06 TOTE £5.60: £2.60, £1.50; EX 18.70 Trifecta £169.10.
Owner Gestut Ammerland **Bred** Newsells Park & Ammerland Gmbh & Co Kg **Trained** Newmarket, Suffolk

FOCUS
Another good handicap. The fourth-favourite made the most of his 8lb weight-for-age allowance to come slightly clear and win well in a good comparative time.

5967 STAN HOLDSTOCK 80TH BIRTHDAY H'CAP — 2m
5:30 (5:33) (Class 3) (0-90,86) 3-Y-O+ **£9,703** (£2,887; £1,443; £721) **Stalls** Low

Form / RPR

663 **1** **Graceful Lady**[24] [5047] 6-8-11 **74**................ DarraghKeenan(5) 3 — 85
(Robert Eddery) *trckd ldrs in slowly run r: wnt 3rd at 1/2-way: led 1f out: pushed along and easily drew rt away* **14/1**

62-5 **2** *6* **Gwafa (IRE)**[36] [4614] 8-9-13 **85**................ FergusSweeney 7 — 89
(Paul Webber) *mde nrly all at mod pce tl rdn and hdd and racing awkwardly 1f out: immediately outpcd by wnr but jst hld on to poor 2nd* **12/1**

1204 **3** *nk* **Ship Of The Fen**[28] [4899] 4-10-0 **86**................(p[1]) WilliamBuick 8 — 89
(Ian Williams) *plld his way into ld after 2f: sn hdd: pressed ldr tl drvn and lost 2nd over 2f out: styd on same pce whn duelling for poor 2nd fnl f* **11/4**[2]

113- **4** *2* **Matchmaking (GER)**[364] [6015] 4-9-10 **82**................ LukeMorris 6 — 83
(Sir Mark Prescott Bt) *dwlt: keen in last pl: sme prog to mod 4th over 2f out: nvr nr ldrs and no imp after* **4/1**[3]

6555 **5** *3 ¼* **October Storm**[15] [5368] 6-9-2 **74**................(p[1]) JamesDoyle 4 — 71
(Mick Channon) *bhd: drvn over 3f out: sn lost tch* **13/2**

0-01 **6** *nk* **Toshima (IRE)**[12] [5496] 4-9-10 **82**................(tp) PatCosgrave 2 — 79
(Robert Stephens) *cl up tl drvn over 3f out: dropped out tamely* **14/1**

4123 **7** *2* **Grenadier Guard (IRE)**[29] [4862] 3-8-12 **83**................(b[1]) FrannyNorton 1 — 77
(Mark Johnston) *rn in snatches and on and off bridle: chsd ldrs tl drvn and nt keen over 4f out: struggling after* **7/4**[1]

3m 22.23s (-6.17) **Going Correction** -0.075s/f (Good)
WFA 3 from 4yo+ 13lb **7** Ran SP% **117.4**
Speed ratings (Par 107): **112,109,108,107,106 106,105**
CSF £164.76 CT £603.96 TOTE £16.70: £6.60, £5.70; EX 184.70 Trifecta £877.20.
Owner Graham & Lynn Knight **Bred** J C Sillett **Trained** Newmarket, Suffolk

FOCUS
A decent staying handicap. They seemed to go steady enough early and the good comparative time is tantamount to how well the winning mare finished off her race. The winner has been rated in line with the better view of her form, and the second similar to his reappearance figure.

T/Plt: £101.90 to a £1 stake. Pool: £60,305.50 - 432.02 winning units T/Qpdt: £30.30 to a £1 stake. Pool: £4,444.40 - 108.52 winning units **Iain Mackenzie**

5553 REDCAR (L-H)
Saturday, August 10

OFFICIAL GOING: Good (good to soft in places; 7.8)
Wind: fairly strong half behind Weather: Showery

5968 BEST FLAT RACES LIVE ON RACING TV (S) STKS — 5f 217y
1:15 (1:16) (Class 5) 2-Y-O
£3,737 (£1,112; £555; £300; £300; £300) **Stalls** Centre

Form / RPR

0560 **1** **Queens Blade**[8] [5618] 2-8-6 53................(b) DuranFentiman 2 — 64
(Tim Easterby) *racd alone against far rail: mde all: rdn 2f out: kpt on wl* **25/1**

3612 **2** *1 ¾* **Calippo (IRE)**[21] [5196] 2-8-5 75................(p) Pierre-LouisJamin(7) 15 — 65+
(Archie Watson) *dwlt sltly: sn prom in centre: rdn along over 2f out: drvn fnl f: kpt on but a hld* **4/1**[2]

225 **3** *¾* **Enjoy The Moment**[10] [5547] 2-8-6 65................ JamesSullivan 1 — 57
(Mick Channon) *dwlt sltly: hld up: rdn along over 2f out: drvn and hdwy over 1f out: kpt on* **7/2**[1]

1063 **4** *3 ½* **Amnaa**[8] [5630] 2-8-5 68................ LauraCoughlan(7) 4 — 52
(Adrian Nicholls) *in tch towards far side of main gp: rdn over 2f out: no ex ins fnl f* **7/1**

2505 **5** *hd* **Gin Gembre (FR)**[21] [5196] 2-8-11 66................ CliffordLee 13 — 50+
(K R Burke) *midfield towards nr side of main gp: rdn over 2f out: drvn over 1f out: one pce and nvr threatened* **20/1**

3303 **6** *1* **Maybellene (IRE)**[8] [5602] 2-8-6 68................ EoinWalsh 6 — 42
(George Scott) *midfield: rdn over 2f out: plugged on: nvr threatened* **5/1**[3]

6540 **7** *nk* **Sparkling Breeze**[17] [5296] 2-8-11 67................ PaulMulrennan 3 — 47
(Michael Dods) *hld up: rdn along over 2f out: kpt on fnl f: nvr threatened* **7/1**

2340 **8** *1* **Mr Fudge**[7] [5668] 2-8-8 71................ SeanDavis(3) 5 — 44
(Richard Fahey) *chsd ldrs: hung repeatedly lft: rdn over 2f out: wknd fnl f* **5/1**[3]

0034 **9** *1 ½* **Beautrix**[8] [5630] 2-8-6 51................ AndrewMullen 10 — 34
(Michael Dods) *prom: rdn over 2f out: wknd over 1f out* **33/1**

606 **10** *¾* **South Light (IRE)**[31] [4778] 2-8-6 49................(t) CamHardie 7 — 32
(Antony Brittain) *prom: rdn over 2f out: wknd over 1f out* **100/1**

600 **11** *1 ¼* **The Mystery Wizard**[10] [5553] 2-8-11 42................ DavidAllan 8 — 33
(Tim Easterby) *hld up: sn pushed along: nvr involved* **66/1**

12 *nse* **Intrinsic Bond** 2-8-11 0................ PhilDennis 9 — 33+
(Tracy Waggott) *v.s.a: a towards rr* **66/1**

13 *5* **Inver Silver** 2-8-6 0................ LiamJones 12 — 13
(Ollie Pears) *hld up: rdn over 2f out: wknd over 1f out* **40/1**

4035 **14** *¾* **Not Another Word**[11] [5514] 2-8-6 50................ RachelRichardson 11 — 11
(Nigel Tinkler) *midfield: rdn along over 3f out: wknd 2f out* **50/1**

0000 **15** *5* **Jakodobro**[17] [5295] 2-8-11 26................(b[1]) RoystonFfrench 14
(Bryan Smart) *sn outpcd and a in rr (jockey said gelding was never travelling)* **100/1**

1m 10.46s (-1.34) **Going Correction** -0.20s/f (Firm) **15** Ran SP% **121.5**
Speed ratings (Par 94): **104,101,100,96,95 94,94,92,90,89 88,87,81,80,73**
CSF £118.65 TOTE £24.20: £6.80, £1.80, £1.80; EX 159.00 Trifecta £826.70.There was no bid for the winner. Calippo was subject to a friendly claim of £6000. Enjoy The Moment was subject to a friendly claim of £6000.
Owner HP Racing Queens Blade & Partner **Bred** Mrs J McMahon & Mickley Stud **Trained** Great Habton, N Yorks

FOCUS
A big field lined up for this seller, but jockey Duran Fentiman was the only one to come down what might have been a quicker part of the track on board the hard to find winner.

5969 CELEBRATE THE LIFE OF ANN ALLPORT MEDIAN AUCTION MAIDEN STKS — 7f
1:45 (1:50) (Class 5) 3-4-Y-O **£4,204** (£1,251; £625; £312) **Stalls** Centre

Form / RPR

0- **1** **Lady Dauphin (IRE)**[291] [8512] 3-8-7 0................ AledBeech(7) 10 — 71
(Charlie Fellowes) *hld up: pushed along and hdwy 3f out: rdn to chal over 1f out: led ins fnl f: edgd lft: kpt on* **5/1**[3]

2 *½* **Ravenscar (IRE)** 3-9-0 0................ TomEaves 2 — 69
(Grant Tuer) *dwlt: hld up: pushed along over 3f out: rdn and hdwy 2f out: chal ins fnl f: kpt on* **20/1**

55 **3** *2 ¼* **Grazeon Roy**[95] [2507] 3-9-5 0................ PaulHanagan 5 — 68
(John Quinn) *prom: rdn over 2f out: kpt on same pce ins fnl f* **9/2**[2]

4 *½* **Eloquent Style (IRE)** 3-9-5 0................ DavidNolan 3 — 67
(Ivan Furtado) *dwlt: led 5f out: rdn over 2f out: hdd ins fnl f: sn no ex* **12/1**

5 *5* **Siena Mia** 4-9-6 0................ PhilDennis 7 — 50
(Philip Kirby) *hld up: hdwy and trckd ldrs over 3f out: rdn over 2f out: edgd lft over 1f out: wknd ins fnl f* **33/1**

3-2 **6** *1 ¼* **Burning Topic (GER)**[24] [5062] 3-9-0 0................ PaulMulrennan 11 — 45
(David Lanigan) *trckd ldrs: pushed along to chal 2f out: drvn over 1f out: wknd ins fnl f (jockey said filly was never travelling)* **5/6**[1]

0-0 **7** *¾* **Littlebitofmagic**[124] [1643] 3-9-0 0................ HarrisonShaw(5) 6 — 48
(Michael Dods) *chsd ldrs: pushed along over 3f out: sn outplcd and btn* **25/1**

8 *½* **Beatrix Enchante** 3-9-0 0................ JamesSullivan 9 — 41
(Ruth Carr) *chsd ldrs: outpcd and btn over 2f out* **50/1**

9 *nk* **Phenakite**[291] [8519] 3-9-5 0................ CamHardie 1 — 46
(Ollie Pears) *hld up: rdn over 3f out: nvr threatened* **16/1**

00 **10** *2 ¼* **Goldfox Grey**[9] [5592] 3-9-5 0................ AndrewMullen 8 — 40
(Robyn Brisland) *led: hdd 5f out: remained prom tl wknd 2f out* **80/1**

0-40 **11** *8* **Farol**[18] [5264] 3-9-0 49................ BarryMcHugh 4 — 13
(James Given) *hld up: wknd and bhd fnl 2f* **50/1**

1m 23.9s (-1.50) **Going Correction** -0.20s/f (Firm)
WFA 3 from 4yo 6lb **11** Ran SP% **119.7**
Speed ratings (Par 103): **100,99,96,96,90 89,88,87,87,84 75**
CSF £102.81 TOTE £6.60: £1.70, £5.00, £1.60; EX 133.10 Trifecta £701.70.
Owner The Johnson'S **Bred** Thomas Hassett **Trained** Newmarket, Suffolk

FOCUS
This didn't have the look a strong race of its type, and it's best rated as modest form until proven otherwise.

5970 JOIN RACING TV NOW H'CAP 7f 219y
2:20 (2:21) (Class 4) (0-80,81) 3-Y-O+

£6,339 (£1,886; £942; £471; £300; £300) Stalls Centre

Form RPR
413 1 **Spiorad (IRE)**[40] 4445 4-9-10 **79**........................(t[1] w) DavidNolan 7 95+
(David O'Meara) *hld up in tch: hdwy over 3f out: led over 2f out: rdn clr over 1f out: kpt on wl* **11/4**[1]
0000 2 5 **Give It Some Teddy**[7] 5693 5-9-7 **76**........................ DuranFentiman 11 80
(Tim Easterby) *hld up: hdwy 3f out: rdn to chse ldr 2f out: outpcd over 1f out: plugged on ins fnl f* **6/1**[3]
-100 3 ¾ **Dancin Boy**[50] 4077 3-9-4 **80**........................ TomEaves 10 81
(Michael Dods) *trckd ldrs: rdn to chal over 2f out: outpcd over 1f out: plugged on ins fnl f* **25/1**
2-62 4 1 ¾ **Cheer The Title (IRE)**[17] 5320 4-9-11 **80**........................ PaulHanagan 5 78
(Tom Clover) *dwlt sltly: sn trckd ldrs racing quite keenly: rdn over 2f out: no ex ins fnl f* **9/2**[2]
3063 5 1 ½ **Zabeel Star (IRE)**[14] 5436 7-9-0 **76**........................(p) LauraCoughlan(7) 6 71
(Karen McLintock) *v.s.a and sn pushed along in rr: plugged on fnl 2f: nvr involved (jockey said gelding was slowly away)* **10/1**
3240 6 shd **Tadaawol**[15] 5398 6-9-12 **81**........................(p) CamHardie 4 76
(Roger Fell) *led: rdn and hdd over 2f out: wknd over 1f out* **14/1**
4523 7 6 **Welcoming (FR)**[17] 5292 3-9-2 **78**........................ RoystonFfrench 2 58
(Mark Johnston) *trckd ldrs: rdn over 3f out: sn wknd (vet said filly lost its right fore shoe)* **9/1**
0456 8 hd **Brother McGonagall**[7] 5693 5-9-5 **79**........................ DannyRedmond(5) 9 59
(Tim Easterby) *trckd ldrs: rdn over 3f out: wknd over 2f out* **9/1**
0-60 9 10 **Armed (IRE)**[77] 3095 4-9-5 **74**........................ PaulMulrennan 1 31
(Phillip Makin) *dwlt: hld up: rdn over 2f out: wknd* **13/2**
6100 10 5 **Tum Tum**[21] 5178 4-9-5 **74**........................(b[1]) PhilDennis 3 20
(Michael Herrington) *dwlt: sn trckd ldrs racing keenly: pushed along and lost pl over 3f out: wknd 2f out (vet said gelding lost both of its front shoes)* **33/1**

1m 34.77s (-1.83) **Going Correction** -0.20s/f (Firm) **10 Ran SP% 115.0**
WFA 3 from 4yo+ 7lb
Speed ratings (Par 105): **101,96,95,93,92 91,85,85,75,70**
CSF £18.88 CT £291.05 TOTE £3.40: £2.50, £1.80, £4.20; EX 17.30 Trifecta £251.00.
Owner Hambleton Racing Ltd XXXVII **Bred** Irish National Stud **Trained** Upper Helmsley, N Yorks

FOCUS
Nothing more than a fair handicap, but the winner was much the best. The third has been rated close to his earlier 1m2f win here.

5971 WATCH RACING TV H'CAP 7f
2:55 (2:56) (Class 3) (0-95,92) 3-Y-O+ £7,762 (£2,310; £1,154; £577) Stalls Centre

Form RPR
0-55 1 **Wahoo**[49] 4127 4-9-8 **86**........................ PaulMulrennan 2 95
(Michael Dods) *prom: pushed along over 2f out: rdn into narrow ld over 1f out: drvn and hld on wl fnl f* **11/1**
0530 2 nk **Whinmoor**[14] 5453 4-9-2 **83**........................(t[1]) RowanScott(3) 3 91
(Nigel Tinkler) *slowly away: sn in tch: trckd ldrs over 2f out: rdn 2f out: chal 110yds out: kpt on* **13/2**[3]
0605 3 nk **Maggies Angel (IRE)**[14] 5453 4-8-7 **74**........................ SeanDavis(3) 1 81
(Richard Fahey) *midfield: rdn along over 2f out: drvn and hdwy over 1f out: chal ins fnl f: kpt on* **12/1**
6115 4 ¾ **Defence Treaty (IRE)**[14] 5434 3-8-10 **80**........................(p) BarryMcHugh 8 83
(Richard Fahey) *trckd ldrs: hung lft and lost pl over 3f out: sn dropped to rr: swtchd lft towards far side and hdwy over 1f out: kpt on ins fnl f* **20/1**
1343 5 nk **Raydiance**[1] 5916 4-10-0 **92**........................ CliffordLee 6 96+
(K R Burke) *trckd ldrs: rdn over 2f out: drvn to chal strly over 1f out: sn edgd rt: one pce fnl 110yds* **4/1**[1]
1101 6 1 **Mutaraffa (IRE)**[17] 5312 3-9-7 **91**........................(h) TomEaves 4 91
(Charles Hills) *led: rdn over 2f out: hdd over 1f out: no ex ins fnl f* **13/2**[3]
4030 7 1 **Hajjam**[7] 5692 5-9-7 **85**........................(p) DavidNolan 11 84
(David O'Meara) *midfield: rdn 2f out: one pce and nvr threatened* **9/1**
5304 8 ¾ **Golden Apollo**[14] 5454 5-9-11 **89**........................(p) DavidAllan 9 86
(Tim Easterby) *midfield: rdn over 2f out: outpcd and btn whn sltly impeded appr fnl f* **7/1**
0052 9 ½ **Presidential (IRE)**[12] 5488 5-9-7 **85**........................ CamHardie 10 81
(Roger Fell) *dwlt: hld up: nvr threatened (jockey said gelding was restless in the stalls and slowly away)* **9/1**
0323 10 1 ¾ **Ulshaw Bridge (IRE)**[30] 4851 4-9-11 **89**........................(b[1]) PaulHanagan 7 80
(James Bethell) *s.i.s: hld up: pushed along and sme hdwy 2f out: rdn and hung rt appr fnl f: sn wknd* **11/2**[2]

1m 22.36s (-3.04) **Going Correction** -0.20s/f (Firm) **10 Ran SP% 115.3**
WFA 3 from 4yo+ 6lb
Speed ratings (Par 107): **109,108,108,107,107 105,104,103,103,101**
CSF £79.82 CT £636.04 TOTE £14.30: £4.20, £2.90, £3.00; EX 91.90 Trifecta £995.20.
Owner J Blackburn & A Turton **Bred** Llety Farms **Trained** Denton, Co Durham

FOCUS
The betting suggested this was an open contest, but it was beneficial to be in the group who were closest to the inside rail. A small pb from the winner, with the fourth to his AW win.

5972 MARKET CROSS JEWELLERS H'CAP 5f 217y
3:30 (3:30) (Class 4) (0-80,80) 3-Y-O+

£6,339 (£1,886; £942; £471; £300; £300) Stalls Centre

Form RPR
0511 1 **Betsey Trotter (IRE)**[17] 5315 4-9-6 **79**........................(p) HarrisonShaw(5) 11 92
(David O'Meara) *dwlt sltly: sn chsd ldrs: pushed into ld over 1f out: kpt on wl to draw clr ins fnl f* **15/2**[3]
0211 2 2 ¾ **Golden Parade**[16] 5335 3-9-2 **74**........................(p) DavidAllan 10 77
(Tim Easterby) *prom: led 3f out: rdn and hdd over 1f out: no ex ins fnl f* **11/8**[1]
646 3 nk **Mr Wagyu (IRE)**[44] 4280 4-9-0 **68**........................(v) PaulMulrennan 9 71
(John Quinn) *chsd ldrs: rdn along 3f out: bit outpcd over 1f out: kpt on ins fnl f* **9/1**
1440 4 hd **Shepherd's Purse**[13] 5478 7-8-9 **63**........................ JamesSullivan 5 66
(Ruth Carr) *stdd s: hld up: pushed along 3f out: kpt on ins fnl f* **15/2**[3]
0504 5 1 ¾ **Nicki's Angel (IRE)**[15] 5399 3-9-3 **78**........................ SeanDavis(3) 3 74
(Richard Fahey) *chsd ldrs: rdn along 3f out: bit outpcd over 1f out: kpt on ins fnl f* **11/1**

4564 6 nk **Everkyllachy (IRE)**[14] 5432 5-8-1 **62**........................(b) LauraCoughlan(7) 8 58
(Karen McLintock) *dwlt: hld up: rdn along 3f out: kpt on ins fnl f: nvr threatened (jockey said gelding was slowly away)* **16/1**
5333 7 nk **Lucky Beggar (IRE)**[16] 5330 9-9-1 **69**........................ PhilDennis 4 64
(David C Griffiths) *midfield: rdn 3f out: outpcd over 1f out: plugged on ins fnl f* **13/2**[2]
-053 8 6 **Laubali**[18] 5281 4-9-7 **75**........................(p) DavidNolan 7 51
(David O'Meara) *racd on far rail: prom: rdn over 2f out: wknd over 1f out (jockey said gelding lost its left fore shoe)* **12/1**
0000 9 4 ½ **Cox Bazar (FR)**[21] 5180 5-9-6 **74**........................(e[1]) TomEaves 6 35
(Ivan Furtado) *led narrowly: hdd 3f out: wknd over 1f out* **66/1**

1m 10.0s (-1.80) **Going Correction** -0.20s/f (Firm) **9 Ran SP% 112.4**
WFA 3 from 4yo+ 4lb
Speed ratings (Par 105): **108,104,103,103,101 100,100,92,86**
CSF £17.57 CT £94.07 TOTE £6.70: £1.80, £1.20, £2.10; EX 13.60 Trifecta £84.90.
Owner F Gillespie **Bred** James Hughes **Trained** Upper Helmsley, N Yorks

FOCUS
This time the whole field raced along the inside rail. The second and third have been rated close to form.

5973 RACING TV STRAIGHT MILE SERIES H'CAP (RACING UK STRAIGHT MILE SERIES QUALIFIER) 1m 2f 1y
4:05 (4:05) (Class 3) (0-90,89) 3-Y-O £7,762 (£2,310; £1,154; £577) Stalls Low

Form RPR
611 1 **Country**[26] 4989 3-9-6 **88**........................(p[1]) LiamJones 7 101+
(William Haggas) *hld up: gd hdwy on outer 3f out: pushed into ld 2f out: rdn briefly ins fnl f: pushed out fnl 110yds* **6/4**[1]
1213 2 ½ **Cardano (USA)**[21] 5194 3-9-1 **83**........................(p) PaulHanagan 3 92
(Ian Williams) *led: hdd over 6f out: remained cl up: rdn to ld again over 2f out: hdd 2f out: kpt on but a hld* **4/1**[3]
3342 3 hd **Noble Prospector (IRE)**[26] 4989 3-8-5 **76**........................ SeanDavis(3) 6 86+
(Richard Fahey) *hld up: sme hdwy and briefly short of room 2f out: rdn over 1f out: kpt on wl fnl f* **16/1**
2163 4 3 ¼ **Emirates Knight (IRE)**[43] 4325 3-9-4 **86**........................ DavidAllan 1 88
(Roger Varian) *trckd ldrs: rdn along 3f out: outpcd 2f out: kpt on ins fnl f* **7/2**[2]
0502 5 ¾ **Loch Ness Monster (IRE)**[23] 5095 3-9-7 **89**......(p[1]) AlistairRawlinson 2 90
(Michael Appleby) *trckd ldrs: rdn along 3f out: no ex fnl f* **6/1**
-545 6 1 ¾ **Billy No Mates (IRE)**[22] 5127 3-9-1 **83**........................ PaulMulrennan 4 80
(Michael Dods) *dwlt: sn midfield: rdn over 2f out: wknd ins fnl f* **12/1**
5-00 7 4 ½ **Off Piste**[83] 2872 3-8-3 **71**........................(t) RachelRichardson 5 59
(Tim Easterby) *prom on outer: racd keenly: led over 6f out: rdn and hdd over 2f out: wknd over 1f out* **50/1**

2m 5.33s (-1.57) **Going Correction** -0.20s/f (Firm) **7 Ran SP% 112.0**
Speed ratings (Par 104): **98,97,97,94,94 92,89**
CSF £7.39 TOTE £2.00: £1.40, £2.10; EX 6.70 Trifecta £58.90.
Owner Sheikh Ahmed Al Maktoum **Bred** Godolphin **Trained** Newmarket, Suffolk

FOCUS
The first race on the round course was run at just an ordinary early gallop. The level is set around the second.

5974 HAPPY WEDDING ANNIVERSARY MR & MRS BROWN H'CAP (DIV I) 1m 5f 218y
4:35 (4:35) (Class 6) (0-65,65) 3-Y-O+

£3,228 (£960; £480; £300; £300; £300) Stalls Low

Form RPR
0302 1 **The Fiddler**[25] 5029 4-9-3 **50**........................ PaulHanagan 1 59
(Chris Wall) *midfield: angled rt to outer over 2f out: pushed along and sn hdwy: led appr fnl f: rdn out ins fnl f* **7/2**[2]
1415 2 2 ¼ **Agravain**[33] 4729 3-9-7 **65**........................ DavidAllan 2 73
(Tim Easterby) *trckd ldrs: rdn to chal over 1f out: styd on but sn hld in 2nd fnl f* **7/4**[1]
5052 3 2 ¼ **Vintage Rose**[13] 5473 3-9-5 **63**........................ AndrewMullen 4 68
(Mark Walford) *midfield: pushed along and hdwy 3f out: led 2f out: sn rdn: hdd appr fnl f: drvn and one pce ins fnl f* **9/1**
0305 4 2 **Lincoln Tale (IRE)**[25] 5028 3-9-5 **63**........................ DavidNolan 8 65
(David O'Meara) *trckd ldrs: rdn to chal 2f out: no ex ins fnl f (vet said filly lost its left fore shoe)* **6/1**[3]
013 5 nk **Nearly There**[20] 5219 6-9-9 **56**........................(t) PaulMulrennan 9 56
(Wilf Storey) *hld up: rdn along over 3f out: plugged on fnl f: nvr threatened* **9/1**
5040 6 3 **So Hi Cardi (FR)**[32] 4769 3-9-1 **59**........................(h[1]) CamHardie 10 57
(Roger Fell) *hld up: pushed along over 3f out: nvr threatened* **33/1**
4-15 7 1 ½ **Casa Comigo (IRE)**[185] 619 4-9-8 **55**........................ KierenFox 5 49
(John Best) *led: rdn and hdd 2f out: wknd over 1f out* **9/1**
633 8 hd **Flower Power**[25] 5019 8-9-13 **60**........................(p) BarryMcHugh 6 53
(Tony Coyle) *dwlt: hld up: rdn over 2f out: sn btn* **20/1**
0043 9 9 **Barb's Prince (IRE)**[19] 5242 3-8-1 **48**........................(p) SeanDavis(3) 7 31
(Ian Williams) *prom: rdn over 2f out: lost pl sltly whn hmpd 2f out: no ch after and eased* **16/1**

3m 5.48s (-1.52) **Going Correction** -0.20s/f (Firm) **9 Ran SP% 116.5**
WFA 3 from 4yo+ 11lb
Speed ratings (Par 101): **96,94,93,92,92 90,89,89,84**
CSF £10.10 CT £49.75 TOTE £4.30: £1.80, £1.10, £2.20; EX 10.20 Trifecta £52.60.
Owner The Equema Partnership **Bred** Genesis Green Stud Ltd **Trained** Newmarket, Suffolk

FOCUS
The first division of a moderate staying handicap, in which the early gallop wasn't strong. The winner has been rated as building on his good Nottingham run.

5975 HAPPY WEDDING ANNIVERSARY MR & MRS BROWN H'CAP (DIV II) 1m 5f 218y
5:05 (5:09) (Class 6) (0-65,66) 3-Y-O+

£3,228 (£960; £480; £300; £300; £300) Stalls Low

Form RPR
-335 1 **Anyonecanhaveitall**[54] 3931 3-9-7 **65**........................ AndrewMullen 1 78
(Mark Johnston) *in tch: hdwy 4f out: pushed into ld 3f out: styd on wl to draw clr fnl 2f: easily* **13/8**[1]
6623 2 6 **Kitty's Cove**[9] 5596 4-9-1 **48**........................(t[1]) DavidAllan 6 51
(Tim Easterby) *dwlt: hld up: hdwy on outer 4f out: rdn to chal 3f out: one pce and sn hld in 2nd fnl 2f* **5/2**[2]
3525 3 3 ¾ **Jan De Heem**[4] 5766 9-8-13 **53**........................(p) EllaMcCain(7) 7 51
(Tina Jackson) *hld up in tch: short of room and lost pl sltly over 3f out: pushed along and sme hdwy over 2f out: plugged on to go poor 3rd appr fnl f (jockey said gelding was denied a clear run app 4f out)* **9/1**

0-65 **4** *nk* **Volcanique (IRE)**[8] 5601 3-8-4 **48**..............(p) JamesSullivan 8 48
(Sir Mark Prescott Bt) *chsd ldr: rdn along over 5f out: edgd rt but led 4f out: hdd 3f out: outpcd and sn btn* **9/2**[3]
0200 **5** *1 1/4* **Miss Ranger (IRE)**[5] 5727 7-9-10 **57**..............(p) CamHardie 9 53
(Roger Fell) *hld up: rdn along 3f out: no imp and sn btn* **33/1**
2130 **6** *58* **Glorious Dane**[36] 4602 3-9-5 **66**.............. SeanDavis(3) 5
(Stef Keniry) *in tch: rdn 4f out: wknd qckly and t.o* **16/1**
0 **7** *40* **Gennaro (IRE)**[36] 4602 3-9-5 **63**..............(t) DavidNolan 3
(Ivan Furtado) *led: racd keenly and clr tl 9f out: rdn and hdd 4f out: wknd qckly and t.o* **18/1**

3m 1.63s (-5.37) **Going Correction** -0.20s/f (Firm)
WFA 3 from 4yo+ 11lb **7 Ran SP% 108.9**
Speed ratings (Par 101): **107,103,101,101,100 67,44**
CSF £5.18 CT £21.33 TOTE £2.10: £1.20, £1.70; EX 5.80 Trifecta £17.40.
Owner Garrett J Freyne **Bred** Newtown Stud And T J Pabst **Trained** Middleham Moor, N Yorks
■ Canford Thompson was withdrawn. Price at time of withdrawal 20-1. Rule 4 does not apply.

FOCUS
The second division of the staying handicap, which was comfortably the quicker of the pair, was taken with ease by the market leader. The form could be rated around 3lb higher.
T/Plt: £883.00 to a £1 stake. Pool: £46,271.36 - 38.25 winning units T/Qpdt: £67.40 to a £1 stake. Pool: £3,675.36 - 40.33 winning units **Andrew Sheret**

5713 DEAUVILLE (R-H)
Saturday, August 10
OFFICIAL GOING: Polytrack: standard; turf: good to soft

5976a PRIX CAVALASSUR (LISTED RACE) (2YO) (STRAIGHT COURSE) (TURF) 5f
2:50 2-Y-O **£27,027** (£10,810; £8,108; £5,405; £2,702)

RPR
1 **Flaming Princess (IRE)**[14] 5411 2-8-10 0 ow1.. ChristopheSoumillon 4 98
(Richard Fahey) *towards rr: swtchd ins and clsd ins fnl 1 1/2f: str run along stands' rail ins fnl f: led fnl 100yds: drvn out: readily* **9/5**[1]
2 *1 1/2* **Kemble (IRE)**[29] 4861 2-8-9 0.............. MickaelBarzalona 2 92
(Richard Hannon) *disp ld: hdd narrowly bef 1/2-way and remained cl up: led 1 1/2f out: drifted rt ent fnl f: hdd fnl 100yds: no ex* **77/10**
3 *1 3/4* **Has D'Emra (FR)**[23] 5116 2-8-13 0..............(b) MaximeGuyon 3 89
(F Rossi, France) **5/2**[2]
4 *1 1/4* **Brand New Day (IRE)**[11] 5539 2-8-9 0..............(b) AntoineHamelin 1 81
(Matthieu Palussiere, France) **43/10**[3]
5 *2* **Great Dame (IRE)**[21] 5185 2-8-9 0.............. AlexisBadel 5 74
(David O'Meara) *chsd ldr: rdn and nt qckn 1 1/2f out: grad dropped away* **11/1**
6 *1 1/4* **Mystic Monarch (FR)**[60] 2-8-9 0.............. CristianDemuro 7 69
(Andrea Marcialis, France) **54/10**

57.15s (-0.35) **6 Ran SP% 118.6**
PARI-MUTUEL (all including 1 euro stake): WIN 2.80; PLACE 1.90, 3.30; SF 12.40.
Owner The Cool Silk Partnership **Bred** Linacre House Limited **Trained** Musley Bank, N Yorks

FOCUS
Not a strong Listed race.

5721 SARATOGA (R-H)
Saturday, August 10
OFFICIAL GOING: Dirt: fast; turf: firm

5977a FOURSTARDAVE H'CAP (GRADE 1) (3YO+) (INNER TURF) (TURF) 1m (T)
10:46 3-Y-O+
£216,535 (£78,740; £47,244; £23,622; £15,748; £2,362)

RPR
1 **Got Stormy (USA)**[7] 4-8-4 0 ow2.............. RicardoSantanaJr 6 113+
(Mark Casse, Canada) *midfield: rdn and gd hdwy fr 2f out: styd on strly fr over 1f out: led 150yds out: sn clr and in command: drvn out: new crse record* **5/1**[3]
2 *2 1/2* **Raging Bull (FR)**[63] 3619 4-8-10 0..............(b) JoseLOrtiz 4 113
(Chad C Brown, U.S.A) *hld up in rr: rdn and hdwy fr 2f out: wd into st: styd on strly fnl f: snatched 2nd cl home: nt rch wnr* **59/20**[2]
3 *hd* **Uni**[42] 5-8-6 0 ow1.............. JoelRosario 3 109
(Chad C Brown, U.S.A) *hld up towards rr: hdwy on inner fr 2f out: rdn 1 1/2f out: nt clr run and forced to switch off rail over 1f out: styd on wl fnl f* **37/20**[1]
4 *hd* **March To The Arch (USA)**[29] 4-8-7 0..............(b) TylerGaffalione 1 109
(Mark Casse, Canada) *towards rr of midfield: rdn over 2f out: drvn and styd on wl fr over 1f out: tk narrow 2nd 75yds out: lost 2 pls cl home* **114/10**
5 *1 1/4* **Made You Look (USA)**[29] 5-8-6 0 ow2.............. JoseLezcano 9 105
(Chad C Brown, U.S.A) *racd in 3rd bhd clr ldr: wnt 2nd over 3f out: clsd on ldr fr over 2f out: rdn under 2f out: led over 1f out: briefly wnt clr: hdd 150yds out: wknd qckly* **153/10**
6 *1/2* **Hembree (USA)**[29] 5-8-5 0..............(b) LuisSaez 8 103
(Michael J Maker, U.S.A) *towards rr: rdn and kpt on fr 2f out: n.d* **157/10**
7 *2 1/2* **Dr. Edgar (USA)**[55] 6-8-6 0..............(b) JulienRLeparoux 2 98
(Barclay Tagg, U.S.A) *chsd clr ldr: dropped to 3rd over 3f out: rdn under 2f out: wknd over 1f out* **19/2**
8 *hd* **Krampus (USA)**[55] 5-8-6 0..............(b) JuniorAlvarado 7 98
(William Mott, U.S.A) *towards rr of midfield: rdn and no imp fr under 2f out* **227/10**
9 *4 1/2* **Gidu (IRE)**[29] 4-8-4 0.............. ManuelFranco 10 85+
(Todd Pletcher, U.S.A) *racd freely: led: sn clr: c bk to field fr over 2f out: rdn 2f out: hdd over 1f out: wknd qckly fnl f* **202/10**
10 *9 3/4* **Ostilio**[84] 2829 4-8-8 0.............. AndreaAtzeni 5 67
(Simon Crisford) *midfield: rdn and outpcd 2 1/2f out: dropped to rr under 2f out: sn struggling* **219/10**

1m 32.0s **10 Ran SP% 120.1**
PARI-MUTUEL (all including 2 unit stake): WIN 12.00; PLACE (1-2) 6.00, 4.30; SHOW (1-2-3) 3.80, 2.80, 2.70; SF 50.00.
Owner Gary Barber & Southern Equine Partners Llc **Bred** Mt Joy Stables, Pope McLean Et Al **Trained** Canada

ARLINGTON PARK (L-H)
Saturday, August 10
OFFICIAL GOING: Polytrack: fast; turf: firm

5978a BEVERLY D. STKS (GRADE 1) (3YO+ FILLIES & MARES) (TURF) 1m 1f 110y
10:53 3-Y-O+
£280,629 (£93,543; £46,771; £23,385; £14,031; £9,354)

RPR
1 **Sistercharlie (IRE)**[28] 4950 5-8-11 0.............. JohnRVelazquez 6 115+
(Chad C Brown, U.S.A) *hld up towards rr: stdy hdwy fr over 3f out: chsd clr ldrs in 3rd whn rdn under 2f out: styd on strly fr over 1f out: led under 1f out: sn clr: comf: new crse record* **2/5**[1]
2 *3* **Awesometank**[28] 4900 4-8-11 0.............. FlorentGeroux 2 109
(William Haggas) *chsd clr ldr in clr 2nd: rdn and kpt on wl fr 1 1/2f out: nt pce of wnr fnl f* **154/10**
3 *2* **Competitionofideas (USA)**[21] 4-8-11 0..............(b) JavierCastellano 3 105
(Chad C Brown, U.S.A) *hld up towards rr: rdn 2f out: styd on fr 1 1/2f out: no imp on front pair fnl f* **6/1**[3]
4 *3/4* **Fleeting (IRE)**[21] 5208 3-8-7 0 ow2.............. RyanMoore 1 108+
(A P O'Brien, Ire) *hld up in rr: hmpd and stmbld after 2f: rdn over 2f out: styd on fr over 1f out: nrst fin* **16/5**[2]
5 *2* **Thais (FR)**[28] 4950 5-8-11 0..............(b) IradOrtizJr 7 99
(Chad C Brown, U.S.A) *led: sn clr: rdn 2f out: reeled in appr fnl f: hdd under 1f out: sn wknd* **19/1**
6 *2 1/2* **Remember Daisy (USA)**[28] 4-8-11 0.............. MitchellMurrill 5 94
(Gary Scherer, U.S.A) *towards rr of midfield: rdn over 2f out: sme hdwy 1 1/2f out: wknd fnl f* **31/1**
7 *4 1/2* **Oh So Terrible (USA)**[28] 5-8-11 0..............(b) JoseValdiviaJr 4 85
(Bradley S Ross, U.S.A) *racd in 3rd at hd of main gp: rdn and lost pl over 2f out: sn struggling* **58/1**

1m 52.43s (-3.04)
WFA 3 from 4yo+ 8lb **7 Ran SP% 125.4**
PARI-MUTUEL (all including 2 unit stake): WIN 2.80; PLACE (1-2) 2.40, 8.00; SHOW (1-2-3) 2.10, 5.20, 3.00; SF 25.60.
Owner Peter M Brant **Bred** Ecurie Des Monceaux **Trained** USA

5979 - (Foreign Racing) - See Raceform Interactive

5547 LEICESTER (R-H)
Sunday, August 11
OFFICIAL GOING: Good to soft
Wind: Fresh across Weather: Showers

5980 LONGINES IRISH CHAMPIONS WEEKEND EBF NOVICE STKS (PLUS 10 RACE) 7f
2:10 (2:10) (Class 4) 2-Y-O **£5,498** (£1,636; £817; £408) **Stalls High**

Form RPR
5 **1** **Surf Dancer (IRE)**[16] 5367 2-9-5 0.............. DanielTudhope 6 87+
(William Haggas) *hld up in tch: led and edgd lft fr over 1f out: r.o: comf* **4/7**[1]
3 **2** *3* **We're Reunited (IRE)**[15] 5447 2-9-5 0.............. EoinWalsh 7 74
(Ronald Harris) *chsd ldr 3f: wnt 2nd again over 2f out: rdn and ev ch over 1f out: styd on same pce ins fnl f* **33/1**
54 **3** *hd* **Can't Stop Now (IRE)**[13] 5501 2-9-5 0.............. AdamKirby 5 74
(Clive Cox) *led: rdn and hdd over 1f out: edgd lft and styd on same pce ins fnl f* **7/2**[2]
045 **4** *5* **Bad Rabbit (IRE)**[29] 4897 2-9-5 69.............. DavidProbert 2 61
(David Loughnane) *prom: chsd ldr 4f out tl rdn over 2f out: edgd lft and wknd over 1f out* **20/1**
5 *nk* **Murraymint (FR)** 2-9-5 0.............. HarryBentley 1 60
(Ralph Beckett) *hld up: pushed along and hdwy over 2f out: wknd over 1f out* **11/1**
55 **6** *2 1/2* **Utopian Lad (IRE)**[13] 5501 2-9-5 0.............. FrannyNorton 3 54
(Tom Dascombe) *s.i.s: hld up: shkn up over 2f out: n.d* **16/1**
06 **7** *1 1/2* **Inflamed**[13] 5493 2-9-5 0.............. LiamKeniry 8 50
(Ed Walker) *hld up: plld hrd: rdn over 1f out: n.d* **50/1**
8 *3/4* **Locked N' Loaded** 2-9-5 0.............. TomMarquand 4 48
(Richard Hannon) *chsd ldrs: rdn over 2f out: wknd over 1f out* **8/1**[3]

1m 26.31s (0.61) **Going Correction** +0.125s/f (Good) **8 Ran SP% 120.9**
Speed ratings (Par 96): **101,97,97,91,91 88,86,85**
CSF £33.69 TOTE £1.30: £1.10, £3.50, £1.20; EX 29.10 Trifecta £96.60.
Owner China Horse Club/Ballylinch Stud **Bred** Skymarc Farm & Qatar Bloodstock Limited **Trained** Newmarket, Suffolk

FOCUS
A breezy run up to a meeting staged on drying ground. A race that lacked anything in the way of strength in depth but a useful performance from the winner, who is the sort to hold his own in better company. The gallop was reasonable.

5981 BLABY (S) STKS 7f
2:45 (2:45) (Class 5) 3-4-Y-O
£3,493 (£1,039; £519; £400; £400; £400) **Stalls High**

Form RPR
4032 **1** **Zoraya (FR)**[10] 5573 4-8-11 71.............. DavidProbert 7 69+
(Paul Cole) *hld up in tch: chsd ldr over 2f out: led over 1f out: pushed clr fnl f: comf* **1/4**[1]
-000 **2** *7* **Hold Your Breath**[8] 5675 4-8-11 40.............. TomMarquand 1 48
(Tony Carroll) *led: rdn and hdd over 1f out: no ex fnl f* **16/1**
0600 **3** *5* **Epaulini**[8] 5695 3-8-10 50.............. TomEaves 2 39
(Michael Dods) *sn prom: rdn over 2f out: wknd over 1f out* **11/2**[2]
-060 **4** *1/2* **Willa's Wish (IRE)**[24] 5084 3-8-5 38.............. KieranO'Neill 6 32
(Tony Carroll) *hld up: rdn over 2f out: wknd over 1f out (jockey said filly ran too freely)* **40/1**
60-0 **5** *1/2* **Willett**[48] 4193 3-8-7 48..............(v[1]) WilliamCox(3) 8 36
(Sarah Hollinshead) *chsd ldr tl rdn over 2f out: wknd over 1f out* **50/1**
5030 **6** *7* **Boxatricks (IRE)**[44] 4336 4-9-0 48.............. SeanKirrane(7) 5 26
(Julia Feilden) *sn pushed along to chse ldrs: lost pl over 4f out: hdwy and hung rt fr over 2f out: sn rdn: wknd fnl f (jockey said gelding was never travelling)* **8/1**[3]
0020 **7** *3/4* **Song Of Summer**[47] 4217 4-8-11 45..............(tp) RossaRyan 3 14
(Phil McEntee) *hld up: rdn over 2f out: wknd over 1f out* **14/1**

4466 8 1 3/4 **Misty Breese (IRE)**15 5421 4-8-11 45 JoeyHaynes 10 9
(Sarah Hollinshead) *s.i.s: hld up: pushed along 4f out: wknd over 2f out* 14/1

1m 25.93s (0.23) **Going Correction** +0.125s/f (Good)
WFA 3 from 4yo 6lb 8 Ran SP% **130.1**
Speed ratings (Par 103): **103,95,89,88,88 80,79,77**
CSF £9.63 TOTE £1.10: £1.02, £3.70, £1.60; EX 10.70 Trifecta £31.40.Zoraya was sold for £10,000.
Owner The Fairy Story Partnership **Bred** Jedburgh Stud & Deepwood Farm Stud **Trained** Whatcombe, Oxon

FOCUS
A lop-sided event with the short-priced market leader and clear form choice proving far too good for some very moderate rivals. The gallop was fair.

5982 COPLOW FILLIES' H'CAP 1m 3f 179y
3:15 (3:19) (Class 4) (0-80,80) 3-Y-O+
£6,080 (£1,809; £904; £452; £400; £400) Stalls Low

Form RPR
6310 1 **Nette Rousse (GER)**15 5458 3-9-7 80 HarryBentley 5 91+
(Ralph Beckett) *s.i.s: pushed along at various stages in rr: hdwy on outer over 3f out: led over 2f out: shkn up and hung rt fr over 1f out: styd on* 3/1[2]

-262 2 2 1/4 **Queen Constantine (GER)**34 4739 3-9-1 74 (h) DavidProbert 6 81
(William Jarvis) *hld up: hdwy to ld 3f out: hdd over 2f out: rdn and edgd lft over 1f out: styd on same pce wl ins fnl f* 13/2

3-50 3 7 **Fannie By Gaslight**10 5571 4-9-11 74 FrannyNorton 4 69
(Mick Channon) *prom: chsd ldr over 8f out tl rdn over 3f out: styd on same pce fr over 1f out* 11/2[3]

153 4 1 1/4 **Kvetuschka**58 3800 3-9-6 79 DanielTudhope 1 73
(Peter Chapple-Hyam) *chsd ldr over 3f: remained handy: rdn over 3f out: wknd fnl f* 9/1

0526 5 3/4 **Overtrumped**5 5785 4-8-11 60 (v) RossaRyan 7 52
(Mike Murphy) *led: rdn and hdd over 3f out: wknd over 1f out* 16/1

5-31 6 nk **Maktabba**25 5048 3-9-1 74 JimCrowley 3 66
(William Haggas) *hld up: hdwy over 5f out: rdn over 3f out: outpcd fr over 2f out* 2/1[1]

533 7 21 **Appointed**15 5458 5-9-9 77 (t) DannyRedmond(5) 2 35
(Tim Easterby) *chsd ldrs: lost pl over 5f out: wknd over 3f out* 8/1

2m 35.41s (0.41) **Going Correction** +0.125s/f (Good)
WFA 3 from 4yo+ 10lb 7 Ran SP% **114.0**
Speed ratings (Par 102): **103,101,96,96,95 95,81**
CSF £22.43 TOTE £3.90: £2.50, £2.60; EX 19.40 Trifecta £81.60.
Owner H H Sheikh Mohammed Bin Khalifa Al Thani **Bred** Gestut Wittekindshof **Trained** Kimpton, Hants

FOCUS
A couple of unexposed sorts in a fair handicap and, although the uneasy market leader disappointed, the first two deserve credit for pulling clear in the last quarter mile. The gallop was reasonable. The second has been rated as running a pb in line with the better view of her form.

5983 RUTLAND H'CAP 6f
3:50 (3:50) (Class 3) (0-90,91) 3-Y-O £12,938 (£3,850; £1,924; £962) Stalls High

Form RPR
2416 1 **Aplomb (IRE)**31 4847 3-9-5 88 TomMarquand 5 98
(William Haggas) *hmpd s: hld up: hdwy over 1f out: rdn: edgd rt and r.o to ld wl ins fnl f* 2/1[1]

5-42 2 nk **Typhoon Ten (IRE)**13 5503 3-8-12 81 RossaRyan 4 90
(Richard Hannon) *hmpd s: plld hrd: trckd ldrs: led over 2f out: shkn up over 1f out: rdn and hdd wl ins fnl f* 4/1[3]

4146 3 1 3/4 **Princess Power (IRE)**15 5442 3-9-4 87 (v) TomEaves 8 90
(Nigel Tinkler) *hld up: hdwy over 2f out: shkn up over 1f out: edgd rt and styd on same pce ins fnl f* 8/1

0210 4 2 **Dominus (IRE)**15 5442 3-9-5 88 JimCrowley 6 85
(Brian Meehan) *hood removed late: chsd ldrs: rdn over 1f out: no ex ins fnl f (jockey said he was slow to remove the blindfold because the colt turned his head and took two attempts to remove it)* 4/1[3]

632 5 14 **Lincoln Park**15 5422 3-9-7 90 JFEgan 7 42
(Michael Appleby) *led: hdd over 4f out: remained w ldr: rdn and ev ch over 2f out: wknd over 1f out* 7/2[2]

2606 6 14 **Obee Jo (IRE)**22 5191 3-8-2 71 oh1 (b1) DuranFentiman 3
(Tim Easterby) *edgd lft s: sn w ldr: racd freely: led over 4f out: hdd & wknd over 2f out (jockey said colt jumped left leaving the stalls and ran too freely)* 16/1

1m 11.92s (-0.18) **Going Correction** +0.125s/f (Good) 6 Ran SP% **112.5**
Speed ratings (Par 104): **106,105,103,100,81 63**
CSF £10.35 CT £49.99 TOTE £2.70: £1.30, £3.00; EX 11.10 Trifecta £39.40.
Owner Ms Fiona Carmichael **Bred** Anglia Bloodstock Ltd & Mr C Humber **Trained** Newmarket, Suffolk

FOCUS
A useful sprint in which the gallop was sound throughout and this form should prove reliable. The third helps set the level.

5984 CROPSTON H'CAP 1m 53y
4:20 (4:20) (Class 4) (0-80,80) 3-Y-O
£6,080 (£1,356; £452; £400; £400) Stalls Low

Form RPR
1631 1 **Kermouster**11 5552 3-8-7 66 SamJames 4 76
(Grant Tuer) *chsd ldr: rdn and edgd lft over 1f out: r.o to ld wl ins fnl f* 10/3[3]

0313 2 nk **Sendeed (IRE)**27 4996 3-9-1 79 (p1) CierenFallon(5) 3 88
(Saeed bin Suroor) *led at stdy pce: shkn up and qcknd over 2f out: rdn and hdd wl ins fnl f* 11/4[1]

4106 2 dht **Greek Hero**30 4895 3-9-3 76 DanielTudhope 1 85
(Declan Carroll) *chsd ldrs: rdn over 1f out: r.o* 11/4[1]

2142 4 3 1/2 **Silkstone (IRE)**24 5104 3-9-7 80 ShaneKelly 5 81
(Pam Sly) *chsd ldrs: rdn over 1f out: no ex ins fnl f* 3/1[2]

0604 5 4 1/2 **Daafr (IRE)**15 5422 3-9-6 79 (p) CamHardie 6 70
(Antony Brittain) *hld up: rdn over 2f out: wknd fnl f* 16/1

41-0 6 3 1/2 **Thorn**62 3647 3-9-3 76 (h1) AdamKirby 2 59
(Peter Hiatt) *hld up: plld hrd: shkn up over 2f out: wknd over 1f out* 16/1

1m 47.98s (1.68) **Going Correction** +0.125s/f (Good) 6 Ran SP% **113.2**
Speed ratings (Par 102): **96,95,95,92,87 84**
WIN: 2.90 Kermouster; PL: 0.60 Sendeed, 0.90 Greek Hero, 2.30 Kermouster; EX: K/S 5.30, K/GH 6.50; CSF: 6.56,; TC: ; TF: K/S/GH 17.80, K/GH/S 21.10;.
Owner D R Tucker **Bred** D R Tucker **Trained** Birkby, N Yorks

FOCUS
A fair handicap but a very ordinary gallop only picked up in the last quarter mile and this bare form may not be entirely reliable. Muddling form.

5985 ROTHERBY H'CAP 6f
4:50 (4:55) (Class 5) (0-70,72) 3-Y-O
£3,428 (£1,020; £509; £400; £400; £400) Stalls High

Form RPR
4136 1 **Eye Of The Water (IRE)**25 5056 3-9-7 68 DavidProbert 1 78
(Ronald Harris) *led 5f out: rdn whn rdr dropped whip over 1f out: edgd lft: styd on* 11/2[3]

3350 2 1 3/4 **Stallone (IRE)**9 5622 3-9-5 66 (v) AdamKirby 10 70
(Richard Spencer) *hld up: hdwy over 2f out: rdn over 1f out: styd on* 4/1[1]

3530 3 1/2 **Moftris**16 5394 3-9-6 72 CierenFallon(5) 7 74+
(William Haggas) *prom: lost pl 4f out: rdn over 1f out: r.o to go 3rd and hung rt towards fin (jockey said gelding ran too freely)* 5/1[2]

-433 4 1 **Tobeeornottobee**14 5478 3-8-10 64 JessicaAnderson(7) 2 63
(Declan Carroll) *chsd wnr after 1f: shkn up over 1f out: no ex ins fnl f* 14/1

5405 5 3/4 **Plumette**22 5176 3-9-7 67 TrevorWhelan 5 65
(David Loughnane) *prom: rdn over 2f out: styd on same pce fnl f (trainer said filly was unsuited by the ground finding it too soft on this occasion)* 12/1

5053 6 1 **One One Seven (IRE)**18 5308 3-8-3 50 CamHardie 6 44
(Antony Brittain) *hld up: hdwy over 2f out: rdn over 1f out: no ex ins fnl f* 16/1

-002 7 1/2 **Great Shout (IRE)**25 5056 3-9-7 68 (t) TomMarquand 9 60
(Amy Murphy) *rrd s: sn prom: rdn and hung rt over 1f out: no ex fnl f* 6/1

0522 8 2 **Kaafy (IRE)**9 5620 3-9-4 65 SamJames 8 51
(Grant Tuer) *hld up: rdn over 1f out: nt trble ldrs* 6/1

0-03 9 3 3/4 **Remission**3 5864 3-7-13 49 oh2 NoelGarbutt(3) 4 23
(Derek Shaw) *led 1f: chsd ldrs: rdn over 3f out: wknd over 1f out* 33/1

1305 10 10 **Aghast**23 5147 3-8-13 60 TomEaves 3 2
(Kevin Ryan) *prom: rdn over 2f out: sn wknd (trainers' rep said, regards poor performance, filly was unsuited by the ground and found it too soft on this occasion)* 5/1[2]

1m 13.21s (1.11) **Going Correction** +0.125s/f (Good) 10 Ran SP% **120.5**
Speed ratings (Par 100): **97,94,94,92,91 90,89,87,82,68**
CSF £28.82 CT £122.24 TOTE £8.00: £1.90, £1.90, £2.30; EX 41.50 Trifecta £248.00.
Owner Malcolm E Wright **Bred** M Fahy **Trained** Earlswood, Monmouths

FOCUS
There was heavy rain on the run up to this race. A modest handicap in which the gallop was sound and this form should work out. The third was the eyecatcher. The second has been rated closer to his earlier form this summer.

5986 THURMASTON H'CAP 5f
5:25 (5:30) (Class 6) (0-65,65) 3-Y-O+
£2,975 (£885; £442; £400; £400; £400) Stalls High

Form RPR
5505 1 **Secret Potion**9 5607 5-9-7 60 DavidProbert 7 69
(Ronald Harris) *s.i.s: hdwy u.p and hung rt fr over 1f out: r.o to ld wl ins fnl f: sn clr* 10/1

0002 2 2 1/4 **One Boy (IRE)**13 5491 8-8-10 49 KieranO'Neill 9 50
(Paul Midgley) *hld up in tch: led stands' side gp and hung rt over 1f out: hdd wl ins fnl f: styd on same pce* 7/1[3]

6053 3 1 1/4 **Toni's A Star**6 5750 7-9-7 60 TomMarquand 6 57
(Tony Carroll) *chsd ldrs: stdd and lost pl 4f out: nt clr run and swtchd rt over 1f out: r.o to go 3rd nr fin* 6/1[2]

0006 4 nk **Minty Jones**11 5551 10-8-4 46 oh1 (b) JaneElliott(3) 3 41
(Michael Mullineaux) *led overall and racd alone fr over 3f out: rdn over 1f out: hdd and no ex wl ins fnl f* 33/1

4520 5 1 1/4 **Atyaaf**9 5629 4-9-1 54 PaddyMathers 5 45
(Derek Shaw) *plld hrd and prom: rdn and edgd rt over 1f out: no ex ins fnl f* 15/2

6006 6 1 3/4 **Qaaraat**12 5515 4-9-10 63 (p1) CamHardie 1 50
(Antony Brittain) *chsd ldr tl swtchd lft and lost pl over 3f out: hdwy and nt clr run over 1f out: styd on same pce fnl f* 6/1[2]

0226 7 1 **Bahuta Acha**1 5952 4-9-12 65 (b) DanielTudhope 11 46
(David Loughnane) *hmpd s: sn pushed along and prom: no ex fr over 1f out* 3/1[1]

0206 8 2 **Ladweb**45 4307 9-9-10 63 JoeyHaynes 2 37
(John Gallagher) *s.i.s: swtchd lft over 3f out: hdwy u.p over 1f out: wknd and eased ins fnl f (jockey said gelding missed the break)* 10/1

2030 9 hd **David's Beauty (IRE)**22 5181 6-9-5 58 (b) JFEgan 10 31
(Brian Baugh) *edgd lft s: led stands' side gp over 3f: wknd fnl f* 12/1

0130 10 10 **Decision Maker (IRE)**20 5244 5-9-4 57 LiamKeniry 8
(Roy Bowring) *chsd ldrs: rdn and wknd over 1f out (jockey said gelding stopped quickly)* 8/1

1m 1.98s (0.18) **Going Correction** +0.125s/f (Good) 10 Ran SP% **117.8**
Speed ratings (Par 101): **103,99,97,96,94 92,90,87,87,71**
CSF £78.98 CT £463.35 TOTE £11.30: £3.30, £2.20, £2.00; EX 100.10 Trifecta £671.80.
Owner RHS Ltd, R Fox, P Charter **Bred** Llety Farms **Trained** Earlswood, Monmouths

FOCUS
A strong gallop to this very ordinary handicap saw the hold up horses come to the fore in the closing stages.
T/Plt: £14.00 to a £1 stake. Pool: £50,956.36 - 3,628.49 winning units T/Qpdt: £13.40 to a £1 stake. Pool: £3,798.40 - 282.17 winning units **Colin Roberts**

5744 WINDSOR (R-H)
Sunday, August 11

OFFICIAL GOING: Good (7.0)
Wind: medium, behind Weather: light cloud

5987 BRENDA BRANT CELEBRATION H'CAP 1m 3f 99y
2:00 (2:03) (Class 6) (0-55,55) 3-Y-O
£2,781 (£827; £413; £400; £400; £400) Stalls Low

Form RPR
0-06 1 **Para Queen (IRE)**48 4177 3-8-6 47 EllieMacKenzie(7) 10 54
(Heather Main) *midfield: rdn and outpcd 3f out: rallied over 1f out: styd on wl ins fnl f to ld last strides (trainer said, regarding the improved form shown, the filly's first run in a handicap and was better suited by the step up in trip from 1m2f to 1m3f)* 25/1

0325 **2** *nk* **Born Leader (FR)**[22] 5175 3-9-6 **54** SeanLevey 12 61
(Hughie Morrison) *chsd ldrs: effrt and ev ch over 3f out: drvn to ld over 1f out: kpt on u.p: hdd last strides* **7/2**[1]

-014 **3** *nk* **Celtic Classic (IRE)**[8] 5648 3-9-4 **52** (b) HectorCrouch 6 58
(Paul Cole) *in tch in midfield: effrt to chse ldrs 3f out: pushed lft over 1f out: edgd rt 1f out: ev ch wl ins fnl f: kpt on* **9/2**[2]

4664 **4** *2* **Tabou Beach Boy**[37] 4587 3-9-5 **53** (p) RichardKingscote 8 56
(Oliver Greenall) *chsd ldrs: effrt ent fnl 3f: edgd lft u.p over 1f out: squeezed for room 1f out: no ex and outpcd fnl 100yds* **14/1**

0404 **5** *1 ¾* **Ideal Grace**[9] 5601 3-8-12 **53** (p) GeorgiaDobie(7) 15 53
(Eve Johnson Houghton) *prom tl chsd ldr 7f out: pushed into ld over 3f out: sn hrd pressed and u.p: hdd over 1f out: no ex and wknd ins fnl f* **10/1**

0300 **6** *¾* **Lady Elysia**[27] 4998 3-9-7 **55** BenCurtis 9 54
(Harry Dunlop) *hld up in last quartet: effrt u.p over 2f out: hdwy over 1f out: kpt on steadily ins fnl f: nvr getting on terms w ldrs* **33/1**

-053 **7** *11* **Cheng Gong**[38] 4568 3-8-13 **47** (p) LukeMorris 5 28
(Tom Clover) *chsd ldrs early: dropped to midfield and rdn 8f out: outpcd and drvn 3f out: nvr threatened to get bk on terms: wknd fnl f (jockey said gelding was never travelling; vet said gelding lost its right hind shoe)* **6/1**[3]

0520 **8** *1 ¾* **Enyama (GER)**[7] 3809 3-9-2 **50** (p[1]) CallumShepherd 4 28
(Michael Attwater) *in tch in midfield: drvn and outpcd 3f out: no threat to ldrs after: wknd fnl f* **66/1**

6-54 **9** *1 ½* **Fame N Fortune**[52] 4038 3-9-7 **55** OisinMurphy 14 31
(Joseph Tuite) *sn stdd and hld up in rr: effrt over 2f out: nvr threatened to get on terms and wl btn whn lft over 1f out* **6/1**[3]

664 **10** *3* **Teemlucky**[17] 5336 3-9-7 **55** MartinDwyer 1 26
(Ian Williams) *s.i.s: hld up towards rr: effrt 3f out: nvr involved and wl btn over 1f out (jockey said filly was slowly away; vet said filly lost its right hind shoe)* **20/1**

-000 **11** *1 ¾* **Breakfast Time**[190] 556 3-9-5 **53** (b[1]) AdamMcNamara 3 21
(Archie Watson) *awkward as stalls opened and s.i.s: a towards rr: u.p 4f out: no rspnse: wl btn fnl 2f (jockey said filly fly leapt from the stalls)* **20/1**

06-0 **12** *shd* **Royal Dancer**[218] 79 3-9-7 **55** DavidEgan 13 23
(Sylvester Kirk) *broke wl: sn retrained and in tch in midfield: rdn 4f out: sn struggling: wl btn fnl 2f* **25/1**

0005 **13** *3 ¾* **Fanny Chenal**[25] 5049 3-8-13 **47** GeraldMosse 11 9
(Jim Boyle) *t.k.h: sn led: hdd over 3f out: struggling and lost pl over 2f out: wknd* **7/1**

0005 **14** *8* **Broughtons Bear (IRE)**[25] 5054 3-8-13 **47** RobHornby 16
(Stuart Williams) *prom: outpcd u.p over 3f out: wl bhd over 1f out* **25/1**

-000 **15** *36* **Arbuckle**[31] 4834 3-8-8 **47** DarraghKeenan(5) 2
(Michael Madgwick) *a towards rr: lost tch over 2f out: t.o and eased fnl f* **66/1**

2m 27.32s (-2.38) **Going Correction** -0.175s/f (Firm) **15** Ran SP% **124.2**
Speed ratings (Par 98): **101,100,100,99,97 97,89,88,86,84 83,83,80,74,48**
CSF £106.00 CT £489.99 TOTE £37.50: £10.90, £1.20, £2.30; EX 184.10 Trifecta £1562.50.
Owner Don Knott And Wetumpka Racing **Bred** Sir E J Loder **Trained** Kingston Lisle, Oxon
■ Stewards' Enquiry : Ellie MacKenzie two-day ban: used whip above the permitted level (Aug 25-26)

FOCUS
Add 9yds. The going was good on a strong drying day. The opener was a low-grade affair and they didn't go flat out, but that didn't stop the shock winner coming from behind.

5988 CON QUINLAN MEMORIAL FILLIES' NOVICE MEDIAN AUCTION STKS (PLUS 10 RACE) 6f 12y
2:30 (2:35) (Class 5) 2-Y-O £3,428 (£1,020; £509; £254) **Stalls** Centre

Form RPR

64 **1** **Angel Grey (IRE)**[16] 5381 2-9-0 0 OisinMurphy 8 78+
(Andrew Balding) *led for 1f: chsd ldr tl pushed into ld again over 1f out: rdn clr 1f out: styd on strly: comf* **9/4**[1]

0426 **2** *3* **Seraphinite (IRE)**[8] 5683 2-9-7 77 CallumShepherd 4 76
(Jamie Osborne) *wnt lft leaving stalls: hdwy to ld after 1f: drvn and hdd over 1f out: nt match pce of wnr but kpt on for clr 2nd ins fnl f* **5/1**[2]

3 *1 ¼* **Pretty In Grey** 2-9-0 0 DavidEgan 2 65
(Marco Botti) *in tch in midfield: pushed along ent fnl 2f: nt clr run wl over 1f out: hung lft and kpt on ins fnl f: no threat to wnr* **14/1**

4 *1 ½* **Letscrackon (IRE)** 2-9-0 0 GeraldMosse 1 61
(Gary Moore) *chsd ldrs: pushed along and struggling whn hung lft over 1f out: no ch w wnr and kpt on same pce ins fnl f* **14/1**

5 *2 ¼* **Inevitable Outcome (IRE)** 2-9-0 0 LouisSteward 10 54+
(David Simcock) *hld up in tch in midfield: swtchd rt and pushed along ent fnl 2f: swtchd lft and reminder ent fnl f: pushed along and kpt on steadily: nvr trbld ldrs* **20/1**

6 *nk* **Belle Anglaise** 2-9-0 0 RichardKingscote 6 53+
(Stuart Williams) *hld up in tch in midfield: nt clr run 3f out: pushed along over 1f out: kpt on steadily ins fnl f: nvr trbld ldrs* **25/1**

7 *2 ½* **Lady Latte (IRE)** 2-9-0 0 BenCurtis 9 46+
(K R Burke) *s.i.s: in rr of main gp: swtchd rt over 1f out: plugged on ins fnl f: nvr trbld ldrs* **16/1**

04 **8** *nk* **You Don't Own Me (IRE)**[6] 5745 2-9-0 0 CharlesBishop 13 45
(Joseph Tuite) *stdd s: t.k.h: hld up in tch in midfield: effrt over 2f out: sn struggling and btn whn hung lft over 1f out: wknd fnl f* **22/1**

9 *3* **Marzipan** 2-9-0 0 RobHornby 3 36
(Jonathan Portman) *t.k.h: hld up in tch in midfield: effrt 2f out: no imp and btn whn rn green and hung lft 1f out: wknd ins fnl f* **20/1**

10 *nk* **Alcance (FR)** 2-9-0 0 HectorCrouch 11 35
(Clive Cox) *chsd ldrs tl 1/2-way: sn struggling u.p: pushed lft and wknd over 1f out* **5/1**[2]

11 *2 ½* **Princess Carly** 2-9-0 0 LukeMorris 7 27
(Ali Stronge) *chsd ldrs early: struggling 1/2-way: hung lft and wknd over 1f out* **40/1**

12 *2* **Loco Dempsey (FR)** 2-9-0 0 SeanLevey 5 21
(Richard Hannon) *s.i.s and hmpd leaving stalls: a bhd (jockey said filly was slowly away)* **6/1**[3]

00 **13** *4* **Lethal Sensation**[45] 4302 2-9-0 0 MartinDwyer 12 9
(Paul Webber) *midfield: rdn and losing pl 1/2-way: bhd over 1f out: wknd* **100/1**

1m 11.17s (-0.93) **Going Correction** -0.175s/f (Firm) **13** Ran SP% **118.8**
Speed ratings (Par 91): **99,95,93,91,88 87,84,84,80,79 76,73,68**
CSF £11.42 TOTE £3.30: £1.40, £1.80, £4.20; EX 10.70 Trifecta £134.90.
Owner J Maldonado **Bred** James F Hanly **Trained** Kingsclere, Hants

FOCUS
A moderate novice sprint and the experienced runners came out on top.

5989 OSSIE AND HUTCH MEMORIAL FILLIES' H'CAP 6f 12y
3:05 (3:05) (Class 4) (0-85,87) 3-Y-O+
£5,207 (£1,549; £774; £400; £400; £400) **Stalls** Centre

Form RPR

4451 **1** **Show Stealer**[13] 5504 6-10-0 **87** RichardKingscote 2 96
(Rae Guest) *hld up in tch in last pair: clsd and nt clr run ent fnl 2f: swtchd lft over 1f out: hdwy to ld jst ins fnl f: r.o wl* **7/4**[1]

0456 **2** *1 ½* **Dizzy G (IRE)**[3] 5839 4-9-2 **75** BenCurtis 1 79
(K R Burke) *trckd ldrs: effrt ent fnl 2f: drvn to ld over 1f out: hdd jst ins fnl f: one pce after* **3/1**[2]

1110 **3** *1 ½* **Alicia Darcy (IRE)**[4] 5813 3-8-11 **74** (b) AdamMcNamara 6 72
(Archie Watson) *dwlt and pushed along early: effrt over 2f out: drvn and ev ch over 1f out: no ex and outpcd fnl 100yds* **11/2**

6620 **4** *1* **Bellevarde (IRE)**[15] 5420 5-9-2 **75** DavidEgan 5 71
(Richard Price) *chsd ldr: drvn and ev ch over 1f out: no ex and wknd ins fnl f* **14/1**

0365 **5** *1 ¾* **Porcelain Girl (IRE)**[24] 5105 3-8-8 **74** CameronNoble(3) 3 63
(Michael Bell) *stdd s: hld up in tch in last pair: swtchd lft and effrt over 1f out: no imp ins fnl f* **6/1**

1505 **6** *5* **Bungee Jump (IRE)**[6] 5746 4-10-0 **87** LukeMorris 4 61
(Grace Harris) *sn led: rdn ent fnl 2f: drvn and hdd over 1f out: btn and eased wl ins fnl f* **5/1**[3]

1m 9.76s (-2.34) **Going Correction** -0.175s/f (Firm)
WFA 3 from 4yo+ 4lb **6** Ran SP% **114.4**
Speed ratings (Par 102): **108,106,104,102,100 93**
CSF £7.44 TOTE £2.20: £1.10, £2.50; EX 7.00 Trifecta £30.70.
Owner Colin Joseph **Bred** Max Weston **Trained** Newmarket, Suffolk

FOCUS
Not much depth to this fillies' sprint in which they went a good clip. The second has been rated to this year's form.

5990 ROYAL WINDSOR RACECOURSE PANORAMIC 1866 RESTAURANT H'CAP 5f 21y
3:35 (3:35) (Class 5) (0-75,77) 3-Y-O+
£3,428 (£1,020; £509; £400; £400; £400) **Stalls** Centre

Form RPR

1501 **1** **Grandfather Tom**[26] 5027 4-9-7 **77** AngusVilliers(7) 1 86
(Robert Cowell) *sn led and mde rest: rdn over 1f out: kpt on wl ins fnl f: holding runner-up and pushed out towards fin* **3/1**[2]

0405 **2** *½* **Glamorous Rocket (IRE)**[16] 5375 4-9-2 **68** CameronNoble(3) 8 75
(Christopher Mason) *chsd ldrs tl chsd ldr wl over 2f out: shkn up 2f out: drvn over 1f out: kpt on: one pce and hld towards fin* **8/1**[3]

5345 **3** *¾* **Restless Rose**[12] 5515 4-9-11 **74** OisinMurphy 3 79+
(Stuart Williams) *chsd ldrs: effrt over 1f out: rdn ins fnl f: swtchd lft nt clrest of runs and kpt on same pce towards fin (jockey said filly was denied a clear run)* **9/4**[1]

6240 **4** *hd* **King Robert**[8] 5661 6-9-13 **76** DavidEgan 2 80
(Charlie Wallis) *chsd ldrs: effrt ent fnl 2f: kpt on same pce u.p ins fnl f* **9/4**[1]

1055 **5** *1 ½* **Solar Park (IRE)**[39] 4507 3-9-8 **74** CallumShepherd 6 71
(Michael Attwater) *dwlt: in tch in midfield: effrt 2f out: unable qck u.p over 1f out: kpt on same pce ins fnl f* **20/1**

0-00 **6** *nk* **Daphinia**[20] 5251 3-9-1 **72** SophieRalston(5) 4 68
(Dean Ivory) *led: sn hdd: chsd wnr tl 1/2-way: edgd lft and unable qck over 1f out: wknd ins fnl f* **20/1**

06-0 **7** *½* **Nautical Haven**[101] 2318 5-9-0 **63** RobertWinston 7 58
(Suzi Best) *a in last pair: effrt ent fnl 2f: kpt on but nvr threatened ldrs* **14/1**

0064 **8** *5* **Autumn Splendour (IRE)**[10] 5581 3-8-12 **69** (t[1]) WilliamCarver(5) 5 45
(Milton Bradley) *s.i.s: a in rr (jockey said gelding was slowly away)* **16/1**

59.19s (-0.91) **Going Correction** -0.175s/f (Firm)
WFA 3 from 4yo+ 3lb **8** Ran SP% **119.7**
Speed ratings (Par 103): **100,99,98,97,95 94,94,86**
CSF £28.62 CT £63.29 TOTE £3.70: £1.40, £1.60, £1.10; EX 27.50 Trifecta £93.60.
Owner J Sargeant **Bred** J Sargeant **Trained** Six Mile Bottom, Cambs

FOCUS
An average sprint. The favourite made all nearest the rail in a bunched finish. The winner has been rated as backing up his Nottingham win, and the third in line with her recent form.

5991 FOLLOW AT THE RACES ON TWITTER H'CAP 1m 31y
4:10 (4:10) (Class 3) (0-95,89) 3-Y-O **£7,246** (£2,168; £1,084; £542; £270) **Stalls** Low

Form RPR

2132 **1** **Spirit Warning**[18] 5312 3-9-4 **89** OisinMurphy 3 94
(Andrew Balding) *t.k.h: chsd ldr: effrt 2f out: drvn and ev ch 1f out: sustained effrt u.p and nosed ahd last strides* **11/8**[1]

0010 **2** *nk* **Arcanada (IRE)**[37] 4607 6-9-8 **86** (p) RichardKingscote 4 91
(Tom Dascombe) *led: rdn and qcknd ent fnl 2f: edgd lft over 1f out: hrd pressed and battled on gamely u.p ins fnl f: hdd last strides* **6/1**[3]

2450 **3** *shd* **Mr Tyrrell (IRE)**[11] 5546 5-9-6 **84** SeanLevey 1 89
(Richard Hannon) *stdd s: hld up in tch in last pair: effrt ent fnl 2f: ev ch 1f out: sustained effrt and kpt on wl ins fnl f: jst hld cl home* **6/1**[3]

5614 **4** *¾* **Sash**[15] 5412 3-9-2 **87** KieranShoemark 2 89
(Amanda Perrett) *t.k.h: trckd ldrs: effrt on inner ent fnl 2f: n.m.r over 1f out: kpt on same pce ins fnl f* **2/1**[2]

2030 **5** *9* **Family Fortunes**[46] 4255 5-9-5 **88** ScottMcCullagh(5) 5 70
(Michael Madgwick) *stdd s: hld up in tch in last pair: effrt ent fnl 2f: no hdwy u.p over 1f out: wknd ins fnl f* **14/1**

1m 42.66s (-1.84) **Going Correction** -0.175s/f (Firm)
WFA 3 from 5yo+ 7lb **5** Ran SP% **110.7**
Speed ratings (Par 107): **102,101,101,100,91**
CSF £10.03 TOTE £2.00: £1.10, £2.30; EX 9.90 Trifecta £38.40.
Owner Kingsclere Racing Club **Bred** Kingsclere Stud **Trained** Kingsclere, Hants

FOCUS
Add 9yds. A tight little handicap in which they sprinted from over two out and the favourite came out best in a three-way photo. The second has been rated to this year's form.

5992 RITA ORA LIVE AT WINDSOR RACECOURSE NOVICE AUCTION STKS 1m 31y
4:40 (4:42) (Class 5) 2-Y-O £3,428 (£1,020; £509; £254) Stalls Low

Form RPR
5 1 **Lucander (IRE)**[18] 5314 2-9-2 0 RobHornby 12 73
(Ralph Beckett) *chsd ldr: effrt ent fnl 2f: rdn to ld over 1f out: hld on wl ins fnl f* **6/1**[3]
4 2 nk **Berkshire Savvy**[11] 5563 2-9-1 0 OisinMurphy 4 71
(Andrew Balding) *t.k.h: hld up in tch in midfield: clsd to chse ldrs 3f out: effrt and chalng over 1f out: awkward hd carriage and a jst hld ins fnl f* **7/4**[1]
51 3 2 **Anniemation (IRE)**[19] 5273 2-9-8 0 JackGarritty 5 74
(Stella Barclay) *led: rdn jst over 2f out: hdd over 1f out: kpt on same pce ins fnl f* **7/1**
0 4 3 **Alibaba**[62] 3644 2-9-2 0 ShelleyBirkett 1 61+
(Julia Feilden) *hld up in midfield: switching lft over 2f out: hdwy over 1f out: kpt on steadily ins fnl f: no threat to ldrs* **20/1**
0 5 ½ **Olivers Pursuit**[94] 2561 2-9-0 0 LukeMorris 11 58
(Gay Kelleway) *chsd ldrs: rdn over 2f out: outpcd over 1f out: no threat to ldrs and kpt on same pce ins fnl f* **50/1**
6 2 ¾ **Big Boris (IRE)** 2-8-13 0 BenCurtis 10 51
(David Evans) *s.i.s: rn green: pushed along and off the pce in last pair: hdwy on outer whn pushed lft over 1f out: kpt on same pce and no imp ins fnl f* **25/1**
7 shd **Island Storm (IRE)** 2-9-0 0 DavidEgan 7 52
(Heather Main) *chsd ldrs: rdn 3f out: sn struggling to qckn: btn whn hung rt over 1f out: wknd ins fnl f* **20/1**
0 8 ½ **Tigerten**[17] 5339 2-9-0 0 CharlesBishop 6 51
(Joseph Tuite) *hld up in rr of main gp: effrt ent fnl 2f: no imp over 1f out: wl hld and one pce ins fnl f* **50/1**
0 9 2 ¼ **Herre Dittery**[18] 5314 2-8-13 0 CharlieBennett 3 45
(Pat Phelan) *midfield: effrt over 2f out: sn struggling and outpcd wl over 1f out: wknd ins fnl f* **66/1**
54 10 1 ¼ **Wallaby (IRE)**[22] 5189 2-8-1 0 AngusVilliers(7) 2 37
(Jonathan Portman) *chsd ldrs: rdn over 2f out: sn struggling and outpcd: btn whn pushed rt over 1f out: wknd ins fnl f* **7/2**[2]
11 1 **Alsukar** 2-8-10 0 MartinDwyer 8 37
(Dean Ivory) *v.s.i.s: wl off the pce in rr: nvr involved and stl in rr whn nt clr run 1f out* **8/1**
12 ½ **No Can Do** 2-9-0 0 CallumShepherd 9 40
(Jamie Osborne) *stdd after s: struggling over 2f out: wl hld whn carried rt over 1f out: wknd ins fnl f* **20/1**

1m 44.81s (0.31) **Going Correction** -0.175s/f (Firm) 12 Ran SP% **120.0**
Speed ratings (Par 94): **91,90,88,85,85 82,82,81,79,78 77,76**
CSF £15.79 TOTE £7.10: £1.70, £1.20, £2.50; EX 21.80 Trifecta £115.00.
Owner Mrs M E Slade & B Ohlsson **Bred** John Connolly **Trained** Kimpton, Hants

FOCUS
Add 9yds. A decent novice and the first three pulled clear.

5993 VISIT ATTHERACES.COM AMATEUR RIDERS' H'CAP 1m 3f 99y
5:10 (5:11) (Class 5) (0-70,72) 4-Y-O+ £3,306 (£1,025; £512; £400; £400; £400) Stalls Low

Form RPR
1432 1 **Broad Appeal**[18] 5316 5-10-12 68 MrJamesHarding 6 74
(Jonathan Portman) *midfield: clsd to chse ldrs 3f out: ev ch 2f out: rdn to ld and edgd rt jst over 1f out: hung lft ins fnl f: kpt on* **7/2**[1]
5306 2 1 **Roy Rocket (FR)**[12] 5528 9-9-13 55 MrRossBirkett 11 59+
(John Berry) *broke wl: sn restrained and hld up off the pce in last trio: clsd 7f out: swtchd lft and effrt 3f out: rdn and hdwy over 1f out: chsd wnr ins fnl f: kpt on* **18/1**
0-6 3 hd **Maroc**[65] 3547 6-10-8 69 (p) MissSarahBowen(5) 13 73
(Nikki Evans) *t.k.h: led and clr tl 7f out: hdd 5f out: styd pressing ldrs: rdn over 3f out: sltly outpcd over 1f out: kpt on again ins fnl f* **16/1**
0000 4 hd **Kismat**[17] 5338 4-9-3 52 (v[1]) MissGeorgiaKing(7) 8 56
(Alan King) *dwlt: midfield: clsd 7f out: effrt over 2f out: hdwy over 1f out: chsng ldrs and keeping on whn n.m.r towards fin* **25/1**
263 5 ½ **Banksy's Art**[17] 5337 4-9-12 61 MrGuyMitchell(7) 7 64
(Amanda Perrett) *midfield: effrt over 3f out: hdwy 2f out: styd on and chsd ldrs ins fnl f: keeping on whn n.m.r nr fin* **11/2**[3]
0510 6 1 ½ **Arctic Sea**[3] 5858 5-11-2 72 (p) MrSimonWalker 2 72
(Paul Cole) *t.k.h: chsd ldr tl 7f out: styd chsng ldrs tl led over 3f out: sn rdn: drvn and hdd jst over 1f out: no ex: lost 2nd ins fnl f: wknd towards fin* **5/1**[2]
2044 7 6 **Country'N'Western (FR)**[101] 2351 7-10-8 69 MrGeorgeEddery(5) 10 59
(Robert Eddery) *midfield: effrt over 2f out: nvr threatened to get on terms w ldrs and wl hld fnl f* **7/1**
36/0 8 1 **Borak (IRE)**[46] 4231 7-10-9 70 (tp) MissJessicaLlewellyn(5) 1 58
(Bernard Llewellyn) *v.s.a: t.k.h: hld up off the pce in last trio: clsd 7f out: effrt over 2f out: no prog and wl hld fnl f (jockey said gelding was slowly away)* **14/1**
-205 9 1 **General Allenby**[16] 5379 5-9-2 51 oh1 MissJenniferPahlman(7) 12 38
(Shaun Keightley) *s.i.s: off the pce in last trio: effrt over 2f out: no imp and wl hld over 1f out* **7/1**
0661 10 1 ¾ **Rocksette**[18] 5310 5-9-8 57 (p) MissSarahWilliams(7) 5 36
(Adam West) *t.k.h: chsd ldrs: chsd ldr over 7f out: led 5f out tl over 3f out: lost pl and bhd over 1f out: wknd fnl f: fin 11th: plcd 10th* **16/1**
00-0 11 14 **Eben Dubai (IRE)**[39] 4498 7-9-2 51 oh6 (b[1]) MissArabellaTucker(7) 4 7
(John Flint) *dwlt: t.k.h: hdwy to go prom in chsng gp 8f out: lost pl and bhd 2f: sn wknd: fin 12th: plcd 11th* **40/1**
6665 D 2 ½ **William Hunter**[17] 5338 7-10-5 68 (t) MrJamieNeild(7) 9 50
(Nigel Twiston-Davies) *midfield: effrt over 2f out: pushed along over 1f out: no imp and btn whn eased ins fnl f: fin 10th: disqualified - jockey failed to draw the correct weight* **10/1**

2m 29.97s (0.27) **Going Correction** -0.175s/f (Firm) 12 Ran SP% **118.3**
Speed ratings (Par 103): **92,91,91,90,90 89,85,84,83,80 70,81**
CSF £70.94 CT £902.90 TOTE £4.10: £1.60, £3.40, £4.80; EX 68.30 Trifecta £961.30.
Owner J G B Portman **Bred** S Dibb & J Repard **Trained** Upper Lambourn, Berks

FOCUS
Add 9yds. An ordinary event and they went a fair gallop. The winner has been rated in line with his recent form.
T/Jkpt: Not Won. T/Plt: £12.10 to a £1 stake. Pool: £100,662.86 - 6,023.80 winning units T/Qpdt: £5.10 to a £1 stake. Pool: £8,595.93 - 1,224.50 winning units **Steve Payne**

5994 - 5996a (Foreign Racing) - See Raceform Interactive

4577 TIPPERARY (L-H)
Sunday, August 11

OFFICIAL GOING: Straight course - soft; round course - soft to heavy

5997a COOLMORE CARAVAGGIO STKS (LISTED RACE) 7f 115y
3:40 (3:40) 2-Y-O £27,905 (£8,986; £4,256; £1,891; £945)

RPR
1 **Justifier (IRE)**[59] 3782 2-9-3 0 (t[1]) ColinKeane 5 103+
(G M Lyons, Ire) *chsd ldr and disp 2nd early: sn settled in 2nd: pushed along into st: sn rdn nr side and disp ld 1 1/2f out: led ins fnl f and drvn clr to assert nr fin* **6/4**[2]
2 1 ½ **Harpocrates (IRE)**[6] 5752 2-9-3 94 SeamieHeffernan 1 100+
(A P O'Brien, Ire) *chsd ldr and disp 2nd early: sn settled in 3rd: pushed along in 3rd after 1/2-way and impr down centre to dispute ld briefly over 1f out: hdd ins fnl f and no imp on wnr nr fin* **5/4**[1]
3 3 ¾ **Rebel Tale (USA)**[52] 4040 2-9-3 85 OisinOrr 6 91
(Andrew Slattery, Ire) *broke wl to ld briefly tl sn hdd and settled towards rr: pushed along in 4th after 1/2-way: rdn into 3rd ent fnl f where no imp on ldrs: kpt on one pce* **10/1**
4 4 ¾ **Lougher (IRE)**[23] 5159 2-8-12 80 RobbieColgan 2 75
(Richard John O'Brien, Ire) *sn led: narrow advantage 3f out stl gng wl: rdn far side under 2f out where jnd and hdd: sn no ex in 4th and wknd ins fnl f* **5/1**[3]
5 6 ½ **Cap D'antibes (IRE)**[13] 5506 2-9-3 0 KillianLeonard 7 64
(John Joseph Murphy, Ire) *dwlt: in rr thrght: drvn and no imp fr 1/2-way: nvr a factor* **33/1**

1m 39.2s 5 Ran SP% **113.1**
CSF £3.88 TOTE £2.50: £1.70, £1.02; DF 5.30 Trifecta £14.80.
Owner Sean Jones/David Spratt/Mrs Lynne Lyons **Bred** Tally-Ho Stud **Trained** Dunsany, Co Meath

FOCUS
A couple of significant defections gave this the look of a match on paper, and those expectations were borne out. A good effort by the winner to master a more experienced opponent from a stable bidding to win this race for the fourth consecutive year.

5998 - 6000a (Foreign Racing) - See Raceform Interactive

5978 ARLINGTON PARK (L-H)
Sunday, August 11

OFFICIAL GOING: Turf: firm

6001a ARLINGTON MILLION XXXVII STKS (GRADE 1) (3YO+) (TURF) 1m 2f
12:12 3-Y-O+
£458,267 (£152,755; £76,377; £38,188; £22,913; £15,275)

RPR
1 **Bricks And Mortar (USA)**[64] 3619 5-9-0 0 IradOrtizJr 3 113+
(Chad C Brown, U.S.A) *midfield on inner: smooth hdwy 2f out: waited for room tl drvn and qcknd to ld fnl 110yds: r.o* **1/2**[1]
2 ¾ **Magic Wand (IRE)**[15] 5414 4-8-11 0 (p) WayneLordan 2 108+
(A P O'Brien, Ire) *racd keenly: a.p: angled out and clsd fr 2f out: chsd ldr 1f out: styd on and getting bttr of ldr as wnr c by fnl 100yds: no ex* **89/10**[3]
3 1 **Bandua (USA)**[29] 4-9-0 0 AdamBeschizza 9 109
(Jack Sisterson, U.S.A) *pushed along to ld: pressed fr 2 1/2f out: drvn and stretched ld over 1 1/2f out: styd on gamely u.p: hdd fnl 100yds: no ex* **169/10**
4 1 **Robert Bruce (CHI)**[64] 3619 5-9-0 0 JavierCastellano 1 107+
(Chad C Brown, U.S.A) *settled in fnl pair on inner: hdwy 1 1/2f out: styd on wl: nvr nrr* **19/5**[2]
5 3 ½ **Pivoine (IRE)**[29] 4935 5-9-0 0 (b) SilvestreDeSousa 6 100
(Andrew Balding) *settled in fnl trio: last and rdn ins fnl 2f: kpt on for press: nt pce to get in contention* **46/1**
6 ½ **Intellogent (IRE)**[77] 3122 4-9-0 0 (b[1]) FlorentGeroux 8 99
(F Chappet, France) *awkward leaving stalls: midfield on outer: angled out and shortlived effrt 2f out: sn rdn and no further imp fnl 1 1/2f* **156/10**
7 hd **Captivating Moon (USA)**[29] 4-9-0 0 JoseValdiviaJr 7 99
(Chris Block, U.S.A) *settled in rr: sme prog 1 1/2f out: wl hld fnl f* **48/1**
8 4 **Hunting Horn (IRE)**[15] 5414 4-9-0 0 (p) RyanMoore 5 91
(A P O'Brien, Ire) *chsd ldr: tried to press 2 1/2f out: rdn and nt qckn 1 1/2f out: wknd fnl f* **132/10**
9 3 ¼ **Catcho En Die (ARG)**[15] 7-9-0 0 SophieDoyle 4 84
(Naipaul Chatterpaul, U.S.A) *chsd ldrs: drvn to go 2nd over 2f out: sn rdn and wknd* **87/1**

1m 59.44s (-2.20) 9 Ran SP% **121.6**
PARI-MUTUEL (all including 2 unit stake): WIN 3.00; PLACE (1-2) 2.40, 6.40; SHOW (1-2-3) 2.10, 4.80, 5.20; SF 19.00.
Owner Klaravich Stables Inc & William H Lawrence **Bred** George Strawbridge Jr **Trained** USA

FOCUS
The third, who had the run of things out in front, limits the level.

5976 DEAUVILLE (R-H)
Sunday, August 11

OFFICIAL GOING: Polytrack: standard; turf: good

6002a PRIX FRANCOIS BOUTIN (LISTED RACE) (2YO) (STRAIGHT COURSE) (TURF) 7f
1:35 2-Y-O £27,027 (£10,810; £8,108; £5,405; £2,702)

RPR
1 **Happy Bere (FR)**[12] 5539 2-9-0 0 MickaelBarzalona 6 101
(A De Watrigant, France) **4/1**[3]
2 2 ½ **Arapaho (FR)**[21] 2-9-0 0 Pierre-CharlesBoudot 4 95
(A Fabre, France) *hmpd and wnt rt leaving stalls: sn trcking ldr: led travelling strly wl over 2f out: drvn appr 1f out: hdd ins fnl f and nt match pce of wnr* **4/5**[1]
3 2 **King's Command**[29] 4920 2-9-0 0 JamesDoyle 1 89
(Charlie Appleby) *in rr early and pushed along: moved up to chse ldrs 3f out: drvn but nt qckn fr 1 1/2f out: kpt on at one pce* **13/5**[2]
4 2 ½ **Get Set (IRE)**[10] 5600 2-9-0 0 (b) AntoineHamelin 5 83
(Matthieu Palussiere, France) **17/1**

5 20 **Muzy (FR)**21 2-9-0 0 (b) DelphineSantiago 2 31
(Andrea Marcialis, France) **27/1**
U **Milltown Star**12 5520 2-9-0 0 MaximeGuyon 3
(Mick Channon) *stmbld and uns rdr stride after leaving stalls* **10/1**
1m 22.05s (-6.25) **6** Ran SP% **121.6**
PARI-MUTUEL (all including 1 euro stake): WIN 5.00; PLACE 1.60, 1.20; SF 10.90.
Owner Haras Du Grand Courgeon **Bred** Sas Regnier & San Gabriel Inv Inc **Trained** France

6003a PRIX MINERVE (GROUP 3) (3YO FILLIES) (ROUND COURSE) (TURF) 1m 4f 110y
2:50 3-Y-O **£36,036** (£14,414; £10,810; £7,207; £3,603)

RPR
1 **Tamniah (FR)**31 3-8-11 0 MickaelBarzalona 6 102
(A Fabre, France) *a cl up on outer: shkn up to ld over 2f out: sn drvn: jnd 1f out and entered hd-to-hd battle: may have been hdd narrowly ins fnl f and again 100yds out: won gamely on the nod* **20/1**
2 shd **Star Terms**28 4964 3-8-11 0 JamesDoyle 2 102
(Richard Hannon) *trckd ldr on inner: chal towards rail fr 2f out: jnd ldr w 1f to run: sustained hd-to-hd run and may have led narrowly ins fnl f and again 100yds out: lost on the nod* **5/2**2
3 hd **Palomba (IRE)**28 4964 3-8-11 0 MaximeGuyon 5 102+
(C Laffon-Parias, France) *fnl pair on outer: pushed along 2 1/2f out: hdwy on outer w 1 1/2f to run: r.o fnl f: nt quite get there* **10/1**
4 1 1/4 **Golden Box (USA)**62 3676 3-8-11 0 ChristopheSoumillon 1 100
(A De Royer-Dupre, France) *midfield on inner: trckd front rnk into st w less than 2 1/2f to run: nt clrest of runs appr fnl f: sn in clr and kpt on at same pce* **42/10**3
5 1/2 **Villa D'Amore (IRE)**42 4429 3-8-11 0 Pierre-CharlesBoudot 7 99
(A Fabre, France) *led: drvn and hdd over 2f out: kpt on for press but nt pce to go w ldrs fnl 1 1/2f* **11/1**
6 shd **Wonderment (IRE)**56 3905 3-8-11 0 StephanePasquier 3 99
(N Clement, France) *fnl pair on inner: last and rowed along wl over 2f out: styd on fnl f: nvr in contention* **23/5**
7 3/4 **Bolleville (IRE)**35 3-8-11 0 CristianDemuro 4 98
(J-C Rouget, France) *midfield on outer: clsd onto heels of ldrs 3f out: pushed along 2f out but no imp: outpcd by ldrs fr over 1f out* **21/10**1
2m 46.94s (0.54) **7** Ran SP% **120.1**
PARI-MUTUEL (all including 1 euro stake): WIN 21.20; PLACE 5.90, 2.20; SF 84.00.
Owner Prince A A Faisal **Bred** Mitaab Abdullah **Trained** Chantilly, France

6004a PRIX DU HARAS DE FRESNAY-LE-BUFFARD JACQUES LE MAROIS (GROUP 1) (3YO+ COLTS, HORSES, F & M) 1m (R)
3:25 3-Y-O+ **£514,774** (£205,945; £102,972; £51,441; £25,765)

RPR
1 **Romanised (IRE)**22 5207 4-9-5 0 WJLee 6 118+
(K J Condon, Ire) *w.w in 5th: clsd 2f out and trckd ldr w 1 1/2f to run: drvn to ld fnl 125yds: qckly asserted: readily* **7/2**2
2 1 1/4 **Shaman (IRE)**54 3951 3-8-13 0 MaximeGuyon 4 115
(C Laffon-Parias, France) *racd keenly: chsd ldng pair under restraint: shkn up to ld wl over 1 1/2f out: hdd fnl 125yds: nt match wnr* **37/10**3
3 nse **Line of Duty (IRE)**71 3345 3-8-13 0 (p) JamesDoyle 7 115+
(Charlie Appleby) *settled in 4th: began to cl on inner 2f out: drvn whn sltly outpcd wl over 1f out: styd on ins fnl f: jst missed 2nd* **78/10**
4 1 1/4 **Watch Me (FR)**51 4051 3-8-9 0 Pierre-CharlesBoudot 1 108
(F-H Graffard, France) *w.w towards rr: tk clsr order 2f out: 3 l 3rd and shkn up over 1f out but no real imp: one pce fnl f* **21/10**1
5 3/4 **Graignes (FR)**35 4705 3-8-13 0 CristianDemuro 5 110
(Y Barberot, France) *dwlt: racd keenly: hld up in rr: clsd over 1 1/2f out: drvn w 1f to run: no further prog fnl f* **16/1**
6 1 **Study Of Man (IRE)**21 4-9-5 0 (b) StephanePasquier 2 108
(P Bary, France) *w.w one fr last: sme mod late hdwy: nvr in contention* **7/2**2
7 4 1/2 **Success Days (IRE)**62 3678 7-9-5 0 NGMcCullagh 3 98
(K J Condon, Ire) *led: sn hdd and trckd new ldr: pushed along over 2f out: sn wknd* **49/1**
8 8 **Vocal Music (IRE)**97 2497 4-9-5 0 TonyPiccone 8 79
(P Bary, France) *sn led: drvn 2f out: hdd wl over 1 1/2f out: wknd qckly* **54/1**
1m 35.16s (-5.64)
WFA 3 from 4yo+ 7lb **8** Ran SP% **119.0**
PARI-MUTUEL (all including 1 euro stake): WIN 4.50; PLACE 2.00, 1.90, 2.70; DF 7.80.
Owner Robert Ng **Bred** Mrs Monica Aherne **Trained** Rathbride, Co Kildare

FOCUS
It's hard to suggest this will be one of the strongest Group 1s to be run this season, but it did contain horses who had won at the highest-level. Run at a respectable gallop thanks to a couple of outsiders striding on from the outset, being close up proved to be an advantage, as take out the pair that led early, the first three home held the three positions just behind them, while the other three made little impact. The second, third and fifth help set the level.

6005a PRIX NUREYEV (LISTED RACE) (3YO) (ROUND COURSE) (TURF) 1m 2f
4:35 3-Y-O **£24,774** (£9,909; £7,432; £4,954; £2,477)

RPR
1 **Alwaab (FR)**33 4770 3-8-13 0 VincentCheminaud 2 99
(A Fabre, France) **22/5**3
2 nk **Flambeur (USA)**42 4431 3-8-13 0 MaximeGuyon 8 98
(C Laffon-Parias, France) **36/5**
3 snk **Volskha (FR)**43 4416 3-9-0 0 AlexisBadel 1 99
(Simone Brogi, France) **14/1**
4 nse **Goya Senora (FR)**33 3-8-13 0 JeromeCabre 4 98
(Y Barberot, France) **12/1**
5 2 1/2 **Chevalier Cathare (FR)**43 3-8-13 0 TheoBachelot 6 93
(S Wattel, France) **11/1**
6 snk **Star Safari**305 8109 3-8-13 0 JamesDoyle 3 93
(Charlie Appleby) *chsd clr ldr: steadily clsd on ldr fr 1/2-way: 2nd whn drvn over 1 1/2f out but nt qckn: dropping away whn sltly impeded between horses fnl f* **31/10**2
7 snk **Idiosa (GER)**77 3121 3-8-9 0 QuentinPerrette 5 88
(Mlle L Kneip, France) **23/1**
8 1/2 **Zarkallani (FR)**70 3390 3-8-13 0 ChristopheSoumillon 7 91
(A De Royer-Dupre, France) **17/10**1
2m 7.72s (-2.48) **8** Ran SP% **119.0**
PARI-MUTUEL (all including 1 euro stake): WIN 5.40; PLACE 2.00, 2.40, 3.60; DF 12.30.
Owner Al Shaqab Racing **Bred** Ecurie Haras Du Cadran, Ecurie La Boetie Et Al **Trained** Chantilly, France

3639 HOPPEGARTEN (R-H)
Sunday, August 11
OFFICIAL GOING: Turf: good

6006a HOPPEGARTENER FLIEGERPREIS/VIERERWETTE MIT 10,000 GARANTIEAUSZAHLUNG - WETTCHANCE DES TAGES (LISTED) 6f
3:15 3-Y-O+ **£12,612** (£5,855; £2,702; £1,351)

RPR
1 **Red Torch (FR)**15 5471 4-9-0 0 OlivierPeslier 2 99
(H-A Pantall, France) **48/10**
2 1 1/4 **Mubaalegh**12 5-9-0 0 JoeFanning 13 95
(J E Hammond, France) *racd keenly: trckd ldr on outer: led wl over 2f out: drvn ins fnl 1 1/2f and styd on: hdd fnl 50yds: no ex* **87/10**
3 1/2 **Big Boots (IRE)**20 3-8-9 0 MarcoCasamento 11 91
(Waldemar Hickst, Germany) **23/5**3
4 1 **Inspired Thought (IRE)**10 5581 3-8-6 0 (p) HollieDoyle 12 85
(Archie Watson) *chsd ldrs on outer: chsd ldr over 2f out: cl 3rd and n.m.r ins fnl f: no ex fnl 75yds: lost 3rd cl home* **17/5**2
5 3/4 **Iron Duke (GER)**39 4534 3-8-9 0 FilipMinarik 8 86
(P Schiergen, Germany) **41/1**
6 3/4 **Julio (GER)**71 3369 4-9-0 0 BauyrzhanMurzabayev 6 85
(Henk Grewe, Germany) **33/10**1
7 1 **Clear For Take Off**39 4534 5-9-0 0 WladimirPanov 1 82
(D Moser, Germany) **144/10**
8 2 **McQueen (FR)**39 4534 7-9-3 0 MichaelCadeddu 5 79
(Yasmin Almenrader, Germany) **181/10**
9 hd **Rope A Dope (IRE)**62 3-8-7 0 ow1 AndraschStarke 9 71
(P Schiergen, Germany) **34/1**
10 1/2 **Dante's Peak**56 3-8-10 0 ow1 (p) SalvatoreSulas 7 72
(Gabor Maronka, Hungary) **52/1**
11 2 1/2 **Politicum (FR)**392 4987 3-8-9 0 (p) MartinLaube 3 63
(Arslangirej Savujev, Czech Republic) **81/1**
12 1/2 **Shining Emerald**71 3369 8-9-3 0 EduardoPedroza 10 67
(A Wohler, Germany) **269/10**
13 7 **Mollys Best (FR)**50 5-9-0 0 (b) PavlinaFilipova 4 41
(Katerina Berthier, Czech Republic) **28/1**
1m 10.55s
WFA 3 from 4yo+ 4lb **13** Ran SP% **118.5**
PARI-MUTUEL (all including 1 euro stake): WIN 5.80 PLACE: 1.50, 2.30, 1.70, 1.40; SF: 22.10.
Owner Sandro V Gianella **Bred** Appapays Racing Club **Trained** France

6007a 129TH LONGINES GROSSER PREIS VON BERLIN (GROUP 1) (3YO+) (TURF) 1m 4f
3:50 3-Y-O+ **£90,090** (£27,027; £13,513; £6,306; £2,702)

RPR
1 **French King**42 4427 4-9-6 0 OlivierPeslier 1 118+
(H-A Pantall, France) *racd keenly: hld up wl in tch: travelled strly into st: angled out ent fnl 2f: qcknd to ld appr fnl f: sn asserted: won cosily* **19/10**2
2 1 **Communique (IRE)**31 4848 4-9-6 0 JoeFanning 4 115
(Mark Johnston) *cl 3rd on outer: led after 3f: kicked for home 2 1/2f out: hdd appr fnl f: styd on gamely but nt match pce of wnr* **3/1**3
3 shd **Old Persian**72 3314 4-9-6 0 WilliamBuick 2 115
(Charlie Appleby) *racd keenly early: a cl up on outer: drvn but no gap between front two ins fnl f: styd on: jst missed 2nd* **13/10**1
4 1 3/4 **Royal Youmzain (FR)**42 4427 4-9-6 0 EduardoPedroza 6 112
(A Wohler, Germany) *hld up in rr: tk clsr order 2f out: kpt on but nt pce to get involved* **112/10**
5 1 1/4 **Alounak (FR)**14 5483 4-9-6 0 MarcoCasamento 5 110
(Waldemar Hickst, Germany) *led: hdd after 3f: sn lost pl: in fnl pair and drvn over 2f out but no imp: kpt on at same pce* **33/1**
6 3 **Andoro (GER)**35 4707 3-8-10 0 BauyrzhanMurzabayev 3 106
(R Dzubasz, Germany) *dwlt sltly: racd in fnl pair: moved up on outer to chse ldrs wl bef 1/2-way: rdn and nt qckn 2f out: grad dropped away* **219/10**
2m 35.16s (5.86)
WFA 3 from 4yo 10lb **6** Ran SP% **118.5**
PARI-MUTUEL (all including 1 euro stake): WIN 2.90; PLACE 2.00, 2.40; SF 6.20.
Owner H H Sheikh Abdulla Bin Khalifa Al Thani **Bred** Umm Qarn Farms **Trained** France

FOCUS
The fourth and fifth anchor the form.

5232 LES LANDES
Sunday, August 11
OFFICIAL GOING: Turf: good, good to firm in places

6008a 2019 RAVENSCROFT JERSEY OAKS (H'CAP) (F&M) (TURF) 1m 2f
3:40 (3:40) 3-Y-O+ **£2,380** (£860; £510)

RPR
1 **Molliana**21 5233 4-9-0 MissSerenaBrotherton 46
(Neil Mulholland) **11/10**1
2 shd **Safira Menina**21 7-9-4 MrFrederickTett 50
(Mrs A Malzard, Jersey) **7/2**3
3 3 3/4 **Island Song (IRE)**21 5-10-7 VictoriaMalzard 59
(Mrs A Malzard, Jersey) **5/4**2
4 10 **Snejinska (FR)**21 5233 5-8-10 oh9 (h) GeorgeRooke 14
(Mrs C Gilbert, Jersey) **5/1**
5 12 **Veronica's Napkin (IRE)**21 8127 7-10-7 DavyDelalande 15
(J Moon, Jersey) **12/1**
6 5 **Koshi**63 3642 4-8-10 oh13 (p) AndrewElliott
(K Kukk, Jersey) **14/1**
7 1 3/4 **Little Lotte (IRE)**51 3642 6-8-10 oh20 (v) RachealKneller
(Mrs A Corson, Jersey) **20/1**
2m 9.0s **7** Ran SP% **150.1**
Owner Dajam Ltd **Bred** Norman Court Stud **Trained** Limpley Stoke, Wilts

6009a LADBROKES LADIES DAY H'CAP (TURF) 1m 100y
4:15 (4:15) (0-60,) 3-Y-O+ £1,780 (£640; £380)

RPR
1 **Brown Velvet**21 5233 7-9-8 GeorgeRooke 33
(Mrs C Gilbert, Jersey) 6/1
2 1 1/2 **Mendacious Harpy (IRE)**37 4684 8-9-0 (p) MrFrederickTett 22
(Mrs A Malzard, Jersey) 5/2[3]
3 1 **Kalani Rose**37 4684 5-8-6 ow1 (b) RachealKneller 12
(Mrs A Corson, Jersey) 16/1
4 1 1/4 **Lyrical Ballad (IRE)**72 3306 3-10-8 (p) HarryReed 45
(Neil Mulholland) 2/1[2]
5 1 **William Booth (IRE)**37 4686 5-10-0 (p) MissSerenaBrotherton 29
(Mrs C Gilbert, Jersey) 6/1
6 nk **Benoordenhout (IRE)**21 8-10-12 DavyDelalande 40
(T Le Brocq, Jersey) 5/1
7 hd **Captain James (FR)**37 4686 9-10-9 MattieBatchelor 36
(Mrs C Gilbert, Jersey) 1/1[1]
8 6 **Drummer Jack (IRE)**37 4684 3-9-4 (t) AndrewElliott 10
(K Kukk, Jersey) 12/1

Owner La Vallette Ltd **Bred** D R Botterill **Trained** Jersey

6010a LADBROKES BEST ODDS GUARANTEED H'CAP (TURF) 1m 4f
4:50 (4:50) 3-Y-O+ £1,780 (£640; £380)

RPR
1 **Aussie Lyrics (FR)**21 9-10-12 MattieBatchelor 67
(Mrs C Gilbert, Jersey) 2/1[2]
2 1 **Hard To Handel**21 5233 7-10-0 MissSerenaBrotherton 53
(Mrs A Malzard, Jersey) 3/1[3]
3 hd **Hidden Depths (IRE)**169 876 4-10-4 HarryReed 57
(Neil Mulholland) 3/1[3]
4 1 1/4 **Kenoughty (FR)**21 3-8-11 GeorgeRooke 45
(J Moon, Jersey) 1/1[1]
5 3 1/4 **Ice Royal (IRE)**21 5233 6-10-3 MrFrederickTett 48
(Mrs A Malzard, Jersey) 7/1
6 1 1/4 **St Ouen (IRE)**21 3-8-12 AndrewElliott 38
(K Kukk, Jersey) 12/1
7 25 **Rainbow Charlie**21 8-8-6 oh27 ow1 RachealKneller
(Mrs A Corson, Jersey) 20/1

Owner White Spot Racing **Bred** Hugh Hogg **Trained** Jersey

5764 CATTERICK (L-H)
Monday, August 12

OFFICIAL GOING: Soft (6.5)
Wind: Moderate against Weather: Sunny periods and showers

6011 RACING CAREERS DAY NOVICE MEDIAN AUCTION STKS 5f
2:15 (2:16) (Class 5) 2-Y-O £4,140 (£1,232; £615; £307) Stalls Low

Form RPR
40 1 **Rapid Russo**17 5388 2-9-2 0 TomEaves 5 79
(Michael Dods) *hld up in rr: hdwy wl over 1f out: rdn to ld and hung lft ins fnl f: kpt on* 20/1
1 2 1 1/2 **Maystar (IRE)**16 5427 2-9-6 0 HollieDoyle 4 77+
(Archie Watson) *cl up: pushed along 1/2-way: rdn 2f out: sn hung lft and outpcd: drvn and ev ch ins fnl f: kpt on same pce* 1/2[1]
42 3 3 **Microscopic (IRE)**27 5026 2-8-11 64 BenCurtis 3 57+
(David Simcock) *t.k.h: slt ld: pushed along 2f out: rdn over 1f out: hdd ins fnl f: hld whn n.m.r on inner ins fnl 100yds* 9/2[3]
3011 4 4 1/2 **Blitzle**20 5279 2-9-1 72 BenRobinson 6 45+
(Ollie Pears) *awkward s and t.k.h: cl up: chal wl over 1f out: sn rdn and ev ch: wknd ent fnl f* 4/1[2]
000 5 4 1/2 **Samsar (IRE)**28 4999 2-9-2 42 (p[1]) TonyHamilton 2 30
(Adrian Nicholls) *trckd ldrs: pushed along over 2f out: sn rdn and wknd over 1f out* 100/1
00 6 17 **Nice One Too**30 4903 2-8-11 0 JohnFahy 1
(David C Griffiths) *trckd ldrs: pushed along bef 1/2-way: sn rdn and outpcd: bhd fnl 2f* 125/1

1m 3.27s (2.77) **Going Correction** +0.525s/f (Yiel) 6 Ran SP% 111.4
Speed ratings (Par 94): **98,95,90,83,76 49**
CSF £30.82 TOTE £20.90: £7.70, £1.10; EX 38.80 Trifecta £113.50.
Owner Mrs C E Dods **Bred** Bolton Grange **Trained** Denton, Co Durham
FOCUS
There was a turn up in this opening 2yo novice race. The winning time indicated the going assessment to be spot on.

6012 RACING TO SCHOOL CLAIMING STKS 1m 4f 13y
2:45 (2:45) (Class 6) 3-Y-O+ £3,105 (£924; £461; £300; £300) Stalls Low

Form RPR
3213 1 **First Flight (IRE)**2 5948 8-9-8 73 BenRobinson 5 78
(Brian Ellison) *trckd ldng pair: hdwy and wd st towards stands' rail: sn chsng ldr: rdn to chal ent fnl f: sn drvn: kpt on u.p to ld nr fin* 5/4[2]
3404 2 shd **Desert Point (FR)**13 5097 7-10-0 79 DanielTudhope 1 84
(Keith Dalgleish) *trckd ldr: hdwy to ld wl over 2f out: racd centre in home st: rdn wl over 1f out: jnd ent fnl f: sn drvn: hdd and no ex nr fin* 5/6[1]
6606 3 20 **Alpasu (IRE)**6 5792 3-9-0 68 (p) TonyHamilton 3 51
(Adrian Nicholls) *led: pushed along and hdd wl over 2f out: racd alone nr stands' rail in home st: sn drvn and one pce* 14/1[3]
3030 4 1 1/2 **Fillydelphia (IRE)**6 5766 8-8-10 45 (p) RhonaPindar(7) 2 41
(Liam Bailey) *dwlt and hld up in rr: hdwy 3f out: chsd ldrs in centre over 2f out: sn rdn: drvn and one pce fnl 2f (vet said mare had a small wound to its right-fore heel)* 25/1
54-0 5 5 **Bold Statement (IRE)**8 5709 4-9-8 57 (t[1]) CamHardie 4 38
(Alan Berry) *trckd ldrs on inner: pushed along 4f out: rdn 3f out: sn wknd* 100/1

2m 46.89s (6.29) **Going Correction** +0.525s/f (Yiel)
WFA 3 from 4yo+ 10lb 5 Ran SP% 110.5
Speed ratings (Par 101): **100,99,86,85,82**
CSF £2.60 TOTE £2.10: £1.30, £1.02; EX 2.50 Trifecta £5.10.
Owner Kristian Strangeway **Bred** Darley **Trained** Norton, N Yorks
FOCUS
The first pair came right away on the stands' side in this uncompetitive claimer.

6013 NATIONAL HORSERACING COLLEGE MEDIAN AUCTION MAIDEN STKS 5f 212y
3:15 (3:20) (Class 6) 3-4-Y-O £3,105 (£924; £461; £230) Stalls Low

Form RPR
3222 1 **Delachance (FR)**14 5492 3-9-5 72 (h) BenCurtis 4 62+
(David Simcock) *cl up: led 4f out: wd st towards stands' side: rdn and clr appr fnl f* 30/100[1]
0260 2 2 1/2 **Isabella Ruby**3 5918 4-8-11 45 (p[1]) GavinAshton(7) 2 50
(Lisa Williamson) *trckd ldrs: hdwy over 2f out: rdn wl over 1f out: sn chsng wnr: no imp fnl f* 12/1[3]
3 4 1/2 **Moudallal** 3-9-0 0 DanielTudhope 1 36
(Robert Cowell) *dwlt: green and outpcd in rr: hdwy 1/2-way: rdn along to chse ldrs wl over 1f out: kpt on same pce* 7/2[2]
5 4 1/2 **Look Who It Isnae (IRE)**9 5669 3-8-9 0 HarrisonShaw(5) 3 34
(Alan Berry) *slt ld 2f: cl up: rdn along 2f out: grad wknd fr over 1f out* 100/1
6000 5 12 **Killer Queen**4 5857 4-9-4 36 (p) JohnFahy 5
(David C Griffiths) *chsd ldrs: rdn along wl over 2f out: sn wknd* 40/1

1m 17.94s (4.34) **Going Correction** +0.525s/f (Yiel)
WFA 3 from 4yo 4lb 5 Ran SP% 110.3
Speed ratings (Par 101): **92,88,82,82,66**
CSF £5.30 TOTE £1.10: £1.10, £2.90; EX 3.20 Trifecta £3.90.
Owner Never Say Die Partnership **Bred** Cocheese Bloodstock & P Chedeville **Trained** Newmarket, Suffolk
FOCUS
A weak maiden sprint and the stands' side was again the place to be.

6014 RACING TV PROFITS RETURNED TO RACING H'CAP 7f 6y
3:45 (3:45) (Class 3) (0-95,96) 4-Y-O+ £8,715 (£2,609; £1,304; £652; £326; £163) Stalls Low

Form RPR
5525 1 **Hells Babe**30 4905 6-9-5 89 HollieDoyle 1 98
(Michael Appleby) *slt ld: wd home st towards stands' rail: rdn wl over 1f out: drvn ins fnl f: kpt on wl towards fin* 9/2[2]
5032 2 2 1/4 **Raselasad (IRE)**40 4511 5-9-5 89 RoystonFfrench 2 92
(Tracy Waggott) *trckd ldng pair: hdwy and wd st: rdn to chse wnr over 1f out: drvn and ev ch jst ins fnl f: kpt on same pce* 6/1[3]
5331 3 1 3/4 **Luis Vaz De Torres (IRE)**21 5246 7-8-10 80 TonyHamilton 7 78
(Richard Fahey) *hld up in tch: hdwy 3f out: wd st: chsd ldrs and n.m.r on inner 2f out: sn rdn: kpt on same pce* 13/2
2406 4 nk **Tadaawol**2 5970 6-8-6 81 (p) PaulaMuir(5) 8 78
(Roger Fell) *cl up: disp ld 3f out: rdn 2f out: sn drvn and kpt on one pce* 10/1
4611 5 2 **Rousayan (IRE)**42 4445 8-9-7 91 (h) BenCurtis 6 83
(Roger Fell) *hld up: effrt and hdwy 2f out: rdn over 1f out: n.d* 7/1
6060 6 2 **Aeolus**14 5488 8-9-1 85 JamesSullivan 3 72
(Ruth Carr) *hld up: hdwy over 2f out: rdn wl over 1f out: n.d* 20/1
-042 7 1/2 **Medahim (IRE)**16 5453 5-9-12 96 DanielTudhope 4 81
(Ivan Furtado) *trckd ldrs: pushed along wl over 2f out: rdn wl over 1f out: sn btn (jockey said gelding ran flat)* 6/4[1]

1m 28.81s (1.41) **Going Correction** +0.525s/f (Yiel) 7 Ran SP% 112.2
Speed ratings (Par 107): **112,109,107,107,104 102,101**
CSF £29.87 CT £171.80 TOTE £5.20: £2.70, £3.10; EX 26.20 Trifecta £252.00.
Owner Mrs Lucinda White **Bred** Mrs Lucinda White (mulbrooke Stud) **Trained** Oakham, Rutland
FOCUS
This feature handicap saw the field again come over stands' side in the home straight. The second has been rated close to form.

6015 EVERY RACE LIVE ON RACING TV H'CAP 7f 6y
4:15 (4:15) (Class 4) (0-80,82) 3-Y-O £6,080 (£1,809; £904; £452; £300) Stalls Low

Form RPR
0403 1 **I Am A Dreamer**4 5862 3-9-9 82 (v) CYHo 3 88
(Mark Johnston) *trckd ldng pair: wd st to centre and sn cl up: rdn to ld jst over 1f out: kpt on wl* 5/1
-000 2 2 3/4 **Fuente**9 5692 3-9-9 82 TomEaves 1 81
(Keith Dalgleish) *cl up on inner: styd alone nr inner rail in home st: rdn along to ld 2f out: hdd and drvn jst over 1f out: kpt on same pce towards fin* 13/2
1545 3 1/2 **Howzer Black (IRE)**28 4980 3-9-1 79 (p) BenSanderson(5) 2 76+
(Keith Dalgleish) *s.i.s and lost 8 l s: tk clsr order 4f out: chsd ldrs over 2f out: rdn wl over 1f out: kpt on same pce fnl f (jockey said gelding missed the break)* 3/1[2]
5311 4 1 **Ollivander (IRE)**19 5297 3-9-2 75 (v) DanielTudhope 4 70
(David O'Meara) *slt ld: wd st to r centre: rdn along and hdd 2f out: drvn over 1f out: sn one pce* 10/3[3]
5415 5 2 **Ramesses**16 5459 3-9-2 75 TonyHamilton 5 64
(Richard Fahey) *hld up in tch: wd st to r alone nr stands' rail: rdn 2f out: drvn over 1f out: sn no imp* 2/1[1]

1m 30.3s (2.90) **Going Correction** +0.525s/f (Yiel) 5 Ran SP% 111.4
Speed ratings (Par 102): **104,100,100,99,96**
CSF £34.14 TOTE £5.70: £2.90, £3.70; EX 43.90 Trifecta £152.20.
Owner M Doyle **Bred** Bearstone Stud Ltd **Trained** Middleham Moor, N Yorks
FOCUS
This wasn't a bad little 3yo handicap. They spread across the track after straightening for home. A small pb from the winner.

6016 WATCH RACING TV NOW H'CAP 1m 7f 189y
4:45 (4:45) (Class 5) (0-70,72) 4-Y-O+ £4,075 (£1,212; £606; £303) Stalls Low

Form RPR
1122 1 **Maid In Manhattan (IRE)**37 4661 5-8-6 60 (h) HarrisonShaw(5) 5 67+
(Rebecca Menzies) *t.k.h: hld up in rr: hdwy and wd st to stands' rail: sn cl up: rdn to ld wl over 1f out: kpt on wl* 6/4[2]
0653 2 1 3/4 **Diodorus (IRE)**25 5097 5-9-8 71 BenCurtis 2 75
(Karen McLintock) *trckd ldr: hdwy and cl up 3f out: wd st towards stands' side: rdn and ev ch 2f out: drvn over 1f out: kpt on same pce* 11/2[3]
110/ 3 5 **Tonto's Spirit**13 8778 7-9-9 72 (h) JamesSullivan 3 70
(Dianne Sayer) *led: pushed along 3f out: styd far side to r alone st: rdn and hdd 2f out: sn drvn and kpt on same pce* 11/8[1]

00-3 4 10 **Cotton Club (IRE)**[19] 5290 8-9-6 **69** JackMitchell 1 55
(George Boughey) *trckd ldng pair: hdwy 3f out: rdn along and wd to r centre in home st: drvn 2f out: sn wknd* **17/2**

3m 46.47s (10.47) **Going Correction** +0.525s/f (Yiel) **4 Ran SP% 108.0**
Speed ratings (Par 103): **94,93,90,85**
CSF £9.13 TOTE £2.30; EX 8.20 Trifecta £11.50.
Owner Stoneleigh Racing **Bred** John Breslin **Trained** Mordon, Durham

FOCUS
A sprint for home developed in this ordinary staying handicap. Form to tread carefully with. It's been rated around the second.

6017 RACING AGAIN 19TH AUGUST H'CAP 5f
5:15 (5:15) (Class 6) (0-60,61) 3-Y-0+ **£3,105** (£924; £461; £300; £300) **Stalls** Low

Form RPR

0035 1 **Seamster**[25] 5084 12-8-12 **56** (t) ThomasGreatrex(5) 4 61
(David Loughnane) *trckd ldrs: hdwy 1/2-way: rdn to chal jst over 1f out: drvn to ld last 100yds: kpt on wl* **6/1**

3501 2 hd **B Fifty Two (IRE)**[6] 5768 10-9-5 **61** 4ex (vt) JaneElliott(3) 5 65
(Marjorie Fife) *slt ld: rdn along 2f out: drvn ent fnl f: hdd last 100yds: kpt on wl towards fin* **2/1**[1]

0400 3 ¾ **Gift In Time (IRE)**[63] 3657 4-9-5 **58** (p) TomEaves 2 60
(Paul Collins) *dwlt: in rr and sn swtchd rt towards stands' side: pushed along and hdwy 2f out: rdn over 1f out: chal and ev ch ent fnl f: sn drvn and kpt on same pce* **7/2**[3]

3540 4 4 ½ **Normal Equilibrium**[23] 5169 9-9-7 **60** (p) BenCurtis 3 45
(Ivan Furtado) *cl up: rdn along 2f out: drvn wl over 1f out: sn wknd* **9/4**[2]

6030 5 11 **North Korea (IRE)**[25] 5084 3-8-4 **46** (p) JamesSullivan 1
(Brian Baugh) *chsd ldng pair: rdn along wl over 2f out: sn wknd* **8/1**

1m 2.65s (2.15) **Going Correction** +0.525s/f (Yiel)
WFA 3 from 4yo+ 3lb **5 Ran SP% 111.7**
Speed ratings (Par 101): **103,102,101,94,76**
CSF £18.66 TOTE £7.20: £2.30, £1.20; EX 22.00 Trifecta £40.10.
Owner Miss Sarah Hoyland **Bred** D G Hardisty Bloodstock **Trained** Tern Hill, Shropshire

FOCUS
There was something of a slow-motion finish to this moderate sprint handicap. The form makes sense rated around the principals.
T/Plt: £47.00 to a £1 stake. Pool: £72,229.28 - 1121.11 winning units T/Qpdt: £28.70 to a £1 stake. Pool: £5,880.28 - 151.41 winning units **Joe Rowntree**

5987 WINDSOR (R-H)
Monday, August 12

OFFICIAL GOING: Good to firm (7.2)
Wind: Light, behind Weather: Fine but cloudy

6018 EXMOOR TRIM - GO ANYWHERE IN COMFORT APPRENTICE H'CAP 6f 12y
5:30 (5:31) (Class 6) (0-60,61) 3-Y-0+
£2,781 (£827; £413; £300; £300; £300) **Stalls** Centre

Form RPR

40-0 1 **Wotadoll**[9] 5678 5-9-11 **61** SebastianWoods 10 68
(Mike Murphy) *taken down early: fast away: led and sn crossed to nr side rail: hdd after 1f: trckd ldr: plld out 2f out: rdn to ld jst over 1f out: kpt on wl* **7/1**

5336 2 ¾ **Under Curfew**[42] 4457 3-9-3 **60** ElishaWhittington(3) 3 64
(Tony Carroll) *wl in tch: rdn and prog on outer 2f out: chsd wnr jst ins fnl f: nt qckn last 100yds (jockey said saddle slipped)* **5/1**[2]

003 3 ½ **Fiery Breath**[26] 5063 4-9-4 **54** (h) DarraghKeenan 9 57
(Robert Eddery) *hld up in towards rr: stdy prog on outer over 2f out: shkn up over 1f out: kpt on to take 3rd last strides* **4/1**[1]

-665 4 ½ **Hellovaqueen**[4] 5837 4-9-5 **60** (b) AngusVilliers(5) 13 62
(Richard Hughes) *racd wd early: crossed to nr side rail and led after 1f: more than 2 l ahd over 2f out: hdd jst over 1f out: no ex* **6/1**

5036 5 1 ¾ **Englishman**[14] 5495 9-9-7 **60** WilliamCarver(3) 12 57
(Milton Bradley) *prom: disp 2nd 2f out: fdd jst over 1f out* **11/2**[3]

0000 6 1 ½ **Aegean Mist**[49] 4185 3-8-11 **56** (p[1]) GeorgeRooke(5) 1 47
(John Bridger) *chsd ldrs: rdn and no prog 2f out: no imp after* **14/1**

-560 7 2 **Lily Of Year (FR)**[51] 4115 4-8-9 **50** MichaelPitt(5) 6 36
(Denis Coakley) *taken down early: t.k.h: hld up in last pair: pushed along and passed rivals fr 2f out: nvr in it* **12/1**

00U0 8 1 ¼ **Indian Affair**[25] 5081 9-8-10 **46** oh1 (bt) PoppyBridgwater 2 28
(Milton Bradley) *a towards rr: no prog 2f out* **16/1**

0050 9 1 **Yet Another (IRE)**[19] 5293 4-8-5 **46** oh1 KeelanBaker(5) 4 25
(Grace Harris) *mostly in last trio: no prog 2f out* **50/1**

-006 10 1 **Crimson Princess**[9] 5678 4-8-7 **46** oh1 GeorgiaDobie(3) 7 22
(Nikki Evans) *taken down early: in tch in midfield: rdn and wknd 2f out* **28/1**

4003 11 3 **Moneta**[26] 5044 3-9-0 **57** (t) TylerSaunders(3) 11 23
(Jonathan Portman) *chsd ldrs 4f: wknd qckly over 1f out* **9/1**

0-00 12 3 **Picket Line**[79] 3089 7-9-9 **59** (b) ScottMcCullagh 8 17
(Geoffrey Deacon) *a wl in rr: nvr a factor* **25/1**

1m 11.61s (-0.49) **Going Correction** -0.075s/f (Good)
WFA 3 from 4yo+ 4lb **12 Ran SP% 118.3**
Speed ratings (Par 101): **100,99,98,97,95 93,90,89,87,86 82,78**
CSF £41.12 CT £163.73 TOTE £7.20: £2.20, £2.10, £1.60; EX 42.30 Trifecta £214.10.
Owner David C Mead **Bred** David C Mead **Trained** Westoning, Beds

FOCUS
Moderate sprinting form, but it was competitive. The winner has been rated in line with the best of last year's form, with the second and third to this year's best.

6019 BRITISH EBF FILLIES' NOVICE STKS (PLUS 10 RACE) 6f 12y
6:00 (6:01) (Class 5) 2-Y-0 **£3,428** (£1,020; £509; £254) **Stalls** Centre

Form RPR

P62 1 **Love Powerful (IRE)**[14] 5500 2-9-0 0 SeanLevey 10 76
(Richard Hannon) *mde all and racd against nr side rail: rdn over 1f out: kpt on wl and fended off chalrs* **6/1**

01 2 ¾ **Company Minx (IRE)**[33] 4798 2-9-4 0 HectorCrouch 6 77
(Clive Cox) *prom: drvn over 1f out: styd on fnl f to snatch 2nd last strides: a hld* **6/1**

10 3 shd **Special Secret**[32] 4840 2-9-4 0 CharlesBishop 5 77
(Eve Johnson Houghton) *prom: rdn wl over 1f out: tried to chal fnl f: kpt on but hld* **10/3**[1]

51 4 ½ **Caspian Queen (IRE)**[28] 4993 2-9-7 0 ShaneKelly 11 79
(Richard Hughes) *mostly chsd wnr: rdn to chal over 1f out: nt qckn and hld fnl f: lost 2 pls after* **8/1**

0 5 nk **Dutch Painting**[24] 5132 2-9-0 0 JasonWatson 4 71
(Michael Bell) *in tch: pushed along and prog 2f out: swtchd to outer and shkn up over 1f out: kpt on but nvr quite able to chal* **16/1**

6 6 nk **Clegane**[33] 4790 2-9-0 0 LiamKeniry 1 70+
(Ed Walker) *nt that wl away: hld up in last trio: sme prog against nr side rail 2f out: no ch whn rdn fnl f: r.o but nvr really in it* **4/1**[3]

52 7 1 ¼ **Onassis (IRE)**[26] 5045 2-9-0 0 StevieDonohoe 2 66
(Charlie Fellowes) *in tch: shkn up to cl on ldrs 2f out: no imp 1f out: fdd* **7/2**[2]

65 8 6 **Egotistic**[9] 5646 2-9-0 0 CallumShepherd 7 48
(David Simcock) *prom gng wl: pushed along and steadily lost pl fr 2f out: wknd fnl f* **50/1**

9 20 **Hot Hot Hot** 2-9-0 0 BrettDoyle 3
(Tony Carroll) *s.s: rcvrd and in tch after 2f: wknd rapidly wl over 1f out: t.o (jockey said filly was slowly away)* **50/1**

10 shd **Half Of Seven** 2-9-0 0 (h[1]) TomMarquand 12
(Jonjo O'Neill) *a wl in rr: t.o* **66/1**

11 2 ¾ **Edge Of The Bay** 2-8-11 0 MitchGodwin(3) 8
(Christopher Mason) *chsd ldrs on outer: hanging lft over 2f out: wknd rapidly wl over 1f out: t.o* **50/1**

004 12 23 **Hot Poppy**[27] 5011 2-9-0 38 (h[1]) JoeyHaynes 9
(John Gallagher) *sn bhd: t.o over 2f out* **100/1**

1m 11.72s (-0.38) **Going Correction** -0.075s/f (Good) **12 Ran SP% 119.2**
Speed ratings (Par 91): **99,98,97,97,96 96,94,86,60,59 56,25**
CSF £41.57 TOTE £6.20: £1.90, £2.00, £1.50; EX 36.50 Trifecta £134.10.
Owner King Power Racing Co Ltd **Bred** Thomas Hassett **Trained** East Everleigh, Wilts

FOCUS
Bit of a bunched finish to this fillies' novice and hard to rate it as anything other than ordinary form.

6020 RITA ORA LIVE AT WINDSOR RACECOURSE NURSERY H'CAP 1m 31y
6:30 (6:30) (Class 4) (0-85,86) 2-Y-O **£4,463** (£1,328; £663; £331) **Stalls** Low

Form RPR

043 1 **Arthur's Court (IRE)**[22] 5212 2-9-2 **76** JamesDoyle 2 81+
(Hugo Palmer) *hld up in last: swift move to press ldng pair over 3f out: drvn 2f out: led over 1f out: styd on* **7/2**

201 2 1 ¾ **Dramatic Sands (IRE)**[41] 4480 2-9-6 **80** AdamMcNamara 1 82+
(Archie Watson) *s.i.s: chsd ldng pair to over 3f out: rdn over 2f out: styd on u.p to take 2nd last 100yds: no imp on wnr* **5/2**[2]

5313 3 ½ **Making History (IRE)**[17] 5382 2-9-12 **86** OisinMurphy 3 86
(Saeed bin Suroor) *led: stl gng wl enough over 2f out: drvn and hdd over 1f out: fnd nil* **7/4**[1]

2315 4 4 **Indian Creak (IRE)**[11] 5587 2-9-6 **80** CallumShepherd 4 71
(Mick Channon) *pressed ldr: upsides over 3f out to wl over 1f out: wknd qckly fnl f* **3/1**[3]

1m 44.22s (-0.28) **Going Correction** -0.075s/f (Good) **4 Ran SP% 112.2**
Speed ratings (Par 96): **98,96,95,91**
CSF £12.53 TOTE £5.80; EX 13.60 Trifecta £18.60.
Owner John Livock, Nat Lacy, Mrs M V Magnier **Bred** Lynch-Bages & Rhinestone Bloodstock **Trained** Newmarket, Suffolk

FOCUS
A fair nursery.

6021 SKY SPORTS RACING ON VIRGIN 535 H'CAP 1m 2f
7:00 (7:01) (Class 3) (0-90,90) 3-Y-0 **£7,246** (£2,168; £1,084; £542; £270) **Stalls** Low

Form RPR

514 1 **Caradoc (IRE)**[16] 5440 4-9-13 **89** OisinMurphy 5 100+
(Ed Walker) *t.k.h: trckd ldr after 2f: led over 2f out gng best: shifted to nr side rail over 1f out: drvn clr fnl f* **11/10**[1]

0064 2 2 ¾ **Mordred (IRE)**[10] 5614 3-9-1 **85** SeanLevey 2 90
(Richard Hannon) *hld up disputing 4th: rdn over 2f out: styd on to take 2nd over 1f out: lft bhd by wnr fnl f* **4/1**[2]

0222 3 ½ **Allegiant (USA)**[11] 5571 4-9-0 **76** JasonWatson 3 80
(Stuart Williams) *trckd ldr 2f: styd cl up: urged along 3f out: drvn to dispute 2nd briefly wl over 1f out: hld whn checked sn after: one pce* **5/1**[3]

3543 4 ½ **Rotherwick (IRE)**[9] 5667 7-9-10 **86** (b) RossaRyan 4 89
(Paul Cole) *hld up disputing 4th: rdn over 3f out: kpt on one pce fnl 2f to press for a pl nr fin* **8/1**

1216 5 5 **Lawn Ranger**[40] 4504 4-9-13 **89** KierenFox 6 82
(Michael Attwater) *sn led: rdn and hdd over 2f out: wknd over 1f out* **14/1**

-404 6 11 **Highbrow**[40] 4504 4-10-0 **90** StevieDonohoe 1 61
(David Simcock) *hld up in last: shkn up 4f out: no rspnse: bhd fnl 2f (jockey said gelding moved poorly throughout)* **9/1**

2m 6.27s (-2.73) **Going Correction** -0.075s/f (Good)
WFA 3 from 4yo+ 8lb **6 Ran SP% 112.1**
Speed ratings (Par 107): **107,104,104,104,100 91**
CSF £5.72 CT £14.37 TOTE £1.90: £1.30, £2.00; EX 6.30 Trifecta £24.80.
Owner P K Siu **Bred** P & B Bloodstock **Trained** Upper Lambourn, Berks

FOCUS
A decent handicap, they went steady enough and the winner was nicely placed to strike. The second has been rated close to his solid Goodwood latest, and the third close to form.

6022 WINDSOR RACECOURSE FIREWORKS, RETURNS 2ND NOVEMBER H'CAP 1m 2f
7:30 (7:32) (Class 5) (0-70,71) 3-Y-0
£3,428 (£1,020; £509; £300; £300; £300) **Stalls** Low

Form RPR

500 1 **Culture (FR)**[62] 3710 3-9-7 **70** (p[1]) AdamKirby 8 80
(George Baker) *trckd ldng pair: chal over 2f out: rdn to ld over 1f out: drew clr fnl f (trainer could offer no explanation for the gelding's apparent improvement in form)* **14/1**

0362 2 3 **Isle Of Wolves**[32] 4836 3-9-2 **65** PatCosgrave 5 69
(Jim Boyle) *trckd ldr: rdn to ld over 2f out: hdd over 1f out: kpt on but no ch w wnr fnl f* **3/1**[1]

02-4 3 2 ¼ **Waterfront (IRE)**[35] 4738 3-9-2 **68** (p[1]) MeganNicholls(3) 9 68
(Simon Crisford) *slowly away: sn in midfield: rdn over 2f out: prog to take 3rd 1f out: no imp on ldng pair* **13/2**

-035 4 1 ¼ **Bartimaeus (IRE)**[34] 4769 3-9-1 **64** OisinMurphy 2 61
(Denis Coakley) *led at mod pce: tried to kick on over 3f out: hdd over 2f out and sn outpcd: one pce after* **13/2**

0541 **5** *hd* **Renardeau**[14] 5497 3-9-8 **71**......(p) TomMarquand 3 68
(Ali Stronge) *hld up in rr: rdn 3f out: prog into midfield 2f out: hrd drvn and no hdwy after* **13/2**

0651 **6** *nse* **Debbonair (IRE)**[18] 5334 3-9-3 **66**......(b) JamesDoyle 6 63
(Hugo Palmer) *hld up in last trio: effrt 3f out: rdn and one pce fnl 2f: nvr a threat* **10/1**

6221 **7** *½* **Bug Boy (IRE)**[11] 5580 3-8-12 **66**......(p) RhiainIngram(5) 1 62
(Paul George) *trckd ldng pair: rdn wl over 2f out: lost pl and btn wl over 1f out* **5/1**[3]

-543 **8** *2* **Closer Than Close**[21] 5249 3-9-2 **65**......(h) JasonWatson 4 57
(Jonathan Portman) *sn in midfield: appeared short of room 6f out and dropped to rr: last over 3f out and swtchd to outer: no prog 2f out: drifted bk towards inner fnl f* **9/2**[2]

0606 **9** *1 ½* **Thunderoad**[14] 5505 3-9-0 **63**...... ShaneKelly 10 52
(Tony Carroll) *hld up in last: effrt on outer 4f out: no prog over 2f out: wknd over 1f out* **40/1**

2m 9.79s (0.79) **Going Correction** -0.075s/f (Good) **9** Ran SP% **118.0**
Speed ratings (Par 100): **93,90,88,87,87 87,87,85,84**
CSF £57.23 CT £310.33 TOTE £15.50: £4.20, £1.70, £2.60; EX 61.20 Trifecta £506.30.
Owner Highclere Thoroughbred Racing - Dream On **Bred** S C E A Haras Du Ma & Elise Drouet **Trained** Chiddingfold, Surrey

FOCUS
Another race in which they didn't go overly fast and it paid to sit prominently. The third has been rated to form.

6023 VISIT ATTHERACES.COM NOVICE STKS 5f 21y
8:00 (8:06) (Class 5) 3-4-Y-O
£3,428 (£1,020; £509; £254) **Stalls** Centre

Form RPR

6- **1** **Bhangra**[439] 3233 3-8-11 0...... OisinMurphy 9 67+
(Robert Cowell) *dwlt sltly: t.k.h and sn trckd ldng pair: wnt 2nd 2f out gng wl: shkn up to ld over 1f out: rdn clr fnl f* **7/2**[3]

0042 **2** *3* **Starchant**[2] 5960 3-8-11 51...... KieranO'Neill 7 56
(John Bridger) *led: rdn and hdd over 1f out: no ch w wnr fnl f but clung on for 2nd* **11/4**[2]

20 **3** *nse* **Grisons (FR)**[32] 4827 3-9-2 0...... AdamKirby 4 61
(Clive Cox) *chsd ldrs: rdn 2f out: tk 3rd fnl f: no ch w wnr but nrly snatched 2nd* **11/10**[1]

3 **4** *3 ½* **Oh So Nice**[19] 5306 3-8-11 0...... BrettDoyle 3 43
(Tony Carroll) *fractious in stalls: pressed ldr: rdn and nt qckn 2f out: lost 2nd and then fdd fnl f* **8/1**

56 **5** *8* **Peggotty**[14] 5494 3-8-11 0...... TomMarquand 2 14
(Tony Carroll) *struggling to keep up by 1/2-way: sn bhd* **25/1**

0000 **6** *¾* **Hornby**[48] 4219 4-9-5 34...... KierenFox 6 18
(Michael Attwater) *sn outpcd: a bhd* **50/1**

6 **7** *1 ½* **Del's Edge**[16] 5448 3-8-8 0...... MitchGodwin(3) 5 6
(Christopher Mason) *chsd ldrs to 1/2-way: wknd qckly* **33/1**

8 *6* **Welsh Warrior** 3-9-2 0...... TrevorWhelan 8
(Nikki Evans) *dwlt: outpcd and a wl bhd* **33/1**

59.41s (-0.69) **Going Correction** -0.075s/f (Good)
WFA 3 from 4yo 3lb **8** Ran SP% **119.3**
Speed ratings (Par 103): **102,97,97,91,78 77,75,65**
CSF £13.83 TOTE £4.30: £1.50, £1.10, £1.10; EX 12.70 Trifecta £29.20.
Owner Manor Farm Stud (rutland) **Bred** Manor Farm Stud (Rutland) **Trained** Six Mile Bottom, Cambs

FOCUS
The market leaders dominated this weak novice. The second has been rated to her shaky last-time-out Lingfield figure.
T/Jkpt: Not won. T/Plt: £67.40 to a £1 stake. Pool: £95,656.69 - 1034.86 winning units T/Qpdt: £20.40 to a £1 stake. Pool: £8,368.62 - 303.19 winning units **Jonathan Neesom**

5629 WOLVERHAMPTON (A.W) (L-H)
Monday, August 12

OFFICIAL GOING: Tapeta: standard
Wind: Light behind Weather: Sunshine and showers

6024 VISIT THEWINNERSENCLOSURE.COM FOR RACING TIPS APPRENTICE H'CAP 7f 36y (Tp)
5:50 (5:50) (Class 6) (0-60,60) 3-Y-O
£2,781 (£827; £413; £300; £300; £300) **Stalls** High

Form RPR

4543 **1** **Deconso**[4] 5869 3-8-7 **51**...... TobyEley(5) 1 61
(Christopher Kellett) *chsd ldrs: led over 2f out: rdn over 1f out: styd on wl: eased nr fin* **13/2**[2]

0525 **2** *3 ½* **Cauthen (IRE)**[122] 1726 3-9-0 **56**...... CierenFallon(3) 11 57
(Ken Cunningham-Brown) *hld up in tch: carried rt over 6f out: rdn to chse wnr and hung lft over 1f out: styd on same pce fnl f (jockey said gelding hung left-handed throughout)* **10/1**

0406 **3** *½* **Lady Lavinia**[17] 5389 3-8-6 **48** ow2...... Pierre-LouisJamin(5) 8 48
(Michael Easterby) *hld up in tch: nt clr run over 6f out: rdn over 1f out: styd on to go 3rd wl ins fnl f* **7/1**[3]

5040 **4** *¾* **Barbarosa (IRE)**[13] 5517 3-9-7 **60**...... PhilDennis 10 58+
(Michael Herrington) *hld up: rdn over 1f out: r.o ins fnl f: nt rch ldrs* **7/2**[1]

1050 **5** *nk* **Lysander Belle (IRE)**[33] 4772 3-9-4 **57**...... WilliamCox 4 54
(Sophie Leech) *chsd ldrs: nt clr run over 2f out: rdn over 1f out: no ex ins fnl f* **16/1**

6502 **6** *4 ½* **Muhallab (IRE)**[22] 5215 3-8-8 **52**...... LauraCoughlan(5) 2 38+
(Adrian Nicholls) *sn led: hdd over 3f out: ev ch over 2f out: wknd fnl f* **7/2**[1]

0004 **7** *1 ¼* **Grey Berry (IRE)**[17] 5389 3-8-13 **55**......(b) DannyRedmond(3) 7 38
(Tim Easterby) *hld up: pushed along over 2f out: nvr on terms* **9/1**

000 **8** *2* **Secret Magic (IRE)**[40] 4518 3-8-2 **46** oh1...... SeanKirrane(5) 9 24
(Mark Loughnane) *s.i.s: rdn over 2f out: n.d* **16/1**

3206 **9** *¾* **Seanjohnsilver (IRE)**[62] 3709 3-9-0 **60**......(t) JessicaAnderson(7) 5 36
(Declan Carroll) *prom: chsd ldr and racd wd over 5f out: led over 3f out: hdd over 2f out: wknd over 1f out* **16/1**

5006 **10** *1* **Smoki Smoka (IRE)**[10] 5632 3-9-0 **58**......(p) EllaMcCain(5) 6 32
(Donald McCain) *sn pushed along and in tch: hmpd and lost pl 6f out: n.d after* **12/1**

0000 **11** *½* **Not So Shy**[4] 5847 3-8-2 **46** oh1...... AledBeech(5) 12 19
(Lisa Williamson) *s.i.s: a in rr* **125/1**

0000 **12** *34* **Hilbre Lake (USA)**[30] 4909 3-8-7 **46** oh1......(v[1]) GabrieleMalune 3
(Lisa Williamson) *s.i.s: sn pushed along into mid-div: wknd over 2f out: eased over 1f out (jockey said gelding had no more to give)* **100/1**

1m 28.94s (0.14) **Going Correction** -0.10s/f (Stan) **12** Ran SP% **116.5**
Speed ratings (Par 98): **95,91,90,89,89 84,82,80,79,78 77,38**
CSF £68.77 CT £477.34 TOTE £6.60: £2.30, £2.00, £2.80; EX 83.70 Trifecta £472.90.
Owner Andy Bell & Fergus Lyons **Bred** Llety Farms **Trained** Lathom, Lancs
■ Stewards' Enquiry : Pierre-Louis Jamin three-day ban: weighed in 2lb over (28-30 Aug); two-day ban: caused interference (26-27 Aug)

FOCUS
A modest apprentice riders' 3yo handicap. The second and third testify to the form not being any better than rated.

6025 FOLLOW @TWENCLOSURE ON TWITTER FILLIES' H'CAP 7f 36y (Tp)
6:20 (6:20) (Class 5) (0-75,75) 3-Y-O+
£3,428 (£1,020; £509; £300; £300; £300) **Stalls** High

Form RPR

5502 **1** **Sonja Henie (IRE)**[38] 4591 3-9-4 **73**...... PJMcDonald 8 80
(David Loughnane) *mde all: qcknd 2f out: rdn over 1f out: jst hld on* **13/2**[3]

2200 **2** *hd* **Turanga Leela**[31] 4879 5-9-1 **69**......(b) TobyEley(5) 3 77
(John Mackie) *chsd wnr 1f: remained handy: chsd wnr again over 2f out: rdn over 1f out: r.o wl* **18/1**

6554 **3** *3 ¾* **Zafaranah (USA)**[32] 4831 5-9-12 **75**...... RobHornby 2 73
(Pam Sly) *hld up in tch: rdn over 1f out: styd on same pce ins fnl f* **7/2**[2]

-500 **4** *1 ¼* **Groupie**[40] 4523 5-8-10 **59**...... CamHardie 4 54
(Tom Tate) *hld up in tch: lost pl over 2f out: rallied over 1f out: styd on same pce ins fnl f* **18/1**

452 **5** *¾* **Lady Alavesa**[54] 4007 4-9-7 **70**...... PhilDennis 1 62
(Michael Herrington) *s.i.s: hld up: hdwy 2f out: sn rdn: no ex ins fnl f* **13/2**[3]

1206 **6** *½* **Eponina (IRE)**[16] 5419 5-9-1 **64**...... LiamJones 9 55
(Michael Appleby) *plld hrd and prom: rdn over 2f out: styd on same pce fr over 1f out* **40/1**

5520 **7** *1 ¼* **Take Fright**[20] 5281 3-8-8 **68**......(t[1]) CierenFallon(5) 7 54
(Hugo Palmer) *s.i.s: hld up: rdn and edgd rt over 1f out: nvr on terms* **14/1**

3233 **8** *hd* **Dashed**[25] 5105 3-9-4 **73**......(b) DavidEgan 6 58
(Roger Varian) *s.i.s: hld up: rdn 1/2-way: n.d* **7/2**[2]

4411 **9** *1 ¼* **Fantastic Flyer**[10] 5632 4-9-2 **70**......(p) SophieRalston(5) 5 54
(Dean Ivory) *s.i.s: racd keenly and hdwy on outer 6f out: shkn up over 2f out: wknd fnl f (jockey said filly was slowly away before then being trapped wide without cover throughout)* **3/1**[1]

1030 **10** *13* **Met By Moonlight**[47] 4247 5-9-7 **70**...... DavidProbert 10 19
(Ron Hodges) *s.i.s: hdwy to chse wnr 6f out tl over 2f out: wknd over 1f out: eased fnl f (jockey said mare stopped quickly)* **33/1**

1m 28.32s (-0.48) **Going Correction** -0.10s/f (Stan)
WFA 3 from 4yo+ 6lb **10** Ran SP% **118.7**
Speed ratings (Par 100): **98,97,93,92,91 90,89,88,87,72**
CSF £117.40 CT £493.44 TOTE £8.70: £2.80, £5.20, £1.90; EX 135.00 Trifecta £450.40.
Owner Sohi & Hoyland **Bred** Diomed Bloodstock Ltd **Trained** Tern Hill, Shropshire

FOCUS
A fair fillies' handicap. The second has been rated back to her January 6f form here.

6026 DOWNLOAD THE HORSETRACKER APP! H'CAP 1m 142y (Tp)
6:50 (6:50) (Class 4) (0-80,81) 3-Y-O+
£5,207 (£1,549; £774; £387; £300; £300) **Stalls** Low

Form RPR

-024 **1** **Engrossed (IRE)**[20] 5283 3-9-2 **75**...... RobHornby 8 82+
(Martyn Meade) *edgd rt s: hld up: shkn up over 3f out: hdwy on outer over 1f out: rdn and r.o to ld post* **13/2**[2]

2134 **2** *hd* **Cape Victory (IRE)**[39] 4565 3-9-6 **79**...... PJMcDonald 4 85
(James Tate) *chsd ldrs: shkn up over 2f out: edgd rt fr over 1f out: led wl ins fnl f: hdd post* **7/2**[1]

5036 **3** *nk* **Dragons Tail (IRE)**[8] 5708 4-10-2 **81**......(p) RichardKingscote 1 86
(Tom Dascombe) *led: rdn and edgd rt over 1f out: hdd wl ins fnl f: styd on (jockey said gelding hung right-handed)* **11/1**

1111 **4** *shd* **Street Poet (IRE)**[20] 5283 6-9-4 **74**...... DannyRedmond(5) 5 79
(Michael Herrington) *chsd ldrs: rdn and ev ch fr over 1f out: styd on* **8/1**

305 **5** *hd* **Mainsail Atlantic (USA)**[18] 5348 4-9-13 **78**......(p) DanielMuscutt 7 83+
(James Fanshawe) *edgd rt s: hld up: hdwy 3f out: nt clr run fr over 1f out: r.o: nvr able to chal (jockey said colt was denied a clear run in the home straight)* **7/1**[3]

1560 **6** *1 ¾* **International Law**[65] 3567 5-9-4 **69**...... CamHardie 3 70
(Antony Brittain) *hld up in tch: rdn over 2f out: styd on* **16/1**

-622 **7** *½* **Fares Poet (IRE)**[33] 4789 3-9-4 **77**...... DavidEgan 6 77
(Marco Botti) *chsd ldr: rdn and ev ch over 1f out: no ex wl ins fnl f* **7/2**[1]

6000 **8** *4* **Critical Thinking (IRE)**[5] 5816 5-9-3 **68**......(tp) DavidProbert 11 59
(David Loughnane) *s.i.s: hld up: rdn over 1f out: nt trble ldrs* **20/1**

1060 **9** *½* **Nezar (IRE)**[20] 5283 8-9-4 **74**...... SophieRalston(5) 10 64
(Dean Ivory) *hld up: rdn on outer 3f out: nvr on terms* **22/1**

4000 **10** *7* **Mr Minerals**[46] 4281 5-9-0 **70**......(p) CierenFallon(5) 2 44
(Alexandra Dunn) *s.i.s: hld up: rdn over 1f out: wknd ins fnl f* **20/1**

4155 **11** *1 ½* **Liliofthelamplight (IRE)**[9] 5688 3-9-3 **76**...... JFEgan 9 47
(Mark Johnston) *s.i.s and hmpd s: hdwy on outer over 5f out: rdn over 3f out: wknd 2f out* **12/1**

1m 49.15s (-0.95) **Going Correction** -0.10s/f (Stan)
WFA 3 from 4yo+ 8lb **11** Ran SP% **117.2**
Speed ratings (Par 105): **100,99,99,99,99 97,97,93,93,87 85**
CSF £28.43 CT £254.91 TOTE £6.70: £1.80, £1.80, £3.50; EX 33.00 Trifecta £232.50.
Owner Mantonbury Stud **Bred** Dubois Holdings Ltd **Trained** Manton, Wilts

FOCUS
The feature contest was a fair handicap. The winning time was comparatively modest from off an even gallop and they finished in a bit of a heap. The fourth and fifth help set the level.

6027 THIS IS GONNA GET TASTY BABY CLAIMING STKS 6f 20y (Tp)
7:20 (7:20) (Class 6) 3-Y-O+
£2,781 (£827; £413; £300; £300; £300) **Stalls** Low

Form RPR

3262 **1** **Mujassam**[6] 5770 7-10-0 74......(v) DavidNolan 8 80
(David O'Meara) *led early: chsd ldr: rdn to ld over 1f out: styd on* **10/3**[1]

0545 **2** *nk* **Harry Beau**[11] 5579 5-9-4 61......(bt) PJMcDonald 1 69
(David Evans) *sn led: rdn and hdd over 1f out: ev ch ins fnl f: styd on* **9/1**

0254 **3** *1 ½* **Lucky Lodge**[20] 5281 9-9-4 70......(b) CamHardie 3 65
(Antony Brittain) *chsd ldrs: rdn over 1f out: styd on same pce wl ins fnl f* **6/1**[3]

4051 **4** 1/2 **The Groove**[34] 4764 6-9-1 68 JackDinsmore(7) 4 67
(David Evans) *hld up: hdwy over 1f out: sn rdn: r.o to go 4th nr fin: nt trble ldrs* **16/1**

5420 **5** hd **Steelriver (IRE)**[12] 5559 9-9-10 77 PhilDennis 9 69
(Michael Herrington) *chsd ldrs: rdn over 1f out: styd on same pce wl ins fnl f* **5/1**[2]

4245 **6** 3/4 **Di Matteo**[10] 5622 3-8-12 69 (p) StefanoCherchi(7) 2 64
(Marco Botti) *s.i.s: hdwy over 2f out: swtchd lft over 1f out: sn rdn: styd on same pce ins fnl f* **5/1**[2]

0026 **7** 1/2 **Duke Cosimo**[18] 5330 9-9-2 59 RobertWinston 5 57
(Michael Herrington) *sn pushed along in rr: styd on fr over 1f out: nt trble ldrs* **8/1**

0360 **8** hd **Zapper Cass (FR)**[3] 5889 6-9-8 71 (p) LiamJones 7 62
(Michael Appleby) *s.i.s: pushed along early in rr: rdn over 1f out: nt rch ldrs* **13/2**

320- **9** 19 **Penniesfromheaven (IRE)**[470] 2161 3-8-9 75 (p[1]) HollieDoyle 6
(Ken Wingrove) *prom: racd keenly: hung rt and lost pl over 3f out: wknd over 2f out (jockey said filly hung badly right-handed)* **28/1**

1m 14.2s (-0.30) **Going Correction** -0.10s/f (Stan)
WFA 3 from 5yo+ 4lb **9 Ran SP% 114.5**
Speed ratings (Par 101): **98,97,95,94,94 93,93,92,67**
CSF £33.87 TOTE £3.70: £1.70, £2.60, £1.90; EX 35.40 Trifecta £216.40.
Owner Thoroughbred British Racing **Bred** Bumble Bs, D F Powell & S Nicholls **Trained** Upper Helmsley, N Yorks
■ Stewards' Enquiry : David Nolan one-day ban: did not keep straight from stalls (Aug 15)

FOCUS
An ordinary claimer. Muddling form.

6028 CELEBRATING 22 YEARS WITHOUT DAVID CHILLERY EBF FILLIES' NOVICE STKS (PLUS 10 RACE) 6f 20y (Tp)
7:50 (7:51) (Class 5) 2-Y-O **£3,428** (£1,020; £509; £254) **Stalls** Low

Form RPR

1 **Melodic Charm (IRE)** 2-9-0 0 PJMcDonald 7 78+
(James Tate) *chsd ldrs: shkn up to ld over 1f out: styd on* **2/1**[1]

42 **2** 3/4 **Dana Forever (IRE)**[20] 5280 2-9-0 0 RichardKingscote 6 76
(Tom Dascombe) *hld up in tch: swtchd rt over 1f out: rdn and r.o to go 2nd post: nt rch wnr* **5/2**[2]

34 **3** hd **Endless Joy**[86] 2840 2-9-0 0 DanielTudhope 1 77
(Archie Watson) *trckd ldrs: nt clr run and swtchd lft over 1f out: chsd wnr ins fnl f: sn rdn: styd on: lost 2nd post* **7/2**[3]

25 **4** 5 **Fair Pass (IRE)**[39] 4557 2-9-0 0 DavidEgan 9 60
(Marco Botti) *led 1f: chsd ldr: rdn and ev ch over 1f out: no ex ins fnl f* **5/1**

05 **5** 1 **Lets Go Lucky**[11] 5577 2-9-0 0 (h) HollieDoyle 5 57
(David Evans) *hld up: hung lft and styd on ins fnl f: nvr nrr (jockey said filly was slowly away and hung left-handed in the home straight)* **50/1**

0 **6** 5 **Lethal Blast**[21] 5250 2-9-0 0 (t[1]) JFEgan 4 42
(Paul George) *led 5f out: rdn and hdd over 1f out: wknd and eased ins fnl f (jockey said filly stopped quickly)* **25/1**

7 nk **Heartstar** 2-8-9 0 TobyEley(5) 3 42
(John Mackie) *s.s: nvr on terms (jockey said filly was slowly away and ran green)* **125/1**

0 **8** nse **Kitos**[7] 5733 2-9-0 0 RyanTate 2 41
(Sir Mark Prescott Bt) *s.s: shkn up on outer 1/2-way: nvr on terms (jockey said filly was slowly away)* **125/1**

4 **9** 1/2 **Carmena (IRE)**[26] 5045 2-9-0 0 DavidProbert 8 40
(Charlie Fellowes) *chsd ldrs: rdn over 2f out: wknd over 1f out* **10/1**

1m 14.43s (-0.07) **Going Correction** -0.10s/f (Stan) **9 Ran SP% 117.3**
Speed ratings (Par 91): **96,95,94,88,86 80,79,79,78**
CSF £7.30 TOTE £3.00: £1.40, £1.10, £1.30; EX 8.50 Trifecta £24.30.
Owner Saeed Manana **Bred** Corduff Stud & T J Rooney **Trained** Newmarket, Suffolk

FOCUS
An ordinary juvenile fillies' novice contest. The favourite won a shade cosily from the right horse in second here on debut. The second and third have been rated as improving.

6029 AN ABSOLUTELY STUPENDOUS PIECE OF CONFECTIONARY NOVICE MEDIAN AUCTION STKS 5f 21y (Tp)
8:20 (8:21) (Class 6) 2-Y-O **£2,781** (£827; £413; £206) **Stalls** Low

Form RPR

1 **1** **He's A Laddie (IRE)**[10] 5635 2-9-9 0 HollieDoyle 5 82
(Archie Watson) *mde all: qcknd 2f out: rdn out* **11/8**[1]

4301 **2** 1 1/4 **Audio**[10] 5602 2-9-4 78 (t) ThoreHammerHansen(5) 6 77
(Richard Hannon) *chsd wnr: rdn and hung lft fnl f: styd on same pce towards fin* **3/1**[3]

4350 **3** 1 **Dynamighty**[23] 5185 2-8-4 69 SeanKirrane(7) 1 61
(Richard Spencer) *chsd ldrs: rdn over 1f out: no ex wl ins fnl f* **12/1**

42 **4** nk **Hot Heels**[16] 5418 2-9-2 0 RichardKingscote 4 65+
(Tom Dascombe) *hld up: pushed along 1/2-way: hdwy on outer over 1f out: sn rdn: r.o: nt rch ldrs* **6/4**[2]

6 **5** 3/4 **Full Spectrum (IRE)**[74] 3257 2-8-11 0 JFEgan 3 58
(Paul George) *s.i.s: hdwy over 1f out: sn rdn and edgd rt: styd on* **16/1**

05 **6** 6 **La Chica Lobo**[10] 5635 2-8-11 0 CamHardie 2 36
(Lisa Williamson) *plld hrd and prom: pushed along 1/2-way: wknd fnl f* **100/1**

00 **7** 1 1/4 **Indra Dawn (FR)**[54] 3990 2-8-9 0 KateLeahy(7) 7 37
(Archie Watson) *s.i.s: outpcd: bhd whn rdn and hung lft over 1f out (jockey said gelding was unsettled in the stalls and was slowly away as a result)* **33/1**

00 **8** nk **Gelsmoor Bay**[9] 5646 2-8-8 0 NoelGarbutt(3) 8 30
(Derek Shaw) *sn outpcd* **100/1**

1m 2.04s (0.14) **Going Correction** -0.10s/f (Stan) **8 Ran SP% 125.6**
Speed ratings (Par 92): **94,92,90,89,88 79,77,76**
CSF £6.87 TOTE £1.80: £1.10, £1.40, £3.10; EX 6.10 Trifecta £31.50.
Owner Arjun Waney **Bred** Kildaragh Stud **Trained** Upper Lambourn, W Berks
■ Stewards' Enquiry : Cam Hardie caution: careless riding

FOCUS
A fair juvenile novice sprint contest. The favourite dictated a tactical gallop, gaining enough of an advantage off the home turn to win neatly. The second has been rated in line with his latest win.

6030 WINNERS ENCLOSURE FOLLOWER SAM DAVIS MAIDEN H'CAP 1m 4f 51y (Tp)
8:50 (8:50) (Class 5) (0-70,72) 3-Y-O **£3,428** (£1,020; £509; £300; £300; £300) **Stalls** Low

Form RPR

3400 **1** **Wanaasah**[37] 4663 3-9-7 69 (h[1]) DavidEgan 9 80
(David Loughnane) *mde all: shkn up and qcknd clr over 2f out: eased ins fnl f* **8/1**

0204 **2** 8 **Say Nothing**[16] 5421 3-9-9 71 PJMcDonald 2 74
(Hughie Morrison) *chsd ldrs: chsd wnr 2f out: rdn over 1f out: no imp* **7/2**[1]

3-05 **3** 1 1/4 **Avenue Foch**[42] 4459 3-9-6 68 GeorgeWood 1 70
(James Fanshawe) *hld up: hdwy 3f out: rdn over 1f out: styd on same pce* **7/2**[1]

-504 **4** 3 **Island Jungle (IRE)**[19] 5311 3-9-6 68 (p) DavidProbert 5 67
(Mark Usher) *hld up: racd keenly: rdn over 2f out: nt trble ldrs* **8/1**

-005 **5** 2 1/2 **Guroor**[18] 5355 3-8-12 67 (b[1]) StefanoCherchi(7) 11 63
(Marco Botti) *stdd s: sn swtchd lft: hld up: effrt on outer over 2f out: nt trble ldrs (jockey said filly hung right-handed)* **7/1**[3]

0000 **6** 2 **Feebi**[21] 5242 3-7-11 50 oh5 PaulaMuir(5) 10 44
(Chris Fairhurst) *chsd ldrs: rdn and outpcd over 3f out: n.d after* **28/1**

0436 **7** 3/4 **Star Talent (IRE)**[9] 5654 3-9-0 67 TobyEley(5) 8 61
(Gay Kelleway) *hld up: rdn over 2f out: n.d (jockey said gelding was never travelling)* **14/1**

-360 **8** 3 1/2 **Flying Moon (GER)**[33] 4787 3-9-0 62 RobHornby 7 52
(Jonathan Portman) *hld up: rdn over 3f out: n.d* **16/1**

00-0 **9** 3 1/4 **Waterproof**[41] 4484 3-8-8 56 JosephineGordon 6 43
(Shaun Keightley) *hld up: rdn over 3f out: n.d* **28/1**

0552 **10** 5 **Arthur Pendragon (IRE)**[16] 5426 3-9-10 72 (b) MartinDwyer 3 54
(Brian Meehan) *chsd wnr: shkn up over 5f out: rdn over 2f out: sn wknd: eased fnl f (jockey said colt was never travelling)* **11/2**[2]

2m 38.13s (-2.67) **Going Correction** -0.10s/f (Stan) **10 Ran SP% 114.0**
Speed ratings (Par 100): **104,98,97,95,94 92,92,90,87,84**
CSF £35.29 CT £115.27 TOTE £8.60: £3.10, £1.40, £1.70; EX 33.40 Trifecta £172.30.
Owner K Sohi **Bred** Shadwell Estate Company Limited **Trained** Tern Hill, Shropshire

FOCUS
An ordinary 3yo middle-distance maiden handicap. The eased-down, wide-margin winner produced the best comparative time on the card. A clear pb from the winner, with the second close to form.
T/Plt: £104.00 to a £1 stake. Pool: £88,932.16 - 623.88 winning units T/Qpdt: £5.70 to a £1 stake. Pool: £11,376.37 - 1463.35 winning units **Colin Roberts**

5926 CLAIREFONTAINE (R-H)
Monday, August 12

OFFICIAL GOING: Turf: good to soft

6031a PRIX CARRUS (H'CAP) (4YO+ FILLIES & MARES) (TURF) 1m 1f
4:55 4-Y-0+ **£11,711** (£4,450; £3,279; £1,873; £936; £702)

RPR

1 **Zaverna (IRE)**[15] 5-9-0 0 MlleCoraliePacaut(3) 5 71
(F Monnier, France) **177/10**

2 nse **Magic Song (FR)**[35] 4747 5-9-2 0 TonyPiccone 16 70
(S Kobayashi, France) **24/1**

3 3/4 **Midgrey (IRE)**[32] 4859 4-9-3 0 (p) MlleAlisonMassin(3) 1 73
(F-X Belvisi, France) **13/1**

4 3 **Montina (FR)**[63] 5-9-4 0 (p) TheoBachelot 7 64
(Werner Glanz, Germany) **21/10**[1]

5 1/2 **Linngaria (FR)**[36] 4-9-2 0 (b) AlexandreRoussel 2 61
(F Foucher, France) **24/1**

6 snk **Flor De Seda (FR)**[83] 2955 4-8-13 0 HugoBesnier(3) 13 61
(Jo Hughes, France) *mid-div on outer: outpcd and pushed along wl over 3f out: rdn over 2f out: responded for press and prog on nr side fr 1 1/2f out: kpt on ins fnl f but n.d* **70/1**

7 3/4 **Caladiyna (FR)**[299] 4-9-2 0 IoritzMendizabal 4 59
(M Planard, France) **46/1**

8 3/4 **Dani Blue (FR)**[11] 6-9-0 0 AnthonyCrastus 3 56
(E Lyon, France) **74/10**[2]

9 nk **Karynia (FR)**[4] 6-8-6 0 (b) EddyHardouin 9 47
(J Parize, France) **27/1**

10 hd **Foulognes (IRE)**[305] 8251 5-9-3 0 (p) CristianDemuro 10 58
(F Vermeulen, France) **17/2**[3]

11 2 1/2 **Rebecamille (FR)**[11] 6-8-6 0 DelphineSantiago(3) 8 45
(H De Nicolay, France) **17/1**

12 1 **Princess Gold (FR)**[36] 4-9-2 0 (b) AugustinMadamet(3) 11 52
(F Rohaut, France) **9/1**

13 1/2 **Crystal Beach Road (FR)**[92] 7-7-10 0 (b) MlleAmbreMolins(7) 14 35
(J Parize, France) **27/1**

14 nk **Alcama Doloise (FR)**[15] 4-8-7 0 (b) MlleAudeDuporte(7) 12 46
(A Bonin, France) **15/1**

15 3 1/2 **Rochenka (FR)**[32] 6-9-1 0 MaximeGuyon 6 39
(M Brasme, France) **10/1**

16 12 **Jasmine A La Plage (FR)**[285] 4-8-0 0 AntoineCoutier 15
(Ludo Van Beylen, Belgium) **27/1**

1m 51.5s **16 Ran SP% 120.3**
PARI-MUTUEL (all including 1 euro stake): WIN 18.70; PLACE 5.40, 7.70, 5.20; DF 158.80.
Owner G Martin, D Paulou & F Monnier **Bred** Ildefonso Leon Sotelo Garcia **Trained** France

5722 CARLISLE (R-H)
Tuesday, August 13

OFFICIAL GOING: Heavy
Wind: Breezy, half against in over 2f of home straight Weather: Cloudy, bright

6032 RACINGTV.COM NURSERY H'CAP 5f
5:10 (5:11) (Class 5) (0-75,76) 2-Y-O **£4,204** (£1,251; £625; £312; £300; £300) **Stalls** Low

Form RPR

0234 **1** **Ventura Flame (IRE)**[8] 5737 2-9-9 76 JoeFanning 2 83
(Keith Dalgleish) *prom: styd w one other on far side ent st: overall ldr 2f out: pushed clr fnl f: comf* **5/1**[2]

4234 **2** 3 1/4 **Mecca's Hot Steps**[24] 5197 2-9-3 70 PaulMulrennan 9 65+
(Michael Dods) *checked and wnt lft s: prom on outside: effrt stands' side and swtchd rt over 1f out: chsd far side wnr ins fnl f: no imp* **11/2**[3]

050 **3** 1/2 **Street Life**[18] 5388 2-8-7 60 (b[1]) PaulHanagan 1 54
(Richard Fahey) *hld up: styd w one other on far side ent st: effrt and rdn 2f out: kpt on same pce fnl f* **9/1**

The Form Book Flat 2019, Raceform Ltd, Newbury, RG14 5SJ

514 **4** *nk* **Auckland Lodge (IRE)**[32] 4889 2-9-2 **74**.................... HarrisonShaw(5) 7 66+
(Ben Haslam) *led: brought to stands' side: hdd by far side wnr 2f out: rallied: one pce ins fnl f* **11/2**[3]

2366 **5** *6* **Bezzas Lad (IRE)**[9] 5703 2-9-5 **72**.................................(b) SamJames 8 43+
(Phillip Makin) *prom on outside tl rdn and wknd in stands' side gp over 1f out* **22/1**

0630 **6** *3/4* **Ice Skate**[7] 5789 2-8-0 **53** oh1.............................. DuranFentiman 4 21+
(Tim Easterby) *dwlt: bhd: swtchd lft bef 1/2-way: effrt stands' side gp over 2f out: no further imp over 1f out* **7/2**[1]

5364 **7** *2 3/4* **Lara Silvia**[11] 5618 2-8-10 **63**.................................. JamieGormley 5 21+
(Iain Jardine) *hld up in tch: rdn in stands' side gp over 2f out: wknd wl over 1f out* **9/1**

3030 **8** *5* **Manolith**[24] 5185 2-9-6 **73**.. DanielTudhope 6 13+
(David O'Meara) *hld up in tch: rdn in stands' side gp over 2f out: sn wknd* **8/1**

366 **9** *2* **Constitutional (IRE)**[54] 4032 2-8-11 **64**........................(v[1]) BenCurtis 3 +
(K R Burke) *restless in stalls: hld up: drvn in stands' side gp over 2f out: sn btn* **14/1**

1m 3.66s (1.56) **Going Correction** +0.30s/f (Good) **9** Ran SP% **111.8**
Speed ratings (Par 94): **99,93,93,92,82 81,77,69,66**
CSF £31.12 CT £236.78 TOTE £6.50: £1.80, £1.70, £3.00; EX 29.70 Trifecta £273.30.
Owner Middleham Park Racing Lxxxiii & Partner **Bred** Emmet Mullins **Trained** Carluke, S Lanarks

FOCUS
A fair nursery. Two horses stuck to their low draws on the heavy ground and finished first and third up the far rail, having taken the shortest route.

6033 RACING TV FILLIES' H'CAP — 5f 193y
5:45 (5:46) (Class 5) (0-70,67) 3-Y-O+
£4,204 (£1,251; £625; £312; £300; £300) **Stalls** Low

Form				RPR

2321 **1** **Bedtime Bella (IRE)**[10] 5669 3-9-2 **64**..........................(v) SeanDavis(3) 4 73
(Michael Appleby) *prom: shkn up and hdwy to ld over 1f out: pushed out fnl f* **5/1**[3]

0202 **2** *2 3/4* **Pearl Of Qatar**[11] 5629 3-8-13 **58**.................................. JasonHart 6 59
(Tristan Davidson) *trckd ldr: led gng wl briefly over 1f out: sn rdn and edgd rt: kpt on same pce ins fnl f* **6/1**

2503 **3** *1/2* **Supaulette (IRE)**[18] 5392 4-9-7 **67**......................(bt) DannyRedmond(5) 1 68
(Tim Easterby) *hld up in tch: effrt and swtchd lft wl over 1f out: rdn and one pce fnl f* **10/1**

3513 **4** *1* **Forever A Lady (IRE)**[3] 5935 6-9-5 **60**.................................. CYHo 2 58
(Keith Dalgleish) *dwlt: bhd: effrt whn carried lft wl over 1f out: sn rdn: one pce fnl f* **9/4**[1]

0221 **5** *hd* **Fox Hill**[13] 5559 3-8-8 **58**.. HarrisonShaw(5) 3 54
(Eric Alston) *trckd ldrs: effrt and edgd lft over 1f out: outpcd fnl f* **11/4**[2]

032 **6** *6* **Blank Canvas**[10] 5669 3-9-1 **60**.. JoeFanning 5 38
(Keith Dalgleish) *t.k.h: led to over 1f out: sn rdn and wknd (jockey said filly stopped quickly)* **8/1**

1m 15.6s (1.00) **Going Correction** +0.30s/f (Good) **6** Ran SP% **108.6**
WFA 3 from 4yo+ 4lb
Speed ratings (Par 100): **105,101,100,99,99 91**
CSF £31.41 TOTE £3.50: £1.80, £2.90; EX 27.00 Trifecta £101.70.
Owner Rod In Pickle Partnership **Bred** Gce Farm Ltd **Trained** Oakham, Rutland

FOCUS
A modest fillies' handicap. They stuck to the far rail following the conclusive evidence the first race provided. The second has been rated to her AW latest.

6034 WATCH RACING TV NOW NOVICE STKS — 1m 1f
6:15 (6:15) (Class 5) 3-Y-O+
£4,204 (£1,251; £625; £312) **Stalls** Low

Form				RPR

2 **1** **Roman Stone (USA)**[38] 4636 3-9-2 0.............................. JoeFanning 7 80+
(Keith Dalgleish) *mde all: shkn up and drew clr fr over 1f out: eased towards fin: readily* **5/1**[3]

3 **2** *3 1/4* **Noble Music (GER)**[136] 1417 3-8-11 0.............................. BenCurtis 4 67+
(Ralph Beckett) *hld up on ins: shkn up and hdwy to chse wnr 2f out: rdn and no imp fnl f* **10/11**[1]

3 *nk* **Goobinator (USA)** 3-9-2 0.. DavidNolan 3 72
(Donald McCain) *t.k.h early: hld up in tch: effrt and green 3f out: kpt on fnl f: nt pce to chal* **28/1**

34 **4** *1 3/4* **Fiery Mission (USA)**[21] 5268 3-9-2 0..........................(t[1]) DanielTudhope 2 68
(Sir Michael Stoute) *hld up in tch: hdwy to dispute 2nd pl over 2f out: sn rdn: one pce appr fnl f* **5/2**[2]

35 **5** *1* **Flash Point (IRE)**[8] 5742 3-9-2 0.............................. CamHardie 5 66
(Tracy Waggott) *chsd wnr to 3f out: rallied: drvn and outpcd fr over 1f out* **125/1**

42 **6** *2 3/4* **Baladio (IRE)**[16] 5477 3-8-11 0.............................. TonyHamilton 6 55
(Richard Fahey) *trckd ldr: wnt 2nd 3f out: drvn and wknd fr 2f out* **9/1**

7 *24* **Jeu De Mots (FR)**[22] 6-9-10 0.............................. PaulMulrennan 1 10
(Dianne Sayer) *s.s: bhd: struggling 4f out: lost tch fr over 2f out* **50/1**

2m 0.54s (1.54) **Going Correction** +0.30s/f (Good) **7** Ran SP% **113.8**
WFA 3 from 6yo 8lb
Speed ratings (Par 103): **105,102,101,100,99 96,75**
CSF £9.95 TOTE £6.10: £2.90, £1.10; EX 13.10 Trifecta £115.50.
Owner Weldspec Glasgow Limited **Bred** Fred W Hertrich III & John D Fielding **Trained** Carluke, S Lanarks

FOCUS
A fair novice contest. The third-favourite relished the heavy ground and won easing down from the front in good style. The fifth, who has been rated in line with the better view of his debut form for now, is perhaps the key to the level.

6035 MATCHBOOK EBF FUTURE STAYERS' NOVICE STKS (PLUS 10 RACE) (SIRE AND DAM RESTRICTED RACE) — 7f 173y
6:45 (6:45) (Class 4) 2-Y-O
£10,350 (£3,080; £1,539) **Stalls** Low

Form				RPR

02 **1** **Frankel's Storm**[18] 5387 2-8-11 0.............................. JoeFanning 1 82+
(Mark Johnston) *mde all: shkn up: edgd lft and drew clr fr over 1f out: v easily* **2/5**[1]

3 **2** *8* **Viceregent**[18] 5396 2-9-2 0.............................. TonyHamilton 5 69
(Richard Fahey) *chsd wnr: effrt and ch briefly over 2f out: hung rt and outpcd fr over 1f out* **9/4**[2]

3 *35* **Holmgarth (FR)** 2-9-2 0.............................. AndrewElliott 3
(Philip Kirby) *green in preliminaries: dwlt: prom: outpcd after 3f: short-lived effrt over 3f out: lost tch fnl 2f* **22/1**[3]

1m 44.42s (4.42) **Going Correction** +0.30s/f (Good) **3** Ran SP% **106.5**
Speed ratings (Par 96): **89,81,46**
CSF £1.56 TOTE £1.30; EX 1.40 Trifecta £1.30.
Owner Nick Bradley Racing 13 **Bred** Normandie Stud Ltd **Trained** Middleham Moor, N Yorks

FOCUS
The feature race was a fair little juvenile novice contest restricted to the progeny of winners over 1m4f plus. The odds-on favourite found far too much for her two opponents from the front. A token rating has been given.

6036 EVERY RACE LIVE ON RACING TV H'CAP — 7f 173y
7:15 (7:17) (Class 6) (0-60,60) 3-Y-O+
£3,234 (£962; £481; £300; £300; £300) **Stalls** Low

Form				RPR

0001 **1** **Dawn Breaking**[6] 5817 4-9-8 **54** 5ex..........................(b) PhilDennis 15 64
(Richard Whitaker) *trckd ldr: led gng wl over 2f out: shkn up and kpt on strly fr over 1f out* **9/2**[1]

0300 **2** *2 3/4* **Muraadef**[21] 5284 4-9-1 **47**.............................. JamieGormley 4 51
(Ruth Carr) *trckd ldrs: effrt and wnt 2nd wl over 1f out: kpt on fnl f: nt pce of wnr* **14/1**

0335 **3** *shd* **Move In Faster**[22] 5239 4-9-12 **58**..........................(v) PaulMulrennan 14 62
(Michael Dods) *hld up in midfield on outside: pushed along over 4f out: rallied 3f out: effrt and hung rt fr wl over 1f out: kpt on ins fnl f* **6/1**[2]

56 **4** *3 1/4* **Searanger (USA)**[13] 5558 6-9-5 **51**.............................. CliffordLee 3 48
(Rebecca Menzies) *t.k.h: hld up in tch: effrt and rdn 2f out: no imp fnl f* **20/1**

3606 **5** *2 1/4* **Mac Ailey**[6] 5816 3-9-7 **60**.............................. RachelRichardson 8 51
(Tim Easterby) *prom: effrt and edgd lft over 2f out: carried rt over 1f out: wknd fnl f* **9/1**

-563 **6** *3/4* **Mr Cool Cash**[26] 5099 7-9-0 **46**..........................(t) SamJames 17 36
(John Davies) *hld up: rdn over 2f out: hdwy over 1f out: kpt on: nvr able to chal: lost hind shoe (vet said gelding lost its right hind shoe)* **12/1**

0020 **7** *nk* **French Flyer (IRE)**[7] 5787 4-9-2 **48**.............................. DanielTudhope 9 37
(Rebecca Bastiman) *led to over 2f out: rdn and wknd over 1f out* **15/2**[3]

0200 **8** *3/4* **Temple Of Wonder (IRE)**[21] 5272 3-9-4 **57**.............................. DavidNolan 16 44
(Liam Bailey) *hld up: drvn over 2f out: sme late hdwy: nvr rchd ldrs* **25/1**

0123 **9** *1* **Cliff Bay (IRE)**[29] 4978 5-9-7 **53**..........................(p) ShaneGray 5 39
(Keith Dalgleish) *hld up in midfield: rdn over 2f out: wknd over 1f out* **9/2**[1]

4000 **10** *1 1/2* **Juals Spirit (IRE)**[63] 3684 3-8-6 **45**..........................(w) AndrewMullen 1 26
(Brian Ellison) *hld up in midfield: drvn and outpcd 3f out: n.d after* **40/1**

3000 **11** *4* **Jagerbond**[16] 5477 3-8-1 **45**..........................(p) AndrewBreslin(5) 7 17
(Andrew Crook) *bhd: drvn along over 3f out: nvr on terms* **14/1**

4420 **12** *1 1/4* **Don't Be Surprised**[22] 5248 4-9-9 **55**..........................(p) PaulHanagan 2 26
(Seb Spencer) *hld up on ins: rdn and outpcd 1/2-way: n.d after* **11/1**

0000 **13** *1 1/4* **Bevsboy (IRE)**[4] 5918 5-8-13 **45**.............................. JasonHart 12 13
(Lynn Siddall) *hld up in tch: drvn and struggling over 2f out: sn btn* **100/1**

-550 **14** *11* **Prosecute (FR)**[38] 4658 6-8-13 **45**.............................. AndrewElliott 11
(Sean Regan) *dwlt: bhd: struggling 3f out: sn btn* **28/1**

00-0 **15** *53* **My Boy Monty**[13] 5552 3-8-6 **45**.............................. CamHardie 6
(Gary Sanderson) *towards rr: struggling 3f out: lost tch fnl 2f: t.o* **100/1**

1m 42.58s (2.58) **Going Correction** +0.30s/f (Good) **15** Ran SP% **118.2**
WFA 3 from 4yo+ 7lb
Speed ratings (Par 101): **99,96,96,92,90 89,89,88,87,86 82,81,79,68,15**
CSF £63.47 CT £391.63 TOTE £4.90: £1.90, £4.50, £2.50; EX 69.50 Trifecta £395.60.
Owner D Gration, G Sutcliffe, N Farman, Jeaton **Bred** Mrs M J Blackburn **Trained** Scarcroft, W Yorks

FOCUS
A modest handicap. It proved hard to make up much ground from off the pace on the testing surface.

6037 JOIN RACING TV NOW H'CAP — 6f 195y
7:45 (7:45) (Class 5) (0-75,76) 3-Y-O+
£4,204 (£1,251; £625; £312; £300; £300) **Stalls** Low

Form				RPR

0044 **1** **Knowing Glance (IRE)**[15] 5488 4-9-4 **67**..........................(h[1]) PaulHanagan 4 76
(Richard Fahey) *mde all: rdn over 2f out: kpt on wl fnl f* **11/4**[1]

2-03 **2** *nk* **Black Friday**[11] 5616 4-9-4 **70**..........................(p) SeanDavis(3) 6 78
(Karen McLintock) *chsd wnr: effrt and drvn along 2f out: kpt on fnl f: hld nr fin* **3/1**[2]

5000 **3** *2 1/4* **Make Me**[11] 5616 4-9-2 **65**..........................(p) JasonHart 8 67
(Tim Easterby) *prom on outside: effrt and disp 2nd pl fr 2f out to ins fnl f: no ex* **3/1**[2]

4630 **4** *2 1/2* **Zoravan (USA)**[8] 5726 6-9-4 **67**..........................(b) CYHo 7 63
(Keith Dalgleish) *hld up: pushed along over 2f out: hdwy over 1f out: sn no imp* **5/1**[3]

1-20 **5** *2 3/4* **Mardle**[59] 3858 3-9-7 **76**..........................(w) BenCurtis 5 63
(K R Burke) *dwlt: hld up in tch: drvn along over 2f out: wknd wl over 1f out* **13/2**

4050 **6** *2 3/4* **Paddy's Pursuit (IRE)**[73] 3354 3-8-7 **62**.............................. PhilDennis 1 41
(David Loughnane) *t.k.h: trckd ldrs: drvn and outpcd over 2f out: wknd over 1f out* **22/1**

1m 30.54s (2.54) **Going Correction** +0.30s/f (Good) **6** Ran SP% **111.0**
WFA 3 from 4yo+ 6lb
Speed ratings (Par 103): **97,96,94,91,88 84**
CSF £11.03 CT £23.73 TOTE £3.20: £1.90, £1.40; EX 9.60 Trifecta £36.90.
Owner Posh John 11 **Bred** Mrs B Gardiner **Trained** Musley Bank, N Yorks

FOCUS
A fair handicap. They finished in market order after a brave, front-running victory from the favourite. The winner has been rated close to his best, with the second to form.

6038 RACING TV H'CAP — 1m 3f 39y
8:15 (8:15) (Class 5) (0-75,77) 3-Y-O+
£4,204 (£1,251; £625; £312; £300; £300) **Stalls** High

Form				RPR

6523 **1** **Flood Defence (IRE)**[4] 5905 5-8-13 **60**.............................. JamieGormley 2 69
(Iain Jardine) *hld up: stdy hdwy over 2f out: shkn up to ld over 1f out: kpt on wl fnl f* **10/3**[2]

2061 **2** *2 1/2* **Beechwood Jude (FR)**[57] 3926 3-9-3 **73**.............................. ShaneGray 7 77
(Keith Dalgleish) *pressed ldr: led and rdn over 2f out: hdd over 1f out: kpt on same pce ins fnl f* **2/1**[1]

2106 **3** *3 3/4* **Auxiliary**[8] 5739 6-9-11 **72**..........................(p) DanielTudhope 3 70
(Liam Bailey) *prom: drvn and outpcd over 2f out: rallied 1f out: kpt on: nt rch first two* **13/2**[3]

2541 **4** *1 3/4* **Trinity Star (IRE)**[10] 5694 8-9-12 **73**..........................(v) CliffordLee 6 68
(Karen McLintock) *trckd ldrs: rdn over 2f out: edgd rt and outpcd over 1f out* **13/2**[3]

0- **5** *1* **Lady Kyria (FR)**[79] 9610 5-9-0 **68**.............................. NickBarratt-Atkin(7) 4 61
(Philip Kirby) *s.i.s: hld up in tch: effrt on outside over 2f out: edgd rt and wknd over 1f out* **40/1**

210 6 8 **Roar (IRE)**[60] 3816 5-10-0 75........................ BarryMcHugh 5 54
(Ed de Giles) *t.k.h: led to over 2f out: rdn and wknd over 1f out* **10/3[2]**

2m 31.78s (2.08) **Going Correction** +0.30s/f (Good)
WFA 3 from 5yo+ 9lb **6 Ran SP% 108.6**
Speed ratings (Par 103): **104,102,99,98,97 91**
CSF £9.71 TOTE £3.20: £2.30, £1.20; EX 9.00 Trifecta £34.90.
Owner Let's Be Lucky Racing 20 **Bred** Mcr Bloodstock Ltd **Trained** Carrutherstown, D'fries & G'way

FOCUS
A fair middle-distance handicap. One of the joint-second favourites won well in a comparatively modest time. The second has been rated to form.
T/Plt: £24.70 to a £1 stake. Pool: £49,776.59 - 1,465.69 winning units T/Qpdt: £5.70 to a £1 stake. Pool: £5,765.61 - 737.52 winning units **Richard Young**

5576 FFOS LAS (L-H)
Tuesday, August 13

OFFICIAL GOING: Good to soft (good in places; 6.7)
Wind: Moderate crosswind Weather: Fine

6039 IWEC ELECTRICAL SERVICES MAIDEN H'CAP FILLIES' STKS 1m 2f (R)
2:15 (2:15) (Class 5) (0-70,70) 3-Y-O+

£3,428 (£1,020; £509; £300; £300; £300) **Stalls Low**

Form RPR

534 1 **Sincerity**[56] 3958 3-9-7 70........................ TomMarquand 6 75+
(James Fanshawe) *hld up: hdwy 3f out: drvn over 2f out: sn chsng ldrs: styd on to ld ins fnl f: pushed out* **11/4[1]**

-200 2 ¾ **Air Force Amy**[94] 2612 3-9-0 68........................ ScottMcCullagh(5) 9 71
(Mick Channon) *chsd ldrs: drvn and hung lft over 2f out: hdd over 1f out: kpt on: no ex towards fin* **4/1[2]**

02 3 hd **Just Once**[61] 3777 3-8-8 57........................ AntonioFresu 1 60
(Mrs Ilka Gansera-Leveque) *s.s: in rr: hdwy and nt clr run 3f out: shkn up 2f out: drvn appr fnl f: styd on wl towards fin* **6/1[3]**

4644 4 hd **Elegant Love**[12] 5580 3-9-2 65........................ HollieDoyle 3 68
(David Evans) *led 1f: remained prom: led again over 2f out: sn rdn: hdd over 1f out: kpt on same pce* **4/1[2]**

/003 5 ½ **Bird To Love**[15] 5499 5-8-6 50........................ WilliamCox(3) 4 51
(Mark Usher) *midfield: tk clsr order 1/2-way: chsng ldrs whn rdn over 2f out: styd on same pce fnl f* **12/1**

5304 6 9 **Be Thankful**[10] 5652 4-8-10 56........................(h) PoppyBridgwater(5) 8 39
(Martin Keighley) *prom: led after 1f tl rdn and hdd over 2f out: wknd over 1f out* **10/1**

-050 7 8 **Peggy McKay**[14] 5528 4-9-5 60........................ RobHornby 7 27
(Andrew Balding) *hld up: rdn 3f out: sn wknd* **16/1**

3-44 8 22 **French Twist**[138] 1385 3-8-13 62........................ DavidEgan 2
(David Loughnane) *midfield: rdn 4f out: wknd 3f out: t.o* **20/1**

0004 9 6 **Arcadienne**[27] 5054 3-8-8 57........................ HarryBentley 5
(Ralph Beckett) *prom: trckd ldr after 3f: rdn and lost 2nd over 3f out: wknd qckly: t.o* **6/1[3]**

2m 10.16s (-2.54) **Going Correction** -0.025s/f (Good)
WFA 3 from 4yo+ 8lb **9 Ran SP% 122.7**
Speed ratings (Par 100): **109,108,108,108,107 100,94,76,71**
CSF £14.78 CT £63.63 TOTE £3.00: £1.20, £2.00, £2.90; EX 18.80 Trifecta £98.20.
Owner Elite Racing Club **Bred** Elite Racing Club **Trained** Newmarket, Suffolk

FOCUS
They went a routine sort of pace in this maiden fillies' handicap and there was a tight five-way finish. The wining time suggested that while it was a drying day, there was still give underfoot. The level is set around the third and fourth, with the second close to her 2yo best.

6040 FFOS LAS WELCOMES JEAN DELARRE NOVICE STKS 7f 80y(R)
2:45 (2:45) (Class 5) 2-Y-O **£3,428** (£1,020; £509; £254) **Stalls Low**

Form RPR

623 1 **Hexagon (IRE)**[31] 4925 2-9-5 79........................ JasonWatson 5 79+
(Roger Charlton) *w ldr: rdn to ld over 2f out: drvn and hrd pressed over 1f out: styd on wl* **6/4[2]**

3 2 1½ **Arabian Moon**[15] 5493 2-9-5 0........................ HarryBentley 2 75
(Ralph Beckett) *s.i.s: sn chsng ldng pair: rdn 3f out: pressed wnr over 1f out: no ex fnl 100yds* **9/2[3]**

2 3 8 **Ventura Bounty (FR)**[25] 5145 2-9-5 0........................ SeanLevey 1 56
(Richard Hannon) *led narrowly: rdn and hdd over 2f out: lost 2nd over 1f out: sn wknd* **11/8[1]**

6 4 8 **Jack Ruby (IRE)**[19] 5345 2-9-5 0........................ TomMarquand 3 36
(Richard Hannon) *a in 4th: rdn over 3f out: wknd 2f out* **12/1**

5 19 **Stop Going On (IRE)** 2-9-0 0........................ HollieDoyle 4
(David Evans) *dwlt: rn green and rdn at times in rr: lost tch 3f out (jockey said filly was never travelling)* **16/1**

1m 34.82s (1.72) **Going Correction** -0.025s/f (Good) **5 Ran SP% 113.9**
Speed ratings (Par 94): **89,87,78,69,47**
CSF £8.94 TOTE £2.30: £1.20, £1.80; EX 8.20 Trifecta £11.40.
Owner Owners Group 032 **Bred** Rathbarry Stud **Trained** Beckhampton, Wilts

FOCUS
The first pair came right away in this fair little juvenile novice event.

6041 PENDINE SANDS HOLIDAY PARK NURSERY H'CAP 5f
3:15 (3:16) (Class 5) (0-70,70) 2-Y-O **£3,428** (£1,020; £509; £300; £300) **Stalls High**

Form RPR

050 1 **Crime Of Passion (IRE)**[45] 4373 2-9-0 63........................ KieranShoemark 5 66
(Jamie Osborne) *hld up: rdn 2f out: hdwy over 1f out: led ent fnl f: edgd lft: rdn out (trainer said, regarding apparent improvement in form, that it was the filly's first run in a handicap and that she also seemed more relaxed in the preliminaries)* **14/1**

5520 2 1¼ **Prissy Missy (IRE)**[21] 5279 2-8-8 57........................ DavidEgan 1 56
(David Loughnane) *disp ld tl led 1/2-way: rdn and hdd over 1f out: kpt on fnl f: edgd lft towards fin* **9/1**

6616 3 nk **Isobar Wind (IRE)**[7] 5789 2-9-7 70........................(b[1]) HarryBentley 2 67
(David Evans) *s.i.s: chsd ldrs: drvn to ld over 1f out: hdd ent fnl f: unable qck (jockey said gelding hung left)* **2/1[2]**

3502 4 ½ **Royal Council (IRE)**[13] 5562 2-9-7 70........................(v[1]) TomMarquand 6 66
(James Tate) *trckd ldng pair: nt clr run 2f out: rdn and ev ch over 1f out: kpt on same pce fnl f* **11/8[1]**

P203 5 9 **Sneaky**[13] 5562 2-9-4 67........................(h) HollieDoyle 4 30
(Archie Watson) *disp ld tl hdd 1/2-way: drvn and qckly lost pl* **7/2[3]**

1m 0.65s (1.65) **Going Correction** -0.025s/f (Good) **5 Ran SP% 114.3**
Speed ratings (Par 94): **85,83,82,81,67**
CSF £114.81 TOTE £18.50: £6.30, £3.80; EX 105.00 Trifecta £325.20.
Owner The Joy Of Six **Bred** Max Morris **Trained** Upper Lambourn, Berks

FOCUS
A modest nursery. With stalls on the stands' side, it was the one who came down the middle who prevailed.

6042 M&M GREENE H'CAP 1m 3f 209y(R)
3:45 (3:49) (Class 6) (0-65,67) 3-Y-O+

£2,781 (£827; £413; £300; £300; £300) **Stalls Low**

Form RPR

-000 1 **Tigerskin**[24] 5175 3-9-3 60........................(bt[1]) HarryBentley 10 73+
(Ralph Beckett) *t.k.h: prom: led over 8f out: drvn over 2f out: drew clr over 1f out: styd on strly: eased nr fin* **14/1**

4553 2 8 **Chinese Alphabet**[12] 5580 3-9-7 64........................(p) JasonWatson 3 64
(William Knight) *s.i.s: sn prom: led after 2f tl over 8f out: bmpd and wnt 2nd again over 3f out: one pce and no ch w easy wnr fr over 1f out: hld modest 2nd* **2/1[2]**

26-0 3 nk **Good Impression**[18] 5378 4-9-7 54........................(p[1]) DavidEgan 5 53
(Dai Burchell) *chsd ldrs: drvn 3f out: unable qck and no ch w easy wnr fr over 1f out: disp modest 2nd ins fnl f* **25/1**

0502 4 1¾ **Risk Mitigation (USA)**[13] 5548 3-8-10 53........................(v) HollieDoyle 7 50
(David Evans) *led 2f: trckd ldr tl drvn: bmpd and lost 2nd over 3f out: one pce and hld after* **9/1**

-321 5 3 **It's How We Roll (IRE)**[15] 5499 5-9-5 52........................(p) JackMitchell 8 43
(John Spearing) *hld up: rdn and sme hdwy over 2f out: 5th and btn whn hung rt appr fnl f (jockey said the gelding hung right in the home straight)* **6/4[1]**

-664 6 1 **Beer With The Boys**[11] 5604 4-10-1 67........................ ScottMcCullagh(5) 9 57
(Mick Channon) *hld up: swtchd rt and rdn over 2f out: no imp (vet said gelding lost his left fore shoe)* **5/1[3]**

6405 7 4½ **Knight Commander**[11] 5604 6-9-8 55........................(b) RaulDaSilva 1 37
(Steve Flook) *chsd ldrs: drvn 3f out: sn wknd* **20/1**

06-0 8 2 **Endean**[18] 5378 4-9-3 50........................ SeanLevey 6 29
(William Muir) *midfield: rdn 3f out: nt run on: wknd wl over 1f out* **40/1**

30-0 9 12 **Born To Please**[92] 2685 5-9-6 53........................ TomMarquand 4 13
(Mark Usher) *hld up towards rr: rdn 4f out: sn wknd* **25/1**

2m 36.98s (-3.22) **Going Correction** -0.025s/f (Good)
WFA 3 from 4yo+ 10lb **9 Ran SP% 121.6**
Speed ratings (Par 101): **109,103,103,102,100 99,96,95,87**
CSF £43.14 CT £739.82 TOTE £15.10: £4.20, £1.20, £7.70; EX 65.30 Trifecta £987.50.
Owner A D G Oldrey & G C Hartigan **Bred** Cheveley Park Stud Ltd **Trained** Kimpton, Hants

FOCUS
A weak handicap.

6043 UNIVERSAL HARDWARE SUPPLIES NOVICE STKS 1m 3f 209y(R)
4:15 (4:26) (Class 5) 3-Y-O+ **£3,428** (£1,020; £509; £254) **Stalls Low**

Form RPR

01 1 **Monica Sheriff**[67] 3553 3-9-4 0........................ TomMarquand 2 81+
(William Haggas) *prom: trckd ldr over 3f out: rdn over 2f out: led ent fnl f: styd on wl* **11/8[2]**

2233 2 3 **Cape Cavalli (IRE)**[53] 4066 3-9-2 83........................(p[1]) JackMitchell 6 73
(Simon Crisford) *led 1f: trckd ldr tl led again 4f out: drvn 2f out: hdd ent fnl f: no ex* **5/6[1]**

00 3 2¼ **Lucy Lou (IRE)**[90] 2731 3-8-11 0........................ KieranShoemark 8 64
(Charles Hills) *hld up: rdn along and hdwy 5f out: rdn again 3f out: styd on to go 3rd over 1f out: no imp fnl f* **12/1**

0 4 1½ **Roving Mission (USA)**[38] 4641 3-8-11 0........................ HarryBentley 4 62
(Ralph Beckett) *hld up: clsd after 4f: drvn over 2f out: sn chsng ldng pair: lost 3rd over 1f out: one pce* **5/1[3]**

P 5 2¼ **Hurry Kane**[43] 4459 3-8-11 0........................ RhiainIngram(5) 5 63?
(Paul George) *t.k.h: prom 2f: hld up in tch after: rdn 3f out: no imp on ldrs: styd on steadily fnl f* **66/1**

00-0 6 22 **De Beau Tant**[90] 2733 4-9-7 38........................ DavidEgan 9 22
(Dai Burchell) *prom: rdn 4f out: wknd over 2f out: t.o* **100/1**

40 7 1¾ **Lady Of Mercia**[12] 5578 3-8-11 0........................ JohnFahy 7 20
(John Flint) *in rr: drvn 4f out: sn lost tch: t.o* **66/1**

8 28 **Tops No**[18] 4-9-7 0........................ SeanLevey 3
(William Muir) *prom: led after 1f to 4f out: wknd qckly: t.o (jockey said filly hung right; vet said filly lost both front shoes)* **33/1**

2m 37.52s (-2.68) **Going Correction** -0.025s/f (Good)
WFA 3 from 4yo 10lb **8 Ran SP% 127.9**
Speed ratings (Par 103): **107,105,103,102,101 86,85,66**
CSF £3.31 TOTE £3.00: £1.10, £1.10, £3.30; EX 3.30 Trifecta £14.80.
Owner Duke Of Devonshire **Bred** The Duke Of Devonshire **Trained** Newmarket, Suffolk
■ Just Champion was withdrawn, price at time of withdrawal 100/1. Rule 4 does not apply.

FOCUS
This was run steadily through the first half, but it is still fair novice form. It's hard to pin down the level, with the third, fourth and fifth all improving.

6044 WHITFORD'S CAFE BAR & LOUNGE H'CAP 1m 6f (R)
4:45 (4:51) (Class 4) (0-85,85) 3-Y-O+

£5,207 (£1,549; £774; £387; £300; £300) **Stalls Low**

Form RPR

6-05 1 **Darksideoftarnside (IRE)**[20] 5321 5-9-9 80........................(p) JasonWatson 2 87
(Ian Williams) *chsd ldrs: rdn over 5f out: led narrowly 2f out: styd on u.p (jockey said gelding hung right)* **6/1**

0060 2 1 **Never Surrender (IRE)**[32] 4884 5-9-7 78........................ KieranShoemark 5 83
(Charles Hills) *hld up: hdwy over 3f out: sn rdn and swtchd lft: no imp on ldrs tl styd on ins fnl f: wnt 2nd last strides (jockey said gelding hung both ways)* **10/1**

6022 3 shd **Diocletian (IRE)**[17] 5423 4-10-0 85........................ RobHornby 6 90
(Andrew Balding) *prom: led 6f out: rdn over 2f out: sn hdd: ev ch after: no ex towards fin and lost 2nd last strides* **5/4[1]**

-223 4 nk **General Zoff**[48] 4257 4-8-13 70........................ TomMarquand 1 74
(William Muir) *hld up: hdwy on outer 7f out: ev ch 2f out tl one pce ins fnl f: lost 3rd cl home* **11/2[3]**

3210 5 19 **Goscote**[17] 5452 4-9-1 72........................ CharlesBishop 3 50
(Henry Candy) *led 1f: remained prom: rdn over 5f out: wknd over 3f out: t.o (jockey said filly stopped quickly)* **7/2[2]**

1502 6 19 **Kashagan**[10] 5694 3-8-11 79........................(b) DavidEgan 7 32
(Archie Watson) *cl up: led after 1f tl hdd 6f out: remained cl up: drvn over 4f out: sn wknd: t.o* **7/1**

3m 6.67s (-1.93) **Going Correction** -0.025s/f (Good)
WFA 3 from 4yo+ 11lb **6 Ran SP% 117.9**
Speed ratings (Par 105): **104,103,103,103,92 81**
CSF £61.85 TOTE £6.00: £2.80, £5.50; EX 47.40 Trifecta £271.80.
Owner Grant Horsfield **Bred** Ballycrighaun Stud **Trained** Portway, Worcs

FOCUS
This modest staying handicap was run at an uneven pace. Muddling form. The third has been rated to his Chester latest and the fourth as back to form.

6045 WALTERS H'CAP 1m (R)
5:15 (5:21) (Class 5) (0-70,70) 3-Y-O+
£3,428 (£1,020; £509; £300; £300; £300) Stalls Low

Form RPR
6631 1 **Greeley (IRE)**[17] 5446 3-9-6 69............................(p) DavidEgan 5 76+
(Rod Millman) *hld up: rdn 3f out: hdwy on outer over 1f out: r.o to ld fnl 75yds: readily* **3/1**[2]
4543 2 1 ¾ **Flying Dragon (FR)**[13] 5561 3-9-7 70.................. TomMarquand 3 73
(Richard Hannon) *prom: rdn to chse ldr over 2f out: kpt on u.p: lost 2nd 100yds out: wnt 2nd again last strides* **2/1**[1]
002 3 hd **Mabo**[15] 5498 4-8-9 51..........................(b) JasonWatson 8 55
(Grace Harris) *s.i.s: sn chsng ldr: rdn to ld over 2f out: 3 l clr appr fnl f: hdd fnl 75yds: lost 2nd last strides (jockey said gelding had no more to give)* **8/1**
025 4 3 **Kodiline (IRE)**[21] 5282 5-9-8 64.................... HarryBentley 7 61
(David Evans) *hld up: hdwy to chse ldrs 3f out: drvn 2f out: fdd fnl f* **5/1**[3]
0000 5 ¾ **Field Of Vision (IRE)**[29] 4994 6-9-2 58.................(p) RobHornby 2 53
(John Flint) *midfield: pushed along over 2f out: hld over 1f out: kpt on towards fin* **11/1**
5564 6 5 **Canoodling**[23] 5214 3-9-2 65........................ KieranShoemark 1 47
(Ian Williams) *t.k.h: prom: rdn over 2f out: wknd appr fnl f* **5/1**[3]
0000 7 hd **Black Truffle (FR)**[41] 4501 9-8-2 51 oh6..........(p) EllieMacKenzie(7) 10 34
(Mark Usher) *t.k.h: sddle sn slipped: hld up in last: pushed along 4f out: no hdwy (jockey said saddle slipped forward)* **50/1**
6306 8 2 ¼ **Tally's Son**[15] 5497 5-8-9 51 oh2.........................(v[1]) JohnFahy 4 29
(Grace Harris) *led tl rdn and hdd over 2f out: wknd over 1f out* **11/1**

1m 43.13s (0.23) **Going Correction** -0.025s/f (Good) 8 Ran SP% **121.4**
WFA 3 from 4yo+ 7lb
Speed ratings (Par 103): **97,95,95,92,91 86,86,83**
CSF £10.15 CT £44.85 TOTE £4.10: £1.50, £1.20, £2.30; EX 10.40 Trifecta £49.10.
Owner The Greeley Syndicate **Bred** Tally-Ho Stud **Trained** Kentisbeare, Devon

FOCUS
Not the worst handicap for the class and they went a fair enough pace. The second and third have been rated to their recent form.
T/Plt: £1,103.30 to a £1 stake. Pool: £66,415.04 - 43.94 winning units T/Qpdt: £185.50 to a £1 stake. Pool: £6,545.38 - 26.11 winning units **Richard Lowther**

5954 LINGFIELD (L-H)
Tuesday, August 13

OFFICIAL GOING: Polytrack: standard
Wind: Light, half behind Weather: Fine

6046 RAY & DI'S GOLDEN WEDDING ANNIVERSARY H'CAP 1m 7f 169y(P)
4:55 (4:55) (Class 6) (0-55,57) 3-Y-O+
£2,781 (£827; £413; £300; £300; £300) Stalls Low

Form RPR
1421 1 **Steel Helmet (IRE)**[17] 5435 5-9-9 50.................. JosephineGordon 4 56
(William Bethell) *t.k.h early: hld up wl in tch in midfield: clsd to chse ldrs 3f out: effrt to chse ldr 2f out: styd on to ld 100yds out: rdn out hands and heels towards fin* **9/4**[1]
030 2 1 ¼ **Beechwood James (FR)**[13] 5548 3-8-8 53. ThoreHammerHansen(5) 14 60
(Richard Hannon) *wnt lft leaving stalls: hld up in tch in midfield: effrt to chse ldrs and hung lft over 1f out: swtchd rt and styd on ins fnl f: snatched 2nd last strides (jockey said colt hung left-handed under pressure)* **12/1**
0552 3 nse **Guaracha**[27] 5053 8-9-1 45..........................(v) JoshuaBryan(3) 3 49
(Alexandra Dunn) *chsd ldrs tl lft chsng ldr 9f out: rdn to ld jst over 2f out: drvn over 1f out: hdd and one pce ins fnl f* **10/1**
3336 4 2 **Yasir (USA)**[21] 5285 11-9-12 53........................ DavidProbert 6 55
(Sophie Leech) *hld up in last quartet: nt clr run over 2f out: hdwy u.p over 1f out: styd on wl ins fnl f: nt rch ldrs* **14/1**
0000 5 nk **Tilsworth Sammy**[12] 5596 4-9-4 45.....................(v[1]) TomQueally 8 47
(J R Jenkins) *hld up in last quartet: hdwy u.p over 1f out: styd on wl ins fnl f: nt rch ldrs* **25/1**
0040 6 ½ **Riverina**[27] 5049 3-8-10 50..........................(h) GeorgeWood 9 53
(Harry Dunlop) *racd in last quartet and pushed along at times: swtchd lft over 2f out: rdn and hdwy on inner over 1f out: styd on wl ins fnl f: nt rch ldrs* **10/1**
5430 7 1 ¼ **Caracas**[27] 2196 5-9-7 48..........................(p) RossaRyan 1 48
(Kevin Frost) *in tch in midfield: effrt and rdn to chse ldrs 3f out: unable qck and outpcd over 1f out: kpt on same pce ins fnl f* **8/1**[3]
10-2 8 2 ½ **Carraigin Aonair (IRE)**[29] 5001 7-9-8 56............. LewisStones(7) 7 53
(Olly Murphy) *hld up in tch in midfield: effrt over 2f out: no imp and kpt on same pce fr over 1f out* **8/1**[3]
40/0 9 ¾ **Swift Blade (IRE)**[6] 5802 11-9-9 57................ RhysClutterbuck(7) 12 53
(Gary Moore) *stdd: short of room and hmpd sn after leaving stalls: hld up in tch in rr: swtchd rt and effrt wl over 1f out: no imp: nvr involved* **33/1**
4400 10 1 ¾ **Millie May**[34] 4796 5-9-4 45........................ KieranO'Neill 2 39
(Jimmy Fox) *led: rdn 3f out: hdd jst over 2f out: outpcd u.p and btn over 1f out: wknd ins fnl f* **25/1**
000- 11 1 ¼ **Mount Cleshar**[162] 9160 5-9-4 45........................ StevieDonohoe 13 37
(John Butler) *hung lft sn after leaving stalls: hld up in rr: nvr involved* **20/1**
500 12 84 **Sleepdancer (IRE)**[24] 5193 3-8-7 52.................(t[1] w) CierenFallon(5) 10
(John Ryan) *t.k.h: chsd ldrs: rdn 4f out: lost pl and bhd over 2f out: sn eased: t.o (jockey said saddle slipped)* **10/1**
000 U **Whims Of Desire**[22] 5242 3-8-3 50........................ GavinAshton(7) 11
(Sir Mark Prescott Bt) *wnt rt leaving stalls: chsd ldr tl ducked sharply rt (paddock exit) and uns rdr 9f out* **7/1**[2]
R-00 R **Threediamondrings**[26] 5106 6-9-5 46.....................(p) NickyMackay 5
(Mark Usher) *ref to r* **20/1**

3m 25.57s (-0.13) **Going Correction** -0.075s/f (Stan) 14 Ran SP% **127.3**
WFA 3 from 4yo+ 13lb
Speed ratings (Par 101): **97,96,96,95,95 94,94,93,92,91 91,49,,**
CSF £30.53 CT £245.67 TOTE £2.60: £1.40, £3.80, £3.20; EX 37.70 Trifecta £195.00.
Owner W A Bethell **Bred** Rabbah Bloodstock Limited **Trained** Arnold, E Yorks

FOCUS
A low-grade staying event but plenty of incident, notably the second favourite running out on the paddock turn and unseating her rider.

6047 VISIT ATTHERACES.COM NOVICE STKS 5f 6y(P)
5:30 (5:35) (Class 5) 2-Y-O
£3,428 (£1,020; £509; £254) Stalls High

Form RPR
320 1 **Cool Sphere (USA)**[13] 5542 2-9-5 81........................ DavidProbert 5 81+
(Robert Cowell) *t.k.h: mde all: clr 2f out: r.o strly and pushed out ins fnl f: v easily* **4/6**[1]
00 2 6 **Blue Venture**[29] 4993 2-9-0........................ BrettDoyle 2 54
(Tony Carroll) *uns rdr and loose bef s: chsd wnr: outpcd 2f out: wl hld after but kpt on to hold 2nd ins fnl f* **50/1**
3 1 **Lady Phyllis** 2-9-0........................ CharlieBennett 3 51+
(Michael Attwater) *s.i.s and rn green early: clsd and in tch whn hung lft over 2f out: outpcd 2f out: pushed along over 1f out: kpt on same pce and no ch w wnr (jockey said colt ran green)* **40/1**
4 nse **Lady Tati (IRE)** 2-9-0........................ StevieDonohoe 4 51
(David Simcock) *trckd ldrs: outpcd 2f out: no ch w wnr and kpt on same pce after* **7/1**[3]
5 2 ¼ **Merchants Breath** 2-9-5........................ ShaneKelly 1 48+
(Shaun Keightley) *v.s.a and green early: clsd and in tch 3f out: nt clr run and outpcd 2f out: swtchd lft over 1f out: no ch after* **20/1**
6 2 **Momentum Swing** 2-9-5........................ PatCosgrave 6 40
(Robert Cowell) *s.i.s: midfield: clsd and in tch after 2f: outpcd 2f out: no ch after (jockey said colt was slowly away)* **9/4**[2]

58.33s (-0.47) **Going Correction** -0.075s/f (Stan) 6 Ran SP% **112.4**
Speed ratings (Par 94): **100,90,88,88,85 81**
CSF £45.65 TOTE £1.40: £1.10, £13.40; EX 29.50 Trifecta £220.40.
Owner The Cool Silk Partnership **Bred** Hinkle Farms **Trained** Six Mile Bottom, Cambs

FOCUS
An uncompetitive novice event in which the pair with experience were dominant, the winner taking full advantage of a big drop in class.

6048 SKY SPORTS RACING ON VIRGIN 535 H'CAP 5f 6y(P)
6:00 (6:02) (Class 6) (0-65,64) 3-Y-O+
£2,781 (£827; £413; £300; £300; £300) Stalls High

Form RPR
0003 1 **Requited (IRE)**[12] 5595 3-9-6 63........................ CharlieBennett 4 70
(Hughie Morrison) *mde virtually all: rdn over 1f out: kpt on wl and holding rivals ins fnl f* **3/1**[1]
2202 2 ¾ **Fairy Fast (IRE)**[8] 5738 3-9-7 64.....................(b) PatCosgrave 7 68
(George Boughey) *short of room leaving stalls: t.k.h: hld up in tch: clsd 2f out: shkn up and hdwy over 1f out: chsd wnr 1f out: drvn and kpt on same pce ins fnl f* **7/1**[3]
-054 3 1 **Roundabout Magic (IRE)**[45] 4374 5-9-9 63........................ NickyMackay 9 65
(Simon Dow) *stdd after s: hld up in tch in rr: swtchd lft over 2f out: hdwy on inner over 1f out: swtchd rt and squeezed through 1f out: drvn and kpt on fnl 100yds* **7/1**[3]
0001 4 hd **Come On Dave (IRE)**[27] 5046 10-9-4 63.............(b) DarraghKeenan(5) 1 64
(John Butler) *taken down early: in tch in midfield: effrt over 1f out: kpt on ins fnl f* **7/2**[2]
1330 5 1 ¼ **Fareeq**[99] 2473 5-9-4 63.....................(bt) WilliamCarver(5) 2 59
(Charlie Wallis) *chsd ldrs: effrt on inner over 1f out: no ex and wknd wl ins fnl f (jockey said gelding hung right-handed in the straight)* **10/1**
0346 6 1 **Pharoh Jake**[4] 5884 11-8-6 46........................ KieranO'Neill 8 39
(John Bridger) *in tch in midfield: wd and outpcd bnd 2f out: kpt on but no threat to ldrs ins fnl f* **14/1**
0000 7 1 **Flowing Clarets**[4] 5884 6-8-9 49........................ LiamJones 10 38
(John Bridger) *taken down early: towards rr and stuck wd: rdn and outpcd bnd 2f out: no threat to ldrs but kpt on ins fnl f* **33/1**
2601 8 1 ¾ **Olaudah**[35] 4763 5-9-8 62........................ DavidProbert 6 45
(Henry Candy) *taken down early: pushed rt leaving stalls: pressed wnr tl unable qck and outpcd over 1f out: wknd ins fnl f* **7/2**[2]
0056 9 3 ¾ **Gifted Zebedee (IRE)**[14] 5532 3-8-9 59.............(t[1]) StefanoCherchi(7) 5 27
(Anthony Carson) *wnt rt leaving stalls: pressed wnr tl unable qck over 1f out: struggling whn squeezed for room 1f out: sn wknd* **20/1**
0436 10 13 **Cookupastorm (IRE)**[40] 4556 3-9-5 62.....................(p) ShaneKelly 3
(Martin Smith) *v free to post: in last pair: swtchd rt over 2f out and eased off: sddle slipped (jockey said filly ran freely to post and his saddle slipped during the race)* **12/1**

58.59s (-0.21) **Going Correction** -0.075s/f (Stan) 10 Ran SP% **125.6**
WFA 3 from 5yo+ 3lb
Speed ratings (Par 101): **98,96,95,94,92 91,89,86,80,60**
CSF £26.95 CT £146.72 TOTE £3.80: £1.90, £2.20, £2.30; EX 33.80 Trifecta £186.30.
Owner H Morrison **Bred** Barry Noonan And Denis Noonan **Trained** East Ilsley, Berks

FOCUS
A modest sprint handicap in which the winner was justifying sustained market support.

6049 WITHEFORD EQUINE BARRIER TRIALS HERE 10TH SEPTEMBER H'CAP 1m 2f (P)
6:30 (6:31) (Class 7) (0-50,51) 3-Y-O+
£2,522 (£750; £375; £187) Stalls Low

Form RPR
0502 1 **Voice Of A Leader (IRE)**[66] 3592 8-9-5 48........................ JoeyHaynes 5 56+
(Chelsea Banham) *taken down early: hld up towards rr: stdy prog 5f out: trcking ldrs and travelling strly ent fnl 2f: swtchd out: effrt and qcknd up to ld ent fnl f: rdn out* **5/1**[2]
0400 2 1 ½ **Cat Royale (IRE)**[49] 4217 6-9-5 48.....................(p) DannyBrock 1 53
(John Butler) *hld up in tch in midfield: nt clr run jst over 2f out: hdwy u.p over 1f out: chsd wnr ins fnl f: kpt on but nvr a threat* **12/1**
-060 3 2 ½ **Grasmere (IRE)**[74] 3298 4-8-13 47.....................(t) DarraghKeenan(5) 3 47
(Alan Bailey) *chsd ldrs: nt clr run ent fnl 2f: swtchd rt and effrt ent fnl f: swtchd lft and styd on ins fnl f: no ch w wnr* **16/1**
306 4 ½ **Ahfad**[63] 3687 4-9-2 45.....................(b) HectorCrouch 13 44
(Gary Moore) *s.i.s and rousted along early: nt clrest of runs over 2f out: swtchd rt and effrt over 1f out: styd on wl ins fnl f: no threat to wnr* **12/1**
3330 5 nk **Captain Marmalade (IRE)**[20] 5310 7-8-11 45 ThoreHammerHansen(5) 2 44
(Jimmy Fox) *s.i.s: hld up in rr: hdwy on inner over 1f out: nt clr run and swtchd rt ins fnl f: styd on towards fin: no threat to wnr* **14/1**
4660 6 hd **Misty Breese (IRE)**[2] 5981 4-8-13 45........................ NoelGarbutt(3) 9 44
(Sarah Hollinshead) *s.i.s: hld up towards rr: effrt but forced wd bnd 2f out: hdwy 1f out: styd on wl ins fnl f: nvr trbld ldrs* **50/1**

4421 **7** *nk* **Born To Reason (IRE)**[6] 5802 5-9-3 **51** 5ex............(p) CierenFallon(5) 11 49
(Alexandra Dunn) *hld up towards rr: nt clr run over 2f out tl effrt and reminder 1f out: swtchd rt and kpt on ins fnl f: nvr trbld ldrs* **9/2**[1]

-600 **8** *1 ¼* **Keep It Country Tv**[54] 4029 3-8-13 **50**............ JFEgan 4 47
(Pat Phelan) *prom: chsd ldr over 6f out: ev ch and drvn over 1f out: nt match pce of wnr 1f out: edgd rt and wknd ins fnl f* **7/1**

1250 **9** *1 ¼* **Nicky Baby (IRE)**[63] 3687 5-9-0 **48**............(b) SophieRalston(5) 8 41
(Dean Ivory) *t.k.h: sn prom: led 8f out tl hdd u.p ent fnl f: wknd ins fnl f* **9/1**

0-0 **10** *1 ½* **Drumshanbo Destiny (FR)**[74] 3299 3-8-13 **50**............ RossaRyan 10 41
(Gary Moore) *in tch in midfield: n.m.r over 2f out: effrt 2f out: drvn and no hdwy over 1f out: nt clrest of runs and wknd ins fnl f* **7/1**

-506 **11** *1* **Classified (IRE)**[29] 4991 5-9-7 **50**............(p) PatCosgrave 6 38
(Ed de Giles) *t.k.h: prom early: settled bk and wl in tch in midfield: clsd to chse ldrs and effrt over 2f out: no ex over 1f out: wknd ins fnl f* **6/1**[3]

0040 **12** *hd* **Far Cry**[68] 3497 6-9-2 **45**............ CharlieBennett 7 33
(Hughie Morrison) *nvr bttr than midfield: no hdwy u.p over 1f out: nvr involved* **20/1**

3500 **13** *10* **Luxford**[10] 5652 5-9-4 **47**............(v[1]) ShaneKelly 12 16
(Gary Moore) *t.k.h: prom early: stdd bk and in tch in midfield: hdwy to chse ldrs over 5f out: lost pl over 2f out: bhd fnl f* **12/1**

2m 5.68s (-0.92) **Going Correction** -0.075s/f (Stan)
WFA 3 from 4yo+ 8lb **13** Ran SP% **126.5**
Speed ratings (Par 97): **100,98,96,96,96 96,95,94,93,92 91,91,83**
CSF £68.17 CT £925.41 TOTE £5.00: £1.80, £4.40, £5.30; EX 67.60 Trifecta £991.60.
Owner Chelsea Banham Pre Training Ltd **Bred** Lynch Bages Ltd **Trained** Cowlinge, Suffolk

FOCUS
Bottom-grade fare with the winner providing Chelsea Banham with her first success as a trainer.

6050 SKY SPORTS RACING ON SKY 415 H'CAP 1m 1y(P)
7:00 (7:03) (Class 5) (0-75,76) 4-Y-O+

£3,428 (£1,020; £509; £300; £300; £300) **Stalls** High

Form RPR

1500 **1** **Lothario**[21] 5267 5-9-2 **70**............ JoeyHaynes 11 79
(Dean Ivory) *pressed ldr tl rdn to ld over 1f out: hld on gamely u.p ins fnl f: all out* **11/2**

-000 **2** *nk* **Merweb (IRE)**[57] 3944 4-9-0 **71**............ JaneElliott(3) 3 79
(Heather Main) *chsd ldrs: effrt over 2f out: hdwy ent fnl f: wnt 2nd ins fnl f: str chal wl ins fnl f: styd on wl but hld cl home* **6/1**

-440 **3** *3* **Dangerous Ends**[40] 4561 5-9-3 **71**............ RossaRyan 5 72+
(Brett Johnson) *stdd s: hld up in rr: hdwy on inner over 1f out: swtchd rt and styd on wl ins fnl f: wnt 3rd cl home: no threat to ldng pair* **8/1**

2166 **4** *nk* **Pheidippides**[117] 1882 4-9-8 **76**............ PatCosgrave 2 77
(Tom Clover) *trckd ldrs: effrt but unable qck over 1f out: wknd ins fnl f: lost 3rd cl home* **9/2**[3]

3-03 **5** *1 ¼* **Glorious Jem**[18] 5373 4-9-2 **70**............(b[1]) DanielMuscutt 9 68
(David Lanigan) *pushed along and in last trio early: hdwy into midfield 5f out: effrt over 2f out: outpcd and swtchd rt 1f out: kpt on but no threat to ldrs ins fnl f* **7/2**[2]

3-15 **6** *nse* **Kitcarina (FR)**[17] 5419 4-9-7 **75**............ DavidProbert 1 73
(Andrew Balding) *led: rdn: hdd and hung lft over 1f out: sn btn and wknd ins fnl f* **11/4**[1]

0410 **7** *nk* **Come On Tier (FR)**[57] 3944 4-9-3 **71**............(v[1]) KierenFox 6 68
(Lee Carter) *t.k.h: hld up in tch towards rr of main gp: effrt 2f out: swtchd rt and kpt on ins fnl f: nvr trbld ldrs* **22/1**

50 **8** *nk* **He's Our Star (IRE)**[18] 5373 4-9-2 **70**............ KieranO'Neill 10 66
(Ali Stronge) *sn towards rr: swtchd rt and effrt over 2f out: swtchd rt and drvn 1f out: kpt on ins fnl f: nvr trbld ldrs* **20/1**

6-06 **9** *11* **Albishr (IRE)**[12] 5574 4-9-2 **70**............(p) NickyMackay 12 41
(Simon Dow) *chsd ldrs: pushed along over 2f out: sn lost pl: bhd and ins fnl f* **33/1**

00-0 **10** *nk* **Sinfonietta (FR)**[21] 5283 7-9-2 **70**............ ShaneKelly 4 40
(Sophie Leech) *midfield: struggling whn swtchd rt bnd 2f out: sn wl btn and bhd ins fnl f* **33/1**

3500 **11** *5* **Tommycole**[41] 4518 4-7-13 **49** oh7............ NoelGarbutt(3) 7 15
(Olly Williams) *s.i.s: nvr travelling wl in last pair: lost tch 2f out* **50/1**

1m 37.12s (-1.08) **Going Correction** -0.075s/f (Stan) **11** Ran SP% **124.8**
Speed ratings (Par 103): **102,101,98,98,97 97,96,96,85,85 80**
CSF £38.51 CT £276.69 TOTE £6.00: £1.70, £2.50, £2.50; EX 36.60 Trifecta £231.70.
Owner Michael & Heather Yarrow **Bred** J Troy, Mrs R Philipps & Highbury Stud **Trained** Radlett, Herts

■ Delicate Kiss was withdrawn, price at time of withdrawal 7/1. Rule 4 applies to board prices prior to withdrawal, but not to SP bets. Deduction of 10p in the pound. New market formed.

FOCUS
A competitive enough contest but little got into it from the rear, the third doing well in the circumstances. A length pb from the winner, with the second rated back to form.

6051 INJURED JOCKEYS FUND H'CAP 7f 1y(P)
7:30 (7:32) (Class 7) (0-50,50) 3-Y-O+ **£2,522** (£750; £375; £187) **Stalls** Low

Form RPR

0350 **1** **Three C's (IRE)**[20] 5293 5-9-3 **47**............(p) PatCosgrave 10 54
(George Boughey) *led: sn hdd: chsd ldrs: effrt over 1f out: drvn to chse ldr 1f out: styd on to ld wl ins fnl f: hld on gamely cl home* **13/2**[3]

0025 **2** *nk* **Vincenzo Coccotti (USA)**[25] 5151 7-9-2 **49**............(p) JoshuaBryan(3) 9 55
(Ken Cunningham-Brown) *broke wl: sn led and gng lft: hdd after 1f and settled in midfield: effrt u.p over 1f out: hung lft but clsd to chal ins fnl f: kpt on: hld cl home* **8/1**

0063 **3** *1* **Cooperess**[15] 5498 6-9-2 **46**............ DavidProbert 6 50
(Adrian Wintle) *sn w ldr: led over 2f out: drvn over 1f out: hdd wl ins fnl f: no ex towards fin* **14/1**

660 **4** *2 ¼* **Spenny's Lass**[11] 5629 4-9-1 **50**............(p) CierenFallon(5) 5 48
(John Ryan) *in tch in midfield: effrt over 2f out: kpt on u.p ins fnl f: nt enough pce to threaten ldrs* **7/1**

0000 **5** *hd* **Stoneyford Lane (IRE)**[11] 5633 5-9-3 **47**............(b) RoystonFfrench 7 44+
(Steph Hollinshead) *dwlt: in rr: swtchd rt: effrt but stl plenty to do over 1f out: styd on strly ins fnl f: nvr trbld ldrs* **33/1**

002 **6** *2* **Billiebrookedit (IRE)**[42] 4481 4-9-2 **46**............ RossaRyan 1 38
(Kevin Frost) *chsd ldrs: unable qck u.p over 1f out: wknd ins fnl f (jockey said gelding was denied a clear run)* **11/2**[2]

0065 **7** *nk* **Catapult**[10] 5678 4-9-2 **46**............ JosephineGordon 2 37
(Shaun Keightley) *pushed along leaving stalls: led after 1f: hdd over 2f out: unable qck over 1f out: wknd ins fnl f* **5/1**[1]

0002 **8** *½* **Essential**[34] 4807 5-9-1 **48**............(b) ConnorMurtagh(3) 4 38
(Olly Williams) *in tch in midfield: bmpd sn after s: effrt over 1f out: nt clr run and swtchd rt ins fnl f: kpt on but no ch w ldrs (jockey said gelding jumped left-handed and lost action)* **8/1**

3200 **9** *nk* **Purple Paddy**[48] 4235 4-9-5 **49**............ KieranO'Neill 11 38
(Jimmy Fox) *chsd ldrs: effrt to press ldr 2f out tl jst over 1f out: wknd ins fnl f* **5/1**[1]

0060 **10** *½* **Hidden Dream (FR)**[11] 5633 4-9-1 **50**............ DarraghKeenan(5) 12 38
(John Butler) *a towards rr: effrt over 2f out: plugged on ins fnl f: nvr trbld ldrs* **10/1**

0030 **11** *2* **Haraz (IRE)**[66] 3592 6-9-3 **47**............ JoeyHaynes 3 30
(Paddy Butler) *a towards rr: effrt over 1f out: no prog and nvr involved* **50/1**

0-00 **12** *shd* **Haabis (USA)**[105] 2240 6-9-4 **48**............ LiamKeniry 13 30
(Patrick Chamings) *midfield: shkn up over 1f out: reminder 1f out: sn wknd* **25/1**

010/ **13** *3 ½* **My Bubba**[964] 8500 7-9-4 **48**............ EoinWalsh 8 21
(Malcolm Saunders) *a towards rr: effrt over 2f out: wd bnd 2f out and wl btn after* **33/1**

0400 **14** *1 ¾* **Ad Valorem Queen (IRE)**[20] 5302 4-9-2 **46**............ TomQueally 14 15
(J R Jenkins) *stdd after s: a towards rr* **40/1**

1m 24.48s (-0.32) **Going Correction** -0.075s/f (Stan) **14** Ran SP% **126.7**
Speed ratings (Par 97): **98,97,96,93,93 91,91,90,90,89 87,87,83,81**
CSF £58.40 CT £728.53 TOTE £8.50: £2.80, £3.00, £4.50; EX 58.60 Trifecta £616.70.
Owner C U Next Wednesday **Bred** Gerry Ross **Trained** Newmarket, Suffolk
■ Stewards' Enquiry : Joshua Bryan one-day ban; failing to ride to draw (Aug 27)

FOCUS
Another lowly event but that will be of scant concern to George Boughey who was saddling his first winner since taking out his training licence.

6052 RACING WELFARE H'CAP 7f 1y(P)
8:00 (8:03) (Class 6) (0-60,62) 3-Y-O

£2,781 (£827; £413; £300; £300; £300) **Stalls** Low

Form RPR

-003 **1** **Fancy Flyer**[26] 5092 3-9-2 **62**............ LukeBacon(7) 10 72+
(Dean Ivory) *early spd and mde all: t.k.h: skipped three l clr 1/2-way: in control over 1f out and pushed out ins fnl f* **10/3**[1]

0040 **2** *3 ½* **Islay Mist**[48] 4244 3-8-9 **48**............(tp) KierenFox 11 49
(Lee Carter) *c across fr wd draw and hmpd rival after 1f: sn trckd ldr: rdn over 2f out: kpt on to take 2nd ins fnl f but no ch* **25/1**

-060 **3** *1* **Powerage (IRE)**[18] 5373 3-8-11 **50**............ DavidProbert 1 48
(Malcolm Saunders) *bhd ldr on inner: sltly hmpd after 1f: rdn to chse ldr over 2f out: kpt on one pce and lost 2nd ins fnl f* **25/1**

-002 **4** *1 ¾* **Harbour Times (IRE)**[18] 5377 3-8-2 **46**............ WilliamCarver(5) 6 41
(Patrick Chamings) *hld up in rr-div: rdn 3f out: sltly hmpd turning into st and a bit to do: stuck on wl fr over 1f out (vet said filly resented the kickback)* **7/2**[2]

5060 **5** *nse* **Orliko (IRE)**[17] 5431 3-9-7 **60**............(bt) RossaRyan 8 54
(Richard Hannon) *hld up in rr: pushed along at 1/2-way and struggling: no imp tl styd on on inner past btn horses fr over 1f out (jockey said gelding was never travelling)* **9/1**

300 **6** *½* **William McKinley**[88] 2795 3-9-9 **62**............(b w) KieranO'Neill 9 54
(Ali Stronge) *trckd ldr: sn leaned on and squeezed up rival after 1f: impr to chse ldr sn after: rdn over 2f out: one pce (vet said gelding lost its left fore shoe)* **10/1**

0644 **7** *6* **So Claire**[17] 5429 3-8-11 **50**............(h[1]) MartinDwyer 7 27
(William Muir) *racd in mid-div and sltly wd: rdn 3f out: no imp over 2f out* **6/1**

3005 **8** *1 ½* **Vino Rosso (IRE)**[8] 5731 3-9-1 **54**............ CharlieBennett 5 27
(Michael Blanshard) *racd in mid-div on inner: hmpd after 1f and swtchd off inner: rdn 3f out: plugged on one pce in st (jockey said filly was denied a clear run)* **16/1**

5002 **9** *½* **True Belief (IRE)**[27] 5044 3-9-6 **59**............(h) DanielMuscutt 4 41+
(Brett Johnson) *taken down early: mid-div on inner: bdly hmpd after 1f and dropped to rr: pushed along and hdwy into mid-div after 3f: gng okay 2f out: fnd little in st* **5/1**[3]

066 **P** **Caesonia**[71] 3421 3-8-9 **53**............ CierenFallon(5) 3
(Charles Hills) *cl up in mid-div between horses: losing grnd bef 1/2-way and p.u over 3f out (jockey said he felt the filly lose action)* **10/1**

1m 24.43s (-0.37) **Going Correction** -0.075s/f (Stan) **10** Ran SP% **118.0**
Speed ratings (Par 98): **99,95,93,91,91 91,84,82,82,**
CSF £86.43 CT £1852.36 TOTE £3.50: £1.40, £7.40, £7.60; EX 66.90 Trifecta £693.30.
Owner Cynthia Smith And Radlett Racing **Bred** Gracelands Stud **Trained** Radlett, Herts
■ Stewards' Enquiry : Kieren Fox seven-day ban; careless riding (Aug 27-31, Sep 1-2)

FOCUS
A winning favourite in the finale, albeit several of his main rivals were hampered in an incident in the early stages.
T/Jkpt: Not Won. T/Plt: £981.30 to a £1 stake. Pool: £67,752.28 - 50.4 winning units T/Qpdt: £234.80 to a £1 stake. Pool: £10,269.98 - 32.36 winning units **Steve Payne**

5780 NOTTINGHAM (L-H)
Tuesday, August 13

OFFICIAL GOING: Good to soft (good in places)
Wind: Fresh across Weather: Cloudy with sunny spells

6053 MANSIONBET NURSERY H'CAP (JOCKEY CLUB GRASSROOTS NURSERY QUALIFIER) 6f 18y
2:00 (2:01) (Class 5) (0-75,76) 2-Y-O

£3,881 (£1,155; £577; £300; £300; £300) **Stalls** Centre

Form RPR

3404 **1** **What A Business (IRE)**[7] 5789 2-8-11 **65**............ BenCurtis 4 72
(Roger Fell) *chsd ldr tl led over 2f out: rdn over 1f out: edgd lft ins fnl f: jst hld on* **7/2**[2]

353 **2** *shd* **Leapers Wood**[22] 5234 2-9-8 **76**............ TomEaves 2 83
(Michael Dods) *sn prom: chsd wnr over 2f out: rdn over 1f out: ev ch ins fnl f: r.o* **3/1**[1]

0503 **3** *3* **Little Ted**[7] 5789 2-8-7 **61**............ JamesSullivan 5 59
(Tim Easterby) *s.i.s: hdwy over 2f out: rdn over 1f out: styd on same pce ins fnl f* **10/1**

3355 **4** *3 ¼* **Stars In The Night (IRE)**[22] 5243 2-9-6 **74**............ KevinStott 6 62
(Kevin Ryan) *awkward s: hdwy over 2f out: rdn over 1f out: styd on same pce* **12/1**

0641 **5** *1 ½* **War Of Clans (IRE)**[7] 5789 2-8-7 **61**............ CliffordLee 3 45
(K R Burke) *sn led: hdd over 2f out: rdn over 1f out: wknd fnl f* **9/2**[3]

000 **6** *1* **Northern Grace**[10] 5689 2-7-11 **54** oh3............ NoelGarbutt(3) 1 35
(Brian Ellison) *broke wl enough: sn pushed along and lost pl: n.d after* **50/1**

2330 **7** 1 ¼ **Coastal Mist (IRE)**[11] 5612 2-9-7 **75**.................... OisinMurphy 10 52
(John Quinn) *hld up: hdwy over 2f out: wknd over 1f out* **3/1**[1]

1330 **8** 4 ½ **Daddies Diva**[24] 5185 2-8-12 **73**.................... OliverSearle(7) 8 37
(Rod Millman) *hld up in tch: wknd over 2f out* **20/1**

000 **9** 2 **Quarrystreetmagic (IRE)**[15] 5501 2-7-10 **57** oh9 ow3(p[1]) ElishaWhittington(7) 7 15
(Brian Meehan) *chsd ldrs: pushed along over 3f out: wknd over 2f out* **125/1**

0415 **10** 2 ¼ **Execlusive (IRE)**[13] 5562 2-9-5 **73**.................... AdamMcNamara 9 24
(Archie Watson) *s.i.s: a in rr: wknd over 2f out (jockey said filly jumped awkwardly from the stalls)* **40/1**

1m 16.16s (2.36) **Going Correction** +0.125s/f (Good) **10** Ran SP% **117.1**
Speed ratings (Par 94): **89,88,84,80,78 77,75,69,66,63**
CSF £14.18 CT £95.74 TOTE £4.70: £1.50, £1.20, £2.80; EX 17.90 Trifecta £115.70.
Owner S Greenhalgh & Northern Marking Ltd **Bred** Chapel Lane Bloodstock **Trained** Nawton, N Yorks

FOCUS
Outer Track, and the rail was out 4yds throughout. The ground was given as on the slow side but it was a largely dry, bright and breezy day, if not warm. A modest nursery to start and they raced up the middle.

6054 MANSIONBET BRITISH EBF NOVICE MEDIAN AUCTION STKS — 1m 75y
2:30 (2:30) (Class 5) 2-Y-O £4,528 (£1,347; £673; £336) **Stalls Centre**

Form RPR

42 **1** **Cloud Drift**[14] 5512 2-9-5 0.................... JamesDoyle 5 75
(Michael Bell) *led: hdd over 5f out: led again over 2f out: rdn over 1f out: styd on* **2/5**[1]

0 **2** nk **Green Book (FR)**[46] 4324 2-9-5 0.................... TomEaves 2 74
(Brian Ellison) *chsd ldrs: shkn up and outpcd over 2f out: swtchd rt over 1f out: r.o ins fnl f: wnt 2nd post* **10/1**[3]

3 nk **Merryweather** 2-9-0 0.................... OisinMurphy 3 69
(Ralph Beckett) *s.i.s: rcvrd to go prom after 1f: rdn to chse wnr over 1f out: styd on: lost 2nd post* **7/2**[2]

0 **4** 6 **Sunshine Fantasy (IRE)**[17] 5433 2-9-0 0.................... AdamMcNamara 4 55+
(Archie Watson) *chsd ldr tl led over 5f out: hdd over 2f out: wknd ins fnl f* **16/1**

0 **5** 7 **Sophar Sogood (IRE)**[27] 5052 2-9-5 0.................... TrevorWhelan 1 45
(Paul D'Arcy) *s.i.s: sn pushed along in rr: lost tch over 2f out (jockey said filly was slowly away)* **100/1**

0 **6** 1 ½ **Bad Attitude**[10] 5676 2-9-5 0.................... EoinWalsh 6 42
(Luke McJannet) *hld up: rdn and wknd over 2f out* **100/1**

00 **7** 12 **Full Strength**[10] 5655 2-9-5 0....................(p[1]) CliffordLee 7 15
(Ivan Furtado) *chsd ldrs: rdn over 3f out: hung lft and wknd over 2f out* **125/1**

1m 48.18s (1.48) **Going Correction** +0.125s/f (Good) **7** Ran SP% **111.4**
Speed ratings (Par 94): **97,96,96,90,83 81,69**
CSF £5.35 TOTE £1.30: £1.02, £3.80; EX 4.70 Trifecta £7.80.
Owner The Queen **Bred** The Queen **Trained** Newmarket, Suffolk

FOCUS
Add 12yds. Probably just ordinary bare form. The winner has been rated just below his Beverley effort.

6055 MANSIONBET BEATEN BY A HEAD H'CAP (A JOCKEY CLUB GRASSROOTS STAYERS SERIES QUALIFIER) — 1m 6f
3:00 (3:01) (Class 5) (0-70,72) 3-Y-O+ £3,735 (£1,118; £559; £300; £300; £300) **Stalls Low**

Form RPR

6600 **1** **Eye Of The Storm (IRE)**[20] 5311 9-9-12 **68**.................... HayleyTurner 2 79
(Conor Dore) *trckd ldrs: racd keenly: shkn up over 2f out: swtchd rt over 1f out: r.o to ld: edgd lft and bmpd wl ins fnl f* **16/1**

0321 **2** hd **Road To Paris (IRE)**[6] 5825 3-8-11 **64** 6ex.................... LukeMorris 6 75
(Sir Mark Prescott Bt) *a.p: chsd ldr over 11f out: shkn up to ld over 2f out: rdn and wandered ins fnl f: hdd and bmpd wl ins fnl f: r.o* **8/15**[1]

66/6 **3** 6 **Be My Sea (IRE)**[63] 3693 8-10-2 **72**.................... GeorgeDowning 8 74
(Tony Carroll) *led at stdy pce after 1f: qcknd over 3f out: hdd over 2f out: no ex ins fnl f* **33/1**

1450 **4** 1 ½ **Motahassen (IRE)**[31] 4914 5-8-7 **56**....................(t) ZakWheatley(7) 10 56
(Declan Carroll) *s.i.s: hld up: shkn up and hung lft 3f out: rdn over 1f out: r.o ins fnl f: nt trble ldrs* **14/1**

-000 **5** ¾ **Bill Cody (IRE)**[24] 5179 4-9-6 **65**.................... ConorMcGovern(3) 5 64
(Julie Camacho) *led 1f: chsd ldrs: rdn over 2f out: styd on same pce fr over 1f out* **20/1**

012- **6** shd **Olympic Odyssey**[121] 4050 4-10-0 **70**....................(w) OisinMurphy 9 69
(Harry Fry) *sn prom: shkn up over 2f out: wknd ins fnl f* **7/2**[2]

-060 **7** ¾ **Brancaster (IRE)**[48] 4257 5-9-10 **66**.................... LiamKeniry 1 64
(David Elsworth) *hld up: hdwy over 2f out: sn rdn: wknd ins fnl f* **8/1**[3]

106/ **8** 6 **Zamoyski**[70] 7624 9-9-9 **72**....................(p) Pierre-LouisJamin(7) 7 62
(Steve Gollings) *s.s: sn pushed along in rr: wknd over 3f out* **40/1**

0/0- **9** 12 **Delannoy**[474] 925 5-9-0 **56**....................(p) DougieCostello 4 29
(Neil Mulholland) *hld up: wknd over 2f out* **100/1**

3m 9.95s (3.55) **Going Correction** +0.125s/f (Good) **9** Ran SP% **122.2**
WFA 3 from 4yo+ 11lb
Speed ratings (Par 103): **94,93,90,89,89 89,88,85,78**
CSF £26.38 CT £352.60 TOTE £24.70: £4.10, £1.02, £6.50; EX 42.20 Trifecta £395.50.
Owner Andrew Page **Bred** Kevin J Molloy **Trained** Frampton Fen, Lincs

FOCUS
Add 24yds. The first two proved well weighted.

6056 BRITISH STALLION STUDS EBF CONDITIONS STKS — 5f 8y
3:30 (3:30) (Class 3) 3-Y-O+ £9,960 (£2,982; £1,491; £745; £372) **Stalls Centre**

Form RPR

16-6 **1** **Kyllang Rock (IRE)**[119] 1839 5-9-0 105.................... OisinMurphy 2 96
(James Tate) *trckd ldrs: shkn up to ld wl ins fnl f: edgd lft nr fin* **2/1**[2]

5165 **2** nk **Peggie Sue**[8] 5736 4-8-4 85.................... TobyEley(5) 3 90
(Adam West) *hld up in tch: nt clr run over 1f out: r.o wl ins fnl f: wnt 2nd post* **18/1**

0/14 **3** nse **Stake Acclaim (IRE)**[66] 3587 7-9-4 107.................... RobertWinston 4 99
(Dean Ivory) *led: shkn up over 1f out: rdn: edgd lft and hdd wl ins fnl f* **7/4**[1]

-430 **4** 1 ½ **Fairy Falcon**[32] 4891 4-8-9 86.................... TomEaves 5 84
(Bryan Smart) *chsd ldr: shkn up over 1f out: rdn: edgd lft and styd on same pce ins fnl f* **10/1**

3030 **5** 3 ¼ **Tarboosh**[46] 4331 6-9-4 104....................(w) DougieCostello 1 82
(Paul Midgley) *plld hrd and prom: rdn over 1f out: wknd ins fnl f (jockey said gelding stopped quickly; vet said that a post-race examination revealed the gelding was showing signs of a prolonged recovery)* **11/4**[3]

1m 0.05s (-0.15) **Going Correction** +0.125s/f (Good) **5** Ran SP% **110.7**
Speed ratings (Par 107): **106,105,105,103,97**
CSF £29.61 TOTE £1.90: £1.10, £5.30; EX 27.10 Trifecta £85.30.
Owner Unknown **Bred** Old Carhue & Graeng Bloodstock **Trained** Newmarket, Suffolk

FOCUS
Muddling form. The time was only 0.23sec quicker than the following Class 5 handicap and the proximity of the runner-up, who had plenty to find, could be used to limit the level although there was a case for her running well. They raced up the middle.

6057 MANSIONBET H'CAP (JOCKEY CLUB GRASSROOTS SPRINT SERIES QUALIFIER) — 5f 8y
4:00 (4:00) (Class 5) (0-70,72) 3-Y-O+ £3,881 (£1,155; £577; £300; £300) **Stalls Centre**

Form RPR

3225 **1** **Afandem (IRE)**[22] 5244 5-9-11 **71**....................(p) NathanEvans 3 79
(Tim Easterby) *restless in stalls: chsd ldr: rdn over 1f out: r.o to ld nr fin* **3/1**[3]

0550 **2** hd **Wrenthorpe**[32] 4894 4-9-5 **72**....................(p) HarryRussell(7) 7 79
(Bryan Smart) *led: rdn over 1f out: edgd lft ins fnl f: hdd nr fin* **2/1**[1]

0404 **3** 1 **Tadaany (IRE)**[7] 5765 7-8-5 **51**....................(p) JamesSullivan 6 55
(Ruth Carr) *chsd ldrs: shkn up over 1f out: rdn ins fnl f: styd on same pce towards fin* **6/1**

0110 **4** ¾ **Gamesome (FR)**[22] 5244 8-9-10 **70**.................... OisinMurphy 5 71
(Paul Midgley) *hld up in tch: shkn up over 1f out: nt trble ldrs* **9/4**[2]

1250 **5** 8 **Hanati (IRE)**[46] 4330 3-8-11 **63**.................... MeganNicholls(3) 2 34
(Brian Ellison) *s.i.s: racd keenly and sn prom: shkn up and lost pl wl over 2f out: wknd over 1f out (jockey said filly stopped quickly)* **14/1**

1m 0.28s (0.08) **Going Correction** +0.125s/f (Good) **5** Ran SP% **110.1**
WFA 3 from 4yo+ 3lb
Speed ratings (Par 103): **104,103,102,100,88**
CSF £9.41 TOTE £3.20: £1.50, £1.50; EX 8.30 Trifecta £33.10.
Owner Reality Partnerships Xi **Bred** Rabbah Bloodstock Limited **Trained** Great Habton, N Yorks

FOCUS
It was hard to make up ground, with the first two on the pace throughout. They raced up the middle. The winner has been rated in line with his C&D form in June, with the second close to last year's C&D win and the third close to his recent form.

6058 MANSIONBET BEST ODDS GUARANTEED H'CAP — 6f 18y
4:30 (4:37) (Class 6) (0-65,67) 3-Y-O+ £3,234 (£962; £481; £300; £300; £300) **Stalls Centre**

Form RPR

-061 **1** **Ugo Gregory**[7] 5786 3-9-7 **64** 6ex.................... NathanEvans 4 73
(Tim Easterby) *hld up: swtchd rt and hdwy over 1f out: rdn and r.o to ld wl ins fnl f* **15/8**[1]

0420 **2** 1 ¼ **Cardaw Lily (IRE)**[7] 5767 4-8-7 **46** oh1.................... JamesSullivan 3 52
(Ruth Carr) *chsd ldrs: led over 1f out: rdn and hdd wl ins fnl f* **10/1**

1212 **3** 2 ¼ **Ninjago**[19] 5330 9-9-12 **65**....................(v) OisinMurphy 5 64
(Paul Midgley) *hld up: hdwy over 2f out: shkn up over 1f out: styd on same pce ins fnl f* **9/2**[2]

1005 **4** ½ **Cupid's Arrow (IRE)**[7] 5768 5-8-13 **52**.................... JackGarritty 2 50
(Ruth Carr) *sn led: rdn and hdd over 1f out: no ex ins fnl f* **13/2**[3]

0315 **5** 2 **Awa Bomba**[20] 5308 3-9-8 **65**.................... GeorgeDowning 6 56
(Tony Carroll) *mid-div rdn over 1f out: styd on same pce fnl f* **33/1**

2400 **6** nse **Soaring Spirits (IRE)**[10] 5675 9-9-4 **57**....................(b) RobertHavlin 10 49
(Dean Ivory) *s.i.s: rdn over 1f out: edgd lft and styd on ins fnl f: nvr nrr* **22/1**

2006 **7** shd **Prestbury Park (USA)**[38] 4630 4-9-13 **66**.................... DougieCostello 9 57
(Paul Midgley) *s.i.s and n.m.r after s: hdwy over 2f out: wknd ins fnl f* **16/1**

0630 **8** 2 ¼ **I Know How (IRE)**[41] 4523 4-9-8 **61**....................(w) KevinStott 13 46
(Julie Camacho) *edgd lft s: nvr nrr* **12/1**

0050 **9** ½ **Tan**[91] 2709 5-9-7 **67**.................... Pierre-LouisJamin(7) 12 50
(Michael Appleby) *hmpd s: prom: hung lft almost thrght: wknd fnl f* **16/1**

006 **10** 2 **Ocean Temptress**[25] 5144 5-8-9 **48**....................(p) LukeMorris 8 25
(Louise Allan) *chsd ldrs: rdn over 2f out: edgd lft and wknd over 1f out* **25/1**

000 **11** hd **Lacan (IRE)**[40] 4566 8-9-2 **62**.................... JoeBradnam(7) 11 38
(Michael Bell) *s.s: outpcd* **66/1**

004 **12** 1 ¼ **Hollander**[41] 4501 5-9-1 **54**....................(tp) HayleyTurner 7 27
(Alexandra Dunn) *chsd ldrs: rdn over 2f out: wknd over 1f out* **16/1**

0006 **13** 2 ¼ **Trust Me (IRE)**[11] 5629 3-8-12 **55**.................... LewisEdmunds 1 20
(Dean Ivory) *s.i.s: a in rr* **14/1**

1m 14.2s (0.40) **Going Correction** +0.125s/f (Good) **13** Ran SP% **120.0**
WFA 3 from 4yo+ 4lb
Speed ratings (Par 101): **102,100,97,96,94 93,93,90,90,87 87,85,82**
CSF £20.86 CT £78.36 TOTE £2.60: £1.10, £2.60, £1.90; EX 21.10 Trifecta £93.90.
Owner F Gillespie **Bred** Brook Stud Bloodstock Ltd **Trained** Great Habton, N Yorks
■ Stewards' Enquiry : Pierre-Louis Jamin one-day ban; late to start (Aug 31)

FOCUS
A modest, truly run handicap and they raced up the middle. The winner has been rated as building on his previous C&D win.

6059 MANSIONBET APPRENTICE H'CAP — 1m 2f 50y
5:00 (5:02) (Class 6) (0-60,62) 4-Y-O+ £3,234 (£962; £481; £300; £300; £300) **Stalls Low**

Form RPR

4042 **1** **Deinonychus**[8] 5743 8-9-2 **59**....................(p) MarcoGhiani(5) 13 68
(Michael Appleby) *a.p: chsd ldr 5f out: led over 2f out: sn hung lft: styd on wl* **3/1**[1]

3455 **2** 2 ½ **Militry Decoration (IRE)**[34] 4787 4-9-4 **61**.................... ZakWheatley(5) 4 66
(Dr Jon Scargill) *chsd ldrs: ev ch over 2f out: styd on same pce ins fnl f* **17/2**

5260 **3** 1 ½ **Tilsworth Lukey**[10] 5653 6-8-3 **46**.................... KeelanBaker(5) 12 48
(J R Jenkins) *hld up: hdwy over 2f out: swtchd lft over 1f out: styd on same pce ins fnl f* **8/1**

0500 **4** 1 ¾ **Inflexiball**[22] 5248 7-8-7 **45**.................... AledBeech 6 44
(John Mackie) *hld up: racd keenly: pushed along over 3f out: styd on ins fnl f: nvr nrr* **25/1**

1440 **5** nk **Majestic Stone (IRE)**[22] 5248 5-8-11 **49**.................... HarryRussell 9 47
(Julie Camacho) *s.i.s: rn wd over 4f out: styd on fr over 1f out: nt rch ldrs* **10/1**

0325 **6** hd **Movie Star (GER)**[39] 4601 4-9-5 **62**.................... AngusVilliers(5) 2 60
(Amy Murphy) *hld up in tch: rdn over 2f out: no ex fnl f* **11/2**[2]

The Form Book Flat 2019, Raceform Ltd, Newbury, RG14 5SJ

5-20 **7** *1* **Frantical**[18] 5378 7-8-8 **49**................................ ElishaWhittington(3) 10 45
(Tony Carroll) *broke wl enough: sn pushed along and lost pl: styd on fnl f: nt trble ldrs* **20/1**

-050 **8** *1 3/4* **Longville Lilly**[26] 5081 4-8-2 **45**................................ IsobelFrancis(5) 11 38
(Trevor Wall) *chsd ldr to 1/2-way: remained handy: ev ch over 2f out: rdn and edgd lft over 1f out: wknd ins fnl f* **66/1**

2400 **9** *6* **Snooker Jim**[7] 5787 4-9-0 **52**................................(t) TobyEley 8 34
(Steph Hollinshead) *hld up: hdwy over 3f out: wknd over 1f out (jockey said gelding had no more to give)* **9/1**

-006 **10** *2 1/2* **I Think So (IRE)**[13] 5549 4-9-7 **59**................................ LauraCoughlan 1 37
(David Loughnane) *chsd ldrs: lost grnd over 5f out: hdwy over 3f out: rdn and wknd over 1f out* **33/1**

3605 **11** *2 1/2* **Lucy's Law (IRE)**[24] 5178 5-9-1 **58**................................ IzzyClifton(5) 7 31
(Tom Tate) *s.i.s: hdwy over 3f out: wknd 2f out* **13/2**[3]

060 **12** *1/2* **Reshaan (IRE)**[42] 4479 4-8-10 **48**................................(p[1]) SeanKirrane 5 20
(Alexandra Dunn) *sn led: hdd & wknd over 2f out* **20/1**

0/00 **13** *8* **Lady Carduros (IRE)**[14] 5528 5-8-7 **45**................................ Pierre-LouisJamin 3 3
(Michael Appleby) *s.i.s: pushed along over 4f out: wknd over 3f out* **66/1**

2m 12.26s (-1.14) **Going Correction** +0.125s/f (Good) **13** Ran SP% **113.7**
Speed ratings (Par 101): **109,107,105,104,104 104,103,101,97,95 93,92,86**
CSF £24.63 CT £181.59 TOTE £2.40: £1.10, £4.00, £2.70; EX 29.10 Trifecta £173.60.
Owner I R Hatton **Bred** Howdale Bloodstock Ltd **Trained** Oakham, Rutland

FOCUS
Add 12yds. A moderate handicap, restricted to apprentices who, prior to August 10, had not ridden more than 25 winners, and they raced middle to far side in the straight.
T/Plt: £18.30 to a £1 stake. Pool: £61,378.81 - 2,441.58 winning units T/Qpdt: £8.80 to a £1 stake. Pool: £4,800.77 - 400.23 winning units **Colin Roberts**

MOULINS (L-H)
Tuesday, August 13

OFFICIAL GOING: Turf: soft

6060a PRIX DES GATEAUX (CLAIMER) (2YO) (STRAIGHT COURSE (2ND POST)) (TURF) 5f
10:55 2-Y-O **£6,756** (£2,702; £2,027; £1,351; £675)

RPR

1 **Cristal Marvelous (FR)**[31] 4949 2-8-9 0................ MlleCoraliePacaut(4) 2 73
(M Boutin, France) **17/10**[1]

2 *1 1/2* **Coply (FR)**[9] 5713 2-9-2 0................................(p) ClementLecoeuvre 6 70
(Matthieu Palussiere, France) **16/5**[2]

3 *3/4* **Shiso (IRE)**[49] 4228 2-8-13 0................................ MickaelBerto 4 65
(R Rohne, Germany) **54/10**

4 *1* **Panthera Tigris**[49] 4228 2-8-8 0................................ RonanThomas 8 56
(Jo Hughes, France) *chsd ldrs on outer: rdn and nt qckn 1 1/2f out: kpt on same pce fnl f* **29/1**

5 *1 1/2* **La Java Bleue (FR)** 2-7-13 0........................ MlleMarieWaldhauser(9) 3 51
(C Escuder, France) **12/1**

6 *2 1/2* **Khalhinkha (FR)** 2-8-8 0................................(p) MickaelForest 1 42
(Simone Brogi, France) **42/10**[3]

7 *dist* **Dalkelef (FR)**[125] 1709 2-9-2 0................................(b) SebastienMaillot 7
(M Boutin, France) **20/1**

8 *dist* **Epona (ITY)** 2-8-7 0 ow1................................ AlexisPouchin(7) 5
(Andrea Marcialis, France) **13/1**

PARI-MUTUEL (all including 1 euro stake): WIN 2.70; PLACE 1.20, 1.40, 1.60; DF 4.90.
Owner Jean-Jacques Boutin **Bred** E Becq **Trained** France

6061a PRIX DES LEVEES (CLAIMER) (3YO) (STRAIGHT COURSE (2ND POST)) (TURF) 5f
11:25 3-Y-O **£6,306** (£2,522; £1,891; £1,261; £630)

RPR

1 **Imotep (FR)**[18] 3-9-0 0................................ MlleCoraliePacaut(3) 1 68
(M Boutin, France) **41/10**[3]

2 *1/4* **Mortirolo (FR)**[30] 4959 3-9-2 0................................(b) AnthonyCrastus 5 66
(Andrea Marcialis, France) **39/10**[2]

3 *1 1/4* **Apotheose (FR)**[34] 3-8-2 0................................ MlleMarieVelon(6) 8 54
(Andrea Marcialis, France) **29/1**

4 *hd* **She's Still Mine**[14] 5538 3-8-13 0................................(b) ClementLecoeuvre 6 58
(Matthieu Palussiere, France) **23/10**[1]

5 *nk* **Hua Hin (IRE)**[131] 1549 3-8-11 0................................(b[1]) JeromeClaudic 9 55
(E Lyon, France) **16/1**

6 *2* **Velvet Vixen (IRE)**[25] 5165 3-8-13 0................................ RonanThomas 7 50
(Jo Hughes, France) *a cl up: led briefly ins first 1 1/2f: shkn up but nt qckn ins fnl 2f: wknd fnl f* **81/10**

7 *nk* **Hit The Track Jack**[25] 5165 3-8-10 0................ JeremieMonteiro(6) 10 52
(D De Waele, France) **43/10**

8 *3 1/2* **Noble Sky (FR)**[63] 3710 3-8-3 0................................(b) AlexisPouchin(5) 4 31
(H Blume, Germany) **20/1**

9 *3 1/2* **Love To Excel (IRE)**[20] 3-8-7 0................................(b) MlleSarahLeger(9) 3 26
(F Foresi, France) **24/1**

10 *2 1/2* **Stuckinthemoment (IRE)**[114] 3-8-11 0................................(b) WilliamSmit 2 12
(D Chenu, France) **74/1**

58.0s **10** Ran SP% **119.5**
PARI-MUTUEL (all including 1 euro stake): WIN 5.10; PLACE 1.70, 1.90, 4.80; DF 11.60.
Owner M Boutin **Bred** M Boutin **Trained** France

6062a PRIX DE MOULINS (MAIDEN) (3YO) (ROUND COURSE (2ND POST) (TURF) 1m
1:42 3-Y-O **£7,207** (£2,882; £2,162; £1,441; £720)

RPR

1 **Arise (FR)**[23] 3-9-2 0................................(p) RonanThomas 5 68
(M Delzangles, France) **30/100**[1]

2 *1/4* **History Wotton (FR)**[20] 5329 3-8-9 0................................ AnthonyCrastus 6 60
(R Martens, France) **10/1**[3]

3 *1* **Danseur D'Argent (FR)**[84] 2954 3-8-9 0................ MlleCoraliePacaut(4) 1 62
(Jo Hughes, France) *settled in fnl trio on inner: last and shkn up 2f fr home: styd on between horses fr 1 1/2f out: tk 3rd cl home: nt trble front pair* **12/1**

4 *nk* **Ghanim (IRE)**[36] 4732 3-8-13 0................................ SoufianeSaadi 4 61
(H-A Pantall, France) **49/10**[2]

5 *1/4* **Gangster Of Love (FR)**[150] 3-8-13 0................................(b) MickaelForest 2 61
(Carmen Bocskai, Germany) **35/1**

6 *shd* **Rush Hour (IRE)**[243] 3-8-3 0................................ MlleLauraGrosso(6) 8 57
(N Clement, France) **15/1**

7 *9 1/2* **Wodanaz (FR)**[44] 3-8-13 0................................ WilliamSmit 7 39
(D Chenu, France) **22/1**

1m 43.8s **7** Ran SP% **124.0**
PARI-MUTUEL (all including 1 euro stake): WIN 1.30; PLACE 1.10, 1.10, 1.10; DF 5.80.
Owner Zak Bloodstock **Bred** Suc. Z Hakam **Trained** France

6063a PRIX DE LA VILLE D'AVERMES (MAIDEN H'CAP) (3YO FILLIES) (ROUND COURSE (2ND POST) (TURF) 1m
2:17 3-Y-O **£7,207** (£2,882; £2,162; £1,441; £720)

RPR

1 **Scarlett Of Tara (GER)**[77] 3-8-9 **0**................................(b) MickaelBerto 14 69
(Karoly Kerekes, Germany) **107/10**

2 *1* **Menthe Pastille (FR)**[33] 3-9-3 **0**................................ SebastienMaillot 11 75
(N Clement, France) **29/10**[1]

3 *nk* **Neelakurinji (FR)** 3-8-8 **0**................................ AnthonyCrastus 4 65
(F Foresi, France) **9/1**

4 *hd* **Brigantine (FR)** 3-7-12 **0**................................ MlleMarieWaldhauser(6) 7 61
(C Escuder, France) **39/10**[2]

5 *1/4* **Caja Primera (GER)**[33] 3-9-6 **0**................................ SoufianeSaadi 1 76
(H-A Pantall, France) **31/5**[3]

6 *1 1/2* **Arbequina (IRE)**[14] 3-8-6 **0**................................ LudovicBoisseau 10 59
(Mlle Y Vollmer, France) **33/1**

7 *nk* **Salty Kiss (FR)**[220] 3-7-11 **0**................................(p) DelphineSantiago(3) 12 52
(F Foresi, France) **25/1**

8 *1 1/4* **Cinephile (FR)** 3-8-7 **0**................................ MickaelForest 13 56
(Mlle Y Vollmer, France) **45/1**

9 *hd* **Jojo (IRE)**[39] 4621 3-9-2 **0**................................ RonanThomas 5 65
(Jo Hughes, France) *sn led: pressed 3f out: hdd appr fnl 2f: outpcd by ldrs 1 1/2f out: wknd ins fnl f* **13/2**

10 *shd* **Hazienda (IRE)**[19] 3-8-9 **0**................................ MlleCoraliePacaut(4) 2 62
(T Castanheira, France) **89/10**

11 *nk* **Chasanas De Bianca (FR)**[12] 3-8-2 **0**................................ MlleMarieVelon(3) 3 53
(M Cesandri, France) **41/1**

12 *11* **Sonoma (FR)**[337] 3-8-8 **0** ow1................................(b) ClementLecoeuvre 6 31
(W Gulcher, Germany) **15/1**

1m 43.7s **12** Ran SP% **119.5**
PARI-MUTUEL (all including 1 euro stake): WIN 11.70; PLACE 3.10, 1.70, 3.20; DF 14.20.
Owner Karoly Kerekes **Bred** Gestut Hachtsee **Trained** Germany

5512 BEVERLEY (R-H)
Wednesday, August 14

OFFICIAL GOING: Good (7.7) changing to good to soft after race 1 (2.00)
Wind: Moderate across Weather: Heavy cloud and showers

6064 WELCOME TO FLEMINGATE LADIES DAY MAIDEN AUCTION STKS 5f
2:00 (2:00) (Class 5) 2-Y-O **£4,463** (£1,328; £663; £331) **Stalls** Low

Form RPR

032 **1** **Kendred Soul (IRE)**[21] 5294 2-9-0 **71**................................ JackGarritty 8 71
(Jedd O'Keeffe) *trckd ldng pair: hdwy 2f out: rdn to ld ent fnl f: kpt on wl* **4/1**[2]

03 **2** *3/4* **Bertie's Princess (IRE)**[15] 5514 2-8-11 0................................ RowanScott(3) 3 68
(Nigel Tinkler) *chsd ldrs: pushed along and hdwy wl over 1f out: sn rdn and styd on wl fnl f* **8/1**

4 **3** *nk* **Reviette**[23] 5243 2-9-0 0................................ DougieCostello 14 67
(Kevin Ryan) *in tch: hdwy 2f out: swtchd lft to outer and rdn over 1f out: kpt on wl fnl f* **7/1**

4 *nse* **Capla Spirit** 2-9-5 0................................(t[1]) JasonHart 5 72+
(Gay Kelleway) *in tch: pushed along 2f out: hdwy on inner over 1f out: rdn and n.m.r ins fnl f: squeezed through and kpt on wl towards fin* **22/1**

32 **5** *1 1/2* **Second Love (IRE)**[48] 4302 2-9-5 0................................ BenCurtis 4 67
(K R Burke) *wnt rt s: cl up: chal 2f out: sn rdn and ev ch: drvn appr fnl f: kpt on same pce* **7/4**[1]

5455 **6** *3 1/4* **Knightcap**[8] 5789 2-9-0 **64**................................ DuranFentiman 1 50
(Tim Easterby) *slt ld: pushed along 2f out: sn rdn: hdd ent fnl f: sn wknd (vet said filly lost it's left-fore shoe)* **9/2**[3]

7 *1/2* **Bella Figlia** 2-9-0 0................................ CamHardie 2 48
(Ollie Pears) *towards rr: pushed along over 2f out: rdn over 1f out: kpt on towards fin* **33/1**

8 *nk* **Brainchild** 2-9-0 0................................ ShaneGray 11 47
(Keith Dalgleish) *towards rr: rdn along 2f out: n.d* **14/1**

50 **9** *1 1/2* **Imperial Eagle (IRE)**[23] 5243 2-9-0 0................................ PhilDennis 6 42
(Lawrence Mullaney) *chsd ldrs: rdn along 2f out: sn wknd* **33/1**

0 **10** *2 1/2* **Hands Down (IRE)**[42] 4517 2-9-0 0................................ TomEaves 9 33
(Nigel Tinkler) *a towards rr* **80/1**

6 **11** *hd* **Wade's Magic**[15] 5514 2-9-5 0................................ RachelRichardson 7 37
(Tim Easterby) *towards rr: pushed along 1/2-way: rdn 2f out: sn wknd* **22/1**

00 **12** *2 1/2* **Tenbobmillionaire**[11] 5689 2-9-0 0................................ DannyRedmond(5) 13 28
(Tim Easterby) *a towards rr* **50/1**

6 **13** *shd* **Blue Lyte**[29] 5017 2-8-7 0................................ IzzyClifton(7) 15 23
(Nigel Tinkler) *a in rr* **50/1**

0 **14** *45* **Violette Szabo (IRE)**[15] 5514 2-8-9 0................ FayeMcManoman(5) 10
(Nigel Tinkler) *rel to r and lost many l s: a t.o (trainer said filly was reluctant to race)* **100/1**

1m 3.76s (0.86) **Going Correction** +0.075s/f (Good) **14** Ran SP% **125.5**
Speed ratings (Par 94): **96,94,94,94,91 86,85,85,82,78 78,74,74,2**
CSF £35.24 TOTE £5.10: £1.70, £2.60, £2.40; EX 48.80 Trifecta £174.50.
Owner Yorkshire Owners Racing Club 1 **Bred** Kildaragh Stud **Trained** Middleham Moor, N Yorks

FOCUS
The going was initially given as good (Going Stick 7.7) but changed to good to soft after the first race. The inside rail between 7.5f and 1.5f was out 2yds. Add 1yd. An ordinary maiden.

6065 BEVERLEY FLEMINGATE SHOPPING CENTRE EBF MAIDEN STKS (PLUS 10 RACE) — 7f 96y
2:30 (2:31) (Class 4) 2-Y-O — £4,463 (£1,328; £663; £331) Stalls Low

Form — RPR

2 **1** **Flylikeaneagle (IRE)**[18] 5433 2-9-5 0 ... JoeFanning 4 80
(Mark Johnston) *mde all: rdn wl over 1f out: kpt on wl* **2/1**[2]

2 **2** 1 1/2 **Yoshimi (IRE)**[19] 5396 2-9-5 0 ... PaulHanagan 2 76
(Richard Fahey) *trckd ldrs on inner: pushed along and hdwy 2f out: swtchd lft and rdn to chse wnr over 1f out: kpt on* **11/4**[3]

3 2 1/4 **Wise Glory (IRE)** 2-9-5 0 ... AndreaAtzeni 3 71+
(Simon Crisford) *awkward and green s: sn hmpd and hld up towards rr on inner: effrt and nt clr run 2f out: swtchd lft to outer over 1f out: sn rdn: styd on strly fnl f* **13/8**[1]

4 1/2 **Strawman (IRE)** 2-9-5 0 ... BarryMcHugh 5 70
(Adrian Nicholls) *dwlt and in rr: hdwy on inner wl over 1f out: sn rdn: kpt on wl fnl f* **40/1**

5 3 1/4 **Sir Charles Punch** 2-9-5 0 ... GrahamLee 7 62
(James Given) *chsd ldrs: rdn along 2f out: sn edgd rt and wknd* **28/1**

50 **6** 3/4 **Hooroo (IRE)**[18] 5433 2-9-5 0 ... BenCurtis 9 60
(K R Burke) *trckd wnr: cl up 1/2-way: rdn along over 2f out: sn wknd* **10/1**

0 **7** 1 1/4 **Fast Track Flyer (IRE)**[8] 5764 2-9-0 0 ... CamHardie 6 52
(Brian Ellison) *chsd ldng pair: rdn along 3f out: sn wknd* **66/1**

6 **8** 2 1/4 **Noble Bertie (USA)**[15] 5512 2-9-5 0 ... DuranFentiman 1 51
(Tim Easterby) *chsd ldrs: rdn along over 2f out: sn wknd* **33/1**

9 5 **Clifftop Heaven** 2-9-5 0 ... DougieCostello 8 39
(Mark Walford) *dwlt and wnt lft s: a in rr (jockey said gelding ran green)* **28/1**

1m 34.68s (2.08) **Going Correction** +0.075s/f (Good) — 9 Ran SP% 121.0
Speed ratings (Par 96): **91,89,86,86,82 81,80,77,71**
CSF £8.08 TOTE £2.70: £1.10, £1.10, £1.30; EX 7.50 Trifecta £11.10.
Owner Barbara & Alick Richmond Racing **Bred** Corduff Stud **Trained** Middleham Moor, N Yorks

FOCUS
Add 8yds. The winner made all and looks useful.

6066 GUEST AND PHILIPS AT FLEMINGATE CLASSIFIED CLAIMING STKS — 7f 96y
3:00 (3:03) (Class 5) 3-Y-O+ — £4,284 (£1,282; £641; £320; £300; £300) Stalls Low

Form — RPR

4144 **1** **Inner Circle (IRE)**[5] 5903 5-9-10 74 ... (p) BenCurtis 4 66+
(Roger Fell) *trckd ldrs: hdwy over 2f out: chal over 1f out: sn rdn: led appr fnl f: drvn out* **4/6**[1]

0000 **2** 1 1/4 **Hippeia (IRE)**[93] 2682 4-9-1 51 ... (v[1]) DannyRedmond(5) 3 59
(Lawrence Mullaney) *led: pushed along 2f out: sn rdn: drvn and hdd appr fnl f: kpt on u.p* **25/1**

3416 **3** 1 1/4 **Muatadel**[15] 5517 6-9-10 65 ... PaulMulrennan 2 60
(John Wainwright) *prom: effrt on inner over 2f out: sn rdn: drvn over 1f out: kpt on same pce* **10/1**

0206 **4** nk **Shortbackandsides (IRE)**[22] 5282 4-9-2 63 ... RachelRichardson 7 51
(Tim Easterby) *prom: hdwy 3f out: rdn along 2f out: drvn over 1f out: kpt on same pce* **8/1**[3]

2066 **5** 1 3/4 **Fard**[5] 5918 4-8-9 57 ... PaulaMuir(5) 8 45
(Roger Fell) *hld up towards rr: hdwy on outer 3f out: rdn along 2f out: drvn over 1f out: no imp* **11/1**

6 shd **Son Of Beauty (IRE)**[74] 3368 3-9-4 71 ... LewisEdmunds 1 53
(Shaun Harris) *in tch on inner: rdn along wl over 2f out: sn drvn and btn* **28/1**

0044 **7** nk **Dream Walker (FR)**[7] 5820 10-9-6 74 ... (tp) DanielTudhope 9 50
(Brian Ellison) *hld up in tch: hdwy wl over 2f out: rdn along wl over 1f out: sn no imp* **3/1**[2]

0603 **8** nk **Henrietta's Dream**[5] 5918 5-8-3 43 ... LauraCoughlan(7) 5 39
(John Wainwright) *a in rr (vet said mare lost it's right-fore shoe)* **66/1**

1m 34.42s (1.82) **Going Correction** +0.075s/f (Good) — 8 Ran SP% 122.3
WFA 3 from 4yo+ 6lb
Speed ratings (Par 103): **92,90,89,88,86 86,86,86**
CSF £27.62 TOTE £1.50: £1.10, £6.50, £2.60; EX 21.10 Trifecta £130.40.Inner Circle was claimed by Mark Loughnane for £10000; Henrietta's Dream was claimed by Mr R. R. Brisland for £3000
Owner MPR, Ventura Racing 6 & Partner **Bred** Anthony Morris **Trained** Nawton, N Yorks

FOCUS
Add 8yds. With his main market rival disappointing, this proved fairly straightforward for the odds-on favourite.

6067 JILL WILLOWS H'CAP — 1m 1f 207y
3:30 (3:32) (Class 4) (0-85,85) 3-Y-O+ — £7,719 (£2,311; £1,155; £577; £300; £300) Stalls Low

Form — RPR

1042 **1** **Gossip Column (IRE)**[10] 5706 4-10-0 85 ... BenCurtis 7 94
(Ian Williams) *cl up: chal over 2f out: rdn to ld 1 1/2f out: drvn ins fnl f: kpt on strly* **11/2**[3]

1331 **2** 1 1/4 **Archie Perkins (IRE)**[33] 4892 4-9-9 83 ... RowanScott(3) 2 89
(Nigel Tinkler) *trckd ldng pair: hdwy 2f out: effrt over 1f out: rdn and n.m.r ent fnl f: sn drvn and chsd wnr: no imp towards fin* **3/1**[1]

0416 **3** 1/2 **Benadalid**[11] 5694 4-9-9 80 ... JoeFanning 1 85
(Chris Fairhurst) *hld up in tch: effrt 2f out: gd hdwy on inner over 1f out: rdn ent fnl f: ev ch: drvn and kpt on same pce last 100yds* **5/1**[2]

5044 **4** 2 **Thomas Cranmer (USA)**[33] 4892 5-9-2 73 ... NathanEvans 3 74
(Tina Jackson) *trckd ldrs: hdwy over 2f out: rdn along wl over 1f out: drvn and kpt on same pce fnl f* **11/2**[3]

0-15 **5** shd **Stonific (IRE)**[123] 1761 6-9-11 82 ... DavidNolan 6 83
(David O'Meara) *hld up in rr: hdwy over 2f out: rdn along on inner over 1f out: kpt on fnl f* **14/1**

0005 **6** 2 **Top Notch Tonto (IRE)**[11] 5694 9-9-0 74 ... MeganNicholls(3) 5 71
(Brian Ellison) *dwlt: hld up in rr: hdwy on outer over 2f out: rdn to chse ldrs over 1f out: sn drvn and no imp* **8/1**

3041 **7** nk **Regal Mirage (IRE)**[17] 5474 5-9-3 74 ... PaulHanagan 9 70
(Tim Easterby) *trckd ldrs: smooth hdwy over 2f out: rdn over 1f out: sn drvn and btn (jockey said gelding ran flat)* **8/1**

040- **8** 1/2 **Invasion Day (IRE)**[18] 5467 3-9-3 82 ... DanielTudhope 4 78
(David O'Meara) *led: rdn along 2f out: hdd 1 1/2f out: cl up and drvn whn edgd lft ent fnl f: sn wknd* **5/1**[2]

026 **9** 12 **International Guy (IRE)**[42] 4520 3-8-8 73 ... PaddyMathers 8 45
(Richard Fahey) *a towards rr: outpcd and bhd fnl 2f* **40/1**

2m 5.19s (-0.51) **Going Correction** +0.075s/f (Good) — 9 Ran SP% 120.4
WFA 3 from 4yo+ 8lb
Speed ratings (Par 105): **105,104,103,102,101 100,100,99,90**
CSF £23.44 CT £90.42 TOTE £6.20: £1.80, £1.50, £2.70; EX 20.40 Trifecta £127.60.
Owner Dr Marwan Koukash **Bred** Peter Reynolds & Robert Dore **Trained** Portway, Worcs

FOCUS
Add 8yds. It didn't pay to be too far off the pace here. The second and third set the level.

6068 WYKELAND/FLEMINGATE H'CAP — 1m 1f 207y
4:00 (4:01) (Class 5) (0-70,71) 3-Y-O+ — £4,347 (£1,301; £650; £325; £300; £300) Stalls Low

Form — RPR

1114 **1** **Dutch Coed**[6] 5850 7-9-3 62 ... RowanScott(3) 2 69
(Nigel Tinkler) *hld up towards rr: hdwy on wd outside over 2f out: rdn to chse ldrs over 1f out: drvn and edgd rt ins fnl f: led last 50yds* **9/2**[3]

2114 **2** nk **Langholm (IRE)**[11] 5654 3-8-13 63 ... (t) PaulHanagan 4 69
(Declan Carroll) *led: pushed along 2f out: rdn over 1f out: drvn ins fnl f: hdd and no ex last 50yds* **9/4**[1]

1344 **3** 1 **Fantastic Ms Fox**[14] 5566 3-8-13 63 ... TonyHamilton 1 67
(Richard Fahey) *chsd ldng pair: tk clsr order 1/2-way: rdn along 2f out: drvn over 1f out: kpt on same pce u.p fnl f* **7/1**

0004 **4** 4 **Showboating (IRE)**[13] 5593 11-9-9 65 ... (p) DougieCostello 7 61
(John Balding) *hld up in rr: hdwy on inner wl over 1f out: sn rdn and kpt on fnl f: nrst fin* **28/1**

-441 **5** 1/2 **Melgate Majeure**[6] 5851 3-8-8 58 ... JamesSullivan 8 53
(Michael Easterby) *trckd ldr: cl up 1/2-way: pushed along 3f out: rdn 2f out: drvn over 1f out: wknd ins fnl f* **5/2**[2]

4633 **6** 1 1/2 **Placebo Effect (IRE)**[14] 5556 4-9-12 68 ... CamHardie 6 60
(Ollie Pears) *in tch: hdwy 3f out: rdn along 2f out: drvn over 1f out: sn wknd* **6/1**

0220 **7** 1 **Spirit Of Lund (IRE)**[22] 5274 3-9-7 71 ... JamieGormley 5 61
(Iain Jardine) *a in rr* **10/1**

2m 5.69s (-0.01) **Going Correction** +0.075s/f (Good) — 7 Ran SP% 116.8
WFA 3 from 4yo+ 8lb
Speed ratings (Par 103): **103,102,101,98,98 97,96**
CSF £15.66 CT £70.15 TOTE £6.30: £2.80, £1.40; EX 19.70 Trifecta £142.80.
Owner Ms Sara Hattersley **Bred** Sara Hattersley **Trained** Langton, N Yorks

FOCUS
Add 8yds. A modest affair run at a good gallop. The third has been rated to form.

6069 PURE BROADBAND MAIDEN H'CAP FILLIES' STKS — 1m 4f 23y
4:30 (4:30) (Class 5) (0-70,70) 3-Y-O+ £4,463 (£1,328; £663; £331; £300) Stalls Low

Form — RPR

3354 **1** **Vindolanda**[8] 5778 3-9-5 68 ... BenCurtis 6 81
(Charles Hills) *trckd ldrs: hdwy to ld over 7f out: jnd and pushed along 3f out: rdn 2f out: drvn jst over 1f out: edgd lft and kpt on gamely fnl f* **6/4**[2]

503 **2** 1 3/4 **Dubious Affair (IRE)**[18] 5421 3-9-7 70 ... DanielTudhope 1 80
(Sir Michael Stoute) *led: hdd over 7f out: trckd wnr: hdwy and cl up 3f out: sn chal: rdn over 1f out: drvn and ev ch ins fnl f: kpt on same pce last 100yds* **1/1**[1]

0363 **3** 8 **Forbidden Dance**[14] 5549 3-9-6 69 ... CharlieBennett 3 66
(Hughie Morrison) *trckd ldng pair: pushed along 3f out: rdn 2f out: kpt on one pce* **13/2**[3]

-500 **4** nk **Reassurance**[37] 4724 4-9-5 63 ... (p) DannyRedmond(5) 2 59
(Tim Easterby) *chsd ldrs: pushed along 3f out: rdn over 2f out: drvn wl over 1f out: one pce* **14/1**

6600 **5** 12 **Just Heather (IRE)**[18] 5421 5-8-2 48 oh3 ... (p) LauraCoughlan(7) 4 24
(John Wainwright) *a in rr* **66/1**

2m 38.81s (0.01) **Going Correction** +0.075s/f (Good) — 5 Ran SP% 111.5
WFA 3 from 4yo+ 10lb
Speed ratings (Par 100): **103,101,96,96,88**
CSF £3.40 TOTE £2.10: £1.10, £1.20; EX 4.20 Trifecta £7.90.
Owner Mrs Fiona Williams **Bred** Mrs F S Williams **Trained** Lambourn, Berks

FOCUS
Add 8yds. The top two in the market pulled well clear, and the winner was the one who wanted it more.

6070 RACING AGAIN TOMORROW H'CAP — 5f
5:05 (5:06) (Class 5) (0-75,75) 3-Y-O — £4,347 (£1,301; £650; £325; £300; £300) Stalls Low

Form — RPR

0-21 **1** **Four Wheel Drive**[9] 5738 3-9-2 70 6ex ... (p) GrahamLee 1 81
(David Brown) *mde all: rdn clr over 1f out: edgd lft ins fnl f: kpt on* **15/8**[1]

3332 **2** 2 1/4 **Diamonique**[5] 5901 3-9-6 74 ... ShaneGray 8 76
(Keith Dalgleish) *prom: chsd wnr 1/2-way: rdn along wl over 1f out: drvn ent fnl f: kpt on same pce* **11/2**

2343 **3** 1 1/4 **Mr Buttons (IRE)**[7] 5826 3-9-6 74 ... (p) TonyHamilton 4 72
(Linda Stubbs) *chsd wnr: rdn along over 2f out: drvn over 1f out: kpt on same pce fnl f* **5/1**[3]

0-00 **4** nk **Swiss Connection**[47] 4335 3-8-10 64 ... (h[1]) RoystonFfrench 10 60
(Bryan Smart) *racd wd: chsd ldrs: swtchd rt and rdn wl over 1f out: kpt on fnl f* **22/1**

-560 **5** 1 1/2 **Essenza (IRE)**[19] 5392 3-8-5 62 ... SeanDavis(3) 7 53
(Richard Fahey) *dwlt and in rr: hdwy on inner to chse ldrs over 2f out: rdn wl over 1f out: sn drvn and kpt on same pce (jockey said filly missed the break)* **16/1**

4405 **6** 1 1/2 **Autumn Flight (IRE)**[12] 5619 3-8-7 61 ... (p) CamHardie 5 47
(Tim Easterby) *in tch: rdn along 2f out: sn drvn and btn* **8/1**

2214 **7** nk **Montalvan (IRE)**[21] 5308 3-8-12 66 ... (p) BenCurtis 9 51
(Roger Fell) *racd wd: chsd ldrs: rdn wl over 1f out: drvn and wknd appr fnl f* **9/2**[2]

2130 **8** 4 **Timetodock**[11] 5660 3-9-3 71 ... (b) JamesSullivan 6 41
(Tim Easterby) *a in rr* **8/1**

1m 2.46s (-0.44) **Going Correction** +0.075s/f (Good) — 8 Ran SP% 117.5
Speed ratings (Par 100): **106,102,100,99,97 95,94,88**
CSF £12.97 CT £45.43 TOTE £2.70: £1.30, £2.00, £1.80; EX 13.40 Trifecta £48.90.
Owner Bratwa **Bred** A C M Spalding **Trained** Averham Park, Notts

FOCUS
Add 1yd. Few got into this, the winner dominating throughout. The second has been rated to form.
T/Plt: £8.90 to a £1 stake. Pool: £65,325.22 - 5,308.68 winning units T/Qpdt: £3.70 to a £1 stake. Pool: £4,887.49 - 967.87 winning units **Joe Rowntree**

5807 KEMPTON (A.W) (R-H)

Wednesday, August 14

OFFICIAL GOING: Polytrack: standard to slow

Weather: drizzle

6071 RACING TV NURSERY H'CAP (JOCKEY CLUB GRASSROOTS NURSERY QUALIFIER) 7f (P)

5:40 (5:41) (Class 6) (0-60,65) 2-Y-O

£3,105 (£924; £461; £300; £300; £300) **Stalls** Low

Form RPR

054 **1** **Lethal Talent**[50] 4222 2-9-2 **62** TylerSaunders(7) 6 67+
(Jonathan Portman) *wnt lft s: sn in tch: pushed along and hdwy to chse ldrs over 1f out: kpt on: led 75yds out* **5/1**[3]

5002 **2** ½ **Luna Wish**[5] 5886 2-8-6 **45** FrannyNorton 7 49
(George Margarson) *squeezed out slightly sn after s: racd keenly and sn prom on outer: pushed along 2f out: rdn into narrow ld 1f out: hdd 75yds out: one pce* **9/2**[2]

3406 **3** 1 ½ **Bacchalot (IRE)**[13] 5576 2-9-9 **62** OisinMurphy 5 62
(Richard Hannon) *midfield: rdn along over 2f out: kpt on ins fnl f: wnt 3rd nr fin* **9/2**[2]

0000 **4** nk **Port Noir**[13] 5576 2-8-8 **47** (t[1]) JohnFahy 14 46
(Grace Harris) *prom: led over 5f out: rdn 2f out: hdd 1f out: no ex ins fnl f: lost 3rd nr fin* **50/1**

006 **5** 1 **Timon (IRE)**[18] 5447 2-8-11 **55** ScottMcCullagh(5) 11 52
(Mick Channon) *led: hdd over 5f out: trckd ldrs: rdn over 2f out: no ex ins fnl f* **20/1**

565 **6** nk **Out Of Here (IRE)**[53] 4125 2-9-7 **60** (p[1]) SeanLevey 8 56+
(Kevin Ryan) *dwlt sltly: hld up: rdn on outer over 2f out: kpt on ins fnl f: nvr threatened ldrs* **7/2**[1]

050 **7** ¾ **Broughtons Compass**[32] 4925 2-8-10 **49** JoeyHaynes 1 43
(Mark Hoad) *midfield: rdn over 2f out: kpt on same pce ins fnl f: nvr threatened ldrs* **25/1**

5453 **8** ¾ **Santorini Sal**[9] 5745 2-8-12 **54** MitchGodwin(3) 12 46
(John Bridger) *trckd ldrs: rdn 2f out: wknd ins fnl f* **16/1**

0300 **9** 1 ¾ **Luscifer**[13] 5576 2-8-11 **50** ShaneKelly 10 37
(Richard Hughes) *dwlt: hld up: pushed along over 2f out: rdn over 1f out: no prog* **25/1**

000 **10** 1 **Premium Bond**[21] 5314 2-8-12 **51** PJMcDonald 3 36
(Richard Hannon) *in tch: rdn over 2f out: wknd ins fnl f* **7/1**

066 **11** 4 **Now I'm A Believer**[13] 5577 2-8-6 **45** HollieDoyle 4 19
(Mick Channon) *hld up: rdn along over 3f out: a towards rr (jockey said filly was never travelling)* **10/1**

064 **12** 8 **Boy George**[20] 5339 2-9-7 **60** LiamKeniry 13 14
(Dominic Ffrench Davis) *hld up: rdn along over 3f out: wknd and bhd over 1f out* **14/1**

1m 27.12s (1.12) **Going Correction** -0.025s/f (Stan) **12 Ran SP% 123.8**
Speed ratings (Par 92): **92,91,89,89,88 87,87,86,84,83 78,69**
CSF £27.90 CT £112.81 TOTE £5.00: £2.00, £1.70, £1.80; EX 24.70 Trifecta £125.50.
Owner Whitcoombe Park Racing **Bred** Bickmarsh Stud **Trained** Upper Lambourn, Berks
■ Stewards' Enquiry : Mitch Godwin three-day ban; careless riding (Aug 28-30)

FOCUS
The going was standard to slow. They went a fair pace in this nursery and two of the market leaders filled the first two places.

6072 JOE O'DONOVAN MEMORIAL/BRITISH STALLION STUDS EBF FILLIES' NOVICE STKS (PLUS 10 RACE) 7f (P)

6:10 (6:11) (Class 5) 2-Y-O **£3,881** (£1,155; £577; £288) **Stalls** Low

Form RPR

5 **1** **Kalsara**[20] 5342 2-9-0 0 OisinMurphy 5 75
(Andrew Balding) *trckd ldr: racd quite keenly: rdn along to chal over 1f out: drvn into narrow ld 1f out: hld on gamely in sustained duel w 2nd* **11/4**[2]

4 **2** shd **African Swift (USA)**[13] 5588 2-9-0 0 FrannyNorton 7 75
(Mark Johnston) *led: rdn along and pressed over 1f out: drvn and hdd 1f out: kpt on but a jst hld in sustained duel w wnr* **1/1**[1]

3 1 ½ **Penpal (IRE)** 2-9-0 0 DanielMuscutt 6 71+
(James Fanshawe) *dwlt sltly: hld up in tch: smooth hdwy 2f out: chsd ldrs over 1f out: kpt on pushed out* **16/1**

0 **4** 4 **Golden Cygnet**[26] 5132 2-9-0 0 RobHornby 3 61
(Ralph Beckett) *midfield: pushed along over 2f out: rdn over 1f out: sn outpcd* **20/1**

0 **5** ½ **Sweet Serenade**[19] 5387 2-9-0 0 PJMcDonald 2 59
(James Tate) *dwlt sltly: sn trckd ldr: rdn 2f out: wknd fnl f* **7/2**[3]

50 **6** 1 ¼ **Pink Tulip**[34] 4840 2-8-9 0 DylanHogan(5) 4 56
(David Simcock) *hld up: pushed along over 2f out: nvr threatened* **40/1**

06 **7** 4 ½ **Little Lulu (IRE)**[49] 4245 2-9-0 0 HollieDoyle 1 44
(Archie Watson) *midfield: pushed along over 2f out: rdn over 1f out: sn wknd* **33/1**

1m 26.88s (0.88) **Going Correction** -0.025s/f (Stan) **7 Ran SP% 114.9**
Speed ratings (Par 91): **94,93,92,87,87 85,80**
CSF £5.89 TOTE £3.70: £2.00, £1.10; EX 6.70 Trifecta £28.30.
Owner James A Oldham **Bred** James A Oldham **Trained** Kingsclere, Hants

FOCUS
There was an exciting finish between the two market leaders in this novice and the second-favourite came out on top.

6073 SUSANNAH & RICH RICCI YOTES COURT VINEYARD NURSERY H'CAP (JC GRASSROOTS NURSERY QUALIFIER) 6f (P)

6:40 (6:40) (Class 4) (0-85,83) 2-Y-O

£5,175 (£1,540; £769; £384; £300; £300) **Stalls** Low

Form RPR

3331 **1** **Endowed**[16] 5501 2-9-5 **81** OisinMurphy 6 93+
(Richard Hannon) *led narrowly: hdd over 3f out: led again 2f out: pushed along and hung rt over 1f out: continued to hang rt but rdn and kpt on to draw clr ins fnl f (jockey said gelding hung right-handed under pressure)* **1/1**[1]

214 **2** 3 ½ **One Hart (IRE)**[25] 5172 2-9-7 **83** FrannyNorton 3 86
(Mark Johnston) *pressed ldr: led over 3f out: hdd 2f out: rdn along and outpcd in 2nd whn hmpd on rail 1f out: kpt on ins fnl f* **5/2**[2]

3231 **3** 4 **Hubert (IRE)**[13] 5577 2-9-3 **79** LukeMorris 4 68
(Sylvester Kirk) *chsd ldrs: rdn over 2f out: outpcd over 1f out: plugged on in 3rd fnl f* **6/1**[3]

100 **4** 1 ¾ **Diligent Deb (IRE)**[18] 5411 2-9-5 **81** PJMcDonald 2 65
(William Muir) *hld up: rdn over 2f out: nvr threatened* **7/1**

360 **5** ½ **Port Winston (IRE)**[28] 5052 2-8-13 **75** TomMarquand 1 57
(Alan King) *chsd ldrs: tk str hold: rdn and outpcd 2f out: wknd fnl f (jockey said gelding ran too free)* **16/1**

535 **6** 12 **Speed Dating (FR)**[11] 5655 2-8-0 **69** AledBeech(7) 5 15
(Derek Shaw) *dwlt sltly: hld up: rdn over 2f out: wknd and bhd* **22/1**

1m 13.16s (0.06) **Going Correction** -0.025s/f (Stan) **6 Ran SP% 115.6**
Speed ratings (Par 96): **98,93,88,85,85 69**
CSF £3.90 TOTE £1.80: £1.10, £1.70; EX 3.90 Trifecta £8.20.
Owner Ben CM Wong **Bred** Aislabie Bloodstock Ltd **Trained** East Everleigh, Wilts

FOCUS
The favourite stormed clear to compete a double in this nursery.

6074 BREEDERS BACKING RACING EBF FILLIES' NOVICE STKS 7f (P)

7:10 (7:12) (Class 5) 3-Y-O+ **£4,916** (£1,463; £731; £365) **Stalls** Low

Form RPR

-01 **1** **Farzeen**[14] 5554 3-9-4 0 JackMitchell 1 91+
(Roger Varian) *mde all: pushed along and qcknd clr over 1f out: eased towards fin: impressive* **8/15**[1]

2 6 **New Angel** 3-8-11 0 RobertHavlin 9 64+
(John Gosden) *dwlt: sn midfield on outer: pushed along over 2f out: kpt on to go 2nd 50yds out: bttr for r* **5/1**[2]

62 **3** ½ **Midas Girl (FR)**[16] 5494 3-8-11 0 LiamKeniry 7 63
(Ed Walker) *trckd ldrs: rdn along over 2f out: kpt on same pce* **14/1**

0- **4** nk **Havana Jane**[243] 9531 4-9-3 0 OisinMurphy 4 64
(Andrew Balding) *dwlt: sn trckd ldrs racing keenly: rdn and outpcd in 2nd over 1f out: no ex ins fnl f and lost 2 pls fnl 50yds (jockey said filly ran too free)* **10/1**

4 **5** 7 **Harbour City (USA)**[22] 5269 3-8-11 0 PJMcDonald 6 43
(James Tate) *trckd ldrs: rdn over 2f out: wknd over 1f out* **11/2**[3]

6 hd **Petit Bay** 3-8-11 0 DavidProbert 5 43
(Sir Mark Todd) *midfield: rdn along over 2f out: sn outpcd and btn* **33/1**

7 shd **Serenading** 3-8-11 0 GeorgeWood 11 42+
(James Fanshawe) *hld up: pushed along over 2f out: kpt on ins fnl f* **22/1**

00 **8** 2 **Pearl Jam**[48] 4305 3-8-11 0 TomMarquand 13 37
(James Fanshawe) *hld up in rr: pushed along 3f out: sme late hdwy* **33/1**

06 **9** 1 ¾ **Tilsworth Diamond**[18] 5428 4-9-3 0 DanielMuscutt 2 34
(Mike Murphy) *midfield on inner: rdn over 2f out: wknd over 1f out* **66/1**

00 **10** nk **Be Together**[28] 5057 3-8-11 0 KieranShoemark 10 32
(Charles Hills) *hld up in midfield: pushed along over 2f out: nvr threatened* **66/1**

6 **11** 4 ½ **Ewell Spring**[74] 3353 3-8-11 0 ShaneKelly 8 19
(Brett Johnson) *hld up in midfield: short of room and snatched up on bnd over 4f out: rdn and hung rt over 1f out: wknd ins fnl f* **100/1**

0 **12** 6 **Keep On Laughing (IRE)**[30] 5004 4-8-12 0 (h) DarraghKeenan(5) 3 5
(John Butler) *pressed ldr: rdn over 2f out: wknd over 1f out* **66/1**

6 **13** 2 ¼ **The Pastoral Bear**[45] 4423 3-8-11 0 LukeMorris 12
(Mark Pattinson) *s.i.s: a towards rr* **66/1**

14 2 ½ **Good Ole Winnie** 3-8-11 0 CharlesBishop 14
(Ali Stronge) *hld up in midfield: rdn over 2f out: sn wknd* **66/1**

1m 25.93s (-0.07) **Going Correction** -0.025s/f (Stan)
WFA 3 from 4yo 6lb **14 Ran SP% 131.7**
Speed ratings (Par 100): **99,92,91,91,83 83,82,80,78,78 73,66,63,60**
CSF £3.93 TOTE £1.40: £1.02, £1.90, £2.60; EX 4.30 Trifecta £30.10.
Owner Helena Springfield Ltd **Bred** Meon Valley Stud **Trained** Newmarket, Suffolk

FOCUS
The hot favourite looked in a different league to her rivals in this novice event. The level is a bit fluid, but it's been rated around the third to her previous two runs.

6075 CELTIC CONTRACTORS H'CAP (LONDON MILE SERIES QUALIFIER) 1m (P)

7:40 (7:42) (Class 5) (0-70,76) 3-Y-O

£3,752 (£1,116; £557; £300; £300; £300) **Stalls** Low

Form RPR

326 **1** **Image Of The Moon**[14] 5561 3-9-1 **69** (p) CierenFallon(5) 8 78
(Shaun Keightley) *prom: drvn into ld over 2f out: rdn in narrow ld over 1f out: strly pressed either side ins fnl f: r.o wl* **14/1**

5411 **2** ½ **Dargel (IRE)**[9] 5731 3-9-13 **76** 6ex AdamKirby 4 84
(Clive Cox) *hld up: drvn and gd hdwy on outer over 1f out: rdn in 3rd ent fnl f: r.o wl into 2nd nr fin but nvr getting to wnr* **10/11**[1]

2461 **3** nk **Universal Effect**[4] 5941 3-9-9 **72** 6ex (h) ShaneKelly 1 79
(David Lanigan) *t.k.h: chsd ldrs: drvn to chal on inner 2f out: rdn and ev ch in cl 2nd ent fnl f: no ex and lost 2nd nr fin* **5/2**[2]

2033 **4** 3 ¼ **Kings Royal Hussar (FR)**[20] 5350 3-9-5 **68** TomMarquand 6 68
(Alan King) *hld up in rr: pushed along over 2f out: drvn and hdwy 1f out: one pce fnl f* **11/1**

4413 **5** 1 ¾ **Rambaldi (IRE)**[41] 4562 3-9-2 **72** (t) StefanoCherchi(7) 7 68
(Marco Botti) *mid-div on outer: tk clsr order 3f out: rdn and lost pl over 1f out: no ex* **10/1**[3]

4166 **6** 1 **Comeonfeeltheforce (IRE)**[13] 5573 3-9-4 **67** (t) PJMcDonald 2 60
(Lee Carter) *mid-div: drvn 3f out: lost pl over 2f out: sn rdn and wknd* **14/1**

560 **7** 1 **Mystical Jadeite**[16] 5497 3-8-4 **53** LukeMorris 5 44
(Grace Harris) *slowly away: hld up: drvn over 2f out: effrt on inner over 1f out: wknd fnl f* **66/1**

65-6 **8** 7 **Lolita Pulido (IRE)**[20] 5350 3-9-5 **68** CharlesBishop 3 43
(Eve Johnson Houghton) *led: drvn and hdd over 2f out: sn rdn and wknd* **25/1**

1m 41.05s (1.25) **Going Correction** -0.025s/f (Stan) **8 Ran SP% 117.1**
Speed ratings (Par 100): **92,91,91,87,86 85,84,77**
CSF £28.04 CT £47.41 TOTE £12.00: £2.30, £1.10, £1.20; EX 21.00 Trifecta £99.80.
Owner Simon Lockyer & Tim Clarke **Bred** Natton House Thoroughbreds **Trained** Newmarket, Suffolk

FOCUS
They went a steady pace and the winner was always prominent. The winner has been rated in line with her earlier AW form, with the second similar to his previous C&D win.

6076 BYRNE GROUP H'CAP 7f (P)

8:10 (8:10) (Class 4) (0-85,87) 3-Y-O+

£6,469 (£1,925; £962; £481; £300; £300) **Stalls** Low

Form RPR

2103 **1** **Jaleel**[11] 5685 3-9-3 **83** (b) JackMitchell 2 87+
(Roger Varian) *slowly away: in rr: pushed along and plenty to do 2f out: rdn and hdwy on outer over 1f out: str run fnl f: led last stride* **10/1**

0610 **2** *nse* **Delilah Park**[22] 5283 5-9-2 **76** .... GeorgeWood 5 82
(Chris Wall) *hld up: pushed along 2f out: hdwy over 1f out: drvn to chal fnl f: sn rdn: r.o to ld fnl 20yds: hdd last stride* **20/1**

53-P **3** *nk* **Brigham Young**[33] 4879 4-9-3 **77** .... LiamKeniry 7 82
(Ed Walker) *trckd ldrs: pushed into ld 2f out: led and rdn 1f out: ld sn reduced ins fnl f: hdd fnl 20yds: no ex* **25/1**

3061 **4** *shd* **Attainment**[22] 5267 3-9-3 **83** .... PJMcDonald 4 86
(James Tate) *led tl hdd after 1f: trckd ldrs: pushed along 2f out: rdn on inner over 1f out: r.o wl fnl f: nt quite get to first three* **5/1**[3]

26 **5** *1 1/4* **Buckingham (IRE)**[21] 5319 3-9-3 **83** .... CharlesBishop 3 83
(Eve Johnson Houghton) *t.k.h: hld up: pushed along 2f out: drvn over 1f out: kpt on wl fnl f: nvr nrr (vet said gelding lost it's right fore shoe)* **16/1**

2231 **6** *3/4* **Franz Kafka (IRE)**[78] 3184 3-9-7 **87** .... RobertHavlin 8 85
(John Gosden) *prom: led after 1f: drvn and hdd 2f out: rdn over 1f out: wknd fnl f* **4/1**[2]

-613 **7** *shd* **Rectory Road**[18] 5412 3-9-7 **87** .... OisinMurphy 6 84
(Andrew Balding) *t.k.h: mid-div on outer: trckd ldrs 3f out: rdn and effrt 1 1/2f out: wknd fnl f* **5/4**[1]

514 **8** *1/2* **Tipperary Jack (USA)**[34] 4827 3-9-3 **83** .... KierenFox 1 83+
(John Best) *hld up: drvn on inner 2f out: sn rdn: nt clr run over 1f out: no ex fnl f* **13/2**

1m 25.08s (-0.92) **Going Correction** -0.025s/f (Stan) 8 Ran SP% **118.0**
WFA 3 from 4yo+ 6lb
Speed ratings (Par 105): **104,103,103,103,102 101,101,100**
CSF £184.57 CT £4808.09 TOTE £10.40: £2.60, £6.60, £6.70; EX 283.00 Trifecta £1225.90.
Owner Abdullatif M Al-Abdulrazzaq **Bred** Jane Allison **Trained** Newmarket, Suffolk
■ Stewards' Enquiry : P J McDonald three-day ban; careless riding (Aug 28-30)

FOCUS
This decent handicap was a race of changing fortunes and there was a thrilling finish. The third has been rated to his 3yo form.

6077 CELTIC CONTRACTS H'CAP 1m 3f 219y(P)
8:40 (8:43) (Class 6) (0-60,60) 3-Y-O+
£3,105 (£924; £461; £300; £300; £300) Stalls Low

Form RPR

0433 **1** **Lauberhorn Rocket (GER)**[62] 3769 4-9-5 **51** .... DavidProbert 12 60
(Tim Vaughan) *hld up: drvn and hdwy on outer 2f out: sn rdn: str run ent fnl f: r.o wl u.p to ld last three strides* **8/1**

1353 **2** *1/2* **Croeso Cymraeg**[22] 5271 5-10-0 **60** .... (h) RaulDaSilva 2 68
(James Evans) *hld up: circled field to go prom 3f out: pushed into ld ent fnl 2f: sn rdn: 2 l ld 1f out: ld sn reduced by wnr: hdd and no ex last three strides* **3/1**[2]

0343 **3** *3* **Hooflepuff (IRE)**[28] 5054 3-8-12 **54** .... GeorgeWood 3 58
(James Fanshawe) *mid-div: pushed along 3f out: drvn and hdwy over 1f out: sn rdn: r.o fnl f: tk 3rd last 25yds* **9/4**[1]

-520 **4** *1 1/4* **Falls Creek (USA)**[181] 721 4-9-0 **46** .... (v[1]) OisinMurphy 1 47
(Andrew Balding) *trckd ldrs: pushed along 2f out: rdn in 2nd over 1f out: no ex and lost two pls fnl f* **14/1**

2623 **5** *3 1/2* **Givepeaceachance**[22] 5285 4-9-9 **55** .... CharlesBishop 5 51
(Denis Coakley) *mid-div: drvn 2f out: rdn over 1f out: one pce fnl f* **7/1**

50-0 **6** *nse* **Highway Bess**[91] 2732 4-9-1 **52** .... WilliamCarver(5) 9 48
(Patrick Chamings) *slowly away: bhd: rdn and effrt 2f out: one pce fnl f* **100/1**

-632 **7** *7* **Aria Rose**[16] 5499 4-9-10 **56** .... LukeMorris 14 41
(Harry Whittington) *chsd ldrs: drvn in 3rd 3f out: rdn and wknd 2f out* **6/1**[3]

0131 **8** *hd* **Kaylen's Mischief**[19] 5378 6-9-3 **54** .... ScottMcCullagh(5) 13 38
(D J Jeffreys) *led: drvn 3f out: rdn over 2f out: sn hdd & wknd* **9/1**

6500 **9** *6* **Presence Process**[134] 1498 5-9-10 **59** .... PaddyBradley(3) 11 34
(Pat Phelan) *hld up: pushed along on inner 2f out: sn rdn and wknd* **50/1**

034- **10** *7* **Malt Teaser (FR)**[442] 3200 5-9-9 **55** .... (t[1]) KierenFox 6 18
(John Best) *chsd ldr: drvn and wknd over 2f out* **16/1**

005 **11** *2 1/2* **Famous Dynasty (IRE)**[35] 4795 5-9-10 **56** .... DanielMuscutt 7 15
(Michael Blanshard) *mid-div: drvn 3f out: rdn 2f out: sn wknd* **33/1**

55-0 **12** *4 1/2* **Rahmah (IRE)**[92] 2720 7-9-11 **57** .... TrevorWhelan 4 9
(Geoffrey Deacon) *slowly away: a bhd (jockey said gelding was slowly away)* **66/1**

000- **13** *5* **Jalingo (IRE)**[262] 5016 8-9-9 **55** .... (tp w) TomMarquand 8
(Ali Stronge) *hld up: rdn and wknd over 3f out* **40/1**

-540 **14** *40* **Ace Cheetah (USA)**[21] 5311 5-10-0 **60** .... DannyBrock 10
(J R Jenkins) *mid-div on outer: drvn and lost pl 4f out: dropped to last 3f out: sn lost tch* **50/1**

2m 33.26s (-1.24) **Going Correction** -0.025s/f (Stan) 14 Ran SP% **128.0**
WFA 3 from 4yo+ 10lb
Speed ratings (Par 101): **103,102,100,99,97 97,92,92,88,84 82,79,76,49**
CSF £33.61 CT £76.68 TOTE £9.60: £2.70, £1.60, £1.40; EX 44.70 Trifecta £193.30.
Owner JRFB Ltd **Bred** Stiftung Gestut Fahrhof **Trained** Aberthin, Vale of Glamorgan

FOCUS
The first two came from some way back in this middle-distance handicap and finished clear of the rest.
T/Plt: £66.90 to a £1 stake. Pool: £60,076.38 - 654.59 winning units. T/Qpdt: £31.80 to a £1 stake. Pool: £6,176.42 - 143.72 winning units. **Andrew Sheret & Keith McHugh**

5446 SALISBURY (R-H)
Wednesday, August 14

OFFICIAL GOING: Good to soft changing to soft after race 2 (2.20)
Wind: Light across Weather: Raining

6078 BRITISH EBF MOLSON COORS NOVICE STKS (PLUS 10 RACE) (DIV I) 6f
1:50 (1:51) (Class 4) 2-Y-O
£4,851 (£1,443; £721; £360) Stalls Low

Form RPR

0 **1** **Ascension**[26] 5131 2-9-5 **0** .... JackMitchell 1 85+
(Roger Varian) *trckd ldrs: led 1f out: shkn up and r.o wl* **13/8**[1]

00 **2** *3 1/2* **Cheat (IRE)**[15] 5523 2-9-5 **0** .... SeanLevey 5 74
(Richard Hannon) *chsd ldr tl led over 1f out: sn rdn and hdd: no ex wl ins fnl f* **8/1**

3 *1 1/2* **Katniss Everdeen (IRE)** 2-9-0 **0** .... HarryBentley 2 65
(Richard Spencer) *mid-div: swtchd lft and hdwy over 2f out: shkn up and hung rt ins fnl f: styd on same pce* **16/1**

4 *2 1/4* **Aweemaweh (IRE)** 2-9-5 **0** .... CharlesBishop 3 63
(Mick Channon) *hld up in tch: shkn up over 2f out: styd on same pce fr over 1f out* **5/1**[3]

56 **5** *nk* **Good Job Power (IRE)**[15] 5523 2-9-5 **0** .... OisinMurphy 8 62
(Richard Hannon) *chsd ldrs: rdn over 1f out: wknd ins fnl f* **5/2**[2]

6 *3 1/2* **Roman Melody** 2-9-5 **0** .... GeraldMosse 9 51+
(David Elsworth) *s.s: rn green in rr: r.o ins fnl f: nvr nrr (jockey said colt was slowly away)* **14/1**

0 **7** *shd* **Woodsmokehill**[23] 5250 2-9-0 **0** .... RobertHavlin 6 46
(Rod Millman) *led over 4f: wknd ins fnl f* **100/1**

8 *1* **Ivadream** 2-9-5 **0** .... AdamMcNamara 7 48
(Roger Charlton) *s.i.s: sn rcvrd into mid-div: rdn over 2f out: wknd over 1f out* **16/1**

6 **9** *8* **Wrath Of Hector**[20] 5339 2-9-5 **0** .... CallumShepherd 4 24
(Tony Newcombe) *sn pushed along in rr: wknd over 2f out* **100/1**

10 *7* **Lady Florence (IRE)** 2-9-0 **0** .... LiamKeniry 12
(Malcolm Saunders) *dwlt and wnt lft s: a in rr: wknd over 2f out (jockey said filly was slowly away)* **66/1**

0 **11** *hd* **Itoldyoutobackit (IRE)**[46] 4373 2-9-5 **0** .... AdamKirby 11
(Jonjo O'Neill) *towards rr on outer: wknd over 2f out* **66/1**

1m 17.18s (2.68) **Going Correction** +0.45s/f (Yiel) 11 Ran SP% **117.8**
Speed ratings (Par 96): **100,95,93,90,89 85,85,83,73,63 63**
CSF £15.97 TOTE £2.40: £1.10, £2.00, £4.10; EX 13.60 Trifecta £129.90.
Owner Highclere T'Bred Racing - Benedict Allen **Bred** Highclere Stud & Partners **Trained** Newmarket, Suffolk

FOCUS
There had been 8mm of rain since 7am but clerk of the course Jeremy Martin said: "It's taken it very well. The worst of the rain was behind us before racing." It was evident the rain had got into the ground in the opener and the winning time indicated it rode more like soft all over. It paid to be handy in this modest juvenile novice event.

6079 BRITISH EBF MOLSON COORS NOVICE STKS (PLUS 10 RACE) (DIV II) 6f
2:20 (2:24) (Class 4) 2-Y-O
£4,851 (£1,443; £721; £360) Stalls Low

Form RPR

4 **1** **Impressor (IRE)**[15] 5523 2-9-5 **0** .... MartinDwyer 3 92+
(Marcus Tregoning) *w ldrs: led over 4f out: brought field over to stands' side over 2f out: shkn up over 1f out: qcknd clr ins fnl f: easily* **13/8**[2]

2 **2** *3 1/2* **Stoweman**[18] 5447 2-9-5 **0** .... AdamKirby 10 79
(Clive Cox) *trckd ldrs: shkn up and hung rt over 3f out: rdn to chse wnr ins fnl f: styd on same pce* **6/4**[1]

2 **3** *4* **Harlequin**[55] 4030 2-9-5 **0** .... DanielMuscutt 2 67
(Luke Dace) *prom: chsd wnr over 3f out: rdn over 1f out: wknd ins fnl f (jockey said colt hung right inside the final 2f)* **16/1**

4 *1 1/2* **North Point** 2-9-5 **0** .... GeraldMosse 7 62
(David Elsworth) *s.i.s: hld up: pushed along over 3f out: styd on ins fnl f: nt trble ldrs* **25/1**

0 **5** *1* **Ruby Power (IRE)**[13] 5588 2-9-0 **0** .... OisinMurphy 11 54
(Richard Hannon) *mid-div: effrt and nt clr run over 1f out: nt trble ldrs* **20/1**

2 **6** *1 1/2* **Bright Valentine**[14] 5550 2-9-0 **0** .... RobHornby 5 50
(Richard Spencer) *chsd ldrs: pushed along 1/2-way: rdn over 1f out: wknd ins fnl f* **7/1**[3]

55 **7** *nk* **Parker's Boy**[30] 4999 2-9-5 **0** .... TrevorWhelan 8 54
(Brian Barr) *led: hdd over 4f out: chsd ldrs: rdn over 1f out: wknd fnl f* **150/1**

8 *2* **Malmesbury Abbey (FR)** 2-9-5 **0** .... LiamKeniry 6 48
(Ed Walker) *s.i.s: hdwy over 2f out: wknd ins fnl f* **16/1**

9 *1* **Alfies Watch** 2-9-5 **0** .... LukeMorris 1 45
(John O'Shea) *uns rdr bhd stalls: s.i.s: pushed along in rr: hdwy on outer over 1f out: wknd fnl f* **100/1**

10 *2 1/4* **Lisbeth Salander (IRE)** 2-9-0 **0** .... HarryBentley 9 33
(Richard Spencer) *s.i.s: sn pushed along in rr: wknd 2f out* **33/1**

0 **11** *7* **Bright Red (IRE)**[16] 5500 2-9-5 **0** .... TomMarquand 4 17
(Richard Hannon) *mid-div: hung rt fr over 4f out: hdwy over 2f out: wknd over 1f out (jockey said colt hung right throughout)* **33/1**

1m 17.38s (2.88) **Going Correction** +0.45s/f (Yiel) 11 Ran SP% **118.5**
Speed ratings (Par 96): **98,93,88,86,84 82,82,79,78,75 65**
CSF £4.14 TOTE £2.80: £1.30, £1.10, £3.40; EX 5.50 Trifecta £28.80.
Owner R C C Villers **Bred** Cottage Bloodstock **Trained** Whitsbury, Hants

FOCUS
They came stands' side in this second division of the 2yo novice event. With the rain continuing to fall the winning time was 0.20sec slower.

6080 S H JONES WINES H'CAP 5f
2:50 (2:53) (Class 4) (0-80,81) 3-Y-O+
£5,692 (£1,694; £846; £423; £300; £300) Stalls Low

Form RPR

3353 **1** **Maid Of Spirit (IRE)**[11] 5659 4-9-2 **70** .... AdamKirby 4 81
(Clive Cox) *mde all: racd alone far side fr over 3f out: rdn and edgd lft over 1f out: styd on* **7/2**[3]

4211 **2** *2 1/4* **Texting**[19] 5372 3-9-7 **78** .... GeraldMosse 11 80+
(Mohamed Moubarak) *s.i.s: c towards stands' side over 3f out: hdwy 1/2-way: rdn to ld that gp and edgd rt ins fnl f: nt rch wnr* **5/2**[1]

0302 **3** *nk* **Gnaad (IRE)**[13] 5595 5-9-2 **75** .... DarraghKeenan(5) 5 77
(Alan Bailey) *half-rrd s: s.i.s: hdwy and racd alone in centre fr over 3f out: rdn over 1f out: styd on* **6/1**

065 **4** *2 1/4* **Just Glamorous (IRE)**[12] 5606 6-9-10 **81** .... CameronNoble(3) 10 75
(Grace Harris) *chsd ldrs: c towards stands' side over 3f out: led that gp 1/2-way: rdn over 1f out: hdd and no ex ins fnl f* **8/1**

2415 **5** *nk* **Rewaayat**[14] 5551 4-9-4 **72** .... JimCrowley 9 65
(Charles Hills) *chsd ldrs: c towards stands; side and led that gp over 3f out: hdd 1/2-way: rdn over 1f out: no ex ins fnl f* **10/3**[2]

3003 **6** *1 1/2* **Joegogo (IRE)**[4] 5959 4-9-8 **76** .... OisinMurphy 7 63
(David Evans) *chsd ldrs: c towards stands' side over 3f out: rdn over 1f out: wknd ins fnl f* **8/1**

1305 **7** *3/4* **Waseem Faris (IRE)**[21] 5318 10-9-12 **80** .... PatDobbs 3 65
(Ken Cunningham-Brown) *rrd s: outpcd (jockey said gelding reared as the stalls opened)* **25/1**

1m 2.3s (1.80) **Going Correction** +0.45s/f (Yiel) 7 Ran SP% **114.2**
WFA 3 from 4yo+ 3lb
Speed ratings (Par 105): **103,99,98,95,94 92,91**
CSF £12.68 CT £49.31 TOTE £3.90: £1.80, £2.50; EX 14.40 Trifecta £53.80.
Owner Con Harrington **Bred** C F Harrington **Trained** Lambourn, Berks

The Form Book Flat 2019, Raceform Ltd, Newbury, RG14 5SJ

FOCUS
The going was officially downgraded to soft all over after the second race. There was a split opinion about where the best ground was in this sprint handicap. The level is a bit fluid.

6081 BRUNTON PUBLICATIONS PEMBROKE H'CAP — 1m
3:20 (3:23) (Class 4) (0-85,85) 3-Y-O

£5,692 (£1,694; £846; £423; £300; £300) Stalls Low

Form — RPR

3611 **1** **Alfred Boucher**[26] 5140 3-9-4 **82** ... DavidProbert 5 — 93+
(Henry Candy) *mde all: shkn up over 1f out: styd on wl: comf* 4/1[2]

0054 **2** *2 1/2* **Oloroso (IRE)**[20] 5351 3-8-10 **74** ... OisinMurphy 4 — 78
(Andrew Balding) *plld hrd and prom: rdn to chse wnr over 1f out: hung rt ins fnl f: styd on same pce* 10/3[1]

656 **3** *1 1/2* **Rudy Lewis (IRE)**[22] 5269 3-8-7 **71** ... HarryBentley 1 — 72
(Charlie Fellowes) *hld up: hdwy and nt clr run over 2f out: rdn over 1f out: styd on same pce ins fnl f* 10/1

-321 **4** *3/4* **Sezim**[47] 4316 3-9-3 **81** ... JackMitchell 3 — 80
(Roger Varian) *hld up: shkn up and nt clr run over 2f out: hdwy over 1f out: sn rdn: styd on same pce fnl f* 10/3[1]

2016 **5** *1 1/2* **Clara Peeters**[15] 5525 3-9-7 **85** ... JimCrowley 2 — 80
(Gary Moore) *racd keenly: prom: chsd wnr over 3f out tl over 1f out: wknd wl ins fnl f* 8/1[3]

152 **6** *11* **Fabulist**[18] 5441 3-9-6 **84** ... RobertHavlin 7 — 54
(John Gosden) *hld up: effrt on outer over 2f out: edgd rt and wknd over 1f out (trainer's rep said filly was unsuited by the soft going and would prefer a firmer surface)* 4/1[2]

1020 **7** *33* **Quick**[32] 4898 3-9-2 **80** ... TomMarquand 6
(Richard Hannon) *sn chsng wnr: pushed along and lost 2nd over 3f out: wknd over 2f out (jockey said filly was never travelling having spread her right fore shoe on the way to post)* 16/1

1m 46.34s (2.84) **Going Correction** +0.45s/f (Yiel) — 7 Ran SP% **112.2**
Speed ratings (Par 102): **103,100,99,98,96 85,52**
CSF £17.02 TOTE £4.90: £2.50, £2.00; EX 18.20 Trifecta £141.90.
Owner Robert Allcock **Bred** Robert Allcock **Trained** Kingston Warren, Oxon

FOCUS
A competitive 3yo handicap and a lively betting heat. This time they kept stands' side. It's been rated at face value, with the second to form.

6082 BRITISH STALLION STUDS EBF UPAVON FILLIES' STKS (LISTED RACE) — 1m 1f 201y
3:50 (3:56) (Class 1) 3-Y-O+

£28,355 (£10,750; £5,380; £2,680; £1,345; £675) Stalls Low

Form — RPR

1301 **1** **Fanny Logan (IRE)**[19] 5397 3-8-8 106 ... (h) RobertHavlin 4 — 112
(John Gosden) *trckd ldrs: led over 2f out: pushed clr fr over 1f out: comf* 1/2[1]

4-03 **2** *7* **Sand Share**[65] 3676 3-8-8 98 ... HarryBentley 2 — 98
(Ralph Beckett) *chsd ldrs: shkn up over 3f out: nt clr run over 2f out: rdn to chse wnr over 1f out: styd on same pce* 4/1[2]

1-40 **3** *3 1/4* **Skill Set (IRE)**[25] 5190 4-9-2 82 ... DavidProbert 8 — 91
(Henry Candy) *led: qcknd over 3f out: hdd over 2f out: rdn and edgd lft over 1f out: wknd ins fnl f* 33/1

6646 **4** *3/4* **Magnolia Springs (IRE)**[25] 5190 4-9-2 94 ... (p[1]) CharlesBishop 3 — 89
(Eve Johnson Houghton) *hld up: hdwy on outer over 1f out: wknd ins fnl f* 10/1[3]

4521 **5** *1 3/4* **Time Change**[7] 5796 4-9-2 80 ... PatDobbs 5 — 86
(Ralph Beckett) *s.i.s: hld up: hdwy over 1f out: wknd fnl f* 25/1

5361 **6** *5* **Queen Of Time**[32] 4930 5-9-2 97 ... (p) KieranShoemark 9 — 76
(Henry Candy) *sn chsng ldr: rdn over 2f out: wknd over 1f out* 11/1

2m 11.97s (1.47) **Going Correction** +0.45s/f (Yiel)
WFA 3 from 4yo+ 8lb — 6 Ran SP% **110.9**
Speed ratings (Par 108): **112,106,103,103,101 97**
CSF £2.71 TOTE £1.30: £1.10, £2.40; EX 3.40 Trifecta £27.60.
Owner HH Sheikha Al Jalila Racing **Bred** Godolphin **Trained** Newmarket, Suffolk

FOCUS
This fillies' Listed event was hit by non-runners. It was run at a fair pace and again the field stuck far side. The second has been rated to her best, with the third to a pb.

6083 CHAMPAGNE JOSEPH PERRIER CONFINED H'CAP (FOR HORSES THAT HAVE NOT WON A FLAT RACE THIS YEAR) — 1m 1f 201y
4:20 (4:26) (Class 5) (0-75,75) 3-Y-O+

£3,737 (£1,112; £555; £300; £300; £300) Stalls Low

Form — RPR

500- **1** **Blistering Bob**[230] 9723 4-9-11 **75** ... (h[1]) WilliamCox(3) 3 — 86
(Roger Teal) *chsd ldrs: led over 1f out: drvn out* 20/1

5024 **2** *2 1/4* **Craneur**[16] 5497 3-8-10 **65** ... JimCrowley 14 — 72
(Harry Dunlop) *prom: racd wd tl jnd main gp and chse ldr over 8f out: led over 3f out: rdn and hdd over 1f out: styd on same pce wl ins fnl f* 6/1[2]

0032 **3** *1/2* **Steeve**[6] 5858 3-9-0 **69** ... (p) LukeMorris 8 — 75
(Rod Millman) *chsd ldrs: rdn and ev ch over 1f out: styd on same pce wl ins fnl f* 4/1[1]

-500 **4** *6* **Thechildren'strust (IRE)**[11] 5667 4-9-12 **73** ... HectorCrouch 5 — 67
(Gary Moore) *led: hdd over 3f out: sn rdn: no ex fnl f: eased nr fin* 9/1

4-33 **5** *6* **Miss Blondell**[14] 5565 6-9-0 **66** ... WilliamCarver(5) 12 — 48
(Marcus Tregoning) *hld up in tch: lost pl and hmpd over 4f out: swtchd lft over 2f out: rdn and hung rt fr over 1f out: nt trble ldrs* 4/1[1]

3304 **6** *2 1/2* **Allocator (FR)**[117] 1928 3-9-5 **74** ... PatDobbs 4 — 51
(Richard Hannon) *hld up: shkn up over 3f out: carried lft over 2f out: n.d* 10/1

4553 **7** *3 1/2* **Glory**[9] 5731 3-9-0 **69** ... TomMarquand 10 — 39
(Richard Hannon) *hld up: rdn over 3f out: wknd wl over 1f out* 12/1

35-0 **8** *1* **Fronsac**[49] 4249 4-9-11 **72** ... RobertWinston 1 — 40
(Daniel Kubler) *chsd ldrs: shkn up over 3f out: edgd lft over 2f out: wknd over 1f out* 14/1

-434 **9** *1/2* **Global Express**[26] 5124 3-9-4 **73** ... GeraldMosse 2 — 41
(Ed Dunlop) *hld up: hdwy over 3f out: wknd and eased over 1f out (trainer's rep said gelding was unsuited by the soft going and would prefer a firmer surface)* 8/1[3]

2553 **10** *14* **Society Guest (IRE)**[8] 5785 3-9-1 **70** ... CallumShepherd 6 — 10
(Mick Channon) *hld up: hdwy over 4f out: wknd 2f out* 12/1

00-6 **11** *15* **Wojood**[21] 5311 3-8-11 **66** ... (bt) JackMitchell 7
(Hugo Palmer) *hld up: hdwy on outer over 4f out: wknd over 3f out (jockey said gelding stopped quickly)* 10/1

2m 13.78s (3.28) **Going Correction** +0.45s/f (Yiel)
WFA 3 from 4yo+ 8lb — 11 Ran SP% **120.4**
Speed ratings (Par 103): **104,102,101,97,92 90,87,86,86,75 63**
CSF £138.87 CT £592.81 TOTE £24.00: £5.60, £2.00, £1.60; EX 247.90 Trifecta £1171.50.
Owner Bex Design & Print Ltd **Bred** M Tuckey T/A Chilling Place Stables **Trained** Lambourn, Berks

FOCUS
A modest handicap and again the far side was favoured. The going seemed to play a big part. The third has been rated close to his latest.

6084 SHADWELL RACING EXCELLENCE APPRENTICE H'CAP (WHIPS SHALL BE CARRIED BUT NOT USED) (DIV I) — 6f 213y
4:50 (4:55) (Class 5) (0-70,72) 3-Y-O+

£4,398 (£1,309; £654; £327; £300; £300) Stalls Low

Form — RPR

0000 **1** **Another Boy**[20] 5351 6-8-5 **54** ... (p) CharlotteBennett(7) 2 — 62
(Ralph Beckett) *chsd ldr: shkn up over 2f out: led 1f out: pushed out (trainer said, regarding the improved form shown, the gelding appreciated the soft going)* 12/1

0200 **2** *3/4* **John Betjeman**[7] 5813 3-9-10 **72** ... EllaMcCain 1 — 76
(Mark Gillard) *chsd ldrs: pushed along and swtchd lft over 2f out: styd on to go 2nd nr fin* 5/1[3]

4002 **3** *1/2* **Arctic Flower (IRE)**[11] 5677 6-8-4 **51** oh6 ... GeorgeRooke(5) 7 — 56
(John Bridger) *led: racd freely: pushed along and hdd 1f out: styd on same pce wl ins fnl f (jockey said mare hung right)* 7/1

2621 **4** *3 1/4* **Stay Forever (FR)**[14] 5561 3-8-13 **66** ... MariePerrault(5) 8 — 60
(Andrew Balding) *dwlt: hld up: hdwy over 2f out: no ex fnl f* 9/2[2]

0234 **5** *nk* **Grey Galleon (USA)**[11] 5677 5-10-0 **70** ... (p) AmeliaGlass 3 — 65
(Clive Cox) *hld up: shkn up and hdwy over 1f out: no imp fnl f (jockey said gelding hung right)* 7/1

-300 **6** *nse* **Keeper's Choice (IRE)**[32] 4902 5-9-8 **71** ... MichaelPitt(7) 6 — 66
(Denis Coakley) *s.i.s: sn pushed along and in tch: outpcd over 2f out: styd on ins fnl f* 8/1

0053 **7** *1 1/2* **Air Of York (IRE)**[13] 5579 7-9-7 **63** ... (p) SeanKirrane 4 — 54
(John Flint) *chsd ldrs: shkn up over 2f out: no ex ins fnl f* 10/1

5364 **8** *4 1/2* **Kinglami**[33] 4872 10-9-4 **63** ... (p) KateLeahy(3) 10 — 43
(John O'Shea) *s.i.s: sn chsng ldrs: pushed along 1/2-way: wknd over 1f out* 20/1

00-3 **9** *1 3/4* **Tell William**[18] 5448 3-9-3 **70** ... (p) GeorgeBass(5) 5 — 43
(Marcus Tregoning) *s.i.s: a bhd* 4/1[1]

6003 **10** *2 1/2* **Bbob Alula**[11] 5677 4-9-10 **66** ... (tp) GavinAshton 9 — 35
(Bill Turner) *bhd fr 1/2-way* 14/1

1m 32.44s (3.74) **Going Correction** +0.45s/f (Yiel)
WFA 3 from 4yo+ 6lb — 10 Ran SP% **119.2**
Speed ratings (Par 103): **96,95,94,90,90 90,88,83,81,78**
CSF £72.62 CT £474.78 TOTE £14.60: £3.90, £2.10, £2.50; EX 97.70 Trifecta £711.10.
Owner Mrs Philip Snow & Partners **Bred** Mrs P Snow & Partners **Trained** Kimpton, Hants

FOCUS
A typically moderate race of its type. The principals came clear. The second has been rated to form, and the third as running her best race since 2017.

6085 SHADWELL RACING EXCELLENCE APPRENTICE H'CAP (WHIPS SHALL BE CARRIED BUT NOT USED) (DIV II) — 6f 213y
5:25 (5:25) (Class 5) (0-70,72) 3-Y-O+

£4,398 (£1,309; £654; £327; £300; £300) Stalls Low

Form — RPR

5502 **1** **Bounty Pursuit**[18] 5446 7-9-5 **64** ... MarcoGhiani(3) 8 — 72
(Michael Blake) *hld up: hdwy on outer over 1f out: shkn up to ld ins fnl f: r.o wl* 9/2[2]

3213 **2** *2* **Crystal Casque**[26] 5137 4-9-9 **70** ... OliverSearle(5) 3 — 73
(Rod Millman) *racd freely: disp ld tl wnt on over 2f out: shkn up and edgd lft over 1f out: hdd and unable qck ins fnl f* 3/1[1]

0-00 **3** *2* **Jean Valjean**[25] 5202 3-9-6 **68** ... (h) SeanKirrane 1 — 64
(Richard Spencer) *racd freely: disp ld to 1/2-way: shkn up over 2f out: ev ch ins fnl f: no ex towards fin* 9/2[2]

6612 **4** *1 1/4* **Misu Pete**[12] 5633 7-9-6 **65** ... (p) IsobelFrancis(3) 5 — 60
(Mark Usher) *hld up: pushed along 1/2-way: hdwy over 2f out: styd on same pce fnl f (jockey said gelding was outpaced in the first half of the race)* 3/1[1]

0305 **5** *1* **Punjab Mail**[33] 4895 3-9-7 **72** ... AngusVilliers(3) 7 — 62
(Ian Williams) *s.i.s: hld up: swtchd lft and hdwy over 2f out: shkn up over 1f out: no ex fnl f* 3/1[1]

0-00 **6** *2 3/4* **Swiper (IRE)**[19] 5377 3-8-8 **59** ... KateLeahy(3) 4 — 42
(John O'Shea) *s.i.s: racd keenly and sn disputing ld tl shkn up over 2f out: wknd fnl f* 25/1[3]

1m 33.15s (4.45) **Going Correction** +0.45s/f (Yiel)
WFA 3 from 4yo+ 6lb — 6 Ran SP% **115.2**
Speed ratings (Par 103): **92,89,87,86,84 81**
CSF £18.95 CT £63.70 TOTE £5.80: £2.80, £2.20; EX 23.90 Trifecta £100.30.
Owner Racing For A Cause **Bred** Cecil And Miss Alison Wiggins **Trained** Trowbridge, Wilts

FOCUS
This second division of the apprentice handicap was slower by 0.71sec. Again they kept far side. The second has been rated close to form.
T/Jkpt: £16,620.30 to a £1 stake. Pool: £46,817.97 - 2.00 winning units T/Plt: £23.30 to a £1 stake. Pool: £63,495.39 - 1,982.82 winning units T/Qpdt: £10.60 to a £1 stake. Pool: £6,370.85 - 441.78 winning units **Colin Roberts**

6086 - 6089a (Foreign Racing) - See Raceform Interactive

5460 **GOWRAN PARK** (R-H)
Wednesday, August 14

OFFICIAL GOING: Yielding to soft

6090a IRISH STALLION FARMS EBF HURRY HARRIET STKS (LISTED RACE) (F&M) **1m 1f 100y**
6:50 (6:52) 3-Y-0+
£29,234 (£9,414; £4,459; £1,981; £990; £495)

RPR
1 **Goddess (USA)**[24] 5223 3-9-0 98 DonnachaO'Brien 12 103+
(A P O'Brien, Ire) *chsd ldrs: tk clsr order in 3rd after 3f: gng wl nr side into st: pushed along to ld under 2f out: sn rdn and kpt on wl ins fnl f: edgd sltly lft nr fin: comf (jockey said filly ran very green)* **14/1**
2 1 1/4 **Tipitena**[47] 4356 4-9-8 90 WJLee 14 99
(W McCreery, Ire) *hld up towards rr early: tk clsr order and disp 8th after 1/2-way: pushed along over 2f out and prog nr side: sn rdn and r.o u.p into 2nd wl ins fnl f: sltly impeded nr fin: a hld* **33/1**
3 1/2 **Who's Steph (IRE)**[61] 3820 4-9-13 108 ColinKeane 2 103
(G M Lyons, Ire) *cl up early tl sn settled bhd ldrs: 4th after 3f: effrt far side under 2f out: no imp on wnr wl ins fnl f where dropped to 3rd: jst hld 3rd* **11/10**[1]
4 hd **Frosty (IRE)**[306] 8146 3-9-0 0 SeamieHeffernan 9 98+
(A P O'Brien, Ire) *dwlt: hld up towards rr: last at 1/2-way: rdn nr side and hdwy 2f out: r.o wl into nvr threatening 4th wl ins fnl f* **16/1**
5 1 1/2 **Camphor (IRE)**[12] 5637 3-9-0 97 ShaneFoley 15 94
(Mrs John Harrington, Ire) *hld up in mid-div: 7th after 3f: rdn and tk clsr order nr side 2f out: no ex bhd ldrs ent fnl f: one pce after* **5/1**[2]
6 2 1/2 **Fresnel**[55] 4014 3-9-0 98 GaryHalpin 5 89
(Jack W Davison, Ire) *led tl jnd after 1f: led narrowly fr 4f out: rdn and hdd under 2f out: sn no imp on wnr u.p in 3rd and one pce ins fnl f* **10/1**[3]
7 1 1/4 **Snapraeceps (IRE)**[28] 5075 3-9-0 93 DeclanMcDonogh 7 87
(Joseph Patrick O'Brien, Ire) *chsd ldrs: rdn far side over 2f out and sn no ex* **12/1**
8 nk **Cnoc An Oir (IRE)**[28] 5075 3-9-0 90 (h) ColmO'Donoghue 3 86
(Joseph Patrick O'Brien, Ire) *mid-div: disp 8th after 3f: hdwy under 3f out: rdn bhd ldrs far side 2f out and wknd u.p fr over 1f out* **33/1**
9 nk **Waitingfortheday (IRE)**[13] 5597 4-9-8 97 (p) NGMcCullagh 8 86
(Joseph Patrick O'Brien, Ire) *chsd ldrs: hmpd sltly between horses into st: rdn and no ex 2f out: wknd* **16/1**
10 4 3/4 **Wisdom Mind (IRE)**[28] 5075 4-9-8 98 (t) ShaneCrosse 13 76
(Joseph Patrick O'Brien, Ire) *w.w towards rr: pushed along into st and nt clr run briefly over 2f out where swtchd rt: sn rdn and no imp over 1f out: kpt on one pce in mod 10th ins fnl f* **33/1**
11 3/4 **Annie Fior (IRE)**[24] 5223 5-9-8 98 PBBeggy 1 74
(B A Murphy, Ire) *v.s.i.s and detached in rr early: hmpd sltly towards rr under 4f out: sme hdwy far side over 2f out: no ex u.p in mid-div under 2f out: sn wknd (trainer said mare showed signs of being in season post race)* **25/1**
12 1 1/4 **Luxuriant**[27] 5113 3-9-0 87 OisinOrr 10 72
(D K Weld, Ire) *hld up: disp 8th after 3f: drvn and no imp over 2f out: wknd* **11/1**
13 3 1/4 **Lady Olenna (IRE)**[18] 5465 3-9-0 88 ChrisHayes 6 65
(R P Cody, Ire) *loaded wout rdr: sn trckd ldr tl disp ld after 1f: hdd narrowly fr 4f out: sn pushed along and no ex 3f out: wknd qckly* **25/1**
14 3 **Coeur D'amour (IRE)**[56] 4011 4-9-8 92 RobbieColgan 4 59
(Madeleine Tylicki, Ire) *hld up: 10th after 3f: short of room and checked between horses under 4f out: pushed along into st and no imp far side under 2f out: wknd* **66/1**

2m 5.06s (-1.94) **14** Ran **SP%** **125.8**
WFA 3 from 4yo+ 8lb
CSF £432.29 TOTE £10.20: £3.50, £9.90, £1.02; DF 299.50 Trifecta £1214.00.
Owner Mrs John Magnier & John G Sikura **Bred** Orpendale & Chelston **Trained** Cashel, Co Tipperary

FOCUS
With conditions in her favour, Who's Steph was a warm order to record her second C&D success but she couldn't give the weight away. Goddess, who looked very good when winning her maiden at Leopardstown last season, has so far yet to replicate that sort of form but looks to be back on track judging by this impressive display. The winner has been rated in line with her latest.

6091 - 6093a (Foreign Racing) - See Raceform Interactive

6031 **CLAIREFONTAINE** (R-H)
Wednesday, August 14

OFFICIAL GOING: Turf: very soft

6094a PRIX LADY CATACLYSM (CLAIMER) (3YO) (TURF) **1m 6f 110y**
2:00 3-Y-O
£8,558 (£3,423; £2,567; £1,711; £855)

RPR
1 **Purple Victory (FR)**[20] 3-8-11 0 (b) AurelienLemaitre 6 80
(F Head, France) **8/5**[1]
2 15 **Holbox (FR)**[12] 5641 3-8-11 0 (b) ThomasTrullier(4) 10 63
(F Vermeulen, France) **26/5**[3]
3 1/2 **Daatis (GER)**[65] 3-9-1 0 AntoineHamelin 7 62
(Waldemar Hickst, Germany) **16/5**[2]
4 1 1/4 **Foxy Power (FR)**[24] 3-9-2 0 (b) MlleMickaelleMichel(3) 3 64
(R Le Gal, France) **14/1**
5 1 1/4 **Chef D'Etat (FR)**[19] 3-8-11 0 (p) IoritzMendizabal 9 55
(J Bertran De Balanda, France) **14/1**
6 snk **Black Abbey (FR)**[19] 3-8-8 0 MlleCoraliePacaut(3) 8 54
(Gavin Hernon, France) **73/10**
7 nk **I Can Dream (FR)**[41] 3-8-6 0 MllePerrineCheyer(9) 4 58
(Yannick Fouin, France) **31/1**
8 15 **Mister Gabriel (FR)**[147] 3-8-6 0 (b) GuillaumeGuedj-Gay(5) 11 33
(J Piednoel, France) **38/1**
9 5 **Miss Fizz (FR)** 3-8-8 0 FabienLefebvre 2 23
(P De Chevigny, France) **33/1**
10 4 1/2 **Delta Bravo (IRE)**[12] 5641 3-8-3 0 AlexisPouchin(5) 5 17
(J S Moore) *broke wl: prom early: mostly racd in 3rd on inner: rdn 2f out: no rspnse and wl btn whn brought to stands' rail 2f out: t.o* **14/1**

3m 14.2s **10** Ran **SP%** **119.1**
PARI-MUTUEL (all including 1 euro stake): WIN 2.60; PLACE 1.20, 1.50, 1.40; DF 5.90.
Owner Ecurie Jean-Louis Bouchard **Bred** Mme M-C Biaudis **Trained** France

6095a PRIX FS CREATION (CONDITIONS) (4YO+) (TURF) **1m 6f 110y**
2:35 4-Y-O+
£12,612 (£4,792; £3,531; £2,018; £1,009; £756)

RPR
1 **Time To Study (FR)**[33] 4884 5-9-2 0 (p) MickaelBarzalona 2 100
(Ian Williams) *trckd ldng pair: pushed along and hdwy to dispute ld 3f out: rdn into narrow ld appr fnl f: drvn clr fnl 100yds* **29/10**[2]
2 3 **Forever Yours (FR)**[42] 4-8-8 0 (p) TheoBachelot 5 88
(S Wattel, France) **7/5**[1]
3 3/4 **Diluvien (FR)**[16] 4-9-4 0 (p) Pierre-CharlesBoudot 3 97
(Gianluca Bietolini, France) **57/10**[3]
4 1 1/4 **Galope Americano (BRZ)**[19] 5-8-11 0 MaximeGuyon 6 88
(Mme Pia Brandt, France) **68/10**
5 3 **Bonaparte Sizing (FR)**[143] 5-8-11 0 IoritzMendizabal 1 84
(J Bertran De Balanda, France) **13/1**
6 4 **Auzebosc (FR)**[16] 4-8-11 0 CristianDemuro 4 78
(S Cerulis, France) **83/10**
7 5 **Fleur Irlandaise (FR)**[38] 4-7-13 0 MllePerrineCheyer(9) 8 68
(Yannick Fouin, France) **55/1**
8 1/2 **Serienschock (GER)**[44] 11-8-3 0 MlleAmbreMolins(8) 7 71
(Mme A Rosa, France) **27/1**

3m 15.2s **8** Ran **SP%** **118.3**
PARI-MUTUEL (all including 1 euro stake): WIN 3.90; PLACE 1.50, 1.20, 1.40; DF 5.10.
Owner K Sohi **Bred** E A R L Haras Du Quesnay **Trained** Portway, Worcs

6064 **BEVERLEY** (R-H)
Thursday, August 15

OFFICIAL GOING: Good to soft (7.7)
Wind: Strong against Weather: Cloudy with sunny periods

6096 EBF FILLIES' NOVICE STKS (PLUS 10 RACE) **5f**
2:00 (2:01) (Class 5) 2-Y-O **£4,032** (£1,207; £603; £302; £150) **Stalls** Low

Form RPR
404 1 **Galadriel**[20] 5387 2-9-0 78 TomEaves 10 77+
(Kevin Ryan) *trckd ldr: cl up 1/2-way: led 2f out: rdn clr over 1f out: kpt on* **2/1**[1]
2 1 1/2 **Say It Simple** 2-9-0 0 PaulHanagan 2 72+
(Richard Fahey) *trckd ldrs: hdwy 2f out: rdn to chse wnr over 1f out: kpt on* **4/1**[3]
3 3/4 **Excel And Succeed (IRE)** 2-9-0 0 PaulMulrennan 11 69+
(Michael Dods) *green and wnt lft s: towards rr: hdwy 2f out: chsd ldrs and swtchd lft over 1f out: kpt on wl fnl f* **16/1**
0 4 1/2 **Bay Filly Rolla**[24] 5243 2-9-0 0 AndrewMullen 8 67
(Michael Dods) *chsd ldrs: hdwy on inner 2f out: rdn over 1f out: kpt on fnl f* **25/1**
4 5 1/2 **Dancing Leopard (IRE)**[122] 1821 2-9-0 0 BenCurtis 4 65+
(K R Burke) *hmpd s and towards rr: hdwy 1/2-way: rdn to chse ldrs wl over 1f out: kpt on same pce fnl f* **5/1**
6 3 1/4 **Astrozone** 2-9-0 0 GrahamLee 12 54
(Bryan Smart) *wnt bdly lft s and towards rr: hdwy and in tch 1/2-way: rdn along 2f out: n.d* **20/1**
56 7 5 **Midnight Mimosa (IRE)**[9] 5788 2-9-0 0 RachelRichardson 5 36
(Tim Easterby) *hmpd s: a in rr* **66/1**
40 8 hd **Sweet Embrace (IRE)**[16] 5514 2-9-0 0 CamHardie 6 35
(John Wainwright) *wnt bdly rt s: chsd ldrs: rdn along over 2f out: sn drvn and wknd* **100/1**
2 9 7 **Band Practice (IRE)**[12] 5681 2-9-0 0 DanielTudhope 3 40+
(Archie Watson) *wnt lft and bmpd s: sddle slipped and rdr lost an iron: sn bhd: sme hdwy 2f out: sn eased (jockey said filly jumped awkwardly leaving stalls, causing him to lose an iron and the saddle slipping)* **5/2**[2]
6 10 20 **Prisma (IRE)**[14] 5590 2-9-0 0 JasonHart 1
(Ivan Furtado) *led: rdn along and hdd 2f out: wknd qckly* **50/1**

1m 5.31s (2.41) **Going Correction** +0.25s/f (Good) **10** Ran **SP%** **117.5**
Speed ratings (Par 91): **90,87,86,85,84 79,71,71,60,28**
CSF £10.04 TOTE £2.50: £1.20, £1.50, £3.90; EX 9.30 Trifecta £93.20.
Owner Sheikh Mohammed Obaid Al Maktoum **Bred** Sheikh Mohammed Obaid Al Maktoum **Trained** Hambleton, N Yorks

FOCUS
The inside rail between 7.5f and 1.5f was dolled out 2yds. They were soon strung out in this interesting fillies' novice event. The winning time suggested plenty of give underfoot. Add 1yd.

6097 HAPPY 90TH BIRTHDAY RONALD GEORGE CLAXTON NURSERY H'CAP **7f 96y**
2:30 (2:30) (Class 5) (0-75,77) 2-Y-O
£4,284 (£1,282; £641; £320; £300; £300) **Stalls** Low

Form RPR
5352 1 **G For Gabrial (IRE)**[9] 5781 2-8-8 62 PaulHanagan 10 68+
(Richard Fahey) *towards rr: hdwy 3f out: chsd ldrs 2f out: rdn to chse ldr ent fnl f: styd on strly to ld fnl 50yds: sn clr* **3/1**[3]
323 2 3 1/4 **Lord Of The Alps (IRE)**[16] 5512 2-9-7 75 JoeFanning 9 73
(Mark Johnston) *trckd ldrs: smooth hdwy and cl up over 2f out: led wl over 1f out: rdn and edgd lft jst ins fnl f: hdd & wknd fnl 50yds* **2/1**[1]
460 3 3/4 **Sir Havelock (IRE)**[35] 4826 2-8-0 57 SeanDavis(3) 2 53
(Richard Fahey) *dwlt and in rr: hdwy over 2f out: rdn to chse ldrs and swtchd rt ent fnl f: kpt on wl towards fin (jockey said colt missed break)* **14/1**
204 4 2 1/4 **Doncaster Rosa**[15] 5547 2-9-3 71 JasonHart 5 62
(Ivan Furtado) *trckd ldng pair: hdwy over 2f out: rdn along wl over 1f out: drvn and kpt on same pce fnl f* **12/1**
3652 5 nk **It's Not My Fault (IRE)**[22] 5295 2-7-12 55 JaneElliott(3) 1 45
(Paul Midgley) *prom: sn trcking ldr on inner: hdwy to ld wl over 2f out: rdn and hdd wl over 1f out: sn drvn and grad wknd* **10/1**
6050 6 1 3/4 **The Trendy Man (IRE)**[22] 5296 2-8-0 54 oh3 (p) AndrewMullen 3 40
(David O'Meara) *chsd ldrs: rdn along wl over 2f out: sn wknd* **33/1**
000 7 1 1/2 **Must Dream**[54] 4106 2-8-0 54 oh1 CamHardie 7 36
(Seb Spencer) *in tch: rdn along over 2f out: n.d* **33/1**
252 8 hd **Northern Hope**[23] 5273 2-9-9 77 DanielTudhope 11 58+
(David O'Meara) *wnt lft s: a in rr (jockey said gelding hung left throughout)* **5/2**[2]

The Form Book Flat 2019, Raceform Ltd, Newbury, RG14 5SJ

000 **9** *12* **Teasel's Rock (IRE)**[15] 5553 2-8-0 **54** oh9..............(p[1]) DuranFentiman 6 6
(Tim Easterby) *led: hdd 3f out: sn rdn and wknd* **50/1**

1m 34.62s (2.02) **Going Correction** +0.25s/f (Good) **9** Ran SP% **118.2**
Speed ratings (Par 94): **98,94,93,90,90 88,86,86,72**
CSF £9.56 CT £72.27 TOTE £3.40: £1.30, £1.30, £3.30; EX 11.00 Trifecta £48.90.
Owner Dr Marwan Koukash **Bred** Mrs Bena Hickey **Trained** Musley Bank, N Yorks

FOCUS
This wasn't a bad nursery and there was plenty of pace on early. Add 8yds.

6098 SUNDAY RACING NEXT ON 25TH AUGUST (S) H'CAP (BEVERLEY MIDDLE DISTANCE SERIES) 1m 4f 23y

3:00 (3:00) (Class 6) (0-60,60) 3-Y-O+

£3,363 (£1,001; £500; £300; £300; £300) **Stalls** Low

Form RPR

5600 **1** **Ezanak (IRE)**[14] 5571 6-9-7 **55**.. BenCurtis 7 61
(Michael Appleby) *prom: hdwy over 2f out: rdn wl over 1f out: drvn appr fnl f: styd on to ld fnl 100yds (trainer rep said, regarding improvement in form, gelding appreciated a drop in grade and the removal of headgear)* **11/2[3]**

0230 **2** *1 1/2* **Loose Chippings (IRE)**[14] 5593 5-9-4 **52**................(p) DougieCostello 4 56
(Ivan Furtado) *sn led: pushed along over 2f out: rdn wl over 1f out: drvn ent fnl f: hdd and no ex fnl 100yds* **13/2**

5040 **3** *1* **Point Of Honour (IRE)**[31] 4990 4-8-12 **46** oh1...........(p[1]) SamJames 10 48
(Phillip Makin) *trckd ldr: hdwy and cl up over 2f out: rdn and ev ch over 1f out: drvn and kpt on same pce fnl f* **3/1[2]**

3400 **4** *1 1/4* **Kalaya (IRE)**[12] 5648 3-8-11 **55**..............................(b[1]) AndrewMullen 6 56
(Archie Watson) *hld up: hdwy over 3f out: rdn along over 2f out: chsd ldrs and drvn over 1f out: kpt on one pce* **9/1**

2331 **5** *1 1/2* **Siyahamba (IRE)**[16] 5513 5-8-13 **47**................................(p) GrahamLee 3 45
(Bryan Smart) *dwlt and towards rr: hdwy to trck ldrs 1/2-way: rdn along wl over 2f out: drvn over 1f out: plugged on one pce (jockey said gelding missed break)* **7/4[1]**

0-06 **6** *nk* **Big Ian**[14] 5580 3-8-6 **50**...(p[1]) PaulHanagan 9 48
(Alan Jones) *in tch: rdn along 3f out: n.d* **16/1**

-004 **7** *5* **Mac O'Polo (IRE)**[143] 1334 5-9-5 **53**................................(p) PaulMulrennan 5 42
(Donald McCain) *prom: rdn along 3f out: drvn over 2f out and sn wknd (jockey said gelding hung right throughout)* **14/1**

0030 **8** *nk* **Royal Liberty**[15] 5555 4-9-2 **50**.. KevinStott 12 39
(Geoffrey Harker) *stdd s: hld up: a in rr* **50/1**

0000 **9** *2 1/2* **Roser Moter (IRE)**[17] 5499 4-8-7 **46**....................(p) TheodoreLadd(5) 11 31
(Michael Appleby) *a towards rr* **50/1**

6005 **10** *3 1/4* **Just Heather (IRE)**[1] 6069 5-8-5 **46** oh1...............(p) LauraCoughlan(7) 1 25
(John Wainwright) *chsd ldrs: pushed along over 4f out: rdn over 3f out: sn outpcd* **80/1**

2m 39.76s (0.96) **Going Correction** +0.25s/f (Good)
WFA 3 from 4yo+ 10lb **10** Ran SP% **117.8**
Speed ratings (Par 101): **106,105,104,103,102 102,98,98,97,94**
CSF £41.33 CT £128.14 TOTE £6.80: £2.10, £1.50, £1.60; EX 49.70 Trifecta £174.90.Ezanak was sold for £4000.
Owner Ian Lawrence **Bred** His Highness The Aga Khan's Studs S C **Trained** Oakham, Rutland

FOCUS
They went a strong pace in this weak selling handicap. Add 8yds.

6099 NIKKI MEADOWS BIRTHDAY DASH H'CAP 5f

3:30 (3:34) (Class 5) (0-70,72) 4-Y-O+

£4,398 (£1,309; £654; £327; £300; £300) **Stalls** Low

Form RPR

5205 **1** **Atyaaf**[4] 5986 4-8-5 **54**... PaddyMathers 8 61
(Derek Shaw) *hld up: hdwy over 1f out: chsd ldrs and n.m.r 1f out: sn rdn and qcknd wl to ld towards fin* **12/1**

6403 **2** *nk* **Sheepscar Lad (IRE)**[30] 5027 5-9-1 **69**............... FayeMcManoman(5) 4 75
(Nigel Tinkler) *hld up: hdwy wl over 1f out: trckd ldrs and n.m.r ent fnl f: sn rdn and slt ld ins fnl f: hdd and no ex towards fin* **11/4[1]**

0562 **3** *hd* **Burtonwood**[16] 5515 7-8-9 **58**.. GrahamLee 11 63
(Julie Camacho) *hld up in tch: hdwy over 1f out: rdn ent fnl f: styd on strly towards fin* **14/1**

0060 **4** *3/4* **Prestbury Park (USA)**[2] 6058 4-9-3 **66**...................... PaulMulrennan 14 68
(Paul Midgley) *trckd ldrs towards outer: hdwy 2f out: rdn over 1f out: drvn and kpt on fnl f* **11/1**

3432 **5** *nk* **Suwaan (IRE)**[8] 5819 5-9-4 **67**..............................(h) JamesSullivan 3 68
(Ruth Carr) *trckd ldrs: hdwy and cl up over 1f out: sn rdn and ev ch: drvn ins fnl f and no ex fnl 100yds* **4/1[2]**

-001 **6** *3/4* **Moonlit Sands (IRE)**[10] 5722 4-8-10 **59** 5ex.............(tp) CamHardie 10 58
(Brian Ellison) *hld up in rr: hdwy wl over 1f out: rdn ent fnl f: kpt on wl towards fin* **20/1**

-045 **7** *3/4* **Young Tiger**[18] 5478 6-8-2 **51** oh2...............................(h) AndrewMullen 2 47
(Tom Tate) *trckd ldrs: hdwy and cl up 2f out: led wl over 1f out: sn rdn: drvn and hdd ins fnl f: wknd towards fin* **11/1**

0003 **8** *3/4* **Guardia Svizzera (IRE)**[10] 5722 5-9-1 **64**......................(h) BenCurtis 6 57
(Roger Fell) *hld up in midfield: effrt and sme hdwy 2f out: rdn over 1f out: kpt on same pce fnl f* **13/2[3]**

0510 **9** *shd* **Point Of Woods**[20] 5393 6-8-6 **60**............................(t) HarrisonShaw(5) 1 53
(Tina Jackson) *towards rr: hdwy on inner wl over 1f out: rdn to chse ldrs appr fnl f: sn drvn and one pce (jockey said gelding was never travelling)* **9/1**

0364 **10** *1/2* **Suitcase 'N' Taxi**[10] 5722 5-8-9 **58**.. JasonHart 15 49
(Tim Easterby) *wnt bdly lft s: racd wd towards stands' rail: sn chsng ldrs: hdwy and cl up 2f out: rdn wl over 1f out: wknd appr fnl f* **22/1**

0100 **11** *1* **Desert Ace (IRE)**[24] 5244 8-9-7 **70**..................................... KevinStott 5 57
(Paul Midgley) *trckd ldrs: hdwy and cl up 2f out: rdn over 1f out: wknd ins fnl f* **16/1**

1-0 **12** *3 1/4* **Mambila (FR)**[21] 5330 5-9-5 **68**.. SamJames 9 44
(Geoffrey Harker) *led: rdn along and hdd wl over 1f out: sn wknd* **25/1**

2250 **13** *12* **Warrior's Valley**[41] 4593 4-9-0 **63**.............................(t) DougieCostello 12
(David C Griffiths) *racd wd towards stands' side: prom: cl up 1/2-way: rdn along wl over 1f out: sn wknd* **25/1**

1m 3.93s (1.03) **Going Correction** +0.25s/f (Good) **13** Ran SP% **123.7**
Speed ratings (Par 103): **101,100,100,99,98 97,96,94,94,93 92,87,67**
CSF £44.31 CT £501.71 TOTE £15.50: £4.50, £2.10, £3.30; EX 60.90 Trifecta £666.00.
Owner Gb Civil Engineering (leicester) Ltd **Bred** Shadwell Estate Company Limited **Trained** Sproxton, Leics

FOCUS
The main action came down the centre in this moderate sprint handicap. Add 1yd. It's been rated as ordinary form, with the third to his C&D latest.

6100 WEATHERBYS TBA H'CAP 2m 32y

4:00 (4:00) (Class 4) (0-85,85) 3-Y-O+ **£6,474** (£1,938; £969; £484) **Stalls** Low

Form RPR

6211 **1** **Platform Nineteen (IRE)**[14] 5596 3-8-4 **74**..............(p) JamesSullivan 2 83+
(Michael Bell) *hld up in tch: hdwy over 2f out: chal wl over 1f out: rdn to ld appr fnl f: kpt on strly towards fin* **2/7[1]**

0603 **2** *2 1/4* **Jukebox Jive (FR)**[17] 5496 5-10-0 **85**......................(t) DougieCostello 4 89
(Jamie Osborne) *slt ld: pushed along and jnd over 2f out: rdn wl over 1f out: hdd appr fnl f: sn drvn and kpt on* **8/1[3]**

1203 **3** *1 1/4* **Echo (IRE)**[44] 4491 4-9-3 **74**...(b) JackGarritty 5 77
(Jedd O'Keeffe) *trckd ldr: hdwy and cl up over 2f out: sn rdn and ev ch: drvn over 1f out: kpt on same pce* **6/1[2]**

5150 **4** *1/2* **Zihaam**[10] 5728 5-8-5 **67**...(p) BenSanderson(5) 6 69
(Roger Fell) *trckd ldng pair: pushed along and sltly outpcd wl over 2f out: sn rdn: kpt on same pce u.p fr over 1f out* **14/1**

3m 40.65s (2.75) **Going Correction** +0.25s/f (Good)
WFA 3 from 4yo+ 13lb **4** Ran SP% **109.8**
Speed ratings (Par 105): **103,101,101,101**
CSF £3.33 TOTE £1.20; EX 3.40 Trifecta £5.80.
Owner The Royal Ascot Racing Club **Bred** Watership Down Stud **Trained** Newmarket, Suffolk
■ Stewards' Enquiry : Ben Sanderson three-day ban: weighed in 2lbs overweight (Aug 18, 29-30)

FOCUS
Add 8yds. Just the four runners and this was predictably tactical. The second has been rated to his latest, and the third close to form.

6101 BEVERLEY ANNUAL BADGEHOLDERS H'CAP 1m 100y

4:30 (4:31) (Class 5) (0-70,69) 3-Y-O

£4,284 (£1,282; £481; £300; £300) **Stalls** Low

Form RPR

2324 **1** **One To Go**[12] 5695 3-8-13 **66**..............................(b) DannyRedmond(5) 6 72
(Tim Easterby) *trckd ldrs: hdwy 3f out: rdn to ld jst over 1f out: drvn out* **9/2[2]**

-350 **2** *1/2* **Alfa Dawn (IRE)**[15] 5556 3-9-4 **66**.. SamJames 1 71
(Phillip Makin) *led: pushed along 2f out: rdn and hdd jst over 1f out: drvn and kpt on wl fnl f* **6/1[3]**

3132 **3** *hd* **Northern Lyte**[22] 5307 3-9-1 **68**........................ FayeMcManoman(5) 8 72
(Nigel Tinkler) *hld up: hdwy 3f out: trckd ldrs 2f out: rdn over 1f out: drvn and kpt on fnl f* **4/1[1]**

0540 **3** *dht* **Osmosis**[15] 5556 3-8-10 **61**.. ConorMcGovern(3) 7 65+
(Jason Ward) *towards rr: pushed along and hdwy 2f out: rdn over 1f out: swtchd rt ent fnl f: styd on strly towards fin* **12/1**

3050 **5** *1* **My Boy Lewis (IRE)**[26] 5176 3-9-5 **67**.. BenCurtis 2 69
(Roger Fell) *dwlt and in rr: hdwy on inner over 2f out: rdn over 1f out: styd on wl towards fin* **22/1**

0444 **6** *nse* **Molly Mai**[23] 5272 3-9-2 **64**.. DanielTudhope 12 66
(Philip McBride) *hld up: hdwy wl over 2f out: in tch and rdn over 1f out: styd on u.p fnl f* **6/1[3]**

3060 **7** *1/2* **Artistic Streak**[41] 4602 3-9-3 **65**.. GrahamLee 9 66
(Donald McCain) *nvr bttr than midfield* **28/1**

5302 **8** *3/4* **Dark Poet**[56] 4029 3-8-9 **57**.. JamesSullivan 3 56
(Ruth Carr) *chsd ldrs: rdn along over 2f out: sn wknd* **20/1**

6630 **9** *nk* **Gunnison**[25] 5215 3-8-2 **53**.. SeanDavis(3) 4 51
(Richard Fahey) *trckd ldng pair: pushed along over 2f out: sn rdn and wknd over 1f out* **33/1**

6423 **10** *1 3/4* **Dreamseller (IRE)**[16] 5517 3-8-6 **54**........................ DuranFentiman 13 49
(Tim Easterby) *in tch on outer: hdwy 3f out: rdn along over 2f out: sn drvn and wknd* **9/1**

2000 **11** *1/2* **Mustadun**[40] 4634 3-9-7 **69**.. JoeFanning 11 63
(Mark Johnston) *a towards rr* **12/1**

3003 **12** *1* **Abie's Hollow**[12] 5695 3-9-0 **62**.. PaulHanagan 10 53
(Tony Coyle) *cl up: pushed along 3f out: rdn 2f out: sn drvn and wknd 9/1*

644 **13** *nk* **Oblate**[29] 5041 3-9-0 **62**.. TomEaves 14 53
(Robyn Brisland) *chsd ldrs: rdn along 3f out: sn wknd* **50/1**

0 **14** *8* **Sauron's Eye**[14] 5594 3-9-0 **62**..(t) DougieCostello 5 35
(Ivan Furtado) *a in rr (jockey said gelding was slowly away)* **66/1**

1m 48.55s (2.15) **Going Correction** +0.25s/f (Good) **14** Ran SP% **121.1**
Speed ratings (Par 100): **99,98,98,98,97 97,96,96,95,93 93,92,92,84**
Place: Northern Lyte £1.00. Osmosis 2.00. Trifecta: OTG/AD/NL £46.80; OTG/AD/O £240.00. Tricast: OTG/AD/NL £61.55; OTG/AD/O £159.90 CSF £29.43 TOTE £5.80: £1.90, £2.10; EX 33.80.
Owner B Valentine & Partner **Bred** Aston Mullins Stud & S Barrow Esq **Trained** Great Habton, N Yorks

FOCUS
Add 8yds. This ordinary 3yo handicap was wide open. It was run at an average pace and saw a tight finish. The first two set the level.

6102 REMEMBERING CHRIS HOGGARD AMATEUR RIDERS' H'CAP (DIV I) 1m 100y

5:05 (5:05) (Class 6) (0-65,67) 4-Y-O+

£2,994 (£928; £464; £300; £300; £300) **Stalls** Low

Form RPR

3122 **1** **Luna Magic**[35] 4838 5-10-11 **62**........................ MissBrodieHampson 1 70
(Archie Watson) *trckd ldr on inner: led 3f out: rdn 2f out: drvn and kpt on strly fnl f* **6/4[1]**

6401 **2** *1 1/4* **Whatwouldyouknow (IRE)**[25] 5213 4-11-2 **67**......... MrSimonWalker 10 72
(Richard Guest) *trckd ldrs: hdwy on inner wl over 2f out: chsd wnr wl over 1f out: sn rdn: drvn and kpt on same pce fnl f* **5/1[2]**

6600 **3** *1 3/4* **Corked (IRE)**[19] 5438 6-9-5 **49** ow2........................ MrConnorWood(7) 9 51
(Alistair Whillans) *towards rr: hdwy on outer wl over 2f out: rdn wl over 1f out: kpt on u.p fnl f* **16/1**

0404 **4** *2 1/4* **Relight My Fire**[15] 5560 9-10-0 **51**........................(b) MissEmilyEasterby 7 48
(Tim Easterby) *towards rr: hdwy 3f out: rdn along to chse ldrs 2f out: sn drvn and no imp fnl f* **16/1**

0401 **5** *2 1/2* **Sumner Beach**[8] 5816 5-10-5 **56** 5ex........................ MrPatrickMillman 6 48
(William Bethell) *in rr: hdwy over 2f out: rdn wl over 1f out: styd on fnl f* **11/2[3]**

0030 **6** *nk* **Prince Consort (IRE)**[16] 5517 4-9-4 **46** oh1......(p) MissSarahBowen(5) 2 37
(John Wainwright) *chsd ldng pair: rdn along 3f out: kpt on same pce fnl 2f* **40/1**

0250 **7** *hd* **Ghazan (IRE)**[23] 5282 4-10-10 **64**............(t[1]) MrMAGalligan(3) 4 55
(Kevin Frost) *chsd ldng pair on outer: rdn along wl over 2f out: sn drvn and wknd* **14/1**
50-0 **8** *1 ¼* **Dose**[15] 5560 6-9-13 **57**............ MrEireannCagney(7) 8 45
(Richard Fahey) *hld up in rr: sme hdwy on inner 2f out: sn rdn: and n.d* **25/1**
0534 **9** *½* **Coviglia (IRE)**[34] 4875 5-11-0 **65**............ MissJoannaMason 5 52
(Jacqueline Coward) *trckd ldrs: smooth hdwy and cl up 3f out: rdn over 2f out: sn drvn and wknd* **5/1**[2]
0500 **10** *8* **Make On Madam (IRE)**[16] 5517 7-9-13 **50**............ MrJamesHarding 3 20
(Les Eyre) *t.k.h: led: pushed along and hdd 3f out: sn rdn and wknd* **16/1**

1m 47.59s (1.19) **Going Correction** +0.25s/f (Good) 10 Ran SP% **119.3**
Speed ratings (Par 101): **104,102,101,98,96 95,95,94,94,86**
CSF £9.25 CT £91.17 TOTE £2.20: £1.10, £2.10, £4.60; EX 8.60 Trifecta £74.50.
Owner Marco Polo **Bred** Lady Jennifer Green **Trained** Upper Lambourn, W Berks

FOCUS
Add 8yds. It paid to be handy in this moderate handicap for amateur riders.

6103 REMEMBERING CHRIS HOGGARD AMATEUR RIDERS' H'CAP (DIV II) 1m 100y
5:40 (5:41) (Class 6) (0-65,65) 4-Y-O+

£2,994 (£928; £464; £300; £300; £300) **Stalls** Low

Form RPR
2036 **1** **Rosy Ryan (IRE)**[9] 5787 9-9-11 **48**............ MissEmmaTodd 3 55
(Tina Jackson) *trckd ldrs: hdwy over 2f out: rdn to ld over 1f out: drvn and kpt on wl towards fin* **5/1**[2]
3530 **2** *2* **Straight Ash (IRE)**[25] 5214 4-10-13 **64**............ MrSimonWalker 6 67
(Ollie Pears) *hld up in tch: hdwy 3f out: chsd ldrs 2f out: rdn and sltly outpcd over 1f out: swtchd lft: drvn and styd on fnl f* **4/1**[1]
3065 **3** *shd* **Espresso Freddo (IRE)**[17] 5497 5-10-3 **59**............(p) MrCraigDowson(5) 10 62
(Robert Stephens) *hld up towards rr: hdwy on outer over 2f out: rdn wl over 1f out: chsd ldrs ent fnl f: kpt on same pce* **11/2**[3]
2566 **4** *½* **Abushamah (IRE)**[15] 5560 8-10-7 **63**............ MissEmilyBullock(5) 2 65
(Ruth Carr) *led: pushed along over 2f out: rdn and hdd over 1f out: wknd fnl f* **4/1**[1]
2140 **5** *2 ¾* **Bollin Ted**[10] 5725 5-11-0 **65**............(p) MissEmilyEasterby 9 61
(Tim Easterby) *sn trcking ldr: pushed along over 2f out: rdn wl over 1f out: sn wknd* **6/1**
0025 **6** *1 ¼* **John Caesar (IRE)**[16] 5518 8-9-9 **46**............(p) MissSerenaBrotherton 5 39
(Rebecca Bastiman) *hld up: a towards rr* **11/2**[3]
3551 **7** *1* **Graceful Act**[16] 5518 11-9-7 **49**............(p) MissAntoniaPeck(5) 7 40
(Ron Barr) *chsd ldng pair: effrt on outer over 2f out: sn rdn and wknd* **17/2**
6650 **8** *14* **Size Matters**[26] 4587 5-9-9 **46** oh1............ MrPatrickMillman 1 8
(Mike Sowersby) *chsd ldrs: pushed along and lost pl 4f out: sn in rr* **25/1**

1m 48.37s (1.97) **Going Correction** +0.25s/f (Good) 8 Ran SP% **116.1**
Speed ratings (Par 101): **100,98,97,97,94 93,92,78**
CSF £25.73 CT £115.18 TOTE £6.10: £1.90, £1.60, £2.60; EX 29.20 Trifecta £138.20.
Owner H L Thompson **Bred** Roger A Ryan **Trained** Liverton, Cleveland

FOCUS
Add 8yds. The second division of the amateur riders' handicap was run at a muddling pace and the time was 0.78sec slower.
T/Plt: £34.80 to a £1 stake. Pool: £59,905.41 - 1,254.05 winning units T/Qpdt: £14.50 to a £1 stake. Pool: £5,155.00 - 262.04 winning units **Joe Rowntree**

5373 CHEPSTOW (L-H)
Thursday, August 15

OFFICIAL GOING: Good to soft (soft in places)
Wind: Light across Weather: Fine

6104 HOVER HELICOPTERS SUPPORTS WALES CHILDREN'S AIR AMBULANCE H'CAP 1m 4f
5:00 (5:00) (Class 5) (0-70,72) 3-Y-O+

£3,428 (£1,020; £509; £300; £300; £300) **Stalls** Low

Form RPR
1320 **1** **Ascot Day (FR)**[61] 3847 5-9-9 **68**............(p) JoshuaBryan(3) 13 77
(Bernard Llewellyn) *chsd ldrs on outer: wnt 2nd over 3f out: drvn over 2f out: chal over 1f out: led narrowly ent fnl f: asserted fnl 75yds (trainer rep said, regarding improvement in form, gelding had benefitted from being ridden with more restraint)* **6/1**[3]
6301 **2** *1 ½* **Harmonise**[10] 5744 5-9-7 **68** 5ex............ ScottMcCullagh(5) 5 75
(Sheena West) *led 2f: remained prom: led wl over 3f out: drvn 2f out: hrd pressed over 1f out: hdd ent fnl f: kpt on and ev ch tl no ex fnl 75yds* **7/1**
620 **3** *2 ¼* **Marengo**[19] 5423 8-9-11 **70**............(b) MitchGodwin(3) 8 73
(Bernard Llewellyn) *hld up: rdn and hdwy on inner over 3f out: wnt 3rd over 1f out: nt run on and no real imp on ldrs (jockey said gelding hung left in home str)* **18/1**
-000 **4** *1* **War Eagle (IRE)**[14] 5594 3-8-13 **70**............(v[1]) ThomasGreatrex(5) 3 72
(Ian Williams) *hld up: rdn and hdwy over 3f out: no further imp tl styd on fnl f* **12/1**
4300 **5** *nk* **General Brook (IRE)**[20] 5378 9-8-8 **57**............(p) KateLeahy(7) 9 58
(John O'Shea) *wnt to post early: hld up: rdn and hdwy over 2f out: styd on fnl f: nvr rchd ldrs* **33/1**
014- **6** *½* **Zillion (IRE)**[289] 7000 5-9-11 **70**............ PageFuller(3) 14 70
(Sue Gardner) *midfield on outer: hdwy over 3f out: sn chsng ldng pair and rdn: kpt on same pce and lost 3rd over 1f out: fdd towards fin* **20/1**
35 **7** *9* **Foresee (GER)**[42] 4547 6-9-0 **56**............ RossaRyan 7 42
(Tony Carroll) *chsd ldrs: rdn over 3f out: wknd 2f out (vet said gelding lost left fore shoe)* **9/2**[2]
1143 **8** *4* **Kingfast (IRE)**[19] 5425 4-9-1 **62**............(v[1]) CierenFallon(5) 2 41
(David Dennis) *t.k.h: prom whn bmpd after 3f: midfield after: rdn 3f out: grad wknd* **4/1**[1]
0205 **9** *nse* **Enmeshing**[13] 5631 6-8-13 **60**............ AndrewBreslin(5) 10 39
(Alexandra Dunn) *dwlt bdly: in tch in rr after 2f: rdn 4f out: wknd 2f out (jockey said gelding was slowly away)* **28/1**
005 **10** *½* **Doune Castle**[84] 2999 3-8-4 **56**............ RaulDaSilva 11 35
(Andrew Balding) *midfield: towards rr by 1/2-way: rdn over 4f out: lost tch 3f out: styd on fnl f* **9/2**[2]
3/05 **11** *4* **Tobougaloo**[21] 5344 8-9-2 **61**............ WilliamCox(3) 1 33
(Stuart Kittow) *wnt to post early: s.i.s: sn prom: rdn over 3f out: wknd wl over 2f out* **9/1**
2142 **12** *10* **Perfect Grace**[8] 5795 3-9-2 **68**............(p[1]) AdamMcNamara 4 25
(Archie Watson) *prom: led after 2f: rdn and hdd wl over 3f out: wknd over 2f out (trainer rep said filly was unsuited by Good to Soft, Soft in places ground and would prefer a firmer surface)* **9/1**
0645 **13** *6* **Puzzle Cache**[117] 1958 5-8-2 **51** oh4............(b) OliverSearle(7) 6
(Rod Millman) *plld hrd: prom: bmpd after 3f: rdn over 3f out: sn wknd* **40/1**

2m 37.75s (-2.55) **Going Correction** +0.175s/f (Good)
WFA 3 from 4yo+ 10lb 13 Ran SP% **129.7**
Speed ratings (Par 103): **110,109,107,106,106 106,100,97,97,97 94,87,83**
CSF £50.23 CT £748.52 TOTE £7.30: £2.30, £2.80, £5.70; EX 44.50 Trifecta £685.00.
Owner Michael Edwards & Partner **Bred** Christophe Jouandou **Trained** Fochriw, Caerphilly

FOCUS
The going was given as good to soft, soft in places (Going Stick 4.9). Distances as advertised. A modest affair. A pb from the winner, and the second has been rated as improving a bit on her Windsor win.

6105 ISTADIA SCREENS SUPPORTS WALES CHILDREN'S AIR AMBULANCE H'CAP 2m
5:35 (5:35) (Class 5) (0-70,72) 4-Y-O+

£3,428 (£1,020; £509; £300; £300; £300) **Stalls** Low

Form RPR
0R02 **1** **Jacob Cats**[44] 4483 10-9-7 **70**............(v) CallumShepherd 8 78
(William Knight) *a.p: tk narrow ld gng wl over 1f out: rdn out fnl f* **12/1**
040 **2** *½* **Norab (GER)**[44] 4483 8-8-6 **58**............(b) WilliamCox(3) 1 65
(Bernard Llewellyn) *led 1f: trckd ldr: drvn 3f out: ev ch 1f out: styd on same pce (jockey said gelding hung left throughout)* **22/1**
4141 **3** *1 ½* **So Near So Farhh**[20] 5379 4-9-2 **70**............ ScottMcCullagh(5) 3 75
(Mick Channon) *hld up: hdwy 7f out: rdn 3f out: chsd ldrs 2f out: styd on same pce fnl f* **5/1**[3]
0162 **4** *nk* **Atomic Jack**[29] 5047 4-9-7 **70**............ PatDobbs 7 75
(George Baker) *half-rrd s: rcvrd to ld after 1f: rdn over 2f out: hdd over 1f out: no ex fnl f: fin lame (vet said gelding finished lame on right fore)* **3/1**[1]
2661 **5** *2 ½* **Make Good (IRE)**[30] 5029 4-8-10 **64**............(bt) CierenFallon(5) 10 66
(David Dennis) *chsd ldrs: rdn 3f out: sltly outpcd 2f out: styd on towards fin* **5/1**[3]
0552 **6** *¾* **Arty Campbell (IRE)**[17] 5496 9-9-1 **67**............(b) JoshuaBryan(3) 12 68
(Bernard Llewellyn) *t.k.h in midfield: rdn over 2f out: styd on same pce (jockey said gelding ran too freely)* **18/1**
6414 **7** *2 ½* **Rosie Royale (IRE)**[22] 5290 7-8-13 **62**............ RossaRyan 4 60
(Roger Teal) *chsd ldrs: rdn over 2f out: unable to chal: wknd ins fnl f* **10/1**
250- **8** *14* **Nordenfelt (IRE)**[14] 7388 6-7-9 **51** oh6............(t) IsobelFrancis(7) 13 32
(Sue Gardner) *midfield tl rdn and wknd over 3f out* **33/1**
4126 **9** *1 ¾* **Master Grey (IRE)**[19] 5452 4-9-9 **72**............ KieranO'Neill 5 51
(Rod Millman) *prom: rdn over 3f out: wknd over 2f out* **4/1**[2]
450- **10** *¾* **War Drums**[101] 8230 5-9-2 **70**............(h) AndrewBreslin(5) 9 48
(Alexandra Dunn) *s.s: hld up: rdn over 3f out: wknd over 2f out* **9/1**
0-50 **11** *5* **Mustaaqeem (USA)**[51] 2718 7-7-13 **55**............(b) KeelanBaker(7) 2 27
(Bernard Llewellyn) *a towards rr: lost tch 4f out: t.o (jockey said gelding was never travelling)* **66/1**
-546 **12** *10* **Noble Behest**[17] 5502 5-9-2 **70**............(p) ThomasGreatrex(5) 6 30
(Ian Williams) *hld up: rdn 5f out: sn lost tch: t.o (jockey said gelding was never travelling)* **14/1**

3m 37.39s (-4.71) **Going Correction** +0.175s/f (Good) 12 Ran SP% **125.8**
Speed ratings (Par 103): **112,111,111,110,109 109,107,100,100,99 97,92**
CSF £259.98 CT £1511.97 TOTE £15.40: £3.40, £6.20, £2.00; EX 357.60 Trifecta £994.70.
Owner Canisbay Bloodstock **Bred** Highclere Stud **Trained** Angmering, W Sussex

FOCUS
The pace was controlled by the favourite and it didn't pay to be too far off it. It's been rated around the winner and third.

6106 DRAGON AIRCON SUPPORTS WALES AIR AMBULANCE EBF NOVICE AUCTION STKS (PLUS 10 RACE) 7f 16y
6:10 (6:11) (Class 4) 2-Y-O **£4,463** (£1,328; £663; £331) **Stalls** Centre

Form RPR
1 **Love Destiny** 2-9-5 0............ DaneO'Neill 4 75
(Mark Johnston) *in tch in midfield: rdn over 2f out: stl 4th ins fnl f: r.o wl on outer fnl 100yds to get up nr fin as ldr faltered* **7/2**[1]
06 **2** *¾* **Junvieve (FR)**[10] 5733 2-9-0 0............ RossaRyan 2 68
(Richard Hannon) *trckd ldrs: rdn over 2f out: wnt 2nd appr fnl f: briefly relegated to cl 3rd towards fin: r.o* **7/2**[1]
2310 **3** *hd* **Space Ace (FR)**[9] 5777 2-9-5 76............(p) AdamMcNamara 5 72
(Archie Watson) *trckd ldr: rdn to ld over 1f out: hung rt appr fnl f: over a l up and keeping on u.p whn jinked rt 75yds out: lost momentum and qckly hdd (vet said filly lost right hind shoe.)* **9/2**[2]
2202 **4** *1* **Nat Love (IRE)**[9] 5777 2-8-11 71............ ScottMcCullagh(5) 8 67
(Mick Channon) *led: rdn 2f out: hdd over 1f out: disputing 2nd whn sltly hmpd appr fnl f: kpt on same pce (jockey said gelding ran too freely and hung both ways)* **9/2**[2]
5 *1 ¾* **Buto** 2-8-11 0............ CierenFallon(5) 6 62
(Eve Johnson Houghton) *hld up towards rr: rdn after 3f: styd on fnl f* **7/1**[3]
6 *2 ½* **Maximilius (GER)** 2-9-5 0............ PatDobbs 7 59
(Ralph Beckett) *chsd ldrs: drvn over 3f out: outpcd 2f out: fdd fnl f* **9/2**[2]
7 *12* **John Leo's Son (IRE)** 2-9-3 0............ CallumShepherd 3 26
(David Evans) *dwlt: rn green and a in rr (jockey said gelding ran green)* **16/1**
05 **8** *11* **Mayflower Lady (IRE)**[30] 5011 2-8-11 0............(h[1]) KieranO'Neill 1
(Ronald Harris) *plld hrd in rr: drvn 4f out: sn lost tch (jockey said filly ran too freely in early stages)* **80/1**

1m 26.54s (2.64) **Going Correction** +0.175s/f (Good) 8 Ran SP% **118.6**
Speed ratings (Par 96): **91,90,89,88,86 83,70,57**
CSF £16.54 TOTE £4.50: £1.70, £1.70, £1.90; EX 17.00 Trifecta £99.10.
Owner M Doyle **Bred** Cheveley Park Stud Ltd **Trained** Middleham Moor, N Yorks

FOCUS
Drama in the closing stages here as the leader threw away certain victory.

6107 MRS IRENE LAUX - 85TH BIRTHDAY CELEBRATION H'CAP 6f 16y
6:40 (6:42) (Class 6) (0-52,52) 3-Y-O+

£2,781 (£827; £413; £300; £300; £300) **Stalls** Centre

Form RPR
0406 **1** **Fantasy Justifier (IRE)**[44] 4481 8-9-7 **51**............(p) KieranO'Neill 5 60+
(Ronald Harris) *s.i.s: in rr: rdn and hdwy on outer over 2f out: led over 1f out: sn hung rt: briefly jnd ins fnl f: r.o (jockey said gelding hung right inside fnl 2f)* **11/2**[2]

-534 **2** 1 ½ **Mad Endeavour**[28] 5083 8-9-7 **51**..........................(b) FergusSweeney 17 56
(Stuart Kittow) *broke wl: led: rdn 2f out: hdd and hung lft over 1f out: ev ch ins fnl f: no ex fnl 100yds (jockey said gelding hung left)* **8/1**

0346 **3** 2 **Cool Strutter (IRE)**[28] 5083 7-8-13 **48**..................(p) ScottMcCullagh(5) 9 47
(John Spearing) *prom: drvn and ev ch 2f out: kpt on same pce in hld 3rd fnl f* **6/1**[3]

4003 **4** nk **Jacksonfire**[15] 5551 7-9-3 **47**..(p) NathanEvans 2 46
(Michael Mullineaux) *hld up: hdwy on outer 1/2-way: drvn and ev ch 2f out: sltly hmpd appr fnl f: no ex* **8/1**

0000 **5** 2 ½ **Alfie's Angel (IRE)**[37] 4765 5-9-3 **47**...................................... RossaRyan 4 37
(Milton Bradley) *hld up: rdn over 2f out: hdwy over 1f out: styd on fnl f: nt rch ldrs* **20/1**

0004 **6** ½ **Twilighting**[6] 5890 3-9-1 **49**.. CharlesBishop 15 37+
(Henry Candy) *dwlt: sn chsng ldrs: rdn over 2f out: trying to chal whn hmpd appr fnl f: nt rcvr* **3/1**[1]

5600 **7** 1 ¼ **Lily Of Year (FR)**[3] 6018 4-8-13 **50**................................ MichaelPitt(7) 7 35
(Denis Coakley) *s.s: rdn along in rr early: drvn over 2f out: no prog tl r.o fnl f* **11/1**

-540 **8** 1 ½ **Langley Vale**[34] 4873 10-9-0 **49**...................................... CierenFallon(5) 16 29
(Roger Teal) *pckd as stalls opened: midfield: rdn over 2f out: no hdwy* **11/2**[2]

605 **9** ½ **Rebecke (IRE)**[22] 5306 3-9-4 **52**..................................... HectorCrouch 11 30
(Clive Cox) *prom: rdn over 2f out: wknd over 1f out* **14/1**

0000 **10** shd **Hellofagame**[38] 4733 4-8-8 **45**.................................... EllieMacKenzie(7) 8 24
(Richard Price) *chsd ldrs: rdn over 2f out: wknd over 1f out* **50/1**

0-00 **11** shd **What A Dazzler**[168] 943 3-8-6 **45**........................ ThoreHammerHansen(5) 1 22
(Bill Turner) *prom: rdn over 3f out: wknd over 1f out* **25/1**

0660 **12** 3 ¾ **Tintern Spirit (IRE)**[106] 2276 3-8-11 **45**.......................... AdamMcNamara 6 11
(Milton Bradley) *t.k.h: rdn over 2f out: a towards rr* **50/1**

0-0 **13** nse **Counterfeit**[54] 4115 4-8-13 **50**......................(p) Pierre-LouisJamin(7) 10 17
(Paul George) *s.i.s: midfield: rdn 1/2-way: sn wknd* **14/1**

0006 **14** 2 ¾ **Swendab (IRE)**[28] 5084 11-8-8 **45**................................(b) KateLeahy(7) 12 4
(John O'Shea) *rrd s and slowly away: sn rcvrd and chsd ldrs: rdn 1/2-way: wknd 2f out (jockey said gelding reared as stalls opened)* **33/1**

1m 13.13s (1.63) **Going Correction** +0.175s/f (Good)
WFA 3 from 4yo+ 4lb **14 Ran SP% 129.4**
Speed ratings (Par 101): **96,94,91,90,87 86,85,83,82,82 82,77,77,73**
CSF £50.58 CT £291.33 TOTE £6.90: £2.40, £4.40, £2.20; EX 48.90 Trifecta £320.60.
Owner Ridge House Stables Ltd **Bred** Denis And Mrs Teresa Bergin **Trained** Earlswood, Monmouths

FOCUS
A low-grade sprint.

6108 DAIKIN AIRCON SUPPORTS WALES CHILDREN'S AIR AMBULANCE H'CAP 6f 16y
7:10 (7:12) (Class 4) (0-80,82) 3-Y-O **£5,207** (£1,549; £774; £387; £300) **Stalls** Centre

Form RPR

3015 **1** **Gambon (GER)**[21] 5343 3-9-4 **76**.. CharlesBishop 4 82
(Eve Johnson Houghton) *hld up: hdwy 2f out: rdn to ld 1f out: r.o* **5/1**

1103 **2** 2 ¾ **Alicia Darcy (IRE)**[4] 5989 3-8-9 **74**..............................(b) KateLeahy(7) 1 71
(Archie Watson) *cl up: led after 1f: drvn 2f out: hdd 1f out: outpcd by wnr fnl 100yds* **9/2**

3554 **3** 2 ¼ **Motagally**[12] 5685 3-9-5 **77**.. DaneO'Neill 5 67
(Charles Hills) *trckd ldng pair: drvn and briefly in 2nd 2f out: one pce appr fnl f* **7/2**[3]

0626 **4** 1 ½ **Cool Reflection (IRE)**[28] 5090 3-9-9 **81**............................ RossaRyan 2 66
(Paul Cole) *hld up: rdn 2f out: sn outpcd by ldrs: kpt on towards fin* **2/1**[1]

4510 **5** ¾ **Pass The Gin**[14] 5589 3-9-7 **82**.. WilliamCox(3) 3 65
(Andrew Balding) *t.k.h: led 1f: remained cl up: rdn and lost 2nd 2f out: sn hung lft and nt run on: fdd fnl f* **3/1**[2]

1m 12.76s (1.26) **Going Correction** +0.175s/f (Good) **5 Ran SP% 115.4**
Speed ratings (Par 102): **98,94,91,89,88**
CSF £27.43 TOTE £6.40: £2.10, £2.40; EX 28.20 Trifecta £130.30.
Owner Anthony Pye-Jeary **Bred** Stiftung Gestut Fahrhof **Trained** Blewbury, Oxon

FOCUS
A fair sprint, and the winner is improving. The second has been rated close to her latest.

6109 BMSSW.COM SUPPORTS WALES CHILDREN'S AIR AMBULANCE H'CAP 6f 16y
7:45 (7:46) (Class 4) (0-80,81) 4-Y-O+
£5,207 (£1,549; £774; £387; £300; £300) **Stalls** Centre

Form RPR

1031 **1** **Major Valentine**[34] 4872 7-9-0 **80**.. KateLeahy(7) 2 93
(John O'Shea) *mde all: pushed along fr 2f out: a in command: comf* **13/2**[3]

0043 **2** 3 ½ **Smokey Lane (IRE)**[17] 5495 5-8-10 **69**..................(v) CallumShepherd 4 71
(David Evans) *in 2nd virtually thrght: rdn over 2f out: hung lft over 1f out: kpt on but little ch w comfortable wnr (jockey said gelding hung left under pressure)* **13/2**[3]

606 **3** 1 ¼ **Doc Sportello (IRE)**[10] 5746 7-9-0 **73**.................................. RobertWinston 1 71
(Tony Carroll) *chsd ldng pair: drvn over 2f out: disp 2nd over 1f out tl ins fnl f* **4/1**[2]

0005 **4** ½ **Naadirr (IRE)**[29] 5038 8-8-11 **75**..................................(p) CierenFallon(5) 6 71
(Kevin Ryan) *dwlt: in rr: drvn over 2f out: sme hdwy over 1f out: hld whn hung rt ins fnl f (jockey said gelding was slowly away)* **10/1**

0260 **5** shd **The Lamplighter (FR)**[49] 4281 4-8-5 **64**.....................(tp) KieranO'Neill 8 60
(George Baker) *wnt lft and bmpd rival leaving stalls: in rr: rdn and sme prog over 2f out: disputing hld 4th whn carried rt ins fnl f* **8/1**

4621 **6** 9 **Atalanta's Boy**[21] 5330 4-8-11 **75**..........................(h) ThomasGreatrex(5) 5 42+
(David Menuisier) *bmpd leaving stalls: plld hrd towards rr: rdn over 2f out: no imp: wknd fnl f: bled fr the nose (vet said gelding bled from nose)* **6/4**[1]

-454 **7** nk **Clear Spring (IRE)**[17] 5503 11-8-13 **72**................................... RyanTate 3 38
(John Spearing) *s.i.s: chsd ldrs tl outpcd over 2f out: wknd over 1f out* **10/1**

1m 11.78s (0.28) **Going Correction** +0.175s/f (Good) **7 Ran SP% 116.0**
Speed ratings (Par 105): **105,100,98,98,97 85,85**
CSF £48.49 CT £191.54 TOTE £4.50: £2.90, £3.60; EX 21.20 Trifecta £121.00.
Owner Pete Smith **Bred** J R Salter **Trained** Elton, Gloucs

FOCUS
Few got into this, the winner in control throughout on the front end. It's hard to pin down the level.

6110 ISTADIA SUPPORTS WALES CHILDREN'S AIR AMBULANCE H'CAP 5f 16y
8:15 (8:15) (Class 5) (0-75,77) 3-Y-O+
£3,428 (£1,020; £509; £300; £300; £300) **Stalls** Centre

Form RPR

1204 **1** **A Sure Welcome**[13] 5606 5-9-12 **77**...................................(p) RyanTate 6 84
(John Spearing) *half-rrd s and slowly away: hld up in tch: rdn over 1f out: wnt 3rd and plenty to do ent fnl f: r.o wl to ld cl home* **11/4**[2]

1201 **2** ½ **Somewhere Secret**[5] 5952 5-9-4 **69** 5ex.....................(p) NathanEvans 7 74
(Michael Mullineaux) *a.p: trckd ldr after 2f: rdn 2f out: led narrowly 75yds out tl hdd cl home* **6/4**[1]

0552 **3** ½ **Secretfact**[47] 4374 6-9-10 **75**.. FergusSweeney 3 78
(Malcolm Saunders) *t.k.h: sn led: taken rt to stands' rail after 2f: rdn over 1f out: hung lft ins fnl f: hdd fnl 75yds* **11/1**

4432 **4** 1 ¾ **Union Rose**[8] 5799 7-9-2 **72**...(p) CierenFallon(5) 2 69
(Ronald Harris) *led early: chsd ldrs tl dropped to last and rdn 2f out: kpt on fnl f* **3/1**[3]

3202 **5** 4 **Jaganory (IRE)**[13] 5607 7-8-1 **57** oh1 ow1..(v) ThoreHammerHansen(5) 1 40
(Christopher Mason) *cl up: rdn and sltly outpcd by ldrs 1/2-way: wknd fnl f* **7/1**

0640 **6** 3 ¾ **Autumn Splendour (IRE)**[4] 5990 3-9-1 **69**.............................. RossaRyan 5 37
(Milton Bradley) *dwlt bdly: in tch in last after 1f: rdn and hdwy on outer 1/2-way: hung lft over 1f out: wknd fnl f (jockey said gelding missed quick and slowly away)* **25/1**

1m 1.59s (2.19) **Going Correction** +0.175s/f (Good)
WFA 3 from 4yo+ 3lb **6 Ran SP% 116.3**
Speed ratings (Par 103): **89,88,87,84,78 72**
CSF £7.69 TOTE £4.00: £1.90, £1.60; EX 8.20 Trifecta £35.30.
Owner Kinnersley Partnership 3 **Bred** Richard Evans Bloodstock **Trained** Kinnersley, Worcs
■ Stewards' Enquiry : Nathan Evans two-day ban: used whip in incorrect place (Aug 29-30)

FOCUS
A modest sprint handicap. A small pb from the winner, with the second rated in line with his Haydock win.
T/Jkpt: Not won. T/Plt: £823.70 to a £1 stake. Pool: £52,808.78 - 46.80 winning units T/Qpdt: £37.10 to a £1 stake. Pool: £8,394.49 - 167.09 winning units **Richard Lowther**

6046 LINGFIELD (L-H)
Thursday, August 15

OFFICIAL GOING: Polytrack: standard
Wind: light to medium, across Weather: fine

6111 VISIT ATTHERACES.COM H'CAP 7f 1y(P)
2:10 (2:10) (Class 5) (0-75,76) 3-Y-O
£3,428 (£1,020; £509; £300; £300; £300) **Stalls** Low

Form RPR

502 **1** **Visionara**[12] 5650 3-9-6 **74**... HollieDoyle 7 82
(Simon Crisford) *chsd ldr tl effrt to ld 2f out: forged ahd and edgd lft ins fnl f: styd on wl* **11/4**[2]

6050 **2** 1 ¾ **Indian Sounds (IRE)**[12] 5651 3-9-1 **69**..........................(b) PJMcDonald 3 72
(Mark Johnston) *led: rdn and hdd 2f out: one pce whn crowded for room and swtchd rt ins fnl f: no imp towards fin* **10/3**[3]

5160 **3** 1 ¾ **Kwela**[19] 5450 3-9-1 **76**...(p) GeorgiaDobie(7) 6 74+
(Eve Johnson Houghton) *t.k.h early: hld up in tch in rr of main gp: nt clr run and swtchd rt over 1f out: hdwy to chse clr ldng pair wl ins fnl f: styng on strly at fin* **20/1**

-056 **4** 2 ¾ **Red Bravo (IRE)**[36] 4793 3-9-7 **75**.................................. KieranShoemark 1 66
(Charles Hills) *chsd ldrs: effrt ent fnl 2f: outpcd and wl hld over 1f out: lost 3rd wl ins fnl f* **6/1**

034P **5** 1 ¼ **Cromwell**[7] 5842 3-7-11 **56** oh1.. RhiainIngram(5) 5 43
(Luke Dace) *hld up in tch in midfield: outpcd ent fnl 2f: wl hld and plugged on same pce ins fnl f* **16/1**

-010 **6** ¾ **Mendoza (IRE)**[31] 5000 3-9-7 **75**...(h) RyanTate 9 60
(James Eustace) *taken down early and led to post: midfield on outer: outpcd and struggling bnd 2f out: wl hld and plugged on same pce ins fnl f* **16/1**

0042 **7** 1 ½ **Excelled (IRE)**[31] 5002 3-9-8 **76**.. DanielMuscutt 4 57
(James Fanshawe) *taken down early: stdd s: hld up in tch in rr of main gp: nt clrest of runs on inner ent fnl 2f: no hdwy over 1f out: nvr involved and wl btn fnl f (jockey said filly moved poorly; post-race examination failed to reveal any abnormality)* **9/4**[1]

2005 **8** 36 **Lady Cosette (FR)**[40] 4653 3-9-4 **72**..............................(b) LukeMorris 8
(Harry Dunlop) *sn dropped to rr: nvr travelling and detached in last: eased fnl f: t.o (jockey said filly was never travelling)* **33/1**

1m 22.9s (-1.90) **Going Correction** -0.15s/f (Stan) **8 Ran SP% 114.3**
Speed ratings (Par 100): **104,102,100,96,95 94,92,51**
CSF £12.38 CT £148.44 TOTE £2.70: £1.30, £1.30, £3.00; EX 12.30 Trifecta £131.30.
Owner W J and T C O Gredley **Bred** W S Farish, Inwood Stable & Bcwt Ltd **Trained** Newmarket, Suffolk

FOCUS
An ordinary 3yo handicap to start and the first two dominated throughout. The second has been rated to this year's form.

6112 WATCH SKY SPORTS RACING IN HD EBF NOVICE STKS 7f 1y(P)
2:40 (2:40) (Class 5) 2-Y-O **£3,428** (£1,020; £509; £254) **Stalls** Low

Form RPR

31 **1** **Hector Loza**[23] 5265 2-9-9 0.. NickyMackay 4 82
(Simon Dow) *taken down early: broke wl: sn restrained and t.k.h: chsd ldrs: wnt 2nd 2f out and sn swtchd rt: clsd u.p to chal ins fnl f: led 50yds out: r.o wl* **4/1**[2]

51 **2** 1 ¼ **Tell Me All**[16] 5512 2-9-9 0.. LukeMorris 5 79
(Sir Mark Prescott Bt) *sn pressing ldr tl led over 5f out: rdn over 1f out: drvn and hrd pressed ins fnl f: hdd 50yds out: no ex and eased nr fin* **8/15**[1]

3 2 ¾ **Transition** 2-9-2 0.. RobertHavlin 6 65
(Amanda Perrett) *rn green and outpcd in last pair: clsd and in tch 3f out: effrt 2f out: chsd clr ldng pair and rdn 1f out: kpt on but no imp* **14/1**

4 8 **Ben Lilly (IRE)** 2-9-2 0.. JosephineGordon 2 44
(Ralph Beckett) *rn green: sn pushed into ld: hdd over 5f out: rdn 3f out: lost 2nd: outpcd and wd bnd 2f out: wknd fnl f* **8/1**[3]

5 2 3/4 **Tantivy** 2-9-2 0 .... SeanLevey 1 37
(Richard Hannon) *rn green: sn outpcd in rr and rdn along: clsd briefly 3f out: sn struggling again: wl btn fnl 2f (jockey said colt was slowly away)* **14/1**

1m 23.93s (-0.87) **Going Correction** -0.15s/f (Stan) **5** Ran SP% **109.7**
Speed ratings (Par 94): **98,96,93,84,81**
CSF £6.57 TOTE £3.90: £1.70, £1.10; EX 6.50 Trifecta £20.90.
Owner Robert Moss **Bred** Saleh Al Homaizi & Imad Al Sagar **Trained** Epsom, Surrey

FOCUS
Two previous winners against three newcomers in this novice and experience told, though not in the order most would have expected. They went a serious pace which played into the hands of the winner.

6113 WITHEFORD EQUINE BARRIER TRIALS AT LINGFIELD PARK NURSERY H'CAP 6f 1y(P)
3:10 (3:10) (Class 5) (0-70,70) 2-Y-O
£3,428 (£1,020; £509; £300; £300; £300) **Stalls Low**

Form RPR
445 1 **Royal Ambition (IRE)**[17] 5500 2-9-6 **69** .... HectorCrouch 3 71+
(Clive Cox) *led: rdn over 2f out: hdd 2f out: battled bk wl to ld again ins fnl f: styd on wl* **7/2**[2]

0335 2 1 **Ossco**[40] 4637 2-9-5 **68** .... SeanLevey 1 67
(Mohamed Moubarak) *chsd ldrs: effrt ent fnl 2f: kpt on wl ins fnl f: snatched 2nd on post* **4/1**[3]

4351 3 *nse* **Fashion Free**[14] 5576 2-9-7 **70** .... HollieDoyle 5 69
(Archie Watson) *dwlt: in tch in rr: hdwy to press wnr over 4f out: rdn to ld narrowly 2f out: drvn ent fnl f: hdd ins fnl f: kpt on same pce and lost 2nd on post* **15/8**[1]

3556 4 1 **Champagne Supanova (IRE)**[27] 5146 2-9-1 **64**.(v[1]) KieranShoemark 2 60
(Richard Spencer) *in tch in rr: effrt ent fnl 2f: no imp over 1f out: hdwy 100yds out: kpt on wl and swtchd rt towards fin* **16/1**

2351 5 *nk* **My Motivate Girl (IRE)**[13] 5630 2-9-5 **68** ....(b) LukeMorris 4 63
(Archie Watson) *dwlt: in tch in last pair: effrt on outer ent fnl 2f: no imp over 1f out: kpt on ins fnl f* **7/1**

034 6 1/2 **Zain Storm (FR)**[56] 4018 2-9-6 **69** .... AndreaAtzeni 6 62
(John Butler) *chsd ldr tl over 4f out: in tch in midfield after: effrt ent fnl 2f: no imp over 1f out: kpt on ins fnl f: nt clr run cl home* **11/2**

1m 12.57s (0.67) **Going Correction** -0.15s/f (Stan) **6** Ran SP% **110.8**
Speed ratings (Par 94): **89,87,87,86,85 85**
CSF £17.16 TOTE £4.30: £2.10, £2.40; EX 17.30 Trifecta £70.10.
Owner J Goddard **Bred** Gus Roche **Trained** Lambourn, Berks

FOCUS
An ordinary nursery and not many got into it.

6114 GMB UNION LONDON REGION MAIDEN FILLIES' STKS 1m 4f (P)
3:40 (3:41) (Class 5) 3-Y-O+
£3,428 (£1,020; £509; £254) **Stalls Low**

Form RPR
-302 1 **Ambling (IRE)**[22] 5311 3-9-0 79 .... RobertHavlin 5 89+
(John Gosden) *taken down early: mde all: travelling best fr 4f out: wnt wl clr 2f out and in n.d whn shkn up over 1f out: v easily and unchal* **8/13**[1]

3 2 9 **Midnights' Gift**[27] 5148 3-9-0 0 .... HollieDoyle 2 75
(Alan King) *t.k.h: chsd wnr for 2f: 3rd and rdn over 4f out: no ch w wnr after: modest 2nd and plugged on same pce fr over 1f out* **10/1**

0-6 3 1 **Honfleur (IRE)**[40] 4641 3-9-0 0 .... PJMcDonald 4 73
(Sir Michael Stoute) *off the pce in 4th: rdn over 4f out: no ch w wnr after: plugged on to go modest 3rd wl ins fnl f* **8/1**[3]

222 4 1 1/2 **The Very Moon**[29] 5048 3-9-0 80 .... AndreaAtzeni 3 71
(Sir Michael Stoute) *squeezed for room leaving stalls: hdwy to chse wnr 10f out: rdn over 4f out: nvr threatened to get on terms w wnr: wl hld and lost 2nd over 1f out: wknd ins fnl f* **11/4**[2]

5 14 **Parisian Affair**[16] 4-9-10 0 .... LukeMorris 1 47
(Neil King) *s.i.s and rousted along leaving stalls: a in rr and nvr on terms: u.p 5f out: wl bhd fnl 3f* **100/1**

2m 28.09s (-4.91) **Going Correction** -0.15s/f (Stan)
WFA 3 from 4yo 10lb **5** Ran SP% **109.8**
Speed ratings (Par 100): **110,104,103,102,93**
CSF £7.80 TOTE £1.80: £1.10, £2.50; EX 6.20 Trifecta £15.20.
Owner Lord Vestey **Bred** Stowell Park Stud **Trained** Newmarket, Suffolk

FOCUS
A one-sided fillies' maiden. The winner has been rated in line with her C&D latest, with the second and third close to form.

6115 SKY SPORTS RACING ON SKY 415 H'CAP 1m 5f (P)
4:10 (4:11) (Class 6) (0-65,71) 3-Y-O+
£2,781 (£827; £413; £300; £300; £300) **Stalls Low**

Form RPR
-541 1 **Mon Frere (IRE)**[12] 5648 3-9-9 **67** ....(p) LukeMorris 1 78
(Sir Mark Prescott Bt) *hld up in tch in midfield: swtchd rt and hdwy to ld and edgd lft ent fnl 2f: forged ahd 1f out: drvn and styd on wl ins fnl f* **6/4**[2]

-030 2 1 1/4 **Ban Shoof**[19] 5425 6-10-0 **62** ....(b) KieranShoemark 5 69
(Gary Moore) *hld up in last trio: effrt and hdwy over 2f out: chsd clr ldng pair over 1f out: styd on wl ins fnl f to go 2nd last strides: nt rch wnr* **8/1**[3]

3351 3 *nk* **Anyonecanhaveitall**[5] 5975 3-9-13 **71** 6ex .... PJMcDonald 7 80
(Mark Johnston) *wl in tch in midfield: edgd out rt and effrt over 2f out: carried lft but kicked on w wnr 2f out tl unable to match pce of wnr 1f out: kpt on same pce after: lost 2nd last strides* **10/11**[1]

6100 4 3 3/4 **Banta Bay**[30] 5029 5-9-3 **51** .... JosephineGordon 2 52
(John Best) *trckd ldrs on inner: nt clr run and swtchd rt over 2f out: effrt jst over 2f out: kpt on same pce fr over 1f out* **22/1**

0000 5 8 **Accessor (IRE)**[22] 5311 4-9-11 **59** .... RobertHavlin 4 48
(Michael Wigham) *s.i.s: hld up in last pair: swtchd rt over 3f out: rdn and outpcd jst over 2f out: no ch after: plugged on to pass btn rivals ins fnl f* **20/1**

0-60 6 1/2 **Pepper Street (IRE)**[29] 5053 4-9-12 **60** ....(p) DanielMuscutt 3 48
(Amy Murphy) *midfield: effrt jst over 2f out: sn outpcd and wl btn over 1f out* **50/1**

23/0 7 *shd* **Jupiter Custos (FR)**[23] 5271 7-9-13 **61** .... NickyMackay 8 49
(Michael Scudamore) *chsd ldr: ev ch and rdn over 2f out: squeezed for room and outpcd 2f out: sn btn and wknd over 1f out* **33/1**

0034 8 1 1/2 **The Wire Flyer**[34] 4868 4-8-11 **45** ....(p) KierenFox 9 31
(John Flint) *s.i.s: hld up in tch in last pair: effrt over 2f out: sn outpcd and wl btn over 1f out* **16/1**

0460 9 4 1/2 **Affair**[30] 5029 5-9-3 **51** .... CharlieBennett 6 30
(Hughie Morrison) *led: rdn and hdd over 2f out: short of room and hmpd ent fnl 2f: sn wknd* **33/1**

2m 45.74s (-0.26) **Going Correction** -0.15s/f (Stan)
WFA 3 from 4yo+ 10lb **9** Ran SP% **126.3**
Speed ratings (Par 101): **94,93,93,90,85 85,85,84,81**
CSF £14.55 CT £17.48 TOTE £2.10: £1.10, £2.00, £1.10; EX 13.40 Trifecta £24.80.
Owner Elite Racing Club **Bred** Elite Racing Club **Trained** Newmarket, Suffolk

FOCUS
A moderate staying handicap with the betting dominated by two bang-in-form 3yos. The went a fair pace and the front four pulled a long way clear of the others.

6116 SKY SPORTS RACING ON VIRGIN 535 H'CAP 7f 1y(P)
4:40 (4:41) (Class 6) (0-65,66) 4-Y-O+
£2,781 (£827; £413; £300; £300; £300) **Stalls Low**

Form RPR
0032 1 **Mochalov**[8] 5807 4-8-7 **56** .... DarraghKeenan(5) 9 66
(Jane Chapple-Hyam) *hld up in midfield: clsd to trck ldrs ent fnl 2f: led wl over 1f out: sn shkn up and asserted: r.o and a in command ins fnl f* **3/1**[1]

0/01 2 1 1/4 **Miss Icon**[28] 5081 5-8-8 **57** .... WilliamCarver(5) 2 64
(Patrick Chamings) *hld up in midfield: clsd to chse ldrs and effrt 2f out: drvn over 1f out: chsd wnr ins fnl f: kpt on but a hld* **3/1**[1]

2042 3 1 1/4 **De Little Engine (IRE)**[7] 5839 5-9-1 **66** ....(p) LukeCatton(7) 5 70
(Alexandra Dunn) *chsd ldr: clsd and trcking ldr whn nt clr run 2f out: effrt on inner over 1f out: chsd wnr ent fnl f: no imp and lost 2nd ins fnl f* **11/2**[2]

0155 4 3/4 **Swissal (IRE)**[28] 5080 4-9-5 **63** ....(p) LukeMorris 10 65
(David Dennis) *s.i.s: off the pce in last quartet: clsd and rdn over 2f out: styd on ins fnl f: nt rch ldrs* **8/1**

4-54 5 1 **Rock Boy Grey (IRE)**[27] 5137 4-9-7 **65** .... PJMcDonald 12 64
(Mark Loughnane) *chsd ldrs: clsd to trck ldr 2f out: ev ch briefly wl over 1f out: unable to match pce of wnr and racd awkwardly and lost 2nd ent fnl f: wknd* **6/1**[3]

-000 6 1 1/4 **Birthday Girl (IRE)**[36] 4776 4-8-2 **46** oh1 ....(t) HollieDoyle 7 42
(Amanda Perrett) *off the pce in midfield: clsd and rdn 3f out: kpt on same pce u.p and no imp fr over 1f out* **66/1**

1002 7 1 3/4 **Blessed To Empress (IRE)**[29] 5051 4-9-3 **61** ......(v) KieranShoemark 1 53
(Amy Murphy) *off the pce in midfield: swtchd rt and effrt 2f out: kpt on ins fnl f: nvr trbld ldrs* **10/1**

0000 8 1 3/4 **Woggle (IRE)**[15] 5565 4-8-2 **46** oh1 .... JosephineGordon 4 33
(Geoffrey Deacon) *chsd clr ldng trio: rdn and losing pl over 2f out: wl hld over 1f out* **20/1**

0000 9 1 1/2 **Farhhmoreexciting**[92] 2738 4-8-1 **52** .... Cameronlles(7) 8 35
(David Elsworth) *s.i.s: a towards rr and racd wd thrght* **20/1**

100- 10 8 **Shoyd**[357] 6439 4-9-2 **60** .... SeanLevey 11 22
(Richard Hannon) *stdd and dropped in bhd after s: a off the pce in rr* **33/1**

3000 11 2 3/4 **Bigshotte**[8] 5807 4-9-1 **59** ....(bt[1]) RobertHavlin 6 14+
(Luke Dace) *racd freely: led and sn clr: hdd wl over 1f out: sn btn and wknd* **12/1**

0 12 36 **Daubney's Dream (IRE)**[41] 4615 4-8-8 **59** ....(vt[1]) GeorgeRooke(7) 3
(Paddy Butler) *restless in stalls: s.i.s: a bhd: lost tch over 2f out: t.o (jockey said gelding was restless in stalls and subsequently was slowly away)* **50/1**

1m 23.65s (-1.15) **Going Correction** -0.15s/f (Stan) **12** Ran SP% **123.5**
Speed ratings (Par 101): **100,98,97,96,95 93,91,89,88,78 75,34**
CSF £11.08 CT £49.90 TOTE £4.10: £1.70, £1.90, £1.70; EX 14.50 Trifecta £59.20.
Owner Mrs Jane Chapple-Hyam **Bred** D H Brailsford **Trained** Dalham, Suffolk

FOCUS
A big field for this moderate handicap. The leaders may have gone off too quick and the field were soon well spread out, but those near the head of the market came to the fore.

6117 RACING WELFARE H'CAP 1m 1y(P)
5:10 (5:13) (Class 6) (0-55,55) 3-Y-O+
£2,781 (£827; £413; £300; £300; £300) **Stalls High**

Form RPR
0000 1 **Good Luck Charm**[41] 4589 10-9-5 **52** ....(b) SeanLevey 12 63
(Gary Moore) *s.i.s and dropped in bhd after s: hld up in rr of main of gp: clsd and jostling w rival ent fnl 2f: str run 1f out to ld ins fnl f: sn clr (trainer said, regarding improvement in form, gelding benefitted from strong pace)* **22/1**

050 2 3 1/4 **Heatherdown (IRE)**[22] 5287 3-9-1 **55** ....(v[1]) PJMcDonald 8 58
(Ian Williams) *chsd ldr after 1f tl over 6f out: chsd ldrs: effrt in 4th ent fnl 2f: hung lft and swtchd rt ins fnl f: kpt on and snatched 2nd last strides: no ch w wnr* **7/2**[1]

0005 3 *hd* **London Pride**[12] 5652 3-8-12 **52** ....(p[1]) LukeMorris 11 54
(Jonathan Portman) *chsd ldr over 6f out: rdn ent fnl 2f: drvn 1f out: nt match pce of wnr and kpt on same pce ins fnl f* **16/1**

0000 4 *hd* **Cuban Spirit**[38] 4733 4-9-4 **51** .... KierenFox 10 54
(Lee Carter) *sn led and crossed to inner: rdn ent fnl 2f: hdd and immediately outpcd ins fnl f: lost 2 pls last strides (jockey said gelding ran too free early on)* **25/1**

2031 5 *nk* **Lippy Lady (IRE)**[22] 5304 3-8-10 **55** ....(h) RhiainIngram(5) 7 56
(Paul George) *taken down early and led part of way to post: s.i.s: hld up off the pce in rr: clsd and swtchd rt over 2f: swtchd lft: effrt but stl plenty to do over 1f out: styd on: nvr trbld ldrs (jockey said filly was slowly away)* **9/2**[2]

3440 6 *hd* **Sea Shack**[84] 3006 5-8-13 **51** ....(tp) WilliamCarver(5) 2 52
(Julia Feilden) *broke wl: chsd ldr for 1f: in tch in midfield: effrt and jostling w rival wl over 1f out: swtchd rt and kpt on ins fnl f: no ch w wnr* **5/1**[3]

0025 7 2 **Caledonia Laird**[13] 5633 8-9-7 **54** ....(e) DanielMuscutt 5 51
(Gay Kelleway) *hld up in midfield: hdwy on outer over 2f out: pressed ldng pair and rdn ent fnl 2f: unable qck over 1f out: wknd ins fnl f* **10/1**

0054 8 3/4 **Gold Flash**[13] 5633 7-9-6 **53** ....(v) KieranShoemark 1 48
(Rod Millman) *rousted along leaving stalls: midfield: effrt and jostling w rival ent fnl 2f: no imp over 1f out: nvr trbld ldrs* **8/1**

0040 9 12 **Pot Luck**[169] 931 3-8-11 **51** .... JosephineGordon 3 18
(Andrew Balding) *nvr travelling wl and a struggling towards rr: wl bhd fnl f* **12/1**

0016 10 3 1/2 **Sussex Solo**[5] 5957 3-8-11 **51** .... RobertHavlin 4 9
(Luke Dace) *t.k.h: chsd ldrs early but sn in midfield: rdn and struggling bnd 2f out: wl bhd ins fnl f* **6/1**

06-0 **11** 3½ **Time Trialist**[38] 4738 3-9-0 **54**................................ CharlieBennett 9 4
(Pat Phelan) *taken down early and led to post: chsd ldrs tl rdn and lost pl over 2f out: wl bhd ins fnl f* **20/1**

1m 37.22s (-0.98) **Going Correction** -0.15s/f (Stan)
WFA 3 from 4yo+ 7lb **11** Ran SP% **118.1**
Speed ratings (Par 101): **98,94,94,94,94 93,91,91,79,75 72**
CSF £96.03 CT £1306.06 TOTE £24.10: £6.00, £1.90, £4.10; EX 151.10 Trifecta £2348.70.
Owner Heart Of The South Racing 101 **Bred** John And Caroline Penny **Trained** Lower Beeding, W Sussex

FOCUS
Another moderate handicap to end and one for the seniors.
T/Plt: £10.90 to a £1 stake. Pool: £52,166.00 - 3,482.75 winning units T/Qpdt: £4.70 to a £1 stake. Pool: £4,773.01 - 741.95 winning units **Steve Payne**

6078 SALISBURY (R-H)
Thursday, August 15

OFFICIAL GOING: Soft (good to soft in places; 7.0) changing to good to soft after race 1 (1.50)
Wind: moderate against Weather: sunny periods

6118 SORVIO INSURANCE BROKERS MAIDEN AUCTION FILLIES' STKS (PLUS 10 RACE) 6f 213y
1:50 (1:55) (Class 4) 2-Y-O **£4,851** (£1,443; £721; £360) **Stalls** Low

Form RPR
36 **1** **Elegant Erin (IRE)**[27] 5132 2-8-9 0................................ TomMarquand 2 74
(Richard Hannon) *compact; trckd ldrs: rdn 2f out: led jst ins fnl f: r.o wl* **7/2**[1]

2 1 **Freyja (IRE)** 2-9-0 0................................ FrannyNorton 12 76
(Mark Johnston) *leggy; sn led: rdn 2f out: hdd jst ins fnl f: kpt on* **6/1**

3 1¼ **Rosardo Senorita** 2-8-7 0................................ RaulDaSilva 5 66
(Rae Guest) *cl-cpld; s.i.s: towards rr: hdwy 3f out: sn rdn: kpt on ins fnl f: wnt 3rd cl home* **40/1**

6425 **4** ¾ **Incognito (IRE)**[14] 5588 2-9-0 **76**................................ GeraldMosse 10 71
(Mick Channon) *in tch: hdwy 3f out: ev ch 2f out: no ex ins fnl f: lost 3rd cl home* **4/1**[2]

5 ½ **Single (IRE)** 2-8-7 0................................(h[1]) DavidEgan 7 63
(Mick Channon) *unfurnished; scope; hld up towards rr: hdwy 2f out: pushed along whn sltly hmpd over 1f out: kpt on nicely ins fnl f wout ever threatening* **14/1**

533 **6** 1 **Zulu Girl**[33] 4897 2-8-9 **68**................................ JimCrowley 9 62
(Eve Johnson Houghton) *towards rr of midfield: hdwy 3f out: nt best of runs over 2f out: sn swtchd lft: kpt on same pce fnl f* **5/1**[3]

7 1½ **Kashmirella (IRE)** 2-9-0 0................................ CharlesBishop 6 63
(Eve Johnson Houghton) *athletic; looked wl; hld up towards rr: pushed along and sme prog 2f out: nvr threatened ldrs: no ex fnl 120yds* **16/1**

8 *shd* **Russian Rumour (IRE)** 2-8-4 0................................ MeganNicholls[(3)] 3 56
(Jonathan Portman) *workmanlike; mid-div: pushed along and hdwy over 2f out: nt pce to get on terms: fdd ins fnl f* **25/1**

560 **9** 9 **Kahpehlo**[54] 4114 2-8-7 **52**................................ KieranO'Neill 13 31
(John Bridger) *trckd ldrs: rdn over 2f out: sn wknd* **150/1**

3 **10** ½ **Moorland Spirit (IRE)**[7] 5838 2-9-0 0................................(b) OisinMurphy 8 37
(Archie Watson) *compact; mid-div: effrt 3f out: wknd over 1f out* **8/1**

11 3½ **Unbridled Light (FR)** 2-8-7 0................................(t[1]) JFEgan 4 21
(Anthony Honeyball) *str; bit bkward; pushed along over 4f out: a towards rr* **50/1**

5 **12** ½ **City Escape (IRE)**[47] 4366 2-8-7 0................................ DavidProbert 1 19
(Rae Guest) *workmanlike; prom: rdn over 2f out: sn wknd* **10/1**

13 7 **Prairie Moppins (USA)** 2-8-9 0................................ RobHornby 11 2
(Sylvester Kirk) *unfurnished; on toes; s.i.s: sn mid-div: rdn 3f out: wknd over 2f out* **25/1**

1m 32.97s (4.27) **Going Correction** +0.525s/f (Yiel) **13** Ran SP% **118.7**
Speed ratings (Par 93): **96,94,93,92,92 90,89,89,78,78 74,73,65**
CSF £23.34 TOTE £4.10: £1.70, £2.00, £12.40; EX 28.80 Trifecta £1261.60.
Owner Pall Mall Partners And Sue Hopgood **Bred** Brian Miller **Trained** East Everleigh, Wilts

FOCUS
Rail erected on the straight course up to 14ft off permanent far side rail. That was done to rail off the damaged ground from the opening day. The going changed prior to the opening race from soft, to soft, good to soft in places. After the race it changed further to good to soft. Probably not the strongest maiden ever but the winner did it nicely. The time wasn't great indicating the ground was still on the soft side.

6119 M J CHURCH NOVICE STKS 6f 213y
2:20 (2:22) (Class 5) 3-Y-O+ **£4,528** (£1,347; £673; £336) **Stalls** Low

Form RPR
-232 **1** **Aluqair (IRE)**[21] 5336 3-9-2 83................................(h) JamesDoyle 9 82
(Simon Crisford) *mde all: rdn whn strly chal 2f out: kpt on wl fnl f: rdn out* **7/4**[2]

452- **2** ¾ **Alrajaa**[330] 7430 3-9-2 83................................ JimCrowley 5 80
(John Gosden) *trckd ldrs: rdn to chal 2f out: kpt on ins fnl f but a being hld* **8/15**[1]

00 **3** 7 **Rifft (IRE)**[23] 5268 4-9-8 0................................ RichardKingscote 6 63
(Lydia Richards) *trckd ldrs: rdn over 2f out: kpt on to go 3rd fnl 120yds but nvr gng pce to trble front pair* **66/1**

05 **4** ¾ **Vipin (FR)**[19] 5428 4-9-5 0................................ GeorgiaCox[(3)] 7 61
(William Muir) *slowly away: trckd wnr tl rdn over 2f out: sn hld by front pair: no ex whn losing 3rd fnl 120yds* **20/1**

00 **5** 4½ **Knightfall**[12] 5650 3-9-2 0................................ StevieDonohoe 4 47
(David Lanigan) *str; in tch: rdn 3f out: nt pce to threaten: wkng whn hmpd by loose horse jst over 1f out* **14/1**[3]

0- **6** 3¼ **Lord Howard (IRE)**[281] 8931 3-8-9 0................................ GeorgeBass[(7)] 3 38
(Mick Channon) *s.i.s: a towards rr* **25/1**

7 11 **Miss Ditsy (IRE)** 3-8-11 0................................ DavidProbert 1 3
(Michael Attwater) *workmanlike; bit bkward; hmpd leaving stalls: sn stdd bk into last pair: rdn 3f out: nvr any imp: wknd over 1f out* **33/1**

8 8 **Auntie June** 3-8-11 0................................ KieranO'Neill 8
(Roy Brotherton) *compact; bit bkward; s.i.s: rdn 3f out: little imp: wknd over 1f out* **66/1**

00 **U** **Four Feet (IRE)**[71] 3464 3-8-9 0................................ EmmaTaff[(7)] 2
(Henry Candy) *workmanlike; awkwardly away whn uns rdr s* **20/1**

1m 31.55s (2.85) **Going Correction** +0.525s/f (Yiel)
WFA 3 from 4yo 6lb **9** Ran SP% **127.6**
Speed ratings (Par 103): **104,103,95,94,89 85,72,63,**
CSF £3.19 TOTE £2.80: £1.10, £1.10, £15.70; EX 2.70 Trifecta £51.00.
Owner Shaikh Duaij Al Khalifa **Bred** Mark Gavin **Trained** Newmarket, Suffolk

FOCUS
This looked a two-horse race beforehand and so it proved in the race itself, as it only concerned the two market leaders from some way out. It was run in a quicker time than the preceding maiden over the same trip. There was drama at the start when Four Feet unseated Emma Taff after she became unbalanced on leaving the stalls. It's been rated around the first two.

6120 FIRST CARLTON FILLIES' H'CAP 6f
2:50 (2:51) (Class 5) (0-70,70) 3-Y-O+
£3,737 (£1,112; £555; £300; £300; £300) **Stalls** Low

Form RPR
-414 **1** **Raincall**[51] 4227 4-9-12 **70**................................ HarryBentley 7 79+
(Henry Candy) *tall; ly; cl up: led wl over 1f out: kpt on wl and a in command fnl f* **10/11**[1]

1346 **2** 1¼ **Maid From The Mist**[13] 5607 3-8-3 **51**................................ DavidEgan 6 55
(John Gallagher) *prom: led briefly 2f out: sn rdn: kpt on gamely but a being hld by wnr fnl f: jst hld on for 2nd* **7/1**

0110 **3** *shd* **Aperitif**[12] 5659 3-9-3 **68**................................ CameronNoble[(3)] 3 72+
(Michael Bell) *hld up last: rdn and hdwy over 1f out: r.o ins fnl f: nrly snatched 2nd fnl stride* **4/1**[2]

1004 **4** *nse* **Lady Monica**[13] 5622 3-9-0 **62**................................ RoystonFfrench 1 66
(John Holt) *trckd ldrs: swtchd lft 2f out: sn rdn: kpt on ins fnl f* **6/1**[3]

6034 **5** 2 **Flying Sakhee**[19] 5430 6-8-7 **51** oh4................................(p) KieranO'Neill 4 50
(John Bridger) *awkwardly away: in last pair: rdn 2f out: no imp tl kpt on ins fnl f* **12/1**

4021 **6** 1½ **Majorette**[114] 2010 5-9-6 **64**................................ TrevorWhelan 2 58
(Brian Barr) *on toes; cl up: rdn over 2f out: nt pce to threaten: fdd fnl 120yds* **16/1**

3-20 **7** 2 **Your Choice**[22] 5309 4-9-7 **65**................................(p) LiamJones 8 52
(Laura Mongan) *hld up in tch: effrt over 2f out: nt pce to get on terms: fdd fnl f* **25/1**

65-0 **8** 5 **Black Lace**[215] 202 4-8-7 **51** oh6................................(v[1]) FrannyNorton 5 22
(Steve Woodman) *led: rdn and hdd 2f out: wknd ent fnl f* **66/1**

1m 18.21s (3.71) **Going Correction** +0.525s/f (Yiel)
WFA 3 from 4yo+ 4lb **8** Ran SP% **118.1**
Speed ratings (Par 100): **96,94,94,94,91 89,86,80**
CSF £8.57 CT £19.22 TOTE £1.70: £1.10, £2.00, £1.40; EX 8.10 Trifecta £31.10.
Owner Rockcliffe Stud **Bred** Rockcliffe Stud **Trained** Kingston Warren, Oxon

FOCUS
A fairly modest handicap. Again it didn't look easy but the favourite ground it out well to successfully concede weight all round. The form makes sense rated at face value.

6121 BOOKER WHOLESALE H'CAP (DIV I) 1m
3:20 (3:22) (Class 6) (0-65,67) 3-Y-O+
£3,058 (£910; £454; £300; £300; £300) **Stalls** Low

Form RPR
05 **1** **Clem A**[16] 5531 3-9-4 **62**................................ OisinMurphy 9 69
(Alan Bailey) *trckd ldr: led over 2f out: sn rdn clr: kpt on wl* **10/1**

0612 **2** 1½ **The Lords Walk**[14] 5570 6-9-11 **67**................................(b[1]) ThoreHammerHansen[(5)] 4 72
(Bill Turner) *hld up in last trio: nt clr run and swtchd lft 2f out: sn rdn: wnt 2nd ent fnl f: kpt on but nvr any threat to wnr* **9/4**[1]

0526 **3** 2½ **Savitar (IRE)**[22] 5309 4-9-9 **60**................................ TomMarquand 7 59
(Jim Boyle) *looked wl; hld up in last trio: hdwy 2f out: sn rdn: wnt 3rd ent fnl f: kpt on same pce* **4/1**[2]

0543 **4** 2¾ **N Over J**[37] 4753 4-9-0 **51**................................(v) DavidEgan 5 44
(William Knight) *trckd ldrs: rdn over 2f out: sn chalng for hld 2nd: no ex ent fnl f* **9/2**[3]

0052 **5** *shd* **Chetan**[22] 5302 7-9-9 **60**................................ RichardKingscote 3 53
(Tony Carroll) *pressed ldr: rdn to dispute 2nd over 2f out: no ex ent fnl f* **9/2**[3]

6-06 **6** 5 **Arabian King**[18] 5477 3-9-7 **65**................................ GeraldMosse 11 45
(David Elsworth) *s.i.s: racd keenly in last trio: outpcd 2f out: n.d (jockey said colt ran too freely)* **9/1**

-400 **7** *hd* **Aye Aye Skipper (IRE)**[44] 4473 9-8-9 **45** oh1................................(b) RobHornby 1 27
(Ken Cunningham-Brown) *mid-div: nt clr run on far rails and swtchd lft 2f out: sn rdn: little imp: wknd fnl f* **33/1**

3400 **8** *nse* **Barrsbrook**[22] 5309 5-9-12 **63**................................(vt) JimCrowley 10 44
(Gary Moore) *s.i.s: mid-div: effrt 3f out: wknd ent fnl f* **16/1**

-360 **9** 13 **Johni Boxit**[20] 5016 4-9-6 **57**................................(p) TrevorWhelan 12 8
(Brian Barr) *racd keenly: led: rdn and hdd over 2f out: sn wknd (jockey said gelding stopped quickly; post-race examination failed to reveal any abnormalities)* **33/1**

1m 47.67s (4.17) **Going Correction** +0.525s/f (Yiel)
WFA 3 from 4yo+ 7lb **9** Ran SP% **118.0**
Speed ratings (Par 101): **100,98,96,93,93 88,87,87,74**
CSF £33.59 CT £107.56 TOTE £10.10: £3.20, £1.50, £1.30; EX 41.70 Trifecta £215.90.
Owner The Skills People Group Ltd **Bred** Charley Knoll Partnership **Trained** Newmarket, Suffolk

FOCUS
A modest handicap but won in clear-cut style by a back-to-form winner.

6122 TATTERSALLS SOVEREIGN STKS (GROUP 3) (C&G) 1m
3:50 (3:51) (Class 1) 3-Y-O+ **£41,310** (£15,783; £7,996; £4,081; £2,146) **Stalls** Low

Form RPR
1000 **1** **Kick On**[56] 4013 3-8-10 107................................ OisinMurphy 7 111
(John Gosden) *sltly on toes; trckd ldrs: chal over 2f out: rdn to take narrow advantage ent fnl f: jst hld on: all out* **9/2**[3]

3R40 **2** *nse* **Accidental Agent**[15] 5543 5-9-3 115................................(p) CharlesBishop 2 112
(Eve Johnson Houghton) *trckd ldrs: nt clr run over 2f out: tried to swtchd lft but hemmed in tl ent fnl f: kpt on wl fnl 120yds: jst failed* **5/1**

6521 **3** ½ **Flashcard (IRE)**[19] 5412 3-8-10 101................................ RobHornby 8 110
(Andrew Balding) *looked wl; hld up bhd ldrs: hdwy 2f out: rdn jst over 1f out: edging rt but kpt on ins fnl f: wnt 3rd towards fin* **3/1**[1]

2030 **4** ½ **Great Scot**[56] 4013 3-8-10 109................................ RichardKingscote 1 109
(Tom Dascombe) *led: rdn whn strly chal 2f out: narrowly hdd ent fnl f: kpt on but no ex whn losing 2 pls cl home* **7/2**[2]

-143 **5** ¾ **King Ottokar (FR)**[56] 4013 3-8-10 106................................ StevieDonohoe 5 107
(Charlie Fellowes) *looked wl; hld up bhd ldrs: nt clr run whn swtchd lft over 1f out: sn rdn: kpt on but nt quite pce to chal* **3/1**[1]

0411 **P** **Marie's Diamond (IRE)**[18] 5475 3-8-10 107................................ FrannyNorton 4
(Mark Johnston) *prom tl appearing to lose action over 3f out: sn p.u (jockey said colt lost its action; post-race examination failed to reveal any abnormalities)* **12/1**

1m 45.81s (2.31) **Going Correction** +0.525s/f (Yiel)
WFA 3 from 5yo+ 7lb **6** Ran SP% **114.8**
Speed ratings (Par 113): **109,108,108,107,107**
CSF £27.31 TOTE £5.00: £2.60, £1.90; EX 24.80 Trifecta £100.10.
Owner Qatar Racing Limited **Bred** Shutford Stud **Trained** Newmarket, Suffolk

FOCUS
A tight Group 3, although possibly not the best renewal, produced a great finish and the result was in some doubt as they passed the line. A length pb from the winner, with the second rated to form.

6123 BOOKER WHOLESALE H'CAP (DIV II) 1m
4:20 (4:23) (Class 6) (0-65,70) 3-Y-O+
£3,058 (£910; £454; £300; £300; £300) Stalls Low

Form RPR
0504 1 **Cuttin' Edge (IRE)**[17] 5498 3-9-7 58 .... TomMarquand 8 69
(William Muir) *mde all: kpt on strly fnl f: drvn out* 6/1[3]
0-42 2 4 ½ **Bruyere (FR)**[14] 5593 3-9-7 65 .... RobertWinston 5 66
(Dean Ivory) *looked wl; racd keenly: hld up: swtchd to centre and hdwy fr over 2f out: chsd wnr jst over 1f out: kpt on but nvr gng pce to get on terms (jockey said filly ran too freely)* 6/4[1]
0000 3 1 **Mrs Benson (IRE)**[22] 5309 4-9-2 53 .... HarryBentley 2 52
(Michael Blanshard) *trckd ldrs tl outpcd over 2f out: making hdwy whn nt clr run briefly over 1f out: kpt on ins fnl f: wnt 3rd towards fin* 25/1
1505 4 ¾ **Sea Of Marengo (IRE)**[8] 5797 3-9-5 63 ....(p[1]) JFEgan 4 59
(Grace Harris) *hld up: rdn and hdwy over 2f out: disp hld 2nd over 1f out tl ent fnl f: kpt on same pce* 16/1
-004 5 1 ¼ **Bakht A Rawan (IRE)**[19] 5446 7-9-11 62 .... DavidProbert 1 57
(Roger Teal) *trckd ldrs: rdn over 2f out: sn chsng wnr: nt pce to get on terms: kpt on tl no ex fnl 75yds* 16/1
0620 6 2 ¾ **My Lady Claire**[33] 4931 3-8-12 56 .... RobHornby 7 43
(Ed Walker) *trckd ldrs: outpcd over 2f out: no threat after* 8/1
2006 7 7 **Dancing Jo**[85] 2965 3-9-9 67 .... FrannyNorton 11 39
(Mick Channon) *in tch: pushed along in last trio over 3f out: wknd over 1f out* 10/1
6300 8 3 **Greyzee (IRE)**[14] 5580 3-9-0 58 .... OisinMurphy 9 23
(Rod Millman) *prom: rdn over 2f out: wknd over 1f out (jockey said gelding lost action; post-race examination failed to reveal any abnormalities)* 9/1
5202 9 ½ **Red Gunner**[30] 5016 5-9-1 52 .... RichardKingscote 10 17
(Mark Loughnane) *trckd ldrs: rdn over 2f out: wknd over 1f out* 5/1[2]

1m 48.44s (4.94) **Going Correction** +0.525s/f (Yiel)
WFA 3 from 4yo+ 7lb 9 Ran SP% **116.8**
Speed ratings (Par 101): **96,91,90,89,88 85,78,75,75**
CSF £15.57 CT £215.53 TOTE £7.60: £2.00, £1.40, £5.10; EX 18.70 Trifecta £208.20.
Owner Purple & Lilac Racing **Bred** P Hyland & C & J McHale **Trained** Lambourn, Berks

FOCUS
This looked open but was turned into a procession. It was the slower of the two divisions and it went to a prominent racer.

6124 BRITISH EBF PREMIER FILLIES' H'CAP 1m 4f 5y
4:55 (4:57) (Class 2) (0-100,95) 3-Y-O+
£18,675 (£5,592; £2,796; £1,398; £699; £351) Stalls Low

Form RPR
4513 1 **Sea Of Faith (IRE)**[27] 5133 3-9-7 95 .... JamesDoyle 6 107
(William Haggas) *str; looked wl; trckd ldrs: led 2f out: styd on strly to assert ins fnl f: rdn out* 3/1[2]
6110 2 3 **Tribal Craft**[15] 5541 3-9-1 89 .... DavidProbert 5 97
(Andrew Balding) *looked wl; led after 2f: rdn and hdd 2f out: styd pressing wnr tl no ex fnl 140yds* 9/2[3]
11 3 6 **Litigious**[19] 5421 3-9-3 91 .... OisinMurphy 2 90
(John Gosden) *ly; t.k.h early: trckd ldrs: pushed along in cl 3rd 4f out: rdn and edgd lft over 2f out: styd on same pce* 1/1[1]
2611 4 nse **Mannaal (IRE)**[15] 5545 3-9-3 94 .... MeganNicholls[(3)] 3 92
(Simon Crisford) *hld up in last pair but in tch: rdn over 3f out: hdwy over 2f out: nvr gng pce to get on terms but styd on fnl f: nrly snatched 3rd fnl stride* 9/1
25-0 5 1 **Thimbleweed**[15] 5545 4-9-9 87 .... HarryBentley 7 82
(Ralph Beckett) *hld up in last pair: rdn and hdwy 3f out: sn disputing 4th: nvr gng pce to get involved but styd on fnl f* 16/1
4310 6 13 **Happy Hiker (IRE)**[26] 5190 3-8-12 86 .... TomMarquand 1 62
(Michael Bell) *led for 2f: trckd ldr: rdn over 3f out: wknd over 2f out* 25/1
1052 7 15 **Katiesheidinlisa**[21] 5332 3-8-11 85 ....(p[1]) RichardKingscote 4 37
(Tom Dascombe) *cl up tl dropped to rr 4f out: sn btn* 33/1

2m 39.53s (1.93) **Going Correction** +0.525s/f (Yiel)
WFA 3 from 4yo 10lb 7 Ran SP% **115.9**
Speed ratings (Par 96): **114,112,108,107,107 98,88**
CSF £17.37 TOTE £3.90: £1.60, £2.50; EX 20.10 Trifecta £46.50.
Owner Sunderland Holding Inc **Bred** Sunderland Holdings Inc **Trained** Newmarket, Suffolk

FOCUS
There were some promising fillies in this, none more so than the winner who did it nicely. The level is a bit fluid, but the race has been rated slightly positively as it stands.

6125 KEVIN HALL & PAT BOAKES MEMORIAL H'CAP 1m 6f 44y
5:30 (5:30) (Class 4) (0-85,77) 3-Y-O £8,927 (£2,656; £1,327; £663; £300) Stalls Far side

Form RPR
4111 1 **Land Of Oz**[8] 5812 3-9-9 77 6ex .... RyanTate 84+
(Sir Mark Prescott Bt) *ly; t.k.h early: hld up bhd ldng quartet: hdwy over 3f out: led 2f out: styd on wl fnl f and a holding runner-up: rdn out* 4/7[1]
0-14 2 ¾ **Whistler Bowl**[24] 5249 3-8-10 64 .... DavidEgan 69
(Gary Moore) *trckd ldrs: nudged along over 4f out: rdn 3f out: styd on ent fnl f: chsd wnr fnl 100yds: a being hld* 7/1[3]
2251 3 1 **Victoriano (IRE)**[8] 5798 3-9-4 72 6ex ....(b) JamesDoyle 76
(Archie Watson) *led: jnd over 4f out: rdn 3f out: hdd 2f out: kpt chsng wnr tl no ex fnl 100yds* 8/1
6361 4 3 ¼ **Young Merlin (IRE)**[15] 5566 3-9-7 75 ....(p) TomMarquand 74
(Roger Charlton) *looked wl; trckd ldrs: rdn 3f out: nt best of runs wl over 1f out but hld: styd on same pce* 8/1
2232 5 3 ¼ **Luck Of Clover**[34] 4862 3-8-11 65 .... OisinMurphy 60
(Andrew Balding) *trckd ldr: disp ld over 4f out: rdn over 2f out: sn hdd: wknd fnl f* 6/1[2]

3m 8.51s (1.91) **Going Correction** +0.525s/f (Yiel) 5 Ran SP% **112.7**
Speed ratings (Par 102): **115,114,114,112,110**
CSF £5.44 TOTE £1.60: £1.10, £2.80; EX 4.70 Trifecta £20.50.
Owner John Brown & Megan Dennis **Bred** Stetchworth & Middle Park Studs Ltd **Trained** Newmarket, Suffolk

FOCUS
A fair finale won by a horse completing a four-timer in little over a month. The second has been rated in line with her Lingfield win, and the third to form.
T/Plt: £27.70 to a £1 stake. Pool: £55,962.99 - 1,474.70 winning units T/Qpdt: £11.00 to a £1 stake. Pool: £4,780.36 - 320.23 winning units **Tim Mitchell**

5864 YARMOUTH (L-H)
Thursday, August 15

OFFICIAL GOING: Good to firm (7.5)
Wind: fresh breeze Weather: sunny intervals; 20 degrees

6126 MANSIONBET BEATEN BY A HEAD H'CAP 5f 42y
4:45 (4:47) (Class 6) (0-55,54) 3-Y-O+
£2,781 (£827; £413; £300; £300; £300) Stalls Centre

Form RPR
0302 1 **Simba Samba**[29] 5064 3-9-3 53 .... RyanMoore 5 60
(Philip McBride) *prom: drvn to ld ins fnl f: in command fnl 100yds* 13/8[1]
6312 2 ¾ **Monarch Maid**[6] 5884 8-8-13 53 .... ElishaWhittington[(7)] 4 58
(Peter Hiatt) *led: pushed along and hdd ins fnl f: kpt on same pce* 13/2
0000 3 1 ¾ **Independence Day (IRE)**[99] 2527 6-9-7 54 .... JoeyHaynes 9 53
(Chelsea Banham) *bhd: rdn and outpcd 2f out: styd on strly ins fnl f: too much to do* 7/2[2]
-550 4 1 ¼ **Camino**[126] 1716 6-8-12 45 ....(p) HayleyTurner 10 40
(Andi Brown) *prom: last of four gng clr 2f out: rdn and no ex 1f out: lost 3rd cl home* 100/1
-003 5 ¾ **Good Business (IRE)**[64] 3738 5-9-7 54 ....(b) SilvestreDeSousa 6 46
(Henry Spiller) *pressed ldrs: drvn 2f out: w ldr briefly 1f out: nt keen and wknd bdly ins fnl f: lost two pls cl home* 8/1
040 6 shd **Royal Mezyan (IRE)**[84] 3001 8-9-5 52 .... LouisSteward 1 43
(Henry Spiller) *wl bhd tl rdn and kpt on ins fnl f: nvr rchd ldrs* 20/1
5100 7 1 **Alisia R (IRE)**[10] 5750 3-9-0 50 ....(h) LewisEdmunds 3 37
(Les Eyre) *chsd ldrs tl rdn and outpcd 2f out* 40/1
3155 8 nse **Tilsworth Rose**[16] 5532 5-9-2 49 ....(b) TonyHamilton 11 37
(J R Jenkins) *uns rdr at s and mounted in stalls: dwlt: sn rdn and outpcd (trainer was informed mare could not run until day after passing a stalls test)* 28/1
0426 9 2 ¾ **Waneen (IRE)**[73] 3425 6-8-7 47 .... MorganCole[(7)] 8 25
(John Butler) *midfield: pushed along and struggling over 2f out* 20/1
2352 10 hd **Arnoul Of Metz**[37] 4765 4-9-2 54 ....(p) DylanHogan[(5)] 7 31
(Henry Spiller) *lost 8 l at s: a bhd: sn struggling (jockey said gelding was slowly away. vet said gelding lost left fore shoe)* 11/2[3]

1m 0.51s (-1.39) **Going Correction** -0.25s/f (Firm)
WFA 3 from 4yo+ 3lb 10 Ran SP% **116.5**
Speed ratings (Par 101): **101,99,97,95,93 93,92,91,87,87**
CSF £11.91 CT £34.10 TOTE £2.20: £1.10, £1.80, £1.90; EX 11.30 Trifecta £57.00.
Owner PMRacing **Bred** J W Mitchell **Trained** Newmarket, Suffolk

FOCUS
Dry, breezy conditions for this seven-race evening card. Races 3 and 4 were increased 10yds in distance by the dolling out of the bottom bend. The stalls were in the centre for this lowly opening sprint handicap, in which it paid to race handily.

6127 EBF STALLIONS NOVICE STKS (PLUS 10 RACE) 7f 3y
5:20 (5:22) (Class 4) 2-Y-O £4,851 (£1,443; £721; £360) Stalls Centre

Form RPR
2 1 **Al Suhail**[34] 4886 2-9-5 0 ....(h[1]) WilliamBuick 2 90+
(Charlie Appleby) *sweating and on his toes: plld hrd and chsd ldr: pushed ahd over 1f out and readily qcknd clr* 1/6[1]
64 2 4 **Imperial Empire**[29] 5059 2-9-5 0 .... BrettDoyle 3 74
(Charlie Appleby) *led and racd freely: pushed along and hdd over 1f out: immediately outpcd by wnr: hung lft ins fnl f (vet said colt lost left hind shoe)* 20/1[3]
3 nk **Tiger Crusade (FR)** 2-9-5 0 .... JamieSpencer 1 73
(David Simcock) *t.k.h: chsd ldng pair: rdn over 1f out: chal for 2nd briefly: rn green and no ex fnl 120yds: wnr wl clr* 20/1[3]
4 4 ½ **Boss Power (IRE)** 2-9-5 0 .... SilvestreDeSousa 4 61
(Sir Michael Stoute) *lost 5 l at s: last mostly: keen early: pushed along 1/2-way: drvn and btn wl over 1f out* 7/1[2]

1m 22.7s (-2.40) **Going Correction** -0.25s/f (Firm) 4 Ran SP% **107.7**
Speed ratings (Par 96): **103,98,98,92**
CSF £4.90 TOTE £1.10; EX 3.20 Trifecta £9.30.
Owner Godolphin **Bred** Meon Valley Stud **Trained** Newmarket, Suffolk

FOCUS
Stalls centre. They raced in single file down the middle of the track at what appeared to be a generous pace, and the winner looks set for better things.

6128 BEST ODDS GUARANTEED AT MANSIONBET H'CAP 1m 3f 104y
5:55 (5:55) (Class 6) (0-65,64) 3-Y-O
£2,781 (£827; £413; £300; £300; £300) Stalls Low

Form RPR
4460 1 **Robert Fitzroy (IRE)**[44] 4484 3-9-6 63 .... CliffordLee 8 69
(Michael Bell) *slowly away: last tl home turn: rdn over 3f out: gd prog on outside 2f out: led over 1f out: hdd fnl 120yds: battled on to repass rival nr post (trainer's rep said, regarding apparent improvement in form, that gelding appeared to benefit from a short break)* 7/1
0002 2 shd **Verify**[14] 5580 3-9-7 64 .... LiamKeniry 2 71+
(Ed Walker) *t.k.h in midfield: trckd ldrs gng wl 3f out: looking for room fr 2f out tl ins fnl f: led u.p 120yds out: wandered rt and hdd fnl strides: should have won* 7/2[2]
5013 3 nk **Hammy End (IRE)**[13] 5601 3-9-1 58 ....(h) MartinDwyer 9 63
(William Muir) *midfield: effrt to go cl up 3f out: rdn to chal ins fnl f: ev ch tl no ex fnl 50yds (vet said gelding lost right hind shoe)* 6/1
-030 4 2 ½ **Minnelli**[22] 5307 3-9-7 64 .... SilvestreDeSousa 3 65
(Philip McBride) *led: drvn over 3f out: hdd 2f out: ev ch 200yds out: sn wknd* 8/1
0321 5 1 ¾ **No Thanks**[13] 5601 3-9-4 61 .... GeorgeWood 12 59
(William Jarvis) *pressed ldr: pushed along to ld 2f out: hdd over 1f out: sn wknd* 11/4[1]
0045 6 nk **Homesick Boy (IRE)**[21] 5354 3-8-13 56 .... PatCosgrave 1 54
(Ed Dunlop) *towards rr: drvn 3f out: swtchd rt over 2f out: plugged on: nvr got in a blow* 10/1
23 7 5 **Miss Green Dream**[47] 4400 3-8-4 47 .... ShelleyBirkett 7 37
(Julia Feilden) *disp 3rd: pushed along and lost pl and n.m.r over 1f out: no ch after* 11/2[3]
0356 8 ¾ **Spirit Of Lucerne (IRE)**[7] 5867 3-8-1 47 .... NoelGarbutt[(3)] 13 35
(Phil McEntee) *disp 3rd: drvn 4f out: fnd nil: btn over 2f out* 33/1

000 **9** *64* **Mazmerize**[12] 5650 3-8-2 **45**....................................(tp) AdrianMcCarthy 10
(Christine Dunnett) *plld hrd: racd in last pair after 2f: drvn over 4f out: sn hopelessly t.o: eased* **100/1**

2m 25.99s (-1.81) **Going Correction** -0.25s/f (Firm) **9** Ran SP% **115.2**
Speed ratings (Par 98): **96,95,95,93,92 92,88,88,41**
CSF £31.65 CT £156.86 TOTE £8.50: £2.80, £1.10, £1.80; EX 38.30 Trifecta £335.60.
Owner The Fitzrovians 2 **Bred** Gerry And John Rowley **Trained** Newmarket, Suffolk

FOCUS
Actual race distance 1m3f114yds, stalls on inner. The first three home all sat a good way off the pace.

6129 VINCE PEARSON SIXTIETH BIRTHDAY H'CAP 1m 2f 23y
6:25 (6:25) (Class 4) (0-80,80) 3-Y-O+
£5,207 (£1,549; £774; £387; £300; £300) **Stalls** Low

Form RPR

0051 **1** **The Corporal (IRE)**[29] 5060 3-9-0 **73**.................................. WilliamBuick 1 86
(Chris Wall) *led 3f: settled cl up: rdn to go 2nd 2f out: led over 1f out: easily strode clr* **5/2**[1]

4233 **2** *4* **Alhaazm**[37] 4760 3-9-7 **80**...(t[1]) RyanMoore 9 85
(Sir Michael Stoute) *pressed ldr after 3f: led over 3f out: sn rdn: hdd over 1f out: immediately outpcd by wnr but clr of rest* **7/2**[2]

6340 **3** *3* **Windsor Cross (IRE)**[24] 5240 4-9-7 **72**.................. TonyHamilton 5 70
(Richard Fahey) *cl up: rdn over 2f out: mod 3rd over 1f out* **20/1**

4103 **4** *½* **Assembled**[19] 5445 3-9-3 **76**.. PatCosgrave 8 74
(Hugo Palmer) *wnt lft s: pressed ldrs: rdn 3f out: outpcd 2f out: mod 4th ins fnl f* **7/1**

631 **5** *2* **The Throstles**[21] 5337 4-9-8 **73**..................................... CliffordLee 3 66
(Kevin Frost) *bhd: effrt over 2f out: sn rdn and no imp: fdd and lost 4th ins fnl f* **10/1**

0022 **6** *2½* **First Response**[27] 5136 4-9-10 **75**............................ ShaneKelly 4 63
(Linda Stubbs) *led after 3f tl rdn and hdd over 3f out: fdd over 2f out* **14/1**

2341 **7** *3* **Beguiling Charm (IRE)**[22] 5307 3-9-0 **73**.................... LiamKeniry 2 56
(Ed Walker) *towards rr: rdn 5f out: sn struggling (jockey said filly ran flat; post-race examination failed to reveal any abnormalities)* **5/1**[3]

3002 **8** *2½* **Balladeer**[20] 5394 3-9-5 **78**.................................(v) HayleyTurner 6 56
(Michael Bell) *towards rr: rdn and struggling fnl 4f: t.o* **13/2**

2614 **9** *6* **Cafe Espresso**[48] 4339 3-9-5 **78**...............................(b) JoeyHaynes 7 44
(Chelsea Banham) *dwlt s and sn hmpd: last and pushed along early: struggling 5f out: t.o* **33/1**

2m 5.29s (-3.51) **Going Correction** -0.25s/f (Firm)
WFA 3 from 4yo 8lb **9** Ran SP% **116.8**
Speed ratings (Par 105): **104,100,98,98,96 94,92,90,85**
CSF £11.33 CT £141.07 TOTE £3.20: £1.60, £1.10, £4.60; EX 11.80 Trifecta £47.30.
Owner Bringloe & Clarke **Bred** Ideal Syndicate **Trained** Newmarket, Suffolk

FOCUS
Actual race distance 1m2f33yds, stalls on inner. A fair handicap, taken apart by a thriving favourite. The second has been rated in line with the better view of his Newbury form.

6130 DOWNLOAD THE MANSIONBET APP H'CAP 1m 3y
6:55 (6:55) (Class 6) (0-60,60) 3-Y-O
£2,781 (£827; £413; £300; £300; £300) **Stalls** Centre

Form RPR

6205 **1** **Purgatory**[9] 5784 3-9-6 **59**.......................................(b[1]) PatCosgrave 7 66+
(Chris Wall) *towards rr: rdn and gd prog 2f out: drvn to ld 120yds out: hung lft but sn in command* **11/1**

0303 **2** *¾* **Ifton**[14] 5575 3-9-7 **60**.. JamieSpencer 10 65
(Ruth Carr) *stdd to give ldr 8 l s: stl had nine to pass ins fnl f: rdn and swtchd rt and fin v strly: too much to do* **7/1**[3]

0001 **3** *¾* **Break Of Day**[5] 5957 3-9-0 **53** 6ex...........................(b) RyanMoore 1 57
(William Haggas) *prom: led 2f out: rdn and hdd 120yds out: carried lft and nt qckn: lost 2nd cl home* **15/8**[1]

4230 **4** *1¼* **Red Archangel (IRE)**[12] 5653 3-8-10 **56**...................(p) SeanKirrane[(7)] 11 57
(Richard Spencer) *prom and t.k.h: rdn 2f out: ev ch ins fnl f: no ex last 100yds* **12/1**

6062 **5** *1½* **Reconnaissance**[16] 5531 3-9-7 **60**.....................(bt) SilvestreDeSousa 8 57
(Tom Clover) *pressed ldrs: drvn to chal over 1f out: no ex ins fnl f* **7/2**[2]

0320 **6** *hd* **Jazz Hands (IRE)**[15] 5552 3-9-0 **53**........................... TonyHamilton 4 50
(Richard Fahey) *chsd ldrs: rdn 2f out: nt qckn over 1f out* **18/1**

0000 **7** *nk* **Princess Florence (IRE)**[8] 5806 3-8-5 **51**............ LauraPearson[(7)] 3 47
(John Ryan) *bhd tl passed btn horses fnl f: no ch w ldrs* **50/1**

060 **8** *hd* **Petite Malle (USA)**[23] 5269 3-9-6 **59**........................ GeorgeWood 2 55
(James Fanshawe) *cl up: drvn 3f out: btn over 1f out* **12/1**

0-00 **9** *3* **Congress Place (IRE)**[27] 5147 3-9-3 **56**................ AlistairRawlinson 12 45
(Michael Appleby) *a towards rr* **33/1**

4056 **10** *3¼* **Salmon Fishing (IRE)**[8] 5807 3-8-13 **59**.................. MarcoGhiani[(7)] 6 40
(Mohamed Moubarak) *chsd ldrs tl rdn and fdd 2f out* **12/1**

2534 **11** *3¼* **Approve The Dream (IRE)**[7] 5867 3-9-2 **55**............... ShelleyBirkett 9 29
(Julia Feilden) *led tl pushed along and hdd 2f out: sn lost pl (jockey said gelding slipped as leaving stalls and moved poorly throughout; post-race examination failed to reveal any abnormalities)* **11/1**

6441 **12** *1¼* **Symphony (IRE)**[47] 4358 3-8-9 **48**.......................... HayleyTurner 13 19
(James Unett) *a bhd* **28/1**

002 **13** *9* **Secret Treaties**[21] 5358 3-8-11 **53**........................ GabrieleMalune[(3)] 5 3
(Christine Dunnett) *prom tl rdn and wknd over 1f out: t.o and eased: fin lame (jockey said filly moved poorly throughout; post-race examination revealed filly lame on left fore. trainer said filly was unsuited by Good to Firm ground, and would prefer an easier surface)* **28/1**

1m 36.29s (-1.91) **Going Correction** -0.25s/f (Firm) **13** Ran SP% **126.3**
Speed ratings (Par 98): **99,98,97,96,94 94,94,94,91,87 84,83,74**
CSF £88.48 CT £222.18 TOTE £13.90: £3.40, £2.90, £1.40; EX 80.40 Trifecta £765.00.
Owner Des Thurlby **Bred** Des Thurlby **Trained** Newmarket, Suffolk

FOCUS
Stalls in centre. They remained well bunched in the middle of the track for most of this modest mile event, in which trainer Chris Wall secured a second consecutive win on the night.

6131 MANSIONBET PROUD TO SUPPORT BRITISH RACING H'CAP 7f 3y
7:30 (7:32) (Class 6) (0-55,55) 3-Y-O+
£2,781 (£827; £413; £300; £300; £300) **Stalls** Centre

Form RPR

-603 **1** **Moretti (IRE)**[73] 3414 4-8-12 **46**............................ LewisEdmunds 13 54
(Les Eyre) *last of three on stands' side early: smooth prog 2f out: led over 1f out: rdn and sn qcknd clr: edgd lft* **12/1**

0000 **2** *2¼* **Garth Rockett**[16] 5526 5-9-7 **55**...........................(tp) HayleyTurner 5 57
(Mike Murphy) *taken down early: bhd: hdwy gng strly 2f out: rdn and chsd wnr over 1f out: sn outpcd* **9/1**[3]

0032 **3** *1¾* **Parknacilla (IRE)**[8] 5797 3-8-5 **48**.....................(p) GabrieleMalune[(3)] 3 43
(Henry Spiller) *midfield: effrt to ld 2f out: rdn and hdd over 1f out: nt qckn ins fnl f* **7/1**[2]

0000 **4** *¾* **Herringswell (FR)**[28] 5081 4-8-5 **46** oh1................... LauraPearson[(7)] 8 41
(Henry Spiller) *bhd: hdwy 2f out: pushed along and kpt on ins fnl f: unable to chal* **20/1**

0001 **5** *1¼* **Spanish Mane (IRE)**[8] 5828 4-9-6 **54** 5ex................. ShelleyBirkett 15 46
(Julia Feilden) *2nd of three on stands' side but off pce of main centre gp: pushed along and kpt on ins fnl f: nt get in a blow (jockey said filly was never travelling)* **7/1**[2]

5066 **6** *1* **Gulland Rock**[22] 5302 8-8-5 **46** oh1..........................(p) MarcoGhiani[(7)] 11 35
(Anthony Carson) *led stands' side trio but off pce of main centre gp: rdn and no ex over 2f out* **25/1**

0343 **7** *nk* **Global Acclamation**[16] 5526 3-9-1 **55**..................(p) SilvestreDeSousa 9 41
(Ed Dunlop) *cl up: drvn 2f out: no ex over 1f out* **7/2**[1]

602 **8** *½* **Little Miss Kodi (IRE)**[28] 5081 6-9-3 **51**.....................(t) ShaneKelly 2 38
(Mark Loughnane) *chsd ldrs tl rdn and btn over 1f out* **10/1**

530 **9** *1½* **Bidding War**[12] 5652 4-9-4 **52**..........................(p) AlistairRawlinson 14 35
(Michael Appleby) *lost 8 l at s: nvr trbld ldrs* **10/1**

0604 **10** *½* **Exning Queen (IRE)**[7] 5864 3-8-1 **46**......................(t) SophieRalston[(5)] 4 26
(Julia Feilden) *lost 10 l at s: pushed along and gd hdwy 2f out: pressed ldrs briefly: wknd over 1f out (jockey said filly was slowly away)* **25/1**

6050 **11** *¾* **Conqueress (IRE)**[7] 5867 5-8-12 **46** oh1....................(p) GeorgeWood 10 26
(Lydia Pearce) *prom tl rdn and lost pl 3f out* **40/1**

0000 **12** *1¾* **My Footsteps**[7] 5842 4-8-12 **46** oh1........................... LiamKeniry 7 21
(Paul D'Arcy) *prom: overall ldr 1/2-way: hdd 2f out: lost pl qckly over 1f out* **40/1**

000- **13** *3¼* **Lottie Deno**[364] 6199 3-8-6 **46**.................................... JoeyHaynes 1 10
(D J Jeffreys) *overall ldr in centre: rdn and hdd 3f out: fdd rapidly wl over 1f out: t.o* **7/2**[1]

646- **14** *nk* **One Flew Over (IRE)**[368] 6064 4-8-5 **46** oh1.(p[1]) ElishaWhittington[(7)] 12 11
(Ian Williams) *chsd ldrs to 1/2-way: t.o* **16/1**

0040 **15** *15* **Tilsworth Prisca**[16] 5526 4-8-7 **46** oh1..........................(h) TobyEley[(5)] 6
(J R Jenkins) *taken down early: sn struggling: t.o* **66/1**

1m 23.26s (-1.84) **Going Correction** -0.25s/f (Firm)
WFA 3 from 4yo+ 6lb **15** Ran SP% **130.0**
Speed ratings (Par 101): **100,97,95,94,93 92,91,91,89,88 87,85,82,81,64**
CSF £116.56 CT £856.91 TOTE £16.40: £3.90, £3.40, £2.30; EX 139.00 Trifecta £812.30.
Owner J L Eyre **Bred** T Boylan **Trained** Catwick, N Yorks

FOCUS
Stalls in centre. Plenty still in with chances 2f out in this weak sprint handicap, but the winner bounded clear.

6132 MANSIONBET AT GREAT YARMOUTH RACECOURSE H'CAP 6f 3y
8:00 (8:04) (Class 5) (0-70,72) 3-Y-O+
£3,428 (£1,020; £509; £300; £300; £300) **Stalls** Centre

Form RPR

0020 **1** **Great Shout (IRE)**[4] 5985 3-9-4 **68**..............................(t) GeorgeWood 6 74
(Amy Murphy) *rrd leaving stalls: dwlt and in last: gd hdwy 2f out: rdn to ld ins fnl f: kpt on wl* **7/1**

3263 **2** *¾* **Lalania**[16] 5532 4-9-6 **66**.. SilvestreDeSousa 5 71
(Stuart Williams) *taken down early: prom: drvn over 2f out: ev ch 1f out: nt qckn and hld by wnr fnl 100yds* **9/4**[1]

5561 **3** *nk* **Cent Flying**[6] 5883 4-9-5 **65** 5ex....................................(t) MartinDwyer 9 69
(William Muir) *bhd and drvn: clsd 2f out: led narrowly over 1f out: hdd ins fnl f: edgd lft and no ex last 100yds* **7/2**[2]

-134 **4** *2¼* **Local History**[20] 5392 3-9-6 **70**.................................... RyanMoore 7 65
(James Tate) *chsd ldrs: rdn over 2f out: chal over 1f out: wknd fnl 100yds: btn whn short of room cl home* **7/2**[2]

2056 **5** *2¾* **Greek Kodiac (IRE)**[19] 5445 3-9-8 **72**.......................(v[1]) PatCosgrave 4 59
(Mick Quinn) *drvn thrght and nvr travelling: struggling 2f out* **5/1**[3]

3006 **6** *¾* **Kraka (IRE)**[21] 5352 4-9-0 **63**..............................(b[1]) GabrieleMalune[(3)] 3 48
(Christine Dunnett) *v free: led and sn 3 l clr: rdn and hdd over 1f out: dropped out qckly* **10/1**

2000 **7** *14* **Bernie's Boy**[124] 1766 6-9-1 **68**............................(tp w) GraceMcEntee[(7)] 1 8
(Phil McEntee) *cl up tl rdn and fdd v rapidly over 2f out: t.o* **25/1**

1m 10.52s (-2.08) **Going Correction** -0.25s/f (Firm)
WFA 3 from 4yo+ 4lb **7** Ran SP% **117.3**
Speed ratings (Par 103): **103,102,101,98,94 93,75**
CSF £24.14 CT £65.97 TOTE £8.20: £3.80, £2.30; EX 27.20 Trifecta £80.90.
Owner Cherry And Whites **Bred** Redpender Stud Ltd **Trained** Newmarket, Suffolk
■ Rotherhithe was withdrawn. Price at time of withdrawal 28/1. Rule 4 does not apply

FOCUS
Stalls in centre. A run-of-the-mill sprint, but the winner rates value for further having reared as the stalls opened.
T/Plt: £18.50 to a £1 stake. Pool: £46,615.22 - 1,837.59 winning units T/Qpdt: £19.80 to a £1 stake. Pool: £6,477.06 - 241.39 winning units **Iain Mackenzie**

6133 - 6136a (Foreign Racing) - See Raceform Interactive

5871
LEOPARDSTOWN (L-H)
Thursday, August 15

OFFICIAL GOING: Good (good to yielding in places)

6137a INVESCO PENSION CONSULTANTS DESMOND STKS (GROUP 3) 1m
7:00 (7:02) 3-Y-O+
£33,486 (£10,783; £5,108; £2,270; £1,135; £567)

RPR

1 **Madhmoon (IRE)**[47] 4414 3-9-0 117........................... ChrisHayes 4 109+
(Kevin Prendergast, Ire) *dwlt and in rr early: 6th 1/2-way: pushed along and hdwy on outer 2f out: rdn in 2nd ins fnl f and r.o wl to sn ld: comf* **4/7**[1]

2 *1½* **Zuenoon (IRE)**[47] 4410 3-9-0 100.....................................(p) OisinOrr 3 105+
(D K Weld, Ire) *hld up towards rr early: last at 1/2-way: prog nr side over 1f out where rdn in 6th: r.o wl into 2nd cl home: nt trble wnr* **25/1**

3 *½* **I Am Superman (IRE)**[22] 5328 3-9-0 107..................... LeighRoche 5 103
(M D O'Callaghan, Ire) *chsd ldrs: 4th 1/2-way: tk clsr order bhd ldrs on outer over 2f out: rdn to ld over 1f out: hdd u.p ins fnl f and no imp on wnr cl home where dropped to 3rd* **5/1**[2]

4 *1½* **Turnberry Isle (IRE)**[11] 5711 3-9-0 100................ DonnachaO'Brien 2 100
(A P O'Brien, Ire) *broke wl to ld briefly tl sn jnd and hdd: settled bhd ldrs: 3rd 1/2-way: pushed along under 2f out where n.m.r and sn swtchd in 5th: rdn and nt clr run ins fnl f: kpt on into 4th cl home* **12/1**

5 *nk* **Pincheck (IRE)**[28] 5112 5-9-7 108........................ ShaneFoley 6 100
(Mrs John Harrington, Ire) *sn disp and led briefly tl settled bhd ldr: clsr 2nd after 1/2-way: rdn to ld briefly 1 1/2f out tl sn hdd: no ex bhd ldrs and wknd ins fnl f* **9/1**

6 *4* **Ancient Spirit (GER)**[28] 5112 4-9-7 110..................(p) KevinManning 7 91
(J S Bolger, Ire) *sn disp and led: 1 l clr at 1/2-way: pressed clly after 1/2-way: rdn and hdd 1 1/2f out: wknd qckly* **8/1**[3]

7 *½* **I Remember You (IRE)**[14] 5598 3-8-11 97.................. SeamieHeffernan 1 86
(A P O'Brien, Ire) *chsd ldrs: 5th 1/2-way: pushed along in 5th under 3f out and no ex u.p in 6th 1 1/2f out: sn wknd* **33/1**

1m 42.01s (-1.79) **Going Correction** +0.20s/f (Good) **7 Ran SP% 115.9**
WFA 3 from 4yo+ 7lb
Speed ratings: **112,110,110,108,108 104,103**
CSF £19.92 TOTE £1.40: £1.02, £8.00; DF 13.80 Trifecta £35.90.
Owner Hamdan Al Maktoum **Bred** Shadwell Estate Company Limited **Trained** Friarstown, Co Kildare

FOCUS
Nothing fancy from Madhmoon but he's got the job done and this should tee him up lovely for the Irish Champion Stakes over an extra two furlongs which should be far more to his liking. He was very much on a hiding to nothing here but connections will be happy. A quote of 12-1 about him for the showpiece on Irish Champions Weekend looks a more than fair offering at this juncture. It's been rated around the fourth.

6138 - 6140a (Foreign Racing) - See Raceform Interactive

6002
DEAUVILLE (R-H)
Thursday, August 15

OFFICIAL GOING: Polytrack: standard; turf: very soft

6141a PRIX DU PORT DE DEAUVILLE (CLAIMER) (2YO) (ALL-WEATHER TRACK) (POLYTRACK) 7f 110y(P)
1:00 2-Y-O £12,162 (£4,864; £3,648; £2,432; £1,216)

RPR

1 **Lalacelle (FR)**[14] 5600 2-8-8 0........................ AurelienLemaitre 7 69
(S Cerulis, France) **57/10**

2 *½* **Mr Shady (IRE)**[13] 5642 2-8-6 0..................(p) AlexisPouchin(5) 1 71
(J S Moore) *s.i.s: bustled along to r in mid-div on inner: prog to dispute over 2f out: sn rdn: unable qck w eventual wnr ent fnl f: kpt on clsng stages* **34/1**

3 *snk* **Kongastet (FR)**[11] 5713 2-8-11 0..................(b) TheoBachelot 8 71+
(S Wattel, France) **3/1**[2]

4 *5* **Lordelio (IRE)**[80] 2-8-11 0........................ PierreBazire 5 59+
(G Botti, France) **5/2**[1]

5 *1 ¼* **Garigliano (FR)** 2-8-10 0..................(b[1]) JeremieMonteiro(8) 3 63+
(N Caullery, France) **11/1**

6 *3* **Clarabola (FR)**[16] 5539 2-8-8 0........................ MaximeGuyon 2 45+
(B De Montzey, France) **7/2**[3]

7 *¾* **Made Guy (USA)**[63] 3760 2-8-11 0..................(b) IoritzMendizabal 4 47+
(J S Moore) *racd in fnl trio: sme prog into mid-div over 1/2-way: asked for effrt 2f out: no imp and sn struggling: wl btn ent fnl f* **22/1**

8 *snk* **Equinozio (IRE)**[65] 3714 2-8-3 0........................ MlleAmbreMolins(8) 6 46+
(A Giorgi, Italy) **68/10**

1m 30.12s **8 Ran SP% 119.1**
PARI-MUTUEL (all including 1 euro stake): WIN 6.70; PLACE 2.30, 7.10, 2.00; DF 102.70.
Owner Stephan Hoffmeister **Bred** Franklin Finance S.A. **Trained** France

6142a ARQANA PRIX DE LIEUREY (GROUP 3) (3YO FILLIES) (ROUND COURSE) (TURF) 1m (R)
2:50 3-Y-O £36,036 (£14,414; £10,810; £7,207; £3,603)

RPR

1 **Fount**[25] 5227 3-8-11 0........................ Pierre-CharlesBoudot 6 109
(A Fabre, France) *prom early: trckd ldr after 1f: nudged along to go upsides 2f out: rdn w narrow ld whn sltly impeded rival ins fnl f: kpt on wl u.p cl home* **76/10**[3]

2 *½* **Twist 'N' Shake**[25] 5227 3-8-11 0........................ OlivierPeslier 8 108
(John Gosden) *sn prom: led after 1f: shkn up on inner w slt advantage 2f out: rdn whn narrowly ins fnl f: kpt on but no ex cl home* **6/4**[1]

3 *nk* **Commes (FR)**[60] 3905 3-9-2 0........................ CristianDemuro 9 112+
(J-C Rouget, France) *trckd ldrs early tl settled in fnl quartet after 2f: dropped to last appr fnl 2f: sn rdn and gd hdwy on outer 1 1/2f out: drvn and clsng qckly to go 3rd ins fnl f: too much to do* **19/10**[2]

4 *snk* **Silva (IRE)**[95] 2669 3-8-11 0........................ TheoBachelot 10 107
(Mme Pia Brandt, France) *disp early: trckd ldr wl in tch after 1f: rdn in 3rd ins fnl 2f: kpt on but nt pce to chal front pair* **50/1**

5 *1 ½* **Matematica (GER)**[47] 4416 3-8-11 0........................ MaximeGuyon 4 103
(C Laffon-Parias, France) *racd midfield: pushed along and cl enough 2f out: rdn and one pce fnl f: nvr threatened ldrs* **9/1**

6 *1* **Noor Sahara (IRE)**[60] 3905 3-8-11 0........................ StephanePasquier 5 101
(F Chappet, France) *hld up in fnl gp: stl gng wl whn prog on outer 2f out: rdn and kpt on fnl 1 1/2f: nt pce to get involved ins fnl f* **12/1**

7 *¾* **Grace Spirit**[23] 3-8-11 0........................ AntoineHamelin 1 99
(A De Royer-Dupre, France) *hld up in fnl quartet: shkn up in rr and plenty to do appr 2f out: rdn and sme prog ins fnl f but nvr able to get involved* **42/1**

8 *snk* **Tifosa (IRE)**[123] 1795 3-8-11 0........................ MickaelBarzalona 2 99
(Mme Pia Brandt, France) *trckd ldrs early tl settled in mid-div after 1f: pushed along 2f out: prog on inner appr fnl f: rdn and wknd ins fnl f* **22/1**

9 *6* **Nooramunga (FR)**[41] 4621 3-8-11 0........................ VincentCheminaud 3 85
(M Delzangles, France) *hld up in fnl gp: pushed along and sme hdwy ins fnl 2f: sn rdn and no rspnse: wl btn and eased fnl f* **27/1**

10 *8* **Stone Tornado**[56] 4047 3-8-11 0........................ JulienAuge 7 67
(C Ferland, France) *t.k.h: racd in midfield: prog on outer and clsr ins fnl 3f: rdn and no rspnse 2f out: sn wl btn: eased ins fnl f* **22/1**

1m 42.95s (2.15) **10 Ran SP% 120.4**
PARI-MUTUEL (all including 1 euro stake): WIN 8.60; PLACE 1.60, 1.20, 1.20; DF 10.10.
Owner K Abdullah **Bred** Juddmonte Farms **Trained** Chantilly, France

FOCUS
The fourth and seventh potentially limit the form.

6143a PRIX GUILLAUME D'ORNANO HARAS DU LOGIS SAINT-GERMAIN (GROUP 2) (3YO) (ROUND COURSE) (TURF) 1m 2f
3:30 3-Y-O £205,405 (£79,279; £37,837; £25,225; £12,612)

RPR

1 **Headman**[46] 4431 3-9-2 0........................ JasonWatson 5 112+
(Roger Charlton) *slt rr s: hld up in last: angled out and shkn up 2f out: edgd rt u.p: styd on wl to ld fnl strides* **3/5**[1]

2 *hd* **Roman Candle**[32] 4963 3-9-2 0........................ MickaelBarzalona 4 110
(A Fabre, France) *sn cl up: drvn along whn pce qckned over 2f out: hdwy to ld over 1 1/2f out: rdn along w narrow ld 1f out: hrd pressed fnl 100yds: hdd cl home: all out* **29/10**[2]

3 *½* **Flop Shot (IRE)**[46] 4431 3-9-2 0........................ MaximeGuyon 3 109
(A Fabre, France) *led 100yds: settled in 3rd: drvn along 2f out: rdn along over 1f out: kpt on wl but nt pce to chal: rdn out* **17/2**

4 *1 ½* **Talk Or Listen (IRE)**[29] 5079 3-9-2 0........................ StephanePasquier 6 106
(F Rossi, France) *led after 100yds: set stdy pce: drvn along and qckned up over 2f out: sn hrd pressed and hdd over 1 1/2f out: rdn along and battled on: wknd fnl 150yds* **15/1**

5 *2 ½* **Taos (FR)**[82] 3108 3-9-2 0........................ ChristopheSoumillon 1 101
(J-C Rouget, France) *settled in 4th: effrt 2f out: in tch tl wkng fnl f: eased cl home* **56/10**[3]

2m 13.1s (2.90) **5 Ran SP% 120.1**
PARI-MUTUEL (all including 1 euro stake): WIN 1.60; PLACE 1.10, 1.10; SF 2.80.
Owner K Abdullah **Bred** Juddmonte Farms (east) Ltd **Trained** Beckhampton, Wilts

FOCUS
They went steady and it turned into a dash for home.

6144a PRIX GONTAUT-BIRON HONG KONG JOCKEY CLUB (GROUP 3) (4YO+) (ROUND COURSE) (TURF) 1m 2f
4:40 4-Y-O+ £36,036 (£14,414; £10,810; £7,207; £3,603)

RPR

1 **Olmedo (FR)**[58] 3948 4-9-0 0........................ CristianDemuro 6 115
(J-C Rouget, France) *racd a little keenly: prom: pushed along to chal 2f out: sn led: kpt on wl u.p ins fnl f: a doing enough* **22/5**[3]

2 *1* **Mountain Angel (IRE)**[33] 4935 5-8-11 0........................ OlivierPeslier 1 110
(Roger Varian) *led: asked to qckn whn pressed 2f out: sn hdd: tried to rally u.p ins fnl f: kpt on clsng stages: a hld* **68/10**

3 *1 ¾* **Trais Fluors**[25] 5-9-0 0........................ Pierre-CharlesBoudot 8 110
(A Fabre, France) *sltly slow into stride: racd in fnl trio: pushed along on outer 2f out: prog fr 1 1/2f out: r.o wl ins fnl f: nvr cl enough to land a blow* **12/5**[1]

4 *¾* **Subway Dancer (IRE)**[29] 5079 7-8-11 0........................ RadekKoplik 5 105
(Z Koplik, Czech Republic) *cl up: shkn up to press ldr over 2f out: sn rdn: unable qck: kpt on same pce fr over 1f out: lost 3rd clsng stages* **36/1**

5 *½* **Royal Julius (IRE)**[29] 5079 6-9-0 0........................ MaximeGuyon 9 107
(J Reynier, France) *mid-div on outer: asked for effrt over 2f out: limited rspnse and rdn 1 1/2f out: one pce ins fnl f: n.d* **12/1**

6 *1 ¾* **King David (DEN)**[41] 4622 4-9-3 0........................ OliverWilson 7 107
(Marc Stott, Denmark) *hld up in rr: pushed along 2f out: nt qckn: passed btn rivals fr 1 1/2f out: kpt on ins fnl f but nvr involved* **9/1**

7 *2 ½* **Diamond Vendome (FR)**[29] 5079 4-9-3 0..................(p) ChristopheSoumillon 4 102
(C Escuder, France) *mid-div on inner: swtchd off rail over 2f out: short-lived effrt 1 1/2f out: sn btn: nvr a factor* **31/5**

8 *6* **Tresorerie (FR)**[57] 4011 4-8-8 0........................ JulienAuge 3 81
(C Ferland, France) *a towards rr: outpcd over 2f out: no imp whn drvn 1 1/2f out: eased clsng stages* **17/1**

9 *¾* **Soleil Marin (IRE)**[29] 5079 5-9-3 0........................ MickaelBarzalona 2 88
(A Fabre, France) *prom on inner: struggling to go pce over 2f out: grad wknd fr over 1 1/2f out: wl btn ent fnl f* **41/10**[2]

2m 6.05s (-4.15) **9 Ran SP% 120.2**
PARI-MUTUEL (all including 1 euro stake): WIN 5.40; PLACE 2.00, 2.00, 1.50; DF 25.10.
Owner Ecurie Antonio Caro & Gerard Augustin-Normand **Bred** Dream With Me Stable **Trained** Pau, France

FOCUS
It's been rated around the balance of the first six.

SAN SEBASTIAN (R-H)
Thursday, August 15

OFFICIAL GOING: Turf: good

6145a COPA DE ORO DE SAN SEBASTIAN - LE DEFI DU GALOP (LISTED RACE) (3YO+) (TURF) 1m 4f
6:40 3-Y-O+ £36,036 (£14,414; £7,207; £3,603)

RPR

1 **Amazing Red (IRE)**[68] 3500 6-9-4 0........................ JoseLuisMartinez 6 95
(Ed Dunlop) *trckd ldrs on ins: pushed along 3f out: rdn and swtchd to ins over 1 1/2f out: r.o and asserted wl ins fnl f* **27/10**[2]

2 *2 ½* **Cnicht (FR)**[77] 5-9-4 0........................ Roberto-CarlosMontenegro 3 91
(D Henderson, France) **5/1**[3]

3 *nk* **Atty Persse (IRE)**[47] 4418 5-9-4 0........................ RicardoSousa 2 91
(Enrique Leon Penate, Spain) **36/5**

4 *½* **Tuvalu**[47] 4418 7-9-4 0........................ JaimeGelabertBautista 1 90
(J-M Osorio, Spain) **164/10**

5 *2 ¼* **Parsifal (SPA)**[47] 4418 6-9-4 0........................ JulienGrosjean 8 86
(G Arizkorreta Elosegui, Spain) **227/10**

6 *½* **Red Onion**[608] 5-9-4 0........................ ClementCadel 11 86
(Gaspar Vaz, Spain) **236/10**

7 *¼* **Liberri (IRE)** 3-8-8 0........................ VaclavJanacek 4 86
(G Arizkorreta Elosegui, Spain) **53/10**

8 *hd* **Zascandil (FR)**[47] 4418 5-9-4 0........................ BorjaFayosMartin 5 85
(C Delcher-Sanchez, France) **23/10**[1]

9 *¼* **Gueraty (FR)**[74] 3-8-8 0........................ MaximeFoulon 7 85
(Angel Imaz-Beloqui, Spain) **43/1**

10 *1 ¼* **Federico**[298] 6-9-4 0........................ AntoineWerle 9 82
(Enrique Leon Penate, Spain) **151/10**

11 *5 ¼* **Falcao Negro**[35] 6-9-4 0........................ Francois-XavierBertras 10 74
(P Vidotto, France) **44/5**

2m 33.28s **11 Ran SP% 134.8**
WFA 3 from 5yo+ 10lb

The Form Book Flat 2019, Raceform Ltd, Newbury, RG14 5SJ

Owner The Hon R J Arculli **Bred** Foursome Thoroughbreds, Muir & Waldron **Trained** Newmarket, Suffolk

[5940]CHELMSFORD (A.W) (L-H)

Friday, August 16

OFFICIAL GOING: Polytrack: standard
Wind: light, behind Weather: rain

6146 BET TOTEPLACEPOT AT TOTESPORT.COM MAIDEN AUCTION FILLIES' STKS 7f (P)

5:40 (5:43) (Class 6) 2-Y-O **£3,169** (£943; £471; £235) **Stalls** Low

Form RPR

033 **1** **Banmi (IRE)**[44] 4502 2-9-0 70........................ OisinMurphy 6 72
(Mohamed Moubarak) *w ldrs tl led after 1f: rdn wl over 1f out: drvn and almost 2 l clr ins fnl f: a holding on towards fin* **4/1**[3]

2 ½ **Restless Endeavour (IRE)** 2-8-13 0........................ HollieDoyle 1 70
(Jamie Osborne) *trckd ldrs: effrt ent fnl 2f: drvn over 1f out: chsd wnr ins fnl f: kpt on wl and clsng towards fin* **7/1**

3 ¾ **Looks Good (IRE)** 2-9-0 0........................ ShaneKelly 3 69+
(Richard Hughes) *led for 1f: w wnr after: effrt over 2f out: unable to match pce of wnr over 1f out: kpt on u.p ins fnl f* **7/2**[2]

3 **4** 7 **Collette (IRE)**[9] 5823 2-8-13 0........................ GeraldMosse 5 50
(Hugo Palmer) *s.i.s: rcvrd and t.k.h in last pair: effrt over 2f out: no imp and hung lft over 1f out: wl btn ins fnl f* **10/11**[1]

0 **5** *nse* **Sea Willow**[36] 4849 2-8-11 0........................ JFEgan 2 47
(Henry Spiller) *stdd after s: t.k.h: hld up in last pair: effrt and outpcd over 2f out: wl hld over 1f out: wknd ins fnl f (jockey said filly ran too free)* **25/1**

1m 28.2s (1.00) **Going Correction** -0.175s/f (Stan) **5 Ran SP% 111.0**
Speed ratings (Par 89): **87,86,85,77,77**
CSF £29.05 TOTE £3.90: £1.40, £2.50; EX 16.50 Trifecta £54.10.
Owner Jaber Ali Alsabah **Bred** Tally-Ho Stud **Trained** Newmarket, Suffolk

FOCUS
With the favourite running miles below expectations, this took little winning. The first three finished in a bit of a heap.

6147 BET TOTEEXACTA AT TOTESPORT.COM NOVICE STKS (PLUS 10 RACE) 5f (P)

6:10 (6:11) (Class 4) 2-Y-O **£5,822** (£1,732; £865; £432) **Stalls** Low

Form RPR

0 **1** **Reassure**[23] 5317 2-8-8 0........................ GeorgiaCox(3) 3 75+
(William Haggas) *t.k.h: trckd ldrs: effrt to chal and hung rt over 1f out: rdn to ld ins fnl f: r.o wl* **5/1**[2]

201 **2** 1 ½ **Cool Sphere (USA)**[3] 6047 2-9-8 81........................ OisinMurphy 4 81
(Robert Cowell) *led and racd keenly in front: rdn and edgd rt over 1f out: drvn and hdd ins fnl f: no ex and outpcd fnl 100yds (vet said colt lost his left-hind shoe)* **4/9**[1]

4631 **3** 2 ¼ **Too Hard To Hold (IRE)**[14] 5618 2-9-8 70........................ CYHo 5 73
(Mark Johnston) *chsd wnr tl unable qck over 1f out: wl hld 3rd and one pce ins fnl f* **8/1**[3]

022 **4** 1 ¾ **Instantly**[13] 5689 2-9-2 69........................ GeraldMosse 6 61
(Robert Cowell) *wnt rt s: in last pair and outpcd after 1f: nvr threatened to get bk on terms: wl hld 4th and kpt on same pce ins fnl f: eased towards fin* **8/1**[3]

00 **5** 3 ¾ **Surrajah (IRE)**[8] 5859 2-9-2 0........................ DaneO'Neill 2 47
(Tom Clover) *stdd after s: t.k.h: hld up in last pair: outpcd after 1f: nvr threatened to get bk on terms w ldrs: wl btn 5th over 1f out* **33/1**

0 **6** 8 **Order Of Merritt (IRE)**[8] 5865 2-9-2 0........................ RyanTate 1 18
(Sir Mark Prescott Bt) *midfield: outpcd after 1f: nvr on terms after: wl bhd over 1f out* **33/1**

59.71s (-0.49) **Going Correction** -0.175s/f (Stan) **6 Ran SP% 114.0**
Speed ratings (Par 96): **96,93,90,87,81 68**
CSF £7.86 TOTE £6.10: £1.70, £1.10; EX 11.80 Trifecta £53.60.
Owner Sheikh Juma Dalmook Al Maktoum **Bred** Rabbah Bloodstock Limited **Trained** Newmarket, Suffolk

FOCUS
They went off hard in this novice contest and the long odds-on favourite appeared to get outstayed. It's been rated at something like face value.

6148 BET TOTEQUADPOT AT TOTESPORT.COM H'CAP 5f (P)

6:40 (6:41) (Class 3) (0-90,89) 3-Y-O **£9,703** (£2,887; £1,443; £721) **Stalls** Low

Form RPR

-124 **1** **Furious**[28] 5143 3-9-7 89........................ OisinMurphy 5 96+
(David Simcock) *squeezed for room leaving stalls: in tch in last trio: clsd to trck ldrs over 2f out: nt clrest of runs over 1f out: effrt to chal 1f out: led ins fnl f: r.o wl* **3/1**[1]

5140 **2** ¾ **Probability (IRE)**[23] 5325 3-9-6 88........................ HollieDoyle 2 92
(Archie Watson) *w ldr tl led on inner over 2f out: drvn over 1f out: hdd and one pce ins fnl f* **9/2**[3]

5065 **3** *nk* **Concierge (IRE)**[15] 5589 3-9-7 89........................(b) GeraldMosse 1 92
(George Scott) *hld up in tch in rr: clsd and nt clr run over 1f out: hdwy u.p 1f out: chsd ldng pair wl ins fnl f: kpt on wl towards fin* **4/1**[2]

232 **4** 1 ¾ **Mercenary Rose (IRE)**[15] 5589 3-8-12 80........................(t) JFEgan 4 77
(Paul Cole) *chsd ldrs: drvn to chal over 1f out tl no ex ins fnl f: wknd towards fin (vet said filly had lost her right-fore shoe)* **4/1**[2]

110 **5** 1 ¼ **Amplify (IRE)**[15] 5589 3-9-2 84........................ JasonWatson 7 76
(Brian Meehan) *edgd lft leaving stalls: hld up in tch in last trio: swtchd rt and effrt over 1f out: no imp u.p over 1f out: wl hld and kpt on same pce ins fnl f* **7/1**

2564 **6** 1 **True Hero**[10] 5791 3-8-9 80........................ RowanScott(3) 6 69
(Nigel Tinkler) *hld up in midfield: unable qck u.p over 1f out: wl hld and one pce ins fnl f* **16/1**

4000 **7** 3 ½ **Blame Roberta (USA)**[15] 5589 3-9-2 84........................(p) DaneO'Neill 3 60
(Robert Cowell) *led: hung rt bnd 3f out: hdd over 2f out: lost pl over 1f out: bhd and eased wl ins fnl f* **8/1**

58.68s (-1.52) **Going Correction** -0.175s/f (Stan) **7 Ran SP% 112.7**
Speed ratings (Par 104): **105,103,103,100,98 96,91**
CSF £16.17 TOTE £3.00: £1.40, £3.50; EX 16.70 Trifecta £59.00.
Owner Qatar Racing Ltd & Kin Hung Kei **Bred** Sir Nicholas & Lady Nugent **Trained** Newmarket, Suffolk

FOCUS
This was run at a strong pace and represents solid form for the level.

6149 BET TOTETRIFECTA AT TOTESPORT.COM H'CAP 5f (P)

7:10 (7:11) (Class 2) (0-105,107) 3-Y-O+ **£12,938** (£3,850; £1,924; £962) **Stalls** Low

Form RPR

0000 **1** **Blue De Vega (GER)**[13] 5661 6-8-8 87........................(tp) PJMcDonald 3 94
(Robert Cowell) *in tch towards rr: effrt over 1f out: hdwy and swtchd rt ins fnl f: str run u.p fnl 100yds to ld cl home* **6/1**

220 **2** *nk* **Puds**[13] 5661 4-8-10 89........................ ShaneKelly 7 95+
(Richard Hughes) *midfield tl stdd and dropped to rr over 3f out: effrt on inner over 1f out: hdwy ins fnl f: str chal wl ins fnl f: wnt 2nd last strides* **6/1**

021 **3** *hd* **Tropics (USA)**[58] 3993 11-9-9 107........................(h) SophieRalston(5) 6 112
(Dean Ivory) *sn pressing ldr: rdn over 1f out: led ent fnl f: kpt on wl ins fnl f tl hdd and lost 2 pls cl home* **8/1**

500 **4** 1 ¾ **Muthmir (IRE)**[34] 4896 9-9-9 102........................(b) DaneO'Neill 2 101
(William Haggas) *sn in tch in midfield: clsd to chse ldrs over 3f out: effrt u.p over 1f out: no ex and wknd wl ins fnl f* **5/1**[3]

1404 **5** *hd* **Jumira Bridge**[7] 5888 5-8-6 92........................ MarcoGhiani(7) 5 90
(Robert Cowell) *squeezed for room leaving stalls: hdwy after 1f: chsd ldrs over 3f out: effrt u.p over 1f out: kpt on same pce ins fnl f* **14/1**

3450 **6** 1 **Caspian Prince (IRE)**[6] 5927 10-9-12 105........................(t) AlistairRawlinson 1 99
(Michael Appleby) *wnt rt leaving stalls: sn led: rdn over 1f out: hdd ent fnl f: no ex and wknd fnl 75yds* **3/1**[1]

0200 **7** 1 ¾ **Encore D'Or**[6] 5927 7-9-7 100........................(v[1]) OisinMurphy 8 88
(Robert Cowell) *chsd ldrs: effrt on outer: unable qck u.p ent fnl f: wknd ins fnl f* **9/1**

1015 **8** 1 ¼ **Corinthia Knight (IRE)**[6] 5927 4-9-10 103........................ HollieDoyle 4 87
(Archie Watson) *midfield tl short of room and lost pl over 3f out: nvr travelling wl after: bhd fnl f* **7/2**[2]

58.37s (-1.83) **Going Correction** -0.175s/f (Stan) **8 Ran SP% 120.2**
Speed ratings (Par 109): **107,106,106,103,103 101,98,96**
CSF £43.83 CT £297.73 TOTE £7.00: £1.60, £2.20, £2.70; EX 45.40 Trifecta £286.50.
Owner Mrs J Morley **Bred** Gestut Ammerland **Trained** Six Mile Bottom, Cambs

FOCUS
This high quality sprint handicap was strongly run and suited the hold up horses.

6150 BET TOTESWINGER AT TOTESPORT.COM H'CAP 1m (P)

7:45 (7:48) (Class 2) (0-105,103) 3-Y-O+ **£12,938** (£3,850; £1,924; £962) **Stalls** Low

Form RPR

/0-5 **1** **Yattwee (USA)**[27] 5188 6-9-8 97........................ CallumShepherd 4 106
(Saeed bin Suroor) *hld up in tch in midfield: effrt over 1f out: hdwy and drvn to chse ldrs 1f out: styd on strly to ld ins fnl f: kpt on wl* **8/1**

0320 **2** ¾ **Nicklaus**[17] 5519 4-9-3 92........................(t) JasonWatson 3 99
(William Haggas) *led: sn hdd and chsd ldr tl over 6f out: styd chsng ldrs tl rdn to chse ldr again over 2f out: drvn and clsd to chal ins fnl f: kpt on but nt quite match pce of wnr wl ins fnl f* **5/1**[2]

-100 **3** *hd* **Ambassadorial (USA)**[16] 5546 5-10-0 103........................ JFEgan 5 109
(Jane Chapple-Hyam) *hld up in midfield on outer: effrt ent fnl 2f: drvn and clsd over 1f out: hdwy to chse ldrs ins fnl f: kpt on to snatch 3rd last stride* **8/1**

4121 **4** *nk* **Star Of Southwold (FR)**[28] 5155 4-8-13 93........................ TheodoreLadd(5) 10 98
(Michael Appleby) *sn led: rdn and kicked on ent fnl 2f: drvn ent fnl f: hdd ins fnl f: no ex towards fin* **7/1**

1210 **5** 3 ¼ **Mubhij (IRE)**[20] 5413 4-9-8 97........................ DaneO'Neill 1 95
(Roger Varian) *hld up in tch in midfield: effrt u.p over 1f out: kpt on same pce u.p ins fnl f* **9/2**[1]

3220 **6** *nk* **Qaroun**[41] 4666 4-9-4 93........................ OisinMurphy 7 90
(Sir Michael Stoute) *chsd ldrs: effrt in 4th ent fnl 2f: drvn and no imp over 1f out: kpt on same pce ins fnl f* **6/1**[3]

0000 **7** 2 ¼ **Blown By Wind**[13] 5666 3-9-3 98........................ CYHo 9 89
(Mark Johnston) *dwlt: swtchd lft sn after s: hld up in last trio: effrt u.p over 2f out: plugged on ins fnl f: nvr trbld ldrs* **25/1**

6124 **8** 3 ¾ **Fields Of Athenry (USA)**[41] 4639 3-8-11 92........................ PJMcDonald 2 74
(James Tate) *in tch in midfield: effrt jst over 2f out: no imp u.p over 1f out: wknd ins fnl f* **6/1**[3]

0000 **9** 5 **Glendevon (USA)**[16] 5546 4-9-4 93........................(h) ShaneKelly 6 65
(Richard Hughes) *stdd bk to rr after s: t.k.h in rr: effrt over 1f out: no prog: nvr involved* **25/1**

0040 **10** *hd* **Key Victory (IRE)**[14] 5610 4-9-13 102........................(p) BrettDoyle 11 73
(Charlie Appleby) *dwlt and swtchd lft sn after s: t.k.h: hld up in last pair: effrt wl over 1f out: no prog and sn wl btn* **10/1**

5000 **11** 4 ½ **Plutonian (IRE)**[17] 5519 5-9-4 93........................(t[1]) HollieDoyle 8 54
(Charles Hills) *pushed along leaving stalls: chsd ldr over 6f out tl lost pl u.p over 2f out: wl bhd ins fnl f (jockey said gelding stopped quickly)* **20/1**

1m 36.61s (-3.29) **Going Correction** -0.175s/f (Stan)
WFA 3 from 4yo+ 6lb **11 Ran SP% 119.7**
Speed ratings (Par 109): **109,108,108,107,104 104,101,98,93,93 88**
CSF £47.40 CT £333.59 TOTE £10.20: £3.30, £2.50, £3.20; EX 57.70 Trifecta £410.30.
Owner Godolphin **Bred** Darley **Trained** Newmarket, Suffolk

FOCUS
This hotly contested handicap was won a shade cosily by the lightly raced Yattwee. Straightforward form, with the fourth helping to set the level.

6151 BET TOTESCOOP6 AT TOTESPORT.COM H'CAP 1m 2f (P)

8:15 (8:17) (Class 3) (0-95,96) 3-Y-O+ **£9,703** (£2,887; £1,443; £721) **Stalls** Low

Form RPR

1454 **1** **Victory Command (IRE)**[15] 5583 3-9-11 96........................ PJMcDonald 2 103
(Mark Johnston) *chsd ldr tl led over 8f out: mde rest: rdn wl over 1f out: styd on wl ins fnl f* **11/4**[2]

1023 **2** 1 **Lexington Empire**[20] 5437 4-9-12 90........................(b) DanielMuscutt 7 95
(David Lanigan) *led for over 1f: chsd ldrs: swtchd rt and effrt ent fnl 2f: str chal over 1f out: kpt on but a hld ins fnl f* **4/1**[3]

00 **3** 3 ¼ **Lush Life (IRE)**[14] 5610 4-10-0 92........................ OisinMurphy 6 91
(Jamie Osborne) *hld up in tch: effrt on inner to chse ldrs over 1f out: no ex 1f out: wknd ins fnl f* **8/1**

6525 **4** 4 ½ **Philamundo (IRE)**[13] 5651 4-8-13 77........................ HollieDoyle 1 67
(Richard Spencer) *stdd and swtchd rt after s: hld up in rr: clsd and effrt on outer to chse ldrs 2f out: unable qck and outpcd over 1f out: wknd ins fnl f* **10/1**

3-52 **5** *1* **Herculean**[20] 5440 4-9-12 **90**.................. JasonWatson 4 78
(Roger Charlton) *chsd ldr over 8f out tl over 7f out: in tch after: effrt over 2f out: unable qck u.p over 1f out: wknd ins fnl f (trainer's rep said that the gelding was unsuited by the Polytrack and racing around a tighter track)* **6/4**[1]

5000 **6** *9* **Cohesion**[13] 5657 6-8-13 **82**.................. PoppyBridgwater(5) 3 52
(David Bridgwater) *rousted along leaving stalls: a towards rr and nvr travelling wl: drvn and wl btn over 1f out* **66/1**

1246 **7** *2 1/2* **Three Weeks (USA)**[139] 1420 4-10-0 **92**.................. DavidProbert 5 57
(David O'Meara) *midfield: hdwy to chse ldr over 8f out tl over 2f out: sn outpcd: wl bhd ins fnl f* **20/1**

2m 4.6s (-4.00) **Going Correction** -0.175s/f (Stan)
WFA 3 from 4yo+ 7lb **7** Ran SP% **113.1**
Speed ratings (Par 107): **109,108,105,102,101 94,92**
CSF £13.86 TOTE £3.40: £1.70, £2.40; EX 11.90 Trifecta £44.90.
Owner Kingsley Park 10 **Bred** J Higgins **Trained** Middleham Moor, N Yorks

FOCUS
This looked competitive beforehand but very few actually featured as the first two drew clear. The first two have been rated close to their best.

6152 MINISTRY OF SOUND THE ANNUAL CLASSICAL H'CAP (DIV I) 1m 2f (P)
8:45 (8:47) (Class 6) (0-55,56) 3-Y-O+

£3,105 (£924; £461; £400; £400; £400) **Stalls** Low

Form RPR

0642 **1** **Sandy Steve**[9] 5803 3-8-13 **54**.................. PJMcDonald 10 65+
(Stuart Williams) *in rr: hdwy on outer 3f out: chsd clr ldng trio 2f out: styd on dourly to ld 100yds out: sn in command and gng away at fin* **6/4**[1]

2353 **2** *1 3/4* **Fair Power (IRE)**[9] 5803 5-9-7 **55**..................(p[1]) OisinMurphy 1 62
(John Butler) *t.k.h: pressed ldr for 2f: chsd ldrs after: effrt between rivals to chal ins fnl f: chsd wnr and one pce fnl 100yds* **11/4**[2]

0004 **3** *1 3/4* **Rainbow Jazz (IRE)**[13] 5653 4-9-3 **51**..................(b) RoystonFfrench 6 54
(Adam West) *rousted along early: hdwy to chse ldr after 2f: led 7f out: hrd drvn over 1f out: hdd 100yds out: no ex* **7/1**[3]

-000 **4** *3 1/4* **Dolly McQueen**[65] 3741 3-8-5 **46** oh1.................. HollieDoyle 2 44
(Anthony Carson) *led tl 7f out: chsd ldr after: rdn and pressing ldr ent fnl 2f: no ex and wknd ins fnl f* **12/1**

2526 **5** *5* **Sharp Operator**[17] 5531 6-9-3 **54**..................(h) JoshuaBryan(3) 8 42
(Charlie Wallis) *stdd and swtchd lft after s: hld up in tch in last quartet: effrt ent fnl 2f: wl hld 5th and no imp fnl f* **8/1**

0050 **6** *2 1/2* **Malaysian Boleh**[8] 5837 9-8-5 **46** oh1..................(p) GraceMcEntee(7) 3 29
(Phil McEntee) *hld up in tch in midfield: nt clr run and shuffled bk towards rr over 2f out: effrt ent fnl 2f: no prog and wl btn fnl f* **33/1**

0060 **7** *1* **Interrogation (FR)**[15] 5596 4-8-12 **46** oh1..................(b) JoeyHaynes 5 27
(Alan Bailey) *in tch in midfield: u.p and outpcd in 4th over 2f out: wl btn over 1f out: wknd* **50/1**

0430 **8** *3/4* **Wynfaul The Wizard (USA)**[10] 5787 4-8-12 **46** oh1......(v) ShaneKelly 9 26
(Laura Morgan) *dwlt: hld up in last quartet: effrt wl over 1f out: no prog and sn wl btn* **50/1**

0000 **9** *1 1/4* **Reformed Character (IRE)**[17] 5531 3-8-5 **46**.......(b[1]) AdrianMcCarthy 4 24
(Lydia Pearce) *s.i.s: a towards rr: nvr involved* **33/1**

0200 **10** *3/4* **Monsieur Fox**[23] 5309 4-9-7 **55**..................(v[1]) CallumShepherd 11 31
(Lydia Richards) *in tch in midfield on outer: effrt over 2f out: sn struggling and lost pl wl over 1f out: wknd* **16/1**

0-43 **11** *10* **Dreamingofdiamonds (IRE)**[20] 5428 3-8-11 **52**......... StevieDonohoe 7 10
(David Lanigan) *pushed along leaving stalls: chsd ldrs tl rdn and lost pl over 2f out: bhd over 1f out: wknd (trainer's rep said that the filly didn't stay the trip of 1m2f)* **12/1**

2m 5.31s (-3.29)
WFA 3 from 4yo+ 7lb **11** Ran SP% **121.3**
CSF £5.55 CT £22.02 TOTE £1.90: £1.10, £1.10, £2.00; EX 5.70 Trifecta £25.30.
Owner J W Parry **Bred** J W Parry **Trained** Newmarket, Suffolk

FOCUS
Modest stuff, but a good effort from Sandy Steve who past everything in the straight to win going away. The winning time was 1.35sec quicker than the second division. The balance of the second and third help set the opening level.

6153 MINISTRY OF SOUND THE ANNUAL CLASSICAL H'CAP (DIV II) 1m 2f (P)
9:15 (9:18) (Class 6) (0-55,55) 3-Y-O+

£3,105 (£924; £461; £400; £400; £400) **Stalls** Low

Form RPR

0012 **1** **Muraaqeb**[6] 5946 5-9-2 **53**..................(p) JoshuaBryan(3) 2 58
(Milton Bradley) *midfield: effrt and clsd over 2f out: swtchd lft and styd on to press ldrs 1f out: ev ch ins fnl f: kpt on to ld last strides* **7/2**[2]

0622 **2** *hd* **Chakrii (IRE)**[13] 5653 3-8-10 **51**..................(p) HayleyTurner 4 57
(Henry Spiller) *hld up in midfield: effrt to chse ldrs and clsng over 2f out: drvn and hdwy to ld 1f out: kpt on wl: hdd last strides* **4/1**[3]

3343 **3** *1/2* **Pike Corner Cross (IRE)**[14] 5633 7-9-3 **51**..................(t) StevieDonohoe 5 55
(David Evans) *midfield: effrt and clsd over 2f out: hdwy u.p over 1f out: chsd ldrs 1f out: kpt on wl ins fnl f* **8/1**

-055 **4** *1/2* **Blowing Dixie**[70] 3528 3-8-12 **53**.................. JFEgan 1 57
(Jane Chapple-Hyam) *prom: effrt to chse ldr and clsng over 2f out: ev ch 1f out: kpt on same pce fnl 100yds* **5/2**[1]

-006 **5** *2 1/4* **Midnight Mood**[22] 5344 6-9-7 **55**.................. OisinMurphy 11 53
(Dominic Ffrench Davis) *hld up towards rr: effrt 2f out: styd on u.p ins fnl f: nt rch ldrs* **6/1**

0066 **6** *2 1/2* **Outlaw Torn (IRE)**[6] 5946 10-8-12 **46** oh1..................(e) BrettDoyle 12 40
(Richard Guest) *chsd ldrs tl hdwy to ld after 2f: clr 7f out: rdn over 1f out: hdd 1f out: wknd ins fnl f* **25/1**

050 **7** *nk* **Margaret J**[6] 5946 3-8-0 **46** oh1..................(p) SophieRalston(5) 7 40
(Phil McEntee) *hld up in last quartet: effrt over 2f out: styd on ins fnl f: nvr trbld ldrs* **33/1**

3R60 **8** *4 1/2* **Principia**[9] 5803 4-9-7 **55**..................(p) DavidProbert 8 40
(Adam West) *s.i.s: in rr: effrt jst over 2f out: hung lft over 1f out: nvr trbld ldrs (jockey said filly hung left-handed in the straight)* **16/1**

000 **9** *nk* **Ximena**[15] 5592 3-8-5 **46**..................(h) HollieDoyle 10 31
(William Jarvis) *s.i.s: t.k.h: hld up in last pair: effrt wl over 1f out: no imp: nvr involved (jockey said filly was slowly into stride and ran too free)* **12/1**

00-0 **10** *2 3/4* **Mister Fawkes**[77] 3299 3-9-0 **55**..................(w) ShaneKelly 6 35
(Richard Hughes) *w ldr for 2f: prom in chsng gp tl lost pl and bhd over 1f out: wknd* **33/1**

2/0- **11** *hd* **Trois Bon Amis (IRE)**[403] 4759 5-8-12 **46** oh1..................(t) PJMcDonald 3 24
(Mark Campion) *t.k.h: led for 2f: chsd ldr: rdn and lost 2nd over 2f out: wknd over 1f out* **50/1**

2m 6.66s (-1.94)
WFA 3 from 4yo+ 7lb **11** Ran SP% **121.5**
CSF £18.05 CT £107.89 TOTE £3.70: £1.60, £1.70, £2.60; EX 16.00 Trifecta £36.20.
Owner E A Hayward **Bred** Peter Winkworth **Trained** Sedbury, Gloucs

FOCUS
This looked the more competitive division of this handicap, though the winning time was 1.35sec slower than the first. Those close up dictate the modest level of the form.
T/Plt: £205.80 to a £1 stake. Pool: £30,218.83 - 146.80 winning units T/Qpdt: £74.60 to a £1 stake. Pool: £4,051.49 - 54.30 winning units **Steve Payne**

5772 NEWBURY (L-H)
Friday, August 16

OFFICIAL GOING: Good to soft (good in places) changing to good to soft (soft in places) after race 3 (2.55) changing to soft after race 6 (4.35)
Wind: strong across Weather: rain

6154 UNIBET EBF MAIDEN STKS (PLUS 10 RACE) 7f (S)
1:50 (1:52) (Class 4) 2-Y-O **£4,463** (£1,328; £663; £331) **Stalls** Centre

Form RPR

1 **Quadrilateral** 2-9-0 **0**.................. JasonWatson 1 82+
(Roger Charlton) *mid-div: pushed along and hdwy 2f out: kpt on wl ins fnl f: led fnl 75yds: rdn out* **7/2**[2]

06 **2** *nk* **Mambo Nights (IRE)**[13] 5665 2-9-5 **0**.................. RossaRyan 6 86
(Richard Hannon) *trckd ldrs: led over 1f out: sn rdn: drifted rt fnl f: kpt on but no ex whn hdd fnl 75yds* **14/1**

52 **3** *3 1/2* **Ottoman Court**[69] 3601 2-9-5 **0**..................(p) WilliamBuick 5 77
(Charlie Appleby) *led: rdn and hdd over 1f out: edgd rt: kpt on same pce fnl f* **8/11**[1]

03 **4** *3 1/4* **Ziggle Pops**[14] 5624 2-9-5 **0**.................. SeanLevey 11 69
(Richard Hannon) *trckd ldrs: rdn over 2f out: kpt on but nt pce to chal: drifted lft ins fnl f* **7/1**[3]

0 **5** *1 1/4* **Honore Daumier (IRE)**[20] 5439 2-9-5 **0**.................. CharlesBishop 2 65
(Henry Candy) *prom: rdn over 2f out: fdd ins fnl f* **100/1**

6 *shd* **Convict** 2-9-5 **0**.................. RichardKingscote 8 65+
(William Haggas) *s.i.s: towards rr: rdn over 2f out: kpt on fnl f but nvr any threat* **12/1**

7 *1 1/2* **Quickstep Lady** 2-9-0 **0**.................. DavidProbert 7 56
(Andrew Balding) *little slowly away: racd green towards rr: sme late prog: nvr on terms* **16/1**

8 *1* **Marion's Boy (IRE)** 2-9-5 **0**.................. AdamKirby 4 59
(Roger Teal) *trckd ldrs: rdn over 2f out: wknd over 1f out* **33/1**

9 *2 1/2* **Arabescato** 2-9-5 **0**.................. KieranShoemark 9 52
(Richard Spencer) *a towards rr* **66/1**

4 **10** *1 3/4* **Mephisto (IRE)**[22] 5345 2-9-5 **0**.................. RobHornby 3 48
(Ralph Beckett) *mid-div: rdn over 2f out: sn wknd* **25/1**

1m 26.88s (-0.12) **Going Correction** +0.225s/f (Good) **10** Ran SP% **122.1**
Speed ratings (Par 96): **109,108,104,100,99 99,97,96,93,91**
CSF £51.81 TOTE £4.00: £1.50, £3.20, £1.10; EX 45.90 Trifecta £97.70.
Owner K Abdullah **Bred** Juddmonte Farms Ltd **Trained** Beckhampton, Wilts

FOCUS
The rails at the 7f and 5f bends were five metres from the inside line, increasing distances of races starting in the back straight. There was 9.5mm of rain two days earlier and race day was rainy, so the ground was given as good to soft, good in places to start. It's hard to know the true worth of this form but the runner-up had already shown fair ability and pulled clear of the others, and the winner is promising. They all started up the middle before edging near side. It's been rated as sound form.

6155 CHRISTOPHER SMITH ASSOCIATES H'CAP 1m (S)
2:25 (2:25) (Class 4) (0-85,84) 3-Y-O+

£5,207 (£1,549; £774; £387; £300; £300) **Stalls** Centre

Form RPR

1041 **1** **Gin Palace**[18] 5505 3-9-3 **79**.................. CharlesBishop 3 89
(Eve Johnson Houghton) *a.p: rdn for str chal fr 2f out: edgd ahd fnl 120yds: kpt on: all out* **12/1**

4514 **2** *hd* **Canal Rocks**[23] 5292 3-9-2 **78**.................. JasonWatson 4 87
(Henry Candy) *a.p: led over 2f out: sn rdn: narrowly hdd fnl 120yds: kpt on gamely* **7/1**[3]

3462 **3** *2 1/2* **Medieval (IRE)**[9] 5804 5-9-7 **77**..................(p) RossaRyan 7 82
(Paul Cole) *s.i.s: sn cl up: swtchd rt over 1f out: sn rdn: r.o ent fnl f: wnt 3rd towards fin* **7/2**[1]

1201 **4** *nk* **Marshal Dan (IRE)**[22] 5343 4-9-3 **80**.................. StefanoCherchi(7) 8 84
(Heather Main) *cl up: rdn over 2f out: chal for 3rd over 1f out: kpt on same pce fnl f* **6/1**[2]

0-25 **5** *nk* **Wufud**[61] 3880 4-9-12 **82**..................(t) RichardKingscote 1 85
(Charles Hills) *s.i.s: sn cl up: hdwy 2f out: rdn over 1f out: chal for 3rd ent fnl f: kpt on tl no ex cl home* **8/1**

4503 **6** *3 1/2* **Mr Tyrrell (IRE)**[5] 5991 5-10-0 **84**.................. SeanLevey 2 79
(Richard Hannon) *cl up: chal for 3rd 2f out: sn rdn: fdd ins fnl f* **12/1**

0112 **7** *1/2* **Los Camachos (IRE)**[165] 1018 4-9-8 **78**.................. HectorCrouch 6 72
(John Gallagher) *disp ld tl rdn over 2f out: fdd fnl f* **40/1**

0243 **8** *6* **Baba Ghanouj (IRE)**[21] 5383 3-9-7 **83**.................. WilliamBuick 10 62
(Ed Walker) *hld up: rdn over 2f out: nvr any imp: wknd over 1f out* **7/1**[3]

0303 **9** *9* **Jackpot Royale**[28] 5150 4-9-13 **83**..................(p) KieranShoemark 5 43
(Michael Appleby) *disp ld tl rdn over 2f out: wkng whn squeezed up over 1f out* **25/1**

0414 **10** *14* **Daddy's Daughter (CAN)**[27] 5195 4-9-13 **83**..................(h) AdamKirby 9 10
(Dean Ivory) *disp ld tl over 2f out: sn wknd (jockey said filly stopped quickly)* **7/2**[1]

1m 39.82s (-0.08) **Going Correction** +0.225s/f (Good)
WFA 3 from 4yo+ 6lb **10** Ran SP% **116.5**
Speed ratings (Par 105): **109,108,106,106,105 102,101,95,86,72**
CSF £93.30 CT £360.87 TOTE £12.00: £3.30, £2.80, £1.60; EX 97.00 Trifecta £385.60.
Owner Mrs Zara Campbell-Harris **Bred** Mrs Z C Campbell-Harris **Trained** Blewbury, Oxon

FOCUS
The action was middle to near side and the first two finishers, for the most part, raced furthest of all away from the near rail, although later evidence didn't point to a bias. The third and fourth have been rated close to form.

6156 ENERGY CHECK H'CAP 1m 5f 61y
2:55 (2:56) (Class 3) (0-90,90) 3-Y-O+ **£5,036**; £1,154; £577**Stalls** Low

Form RPR

5410 **1** **Frontispiece**[9] 5811 5-9-10 **85**.................. KieranShoemark 3 92
(Amanda Perrett) *led: swtchd to stands' side ent st: rdn and strly chal fr over 2f out: narrowly hdd towards fin: drvn bk to dead-heat fnl stride* **13/2**

0241 **1** *dht* **Emenem**[23] 5321 5-9-0 **82** .... LeviWilliams(7) 4 89
(Simon Dow) *in tch: swtchd towards stands' side ent st: pushed along over 2f out: rdn and hdwy whn nt clr run briefly jst ins fnl f: kpt on wl to take narrow advantage towards fin: jnd on line* **8/1**

2300 **3** *2 ½* **Mandalayan (IRE)**[23] 5321 4-9-8 **83** .... RobHornby 2 86
(Jonathan Portman) *trckd ldr: swtchd to stands' side ent st: rdn to chal 3f out: stl gd ch ent fnl f: sn drifted lft and no ex* **14/1**

2352 **4** *2 ½* **War Brigade (FR)**[11] 5739 5-8-9 **70** oh1 .... (p) JasonWatson 6 70
(Ian Williams) *in tch: swtchd towards stands' side ent st: rdn and ev ch over 2f out tl ent fnl f: no ex* **5/2**[1]

6 **5** *3* **Walter White (FR)**[37] 4792 4-9-1 **76** .... DavidProbert 5 71
(Alan King) *s.i.s: in tch: kpt to centre home st: chal gng wl over 2f out: sn rdn: hld ent fnl f: wknd fnl 120yds* **11/4**[2]

1241 **6** *3 ¼* **Battle Of Wills (IRE)**[27] 5201 3-9-6 **90** .... (p) AdamKirby 1 82
(James Tate) *trckd ldr: kpt to centre home st: rdn and ev ch over 2f out tl over 1f out: wknd fnl f* **3/1**[3]

2m 55.97s (1.57) **Going Correction** +0.225s/f (Good)
WFA 3 from 4yo+ 9lb **6 Ran SP% 111.3**
Speed ratings (Par 107): **104,104,102,100,99 97**
WIN: 3.80 Frontispiece, 3.50 Emenem; PL: 3.40 Frontispiece, 3.10 Emenem; EX: F/E 29.40, E/F 30.80; CSF: F/E 26.39, E/F 27.57; TF: F/E/M 180.00, E/F/M 166.10;.

Owner Frontispiece Partnership **Bred** The Queen **Trained** Pulborough, W Sussex

Owner Robert Moss **Bred** D R Tucker **Trained** Epsom, Surrey

FOCUS
Add 18yds. After this race the going was changed to good to soft, soft in places. Most of these headed near side in the straight. But the two who stayed away from the fence, more up the middle for the most part, filled in the last two places - that outcome went against what happened in the preceding race, so a hard track to read. It's been rated as modest form.

6157 BYERLEY STUD STKS (REGISTERED AS THE ST HUGH'S STAKES) (LISTED RACE) (FILLIES) 5f 34y

3:30 (3:30) (Class 1) 2-Y-O

£14,461 (£5,482; £2,743; £1,366; £685; £344) **Stalls** Centre

Form RPR

5414 **1** **Orlaith (IRE)**[16] 5544 2-9-0 89 .... PaulMulrennan 1 97
(Iain Jardine) *mid-div: hdwy over 2f out: nt clr run briefly over 1f out: qcknd up wl jst ins fnl f: led fnl 75yds: r.o* **14/1**

2541 **2** *¾* **Al Raya**[13] 5681 2-9-0 94 .... DavidProbert 5 94
(Simon Crisford) *trckd ldrs: rdn to ld over 1f out: kpt on but no ex whn hdd fnl 75yds* **4/1**[2]

210 **3** *1 ¾* **Dr Simpson (FR)**[16] 5542 2-9-0 89 .... RichardKingscote 2 88
(Tom Dascombe) *prom: rdn over 1f out: kpt on but nt pce of front pair ins fnl f* **5/1**[3]

61 **4** *¾* **Jouska**[23] 5317 2-9-0 0 .... CharlesBishop 3 85
(Henry Candy) *mid-div: nt clr run over 1f out: sn shkn up: r.o ins fnl f: wnt 4th fnl 120yds* **6/1**

0616 **5** *1 ½* **Glamorous Anna**[16] 5544 2-9-0 80 .... WilliamCox 8 80
(Christopher Mason) *led: rdn and hdd over 1f out: kpt on same pce fnl f* **66/1**

4404 **6** *nse* **American Lady (IRE)**[11] 5751 2-9-0 0 .... ConorMaxwell 11 80
(J A Stack, Ire) *hld up: rdn 2f out: nt pce to get involved but kpt on fnl f* **25/1**

2115 **7** *shd* **Good Vibes**[20] 5411 2-9-3 96 .... AdamKirby 12 84+
(David Evans) *hld up: rdn 2f out: kpt on fnl f but little imp on ldrs (jockey said filly was denied a clear run; trainer said filly was unsuited by the going and would prefer a faster surface)* **3/1**[1]

1351 **8** *½* **Ocasio Cortez (IRE)**[20] 5418 2-9-0 84 .... SeanLevey 10 78
(Richard Hannon) *trckd ldr: rdn 2f out: nt pce to chal: wknd fnl f* **10/1**

1 **9** *5* **Seize The Time (IRE)**[25] 5243 2-9-0 0 .... CliffordLee 7 60
(K R Burke) *s.i.s: towards rr: rdn over 2f out: little imp: wknd fnl f* **10/1**

1 **10** *3* **Ishvara**[15] 5590 2-9-0 0 .... KieranShoemark 9 49
(Robert Cowell) *in tch: effrt wl over 1f out: wknd fnl f* **11/1**

1m 2.69s (1.19) **Going Correction** +0.225s/f (Good) **10 Ran SP% 114.5**
Speed ratings (Par 99): **99,97,95,93,91 91,91,90,82,77**
CSF £68.09 TOTE £15.70: £4.50, £2.20, £2.30; EX 84.50 Trifecta £394.90.

Owner James Fyffe & Scott Fyffe **Bred** Grange Stud **Trained** Carrutherstown, D'fries & G'way

FOCUS
This looked an ordinary fillies' Listed race. They all raced near side but there was no golden rail this time. The second, third, fourth and fifth have been rated close to their pre-race marks.

6158 PEPPER PINK GIN NURSERY H'CAP 5f 34y

4:00 (4:00) (Class 4) (0-85,79) 2-Y-O

£5,207 (£1,549; £774; £387; £300; £300) **Stalls** Centre

Form RPR

3150 **1** **Bushtucker Trial (IRE)**[21] 5390 2-9-1 **73** .... CliffordLee 6 77
(Michael Bell) *trckd ldrs: sltly outpcd over 1f out: str run ins fnl f: led towards fin* **3/1**[1]

1663 **2** *nk* **Shammah (IRE)**[12] 5703 2-9-6 **78** .... SeanLevey 7 81
(Richard Hannon) *trckd ldrs: rdn to chal over 1f out: led ent fnl f: kpt on: hdd towards fin* **4/1**[3]

010 **3** *¾* **Dark Optimist (IRE)**[41] 4647 2-9-7 **79** .... (t[1]) KieranShoemark 4 79
(David Evans) *nt the best away: last: rdn whn outpcd 2f out: hdwy ent fnl f: r.o wl: wnt 3rd towards fin* **9/1**

663 **4** *¾* **Queen Aya**[32] 4993 2-8-5 **66** .... WilliamCox(3) 1 64
(Ed Walker) *trckd ldr: rdn and ev ch ent fnl f: kpt on same pce fnl 120yds* **4/1**[3]

4254 **5** *½* **Swinley (IRE)**[18] 5500 2-8-10 **75** .... AngusVilliers(7) 3 71
(Richard Hughes) *trckd ldrs: rdn over 1f out: kpt on fnl f but nt pce to chal* **10/3**[2]

352 **6** *1* **Point Of Order**[15] 5577 2-9-6 **78** .... AdamMcNamara 8 70
(Archie Watson) *led: rdn over 1f out: hdd ent fnl f: no ex fnl 120yds (jockey said colt hung right-handed throughout)* **11/2**

1m 4.44s (2.94) **Going Correction** +0.225s/f (Good) **6 Ran SP% 113.5**
Speed ratings (Par 96): **85,84,83,82,81 79**
CSF £15.50 CT £94.06 TOTE £4.10: £2.20, £2.20; EX 16.70 Trifecta £96.90.

Owner Christopher Wright & David Kilburn **Bred** Ambrose Madden **Trained** Newmarket, Suffolk

FOCUS
This was run at an overly strong pace. They all raced near side early but slightly off the rail before all bar one of them drifted to the middle late on - the solo runner in the concluding stages was the winner, who switched onto the fence and surged home from a hopeless looking position. Straightforward form.

6159 TOM MITCHELL 65TH BIRTHDAY BRITISH EBF FILLIES' NOVICE STKS (PLUS 10 RACE) 6f

4:35 (4:35) (Class 4) 2-Y-O **£5,757** (£1,713; £856; £428) **Stalls** Centre

Form RPR

23 **1** **Game And Set**[21] 5366 2-9-0 0 .... DavidProbert 6 86
(Andrew Balding) *a.p: led 2f out: kpt on strly fnl f: rdn out* **4/1**[3]

2 **2** *2* **Star In The Making**[88] 2915 2-9-0 0 .... HectorCrouch 5 80
(Clive Cox) *trckd ldrs: rdn to chse wnr over 1f out: kpt on but a being hld fnl f* **2/1**[1]

3 *4 ½* **Woodhouse** 2-9-0 0 .... WilliamBuick 4 67+
(Sir Michael Stoute) *s.i.s: last but in tch: hdwy over 1f out: kpt on into 3rd ins fnl f wout ever threatening to get on terms w front pair* **9/2**

2 **4** *3* **Breath Of Joy**[37] 4790 2-9-0 0 .... RichardKingscote 3 58
(Amy Murphy) *trckd ldrs: rdn to chse wnr briefly over 1f out: sn hung lft: wknd fnl f* **7/2**[2]

3 **5** *2 ½* **Kodiellen (IRE)**[7] 5906 2-9-0 0 .... SeanLevey 1 50
(Richard Hannon) *in tch: effrt 2f out: nt pce to get involved: wknd fnl f* **6/1**

6 *15* **Don'tyouwantmebaby (IRE)** 2-9-0 0 .... PaulMulrennan 2
(Richard Spencer) *s.i.s: in tch: rdn over 2f out: sn wknd* **16/1**

00 **7** *2* **Spurofthemoment**[8] 5859 2-9-0 0 .... KieranShoemark 7
(Charles Hills) *led tl 2f out: sn wknd* **33/1**

1m 14.8s (1.60) **Going Correction** +0.225s/f (Good) **7 Ran SP% 116.8**
Speed ratings (Par 93): **98,95,89,85,82 62,59**
CSF £12.94 TOTE £4.90: £2.60, £1.60; EX 11.80 Trifecta £62.80.
Owner Nicholas Jones **Bred** Coln Valley Stud **Trained** Kingsclere, Hants

FOCUS
A race run in murky conditions, afterwards the ground was eased again to soft. The first two had already shown fair ability and there was a promising newcomer in third. They all raced near side. The winner has been rated as building on her Ascot form.

6160 MOBILE PIMM'S BARS APPRENTICE H'CAP 1m 1f

5:05 (5:06) (Class 5) (0-75,78) 3-Y-O+

£3,428 (£1,020; £509; £300; £300; £300) **Stalls** Low

Form RPR

6450 **1** **Kheros**[17] 5516 3-9-1 **74** .... (p) Pierre-LouisJamin(3) 10 86
(Archie Watson) *mde virtually all: rdn 3f out: edgd rt over 1f out: drifted lft whn strly chal thrght fnl f: styd on v gamely: all out* **20/1**

-100 **2** *hd* **Freckles**[21] 5373 4-8-13 **65** .... (h[1]) WilliamCarver(3) 6 76+
(Marcus Tregoning) *hld up bhd: rdn and hdwy fr 3f out: str chal ins fnl f: styd on: hld cl home* **10/1**

-526 **3** *½* **Skyman**[37] 4789 3-9-3 **73** .... ThomasGreatrex 9 83
(Roger Charlton) *hld up towards rr: rdn and hdwy over 2f out: wnt 3rd ins fnl f: styd on: fin wl (jockey said gelding was slowly away)* **5/1**[3]

3316 **4** *2 ¼* **Stormingin (IRE)**[29] 5089 6-9-6 **76** .... LouisGaroghan(7) 2 81
(Gary Moore) *hld up towards rr: rdn and hdwy fr 3f out: hmpd in 3rd over 1f out: styd on same pce fnl f* **7/1**

2151 **5** *4 ½* **Saikung (IRE)**[10] 5782 3-9-8 **78** 6ex .... SebastianWoods 11 74
(Charles Hills) *racd keenly: trckd ldrs: rdn 3f out: disp 2nd wl over 1f out: wknd ent fnl f* **7/2**[1]

3-06 **6** *3 ¼* **Settle Petal**[15] 5570 5-9-2 **65** .... SeamusCronin 5 54
(Pat Phelan) *trckd ldrs: rdn over 2f out: wkng whn hmpd over 1f out* **8/1**

0441 **7** *5* **Baashiq (IRE)**[9] 5807 5-8-12 **66** 5ex .... (p) StefanoCherchi(5) 1 44
(Peter Hiatt) *mid-div: hdwy over 5f out: chal over 4f out: rdn over 3f out: wknd 2f out (jockey said gelding was unsuited by the going and would prefer a faster surface)* **4/1**[2]

2345 **8** *1 ½* **Bond Angel**[20] 5446 4-8-11 **65** .... JackDinsmore(5) 7 40
(David Evans) *prom tl wknd over 3f out* **33/1**

120 **9** *nk* **Club Tropicana**[14] 5626 4-9-5 **71** .... (tp) SeanKirrane(3) 4 46
(Richard Spencer) *s.i.s: sn mid-div: effrt over 2f out: wknd over 1f out (jockey said filly missed the break)* **12/1**

0-20 **10** *27* **Le Maharajah (FR)**[47] 4426 4-9-3 **66** .... (p[1]) ScottMcCullagh 3
(Tom Clover) *mid-div tl wknd over 3f out: t.o (jockey said gelding stopped quickly)* **15/2**

1m 58.8s (3.10) **Going Correction** +0.225s/f (Good)
WFA 3 from 4yo+ 7lb **10 Ran SP% 118.8**
Speed ratings (Par 103): **95,94,94,92,88 85,81,79,79,55**
CSF £209.04 CT £1169.16 TOTE £21.10: £5.40, £2.90, £2.20; EX 345.60 Trifecta £2307.00.
Owner W J A Nash & Partner **Bred** Whitwell Bloodstock **Trained** Upper Lambourn, W Berks
■ Stewards' Enquiry : William Carver four-day ban: used whip above the permitted level (Aug 30-31, Sep 1-2)

FOCUS
Add 18yds. A modest handicap but the winner looked to do extremely well. They raced middle to near side in the straight. The winner has been rated back to form, with the third running a small pb in line with his Nottingham second.
T/Jkpt: Not Won. T/Plt: £119.90 to a £1 stake. Pool: £70,771.01 - 430.69 winning units T/Qpdt: £33.90 to a £1 stake. Pool: £6,359.87 - 138.76 winning units **Tim Mitchell**

5961 NEWMARKET (R-H)

Friday, August 16

OFFICIAL GOING: Good changing to good to soft after race 3 (6.20)
Wind: breezy Weather: light rain; 17 degrees

6161 WSG SPORTS SIGNAGE BRITISH EBF NOVICE AUCTION STKS (PLUS 10 RACE) 7f

5:15 (5:15) (Class 4) 2-Y-O **£5,175** (£1,540; £769; £384) **Stalls** High

Form RPR

0 **1** **Ten Thousand Stars**[20] 5433 2-8-10 0 .... BarryMcHugh 6 70
(Adrian Nicholls) *pressed ldrs: rdn to ld over 1f out: hld on gamely cl home* **16/1**

4454 **2** *½* **Hashtagmetoo (USA)**[10] 5777 2-8-8 70 .... ThoreHammerHansen(5) 1 72+
(Jamie Osborne) *bhd: drvn and outpcd 2f out: stl 7th 1f out: kpt on v gamely to snatch 2nd but nt quite rch wnr* **3/1**[2]

3 *hd* **Take Me To The Sky** 2-9-2 0 .... JamieSpencer 8 74
(Ed Dunlop) *lost 10 l s: rdn and gd hdwy 2f out: pressed ldrs and ev ch fnl f: no ex cl home: lost 2nd fnl stride* **14/1**

The Form Book Flat 2019, Raceform Ltd, Newbury, RG14 5SJ

335 **4** *nk* **Swinley Forest (IRE)**[29] 5082 2-9-5 77 JamesDoyle 9 77
(Brian Meehan) *wnt rt s: t.k.h: led after 1f: rdn over 2f out: hdd over 1f out: kpt on steadily but hld by wnr after: lost 3rd fnl strides* **6/4**[1]

5 **5** *3/4* **Webuyanyhorse**[13] 5676 2-9-5 0 TrevorWhelan 3 75
(Jamie Osborne) *towards rr: rdn and hdwy over 1f out: styd on wl cl home* **14/1**

6 **6** *3 1/4* **Jack Ryan (IRE)**[24] 5273 2-9-1 0 AdrianMcCarthy 11 62
(John Ryan) *prom: rdn and ev ch over 1f out: fdd fnl 100yds* **20/1**

6 **7** *1/2* **Glen Esk**[13] 5655 2-9-2 0 GeorgeWood 5 62
(Chris Wall) *midfield: drvn over 2f out: btn 1f out* **10/1**

00 **8** *2* **Fair Warning**[71] 3491 2-8-10 0 DylanHogan(5) 7 56
(Henry Spiller) *chsd ldrs: rdn 1/2-way: sn btn* **66/1**

6 **9** *1/2* **Disarming (IRE)**[25] 5250 2-8-11 0 KierenFox 4 51
(Dr Jon Scargill) *bhd and sn pushed along: a outpcd* **20/1**

66 **10** *2 3/4* **Aldrich Bay (IRE)**[23] 5314 2-9-1 0 LiamKeniry 2 47
(William Knight) *s.s: sn drvn in rr: a outpcd* **14/1**

06 **11** *1 1/2* **Bad Attitude**[3] 6054 2-9-1 0 EoinWalsh 10 43
(Luke McJannet) *struggling fr 1/2-way* **100/1**

12 *1/2* **Ventura Star (IRE)** 2-9-3 0 StevieDonohoe 13 44
(David Lanigan) *sn drvn: struggling towards rr after 3f* **5/1**[3]

0 **13** *9* **Early Morning Mist (IRE)**[30] 5052 2-8-6 0 DarraghKeenan(5) 12 15
(Amy Murphy) *t.k.h: led 1f: drvn and fdd over 2f out: t.o and eased* **50/1**

1m 28.11s (2.41) **Going Correction** +0.35s/f (Good) **13 Ran SP% 130.6**
Speed ratings (Par 96): **100,99,99,98,98 94,93,91,90,87 86,85,75**
CSF £67.49 TOTE £26.90: £5.30, £1.60, £2.90; EX 115.10 Trifecta £788.00.
Owner Saxtead Livestock Ltd **Bred** Saxtead Livestock Ltd **Trained** Sessay, N Yorks

FOCUS
Far side course used. Stalls: far side, except 1m2f: centre. No less than 12mm of rain had fallen in the preceding 48 hours which turned the official going Good, with a GoingStick reading of 7.8. An overcast meeting and cooler than of late with temperatures around 17C. A novice with little strength in depth and they came up the centre of the track off a modest pace. The second and fourth set the opening level.

6162 WSG SPORTS SIGNAGE SUPPORTS #SUPERJOSH CHARITY H'CAP 6f

5:50 (5:50) (Class 4) (0-85,87) 3-Y-0+

£5,822 (£1,732; £865; £432; £400; £400) **Stalls High**

Form RPR

5613 **1** **Cent Flying**[1] 6132 4-8-7 66 5ex (t) MartinDwyer 2 77
(William Muir) *towards rr: rdn 2f out: clsd to ld over 1f out: sn clr* **8/1**

0214 **2** *1 1/4* **Hart Stopper**[8] 5868 5-9-10 83 (t) JamieSpencer 4 89
(Stuart Williams) *lost 7 l s: t.k.h in rr: drvn and hdwy over 1f out: wnt 2nd cl home: nt rch wnr* **8/1**

4 **3** *3/4* **That's Not Me (IRE)**[33] 4952 3-8-10 72 DavidEgan 3 76
(Anthony McCann, Ire) *led: drvn 2f out: hdd over 1f out: no ex and lost 2nd cl home* **6/1**[3]

3305 **4** *shd* **Martineo**[8] 5862 4-9-2 80 DarraghKeenan(5) 8 83+
(John Butler) *bhd: rdn 1/2-way: last over 1f out: n.m.r but got through late and fin stoutly: nrly snatched 3rd (jockey said gelding was denied a clear run)* **5/1**[2]

4124 **5** *1/2* **Suzi's Connoisseur**[14] 5628 8-9-1 77 (v) TimClark(3) 1 79
(Jane Chapple-Hyam) *plld hrd: last early: pushed along 1/2-way: n.m.r but kpt on ins fnl f: nvr looked like rching ldrs (jockey said gelding was denied a clear run)* **10/1**

1215 **6** *3/4* **Gold At Midnight**[7] 5882 3-9-2 78 LiamKeniry 6 77
(William Stone) *dwlt: sn rcvrd to press ldr: rdn and lost 2nd over 1f out: no ex* **7/1**

0330 **7** *3/4* **Normandy Barriere (IRE)**[20] 5416 7-9-5 85 (p) IzzyClifton(7) 9 82
(Nigel Tinkler) *midfield: drvn and btn over 1f out* **5/1**[2]

0222 **8** *1 1/2* **Han Solo Berger (IRE)**[17] 5532 4-9-1 74 (p) GeorgeWood 5 66
(Chris Wall) *t.k.h: nvr bttr than midfield: rdn and btn over 1f out* **9/2**[1]

0002 **9** *2* **Captain Colby (USA)**[20] 5444 7-9-7 85 TobyEley(5) 7 71
(Paul Midgley) *prom: rdn 1/2-way: sn lost pl (jockey said gelding stopped quickly)* **9/1**

1m 13.14s (1.04) **Going Correction** +0.35s/f (Good)
WFA 3 from 4yo+ 3lb **9 Ran SP% 119.6**
Speed ratings (Par 105): **107,105,104,104,103 102,101,99,96**
CSF £72.56 CT £418.05 TOTE £8.20: £2.10, £2.30, £2.10; EX 39.00 Trifecta £286.70.
Owner Clarke, Edginton, Niven **Bred** Frank Brady **Trained** Lambourn, Berks

FOCUS
Ordinary for the grade and the pace was fair for the conditions. They raced towards the far side and they finished tightly-grouped behind the winner. Straightforward form, with the second rated to form.

6163 HEATH COURT HOTEL BRITISH EBF NOVICE STKS (PLUS 10 RACE) 1m

6:20 (6:22) (Class 4) 2-Y-0 **£5,175** (£1,540; £769; £384) **Stalls High**

Form RPR

1 **Sound Of Cannons** 2-9-2 0 LiamKeniry 8 85+
(Brian Meehan) *cl up: rdn to ld over 1f out: hrd pressed after but hung on v tenaciously: jst lasted* **5/1**[3]

2 *hd* **Discovery Island** 2-9-2 0 JamesDoyle 6 85+
(Charlie Appleby) *chsd ldrs: rdn over 2f out: wnt 3rd 1f out: sustained chal and gaining fnl 100yds: snatched 2nd but nt quite pass wnr* **5/2**[1]

3 *nk* **Shandoz** 2-9-2 0 DavidEgan 7 84+
(Roger Varian) *cl up: rdn over 1f out: ev ch and kpt on thrght fnl f: nt qckn fnl 50yds and jst lost 2nd* **15/2**

4 *8* **Caledonian Crusade (IRE)** 2-9-2 0 JamieSpencer 3 66
(David Simcock) *bhd: pushed along 3f out: btn over 2f out: snatched poor 4th* **12/1**

16 **5** *shd* **Wild Thunder (IRE)**[34] 4920 2-9-8 0 StevieDonohoe 1 72
(Richard Hannon) *prom: rdn to ld 2f out: hdd over 1f out: wknd qckly* **5/2**[1]

6 *3/4* **Diyari (IRE)** 2-9-2 0 MartinDwyer 4 64
(John Gosden) *bhd: in last and rdn 1/2-way: sn struggling* **9/2**[2]

0 **7** *2 3/4* **Today Power (IRE)**[51] 4252 2-9-2 0 RossaRyan 2 58
(Richard Hannon) *led: rdn and hdd 2f out: fdd over 1f out* **25/1**

1m 43.7s (3.70) **Going Correction** +0.35s/f (Good) **7 Ran SP% 115.3**
Speed ratings (Par 96): **95,94,94,86,86 85,82**
CSF £18.24 TOTE £6.00: £2.60, £1.60; EX 25.30 Trifecta £121.80.
Owner Centurion Thoroughbreds **Bred** Cheveley Park Stud Ltd **Trained** Manton, Wilts

FOCUS
Won in the past by the likes of Roaring Lion (2017) and by Frankel nine years ago when it was a maiden, this renewal again contained some nice types who will likely go on to better things. They were spread across the track and the first three, all debutants, finished close together, drawing clear of the remainder.

6164 FIRESTONE BUILDING PRODUCTS H'CAP 1m

6:50 (6:53) (Class 5) (0-75,77) 3-Y-0+

£4,528 (£1,347; £673; £400; £400; £400) **Stalls High**

Form RPR

3620 **1** **Calvados Spirit**[13] 5693 6-10-0 75 JamieSpencer 11 83
(Richard Fahey) *awkward leaving stalls: bhd: hdwy and disputing 4th 1f out: drvn ahd fnl 100yds: kpt on wl (trainer's rep said, regarding the improved form shown, the gelding appeared to appreciate the drop in class)* **7/2**[1]

5 **2** *3/4* **Mutadaawel (IRE)**[71] 3522 4-9-12 73 (p[1]) DavidEgan 12 79
(Anthony McCann, Ire) *rdn in midfield 1/2-way: effrt wl over 1f out: wnt 2nd and ch 100yds out: hld cl home* **6/1**

3632 **3** *1/2* **Catch My Breath**[8] 5866 3-8-10 63 (p[1]) StevieDonohoe 6 67
(John Ryan) *prom: rdn to ld over 1f out: hdd and nt qckn fnl 100yds* **5/1**[2]

6253 **4** *3/4* **Creek Island (IRE)**[16] 5557 3-8-13 71 AndrewBreslin(5) 4 73
(Mark Johnston) *bhd and sn pushed along: hdwy over 1f out: kpt on ins fnl f but nvr quite rchd ldrs* **8/1**

4024 **5** *1/2* **Robero**[56] 4078 7-9-9 75 (p) TobyEley(5) 9 77
(Gay Kelleway) *prom and t.k.h: rdn and chal 1f out: ev ch 100yds out: wknd cl home (jockey said gelding ran too freely)* **14/1**

5613 **6** *nse* **Trulee Scrumptious**[9] 5870 10-8-4 58 (v) AledBeech(7) 1 60
(Peter Charalambous) *swtchd to stands' rails to ld: sn 3 l clr: rdn and hdd over 1f out: hld but kpt on gamely after* **7/1**

5650 **7** *1 3/4* **Letsbe Avenue (IRE)**[36] 4838 4-9-12 73 JamesDoyle 3 71
(Richard Hannon) *bhd: rdn and plugged on fnl f: nvr rchd ldrs* **10/1**

0406 **8** *1 3/4* **Burguillos**[69] 3597 6-9-6 72 (h[1]) DarraghKeenan(5) 5 66
(John Butler) *taken down early: chsd ldrs: rdn over 2f out: sn wl btn* **16/1**

6423 **9** *8* **Moxy Mares**[17] 5537 4-9-10 76 (p) DylanHogan(5) 8 51
(Mark Loughnane) *prom: rdn and fdd over 2f out: sn wl bhd (jockey said gelding stopped quickly)* **11/2**[3]

4115 **10** *25* **Mitigator**[14] 5632 3-8-12 65 (b) RobHornby 10
(Lydia Pearce) *unruly stalls: lost 6 l s: rdn and nvr travelling in rr: t.o over 2f out: eased* **14/1**

1m 41.72s (1.72) **Going Correction** +0.35s/f (Good)
WFA 3 from 4yo+ 6lb **10 Ran SP% 120.5**
Speed ratings (Par 103): **105,104,103,103,102 102,100,98,90,65**
CSF £25.35 CT £109.99 TOTE £4.10: £1.80, £2.50, £1.80; EX 27.10 Trifecta £126.80.
Owner Aidan J Ryan & Partner **Bred** Newsells Park Stud **Trained** Musley Bank, N Yorks

FOCUS
Fairly competitive for the grade and the pace was genuine. They came towards the stands' side and the winner came from off the pace. Straightforward form, with the winner rated to this year's form, and third running as well as ever.

6165 FIRESTONE RUBBERGARD H'CAP 1m 2f

7:20 (7:21) (Class 5) (0-75,76) 3-Y-0+

£4,528 (£1,347; £673; £400; £400; £400) **Stalls Centre**

Form RPR

2223 **1** **Allegiant (USA)**[4] 6021 4-10-1 76 JamieSpencer 3 89
(Stuart Williams) *t.k.h in 2nd pl: taken to ld four others up centre after 3f: led overall 1/2-way: drvn over 1f out and sn clr: edgd rt cl home* **5/2**[1]

1344 **2** *4* **Water's Edge (IRE)**[22] 5348 3-9-1 74 CierenFallon(5) 8 79
(George Baker) *last of five up centre after 3f: rdn over 2f out: kpt on steadily to go v wl hld 2nd 120yds out* **9/2**[3]

4416 **3** *1 1/4* **Indomeneo**[11] 5725 4-9-12 76 ConnorMurtagh(3) 5 79
(Richard Fahey) *chsd wnr in centre after 3f: rdn over 1f out: easily outpcd by him after: lost 2nd fnl 120yds* **7/1**

0001 **4** *2 1/4* **Capriolette (IRE)**[10] 5785 4-9-12 73 5ex LiamKeniry 9 71
(Ed Walker) *t.k.h: sn led on outside: wnt to stands' rails after 3f: hdd 5f out: drvn and outpcd over 1f out* **6/1**

625- **5** *2 1/2* **Swilly Sunset**[47] 5592 6-9-9 75 DarraghKeenan(5) 6 68
(Anthony Carson) *pressed ldrs in centre after 3f tl rdn and wknd 2f out* **12/1**

4003 **6** *1/2* **Guildhall**[28] 5124 3-9-8 76 (b[1]) RobHornby 1 68
(Ralph Beckett) *chsd only other to opt for stands' rails after 3f: rdn and btn 2f out (trainer's rep could offer no explanation for the gelding's performance)* **7/2**[2]

4310 **7** *1/2* **Maqaadeer**[25] 5245 3-9-5 73 LouisSteward 7 64
(Ed Dunlop) *towards rr in centre after 3f: drvn over 2f out: sn btn* **8/1**

2m 11.31s (4.21) **Going Correction** +0.35s/f (Good)
WFA 3 from 4yo+ 7lb **7 Ran SP% 114.6**
Speed ratings (Par 103): **97,93,92,91,89 88,88**
CSF £14.07 CT £68.41 TOTE £2.60: £1.80, £2.30; EX 12.40 Trifecta £48.20.
Owner T W Morley & Partner **Bred** Juddmonte Farms Inc **Trained** Newmarket, Suffolk

FOCUS
Rail realignment added 17yds to the distance. Fairly competitive for the grade and the winner was always to the fore. The second and third have been rated close to form.

6166 FIRESTONE RUBBERCOVER H'CAP 1m

7:55 (7:55) (Class 3) (0-95,90) 3-Y-0+ **£9,703** (£2,887; £1,443; £721) **Stalls High**

Form RPR

6051 **1** **Humble Gratitude**[12] 5708 4-9-2 83 5ex (p) CierenFallon(5) 3 92
(Ian Williams) *racd in last pl: drvn and looked outpcd over 2f out: styd on to go 3rd over 1f out and 2nd fnl 120yds: hung fire briefly: carried sltly rt but galvanised to ld cl home: gd ride* **5/1**

1302 **2** *1/2* **Pinnata (IRE)**[20] 5445 5-9-1 77 (t) JamieSpencer 4 85
(Stuart Williams) *led over 5f out: travelled easily tl shkn up and pressed 120yds out: drvn and edgd sltly rt and hdd nr fin* **10/3**[3]

4553 **3** *3* **Enigmatic (IRE)**[28] 5155 5-9-8 89 DarraghKeenan(5) 5 90
(Alan Bailey) *trckd ldrs: wnt 2nd 3f out: drvn 2f out: one pce whn lost 2nd 120yds out* **11/4**[1]

5133 **4** *6* **Mr Top Hat**[10] 5776 4-10-0 90 DavidEgan 2 77
(David Evans) *led for over 2f: lost 2nd 3f out: sn drvn: lost 3rd and fdd over 1f out* **7/2**

0221 **5** *21* **Siglo Six**[22] 5336 3-9-2 84 (h) JamesDoyle 1 22
(Hugo Palmer) *racd in last pair: rdn and labouring over 2f out: sn t.o and eased (jockey said gelding stopped quickly)* **3/1**[2]

1m 41.88s (1.88) **Going Correction** +0.35s/f (Good)
WFA 3 from 4yo+ 6lb **5 Ran SP% 113.6**
Speed ratings (Par 107): **104,103,100,94,73**
CSF £22.05 TOTE £6.30: £1.90, £1.90; EX 23.10 Trifecta £101.00.

Owner Dr Marwan Koukash **Bred** Whitsbury Manor Stud **Trained** Portway, Worcs

FOCUS

A weak handicap for the grade and the pace was ordinary. The winner came from off the pace. A small pb from the winner.

T/Plt: £159.40 to a £1 stake. Pool: £47,891.53 - 219.27 winning units T/Qpdt: £18.10 to a £1 stake. Pool: £5,769.32 - 235.0 winning units **Iain Mackenzie**

6053 NOTTINGHAM (L-H)

Friday, August 16

OFFICIAL GOING: Soft changing to heavy after race 2 (2.35)

Wind: Light, half against in straight of over 4f Weather: Rain

6167 MANSIONBET EBF MAIDEN STKS — 6f 18y

2:00 (2:01) (Class 5) 2-Y-O — **£3,881** (£1,155; £577; £288) **Stalls** High

Form — RPR

1 **Danyah (IRE)** 2-9-5 0 ... JimCrowley 7 — 84+
(Owen Burrows) *trckd ldrs: swtchd lft and effrt over 1f out: r.o to ld fnl 120yds: pushed out towards fin* **11/4**[2]

435 2 1¼ **Upstate New York (IRE)**[34] 4903 2-9-5 79 ... DanielTudhope 3 — 78
(Richard Fahey) *stdd s: hld up: in tch: angled out 2f out: led over 1f out and edgd rt: hdd fnl 120yds: nt pce of wnr towards fin* **12/1**[3]

3 3½ **Panic Room (IRE)** 2-9-5 0 ... PJMcDonald 1 — 68+
(Tom Dascombe) *wnt lft s: rn green and towards rr: outpcd and pushed along: styd on fnl 100yds: tk 3rd cl home: no ch w front two* **20/1**

23 4 ¾ **Clan Royale**[85] 3008 2-9-5 0 ... DavidEgan 5 — 65
(Roger Varian) *racd keenly: trckd ldrs: led 2f out: sn rdn: hdd over 1f out: sltly intimidated ent fnl f: no ex fnl 75yds* **11/8**[1]

3432 5 2 **No Mercy**[21] 5390 2-9-5 78 ... BenCurtis 2 — 59
(K R Burke) *w ldr: led 1/2-way: rdn and hdd 2f out: wknd fnl 100yds* **11/4**[2]

00 6 10 **Pull Harder Con**[10] 5780 2-9-5 0 ... DavidNolan 4 — 29
(Robyn Brisland) *bhd: outpcd: nvr on terms* **100/1**

24 7 11 **Lilkian**[17] 5527 2-9-5 0 ... HayleyTurner 6
(Shaun Keightley) *led: pushed along and hdd 1/2-way: wknd ent fnl 2f* **33/1**

1m 19.65s (5.85) **Going Correction** +1.15s/f (Soft) — 7 Ran SP% **111.8**

Speed ratings (Par 94): **107,105,100,99,97 83,69**

CSF £31.07 TOTE £2.90: £1.30, £4.70; EX 27.40 Trifecta £140.60.

Owner Hamdan Al Maktoum **Bred** Shadwell Estate Company Limited **Trained** Lambourn, Berks

FOCUS

Outer track used. This was run in heavy rain, and afterwards Jim Crowley described it as "proper soft ground." Impressive from Danyah, whose owner won this maiden in 2017 with subsequent Commonwealth Cup winner Eqtidaar.

6168 MANSIONBET BEATEN BY A HEAD H'CAP — 5f 8y

2:35 (2:36) (Class 6) (0-60,61) 3-Y-O+

£3,234 (£962; £481; £300; £300; £300) **Stalls** High

Form — RPR

0022 1 **One Boy (IRE)**[5] 5986 8-8-10 49 ... JasonHart 7 — 58
(Paul Midgley) *hld up: travelling wl and hdwy over 2f out: chsd ldr over 1f out: chalng wl ins fnl f: kpt on for press to ld nr fin* **2/1**[1]

6462 2 hd **Valentino Sunrise**[27] 5169 3-9-3 58 ... DanielTudhope 11 — 66
(Mick Channon) *a.p: led 2f out: rdn over 1f out: strly pressed wl ins fnl f: hdd nr fin* **2/1**[1]

300 3 6 **Tizwotitiz**[38] 4763 3-8-13 54 ...(v) HayleyTurner 5 — 40
(Steph Hollinshead) *hld up early: bhd and pushed along over 3f out: hdwy u.p ins fnl f: styd on to take 3rd towards fin: no ch w front pair* **14/1**

00 4 nk **The Golden Cue**[6] 5952 4-9-6 59 ... PatCosgrave 8 — 44
(Steph Hollinshead) *sluggish s: hld up: rdn 2f out: hdwy u.p over 1f out: no imp on ldrs: styd on same pce fnl 100yds (jockey said gelding hung right in the closing stages)* **5/1**[2]

0602 5 4 **Celerity (IRE)**[7] 5893 5-8-5 47 ...(v) NoelGarbutt(3) 10 — 18
(Lisa Williamson) *prom: rdn over 2f out: outpcd by ldrs over 1f out: wknd fnl 75yds* **20/1**

0252 6 3¾ **Bronze Beau**[9] 5822 12-9-2 58 ...(tp) CameronNoble(3) 2 — 15
(Linda Stubbs) *led: rdn and hdd 2f out: wknd fnl 100yds* **12/1**[3]

0200 7 ¾ **Bluella**[10] 5765 4-8-2 45 oh1 ...(vt) PaulaMuir(5) 3
(Robyn Brisland) *chsd ldrs: rdn over 2f out: stl there over 1f out: wknd ins fnl f* **14/1**

050/ 8 nk **Mysterious Look**[629] 8953 6-9-5 58 ... JoeyHaynes 4 — 12
(Sarah Hollinshead) *in tch: lost pl over 2f out: no real imp after* **40/1**

2-30 9 8 **Alban's Dream**[193] 605 3-9-1 61 ... AndrewBreslin(5) 9
(Robert Eddery) *wnt lft s: chsd ldrs: pushed along and lost pl over 2f out: sn wknd* **33/1**

1m 5.6s (5.40) **Going Correction** +1.15s/f (Soft)

WFA 3 from 4yo+ 2lb — 9 Ran SP% **114.5**

Speed ratings (Par 101): **102,101,92,91,85 79,78,77,64**

CSF £5.42 CT £40.31 TOTE £2.50: £1.10, £1.10, £3.30; EX 7.10 Trifecta £54.30.

Owner Ta Stephenson M Ezro & I Massheder **Bred** Tom Radley **Trained** Westow, N Yorks

FOCUS

The two market leaders drew clear in this low-grade sprint, in which the main action took place near the stands' rail. The second has been rated in line with last year's best in similar conditions.

6169 MANSIONBET BEST ODDS GUARANTEED MAIDEN STKS — 1m 75y

3:05 (3:08) (Class 5) 3-Y-O+ — **£3,881** (£1,155; £577; £288) **Stalls** Centre

Form — RPR

-052 1 **Ghaly**[24] 5268 3-9-5 85 ... PatCosgrave 1 — 79+
(Saeed bin Suroor) *mde all: shkn up to draw clr over 1f out: eased down wl ins fnl f* **4/6**[1]

64 2 2 **Olympic Conqueror (IRE)**[19] 5477 3-9-5 0 ... DanielMuscutt 10 — 65
(James Fanshawe) *chsd ldrs: rdn over 2f out: chsng wnr in vain over 1f out: styd on towards fin whn no ch (flattered)* **11/1**[3]

3 ½ **Court Order** 3-9-5 0 ... PJMcDonald 3 — 64+
(James Tate) *missed break: hld up: rdn and hdwy over 2f out: styd on ins fnl f: gng on at fin: no ch w wnr (flattered)* **9/4**[2]

00 4 3 **Elena Osorio (IRE)**[14] 5627 3-9-0 0 ... HayleyTurner 8 — 52
(David Elsworth) *racd keenly: in tch: rdn and outpcd over 2f out: kpt on towards fin but no ch* **18/1**

4 5 ½ **Sally Hope**[15] 5592 3-9-0 0 ... RoystonFfrench 2 — 51
(John Gallagher) *chsd wnr: rdn over 2f out: lost 2nd over 1f out: wknd ins fnl f* **25/1**

0 6 4 **Aspiring Diva**[9] 5808 3-9-0 0 ... JasonHart 5 — 42
(Mohamed Moubarak) *hld up: pushed along and outpcd 3f out: nvr a threat* **80/1**

60- 7 4 **Dark Mystique**[347] 6881 3-9-5 0 ... JoeyHaynes 4 — 37
(Dean Ivory) *racd keenly: prom: rdn 4f out: wknd over 2f out* **20/1**

1m 58.76s (12.06) **Going Correction** +1.15s/f (Soft)

WFA 3 from 5yo 6lb — 7 Ran SP% **114.2**

Speed ratings (Par 103): **85,83,82,79,79 75,71**

CSF £9.65 TOTE £1.40: £1.10, £3.10; EX 7.40 Trifecta £17.90.

Owner Godolphin **Bred** Godolphin **Trained** Newmarket, Suffolk

FOCUS

Add 18yds. This was run in a time 17.36sec outside the standard, in very testing conditions with the ground description having changed to heavy before this race. The level is a bit fluid, but the second, fourth and fifth have been rated close to their previous form for now.

6170 MANSIONBET FILLIES' H'CAP — 1m 75y

3:40 (3:41) (Class 4) (0-80,81) 3-Y-O+

£6,469 (£1,925; £962; £481; £300; £300) **Stalls** Centre

Form — RPR

6363 1 **Romola**[9] 5827 3-9-9 81 ...(v[1]) DanielTudhope 5 — 95
(Sir Michael Stoute) *in tch on outer: wnt 2nd 2f out: rdn to ld wl over 1f out: styd on wl to draw clr ins fnl f: eased towards fin* **10/1**

3244 2 8 **Queen Penn**[26] 5218 4-9-7 73 ... DavidNolan 9 — 70
(Richard Fahey) *led after 1f: rdn over 2f out: hdd wl over 1f out: no ch w wnr fnl f* **8/1**

1021 3 1¾ **Classic Charm**[15] 5593 4-9-6 72 ... JoeyHaynes 7 — 65
(Dean Ivory) *sn led: hdd after 1f: remained prom: pushed along 4f out: rdn and ev ch 3f out: one pce u.p fr over 1f out* **9/4**[1]

243 4 ½ **Material Girl**[15] 5573 3-8-12 73 ...(v) MeganNicholls(3) 3 — 64
(Richard Spencer) *hld up towards rr: rdn and hdwy over 2f out: plugged on for press ins fnl f: no ch w wnr* **8/1**

1222 5 6 **Polyphony (IRE)**[31] 5030 4-9-7 73 ...(h) JasonHart 8 — 51
(John Mackie) *broke wl and led early: racd keenly: remained prom: rdn and wknd over 2f out (trainer said filly was unsuited by the heavy going and would prefer a quicker surface)* **3/1**[2]

2006 6 1¾ **Kimblewick (IRE)**[31] 5030 3-9-8 80 ...(p[1]) NickyMackay 6 — 53
(John Gosden) *sn pushed along and bhd: drvn over 3f out: nvr able to get involved* **12/1**

-423 7 2 **Eula Varner**[13] 5688 5-9-10 76 ... JimCrowley 4 — 45
(Henry Candy) *hld up in tch: drvn and wknd over 3f out* **7/1**[3]

-146 8 1¼ **Geizy Teizy (IRE)**[25] 5253 3-9-4 76 ... DanielMuscutt 1 — 42
(Marco Botti) *taken bk early: hld up: effrt to chse ldrs 3f out: no imp 2f out: wknd over 1f out (trainer's rep said filly was unsuited by the heavy going and would prefer a quicker surface)* **16/1**

1m 52.31s (5.61) **Going Correction** +1.15s/f (Soft)

WFA 3 from 4yo+ 6lb — 8 Ran SP% **113.2**

Speed ratings (Par 102): **111,103,101,100,94 93,91,89**

CSF £84.20 CT £244.48 TOTE £9.90: £2.50, £1.70, £1.40; EX 71.60 Trifecta £855.10.

Owner Cheveley Park Stud **Bred** Cheveley Park Stud Ltd **Trained** Newmarket, Suffolk

FOCUS

Add 18yds. They finished strung out behind the easy winner in this fair fillies' handicap. The level is hard to pin down.

6171 MANSIONBET COLWICK CUP H'CAP — 1m 6f

4:10 (4:10) (Class 3) (0-95,96) 3-Y-O+

£21,787 (£6,524; £3,262; £1,631; £815; £409) **Stalls** Low

Form — RPR

1242 1 **Laafy (USA)**[11] 5734 3-8-10 85 ...(v[1]) JimCrowley 9 — 96
(Sir Michael Stoute) *chsd ldr most of way: chalng 4f out: rdn over 2f out: led over 1f out: styd on to draw clr towards fin* **2/1**[1]

-044 2 2¾ **Not So Sleepy**[35] 4884 7-10-0 93 ...(t) DanielTudhope 3 — 100
(Hughie Morrison) *hld up in rr: hdwy over 3f out: chsd front pair 2f out: no imp tl styd on ins fnl f: tk 2nd fnl strides: nt trble wnr* **4/1**[3]

3211 3 hd **Rochester House (IRE)**[10] 5769 3-9-4 93 6ex ... JoeFanning 1 — 100
(Mark Johnston) *prom: led after 3f: pressed fr 4f out: rdn over 2f out: hdd over 1f out: stl ch ins fnl f: no ex towards fin and lost 2nd fnl strides* **10/3**[2]

1-03 4 9 **Twin Star (IRE)**[63] 3799 5-10-0 93 ...(t) DanielMuscutt 2 — 87
(Noel Williams) *in tch: drvn whn chsng ldrs over 3f out: one pce u.p 2f out: n.d after* **25/1**

-154 5 6 **Brasca**[35] 4862 3-8-7 82 ... HarryBentley 4 — 70
(Ralph Beckett) *hld up: effrt over 4f out: sn no imp: wknd over 2f out* **8/1**

03 6 13 **Litterale Ci (FR)**[18] 5508 6-9-9 91 ... MeganNicholls(3) 8 — 59
(Harry Fry) *hld up: hdwy over 4f out: wknd over 2f out: eased whn wl btn ins fnl f (trainer's rep said filly mare was unsuited by the heavy going and would prefer a quicker surface)* **6/1**

0206 7 16 **Al Kout**[6] 5928 5-9-6 85 ...(h) JoeyHaynes 7 — 30
(Heather Main) *trckd ldrs: rdn 6f out: lost pl 5f out: bhd over 4f out: eased whn wl btn over 1f out* **25/1**

13-5 8 23 **African Jazz (IRE)**[20] 5443 4-9-12 91 ...(tp) BrettDoyle 5 — 4
(Charlie Appleby) *led: hdd after 3f: remained prom: rdn 6f out: wknd 4f out: eased whn wl btn over 1f out: t.o (jockey said gelding stopped quickly)* **20/1**

3m 19.17s (12.77) **Going Correction** +1.15s/f (Soft)

WFA 3 from 4yo+ 10lb — 8 Ran SP% **114.3**

Speed ratings (Par 107): **109,107,107,102,98 91,82,69**

CSF £9.87 CT £23.91 TOTE £2.90: £1.20, £1.70, £1.70; EX 12.90 Trifecta £53.80.

Owner Salem Bel Obaida **Bred** Michael Edward Connelly **Trained** Newmarket, Suffolk

FOCUS

Add 42yds. The fifth running of this valuable handicap, and they came home at wide intervals behind the first three. The runners made for the centre in the home straight. The second has been rated in line with his latest.

6172 BRITISH STALLION STUDS EBF FILLIES' H'CAP — 1m 2f 50y

4:45 (4:45) (Class 3) (0-95,89) 3-Y-O+ **£16,172** (£4,812; £2,405; £1,202) **Stalls** Low

Form — RPR

351 1 **Ojooba**[28] 5148 3-9-4 86 ... JimCrowley 4 — 100
(Owen Burrows) *chsd ldrs: wnt 2nd over 3f out: led over 2f out: edgd lft ent fnl f: styd on wl to draw clr* **11/4**[2]

0042 2 5 **Empress Ali (IRE)**[11] 5741 8-9-2 77 ... JamesSullivan 7 — 81
(Tom Tate) *chsd ldr: pushed along and lost pl over 3f out: chsd wnr u.p fnl f but no imp* **12/1**

5042 3 ¾ **Red Hot (FR)**[20] 5458 3-9-6 88 ... DanielTudhope 6 — 91
(Richard Fahey) *in tch: dropped to rr over 5f out: effrt over 2f out: styd on same pce u.p fnl f* **9/2**[3]

2211 4 2¾ **Birdcage Walk**[25] 5253 3-9-3 85 ...(h) PatCosgrave 2 — 82
(Hugo Palmer) *led: rdn and hdd over 2f out: kpt on u.p after: wknd ins fnl f* **11/2**

2121 **5** ½ **Teodora De Vega (IRE)**16 5549 3-8-9 77............ HarryBentley 3 73
(Ralph Beckett) *s.i.s: hld up: clsd 6f out: trckd ldrs: rdn over 3f out: no imp after: wknd ins fnl f* **11/8**1

2m 22.82s (9.42) **Going Correction** +1.15s/f (Soft) 5 Ran SP% **110.0**
WFA 3 from 8yo 7lb
Speed ratings (Par 104): **108,104,103,101,100**
CSF £29.62 TOTE £3.70: £1.80, £4.30; EX 30.40 Trifecta £74.80.
Owner Hamdan Al Maktoum **Bred** Shadwell Estate Company Limited **Trained** Lambourn, Berks

FOCUS
Add 18yds. A worthwhile prize and a dominant performance from the winner. They came up the middle in the home straight. The second has been rated close to her latest.

6173 AJA NOVICE FLAT AMATEUR RIDERS' H'CAP (FOR NOVICE AMATEUR RIDERS) 1m 2f 50y
5:20 (5:20) (Class 6) (0-65,66) 3-Y-O+
£3,119 (£967; £483; £300; £300; £300) **Stalls** Low

Form RPR
3642 **1** **Gravity Wave (IRE)**22 5338 5-11-5 63............(p) MissImogenMathias 2 71
(John Flint) *hld up: hdwy over 2f out: chsd ldr 1f out: styd on to ld fnl 150yds: in command after* **6/1**3
2146 **2** 1¾ **Elsie Violet (IRE)**22 5337 3-10-10 61............(p) MrGeorgeEddery 7 67
(Robert Eddery) *led: pushed along over 2f out: hung lft wl over 1f out: hdd fnl 150yds: styd on same pce towards fin* **8/1**
2563 **3** 1¾ **Dolly Dupree**16 5552 3-9-8 48............ MrOliverDaykin(3) 6 51
(Paul D'Arcy) *chsd ldr: ev ch over 3f out: edgd lft 2f out: no imp: lost 2nd 1f out: kpt on same pce ins fnl f* **10/1**
5263 **4** 9 **Dark Devil (IRE)**12 5709 6-11-5 66............ MrEireannCagney(3) 4 52
(Richard Fahey) *midfield: hdwy over 4f out: chsd ldrs over 3f out: no imp 2f out: wknd over 1f out* **9/4**1
0000 **5** 2½ **Dutch Artist (IRE)**16 5560 7-10-2 49............ MissBelindaJohnson(3) 1 30
(Nigel Tinkler) *hld up: outpcd over 2f out: nvr a threat* **16/1**
5524 **6** 1 **Light Of Air (FR)**15 5570 6-11-0 61............(b) MissKatyBrooks(3) 3 40
(Gary Moore) *chsd ldrs: pushed along and no imp over 2f out: wknd over 1f out* **3/1**2
236 **7** 11 **Atalanta Queen**55 4115 4-10-8 52............(v) MissSarahBowen 10 12
(Robyn Brisland) *chsd ldrs tl rdn and wknd over 2f out* **6/1**3
140- **8** 17 **Angel Of The North (IRE)**42 6236 4-10-5 52....(t1) MrFinbarMulrine(3) 5
(Robin Dickin) *hld up: lft bhd over 5f out* **33/1**
00-0 **9** 35 **Monzino (USA)**22 5043 11-10-1 48 oh1 ow2............ MrHakanSensoy(3) 8
(Michael Chapman) *hld up on outer: wl bhd 6f out: t.o* **150/1**

2m 29.35s (15.95) **Going Correction** +1.15s/f (Soft) 9 Ran SP% **114.0**
WFA 3 from 4yo+ 7lb
Speed ratings (Par 101): **82,80,79,72,70 69,60,46,18**
CSF £52.29 CT £470.29 TOTE £6.30: £2.90, £2.10, £2.10; EX 50.80 Trifecta £283.90.
Owner Mel Mathias **Bred** Paget Bloodstock & Eadling Farm **Trained** Kenfig Hill, Bridgend

FOCUS
Add 18yds. A slow-motion finish to this lowly handicap, which was run in the worst of the ground. It's been rated with feet on the ground around the second.
T/Plt: £39.80 to a £1 stake. Pool: £50,118.33 - 917.31 winning units T/Qpdt: £11.10 to a £1 stake. Pool: £5,802.62 - 383.45 winning units **Darren Owen**

5912THIRSK (L-H)
Friday, August 16

OFFICIAL GOING: Soft (good to soft in places) changing to soft after race 2 (5.25)
Wind: light across Weather: Rain, stopped before race 4

6174 LADIES' DAY @THIRSKRACES SATURDAY 7TH SEPTEMBER BOOK NOW H'CAP (FOR LADY AMATEUR RIDERS) 6f
4:55 (4:56) (Class 6) (0-60,61) 3-Y-O+
£2,950 (£915; £457; £400; £400; £400) **Stalls** Centre

Form RPR
3005 **1** **I'll Be Good**7 5892 10-9-8 47............ MissAmieWaugh 4 55
(Alan Berry) *chsd ldrs towards far side: rdn to ld appr fnl f: edgd lft: kpt on* **25/1**
5410 **2** 1 **Mr Greenlight**10 5768 4-10-6 59............ MissEmilyEasterby 6 64
(Tim Easterby) *chsd ldrs: edgd rt and led 2f out: sn rdn: hdd appr fnl f: kpt on* **10/1**
5012 **3** 1¼ **B Fifty Two (IRE)**4 6017 10-10-8 61 4ex............(tp) MissBeckySmith 5 62
(Marjorie Fife) *midfield: rdn over 2f out: sme hdwy over 1f out: kpt on to go 3rd ins fnl f* **7/1**2
5130 **4** 1¾ **Space War**52 4207 12-9-11 57............(t) MissMaisieSharp(7) 19 53
(Michael Easterby) *chsd ldrs towards stands' side: rdn over 2f out: plugged on ins fnl f* **25/1**
6502 **5** ½ **Patrick (IRE)**8 5857 7-9-10 54............ MissAmyCollier(5) 2 50
(Paul Midgley) *chsd ldrs towards far side: rdn 2f out: one pce ins fnl f: jockey briefly stopped riding 75yds out (jockey said that her saddle slipped shortly after the 1f marker, but having managed to readjust it into position ½ a furlong out, she was then able to ride out to the line; vet said gelding lost its right hind shoe)* **6/1**1
2355 **6** 2½ **Bobby Joe Leg**125 1766 5-10-2 60............(b) MissEmilyBullock(5) 8 47
(Ruth Carr) *outpcd towards rr tl plugged on fr over 1f out* **14/1**
0600 **7** nse **Mitchum**10 5767 10-9-2 46 oh1............(p) SophieSmith(5) 7 33
(Ron Barr) *chsd ldrs: rdn along and lost pl 3f out: plugged on fnl f* **28/1**
0020 **8** hd **Essential**3 6051 5-9-4 48............ MissCharlotteCrane(5) 10 34
(Olly Williams) *chsd ldrs: rdn over 2f out: wknd ins fnl f* **7/1**2
1664 **9** 2 **Lincoln Red**7 5914 3-9-10 57............(p1) MissAntoniaPeck(5) 14 37
(Olly Williams) *dwlt: sn in tch: rdn over 2f out: wknd over 1f out* **17/2**
6500 **10** ¾ **Coastal Cyclone**23 5302 5-9-0 46............(p) MissRachelDavies(7) 11 24
(Harry Dunlop) *sn outpcd towards rr: nvr involved* **22/1**
0004 **11** 1¼ **Gun Case**32 4979 7-9-11 50............(p) MissEmmaTodd 1 24
(Alistair Whillans) *dwlt: a towards rr* **20/1**
5020 **12** 1 **Just An Idea (IRE)**23 5302 5-9-8 54............(b) MissCamillaSwift(7) 16 25
(Roger Ingram) *midfield: rdn along 3f out: wknd over 1f out* **16/1**
0040 **13** 1¼ **Racquet**10 5765 6-9-2 46 oh1............(b) MissShannonWatts(5) 15 14
(Ruth Carr) *led: racd more towards stands' side: rdn and hdd 2f out: wknd* **16/1**
6004 **14** ¾ **Peachey Carnehan**30 5051 5-10-3 56........(b) MissMichelleMullineaux 9 21
(Michael Mullineaux) *s.i.s: a outpcd in rr* **10/1**
4235 **15** 1½ **Jacob's Pillow**6 5935 8-10-3 56............(p) MissSerenaBrotherton 13 17
(Rebecca Bastiman) *chsd ldrs tl wknd 2f out* **8/1**3
4006 **16** nk **Just A Rumour (IRE)**7 5904 3-8-11 46 oh1...(p) MissPaigeHopper(7) 18 6
(Noel Wilson) *chsd ldrs: rdn over 2f out: hung lft and wknd over 1f out (jockey said filly hung left-handed throughout)* **50/1**
60-0 **17** 3¼ **Red Hot Fusion (IRE)**74 3416 5-9-0 46 oh1............ MissAlexGarven(7) 12
(Alan Berry) *a towards rr (vet said gelding had lost its left fore shoe)* **100/1**

1m 17.27s (4.47) **Going Correction** +0.825s/f (Soft) 17 Ran SP% **120.7**
WFA 3 from 4yo+ 3lb
Speed ratings (Par 101): **103,101,100,97,97 93,93,93,90,89 88,86,85,84,82 81,77**
CSF £240.58 CT £1255.02 TOTE £27.30: £5.10, £2.20, £1.70, £5.50; EX 480.60 Trifecta £713.90.
Owner Alan Berry **Bred** Cobhall Court Stud **Trained** Cockerham, Lancs

FOCUS
Both bends out to provide fresh ground which extended distances to races over 7f plus. A wet day and the ground was officially given as soft, good to soft in places before the first. \n\x\x A big field for this lady amateur riders' handicap and those drawn low looked to be at an advantage. Straightforward form, with the winner rated in line with his best efforts in recent years.

6175 BRITISH EBF NOVICE STKS (PLUS 10 RACE) 6f
5:25 (5:28) (Class 4) 2-Y-O
£6,469 (£1,925; £962; £481) **Stalls** Centre

Form RPR
1020 **1** **Three Coins**13 5683 2-9-3 74............ TonyHamilton 6 78
(Richard Fahey) *trckd ldrs: pushed into ld appr fnl f: rdn and kpt on* **6/1**3
3 **2** 1¾ **Soaring Star (IRE)**36 4826 2-9-5 0............ KevinStott 3 75
(Kevin Ryan) *s.i.s: sn in tch: pushed along and hdwy over 1f out: chal appr fnl f: drvn ins fnl f: edgd lft and one pce* **15/8**1
3 ½ **Poet's Lady** 2-9-0 0............ BenRobinson 13 68
(David Barron) *s.i.s: hld up: pushed along and hdwy over 1f out: chsd ldrs 1f out: rdn and kpt on* **25/1**
605 **4** ¾ **Light The Fuse (IRE)**23 5294 2-9-5 0............ AndrewMullen 1 71
(K R Burke) *wnt lft s: sn midfield: pushed along and hdwy over 1f out: kpt on ins fnl f* **40/1**
3 **5** ¾ **Red Treble**43 4550 2-9-0 0............(h1) PaulHanagan 10 64
(Rebecca Menzies) *midfield: rdn along 2f out: edgd lft 1f out: kpt on ins fnl f* **9/1**
5 **6** 1¼ **Cold Light Of Day**16 5553 2-9-0 0............ CamHardie 8 60+
(Michael Dods) *in tch: pushed along 2f out: swtchd rt ins fnl f: styd on* **9/1**
7 1¾ **Seven Emirates (IRE)** 2-9-5 0............ BenCurtis 4 60
(K R Burke) *trckd ldrs: rdn over 1f out: wknd ins fnl f* **11/2**2
8 ¾ **Twist Of Hay** 2-9-0 0............ TomEaves 7 53
(Michael Dods) *dwlt: hld up: pushed along and sme hdwy over 1f out: wknd fnl 110yds* **10/1**
05 **9** 2 **Idoapologise**21 5396 2-9-2 0............(h1) SeanDavis(3) 5 52
(James Bethell) *led: rdn 2f out: hdd appr fnl f: wknd* **50/1**
52 **10** 4 **Fast Deal**10 5764 2-9-5 0............ RachelRichardson 11 40
(Tim Easterby) *trckd ldrs: rdn 2f out: wknd appr fnl f* **16/1**
00 **11** 5 **Redzone**16 5553 2-9-5 0............ GrahamLee 16 25
(Bryan Smart) *s.i.s: a towards rr* **33/1**
0 **12** 1 **Slaidburn**19 5472 2-9-5 0............ PhilDennis 14 22
(Tim Easterby) *hld up: rdn along 2f out: sn wknd* **16/1**
0 **13** 5 **Norton Lad**13 5689 2-9-0 0............ DannyRedmond(5) 2 7
(Tim Easterby) *prom: rdn over 2f out: wknd over 1f out* **80/1**
14 3 **New Man** 2-9-5 0............ NathanEvans 9
(Tim Easterby) *a in rr* **40/1**

1m 17.19s (4.39) **Going Correction** +0.825s/f (Soft) 14 Ran SP% **120.2**
Speed ratings (Par 96): **103,100,100,99,98 96,94,93,90,85 78,77,70,66**
CSF £16.67 TOTE £7.50: £2.30, £1.40, £7.30; EX 19.90 Trifecta £861.60.
Owner Bearstone Stud Limited **Bred** Bearstone Stud **Trained** Musley Bank, N Yorks

FOCUS
On paper, this had the appearance of a fair novice for the course but not all of them handled conditions. It was slightly quicker than the modest opening handicap.

6176 SCOUTING FOR GIRLS - LIVE TONIGHT @THIRSKRACES H'CAP 7f
5:55 (5:57) (Class 5) (0-70,75) 3-Y-O
£4,078 (£1,213; £606; £400; £400; £400) **Stalls** Centre

Form RPR
5456 **1** **Ey Up Its Mick**10 5771 3-8-8 57............(b) PaulHanagan 9 64
(Tony Coyle) *s.i.s: swtchd lft and sn midfield: pushed along to chse and hdwy to chse ldrs over 2f out: rdn into narrow ld appr fnl f: edgd lft ins fnl f: drvn all out (trainer said, regarding the improved form shown, the gelding appreciated the softer ground)* **9/1**3
-011 **2** shd **Alotabottle**10 5771 3-9-9 75 6ex............ SeanDavis(3) 5 81
(Kevin Ryan) *trckd ldrs: rdn over 2f out: drvn over 2f out: kpt on ins fnl f to chal towards fin* **9/4**1
0164 **3** ¾ **Primeiro Boy (IRE)**14 5632 3-9-0 63............ TonyHamilton 3 67
(Richard Fahey) *trckd ldrs: drvn to chal strly appr fnl f: one pce towards fin* **22/1**
5004 **4** ½ **Uncle Norman (FR)**10 5771 3-8-2 51............(b) CamHardie 7 54
(Tim Easterby) *s.i.s: hld up towards inner: rdn along and sme hdwy 2f out: drvn over 1f out: swtchd rt ins fnl f: styd on* **9/1**3
0030 **5** ½ **Abie's Hollow**1 6101 3-8-13 62............ TomEaves 10 66+
(Tony Coyle) *hld up: hdwy on inner over 2f out: rdn over 1f out: chsd ldr whn hmpd on rail 110yds out: kpt on* **7/1**2
2-50 **6** 1 **Evolutionary (IRE)**44 4507 3-9-4 67............ JamieGormley 1 66
(Iain Jardine) *led: rdn over 2f out: hdd appr fnl f: no ex fnl 110yds* **50/1**
6000 **7** 3¾ **Turquoise Friendly**59 3964 3-8-10 59............(t1) KevinStott 13 47
(Michael Easterby) *hld up: rdn along 2f out: nvr threatened* **66/1**
0550 **8** 1½ **House Deposit**7 5914 3-8-12 61............ BenCurtis 8 45
(Roger Fell) *midfield: rdn over 2f out: wknd over 1f out* **7/1**2
5342 **9** 1 **Dream Of Honour (IRE)**41 4629 3-9-7 70............ RachelRichardson 11 52
(Tim Easterby) *midfield on outer: rdn over 2f out: wknd over 1f out* **16/1**
0054 **10** 1½ **Torque Of The Town (IRE)**27 5202 3-8-4 53............ PhilDennis 2 31
(Noel Wilson) *prom: rdn over 2f out: wknd over 1f out* **33/1**
0344 **11** hd **Stronsay (IRE)**22 5335 3-9-7 70............(p) GrahamLee 14 47
(Bryan Smart) *hld up: pushed along over 2f out: rdn over 1f out: edgd lft and wknd* **7/1**2
300 **12** 9 **Paradise Papers**110 2148 3-9-3 66............ BenRobinson 12 19
(David Barron) *hld up: rdn along over 3f out: wknd and sn bhd* **28/1**
4606 **13** 48 **Socru (IRE)**13 5692 3-9-7 70............(h) NathanEvans 4 +
(Michael Easterby) *rrd: blindfold removed late and lost several l s: a t.o (trainer said the gelding became agitated in the stalls, reared then lunged forward, resulting in the rider being unable to remove the blindfold)* **10/1**

1m 33.75s (6.15) **Going Correction** +0.825s/f (Soft) 13 Ran SP% **117.4**
Speed ratings (Par 100): **97,96,96,95,94 93,89,87,86,84 84,74,19**
CSF £27.67 CT £445.72 TOTE £10.40: £2.90, £1.50, £5.20; EX 42.30 Trifecta £850.60.
Owner Mrs M Lingwood **Bred** Mrs M Lingwood **Trained** Norton, N Yorks

FOCUS
There was 20yds added and the official description was changed to soft before the race. A close finish to this modest handicap, with the favourite just edged out.

6177 IRISH STALLION FARMS EBF NOVICE STKS 7f
6:30 (6:38) (Class 4) 3-Y-O+ £6,469 (£1,925; £962; £481) Stalls Centre

Form RPR
3- **1** **Montatham**[294] 8606 3-9-2 0 PaulHanagan 9 88+
(William Haggas) *prom: pushed into ld over 1f out: edgd lft: kpt on pushed out* 1/3[1]
662 **2** 2 **Mogsy (IRE)**[28] 5128 3-8-13 85 JaneElliott(3) 2 83
(Tom Dascombe) *led: rdn along over 2f out: drvn and hdd over 1f out: kpt on but a hld* 9/4[2]
0 **3** 10 **Itmakesyouthink**[30] 5057 5-9-4 0 (h) SeanDavis(3) 6 59
(Mark Loughnane) *dwlt: sn in tch: pushed along 3f out: rdn to go 3rd 2f out: sn wknd* 25/1
00 **4** 4 1/2 **Spotton (IRE)**[19] 5477 3-9-2 0 LewisEdmunds 4 45
(Rebecca Bastiman) *trckd ldrs: rdn over 2f out: wknd over 1f out* 40/1
00 **5** 6 **Hunters Step**[13] 5690 3-9-2 0 PhilDennis 7 30
(Noel Wilson) *dwlt: hld up: rdn over 2f out: sn wknd* 80/1
0 **6** 2 3/4 **Rent's Dew (IRE)**[13] 5690 3-9-2 0 RachelRichardson 3 23
(Tim Easterby) *slowly away: a towards rr* 22/1[3]
1m 32.73s (5.13) **Going Correction** +0.825s/f (Soft)
WFA 3 from 4yo+ 5lb **6** Ran SP% **117.7**
Speed ratings (Par 105): **103,100,89,84,77 74**
CSF £1.46 TOTE £1.20: £1.10, £1.10; EX 1.20 Trifecta £2.70.
Owner Hamdan Al Maktoum **Bred** Worksop Manor Stud **Trained** Newmarket, Suffolk
■ Bayraat (20-1), Sils Maria (50-1) and Thornaby Spirit (28-1) were all withdrawn. Rule 4 does not apply.

FOCUS
20yds added. Three horses withdrawn late but it made little difference to the strength of the race. The market got this spot on, with the avalanche of late money on the favourite proving well placed.

6178 DEARNLEYS HIGH QUALITY SOLAR SHADING SOLUTIONS H'CAP 5f
7:00 (7:08) (Class 4) (0-80,82) 4-Y-O+ £5,433 (£1,617; £808; £404; £400; £400) Stalls Centre

Form RPR
5362 **1** **Our Little Pony**[13] 5691 4-8-9 73 FayeMcManoman(5) 2 86
(Lawrence Mullaney) *hld up centre: rdn and hdwy over 1f out: led 1f out: kpt on wl to draw clr* 5/1[1]
4120 **2** 3 **Music Society (IRE)**[48] 4406 4-9-4 77 NathanEvans 11 79+
(Tim Easterby) *trckd ldrs stands' side: led gp 3f out: rdn and edgd lft to join centre gp over 1f out: sn chsd ldr: kpt on same pce in 2nd fnl f: 1st of 4 in gp* 5/1[1]
0101 **3** 3 **Show Palace**[15] 5595 6-9-3 76 (p) DavidNolan 7 67
(Jennie Candlish) *prom centre: rdn to ld over 1f out: hdd 1f out: no ex: 2nd of 7 in gp* 10/1
205 **4** 1 1/4 **Bowson Fred**[13] 5691 7-9-2 75 (t[1]) CamHardie 5 62
(Michael Easterby) *chsd ldrs centre: rdn over 2f out: no ex fnl f: 3rd of 7 in gp* 14/1
4611 **5** nk **Boudica Bay (IRE)**[14] 5620 4-8-5 64 ShelleyBirkett 8 50
(Eric Alston) *chsd ldrs centre: rdn 2f out: no ex fnl f: 4th of 7 in gp* 9/1
5001 **6** 1/2 **Hawaam (IRE)**[13] 5691 4-9-9 82 (p) BenCurtis 6 66
(Roger Fell) *racd centre: led: rdn and hdd over 1f out: wknd fnl f: 5th of 7 in gp* 15/2[2]
342 **7** hd **Gorgeous General**[11] 5722 4-7-13 61 oh4 SeanDavis(3) 1 44
(Lawrence Mullaney) *in tch centre: rdn over 2f out: hung lft and btn over 1f out: 6th of 7 in gp* 20/1
0341 **8** 1 **Red Pike (IRE)**[7] 5901 8-9-1 74 4ex GrahamLee 3 54
(Bryan Smart) *hld up centre: rdn over 2f out: nvr threatened: last of 7 in gp* 8/1[3]
3212 **9** 4 1/2 **Nibras Again**[40] 4691 5-9-7 80 KevinStott 12 43
(Paul Midgley) *swtchd rt s to r against stands' rail: chsd ldrs: rdn over 2f out: sn wknd: 2nd of 4 in gp* 8/1[3]
5426 **10** 2 1/4 **Merry Banter**[23] 5298 5-9-9 82 BenRobinson 9 37
(Paul Midgley) *led quarter stands' side: hdd in gp 3f out: rdn along 2f out: sn btn: 3rd of 4 in gp (jockey said that the mare anticipated the start and missed the break)* 11/1
41-3 **11** 6 **Thirlmere**[36] 4827 4-8-13 72 JasonHart 13 6
(Julie Camacho) *racd stands' side: trckd ldr: rdn 2f out: edgd lft and wknd (trainer's rep said that the filly was unsuited by the soft ground, which in their opinion was riding slower and would prefer a faster surface)* 15/2[2]
1m 1.49s (2.09) **Going Correction** +0.825s/f (Soft) **11** Ran SP% **117.9**
Speed ratings (Par 105): **109,104,99,97,96 96,95,94,87,83 73**
CSF £28.57 CT £247.83 TOTE £5.00: £2.00, £2.30, £3.50; EX 30.80 Trifecta £683.60.
Owner Richard Swift **Bred** Mel Roberts & Ms Nicola Meese **Trained** Great Habton, N Yorks

FOCUS
Only exposed performers in this sprint, but it was wide open and it's fair form. They initially raced in two groups with those who remained centre doing the best.

6179 CLIFF STUD REARING WINNERS H'CAP 7f 218y
7:30 (7:32) (Class 4) (0-80,84) 3-Y-O+ £5,433 (£1,617; £808; £404; £400; £400) Stalls Centre

Form RPR
4131 **1** **Spiorad (IRE)**[6] 5970 4-10-4 84 5ex (t) DanielTudhope 9 97+
(David O'Meara) *dwlt: hld up in rr: brought wd to centre st: pushed along and gd hdwy over 2f out: rdn to ld appr fnl f: edgd lft: pushed out towards fin: shade cosily* 11/8[1]
0652 **2** 1 1/2 **Al Erayg (IRE)**[6] 5948 6-9-8 74 (p) JasonHart 12 82
(Tim Easterby) *trckd ldrs: brought wd to centre st: rdn to ld wl over 1f out: sn drvn: hdd appr fnl f: kpt on same pce* 3/1[2]
2265 **3** nk **Zip**[16] 5557 3-8-11 72 SeanDavis(3) 1 78
(Richard Fahey) *hld up in midfield: hdwy and chsd ldr over 2f out: sn rdn: drvn and ev ch 1f out: kpt on same pce ins fnl f* 16/1
0040 **4** 7 **Florenza**[36] 4828 6-10-1 81 TomEaves 4 72
(Chris Fairhurst) *trckd ldrs: rdn along 3f out: wknd fnl f* 28/1
13-0 **5** 3/4 **Parole (IRE)**[12] 5709 7-9-3 69 (t) RachelRichardson 6 58
(Tim Easterby) *dwlt: hld up: rdn over 2f out: nvr threatened* 50/1
0404 **6** 4 **Confrontational (IRE)**[12] 5709 5-9-11 77 AndrewMullen 3 57
(Jennie Candlish) *midfield: brought wd to centre st: rdn over 2f out: edgd lft and wknd* 16/1
0001 **7** 1 3/4 **Start Time (IRE)**[18] 5488 6-9-8 74 KevinStott 7 50
(Paul Midgley) *led: rdn and hdd wl over 1f out: wknd* 6/1[3]
0001 **8** 15 **Alfa McGuire (IRE)**[32] 4982 4-9-10 76 (p[1]) GrahamLee 2 18
(Phillip Makin) *in tch: brought wd to centre st: rdn over 2f out: sn wknd (trainer could offer no explanation for the gelding's performance)* 22/1
035- **9** 3 1/2 **Elusive Heights (IRE)**[240] 9614 6-9-7 73 BenCurtis 11 7
(Roger Fell) *prom: brought wd to outer st: rdn over 2f out: wknd* 16/1
1m 48.46s (6.76) **Going Correction** +0.825s/f (Soft)
WFA 3 from 4yo+ 6lb **9** Ran SP% **108.8**
Speed ratings (Par 105): **99,97,97,90,89 85,83,68,65**
CSF £4.66 CT £34.47 TOTE £1.80: £1.10, £1.20, £2.40; EX 5.00 Trifecta £45.30.
Owner Hambleton Racing Ltd XXXVII **Bred** Irish National Stud **Trained** Upper Helmsley, N Yorks
■ Donnelly's Rainbow was withdrawn. Price at time of withdrawal 12-1. Rule 4 applies to all bets. Deduction - 5p in the pound.

FOCUS
20yds added in this fair handicap, where they went a good pace, considering the conditions.

6180 THIRSK RACECOURSE - IDEAL VENUE FOR INDOOR & OUTDOOR EVENTS H'CAP 1m 4f 8y
8:05 (8:07) (Class 6) (0-65,65) 3-Y-O+ £3,398 (£1,011; £505; £400; £400; £400) Stalls High

Form RPR
0-00 **1** **Near Kettering**[69] 3568 5-9-11 62 (t) CamHardie 12 68
(Sam England) *led for 2f: prom: pushed along to ld again over 1f out: sn rdn: drvn out ins fnl f* 9/2[2]
2652 **2** 1/2 **Dew Pond**[7] 5905 7-9-5 56 (bt) NathanEvans 4 61
(Tim Easterby) *hld up in midfield: hdwy over 2f out: gng wl but short of room bhd ldrs appr fnl f: drvn ins fnl f: kpt on wl* 7/1[3]
0000 **3** shd **Half Bolly**[7] 5898 3-8-9 55 JasonHart 15 61
(Mark Walford) *trckd ldrs on outer: rdn and ev ch over 1f out: styd on ins fnl f* 25/1
0-11 **4** 2 **True Romance (IRE)**[10] 5766 5-9-9 60 5ex GrahamLee 7 62
(Julia Brooke) *in tch: pushed along and hdwy to chse ldrs 2f out: drvn and one pce fnl f* 6/4[1]
0056 **5** hd **Seaborough (IRE)**[16] 5556 4-8-12 56 RhonaPindar(7) 13 58
(David Thompson) *midfield: hdwy and prom over 7f out: rdn 2f out: edgd lft and no ex fnl 110yds* 16/1
5500 **6** 2 1/4 **Beaufort (IRE)**[10] 5784 3-9-2 62 DavidNolan 1 61
(Michael Dods) *hld up in midfield: rdn along over 2f out: plugged on ins fnl f* 14/1
3352 **7** 1 1/4 **Majeste**[11] 5728 5-9-9 65 DannyRedmond(5) 9 61
(Rebecca Bastiman) *in tch: trckd ldrs 6f out: rdn over 2f out: outpcd over 1f out* 9/1
6515 **8** 1 3/4 **Ninepin Bowler**[42] 4587 5-9-9 60 DanielTudhope 10 54
(Ann Duffield) *racd keenly: led after 2f out: rdn along and hdd over 1f out: wknd ins fnl f* 8/1
0034 **9** 4 **Ad Libitum**[16] 5556 4-9-13 64 (p) BenCurtis 8 52
(Roger Fell) *dwlt: hld up: nvr threatened (jockey said gelding ran flat)* 9/1
0245 **10** 3/4 **Farhh Away**[26] 5213 4-10-0 65 (p) TomEaves 2 52
(Michael Dods) *trckd ldrs: rdn over 2f out: wknd over 1f out* 16/1
040 **11** 21 **Dr Richard Kimble (IRE)**[39] 4724 4-9-9 63 JaneElliott(3) 14 18
(Marjorie Fife) *a towards rr* 33/1
0010 **12** 2 3/4 **Strategic (IRE)**[32] 4990 4-8-9 46 (h) ShelleyBirkett 5
(Eric Alston) *midfield: wknd over 2f out (jockey said gelding ran too free)* 16/1
00-0 **13** 2 1/4 **Bigdabog**[25] 5248 4-8-9 46 oh1 JamieGormley 11
(Stella Barclay) *a in rr* 50/1
2m 52.23s (12.23) **Going Correction** +0.825s/f (Soft)
WFA 3 from 4yo+ 9lb **13** Ran SP% **134.9**
Speed ratings (Par 101): **92,91,91,90,90 88,87,86,83,83 69,67,66**
CSF £40.87 CT £761.65 TOTE £6.90: £3.40, £1.60, £14.30; EX 56.60 Trifecta £1806.00.
Owner Redivivus Racing **Bred** Michael E Broughton **Trained** Guiseley, W Yorks

FOCUS
30yds added. A proper stamina test, they were well grouped up the straight and only weak form.
T/Plt: £34.10 to a £1 stake. Pool: £39,256.16 - 839.31 winning units T/Qpdt: £5.20 to a £1 stake. Pool: £5,069.94 - 717.01 winning units **Andrew Sheret**

6024 WOLVERHAMPTON (A.W) (L-H)
Friday, August 16

OFFICIAL GOING: Tapeta: standard
Wind: Fresh behind Weather: Showers

6181 SUPPORT MISS GARGAR IN THE FIRST H'CAP 6f 20y (Tp)
1:40 (1:42) (Class 6) (0-60,62) 3-Y-O £2,781 (£827; £413; £300; £300; £300) Stalls Low

Form RPR
0505 **1** **Lysander Belle (IRE)**[4] 6024 3-9-5 57 CallumShepherd 4 64
(Sophie Leech) *chsd ldrs: led over 1f out: rdn out* 10/3[2]
240 **2** 1 1/2 **Casarubina (IRE)**[70] 3532 3-9-7 59 (t) JosephineGordon 3 61
(Nick Littmoden) *hld up: hdwy over 1f out: styd on to go 2nd nr fin* 16/1
635 **3** shd **Miss Gargar**[7] 5890 3-9-2 54 (v) RobertHavlin 9 56
(Harry Dunlop) *a.p: chsd ldr over 1f out: sn rdn and ev ch: styd on same pce wl ins fnl f* 10/1
0402 **4** nk **Maid Millie**[7] 5890 3-8-11 54 (v) CierenFallon(5) 1 55
(Robert Cowell) *s.s: hmpd wl over 5f out: hdwy over 1f out: r.o: nt rch ldrs (jockey said filly was slowly away)* 9/4[1]
0560 **5** 1 **No More Regrets (IRE)**[20] 5419 3-9-5 62 HarrisonShaw(5) 8 60
(Patrick Morris) *chsd ldr tl led 2f out: rdn and hdd over 1f out: styd on same pce ins fnl f* 6/1
0060 **6** 1/2 **Brother Bentley**[45] 4481 3-9-1 53 (p) LukeMorris 7 49
(Ronald Harris) *chsd ldrs: pushed along over 3f out: rdn and nt clr run over 1f out: kpt on* 25/1
5-04 **7** nk **Molly Blake**[30] 5044 3-9-7 59 OisinMurphy 10 54
(Clive Cox) *hld up in tch: plld hrd: rdn on outer over 1f out: edgd rt: no imp ins fnl f (jockey said filly ran too freely)* 4/1[3]
6500 **8** 1 1/2 **Supreme Dream**[16] 5558 3-8-4 45 (v[1]) GabrieleMalune(3) 12 36
(Shaun Harris) *hld up in tch on outer: stdd and lost pl 4f out: rdn over 1f out: nt trble ldrs* 50/1
5400 **9** 3/4 **Boorowa**[18] 5498 3-9-0 52 (b[1]) TomMarquand 2 41
(Ali Stronge) *hld up: rdn and rn wd wl over 1f out: r.o ins fnl f: nvr nrr* 12/1
0000 **10** 1 **Andies Armies**[8] 5847 3-8-0 45 (v[1]) GavinAshton(7) 11 31
(Lisa Williamson) *s.i.s: hdwy over 1f out: wknd fnl f* 100/1
000 **11** 3 3/4 **Shawwaslucky**[42] 4592 3-8-7 45 PaddyMathers 5 19
(Derek Shaw) *hld up: rdn over 2f out: a in rr* 100/1

0U00 **12** 9 **Quarto Cavallo**[9] 5806 3-8-7 **45**....................(b) RaulDaSilva 6
(Adam West) *led 4f: wknd over 1f out* **33/1**

1m 14.71s (0.21) **Going Correction** 0.0s/f (Stan) 12 Ran SP% **121.5**
Speed ratings (Par 98): **98,96,95,95,94 93,93,91,90,88 83,71**
CSF £54.82 CT £501.85 TOTE £3.80: £1.10, £4.30, £2.90; EX 72.00 Trifecta £471.20.
Owner Mike Harris Racing Club **Bred** Mattock Stud **Trained** Elton, Gloucs

FOCUS
A moderate sprint. Ordinary form, with the third and fourth helping to pin the opening level.

6182 JOIN THE BRITISH RACING CLUB TODAY NURSERY H'CAP 5f 21y (Tp)
2:10 (2:10) (Class 6) (0-60,62) 2-Y-O
£2,781 (£827; £413; £300; £300; £300) **Stalls** Low

Form RPR

600 **1** **Queenoftheclyde (IRE)**[32] 4992 2-8-12 **54**.............. HarrisonShaw(5) 5 56
(K R Burke) *s.i.s: hld up: racd keenly: hdwy over 1f out: led ins fnl f: rdn out* **6/1**[3]

460 **2** ½ **Call Me Cheers**[24] 5280 2-9-7 **58**.................... RobertWinston 8 58
(David Evans) *chsd ldrs on outer: pushed along 1/2-way: rdn over 1f out: r.o* **18/1**

344 **3** ¾ **Ma Boy Harris (IRE)**[19] 5472 2-9-10 **61**.................. LewisEdmunds 6 59
(Phillip Makin) *chsd ldrs: rdn and ev ch over 1f out: sn edgd lft: styd on* **6/1**[3]

0406 **4** hd **Comeatchoo (IRE)**[14] 5618 2-9-2 **53**....................(b[1]) DuranFentiman 4 50
(Tim Easterby) *hld up in tch: rdn and ev ch over 1f out: styd on same pce towards fin* **25/1**

0065 **5** nk **Invincible Bertie (IRE)**[14] 5618 2-9-2 **56**.............. RowanScott(3) 10 52
(Nigel Tinkler) *hld up in tch on outer: lost pl over 3f out: rdn: hung lft and r.o ins fnl f: nt rch ldrs* **7/1**

3326 **6** shd **Beignet (IRE)**[16] 5562 2-9-11 **62**........................ OisinMurphy 7 57
(Richard Hannon) *sn led: hdd 4f out: led again over 1f out: sn rdn: hdd ins fnl f: no ex towards fin* **3/1**[1]

664 **7** 1¼ **Hollywood Waltz**[14] 5602 2-9-4 **55**...................... CallumShepherd 2 47
(Mick Channon) *chsd ldrs: shkn up and nt clr run over 1f out: nt clr run again ins fnl f: styd on same pce* **12/1**

004 **8** 1¾ **Oribi**[20] 5427 2-9-4 **55**................................ TomMarquand 9 40
(William Haggas) *prom: nt clr run and lost pl over 3f out: rdn 1/2-way: n.d after* **7/2**[2]

0340 **9** nk **Beautrix**[6] 5968 2-9-0 **51**.............................. ShaneGray 3 34
(Michael Dods) *s.i.s: hdwy 1/2-way: rdn and nt clr run over 1f out: no ex ins fnl f* **10/1**

0050 **10** 2¾ **Walton Thorns (IRE)**[28] 5146 2-9-2 **58**.................. CierenFallon(5) 1 32
(Charles Hills) *sn pushed along and prom: led 4f out: rdn and hdd over 1f out: nt clr run and eased ins fnl f* **12/1**

1m 3.39s (1.49) **Going Correction** 0.0s/f (Stan) 10 Ran SP% **121.9**
Speed ratings (Par 92): **88,87,86,85,85 85,83,80,79,75**
CSF £111.84 CT £687.96 TOTE £6.50: £1.90, £8.40, £3.10; EX 178.40 Trifecta £1219.10.
Owner Men Fae The Clyde & E Burke **Bred** Miss Joanne Comer **Trained** Middleham Moor, N Yorks

FOCUS
They went pretty steady in the early stages, were well bunched turning in and finished in a bit of a heap. It's been rated as ordinary form, with the second and third among those that fit.

6183 SPILLARD SAFETY SYSTEMS H'CAP 5f 21y (Tp)
2:45 (2:45) (Class 5) (0-70,70) 3-Y-O
£3,428 (£1,020; £509; £300; £300; £300) **Stalls** Low

Form RPR

1404 **1** **Dream House**[7] 5904 3-8-12 **61**......................(b[1]) DuranFentiman 1 68
(Tim Easterby) *hld up in tch: swtchd lft over 1f out: rdn and r.o to ld wl ins fnl f* **14/1**

1302 **2** nk **Thegreyvtrain**[14] 5603 3-8-13 **62**........................ LukeMorris 8 68
(Ronald Harris) *led: shkn up over 1f out: rdn: edgd lft and hdd wl ins fnl f* **25/1**

0204 **3** nse **Scale Force**[13] 5660 3-9-7 **70**..........................(v) OisinMurphy 6 76
(Gay Kelleway) *chsd ldr 2f: rdn to chse ldr again over 1f out: r.o* **5/2**[1]

6454 **4** 1¾ **Lorna Cole (IRE)**[11] 5736 3-9-1 **69**...................... CierenFallon(5) 5 69
(William Muir) *chsd ldrs: rdn over 1f out: styd on* **7/2**[3]

2022 **5** ¾ **Fairy Fast (IRE)**[3] 6048 3-9-1 **64**......................(b) TomMarquand 2 61
(George Boughey) *s.i.s: hdwy on outer over 1f out: r.o: nt rch ldrs* **3/1**[2]

3340 **6** 1½ **Sing Bertie (IRE)**[10] 5765 3-8-2 **51** oh6.................. PaddyMathers 4 42
(Derek Shaw) *s.i.s and edgd rt s: hld up: racd keenly: hdwy over 1f out: nt rch ldrs* **40/1**

0042 **7** ½ **Phoenix Star (IRE)**[9] 5826 3-9-4 **67**.................. JosephineGordon 7 57
(Nick Littmoden) *s.i.s: pushed along over 3f out: nvr nrr (jockey said gelding jumped awkwardly from the stalls and shortly afterwards clipped the heels of Thegreyvtrain)* **11/1**

2410 **8** 4 **Superseded (IRE)**[35] 4894 3-9-5 **68**...................... RobertWinston 3 43
(John Butler) *chsd ldrs: wnt 2nd 3f out tl rdn over 1f out: wknd ins fnl f (jockey said gelding lost its action entering the home straight)* **9/2**

1m 2.22s (0.32) **Going Correction** 0.0s/f (Stan) 8 Ran SP% **115.3**
Speed ratings (Par 100): **97,96,96,93,92 90,89,82**
CSF £292.18 CT £1170.92 TOTE £18.30: £3.90, £3.30, £1.30; EX 61.40 Trifecta £1043.30.
Owner Ontoawinner, SDH Project Services Ltd 2 **Bred** Whitsbury Manor Stud **Trained** Great Habton, N Yorks

FOCUS
A modest affair, but a nice performance from the winner in first-time headgear. It's been rated around the second and third.

6184 BRC IS TURNING FANS INTO OWNERS NURSERY H'CAP 7f 36y (Tp)
3:15 (3:15) (Class 4) (0-85,85) 2-Y-O
£4,463 (£1,328; £663) **Stalls** High

Form RPR

121 **1** **Above (FR)**[14] 5615 2-9-7 **85**............................ OisinMurphy 3 94+
(Archie Watson) *chsd ldr tl led over 2f out: pushed clr over 1f out: comf* **11/10**[1]

0346 **2** 6 **Dark Silver (IRE)**[14] 5612 2-8-11 **75**.................... LukeMorris 2 69
(Ed Walker) *chsd ldrs: shkn up 1/2-way: rdn 2f out: sn outpcd: wnt 2nd wl ins fnl f* **7/1**[2]

5411 **3** 1½ **Rich Belief**[7] 5896 2-9-0 **78**............................ RobertWinston 1 69
(James Bethell) *pushed along to ld: shkn up and hdd over 2f out: sn outpcd: lost 2nd wl ins fnl f: eased nr fin* **11/10**[1]

1m 28.14s (-0.66) **Going Correction** 0.0s/f (Stan) 3 Ran SP% **107.7**
Speed ratings (Par 96): **103,96,94**
CSF £6.88 TOTE £2.20; EX 6.20 Trifecta £10.60.
Owner Qatar Racing Limited **Bred** J Kilpatrick & Mme D Ades Hazan **Trained** Upper Lambourn, W Berks

FOCUS
This proved rather uncompetitive, the winner scooting home in good style for an easy win.

6185 VISIT THE BRITISHRACINGCLUB.COM EBF MAIDEN STKS (PLUS 10 RACE) 1m 142y (Tp)
3:50 (3:51) (Class 4) 2-Y-O
£4,787 (£1,424; £711; £355) **Stalls** Low

Form RPR

43 **1** **Dubai Souq (IRE)**[16] 5563 2-9-0 0.......................... CierenFallon(5) 7 82
(Saeed bin Suroor) *chsd ldrs: led over 2f out: sn edgd lft: rdn clr over 1f out* **15/8**[2]

5206 **2** 3¾ **Mass Media**[15] 5572 2-9-5 **78**..........................(b[1]) RobertHavlin 2 74
(John Gosden) *sn led: hdd and hmpd over 2f out: rdn: hung lft and styd on same pce ins fnl f* **7/2**[3]

3 4½ **Dark Heart** 2-9-5 0.................................... FrannyNorton 8 65+
(Mark Johnston) *s.i.s: sn pushed along in rr: r.o to go 3rd wl ins fnl f: nt trble ldrs* **12/1**

5 **4** 1¼ **Star Of Wells (IRE)**[22] 5345 2-9-5 0...................... TomMarquand 4 62
(William Haggas) *hld up in tch: chsd ldr over 3f out tl over 2f out: wknd fnl f* **6/4**[1]

0 **5** 4 **Sky Flyer**[28] 5131 2-9-5 0............................ JosephineGordon 5 54
(Ralph Beckett) *s.i.s: pushed along in rr: hdwy over 2f out: wknd wl over 1f out* **10/1**

64 **6** hd **Gloryana**[11] 5732 2-9-0 0.................................. LukeMorris 1 48
(Archie Watson) *led early: chsd ldr tl over 6f out: wnt 2nd again over 4f out tl over 3f out: rdn over 2f out: wknd wl over 1f out* **16/1**

P0P **7** 22 **Austin Taetious**[36] 4832 2-9-5 0.......................... CharlieBennett 6 7
(Adam West) *broke wl enough: sn lost pl and pushed along: bhd fnl 4f* **100/1**

0 **8** 30 **Puzzlebook**[18] 5493 2-9-0 0.............................. RobertWinston 3
(David Evans) *sn prom: chsd ldr over 6f out tl rdn over 4f out: wknd over 3f out: eased over 1f out (jockey said filly lost its action approximately 3f out)* **66/1**

1m 48.62s (-1.48) **Going Correction** 0.0s/f (Stan) 8 Ran SP% **122.2**
Speed ratings (Par 96): **106,102,98,97,94 93,74,47**
CSF £9.82 TOTE £2.30: £1.10, £1.20, £3.70; EX 7.40 Trifecta £53.50.
Owner Godolphin **Bred** Godolphin **Trained** Newmarket, Suffolk

FOCUS
They went a good gallop and finished strung out in this maiden. The opening level is fluid.

6186 FOLLOW ON TWITTER #BRITRACINGCLUB H'CAP 1m 1f 104y (Tp)
4:20 (4:22) (Class 5) (0-75,76) 3-Y-O
£3,428 (£1,020; £509; £300; £300; £300) **Stalls** Low

Form RPR

-232 **1** **Shrewdness**[51] 4234 3-9-5 **73**............................ TomMarquand 3 85+
(William Haggas) *s.i.s: sn prom: nt clr run and lost pl over 7f out: hdwy on outer over 1f out: rdn to ld and hung lft ins fnl f: r.o: comf* **11/4**[2]

0500 **2** 3½ **Prairie Spy (IRE)**[16] 5565 3-9-5 **73**...................... FrannyNorton 5 77
(Mark Johnston) *hmpd s: sn prom: pushed along over 5f out: rdn to ld over 1f out: hdd ins fnl f: styd on same pce* **9/1**

5613 **3** ¾ **Alma Linda**[6] 5941 3-9-5 **73**............................(p) LukeMorris 2 75
(Sir Mark Prescott Bt) *trckd ldrs: racd keenly: nt clr run over 2f out: rdn and hung lft over 1f out: styd on* **5/2**[1]

32 **4** ½ **Little India (FR)**[42] 4602 3-9-0 **73**...................... HarrisonShaw(5) 8 74
(K R Burke) *hmpd s: sn chsng ldrs: led wl over 1f out: sn rdn: edgd lft and hdd: no ex wl ins fnl f* **5/1**[3]

2100 **5** shd **My Dear Friend**[20] 5445 3-9-8 **76**..................(b[1]) JosephineGordon 6 77
(Ralph Beckett) *hmpd s: hld up: racd keenly: rdn and hung lft fr over 1f out: r.o ins fnl f: nt rch ldrs* **10/1**

3-20 **6** 1¼ **Characteristic (IRE)**[24] 5270 3-9-7 **75**.................. RobertHavlin 1 73
(Tom Clover) *restless in stalls: s.i.s: hld up: hdwy over 3f out: nt clr run and swtchd lft wl over 1f out: styd on same pce ins fnl f* **8/1**

4354 **7** ¾ **Kuwait Station (IRE)**[16] 5557 3-9-6 **74**..................(b[1]) ShaneGray 9 71
(David O'Meara) *hld up: nt clr run over 1f out: hung lft ins fnl f: nt trble ldrs* **12/1**

1060 **8** 6 **Fenjal (IRE)**[12] 4215 3-9-2 **70**..........................(b) RobertWinston 4 54
(Gay Kelleway) *wnt rt s: sn led: hdd 4f out: sn drvn along: led again 2f out: sn hdd: wknd ins fnl f* **16/1**

4010 **9** 13 **Al Daayen (FR)**[13] 5679 3-8-3 **57**.......................... JimmyQuinn 7 14
(Conrad Allen) *hmpd s: hdwy over 7f out: chsd ldr over 6f out: led 4f out: rdn and hdd 2f out: wknd wl over 1f out* **20/1**

2m 0.13s (-0.67) **Going Correction** 0.0s/f (Stan) 9 Ran SP% **120.4**
Speed ratings (Par 100): **102,98,98,97,97 96,95,90,79**
CSF £29.30 CT £71.07 TOTE £3.40: £1.50, £3.40, £1.30; EX 34.50 Trifecta £153.80.
Owner The Queen **Bred** The Queen **Trained** Newmarket, Suffolk

FOCUS
A fairly competitive handicap but the winner did it well. The third and fourth help set the level.

6187 FOLLOW ON FACEBOOK @BRITISHRACINGCLUB FILLIES' NOVICE STKS 1m 1f 104y (Tp)
4:50 (4:52) (Class 5) 3-Y-O+
£3,428 (£1,020; £509; £254) **Stalls** Low

Form RPR

12 **1** **Sweet Promise**[28] 5148 3-9-4 0.......................... TomMarquand 2 92+
(James Fanshawe) *hld up in tch: shkn up to ld ins fnl f: pushed clr: comf* **15/8**[2]

3-2 **2** 3 **Maximum Effect**[24] 5269 3-8-11 0........................ RobertHavlin 8 76
(John Gosden) *edgd rt s: led at stdy pce over 7f out: qcknd over 2f out: rdn: edgd rt and hdd ins fnl f: styd on same pce* **6/5**[1]

3-5 **3** nk **Dubai Discovery (USA)**[14] 5627 3-8-8 0................ GabrieleMalune(3) 7 75
(Saeed bin Suroor) *a.p: chsd ldr 7f out: rdn over 1f out: nt clr run ins fnl f: styd on same pce* **5/2**[3]

05 **4** 5 **Storm Eleanor**[15] 5592 3-8-11 0.......................... CharlieBennett 4 65
(Hughie Morrison) *hld up: hdwy over 5f out: shkn up over 1f out: styd on same pce* **50/1**

4550 **5** 3½ **Tarbeyah (IRE)**[15] 5593 4-8-13 **63**....................(t[1]) HarrisonShaw(5) 1 58
(Kevin Frost) *chsd ldrs: rdn and outpcd over 2f out: hung lft over 1f out: styd on ins fnl f* **28/1**

00 **6** hd **Your Thoughts (FR)**[28] 5141 3-8-11 0...................... FrannyNorton 3 57
(Paul Webber) *hld up: racd keenly: hdwy over 2f out: shkn up and outpcd over 1f out* **100/1**

6 **7** 13 **Amber Jet (IRE)**[42] 4597 3-8-11 0.......................... JimmyQuinn 5 30
(John Mackie) *sn pushed along in rr: wknd 3f out* **100/1**

6 **8** 4½ **Phoebe Agnes**[30] 5062 3-8-11 0.......................... RaulDaSilva 6 20
(Shaun Harris) *sn led: hdd after 1f: chsd ldrs tl rdn and wknd over 2f out* **100/1**

55 **P** **Lope Scholar (IRE)**[27] 5193 3-8-11 0........................ JosephineGordon 9
(Ralph Beckett) *restless in stalls: dwlt: sn pushed along in rr: wknd over 3f out: bhd whn p.u and dismntd over 2f out (jockey said filly lost its action)* **10/1**

2m 2.3s (1.50) **Going Correction** 0.0s/f (Stan)
WFA 3 from 4yo 7lb **9** Ran SP% **126.3**
Speed ratings (Par 100): **93,90,90,85,82 82,70,66,**
CSF £5.04 TOTE £2.70: £1.10, £1.10, £1.20; EX 4.90 Trifecta £8.80.
Owner A Boyd-Rochfort **Bred** Mr & Mrs G Middlebrook **Trained** Newmarket, Suffolk
FOCUS
This was steadily run and turned into a bit of a dash for home. Muddling form. It's been rated around the second.
T/Plt: £486.30 to a £1 stake. Pool: £55,864.50 - 83.85 winning units T/Qpdt: £17.20 to a £1 stake. Pool: £7,594.41 - 326.22 winning units **Colin Roberts**

6188 - 6189a (Foreign Racing) - See Raceform Interactive

5919 CURRAGH (R-H)
Friday, August 16

OFFICIAL GOING: Round course - yielding to soft; straight course - soft

6190a RYANS CLEANING EVENT SPECIALIST CURRAGH STKS (LISTED RACE) 5f
5:45 (5:45) 2-Y-O
£24,981 (£8,045; £3,810; £1,693; £846; £423) **Stalls** Centre

RPR

1 **Millisle (IRE)**[21] 5400 2-8-12 0........................ ShaneFoley 7 100
(Mrs John Harrington, Ire) *cl up bhd ldr and disp 2nd early: pushed along nr side at 1/2-way: rdn in 3rd 1 1/2f out and wnt 2nd ent fnl f: r.o wl u.p wl ins fnl f to ld fnl strides* **11/2**

2 1/2 **Isabeau (IRE)**[22] 5361 2-8-12 92........................(b) LeighRoche 2 98
(M D O'Callaghan, Ire) *sn led narrowly far side: pushed along 2f out and extended advantage over 1f out: reduced advantage u.p wl ins fnl f where strly pressed and hdd fnl strides* **13/2**

3 2 1/2 **Lil Grey (IRE)**[27] 5206 2-8-12 95........................ RobbieColgan 5 89
(Ms Sheila Lavery, Ire) *chsd ldrs: rdn in 4th fr 2f out and no imp on ldr ent fnl f: kpt on same pce into 3rd wl ins fnl f: nvr trbld ldrs* **11/8**[1]

4 2 1/4 **Real Appeal (GER)**[27] 5206 2-9-6 0........................(b) KevinManning 4 89
(J S Bolger, Ire) *cl up bhd ldr and disp 2nd early: pushed along after 2f out and sn no ex u.p: no imp on ldr in 3rd ent fnl f: wknd into 4th wl ins fnl f* **10/1**

5 1 1/4 **King Neptune (USA)**[15] 5584 2-9-3 96........................ RyanMoore 3 82
(A P O'Brien, Ire) *w.w in rr: drvn fr 1/2-way and no imp u.p 1 1/2f out: impr into 5th ins fnl f and kpt on: nvr trbld ldrs* **4/1**[2]

6 2 1/2 **Air Force Jet**[16] 5542 2-9-3 99........................ DonnachaO'Brien 6 73
(Joseph Patrick O'Brien, Ire) *prom early tl sn settled bhd ldrs: drvn fr 1/2-way and sn no ex u.p in 5th: wknd to rr ins fnl f: eased nr fin* **9/2**[3]

1m 1.2s (0.80) **Going Correction** +0.475s/f (Yiel) **6** Ran SP% **118.1**
Speed ratings: **106,105,101,97,95 91**
CSF £41.41 TOTE £2.70: £1.80, £3.60; DF 36.30 Trifecta £194.30.
Owner Stonethorn Stud Farms Limited **Bred** Stonethorn Stud Farms Ltd **Trained** Moone, Co Kildare
FOCUS
A dramatic finish to proceedings, with the Group 1 Juddmonte Cheveley Park Stakes-entered filly lunging late to come out on top.

6191a COMER GROUP INTERNATIONAL IRISH ST LEGER TRIAL STKS (GROUP 3) 1m 6f
6:15 (6:15) 3-Y-O+
£53,153 (£17,117; £8,108; £3,603; £1,801; £900)

RPR

1 **Southern France (IRE)**[17] 5522 4-9-8 112........................ RyanMoore 2 115
(A P O'Brien, Ire) *sweated up befhand: hld up bhd ldrs in 3rd: impr into 2nd fr 3f out gng wl: sn pushed along: led nr side 1 1/2f out and rdn: styd on wl u.p to assert ins fnl f* **5/2**[1]

2 2 **Downdraft (IRE)**[21] 5404 4-9-8 101........................(t) DonnachaO'Brien 4 112
(Joseph Patrick O'Brien, Ire) *w.w in rr: last at 1/2-way: hdwy gng wl nr side under 3f out into 3rd 2f out and pushed along: rdn into 2nd ins fnl f and kpt on wl: a hld by wnr* **11/2**

3 2 **Master Of Reality (IRE)**[57] 4015 4-9-11 118........................ WayneLordan 3 112
(Joseph Patrick O'Brien, Ire) *led narrowly early: 1 l clr after 4f: pushed along over 2f out and pressed: rdn and hdd 1 1/2f out: no imp on wnr u.p ins fnl f where dropped to 3rd: kpt on same pce to jst hold 3rd* **3/1**[2]

4 hd **Capri (IRE)**[57] 4015 5-9-8 113........................ SeamieHeffernan 1 109
(A P O'Brien, Ire) *w.w towards rr: 5th 1/2-way: dropped to rr briefly under 3f out: sn swtchd rt and impr between horses into 4th under 2f out and rdn: no imp on ldrs ins fnl f: kpt on nr fin: jst failed for 3rd* **7/2**[3]

5 9 1/2 **Cimeara (IRE)**[36] 4856 4-9-5 101........................ ChrisHayes 5 93
(Joseph Patrick O'Brien, Ire) *chsd ldrs in 4th: drvn into 3rd briefly fr 3f out tl no ex and lost pl 2f out: sn wknd* **14/1**

6 9 **Eminent Authority (IRE)**[58] 3984 3-8-12 98........(t) DeclanMcDonogh 6 85
(Joseph Patrick O'Brien, Ire) *on toes befhand: pushed along briefly fr s: sn settled bhd ldr in 2nd: pushed along in 2nd under 4f out and dropped to 4th fr 3f out: sn rdn and wknd u.p to rr over 2f out: eased nr fin* **6/1**

3m 10.48s (2.58) **Going Correction** +0.475s/f (Yiel)
WFA 3 from 4yo+ 10lb **6** Ran SP% **112.1**
Speed ratings: **108,106,105,105,100 95**
CSF £16.42 TOTE £2.90: £1.30, £2.20; DF 18.90 Trifecta £50.60.
Owner Derrick Smith & Mrs John Magnier & Michael Tabor **Bred** Lynch-Bages & Rhinestone Bloodstock **Trained** Cashel, Co Tipperary
FOCUS
A good performance from the winner, who should gain confidence from a first success since May 2018. The second has been rated in line with the best view of his latest effort, with the winner close to his best.

6192a ROYAL WHIP STKS (GROUP 3) 1m 2f
6:45 (6:49) 3-Y-O+
£31,891 (£10,270; £4,864; £2,162; £1,081; £540)

RPR

1 **Buckhurst (IRE)**[48] 4411 3-9-2 109........................ DonnachaO'Brien 2 115
(Joseph Patrick O'Brien, Ire) *sn led tl hdd after 2f: cl 2nd at 1/2-way: gng wl bhd ldr over 2f out: sn pushed along and led 1 1/2f out: sn rdn and strly pressed w reduced ld wl ins fnl f: hld on wl* **11/2**[2]

2 hd **Leo De Fury (IRE)**[15] 5585 3-8-13 105........................ ShaneFoley 1 112+
(Mrs John Harrington, Ire) *chsd ldrs: 4th 1/2-way: impr into 3rd over 3f out and pushed along into st: rdn 2f out and clsd u.p nr side into 2nd ins fnl f: strly pressed wnr wl ins fnl f: jst hld* **7/1**[3]

3 1 1/2 **Guaranteed (IRE)**[8] 5874 3-8-13 109........................(t) KevinManning 4 109
(J S Bolger, Ire) *chsd ldrs tl impr to ld after 2f: narrow advantage at 1/2-way: rdn over 2f out and strly pressed: hdd far side 1 1/2f out: no imp on wnr ins fnl f where dropped to 3rd* **12/1**

4 1 1/4 **Sir Dragonet (IRE)**[76] 3345 3-9-2 117........................ RyanMoore 7 109
(A P O'Brien, Ire) *w.w in rr: tk clsr order in 6th bef 1/2-way: lft 4th over 3f out: pushed along over 2f out and n.m.r over 1f out where rdn in clsr 4th: no imp on ldrs wl ins fnl f: eased cl home* **4/9**[1]

5 5 1/2 **Nickajack Cave (IRE)**[49] 4356 3-8-13 90........................ ColinKeane 6 95
(G M Lyons, Ire) *hld up in 6th early: dropped to rr bef 1/2-way: lft 6th 3f out and pushed along: rdn in mod 5th under 2f out and no imp on ldrs: one pce after* **33/1**

6 3 1/2 **Shelir (IRE)**[83] 3104 3-8-13 100........................ ChrisHayes 5 88
(D K Weld, Ire) *chsd ldrs: 5th 1/2-way: dropped to 6th briefly over 3f out tl sn lft 5th: pushed along under 3f out and wknd to rr under 2f out* **14/1**

P **Zabriskie (IRE)**[17] 5535 4-9-6 89........................ SeamieHeffernan 3
(Luke Comer, Ire) *prom tl sn settled bhd ldr early: 3rd at 1/2-way: pushed along over 3f out where dropped to 4th and sn p.u: fatally injured* **100/1**

2m 13.99s (2.49) **Going Correction** +0.475s/f (Yiel)
WFA 3 from 4yo 7lb **7** Ran SP% **115.4**
Speed ratings: **106,105,104,103,99 96,**
CSF £43.40 TOTE £5.70: £2.30, £3.30; DF 35.10 Trifecta £140.20.
Owner Lloyd J Williams **Bred** Denford Stud Ltd **Trained** Owning Hill, Co Kilkenny
FOCUS
Back-to-back C&D Group 3s for Buckhurst, an improving colt who can go further. Personal bests from the first two, with the third rated to his mark.

6193 - 6195a (Foreign Racing) - See Raceform Interactive

6094 CLAIREFONTAINE (R-H)
Friday, August 16

OFFICIAL GOING: Turf: good to soft

6196a PRIX EQUIDARMOR - TRM (CLAIMER) (2YO) (TURF) 7f
12:45 2-Y-O **£8,558** (£3,423; £2,567; £1,711; £855)

RPR

1 **Silencious (FR)**[17] 2-8-6 0........................ HugoBesnier(5) 9 65
(S Cerulis, France) **101/10**

2 3/4 **Another Planet (FR)**[11] 5763 2-9-2 0........................(b) EddyHardouin 2 68
(Matthieu Palussiere, France) **61/10**[2]

3 1 3/4 **Gin Gembre (FR)**[6] 5968 2-9-1 0........................ TonyPiccone 12 62
(K R Burke) *early spd fr wd draw: trckd ldng pair on outer: pushed along in 3rd appr 2f out: rdn and wnt 2nd ins fnl 1 1/2f: kpt on wout quite chalng ldr: lost 2nd fnl 50yds* **61/10**[2]

4 1 1/4 **Makeno (FR)** 2-9-4 0........................ Pierre-CharlesBoudot 6 62
(D Guillemin, France) **21/10**[1]

5 1 1/2 **Spinning Mist**[14] 2-8-6 0........................(b[1]) MlleLeaBails(9) 7 55
(Andrea Marcialis, France) **16/1**

6 3/4 **Pic Cel (FR)**[11] 5759 2-9-1 0........................(b) HugoJourniac 8 53
(J-C Rouget, France) **9/1**

7 1 3/4 **Kamran (GER)** 2-8-11 0........................(p) ClementLecoeuvre 1 44
(Henk Grewe, Germany) **13/2**[3]

8 2 **Fact Or Fable (IRE)**[12] 5713 2-8-6 0........................ AlexisPouchin(5) 4 39
(J S Moore) *racd in rr of midfield: rdn and sme prog to chse ldrs ins fnl 2f: wknd and wl btn fnl f* **26/1**

9 3/4 **Wardachan (FR)**[15] 2-8-8 0........................ FabriceVeron 13 34
(Laurent Loisel, France) **53/1**

10 nk **Carmague (IRE)**[15] 5600 2-8-11 0........................ GregoryBenoist 5 36
(J S Moore) *wl away: sn prom: trckd ldrs wl in tch: rdn along and lost pl ins fnl 3f: no imp and wl btn fr 2f out* **19/1**

11 2 1/2 **Get The Look (IRE)**[11] 5759 2-8-8 0........................ MickaelBarzalona 11 27
(J S Moore) *towards rr on outer: pushed along 1/2-way: sn rdn and no imp: wl btn fnl 2f: eased ins fnl f* **19/1**

12 snk **Happy Star (FR)**[37] 2-9-1 0........................(p) MaximeGuyon 10 34
(C Escuder, France) **20/1**

1m 25.3s **12** Ran SP% **119.0**
PARI-MUTUEL (all including 1 euro stake): WIN 11.10; PLACE 3.20, 2.40, 2.80; DF 32.00.
Owner Stephan Hoffmeister **Bred** Haras Des Evees **Trained** France

5793 BATH (L-H)
Saturday, August 17

OFFICIAL GOING: Good to soft (soft in places; 6.5)
Wind: Fresh across, easing as the night went on Weather: Fine

6197 ASTON MANOR CIDER H'CAP 5f 10y
4:40 (4:41) (Class 5) (0-75,72) 3-Y-O **£3,428** (£1,020; £509; £400; £400) **Stalls** Centre

Form RPR

4431 **1** **Kodiak Attack (IRE)**[7] 5960 3-9-0 **65**........................ TomMarquand 5 71
(Sylvester Kirk) *chsd ldr: rdn to ld over 1f out: styd on u.p* **9/4**[2]

4031 **2** nk **Society Star**[8] 5917 3-8-2 **60**........................(p) AngusVilliers(7) 2 65
(Robert Cowell) *prom: pushed along 1/2-way: rdn and ev ch ins fnl f: styd on* **5/2**[3]

-240 **3** 3 3/4 **Bluebell Time (IRE)**[88] 2939 3-8-10 **61**........................ JFEgan 4 52
(Malcolm Saunders) *led: rdn and hdd over 1f out: no ex ins fnl f* **5/1**

0556 **4** 1/2 **Michaels Choice**[8] 5882 3-9-7 **72**........................ RyanTate 1 62
(William Jarvis) *chsd ldrs: rdn over 1f out: styd on same pce fnl f* **2/1**[1]

40-4 **5** 2 **Disruptor (FR)**[10] 5826 3-8-13 **67**........................ JoshuaBryan(3) 3 49
(Charlie Wallis) *s.i.s: hld up: rdn over 1f out: nt trble ldrs* **16/1**

1m 3.77s (1.77) **Going Correction** +0.375s/f (Good) **5** Ran SP% **115.2**
Speed ratings (Par 100): **100,99,93,92,89**
CSF £8.74 TOTE £2.90: £1.60, £1.70; EX 9.50 Trifecta £21.30.
Owner Mrs J Fowler **Bred** Tally-Ho Stud **Trained** Upper Lambourn, Berks

FOCUS
After 20mm of rain the going was good to soft, soft in places with a reading of 6.5. A low-key start with a Class 5 3yo sprint handicap but a game and progressive winner. The second has been rated to form.

6198 ASTON MANOR MAIDEN STKS 5f 160y
5:15 (5:16) (Class 4) 3-Y-O+ £5,072 (£1,518; £759; £379; £189) Stalls Centre

Form RPR
203 1 **Grisons (FR)**[5] 6023 3-9-2 0 WilliamCox(3) 2 63
(Clive Cox) *mde virtually all: rdn over 1f out: styd on: idled towards fin (vet said colt lost its right fore shoe)* 13/8[2]
0- 2 hd **A Place To Dream**[253] 9443 3-9-5 0 DanielMuscutt 4 62
(Mike Murphy) *prom: rdn over 1f out: chsd wnr wl ins fnl f: r.o* 12/1[3]
3 3 2 1/2 **Mofaaji**[48] 4421 3-9-5 0 PatCosgrave 3 54
(Simon Crisford) *trckd ldrs: racd keenly: wnt 2nd 3f out: rdn and ev ch over 1f out: no ex wl ins fnl f* 4/6[1]
4 4 hd **Excelinthejungle (IRE)**[7] 5960 3-9-5 0 TomMarquand 1 53
(Seamus Durack) *s.i.s: hdwy 1/2-way: rdn over 1f out: styd on same pce ins fnl f* 16/1
04 5 4 1/2 **Disey's Edge**[21] 5448 3-9-0 0 TrevorWhelan 5 34
(Christopher Mason) *chsd wnr tl rdn 3f out: wkng whn edgd lft fnl f* 33/1
1m 13.61s (2.51) **Going Correction** +0.375s/f (Good) 5 Ran SP% 114.6
Speed ratings (Par 105): **98,97,94,94,88**
CSF £19.69 TOTE £2.40: £1.20, £5.50; EX 22.10 Trifecta £29.60.
Owner China Horse Club International Limited **Bred** S A R L Eds Stud Ltd **Trained** Lambourn, Berks

FOCUS
A 3yo+ maiden in name but only contested by 3yos. The consistent second favourite just hung on to get off the mark at the 4th time of asking. The winner has been rated to form.

6199 KINGSTONE PRESS APPLE MAIDEN H'CAP 5f 160y
5:50 (5:52) (Class 6) (0-60,48) 4-Y-O+
£2,781 (£827; £413; £400; £400; £400) Stalls Centre

Form RPR
6003 1 **Kellington Kitty (USA)**[10] 5806 4-9-2 45 (p) DanielMuscutt 6 53
(Mike Murphy) *broke wl enough out wd: lost pl over 4f out: hdwy over 2f out: rdn to ld and edgd rt over 1f out: wnt clr ins fnl f* 7/2[2]
0045 2 6 **Praxedis**[9] 5864 4-9-5 48 (v[1]) PatCosgrave 4 36
(Robert Cowell) *pushed along to chse ldrs: rdn and ev ch over 1f out: no ex ins fnl f* 4/1[3]
050- 3 nk **Dollywaggon Pike**[383] 5554 5-8-11 45 TobyEley(5) 3 32
(J R Jenkins) *chsd ldr tl led over 2f out: rdn: edgd rt and hdd over 1f out: no ex ins fnl f (jockey said mare hung right)* 18/1
0232 4 2 **Prince Rock (IRE)**[25] 5264 4-9-3 46 (h) TomMarquand 1 27
(Simon Dow) *s.i.s: hdwy over 4f out: rdn over 1f out: wknd ins fnl f* 11/10[1]
0505 5 4 1/2 **Raise A Little Joy**[10] 5822 4-8-13 45 (v) JoshuaBryan(3) 2 11
(J R Jenkins) *led 3f: sn rdn: wknd fnl f* 14/1
0000 6 hd **Tally's Song**[36] 4873 6-9-2 45 (p) JFEgan 7 10
(Grace Harris) *sn outpcd* 20/1
0000 7 3 1/4 **Woggle (IRE)**[2] 6116 4-9-2 45 TrevorWhelan 5
(Geoffrey Deacon) *broke wl enough: sn pushed along and lost pl: rdn and wknd 1/2-way (jockey said filly jumped awkwardly from the stalls)* 7/1
1m 13.11s (2.01) **Going Correction** +0.375s/f (Good) 7 Ran SP% 119.0
Speed ratings (Par 101): **101,93,92,89,83 83,79**
CSF £18.97 CT £224.18 TOTE £3.80: £2.30, £1.90; EX 14.40 Trifecta £100.40.
Owner Lemon, Papworth, Hazelwood & Sullivan **Bred** Kenneth L Ramsey And Sarah K Ramsey **Trained** Westoning, Beds

FOCUS
A 0-60 but the top one was only rated 48. An uncompetitive looking sprint handicap with an 11-10 favourite who is now 0-17.

6200 KINGSTONE PRESS APPLE H'CAP (VALUE RATER RACING CLUB BATH SUMMER STAYERS SERIES QUALIFIER) 1m 5f 11y
6:20 (6:20) (Class 5) (0-75,74) 4-Y-O+
£3,428 (£1,020; £509; £400; £400; £400) Stalls High

Form RPR
6330 1 **Miss Latin (IRE)**[17] 5540 4-9-2 74 DylanHogan(5) 1 81
(David Simcock) *hld up: hdwy 1/2-way: rdn to ld and edgd lft over 1f out: styd on* 13/2
2320 2 nse **Singing The Blues (IRE)**[16] 5571 4-9-5 72 DanielMuscutt 6 79
(Rod Millman) *led: rdn and hdd over 1f out: rallied ins fnl f: styd on* 5/4[1]
0200 3 2 3/4 **The Detainee**[42] 4661 6-8-12 65 (v[1]) TrevorWhelan 2 68
(Neil Mulholland) *chsd ldrs: rdn over 2f out: styd on same pce wl ins fnl f* 20/1
2533 4 1/2 **Panatos (FR)**[22] 5379 4-8-11 64 ow1 RossaRyan 4 66
(Alexandra Dunn) *pushed along to chse ldr: rdn and lost 2nd over 1f out: styd on same pce ins fnl f* 5/2[2]
4322 5 3 **Royal Flag**[12] 5727 9-8-11 64 BenRobinson 9 62
(Brian Ellison) *s.i.s: hld up: rdn over 3f out: nt rch ldrs (jockey said gelding was never travelling)* 5/1[3]
6-06 6 13 **Lady Natasha (IRE)**[32] 5012 6-8-2 60 oh15 (t) SophieRalston(5) 8 38
(James Grassick) *chsd ldrs: pushed along 1/2-way: rdn over 3f out: wknd 2f out* 66/1
126- 7 13 **Zoffany Bay (IRE)**[117] 6897 5-9-4 71 (p) TomMarquand 7 30
(Ali Stronge) *s.i.s: hld up: rdn over 3f out: wknd over 2f out* 9/1
2m 53.05s (0.25) **Going Correction** +0.10s/f (Good) 7 Ran SP% 119.3
Speed ratings (Par 103): **103,102,101,100,99 91,83**
CSF £16.05 CT £162.21 TOTE £8.40: £3.10, £1.40; EX 20.00 Trifecta £114.80.
Owner Mrs Fitri Hay **Bred** Lynch Bages **Trained** Newmarket, Suffolk

FOCUS
Race distance 10yds further than advertised. A thrilling finish to a 0-75 staying handicap. The third and fourth have been rated close to their recent form.

6201 SAMWORTH BROTHERS H'CAP 1m
6:50 (6:55) (Class 4) (0-80,82) 4-Y-O+
£5,207 (£1,549; £774; £400; £400; £400) Stalls Low

Form RPR
-420 1 **Secret Return (IRE)**[42] 4639 6-9-4 77 JFEgan 2 83
(Paul George) *chsd ldrs: rdn over 2f out: led over 1f out: edgd rt ins fnl f: jst hld on (starter reported that the mare was unruly at the start and reluctant to load; trainer was informed that the filly could not run until the day after passing a stalls test)* 2/1[1]
4241 2 nk **Tukhoom (IRE)**[10] 5820 6-9-8 81 (p) TomMarquand 4 86
(David O'Meara) *chsd ldrs: rdn over 2f out: ev ch over 1f out: r.o* 9/2[2]
4231 3 nse **Pickett's Charge**[9] 5839 6-8-11 70 (t) BenRobinson 7 75
(Brian Ellison) *broke wl: lost pl after 1f: rdn over 2f out: hdwy over 1f out: r.o* 11/1
3630 4 1 1/2 **Rogue**[17] 5564 4-9-4 82 SebastianWoods(5) 9 84
(Alexandra Dunn) *sn led: rdn and hdd over 1f out: edgd lft ins fnl f: no ex towards fin* 10/1
0002 5 3/4 **Merweb (IRE)**[4] 6050 4-8-12 71 JoeyHaynes 6 71
(Heather Main) *hld up: shkn up over 2f out: edgd lft and nt clr run over 1f out: r.o ins fnl f: nvr nr to chal* 5/1[3]
3224 6 3/4 **Sir Roderic (IRE)**[16] 5579 6-9-1 74 DanielMuscutt 8 72
(Rod Millman) *plld hrd and prom: settled to trck ldrs after 1f: rdn and ev ch over 1f out: styd on same pce ins fnl f* 8/1
2330 7 1 1/4 **Regimented (IRE)**[38] 4786 4-9-5 78 RossaRyan 5 73
(Richard Hannon) *s.i.s: hld up: rdn over 1f out: nt trble ldrs* 8/1
1306 8 1 1/4 **Here's Two**[62] 3892 6-8-10 72 WilliamCox(3) 1 65
(Ron Hodges) *chsd ldr: rdn over 2f out: no ex ins fnl f* 25/1
1-45 9 2 1/4 **Arabian Jazz (IRE)**[35] 4902 4-9-4 77 (h) JasonWatson 3 64
(Michael Bell) *hld up: racd keenly: hdwy over 2f out: wknd fnl f* 6/1
1m 41.85s (0.15) **Going Correction** +0.10s/f (Good) 9 Ran SP% 126.0
Speed ratings (Par 105): **103,102,102,101,100 99,98,97,94**
CSF £12.28 CT £86.50 TOTE £2.80: £1.40, £1.90, £2.40; EX 12.80 Trifecta £132.50.
Owner Cross Channel Racing Club **Bred** Holburn Trust Co **Trained** Crediton, Devon

FOCUS
Race distance 10yds further than advertised. A competitive Class 4 handicap and a gamble landed. The second and third have been rated to their recent form.

6202 KINGSTONE PRESS WILD BERRY H'CAP 1m 2f 37y
7:20 (7:22) (Class 6) (0-60,61) 3-Y-O
£2,781 (£827; £413; £400; £400; £400) Stalls Low

Form RPR
0043 1 **Ragstone Cowboy (IRE)**[11] 5784 3-9-5 57 (v[1]) ShaneKelly 7 63
(Gary Moore) *hld up in tch: shkn up over 2f out: rdn to ld wl ins fnl f: edgd lft: styd on* 9/2
3323 2 3/4 **Queen's Soldier (GER)**[19] 5497 3-9-4 61 WilliamCarver(5) 9 66
(Andrew Balding) *hld up in tch on outer: rdn to ld and edgd lft over 1f out: hdd wl ins fnl f: kpt on (jockey said gelding hung left in the home straight)* 5/2[1]
0-00 3 1/2 **Tamok (IRE)**[79] 3277 3-8-9 47 (v[1]) JasonWatson 2 51
(Michael Bell) *pushed along to go prom after 1f: rdn over 2f out: ev ch wl ins fnl f: unable qck towards fin* 11/1
0500 4 shd **Mr Nice Guy (IRE)**[11] 5778 3-9-0 57 PoppyBridgwater(5) 8 60
(Sylvester Kirk) *pushed along early in rr: rdn and hung lft over 1f out: r.o ins fnl f: nt rch ldrs* 20/1
0042 5 1 **Goodwood Sonnet (IRE)**[26] 5249 3-8-13 51 (v) TomMarquand 6 53
(William Knight) *s.i.s: hld up: hdwy over 1f out: hung lft ins fnl f: styd on (vet said gelding lost his left fore shoe)* 4/1[3]
0046 6 1/2 **Max Guevara (IRE)**[24] 5304 3-9-7 59 JFEgan 3 60
(William Muir) *hld up: racd keenly: hdwy over 1f out: rdn and ev ch wl ins fnl f: styd on same pce: eased towards fin (jockey said gelding was crowded for room by Tamok, forcing him to stop riding and being eased in the last fifty yards)* 20/1
4522 7 2 3/4 **Uncertain Smile (IRE)**[11] 5784 3-9-6 61 (h) WilliamCox(3) 1 57
(Clive Cox) *trckd ldrs: plld hrd: wnt 2nd after 1f tl over 6f out: remained handy: shkn up: nt clr run and lost pl over 2f out: nt clr run again and wknd ins fnl f* 7/2[2]
4000 8 1 1/4 **Another Approach (FR)**[26] 5249 3-8-12 50 (p) MartinDwyer 4 43
(Amanda Perrett) *led: rdn and hdd over 1f out: wknd ins fnl f* 20/1
1634 9 2 3/4 **Bader**[10] 5803 3-9-2 54 (b) RossaRyan 5 42
(Richard Hannon) *chsd ldr 1f: wnt 2nd again over 6f out tl rdn over 2f out: wknd fnl f (jockey said gelding was never travelling; vet said gelding lost his left hind shoe)* 10/1
2m 12.33s (1.23) **Going Correction** +0.10s/f (Good) 9 Ran SP% 120.7
Speed ratings (Par 98): **99,98,98,97,97 96,94,93,91**
CSF £16.47 CT £112.69 TOTE £4.60: £1.60, £1.30, £3.60; EX 19.60 Trifecta £258.30.
Owner Gallagher Bloodstock Limited **Bred** M P & R J Coleman **Trained** Lower Beeding, W Sussex
■ Stewards' Enquiry : Shane Kelly two-day ban: used whip above the permitted level (Aug 31, Sep 1)

FOCUS
Race distance 10yds further than advertised. A tight 3yo handicap and not much in it at the death. Limited form.

6203 KINGSTONE PRESS APPLE CIDER H'CAP (VALUE RATER RACING CLUB BATH SUMMER SPRINT SERIES QUALIFIER) 5f 160y
7:50 (7:54) (Class 5) (0-75,74) 4-Y-O+
£3,428 (£1,020; £509; £400; £400; £400) Stalls Centre

Form RPR
-636 1 **Sweet Pursuit**[12] 5736 5-9-2 72 FinleyMarsh(3) 1 78
(Rod Millman) *hld up: pushed along over 3f out: nt clr run and swtchd rt over 1f out: str run ins fnl f to ld post* 10/1
0124 2 hd **Delagate This Lord**[24] 5318 5-9-7 74 TomMarquand 8 79
(Michael Attwater) *w ldrs 1f: remained handy: rdn to ld wl ins fnl f: hdd post* 7/2[1]
5242 3 1/2 **Princely**[36] 4872 4-8-11 64 MartinDwyer 5 67
(Tony Newcombe) *w ldr tl led over 2f out: rdn and hdd wl ins fnl f: styd on* 7/1
2204 4 nk **Big Lachie**[8] 5882 5-9-6 73 JasonWatson 9 75
(Mark Loughnane) *s.i.s: hdwy on outer over 2f out: rdn and ev ch wl ins fnl f: styd on* 5/1[3]
0300 5 3/4 **Met By Moonlight**[5] 6025 5-9-0 70 WilliamCox(3) 7 70
(Ron Hodges) *chsd ldrs: rdn over 1f out: styd on* 14/1
5051 6 1 1/2 **Secret Potion**[6] 5986 5-8-12 65 5ex LiamKeniry 6 60
(Ronald Harris) *chsd ldrs: rdn and ev ch wl over 1f out: styd on same pce ins fnl f* 5/1[3]
3602 7 shd **Madrinho (IRE)**[12] 5723 6-8-12 72 ElishaWhittington(7) 4 67
(Tony Carroll) *prom: lost pl over 4f out: sn pushed along: hdwy over 1f out: styd on* 8/1
-12 8 27 **Nigg Bay (IRE)**[19] 5495 5-9-6 73 (v) ShaneKelly 2
(J F Levins, Ire) *restless in stalls: s.i.s: hdwy over 4f out: rdn over 2f out: wknd and eased fnl f (starter reported that the gelding was unruly at the start; trainers' rep was informed that the gelding could not run until the day after passing a stalls test)* 4/1[2]

000- **9** *9* **Titus Secret**[313] 8047 7-9-0 **67**........................ JFEgan 3
(Malcolm Saunders) *led: hdd over 2f out: wknd fnl f (jockey said gelding stopped quickly)* **16/1**

1m 11.5s (0.40) **Going Correction** +0.375s/f (Good) **9** Ran SP% **120.8**
Speed ratings (Par 103): **108,107,107,106,105 103,103,67,55**
CSF £47.17 CT £272.45 TOTE £10.50: £3.20, £1.60, £2.20; EX 66.80 Trifecta £392.90.
Owner Always Hopeful Partnership **Bred** Tom Chadney & Peter Green **Trained** Kentisbeare, Devon

FOCUS
A very tight sprint handicap and another late swooping winner. Sound form rated around the second.
T/Plt: £67.10 to a £1 stake. Pool: £41,543.34 - 451.75 winning units T/Qpdt: £16.80 to a £1 stake. Pool: £7,566.72 - 331.99 winning units **Colin Roberts**

5654 DONCASTER (L-H)

Saturday, August 17

OFFICIAL GOING: Soft (good to soft in places; 6.7)
Wind: Moderate against Weather: Cloudy with sunny periods

6204 DONCASTER GROUNDWORKS H'CAP 7f 6y
1:10 (1:13) (Class 5) (0-70,70) 3-Y-O+
£3,428 (£1,020; £509; £300; £300; £300) **Stalls** Low

Form RPR

2011 **1** **Red Seeker**[18] 5517 4-9-4 **67**........................(t) DannyRedmond(5) 6 76
(Tim Easterby) *hld up in tch: hdwy to ld 2f out: jnd and rdn over 1f out: drvn ins fnl f: hld on wl towards fin* **7/1**[3]

666 **2** *hd* **Valley Of Fire**[26] 5238 7-9-5 **63**........................(p) LewisEdmunds 4 71
(Les Eyre) *in tch: hdwy over 2f out: rdn to chal over 1f out: drvn and ev ch ins fnl f: no ex towards fin* **14/1**

4143 **3** *1* **Poet's Pride**[29] 5123 4-9-9 **67**........................ BenCurtis 18 72+
(David Barron) *hld up towards rr: swtchd rt and hdwy on stands' side wl over 1f out: sn rdn: styd on wl fnl f (jockey said gelding hung left in the final furlong)* **17/2**

-000 **4** *1 ¼* **Al Suil Eile (FR)**[60] 3970 3-9-6 **69**........................ RobbieDowney 7 69
(John Quinn) *hld up: hdwy over 2f out: rdn to chse ldrs over 1f out: drvn and kpt on same pce fnl f* **33/1**

4500 **5** *¾* **Deansgate (IRE)**[49] 4365 6-9-7 **70**........................ HarrisonShaw(5) 3 70
(Julie Camacho) *dwlt and hld up in rr: hdwy on inner wl over 2f out: rdn to chse ldrs over 1f out: drvn and kpt on same pce fnl f (jockey said gelding missed the break)* **16/1**

530 **6** *2* **In The Cove (IRE)**[14] 5651 3-9-6 **69**........................ RossaRyan 15 62
(Richard Hannon) *in tch towards stands' side: hdwy 2f out: rdn wl over 1f out: drvn and no imp fnl f* **14/1**

0500 **7** *1 ¾* **Mutafarrid (IRE)**[47] 4440 4-9-12 **70**........................ KevinStott 5 60
(Paul Midgley) *hld up in midfield: hdwy to chse ldrs 2f out: sn rdn and kpt on same pce appr fnl f* **33/1**

3400 **8** *hd* **Flying Raconteur**[17] 5556 5-9-4 **65**........................(t) RowanScott(3) 8 55
(Nigel Tinkler) *prom: rdn along over 2f out: sn drvn and grad wknd* **12/1**

1603 **9** *½* **Verdigris (IRE)**[27] 5218 4-9-8 **66**........................ AndrewMullen 17 55+
(Ruth Carr) *t.k.h: hld up in rr: sme hdwy whn sltly hmpd wl over 1f out: sn rdn and n.d (jockey said filly was denied a clear run on a couple of occasions in the final furlong)* **14/1**

5306 **10** *nse* **Sirius Slew**[15] 5622 3-9-6 **69**........................(p) HayleyTurner 21 56
(Alan Bailey) *chsd ldrs towards stands' side: swtchd lft and rdn along 2f out: sn wknd* **28/1**

2402 **11** *6* **Logi (IRE)**[8] 5903 5-9-9 **67**........................(b) JamieGormley 22 40
(Rebecca Bastiman) *cl up towards stands' side: rdn along over 2f out: sn drvn and wknd* **17/2**

0221 **12** *1 ¼* **Strong Steps**[19] 5490 7-9-11 **69**........................(p) JimCrowley 9 39
(Jim Goldie) *trckd ldrs centre: pushed along wl over 2f out: sn rdn and wknd* **6/1**[2]

-363 **13** *¾* **Pamper**[16] 5592 3-9-6 **69**........................ OisinMurphy 20 35
(James Fanshawe) *towards rr: pushed along 1/2-way: rdn over 2f out: n.d* **11/2**[1]

0030 **14** *shd* **Mudawwan (IRE)**[45] 4523 5-9-7 **65**........................(p) PaulHanagan 10 32
(James Bethell) *racd centre: led: pushed along 3f out: rdn along and hdd 2f out: sn wknd* **20/1**

1406 **15** *shd* **Newstead Abbey**[136] 1522 9-8-11 **60**........................ TheodoreLadd(5) 11 27
(Rebecca Bastiman) *midfield: effrt whn jampered wl over 1f out: n.d* **50/1**

-600 **16** *5* **Allsfineandandy (IRE)**[17] 5554 3-7-11 **51** oh4........................(b[1]) PaulaMuir(5) 2 3
(Lynn Siddall) *a in rr: outpcd and bhd fnl 2f (jockey said gelding was never travelling; trainer said gelding would be suited by a step up in trip)* **100/1**

0043 **17** *¾* **Gavi Di Gavi (IRE)**[25] 5282 4-9-0 **58**........................ TomQueally 19 10
(Alan King) *prom: cl up over 3f out: rdn along wl over 2f out: sn wknd* **16/1**

1m 29.6s (3.20) **Going Correction** +0.525s/f (Yiel)
WFA 3 from 4yo+ 5lb **17** Ran SP% **119.7**
Speed ratings (Par 103): **102,101,100,99,98 96,94,93,93,93 86,84,84,83,83 78,77**
CSF £88.01 CT £768.07 TOTE £7.50: £2.00, £3.50, £2.40, £8.40; EX 155.10 Trifecta £934.70.
Owner Brian Valentine **Bred** Aunty Ifl **Trained** Great Habton, N Yorks
■ Mywayistheonlyway was withdrawn. Price at time of withdrawal 10/1. Rule 4 applies to all bets - deduction 5p in the £.
■ Stewards' Enquiry : Danny Redmond four-day ban: used whip above the permitted level (Aug 31, Sep 1-3)
Hayley Turner two-day ban: interference & careless riding (Aug 31, Sep 1)

FOCUS
This looked ultra competitive despite five absentees. They all raced towards the centre. The second has been rated to his reappearance effort, with the third to form.

6205 WAVIN HEP20 EBF MAIDEN FILLIES' STKS (PLUS 10 RACE) 1m (S)
1:40 (1:41) (Class 5) 2-Y-O **£3,428** (£1,020; £509; £254) **Stalls** Low

Form RPR

2 **1** **Alpen Rose (IRE)**[29] 5139 2-9-0 0........................ BrettDoyle 6 77+
(Charlie Appleby) *mde all: clr whn green and idled over 1f out: jnd and rdn ent fnl f: kpt on wl* **8/11**[1]

5 **2** *1* **Stars In The Sky**[22] 5366 2-9-0 0........................ OisinMurphy 7 74+
(William Haggas) *trckd wnr: pushed and hdwy over 1f out: rdn to chal ent fnl f: ev ch tl kpt on same pce last 100yds* **2/1**[2]

0 **3** *5* **Good Reason**[16] 5588 2-9-0 0........................ TomQueally 1 62+
(Saeed bin Suroor) *awkward s and dwlt: t.k.h in rr: hdwy 3f out: chsd ldng pair over 2f out: rdn along wl over 1f out: kpt on same pce* **12/1**

4 *3 ½* **Ruby Shield (USA)** 2-9-0 0........................ JackGarritty 8 56+
(Richard Fahey) *t.k.h and hld up in rr: hdwy over 2f out: chsd ldrs wl over 1f out: n.d* **9/1**[3]

06 **5** *3 ¼* **Pearl Beach**[30] 5088 2-9-0 0........................ JimCrowley 2 47
(William Knight) *t.k.h: chsd ldrs: rdn along wl over 2f out: sn wknd* **50/1**

0 **6** *1* **Loco Dempsey (FR)**[6] 5988 2-9-0 0........................ RossaRyan 3 45
(Richard Hannon) *a in rr: outpcd and bhd fnl 3f* **28/1**

6 **7** *14* **Mrs Tiffen**[13] 5704 2-8-7 0........................ GavinAshton(7) 4 14
(Lisa Williamson) *t.k.h: chsd ldng pair: rdn along over 3f out: sn wknd* **100/1**

1m 45.26s (5.06) **Going Correction** +0.525s/f (Yiel) **7** Ran SP% **115.3**
Speed ratings (Par 91): **95,94,89,85,82 81,67**
CSF £2.43 TOTE £1.50: £1.10, £1.50; EX 2.50 Trifecta £7.40.
Owner Godolphin **Bred** Sunderland Holdings Inc **Trained** Newmarket, Suffolk

FOCUS
This maiden revolved around to big two in the market.

6206 ETICO MORTGAGE CLAIMS NOVICE STKS 6f 2y
2:15 (2:15) (Class 5) 3-Y-O+ **£3,428** (£1,020; £509; £254) **Stalls** Low

Form RPR

1 **Mutafawwig** 3-9-2 0........................ HectorCrouch 5 85+
(Saeed bin Suroor) *t.k.h early: mde all: qcknd clr wl over 1f out: kpt on strly* **5/4**[1]

02 **2** *3 ½* **Marvel**[8] 5917 3-8-11 0........................ HarrisonShaw(5) 6 71
(Julie Camacho) *awkward s: keen and hld up: hdwy over 2f out: rdn to chse wnr ent fnl f: kpt on: no imp* **12/1**

0- **3** *2 ½* **Buniann (IRE)**[313] 8041 3-9-2 0........................ KevinStott 1 63
(Paul Midgley) *trckd ldrs: hdwy 3f out: rdn along 2f out: drvn wl over 1f out: kpt on same pce* **9/1**

56 **4** *hd* **Gleniffer**[17] 5554 3-9-2 0........................ JamieGormley 3 62
(Jim Goldie) *hld up in rr: hdwy 2f out: rdn wl over 1f out: kpt on fnl f* **16/1**

5 *2* **Futuristic (IRE)** 3-9-2 0........................ OisinMurphy 2 56
(James Tate) *trckd wnr: pushed along over 2f out: rdn wl over 1f out: wknd appr fnl f* **2/1**[2]

6 *1 ¾* **Double Martini (IRE)**[91] 2850 3-9-9 0........................ BenCurtis 7 57
(Roger Fell) *trckd ldng pair: pushed along over 2f out: sn rdn and wknd wl over 1f out* **5/1**[3]

0 **7** *nk* **Loretta (IRE)**[61] 3920 3-8-11 0........................ PaulHanagan 4 44
(Julie Camacho) *t.k.h: chsd ldrs: pushed along 1/2-way: rdn and wknd over 2f out* **25/1**

1m 16.39s (3.69) **Going Correction** +0.525s/f (Yiel) **7** Ran SP% **121.9**
Speed ratings (Par 103): **96,91,88,87,85 82,82**
CSF £20.00 TOTE £1.90: £1.30, £3.60; EX 16.20 Trifecta £133.90.
Owner Godolphin **Bred** Godolphin **Trained** Newmarket, Suffolk

FOCUS
An informative novice and an impressive debut from the winner. The level is fluid.

6207 ALAN SMITH MEMORIAL H'CAP 7f 6y
2:50 (2:50) (Class 2) (0-105,103) 3-Y-O+
£12,450 (£3,728; £1,864; £932; £466; £234) **Stalls** Low

Form RPR

5326 **1** **Breanski**[21] 5434 5-8-7 **84** oh1........................ AntonioFresu 5 92
(Jedd O'Keeffe) *hld up towards rr: gd hdwy on inner over 2f out: chal over 1f out: rdn to ld ent fnl f: drvn and kpt on wl towards fin* **9/1**

0520 **2** *nk* **Presidential (IRE)**[7] 5971 5-8-8 **85**........................(p[1]) BenCurtis 7 92
(Roger Fell) *hld up towards rr: hdwy towards outer 2f out: rdn over 1f out: chsd wnr ins fnl f: sn drvn and kpt on* **11/2**[3]

3001 **3** *¾* **Rum Runner**[15] 5626 4-8-11 **88**........................ RossaRyan 10 93
(Richard Hannon) *hld up in rr: hdwy on outer wl over 1f out: rdn appr fnl f: kpt on wl* **14/1**

1051 **4** *½* **Finoah (IRE)**[7] 5953 3-8-8 **93**........................(v) JaneElliott(3) 2 95
(Tom Dascombe) *t.k.h early: trckd ldrs: hdwy on inner over 2f out: rdn to chal wl over 1f out: led narrowly briefly jst over 1f out: hdd ent fnl f: drvn: edgd rt and kpt on same pce fnl f* **12/1**

132 **5** *3 ¾* **That Is The Spirit**[22] 5386 8-8-4 **86**........................ TheodoreLadd(5) 3 80
(Michael Appleby) *t.k.h: led: pushed along 2f out: sn rdn: drvn and hdd appr fnl f: sn wknd* **7/1**

32-2 **6** *1 ½* **Double Kodiac (IRE)**[121] 1888 3-8-3 **85**........................ HayleyTurner 11 72
(Simon Crisford) *trckd ldr: effrt 2f out: sn rdn and wknd* **9/4**[1]

4P44 **7** *¾* **Remarkable**[8] 5916 6-9-7 **98**........................(b) RobbieDowney 9 85
(David O'Meara) *s.i.s and lost 6 l at s: a bhd (jockey said gelding was restless in the stalls and slowly away)* **20/1**

1105 **8** *2 ¼* **Motafaawit (IRE)**[37] 4850 3-9-7 **103**........................ JimCrowley 8 82
(Richard Hannon) *trckd ldrs: hdwy over 2f out: rdn wl over 1f out: sn wknd* **4/1**[2]

2- **9** *7* **Nordic Fire**[51] 3-8-8 **90**........................ OisinMurphy 4 50
(David O'Meara) *t.k.h: trckd ldrs: pushed along over 2f out: sn rdn and wknd* **8/1**

3530 **10** *22* **Celebrity Dancer (IRE)**[36] 4895 3-8-3 **85**........................ AndrewMullen 1
(Kevin Ryan) *t.k.h: trckd ldng pair: rdn along 2f out: sn wknd (jockey said gelding stopped quickly)* **20/1**

1m 28.67s (2.27) **Going Correction** +0.525s/f (Yiel)
WFA 3 from 4yo+ 5lb **10** Ran SP% **123.6**
Speed ratings (Par 109): **108,107,106,106,101 100,99,96,88,63**
CSF £61.51 CT £700.18 TOTE £11.30: £3.10, £2.20, £3.40; EX 66.70 Trifecta £1422.70.
Owner Quantum **Bred** Mrs P Good **Trained** Middleham Moor, N Yorks

FOCUS
With just one of these rated in excess of 100, this wasn't a particularly strong race for the grade. The first three have been rated to their best.

6208 HAPPY BIRTHDAY DEBBIE JEFFERSON H'CAP 5f 3y
3:25 (3:26) (Class 3) (0-95,91) 3-Y-O+ **£7,762** (£2,310; £1,154; £577) **Stalls** Low

Form RPR

0456 **1** **Orvar (IRE)**[21] 5420 6-9-6 **87**........................ OisinMurphy 4 98
(Paul Midgley) *hld up: hdwy wl over 1f out: rdn to ld ins fnl f: kpt on strly (trainer could offer no explanation for the gelding's improved form)* **10/3**[1]

0040 **2** *1 ½* **Saaheq**[18] 5524 5-9-7 **88**........................ AlistairRawlinson 1 94
(Michael Appleby) *hld up towards rr: hdwy wl over 1f out: chsd ldrs appr fnl f: sn rdn and kpt on wl towards fin* **7/1**

2034 **3** *hd* **Acclaim The Nation (IRE)**[21] 5420 6-8-13 **85**.....(p) HarrisonShaw(5) 11 90
(Eric Alston) *set str pce: rdn wl over 1f out: jnd and drvn 1f out: hdd ins fnl f: kpt on same pce* **5/1**[3]

6002 **4** *nse* **The Daley Express (IRE)**[26] 5252 5-9-5 **86**........................ AndrewMullen 3 91
(Ronald Harris) *chsd ldng pair: rdn along wl over 1f out: drvn ent fnl f: kpt on same pce* **12/1**

-300 **5** *1 ¼* **Kick On Kick On**[22] 5371 4-9-3 **91**........................ AmeliaGlass(7) 6 91
(Clive Cox) *hld up towards rr: hdwy on outer over 2f out: rdn to chse ldrs over 1f out: drvn: edgd lft and kpt on same pce ins fnl f* **9/1**

1150 **6** ½ **Dapper Man (IRE)**[22] 5371 5-9-1 **87**........ BenSanderson(5) 13 85
(Roger Fell) *cl up: rdn along 2f out: drvn over 1f out: grad wknd* **16/1**

3234 **7** ½ **Roundhay Park**[14] 5691 4-9-4 **85**........(t[1]) LewisEdmunds 12 82
(Nigel Tinkler) *awkward s: a towards rr (jockey said gelding fly leapt leaving the stalls)* **9/2[2]**

5303 **8** 8 **Tommy G**[14] 5661 6-8-10 **77**........ JamieGormley 2 45
(Jim Goldie) *trckd ldrs: hdwy over 2f out: rdn along wl over 1f out: sn wknd (trainer's rep said gelding was unsuited by the going and would prefer a quicker surface)* **5/1[3]**

-500 **9** 7 **Dancing Warrior**[16] 5589 3-9-2 **85**........ JimCrowley 8 28
(William Knight) *chsd ldrs: rdn along over 2f out: sn drvn and wknd* **14/1**

1m 0.91s (1.31) **Going Correction** +0.525s/f (Yiel)
WFA 3 from 4yo+ 2lb **9** Ran SP% **117.3**
Speed ratings (Par 107): **110,107,107,107,105 104,103,90,79**
CSF £27.56 CT £117.05 TOTE £4.10: £1.60, £2.70, £1.80; EX 28.40 Trifecta £142.50.
Owner Taylor's Bloodstock Ltd **Bred** David Harrison **Trained** Westow, N Yorks

FOCUS
This was strongly run and was won with some authority by Orvar for the second year in succession. Solid form rated around the second, third and fourth.

6209 EXPERIENCE YORKSHIRE'S CLASSIC 11-14 SEPTEMBER H'CAP 1m 2f 43y
4:00 (4:00) (Class 4) (0-85,83) 3-Y-O **£5,207** (£1,549; £774; £387; £300) **Stalls** High

Form RPR

3315 **1** **Moll Davis (IRE)**[17] 5545 3-9-5 **81**........ HayleyTurner 1 97+
(George Scott) *hld up in rr: smooth hdwy on inner over 3f out: led on bit 2f out: sn pushed clr: easily* **4/5[1]**

5-13 **2** 4 ½ **Proton (IRE)**[57] 4076 3-9-6 **82**........ PaulHanagan 5 86
(Jedd O'Keeffe) *trckd ldr: hdwy to take narrow ld 3f out: sn rdn: hdd 2f out: sn drvn: kpt on same pce (vet said gelding lost its right fore shoe)* **13/2[3]**

3040 **3** 1 ¼ **Kingson (IRE)**[26] 5245 3-8-8 **70**........ AndrewMullen 2 71
(Richard Fahey) *hld up: hdwy over 3f out: rdn 2f out: chsd wnr briefly over 1f out: sn drvn: edgd lft and kpt on one pce* **7/1**

3132 **4** 12 **Tabassor (IRE)**[14] 5687 3-9-4 **80**........ JimCrowley 4 57
(Charles Hills) *led: pushed along 4f out: rdn and hdd 3f out: sn wknd* **3/1[2]**

0 **5** 2 **Jupiter Road**[17] 5557 3-9-0 **83**........(tp) IzzyClifton(7) 3 56
(Nigel Tinkler) *trckd ldng pair: hdwy and cl up 3f out: rdn along over 2f out: sn drvn and wknd over 1f out* **16/1**

2m 15.3s (3.00) **Going Correction** +0.525s/f (Yiel) **5** Ran SP% **112.3**
Speed ratings (Par 102): **109,105,104,94,93**
CSF £6.86 TOTE £1.70: £1.10, £2.50; EX 7.10 Trifecta £16.60.
Owner Sonia M Rogers & Anthony Rogers **Bred** Airlie Stud & Mrs S M Rogers **Trained** Newmarket, Suffolk

FOCUS
Add 18 yards. This was won in effortless fashion by the rapidly improving favourite. The third has been rated to form.

6210 DONCASTER RACECOURSE SUPPORTING DONCASTER PRIDE APPRENTICE H'CAP 1m 2f 43y
4:35 (4:35) (Class 5) (0-75,75) 4-Y-O+
£3,428 (£1,020; £509; £300; £300; £300) **Stalls** High

Form RPR

0564 **1** **Delph Crescent (IRE)**[12] 5741 4-9-7 **70**........(v) PaulaMuir 8 80
(Richard Fahey) *hld up in rr: smooth hdwy on outer 3f out: sn trcking ldrs: rdn to ld over 1f out: kpt on strly* **5/2[1]**

/600 **2** 3 **Tommy Hallinan (IRE)**[148] 1271 5-8-8 **60**........(w) HarryRussell(3) 7 64
(Brian Ellison) *led: pushed along 3f out: sn hdd and rdn: drvn and kpt on fnl f* **14/1**

-633 **3** ½ **Elhafei (USA)**[18] 5529 4-9-9 **72**........ TheodoreLadd 1 75
(Michael Appleby) *trckd ldr: pushed along over 3f out: rdn over 2f out: sn drvn and kpt on same pce* **3/1[3]**

0033 **4** 2 **Detachment**[18] 5516 6-9-12 **75**........ BenSanderson 4 74
(Roger Fell) *hld up in tch: hdwy 3f out: shkn up 2f out: rdn over 1f out: sn no imp* **11/4[2]**

-400 **5** nk **Kaser (IRE)**[31] 5055 4-9-9 **75**........ LauraCoughlan(3) 2 73
(David Loughnane) *trckd ldng pair: hdwy over 3f out: slt ld 2f out: sn rdn: drvn and hdd over 1f out: plugged on same pce* **14/1**

0063 **6** 2 ½ **Bhodi (IRE)**[10] 5807 4-8-12 **61**........ HarrisonShaw 5 54
(Kevin Frost) *trckd ldrs: effrt on inner 4f out: rdn along 3f out: sn btn* **20/1**

3354 **7** 7 **Archippos**[28] 5179 6-9-8 **71**........ DannyRedmond 6 50
(Michael Herrington) *hld up towards rr: stdy hdwy on outer over 3f out: chsd ldrs wl over 2f out: sn rdn and wknd* **4/1**

2m 19.49s (7.19) **Going Correction** +0.525s/f (Yiel) **7** Ran SP% **118.3**
Speed ratings (Par 103): **92,89,89,87,87 85,79**
CSF £38.84 CT £111.82 TOTE £2.90: £1.90, £4.60; EX 35.50 Trifecta £103.40.
Owner Withernsea Thoroughbred Limited **Bred** Knocktoran Stud **Trained** Musley Bank, N Yorks

FOCUS
Add 18 yards. Another decisive winning favourite on the card. The third has been rated close to his recent form.
T/Plt: £104.60 to a £1 stake. Pool: £65,068.04 - 453.90 winning units. T/Qpdt: £30.80 to a £1 stake. Pool: £4,443.81 - 106.56 winning units. **Joe Rowntree**

6154 NEWBURY (L-H)
Saturday, August 17

OFFICIAL GOING: Soft (5.9)
Wind: moderate against Weather: cloudy periods

6211 ENERGY CHECK H'CAP (DIV I) 1m 2f
1:15 (1:15) (Class 4) (0-85,85) 3-Y-O+
£5,207 (£1,549; £774; £387; £300; £300) **Stalls** Low

Form RPR

-315 **1** **Qarasu (IRE)**[28] 5194 3-9-7 **85**........ JasonWatson 9 100
(Roger Charlton) *trckd ldrs: shkn up to ld 2f out: wandered u.p fr over 1f out: kpt on strly fnl f: rdn out* **9/4[1]**

0204 **2** 4 **Sputnik Planum (USA)**[28] 5174 5-9-13 **84**........(t) PJMcDonald 5 91
(Michael Appleby) *mid-div: hdwy over 3f out: rdn over 2f out: wnt 2nd wl over 1f out: kpt on but nt pce to chal wnr* **7/1[3]**

242 **3** 3 ½ **Caravan Of Hope (IRE)**[15] 5634 3-9-3 **81**........ JamesDoyle 10 81
(Hugo Palmer) *pressed ldr tl outpcd over 2f out: hmpd over 1f out: kpt on again fnl f: wnt 3rd towards fin* **4/1[2]**

53-1 **4** ½ **Murray River (USA)**[196] 567 3-9-5 **83**........(b) RobertHavlin 3 82
(John Gosden) *in last pair: struggling 4f out: no imp tl styd on fnl f: snatched 4th cl home* **4/1[2]**

3606 **5** ½ **Uther Pendragon (IRE)**[10] 5796 4-9-2 **73**........(p) JamieSpencer 4 71
(J S Moore) *hld up towards rr: hdwy over 2f out: rdn int 3rd over 1f out but hanging lft: no ex whn losing 2 pls ins fnl 140yds* **16/1**

2210 **6** nk **Sashenka (GER)**[11] 5779 3-8-11 **75**........ LiamKeniry 6 72
(Sylvester Kirk) *hld up towards rr: hdwy over 3f out: rdn to chse ldrs over 2f out: kpt on same pce* **11/1**

0030 **7** 2 ¼ **Secret Art (IRE)**[64] 3806 9-9-8 **79**........ SilvestreDeSousa 2 72
(Gary Moore) *trckd ldrs: rdn 3f out: hld whn sltly hmpd over 1f out: wknd fnl f* **20/1**

042 **8** hd **Hazm (IRE)**[21] 5451 4-9-10 **81**........ TomMarquand 8 74
(Tim Vaughan) *led: rdn and hdd 2f out: wknd ent fnl f* **14/1**

51-5 **9** 5 **Monoxide**[116] 2022 4-9-12 **83**........ RobHornby 1 66
(Martyn Meade) *mid-div tl outpcd over 2f out: nvr bk on terms: wknd fnl f* **12/1**

2m 12.86s (3.16) **Going Correction** +0.425s/f (Yiel)
WFA 3 from 4yo+ 7lb **9** Ran SP% **116.6**
Speed ratings (Par 105): **104,100,98,97,97 96,95,95,91**
CSF £18.86 CT £60.18 TOTE £3.00: £1.40, £1.90, £1.40; EX 18.30 Trifecta £57.50.
Owner H H Sheikh Mohammed Bin Khalifa Al Thani **Bred** Al Shahania Stud **Trained** Beckhampton, Wilts

FOCUS
The rails at the far bends had been moved in to provide fresh ground. All distances as advertised. There was 12mm of rain the previous day, so soft going, but race day was mainly dry. Jockeys described conditions as 'tacky', 'holding' and 'like glue'. They raced up the middle in the straight. The second has been rated as running as well as ever.

6212 DENFORD STKS (LISTED RACE) (FORMERLY THE WASHINGTON SINGER STAKES) 7f (S)
1:50 (1:51) (Class 1) 2-Y-O **£22,684** (£8,600; £4,304; £2,144; £1,076) **Stalls** Centre

Form RPR

11 **1** **Thunderous (IRE)**[27] 5212 2-9-1 **91**........ FrannyNorton 2 100
(Mark Johnston) *a.p: led over 1f out: sn strly chal: drifted lft ins fnl f: kpt on wl: asserting at fin: rdn out (vet said colt lost its left hind shoe)* **11/8[1]**

2141 **2** 1 **Sesame Birah (IRE)**[11] 5774 2-8-10 **91**........ TomMarquand 3 93
(Richard Hannon) *trckd ldrs: rdn to press wnr jst over 1f out: kpt on ins fnl f tl no ex nring fin* **16/1**

5142 **3** nk **Sun Power (FR)**[21] 5415 2-9-1 **102**........ SilvestreDeSousa 4 97
(Richard Hannon) *racd keenly trcking ldrs: rdn in cl 3rd jst over 1f out: sn hung lft: kpt on but nt quite pce to chal ins fnl f (jockey said colt hung left-handed)* **15/8[2]**

1 **4** 2 ¼ **Pyledriver**[35] 4925 2-9-1 **0**........ MartinDwyer 5 91
(William Muir) *hld up bhd ldrs: pushed along over 3f out: hdwy 2f out: sn rdn: drifted lft and one pce fnl f* **7/1**

021 **5** 8 **Frankel's Storm**[4] 6035 2-8-10 **0**........ PJMcDonald 6 66
(Mark Johnston) *led: rdn and hdd over 1f out: wknd ent fnl f* **6/1[3]**

1m 30.07s (3.07) **Going Correction** +0.425s/f (Yiel) **5** Ran SP% **109.6**
Speed ratings (Par 102): **99,97,97,94,85**
CSF £20.91 TOTE £2.10: £1.30, £5.00; EX 19.00 Trifecta £41.10.
Owner Highclere T'Bred Racing - George Stubbs **Bred** Rabbah Bloodstock Limited **Trained** Middleham Moor, N Yorks

FOCUS
In the absence of Juan Elcano, who was set to be a short-priced favourite, this form is probably best viewed through the runner-up, with the third too keen and hanging, so it looks ordinary for the grade. They raced up the middle. It's been rated as par for the grade, with the second just above her French Listed form.

6213 UNIBET GEOFFREY FREER STKS (GROUP 3) 1m 5f 61y
2:25 (2:25) (Class 1) 3-Y-O+ **£34,026** (£12,900; £6,456; £3,216; £1,614) **Stalls** Low

Form RPR

2516 **1** **Technician (IRE)**[16] 5585 3-8-10 **103**........ RobHornby 2 113
(Martyn Meade) *trckd ldrs: pushed along to hold pce over 5f out: hdwy 2f out: rdn jst outside fnl f: styd on wl to ld towards fin* **10/1**

1040 **2** ¾ **Morando (FR)**[21] 5414 6-9-8 **113**........ SilvestreDeSousa 4 115
(Andrew Balding) *trckd ldrs: pushed along over 3f out: led wl over 2f out: drifted rt u.p ent fnl f: styd on but no ex whn hdd towards fin* **11/8[1]**

4112 **3** 6 **Durston**[17] 5541 3-8-10 **94**........ JamieSpencer 1 103
(David Simcock) *hld up 5th wl in tch: tk clsr order over 3f out: wnt 2nd briefly jst ins 2f out: edgd lft: sn rdn and hld: no ex fnl f* **3/1[2]**

1411 **4** 6 **Sextant**[22] 5370 4-9-5 **103**........ RyanMoore 5 94
(Sir Michael Stoute) *slowly away: sn trcking ldrs: disp 2nd over 6f out: rdn and ev ch briefly over 2f out: hld whn taking a false step over 1f out: wknd fnl f* **4/1[3]**

2011 **5** 33 **Sameem (IRE)**[29] 5121 3-8-10 **96**........ PJMcDonald 3 45
(James Tate) *led: rdn and hdd wl over 2f out: sn wknd (trainer could offer no explanation for the colt's performance)* **13/2**

2m 55.7s (1.30) **Going Correction** +0.425s/f (Yiel)
WFA 3 from 4yo+ 9lb **5** Ran SP% **109.5**
Speed ratings (Par 113): **113,112,108,105,84**
CSF £24.24 TOTE £12.30: £3.30, £1.40; EX 27.70 Trifecta £74.30.
Owner Team Valor 1 **Bred** Barronstown Stud **Trained** Manton, Wilts

FOCUS
An improved display from the winner, even with the runner-up probably below his peak. The action was middle to near side in the closing stages. The second has been rated to his best outside of his Chester win.

6214 UNIBET H'CAP 7f (S)
3:00 (3:00) (Class 3) (0-95,95) 3-Y-O+
£12,450 (£3,728; £1,864; £932; £466; £234) **Stalls** Centre

Form RPR

0305 **1** **Pattie**[7] 5944 5-9-4 **86**........ GeraldMosse 6 95
(Mick Channon) *trckd ldrs: rdn to ld jst over 1f out: drifted lft: r.o wl* **9/2**

5064 **2** hd **Ripp Orf (IRE)**[21] 5413 5-9-10 **92**........(t) JasonWatson 9 100
(David Elsworth) *hld up: hdwy 2f out: rdn for str chal ins fnl f: r.o: jst hld* **4/1[3]**

0505 **3** 1 ¾ **Love Dreams (IRE)**[13] 5708 5-9-13 **95**........(p) FrannyNorton 7 99
(Mark Johnston) *prom: disp ld 2f out: sn rdn: hdd jst over 1f out: kpt on same pce ins fnl f* **9/1**

0521 **4** 1 ¾ **Graphite Storm**[22] 5386 5-9-4 **86**........ AdamKirby 5 85
(Clive Cox) *trckd ldrs: rdn 2f out: nt pce to chal but kpt on ins fnl f to go 4th cl home* **7/2[2]**

20-0 **5** nk **Piece Of History (IRE)**[28] 5173 4-9-10 **92**........ TomMarquand 3 91
(Saeed bin Suroor) *trckd ldr: disp ld 2f out: sn rdn: hdd jst over 1f out: sn no ex: lost 4th cl home* **7/1**

0-52 **6** 1 3/4 **George William**[28] 5188 6-9-11 **93** AndreaAtzeni 2 87
(Ed Walker) *in tch: tk clsr order over 2f out: effrt wl over 1f out: wknd ent fnl f* **3/1**[1]

1400 **7** 18 **Toy Theatre**[109] 2252 5-9-2 **84** SilvestreDeSousa 4 31
(Michael Appleby) *led: rdn and hdd 2f out: sn wknd* **16/1**

1m 28.94s (1.94) **Going Correction** +0.425s/f (Yiel)
WFA 3 from 4yo+ 5lb **7 Ran SP% 113.8**
Speed ratings (Par 107): **105,104,102,100,100 98,77**
CSF £22.49 CT £153.45 TOTE £5.30: £2.70, £2.30; EX 26.90 Trifecta £164.90.
Owner M Channon **Bred** Mike Channon Bloodstock Ltd **Trained** West Ilsley, Berks

FOCUS
The first four were handily weighted on their best so probably okay form. They raced up the middle. Straightforward form, with the winner rated to her turf best and the second to this year's form.

6215 UNIBET HUNGERFORD STKS (GROUP 2) 7f (S)
3:35 (3:37) (Class 1) 3-Y-O+
£56,710 (£21,500; £10,760; £5,360; £2,690; £1,350) **Stalls Centre**

Form RPR

0220 **1** **Glorious Journey**[35] 4923 4-9-6 108 JamesDoyle 1 114
(Charlie Appleby) *trckd ldr: led over 1f out: drifted lft but kpt on wl fnl f: rdn out* **10/3**[2]

000- **2** 1/2 **Librisa Breeze**[280] 9003 7-9-6 105 JoeyHaynes 4 113
(Dean Ivory) *hld up: hdwy over 2f out: rdn over 1f out: pressed wnr jst ins fnl f: kpt on but a being jst hld* **16/1**

1113 **3** 1 **Safe Voyage (IRE)**[28] 5207 6-9-6 113 JasonHart 3 110
(John Quinn) *trckd ldrs: rdn over 2f out: kpt on but nvr gng pce to get on terms fnl f* **5/2**[1]

-041 **4** 3 1/2 **Sir Dancealot (IRE)**[18] 5521 5-9-9 115 GeraldMosse 7 104
(David Elsworth) *hld up: rdn over 2f out: hdwy over 1f out: kpt on same pce fnl f* **9/2**[3]

1122 **5** 2 1/4 **Hey Gaman**[18] 5521 4-9-6 113 PJMcDonald 8 95
(James Tate) *trckd ldr: rdn 2f out: nt pce to chal: wknd fnl f* **9/2**[3]

6240 **6** 2 1/4 **Donjuan Triumphant (IRE)**[18] 5521 6-9-6 108 SilvestreDeSousa 6 89
(Andrew Balding) *led: drifting rt u.p whn hdd over 1f out: sn wknd (jockey said horse hung right-handed)* **8/1**

01-5 **7** 6 **Flaming Spear (IRE)**[18] 5521 7-9-6 109 MartinDwyer 5 74
(Dean Ivory) *hld up: rdn over 2f out: nvr threatened: wknd over 1f out (jockey said gelding moved poorly)* **10/1**

1m 27.3s (0.30) **Going Correction** +0.425s/f (Yiel)
WFA 3 from 4yo+ 5lb **7 Ran SP% 114.1**
Speed ratings (Par 115): **115,114,113,109,106 104,97**
CSF £51.24 CT £153.41 TOTE £4.20: £2.40, £6.20; EX 59.60 Trifecta £178.60.
Owner HH Sheikha Al Jalila Racing **Bred** Normandie Stud Ltd **Trained** Newmarket, Suffolk

FOCUS
Most of these were below their best for one reason or another but still a smart performance from the winner, who is still developing his game. They raced middle to near side for the most part. The second has been rated as running his best race since his 2017 Champions Sprint win.

6216 FRONTIER BRITISH EBF MAIDEN STKS (PLUS 10 RACE) 1m 4f
4:10 (4:10) (Class 3) 3-Y-O **£9,703** (£2,887; £1,443; £721) **Stalls Low**

Form RPR

3203 **1** **Rhythmic Intent (IRE)**[23] 5341 3-9-5 81 JamesDoyle 5 92
(Stuart Williams) *trckd ldr: led over 2f out: sn rdn clr: styd on wl: comf* **4/1**[3]

5 **2** 4 **Arabist**[92] 2795 3-9-5 0 RobertHavlin 2 86
(John Gosden) *trckd ldr: rdn 3f out: nt pce to get on terms: styd on to go 2nd wl ins fnl f: no ch w wnr* **6/1**

2535 **3** 2 **High Commissioner (IRE)**[15] 5614 3-9-5 84 PJMcDonald 3 82
(Paul Cole) *led: rdn and hdd over 2f out: sn hld by wnr: no ex whn lost 2nd wl ins fnl f* **3/1**[2]

5 **4** 25 **Paintball Wizard (IRE)**[11] 5783 3-9-5 0 ShelleyBirkett 4 42
(Julia Feilden) *s.i.s: last of 5 but in tch tl outpcd over 3f out: wnt modest 4th cl home* **20/1**

2 **5** 1 **Adonijah**[22] 5384 3-9-5 0 JasonWatson 1 41
(Henry Candy) *trckd ldrs: rdn over 2f out: wknd wl over 1f out: lost modest 4th cl home (trainer said colt may have been unsuited by the going and would prefer a faster surface)* **1/1**[1]

2m 40.7s (2.70) **Going Correction** +0.425s/f (Yiel) **5 Ran SP% 114.0**
Speed ratings (Par 104): **108,105,104,87,86**
CSF £26.81 TOTE £4.90: £1.80, £2.80; EX 24.30 Trifecta £59.10.
Owner Happy Valley Racing & Breeding Limited **Bred** Fermoir Ltd **Trained** Newmarket, Suffolk

FOCUS
The favourite flopped, the third was below form and the second is still a work in progress, but nevertheless the winner is pretty useful. They stayed far side in the straight. The level is a bit fluid.

6217 ENERGY CHECK H'CAP (DIV II) 1m 2f
4:45 (4:45) (Class 4) (0-85,84) 3-Y-O+
£5,207 (£1,549; £774; £387; £300; £300) **Stalls Low**

Form RPR

0000 **1** **Torcello (IRE)**[10] 5811 5-8-11 **74** ElishaWhittington(7) 8 82
(Shaun Lycett) *led tl rdn over 2f out: rallied to regain ld jst ins fnl f: kpt on gamely: rdn out (trainer said, regarding the improved form shown, the gelding had benefitted from getting an easy lead on the soft ground)* **25/1**

6431 **2** 3/4 **Ritchie Valens (IRE)**[11] 5779 3-9-3 **80** AndreaAtzeni 5 86
(Richard Hannon) *s.i.s: in last pair: hdwy over 2f out: sn rdn: kpt on ins fnl f: wnt 2nd fnl 120yds: a being hld by wnr* **4/1**[3]

1316 **3** hd **Ocala**[17] 5545 4-9-9 **84** WilliamCarver(5) 2 89
(Andrew Balding) *s.i.s: mid-div: hdwy over 3f out: travelling wl enough whn nt clr run over 2f out: rdn and hdwy over 1f out: cl 3rd ent fnl f: kpt on* **7/2**[2]

4622 **4** 1 3/4 **Zzoro (IRE)**[16] 5594 6-9-8 **78** JasonWatson 3 80
(Amanda Perrett) *trckd ldrs: led over 2f out: sn rdn: hdd jst ins fnl f: kpt on same pce* **11/2**

4152 **5** 1 **Pour Me A Drink**[63] 3859 3-9-2 **79** AdamKirby 9 84+
(Clive Cox) *racd keenly in midfield: nt clr run 4f out and again whn rdn over 2f out: nt pce to qckn whn gap appeared over 1f out: hmpd again ent fnl f: no ch after (jockey said gelding was denied a clear run; vet said gelding was struck into on its left fore)* **5/2**[1]

3630 **6** 3 **C Note (IRE)**[14] 5667 6-9-10 **80** (bt) PJMcDonald 7 74
(Heather Main) *prom: rdn over 2f out: wknd jst over 1f out* **12/1**

3030 **7** 19 **Jackpot Royale**[1] 6155 4-9-13 **83** (p) GeraldMosse 4 39
(Michael Appleby) *a towards rr* **12/1**

0333 **8** 14 **Power Of States (IRE)**[14] 5694 3-9-1 **78** JamesDoyle 1 7
(Hugo Palmer) *little slowly away: sn trcking ldrs: chal 3f out: sn rdn: wknd wl over 1f out (jockey said colt stopped quickly)* **7/1**

2m 11.1s (1.40) **Going Correction** +0.425s/f (Yiel)
WFA 3 from 4yo+ 7lb **8 Ran SP% 117.9**
Speed ratings (Par 105): **111,110,110,108,108 105,90,79**
CSF £125.83 CT £450.73 TOTE £39.50: £7.80, £1.70, £1.50; EX 208.90 Trifecta £1618.70.
Owner Dan Gilbert **Bred** Rathasker Stud **Trained** Leafield, Oxon

FOCUS
A fair handicap, leg two. They stayed far side in the straight. The form looks sound rated around the second and third.

6218 RACING TV H'CAP (FOR LADY AMATEUR RIDERS) 1m 4f
5:20 (5:20) (Class 4) (0-80,79) 3-Y-O+
£5,552 (£1,722; £860; £430; £300; £300) **Stalls Low**

Form RPR

1116 **1** **Gas Monkey**[21] 5436 4-10-1 **78** (h) MissSarahBowen(5) 8 88
(Julia Feilden) *travelled wl virtually thrght: trckd ldrs: led over 2f out: in command fnl f: pushed out* **5/2**[1]

-565 **2** 1/2 **Landa Beach (IRE)**[78] 3295 3-9-4 **78** (p[1]) MissClaudiaMetaireau(7) 5 86
(Andrew Balding) *hld up last: pushed along over 2f out: gd hdwy over 1f out: wnt 2nd ins fnl f: kpt on and clsng on wnr at fin but a being hld* **6/1**[3]

1006 **3** 3 1/2 **Restive (IRE)**[17] 5555 6-9-5 **63** (t) MissSerenaBrotherton 1 64
(Michael Appleby) *racd keenly: trckd ldrs: rdn to chse wnr over 1f out tl jst ins fnl f: kpt on same pce* **10/1**

241 **4** nk **Nabhan**[19] 4543 7-9-9 **72** (tp) MissJessicaLlewellyn(5) 2 72
(Bernard Llewellyn) *hld up: pushed along and stdy prog fr 3f out: chal for 3rd ins fnl f: kpt on same pce* **8/1**

610 **5** 1 3/4 **Rake's Progress**[52] 4241 5-10-4 **76** MissBrodieHampson 7 73
(Heather Main) *hld up in tch: rdn and hdwy over 2f out: sn chalng for 3rd: hung lft over 1f out: fdd ins fnl f* **9/2**[2]

0611 **6** 2 1/2 **Breathable**[12] 5728 4-10-3 **75** MissEmilyEasterby 3 67
(Tim Easterby) *prom: rdn 3f out: wknd over 1f out* **9/2**[2]

/0-0 **7** 5 **Sea Sovereign (IRE)**[24] 5320 6-9-9 **67** MissBeckySmith 6 49
(Ian Williams) *led tl rdn over 2f out: sn wknd* **8/1**

1443 **8** 20 **Cry Wolf**[108] 2278 6-10-4 **79** MissHannahWelch(3) 4 21
(Alexandra Dunn) *trckd ldrs tl rdn over 3f out: sn btn* **10/1**

2m 41.12s (3.12) **Going Correction** +0.425s/f (Yiel)
WFA 3 from 4yo+ 9lb **8 Ran SP% 119.6**
Speed ratings (Par 105): **106,105,103,103,101 100,96,83**
CSF £18.92 CT £131.58 TOTE £3.30: £1.40, £2.10, £3.10; EX 17.90 Trifecta £203.80.
Owner Newmarket Equine Tours Racing Club **Bred** Julia Feilden **Trained** Exning, Suffolk

FOCUS
The main action was up the middle in the closing stages. The third has been rated close to form.
T/Plt: £415.40 to a £1 stake. Pool: £97,274.84 - 170.91 winning units. T/Qpdt: £171.90 to a £1 stake. Pool: £7,322.74 - 31.52 winning units. **Tim Mitchell**

6161 NEWMARKET (R-H)
Saturday, August 17

OFFICIAL GOING: Good (good to soft in places; 7.2)
Wind: medium, across Weather: fine

6219 32RED BRITISH EBF NOVICE STKS (PLUS 10 RACE) 6f
2:10 (2:10) (Class 4) 2-Y-O **£5,175** (£1,540; £769; £384) **Stalls Low**

Form RPR

63 **1** **Powertrain (IRE)**[19] 5501 2-9-5 0 JackMitchell 2 88
(Hugo Palmer) *trckd ldrs on stands' rail: nt clr run: swtchd lft and squeezed through over 1f out: sn pressing ldr: styd on gamely u.p to ld last strides* **7/2**[2]

2 hd **Premier Power** 2-9-5 0 DavidEgan 4 87+
(Roger Varian) *t.k.h: w ldr tl led after 1f out: rdn over 1f out: kpt on under mainly hands and heels riding ins fnl f: grad worn down fnl 100yds: hdd last strides* **1/1**[1]

033 **3** 6 **Colonel Whitehead (IRE)**[9] 5859 2-9-5 71 LukeMorris 7 69
(Heather Main) *chsd ldrs: clsd to press ldrs 4f out: effrt 3f out: chsd ldr briefly over 1f out: 3rd and outpcd 1f out: wknd ins fnl f* **14/1**

4 1/2 **More Than A Prince** 2-9-5 0 PatDobbs 8 68
(Richard Hannon) *stdd s: hld up in tch: shkn up 2f out: no imp over 1f out: wl hld and plugged on same pce ins fnl f* **17/2**

5 1/2 **Rondo (USA)** 2-9-5 0 KieranShoemark 6 66
(Charles Hills) *stdd s: hld up in tch in rr: effrt ent fnl 2f: swtchd lft over 1f out: no imp: wl hld and plugged on same pce ins fnl f* **12/1**

4 **6** 2 1/2 **Robert Guiscard (IRE)**[9] 5865 2-9-5 0 HarryBentley 5 60
(Mark Johnston) *led for 1f: pressed ldr: jst getting outpcd and lost 2nd whn squeezed for room and hmpd over 1f out: wknd ins fnl f* **6/1**[3]

00 **7** 6 **Wizardry (FR)**[15] 5624 2-9-5 0 GeorgeWood 1 41
(George Scott) *dwlt: hld up in tch in rr: effrt ent fnl 2f: sn struggling and outpcd over 1f out: wknd ins fnl f* **66/1**

1m 12.22s (0.12) **Going Correction** -0.075s/f (Good) **7 Ran SP% 112.9**
Speed ratings (Par 96): **96,95,87,87,86 83,75**
CSF £7.17 TOTE £4.70: £2.00, £1.20; EX 8.20 Trifecta £42.50.
Owner Isa Salman **Bred** Coolmore **Trained** Newmarket, Suffolk

FOCUS
Far side course. Stalls: all races stands' side. The going was given as good, good to soft in places (GoingStick 7.2). The re-positioning of the bend into the home straight increased the distance of the 1m4f & 1m6f races by 17yds. The first two pulled well clear and look useful sorts.

6220 UNIBET GREY HORSE H'CAP 6f
2:45 (2:45) (Class 4) (0-85,86) 3-Y-O+
£13,196 (£3,927; £1,962; £981; £300; £300) **Stalls Low**

Form RPR

0523 **1** **Case Key**[10] 5799 6-8-5 **66** (b) JimmyQuinn 4 75
(Michael Appleby) *mde all: rdn over 1f out: kpt on gamely u.p ins fnl f* **16/1**

3431 **2** 1 1/4 **Chatham House**[11] 5773 3-9-7 **85** SeanLevey 10 90
(Richard Hannon) *in tch in midfield: effrt 2f out: hdwy u.p 1f out: chse wnr ins fnl f: no imp towards fin* **5/1**[1]

4553 **3** 1/2 **My Style (IRE)**[19] 5494 3-8-2 **72** ow1 GeorgiaDobie(7) 16 76+
(Eve Johnson Houghton) *in tch in midfield: edgd out lft and effrt ent fnl 2f: hdwy 1f out: kpt on wl to go 3rd towards fin: nvr getting to wnr* **16/1**

2232 **4** 1/2 **Lethal Angel**[12] 5750 4-8-9 **70** (p) HarryBentley 6 72
(Stuart Williams) *chsd ldrs: effrt over 1f out: drvn to chse wnr ent fnl f: kpt on same pce and no imp: lost 2 pls ins fnl f* **7/1**[2]

6060 **5** *hd* **Buccaneers Vault (IRE)**[18] 5515 7-8-7 **68**.................... LukeMorris 3 69
(Paul Midgley) *short of room sn after s: in tch in midfield: rdn 3f out: hrd drvn over 1f out: kpt on ins fnl f* **16/1**

3330 **6** *nse* **Lucky Beggar (IRE)**[7] 5972 9-8-6 **67**.................... GeorgeWood 13 68
(David C Griffiths) *taken down early: chsd wnr: effrt over 1f out: lost 2nd ent fnl f: kpt on same pce u.p ins fnl f* **16/1**

2521 **7** *nk* **Zumurud (IRE)**[31] 5040 4-9-9 **84**.................... DavidProbert 15 84
(Rebecca Bastiman) *in tch in midfield: clsd to chse ldrs 3f out: effrt 2f out: drvn 1f out: kpt on same pce and no imp ins fnl f* **10/1**

1260 **8** *1* **Came From The Dark (IRE)**[7] 5951 3-9-4 **82**....... RichardKingscote 11 79
(Ed Walker) *hld up in tch towards rr: effrt over 1f out: drvn ent fnl f: kpt on but nvr threatening ldrs: nt clrest of runs and eased towards fin* **5/1**[1]

1143 **9** *nse* **Glenn Coco**[28] 5195 5-9-3 **85**....................(t) MarcoGhiani[(7)] 8 82
(Stuart Williams) *wl in tch in midfield: effrt over 1f out: kpt on u.p ins fnl f: nvr trbld ldrs* **7/1**[2]

1645 **10** *1* **Global Tango (IRE)**[14] 5649 4-9-5 **85**....................(b) CierenFallon[(5)] 14 78
(Luke McJannet) *t.k.h: chsd ldrs early: settled bk and wl in tch in midfield: hdwy to chse ldrs over 1f out: hung bdly lft 1f out: no prog fnl f (jockey said gelding hung left-handed under pressure)* **16/1**

0062 **11** *1 1/4* **Harbour Vision**[14] 5688 4-8-10 **71**....................(v) PaddyMathers 12 60
(Derek Shaw) *taken down early: hld up wl in tch towards rr: effrt ent fnl 2f: drvn over 1f out: nvr trbld ldrs* **16/1**

5356 **12** *hd* **Le Manege Enchante (IRE)**[8] 5892 6-7-11 **61** oh15(v) NoelGarbutt[(3)] 1 50
(Derek Shaw) *stdd s: hld up in tch in rr: effrt ent fnl 2f: nvr trbld ldrs* **66/1**

400 **13** *nk* **Aim Power (IRE)**[35] 4922 3-9-8 **86**.................... PatDobbs 9 74
(Richard Hannon) *chsd ldrs: rdn ent fnl 2f: sn struggling and lost pl over 1f out: wknd ins fnl f* **14/1**

6500 **14** *hd* **Bengali Boys (IRE)**[51] 4303 4-8-12 **73**....................(b[1]) GeorgeDowning 7 60
(Tony Carroll) *hld up in tch towards rr: effrt over 2f out: no imp u.p and wknd ins fnl f* **25/1**

2140 **15** *1 1/2* **Revolutionise (IRE)**[21] 5442 3-8-13 **77**....................(p[1]) DavidEgan 5 59
(Roger Varian) *t.k.h: wl in tch in midfield: effrt over 2f out: lost pl u.p over 1f out: wknd ins fnl f* **9/1**[3]

5410 **16** *1 1/2* **Stewardess (IRE)**[22] 5392 4-8-8 **72**.................... SeanDavis[(3)] 2 50
(Richard Fahey) *hld up wl in tch towards rr: effrt over 2f out: edgd lft and no hdwy over 1f out: bhd ins fnl f* **25/1**

1m 11.17s (-0.93) **Going Correction** -0.075s/f (Good) **16 Ran SP% 128.6**
WFA 3 from 4yo+ 3lb
Speed ratings (Par 105): **103,101,100,100,99 99,99,97,97,96 94,94,94,93,91 89**
CSF £97.54 CT £1408.77 TOTE £19.30: £4.20, £1.90, £4.00, £1.60; EX 181.90 Trifecta £2924.60.
Owner Terry Pryke **Bred** Lady Cobham **Trained** Oakham, Rutland

FOCUS
A wide open handicap but the winner, who was competing in this race for the third time, made all to repeat his success two years ago. The winner has been rated close to his 2018 form.

6221 UNIBET FILLIES' NURSERY H'CAP — 7f

3:20 (3:20) (Class 2) 2-Y-O

£11,644 (£3,465; £1,731; £865) **Stalls Low**

Form RPR

4341 **1** **Lady Red Moon**[8] 5885 2-8-3 **71**.................... StefanoCherchi[(7)] 2 74
(Marco Botti) *racd in nr side quartet: hld up in tch in rr: effrt ent fnl 2f: styd on wl ins fnl f to ld last strides* **12/1**

423 **2** *nk* **Imperial Gloriana (IRE)**[22] 5387 2-9-2 **77**.................... HarryBentley 4 80
(David O'Meara) *racd in nr side quartet: hld up in tch: effrt ent fnl 2f: swtchd rt over 1f out: kpt on u.p to chse ldr ins fnl f: clsd to ld towards fin: hdd last strides* **3/1**[2]

221 **3** *1* **Mild Illusion (IRE)**[12] 5745 2-8-12 **73**.................... LukeMorris 1 73
(Jonathan Portman) *racd in nr side quartet: overall ldr: effrt and hung lft over 1f out: edgd bk rt u.p but kpt on ins fnl f: hdd and lost 2 pls towards fin (jockey said filly hung left-handed under pressure)* **11/2**

2461 **4** *1 1/2* **Miss Villanelle**[11] 5777 2-9-3 **78**.................... KieranShoemark 7 74+
(Charles Hills) *restless in stalls: dwlt: racd in centre quartet: led gp after 1f and chsd ldr overall: effrt ent fnl 2f: drvn and stl pressing ldr over 1f out: no ex and outpcd wl ins fnl f (jockey said filly was slowly away)* **6/1**

1165 **5** *1* **Go Well Spicy (IRE)**[14] 5683 2-9-1 **76**.................... DavidEgan 3 69
(Mick Channon) *racd in nr side quartet: stdd to rr sn after s: hdwy 1/2-way: effrt ent fnl 2f: unable qck 1f out: kpt on same pce ins fnl f* **5/1**[3]

0612 **6** *3/4* **Constanzia**[8] 5885 2-8-5 **66**.................... JimmyQuinn 5 57+
(Jamie Osborne) *racd in centre quartet: chsd ldrs overall: effrt over 1f out: no ex u.p 1f out: wknd wl ins fnl f* **33/1**

5226 **7** *3 1/4* **Blausee (IRE)**[28] 5189 2-8-6 **70**.................... SeanDavis[(3)] 6 53+
(Philip McBride) *racd in centre quartet: hld up wl in tch: effrt wl over 2f out: unable qck and btn over 1f out: wknd ins fnl f* **16/1**

1041 **8** *1 3/4* **Graceful Magic**[14] 5683 2-9-7 **82**.................... CharlesBishop 8 60+
(Eve Johnson Houghton) *racd in centre quartet: in tch: effrt ent fnl 2f: unable qck over 1f out: wknd ins fnl f (trainer said filly was unsuited by the ground and would prefer a quicker surface)* **5/2**[1]

1m 25.38s (-0.32) **Going Correction** -0.075s/f (Good) **8 Ran SP% 116.4**
Speed ratings (Par 97): **98,97,96,94,93 92,89,87**
CSF £48.98 CT £226.85 TOTE £11.30: £2.70, £1.40, £2.00; EX 47.40 Trifecta £302.60.
Owner Giulio Spozio & Partner **Bred** Mrs C E Cone **Trained** Newmarket, Suffolk

FOCUS
They went a good gallop and the stands' rail proved an advantage. The winner has been rated up slightly on her Chelmsford win.

6222 UNIBET H'CAP — 6f

3:55 (3:55) (Class 2) (0-105,102) 3-Y-O

£28,012 (£8,388; £4,194; £2,097; £1,048; £526) **Stalls Low**

Form RPR

2163 **1** **Dazzling Dan (IRE)**[37] 4847 3-9-4 **99**.................... DavidProbert 7 107
(Pam Sly) *w ldr: rdn to ld ent fnl f: r.o wl and holding chalr towards fin* **10/3**[2]

1264 **2** *1/2* **Oxted**[14] 5658 3-9-2 **102**.................... CierenFallon[(5)] 2 108+
(Roger Teal) *t.k.h: chsd ldrs: n.m.r and shuffled bk to midfield over 1f out: hdwy to chse wnr ins fnl f: pressing wnr but hld towards fin (jockey said gelding ran too freely early in the race)* **6/1**[3]

4203 **3** *1 3/4* **Woven**[7] 5932 3-8-12 **93**.................... StevieDonohoe 8 94
(David Simcock) *stdd and dropped in bhd after s: hld up in tch in rr: clsd and nt clrest of runs over 1f out: hdwy ins fnl f: r.o to go 3rd last strides* **16/1**

4161 **4** *nk* **Aplomb (IRE)**[6] 5983 3-8-13 **94** 6ex.................... RichardKingscote 3 94
(William Haggas) *chsd ldrs: effrt over 1f out: no ex u.p ins fnl f: outpcd towards fin* **7/4**[1]

0-01 **5** *hd* **Lihou**[101] 2525 3-8-2 **83**.................... DavidEgan 4 82
(David Evans) *led: rdn over 1f out: hdd ent fnl f: edgd lft and no ex ins fnl f: outpcd towards fin* **16/1**

2140 **6** *1 3/4* **Tinto**[14] 5661 3-8-1 **87**.................... DarraghKeenan[(5)] 1 81
(Amanda Perrett) *hld up wl in tch in midfield: nt clr run over 1f out: swtchd lft 1f out: stl n.m.r: squeezed for room ins fnl f: no imp after (jockey said gelding was denied a clear run)* **16/1**

3014 **7** *3/4* **Kinks**[7] 5932 3-8-13 **94**.................... CharlesBishop 6 85
(Mick Channon) *chsd ldrs: effrt over 1f out: no ex u.p 1f out: wknd ins fnl f* **7/1**

1410 **8** *1 1/4* **Gabrial The Wire**[37] 4847 3-8-7 **91**.................... SeanDavis[(3)] 9 78
(Richard Fahey) *hld up in tch towards rr: effrt 2f out: no imp u.p over 1f out: wknd ins fnl f* **16/1**

-050 **9** *13* **Dave Dexter**[63] 3865 3-9-0 **95**.................... HarryBentley 5 41
(Ralph Beckett) *t.k.h: hld up in tch: lost pl u.p and btn over 1f out: wknd fnl f* **12/1**

1m 10.68s (-1.42) **Going Correction** -0.075s/f (Good) **9 Ran SP% 117.4**
Speed ratings (Par 106): **106,105,103,102,102 100,99,97,80**
CSF £24.22 CT £283.33 TOTE £4.20: £1.40, £2.00, £4.50; EX 26.20 Trifecta £274.30.
Owner Thorney Racing Partners **Bred** Peter & Hugh McCutcheon **Trained** Thorney, Cambs

FOCUS
The early pace wasn't strong and it was an advantage to be handy. The stands' rail once again proved an advantage. A length pb from the winner, with the third rated close to his latest.

6223 TBA SUPPORTING BRITISH BREEDERS FILLIES' H'CAP — 1m 6f

4:30 (4:32) (Class 2) (0-105,94) 3-Y-O+

£24,900 (£7,456; £3,728; £1,864; £932; £468) **Stalls Low**

Form RPR

3663 **1** **I'll Have Another (IRE)**[12] 5735 3-9-6 **94**.................... CYHo 1 102
(Mark Johnston) *led for over 1f: chsd ldr: effrt and ev ch over 1f out: drvn to ld ins fnl f: hld on wl towards fin* **6/1**

0411 **2** *nk* **Oydis**[21] 5452 3-9-1 **89**.................... HarryBentley 2 96
(Ralph Beckett) *chsd wnr tl led after over 1f: rdn ent fnl 2f: edgd lft u.p and hdd ins fnl f: kpt on u.p but hld towards fin* **7/4**[1]

1651 **3** *5* **Jedhi**[29] 5133 4-9-3 **86**.................... CierenFallon[(5)] 4 86
(Hughie Morrison) *hld up in 5th: clsd to chse ldrs 3f out: sn rdn: no ex u.p 1f out: wknd ins fnl f* **3/1**[2]

251 **4** *9* **Lady Of Shalott**[49] 4391 4-10-0 **92**....................(h) StevieDonohoe 6 79
(David Simcock) *hld up in rr: effrt over 3f out: sn struggling and outpcd: no ch w ldrs fnl 2f: plugged on to pass btn rivals ins fnl f* **11/2**[3]

4236 **5** *3 1/4* **Vampish**[14] 5682 4-8-10 **74**.................... DavidProbert 3 56
(Philip McBride) *chsd ldrs: effrt over 2f out: outpcd and btn over 1f out: wknd fnl f* **14/1**

1514 **6** *3 1/4* **Moment Of Hope (IRE)**[17] 5545 3-7-13 **76**.................... SeanDavis[(3)] 5 54
(David Simcock) *stdd s: hld up in 4th: clsd to chse ldrs 3f out: rdn over 2f out: sn struggling and btn over 1f out: wknd fnl f* **7/1**

2m 56.39s (-3.51) **Going Correction** -0.075s/f (Good) **6 Ran SP% 110.2**
WFA 3 from 4yo 10lb
Speed ratings (Par 96): **107,106,103,98,96 95**
CSF £16.36 TOTE £7.30: £2.60, £1.40; EX 22.50 Trifecta £97.10.
Owner Paul & Clare Rooney **Bred** Manister House Stud **Trained** Middleham Moor, N Yorks

FOCUS
Add 17yds. Few got into this, the two up front having it between them. The second confirmed the merit of her Salisbury win.

6224 32RED H'CAP — 1m 4f

5:05 (5:08) (Class 4) (0-80,82) 3-Y-O+

£5,822 (£1,732; £865; £432; £300; £300) **Stalls Low**

Form RPR

0432 **1** **Oh It's Saucepot**[19] 5502 5-9-11 **77**.................... JackMitchell 5 86
(Chris Wall) *t.k.h: led for 2f: chsd ldr tl 8f out: styd handy: effrt to chal over 1f out: rdn to ld 1f out: doing little in front but forged ahd 100yds out: styd on* **3/1**[2]

2524 **2** *1 1/4* **Australis (IRE)**[21] 5452 3-9-0 **75**....................(b[1]) DavidEgan 8 82
(Roger Varian) *t.k.h early: pressed ldr tl chsd ldr 8f out: reminder 4f out: drvn 3f out: kpt on same pce u.p fnl f* **3/1**[2]

12-6 **3** *nk* **Cubswin (IRE)**[19] 1291 5-9-12 **78**.................... JimmyQuinn 3 84
(Neil King) *s.i.s and swtchd lft sn after s: hdwy to ld after 2f: rdn over 2f out: hdd 1f out: kpt on same pce ins fnl f* **10/1**

0626 **4** *4* **Jawshan (USA)**[16] 5571 4-9-0 **66**....................(p) PaddyMathers 9 65
(Ian Williams) *hld up wl in tch in last pair: effrt over 2f out: no imp over 1f out: wl hld and plugged on same pce fnl f* **33/1**

6222 **5** *nk* **Holy Kingdom (IRE)**[70] 3604 3-9-7 **82**.................... LukeMorris 6 81
(Tom Clover) *t.k.h early: hld up in tch in midfield: effrt over 2f out: unable qck u.p over 1f out: wl hld and plugged on same pce fnl f* **11/4**[1]

1605 **6** *20* **Winged Spur (IRE)**[24] 5305 4-9-13 **79**.................... HarryBentley 4 46
(Mark Johnston) *in tch in midfield: pushed along over 2f out: sn outpcd: wl btn over 1f out: eased ins fnl f (trainer's rep could offer no explanation for the filly's performance)* **12/1**

500 **7** *6* **Great Hall**[56] 4118 9-9-9 **80**.................... DarraghKeenan[(5)] 2 37
(Mick Quinn) *taken down early: hld up in rr: effrt 4f out: sn struggling and wl btn fnl 2f (jockey said gelding was never travelling)* **25/1**

1010 **R** **Buckland Boy (IRE)**[28] 5179 4-9-6 **72**.................... StevieDonohoe 1
(Charlie Fellowes) *ref to r* **6/1**[3]

2m 33.08s (-0.82) **Going Correction** -0.075s/f (Good) **8 Ran SP% 114.5**
WFA 3 from 4yo+ 9lb
Speed ratings (Par 105): **99,98,97,95,95 81,77,**
CSF £12.50 CT £77.50 TOTE £3.80: £1.30, £1.50, £1.80; EX 13.60 Trifecta £175.10.
Owner The Eight Of Diamonds **Bred** Mrs C J Walker **Trained** Newmarket, Suffolk

FOCUS
Add 17yds. The first three pulled clear and once again the stands' rail proved an advantage. The second has been rated to form.

6225 32RED CASINO H'CAP — 7f

5:35 (5:37) (Class 4) (0-85,87) 3-Y-O

£5,822 (£1,732; £865; £432; £300; £300) **Stalls Low**

Form RPR

211 **1** **Mutamaasik**[14] 5650 3-9-9 **87**.................... DaneO'Neill 5 102+
(Roger Varian) *led and crossed to r against stands' rail: hdd after over 1f: chsd ldr: rdn 2f out: led over 1f out: clr and styd on strly ins fnl f: comf* **6/4**[1]

3334 **2** *2 3/4* **Nubough (IRE)**[12] 5724 3-9-2 **83**.................... SeanDavis[(3)] 7 87
(Iain Jardine) *hdwy to ld after over 1f out: rdn and hdd over 1f out: nt match pce of wnr but kpt on to hold 2nd ins fnl f* **7/1**

0606 **3** *3/4* **Fintas**[14] 5666 3-9-8 **86**....................(t) HarryBentley 8 88
(David O'Meara) *t.k.h: hld up in tch in last pair: effrt 2f out: edgd rt and drvn 1f out: no ch w wnr but kpt on to go 3rd wl ins fnl f* **5/2**[2]

312 **4** *1* **Fashionesque (IRE)**[23] 5357 3-8-6 **70**.............................. LukeMorris 2 69
(Rae Guest) *t.k.h early: trckd ldrs: swtchd lft and effrt 2f out: no imp u.p 1f out: wl hld and one pce ins fnl f* **9/1**

2105 **5** *3 ¾* **After John**[11] 5773 3-9-4 **82**.............................. CallumShepherd 1 71
(Mick Channon) *hld up in tch in rr: effrt ent fnl 2f: drvn and no hdwy over 1f out: wl hld ins fnl f* **4/1**[3]

00-6 **6** *15* **Isle Of Innisfree (USA)**[14] 5649 3-9-6 **84**.....................(t[1]) SeanLevey 4 33
(Paul D'Arcy) *taken down early: t.k.h: chsd ldrs: rdn over 2f out: lost pl over 1f out: bhd ins fnl f* **25/1**

1m 24.59s (-1.11) **Going Correction** -0.075s/f (Good) **6** Ran SP% **114.9**
Speed ratings (Par 102): **103,99,99,97,93 76**
CSF £13.23 CT £24.79 TOTE £2.10: £1.40, £3.20; EX 11.10 Trifecta £40.40.
Owner Hamdan Al Maktoum **Bred** Shadwell Estate Company Limited **Trained** Newmarket, Suffolk

FOCUS
The early pace was controlled and that favoured the two up front. The form makes sense rated around the second and third.
T/Plt: £65.10 to a £1 stake. Pool: £70,428.22 - 789.26 winning units T/Qpdt: £24.40 to a £1 stake. Pool: £4,626.95 - 139.97 winning units **Steve Payne**

5787 RIPON (R-H)
Saturday, August 17

OFFICIAL GOING: Soft (6.8)
Wind: Moderate, across in straight of over 4f Weather: Fine

6226 FOLLOW @WILLHILLRACING ON TWITTER NOVICE AUCTION STKS (PLUS 10 RACE) 1m
1:30 (1:30) (Class 4) 2-Y-O **£4,528** (£1,347; £673; £336) **Stalls** Low

Form RPR

421 **1** **King's Caper**[42] 4623 2-9-5 87.............................. JoeFanning 4 85
(Mark Johnston) *mde all: rdn over 2f out: styd on to draw clr ins fnl f: eased cl home* **4/6**[1]

2 *3 ¼* **Manzo Duro (IRE)** 2-9-4 0.............................. DavidNolan 1 73+
(David O'Meara) *dwlt: midfield: rdn 3f out: hdwy over 2f out: angled out over 1f out: styd on ins fnl f: tk 2nd fnl 60yds: nt trble wnr* **4/1**[2]

034 **3** *1 ¼* **Harswell Approach (IRE)**[15] 5615 2-8-10 68.............................. SamJames 7 62
(Liam Bailey) *chsd wnr: rdn over 2f out: unable qck over 1f out: sn hung rt whn no ch: no ex and lost 2nd fnl 60yds* **16/1**

4 *nk* **Arch Moon** 2-9-2 0.............................. PaulMulrennan 9 67
(Michael Dods) *dwlt: hld up on inner: rdn over 2f out: sn plld off rail and hdwy: kpt on ins fnl f: nt pce to chal* **10/1**

0 **5** *nk* **Phantom Bride (IRE)**[16] 5588 2-8-13 0.............................. CliffordLee 2 64
(K R Burke) *chsd ldrs: drvn over 2f out: nt pce of front two over 1f out: swtchd lft ins fnl f: no ex towards fin* **5/1**[3]

55 **6** *14* **Bye Bye Euro (IRE)**[25] 5273 2-8-5 0.............................. JamesSullivan 8 25
(Keith Dalgleish) *midfield: swtchd lft over 3f out: sn rdn: wknd 2f out* **16/1**

7 *1 ¼* **Ventura Destiny (FR)** 2-8-9 0.............................. ShaneGray 6 26
(Keith Dalgleish) *in rr: niggled along over 5f out: sme hdwy u.p over 3f out: no imp on ldrs: wknd ent fnl 2f* **25/1**

00 **8** *8* **Two Sox**[14] 5655 2-8-12 0.............................. DavidAllan 5 12
(Tim Easterby) *hld up: rdn over 3f out: lft bhd over 2f out* **16/1**

6 **9** *1* **Swift Arion (IRE)**[61] 3919 2-8-12 0.............................. BarryMcHugh 3 9
(John Quinn) *trckd ldrs: rdn over 3f out: sn outpcd: wknd 2f out* **66/1**

1m 46.14s (5.14) **Going Correction** +0.65s/f (Yiel) **9** Ran SP% **128.7**
Speed ratings (Par 96): **98,94,93,93,92 78,77,69,68**
CSF £4.42 TOTE £1.50: £1.10, £2.10, £3.60; EX 5.40 Trifecta £35.40.
Owner Kingsley Park 13 **Bred** Highclere Stud **Trained** Middleham Moor, N Yorks

FOCUS
After riding in the opener Jimmy Sullivan said: "The ground is soft," Joe Fanning said: "It's very testing" and Barry McHugh said: "It's hard work." There wasn't a great deal of depth to this novice event, which provided easy pickings for the favourite. It was run over an additional 4yds. The third helps set the level.

6227 WILLIAM HILL SILVER TROPHY H'CAP (CONSOLATION RACE FOR THE WILLIAM HILL GREAT ST WILFRID STKS) 6f
2:05 (2:06) (Class 2) 3-Y-O+
£12,450 (£3,728; £1,864; £932; £466; £234) **Stalls** High

Form RPR

2000 **1** **Growl**[14] 5664 7-9-9 **89**.............................. TonyHamilton 18 100
(Richard Fahey) *racd in nrside gp: a.p: led gp ent fnl 2f: possibly led overall 1f out: r.o wl and wnt clr of nrside rivals: 1st of 7 in gp* **9/1**[2]

0000 **2** *nk* **Hyperfocus (IRE)**[14] 5664 5-9-9 **89**.....................(p) DavidAllan 8 99
(Tim Easterby) *led far side gp narrowly and possibly overall: kicked on and rdn over 1f out: sn edgd rt: possibly hdd overall 1f out: r.o u.p ins fnl f but hld towards fin: 1st of 12 in gp* **9/1**[2]

4433 **3** *2 ¾* **Mark's Choice (IRE)**[23] 5335 3-8-13 **82**.............................. SamJames 11 83
(Ruth Carr) *racd far side: chsd ldrs: rdn over 2f out: kpt on to chse gp ldr ins fnl f but no real imp: 2nd of 12 in gp* **12/1**

21-0 **4** *1 ¼* **Airglow (IRE)**[14] 5670 4-9-0 **80**.....................(h) NathanEvans 20 77
(Michael Easterby) *racd in nrside gp: led gp: rdn 1/2-way: hdd in gp ent fnl 2f: kpt on ins fnl f: nt pce of ldrs: 2nd of 7 in gp* **33/1**

3603 **5** *½* **Lucky Lucky Man (IRE)**[14] 5670 4-8-9 **78**.............. ConnorMurtagh(3) 16 74
(Richard Fahey) *racd in nrside gp: chsd ldrs: rdn 1/2-way: hung rt over 1f out: styd on same pce ins fnl f: 3rd of 7 in gp* **14/1**

0004 **6** *nk* **Royal Brave (IRE)**[15] 5617 8-9-4 **84**.............................. RoystonFfrench 17 79
(Rebecca Bastiman) *racd in nr side gp: in rr: rdn over 2f out: hdwy ins fnl f: kpt on: nvr able to chal: 4th of 7 in gp* **33/1**

4100 **7** *1 ¼* **Whataguy**[16] 5589 3-8-7 **79**.....................(p) MeganNicholls(3) 1 70
(Paul Nicholls) *racd far side: midfield: plld out and hdwy over 2f out: chsd ldrs u.p over 1f out: styd on same pce fnl 100yds: nt pce to chal: 3rd of 12 in gp* **25/1**

1003 **8** *hd* **Dalton**[12] 5740 5-9-5 **85**.............................. GrahamLee 14 75
(Julie Camacho) *racd in nrside gp: chsd ldrs: rdn over 2f out: unable qck over 1f out: no ex ins fnl f: 5th of 7 in gp* **10/1**[3]

4100 **9** *hd* **Bossipop**[12] 5740 6-9-4 **84**.....................(b) CamHardie 7 73
(Tim Easterby) *racd far side: w ldr: rdn and ev ch over 2f out: unable qck over 1f out: lost pl ins fnl f: no ex fnl 150yds: 4th of 12 in gp* **33/1**

1106 **10** *1* **Tomily (IRE)**[8] 5888 5-9-7 **87**.............................. DavidNolan 13 73
(David O'Meara) *racd far side: in rr: rdn over 2f out: hdwy over 1f out: styd on ins fnl f: nt trble ldrs: 5th of 12 in gp* **22/1**

10-2 **11** *¾* **Alaadel**[65] 3770 6-9-9 **89**.....................(t) ConnorBeasley 4 73
(Stuart Williams) *s.i.s: racd far side: bhd: swtchd lft over 2f out: hdwy over 1f out: styd on ins fnl f: no further prog nr fin: 6th of 12 in gp (jockey said gelding was never travelling)* **7/1**[1]

4050 **12** *½* **Flying Pursuit**[14] 5692 6-9-9 **89**.....................(p) RachelRichardson 5 71
(Tim Easterby) *racd far side: in tch: drvn over 2f out: kpt on same pce ins fnl f: 7th of 12 in gp* **7/1**[1]

5500 **13** *nk* **Brian The Snail (IRE)**[14] 5661 5-9-7 **87**.............................. JosephineGordon 2 68
(Richard Fahey) *racd far side: in rr: outpcd over 2f out: swtchd lft ins fnl f: kpt on: nvr able to trble ldrs: 8th of 12 in gp* **12/1**

0103 **14** *3 ¼* **Orion's Bow**[8] 5901 8-8-11 **77**.....................(tp) PhilDennis 6 48
(Tim Easterby) *racd far side: chsd ldrs: rdn over 2f out: unable qck over 1f out: wknd ins fnl f: 9th of 12 in gp* **33/1**

4404 **15** *hd* **Shepherd's Purse**[7] 5972 7-8-0 **63** oh3.............................. JamesSullivan 10 36
(Ruth Carr) *racd far side: midfield: rdn over 2f out: wknd over 1f out: 10th of 12 in gp* **33/1**

616 **16** *2 ¼* **Tawny Port**[15] 5628 5-9-6 **86**.............................. ShaneGray 15 49
(Stuart Williams) *racd nrside: in rr: rdn and outpcd 1/2-way: nvr a threat: 6th of 7 in gp* **16/1**

6101 **17** *1 ¼* **Royal Prospect (IRE)**[27] 5217 4-9-8 **88**.............................. PaulMulrennan 12 47
(Julie Camacho) *racd far side: midfield: rdn over 2f out: wknd over 1f out: 11th of 12 in gp* **11/1**

2055 **18** *½* **Yousini**[29] 5120 3-9-8 **91**.............................. TomEaves 19 48
(Kevin Ryan) *racd nrside: prom: rdn over 2f out: wknd over 1f out: 7th of 7 in gp* **14/1**

0305 **19** *6* **Paddy Power (IRE)**[14] 5661 6-9-0 **80**.............................. JoeFanning 9 18
(Richard Fahey) *racd far side: hld up: rdn over 2f out: wl btn over 1f out: 12th of 12 in gp* **11/1**

1m 15.5s (3.00) **Going Correction** +0.60s/f (Yiel)
WFA 3 from 4yo+ 3lb **19** Ran SP% **128.3**
Speed ratings (Par 109): **104,103,99,98,97 97,95,95,95,93 92,92,91,87,87 84,82,81,73**
CSF £83.85 CT £1002.48 TOTE £9.80: £2.40, £3.20, £3.30, £10.30; EX 142.20 Trifecta £916.60.
Owner Dr Marwan Koukash **Bred** Kincorth Investments Inc **Trained** Musley Bank, N Yorks

FOCUS
There didn't appear any sort of draw bias in this very competitive event. They split into two groups and it was the smaller bunch of seven which produced the winner, with the runner-up racing on the other flank. The first two finished clear. The second has been rated back to his June C&D form on softish ground.

6228 WILLIAM HILL RIPON HORNBLOWER CONDITIONS STKS (PLUS 10 RACE) 6f
2:40 (2:41) (Class 2) 2-Y-O **£9,337** (£2,796; £1,398; £699; £349) **Stalls** High

Form RPR

1 **1** **Ventura Lightning (FR)**[22] 5388 2-9-2 0.............................. TonyHamilton 3 73+
(Richard Fahey) *prom: effrt and lugged rt fr ent fnl 2f: led narrowly jst over 1f out: pressed by rival tl edgd lft and asserted towards fin* **6/5**[1]

3110 **2** *1 ¾* **Eton College (IRE)**[15] 5612 2-9-5 87.............................. JoeFanning 4 73
(Mark Johnston) *led: rdn over 1f out: sn hdd narrowly: continued to chal ins fnl f: checked sltly whn hld towards fin: no ex* **5/4**[2]

506 **3** *1 ¼* **Wots The Wifi Code**[35] 4937 2-9-2 57.............................. BarryMcHugh 2 64
(Tony Coyle) *hld up: effrt over 2f out: chsd ldrs over 1f out: kpt on ins fnl f: nvr able to chal* **20/1**

4 *6* **Borsdane Wood** 2-8-11 0.............................. CliffordLee 5 41
(K R Burke) *chsd ldrs: rdn over 2f out: outpcd over 1f out: wl hld after* **11/2**[3]

0600 **5** *½* **Tiltilys Rock (IRE)**[11] 5764 2-9-2 47.............................. AndrewElliott 1 45
(Andrew Crook) *prom tl rdn and wknd over 1f out* **66/1**

1m 15.8s (3.30) **Going Correction** +0.60s/f (Yiel) **5** Ran SP% **111.5**
Speed ratings (Par 100): **102,99,98,90,89**
CSF £3.07 TOTE £1.90: £1.10, £1.10; EX 3.00 Trifecta £14.00.
Owner Middleham Park Racing LXXXI & Partner **Bred** Snowdrop Stud Corporation Limited **Trained** Musley Bank, N Yorks

FOCUS
The latest edition of this long-established race had the look of a match, and the market leaders duly contested the finish. The third, fifth and time mean this race can't be rated much higher.

6229 WILLIAM HILL GREAT ST WILFRID H'CAP 6f
3:15 (3:15) (Class 2) 3-Y-O+
£46,687 (£13,980; £6,990; £3,495; £1,747; £877) **Stalls** High

Form RPR

0-51 **1** **Dakota Gold**[21] 5454 5-9-7 **99**.............................. ConnorBeasley 15 113
(Michael Dods) *racd nrside: mde all: rdn over 2f out: hung rt over 1f out: sn kicked clr of gp: r.o wl and in command ins fnl f: 1st of 7 in gp* **5/1**[1]

534 **2** *2 ¼* **Summerghand (IRE)**[14] 5664 5-9-8 **100**.............................. DanielTudhope 5 107+
(David O'Meara) *racd far side: hld up: rdn and hdwy over 2f out: styd on ins fnl f: led gp fnl 130yds: nt pce of wnr: 1st of 9 in gp* **15/2**

1031 **3** *1 ¾* **Citron Major**[12] 5746 4-8-9 **90**.....................(t[1]) RowanScott(3) 1 91
(Nigel Tinkler) *racd far side: in tch: effrt to chse ldrs over 2f out: ev ch in gp ins fnl f: styd on same pce towards fin: nt pce of front two: 2nd of 9 in gp* **18/1**

4222 **4** *¾* **Muscika**[12] 5740 5-8-11 **92**.....................(v) ConorMcGovern(3) 6 91
(David O'Meara) *racd far side and led gp: rdn over 2f out: nt pce of wnr over 1f out: hdd in gp fnl 130yds: no ex towards fin: 3rd of 9 in gp* **14/1**

0130 **5** *1 ¼* **Staxton**[21] 5454 4-9-7 **99**.....................(p) DuranFentiman 20 94
(Tim Easterby) *racd nrside: chsd ldrs: rdn 1/2-way: wnt 2nd in gp over 1f out: kpt on ins fnl f but nt pce to trble wnr: 2nd of 7 in gp* **18/1**

651 **6** *2 ¼* **Lahore (USA)**[12] 5740 5-9-1 **93**.............................. PaulMulrennan 19 81
(Phillip Makin) *racd nrside: chsd wnr tl unable qck over 1f out: styd on same pce ins fnl f: 3rd of 7 in gp* **7/1**[3]

2630 **7** *¾* **Ice Age (IRE)**[19] 5504 6-9-4 **96**.............................. TomEaves 14 81
(Eve Johnson Houghton) *racd nrside: chsd ldrs: rdn 1/2-way: one pce fr over 1f out: no imp after: 4th of 7 in gp* **20/1**

5200 **8** *1 ½* **Lake Volta (IRE)**[14] 5664 4-9-7 **99**.............................. JoeFanning 13 79
(Mark Johnston) *racd nrside: midfield: rdn 1/2-way: outpcd 2f out: wl hld ins fnl f: 5th of 7 in gp* **7/1**[3]

0321 **9** *2* **Poyle Vinnie**[14] 5661 9-8-12 **90**.....................(p) JamesSullivan 8 64
(Ruth Carr) *wnt to post early: racd far side: hld up: hdwy over 2f out: rdn to chse ldrs over 1f out: one pce ins fnl f: 4th of 9 in gp* **25/1**

-046 **10** *hd* **Lancelot Du Lac (ITY)**[7] 5927 9-9-5 **97**.....................(h) RobertWinston 10 70
(Dean Ivory) *wnt to post early: racd far side: chsd ldrs: rdn over 2f out: outpcd over 1f out: n.d after: 5th of 9 in gp* **33/1**

6000 **11** *1 ¼* **George Bowen (IRE)**[14] 5664 7-9-7 **99**.....................(v) TonyHamilton 4 68
(Richard Fahey) *racd far side: midfield: rdn and lost pl over 1f out: n.d after: 6th of 9 in gp* **28/1**

4106 **12** *¾* **Gulliver**[14] 5664 5-9-7 **99**.....................(tp) ShaneGray 18 66
(David O'Meara) *racd nrside: hld up: rdn over 2f out: no imp: 6th of 7 in gp* **28/1**

4240 **13** 1 1/2 **Reputation (IRE)**[21] 5413 6-9-4 **96** .... BarryMcHugh 11 58
(Ruth Carr) *racd in centre of trck: carried rt briefly after 1f: racd alone after: rdn over 2f out: wknd jst over 1f out: eased whn btn fnl 100yds* **18/1**

330 **14** 1 3/4 **Great Prospector (IRE)**[49] 4402 4-8-13 **94** .... MeganNicholls(3) 7 51
(Richard Fahey) *racd far side: hld up: rdn and hdwy over 2f out: nvr able to trble ldrs: wknd over 1f out: 7th of 9 in gp (jockey said gelding was never travelling)* **6/1**[2]

-013 **15** 3/4 **Richenza (FR)**[62] 3891 4-9-4 **96** .... JosephineGordon 9 50
(Ralph Beckett) *racd far side: prom: rdn over 2f out: wknd over 1f out: 8th of 9 in gp* **14/1**

1033 **16** 1 **Belated Breath**[19] 5504 4-8-13 **91** .... CharlieBennett 16 42
(Hughie Morrison) *missed break: racd nrside: hld up: rdn over 2f out: lft bhd over 1f out: 7th of 7 in gp (trainer's rep could offer no explanation for the poor form shown)* **14/1**

4505 **17** 12 **Vintage Brut**[13] 5705 3-9-7 **102** ....(b[1]) DavidAllan 12 15
(Tim Easterby) *wnt to post early: sed in centre of trck: swtchd rt to r in far side gp after 1f: prom: rdn and wknd over 2f out: eased whn wl btn over 1f out: 9th of 9 in gp* **16/1**

1m 14.56s (2.06) **Going Correction** +0.60s/f (Yiel)
WFA 3 from 4yo+ 3lb **17 Ran SP% 127.8**
Speed ratings (Par 109): **110,107,104,103,102 99,98,96,93,93 91,90,88,86,85 83,67**
CSF £39.96 CT £673.19 TOTE £7.40: £2.40, £2.20, £4.10, £2.80; EX 64.70 Trifecta £1267.50.

Owner Doug Graham & Ian Davison **Bred** Redgate Bstock & Peter Bottowley Bstock **Trained** Denton, Co Durham

FOCUS
A winning favourite in this valuable and prestigious handicap, in a time almost a second quicker than the earlier consolation race. Again the winner came out of a seven-strong group on the stands' side, with the runner-up (and the next two home) racing on the far side. Last year's winner Gunmetal was a late absentee. The second has been rated close to form.

6230 BRITISH STALLION STUDS EBF FILLIES' H'CAP 1m 1f 170y
3:50 (3:51) (Class 4) (0-80,80) 3-Y-O+

£6,339 (£1,886; £942; £471; £300; £300) Stalls Low

Form RPR

0221 **1** **Anna Bunina (FR)**[43] 4585 3-9-4 **77** .... JackGarritty 5 85
(Jedd O'Keeffe) *racd keenly: prom: nosed ahd over 3f out: rdn and hdd over 1f out: continued to chal: rallied to regain ld fnl 110yds: kpt on gamely towards fin* **11/4**[1]

525 **2** nk **Lady Alavesa**[5] 6025 4-8-11 **63** .... PhilDennis 6 70
(Michael Herrington) *hld up: hdwy over 2f out: led and hung rt over 1f out: continued to hang rt ins fnl f whn pressed: hdd fnl 110yds: kpt on towards fin but hld* **11/2**

6123 **3** 1 3/4 **Railport Dolly**[20] 5474 4-9-9 **75** ....(h) GrahamLee 4 78
(David Barron) *cl up: effrt to chal 2f out: unable qck over 1f out: styd on same pce ins fnl f* **5/1**

330 **4** nk **Appointed**[6] 5982 5-9-11 **77** ....(t) DavidAllan 3 80
(Tim Easterby) *hld up: rdn over 2f out: kpt on ins fnl f: nvr able to chal* **7/2**[3]

3310 **5** 20 **Quintada**[15] 5614 3-9-7 **80** .... JoeFanning 1 43
(Mark Johnston) *led: hdd over 3f out: wknd qckly over 2f out* **3/1**[2]

0525 **6** 25 **Lola's Theme**[21] 5424 3-8-13 **72** ....(p) PaulMulrennan 2
(Tom Dascombe) *trckd ldrs: drvn 4f out: lost pl over 3f out: sn wknd: t.o* **12/1**

2m 9.36s (4.76) **Going Correction** +0.60s/f (Yiel)
WFA 3 from 4yo+ 7lb **6 Ran SP% 113.6**
Speed ratings (Par 102): **105,104,103,103,87 67**
CSF £18.36 TOTE £3.00: £2.10, £2.60; EX 15.40 Trifecta £54.30.

Owner Highbeck Racing 3 **Bred** Dermot Cantillon **Trained** Middleham Moor, N Yorks

FOCUS
Add 4yds. A fair fillies' handicap. The second has been rated to her turf best, with the third close to form.

6231 VISIT ATTHERACES.COM H'CAP 1m
4:25 (4:27) (Class 3) (0-90,91) 3-Y-O-£9,451 (£2,829; £1,414; £708; £352) Stalls Low

Form RPR

5053 **1** **Hortzadar**[19] 5489 4-10-0 **91** .... DanielTudhope 6 100
(David O'Meara) *chsd ldrs: effrt on outer over 2f out: led over 1f out: kpt on gamely ins fnl f* **2/1**[1]

02 **2** 1/2 **Donncha (IRE)**[12] 5726 8-9-9 **86** .... CamHardie 12 93
(Seb Spencer) *hld up: rdn and hdwy 2f out: styd on to take 2nd wl ins fnl f: clsd on wnr nr fin* **10/1**

5005 **3** 1 1/2 **Garden Oasis**[22] 5398 4-8-12 **75** .... DuranFentiman 11 79
(Tim Easterby) *chsd ldr: rdn and ev ch ent fnl 2f: stl cl up ins fnl f but unable qck: styd on same pce ins fnl 100yds* **16/1**

3520 **4** 1 1/2 **Ayutthaya (IRE)**[19] 5489 4-9-9 **86** .... TomEaves 8 86
(Kevin Ryan) *led: rdn over 2f out: hdd over 1f out: stl wl there ins fnl f: no ex fnl 100yds* **3/1**[2]

2600 **5** 1/2 **Fennaan (IRE)**[14] 5693 4-9-8 **85** .... SamJames 9 84
(Phillip Makin) *missed break: in rr: rdn wl over 1f out and hdwy: kpt on ins fnl f: nvr able to trble ldrs (jockey said gelding hung right-handed)* **11/2**

3000 **6** 1/2 **Hayadh**[14] 5693 6-9-11 **88** .... PhilDennis 7 86
(Rebecca Bastiman) *midfield: rdn 3f out: no imp on ldrs* **11/1**

0140 **7** 8 **Reggae Runner (FR)**[14] 5667 3-9-1 **84** .... JoeFanning 10 62
(Mark Johnston) *trckd ldrs: rdn 3f out: wknd 2f out* **11/1**

0542 **8** 2 1/2 **Storm Ahead (IRE)**[10] 5820 6-9-0 **77** ....(b) DavidAllan 5 51
(Tim Easterby) *in rr: pushed along over 3f out: nvr able to get involved (jockey said gelding became unbalanced on the undulations of the track)* **9/2**[3]

1m 44.44s (3.44) **Going Correction** +0.60s/f (Yiel)
WFA 3 from 4yo+ 6lb **8 Ran SP% 123.5**
Speed ratings (Par 107): **106,105,104,102,102 101,93,91**
CSF £25.87 CT £270.82 TOTE £3.00: £1.20, £2.60, £5.00; EX 25.10 Trifecta £358.80.

Owner Akela Construction Ltd **Bred** The Aston House Stud **Trained** Upper Helmsley, N Yorks

■ Gentle Look was withdrawn. Price at time of withdrawal 5/1. Rule 4 applies to board prices prior to withdrawal - deduction 15p in the pound. New market formed.

FOCUS
Add 4yds. Four non-runners altered the complexion of this event, and it wasn't a strong race for the grade. The winner has been rated back to his early season form.

6232 WILLIAM HILL LEADING RACECOURSE BOOKMAKER H'CAP 1m 4f 10y
4:55 (4:58) (Class 5) (0-75,76) 3-Y-O

£4,398 (£1,309; £654; £327; £300; £300) Stalls Centre

Form RPR

3321 **1** **Euro Implosion (IRE)**[8] 5905 3-9-1 **68** .... GrahamLee 5 77+
(Keith Dalgleish) *prom: upsides 4f out: led 3 out: rdn over 2f out: kpt on wl towards fin* **3/1**[1]

1153 **2** 1 1/2 **Potenza (IRE)**[8] 5898 3-8-10 **66** .... GabrieleMalune(3) 4 72
(Stef Keniry) *hld up: rdn over 3f out: hdwy over 2f out: chsd wnr over 1f out: tried to chal ins fnl f: styd on same pce fnl 100yds* **11/2**

2111 **3** 1/2 **Funny Man**[21] 5426 3-9-7 **74** ....(b) DanielTudhope 7 79
(David O'Meara) *hld up: pushed along over 4f out: no imp 3f out: styd on ins fnl f: gng on at fin (jockey said gelding was never travelling)* **4/1**[2]

4554 **4** nk **Cuba Ruba**[8] 5915 3-8-5 **58** ....(p[1]) DuranFentiman 2 63
(Tim Easterby) *prom: rdn over 2f out: unable qck over 1f out: kpt on same pce ins fnl f* **10/1**

0611 **5** 1 1/4 **Five Helmets (IRE)**[41] 4689 3-9-7 **74** ....(p) JamieGormley 6 77
(Iain Jardine) *chsd ldrs: cl up wl over 3f out: sn rdn: outpcd over 1f out: kpt on u.p ins fnl f but unable to chal: one pce towards fin* **6/1**

3115 **6** 11 **Mister Chiang**[9] 5840 3-9-9 **76** ....(b) JoeFanning 1 61
(Mark Johnston) *led: jnd 4f out: pushed along and hdd 3f out: u.p whn checked sltly jst over 2f out: wknd wl over 1f out: eased whn btn ins fnl f* **9/2**[3]

-064 **7** 18 **Philonikia**[28] 5175 3-9-0 **67** ....(p[1]) KevinStott 3 24
(Ralph Beckett) *hld up: drvn and outpcd over 3f out: lft bhd 2f out: eased whn wl btn over 1f out (jockey said filly was never travelling)* **5/1**

2m 43.95s (7.65) **Going Correction** +0.60s/f (Yiel) **7 Ran SP% 118.6**
Speed ratings (Par 100): **98,97,96,96,95 88,76**
CSF £20.96 TOTE £3.60: £1.80, £4.70; EX 22.50 Trifecta £143.40.
Owner J S Morrison **Bred** Aaron Boland **Trained** Carluke, S Lanarks

FOCUS
Add 4yds. A decent little handicap, but the first five finished in a bit of a heap. The time was over 12sec slower than standard. Muddling form, but the second has been credited with a small pb, and the third as running close to form.
T/Jkpt: £441.60 to a £1 stake. Pool: £14,084.51 - 22.64 winning units T/Plt: £24.50 to a £1 stake. Pool: £88,157.91 - 2,624.65 winning units T/Qpdt: £5.80 to a £1 stake. Pool: £6,074.70 - 773.08 winning units **Darren Owen**

6233 - 6234a (Foreign Racing) - See Raceform Interactive

3817
CORK (R-H)
Saturday, August 17

OFFICIAL GOING: Straight course - good; round course - yielding to soft (yielding in places)

6235a MATCHBOOK STRAIGHT SEVEN PLATINUM STKS (LISTED RACE) 7f
2:35 (2:38) 3-Y-O+

£25,247 (£8,130; £3,851; £1,711; £855; £427)

RPR

1 **Flight Risk (IRE)**[28] 5207 8-10-0 109 .... KevinManning 7 112+
(J S Bolger, Ire) *w.w in rr: prog nr side 2f out: rdn to ld over 1f out and styd on wl to assert ins fnl f: comf* **13/8**[1]

2 2 1/2 **Black Magic Woman (IRE)**[16] 5598 3-8-13 95 .... RonanWhelan 6 93
(Jack W Davison, Ire) *on toes befhand: hld up in tch: swtchd rt 2f out and tk clsr order: effrt far side over 1f out: sn rdn in 2nd and no imp on wnr ins fnl f: kpt on wl* **4/1**[2]

3 3/4 **Chocolate Music (IRE)**[16] 5598 3-8-13 92 .... ShaneFoley 1 91
(Mrs John Harrington, Ire) *chsd ldrs: drvn bhd ldrs over 2f out: no imp on wnr u.p in 3rd ins fnl f: kpt on wl* **5/1**[3]

4 2 3/4 **Rhydwyn (IRE)**[32] 5032 3-9-4 87 ....(t[1]) ColinKeane 8 89
(T Hogan, Ire) *sn led narrowly tl jnd briefly fr 1/2-way: regained advantage under 2f out and rdn: hdd u.p over 1f out and sn no ex in 4th* **14/1**

5 1/2 **Drombeg Dream (IRE)**[64] 3828 4-9-4 99 .... WayneLordan 5 84
(Augustine Leahy, Ire) *chsd ldrs: pushed along bhd ldrs over 2f out and hmpd sltly 1 1/2f out: sn rdn in 6th and flashed tail over 1f out: kpt on one pce into 5th nr fin: nvr trbld ldrs* **12/1**

6 1/2 **Manjeer (IRE)**[32] 5032 3-9-4 92 .... RossCoakley 9 86
(John M Oxx, Ire) *wnt sltly lft s: cl up: disp ld fr 1/2-way tl pushed along over 2f out and sn hdd u.p: wknd over 1f out* **10/1**

7 3 **Opening Verse (IRE)**[10] 5833 3-9-4 82 .... KillianLeonard 2 78
(John Joseph Murphy, Ire) *w.w towards rr: drvn over 2f out and no imp u.p over 1f out: one pce after and eased nr fin* **16/1**

8 2 3/4 **Marshall Jennings (IRE)**[18] 5535 7-9-9 100 .... TomMadden 3 72
(Mrs John Harrington, Ire) *chsd ldrs: drvn bhd ldrs over 2f out and wknd over 2f out: eased nr fin* **8/1**

1m 23.12s
WFA 3 from 4yo+ 5lb **8 Ran SP% 115.2**
CSF £8.15 TOTE £2.00: £1.02, £1.60, £1.80; DF 10.60 Trifecta £31.20.
Owner Mrs J S Bolger **Bred** James F Hanly **Trained** Coolcullen, Co Carlow

FOCUS
An excellent display from a rock solid performer in Listed and Group company, albeit he held an edge over these rivals on ratings.

6236a-6238a (Foreign Racing) - See Raceform Interactive

6239a IRISH STALLION FARMS EBF GIVE THANKS STKS (GROUP 3) (F&M) 1m 4f
4:55 (4:55) 3-Y-O+ £39,864 (£12,837; £6,081; £2,702; £1,351; £675)

RPR

1 **Tarnawa (IRE)**[78] 3316 3-9-3 102 .... ChrisHayes 6 111+
(D K Weld, Ire) *hld up towards rr: tk clsr order in 4th fr 1/2-way: travelling wl bhd ldrs over 2f out: led 1 1/2f out and rdn clr ent fnl f: styd on strly: comf* **7/2**[3]

2 2 1/2 **Simply Beautiful (IRE)**[23] 5364 3-9-0 95 .... DonnachaO'Brien 4 104
(A P O'Brien, Ire) *chsd ldrs in 4th early: 5th fr 1/2-way: tk clsr order gng wl 3f out: swtchd rt over 2f out: sn rdn into 2nd over 1f out: no imp on wnr ins fnl f: kpt on same pce: jst hld 2nd (jockey said filly hung slightly)* **5/2**[1]

The Form Book Flat 2019, Raceform Ltd, Newbury, RG14 5SJ

3 *hd* **Delphinia (IRE)**78 3316 3-9-0 104 .... SeamieHeffernan 3 104+
(A P O'Brien, Ire) *hld up in rr: last at 1/2-way: stl gng wl 3f out: pushed along in 5th 2f out: sn rdn and r.o into nvr threatening 3rd ins fnl f: jst failed for 2nd: nt trble easy wnr* **3/1**2

4 *5 1/2* **Moteo (IRE)**37 4856 4-9-9 99 .... RonanWhelan 5 94
(John M Oxx, Ire) *trckd ldr early: dropped to 3rd after 3f: 3rd at 1/2-way: effrt nr side and led briefly 2f out: sn hdd u.p and no ex in 3rd 1f out: wknd into 4th ins fnl f* **4/1**

5 *3* **Credenza (IRE)**98 2642 3-9-0 93 .... PBBeggy 2 90
(A P O'Brien, Ire) *chsd ldrs in 3rd early tl wnt 2nd after 3f: clsr 2nd bef st: drvn to ld briefly over 2f out where hung sltly tl sn hdd: wknd between horses 1 1/2f out* **14/1**

6 *19* **Invitation (IRE)**15 5638 3-9-0 85 .... (b) WayneLordan 1 60
(A P O'Brien, Ire) *sweated up befhand: broke wl to ld: racd keenly early and sn extended advantage: reduced ld bef st: hdd over 2f out and wknd qckly: eased ins fnl f* **10/1**

2m 41.76s (-6.14)
WFA 3 from 4yo 9lb **6 Ran SP% 111.6**
CSF £12.50 TOTE £5.20: £1.80, £1.70; DF 13.30 Trifecta £57.00.
Owner H H Aga Khan **Bred** His Highness The Aga Khan's Studs S C **Trained** Curragh, Co Kildare

FOCUS
Since 2012, this race has either gone the way of Dermot Weld or Aidan O'Brien and history repeated itself once again. Visually, it seemed that they didn't hang around in front and the winner proved her class. The second has been rated to the best view of her latest form.

6240 - 6247a (Foreign Racing) - See Raceform Interactive

6141

DEAUVILLE (R-H)

Saturday, August 17

OFFICIAL GOING: Polytrack: standard; turf: soft

6248a SHADWELL PRIX DU CALVADOS (GROUP 2) (2YO FILLIES) (STRAIGHT COURSE) (TURF) 7f

1:35 2-Y-O **£66,756** (£25,765; £12,297; £8,198)

RPR

1 **Tropbeau**21 5469 2-8-11 0 .... MickaelBarzalona 4 111
(A Fabre, France) *a cl up on outer: pressed ldr fr 2f out: led ent fnl 1 1/2f: asserted ins fnl f: drvn out: readily* **7/10**1

2 *2 1/2* **Marieta (FR)**35 4947 2-8-11 0 .... TonyPiccone 1 104
(M Delcher Sanchez, France) *racd keenly: hld up in 4th: angled out and forged between horses over 1f out: kpt on but nt pce of wnr* **18/5**3

3 *1 1/4* **Walk In Marrakesh (IRE)**23 5346 2-8-11 0 .... WilliamBuick 2 101
(Mark Johnston) *dwlt sltly: sn led on inner: niggled along 2 1/2f out: hdd ent fnl 1 1/2f: kpt on at one pce* **27/10**2

4 *nk* **Schwesterherz (FR)**20 2-8-11 0 .... AntoineHamelin 3 100
(Henk Grewe, Germany) *pressed ldr early: dropped in bhd front two appr 1/2-way: rdn and nt qckn 1 1/2f out: one pce fnl f* **69/10**

1m 24.1s (-4.20) **4 Ran SP% 120.2**
PARI-MUTUEL (all including 1 euro stake): WIN 1.70; PLACE 1.10, 1.20; SF 4.30.
Owner Lady Bamford **Bred** Lord Margadale **Trained** Chantilly, France

FOCUS
The level is a bit fluid.

6249a SHADWELL PRIX DAPHNIS (GROUP 3) (3YO) (ROUND COURSE) (TURF) 1m (R)

2:50 3-Y-O **£36,036** (£14,414; £10,810; £7,207; £3,603)

RPR

1 **Delaware**20 5480 3-9-0 0 .... VincentCheminaud 7 112+
(A Fabre, France) *led: hdd appr 1/2-way: trckd new ldr: eased to the front 2f out: kicked clr fr 1 1/2f out: in command fnl f: comf* **8/5**1

2 *4* **Dave (FR)**20 5480 3-9-0 0 .... MaximeGuyon 1 102
(Mme Pia Brandt, France) *cl up on inner: 3rd and drvn 1 1/2f out: chsd clr ldr ins fnl f: kpt on to hold 2nd but no match for wnr* **56/10**

3 *1/2* **Paramount (FR)**21 5470 3-8-10 0 .... JulienAuge 6 97
(C Ferland, France) *in rr: hdwy fr 2f out: styd on to chal for pls ins fnl f: nvr nrr* **23/1**

4 *1/2* **Go To Hollywood (FR)**20 5480 3-9-0 0 .... JeromeCabre 3 100
(Y Barberot, France) *w.w in fnl pair: tk clsr order 1 1/2f out: styd on u.p fnl f: nt pce to get on terms* **19/1**

5 *2* **Shendam (FR)**34 3-9-0 0 .... ChristopheSoumillon 4 95
(M Delzangles, France) *racd keenly: trckd ldr: cl 4th and travelling wl 3f out: rdn along to chse eventual wnr over 1 1/2f out: wknd fnl f* **12/5**2

6 *3 1/2* **Icefinger (IRE)**44 3-9-0 0 .... StephanePasquier 5 87
(Gavin Hernon, France) *settled in fnl trio: pushed along fr 3f out: no imp turning for home: wl hld fnl 1 1/2f* **10/1**

7 *5* **Urwald**41 4705 3-9-0 0 .... Pierre-CharlesBoudot 2 76
(A Fabre, France) *plld hrd: heavily restrained in midfield: allowed to go on and led bef 1/2-way: hdd w 2f to run: wknd wl over 1f out* **42/10**3

1m 45.56s (4.76) **7 Ran SP% 120.5**
PARI-MUTUEL (all including 1 euro stake): WIN 2.60; PLACE 1.50, 2.10; SF 8.90.
Owner K Abdullah **Bred** Juddmonte Farms **Trained** Chantilly, France

FOCUS
The second to the fifth set the level.

6250a SHADWELL PRIX DE LA NONETTE (GROUP 2) (3YO FILLIES) (ROUND COURSE) (TURF) 1m 2f

3:25 3-Y-O **£66,756** (£25,765; £12,297; £8,198; £4,099)

RPR

1 **Terebellum (IRE)**65 3762 3-9-0 0 .... MickaelBarzalona 5 111+
(John Gosden) *chsd ldrs: dropped towards rr bef 1/2-way: clsd fr 2 1/2f out: led ins fnl 1 1/2f: drvn clr ent fnl f: comf* **69/10**

2 *1 3/4* **Mutamakina**33 5008 3-9-0 0 .... OlivierPeslier 1 107+
(C Laffon-Parias, France) *racd keenly: hld up in midfield on inner: shuffled bk w 3f to run: n.m.r 2 1/2f out or again w 2f to run: angled out over 1f out: styd on fnl f: tk 2nd cl home: n.d to wnr* **68/10**

3 *1/2* **Cartiem (FR)**21 5470 3-9-0 0 .... CristianDemuro 4 106
(J-C Rouget, France) *racd keenly: squeezed out of midfield after 1 1/2f: hld up towards rr: shkn up and angled out w 2f to run: styd on u.p fnl f: nrest at fin* **22/1**

4 *1 1/4* **Suphala (FR)**49 4416 3-9-0 0 .... Pierre-CharlesBoudot 6 104
(A Fabre, France) *chsd ldrs on outer: cl 2nd w 3f to run: shkn up to ld 2f out: hdd ins fnl 1 1/2f: no ex* **19/5**2

5 *1/2* **Platane**62 3905 3-9-0 0 .... MaximeGuyon 2 103
(C Laffon-Parias, France) *led: hdd after 1f: remained cl up on inner: 3rd and shkn up 2 1/2f fr home: sltly impeded 2f out: sn rdn and no further imp: grad lft bhd ins fnl f* **10/1**

6 *2 1/2* **Etoile (FR)**62 3905 3-9-0 0 .... ChristopheSoumillon 8 98
(J-C Rouget, France) *w.w in fnl pair: moved into midfield on outer bef 1/2-way: short-lived effrt 1 1/2f fr home: sn rdn and btn* **8/5**1

7 *3 1/2* **Divine Image (USA)**140 1443 3-9-0 0 .... WilliamBuick 7 91
(Charlie Appleby) *cl up: led after 1f: drvn for home 2 1/2f out: hdd 2f fr home: sn wknd* **48/10**3

8 *15* **Phoceene (FR)**33 5008 3-9-0 0 .... StephanePasquier 3 61
(F Rossi, France) *sltly outpcd early: in rr: last and drvn 3f out: lost tch ins fnl 2f: eased fnl f* **26/1**

2m 10.49s (0.29) **8 Ran SP% 119.2**
PARI-MUTUEL (all including 1 euro stake): WIN 7.90; PLACE 3.20, 2.30, 4.50; DF 20.10.
Owner HRH Princess Haya Of Jordan **Bred** Alan O'Flynn **Trained** Newmarket, Suffolk

FOCUS
The first three have been rated as improving.

6251a CRITERIUM DU FONDS EUROPEEN DE L'ELEVAGE (LISTED RACE) (2YO) (ROUND COURSE) (TURF) 1m (R)

4:00 2-Y-O **£54,954** (£21,981; £16,486; £10,990; £5,495)

RPR

1 **Helter Skelter (FR)**34 4961 2-9-0 0 .... ChristopheSoumillon 5 103+
(J-C Rouget, France) **9/10**1

2 *3 1/2* **Saqqara King (USA)**34 4961 2-9-0 0 .... (p) WilliamBuick 2 95
(Charlie Appleby) *chsd ldr on outer: virtually upsides fr 3f out: led 2f fr home: drvn over 1 1/2f out: sn rdn and hdd ent fnl f: no ex* **39/10**2

3 *snk* **Shared Belief (IRE)**35 4920 2-9-0 0 .... HollieDoyle 1 95
(Archie Watson) *led: pushed along and hdd 2f out: rallied u.p 1 1/2f out: kpt on gamely fnl f* **54/10**3

4 *3 1/2* **Chill Chainnigh (FR)**9 2-9-0 0 .... Pierre-CharlesBoudot 4 87
(Y Barberot, France) **11/2**

5 *3/4* **Patzefredo (FR)**14 2-9-0 0 .... FranckBlondel 3 86
(F Rossi, France) **13/1**

6 *20* **Assier**12 5759 2-9-0 0 .... MaximeGuyon 6 42
(Simone Brogi, France) **11/1**

1m 46.22s (5.42) **6 Ran SP% 119.5**
PARI-MUTUEL (all including 1 euro stake): WIN 1.90; PLACE 1.40, 2.00; SF 4.40.
Owner Ecuries Serge Stempniak **Bred** L Jamault **Trained** Pau, France

6252a PRIX ETALON TASLEET (CONDITIONS) (3YO) (STRAIGHT COURSE) (TURF) 6f

4:35 3-Y-O

£15,765 (£5,990; £4,414; £2,522; £1,261; £945)

RPR

1 **Trois Mille (FR)**23 3-8-13 0 .... StephanePasquier 2 108
(S Cerulis, France) **67/10**

2 *1 1/2* **Milord's Song (FR)**41 4703 3-8-13 0 .... (p) TheoBachelot 3 104
(S Wattel, France) **19/10**1

3 *1/2* **Nashirah**26 3-8-9 0 .... MickaelBarzalona 1 98
(H-A Pantall, France) *w.w in rr: shkn up to cl wl over 1 1/2f out: chsd ldrs into fnl f: kpt on but run flattened out fnl 75yds* **23/5**

4 *1 1/4* **True Mason**14 5664 3-8-13 0 .... (b1) TonyPiccone 5 98
(K R Burke) *rowed along fr stalls: sn led: clr bef 1/2-way: drvn and edgd lft fr 1 1/2f out: on stands' rail whn hdd last 125yds: no ex* **43/10**3

5 *4* **Axcelerator (IRE)** 3-8-13 0 .... JulienAuge 4 85
(C Ferland, France) **11/1**

6 *2 1/2* **Cigalera (FR)**59 3-8-9 0 .... VincentCheminaud 7 73
(M Delcher Sanchez, France) **15/1**

7 *10* **Wind Test**22 3-8-13 0 .... (b) CristianDemuro 6 45
(Andrea Marcialis, France) **39/10**2

1m 9.77s (-1.23) **7 Ran SP% 119.2**
PARI-MUTUEL (all including 1 euro stake): WIN 7.70; PLACE 2.80, 1.70; SF 29.90.
Owner Stephan Hoffmeister **Bred** P Boudengen **Trained** France

6253 - (Foreign Racing) - See Raceform Interactive

5814

PONTEFRACT (L-H)

Sunday, August 18

OFFICIAL GOING: Good (good to soft in places)
Wind: Light across Weather: Cloury with sunny periods

6254 TREVOR WOODS MEMORIAL BRITISH EBF NOVICE STKS (PLUS 10 RACE) 5f 3y

2:00 (2:04) (Class 4) 2-Y-O **£4,528** (£1,347; £673; £336) **Stalls** Low

Form RPR

2 1 **Queen's Order**21 5472 2-8-11 0 .... DanielTudhope 3 76+
(Kevin Ryan) *mde all: pushed along over 1f out: rdn and kpt on wl fnl f* **2/7**1

53 2 *2* **Arriba Arriba (IRE)**46 4509 2-9-2 0 .... GrahamLee 4 71
(Rebecca Menzies) *chsd wnr: rdn along wl over 1f out: drvn and kpt on fnl f* **10/1**3

3 *nk* **Lady Nectar (IRE)** 2-8-11 0 .... FrannyNorton 2 65
(Ann Duffield) *chsd ldng pair: hdwy 2f out: sn rdn: drvn and kpt on same pce fnl f* **33/1**

4 *5* **Moon Power** 2-8-11 0 .... SilvestreDeSousa 5 47
(K R Burke) *dwlt: green and t.k.h early: in tch: hdwy over 2f out: sn rdn along and no imp* **3/1**2

0 5 *6* **Serious Jockin**12 5775 2-9-2 0 .... BenCurtis 6 30
(Mick Channon) *in rr: outpcd and pushed along wl over 2f out: sn rdn: n.d* **12/1**

05 6 *3/4* **Maurice Dancer**15 5689 2-9-2 0 .... PaulMulrennan 7 28
(Julie Camacho) *chsd ldrs: rdn along wl over 2f out: sn wknd* **20/1**

05 7 *27* **Last Date**26 5280 2-9-2 0 .... DougieCostello 8
(Ivan Furtado) *dwlt: a in rr: outpcd and bhd whn eased fnl f* **66/1**

1m 3.29s (-0.61) **Going Correction** +0.025s/f (Good) **7 Ran SP% 128.7**
Speed ratings (Par 96): **105,101,101,93,83 82,39**
CSF £6.26 TOTE £1.20: £1.10, £3.20; EX 6.80 Trifecta £67.10.
Owner Clipper Logistics **Bred** Aspire Bloodstock **Trained** Hambleton, N Yorks
■ Gypsy Traveller was withdrawn. Price at time of withdrawal 33/1. Rule 4 does not apply

FOCUS
There was 14mm of rain on Friday giving 20.5 mm in total throughout the week, but race day was mainly dry and breezy, with sunny spells. In an uncompetitive novice, the first three filled those spots throughout, with the winner making all - she's quite useful.

6255 PAUL CRAGG 50TH BIRTHDAY H'CAP — 1m 4f 5y
2:30 (2:32) (Class 3) (0-90,91) 3-Y-O+

£7,470 (£2,236; £1,118; £559; £279; £140) Stalls Low

Form — RPR

6131 **1** **Hereby (IRE)**[14] 5706 3-8-7 75 .... HarryBentley 1 — 83
(Ralph Beckett) *trckd ldr: cl up 3f out: slt ld 2f out: rdn over 1f out: strly chal and drvn ins fnl f: kpt on wl towards fin* **1/1**[1]

6244 **2** ½ **Doctor Cross (IRE)**[13] 5743 5-8-11 73 .... ConnorMurtagh(3) 2 — 80
(Richard Fahey) *trckd ldng pair: hdwy over 2f out: rdn to chal over 1f out: drvn to dispute ld and ev ch ins fnl f tl no ex fnl 75yds* **10/1**

4443 **3** 1¼ **Final**[13] 5739 7-9-6 79 .... FrannyNorton 8 — 84+
(Mark Johnston) *in rr: pushed along over 3f out: hdwy on outer wl over 1f out: sn rdn and styd on strly fnl f* **20/1**

4206 **4** ¾ **Asian Angel (IRE)**[8] 5931 3-9-2 84 .... JoeFanning 7 — 88
(Mark Johnston) *hld up towards rr: hdwy 3f out: rdn along to chse ldrs over 1f out: drvn ins fnl f: kpt on* **5/1**[2]

0060 **5** 1½ **Multellie**[15] 5694 7-9-3 76 .... DavidAllan 6 — 77
(Tim Easterby) *led: rdn along 3f out: hdd 2f out: sn drvn and wknd appr fnl f* **20/1**

0504 **6** 1¼ **Dance King**[15] 5694 9-9-4 77 ....(tp) PaulMulrennan 4 — 76
(Tim Easterby) *trckd ldrs: hdwy 3f out: rdn along 2f out: drvn over 1f out: kpt on one pce* **20/1**

2262 **7** ½ **Jabbaar**[9] 5902 6-10-0 87 .... JamieGormley 3 — 86
(Iain Jardine) *hld up: a towards rr* **11/2**[3]

5662 **8** 7 **Busy Street**[36] 4899 7-9-13 91 .... CierenFallon(5) 9 — 78
(Michael Appleby) *trckd ldrs on outer: hdwy and cl up 3f out: rdn along wl over 1f out: sn btn* **12/1**

2m 39.45s (-1.65) **Going Correction** +0.025s/f (Good)
WFA 3 from 5yo+ 9lb — 8 Ran SP% **113.1**
Speed ratings (Par 107): **106,105,104,104,103 102,102,97**
CSF £11.39 CT £120.78 TOTE £1.80: £1.10, £2.80, £4.20; EX 12.20 Trifecta £113.60.
Owner J H Richmond-Watson **Bred** Lawn Stud **Trained** Kimpton, Hants

FOCUS
A fair handicap.

6256 MOOR TOP FARM SHOP HEMSWORTH H'CAP — 2m 1f 27y
3:00 (3:00) (Class 5) (0-75,76) 3-Y-O+

£3,881 (£1,155; £577; £400; £400; £400) Stalls Low

Form — RPR

0-26 **1** **Forewarning**[20] 5487 5-9-6 65 .... CamHardie 2 — 72
(Julia Brooke) *hld up in rr: hdwy on outer over 2f out: chsd ldrs over 1f out: rdn to chal ent fnl f: styd on wl to ld towards fin* **11/2**[2]

1143 **2** ½ **Champarisi**[56] 4146 4-10-3 76 .... SamJames 3 — 82
(Grant Tuer) *trckd ldr: hdwy to ld 3f out: rdn along wl over 1f out: jnd and drvn ent fnl f: hdd and no ex towards fin* **11/2**[2]

0011 **3** 2¼ **Stormin Norman**[13] 5727 4-9-5 64 .... FrannyNorton 5 — 68
(Micky Hammond) *trckd ldrs: niggled along bef 1/2-way: pushed along 5f out: rdn along 3f out: kpt on u.p fr over 1f out* **6/5**[1]

0206 **4** ½ **St Andrews (IRE)**[13] 5727 6-8-9 54 ....(v) PhilDennis 1 — 57
(Gillian Boanas) *trckd ldrs: hdwy to chse ldr over 2f out: rdn along wl over 1f out: sn drvn and kpt on same pce* **8/1**[3]

4066 **5** 4½ **Valkenburg**[23] 5391 4-9-5 64 ....(p) JoeFanning 4 — 62
(William Bethell) *prom: cl up 3f out: rdn along 2f out: drvn over 1f out: grad wknd* **10/1**

-563 **6** 10 **Gemini**[16] 5604 4-9-6 65 .... JasonHart 7 — 52
(John Quinn) *hld up towards rr: effrt and sme hdwy on inner over 2f out: sn rdn along and wknd wl over 1f out* **16/1**

6232 **7** 6 **Remember The Days (IRE)**[23] 5391 5-10-0 73 .... GrahamLee 6 — 53
(Jedd O'Keeffe) *led: rdn along and hdd 3f out: sn wknd* **9/1**

3m 49.37s (0.17) **Going Correction** +0.025s/f (Good) — 7 Ran SP% **112.3**
Speed ratings (Par 103): **99,98,97,97,95 90,87**
CSF £33.94 TOTE £6.50: £3.80, £3.00; EX 28.90 Trifecta £98.00.
Owner Ladsdoracing & Partner **Bred** Juddmonte Farms Ltd **Trained** Middleham, N Yorks

FOCUS
A modest staying handicap.

6257 EBF STALLIONS HIGHFIELD FARM FLYING FILLIES' STKS (LISTED RACE) — 6f
3:30 (3:32) (Class 1) 3-Y-O+

£33,612 (£12,798; £6,408; £3,198; £1,602; £804) Stalls Low

Form — RPR

0022 **1** **Perfection**[16] 5608 4-9-2 105 ....(v[1]) SilvestreDeSousa 9 — 106
(David O'Meara) *trckd ldr: cl up 2f out: rdn to take slt ld appr fnl f: drvn out* **5/2**[1]

3212 **2** ½ **Shades Of Blue (IRE)**[37] 4891 3-8-13 105 .... HollieDoyle 8 — 104+
(Clive Cox) *trckd ldrs: hdwy 2f out: sn chsng ldng pair: rdn to chse wnr ins fnl f: sn drvn and no imp towards fin* **11/4**[2]

-013 **3** 1½ **Miss Celestial (IRE)**[14] 5705 3-8-13 97 ....(p) LukeMorris 11 — 100+
(Sir Mark Prescott Bt) *towards rr: hdwy on outer 2f out: rdn over 1f out: styd on wl fnl f* **20/1**

-061 **4** ¾ **Princes Des Sables**[10] 5846 3-8-13 96 .... SamJames 3 — 97
(Kevin Ryan) *led: rdn along and jnd 2f out: drvn and hdd appr fnl f: grad wknd* **11/2**

2413 **5** 1 **Maygold**[19] 5524 4-9-2 86 .... LiamKeniry 10 — 94
(Ed Walker) *awkward s: t.k.h and hld up in rr: hdwy over 2f out: rdn wl over 1f out: kpt on: nrst fin* **40/1**

0166 **6** nk **Yolo Again (IRE)**[14] 5705 3-8-13 89 .... BenCurtis 7 — 93
(Roger Fell) *chsd ldrs: rdn along and hdwy over 2f out: drvn over 1f out: kpt on same pce* **66/1**

2211 **7** 3 **Tapisserie**[53] 4242 3-8-13 100 .... PaulHanagan 4 — 83
(William Haggas) *trckd ldng pair: effrt over 2f out: sn rdn: wknd over 1f out (vet said filly finished slightly lame on its right hind)* **9/2**[3]

10-3 **8** nk **Red Balloons**[37] 4891 3-8-13 95 .... DanielTudhope 6 — 82
(Richard Fahey) *hld up: a towards rr* **12/1**

6014 **9** 2¼ **Sunday Star**[14] 5714 3-8-13 100 .... RichardKingscote 5 — 91+
(Ed Walker) *a in rr (jockey said filly was denied a clear run in the home straight)* **10/1**

31-0 **10** 4½ **Stage Play (IRE)**[16] 5608 3-8-13 97 .... HayleyTurner 1 — 61
(Michael Bell) *in tch on inner: rdn along over 2f out: sn wknd* **33/1**

1m 15.55s (-1.55) **Going Correction** +0.025s/f (Good)
WFA 3 from 4yo 3lb — 10 Ran SP% **117.2**
Speed ratings (Par 108): **111,110,108,107,106 105,101,101,98,92**
CSF £9.27 TOTE £3.40: £1.20, £1.30, £5.00; EX 11.00 Trifecta £104.30.
Owner Cheveley Park Stud **Bred** Cheveley Park Stud Ltd **Trained** Upper Helmsley, N Yorks

FOCUS
A good fillies' Listed race.

6258 WILLIAM HILL LEADING RACECOURSE BOOKMAKER H'CAP — 1m 6y
4:00 (4:01) (Class 3) (0-95,95) 3-Y-O

£7,470 (£2,236; £1,118; £559; £279; £140) Stalls Low

Form — RPR

2146 **1** **Smile A Mile (IRE)**[18] 5564 3-9-0 88 .... JoeFanning 1 — 97
(Mark Johnston) *mde all: rdn along 2f out: styd on strly fnl f (trainer's rep could offer no explanation for geldings improved form)* **9/1**

5310 **2** 2½ **Dalaalaat (IRE)**[17] 5583 3-8-10 89 .... CierenFallon(5) 3 — 92
(William Haggas) *trckd wnr: hdwy over 2f out: rdn wl over 1f out: drvn and no imp fnl f* **11/8**[1]

1110 **3** 1 **Global Gift (FR)**[29] 5192 3-9-2 90 ....(h) BenCurtis 2 — 91
(Ed Dunlop) *trckd ldrs on inner: effrt over 2f out: sn rdn along: drvn and kpt on fnl f* **6/1**[3]

3340 **4** 2 **Amadeus Grey (IRE)**[23] 5394 3-8-6 80 ....(t) DuranFentiman 6 — 76
(Tim Easterby) *hld up in rr: hdwy over 2f out: rdn to chse ldrs over 1f out: sn drvn and no imp* **25/1**

3234 **5** 1¼ **Lightning Attack**[51] 4316 3-8-2 76 oh2 ....(p) PaddyMathers 5 — 69
(Richard Fahey) *a towards rr* **12/1**

21 **6** 2¼ **Global Hunter (IRE)**[22] 5451 3-9-2 95 .... ThomasGreatrex(5) 4 — 83
(Saeed bin Suroor) *trckd ldrs on outer: pushed along over 2f out: sn rdn and btn wl over 1f out (jockey said colt ran too freely; vet said colt had lost its right fore and left hind shoes)* **2/1**[2]

1m 45.19s (-0.71) **Going Correction** +0.025s/f (Good) — 6 Ran SP% **111.3**
Speed ratings (Par 104): **104,101,100,98,97 95**
CSF £21.63 TOTE £8.00: £3.20, £1.30; EX 27.40 Trifecta £86.70.
Owner Sheikh Hamdan bin Mohammed Al Maktoum **Bred** Godolphin **Trained** Middleham Moor, N Yorks

FOCUS
The winner got the run of the race in front.

6259 FOLLOW @WILLHILLRACING ON TWITTER NOVICE STKS — 1m 6y
4:30 (4:30) (Class 4) 3-Y-O+ — £5,207 (£1,549; £774; £387) Stalls Low

Form — RPR

3245 **1** **Storting**[15] 5667 3-9-2 78 .... SilvestreDeSousa 5 — 82+
(Mick Channon) *in tch: gd hdwy on outer 3f out: sn cl up: chal 1 1/2f out: sn led and rdn clr: styd on strly (trainer was informed that the gelding could not run until the day after passing a stalls test)* **7/4**[1]

31 **2** 3¾ **Eva Maria**[15] 5690 3-9-3 0 .... PaulHanagan 7 — 74
(Richard Fahey) *trckd ldng pair: hdwy over 2f out: rdn to ld briefly 1 1/2f out: sn hdd and drvn: kpt on same pce* **15/8**[2]

5/50 **3** 7 **Ningaloo (GER)**[15] 5656 5-9-8 55 .... PhilDennis 4 — 58
(Rebecca Bastiman) *dwlt and in rr: rdn along and hdwy wl over 1f out: sn swtchd rt to outer: kpt on wl fnl f* **100/1**

4 hd **Beethoven's Gal**[219] 190 3-8-11 0 ....(w) TonyHamilton 3 — 52
(Richard Fahey) *chsd ldrs: rdn along over 2f out: drvn over 1f out: plugged on one pce* **20/1**

0 **5** ½ **Cheerful**[16] 5627 3-8-11 0 .... JasonHart 8 — 51
(Philip McBride) *midfield on inner: pushed along 3f out: rdn over 2f out: plugged on: n.d* **100/1**

25 **6** 4 **Gazton**[21] 5477 3-9-2 0 ....(h) DougieCostello 2 — 46
(Ivan Furtado) *chsd ldrs: rdn along over 2f out: sn wknd* **25/1**

24 **7** 1½ **Sorbonne**[18] 5554 3-9-2 0 .... GrahamLee 1 — 43
(David Barron) *in tch: rdn along wl over 2f out: n.d* **16/1**

05- **8** 5 **Poetic Legacy (IRE)**[288] 8833 3-8-11 0 .... DanielTudhope 6 — 27
(Mark Johnston) *slt ld: pushed along over 2f out: sn rdn: hdd 1 1/2f out: sn wknd* **25/1**

60 **9** 1¾ **Inner Charm**[95] 3-8-11 68 ....(h[1]) SamJames 9 — 22
(Kevin Ryan) *a in rr* **50/1**

4- **10** 16 **Reaction Time**[428] 3867 4-9-8 0 .... PatCosgrave 10
(Saeed bin Suroor) *cl up: rdn along over 2f out: sn wknd: bhd and eased fnl f* **3/1**[3]

1m 45.35s (-0.55) **Going Correction** +0.025s/f (Good)
WFA 3 from 4yo+ 6lb — 10 Ran SP% **118.4**
Speed ratings (Par 105): **103,99,92,92,91 87,86,81,79,63**
CSF £5.09 TOTE £2.50: £1.10, £1.20, £12.80; EX 5.00 Trifecta £226.70.
Owner Jon and Julia Aisbitt **Bred** Jon And Julia Aisbitt **Trained** West Ilsley, Berks

FOCUS
Only three serious contenders according to the betting, one of them flopped, and the pace looked overly strong, which suited the winner - but he is useful.

6260 NOVA DISPLAY H'CAP (DIV I) — 6f
5:00 (5:00) (Class 5) (0-75,78) 3-Y-O+

£3,881 (£1,155; £577; £400; £400; £400) Stalls Low

Form — RPR

2251 **1** **Inexes**[18] 5551 7-9-6 71 ....(p) JasonHart 3 — 80+
(Ivan Furtado) *trckd ldrs gng wl: effrt and nt clr run wl over 1f out: hdwy 1f out: rdn and qcknd to ld ins fnl f: kpt on* **7/2**[2]

1644 **2** ½ **Penny Pot Lane**[11] 5821 6-9-0 65 ....(p) PhilDennis 8 — 71
(Richard Whitaker) *trckd ldng pair: hdwy on outer 2f out: rdn to ld 1f out: sn drvn: hdd ins fnl f: kpt on* **5/1**[3]

0133 **3** 1¼ **Magical Effect (IRE)**[11] 5821 7-9-13 78 .... JamieGormley 2 — 80
(Ruth Carr) *led: rdn along 2f out: drvn and hdd 1f out: kpt on same pce* **13/8**[1]

5033 **4** 2½ **Supaulette (IRE)**[5] 6033 4-9-2 67 ....(bt) DavidAllan 6 — 61
(Tim Easterby) *trckd ldrs: pushed along 2f out: rdn over 1f out: kpt on one pce* **7/1**

0564 **5** 1¾ **Tathmeen (IRE)**[114] 2079 4-9-8 73 .... CamHardie 5 — 61
(Antony Brittain) *cl up: rdn along 2f out: drvn over 1f out: grad wknd* **20/1**

6430 **6** 1¾ **Van Gerwen**[73] 3504 6-9-5 70 .... LewisEdmunds 9 — 53
(Les Eyre) *hld up towards rr: hdwy 2f out: rdn over 1f out: no imp fnl f* **14/1**

-500 **7** ¾ **Almurr (IRE)**[15] 5691 3-9-7 75 ....(h[1]) SamJames 1 — 55
(Phillip Makin) *sn outpcd and bhd: hdwy wl over 1f out: sn rdn: kpt on nr fnl f (jockey said gelding was never travelling)* **14/1**

215- **8** 1 1/4 **Crash Helmet**[306] 8301 4-9-2 **67** .... FrannyNorton 4 43
(Micky Hammond) *chsd ldrs: rdn along on inner over 2f out: sn wknd* **14/1**

1m 17.04s (-0.06) **Going Correction** +0.025s/f (Good)
WFA 3 from 4yo+ 3lb 8 Ran SP% **114.2**
Speed ratings (Par 103): **101,100,98,95,93 90,89,88**
CSF £21.32 CT £37.85 TOTE £4.00: £1.40, £1.70, £1.10; EX 20.00 Trifecta £49.00.
Owner 21st Century Racing **Bred** Meon Valley Stud **Trained** Wiseton, Nottinghamshire

FOCUS
The first five finishers filled the first five positions for much of the way in a race run 0.93sec slower than the second division.

6261 NOVA DISPLAY H'CAP (DIV II) 6f
5:30 (5:30) (Class 5) (0-75,76) 3-Y-0+

£3,881 (£1,155; £577; £400; £400; £400) Stalls Low

Form RPR

2421 **1** **Springwood Drive**[9] 5893 3-9-0 **68** .... DavidAllan 2 78+
(Tim Easterby) *trckd ldrs: pushed along 2f out: swtchd rt and rdn over 1f out: styd on to chal ins fnl f: led fnl100yds* **9/4**[1]

0065 **2** 1 1/4 **Saluti (IRE)**[43] 4649 5-9-11 **76** .... GrahamLee 1 82
(Paul Midgley) *in tch: hdwy wl over 1f out: rdn to chse ldrs ent fnl f: kpt on wl towards fin* **7/1**

4463 **3** 1 3/4 **Juanito Chico (IRE)**[10] 5863 5-9-6 **71** ....(p) SilvestreDeSousa 7 71
(Stuart Williams) *dwlt and in rr: hdwy on outer over 2f out: rdn wl over 1f out: kpt on u.p fnl f* **5/1**[3]

0005 **4** 1/2 **Militia**[11] 5819 4-9-2 **67** .... PaulHanagan 5 66
(Richard Fahey) *led: rdn clr wl over 1f out: jnd and drvn ent fnl f: hdd & wknd fnl 100yds* **10/1**

2235 **5** 1 3/4 **Esprit De Corps**[15] 5692 5-9-2 **72** .... CierenFallon(5) 3 65
(David Barron) *in rr: pushed along and outpcd over 3f out: rdn 2f out: kpt on fnl f: n.d* **4/1**[2]

1512 **6** 3/4 **Dancing Rave**[15] 5670 3-9-7 **75** .... DanielTudhope 6 66
(David O'Meara) *chsd ldrs on outer: hdwy over 2f out: rdn to chse ldr and edgd lft over 1f out: sn drvn and wknd* **7/1**

6463 **7** 5 **Mr Wagyu (IRE)**[8] 5972 4-9-3 **68** ....(v) JasonHart 8 43
(John Quinn) *chsd ldr: rdn along over 2f out: drvn wl over 1f out: sn wknd* **12/1**

0504 **8** 2 1/2 **Another Angel (IRE)**[57] 4103 5-9-8 **73** .... CamHardie 4 40
(Antony Brittain) *chsd ldng pair: hdwy over 2f out: rdn wl over 1f out: sn drvn and wknd* **16/1**

1m 16.11s (-0.99) **Going Correction** +0.025s/f (Good)
WFA 3 from 4yo+ 3lb 8 Ran SP% **115.1**
Speed ratings (Par 103): **107,105,103,102,100 99,92,89**
CSF £18.77 CT £71.67 TOTE £2.70: £1.30, £2.40, £1.90; EX 21.10 Trifecta £93.30.
Owner David W Armstrong **Bred** Highfield Farm Llp **Trained** Great Habton, N Yorks

FOCUS
The winner, off a strong-looking pace, did this smoothly in a time almost a second faster than the first leg.
T/Jkpt: £1,818.10 to a £1 stake. Pool: £14,084.51 T/Plt: £22.70 to a £1 stake. Pool: £92,926.56 - 2,975.51 winning units T/Qpdt: £11.70 to a £1 stake. Pool: £7,347.48 - 464.57 winning units
Joe Rowntree

6248 DEAUVILLE (R-H)
Sunday, August 18

OFFICIAL GOING: Turf: heavy; polytrack: standard

6262a PRIX D'EXMES (MAIDEN) (2YO COLTS & GELDINGS) (STRAIGHT COURSE) (TURF) 6f
1:00 2-Y-0 £12,162 (£4,864; £3,648; £2,432; £1,216)

RPR

1 **Golden Boy (FR)**[22] 5468 2-9-2 0 .... TheoBachelot 4 83+
(S Wattel, France) **6/4**[1]

2 2 1/2 **Matello (FR)**[19] 2-8-10 0 .... AugustinMadamet(6) 3 76
(C Laffon-Parias, France) **48/10**[3]

3 2 **Lin Chong**[23] 5374 2-9-2 0 .... OlivierPeslier 2 70
(Paul Cole) *trckd ldrs: wnt 2nd whn rdn over 1 1/2f out: no ex towards fin* **61/10**

4 2 1/2 **Chambonas (FR)**[19] 2-9-2 0 .... AlexisBadel 5 62
(S Cerulis, France) **12/1**

5 2 **Panda Seven (FR)**[31] 2-9-2 0 .... Pierre-CharlesBoudot 8 56
(Gavin Hernon, France) **18/5**[2]

6 5 **Zabarqan (IRE)**[22] 5468 2-9-2 0 .... ChristopheSoumillon 1 57
(J-C Rouget, France) *trckd ldr on ins: bmpd sltly and lost grnd ins first f: rdn over 2f out: no ex and wknd ins fnl f* **67/10**

7 5 **Vinyl Track (IRE)**[31] 5116 2-9-2 0 .... CristianDemuro 7 26
(G Botti, France) **14/1**

1m 13.66s (2.66) 7 Ran SP% **120.4**
PARI-MUTUEL (all including 1 euro stake): WIN 2.50; PLACE 1.20, 1.60, 1.70; DF 7.70.
Owner Ecurie Jean-Louis Bouchard **Bred** S Boucheron **Trained** France

6263a DARLEY PRIX DE POMONE (GROUP 2) (3YO+ FILLIES & MARES) (ROUND COURSE) (TURF) 1m 4f 110y
1:35 3-Y-0+ £66,756 (£25,765; £12,297; £8,198; £4,099)

RPR

1 **Dame Malliot**[29] 5190 3-8-9 0 .... FrankieDettori 2 110+
(Ed Vaughan) *chsd ldr on outer: disp ld ins fnl 2 1/2f: drvn and hdd 2f out: styd on u.p to grad reel in ldr fnl f: led cl home* **7/5**[1]

2 hd **Love So Deep (JPN)**[15] 5682 3-8-9 0 .... JFEgan 3 109
(Jane Chapple-Hyam) *chsd ldrs on inner: angled out rnd ldr to dispute ldr ins fnl 2 1/2f out: drvn to ld 2f out: styd on but strly rdn ins fnl f: hdd cl home* **24/1**

3 2 **Klassique**[43] 4645 4-9-4 0 .... JamesDoyle 5 104
(William Haggas) *prom on outer: rdn to chse two ldrs 2f out: kpt on but no imp on front two ins fnl f* **31/10**[2]

4 3/4 **Ligne D'Or**[35] 4962 4-9-4 0 .... VincentCheminaud 6 103
(A Fabre, France) *settled one fr last: hdwy over 2f out: styd on u.p but nvr on terms: run flattened out last 75yds* **9/1**

5 1 1/4 **Hermaphrodite (FR)**[20] 5510 4-9-4 0 .... Pierre-CharlesBoudot 8 101
(F-H Graffard, France) *midfield: rdn but no imp over 2f out: kpt on at same pce: nvr threatened ldrs* **10/1**

6 3/4 **Fira (FR)**[28] 5229 4-9-4 0 .... CristianDemuro 9 100
(S Dehez, France) *towards rr: rdn over 2f out: kpt on fnl f: nvr trbld ldrs* **30/1**

7 1 1/2 **Listen In (IRE)**[20] 5510 5-9-4 0 .... AurelienLemaitre 10 97
(F Head, France) *w.w in rr: hdwy on outer 2f fr home: no further imp ins fnl 1 1/2f* **9/1**

8 1 1/2 **South Sea Pearl (IRE)**[15] 5663 3-8-9 0 .... RyanMoore 1 97
(A P O'Brien, Ire) *towards rr: pushed along 3f out: last and rdn 2f out: nvr involved* **73/10**[3]

9 2 1/2 **Peach Tree (IRE)**[15] 5663 3-8-9 0 .... WayneLordan 7 93
(A P O'Brien, Ire) *led: hdd ins fnl 2 1/2f: sn wknd* **44/1**

10 6 **Abadan**[50] 5-9-4 0 ....(p) LukasDelozier 4 81
(Henk Grewe, Germany) *prom on inner: outpcd and rowed along 2 1/2f out: wknd 1 1/2f out and eased* **36/1**

2m 46.23s (-0.17)
WFA 3 from 4yo+ 9lb 10 Ran SP% **119.3**
PARI-MUTUEL (all including 1 euro stake): WIN 2.40; PLACE 1.30, 3.90, 1.70; DF 18.10.
Owner A E Oppenheimer **Bred** Hascombe And Valiant Studs **Trained** Newmarket, Suffolk

FOCUS
It's been rated around the balance of the second to the sixth.

6264a DARLEY PRIX MORNY - FINALE DES DARLEY SERIES (GROUP 1) (2YO COLTS & FILLIES) (STR COURSE) (TURF) 6f
2:50 2-Y-0 £180,171 (£72,081; £36,040; £18,004; £9,018)

RPR

1 **Earthlight (IRE)**[21] 5481 2-9-0 0 .... MickaelBarzalona 5 119
(A Fabre, France) *settled midfield: shkn up and clsd on ldr fr 1 1/2f out: led ent fnl f: sn rdn and drifted rt: r.o* **12/5**[2]

2 nk **Raffle Prize (IRE)**[37] 4883 2-8-10 0 .... FrankieDettori 2 114
(Mark Johnston) *led field towards centre of trck: shkn up 1 1/2f out: hdd ent fnl f: carried rt as wnr drifted: r.o: pair clr* **19/10**[1]

3 2 1/2 **Golden Horde (IRE)**[17] 5584 2-9-0 0 .... AdamKirby 4 111
(Clive Cox) *a cl up: 3rd and rdn wl over 1f out: readily outpcd by front two fr 1f out: kpt on for 3rd* **13/1**

4 2 **Arizona (IRE)**[61] 3949 2-9-0 0 .... RyanMoore 3 105
(A P O'Brien, Ire) *chsd ldr on ins of gp: drvn and no imp appr 2f out: rdn whn wandered 1f out: kpt on fnl f: n.d* **56/10**

5 hd **A'Ali (IRE)**[28] 5228 2-9-0 0 .... JamesDoyle 8 104
(Simon Crisford) *prom on outer: pushed along and effrt 2f out: outpcd appr fnl f: sn dropped away* **42/10**[3]

6 1 1/4 **Aroha (IRE)**[22] 5411 2-8-10 0 .... WilliamBuick 7 96
(Brian Meehan) *towards rr on outer: short-lived effrt over 1 1/2f out: sn btn* **44/1**

7 1 3/4 **Royal Dornoch (IRE)**[17] 5584 2-9-0 0 .... DonnachaO'Brien 6 95
(A P O'Brien, Ire) *w.w in rr: no imp u.p fr 2f out: nvr in contention* **45/1**

8 1 1/4 **Devil (IRE)**[22] 5468 2-9-0 0 .... MaximeGuyon 1 91
(F Head, France) *prom on inner: lost pl more than 2f out: wl hld fnl f* **9/1**

1m 12.0s (1.00) 8 Ran SP% **119.8**
PARI-MUTUEL (all including 1 euro stake): WIN 3.40; PLACE 1.40, 1.30, 2.40; DF 4.40.
Owner Godolphin SNC **Bred** Godolphin **Trained** Chantilly, France

FOCUS
James Doyle described the ground as "pretty desperate" while Frankie Dettori called it "sticky and soft". This was a high-class renewal of the Morny with a trio of Royal Ascot winners taking on the Richmond winner and a promising unbeaten colt representing the home team. It was the latter who came out on top in a truly-run affair, giving France only its second Morny winner in the last fifteen years and Andre Fabre his first since Zafonic in 1992. The first two came clear. The third has been rated to his Richmond form.

6265a DARLEY PRIX JEAN ROMANET (GROUP 1) (4YO+ FILLIES & MARES) (ROUND COURSE) (TURF) 1m 2f
3:25 4-Y-0+ £128,693 (£51,486; £25,743; £12,860; £6,441)

RPR

1 **Coronet**[49] 4430 5-9-0 0 .... FrankieDettori 1 115+
(John Gosden) *a cl up on inner: qcknd to ld 1 1/2f out: edgd lft fr 1f out: styd on fnl f: a holding runner-up* **17/10**[1]

2 3/4 **With You**[21] 5479 4-9-0 0 ....(b) AurelienLemaitre 7 114+
(F Head, France) *cl up on outer: 4th and drvn w 2f to run: styd on u.p fnl f: a hld by wnr* **41/10**[3]

3 1 3/4 **Red Tea**[28] 5223 6-9-0 0 .... DonnachaO'Brien 8 110
(Joseph Patrick O'Brien, Ire) *a little slow to stride: moved up qckly to trck ldr after 1 1/2f: shkn up to chal ins fnl 2f: kpt on at same pce* **34/1**

4 3/4 **I Can Fly**[18] 5543 4-9-0 0 .... RyanMoore 6 109
(A P O'Brien, Ire) *hld up in fnl pair: last and shkn up more than 1 1/2f out: styd on fnl f: nrest at fin* **41/5**

5 1/2 **Spirit Of Nelson (IRE)**[28] 5229 4-9-0 0 .... MaximeGuyon 5 108
(J Reynier, France) *w.w in fnl pair: styd on fr 1 1/2f out: nt pce to trble ldrs* **15/1**

6 nk **Wild Illusion**[51] 4354 4-9-0 0 ....(p) WilliamBuick 4 107
(Charlie Appleby) *led: drvn 2f out: hdd 1 1/2f out: grad dropped away fnl f* **16/5**[2]

7 3/4 **Musis Amica (IRE)**[28] 5229 4-9-0 0 .... MickaelBarzalona 2 105
(A Fabre, France) *settled towards rr: scrubbed along 2 1/2f out but no imp: wl hld fnl f* **58/10**

8 nk **Worth Waiting**[51] 4354 4-9-0 0 .... JamesDoyle 9 105
(David Lanigan) *towards rr on outer: pushed along 2 1/2f out: n.m.r and bmpd whn struggling 1 1/2f out: nvr in contention* **25/1**

2m 9.95s (-0.25) 8 Ran SP% **119.0**
PARI-MUTUEL (all including 1 euro stake): WIN 2.70; PLACE 1.30, 1.90, 5.20; DF 6.40.
Owner Denford Stud **Bred** Denford Stud Ltd **Trained** Newmarket, Suffolk

FOCUS
Not an overly strong edition of this Group 1 but a worthy and decisive winner in a race which was run at a fairly even gallop. The third has been rated to her best.

6266a DARLEY PRIX KERGORLAY (GROUP 2) (3YO+) (ROUND COURSE) (TURF) 1m 7f
4:00 3-Y-0+ £66,756 (£25,765; £12,297; £8,198; £4,099)

RPR

1 **Marmelo**[35] 4962 6-9-4 0 .... ChristopheSoumillon 5 109+
(Hughie Morrison) *w.w towards rr: stdy prog to chse ldng pair into st: edgd lft and clsd to ld over 1f out: shkn up and edgd rt ins fnl f: styd on wl: readily* **4/5**[1]

2 3/4 **Call The Wind**[35] 4962 5-9-8 0 .... AurelienLemaitre 9 112+
(F Head, France) *hld up in fnl pair: last and going along 3 1/2f fr home: hdwy 2 1/2f out: styd on to chse ldr fnl f: no ex late on* **39/10**[2]

3 3 **Haky (IRE)**[26] 5-9-4 0 GeraldMosse 7 104
(J E Hammond, France) *fly-jmpd leaving stalls: trckd ldr: led after 3f but hdd sn after: chsd ldr: drvn and ev ch ins fnl 1 1/2f: kpt on same pce fnl f* **16/1**

4 2 **Mille Et Mille**[23] 5409 9-9-4 0 CristianDemuro 8 102
(C Lerner, France) *led: hdd after 3f but regained ld after anther f: hdd over 1f out: sn lft bhd* **10/1**

5 4 **Palpitator (FR)**[23] 5409 5-9-4 0 SebastienMaillot 4 97
(C Bresson, France) *w.w in fnl pair: sme late prog past btn horses: nvr figured* **8/1**[3]

6 3 1/2 **Khan (GER)**[105] 2455 5-9-4 0 (p) LukasDelozier 2 93
(Henk Grewe, Germany) *chsd ldrs: rdn and nt qckn 2f out: sn wknd* **30/1**

7 2 1/2 **Lillian Russell (IRE)**[23] 5409 4-9-1 0 MickaelBarzalona 1 87
(H-A Pantall, France) *w.w towards rr on inner: tk clsr order 1/2-way: wknd ins fnl 2f* **15/1**

8 30 **Pallasator**[57] 4096 10-9-4 0 JamieSpencer 6
(Gordon Elliott, Ire) *w.w in midfield: outpcd and drvn 2 1/2f out: sn lost tch and eased* **12/1**

3m 18.1s (-1.00) **8 Ran SP% 119.2**
PARI-MUTUEL (all including 1 euro stake): WIN 1.80; PLACE 1.10, 1.30, 1.80; DF 2.60.
Owner The Fairy Story Partnership & Aziz Kheir **Bred** Deepwood Farm Stud **Trained** East Ilsley, Berks

6267a PRIX DE CAGNY (H'CAP) (3YO+) (STRAIGHT COURSE) (TURF) 6f

4:35 3-Y-O+
£12,612 (£4,792; £3,531; £2,018; £1,009; £756)

RPR

1 **George The Prince (FR)**[42] 4704 5-9-6 0 (b) CristianDemuro 8 91
(G Doleuze, France) **8/1**[3]

2 2 **Gone Solo (IRE)**[10] 4-8-10 0 EddyHardouin 2 75
(Robert Collet, France) **19/1**

3 1 1/2 **Tallinski (IRE)**[89] 2956 5-9-1 0 AurelienLemaitre 15 75
(Sofie Lanslots, France) **14/1**

4 nk **Canouville (FR)**[67] 4-8-11 0 (p) GregoryBenoist 9 70
(Mlle Y Vollmer, France) **10/1**

5 1 **Xenophanes (IRE)**[77] 9-8-8 0 MlleCoraliePacaut(3) 7 67
(M Boutin, France) **14/1**

6 1 **Mandolin Wind (FR)**[17] 5-9-3 0 (b[1]) FabriceVeron 16 70
(E J O'Neill, France) **16/1**

7 shd **Blue Tango (GER)**[77] 4-8-11 0 AugustinMadamet(4) 5 68
(M Munch, Germany) **11/1**

8 1 **Dream Life (FR)**[23] 3-9-4 0 GeraldMosse 10 70
(J-P Dubois, France) **6/1**[2]

9 nk **Tenorio (FR)**[89] 6-8-10 0 (b) MickaelBarzalona 3 58
(Mlle V Dissaux, France) **11/1**

10 1 1/2 **Achille Des Aigles (FR)**[89] 5-8-10 0 MlleFriedaValleSkar(7) 18 61
(Mme C Barande-Barbe, France) **9/1**

11 nse **Matista (IRE)**[46] 3-9-2 0 VincentCheminaud 12 62
(H-A Pantall, France) **11/1**

12 1 1/4 **Beyond My Dreams (IRE)**[24] 4-9-3 0 (b) ChristopheSoumillon 17 56
(F Vermeulen, France) **51/10**[1]

13 1 1/2 **Never Without You (FR)**[19] 5-8-3 0 ow3 RosarioMangione 11 38
(P Capelle, France) **79/1**

14 1 1/2 **Marvellous Night (FR)**[12] 4-8-13 0 (p) HugoJourniac 13 43
(H De Nicolay, France) **24/1**

15 1 1/4 **Champion Brogie (IRE)**[16] 5644 3-7-12 0 AlexisPouchin(4) 1 31
(J S Moore) *trckd ldr in stands' side gp: u.p and pushed along over 2f out: no imp and eased wl ins fnl f* **18/1**

1m 12.81s (1.81)
WFA 3 from 4yo+ 3lb **15 Ran SP% 120.6**
PARI-MUTUEL (all including 1 euro stake): WIN 9.00; PLACE 4.00, 6.60, 4.90; DF 95.30.
Owner Mlle Claire Stephenson & Guy Nabet **Bred** Mlle C Stephenson **Trained** France

6268a - 6269a (Foreign Racing) - See Raceform Interactive

5719 DUSSELDORF (R-H)

Sunday, August 18

OFFICIAL GOING: Turf: soft

6270a GROSSER SPARKASSENPREIS - PREIS DER STADTSPARKASSE DUSSELDORF (LISTED RACE) (3YO+ FILLIES & MARES) 7f

4:20 3-Y-O+
£15,765 (£6,306; £4,504; £2,702; £1,351; £900)

RPR

1 **Emerita (GER)**[48] 4461 4-9-2 0 AndraschStarke 8 101
(H-J Groschel, Germany) **23/5**[3]

2 1 1/4 **Gypsy Spirit**[16] 5608 3-8-11 0 JackMitchell 1 96
(Tom Clover) *trckd ldr on inner: rdn and ev ch over 2f out: led briefly 1 1/2f out: styd on: nt match wnr* **29/10**[2]

3 1 1/2 **K Club (IRE)**[71] 3-8-11 0 AlexanderPietsch 9 92
(J Hirschberger, Germany) **79/10**

4 1 1/2 **Caesara**[48] 4461 4-9-2 0 MichaelCadeddu 7 90
(Jean-Pierre Carvalho, Germany) **25/1**

5 shd **Peace Of Paris (GER)**[48] 4461 3-8-11 0 MartinSeidl 2 88
(Markus Klug, Germany) **11/1**

6 2 **Cabarita (GER)**[48] 4461 4-9-2 0 AndreBest 4 84
(H-J Groschel, Germany) **232/10**

7 1 **Magic Image**[57] 3-8-11 0 JulienGuillochon 5 80
(H-A Pantall, France) *mid-div: rdn over 2f out: no ex and dropped to 7th ins fnl f* **13/10**[1]

8 7 **Skrei (IRE)**[69] 4-9-2 0 (b) RenePiechulek 6 63
(Dr A Bolte, Germany) **187/10**

1m 28.34s
WFA 3 from 4yo 5lb **8 Ran SP% 119.6**
PARI-MUTUEL (all including 1 euro stake): WIN 5.60 PLACE: 1.60, 1.50, 2.30; SF: 21.70.
Owner Gestut Paschberg **Bred** Gestut Paschberg **Trained** Germany

6011 CATTERICK (L-H)

Monday, August 19

OFFICIAL GOING: Soft (good to soft in places; 6.3)
Wind: Fresh half against Weather: Cloudy and blustery with sunny periods

6271 CARNIVAL FAMILY DAY (S) STKS 7f 6y

2:00 (2:02) (Class 6) 2-Y-O **£3,105** (£924; £461; £300; £300) **Stalls** Low

Form RPR

0300 1 **Our Dave**[26] 5295 2-8-12 53 (v[1]) JasonHart 4 55
(John Quinn) *trckd ldrs: pushed along on inner 1/2-way: hdwy wl over 2f out: chsd ldr and rdn wl over 1f out: led jst over 1f out: kpt on* **8/1**

2253 2 2 3/4 **Enjoy The Moment**[9] 5968 2-8-7 64 BenCurtis 1 43
(Mick Channon) *led: pushed along 3f out: rdn over 2f out: drvn and hdd jst over 1f out: sn one pce (jockey said filly hung right throughout)* **4/6**[1]

0000 3 1 3/4 **Fulbeck Rose**[13] 5789 2-8-7 37 (t) AndrewMullen 2 38+
(Nigel Tinkler) *s.i.s and lost 5 l s: tk clsr order 4f out: rdn along to chse ldrs over 2f out: drvn wl over 1f out: kpt on same pce (jockey said filly was slowly away)* **33/1**

600 4 1 **Grimbold**[16] 5655 2-8-5 62 (b) RhonaPindar(7) 6 41
(K R Burke) *cl up on outer: edgd rt home turn: sn rdn along and outpcd 2f out: plugged on u.p after* **5/1**[2]

0630 5 10 **Schumli**[13] 5789 2-8-7 59 CamHardie 3 10
(David O'Meara) *cl up: rdn along over 2f out: sn drvn and wknd wl over 1f out (jockey said filly weakened quickly from two furlongs out)* **11/2**[3]

1m 32.38s (4.98) **Going Correction** +0.375s/f (Good) **5 Ran SP% 106.1**
Speed ratings (Par 92): **86,82,80,79,68**
CSF £13.12 TOTE £7.00: £2.70, £1.10; EX 15.30 Trifecta £120.00.There was no bid for the winner.
Owner Ryedale Racing **Bred** Sledmere Bloodstock **Trained** Settrington, N Yorks

FOCUS
It paid to be handy in this desperately weak 2yo seller and, as they kept far side, a headwind was evident in the home straight.

6272 LIKE RACING TV ON FACEBOOK NURSERY H'CAP 5f 212y

2:30 (2:31) (Class 4) (0-85,84) 2-Y-O
£6,080 (£1,809; £904; £452; £300; £300) **Stalls** Low

Form RPR

4556 1 **Knightcap**[5] 6064 2-8-1 **64** DuranFentiman 2 72+
(Tim Easterby) *trckd ldrs on inner: hdwy over 2f out: rdn to ld wl over 1f out: sn clr: readily* **13/2**[3]

6504 2 3 1/4 **Bob's Oss (IRE)**[15] 5703 2-8-0 **63** oh4 CamHardie 3 61
(Alan Berry) *in rr: rdn along over 2f out: styd on u.p fr over 1f out: tk 2nd towards fin* **50/1**

0341 3 3/4 **Good Night Mr Tom (IRE)**[16] 5668 2-9-7 **84** JoeFanning 4 80
(Mark Johnston) *trckd ldng pair: hdwy wl over 2f out: rdn and ev ch wl over 1f out: sn drvn and kpt on same pce* **5/4**[1]

2024 4 shd **Exclusively**[27] 5275 2-9-6 **83** (p[1]) BenCurtis 5 78
(Archie Watson) *cl up: disp ld 2 1/2f out: sn rdn along and ev ch tl drvn over 1f out and kpt on same pce* **4/1**[2]

0210 5 2 1/2 **Infinite Grace**[16] 5683 2-9-3 **80** DanielTudhope 1 68
(David O'Meara) *led: jnd and rdn along wl over 2f out: drvn and hdd wl over 1f out: grad wknd* **4/1**[2]

436 6 1 **Woven Quality (IRE)**[13] 5764 2-8-11 **74** AndrewMullen 8 59
(Donald McCain) *cl up on outer: rdn along wl over 2f out: sn drvn and wknd* **12/1**

5140 7 1/2 **Gold Venture (IRE)**[16] 5683 2-8-2 **65** JimmyQuinn 6 48
(Philip Kirby) *a towards rr* **25/1**

0030 8 1 **She's Easyontheeye (IRE)**[20] 5514 2-8-1 **67** SeanDavis(3) 7 47
(John Quinn) *a towards rr* **33/1**

1m 16.24s (2.64) **Going Correction** +0.375s/f (Good) **8 Ran SP% 114.2**
Speed ratings (Par 96): **97,92,91,91,88 86,86,84**
CSF £263.53 CT £657.19 TOTE £7.10: £1.70, £12.70, £1.10; EX 168.10 Trifecta £548.10.
Owner Lovely Bubbly Racing **Bred** Mrs D O'Brien **Trained** Great Habton, N Yorks

FOCUS
They explored the centre of the home straight in this modest nursery, and it looked hard enough work.

6273 FOLLOW @RACINGTV ON TWITTER H'CAP 5f 212y

3:00 (3:00) (Class 6) (0-60,60) 3-Y-O+
£3,105 (£924; £461; £300; £300; £300) **Stalls** Low

Form RPR

/001 1 **Night Law**[13] 5767 5-8-12 **51** (b) PhilDennis 6 58
(Katie Scott) *trckd ldr: led 1/2-way: rdn clr wl over 1f out: drvn and kpt on towards fin* **7/1**

0123 2 3/4 **B Fifty Two (IRE)**[3] 6174 10-9-4 **60** (tp) JaneElliott(3) 1 65
(Marjorie Fife) *towards rr on inner: pushed along 1/2-way: hdwy 2f out: rdn wl over 1f out: kpt on fnl f (jockey said gelding missed the break)* **11/2**[3]

6430 3 1 3/4 **Spirit Of Zebedee (IRE)**[19] 5558 6-8-9 **48** (v) JasonHart 5 48
(John Quinn) *trckd ldng pair: hdwy over 2f out: rdn to chse wnr wl over 1f out: sn drvn and kpt on same pce* **5/1**[2]

0050 4 nk **Carlovian**[9] 5938 6-8-13 **52** (p) DougieCostello 9 51
(Mark Walford) *chsd ldrs: wd st towards stands' rail: rdn along 2f out: drvn over 1f out: kpt on fnl f* **20/1**

4102 5 1 1/4 **Mr Greenlight**[3] 6174 4-9-6 **59** DavidAllan 7 54
(Tim Easterby) *in tch: hdwy over 2f out: rdn to chse ldrs wl over 1f out: sn drvn and no imp* **3/1**[1]

0366 6 3/4 **Santafiora**[16] 5659 5-9-0 **53** KevinStott 4 46
(Julie Camacho) *trckd ldrs: hdwy over 2f out: rdn along wl over 1f out: sn drvn and one pce* **11/2**[3]

5100 7 4 1/2 **Point Of Woods**[4] 6099 6-9-7 **60** (t[1]) JamesSullivan 3 39
(Tina Jackson) *midfield: hdwy over 2f out: sn chsng ldrs and rdn: sn no imp* **25/1**

0002 8 4 **Deeds Not Words (IRE)**[13] 5767 8-9-4 **57** (p) BenCurtis 2 24
(Tracy Waggott) *nvr bttr than midfield* **12/1**

0350 9 shd **Little Miss Muffin**[13] 5771 3-8-8 **57** HarryRussell(7) 8 24
(Sam England) *a in rr* **33/1**

5000 10 nk **Just For The Craic (IRE)**[17] 5629 4-8-10 **52** (t[1]) SeanDavis(3) 11 18
(Neil Mulholland) *a in rr* **33/1**

0000 11 1/2 **Super Florence (IRE)**[26] 5300 4-8-12 **56** (h) HarrisonShaw(5) 10 20
(Iain Jardine) *led: hdd 1/2-way: sn rdn along and wknd (jockey said filly weakened quickly in the home straight)* **12/1**

-000 12 2 **Capla Demon**[182] 788 4-9-7 **60**........................(p) CamHardie 12 18
(Antony Brittain) *a in rr* **33/1**

1m 16.05s (2.45) **Going Correction** +0.375s/f (Good)
WFA 3 from 4yo+ 3lb **12** Ran SP% **117.8**
Speed ratings (Par 101): **98,97,94,94,92 91,85,80,80,79 79,76**
CSF £42.04 CT £211.49 TOTE £6.90: £2.10, £2.20, £2.00; EX 42.00 Trifecta £157.70.
Owner B T McDonald **Bred** George Strawbridge **Trained** Galasheils, Scottish Borders

FOCUS
Again the far side was shunned in this moderate sprint handicap.

6274 MINSTER FM NOVICE STKS 1m 4f 13y
3:30 (3:30) (Class 5) 3-Y-O+
£4,140 (£1,232; £615; £307) **Stalls** Low

Form RPR

3 1 **Ahorsewithnoname**[73] 3553 4-9-6 0........................ DanielTudhope 6 87+
(Brian Ellison) *trckd ldrs: hdwy to ld 1/2-way: pushed clr wl over 3f out: readily* **10/11**[1]

22- 2 4 **Wolf Prince (IRE)**[305] 8336 3-9-2 0........................ BenCurtis 5 82
(Amy Murphy) *trckd ldrs: chsd wnr fr 1/2-way: rdn along over 3f out: drvn 2f out: kpt on: no imp* **7/2**[2]

4 3 5 **Gabrials Boy**[16] 5656 3-9-2 0........................ TonyHamilton 4 74
(Richard Fahey) *in tch: hdwy to chse ldng pair 5f out: rdn along 3f out: drvn 2f out plugged on one pce* **5/1**[3]

0 4 21 **Detonation**[22] 5477 3-9-2 0........................ RaulDaSilva 8 40
(Shaun Harris) *bhd: rdn along over 4f out: plodded on fnl 3f: nvr a factor* **125/1**

5 3 1/4 **Wadacre Galoubet** 3-9-2 0........................ JoeFanning 7 35
(Mark Johnston) *green and hmpd s: a in rr: outpcd fr over 4f out: bhd fnl 2f* **6/1**

50 6 12 **Magic Act (IRE)**[14] 5742 3-8-11 0........................ AndrewBreslin(5) 1 16
(Mark Johnston) *slt ld: hdd 1/2-way: sn outpcd and bhd fnl 4f* **28/1**

0 7 83 **Double Esprit**[16] 5656 3-9-2 0........................ GrahamLee 3
(Donald McCain) *chsd ldrs: pushed along 1/2-way: rdn and outpcd fr over 4f out: t.o fnl 3f* **18/1**

6 U **Pound Off You**[14] 5742 3-8-11 0........................ PhilDennis 2
(Gillian Boanas) *cl up tl rn wd and uns rdr bnd after 3f* **100/1**

2m 41.82s (1.22) **Going Correction** +0.375s/f (Good)
WFA 3 from 4yo 9lb **8** Ran SP% **116.1**
Speed ratings (Par 103): **108,105,102,88,85 77,22,**
CSF £4.42 TOTE £1.70: £1.10, £1.20, £1.30; EX 3.70 Trifecta £10.30.
Owner D J Burke & P Alderson **Bred** Whitley Stud **Trained** Norton, N Yorks

FOCUS
This uncompetitive novice event proved a thorough test. The winner has been rated as improving, with the second and third close to form.

6275 WATCH RACING TV NOW H'CAP (DIV I) 7f 6y
4:00 (4:05) (Class 6) (0-60,60) 3-Y-O+
£4,075 (£1,212; £606; £303; £300; £300) **Stalls** Low

Form RPR

0501 1 **Chaplin Bay (IRE)**[9] 5938 7-9-0 **53**........................ JamesSullivan 4 61
(Ruth Carr) *trckd ldrs: hdwy and wd st: cl up 2f out: rdn to chal over 1f out: drvn ins fnl f: kpt on wl to ld nr fin* **11/1**

0005 2 nk **Sophia Maria**[13] 5767 3-8-8 **55**........................(p) JaneElliott(3) 2 60
(James Bethell) *trckd ldrs: hdwy and wd st: led wl over 1f out: sn rdn: drvn ins fnl f: hdd and no ex nr fin* **18/1**

-522 3 2 **Radjash**[10] 5918 5-8-8 **54**........................(t) ZakWheatley(7) 12 56
(Declan Carroll) *in tch: hdwy and wd st: chsd ldrs 2f out: rdn: nt clr run and swtchd lft ent fnl f: kpt on* **5/1**[2]

1040 4 3/4 **Tarnhelm**[11] 5857 4-8-8 **54**........................ RhonaPindar(7) 5 54
(Wilf Storey) *dwlt and bhd: wd st: hdwy 2f out: nt clr run and swtchd rt to stands' rail over 1f out: kpt on fnl f* **22/1**

0006 5 1 1/4 **Hitman**[18] 5593 6-9-7 **60**........................ LewisEdmunds 10 57
(Rebecca Bastiman) *dwlt and bhd: hdwy over 2f out: rdn over 1f out: styd on fnl f* **16/1**

0665 6 2 1/2 **Fard**[5] 6066 4-9-2 **55**........................(b[1]) BenCurtis 15 45
(Roger Fell) *in tch: hdwy over 2f out: rdn wl over 1f out: no imp fnl f* **18/1**

0322 7 1/2 **Perfect Swiss**[19] 5558 3-8-11 **55**........................ DavidAllan 6 42+
(Tim Easterby) *s.i.s and bhd: hdwy on inner over 2f out: sn rdn and kpt on fnl f (jockey said gelding reared as the stalls opened)* **9/2**[1]

026 8 nse **Billiebrookedit (IRE)**[6] 6051 4-8-7 **46**........................ CamHardie 8 36
(Kevin Frost) *chsd ldrs: wd st: rdn along and n.m.r over 1f out: kpt on same pce* **11/1**

020 9 1 1/4 **Billy Wedge**[23] 5438 4-8-13 **52**........................ ConnorBeasley 9 38
(Tracy Waggott) *led: wd to stands' rail: rdn along over 2f out: hdd wl over 1f out: sn wknd* **6/1**[3]

64 10 nk **Searanger (USA)**[6] 6036 6-8-12 **51**........................ CliffordLee 1 36
(Rebecca Menzies) *chsd ldrs: rdn along on inner over 2f out: drvn wl over 1f out: wknd appr fnl f* **8/1**

5005 11 2 **De Latour**[14] 5738 3-8-1 **48** oh1 ow2........................ SeanDavis(3) 14 26
(Jason Ward) *cl up: rdn along and wd st: wknd 2f out* **66/1**

4202 12 1 **Mightaswellsmile**[13] 5768 5-8-0 **46**........................ AledBeech(7) 7 23
(Ron Barr) *a towards rr* **16/1**

-006 13 8 **Vicky Cristina (IRE)**[31] 5147 4-8-7 **46** oh1........................ RoystonFfrench 3 2
(John Holt) *a towards rr* **40/1**

06-6 14 1 1/4 **Mr Sundowner (USA)**[29] 5214 7-9-6 **59**........................ PhilDennis 13 12
(Michael Herrington) *a towards rr* **16/1**

-000 15 11 **Kings Academy**[31] 5151 5-9-0 **53**........................(v) JimmyQuinn 11
(John Mackie) *dwlt: a in rr* **40/1**

1m 30.2s (2.80) **Going Correction** +0.375s/f (Good)
WFA 3 from 4yo+ 5lb **15** Ran SP% **115.8**
Speed ratings (Par 101): **99,98,96,95,94 91,90,90,89,88 86,85,76,74,62**
CSF £180.83 CT £1141.68 TOTE £12.10: £3.10, £5.90, £1.70; EX 157.70 Trifecta £2853.80.
Owner Miss B Houlston,Mrs M Chapman,Mrs R Carr **Bred** Stonethorn Stud Farms Ltd **Trained** Huby, N Yorks

FOCUS
A wide-open looking handicap. The first pair fought it out on the stands' side.

6276 WATCH RACING TV NOW H'CAP (DIV II) 7f 6y
4:30 (4:33) (Class 6) (0-60,60) 3-Y-O+
£4,075 (£1,212; £606; £303; £300; £300) **Stalls** Low

Form RPR

5404 1 **Our Charlie Brown**[40] 4784 5-9-5 **58**........................(p) JamesSullivan 4 72
(Tim Easterby) *trckd ldrs: hdwy and wd st: cl up over 2f out: rdn to ld 1 1/2f out: clr ins fnl f* **13/2**[2]

5111 2 3 1/4 **Kodimoor (IRE)**[23] 5430 6-9-0 **53**........................(p) DougieCostello 13 59
(Mark Walford) *cl up: wd st and led over 2f out: jnd and rdn wl over 1f out: sn hdd and drvn: kpt on same pce* **12/1**

6200 3 1/2 **Ghathanfar (IRE)**[16] 5695 3-8-13 **57**........................ RoystonFfrench 14 59
(Tracy Waggott) *trckd ldrs: wd st: rdn along 2f out: drvn over 1f out: kpt on same pce fnl f* **22/1**

3450 4 1/2 **The Stalking Moon (IRE)**[13] 5770 5-9-7 **60**........................ AndrewMullen 6 63
(Adrian Nicholls) *towards rr: pushed along 1/2-way: hdwy over 2f out: rdn to chse ldrs over 1f out: sn drvn and no imp* **8/1**

4000 5 1 **Muqarred (USA)**[11] 5852 7-8-10 **49**........................ ShaneGray 12 49
(Karen Tutty) *chsd ldrs: rdn along over 2f out: drvn wl over 1f out: kpt on same pce* **40/1**

0005 6 3/4 **Chickenfortea (IRE)**[13] 5767 5-8-11 **50**........................ JasonHart 10 48
(Eric Alston) *dwlt and towards rr: wd st: hdwy 2f out: rdn and kpt on fnl f (jockey said gelding stumbled leaving the stalls and ran too free)* **12/1**

0401 7 1/2 **Ingleby Molly (IRE)**[11] 5857 4-8-4 **46** oh1........(h) ConnorMcGovern(3) 9 43
(Jason Ward) *prom: wd st: cl up over 2f out: sn rdn and wknd over 1f out* **16/1**

0505 8 6 **Eldelbar (SPA)**[13] 5770 5-9-1 **54**........................(h) PaddyMathers 15 36
(Geoffrey Harker) *blind removed late and dwlt: in rr tl styd on fnl 2f (jockey was slow to remove the blindfold explaining that it became stuck on the gelding's hood and took three attempts to remove)* **20/1**

0551 9 nk **Bee Machine (IRE)**[62] 3970 4-8-9 **55**........................(t) ZakWheatley(7) 8 36
(Declan Carroll) *towards rr: rdn along and sme hdwy 2f out: n.d* **8/1**

5355 10 7 **Dominannie (IRE)**[10] 5918 6-8-7 **46**........................ NathanEvans 3 9
(Ron Barr) *a in rr* **33/1**

0006 11 3/4 **Naples Bay**[35] 4978 5-8-13 **52**........................ PhilDennis 11 13
(Katie Scott) *slt ld: wd st: rdn and hdd over 2f out: sn wknd* **18/1**

0002 12 4 1/2 **Hippeia (IRE)**[5] 6066 4-8-12 **51**........................(v) DanielTudhope 7
(Lawrence Mullaney) *trckd ldrs on inner: pushed along 3f out: sn rdn and wknd over 2f out (jockey said filly was unsuited by not being able to dominate on this occasion)* **9/2**[1]

2322 13 11 **Macs Blessings (IRE)**[9] 5935 3-8-12 **59**........................(v) SeanDavis(3) 5
(Stef Keniry) *a in rr (jockey said gelding became unbalanced in the home straight)* **15/2**[3]

6034 P **Leeshaan (IRE)**[28] 5238 4-8-7 **46**........................ JamieGormley 1
(Rebecca Bastiman) *in tch on inner: lost pl over 4f out: lost action and bhd whn p.u 3f out (jockey said gelding lost it's action)* **15/2**[3]

1m 29.6s (2.20) **Going Correction** +0.375s/f (Good)
WFA 3 from 4yo+ 5lb **14** Ran SP% **118.3**
Speed ratings (Par 101): **102,98,97,97,96 95,94,87,87,79 78,73,60,**
CSF £76.95 CT £1668.76 TOTE £6.50: £2.30, £2.50, £7.40; EX 53.50 Trifecta £1254.70.
Owner Ontoawinner, SDH Project Services Ltd 2 **Bred** North Bradon Stud & D R Tucker **Trained** Great Habton, N Yorks

FOCUS
The second division of the 7f handicap was run in a 0.60secs quicker time. Again they came stands' side. Straightforward form with the third to his mark.

6277 RACINGTV.COM H'CAP 5f
5:00 (5:03) (Class 6) (0-60,60) 3-Y-O+
£3,105 (£924; £461; £300; £300; £300) **Stalls** Low

Form RPR

0032 1 **The Grey Zebedee**[13] 5765 3-9-2 **55**........................(b) DuranFentiman 11 63
(Tim Easterby) *sltly hmpd s: trckd ldrs stands' side: hdwy 3f out: cl up over 2f out: rdn to ld over 1f out: sn edgd rt: styd on wl fnl f* **7/1**[3]

2002 2 1 3/4 **Teepee Time**[10] 5892 6-8-13 **50**........................(b) JackGarritty 10 52
(Michael Mullineaux) *sltly hmpd s: sn cl up nr stands' rail: led 2f out: sn rdn: hdd over 1f out: n.m.r and swtchd lft ent fnl f: sn drvn and kpt on* **12/1**

0606 3 3/4 **Trulove**[32] 5094 6-8-8 **45**........................(p) JamieGormley 14 44
(John David Riches) *in tch towards stands' side: hdwy 2f out: rdn over 1f out: kpt on fnl f* **80/1**

0051 4 1/2 **I'll Be Good**[3] 6174 10-8-11 **51** 4ex........................ ConnorMurtagh(3) 13 49
(Alan Berry) *racd nr stands' rail: prom whn stmbld sltly and sddle slipped after 1f: chsd ldrs: rdn along and n.m.r over 1f out: kpt on fnl f (jockey said saddle slipped)* **7/1**[3]

0010 5 1/2 **Amelia R (IRE)**[16] 5659 3-9-7 **60**........................ ConnorBeasley 3 56+
(Ray Craggs) *trckd ldrs centre: hdwy 2f out: rdn and ev ch over 1f out: sn drvn and wknd fnl f* **9/2**[2]

6323 6 nk **Amazing Alba**[10] 5904 3-9-7 **60**........................(h) KevinStott 15 55
(Alistair Whillans) *racd nr stands' rail: in tch: hdwy 2f out: swtchd lft and rdn wl over 1f out: kpt on* **11/1**

4000 7 1 **Astraea**[11] 5857 4-9-1 **52**........................(b) NathanEvans 2 43+
(Michael Easterby) *racd centre: dwlt and towards rr tl styd on fnl 2f* **22/1**

0650 8 3/4 **Paco Escostar**[22] 5478 4-8-12 **49**........................(v) CamHardie 1 37+
(Julie Camacho) *racd centre: in tch: hdwy 2f out: sn rdn: edgd lft ent fnl f: no imp* **9/1**

6000 9 shd **Thornaby Princess**[11] 5857 8-8-6 **46** ow1........(p) ConnorMcGovern(3) 7 34
(Jason Ward) *wnt rt s: in tch towards stands' side: rdn along 1/2-way: n.d* **33/1**

1003 10 1/2 **Cuppacoco**[24] 5393 4-9-5 **56**........................ JoeFanning 6 42
(Ann Duffield) *prom centre: rdn along wl over 1f out: sn wknd* **11/1**

4003 11 hd **Gift In Time (IRE)**[7] 6017 4-9-7 **58**........................(p) DavidAllan 12 43
(Paul Collins) *racd towards stands' side: dwlt and a towards rr* **4/1**[1]

6505 12 2 **Gorgeous Gobolina**[11] 5854 3-9-4 **57**........................ PhilDennis 9 35
(Susan Corbett) *sltly hmpd s: racd towards centre and led: pushed along 1/2-way: rdn and hdd 2f out: sn drvn and wknd appr fnl f* **25/1**

0064 13 1 **Minty Jones**[8] 5986 10-8-5 **45**........................(b) JaneElliott(3) 8 20
(Michael Mullineaux) *hmpd s: in tch towards stands' side: rdn along over 2f out: sn wknd* **33/1**

6304 14 3/4 **Champagne Mondays**[14] 5738 3-8-6 **45**........................(b) JamesSullivan 5 17
(Scott Dixon) *racd centre: cl up: rdn along 2f out: sn drvn and wknd* **22/1**

604 15 4 **Final Legacy**[10] 5917 3-8-6 **45**........................ PaddyMathers 4 3
(Derek Shaw) *racd centre: dwlt: a towards rr* **50/1**

1m 1.21s (0.71) **Going Correction** +0.375s/f (Good)
WFA 3 from 4yo+ 2lb **15** Ran SP% **119.2**
Speed ratings (Par 101): **109,106,105,104,103 102,101,100,99,99 98,95,94,92,86**
CSF £80.17 CT £6076.61 TOTE £5.70: £1.90, £3.40, £32.10; EX 53.60 Trifecta £1836.90.
Owner The Geordie Boys & Partner **Bred** D R Botterill **Trained** Great Habton, N Yorks

FOCUS
Another open-looking sprint handicap and the far side was shunned once more. Straightforward form with the runner-up to her latest.

6278 28TH AUGUST IS LADIES' DAY AMATEUR RIDERS' H'CAP 1m 4f 13y
5:35 (5:36) (Class 5) (0-70,72) 4-Y-O+
£3,930 (£1,219; £609; £304; £300; £300) Stalls Low

Form RPR
1502 1 **Percy Prosecco**[20] 5528 4-10-5 61 MissBrodieHampson 5 70
(Archie Watson) *trckd ldrs: hdwy 4f out: led 3f out and wd st: rdn clr wl over 1f out: kpt on* 6/1[3]
5253 2 1 **Jan De Heem**[9] 5975 9-9-9 51 (v) MissEmmaTodd 10 58
(Tina Jackson) *wnt bdly rt s and lost 4 l: in rr: hdwy 7f out: in tch 5f out: chsd ldrs over 2f out: rdn wl over 1f out: styd on fnl f* 9/1
1315 3 2 ½ **Be Perfect (USA)**[17] 5621 10-10-9 70 MissEmilyBullock(5) 9 73
(Ruth Carr) *trckd ldrs: hdwy 4f out: wd st to stands' rail and sn prom: rdn along 2f out: drvn over 1f out: kpt on same pce* 15/2
4426 4 nk **Snookered (IRE)**[15] 5712 5-10-7 70 (p) MrMattBrown(7) 2 73
(Brian Ellison) *trckd ldrs: hdwy over 3f out: wd st: rdn over 2f out: chsd wnr wl over 1f out: sn drvn: kpt on same pce fnl f* 9/2[2]
1 5 2 ¼ **Mauricio (IRE)**[12] 5824 5-10-13 69 MissSerenaBrotherton 7 68
(Dr Richard Newland) *t.k.h: trckd ldr: pushed along over 3f out: rdn along wl over 2f out: sn drvn and one pce* 2/1[1]
6640 6 2 ½ **Tapis Libre**[14] 5727 11-10-12 68 (v) MissJoannaMason 8 63
(Jacqueline Coward) *led: pushed along 4f out: rdn over 3f out: sn hdd: wknd fnl 2f* 17/2
6336 7 nse **Duke Of Yorkshire**[17] 5621 9-10-1 57 (p) MissEmilyEasterby 3 52
(Tim Easterby) *trckd ldng pair on inner: rdn along over 3f out: plugged on one pce fnl 2f* 22/1
0003 8 3 ¾ **Galactic Spirit**[17] 5625 4-10-7 70 (p) MrRobertLaw-Eadie(7) 4 59
(James Evans) *hld up: a in rr* 16/1
6200 9 4 **Strictly Art (IRE)**[55] 4216 6-9-10 59 MissEmmaJack(7) 6 41
(Alan Bailey) *a towards rr* 25/1
00 10 12 **Rayna's World (IRE)**[66] 3816 4-10-9 72 MrHenryNewcombe(7) 1 35
(Philip Kirby) *a in rr* 33/1

2m 46.97s (6.37) **Going Correction** +0.375s/f (Good) 10 Ran SP% 115.1
Speed ratings (Par 103): **93,92,90,90,88 87,87,84,82,74**
CSF £56.42 CT £410.54 TOTE £7.20: £2.20, £2.80, £1.70; EX 57.50 Trifecta £299.00.
Owner The Real Quiz **Bred** Clive Dennett **Trained** Upper Lambourn, W Berks
■ Stewards' Enquiry : Mr Matt Brown two-day ban; misuse of whip (tba)

FOCUS
A modest, muddling race, but this rates a pb from the winner with the runner-up to form.
T/Plt: £23.60 to a £1 stake. Pool: £62,610.69 - 1932.11 winning units T/Qpdt: £14.40 to a £1 stake. Pool: £5,925.27 - 303.98 winning units **Joe Rowntree**

6111
LINGFIELD (L-H)
Monday, August 19

OFFICIAL GOING: Polytrack: standard
Wind: medium, strong at times, across Weather: cloudy, showers

6279 INJURED JOCKEYS FUND H'CAP 1m 2f (P)
2:15 (2:17) (Class 6) (0-60,60) 3-Y-O
£2,781 (£827; £413; £300; £300; £300) Stalls Low

Form RPR
000 1 **Quemonda**[109] 2340 3-9-1 54 PatDobbs 14 60
(Ken Cunningham-Brown) *hld up in tch in midfield: nt clr run over 2f out: rdn and hdwy over 1f out: styd on strly ins fnl f to ld 50yds out: sn in command* 33/1
540 2 1 ¼ **Fame N Fortune**[8] 5987 3-9-2 55 (b[1]) RobHornby 3 59
(Joseph Tuite) *sn led: rdn wl over 1f out: pressed ins fnl f: hdd and no ex 50yds out* 8/1
6500 3 hd **Forty Four Sunsets (FR)**[19] 5552 3-8-10 49 RossaRyan 5 53
(Richard Hannon) *hld up in tch in midfield: nt clr run over 2f out: swtchd lft and hdwy over 1f out: chsd ldr ins fnl f: ev ch 100yds out: nt match pce of wnr fnl 50yds* 14/1
-050 4 3 ¼ **Asensio**[19] 5552 3-9-6 59 (t[1]) GeraldMosse 6 57
(Mohamed Moubarak) *s.i.s: in rr: hdwy on outer 6f out: effrt to chse ldrs over 2f out: chsd ldr over 1f out: no imp and lost 2 pls ins fnl f: eased towards fin* 16/1
0013 5 nk **Sir Canford (IRE)**[16] 5679 3-9-7 60 (p) CharlesBishop 10 58
(Ali Stronge) *hmpd and dropped to rr sn after s: hld up towards rr: lost nr side cheekpiece over 4f out: effrt over 2f out: nt clr run and swtchd rt over 1f out: styd on wl ins fnl f: nvr trbld ldrs* 7/1[3]
-053 6 1 **Ramatuelle**[12] 5795 3-8-7 46 (p[1]) LukeMorris 7 41
(Sir Mark Prescott Bt) *midfield and rousted along early: rdn over 3f out: nt clrest of runs over 2f out: plugged on u.p fr over 1f out: nvr enough pce to threaten ldrs* 9/2[1]
5034 7 1 **Four Mile Bridge (IRE)**[32] 5085 3-9-5 58 FergusSweeney 2 51
(Mark Usher) *s.i.s and pushed along early: hld up in rr: effrt over 2f out: v wd bnd 2f out: hdwy 1f out: styd on wl ins fnl f: nvr trbld ldrs* 5/1[2]
050 8 nk **Savoy Brown**[9] 5957 3-8-11 50 KierenFox 12 42
(Michael Attwater) *t.k.h: hld up in tch in midfield: effrt on inner 2f out: swtchd rt wl over 1f out: plugged on same pce and no threat to ldrs fnl f* 28/1
606 9 1 ½ **Necoleta**[14] 5748 3-8-7 46 oh1 DavidEgan 1 35
(Sylvester Kirk) *hld up in last quintet: effrt over 2f out: nt clrest of runs over 1f out: plugged on but nvr trbld ldrs* 16/1
0644 10 ½ **Padura Brave**[14] 5731 3-9-7 60 (v[1]) DavidProbert 11 48
(Mark Usher) *sn chsng ldr: lost 2nd u.p over 1f out and sn btn: fdd ins fnl f (jockey said filly hung left-handed under pressure)* 12/1
0006 11 1 ½ **Lynchpin (IRE)**[11] 5866 3-9-4 57 (b[1]) BrettDoyle 9 42
(Lydia Pearce) *s.i.s: t.k.h: hld up in last quintet: effrt on outer over 2f out: nvr involved* 25/1
40-5 12 4 **Milldean Felix (IRE)**[16] 5679 3-9-0 53 (v) RobertWinston 4 31
(Suzi Best) *midfield and pushed along early: steadily lost pl: bhd over 2f out* 17/2
0040 13 2 ½ **Arcadienne**[6] 6039 3-9-4 57 (b[1]) HarryBentley 13 30
(Ralph Beckett) *t.k.h: chsd ldrs: rdn over 2f out: sn struggling and lost pl over 1f out: sn wknd* 14/1
0542 14 7 **Zappiness (USA)**[16] 5652 3-9-5 58 JackMitchell 8 18+
(Peter Chapple-Hyam) *chsd ldrs: rdn over 3f out: struggling and losing pl whn short of room and hmpd wl over 1f out: sn wknd (trainers' rep could offer no explanation for the poor performance)* 5/1[2]

2m 5.35s (-1.25) **Going Correction** -0.10s/f (Stan) 14 Ran SP% 128.7
Speed ratings (Par 98): **101,100,99,97,97 96,95,95,93,93 92,89,87,81**
CSF £293.33 CT £3910.95 TOTE £49.00: £12.50, £2.60, £4.80; EX 675.60 Trifecta £3831.50.
Owner Mrs E A Bass **Bred** Newsells Park Stud **Trained** Danebury, Hants

FOCUS
A weak affair even for this grade although the tempo was decent enough.

6280 WITHEFORD EQUINE BARRIER TRIALS AT LINGFIELD PARK FILLIES' H'CAP 1m 2f (P)
2:45 (2:45) (Class 4) (0-80,81) 3-Y-O+
£5,207 (£1,549; £774; £387; £300; £300) Stalls Low

Form RPR
-035 1 **Cantiniere (USA)**[27] 5267 4-9-12 80 (p[1]) HayleyTurner 5 90
(Saeed bin Suroor) *wnt rt leaving stalls: in tch in midfield: effrt to chse ldrs over 1f out: clsd u.p and drvn to chal ins fnl f: led wl ins fnl f: styd on* 7/4[1]
6-02 2 ½ **Scheme**[11] 5855 3-8-10 71 (p[1]) LukeMorris 3 80
(Sir Mark Prescott Bt) *pressed ldr: rdn and ev ch 2f out: drvn to ld jst over 1f out: hdd wl ins fnl f: kpt on but hld towards fin* 6/1
1355 3 2 ¼ **Geetanjali (IRE)**[35] 4997 4-9-6 77 (p) CameronNoble(3) 6 81
(Michael Bell) *hood removed late: hld up in tch in last trio: effrt 2f out: hdwy u.p over 1f out: chsd ldng pair ins fnl f: no imp (jockey was slow to remove the blindfold explaining that it had got caught on the cheek-pieces and took two attempts to remove it)* 16/1
0123 4 ¾ **Manorah (IRE)**[16] 5687 3-9-5 80 JackMitchell 4 83
(Roger Varian) *hld up in tch: effrt ent fnl 2f: drvn over 1f out: kpt on ins fnl f: no threat to ldng pair* 9/4[2]
4554 5 1 ¾ **Elisheba (IRE)**[16] 5687 3-9-6 81 (p) RobertHavlin 1 80
(John Gosden) *led: rdn and hrd pressed 2f out: hdd jst over 1f out: no ex and wknd ins fnl f* 5/1[3]
2-30 6 1 ½ **Snowdon**[30] 5198 4-9-7 75 (p) TomMarquand 2 71
(Michael Dods) *chsd ldrs: effrt over 2f out: unable qck and outpcd over 1f out: wknd ins fnl f* 16/1
4653 7 13 **Narjes**[18] 5574 5-9-1 69 (h) HectorCrouch 7 39
(Laura Mongan) *s.i.s: hld up in tch in last trio: rdn over 2f out: sn struggling and lost tch over 1f out (jockey said mare was slowly away)* 16/1

2m 3.69s (-2.91) **Going Correction** -0.10s/f (Stan) 7 Ran SP% 115.7
WFA 3 from 4yo+ 7lb
Speed ratings (Par 102): **107,106,104,104,102 101,91**
CSF £13.31 TOTE £2.60: £1.30, £2.50; EX 14.20 Trifecta £98.30.
Owner Godolphin **Bred** Ranjan Racing Inc **Trained** Newmarket, Suffolk

FOCUS
Fairly competitive for the small field but only a modest pace. The winner has been rated as improving.

6281 WATCH SKY SPORTS RACING IN HD FILLIES' NOVICE AUCTION STKS 1m 1y(P)
3:15 (3:16) (Class 6) 2-Y-O
£2,781 (£827; £413; £206) Stalls High

Form RPR
612 1 **Little Bird (IRE)**[26] 5314 2-9-3 77 SeanLevey 4 74+
(Richard Hannon) *led for 2f: styd chsng ldr tl pushed into ld again ent fnl 2f: rdn and asserted 1f out: in command and kpt on wl ins fnl f* 8/11[1]
2 1 ¼ **Her Indoors (IRE)** 2-9-0 0 TomMarquand 1 68+
(Alan King) *s.i.s and flashing tail leaving stalls: rn green: in tch in rr: effrt on inner ent fnl 2f: hdwy 1f out: chsd wnr ins fnl f: kpt on* 14/1[3]
02 3 1 ¾ **Hiconic**[17] 5630 2-8-8 0 LukeMorris 3 58
(Alex Hales) *chsd ldrs: effrt and nt clr run over 2f out: effrt u.p to chse wnr ent fnl f: no imp and lost 2nd ins fnl f* 20/1
5 4 1 **Um Elnadim (FR)**[17] 5615 2-8-12 0 FrannyNorton 6 60
(Mark Johnston) *uns rdr on way to s: dwlt and pushed along leaving stalls: sn rcvrd and wl in tch on outer: rdn and outpcd over 1f out: wl hld and one pce ins fnl f* 7/4[2]
00 5 3 ¼ **Loretta Lass**[14] 5732 2-8-10 0 DavidProbert 2 50
(Adam West) *dwlt and rdn early: hdwy to ld after 2f: rdn and hdd ent fnl 2f: outpcd over 1f out: sn wknd: eased towards fin* 66/1
5 6 1 ¼ **Fair Sabra**[9] 5961 2-8-8 0 HollieDoyle 5 45
(David Elsworth) *in tch: n.m.r over 2f out: sn rdn and outpcd over 1f out: bhd ins fnl f* 14/1[3]

1m 38.89s (0.69) **Going Correction** -0.10s/f (Stan) 6 Ran SP% 113.9
Speed ratings (Par 89): **92,90,89,88,84 83**
CSF £13.41 TOTE £1.40: £1.10, £4.50; EX 9.60 Trifecta £33.60.
Owner Michael Pescod & Justin Dowley **Bred** Springbank Way Stud **Trained** East Everleigh, Wilts

FOCUS
An interesting novice auction race for fillies and the gallop was not strong. The winner didn't need to match her recent turf form at this venue.

6282 GOODBYE & GOOD LUCK WILL HUDSON H'CAP 1m 1y(P)
3:45 (3:46) (Class 4) (0-80,82) 3-Y-O
£5,207 (£1,549; £774; £387) Stalls High

Form RPR
-212 1 **Shawaaheq (IRE)**[27] 5270 3-9-7 77 JimCrowley 3 84
(Ed Dunlop) *mde all and dictated gallop: rdn and qcknd 2f out: drvn over 1f out: styd on and a doing enough ins fnl f* 5/2[3]
4110 2 ¾ **Al Messila**[20] 5525 3-9-12 82 PatDobbs 1 87
(Richard Hannon) *t.k.h: chsd wnr for 1f: styd chsng ldrs: effrt on inner wl over 1f out: kpt on u.p but hld by wnr ins fnl f: wnt 2nd cl home* 9/4[2]
3421 3 nse **Eligible (IRE)**[25] 5350 3-9-12 82 AdamKirby 4 87
(Clive Cox) *restless in stalls: dwlt: chsd wnr after 1f: effrt ent fnl 2f: drvn over 1f out: kpt on same pce u.p ins fnl f: lost 2nd cl home* 11/8[1]
5305 4 1 ½ **Tronada**[25] 5349 3-9-0 70 TomMarquand 2 71
(Alan King) *s.i.s: wl in tch in rr: effrt ent fnl 2f: kpt on but no imp fnl f* 10/1

1m 38.78s (0.58) **Going Correction** -0.10s/f (Stan) 4 Ran SP% 110.5
Speed ratings (Par 102): **93,92,92,90**
CSF £8.50 TOTE £2.50; EX 7.10 Trifecta £13.40.
Owner Hamdan Al Maktoum **Bred** Shadwell Estate Company Limited **Trained** Newmarket, Suffolk

The Form Book Flat 2019, Raceform Ltd, Newbury, RG14 5SJ

FOCUS
Competitive despite the paucity of runners and the winner dictated under a well-judged ride. The early pace was modest. This rates a length pb from the winner, with the second and third pretty much to their marks.

6283 RACING WELFARE NOVICE STKS — 7f 1y(P)
4:15 (4:18) (Class 5) 3-Y-O+ £3,428 (£1,020; £509; £254) Stalls Low

Form RPR

4-5 **1** **Lady Bowthorpe**[16] 5650 3-9-0 0 ... KieranShoemark 5 76
(William Jarvis) *mde all: pushed along and kicked clr ent fnl 2f: rdn over 1f out: styd on wl and in command ins fnl f: comf* 11/8[1]

3 **2** 2 **Sloane Garden**[25] 5357 3-9-0 0 ... OisinMurphy 6 71
(James Tate) *chsd wnr thrght: effrt and wnt clr w wnr whn drifted rt bnd 2f out: kpt on same pce fnl f* 9/4[2]

3 8 **Alameery** 3-9-5 0 ... JimCrowley 3 54
(Ed Dunlop) *chsd ldng pair: effrt over 2f out: sn outpcd by ldng pair: wl hld 3rd fr over 1f out* 4/1[3]

00 **4** 2 **A Hundred Echoes**[94] 2794 3-9-5 0 ... DavidEgan 7 49
(Roger Varian) *t.k.h: hld up in midfield: hdwy to chse ldng trio over 5f out: effrt and outpcd over 2f out: wl hld and plugged on same pce fr over 1f out* 14/1

50 **5** nk **Young General (IRE)**[12] 5808 3-9-5 0 ... FergusSweeney 2 48
(Richard Hannon) *hld up in last trio: outpcd over 2f out: no ch w ldrs but sme modest hdwy over 1f out: nvr involved* 9/1

0 **6** 2 ½ **Urban Scene**[14] 5748 3-9-0 0 ... CallumShepherd 4 36
(Linda Jewell) *dwlt: hld up in last trio: outpcd and nt clr run over 2f out: no ch and swtchd rt over 1f out: plugged on ins fnl f* 66/1

0 **7** 2 ½ **Noverre Dancer (IRE)**[157] 1217 3-9-2 0 ... JoshuaBryan(3) 1 34
(Nick Littmoden) *in tch in midfield: rdn and outpcd over 2f out: wknd over 1f out* 33/1

8 hd **Global Challenger (IRE)** 3-9-5 0 ... GeraldMosse 9 34
(Gay Kelleway) *restless in stalls: s.i.s: a towards rr: outpcd over 2f out: sn wl btn* 14/1

0-0 **9** 17 **Formally**[172] 943 3-9-5 0 ... BrettDoyle 10
(Tony Carroll) *chsd ldng trio on outer for over 1f out: outpcd and wl btn whn v wd bnd 2f out: wl bhd ins fnl f (vet said colt lost it's right fore shoe)* 100/1

1m 23.61s (-1.19) **Going Correction** -0.10s/f (Stan) 9 Ran SP% 121.6
Speed ratings (Par 103): **102,99,90,88,87 85,82,82,62**
CSF £4.92 TOTE £2.20: £1.10, £1.20, £1.60; EX 5.70 Trifecta £16.20.
Owner Ms E L Banks **Bred** Scuderia Archi Romani **Trained** Newmarket, Suffolk

FOCUS
Not much strength in depth and the market spoke correctly, with the first two in the market having it to themselves throughout, and they have been rated as improving.

6284 SKY SPORTS RACING ON SKY 415 H'CAP — 6f 1y(P)
4:45 (4:46) (Class 6) (0-55,55) 3-Y-O+
£2,781 (£827; £413; £300; £300; £300) Stalls Low

Form RPR

0R45 **1** **Dandilion (IRE)**[10] 5884 6-8-12 49 ... JoshuaBryan(3) 4 55
(Alex Hales) *midfield: effrt ent fnl 2f: swtchd rt and hdwy u.p over 1f out: styd on strly ins fnl to ld towards fin* 6/1

4221 **2** ½ **Tarseekh**[27] 5264 6-9-1 54 ...(b) WilliamCarver(5) 9 59
(Charlie Wallis) *broke fast: led and crossed to inner: rdn 2f out: drvn over 1f out: kpt on u.p: hdd and no ex towards fin* 4/1[2]

2324 **3** nk **Prince Rock (IRE)**[2] 6199 4-8-5 46 ...(h) LeviWilliams(7) 6 50
(Simon Dow) *hld up in rr of main gp: effrt 2f out: clsng whn nt clr run and swtchd rt 1f out: styd on strly ins fnl f: nt quite rch wnr (jockey said gelding was denied a clear run)* 7/1

0000 **4** nse **Mercers**[33] 5046 5-9-4 52 ...(b) CallumShepherd 10 55
(Paddy Butler) *midfield: effrt 2f out: hdwy u.p over 1f out: styd on to press ldrs wl ins fnl f: keeping on same pce whn squeezed for room nr fin* 40/1

5043 **5** 1 ½ **Quick Recovery**[27] 5264 4-8-12 53 ...(b) IsobelFrancis(7) 3 52
(Jim Boyle) *taken down early: chsd ldrs: effrt u.p on inner over 1f out: kpt on same pce ins fnl f (jockey said filly hung right-handed)* 7/2[1]

0020 **6** nk **Gold Club**[33] 5050 8-8-10 49 ... DarraghKeenan(5) 1 47
(Lee Carter) *chsd ldr: pressing ldr and effrt ent fnl 2f: no ex u.p and wknd wl ins fnl f* 14/1

0050 **7** 2 ¼ **Such Promise**[23] 5430 3-9-1 52 ...(v) RossaRyan 11 43
(Mike Murphy) *swtchd lft after s: hld up in rr of main gp: effrt 2f out: kpt on ins fnl f: nvr trbld ldrs* 12/1

4001 **8** ½ **Classy Cailin (IRE)**[33] 5063 4-9-4 52 ...(v) ShaneKelly 8 42
(Pam Sly) *chsd ldrs: pressing ldng pair and rdn jst over 2f out: lost pl u.p and btn over 1f out: wknd ins fnl f* 11/2[3]

0045 **9** ½ **Invincible One (IRE)**[9] 5957 3-8-12 49 ...(p) JasonWatson 5 37
(Sylvester Kirk) *hld up in midfield: effrt 2f out: no imp over 1f out: wl hld and one pce ins fnl f* 7/1

4-53 **10** 11 **Meraki**[32] 5102 3-8-7 49 ...(b) TheodoreLadd(5) 2 4
(Tim Pinfield) *a in rr of main gp: lost tch over 1f out* 12/1

-000 **11** 11 **Dutiful Son (IRE)**[33] 5051 9-9-7 55 ... EoinWalsh 7
(Emma Owen) *sn detached in last: wl bhd 1/2-way (jockey said gelding was never travelling)* 33/1

1m 10.78s (-1.12) **Going Correction** -0.10s/f (Stan)
WFA 3 from 4yo+ 3lb 11 Ran SP% 124.3
Speed ratings (Par 101): **103,102,101,101,99 99,96,95,95,80 65**
CSF £32.11 CT £182.00 TOTE £7.00: £2.60, £1.60, £2.80; EX 41.90 Trifecta £342.30.
Owner Golden Equinox Racing **Bred** Ballyhane Stud **Trained** Edgcote, Northamptonshire

FOCUS
A weak handicap.

6285 SKY SPORTS RACING ON VIRGIN 535 H'CAP — 5f 6y(P)
5:15 (5:15) (Class 6) (0-55,55) 3-Y-O+
£2,781 (£827; £413; £300; £300; £300) Stalls High

Form RPR

4113 **1** **Aquadabra (IRE)**[23] 5449 4-9-7 55 ... CallumShepherd 7 60
(Christopher Mason) *restless in stalls: chsd ldrs: effrt wl over 1f out: clsd and drvn to chal 1f out: led ins fnl f: kpt on: all out* 5/2[1]

455- **2** shd **Katherine Place**[404] 4803 4-8-13 47 ...(t) RyanTate 9 52
(Bill Turner) *midfield: hdwy to press ldr over 3f out: ev ch and effrt wl over 1f out: kpt on wl u.p: jst hld* 25/1

0000 **3** hd **Flowing Clarets**[6] 6048 6-8-12 46 ... LiamJones 3 50
(John Bridger) *taken down early: in tch tl short of room and dropped to last trio after 1f: effrt over 1f out: clsd u.p ins fnl f: styd on wl u.p towards fin* 8/1

0005 **4** ¾ **Sandfrankskipsgo**[33] 5046 10-9-6 54 ... ShaneKelly 1 55
(Peter Crate) *in tch: effrt over 1f out: drvn to chse ldrs ins fnl f: kpt on same pce towards fin* 6/1[3]

0522 **5** ½ **Terri Rules (IRE)**[26] 5315 4-9-6 54 ... KierenFox 8 53
(Lee Carter) *hld up in tch in last trio: effrt and hdwy on inner over 1f out: chsd ldrs and kpt on same pce ins fnl f* 7/2[2]

0504 **6** nse **Ask The Guru**[10] 5884 9-8-12 46 oh1 ...(p) RobertHavlin 4 46
(Michael Attwater) *chsd ldr tl over 3f out: styd chsng ldrs: nt clr run 1f out: nvr enough room ins fnl f: kpt on same pce towards fin* 14/1

004R **7** nk **Knockabout Queen**[10] 5884 3-9-4 54 ... EoinWalsh 2 52
(Tony Carroll) *s.i.s: in rr: effrt and hung rt bnd 2f: kpt on u.p ins fnl f: nt rch ldrs (jockey said filly was slowly away)* 16/1

2106 **8** nk **Brogans Bay (IRE)**[33] 5046 4-9-7 55 ... JFEgan 6 52
(Simon Dow) *dwlt: in tch: wd bnd 2f out: kpt on u.p ins fnl f* 7/2[2]

4306 **9** nk **Awake In Asia**[33] 5044 3-9-2 55 ...(p) JoshuaBryan(3) 5 51
(Charlie Wallis) *led: rdn over 1f out: drvn and hdd ins fnl f: wknd towards fin* 16/1

58.84s (0.04) **Going Correction** -0.10s/f (Stan)
WFA 3 from 4yo+ 2lb 9 Ran SP% 120.7
Speed ratings (Par 101): **95,94,94,93,92 92,91,91,91**
CSF £72.37 CT £458.51 TOTE £3.20: £1.30, £10.30, £2.20; EX 78.40 Trifecta £532.40.
Owner Brian Hicks **Bred** Rathasker Stud **Trained** Caewent, Monmouthshire

FOCUS
The lack of early pace resulted in a bunched finish. A moderate race.
T/Plt: £139.40 to a £1 stake. Pool: £67,877.10 - 355.25 winning units T/Qpdt: £8.00 to a £1 stake. Pool: £8.368.57 - 766.87 winning units **Steve Payne**

6018 WINDSOR (R-H)
Monday, August 19

OFFICIAL GOING: Good (good to soft in places; 6.9)
Wind: Fresh, behind Weather: Fine

6286 SKY SPORTS RACING ON SKY 415 H'CAP — 6f 12y
5:30 (5:32) (Class 5) (0-70,75) 3-Y-O
£3,428 (£1,020; £509; £300; £300; £300) Stalls Centre

Form RPR

1361 **1** **Eye Of The Water (IRE)**[8] 5985 3-9-11 74 6ex ... DavidProbert 12 86
(Ronald Harris) *w ldrs: narrow ld 1/2-way: drvn over 1f out: kpt on wl and asserted last 75yds (vet said gelding lost right fore shoe)* 8/1

5021 **2** ½ **Sonja Henie (IRE)**[7] 6025 3-9-7 75 6ex ... ThomasGreatrex(5) 7 85
(David Loughnane) *mde most to 1/2-way: w wnr after and clr of rest fr 2f out: upsides and drvn fnl f: nt qckn last 100yds* 15/2[3]

-021 **3** 4 ½ **Foxy Femme**[44] 4651 3-9-5 68 ... JoeyHaynes 1 64
(John Gallagher) *pushed along towards rr bef 1/2-way: styd on u.p over 1f out: snatched 3rd last stride* 4/1[1]

1365 **4** shd **Ever Rock (IRE)**[12] 5793 3-8-3 59 ... LauraCoughlan(7) 10 54
(J S Moore) *wl in rr: prog on wd outside over 2f out: rdn to chse clr ldng pair ins fnl f: no imp and lost 3rd last stride* 25/1

3212 **5** shd **Quirky Gertie (IRE)**[18] 5575 3-9-4 72 ... ScottMcCullagh(5) 11 67
(Mick Channon) *wl in rr: rdn and prog over 2f out: nt clr run and swtchd lft 1f out: styd on and nrly grabbed a pl* 9/1

3362 **6** nk **Under Curfew**[7] 6018 3-8-11 60 ... TomMarquand 3 54
(Tony Carroll) *in tch: rdn over 2f out: hrd drvn and ch of 3rd pl fnl f but no ch of winning: one pce nr fin* 13/2[2]

0006 **7** ¾ **Aegean Mist**[7] 6018 3-8-7 56 ...(p) HollieDoyle 8 48
(John Bridger) *w ldrs to over 2f out: lost pl and outpcd: kpt on again ins fnl f* 25/1

0512 **8** 3 ½ **Tone The Barone**[25] 5356 3-9-6 69 ...(t) SilvestreDeSousa 6 49
(Stuart Williams) *in tch: drvn over 2f out: no imp on ldrs u.p over 1f out: wknd fnl f (trainer reported gelding made a noise)* 4/1[1]

3033 **9** ½ **Devils Roc**[26] 5289 3-9-5 68 ... RobHornby 15 47
(Jonathan Portman) *w ldrs to 2f out: wknd over 1f out* 20/1

5204 **10** 2 **Alliseeisnibras (IRE)**[33] 5050 3-9-6 69 ... SeanLevey 14 41
(Ismail Mohammed) *dwlt: sn chsd ldrs: rdn over 2f out: wknd qckly over 1f out* 10/1

04-0 **11** 1 ¾ **Intricate**[53] 4285 3-9-3 66 ... HectorCrouch 2 33
(Clive Cox) *w ldrs 2f: unable to hold pl and rdn in midfield 1/2-way: sn struggling* 20/1

3060 **12** 1 ¾ **Painted Dream**[17] 5622 3-8-11 65 ... CierenFallon(5) 4 26
(George Margarson) *nvr gng the pce and a struggling in rr* 25/1

1453 **13** 7 **Halle's Harbour**[108] 2357 3-8-2 56 ...(v) RhiainIngram(5) 5
(Paul George) *a wl in rr: hanging and wknd 2f out: eased* 25/1

000- **14** 6 **Tru Grit (IRE)**[241] 9669 3-8-13 62 ... LukeMorris 9
(Tom Clover) *in tch to 1/2-way: sn wknd: bhd and eased fnl f* 50/1

1m 11.75s (-0.35) **Going Correction** +0.10s/f (Good) 14 Ran SP% 122.2
Speed ratings (Par 100): **106,105,99,99,99 98,97,93,92,89 87,85,75,67**
CSF £61.31 CT £289.54 TOTE £9.50: £2.90, £3.00, £2.00; EX 86.20 Trifecta £326.70.
Owner Malcolm E Wright **Bred** M Fahy **Trained** Earlswood, Monmouths

FOCUS
Two recent scorers dominated this sprint handicap, pulling right away from over 1f out near to the stands' rail, and they are progressive.

6287 BRITISH STALLION STUDS EBF MAIDEN STKS (PLUS 10 RACE) — 6f 12y
6:00 (6:03) (Class 4) 2-Y-O £4,463 (£1,328; £663; £331) Stalls Centre

Form RPR

06 **1** **Winning Streak**[17] 5624 2-8-12 0 ...(t[1]) MarcoGhiani(7) 2 82
(Stuart Williams) *trckd ldng pair: pushed along over 2f out: chsd ldr over 1f out: grad clsd after: shkn up to ld last 100yds: readily* 28/1

23 **2** 1 **Lost In Time**[20] 5523 2-9-5 0 ... OisinMurphy 3 79
(Saeed bin Suroor) *disp ld tl def advantage over 2f out: looked in command over 1f out: rdn fnl f: hdd and outpcd last 100yds* 4/7[1]

320 **3** 5 **Written Broadcast (IRE)**[20] 5523 2-9-5 80 ... SeanLevey 12 64
(Richard Hannon) *chsd ldrs: pushed along 1/2-way: sn outpcd: kpt on over 1f out to take modest 3rd last stride* 4/1[2]

43 **4** shd **Three Fans (FR)**[12] 5815 2-9-5 0 ... RichardKingscote 1 64
(Tom Dascombe) *disp ld to over 2f out: chsd ldr to over 1f out: wknd fnl f: lost 3rd last stride* 13/2[3]

5 **5** 3 ½ **Bryn Du**[18] 5591 2-9-5 0 ... TomMarquand 8 53
(William Haggas) *chsd ldrs: urged along and outpcd sn after 1/2-way: no prog after* 16/1

6 ¾ **Wilfy** 2-9-5 0 ... LiamKeniry 6 51
(Sylvester Kirk) *s.s: wl off the pce in rr: sme prog over 2f out: nvr a factor but kpt on fnl f (jockey said colt was slowly away and hung right-handed)* 40/1

The Form Book Flat 2019, Raceform Ltd, Newbury, RG14 5SJ

0 **7** 2 ¾ **Arabian Dream**[13] 5772 2-9-0 0 .... HarryBentley 11 38
(Ralph Beckett) *nt that wl away: a towards rr: outpcd fr 1/2-way: no ch fnl 2f* **20/1**

65 **8** 4 **Full Spectrum (IRE)**[7] 6029 2-9-0 0 .... (p[1]) LukeMorris 10 26
(Paul George) *t.k.h: hld up in rr: brief effrt 2f out: no ch whn impeded over 1f out: wknd* **80/1**

9 4 **Gift Of Youth** 2-9-5 0 .... CharlesBishop 9 19
(Amanda Perrett) *a off the pce: wknd 2f out* **40/1**

10 1 ½ **Erika** 2-9-0 0 .... GeraldMosse 7 9
(Neil Mulholland) *gd spd to press ldrs to 1/2-way: wknd qckly 2f out* **100/1**

5 **11** 39 **Island Warrior (IRE)**[25] 5339 2-9-5 0 .... (t[1]) DavidEgan 5
(Heather Main) *dwlt: a bhd: t.o* **20/1**

1m 12.21s (0.11) **Going Correction** +0.10s/f (Good) **11** Ran SP% **122.9**
Speed ratings (Par 96): **103,101,95,94,90 89,85,80,74,72 20**
CSF £45.38 TOTE £49.60: £7.30, £1.02, £1.60; EX 107.50 Trifecta £423.10.
Owner T W Morley **Bred** Mrs Fiona Denniff **Trained** Newmarket, Suffolk

FOCUS
Bit of a turn up in this maiden, with the front two clear. The runner-up has been rated to his Goodwood form.

6288 ODDFELLOWS H'CAP — 5f 21y

6:30 (6:30) (Class 4) (0-80,82) 3-Y-O+
£5,207 (£1,549; £774; £387; £300; £300) **Stalls** Centre

Form RPR

5260 **1** **Harry Hurricane**[20] 5524 7-9-5 **79** .... (p) CierenFallon(5) 7 87
(George Baker) *disp ld to over 1f out: sn shkn up and pressed ldr: rdn to ld ins fnl f: styd on* **9/2**[3]

3001 **2** ¾ **Look Surprised**[14] 5750 6-8-12 **70** .... WilliamCox(3) 6 75
(Roger Teal) *disp ld: narrow advantage over 1f out: rdn and hdd ins fnl f: nt qckn* **4/1**[2]

4531 **3** 1 ¾ **Indian Raj**[26] 5318 5-9-6 **75** .... (t) OisinMurphy 8 74
(Stuart Williams) *hld up in 5th: shkn up 2f out: tried to cl over 1f out but nt qckn: kpt on to take 3rd last strides* **11/10**[1]

305 **4** hd **Kodiac Express (IRE)**[11] 5843 4-9-2 **71** .... RossaRyan 9 69
(Mike Murphy) *taken down early: w ldrs to 1/2-way: rdn 2f out: kpt on one pce after* **11/1**

4350 **5** 5 **Pettochside**[28] 5252 10-8-12 **67** .... HollieDoyle 3 47
(John Bridger) *rousted s: disp ld to jst over 2f out: wknd over 1f out* **6/1**

0555 **6** 10 **Solar Park (IRE)**[8] 5990 3-9-3 **74** .... RobHornby 4 18
(Michael Attwater) *sltly awkward s: a last: struggling fr 1/2-way: t.o* **25/1**

59.67s (-0.43) **Going Correction** +0.10s/f (Good)
WFA 3 from 4yo+ 2lb **6** Ran SP% **112.3**
Speed ratings (Par 105): **107,105,103,102,94 78**
CSF £22.46 CT £31.94 TOTE £5.50: £2.40, £1.70; EX 19.70 Trifecta £56.70.
Owner Dare To Dream Racing **Bred** Selwood Bloodstock, Hoskins & Lowry **Trained** Chiddingfold, Surrey

FOCUS
The winner has been rated in line with this year's form, with the runner-up to form.

6289 WINDSOR RACECOURSE FIREWORKS, RETURNS 2ND NOVEMBER H'CAP — 1m 2f

7:00 (7:00) (Class 4) (0-80,81) 4-Y-O+
£5,207 (£1,549; £774; £387; £300; £300) **Stalls** Low

Form RPR

3134 **1** **Black Lotus**[61] 4007 4-9-7 **80** .... GeorgeWood 7 90+
(Chris Wall) *hld up in rr: gng strly whn waiting for room 3f out: impeded on outer over 2f out: prog over 1f out: swept into the ld ins fnl f: sn clr: comf* **3/1**[1]

5211 **2** 2 ¼ **The Jean Genie**[121] 1934 5-9-8 **81** .... HollieDoyle 3 85
(William Stone) *led 2f: trckd ldrs after: rdn over 2f out: led over 1f out: hdd and readily outpcd ins fnl f* **8/1**

4501 **3** ½ **High Acclaim (USA)**[14] 5747 5-9-1 **74** .... SilvestreDeSousa 2 77
(Roger Teal) *s.i.s: sn chsd ldrs: urged along over 3f out: styd cl up and stl ch 1f out: kpt on same pce* **7/2**[2]

1255 **4** ¾ **Global Art**[23] 5436 4-9-8 **81** .... (b) AdamKirby 9 83
(Ed Dunlop) *dwlt: hld up in last pair: prog on outer wl over 2f out: drvn to chal jst over 1f out: fdd ins fnl f* **16/1**

6016 **5** ¾ **Medalla De Oro**[11] 5849 5-9-7 **80** .... (h) JackMitchell 6 80
(Tom Clover) *led after 2f: urged along to go for home 3f out: hdd over 1f out: steadily outpcd* **11/2**[3]

0062 **6** 2 **Perfect Refuge**[14] 5747 4-8-11 **70** .... HectorCrouch 5 66
(Clive Cox) *hld up in last: shkn up and prog over 2f out: chsd ldrs over 1f out: one pce after* **7/1**

-542 **7** 2 ¼ **Statuario**[30] 5178 4-9-6 **79** .... (p) LukeMorris 4 71
(Richard Spencer) *trckd ldr after 3f: urged along over 3f out: lost 2nd wl over 1f out: wknd u.p* **13/2**

3-00 **8** 1 ¼ **Sing Out Loud (IRE)**[47] 4506 4-8-13 **77** .... ScottMcCullagh(5) 1 66
(Michael Madgwick) *hld up towards rr: shkn up over 2f out: no real prog* **20/1**

5010 **9** 6 **Prevent**[30] 5178 4-9-3 **76** .... (p) JimCrowley 10 53
(Ian Williams) *chsd ldrs: rdn over 2f out: nt qckn wl over 1f out: wknd qckly* **12/1**

0005 **10** 13 **Rock Icon**[73] 3529 6-8-12 **71** .... CharlesBishop 8 22
(Ali Stronge) *sn hld up in midfield: lost pl over 3f out: sn in last and wkng: t.o* **33/1**

2m 9.72s (0.72) **Going Correction** +0.10s/f (Good) **10** Ran SP% **120.8**
Speed ratings (Par 105): **68,66,65,65,64 63,61,60,55,45**
CSF £28.90 CT £90.06 TOTE £3.70: £1.40, £2.30, £1.70; EX 39.50 Trifecta £112.70.
Owner Ms Aida Fustoq **Bred** Deerfield Farm **Trained** Newmarket, Suffolk

FOCUS
Add 18yds. Fair form, the gallop was ordinary and the favourite overcame trouble in running to win readily, resuming her progress.

6290 RITA ORA LIVE AT WINDSOR RACECOURSE NOVICE STKS — 1m 2f

7:30 (7:31) (Class 5) 3-4-Y-O
£3,428 (£1,020; £509; £254) **Stalls** Low

Form RPR

23 **1** **Passion And Glory (IRE)**[24] 5384 3-9-2 0 .... OisinMurphy 6 84+
(Saeed bin Suroor) *mde virtually all: stl gng strly over 2f out: shkn up and pressed over 1f out: styd on and in command fnl f* **8/11**[1]

10 **2** 1 ¾ **El Misk**[124] 1856 3-9-9 0 .... RobertHavlin 15 87
(John Gosden) *sn trckd wnr: rdn and lost 2nd 2f out: kpt on same pce to regain 2nd last stride* **3/1**[2]

3 shd **Shauyra (IRE)** 3-8-8 0 .... GeorgiaCox(3) 1 76+
(William Haggas) *dwlt but sn v prom: chsd wnr 2f out: rdn and tried to chal over 1f out: hld fnl f: eased fnl strides and lost 2nd post* **18/1**

03 **4** 4 **Dobrianka**[184] 761 3-8-11 0 .... HarryBentley 11 67
(Ralph Beckett) *chsd ldrs: shkn up over 2f out: steadily outpcd after: should do bttr* **6/1**[3]

06 **5** 6 **Zest Of Zambia (USA)**[18] 5578 3-8-11 0 .... DavidEgan 2 55
(Dai Burchell) *wl in tch: rdn and stl chsng ldrs over 2f out: wknd over 1f out* **100/1**

03 **6** 1 ¼ **Cochise**[18] 5578 3-9-2 0 .... JasonWatson 14 58+
(Roger Charlton) *fractious to post: t.k.h: hld up in midfield: shkn up and outpcd over 3f out: kpt on over 1f out* **20/1**

5 **7** 1 ¼ **Gibraltarian (IRE)**[14] 5748 3-8-11 0 .... CharlieBennett 4 50
(Jim Boyle) *in tch in midfield: outpcd by ldrs over 3f out: reminder over 2f out: no prog after: nt disgraced* **100/1**

8 2 **Torbellino** 3-8-11 0 .... KierenFox 3 46
(John Best) *dwlt: quick prog after 3f to trck ldng pair: rdn 3f out: wknd over 2f out* **100/1**

0-5 **9** 2 **Jeweller**[110] 2289 3-9-2 0 .... LouisSteward 7 47
(Sir Michael Stoute) *hld up towards rr: modest prog over 3f out: pushed along and no hdwy over 2f out: nvr really in it* **25/1**

0 **10** 1 ¼ **Star Guide (GER)**[142] 1417 3-8-11 0 .... (h) ThomasGreatrex(5) 12 45
(David Menuisier) *mostly wl in rr: lft bhd over 3f out: passed a few late on: nvr in it* **40/1**

0 **11** ¾ **Capla Huntress**[16] 5656 3-8-11 0 .... JackMitchell 8 38
(Chris Wall) *hld up and last after 3f: rn green whn shkn up over 3f out: swtchd rt jst over 1f out: no real prog but sing to run on nr fin* **50/1**

12 1 **Devizes (IRE)**[152] 3-9-2 0 .... JFEgan 16 41
(Pat Phelan) *hld up in last: prog after 3f but stl towards rr: brief effrt over 3f out: wknd over 2f out* **100/1**

4 **13** nk **Viking Prince (IRE)**[13] 5783 3-9-2 0 .... RichardKingscote 13 40
(Ian Williams) *a wl in rr: pushed along and lft bhd over 3f out: nvr in it* **66/1**

0 **14** hd **Binmar's Sexy Lexy (CAN)**[23] 5451 3-8-8 0 .... WilliamCox(3) 10 35
(Stuart Kittow) *t.k.h early: sn towards rr: struggling 3f out* **100/1**

15 7 **Sea It My Way (IRE)** 3-9-2 0 .... GeorgeWood 5 26
(James Fanshawe) *slowly away: nvr beyond midfield: wknd u.p 3f out* **16/1**

16 16 **Olaf** 3-9-2 0 .... LiamJones 9
(John Bridger) *rn v green: sn pushed along: a in rr: t.o* **100/1**

2m 11.17s (2.17) **Going Correction** +0.10s/f (Good) **16** Ran SP% **128.8**
Speed ratings (Par 103): **95,93,93,90,85 84,83,81,80,79 78,77,77,77,71 59**
CSF £2.97 TOTE £1.50: £1.10, £1.50, £4.40; EX 3.90 Trifecta £31.50.
Owner Godolphin **Bred** Godolphin **Trained** Newmarket, Suffolk
■ Stewards' Enquiry : Georgia Cox ten-day ban: failed to achieve best possible placing (Sep 2nd-11th)

FOCUS
Add 18yds. A useful novice, but little got into it with the market leaders dominating and the winner didn't have to run to his best.

6291 SKY SPORTS RACING ON VIRGIN 535 H'CAP — 1m 3f 99y

8:00 (8:00) (Class 4) (0-80,80) 3-Y-O+
£5,207 (£1,549; £774; £387; £300; £300) **Stalls** Low

Form RPR

5233 **1** **Tammooz**[13] 5779 3-9-5 **79** .... DavidEgan 6 91+
(Roger Varian) *hld up disputing 3rd and off the pce: shkn up to chse clr ldr over 2f out: grad clsd: drvn to chal fnl f: led nr fin* **5/2**[2]

-621 **2** hd **Zoffee**[21] 5502 3-9-6 **80** .... SilvestreDeSousa 7 91
(Tom Dascombe) *racd freely: led and clr w one rival: sent for home 3f out and sn 4 l ahd: rdn over 2f out: kpt on but worn down nr fin* **5/4**[1]

5140 **3** 10 **King Of The Sand (IRE)**[46] 4543 4-9-11 **77** .... AdamKirby 3 70
(Gary Moore) *trckd ldr and wl ahd of rest: rdn over 3f out: lost 2nd over 2f out: steadily lft bhd* **8/1**[3]

3006 **4** 1 ¾ **Central City (IRE)**[11] 5858 4-10-0 **80** .... JimCrowley 4 70
(Ian Williams) *hld up disputing 3rd and off the pce: pushed along and no prog over 2f out: no ch whn rdn over 1f out* **12/1**

P050 **5** ½ **Tribal Commander**[30] 5175 3-8-4 **64** .... LukeMorris 1 54
(Ian Williams) *stdd s: hld up in last and wl off the pce: nvr a factor* **20/1**

1543 **6** ½ **Miss M (IRE)**[25] 5344 5-8-12 **64** .... JFEgan 2 52
(William Muir) *dwlt: hld up in 5th and off the pce: rdn and sme prog to chse clr ldng pair over 1f out: wknd ins fnl f* **8/1**[3]

5155 **7** 9 **El Borracho (IRE)**[32] 5091 4-9-8 **74** .... (h) TomMarquand 5 47
(Simon Dow) *stdd s: hld up in last pair: rdn and struggling 3f out: sn bhd* **16/1**

2m 29.59s (-0.11) **Going Correction** +0.10s/f (Good)
WFA 3 from 4yo+ 8lb **7** Ran SP% **113.6**
Speed ratings (Par 105): **104,103,96,95,94 94,88**
CSF £5.90 TOTE £3.10: £1.70, £1.30; EX 7.20 Trifecta £37.90.
Owner Sheikh Ahmed Al Maktoum **Bred** Bartisan Racing Ltd **Trained** Newmarket, Suffolk

FOCUS
Add 18yds. A fair handicap, they were strung out from an early stage and the two market leaders pulled well clear.
T/Jkpt: Not won. T/Plt: £21.50 to a £1 stake. Pool: £95,654.58 - 3234.03 winning units T/Qpdt: £8.40 to a £1 stake. Pool: £8,841.17 - 773.08 winning units **Jonathon Neesom**

6292 - 6298a (Foreign Racing) - See Raceform Interactive

5878 BRIGHTON (L-H)

Tuesday, August 20

OFFICIAL GOING: Good to firm (7.9)
Wind: virtually nil Weather: warm and sunny

6299 ANTIQUES VINTAGE & COLLECTABLES FAIR 25 AUG H'CAP — 5f 60y

1:40 (1:45) (Class 5) (0-75,68) 3-Y-O+ **£3,428** (£1,020; £509; £300; £300) **Stalls** Centre

Form RPR

6232 **1** **Big Time Maybe (IRE)**[13] 5793 4-8-11 **60** .... (p) CierenFallon(5) 3 67
(Michael Attwater) *settled wl in 3rd: effrt to chse ldr 2f out: rdn and almost upsides 1f out: drvn to ld fnl 75yds* **13/8**[1]

4052 **2** nk **Glamorous Rocket (IRE)**[9] 5990 4-9-10 **68** .... CharlesBishop 2 74
(Christopher Mason) *led and racd keenly: rdn and hung rt 1f out: drvn and hdd by wnr fnl 75yds (jockey said filly hung right-handed throughout)* **5/2**[2]

546 **3** 2 **Pink Iceburg (IRE)**[27] 5318 3-9-7 **67** .... TomQueally 5 66
(Peter Crate) *chsd ldr: rdn along and outpcd by front pair over 1f out: one pce fnl f* **7/1**

The Form Book Flat 2019, Raceform Ltd, Newbury, RG14 5SJ

2202 **4** 4 1/2 **Ghepardo**[24] 5449 4-9-5 63 TomMarquand 1 46
(Patrick Chamings) *settled in 4th: pushed along and no imp 2f out: rdn and one pce fnl f* 11/4[3]

0000 **5** 2 **The Lacemaker**[11] 5892 5-9-4 62 (p) JFEgan 4 38
(Milton Harris) *dwlt bdly and racd in last: latched on to main gp 1/2-way: sn rdn and outpcd 2f out: one pce after* 33/1

1m 2.73s (-0.27) **Going Correction** +0.025s/f (Good)
WFA 3 from 4yo+ 2lb 5 Ran SP% **108.8**
Speed ratings (Par 103): **103,102,99,92,88**
CSF £5.81 TOTE £2.10: £1.20, £1.70; EX 5.00 Trifecta £14.40.
Owner Dare To Dream Racing **Bred** Joe Fogarty **Trained** Epsom, Surrey

FOCUS
The rail was moved out 2yds from the 6f start down to the 5f, then 1m round the bend to the 2.2f. This wasn't a bad little sprint handicap for the class. The winner rates to his penultimate Sandown form. Add 9yds.

6300 SUMMERTIMELIVE.CO.UK CLASSIC IBIZA 7 SEPT NOVICE MEDIAN AUCTION STKS 5f 215y
2:10 (2:15) (Class 5) 2-Y-O £3,428 (£1,020; £509; £254) **Stalls** Centre

Form RPR
55 **1** **Punchbowl Flyer (IRE)**[14] 5774 2-9-5 0 CharlesBishop 1 77+
(Eve Johnson Houghton) *racd in rr of midfield: hdwy to chse ldrs 2f out and hung lft: sn rdn and kpt on wl to ld fnl 50yds despite hanging lft again (jockey said colt hung left-handed)* 4/1[2]

22 **2** 1/2 **Laikaparty (IRE)**[25] 5381 2-9-5 0 (p[1]) HollieDoyle 8 72
(Archie Watson) *led: rdn and strly pressed 2f out: drvn and kpt on wl for press 1f out: no ex whn hdd by wnr fnl 50yds* 4/9[1]

0 **3** 3/4 **Gleeds Girl**[14] 5772 2-9-0 0 TomMarquand 2 65
(Mick Channon) *racd in midfield: pushed along 2f out: sn rdn and kpt on wl fnl f: nt rch wnr* 20/1

5 **4** 1/2 **Music Therapist (IRE)**[11] 5913 2-9-5 0 PatCosgrave 9 68
(George Scott) *restless in stalls: chsd ldr: rdn upsides and ev ch 1f out: one pce fnl f* 10/1

3 **5** 1 1/2 **Global Agreement**[11] 5879 2-9-5 0 JFEgan 4 64
(Milton Harris) *trckd ldr: rdn along and no imp 2f out: one pce fnl f* 6/1[3]

0 **6** 1 3/4 **Hootenanny (IRE)**[14] 5780 2-9-5 0 JimmyQuinn 6 58
(Adam West) *hld up: pushed along in rr 2f out: one pce fnl f* 50/1

0 **7** 1 **Alcance (FR)**[9] 5988 2-9-0 0 HectorCrouch 5 50
(Clive Cox) *racd in midfield: rdn along and outpcd over 1f out: one pce fnl f* 14/1

8 2 1/2 **Scallywagtail (IRE)** 2-9-5 0 TomQueally 7 47
(Gary Moore) *hld up: rdn in rr on outer 2f out: nvr on terms* 20/1

1m 11.25s (0.15) **Going Correction** +0.025s/f (Good) 8 Ran SP% **130.8**
Speed ratings (Par 94): **100,99,98,97,95 93,92,88**
CSF £7.00 TOTE £7.50: £1.50, £1.02, £4.40; EX 8.50 Trifecta £52.70.
Owner The Punch Bunch **Bred** Castle Estates Ltd **Trained** Blewbury, Oxon

FOCUS
This modest novice event was run at a decent pace. Add 9yds.

6301 ABF THE SOLDIERS CHARITY H'CAP 5f 215y
2:40 (2:45) (Class 4) (0-80,82) 3-Y-O+
£5,207 (£1,549; £774; £387; £300; £300) **Stalls** Centre

Form RPR
1032 **1** **Alicia Darcy (IRE)**[5] 6108 3-8-9 74 (b) KateLeahy(7) 1 80
(Archie Watson) *racd in midfield: effrt to chse ldng pair over 1f out: sn rdn and kpt on wl to ld cl home* 11/2

3031 **2** nk **Tin Hat (IRE)**[11] 5882 3-9-3 82 (p) GeorgiaDobie(7) 3 87
(Eve Johnson Houghton) *led at stdy pce: effrt to qckn tempo 2f out: rdn and hdd over 1f out: kpt on wl for press fnl f to regain 2nd fnl strides* 5/1[3]

512 **3** shd **Pink Flamingo**[25] 5372 3-9-4 81 CierenFallon(5) 4 86
(Michael Attwater) *trckd ldr: rdn along to take a narrow ld over 1f out: no ex whn hdd and lost 2 pls cl home* 11/4[1]

4650 **4** 2 1/4 **Lightning Charlie**[17] 5661 7-9-1 75 ScottMcCullagh(5) 7 72
(Amanda Perrett) *racd in midfield: pushed along and no imp 2f out: one pce fnl f* 6/1

1134 **5** 3/4 **Spanish Star (IRE)**[40] 4844 4-9-5 74 HectorCrouch 2 69
(Patrick Chamings) *trckd ldr on inner: pushed along and no imp 2f out: sn rdn over 1f out: one pce fnl f* 9/2[2]

2661 **6** nk **Enthaar**[12] 5843 4-9-4 73 (tp) TomMarquand 6 67
(Stuart Williams) *hld up: rdn and outpcd 2f out: no imp fnl f* 8/1

5003 **7** 1/2 **Pour La Victoire (IRE)**[11] 5882 9-9-2 71 GeorgeDowning 5 64
(Tony Carroll) *wnt to post early: hld up: rdn in last over 1f out: nvr on terms* 11/1

1m 11.06s (-0.04) **Going Correction** +0.025s/f (Good)
WFA 3 from 4yo+ 3lb 7 Ran SP% **110.6**
Speed ratings (Par 105): **101,100,100,97,96 96,95**
CSF £30.54 TOTE £5.60: £2.90, £2.70; EX 25.80 Trifecta £93.90.
Owner Boadicea Bloodstock **Bred** Tally-Ho Stud **Trained** Upper Lambourn, W Berks

FOCUS
Racing handily was a must in this ordinary sprint handicap. Add 9yds.

6302 SUSSEX ART FAIRS (EAST) 12 OCT MEDIAN AUCTION MAIDEN STKS 6f 210y
3:10 (3:15) (Class 6) 3-5-Y-O £2,781 (£827; £413; £206) **Stalls** Low

Form RPR
-306 **1** **So Macho (IRE)**[13] 5817 4-9-10 64 JackMitchell 4 68
(Grant Tuer) *mde all: pushed along to qckn tempo 2f out: rdn w 1 l ld 1f out: drvn out fnl f* 8/11[1]

6056 **2** 1 1/2 **Ecstasea (IRE)**[12] 5869 3-9-0 57 JFEgan 5 57
(Rae Guest) *hld up: hdwy u.p 2f out: rdn and styd on wl fnl f: nt rch wnr* 10/1

5-00 **3** nk **Dependable (GER)**[27] 5309 4-9-0 57 CierenFallon(5) 6 58
(Charles Hills) *chsd wnr: rdn and outpcd 2f out: kpt on fnl f but no imp* 13/2[2]

000- **4** 3 1/4 **Penwood (FR)**[269] 9244 4-9-5 57 TomMarquand 3 49
(Joseph Tuite) *racd in midfield: rdn along and no imp 2f out: wknd fnl f* 15/2

3560 **5** 1 3/4 **Spirit Of Lucerne (IRE)**[5] 6128 3-8-7 46 GraceMcEntee(7) 7 43
(Phil McEntee) *midfield: effrt to chse wnr 2f out: rdn and sn wknd 1f out* 20/1

44 **6** 15 **Brambledown**[10] 5955 3-9-5 0 HectorCrouch 2 7
(Gary Moore) *trckd wnr on inner: rdn and lost pl over 2f out: sn detached (trainer said gelding was outpaced on drop back in trip)* 7/1[3]

1m 24.8s (1.00) **Going Correction** +0.025s/f (Good)
WFA 3 from 4yo 5lb 6 Ran SP% **109.4**
Speed ratings (Par 101): **95,93,92,89,87 70**
CSF £8.37 TOTE £1.40: £1.10, £4.20; EX 8.10 Trifecta £26.90.
Owner J A Swinbank And G F Tuer **Bred** Northern Bloodstock Agency Ltd **Trained** Birkby, N Yorks

FOCUS
A weak maiden, rated as straightforward form. Add 9yds.

6303 INJURED JOCKEYS FUND H'CAP 1m 3f 198y
3:40 (3:46) (Class 6) (0-65,65) 4-Y-O+
£2,781 (£827; £413; £300; £300; £300) **Stalls** High

Form RPR
0534 **1** **Esspeegee**[33] 5106 6-8-10 59 (v[1]) DarraghKeenan(5) 7 68
(Alan Bailey) *racd in midfield: pushed along on outer 2f out to take clsr order: rdn to ld 1f out: styd on strly* 9/2[3]

0-36 **2** 3 3/4 **Star Of Athena**[66] 3834 4-9-0 58 PatCosgrave 10 62
(Ali Stronge) *hld up: hdwy u.p 2f out: rdn to chse wnr over 1f out: kpt on* 18/1

-100 **3** 2 1/4 **Kirtling**[21] 5528 8-8-13 57 (t) JackMitchell 9 56
(Andi Brown) *dwlt and racd in rr: hdwy gng keenly on inner over 2f out: swtchd lft to far rail and rdn to ld 2f out: drvn and hdd by wnr 1f out: no ex (jockey said gelding was slowly away)* 20/1

4210 **4** 2 1/2 **Born To Reason (IRE)**[7] 6049 5-8-6 50 (p) HollieDoyle 12 45
(Alexandra Dunn) *trckd ldr: rdn along to chse wnr over 1f out: one pce fnl f* 4/1[2]

6300 **5** nse **King Athelstan (IRE)**[36] 4991 4-8-12 56 (b) HectorCrouch 5 51
(Gary Moore) *racd in midfield: hdwy u.p 2f out: sn rdn and ev ch 1f out: wknd fnl f* 13/2

0401 **6** nk **Contingency Fee**[17] 5679 4-8-9 60 (p) GraceMcEntee(7) 6 55
(Phil McEntee) *led: rdn along and hdd 2f out: wknd fnl f* 14/1

3062 **7** 4 1/2 **Roy Rocket (FR)**[9] 5993 9-8-11 55 JFEgan 8 43
(John Berry) *hld up in rr: hdwy on outer 3f out: sn rdn and no imp over 1f out: one pce after* 7/1

0463 **8** nk **Paddy The Chef (IRE)**[21] 5528 4-9-2 65 (p) CierenFallon(5) 3 52
(Ian Williams) *in tch in 3rd: pushed along to chse ldr 2f out: sn rdn and fnd little: one pce fnl f* 7/2[1]

4-04 **9** 5 **Amanto (GER)**[19] 5571 9-9-7 65 (tp) TomMarquand 1 44
(Ali Stronge) *hld up: rdn and outpcd over 2f out: n.d* 12/1

4230 **10** 1 1/4 **Rose Crown**[27] 5301 5-8-11 60 ScottMcCullagh(5) 11 37
(Mick Channon) *racd in midfield: rdn and lost pl 2f out: wknd fnl f* 20/1

0000 **11** shd **River Dart (IRE)**[47] 4543 7-8-13 62 TobyEley(5) 4 39
(Tony Carroll) *hld up: rdn and detached over 2f out (jockey said gelding was never travelling and hung right-handed)* 28/1

2m 32.68s (-3.32) **Going Correction** +0.025s/f (Good) 11 Ran SP% **118.8**
Speed ratings (Par 101): **109,106,105,103,103 103,100,99,96,95 95**
CSF £80.05 CT £1481.99 TOTE £5.90: £2.00, £5.70, £5.80; EX 129.20 Trifecta £2275.80.
Owner The Skills People Group Ltd **Bred** Trinity Park Stud **Trained** Newmarket, Suffolk

FOCUS
This moderate handicap was run at a sound tempo. Add 9yds.

6304 SKY SPORTS RACING ON SKY 415 MAIDEN H'CAP 1m 1f 207y
4:10 (4:17) (Class 5) (0-70,71) 3-Y-O+
£3,428 (£1,020; £509; £300; £300; £300) **Stalls** High

Form RPR
5423 **1** **Lady Mascara**[26] 5349 3-9-7 70 TomMarquand 3 79+
(James Fanshawe) *settled wl in midfield: clsd on ldrs gng wl on inner 2f out: rdn along to ld over 1f out: styd on strly* 2/1[1]

0060 **2** 1 3/4 **Circle Of Stars (IRE)**[90] 2965 3-9-0 63 JackMitchell 8 67
(Charlie Fellowes) *in rr of midfield: effrt to cl on outer 2f out: sn rdn and drifted lft u.p 1f out: kpt on wl: nt rch wnr* 11/1

4-05 **3** 1 1/4 **Slade King (IRE)**[40] 4836 3-9-5 68 TomQueally 5 70
(Gary Moore) *in rr of midfield: rdn and little imp 2f out: drvn and kpt on one pce fnl f* 16/1

2002 **4** 1/2 **Air Force Amy**[7] 6039 3-9-0 68 ScottMcCullagh(5) 6 69
(Mick Channon) *hld up in rr: effrt on inner to chse wnr 2f out: sn rdn and kpt on one pce fnl f* 9/4[2]

0024 **5** 2 1/2 **Tattenhams**[14] 5784 3-8-2 51 oh3 JimmyQuinn 1 47
(Adam West) *led: rdn along and hdd by wnr over 1f out: wknd fnl f* 18/1

2333 **6** 1 **Sarasota (IRE)**[15] 5747 4-8-9 58 GeorgeRooke(7) 9 51
(Mark Gillard) *midfield: gd prog to chse ldr 2f out: sn rdn and fnd little: wknd fnl f* 10/1

5506 **7** 6 **God Has Given**[33] 5104 3-8-9 63 (p) CierenFallon(5) 7 45
(Ian Williams) *trckd ldr: rdn along and lost pl 2f out: sn struggling* 7/1[3]

-522 **8** 17 **Temujin (IRE)**[73] 3594 3-8-12 61 PatCosgrave 2 9
(Ali Stronge) *trckd ldr: rdn along and lost pl 2f out: eased fnl f* 9/1

2m 4.42s (-0.58) **Going Correction** +0.025s/f (Good)
WFA 3 from 4yo 7lb 8 Ran SP% **115.2**
Speed ratings (Par 103): **103,101,100,100,98 97,92,79**
CSF £25.16 CT £277.29 TOTE £2.40: £1.10, £3.00, £3.50; EX 25.60 Trifecta £192.50.
Owner Helena Springfield Ltd **Bred** Meon Valley Stud **Trained** Newmarket, Suffolk

FOCUS
A maiden handicap but competitive nonetheless. Add 9yds.

6305 RACINGWELFARE.CO.UK APPRENTICE H'CAP (RACING EXCELLENCE APPRENTICE TRAINING SERIES) 7f 211y
4:40 (4:45) (Class 6) (0-60,61) 4-Y-O+
£2,781 (£827; £413; £300; £300; £300) **Stalls** Low

Form RPR
-003 **1** **Maldonado (FR)**[21] 5518 5-9-8 58 ScottMcCullagh 8 63
(Michael Easterby) *trckd ldr: pushed along to ld 2f out: sn rdn and strly pressed 1f out: kpt on gamely: all out* 7/2[1]

525 **2** shd **Silverturnstogold**[74] 3533 4-9-10 60 TobyEley 9 65
(Tony Carroll) *hld up: hdwy on outer 2f out: sn rdn and no immediate imp: drvn and styd on strly fnl f: jst failed (jockey said gelding ran too free in the early stages)* 7/2[1]

0001 **3** hd **Good Luck Charm**[5] 6117 10-9-3 61 4ex (b) RhysClutterbuck(8) 3 65
(Gary Moore) *hld up: gd hdwy on outer over 2f out: rdn upsides and ev ch 1f out: nt quite rch wnr* 6/1

3410 **4** nk **Harlequin Rose (IRE)**[13] 5806 5-8-13 49 (v) WilliamCarver 7 53
(Patrick Chamings) *racd in midfield: pushed along to cl 2f out: briefly short of room over 1f out: sn rdn and kpt on fnl f* 4/1[2]

The Form Book Flat 2019, Raceform Ltd, Newbury, RG14 5SJ

0445 **5** 1 1/2 **Duke Of North (IRE)**[19] 5574 7-8-9 **53**........................(p) IsobelFrancis(8) 2 53
(Jim Boyle) *midfield on inner: clsd gng wl over 2f out: rdn and ev ch 1f out: one pce fnl f* **15/2**

1400 **6** 1 **Hedging (IRE)**[13] 5804 5-9-8 **61**.....................................(b) GeorgiaDobie(3) 5 59
(Eve Johnson Houghton) *trckd ldr: pushed along over 2f out: rdn and no imp over 1f out: one pce fnl f* **5/1**[3]

0663 **7** 1/2 **Ramblow**[12] 5842 6-8-10 **46** oh1...(vt) CierenFallon 4 44
(Alexandra Dunn) *led: rdn along and hdd by wnr 2f out: wknd ins fnl f (jockey said mare ran too free in early the stages)* **20/1**

2004 **8** 3 3/4 **Don't Cry About It (IRE)**[12] 5837 4-8-8 **49**..................(bt) AngusVilliers(5) 6 37
(Ali Stronge) *racd in midfield: rdn along and lost pl 2f out: sn bhd* **20/1**

1m 37.37s (0.47) **Going Correction** +0.025s/f (Good) **8** Ran SP% **116.7**
Speed ratings (Par 101): **98,97,97,97,95 94,94,90**
CSF £16.27 CT £68.95 TOTE £4.50: £1.60, £1.40, £2.20; EX 22.00 Trifecta £84.40.
Owner A Saha **Bred** Snowdrop Stud Co Ltd **Trained** Sheriff Hutton, N Yorks

FOCUS
A typically moderate race of its type and it threw up a tight finish. Add 9yds.
T/Plt: £80.30 to a £1 stake. Pool: £69,034.33 - 627.51 winning units T/Qpdt: £51.50 to a £1 stake. Pool: £5,962.72 - 85.66 winning units **Mark Grantham**

5668 HAMILTON (R-H)

Tuesday, August 20

6306 Meeting Abandoned - false ground

6071 KEMPTON (A.W) (R-H)

Tuesday, August 20

OFFICIAL GOING: Polytrack: standard to slow (watering)
Wind: Fresh, across (away from stands) Weather: Fine

6313 MATCHBOOK BETTING EXCHANGE NURSERY H'CAP (JOCKEY CLUB GRASSROOTS NURSERY QUALIFIER) 6f (P)

2:00 (2:00) (Class 6) (0-60,61) 2-Y-O

£3,105 (£924; £461; £300; £300; £300) **Stalls** Low

Form RPR

4532 **1** **Come On Girl**[10] 5958 2-9-2 **55**.. RaulDaSilva 5 62
(Tony Carroll) *trckd ldrs: wnt 2nd over 2f out: rdn to chal on inner over 1f out: pressed new ldr after: kpt on wl to ld last 75yds* **7/2**[1]

645 **2** nk **Red Jasper**[12] 5865 2-9-6 **59**.. LiamJones 6 65
(Michael Appleby) *trckd ldrs: rdn and clsd over 2f out: drvn ahd over 1f out: kpt on and clr w wnr but hdd and no ex last 75yds* **10/1**

664 **3** 6 **Positive Light (IRE)**[12] 5838 2-9-0 **60**.............................. GavinAshton(7) 9 48
(Sir Mark Prescott Bt) *slowly away and impeded s: long way bhd in last pair: sme prog 2f out: reminders 1f out: styd on wl to take 3rd last strides* **12/1**

0044 **4** 3/4 **Grace Plunkett**[10] 5958 2-9-0 **53**...................................(b) HarryBentley 8 39
(Richard Spencer) *bmpd s: prom: rdn to chse clr ldng trio 2f out: kpt on to press for 3rd fnl f: nvr pce to threaten* **10/1**

005 **5** 1/2 **Sir Rodneyredblood**[53] 4344 2-9-2 **55**.............................. DavidProbert 12 39+
(J R Jenkins) *led fr wdst draw and crossed sharply to inner: led at furious pce but pressed: hdd over 1f out and impeded: wknd (jockey said gelding jumped right-handed when leaving the stalls)* **40/1**

5560 **6** 1 1/2 **Interrupted Dream**[20] 5562 2-9-8 **61**.............................. FrannyNorton 7 41
(Mark Johnston) *outpcd and bhd: rdn wl over 2f out and tried to make prog: nvr able to figure* **8/1**

064 **7** 1/2 **Pearl Stream**[22] 5485 2-9-8 **61**.............................. PaulMulrennan 1 39
(Michael Dods) *slowly away: mostly in last pair and bdly outpcd: passed a few late on but nvr a factor (jockey said filly was never travelling)* **4/1**[2]

006 **8** 3 **Hot Date**[15] 5745 2-8-6 **45**.. DavidEgan 10 14
(George Margarson) *sltly impeded s: chsd ldrs tl wknd 2f out* **10/1**

066 **9** hd **Mungo's Quest (IRE)**[61] 4030 2-8-5 **51**.............................. LeviWilliams(7) 4 20
(Simon Dow) *dwlt: outpcd and bhd: rdn and brief effrt over 2f out: sn no hdwy* **16/1**

050 **10** nk **Resplendent Rose**[10] 5956 2-8-3 **45**..........................(p[1]) WilliamCox(3) 2 13
(Michael Madgwick) *outpcd and bhd: nvr able to make any prog* **25/1**

045 **11** nse **Yorkshire Grey (IRE)**[13] 5815 2-9-7 **60**.............................. AdamKirby 3 28
(Ann Duffield) *chsd ldrs: drvn in 7th bef 1/2-way and struggling after* **6/1**[3]

0000 **12** 10 **Quarrystreetmagic (IRE)**[7] 6053 2-8-6 **45**..............(b[1]) HayleyTurner 11 +
(Brian Meehan) *spd fr wd draw to press ldr at furious pce: lost 2nd and wknd rapidly over 2f out: t.o* **50/1**

1m 14.15s (1.05) **Going Correction** +0.025s/f (Slow) **12** Ran SP% **116.7**
Speed ratings (Par 92): **94,93,85,84,83 81,81,77,77,76 76,63**
CSF £37.80 CT £380.64 TOTE £4.00: £1.40, £3.10, £3.30; EX 31.20 Trifecta £114.30.
Owner Mrs Donna Hopkins **Bred** Kirtlington Stud Ltd **Trained** Cropthorne, Worcs

FOCUS
A weak nursery but one run at a blistering gallop and the kickback looked pretty severe for those who struggled to go early speed.

6314 MATCHBOOK 2% NET WIN NOVICE AUCTION STKS 1m (P)

2:30 (2:30) (Class 5) 2-Y-O **£3,881** (£1,155; £577; £288) **Stalls** Low

Form RPR

1 **Bronze River** 2-9-2 0.. WilliamCox(3) 7 77+
(Andrew Balding) *s.s: sn trckd ldrs on outer: clsd to take 2nd 2f out and sn chalng: looked narrowly hld fnl f and briefly carried lft: styd on fnl 75yds to ld last strides* **5/1**[2]

02 **2** hd **Overpriced Mixer**[49] 4480 2-9-5 0.. OisinMurphy 8 77
(Jamie Osborne) *trckd ldr after 2f: led over 2f out: hrd pressed over 1f out: edgd lft fnl f but looked like holding on: hdd last strides* **8/15**[1]

0 **3** 1 1/2 **Island Storm (IRE)**[9] 5992 2-9-5 0.. DavidEgan 2 74
(Heather Main) *led 1f: styd prom but pushed along at times: rdn to chse ldng pair over 1f out: kpt on but nvr able to chal: hung lft nr fin* **11/2**[3]

0 **4** 7 **No Can Do**[9] 5992 2-9-5 0..(t[1]) ShaneKelly 3 57
(Jamie Osborne) *led after 1f and set mod pce: hdd over 2f out: wknd over 1f out* **20/1**

5 3 **Gweedore** 2-9-5 0.. GeraldMosse 1 51
(Jason Ward) *dwlt: hld up in rr: pushed along and in tch over 2f out: sn outpcd and btn* **16/1**

6 shd **Opine (IRE)** 2-9-5 0.. HayleyTurner 4 50
(Michael Bell) *in tch but rn green: shkn up 3f out: carried hd awkwardly and lft bhd over 2f out* **10/1**

00 **7** 1/2 **Early Morning Mist (IRE)**[4] 6161 2-8-11 0.............. GabrieleMalune(3) 6 44
(Amy Murphy) *dwlt: in tch in rr: outpcd over 2f out: no prog after* **66/1**

0 **8** 11 **Havana Princess**[41] 4790 2-9-0 0.. KierenFox 5 19
(Dr Jon Scargill) *hld up in last: pushed along and lost tch over 2f out: t.o* **50/1**

1m 40.97s (1.17) **Going Correction** +0.025s/f (Slow) **8** Ran SP% **120.5**
Speed ratings (Par 94): **95,94,93,86,83 83,82,71**
CSF £8.44 TOTE £6.80: £1.50, £1.02, £2.00; EX 11.70 Trifecta £29.90.
Owner I A Balding **Bred** Meon Valley Stud **Trained** Kingsclere, Hants

FOCUS
Little depth to this and the front three, who came clear, look the ones to focus on.

6315 MATCHBOOK NOVICE STKS (DIV I) 1m (P)

3:00 (3:00) (Class 5) 3-Y-O+ **£3,881** (£1,155; £577; £288) **Stalls** Low

Form RPR

-4 **1** **Albadr (USA)**[96] 2764 3-9-2 0.. JimCrowley 4 85+
(John Gosden) *hld up in rr: shkn up in 7th over 2f out: prog over 1f out: rdn to chse wnr ins fnl f: clsd nr fin: led last stride* **4/1**[3]

22 **2** nse **Loving Glance**[18] 5627 3-8-11 0.. RobHornby 1 80
(Martyn Meade) *trckd ldng pair: rdn to ld over 1f out: styd on fnl f but hdd last stride* **11/10**[1]

50 **3** 2 3/4 **Mr Carpenter (IRE)**[29] 5254 3-9-2 0.. DanielMuscutt 2 79
(David Lanigan) *trckd ldrs: shkn up over 2f out: styd on to take 2nd briefly jst ins fnl f: one pce after (jockey said gelding hung left-handed on bend; vet said gelding lost right hind shoe)* **25/1**

01- **4** 1/2 **Mostawaa**[286] 8922 3-9-0 0.. EllieMacKenzie(7) 8 83
(Heather Main) *w ldr: led after 3f: rdn and hdd over 1f out: steadily fdd fnl f* **5/1**

43 **5** 2 1/2 **Happy Face (IRE)**[17] 5690 3-8-11 0..................................(t) HarryBentley 5 67
(Hugo Palmer) *chsd ldrs: shkn up over 2f out: one pce and nvr able to chal* **16/1**

5 **6** 3 **Uzincso**[36] 5004 3-9-2 0.. LiamKeniry 10 65
(John Butler) *hld up in last pair: rdn on inner and brief prog over 2f out: no hdwy and btn over 1f out* **100/1**

6 **7** 1 1/4 **Shark (FR)**[53] 4334 3-9-2 0.. OisinMurphy 7 62+
(James Fanshawe) *hld up and sn in last: wl adrift over 2f out: kpt on steadily over 1f out: nvr in it: do bttr* **7/2**[2]

8 5 **Brute Force** 3-9-2 0.. RobertWinston 6 51
(Daniel Kubler) *led 3f: pressed ldr: rdn 3f out: wknd 2f out* **100/1**

00 **9** 21 **Misread**[24] 5428 3-8-11 0.. TrevorWhelan 3
(Geoffrey Deacon) *sn towards rr: dropped to last and struggling bef 1/2-way: t.o* **250/1**

00 **10** 5 **Winalotwithalittle (IRE)**[15] 5748 3-8-11 0.............................. NickyMackay 9
(J R Jenkins) *t.k.h early: chsd ldrs: wknd rapidly over 2f out: t.o* **250/1**

1m 39.39s (-0.41) **Going Correction** +0.025s/f (Slow) **10** Ran SP% **119.0**
Speed ratings (Par 103): **103,102,100,99,97 94,92,87,66,61**
CSF £9.04 TOTE £4.30: £1.20, £1.10, £5.90; EX 10.20 Trifecta £114.40.
Owner Hamdan Al Maktoum **Bred** Shadwell Farm LLC **Trained** Newmarket, Suffolk

FOCUS
A good-quality novice event for the time of year and winners should come out of this, although the winner looks likely to prove the best of these in the long term.

6316 MATCHBOOK NOVICE STKS (DIV II) 1m (P)

3:30 (3:30) (Class 5) 3-Y-O+ **£3,881** (£1,155; £577; £288) **Stalls** Low

Form RPR

633 **1** **Magical Rhythms (USA)**[18] 5627 3-8-13 83........................ DavidEgan 7 81+
(John Gosden) *trckd ldrs: shkn up and prog over 2f out: led over 1f out: rdn and out and in command fnl f* **3/1**[2]

6 **2** 3/4 **Mayne (IRE)**[17] 5650 3-9-4 0.. OisinMurphy 9 84
(Andrew Balding) *racd freely: led: rdn and hdd over 1f out: kpt on wl but readily hld ins fnl f* **2/1**[1]

3 **3** 3 **Knockacullion (USA)**[28] 5269 3-9-4 0.............................. ShaneKelly 4 77
(Richard Hughes) *pressed ldr to 2f out: sn outpcd: styd on again ins fnl f wout threatening ldng pair* **9/2**[3]

62 **4** 2 1/4 **Al Moataz (IRE)**[19] 5592 3-9-4 0.. DanielMuscutt 8 72
(Marco Botti) *trckd ldng pair: disp 2nd 2f out: sn outpcd: fdd ins fnl f* **20/1**

5 2 3/4 **Loveheart** 3-8-13 0.. HayleyTurner 1 61
(Michael Bell) *a in midfield: pushed along and outpcd 2f out: kpt on same pce after* **25/1**

6 1 **Ghadbbaan** 3-9-4 0..(w) JimCrowley 2 63+
(Sir Michael Stoute) *s.s and urged along: mostly in last pair: nvr a factor but kpt on over 1f out* **3/1**[2]

0 **7** 4 1/2 **High Gloss**[20] 5554 3-8-13 0.. HarryBentley 6 48
(James Fanshawe) *rrd bdly s: a in rr: shkn up over 2f out: no prog* **16/1**

00 **8** 5 **Keep On Laughing (IRE)**[6] 6074 4-9-2 0..................(t[1]) GeorgiaCox(3) 3 38
(John Butler) *chsd ldrs tl wknd jst over 2f out* **200/1**

0- **9** 6 **Celestial**[316] 8040 3-8-13 0.. DavidProbert 5 23
(Michael Blanshard) *sn in last pair: no prog over 2f out: bhd after* **150/1**

1m 39.09s (-0.71) **Going Correction** +0.025s/f (Slow)
WFA 3 from 4yo 6lb **9** Ran SP% **117.2**
Speed ratings (Par 103): **104,103,100,98,95 94,89,84,78**
CSF £9.39 TOTE £3.80: £1.30, £1.30, £1.70; EX 10.70 Trifecta £32.70.
Owner Prince A A Faisal **Bred** Nawara Stud Company Ltd **Trained** Newmarket, Suffolk

FOCUS
Not as strong as the first division but the winner set a useful enough standard, not needing to improve, although whether she turns out to be the best of these in the long term is another question.

6317 GET SWITCHED ON WITH MATCHBOOK H'CAP 1m (P)

4:00 (4:00) (Class 5) (0-70,70) 3-Y-O+

£3,752 (£1,116; £557; £300; £300; £300) **Stalls** Low

Form RPR

-320 **1** **Highfaluting (IRE)**[70] 3700 5-9-8 **66**.............................. GeraldMosse 8 76+
(James Eustace) *wl in tch towards outer: rdn and prog 2f out: led jst over 1f out: drvn fnl f: jst hld on* **12/1**

2310 **2** nse **Toro Dorado**[13] 5797 3-9-2 **66**.. OisinMurphy 5 73
(Ed Dunlop) *hld up in rr: prog over 2f out: rdn over 1f out: chsd wnr ins fnl f: clsd nr fin: jst failed* **5/1**[2]

5064 **3** 1 **Makambe (IRE)**[13] 5824 4-9-5 **63**..................................(p) JoeyHaynes 11 69
(Chelsea Banham) *hld up in midfield: rdn and prog jst over 2f out: styd on over 1f out to take 3rd last 50yds: nt quite pce to chal* **11/1**

-121 **4** 3/4 **Kendergarten Kop (IRE)**[27] 5309 4-9-10 **68**..............(p) DavidProbert 1 72
(David Flood) *trckd ldrs: prog 2f out: drvn to ld briefly over 1f out: one pce fnl f* **5/2**[1]

4045 **5** 1 3/4 **Cashel (IRE)**[13] 5807 4-9-5 **63** .... AlistairRawlinson 3 63
(Michael Appleby) *trckd ldrs: rdn over 2f out: nt qckn over 1f out: kpt on same pce fnl f* **7/1**[3]

-440 **6** 3/4 **French Twist**[7] 6039 3-8-12 **62** .... DavidEgan 12 60
(David Loughnane) *pressed ldr: hrd rdn and lost pl 2f out: one pce after* **66/1**

0000 **7** 1 1/4 **Weloof (FR)**[18] 5632 5-9-2 **63** .... GeorgiaCox(3) 4 59
(John Butler) *stdd s: hld up in last: passed wkng rivals over 1f out: nvr remotely involved (jockey said gelding was slowly away)* **100/1**

01-0 **8** 3/4 **Deleyll**[28] 5282 5-9-6 **64** .... SeanLevey 2 58
(John Butler) *nvr beyond midfield: rdn over 2f out: no imp on ldrs on inner over 1f out* **20/1**

540 **8** *dht* **Kafeel (USA)**[33] 5081 8-8-6 **53** .... (p) WilliamCox(3) 10 47
(Alexandra Dunn) *sn led fr wd draw: shkn up over 2f out: hdd over 1f out: wknd qckly fnl f* **80/1**

3206 **10** *hd* **Choral Music**[17] 5677 4-9-12 **70** .... RobHornby 6 63
(John E Long) *hld up in rr: prog on inner over 2f out: no hdwy over 1f out: fdd fnl f* **7/1**[3]

000 **11** *nk* **Vixen (IRE)**[19] 5593 5-9-5 **68** .... (h) ThomasGreatrex(5) 7 61
(Emma Lavelle) *prom: rdn over 2f out and sn lost pl: no ch over 1f out* **25/1**

066- **12** 3 1/2 **Professor**[475] 2279 9-9-7 **65** .... KierenFox 9 50
(William Knight) *a in rr: rdn and no prog wl over 2f out* **33/1**

054- **13** 1 3/4 **Rusper's Gift (IRE)**[241] 9683 3-9-4 **68** .... DougieCostello 13 48
(Jamie Osborne) *a in rr: rdn and struggling 3f out* **33/1**

4200 **14** 10 **Subliminal**[19] 5570 4-9-5 **63** .... (b) AdamKirby 14 21
(Simon Dow) *prom on outer tl wknd rapidly over 2f out: t.o* **8/1**

1m 39.22s (-0.58) **Going Correction** +0.025s/f (Slow)
WFA 3 from 4yo+ 6lb **14** Ran SP% **115.6**
Speed ratings (Par 103): **103,102,101,101,99 98,97,96,96,96 96,92,90,80**
CSF £64.63 CT £704.67 TOTE £13.10: £4.40, £2.20, £3.40; EX 79.90 Trifecta £685.90.
Owner David Batten **Bred** Bloomsbury Stud **Trained** Newmarket, Suffolk

FOCUS
A modest handicap in which they didn't go a breakneck gallop, and the winner improved.

6318 MATCHBOOK BETTING PODCAST H'CAP 7f (P)
4:30 (4:30) (Class 3) (0-90,90) 3-Y-O+

£9,337 (£2,796; £1,398; £699; £349; £175) **Stalls** Low

Form RPR

21-4 **1** **Lethal Lunch**[164] 1097 4-9-12 **90** .... AdamKirby 6 98
(Clive Cox) *hld up in last in modly run r: prog and threaded between rivals over 1f out: rdn to ld jst ins fnl f: hung lft after: drvn out* **7/2**[2]

5160 **2** *nk* **Diocles Of Rome (IRE)**[24] 5413 4-9-8 **86** .... HarryBentley 2 93
(Ralph Beckett) *trckd ldrs: waiting for a gap 2f out: drvn and clsd fnl f: tk 2nd last 100yds: styd on but jst hld* **13/8**[1]

026- **3** 1 1/4 **Tadleel**[381] 5753 4-9-6 **84** .... JimCrowley 8 89
(Ed Dunlop) *pressed ldr: shkn up to ld 2f out: drvn and hdd jst ins fnl f: hld whn sltly checked last strides* **25/1**

2252 **4** *hd* **Quick Breath**[18] 5626 4-8-12 **83** .... TylerSaunders(7) 5 86
(Jonathan Portman) *hld up: quick move on outer to press ldng pair 4f out: rdn and nt qckn 2f out: kpt on again ins fnl f* **9/2**[3]

-245 **5** 1 **Miracle Of Medinah**[18] 5628 8-9-2 **87** .... EllieMacKenzie(7) 1 87
(Mark Usher) *hld up in cl tch: effrt on inner 2f out: tried to cl jst over 1f out: one pce fnl f* **18/1**

4010 **6** 1/2 **Assimilation (IRE)**[14] 5773 3-8-12 **81** .... LiamKeniry 4 78
(Ed Walker) *t.k.h early and hld up in tch: pushed along 1/2-way: nt keen and dropped to last over 1f out: r.o again last 50yds* **7/1**

2541 **7** *nk* **Chica De La Noche**[19] 5573 5-8-12 **76** .... (p) OisinMurphy 7 74
(Simon Dow) *led at mod pce: shkn up and hdd 2f out: lost pl and fdd fnl f* **10/1**

1m 27.22s (1.22) **Going Correction** +0.025s/f (Slow)
WFA 3 from 4yo+ 5lb **7** Ran SP% **109.2**
Speed ratings (Par 107): **94,93,92,92,90 90,89**
CSF £8.69 CT £101.47 TOTE £2.50: £1.60, £1.60; EX 9.60 Trifecta £108.70.
Owner The Rat Pack Partnership 2017 **Bred** Horizon Bloodstock Limited **Trained** Lambourn, Berks
■ Stewards' Enquiry : Adam Kirby two-day ban: careless riding (Sep 3rd-4th)

FOCUS
Quite a competitive little handicap and although they didn't go a particularly strong gallop, the winner showed a bright turn of foot to come from the back of the field. The first two have been rated as improving.

6319 MATCHBOOK VIP H'CAP 6f (P)
5:05 (5:05) (Class 4) (0-85,85) 3-Y-O+

£6,469 (£1,925; £962; £481; £300; £300) **Stalls** Low

Form RPR

1-50 **1** **Power Link (USA)**[28] 5266 3-9-4 **80** .... (p) OisinMurphy 8 98
(James Tate) *chsd clr ldng pair: tk 2nd over 1f out and sn clsd qckly to ld: rdn clr fnl f and styd on wl* **16/1**

630 **2** 3 3/4 **Busby (IRE)**[10] 5942 4-9-3 **76** .... (p) MartinDwyer 2 82
(Conrad Allen) *chsd clr ldr: pushed along 1/2-way: lost 2nd over 1f out: styd on to chse wnr jst ins fnl f but easily lft bhd* **6/1**[3]

3303 **3** *hd* **Lady Dancealot (IRE)**[18] 5628 4-9-9 **82** .... GeraldMosse 1 87
(David Elsworth) *chsd clr ldrs: rdn over 2f out: styd on over 1f out to take 3rd last 150yds: pressed runner-up nr fin* **5/4**[1]

030 **4** 2 1/2 **Private Matter**[13] 5821 5-9-2 **75** .... DavidProbert 3 72
(Amy Murphy) *hld up off the pce towards rr: shkn up over 2f out: kpt on one pce to take modest 4th ins fnl f* **16/1**

135- **5** 1 3/4 **Sparkalot**[452] 3054 5-9-5 **85** .... LeviWilliams(7) 4 77
(Simon Dow) *t.k.h: hld up in last pair: shkn up over 2f out: no real prog* **14/1**

-304 **6** 2 **Airshow**[17] 5649 4-9-12 **85** .... AlistairRawlinson 7 70
(Michael Appleby) *tore off in front and sn 4 l clr: hdd & wknd rapidly jst over 1f out (jockey said gelding ran too free and hung right-handed)* **14/1**

3404 **7** 1 1/4 **Givinitsum (SAF)**[12] 5862 4-9-9 **82** .... CharlesBishop 11 63
(Eve Johnson Houghton) *hld up in last pair: rdn and struggling over 2f out* **33/1**

0342 **8** *shd* **Katheefa (USA)**[10] 5942 5-9-10 **83** .... JackGarritty 6 64
(Ruth Carr) *hld up in midfield and off the pce: rdn and no prog over 2f out: no ch after* **16/1**

-422 **9** 1/2 **Typhoon Ten (IRE)**[9] 5983 3-9-5 **81** .... SeanLevey 9 60
(Richard Hannon) *chsd clr ldrs: rdn and no prog 2f out: wknd over 1f out* **7/2**[2]

1m 11.72s (-1.38) **Going Correction** +0.025s/f (Slow)
WFA 3 from 4yo+ 3lb **9** Ran SP% **114.9**
Speed ratings (Par 105): **110,105,104,101,99 96,94,94,93**
CSF £108.01 CT £210.15 TOTE £11.30: £2.80, £2.20, £1.10; EX 131.20 Trifecta £311.10.
Owner Sheikh Rashid Dalmook Al Maktoum **Bred** SF Bloodstock LLC **Trained** Newmarket, Suffolk
■ Last Page was withdrawn. Price at time of withdrawal 25-1. Rule 4 does not apply.

FOCUS
This was won in good style by an improver.

6320 MATCHBOOK CASINO H'CAP 1m 3f 219y(P)
5:40 (5:40) (Class 5) (0-70,75) 3-Y-O+

£3,752 (£1,116; £557; £300; £300; £300) **Stalls** Low

Form RPR

-114 **1** **Sir Prize**[185] 754 4-10-0 **68** .... RobertWinston 1 75
(Dean Ivory) *hld up in last: cajoled along and stl there over 2f out: gd prog on outer to chse ldr over 1f out: clsd to ld last 150yds: styd on wl* **3/1**[2]

4001 **2** 1 1/2 **Wanaasah**[8] 6030 3-9-12 **75** 6ex .... (h) DavidEgan 5 80
(David Loughnane) *led: kicked for home wl over 2f out: hdd and outpcd last 150yds* **7/4**[1]

1335 **3** 1 **Murhib (IRE)**[28] 5271 7-9-3 **57** .... (h) RichardKingscote 8 60
(Lydia Richards) *chsd ldr: shkn up over 3f out: lost 2nd over 1f out: one pce and wl hld after* **9/1**[3]

5265 **4** *nse* **Mullarkey**[27] 5309 5-9-4 **58** .... (t) KierenFox 4 61
(John Best) *hld up in rr: shkn up and prog jst over 2f out: drvn on inner fnl f: kpt on to press for 3rd but nt pce to threaten* **14/1**

5044 **5** 1/2 **Island Jungle (IRE)**[8] 6030 3-9-5 **68** .... (p) FergusSweeney 3 70
(Mark Usher) *trckd ldrs: rdn over 2f out: one pce over 1f out and pressed for a pl fnl f* **22/1**

060 **6** 5 **Champ Ayr**[19] 5578 3-8-13 **62** .... DavidProbert 6 56
(David Menuisier) *dwlt: hld up in rr: effrt over 2f out: no prog over 1f out: wknd fnl f* **33/1**

4215 **7** *shd* **Gold Arch**[14] 5792 3-9-3 **66** .... (b) DanielMuscutt 7 60
(David Lanigan) *trckd ldrs on outer: shkn up over 2f out: no prog whn impeded over 1f out: wknd (jockey said gelding hung right-handed throughout)* **3/1**[2]

113- **8** 16 **Zarrar (IRE)**[241] 9687 4-9-6 **65** .... (bt) RobJFitzpatrick(5) 2 33
(Camilla Poulton) *rousted early: prom: rdn wl over 2f out: wknd rapidly wl over 1f out: t.o (jockey said gelding was slowly away)* **20/1**

2m 35.36s (0.86) **Going Correction** +0.025s/f (Slow)
WFA 3 from 4yo+ 9lb **8** Ran SP% **115.1**
Speed ratings (Par 103): **98,97,96,96,95 92,92,81**
CSF £8.50 CT £40.19 TOTE £3.80: £1.20, £1.10, £2.60; EX 10.60 Trifecta £53.40.
Owner Michael & Heather Yarrow **Bred** Chippenham Lodge Stud **Trained** Radlett, Herts

FOCUS
Not a bad little 0-70 and it was run at what appeared quite an even tempo. The winner remains on the upgrade, with the third and fourth helping to set the standard.
T/Jkpt: Not won. T/Plt: £13.70 to a £1 stake. Pool: £59,337.07 - 3,152.42 winning units T/Qpdt: £5.90 to a £1 stake. Pool: £6,310.15 - 779,89 winning units **Jonathan Neesom**

6126 YARMOUTH (L-H)
Tuesday, August 20

OFFICIAL GOING: Good to firm (watered; 7.4)
Wind: light to medium across Weather: fine

6321 MANSIONBET BEATEN BY A HEAD H'CAP 5f 42y
4:55 (4:56) (Class 6) (0-60,60) 3-Y-O+

£2,781 (£827; £413; £300; £300; £300) **Stalls** Centre

Form RPR

0000 **1** **Dark Side Dream**[11] 5889 7-9-7 **60** .... (p) SilvestreDeSousa 7 66
(Charlie Wallis) *in tch in midfield: hdwy u.p over 1f out: ev ch ins fnl f: styd on wl to ld nr fin* **14/1**

3430 **2** *hd* **Archimedes (IRE)**[48] 4494 6-9-5 **58** .... (vt) JasonWatson 1 63
(David C Griffiths) *led and crossed towards stands' rail: drvn over 1f out: kpt on wl u.p tl hdd and no ex nr fin* **14/1**

503 **3** *hd* **Swell Song**[13] 5822 3-8-8 **49** .... (p) JosephineGordon 4 54
(Robert Cowell) *pushed along leaving stalls: chsd ldrs: wnt 2nd and effrt ent fnl 2f: drvn and ev ch over 1f out: kpt on wl u.p: no ex nr fin* **20/1**

3122 **4** 1 1/4 **Monarch Maid**[5] 6126 8-8-7 **53** .... ElishaWhittington(7) 2 53
(Peter Hiatt) *chsd ldr tl ent fnl 2f: sn rdn: stl pressing ldrs u.p 1f out: no ex and outpcd fnl 100yds* **7/2**[3]

5-00 **5** 2 1/2 **Dahik (IRE)**[45] 4632 4-9-2 **55** .... CamHardie 5 46
(Michael Easterby) *sltly awkward leaving stalls: hld up in tch in midfield: effrt over 2f out: unable qck u.p over 1f out: wl hld and plugged on same pce ins fnl f* **11/4**[2]

3021 **6** 3 1/2 **Simba Samba**[5] 6126 3-8-13 **59** 6ex .... DylanHogan(5) 6 37+
(Philip McBride) *bmpd leaving stalls: in tch towards rr: effrt over 2f out: clsd u.p to chse ldrs whn sltly impeded 1f out: sn eased: sddle slipped (jockey said saddle slipped approx two furlongs out)* **6/4**[1]

0560 **7** 1/2 **Gifted Zebedee (IRE)**[7] 6048 3-8-11 **59** .... StefanoCherchi(7) 3 36
(Anthony Carson) *in tch in last trio: effrt jst over 2f out: unable qck and outpcd over 1f out: wl btn ins fnl f* **33/1**

0350 **8** 1/2 **Awarded**[34] 5064 3-8-10 **51** .... (p) BrettDoyle 8 26
(Robert Cowell) *hld up in tch in last trio: shkn up 2f out: edgd rt and no imp u.p over 1f out: wl btn ins fnl f (jockey said filly hung right approx two furlongs out)* **66/1**

1m 0.17s (-1.73) **Going Correction** -0.175s/f (Firm)
WFA 3 from 4yo+ 2lb **8** Ran SP% **111.4**
Speed ratings (Par 101): **106,105,105,103,99 93,92,92**
CSF £171.03 CT £3814.60 TOTE £15.40: £3.90, £2.80, £3.90; EX 96.60 Trifecta £794.50.
Owner M M Foulger & Mrs Shelley Dwyer **Bred** Newsells Park Stud **Trained** Ardleigh, Essex

FOCUS
A lowly sprint, they were spread middle to stands' side.

6322 BEST ODDS GUARANTEED AT MANSIONBET APP FILLIES' NOVICE STKS (PLUS 10 RACE) 1m 3y
5:25 (5:25) (Class 5) 2-Y-O

£3,428 (£1,020; £509; £254) **Stalls** Centre

Form RPR

4 **1** **Festive Star**[17] 5684 2-9-0 0 .... SilvestreDeSousa 6 79
(Simon Crisford) *trckd ldrs: clsd to press ldr 3f out: rdn and ev ch jst over 2f out: rdn to ld narrowly over 1f out: edgd lft but forged ahd wl ins fnl f: styd on wl (jockey said filly lugged left under pressure)* **7/2**[3]

3 **2** 3/4 **Amber Island (IRE)**[17] 5684 2-9-0 0 .... WilliamBuick 5 77
(Charlie Appleby) *bmpd leaving stalls: sn led: jnd 3f out: rdn ent fnl 2f: hdd narrowly over 1f out: kpt on u.p: no ex and jst outpcd wl ins fnl f* **11/8**[1]

3 *1* **Pocket Square** 2-9-0 0................................ JasonWatson 7 75+
(Roger Charlton) *hld up in tch in last pair: effrt over 2f out: rdn to chse ldng pair over 1f out: kpt on ins fnl f: nvr quite enough pce to get on terms* **9/4**[2]

4 *1 1/4* **Dubai Life (USA)** 2-9-0 0................................ GeorgeWood 1 72+
(Saeed bin Suroor) *in tch in midfield: effrt ent fnl 2f: rn green and edgd lft over 1f out: kpt on same pce ins fnl f* **6/1**

4 **5** *4* **Itmusthavebeenlove (IRE)**[32] 5139 2-9-0 0................ JamieSpencer 4 63
(Michael Bell) *squeezed for room leaving stalls: clsd and effrt 2f out: outpcd and rdn over 1f out: wknd ins fnl f* **16/1**

00 **6** *17* **Lily Bonnette**[48] 4502 2-9-0 0................................ ShelleyBirkett 2 24
(Julia Feilden) *chsd ldr tl 3f out: sn rdn and struggling: bhd over 1f out* **250/1**

1m 36.52s (-1.68) **Going Correction** -0.175s/f (Firm) 6 Ran SP% **115.7**
Speed ratings (Par 91): **101,100,99,98,94 77**
CSF £9.14 TOTE £4.60: £2.30, £1.20; EX 10.10 Trifecta £24.80.
Owner Rabbah Racing **Bred** Sun Kingdom Pty Ltd **Trained** Newmarket, Suffolk

FOCUS
Little got into this fair novice. They raced centre-field. This has been rated conservatively to start.

6323 DOWNLOAD THE MANSIONBET APP H'CAP 1m 3f 104y
5:55 (5:56) (Class 5) (0-75,77) 3-Y-O+ £3,428 (£1,020; £509; £300; £300) Stalls Low

Form RPR

6234 **1** **Potters Lady Jane**[18] 5623 7-9-5 **70**...........................(p) JamieSpencer 2 76
(Lucy Wadham) *led and set stdy gallop for 4f: chsd ldr tl rdn to ld again 1f out: styd on wl ins fnl f* **8/1**

0321 **2** *1 1/4* **Knowing**[21] 5529 3-9-2 **75**................................ GeorgeWood 5 80
(James Fanshawe) *in tch: clsd to trck ldrs 2f out: barging match w rival over 1f out: effrt ent fnl f: kpt on u.p ins fnl f: snatched 2nd last strides* **11/8**[1]

1-33 **3** *nk* **Albanita**[10] 5954 3-9-3 **76**................................(p) LukeMorris 1 80
(Sir Mark Prescott Bt) *chsd ldng pair: hemmed in 2f out: rdr trying to force way out and barging match w rival over 1f out: swtchd lft and effrt between ldng pair ent fnl f: wnt 2nd ins fnl f: no imp: lost 2nd last strides* **9/2**[3]

-045 **4** *1* **Bartholomew J (IRE)**[47] 4569 5-9-5 **70**................(p) RoystonFfrench 3 73
(Lydia Pearce) *hld up in tch in rr: reminder 3f out: rdn and swtchd rt 2f out: rallied 1f out: kpt on ins fnl f* **33/1**

5254 **5** *1 1/2* **Fraser Island (IRE)**[12] 5840 3-9-4 **77**..................(b[1]) SilvestreDeSousa 4 77
(Mark Johnston) *chsd ldr tl led 8f out: rdn over 2f out: hdd over 1f out: no ex and wknd ins fnl f* **15/8**[2]

2m 27.19s (-0.61) **Going Correction** -0.175s/f (Firm)
WFA 3 from 5yo+ 8lb 5 Ran SP% **109.1**
Speed ratings (Par 103): **95,94,93,93,92**
CSF £19.32 TOTE £7.90: £3.10, £1.10; EX 17.80 Trifecta £46.80.
Owner Mrs J May **Bred** Mrs J May **Trained** Newmarket, Suffolk
■ Stewards' Enquiry : Luke Morris five-day ban; improper conduct (Sept 3-7)

FOCUS
Bit of a bunched finish to this ordinary handicap. The early pace was steady but they got racing a fair way out. Add 10yds.

6324 MANSIONBET YOUR FAVOURITE PLACE TO BET H'CAP 1m 2f 23y
6:25 (6:25) (Class 6) (0-60,62) 4-Y-O+
£2,781 (£827; £413; £300; £300; £300) Stalls Low

Form RPR

0003 **1** **Contrast (IRE)**[45] 4658 5-9-6 **59**................................ CamHardie 8 65
(Michael Easterby) *s.i.s: hld up in last trio: effrt 3f out: clsd u.p to chse ldrs 1f out: str chal ins fnl f: styd on wl to ld cl home* **9/4**[1]

5325 **2** *hd* **Apache Blaze**[15] 5728 4-9-9 **62**..........................(p) JasonWatson 7 68
(Robyn Brisland) *chsd ldng trio: edgd out rt and effrt over 2f out: drvn to ld over 1f out: hrd pressed and kpt on wl but edgd rt u.p ins fnl f: hdd cl home (jockey said filly hung both left and right under pressure)* **9/2**[3]

5332 **3** *hd* **Percy Toplis**[12] 5867 5-8-8 **47**..........................(b) EoinWalsh 1 52
(Christine Dunnett) *s.i.s: bhd and cajoled along early: rdn 3f out: hdwy u.p over 1f out: styd on wl to press ldrs towards fin: nt quite rch ldng pair (jockey said gelding was never travelling)* **10/1**

06/0 **4** *2 1/4* **Saga Sprint (IRE)**[148] 1333 6-8-7 **46** oh1.................. AdrianMcCarthy 6 47
(J R Jenkins) *in tch in midfield: effrt and hdwy over 2f out: chsd ldrs and drvn over 1f out: ev ch ins fnl f: no ex and outpcd fnl 100yds* **100/1**

0040 **5** *1 1/2* **Windsorlot (IRE)**[22] 5499 6-8-0 **46**.................... ElishaWhittington[(7)] 4 44
(Tony Carroll) *pushed along leaving stalls: racd in last trio: clsd on inner and nt clr run over 2f out: sn swtchd rt: effrt to chse ldrs 1f out: no ex and outpcd ins fnl f* **16/1**

0400 **6** *6* **Nordic Flight**[27] 5316 4-9-7 **60**................................ LukeMorris 3 47
(James Eustace) *in tch in midfield: rdn: nt clrest of runs and outpcd over 2f out: no threat to ldrs after: wknd fnl f* **9/1**

3256 **7** *1/2* **Movie Star (GER)**[7] 6059 4-9-9 **62**......................(v[1]) SilvestreDeSousa 9 48
(Amy Murphy) *chsd ldrs after 1f: wnt 2nd 1/2-way tl rdn to ld over 2f out: hdd over 1f out: sn btn and wknd ins fnl f (trainers' rep said filly did not face the application of a first-time visor)* **4/1**[2]

60-2 **8** *nk* **Lily Ash (IRE)**[17] 5679 6-9-3 **56**................................ RossaRyan 10 41
(Mike Murphy) *led after 1f: rdn and hdd over 2f out: lost pl and btn over 1f out: wknd ins fnl f* **20/1**

0006 **9** *14* **Star Attraction (FR)**[17] 5675 4-8-7 **46** oh1..................(t) BrettDoyle 2 5
(Tony Carroll) *midfield: rdn 3f out: lost pl and bhd over 1f out: wknd* **40/1**

-000 **10** *3* **Right About Now (IRE)**[26] 5354 5-9-9 **62**.........(b w) JosephineGordon 5 15
(Charlie Wallis) *led for 1f: chsd ldrs: effrt 3f out: lost pl over 1f out: sn wknd* **25/1**

2m 6.67s (-2.13) **Going Correction** -0.175s/f (Firm) 10 Ran SP% **119.4**
Speed ratings (Par 101): **101,100,100,98,97 92,92,92,81,78**
CSF £12.67 CT £86.08 TOTE £3.60: £1.60, £1.30, £2.20; EX 18.40 Trifecta £74.40.
Owner A Saha Racing **Bred** Lynn Lodge Stud **Trained** Sheriff Hutton, N Yorks

FOCUS
Moderate handicap form, there was near enough four in a line with a furlong to run. Add 10yds.

6325 MANSIONBET AT YARMOUTH RACECOURSE MEDIAN AUCTION MAIDEN STKS 6f 3y
6:55 (6:55) (Class 6) 3-4-Y-O £2,781 (£827; £413; £206) Stalls Centre

Form RPR

435/ **1** **Society Prince (IRE)**[661] 8432 4-9-8 70................................ GeorgeWood 2 72
(James Fanshawe) *s.i.s: midfield: clsd to chse ldrs jst over 2f out: chsd ldr jst ins fnl f: styd on wl u.p fnl 100yds to ld last strides* **11/4**[2]

230- **2** *hd* **Sky Patrol (IRE)**[334] 7469 3-9-5 71................................ JasonWatson 6 71
(Lucy Wadham) *chsd ldr tl led 3f out: rdn over 2f out: drvn 1f out: kpt on but hdd last strides* **5/4**[1]

3 *1 1/4* **Capla Berry** 3-9-0 0................................ SilvestreDeSousa 3 63+
(Rae Guest) *s.i.s: rn green and off the pce in last pair: rdn over 2f out: sme hdwy and swtchd lft over 1f out: wnt 3rd ins fnl f and gng on fin: nt rch ldrs* **11/4**[2]

300 **4** *2* **Moveonup (IRE)**[15] 5730 3-9-5 63................................(p) LukeMorris 4 62
(Gay Kelleway) *chsd ldrs tl pressed ldr over 2f out: drvn over 1f out: no ex and lost 2nd jst ins fnl f: wknd and eased cl home* **10/1**[3]

6006 **5** *12* **Diamond Cara**[10] 5960 3-9-0 29................................ CallumShepherd 1 21
(Stuart Williams) *broke fast: led and racd along in centre: rdn and hdd 3f out: lost pl and wl btn over 1f out: wknd fnl f* **40/1**

6 *nse* **Forgotten Girl** 3-9-0 0................................ AdrianMcCarthy 5 21
(Christine Dunnett) *s.i.s: off the pce in last pair: nvr involved* **40/1**

1m 11.78s (-0.82) **Going Correction** -0.175s/f (Firm)
WFA 3 from 4yo 3lb 6 Ran SP% **111.7**
Speed ratings (Par 101): **98,97,96,93,77 77**
CSF £6.53 TOTE £3.90: £1.60, £1.20; EX 6.60 Trifecta £16.20.
Owner Fred Archer Racing - Melton **Bred** Tally-Ho Stud **Trained** Newmarket, Suffolk

FOCUS
Modest maiden form and the only 4yo in the field came out on top, but he showed slight progress to do so.

6326 MANSIONBET PROUD TO SUPPORT BRITISH RACING H'CAP 7f 3y
7:25 (7:26) (Class 4) (0-80,80) 3-Y-O+
£5,207 (£1,549; £774; £387; £300; £300) Stalls Centre

Form RPR

0243 **1** **Queen Of Burgundy**[17] 5647 3-9-2 **76**...................... SilvestreDeSousa 6 81
(Christine Dunnett) *mde all: rdn ent fnl 2f: drvn over 1f out: hld on gamely ins fnl f: all out* **7/2**[2]

6025 **2** *shd* **Masked Identity**[27] 5320 4-9-11 **80**...................... JosephineGordon 7 86
(Shaun Keightley) *chsd ldrs: effrt ent fnl 2f: drvn and pressed wnr 1f out: str chal ins fnl f: kpt on wl: jst hld* **8/1**

0004 **3** *2 1/4* **Sir Titan**[18] 5626 5-9-11 **80**................................ HayleyTurner 5 80
(Tony Carroll) *chsd wnr: rdn over 2f out: lost 2nd and unable qck 1f out: kpt on same pce ins fnl f* **3/1**[1]

6445 **4** *nk* **Young John (IRE)**[22] 5503 6-9-6 **75**................................ RossaRyan 3 74
(Mike Murphy) *t.k.h: hld up wl in tch in midfield: effrt 2f out: drvn over 1f out: kpt on same pce and no imp ins fnl f* **11/2**

4003 **5** *hd* **Nick Vedder**[12] 5868 5-9-4 **73**..........................(b) JamieSpencer 4 72
(Michael Wigham) *stdd s: hld up in tch in rr: effrt and swtchd rt over 1f out: kpt on same pce and no imp ins fnl f* **9/1**

6422 **6** *2* **Roman Spinner**[13] 5828 4-9-2 **71**..........................(t) LukeMorris 2 64
(Rae Guest) *in tch in last pair: rdn over 2f out: drvn over 1f out: no imp 1f out: wknd ins fnl f* **8/1**

-115 **7** *3/4* **Keepup Kevin**[27] 5303 5-9-7 **76**................................ CallumShepherd 1 67
(Pam Sly) *chsd ldrs: rdn ent fnl 2f: unable qck over 1f out: wknd ins fnl f* **4/1**[3]

1m 22.98s (-2.12) **Going Correction** -0.175s/f (Firm)
WFA 3 from 4yo+ 5lb 7 Ran SP% **114.8**
Speed ratings (Par 105): **105,104,102,101,101 99,98**
CSF £31.11 TOTE £4.90: £1.90, £4.60; EX 37.40 Trifecta £120.00.
Owner Trevor Milner **Bred** Cheveley Park Stud Ltd **Trained** Hingham, Norfolk

FOCUS
An ordinary handicap run at a steady gallop and it paid to race prominently.

6327 MANSIONBET AT GREAT YARMOUTH RACECOURSE H'CAP 1m 3y
7:55 (7:55) (Class 6) (0-55,57) 4-Y-O+
£2,781 (£827; £413; £300; £300; £300) Stalls Centre

Form RPR

6046 **1** **Top Offer**[12] 5851 10-8-9 **45** oh1..........................(p) MeganNicholls[(3)] 6 52
(Patrick Morris) *stdd s: hld up in tch towards rr: effrt 2f out: hdwy and rdn to press ldrs 1f out: led ins fnl f: r.o wl* **20/1**

0306 **2** *1/2* **Lunar Deity**[13] 5824 10-9-0 **55**................................ MarcoGhiani[(7)] 11 60
(Stuart Williams) *hld up in tch in midfield: effrt ent fnl 2f: rdn and clsd over 1f out: ev ch 1f out: chsd wnr and kpt on fnl 100yds* **5/1**[2]

2400 **3** *1 1/2* **Hi Ho Silver**[34] 5051 5-9-2 **50**................................ GeorgeWood 14 51
(Chris Wall) *t.k.h: chsd ldrs tl led 3f out: rdn ent fnl 2f: hdd ins fnl f: no ex and outpcd fnl 100yds* **7/2**[1]

500 **4** *hd* **Steal The Scene (IRE)**[21] 5526 7-9-9 **57**......................(t[1]) RossaRyan 7 58
(Kevin Frost) *hld up in tch towards rr: clsd over 1f out: chsd ldrs and swtchd lft 1f out: kpt on ins fnl f* **16/1**

0600 **5** *1/2* **Pumaflor (IRE)**[35] 5024 7-9-4 **52**..........................(p) CallumShepherd 3 52
(Philip Kirby) *led tl 3f out: styd prom: rdn ent fnl 2f: stl ev ch 1f out: no ex and outpcd fnl 100yds* **25/1**

6043 **6** *hd* **Agent Of Fortune**[21] 5531 4-9-8 **56**..........................(p) SilvestreDeSousa 2 55
(Christine Dunnett) *hld up in tch in midfield: swtchd lft and effrt over 2f out: drvn and pressing ldrs over 1f out: ev ch 1f out: no ex and outpcd fnl 100yds* **7/2**[1]

0600 **7** *nse* **Alexandrakollontai (IRE)**[12] 5844 9-9-8 **56**.............(b) CamHardie 10 55
(Alistair Whillans) *in tch in rr but niggled along hdwy u.p 1f out: styd on ins fnl f: nvr trbld ldrs* **18/1**

2545 **8** *1 1/2* **Seaquinn**[63] 3966 4-8-12 **45** oh1................................ JosephineGordon 12 42
(John Best) *hld up in tch: effrt nr stands' rail over 1f out: kpt on ins fnl f: no threat to ldrs* **14/1**

0353 **9** *1/2* **Takiah**[12] 5867 4-8-12 **46**..........................(b[1]) LukeMorris 15 41
(Peter Hiatt) *in tch: rdn and hdwy to press ldrs 2f out: unable qck over 1f out: wknd ins fnl f* **12/1**

65-0 **10** *3* **Tallulah's Quest (IRE)**[17] 5675 5-8-10 **51**.................... SeanKirrane[(7)] 4 39
(Julia Feilden) *t.k.h: wl in tch in midfield: effrt jst over 2f out: unable qck and btn over 1f out: wknd ins fnl f* **16/1**

-020 **11** *1 1/4* **Sir Magnum**[18] 5633 4-9-3 **51**................................ BrettDoyle 5 36
(Tony Carroll) *stdd s: hld up in tch: shuffled bk towards rr and nt clr run over 2f out: shifting and trying to rally 1f out: no imp and no threat to ldrs fnl f* **11/1**

5000 **12** *3/4* **Silvington**[27] 5302 4-8-12 **45** oh1..........................(v) EoinWalsh 9 29
(Mark Loughnane) *prom: rdn over 2f out: lost pl and btn over 1f out: wknd ins fnl f* **66/1**

0605 **13** *6* **Pinchpoint (IRE)**[47] 4568 4-8-11 **50**..........................(p[1]) DylanHogan[(5)] 1 19
(John Butler) *t.k.h: wl in tch in midfield: rdn over 2f out: losing pl and btn over 1f out: wknd ins fnl f* **8/1**[3]

05-0 **14** *5* **General Patton**[12] 5867 5-8-12 **45** oh1..........................(p) RoystonFfrench 8 4
(Lydia Pearce) *chsd ldrs: rdn 1/2-way and sn struggling to hold pl: bhd fnl f* **100/1**

1m 37.22s (-0.98) **Going Correction** -0.175s/f (Firm) 14 Ran SP% **123.0**
Speed ratings (Par 101): **97,96,95,94,94 94,94,92,92,89 87,87,81,76**
CSF £117.42 CT £458.34 TOTE £29.80: £7.20, £1.50, £1.80; EX 293.80 Trifecta £673.10.
Owner Matt Watkinson **Bred** Juddmonte Farms Ltd **Trained** Prescot, Merseyside

FOCUS
In contrast to some of the earlier races the closers were seen to best effect this time; compressed, ordinary form.
T/Plt: £314.00 to a £1 stake. Pool: £61,566.14 - 143.11 winning units T/Qpdt: £15.60 to a £1 stake. Pool: £8,588.65 - 406.82 winning units **Steve Payne**

6262 DEAUVILLE (R-H)
Tuesday, August 20
OFFICIAL GOING: Polytrack: standard; turf: soft

6328a PRIX D'ISIGNY - CATEGORIE PERSONNEL ADMINISTRATIF (CLAIMER) (3YO) (ALL-WEATHER TRACK) (POLYTRACK) 1m 1f 110y(P)
2:50 3-Y-O £8,558 (£3,423; £2,567; £1,711; £855)

RPR
1 **Aniel (FR)**78 3-9-1 0 MaximeGuyon 5 75
(Simone Brogi, France) **19/2**
2 hd **Salina (FR)**21 3-8-5 0 MlleCoraliePacaut(3) 10 68
(J-C Rouget, France) **12/5**1
3 ½ **Ticklish (FR)**34 5055 3-8-8 0 MickaelBarzalona 3 67
(Mark Johnston) *qckly away: led: asked to qckn over 2f out: rdn 1 1/2f out: chal ent fnl f: hdd fnl 50yds: no ex towards fin* **7/2**2
4 1½ **Black And Blue (FR)**265 3-8-8 0 AurelienLemaitre 11 64
(Mario Hofer, Germany) **26/1**
5 ¾ **Fire Of Beauty (FR)**23 3-8-13 0 ow2 ChristopheSoumillon 4 67
(Andrea Marcialis, France) **22/5**3
6 hd **Mirasch (FR)**62 3-8-11 0 TheoBachelot 12 65
(Waldemar Hickst, Germany) **20/1**
7 nse **Chacha Boy (FR)**23 3-8-4 0 (b) ClementGuitraud(7) 6 65
(Y Barberot, France) **20/1**
8 4½ **Lauderdale (FR)**7 3-9-1 0 PierantonioConvertino 9 60
(Charley Rossi, France) **38/1**
9 9 **Swingy (FR)**18 5641 3-9-1 0 (b) CristianDemuro 1 41
(D Smaga, France) **13/1**
10 2½ **Brandon (FR)**23 3-8-11 0 PierreBazire 7 32
(G Botti, France) **20/1**
11 5 **San Paolo (FR)**43 3-8-7 0 (p) MlleFriedaValleSkar(9) 8 27
(C Lerner, France) **84/10**
12 2 **Pinaclouddown (IRE)**25 5407 3-8-8 0 (b) AlexandreChesneau(3) 2 18
(J-Y Artu, France) **93/1**
1m 58.03s 12 Ran SP% 119.1
PARI-MUTUEL (all including 1 euro stake): WIN 10.50; PLACE 2.30, 1.40, 1.70; DF 14.70.
Owner Khalifa Mohammed Al Attiyah **Bred** J Krauze **Trained** France

6197 BATH (L-H)
Wednesday, August 21
OFFICIAL GOING: Good (good to firm in places; 7.2)
Wind: light across Weather: sunny periods

6329 VISIT VALUERATER.CO.UK FOR BEST FREE TIPS H'CAP (VALUE RATER RACING CLUB SUMMER SPRINT SERIES) 5f 160y
1:45 (1:47) (Class 6) (0-60,61) 3-Y-O+
£2,781 (£827; £413; £300; £300; £300) Stalls Centre

Form RPR
0-32 1 **Tawaafoq**12 5883 5-9-1 56 (h) FinleyMarsh(3) 3 62
(Adrian Wintle) *chsd ldrs: rdn for str chal over 1f out: kpt on ins fnl f: led cl home* **11/1**
44-P 2 hd **Catheadans Fury**152 1265 5-9-7 59 (t) GeorgeWood 9 64
(Martin Bosley) *mid-div: hdwy over 2f out: sn rdn: tk narrow advantage and edgd rt over 1f out: kpt on ins fnl f: hdd cl home* **28/1**
5452 3 nk **Harry Beau**9 6027 5-9-9 61 (bt) HarryBentley 2 65
(David Evans) *rousted along leaving stalls: sn chsng ldrs: rdn over 2f out: kpt on ins fnl f* **9/2**3
2104 4 hd **Papa Delta**12 5889 5-9-3 55 GeorgeDowning 10 59
(Tony Carroll) *mid-div: hdwy over 2f out: sn rdn to take narrow advantage: hmpd and hdd over 1f out: kpt on fnl f* **4/1**2
2501 5 ¾ **Red Tycoon (IRE)**19 5607 7-9-6 58 (b) HectorCrouch 15 59
(Ken Cunningham-Brown) *s.i.s: towards rr: hdwy over 2f out: rdn and ev ch whn edging lft over 1f out: no ex fnl 120yds* **12/1**
0-01 6 ½ **Wotadoll**9 6018 5-9-4 61 SebastianWoods(5) 11 61
(Mike Murphy) *mid-div on outer: hdwy over 2f out: sn rdn: ev ch over 1f out: kpt on same pce ins fnl f* **9/4**1
5252 7 ½ **Cauthen (IRE)**9 6024 3-9-1 56 PatDobbs 16 54
(Ken Cunningham-Brown) *s.i.s: towards rr: hdwy over 1f out: kpt on but no threat fnl f* **10/1**
0-34 8 2¾ **Amberine**89 3036 5-8-9 47 EoinWalsh 13 36
(Malcolm Saunders) *s.i.s: towards rr: sme late prog: n.d* **20/1**
0000 9 1½ **Burauq**34 5081 7-8-7 45 RaulDaSilva 1 29
(Milton Bradley) *led: rdn and hdd over 2f out: wknd fnl f* **66/1**
2025 10 2 **Jaganory (IRE)**6 6110 7-9-3 55 (v) CallumShepherd 5 32
(Christopher Mason) *mid-div: hdwy over 2f out: sn rdn to chse ldrs: wknd fnl f (jockey said gelding moved poorly)* **14/1**
1640 11 2¾ **Toolatetodelegate**12 5884 5-9-0 52 (tp) TrevorWhelan 8 20
(Brian Barr) *s.i.s: a towards rr* **25/1**
6300 12 1 **Grandstand (IRE)**33 5147 3-9-0 55 LukeMorris 12 20
(Richard Price) *mid-div: pushed along over 3f out: rdn over 2f out: wknd over 1f out (vet said gelding lost left fore shoe)* **33/1**
0000 13 32 **Spring Holly (IRE)**20 5582 3-8-4 45 JimmyQuinn 6
(Milton Bradley) *prom: rdn over 2f out: wknd over 1f out* **100/1**
1m 10.84s (-0.26) **Going Correction** -0.075s/f (Good)
WFA 3 from 4yo+ 3lb 13 Ran SP% 118.2
Speed ratings (Par 101): **98,97,97,97,96 95,94,91,89,86 82,81,38**
CSF £293.20 CT £1590.53 TOTE £10.00: £3.30, £8.20, £1.90; EX 292.10 Trifecta £1655.20.
Owner S R Whistance **Bred** Whitsbury Manor Stud **Trained** Westbury-On-Severn, Gloucs

FOCUS
The rails were moved out 3 yards on the bend into the home straight adding approximately 10 yards to all races on the round course. This opening sprint was a competitive race for the grade and there was a bunched finish.

6330 SOUNDS COMMERCIAL BRISTOL MAIDEN STKS 5f 10y
2:15 (2:16) (Class 5) 2-Y-O £3,428 (£1,020; £509; £254) Stalls Centre

Form RPR
1 **Brad The Brief** 2-9-5 0 DavidProbert 8 77+
(Tom Dascombe) *s.i.s: sn pushed along towards rr: hdwy over 2f out: drifted lft but r.o wl fnl f: led fnl 100yds: rdn out* **8/1**
42 2 ¾ **Sand Diego (IRE)**13 5859 2-9-5 0 PatDobbs 1 74
(Peter Crate) *racd keenly: sn led: rdn ent fnl f: kpt on but no ex whn hdd fnl 100yds* **9/4**2
3 2¼ **Tommy Rock (IRE)** 2-9-5 0 AdamKirby 9 66+
(Clive Cox) *towards rr: hdwy over 2f out: kpt on under hands and heels ins fnl f: snatched 3rd cl home* **2/1**1
6 4 hd **Big Impact**26 5381 2-9-5 0 EoinWalsh 5 65
(Luke McJannet) *chsd ldrs: rdn to chal over 1f out: kpt on same pce ins fnl f: lost 3rd cl home* **25/1**
5 ½ **Barking Mad** 2-9-5 0 HarryBentley 6 63
(David Evans) *towards rr: rdn over 2f out: hdwy over 1f out: kpt on ins fnl f* **25/1**
4650 6 1¾ **Falconidae (IRE)**18 5683 2-9-0 70 SeanLevey 4 52
(Richard Hannon) *chsd ldrs: rdn 2f out: one pce fnl f* **8/1**
4 7 nk **Aweemaweh (IRE)**7 6078 2-9-5 0 CharlesBishop 7 56
(Mick Channon) *mid-div: rdn over 2f out: kpt on but nt pce to get involved* **5/1**3
6 8 ½ **Calbuco**14 5794 2-9-5 0 HectorCrouch 11 54
(Rod Millman) *in tch: hdwy over 2f out: effrt over 1f out: fdd fnl f* **100/1**
02 9 4½ **Force Of Impact (IRE)**16 5729 2-9-5 0 LukeMorris 10 38
(Paul George) *prom: rdn over 2f out: wknd over 1f out* **20/1**
10 4½ **Handful Of Gold (IRE)** 2-9-0 0 JohnFahy 2 17
(Kevin Bishop) *s.i.s: a in rr* **100/1**
0 11 5 **Lady Florence (IRE)**7 6078 2-9-0 0 JimmyQuinn 3
(Malcolm Saunders) *mid-div: rdn over 2f out: wknd over 1f out (jockey said filly ran greenly and hung left-handed from halfway)* **100/1**
1m 2.15s (0.15) **Going Correction** -0.075s/f (Good) 11 Ran SP% 118.4
Speed ratings (Par 94): **95,93,90,89,89 86,85,85,77,70 62**
CSF £25.46 TOTE £6.50: £1.90, £1.20, £2.60; EX 28.10 Trifecta £139.60.
Owner Chasemore Farm **Bred** Chasemore Farm **Trained** Malpas, Cheshire

FOCUS
A promising newcomer stayed on strongly to beat the two market leaders in this maiden.

6331 WEATHERBYS RACING BANK FOREIGN EXCHANGE H'CAP 1m 2f 37y
2:50 (2:50) (Class 4) (0-80,81) 3-Y-O+
£5,207 (£1,549; £774; £387; £300; £300) Stalls Low

Form RPR
240 1 **Champs De Reves**57 4220 4-8-13 69 MeganNicholls(3) 8 77
(Michael Blake) *hld up last: hdwy fr over 2f out: rdn to ld over 1f out: drifted lft fnl f: kpt on wl: comf (regarding the apparent improvement in form, trainer's rep said gelding had benefitted from a 57 day break)* **13/2**
5245 2 1¼ **Carp Kid (IRE)**20 5571 4-9-3 73 (p) FinleyMarsh(3) 4 78
(John Flint) *led: rdn whn strly chal 2f out: hdd over 1f out: kpt on same pce fnl f* **8/1**
6311 3 ½ **Greeley (IRE)**8 6045 3-9-1 75 6ex (p) DavidEgan 2 79
(Rod Millman) *hld up in last pair: hdwy over 2f out: rdn upsides wl over 1f out tl jst over 1f out: no ex fnl 100yds* **7/1**
1-54 4 5 **Let Rip (IRE)**28 5320 5-9-11 78 AdamKirby 5 72
(Henry Candy) *hld up in tch: rdn into 4th 2f out: nt pce to get on terms* **5/2**1
5120 5 2¾ **El Picador (IRE)**20 5594 3-9-2 76 (v) PatDobbs 6 64
(Sir Michael Stoute) *hld up in tch: rdn whn sltly hmpd 2f out: sn one pce* **5/1**3
643 6 5 **Gallatin**16 5748 3-8-12 72 DavidProbert 9 50
(Andrew Balding) *trckd ldr tl rdn over 2f out: wknd over 1f out* **7/2**2
-126 7 2¼ **Livvys Dream (IRE)**16 5741 4-9-12 79 (h) CallumShepherd 1 53
(Charles Hills) *s.i.s: plld hrd: trckd ldrs after 2f: rdn over 2f out: wknd over 1f out (jockey said filly ran too free)* **7/1**
4513 8 ½ **Gendarme (IRE)**12 5881 4-9-4 76 (b) SebastianWoods(5) 7 49
(Alexandra Dunn) *trckd ldrs: rdn over 2f out: wknd over 1f out* **16/1**
2m 8.13s (-2.97) **Going Correction** -0.075s/f (Good)
WFA 3 from 4yo+ 7lb 8 Ran SP% 122.8
Speed ratings (Par 105): **106,105,104,100,98 94,92,92**
CSF £61.04 CT £384.90 TOTE £9.40: £2.30, £2.30, £1.70; EX 73.10 Trifecta £570.70.
Owner Staverton Owners Group **Bred** Redgate Bstock & Peter Bottowley Bstock **Trained** Trowbridge, Wilts
■ Athmad was withdrawn. Price at time of withdrawal 4/1. Rule 4 applies to all bets struck prior to withdrawal, but not to SP bets. Deduction - 20p in the £. New market formed

FOCUS
Race distance increased by 10yds. The winner posted a pb.

6332 WEATHERBYS RACING BANK H'CAP 5f 10y
3:25 (3:25) (Class 3) (0-90,89) 3-Y-O+ £7,439 (£2,213; £1,106; £553) Stalls Centre

Form RPR
1105 1 **Amplify (IRE)**5 6148 3-9-5 84 HarryBentley 4 95
(Brian Meehan) *chsd ldrs: outpcd over 2f out: sn swtchd rt: hdwy over 1f out: str run to ld fnl 120yds: readily* **3/1**2
5523 2 2 **Secretfact**6 6110 6-8-12 75 JimmyQuinn 8 79
(Malcolm Saunders) *racd keenly: in tch: hdwy over 2f out: led jst over 1f out: sn rdn: hdd fnl 120yds: nt pce of wnr* **12/1**
5112 3 1¼ **Heritage**28 5291 3-9-10 89 (p) AdamKirby 1 89
(Clive Cox) *trckd ldrs: chal 2f out: rdn and ev ch jst over 1f out: kpt on same pce ins fnl f* **2/1**1
0024 4 1 **The Daley Express (IRE)**4 6208 5-9-9 86 DavidProbert 3 82
(Ronald Harris) *led: rdn and hdd 2f out: kpt on tl no ex fnl 140yds (jockey said gelding ran too free)* **7/2**3
0616 5 1¾ **Little Legs**26 5399 3-8-12 84 HarryRussell(7) 9 74
(Brian Ellison) *trckd ldrs: led 2f out: sn rdn: hdd jst over 1f out: no ex fnl f* **16/1**
6300 6 ¾ **Line Of Reason (IRE)**22 5524 9-9-8 85 LukeMorris 6 72
(Paul Midgley) *s.i.s: in tch but sn pushed along: kpt on but nvr gng pce to get on terms* **7/1**
0-40 7 3 **Glory Fighter**20 5589 3-9-3 82 GeraldMosse 7 58
(Charles Hills) *prom: rdn over 2f out: wknd over 1f out* **22/1**

11-5 **8** *10* **Laith Alareen**[25] 5444 4-9-8 **85**....................(t) DougieCostello 5 25
(Ivan Furtado) *prom: rdn over 2f out: wknd over 1f out (jockey said gelding stopped quickly)* **25/1**

1m 0.83s (-1.17) **Going Correction** -0.075s/f (Good)
WFA 3 from 4yo+ 2lb 8 Ran SP% **114.8**
Speed ratings (Par 107): **106,102,100,99,96 95,90,74**
CSF £38.30 CT £88.06 TOTE £4.00: £1.40, £3.10, £1.10; EX 41.20 Trifecta £127.90.
Owner Manton Thoroughbreds III **Bred** Drumlin Bloodstock **Trained** Manton, Wilts

FOCUS
They were spread across the track in this good handicap and the winner came widest of all, posting a pb.

6333 PLAY "FOUR FROM THE TOP" AT VALUERATER.CO.UK H'CAP (VALUE RATER CLUB SUMMER STAYERS' SERIES) 1m 6f
4:05 (4:05) (Class 5) (0-70,70) 3-Y-O+
£3,428 (£1,020; £509; £300; £300; £300) **Stalls** High

Form RPR
3212 **1** **Road To Paris (IRE)**[8] 6055 3-8-12 **64**....................(p[1]) LukeMorris 5 69+
(Sir Mark Prescott Bt) *rousted along leaving stalls: sn trcking ldr: chal 3f out: led 2f out: styd on: drvn out* **4/7**[1]

4140 **2** *½* **Rosie Royale (IRE)**[6] 6105 7-9-6 **62**.................... GeorgeWood 1 65
(Roger Teal) *trckd ldrs: rdn over 2f out: chal for 2nd ent fnl f: styd on wl cl home* **8/1**[3]

24-5 **3** *hd* **Hope Is High**[28] 5316 6-9-10 **66**.................... JFEgan 9 69
(John Berry) *mid-div: hdwy 3f out: sn rdn: chal for 2nd ent fnl f: styd on wl towards fin* **7/1**[2]

6/00 **4** *nk* **Borak (IRE)**[10] 5993 7-9-11 **70**....................(p) JoshuaBryan[(3)] 6 72
(Bernard Llewellyn) *hld up in tch: rdn and hdwy over 2f out: chal for 2nd ent fnl f: styd on* **25/1**

3522 **5** *hd* **Filament Of Gold (USA)**[28] 5290 8-8-10 **52**....................(b) DavidProbert 2 54
(Roy Brotherton) *hld up in last pair: hdwy over 2f out: sn rdn: chal for 2nd ent fnl f: styd on* **16/1**

4134 **6** *1 ½* **Becky Sharp**[16] 5744 4-8-9 **51** oh1....................(b) CharlieBennett 7 51
(Jim Boyle) *led: rdn whn strly chal 3f out: hdd 2f out: styd on tl no ex fnl 100yds* **12/1**

004 **7** *5* **Conkering Hero (IRE)**[42] 4791 5-9-9 **70**.................... ScottMcCullagh[(5)] 4 63
(Joseph Tuite) *trckd ldrs tl lost pl over 5f out: struggling over 3f out: nvr bk on terms* **16/1**

160 **8** *2 ½* **Swordbill**[46] 4661 4-9-13 **69**....................(p) AdamKirby 8 58
(Ian Williams) *s.i.s and squeezed up s: in last pair: rdn over 2f out: nvr threatened: wknd fnl f* **7/1**[2]

3m 6.98s (0.88) **Going Correction** -0.075s/f (Good)
WFA 3 from 4yo+ 10lb 8 Ran SP% **123.1**
Speed ratings (Par 103): **94,93,93,93,93 92,89,88**
CSF £7.00 CT £21.44 TOTE £1.40: £1.10, £2.20, £2.20; EX 7.30 Trifecta £32.20.
Owner Jones, Julian, Lee, Royle & Wicks **Bred** Rabbah Bloodstock Limited **Trained** Newmarket, Suffolk

FOCUS
Race distance increased by 10yds. There was a bunched finish in this staying handicap but they went a fair pace and the hot favourite came out on top.

6334 JANE LOWNDES WHINNEY H'CAP 1m
4:40 (4:40) (Class 6) (0-65,65) 4-Y-O+
£2,781 (£827; £413; £300; £300; £300) **Stalls** Low

Form RPR
5463 **1** **Zefferino**[60] 4115 5-9-0 **58**....................(t) GeorgeWood 1 64
(Martin Bosley) *hld up towards rr: nt best of runs wl over 1f out: hdwy sn after: str run ins fnl f: disp ld towards fin: won on nod* **8/1**[3]

0306 **2** *shd* **Sir Plato (IRE)**[37] 4994 5-9-4 **65**....................(v[1]) FinleyMarsh[(3)] 10 71
(Rod Millman) *trckd ldrs: pushed along over 4f out: rdn over 2f out: led jst ins fnl f: jnd towards fin: lost on nod* **5/1**[2]

5041 **3** *nk* **Cuttin' Edge (IRE)**[6] 6123 5-9-5 **63** 5ex.................... HarryBentley 5 68
(William Muir) *led: rdn whn strly chal over 2f out: hdd jst ins fnl f: kpt on* **7/4**[1]

3303 **4** *1* **Accomplice**[18] 5675 5-8-11 **55**.................... CharlieBennett 9 58
(Michael Blanshard) *hld up towards rr: hdwy in centre over 2f out: sn rdn: kpt on fnl f but nt quite pce to chal* **16/1**

4204 **5** *1 ¼* **Takeonefortheteam**[28] 5309 4-9-4 **62**.................... LiamJones 2 62
(Mark Loughnane) *in tch: tk clsr order over 3f out: rdn over 2f out: ev ch ent fnl f: no ex fnl 120yds* **10/1**

023 **6** *nk* **Mabo**[8] 6045 4-8-7 **51**....................(b) JFEgan 3 50
(Grace Harris) *trckd ldrs: rdn and ev ch over 1f out: no ex ins fnl f* **20/1**

2020 **7** *nk* **Red Gunner**[6] 6123 5-8-8 **52**.................... CallumShepherd 6 51
(Mark Loughnane) *dwlt: towards rr: swtchd to centre wl over 2f out: sn rdn: kpt on fnl f but nvr any threat* **16/1**

3635 **8** *1* **Mister Musicmaster**[26] 5373 10-8-11 **58**.................... MeganNicholls[(3)] 14 54
(Ron Hodges) *mid-div: rdn over 2f out: sn one pce* **16/1**

4545 **9** *nse* **Edge (IRE)**[13] 5867 8-8-10 **54**....................(b) DavidProbert 4 50+
(Bernard Llewellyn) *mid-div: rdn and hdwy over 2f out: styng on in cl 5th whn nt clr run on far rails and snatched up ins fnl f: no ch after* **12/1**

0-40 **10** *½* **Outer Space**[56] 4235 8-9-2 **63**....................(p) WilliamCox[(3)] 7 58
(John Flint) *a towards rr* **20/1**

100 **11** *2 ¼* **Medici Moon**[102] 2631 5-8-1 **50** ow1..........(p) ThoreHammerHansen[(5)] 13 40
(Richard Price) *pressed ldr: rdn wl over 2f out: sn hld: wknd ent fnl f* **25/1**

040 **12** *4 ½* **Gates Pass**[29] 5284 4-9-2 **60**....................(t) TrevorWhelan 12 39
(Brian Barr) *mid-div: hdwy over 2f out: sn rdn: wknd over 1f out* **20/1**

1m 41.08s (-0.62) **Going Correction** -0.075s/f (Good) 12 Ran SP% **116.7**
Speed ratings (Par 101): **100,99,99,98,97 97,96,95,95,95 92,88**
CSF £44.04 CT £104.01 TOTE £11.10: £3.10, £2.10, £1.20; EX 71.90 Trifecta £292.30.
Owner John Carey **Bred** Saleh Al Homaizi & Imad Al Sagar **Trained** Chalfont St Giles, Bucks

FOCUS
Race distance increased by 10yds. They went a decent pace and there was an exciting finish in this handicap

6335 UNIVERSITY AND LITERARY CLUB VETERANS' H'CAP 5f 160y
5:15 (5:15) (Class 5) (0-75,76) 6-Y-O+
£3,428 (£1,020; £509; £300; £300; £300) **Stalls** Centre

Form RPR
4324 **1** **Union Rose**[6] 6110 7-9-4 **72**....................(v) RaulDaSilva 5 81
(Ronald Harris) *trckd ldr: reminder over 3f out: rdn over 2f out: led ent fnl f: drifted lft: r.o wl: asserting towards fin* **4/1**[2]

0054 **2** *1 ¼* **Naadirr (IRE)**[6] 6109 8-9-7 **75**....................(v) DougieCostello 2 80
(Kevin Ryan) *s.i.s: sn mid-div: hdwy wl over 1f out: sn rdn: pressed wnr ins fnl f: a being hld* **13/2**

6562 **3** *2* **La Fortuna**[36] 5013 6-8-12 **66**....................(t) CallumShepherd 8 64
(Charlie Wallis) *hld up in last pair: hdwy over 2f out: rdn in cl 3rd ent fnl f: kpt on same pce* **6/1**

5620 **4** *1* **Little Palaver**[71] 3701 7-8-11 **72**....................(p) AmeliaGlass[(7)] 1 67
(Clive Cox) *mid-div: rdn over 2f out: kpt on but nt pce to chal* **6/1**

0115 **5** *½* **Storm Melody**[28] 5291 6-9-8 **76**....................(p) HarryBentley 10 69
(Ali Stronge) *trckd ldrs: rdn 3f out: ev ch over 1f out: fdd fnl f* **5/1**[3]

00 **6** *2 ½* **Pea Shooter**[35] 5038 10-8-9 **70**.................... HarryRussell[(7)] 7 55
(Brian Ellison) *trckd ldrs: rdn in cl 3rd over 2f out: wknd jst over 1f out* **20/1**

1442 **7** *½* **King Crimson**[13] 5843 7-8-13 **72**....................(t) DarraghKeenan[(5)] 4 55
(John Butler) *led: rdn over 1f out: hdd ent fnl f: wknd* **8/1**

0420 **8** *4 ½* **George Dryden (IRE)**[22] 5532 7-9-3 **71**.................... JackMitchell 6 40
(George Boughey) *s.i.s: a towards rr (jockey said gelding ran too free)* **7/2**[1]

1m 9.9s (-1.20) **Going Correction** -0.075s/f (Good) 8 Ran SP% **116.7**
Speed ratings: **105,103,100,99,98 95,94,88**
CSF £30.70 CT £156.79 TOTE £3.80: £1.60, £2.20, £1.90; EX 28.90 Trifecta £131.50.
Owner Adrian Evans **Bred** Home Farm **Trained** Earlswood, Monmouths

FOCUS
They went a strong pace in this veterans' handicap and one of the market leaders scored in decent style.
T/Plt: £42.00 to a £1 stake. Pool: £50,617.22 - 879.70 winning units T/Qpdt: £8.70 to a £1 stake. Pool: £5,238.74 - 444.50 winning units **Tim Mitchell**

6032 CARLISLE (R-H)
Wednesday, August 21

OFFICIAL GOING: Good to soft (soft in places; 6.2)
Wind: fairly strong against Weather: fine

6336 BRITISH STALLION STUDS EBF MAIDEN STKS (DIV I) 5f 193y
2:05 (2:08) (Class 5) 2-Y-O **£4,204** (£1,251; £625; £312) **Stalls** Low

Form RPR
1 **Deb's Delight** 2-9-5 0.................... DavidNolan 6 87+
(Richard Fahey) *dwlt: rcvrd to sn chse ldrs: pushed along to chal over 1f out: led 1f out: kpt on wl pushed out* **10/3**[2]

3532 **2** *3* **Leapers Wood**[8] 6053 2-9-5 76.................... GrahamLee 5 78
(Michael Dods) *led narrowly: stl on bit 2f out: pushed along over 1f out: hdd 1f out: drvn and sn no ex* **4/6**[1]

3 *½* **Dandy's Angel (IRE)** 2-8-11 0.................... SeanDavis[(3)] 1 71+
(John Wainwright) *hld up: rdn along over 3f out: hdwy over 1f out: wnt 3rd ins fnl f: kpt on wl* **25/1**

0 **4** *3 ½* **Lasting Legacy**[21] 5553 2-9-0 0.................... MichaelStainton 2 61
(Chris Fairhurst) *chsd ldrs: rdn along over 3f out: plugged on* **12/1**

5 *1 ¾* **Cassy O (IRE)** 2-9-5 0.................... DuranFentiman 4 60
(Tim Easterby) *midfield: pushed along over 1f out: kpt on ins fnl f* **50/1**

0 **6** *1 ¼* **Herbert Pocket**[97] 2780 2-9-5 0.................... DavidAllan 12 57
(Tim Easterby) *dwlt: hld up: sn pushed along: sme hdwy: nvr threatened ldrs* **40/1**

7 *1* **Alioski** 2-9-5 0.................... KevinStott 10 54
(Kevin Ryan) *sn pressed ldr: rdn over 2f out: wknd over 1f out* **7/1**[3]

66 **8** *½* **Honnold**[33] 5152 2-9-2 0.................... ConnorMurtagh[(3)] 8 52
(Donald McCain) *midfield: rdn along over 2f out: wknd over 1f out* **80/1**

9 *3* **Get Boosting** 2-9-5 0.................... ShaneGray 3 43
(Keith Dalgleish) *w ldrs: rdn over 2f out: wknd over 1f out* **33/1**

10 *1 ¼* **Somekindasuperstar** 2-9-0 0.................... JamesSullivan 7 34
(Paul Collins) *a outpcd in rr* **66/1**

0 **11** *¾* **Bal Mal (FR)**[28] 5294 2-9-5 0.................... JasonHart 11 37
(John Quinn) *hld up in midfield: pushed along 2f out: wknd ins fnl f* **16/1**

1m 16.93s (2.33) **Going Correction** +0.35s/f (Good) 11 Ran SP% **123.1**
Speed ratings (Par 94): **98,94,93,88,86 84,83,82,78,77 76**
CSF £5.98 TOTE £4.80: £1.50, £1.02, £10.40; EX 7.30 Trifecta £90.20.
Owner Mr & Mrs N Wrigley **Bred** Mr & Mrs N Wrigley **Trained** Musley Bank, N Yorks

FOCUS
The ground was drying out. This was the first division of a juvenile maiden in which most were lightly raced or newcomers. It was run at a sound gallop with the field racing towards the inside.

6337 BRITISH STALLION STUDS EBF MAIDEN STKS (DIV II) 5f 193y
2:35 (2:39) (Class 5) 2-Y-O **£4,204** (£1,251; £625; £312) **Stalls** Low

Form RPR
1 **Amaysmont** 2-9-2 0.................... SeanDavis[(3)] 8 87+
(Richard Fahey) *dwlt: sltly hld up in midfield: pushed along 3f out: angled lft to outer 2f out: sn gd hdwy: rdn to ld 1f out: kpt on wl to draw clr* **10/3**[1]

22 **2** *4 ½* **Alix James**[37] 4976 2-9-5 0.................... JamieGormley 11 73
(Iain Jardine) *prom: rdn 2f out: led over 1f out: hung rt and hdd 1f out: sn no ex* **9/2**[3]

42 **3** *2 ½* **Ainsdale**[14] 5815 2-9-5 0.................... CliffordLee 1 65
(K R Burke) *led narrowly: rdn and edgd rt 2f out: hdd over 1f out: wknd ins fnl f* **4/1**[2]

3223 **4** *1* **Cruising**[21] 5553 2-9-5 75.................... DavidNolan 10 62
(David Brown) *chsd ldrs towards outer: rdn 2f out: edgd rt over 1f out: drvn and wknd ins fnl f* **8/1**

5 *nk* **Hartswood** 2-9-2 0.................... ConnorMurtagh[(3)] 4 61+
(Richard Fahey) *dwlt: hld up: pushed along and bit clsr 2f out: rdn over 1f out: kpt on pushed out ins fnl f (An inquiry was held into the running and riding of the colt which appeared to be tenderly handled in the final furlong; the rider was interviewed and shown recordings of the race and the Veterinary Officer reported a post-race examination failed to reve* **14/1**

6 *2 ½* **Dilithium (FR)** 2-9-5 0.................... KevinStott 2 54
(Kevin Ryan) *chsd ldrs: rdn 2f out: wknd ins fnl f* **10/1**

7 *½* **Jerbourg** 2-9-5 0.................... DavidAllan 6 52
(Tim Easterby) *midfield on inner: quite keenly early: pushed along 2f out: one pce and nvr threatened ldrs (jockey said colt ran too free)* **17/2**

06 **8** *1 ½* **Proclaimer**[21] 5553 2-9-5 0.................... CamHardie 12 48
(Julie Camacho) *dwlt: hld up towards outer: pushed along over 3f out: nvr threatened* **25/1**

03 **9** *1 ½* **Angels Faces (IRE)**[12] 5895 2-9-0 0.................... SamJames 3 38
(Grant Tuer) *chsd ldrs: pushed along and outpcd over 2f out: wknd over 1f out* **7/1**

6440 **10** *2 ¼* **King Lenox**[60] 4125 2-9-2 66.................... RowanScott[(3)] 7 36
(Nigel Tinkler) *hld up in midfield: pushed along 3f out: wknd over 1f out* **50/1**

11 *11* **Jems Bond** 2-9-5 0 PhilDennis 5 3
(Alan Brown) *dwlt: a in rr* **100/1**
1m 16.2s (1.60) **Going Correction** +0.35s/f (Good) **11** Ran SP% **118.0**
Speed ratings (Par 94): **103,97,93,92,91 88,87,85,83,80 66**
CSF £18.11 TOTE £4.20: £2.00, £2.00, £1.50; EX 18.80 Trifecta £42.40.
Owner G J Paver **Bred** Mrs Glenda Swinglehurst **Trained** Musley Bank, N Yorks

FOCUS
The second and marginally faster division of the 6f juvenile maiden in which the pace was decent and, though the field raced towards the far side, the winner was widest of all and was more in the centre.

6338 RACINGTV H'CAP (JOCKEY CLUB GRASSROOTS SPRINT SERIES QUALIFIER) 5f 193y
3:10 (3:13) (Class 5) (0-70,71) 3-Y-O

£4,204 (£1,251; £625; £312; £300; £300) **Stalls** Low

Form RPR
3152 **1** **Mina Velour**[41] 4822 3-9-6 **68** (h) GrahamLee 5 75+
(Bryan Smart) *midfield: styd far side st: pushed along and hdwy to chse ldr over 1f out: rdn to chal ins fnl f: kpt on to ld towards fin* **6/1**[3]
4056 **2** *½* **Autumn Flight (IRE)**[7] 6070 3-8-13 **61** (b[1]) DavidAllan 8 66
(Tim Easterby) *dwlt sltly: rapid hdwy and led on outside after 1f: angled lft to r stands' side over 2f out: drvn over 1f out: strly pressed ins fnl f: hdd towards fin* **12/1**
3211 **3** *hd* **Bedtime Bella (IRE)**[8] 6033 3-9-5 **70** 6ex (v) SeanDavis(3) 9 74
(Michael Appleby) *sltly awkward s: midfield: swtchd lft to r stands' side over 2f out: hdwy and sn chsd ldr: drvn over 1f out: kpt on ins fnl f* **9/2**[2]
0255 **4** *1 ¾* **Popping Corks (IRE)**[23] 5491 3-8-3 **51** JamesSullivan 6 50
(Linda Perratt) *hld up in midfield: styd far side st: hdwy and chsd ldrs over 1f out: rdn ins fnl f: sn one pce* **33/1**
-000 **5** *¾* **Kyllachy Castle**[12] 5914 3-8-2 **50** oh5 CamHardie 10 46
(Lynn Siddall) *dwlt: hld up: sn pushed along: styd far side st: r.o ins fnl f: nrst fin* **150/1**
0611 **6** *2 ¾* **Ugo Gregory**[8] 6058 3-9-9 **71** 6ex NathanEvans 3 59
(Tim Easterby) *chsd ldrs: styd far side st: rdn 2f out: no ex ins fnl f* **11/4**[1]
2405 **7** *2* **Sarasota Bay**[12] 5893 3-9-3 **65** (v[1]) RobbieDowney 2 46
(John Quinn) *chsd ldrs: styd far side st: rdn 2f out: wknd fnl f* **16/1**
0233 **8** *7* **Kolossus**[16] 5724 3-9-7 **69** DavidNolan 4 28
(Michael Dods) *led for 1f: prom: styd far side st: rdn 2f out: wknd fnl f* **9/2**[2]
0003 **9** *9* **Princess Palliser (IRE)**[12] 5914 3-8-10 **58** (p) JasonHart 7
(John Quinn) *chsd ldrs: styd far side st: rdn and edgd lft over 1f out: sn wknd* **10/1**
3220 **10** *12* **Macs Blessings (IRE)**[2] 6276 3-8-8 **59** (b) GabrieleMalune(3) 1
(Stef Keniry) *a in rr: eased fnl f (jockey said gelding was never travelling)* **8/1**
1m 17.31s (2.71) **Going Correction** +0.35s/f (Good) **10** Ran SP% **114.7**
Speed ratings (Par 100): **95,94,94,91,90 87,84,75,63,47**
CSF £74.10 CT £353.73 TOTE £6.30: £2.10, £4.10, £1.70; EX 74.00 Trifecta £348.30.
Owner P Sutherland **Bred** Whatton Manor Stud **Trained** Hambleton, N Yorks

FOCUS
A competitive 0-70 sprint and the first two in the market had both won their last two races. On this occasion the field split into two groups with the second and third the only two to race against the stands' side rail. Once again near the far side rail seemed to be the worst ground. Interestingly the time was slower than for either of the two juvenile maidens.

6339 RACINGTV.COM H'CAP 5f
3:45 (3:47) (Class 4) (0-85,86) 3-Y-O+

£7,115 (£2,117; £1,058; £529; £300; £300) **Stalls** Low

Form RPR
1202 **1** **Music Society (IRE)**[5] 6178 4-9-3 **76** NathanEvans 1 86
(Tim Easterby) *trckd ldrs: pushed into ld over 1f out: edgd lft to rail: kpt on wl: comf* **15/8**[1]
4040 **2** *1 ¾* **Stoney Lane**[18] 5692 4-9-0 **73** (p[1]) PhilDennis 6 77
(Richard Whitaker) *chsd ldrs: drvn to chse wnr 1f out: edgd rt and kpt on same pce* **4/1**[2]
-211 **3** *hd* **Four Wheel Drive**[7] 6070 3-8-13 **74** 6ex (p) GrahamLee 8 77
(David Brown) *chsd ldrs: rdn along 2f out: briefly n.m.r appr fnl f: drvn and kpt on ins fnl f* **6/1**[3]
0123 **4** *hd* **Heath Charnock**[18] 5658 3-9-11 **86** AndrewMullen 4 89
(Michael Dods) *dwlt sltly: hld up in tch: pushed along over 1f out: drvn and kpt on fnl f* **11/1**
4000 **5** *½* **Gracious John (IRE)**[49] 4521 6-9-5 **85** AngusVilliers(7) 5 86
(Ian Williams) *outpcd in rr tl kpt on towards wd outside fr appr fnl f* **12/1**
6206 **6** *4 ½* **Manshood (IRE)**[18] 5691 6-9-10 **83** (v) JasonHart 3 68
(Paul Midgley) *hld up: rdn over 1f out: sn btn* **8/1**
-500 **7** *shd* **Adam's Ale**[16] 5723 10-8-11 **70** (p) JamesSullivan 9 54
(Marjorie Fife) *midfield: rdn along over 2f out: sn outpcd and dropped to rr: swtchd rt to outer and plugged on past btn horses ins fnl f* **50/1**
1000 **8** *1 ¼* **Bossipop**[4] 6227 6-9-6 **84** (b) DannyRedmond(5) 2 64
(Tim Easterby) *prom: rdn 2f out: wknd fnl f* **14/1**
0054 **9** *1 ¾* **Militia**[3] 6261 4-8-5 **67** ConnorMurtagh(3) 7 40
(Richard Fahey) *led: racd quite keenly: rdn and hdd over 1f out: sn wknd* **7/1**
1m 3.02s (0.92) **Going Correction** +0.35s/f (Good)
WFA 3 from 4yo+ 2lb **9** Ran SP% **117.3**
Speed ratings (Par 105): **106,103,102,102,101 94,94,92,89**
CSF £9.39 CT £37.94 TOTE £2.70: £1.40, £1.60, £1.50; EX 12.30 Trifecta £64.20.
Owner Richard Taylor & Philip Hebdon **Bred** Pier House Stud **Trained** Great Habton, N Yorks

FOCUS
A competitive 5f handicap in which the whole field raced towards the stands' side with the decisive winner fairly sprinting away having bagged the rail in the closing stages. The winner rates to his turf best; sound form around the next three finishers.

6340 EVERY RACE LIVE ON RACING TV H'CAP (JOCKEY CLUB GRASSROOTS STAYERS' SERIES QUALIFIER) 1m 6f 32y
4:25 (4:26) (Class 4) (0-85,81) 3-Y-O+

£7,115 (£2,117; £1,058; £529; £300; £300) **Stalls** Low

Form RPR
3-22 **1** **Navajo Pass**[16] 5742 3-9-6 **81** GrahamLee 8 92
(Donald McCain) *trckd ldr: pushed along to chal over 3f out: led narrowly over 2f out: drvn over 1f out: hld on gamely in sustained duel w 2nd* **2/1**[1]
5132 **2** *shd* **Celestial Force (IRE)**[13] 5849 4-10-0 **79** CliffordLee 3 89
(Tom Dascombe) *led: jnd over 3f out: rdn and hdd narrowly over 2f out: styd on wl in sustained duel w wnr but a jst hld* **6/1**
0221 **3** *6* **Contrebasse**[12] 5897 4-9-6 **71** DavidAllan 7 73
(Tim Easterby) *midfield: rdn over 2f out: styd on into 3rd fnl 2f* **8/1**
1230 **4** *6* **Grenadier Guard (IRE)**[11] 5967 3-9-6 **81** (b) FrannyNorton 6 74
(Mark Johnston) *dwlt and reminders sn after s: sn midfield: wnt in snatches: hdwy and chsd ldrs over 4f out: rdn over 3f out: outpcd and btn over 2f out: plugged on ins fnl f* **5/1**[3]
0612 **5** *5* **Beechwood Jude (FR)**[8] 6038 3-8-12 **73** ShaneGray 5 59
(Keith Dalgleish) *hld up: rdn along 4f out: sme hdwy over 2f out: wknd fnl f* **4/1**[2]
3225 **6** *8* **Royal Flag**[4] 6200 9-8-13 **64** JasonHart 2 39
(Brian Ellison) *hld up: rdn along over 4f out: drvn over 3f out: sn wknd* **16/1**
620 **7** *½* **Cormier (IRE)**[32] 5175 3-8-5 **69** GabrieleMalune(3) 1 45
(Stef Keniry) *trckd ldr: rdn along and lost pl over 3f out: wknd over 2f out (jockey said gelding weakened quickly final 2f)* **13/2**
3m 12.24s (0.64) **Going Correction** +0.35s/f (Good)
WFA 3 from 4yo+ 10lb **7** Ran SP% **114.6**
Speed ratings (Par 105): **108,107,104,101,98 93,93**
CSF £14.59 CT £78.33 TOTE £2.90: £2.20, £1.90; EX 12.60 Trifecta £38.60.
Owner T G Leslie **Bred** Natton House Thoroughbreds & Mr G Bishop **Trained** Cholmondeley, Cheshire

FOCUS
A staying handicap run at a fair gallop in which they all came stands' side in the straight and the first two were clear. The winner improved. Add 8yds.

6341 WATCH RACING TV NOW H'CAP (JOCKEY CLUB GRASSROOTS FLAT MIDDLE DISTANCE SERIES QUALIFIER) 1m 1f
4:55 (4:58) (Class 5) (0-70,69) 3-Y-O+

£4,204 (£1,251; £625; £312; £300; £300) **Stalls** Low

Form RPR
0054 **1** **Royal Shaheen (FR)**[16] 5726 6-9-11 **66** (v) GrahamLee 6 76
(Alistair Whillans) *trckd ldrs: chal gng wl 2f out: pushed into ld over 1f out: rdn and kpt on wl* **9/1**[3]
6150 **2** *1 ¾* **Home Before Dusk**[30] 5239 4-9-9 **64** ShaneGray 5 70
(Keith Dalgleish) *slowly away: hld up: rdn along over 3f out: styd on wl on outer fr over 1f out: wnt 2nd 75yds out: no threat to wnr* **20/1**
0122 **3** *½* **Firewater**[12] 5898 3-9-2 **67** (p) SeanDavis(3) 15 72
(Richard Fahey) *in tch: rdn along over 3f out: lost pl over 2f out: styd on fr appr fnl f: wnt 3rd 75yds out* **9/1**[3]
0413 **4** *½* **Remember Rocky**[34] 5096 10-9-2 **62** (b) PaulaMuir(5) 1 66
(Lucy Normile) *outpcd towards rr: styd on fr outside appr fnl f* **16/1**
0242 **5** *1 ¼* **Iconic Code**[13] 5844 4-9-4 **64** AndrewBreslin(5) 9 65
(Keith Dalgleish) *midfield: rdn over 3f out: hdwy and chsd ldrs 2f out: no ex fnl 75yds* **10/1**
5234 **6** *hd* **Ghayyar (IRE)**[16] 5725 5-9-9 **69** (tp) DannyRedmond(5) 7 70
(Tim Easterby) *trckd ldrs: rdn over 2f out: no ex fnl 75yds* **11/2**[1]
0033 **7** *nk* **Carey Street (IRE)**[20] 5593 3-9-4 **66** JasonHart 16 66
(John Quinn) *dwlt: hld up: rdn along 2f out: angled rt 1f out: styd on pushed out ins fnl f* **15/2**[2]
4060 **8** *1 ¼* **Gworn**[11] 5937 9-9-2 **57** LewisEdmunds 2 55
(R Mike Smith) *nvr much bttr than midfield* **28/1**
6300 **9** *1 ½* **Najashee (IRE)**[23] 5490 5-9-12 **67** (p[1]) KevinStott 12 61
(Roger Fell) *hld up in midfield: rdn along 3f out: plugged on fnl f: nvr trbld ldrs* **18/1**
1014 **10** *1 ½* **Spirit Of Sarwan (IRE)**[11] 5933 5-9-7 **65** (b) GabrieleMalune(3) 13 56
(Stef Keniry) *v.s.a and in rr: minor late hdwy: nvr involved (jockey said gelding was slowly away)* **28/1**
4425 **11** *¾* **Ventura Bay (IRE)**[34] 5102 3-8-13 **64** ConnorMurtagh(3) 8 54
(Richard Fahey) *prom: rdn to ld 2f out: sn wandered: hdd over 1f out: wknd fnl f* **12/1**
3015 **12** *nk* **Beverley Bullet**[16] 5726 6-9-10 **65** (p) PhilDennis 14 54
(Lawrence Mullaney) *trckd ldrs: rdn over 2f out: wknd fnl f* **11/2**[1]
3320 **13** *2 ½* **Chinese Spirit (IRE)**[11] 5938 5-9-9 **64** DavidNolan 3 48
(Linda Perratt) *midfield: rdn and hdwy to chse ldrs on outer 2f out: wknd ins fnl f* **9/1**[3]
0-00 **14** *6* **Crimson Skies (IRE)**[18] 5694 4-9-7 **62** SamJames 11 33
(John Davies) *led: rdn and hdd 2f out: already wkng whn short of room on rail over 1f out* **100/1**
3-05 **15** *½* **Parole (IRE)**[5] 6179 7-9-12 **67** (t) RachelRichardson 10 37
(Tim Easterby) *prom: lost pl over 2f out: rdn and wknd over 1f out* **14/1**
4604 **16** *2* **Guvenor's Choice (IRE)**[47] 4602 4-9-8 **63** (t) JamesSullivan 4 29
(Marjorie Fife) *hld up in midfield: rdn over 2f out: wknd fnl f* **25/1**
2m 2.32s (3.32) **Going Correction** +0.35s/f (Good)
WFA 3 from 4yo+ 7lb **16** Ran SP% **123.6**
Speed ratings (Par 103): **99,97,97,96,95 95,95,93,92,91 90,90,88,82,82 80**
CSF £187.69 CT £1753.91 TOTE £9.90: £2.80, £3.90, £2.40, £3.10; EX 90.30 Trifecta £728.60.
Owner Frank Lowe **Bred** SF Bloodstock LLC **Trained** Newmill-On-Slitrig, Borders

FOCUS
Mainly exposed sorts in this handicap which was run at a fair gallop and the field came across to the stands' side rail. Straightforward form. Add 8yds.

6342 JOIN RACING TV NOW H'CAP 7f 173y
5:25 (5:27) (Class 5) (0-70,70) 3-Y-O

£4,204 (£1,251; £625; £312; £300; £300) **Stalls** Low

Form RPR
0603 **1** **Sootability (IRE)**[13] 5844 3-8-10 **62** SeanDavis(3) 6 75
(Richard Fahey) *in tch: rdn along over 3f out: rdn to chse ldrs over 1f out: drvn to ld 110yds: styd on wl* **3/1**[1]
3330 **2** *2 ¾* **Power Player**[12] 5898 3-9-5 **68** CliffordLee 9 74
(K R Burke) *hld up in midfield: rdn over 2f out: styd on wl fnl f: wnt 2nd post* **8/1**
6510 **3** *shd* **Mecca's Gift (IRE)**[43] 4761 3-9-7 **70** (b) GrahamLee 3 76
(Michael Dods) *trckd ldrs: pushed along over 2f out: rdn to ld appr fnl f: drvn and hdd 110yds: no ex: lost 2nd post (vet said filly lost its left hind shoe)* **12/1**
-060 **4** *¾* **Iron Mike**[41] 4820 3-8-12 **61** ShaneGray 5 65+
(Keith Dalgleish) *w ldr: rdn over 2f out: no ex ins fnl f* **7/2**[2]
3650 **5** *nse* **Curfewed (IRE)**[57] 4210 3-9-1 **64** (p) CamHardie 8 68
(Tracy Waggott) *hld up: pushed along 3f out: swtchd rt to outer 2f out: rdn and sn hdwy: styd on fnl f* **28/1**
0505 **6** *3 ¾* **My Boy Lewis (IRE)**[6] 6101 3-9-4 **67** (p[1]) KevinStott 1 62
(Roger Fell) *dwlt: hld up in midfield: rdn and hdwy on outer over 2f out: sn chsd ldrs: wknd ins fnl f* **7/1**[3]

5060 **7** 1 **Sir Victor (IRE)**[14] 5817 3-9-4 **67**...........(b[1]) FrannyNorton 11 60
(Tom Dascombe) *trckd ldrs: racd keenly: hung lft and lost pl over 2f out: sn btn (jockey said gelding hung left turning into home straight)* **8/1**

4230 **8** ¾ **Juniors Fantasy (IRE)**[14] 5817 3-8-7 **56**...........(t) DuranFentiman 10 47
(Tim Easterby) *trckd ldrs: pushed along to ld 2f out: sn rdn: hdd appr fnl f: wknd qckly fnl 110yds* **8/1**

5006 **9** 3¾ **Constant**[15] 5786 3-9-7 **70**...........(v[1]) DavidNolan 4 53
(David O'Meara) *hld up: racd keenly: rdn over 3f out: sn btn* **16/1**

5-00 **10** 8 **Sesame (IRE)**[71] 3683 3-8-11 **60**........... AlistairRawlinson 12 24
(Michael Appleby) *led narrowly: rdn and hdd 2f out: wknd appr fnl f* **40/1**

0-00 **11** *hd* **Coco Motion (IRE)**[64] 3972 3-8-11 **60**........... AndrewMullen 7 24
(Michael Dods) *s.i.s: hld up: rdn over 3f out: sn wknd* **50/1**

1m 43.86s (3.86) **Going Correction** +0.35s/f (Good) **11** Ran SP% **114.5**
Speed ratings (Par 100): **94,91,91,90,90 86,85,84,81,73 72**
CSF £26.24 CT £254.59 TOTE £2.90: £1.40, £2.20, £3.00; EX 19.40 Trifecta £186.30.
Owner Mrs H Steel **Bred** Mighty Universe Ltd **Trained** Musley Bank, N Yorks

FOCUS
A run-of-the-mill handicap run at a fair gallop with, once again, the field edging towards the stands' side. On this occasion the first three ended up racing more towards the centre. Add 8yds.

6343 AJA NOVICE FLAT AMATEUR RIDERS' H'CAP (FOR NOVICE AMATEUR RIDERS) 1m 3f 39y
5:55 (5:55) (Class 6) (0-65,68) 4-Y-O+
£3,119 (£967; £483; £300; £300; £300) **Stalls** High

Form RPR

4226 **1** **Hugoigo**[11] 5939 5-10-8 **52**...........(p) MissShannonWatts 2 60
(Jim Goldie) *midfield: pushed along and hdwy over 2f out: chsd ldr over 1f out: chal 110yds out: styd on to ld towards fin* **20/1**

00/0 **2** ½ **Frightened Rabbit (USA)**[30] 3686 7-10-2 **46** oh1........... MissAmyCollier 5 53
(Dianne Sayer) *trckd ldrs: led 2f out: sn rdn along: pressed 110yds out: one pce and hdd towards fin* **17/2**

6421 **3** 3 **Gravity Wave (IRE)**[5] 6173 5-11-10 **68** 5ex......(p) MissImogenMathias 1 70
(John Flint) *hld up: rdn and hdwy over 1f out: styd on fnl f* **6/1[3]**

5050 **4** 1¾ **Grandscape**[16] 5728 4-11-6 **64**...........(v[1]) SophieSmith 10 64
(Ed Dunlop) *s.i.s: hld up: gd hdwy 3f out to chal 2f out: sn rdn: edgd rt and no ex ins fnl f* **20/1**

1405 **5** ¾ **Bollin Ted**[6] 6103 5-11-7 **65**........... MissJessicaGillam 3 63
(Tim Easterby) *in tch: rdn over 2f out: no imp* **20/1**

02-0 **6** 1½ **Knightly Spirit**[33] 5156 4-11-3 **64**........... MrEireannCagney(3) 9 60
(Iain Jardine) *hld up in midfield: pushed along over 2f out: no imp* **40/1**

-000 **7** ½ **Excalibur (POL)**[16] 5727 6-10-2 **46** oh1...........(p) AidanMacdonald 8 41
(Micky Hammond) *hld up: minor hdwy over 1f out: nvr involved* **33/1**

3520 **8** 3¾ **Majeste**[5] 6180 5-11-7 **65**........... MrMatthewEnnis 12 54
(Rebecca Bastiman) *trckd ldrs: racd keenly: rdn over 2f out: wknd fnl f* **8/1**

9 ¾ **Lucky Icon (IRE)**[19] 4719 5-9-13 **46** oh1......... MrHenryNewcombe(3) 11 34
(Philip Kirby) *trckd ldrs: rdn along over 3f out: wknd over 1f out* **11/10[1]**

6650 **10** ¾ **Can Can Sixty Two**[11] 5937 4-10-13 **60**........... MissPaigeHopper(3) 6 47
(R Mike Smith) *prom: racd keenly: led over 3f out: hdd 2f out: sn wknd* **33/1**

3454 **11** 7 **Iolani (GER)**[16] 5728 7-10-13 **60**........... MissRachelSharpe(3) 4 36
(Dianne Sayer) *slowly away: a in rr* **11/2[2]**

4-05 **12** 10 **Bold Statement (IRE)**[9] 6012 4-10-10 **54**......(t) MrThomasGreenwood 7 14
(Alan Berry) *led: hdd over 3f out: wknd and bhd* **100/1**

2m 33.88s (4.18) **Going Correction** +0.35s/f (Good) **12** Ran SP% **122.5**
Speed ratings (Par 101): **98,97,95,94,93 92,92,89,88,88 83,76**
CSF £174.47 CT £1168.37 TOTE £22.60: £4.40, £2.10, £2.50; EX 140.20 Trifecta £1643.60.
Owner Johnnie Delta Racing **Bred** Jim Goldie **Trained** Uplawmoor, E Renfrews

FOCUS
A handicap for amateur riders. The gallop was strong and the winner came from some way back. Add 8yds.
T/Plt: £21.60 to a £1 stake. Pool: £42,956.63 - 1,450.89 winning units T/Qpdt: £13.70 to a £1 stake. Pool: £3,387.73 - 182.82 winning units **Andrew Sheret**

6313 KEMPTON (A.W) (R-H)
Wednesday, August 21
OFFICIAL GOING: Polytrack: standard to slow (watered)

6344 RACINGTV.COM NOVICE AUCTION STKS (PLUS 10 RACE) 7f (P)
5:45 (5:46) (Class 4) 2-Y-O
£5,822 (£1,732; £865; £432) **Stalls** Low

Form RPR

2 **1** **Restless Endeavour (IRE)**[5] 6146 2-8-9 0........... HollieDoyle 8 69
(Jamie Osborne) *w ldr and rn green on bnd 4f out: rdn 2f out: led ent fnl f: strly pressed last strides: fought bk and jst prevailed* **5/1[3]**

5 **2** *nse* **Lyricist Voice**[25] 5433 2-8-11 0........... ShaneKelly 5 71
(Marco Botti) *hld up in rr-div: gng wl over 2f out: rdn wl over 1f out w a bit to do in 6th: styd on strly between horses ins fnl f: jst failed* **9/4[2]**

3 *nk* **Jalwan (USA)** 2-9-1 0........... RobertHavlin 1 74
(John Butler) *trckd ldr on inner: effrt 2f out: ev ch ent fnl f: kpt on wl fnl 200yds but nt pce of front pair cl home* **33/1**

02 **4** *nk* **Rajguru**[12] 5887 2-8-12 0........... PatCosgrave 3 70
(Tom Clover) *trckd ldng pair on outer: rdn over 2f out: ev ch on outer over 1f out: kpt on wl fnl f wout matching ldrs* **6/1**

01 **5** 6 **D Day (IRE)**[15] 5775 2-9-5 0........... SeanLevey 2 61
(Richard Hannon) *blindfolded to load: awkward leaving stalls but sn led: shkn up 2f out: rdn 2f out: fnd nil over 1f out: sn hdd and fdd tamely fnl f (jockey said colt stopped quickly; trainer's rep said colt was possibly unsuited by the all-weather surface)* **11/10[1]**

43 **6** *nk* **Robert Frost (USA)**[12] 5887 2-8-9 0........... CameronNoble(3) 4 54
(Jane Chapple-Hyam) *hld up in rr-div: effrt fr 2f out on inner: no imp over 1f out and pushed out* **20/1**

7 2¼ **Glencoe Boy (IRE)** 2-9-2 0........... DavidEgan 6 52
(David Flood) *in rr and sltly keen thrght: effrt over 2f out: plugged on being shuffled along fr over 1f out (jockey said colt was slowly away)* **33/1**

8 1½ **Go Bob Go (IRE)** 2-9-2 0........... CharlesBishop 7 48
(Eve Johnson Houghton) *sltly missed break: green in rr: shuffled along out fr 2f out* **20/1**

1m 28.21s (2.21) **Going Correction** +0.125s/f (Slow) **8** Ran SP% **124.7**
Speed ratings (Par 96): **92,91,91,91,84 84,81,79**
CSF £17.63 TOTE £6.50: £1.70, £1.30, £11.50; EX 25.70 Trifecta £454.80.
Owner The 10 For 10 Partnership **Bred** John & Anne-Marie O'Connor **Trained** Upper Lambourn, Berks

FOCUS
A novice auction with little depth and the first four finished in a heap.

6345 100% PROFIT BOOST AT 32REDSPORT.COM NOVICE MEDIAN AUCTION STKS 1m 3f 219y(P)
6:15 (6:18) (Class 4) 3-5-Y-O
£5,822 (£1,732; £865; £432) **Stalls** Low

Form RPR

2352 **1** **Inclyne**[25] 5421 3-8-11 **78**........... OisinMurphy 6 78+
(Andrew Balding) *trckd ldrs: shkn up and clsd on ldrs 2f out: sn rdn and led ent fnl f: in control fnl 200yds and pushed out* **4/7[1]**

0-2 **2** 3¼ **Mojave**[100] 2690 3-9-2 0........... AdamMcNamara 4 78
(Roger Charlton) *w ldr: shkn up and led 2f out: sn rdn: hdd ent fnl f: sn hld and plugged on* **5/2[2]**

43 **3** 7 **Voice Of Calm**[11] 5955 3-8-11 0........... RobertHavlin 2 62
(Harry Dunlop) *led and allowed to dictate pce: slowed tempo in bk st: rdn over 2f out: nt qckn and sn hdd: plugged on one pce fr over 1f out* **6/1[3]**

6 **4** 1¾ **Allocated (IRE)**[51] 4459 3-9-2 0........... SeanLevey 5 64
(John Butler) *trckd ldng pair: effrt over 2f out: kpt on one pce* **50/1**

5 **5** 2½ **Parisian Affair**[6] 6114 4-9-6 0........... FergusSweeney 8 55
(Neil King) *hld up in last pair: tk clsr order into mid-div in bk st: kpt on one pce (jockey said filly was slowly away)* **66/1**

4 **6** *nk* **Sible Hedingham**[43] 4760 3-8-11 0........... HollieDoyle 3 55
(James Eustace) *mid-div on inner: rdn over 2f out: lft bhd wl over 1f out: pushed out (jockey said filly ran in snatches)* **8/1**

0 **7** 1¼ **Melburnian**[14] 5808 3-9-1 0 ow2........... PaddyBradley(3) 1 60
(Jane Chapple-Hyam) *hld up in rr-div: effrt 2f out: no imp and pushed out fr wl over 1f out* **33/1**

0-0 **8** 68 **Miss Firecracker (IRE)**[47] 4592 3-8-11 0........... ShaneKelly 7
(Dr Jon Scargill) *a in rr: eased fr 2f out: t.o: lame (vet said filly was lame behind)* **100/1**

2m 33.24s (-1.26) **Going Correction** +0.125s/f (Slow)
WFA 3 from 4yo 9lb **8** Ran SP% **125.0**
Speed ratings (Par 105): **109,106,102,101,99 99,98,52**
CSF £2.66 TOTE £1.40: £1.02, £1.10, £1.70; EX 2.50 Trifecta £5.60.
Owner Kingsclere Racing Club **Bred** Kingsclere Stud **Trained** Kingsclere, Hants

FOCUS
A weak novice and a sluggish gallop. It turned into something of a sprint and they finished strung out. The didn't need her best, rated around the second.

6346 32RED ON THE APP STORE FILLIES' H'CAP 7f (P)
6:45 (6:45) (Class 4) (0-85,85) 3-Y-O
£6,469 (£1,925; £962; £481; £300; £300) **Stalls** Low

Form RPR

0266 **1** **Turn 'n Twirl (USA)**[26] 5386 3-9-7 **85**........... PatCosgrave 6 92
(Simon Crisford) *trckd ldr and t.k.h early: shkn up and cruised up to ld wl over 1f out: pushed along fr over 1f out: rdn out fnl f* **5/1[3]**

5022 **2** ¾ **Strict Tempo**[15] 5773 3-9-4 **82**........... OisinMurphy 5 87+
(Andrew Balding) *racd in mid-div: shkn up 2f out and travelling wl: tried to angle to outer over 1f out: racd awkwardly and dropped to 5th sn after: fnd stride fnl f and fin strly to take 2nd cl home: too much to do* **7/4[1]**

3-64 **3** 1¼ **To The Moon**[69] 3761 3-9-0 **78**........... RobertHavlin 1 80
(John Gosden) *led: rdn over 2f out: hdd over 1f out: kpt on chsng wnr tl lost 2nd cl home* **11/4[2]**

311 **4** 2¼ **Lapidary**[16] 5736 3-9-0 **78**........... LukeMorris 3 74
(Heather Main) *bhd ldr on inner: rdn over 2f out and wnt to inner: styd on tl no ex fnl f* **5/1[3]**

6103 **5** ¾ **Shorter Skirt**[15] 5773 3-9-2 **80**........... CharlesBishop 2 74
(Eve Johnson Houghton) *in rr and tk sltly t.k.h: rdn over 2f out: plugged on fr over 1f out* **10/1**

61-2 **6** 2½ **Angel Mead**[25] 5448 3-9-3 **81**........... FergusSweeney 4 68
(Joseph Tuite) *awkward s: in rr and t.k.h early: effrt over 2f out: no imp over 1f out (jockey said filly jumped right-handed from the stalls)* **16/1**

1m 26.34s (0.34) **Going Correction** +0.125s/f (Slow) **6** Ran SP% **111.3**
Speed ratings (Par 99): **103,102,100,98,97 94**
CSF £13.99 TOTE £5.00: £1.80, £1.80; EX 14.10 Trifecta £45.10.
Owner Sheikh Juma Dalmook Al Maktoum **Bred** O Gentry, O Trevino & Fox-Straus Ky **Trained** Newmarket, Suffolk

FOCUS
With the lack of a genuine pace, this fair fillies' handicap turned into a bit of a sprint.

6347 32RED H'CAP (LONDON MILE SERIES QUALIFIER) 1m (P)
7:15 (7:20) (Class 3) (0-90,90) 3-Y-O+
£9,337 (£2,796; £1,398; £699; £349; £175) **Stalls** Low

Form RPR

0455 **1** **Kuwait Currency (USA)**[11] 5948 3-9-6 **89**...........(t) PatDobbs 2 98
(Richard Hannon) *trckd ldrs: smooth hdwy wl over 1f out and swtchd to outer: sn rdn: styd on wl ins fnl f to ld 110yds out: comf* **8/1**

-165 **2** 1½ **Pesto**[21] 5564 3-9-7 **90**........... SeanLevey 9 95+
(Richard Hannon) *hld up in rr-div: shkn up wl over 3f out: rdn on inner 2f out: sustained run fr over 1f out: tk 2nd cl home* **16/1**

3042 **3** *shd* **Al Jellaby**[26] 5383 4-9-10 **87**...........(h) AdamKirby 1 93
(Clive Cox) *sn led: narrowly hdd over 2f out: rdn sn after: kpt on wl ent fnl f: briefly nosed bk into ld 150yds out: lost 2nd cl home* **5/1[3]**

4520 **4** ½ **Felix The Poet**[25] 5422 3-9-5 **88**...........(b) HollieDoyle 12 92
(Archie Watson) *w ldr: nosed into ld over 2f out: sn rdn: kpt on wl tl hdd 150yds out: dropped to 4th sn after* **20/1**

1333 **5** 1 **Freerolling**[32] 5174 4-9-8 **85**........... DavidProbert 7 88+
(Charlie Fellowes) *hld up in rr-div: clsr over 2f out: rdn 2f out: styd on over 1f out: one pce fnl 150yds* **7/2[2]**

0410 **6** ¾ **Harbour Spirit (FR)**[18] 5667 3-9-2 **85**........... ShaneKelly 3 85
(Richard Hughes) *s.s: sn pushed up into mid-div on inner: gng okay wl over 1f out: rdn sn after and kpt on one pce fnl f* **10/1**

P065 **7** 1½ **He's Amazing (IRE)**[15] 5776 4-9-3 **80**........... HectorCrouch 8 77
(Ed Walker) *racd in mid-div between horses and urged along fr 1/2-way: rdn over 2f out: kpt on* **14/1**

0305 **8** ¾ **Family Fortunes**[10] 5991 5-9-6 **88**........... ScottMcCullagh(5) 6 84
(Michael Madgwick) *hld up in rr: gng wl 2f out: shuffled along w plenty to do over 1f out: nvr involved (jockey said gelding was denied a clear run)* **25/1**

-350 **9** *hd* **Leader Writer (FR)**[41] 4851 7-9-4 **81**...........(p) GeraldMosse 5 76
(David Elsworth) *missed break and in last: rdn over 2f out: plugged on fr over 1f out (jockey said horse was slowly away)* **8/1**

215- **10** 1¾ **Alfurat River**[299] 8590 3-9-5 **88**........... OisinMurphy 10 78
(Saeed bin Suroor) *rrd leaving stalls: sn in mid-div on outer: rdn over 2f out: no imp over 1f out (jockey said gelding reared leaving the stalls)* **2/1[1]**

2310 **11** *10* **In The Red (IRE)**[18] 5667 6-9-2 **79**....................(p) EoinWalsh 11 47
(Martin Smith) *trckd ldrs on outer: rousted along 3f out: wknd fr over 2f out* **40/1**

1m 39.33s (-0.47) **Going Correction** +0.125s/f (Slow)
WFA 3 from 4yo+ 6lb **11** Ran SP% **127.1**
Speed ratings (Par 107): **107,105,105,104,103 103,101,100,100,98 88**
CSF £134.61 CT £734.34 TOTE £9.50: £2.30, £4.70, £2.20; EX 148.90 Trifecta £1690.20.
Owner Sheikh Abdullah Almalek Alsabah **Bred** Kenneth L Ramsey & Sarah K Ramsey **Trained** East Everleigh, Wilts

■ Mawakib was withdrawn. Price at time of withdrawal 3/1. Rule 4 applies to all bets struck prior to withdrawal, but not to SP bets. Deduction - 25p in the £. New market formed

FOCUS
Fairly competitive for the grade, despite the withdrawal of Mawakib before the start, and while the pace was modest, it held up and few got into it, with the Hannon yard gaining a one-two. The third helps set the standard.

6348 32RED CASINO H'CAP 1m 7f 218y(P)
7:45 (7:47) (Class 4) (0-85,85) 4-Y-O+ **£6,469** (£1,925; £962; £481; £300) **Stalls Low**

Form RPR

-111 **1** **Distant Chimes (GER)**[19] 5631 4-9-7 **85**....................(p) LukeMorris 4 97+
(Sir Mark Prescott Bt) *t.k.h early and restrained into rr: shkn up in last wl over 3f out: effrtless prog through rivals fr over 1f out: sn cruising upsides ldr: cantered into ld fnl 150yds: easily* **4/9**[1]

2234 **2** *1* **General Zoff**[8] 6044 4-8-6 **70**.................... JFEgan 3 74
(William Muir) *led tl hdd on bnd appr bk st: rdn in 2nd over 2f out: regained ld 2f out: kpt on tl wnr cantered by fnl 150yds* **9/2**[2]

-016 **3** *1 ¼* **Toshima (IRE)**[11] 5967 4-9-4 **82**....................(tp) OisinMurphy 2 84
(Robert Stephens) *trckd ldrs: rdn over 2f out: plugged on* **7/1**[3]

0620 **4** *½* **Baydar**[67] 3861 6-8-9 **73**....................(p w) DavidProbert 5 74
(Ivan Furtado) *slow s: in rr tl clsr at 1/2-way: rdn over 2f out: plugged on one pce fr over 1f out* **33/1**

-013 **5** *13* **Highland Sky (IRE)**[14] 5825 4-8-5 **69**....................(h) HollieDoyle 1 55
(David Simcock) *hld up: sweeping move on bnd appr bk st to ld: rdn wl over 2f out: hdd 2f out: no ex sn after (jockey said gelding hung left-handed throughout and ran too free)* **16/1**

3m 33.68s (3.58) **Going Correction** +0.125s/f (Slow) **5** Ran SP% **108.8**
Speed ratings (Par 105): **96,95,94,94,88**
CSF £2.70 TOTE £1.20: £1.02, £2.00; EX 2.30 Trifecta £5.10.
Owner Phil Fry - Osborne House **Bred** Gestut Wiesengrund **Trained** Newmarket, Suffolk

FOCUS
A messy race and weak for the grade but the winner could not have done it any more easily off a pedestrian pace. The runner-up has been rated to form.

6349 32RED.COM H'CAP 1m 3f 219y(P)
8:15 (8:15) (Class 3) (0-95,95) 3-Y-O **£9,337** (£2,796; £1,398; £699; £349) **Stalls Low**

Form RPR

-220 **1** **Deal A Dollar**[19] 5614 3-8-9 **83**....................(bt[1]) PatDobbs 1 90+
(Sir Michael Stoute) *hld up in last: shkn up and swtchd to outer over 2f out: rdn over 1f out and clsng ent fnl f: pushed out to ld last strides under wl timed ride: cosily* **7/2**[2]

0 **2** *1* **Grey D'Ars (FR)**[19] 5614 3-8-5 **79**.................... HollieDoyle 3 84
(Nick Littmoden) *led: rdn wl over 2f out: kpt on pluckily fr over 1f out and drifted to inner: hdd last strides* **4/1**[3]

0600 **3** *nk* **Severance**[21] 5541 3-9-3 **91**....................(h) CallumShepherd 5 95
(Mick Channon) *t.k.h in 4th: rdn over 2f out: kpt on one pce fnl f* **9/2**

-145 **4** *½* **Travel On**[104] 2553 3-9-7 **95**....................(p[1]) RobertHavlin 4 98
(John Gosden) *trckd ldr on outer and tk sltly t.k.h: rdn over 2f out: kpt on fr over 1f out: no ex ins fnl f* **6/1**

6315 **5** *1 ½* **Zuba**[11] 5931 3-8-6 **80**.................... DavidEgan 2 81
(Amanda Perrett) *racd in 3rd: rdn over 2f out: styd on fr over 1f out: no imp fnl f* **7/4**[1]

2m 34.28s (-0.22) **Going Correction** +0.125s/f (Slow) **5** Ran SP% **111.1**
Speed ratings (Par 104): **105,104,104,103,102**
CSF £17.37 TOTE £4.60: £1.80, £2.30; EX 17.20 Trifecta £55.70.
Owner Saeed Suhail **Bred** Rabbah Bloodstock Limited **Trained** Newmarket, Suffolk

FOCUS
Modest for the grade and the pace was ordinary. The winner came from last to first up the centre of the track under a well-timed ride, posting a clear pb.

6350 WISE BETTING AT RACINGTV.COM H'CAP 7f (P)
8:45 (8:47) (Class 5) (0-75,77) 3-Y-O+

£3,752 (£1,116; £557; £300; £300; £300) **Stalls Low**

Form RPR

0002 **1** **Indian Viceroy**[14] 5813 3-9-7 **75**.................... OisinMurphy 4 84
(Hughie Morrison) *dipped leaving stalls: sn bhd ldrs: rdn 2f out: kpt on wl ent fnl f: led 110yds out: edgd lft last strides* **5/2**[1]

0034 **2** *hd* **Lady Of Aran (IRE)**[18] 5651 4-9-9 **72**.................... DavidProbert 7 82
(Charlie Fellowes) *bhd ldr on outer: rdn 2f out: led over 1f out: strly pressed fnl f and hdd 110yds out: no ex last strides* **7/2**[3]

022 **3** *1* **Stormbomber (CAN)**[16] 5730 3-9-0 **68**.................... LiamKeniry 6 73
(Ed Walker) *cl up in mid-div: swtchd to outer and rdn 2f out: kpt on wl and ev ch tl no ex last 150yds* **11/4**[2]

0056 **4** *nk* **Kamikaze Lord (USA)**[18] 5647 3-9-4 **72**....................(t) RobertHavlin 2 76+
(John Butler) *cl up in mid-div: gng wl on heels of ldrs fr over 1f: nt clr run thrght whole of fnl f: unlucky (jockey said colt was denied a clear run on several occasions inside the final furlong)* **8/1**

6334 **5** *3* **Coverham (IRE)**[13] 5870 5-9-10 **73**....................(p) RyanTate 9 71
(James Eustace) *hld up in rr: rdn 2f out: plugged on one pce* **12/1**

360 **6** *1* **Powerful Star (IRE)**[54] 4341 3-9-4 **72**.................... DanielMuscutt 1 66
(David Lanigan) *hld up in rr-div: rdn 2f out: no imp* **16/1**

-110 **7** *1 ¼* **Astrospeed (IRE)**[138] 1560 4-9-8 **71**....................(h) GeorgeWood 8 63
(James Fanshawe) *tk fierce hold early in rr: rdn 2f out: plugged on* **12/1**

1/0- **8** *½* **Epic Adventure (FR)**[357] 4-10-0 **77**....................(p) GeraldMosse 5 68
(Roger Teal) *led: rdn wl over 2f out: hdd over 1f out: wknd qckly fnl f* **33/1**

20 **9** *8* **The Establishment**[50] 4479 4-9-6 **69**....................(h) EoinWalsh 3 38
(John Butler) *a in rr (jockey said gelding stopped quickly)* **33/1**

1m 26.27s (0.27) **Going Correction** +0.125s/f (Slow)
WFA 3 from 4yo+ 5lb **9** Ran SP% **115.7**
Speed ratings (Par 103): **103,102,101,101,97 96,95,94,85**
CSF £11.55 CT £24.24 TOTE £3.70: £1.50, £1.20, £1.60; EX 13.10 Trifecta £46.50.
Owner Mr & Mrs S Malcolm & & Mrs H Parkes **Bred** The Lavington Stud **Trained** East Ilsley, Berks

FOCUS
An ordinary handicap and the pace was steady. The winner rates back to his 2yo form.
T/Plt: £80.80 to a £1 stake. Pool: £55,850.96 - 504.22 winning units T/Qpdt: £25.20 to a £1 stake. Pool: £6,365.30 - 186.81 winning units **Cathal Gahan**

5453 YORK (L-H)
Wednesday, August 21

OFFICIAL GOING: Good (6.9, stands' side 6.8)
Wind: Moderate half behind Weather: Cloudy with sunny periods

6351 SKY BET AND SYMPHONY GROUP H'CAP 5f 89y
1:55 (1:57) (Class 2) (0-105,104) 3-Y-O+

£43,575 (£13,048; £6,524; £3,262; £1,631; £819) **Stalls** Centre

Form RPR

-511 **1** **Dakota Gold**[4] 6229 5-9-10 **104** 5ex.................... ConnorBeasley 10 113
(Michael Dods) *looked wl; trckd ldr centre: hdwy to chal over 1f out: rdn to ld ent fnl f: sn drvn and hld on wl towards fin* **4/1**[1]

3000 **2** *¾* **Marnie James**[39] 4896 4-9-6 **100**.................... JamieSpencer 6 106
(Jedd O'Keeffe) *racd centre: hld up in midfield: hdwy 2f out: swtchd rt and rdn to chse ldrs over 1f out: drvn and kpt on strly fnl f* **11/1**

1220 **3** *shd* **Arecibo (FR)**[18] 5664 4-9-4 **98**.................... DanielTudhope 3 104
(David O'Meara) *racd centre: hld up in rr: hdwy over 2f out: chsd ldrs and swtchd lft over 1f out: sn rdn: styd on wl fnl f* **11/1**

1210 **4** *nk* **Makanah**[54] 4331 4-9-2 **96**.................... PaulHanagan 9 101+
(Julie Camacho) *looked wl; racd centre: in rr: hdwy 2f out: rdn over 1f out: kpt on fnl f* **40/1**

0033 **5** *nk* **Watchable**[11] 5942 9-9-3 **97**....................(p) FrankieDettori 15 101
(David O'Meara) *racd centre: chsd ldng pair: rdn along over 1f out: drvn ent fnl f: kpt on same pce towards fin* **20/1**

3000 **6** *shd* **A Momentofmadness**[22] 5524 6-9-1 **95**....................(h) WilliamBuick 7 98
(Charles Hills) *racd centre: qckly away and set str pce: rdn along and jnd over 1f out: hdd and drvn ent fnl f: edgd lft and kpt on same pce* **22/1**

4561 **7** *nk* **Orvar (IRE)**[4] 6208 6-8-12 **92** 5ex.................... JasonWatson 13 94
(Paul Midgley) *racd centre: hld up towards rr: hdwy 2f out: rdn to chse ldrs over 1f out: keeping on whn n.m.r jst ins fnl f* **14/1**

0305 **8** *½* **Tarboosh**[8] 6056 6-9-10 **104**.................... TonyHamilton 19 104
(Paul Midgley) *racd towards stands' side: hld up towards rr: hdwy 1/2-way: rdn to chse ldrs over 1f out: drvn and edgd lft jst ins fnl f: kpt on same pce (vet said gelding lost its right-fore shoe)* **33/1**

-005 **9** *1* **Justanotherbottle (IRE)**[18] 5664 5-9-2 **96**.................... JamesDoyle 12 93
(Declan Carroll) *chsd ldrs centre: rdn along wl over 1f out: sn drvn and no imp* **7/1**[2]

5316 **10** *nk* **Camacho Chief (IRE)**[25] 5454 4-9-5 **99**.................... PaulMulrennan 1 95
(Michael Dods) *chsd ldrs centre: rdn along 2f out: sn drvn and grad wknd* **16/1**

4565 **11** *nk* **Lord Riddiford (IRE)**[22] 5524 4-8-5 **90**.................... CierenFallon(5) 11 85
(John Quinn) *looked wl; chsd ldrs centre: rdn along 2f out: grad wknd (jockey said gelding hung left throughout)* **25/1**

1221 **12** *½* **Jabbarockie**[19] 5617 6-8-9 **94**.................... HarrisonShaw(5) 20 87
(Eric Alston) *racd nr stands' rail: prom: rdn along wl over 1f out: sn drvn and wknd appr fnl f* **18/1**

5460 **13** *hd* **Gunmetal (IRE)**[18] 5664 6-9-7 **101**.................... JoeFanning 4 93
(David Barron) *racd centre: hld up in rr: n.d* **8/1**[3]

0040 **14** *¾* **Duke Of Firenze**[18] 5661 10-8-11 **91**.................... TomMarquand 5 81
(David C Griffiths) *looked wl; dwlt and n.m.r s: a in rr centre* **25/1**

0310 **15** *¾* **Fool For You (IRE)**[39] 4896 4-8-12 **92**.................... PJMcDonald 21 79
(Richard Fahey) *racd towards stands' side: in tch: pushed along and sme hdwy 2f out: sn rdn and btn* **33/1**

4506 **16** *nk* **Caspian Prince (IRE)**[5] 6149 10-9-9 **103**....................(t[1]) AlistairRawlinson 18 89
(Michael Appleby) *racd nr stands' rail: prom: rdn along wl over 1f out: grad wknd* **33/1**

1036 **17** *shd* **Queen Of Desire (IRE)**[40] 4891 4-9-2 **96**.................... AndreaAtzeni 22 82
(Roger Varian) *looked wl; racd stands' side: a in rr* **25/1**

0200 **18** *¾* **Foolaad**[11] 5927 8-9-3 **97**....................(t) RobertWinston 8 80
(Roy Bowring) *chsd ldrs centre: rdn along wl over 1f out: sn drvn and wknd* **33/1**

0601 **19** *½* **Stone Of Destiny**[11] 5927 4-9-5 **99**.................... SilvestreDeSousa 14 80
(Andrew Balding) *looked wl; racd towards stands' side: a towards rr* **12/1**

50-5 **20** *½* **Mythmaker**[102] 2614 7-9-3 **97**.................... JackGarritty 2 77
(Bryan Smart) *racd towards far side: in tch: rdn along over 2f out: sn wknd* **80/1**

1230 **21** *nse* **Harome (IRE)**[26] 5371 5-8-10 **90**.................... BenCurtis 16 69
(Roger Fell) *racd nr stands' rail: prom: rdn along over 2f out: sn wknd* **40/1**

2222 **22** *2* **Final Venture**[11] 5927 7-9-10 **104**.................... OisinMurphy 17 76
(Paul Midgley) *racd towards stands' side: hld up: effrt and sme hdwy 1/2-way: rdn along 2f out: sn wknd (jockey said gelding jumped awkwardly)* **12/1**

1m 1.89s (-1.71) **Going Correction** 0.0s/f (Good) **22** Ran SP% **132.0**
Speed ratings (Par 109): **113,111,111,111,110 110,110,109,107,107 106,105,105,104,103 102,102,101,100,99 99,96**
CSF £41.29 CT £485.65 TOTE £4.30: £1.80, £3.60, £3.40, £10.70; EX 51.40 Trifecta £585.70.
Owner Doug Graham & Ian Davison **Bred** Redgate Bstock & Peter Bottowley Bstock **Trained** Denton, Co Durham

FOCUS
The time of the opener was only 0.17sec outside the course record, suggesting conditions were on the quick side. Wind: SW 12mph. The rail was out ten metres from its innermost line on the home bend from 1m1f to the entrance to the home straight, adding 32yds to races beyond 1m1f. They split into two groups in this big-field sprint, the smaller one which contained seven horses racing towards the stands' side. The best of them could only finish eighth, with the main action developing up the centre of the track. The winner rates better than ever.

6352 TATTERSALLS ACOMB STKS (GROUP 3) 7f
2:25 (2:26) (Class 1) 2-Y-O

£56,710 (£21,500; £10,760; £5,360; £2,690; £1,350) **Stalls Low**

Form RPR

31 **1** **Valdermoro (USA)**[27] 5331 2-9-1 0.................... TonyHamilton 1 108+
(Richard Fahey) *unfurnished: scope; trckd ldrs: hdwy to chse ldr wl over 2f out: pushed along wl over 1f out: sn rdn: styd on wl u.p ins fnl f to ld nr fin* **9/2**[2]

52 **2** *nk* **Harpocrates (IRE)**[10] 5997 2-9-1 0....................(b[1]) RyanMoore 2 108
(A P O'Brien, Ire) *sn led: qcknd clr over 2f out: rdn over 1f out: drvn ins fnl f: hdd and no ex towards fin* **7/1**

4643 **3** *2 ½* **Ropey Guest**[25] 5415 2-9-1 **97**.................... TomQueally 6 101
(George Margarson) *hld up towards rr: hdwy on outer wl over 1f out: sn rdn: styd on wl fnl f* **25/1**

	4	nk	**Vitalogy**[28] 5323 2-9-1 0........ DonnachaO'Brien 8 100 (Joseph Patrick O'Brien, Ire) *unfurnished; trckd ldrs: hdwy over 3f out: rdn along wl over 1f out: sn drvn and kpt on same pce* **9/2**[2]
51	5	2 1/4	**Morisco (IRE)**[25] 5433 2-9-1 0........ RichardKingscote 10 94 (Tom Dascombe) *str; dwlt and swtchd lft s: in rr: hdwy 3f out: rdn along 2f out: sn drvn and kpt on: n.d* **28/1**
1	6	1 1/2	**Persuasion (IRE)**[18] 5665 2-9-1 0........ JamesDoyle 4 90 (Charles Hills) *athletic; trckd ldrs on outer: hdwy 3f out: rdn to chse ldng pair over 1f out: sn drvn and wknd* **5/2**[1]
1	7	1 1/2	**Yorkshire Gold**[21] 5550 2-9-1 0........ AndreaAtzeni 9 87 (Kevin Ryan) *leggy: athletic; cl up: pushed along 3f out: rdn 2f out: sn drvn and wknd over 1f out* **14/1**
31	8	1 3/4	**Kingbrook**[39] 4897 2-9-1 0........ JoeFanning 3 82+ (Mark Johnston) *str; sweating; dwlt and n.m.r s: hld up towards rr: effrt and sme hdwy on inner 3f out: rdn along over 2f out: sn edgd lft and n.d* **6/1**[3]
21	9	1 1/2	**Ethic**[25] 5447 2-9-1 0........ TomMarquand 5 78+ (William Haggas) *str; hld up towards rr: pushed along 3f out: sn rdn and outpcd fnl 2f* **10/1**

1m 24.09s (-0.51) **Going Correction** 0.0s/f (Good) **9** Ran SP% **114.8**
Speed ratings (Par 104): **102,101,98,98,95 94,92,90,88**
CSF £35.70 TOTE £5.30: £1.70, £1.80, £4.90; EX 31.00 Trifecta £423.90.

Owner M J Macleod **Bred** Cesa Farm & Laberinto Farm & Racing Corp **Trained** Musley Bank, N Yorks

FOCUS
This didn't look up to par on pre-race profiles but the third has been credited with his Coventry figure so it looks an okay renewal. They came centre-field in the straight.

6353 SKY BET GREAT VOLTIGEUR STKS (GROUP 2) (C&G) 1m 3f 188y

3:00 (3:00) (Class 1) 3-Y-O **£96,407** (£36,550; £18,292; £9,112; £4,573) **Stalls** Centre

Form			RPR
111	1		**Logician**[48] 4559 3-9-0 101........ FrankieDettori 2 119+ (John Gosden) *str; gd-bodied; trckd ldng pair: hdwy 3f out: led 2f out: sn rdn: pushed out and clr ins fnl f: kpt on strly* **10/11**[1]
-122	2	1 3/4	**Constantinople (IRE)**[20] 5585 3-9-0 110........ RyanMoore 1 115 (A P O'Brien, Ire) *sweating; hld up in rr: smooth hdwy over 3f out: cl up 2f out: sn chsng wnr: rdn wl over 1f out: drvn and edgd lft ins fnl f: kpt on same pce* **5/2**[2]
0030	3	7	**Norway (IRE)**[25] 5414 3-9-0 104........ DonnachaO'Brien 5 104 (A P O'Brien, Ire) *led: pushed along 3f out: sn rdn hdd 2f out: sn drvn and kpt on one pce* **10/1**
0230	4	1 1/4	**Jalmoud**[20] 5585 3-9-0 108........(h) WilliamBuick 4 102 (Charlie Appleby) *trckd ldr: hdwy over 3f out: rdn to take slt ld over 2f out: sn hdd and drvn wknd wl over 1f out* **12/1**
5321	5	3	**Nayef Road (IRE)**[20] 5585 3-9-0 108........ SilvestreDeSousa 3 97 (Mark Johnston) *hld up in tch: hdwy over 3f out: rdn along wl over 2f out: sn drvn and btn* **15/2**[3]

2m 27.91s (-5.29) **Going Correction** 0.0s/f (Good) **5** Ran SP% **109.5**
Speed ratings (Par 112): **114,112,108,107,105**
CSF £3.33 TOTE £1.60: £1.10, £1.60; EX 3.40 Trifecta £12.10.

Owner K Abdullah **Bred** Juddmonte Farms Ltd **Trained** Newmarket, Suffolk

FOCUS
Add 32yds. This wasn't the deepest Voltigeur, but it was run at a good gallop and proved a proper test. The winner posted a figure close to the leading 1m4f 3yos.

6354 JUDDMONTE INTERNATIONAL STKS (BRITISH CHAMPIONS SERIES) (GROUP 1) 1m 2f 56y

3:35 (3:35) (Class 1) 3-Y-O+

£602,543 (£228,437; £114,325; £56,950; £28,581; £14,343) **Stalls** Low

Form			RPR
4311	1		**Japan**[38] 4963 3-8-13 117........ RyanMoore 7 125 (A P O'Brien, Ire) *trckd ldrs: hdwy over 2f out: rdn to chal jst over 1f out: drvn to take slt ld ins fnl f: hdd last 50yds: hrd drvn and led again nr line* **5/1**[3]
1112	2	hd	**Crystal Ocean**[25] 5414 5-9-6 127........ JamesDoyle 4 124 (Sir Michael Stoute) *looked wl; trckd ldr: hdwy 3f out: chal over 2f out: sn led: jnd and rdn over 1f out: drvn and hdd narrowly ins fnl f: rallied gamely to take slt ld last 50yds: hdd and no ex nr line* **11/10**[1]
1311	3	1	**Elarqam**[25] 5455 4-9-6 118........ JimCrowley 2 122+ (Mark Johnston) *sweating; trckd ldng pair: pushed along 3f out: rdn and sltly outpcd over 2f out: drvn over 1f out: styng on whn n.m.r ins fnl f: swtchd rt and kpt on wl towards fin (jockey said colt was denied a clear run in the final furlong)* **8/1**
-112	4	3/4	**King Of Comedy (IRE)**[64] 3951 3-8-13 116........ FrankieDettori 1 121+ (John Gosden) *dwlt: hld up: hdwy 3f out: rdn along 2f out: drvn and styd on to chse ldng pair ins fnl f: sn n.m.r and kpt on same pce towards fin* **4/1**[2]
3134	5	1 3/4	**Regal Reality**[25] 5455 4-9-6 120........ RichardKingscote 8 118+ (Sir Michael Stoute) *dwlt: hld up: hdwy 3f out: rdn along to chse ldrs over 1f out: sn drvn and kpt on same pce ins fnl f* **20/1**
3015	6	nk	**Lord Glitters (FR)**[21] 5543 6-9-6 117........ DanielTudhope 9 116 (David O'Meara) *awkward s: hld up towards rr: pushed along over 3f out: rdn over 2f out: styd on fr over 1f out* **25/1**
1612	7	3/4	**Circus Maximus (IRE)**[21] 5543 3-8-13 118........(b) DonnachaO'Brien 6 115 (A P O'Brien, Ire) *led: rdn along 3f out: hdd 2f out: sn drvn: wknd ent fnl f* **12/1**
4-26	8	1 1/4	**Cheval Grand (JPN)**[25] 5414 7-9-6 119........ OisinMurphy 5 112 (Yasuo Tomomichi, Japan) *looked wl; hld up in tch: pushed along over 3f out: rdn wl over 2f out: sn drvn and wknd* **28/1**
-030	9	3 1/2	**Thundering Blue (USA)**[52] 4430 6-9-6 112........ JasonWatson 3 105 (David Menuisier) *hld up in rr: effrt and sme hdwy on inner 3f out: rdn 2f out: sn drvn and n.d* **66/1**

2m 7.77s (-2.53) **Going Correction** 0.0s/f (Good)
WFA 3 from 4yo+ 7lb **9** Ran SP% **116.6**
Speed ratings (Par 117): **110,109,109,108,107 106,106,105,102**
CSF £10.63 CT £43.62 TOTE £5.40: £1.70, £1.10, £2.50; EX 12.50 Trifecta £76.80.

Owner Derrick Smith & Mrs John Magnier & Michael Tabor **Bred** Newsells Park Stud **Trained** Cashel, Co Tipperary

FOCUS
Add 32yds. A cracking line-up and the right horses came to the fore but there's little doubt Crystal Ocean ran below his best and, with the pace a steady enough one, especially early, there was little over 4l covering the first seven at the line. They stayed far side in the straight.

6355 SKY BET H'CAP 2m 56y

4:15 (4:15) (Class 2) (0-105,102) 4-Y-O+

£43,575 (£13,048; £6,524; £3,262; £1,631; £819) **Stalls** Low

Form			RPR
3501	1		**Eddystone Rock (IRE)**[11] 5928 7-9-3 95........ JamesDoyle 8 105 (John Best) *hld up in rr: hdwy over 2f out: swtchd rt to outer and rdn over 1f out: styd on strly fnl f to ld towards fin* **8/1**
1025	2	nk	**Rare Groove (IRE)**[32] 5183 4-9-4 96........ PJMcDonald 13 105 (Jedd O'Keeffe) *trckd ldrs: hdwy to ld wl over 2f out: rdn wl over 1f out: drvn and edgd lft ins fnl f: hdd and no ex towards fin* **12/1**
-413	3	1 1/4	**Infrastructure**[25] 5443 4-9-0 92........ RobHornby 15 99 (Martyn Meade) *hld up in rr: hdwy 3f out: rdn wl over 1f out: chsd ldr ent fnl f: sn drvn and kpt on wl towards fin* **10/1**
0000	4	1 1/4	**Melting Dew**[11] 5929 5-8-13 91........(p) RyanMoore 12 97 (Sir Michael Stoute) *hld up towards rr: hdwy 3f out: rdn along 2f out: drvn over 1f out: kpt on fnl f* **16/1**
1110	5	nk	**Carnwennan (IRE)**[32] 5183 4-9-2 94........ StevieDonohoe 3 99 (Charlie Fellowes) *looked wl; hld up in midfield: hdwy 3f out: chsd ldrs 2f out: rdn to chse ldng pair over 1f out: sn drvn and kpt on same pce* **7/1**[2]
6523	6	hd	**Claire Underwood (IRE)**[12] 5902 4-8-8 86........ PaddyMathers 17 91 (Richard Fahey) *trckd ldng pair: hdwy 3f out: sn cl up: rdn along 2f out: drvn over 1f out: kpt on same pce* **25/1**
050-	7	nse	**Clever Cookie**[333] 7542 11-9-2 94........ RobertWinston 5 99 (Peter Niven) *hld up in midfield: hdwy 3f out: effrt and nt clr run 2f out: sn rdn and styd on fnl f* **66/1**
2302	8	1	**Sleeping Lion (USA)**[26] 5368 4-9-0 92........ JamieSpencer 1 96 (James Fanshawe) *looked wl; hld up towards rr: hdwy 3f out: rdn along 2f out: styd on fnl f* **15/2**[3]
0415	9	nk	**Charles Kingsley**[18] 5662 4-9-8 100........ JoeFanning 9 103 (Mark Johnston) *looked wl; led: pushed along over 3f out: rdn and hdd wl over 2f out: sn drvn: wknd appr fnl f* **8/1**
004	10	nk	**Blakeney Point**[12] 5909 6-9-7 99........(bt) JasonWatson 2 102 (Roger Charlton) *trckd ldrs: hdwy and cl up 3f out: rdn to chal and ev ch over 1f out: sn drvn: edgd lft and kpt on one pce (jockey said gelding hung left under pressure)* **14/1**
2010	11	shd	**Mancini**[21] 5540 5-9-2 94........ RichardKingscote 14 97 (Jonathan Portman) *trckd ldrs: pushed along and hdwy over 3f out: rdn wl over 2f out: drvn and one pce fr wl over 1f out* **12/1**
2-20	12	3 1/4	**Dubawi Fifty**[21] 5540 6-9-10 102........(p) FrankieDettori 6 101 (Karen McLintock) *trckd ldrs: hdwy on outer and cl up 1/2-way: rdn along 3f out: drvn over 2f out: sn wknd* **6/1**[1]
5622	13	1/2	**Makawee (IRE)**[25] 5457 4-9-0 92........ DanielTudhope 7 90 (David O'Meara) *a towards rr* **9/1**
020	14	3/4	**My Reward**[14] 5818 7-8-10 88........ ConnorBeasley 11 86 (Tim Easterby) *in tch: pushed along on outer 3f out: rdn over 2f out: sn wknd* **50/1**
5030	15	2 1/4	**Blue Laureate**[11] 5928 4-8-10 88........ PaulHanagan 16 83 (Ian Williams) *a in rr* **20/1**
2140	16	2 1/2	**Bartholomeu Dias**[18] 5662 4-9-5 97........ KieranShoemark 10 89 (Charles Hills) *trckd ldrs: pushed along over 3f out: sn rdn: drvn 2f out and sn wknd* **33/1**
6005	17	2 1/4	**Aircraft Carrier (IRE)**[11] 5928 4-9-3 95........(v) JimCrowley 4 84 (John Ryan) *looked wl; a towards rr (jockey said gelding hung left in the closing stages)* **40/1**

3m 33.22s (-0.68) **Going Correction** 0.0s/f (Good) **17** Ran SP% **125.2**
Speed ratings (Par 109): **101,100,100,99,99 99,99,98,98,98 98,96,96,96,95 93,92**
CSF £96.28 CT £991.92 TOTE £7.80: £2.40, £2.90, £3.00, £4.30; EX 96.40 Trifecta £922.00.

Owner Curtis, Malt & Williams **Bred** Ballygallon Stud Limited **Trained** Oad Street, Kent

FOCUS
Add 32yds. An open staying handicap. They went fairly steady early on, but the pace picked up a fair way out and, bar the runner-up, the closers dominated the finish. Solid form, with the winner rated back to his best.

6356 SKY BET NURSERY H'CAP 6f

4:50 (5:01) (Class 2) 2-Y-O

£43,575 (£13,048; £6,524; £3,262; £1,631; £819) **Stalls** High

Form			RPR
4310	1		**Owney Madden**[19] 5612 2-8-8 80........ RobHornby 2 88 (Martyn Meade) *trckd ldrs centre: hdwy to chal over 1f out: rdn ins fnl f: drvn and kpt on wl to ld towards fin* **20/1**
2111	2	nk	**Troubador (IRE)**[26] 5390 2-9-7 93........ PaulMulrennan 7 100 (Michael Dods) *trckd ldr centre: cl up 2f out: rdn to ld over 1f out: sn jnd and drvn: hdd and no ex towards fin* **12/1**
2051	3	nk	**Rose Of Kildare (IRE)**[18] 5683 2-9-1 87........ JoeFanning 8 93 (Mark Johnston) *looked wl; chsd ldrs centre: rdn along wl over 1f out: drvn and kpt on wl fnl f* **18/1**
1033	4	2 3/4	**Monoski (USA)**[17] 5707 2-9-7 93........ SilvestreDeSousa 5 91 (Mark Johnston) *sweating; hld up towards rr: hdwy towards far side 2f out: rdn over 1f out: styd on fnl f* **14/1**
5115	5	1/2	**Hard Nut (IRE)**[19] 5612 2-8-13 85........ RyanMoore 4 81 (Richard Hannon) *in tch towards far side: hdwy to chse ldrs 2f out: sn rdn: drvn and kpt on same pce fnl f* **9/1**[3]
215	6	1	**Buhturi (IRE)**[25] 5415 2-9-2 88........ JimCrowley 12 81 (Charles Hills) *midfield: hdwy over 2f out: rdn to chse ldrs wl over 1f out: sn drvn and kpt on same pce fnl f* **20/1**
111	7	nk	**Oti Ma Boati**[32] 5171 2-8-9 81........ ChrisHayes 6 74 (William Haggas) *looked wl; dwlt and towards rr: pushed along and hdwy 2f out: sn rdn and kpt on fnl f (jockey said filly jumped awkwardly)* **11/4**[1]
0260	8	shd	**Separate**[19] 5612 2-8-11 79........(b[1]) AndreaAtzeni 11 75 (Richard Hannon) *chsd ldrs centre: rdn along and outpcd over 2f out: styd on u.p fr over 1f out* **25/1**
4323	9	1/2	**Born To Destroy**[19] 5612 2-8-7 79........ MartinDwyer 19 70+ (Richard Spencer) *racd towards stands' side: chsd ldrs: rdn along 2f out: sn drvn and wknd* **33/1**
626	10	1/2	**Streaker**[14] 5815 2-8-5 77........ JosephineGordon 13 66 (Kevin Ryan) *chsd ldrs centre: rdn along 2f out: drvn and wknd over 1f out* **100/1**
3114	11	hd	**Praxeology (IRE)**[19] 5612 2-9-2 88........ FrankieDettori 9 77 (Mark Johnston) *looked wl; led centre: jnd and shkn up wl over 1f out: sn rdn and hdd: wknd fnl f* **8/1**[2]

6220 **12** 1 1/2 **Vardon Flyer**[40] 4878 2-8-7 **79** (t[1]) BenCurtis 17 63+
(Michael Easterby) *r towards stands' side: chsd ldrs: rdn along 2f out: sn wknd* **33/1**

1105 **13** 1 **Hurstwood**[17] 5707 2-9-3 **89** DanielTudhope 14 70
(Tim Easterby) *chsd ldrs centre: rdn along 2f out: sn drvn and wknd* **40/1**

1022 **14** nk **Bill Neigh**[17] 5707 2-8-12 **89** CierenFallon(5) 15 69+
(John Ryan) *midfield: rdn along over 2f out: sn wknd (vet said colt lost its left-fore shoe)* **25/1**

211 **15** 10 **Pop Dancer (IRE)**[12] 5900 2-9-4 **90** TonyHamilton 22 40+
(Richard Fahey) *racd towards strnds side: a in rr* **8/1**[2]

2341 **16** 1 3/4 **Ventura Flame (IRE)**[8] 6032 2-8-7 **79** 6ex PaulHanagan 20 24+
(Keith Dalgleish) *racd towards stands' side: chsd ldrs: rdn over 2f out: sn wknd* **40/1**

4211 **17** 1 3/4 **Homespin (USA)**[19] 5612 2-9-7 **93** JamesDoyle 21 33+
(Mark Johnston) *racd towards stands' side: a in rr (jockey said colt slipped leaving the stalls)* **12/1**

531 **18** 3/4 **Otago**[54] 4344 2-8-8 **80** HayleyTurner 16 18+
(Michael Bell) *dwlt and bmpd s: a in rr* **25/1**

234 **19** 2 **Mr Jones And Me**[17] 5707 2-8-3 **78** JaneElliott(3) 10 10
(Tom Dascombe) *a in rr (jockey said colt was never travelling; vet said volt to be lame on its left hind)* **33/1**

11 **20** 1/2 **Malvern**[12] 5879 2-9-0 **86** RossaRyan 1 16
(Richard Hannon) *racd towards far side: in rr and rdn whn hung bdly rt 2f out: sn bhd (jockey said colt hung right)* **14/1**

1m 10.95s (-0.65) **Going Correction** 0.0s/f (Good) **20** Ran SP% **128.6**
Speed ratings (Par 100): **104,103,103,99,98 97,97,97,96,95 95,93,92,91,78 76,73,72,70,69**
CSF £226.55 CT £4401.22 TOTE £20.40: £4.30, £2.60, £3.80, £3.50; EX 300.60 Trifecta £3968.80.
Owner Chelsea Thoroughbreds - Owney Madden 1 **Bred** Simon W Clarke **Trained** Manton, Wilts

FOCUS
Three pulled clear late in this useful nursery, with the low-drawn runners dominating. The main action late on took place down the centre.
T/Jkpt: Not won. T/Plt: £342.00 to a £1 stake. Pool: £284,928.61 - 608.18 winning units T/Qpdt: £28.20 to a £1 stake. Pool: £21,516.71 - 563.70 winning units **Joe Rowntree**

6357 - 6360a (Foreign Racing) - See Raceform Interactive

6104 CHEPSTOW (L-H)

Thursday, August 22

OFFICIAL GOING: Good (good to soft in places; 5.6)
Wind: Slight across Weather: Cloudy

6361 BETAID.ORG RESPONSIBLE GAMBLING H'CAP 1m 14y

1:45 (1:49) (Class 6) (0-60,60) 3-Y-O
£2,781 (£827; £413; £300; £300; £300) **Stalls** Centre

Form RPR

0000 **1** **Set Point Charlie (IRE)**[14] 5867 3-9-1 **54** (t[1]) TomQueally 14 63+
(Seamus Durack) *hld up: hdwy on stands' rail 2f out: led 1f out: pushed clr: comf (regarding the apparent improvement in form, trainer's rep said gelding wore a first time tongue strap and appreciated the easier ground)* **16/1**

0-05 **2** 2 1/4 **Willett**[11] 5981 3-8-6 **48** (v) WilliamCox(3) 15 50
(Sarah Hollinshead) *cl up: led after 2f: drvn over 2f out: hdd 1f out: qckly outpcd by wnr* **50/1**

5024 **3** 1 1/4 **Risk Mitigation (USA)**[9] 6042 3-9-0 **53** LiamKeniry 9 52
(David Evans) *prom: drvn 3f out: sn outpcd and lost pl: swtchd rt over 1f out: r.o fnl f: wnt 3rd towards fin* **9/2**[2]

5-05 **4** 3/4 **Carlow Boy (IRE)**[14] 5866 3-8-7 **45** oh1 (b[1]) LukeMorris 12 43
(Christopher Kellett) *prom: rdn over 2f out: lost 2nd over 1f out: one pce* **14/1**

-054 **5** 1 1/4 **Forthwith**[15] 5797 3-8-7 **45** oh1 (h) RaulDaSilva 4 40+
(Tony Carroll) *led 2f: remained prom: drvn over 2f out: edgd lft over 1f out: kpt on same pce* **11/2**[3]

0603 **6** hd **Powerage (IRE)**[9] 6052 3-8-11 **50** DavidProbert 7 44
(Malcolm Saunders) *chsd ldrs: rdn over 2f out: kpt on same pce* **8/1**

-006 **7** 3/4 **Swiper (IRE)**[8] 6085 3-9-6 **59** (p[1]) RossaRyan 8 51
(John O'Shea) *midfield: rdn over 2f out: styd on 1f out: nvr able to chal* **20/1**

6600 **8** 1 3/4 **Tintern Spirit (IRE)**[7] 6107 3-8-2 **45** oh1 WilliamCarver(5) 16 34
(Milton Bradley) *midfield: rdn and sme prog over 2f out: fdd ins fnl f (vet said filly lost left fore shoe)* **66/1**

6440 **9** 2 1/4 **So Claire**[9] 6052 3-8-8 **50** (b[1]) GeorgiaCox(3) 11 33
(William Muir) *s.s: towards rr: rdn and sme prog over 3f out: no hdwy fnl 2f (jockey said filly was slowly away)* **11/1**

0500 **10** 1/2 **Grey Hare**[27] 5377 3-8-10 **48** oh1 ow3 (t) GeorgeDowning 1 31+
(Tony Carroll) *s.i.s: hld up: rdn 3f out: no ch fnl 2f* **14/1**

555 **11** 2 1/4 **Charlie Arthur (IRE)**[30] 5284 3-9-4 **60** (b[1]) FinleyMarsh(3) 2 37+
(Richard Hughes) *midfield: rdn over 2f out: wkng whn hung lft over 1f out* **3/1**[1]

0050 **12** 1 **Vino Rosso (IRE)**[9] 6052 3-8-12 **51** CharlieBennett 10 25
(Michael Blanshard) *chsd ldrs: rdn 2f out: wknd over 1f out* **20/1**

0-00 **13** 1 **Dream Model (IRE)**[59] 4196 3-9-0 **53** EoinWalsh 6 25
(Mark Loughnane) *in rr: rdn along on outer after 2f: wknd u.p over 2f out (jockey said filly ran too free to post)* **28/1**

0605 **14** 18 **Orliko (IRE)**[9] 6052 3-9-7 **60** (bt) PatDobbs 5
(Richard Hannon) *in rr: lost tch 3f out: t.o (jockey said gelding hung left)* **7/1**

0-00 **15** 24 **Poet Pete (IRE)**[129] 1824 3-8-7 **45** oh1 PhilipPrince 3 +
(Mark Usher) *s.i.s: sn bhd: t.o fr 1/2-way* **25/1**

1m 36.09s (0.09) **Going Correction** -0.125s/f (Firm) **15** Ran SP% **130.0**
Speed ratings (Par 98): **94,91,90,89,88 88,87,85,83,83 80,79,78,60,36**
CSF £694.20 CT £4184.97 TOTE £18.60: £4.40, £15.20, £2.20; EX 804.60 Trifecta £1262.70.
Owner Mrs Pao, Stafford & Tucker **Bred** Kevin J Molloy **Trained** Upper Lambourn, Berkshire

FOCUS
Following a drying day on Wednesday the going was given as good, good to soft in places (Going Stick 5.6). A fairly run low-grade handicap in which track position had a major impact, the first two always close to the stands' rail, which seemed favoured. As such, it's best to take a cautious view of the form, with those stuck towards the middle of the track worth excusing.

6362 COMPAREBETTINGSITES.COM ONLINE BETTING FILLIES' H'CAP 1m 14y

2:15 (2:17) (Class 5) (0-75,74) 3-Y-O+
£3,428 (£1,020; £509; £300; £300; £300) **Stalls** Centre

Form RPR

6343 **1** **Amorously (IRE)**[15] 5813 3-9-4 **72** PatDobbs 8 79
(Richard Hannon) *racd alone 1f bef joining stands' side gp: in tch: clsd over 2f out: led wl over 1f out: drvn out fnl f* **5/1**[2]

0305 **2** 3/4 **Madeleine Bond**[16] 5782 5-9-5 **70** GeorgiaCox(3) 10 76
(Henry Candy) *hld up on stands' side: rdn over 2f out: hdwy to chse ldrs over 1f out: wnt 2nd ins fnl f: unable qck towards fin* **9/2**[1]

4446 **3** 1/2 **Regal Banner**[12] 5941 3-9-4 **72** (p[1]) JackMitchell 2 76
(Roger Varian) *hld up in centre: rdn and hdwy over 3f out: led narrowly over 2f out tl wl over 1f out: sn edgd rt: kpt on fnl f* **13/2**[3]

0400 **4** hd **Daryana**[16] 5779 3-8-6 **67** GeorgiaDobie(7) 1 70+
(Eve Johnson Houghton) *s.i.s: towards rr in centre: rdn over 3f out: hdwy whn nt clr run wl over 1f out: styd on wl fnl f* **11/1**

0510 **5** shd **Kyllachys Tale (IRE)**[19] 5677 5-9-0 **62** RossaRyan 12 66
(Roger Teal) *led gp on stands' side and prom overall: drvn 2f out: kpt on* **5/1**[2]

1006 **6** 2 **Nightingale Valley**[18] 5709 6-9-12 **74** (v[1]) TomQueally 9 74
(Stuart Kittow) *hld up on stands' side: rdn 3f out: hdwy over 2f out: unbalanced appr fnl f: hld after* **20/1**

3450 **7** 3 3/4 **Bond Angel**[6] 6160 4-9-3 **65** LiamKeniry 4 56
(David Evans) *t.k.h: in tch in centre: drvn 3f out: outpcd 2f out: sme late prog* **20/1**

3561 **8** 1 **I'lletyougonow**[17] 5749 3-9-6 **74** (p) CallumShepherd 6 62
(Mick Channon) *led gp in centre and overall: rdn 3f out: hdd over 2f out: wknd over 1f out* **7/1**

0234 **9** 2 **Elena**[22] 5549 3-8-11 **65** LukeMorris 7 48
(Charles Hills) *trckd ldrs in centre: rdn over 2f out: wknd over 1f out (vet said filly had a small, old wound on the right fore which was reopened during the race)* **10/1**

/000 **10** 1 1/4 **Chiavari (IRE)**[17] 5761 5-9-0 **65** FinleyMarsh(3) 11 46
(Alexandra Dunn) *prom on stands' side: drvn 2f out: wkng whn hmpd over 1f out: bled fr the nose (vet said mare bled from nose)* **12/1**

2051 **11** 94 **Red Romance**[26] 5429 3-9-5 **73** HectorCrouch 5
(Clive Cox) *trckd ldrs in centre: rdn 3f out: sn wknd: virtually p.u fnl 2f: t.o: bled fr the nose (vet said filly bled from nose)* **8/1**

1m 34.81s (-1.19) **Going Correction** -0.125s/f (Firm)
WFA 3 from 4yo+ 6lb **11** Ran SP% **123.1**
Speed ratings (Par 100): **100,99,98,98,98 96,92,91,89,88**
CSF £29.25 CT £152.56 TOTE £4.20: £1.60, £3.10, £2.50; EX 32.10 Trifecta £222.90.
Owner Ali Bahbahani **Bred** Haras Don Alberto **Trained** East Everleigh, Wilts

FOCUS
A fair fillies' handicap in which the draw wasn't quite so influential as the previous race over the same C&D but the finish was still fought out by a pair that raced in the group that came towards the stands' rail. The pace was sound and, overall, the form has a reliable look to it. This rates a pb from the winner.

6363 NEIL CALVERT'S RETIREMENT CELEBRATIONS H'CAP 7f 16y

2:50 (2:51) (Class 6) (0-65,64) 3-Y-O+
£2,781 (£827; £413; £300; £300; £300) **Stalls** Centre

Form RPR

5021 **1** **Bounty Pursuit**[8] 6085 7-9-5 **64** MarcoGhiani(7) 2 74
(Michael Blake) *a.p: led gng wl 2f out: shkn up over 1f out: r.o* **4/1**[1]

061 **2** 1 3/4 **Fantasy Justifier (IRE)**[7] 6107 8-9-3 **55** 4ex (p) LukeMorris 16 63+
(Ronald Harris) *s.i.s: t.k.h in rr: n.m.r after 3f: rdn over 2f out: nt clr run over 1f out: r.o wl fnl f: wnt 2nd fnl 75yds: nt rch wnr (jockey said gelding was denied a clear run)* **10/1**

0633 **3** 1 1/2 **Cooperess**[9] 6051 6-8-8 **46** DavidProbert 11 48
(Adrian Wintle) *chsd ldrs: rdn and n.m.r 2f out: r.o fnl f* **15/2**

0614 **4** 3/4 **Secondo (FR)**[24] 5495 9-9-6 **63** (v) DarraghKeenan(5) 4 63
(Robert Stephens) *hld up towards rr: clsd over 3f out: rdn 2f out: wnt 2nd early ins fnl f tl no ex fnl 75yds* **14/1**

0005 **5** nk **Alfie's Angel (IRE)**[7] 6107 5-8-9 **47** RaulDaSilva 12 46
(Milton Bradley) *sltly hmpd leaving stalls: t.k.h: sn chsng ldrs: rdn 2f out: hanging lft fr 2f out and unable to chal: r.o nr fin* **25/1**

0600 **6** 1/2 **Reshaan (IRE)**[9] 6059 4-8-5 **48** (p) ThoreHammerHansen(5) 8 46
(Alexandra Dunn) *cl up: led over 4f out: rdn 3f out: hdd 2f out: fdd ins fnl f (jockey said gelding hung right under pressure)* **20/1**

1044 **7** 1 **Papa Delta**[1] 6329 5-9-3 **55** GeorgeDowning 6 50
(Tony Carroll) *midfield: rdn 3f out: sn chsng ldrs: wknd fnl f* **5/1**[2]

3065 **8** nse **Rosamour (IRE)**[21] 5575 3-8-12 **62** (b[1]) GeorgeRooke(7) 15 55
(Richard Hughes) *wnt lft leaving stalls: towards rr: hdwy 3f out: rdn 2f out: fdd fnl f* **11/2**[3]

0U00 **9** hd **Indian Affair**[10] 6018 9-8-2 **45** (tp) WilliamCarver(5) 17 39
(Milton Bradley) *towards rr on stands' rail: rdn over 3f out: no real hdwy* **33/1**

6 **10** shd **Satchville Flyer**[43] 4797 8-9-10 **62** LiamKeniry 10 61
(David Evans) *hld up: pushed along over 2f out: no hdwy tl r.o ins fnl f: n.m.r and eased cl home (jockey said gelding was denied a clear run)* **25/1**

0450 **11** 3/4 **Test Valley (IRE)**[76] 3533 4-9-5 **57** JohnFahy 13 49
(Tracey Barfoot-Saunt) *s.i.s: sltly hmpd leaving stalls: drvn over 2f out: a in rr* **16/1**

-350 **12** shd **Secret Glance**[61] 4115 7-8-4 **45** JaneElliott(3) 5 37
(Adrian Wintle) *cl up on outer: led after 2f tl over 4f out: remained prom: drvn 3f out: wknd ins fnl f* **16/1**

10/0 **13** 10 **My Bubba**[9] 6051 7-8-10 **48** EoinWalsh 1 14
(Malcolm Saunders) *hld up: drvn over 3f out: wknd 2f out (jockey said gelding was never travelling)* **50/1**

502 **14** hd **Master Poet**[26] 5430 4-9-1 **53** HectorCrouch 7 18
(Gary Moore) *led 2f: cl up: drvn 3f out: wknd over 1f out (jockey said gelding hung left throughout)* **4/1**[1]

1m 23.29s (-0.61) **Going Correction** -0.125s/f (Firm)
WFA 3 from 4yo+ 5lb **14** Ran SP% **128.7**
Speed ratings (Par 101): **98,96,94,93,93 92,91,91,91,90 90,90,78,78**
CSF £45.65 CT £312.77 TOTE £4.30: £2.40, £3.40, £2.30; EX 38.10 Trifecta £169.00.
Owner Racing For A Cause **Bred** Cecil And Miss Alison Wiggins **Trained** Trowbridge, Wilts

FOCUS
The whole field edged across to the stands' side quite early and the pace was even throughout, so this looks like a fair result acknowledging the runner-up didn't get a clear run through. He and the winner are in great order and this is stronger form than the average 0-65 here.

6364 COMPAREBETTINGSITES.COM FREE BETS EBF NOVICE STKS 5f 16y

3:25 (3:27) (Class 5) 2-Y-O
£3,428 (£1,020; £509; £254) **Stalls** Centre

Form RPR

4 **1** **Lexington Rebel (FR)**[21] 5577 2-9-2 0 PatDobbs 3 84
(Richard Hannon) *s.i.s: chsd duelling ldrs: clsd on them over 2f out: sn shkn up: led 1f out: hung lft early ins fnl f: comf* **5/2**[3]

610 **2** 1 1/4 **Don't Stop Dancing (IRE)**[21] 5584 2-9-6 87 LukeMorris 1 83
(Ronald Harris) *disp ld: rdn 2f out: def advantage over 1f out tl hung lft and hdd 1f out: unable qck* **2/1**[2]

2420 **3** 3¾ **When Comes Here (IRE)**[21] 5587 2-9-2 **80**.................... DavidProbert 2 66
(Andrew Balding) *disp ld: rdn 2f out: dropped to 3rd over 1f out: wknd fnl f* **11/8**[1]

4 5 **Indyzeb (IRE)** 2-8-11 0.. RaulDaSilva 4 43+
(Seamus Mullins) *dwlt: s.i.s and sn wl bhd: r.o fnl f* **20/1**

1m 0.16s (0.76) **Going Correction** -0.125s/f (Firm) **4** Ran SP% **108.8**
Speed ratings (Par 94): **88,86,80,72**
CSF £7.80 TOTE £3.50; EX 7.10 Trifecta £9.90.
Owner Middleham Park Racing X **Bred** Erich Schmid **Trained** East Everleigh, Wilts

FOCUS
Just an average sprint novice for juveniles. The second and third softened each other up by duelling through the first half of the race, which played out nicely for the more patiently ridden winner.

6365 JOHN LOVELL & MARTIN DAVIES ONCOURSE BOOKMAKERS CHEPSTOW H'CAP 5f 16y
4:00 (4:00) (Class 6) (0-65,65) 3-Y-O+

£2,781 (£827; £413; £300; £300; £300) **Stalls** Centre

Form RPR
0516 **1** **Secret Potion**[5] 6203 5-10-1 **65** 5ex.......................... DavidProbert 1 72
(Ronald Harris) *hld up: rdn and hdwy over 1f out: led ent fnl f: sn edgd rt: r.o* **11/4**[2]

-006 **2** ¾ **Atty's Edge**[15] 5799 3-8-11 **52**.......................... WilliamCox(3) 8 56
(Christopher Mason) *cl up: led 1/2-way: rdn over 1f out: hdd ent fnl f: r.o* **20/1**

3202 **3** 1¾ **Spot Lite**[21] 5582 4-9-6 **56**..........................(p) DanielMuscutt 2 54
(Rod Millman) *prom: drvn over 1f out: sn ev ch: outpcd by ldng pair towards fin* **8/1**

2022 **4** 1½ **Pearl Of Qatar**[9] 6033 3-9-6 **58**.......................... LukeMorris 6 51
(Tristan Davidson) *trckd ldrs: rdn and nt clr run 2f out: sn swtchd lft: kpt on fnl f* **5/2**[1]

4622 **5** nk **Valentino Sunrise**[6] 6168 3-9-1 **58**.......................... ScottMcCullagh(5) 4 50
(Mick Channon) *led to 1/2-way: remained cl up: rdn 2f out: fdd fnl f* **5/2**[1]

0060 **6** hd **Crimson Princess**[10] 6018 4-8-9 **45**.......................... JohnFahy 5 36
(Nikki Evans) *s.i.s: in rr: rdn ins fnl f: r.o wl towards fin* **40/1**

001 **7** ½ **Compton Poppy**[27] 5375 5-9-10 **60**..........................(b) GeorgeDowning 7 50
(Tony Carroll) *hld up: clsd on ldrs 2f out: nt clr run over 1f out: rdn ent fnl f: unable qck (jockey said mare was denied a clear run)* **6/1**[3]

59.07s (-0.33) **Going Correction** -0.125s/f (Firm)
WFA 3 from 4yo+ 2lb **7** Ran SP% **116.4**
Speed ratings (Par 101): **97,95,93,90,90 89,89**
CSF £53.20 CT £398.28 TOTE £4.80: £3.10, £9.00; EX 80.70 Trifecta £404.60.
Owner RHS Ltd, R Fox, P Charter **Bred** Llety Farms **Trained** Earlswood, Monmouths

FOCUS
A weak sprint handicap in which the front pair were the only ones to truly give their running. The field again edged over to the stands' side and there was no obvious bias.

6366 COMPAREBETTINGSITES.COM BETTING H'CAP 2m 2f
4:30 (4:34) (Class 6) (0-65,67) 3-Y-O+

£2,781 (£827; £413; £300; £300; £300) **Stalls** Low

Form RPR
5526 **1** **Arty Campbell (IRE)**[7] 6105 9-10-2 **67**..........................(p) ScottMcCullagh(5) 8 75
(Bernard Llewellyn) *hld up in last: hdwy 7f out: disp ld 3f out: sn rdn: duelled after tl on top last strides (jockey said gelding hung left)* **9/1**

402 **2** hd **Norab (GER)**[7] 6105 8-9-12 **58**..........................(b) DanielMuscutt 1 66
(Bernard Llewellyn) *prom: drvn to dispute ld 3f out: duelled u.p tl jst hld last strides* **4/1**[2]

0-32 **3** 6 **Danglydontask**[27] 5379 8-9-3 **49**..........................(b) RossaRyan 4 50
(Mike Murphy) *chsd ldrs: rdn and sltly outpcd 3f out: styd on to go 3rd over 1f out: no further imp* **11/2**[3]

-654 **4** 3¾ **Volcanique (IRE)**[12] 5975 3-8-3 **48**..........................(b[1]) LukeMorris 9 48
(Sir Mark Prescott Bt) *prom: trckd ldr 9f out tl rdn and lost 2nd 3f out: one pce* **10/3**[1]

0-00 **5** 7 **Tsundoku (IRE)**[33] 1429 8-8-13 **45**.......................... JohnFahy 6 33
(Alexandra Dunn) *s.i.s: in rr: hdwy on outer after 3f: led 9f out tl rdn and hdd 3f out: wknd 2f out (jockey said mare hung left throughout)* **7/1**

5044 **6** 6 **Demophon**[13] 5891 5-8-13 **45**.......................... RaulDaSilva 11 26
(Steve Flook) *mde most tl hdd 9f out: drvn 4f out: wknd over 2f out* **12/1**

5-00 **7** 5 **Crindle Carr (IRE)**[41] 4868 5-9-1 **47**..........................(p) LiamJones 5 22
(John Flint) *prom: led briefly after 2f: rdn 4f out: wknd 3f out* **28/1**

-000 **8** 3 **Everlasting Sea**[37] 5029 5-8-13 **45**.......................... JosephineGordon 3 16
(Stuart Kittow) *hld up: rdn over 3f out: sn btn* **33/1**

-500 **9** 2¼ **Mustaaqeem (USA)**[7] 6105 7-9-6 **55**..........................(b) WilliamCox(3) 7 23
(Bernard Llewellyn) *s.i.s: in rr: struggling 6f out: sn lost tch (jockey said gelding was never travelling)* **50/1**

50-0 **10** 26 **Nordenfelt (IRE)**[7] 6105 6-8-13 **45**.......................... LiamKeniry 10
(Sue Gardner) *in tch towards rr tl rdn and wknd over 4f out: t.o* **25/1**

6034 **11** 2½ **Constraint**[21] 5596 3-9-5 **64**.......................... DavidProbert 2 2
(Andrew Balding) *midfield: rdn 4f out: wknd qckly: t.o (jockey said filly stopped quickly)* **10/3**[1]

3m 59.15s (-10.75) **Going Correction** -0.125s/f (Firm)
WFA 3 from 5yo+ 13lb **11** Ran SP% **123.9**
Speed ratings (Par 101): **101,100,98,96,93 90,88,87,86,74 73**
CSF £46.09 CT £226.25 TOTE £6.40: £2.20, £1.70, £2.20; EX 45.30 Trifecta £149.70.
Owner Alex James & B J Llewellyn **Bred** Airlie Stud **Trained** Fochriw, Caerphilly

FOCUS
Disappointing efforts from the 3yos left it to a couple of veterans to fight this out after a sound gallop had ensured a thorough test of stamina.

6367 INTERBET.COM FOOTBALL BETTING H'CAP 1m 4f
5:05 (5:06) (Class 6) (0-65,65) 3-Y-O

£2,781 (£827; £413; £300; £300; £300) **Stalls** Low

Form RPR
1521 **1** **Trouble Shooter (IRE)**[13] 5915 3-8-9 **53**..........................(v) JosephineGordon 1 64+
(Shaun Keightley) *trckd ldrs: led gng wl 3f out: shkn up 2f out: styd on wl: eased nr fin* **2/1**[1]

00-4 **2** 2½ **Aussie Breeze**[27] 5378 3-8-4 **48**.......................... RoystonFfrench 6 53
(Tom George) *chsd ldrs: rdn to go 2nd over 2f out: outpcd by wnr over 1f out: kpt on but no imp* **4/1**[2]

0456 **3** 2¾ **Ocean Reach**[16] 5784 3-7-11 **46**.......................... SophieRalston(5) 3 47
(Richard Price) *cl up 2f: sn hld up towards rr: last whn shkn up over 3f out: swtchd rt over 2f out: styd on to go 3rd fnl 75yds: no ch w ldng pair (jockey said filly was denied a clear run)* **8/1**

050 **4** 2¼ **Hermosura**[19] 5656 3-9-7 **65**.......................... PatDobbs 7 62
(Ralph Beckett) *s.i.s: hld up: hdwy into midfield 1/2-way: rdn over 3f out: styd on: in hld 3rd 1f out tl 75yds out* **11/2**[3]

000 **5** 1 **Pecorino**[66] 3946 3-8-13 **60**.......................... FinleyMarsh(3) 4 56
(Richard Hughes) *midfield: chsng ldrs whn rdn 3f out: sn one pce and hld* **8/1**

000 **6** ½ **Capricorn Prince**[21] 5592 3-7-11 **46** oh1.......................... RhiainIngram(5) 5 41
(Gary Moore) *towards rr: rdn and hdwy on outer to chse ldrs over 2f out: wknd appr fnl f (trainer's rep said gelding was not suited by the undulations of the track)* **33/1**

000 **7** ½ **Mini Milk**[26] 5451 3-8-12 **63**.......................... TylerSaunders(7) 2 57
(Jonathan Portman) *s.i.s: in rr: rdn and sme prog over 3f out: no imp fnl 2f* **28/1**

5430 **8** 8 **Closer Than Close**[10] 6022 3-9-7 **65**.......................... DanielMuscutt 8 46
(Jonathan Portman) *carried lft leaving stalls: midfield: impr to chse ldrs 6f out: rdn 4f out: wknd wl over 1f out (trainer's rep said gelding was not suited by the undulations of the track)* **7/1**

064 **9** 6 **Voice Of Salsabil**[21] 5578 3-8-13 **57**.......................... LiamKeniry 10 29
(David Evans) *midfield: hdwy on outer into 2nd after 3f: drvn and lost 2nd over 2f out: wknd over 1f out* **25/1**

00U **10** 17 **Whims Of Desire**[9] 6046 3-8-6 **50**..........................(v[1]) LukeMorris 9
(Sir Mark Prescott Bt) *wnt lft leaving stalls: led tl rdn and hdd 3f out: wknd qckly: t.o* **14/1**

2m 36.61s (-3.69) **Going Correction** -0.125s/f (Firm) **10** Ran SP% **120.3**
Speed ratings (Par 98): **107,105,103,102,101 101,100,95,91,80**
CSF £9.96 CT £54.34 TOTE £2.90: £1.30, £1.80, £3.10; EX 12.30 Trifecta £83.20.
Owner Simon Lockyer **Bred** Kildaragh Stud & M Downey **Trained** Newmarket, Suffolk

FOCUS
This was well-run and the front pair are going the right way, so it's form to take a positive view of.
T/Plt: £1,017.00 to a £1 stake. Pool: £44,650.52 - 32.05 winning units T/Qpdt: £70.50 to a £1 stake. Pool: £4,521.18 - 47.41 winning units **Richard Lowther**

5980 LEICESTER (R-H)
Thursday, August 22

OFFICIAL GOING: Good (7.0)
Wind: Fresh half-behind Weather: Overcast

6368 GLEBE NOVICE MEDIAN AUCTION STKS 7f
5:30 (5:31) (Class 5) 2-Y-O **£3,881** (£1,155; £577; £288) **Stalls** High

Form RPR
5 **1** **Escape Proof**[36] 5052 2-8-11 0.......................... AdamMcNamara 6 70
(Roger Charlton) *mde virtually all: rdn over 1f out: styd on* **11/4**[2]

5 **2** 1½ **Rocket Dancer**[70] 3760 2-9-2 0.......................... RobertHavlin 5 71
(Sylvester Kirk) *s.i.s: hdwy over 3f out: chsd wnr over 1f out: styd on* **14/1**[3]

1 **3** ½ **Wyclif**[19] 5655 2-9-9 0.......................... KevinStott 9 77
(Ralph Beckett) *s.s: pushed along and hdwy over 2f out: rdn over 1f out: styd on* **8/15**[1]

4 **4** nk **Trumpets Call (IRE)**[13] 5894 2-9-2 0.......................... DavidEgan 7 69
(David Loughnane) *prom: rdn over 3f out: styd on* **50/1**

5 **5** 1½ **Internationaltiger**[26] 5456 2-9-2 0.......................... JackGarritty 14 65+
(Richard Fahey) *hld up: hdwy over 3f out: shkn up over 2f out: styd on* **25/1**

0 **6** 1 **Clifftop Heaven**[8] 6065 2-9-2 0.......................... DougieCostello 3 62
(Mark Walford) *w wnr over 3f: sn rdn: styd on same pce fnl f* **66/1**

50 **7** 7 **Castel Angelo (IRE)**[14] 5859 2-9-2 0.......................... DaneO'Neill 2 44
(Henry Candy) *prom: racd keenly and wd: chsd wnr over 2f out tl over 1f out: wknd fnl f* **16/1**

5 **8** 2 **Fedora Fits**[16] 5780 2-8-8 0.......................... MeganNicholls(3) 16 34
(Mark Loughnane) *prom: rdn 1/2-way: hung rt over 2f out: sn wknd* **33/1**

05 **9** nse **Sophar Sogood (IRE)**[9] 6054 2-9-2 0.......................... TrevorWhelan 10 39
(Paul D'Arcy) *mid-div: pushed along and lost pl 1/2-way: n.d after* **100/1**

06 **10** 2 **Hermano Bello (FR)**[26] 5439 2-9-2 0.......................... SeanLevey 15 34
(Richard Hannon) *hld up: rdn over 2f out: nvr on terms* **25/1**

11 2¼ **Compensate** 2-9-2 0.......................... KieranShoemark 11 28
(Andrew Balding) *s.i.s: nvr nrr* **20/1**

04 **12** ¾ **Thomas Hawk**[18] 5704 2-9-2 0.......................... AndrewMullen 17 26
(Alan Brown) *s.i.s: hld up: rdn over 2f out: nvr on terms* **100/1**

66 **13** 4 **Activius (IRE)**[76] 3542 2-9-2 0.......................... JFEgan 4 15
(Brian Meehan) *s.i.s: hld up: rdn over 2f out: n.d* **33/1**

14 7 **Screeching Dragon (IRE)** 2-9-2 0.......................... CliffordLee 8
(Kevin Frost) *in rr and pushed along over 4f out: n.d* **80/1**

0 **15** nse **Apachito**[81] 3371 2-9-2 0.......................... RyanPowell 12
(Kevin Frost) *s.i.s: a in rr* **100/1**

16 ¾ **Casablanca Kid (IRE)** 2-9-2 0.......................... PaulMulrennan 18
(Denis Quinn) *sn pushed along in rr: n.d* **66/1**

00 **17** 8 **Khalaty**[16] 5780 2-8-11 0..........................(p[1]) GrahamLee 13
(James Given) *hld up in tch: rdn and wknd over 2f out* **100/1**

0 **18** 18 **Paisley's Promise (IRE)**[23] 5527 2-8-8 0.......................... GabrieleMalune(3) 1
(Mike Murphy) *s.i.s: a in rr: bhd fr 1/2-way: eased over 1f out* **100/1**

1m 25.04s (-0.66) **Going Correction** -0.15s/f (Firm) **18** Ran SP% **133.9**
Speed ratings (Par 94): **97,95,94,94,92 91,83,81,81,78 76,75,70,62,62 61,52,32**
CSF £41.27 TOTE £4.30: £1.10, £3.60, £1.10; EX 56.10 Trifecta £113.80.
Owner K Abdullah **Bred** Juddmonte Farms Ltd **Trained** Beckhampton, Wilts

FOCUS
Overcast and blustery but dry conditions, and ground which had dried out from the previous evening's good to soft, good in places. Only two were seriously fancied in the market for this big-field opener, in which the winner came down the centre.

6369 IRISH STALLION FARMS EBF FILLIES' NURSERY H'CAP 6f
6:00 (6:00) (Class 4) (0-80,76) 2-Y-O

£6,727 (£2,002; £1,000; £500; £300; £300) **Stalls** High

Form RPR
2240 **1** **Insania**[21] 5587 2-9-7 **76**.......................... CliffordLee 8 84
(K R Burke) *hmpd s: chsd ldrs: rdn over 2f out: wnt 2nd over 1f out: led ins fnl f: r.o* **4/1**[2]

5561 **2** 1¾ **Knightcap**[3] 6272 2-9-1 **70** 6ex.......................... DuranFentiman 6 73
(Tim Easterby) *stdd s: hld up: hdwy on outer over 3f out: led over 2f out: rdn over 1f out: edgd lft and hdd ins fnl f: no ex towards fin* **5/2**[1]

5414 **3** 1¼ **Havana Dawn**[47] 4647 2-9-1 **70**.......................... PaulMulrennan 4 69
(Phillip Makin) *chsd ldrs: swtchd rt over 2f out: sn rdn: styd on same pce ins fnl f* **6/1**[3]

415 **4** *nse* **Mitty's Smile (IRE)**[12] 5934 2-9-4 **73**........................ AdamMcNamara 9 72
(Archie Watson) *prom: lost pl after 1f: sn pushed along: hdwy u.p over 1f out: nt rch ldrs* **10/1**
1340 **5** *4 1/2* **Brazen Safa**[33] 5189 2-9-3 **75**........................ CameronNoble(3) 7 60
(Michael Bell) *edgd lft s: hld up in tch: rdn over 2f out: styng on same pce whn nt clr run over 1f out* **9/1**
330 **6** *3/4* **Atmospheric**[33] 5189 2-9-7 **76**........................ HectorCrouch 2 59
(Clive Cox) *chsd ldrs: rdn and ev ch over 2f out: wknd ins fnl f* **6/1**[3]
4316 **7** *2 1/2* **Bartat**[12] 5958 2-8-12 **67**........................ DavidEgan 5 43
(Mick Channon) *led over 3f: sn rdn: wknd fnl f* **11/1**
433 **8** *1 3/4* **Feel Good Factor**[20] 5635 2-8-7 **65**........................ MeganNicholls(3) 3 35
(Richard Fahey) *plld hrd and prom: rdn over 2f out: wknd over 1f out* **8/1**

1m 11.93s (-0.17) **Going Correction** -0.15s/f (Firm) **8** Ran SP% **115.7**
Speed ratings (Par 93): **95,92,91,90,84 83,80,78**
CSF £14.64 CT £59.29 TOTE £4.30: £1.20, £1.50, £2.20; EX 16.00 Trifecta £79.30.
Owner Titanium Racing Club **Bred** Grovewood Stud **Trained** Middleham Moor, N Yorks

FOCUS
Stalls on stands side. A wide-open fillies' nursery and a pb from the winner.

6370 IRISH THOROUGHBRED MARKETING BOARD H'CAP 1m 53y
6:30 (6:31) (Class 4) (0-80,81) 3-Y-0+

£5,207 (£1,549; £774; £387; £300; £300) **Stalls** Low

Form RPR
3022 **1** **Pinnata (IRE)**[6] 6166 5-9-9 **77**........................(t) SeanLevey 3 85
(Stuart Williams) *racd keenly: wnt 2nd after 1f: rdn to ld over 1f out: edgd lft wl ins fnl f: styd on* **7/4**[1]
0262 **2** *3/4* **Dubai Acclaim (IRE)**[16] 5782 4-9-0 **68**........................ BarryMcHugh 4 74
(Richard Fahey) *trckd ldrs: plld hrd: rdn to chse wnr ins fnl f: sn ev ch: unable qck nr fin* **9/1**
5334 **3** *1 1/4* **Eesha's Smile (IRE)**[34] 5138 3-8-3 **66**........................(p) GabrieleMalune(3) 2 68
(Ivan Furtado) *led at stdy pce 7f out: qcknd 3f out: rdn and hdd over 1f out: edgd lft and styd on same pce wl ins fnl f* **10/1**
5420 **4** *hd* **Storm Ahead (IRE)**[5] 6231 6-9-9 **77**........................(b) DavidAllan 5 80
(Tim Easterby) *hld up: hdwy over 3f out: rdn over 1f out: styd on* **10/1**
3523 **5** *2 1/2* **Kannapolis (IRE)**[17] 5725 4-9-3 **71**........................ NathanEvans 8 68
(Michael Easterby) *pushed along leaving stalls: in rr: hdwy over 2f out: rdn over 1f out: styd on same pce ins fnl f* **4/1**[2]
2100 **6** *1* **Stringybark Creek**[21] 5597 5-9-5 **80**........................ LauraCoughlan(7) 10 75
(David Loughnane) *hld up: hdwy u.p on outer over 1f out: sn hung rt: no ex ins fnl f* **20/1**
6313 **7** *3* **Venusta (IRE)**[60] 4147 3-8-12 **72**........................(w) DavidEgan 1 59
(Mick Channon) *s.i.s: in rr: rdn over 2f out: nvr on terms* **16/1**
2100 **8** *shd* **Mister Music**[26] 5416 10-8-13 **74**........................ ElishaWhittington(7) 9 61
(Tony Carroll) *s.i.s: in rr: rdn over 2f out: nt trble ldrs* **33/1**
0-24 **9** *2 1/4* **Baalbek (USA)**[73] 3648 3-9-3 **77**........................ DaneO'Neill 6 58
(Owen Burrows) *s.i.s: sn pushed along to go prom then plld hrd: rdn over 2f out: wknd over 1f out* **6/1**[3]
0314 **10** *8* **Wild Hope**[17] 5749 3-9-7 **81**........................ KevinStott 7 44
(Kevin Ryan) *led 1f: chsd ldrs: rdn over 2f out: wknd over 1f out* **8/1**

1m 44.53s (-1.77) **Going Correction** -0.15s/f (Firm)
WFA 3 from 4yo+ 6lb **10** Ran SP% **123.5**
Speed ratings (Par 105): **102,101,100,99,97 96,93,93,90,82**
CSF £20.34 CT £127.82 TOTE £2.60: £1.10, £2.70, £3.60; EX 22.10 Trifecta £131.00.
Owner David N Reynolds & C D Watkins **Bred** Ammerland Verwaltung Gmbh & Co Kg **Trained** Newmarket, Suffolk

FOCUS
Stalls on inner. A refusal to settle proved no bar to the first two home finishing a little clear of the remainder. The winner has been rated to his latest form.

6371 NOD NEWNHAM FILLIES' H'CAP 1m 3f 179y
7:00 (7:04) (Class 5) (0-70,70) 3-Y-0+

£3,428 (£1,020; £509; £300; £300; £300) **Stalls** Low

Form RPR
3012 **1** **Harmonise**[7] 6104 5-9-12 **66**........................ HectorCrouch 6 75+
(Sheena West) *a.p: chsd ldr over 9f out: led over 3f out: rdn and edgd lft over 1f out: bmpd ins fnl f: styd on gamely* **6/4**[1]
0543 **2** *3/4* **Sempre Presto (IRE)**[25] 5473 4-9-11 **65**........................ DavidNolan 5 72
(Richard Fahey) *hld up: hdwy over 2f out: rdn over 1f out: ev ch whn edgd rt and bmpd ins fnl f: unable qck nr fin* **13/2**
3054 **3** *5* **Lincoln Tale (IRE)**[12] 5974 3-8-13 **62**........................ ShaneGray 8 61
(David O'Meara) *hld up: hdwy over 7f out: rdn over 1f out: styd on same pce ins fnl f* **9/1**
0-50 **4** *nk* **Lady Navarra (IRE)**[48] 4592 3-8-10 **59**........................ CliffordLee 3 58
(Gay Kelleway) *led: racd keenly: hdd over 3f out: sn rdn: ev ch over 1f out: no ex ins fnl f* **25/1**
5-33 **5** *1* **Konigin**[15] 5824 4-9-8 **62**........................(t) JFEgan 7 59
(John Berry) *hld up: hdwy on outer over 3f out: rdn and edgd rt over 1f out: no ex fnl f* **4/1**[2]
P460 **6** *6* **Raven's Raft (IRE)**[18] 5706 4-9-7 **61**........................ DavidEgan 1 48
(David Loughnane) *chsd ldr over 2f: remained handy: rdn over 3f out: outpcd over 2f out: n.d after* **14/1**
6420 **7** *8* **Princess Harley (IRE)**[30] 5271 4-9-9 **63**........................ FrannyNorton 2 38
(Mick Quinn) *prom: lost pl over 5f out: rdn over 3f out: wknd over 2f out* **12/1**
2042 **8** *17* **Say Nothing**[10] 6030 3-9-7 **70**........................ DaneO'Neill 4 17
(Hughie Morrison) *prom: lost pl over 6f out: rdn and wknd over 2f out* **6/1**[3]

2m 34.05s (-0.95) **Going Correction** -0.15s/f (Firm)
WFA 3 from 4yo+ 9lb **8** Ran SP% **115.8**
Speed ratings (Par 100): **97,96,93,92,92 88,82,71**
CSF £12.04 CT £66.21 TOTE £2.40: £1.30, £1.50, £2.50; EX 11.60 Trifecta £64.60.
Owner Ian Poysden **Bred** J Repard & S Dibb **Trained** Falmer, E Sussex

FOCUS
Stalls on inner. A most courageous effort from the in-form topweight in a race delayed by Konigin's reluctance to load.

6372 GALLOWGATE NURSERY H'CAP 7f
7:30 (7:33) (Class 5) (0-70,72) 2-Y-0

£3,428 (£1,020; £509; £300; £300; £300) **Stalls** High

Form RPR
530 **1** **Diva Rock**[21] 5588 2-9-5 **68**........................ PatCosgrave 5 72
(George Baker) *hld up: racd keenly: hdwy over 4f out: led over 1f out: sn rdn: jst hld on* **6/1**[3]
0404 **2** *shd* **We Owen A Dragon**[16] 5781 2-8-10 **62**........................ JaneElliott(3) 11 66
(Tom Dascombe) *chsd ldrs: shkn up over 2f out: r.o* **16/1**
6126 **3** *2 1/4* **Constanzia**[5] 6221 2-9-3 **66**........................ DavidEgan 2 64
(Jamie Osborne) *w ldrs: led 4f out: rdn and hdd over 1f out: no ex wl ins fnl f* **11/1**
5616 **4** *1 1/4* **Ebony Adams**[13] 5912 2-9-3 **66**........................ RobertWinston 8 61
(Brian Meehan) *led: hdd over 5f out: chsd ldrs: rdn over 1f out: styd on same pce ins fnl f* **20/1**
1540 **5** *3/4* **Bella Brazil (IRE)**[19] 5683 2-9-6 **69**........................ JFEgan 4 62
(David Barron) *chsd ldrs: rdn over 1f out: styd on same pce ins fnl f* **12/1**
0304 **6** *2 1/2* **Richard R H B (IRE)**[35] 5101 2-9-7 **70**........................ TrevorWhelan 9 57
(David Loughnane) *chsd ldrs: pushed along 1/2-way: rdn over 1f out: hung rt and no ex ins fnl f* **25/1**
504 **7** *shd* **Zingaro Boy (IRE)**[15] 5809 2-9-9 **72**........................ JackMitchell 10 59
(Hugo Palmer) *hld up: hdwy 1/2-way: rdn over 1f out: wknd ins fnl f* **4/1**[1]
535 **8** *2* **London Calling (IRE)**[16] 5777 2-9-7 **70**........................(h) KieranShoemark 12 52
(Richard Spencer) *pushed along early in rr: rdn over 2f out: nt rch ldrs* **10/1**
5033 **9** *3/4* **Little Ted**[9] 6053 2-9-0 **63**........................ DavidAllan 7 43
(Tim Easterby) *hld up: hdwy 1/2-way: nt clr run over 2f out: n.d after* **8/1**
050 **10** *3 1/4* **Just Norman**[20] 5624 2-8-13 **62**........................(b[1]) TomQueally 15 34
(Paul D'Arcy) *s.i.s: hld up: rdn over 2f out: sme hdwy over 1f out: wknd ins fnl f* **50/1**
536 **11** *3/4* **Outtake**[26] 5456 2-9-5 **68**........................ SeanLevey 14 38
(Richard Hannon) *hld up: rdn over 2f out: n.d* **14/1**
360 **12** *nk* **Breck's Selection (FR)**[30] 5273 2-9-5 **68**........................ FrannyNorton 13 37
(Mark Johnston) *prom: lost pl 3f out: wknd over 2f out* **20/1**
6600 **13** *3* **Van Dijk**[44] 4756 2-8-10 **59**........................(b) CamHardie 6 21
(Antony Brittain) *s.i.s: hld up: rdn over 2f out: n.d* **50/1**
0134 **14** *6* **Ambyfaeirvine (IRE)**[29] 5296 2-9-7 **70**........................ DavidNolan 1 17
(Ivan Furtado) *w ldrs: led over 5f out tl 4f out: rdn over 2f out: wknd over 1f out* **8/1**
4263 **15** *15* **Yarrow Gate**[19] 5668 2-9-7 **70**........................ GrahamLee 3
(Michael Dods) *plld hrd and prom: shkn up and wknd over 2f out* **6/1**[3]

1m 24.87s (-0.83) **Going Correction** -0.15s/f (Firm) **15** Ran SP% **131.3**
Speed ratings (Par 94): **98,97,95,93,93 90,90,87,86,83 82,82,78,71,54**
CSF £100.70 CT £1087.95 TOTE £5.40: £2.40, £7.20, £4.50; EX 203.10 Trifecta £1597.40.
Owner FTP Equine Holdings Ltd **Bred** Saleh Al Homaizi & Imad Al Sagar **Trained** Chiddingfold, Surrey

FOCUS
Stalls on stands side. Most still appeared to hold a chance nearing the 2f pole, but the first two came clear up the centre. The winner rates an improver.

6373 CHARLES STREET H'CAP 6f
8:00 (8:01) (Class 5) (0-70,72) 3-Y-0+

£3,428 (£1,020; £509; £300; £300; £300) **Stalls** High

Form RPR
0456 **1** **Final Frontier (IRE)**[46] 4693 6-8-13 **62**........................ JackGarritty 7 74
(Ruth Carr) *sn pushed along in rr: hdwy over 2f out: led and edgd lft over 1f out: styd on wl* **7/1**
3306 **2** *2 1/2* **Lucky Beggar (IRE)**[5] 6220 9-9-4 **67**........................ DavidAllan 10 71
(David C Griffiths) *chsd ldrs: led over 2f out: rdn and hdd over 1f out: styd on same pce ins fnl f* **6/1**[3]
-005 **3** *nk* **Absolute Dream (IRE)**[16] 5786 3-9-4 **70**........................ BarryMcHugh 8 73
(Richard Fahey) *sn pushed along in rr: rdn over 2f out: r.o ins fnl f: nt rch ldrs* **12/1**
-354 **4** *hd* **Mykindofsunshine (IRE)**[59] 4185 3-9-5 **71**........................ HectorCrouch 9 73
(Clive Cox) *hld up: pushed along 1/2-way: rdn and r.o ins fnl f: nt rch ldrs* **8/1**
3414 **5** *3/4* **Evening Attire**[22] 5551 8-9-2 **65**........................ PatCosgrave 2 65
(William Stone) *chsd ldrs: pushed along over 2f out: styd on same pce ins fnl f* **3/1**[1]
4204 **6** *3/4* **Mutabaahy (IRE)**[28] 5330 4-9-4 **67**........................ CamHardie 11 65
(Antony Brittain) *trckd ldrs: rdn over 1f out: styd on same pce ins fnl f* **11/2**[2]
0340 **7** *1 3/4* **Kenny The Captain (IRE)**[17] 5723 8-8-13 **62**........................ RachelRichardson 1 54
(Tim Easterby) *prom: rdn over 1f out: no ex ins fnl f* **11/1**
540 **8** *1/2* **Scuzeme**[19] 5670 5-9-7 **70**........................(h) SamJames 12 60
(Phillip Makin) *led over 3f: sn rdn: edgd lft over 1f out: no ex* **10/1**
0006 **9** *3/4* **Gunmaker (IRE)**[14] 5852 5-8-7 **56** oh1........................ NathanEvans 5 44
(Ruth Carr) *s.i.s: hld up: hdwy u.p over 1f out: wknd wl ins fnl f* **14/1**
46-6 **10** *2 1/2* **Allen A Dale (IRE)**[58] 4207 3-9-6 **72**........................ DavidNolan 13 52
(Richard Fahey) *hld up: rdn over 2f out: wknd over 1f out* **12/1**
4100 **11** *4 1/2* **Murqaab**[77] 3516 3-9-1 **67**........................(t[1] w) LewisEdmunds 4 33
(John Balding) *hld up: shkn up over 2f out: n.d* **33/1**
1/00 **12** *1/2* **Gustavo Fring (IRE)**[50] 4501 5-9-4 **67**........................(h[1]) KieranShoemark 6 31
(Richard Spencer) *w ldr: rdn and ev ch over 2f out: wknd and eased fnl f* **16/1**

1m 11.01s (-1.09) **Going Correction** -0.15s/f (Firm)
WFA 3 from 4yo+ 3lb **12** Ran SP% **126.6**
Speed ratings (Par 103): **101,97,97,97,96 95,92,91,87 81,81**
CSF £52.21 CT £516.04 TOTE £8.00: £2.40, £2.10, £2.60; EX 58.90 Trifecta £931.90.
Owner Vimal Khosla **Bred** Vimal And Gillian Khosla **Trained** Huby, N Yorks

FOCUS
Stalls on stands side. A run of the mill sprint handicap to finish, but a clear-cut scorer rejuvenated by the drop in trip.
T/Plt: £135.40 to a £1 stake. Pool: £51,880.48 - 279.67 winning units T/Qpdt: £74.50 to a £1 stake. Pool: £5,843.67 - 58.01 winning units **Colin Roberts**

6351 YORK (L-H)
Thursday, August 22

OFFICIAL GOING: Good (good to firm in places; overall 7.1, home straight: far side 7.0, centre 7.0, stands' side 6.9)
Wind: Fresh half behind Weather: Light showers

6374 SKY BET LOWTHER STKS (GROUP 2) (FILLIES) 6f
1:55 (1:55) (Class 1) 2-Y-O

£134,828 (£51,116; £25,581; £12,743; £6,395; £3,209) **Stalls** High

Form RPR
313 **1** **Living In The Past (IRE)**[26] 5411 2-9-0 **100**........................ DanielTudhope 1 110
(K R Burke) *looked wl; mde all: rdn clr over 1f out: kpt on wl* **12/1**
1411 **2** *3/4* **Liberty Beach**[22] 5542 2-9-0 **105**........................ JasonHart 9 108+
(John Quinn) *hld up in tch: hdwy 2f out: rdn over 1f out: chsd wnr ins fnl f: sn drvn and kpt on* **15/8**[1]

The Form Book Flat 2019, Raceform Ltd, Newbury, RG14 5SJ

1150 **3** *1* **Good Vibes**[6] 6157 2-9-0 96 .... HarryBentley 8 105
(David Evans) *looked wl; t.k.h early: hld up: hdwy 2f out: n.m.r jst over 1f out: sn rdn and kpt on wl fnl f* **20/1**

11 **4** *hd* **Under The Stars (IRE)**[26] 5411 2-9-0 102 .... PJMcDonald 5 104+
(James Tate) *str; looked wl; trckd ldng pair: hdwy 2f out: rdn over 1f out: drvn and kpt on same pce fnl f* **5/1[2]**

1 **5** *½* **Wejdan (FR)**[16] 5772 2-9-0 0 .... JamesDoyle 10 103+
(William Haggas) *str; hld up in rr: hdwy over 2f out: rdn over 1f out: kpt on wl fnl f* **6/1[3]**

524 **6** *1* **Precious Moments (IRE)**[28] 5361 2-9-0 0 .... RyanMoore 7 100
(A P O'Brien, Ire) *sweating; trckd ldrs: pushed along 2f out: sn rdn and grad wknd* **9/1**

320 **7** *2 ¼* **Celtic Beauty (IRE)**[17] 5751 2-9-0 0 ....(t) WJLee 2 93
(K J Condon, Ire) *chsd ldrs on outer: rdn along over 2f out: sn wknd* **8/1**

21 **8** *¾* **Nasaiym (USA)**[34] 5132 2-9-0 0 .... OisinMurphy 3 91
(James Tate) *ly: looked wl; chsd wnr: rdn along 2f out: drvn wl over 1f out: sn wknd* **8/1**

1103 **9** *1 ¼* **Flippa The Strippa (IRE)**[22] 5544 2-9-0 94 .... SilvestreDeSousa 6 87
(Charles Hills) *a in rr* **25/1**

30 **10** *14* **Moon Of Love (IRE)**[62] 4048 2-9-0 0 .... BarryMcHugh 4 45
(Richard Fahey) *plld hrd early: chsd ldng pair: lost pl 1/2-way: bhd fnl 2f* **50/1**

1m 10.74s (-0.86) **Going Correction** -0.05s/f (Good) **10 Ran SP% 116.2**
Speed ratings (Par 103): **103,102,100,100,99 98,95,94,92,74**
CSF £34.10 CT £474.39 TOTE £12.70: £3.00, £1.30, £5.10; EX 36.20 Trifecta £427.40.

Owner Clipper Logistics **Bred** Newlands House Stud & Mrs A M Burns **Trained** Middleham Moor, N Yorks

FOCUS
The forecast going was altered in the morning from the overnight good to good, good to firm in places. This race always produces a classy winner, with quite a few in the past decade going on to land the Group 1 Cheveley Park Stakes, like Fairyland did in 2018. The time was fractionally slower than the sales race that followed it. This rates further improvement from the winner, although she had the run of the race.

6375 GOFFS UK PREMIER YEARLING STKS — 6f

2:25 (2:29) (Class 2) 2-Y-O

£147,540 (£59,040; £29,520; £14,730; £7,380; £7,380) **Stalls** High

Form — RPR

1 **1** **Mums Tipple (IRE)**[27] 5367 2-9-5 0 .... RyanMoore 14 119+
(Richard Hannon) *looked wl; mde all: pushed along and qcknd wl clr over 1f out: drvn out* **7/2[1]**

1030 **2** *11* **Rayong**[32] 5228 2-9-0 98 .... SilvestreDeSousa 22 81
(K R Burke) *hld up in tch: hdwy over 2f out: rdn wl over 1f out: styd on fnl f: no ch w wnr (jockey said colt hung left under pressure)* **10/1**

4 **3** *nk* **Klopp Of The Kop (IRE)**[132] 1733 2-9-0 0 .... AdamKirby 16 80+
(Clive Cox) *towards rr and pushed along 1/2-way: rdn over 2f out: hdwy to chse ldrs and swtchd rt over 1f out: sn drvn: fin strly* **20/1**

4 *nse* **Piece Of Paradise (IRE)**[11] 5994 2-8-12 0 ....(bt) FrankieDettori 12 78
(J A Stack, Ire) *athletic; hld up: hdwy 1/2-way: rdn 2f out: styd on u.p fnl f* **12/1**

421 **5** *½* **National League (IRE)**[41] 4876 2-9-0 79 .... PaulHanagan 3 78
(Richard Fahey) *trckd ldrs: chsd wnr over 2f out: rdn wl over 1f out: drvn and kpt on same pce fnl f* **16/1**

3216 **6** *1 ½* **Raahy**[22] 5542 2-9-0 96 .... HarryBentley 13 74
(George Scott) *chsd ldrs: hdwy 2f out: sn rdn: drvn and kpt on same pce fnl f* **7/1[3]**

3222 **7** *shd* **Sermon (IRE)**[18] 5703 2-9-0 80 ....(p[1]) RichardKingscote 10 73
(Tom Dascombe) *chsd ldrs: rdn along 2f out: swtchd lft and drvn jst over 1f out: one pce fnl f* **40/1**

3124 **8** *nk* **Sir Arthur Dayne (IRE)**[12] 5962 2-9-0 80 ....(v[1]) GeraldMosse 19 72
(Mick Channon) *looked wl; towards rr and rdn along 1/2-way: hdwy wl over 1f out: styd on fnl f* **50/1**

5312 **9** *1* **St Ives**[14] 5853 2-9-0 79 .... JamesDoyle 4 69
(William Haggas) *towards rr: hdwy wl over 2f out: rdn to chse ldrs over 1f out: no imp* **6/1[2]**

2353 **10** *½* **Top Buck (IRE)**[72] 3695 2-9-0 78 .... JasonWatson 7 68
(Brian Meehan) *midfield: hdwy 2f out: sn rdn and n.d* **66/1**

5120 **11** *nk* **Mia Diva**[19] 5683 2-8-9 76 ....(t[1]) JasonHart 9 62
(John Quinn) *chsd ldrs: rdn along 2f out: wkng and hld whn n.m.r and sltly hmpd over 1f out* **40/1**

12 *¾* **Latin Five (IRE)**[17] 5752 2-9-0 0 .... SeamieHeffernan 15 65
(Joseph Patrick O'Brien, Ire) *in tch: rdn along over 2f out: drvn wl over 1f out: no hdwy* **33/1**

032 **13** *¾* **Barbarella (IRE)**[22] 5547 2-8-9 76 .... ShaneGray 1 57
(Kevin Ryan) *str; chsd ldrs: rdn along over 2f out: sn drvn and wknd* **25/1**

2242 **14** *1* **Sword Beach (IRE)**[21] 5587 2-9-0 84 .... TomMarquand 17 59
(Eve Johnson Houghton) *a towards rr* **20/1**

210 **15** *½* **Fleeting Prince (IRE)**[21] 5584 2-9-0 97 .... KieranShoemark 6 58
(Charles Hills) *in tch: hdwy to chse ldrs 2f out: sn rdn and wknd over 1f out* **8/1**

1 **16** *nse* **Love Destiny**[7] 6106 2-9-0 0 .... FrannyNorton 20 58
(Mark Johnston) *looked wl; dwlt: a in rr* **28/1**

5223 **17** *1 ¾* **Show Me Show Me**[22] 5542 2-9-3 101 .... PaddyMathers 5 56
(Richard Fahey) *dwlt: a towards rr* **7/1[3]**

0600 **18** *2 ¼* **Too Shy Shy (IRE)**[48] 4583 2-8-9 79 ....(h[1]) MartinDwyer 2 41
(Richard Spencer) *midfield: rdn along wl over 2f out: sn outpcd* **100/1**

002 **19** *2 ¼* **Cheat (IRE)**[8] 6078 2-9-0 0 .... OisinMurphy 11 39
(Richard Hannon) *dwlt: a towards rr* **40/1**

524 **20** *1* **Spygate**[40] 4910 2-9-0 76 .... DanielTudhope 18 36
(Richard Fahey) *chsd ldrs: rdn along 2f out: sn wknd* **66/1**

2430 **21** *5* **Corndavon Lad (IRE)**[27] 5390 2-9-0 72 ....(v[1]) BarryMcHugh 8 21
(Richard Fahey) *a in rr* **100/1**

1m 9.32s (-2.28) **Going Correction** -0.05s/f (Good) **21 Ran SP% 129.3**
Speed ratings (Par 100): **113,98,97,97,97 95,95,94,93,92 92,91,90,88,88 88,85,82,79,78 71**
CSF £35.13 TOTE £4.00: £2.00, £4.00, £6.00; EX 57.10 Trifecta £1792.90.

Owner Marian Lyons & Patricia Zanelli **Bred** Abbey Bloodstock Limited **Trained** East Everleigh, Wilts

■ Stewards' Enquiry : Ryan Moore two-day ban: used whip when clearly winning (5-6 Sep)

FOCUS
A rare sight in one of these big-field, often competitive sales races with the winner absolutely bolting up to score by a double-figure margin. It was most impressive visually, but the runner-up clearly didn't run to his mark of 98.

6376 CLIPPER LOGISTICS H'CAP — 7f 192y

3:00 (3:01) (Class 2) 3-Y-O+

£52,912 (£15,844; £7,922; £3,961; £1,980; £994) **Stalls** Low

Form — RPR

1030 **1** **What's The Story**[20] 5610 5-9-6 103 ....(p) JoeFanning 14 112
(Keith Dalgleish) *hld up towards rr: stdy hdwy over 3f out: chsd ldrs 2f out: rdn to chal ent fnl f: drvn and kpt on wl to ld nr fin* **12/1**

0102 **2** *hd* **Vale Of Kent (IRE)**[20] 5610 4-9-7 104 .... FrankieDettori 20 113
(Mark Johnston) *looked wl; led: pushed along and jnd 2f out: rdn wl over 1f out: drvn ins fnl f: hdd and no ex nr fin* **10/1**

-225 **3** *2 ¼* **Kynren (IRE)**[64] 3987 5-9-4 101 .... RobertWinston 8 106+
(David Barron) *in tch: hdwy 3f out: chsd ldrs 2f out: rdn over 1f out: drvn and keeping on whn n.m.r ins fnl f: one pce after* **7/2[1]**

2016 **4** *1 ¼* **Firmament**[26] 5413 7-9-2 99 ....(p) AdamKirby 12 100
(David O'Meara) *looked wl; hld up towards rr: swtchd rt and hdwy over 2f out: rdn along to chse ldrs 1 1/2f out: drvn and kpt on fnl f* **12/1**

05-1 **5** *nk* **Silver Line (IRE)**[34] 5150 5-9-5 107 .... CierenFallon[(5)] 2 107
(Saeed bin Suroor) *looked wl; trckd ldrs on inner: smooth hdwy and cl up 3f out: ev ch over 1f out: styd on same pce fnl f* **11/1**

4211 **6** *1* **Qaysar (FR)**[12] 5965 4-9-3 100 .... JamesDoyle 1 98
(Richard Hannon) *hld up towards rr: hdwy 3f out: rdn along 2f out: drvn and kpt on fnl f* **15/2[2]**

2000 **7** *½* **So Beloved**[20] 5610 9-9-5 102 .... DavidNolan 15 99
(David O'Meara) *hld up in rr: pushed along 3f out: hdwy 2f out: sn rdn and kpt on fnl f* **33/1**

1000 **8** *½* **Waarif (IRE)**[12] 5930 6-8-13 96 .... RobbieDowney 16 92
(David O'Meara) *prom: pushed along over 3f out: rdn over 2f out: sn drvn and wknd* **50/1**

4202 **9** *1 ¼* **Thrave**[33] 5192 4-8-13 96 .... HarryBentley 7 89
(Henry Candy) *looked wl; midfield: pushed along and hdwy 3f out: rdn over 2f out: sn drvn and no imp fnl f* **8/1[3]**

2010 **10** *½* **Blackheath**[22] 5546 4-8-6 89 .... PaulHanagan 3 81
(Ed Walker) *nvr bttr than midfield* **12/1**

2025 **11** *hd* **Baltic Baron (IRE)**[20] 5610 4-9-2 99 ....(v) DanielTudhope 17 90
(David O'Meara) *hld up towards rr: effrt and sme hdwy on outer 3f out: sn rdn and n.d* **12/1**

6440 **12** *1* **Arbalet (IRE)**[26] 5413 4-9-2 99 ....(t) PatCosgrave 13 88
(Hugo Palmer) *looked wl; a towards rr* **25/1**

-022 **13** *shd* **Wafy (IRE)**[16] 5776 4-8-7 90 .... AndreaAtzeni 11 79
(Charles Hills) *chsd ldrs: rdn along 3f out: sn wknd* **10/1**

1403 **14** *½* **Petrus (IRE)**[47] 4666 4-9-2 99 ....(p) MartinDwyer 4 86
(Brian Meehan) *looked wl; a towards rr* **14/1**

0100 **15** *½* **History Writer (IRE)**[20] 5610 4-9-0 97 ....(t) JasonWatson 18 83
(David Menuisier) *hld up: a towards rr* **25/1**

1666 **16** *4 ½* **Via Serendipity**[12] 5930 5-8-11 94 ....(t) OisinMurphy 6 70
(Stuart Williams) *chsd ldrs: rdn along wl over 2f out: drvn and wknd wl over 1f out* **14/1**

5124 **17** *3* **Club Wexford (IRE)**[12] 5948 8-8-11 94 .... BenCurtis 5 63
(Roger Fell) *prom: cl up over 3f out: sn pushed along: rdn wl over 2f out and sn wknd* **33/1**

1U36 **F** **Crownthorpe**[27] 5398 4-8-5 91 ....(p) SeanDavis[(3)] 9
(Richard Fahey) *racd awkwardly: hld up in rr whn stmbld and fell over 5f out* **66/1**

1m 36.14s (-1.36) **Going Correction** -0.05s/f (Good) **18 Ran SP% 132.7**
Speed ratings (Par 109): **104,103,101,100,100 99,98,98,96,96 96,95,94,94,93 89,86,**
CSF £129.33 CT £543.04 TOTE £12.40: £3.00, £2.10, £1.70, £3.30; EX 139.80 Trifecta £994.10.

Owner Weldspec Glasgow Limited **Bred** Mrs Liz Nelson Mbe **Trained** Carluke, S Lanarks

■ Stewards' Enquiry : Joe Fanning four-day ban: used whip above permitted level (5-6 & 8-9 Sep)

FOCUS
Always a big field, this handicap for smart performers featured runners from all the major 7f-1m races of the season so far. There didn't look any hard-luck stories, so the form should be reliable. The first two have been rated as improving. Add 36yds.

6377 DARLEY YORKSHIRE OAKS (GROUP 1) (BRITISH CHAMPIONS SERIES) (F&M) — 1m 3f 188y

3:35 (3:35) (Class 1) 3-Y-O+

£241,017 (£91,375; £45,730; £22,780) **Stalls** Centre

Form — RPR

1-11 **1** **Enable**[26] 5414 5-9-7 126 .... FrankieDettori 1 128+
(John Gosden) *sweating; mde all: shkn up 2f out: rdn over 1f out: styd on strly* **1/4[1]**

1122 **2** *2 ¾* **Magical (IRE)**[47] 4668 4-9-7 122 .... RyanMoore 4 123
(A P O'Brien, Ire) *trckd ldng pair: hdwy over 3f out: chsd wnr and cl up 2f out: rdn to chal over 1f out: drvn and kpt on same pce fnl f* **4/1[2]**

-163 **3** *10* **Lah Ti Dar**[53] 4430 4-9-7 113 .... WilliamBuick 2 107
(John Gosden) *trckd ldr: hdwy over 3f out: cl up over 2f out: sn rdn and one pce fr wl over 1f out* **11/1[3]**

4130 **4** *1 ½* **South Sea Pearl (IRE)**[4] 6263 3-8-12 101 .... SeamieHeffernan 3 105
(A P O'Brien, Ire) *hld up: a in rr* **100/1**

2m 29.9s (-3.30) **Going Correction** -0.05s/f (Good) **4 Ran SP% 109.3**
WFA 3 from 4yo+ 9lb
Speed ratings (Par 117): **109,107,100,99**
CSF £1.66 TOTE £1.10; EX 1.60 Trifecta £1.40.

Owner K Abdullah **Bred** Juddmonte Farms Ltd **Trained** Newmarket, Suffolk

FOCUS
Distance increased by 43yds. A final chance to see Enable, one of the all-time greats, strut her stuff on home soil and she didn't disappoint, making all and staying on strongly to see off old rival Magical. The winner has been rated to this year's form.

6378 BRITISH EBF & SIR HENRY CECIL GALTRES STKS (LISTED RACE) (F&M) — 1m 3f 188y

4:15 (4:16) (Class 1) 3-Y-O+

£39,697 (£15,050; £7,532; £3,752; £1,883; £945) **Stalls** Centre

Form — RPR

4 **1** **Search For A Song (IRE)**[33] 5208 3-8-12 104 .... OisinMurphy 9 108
(D K Weld, Ire) *ly: looked wl; racd wd early: cl up: led after 2f: hdd after 3f: trckd ldng pair: hdwy 3f out: led 2f out: sn rdn: drvn ins fnl f and kpt on strly* **3/1[1]**

The Form Book Flat 2019, Raceform Ltd, Newbury, RG14 5SJ

1142 **2** 1 ¾ **Vivionn**[22] [5545] 3-8-12 95........................ WilliamBuick 5 105
(Sir Michael Stoute) *trckd ldrs: hdwy on inner 3f out: chsd ldng pair 2f out: rdn to chse wnr ent fnl f: sn drvn and no imp towards fin* **11/2[3]**

1424 **3** hd **Spirit Of Appin**[19] [5682] 4-9-7 97........................ MartinDwyer 8 105
(Brian Meehan) *looked wl; t.k.h: led 2f: prom: led again 3f out: rdn and hdd 2f out: cl up and drvn over 1f out: kpt on fnl f* **20/1**

1041 **4** 3 ¼ **Hameem**[17] [5735] 4-9-7 101........................ JimCrowley 11 99
(John Gosden) *trckd ldrs: hdwy 3f out: rdn along 2f out: drvn over 1f out: sn no imp* **12/1**

1112 **5** 2 ¼ **Bella Vita**[19] [5682] 3-8-12 98........................ CharlesBishop 10 96
(Eve Johnson Houghton) *hld up towards rr: hdwy on outer wl over 2f out: sn rdn and plugged on fnl f* **8/1**

1-20 **6** 1 ¾ **Tauteke**[83] [3316] 3-8-12 90........................ AndreaAtzeni 6 93
(Roger Varian) *looked wl; trckd ldrs: pushed along over 3f out: rdn wl over 2f out: sn drvn and wknd* **20/1**

2203 **7** 3 ¼ **Shambolic (IRE)**[19] [5682] 3-8-12 97........................ FrankieDettori 2 88
(John Gosden) *hld up: a towards rr* **6/1**

2663 **8** 2 ½ **Frankellina**[27] [5397] 3-8-12 105........................ JamesDoyle 7 84
(William Haggas) *dwlt: plld hrd and sn chsng ldrs: led after 3f: hdd and pushed along 3f out: rdn over 2f out: sn btn (jockey said filly ran too free)* **9/2[2]**

6-13 **9** ½ **Naqaawa (IRE)**[22] [5545] 4-9-7 93........................ TomMarquand 1 83
(William Haggas) *dwlt: a in rr* **25/1**

0-4 **10** 5 **Frosty (IRE)**[8] [6090] 3-8-12 0........................ RyanMoore 3 75
(A P O'Brien, Ire) *dwlt: a in rr* **7/1**

2m 30.3s (-2.90) **Going Correction** -0.05s/f (Good)
WFA 3 from 4yo 9lb **10 Ran SP% 117.5**
Speed ratings (Par 111): **107,105,105,103,102 100,98,97,96,93**
CSF £19.00 TOTE £3.50: £1.60, £1.90, £5.10; EX 20.10 Trifecta £535.40.
Owner Moyglare Stud Farm **Bred** Moyglare Stud Farm Ltd **Trained** Curragh, Co Kildare
■ Stewards' Enquiry : Martin Dwyer four-day ban: used whip above permitted level (5-6 & 8-9 Sep)

FOCUS
Add 43yds. Good form for the grade with the unexposed winner building on her Irish Oaks promise. The third helps set the standard.

6379 BRITISH STALLION STUDS EBF FILLIES' H'CAP 7f
4:50 (4:51) (Class 2) (0-105,102) 3-Y-O+
£43,575 (£13,048; £6,524; £3,262; £1,631; £819) **Stalls** Low

Form RPR

-530 **1** **Excellent Times**[69] [3815] 4-8-6 **84**........................ PhilDennis 16 93
(Tim Easterby) *towards rr: hdwy over 2f out: rdn wl over 1f out: styd on strly ent fnl f: led towards fin* **66/1**

1223 **2** hd **Agincourt (IRE)**[44] [4758] 4-9-0 **92**........................ DanielTudhope 7 100
(David O'Meara) *trckd ldrs: cl up 3f out: led wl over 1f out: drvn and edgd rt ent fnl f: hdd and no ex nr fin* **9/1[3]**

1-43 **3** nk **Chaleur**[23] [5525] 3-9-1 **98**........................ HarryBentley 13 104
(Ralph Beckett) *trckd ldrs: hdwy 3f out: cl up 2f out: sn rdn: drvn and ev ch ins fnl f: kpt on* **10/1**

2 **4** nk **Salayel**[40] [4922] 3-8-8 **91**........................ AndreaAtzeni 5 96
(Roger Varian) *looked wl; trckd ldrs on inner: hdwy over 2f out: cl up and rdn wl over 1f out: drvn and ev ch ins fnl f: kpt on* **3/1[1]**

3101 **5** 1 ¼ **Breathtaking Look**[26] [5441] 4-9-0 **92**........................ PJMcDonald 11 95
(Stuart Williams) *trckd ldrs: hdwy over 2f out: rdn wl over 1f out: drvn ent fnl f: kpt on same pce* **16/1**

-111 **6** nse **Mubtasimah**[13] [5910] 3-8-12 **95**........................ JamesDoyle 12 96
(William Haggas) *in tch: hdwy over 2f out: rdn wl over 1f out: kpt on same pce fnl f* **7/2[2]**

46-1 **7** hd **Crafty Madam (IRE)**[33] [5204] 5-8-11 **89**........................(t) WJLee 8 92
(K J Condon, Ire) *hld up: hdwy over 2f out: rdn to chse ldrs jst over 1f out: ch whn n.m.r ent fnl f: drvn and kpt on same pce after* **12/1**

0250 **8** 1 **Clon Coulis (IRE)**[20] [5610] 5-9-10 **102**........................(h) JamieSpencer 1 102
(David Barron) *towards rr on inner: hdwy over 2f out: rdn wl over 1f out: kpt on fnl f* **16/1**

5-10 **9** 1 **Lyzbeth (FR)**[20] [5608] 3-8-13 **96**........................ RobHornby 17 91+
(Martyn Meade) *blindfold removed late and dwlt: towards rr and sn swtchd lft: swtchd rt to outer and hdwy wl over 2f out: rdn and chsd ldrs wl over 1f out: no imp fnl f (jockey said he was slow to remove the blindfold, resulting in his horse being slow to start)* **14/1**

1631 **10** ½ **Rux Ruxx (IRE)**[13] [5903] 4-8-2 **80**........................(p) JamieGormley 2 76
(Tim Easterby) *in tch on inner: pushed along and hdwy wl over 2f out: rdn wl over 1f out: kpt on u.p fnl f* **33/1**

6-00 **11** ½ **Dance Diva**[23] [5525] 4-8-12 **90**........................ PaulHanagan 4 85
(Richard Fahey) *in tch on inner: rdn along over 2f out: sn drvn and btn* **16/1**

4566 **12** hd **Whitefountainfairy (IRE)**[22] [5546] 4-8-7 **85**........... SilvestreDeSousa 18 79
(Andrew Balding) *looked wl; in tch: pushed along and chsd ldrs over 2f out: drvn wl over 1f out: grad wknd* **9/1[3]**

3621 **13** 1 ½ **Our Little Pony**[6] [6178] 4-7-12 **81** 5ex ow3........... FayeMcManoman[(5)] 3 71
(Lawrence Mullaney) *in tch: rdn along wl over 2f out: n.d* **25/1**

2000 **14** nk **Starlight Romance (IRE)**[26] [5453] 5-8-7 **85**........................ PaddyMathers 20 74
(Richard Fahey) *a towards rr* **50/1**

0462 **15** 1 **Divinity**[16] [5790] 3-8-7 **90**........................ BenCurtis 10 75
(K R Burke) *led: rdn along 3f out: hdd 2f out: sn wknd* **40/1**

3401 **16** 1 ½ **Kylie Rules**[19] [5693] 4-8-8 **86**........................ JamesSullivan 14 69
(Ruth Carr) *t.k.h: hld up: a in rr* **25/1**

4540 **17** 1 ¾ **New Day Dawn (IRE)**[12] [5949] 4-9-0 **92**........................ RichardKingscote 6 70
(Tom Dascombe) *looked wl; a in rr* **40/1**

0050 **18** 3 ¾ **Stay Classy (IRE)**[18] [5705] 3-8-9 **92**........................ MartinDwyer 19 58
(Richard Spencer) *dwlt: a in rr* **50/1**

1232 **19** ¾ **Warning Fire**[15] [5805] 3-8-5 **88**........................ JoeFanning 9 52
(Mark Johnston) *chsd ldrs: rdn along wl over 2f out: sn drvn and wknd wl over 1f out* **25/1**

1m 21.95s (-2.65) **Going Correction** -0.05s/f (Good)
WFA 3 from 4yo+ 5lb **19 Ran SP% 133.1**
Speed ratings (Par 96): **113,112,112,112,110 110,110,109,108,107 106,106,105,104,103 101,99,95,94**
CSF £596.91 CT £6569.36 TOTE £77.30: £14.10, £2.40, £2.70, £1.50; EX 1421.50.
Owner Times Of Wigan **Bred** Times Of Wigan Ltd **Trained** Great Habton, N Yorks

FOCUS
A massive turn up here with the complete outsider striking at 66-1. They headed centre-field and loads had their chance.
T/Jkpt: Not Won. T/Plt: £31.10 to a £1 stake. Pool: £273,944.35 - 6,416.06 winning units T/Qpdt: £8.40 to a £1 stake. Pool: £21,020.95 - 1,836.13 winning units **Joe Rowntree/Darren Owen**

6380 - 6383a (Foreign Racing) - See Raceform Interactive

6196
CLAIREFONTAINE (R-H)
Thursday, August 22
OFFICIAL GOING: Flat: good; hurdles/chase: soft

6384a PRIX FERME DE LA VALLEE AU TANNEUR - G. & J.L. CENIER (H'CAP) (2YO) (TURF) 7f
3:20 2-Y-O **£11,261** (£4,504; £3,378; £2,252; £1,126)

RPR

1 **Grey Mystere**[23] 2-9-1 0........................ MlleCoralie Pacaut[(3)] 1 97+
(J-C Rouget, France) **8/5[1]**

2 5 ½ **Pink Princess**[18] [5713] 2-8-7 0........................ MickaelBarzalona 5 71
(P Monfort, France) **43/5**

3 hd **Marselha Prince (FR)** 2-9-1 0........................ TheoBachelot 9 78
(Cedric Rossi, France) **10/1**

4 4 ½ **Ammobaby (FR)**[23] 2-8-13 0........................ MaximeGuyon 8 64
(H De Nicolay, France) **57/10[3]**

5 ¾ **Forwardly (FR)**[117] 2-8-11 0........................(b[1]) PierantonioConvertino 10 60
(Charley Rossi, France) **13/1**

6 ¾ **All Revved Up (IRE)**[18] [5713] 2-8-5 0........................ SebastienMaillot 3 52
(C Boutin, France) **43/1**

7 1 ¼ **My Premier County (FR)**[18] [5713] 2-8-9 0........................(b) AntoineHamelin 4 53
(Matthieu Palussiere, France) **18/1**

8 nk **Vereny Ka (FR)**[18] [5713] 2-7-11 0........................ MlleAlisonMassin[(3)] 13 43
(C Lerner, France) **28/1**

9 ½ **Wedding Proposal (FR)**[83] 2-8-7 0........................ AlexisBadel 12 52+
(D & P Prod'Homme, France) **35/1**

10 ¾ **Morgenstern (FR)**[17] [5763] 2-8-5 0........................(p) VincentCheminaud 7 48+
(D Windrif, France) **14/1**

11 2 **Fact Or Fable (IRE)**[6] [6196] 2-8-2 0........................ AlexisPouchin[(3)] 6 39
(J S Moore) *hld up towards rr: outpcd and pushed along on nr side rail over 2f out: rdn 1 1/2f out: no imp and wl btn ent fnl f* **78/1**

12 nk **Coply (FR)**[9] [6060] 2-8-5 0........................(p) CristianDemuro 11 38
(R Chotard, France) **48/10[2]**

13 4 **Carmague (IRE)**[6] [6196] 2-8-5 0........................(p) AntoineCoutier 2 28
(J S Moore) *prom: asked for effrt over 2f out: nt qckn and sn struggling: wknd into last over 1f out: eased clsng stages* **91/1**

1m 20.5s **13 Ran SP% 120.1**
PARI-MUTUEL (all including 1 euro stake): WIN 2.60; PLACE 1.40, 2.40, 2.80; DF 14.50.
Owner Laurent Dassault **Bred** Ecurie La Vallee Martigny Earl **Trained** Pau, France

6385a GRAND PRIX DE CLAIREFONTAINE (LISTED RACE) (3YO) (TURF) 1m 4f
4:05 3-Y-O **£24,774** (£9,909; £7,432; £4,954; £2,477)

RPR

1 **Surrey Thunder (FR)**[12] [5950] 3-9-0 0........................ AlexisBadel 2 104
(Joseph Tuite) *racd in fnl quartet: asked to improve 3f out: prog to chal 2f out: sn led: styd on strly ins fnl f: readily* **19/10[1]**

2 1 ¼ **Eliade (FR)**[81] [3391] 3-8-10 0........................ OlivierPeslier 8 98
(F Rohaut, France) **67/10[3]**

3 3 **Styledargent (FR)**[37] 3-9-0 0........................(p) Pierre-CharlesBoudot 6 97
(J-P Gauvin, France) **10/1**

4 snk **Mister Nino (FR)**[18] [5717] 3-9-0 0........................ MickaelBarzalona 1 97
(J-M Beguigne, France) **9/1**

5 1 **Scarlet Tufty (FR)**[24] 3-9-0 0........................ JulienAuge 7 95
(C Ferland, France) **11/1**

6 nse **Secret Potion (GER)**[60] 3-9-0 0........................(p) LukasDelozier 5 95
(Henk Grewe, Germany) **31/1**

7 1 ¾ **Idiosa (GER)**[11] [6005] 3-8-10 0........................ GregoryBenoist 4 88
(Mlle L Kneip, France) **46/1**

8 2 **No Tinc Por**[34] [5167] 3-8-10 0........................(b[1]) StephanePasquier 9 85
(N Clement, France) **24/1**

9 20 **Rudimental (FR)**[28] 3-9-0 0........................ CristianDemuro 10 57
(C Lerner, France) **10/1**

10 4 **Kasaman (FR)**[39] [4963] 3-9-0 0........................(p) ChristopheSoumillon 3 51
(M Delzangles, France) **27/10[2]**

2m 30.9s (-7.00) **10 Ran SP% 120.3**
PARI-MUTUEL (all including 1 euro stake): WIN 2.90; PLACE 1.50, 1.90, 2.30; DF 13.20.
Owner Surrey Racing (th) **Bred** Patrick Chedeville Et Al **Trained** Lambourn, Berks

PORNICHET-LA BAULE
Thursday, August 22
OFFICIAL GOING: Viscoride: standard

6386a PRIX DE BEXBACH (CLAIMER) (2YO) (VISCORIDE) 1m
5:44 2-Y-O **£5,405** (£2,162; £1,621; £1,081; £540)

RPR

1 **Mrs Dukesbury (FR)**[13] [5912] 2-8-5 0........................(b[1]) HollieDoyle[(3)] 9 70
(Archie Watson) *drvn along early to ld after 100yds: 2 l clr and shkn up over 2f out: sn 5 l clr: kpt on wl: comf* **21/10[1]**

2 4 ½ **Lady Minx**[83] 2-8-8 0........................ AlexandreRoussel 2 60
(Edouard Monfort, France) **18/5[3]**

3 ¾ **Molino (FR)**[62] 2-9-1 0........................(b[1]) TonyPiccone 8 65
(C Ferland, France) **23/10[2]**

4 3 **Terre De France (FR)** 2-9-1 0........................ AntonioPolli 7 58
(M Delcher Sanchez, France) **87/10**

5 nse **Be The Mam (FR)**[21] 2-8-10 0........................(p) MaximilienJustum[(8)] 3 61
(N Leenders, France) **24/1**

6 3 **Holy Bere (FR)**[12] 2-8-8 0........................ MathieuAndrouin 6 44
(Edouard Monfort, France) **34/1**

7 12 **Harmonie Royale (FR)** 2-8-11 0........................ RichardJuteau 1 19
(P Monfort, France) **18/1**

8 2 ½ **Linked (IRE)**[24] 2-8-11 0........................(p) FabriceVeron 4 14
(E J O'Neill, France) **9/1**

9 6 **Kiastep (FR)**[158] [1240] 2-9-1 0........................ JeromeCabre 5 4
(Mme E Vibert, France) **25/1**

1m 38.6s **9 Ran SP% 120.6**
PARI-MUTUEL (all including 1 euro stake): WIN 3.10; PLACE 1.30, 1.30, 1.30; DF 6.90.
Owner W J A Nash & Partner **Bred** S C Ecurie Jema **Trained** Upper Lambourn, W Berks

6146 **CHELMSFORD (A.W)** (L-H)

Friday, August 23

OFFICIAL GOING: Polytrack: standard

Wind: light, behind Weather: sunny and warm

6387 BET AT TOTESPORT.COM NURSERY H'CAP — 6f (P)

5:45 (5:46) (Class 6) (0-65,67) 2-Y-O

£3,266 (£972; £485; £400; £400; £400) **Stalls** Centre

Form RPR

5564 1 **Champagne Supanova (IRE)**[8] 6113 2-9-6 **64**.......(v) RobertWinston 5 73+
(Richard Spencer) chsd ldrs: clsd to press ldr wl over 2f out: pushed into ld over 1f out: sn in command and clr ins fnl f: eased towards fin **8/1**

033 2 4 **Elpheba (IRE)**[31] 5280 2-9-0 **63**........................ ThomasGreatrex(5) 1 60
(David Loughnane) led for almost 1f: chsd ldr tl wl over 2f out: effrt whn nt clr run and swtchd rt over 1f out: hung rt 1f out: kpt on same pce to go 2nd wl ins fnl f: no ch w wnr **7/2[2]**

5601 3 3/4 **Foad**[13] 5958 2-9-7 **65**..(b) HollieDoyle 3 60
(Ed Dunlop) t.k.h: led after almost 1f: rdn: edgd lft and hdd over 1f out: wknd and lost 2nd wl ins fnl f **1/1[1]**

404 4 1 3/4 **Red Maharani**[76] 3579 2-9-2 **60**..............................(b1) AndrewMullen 6 50
(James Given) wnt rt leaving stalls and s.i.s: rousted along early: clsd and in tch 1/2-way: effrt on outer over 2f out: modest 4th and kpt on same pce ins fnl f (jockey said filly missed the break) **16/1**

0503 5 1 1/2 **Leg It Lenny (IRE)**[14] 5885 2-9-6 **64**...........................(v1) LukeMorris 2 49
(Robert Cowell) broke okay but racd awkwardly: sn dropped to rr and rousted along: clsd and in tch 1/2-way: hung lft: impeded and swtchd rt over 1f out: wl hld and hung lft ins fnl f (trainer's rep said colt did not face the first time visor) **5/1[3]**

056 6 1 **Twittering (IRE)**[21] 5635 2-9-9 **67**........................ JosephineGordon 4 49
(Jamie Osborne) chsd ldrs tl 1/2-way: sn outpcd and struggling in rr whn short of room and impeded over 1f out: no ch after **16/1**

1m 12.92s (-0.78) **Going Correction** -0.275s/f (Stan) **6 Ran SP% 111.8**

Speed ratings (Par 92): **94,88,87,85,83 82**

CSF £35.30 TOTE £9.80: £3.80, £1.80; EX 53.50 Trifecta £144.70.

Owner Phil Cunningham **Bred** Ballyphilip Stud **Trained** Newmarket, Suffolk

FOCUS

A modest sprint nursery, but one run at a good gallop and one that threw up an impressive winner.

6388 TOTEPOOL CASH BACK CLUB AT TOTESPORT.COM NOVICE STKS — 6f (P)

6:15 (6:17) (Class 5) 3-Y-O+

£4,948 (£1,472; £735; £367) **Stalls** Centre

Form RPR

41 1 **Aljari**[37] 5057 3-9-9 0.. LukeMorris 3 87+
(Marco Botti) chsd ldrs: effrt 2f out: clsd u.p to press ldrs 1f out: styd on to ld ins fnl f: sn in command and eased towards fin **2/7[1]**

1 2 1 3/4 **Whisper Aloud**[165] 1142 3-9-4 0...................................... HollieDoyle 5 76
(Archie Watson) awkward and wnt rt leaving stalls: led: drvn over 1f out: hrd pressed and wandered jst ins fnl f: sn hdd and outpcd **7/2[2]**

534- 3 6 **Lucky Charm**[366] 6404 3-8-11 73........................... JosephineGordon 4 50
(Chris Wall) awkward leaving stalls: led: drvn and hdd over 1f out: fdd ins fnl f **10/1[3]**

06 4 nk **Annakonda (IRE)**[35] 5141 3-8-11 0.................................. BrettDoyle 1 49
(Peter Chapple-Hyam) pushed along leaving stalls: chsd ldrs tl 4th and outpcd u.p over 1f out: wl btn fnl f **25/1**

5 34 **Waffleton** 3-8-8 0.. NoelGarbutt(3) 2
(Derek Shaw) v.s.a: a t.o **50/1**

1m 12.16s (-1.54) **Going Correction** -0.275s/f (Stan) **5 Ran SP% 114.9**

Speed ratings (Par 103): **99,96,88,88,42**

CSF £1.85 TOTE £1.10: £1.10, £1.20; EX 1.80 Trifecta £2.80.

Owner Raed El Youssef **Bred** Newsells Park Stud **Trained** Newmarket, Suffolk

FOCUS

Not a bad little novice event, but the pace was pressured and that set things up for Aljari to swoop in the final furlong.

6389 EXTRA PLACES AT TOTESPORT.COM H'CAP — 7f (P)

6:45 (6:46) (Class 6) (0-60,61) 3-Y-O

£3,266 (£972; £485; £400; £400; £400) **Stalls** Low

Form RPR

040 1 **Sharp Talk (IRE)**[22] 5592 3-9-5 **58**...................... JosephineGordon 3 65
(Shaun Keightley) t.k.h: chsd ldr tl over 2f out: styd handy: effrt to chal over 1f out: led and wnt rt ins fnl f: styd on wl (trainer could offer no explanation for the gelding's improved form; jockey said gelding lugged right-handed from 2f out) **25/1**

0001 2 3/4 **Dutch Story**[15] 5869 3-9-1 **54**..............................(p) RobertWinston 12 59
(Amanda Perrett) in tch in midfield: clsd to chse ldrs and effrt 2f out: ev ch u.p over 1f out: chsd wnr and kpt on same pce ins fnl f **9/2[3]**

5026 3 2 **Muhallab (IRE)**[11] 6024 3-8-13 **52**............................. AndrewMullen 13 52
(Adrian Nicholls) sn led: rdn and hrd pressed over 1f out: hdd ins fnl f: no ex and wknd towards fin **8/1**

366 4 1/2 **Penarth Pier (IRE)**[24] 5526 3-9-5 **58**................................ HollieDoyle 5 57
(Christine Dunnett) chsd ldrs tl wnt 2nd and rdn over 2f out: unable qck: outpcd and n.m.r over 1f out: kpt on same pce ins fnl f **10/1**

0424 5 1/2 **Miss Liberty Belle (AUS)**[24] 5526 3-9-4 **57**...........(p) AdrianMcCarthy 7 54+
(William Jarvis) s.i.s: hld up in rr of main gp: effrt on outer 2f out: hung lft and kpt on ins fnl f: nvr trbld ldrs **10/1**

4522 6 shd **Classic Star**[13] 5957 3-9-8 **61**.................................... JoeyHaynes 4 58+
(Dean Ivory) hld up in rr of main gp: effrt 2f out: kpt on ins fnl f: nvr a threat to ldrs **5/2[1]**

5431 7 1 **Deconso**[11] 6024 3-8-5 **49**.. TobyEley(5) 8 43
(Christopher Kellett) in tch in midfield: effrt but unable qck over 1f out: wl hld and kpt on same pce ins fnl f (jockey said ran flat) **4/1[2]**

000 8 3 **Congress Place (IRE)**[8] 6130 3-8-12 **56**...........(v1) TheodoreLadd(5) 10 43
(Michael Appleby) midfield: unable qck and btn over 1f out: wknd ins fnl f **14/1**

-050 9 1/2 **Denis The Diva**[16] 5797 3-9-7 **60**................................ LukeMorris 11 45
(Rae Guest) towards rr of main gp: hdwy into midfield 1/2-way: unable qck u.p and btn over 1f out: wknd ins fnl f **16/1**

0060 10 11 **Sittin Handy (IRE)**[15] 5867 3-8-2 **46** oh1...............(p) SophieRalston(5) 14 3
(Dean Ivory) sn bhd: detached last 1/2-way: no ch after (jockey said gelding was slowly away) **25/1**

-010 11 1 3/4 **Rita's Folly**[15] 5869 3-9-0 **58**.........................(p1) DarraghKeenan(5) 2 10
(Anthony Carson) pushed along leaving stalls: chsd ldrs: nt clrest of runs and shuffled bk over 2f out: rdn over 1f out: sn bhd and eased ins fnl f **16/1**

0000 12 5 **Shawwaslucky**[7] 6181 3-8-4 **46** oh1.............................. NoelGarbutt(3) 1
(Derek Shaw) pushed along in midfield: dropped to rr of main gp and rdn over 2f out: wknd over 1f out **66/1**

1m 25.39s (-1.81) **Going Correction** -0.275s/f (Stan) **12 Ran SP% 123.7**

Speed ratings (Par 98): **99,98,95,95,94 94,93,90,89,76 74,69**

CSF £138.33 CT £1034.02 TOTE £37.80: £7.70, £1.80, £2.40; EX 230.30 Trifecta £931.70.

Owner Simon Lockyer **Bred** James Keville **Trained** Newmarket, Suffolk

FOCUS

A couple of last-time out winners but not a deep race, routine form for the grade.

6390 IRISH LOTTO AT TOTESPORT.COM H'CAP — 1m 2f (P)

7:15 (7:17) (Class 4) (0-85,85) 3-Y-O+ **£7,051** (£2,098; £1,048; £524) **Stalls** Low

Form RPR

0300 1 **Secret Art (IRE)**[6] 6211 9-9-7 **82**.................................... LukeMorris 1 88
(Gary Moore) trckd ldrs: nt clr run over 2f out: effrt on inner over 1f out: str chal u.p ins fnl f: styd on wl to ld nr fin (trainer said regarding apparent improvement in form that the gelding appeared to appreciate the return to an all-weather surface on this occasion) **12/1**

3635 2 shd **Michele Strogoff**[16] 5796 6-9-2 **82**........................ TheodoreLadd(5) 3 87
(Michael Appleby) taken down early: led: rdn and bmpd wl over 1f out: drvn and hrd pressed ins fnl f: hdd nr fin **9/2[3]**

1240 3 nk **Sophosc (IRE)**[13] 5931 3-9-2 **84**................................... RobHornby 5 88
(Joseph Tuite) stdd s: hld up in tch: effrt whn lft 4th and impeded wl over 1f out: hung lft and stl pressing ldr 1f out: nt quite rch ldng pair **10/1**

-544 4 3/4 **Let Rip (IRE)**[2] 6331 5-9-3 **78**.................................... JasonWatson 4 81
(Henry Candy) chsd ldr for 2f: styd chsng ldrs: effrt to press ldr whn impeded wl over 1f out: hung lft and stl pressing ldr 1f out: no ex and jst outpcd wl ins fnl f (jockey said gelding hung badly left-handed; vet said gelding sustained a wound to its left hind) **7/4[2]**

2422 F **Alnadir (USA)**[15] 5841 3-9-3 **85**........................(h) SilvestreDeSousa 2
(Simon Crisford) taken down early: s.i.s: swtchd rt sn after s and hdwy to chse ldr after 2f: effrt and ev ch over 2f out: squeezed for room: stmbld and fell wl over 1f out **11/8[1]**

2m 4.58s (-4.02) **Going Correction** -0.275s/f (Stan) **5 Ran SP% 113.4**

WFA 3 from 5yo+ 7lb

Speed ratings (Par 105): **105,104,104,104,**

CSF £62.48 TOTE £12.30: £4.40, £2.10; EX 56.00 Trifecta £94.10.

Owner Excel Racing **Bred** Grange Stud **Trained** Lower Beeding, W Sussex

■ Stewards' Enquiry : Theodore Ladd ten-day ban; careless riding (Sep 6-15)

FOCUS

A tight little handicap, but a race marred by the terrible incident off the home turn where Alnadir took a horrific fall. The gallop didn't look particularly strong and the four finishers were covered by just over a length at the line.

6391 LILIAN THOMPSON "BEST MUM" OPTIONAL CLAIMING H'CAP — 1m (P)

7:45 (7:50) (Class 2) 4-Y-O+ **£19,407** (£5,775; £2,886; £1,443) **Stalls** Low

Form RPR

1214 1 **Star Of Southwold (FR)**[7] 6150 4-8-13 **91**............ TheodoreLadd(5) 4 100
(Michael Appleby) pressed ldr tl over 5f out: styd chsng ldrs: effrt wl over 1f out: led 1f out: rdn and styd on wl **15/8[2]**

4063 2 1 1/2 **Glory Awaits (IRE)**[20] 5651 9-8-0 **73** oh1.......................(b) HollieDoyle 1 79
(David Simcock) led: rdn 2f out: hdd 1f out: kpt on same pce after **20/1**

244 3 nse **Seniority**[21] 5610 5-10-0 **101**.. JasonWatson 2 107
(William Haggas) trckd ldrs: swtchd lft and n.m.r on inner over 1f out: kpt on same pce u.p ins fnl f **6/4[1]**

4003 4 2 3/4 **Zwayyan**[13] 5930 6-9-12 **99**..(v) RobHornby 3 99
(Andrew Balding) hld up in tch towards rr of main gp: effrt wl over 1f out: kpt on ins fnl f: nvr trbld ldrs **9/2[3]**

0000 5 1 **Another Batt (IRE)**[13] 5930 4-9-3 **97**........................ AngusVilliers(7) 9 94
(Richard Hughes) hld up in tch on outer: effrt wl over 1f out: kpt on same pce and no imp ins fnl f **25/1**

-200 6 1/2 **Azzeccagarbugli (IRE)**[69] 3857 6-8-9 **82**..........(p) JosephineGordon 8 78
(Mike Murphy) chsd ldrs tl clsd to press ldr over 5f out: unable qck and lost pl over 1f out: wknd ins fnl f **33/1**

100 7 1/2 **Breden (IRE)**[13] 5930 9-9-12 **99**.................................... RobertWinston 6 94
(Linda Jewell) hld up in tch in rr of main gp: effrt ent fnl 2f: no imp u.p over 1f out: kpt on same pce fnl f **20/1**

5053 8 hd **Love Dreams (IRE)**[6] 6214 5-9-8 **95**............................(p) DavidEgan 7 90
(Mark Johnston) rdr struggling to remove hood and walked out of stalls: a towards rr: nvr involved (jockey said that he lost his grip at the first attempt to remove blindfold and was delayed in making a second attempt as the gelding had broken from the stalls and stumbled, causing him to become unbalanced before successfully removing the blindfold) **16/1**

0334 9 25 **Salateen**[13] 5965 7-10-0 **101**.......................................(tp) DavidNolan 5 38
(David O'Meara) chsd ldrs: rdn over 2f out: lost pl and wl bhd ins fnl f **33/1**

1m 35.64s (-4.26) **Going Correction** -0.275s/f (Stan) **9 Ran SP% 118.1**

Speed ratings (Par 109): **110,108,108,105,104 104,103,103,78**

CSF £43.60 CT £69.16 TOTE £2.70: £1.10, £5.90, £1.10; EX 32.70 Trifecta £110.30.

Owner Middleham Park Racing XXXIII **Bred** S C Snig Elevage **Trained** Oakham, Rutland

FOCUS

Not a strong race for the grade and contested by mainly exposed types. However, it was run at an even tempo and was run in a good time, so the form is solid enough, with this rating a small pb from the winner. The front three all race close to the pace.

6392 DOUBLE DELIGHT HAT-TRICK HEAVEN AT TOTESPORT.COM H'CAP — 1m 6f (P)

8:15 (8:18) (Class 5) (0-75,75) 3-Y-O **£5,175** (£1,540; £769; £400; £400) **Stalls** Low

Form RPR

0142 1 **Manton Warrior (IRE)**[16] 5825 3-9-5 **68**.................(t1) StevieDonohoe 4 77
(Charlie Fellowes) in tch in last pair: rdn over 3f out: clsd u.p over 1f out: led and edgd lft ins fnl f: styd on strly **5/1**

5411 2 1 1/4 **Mon Frere (IRE)**[8] 6115 3-9-10 **73** 6ex..........................(p) LukeMorris 1 80
(Sir Mark Prescott Bt) chsd ldr: effrt ent fnl 2f: rdn to ld over 1f out: hdd and one pce ins fnl f **2/1[2]**

0012 3 2 3/4 **Wanaasah**[3] 6320 3-9-12 **75** 6ex......................................(h) DavidEgan 2 78
(David Loughnane) led: rdn wl over 2f out: hdd over 1f out: no ex and one pce ins fnl f **7/2[3]**

0001 4 4 1/2 **Samba Saravah (USA)**[57] 4291 3-9-5 **68**.........................(t) JasonWatson 3 65
(Charlie Fellowes) t.k.h to post: awkward leaving stalls: chsd ldrs after over 1f: effrt wl over 2f out: no ex u.p over 1f out: wknd ins fnl f **15/8[1]**

4-05 5 3 1/4 **Strindberg**[53] 4443 3-9-2 65 ....(b[1]) HayleyTurner 5 57
(Marcus Tregoning) *chsd ldrs for over 1f: in tch in last pair after tl outpcd u.p over 2f out: wl btn fnl f* 14/1
2m 58.54s (-4.66) **Going Correction** -0.275s/f (Stan) 5 Ran SP% **113.7**
Speed ratings (Par 100): **102,101,99,97,95**
CSF £15.93 TOTE £6.10: £2.60, £1.60; EX 19.30 Trifecta £48.50.
Owner Second Chancers **Bred** Glashare House Stud **Trained** Newmarket, Suffolk
FOCUS
A strong race for the grade, with a couple of these on the up, and there were no excuses for the beaten horses.

6393 BOOK TICKETS AT CHELMSFORDCITYRACECOURSE.COM H'CAP 1m 2f (P)
8:45 (8:50) (Class 5) (0-70,72) 3-Y-O

£5,175 (£1,540; £769; £400; £400; £400) **Stalls** Low

Form RPR
4-60 1 **The Dancing Poet**[23] 5561 3-9-6 67 ....(p[1]) HollieDoyle 4 75
(Ed Vaughan) *mde virtually all: rdn wl over 1f out: sustained duel w runner-up: kpt on wl: jst prevailed cl home* 8/1
2001 2 nk **Junior Rip (IRE)**[13] 5946 3-9-7 68 .... JasonWatson 7 75
(Roger Charlton) *t.k.h: w wnr: effrt wl over 1f out: sn drvn and sustained duel w wnr after: jst outpcd cl home* 15/8[1]
5443 3 2 **Canasta**[31] 5284 3-8-8 62 .... LorenzoAtzori(7) 9 65+
(James Fanshawe) *stdd after s and dropped in bhd: clsd on inner and nt clr run 2f out: hdwy ent fnl f: chsd ldng pair and r.o wl ins fnl f: nt rch ldrs (jockey said filly was denied a clear run for some distance early in the home straight)* 12/1
3352 4 1 1/4 **Corinthian Girl (IRE)**[18] 5731 3-9-5 66 .... StevieDonohoe 2 67
(David Lanigan) *s.i.s: in tch towards rr: effrt and hdwy 2f out: chsd ldrs and kpt on ins fnl f: no threat to ldrs* 5/1[3]
0310 5 1 **Spirit Of Angel (IRE)**[87] 3204 3-9-4 65 ....(p[1]) HayleyTurner 8 64
(Marcus Tregoning) *chsd ldrs: effrt over 2f out: unable qck over 1f out: kpt on same pce ins fnl f* 10/1
0-30 6 1 **Social Network (IRE)**[21] 5627 3-9-3 64 .... DavidEgan 1 61
(James Tate) *trckd ldrs: unable qck and edgd rt over 1f out: wl hld and one pce ins fnl f* 4/1[2]
0060 7 1/2 **Love Your Work (IRE)**[20] 5651 3-9-11 72 .... RoystonFfrench 5 68
(Adam West) *t.k.h: hld up in tch in midfield: effrt over 2f out: no imp whn nt clrest of runs over 1f out: kpt on same pce ins fnl f* 16/1
4323 8 3/4 **Better Than Ever (IRE)**[27] 5424 3-9-7 71 .... AaronJones(3) 3 65
(Marco Botti) *hld up in tch towards rr: effrt and nt clrest of runs wl over 1f out: no imp fnl f: nvr threatened ldrs* 8/1
9 10 **Dreamboat Dave (IRE)**[93] 2983 3-8-13 60 ....(b) ShelleyBirkett 6 34
(Sarah Humphrey) *s.i.s: t.k.h: hld up in tch on outer: effrt over 2f out: hung lft and wknd over 1f out* 16/1
2m 7.21s (-1.39) **Going Correction** -0.275s/f (Stan) 9 Ran SP% **122.2**
Speed ratings (Par 100): **94,93,92,91,90 89,89,88,80**
CSF £24.85 CT £190.84 TOTE £9.80: £2.60, £1.20, £2.30; EX 34.50 Trifecta £311.10.
Owner Mohammed Rashid **Bred** Rabbah Bloodstock Limited **Trained** Newmarket, Suffolk
FOCUS
A muddling race with no early pace, but the first two have been rated as improving.
T/Plt: £213.20 to a £1 stake. Pool: £30,608.96 - 143.51 winning units T/Qpdt: £70.20 to a £1 stake. Pool: £3,789.91 - 53.97 winning units **Steve Payne**

6039 FFOS LAS (L-H)
Friday, August 23

OFFICIAL GOING: Good (good to soft in places)
Wind: Slight across Weather: Fine and warm

6394 R J FINANCIAL PLANNING NURSERY H'CAP 7f 80y(R)
1:45 (1:46) (Class 6) (0-65,67) 2-Y-O

£2,781 (£827; £413; £300; £300; £300) **Stalls** Centre

Form RPR
0001 1 **Mac McCarthy (IRE)**[14] 5886 2-9-2 63 .... FinleyMarsh(3) 8 73+
(Richard Hughes) *trckd ldrs: shkn up to ld appr fnl f: sn c clr: comf* 7/1
005 2 3 3/4 **Jungle Book (GER)**[45] 4766 2-8-12 63 .... TylerSaunders(7) 12 64
(Jonathan Portman) *prom: led over 5f out: rdn over 2f out: hdd appr fnl f: outpcd by comfortable wnr* 9/2[1]
005 3 1 3/4 **Speed Merchant (IRE)**[28] 5381 2-9-5 63 .... MartinDwyer 4 60
(Brian Meehan) *midfield: rdn and clsd 2f out: ev ch 1f out: unable qck fnl f* 5/1[2]
4042 4 1 1/4 **Lexington Quest (IRE)**[14] 5907 2-9-6 64 .... FergusSweeney 9 58
(Richard Hannon) *led tl hdd over 5f out: chsd ldr: rdn over 2f out: sn lost 2nd: kpt on same pce* 6/1[3]
040 5 nk **Buy Nice Not Twice (IRE)**[28] 5366 2-8-9 53 .... JohnFahy 5 46
(Richard Hannon) *hld up: stl in rr whn rdn over 2f out: swtchd rt over 1f out: r.o fnl f* 7/1
660 6 1 1/4 **Ten Chants**[17] 5780 2-9-9 67 .... LouisSteward 1 57
(Ed Dunlop) *midfield: rdn over 2f out: sn outpcd by ldrs: styd on steadily fnl f* 9/1
040 7 shd **Clandestine Affair (IRE)**[13] 5956 2-9-4 62 .... ShaneKelly 10 52
(Jamie Osborne) *prom: drvn over 2f out: outpcd by ldrs over 1f out (jockey said colt hung left)* 14/1
050 8 1 **Son Of Prancealot (IRE)**[17] 5775 2-9-3 61 ....(t) EoinWalsh 6 48
(David Evans) *s.i.s: sn in midfield: rdn over 4f out: no prog after* 25/1
0244 9 3/4 **Chromium**[22] 5576 2-9-0 65 ....(p) EllieMacKenzie(7) 3 50
(Mark Usher) *hld up: rdn over 2f out: styd on same pce: nvr able to chal* 9/1
406 10 hd **Precision Storm**[15] 5848 2-9-2 63 .... MeganNicholls(3) 7 48
(Mark Loughnane) *towards rr: rdn over 2f out: sme prog over 1f out: wknd ins fnl f* 14/1
005 11 4 **Kentucky Hardboot (IRE)**[16] 5801 2-9-5 63 .... CallumShepherd 2 38
(Mick Channon) *a towards rr* 8/1
0004 12 2 3/4 **Pilsdon Pen**[14] 5886 2-9-2 60 ....(b[1]) LiamKeniry 11 28
(Joseph Tuite) *t.k.h: chsd ldrs tl rdn and wknd over 2f out* 22/1
1m 32.98s (-0.12) **Going Correction** -0.025s/f (Good) 12 Ran SP% **126.8**
Speed ratings (Par 92): **99,94,92,91,90 89,89,88,87,87 82,79**
CSF £41.36 CT £182.33 TOTE £8.50: £3.20, £2.80, £2.50; EX 57.80 Trifecta £360.90.
Owner R Gander & Partner **Bred** Ballyphilip Stud **Trained** Upper Lambourn, Berks

FOCUS
Race distance plus 11 yards. A competitive heat for this modest nursery where it was beneficial to be up with the pace, and this rates a nice step forward from the winner.

6395 FLY TUI FROM CARDIFF AIRPORT/EBF NOVICE STKS 7f 80y(R)
2:15 (2:16) (Class 5) 2-Y-O

£3,428 (£1,020; £509; £254) **Stalls** Centre

Form RPR
4 1 **Tritonic**[34] 5177 2-9-2 0 .... MeganNicholls(3) 10 78
(Alan King) *s.i.s: hld up: rdn over 2f out: hdwy over 1f out: stl 4th ent fnl f: styd on to ld last strides* 3/1[2]
5 2 1/2 **Skontonovski**[21] 5624 2-9-5 0 .... MartinDwyer 7 77+
(Richard Spencer) *led: qcknd over 3f out: shkn up over 1f out: stl 3 l clr whn rdn ins fnl f: hdd last strides* 5/2[1]
32 3 1 1/4 **We're Reunited (IRE)**[12] 5980 2-9-5 0 .... EoinWalsh 9 74
(Ronald Harris) *t.k.h: trckd ldr: drvn 2f out: kpt on same pce and lost 2nd ins fnl f: carried slty lft towards fin* 5/1
03 4 nk **Protagonist (FR)**[16] 5809 2-9-5 0 .... CallumShepherd 3 73
(Jamie Osborne) *chsd ldrs: rdn 3f out: styd on to chal for 2nd briefly ins fnl f: unable qck* 7/2[3]
5 2 1/4 **Tafish (IRE)** 2-9-5 0 .... ShaneKelly 2 68+
(Richard Hughes) *trckd ldrs: rdn over 2f out: wknd fnl f* 10/1
04 6 6 **Slavonic Dance (IRE)**[16] 5801 2-9-0 0 .... LouisSteward 6 48
(Ralph Beckett) *midfield: rdn over 2f out: outpcd by ldrs over 1f out* 20/1
7 nk **Campari** 2-9-5 0 .... AdamMcNamara 11 52
(Roger Charlton) *s.s: in rr: rdn 3f out: no hdwy tl styd on fnl f (jockey said colt ran green)* 16/1
0 8 1 **Grimsthorpe Castle**[17] 5774 2-9-5 0 .... LiamKeniry 8 50
(Ed Walker) *midfield: shkn up over 2f out: sn outpcd by ldrs and no ch* 33/1
9 2 3/4 **Werewolf** 2-9-5 0 .... GeorgeWood 1 43
(Archie Watson) *chsd ldrs: rdn over 2f out: wknd over 1f out* 12/1
6 10 1 3/4 **Big Boris (IRE)**[12] 5992 2-9-5 0 .... JohnFahy 4 39
(David Evans) *s.i.s: in rr: wl adrift whn nudged along over 2f out: r.o fnl f* 33/1
0 11 28 **John Leo's Son (IRE)**[8] 6106 2-9-0 0 .... RhiainIngram(5) 5
(David Evans) *a in rr: lost tch 3f out: t.o* 50/1
1m 34.04s (0.94) **Going Correction** -0.025s/f (Good) 11 Ran SP% **127.7**
Speed ratings (Par 94): **93,92,91,90,88 81,80,79,76,74 42**
CSF £11.67 TOTE £3.90: £1.50, £1.50, £2.00; EX 18.20 Trifecta £96.70.
Owner Mcneill Family & Ian Dale **Bred** Miss K Rausing **Trained** Barbury Castle, Wilts
FOCUS
Race distance plus 11 yards. A decent novice event run at a sound gallop with the favourite just being collared on the line. This has been rated around the balance of the front four.

6396 PLUMBASE H'CAP 6f
2:50 (2:51) (Class 3) (0-95,93) 3-Y-O **£7,246** (£2,168; £1,084; £542; £270) **Stalls** High

Form RPR
1-62 1 **Bernardo O'Reilly**[20] 5658 5-9-9 90 .... MartinDwyer 7 100
(Richard Spencer) *hld up: rdn over 2f out: hdwy over 1f out: r.o to ld fnl 50yds* 7/2[2]
0220 2 1/2 **Sunsprite (IRE)**[25] 5504 3-9-9 93 ....(p) ShaneKelly 4 101
(Richard Hughes) *racd keenly: prom: rdn over 2f out: ev ch ins fnl f: unable qck towards fin* 8/1
32U1 3 nk **Royal Residence**[24] 5530 4-9-10 91 .... CallumShepherd 5 98
(James Tate) *chsd ldrs: rdn 2f out: led narrowly ins fnl f tl hdd fnl 50yds* 5/1
110 4 nse **Molls Memory**[25] 5504 4-9-2 83 .... LiamKeniry 8 90
(Ed Walker) *hld up: rdn 2f out: hdwy over 1f out: r.o ins fnl f* 3/1[1]
5400 5 1 1/4 **Diamond Dougal (IRE)**[26] 5476 4-9-1 87 .... ScottMcCullagh(5) 2 90
(Mick Channon) *hld up: rdn and clsd over 1f out: nt clr run briefly appr fnl f: styd on (jockey said gelding was denied a clear run)* 14/1
5035 6 1/2 **Breath Of Air**[20] 5666 3-9-5 89 .... AdamMcNamara 6 90
(Charles Hills) *trckd ldr: rdn wl over 1f out: ev ch 1f out: fdd ins fnl f* 9/2[3]
6220 7 nse **Ballyquin (IRE)**[20] 5661 4-8-11 81 .... WilliamCox(3) 1 82
(Andrew Balding) *led: drvn 2f out: sn hrd pressed: hdd ins fnl f: wknd* 9/1
4000 8 1 **Freescape**[34] 5205 4-9-10 91 .... LouisSteward 3 89
(David Marnane, Ire) *midfield: rdn over 2f out: fdd fnl f* 12/1
0516 9 1 **Beyond Equal**[49] 4609 4-9-8 89 .... FergusSweeney 9 84
(Stuart Kittow) *t.k.h: hld up in midfield: hdwy to trck ldrs 1/2-way: rdn wl over 1f out: wknd appr fnl f* 12/1
1m 10.61s (-0.29) **Going Correction** -0.025s/f (Good)
WFA 3 from 4yo+ 3lb 9 Ran SP% **125.2**
Speed ratings (Par 107): **100,99,98,98,97 96,96,95,93**
CSF £34.74 CT £146.60 TOTE £4.60: £1.70, £2.60, £1.70; EX 41.50 Trifecta £264.70.
Owner Rebel Racing (2) **Bred** Chasemore Farm **Trained** Newmarket, Suffolk
FOCUS
A strongly run handicap where the winner came from last to first to just get up. The winning jockey stated the ground was riding softer than the official going description of good, good to soft in places.

6397 HONEYWELL H'CAP 5f
3:25 (3:25) (Class 6) (0-65,69) 3-Y-O

£2,781 (£827; £413; £300; £300; £300) **Stalls** High

Form RPR
031 1 **Gilt Edge**[16] 5799 3-8-13 60 .... RhiainIngram(5) 4 66
(Christopher Mason) *s.i.s: sn chsng ldrs: hdwy whn carried lft over 1f out: sn drvn: edgd rt and pressed ldr ins fnl f: r.o to ld last strides* 7/4[1]
4544 2 hd **Lorna Cole (IRE)**[7] 6183 3-9-11 67 ....(b[1]) MartinDwyer 6 72
(William Muir) *hld up: hdwy to ld narrowly over 1f out: drvn fnl f: hdd last strides (vet said filly lost her right hind shoe)* 2/1[2]
5040 3 1 1/4 **Mayfair Madame**[34] 5181 3-8-13 55 .... ShaneKelly 1 56
(Stuart Kittow) *hld up: pushed along and slty outpcd 1/2-way: rdn and stl last ent fnl f: r.o wl and wnt 3rd fnl 50yds: gng on fin* 10/1
053 4 1 3/4 **Skeetah**[18] 5738 3-9-1 60 .... MeganNicholls(3) 5 54
(John Quinn) *trckd ldrs: rdn over 1f out: kpt on same pce* 5/1
0000 5 1/2 **Solesmes**[55] 4376 3-8-1 46 ....(b[1]) WilliamCox(3) 7 39
(Tony Newcombe) *cl up: led and hung bdly lft over 1f out: sn hdd: drvn and unable qck: lost 2 pls towards fin* 22/1
3022 6 6 **Thegreyvtrain**[7] 6183 3-9-6 62 .... RaulDaSilva 2 40+
(Ronald Harris) *led: rdn 2f out: sn hmpd: carried bdly lft and lost pl: wknd* 7/2[3]
58.56s (-0.44) **Going Correction** -0.025s/f (Good) 6 Ran SP% **122.0**
Speed ratings (Par 98): **102,101,99,96,96 86**
CSF £6.29 TOTE £3.50: £3.00, £1.30; EX 5.50 Trifecta £37.70.
Owner S Bishop And C Mason **Bred** Christopher & Annabelle Mason **Trained** Caewent, Monmouthshire

FOCUS
A modest sprint handicap fought out by the two market principals. The winner has been rated in line with her Bath form.

6398 BRITISH STALLION STUDS EBF FILLIES' H'CAP — 1m 2f (R)
4:00 (4:00) (Class 3) (0-95,90) 3-Y-0+ — **£9,451** (£2,829; £1,414) **Stalls** Centre

Form — RPR

11 **1** **Last Look (IRE)**[17] 5783 3-9-4 **90** .... GabrieleMalune(3) 3 — 103+
(Saeed bin Suroor) *s.i.s: sn led and mde rest: increased tempo 4f out: shkn up 2f out: rdn and r.o wl fnl f* — **4/9**[1]

5251 **2** 2 3/4 **Norma**[23] 5565 3-9-2 **85** .... GeorgeWood 2 — 92
(James Fanshawe) *led early: trckd wnr: rdn over 1f out: swtchd lft ent fnl f: sn outpcd: no ex fnl 100yds* — **11/4**[2]

4241 **3** 3 1/2 **Clarion**[20] 5687 3-9-1 **84** .... LouisSteward 1 — 84
(Sir Michael Stoute) *hld up last of 3: rdn over 2f out: outpcd and btn over 1f out* — **4/1**[3]

2m 14.62s (1.92) **Going Correction** -0.025s/f (Good) — **3** Ran SP% **115.9**
Speed ratings (Par 104): **91,88,86**
CSF £2.33 TOTE £1.30; EX 3.10 Trifecta £2.70.
Owner Godolphin **Bred** Godolphin **Trained** Newmarket, Suffolk

FOCUS
Race distance plus 11 yards. A small, but good quality, field for the feature race on the card won in straightforward fashion by the well-bred odds-on favourite.

6399 VIESSMANN NOVICE STKS — 1m (R)
4:35 (4:36) (Class 5) 3-Y-0+ — **£3,428** (£1,020; £509; £254) **Stalls** Centre

Form — RPR

43 **1** **Motfael (IRE)**[20] 5650 3-9-5 0 .... MartinDwyer 4 — 87+
(Owen Burrows) *hld up bhd ldng pair: shkn up over 2f out: hung lft and led wl over 1f out: pushed clr fnl f* — **4/6**[1]

020 **2** 6 **Hawridge Storm (IRE)**[13] 5947 3-9-5 80 ....(v[1]) LiamKeniry 1 — 73
(Rod Millman) *dwlt: bhd: clsd and in tch after 2f: drvn in last over 2f out: styd on to go modest 2nd towards fin* — **5/2**[2]

-305 **3** 1 1/2 **Penrhos**[57] 4306 3-9-5 70 .... CallumShepherd 2 — 70
(Charles Hills) *led: jnd over 3f out: rdn and hdd wl over 1f out: fnd little and grad wknd: lost 3rd towards fin* — **7/2**[3]

4 9 **Wings Of Dubai (IRE)** 3-9-0 0 ....(p[1]) RaulDaSilva 3 — 44
(Ismail Mohammed) *t.k.h: trckd ldr: disp ld over 3f out: rdn 2f out: 3rd whn carried lft over 1f out: continued to hang lft and wknd (jockey said filly hung left)* — **11/1**

1m 43.04s (0.14) **Going Correction** -0.025s/f (Good) — **4** Ran SP% **119.1**
Speed ratings (Par 103): **98,92,90,81**
CSF £3.15 TOTE £1.50; EX 4.10 Trifecta £4.50.
Owner Sheikh Ahmed Al Maktoum **Bred** Fidelite Syndicate & Irish National Stud **Trained** Lambourn, Berks

FOCUS
Race distance plus 11 yards. A weak novice event won in workmanlike fashion by the odds-on favourite.

6400 HEATFORCE H'CAP — 1m 6f (R)
5:05 (5:07) (Class 6) (0-60,66) 3-Y-0+ — **£2,781** (£827; £413; £300; £300; £300) **Stalls** Low

Form — RPR

0001 **1** **Tigerskin**[10] 6042 3-9-11 **66** 6ex ....(bt) LouisSteward 13 — 78+
(Ralph Beckett) *t.k.h: sn trcking ldrs: led 2f out: rdn and qckly c clr: easily* — **6/4**[1]

5444 **2** 5 **Spring Run**[32] 5242 3-8-6 **54** .... TylerSaunders(7) 8 — 58
(Jonathan Portman) *midfield: hdwy on outer 3f out: sn rdn: wnt 2nd appr fnl f: kpt on but no ch w easy wnr* — **11/1**

0050 **3** 1 1/2 **Bambys Boy**[31] 5269 8-9-13 **58** ....(h[1]) LiamKeniry 15 — 57
(Neil Mulholland) *wnt to post early: s.i.s: t.k.h towards rr: hdwy on outer to chse ldrs after 3f: rdn over 2f out: hung lft and hmpd wl over 1f out: styd on fnl f (jockey said gelding hung left)* — **16/1**

0056 **4** 1 1/2 **Dancing Lilly**[28] 5378 4-9-0 **50** .... RachealKneller(5) 10 — 47
(Debbie Hughes) *chsd ldrs: nt clr run and lost pl over 2f out: styd on fnl f (jockey said filly hung right)* — **20/1**

4/0- **5** 2 **Boutan**[52] 546 6-9-7 **55** .... WilliamCox(3) 11 — 49
(Grace Harris) *prom: rdn over 2f out: styd on same pce* — **50/1**

-053 **6** hd **Purple Jazz (IRE)**[28] 5378 4-9-3 **53** ....(t) ScottMcCullagh(5) 5 — 47
(Jeremy Scott) *hld up: hdwy over 2f out: sn cl up and rdn: lost hld 2nd appr fnl f: wknd* — **10/1**[3]

0003 **7** 3/4 **Half Bolly**[7] 6180 3-8-5 **49** .... MeganNicholls(3) 16 — 44
(Mark Walford) *prom: disp ld after 5f: led 4f out: rdn over 2f out: sn hdd: wknd appr fnl f (jockey said gelding jumped left upon leaving the stalls)* — **5/1**[2]

005 **8** 1 1/4 **Zaydanides (FR)**[22] 5578 7-10-0 **59** .... GeorgeWood 2 — 50
(Tim Pinfield) *hld up: nt clr run over 2f out: sn rdn: swtchd lft over 1f out: modest late prog* — **50/1**

3000 **9** 1/2 **Spirit Of Nicobar**[20] 5648 3-8-9 **50** .... MartinDwyer 12 — 42
(Andrew Balding) *midfield: rdn 4f out: one pce and no ch fnl 3f* — **14/1**

3252 **10** nk **Born Leader (FR)**[12] 5987 3-8-13 **54** .... CharlieBennett 7 — 46
(Hughie Morrison) *chsd ldrs: rdn 3f out: wknd over 1f out* — **5/1**[2]

6000 **11** 1 **Triple Genius (IRE)**[22] 5596 3-8-3 **47** ....(b[1]) GabrieleMalune(3) 3 — 38
(Ed Dunlop) *hld up: rdn over 4f out: sme hdwy 3f out: edgd lft and btn over 2f out* — **33/1**

0600 **12** shd **Miss Harriett**[28] 5378 3-8-11 **52** .... FergusSweeney 4 — 43
(Stuart Kittow) *midfield: rdn 3f out: wknd over 1f out* — **25/1**

-030 **13** 1 1/4 **Carnage**[28] 5378 4-9-4 **49** .... JohnFahy 6 — 36
(Nikki Evans) *towards rr: rdn over 2f out: wknd over 1f out* — **16/1**

5213 **14** 33 **Bird For Life**[21] 5631 5-9-1 **53** ....(p) EllieMacKenzie(7) 1
(Mark Usher) *towards rr: rdn 3f out: lost tch 2f out: t.o* — **10/1**[3]

0043 **15** 12 **Antidote (IRE)**[20] 5648 3-9-0 **55** ....(p) ShaneKelly 9
(Richard Hughes) *led: jnd after 5f: rdn and hdd 4f out: wknd over 2f out: t.o* — **12/1**

3m 5.22s (-3.38) **Going Correction** -0.025s/f (Good)
WFA 3 from 4yo+ 10lb — **15** Ran SP% **141.4**
Speed ratings (Par 101): **108,105,104,103,102 102,101,101,100,100 100,99,99,80,73**
CSF £23.51 CT £237.46 TOTE £2.80: £1.70, £4.10, £6.60; EX 28.00 Trifecta £508.80.
Owner A D G Oldrey & G C Hartigan **Bred** Cheveley Park Stud Ltd **Trained** Kimpton, Hants

FOCUS
Race distance plus 11 yards. A modest long-distance handicap taken apart by the well-in favourite.
T/Plt: £27.00 to a £1 stake. Pool: £46,967.90 - 1,268.16 winning units T/Qpdt: £9.20 to a £1 stake. Pool: £3,493.70 - 278.08 winning units **Richard Lowther**

5661 GOODWOOD (R-H)
Friday, August 23

OFFICIAL GOING: Good (good to soft in places; 6.8)
Wind: Virtually nil Weather: Warm and sunny

6401 LADBROKES 1-2-FREE ON FOOTBALL APPRENTICE H'CAP — 6f
5:00 (5:00) (Class 5) (0-70,70) 3-Y-0+ — **£4,787** (£1,424; £711; £400; £400; £400) **Stalls** High

Form — RPR

2605 **1** **The Lamplighter (FR)**[8] 6109 4-9-6 **64** ....(tp) CierenFallon 8 — 78
(George Baker) *trckd ldr on stands' rail: rdn and mde hdwy over 1f out: led 1f out: styd on wl* — **7/1**

2422 **2** 3 3/4 **Seprani**[13] 5959 5-9-7 **70** .... StefanoCherchi(5) 5 — 72
(Amy Murphy) *racd in midfield: effrt to ld 2f out: rdn along and hdd 1f out: kpt on one pce fnl f* — **11/2**[2]

2324 **3** shd **Lethal Angel**[6] 6220 4-9-7 **70** ....(p) MarcoGhiani(5) 4 — 72
(Stuart Williams) *trckd ldr: rdn along and outpcd 2f out: kpt on again ins fnl f* — **7/4**[1]

6020 **4** 1 **Lilbourne Star (IRE)**[29] 5352 4-9-7 **68** .... Pierre-LouisJamin(3) 3 — 66
(Clive Cox) *hld up: pushed along and no hdwy over 2f out: sn rdn and kpt on fnl f* — **6/1**[3]

2345 **5** 3/4 **Grey Galleon (USA)**[9] 6084 5-9-7 **70** ....(p) AmeliaGlass(5) 7 — 66
(Clive Cox) *hld up: rdn along and no imp 2f out: kpt on one pce fnl f* — **6/1**[3]

0060 **6** hd **Aegean Mist**[4] 6286 3-8-9 **56** ....(v[1]) PoppyBridgwater 6 — 51
(John Bridger) *led: rdn along and hdd 2f out: one pce fnl f* — **14/1**

0365 **7** 3/4 **Englishman**[11] 6018 9-8-13 **60** ....(p) SeanKirrane(3) 1 — 53
(Milton Bradley) *racd in midfield on outer: rdn on outer 2f out: wknd fnl f* — **10/1**

0600 **8** 9 **Wiff Waff**[43] 4844 4-9-5 **63** .... DylanHogan 2 — 27
(Chris Gordon) *dwlt sltly and racd in rr of midfield: pushed along and outpcd 2f out: wknd fnl f* — **12/1**

1m 11.21s (-0.89) **Going Correction** +0.025s/f (Good)
WFA 3 from 4yo+ 3lb — **8** Ran SP% **116.3**
Speed ratings (Par 103): **106,101,100,99,98 98,97,85**
CSF £45.79 CT £98.15 TOTE £7.00: £1.80, £2.00, £1.20; EX 47.00 Trifecta £115.30.
Owner The Lamplighter Syndicate **Bred** E A R L Ecurie Haras Du Cadran Et Al **Trained** Chiddingfold, Surrey

FOCUS
The ground had been drying through the week. The rail on the bottom bend had been dolled out 3yds. This was rather steadily run in sprinting terms and as such, turned out to be messy, the winner always well placed against the stands' rail while a couple of the more fancied ones didn't get going soon enough from further back. The winner has been rated to his turf best.

6402 BRITISH EUROPEAN BREEDERS FUND EBF NOVICE STKS (PLUS 10 RACE) — 1m
5:35 (5:38) (Class 4) 2-Y-O — **£6,404** (£1,905; £952; £476) **Stalls** Low

Form — RPR

2 **1** **Volkan Star (IRE)**[14] 5908 2-9-5 0 .... WilliamBuick 5 — 88+
(Charlie Appleby) *mde all: pushed along and easily drew clr over 1f out: v easily* — **1/3**[1]

0 **2** 6 **Hold Fast (IRE)**[22] 5588 2-9-0 0 .... DavidProbert 6 — 67+
(Andrew Balding) *settled wl in midfield: effrt to cl 2f out: sn rdn and kpt on wl to gain remote 2nd fnl f* — **4/1**[2]

66 **3** 1 **Oslo**[16] 5809 2-9-5 0 .... DanielMuscutt 8 — 70
(Sir Michael Stoute) *trckd wnr: rdn along and outpcd over 1f out: kpt on one pce fnl f: lost remote 2nd fnl half f* — **4/1**[2]

05 **4** 8 **Selsey Sizzler**[62] 4117 2-8-12 0 .... Pierre-LouisJamin(7) 7 — 52
(William Knight) *racd in rr: pushed along after 2f: rdn in rr and readily outpcd 3f out: plugged on* — **14/1**[3]

0 **5** hd **Debt Of Honour**[14] 5908 2-9-2 0 .... CameronNoble(3) 4 — 51
(Michael Bell) *hld up: rdn along in rr over 2f out: kpt on one pce* — **33/1**

0 **6** 3 3/4 **Dazzling Darren (IRE)**[20] 5676 2-9-5 0 .... JimmyQuinn 2 — 42
(Adam West) *racd in midfield: rdn and outpcd over 2f out: sn bhd* — **50/1**

0 **7** 1 1/2 **Locked N' Loaded**[12] 5980 2-9-5 0 .... RossaRyan 3 — 39
(Richard Hannon) *v keen to post: prom and racd keenly: rdn and no imp 2f out: wknd fnl f* — **20/1**

0 **R** **Great Fengshui (IRE)**[27] 5439 2-9-5 0 .... PatDobbs 1 — +
(Richard Hannon) *rrd and got stuck in stalls as they opened (trainer was informed that the colt could not run until the day after passing a stalls test)* — **20/1**

1m 40.29s (1.09) **Going Correction** +0.025s/f (Good) — **8** Ran SP% **136.1**
Speed ratings (Par 96): **95,89,88,80,79 76,74,**
CSF £3.05 TOTE £1.30: £1.02, £1.60, £1.70; EX 3.20 Trifecta £6.00.
Owner Godolphin **Bred** Forenaghts Stud & S Mencoff **Trained** Newmarket, Suffolk

FOCUS
Add 6yds. Straightforward form to assess with the winner, who was a cut above, easily going clear after dictating a steady pace. He's a pattern performer in the making but several of those in behind have varying degrees of potential, too.

6403 CHICHESTER OBSERVER NURSERY H'CAP — 7f
6:05 (6:07) (Class 4) (0-80,80) 2-Y-O — **£6,016** (£1,790; £894; £447; £400) **Stalls** Low

Form — RPR

3154 **1** **Indian Creak (IRE)**[11] 6020 2-9-7 **80** .... DavidProbert 1 — 84
(Mick Channon) *mde all: qcknd 2 l clr 2f out: rdn and wandered arnd u.p over 1f out: pushed out whn wl in command fnl f: nvr chal* — **9/4**[2]

450 **2** 2 1/2 **Qaaddim (IRE)**[21] 5624 2-8-11 **75** ....(p[1]) CierenFallon(5) 4 — 72+
(Roger Varian) *restrained in last: rdn along in rr over 2f out: wnt 4th over 1f out: kpt on wl u.p fnl f to go 2nd cl home* — **10/3**[3]

022 **3** nk **Cotai Again (IRE)**[14] 5879 2-9-5 **78** ....(h[1]) DanielMuscutt 5 — 74
(Charles Hills) *trckd wnr: pushed along 3f out: rdn to chse wnr 2f out: kpt on one pce fnl f: lost 2nd fnl strides* — **6/1**

055 **4** 1 1/4 **Bowling Russian (IRE)**[24] 5523 2-8-11 **70** .... HectorCrouch 6 — 63
(George Baker) *settled in midfield: rdn and no immediate imp over 2f out: kpt on one pce fnl f* — **6/4**[1]

006 **5** 12 **Barry Magoo**[84] 3312 2-8-5 **64** .... JimmyQuinn 3 — 25
(Adam West) *trckd wnr on inner: rdn and lost pl over 2f out: sn bhd* — **33/1**

1m 27.55s (0.85) **Going Correction** +0.025s/f (Good) — **5** Ran SP% **111.1**
Speed ratings (Par 96): **96,93,92,91,77**
CSF £10.13 TOTE £2.80: £1.50, £1.70; EX 9.20 Trifecta £29.80.
Owner Peter Taplin & Susan Bunney **Bred** Mount Coote Stud & New England Stud **Trained** West Ilsley, Berks

FOCUS
Add 6yds. Experience and professionalism won the day with the winner, who was allowed an easy lead, away and gone before the others got themselves fully organised. The second is the one take from the race.

6404 LEVIN DOWN H'CAP 6f
6:35 (6:35) (Class 2) (0-105,97) 3-Y-O+ £13,903 (£5,658; £2,829; £1,416; £705) Stalls High

Form | | | | RPR
0051 1 **Green Power**[24] 5524 4-9-6 96 HectorCrouch 3 102
(John Gallagher) *mde all: shkn up 2f out: sn rdn and strly pressed 1f out: kpt on gamely fnl f: all out* 4/1[3]
1450 2 *nse* **Embour (IRE)**[20] 5664 4-9-5 95 RossaRyan 2 101
(Richard Hannon) *trckd wnr: effrt to chse wnr 2f out: rdn upsides and ev ch 1f out: kpt on wl: jst failed* 7/2[2]
4511 3 *nk* **Show Stealer**[12] 5989 6-9-2 92 5ex (p) DavidProbert 7 97+
(Rae Guest) *racd in midfield: hdwy on heels of ldng pair 2f out: swtchd rt and rdn 1f out: kpt on wl* 7/1
1222 4 *nk* **Open Wide (USA)**[20] 5664 5-9-7 97 (b) PatDobbs 5 101
(Amanda Perrett) *trckd wnr on rail: pushed along and n.m.r over 1f out: rdn once in clr fnl f: styd on wl* 15/8[1]
060 5 *nse* **Sir Maximilian (IRE)**[20] 5664 10-8-11 92 (v) CierenFallon(5) 4 96
(Ian Williams) *racd in midfield: rdn along on outer 2f out: kpt on fnl f* 8/1
6000 6 5 **Glenamoy Lad**[183] 843 5-9-3 93 (t) JimmyQuinn 6 81
(Michael Wigham) *hld up: rdn in rr and outpcd 2f out: nvr able to chal* 12/1
1-46 7 2 **Ice Lord (IRE)**[14] 5911 7-9-2 92 DanielMuscutt 1 73
(Chris Wall) *racd in midfield: effrt on outer to chse wnr 2f out: wknd fnl f (jockey said gelding hung right-handed)* 14/1

1m 11.17s (-0.93) **Going Correction** +0.025s/f (Good) 7 Ran SP% 115.0
Speed ratings (Par 109): **107,106,106,106,106 99,96**
CSF £18.58 TOTE £4.80: £2.10, £2.20; EX 18.20 Trifecta £126.50.
Owner Nino's Partnership **Bred** Crossfields Bloodstock Ltd **Trained** Chastleton, Oxon

FOCUS
A tight finish and the principals have been rated pretty much to form.

6405 LADBROKES H'CAP 2m
7:05 (7:06) (Class 5) (0-70,69) 3-Y-O £4,787 (£1,424; £711; £400; £400) Stalls Low

Form | | | | RPR
-123 1 **Blame It On Sally (IRE)**[16] 5798 3-9-3 65 (v[1]) RyanTate 4 79
(Sir Mark Prescott Bt) *mde all: shkn up to extend advantage over 2f out: sn wl in command: pushed out fnl f: comf* 7/4[2]
-142 2 4 **Whistler Bowl**[8] 6125 3-9-2 64 HectorCrouch 1 72
(Gary Moore) *hld up: wnt 4th 7f out: pushed along to take clsr order 3f out: rdn to go 2nd over 2f out: kpt on fnl f but no ch w easy wnr* 5/6[1]
5266 3 8 **Sea Art**[32] 5249 3-9-1 63 (v) PatDobbs 2 61
(William Knight) *racd in midfield: wnt 2nd 7f out: pushed along and outpcd over 2f out: sn wknd* 9/1[3]
6205 4 2 **Fayetta**[13] 5954 3-9-7 69 (b) TrevorWhelan 5 65
(David Loughnane) *trckd wnr: rdn and outpcd over 2f out: sn bhd* 20/1
2050 5 19 **Vin D'Honneur (IRE)**[21] 5623 3-8-8 56 (p) DavidProbert 3 29
(Stuart Williams) *settled in 4th: niggled along sn after s: rdn on outer 3f out: sn wknd and bhd (jockey said filly hung left-handed throughout)* 16/1

3m 29.15s (-1.75) **Going Correction** +0.025s/f (Good) 5 Ran SP% 111.6
Speed ratings (Par 100): **105,103,99,98,88**
CSF £3.61 TOTE £2.50: £1.40, £1.10; EX 3.30 Trifecta £7.30.
Owner Mr & Mrs John Kelsey-Fry **Bred** John Kelsey-Fry **Trained** Newmarket, Suffolk

FOCUS
Add 3yds. The pair with the most appealing profiles came to the fore, with the winner much improved in a first-time visor and the second worthy of some credit for pulling a long way clear of the others. The pace was sound, making for a true test.

6406 BRITISH EUROPEAN BREEDERS FUND SUPPORTS RACING WELFARE EBF FILLIES' H'CAP 1m
7:35 (7:35) (Class 3) (0-95,94) 3-Y-O+ £9,451 (£2,829; £1,414; £708; £352) Stalls Low

Form | | | | RPR
2215 1 **Audarya (FR)**[27] 5458 3-8-13 87 DanielMuscutt 5 95+
(James Fanshawe) *settled wl in 4th: hdwy on outer over 2f out: sn rdn and styd on wl to ld wl ins fnl f* 10/3[2]
3134 2 1 **Infanta Isabella**[24] 5525 5-9-5 92 (t) CierenFallon(5) 3 99
(George Baker) *trckd ldr: pushed along to ld over 1f out: rdn and hung rt whn hdd ins fnl f: no ex (jockey said mare hung left-handed throughout)* 13/8[1]
2205 3 1 ¼ **Hateya (IRE)**[24] 5525 4-9-7 94 DylanHogan(5) 2 98
(Jim Boyle) *trckd ldr: rdn along and ev ch over 1f out: one pce whn sltly short of room ins fnl f* 8/1
0-11 4 ¾ **Ghaziyah**[31] 5269 3-8-12 89 GeorgiaCox(3) 4 91
(William Haggas) *led: shkn up over 2f out: rdn along and hdd by wnr over 1f out: wkng whn hmpd by rival wl ins fnl f* 4/1
-214 5 5 **Loolwah (IRE)**[41] 4898 3-8-10 84 (v[1]) DavidProbert 1 74
(Sir Michael Stoute) *hld up in last and racd freely: rdn in rr 2f out and fnd little: n.d (jockey said filly hung both ways)* 7/2[3]

1m 39.05s (-0.15) **Going Correction** +0.025s/f (Good)
WFA 3 from 4yo+ 6lb 5 Ran SP% 114.5
Speed ratings (Par 104): **101,100,98,98,93**
CSF £9.64 TOTE £4.00: £1.70, £1.50; EX 10.30 Trifecta £28.20.
Owner Mrs A M Swinburn **Bred** Haras D'Ecouves **Trained** Newmarket, Suffolk

FOCUS
Add 6yds. There were a couple of mild disappointments but the winner is going the right way and the next pair home are both reliable sorts, so it looks like solid form. The pace was even and there were no hard-luck stories.
T/Plt: £13.90 to a £1 stake. Pool: £32,153.81 - 2,304.62 winning units T/Qpdt: £7.80 to a £1 stake. Pool: £2,849.28 - 362.68 winning units **Mark Grantham**

6219 NEWMARKET (R-H)
Friday, August 23

OFFICIAL GOING: Good to firm
Wind: Nil Weather: Fine

6407 C J MURFITT LTD FILLIES' NOVICE STKS (PLUS 10 RACE) 7f
2:05 (2:06) (Class 4) 2-Y-O £5,175 (£1,540; £769; £384) Stalls High

Form | | | | RPR
1 **Powerful Breeze** 2-9-0 0 DavidEgan 8 91+
(Hugo Palmer) *hld up: shkn up and hdwy over 2f out: led over 1f out: rdn and edgd rt ins fnl f: r.o* 20/1
2 2 ¾ **Broadbeach (IRE)** 2-9-0 0 HayleyTurner 4 84
(David Simcock) *hld up in tch: rdn and edgd rt over 1f out: styd on same pce ins fnl f* 33/1
54 3 4 ½ **Masaakin**[20] 5646 2-9-0 0 DaneO'Neill 6 71
(Richard Hannon) *sn led: racd keenly: hdd 3f out: led again over 2f out: rdn: edgd rt and hdd over 1f out: wknd ins fnl f* 14/1
4 3 ¼ **Tomouh (IRE)** 2-9-0 0 PatCosgrave 3 63
(Saeed bin Suroor) *wnt rt s: sn chsng ldrs: shkn up over 1f out: sn wknd* 2/1[2]
0 5 ¾ **Parikarma (IRE)**[20] 5684 2-9-0 0 TomQueally 7 61
(Ed Dunlop) *chsd ldrs: shkn up over 2f out: wknd over 1f out* 16/1
2 6 ½ **Thread Of Silver**[13] 5961 2-9-0 0 (h) WilliamBuick 1 59
(Charlie Appleby) *wnt rt s: sn pulling hrd in 2nd: led 3f out: hdd over 2f out: rdn over 1f out: sn wknd (trainer said filly ran too free)* 6/5[1]
7 1 ½ **Fashion Royalty** 2-9-0 0 JasonWatson 2 55
(Roger Charlton) *wnt rt s: in rr: rdn over 2f out: wknd over 1f out* 5/1[3]
8 23 **Chiarodiluna** 2-9-1 0 ow1 RobHornby 5
(Philip McBride) *hld up: rdn 1/2-way: wknd over 2f out* 50/1

1m 25.34s (-0.36) **Going Correction** -0.05s/f (Good) 8 Ran SP% 117.7
Speed ratings (Par 93): **100,96,91,88,87 86,84,58**
CSF £470.97 TOTE £22.80: £7.60, £7.70, £3.60; EX 294.30 Trifecta £1019.30.
Owner Dr Ali Ridha **Bred** Rabbah Bloodstock Limited **Trained** Newmarket, Suffolk

FOCUS
A novice event for juvenile fillies, with Godolphin being responsible for the first two in the market, though they both ran below expectations. They finished strung out.

6408 GALICUIX FILLIES' H'CAP 7f
2:40 (2:41) (Class 4) (0-85,86) 3-Y-O+
£6,469 (£1,925; £962; £481; £300; £300) Stalls High

Form | | | | RPR
1036 1 **Astrologer**[27] 5459 3-9-11 86 JasonWatson 4 93
(David O'Meara) *mde all: rdn and hung rt over 1f out: sn clr: styd on* 3/1[2]
3364 2 1 ¼ **Hunni**[22] 5573 4-9-3 73 DavidEgan 3 79
(Tom Clover) *chsd ldrs: rdn over 2f out: chsd wnr over 1f out: styd on* 7/2[3]
5415 3 ¾ **Dream World (IRE)**[15] 5870 4-9-4 74 AlistairRawlinson 6 78
(Michael Appleby) *chsd ldrs: rdn and hung lft over 1f out: styd on same pce towards fin (jockey said filly hung left in the final furlong)* 13/2
3233 4 2 **Chloellie**[16] 5828 4-9-0 70 TomQueally 1 69
(J R Jenkins) *prom: lost pl over 4f out: rdn over 2f out: styd on ins fnl f* 12/1
4503 5 4 **Conga**[27] 5419 3-9-2 77 SamJames 5 63
(Kevin Ryan) *w wnr tl shkn up over 2f out: carried lft over 1f out: wknd fnl f (trainer's rep said filly was unsuited by the going and would prefer an easier surface and may have been unsuited by the 7f trip)* 7/2[3]
0321 6 9 **Alnaseem**[20] 5688 3-9-7 82 (h) DaneO'Neill 2 43
(Luke McJannet) *s.i.s: hdwy over 4f out: hung lft and rdn over 2f out: wknd and eased over 1f out (jockey said filly had no more to give)* 11/4[1]

1m 25.43s (-0.27) **Going Correction** -0.05s/f (Good)
WFA 3 from 4yo 5lb 6 Ran SP% 117.1
Speed ratings (Par 102): **99,97,96,94,89 79**
CSF £14.65 TOTE £4.00: £1.80, £2.30; EX 16.20 Trifecta £79.30.
Owner Cheveley Park Stud **Bred** Cheveley Park Stud Ltd **Trained** Upper Helmsley, N Yorks

FOCUS
A handicap for fillies run at just an ordinary gallop, and the winner resumed her progress.

6409 CJMURFITT.COM BRITISH STALLION STUDS EBF NOVICE STKS (PLUS 10 RACE) (C&G) 7f
3:15 (3:17) (Class 4) 2-Y-O £5,175 (£1,540; £769; £384) Stalls High

Form | | | | RPR
1 **Royal Crusade** 2-9-0 0 WilliamBuick 2 83+
(Charlie Appleby) *s.i.s and wnt rt s: hld up: hdwy over 2f out: led over 1f out: shkn up and edgd lft ins fnl f: styd on: comf* 5/6[1]
2 *nk* **Hot Summer** 2-9-0 0 AndrewMullen 4 82+
(Richard Hannon) *hld up in tch: shkn up and swtchd lft over 1f out: sn chsng wnr: r.o* 25/1
3 3 ¼ **Never Alone** 2-9-0 0 BrettDoyle 3 74+
(Charlie Appleby) *wnt rt s: sn prom: shkn up: nt clr run and swtchd rt over 1f out: edgd lft and styd on ins fnl f* 13/2[3]
4 3 ¼ **Striking Approach** 2-9-0 0 JasonWatson 7 65
(Roger Charlton) *chsd ldrs: rdn and ev ch over 1f out: wknd ins fnl f* 16/1
5 *nk* **Robert Walpole** 2-9-0 0 HayleyTurner 9 65
(George Scott) *chsd ldr tl led over 4f out: rdn and hdd over 1f out: wknd ins fnl f* 20/1
6 5 **Plunkett** 2-9-0 0 RobertHavlin 8 52
(Ed Dunlop) *hld up: shkn up over 2f out: wknd over 1f out* 50/1
7 ¾ **Draw Lots (IRE)** 2-9-0 0 DavidEgan 5 50
(Brian Meehan) *wnt rt s: sn led: hdd over 4f out: remained w ldr: rdn and ev ch over 1f out: wknd fnl f* 25/1
8 3 ¼ **Great Image (IRE)** 2-9-0 0 PatCosgrave 1 41
(Saeed bin Suroor) *wnt rt s: racd keenly and sn prom: rdn and ev ch over 1f out: wknd fnl f* 7/2[2]
9 2 ¾ **Prince Imperial (USA)** 2-9-0 0 TomQueally 10 34
(Sir Michael Stoute) *s.i.s: rn green in rr: wknd over 2f out* 7/1

1m 25.78s (0.08) **Going Correction** -0.05s/f (Good) 9 Ran SP% 122.9
Speed ratings (Par 96): **97,96,92,89,88 83,82,78,75**
CSF £35.02 TOTE £1.70: £1.10, £5.60, £1.80; EX 37.50 Trifecta £195.70.
Owner Godolphin **Bred** Godolphin **Trained** Newmarket, Suffolk

FOCUS
A 7f juvenile novice for colts and geldings in which all nine were newcomers. The winner was the well-backed favourite but the time was the slowest of the three 7f races.

6410 PANTILE STUD H'CAP 1m
3:50 (3:51) (Class 4) (0-85,86) 3-Y-O £6,469 (£1,925; £962; £481; £300) Stalls High

Form | | | | RPR
3631 1 **Romola**[7] 6170 3-9-8 84 6ex (v) DavidEgan 1 95
(Sir Michael Stoute) *chsd ldrs: rdn to ld over 1f out: sn hdd: edgd and carried lft ins fnl f: rallied to ld nr fin* 5/4[1]
324 2 *nse* **Sandret (IRE)**[17] 5790 3-9-4 80 AndrewMullen 2 91
(Ben Haslam) *s.i.s: hld up: shkn up over 2f out: hdwy u.p to ld over 1f out: sn hung lft: hdd nr fin* 7/1
6063 3 5 **Fintas**[6] 6225 3-9-10 86 (t) JasonWatson 3 86
(David O'Meara) *led: shkn up and qckn over 2f out: rdn and hdd over 1f out: no ex ins fnl f* 2/1[2]

0512 **4** *shd* **Battle Of Waterloo (IRE)**[21] 5619 3-9-5 **81**........................ BrettDoyle 6 80
(John Ryan) *hld up: hdwy over 2f out: rdn and ev ch over 1f out: edgd lft and no ex ins fnl f* **6/1**[3]

4-45 **5** *17* **Aussie View (IRE)**[18] 5749 3-9-6 **82**........................ TomQueally 4 42
(George Margarson) *chsd ldr: wnt upsides over 5f out tl shkn up over 2f out: wknd over 1f out* **16/1**

1m 38.22s (-1.78) **Going Correction** -0.05s/f (Good) **5** Ran SP% **110.4**
Speed ratings (Par 102): **106,105,100,100,83**
CSF £10.43 TOTE £1.60: £1.20, £3.00; EX 9.60 Trifecta £17.90.
Owner Cheveley Park Stud **Bred** Cheveley Park Stud Ltd **Trained** Newmarket, Suffolk

FOCUS
The well-in winner didn't have to match the form of her Nottingham success.

6411 ANDY WRIGHT MEMORIAL H'CAP 1m 4f
4:25 (4:26) (Class 4) (0-85,87) 3-Y-O+
£6,469 (£1,925; £962; £481; £300; £300) **Stalls** Centre

Form RPR

421 **1** **Dramatic Device**[36] 5103 4-9-12 **82**........................ PatCosgrave 7 92
(Chris Wall) *a.p: shkn up to ld and edgd rt over 1f out: rdn and edgd lft ins fnl f: styd on* **9/2**

-316 **2** *2 1/2* **Fox Vardy (USA)**[21] 5614 3-9-4 **83**........................ RobHornby 4 90
(Martyn Meade) *chsd ldrs: rdn and hung lft over 2f out: styd on same pce ins fnl f* **9/4**[1]

1222 **3** *2* **Takumi (IRE)**[53] 4450 3-9-6 **85**........................ DavidEgan 3 89
(Roger Varian) *hld up: hdwy over 2f out: shkn up to ld over 1f out: sn rdn: hung lft and hdd: hung rt ins fnl f: no ex* **3/1**[2]

4136 **4** *nk* **Great Bear**[56] 4327 3-9-2 **81**........................(p[1]) JasonWatson 2 84
(Roger Charlton) *led: shkn up over 2f out: rdn: edgd lft and hdd over 1f out: styd on same pce* **4/1**[3]

0001 **5** *3* **Stamford Raffles**[20] 5686 6-10-0 **87**........................ TimClark(3) 5 85
(Jane Chapple-Hyam) *hld up: rdn and swtchd lft over 2f out: wknd ins fnl f (jockey said gelding hung left throughout)* **16/1**

1-56 **6** *3 1/4* **Ginistrelli (IRE)**[63] 4063 3-9-1 **80**........................ RobertHavlin 6 73
(Ed Walker) *chsd ldr tl rdn and hung lft over 2f out: wknd over 1f out* **13/2**

2m 32.26s (-1.64) **Going Correction** -0.05s/f (Good) **6** Ran SP% **113.2**
WFA 3 from 4yo+ 9lb
Speed ratings (Par 105): **103,101,100,99,97 95**
CSF £15.30 TOTE £6.10: £3.20, £1.50; EX 21.30 Trifecta £45.00.
Owner The Clodhoppers **Bred** Godolphin **Trained** Newmarket, Suffolk

FOCUS
This rates a good little race.

6412 RACING WELFARE FILLIES' H'CAP 1m 2f
4:55 (4:58) (Class 5) (0-70,71) 3-Y-O+
£4,528 (£1,347; £673; £336; £300; £300) **Stalls** Centre

Form RPR

001 **1** **Geranium**[30] 5316 4-9-10 **65**........................ DaneO'Neill 1 82+
(Hughie Morrison) *chsd ldrs: shkn up to ld over 1f out: edgd rt: pushed clr fnl f: easily* **11/4**[1]

22 **2** *6* **Mina Vagante**[23] 5556 3-9-9 **71**........................ PatCosgrave 3 74
(Hugo Palmer) *hld up: hdwy over 2f out: rdn to chse wnr ins fnl f: styd on same pce* **11/4**[1]

6136 **3** *3 3/4* **Trulee Scrumptious**[7] 6164 10-8-10 **58**........................(v) AledBeech(7) 2 53
(Peter Charalambous) *led: rdn: edgd lft and hdd over 1f out: wknd fnl f* **6/1**[3]

5024 **4** *nk* **Scenesetter (IRE)**[15] 5855 3-9-2 **64**........................(p) DavidEgan 7 59
(Marco Botti) *chsd ldr 9f out: rdn over 2f out: ev ch over 1f out: sn edgd rt: wknd ins fnl f* **7/1**

4443 **5** *8* **Winter Snowdrop (IRE)**[15] 5866 3-8-2 **50** oh5........................ ShelleyBirkett 5 29
(Julia Feilden) *chsd ldrs: rdn over 3f out: wknd over 2f out* **33/1**

2013 **6** *hd* **Cape Cyclone (IRE)**[28] 5380 4-8-13 **54**........................ JasonWatson 6 32
(Stuart Williams) *chsd ldrs: lost pl over 8f out: hdwy over 4f out: rdn and wknd 2f out (trainer said filly boiled over in the preliminaries and was keen in the early stages of the race)* **7/2**[2]

000 **7** *45* **Bated Beauty (IRE)**[60] 4194 4-9-8 **63**........................ TomQueally 8
(John Butler) *hld up: shkn up over 4f out: wknd 3f out* **16/1**

-100 **8** *4* **Pushmi Pullyu (IRE)**[18] 5730 3-8-13 **64**........................ TimClark(3) 9
(Jane Chapple-Hyam) *hld up: racd wd fr over 7f out: hdwy over 5f out: wknd over 3f out (jockey said filly hung right; trainer's rep said filly was unsuited by the going and would prefer an easier surface)* **16/1**

2m 6.56s (-0.54) **Going Correction** -0.05s/f (Good) **8** Ran SP% **117.0**
WFA 3 from 4yo+ 7lb
Speed ratings (Par 100): **100,95,92,91,85 85,49,46**
CSF £10.69 CT £41.37 TOTE £3.00: £1.50, £1.60, £2.00; EX 10.00 Trifecta £39.90.
Owner Trenchard, Morrison & Margadale **Bred** Viscountess Trenchard **Trained** East Ilsley, Berks

FOCUS
The rates a clear pb from the winner, rated around the runner-up.

6413 RACING TV H'CAP 6f
5:30 (5:30) (Class 3) (0-90,89) 3-Y-O
£9,056 (£2,695; £1,346; £673) **Stalls** High

Form RPR

661- **1** **Total Commitment (IRE)**[261] 9395 3-8-9 **77**........................ JasonWatson 7 83
(Roger Charlton) *sn chsng ldr: rdn over 1f out: r.o to ld wl ins fnl f* **14/1**

11 **2** *nk* **Drummond Warrior (IRE)**[54] 4421 3-9-3 **85**........................ RobHornby 2 90
(Pam Sly) *s.i.s: sn rcvrd to ld: shkn up and qcknd over 2f out: rdn and hung rt fr over 1f out: hdd wl ins fnl f: r.o* **4/1**[2]

1406 **3** *nse* **Tinto**[6] 6222 3-9-5 **87**........................ RobertHavlin 3 92+
(Amanda Perrett) *stdd s: hld up: swtchd rt and hdwy over 1f out: rdn ins fnl f: r.o* **8/1**

-451 **4** *1 1/4* **Monsieur Noir**[27] 5448 3-9-2 **84**........................ DavidEgan 5 85
(Roger Varian) *chsd ldrs: shkn up over 2f out: nt clr run over 1f out: styd on* **9/2**[3]

2104 **5** *3/4* **Dominus (IRE)**[12] 5983 3-9-6 **88**........................(t[1]) JFEgan 4 87
(Brian Meehan) *hood removed late: s.s: hdwy over 4f out: rdn over 1f out: styd on same pce ins fnl f* **5/1**

5012 **6** *3/4* **Majaalis (FR)**[24] 5530 3-9-4 **86**........................ DaneO'Neill 6 82
(William Haggas) *s.i.s: hld up: rdn over 1f out: nt trble ldrs* **2/1**[1]

0653 **7** *1/2* **Concierge (IRE)**[7] 6148 3-9-7 **89**........................(b) HayleyTurner 1 84
(George Scott) *broke wl and led early: stdd to trck ldrs: racd keenly: shkn up and nt clr run over 1f out: no ex ins fnl f* **17/2**

1m 14.93s (2.83) **Going Correction** -0.05s/f (Good) **7** Ran SP% **116.5**
Speed ratings (Par 104): **79,78,78,76,75 74,74**
CSF £70.77 TOTE £14.10: £5.50, £3.10; EX 82.40 Trifecta £477.90.
Owner Brook Farm Bloodstock **Bred** Watership Down Stud **Trained** Beckhampton, Wilts

FOCUS
A decent 3yo sprint handicap. The fourth helps set the standard.

T/Plt: £1,117.70 to a £1 stake. Pool: £52,795.87 - 34.48 winning units T/Qpdt: £5.00. to a £1 stake. Pool: £6,688.67 - 988.07 winning units **Colin Roberts**

6118 SALISBURY (R-H)
Friday, August 23

OFFICIAL GOING: Good (8.0)
Wind: light against Weather: sunny

6414 SHIPSEYS MARQUEES AMATEUR RIDERS' H'CAP 1m
5:15 (5:17) (Class 5) (0-70,72) 3-Y-O+
£3,606 (£1,118; £558; £400; £400; £400) **Stalls** Low

Form RPR

0300 **1** **Haraz (IRE)**[10] 6051 6-9-2 **50** oh3........................ MissMeganTrainor(7) 5 56
(Paddy Butler) *mde all: kpt on wl: pushed out (trainer said regarding apparent improvement in form that the gelding benefitted from an easy lead)* **100/1**

4161 **2** *nk* **Imperial Act**[38] 5016 4-10-1 **63**........................ MissMeganFox(7) 3 68
(Andrew Balding) *hld up in tch: hdwy to chse wnr over 1f out: kpt on ins fnl f but nvr quite getting there* **8/1**

212 **3** *2 1/2* **Amor Fati (IRE)**[14] 5881 4-10-10 **72**........................ MrPhilipThomas(7) 7 71
(David Evans) *hld up: rdn over 2f out: no imp tl hdwy into 3rd over 1f out: kpt on same pce fnl f* **7/1**[3]

6310 **4** *3* **Mandocello (FR)**[17] 5779 3-10-9 **70**........................ MrPatrickMillman 6 61
(Rod Millman) *stdd s: in last pair: hdwy 4f out: disp 2nd 3f out: sn rdn: nt gng pce to chal: no ex ent fnl f* **15/8**[1]

4006 **5** *1 1/4* **Hedging (IRE)**[3] 6305 5-9-13 **61**........................(b) MissNynkeSchilder(7) 1 50
(Eve Johnson Houghton) *nvr really travelling: sn dropped to rr: sme late prog: nvr on terms* **10/1**

4135 **6** *2 1/2* **Fieldsman (USA)**[23] 5560 7-10-9 **69**........................ MissSarahBowen(5) 4 53
(Tony Carroll) *trckd ldrs: disp 2nd 3f out: sn rdn: nt pce to chal: wknd ent fnl f* **5/2**[2]

1254 **7** *3/4* **Waqt (IRE)**[18] 5760 5-11-0 **72**........................(p) MissHannahWelch(3) 2 54
(Alexandra Dunn) *trckd wnr: rdn over 2f out: wknd ent fnl f* **15/2**

1m 44.74s (1.24) **Going Correction** +0.05s/f (Good) **7** Ran SP% **108.8**
WFA 3 from 4yo+ 6lb
Speed ratings (Par 103): **95,94,92,89,87 85,84**
CSF £679.28 TOTE £106.50: £20.10, £2.70; EX 307.20 Trifecta £4625.40.
Owner Christopher W Wilson & Partner **Bred** His Highness The Aga Khan's Studs S C **Trained** East Chiltington, E Sussex

FOCUS
The going was good (GoingStick: 8.0). Rail up to 18ft off permanent far side rail between 1m start and winning line. A modest amateurs' event to start and a huge surprise. The runner-up has been rated to her latest form.

6415 DRAINTECH TANKERS EBF NOVICE AUCTION STKS (PLUS 10 RACE) 6f
5:50 (5:50) (Class 4) 2-Y-O
£4,851 (£1,443; £721; £360) **Stalls** Low

Form RPR

51 **1** **Hamish Macbeth**[28] 5381 2-9-5 0........................ JackMitchell 6 88+
(Hugo Palmer) *travelled wl: trckd ldrs: led wl over 1f out: edgd rt but sn qcknd clr: comf* **1/2**[1]

2 **2** *1 3/4* **Cosmic Power (IRE)**[28] 5374 2-8-13 0........................ CharlesBishop 8 75+
(Eve Johnson Houghton) *sn outpcd in last pair but kpt in tch: hdwy over 1f out: chsd wnr jst ins fnl f: kpt on but nt gng pce to get on terms* **9/2**[2]

0 **3** *2* **Progressive Rating**[85] 3274 2-8-11 0........................ FrannyNorton 5 67
(William Knight) *chsd ldrs tl outpcd over 2f out: hdwy over 1f out: wnt 3rd ins fnl f: kpt on wout ever threatening* **10/1**

4035 **4** *2 1/2* **The Blue Bower (IRE)**[15] 5838 2-8-1 **68**........................ JaneElliott(3) 9 52
(Suzy Smith) *sn prom: chal over 2f out: sn rdn: outpcd by wnr over 1f out: no ex ins fnl f* **28/1**

6 **5** *1* **Ocho Grande (IRE)**[23] 5563 2-8-6 0........................ GeorgiaDobie(7) 3 58
(Eve Johnson Houghton) *sn pushed along in last pair: nvr gng pce to get involved* **33/1**

64 **6** *1/2* **Dreamy Rascal (IRE)**[30] 5288 2-8-1 **63**........ ThoreHammerHansen(5) 1 50
(Richard Hannon) *led: rdn and hdd wl over 1f out: sn outpcd by wnr: wknd ins fnl f* **20/1**

7 *4* **Rapidash** 2-8-11 0........................ SeanLevey 2 43
(Richard Hannon) *trckd ldrs: effrt 2f out: wknd ent fnl f* **8/1**[3]

1m 15.05s (0.55) **Going Correction** +0.05s/f (Good) **7** Ran SP% **116.2**
Speed ratings (Par 96): **98,95,93,89,88 87,82**
CSF £3.15 TOTE £1.30: £1.10, £1.90; EX 3.40 Trifecta £15.10.
Owner Hunscote Stud Ltd & Mrs Lynne Maclennan **Bred** Whitsbury Manor Stud & R J Cornelius **Trained** Newmarket, Suffolk

FOCUS
This looked a two-horse race and they filled the first two places.

6416 SIGNS IN MOTION NURSERY H'CAP 1m
6:20 (6:21) (Class 5) (0-75,77) 2-Y-O
£3,737 (£1,112; £555; £400; £400; £400) **Stalls** Low

Form RPR

601 **1** **Walkonby**[14] 5907 2-8-9 **61**........................ FrannyNorton 7 67
(Mick Channon) *trckd ldrs: rdn for str chal over 1f out: led fnl 120yds: r.o* **4/1**[3]

0343 **2** *1 1/2* **Always Fearless (IRE)**[13] 5956 2-9-7 **73**........................ SeanLevey 2 76
(Richard Hannon) *trckd ldr: rdn to ld over 1f out: hdd fnl 120yds: kpt on but no ex* **7/2**[2]

4063 **3** *1* **Bacchalot (IRE)**[9] 6071 2-8-7 **62**........................ JaneElliott(3) 1 63
(Richard Hannon) *hld up: pushed along and hdwy 2f out: rdn and ev ch over 1f out: kpt on same pce fnl 120yds* **10/1**

4213 **4** *1/2* **Incinerator**[13] 5962 2-9-10 **76**........................(t) JackMitchell 6 76
(Hugo Palmer) *racd keenly: hld up: hdwy over 2f out: sn rdn: nt pce to get on terms but kpt on ins fnl f* **6/4**[1]

0454 **5** *8* **Bad Rabbit (IRE)**[12] 5980 2-9-3 **69**........................ CharlesBishop 3 50
(David Loughnane) *led: rdn and hdd over 1f out: sn wknd* **10/1**

0460 **6** *hd* **Pitcher**[22] 5587 2-8-11 **68**........................ ThoreHammerHansen(5) 4 49
(Richard Hannon) *trckd ldr: chal over 2f out: sn rdn: hld over 1f out: wknd ent fnl f* **9/1**

4315 **7** *1 1/2* **Fantom Force (IRE)**[14] 5896 2-9-4 **77**........................ LukeCatton(7) 5 54
(Richard Hannon) *nvr really travelling: struggling over 3f out: a last* **16/1**

1m 44.56s (1.06) **Going Correction** +0.05s/f (Good) **7** Ran SP% **116.3**
Speed ratings (Par 94): **96,94,93,93,85 84,83**
CSF £18.98 TOTE £3.80: £2.10, £2.10; EX 22.80 Trifecta £70.10.
Owner M Channon **Bred** Mike Channon Bloodstock Limited **Trained** West Ilsley, Berks

FOCUS
An ordinary nursery in which Richard Hannon saddled four of the seven runners, but the prize went elsewhere. This has been rated a shade cautiously around the second and third.

6417 LONGINES IRISH CHAMPIONS WEEKEND EBF STONEHENGE STKS (LISTED RACE) 1m
6:50 (6:52) (Class 1) 2-Y-O

£17,013 (£6,450; £3,228; £1,608; £807; £405) **Stalls** Low

Form RPR

1 **Mohican Heights (IRE)**[98] 2812 2-9-1 0........................ JamieSpencer 2 100+
(David Simcock) *trckd ldrs: rdn to ld over 1f out: kpt on wl and in command fnl f* **6/1**

2216 **2** *2* **Subjectivist**[27] 5415 2-9-1 91........................ JackMitchell 3 95
(Mark Johnston) *trckd ldrs: rdn 2f out: chsd wnr ent fnl f: kpt on but nt pce to get on terms* **11/2**

51 **3** *3/4* **Berlin Tango**[25] 5493 2-9-1 0........................ OisinMurphy 1 94
(Andrew Balding) *hld up bhd ldrs: hdwy 2f out: sn rdn: wnt 4th over 1f out: pressed for 2nd ins fnl f: kpt on but no ex nring fin* **7/2**[3]

1 **4** *1/2* **Man Of The Night (FR)**[50] 4558 2-9-1 0........................ SeanLevey 4 93
(Richard Hannon) *hld up last but in tch: swtchd lft for effrt over 2f out: sn edging lft u.p: kpt on into 4th ins fnl f but nvr gng pce to get on terms (jockey said colt hung left handed)* **9/4**[1]

41 **5** *2 1/4* **Passing Fashion (IRE)**[20] 5676 2-9-1 0........................ TomMarquand 6 87
(Ralph Beckett) *prom: led 2f out: rdn and hdd over 1f out: sn hung lft: wknd ent fnl f (jockey said gelding hung left-handed under pressure)* **25/1**

5111 **6** *7* **Governor Of Punjab (IRE)**[22] 5587 2-9-1 91........................ FrannyNorton 5 71
(Mark Johnston) *racd freely: led: rdn and hdd 2f out: sn wknd (jockey said colt ran too free to post and during the race)* **3/1**[2]

1m 42.74s (-0.76) **Going Correction** +0.05s/f (Good) **6 Ran SP% 111.5**
Speed ratings (Par 102): **105,103,102,101,99 92**
CSF £36.99 TOTE £6.00: £3.00, £2.90; EX 29.30 Trifecta £133.60.
Owner Qatar Racing Ltd & Sun Bloodstock Sarl **Bred** Kevin J Molloy **Trained** Newmarket, Suffolk

FOCUS
An interesting Listed event with five of the six runners successful last time out, but it has been rated a bit below the recent race average. The whole field were spread right across the track coming to the last furlong.

6418 EDWARDS FORD FORAY MOTOR GROUP H'CAP 6f 213y
7:20 (7:20) (Class 5) (0-75,77) 3-Y-O

£3,737 (£1,112; £555; £400; £400; £400) **Stalls** Low

Form RPR

1024 **1** **Song Of The Isles (IRE)**[28] 5380 3-8-9 66........................ JaneElliott(3) 6 78
(Heather Main) *trckd ldrs: rdn to ld over 1f out: kpt on strly and sn in command* **16/1**

-225 **2** *3* **Quarry Beach**[15] 5863 3-9-3 71........................ CharlesBishop 5 75
(Henry Candy) *racd keenly in tch: rdn and hdwy over 1f out: r.o to go 2nd fnl 120yds: no threat to wnr* **5/1**[3]

3624 **3** *2 1/4* **James Park Woods (IRE)**[20] 5688 3-9-7 75........................ JamieSpencer 1 73
(Ralph Beckett) *slowly away: sn rousted along: led after 1f: rdn over 2f out: hdd over 1f out: no ex fnl 120yds* **5/2**[1]

3025 **4** *1 1/4* **Balata Bay**[16] 5813 3-9-4 72........................(b) SeanLevey 7 67
(Richard Hannon) *hld up: rdn and stdy prog fnl 2f: nvr gng pce to get involved but kpt on to go 4th nring fin* **8/1**

6302 **5** *hd* **Hey Ho Let's Go**[27] 5431 3-8-9 63........................(h) OisinMurphy 4 57
(Clive Cox) *led for 1f: trckd ldr: rdn over 2f out: kpt on same pce fnl f: lost 4th nring fin* **11/2**

1555 **6** *2 1/4* **Jungle Juice (IRE)**[22] 5573 3-9-9 77........................ FrannyNorton 3 65
(Mick Channon) *trckd ldrs: rdn over 2f out: sn one pce: fdd ins fnl f* **14/1**

5-32 **7** *12* **Just My Type**[50] 4554 3-9-6 74........................ JackMitchell 2 30
(Roger Varian) *trckd ldrs: rdn over 2f out: sn wknd (jockey said filly was never travelling)* **3/1**[2]

3-56 **8** *3/4* **Deference**[16] 5813 3-9-4 72........................ TomMarquand 8 26
(Amanda Perrett) *in last pair: struggling over 3f out: sn btn* **16/1**

1m 28.3s (-0.40) **Going Correction** +0.05s/f (Good) **8 Ran SP% 115.2**
Speed ratings (Par 100): **104,100,98,96,96 93,80,79**
CSF £94.17 CT £274.37 TOTE £14.60: £3.70, £1.70, £1.40; EX 82.40 Trifecta £761.70.
Owner Donald M Kerr **Bred** Seamus Phelan **Trained** Kingston Lisle, Oxon

FOCUS
An ordinary 3yo handicap but a clear pb from the winner, rated around the second.

6419 VENTURE SECURITY H'CAP 1m 6f 44y
7:50 (7:50) (Class 5) (0-75,74) 3-Y-O+

£3,737 (£1,112; £555; £400; £400; £400) **Stalls** Far side

Form RPR

0141 **1** **Cambric**[21] 5623 3-9-6 74........................ OisinMurphy 84+
(Roger Charlton) *in tch: hdwy 3f out: led wl over 1f out: styd on strly fnl f: rdn out* **5/6**[1]

0403 **2** *3/4* **Cogital**[18] 5744 4-9-6 64........................(h) SeanLevey 71
(Amanda Perrett) *hld up in last trio: pushed along and stdy prog fr over 2f out: rdn into 3rd ent fnl f: styd on to go 2nd nring fin* **7/1**[3]

2610 **3** *3/4* **Sufi**[27] 5452 5-9-11 72........................ CameronNoble(3) 78
(Ken Cunningham-Brown) *trckd ldrs: rdn to ld briefly 2f out: styd on but a being hld by wnr fnl f: no ex whn losing 2nd nring fin* **8/1**

2513 **4** *2 1/2* **Victoriano (IRE)**[8] 6125 3-9-5 73........................(b) AdamMcNamara 76
(Archie Watson) *disp ld most of way: rdn over 3f out: hdd 2f out: styd on same pce* **7/2**[2]

3430 **5** *2 3/4* **Fields Of Fortune**[15] 5840 5-9-7 65........................(p) TomMarquand 64
(Alan King) *hld up in last pair: hdwy over 2f out: sn rdn: nt quite pce to mount serious chal: fdd ins fnl f* **9/1**

-00R **6** *4* **Threediamondrings**[10] 6046 6-8-6 53 oh8........................ JaneElliott(3) 46
(Mark Usher) *racd keenly in tch: trckd ldrs over 6f out: rdn over 2f out: ev ch wl over 1f out: wknd ent fnl f* **33/1**

006- **7** *2 1/2* **Bostonian**[63] 1723 9-8-11 62........................(t) ElishaWhittington(7) 52
(Shaun Lycett) *disp ld: rdn 3f out: hdd 2f out: sn wknd (jockey said gelding hung left-handed)* **25/1**

00R0 **8** *1* **Camakasi (IRE)**[59] 4220 8-9-5 63........................(p) CharlesBishop 51
(Ali Stronge) *hld up in rr: rdn 3f out: nvr any imp* **40/1**

3m 10.78s (4.18) **Going Correction** +0.05s/f (Good)
WFA 3 from 4yo+ 10lb **8 Ran SP% 119.6**
Speed ratings (Par 103): **90,89,89,87,86 83,82,81**
CSF £7.96 CT £31.55 TOTE £1.80: £1.10, £2.00, £2.40; EX 7.20 Trifecta £28.40.
Owner D J Deer **Bred** D J And Mrs Deer **Trained** Beckhampton, Wilts

FOCUS
An ordinary staying handicap, but the pace seemed honest enough. The winner is on the upgrade, with the second and third setting the standard.
T/Plt: £425.80 to a £1 stake. Pool: £33,972.49 - 54.77 winning units T/Qpdt: £39.30 to a £1 stake. Pool: £4,786.73 - 90.06 winning units **Tim Mitchell**

6374

YORK (L-H)
Friday, August 23

OFFICIAL GOING: Good to firm (good in places) changing to good to firm after race 2 (2.25)
Wind: Moderate behind Weather: Warm and sunny

6420 SKY BET H'CAP 1m 3f 188y
1:55 (1:55) (Class 2) (0-105,105) 3-Y-O+

£43,575 (£13,048; £6,524; £3,262; £1,631; £819) **Stalls** Centre

Form RPR

2132 **1** **Tamreer**[49] 4599 4-8-8 89........................(h) BenCurtis 9 97
(Roger Fell) *trckd ldrs: hdwy over 2f out: rdn to ld 1 1/2f out: drvn ins fnl f: hld on gamely towards fin* **33/1**

-202 **2** *hd* **Corelli (USA)**[14] 5909 4-9-5 100........................(t) FrankieDettori 13 107
(John Gosden) *looked wl; trckd ldrs: hdwy over 2f out: rdn to chal over 1f out: drvn and ev ch ins fnl f: no ex nr fin* **6/1**[2]

5141 **3** *hd* **Caradoc (IRE)**[11] 6021 4-8-13 94 5ex........................ OisinMurphy 2 101
(Ed Walker) *looked wl; hld up in rr: hdwy 3f out: chsd ldrs over 1f out: sn rdn: styd on strly to chal wl ins fnl f: kpt on (jockey said gelding ran too freely)* **4/1**[1]

31/P **4** *1 1/2* **Gibbs Hill (GER)**[55] 4382 6-9-10 105........................ AndreaAtzeni 7 109+
(Roger Varian) *hld up towards rr: hdwy 4f out: pushed along over 2f out: rdn to chse ldrs over 1f out: drvn and ch ent fnl f: kpt on same pce* **16/1**

1203 **5** *shd* **Epaulement (IRE)**[48] 4646 4-9-7 102........................ RichardKingscote 19 106
(Tom Dascombe) *sweating; led 2f: trckd ldr: led again over 2f out: sn rdn: hdd 1 1/2f out: sn drvn and kpt on same pce* **14/1**

20-4 **6** *1 1/2* **Eynhallow**[13] 5966 5-9-1 96........................ JamesDoyle 12 98
(Charlie Appleby) *sweating; chsd ldng trio: rdn along over 2f out: drvn over 1f out: grad wknd* **10/1**

4026 **7** *nk* **Persian Moon (IRE)**[23] 5541 3-8-9 99........................ SilvestreDeSousa 4 101
(Mark Johnston) *in tch: pushed along on inner 3f out: rdn over 2f out: kpt on same pce* **9/1**

6041 **8** *1 3/4* **Indianapolis (IRE)**[13] 5929 4-9-3 98........................(p) PaulMulrennan 5 96
(James Given) *hld up in midfield: effrt and sme hdwy 3f out: rdn along 2f out: sn drvn and no imp (vet said colt was struck into and lost its right hind shoe)* **16/1**

2102 **9** *1/2* **Jazeel (IRE)**[24] 5519 4-9-2 97........................ JamieSpencer 14 95
(Jedd O'Keeffe) *hld up and bhd: niggled along 4f out: rdn 3f out: hdwy over 2f out: styd on fr over 1f out: nvr nr ldrs* **8/1**

0406 **10** *2 3/4* **Hermoso Mundo (SAF)**[20] 5662 7-9-0 95........................ DavidAllan 8 88
(Hughie Morrison) *chsd ldrs: rdn along 4f out: wknd 3f out* **25/1**

-204 **11** *1/2* **Scarlet Dragon**[20] 5662 6-9-6 101........................(h) TomMarquand 17 93
(Alan King) *hld up: a towards rr* **14/1**

5042 **12** *3/4* **Genetics (FR)**[13] 5929 5-8-12 93........................ GrahamLee 18 84
(Andrew Balding) *prom: led after 2f: rdn along 3f out: sn hdd & wknd* **25/1**

2113 **13** *1* **Mandarin (GER)**[13] 5929 5-8-12 93........................ PJMcDonald 6 83
(Ian Williams) *looked wl; trckd ldrs: pushed along 3f out: rdn over 2f out: sn drvn and wknd (vet said gelding to be lame on its right fore)* **7/1**[3]

2116 **14** *hd* **Anythingtoday (IRE)**[28] 5370 5-9-2 97........................(p) DanielTudhope 10 86
(David O'Meara) *a towards rr* **25/1**

0005 **15** *2* **Restorer**[13] 5929 7-8-13 94........................ JimCrowley 1 80
(Ian Williams) *midfield: effrt on inner over 4f out: rdn along over 3f out: sn btn* **28/1**

5341 **16** *1/2* **Western Duke (IRE)**[27] 5417 5-8-6 87........................ PaddyMathers 20 72
(Ian Williams) *looked wl; hld up: a towards rr* **33/1**

2m 25.4s (-7.80) **Going Correction** -0.15s/f (Firm) course record
WFA 3 from 4yo+ 9lb **16 Ran SP% 123.0**
Speed ratings (Par 109): **109,108,108,107,107 106,106,105,104,103 102,102,101,101,100 99**
CSF £210.70 CT £990.13 TOTE £36.80: £5.80, £2.10, £1.70, £3.70; EX 268.00 Trifecta £3221.30.
Owner Arcane Racing Partnership **Bred** Shadwell Estate Company Limited **Trained** Nawton, N Yorks

FOCUS
With only 10.6mm of rainfall over the past week, conditions were officially described as good to firm (Going Stick reading of 7.3 at 8.30am). Fresh ground was provided with the rail place on its innermost line. Another strong edition of this valuable middle-distance handicap. The winner showed her earlier Listed form did not flatter her, rated to that level.

6421 WEATHERBYS HAMILTON LONSDALE CUP STKS (GROUP 2) (BRITISH CHAMPIONS SERIES) 2m 56y
2:25 (2:25) (Class 1) 3-Y-O+ **£127,597** (£48,375; £24,210; £12,060) **Stalls** Low

Form RPR

-111 **1** **Stradivarius (IRE)**[24] 5522 5-9-6 121........................ FrankieDettori 3 119+
(John Gosden) *trckd ldng pair: hdwy over 2f out: swtchd rt to stands' rail and effrt wl over 1f out: sn led: rdn appr fnl f: kpt on strly* **4/9**[1]

1122 **2** *1 1/4* **Dee Ex Bee**[24] 5522 4-9-3 119........................ SilvestreDeSousa 4 113
(Mark Johnston) *looked wl; set stdy early clip: increased pce after 6f: pushed along and qckdn pce 7f out: rdn along qckdn over 4f out: jnd 3f out: hdd over 2f out: sn drvn: rallied wl u.p fnl f: regained 2nd nr line (vet said colt to have bled from its right nostril in the wash down area, and subsequently on return to the stable yard, was found to have bled from both nostrils)* **3/1**[2]

2-0 **3** *nse* **Il Paradiso (USA)**[33] 5226 3-8-5 103........................(p) WayneLordan 5 113
(A P O'Brien, Ire) *str: looked wl; trckd ldr: hdwy 4f out: cl up 3f out: rdn to take slt ld 2f out: drvn and hdd over 1f out: kpt on u.p fnl f: lost 2nd nr line* **20/1**

3-1 **4** *16* **Falcon Eight (IRE)**[48] 4670 4-9-3 111........................(p) OisinMurphy 2 94
(D K Weld, Ire) *hld up in tch: pushed along over 4f out: sn rdn along and outpcd fnl 3f (vet said colt had a small amount of blood in its right nostril)* **12/1**[3]

3m 27.06s (-6.84) **Going Correction** -0.15s/f (Firm) course record
WFA 3 from 4yo+ 12lb **4 Ran SP% 106.7**
Speed ratings (Par 115): **111,110,110,102**
CSF £1.96 TOTE £1.20; EX 1.70 Trifecta £6.30.
Owner B E Nielsen **Bred** Bjorn Nielsen **Trained** Newmarket, Suffolk

The Form Book Flat 2019, Raceform Ltd, Newbury, RG14 5SJ

FOCUS
Little else should have been expected other than another win for staying great Stradivarius, who completed the Weatherby's Hamilton's 1,000,000GBP bonus for a second straight season. The level is a bit fluid. If the runner-up was to be rated to form then the third would be among the leading middle-distance 3yos, so the race has been rated cautiously with the winner not need to improve despite carrying a penalty. The third is the key.

6422 AL BASTI EQUIWORLD DUBAI GIMCRACK STKS (GROUP 2) (C&G) 6f

3:00 (3:02) (Class 1) 2-Y-O

£127,597 (£48,375; £24,210; £12,060; £6,052; £3,037) **Stalls** High

Form RPR

122 **1** **Threat (IRE)**[22] 5584 2-9-0 111........................ OisinMurphy 6 112
(Richard Hannon) *trckd ldrs: smooth hdwy over 2f out: sn cl up: rdn to ld jst over 1f out: kpt on strly* **11/10**[1]

1061 **2** 1 1/4 **Lord Of The Lodge (IRE)**[15] 5845 2-9-0 95........................ BenCurtis 8 108
(K R Burke) *led: rdn along over 2f out: drvn and hdd jst over 1f out: kpt on u.p fnl f* **16/1**

14 **3** 2 3/4 **Repartee (IRE)**[35] 5134 2-9-0 0........................ AndreaAtzeni 5 100
(Kevin Ryan) *compact; cl up: rdn along 2f out: sn ev ch: drvn over 1f out: kpt on same pce (jockey said colt hung right under pressure)* **11/2**[2]

11 **4** 1 **Malotru**[61] 4172 2-9-0 0........................ GeraldMosse 10 97+
(Marco Botti) *str; looked wl; towards rr: hdwy 2f out: swtchd rt and rdn over 1f out: styd on wl fnl f* **20/1**

316 **5** 1 **Summer Sands**[65] 3988 2-9-0 96........................ BarryMcHugh 12 94
(Richard Fahey) *chsd ldrs: rdn along and outpcd wl over 1f out: kpt on u.p fnl f* **16/1**

6 **6** nk **Pistoletto (USA)**[34] 5206 2-9-0 0........................ RyanMoore 4 93
(A P O'Brien, Ire) *str; hld up towards rr: smooth hdwy on outer 1/2-way: chsd ldrs 2f out: sn cl up: rdn and wknd fnl f* **16/1**

21 **7** 2 3/4 **Byline**[35] 5118 2-9-0 0........................ KevinStott 1 85
(Kevin Ryan) *athletic; chsd ldrs: rdn along over 2f out: sn drvn and wknd* **25/1**

411 **8** 1/2 **Spartan Fighter**[42] 4889 2-9-0 94........................ DanielTudhope 7 83
(Declan Carroll) *str; looked wl; hld up towards rr: effrt and sme hdwy over 2f out: sn rdn: n.d* **10/1**[3]

3026 **9** 1 3/4 **Misty Grey (IRE)**[22] 5584 2-9-0 99........................ JoeFanning 11 78
(Mark Johnston) *chsd ldrs: rdn along wl over 2f out: sn wknd* **33/1**

101 **10** 2 **Iffraaz (IRE)**[50] 4564 2-9-0 90........................ JamesDoyle 2 72
(Mark Johnston) *towards rr: rdn along bef 1/2-way: sn outpcd* **20/1**

2133 **11** 14 **Dubai Station**[26] 5481 2-9-0 101........................ FrankieDettori 13 30
(K R Burke) *in tch: rdn along 1/2-way: sn wknd (jockey said colt lost its action; vet said colt to be lame on its right hind)* **12/1**

21 **12** 9 **Abstemious**[27] 5456 2-9-0 0........................ JamieSpencer 14 +
(Kevin Ryan) *tall; cl up: rdn along wl over 2f out: sn wknd (trainer's rep said gelding found the good to firm ground too quick)* **14/1**

1m 9.62s (-1.98) **Going Correction** -0.15s/f (Firm) **12 Ran SP% 120.4**
Speed ratings (Par 106): **107,105,101,100,99 98,94,94,91,89 70,58**
CSF £20.49 CT £77.94 TOTE £1.90: £1.10, £4.10, £1.80; EX 21.50 Trifecta £114.90.

Owner Cheveley Park Stud **Bred** La Lumiere Partnership **Trained** East Everleigh, Wilts

FOCUS
This revolved around Threat, who was clear on ratings and had twice gone close at this level. The further he went, the better and he looks a likely candidate for next year's 2,000 Guineas. He has been rated to the ten-year race par.

6423 COOLMORE NUNTHORPE STKS (GROUP 1) (BRITISH CHAMPIONS SERIES) 5f

3:35 (3:37) (Class 1) 2-Y-O+

£226,840 (£86,000; £43,040; £21,440; £10,760; £5,400) **Stalls** Centre

Form RPR

-121 **1** **Battaash (IRE)**[21] 5611 5-9-11 123........................ JimCrowley 1 129
(Charles Hills) *sweating; cl up: led 2f out: rdn and qcknd clr over 1f out: impressive* **7/4**[2]

-334 **2** 3 3/4 **Soldier's Call**[33] 5222 3-9-9 114........................ DanielTudhope 4 116
(Archie Watson) *cl up: led 3f out: rdn along and jnd over 2f out: sn hdd: chsd wnr and drvn ins fnl f: no imp* **20/1**

1050 **3** 1 **So Perfect (USA)**[19] 5716 3-9-6 106........................ WayneLordan 6 109+
(A P O'Brien, Ire) *towards rr: hdwy 2f out: rdn wl over 1f out: kpt on fnl f* **25/1**

-134 **4** 1 **Mabs Cross**[66] 3950 5-9-8 114........................ GeraldMosse 5 105
(Michael Dods) *towards rr: rdn along 1/2-way: hdwy wl over 1f out: kpt on fnl f* **5/1**[3]

0210 **5** 1/2 **Copper Knight (IRE)**[21] 5611 5-9-11 106........................(t) DavidAllan 7 107
(Tim Easterby) *chsd ldrs: rdn along 2f out: sn drvn and kpt on one pce* **40/1**

-541 **6** 1 1/4 **Ten Sovereigns (IRE)**[41] 4923 3-9-9 122........................ RyanMoore 11 102
(A P O'Brien, Ire) *trckd ldrs: hdwy to chse ldng pair 2f out: rdn over 1f out: sn drvn and wknd* **13/8**[1]

1630 **7** 1 **Ornate**[20] 5664 6-9-11 103........................ PhilDennis 3 98
(David C Griffiths) *sweating; led 2f: cl up: rdn along over 2f out: grad wknd* **66/1**

1125 **8** 2 1/4 **El Astronaute (IRE)**[21] 5611 6-9-11 109........................ JasonHart 9 90
(John Quinn) *chsd ldrs: rdn along over 2f out: sn drvn and wknd* **33/1**

-004 **9** nk **Rumble Inthejungle (IRE)**[21] 5611 3-9-9 104........................ OisinMurphy 10 89
(Richard Spencer) *a towards rr* **66/1**

5653 **10** 2 1/2 **Fairyland (IRE)**[41] 4923 3-9-6 110........................ DonnachaO'Brien 2 77
(A P O'Brien, Ire) *dwlt: a towards rr* **11/1**

1123 **11** 1 1/4 **Garrus (IRE)**[33] 5222 3-9-9 109........................ KieranShoemark 12 76
(Charles Hills) *dwlt: a in rr* **33/1**

55.9s (-2.30) **Going Correction** -0.15s/f (Firm) course record **11 Ran SP% 119.4**
WFA 3 from 5yo+ 2lb
Speed ratings: **112,106,104,102,102 100,98,94,94,90 88**
CSF £41.36 CT £684.36 TOTE £2.50: £1.20, £4.10, £5.80; EX 37.90 Trifecta £432.90.

Owner Hamdan Al Maktoum **Bred** Ballyphilip Stud **Trained** Lambourn, Berks

FOCUS
This is a test for only the purest of speedsters when the ground is quick and two of those came to the fore here, with the King's Stand two-three finishing one-two this time. It wasn't close, though, with the winner bolting up - in a new course record, lowering Dayjur's mark from 1990 by 0.26sec - and he has been rated back to his best. There is even a case for rating this a bit higher and this was the best figure in the race since Oasis Dream in 2003.

6424 BRITISH STALLION STUDS EBF CONVIVIAL MAIDEN STKS (PLUS 10 RACE) 7f

4:15 (4:17) (Class 2) 2-Y-O

£43,575 (£13,048; £6,524; £3,262; £1,631; £819) **Stalls** Low

Form RPR

2 **1** **Molatham**[28] 5367 2-9-5 0........................ JimCrowley 5 90+
(Roger Varian) *looked wl; trckd ldrs: hdwy on inner and cl up over 2f out: chal and rdn over 1f out: drvn to ld ins fnl f: kpt on wl towards fin* **2/1**[1]

02 **2** nk **Celtic Art (FR)**[20] 5665 2-9-5 0........................ PJMcDonald 7 89
(Paul Cole) *str; chsd ldr: hdwy and cl up over 2f out: led wl over 1f out: sn jnd and rdn: drvn and hdd ins fnl f: kpt on wl u.p towards fin* **9/1**

2 **3** 2 1/4 **Dubai Mirage (IRE)**[15] 5860 2-9-5 0........................ OisinMurphy 14 83+
(Saeed bin Suroor) *compact; in tch: hdwy on outer over 2f out: rdn wl over 1f out: styd on to chse ldng pair ins fnl f: sn edgd lft and no imp (jockey said colt hung left)* **7/2**[3]

4 4 1/2 **Pot Of Paint** 2-9-5 0........................ RichardKingscote 12 71+
(Tom Dascombe) *athletic; green and in rr: hdwy over 2f out: pushed along wl over 1f out: n.m.r over 1f out: styd on strly fnl f: nrst fin (jockey said colt ran green)* **66/1**

42 **5** 1 **African Swift (USA)**[9] 6072 2-9-0 0........................ JoeFanning 16 63
(Mark Johnston) *wnt rt s: chsd ldrs on outer: rdn along 2f out: drvn over 1f out: grad wknd* **40/1**

6 1/2 **Gift Of Kings** 2-9-5 0........................ JamieSpencer 4 67+
(Kevin Ryan) *str; towards rr: hdwy over 2f out: sn rdn and kpt on fnl f* **33/1**

444 **7** 1 1/4 **Zuckerberg (IRE)**[17] 5764 2-9-5 70........................ TomMarquand 8 64
(Ivan Furtado) *led: rdn along and jnd over 2f out: sn hdd: drvn and wknd* **100/1**

0 **8** 1/2 **Station To Station**[34] 5186 2-9-5 0........................ AdamKirby 6 62
(Clive Cox) *unfurnished; in tch: hdwy to chse ldrs over 2f out: sn rdn and wknd over 1f out* **33/1**

9 1 3/4 **Western Hero (IRE)** 2-9-5 0........................ DanielTudhope 13 60+
(Kevin Ryan) *compact; chsd ldrs: rdn along over 2f out: sn wknd (jockey said colt hung left)* **20/1**

3 **10** 1 1/2 **Fox Duty Free (IRE)**[34] 5186 2-9-5 0........................ SilvestreDeSousa 11 53
(Andrew Balding) *str; looked wl; dwlt and in rr: hdwy over 2f out: rdn along wl over 1f out: kpt on: n.d* **3/1**[2]

3 **11** 1/2 **Afro Blue (IRE)**[14] 5908 2-9-5 0........................ AndreaAtzeni 9 52
(Richard Hannon) *compact; chsd ldrs: rdn along 3f out: sn wknd* **20/1**

12 nk **Cruyff** 2-9-5 0........................ HarryBentley 2 51
(Richard Spencer) *str; nvr bttr than midfield* **25/1**

13 1/2 **Kumasi** 2-9-5 0........................ JamesDoyle 15 50
(David O'Meara) *str; bit bkward; a towards rr* **33/1**

14 5 **Cabot Cliffs (IRE)** 2-9-5 0........................ PaulHanagan 10 36
(Charles Hills) *athletic; a towards rr* **66/1**

1m 23.04s (-1.56) **Going Correction** -0.15s/f (Firm) **14 Ran SP% 119.2**
Speed ratings (Par 100): **102,101,99,93,92 92,90,90,88,86 85,85,85,79**
CSF £18.83 TOTE £2.70: £1.30, £2.30, £1.50; EX 19.10 Trifecta £62.00.

Owner Hamdan Al Maktoum **Bred** Cheveley Park Stud Ltd **Trained** Newmarket, Suffolk

■ Dulas was withdrawn. Price at time of withdrawal 16-1. Rule 4 does not apply

FOCUS
The richest maiden run anywhere in Britain. The first three pulled clear and it looks strong form.

6425 NATIONWIDE ACCIDENT REPAIR SERVICES H'CAP 7f 192y

4:50 (4:52) (Class 2) (0-105,103) 3-Y-O

£43,575 (£13,048; £6,524; £3,262; £1,631; £409) **Stalls** Low

Form RPR

1000 **1** **Pogo (IRE)**[20] 5666 3-9-3 **99**........................ KieranShoemark 3 108
(Charles Hills) *trckd ldrs: hdwy and cl up over 2f out: rdn to chal over 1f out: drvn ins fnl f: kpt on gamely to ld nr fin* **12/1**

114 **2** nk **Vitralite (IRE)**[35] 5128 3-8-12 **94**........................ BenCurtis 10 102
(K R Burke) *str; led: pushed along over 2f out: rdn and jnd over 1f out: drvn ins fnl f: edgd lft: hdd and no ex nr fin* **11/1**

0430 **3** 1 **Fanaar (IRE)**[27] 5413 3-9-4 **100**........................(bt) JimCrowley 7 106+
(William Haggas) *looked wl; hld up in rr: hdwy 3f out: rdn to chse ldrs over 1f out: drvn and ev ch ins fnl f: kpt on same pce towards fin* **8/1**[2]

-511 **4** 1 3/4 **Seductive Moment (GER)**[27] 5445 3-8-12 **94**........................ JoeFanning 13 96
(Mark Johnston) *trckd ldr: rdn along over 2f out: drvn over 1f out: kpt on same pce* **14/1**

1210 **5** hd **Biometric**[21] 5609 3-9-5 **101**........................ HarryBentley 16 102
(Ralph Beckett) *trckd ldrs on outer: pushed along and hdwy over 2f out: rdn wl over 1f out: drvn ent fnl f: kpt on same pce* **8/1**[2]

4040 **6** 1/2 **Dark Vision (IRE)**[21] 5610 3-9-7 **103**........................(b) JamesDoyle 4 103
(Mark Johnston) *t.k.h and hmpd sn after s: in rr: hdwy on inner 3f out: chsd ldrs 2f out: rdn and ch over 1f out: sn drvn and grad wknd fnl f* **4/1**[1]

-253 **6** dht **Boston George (IRE)**[25] 5488 3-8-5 **87**........................ ShaneGray 2 87+
(Keith Dalgleish) *hld up towards rr: hdwy 3f out: chsd ldrs 2f out: rdn over 1f out: drvn and no imp fnl f* **16/1**

1160 **8** nse **Coolagh Forest (IRE)**[22] 5583 3-8-9 **91**........................ PaulHanagan 5 91
(Richard Fahey) *t.k.h: chsd ldrs: n.m.r and hmpd 1/2-way: rdn along over 2f out: sn drvn and kpt on same pce* **25/1**

0511 **9** 3/4 **Edaraat**[23] 5557 3-8-7 **89**........................ AndreaAtzeni 12 87
(Roger Varian) *hld up in rr: n.m.r and hmpd 1/2-way: sn swtchd rt to outer: hdwy and in tch over 2f out: rdn wl over 1f out: kpt on same pce* **9/1**[3]

2420 **10** shd **King Of Tonga (IRE)**[55] 4403 3-8-6 **88**........................ CamHardie 8 86
(David O'Meara) *hld up: a towards rr* **28/1**

51-6 **11** 1 **Jonah Jones (IRE)**[13] 5953 3-8-11 **93**........................ RichardKingscote 1 89
(Tom Dascombe) *chsd ldrs: rdn along 3f out: drvn 2f out: sn wknd* **14/1**

2432 **12** hd **Hold Still (IRE)**[18] 5749 3-7-12 **85** oh2 ow3........................ FayeMcManoman[(5)] 6 80
(William Muir) *t.k.h: chsd ldrs: n.m.r and hmpd 5f out: pushed along over 3f out: sn rdn and wknd 2f out (jockey said colt was short of room in the early stages)* **28/1**

2145 **13** 1/2 **Archaeology**[56] 4325 3-8-0 **82**........................(w) PaddyMathers 15 76
(Jedd O'Keeffe) *rrd and dwlt s: sn swtchd lft: hld up: a in rr* **16/1**

3242 **14** nk **Fastman (IRE)**[20] 5685 3-8-8 **90**........................ JasonHart 9 83
(David O'Meara) *looked wl; hld up: hdwy 3f out: rdn over 2f out: sn drvn and n.d* **11/1**

1321 **15** *shd* **Spirit Warning**[12] 5991 3-8-8 95 6ex.................... WilliamCarver(5) 11 88
(Andrew Balding) *hld up: effrt and sme hdwy 3f out: rdn along over 2f out: n.d (jockey said gelding ran too freely)* **16/1**

0211 **16** *7* **Irv (IRE)**[28] 5398 3-8-3 85.................... JamesSullivan 14 62
(Micky Hammond) *looked wl; plld hrd: chsd ldrs: hung lft and rt 5f out: sn lost pl: hung lft 4f out: sn outpcd (jockey said gelding ran too freely)* **10/1**

1m 34.95s (-2.55) **Going Correction** -0.15s/f (Firm) course record **16 Ran SP% 127.4**
Speed ratings (Par 106): 106,105,104,102,102 102,102,102,101,101 100,100,99,99,99 92
CSF £141.15 CT £1183.17 TOTE £16.60: £3.40, £3.50, £2.80, £2.10; EX 184.10 Trifecta £2000.40.
Owner Gary And Linnet Woodward **Bred** Thomas Foy **Trained** Lambourn, Berks

FOCUS
A good-quality, competitive 3yo handicap in which it paid to race prominently. The third, therefore, can have his effort upgraded.
T/Jkpt: £31,960.00 to a £1 stake. Pool: £45,014.18 - 1 winning unit T/Plt: £58.60 to a £1 stake. Pool: £258,224.10 - 3,214.86 winning units T/Qpdt: £20.60 to a £1 stake. Pool: £21,033.80 - 753.58 winning units **Joe Rowntree**

6426 - 6428a (Foreign Racing) - See Raceform Interactive

6188 CURRAGH (R-H)
Friday, August 23

OFFICIAL GOING: Straight course - yielding; round course - good to yielding

6429a DEBUTANTE STKS (GROUP 2) (FILLIES) 7f
6:40 (6:41) 2-Y-O
£61,126 (£19,684; £9,324; £4,144; £2,072; £1,036)

RPR

1 **Alpine Star (IRE)**[21] 5636 2-9-0 0.................... ShaneFoley 2 107
(Mrs John Harrington, Ire) *chsd ldrs: 4th 3f out: effrt far side under 2f out: r.o wl u.p in 2nd wl ins fnl f to ld fnl strides* **2/1**[2]

2 *shd* **Petite Mustique (IRE)**[24] 5533 2-9-0 0.................... DonnachaO'Brien 8 107
(A P O'Brien, Ire) *chsd ldrs: 3rd 3f out: hdwy nr side to chal over 1f out and sn led narrowly: strly pressed wl ins fnl f and hdd fnl strides* **9/1**[3]

3 *¾* **Soul Search (IRE)**[34] 5206 2-9-0 0.................... ColinKeane 1 105
(G M Lyons, Ire) *dwlt sltly: settled in rr of mid-div: 7th bef 1/2-way: swtchd rt over 2f out and tk clsr order: sn rdn bhd ldrs and almost on terms u.p far side ins fnl f: no ex in 3rd nr fin* **10/1**

4 *1* **So Wonderful (USA)**[29] 5361 2-9-0 95.................... WayneLordan 9 102
(A P O'Brien, Ire) *hld up in mid-div: 6th 3f out: drvn 1 1/2f out and r.o u.p ins fnl f into 4th: nvr trbld ldrs* **20/1**

5 *1* **Love (IRE)**[29] 5361 2-9-0 105.................... RyanMoore 5 100
(A P O'Brien, Ire) *prom tl sn settled bhd ldr in cl 2nd: disp ld fr 1/2-way: drvn to ld 2f out tl hdd u.p ent fnl f: no ex and wknd ins fnl f: jst hld 5th* **6/4**[1]

6 *shd* **Tango (IRE)**[56] 4352 2-9-0 92.................... SeamieHeffernan 7 99
(A P O'Brien, Ire) *settled in rr: pushed along 3f out and no imp u.p in 8th over 1f out: r.o far side ins fnl f: jst failed for 5th: nrst fin* **16/1**

7 *½* **Know It All**[14] 5921 2-9-0 0.................... ChrisHayes 3 98
(J P Murtagh, Ire) *hld up in mid-div: 5th 3f out: swtchd rt under 2f out and sn rdn bhd ldrs: n.m.r briefly ins fnl f where swtchd: no ex nr fin where dropped to 7th* **20/1**

8 *5 ½* **Windracer (IRE)**[29] 5361 2-9-0 0.................... NGMcCullagh 6 84
(Mrs John Harrington, Ire) *sn led tl jnd fr 1/2-way: drvn and hdd 2f out: no ex u.p over 1f out: sn wknd* **14/1**

9 *½* **French Rain (IRE)**[33] 5220 2-9-0 0.................... GaryCarroll 4 82
(G M Lyons, Ire) *towards rr: 8th 3f out: drvn and swtchd rt over 2f out: no ex u.p under 2f out: sn wknd* **16/1**

1m 27.08s (2.08) **Going Correction** +0.475s/f (Yiel) **9 Ran SP% 120.4**
Speed ratings: 107,106,106,104,103 103,103,96,96
CSF £21.86 TOTE £2.70: £1.20, £2.90, £2.80; DF 26.00 Trifecta £116.90.
Owner Niarchos Family **Bred** Niarchos Family **Trained** Moone, Co Kildare

FOCUS
A tremendous finish served up by two talented fillies and the winner got the job done despite looking outpaced most of the way. She got a quote of 33-1 for next year's 1,000 Guineas but, at this juncture, she'd look to be more of an Oaks type. The first four have been rated as progressing significantly.

6430a GALILEO IRISH EBF FUTURITY STKS (GROUP 2) 7f
7:10 (7:12) 2-Y-O
£69,099 (£22,252; £10,540; £4,684; £2,342; £1,171)

RPR

1 **Armory (IRE)**[29] 5362 2-9-3 108.................... RyanMoore 4 110+
(A P O'Brien, Ire) *chsd ldrs: disp 4th at 1/2-way: pushed along and tk clsr order between horses 2f out: rdn and qcknd wl to ld 1 1/2f out: kpt on wl ins fnl f* **4/6**[1]

2 *¾* **Rebel Tale (USA)**[12] 5997 2-9-3 88.................... BenCoen 3 108
(Andrew Slattery, Ire) *chsd ldrs early: 6th 1/2-way: pushed along bhd ldrs over 2f out where n.m.r briefly: sn rdn and r.o wl to press wnr in 2nd wl ins fnl f: a hld* **50/1**

3 *1* **Geometrical (IRE)**[9] 6087 2-9-3 0.................... KevinManning 9 105
(J S Bolger, Ire) *w.w: disp 4th at 1/2-way: drvn over 2f out and no imp on wnr u.p disputing 3rd nr side wl ins fnl f where edgd sltly rt: kpt on wl* **14/1**

4 *½* **Roman Turbo (IRE)**[34] 5206 2-9-3 100.................... RonanWhelan 5 104
(M Halford, Ire) *chsd ldrs and racd keenly early: 7th 1/2-way: stl gng wl under 2f out where n.m.r briefly: hdwy over 1f out where rdn: wnt 2nd briefly ins fnl f tl sn no ex and dropped to 4th* **9/1**

5 *2* **Justifier (IRE)**[12] 5997 2-9-3 0....................(t) ColinKeane 6 100
(G M Lyons, Ire) *sn chsd ldrs: clsr in 3rd at 1/2-way: drvn nr side 2f out and no ex u.p ins fnl f: one pce in 5th wl ins fnl f where sltly hmpd* **11/2**[3]

6 *2* **Jungle Cove (IRE)**[34] 5203 2-9-3 0.................... ShaneFoley 8 94
(Mrs John Harrington, Ire) *dwlt: settled in rr: last at 1/2-way: pushed along under 2f out and sme hdwy u.p into 6th ins fnl f: no ex and one pce clsng stages* **25/1**

7 *3 ½* **Iberia (IRE)**[34] 5203 2-9-3 0.................... DonnachaO'Brien 2 87
(A P O'Brien, Ire) *prom tl sn settled bhd ldr: cl 2nd at 1/2-way: pushed along and led narrowly fr 2f out: sn rdn and hdd 1 1/2f out: wknd ins fnl f where hmpd and checked: eased in 7th clsng stages* **4/1**[2]

8 *2* **Toronto (IRE)**[29] 5362 2-9-3 97.................... SeamieHeffernan 1 79
(A P O'Brien, Ire) *sn led: narrow advantage at 1/2-way: pushed along and hdd fr 2f out: sn rdn and wknd over 1f out: eased in rr ins fnl f* **20/1**

1m 28.03s (3.03) **Going Correction** +0.475s/f (Yiel) **8 Ran SP% 122.6**
Speed ratings: 101,100,99,98,96 93,89,87
CSF £61.41 TOTE £1.40: £1.02, £6.90, £3.80; DF 45.50 Trifecta £395.80.
Owner Mrs John Magnier & Michael Tabor & Derrick Smith **Bred** Coolmore **Trained** Cashel, Co Tipperary

FOCUS
Aidan O'Brien has won this race with high-class colts Anthony Van Dyck, Gleneagles and Giant's Causeway, and Armory completed Futurity win number 13 for team Ballydoyle with something. This rates an average renewal but the winner looks like he has more to offer.

6431 - 6432a (Foreign Racing) - See Raceform Interactive

6328 DEAUVILLE (R-H)
Friday, August 23

OFFICIAL GOING: Polytrack: standard; turf: good

6433a PRIX DU QUARTIER SAINT-FRANCOIS (MAIDEN) (2YO COLTS & GELDINGS) (ROUND COURSE) (TURF) 1m (R)
1:20 2-Y-O
£11,261 (£4,504; £3,378; £2,252; £1,126)

RPR

1 **Wally (IRE)**[21] 5642 2-9-2 0.................... ChristopheSoumillon 7 85+
(J-C Rouget, France) **8/5**[1]

2 *hd* **Dyami (FR)**[20] 5665 2-9-2 0.................... TheoBachelot 6 84+
(George Baker) *broke wl: sn led: rdn w 1 l ld 1f out: kpt on bravely whn jnd ins fnl f: hdd last stride* **8/1**

3 *3 ½* **Lionel (FR)**[21] 5642 2-9-2 0....................(p) FabriceVeron 1 76
(C Lerner, France) **11/1**

4 *¾* **Firstman (FR)**[32] 2-9-2 0.................... CristianDemuro 5 75
(J-C Rouget, France) **12/5**[2]

5 *¾* **Inca Man (FR)**[22] 5572 2-9-2 0.................... TonyPiccone 4 73
(Paul Cole) *reluctant to enter stalls: wl away: sn taken bk to midfield: outpcd and pushed along in fnl trio 3f out: rdn and swtchd lft 1 1/2f out: late hdwy fnl 100yds: nt trble ldrs* **39/10**[3]

6 *1 ¼* **Mr Shady (IRE)**[8] 6141 2-8-10 0....................(p) AlexisPouchin(6) 3 70
(J S Moore) *racd in midfield: nudged along in fnl trio 3f out: rdn and no imp fnl 2f: styd on one pce* **29/1**

7 *5* **Reux**[17] 2-9-2 0.................... AurelienLemaitre 2 59
(F Head, France) **10/1**

1m 41.39s (0.59) **7 Ran SP% 120.2**
PARI-MUTUEL (all including 1 euro stake): WIN 2.60; PLACE 1.40, 2.50, 2.30; DF 8.60.
Owner Ecurie Jean-Pierre Barjon **Bred** Ecurie Haras Du Cadran, Sas I.E.I. & C Lerner **Trained** Pau, France

6434a PRIX TOM LANE (CONDITIONS) (APPRENTICE & YOUNG JOCKEYS) (4YO+) (ALL-WEATHER TRACK) (POLYTRACK) 7f 110y(P)
5:25 4-Y-0+
£9,009 (£3,603; £2,702; £1,801; £900)

RPR

1 **Be My Prince (GER)**[113] 5-8-6 0.................... HugoBesnier(5) 5 75
(Frau S Weis, Germany) **22/1**

2 *1 ½* **Cassard (FR)**[63] 4-8-8 0....................(b) DamienBoche(6) 11 74
(P Monfort, France) **9/1**

3 *3* **Patchewollock (IRE)**[141] 5-8-6 0.................... AugustinMadamet(5) 4 64
(G Nicot, France) **43/5**

4 *nk* **Cape Greco (USA)**[46] 4747 4-8-13 0.................... MathieuPelletan(3) 8 68
(Jo Hughes, France) *hld up towards rr of midfield: pushed along 2 1/2f out: sn rdn and styd on: nt pce to get on terms w ldrs: drvn out* **15/1**

5 *¾* **Its All Class (FR)**[416] 9-8-7 0....................(p) MlleAmbreMolins(9) 3 66
(J Reynier, France) **68/10**[3]

6 *¾* **We Ride The World (IRE)**[13] 4-9-3 0....................(p) QuentinPerrette(5) 10 70
(Amandine Baudron, France) **14/1**

7 *1 ½* **Pegasus**[47] 4-9-1 0.................... ThomasTrullier(3) 7 63
(A Kleinkorres, Germany) **43/10**[2]

8 *4* **Jeremiade (FR)**[71] 4-8-5 0.................... BenjaminMarie(5) 9 45
(Mme J Hendriks, Holland) **42/1**

9 *2 ½* **Shams Brazilero (IRE)**[494] 5-8-3 0.................... MlleLeaBails(8) 6 39
(Andrea Marcialis, France) **21/10**[1]

10 *3 ½* **Beaupreau**[13] 7-9-7 0....................(b) MlleAnnaVanDenTroost(4) 2 45
(T Van Den Troost, Belgium) **7/1**

11 *10* **Signs Of Success (IRE)**[55] 6-8-8 0....................(p) JenteMarien(6) 1 9
(Mme J Hendriks, Holland) **33/1**

1m 27.68s **11 Ran SP% 119.4**
PARI-MUTUEL (all including 1 euro stake): WIN 23.10; PLACE 5.60, 3.30, 2.90; DF 128.60.
Owner Lebeau Racing **Bred** Frau Marlene Haller **Trained** Germany

6387 CHELMSFORD (A.W) (L-H)
Saturday, August 24

OFFICIAL GOING: Polytrack: standard
Wind: light breeze Weather: mostly sunny, very warm

6435 BET TOTEPLACEPOT AT TOTESPORT.COM NURSERY H'CAP 1m (P)
2:00 (2:01) (Class 6) (0-60,55) 2-Y-O
£3,428 (£1,020; £509; £300; £300; £300) Stalls Low

Form RPR

0022 **1** **Luna Wish**[10] 6071 2-9-1 49.................... JimmyQuinn 6 61+
(George Margarson) *prom: led 2f out: drvn 3 l clr 1f out: c further clr fnl f: easily* **7/4**[1]

060 **2** *4* **Inflamed**[13] 5980 2-9-7 55.................... LiamKeniry 2 57
(Ed Walker) *trckd ldr: pushed along over 2f out: rdn in 3rd over 1f out: kpt on into 2nd fnl f: nvr nr wnr* **2/1**[2]

0500 **3** *2 ½* **Broughtons Compass**[10] 6071 2-8-13 47.................... JoeyHaynes 5 43
(Mark Hoad) *hld up: drvn in 4th 2f out: rdn over 1f out: kpt on into 3rd fnl f* **10/1**

0065 **4** *nk* **Timon (IRE)**[10] 6071 2-9-6 54....................(p[1]) AdamMcNamara 4 50
(Mick Channon) *led: pushed along over 2f out: rdn and hdd 2f out: grad wknd* **4/1**[3]

056 **5** *2* **Halfacrown (IRE)**[15] 5887 2-9-4 52.................... GeorgeWood 1 43
(Jamie Osborne) *hld up: drvn 2f out: rdn over 1f out: no imp* **8/1**

006 **6** *10* **Cersei Lannister (IRE)**[31] 5295 2-8-12 46....................(v) KieranO'Neill 3 14
(Adrian Nicholls) *slowly away: bhd: rdn on outer over 2f out: lost tch over 1f out* **11/1**

1m 39.82s (-0.08) **Going Correction** -0.225s/f (Stan) **6 Ran SP% 118.2**
Speed ratings (Par 92): 91,87,84,84,82 72
CSF £6.00 TOTE £2.10: £1.40, £1.30; EX 8.80 Trifecta £25.70.
Owner F Butler **Bred** E Cantillon **Trained** Newmarket, Suffolk

FOCUS
This weak nursery was won easily by the market leader.

6436 BET TOTEEXACTA AT TOTESPORT.COM NURSERY H'CAP 5f (P)
2:35 (2:35) (Class 4) (0-80,81) 2-Y-O
£6,145 (£1,828; £913; £456; £300; £300) **Stalls Low**

Form | RPR
563 **1** **She Can Dance**[43] 4889 2-9-7 **77**........ SamJames 5 84
(Kevin Ryan) *hld up on outer: pushed along and hdwy 1 1/2f out: rdn to ld ent fnl f: sn clr: comf* **4/1**[3]
4100 **2** 2 1/4 **Dazzling Des (IRE)**[32] 5275 2-9-11 **81**........ LiamKeniry 3 80
(David O'Meara) *hld up in rr: drvn and hdwy 1 1/2f out: rdn to chal 1f out: kpt on fnl f: nt pce of wnr* **9/2**
0501 **3** hd **Crime Of Passion (IRE)**[11] 6041 2-8-11 **67**........ GeorgeWood 2 65
(Jamie Osborne) *hld up: trckd ldrs 2f out: drvn to chal 1 1/2f out: rdn and ev ch 1f out: one pce fnl f* **4/1**[3]
3526 **4** 1 1/4 **Point Of Order**[8] 6158 2-9-6 **76**........ AdamMcNamara 4 70
(Archie Watson) *disp ld tl rdn to ld on own 1 1/2f out: hdd ent fnl f: wknd last 150yds* **7/2**[2]
1521 **5** 1 **Dandizette (IRE)**[32] 5275 2-8-11 **74**........ LauraCoughlan(7) 6 64
(Adrian Nicholls) *disp ld tl rdn and hdd 1 1/2f out: sn wknd* **11/4**[1]
0645 **6** 1/2 **Hollaback Girl**[17] 5800 2-8-4 **60**........(p) KieranO'Neill 1 48
(Richard Spencer) *trckd ldrs on inner: drvn 2f out: sn rdn: cl up over 1f out: wknd fnl f* **12/1**

59.45s (-0.75) **Going Correction** -0.225s/f (Stan) 6 Ran SP% **114.8**
Speed ratings (Par 96): **97,93,93,91,89 88**
CSF £22.58 TOTE £4.80: £2.90, £2.70; EX 22.60 Trifecta £137.00.
Owner Clipper Logistics **Bred** Branton Court Stud **Trained** Hambleton, N Yorks

FOCUS
An open looking nursery and an improved winner.

6437 BET TOTEQUADPOT AT TOTESPORT.COM H'CAP 1m 5f 66y(P)
3:10 (3:11) (Class 3) (0-90,90) 3-Y-O+ £10,350 (£3,080; £1,539; £769) **Stalls Low**

Form | RPR
0411 **1** **Calculation**[36] 5127 3-8-13 **84**........(v) LouisSteward 1 97+
(Sir Michael Stoute) *mde all: pushed along in 2 l ld 2f out: reminder in 3 l ld 1f out: pushed out fnl f: sn wl clr: easily* **4/5**[1]
13-4 **2** 6 **Matchmaking (GER)**[14] 5967 4-9-6 **82**........ RyanTate 2 84
(Sir Mark Prescott Bt) *hld up in last: drvn and hdwy on outer over 2f out: 3 l 2nd 1f out: one pce fnl f: no ch w wnr* **9/4**[2]
2411 **3** 1 **Emenem**[8] 6156 5-9-2 **85**........ LeviWilliams(7) 4 86
(Simon Dow) *trckd ldr: drvn and dropped to last over 2f out: rdn into 3rd over 1f out: no ex fnl f* **4/1**[3]
2400 **4** 19 **Exceeding Power**[56] 4381 8-10-0 **90**........ GeorgeWood 3 63
(Martin Bosley) *trckd ldr: pushed along in 3rd 2f out: sn rdn: dropped to last and lost tch* **20/1**

2m 50.49s (-3.11) **Going Correction** -0.225s/f (Stan) 4 Ran SP% **111.1**
WFA 3 from 4yo+ 9lb
Speed ratings (Par 107): **100,96,95,84**
CSF £3.00 TOTE £1.50; EX 2.60 Trifecta £4.90.
Owner The Queen **Bred** The Queen **Trained** Newmarket, Suffolk

FOCUS
This feature was dominated throughout by the positively ridden Calculation, who landed a hat-trick in some style.

6438 BET TOTETRIFECTA AT TOTESPORT.COM BRITISH EBF FILLIES' NOVICE STKS 1m 2f (P)
3:45 (3:50) (Class 4) 3-Y-O+ £6,501 (£1,934; £966; £483) **Stalls Low**

Form | RPR
2425 **1** **Inference**[49] 4641 3-9-0 82........ NickyMackay 3 90
(John Gosden) *disp ld tl led on own after 1f: mde rest: pushed along in 2 l ld 2f out: rdn in 3 l ld 1f out: rdn further clr fnl f: comf* **10/3**[3]
2 **2** 5 **Strelka**[19] 5748 3-9-0 0........ LouisSteward 4 83
(Ralph Beckett) *chsd ldrs: wnt 2nd 3f out: pushed along in 2 l 2nd 2f out: rdn over 1f out: no ex fnl f* **9/4**[1]
2-3 **3** 7 **Stratification (USA)**[100] 2771 3-9-0 0........ KieranO'Neill 6 67
(John Gosden) *hld up in last: hdwy on outer 3f out: drvn in 3rd 2f out: rdn over 1f out: no imp* **5/2**[2]
3242 **4** 2 **Infuse (IRE)**[25] 5529 3-9-0 77........ AdamMcNamara 2 63
(Roger Charlton) *t.k.h: hld up: rdn in 5th over 2f out: plugged on into 4th fnl f* **5/1**
56 **5** 2 **Hazaranda**[36] 5148 3-9-0 0........(t[1]) JimmyQuinn 1 60
(Sir Michael Stoute) *trckd ldrs: rdn in 4th 2f out: grad wknd: lost 4th ins fnl f* **14/1**
60 **6** 29 **Brass (FR)**[44] 4842 3-9-0 0........ GeorgeWood 7
(Paul Webber) *awkward leaving stalls and slowly away: bhd: drvn and lost tch 3f out* **50/1**
5 **7** 2 **Baaqiah**[17] 5810 3-9-0 0........ JackMitchell 5
(Roger Varian) *disp ld tl trckd ldr after 1f: drvn and lost pl 3f out: sn wl bhd: eased over 1f out* **7/1**

2m 2.83s (-5.77) **Going Correction** -0.225s/f (Stan) 7 Ran SP% **120.2**
Speed ratings (Par 102): **114,110,104,102,101 78,76**
CSF £12.15 TOTE £3.60: £2.40, £1.30; EX 14.50 Trifecta £34.30.
Owner Cheveley Park Stud **Bred** Cheveley Park Stud Ltd **Trained** Newmarket, Suffolk

FOCUS
An informative contest, the first five in the betting all having shown ability from limited starts. It developed into a match in the straight.

6439 VICTORIA BASS H'CAP 1m 2f (P)
4:20 (4:23) (Class 5) (0-70,71) 3-Y-O+
£5,433 (£1,617; £808; £404; £300; £300) **Stalls Low**

Form | RPR
3424 **1** **Perfecimperfection (IRE)**[72] 3773 3-8-12 **68**........ StefanoCherchi(7) 9 75+
(Marco Botti) *trckd ldrs: led 2f out: rdn in 1 l ld 1f out: r.o wl fnl f* **8/1**
0053 **2** 1 1/4 **Bayston Hill**[23] 5570 5-9-8 **67**........(p) FinleyMarsh(3) 2 71
(Mark Usher) *trckd ldr: pushed along 2f out: drvn 1 1/2f out: rdn into 2nd fnl f: kpt on wl: lost shoe* **6/1**[3]
2-43 **3** 2 **Waterfront (IRE)**[12] 6022 3-9-3 **66**........(v[1]) AntonioFresu 8 67
(Simon Crisford) *slowly away but sn racing in mid-div: drvn on outer 2f out: rdn over 1f out: r.o fnl f: tk 3rd last few strides* **6/1**[3]
4300 **4** nk **Fiction Writer (USA)**[19] 5731 3-9-2 **65**........ ConnorBeasley 5 65
(Mark Johnston) *led: rdn and hdd 2f out: grad wknd: lost 3rd last few strides: lost shoe* **16/1**
6425 **5** 1/2 **Kingdom Of Dubai (FR)**[64] 4071 3-9-4 **67**........ JackMitchell 4 66
(Roger Varian) *hld up: drvn and plenty to do on outer 2f out: rdn over 1f out: r.o past btn rivals ins fnl f* **3/1**[1]
-601 **6** 3/4 **Go Fox**[30] 5354 4-10-0 **70**........ GeorgeWood 3 67
(Tom Clover) *hld up: pushed along 2f out: sn drvn: rdn over 1f out: no imp* **5/1**[2]
3300 **7** shd **Paco's Prince**[59] 4250 4-9-7 **70**........ AledBeech(7) 7 67
(Nick Littmoden) *chsd ldrs: drvn in 4th 2f out: rdn and wknd over 1f out* **20/1**
1653 **8** nse **Tangramm**[18] 5782 7-9-13 **69**........(p) RyanTate 1 66
(Dean Ivory) *mid-div: drvn 2f out: rdn over 1f out: wknd fnl f* **8/1**
4403 **9** nse **Dangerous Ends**[11] 6050 5-9-10 **71**........ WilliamCarver(5) 6 68
(Brett Johnson) *slowly away: bhd: effrt on inner 2f out: sn drvn: rdn and wknd fnl f* **5/1**[2]

2m 5.95s (-2.65) **Going Correction** -0.225s/f (Stan) 9 Ran SP% **119.8**
WFA 3 from 4yo+ 7lb
Speed ratings (Par 103): **101,100,98,98,97 97,97,97,97**
CSF £57.37 CT £374.85 TOTE £8.70: £2.70, £1.80, £1.80; EX 72.50 Trifecta £423.20.
Owner R Bruni & Partner **Bred** Manister House & Grange Stud **Trained** Newmarket, Suffolk

FOCUS
Modest handicap form.

6440 BET TOTESWINGER AT TOTESPORT.COM H'CAP 7f (P)
4:50 (4:52) (Class 4) (0-85,87) 3-Y-O+
£6,016 (£1,790; £894; £447; £300; £300) **Stalls Low**

Form | RPR
0614 **1** **Attainment**[10] 6076 3-9-5 **83**........ JoeyHaynes 1 89
(James Tate) *chsd ldrs: drvn into 2nd over 2f out: rdn to ld 1f out: r.o wl fnl f* **2/1**[1]
6320 **2** 3/4 **Zeyzoun (FR)**[22] 5626 5-9-4 **77**........(h) GeorgeWood 6 83
(Chris Wall) *mid-div: drvn 2f out: hdwy into 3rd over 1f out: swtchd and wnt 2nd ins fnl f: rdn and r.o wl: a hld* **9/2**[3]
0430 **3** 2 **Uncle Jerry**[63] 4103 3-8-13 **77**........(p[1]) JackMitchell 7 76
(Mohamed Moubarak) *hld up: drvn on outer 2f out: rdn and hdwy over 1f out: kpt on fnl f* **16/1**
6450 **4** 2 3/4 **Global Tango (IRE)**[7] 6220 4-9-9 **85**........(b) WilliamCox(3) 8 78
(Luke McJannet) *hld up: drvn in 7th 2f out: rdn over 1f out: kpt on into 4th fnl f* **16/1**
265 **5** 1/2 **Buckingham (IRE)**[10] 6076 3-8-11 **82**........ GeorgiaDobie(7) 5 72
(Eve Johnson Houghton) *hld up: drvn and effrt 2f out: sn rdn: wknd fnl f* **7/2**[2]
1000 **6** hd **Sword Exceed (GER)**[18] 5770 5-9-4 **77**........ KieranO'Neill 3 68
(Ivan Furtado) *led: drvn in 2 l ld 2f out: rdn and hdd 1f out: wknd fnl f* **10/1**
4031 **7** 3 **I Am A Dreamer**[12] 6015 3-9-9 **87**........(v) ConnorBeasley 2 68
(Mark Johnston) *prom: drvn and lost pl over 2f out: sn rdn and wknd* **9/2**[3]
63P5 **8** 49 **You Never Can Tell (IRE)**[31] 5312 3-9-0 **85**........(b) SeanKirrane(7) 4
(Richard Spencer) *slowly away: bhd: rdn over 3f out: sn lost tch* **25/1**

1m 24.36s (-2.84) **Going Correction** -0.225s/f (Stan) 8 Ran SP% **116.6**
WFA 3 from 4yo+ 5lb
Speed ratings (Par 105): **107,106,103,100,100 99,96,40**
CSF £11.57 CT £112.52 TOTE £2.60: £1.10, £1.60, £3.90; EX 11.10 Trifecta £94.70.
Owner Saeed Manana **Bred** Rabbah Bloodstock Limited **Trained** Newmarket, Suffolk

FOCUS
With all of the runners rated 77 or higher, there was plenty of depth to this handicap and this is straightforward form around the front pair.

6441 BET TOTESCOOP6 AT TOTESPORT.COM H'CAP 7f (P)
5:25 (5:27) (Class 6) (0-60,62) 3-Y-O+
£3,428 (£1,020; £509; £300; £300; £300) **Stalls Low**

Form | RPR
0252 **1** **Vincenzo Coccotti (USA)**[11] 6051 7-8-12 **51**........(p) FinleyMarsh(3) 4 63
(Ken Cunningham-Brown) *chsd ldrs: drvn and hdwy on outer 1 1/2f out: rdn to chal 1f out: led 1/2f out: sn clr* **6/1**[3]
2231 **2** 2 1/4 **Magicinthemaking (USA)**[66] 3996 5-9-7 **57**........ KieranO'Neill 8 63
(John E Long) *mid-div on outer: hdwy over 2f out: sn cl up: rdn over 1f out: led ent fnl f: hdd 1/2f out: no ex* **4/1**[1]
0604 **3** 1 **Red Skye Delight (IRE)**[32] 5264 3-8-10 **51**........(h[1]) JackMitchell 11 52
(Luke McJannet) *chsd ldrs: drvn to ld 2f out: rdn over 1f out: hdd ent fnl f: no ex* **14/1**
0650 **4** 3/4 **Catapult**[11] 6051 4-8-3 **46** oh1........ MorganCole(7) 6 47
(Shaun Keightley) *prom: trckd ldrs 2f out: n.m.r 1 1/2f out: in clr: cl up and drvn 1f out: wknd wl ins fnl f* **9/1**
-060 **5** 1/2 **Majdool (IRE)**[32] 5282 6-9-9 **59**........(e) ConnorBeasley 1 59
(Noel Wilson) *hld up: drvn and hdwy over 1f out: sn rdn: no ex fnl f* **9/1**
-120 **6** hd **Kennocha (IRE)**[25] 5526 3-9-4 **59**........(t) GeorgeWood 2 56
(Amy Murphy) *hld up: drvn 2f out: sn rdn: no imp* **8/1**
2066 **7** 2 **Miaella**[72] 3781 4-9-10 **60**........ JoeyHaynes 3 54
(Chelsea Banham) *hld up: drvn 2f out: rdn over 1f out: no imp* **5/1**[2]
306 **8** nse **Obsession For Gold (IRE)**[15] 5890 3-8-13 **54**........(t) AntonioFresu 9 46
(Mrs Ilka Gansera-Leveque) *slowly away: bhd: drvn and effrt over 1f out: rdn fnl f: one pce* **16/1**
2050 **9** 3 1/4 **Holy Tiber (IRE)**[36] 5144 4-9-6 **56**........ RyanTate 5 41
(Chelsea Banham) *hld up: rdn on outer 2f out: no imp: eased fnl f* **5/1**[2]
2655 **10** 3/4 **Pearl Spectre (USA)**[21] 5677 8-9-5 **62**........(v) GraceMcEntee(7) 7 45
(Phil McEntee) *mid-div: drvn and lost pl over 2f out: sn rdn and wknd* **8/1**
00-0 **11** 2 **Amaranth (IRE)**[226] 155 6-8-10 **46** oh1........ NickyMackay 10 24
(Simon Dow) *led: rdn and hdd 2f out: wknd* **10/1**

1m 25.4s (-1.80) 11 Ran SP% **131.5**
WFA 3 from 4yo+ 5lb
CSF £34.13 CT £350.70 TOTE £6.60: £2.10, £1.90, £4.80; EX 17.90 Trifecta £205.70.
Owner David Henery **Bred** Gainesway Thoroughbreds Ltd Et Al **Trained** Danebury, Hants

FOCUS
A moderate but competitive handicap and the winner has been rated within 5lb of last year's best.
T/Plt: £47.20 to a £1 stake. Pool: £20,964.87 - 443.64 winning units T/Qpdt: £12.70 to a £1 stake. Pool: £1,374.23 - 108.10 winning units **Keith McHugh**

6401 **GOODWOOD** (R-H)

Saturday, August 24

OFFICIAL GOING: Good (7.0)

Wind: Virtually nil Weather: Warm and sunny

6442 BET ON RACING WITH LADBROKES EBF FILLIES' NOVICE AUCTION STKS (PLUS 10 RACE) 6f

1:30 (1:30) (Class 4) 2-Y-O £6,404 (£1,905; £952; £476) Stalls High

Form RPR

52 1 **Epsom Faithfull**[19] 5745 2-8-11 0 CharlieBennett 3 72
(Pat Phelan) *trckd ldr: shkn up to take narrow ld 2f out: rdn and strly pressed by rival 1f out: styd on wl (vet said filly lost its right hind shoe)* **8/1**

02 2 ½ **Strawberry Hind (IRE)**[15] 5906 2-9-0 0 DavidEgan 5 74
(Mick Channon) *cl up: rdn along to chse wnr 2f out: almost upsides and ev ch 1f out: no ex fnl 100yds* **7/2**[3]

10 3 nk **Odyssey Girl (IRE)**[35] 5185 2-9-4 0 HarryBentley 6 77
(Richard Spencer) *trckd wnr: effrt to cl whn short of room over 1f out: rdn once in clr ins fnl f: kpt on* **2/1**[1]

6 4 1 ¾ **Pettinger**[24] 5547 2-8-12 0 KieranShoemark 4 66
(Charles Hills) *hld up: effrt on outer 2f out: rdn and hung rt 1f out: one pce fnl f* **16/1**

5 ¾ **Mrs Merton** 2-9-0 0 OisinMurphy 1 66
(William Knight) *s.i.s and racd in last: hdwy into midfield 2f out: sn rdn and hung lft 1f out: one pce after* **10/1**

6 ½ **Miss Thoughtful** 2-8-11 0 TomMarquand 9 61
(Jamie Osborne) *racd in midfield: dropped to last 1/2-way: kpt on again under hands and heels fnl f* **25/1**

242 7 1 **Feelinlikeasomeone**[19] 5737 2-8-13 76 FrannyNorton 8 60
(Mark Johnston) *led: rdn along and hdd by wnr 2f out: wknd fnl f* **5/2**[2]

00 8 1 ¼ **Bockos Amber (IRE)**[18] 5772 2-9-0 0 RossaRyan 7 57
(Roger Teal) *in rr of midfield: rdn and no imp 2f out: wknd fnl f* **50/1**

1m 11.96s (-0.14) **Going Correction** 0.0s/f (Good) 8 Ran SP% **116.0**
Speed ratings (Par 93): **100,99,98,96,95 94,93,91**
CSF £36.71 TOTE £9.10: £1.80, £1.30, £1.30; EX 40.50 Trifecta £126.80.
Owner Epsom Racegoers No. 2 **Bred** James Patton **Trained** Epsom, Surrey

FOCUS
A warm summer's day and the ground had dried out since Friday evening's card. Ordinary form for the track but the front three have been rated as improving.

6443 LADBROKES CELEBRATION MILE STKS (GROUP 2) 1m

2:05 (2:05) (Class 1) 3-Y-O+
£75,849 (£28,756; £14,391; £7,169; £3,597; £1,805) Stalls Low

Form RPR

0511 1 **Duke Of Hazzard (FR)**[22] 5609 3-8-12 111 (b) RossaRyan 3 115
(Paul Cole) *trckd ldr: rdn to chse ldr over 1f out: kpt on wl for press to ld fnl 75yds: a doing enough* **3/1**[2]

3524 2 ¾ **Turgenev**[44] 4850 3-8-12 108 (p[1]) RobertHavlin 5 113
(John Gosden) *hld up: clsd on outer gng wl over 1f out: sn rdn and kpt on fnl f: nt rch wnr* **10/1**

3104 3 hd **Happy Power (IRE)**[24] 5543 3-8-12 115 OisinMurphy 6 113
(Andrew Balding) *trckd ldr: shkn up to ld over 1f out: sn rdn and hdd by wnr fnl 75yds: no ex* **4/1**[3]

1344 4 ¾ **Skardu**[67] 3951 3-8-12 114 TomMarquand 1 111
(William Haggas) *settled in 4th: pushed along and no imp 2f out: sn rdn and kpt on one pce fr 1f out* **2/1**[1]

4111 5 ¾ **Beat Le Bon (FR)**[22] 5610 3-8-12 110 PatDobbs 4 109
(Richard Hannon) *dwlt and racd keenly in rr: pushed along on inner over 1f out: kpt on under hands and heels ins fnl f (jockey said colt was slowly away)* **4/1**[3]

0246 6 2 **Nyaleti (IRE)**[23] 5586 4-9-1 105 FrannyNorton 2 103
(Mark Johnston) *led and racd keenly: rdn along and hdd over 1f out: wknd fnl f (vet said filly was lame on its left fore)* **20/1**

1m 37.47s (-1.73) **Going Correction** 0.0s/f (Good)
WFA 3 from 4yo 6lb 6 Ran SP% **112.2**
Speed ratings (Par 115): **108,107,107,106,105 103**
CSF £30.66 TOTE £3.60: £1.90, £4.00; EX 31.70 Trifecta £74.60.
Owner Mrs Fitri Hay **Bred** Runnymede Farm Inc & Catesby W Clay **Trained** Whatcombe, Oxon

FOCUS
Add 6yds. A decent renewal of this Group 2, but the first five - all 3yo colts - were covered by less than 2.5l at the line. The initial pace didn't appear a strong one, a couple pulling for their heads. The winner has been rated in line with his recent victories, and a small pb from the second.

6444 LADBROKES PRESTIGE STKS (GROUP 3) (FILLIES) 7f

2:40 (2:40) (Class 1) 2-Y-O
£28,355 (£10,750; £5,380; £2,680; £1,345; £675) Stalls Low

Form RPR

41 1 **Boomer**[30] 5342 2-9-0 0 RichardKingscote 1 103
(Tom Dascombe) *trckd ldr and a little free early: sn settled: shkn up to ld over 1f out: mostly hands and heels ins fnl f: cosily* **5/2**[1]

2143 2 nk **Dark Lady**[14] 5964 2-9-0 96 PatDobbs 4 102
(Richard Hannon) *hld up: smooth hdwy onto heels of ldrs 2f out: rdn to chse wnr 1f out: kpt on but a hld* **5/1**[3]

101 3 ¾ **Shadn (IRE)**[36] 5134 2-9-0 96 OisinMurphy 2 100
(Andrew Balding) *racd in midfield on inner: effrt to chse wnr over 1f out: briefly short of room and swtchd rt to rail 1f out: sn rdn and kpt on wl* **3/1**[2]

32 4 ¾ **Stylistique**[19] 5733 2-9-0 0 DavidEgan 9 98
(Roger Varian) *trckd ldr on outer: pushed along to ld 2f out: sn rdn and hdd by wnr over 1f out: no ex fnl f* **14/1**

3144 5 2 ¼ **Romsey**[14] 5964 2-9-0 93 TomMarquand 5 92
(Hughie Morrison) *led: rdn along and hdd 2f out: wknd fnl f* **11/1**

1 6 1 ¾ **Alpinista**[37] 5088 2-9-0 0 AdamKirby 8 88
(Sir Mark Prescott Bt) *restless in stalls and dwlt: racd in rr: niggled along and sltly detached 1/2-way: mde sme late hdwy* **3/1**[2]

41 7 5 **Angel Of Delight (IRE)**[21] 5684 2-9-0 0 PatCosgrave 6 75
(Hugo Palmer) *racd in rr of midfield: rdn along and no imp over 2f out: wknd 1f out* **16/1**

1m 26.49s (-0.21) **Going Correction** 0.0s/f (Good) 7 Ran SP% **116.1**
Speed ratings (Par 101): **101,100,99,98,96 94,88**
CSF £15.97 TOTE £3.20: £1.80, £2.30; EX 13.70 Trifecta £30.60.
Owner Chasemore Farm **Bred** Chasemore Farm **Trained** Malpas, Cheshire

FOCUS
Add 6yds. Probably an ordinary edition of this Group 3 event, which produced the 1,000 Guineas heroine Billesdon Brook in 2017.

6445 LADBROKES WHERE THE NATION PLAYS H'CAP 7f

3:15 (3:16) (Class 2) 3-Y-O+
£46,687 (£13,980; £6,990; £3,495; £1,747; £877) Stalls Low

Form RPR

2002 1 **Salute The Soldier (GER)**[24] 5546 4-9-0 98 AdamKirby 9 106
(Clive Cox) *racd in 4th: hdwy on outer over 1f out: sn rdn and drifted rt u.p: led ins fnl f: drvn out* **5/1**[1]

1-46 2 nk **Tabarrak (IRE)**[56] 4389 6-9-10 108 OisinMurphy 5 115
(Richard Hannon) *racd keenly in midfield: clsd on ldrs gng wl 2f out: briefly short of room over 1f out: rdn and kpt on wl once in clr: jst failed* **13/2**[3]

5002 3 ½ **Zhui Feng (IRE)**[14] 5930 6-9-0 98 (p) KieranShoemark 8 104
(Amanda Perrett) *led: rdn along and hdd jst ins fnl f: no ex fnl 100yds* **12/1**

0334 4 ½ **Cliffs Of Capri**[24] 5546 5-8-10 94 (p) DougieCostello 1 101
(Jamie Osborne) *racd in midfield: stl gng wl on heels of ldrs whn short of room over 1f out: boxed in fnl f and unable to chal (jockey said gelding was denied a clear run)* **10/1**

000 5 nk **Sanaadh**[42] 4921 6-8-9 93 (t) RobertHavlin 11 97
(Michael Wigham) *hld up: rdn along and no immediate imp 2f out: drvn and styd on strly fnl f* **28/1**

6200 6 shd **Kimifive (IRE)**[21] 5664 4-8-8 92 HarryBentley 7 96
(Joseph Tuite) *racd in midfield: hdwy on outer over 2f out: sn rdn and kpt on fnl f: nt rch ldrs* **5/1**[1]

3051 7 ½ **Pattie**[7] 6214 5-8-5 89 DavidEgan 4 91
(Mick Channon) *restless in stalls: hld up: pushed along in rr 2f out: n.d* **12/1**

2000 8 shd **Lake Volta (IRE)**[7] 6229 4-8-13 97 FrannyNorton 10 99
(Mark Johnston) *trckd ldr: rdn along to chse ldr 2f out: wkng whn hmpd 1f out: nt rcvr* **6/1**[2]

3625 9 nse **Oh This Is Us (IRE)**[27] 5475 6-9-7 105 PatDobbs 2 108+
(Richard Hannon) *settled wl in midfield on inner: making hdwy whn short of room over 1f out: boxed in and nvr able to chal fnl f (jockey said horse was denied a clear run)* **8/1**

1110 10 ½ **Gossiping**[22] 5610 7-8-13 97 ShaneKelly 3 100
(Gary Moore) *trckd ldr in 3rd: rdn along to chse ldr 2f out: wkng whn hmpd over 1f out: nt rcvr* **5/1**[1]

5202 11 1 ¾ **Presidential (IRE)**[7] 6207 5-8-3 87 (p) CamHardie 12 83
(Roger Fell) *hld up: pushed along in rr over 2f out: nvr on terms* **25/1**

56-0 12 2 ½ **Dutch Treat**[133] 1751 3-8-5 94 JosephineGordon 6 82
(Andrew Balding) *hld up: pushed along in rr 3f out: a in bhd* **33/1**

1m 25.7s (-1.00) **Going Correction** 0.0s/f (Good)
WFA 3 from 4yo+ 5lb 12 Ran SP% **123.4**
Speed ratings (Par 109): **105,104,104,103,103 103,102,102,102,101 99,96**
CSF £38.05 CT £382.41 TOTE £7.20: £2.30, £2.50, £2.90; EX 48.00 Trifecta £445.50.
Owner Mr & Mrs P Hargreaves & A D Spence **Bred** A Spence **Trained** Lambourn, Berks

FOCUS
Add 6yds. This valuable handicap didn't attract as large a field as it does usually. It produced a bunch finish and there were several what-might-have beens.

6446 LADBROKES MARCH STKS (GROUP 3) (IN MEMORY OF JOHN DUNLOP) 1m 6f

3:50 (3:53) (Class 1) 3-Y-O £56,710 (£21,500; £10,760; £5,360; £2,690) Stalls Low

Form RPR

1011 1 **Sir Ron Priestley**[24] 5541 3-9-2 105 FrannyNorton 1 109
(Mark Johnston) *mde virtually all: shkn up w short ld 2f out: rdn and styd on strly ins fnl f: won gng away* **1/1**[1]

31 2 1 ¼ **Promissory (IRE)**[50] 4600 3-8-13 0 RobertHavlin 4 104
(John Gosden) *trckd wnr: effrt to chse wnr 2f out: rdn upsides and ev ch jst over 1f out: kpt on but unable to match wnr fnl f* **7/2**[2]

2452 3 1 ½ **Manuela De Vega (IRE)**[21] 5663 3-8-13 105 HarryBentley 2 102
(Ralph Beckett) *trckd wnr: swtchd lft off heels over 2f out: rdn and outpcd by ldng pair over 1f out: kpt on* **7/2**[2]

5055 4 1 ¾ **Blue Gardenia (IRE)**[21] 5682 3-8-13 95 (p) KieranShoemark 3 100
(David O'Meara) *hld up: pushed along to chse wnr on inner 2f out: rdn and no imp fnl f* **33/1**

-115 5 15 **Dal Horrisgle**[23] 5585 3-9-2 102 TomMarquand 5 84
(William Haggas) *hld up: pushed along over 3f out: rdn and lost pl 2f out (trainer's rep could offer no explanation for the gelding's performance)* **11/2**[3]

3m 1.21s (-2.49) **Going Correction** 0.0s/f (Good) 5 Ran SP% **112.8**
Speed ratings (Par 110): **107,106,105,104,95**
CSF £5.04 TOTE £1.90: £1.10, £2.00; EX 5.00 Trifecta £12.10.
Owner Paul Dean **Bred** Mascalls Stud **Trained** Middleham Moor, N Yorks

FOCUS
The second running of this as a Group 3, and there was little change in the order. The winner probably didn't need to improve.

6447 LADBROKES SUPPORTING CHILDREN WITH CANCER H'CAP 1m 1f 11y

4:25 (4:25) (Class 3) (0-90,91) 3-Y-O+ £9,056 (£2,695; £1,346; £673) Stalls Low

Form RPR

2165 1 **Lawn Ranger**[12] 6021 4-9-10 88 HarryBentley 5 98
(Michael Attwater) *mde all: shkn up over 2f out: rdn whn pressed by rival over 1f out: drvn and kpt on strly fnl f: won gng away* **12/1**

3622 2 3 ½ **You're Hired**[21] 5667 6-9-4 87 (p) ScottMcCullagh[(5)] 6 90
(Amanda Perrett) *trckd wnr: rdn to chse wnr 2f out: ev ch over 1f out: unable to sustain effrt fnl f* **3/1**[2]

5434 3 ½ **Rotherwick (IRE)**[12] 6021 7-9-7 85 (b) PatDobbs 7 87+
(Paul Cole) *hld up: rdn in rr over 2f out: sme late hdwy passed btn horses* **8/1**

3023 4 3 **Dark Red (IRE)**[28] 5440 7-9-12 90 (b) KieranShoemark 4 86
(Ed Dunlop) *racd in midfield: pushed along 3f out: rdn and no imp 2f out: one pce fnl f* **7/1**[3]

2111 5 1 ¼ **Chance**[29] 5394 3-9-6 91 AdamKirby 1 85
(Simon Crisford) *settled in 3rd: rdn and outpcd by front pair over 2f out: wknd fnl f* **1/1**[1]

6065 6 2 ½ **Uther Pendragon (IRE)**[7] 6211 4-8-8 72 (p) DavidEgan 2 61
(J S Moore) *hld up: rdn along over 2f out: nvr on terms* **20/1**

1m 54.61s (-2.79) **Going Correction** 0.0s/f (Good)
WFA 3 from 4yo+ 7lb 6 Ran SP% **111.1**
Speed ratings (Par 107): **112,108,108,105,104 102**
CSF £46.54 TOTE £14.60: £4.20, £1.70; EX 48.50 Trifecta £206.00.

The Form Book Flat 2019, Raceform Ltd, Newbury, RG14 5SJ

Owner Canisbay Bloodstock **Bred** Jacqueline Doyle **Trained** Epsom, Surrey
FOCUS
Add 6yds. This rates a significant pb from the winner.

6448 LADBROKES COMMITTED TO SAFER GAMBLING H'CAP — 1m 6f
5:00 (5:00) (Class 4) (0-85,85) 4-Y-O+
£6,274 (£1,867; £933; £466; £300; £300) Stalls Low

Form				RPR
0532	1		**Past Master**[22] 5625 6-9-0 78 ... AdamKirby 6 (Henry Candy) *dwlt and racd in midfield: effrt on outer to cl on ldr over 2f out: rdn along to ld narrowly over 1f out: drvn out fnl f* 9/4[1]	88
3116	2	nk	**Berrahri (IRE)**[28] 5423 8-9-1 79 ... JosephineGordon 1 (John Best) *led: shkn up w short ld 2f out: rdn along and hdd by wnr over 1f out: rallied wl u.p fnl f: jst hld* 8/1	89
2130	3	10	**Age Of Wisdom (IRE)**[24] 5540 6-8-7 71 ... (p) HarryBentley 7 (Gary Moore) *broke wl and restrained in rr: pushed along on outer over 2f out: rdn and wnt 3rd over 1f out: one pce fnl f* 5/1[3]	68
-144	4	½	**Rydan (IRE)**[71] 3799 8-9-0 78 ... (v) PatDobbs 2 (Gary Moore) *hld up: sltly hmpd after 2f out: clsd on ldrs gng wl over 2f out: sn rdn and fnd little: one pce after* 7/1	74
6646	5	3½	**Beer With The Boys**[11] 6042 4-8-2 66 oh1 ... DavidEgan 8 (Mick Channon) *trckd ldr: rdn to chse ldr over 2f out: wknd fnl f* 13/2	57
0602	6	5	**Never Surrender (IRE)**[11] 6044 5-9-0 78 ... KieranShoemark 4 (Charles Hills) *midfield in tch: rdn along to chse ldr over 2f out: wknd fnl f* 11/2	63
2254	7	1¾	**Orin Swift (IRE)**[28] 5457 5-8-12 83 ... TylerSaunders(7) 5 (Jonathan Portman) *in rr of midfield: pushed along in rr 3f out: nvr on terms* 9/2[2]	66

3m 1.6s (-2.10) **Going Correction** 0.0s/f (Good) 7 Ran SP% 117.9
Speed ratings (Par 105): **106,105,100,99,97 94,93**
CSF £22.24 CT £83.64 TOTE £3.10: £1.80, £4.50; EX 23.20 Trifecta £99.20.
Owner D B Clark/A R Bentall/H Candy **Bred** Bugley Stud (millestan) Partnership **Trained** Kingston Warren, Oxon
■ Stewards' Enquiry : Josephine Gordon two-day ban; misuse of whip (Sep 8-9)
Tyler Saunders five-day ban; careless riding (Sep 7-11)
FOCUS
The first two pulled clear, in a time only 0.39sec slower than the Group 3 March Stakes, and both have been rated as improving slightly.
T/Jkpt: Not Won. T/Plt: £219.10 to a £1 stake. Pool: £250,708.14 - 250.41 winning units T/Qpdt: £29.70 to a £1 stake. Pool: £20,284.15 - 147.34 winning units **Mark Grantham**

6407 NEWMARKET (R-H)
Saturday, August 24

OFFICIAL GOING: Good to firm (watered; 7.5)
Wind: Light across Weather: Fine

6449 PRICE BAILEY "IT'S ALL ABOUT YOU" BRITISH EBF NOVICE STKS (PLUS 10 RACE) — 6f
1:40 (1:42) (Class 4) 2-Y-O
£5,175 (£1,540; £769; £384) Stalls Low

Form				RPR
1	1		**Huraiz (IRE)**[16] 5856 2-9-5 0 ... DaneO'Neill 5 (Mark Johnston) *led: hdd over 3f out: led again 2f out: sn rdn: jst hld on* 2/1[2]	83
223	2	shd	**Electrical Storm**[64] 4069 2-9-2 86 ... CallumShepherd 8 (Saeed bin Suroor) *chsd ldrs on outer: rdn over 1f out: chsd wnr ins fnl f: r.o* 11/10[1]	80
0	3	3	**Many A Star (IRE)**[15] 5908 2-9-2 0 ... TomQueally 6 (James Given) *racd keenly in 2nd tl led over 3f out: hdd 2f out: rdn over 1f out: no ex ins fnl f* 9/1	71
	4	nk	**One Night Stand** 2-9-2 0 ... AdrianMcCarthy 4 (William Jarvis) *plld hrd and prom: rdn over 1f out: swtchd lft ins fnl f: styd on same pce (jockey said gelding ran too freely)* 20/1	70
0	5	¾	**Fighting Don (FR)**[36] 5131 2-9-2 0 ... SeanLevey 3 (Harry Dunlop) *chsd ldrs: pushed along 1/2-way: rdn and swtchd lft over 1f out: styd on same pce fnl f* 50/1	68+
	6	hd	**Badri** 2-9-2 0 ... DavidProbert 10 (Charles Hills) *s.i.s: hld up: hdwy 2f out: edgd rt and no ex ins fnl f* 5/1[3]	67
05	7	1	**Boasty (IRE)**[77] 3579 2-8-9 0 ... AledBeech(7) 2 (Charlie Fellowes) *unruly bhd stalls: hld up: shkn up over 2f out: sme hdwy over 1f out: nt clr run and wknd ins fnl f* 40/1	65
	8	¾	**Mums The Law** 2-8-11 0 ... ConnorBeasley 7 (Jane Chapple-Hyam) *s.s: rdn over 2f out: nt trble ldrs* 33/1	57
5	9	8	**William Thomas (IRE)**[15] 5887 2-9-2 0 ... EoinWalsh 1 (Robert Eddery) *s.s: a in rr* 50/1	38

1m 13.91s (1.81) **Going Correction** +0.15s/f (Good) 9 Ran SP% 121.7
Speed ratings (Par 96): **93,92,88,88,87 87,85,84,74**
CSF £4.66 TOTE £2.90: £1.20, £1.10, £2.60; EX 4.20 Trifecta £17.00.
Owner Hamdan Al Maktoum **Bred** Shadwell Estate Company Limited **Trained** Middleham Moor, N Yorks
■ Stewards' Enquiry : Callum Shepherd two-day ban; misuse of whip (Sep 8-9)
FOCUS
The last meeting of the year on the July Course. The opener was a decent novice won by the smart Jash last year, and they raced towards the stands' rail.

6450 PRICE BAILEY INTERNATIONAL NURSERY H'CAP — 7f
2:10 (2:10) (Class 3) (0-95,83) 2-Y-O
£9,056 (£2,695; £1,346; £673) Stalls Low

Form				RPR
131	1		**Hariboux**[17] 5801 2-9-6 82 ... (h) JackMitchell 1 (Hugo Palmer) *trckd ldrs: racd keenly: swtchd lft over 2f out: shkn up to ld and abt to be rdn whn rdr dropped whip over 1f out: r.o wl* 5/1[3]	93
2312	2	4	**Visible Charm (IRE)**[14] 5962 2-9-7 83 ... WilliamBuick 3 (Charlie Appleby) *w ldr tl led over 2f out: rdn: edgd rt and hdd over 1f out: no ex ins fnl f* 11/10[1]	83
3222	3	7	**Saint Of Katowice (IRE)**[22] 5615 2-9-2 78 ... BarryMcHugh 4 (Richard Fahey) *w ldrs: rdn and ev ch over 1f out: wknd ins fnl f* 7/4[2]	59
0532	4	6	**Road Rage (IRE)**[15] 5896 2-8-13 75 ... (p) ConnorBeasley 2 (Michael Dods) *led: rdn and hdd over 2f out: wknd over 1f out* 8/1	40

1m 27.0s (1.30) **Going Correction** +0.15s/f (Good) 4 Ran SP% 111.8
Speed ratings (Par 98): **98,93,85,78**
CSF £11.43 TOTE £5.60; EX 11.10 Trifecta £13.90.
Owner Kremlin Cottage Ix **Bred** Lady Gillian Brunton **Trained** Newmarket, Suffolk
FOCUS
A tight nursery won by some decent performers down the years, and they went a fair clip before the winner came from behind.

6451 PRICE BAILEY "RIGHT ADVICE FOR LIFE" H'CAP — 7f
2:45 (2:47) (Class 3) (0-90,91) 3-Y-O
£9,056 (£2,695; £1,346; £673) Stalls Low

Form				RPR
4321	1		**Posted**[28] 5450 3-9-2 85 ... (h) SeanLevey 2 (Richard Hannon) *s.i.s: hld up: hdwy over 1f out: sn swtchd rt: led wl ins fnl f: r.o* 9/4[1]	93+
1533	2	1¼	**Cristal Breeze (IRE)**[28] 5442 3-9-0 83 ... WilliamBuick 1 (William Haggas) *led: shkn up over 2f out: rdn and edgd lft over 1f out: hdd ins fnl f: styd on* 3/1[3]	88
55-6	3	hd	**Canton Queen (IRE)**[126] 1939 3-9-7 90 ... TomQueally 7 (Richard Hannon) *chsd ldrs: rdn to ld and edgd rt ins fnl f: sn hdd: styd on same pce* 25/1	94
3342	4	2	**Nubough (IRE)**[7] 6225 3-8-11 83 ... ConorMcGovern(3) 3 (Iain Jardine) *chsd ldrs: rdn and ev ch fr over 1f out tl nt clr run and no ex ins fnl f* 11/2	82
1532	5	hd	**Tenax (IRE)**[19] 5724 3-8-11 85 ... FayeMcManoman(5) 8 (Nigel Tinkler) *rrd s: bhd: hdwy over 1f out: rdn and edgd rt ins fnl f: styd on same pce* 9/1	83
1401	6	11	**Moraawed**[31] 5319 3-9-8 91 ... DaneO'Neill 6 (Roger Varian) *chsd ldrs: rdn whn hmpd over 1f out: wknd ins fnl f (trainer's rep could offer no explanation for the gelding's performance)* 11/4[2]	59

1m 25.24s (-0.46) **Going Correction** +0.15s/f (Good) 6 Ran SP% 111.7
Speed ratings (Par 104): **108,106,106,104,103 91**
CSF £9.19 CT £121.44 TOTE £3.10: £2.00, £2.10; EX 10.30 Trifecta £85.50.
Owner R Barnett **Bred** W & R Barnett Ltd **Trained** East Everleigh, Wilts
■ After John was withdrawn. Price at time of withdrawal 16/1. Rule 4 does not apply.
FOCUS
A fair handicap and they went a good gallop up the stands' side.

6452 PRICE BAILEY "FIRM OF THE YEAR" H'CAP — 1m 6f
3:20 (3:21) (Class 2) (0-105,104) 3-Y-O+
£28,012 (£8,388; £4,194; £2,097; £1,048; £526) Stalls Low

Form				RPR
5-41	1		**Saroog**[42] 4899 5-9-2 96 ... WilliamBuick 6 (Simon Crisford) *sn chsng ldr: led over 3f out: rdn and hung lft fr over 1f out: styd on gamely* 11/8[1]	103
2051	2	1¼	**Themaxwecan (IRE)**[29] 5368 3-8-7 97 ... CliffordLee 2 (Mark Johnston) *led: hdd over 3f out: rdn over 2f out: hung lft over 1f out: styd on* 9/4[2]	104
5-04	3	hd	**Breath Caught**[43] 4863 4-8-10 90 ... CallumShepherd 4 (David Simcock) *hld up: hdwy over 2f out: rdn and hung lft fr over 1f out: styd on* 10/1	95
0200	4	½	**Byron Flyer**[49] 4646 8-9-10 104 ... (p) DavidProbert 7 (Ian Williams) *hld up: hdwy over 3f out: rdn and hung lft over 1f out: ev ch ins fnl f: styd on same pce towards fin* 11/1	108
1660	5	½	**Island Brave (IRE)**[21] 5662 5-9-4 98 ... AlistairRawlinson 5 (Heather Main) *hld up: hdwy over 3f out: rdn and edgd lft over 1f out: ev ch ins fnl f: no ex towards fin* 10/1	101
0050	6	1½	**Aircraft Carrier (IRE)**[3] 6355 4-9-1 95 ... (p) TomQueally 3 (John Ryan) *s.i.s: sn chsng ldrs: rdn over 2f out: hung lft and outpcd over 1f out: styd on ins fnl f* 25/1	96
310/	7	½	**Fiesole**[105] 7230 7-8-2 82 ... HayleyTurner 1 (Olly Murphy) *chsd ldrs: carried lft over 1f out: rdn and ev ch ins fnl f: wknd towards fin* 7/1[3]	83

3m 5.2s (5.30) **Going Correction** +0.15s/f (Good) 7 Ran SP% 115.7
WFA 3 from 4yo+ 10lb
Speed ratings (Par 109): **90,89,89,88,88 87,87**
CSF £4.75 TOTE £2.10: £1.50, £1.50; EX 5.50 Trifecta £19.80.
Owner Abdulla Al Mansoori **Bred** Ammerland Verwaltung Gmbh & Co Kg **Trained** Newmarket, Suffolk
FOCUS
A good staying handicap and the form looks solid, with the third helping to set a straightforward level and the first two in the betting coming to the fore. The same pair took them along at fair pace, and they finished fairly close up on the far side.

6453 PRICE BAILEY CHARTERED ACCOUNTANTS HOPEFUL STKS (LISTED RACE) — 6f
3:55 (4:00) (Class 1) 3-Y-O+
£20,982 (£7,955; £3,981; £1,983; £995; £499) Stalls Low

Form				RPR
6413	1		**Raucous**[21] 5664 6-9-1 105 ... (tp) AlistairRawlinson 2 (Robert Cowell) *sn chsng ldrs: shkn up over 2f out: rdn and hung lft fr over 1f out: styd on to ld towards fin (jockey said gelding hung left-handed)* 10/1	108
2046	2	hd	**Pretty Pollyanna**[20] 5716 3-8-7 109 ... HayleyTurner 4 (Michael Bell) *led early: trckd ldrs: rdn to ld ins fnl f: edgd lft: hdd towards fin (vet said filly lost its left fore shoe)* 10/11[1]	102
0022	3	nk	**Rock On Baileys**[20] 5705 4-8-10 94 ... (b) BarryMcHugh 10 (Amy Murphy) *hld up: hdwy over 1f out: rdn and ev ch ins fnl f: styd on* 33/1	101
5550	4	2¼	**Sir Thomas Gresham (IRE)**[112] 2409 4-9-1 101 ... (t) RobertWinston 3 (Tim Pinfield) *sn led: rdn over 1f out: hdd ins fnl f: edgd lft and no ex* 25/1	99
5111	5	hd	**Land Of Legends (IRE)**[21] 5666 3-8-12 104 ... CallumShepherd 8 (Saeed bin Suroor) *s.i.s: hmpd sn after s: hld up: hdwy over 2f out: rdn and nt clr run over 1f out: styd on same pce ins fnl f* 11/4[2]	99+
00	6	1	**Fille De Reve**[43] 4891 4-8-10 90 ... CliffordLee 6 (Ed Walker) *hld up: rdn and hung lft over 1f out: nt trble ldrs (jockey said filly hung left-handed under pressure)* 40/1	91
0-52	7	1½	**Enjazaat**[49] 4648 4-9-1 100 ... DaneO'Neill 9 (Owen Burrows) *s.i.s: hld up: hdwy u.p over 1f out: wknd ins fnl f* 12/1	91
0001	8	¾	**Good Effort (IRE)**[15] 5911 4-9-1 98 ... SeanLevey 7 (Ismail Mohammed) *hmpd after s: racd keenly and sn prom: rdn and ev ch over 1f out: wknd wl ins fnl f* 9/1[3]	89
116	9	3¾	**I Could Do Better (IRE)**[22] 5609 3-8-12 95 ... DavidProbert 1 (Ian Williams) *s.i.s: sn chsng ldrs: rdn over 2f out: edgd lft and wknd over 1f out (jockey said gelding was restless in the stalls)* 22/1	78

1220 **10** 23 **Emily Goldfinch**[14] 5944 6-8-10 92........................(p) RachelRichardson 5 4
(Phil McEntee) *wnt lft sn after s: jnd ldr over 5f out tl over 3f out: wknd over 2f out* **50/1**

1m 11.75s (-0.35) **Going Correction** +0.15s/f (Good)
WFA 3 from 4yo+ 3lb **10** Ran SP% **121.4**
Speed ratings (Par 111): **108,107,107,104,104 102,100,99,94,64**
CSF £19.67 TOTE £11.10: £2.40, £1.10, £6.90; EX 37.20 Trifecta £573.60.
Owner T W Morley **Bred** Saleh Al Homaizi & Imad Al Sagar **Trained** Six Mile Bottom, Cambs

FOCUS
A quality sprint and they came down the middle. It paid to race prominently and the third is possibly the key to the form.

6454 "GROW WITH PRICE BAILEY" H'CAP 1m 2f
4:30 (4:30) (Class 4) (0-85,85) 3-Y-O **£5,822** (£1,732; £865; £432) **Stalls** Centre

Form RPR
2132 **1** **Cardano (USA)**[14] 5973 3-9-7 **85**........................(p) RobertWinston 5 93
(Ian Williams) *trckd ldrs: racd keenly: wnt 2nd over 3f out: led over 2f out: rdn over 1f out: edgd lft ins fnl f: styd on* **15/8**[1]

2414 **2** nk **Bint Soghaan**[22] 5605 3-9-3 **81**........................ DaneO'Neill 3 88
(Richard Hannon) *stdd s: hld up: hdwy over 1f out: chsd wnr over 1f out: sn rdn and ev ch: edgd lft ins fnl f: styd on* **9/2**[3]

363 **3** 11 **Fearless Warrior (FR)**[47] 4739 3-9-0 **78**........................ DavidProbert 1 65
(Eve Johnson Houghton) *racd keenly: led 1f: remained w ldr tl shkn up over 3f out: rdn and wknd over 1f out* **4/1**[2]

02 **4** 2½ **Grey D'Ars (FR)**[3] 6349 3-9-1 **79**........................ CallumShepherd 2 61
(Nick Littmoden) *racd keenly: led after 1f: rdn and hdd over 2f out: wknd over 1f out* **15/8**[1]

2m 5.94s (-1.16) **Going Correction** +0.15s/f (Good) **4** Ran SP% **107.7**
Speed ratings (Par 102): **110,109,100,98**
CSF £9.96 TOTE £2.70; EX 7.80 Trifecta £11.80.
Owner Sohi & Sohi **Bred** Mt Brilliant Broodmares II Llc **Trained** Portway, Worcs

FOCUS
A fair handicap. The first two came clear and the form looks solid.

6455 PRICE BAILEY NEWMARKET OFFICE H'CAP 5f
5:05 (5:06) (Class 4) (0-85,87) 3-Y-O+
£5,822 (£1,732; £865; £432; £300; £300) **Stalls** Low

Form RPR
2220 **1** **Han Solo Berger (IRE)**[8] 6162 4-9-1 **73**........................(p) TomQueally 11 80
(Chris Wall) *hld up: hdwy 1/2-way: rdn and edgd rt over 1f out: led ins fnl f: r.o* **6/1**[2]

622 **2** nk **War Whisper (IRE)**[22] 5617 6-9-10 **82**........................ DavidProbert 9 88
(Paul Midgley) *trckd ldrs: rdn and ev ch whn n.m.r over 1f out: r.o* **8/1**

0410 **3** nse **Secretinthepark**[21] 5661 9-9-4 **76**........................(b) RobertWinston 2 82
(Michael Mullineaux) *sn w ldr: led 1/2-way: rdn and hdd ins fnl f: r.o* **7/1**[3]

1226 **4** ½ **Equitation**[26] 5504 5-10-1 **87**........................(t) DaneO'Neill 7 91
(Stuart Williams) *hld up: rdn and hung lft fr over 1f out: r.o: nt rch ldrs* **7/2**[1]

153 **5** ½ **Foxy Forever (IRE)**[22] 5606 9-9-9 **81**........................(bt) SeanLevey 4 83
(Michael Wigham) *hld up in tch: nt clr run and swtchd rt over 1f out: r.o* **7/1**[3]

4350 **6** ¾ **Leo Minor (USA)**[21] 5647 5-8-11 **69**........................(p) CliffordLee 8 68
(Robert Cowell) *chsd ldrs: rdn and ev ch over 1f out: no ex wl ins fnl f* **10/1**

1143 **7** ½ **Jack The Truth (IRE)**[28] 5444 5-9-10 **82**........................(h[1]) LouisSteward 10 80
(George Scott) *s.i.s: hld up: nt clr run over 1f out: r.o ins fnl f: nvr nrr* **10/1**

36 **8** 1¼ **Excessable**[22] 5617 6-9-3 **75**........................(t) RachelRichardson 1 68
(Tim Easterby) *chsd ldrs: rdn over 1f out: no ex ins fnl f* **8/1**

2120 **9** nk **Nibras Again**[8] 6178 5-9-8 **80**........................ HayleyTurner 6 72
(Paul Midgley) *s.i.s: hld up: nvr on terms* **6/1**[2]

0056 **10** 12 **Sandridge Lad (IRE)**[38] 5064 3-8-6 **66**........................ AdrianMcCarthy 3 15
(John Ryan) *hld up: pushed along 1/2-way: wknd over 1f out (jockey said gelding stumbled when leaving the stalls)* **40/1**

4006 **11** 7 **Victory Angel (IRE)**[25] 5530 5-9-12 **84**........................(v) CallumShepherd 5 8
(Robert Cowell) *led to 1/2-way: wknd and eased fnl f (jockey said filly stopped quickly)* **18/1**

58.75s (0.05) **Going Correction** +0.15s/f (Good)
WFA 3 from 4yo+ 2lb **11** Ran SP% **123.9**
Speed ratings (Par 105): **105,104,104,103,102 101,100,98,98,79 67**
CSF £56.52 CT £360.34 TOTE £6.70: £2.30, £3.20, £2.50; EX 60.50 Trifecta £670.40.
Owner Mrs B Berresford **Bred** Irish National Stud **Trained** Newmarket, Suffolk

FOCUS
A competitive sprint and they came down the middle, the first two emerging more towards the far side. The winner has been rated in line with this year's form.
T/Plt: £55.10 to a £1 stake. Pool: £55,516.66 - 734.70 winning units T/Qpdt: £6.20 to a £1 stake. Pool: £3,785.70 - 445.81 winning units **Colin Roberts**

5968 REDCAR (L-H)
Saturday, August 24

OFFICIAL GOING: Good to firm (good in places; 8.7)
Wind: virtually nil Weather: Hot and sunny

6456 JOIN RACING TV NOW H'CAP (FOR LADY AMATEUR RIDERS) 1m 2f 1y
4:55 (4:55) (Class 5) (0-75,75) 3-Y-O+
£3,619 (£1,122; £560; £400; £400; £400) **Stalls** Low

Form RPR
0-36 **1** **Regal Director (IRE)**[70] 3861 4-10-7 **75**........................ MissBrodieHampson 3 85+
(Archie Watson) *trckd ldrs: pushed into ld over 2f out: rdn and styd on wl* **6/4**[1]

0000 **2** 3 **Capton**[17] 5820 6-10-5 **73**........................ MissJoannaMason 7 75
(Michael Easterby) *prom: led over 3f out: rdn and hdd over 2f out: styd on same pce* **6/1**[3]

0300 **3** ½ **Firby (IRE)**[19] 5728 4-9-7 **68**........................ MissRachelTaylor(7) 8 69
(Michael Dods) *hld up in rr: hdwy over 2f out: reminder and chsd ldr over 1f out: kpt on same pce* **16/1**

0444 **4** 2¾ **Thomas Cranmer (USA)**[10] 6067 5-10-4 **72**.... MissSerenaBrotherton 6 68
(Tina Jackson) *trckd ldrs: rdn along 3f out: sn one pce* **5/2**[2]

4123 **5** nse **Thorntoun Care**[19] 5728 8-9-10 **69**........................(p) MissAmyCollier(5) 10 65
(Karen Tutty) *hld up: pushed along and hdwy 2f out: kpt on same pce* **11/1**

0444 **6** 7 **Quoteline Direct**[17] 5817 6-9-7 **61**........................(h) MissBeckySmith 5 43
(Micky Hammond) *hld up in midfield: rdn along 3f out: wknd over 1f out* **9/1**

0000 **7** 2½ **Squire**[21] 5653 8-8-11 **56** oh2........................(tp) SophieSmith(5) 11 34
(Marjorie Fife) *led: rdn and hdd over 3f out: sn wknd* **50/1**

1336 **8** 3¾ **Ventura Gold (IRE)**[59] 4239 4-10-6 **74**........................ MissAmieWaugh 1 45
(Steve Gollings) *hld up: rdn along 3f out: sn wknd* **11/1**

5215 **9** 10 **Bollin Joan**[16] 5849 4-10-4 **72**........................(p) MissEmilyEasterby 12 24
(Tim Easterby) *in tch on outer: rdn over 3f out: sn wknd* **12/1**

2m 3.22s (-3.68) **Going Correction** -0.325s/f (Firm) **9** Ran SP% **125.1**
Speed ratings (Par 103): **101,98,98,96,95 90,88,85,77**
CSF £12.56 CT £114.47 TOTE £2.50: £1.30, £2.60, £5.80; EX 16.00 Trifecta £209.80.
Owner The Real Quiz **Bred** Sheikh Mohammed Obaid Al Maktoum **Trained** Upper Lambourn, W Berks
■ Railport Dolly was withdrawn. Price at time of withdrawal 4/1. Rule 4 applies to board prices prior to withdrawal - deduction 20p in the pound. New market formed

FOCUS
Fast ground in evidence for this meeting. This was a handicap for women amateur riders featuring mainly exposed sorts run at a fair gallop, but the winner could do better still.

6457 BEST FLAT RACES LIVE ON RACING TV NOVICE AUCTION STKS 5f 217y
5:30 (5:31) (Class 5) 2-Y-O **£4,204** (£1,251; £625; £312) **Stalls** Centre

Form RPR
1 **Bond's Boy** 2-8-12 0........................ ConnorMurtagh(3) 10 74+
(Richard Fahey) *hld up: pushed along and gd hdwy 2f out: led ins fnl f: kpt on wl* **16/1**

0344 **2** 2½ **Paddy Elliott (IRE)**[40] 4999 2-9-3 71........................ BenRobinson 6 68
(Brian Ellison) *prom: rdn over 2f out: led jst ins fnl f: sn hdd: one pce* **4/1**[2]

3 1 **Challet (IRE)** 2-9-5 0........................ AndrewMullen 13 67
(Michael Dods) *trckd ldrs: rdn along over 2f out: kpt on same pce* **20/1**

60 **4** ½ **Wade's Magic**[10] 6064 2-9-5 0........................ JamieGormley 12 65
(Tim Easterby) *trckd ldrs: rdn 2f out: kpt on ins fnl f* **33/1**

5 nse **Dream Together (IRE)** 2-9-3 0........................ JackGarritty 4 63+
(Jedd O'Keeffe) *s.i.s: hld up: pushed along 2f out: r.o wl fnl 150yds: nrst fin* **22/1**

6 shd **Um Aljadeela (IRE)** 2-9-0 0........................ ShaneGray 8 60
(Kevin Ryan) *midfield: pushed along over 2f out: kpt on ins fnl f: briefly short of room 75yds out* **11/1**

02 **7** nse **Abbey Wharf (IRE)**[28] 5456 2-8-9 0........................ RowanScott(3) 1 58
(Nigel Tinkler) *in tch: rdn and outpcd over 2f out: kpt on fnl f* **9/2**[3]

3 **8** nk **Tyler Durden (IRE)**[16] 5865 2-9-5 0........................(h) PaulMulrennan 9 64
(Richard Spencer) *chsd ldrs: rdn and edgd lft over 2f out: drvn over 1f out: no ex ins fnl f* **2/1**[1]

9 1½ **Joshua R (IRE)** 2-9-1 0........................ KevinStott 5 55
(David Barron) *led: rdn 3 l clr over 2f out: edgd lft over 1f out: drvn and hdd jst ins fnl f: wknd* **16/1**

10 2½ **Ventura Express** 2-9-2 0........................ SeanDavis(3) 2 51+
(Richard Fahey) *v.s.a and bhd: sme late hdwy* **8/1**

11 1 **Rosa P** 2-8-12 0........................ RoystonFfrench 7 41
(Steph Hollinshead) *hld up: nvr threatened* **50/1**

00 **12** 6 **Hands Down (IRE)**[10] 6064 2-9-0 0........................ LewisEdmunds 11 23
(Nigel Tinkler) *hld up: nvr threatened* **100/1**

1m 9.46s (-2.34) **Going Correction** -0.325s/f (Firm) **12** Ran SP% **117.7**
Speed ratings (Par 94): **106,102,101,100,100 100,100,100,98,94 93,85**
CSF £75.07 TOTE £20.80: £5.00, £1.40, £7.10; EX 85.60 Trifecta £1019.60.
Owner Crown Select **Bred** David Hoigate **Trained** Musley Bank, N Yorks

FOCUS
A novice auction for 2yos in which seven of the 12 were making their debuts. This has been rated ordinary form.

6458 BAKERS TAILORING AND FORMAL HIRE FILLIES' NOVICE AUCTION STKS (PLUS 10 RACE) 7f
6:00 (6:01) (Class 5) 2-Y-O **£4,204** (£1,251; £625; £312) **Stalls** Centre

Form RPR
21 **1** **Nirodha (IRE)**[30] 5353 2-9-4 0........................ SeanDavis(3) 4 74
(Amy Murphy) *mde all: rdn over 2f out: hung lft over 1f out: drvn out* **5/1**

3425 **2** ¾ **Lexi The One (IRE)**[20] 5703 2-8-11 66........................ ConnorMurtagh(3) 6 65
(Richard Fahey) *trckd ldr: rdn and outpcd in 4th over 2f out: kpt on ins fnl f to go 2nd fnl 110yds* **9/2**[3]

032 **3** 2 **Bertie's Princess (IRE)**[10] 6064 2-8-11 68........................ RowanScott(3) 2 60
(Nigel Tinkler) *trckd ldr: rdn over 2f out: kpt on same pce* **3/1**[2]

3 **4** 1¾ **Katniss Everdeen (IRE)**[10] 6078 2-9-0 0........................ PaulMulrennan 1 56
(Richard Spencer) *trckd ldr: keen early: rdn over 2f out: no ex fnl 110yds* **6/4**[1]

06 **5** 3¼ **Carriage Clock**[15] 5895 2-9-0 0........................ RoystonFfrench 7 46
(Steph Hollinshead) *hld up: pushed along over 2f out: nvr threatened* **33/1**

00 **6** 9 **Boulevard Beauty (IRE)**[15] 5895 2-9-0 0........................ JasonHart 3 22
(Tim Easterby) *hld up: rdn over 2f out: sn wknd* **50/1**

250 **7** 9 **Just Jean (IRE)**[52] 4517 2-9-0 61........................ AndrewMullen 8
(Micky Hammond) *hld up: rdn over 2f out: sn wknd (jockey said filly lost its action)* **14/1**

1m 24.7s (-0.70) **Going Correction** -0.325s/f (Firm) **7** Ran SP% **111.4**
Speed ratings (Par 91): **91,90,87,85,82 71,61**
CSF £26.05 TOTE £11.00: £3.20, £1.40; EX 23.70 Trifecta £51.30.
Owner Daniel Macauliffe & Anoj Don **Bred** Leaf Stud **Trained** Newmarket, Suffolk

FOCUS
An ordinary novice auction for juvenile fillies.

6459 MARKET CROSS JEWELLERS H'CAP 1m 5f 218y
6:30 (6:31) (Class 4) (0-80,79) 3-Y-O **£6,080** (£1,809; £904; £452; £400) **Stalls** Low

Form RPR
2233 **1** **Selino**[19] 5734 3-9-7 **79**........................(v[1]) DanielMuscutt 3 87
(James Fanshawe) *hld up: rdn and hdwy on outer over 2f out: drvn to chse ldrs over 1f out: chal strly fnl 50yds: led post* **10/3**[3]

1113 **2** nse **Funny Man**[7] 6232 3-9-2 **74**........................(b) DanielTudhope 2 82
(David O'Meara) *hld up in tch: rdn along and hdwy over 2f out: chal over 1f out: drvn into ld ins fnl f: strly pressed fnl 50yds: hdd post* **11/4**[2]

4152 **3** 2 **Agravain**[14] 5974 3-8-8 **66**........................ DavidAllan 5 71
(Tim Easterby) *led: rdn and pressed over 2f out: drvn and hdd ins fnl f: no ex fnl 110yds* **5/1**

3513 **4** 2½ **Anyonecanhaveitall**[9] 6115 3-9-1 **73**........................ JoeFanning 4 75
(Mark Johnston) *trckd ldrs: rdn to chal over 2f out: outpcd and hld in 4th appr fnl f* **7/4**[1]

3122 **5** 6 **Well Funded (IRE)**[23] 5596 3-8-4 **65**........................ SeanDavis(3) 6 59
(James Bethell) *prom: rdn along over 3f out: wknd over 1f out* **12/1**

2m 59.92s (-7.08) **Going Correction** -0.325s/f (Firm) **5** Ran SP% **110.5**
Speed ratings (Par 102): **107,106,105,104,100**
CSF £12.80 TOTE £3.10: £1.30, £1.90; EX 10.50 Trifecta £45.50.
Owner Dr Catherine Wills **Bred** St Clare Hall Stud **Trained** Newmarket, Suffolk

FOCUS
Mainly progressive sorts in this. The pace was fair and the first two were the last two turning for home.

6460 RACING TV STRAIGHT MILE SERIES H'CAP (RACING UK STRAIGHT MILE SERIES QUALIFIER) 7f 219y

7:00 (7:00) (Class 3) (0-90,88) 3-Y-O+ £7,762 (£2,310; £1,154; £577) Stalls Centre

Form RPR

0440 **1** **Universal Gleam**[21] 5693 4-9-13 **87**......JoeFanning 2 95
(Keith Dalgleish) *stdd s: hld up: stdy hdwy over 3f out: pushed along to chse ldrs over 1f out: rdn to ld fnl 75yds* **9/2**[2]

1215 **2** ¾ **Star Shield**[21] 5693 4-9-8 **82**......DanielTudhope 14 88
(David O'Meara) *trckd ldrs: racd quite keenly: pushed along over 1f out: drvn to chal ins fnl f: kpt on* **3/1**[1]

0002 **3** nk **Give It Some Teddy**[14] 5970 5-9-2 **76**......DuranFentiman 8 81
(Tim Easterby) *hld up in midfield: rdn and hdwy over 1f out: kpt on wl fnl f* **6/1**[3]

030 **4** ¾ **Scottish Summit (IRE)**[19] 5741 6-9-6 **80**......KevinStott 16 84
(Geoffrey Harker) *prom: rdn to ld 2f out: edgd lft over 1f out: drvn fnl f: hdd 75yds out: no ex* **22/1**

0330 **5** nse **Algaffaal (USA)**[28] 5445 4-9-2 **76**......(p) BenRobinson 17 79
(Brian Ellison) *s.i.s: hld up: rdn along 3f out: sme hdwy over 1f out: styd on wl fnl 110yds* **33/1**

066- **6** ½ **Tangled (IRE)**[253] 9532 4-9-8 **85**......GemmaTutty(3) 3 87
(Karen Tutty) *midfield: racd keenly: hdwy and prom 3f out: rdn over 1f out: kpt on same pce ins fnl f* **18/1**

5250 **7** nk **Kripke (IRE)**[21] 5693 4-9-8 **82**......BenCurtis 1 84
(David Barron) *chsd ldrs: rdn and outpcd over 2f out: kpt on ins fnl f* **6/1**[3]

5-20 **8** 5 **Young Fire (FR)**[14] 5948 4-10-0 **88**......DavidNolan 18 78
(David O'Meara) *midfield: pushed along 3f out: wknd ins fnl f* **11/1**

3056 **9** 2¼ **Rashdan (FR)**[26] 5489 4-8-13 **73**......JamieGormley 4 58
(Iain Jardine) *dwlt: hld up: nvr threatened (jockey said gelding anticipated the start and missed the break)* **12/1**

2210 **10** nk **Strong Steps**[7] 6204 7-8-6 **69**......(p) SeanDavis(3) 13 53
(Jim Goldie) *prom: rdn over 2f out: wknd over 1f out* **25/1**

-006 **11** 1¼ **Banksea**[48] 4692 6-9-10 **87**......(h) ConnorMurtagh(3) 6 68
(Marjorie Fife) *hld up: rdn over 3f out: sn wknd* **25/1**

04-0 **12** 2¾ **Destroyer**[29] 5398 6-8-12 **72**......JamesSullivan 15 47
(Tom Tate) *led: rdn and hdd 2f out: wknd* **40/1**

5302 **13** 13 **Whinmoor**[14] 5971 4-9-7 **84**......(t) RowanScott(3) 9 29
(Nigel Tinkler) *trckd ldrs: rdn and lost pl 3f out: wknd over 1f out* **7/1**

1m 36.01s (-0.59) **Going Correction** -0.325s/f (Firm) **13 Ran SP% 123.0**
Speed ratings (Par 107): **89,88,87,87,87 86,86,81,79,78 77,74,61**
CSF £17.74 CT £87.81 TOTE £5.50: £2.60, £1.70, £2.00; EX 27.00 Trifecta £125.80.
Owner Weldspec Glasgow Limited **Bred** Mrs D O'Brien **Trained** Carluke, S Lanarks

FOCUS
Straightforward form with a few regulars running close to their recent levels and the winner rates back to his best.

6461 EVERY RACE LIVE ON RACING TV H'CAP 7f

7:30 (7:32) (Class 5) (0-75,75) 3-Y-O+ £3,755 (£1,117; £558; £400; £400; £400) Stalls Centre

Form RPR

6662 **1** **Valley Of Fire**[7] 6204 7-9-3 **66**......(p) LewisEdmunds 8 72
(Les Eyre) *dwlt: hld up: rdn and hdwy over 1f out: kpt on wl: led 50yds out* **15/2**

0015 **2** ½ **Strawberryandcream**[17] 5816 4-9-0 **63**......PaulHanagan 6 68
(James Bethell) *prom: rdn 2f out: led 1f out: sn drvn: hdd 50yds out: kpt on* **20/1**

003 **3** shd **Mostahel**[49] 4660 5-9-5 **68**......PaulMulrennan 4 72
(Paul Midgley) *trckd ldrs: pushed along and bit short of room over 1f out: swtchd rt appr fnl f: rdn and kpt on* **20/1**

4013 **4** ½ **Twin Appeal (IRE)**[18] 5770 8-9-9 **75**......GemmaTutty(3) 1 78
(Karen Tutty) *hld up: hdwy 2f out: rdn and kpt on fnl f* **6/1**[2]

2355 **5** ½ **Esprit De Corps**[6] 6261 5-9-9 **72**......DanielMuscutt 9 74
(David Barron) *s.i.s: hld up: prog into midfield over 3f out: rdn to chse ldrs appr fnl f: kpt on (jockey said gelding stumbled leaving the stalls)* **7/1**[3]

0003 **6** ½ **Make Me**[11] 6037 4-9-0 **63**......(b[1]) JasonHart 7 63
(Tim Easterby) *led: rdn over 2f out: hdd 1f out: one pce* **6/1**[2]

1433 **7** shd **Poet's Pride**[7] 6204 4-9-5 **68**......BenCurtis 2 68
(David Barron) *racd keenly in midfield: hdwy and chse ldrs 2f out: drvn to chal appr fnl f: no ex fnl 50yds* **3/1**[1]

5005 **8** 2½ **Deansgate (IRE)**[7] 6204 6-9-2 **68**......ConnorMurtagh(3) 13 61
(Julie Camacho) *dwlt: sn midfield: rdn along 3f out: no imp* **20/1**

5000 **9** nk **Mutafarrid (IRE)**[7] 6204 4-9-3 **66**......KevinStott 12 59
(Paul Midgley) *prom: rdn over 2f out: wknd over 1f out* **12/1**

6030 **10** ½ **Verdigris (IRE)**[7] 6204 4-9-2 **65**......TomEaves 15 56
(Ruth Carr) *slowly away: hld up: rdn 2f out: nvr threatened* **11/1**

1250 **11** ½ **Mr Strutter (IRE)**[16] 5852 5-9-1 **69**......BenSanderson(5) 14 59
(Ronald Thompson) *hld up in midfield: rdn over 2f out: nvr threatened* **16/1**

5433 **12** ¾ **Yes You (IRE)**[21] 5670 5-9-10 **73**......JamieGormley 19 61
(Iain Jardine) *trckd ldrs: rdn over 2f out: wknd over 1f out* **22/1**

0001 **13** 2¾ **Insurplus (IRE)**[24] 5560 6-8-2 **58**......CoreyMadden(7) 17 38
(Jim Goldie) *midfield: rdn over 2f out: wknd over 1f out* **25/1**

1m 23.39s (-2.01) **Going Correction** -0.325s/f (Firm) **13 Ran SP% 122.2**
WFA 3 from 4yo+ 5lb
Speed ratings (Par 103): **98,97,97,96,96 95,95,92,92,91 91,90,87**
CSF £155.91 CT £2886.93 TOTE £8.90: £3.10, £6.90, £6.20; EX 196.60 Trifecta £1992.60.
Owner Billy Parker & Steven Parker **Bred** Bearstone Stud Ltd **Trained** Catwick, N Yorks
■ Stewards' Enquiry : Lewis Edmunds three-day ban; careless riding (Sep 8-10)
Paul Hanagan two-day ban; misuse of whip (Sep 8-9)

FOCUS
A run-of-the-mill 7f handicap with the vast majority fully exposed.

6462 THANK YOU AND GOOD LUCK BECKY SHAW H'CAP 5f 217y

8:00 (8:02) (Class 6) (0-55,57) 3-Y-O+ £3,500 (£1,041; £520; £400; £400; £400) Stalls Centre

Form RPR

-005 **1** **Dahik (IRE)**[4] 6321 4-9-2 **55**......(b[1]) GerO'Neill(5) 10 62
(Michael Easterby) *mde all: sn clr: pushed along over 1f out: rdn ins fnl f: reduced advantage towards fin but nvr in danger* **4/1**[1]

3003 **2** 1 **Tizwotitiz**[8] 6168 3-9-1 **52**......(h) JasonHart 5 56
(Steph Hollinshead) *chsd clr ldr: rdn over 2f out: kpt on fnl f* **7/1**

0500 **3** 1¼ **Alqaab**[15] 5918 4-9-6 **54**......(h) JamesSullivan 8 54
(Ruth Carr) *midfield: rdn over 2f out: kpt on fnl f* **9/1**

005 **4** 1½ **Nifty Niece (IRE)**[24] 5558 5-8-12 **46** oh1......JoeFanning 2 41
(Ann Duffield) *dwlt: hld up: rdn along 3f out: hdwy over 1f out: kpt on* **16/1**

0600 **5** nse **Tavener**[38] 5038 7-9-3 **51**......(t) DavidNolan 13 46
(Declan Carroll) *chsd clr ldr: rdn over 2f out: edgd lft and no ex ins fnl f* **12/1**

0012 **6** shd **Grimsdyke**[15] 5914 3-9-1 **52**......DuranFentiman 20 47
(Tim Easterby) *midfield: rdn over 2f out: kpt on same pce and nvr threatened* **9/2**[2]

0044 **7** ½ **Caledonian Gold**[15] 5918 6-8-5 **46** oh1......GavinAshton(7) 15 39
(Lisa Williamson) *midfield: rdn along 3f out: plugged on: nvr threatened* **28/1**

2000 **8** 1¼ **Dalness Express**[43] 4873 6-8-6 **47**......(t) Pierre-LouisJamin(7) 17 36
(Archie Watson) *dwlt: sn pushed along and nvr bttr than midfield* **5/1**[3]

0020 **9** nk **Deeds Not Words (IRE)**[5] 6273 8-9-9 **57**......(p) RoystonFrench 19 45
(Tracy Waggott) *nvr bttr than midfield (jockey said gelding was never travelling)* **25/1**

000 **10** 1 **Lord Of The Glen**[81] 3452 4-9-1 **52**......SeanDavis(3) 18 37
(Jim Goldie) *hld up: nvr threatened* **25/1**

0304 **11** ¾ **Jessie Allan (IRE)**[14] 5935 8-8-5 **46** oh1......CoreyMadden(7) 11 29
(Jim Goldie) *dwlt: hld up: nvr threatened* **16/1**

00-0 **12** 3½ **Hey Jazzy Lady (IRE)**[15] 5914 3-8-13 **50**......DavidAllan 16 21
(Andrew Crook) *midfield: rdn over 2f out: wknd over 1f out* **50/1**

6003 **13** 2 **Epaulini**[13] 5981 3-8-11 **48**......(p[1]) TomEaves 12 13
(Michael Dods) *chsd clr ldr: rdn 3f out: wknd over 1f out* **14/1**

0-00 **14** 6 **Jessinamillion**[18] 5787 5-9-1 **49**......(p) PaulHanagan 14
(James Bethell) *dwlt: a in rr* **12/1**

0-00 **15** 10 **Sandytown (IRE)**[56] 4367 4-9-2 **50**......PhilDennis 1
(David C Griffiths) *a in rr* **33/1**

1m 9.89s (-1.91) **Going Correction** -0.325s/f (Firm) **15 Ran SP% 127.2**
WFA 3 from 4yo+ 3lb
Speed ratings (Par 101): **103,101,100,98,97 97,97,95,95,93 92,88,85,77,64**
CSF £31.70 CT £206.84 TOTE £5.10: £2.60, £2.20, £3.70; EX 34.60 Trifecta £243.30.
Owner A Saha **Bred** Tally-Ho Stud **Trained** Sheriff Hutton, N Yorks

FOCUS
A low-grade race but quite an interesting winner.
T/Plt: £1,086.80 to a £1 stake. Pool: £40,942.00 - 27.50 winning units T/Qpdt: £85.40 to a £1 stake. Pool: £6,098.94 - 52.84 winning units **Andrew Sheret**

6286 WINDSOR (R-H)

Saturday, August 24

OFFICIAL GOING: Good to firm (watered; 7.4)
Wind: Almost nil Weather: Sunny, hot

6463 MPM FLOORING H'CAP 1m 3f 99y

4:40 (4:43) (Class 5) (0-75,75) 3-Y-O £3,428 (£1,020; £509; £400; £400; £400) Stalls Low

Form RPR

3-62 **1** **Fantastic Blue**[18] 5779 3-9-6 **74**......PatCosgrave 4 88
(Ismail Mohammed) *hld up in 4th: shkn up 3f out: prog over 2f out: rdn to ld over 1f out: styd on to draw clr fnl f* **6/4**[1]

3522 **2** 3 **Starfighter**[30] 5355 3-9-7 **75**......LiamKeniry 2 84
(Ed Walker) *hld up in last pair: shkn up and prog 3f out: rdn to chal and w wnr over 1f out: kpt on one pce fnl f* **3/1**[2]

1145 **3** 6 **Cherry Cola**[18] 5778 3-9-1 **69**......TrevorWhelan 3 69
(Sheena West) *hld up in last pair: swift move on inner to ld wl over 2f out: sn rdn: hdd & wknd over 1f out* **8/1**

214 **4** 1¾ **Mukha Magic**[26] 5502 3-9-0 **68**......(v) GeorgeDowning 5 65
(Gay Kelleway) *chsd ldr 2f: rdn over 3f out and tried to chal: lost pl and n.m.r 2f out: wknd* **6/1**[3]

4112 **5** hd **Sadlers Beach (IRE)**[22] 5601 3-8-10 **64**......(h) MartinDwyer 1 60
(Marcus Tregoning) *awkward s: quick rcvry to chse clr ldr after 2f: rdn to chal over 3f out: stl upsides over 2f out: wknd wl over 1f out* **6/1**[3]

3046 **6** 7 **Allocator (FR)**[10] 6083 3-9-2 **70**......RossaRyan 6 55
(Richard Hannon) *led and sn clr: c bk to rivals 4f out: hdd & wknd qckly wl over 2f out (jockey said gelding ran too freely)* **16/1**

2m 25.62s (-4.08) **Going Correction** -0.125s/f (Firm) **6 Ran SP% 110.6**
Speed ratings (Par 100): **109,106,102,101,101 95**
CSF £5.93 TOTE £2.10: £1.50, £1.80; EX 5.80 Trifecta £23.20.
Owner Nabil Mourad **Bred** Whitwell Bloodstock **Trained** Newmarket, Suffolk

FOCUS
A wide open 0-75 but the market got this right with the well-backed Fantastic Blue doing the business despite still not looking anything like the finished article.

6464 MPM FLOORING NOVICE STKS 6f 12y

5:15 (5:18) (Class 5) 2-Y-O £3,428 (£1,020; £509; £254) Stalls Centre

Form RPR

61 **1** **Golden Dragon (IRE)**[26] 5500 2-9-9 0......PatCosgrave 7 89
(Stuart Williams) *trckd ldng pair: shkn up 2f out: led on outer 1f out: hung lft fnl f: jst hld on* **4/1**[3]

2 shd **King's Lynn** 2-9-2 0......OisinMurphy 6 82+
(Andrew Balding) *dwlt: in tch towards rr: pushed along and prog 2f out: styd on wl fnl f: tk 2nd nr fin and clsd qckly on wnr: jst failed* **9/1**

15 **3** ¾ **Old News**[36] 5134 2-9-9 0......ShaneKelly 1 86
(Richard Hughes) *racd against rail: mde most: rdn and hdd 1f out: styd on same pce* **7/2**[2]

4 **4** ½ **Phuket Power (IRE)**[16] 5859 2-9-2 0......RichardKingscote 4 78
(Tom Dascombe) *w ldr: rdn 2f out: stl ev ch 1f out: kpt on same pce* **7/4**[1]

5 3¼ **Bill The Butcher (IRE)** 2-9-2 0......MartinDwyer 3 68
(Richard Spencer) *slowly away: t.k.h and sn chsd ldrs: hanging lft fr wl over 1f out: one pce after (jockey said colt hung left)* **14/1**

04 **6** 5 **Desert Palms**[36] 5131 2-9-2 0......RossaRyan 10 53
(Richard Hannon) *dwlt: in tch on outer but nt gng that wl: rdn over 2f out: wknd over 1f out* **5/1**

0 **7** ½ **Awesome Gary**[40] 4992 2-9-2 0......BrettDoyle 5 52
(Tony Carroll) *chsd ldrs to 1/2-way: wknd over 2f out* **66/1**

8 1¼ **Thunder Flash** 2-9-2 0......LiamKeniry 2 48
(Ed Walker) *dwlt: a in rr: wknd 2f out* **25/1**

05 **9** *31* **Serious Jockin**[6] 6254 2-9-2 0 .... GeorgeDowning 8
(Mick Channon) *a in rr: wknd 1/2-way: eased 2f out: t.o (jockey said colt ran too free to post)* **66/1**

1m 12.27s (0.17) **Going Correction** -0.125s/f (Firm) **9** Ran SP% **118.8**
Speed ratings (Par 94): **93,92,91,91,86 80,79,77,36**
CSF £40.16 TOTE £5.20: £1.60, £3.10, £1.30; EX 38.20 Trifecta £151.10.

Owner Happy Valley Racing & Breeding Limited **Bred** Ms Morna McDowall **Trained** Newmarket, Suffolk

FOCUS
Not a bad little novices' contest featuring some interesting newcomers, but experience proved key, with the penalised runners finishing first and third. The winner rates an improver.

6465 WATCH SKY SPORTS RACING IN HD H'CAP — 6f 12y
5:50 (5:52) (Class 4) (0-80,82) 3-Y-O+
£5,207 (£1,549; £774; £400; £400; £400) **Stalls** Centre

Form — RPR

0011 **1** **Yimou (IRE)**[16] 5868 4-9-4 **78** .... MartinDwyer 7 91
(Dean Ivory) *mde all: shkn up over 1f out: clr and in command fnl f: rdn out* **13/8**[1]

3602 **2** *2 1/2* **Iconic Knight (IRE)**[29] 5395 4-9-4 **78** .... ShaneKelly 4 83
(Ed Walker) *prom: rdn to chse wnr wl over 1f out: no imp u.p fnl f (vet said gelding lost his left hind shoe)* **6/1**[3]

2312 **3** *shd* **Baby Steps**[17] 5821 3-9-2 **79** .... RichardKingscote 6 84
(David Loughnane) *prom: rdn and nt qckn 2f out: styd on again fnl f to press for 2nd nr fin* **11/2**[2]

4313 **4** *2 1/4* **Oeil De Tigre (FR)**[16] 5839 8-9-0 **81** .... ElishaWhittington(7) 5 78
(Tony Carroll) *sn hld up: pushed along 1/2-way: effrt on outer 2f out: nt qckn over 1f out: fdd ins fnl f* **8/1**

-664 **5** *nk* **Silca Mistress**[37] 5105 4-9-4 **78** .... LiamKeniry 8 75
(Clive Cox) *taken down away fr crowd: hld up: rdn on outer over 2f out: effrt wl over 1f out: sn no prog* **20/1**

0/6 **6** *1* **Duplication (IRE)**[14] 5965 5-9-6 **80** .... RobertHavlin 1 73
(John Ryan) *hld up in tch: cajoled along wl over 1f out: no real prog and nvr in it* **33/1**

0312 **7** *hd* **Tin Hat (IRE)**[4] 6301 3-9-5 **82** ....(p) GeorgeDowning 2 75
(Eve Johnson Houghton) *mostly chsd wnr to wl over 1f out: wknd* **6/1**[3]

0503 **8** *1/2* **Swiss Knight**[15] 5911 4-9-6 **80** ....(t) OisinMurphy 3 71
(Stuart Williams) *hld up in rr: shkn up 2f out: no prog and nvr in it (jockey said gelding stopped quickly)* **13/2**

1m 11.28s (-0.82) **Going Correction** -0.125s/f (Firm)
WFA 3 from 4yo+ 3lb **8** Ran SP% **114.2**
Speed ratings (Par 105): **100,96,96,93,93 91,91,90**
CSF £11.71 CT £43.08 TOTE £2.40: £1.10, £1.80, £1.80; EX 11.00 Trifecta £40.90.

Owner Andrew L Cohen **Bred** Alexander Bloodstock **Trained** Radlett, Herts

FOCUS
Some in-form horses in here but the most progressive runner in the field ran out an authoritative winner.

6466 SRI LANKA AUGUST STKS (LISTED RACE) — 1m 3f 99y
6:20 (6:20) (Class 1) 3-Y-O+ **£20,982** (£7,955; £3,981; £1,983; £995) **Stalls** Low

Form — RPR

0-05 **1** **Raakib Alhawa (IRE)**[71] 3814 3-8-11 98 .... JamieSpencer 5 109
(David Simcock) *stdd s: hld up in last: prog on outer over 2f out: shkn up to ld 1f out: rdn and edgd rt ins fnl f: styd on* **7/2**[2]

1-40 **2** *1 1/4* **Grace And Danger (IRE)**[93] 3012 3-8-8 94 ow2 .... OisinMurphy 2 104
(Andrew Balding) *t.k.h: cl up: pushed along and nt qckn 3f out: renewed effrt 2f out: chal jst over 1f out: hld whn sltly impeded ins fnl f* **11/2**

5202 **3** *1/2* **Lucius Tiberius (IRE)**[49] 4646 4-9-5 106 ....(t[1]) WilliamBuick 6 106
(Charlie Appleby) *trckd ldr: pushed along to chal 3f out: narrow ld wl over 1f out to fnl f: hld whn tightened up ins fnl f: kpt on* **5/4**[1]

0352 **4** *nse* **Crowned Eagle**[62] 4173 5-9-5 106 .... TomMarquand 4 105
(Marco Botti) *led: sent for home 3f out: drvn and narrowly hdd wl over 1f out: short of room briefly ins fnl f: kpt on* **4/1**[3]

-240 **5** *9* **Big Country (IRE)**[147] 1420 6-9-5 109 ....(w) LukeMorris 1 91
(Michael Appleby) *t.k.h hld up in 4th: rdn over 2f out: wknd over 1f out: eased* **8/1**

2m 25.23s (-4.47) **Going Correction** -0.125s/f (Firm)
WFA 3 from 4yo+ 8lb **5** Ran SP% **113.2**
Speed ratings (Par 111): **111,110,109,109,103**
CSF £22.12 TOTE £4.20: £2.00, £2.60; EX 20.60 Trifecta £72.20.

Owner Khalifa Dasmal **Bred** Springbank Way Stud **Trained** Newmarket, Suffolk

■ Stewards' Enquiry : Jamie Spencer two-day ban; careless riding (Sep 8-9)

FOCUS
The first two have been rated as improving but this was a messy renewal so it's difficult to have confidence in the form.

6467 SKY SPORTS RACING WINTER HILL STKS (GROUP 3) — 1m 2f
6:50 (6:51) (Class 1) 3-Y-O+ **£34,026** (£12,900; £6,456; £3,216; £1,614) **Stalls** Low

Form — RPR

0031 **1** **Desert Encounter (IRE)**[22] 5613 7-9-8 116 ....(h) JamieSpencer 1 119
(David Simcock) *hld up in last: cajoled along and prog against rail 2f out to chse ldr over 1f out: clsd to ld last 100yds: styd on wl* **4/1**[3]

0150 **2** *1/2* **Matterhorn (IRE)**[27] 5483 4-9-5 110 .... FrannyNorton 2 115
(Mark Johnston) *led: stretched on 3f out: drvn over 1f out: hdd last 100yds: tried to respond but no ex nr fin* **3/1**[2]

R402 **3** *5* **Accidental Agent**[9] 6122 5-9-5 112 ....(p) CharlesBishop 5 106
(Eve Johnson Houghton) *hld up in 4th: shkn up 3f out: no imp on ldr but disp 2nd briefly over 1f out: fdd ins fnl f* **12/1**

-214 **4** *shd* **Queen Power (IRE)**[65] 4014 3-8-9 104 .... OisinMurphy 3 103
(Sir Michael Stoute) *t.k.h: trckd ldng pair: shkn up 3f out: drvn to dispute 2nd briefly over 1f out but no imp on wnr: fdd ins fnl f* **11/8**[1]

1-10 **5** *nk* **Star Of Bengal**[67] 3953 4-9-5 107 ....(p) RobertHavlin 4 105
(John Gosden) *trckd ldr: rdn over 2f out and no imp: lost 2nd and fdd over 1f out* **9/2**

2m 4.24s (-4.76) **Going Correction** -0.125s/f (Firm) course record
WFA 3 from 4yo+ 7lb **5** Ran SP% **113.0**
Speed ratings (Par 113): **114,113,109,109,109**
CSF £16.53 TOTE £4.70: £1.60, £2.00; EX 16.10 Trifecta £36.10.

Owner Abdulla Al Mansoori **Bred** Tally-Ho Stud **Trained** Newmarket, Suffolk

FOCUS
Quite a competitive Group 3 despite the small field. The winner has been rated to his best.

6468 WINDSOR RACECOURSE FIREWORKS RETURN - 2ND NOVEMBER H'CAP — 1m 31y
7:20 (7:21) (Class 4) (0-85,85) 3-Y-O+
£5,207 (£1,549; £774; £400; £400; £400) **Stalls** Low

Form — RPR

5114 **1** **City Wanderer (IRE)**[23] 5574 3-8-12 **75** ....(p[1]) TomMarquand 4 82
(Mick Channon) *led 100yds: chsd ldr after: pushed along 3f out: narrow ld wl over 1f out: jnd ins fnl f: styd on wl last 100yds* **10/1**

2321 **2** *1 1/4* **Rock The Cradle (IRE)**[16] 5863 3-9-1 **78** .... JamieSpencer 5 82
(Ed Vaughan) *t.k.h: hld up in last: prog on outer over 2f out: chsd wnr jst over 1f out and sn chalng: upsides ins fnl f: nt qckn last 100yds* **5/2**[1]

2014 **3** *1 1/4* **Marshal Dan (IRE)**[8] 6155 4-9-2 **80** .... StefanoCherchi(7) 1 83
(Heather Main) *trckd ldng pair: gng wl whn waiting for room over 2f out: swtchd lft wl over 1f out but gap clsd: rdn and n.m.r fnl f: styd on to take 3rd nr fin* **11/2**

4623 **4** *shd* **Medieval (IRE)**[8] 6155 5-9-6 **77** ....(p) RossaRyan 3 80
(Paul Cole) *hld up in 4th: pushed along 3f out: brought to chal over 1f out: nt qckn and hld whn short of room ins fnl f* **7/2**[2]

0542 **5** *1 1/2* **Oloroso (IRE)**[10] 6081 3-8-11 **74** .... OisinMurphy 6 72
(Andrew Balding) *led after 100yds: rdn and hdd wl over 1f out: grad fdd* **4/1**[3]

1020 **6** *nk* **La Maquina**[24] 5546 4-10-0 **85** ....(t) HarryBentley 2 83
(George Baker) *hld up in 5th: nt gng as wl as others fr 3f out: no real prog fnl 2f* **9/2**

1m 42.04s (-2.46) **Going Correction** -0.125s/f (Firm)
WFA 3 from 4yo+ 6lb **6** Ran SP% **113.5**
Speed ratings (Par 105): **107,105,104,104,102 102**
CSF £35.78 TOTE £8.90: £3.40, £1.70; EX 20.50 Trifecta £109.10.

Owner George Materna & Roger Badley **Bred** Kildaragh Stud **Trained** West Ilsley, Berks

FOCUS
Reasonably competitive for the grade and an open looking heat on paper. This rates a minor pb from the winner.

6469 FOLLOW AT THE RACES ON TWITTER H'CAP — 1m 31y
7:50 (7:51) (Class 5) (0-75,77) 3-Y-O+
£3,428 (£1,020; £509; £400; £400; £400) **Stalls** Low

Form — RPR

2236 **1** **Kingston Kurrajong**[21] 5667 6-9-11 **74** .... OisinMurphy 1 81
(William Knight) *trckd ldrs: plld out over 1f out: sn clsd: drvn to ld ins fnl f: edgd lft but hld on wl* **11/4**[1]

6644 **2** *nk* **Recondite (IRE)**[18] 5782 3-9-2 **71** .... HarryBentley 2 76
(Ralph Beckett) *trckd ldrs: drvn wl over 1f out: clsd to chal fnl f: jst hld last 50yds* **4/1**[2]

3235 **3** *3/4* **Jack D'Or**[18] 5779 3-9-4 **73** .... LiamKeniry 7 77
(Ed Walker) *trckd ldr: stl gng strly 2f out: rdn to chal over 1f out: fnd little and outpcd ins fnl f* **9/2**[3]

-530 **4** *3/4* **Water Diviner (IRE)**[17] 5804 3-9-8 **77** .... RossaRyan 5 79
(Richard Hannon) *led: rdn 2f out: hanging lft over 1f out: hdd and no ex ins fnl f (jockey said colt ran freely early on)* **14/1**

2225 **5** *1* **Amaretto**[23] 5570 4-8-9 **58** .... CharlieBennett 6 59
(Jim Boyle) *hld up in last pair: gng strly but same pl 2f out: shkn up over 1f out: styd on to take 5th nr fin: nvr cl enough to threaten* **14/1**

1052 **6** *hd* **Delicate Kiss**[30] 5351 5-9-8 **71** ....(b) LiamJones 3 71
(John Bridger) *towards rr: rdn over 2f out: no imp on ldrs over 1f out: one pce* **12/1**

0600 **7** *1 3/4* **Ghayadh**[58] 4300 4-9-12 **75** ....(h) JamieSpencer 8 71
(George Boughey) *s.s: hld up in last: stl there on outer 2f out but yet to be asked for effrt: no prog and swtchd ins fnl f: passed a few late on (jockey said gelding hung left causing his saddle to slip and rotate preventing him from riding an effective finish)* **12/1**

4062 **8** *nk* **Noble Fox**[26] 5505 3-8-11 **69** ....(p[1]) WilliamCox(3) 9 63
(Clive Cox) *nvr bttr than midfield: rdn over 2f out: no prog over 1f out* **15/2**

6500 **9** *1 1/4* **Letsbe Avenue (IRE)**[8] 6164 4-9-7 **70** .... TomMarquand 4 63
(Richard Hannon) *a towards rr: rdn and no prog over 2f out* **12/1**

3006 **10** *3 3/4* **Keeper's Choice (IRE)**[10] 6084 5-9-5 **68** .... ShaneKelly 10 52
(Denis Coakley) *prom: lost pl 1/2-way: cl up again over 2f out: drvn and wknd wl over 1f out* **16/1**

1m 43.48s (-1.02) **Going Correction** -0.125s/f (Firm)
WFA 3 from 4yo+ 6lb **10** Ran SP% **118.9**
Speed ratings (Par 103): **100,99,98,98,97 97,95,94,93,89**
CSF £13.75 CT £49.49 TOTE £3.30: £1.50, £2.10, £1.80; EX 16.00 Trifecta £93.70.

Owner Canisbay Bloodstock **Bred** Kingston Park Studs Pty Ltd **Trained** Angmering, W Sussex

FOCUS
A wide-open handicap run and the winner rates in line with his best turf form of recent years.
T/Plt: £198.10 to a £1 stake. Pool: £41,270.77 - 152.06 winning units T/Qpdt: £45.10 to a £1 stake. Pool: £6,025.12 - 98.69 winning units **Jonathon Neesom**

6420 YORK (L-H)
Saturday, August 24

OFFICIAL GOING: Good to firm (watered; overall 7.4, home straight: far side 7.3, centre 7.3, stands' side 7.2)
Wind: Moderate behind Weather: Warm and sunny

6470 SKY BET AND SYMPHONY GROUP STRENSALL STKS (GROUP 3) — 1m 177y
1:50 (1:50) (Class 1) 3-Y-O+
£56,710 (£21,500; £10,760; £5,360; £2,690; £1,350) **Stalls** Low

Form — RPR

1120 **1** **Zaaki**[25] 5521 4-9-8 112 .... RyanMoore 5 114
(Sir Michael Stoute) *racd keenly: trckd ldrs: rdn over 2f out: led wl over 1f out: kpt on gamely* **7/2**[2]

1025 **2** *nk* **Bangkok (IRE)**[28] 5455 3-9-1 109 .... JamesDoyle 6 113
(Andrew Balding) *hld up: effrt 3f: hdwy to ld briefly over 1f out: hdd ent fnl 1f: sn drvn: kpt on* **7/1**[3]

3016 **3** *1/2* **Space Traveller**[25] 5521 3-9-1 113 .... DanielTudhope 2 112
(Richard Fahey) *t.k.h: hld up: rdn over 3f out: drvn to chal over 1f out: kpt on same pce* **10/1**

-112 **4** *1 1/4* **Wissahickon (USA)**[127] 1921 4-9-8 115 .... FrankieDettori 1 110
(John Gosden) *trckd ldr: rdn to ld over 2f out: hdd wl over 1f out: one pce fnl 1f* **1/1**[1]

213 **5** *nk* **Escobar (IRE)**[22] 5610 5-9-5 104....................(t) JamieSpencer 3 106
(David O'Meara) *hld up in rr: hdwy 3f out: rdn along 2f out: kpt on same pce (gelding arrived at the start with blood in its mouth having bitten its tongue and was deemed fit to race)* **8/1**

0216 **6** *nk* **Forest Ranger (IRE)**[28] 5455 5-9-10 112.................... TonyHamilton 4 110
(Richard Fahey) *led: hdd over 2f out: sn drvn: wknd fnl 1f* **12/1**

1m 48.68s (-1.72) **Going Correction** -0.125s/f (Firm)
WFA 3 from 4yo+ 7lb **6** Ran SP% **112.6**
Speed ratings (Par 113): **102,101,101,100,99 99**
CSF £27.12 TOTE £4.20: £1.90, £2.50; EX 25.80 Trifecta £132.30.
Owner Ahmad Alotaibi **Bred** Miss K Rausing **Trained** Newmarket, Suffolk

FOCUS
The rail was out three metres from the innermost position providing fresh ground from 1m1f to the entrance to the home straight, adding 9yds to this distance. There was 3mm-4mm of water put on overnight and it was another warm, sunny day. This was a solid, competitive Group 3 in which all bar the fifth horse were penalised for winning in Group company this year. They raced up the middle in the straight.

6471 SKY BET MELROSE H'CAP (HERITAGE HANDICAP) 1m 5f 188y
2:25 (2:26) (Class 2) (0-105,96) 3-Y-O
£77,812 (£23,300; £11,650; £5,825; £2,912; £1,462) **Stalls** Low

Form RPR

213 **1** **Hamish**[44] 4842 3-9-3 **92**.................... JamesDoyle 6 103+
(William Haggas) *hld up towards rr: pushed along and hdwy towards outer 3f out: chsd ldrs over 1f out: sn rdn to chal: drvn and kpt on wl to ld ins fnl f* **7/1**

211 **2** *3/4* **First In Line**[21] 5656 3-9-7 **96**.................... FrankieDettori 5 106+
(John Gosden) *trckd ldr: wd st towards stands' side: cl up 3f out: rdn to take slt ld nr stands' rail 1 1/2f out: drvn and hdd ins fnl f: kpt on* **3/1**[1]

1111 **3** *1 1/4* **Land Of Oz**[9] 6125 3-8-7 **82**.................... LukeMorris 1 90
(Sir Mark Prescott Bt) *trckd ldrs: hdwy and cl up over 2f out: sn rdn: drvn and ev ch jst over 1f out: kpt on same pce ins fnl f* **5/1**[2]

5541 **4** *nse* **Skymax (GER)**[36] 5135 3-8-13 **88**....................(b) AndreaAtzeni 4 96
(Ralph Beckett) *sn led: pushed along 3f out: rdn and hdd over 2f out: cl up: drvn over 1f out: edgd rt ent fnl f: kpt on same pce* **16/1**

4311 **5** *1 1/4* **Just Hubert (IRE)**[30] 5347 3-8-11 **86**.................... PJMcDonald 7 92
(William Muir) *chsd ldrs: hdwy 3f out: rdn along 2f out: drvn over 1f out: kpt on one pce* **20/1**

0545 **6** *nk* **Almania (IRE)**[23] 5583 3-9-6 **95**.................... DanielTudhope 10 101
(Sir Michael Stoute) *hld up towards rr: hdwy on inner 3f out: chsd ldrs wl over 1f out: sn rdn and ch appr fnl f: sn drvn and one pce* **8/1**

2123 **7** *1/2* **Kiefer**[28] 5417 3-8-13 **88**.................... CharlesBishop 9 93+
(Eve Johnson Houghton) *hld up in tch: hdwy 3f out: rdn along 2f out: sn drvn and no imp appr fnl f (vet said colt was showing signs of post-race heat stress)* **7/1**

-33 **8** *nk* **Eminence (IRE)**[24] 5541 3-9-7 **96**.................... RyanMoore 8 101
(A P O'Brien, Ire) *hld up in midfield: stdy hdwy on inner 3f out: chsd ldrs 2f out: rdn to dispute ld over 1f out: drvn and wknd ent fnl f* **6/1**[3]

2211 **9** *1/2* **Starczewski (USA)**[14] 5943 3-8-5 **80**.................... HollieDoyle 11 84
(David Simcock) *hld up in rr: effrt over 3f out: rdn along and chsng ldrs whn n.m.r over 1f out: sn drvn and no imp* **14/1**

-131 **10** *3/4* **Universal Order**[22] 5605 3-8-13 **88**.................... JamieSpencer 13 91
(David Simcock) *hld up in rr: hdwy wl over 2f out: sn rdn: drvn and no imp fr over 1f out* **16/1**

2113 **11** *2* **Rochester House (IRE)**[8] 6171 3-9-7 **96**.................... JoeFanning 3 96
(Mark Johnston) *trckd ldng pair: hdwy over 3f out: led over 2f out: sn rdn: hdd 1 1/2f out: sn drvn and wknd* **22/1**

2 **12** *30* **King's Vow (FR)**[22] 5637 3-9-7 **96**....................(t[1]) DonnachaO'Brien 2 56+
(Joseph Patrick O'Brien, Ire) *chsd ldrs: pushed along over 4f out: rdn over 3f out: wknd over 2f out: bhd and eased fnl f (trainer could offer no explanation for the colt's performance)* **20/1**

2m 56.08s (-4.12) **Going Correction** -0.125s/f (Firm) **12** Ran SP% **124.4**
Speed ratings (Par 106): **106,105,104,104,104 103,103,103,103,102 101,84**
CSF £28.83 CT £120.58 TOTE £8.80: £2.80, £1.70, £1.70; EX 41.80 Trifecta £346.10.
Owner B Haggas **Bred** J B Haggas **Trained** Newmarket, Suffolk

FOCUS
Add 11yds. A 'win and you're in' for next year's Ebor, this was a strong 3yo staying handicap with a number of these looking well handicapped including the first three finishers. They were spread out across the track in the straight but middle-to-near side looked best.

6472 SKY BET CITY OF YORK STKS (GROUP 2) 7f
3:00 (3:00) (Class 1) 3-Y-O+
£127,597 (£48,375; £24,210; £12,060; £6,052; £3,037) **Stalls** Low

Form RPR

3-16 **1** **Shine So Bright**[112] 2411 3-9-1 111.................... JamesDoyle 2 114
(Andrew Balding) *mde all: rdn wl over 1f out: drvn ins fnl f: hld on gamely nr fin* **6/1**

-261 **2** *nse* **Laurens (FR)**[27] 5479 4-9-8 116.................... PJMcDonald 6 117
(K R Burke) *trckd wnr: effrt 2f out: sn rdn along and chal over 1f out: drvn ins fnl f: kpt on wl towards fin: jst hld* **2/1**[1]

-110 **3** *2* **Cape Byron**[42] 4923 5-9-6 113.................... AndreaAtzeni 8 110
(Roger Varian) *chsd ldng pair: pushed along over 2f out: rdn wl over 1f out: drvn fnl f: no imp* **9/2**[2]

-244 **4** *1* **Speak In Colours**[25] 5521 4-9-6 111....................(t) DonnachaO'Brien 1 107
(Joseph Patrick O'Brien, Ire) *chsd ldrs: rdn along over 2f out: drvn over 1f out: kpt on same pce* **7/1**

0414 **5** *1* **Sir Dancealot (IRE)**[7] 6215 5-9-9 114.................... GeraldMosse 10 107+
(David Elsworth) *hld up in rr: hdwy 3f out: rdn to chse ldrs wl over 1f out: sn drvn and kpt on same pce* **7/1**

3343 **6** *1 1/2* **Gordon Lord Byron (IRE)**[15] 5923 11-9-6 106.................... ColinKeane 3 100
(T Hogan, Ire) *chsd ldrs: rdn along 3f out: drvn wl over 1f out: sn no imp* **33/1**

5550 **7** *1/2* **Le Brivido (FR)**[20] 5716 5-9-6 113.................... RyanMoore 9 99
(A P O'Brien, Ire) *hld up: a towards rr* **5/1**[3]

-216 **8** *1 1/2* **Servalan (IRE)**[15] 5923 3-8-12 99.................... ShaneFoley 4 90
(Mrs John Harrington, Ire) *a towards rr* **25/1**

1660 **9** *1* **Mr Lupton (IRE)**[20] 5716 6-9-9 110.................... PaulHanagan 7 95
(Richard Fahey) *in tch: pushed along over 3f out: rdn wl over 2f out: sn drvn and wknd* **33/1**

1m 21.0s (-3.60) **Going Correction** -0.125s/f (Firm) course record
WFA 3 from 4yo+ 5lb **9** Ran SP% **117.2**
Speed ratings (Par 115): **115,114,112,111,110 108,108,106,105**
CSF £18.41 CT £59.27 TOTE £7.10: £2.00, £1.20, £1.60; EX 18.30 Trifecta £97.60.
Owner King Power Racing Co Ltd **Bred** Miss K Rausing **Trained** Kingsclere, Hants

FOCUS
Newly upgraded to Group 2, this was a good race but the 1-2-3-4 raced in that order for most of the way. The action was middle-to-near side in the straight and the track record was lowered.

6473 SKY BET EBOR H'CAP (HERITAGE HANDICAP) 1m 5f 188y
3:40 (3:45) (Class 2) 4-Y-O+
£600,000 (£179,900; £95,000; £50,000; £28,600; £15,000) **Stalls** Low

Form RPR

0235 **1** **Mustajeer**[57] 4351 6-9-5 **108**....................(h) ColinKeane 2 114
(G M Lyons, Ire) *hld up in midfield: hdwy over 3f out: chsd ldrs 2f out: sn chal: rdn to ld over 1f out: drvn and edgd rt ins fnl f: kpt on wl towards fin* **16/1**

0010 **2** *3/4* **Red Galileo**[56] 4382 8-9-1 **109**....................(h) CierenFallon(5) 12 114
(Saeed bin Suroor) *hld up in midfield: hdwy and wd st: chsd ldrs nr stands' rail 3f out: rdn 2f out: ev ch over 1f out: drvn ent fnl f: kpt on* **25/1**

5030 **3** *1/2* **Desert Skyline (IRE)**[21] 5662 5-9-5 **108**....................(v[1]) GeraldMosse 15 112
(David Elsworth) *hld up towards rr: hdwy into midfield and wd st towards stands' rail: hdwy 3f out: nt clr run and swtchd lft 2f out: sn rdn: drvn jst over 1f out: kpt on wl fnl f* **25/1**

6230 **4** *3/4* **Raymond Tusk (IRE)**[65] 4015 4-9-8 **111**.................... JamieSpencer 21 114
(Richard Hannon) *hld up in rr: hdwy towards centre wl over 2f out: rdn and n.m.r wl over 1f out: styng on whn nt clr run jst over 1f out: rdn and kpt on strly fnl f* **16/1**

-333 **5** *1/2* **Barsanti (IRE)**[56] 4390 7-9-4 **107**....................(b[1]) AndreaAtzeni 8 111
(Roger Varian) *hld up in rr: hdwy and wd st: effrt nr stands' rail whn nt clr run 2f out: sn swtchd lft and rdn: n.m.r over 1f out: styd on wl fnl f* **25/1**

1-20 **6** *1/2* **True Self (IRE)**[44] 4856 6-9-7 **110**.................... DonnachaO'Brien 5 112
(W P Mullins, Ire) *hld up in tch on inner: hdwy 4f out: sn trcking ldrs: led over 2f out: sn jnd and rdn: hdd over 1f out: sn drvn: edgd rt and wknd ins fnl f* **14/1**

3-20 **7** *1 3/4* **Ben Vrackie**[43] 4884 4-9-5 **108**.................... FrankieDettori 22 108
(John Gosden) *wnt rt s: cl up: led after 2f: pushed along over 3f out: sn rdn: hdd over 2f out: sn drvn and grad wknd (trainer was asked to explain why he was running the colt here on going described as Good to Firm, having reported that the colt would prefer an easier surface following its run at Newmarket on 12 July 2019. Trainer said that in hindsight he felt it may* **8/1**[3]

-405 **8** *hd* **Prince Of Arran**[22] 5613 6-9-7 **110**.................... StevieDonohoe 16 110
(Charlie Fellowes) *in tch: hdwy 4f out: rdn along to chse ldrs wl over 2f out: drvn wl over 1f out: kpt on same pce fnl f* **33/1**

4-23 **9** *2* **Raheen House (IRE)**[42] 4933 5-9-8 **111**.................... JamesDoyle 9 108
(William Haggas) *hld up in rr: hdwy on inner 3f out: rdn along to chse ldrs wl over 1f out: sn drvn and no imp* **5/1**[1]

-202 **10** *1/2* **Mekong**[49] 4670 4-9-7 **110**.................... RyanMoore 3 106
(Sir Michael Stoute) *hld up towards rr on inner: effrt over 3f out: rdn along over 2f out: kpt on one pce* **14/1**

3613 **11** *3 3/4* **Cleonte (IRE)**[49] 4670 6-9-2 **105**.................... RobHornby 1 96
(Andrew Balding) *trckd ldrs: pushed along over 3f out: rdn over 2f out: sn drvn and one pce* **50/1**

60-3 **12** *3* **Max Dynamite (FR)**[36] 5164 9-9-7 **110**....................(p) RonanWhelan 10 98
(W P Mullins, Ire) *hld up towards rr: hdwy over 3f out: rdn along wl over 2f out: sn btn* **33/1**

10-1 **13** *hd* **Withhold**[35] 5183 6-9-10 **113**....................(p) JasonWatson 6 100
(Roger Charlton) *wnt lft s: slt ld 2f: trckd ldng pair: effrt and cl up over 3f out: rdn along wl over 2f out: sn drvn and grad wknd* **10/1**

1561 **14** *1 1/2* **Red Verdon (USA)**[42] 4933 6-9-9 **112**....................(b) ShaneFoley 14 97
(Ed Dunlop) *hld up towards rr: hdwy over 3f out: rdn along to chse ldrs 2f out: drvn over 1f out: wknd* **22/1**

4-10 **15** *1 1/4* **Wells Farhh Go (IRE)**[25] 5522 4-9-9 **112**.................... DavidAllan 13 96
(Tim Easterby) *hld up in rr: pushed along over 4f out: sn rdn and nvr a factor* **10/1**

-010 **16** *1 3/4* **The Grand Visir**[35] 5183 5-9-2 **105**....................(p) JimCrowley 7 86
(Ian Williams) *in tch: pushed along 4f out: rdn over 3f out: sn wknd* **50/1**

1153 **17** *7* **Baghdad (FR)**[22] 5613 4-9-6 **109**.................... PJMcDonald 18 81
(Mark Johnston) *chsd ldrs: rdn along over 3f out: drvn over 2f out: sn wknd* **10/1**

1611 **18** *7* **King's Advice**[21] 5662 5-9-9 **112** 4ex.................... JoeFanning 19 75
(Mark Johnston) *in tch on outer: pushed along over 4f out: rdn over 3f out: sn wknd (jockey said horse was never travelling)* **7/1**[2]

2151 **19** *5* **Kelly's Dino (FR)**[15] 5909 6-9-6 **109** 4ex....................(p) BenCurtis 24 66+
(K R Burke) *chsd ldrs: rdn along over 3f out: wkng whn n.m.r 2f out* **25/1**

-614 **20** *10* **Weekender**[42] 4933 5-9-8 **111**.................... GrahamLee 23 55
(John Gosden) *hmpd s: racd wd early: sn prom: wd st: rdn along nr stands' rail over 3f out: wknd 2f out (jockey said gelding ran flat)* **14/1**

4600 **P** **Making Miracles**[35] 5183 4-9-3 **106**.................... JasonHart 4
(Mark Johnston) *dwlt and hmpd s: a in rr: rdn along over 4f out: detached whn p.u wl over 2f out (jockey said gelding stopped quickly; vet said the gelding to be displaying a prolonged recovery, lame on its left fore and it was treated for postrace heat stress)* **66/1**

0120 **P** **Dramatic Queen (USA)**[21] 5663 4-9-4 **107**.................... DanielTudhope 11
(William Haggas) *cl up: pushed along over 4f out: rdn wl over 3f out: sn lost pl and p.u over 1f out (trainer's rep could offer no explanation for the filly's performance)* **20/1**

2m 52.97s (-7.23) **Going Correction** -0.125s/f (Firm) course record **22** Ran SP% **135.1**
Speed ratings (Par 109): **115,114,114,113,113 113,112,112,111,110 108,106,106,105,105 104,100,96,93,87**
CSF £389.63 CT £9604.85 TOTE £19.80: £5.00, £5.80, £6.30, £4.30; EX 755.30 Trifecta £19135.70.
Owner David Spratt **Bred** Shadwell Estate Company Limited **Trained** Dunsany, Co Meath
■ Stewards' Enquiry : Gerald Mosse seven-day ban; misuse of whip (Sep 7-13); £650.00 fine; misuse of whip

FOCUS
Add 11yds. The first million-pound Ebor, handicaps don't get much stronger than this, with the bottom horse rated 105, and if anything it had the look and feel of a competitive Group race, with just 8lb separating the 22 runners. The main action unfolded more towards the stands' side late on and the winner lowered the track record in a time 3.11sec quicker than the earlier Melrose.

6474 JULIA GRAVES ROSES STKS (LISTED RACE) 5f
4:10 (4:16) (Class 1) 2-Y-O
£39,697 (£15,050; £7,532; £3,752; £1,883; £945) **Stalls** High

Form RPR

2 **1** **Alligator Alley**[24] 5542 2-9-0 0.................... DonnachaO'Brien 10 101+
(Joseph Patrick O'Brien, Ire) *hmpd s: hld up: rdn over 1f out: styng on wl whn sltly hmpd ins fnl f: sn led and clr towards fin: readily* **11/8**[1]

103 **2** 1 **Dr Simpson (FR)**[8] 6157 2-8-9 92........................ PaulHanagan 6 92+
(Tom Dascombe) *a.p: rdn 2f: responded to driving and kpt on gamely fnl f* **16/1**

11 **3** shd **Streamline**[19] 5729 2-9-0 89........................(h) HectorCrouch 4 97
(Clive Cox) *hld up: rdn 3f out: drvn wl over 1f out: kpt on* **25/1**

5 **4** 1/2 **Think Big (IRE)**[15] 5922 2-9-0 0........................ ColinKeane 13 95
(John Joseph Murphy, Ire) *hld up: outpcd 1/2-way: rdn over 2f out: styd on wl fnl f: nrst fin* **20/1**

6232 **5** nk **Mighty Spirit (IRE)**[24] 5544 2-8-9 93........................ PJMcDonald 9 89
(Richard Fahey) *hld up: rdn whn nt clr run 2f out: drvn over 1f out: kpt on fnl f* **7/1[3]**

1052 **6** 1 **Kemble (IRE)**[14] 5976 2-8-9 95........................ AndreaAtzeni 7 85
(Richard Hannon) *prom: rdn and sltly outpcd 2f out: styd on fnl f* **20/1**

05 **7** 1/2 **Daughter In Law (IRE)**[24] 5544 2-8-9 87................(b) JasonWatson 12 84
(Roger Charlton) *wnt lft s: led: rdn and clr over 1f out: drvn and edgd rt ins fnl f: sn hdd & wknd (jockey said filly hung left in the final furlong)* **33/1**

3201 **8** 1 **Dream Shot (IRE)**[15] 5887 2-9-0 96........................ DanielTudhope 11 85
(James Tate) *hmpd s: towards rr: hdwy whn n.m.r and bmpd wl over 1f out: kpt on same pce after (jockey said colt hung left)* **16/1**

11 **9** 2 1/4 **He's A Laddie (IRE)**[12] 6029 2-9-0 85........................ HollieDoyle 8 80
(Archie Watson) *awkward leaving stalls: racd keenly: chsd ldrs: rdn 2f out: grad wknd* **20/1**

1022 **10** 3/4 **Dylan De Vega**[22] 5612 2-9-0 92........................(p[1]) TonyHamilton 3 74
(Richard Fahey) *prom: rdn 2f out: drvn ent over 1f out: sn one pce* **12/1**

31 **11** 1 1/4 **Treble Treble (IRE)**[36] 5125 2-9-0 0........................ TomEaves 1 70
(Kevin Ryan) *chsd ldrs: rdn wl over 2f out: grad wknd* **9/1**

1 **12** 3/4 **Wonderwork (IRE)**[21] 5689 2-9-0 0........................ BenCurtis 2 67
(K R Burke) *racd keenly: cl up on outer: rdn 2f out: sn wknd* **5/1[2]**

57.69s (-0.51) **Going Correction** -0.125s/f (Firm) **12 Ran SP% 121.8**
Speed ratings (Par 102): **99,97,97,96,95 94,93,91,88,87 85,83**
CSF £25.05 TOTE £2.10: £1.20, £4.30, £6.90; EX 27.50 Trifecta £349.30.
Owner Smith/Magniers/Shanahan/Carthy **Bred** Whatton Manor Stud **Trained** Owning Hill, Co Kilkenny

FOCUS
Not a terribly strong Listed event and the best horse in the race overcame interference to win, rated 3lb off his best. The leaders did too much and the hold-up horses came to the fore late on.

6475 SKY BET H'CAP — 1m 2f 56y
4:45 (4:47) (Class 2) (0-105,100) 3-Y-O+
£43,575 (£13,048; £6,524; £3,262; £1,631; £819) **Stalls** Low

Form RPR

2141 **1** **Forest Of Dean**[23] 5583 3-9-3 100........................ FrankieDettori 1 116+
(John Gosden) *trckd ldrs on inner: hdwy over 3f out: led 2f out: rdn over 1f out: kpt on wl* **6/4[1]**

06 **2** 1 1/2 **Johnny Drama (IRE)**[25] 5519 4-9-7 97........................ JasonWatson 15 106
(Andrew Balding) *slt ld: rdn along 3f out: hdd 2f out: cl up and drvn over 1f out: kpt on same pce fnl f* **9/1**

4405 **3** 3/4 **Ventura Knight (IRE)**[14] 5966 4-9-4 94........................(b[1]) RyanMoore 2 101
(Mark Johnston) *hld up towards rr: hdwy 3f out: rdn along 2f out: chsd ldrs and drvn over 1f out: kpt on fnl f* **20/1**

1221 **4** 1 1/4 **Rise Hall**[28] 5440 4-9-9 99........................(b) RobHornby 6 104
(Martyn Meade) *hld up towards rr: hdwy on inner wl over 2f out: rdn wl over 1f out: kpt on same pce fnl f* **9/2[2]**

4541 **5** 1 **Victory Command (IRE)**[8] 6151 3-9-3 100........................ PJMcDonald 4 103
(Mark Johnston) *cl up: disp ld over 3f out: rdn along over 2f out: drvn wl over 1f out: grad wknd* **16/1**

2021 **6** nk **Furzig**[28] 5436 4-8-12 88........................ PaulHanagan 14 90
(Richard Fahey) *towards rr: hdwy 3f out and sn pushed along: rdn 2f out: drvn over 1f out: kpt on fnl f* **14/1**

2005 **7** nk **Society Red**[28] 5440 5-8-9 88........................ MeganNicholls(3) 16 89
(Richard Fahey) *chsd ldng pair: pushed along 3f out: rdn over 2f out: sn drvn and wknd over 1f out* **20/1**

/52- **8** 2 1/4 **Tudor City (IRE)**[23] 4855 7-8-5 81........................(t) JFEgan 3 78
(A J Martin, Ire) *hld up towards rr: pushed along and hdwy 3f out: rdn to chse ldrs wl over 1f out: drvn and wknd appr fnl f (jockey said gelding ran flat)* **6/1[3]**

5123 **9** 1/2 **Cockalorum (IRE)**[19] 5741 4-8-11 87........................(b[1]) BenCurtis 17 83
(Roger Fell) *chsd ldrs on outer: wd st to r nr stands' rail: rdn along over 2f out: sn drvn and wknd* **25/1**

5443 **10** 2 **Glasses Up (USA)**[16] 5849 4-8-3 79........................(v[1]) PaddyMathers 9 71
(R Mike Smith) *t.k.h: chsd ldrs: rdn along 3f out: wknd 2f out* **33/1**

3516 **11** 1 1/2 **Poet's Dawn**[56] 4403 4-8-8 84........................ DuranFentiman 5 73
(Tim Easterby) *prom: rdn along 3f out: drvn and wknd 2f out* **50/1**

5025 **12** 4 **Beringer**[25] 5519 4-9-9 99........................(p) AndreaAtzeni 12 80
(Alan King) *hld: a in rr (jockey said gelding ran flat)* **9/1**

000- **13** 9 **Star Archer**[329] 7758 5-9-2 92........................ NathanEvans 13 55
(Michael Easterby) *a in rr: rdn along 4f out: sn outpcd and bhd* **50/1**

-421 **14** 88 **Dragon Mall (USA)**[199] 625 6-9-2 92........................(t) StevieDonohoe 8
(Rebecca Menzies) *s.i.s and lost several l s: a bhd: wl detached fr 1/2-way (jockey said gelding moved poorly)* **50/1**

2m 6.06s (-4.24) **Going Correction** -0.125s/f (Firm) **14 Ran SP% 127.2**
WFA 3 from 4yo+ 7lb
Speed ratings (Par 109): **111,109,109,108,107 107,106,105,104,103 101,98,91,21**
CSF £15.82 CT £210.68 TOTE £2.20: £1.30, £2.90, £6.10; EX 16.90 Trifecta £178.00.
Owner HRH Princess Haya Of Jordan **Bred** Car Colston Hall Stud **Trained** Newmarket, Suffolk

FOCUS
Add 11yds. A useful handicap but the improving winner had plenty in hand. Again, the main action was middle-to-near side in the straight.

6476 SKY BET APPRENTICE H'CAP — 5f
5:20 (5:21) (Class 2) (0-105,104) 3-Y-O
£43,575 (£13,048; £6,524; £3,262; £1,631; £819) **Stalls** Centre

Form RPR

0341 **1** **Que Amoro (IRE)**[29] 5399 3-8-7 90........................(p) PhilDennis 2 102+
(Michael Dods) *racd centre: chsd ldr: led after 1f: clr 2f out: rdn over 1f out: kpt on wl* **9/1**

2112 **2** 1 3/4 **Moss Gill (IRE)**[44] 4847 3-7-12 88........................ AngusVilliers(7) 6 94
(James Bethell) *t.k.h: trckd ldrs centre: hdwy to chse wnr wl over 1f out: drvn and no imp fnl f* **7/2[1]**

-131 **3** shd **Roulston Scar (IRE)**[75] 3654 3-8-5 88........................ MeganNicholls 1 94
(Kevin Ryan) *racd centre: prom: chsd wnr 1/2-way: rdn along wl over 1f out: drvn and kpt on same pce fnl f* **8/1[3]**

1463 **4** 3/4 **Princess Power (IRE)**[13] 5983 3-7-11 87........................(v) IzzyClifton(7) 7 90
(Nigel Tinkler) *dwlt: sn trcking ldrs centre: hdwy 1/2-way: rdn along to chse ldng pair 2f out: drvn over 1f out: kpt on same pce* **14/1**

1122 **5** 2 1/4 **Pass The Vino (IRE)**[14] 5932 3-8-12 98........................ DarraghKeenan(3) 17 93+
(Paul D'Arcy) *racd towards stands' side: towards rr: hdwy 2f out: sn rdn: styd on wl fnl f* **6/1[2]**

1333 **6** nk **Wedding Date**[29] 5371 3-8-3 89........................ ThoreHammerHansen(3) 8 83
(Richard Hannon) *racd centre: in rr: pushed along and hdwy over 2f out: sn rdn: styd on fnl f: nrst fin (vet said filly was lame right fore and left hind)* **12/1**

4400 **7** 1/2 **Alfie Solomons (IRE)**[23] 5589 3-7-11 83 oh2........................(vt[1]) PaulaMuir(3) 3 75
(Richard Spencer) *chsd ldrs centre: rdn along 2f out: grad wknd* **16/1**

0610 **8** 1 **Free Love**[26] 5504 3-8-3 89........................ TheodoreLadd(3) 18 77+
(Michael Appleby) *racd towards stands' side: in tch: rdn along 2f out: sn no imp* **33/1**

1204 **9** nk **She Can Boogie (IRE)**[56] 4359 3-8-9 92........................ JaneElliott 4 79
(Tom Dascombe) *racd centre: led 1f: chsd wnr: rdn over 2f out: sn wknd* **25/1**

0423 **10** 3/4 **Lufricia**[23] 5589 3-8-4 87........................ GeorgiaCox 13 72
(Roger Varian) *racd centre: towards rr: pushed along and hdwy over 2f out: rdn and n.m.r over 1f out: sn swtchd lft and kpt on: n.d* **16/1**

1100 **11** 3/4 **Rathbone**[44] 4847 3-8-6 92........................ DylanHogan(3) 14 74+
(Kevin Ryan) *towards rr tl sme late hdwy* **25/1**

6165 **12** 1/2 **Little Legs**[3] 6332 3-8-1 84........................(p[1]) GabrieleMalune 5 64
(Brian Ellison) *chsd ldrs centre: rdn along over 2f out: sn drvn and wknd* **20/1**

0104 **13** nse **Recon Mission (IRE)**[14] 5927 3-9-4 104........................ CierenFallon(3) 11 84
(Tony Carroll) *chsd ldrs centre: rdn along 2f out: sn edgd lft and wknd (jockey said colt hung left throughout)* **10/1**

4-0 **14** shd **Mid Winster**[31] 5325 3-8-7 90........................ BenCoen 10 70
(Andrew Slattery, Ire) *towards rr: effrt and sme hdwy over 2f out: sn n.m.r: sn rdn and n.d* **25/1**

60-1 **15** 1/2 **Count D'orsay (IRE)**[18] 5791 3-7-11 83 oh2........................ RhiainIngram(3) 15 61+
(Tim Easterby) *racd towards stands' side: in tch: rdn along over 2f out: sn wknd* **16/1**

1051 **16** 1/2 **Amplify (IRE)**[3] 6332 3-8-6 89 6ex........................ CameronNoble 16 65+
(Brian Meehan) *racd towards stands' side: a towards rr* **11/1**

2000 **17** nk **Street Parade**[14] 5927 3-8-7 97........................(t) MarcoGhiani(7) 12 72+
(Stuart Williams) *a towards rr* **33/1**

2302 **18** 2 1/2 **James Watt (IRE)**[18] 5791 3-7-13 85........................ AndrewBreslin(3) 19 51+
(Michael Bell) *racd towards stands' side: a towards rr* **33/1**

-020 **19** 6 **Junius Brutus (FR)**[14] 5932 3-8-11 97........................ ThomasGreatrex(3) 20 41+
(Ralph Beckett) *racd nr stands' rail: prom: rdn along over 2f out: sn wknd (jockey said gelding was never travelling)* **33/1**

56.52s (-1.68) **Going Correction** -0.125s/f (Firm) **19 Ran SP% 135.1**
Speed ratings (Par 106): **108,105,105,103,100 99,98,97,96,95 94,93,93,93,92 91,91,87,77**
CSF £39.73 CT £228.44 TOTE £9.90: £2.60, £1.70, £2.70, £3.60; EX 45.90 Trifecta £336.00.
Owner P Appleton & Mrs Anne Elliott **Bred** Rathasker Stud **Trained** Denton, Co Durham

FOCUS
A useful 3yo sprint won in good style by an improving filly.
T/Jkpt: Not Won. T/Plt: £239.80 to a £1 stake. Pool: £250,708.14 - 762.95 winning units T/Qpdt: £52.10 to a £1 stake. Pool: £20,284.15 - 288.03 winning units **Joe Rowntree/Jonathan Doidge**

6477 - 6484a (Foreign Racing) - See Raceform Interactive

2890
SAINT-MALO (L-H)
Saturday, August 24

OFFICIAL GOING: Turf: good to soft

6485a PRIX JACQUES CARTIER (CLAIMER) (2YO) (TURF) — 5f 110y
10:00 2-Y-O
£5,855 (£2,342; £1,756; £1,171; £585)

RPR

1 **Spinning Mist**[8] 6196 2-8-11 0........................(b) FabriceVeron 5 67+
(Andrea Marcialis, France) **77/10**

2 2 **Skip The Queue (IRE)**[19] 5763 2-8-11 0........................(b) AntoineCoutier 1 60
(Matthieu Palussiere, France) **23/10[2]**

3 1 **Panthera Tigris**[11] 6060 2-8-6 0........................ DamienBoche(5) 2 57
(Jo Hughes, France) *broke wl: chsd ldr on inner: pushed along to cl on ldng pair 2 1/2f out: sn rdn: styd on wl u.p fnl f* **14/1**

4 2 **Trou Aux Biches (FR)**[23] 5600 2-8-0 0........................(b) ClementGuitraud(8) 6 47
(Y Barberot, France) **13/2[3]**

5 1/2 **Jayadeeva (FR)**[20] 5713 2-9-1 0........................ MlleCoraliePacaut(3) 8 56
(A Giorgi, Italy) **7/5[1]**

6 2 **Happy Chrisnat (FR)**[25] 2-8-13 0........................(b) SebastienPrugnaud(5) 4 49
(C Plisson, France) **20/1**

7 6 **Cormolain (FR)** 2-9-1 0........................ LudovicBoisseau 7 26
(Andrea Marcialis, France) **11/1**

8 1 **Bois D'Argile** 2-9-4 0........................ MickaelForest 3 26
(C Plisson, France) **25/1**

1m 3.92s **8 Ran SP% 120.4**
PARI-MUTUEL (all including 1 euro stake): WIN 8.70; PLACE 2.50, 1.80, 3.40; DF 10.20.
Owner Montgomery Motto **Bred** Newsells Park Stud **Trained** France

6486a PRIX ROBERT SURCOUF (MAIDEN) (3YO) (TURF) — 1m 1f
11:30 3-Y-O
£6,756 (£2,702; £2,027; £1,351; £675)

RPR

1 **Dragoness**[15] 3-8-13 0........................(p) RonanThomas 6
(F-H Graffard, France) **11/10[1]**

2 1 **Pearl Of Freedom**[16] 3-8-13 0........................ JulienGuillochon 8
(H-A Pantall, France) *racd on outer: pushed along 2f out: sn drvn to chal: styd on u.p fnl f: a hld by wnr* **29/10[2]**

3 nse **Indian Pacific (FR)**[25] 3-9-2 0........................ FabriceVeron 7
(Louis Baudron, France) **78/10**

4 1/4 **Showmethemoon** 3-8-5 0........................ MlleCoraliePacaut(3) 3
(J-C Rouget, France) **54/10[3]**

5 6 1/2 **Nefyn Beach (IRE)**[31] 5329 3-8-13 0........................ MorganDelalande 5
(Jo Hughes, France) *settled bhd ldng trio: pushed along 3f out: wknd u.p ins fnl 2f* **22/1**

6 1/4 **Queen Flawless (FR)**[39] 3-8-8 0........................ MickaelForest 2
(J-P Dubois, France) **40/1**

7 4 **Saam (FR)**[25] 3-9-2 0........................ MathieuAndrouin 1
(Mme P Butel & J-L Beaunez, France) **15/2**

1m 54.15s **7 Ran SP% 118.8**
PARI-MUTUEL (all including 1 euro stake): WIN 2.10; PLACE 1.10, 1.10, 1.30; DF 3.20.
Owner Al Asayl France **Bred** Al Asayl Bloodstock Ltd **Trained** France

The Form Book Flat 2019, Raceform Ltd, Newbury, RG14 5SJ

3385 BADEN-BADEN (L-H)

Saturday, August 24

OFFICIAL GOING: Turf: good

6487a 64TH PREIS DER SPARKASSEN FINANZGRUPPE (GROUP 3) (3YO+) (TURF) 1m 2f

3:50 3-Y-O+ £28,828 (£10,810; £5,405; £2,702; £1,801)

RPR

1 **Alounak (FR)**13 6007 4-8-11 0 .... ClementLecoeuvre 7 110
(Waldemar Hickst, Germany) *chsd ldng pair on outer: sltly outpcd and rousted along over 2f out: styd on to chse ldr appr fnl f: r.o u.p: led post* **139/10**

2 *shd* **Be My Sheriff (GER)**111 2455 5-9-0 0 .... LukasDelozier 1 113
(Henk Grewe, Germany) *led on inner: kicked for home 2 1/2f out: jst over 1 l clr and hrd rdn appr fnl f: styd on determinedly: hdd fnl stride* **23/5**3

3 *1 1/4* **Royal Youmzain (FR)**13 6007 4-9-0 0 .... EduardoPedroza 4 111
(A Wohler, Germany) *settled in fnl trio: clsd a little 4f out: 3rd and scrubbed along w 2f to run: styd on u.p fnl f but nt match front two* **2/1**1

4 *nse* **Itobo (GER)**50 4622 7-9-4 0 .... MarcoCasamento 5 114
(H-J Groschel, Germany) *racd in fnl pair: hdwy on outer 2 1/2f out: c wd into st: styd on relentlessly u.p fnl 1 1/2f: nt pce to chal* **79/10**

5 *1/2* **Wai Key Star (GER)**27 5483 6-9-0 0 ....(b) AdriedeVries 6 109
(Frau S Steinberg, Germany) *w.w in rr: clsd u.p ins last 2f: styd on fnl f: nvr able to chal* **4/1**2

6 *6* **Dato**48 3-8-5 0 .... BayarsaikhanGanbat 8 96
(S Smrczek, Germany) *settled in midfield: lost pl 4f out: wl hld fnl 1 1/2f* **167/10**

7 *3/4* **Sibelius (GER)**24 3-8-5 0 .... MaximPecheur 2 95
(Markus Klug, Germany) *chsd ldng pair on inner: 2nd and rdn 2f out: lost pl 1 1/2f fr home: wknd fnl f* **125/10**

8 *9* **Ismene (GER)**20 5720 3-8-4 0 .... FilipMinarik 3 76
(Jean-Pierre Carvalho, Germany) *racd keenly: restrained in 2nd: drvn and no imp wl over 2f out: sn began to labour and lost pl: wknd ins fnl f* **49/10**

2m 1.67s (-3.32) **8 Ran SP% 119.1**
WFA 3 from 4yo+ 7lb
PARI-MUTUEL (all including 1 euro stake): WIN 14.90 PLACE: 2.60, 1.90, 1.20; SF: 60.50.
Owner Darius Racing **Bred** Framont Limited & S.C.E.A. Des Prairies **Trained** Germany

6488 - 6490a (Foreign Racing) - See Raceform Interactive

6253 SARATOGA (R-H)

Saturday, August 24

OFFICIAL GOING: Dirt: fast; turf: firm

6491a WOODFORD RESERVE BALLSTON SPA STKS (GRADE 2) (3YO+ FILLIES & MARES) (MELLON COURSE) (TURF) 1m 110y(T)

8:35 3-Y-O+ £173,228 (£62,992; £37,795; £18,897; £9,448; £6,299)

RPR

1 **Significant Form (USA)**34 4-8-8 0 .... JohnRVelazquez 4 104
(Chad C Brown, U.S.A) *chsd ldr on inner: moved outside turning for home and chsd ldr fnl 1 1/2f: r.o u.p fnl f: got up fnl strides* **73/10**

2 *nk* **Indian Blessing**34 5230 5-8-8 0 .... FlorentGeroux 5 103
(Ed Walker) *racd keenly: hld up in midfield: hdwy on inner 1 1/2f out: str run u.p fnl f: led ins last 100yds and r.o: hdd fnl strides* **101/10**

3 *nk* **Starship Jubilee (USA)**56 6-8-10 0 .... JoseLezcano 8 104
(Kevin Attard, Canada) *racd keenly: a.p on outer: pushed along fr 2 1/2f out: styd on strly fnl f while edging rt: jst missed* **68/10**

4 *nse* **Fifty Five (USA)**53 5-8-6 0 .... JavierCastellano 2 100
(Chad C Brown, U.S.A) *towards rr on inner: drvn and angled out to cl more than 2f out: styd on strly while cariied sltly rt by rival ins: jst failed* **73/20**3

5 *nk* **Conquest Hardcandy (USA)**43 5-8-6 0 .... TylerGaffalione 6 100
(James T Ryerson, U.S.A) *led: drvn for home more than 1 1/2f out: hrd pressed ins fnl f: hdd ins last 100yds: no ex* **41/1**

6 *1 1/2* **Hogans Holiday (USA)**69 4-8-6 0 .... RicardoSantanaJr 1 96
(Robert N Falcone Jr, U.S.A) *midfield on inner: lost pl 1/2-way: rdn and effrt 1 1/2f out: kpt on fnl f: nt pce to get on terms* **47/1**

7 *hd* **Scottish Jig (USA)**50 4-8-6 0 .... JoelRosario 7 96
(William Mott, U.S.A) *chsd ldr on outer: drvn and nt qckn ins last 2f: readily outpcd fnl f* **114/10**

8 *1/2* **Secret Message (USA)**42 4950 4-8-10 0 ....(b) JoseLOrtiz 3 99
(H Graham Motion, U.S.A) *racd keenly: hld up in rr: kpt on u.p fr 1 1/2f out: nvr in contention* **61/20**2

9 *2 1/2* **Mascha (FR)**24 4-8-6 0 .... IradOrtizJr 9 89
(Chad C Brown, U.S.A) *towards rr on outer: drvn 2 1/2f out but no imp: kpt on at same pce last 1 1/2f: nvr figured* **27/10**1

1m 41.39s **9 Ran SP% 119.6**
PARI-MUTUEL (all including 2 unit stake): WIN 16.60; PLACE (1-2) 8.00, 9.90; SHOW (1-2-3) 5.90, 7.60, 5.20; SF 186.00.
Owner Stephanie Seymour Brant **Bred** Brereton C Jones **Trained** USA

6492 - 6495a (Foreign Racing) - See Raceform Interactive

6096 BEVERLEY (R-H)

Sunday, August 25

OFFICIAL GOING: Good to firm (good in places; watered; 7.7)
Wind: Moderate behind Weather: Hot & sunny

6496 JOHN JENKINS MEMORIAL CLAIMING STKS 7f 96y

2:10 (2:10) (Class 5) 3-Y-O+ £3,780 (£1,131; £565; £283; £141) **Stalls Low**

Form RPR

2412 1 **Tukhoom (IRE)**8 6201 6-9-5 82 ....(v) HarrisonShaw(5) 5 88
(David O'Meara) *mde all: rdn along over 2f out: drvn over 1f out: kpt on strly* **6/4**2

0005 2 *3 3/4* **Carry On Deryck**25 5555 7-9-1 77 .... CamHardie 4 70
(Ollie Pears) *trckd ldng pair: pushed along over 2f out: rdn over 1f out: styd on fnl f: no ch w wnr* **10/1**3

6115 3 *1/2* **Rousayan (IRE)**13 6014 8-9-10 91 ....(h) BenCurtis 6 78
(Roger Fell) *trckd wnr: hdwy 3f out: chal over 2f out: rdn wl over 1f out: sn drvn and kpt on one pce* **1/1**1

4163 4 *8* **Muatadel**11 6066 6-9-6 65 .... PaulMulrennan 1 54
(John Wainwright) *hld up: hdwy 3f out: in tch and rdn along over 2f out: sn one pce* **28/1**

0100 5 *4 1/2* **Zodiakos (IRE)**27 5490 6-9-1 71 ....(p) BenSanderson(5) 3 43
(Roger Fell) *dwlt and towards rr: pushed along 1/2-way: rdn wl over 2f out: sn drvn and wknd* **18/1**

1m 31.15s (-1.45) **Going Correction** -0.175s/f (Firm) **5 Ran SP% 107.8**
Speed ratings (Par 103): **101,96,96,87,81**
CSF £14.68 TOTE £2.60: £1.30, £2.90; EX 12.70 Trifecta £18.50.
Owner R Bremer **Bred** Kabansk Ltd & Rathbarry Stud **Trained** Upper Helmsley, N Yorks

FOCUS
A warm run up to a meeting staged on watered ground. A couple of useful types but not a competitive contest and a race in which the market leader underperformed. The steady pace means this form isn't overly reliable.

6497 EBF MAIDEN AUCTION STKS 7f 96y

2:40 (2:42) (Class 5) 2-Y-O £3,881 (£1,155; £577; £288) **Stalls Low**

Form RPR

40 1 **Magna Moralia (IRE)**19 5764 2-9-5 0 .... JasonHart 6 71
(John Quinn) *chsd ldr: hdwy over 2f out: rdn and cl up wl over 1f out: sn chal: drvn ent fnl f: kpt on wl u.p to ld last stride* **11/1**

04 2 *shd* **Alibaba**14 5992 2-9-5 0 .... ShelleyBirkett 2 71
(Julia Feilden) *led: pushed along and jnd wl over 1f out: slt ld and rdn ent fnl f: edgd lft and kpt on gamely: hdd last stride* **14/1**

66 3 *2* **Abbotside**17 5856 2-9-5 0 .... PaulMulrennan 9 66
(James Bethell) *chsd ldng pair: hdwy 2f out: rdn over 1f out: drvn and kpt on same pce fnl f* **10/1**3

4 *2 1/2* **Reggino (FR)** 2-9-4 0 .... PJMcDonald 3 59+
(Jedd O'Keeffe) *hld up in rr: hdwy over 2f out: rdn along over 1f out: kpt on fnl f* **6/1**1

5 *shd* **First Impression (IRE)** 2-9-4 0 .... RobbieDowney 1 59
(John Quinn) *chsd ldrs: rdn along wl over 2f out: sn drvn and kpt on same pce* **16/1**

060 6 *3/4* **Carriesmatic**30 5387 2-8-10 58 .... AndrewMullen 5 49
(David Barron) *in tch: hdwy to chse ldrs wl over 2f out: rdn wl over 1f out: drvn and no imp fnl f* **28/1**

7 *7* **Take That** 2-9-4 0 .... TonyHamilton 4 40
(Richard Fahey) *a towards rr* **8/1**2

60 8 *6* **Blue Lyte**11 6064 2-8-5 0 .... FayeMcManoman(5) 8 17
(Nigel Tinkler) *a in rr* **100/1**

1m 32.39s (-0.21) **Going Correction** -0.175s/f (Firm) **8 Ran SP% 59.8**
Speed ratings (Par 94): **94,93,91,88,88 87,79,72**
CSF £37.56 TOTE £7.10: £1.80, £1.90, £1.50; EX 43.60 Trifecta £101.80.
Owner The Desperados **Bred** Rathasker Stud **Trained** Settrington, N Yorks
■ Yoshimi was withdrawn. Price at time of withdrawal 4-6f. Rule 4 applies to all bets - deduction 55p in the pound.

FOCUS
No more than a modest maiden and one that lost much of its interest with the late withdrawal of the short-priced market leader Yoshimi, whose stall opened prematurely. The gallop was an ordinary one and those held up were at a disadvantage.

6498 COVERS33 FOR ALL YOUR VINYL NEEDS NURSERY H'CAP 5f

3:15 (3:15) (Class 3) (0-95,87) 2-Y-O £6,301 (£1,886; £943; £472; £235) **Stalls Low**

Form RPR

1501 1 **Bushtucker Trial (IRE)**9 6158 2-8-10 **76** .... CliffordLee 3 77
(Michael Bell) *in rr: rdn along and outpcd 1/2-way: hdwy over 1f out: styd on strly and squeezed through on inner to ld nr fin* **4/1**2

3135 2 *nk* **Tom Tulliver**33 5275 2-8-13 **79** .... TomEaves 2 79
(Declan Carroll) *chsd ldrs: rdn along and outpcd over 2f out: hdwy over 1f out: drvn and styd on wl fnl f* **8/1**

163 3 *hd* **Proper Beau**16 5900 2-9-4 **84** ....(t) GrahamLee 5 83
(Bryan Smart) *cl up: chal 2f out: rdn along wl over 1f out: drvn to take slt ld ins fnl f: hdd and no ex nr fin* **5/1**3

211 4 *3/4* **Harry Love (IRE)**26 5514 2-9-2 **82** .... BenRobinson 1 78
(Ollie Pears) *cl up on inner: rdn to take narrow advantage wl over 1f out: drvn ent fnl f: sn hdd and ev ch: edgd lft and no ex towards fin* **4/6**1

5505 5 *2 1/4* **Great Dame (IRE)**15 5976 2-9-2 **87** .... HarrisonShaw(5) 4 75
(David O'Meara) *slt ld: pushed along 1/2-way: rdn and hdd wl over 1f out: sn drvn and wknd appr fnl f* **14/1**

1m 1.5s (-1.40) **Going Correction** -0.175s/f (Firm) **5 Ran SP% 114.4**
Speed ratings (Par 98): **104,103,103,102,98**
CSF £32.78 TOTE £4.40: £1.50, £3.10; EX 27.40 Trifecta £85.20.
Owner Christopher Wright & David Kilburn **Bred** Ambrose Madden **Trained** Newmarket, Suffolk

FOCUS
Straightforward form with most of the field rated near their marks.

6499 BEVERLEY LIONS H'CAP (DIV I) 1m 1f 207y

3:50 (3:50) (Class 6) (0-55,56) 3-Y-O+ £2,587 (£770; £384; £192) **Stalls Low**

Form RPR

4203 1 **Brutalab**18 5814 3-9-2 **52** ....(p1) DavidAllan 13 62+
(Tim Easterby) *led 3f: trckd ldr: hdwy to ld wl 3f out: rdn clr 2f out: drvn and kpt on fnl f* **15/8**1

2500 2 *1 3/4* **Kodi Koh (IRE)**17 5851 4-9-0 **46** .... RowanScott(3) 6 52
(Simon West) *t.k.h: hld up in rr: hdwy on inner over 2f out: rdn over 1f out: styd on fnl f: swtchd lft and kpt on last 75yds to take 2nd on line (jockey said filly was denied a clear run approaching 2f out until 1 1/2f out)* **20/1**

0006 3 *shd* **Star Ascending (IRE)**20 5728 7-9-13 **56** ....(p) JoeFanning 11 62
(Jennie Candlish) *trckd ldrs: hdwy 3f out: chsd wnr over 2f out: rdn wl over 1f out: drvn and kpt on same pce fnl f: lost 2nd on line* **9/1**3

0256 4 *2* **John Caesar (IRE)**10 6103 8-9-2 **45** ....(p) PhilDennis 14 47
(Rebecca Bastiman) *in rr: hdwy over 2f out: rdn wl over 1f out: styd on fnl f: nrst fin* **16/1**

500- 5 *2 3/4* **Call Me Madam**253 9551 4-9-7 **50** .... PJMcDonald 10 47
(James Bethell) *in rr: hdwy over 2f out: sn rdn: kpt on fnl f: nrst fin* **14/1**

2300 6 *3/4* **Foxrush Take Time (FR)**22 5653 4-8-9 **45** ....(e) HarryRussell(7) 7 40
(Richard Guest) *chsd ldrs: rdn along 2f out: sn drvn and one pce* **16/1**

0060 7 *hd* **Furyan**22 5695 3-8-10 **46** .... TomEaves 4 42
(Nigel Tinkler) *in tch: effrt and hdwy wl over 2f out: sn rdn and n.d* **16/1**

The Form Book Flat 2019, Raceform Ltd, Newbury, RG14 5SJ

3620 **8** 2 3/4 **Clive Clifton (IRE)**[39] 5049 6-9-3 **46**..............................(p) CliffordLee 12 36
(Kevin Frost) *prom: led after 3f: hdd wl over 3f out: rdn along wl over 2f out: sn drvn and wknd* **16/1**

-050 **9** *nk* **Jimmy Krankyar (USA)**[19] 5766 3-8-10 **46**......................(p) BenCurtis 5 36
(Phillip Makin) *nvr bttr than midfield* **9/1**[3]

0060 **10** 1 1/4 **Intense Pleasure (IRE)**[25] 5556 4-9-2 **45**.................. JamesSullivan 1 32
(Ruth Carr) *in tch on inner: rdn along and hdwy wl over 2f out: drvn and wknd wl over 1f out* **16/1**

6013 **11** 1 1/4 **Metronomic (IRE)**[19] 5766 5-8-10 **46**...................... ZakWheatley(7) 2 30
(Peter Niven) *dwlt: stdy hdwy 1/2-way: chsd ldrs 4f out: rdn along wl over 2f out: sn wknd (jockey said gelding reared as the stalls opened and was slowly away)* **11/2**[2]

010 **12** 3 1/2 **Bob's Girl**[20] 5725 4-9-5 **48**..............................(b) NathanEvans 8 26
(Michael Mullineaux) *trckd ldrs: rdn along 3f out: wknd over 2f out* **12/1**

0050 **13** 21 **Just Heather (IRE)**[10] 6098 5-8-9 **45**......................(p) LauraCoughlan(7) 9
(John Wainwright) *a towards rr* **80/1**

2m 4.27s (-1.43) **Going Correction** -0.175s/f (Firm)
WFA 3 from 4yo+ 7lb **13** Ran SP% **119.9**
Speed ratings (Par 101): **98,96,96,94,92 92,91,89,89,88 87,84,67**
CSF £46.32 CT £287.03 TOTE £2.60: £1.30, £5.70, £2.70; EX 44.80 Trifecta £234.90.
Owner Ontoawinner 10 **Bred** D R Tucker **Trained** Great Habton, N Yorks

FOCUS
An ordinary handicap. The gallop was reasonable.

6500 BEVERLEY H'CAP — 1m 1f 207y
4:25 (4:25) (Class 5) (0-75,74) 3-Y-O+ **£5,040** (£1,508; £754; £377; £188) **Stalls** Low

Form RPR

6115 **1** **Five Helmets (IRE)**[8] 6232 3-9-7 **74**..............................(p) JamieGormley 1 81
(Iain Jardine) *hld up in rr: hdwy wl over 1f out: trckd ldrs ent fnl f: rdn and qcknd wl to ld towards fin* **9/4**[1]

0226 **2** 1/2 **First Response**[10] 6129 4-10-0 **74**.................................. TonyHamilton 3 79
(Linda Stubbs) *trckd ldrs: hdwy on inner over 1f out: rdn to chal ent fnl f: slt ld last 100yds: drvn: hdd and no ex nr fin* **10/1**

4020 **3** 3/4 **Ideal Candy (IRE)**[20] 5725 4-9-7 **70**..........................(h) GemmaTutty(3) 4 74
(Karen Tutty) *led: pushed along 2f out: jnd and rdn over 1f out: drvn ent fnl f: hdd last 100yds: no ex* **5/1**

1141 **4** 1 1/2 **Dutch Coed**[11] 6068 7-9-2 **65**.. RowanScott(3) 6 66
(Nigel Tinkler) *hld up: hdwy on outer over 2f out: rdn over 1f out: chal and ev ch ent fnl f: drvn and kpt on same pce last 100yds* **4/1**[3]

2225 **5** 8 **Lady Scatterley (FR)**[19] 5785 3-9-1 **68**.......................... DavidAllan 7 55
(Tim Easterby) *t.k.h: rn in snatched: chsd ldrs: awkward bnd over 4f out: rdn along wl over 2f out: sn wknd (jockey said filly hung left-handed)* **7/2**[2]

0613 **6** 1 1/2 **Kwanza**[16] 5899 4-9-5 **65**.. JoeFanning 5 48
(Mark Johnston) *trckd ldr: hdwy and cl up over 2f out: sn rdn: drvn wl over 1f out: sn btn* **5/1**

2m 3.77s (-1.93) **Going Correction** -0.175s/f (Firm)
WFA 3 from 4yo+ 7lb **6** Ran SP% **115.4**
Speed ratings (Par 103): **100,99,99,97,91 90**
CSF £25.78 TOTE £2.90: £1.40, £5.90; EX 25.90 Trifecta £101.60.
Owner Brendan Keogh **Bred** Ms Natalie Cleary **Trained** Carrutherstown, D'fries & G'way

FOCUS
A fair handicap run at just a modest gallop but the winner is a bit better than the bare form.

6501 BEVERLEY ANNUAL BADGEHOLDERS H'CAP — 1m 100y
5:00 (5:01) (Class 4) (0-80,82) 3-Y-O **£5,040** (£1,508; £754; £377; £188) **Stalls** Low

Form RPR

323 **1** **Northern Lyte**[10] 6101 3-8-5 **68**..............................(t) FayeMcManoman(5) 4 75
(Nigel Tinkler) *hld up in rr: hdwy 2f out: rdn to chse ldrs over 1f out: chal ent fnl f: led last 100yds* **10/3**[3]

3241 **2** 3/4 **One To Go**[10] 6101 3-8-10 **68**..............................(b) DavidAllan 2 74
(Tim Easterby) *trckd ldng pair: hdwy 2f out: sn chsng ldrs: rdn to chal and ev ch over 1f out: drvn ins fnl f: kpt on same pce last 100yds* **6/4**[1]

40-0 **3** 2 1/2 **Invasion Day (IRE)**[11] 6067 3-9-10 **82**......................(p) ShaneGray 3 82
(David O'Meara) *led: pushed along 2f out: rdn over 1f out: drvn ent fnl f: hdd and kpt on same pce last 100yds* **20/1**

223 **4** 2 1/2 **Jomrok**[22] 5656 3-9-7 **79**.. DaneO'Neill 7 74
(Owen Burrows) *trckd ldr: hdwy and cl up over 2f out: rdn along wl over 1f out: sn drvn and btn* **3/1**[2]

0020 **5** 11 **Balladeer**[10] 6129 3-9-3 **78**..............................(b[1]) CameronNoble(3) 6 48
(Michael Bell) *trckd ldrs: pushed along over 3f out: sn rdn and wknd (jockey said gelding stopped quickly)* **7/1**

1m 43.89s (-2.51) **Going Correction** -0.175s/f (Firm) **5** Ran SP% **105.3**
Speed ratings (Par 102): **105,104,101,99,88**
CSF £7.79 TOTE £3.40: £1.50, £1.20; EX 7.20 Trifecta £26.60.
Owner Exors Of The Late Miss C Wright **Bred** The Glanvilles Stud **Trained** Langton, N Yorks
■ Joe The Beau was withdrawn. Price at time of withdrawal 8-1. Rule 4 \n\x\x applies to all bets - deduction 10p in the poun

FOCUS
A weakly contested race for the grade. An ordinary gallop picked up in the last quarter mile.

6502 BEVERLEY LIONS H'CAP (DIV II) — 1m 1f 207y
5:30 (5:31) (Class 6) (0-55,55) 3-Y-O+ **£2,587** (£770; £384; £192) **Stalls** Low

Form RPR

520 **1** **Melabi (IRE)**[38] 5106 6-8-12 **46** oh1.................................. CamHardie 2 54
(Stella Barclay) *in tch on inner: hdwy over 2f out: rdn over 1f out: styd on to ld ins fnl f (trainer could offer no explanation for the gelding's improved form)* **8/1**

4014 **2** 1 1/4 **Blyton Lass**[34] 5248 4-9-1 **49**.. PJMcDonald 8 55
(James Given) *prom: cl up 4f out: led 3f out: rdn wl over 1f out: drvn and hdd ins fnl f: kpt on same pce* **15/8**[1]

3000 **3** 1 1/2 **Splash Of Verve (IRE)**[17] 5851 7-8-5 **46**.................. AledBeech(7) 10 49
(David Thompson) *hld up in rr: hdwy over 2f out: rdn along on inner over 1f out: drvn and kpt on fnl f (jockey said gelding was denied a clear run approaching the 2f marker; vet said gelding lost its right fore shoe)* **16/1**

3040 **4** *nk* **Fitzy**[25] 5556 3-9-0 **55**..(p) GrahamLee 9 59
(David Brown) *dwlt: hld up in rr: hdwy on outer 2f out: rdn over 1f out: drvn and kpt on fnl f* **9/1**

0306 **5** 2 3/4 **Prince Consort (IRE)**[10] 6102 4-9-0 **48** oh1 ow2.....(p) PaulMulrennan 1 45
(John Wainwright) *trckd ldrs: hdwy over 3f out: rdn to chse ldr 2f out: drvn over 1f out: grad wknd* **22/1**

5060 **6** 1/2 **King Of Naples**[17] 5851 6-9-7 **55**..............................(h) JamesSullivan 4 51
(Ruth Carr) *dwlt and hld up in rr: hdwy over 2f out: rdn along wl over 1f out: n.d* **10/1**

0666 **7** 1 1/4 **Outlaw Torn (IRE)**[9] 6153 10-8-7 **48** oh1 ow2.........(e[1]) HarryRussell(7) 7 42
(Richard Guest) *chsd ldrs: hdwy over 2f out: sn rdn along wl over 1f out: sn drvn and wknd* **25/1**

0260 **8** 1 1/4 **Bigbadboy (IRE)**[19] 5787 6-8-12 **46** oh1.......................... AndrewMullen 12 38
(Clive Mulhall) *prom: effrt to chse ldr 2 1/2f out: rdn wl over 1f out: sn drvn and wknd* **6/1**[3]

006 **9** 1 **The Mekon**[68] 3970 4-9-5 **53**.. PhilDennis 11 43
(Noel Wilson) *a towards rr* **20/1**

0000 **10** 8 **Jagerbond**[12] 6036 3-8-3 **49** oh1 ow3..............(b[1]) FayeMcManoman(5) 13 25
(Andrew Crook) *chsd ldrs on outer: rdn along over 3f out: sn wknd* **40/1**

0040 **11** 3 **Grey Berry (IRE)**[13] 6024 3-8-12 **53**..............................(b) DavidAllan 6 23
(Tim Easterby) *led: rdn along and hdd 3f out: wknd over 2f out* **9/2**[2]

0-00 **12** 29 **Stainforth Swagger**[30] 5389 3-8-0 **46**..................(p[1]) AndrewBreslin(5) 5
(Ronald Thompson) *a in rr* **50/1**

2m 4.82s (-0.88) **Going Correction** -0.175s/f (Firm)
WFA 3 from 4yo+ 7lb **12** Ran SP% **120.7**
Speed ratings (Par 101): **96,95,93,93,91 90,89,88,88,81 79,56**
CSF £22.39 CT £247.30 TOTE £10.50: £3.00, £1.30, £5.70; EX 38.90 Trifecta £287.70.
Owner J H Chrimes **Bred** Barronstown Stud **Trained** Garstang, Lancs

FOCUS
Routine form for the grade with the one-two dictating an ordinary level.

6503 PURE BROADBAND H'CAP — 5f
6:00 (6:02) (Class 6) (0-60,62) 3-Y-O+ **£2,587** (£770; £384; £192) **Stalls** Low

Form RPR

4302 **1** **Archimedes (IRE)**[5] 6321 6-9-6 **58**..............................(vt) DavidAllan 15 67
(David C Griffiths) *qckly away: mde all: rdn and kpt on strly fnl f* **6/1**[2]

5623 **2** 1 1/2 **Burtonwood**[10] 6099 7-9-7 **59**.. GrahamLee 13 63
(Julie Camacho) *in tch: hdwy wl over 1f out: swtchd lft and rdn appr fnl f: styd on wl towards fin* **7/1**[3]

6-60 **3** 1 **Tick Tock Croc (IRE)**[25] 5559 3-8-11 **51**..................(h) RoystonFfrench 6 51
(Bryan Smart) *chsd wnr: rdn along wl over 1f out: sn drvn and kpt on same pce* **9/1**

3003 **4** *nk* **Storm Lightning**[38] 5084 10-8-7 **45**.................................... CliffordLee 1 44
(Kevin Frost) *midfield: hdwy wl over 1f out: rdn and n.m.r appr fnl f: kpt on wl towards fin* **16/1**

0553 **5** 2 **Poeta Brasileiro (IRE)**[16] 5889 4-9-10 **62**..............(b) PaulMulrennan 10 54
(David Brown) *chsd ldng pair: rdn wl over 1f out: grad wknd* **11/2**[1]

3253 **6** 1/2 **War Ensign (IRE)**[16] 5917 4-8-12 **50**..................(p) RachelRichardson 2 40
(Tim Easterby) *in rr: hdwy over 1f out: sn rdn and kpt on fnl f* **11/2**[1]

0016 **7** 1 **Oriental Splendour (IRE)**[20] 5722 7-8-13 **51**..........(b) JamesSullivan 12 37
(Ruth Carr) *towards rr: hdwy wl over 1f out: n.m.r and swtchd lft over 1f out: sn rdn and no imp* **16/1**

204 **8** 1 1/2 **Arnold**[26] 5515 5-9-9 **61**..(p) JoeFanning 11 42
(Ann Duffield) *a towards rr* **6/1**[2]

0030 **9** 3/4 **Computable**[33] 5276 5-9-4 **61**..............................(e) DannyRedmond(5) 3 39
(Tim Easterby) *chsd ldrs on inner: rdn along wl over 1f out: sn wknd* **8/1**

0000 **10** 12 **Astraea**[6] 6277 4-8-9 **52**..(b) GerO'Neill(5) 7 +
(Michael Easterby) *hmpd s: a bhd (jockey said filly was slowly away and never travelling)* **9/1**

1m 1.32s (-1.58) **Going Correction** -0.175s/f (Firm)
WFA 3 from 4yo+ 2lb **10** Ran SP% **114.7**
Speed ratings (Par 101): **105,102,101,100,97 96,94,92,91,72**
CSF £46.79 CT £384.19 TOTE £6.40: £2.30, £2.80, £2.20; EX 46.00 Trifecta £388.10.
Owner Ladies And The Tramps **Bred** Paddy Twomey & Irish National Stud **Trained** Bawtry, S Yorks

FOCUS
Exposed performers in an ordinary handicap notable for a glut of non-runners. The winner rates back to last year's best, with the runner-up basically to recent form.
T/Plt: £986.10 to a £1 stake. Pool: £60,103.89 - 44.49 winning units T/Qpdt: £52.90 to a £1 stake. Pool: £6,216.43 - 86.89 winning units **Joe Rowntree**

6442 GOODWOOD (R-H)
Sunday, August 25

OFFICIAL GOING: Good (good to firm in places; 7.3)
Wind: Virtually Nil Weather: Hot and sunny

6504 LADBROKES WHERE THE NATION PLAYS MAIDEN AUCTION STKS (PLUS 10 RACE) — 1m
2:00 (2:01) (Class 4) 2-Y-O **£4,787** (£1,424; £711; £355) **Stalls** Low

Form RPR

0 **1** **Luigi Vampa (FR)**[19] 5775 2-9-4 0.................................. JasonWatson 2 79+
(David Menuisier) *str; trckd ldr: swtchd lft off heels over 2f out: sn rdn and gd hdwy over 1f out: styd on wl to ld 100yds out: pushed out (jockey said colt hung right-handed)* **25/1**

4542 **2** 1 1/4 **Hashtagmetoo (USA)**[9] 6161 2-9-0 70.......................... TomMarquand 6 72
(Jamie Osborne) *led: shkn up and extended advantage over 1f out: sn rdn and hdd by wnr fnl 100yds: kpt on* **3/1**[2]

5 **3** 2 **Single (IRE)**[10] 6118 2-8-10 0..............................(h) OisinMurphy 3 63
(Mick Channon) *looked wl; racd in midfield: rdn along and no imp over 2f out: little green u.p 1f out: kpt on fnl f* **5/4**[1]

062 **4** 5 **Junvieve (FR)**[10] 6106 2-8-13 69.. SeanLevey 8 55
(Richard Hannon) *trckd ldr: rdn to chse ldr 2f out: wknd fnl f* **9/2**[3]

5 1/2 **Sweet Reward (IRE)** 2-9-5 0.. RobHornby 1 60
(Jonathan Portman) *tall; towards rr of midfield: rdn along and outpcd 2f out: kpt on one pce fnl f* **14/1**

5 **6** 1 1/2 **Murraymint (FR)**[14] 5980 2-9-4 0...................................... HarryBentley 4 55
(Ralph Beckett) *leggy; athletic; hld up: pushed along in rr over 3f out: sn rdn and no imp 2f out: one pce after* **15/2**

7 24 **The Simple Truth (FR)** 2-8-11 0.............................. MeganNicholls(3) 5
(John Berry) *workmanlike; bit bkward; racd in midfield on outer: pushed along in rr 3f out: sn detached (jockey said gelding hung left-handed throughout; vet said that the gelding was treated for post-race ataxia)* **33/1**

1m 40.59s (1.39) **Going Correction** +0.025s/f (Good) **7** Ran SP% **112.8**
Speed ratings (Par 96): **94,92,90,85,85 83,59**
CSF £96.05 TOTE £23.40: £7.30, £1.50; EX 117.90 Trifecta £185.90.
Owner Shinco Racing Limited **Bred** Haras De Saint Julien & Mme A Tamagni **Trained** Pulborough, W Sussex
■ Stewards' Enquiry : Jason Watson two-day ban; careless riding (Sep 8-9)

FOCUS
One of the hottest days of the year, and slightly quicker ground than on Saturday. This rates straightforward form, with the winner taking a nice step forward. Add 6yds.

6505 CHICHESTER CITY (S) STKS 1m 3f 44y
2:30 (2:30) (Class 3) 3-Y-O **£9,703** (£2,887; £1,443; £721) **Stalls** High

Form RPR
3232 **1** **Queen's Soldier (GER)**[8] 6202 3-9-0 61 OisinMurphy 7 70
(Andrew Balding) *settled wl in midfield: smooth hdwy on outer 2f out: pushed along to ld over 1f out: sn in command: pushed out* **5/4**[1]
6444 **2** *3 ¾* **Elegant Love**[12] 6039 3-8-9 65 HarryBentley 3 59
(David Evans) *trckd ldr early: led over 4f out: shkn up 2f out: sn rdn and hdd by wnr over 1f out: kpt on one pce fnl f* **9/4**[2]
0240 **3** *1 ½* **Watch And Learn**[19] 5766 3-8-9 54 FrannyNorton 1 57
(Donald McCain) *hld up in rr: hdwy into midfield 3f out: rdn and no immediate imp 2f out: kpt on wl enough fnl f* **14/1**
0-40 **4** *nk* **Limelighter**[11] 4836 3-9-0 62 TrevorWhelan 2 61
(Sheena West) *trckd ldr: rdn along to chse ldr 2f out: one pce fnl f* **16/1**
5550 **5** *1 ½* **Canford Dancer**[35] 4247 3-8-9 65 (p) ShaneKelly 6 54
(Richard Hughes) *towards rr of midfield: pushed along and no imp over 2f out: rdn and kpt on one pce fnl f* **14/1**
0-6 **6** *4 ½* **Lord Howard (IRE)**[10] 6119 3-9-0 0 DavidProbert 8 52
(Mick Channon) *compact; midfield: effrt to chse ldr 2f out: rdn and no hdwy over 1f out: one pce fnl f* **12/1**[3]
0330 **7** *1* **Hen (IRE)**[11] 3418 3-8-9 58 TomMarquand 5 45
(Jamie Osborne) *dwlt bdly and racd in rr: nvr on terms (jockey said filly was slowly away)* **12/1**[3]
00 **8** *6* **Drumshanbo Destiny (FR)**[12] 6049 3-9-0 47 (p[1]) SeanLevey 10 40
(Gary Moore) *hld up: pushed along in rr on outer 3f out: nvr on terms* **16/1**
0000 **9** *24* **Hilbre Lake (USA)**[13] 6024 3-8-7 37 GavinAshton(7) 4 2
(Lisa Williamson) *racd in midfield: rdn along and lost pl over 2f out: sn bhd* **100/1**
0 **10** *98* **Blue Laurel**[33] 5268 3-8-11 0 (t[1]) FinleyMarsh(3) 9
(Richard Hughes) *compact: bit bkward; led: rdn and hdd over 4f out: sn lost pl and bhd (trainer's rep said gelding had a breathing problem; vet reported that the gelding suffered from post-race ataxia)* **33/1**

2m 27.95s (-0.35) **Going Correction** +0.025s/f (Good) **10** Ran SP% **119.6**
Speed ratings (Par 104): **97,94,93,92,91 88,87,83,66,**
CSF £4.15 TOTE £2.00: £1.10, £1.30, £3.50; EX 3.70 Trifecta £31.70.The winner was sold to Alastair Ralph for £24,000.
Owner Martin & Valerie Slade & Partner **Bred** Gestut Gorlsdorf **Trained** Kingsclere, Hants

FOCUS
Add 6yds. A valuable seller, and a minor pb from the winner.

6506 LADBROKES H'CAP 1m 1f 197y
3:00 (3:01) (Class 2) (0-100,96) 3-Y-O **£24,900** (£7,456; £3,728; £1,864) **Stalls** Low

Form RPR
-114 **1** **Le Don De Vie**[25] 5541 3-9-7 **96** OisinMurphy 1 106
(Hughie Morrison) *looked wl; settled in 3rd: clsd gng wl 2f out: rdn once gap opened between rivals 1f out: styd on wl to ld fnl 100yds: cosily* **2/1**[1]
3141 **2** *½* **Great Example**[37] 5149 3-9-7 **96** JasonWatson 5 105
(Saeed bin Suroor) *hld up: hdwy on outer over 2f out: rdn to ld over 1f out: kpt on but hdd by wnr fnl 100yds: no ex (jockey said colt hung left-handed)* **5/2**[2]
2213 **3** *5* **Harrovian**[23] 5614 3-9-2 **91** (v[1]) RobertHavlin 3 91
(John Gosden) *trckd ldr: pushed along to ld over 2f out: sn rdn and hdd over 1f out: wknd fnl f* **3/1**[3]
431 **4** *3 ¼* **Joyful Mission (USA)**[28] 5477 3-9-3 **92** (h) DanielTudhope 6 85
(Sir Michael Stoute) *free to post; led and racd freely: rdn along and hdd over 2f out: grad wknd fr over 1f out* **10/3**

2m 4.72s (-4.18) **Going Correction** +0.025s/f (Good) **4** Ran SP% **110.0**
Speed ratings (Par 106): **112,111,107,105**
CSF £7.30 TOTE £2.90; EX 6.90 Trifecta £12.00.
Owner Aziz Kheir **Bred** Miss K Rausing **Trained** East Ilsley, Berks

FOCUS
A classy little handicap.

6507 GOODWOOD AMATEUR RIDERS' H'CAP (IN MEMORY OF GAY KINDERSLEY) 1m 1f 11y
3:35 (3:35) (Class 5) (0-70,72) 4-Y-O+
£5,240 (£1,625; £812; £406; £400; £400) **Stalls** Low

Form RPR
2056 **1** **Brother In Arms (IRE)**[18] 5806 5-9-4 **48** oh3 MissSarahBowen(5) 8 55
(Tony Carroll) *hld up wl off pce: pushed along in rr over 2f out: rdn and gd hdwy over 1f out: drvn and styd on strly to ld post* **20/1**
1221 **2** *nk* **Luna Magic**[10] 6102 5-11-0 **67** MissBrodieHampson 2 73
(Archie Watson) *looked wl; racd in midfield: gd hdwy to ld 2f out: sn rdn and drifted rt 1f out: hdd by wnr post* **5/4**[1]
0404 **3** *2 ¾* **Jumping Jack (IRE)**[38] 5091 5-10-12 **65** MrSimonWalker 10 66
(Chris Gordon) *racd in midfield: effrt on outer 2f out: rdn and no imp 1f out: kpt on one pce* **13/2**[2]
0653 **4** *nk* **Espresso Freddo (IRE)**[10] 6103 5-10-1 **59** (p) MrCraigDowson(5) 6 59
(Robert Stephens) *midfield: effrt on inner 2f out: rdn and outpcd by front pair 1f out: kpt on* **7/1**[3]
0563 **5** *2* **Topology**[83] 3429 6-9-12 **58** MissMatildaBlundell(7) 9 54
(Joseph Tuite) *trckd ldr for 2f then led: rdn along and hdd 2f out: wknd fnl f* **14/1**
5434 **6** *nk* **N Over J**[10] 6121 4-9-10 **49** (v) MrPatrickMillman 7 44
(William Knight) *led for 2f then trckd ldr: rdn and unable qck 2f out: one pce fnl f* **7/1**[3]
0461 **7** *7* **Creative Talent (IRE)**[18] 5803 7-10-2 **62** MissSophieColl(7) 4 43
(Tony Carroll) *dwlt bdly and racd in rr: nvr on terms (jockey said gelding was slowly away)* **13/2**[2]
0010 **8** *12* **Guardiola (USA)**[17] 5867 4-9-4 **48** oh1 (tp) MissJessicaLlewellyn(5) 1 5
(Bernard Llewellyn) *v.s.a and detached: a bhd (gelding was found to have bitten its tongue having arrived at the start and was deemed fit to race; jockey said gelding was slow into stride)* **12/1**

1m 57.21s (-0.19) **Going Correction** +0.025s/f (Good) **8** Ran SP% **115.2**
Speed ratings (Par 103): **101,100,98,98,96 95,89,79**
CSF £46.16 CT £194.56 TOTE £21.80: £4.20, £1.10, £2.00; EX 76.10 Trifecta £514.80.
Owner Cover Point Racing **Bred** Patrick Roche **Trained** Cropthorne, Worcs

FOCUS
Add 6yds. A moderate race. The winner rates back to last year's best.

6508 WEATHERBYS RACING BANK SUPREME STKS (GROUP 3) 7f
4:10 (4:10) (Class 1) 3-Y-O+
£34,026 (£12,900; £6,456; £3,216; £1,614; £810) **Stalls** Low

Form RPR
2333 **1** **Suedois (FR)**[26] 5521 8-9-3 110 (p) DanielTudhope 8 113
(David O'Meara) *trckd ldr: shkn up to ld over 1f out: sn rdn and kpt on wl fnl f: a doing enough* **5/1**[3]
0623 **2** *nk* **Momkin (IRE)**[23] 5609 3-8-12 107 (b) OisinMurphy 6 110
(Roger Charlton) *looked wl; racd in midfield: hdwy on outer 2f out: rdn 1f out: styd on strly: nt rch wnr* **3/1**[2]
2040 **3** *hd* **Larchmont Lad (IRE)**[29] 5413 5-9-3 105 CharlesBishop 3 112
(Joseph Tuite) *looked wl; trckd ldr: pushed along 2f out: rdn and outpcd by wnr over 1f out: kpt on all the way to the line: nt rch wnr* **14/1**
0532 **4** *1 ½* **Di Fede (IRE)**[28] 5475 4-9-0 102 HarryBentley 1 106
(Ralph Beckett) *racd in midfield: effrt on inner 2f out: clsng whn short of room on inner over 1f out: rdn once in the clr and kpt on fnl f* **16/1**
3050 **5** *1 ½* **Breton Rock (IRE)**[26] 5521 9-9-3 103 StevieDonohoe 2 104
(David Simcock) *hld up: rdn in rr and no imp over 1f out: sme late hdwy passed btn horses* **50/1**
-410 **6** *½* **Limato (IRE)**[43] 4923 7-9-6 114 JamesDoyle 9 106
(Henry Candy) *looked wl; racd in midfield: clsd on bit on outer 2f out: sn rdn and fnd little: wknd fnl f* **5/2**[1]
1030 **7** *½* **Fox Champion (IRE)**[21] 5716 3-9-3 108 SeanLevey 5 104
(Richard Hannon) *looked wl; led: rdn along and hdd by wnr over 1f out: wknd fnl f* **7/1**
2060 **8** *½* **Mot Juste (USA)**[23] 5608 3-8-9 102 DavidEgan 4 95
(Roger Varian) *racd in midfield: rdn along and no imp over 2f out: wknd fnl f* **16/1**
2165 **9** *1 ½* **Anna Nerium**[30] 5369 4-9-3 107 TomMarquand 7 96
(Richard Hannon) *hld up: pushed along on outer over 3f out: rdn 2f out: no imp over 1f out* **12/1**
4430 **10** *hd* **Angel's Hideaway (IRE)**[23] 5608 3-8-9 106 (p[1]) RobertHavlin 10 91
(John Gosden) *restrained in last fr wd draw: a in rr* **12/1**

1m 24.99s (-1.71) **Going Correction** +0.025s/f (Good)
WFA 3 from 4yo+ 5lb **10** Ran SP% **118.5**
Speed ratings (Par 113): **110,109,109,107,106 105,104,104,102,102**
CSF £20.75 TOTE £6.50: £1.70, £1.40, £3.50; EX 24.20 Trifecta £219.80.
Owner George Turner & Clipper Logistics **Bred** Elisabeth Vidal **Trained** Upper Helmsley, N Yorks

FOCUS
Add 6yds. A competitive edition of this event, and solid Group 3 form.

6509 LADBROKES SUPPORTING CHILDREN WITH CANCER FILLIES' H'CAP 1m 3f 218y
4:45 (4:45) (Class 3) (0-90,90) 3-Y-O+ **£12,602** (£3,772; £1,886; £944; £470) **Stalls** High

Form RPR
4-43 **1** **Alemagna**[18] 5810 3-8-6 **77** HarryBentley 6 86+
(David Simcock) *str: looked wl; hld up: hdwy on outer under hands and heels 2f out: rdn to ld 1f out: asserted wl ins fnl f* **10/11**[1]
-346 **2** *2* **Quicksand (IRE)**[32] 5305 4-9-2 **78** DanielTudhope 2 83
(Hughie Morrison) *led: rdn along and hdd by wnr 1f out: kpt on one pce fnl f* **6/1**[3]
0304 **3** *5* **Mazzuri (IRE)**[57] 4391 4-10-0 **90** JasonWatson 1 87
(Amanda Perrett) *hld up: effrt to go 3rd 2f out: sn rdn and unable to match pce of wnr 1f out: kpt on* **14/1**
-503 **4** *12* **Fannie By Gaslight**[14] 5982 4-8-10 **72** FrannyNorton 4 50
(Mick Channon) *trckd ldr early: pushed along and no imp over 2f out: sn rdn and fnd little: wknd fnl f* **4/1**[2]
6024 **5** *1 ¾* **Spanish Aria**[19] 5785 3-8-11 **82** (b[1]) NickyMackay 3 58
(John Gosden) *trckd ldr and racd freely: pushed along to chse ldr 3f out: rdn and lost pl 2f out: sn wknd (jockey said filly ran too free)* **4/1**[2]

2m 35.13s (-4.47) **Going Correction** +0.025s/f (Good)
WFA 3 from 4yo 9lb **5** Ran SP% **113.3**
Speed ratings (Par 104): **110,108,105,97,96**
CSF £7.25 TOTE £1.80: £1.10, £2.90; EX 6.40 Trifecta £30.40.
Owner Miss K Rausing **Bred** Miss K Rausing **Trained** Newmarket, Suffolk

FOCUS
This was run at a fair gallop and the form level is fluid.

6510 LADBROKES COMMITTED TO SAFER GAMBLING H'CAP 5f
5:20 (5:20) (Class 5) (0-70,72) 3-Y-O+
£5,433 (£1,617; £808; £404; £400; £400) **Stalls** High

Form RPR
3532 **1** **Red Stripes (USA)**[15] 5952 7-8-7 **55** (b) GavinAshton(7) 3 61
(Lisa Williamson) *chsd ldr: rdn upsides ldr 1f out: drvn and led narrowly fnl 50yds: hld on wl* **3/1**[2]
4015 **2** *nk* **Zac Brown (IRE)**[16] 5888 8-10-2 **71** (t) DavidEgan 7 76
(Charlie Wallis) *led on stands' rail: rdn along and hdd over 1f out: rallied wl u.p fnl f* **5/2**[1]
4405 **3** *½* **Firenze Rosa (IRE)**[20] 5750 4-8-0 **46** oh1 RhiainIngram(5) 1 49
(John Bridger) *chsd ldr: rdn to ld over 1f out: hdd and lost 2 pls fnl 50yds* **8/1**
0003 **4** *½* **Flowing Clarets**[6] 6285 6-8-7 **48** LiamJones 8 49
(John Bridger) *trckd ldr: rdn along and no imp 2f out: kpt on wl for press fnl f and no racing room fnl 100yds* **8/1**
25-4 **5** *3 ½* **Broughton Excels**[18] 5822 4-8-11 **52** HayleyTurner 4 41
(Stuart Williams) *hld up: rdn and outpcd 1/2-way: n.d* **3/1**[2]
6000 **6** *1* **Wiff Waff**[2] 6401 4-9-8 **63** CharlesBishop 2 48
(Chris Gordon) *restless in stalls: hld up: outpcd 1/2-way: nvr on terms* **7/1**[3]

58.08s (-0.02) **Going Correction** +0.025s/f (Good) **6** Ran SP% **113.3**
Speed ratings (Par 103): **101,100,99,98,93 91**
CSF £11.13 CT £51.76 TOTE £2.80: £1.90, £2.10; EX 10.40 Trifecta £61.50.
Owner E H Jones (paints) Ltd **Bred** Tim Ahearn **Trained** Taporley, Wrexham

FOCUS
A poorly contested Class 5.

6511 SILK SERIES LADY RIDERS' H'CAP (PRO-AM LADY RIDERS' RACE) 1m 3f 218y
5:50 (5:51) (Class 4) (0-80,78) 3-Y-O+
£6,727 (£2,002; £1,000; £500; £400; £400) **Stalls** High

Form				RPR
2112	1		**Blue Medici**[17] 5850 5-9-10 **72** MissBeckySmith(5) 4 (Mark Loughnane) *hld up: smooth hdwy 2f out: shkn up to ld over 1f out: sn rdn and battled on gamely fnl f: jst hld on* **5/2**[1]	79
3531	2	shd	**Lightening Dance**[31] 5344 5-10-4 **75** (b) HayleyTurner 2 (Amanda Perrett) *hld up: hdwy u.p 2f out: rdn to chal wnr 1f out: kpt on wl: jst failed* **5/2**[1]	82
6-00	3	6	**Royal Dancer**[14] 5987 3-8-0 **59** oh7 ElinorJones(7) 7 (Sylvester Kirk) *trckd ldr: upsides 4f out: sn rdn and unable qck over 2f out: one pce fnl f* **20/1**	57
3201	4	1	**Ascot Day (FR)**[10] 6104 5-9-8 **72** (p) MissJessicaLlewellyn(7) 5 (Bernard Llewellyn) *led: pushed along and jnd by rivals 4f out: rdn w narrow advantage 3f out: hdd 2f out: wknd fnl f* **4/1**[2]	68
3025	5	nse	**French Mix (USA)**[17] 5858 5-10-0 **78** MissHannahWelch(7) 3 (Alexandra Dunn) *settled in 3rd: hdwy to press ldr 4f out: rdn along to ld 2f out: sn hdd by wnr: wknd fnl f* **13/2**	74
4004	6	3 ¼	**Last Enchantment (IRE)**[44] 4869 4-9-5 **69** (t) MissMillieWonnacott(7) 1 (Neil Mulholland) *racd in midfield: outpcd 3f out: sn rdn and nvr able to get on terms* **16/1**	59
6636	7	7	**Surrey Blaze (IRE)**[21] 1518 4-10-1 **75** MeganNicholls(3) 6 (Joseph Tuite) *hld up: rdn and no imp over 2f out: a in rr* **11/2**[3]	54

2m 40.3s (0.70) **Going Correction** +0.025s/f (Good)
WFA 3 from 4yo+ 9lb **7 Ran SP% 116.5**
Speed ratings (Par 105): **93,92,88,88,88 86,81**
CSF £9.11 TOTE £3.20: £2.10, £1.80; EX 8.20 Trifecta £168.20.
Owner Laurence Bellman **Bred** Kirtlington Stud Ltd **Trained** Rock, Worcs

FOCUS
Another poorly contested race for the grade, but the first two rate as improvers.
T/Jkpt: Not Won. T/Plt: £36.40 to a £1 stake. Pool: £86,160.57 - 1,725.72 winning units T/Qpdt: £14.40 to a £1 stake. Pool: £6,868.05 - 351.1 winning units **Mark Grantham**

6321 YARMOUTH (L-H)
Sunday, August 25

OFFICIAL GOING: Firm (7.6)
Wind: Light, half against Weather: Hot

6512 MANSIONBET BEATEN BY A HEAD APPRENTICE H'CAP 1m 2f 23y
2:20 (2:20) (Class 5) (0-75,77) 4-Y-O+
£3,752 (£1,116; £557; £400; £400; £400) **Stalls** Low

Form				RPR
3553	1		**Geetanjali (IRE)**[6] 6280 4-9-3 **77** (v1) JoeBradnam(7) 7 (Michael Bell) *t.k.h: hld up in tch in midfield: clsd to go prom in chsng gp 5f out: steadily clsd and led over 1f out: shkn up and readily asserted ins fnl f: comf* **11/2**	86
3544	2	2 ¾	**Sudona**[26] 5529 4-9-5 **72** (v1) MarkCrehan 3 (Hugo Palmer) *handy in chsng gp on inner: grad clsd fr 3f out: swtchd and effrt over 1f out: kpt on same pce to snatch 2nd last strides: no ch w wnr* **7/2**[2]	76
6333	3	nk	**Elhafei (USA)**[8] 6210 4-9-4 **71** WilliamCarver 4 (Michael Appleby) *sn led: hdd 7f out and chsd clr ldr: effrt and clsd over 2f out: drvn and ev ch briefly over 1f out: nt pce of wnr ins fnl f: lost 2nd last strides* **9/4**[1]	74
6433	4	½	**Brittanic (IRE)**[18] 5811 5-8-10 **68** AngusVilliers(5) 1 (David Simcock) *hld up in last pair: detached and effrt in centre 3f out: hdwy over 1f out: stvd on ins fnl f: no threat to wnr* **5/1**[3]	70
25-5	5	½	**Swilly Sunset**[9] 6165 6-9-3 **73** MarcoGhiani(3) 5 (Anthony Carson) *chsd ldrs early: steadily lost pl and detached in rr 4f out: effrt in centre 3f out: hdwy over 1f out: styd on ins fnl f: no threat to wnr* **20/1**	75
3456	6	2	**Wimpole Hall**[31] 5348 6-9-3 **77** (p) GaiaBoni(7) 2 (William Jarvis) *dwlt: t.k.h: hld up towards rr: hdwy to prom in chsng gp 1/2-way: rdn over 2f out: outpcd and btn over 1f out: wknd ins fnl f* **14/1**	75
0404	7	2 ¾	**Double Reflection**[17] 5841 4-9-4 **74** (v1) RhonaPindar(3) 6 (K R Burke) *sn chsng ldr tl led 7f out: clr 6f out: rdn over 2f out: hdd over 1f out: sn btn and wknd ins fnl f* **11/2**	67

2m 5.46s (-3.34) **Going Correction** -0.175s/f (Firm) **7 Ran SP% 111.9**
Speed ratings (Par 103): **106,103,103,103,102 101,98**
CSF £23.85 TOTE £6.00: £3.20, £2.40; EX 28.00 Trifecta £84.40.
Owner Hugo Merry **Bred** G S K International **Trained** Newmarket, Suffolk

FOCUS
Add 10yds. A modest contest for apprentice riders, in which two of the three wearing a first-time visor came to the fore. This rates a minor pb from the winner.

6513 BEST ODDS GUARANTEED AT MANSIONBET APP H'CAP 1m 2f 23y
2:50 (2:53) (Class 2) (0-100,101) 3-Y-O+
£13,695 (£4,100; £2,050; £1,025; £512; £257) **Stalls** Low

Form				RPR
0-05	1		**Protected Guest**[30] 5370 4-9-5 **89** TomQueally 9 (George Margarson) *stdd after s: hld up in tch: clsd and travelling strly over 1f out: pushed along to chal ins fnl f: qcknd and fnd enough under tender handling to ld cl home* **16/1**	99+
2-11	2	nk	**Gifts Of Gold (IRE)**[22] 5667 4-9-12 **101** CierenFallon(5) 5 (Saeed bin Suroor) *hld up wl in tch in midfield: clsd to press ldrs 3f out: rdn to ld 2f out: hung lft ins fnl f: hdd cl home (jockey said gelding hung left-handed throughout)* **11/10**[1]	110
1623	3	3	**Oasis Prince**[19] 5790 3-9-5 **96** JamieSpencer 7 (Mark Johnston) *sn led: rdn and hdd 2f out: drvn over 1f out: no ex and outpcd ins fnl f* **7/2**[3]	99
4010	4	nk	**Certain Lad**[21] 5711 3-9-7 **98** CallumShepherd 6 (Mick Channon) *taken down early: t.k.h: pressed ldrs tl chsd ldr after 2f tl over 2f out: hung lft and swtchd rt over 1f out: unable qck and one pce ins fnl f* **10/1**	100
-106	5	2	**Elector**[51] 4613 4-9-11 **95** (p1) RyanMoore 3 (Sir Michael Stoute) *stdd after s: hld up in tch in last pair: effrt over 2f out: hung lft and no imp over 1f out: wl hld and one pce ins fnl f* **3/1**[2]	93
-555	6	4	**Cote D'Azur**[111] 2486 6-8-12 **82** LewisEdmunds 2 (Les Eyre) *t.k.h: led for 1f: chsd ldrs: lost pl and bhd over 1f out: wknd ins fnl f* **22/1**	72

2m 8.29s (-0.51) **Going Correction** -0.175s/f (Firm)
WFA 3 from 4yo+ 7lb **6 Ran SP% 114.2**
Speed ratings (Par 109): **95,94,92,90,90 87**
CSF £35.43 CT £80.95 TOTE £19.00: £6.30, £1.10; EX 39.90 Trifecta £121.70.
Owner John Guest Racing **Bred** Rabbah Bloodstock Limited **Trained** Newmarket, Suffolk

FOCUS
Add 10yds. A decent race even though three came out, but the early gallop was nothing more than a dawdle. It quickened up from the 4f marker.

6514 BRITISH STALLION STUDS EBF MAIDEN FILLIES' STKS (PLUS 10 RACE) 6f 3y
3:25 (3:26) (Class 4) 2-Y-O
£4,787 (£1,424; £711; £355) **Stalls** Centre

Form				RPR
3	1		**Jovial**[22] 5646 2-9-0 0 RyanMoore 9 (Sir Michael Stoute) *hld up in tch in midfield: effrt 2f out: sn swtchd rt and rdn to ld over 1f out: edging lft but styd on strly ins fnl f: gng away at fin* **10/11**[1]	82
	2	1 ¼	**Faakhirah (IRE)** 2-9-0 0 CallumShepherd 2 (Saeed bin Suroor) *chsd ldrs: effrt 2f out: rdn and ev ch over 1f out: kpt on ins fnl f: no ex towards fin* **12/1**	78+
5	3	2 ¼	**Charming Spirit (IRE)**[19] 5772 2-9-0 0 JackMitchell 10 (Roger Varian) *chsd ldng pair: effrt jst over 2f out: unable qck over 1f out: kpt on same pce ins fnl f* **3/1**[2]	71
	4	4 ½	**Varsha** 2-9-0 0 LukeMorris 1 (Ismail Mohammed) *led: rdn 2f out: hdd over 1f out: no ex and wknd ins fnl f* **28/1**	56
00	5	1	**Clever Candy**[16] 5906 2-9-0 0 HollieDoyle 3 (Michael Bell) *t.k.h: hld up towards rr: pushed along and hdwy into midfield over 1f out: no threat to ldrs but kpt on ins fnl f* **50/1**	53
	6	½	**Jaaneh** 2-9-0 0 JimCrowley 7 (William Haggas) *s.i.s and sltly impeded leaving stalls: a towards rr: rdn 2f out: sn outpcd and wl hld over 1f out* **7/2**[3]	52
	7	6	**Sarayaat (IRE)** 2-9-0 0 DanielMuscutt 5 (James Fanshawe) *stdd after s: hld up in tch in midfield: outpcd ent fnl 2f: sn btn* **16/1**	32
00	8	¾	**Red Hottie**[32] 5317 2-9-0 0 AlistairRawlinson 6 (Michael Appleby) *broke wl: restrained and in tch in midfield: rdn over 2f out: sn outpcd and wl btn over 1f out* **80/1**	30
00	9	15	**Farewell Kiss (IRE)**[19] 5772 2-9-0 0 JamieSpencer 8 (Michael Bell) *stdd and wnt sharply lft leaving stalls: hld up in last pair: effrt 2f out: sn btn and hung rt: wl bhd ins fnl f (jockey said filly hung right-handed throughout; trainer's rep said the filly was unsuited by the Firm going on this occasion and would prefer an easier surface)* **33/1**	

1m 10.49s (-2.11) **Going Correction** -0.175s/f (Firm) **9 Ran SP% 122.8**
Speed ratings (Par 93): **107,105,102,96,95 94,86,85,65**
CSF £15.61 TOTE £1.60: £1.10, £2.60, £1.30; EX 13.50 Trifecta £32.60.
Owner K Abdullah **Bred** Juddmonte Farms Ltd **Trained** Newmarket, Suffolk

FOCUS
Probably a decent event and the market leader got the job done, this rating a nice step forward.

6515 DOWNLOAD THE MANSIONBET APP NURSERY H'CAP 6f 3y
4:00 (4:01) (Class 4) (0-85,87) 2-Y-O
£4,787 (£1,424; £711; £400) **Stalls** Centre

Form				RPR
3114	1		**War Storm**[44] 4878 2-9-7 **83** (p) HollieDoyle 3 (Archie Watson) *rousted along leaving stalls: led tl 4f out: led again 2f out and sn rdn: pressed and drvn ins fnl f: styd on and holding chalr towards fin* **4/9**[1]	86
200	2	½	**Taste The Nectar (USA)**[81] 3461 2-8-7 **69** (p1) JosephineGordon 4 (Robert Cowell) *hld up in tch in rr: clsd and nt clr run over 1f out: swtchd lft and effrt 1f out: pressed wnr and drvn ins fnl f: kpt on but hld towards fin* **11/1**	70
603	3	3 ¾	**Little Brown Trout**[37] 5145 2-8-6 **75** MarcoGhiani(7) 2 (William Stone) *dwlt: sn rcvrd: t.k.h and pressed wnr: led 4f out: hdd 2f out: sn rdn: no ex and wknd ins fnl f* **9/2**[2]	64
103	4	1 ¾	**Dark Optimist (IRE)**[9] 6158 2-9-3 **79** (t) JFEgan 1 (David Evans) *chsd ldng pair: effrt ent fnl 2f: unable qck u.p ent fnl f: no ex and wknd ins fnl f* **6/1**[3]	63

1m 11.41s (-1.19) **Going Correction** -0.175s/f (Firm) **4 Ran SP% 110.1**
Speed ratings (Par 96): **100,99,94,92**
CSF £6.16 TOTE £1.20; EX 6.60 Trifecta £13.30.
Owner Saeed Bin Mohammed Al Qassimi **Bred** Gary Hodson & Peter Moule **Trained** Upper Lambourn, W Berks

FOCUS
The favourite was really well backed close to the off and didn't give his supporters too many worries, posting a minor pb.

6516 ROBERT BROWN MEMORIAL H'CAP 1m 3y
4:35 (4:35) (Class 3) (0-95,94) 3-Y-O+ **£9,766** (£2,923; £1,461; £731; £364) **Stalls** Centre

Form				RPR
420	1		**Bless Him (IRE)**[26] 5519 5-9-12 **92** (h) JamieSpencer 2 (David Simcock) *stdd and dropped in bhd after s: hld up in tch: clsd and cruised upsides rivals jst over 1f out: led ins fnl f: shkn up and readily asserted: nt extended* **11/4**[2]	101+
1002	2	1 ½	**Solid Stone (IRE)**[25] 5564 3-9-8 **94** RyanMoore 5 (Sir Michael Stoute) *chsd ldrs: effrt to press ldrs ent fnl 2f: drvn and ev ch over 1f out: nt match pce of wnr and kpt on same pce ins fnl f* **10/11**[1]	99
0421	3	shd	**Arigato**[30] 5383 4-9-0 **80** (p) JosephineGordon 1 (William Jarvis) *led: rdn over 1f out: drvn and hdd ins fnl f: nt match pce of wnr and kpt on same pce ins fnl f* **8/1**	85
205	4	½	**Balgair**[30] 5383 5-9-4 **84** (h) LukeMorris 3 (Tom Clover) *chsd ldrs: effrt jst over 2f out: drvn and stl pressing ldrs 1f out: no match pce of wnr and one pce ins fnl f* **12/1**	88
1461	5	8	**Smile A Mile (IRE)**[7] 6258 3-9-8 **94** 6ex JimCrowley 6 (Mark Johnston) *pressed ldr: rdn and ev ch over 2f out: outpcd and btn over 1f out: wknd ins fnl f (trainer could offer no explanation for the gelding's performance)* **13/2**[3]	79

1m 35.86s (-2.34) **Going Correction** -0.175s/f (Firm)
WFA 3 from 4yo+ 6lb **5 Ran SP% 111.2**
Speed ratings (Par 107): **104,102,102,101,93**
CSF £5.75 TOTE £3.90: £1.60, £1.10; EX 6.60 Trifecta £16.80.
Owner Tony Perkins & Partners **Bred** Knocklong House Stud **Trained** Newmarket, Suffolk

FOCUS
This developed into a dash after the early stages.

6517 MANSIONBET YOUR FAVOURITE PLACE TO BET H'CAP 7f 3y
5:10 (5:10) (Class 3) (0-95,95) 3-Y-O+ £9,766 (£2,923; £1,461; £731) Stalls Centre

Form RPR
5340 1 **Spanish City**[22] 5664 6-9-12 **95**............ JackMitchell 5 101
(Roger Varian) *hld up in tch: effrt and shkn up over 1f out: clsd u.p to ld ins fnl f: r.o wl* **7/4**[2]
0065 2 3/4 **Haddaf (IRE)**[23] 5626 4-8-4 **80**............(t) MarcoGhiani(7) 2 84
(Stuart Williams) *led: rdn over 1f out: hdd ins fnl f: kpt on same pce u.p towards fin* **11/1**
0530 3 1 1/4 **Love Dreams (IRE)**[2] 6391 5-9-11 **94**............(p) RyanMoore 6 95
(Mark Johnston) *chsd ldr: effrt and ev ch over 1f out: no ex and one pce fnl 100yds* **5/2**[3]
-310 4 4 1/2 **Light And Dark**[25] 5546 3-9-5 **93**............ CallumShepherd 3 79
(Saeed bin Suroor) *in tch in rr: clsd jst over 2f out: effrt to press ldrs over 1f out: edgd lft and no ex 1f out: sn btn and eased towards fin (jockey said colt stopped quickly)* **13/8**[1]

1m 22.85s (-2.25) **Going Correction** -0.175s/f (Firm) 4 Ran SP% **111.4**
WFA 3 from 4yo+ 5lb
Speed ratings (Par 107): **105,104,102,97**
CSF £16.33 TOTE £2.30; EX 17.40 Trifecta £38.30.
Owner Merry Fox Stud Limited **Bred** Merry Fox Stud Limited **Trained** Newmarket, Suffolk

FOCUS
Not form to rely on given the small field but a nice performance from the winner.

6518 MANSIONBET AT YARMOUTH RACECOURSE H'CAP 7f 3y
5:40 (5:43) (Class 5) (0-70,71) 3-Y-O+
£3,816 (£1,135; £567; £400; £400; £400) Stalls Centre

Form RPR
6031 1 **Moretti (IRE)**[10] 6131 4-8-10 **53**............ LewisEdmunds 7 60
(Les Eyre) *stdd s: hld up in tch in rr: effrt 2f out: hdwy and rdn to ld 1f out: r.o wl u.p ins fnl f* **9/2**[2]
4260 2 1/2 **Atletico (IRE)**[15] 5945 7-9-10 **67**............ HollieDoyle 3 73
(David Evans) *broke wl: sn restrained and hld up in last pair: effrt and hdwy over 1f out: rdn to chal 1f out: kpt on but hld towards fin* **3/1**[1]
5321 3 1 1/2 **Global Hope (IRE)**[17] 5864 4-9-9 **66**............(tp) LukeMorris 5 68
(Gay Kelleway) *taken down early: stdd after leaving stalls: chsd ldrs: effrt 2f out: hrd drvn and ev ch jst over 1f out: kpt on same pce ins fnl f* **11/2**
3055 4 3/4 **Punjab Mail**[11] 6085 3-9-8 **70**............ RyanMoore 6 68
(Ian Williams) *hld up in tch in midfield: effrt 2f out: nt clr run and swtchd rt 1f out: kpt on ins fnl f: unable to threaten ldrs* **5/1**[3]
5034 5 1 1/4 **Bint Dandy (IRE)**[18] 5827 8-9-12 **69**............(b) CallumShepherd 1 65
(Charlie Wallis) *sn led: rdn 2f out: drvn and hdd 1f out: no ex and wknd fnl 100yds* **16/1**
5226 6 2 3/4 **Dancingwithwolves (IRE)**[36] 5202 3-9-9 **71**............ JimCrowley 2 58
(Ed Dunlop) *sn chsng ldr: effrt and ev ch over 1f out: sn struggling to qckn and btn 1f out: wknd ins fnl f* **9/2**[2]
2455 7 4 1/2 **Royal Welcome**[25] 5554 3-9-9 **71**............(v[1]) JamieSpencer 4 46
(James Tate) *hld up in tch in midfield: effrt jst over 2f out: unable qck and btn 1f out: eased ins fnl f (trainer's rep could offer no explanation for the filly's performance)* **5/1**[3]

1m 23.35s (-1.75) **Going Correction** -0.175s/f (Firm) 7 Ran SP% **116.0**
WFA 3 from 4yo+ 5lb
Speed ratings (Par 103): **103,102,100,99,98 95,90**
CSF £18.94 CT £75.66 TOTE £5.10: £2.80, £2.10; EX 21.60 Trifecta £116.80.
Owner J L Eyre **Bred** T Boylan **Trained** Catwick, N Yorks

FOCUS
A modest event. Most had some sort of chance 2f from home and the winner is in the form of her life.
T/Plt: £36.90 to a £1 stake. Pool: £76,076.51 - 1,504.77 winning units T/Qpdt: £6.30 to a £1 stake. Pool: £6,737.51 - 785.88 winning units **Steve Payne**

6487 BADEN-BADEN (L-H)
Sunday, August 25

OFFICIAL GOING: Turf: good

6519a 149TH CASINO BADEN-BADEN GOLDENE PEITSCHE (GROUP 2) (3YO+) (TURF) 6f
4:10 3-Y-O+ £36,036 (£13,963; £7,207; £3,603; £2,252)

RPR
1 **Royal Intervention (IRE)**[23] 5608 3-8-11 0............ GeraldMosse 5 107+
(Ed Walker) *disp ld: pushed along over 2f out: sn led: rdn appr fnl f: kpt on wl* **9/5**[2]
2 1 1/2 **Waldpfad (GER)**[36] 5184 5-9-4 0............ MaximPecheur 1 106+
(D Moser, Germany) *trckd ldng pair on inner: nudged along 3f out: rdn and r.o ins fnl f: nt rch wnr* **13/10**[1]
3 1 3/4 **Big Boots (IRE)**[14] 6006 3-9-1 0............ MarcoCasamento 2 101
(Waldemar Hickst, Germany) *disp ld: hdd wl over 2f out: rdn 1 1/2f out: kpt on one pce* **15/2**
4 nk **Namos (GER)**[21] 5716 3-9-1 0............ WladimirPanov 7 100
(D Moser, Germany) *chsd ldrs on outer: rdn over 2f out: no imp* **11/2**[3]
5 nk **Zargun (GER)**[70] 3907 4-9-4 0............(p) LukasDelozier 3 99
(Henk Grewe, Germany) *trckd ldrs: rdn 2 1/2f out: kpt on one pce* **221/10**
6 3/4 **Iron Duke (GER)**[14] 6006 3-9-1 0............ FilipMinarik 4 96
(P Schiergen, Germany) *chsd ldrs: outpcd sltly at 1/2-way: sn rdn: no imp and wknd* **217/10**
7 3 1/2 **K Club (IRE)**[7] 6270 3-8-11 0............ AlexanderPietsch 6 81
(J Hirschberger, Germany) *towards rr: pushed along over 2 1/2f out: nvr a factor* **28/1**

1m 8.49s (-1.80) 7 Ran SP% **118.5**
WFA 3 from 4yo+ 3lb
PARI-MUTUEL (all including 1 euro stake): WIN 2.80 PLACE: 1.40, 1.50; SF: 3.80.
Owner Lord Lloyd Webber And W S Farish **Bred** Exciting Times Partnership **Trained** Upper Lambourn, Berks

6433 DEAUVILLE (R-H)
Sunday, August 25

OFFICIAL GOING: Polytrack: standard; turf: good

6520a PRIX DE MEAUTRY BARRIERE (GROUP 3) (3YO+) (STRAIGHT COURSE) (TURF) 6f
1:35 3-Y-O+ £36,036 (£14,414; £10,810; £7,207; £3,603)

RPR
1 **Spinning Memories (IRE)**[21] 5716 4-9-0 0 ow1 ChristopheSoumillon 8 115+
(P Bary, France) *prom: swtchd lft and pushed along 1 1/2f out: rdn to chal ent fnl f: sn led: r.o strly: gng away at fin* **2/1**[1]
2 3 1/2 **Stake Acclaim (IRE)**[12] 6056 7-9-3 0 ow1............ FrankieDettori 5 107
(Dean Ivory) *cl up: pushed along jst under 2f out: upsides ldr whn rdn over 1f out: kpt on ins fnl f: no ch w clr wnr* **10/1**
3 1/2 **Tertius (FR)**[21] 5714 3-9-0 0 ow1............ TheoBachelot 10 105
(M Nigge, France) *hld up towards rr: pushed along and effrt outside rivals fr 2f out: rdn over 1f out: kpt on: nvr gng pce to chal* **24/1**
4 1 **Poetry**[43] 4932 3-8-10 0 ow1............ MickaelBarzalona 6 98
(Michael Bell) *racd in fnl quartet: pushed along 2f out: rdn ent fnl f: responded for press clsng stages: r.o into modest 4th cl home* **12/1**
5 snk **Comedia Eria (FR)**[43] 4948 7-9-0 0 ow1............ StephanePasquier 9 99
(P Monfort, France) *midfield: asked for effrt 2f out: unable qck: kpt on same pce ins fnl f: n.d* **24/1**
6 1 1/4 **Keystroke**[36] 5184 7-9-5 0 ow1............(b[1]) AdamKirby 7 100
(Stuart Williams) *s.i.s: in rr: pushed along and sme prog fr 2f out: rdn over 1f out: kpt on same pce ins fnl f* **33/10**[3]
7 hd **Big Brothers Pride (FR)**[23] 5611 3-8-13 0 ow2 Pierre-CharlesBoudot 2 96
(F Rohaut, France) *led: asked to qckn whn pressed jst under 2f out: jnd over 1f out: sn hdd: grad wknd ins fnl f: no ex* **31/10**[2]
8 3 1/2 **Viscount Barfield**[7] 6-9-3 0 ow1............ CristianDemuro 1 86
(Mme Pia Brandt, France) *racd in fnl pair: outpcd and dropped to rr over 2f out: passed btn rival whn wl hld over 1f out: nvr a factor* **14/1**
9 6 **Ilanga (FR)**[108] 2564 3-8-13 0 ow2............ AlexandreGavilan 3 65
(D Guillemin, France) *midfield: struggling to go pce and lost position over 2f out: sn wl btn and dropped to rr over 1f out* **14/1**

1m 8.89s (-2.11) 9 Ran SP% **119.1**
WFA 3 from 4yo+ 3lb
PARI-MUTUEL (all including 1 euro stake): WIN 3.00; PLACE 1.30, 2.30, 3.90; DF 8.00.
Owner Sutong Pan Racing Bloodstock **Bred** Mubarak Al Naemi **Trained** Chantilly, France

FOCUS
A pb from the winner, with the second to fifth helping to set the standard.

6521a PRIX CASINO BARRIERE DEAUVILLE (H'CAP) (3YO+) (ROUND COURSE) (TURF) 2m
2:15 3-Y-O+
£31,531 (£11,981; £8,828; £5,045; £2,522; £1,891)

RPR
1 **Diluvien (FR)**[11] 6095 4-9-7 0 ow1............ StephanePasquier 16 90
(Gianluca Bietolini, France) **175/10**
2 1/2 **Karlstad (FR)**[64] 4-9-4 0 ow1............ MickaelBarzalona 12 86
(Mme Pia Brandt, France) **19/5**[1]
3 1/2 **Spirit's Revench (FR)**[87] 9-8-9 0 ow1............ AurelienLemaitre 1 76
(P Demercastel, France) **19/1**
4 3/4 **Bosquentin (FR)**[110] 4-8-10 0 ow1............(p) ThierryThulliez 4 77
(S Cerulis, France) **19/1**
5 hd **Vasy Sakhee (FR)**[64] 6-8-11 0 ow1............(b) TheoBachelot 2 77
(Y Barberot, France) **13/2**[2]
6 3/4 **Magical Forest (IRE)**[54] 5-9-3 0 ow1............ ChristopheSoumillon 10 83
(H Blume, Germany) **83/10**[3]
7 1 **Oriental Queen (FR)**[24] 4-8-10 0 ow1............ HugoJourniac 15 74
(M Nigge, France) **16/1**
8 2 1/2 **Investor (FR)**[27] 4-9-6 0 ow1............ AnthonyCrastus 13 82
(Carmen Bocskai, Germany) **21/1**
9 hd **Coulonces (FR)**[30] 4-9-1 0 ow1............ CristianDemuro 14 77
(M Delzangles, France) **9/1**
10 5 **Rannan (FR)**[27] 4-9-4 0 ow1............ OlivierPeslier 7 74
(R Martens, France) **18/1**
11 snk **Luminosa (FR)**[24] 4-8-9 0 ow1............(b) AlexisBadel 9 65
(D Smaga, France) **23/1**
12 3/4 **Elysian Star (FR)**[53] 5-8-8 0 ow1............ IoritzMendizabal 5 63
(B Moreno-Navarro, France) **21/1**
13 9 **Desert Warrior (IRE)**[40] 5035 6-8-11 0 ow1............(p) FranckBlondel 3 56
(F Foresi, France) **24/1**
14 2 1/2 **Show The Way (IRE)**[40] 5035 5-8-8 0 ow1............ RonanThomas 11 50
(F Foresi, France) **35/1**
15 7 **Culmination**[30] 5410 7-9-6 0 ow1............ AntoineHamelin 8 55
(Jo Hughes, France) *settled in mid-div on outer: struggling to go pce and bustled along over 5f out: grad wknd to fnl pair 3f out: wl btn over 2f out* **11/1**
16 2 **Carnageo (FR)**[110] 6-8-9 0 ow1............(b) FabriceVeron 6 41
(P Monfort, France) **9/1**

3m 23.58s (203.58) 16 Ran SP% **119.8**
PARI-MUTUEL (all including 1 euro stake): WIN 18.50; PLACE 5.10, 2.10, 5.10; DF 35.60.
Owner Stefano Bacci & Antonio Pierini **Bred** Wertheimer & Frere **Trained** France

6522a LUCIEN BARRIERE GRAND PRIX DE DEAUVILLE (GROUP 2) (3YO+) (ROUND COURSE) (TURF) 1m 4f 110y
3:30 3-Y-O+ £102,702 (£39,639; £18,918; £12,612; £6,306)

RPR
1 **Ziyad**[56] 4430 4-9-4 0 ow1............ OlivierPeslier 2 114+
(C Laffon-Parias, France) *settled in 2nd: rdn 2f out: sn led: styd on ins fnl f: a doing enough* **2/1**[2]
2 1/2 **Soft Light (FR)**[42] 4963 3-8-9 0 ow1............ CristianDemuro 6 114+
(J-C Rouget, France) *hld up in rr: slt hdwy over 2f out: sn rdn: r.o ins fnl f: nt rch wnr* **61/10**[3]
3 2 **Nagano Gold**[64] 4093 5-9-4 0 ow1............ ChristopheSoumillon 5 109
(Vaclav Luka Jr, Czech Republic) *towards rr: smooth hdwy and ev ch ent st: rdn 2f out: kpt on one pce* **17/10**[1]
4 1/2 **Villa Rosa (FR)**[63] 4159 4-9-1 0 ow1............ AlexisBadel 7 105
(H-F Devin, France) *mid-div: rdn 2 1/2f out: kpt on one pce* **32/5**

The Form Book Flat 2019, Raceform Ltd, Newbury, RG14 5SJ

5 3 **Master's Spirit (IRE)**[21] 5718 8-9-4 0 ow1......... Pierre-CharlesBoudot 3 103
(J Reynier, France) *chsd ldrs on inner: rdn 1 1/2f out: squeezed by rival appr fnl f: styd on under hands and heels ride* **15/1**

6 12 **Premier Lion (FR)**[27] 4-9-4 0 ow1............................(b) AntoineHamelin 1 84
(Vaclav Luka Jr, Czech Republic) *led: pushed along over 3f out: sn fdd* **62/1**

7 15 **Tiberian (FR)**[63] 4159 7-9-4 0 ow1.......................... FrankieDettori 4 60
(Mlle L Kneip, France) *chsd ldrs: hrd rdn 3f out: no imp* **14/1**

8 3/4 **Gyllen (USA)**[21] 5718 4-9-4 0 ow1........................ MickaelBarzalona 8 59
(A Fabre, France) *towards rr on outer: rdn over 2f out: nvr a factor* **14/1**

2m 38.2s (-8.20)
WFA 3 from 4yo+ 9lb **8** Ran SP% **119.1**
PARI-MUTUEL (all including 1 euro stake): WIN 3.00; PLACE 1.10, 1.50, 1.30; DF 8.20.
Owner Wertheimer & Frere **Bred** Wertheimer Et Frere **Trained** Chantilly, France

4419 OVREVOLL (R-H)

Sunday, August 25

OFFICIAL GOING: Turf: good

6523a GIANT SANDMAN POLAR CUP (GROUP 3) (3YO+) (TURF) 6f 187y

2:55 3-Y-O+ £31,731 (£13,599; £6,527; £4,351; £2,719)

RPR

1 **Duca Di Como (IRE)**[25] 4-9-4 0.............................. ElioneChaves 5 100
(Cathrine Erichsen, Norway) *settled in mid-div: pushed along 2f out: rdn over 1f out: r.o wl* **4/5**[1]

2 1 **Captain America (SWE)**[70] 9-9-4 0.......................... CarlosLopez 7 97
(Annike Bye Hansen, Norway) *in rr: outpcd over 3f out: rdn: kpt on ins fnl f to go 2nd cl home* **7/1**

3 hd **Brian Ryan**[70] 3907 4-9-8 0.............................. Jan-ErikNeuroth 3 100
(Wido Neuroth, Norway) *mid-div on inner: rdn over 2f out: styd on* **19/5**[2]

4 1/4 **Land's End (DEN)**[42] 7-9-4 0.............................. MartinRodriguez 6 96
(Francisco Castro, Sweden) *sltly outpcd in rr: clsd up to main gp: rdn over 2f out: kpt on* **176/10**

5 1 **Backcountry**[25] 7-9-4 0.......................................(b) OliverWilson 10 93
(Annette Stjernstrand, Sweden) *chsd ldr: effrt over 2f out: kpt on one pce* **134/10**

6 1 **Fiftyshadesfreed (IRE)**[711] 8-9-4 0...................(b) Per-AndersGraberg 8 89
(Lennart Jarven, Sweden) *cl up on outer: rdn ent st: no imp* **68/10**[3]

7 1/4 **Pal O'Mine (IRE)**[322] 9-9-4 0........................ KaiaSofieIngolfsland 9 89
(Tina Smith, Norway) *led: rdn to assert 2f out: no ex ins fnl f: wknd* **47/1**

8 3/4 **No Comment (DEN)**[60] 6-9-4 0...........................(b) RafaeldeOliveira 1 86
(Bent Olsen, Denmark) *chsd ldr on inner: rdn over 1 1/2f out: no imp and wknd* **39/1**

9 6 1/4 **Anachronist (FR)** 5-9-4 0.............................. ManuelMartinez 4 67
(Isidro Vergara, Norway) *racd in 2nd: u.p 3f out: no imp thereafter* **269/10**

10 3 1/4 **Sarookh (USA)**[70] 4-9-4 0.............................. ShaneKarlsson 2 57
(Jessica Long, Sweden) *towards rr on inner: rdn over 1 1/2f out: no imp and wknd* **153/10**

1m 19.5s **10** Ran SP% **128.3**
TOTE (all including 1 unit stake): WIN 1.89; PLACE: 1.69, 2.35, 1.91; SF 418.30.
Owner Stall Como **Bred** Crone Stud Farms Ltd **Trained** Norway

6524a MARIT SVEAAS MINNELOP (GROUP 3) (3YO+) (TURF) 1m 1f

3:20 3-Y-O+ £72,529 (£23,572; £10,879; £6,527; £4,351)

RPR

1 **Square De Luynes (FR)**[57] 4419 4-9-6 0................... PatCosgrave 9 110
(Niels Petersen, Norway) *mde virtually all: shkn up and readily qcknd clr fr 1 1/2f out: on strly ins fnl f: easily* **3/5**[1]

2 8 3/4 **Buddy Bob (IRE)** 4-9-4 0..(p) DaleSwift 10 90
(Wido Neuroth, Norway) *hld up towards rr: pushed along ins fnl 3f: prog fr 2f out: kpt on strly u.p fr 1f out: snatched 2nd fnl strides* **39/1**

3 nse **Appelina (DEN)**[24] 6-9-1 0.............................. Jan-ErikNeuroth 2 87
(Wido Neuroth, Norway) *prom: pushed along to chse ldr over 2 1/2f out: drvn in 2nd fr 1 1/2f out: kpt on same pce ins fnl f: lost 2nd fnl strides* **43/10**[2]

4 3/4 **Trouble Of Course (FR)**[15] 5-9-4 0......................... ShaneKarlsson 5 88
(Niels Petersen, Norway) *racd in fnl trio: pushed along on far side rail fr over 2 1/2f out: prog fr 2f out: styd on wl ins fnl f* **156/10**

5 1 **Learn By Heart**[15] 4-9-6 0.............................. RafaeldeOliveira 3 88
(Bent Olsen, Denmark) *midfield on inner: pushed along 3f out: limited rspnse and sn drvn: kpt on in modest 5th fr over 1f out* **165/10**

6 1/2 **Swedish Dream (FR)**[70] 3902 5-9-4 0........................ CarlosLopez 4 85
(Annike Bye Hansen, Norway) *midfield: swtchd rt and asked for effrt on nr side fr 3f out: sn drvn: unable qck: kpt on same pce ins fnl f* **73/10**[3]

7 2 **Cockney Cracker (FR)**[15] 8-9-4 0.............................. OliverWilson 8 81
(Niels Petersen, Norway) *racd in fnl pair: pushed along on far side rail fr over 3f out: no imp: mod prog fr 1 1/2f out: nvr a factor* **245/10**

8 nk **Victor Kalejs (USA)**[25] 5-9-4 0........................ Per-AndersGraberg 11 80
(Roy Arne Kvisla, Sweden) *midfield on outer: struggling to go pce and pushed along over 3f out: no rspnse and wl btn fr 2f out* **24/1**

9 2 1/4 **Jubilance (IRE)**[56] 10-9-4 0.............................. ElioneChaves 6 76
(Bent Olsen, Denmark) *a towards rr: outpcd fr over 3f out: passed btn rival ins fnl f: nvr a factor* **186/10**

10 3 **Quarterback (GER)**[855] 1957 7-9-4 0.....................(p) ManuelGMartinez 1 69
(Yvonne Durant, Norway) *cl up: shortlived effrt over 3f out: sn wknd and wl btn over 2f out* **132/10**

1m 47.1s (-2.80) **10** Ran SP% **127.7**
TOTE (all including 1 unit stake): WIN 1.66; PLACE 1.33, 4.92, 1.53; DF 224.07.
Owner Stall Power Girls **Bred** Jacques Beres **Trained** Norway

6361 CHEPSTOW (L-H)

Monday, August 26

OFFICIAL GOING: Good (good to firm in places; watered; 5.8)
Wind: Fine and warm Weather: Gentle headwind

6525 BETAID.ORG RESPONSIBLE GAMBLING H'CAP 6f 16y

2:00 (2:00) (Class 4) (0-85,87) 3-Y-O+
£5,207 (£1,549; £774; £387; £300; £300) **Stalls** Centre

Form RPR

0311 1 **Major Valentine**[11] 6109 7-9-3 **87**.............................. KateLeahy(7) 6 93
(John O'Shea) *s.i.s: sn trcking ldr: led after 2f: pushed along over 2f out: hrd pressed ins fnl f: jst hld on* **11/4**[1]

2041 2 shd **A Sure Welcome**[11] 6110 5-8-12 **80**....................(p) ScottMcCullagh(5) 3 86
(John Spearing) *chsd ldng pair: drvn to go 2nd over 1f out: clsd on wnr ins fnl f: ev ch towards fin: jst failed* **8/1**

5056 3 4 **Bungee Jump (IRE)**[15] 5989 4-9-8 **85**.............................. RossaRyan 5 79
(Grace Harris) *led: sn taken rt to stands' rail: hdd after 2f: drvn over 1f out: sn lost 2nd: fdd ins fnl f* **9/2**[2]

1420 4 1 **Dark Shadow (IRE)**[28] 5504 3-9-6 **86**.............................. HectorCrouch 2 77
(Clive Cox) *chsd ldrs: rdn 1/2-way: kpt on but nvr able to chal* **5/1**[3]

0151 5 1 **Gambon (GER)**[11] 6108 3-9-2 **82**.............................. CharlesBishop 4 70
(Eve Johnson Houghton) *s.i.s: in rr: rdn 2f out: no real imp* **11/4**[1]

0362 6 3 1/4 **Red Alert**[17] 5882 5-9-4 **81**...(p) TomMarquand 1 59
(Tony Carroll) *hld up: rdn over 2f out: wknd over 1f out* **8/1**

1m 10.28s (-1.22) **Going Correction** -0.175s/f (Firm)
WFA 3 from 4yo+ 3lb **6** Ran SP% **110.4**
Speed ratings (Par 105): **101,100,95,94,92 88**
CSF £23.93 TOTE £2.90: £2.00, £3.20; EX 31.90 Trifecta £82.20.
Owner Pete Smith **Bred** J R Salter **Trained** Elton, Gloucs
■ Stewards' Enquiry : Scott McCullagh two-day ban: used whip above permitted level (Sep 9-10)

FOCUS
Racing stands' side, little got into this sprint and the front two came clear late on. The second has been credited with a marginal pb.

6526 COMPAREBETTINGSITES.COM ONLINE BETTING APPRENTICE (S) STKS 6f 16y

2:35 (2:35) (Class 6) 3-5-Y-O £2,781 (£827; £413; £300; £300) **Stalls** Centre

Form RPR

2404 1 **Diamond Shower (IRE)**[17] 5893 3-8-5 65...................... SeanKirrane(3) 2 58+
(Richard Fahey) *hld up: prog 1/2-way: wnt 2nd over 2f out: sn drvn: led appr fnl f: qckly in command: comf* **11/10**[1]

6654 2 3 1/2 **Hellovaqueen**[14] 6018 4-8-11 58...............................(b) AngusVilliers(5) 6 53
(Richard Hughes) *led and claimed stands' rail: rdn over 2f out: hdd appr fnl f: sn outpcd by wnr* **6/4**[2]

U460 3 2 3/4 **Mooroverthebridge**[45] 4870 5-9-2 54........................(p[1]) ScottMcCullagh 1 44
(Grace Harris) *s.s: in rr: rdn and clsd 2f out: wnt 3rd over 1f out: styd on but no further imp (jockey said mare missed break)* **5/1**[3]

0500 4 2 1/4 **Yet Another (IRE)**[14] 6018 4-8-11 35........................(b[1]) KeelanBaker(5) 5 38
(Grace Harris) *chsd ldrs: drvn over 2f out: sn outpcd and no ch (jockey said gelding jumped right-handed from stalls)* **33/1**

-000 5 1 **What A Dazzler**[11] 6107 3-8-8 42............................(p[1]) DarraghKeenan 3 30
(Bill Turner) *chsd ldr tl rdn and lost 2nd over 2f out: wknd over 1f out* **33/1**

1m 11.25s (-0.25) **Going Correction** -0.175s/f (Firm)
WFA 3 from 4yo+ 3lb **5** Ran SP% **110.2**
Speed ratings (Par 101): **94,89,85,82,81**
CSF £3.02 TOTE £1.90: £1.10, £1.50; EX 3.10 Trifecta £3.80.The winner was sold to John Flint for £7,000
Owner Paul C Garner **Bred** Mrs C Hartery **Trained** Musley Bank, N Yorks

FOCUS
A lowly seller that looked a match and the two clear market leaders had it between them from 2f out. Ultimately the favourite won tidily. The fourth and fifth limit the level.

6527 COMPAREBETTINGSITES.COM ONLINE BETTING FILLIES' NOVICE AUCTION STKS (PLUS 10 RACE) 7f 16y

3:10 (3:10) (Class 5) 2-Y-O £3,428 (£1,020; £509; £254) **Stalls** Centre

Form RPR

36 1 **Gert Lush (IRE)**[62] 4222 2-9-0 0.............................. RossaRyan 5 64+
(Roger Teal) *hld up in tch: hdwy and hung rt over 2f out: led over 1f out: drvn and hung lft ins fnl f: rn green but a doing enough* **11/4**[2]

3103 2 3/4 **Space Ace (FR)**[11] 6106 2-9-7 76........................(b[1]) AdamMcNamara 3 69
(Archie Watson) *t.k.h: led: rdn 2f out: drvn and hdd over 1f out: kpt on same pce and hld after* **2/5**[1]

0 3 1 3/4 **Annie Quickstep (IRE)**[21] 5745 2-9-0 0.............................. RobHornby 2 57
(Jonathan Portman) *cl up: rdn over 2f out: lost 2nd over 1f out: edgd rt fnl f: styd on same pce (vet said filly lost right hind shoe)* **11/1**[3]

0 4 13 **Diligent Lass**[33] 5314 2-9-0 0.............................. DanielMuscutt 1 22
(Michael Blanshard) *wnt lft leaving stalls: sn in tch: pushed along over 2f out: qckly outpcd by ldrs: wknd over 1f out (jockey said filly jumped left leaving stalls; vet said filly lost left hind shoe)* **50/1**

0 5 nk **Unbridled Light (FR)**[11] 6118 2-8-7 0.............................. KateLeahy(7) 4 21
(Anthony Honeyball) *cl up: rdn 3f out: sn lost pl: in rr whn swvd rt wl over 1f out (jockey said filly ran green)* **33/1**

1m 24.29s (0.39) **Going Correction** -0.175s/f (Firm) **5** Ran SP% **111.3**
Speed ratings (Par 91): **90,89,87,72,71**
CSF £4.29 TOTE £3.50: £1.30, £1.10; EX 3.20 Trifecta £9.10.
Owner Mrs Muriel Forward & Dr G C Forward **Bred** Rathbarry Stud **Trained** Lambourn, Berks

FOCUS
Bit of a turn up in this novice, with the red-hot favourite turned over. They headed centre-field this time.

6528 COMPAREBETTINGSITES.COM BETTING EBF NOVICE STKS (PLUS 10 RACE) (C&G) 7f 16y

3:45 (3:47) (Class 4) 2-Y-O £4,851 (£1,443; £721; £360) **Stalls** Centre

Form RPR

22 1 **Stoweman**[12] 6079 2-9-0 0.............................. HectorCrouch 2 79
(Clive Cox) *mde all: drvn wl over 1f out: styd on wl* **13/8**[1]

51 2 1 3/4 **Bodyline (IRE)**[25] 5572 2-9-6 0.............................. LukeMorris 3 80
(Sir Mark Prescott Bt) *s.i.s: sn chsng wnr: rdn over 2f out: hung lft fr over 1f out: unable to chal but kpt on to hold 2nd* **6/1**

5 3 nk **Impatient**[19] 5809 2-9-0 0.............................. RobHornby 6 73
(Ralph Beckett) *t.k.h: chsd ldrs: rdn 2f out: styd on steadily fnl f: jst missed 2nd* **9/4**[2]

63 **4** *nk* **Fantasy Believer (IRE)**[20] 5774 2-9-0 0.......................... KieranShoemark 5 73
(Charles Hills) *chsd ldrs: rdn over 1f out: kpt on fnl f: unable to chal* **11/2**[3]

5 *3* **Intrepid Italian** 2-9-0 0.......................... RossaRyan 8 65
(Richard Hannon) *t.k.h bhd ldrs: rdn to dispute 2nd 2f out: wknd fnl f (jockey said colt hung left)* **16/1**

6 *4 1/2* **HMS President (IRE)** 2-9-0 0.......................... TomMarquand 7 52
(Eve Johnson Houghton) *s.i.s: carried rt sn after s: in rr: rdn 3f out: no ch fnl 2f* **12/1**

35 **7** *5* **Global Agreement**[6] 6300 2-9-0 0.......................... LiamKeniry 4 39
(Milton Harris) *hld up: swtchd rt sn after s: rdn over 2f out: sn btn* **33/1**

6 **8** *3 3/4* **Cappella Fella (IRE)**[45] 4876 2-8-11 0.......................... WilliamCox(3) 1 29
(Sarah Hollinshead) *t.k.h: prom on outer: lost pl 1/2-way: sn in rr* **80/1**

1m 22.8s (-1.10) **Going Correction** -0.175s/f (Firm) **8** Ran SP% **116.3**
Speed ratings (Par 96): **99,97,96,96,92 87,82,77**
CSF £12.46 TOTE £2.50: £1.10, £2.20, £1.10; EX 12.60 Trifecta £25.80.
Owner Alan G Craddock **Bred** Alan Craddock **Trained** Lambourn, Berks

FOCUS
Racing stands' side for this novice, little got into it with the winner making all. It's been rated at face value.

6529 HOT TUBS SPLASH AND DASH H'CAP — 7f 16y
4:20 (4:21) (Class 6) (0-65,65) 3-Y-0+

£2,781 (£827; £413; £300; £300; £300) **Stalls** Centre

Form RPR

532 **1** **Captain Sedgwick (IRE)**[23] 5675 5-8-6 **48**.......................... JaneElliott(3) 14 55
(John Spearing) *wnt to post early: a.p: led wl over 2f out: sn drvn: hrd pressed over 1f out: hld on wl towards fin* **3/1**[1]

/012 **2** *nk* **Miss Icon**[11] 6116 5-9-6 **59**.......................... LiamKeniry 7 65
(Patrick Chamings) *hld up: hdwy 1/2-way: sltly hmpd wl over 2f out: sn drvn: ev ch over 1f out: unable qck towards fin* **9/2**[2]

3031 **3** *1 1/4* **Jupiter**[23] 5675 4-8-11 **57**..........................(v) LukeCatton(7) 12 60
(Alexandra Dunn) *led 2f: chsd ldr: rdn and ev ch 2f out: lost 2nd over 1f out: kpt on (vet said gelding had bitten his tongue)* **11/1**

051 **4** *2 1/4* **Clem A**[11] 6121 3-9-4 **65**.......................... DarraghKeenan(3) 5 60
(Alan Bailey) *chsd ldrs: rdn 3f out: sltly outpcd over 1f out: styd on (vet said gelding lost left fore shoe)* **5/1**[3]

1-50 **5** *shd* **Wild Dancer**[32] 5351 6-9-9 **62**.......................... DanielMuscutt 8 58
(Patrick Chamings) *chsd ldrs: rdn over 2f out: kpt on same pce fnl f* **12/1**

6333 **6** *4 1/2* **Cooperess**[4] 6363 6-8-4 **46**.......................... MeganNicholls(3) 2 30
(Adrian Wintle) *hld up: rdn and hdwy on outer over 2f out: no further prog* **5/1**[3]

0005 **7** *1/2* **Field Of Vision (IRE)**[13] 6045 6-9-2 **55**..........................(p) RobHornby 11 38
(John Flint) *prom: rdn over 2f out: wknd fnl f* **14/1**

0323 **8** *3 1/2* **Masquerade Bling (IRE)**[55] 4479 5-9-4 **57**..........................(p) LukeMorris 4 31
(Neil Mulholland) *hld up: rdn and sme prog 3f out: hld fnl 2f* **12/1**

5400 **9** *2* **Langley Vale**[11] 6107 10-8-5 **47**.......................... WilliamCox(3) 3 15
(Roger Teal) *wnt to post early: hld up: rdn 3f out: sn outpcd and btn* **33/1**

/000 **10** *1/2* **Lady Carduros (IRE)**[13] 6059 5-8-7 **46** oh1..........................(v[1]) LiamJones 13 13
(Michael Appleby) *s.i.s: sn chsng ldrs: led after 2f: rdn and hung lft 3f out: sn hdd: wknd qckly* **50/1**

4002 **11** *3 1/4* **Bold Show**[18] 5847 3-9-0 **58**..........................(v) TonyHamilton 9 14
(Richard Fahey) *midfield: rdn over 3f out: sn wknd* **12/1**

0002 **12** *6* **Hold Your Breath**[15] 5981 4-8-7 **46**..........................(h) JohnFahy 6
(Tony Carroll) *wnt to post early: chsd ldrs 2f: towards rr by 1/2-way: wknd over 2f out* **25/1**

1m 22.27s (-1.63) **Going Correction** -0.175s/f (Firm) **12** Ran SP% **123.3**
WFA 3 from 4yo+ 5lb
Speed ratings (Par 101): **102,101,100,97,97 92,91,87,85,84 81,74**
CSF £16.45 CT £138.43 TOTE £4.00: £1.50, £2.00, £3.10; EX 17.70 Trifecta £147.70.
Owner Oakridge Racing **Bred** Yeomanstown Stud **Trained** Kinnersley, Worcs

FOCUS
A moderate handicap, the main action unfolded near to the stands' side late on. Straightforward form rated around the principals.

6530 SIR GORDON RICHARDS H'CAP (SPONSORED BY HEATH HOUSE STABLES) — 2m
4:55 (4:55) (Class 3) (0-90,91) 3-Y-0+

£7,246 (£2,168; £1,084) **Stalls** Low

Form RPR

421 **1** **Charlie D (USA)**[24] 5604 4-8-13 **80**..........................(tp) JaneElliott(3) 3 84
(Tom Dascombe) *mde all: set stdy pce tl qcknd tempo 4f out: pushed along 3f out: hrd pressed 2f out: edgd rt ins fnl f: hld on u.p* **4/1**[3]

631 **2** *nk* **Graceful Lady**[16] 5967 6-9-0 **81**.......................... DarraghKeenan(3) 1 85
(Robert Eddery) *trckd wnr: rdn over 3f out: lost 2nd over 2f out: rallied to go 2nd again ins fnl f: styd on: jst hld* **7/2**[2]

1111 **3** *1 1/4* **Distant Chimes (GER)**[5] 6348 4-9-12 **90** 5ex..........................(p) LukeMorris 4 93
(Sir Mark Prescott Bt) *s.s: hld up in tch in last of 3: rdn over 3f out: wnt 2nd over 2f out: sn ev ch: one pce over 1f out: lost 2nd ins fnl f* **1/2**[1]

3m 35.15s (-6.95) **Going Correction** -0.175s/f (Firm) **3** Ran SP% **108.9**
Speed ratings (Par 107): **110,109,109**
CSF £13.63 TOTE £2.00; EX 6.80 Trifecta £19.30.
Owner D R Passant & T Dascombe **Bred** Rabbah Bloodstock Ltd **Trained** Malpas, Cheshire

FOCUS
Just the three of them in what was a decent staying handicap and they finished in reverse market order. The third has been rated in line with his AW form.

6531 INTERBET.COM H'CAP — 1m 4f
5:30 (5:31) (Class 6) (0-60,60) 3-Y-0

£2,781 (£827; £413; £300; £300; £300) **Stalls** Low

Form RPR

060 **1** **Kasuku**[19] 5808 3-8-7 **46**..........................(b[1]) RobHornby 6 54+
(Ralph Beckett) *chsd along towards rr early: hdwy to ld after 3f: drvn over 2f out: styd on wl* **12/1**

0143 **2** *1 1/4* **Celtic Classic (IRE)**[15] 5987 3-9-0 **53**..........................(b) RossaRyan 2 59
(Paul Cole) *prom: rdn 4f out: sn sltly outpcd: styd on to go 2nd nr fin* **9/4**[1]

-003 **3** *nk* **Tamok (IRE)**[9] 6202 3-8-8 **47**..........................(v) TomMarquand 13 53
(Michael Bell) *prom: wnt 2nd 7f out: rdn 3f out: kpt on u.p: unable to chal wnr fnl f: lost 2nd nr fin* **5/1**[3]

6232 **4** *1 1/2* **Sinndarella (IRE)**[19] 5798 3-8-6 **48**.......................... NoelGarbutt(3) 10 51
(Sarah Hollinshead) *hld up towards rr: n.m.r on inner 5f out: rdn over 3f out: hdwy 2f out: sn chsng ldrs: styd on same pce fnl f* **7/1**

0-34 **5** *1 1/2* **Estrela Star (IRE)**[23] 5680 3-9-3 **56**.......................... CharlesBishop 11 57
(Ali Stronge) *t.k.h in midfield: rdn 3f out: no real imp tl styd on fnl f* **14/1**

2330 **6** *4* **Mongolia**[71] 3888 3-9-2 **55**.......................... LukeMorris 9 49
(Michael Appleby) *sn trcking ldrs: pushed along 5f out: rdn 3f out: kpt on same pce tl wknd fnl f* **10/1**

5423 **7** *1* **Menin Gate (IRE)**[20] 5792 3-9-7 **60**..........................(p) TonyHamilton 8 53
(Richard Fahey) *prom: led after 1f tl after 3f: drvn 3f out: fdd fr over 1f out* **3/1**[2]

00-0 **8** *19* **Miss Swift**[87] 3324 3-8-0 **46** oh1.......................... AngusVilliers(7) 12 8
(Marcus Tregoning) *led 1f: remained prom tl rdn and outpcd 3f out: wknd over 1f out: t.o (jockey said filly ran green)* **22/1**

0-00 **9** *16* **Redemptress (IRE)**[152] 1352 3-8-7 **46** oh1.......................... LiamJones 1
(John O'Shea) *a towards rr: struggling 5f out: t.o* **50/1**

5640 **10** *5* **Lucky Lou (IRE)**[84] 3418 3-9-5 **58**..........................(h) LiamKeniry 4
(Ken Cunningham-Brown) *hld up: rdn 3f out: sn wknd: t.o* **20/1**

0306 **11** *20* **Coastguard Watch (FR)**[52] 4684 3-9-2 **55**.......................... HectorCrouch 14
(Natalie Lloyd-Beavis) *t.k.h in rr: rdn 3f out: sn wknd: t.o (vet said gelding lost left fore shoe)* **50/1**

2m 35.81s (-4.49) **Going Correction** -0.175s/f (Firm) **11** Ran SP% **121.4**
Speed ratings (Par 98): **107,106,105,104,103 101,100,87,77,73 60**
CSF £39.30 CT £160.73 TOTE £16.50: £3.60, £1.50, £1.80; EX 58.90 Trifecta £270.80.
Owner Larksborough Stud Limited **Bred** Larksborough Stud Limited **Trained** Kimpton, Hants

FOCUS
Lowly 3yo form and another race where it paid to be prominent. The pace was a steady one. Straightforward form.
T/Plt: £31.20 to a £1 stake. Pool: £47,589.76 - 1,112.51 winning units T/Qpdt: £9.20 to a £1 stake. Pool: £3,885.90 - 309.25 winning units **Richard Lowther**

5570 EPSOM (L-H)
Monday, August 26

OFFICIAL GOING: Good (good to firm in places; watered; 6.6)
Wind: Light, behind Weather: Hot

6532 BRITISH STALLION STUDS EBF MAIDEN AUCTION STKS (PLUS 10 RACE) — 7f 3y
1:55 (1:57) (Class 4) 2-Y-O

£4,851 (£1,443; £721; £360) **Stalls** Low

Form RPR

2024 **1** **Nat Love (IRE)**[11] 6106 2-9-0 73.......................... PatDobbs 2 72+
(Mick Channon) *sn w ldrs: led over 4f out: shkn up 2f out: sn clr: r.o wl ins fnl f: comf* **8/15**[1]

05 **2** *4* **Olivers Pursuit**[15] 5992 2-9-2 0.......................... ShaneKelly 4 64
(Gay Kelleway) *sn trcking ldng pair: effrt 3f out: sn rdn: chsd clr wnr and edgd lft over 1f out: no imp but kpt on for clr 2nd* **13/2**[3]

30 **3** *3 3/4* **Moorland Spirit (IRE)**[11] 6118 2-8-11 0..........................(b) SeanDavis(3) 6 52
(Archie Watson) *broke wl: led: sn hdd and chsd ldng trio: rdn over 3f out: outpcd and wl hld whn swtchd rt over 1f out: plugged on same pce to go modest 3rd ins fnl f* **6/1**[2]

4 *1* **Kuwaity** 2-9-2 0.......................... JasonWatson 5 51
(Mohamed Moubarak) *sn led: hdd over 4f out: chsd wnr: rdn over 2f out: nt match pce of wnr and lost 2nd over 1f out: wknd ins fnl f* **6/1**[2]

0 **5** *1 1/4* **Pure Purfection (IRE)**[28] 5500 2-8-9 0.......................... CharlieBennett 7 41+
(Jim Boyle) *midfield: outpcd 4f out: no threat to ldrs after but kpt on ins fnl f* **40/1**

00 **6** *1/2* **Herre Dittery**[15] 5992 2-8-7 0.......................... EllaBoardman(7) 3 45
(Pat Phelan) *s.i.s: wl off the pce in last trio: pushed along over 2f out: edgd lft over 1f out: kpt on ins fnl f: nvr trbld ldrs* **40/1**

04 **7** *8* **No Can Do**[6] 6314 2-9-2 0..........................(t) RobertHavlin 8 26
(Jamie Osborne) *dropped in bhd after s: a towards rr* **16/1**

8 *hd* **Am I Dreaming (IRE)** 2-8-9 0.......................... GeorgeWood 1 18
(Adam West) *v.s.a: rn green and a bhd (jockey said filly was slowly away and ran green)* **16/1**

1m 23.1s (-0.30) **Going Correction** -0.05s/f (Good) **8** Ran SP% **123.8**
Speed ratings (Par 96): **99,94,90,89,87 87,77,77**
CSF £5.57 TOTE £1.30: £1.02, £1.60, £2.10; EX 4.40 Trifecta £18.80.
Owner Mrs T Burns **Bred** Rathasker Stud **Trained** West Ilsley, Berks

FOCUS
The watered ground was given as good, good to firm in places (Going Stick 6.6). The rail was out 5yds from 1m to the winning post. Add 12yds. Just an ordinary maiden. The winner has been rated to his previous best.

6533 POUNDLAND FAMILY FAVOURITE H'CAP (JOCKEY CLUB GRASSROOTS SPRINT SERIES QUALIFIER) — 6f 3y
2:30 (2:33) (Class 5) (0-75,79) 3-Y-O

£5,175 (£1,540; £769; £384; £300; £300) **Stalls** High

Form RPR

0212 **1** **Sonja Henie (IRE)**[7] 6286 3-9-1 **74**.......................... ThomasGreatrex(5) 6 84
(David Loughnane) *pressed ldrs: upsides ldr and travelling bttr ent fnl 2f: pushed into ld ent fnl f: rdn and r.o wl ins fnl f* **2/1**[1]

-214 **2** *1 3/4* **Orange Blossom**[23] 5659 3-9-1 **69**.......................... BarryMcHugh 1 74
(Richard Fahey) *sn led: hrd pressed and rdn ent fnl 2f: hdd ent fnl f: kpt on same pce ins fnl f (trainer was informed filly could not run until the day after passing a stalls test)* **4/1**[3]

2112 **3** *1/2* **Golden Parade**[16] 5972 3-9-7 **75**..........................(p) DavidAllan 4 78
(Tim Easterby) *t.k.h: chsd ldng pair: effrt over 1f out: kpt on same pce ins fnl f (jockey said gelding ran too free)* **9/4**[2]

0201 **4** *3/4* **Great Shout (IRE)**[11] 6132 3-9-3 **71**..........................(t) GeorgeWood 7 72
(Amy Murphy) *t.k.h: hld up in tch in last pair: effrt wl over 1f out: kpt on ins fnl f: no threat to wnr (jockey said filly ran too free)* **6/1**

4122 **5** *2* **Swiss Pride (IRE)**[23] 5647 3-9-8 **76**.......................... ShaneKelly 5 71
(Richard Hughes) *hld up wl in tch in midfield: effrt over 1f out: drvn and unable qck 1f out: wknd ins fnl f* **16/1**

0321 **6** *3 1/2* **Alicia Darcy (IRE)**[6] 6301 3-9-8 **79** 6ex..........................(b) SeanDavis(3) 2 64
(Archie Watson) *t.k.h: hld up in tch in last pair: effrt ent fnl 2f: no imp u.p over 1f out: wknd ins fnl f* **9/1**

1m 8.58s (-1.32) **Going Correction** -0.05s/f (Good) **6** Ran SP% **114.3**
Speed ratings (Par 100): **106,103,103,102,99 94**
CSF £10.72 TOTE £2.80: £1.60, £2.10; EX 12.40 Trifecta £37.60.
Owner Sohi & Hoyland **Bred** Diomed Bloodstock Ltd **Trained** Tern Hill, Shropshire
■ Molaaheth was withdrawn. Price at time of withdrawal 20/1. Rule 4 does not apply.

FOCUS
Add 8yds. The early gallop wasn't that strong and it paid to be up with the pace. The winner backed up her recent form, and the third has been rated to his recent level.

6534 POUNDHOUND DOGGY DASH H'CAP 5f
3:05 (3:06) (Class 2) (0-100,96) 3-Y-O+
£11,827 (£3,541; £1,770; £885; £442; £222) **Stalls** High

Form RPR
4260 **1** **Merry Banter**[10] 6178 5-8-8 **80** HarryBentley 6 88
(Paul Midgley) *chsd ldr: effrt and swtchd lft jst over 1f out: rdn and clsd to ld 100yds out: styd on wl* **9/2**[2]
0400 **2** 1 **Duke Of Firenze**[5] 6351 10-9-5 **91** DavidAllan 5 95
(David C Griffiths) *chsd ldrs: effrt and swtchd jst over 1f out: hdwy and rdn ton press wnr wl ins fnl f: kpt on same pce towards fin* **6/1**[3]
6516 **3** 1/2 **Harrogate (IRE)**[24] 5606 4-8-6 **78** (b) CharlieBennett 7 81
(Jim Boyle) *led: rdn jst over 1f out: hdd 100yds out: no ex and one pce towards fin* **14/1**
0360 **4** 1 1/2 **Queen Of Desire (IRE)**[5] 6351 4-9-10 **96** JackMitchell 2 93
(Roger Varian) *midfield: effrt 2f out: unable qck over 1f out: kpt on same pce and no imp ins fnl f* **4/1**[1]
0001 **5** 1/2 **Blue De Vega (GER)**[10] 6149 6-8-12 **89** (tp) CierenFallon(5) 8 84
(Robert Cowell) *hld up in rr: short of room after 1f out: sn swtchd lft: hdwy 1/2-way: rdn over 1f out: no imp ins fnl f: eased towards fin* **4/1**[1]
2300 **6** 2 **Harome (IRE)**[5] 6351 5-8-13 **90** PaulaMuir(5) 4 78
(Roger Fell) *stdd s: t.k.h: hld up towards rr: effrt and edgd lft over 1f out: no imp: nvr trbld ldrs* **5/1**
3310 **7** 1 3/4 **Shamshon (IRE)**[28] 5504 8-8-11 **83** JasonWatson 1 65
(Stuart Williams) *midfield: effrt 2f out: unable qck over 1f out: wknd ins fnl f* **12/1**
5000 **8** 3/4 **Koditime (IRE)**[27] 5524 4-9-1 **87** ShaneKelly 3 66
(Clive Cox) *hld up towards rr: effrt 2f out: no imp whn nt clr run over 1f out: nvr involved* **9/1**
54.2s (-1.10) **Going Correction** -0.05s/f (Good) **8** Ran SP% **116.8**
Speed ratings (Par 109): **106,104,103,101,100 97,94,93**
CSF £32.24 CT £351.63 TOTE £5.50: £1.60, £2.00, £4.40; EX 34.70 Trifecta £489.80.
Owner H Thornton & P T Midgley **Bred** Jeremy Green And Sons **Trained** Westow, N Yorks
FOCUS
Not many got into this, the first two being the closest challengers to the clear leader from early on in the race, and all three raced next to the stands' rail most of the way. Straightforward form rated around the first three.

6535 AMATEURS' DERBY H'CAP (FOR GENTLEMAN AMATEUR RIDERS) 1m 4f 6y
3:40 (3:42) (Class 4) (0-85,87) 4-Y-O+
£7,486 (£2,322; £1,160; £580; £300; £300) **Stalls** Centre

Form RPR
5236 **1** **C'Est No Mour (GER)**[18] 5840 6-10-12 **76** (v[1]) MrSimonWalker 4 83
(Peter Hedger) *dwlt: sn rcvrd and wl in tch in midfield: clsd to ld and travelling strly over 2f out: rdn over 1f out: kpt on wl and a doing enough ins fnl f* **5/2**[2]
2231 **2** 1/2 **Allegiant (USA)**[10] 6165 4-11-3 **81** MrPatrickMillman 8 87
(Stuart Williams) *chsd ldr: ev ch and rdn jst over 2f out: kpt on wl u.p ins fnl f: a hld by wnr* **2/1**[1]
2055 **3** 1/2 **Mistiroc**[26] 4877 8-11-9 **87** (v) MrJJCodd 6 92
(John Quinn) *chsd ldrs early but mostly midfield: dropped to rr and stl wl in tch 7f out: effrt whn edgd lft and bumping w rival 2f out: chsd ldrs over 1f out: kpt on wl ins fnl f* **7/2**[3]
0600 **4** 4 1/2 **Brancaster (IRE)**[13] 6055 5-9-12 **66** oh2 MrGeorgeEddery(4) 7 64
(David Elsworth) *hld up in tch: effrt whn edgd rt and bumping w rival 2f out: no imp and edging lft over 1f out: wl hld ins fnl f* **16/1**
1310 **5** 6 **Ashazuri**[25] 5571 5-10-11 **75** (h) MrJamesHarding 5 64
(Jonathan Portman) *mde most tl rdn and hdd over 2f out: sn outpcd and wl btn over 1f out: wknd fnl f* **8/1**
0202 **6** 1 3/4 **Fairy Tale (IRE)**[23] 5686 4-11-7 **85** MrRossBirkett 3 72
(Gay Kelleway) *stdd after s: hld up in tch: effrt whn squeezed for room and hmpd 2f out: no ch after (jockey said gelding suffered interference approx 2f out)* **9/1**
5046 **7** 1 1/2 **Dance King**[8] 6255 9-10-13 **77** (tp) MrWilliamEasterby 1 60
(Tim Easterby) *trckd ldrs: effrt on inner over 2f out: no imp and wl btn over 1f out: wknd fnl f* **20/1**
2m 40.76s (-0.04) **Going Correction** -0.05s/f (Good) **7** Ran SP% **115.9**
Speed ratings (Par 105): **98,97,97,94,90 89,88**
CSF £8.18 CT £16.58 TOTE £3.40: £1.80, £1.60; EX 9.10 Trifecta £26.40.
Owner D Wilbrey **Bred** Graf U Grafin V Stauffenberg **Trained** Hook, Hampshire
FOCUS
Add 14yds. A couple of course specialists led them home here. The winner has been rated in line with the best of this year's form.

6536 WALTER NIGHTINGALL CONDITIONS STKS 1m 2f 17y
4:15 (4:15) (Class 3) 3-Y-O+ **£9,337** (£2,796; £1,398) **Stalls** Low

Form RPR
4123 **1** **Setting Sail**[27] 5519 4-9-7 106 WilliamBuick 2 112
(Charlie Appleby) *mde all: rdn 3f out: clr and in command over 1f out: styd on strly: eased towards fin* **4/6**[1]
26-0 **2** 4 1/2 **Crossed Baton**[124] 2033 4-9-2 103 (bt[1]) RobertHavlin 3 95
(John Gosden) *pressed wnr: effrt 3f out: drvn and nt match pce of wnr over 1f out: wl hld and kpt on same pce fnl f* **9/2**[3]
3424 **3** 129 **Desert Fire (IRE)**[23] 5657 4-9-7 102 (p) JasonWatson 1
(Saeed bin Suroor) *stmbld bdly leaving stalls: rdr lost irons: no ch to rcvr irons and hacked rnd in rr: t.o (jockey said colt stumbled leaving stalls causing him to lose his irons which he was unable to regain)* **9/4**[2]
2m 9.49s (-0.51) **Going Correction** -0.05s/f (Good) **3** Ran SP% **108.9**
Speed ratings (Par 107): **100,96,**
CSF £3.82 TOTE £1.50; EX 3.30 Trifecta £2.90.
Owner Godolphin **Bred** Godolphin **Trained** Newmarket, Suffolk
FOCUS
Add 14yds. A lot of the interest was lost when the second-favourite lost his race at the start, and the favourite had no issues seeing off his one rival. A token rating has been given.

6537 POUNDLAND SUMMER BLOW OUT H'CAP 1m 2f 17y
4:50 (4:50) (Class 3) (0-90,90) 3-Y-O+ **£9,337** (£2,796; £1,398; £699) **Stalls** Low

Form RPR
3513 **1** **Victory Chime (IRE)**[16] 5966 4-9-9 **87** (v) HarryBentley 3 95
(Ralph Beckett) *mde all: rdn ent fnl 2f: rdn over 1f out: styd on wl ins fnl f: rdn out* **2/1**[2]
1001 **2** 1 3/4 **Stealth Fighter (IRE)**[56] 4450 4-9-7 **90** CierenFallon(5) 5 95
(Saeed bin Suroor) *chsd ldrs tl chsd wnr after 2f: effrt over 2f out: pressing wnr and edging lft over 1f out: no ex and one pce ins fnl f* **15/8**[1]
3010 **3** 3 3/4 **Mr Scaramanga**[23] 5667 5-9-7 **85** WilliamBuick 1 83
(Simon Dow) *chsd wnr for 2f: chsd ldng pair after: effrt jst over 2f out: outpcd and edging lft over 1f out: swtchd rt and wl hld fnl f* **2/1**[2]
3006 **4** 2 3/4 **Pactolus (IRE)**[33] 5320 8-9-3 **81** (t) JasonWatson 4 73
(Stuart Williams) *hld up in rr: effrt jst over 2f out: no imp and wl hld whn hung lft fnl f* **9/1**[3]
2m 7.01s (-2.99) **Going Correction** -0.05s/f (Good)
WFA 3 from 4yo+ 7lb **4** Ran SP% **111.4**
Speed ratings (Par 107): **109,107,104,102**
CSF £6.30 TOTE £3.30; EX 6.20 Trifecta £9.60.
Owner A Nevin **Bred** M Downey & Kildaragh Stud **Trained** Kimpton, Hants
FOCUS
Add 14yds. They went steady early and the winner saved plenty in front. It's been rated with feet on the ground.

6538 POUNDLAND SAVES THE DAY H'CAP 1m 113y
5:25 (5:26) (Class 4) (0-80,80) 3-Y-O+
£7,115 (£2,117; £1,058; £529; £300; £300) **Stalls** Low

Form RPR
6-00 **1** **Surrey Hope (USA)**[20] 5776 5-9-12 **80** JasonWatson 2 89
(Hughie Morrison) *mde all: rdn ent fnl 2f: 2 l clr over 1f out: styd on wl and a doing enough ins fnl f (trainer could offer no explanation for gelding's improvement in form)* **5/2**[2]
0321 **2** 1 3/4 **Data Protection**[25] 5574 4-9-7 **75** (t) HarryBentley 4 80
(William Muir) *t.k.h: chsd ldng pair tl over 4f out: hdwy u.p to chse wnr over 1f out: kpt on but a hld ins fnl f* **9/4**[1]
3314 **3** 2 **Angel's Whisper (IRE)**[38] 5144 4-9-0 **71** SeanDavis(3) 5 72
(Amy Murphy) *hld up in tch in midfield: effrt over 2f out: kpt on u.p to go 3rd ins fnl f: no threat to wnr* **13/2**
0055 **4** 1 1/4 **Hackle Setter (USA)**[28] 5505 3-8-7 **73** PoppyBridgwater(5) 7 71
(Sylvester Kirk) *s.i.s: sn swtchd lft and rousted along early: in rr of main gp: shkn up 2f out: pushed along over 1f out: kpt on ins fnl f: nvr trbld ldrs* **11/1**
4003 **5** 1 **Sweet Charity**[44] 4898 4-8-12 **71** CierenFallon(5) 3 67
(Denis Coakley) *wl in tch in midfield: chsd ldng pair over 4f out: nt clrest of runs on inner ent fnl 2f: 3rd and no imp 1f out: wknd ins fnl f* **6/1**
4051 **6** hd **Plunger**[24] 5643 4-9-12 **80** (b) PatDobbs 6 75
(Paul Cole) *sn chsng wnr: effrt over 2f out: lost pl and changed legs over 1f out: wknd ins fnl f* **4/1**[3]
6530 **7** 19 **Narjes**[7] 6280 5-8-12 **66** (h) RobertHavlin 1 20+
(Laura Mongan) *v s.i.s: detached in last: clsd a little 4f out but nvr on terms w ldrs: lost tch 2f out: wl bhd over 1f out (jockey said mare was slowly away)* **16/1**
1m 42.91s (-3.49) **Going Correction** -0.05s/f (Good)
WFA 3 from 4yo+ 7lb **7** Ran SP% **121.2**
Speed ratings (Par 105): **113,111,109,108,107 107,90**
CSF £9.36 TOTE £3.80: £2.10, £1.60; EX 10.90 Trifecta £73.30.
Owner Surrey Racing (sh) **Bred** Nancy Mazzoni **Trained** East Ilsley, Berks
FOCUS
Add 14yds. Another all-the-way winner. The second and third have been rated to their recent levels.
T/Plt: £78.00 to a £1 stake. Pool: £53,616.88 - 501.26 winning units T/Qpdt: £31.40 to a £1 stake. Pool: £3,771.33 - 88.82 winning units **Steve Payne**

6226 RIPON (R-H)
Monday, August 26
OFFICIAL GOING: Good (good to firm in places; 7.8)
Wind: Almost nil Weather: Hot and Sunny

6539 TONY PYKE 60TH BIRTHDAY (S) STKS 6f
2:10 (2:15) (Class 6) 2-Y-O
£3,105 (£924; £461; £300; £300; £300) **Stalls** High

Form RPR
5601 **1** **Queens Blade**[16] 5968 2-8-13 67 (b) DuranFentiman 4 57
(Tim Easterby) *racd far side: chsd ldr: led overall over 2f out: sn rdn: hdd over 1f out: continued to chal ins fnl f: rallied to regain overall ld post: 1st of 3 in gp* **4/1**[2]
6332 **2** shd **Two Hearts**[24] 5618 2-9-0 49 SamJames 2 58
(Grant Tuer) *racd far side: hld up in trio: effrt over 2f out: led overall over 1f out: strly pressed thrght fnl f: hdd post: 2nd of 3 in gp* **6/1**
5400 **3** 1 3/4 **Sparkling Breeze**[16] 5968 2-9-0 64 (p[1]) ConnorBeasley 5 53
(Michael Dods) *racd in nrside gp: prom: led gp 1/2-way: sn rdn: hdd over 2f out: stl there u.p: styd on to ld gp towards fin: nt pce of front two: 1st of 8 in gp* **11/2**
3036 **4** nk **Maybellene (IRE)**[16] 5968 2-8-9 65 (v[1]) OisinMurphy 6 47
(George Scott) *racd in nrside gp: chsd ldrs: effrt to ld gp over 2f out: styd on same pce ins fnl f: nt pce of overall ldrs: hdd in gp towards fin: 2nd of 8 in gp* **11/4**[1]
0604 **5** 3/4 **The Ginger Bullet**[17] 5896 2-9-0 57 PaulHanagan 9 50
(Richard Fahey) *racd in nrside gp: midfield: drvn over 2f out: hdwy u.p 1f out: styd on towards fin: nvr able to chal: 3rd of 8 in gp (vet said colt lost left fore shoe)* **6/1**
0000 **6** 2 3/4 **Teasel's Rock (IRE)**[11] 6097 2-8-9 36 (p) RachelRichardson 7 36
(Tim Easterby) *racd in nrside gp and led gp: hdd 1/2-way: rdn over 2f out: one pce fr over 1f out: 4th of 8 in gp* **50/1**
0005 **7** 1 **Samsar (IRE)**[14] 6011 2-8-7 42 LauraCoughlan(7) 11 38
(Adrian Nicholls) *missed break: racd in nrside gp: in tch: rdn and unable qck over 2f out: one pce fnl f: 5th of 8 in gp* **50/1**
5655 **8** 1/2 **Callipygian**[17] 5912 2-8-9 60 (t[1]) PJMcDonald 8 32
(James Given) *racd in nrside gp: prom early: chsd ldrs after: rdn over 2f out: hung rt and outpcd over 1f out: wknd ins fnl f: 6th of 8 in gp* **5/1**[3]
0003 **9** 1 1/4 **Fulbeck Rose**[7] 6271 2-8-6 37 (t) RowanScott(3) 3 28
(Nigel Tinkler) *s.v.s: sn swtchd lft to r in nrside gp: bhd: sme hdwy u.p over 2f out: nvr a threat: 7th of 8 in gp (jockey said filly missed break)* **33/1**
000 **10** 6 **Tenbobmillionaire**[12] 6064 2-9-0 55 (b[1]) JasonHart 1 15
(Tim Easterby) *racd far side: led overall: drvn and hdd over 2f out: wknd over 1f out: 3rd of 3 in gp* **20/1**

05U0 **11** *7* **Champagne Victory (IRE)**[38] 5145 2-8-9 52..............(p[1]) CamHardie 13
(Brian Ellison) *racd in nrside gp: towards rr: sn pushed along and outpcd: lft bhd over 2f out: 8th of 8 in gp* **40/1**

1m 12.55s (0.05) **Going Correction** -0.225s/f (Firm) **11** Ran SP% **121.4**
Speed ratings (Par 92): **90,89,87,87,86 82,81,80,78,70 61**
CSF £27.87 TOTE £3.70: £1.60, £2.10, £2.10; EX 15.30 Trifecta £114.80.The winner was bought in for £5,000
Owner HP Racing Queens Blade & Partner **Bred** Mrs J McMahon & Mickley Stud **Trained** Great Habton, N Yorks

FOCUS
All rails on innermost positions, no added yards. There was a split opinion as to where the best ground was in this opening 2yo seller. The far side proved the place to be. The sixth and seventh help set the level.

6540 YORKSHIRE AIR AMBULANCE H'CAP 1m 1f 170y
2:45 (2:47) (Class 5) (0-75,74) 3-Y-O
£4,075 (£1,212; £606; £303; £300; £300) **Stalls** Low

Form RPR
4335 **1** **Fragrant Dawn**[21] 5734 3-9-3 **70**..............................(h) JimCrowley 2 77
(Charles Hills) *led: rdn whn pressed over 2f out: hdd narrowly 1f out: rallied to regained ld fnl 100yds: kpt on wl* **2/1**[1]
0404 **2** *nk* **Barbarosa (IRE)**[14] 6024 3-8-5 **58**.............................. PhilDennis 3 64
(Michael Herrington) *restless in stalls: hld up: nt clr run over 2f out: effrt sn after: led narrowly 1f out: hdd fnl 100yds: kpt on but hld after* **17/2**
5620 **3** *1* **Smeaton (IRE)**[23] 5695 3-8-8 **61**.............................. JasonHart 1 65
(Roger Fell) *trckd ldrs: lost pl 3f out: shkn up jst bhd ldrs whn nt clr run over 2f out: rdn whn wl there on rail over 1f out: swtchd lft ins fnl f: styd on towards fin (jockey said gelding denied clear run approaching fnl f)* **5/1**
3236 **4** *7* **Highwaygrey**[17] 5898 3-9-0 **67**.............................. DuranFentiman 6 58
(Tim Easterby) *restless in stalls: racd keenly wout cover: prom: rdn and ev ch over 2f out: checked whn u.p over 1f out: hung rt and wknd ins fnl f* **4/1**[2]
5432 **5** *3 1/2* **Flying Dragon (FR)**[13] 6045 3-9-3 **70**.............................. SeanLevey 4 54
(Richard Hannon) *handy: effrt 3f out: rdn and ev ch over 2f out: wknd and edgd rt over 1f out* **9/2**[3]
5002 **6** *14* **Prairie Spy (IRE)**[10] 6186 3-9-7 **74**..............................(v[1]) JoeFanning 5 31
(Mark Johnston) *sluggish s: racd keenly: hld up: hdwy over 3f out: rdn and chsd ldrs on outer over 2f out: wknd over 1f out* **9/1**

2m 2.71s (-1.89) **Going Correction** -0.225s/f (Firm) **6** Ran SP% **108.7**
Speed ratings (Par 100): **98,97,96,91,88 77**
CSF £17.43 TOTE £2.50: £1.70, £4.00; EX 20.50 Trifecta £97.00.
Owner Abdulla Al Khalifa **Bred** Sheikh Abdulla Bin Isa Al-Khalifa **Trained** Lambourn, Berks
■ Fume was withdrawn. Price at time of withdrawal 9/1. Rule 4 applies to all bets - deduction 10p in the £.

FOCUS
This modest 3yo handicap was run at an ordinary pace. It's been rated as ordinary straightforward form.

6541 BILLY NEVETT MEMORIAL H'CAP 1m 1f 170y
3:20 (3:21) (Class 3) (0-90,90) 3-Y-O **£7,762** (£2,310; £1,154; £577) **Stalls** Low

Form RPR
1251 **1** **Southern Rock (IRE)**[21] 5741 3-9-6 **89**.............................. DanielTudhope 5 95
(David O'Meara) *wnt to post early: chsd ldr: rdn to chal over 2f out: sn upsides: r.o gamely to ld post* **5/6**[1]
5200 **2** *shd* **The Trader (IRE)**[25] 5583 3-9-7 **90**.............................. JoeFanning 3 96
(Mark Johnston) *led: rdn whn jnd 2f out: edgd lft u.p over 1f out: continually strly pressed: hdd post* **2/1**[2]
1360 **3** *4 1/2* **Amber Spark (IRE)**[16] 5931 3-8-11 **80**.............................. PaulHanagan 2 77
(Richard Fahey) *hld up: effrt to chse ldrs over 2f out: no imp ins fnl f: kpt on same pce* **7/1**[3]
-526 **4** *hd* **Madeeh**[51] 4671 3-8-9 **78**..............................(t) PJMcDonald 4 75
(Philip Kirby) *prom: rdn 3f out: outpcd by ldrs over 2f out: kpt on u.p towards fin but no ch* **20/1**
05 **5** *3 3/4* **Jupiter Road**[9] 6209 3-8-6 **80**..............................(t) FayeMcManoman(5) 1 70?
(Nigel Tinkler) *hld up: pushed along and outpcd 3f out: nvr a threat* **16/1**

2m 0.96s (-3.64) **Going Correction** -0.225s/f (Firm) **5** Ran SP% **111.0**
Speed ratings (Par 104): **105,104,101,101,98**
CSF £2.76 TOTE £1.70: £1.10, £1.60; EX 2.70 Trifecta £7.10.
Owner O T I Racing & Middleham Park Racing Vi **Bred** Godolphin **Trained** Upper Helmsley, N Yorks
■ Stewards' Enquiry : Daniel Tudhope two-day ban: used whip down shoulder (Sep 9-10)

FOCUS
The two market leaders dominated this tidy little 3yo handicap. The second's Epsom form could be rated this good.

6542 BRITISH STALLION STUDS EBF RIPON CHAMPION TWO YRS OLD TROPHY STKS (LISTED RACE) 6f
3:55 (3:59) (Class 1) 2-Y-O
£17,013 (£6,450; £3,228; £1,608; £807; £405) **Stalls** High

Form RPR
1225 **1** **Platinum Star (IRE)**[27] 5520 2-9-3 106.............................. CallumShepherd 7 108
(Saeed bin Suroor) *trckd ldrs: led ent fnl 2f: rdn over 1f out: edgd lft ins fnl f: r.o wl: comf* **6/4**[1]
1104 **2** *3 1/2* **Lambeth Walk**[45] 4883 2-8-12 96.............................. OisinMurphy 6 93
(Archie Watson) *led for nrly 2f: trckd ldrs after: pushed along over 2f out: angled out and effrt over 1f out: sn chsd wnr: no imp ins fnl f* **9/2**[3]
2141 **3** *1/2* **Oh Purple Reign (IRE)**[22] 5707 2-9-3 97.............................. SeanLevey 4 96
(Richard Hannon) *in tch: pushed along 4f out: outpcd over 3f out: drvn to cl 2f out: kpt on u.p ins fnl f but nt pce of wnr: one pce fnl 50yds* **11/4**[2]
311 **4** *2 1/2* **Sir Boris (IRE)**[20] 5780 2-9-3 90.............................. RichardKingscote 5 89
(Tom Dascombe) *prom: led after nrly 2f: rdn over 2f out: hdd ent fnl 2f: sn got unbalanced: one pce fnl f* **5/1**
2111 **5** *1 1/4* **Bettys Hope**[37] 5185 2-8-12 90.............................. DavidEgan 3 80
(Rod Millman) *prom on outer: rdn over 2f out: unable qck over 1f out: wknd ins fnl f* **14/1**
3211 **6** *8* **Keep Busy (IRE)**[51] 4647 2-8-12 78.............................. JasonHart 2 56
(John Quinn) *sn swtchd lft and s.i.s: in rr: pushed along 3f out: nvr gng pce to get involved* **20/1**

1m 10.42s (-2.08) **Going Correction** -0.225s/f (Firm) **6** Ran SP% **112.9**
Speed ratings (Par 102): **104,99,98,95,93 83**
CSF £8.83 TOTE £2.30: £1.40, £2.20; EX 9.90 Trifecta £26.00.
Owner Godolphin **Bred** Corduff Stud & Farmleigh Bloodstock Ltd **Trained** Newmarket, Suffolk

FOCUS
The feature 2yo Listed event saw the field stick stands' side and there was a brisk pace on. It was a decent winning time.

6543 RIPON ROWELS H'CAP 1m
4:30 (4:32) (Class 2) (0-100,100) 3-Y-O+
£15,562 (£4,660; £2,330; £1,165; £582; £292) **Stalls** Low

Form RPR
0642 **1** **Ibraz**[16] 5965 4-9-5 **93**.............................. JimCrowley 6 101+
(Roger Varian) *chsd ldr: led over 2f out: edgd lft ins fnl f: drvn out and r.o* **9/5**[1]
-014 **2** *1 1/2* **Alfred Richardson**[23] 5693 5-9-1 **89**.............................. OisinMurphy 5 94
(John Davies) *chsd ldrs: rdn over 2f out: wnt 2nd ins fnl f: no real imp on wnr* **5/1**[3]
4031 **3** *nk* **Fayez (IRE)**[27] 5519 5-9-12 **100**.............................. DanielTudhope 3 104
(David O'Meara) *s.i.s: hld up: angled out and hdwy over 1f out: styd on ins fnl f: nt trble wnr* **7/2**[2]
5231 **4** *1 1/4* **Mikmak**[16] 5948 6-8-13 **87**..............................(p) DuranFentiman 2 88
(Tim Easterby) *racd keenly: midfield: effrt to chse ldrs over 2f out: styd on same pce fnl f* **9/1**
3102 **5** *hd* **Helovaplan (IRE)**[35] 5246 5-8-12 **86**.............................. GrahamLee 1 87
(Bryan Smart) *wnt to post early: led: rdn and hdd over 2f out: nt pce of wnr over 1f out: wnt lft u.p ins fnl f: kpt on same pce* **16/1**
5130 **6** *1/2* **Irreverent**[23] 5693 3-8-8 **88**.............................. PaulHanagan 4 86
(Richard Fahey) *hld up: rdn over 2f out: kpt on u.p ins fnl f: nvr able to chal* **7/1**
3230 **7** *5* **Ulshaw Bridge (IRE)**[16] 5971 4-9-0 **88**..............................(p) PJMcDonald 7 76
(James Bethell) *hld up: pushed along 3f out: one pce and no imp over 1f out: wknd fnl 100yds* **10/1**
1153 **8** *1* **Rousayan (IRE)**[1] 6496 8-8-12 **91**..............................(h) BenSanderson(5) 9 77
(Roger Fell) *chsd ldrs: rdn over 2f out: wknd over 1f out* **20/1**

1m 37.28s (-3.72) **Going Correction** -0.225s/f (Firm)
WFA 3 from 4yo+ 6lb **8** Ran SP% **116.8**
Speed ratings (Par 109): **109,107,107,105,105 105,100,99**
CSF £11.42 CT £28.96 TOTE £2.30: £1.40, £1.40, £1.50; EX 12.30 Trifecta £44.10.
Owner Hamdan Al Maktoum **Bred** Rabbah Bloodstock Limited **Trained** Newmarket, Suffolk

FOCUS
There was a fair enough pace on in this good-quality handicap. Solid form. The second and third set a straightforward level.

6544 THEAKSTONS BEER 'N' BBQ FESTIVAL 28TH SEPTEMBER MAIDEN STKS 1m 1f 170y
5:05 (5:11) (Class 5) 3-Y-O+ **£4,528** (£1,347; £673; £336) **Stalls** Low

Form RPR
43 **1** **Gabrials Boy**[7] 6274 3-9-5 0.............................. PaulHanagan 5 88+
(Richard Fahey) *trckd ldrs: outpcd by front two over 3f out: clsd to take 2nd jst over 2f out: r.o ins fnl f to ld fnl 100yds: gamely* **5/1**[2]
32-2 **2** *nk* **Narynkol**[20] 5783 4-9-12 84.............................. DavidEgan 4 86
(Roger Varian) *w ldr: led over 3f out: rdn over 2f out: hdd fnl 100yds: hld nr fin* **2/9**[1]
4240 **3** *14* **Double Honour**[26] 5557 3-9-5 75..............................(p[1]) PJMcDonald 3 60
(James Bethell) *led: hdd over 3f out: sn rdn: lost 2nd jst over 2f out: wknd over 1f out* **11/2**[3]
0-5 **4** *9* **Art Of Diplomacy**[213] 405 3-9-5 0.............................. CamHardie 6 42
(Michael Easterby) *in rr: niggled along 6f out: drvn and outpcd over 3f out: kpt on to take 4th ins fnl f: nvr involved* **25/1**
6U **5** *5* **Pound Off You**[7] 6274 3-9-0 0.............................. PhilDennis 1 27
(Gillian Boanas) *trckd ldrs: outpcd by front pair over 3f out: wknd over 2f out* **100/1**
6 *34* **Sandy Street** 3-9-5 0.............................. GrahamLee 2
(Donald McCain) *s.i.s: hld up: pushed along over 4f out: wknd over 3f out: lft bhd over 2f out: t.o* **33/1**
0 **U** **Profile Prince**[21] 5742 3-9-5 0.............................. JackGarritty 7
(Micky Hammond) *hld up: shkn up bef wnt wrong and uns rdr over 3f out* **150/1**

2m 1.26s (-3.34) **Going Correction** -0.225s/f (Firm)
WFA 3 from 4yo 7lb **7** Ran SP% **122.3**
Speed ratings (Par 103): **104,103,92,85,81 54,**
CSF £7.21 TOTE £6.90: £1.90, £1.10; EX 12.50 Trifecta £17.80.
Owner Dr Marwan Koukash **Bred** Newsells Park Stud **Trained** Musley Bank, N Yorks

FOCUS
A weak maiden. It's been rated at face value.

6545 AJA NOVICE FLAT AMATEUR RIDERS' H'CAP 1m 2f 190y
5:40 (5:43) (Class 6) (0-60,62) 4-Y-O+
£2,994 (£928; £464; £300; £300; £300) **Stalls** Low

Form RPR
0502 **1** **Sulafaat (IRE)**[18] 5851 4-9-13 **48**..............................(p) MissJessicaBedi(5) 7 55
(Rebecca Menzies) *chsd ldrs: wnt 2nd 2f out: rdn over 1f out: led ins fnl f: r.o* **8/1**
5510 **2** *2 3/4* **Graceful Act**[11] 6103 11-10-5 **49**.............................. SophieSmith 1 51
(Ron Barr) *in tch: clsd to ld after 3f: pushed along over 2f out: hdd ins fnl f: no ex towards fin* **7/1**
4560 **3** *1* **Barney Bullet (IRE)**[20] 5787 4-9-10 **45**..............(e) MissPaigeHopper(5) 8 45
(Noel Wilson) *hld up: impr to trck ldrs 7f out: outpcd over 3f out: rallied 2f out: styd on towards fin* **18/1**
6001 **4** *3* **Ezanak (IRE)**[11] 6098 6-11-0 **58**.............................. MissSarahBowen 10 53
(John Wainwright) *in tch: taken bk after 2f: pushed along 5f out: hdwy 4f out: chsd ldrs 3f out: unable to land a blow: one pce fnl f* **5/1**[2]
0051 **5** *1 1/2* **Zealous (IRE)**[21] 5725 6-10-13 **62**..............................(p) MrConnorWood(5) 5 54
(Alistair Whillans) *racd keenly: handy: led after 2f: hdd after 3f: continued to chse ldr tl 2f out: edgd rt and unable qck u.p over 1f out: wknd ins fnl f* **5/4**[1]
0464 **6** *4 1/2* **Optima Petamus**[18] 5851 7-10-1 **45**..............................(b) MissShannonWatts 4 29
(Liam Bailey) *s.v.s: bhd: coasted past btn rivals ins fnl f: nvr on terms: lame (jockey said gelding missed break; post-race examination revealed gelding lame right hind)* **13/2**[3]
1/05 **7** *4 1/2* **Khismet**[12] 3571 6-10-8 **52**..............................(p) MissImogenMathias 9 28
(John Flint) *prom on outer: taken bk after 3f: towards rr 5f out: outpcd over 4f out: n.d after* **7/1**
-050 **8** *3* **Bold Statement (IRE)**[5] 6343 4-10-0 **49**..............(t) MrEireannCagney(5) 3 20
(Alan Berry) *hld up: rdn over 2f out: nvr a threat* **33/1**

0-0 **9** *26* **Carta Blanca (IRE)**[21] 5728 6-10-1 **45**........................ MissAmyCollier 6
(David Thompson) *racd keenly: led for 2f: remained prom: wknd over 4f out* **25/1**

2m 19.81s (0.81) **Going Correction** -0.225s/f (Firm) **9** Ran SP% **122.6**
Speed ratings (Par 101): **88,86,85,83,82 78,75,73,54**
CSF £66.65 CT £999.75 TOTE £8.60: £2.50, £2.40, £5.50; EX 80.60 Trifecta £891.70.
Owner A Lister **Bred** Shadwell Estate Company Limited **Trained** Mordon, Durham
■ Shakiah was withdrawn. Price at time of withdrawal 25/1. Rule 4 does not apply.

FOCUS
A moderate handicap, confined to amateur riders, in which there was an injection of pace around 3f out. The winner has been rated to this year's best.
T/Plt: £10.50 to a £1 stake. Pool: £60,178.11 - 4,181.35 winning units T/Qpdt: £1.70 to a £1 stake. Pool: £5,360.60 - 2,253.91 winning units **Darren Owen**

3204 SOUTHWELL (L-H)

Monday, August 26

OFFICIAL GOING: Fibresand: standard (watered)
Wind: Virtually nil Weather: Warm and sunny

6546 SKY SPORTS RACING ON SKY 415 H'CAP 7f 14y(F)
1:50 (1:54) (Class 6) (0-60,60) 3-Y-O+
£2,781 (£827; £413; £300; £300; £300) **Stalls** Low

Form RPR
3000 **1** **Break The Silence**[59] 4346 5-8-5 **48**........................(b) JonathanFisher(7) 3 56
(Scott Dixon) *cl up: led after 1f: rdn along 2f out: drvn over 1f out: kpt on gamely fnl f* **14/1**
0000 **2** *½* **Mister Freeze (IRE)**[42] 5003 5-9-0 **50**........................(vt) DavidProbert 10 57
(Patrick Chamings) *trckd ldrs whn n.m.r and lost pl after 1f: towards rr: hdwy 2f out: sn rdn: styd on strly ent fnl f: jst hld* **16/1**
2003 **3** *nse* **Ticks The Boxes (IRE)**[18] 5857 7-9-6 **56**........................ BenRobinson 9 63
(Brian Ellison) *prom: cl up 3f out: rdn along 2f out: sn edgd rt: drvn to chse wnr and edgd lft ins fnl f: kpt on* **5/1**[2]
1102 **4** *1½* **Fly True**[24] 5632 6-9-10 **60**........................ NickyMackay 13 62
(Ivan Furtado) *sn cl up on outer: chal 1/2-way: rdn along 2f out: drvn over 1f out: kpt on same pce fnl f* **11/1**
140 **5** *1* **Queen Of Kalahari**[27] 5517 4-8-13 **49**........................(p) LewisEdmunds 4 49
(Les Eyre) *trckd ldrs: hdwy over 2f out: rdn wl over 1f out: drvn and kpt on same pce fnl f* **14/1**
0002 **6** *2¼* **Rock In Society (IRE)**[18] 5837 4-9-4 **54**........................(b) JoeyHaynes 7 48
(John Butler) *trckd ldrs: hdwy over 2f out: rdn along wl over 1f out: n.m.r ent fnl f: kpt on one pce* **18/1**
0420 **7** *hd* **Filbert Street**[80] 3527 4-9-0 **50**........................ AlistairRawlinson 6 43+
(Michael Appleby) *dwlt and towards rr: wd st: rdn along and n.m.r 2f out: sn swtchd lft and edgd across to inner: kpt on fnl f: nvr nr ldrs (jockey said gelding was never travelling)* **11/8**[1]
-130 **8** *nk* **Quick Monet (IRE)**[35] 5247 6-8-12 **48**........................ BenCurtis 2 40
(Shaun Harris) *dwlt: a towards rr (jockey said gelding was slowly away)* **25/1**
2360 **9** *½* **Atalanta Queen**[10] 6173 4-9-0 **50**........................(v) HollieDoyle 1 41
(Robyn Brisland) *slt ld 1f: cl up on inner: rdn along 3f out: wknd 2f out* **9/1**[3]
4561 **10** *hd* **Ey Up Its Mick**[10] 6176 3-9-5 **60**........................(b) TomEaves 11 48
(Tony Coyle) *dwlt and towards rr: wd st: n.d* **16/1**
5510 **11** *6* **Bee Machine (IRE)**[7] 6276 4-8-12 **55**........................(t) ZakWheatley(7) 8 29
(Declan Carroll) *a towards rr* **10/1**
040 **12** *9* **Hollander**[13] 6058 5-8-11 **52**........................(tp) HarrisonShaw(5) 14 2
(Alexandra Dunn) *dwlt: a in rr* **33/1**
0200 **13** *12* **Essential**[10] 6174 5-8-8 **47**........................(b) ConnorMurtagh(3) 12
(Olly Williams) *in tch: rdn along 1/2-way: sn lost pl and bhd (jockey said colt hung left throughout)* **33/1**

1m 29.32s (-0.98) **Going Correction** -0.10s/f (Stan) **13** Ran SP% **126.3**
WFA 3 from 4yo+ 5lb
Speed ratings (Par 101): **101,100,100,98,97 94,94,94,93,93 86,76,62**
CSF £227.94 CT £1331.92 TOTE £19.40: £5.10, £5.70, £1.80; EX 372.70 Trifecta £1390.40.
Owner Winning Connections Racing **Bred** Richard Moses Bloodstock **Trained** Babworth, Notts
■ Port Soif was withdrawn, price at time of withdrawal 12/1. Rule 4 applies to all bets struck prior to withdrawal, but not to SP bets. Deduction of 5p in the pound. New market formed.

FOCUS
A modest handicap on watered, standard Fibresand on a hot afternoon.

6547 MSR NEWSGROUP H'CAP 6f 16y(F)
2:25 (2:27) (Class 5) (0-70,70) 3-Y-O+
£3,428 (£1,020; £509; £300; £300; £300) **Stalls** Low

Form RPR
400 **1** **Scuzeme**[4] 6373 5-9-10 **70**........................(h) BenCurtis 2 83
(Phillip Makin) *mde all: rdn clr wl over 1f out: kpt on strly* **11/4**[2]
0500 **2** *4½* **Tan**[13] 6058 5-9-0 **65**........................ TheodoreLadd(5) 11 64
(Michael Appleby) *dwlt: sn chsng ldrs on outer: rdn along over 2f out: chsd wnr over 1f out: drvn and no imp fnl f* **5/2**[1]
420 **3** *1¼* **Gorgeous General**[10] 6178 4-8-13 **59**........................ PaulMulrennan 10 54
(Lawrence Mullaney) *cl up: ev ch 2f out: sn rdn: drvn over 1f out: kpt on same pce* **11/2**[3]
6060 **4** *1¾* **Beechwood Izzy (IRE)**[20] 5786 3-8-13 **62**........................ ShaneGray 8 51+
(Keith Dalgleish) *towards rr: wd st and hdwy over 2f out: rdn wl over 1f out: kpt on fnl f: n.d* **14/1**
0105 **5** *nk* **Amelia R (IRE)**[7] 6277 3-8-11 **60**........................ JimmyQuinn 9 48
(Ray Craggs) *cl up: rdn along over 2f out: drvn and edgd lft over 1f out: kpt on same pce* **8/1**
-003 **6** *2¼* **Chez Vegas**[39] 5107 6-8-5 **51** oh1........................(b[1]) JamesSullivan 1 32
(Scott Dixon) *chsd ldrs: rdn along on inner wl over 2f out: sn drvn and grad wknd* **18/1**
4/ **7** *2* **Caso Do Lago (IRE)**[1518] 3746 8-8-11 **57**........................ AdrianMcCarthy 3 31
(Robyn Brisland) *towards rr: hdwy on inner over 2f out: sn rdn along and n.d* **50/1**
0000 **8** *¾* **Inaam (IRE)**[34] 5283 6-9-7 **70**........................ GeorgiaCox(3) 4 42
(John Butler) *a towards rr* **25/1**
5000 **9** *1* **Bengali Boys (IRE)**[9] 6220 4-9-10 **70**........................(b) GeorgeDowning 5 39
(Tony Carroll) *a in rr* **12/1**
31-0 **10** *1* **Declamation (IRE)**[19] 5807 9-9-1 **61**........................ JoeyHaynes 6 27
(John Butler) *a in rr (jockey said gelding didn't face kickback)* **14/1**
1006 **11** *½* **Optimickstickhill**[20] 5765 4-8-5 **51** oh3........................(b) PaddyMathers 7 15
(Scott Dixon) *chsd ldrs: rdn along bef 1/2-way: sn wknd* **25/1**

1m 14.92s (-1.58) **Going Correction** -0.10s/f (Stan)
WFA 3 from 4yo+ 3lb **11** Ran SP% **117.7**
Speed ratings (Par 103): **106,100,98,96,95 92,89,88,87,86 85**
CSF £9.83 CT £35.50 TOTE £3.40: £1.20, £2.30, £2.20; EX 10.80 Trifecta £40.70.
Owner P J Makin **Bred** R S Hoskins & Hermes Services **Trained** Easingwold, N Yorks

FOCUS
An ordinary handicap. The second-favourite decisively made all in a good comparative time.

6548 VISIT ATTHERACES.COM EBF NOVICE STKS 4f 214y(F)
3:00 (3:00) (Class 5) 2-Y-O **£3,428** (£1,020; £509; £254) **Stalls** Centre

Form RPR
12 **1** **Maystar (IRE)**[14] 6011 2-9-9 0........................ HollieDoyle 8 79
(Archie Watson) *slt ld centre: rdn along over 1f out: hdd narrowly ent fnl f and sn drvn: rallied gamely to ld again fnl 50yds* **9/4**[2]
53 **2** *¾* **Augustus Caesar (USA)**[29] 5472 2-8-11 0........................ HarrisonShaw(5) 10 69
(David O'Meara) *cl up centre: rdn over 1f out: slt ld ent fnl f: sn drvn: hdd and no ex fnl 50yds* **11/2**[3]
241 **3** *nk* **Strong Power (IRE)**[115] 2362 2-9-9 86........................ HayleyTurner 1 75
(George Scott) *cl up centre: effrt ent fnl f: sn rdn and ev ch: drvn and kpt on same pce fnl 50yds* **11/8**[1]
4 *1½* **Royal Context (IRE)** 2-9-2 0........................ PaulMulrennan 3 64+
(Michael Dods) *trckd ldrs centre: hdwy 2f out: swtchd rt and rdn over 1f out: kpt on same pce fnl f* **20/1**
0415 **5** *3¼* **One Bite (IRE)**[23] 5668 2-9-9 76........................ TomEaves 7 62
(Keith Dalgleish) *cl up centre: rdn along 2f out: sn edgd lft towards inner rail and wknd* **9/1**
5 **6** *1* **Merchants Breath**[13] 6047 2-9-2 0........................ JosephineGordon 9 48
(Shaun Keightley) *in tch centre: rdn along 1/2-way: sn one pce* **20/1**
7 *¾* **Abbaleka** 2-9-2 0........................ AlistairRawlinson 4 45
(Michael Appleby) *dwlt and bhd tl sme hdwy fnl 2f* **33/1**
8 *shd* **Pearl Of India** 2-8-11 0........................ DavidProbert 2 39
(Robyn Brisland) *dwlt: in rr tl styd on fnl 2f* **50/1**
9 *1* **Triple Spear** 2-8-11 0........................ TheodoreLadd(5) 5 41
(Michael Appleby) *a in rr* **25/1**
00 **10** *2¾* **Kitos**[14] 6028 2-8-4 0........................ GavinAshton(7) 6 26
(Sir Mark Prescott Bt) *a in rr* **100/1**
06 **11** *3* **Order Of Merritt (IRE)**[10] 6147 2-9-2 0........................ RyanTate 11 20
(Sir Mark Prescott Bt) *racd towards stands' side: in tch: rdn along bef 1/2-way: sn outpcd* **100/1**

58.87s (-0.83) **Going Correction** -0.10s/f (Stan) **11** Ran SP% **118.5**
Speed ratings (Par 94): **102,100,100,97,92 91,89,89,88,83 78**
CSF £14.09 TOTE £2.60: £1.20, £1.20, £1.50; EX 13.60 Trifecta £30.50.
Owner Hambleton Racing Ltd XXXVI **Bred** Ballinvana House Stud **Trained** Upper Lambourn, W Berks

FOCUS
A fairly decent juvenile novice sprint contest. The second-favourite pulled out more to see off two persistent rivals in the final 100 yards. It's been rated as straightforward form.

6549 DARREN & EVELYN LAKE MEMORIAL H'CAP 4f 214y(F)
3:35 (3:36) (Class 3) (0-90,88) 4-Y-O+ **£8,086** (£2,406; £1,202; £601) **Stalls** Centre

Form RPR
0066 **1** **Crosse Fire**[20] 5768 7-8-8 **75**........................(b) JamesSullivan 1 87
(Scott Dixon) *racd towards centre: cl up: rdn to ld over 1f out: kpt on strly fnl f* **11/1**
0212 **2** *1½* **Fantasy Keeper**[16] 5951 5-8-13 **80**........................ AndrewMullen 7 87
(Michael Appleby) *racd towards stands' side: trckd ldrs: hdwy 1/2-way: rdn to chal over 1f out: drvn and edgd lft ins fnl f: kpt on same pce towards fin* **3/1**[1]
0200 **3** *1¾* **Dark Shot**[23] 5661 6-9-6 **87**........................(p) DavidProbert 5 87
(Scott Dixon) *trckd ldrs centre: hdwy 1/2-way: rdn over 1f out: drvn and kpt on same pce fnl f* **11/1**
2500 **4** *½* **Warrior's Valley**[11] 6099 4-8-6 **73**........................(tp) JosephineGordon 9 72
(David C Griffiths) *racd towards stands' side: led: rdn along over 2f out: hdd over 1f out: drvn and wknd fnl f* **16/1**
-400 **5** *shd* **Lomu (IRE)**[38] 5120 5-9-3 **84**........................ TomEaves 3 82
(Keith Dalgleish) *dwlt and towards rr: sn swtchd lft towards far side: hdwy over 2f out: chsd ldrs and rdn over 1f out: kpt on same pce fnl f (vet said gelding lost right hind shoe)* **8/1**
1-04 **6** *½* **Airglow (IRE)**[9] 6227 4-8-8 **80**........................(h) GerO'Neill(5) 8 76
(Michael Easterby) *racd stands' side: chsd ldrs: rdn along 2f out: drvn over 1f out: no imp fnl f* **13/2**
6426 **7** *3* **Zylan (IRE)**[28] 5488 7-9-7 **88**........................(p) BenCurtis 4 74
(Roger Fell) *chsd ldrs centre: rdn along and lost pl 1/2-way: n.d* **7/2**[2]
1632 **8** *3¼* **Samovar**[81] 3504 4-8-7 **74**........................ PaddyMathers 2 48
(Scott Dixon) *racd towards far side: prom: rdn along 2f out: sn wknd* **5/1**[3]
00-0 **9** *1* **Ebitda**[46] 4829 5-7-11 **66** oh3........................ SophieRalston(5) 6 39
(Scott Dixon) *racd towards stands' side: prom: rdn along bef 1/2-way: sn outpcd* **33/1**

58.14s (-1.56) **Going Correction** -0.10s/f (Stan) **9** Ran SP% **113.8**
Speed ratings (Par 107): **108,105,102,102,101 101,96,91,89**
CSF £43.47 CT £379.01 TOTE £13.40: £3.70, £1.60, £3.10; EX 58.80 Trifecta £250.10.
Owner Paul J Dixon & Darren Lucas **Bred** Dr A Gillespie **Trained** Babworth, Notts

FOCUS
The feature contest was a decent sprint handicap and a C&D specialist won well towards the far side in marginally the best comparative time on the card. The second has been rated near his recent turf form.

6550 SKY SPORTS RACING ON VIRGIN 535 H'CAP 1m 4f 14y(F)
4:10 (4:11) (Class 6) (0-55,56) 3-Y-O+
£2,781 (£827; £413; £300; £300; £300) **Stalls** Low

Form RPR
0554 **1** **Blowing Dixie**[10] 6153 3-9-2 **53**........................ JFEgan 12 65+
(Jane Chapple-Hyam) *trckd ldrs: hdwy and cl up over 5f out: led 4f out: pushed along and clr 2f out: rdn over 1f out: styd on strly* **11/4**[2]
5633 **2** *5* **Dolly Dupree**[10] 6173 3-8-13 **55**........................ TheodoreLadd(5) 6 58
(Paul D'Arcy) *prom: effrt to chse wnr over 2f out: sn rdn: drvn over 1f out: kpt on: no imp* **6/1**[3]
4331 **3** *11* **Lauberhorn Rocket (GER)**[12] 6077 4-10-0 **56**........................ DavidProbert 8 40
(Tim Vaughan) *in tch: hdwy to trck ldrs 5f out: rdn along to chse ldng pair over 2f out: sn drvn and one pce (jockey said gelding hung left)* **5/4**[1]
0005 **4** *16* **Tyrsal (IRE)**[16] 5946 8-9-3 **45**........................(v) JosephineGordon 2
(Shaun Keightley) *hld up towards rr: hdwy and in tch 1/2-way: rdn along to chse ldrs 4f out: plugged on u.p fnl 2f* **25/1**

The Form Book Flat 2019, Raceform Ltd, Newbury, RG14 5SJ

3000 **5** *1 3/4* **Albert Boy (IRE)**[21] 5743 6-9-0 **49** ...... JonathanFisher(7) 11 5
(Scott Dixon) *cl up: rdn along 5f out: drvn 3f out: sn outpcd* **18/1**

2005 **6** *5* **Miss Ranger (IRE)**[16] 5975 7-9-10 **52** ...... (b) BenCurtis 7
(Roger Fell) *led: rdn along 5f out: hdd 4f out: sn drvn and wknd 3f out* **10/1**

0630 **7** *hd* **Harry The Norseman**[25] 5596 3-9-5 **56** ...... DougieCostello 5 5
(Jonjo O'Neill) *chsd ldrs: rdn along 5f out: sn outpcd* **20/1**

6060 **8** *25* **Shamitsar**[56] 4435 5-9-3 **45** ...... (p1) JimmyQuinn 1
(Ray Craggs) *a in rr: outpcd and wl bhd fnl 3f (trainer said gelding had a breathing problem)* **28/1**

000 **9** *46* **Bannockburn (IRE)**[143] 1570 3-9-4 **55** ...... (w) ShaneGray 4
(Keith Dalgleish) *chsd ldrs: rdn along bef 1/2-way: sn lost pl and towards rr: wl bhd fnl 3f* **14/1**

2m 39.89s (-1.11) **Going Correction** -0.10s/f (Stan)
WFA 3 from 4yo+ 9lb **9** Ran SP% **118.5**
Speed ratings (Par 101): **99,95,88,77,76 73,73,56,25**
CSF £19.74 CT £29.95 TOTE £3.20: £1.30, £1.30, £1.10; EX 19.50 Trifecta £45.00.

Owner Mohammed Alenezi **Bred** Merry Fox Stud Limited **Trained** Dalham, Suffolk

FOCUS
A moderate middle-distance handicap. The second-favourite's winning time was modest but he pulled well clear of this opposition in the final furlong. A minor pb from the winner, with the second rated to her recent best.

6551 FOLLOW AT THE RACES ON TWITTER NOVICE STKS — 4f 214y(F)
4:45 (4:46) (Class 5) 3-Y-O+ **£3,428** (£1,020; £509; £254) **Stalls** Centre

Form RPR

2000 **1** **Bluella**[10] 6168 4-8-13 41 ...... (bt1) HollieDoyle 2 54
(Robyn Brisland) *racd centre: slt ld: rdn along 2f out: drvn ent fnl f: hld on gamely nr fin (trainer said, regarding improvement in form, filly appreciated a return to Southwell, where the filly has been placed previously and what he considered to be a weak race against opponents who were running on the all-weather for the first time)* **25/1**

04 **2** *shd* **Lyons Lane**[23] 5669 3-8-11 0 ...... TomEaves 1 54
(Michael Dods) *racd centre: trckd wnr: hdwy 2f out: rdn to chal over 1f out: drvn and ev ch ins fnl f: edgd lft and no ex towards fin* **18/1**

0 **3** *7* **Bluetta**[68] 4010 3-8-11 0 ...... AdrianMcCarthy 6 28
(Robyn Brisland) *racd towards stands' side: chsd ldrs: rdn along 2f out: sn drvn and kpt on one pce* **50/1**

6 **4** *3/4* **Double Martini (IRE)**[9] 6206 3-9-9 0 ...... BenCurtis 5 38
(Roger Fell) *sn outpcd and bhd: hdwy wl over 1f out: kpt on fnl f* **5/1**[3]

23- **5** *1 1/4* **Quickly Does It**[353] 7041 3-8-11 0 ...... (w) BenRobinson 3 21
(Brian Ellison) *sn outpcd and rdn along in rr: sme late hdwy (jockey said gelding was never travelling)* **2/1**[2]

6-1 **6** *1/2* **Bhangra**[14] 6023 3-9-4 0 ...... DavidProbert 4 26
(Robert Cowell) *racd centre: cl up effrt and ev ch 2f out: sn rdn and wknd qckly appr fnl f (jockey said filly hung right in fnl f and stopped quickly; post-race examination reveal filly had tyed up)* **10/11**[1]

59.21s (-0.49) **Going Correction** -0.10s/f (Stan)
WFA 3 from 4yo 2lb **6** Ran SP% **113.5**
Speed ratings (Par 103): **99,98,87,86,84 83**
CSF £341.62 TOTE £21.50: £7.40, £6.70; EX 128.80 Trifecta £770.10.

Owner M J Golding **Bred** M J Golding **Trained** Danethorpe, Notts

FOCUS
An ordinary novice sprint contest. The front three in the market all disappointed to differing degrees and a filly with an official rating of 41 won narrowly.

6552 WATCH SKY SPORTS RACING IN HD H'CAP — 2m 102y(F)
5:20 (5:21) (Class 6) (0-55,55) 3-Y-O+
£2,781 (£827; £413; £300; £300; £300) **Stalls** Low

Form RPR

-312 **1** **Thahab Ifraj (IRE)**[82] 3205 6-9-5 **50** ...... DavidProbert 6 61+
(Alexandra Dunn) *trckd ldrs: smooth hdwy over 3f out: led wl over 1f out: sn rdn clr: readily* **9/4**[1]

0040 **2** *3* **Thornton Le Clay**[35] 5248 3-8-3 **45** oh1 ...... JamesSullivan 8 53
(Michael Easterby) *prom: effrt 4f out and sn cl up: rdn to ld over 2f out: hdd wl over 1f out: sn drvn and kpt on: no imp* **12/1**

0302 **3** *12* **Beechwood James (FR)**[13] 6046 3-8-6 **54** ... ThoreHammerHansen(5) 7 46
(Richard Hannon) *cl up: led over 4f out: rdn along over 3f out: hdd wl over 2f out: sn drvn and plugged on one pce* **3/1**[2]

0005 **4** *2 1/2* **Tilsworth Sammy**[13] 6046 4-9-1 **45** oh1 ...... (b1) TomQueally 9 33
(J R Jenkins) *trckd ldrs: hdwy and cl up on outer over 4f out: rdn along over 3f out: drvn wl over 2f out: sn wknd* **14/1**

211 **5** *5* **Steel Helmet (IRE)**[13] 6046 5-9-9 **54** ...... JosephineGordon 2 35
(William Bethell) *led: pushed along over 5f out: hdd over 4f out: sn rdn along and lost pl over 3f out: sn bhd* **3/1**[2]

)00 **6** *1* **Breakfast Time**[15] 5987 3-8-8 **51** ...... (b) HollieDoyle 5 33
(Archie Watson) *hld up in rr: pushed along over 5f out: sn rdn and wknd* **12/1**

)6 **7** *17* **So Hi Cardi (FR)**[16] 5974 3-8-11 **54** ...... (h) BenCurtis 3 15
(Roger Fell) *hld up: a in rr: outpcd and bhd fnl 4f* **10/1**[3]

) **8** *62* **Mount Cleshar**[13] 6046 5-9-1 **45** oh1 ...... (t1) JFEgan 1
(John Butler) *trckd ldrs: pushed along on inner over 6f out: sn lost pl and bhd fnl 4f* **20/1**

3m 4.91s (-0.59) **Going Correction** -0.10s/f (Stan)
WFA 3 from 4yo+ 12lb **8** Ran SP% **116.7**
Speed ratings (Par 101): **97,95,89,88,85 85,76,45**
CSF £31.50 CT £83.39 TOTE £3.00: £1.20, £4.40, £1.10; EX 36.20 Trifecta £161.60.

Owner The Dunnitalls **Bred** P G Lyons **Trained** West Buckland, Somerset

■ Stewards' Enquiry : Tom Queally three-day ban: weighed in 2lb overweight (Sep 9-11)

FOCUS
A moderate staying handicap. The favourite won with his head in his chest from off a modest gallop.

T/Jkpt: Not Won. T/Plt: £463.60 to a £1 stake. Pool: £69,833.25 - 109.95 winning units T/Qpdt: £81.60 to a £1 stake. Pool: £6,284.05 - 56.93 winning units **Joe Rowntree**

6008 LES LANDES
Monday, August 26

OFFICIAL GOING: Good to firm (firm in places)

6553a SUE & NIGEL PRITCHARD H'CAP SPRINT — 5f 100y
3:05 (3:05) 3-Y-O+ **£1,780** (£640; £380)

RPR

1 **Man Of The Sea (IRE)**[36] 5232 3-10-6 0 ...... (tp) BrendanPowell 62
(Neil Mulholland) *trckd ldrs: outpcd turn over 2f out: sn drvn: styd on strly to ld cl home: all out* **5/4**[1]

2 *nk* **Sing Something**[15] 6-10-2 0 ...... GeorgeRooke 55
(Mrs C Gilbert, Jersey) *missed break: last into st: sn swtchd wd to chal: drvn and led briefly ins fnl f: no ex whn hdd cl home* **9/2**

3 *2* **Chapeau Bleu (IRE)**[15] 7-9-5 0 ...... MissSerenaBrotherton 37
(Mrs C Gilbert, Jersey) *trckd ldrs: outpcd turn 3f out: drvn to chal and ev ch over 1f out: kpt on one pce* **7/2**[3]

4 *3/4* **Relaxed Boy (FR)**[15] 6-10-12 0 ...... (t) MrFrederickTett 56
(Mrs A Malzard, Jersey) *led to 3f out: stl ev ch 1f out: wknd cl home* **3/1**[2]

5 *2 1/4* **Fruit Salad**[36] 5232 6-10-0 0 ...... (b) MarkQuinlan 37
(K Kukk, Jersey) *trckd ldrs: wnt on 3f out: wknd whn hdd ins fnl f* **9/2**

6 *3* **Country Blue (FR)**[36] 5232 10-9-8 0 ...... (p) VictoriaMalzard 21
(Mrs A Malzard, Jersey) *hld up: t.k.h and plld way into 2nd 3f out: wknd fr wl over 1f out* **9/1**

Owner Dajam Ltd **Bred** Stephanie Hanly **Trained** Limpley Stoke, Wilts

6554a 2019 OAKBRIDGE CLARENDON H'CAP — 1m 4f
3:40 (3:40) 3-Y-O+ **£2,380** (£860; £510)

RPR

1 **Molliana**[15] 6008 4-9-4 0 ...... BrendanPowell 49
(Neil Mulholland) *trckd ldrs: hdwy to chal fr over 3f out: led 1f out: drvn out* **13/8**[1]

2 *2 1/4* **Island Song (IRE)**[15] 6008 5-10-7 0 ...... MrFrederickTett 62
(Mrs A Malzard, Jersey) *trckd ldr: wnt on 3f out: sn drvn: hdd 1f out: no ex* **11/2**

3 *3 1/4* **Aussie Lyrics (FR)**[15] 6010 9-10-12 0 ...... MattieBatchelor 62
(Mrs C Gilbert, Jersey) *trckd ldrs: hdwy to chal fr over 3f out: ev ch 2f out: one pce* **2/1**[2]

4 *1/2* **Hard To Handel**[15] 6010 7-9-12 0 ...... MissSerenaBrotherton 47
(Mrs A Malzard, Jersey) *hld up: hdwy to cl fr over 3f out: nvr able to chal* **13/2**

5 *30* **Gabster (IRE)**[15] 4687 6-9-4 0 ...... (b) PhilipPrince
(K Kukk, Jersey) *led: sn clr: rdn fr 5f out: hdd 3f out: wknd rapidly: t.o* **11/1**

6 *2 1/4* **Kenoughty (FR)**[15] 6010 3-8-10 0 ...... GeorgeRooke
(J Moon, Jersey) *a bhd: nvr a factor: t.o* **11/4**[3]

Owner Dajam Ltd **Bred** Norman Court Stud **Trained** Limpley Stoke, Wilts

6555a BLOODSTOCK ADVISORY SERVICES H'CAP MILE — 1m 100y
4:50 (4:50) 3-Y-O+ **£1,780** (£640; £380)

RPR

1 **African Showgirl**[228] 155 6-9-1 0 ...... TimClark 35
(Eve Johnson Houghton) *hld up: 5th in st: drvn to ld fnl 75yds* **6/1**

2 *1* **Brown Velvet**[15] 6009 7-9-3 0 ...... GeorgeRooke 35
(Mrs C Gilbert, Jersey) *hld up: hdwy to go 3rd 3f out: drvn to ld briefly wl ins fnl f: no ex whn hdd fnl 75yds* **5/2**[3]

3 *1/2* **Honcho (IRE)**[15] 7-10-9 0 ...... VictoriaMalzard 54
(Mrs A Malzard, Jersey) *led: strly chal fr 2f out: hdd wl ins fnl f: no ex* **9/4**[2]

4 *8* **Snejinska (FR)**[15] 6008 5-9-2 0 ...... (h) MissSerenaBrotherton 15
(Mrs C Gilbert, Jersey) *hld up: 7th into st: styd on through btn horses but n.d* **8/1**

5 *3/4* **Lyrical Ballad (IRE)**[15] 6009 3-10-1 0 ...... (p) BrendanPowell 31
(Neil Mulholland) *trckd ldr in cl 2nd: wknd fr over 1f out* **6/4**[1]

6 *8* **Ice Royal (IRE)**[15] 6010 6-10-12 0 ...... MrFrederickTett 20
(Mrs A Malzard, Jersey) *hld up: 6th into st: nvr a factor* **11/2**

7 *2* **Kalani Rose**[15] 6009 5-8-5 0 oh8 ...... (v) PhilipPrince
(Mrs A Corson, Jersey) *trckd ldrs in 3rd: drvn and 4th into st: wknd rapidly* **11/1**

8 *11* **Jersey Jack (JER)**[15] 3-10-6 0 ...... MarkQuinlan
(K Kukk, Jersey) *trckd ldrs: wknd rapidly fr 3f out: t.o* **16/1**

Owner Miss Vanda Ohlidalova **Bred** Ballabeg Stables **Trained** Blewbury, Oxon

6329 BATH (L-H)
Tuesday, August 27

OFFICIAL GOING: Good to firm (firm in places; 8.8)
Wind: Light half across Weather: Sunny periods

6556 SKY SPORTS RACING ON SKY 415 "HANDS AND HEELS" APPRENTICE H'CAP (HANDS N HEEL SERIES) — 2m 1f 24y
4:45 (4:45) (Class 5) (0-75,75) 4-Y-O+ **£3,428** (£1,020; £509; £300; £300) **Stalls** Centre

Form RPR

0-34 **1** **Cotton Club (IRE)**[15] 6016 8-9-5 **68** ...... MarcoGhiani 3 82
(George Boughey) *trckd ldrs early: in last pair after 4f: clsd on ldng pair over 3f out: led over 2f out: sn clr: pushed out* **10/3**[3]

1062 **2** *13* **Sacred Sprite**[18] 5891 4-8-11 **60** ...... GeorgiaDobie 5 58
(John Berry) *hld up in last pair: hdwy over 2f out: sn rdn: kpt on into 2nd over 1f out but no ch w wnr* **5/6**[1]

4016 **3** *15* **Contingency Fee**[7] 6303 4-8-11 **60** ...... (p) GraceMcEntee 4 40
(Phil McEntee) *prom: led after 3f: rdn and hdd over 2f out: wknd over 1f out* **3/1**[2]

The Form Book Flat 2019, Raceform Ltd, Newbury, RG14 5SJ

066 **4** *12* **Lady Natasha (IRE)**[10] 6200 6-8-4 **56** oh11..................(t) LukeBacon(3) 2 22
(James Grassick) *trckd ldrs: pressed ldr over 7f out: rdn and ev ch over 3f out tl over 2f out: wknd over 1f out* **66/1**

000- **5** *20* **Silver Character (IRE)**[36] 7083 4-9-12 **75**......................(b1) EllaMcCain 1 17
(Donald McCain) *led for 3f: chsd ldr: pushed along over 9f out: dropped to last over 3f out: sn wknd: t.o* **16/1**

3m 44.35s (-7.05) **Going Correction** -0.15s/f (Firm) **5** Ran SP% **110.0**
Speed ratings (Par 103): **106,99,92,87,77**
CSF £6.57 TOTE £4.60: £1.60, £1.10; EX 8.80 Trifecta £11.60.
Owner Boughey **Bred** Patrick Gleeson **Trained** Newmarket, Suffolk

FOCUS
A fair apprentice riders' staying handicap.

6557 SKY SPORTS RACING ON VIRGIN 535 NURSERY H'CAP 5f 10y
5:20 (5:21) (Class 5) (0-70,71) 2-Y-O
£3,428 (£1,020; £509; £300; £300; £300) **Stalls** Centre

Form RPR
442 **1** **Aryaaf (IRE)**[20] 5794 2-9-7 **69**.................................. JimCrowley 5 73+
(Simon Crisford) *squeezed up s: in last pair: hdwy fr 3f out: led narrowly 2f out: kpt on wl fnl f: rdn out* **6/4**[1]

5202 **2** *3/4* **Prissy Missy (IRE)**[14] 6041 2-8-9 **57**.............................. DavidEgan 3 57
(David Loughnane) *led: rdn and hdd 2f out: kpt on gamely ins fnl f: regained 2nd cl home (vet said filly lost its left hind shoe)* **7/2**[2]

3052 **3** *shd* **Airbrush (IRE)**[20] 5800 2-9-7 **69**............................... OisinMurphy 2 69
(Richard Hannon) *travelled wl most of way: trckd ldrs: chal 2f out: rdn jst over 1f out: kpt on w ev ch tl no ex nring fin* **7/2**[2]

4602 **4** *2* **Call Me Cheers**[11] 6182 2-8-12 **60**.......................... KieranShoemark 6 53
(David Evans) *wnt lft s: prom: rdn and ev ch 2f out: sn hld: kpt on same pce fnl f* **8/1**[3]

4150 **5** *1 1/4* **Exclusive (IRE)**[14] 6053 2-9-9 **71**............................. AdamMcNamara 1 59
(Archie Watson) *sn pushed along in tch: rdn over 2f out: nt pce to get on terms* **12/1**

0500 **6** *1 1/4* **Walton Thorns (IRE)**[11] 6182 2-8-7 **55**........................ MartinDwyer 4 39
(Charles Hills) *hld up: rdn over 2f out: little imp* **20/1**

1m 1.6s (-0.40) **Going Correction** -0.15s/f (Firm) **6** Ran SP% **108.0**
Speed ratings (Par 94): **97,95,95,92,90 88**
CSF £6.32 TOTE £2.10: £1.20, £2.10; EX 6.20 Trifecta £16.00.
Owner Hamdan Al Maktoum **Bred** Mrs Noreen Clibborn **Trained** Newmarket, Suffolk

FOCUS
An ordinary nursery sprint.

6558 FROME SCAFFOLDING H'CAP 1m
5:50 (5:50) (Class 5) (0-70,72) 3-Y-O **£3,428** (£1,020; £509; £300; £300) **Stalls** Low

Form RPR
0-30 **1** **Tell William**[13] 6084 3-9-6 **68**....................................(b1) MartinDwyer 1 76
(Marcus Tregoning) *sn chsng ldr: rdn over 2f out: styd on ins fnl f: led fnl 110yds: rdn out* **7/1**[3]

0531 **2** *1/2* **Lucky Number**[20] 5797 3-9-7 **72**.................................. GeorgiaCox(3) 3 79
(William Haggas) *led after 1f: rdn over 1f out: styd on but no ex whn hdd fnl 110yds* **2/1**[1]

3612 **3** *6* **Conspiritor**[34] 5292 3-9-10 **72**.............................. KieranShoemark 2 65
(Charles Hills) *led for 1f: trckd ldrs: rdn over 2f out: sn one pce* **2/1**[1]

336 **4** *3 1/2* **Abr Al Hudood (JPN)**[25] 5627 3-9-10 **72**......................... OisinMurphy 5 57
(Hugo Palmer) *hld up bhd ldrs: rdn over 2f out: nt pce to chal: wknd ent fnl f* **5/2**[2]

5-60 **5** *19* **Lolita Pulido (IRE)**[13] 6075 3-8-9 **64**.......................... GeorgiaDobie(7) 4
(Eve Johnson Houghton) *dwlt: in last pair but in tch: rdn 3f out: sn outpcd (trainer's rep said filly had a breathing problem)* **20/1**

1m 39.4s (-2.30) **Going Correction** -0.15s/f (Firm) **5** Ran SP% **112.5**
Speed ratings (Par 100): **105,104,98,95,76**
CSF £21.83 TOTE £8.50: £3.40, £2.00; EX 24.00 Trifecta £50.60.
Owner R C C Villers **Bred** Lordship Stud **Trained** Whitsbury, Hants

FOCUS
An ordinary 3yo handicap.

6559 SKY SPORTS RACING ON VIRGIN 535 FILLIES' NOVICE STKS 1m
6:20 (6:21) (Class 5) 3-Y-O+ **£3,428** (£1,020; £509; £254) **Stalls** Low

Form RPR
3424 **1** **Alandalos**[21] 5779 3-8-12 **75**.................................. JimCrowley 1 75
(Charles Hills) *led: rdn and hdd over 1f out: kpt on u.str driving ins fnl f: led fnl 70yds* **4/6**[1]

2 *nk* **Brown Honey** 3-8-12 0.. SeanLevey 3 74
(Ismail Mohammed) *hld up 5th: hdwy over 2f out: led over 1f out: sn rdn: kpt on whn hdd fnl 70yds: hld cl home (jockey said gelding hung right-handed)* **7/1**

0-1 **3** *2* **Lady Dauphin (IRE)**[17] 5969 3-9-3 0............................ StevieDonohoe 2 75
(Charlie Fellowes) *trckd ldrs: rdn over 2f out: sn edging lft: kpt on ins fnl f to go 3rd: nt pce to threaten front pair* **4/1**[2]

506 **4** *1 1/4* **Love Explodes**[60] 4326 3-8-12 **77**.............................. OisinMurphy 4 67
(Ed Vaughan) *trckd ldrs: rdn to dispute jst over 2f out: hdd over 1f out: no ex ins fnl f* **9/2**[3]

00 **5** *44* **Little Lady Luck**[17] 5955 3-8-5 0............................ EllieMacKenzie(7) 5
(Mark Usher) *pressed wnr tl pushed along over 3f out: sn hung bdly rt and drifted to stands' side rail: sn wknd: t.o (jockey said filly hung right-handed)* **100/1**

1m 39.87s (-1.83) **Going Correction** -0.15s/f (Firm) **5** Ran SP% **111.7**
Speed ratings (Par 100): **103,102,100,99,55**
CSF £6.25 TOTE £1.50: £1.10, £2.60; EX 6.10 Trifecta £15.70.
Owner Hamdan Al Maktoum **Bred** Shadwell Estate Company Limited **Trained** Lambourn, Berks

FOCUS
A fair 3yo fillies' novice contest. The winning time was slower than the previous C&D 3yo handicap from off another initially muddling gallop. The winner has been rated near her pre-race best.

6560 PLAY "FOUR FROM THE TOP" AT VALUERATER.CO.UK H'CAP (VALUE RATER RACING CLUB STAYERS' SERIES) 1m 2f 37y
6:50 (6:52) (Class 6) (0-60,60) 4-Y-O+
£2,781 (£827; £413; £300; £300; £300) **Stalls** Low

Form RPR
000 **1** **Valentine Mist (IRE)**[20] 5795 7-8-2 **46** oh1................ SophieRalston(5) 3 51
(James Grassick) *mde all: drifted lft but styd on gamely fnl f: rdn out (trainer said regarding apparent improvement in from that the mare had benefitted from a more positive ride on this occasion)* **100/1**

-200 **2** *1* **Frantical**[14] 6059 7-8-2 **48**................................ ElishaWhittington(7) 4 51
(Tony Carroll) *hld up: hdwy over 2f out: sn rdn: nt clr run briefly over 1f out: kpt on ins fnl f: wnt 2nd fnl 70yds (jockey said gelding was denied a clear run on the run to the line)* **8/1**

4050 **3** *1/2* **Taurean Dancer (IRE)**[25] 5631 4-9-7 **60**........................ OisinMurphy 7 62
(Roger Teal) *trckd ldrs: rdn over 2f out: sn chsng wnr: kpt on ins fnl f: hld in 3rd whn tight for room and snatched up cl home* **5/1**[3]

3166 **4** *nk* **Khaan**[32] 5373 4-8-11 **50**...................................... MartinDwyer 6 52
(Michael Appleby) *racd keenly: hld up: midfield 7f out: rdn whn nt clr run over 1f out: sn swtchd rt: kpt on ins fnl f: wnt 4th towards fin (vet said colt lost its right hind shoe)* **3/1**[1]

0053 **5** *1/2* **Sussex Girl**[20] 5802 5-8-9 **48**................................ FrannyNorton 8 49
(John Berry) *racd keenly in tch: in last trio 3f out: hdwy over 2f out: rdn whn carried rt over 1f out: kpt on ins fnl f* **7/1**

6320 **6** *3/4* **War Of Succession**[19] 5858 5-8-12 **58**.......................... MarcoGhiani(7) 5 57
(Tony Newcombe) *s.i.s: racd keenly and sn in tch: rdn to chse wnr whn hung lft over 1f out: no ex ins fnl f* **7/2**[2]

6450 **7** *3/4* **Puzzle Cache**[12] 6104 5-8-7 **46** oh1.............................(b) JoeyHaynes 2 44
(Rod Millman) *racd keenly: in tch: trckd ldrs 6f out: rdn over 2f out: disp 2nd over 1f out: no ex ins fnl f* **33/1**

6610 **8** *nk* **Rocksette**[16] 5993 5-8-12 **56**....................................(h1) TobyEley(5) 10 53
(Adam West) *dwlt: reminders: in rr: hdwy on outer over 3f out: effrt chsng ldrs over 2f out: sltly hmpd over 1f out: one pce fnl f (jockey said mare was slowly away and suffered interference app 1½f out)* **20/1**

3335 **9** *1/2* **Prerogative (IRE)**[20] 5802 5-8-7 **46** oh1...........................(p) DavidEgan 1 42
(Tony Carroll) *trckd wnr tl outpcd over 2f out: no threat after* **8/1**

0464 **10** *2 3/4* **Buzz Lightyere**[17] 5946 6-9-2 **55**..............................(b) DanielMuscutt 9 46
(Patrick Chamings) *hld up: rdn over 2f out: nt pce to get involved* **12/1**

2m 10.58s (-0.52) **Going Correction** -0.15s/f (Firm) **10** Ran SP% **115.0**
Speed ratings (Par 101): **96,95,94,94,94 93,92,92,92,90**
CSF £758.84 CT £4739.20 TOTE £59.30: £12.40, £2.30, £2.10; EX 2758.20 Trifecta £1874.00.
Owner J Grassick **Bred** Victor Stud Bloodstock Ltd **Trained** Cheltenham, Gloucs

FOCUS
A modest handicap. The complete outsider made all off a slow gallop.

6561 SKY SPORTS RACING ON SKY 415 NOVICE STKS 5f 160y
7:20 (7:21) (Class 5) 3-Y-O+ **£3,428** (£1,020; £509; £254) **Stalls** Centre

Form RPR
12 **1** **Whisper Aloud**[4] 6388 3-9-5 0.................................. OisinMurphy 2 79
(Archie Watson) *a.p: led 2f out: rdn clr ent fnl f: comf* **1/4**[1]

0443 **2** *8* **Zaula**[18] 5878 3-8-12 47..................................... DavidEgan 5 45
(Mick Channon) *chsd ldrs: pushed along over 3f out: rdn over 2f out: kpt on to go 2nd jst ins fnl f: nvr any ch w wnr (vet said filly lost its left hind shoe)* **5/1**[2]

3 *5* **Bithiah (IRE)** 3-8-12 0.. SeanLevey 4 28
(Ismail Mohammed) *hung rt thrght: trckd ldrs: rdn to chal over 2f out tl over 1f out: lost 2nd jst ins fnl f: fdd* **5/1**[2]

60 **4** *2 1/4* **Del's Edge**[15] 6023 3-8-9 0................................ WilliamCox(3) 3 20
(Christopher Mason) *led: rdn and hdd 2f out: wknd fnl f* **33/1**[3]

0 **5** *3/4* **Welsh Warrior**[15] 6023 3-9-3 0................................ JohnFahy 1 23
(Nikki Evans) *awkwardly away: chsd ldng quartet: rdn over 2f out: nt pce to get involved* **50/1**

1m 10.82s (-0.28) **Going Correction** -0.15s/f (Firm) **5** Ran SP% **118.2**
Speed ratings (Par 103): **95,84,77,74,73**
CSF £2.53 TOTE £1.10: £1.10, £2.10; EX 2.20 Trifecta £3.00.
Owner Clipper Logistics **Bred** Lordship Stud **Trained** Upper Lambourn, W Berks

FOCUS
A fair, if uncompetitive, 3yo novice sprint.

6562 VISIT VALUERATER.CO.UK FOR BEST FREE TIPS H'CAP (VALUE RATER RACING CLUB SPRINT SERIES) 5f 10y
7:50 (7:50) (Class 5) (0-70,69) 3-Y-O+
£3,428 (£1,020; £509; £300; £300; £300) **Stalls** Centre

Form RPR
0411 **1** **Awsaaf**[85] 3425 4-9-8 **67**..(t) FrannyNorton 2 77
(Michael Wigham) *wnt sltly lft s: outpcd in last: gd hdwy over 1f out: led fnl 100yds: r.o wl* **5/1**[3]

0226 **2** *1/2* **Thegreyvtrain**[4] 6397 3-8-8 **62**.............................. MarcoGhiani(7) 5 70
(Ronald Harris) *led: rdn over 1f out: kpt on but no ex whn hdd fnl 100yds* **9/2**[2]

2423 **3** *6* **Princely**[10] 6203 4-9-4 **63**....................................... MartinDwyer 4 50
(Tony Newcombe) *trckd ldrs: effrt 2f out: outpcd by front pair fnl f* **11/8**[1]

2504 **4** *3/4* **Essaka (IRE)**[19] 5843 7-9-1 **65**............................. SophieRalston(5) 6 49
(Tony Carroll) *trckd ldrs on outer: effrt 2f out: kpt on same pce fnl f* **10/1**

0051 **5** *1 1/4* **Haveoneyerself (IRE)**[20] 5822 4-9-1 **63**..........(p) DarraghKeenan(3) 1 42
(John Butler) *carried sltly lft s: sn chsng ldrs: rdn 2f out: fdd ins fnl f (jockey said gelding hung right-handed)* **9/1**

606U **6** *1* **Arzaak (IRE)**[28] 5532 5-9-8 **67**..................................(b) DavidEgan 3 43
(Charlie Wallis) *trckd ldrs: rdn over 2f out: fdd fnl f* **12/1**

6110 **7** *3 1/2* **Perfect Charm**[20] 5822 3-9-8 **69**.............................(b) OisinMurphy 7 32
(Archie Watson) *trckd ldr tl rdn over 2f out: wknd over 1f out (jockey said filly was unsuited by the fast early pace)* **9/1**

1m 1.49s (-0.51) **Going Correction** -0.15s/f (Firm)
WFA 3 from 4yo+ 2lb **7** Ran SP% **113.7**
Speed ratings (Par 103): **98,97,87,86,84 82,77**
CSF £27.20 TOTE £6.00: £2.70, £3.20; EX 31.50 Trifecta £62.80.
Owner Tugay Akman & Ms I D Heerowa **Bred** Lordship Stud **Trained** Newmarket, Suffolk

FOCUS
An ordinary sprint handicap. The third-favourite came through late to win well. At least a minor pb from the second.

T/Plt: £29.80 to a £1 stake. Pool: £37,785.37 - 923.34 winning units T/Qpdt: £22.30 to a £1 stake. Pool: £5,193.00 - 172.3 winning units **Tim Mitchell**

6532 **EPSOM** (L-H)

Tuesday, August 27

OFFICIAL GOING: Good to firm (good in places; watered; 6.9)

Wind: Light, half behind Weather: Hot

6563 CHANTILLY NURSERY H'CAP (JOCKEY CLUB GRASSROOTS NURSERY QUALIFIER) 7f 3y

2:10 (2:10) (Class 5) (0-70,71) 2-Y-O

£4,528 (£1,347; £673; £336; £300; £300) **Stalls** Low

Form RPR

565 **1** **Good Job Power (IRE)**[13] 6078 2-9-13 **71**........................ PatDobbs 7 76+
(Richard Hannon) mde all and dictated gallop: travelling best 2f out: readily wnt clr over 1f out: pushed along and a doing enough ins fnl f **9/4**[1]

6054 **2** 3/4 **Light The Fuse (IRE)**[11] 6175 2-9-8 **71**.................. HarrisonShaw(5) 3 72
(K R Burke) t.k.h: chsd wnr tl 5f out: styd trcking ldrs: effrt over 2f out: chsd wnr and hung lft 1f out: kpt on but stl hanging ins fnl f **5/2**[2]

400 **3** 4 **Krishmaya (IRE)**[34] 5317 2-8-1 **50**.................. RhiainIngram(5) 5 41
(Adam West) stdd s: t.k.h: hld up in tch: hdwy to join wnr after 2f: rdn 2f out: sn outpcd and btn whn lost 2nd 1f out: wknd ins fnl f **25/1**

0654 **4** 1/2 **Timon (IRE)**[3] 6435 2-8-10 **54**........................(p) FrannyNorton 2 43
(Mick Channon) restless in stalls: dwlt and hmpd sn after leaving stalls: in rr: effrt wl 2f out: styd on to pass btn horses ins fnl f: nvr trbld ldrs **11/4**[3]

4004 **5** 3/4 **Geepower (IRE)**[20] 5800 2-9-0 **58**........................(b) JamesSullivan 4 45
(Brian Ellison) t.k.h: hld up in tch: effrt jst over 2f out: unable qck and sn outpcd: wl hld fnl f **14/1**

5356 **6** 3/4 **Speed Dating (FR)**[13] 6073 2-9-0 **65**........................ AledBeech(7) 6 50
(Derek Shaw) t.k.h: hld up in tch in midfield: effrt and hung lft 2f out: sn outpcd and wl hld after (jockey said gelding hung left handed) **10/1**

0146 **7** 3 **Shani**[41] 5045 2-9-4 **62**........................ LiamJones 1 40
(John Bridger) hld up in tch: effrt jst over 2f out: sn struggling and outpcd: bhd ins fnl f **14/1**

1m 23.68s (0.28) **Going Correction** -0.275s/f (Firm) 7 Ran SP% **112.3**
Speed ratings (Par 94): **87,86,81,81,80 79,75**
CSF £7.84 TOTE £2.80: £2.00, £1.40; EX 7.30 Trifecta £78.50.
Owner King Power Racing Co Ltd **Bred** Rathbarry Stud **Trained** East Everleigh, Wilts

FOCUS
The watered ground (2.5mm applied to the home straight and back straight after racing the previous day) was given as good to firm, good in places (GoingStick 6.9). The rail was at its innermost configuration and all distances were as advertised. Following on from the pattern established the previous day, it paid to be on the front end in this opening nursery.

6564 BRITISH STALLION STUDS EBF MAIDEN STKS (PLUS 10 RACE) 1m 113y

2:45 (2:46) (Class 4) 2-Y-O

£4,787 (£1,424; £711; £355) **Stalls** Low

Form RPR

030 **1** **Gold Souk (IRE)**[24] 5665 2-9-5 83........................ FrannyNorton 3 83+
(Mark Johnston) mde all: pushed along ent fnl 2f: kpt on and a in command fnl f **5/2**[2]

5 **2** 2 3/4 **South Coast (USA)**[22] 5732 2-9-0 0........................ HectorCrouch 7 72
(Saeed bin Suroor) chsd wnr: effrt jst over 2f out: hung lft over 1f out: stl hanging and kpt on same pce ins fnl f (jockey said filly hung left-handed) **4/1**[3]

5 **3** 2 1/2 **Baptism (IRE)**[18] 5908 2-9-5 0........................ RobertHavlin 1 71
(John Gosden) chsd ldrs: effrt over 2f out: outpcd and shifted rt over 1f out: pushed along and kpt on ins fnl f: no threat to wnr **7/4**[1]

05 **4** 1 3/4 **Sky Flyer**[11] 6185 2-9-5 0........................ HarryBentley 4 67+
(Ralph Beckett) midfield: rdn 3f out: sn outpcd: modest 4th over 1f out: kpt on ins fnl f: no threat to ldrs **11/1**

4 **5** 10 **Red For All**[17] 5956 2-9-5 0........................ TomMarquand 5 44
(Ed Dunlop) hld up in rr of main gp: rdn over 3f out: sn outpcd and no ch fnl 2f **8/1**

00 **6** 2 1/2 **Today Power (IRE)**[11] 6163 2-9-5 0........................ SeanLevey 8 38
(Richard Hannon) chsd ldrs: rdn over 2f out: outpcd and btn 5th over 1f out: wknd fnl f **33/1**

7 8 **Moulmein** 2-9-5 0........................ JasonWatson 6 20
(Sylvester Kirk) towards rr of main gp: j. path after 1f and nvr travelling after: rdn and outpcd whn wd bnd over 3f out: no ch after (trainer's rep said colt lost its action after jumping the road crossing and found the going too quick and would prefer an easier surface) **12/1**

8 27 **Noafence (IRE)** 2-9-0 0........................ CharlieBennett 2
(Adam West) rn green and sn outpcd in rr: lost tch 5f out: t.o (jockey said filly ran green) **50/1**

1m 43.68s (-2.72) **Going Correction** -0.275s/f (Firm) 8 Ran SP% **117.0**
Speed ratings (Par 96): **101,98,96,94,85 83,76,52**
CSF £13.40 TOTE £3.10: £1.20, £1.50, £1.10; EX 14.40 Trifecta £33.60.
Owner Sheikh Hamdan bin Mohammed Al Maktoum **Bred** Godolphin **Trained** Middleham Moor, N Yorks

FOCUS
Another all-the-way winner.

6565 TERRY MILLS & JOHN AKEHURST H'CAP 6f 3y

3:15 (3:16) (Class 3) (0-90,91) 3-Y-O+

£9,337 (£2,796; £1,398; £699; £349; £175) **Stalls** High

Form RPR

0302 **1** **Mokaatil**[22] 5746 4-8-13 **86**........................(p) AngusVilliers(7) 7 92
(Ian Williams) t.k.h: in tch on outer: effrt over 1f out: str chal ins fnl f: r.o wl to ld wl ins fnl f **10/1**

1062 **2** 1/2 **Count Otto (IRE)**[18] 5911 4-9-10 **90**........................(h) PatDobbs 3 95
(Amanda Perrett) hld up in rr: effrt 2f out: hdwy ins fnl f: styd on wl towards fin to snatch 2nd last strides: nvr quite getting to wnr **5/1**

1524 **3** nk **Little Boy Blue**[22] 5746 4-9-6 **91**..................(h) ThoreHammerHansen(5) 6 95
(Bill Turner) w ldr tl led and edgd lft 4f out: rdn over 1f out: drvn and hrd pressed ins fnl f: hdd and no ex wl ins fnl f: lost 2nd last strides **7/2**[2]

3011 **4** 1 1/2 **Thegreatestshowman**[24] 5647 3-9-3 **86**........................ JackMitchell 2 85
(Amy Murphy) mounted in chute: led: sn hdd and t.k.h in midfield: swtchd lft and effrt wl over 1f out: pressing ldrs 1f out: no ex ins fnl f **11/4**[1]

4562 **5** nse **Dizzy G (IRE)**[16] 5989 4-8-4 **75**........................ HarrisonShaw(5) 4 74
(K R Burke) mounted in chute and taken down early: sn led: hdd and hmpd 4f out: effrt on inner 2f out: no ex and ins fnl f **9/2**[3]

3210 **6** 1 1/2 **Poyle Vinnie**[10] 6229 9-9-10 **90**........................(p) JamesSullivan 1 86
(Ruth Carr) t.k.h: in tch: swtchd rt and hdwy to chse ldrs over 3f out: shkn up and nt clr run over 1f out: swtchd lft and dropped to rr 1f out: no imp fnl f **9/2**[3]

1m 7.64s (-2.26) **Going Correction** -0.275s/f (Firm)
WFA 3 from 4yo+ 3lb 6 Ran SP% **111.0**
Speed ratings (Par 107): **104,103,102,100,100 98**
CSF £56.02 TOTE £12.30: £4.70, £2.30; EX 69.90 Trifecta £348.90.
Owner Midtech **Bred** Biddestone Stud **Trained** Portway, Worcs

FOCUS
This looked a competitive sprint handicap on paper, and they finished in a bit of a heap. The early pace wasn't that strong and several failed to settle. The form could be rated a pound higher through the second and third.

6566 STANLEY WOOTTON H'CAP (JOCKEY CLUB GRASSROOTS FLAT MIDDLE DISTANCE SERIES QUALIFIER) 1m 4f 6y

3:50 (3:52) (Class 5) (0-70,72) 3-Y-O+

£4,528 (£1,347; £673; £336; £300; £300) **Stalls** Centre

Form RPR

4131 **1** **Peace Prevails**[26] 5571 4-9-0 **63**........................(p) IsobelFrancis(7) 2 70
(Jim Boyle) hld up in last pair: effrt in centre and stl plenty to do 3f out: clsd u.p over 1f out: styd on relentlessly to ld wl ins fnl f **7/4**[1]

2654 **2** 1/2 **Mullarkey**[7] 6320 5-9-2 **58**........................(t) KierenFox 8 64
(John Best) in tch in midfield: effrt over 2f out: chal over 1f out: kpt on but nt quite match pce of wnr wl ins fnl f **5/1**[3]

1131 **3** nk **Junoesque**[18] 5881 5-9-11 **67**........................(p) HectorCrouch 6 73
(John Gallagher) in tch in midfield tl chsd ldrs 8f out: chsd ldr over 3f out: rdn to ld 2f out: kpt on u.p tl hdd and no ex wl ins fnl f **5/1**[3]

0302 **4** 3 **Ban Shoof**[12] 6115 6-9-9 **65**........................(b) AdamKirby 4 66
(Gary Moore) rn in snatches: in tch in last pair: effrt over 2f out: swtchd lft 1f out: kpt on ins fnl f: nvr trbld ldrs **4/1**[2]

4506 **5** 2 1/2 **Hatsaway (IRE)**[24] 5679 8-8-13 **58**........................(p) PaddyBradley(3) 5 55
(Pat Phelan) led for 1f: dropped to midfield but stl wl in tch 8f out: clsd to chse ldrs over 2f out: struggling to qckn u.p whn rdr dropped whip over 1f out: sn hung lft and wknd ins fnl f **20/1**

6264 **6** 3 1/2 **Jawshan (USA)**[10] 6224 4-9-9 **65**........................(p) AndreaAtzeni 1 56
(Ian Williams) led after 1f: rdn over 2f out: hdd 2f out: no ex over 1f out: wknd fnl f **5/1**[3]

062- **7** 27 **Takbeer (IRE)**[107] 5202 7-10-2 **72**........................(p) CharlesBishop 7 20
(Nikki Evans) chsd ldr over 10f out: rdn 5f out: lost pl over 3f out: wl bhd and eased ins fnl f: t.o (jockey said gelding found the good to firm, good in places going too quick and would prefer an easier surface) **33/1**

2m 36.82s (-3.98) **Going Correction** -0.275s/f (Firm) 7 Ran SP% **114.1**
Speed ratings (Par 103): **102,101,101,99,97 95,77**
CSF £10.89 CT £36.08 TOTE £2.40: £1.50, £2.40; EX 9.90 Trifecta £38.10.
Owner Epsom Equine Spa Partnership **Bred** W A Tinkler **Trained** Epsom, Surrey

FOCUS
They went a solid gallop here and it set up for a closer. Straightforward form.

6567 BACK TO THE 80S NYE PARTY H'CAP 7f 3y

4:20 (4:23) (Class 4) (0-80,82) 3-Y-O+

£7,115 (£2,117; £1,058; £529; £300; £300) **Stalls** Low

Form RPR

2436 **1** **Key Player**[20] 5804 4-9-13 **81**........................(p) CharlesBishop 1 90
(Eve Johnson Houghton) mde virtually all: kicked clr w rival and rdn ent fnl 2f: hung rt over 1f out: kpt on gamely ins fnl f (jockey said gelding hung right-handed) **8/1**

4633 **2** 1 1/4 **Juanito Chico (IRE)**[9] 6261 5-9-3 **71**........................(p) DavidProbert 2 77
(Michael Attwater) chsd ldrs: outpcd over 2f out: rallied u.p 1f out: drvn and chsd wnr wl ins fnl f: kpt on but nvr getting on terms **7/1**

4330 **3** 1 3/4 **Highland Acclaim (IRE)**[30] 5476 8-9-6 **74**........................ HarryBentley 11 75
(David O'Meara) broke wl fr wd draw: chsd wnr: kicked clr w wnr and rdn jst over 2f out: unable qck u.p 1f out: lost 2nd wl ins fnl f: wknd towards fin **13/2**[3]

5150 **4** nk **Black Medick**[24] 5651 3-8-12 **71**........................ HectorCrouch 7 69+
(Laura Mongan) hld up in midfield: effrt towards inner over 2f out: hdwy u.p to chse ldrs 1f out: kpt on same pce and no imp ins fnl f **25/1**

6444 **5** 1 **Maksab (IRE)**[17] 5945 4-9-8 **81**........................ ScottMcCullagh(5) 9 79+
(Mick Channon) hld up in midfield: effrt ent fnl 2f: drvn over 1f out: kpt on ins fnl f: nvr getting to ldrs **7/1**

0151 **6** nk **Swift Approval (IRE)**[19] 5862 7-10-0 **82**........................ AndreaAtzeni 4 79
(Stuart Williams) wl in tch in midfield: rdn and outpcd over 2f out: drvn over 1f out: kpt on but no threat to ldrs ins fnl f **9/2**[1]

3025 **7** nse **Mamillius**[19] 5839 6-9-12 **80**........................ PatCosgrave 3 77+
(George Baker) stdd s: hld up in last quartet: effrt ent fnl 2f: kpt on ins fnl f: nvr trbld ldrs **11/2**[2]

0330 **8** shd **Dream Catching (IRE)**[18] 5882 4-9-2 **75**...............(b) WilliamCarver(5) 6 72+
(Andrew Balding) hld up in last quartet: effrt jst over 2f out: kpt on ins fnl f: nvr trbld ldrs **11/2**[2]

101 **9** 1/2 **Kachumba**[20] 5805 4-9-8 **76**........................ AdamKirby 5 71+
(Rae Guest) dwlt: hld up in last quartet: effrt over 2f out: kpt on ins fnl f: nvr trbld ldrs **9/1**

2621 **10** 3/4 **Mujassam**[15] 6027 7-9-2 **75**........................(b) CierenFallon(5) 8 68
(Sophie Leech) chsd ldrs: outpcd over 2f out: lost pl over 1f out: wl hld ins fnl f **12/1**

0301 **11** 2 1/2 **Incentive**[29] 5498 5-8-11 **65**........................(p) LiamKeniry 10 52+
(Stuart Kittow) dwlt: a towards rr: nvr involved **25/1**

1m 20.16s (-3.24) **Going Correction** -0.275s/f (Firm)
WFA 3 from 4yo+ 5lb 11 Ran SP% **123.8**
Speed ratings (Par 105): **107,105,103,103,102 101,101,101,101,100 97**
CSF £66.52 CT £398.84 TOTE £8.80: £2.50, £2.50, £2.20; EX 67.60 Trifecta £699.00.
Owner Raw, Reeve & Wollaston **Bred** Heather Raw **Trained** Blewbury, Oxon

FOCUS
The pace held up well here, nothing really getting involved from behind. The winner has been rated back in line with his best.

6568 JOIN RACING TV NOW H'CAP 1m 2f 17y

4:55 (4:56) (Class 5) (0-70,69) 3-Y-O+

£4,528 (£1,347; £673; £336; £300; £300) **Stalls** Low

Form RPR

3622 **1** **Isle Of Wolves**[15] 6022 3-9-4 **66**........................ PatCosgrave 2 75
(Jim Boyle) chsd ldr: clsd and ev ch ent fnl 2f: rdn to ld over 1f out: drvn and asserted ins fnl f: styd on wl **1/1**[1]

The Form Book Flat 2019, Raceform Ltd, Newbury, RG14 5SJ

4455 **2** 2 3/4 **Duke Of North (IRE)**[7] 6305 7-8-5 **53**......................(p) IsobelFrancis(7) 8 56
(Jim Boyle) *stdd after s: t.k.h: hld up in rr: hdwy on outer 4f out: led 2f out: hdd and rdn over 1f out: no ex and outpcd ins fnl f: wknd towards fin (jockey said gelding ran too freely)* **10/1**

1504 **3** *shd* **Couldn't Could She**[20] 5795 4-9-9 **64**........................ CharlieBennett 6 68
(Adam West) *hld up in last pair: clsd on inner and nt clr run ent fnl 2f: swtchd rt and effrt to chse ldrs over 1f out: edgd rt and kpt on same pce ins fnl f (jockey said filly hung right-handed up the camber)* **9/1**

0523 **4** 1 1/2 **Grange Walk (IRE)**[34] 5316 4-9-8 **63**........................ TomMarquand 3 63
(Pat Phelan) *chsd ldrs: effrt ent fnl 2f: struggling to qckn and sltly impeded over 1f out: kpt on same pce and no imp ins fnl f* **4/1**[2]

0630 **5** 2 **Sweet Nature (IRE)**[20] 5807 4-8-6 **50**........................ MeganNicholls(3) 5 46
(Laura Mongan) *in tch in midfield: effrt ent fnl 2f: no imp over 1f out: wl hld ins fnl f* **16/1**

63 **6** 2 1/4 **Maroc**[16] 5993 6-10-0 **69**........................(p) CharlesBishop 1 61
(Nikki Evans) *led and sn clr: rdn over 2f out: hdd 2f out: sn lost pl and bhd whn changed legs over 1f out: wknd fnl f (trainer said gelding was unsuited by the undulations here at Epsom and would prefer a flatter track)* **5/1**[3]

2m 6.95s (-3.05) **Going Correction** -0.275s/f (Firm)
WFA 3 from 4yo+ 7lb **6 Ran SP% 111.6**
Speed ratings (Par 103): **101,98,98,97,95 94**
CSF £11.97 CT £56.62 TOTE £1.70: £1.10, £3.80; EX 8.90 Trifecta £35.80.
Owner Inside Track Racing Club **Bred** Emma Capon Bloodstock **Trained** Epsom, Surrey

FOCUS
A modest affair. The second has been rated near his recent better figures.

6569 SPECTACULAR CHRISTMAS PARTIES AT EPSOM DOWNS H'CAP 7f 3y
5:25 (5:28) (Class 6) (0-65,67) 3-Y-O

£3,881 (£1,155; £577; £300; £300; £300) **Stalls** Low

Form RPR

3060 **1** **Sirius Slew**[10] 6204 3-9-4 **67**........................(p) CierenFallon(5) 4 74
(Alan Bailey) *chsd ldrs: effrt over 2f out: hdwy over 1f out and str chal u.p 1f out: led 100yds out: hld on cl home (trainer said regarding apparent improvement in from that the gelding benefited from a clear run and probably appreciated a drop in class)* **9/2**[2]

0024 **2** *nk* **Poet's Magic**[26] 5575 3-9-4 **62**........................ DavidProbert 9 68
(Jonathan Portman) *midfield: effrt over 2f out: hdwy over 1f out and chsd ldrs 1f out: styd on wl u.p fnl 100yds: wnt 2nd cl home: nt quite rch wnr* **7/1**

-433 **3** 1/2 **Threefeetfromgold (IRE)**[24] 5678 3-9-7 **65**..............(h) HectorCrouch 7 70
(Martin Smith) *led: rdn ent fnl 2f: drvn and hrd pressed 1f out: hdd 100yds out: kpt on but hld after: lost 2nd cl home* **12/1**

3532 **4** 3/4 **Arriba De Toda (IRE)**[19] 5842 3-8-3 **47**........................ JamesSullivan 13 50
(Brian Ellison) *chsd ldrs: effrt on inner over 2f out: chsd wnr briefly wl over 1f out: edgd lft and kpt on same pce ins fnl f* **10/1**

0506 **5** 1 1/4 **Paddy's Pursuit (IRE)**[14] 6037 3-8-8 **57**........................ ThomasGreatrex(5) 15 57
(David Loughnane) *dwlt: off the pce towards rr: rdn 3f out: edgd lft but sme prog over 1f out: kpt on wl ins fnl f: nt rch ldrs (jockey said gelding was slowly away)* **50/1**

2560 **6** *nk* **Aubretia (IRE)**[21] 5779 3-9-8 **66**........................ PatDobbs 11 65
(Richard Hannon) *off the pce in midfield: effrt over 2f out: nt clr run wl over 1f out: sn swtchd lft and hdwy 1f out: kpt on wl ins fnl f: nt rch ldrs* **15/2**

0044 **7** 2 1/2 **Lady Monica**[12] 6120 3-9-4 **62**........................ RoystonFfrench 1 54
(John Holt) *chsd ldr for over 1f: chsd ldrs: effrt to chse ldr again over 2f out tl wl over 1f out: lost pl ent fnl f: wknd ins fnl f* **12/1**

504 **8** 1/2 **Moon Artist (FR)**[19] 5842 3-7-11 **46** oh1........................ RhiainIngram(5) 5 37
(Michael Blanshard) *off the pce in midfield: effrt over 2f out: hung lft but sme prog over 1f out: kpt on ins fnl f: nvr trbld ldrs* **33/1**

0013 **9** 1 1/4 **Break Of Day**[12] 6130 3-8-10 **54**........................(b) TomMarquand 3 42
(William Haggas) *midfield: effrt over 2f out: no imp u.p and btn over 1f out: wknd ins fnl f* **4/1**[1]

0024 **10** 1/2 **Harbour Times (IRE)**[14] 6052 3-7-9 **46**........................ IsobelFrancis(7) 6 33
(Patrick Chamings) *dwlt: off the pce towards rr: c centre and effrt over 3f out: kpt on but nvr involved (jockey said filly was outpaced)* **16/1**

0000 **11** *shd* **Confab (USA)**[31] 5431 3-8-13 **57**........................ PatCosgrave 2 43
(George Baker) *s.i.s: wl off the pce towards rr: c towards centre and effrt over 3f out: kpt on but nvr involved* **33/1**

60-4 **12** 3 1/4 **Geneva Spur (USA)**[33] 5357 3-9-5 **63**........................ AndreaAtzeni 8 41
(Roger Varian) *midfield: effrt and edgd rt over 2f out: no imp and btn over 1f out: wknd fnl f: eased towards fin* **11/2**[3]

-060 **13** 4 1/2 **Crimson Kiss (IRE)**[27] 5561 3-8-8 **52**........................(p[1]) CharlieBennett 10 18
(Pat Phelan) *dwlt: a off the pce towards rr: n.d* **33/1**

6020 **14** 2 1/4 **Recuerdame (USA)**[22] 5731 3-9-6 **64**........................ AdamKirby 14 24
(Simon Dow) *chsd ldr after 1f tl over 2f out: steadily lost pl: bhd ins fnl f* **12/1**

1m 21.08s (-2.32) **Going Correction** -0.275s/f (Firm) **14 Ran SP% 126.7**
Speed ratings (Par 98): **102,101,101,100,98 98,95,95,93,93 92,89,84,81**
CSF £37.25 CT £370.62 TOTE £6.30: £2.30, £2.50, £3.90; EX 37.70 Trifecta £456.70.
Owner Trevor Milner **Bred** Dachel Stud **Trained** Newmarket, Suffolk

FOCUS
An ordinary handicap, but a competitive one.
T/Plt: £40.80 to a £1 stake. Pool: £68,540.27 - 1,224.24 winning units T/Qpdt: £38.30 to a £1 stake. Pool: £5,581.23 - 107.67 winning units **Steve Payne**

5899 MUSSELBURGH (R-H)
Tuesday, August 27

OFFICIAL GOING: Good to firm (good in places; watered; 7.4)
Wind: Light, across Weather: Overcast, rain from races 3-4

6570 WATCH RACINGTV NOW MAIDEN AUCTION FILLIES' STKS 7f 33y
5:00 (5:01) (Class 6) 2-Y-O **£3,105** (£924; £461; £230) **Stalls** Low

Form RPR

35 **1** **Red Treble**[11] 6175 2-8-9 **0**........................(h) CamHardie 3 73+
(Rebecca Menzies) *mde all: set stdy pce: shkn up and qcknd clr over 1f out: kpt on wl fnl f: unchal* **7/2**[3]

3 **2** 2 1/2 **Rosardo Senorita**[12] 6118 2-7-10 **0**........................ AndrewBreslin(5) 4 58
(Rae Guest) *dwlt: sn prom on outside: hdwy over 2f out: chsd wnr and hung rt over 1f out: sn one pce* **6/4**[1]

3 1 1/4 **Handlebars (IRE)** 2-8-11 **0**........................ JoeFanning 2 65
(Keith Dalgleish) *dwlt: t.k.h and sn trcking wnr: drvn over 2f out: outpcd fr over 1f out* **3/1**[2]

45 **4** 7 **Dancing Leopard (IRE)**[12] 6096 2-8-7 **0**........................ BenCurtis 1 42
(K R Burke) *trckd ldrs: rdn over 2f out: wknd wl over 1f out* **7/2**[3]

1m 30.17s (1.17) **Going Correction** +0.10s/f (Good) **4 Ran SP% 109.4**
Speed ratings (Par 89): **97,94,92,84**
CSF £9.24 TOTE £4.20; EX 8.10 Trifecta £22.20.
Owner Flying High **Bred** Biddestone Stud Ltd **Trained** Mordon, Durham

FOCUS
A modest small-field maiden and the winner made all.

6571 LIVE RACING TV ON FACEBOOK NURSERY H'CAP 7f 33y
5:30 (5:30) (Class 6) (0-65,67) 2-Y-O

£3,105 (£924; £461; £300; £300; £300) **Stalls** Low

Form RPR

5023 **1** **Out Of Breath**[18] 5896 2-9-7 **65**........................ SamJames 2 69
(Grant Tuer) *mde all: rdn and hrd pressed fr 2f out: kpt on wl to assert fnl 150yds* **10/3**[2]

0600 **2** 1 1/4 **Never Said Nothing (IRE)**[34] 5296 2-8-13 **57**........................ BenRobinson 3 58
(Brian Ellison) *pressed wnr thrght: effrt and chal 2f out to 1f out: kpt on same pce fnl 150yds* **10/1**

4636 **3** 3 **Rusalka (IRE)**[34] 5296 2-8-13 **57**........................ DuranFentiman 4 50
(Tim Easterby) *t.k.h: in tch: stdy hdwy whn n.m.r briefly over 2f out: rdn over 1f out: sn one pce* **6/1**

455 **4** 3 1/4 **Spanish Time**[51] 4688 2-9-9 **67**........................ JasonHart 1 52
(Keith Dalgleish) *dwlt: t.k.h and sn prom: rdn over 2f out: outpcd fr over 1f out* **3/1**[1]

060 **5** 3/4 **Baileys Prayer (FR)**[78] 3644 2-8-3 **50**........................ SeanDavis(3) 7 33
(Richard Fahey) *s.i.s: sn pushed along in rr: drvn along and outpcd over 2f out: sme late hdwy: nvr rchd ldrs* **10/1**

0625 **6** *nk* **Percy Green (IRE)**[18] 5886 2-9-3 **61**........................ BenCurtis 5 43
(K R Burke) *s.i.s: hld up: effrt and rdn over 2f out: no further imp fr over 1f out* **9/2**[3]

5606 **7** 18 **Interrupted Dream**[7] 6313 2-9-3 **61**........................ JoeFanning 6
(Mark Johnston) *prom on outside: rdn over 2f out: wknd wl over 1f out* **6/1**

1m 29.47s (0.47) **Going Correction** +0.10s/f (Good) **7 Ran SP% 113.0**
Speed ratings (Par 92): **101,99,96,92,91 91,70**
CSF £34.42 TOTE £4.30: £4.50, £6.30; EX 35.30 Trifecta £456.70.
Owner Moment of Madness **Bred** Faisal Meshrf Alqahtani **Trained** Birkby, N Yorks

FOCUS
Modest nursery form, with the prominent racers favoured.

6572 MAGNERS GB H'CAP 7f 33y
6:00 (6:01) (Class 6) (0-60,63) 4-Y-O+

£2,781 (£827; £413; £300; £300; £300) **Stalls** Low

Form RPR

0000 **1** **Echo Of Lightning**[20] 5820 9-9-7 **60**........................(p) BenCurtis 9 71
(Roger Fell) *mde all: rdn over 1f out: drew clr ins fnl f (trainer's rep said regarding apparent improvement in form that the gelding may have appreciated the return to Musselburgh, where the gelding has won previously)* **18/1**

0600 **2** 3 1/4 **Robben Rainbow**[19] 5852 5-8-13 **52**........................ JasonHart 2 55
(Katie Scott) *chsd ldrs: effrt and wnt 2nd over 2f out: rdn and edgd lft over 1f out: kpt on same pce fnl f* **12/1**

6222 **3** *shd* **Be Bold**[17] 5933 7-8-11 **53**........................(b) RowanScott(3) 4 55
(Rebecca Bastiman) *s.i.s: hld up: rdn over 2f out: gd hdwy fnl f: fin wl* **10/1**

4041 **4** 1 1/4 **Our Charlie Brown**[8] 6276 5-9-5 **63** 5ex..............(p) DannyRedmond(5) 5 62
(Tim Easterby) *t.k.h: trckd ldrs: effrt and drvn along 2f out: sn one pce* **11/8**[1]

0425 **5** 3/4 **Let Right Be Done**[43] 4979 7-8-7 **46** oh1..................(b) AndrewMullen 1 43
(Linda Perratt) *t.k.h: in tch: rdn over 2f out: kpt on same pce fr over 1f out* **28/1**

4560 **6** 4 1/2 **Tellovoi (IRE)**[92] 3142 11-8-8 **47**........................(p) PaddyMathers 6 32
(Richard Guest) *dwlt: bhd: rdn over 2f out: sme late hdwy: nvr rchd ldrs* **40/1**

7 1/2 **Fascinating Spirit (IRE)**[72] 3898 4-8-7 **49**........................(vt[1]) SeanDavis(3) 12 33
(A J Martin, Ire) *hld up: rdn over 2f out: hdwy and edgd lft over 1f out: nvr rchd ldrs* **14/1**

5134 **8** 4 **Forever A Lady (IRE)**[14] 6033 6-9-7 **60**........................ JoeFanning 10 34
(Keith Dalgleish) *hld up on outside: rdn over 2f out: wknd over 1f out* **8/1**[3]

0210 **9** 1/2 **Etikaal**[25] 5616 5-9-7 **60**........................ SamJames 11 32
(Grant Tuer) *s.i.s: sn rcvrd to chse wnr: rdn over 2f out: wknd over 1f out* **15/2**[2]

4545 **10** 1 **Colour Contrast (IRE)**[25] 5616 6-9-6 **59**........................(b) JamieGormley 8 29
(Iain Jardine) *s.i.s: bhd: rdn along over 2f out: nvr on terms* **8/1**[3]

6604 **11** *nk* **Spenny's Lass**[14] 6051 4-8-9 **48**........................(p) CamHardie 7 17
(John Ryan) *prom: lost grnd after 3f: rdn and wknd over 2f out* **16/1**

5050 **12** 4 **Bareed (USA)**[36] 5238 4-8-2 **46** oh1........................(p) AndrewBreslin(5) 3 5
(Linda Perratt) *dwlt: bhd: struggling after 3f: nvr on terms* **40/1**

1m 28.78s (-0.22) **Going Correction** +0.10s/f (Good) **12 Ran SP% 119.0**
Speed ratings (Par 101): **105,101,101,99,98 93,93,88,88,86 86,81**
CSF £215.78 CT £2320.41 TOTE £22.20: £5.80, £4.60, £2.10; EX 318.60 Trifecta £3296.30.
Owner Victoria Greetham & Emily Beasley **Bred** Gracelands Stud **Trained** Nawton, N Yorks

FOCUS
Moderate handicap form with the favourite disappointing.

6573 BOOKIE IN THE MORNING H'CAP 1m 208y
6:30 (6:32) (Class 5) (0-70,72) 4-Y-O+

£3,752 (£1,116; £557; £300; £300; £300) **Stalls** Low

Form RPR

204 **1** **Ventura Royal (IRE)**[45] 4917 4-8-13 **62**........................(h) RobbieDowney 2 72
(David O'Meara) *trckd ldr: rdn to ld over 1f out: kpt on strly fnl f* **11/1**

1253 **2** 2 1/4 **How Bizarre**[18] 5903 4-9-9 **72**........................ DavidNolan 9 78
(Liam Bailey) *led: rdn and hdd over 1f out: kpt on same pce fnl f* **9/2**[1]

4012 **3** 2 1/4 **Whatwouldyouknow (IRE)**[12] 6102 4-9-6 **69**........................ PaulMulrennan 7 70
(Richard Guest) *trckd ldrs: drvn along over 2f out: no ex fr over 1f out* **9/2**[1]

2346 **4** 3 **Ghayyar (IRE)**[6] 6341 5-9-1 **69**........................(tp) DannyRedmond(5) 8 64
(Tim Easterby) *in tch on outside: effrt over 2f out: hung rt and wknd over 1f out* **13/2**[2]

3504 **5** 1 **Zeshov (IRE)**[18] 5899 8-8-13 **65**........................(p) RowanScott(3) 6 58
(Rebecca Bastiman) *dwlt: hld up: drvn along over 2f out: no imp fr over 1f out* **16/1**

5302 **6** 3/4 **Straight Ash (IRE)**[12] 6103 4-9-1 **64**........................ BenRobinson 1 56
(Ollie Pears) *hld up on ins: rdn and outpcd over 2f out: sme late hdwy: nvr rchd ldrs* **7/1**[3]

The Form Book Flat 2019, Raceform Ltd, Newbury, RG14 5SJ

3000 **7** *2 ½* **Jacob Black**[25] 5616 8-9-7 **70**........(v) JoeFanning 3 57
(Keith Dalgleish) *dwlt: hld up: shkn up over 2f out: sn no imp: btn over 1f out* **12/1**

4524 **8** *hd* **Battle Of Marathon (USA)**[25] 5625 7-9-9 **72**........(p) CamHardie 4 60
(John Ryan) *slowly away: bhd: drvn 3f out: no imp whn hmpd ins fnl f (jockey said gelding was slowly away then denied a clear run approaching the final half furlong)* **12/1**

505 **9** *hd* **Lucky Violet (IRE)**[18] 5899 7-8-11 **60**........(h) JamieGormley 5 46
(Linda Perratt) *prom: rdn over 3f out: wknd fnl 2f* **7/1**[3]

2634 **10** *1* **Dark Devil (IRE)**[11] 6173 6-8-12 **64**........(p) SeanDavis(3) 10 48
(Richard Fahey) *slowly away: bhd: rdn and hung rt over 2f out: sn btn* **9/1**

1m 53.8s (0.70) **Going Correction** +0.10s/f (Good) **10** Ran SP% **114.3**
Speed ratings (Par 103): **100,98,96,93,92 91,89,89,89,88**
CSF £58.77 CT £263.82 TOTE £11.20: £4.40, £3.40, £1.10; EX 84.90 Trifecta £592.90.
Owner Middleham Park Racing CXVII **Bred** Rabbah Bloodstock Limited **Trained** Upper Helmsley, N Yorks

FOCUS
Little got into this modest handicap, with the prominent racers again seen to best effect. A minor pb from the winner.

6574 WATCH RACING TV NOW H'CAP — 5f 1y
7:00 (7:02) (Class 6) (0-55,57) 4-Y-O+

£2,781 (£827; £413; £300; £300; £300) **Stalls** High

Form RPR

0000 **1** **Thornaby Princess**[8] 6277 8-9-0 **45**........(p) TomEaves 9 51
(Jason Ward) *trckd ldrs: rdn to ld over 1f out: kpt on wl fnl f* **28/1**

0006 **2** *¾* **Corton Lass**[29] 5491 4-9-0 **45**........ JoeFanning 12 48
(Keith Dalgleish) *slowly away: t.k.h in rr: effrt whn nt clr run and swtchd rt over 1f out: chsd wnr ins fnl f: r.o (jockey said filly was denied a clear run 1½f out)* **20/1**

0- **3** *½* **Zeb City (IRE)**[101] 2851 4-9-0 **45**........ BenCurtis 1 47
(Mark L Fagan, Ire) *prom on outside: effrt and chsd wnr over 1f out to ins fnl f: kpt on same pce* **14/1**

0000 **4** *nk* **Super Florence (IRE)**[8] 6273 4-9-11 **56**........(h) JamieGormley 14 56+
(Iain Jardine) *cl up: n.m.r briefly 1/2-way: rdn and outpcd over 1f out: r.o ins fnl f (jockey said that his saddle slipped)* **13/2**[3]

0545 **5** *hd* **Star Cracker (IRE)**[22] 5722 7-9-0 **45**........(p) PaulMulrennan 7 45
(Jim Goldie) *midfield: rdn 1/2-way: hdwy over 1f out: drvn and one pce ins fnl f* **16/1**

000 **6** *½* **Lord Of The Glen**[3] 6462 4-9-7 **52**........(v) PaddyMathers 2 50
(Jim Goldie) *s.i.s: bhd and outpcd: hdwy appr fnl f: kpt on: nrst fin* **12/1**

3001 **7** *1 ½* **Mr Shelby (IRE)**[17] 5935 5-9-9 **57**........(p) SeanDavis(3) 10 50
(S Donohoe, Ire) *trckd ldrs: n.m.r briefly wl over 1f out: sn rdn: no ex ins fnl f: b.b.v (vet said gelding bled from the nose)* **7/1**

3046 **8** *1* **Jeffrey Harris**[25] 5620 4-9-0 **52**........(t[1]) CoreyMadden(7) 11 45+
(Jim Goldie) *rrd and lost several l s: hdwy and tagged onto bk of gp 1/2-way: effrt whn nt clr run over 1f out: keeping on whn n.m.r ins fnl f: no imp (jockey said gelding reared as the stalls opened and was then denied a clear run in the final half furlong)* **4/1**[2]

050 **9** *3 ½* **Lady Joanna Vassa (IRE)**[29] 5491 6-9-0 **45**........(b[1]) AndrewMullen 5 21
(Richard Guest) *w ldrs: led 1/2-way to over 1f out: sn wknd (jockey said mare hung left from 2f out)* **40/1**

2526 **10** *3* **Bronze Beau**[11] 6168 12-9-7 **57**........(tp) FayeMcManoman(5) 6 23
(Linda Stubbs) *led to 1/2-way: rdn and wknd over 1f out* **18/1**

2536 **11** *1 ¼* **War Ensign (IRE)**[2] 6503 4-9-5 **50**........(p) JasonHart 8 11
(Tim Easterby) *towards rr: drvn along 1/2-way: sn no imp: btn over 1f out (jockey said gelding was never travelling)* **11/4**[1]

-400 **12** *1* **Raise A Billion**[29] 5491 8-8-11 **45**........ ConnorMurtagh(3) 4 2
(Alan Berry) *bhd and sn outpcd: nvr on terms (jockey said gelding was never travelling)* **50/1**

2600 **13** *19* **Angel Eyes**[27] 5558 4-9-1 **46**........ DannyBrock 3
(John David Riches) *bhd on outside: struggling 1/2-way: btn and eased fnl f* **18/1**

1m 1.03s (1.33) **Going Correction** +0.10s/f (Good) **13** Ran SP% **115.9**
Speed ratings (Par 101): **93,91,91,90,90 89,87,85,79,75 73,71,41**
CSF £474.25 CT £8189.69 TOTE £30.60: £8.40, £7.30, £5.70; EX 521.00 Trifecta £2443.00.
Owner Ingleby Bloodstock Limited **Bred** Dave Scott **Trained** Sessay, N Yorks

FOCUS
Two of the outsiders came to the fore in this moderate sprint.

6575 FOLLOW @RACINGTV ON TWITTER H'CAP — 7f 33y
7:30 (7:32) (Class 6) (0-60,60) 3-Y-O

£2,781 (£827; £413; £300; £300; £300) **Stalls** Low

Form RPR

0263 **1** **Muhallab (IRE)**[4] 6389 3-8-13 **52**........ AndrewMullen 5 59
(Adrian Nicholls) *t.k.h early: trckd ldrs: effrt and swtchd rt 2f out: led ent fnl f: edgd lft: kpt on strly* **3/1**[2]

4001 **2** *2 ¼* **Jack Randall**[19] 5847 3-9-5 **58**........ DuranFentiman 6 59
(Tim Easterby) *t.k.h: prom: rdn to ld over 1f out: edgd rt and hdd ent fnl f: sn one pce* **11/4**[1]

366 **3** *3* **God Of Dreams**[35] 5272 3-9-4 **57**........ PaulMulrennan 11 53
(Iain Jardine) *s.i.s: hld up on ins: effrt whn checked 2f out: rallied and chsd clr ldng pair ins fnl f: r.o* **14/1**

6015 **4** *½* **Sharrabang**[19] 5852 3-9-2 **55**........ CamHardie 9 47
(Stella Barclay) *led: rdn and hdd over 1f out: outpcd fnl f (jockey said gelding hung left throughout)* **5/1**[3]

5140 **5** *1 ¾* **Lethal Laura**[32] 5389 3-8-12 **51**........ PaddyMathers 7 39
(R Mike Smith) *in tch on outside: effrt and drvn along 2f out: wknd ins fnl f* **10/1**

004 **6** *½* **Spotton (IRE)**[11] 6177 3-8-6 **48**........ RowanScott(3) 2 34
(Rebecca Bastiman) *s.s: hld up: pushed along over 2f out: hdwy over 1f out: no further imp fnl 100yds* **16/1**

0326 **7** *4 ½* **Blank Canvas**[14] 6033 3-9-6 **59**........ JoeFanning 8 34
(Keith Dalgleish) *t.k.h: cl up: rdn over 2f out: wknd over 1f out* **8/1**

-505 **8** *½* **Darwina**[21] 5771 3-8-13 **52**........(h) JasonHart 1 25
(Alistair Whillans) *hld up in midfield on ins: effrt over 2f out: wknd over 1f out* **10/1**

005 **9** *2 ½* **Hunters Step**[11] 6177 3-8-4 **48**........ AndrewBreslin(5) 10 15
(Noel Wilson) *s.i.s: bhd: drvn over 2f out: wknd over 1f out* **50/1**

2505 **10** *8* **Hanati (IRE)**[14] 6057 3-9-7 **60**........ BenRobinson 3 6
(Brian Ellison) *hld up on ins: struggling over 2f out: sn btn (jockey said filly hung left throughout)* **25/1**

000- **11** *2* **Miss Maben**[385] 5816 3-8-7 **46** oh1........ JamieGormley 4
(Iain Jardine) *t.k.h: hld up bhd ldng gp: rdn over 2f out: sn wknd* **40/1**

1m 30.29s (1.29) **Going Correction** +0.10s/f (Good) **11** Ran SP% **118.4**
Speed ratings (Par 98): **96,93,90,89,87 86,81,81,78,69 66**
CSF £11.59 CT £102.40 TOTE £3.60: £1.60, £1.50, £3.90; EX 12.50 Trifecta £131.80.
Owner J Aljunaibi **Bred** Alan D Gray **Trained** Sessay, N Yorks

FOCUS
Moderate 3yo form.

6576 RACINGTV.COM H'CAP — 1m 4f 104y
8:00 (8:00) (Class 4) (0-85,84) 3-Y-O+

£5,692 (£1,694; £846; £423; £300; £300) **Stalls** Low

Form RPR

2505 **1** **Mutamaded (IRE)**[20] 5818 6-10-0 **82**........ PaulMulrennan 5 89
(Ruth Carr) *checked s: in tch: gd hdwy to ld over 3f out: rdn 2f out: r.o wl* **9/2**[3]

4351 **2** *2* **Four Kingdoms (IRE)**[19] 5850 5-9-7 **75**........ PaddyMathers 4 79
(R Mike Smith) *chsd ldr to 1/2-way: cl up: drvn and outpcd over 3f out: rallied to chse wnr over 1f out: r.o* **9/2**[3]

6/0 **3** *hd* **Acclamatio (IRE)**[23] 5712 5-9-4 **72**........(t) BenCurtis 6 75
(A J Martin, Ire) *plld hrd: in tch: rdn and outpcd over 2f out: rallied over 1f out: r.o fnl f* **9/4**[1]

6265 **4** *1 ¾* **Low Profile**[30] 5473 4-8-9 **66**........(p) RowanScott(3) 7 67
(Rebecca Bastiman) *cl up: wnt 2nd 1/2-way to over 3f out: rdn and outpcd over 2f out: rallied fnl f: no imp* **11/1**

4166 **5** *1 ½* **Maulesden May (IRE)**[17] 5937 6-9-3 **74**........ SeanDavis(3) 3 72
(Keith Dalgleish) *hld up: hdwy and prom over 4f out: rdn: edgd rt and wknd over 1f out* **12/1**

1606 **6** *4 ½* **Cape Islay (FR)**[23] 5706 3-9-7 **84**........ JoeFanning 2 76
(Mark Johnston) *led at modest gallop: rdn and hdd over 3f out: rallied and chsd wnr to over 1f out: wknd fnl f* **11/4**[2]

56-0 **7** *4* **An Fear Ciuin (IRE)**[87] 3361 8-9-5 **73**........ JamieGormley 1 58
(R Mike Smith) *hld up: pushed along briefly 1/2-way: drvn over 3f out: wknd over 2f out* **33/1**

2m 50.16s (5.66) **Going Correction** +0.10s/f (Good) **7** Ran SP% **112.8**
WFA 3 from 4yo+ 9lb
Speed ratings (Par 105): **85,83,83,82,81 78,75**
CSF £24.14 TOTE £3.90: £2.90, £1.40; EX 18.50 Trifecta £67.20.
Owner The Bottom Liners & Mrs R Carr **Bred** Shadwell Estate Company Limited **Trained** Huby, N Yorks

FOCUS
An ordinary handicap won in good style by the top weight. The winner has been rated near this year's form.
T/Jkpt: Not Won. T/Plt: £23,843.50 to a £1 stake. Pool: £40,828.05 - 1.25 winning units T/Qpdt: £835.30 to a £1 stake. Pool: £8,578.93 - 7.6 winning units **Richard Young**

6539 RIPON (R-H)
Tuesday, August 27

OFFICIAL GOING: Good (good to firm in places; 8.0)
Wind: Nil Weather: Hot and Sunny

6577 DOWNLOAD THE FREE AT THE RACES APP EBF FILLIES' NOVICE STKS (PLUS 10 RACE) — 5f
1:55 (1:56) (Class 5) 2-Y-O

£3,881 (£1,155; £577; £288) **Stalls** High

Form RPR

62 **1** **Hot Affair**[21] 5788 2-9-0 0........ DanielTudhope 6 86
(Tom Dascombe) *mde all: shkn up over 1f out: r.o wl to draw clr fnl 100yds* **7/4**[2]

322 **2** *3 ¼* **Poets Dance**[26] 5590 2-9-0 79........ DavidAllan 4 74
(Rae Guest) *wnt rt s: chsd wnr: pushed along over 2f out: no imp ins fnl f* **6/5**[1]

10 **3** *3 ¾* **Ultra Violet**[17] 5964 2-9-7 0........ RobHornby 3 68+
(Ed Vaughan) *wnt rt s: chsd ldrs: rdn and outpcd ent fnl 2f: one pce whn no ch fnl f (trainer's rep said filly was unsuited by drop in trip)* **7/2**[3]

0 **4** *½* **Brainchild**[13] 6064 2-9-0 0........ ShaneGray 2 59
(Keith Dalgleish) *s.i.s: rn green: in rr and pushed along: hdwy over 3f out: chsd ldrs jst over 1f out: nvr gng pce to get seriously involved* **33/1**

65 **5** *15* **Led Astray**[22] 5737 2-9-0 0........ CliffordLee 1 5
(Michael Bell) *s.i.s: carried rt s: rn green: in rr and pushed along: nvr able to get to ldrs: hung rt over 1f out: wl btn* **22/1**

006 **6** *32* **Nice One Too**[15] 6011 2-9-0 11........(v[1]) PhilDennis 5
(David C Griffiths) *drvn along thrght: chsd ldrs: lost pl over 3f out: sn bhd: lost tch over 1f out: t.o* **200/1**

58.29s (-1.11) **Going Correction** -0.25s/f (Firm) **6** Ran SP% **111.8**
Speed ratings (Par 91): **98,92,86,86,62 10**
CSF £4.17 TOTE £2.70: £1.70, £1.10; EX 3.70 Trifecta £6.70.
Owner Clipper Logistics **Bred** Miss K J Keir **Trained** Malpas, Cheshire

FOCUS
All rails on innermost positions, no added yards. The first pair dominated this fair fillies' novice, having kept stands' side.

6578 FREE TIPS AVAILABLE ON ATTHERACES.COM (S) STKS — 1m 1f 170y
2:30 (2:31) (Class 6) 3-4-Y-O

£3,105 (£924; £461; £300; £300; £300) **Stalls** Low

Form RPR

2-06 **1** *nse* **Knightly Spirit**[6] 6343 4-9-2 64........ DavidAllan 2 56+
(Iain Jardine) *trckd ldrs: nt clr run over 2f out: angled out over 1f out: edgd lft ins fnl f: sn bmpd by rival whn chalng: jst denied on the nod in driving fin: awrdd r* **7/4**[1]

0630 **2** **Amity Island**[28] 5518 4-9-2 46........ LewisEdmunds 8 56
(Ollie Pears) *in rr: hdwy u.p 2f out: edgd rt whn bmpd rival and led narrowly ins fnl f: jst prevailed on the nod in driving fin: disqualified and plcd 2nd - caused interference* **11/1**

-040 **3** *1 ¾* **Ride The Monkey (IRE)**[39] 5124 3-8-9 72........ CliffordLee 7 54
(Michael Dods) *racd keenly: prom: rdn to ld jst over 2f out: hdd ins fnl f: styd on same pce towards fin* **3/1**[2]

0502 **4** *1* **Smashing Lass (IRE)**[32] 5389 3-8-4 46........(p) NathanEvans 5 47
(Ollie Pears) *hld up: pushed along over 4f out: hdwy u.p 2f out: chsd ldrs ins fnl f: kpt on u.p: nt quite pce to mount serious chal* **15/2**

0 **5** *½* **Phenakite**[17] 5969 3-8-6 0........ ConorMcGovern(3) 4 51
(Ollie Pears) *w ldr: rdn to ld over 2f out: sn hdd: stl there 1f out: no ex fnl 75yds* **25/1**

0000 **6** *6* **Dothraki (IRE)**[27] 5559 3-8-9 43..............................(v[1]) PhilDennis 3 39
(Ronald Thompson) *trckd ldrs: pushed along over 3f out: sn lost pl: kpt on modly ins fnl f: no imp* **66/1**

3445 **7** *2 1/4* **Tails I Win (CAN)**[32] 5389 3-8-4 54..............................(p[1]) LukeMorris 9 30
(Roger Fell) *racd on outer: cl up: dropped in bhd ldrs 6f out: effrt 3f out: rdn and ev ch 2f out: one pce over 1f out: edgd rt ins fnl f: sn wknd* **7/2[3]**

3065 **8** *2 3/4* **Prince Consort (IRE)**[2] 6502 4-9-2 45..............................(b[1]) GrahamLee 1 29
(John Wainwright) *led: rdn and hdd over 2f out: wknd over 1f out* **20/1**

00 **9** *34* **Graciarose**[27] 5554 3-8-4 0..............................(p[1]) ShaneGray 6
(Tracy Waggott) *midfield: pushed along 6f out: lost pl over 4f out: bhd 3f out* **100/1**

2m 2.93s (-1.67) **Going Correction** -0.25s/f (Firm)
WFA 3 from 4yo 7lb **9** Ran SP% **114.8**
Speed ratings (Par 101): **95,96,94,93,93 88,86,84,57**
CSF £21.81 TOTE £2.30: £2.70, £1.10, £2.10; EX 18.20 Trifecta £97.40.There was no bid for the winner.
Owner Ibrahim Rachid **Bred** Cheveley Park Stud Ltd **Trained** Carrutherstown, D'fries & G'way
■ Stewards' Enquiry : David Allan two-day ban: used whip above permitted level (10-11 Sep)

FOCUS
There was a rough finish to this moderate seller.

6579 21 ENGINEER REGIMENT SAPPER NURSERY H'CAP 1m
3:00 (3:00) (Class 4) (0-85,81) 2-Y-O £4,722 (£1,405; £702; £351) Stalls Low

Form RPR

313 **1** **World Title (IRE)**[49] 4750 2-9-7 **81**.............................. DanielTudhope 2 85+
(Archie Watson) *mde all: rdn over 1f out: kpt on wl fnl f* **5/4[1]**

520 **2** *1* **Fast Deal**[11] 6175 2-8-11 **71**.............................. DavidAllan 3 71
(Tim Easterby) *trckd ldrs: nt clr run ent fnl 3f: effrt over 2f out: kpt on ins fnl f to take 2nd fnl 75yds: nt quite pce of wnr* **9/1**

3521 **3** *1/2* **G For Gabrial (IRE)**[12] 6097 2-8-10 **70**.............................. PaulHanagan 4 69
(Richard Fahey) *chsd wnr: pushed along over 3f out: rdn and ev ch 2f out: unable qck 1f out: lost 2nd fnl 75yds: kpt on same pce* **7/4[2]**

3223 **4** *4* **Breguet Man (IRE)**[19] 5853 2-8-12 **72**..............................(p[1]) ShaneGray 1 61
(Keith Dalgleish) *hld up in rr: rdn over 2f out: outpcd over 1f out: nvr able to chal* **9/2[3]**

1m 39.22s (-1.78) **Going Correction** -0.25s/f (Firm) **4** Ran SP% **109.0**
Speed ratings (Par 96): **98,97,96,92**
CSF £11.25 TOTE £2.40; EX 10.70 Trifecta £38.40.
Owner Clipper Logistics **Bred** Oghill House Stud & Joseph M Burke **Trained** Upper Lambourn, W Berks

FOCUS
Just the four runners and unsurprisingly this modest nursery proved tactical.

6580 ATTHERACES.COM CITY OF RIPON H'CAP 1m 1f 170y
3:35 (3:35) (Class 3) (0-90,88) 4-Y-O+
£9,337 (£2,796; £1,398; £699; £349; £175) Stalls Low

Form RPR

4163 **1** **Benadalid**[13] 6067 4-8-13 **80**.............................. DanielTudhope 6 88
(Chris Fairhurst) *hld up: hdwy 3f out: led 2f out: kpt on wl fnl f* **9/4[1]**

6005 **2** *3/4* **Fennaan (IRE)**[10] 6231 4-9-2 **83**..............................(h) GrahamLee 2 90
(Phillip Makin) *hld up in rr: hdwy over 3f out: sn rdn: wnt 2nd fnl 110yds: styd on towards fin: nvr really able to chal wnr* **7/2[2]**

0053 **3** *3/4* **Garden Oasis**[10] 6231 4-8-7 **74**.............................. RachelRichardson 4 79
(Tim Easterby) *chsd ldrs: rdn over 2f out: sn trying to chal: edgd rt over 1f out and unable qck: styd on same pce ins fnl f* **15/2**

0505 **4** *3* **Sands Chorus**[22] 5741 7-8-3 **70**..............................(p) LukeMorris 1 69
(Scott Dixon) *wnt to post early: led: rdn 3f out: hdd 2f out: nt pce of ldrs over 1f out: no ex ins fnl f* **6/1[3]**

2500 **5** *2 1/2* **Aiya (IRE)**[24] 5667 4-8-11 **78**..............................(h) DavidAllan 7 73
(Tim Easterby) *racd keenly: chsd ldrs: wnt 2nd over 4f out: rdn 3f out: ev ch over 2f out: wknd over 1f out* **6/1[3]**

0230 **6** *4 1/2* **Dawaaleeb (USA)**[21] 5776 5-9-6 **87**.............................. LewisEdmunds 5 73
(Les Eyre) *midfield: rdn and lost pl over 3f out: n.d after (jockey said gelding was never travelling)* **13/2**

1100 **7** *2* **Mulligatawny (IRE)**[24] 5657 6-9-2 **88**..............................(p) BenSanderson(5) 3 70
(Roger Fell) *chsd ldr tl over 4f out: rdn 3f out: wknd over 2f out* **16/1**

2m 0.84s (-3.76) **Going Correction** -0.25s/f (Firm) **7** Ran SP% **112.5**
Speed ratings (Par 107): **105,104,103,101,99 95,94**
CSF £9.85 TOTE £3.10: £1.60, £2.30; EX 11.40 Trifecta £57.40.
Owner Mrs Shirley France **Bred** P Balding **Trained** Middleham, N Yorks

FOCUS
The principals came clear off a solid pace in this fair handicap. It's been rated around the first three, with the third near his recent best.

6581 WATCH SKY SPORTS RACING IN HD H'CAP 6f
4:05 (4:05) (Class 4) (0-85,87) 4-Y-O+
£5,692 (£1,694; £846; £423; £300; £300) Stalls High

Form RPR

0003 **1** **Gullane One (IRE)**[22] 5723 4-8-2 **66**..............................(p) RachelRichardson 10 72
(Tim Easterby) *mde all: rdn over 1f out: r.o gamely whn pressed: kpt finding nr fin* **14/1**

5111 **2** *nk* **Betsey Trotter (IRE)**[17] 5972 4-9-9 **87**..............................(p) DanielTudhope 7 92
(David O'Meara) *chsd wnr: rdn and chalng over 1f out: r.o ins fnl f: jst hld* **7/2[2]**

5000 **3** *hd* **Brian The Snail (IRE)**[10] 6227 5-9-7 **85**.............................. TonyHamilton 9 90
(Richard Fahey) *chsd ldrs: rdn over 2f out: r.o u.p ins fnl f: clsd towards fin* **6/1**

145 **4** *1 1/4* **Equiano Springs**[32] 5395 5-9-2 **80**.............................. GrahamLee 4 81+
(Tom Tate) *wnt to post early: in rr: pushed along over 3f out: rdn and hdwy over 1f out: styd on u.p fnl 100yds: nvr able to chal ldrs* **5/2[1]**

0605 **5** *3 1/4* **Buccaneers Vault (IRE)**[10] 6220 7-8-0 **67**.............................. JaneElliott(3) 6 58
(Paul Midgley) *in tch: rdn over 2f out: one pce fr over 1f out: no imp after* **11/2[3]**

2004 **6** *3/4* **Upstaging**[22] 5740 7-8-11 **75**.............................. BarryMcHugh 8 64
(Noel Wilson) *hld up: pushed along 1/2-way: nvr able to trble ldrs* **22/1**

5405 **7** *1 3/4* **Pipers Note**[22] 5740 9-9-5 **83**.............................. JackGarritty 1 67
(Ruth Carr) *chsd ldrs: rdn over 2f out: wknd ins fnl f* **8/1**

0-04 **8** *9* **Big Les (IRE)**[30] 5476 4-9-4 **82**.............................. LukeMorris 2 39
(Karen McLintock) *nvr bttr than midfield: pushed along 4f out: wknd 2f out: lame (vet said gelding finished lame right fore)* **8/1**

1m 10.27s (-2.23) **Going Correction** -0.25s/f (Firm) **8** Ran SP% **113.7**
Speed ratings (Par 105): **104,103,103,101,97 96,94,82**
CSF £61.87 CT £331.39 TOTE £16.00: £3.50, £2.00, £1.30; EX 76.40 Trifecta £454.00.
Owner Mount Pleasant Racing **Bred** E Phelan & Dream Ahead Syndicate **Trained** Great Habton, N Yorks

FOCUS
Not a bad sprint handicap. Again the stands' side was favoured. It's been rated as straightforward form, with the second to her recent form.

6582 WATCH FREE RACE REPLAYS ON ATTHERACES.COM H'CAP 1m
4:35 (4:35) (Class 5) (0-75,75) 3-Y-O+
£3,752 (£1,116; £557; £300; £300; £300) Stalls Low

Form RPR

4000 **1** **Flying Raconteur**[10] 6204 5-9-1 **63**..............................(t) LewisEdmunds 7 73
(Nigel Tinkler) *hld up in midfield: hdwy 3f out: rdn to ld narrowly 1f out: r.o gamely: asserted nr fin* **13/2[3]**

1136 **2** *1* **Salam Zayed**[27] 5557 3-9-3 **71**.............................. PaulHanagan 2 78
(Richard Fahey) *trckd ldrs: effrt over 3f out: ev ch over 1f out: str chal ins fnl f: r.o u.p: no ex towards fin* **5/1[2]**

3320 **3** *2* **Morning Duel (IRE)**[24] 5690 3-9-7 **75**..............................(t) DanielTudhope 1 77
(David O'Meara) *led: rdn 2f out: hdd 1f out: stl there ins fnl f: no ex fnl 100yds* **4/1[1]**

6505 **4** *1 1/2* **Curfewed (IRE)**[6] 6342 3-8-10 **64**..............................(p) LukeMorris 4 63
(Tracy Waggott) *trckd ldrs: rdn and lost pl over 3f out: rallied 2f out: edgd lft ins fnl f: kpt on u.p: nvr able to chal* **14/1**

5543 **5** *2 3/4* **Zafaranah (USA)**[15] 6025 5-9-5 **67**.............................. RobHornby 9 60
(Pam Sly) *hld up: hdwy over 3f out: rdn to chse ldrs over 2f out: hung rt ins fnl f: kpt on same pce* **4/1[1]**

500- **6** *hd* **Shouranour (IRE)**[339] 7522 9-8-11 **62**..............................(p) ConorMcGovern(3) 5 55
(Peter Niven) *in tch: hdwy over 3f out: rdn to chse ldrs over 2f out: kpt on same pce ins fnl f* **16/1**

5664 **7** *1/2* **Abushamah (IRE)**[12] 6103 8-9-0 **62**.............................. JackGarritty 6 54
(Ruth Carr) *w ldr tl rdn wl over 2f out: hung rt and wknd over 1f out* **10/1**

5206 **8** *5* **Diviner (IRE)**[25] 5619 3-8-8 **65**.............................. JaneElliott(3) 3 44
(Mark Johnston) *no bttr than midfield: niggled along 6f out: pushed along and outpcd over 3f out: n.d after* **20/1**

6000 **9** *4* **New Look (FR)**[22] 5726 4-9-8 **70**..............................(p) DavidAllan 8 41
(Tim Easterby) *hld up in rr: swtchd lft and pushed along over 4f out: nvr able to get on terms w ldrs* **9/1**

3365 **10** *1 1/2* **Roller**[20] 5804 6-9-9 **71**..............................(p) ShaneGray 10 39
(Mark Loughnane) *hld up in rr: pushed along over 3f out: nvr a threat (jockey said gelding boiled over in preliminaries)* **10/1**

1m 37.31s (-3.69) **Going Correction** -0.25s/f (Firm)
WFA 3 from 4yo+ 6lb **10** Ran SP% **115.5**
Speed ratings (Par 103): **108,107,105,103,100 100,100,95,91,89**
CSF £38.62 CT £150.21 TOTE £7.40: £2.20, £1.60, £1.20; EX 49.40 Trifecta £565.10.
Owner David Aarons **Bred** Jocelyn Targett **Trained** Langton, N Yorks

FOCUS
This wide-open looking handicap was run at a brisk pace.

6583 SKY SPORTS RACING ON SKY 415 STAYERS H'CAP 2m
5:05 (5:07) (Class 6) (0-65,67) 3-Y-O+ £3,105 (£924; £461; £300; £300) Stalls High

Form RPR

1101 **1** **Clearance**[17] 5939 5-9-13 **60**.............................. GrahamLee 4 69+
(Iain Jardine) *a.p: wnt 2nd over 5f out: led narrowly on bit 3f out: a travelling strly and confidently rdn: shkn up ins fnl f: easily* **1/1[1]**

5300 **2** *2 1/4* **Buyer Beware (IRE)**[29] 5487 7-10-0 **61**..............................(v[1]) DanielTudhope 2 66
(Liam Bailey) *led: hdd narrowly 3f out: sn rdn and a fighting losing battle: styd on same pce ins fnl f and no ch w wnr* **3/1[2]**

-066 **3** *5* **Rockliffe**[21] 5766 6-8-12 **45**.............................. PaulHanagan 3 44
(Micky Hammond) *hld up in rr: rdn and hdwy 4f out: chsd ldrs after: kpt on u.p fnl 3f: no further imp fnl 100yds (jockey said gelding lost right hind shoe)* **11/1**

343- **4** *16* **Uptown Funk (IRE)**[10] 4067 5-10-6 **67**..............................(p) ShaneGray 6 47
(Keith Dalgleish) *chsd ldr after 2f tl rdn over 5f out: drvn over 4f out: sn wknd: eased whn wl btn fnl f* **4/1[3]**

003 **5** *39* **Simul Amicis**[47] 4818 3-8-3 **48** ow3.............................. NathanEvans 5
(Dianne Sayer) *racd keenly: prom: stdd after 2f: hld up: rdn 5f out: wknd over 3f out: eased whn wl btn fnl f: t.o* **14/1**

3m 29.72s (-2.68) **Going Correction** -0.25s/f (Firm)
WFA 3 from 4yo+ 12lb **5** Ran SP% **110.0**
Speed ratings (Par 101): **96,94,92,84,64**
CSF £4.23 TOTE £1.80: £1.10, £1.80; EX 4.60 Trifecta £15.70.
Owner Kildonan Gold Racing 2 & Partner **Bred** Richard W Farleigh **Trained** Carrutherstown, D'fries & G'way

FOCUS
They finished strung out in this staying handicap and the market got it right.
T/Plt: £25.50 to a £1 stake. Pool: £65,847.12 - 1,878.66 winning units T/Qpdt: £10.90 to a £1 stake. Pool: £4,532.95 - 307.35 winning units **Darren Owen**

6520 DEAUVILLE (R-H)
Tuesday, August 27
OFFICIAL GOING: Polytrack: standard

6584a PRIX DINAROBIN BEACHCOMBER GOLF RESORT & SPA (CLAIMER) (2YO) (POLYTRACK) 6f 110y(P)
4:10 2-Y-O £10,360 (£4,144; £3,108; £2,072; £1,036)

RPR

1 **Coronado Beach**[17] 2-9-5 0 ow1.............................. TheoBachelot 6 80
(A Giorgi, Italy) **107/10**

2 *2* **Lalacelle (FR)**[12] 6141 2-9-0 0 ow1.............................. AurelienLemaitre 5 69
(S Cerulis, France) **5/1[3]**

3 *snk* **White Elusive (FR)**[7] 2-8-13 0 ow2.............................. StephanePasquier 4 68
(F Rossi, France) **18/5[2]**

4 *3 1/2* **Silencious (FR)**[11] 6196 2-8-7 0 ow1.............................. HugoBesnier(5) 7 57
(M Boutin, France) **76/10**

5 *3 1/2* **Abundancia (FR)** 2-9-2 0 ow1.............................. AlexandreGavilan 9 51
(D Guillemin, France) **12/1**

6 *snk* **Get The Look (IRE)**[11] 6196 2-8-9 0 ow1.............................. IoritzMendizabal 3 43
(J S Moore) *towards rr of midfield: rdn 2 1/2f out: minor prog fr 2f out: no ex and kpt on same pce ins fnl f: nvr threatened* **49/1**

7 *3 1/2* **Calippo (IRE)**[17] 5968 2-8-6 0 ow1..............................(p) HollieDoyle(3) 8 34+
(Archie Watson) *bustled along to trck ldr: disp ld bef 1/2-way: sn led: asked to qckn 3f out: hdd jst under 2f out: grad wknd u.p fr over 1f out* **8/5[1]**

The Form Book Flat 2019, Raceform Ltd, Newbury, RG14 5SJ

8 3 1/2 **Butterfly Pose (IRE)**[20] 5794 2-8-7 0 ow1......................(p) AlexisPouchin(5) 10 27
(J S Moore) *in rr: outpcd and pushed along 2 1/2f out: rdn 1 1/2f out: passed btn rivals fr over 1f out: nvr a factor* **36/1**

9 7 **Mehanydream (FR)**[14] 2-9-2 0 ow1........................ SebastienMaillot 1 11
(C Boutin, France) **13/1**

10 4 **Boundless**[69] 2-8-13 0 ow2..................................(p) FabriceVeron 2 +
(E J O'Neill, France) **48/1**

1m 17.55s **10 Ran SP% 118.6**
PARI-MUTUEL (all including 1 euro stake): WIN 11.70; PLACE 3.00, 1.90, 1.90; DF 26.00.
Owner Pietro Sinistri **Bred** Team Hogdala A.B. **Trained** Italy

6271 CATTERICK (L-H)

Wednesday, August 28

OFFICIAL GOING: Good (good to firm in places; 7.9) changing to good after race 1 (2.20)
Wind: light behind Weather: overcast, odd shower

6585 OOPS A DAISY FLORISTS MEDIAN AUCTION MAIDEN STKS 5f
2:20 (2:21) (Class 5) 2-Y-0 **£4,140** (£1,232; £615; £307) **Stalls** Low

Form RPR

0 1 **Romantic Vision (IRE)**[25] 5689 2-9-5 0........................ DanielTudhope 6 69
(Kevin Ryan) *pressed ldr towards outer: rdn along 2f out: drvn ins fnl f: kpt on to ld nr fin* **5/4[1]**

6 2 1/2 **Astrozone**[13] 6096 2-9-0 0.............................. GrahamLee 5 63
(Bryan Smart) *squeezed out sltly s: sn prom: pushed into narrow ld over 1f out: drvn ins fnl f: one pce and hdd towards fin* **7/1**

0025 3 1 1/4 **Ellenor Gray (IRE)**[31] 5472 2-9-0 70.......................... PaulHanagan 1 58
(Richard Fahey) *led narrowly: drvn and hdd over 1f out: kpt on same pce ins fnl f* **3/1[2]**

4 nk **Breguet Boy (IRE)** 2-9-5 0...................................... JasonHart 3 62+
(Keith Dalgleish) *hld up: pushed along and outpcd towards rr 3f out: rdn over 1f out: kpt on wl fnl f: nrst fin* **4/1[3]**

056 5 shd **La Chica Lobo**[16] 6029 2-8-7 49.......................... GavinAshton(7) 4 57
(Lisa Williamson) *wnt rt s: sn chsd ldrs: pushed along and bit outpcd 2f out: rdn and kpt on ins fnl f* **50/1**

00 6 7 **Norton Lad**[12] 6175 2-9-5 0........................... RachelRichardson 8 36
(Tim Easterby) *hld up: pushed along over 2f out: wknd over 1f out* **40/1**

7 4 **Max L (IRE)** 2-9-5 0...................................... PaulMulrennan 2 22
(Alistair Whillans) *s.i.s: a in rr* **16/1**

1m 1.05s (0.55) **Going Correction** +0.30s/f (Good) **7 Ran SP% 112.2**
Speed ratings (Par 94): **107,106,104,103,103 92,85**
CSF £10.56 TOTE £2.20: £1.90, £1.70; EX 13.30 Trifecta £23.70.
Owner Roger Peel & Clipper Logistics **Bred** Messrs J, R & J Hyland **Trained** Hambleton, N Yorks

FOCUS
The bend into home straight was dolled out 3yds, while the rail in back the straight from 6f moved out 2yds, and rail in home straight moved out 3yds. It paid to be handy in this modest 2yo maiden. The winner has been rated as improving on his debut.

6586 YORKSHIRE DALES DISTILLERY H'CAP 1m 5f 192y
2:50 (2:50) (Class 5) (0-70,72) 3-Y-0+ **£4,075** (£1,212; £606; £303; £300; £300) **Stalls** Low

Form RPR

4622 1 **Kensington Art**[37] 5242 3-8-9 60.......................(p) PaulHanagan 5 76
(Richard Fahey) *trckd ldr: sn arnd 5 l clr of rest: led wl over 2f out: rdn and sn in command: hung lft fr over 1f out but stl drew further clr* **3/1[2]**

4601 2 16 **Robert Fitzroy (IRE)**[13] 6128 3-9-1 66......................... CliffordLee 6 60
(Michael Bell) *midfield: rdn along 3f out: styd on to go remote 2nd appr fnl f: no ch w wnr* **11/4[1]**

4041 3 3/4 **Stormin Tom (IRE)**[23] 5739 7-9-8 68..................... DannyRedmond(5) 4 59
(Tim Easterby) *midfield: plugged on to go remote 3rd appr fnl f: nvr threatened* **7/2[3]**

6055 4 6 **Maghfoor**[28] 5556 5-8-12 58.............................(p) HarrisonShaw(5) 3 40
(Eric Alston) *hld up in midfield: rdn along 3f out: nvr threatened* **9/2**

000 5 3 1/2 **Midnight Warrior**[35] 5301 9-8-4 50 oh5......................(t) PaulaMuir(5) 8 27
(Ron Barr) *chsd clr ldng pair: rdn over 2f out: wknd over 1f out* **40/1**

00-0 6 1 1/4 **Paris Protocol**[188] 272 6-10-0 69........................ DougieCostello 2 45
(Mark Walford) *hld up: rdn along 4f out: sn btn* **25/1**

5150 7 nk **Ninepin Bowler**[12] 6180 5-9-4 59.......................... DanielTudhope 7 34
(Ann Duffield) *led: rdn along and hdd wl over 2f out: wknd over 1f out* **9/1**

-040 8 74 **Moving Forward (IRE)**[20] 5849 4-10-3 72....................(p[1]) PaulMulrennan 1
(Tony Coyle) *a in rr: eased and t.o fnl 4f (jockey said gelding was never travelling)* **22/1**

3m 6.59s (-1.01) **Going Correction** +0.30s/f (Good) **8 Ran SP% 112.7**
WFA 3 from 4yo+ 10lb
Speed ratings (Par 103): **108,98,98,95,93 92,92,49**
CSF £11.23 CT £28.45 TOTE £3.00: £1.10, £1.30, £2.70; EX 10.50 Trifecta £23.90.
Owner Mrs H Steel **Bred** Mrs H Steel **Trained** Musley Bank, N Yorks

FOCUS
The going was downgraded to good all over after the first, with some jockeys reporting it rode even easier than that. Few landed a blow in this ordinary staying handicap and it's form to treat with some caution. Add 9yds.

6587 SECRET SPA FILLIES' NOVICE STKS 7f 6y
3:20 (3:21) (Class 5) 3-Y-0+ **£4,140** (£1,232; £615; £307) **Stalls** Low

Form RPR

1 **Toronado Queen (IRE)** 3-8-11 0......................... ConnorMurtagh(3) 7 76+
(Richard Fahey) *hld up: pushed along and gd hdwy on outer over 2f out: rdn to ld ins fnl f: edgd lft: kpt on wl to draw clr towards fin* **13/2[3]**

03 2 3 1/4 **Narak**[28] 5554 3-9-0 0.................................. ConnorBeasley 5 67
(George Scott) *led for 2f: prom: rdn to ld again 2f out: drvn and hdd ins fnl f: no ex fnl 75yds* **5/4[1]**

65 3 5 **Friday Fizz (IRE)**[42] 5057 3-9-0 0......................... PaulHanagan 6 54
(Mark Loughnane) *trckd ldrs: led 5f out: rdn and hdd 2f out: wknd appr fnl f* **12/1**

5 4 1 **Loveheart**[8] 6316 3-9-0 0............................... DanielTudhope 4 51
(Michael Bell) *trckd ldrs: rdn 2f out: wknd appr fnl f* **7/4[2]**

5 1/2 **Calima Calling (IRE)** 3-8-9 0........................ TheodoreLadd(5) 2 49
(Michael Appleby) *dwlt: hld up: pushed along and sme hdwy over 2f out: no ex ins fnl f* **33/1**

-400 6 6 **Farol**[18] 5969 3-9-0 47.......................................(b[1]) GrahamLee 3 33
(James Given) *trckd ldrs: rdn along and lost pl over 2f out: wknd over 1f out* **66/1**

7 3 **Strictly Legal (IRE)** 3-8-9 0........................ RobJFitzpatrick(5) 1 25
(David O'Meara) *dwlt: hld up: rdn over 2f out: sn wknd* **18/1**

1m 29.72s (2.32) **Going Correction** +0.30s/f (Good) **7 Ran SP% 111.5**
Speed ratings (Par 100): **98,94,88,87,86 80,76**
CSF £14.35 TOTE £4.60: £1.90, £1.50; EX 13.80 Trifecta £89.70.
Owner Richard Fahey Ebor Racing Club Ltd **Bred** Deer Forest Stud **Trained** Musley Bank, N Yorks

FOCUS
The went a solid pace in this 3yo run-of-the-mill fillies' novice contest. Add 9yds. The third and the time suggest the bare form is limited.

6588 ERNEST NORRIS (1919-1992) MEMORIAL H'CAP 7f 6y
3:50 (3:50) (Class 4) (0-85,87) 3-Y-0+ **£6,080** (£1,809; £904; £452; £300; £300) **Stalls** Low

Form RPR

4534 1 **Sparklealot (IRE)**[32] 5459 3-9-2 81.......................(p) TrevorWhelan 9 92
(Ivan Furtado) *mde all: pushed along over 2f out: rdn over 1f out: kpt on wl* **6/1**

0660 2 1 3/4 **Parys Mountain (IRE)**[25] 5692 5-8-12 77..............(t) DannyRedmond(5) 4 85
(Tim Easterby) *hld up: pushed along and hdwy on outer over 2f out: rdn to chse ldr over 1f out: kpt on* **13/2**

3313 3 2 **Luis Vaz De Torres (IRE)**[16] 6014 7-9-6 80..................... PaulHanagan 8 83
(Richard Fahey) *midfield: chsd ldr 3f out: rdn over 2f out: no ex fnl 110yds* **4/1[2]**

0002 4 2 **Fuente**[16] 6015 3-9-3 82................................... JasonHart 1 77
(Keith Dalgleish) *in tch: pushed along and lost pl over 2f out: rdn and hdwy to chse appr fnl f: no ex ins fnl f* **5/1**

103 5 2 **Lamloom (IRE)**[37] 5246 5-9-13 87.......................... DanielTudhope 6 79
(David O'Meara) *trckd ldr: racd keenly: rdn over 2f out: wknd fnl f* **7/2[1]**

2420 6 1/2 **Saisons D'Or (IRE)**[37] 5246 4-9-7 81........................ JackGarritty 2 72
(Jedd O'Keeffe) *dwlt: hld up: rdn over 2f out: nvr threatened (jockey said gelding was slowly into stride)* **9/2[3]**

0050 7 4 **Regulator (IRE)**[132] 1880 4-9-3 77.......................(p) RossaRyan 3 57
(Alexandra Dunn) *prom: hung lft and lost pl on bnd over 2f out: wknd over 1f out (jockey said gelding stumbled coming off the final bend)* **25/1**

0650 8 11 **Ower Fly**[21] 5821 6-9-3 77................................ JamesSullivan 5 27
(Ruth Carr) *s.i.s: a in rr (jockey said gelding was never travelling)* **20/1**

1m 28.92s (1.52) **Going Correction** +0.30s/f (Good) **8 Ran SP% 113.3**
WFA 3 from 4yo+ 5lb
Speed ratings (Par 105): **103,101,98,96,94 93,89,76**
CSF £43.47 CT £174.30 TOTE £4.90: £1.50, £3.00, £1.20; EX 38.70 Trifecta £119.80.
Owner John Marriott **Bred** Lynnlodge Stud & Arthur Finnan **Trained** Wiseton, Nottinghamshire

FOCUS
An open-looking handicap and predictably it was frantically run. Add 9yds. A pb from the winner, and the ratings might have to go up.

6589 LA FILLE ROUGE H'CAP (A QUALIFIER FOR THE CATTERICK TWELVE FURLONG SERIES FINAL) 1m 4f 13y
4:20 (4:20) (Class 4) (0-85,77) 3-Y-0 **£6,080** (£1,809; £904; £452) **Stalls** Centre

Form RPR

3211 1 **Euro Implosion (IRE)**[11] 6232 3-9-2 72........................ GrahamLee 5 78+
(Keith Dalgleish) *trckd ldr in 2nd: pushed along to chal over 2f out: led narrowly over 1f out: sn drvn: asserted 1f out: hld on towards fin* **11/4[2]**

333 2 1/2 **Dante's View (IRE)**[53] 4636 3-9-7 77..................(v[1]) DanielTudhope 4 82
(Sir Michael Stoute) *in tch in 3rd: pushed along to chse ldng pair over 2f out: swtchd rt 2f out: hrd drvn over 1f out: looked bit awkward: styd on towards fin* **2/1[1]**

3443 3 1/2 **Fantastic Ms Fox**[14] 6068 3-8-7 63......................... PaulHanagan 1 67
(Richard Fahey) *hld up in tch in 4th: rdn along and outpcd over 2f out: drvn and styd on fnl f (jockey said filly stumbled shortly after the crossing in the back straight)* **7/2[3]**

3123 4 2 **Conundrum**[44] 4988 3-9-7 77............................... JackGarritty 2 78
(Jedd O'Keeffe) *led: rdn along and pressed over 2f out: hdd over 1f out: no ex ins fnl f* **11/4[2]**

2m 45.91s (5.31) **Going Correction** +0.30s/f (Good) **4 Ran SP% 108.9**
Speed ratings (Par 102): **94,93,93,92**
CSF £8.54 TOTE £2.80; EX 5.60 Trifecta £12.80.
Owner J S Morrison **Bred** Aaron Boland **Trained** Carluke, S Lanarks

FOCUS
This tight 3yo handicap proved a tactical affair. Add 9yds. The third helps set the level.

6590 BLACK BULL INN MOULTON H'CAP 5f 212y
4:55 (4:59) (Class 6) (0-60,58) 3-Y-0+ **£3,105** (£924; £461; £300; £300; £300) **Stalls** Low

Form RPR

0103 1 **Someone Exciting**[22] 5768 6-8-11 53..................... HarrisonShaw(5) 8 60
(David Thompson) *hld up: rdn and hdwy on outer over 1f out: led 110yds out: kpt on* **11/2[2]**

054 2 3/4 **Nifty Niece (IRE)**[4] 6462 5-8-10 47 ow2.................... ConnorBeasley 11 52
(Ann Duffield) *s.i.s: hld up in rr: rdn and hdwy on outside over 1f out: r.o fnl f* **9/1**

5040 3 3/4 **Vallarta (IRE)**[28] 5559 9-8-9 46.......................... JamesSullivan 7 49
(Ruth Carr) *led: rdn and strly pressed over 1f out: hdd 110yds out: one pce* **7/1[3]**

2602 4 nse **Isabella Ruby**[16] 6013 4-8-1 45.......................(h) GavinAshton(7) 1 47
(Lisa Williamson) *dwlt: midfield on inner: pushed along and hdwy over 1f out: ev ch 1f out: kpt on* **14/1**

2020 5 1/2 **Mightaswellsmile**[9] 6275 5-8-4 46........................ PaulaMuir(5) 12 47
(Ron Barr) *chsd ldr on outer: rdn over 2f out: chal strly over 1f out: one pce ins fnl f* **7/1[3]**

4303 6 1 1/2 **Spirit Of Zebedee (IRE)**[9] 6273 6-8-11 48....................(v) JasonHart 2 44
(John Quinn) *prom: rdn over 2f out: no ex fnl 110yds* **3/1[1]**

5004 7 nk **Groupie**[16] 6025 5-9-5 56................................ GrahamLee 5 51
(Tom Tate) *chsd ldrs: rdn over 2f out: no ex fnl 110yds* **11/2[2]**

2430 8 2 1/2 **Extrasolar**[35] 5300 9-9-1 57...........................(t) BenSanderson(5) 6 45
(Geoffrey Harker) *hld up in midfield: rdn over 2f out: nvr threatened* **8/1**

0351 9 1 1/4 **Seamster**[16] 6017 12-9-2 58.......................(t) ThomasGreatrex(5) 3 42
(David Loughnane) *midfield: rdn 2f out: wknd ins fnl f* **14/1**

000 10 17 **Lambrini Lullaby**[39] 5181 4-8-5 45.....................(v[1]) ConnorMurtagh(3) 9
(Lisa Williamson) *prom: rdn over 2f out: wknd over 1f out* **50/1**

1m 15.8s (2.20) **Going Correction** +0.30s/f (Good) **10 Ran SP% 117.2**
WFA 3 from 4yo+ 3lb
Speed ratings (Par 101): **97,96,95,94,94 92,91,88,86,64**
CSF £54.47 CT £353.37 TOTE £7.30: £2.40, £2.60, £2.60; EX 61.30 Trifecta £517.10.
Owner Jordan Souster **Bred** Trebles Holford Farm Thoroughbreds **Trained** Bolam, Co Durham

FOCUS
A weak sprint handicap in which the main action developed down the centre. Add 9yds.

6591 MILLBRY HILL COUNTRY STORE H'CAP 5f 212y
5:25 (5:26) (Class 5) (0-75,75) 3-Y-O+
£4,075 (£1,212; £606; £303; £300; £300) Stalls Low

Form RPR
0-02 1 **Six Strings**[225] 249 5-9-9 **74**.. AlistairRawlinson 7 85
(Michael Appleby) *midfield: rdn and hdwy over 1f out: kpt on to ld fnl 75yds* 4/1[2]
3061 2 2 ¾ **Redrosezorro**[23] 5723 5-9-0 **70**........................(h) HarrisonShaw(5) 4 73
(Eric Alston) *led: rdn 3 l clr 2f out: reduced advantage ins fnl f: hdd 75yds out: no ex* 11/4[1]
0235 3 hd **Amazing Grazing (IRE)**[34] 5330 5-9-2 **67**..................(p[1]) PhilDennis 12 69
(Rebecca Bastiman) *midfield on outside: rdn over 2f out: kpt on ins fnl f* 14/1
0623 4 ½ **Woodside Wonder**[26] 5619 3-9-6 **74**........................(v) GrahamLee 10 75
(Keith Dalgleish) *slowly away: outpcd in rr tl kpt on fnl f* 16/1
0662 5 1 ¼ **Rose Marmara**[42] 5040 6-8-13 **67**........................(tp) ConnorMurtagh(3) 9 64
(Brian Rothwell) *chsd ldrs: rdn over 2f out: no ex ins fnl f* 25/1
3062 6 ½ **Lucky Beggar (IRE)**[6] 6373 9-9-1 **66**........................ ConnorBeasley 8 61
(David C Griffiths) *hld up in midfield: rdn over 2f out: one pce fnl f: nvr threatened* 15/2
2504 7 shd **Spirit Of Wedza (IRE)**[32] 5444 7-9-0 **72**...................... VictorSantos(7) 2 67
(Julie Camacho) *hld up: rdn over 2f out: kpt on fnl f: nvr threatened* 20/1
2354 8 shd **Indian Pursuit (IRE)**[19] 5892 6-8-12 **63**........................(v) JasonHart 11 58
(John Quinn) *midfield: rdn and sme hdwy on outer 2f out: no ex fnl 110yds* 12/1
0542 9 4 ½ **Naadirr (IRE)**[7] 6335 8-9-8 **73**........................(v) DougieCostello 5 54
(Kevin Ryan) *dwlt: hld up: nvr threatened* 10/1
43 10 1 ¾ **That's Not Me (IRE)**[12] 6162 3-9-3 **71**........................ RobbieDowney 6 47
(Anthony McCann, Ire) *chsd ldr: rdn over 2f out: wknd fnl f (jockey said filly hung right)* 5/1[3]
5000 11 3 ¼ **Almurr (IRE)**[10] 6260 3-9-7 **75**........................(h) PaulMulrennan 1 41
(Phillip Makin) *chsd ldr: rdn over 2f out: wknd over 1f out* 33/1

1m 15.54s (1.94) **Going Correction** +0.30s/f (Good)
WFA 3 from 4yo+ 3lb **11 Ran SP% 116.0**
Speed ratings (Par 103): **99,95,95,94,92 92,91,91,85,83 79**
CSF £14.73 CT £142.02 TOTE £4.60: £1.60, £1.60, £4.00; EX 17.80 Trifecta £251.30.
Owner S & R Racing Partnership **Bred** Andrew W Robson **Trained** Oakham, Rutland

FOCUS
They went hard early on in this modest sprint handicap. Again the far side was shunned. Add 9yds. The winner has been rated back to last year's best.
T/Plt: £115.40 to a £1 stake. Pool: £43,945.30 - 277.81 winning units T/Qpdt: £45.30 to a £1 stake. Pool: £3,937.24 - 64.22 winning units **Andrew Sheret**

6344 KEMPTON (A.W) (R-H)
Wednesday, August 28
OFFICIAL GOING: Polytrack: standard to slow (watered)
Wind: Moderate, across (away from stands) Weather: Fine but cloudy, warm

6592 BRITISH STALLION STUDS EBF FILLIES' NOVICE STKS (PLUS 10 RACE) 1m (P)
5:55 (5:57) (Class 5) 2-Y-O
£3,881 (£1,155; £577; £288) Stalls Low

Form RPR
34 1 **Run Wild (GER)**[23] 5733 2-9-0 0........................ OisinMurphy 2 91+
(John Gosden) *trckd ldng pair: clsd qckly to ld over 1f out: pushed along and drew rt away: impressive* 9/2[3]
3 2 6 **Tanita**[23] 5733 2-9-0 0........................ RyanMoore 6 77
(Sir Michael Stoute) *trckd ldr: led jst over 2f out and sent for home: hdd over 1f out and swiftly outpcd by wnr* 10/11[1]
4 3 2 **Virgin Snow**[39] 5170 2-9-0 0........................ JimCrowley 4 73
(Ed Dunlop) *chsd ldrs: shkn up and outpcd 2f out: kpt on steadily to take modest 3rd fnl f* 14/1
3 4 1 ¼ **National Treasure (IRE)**[40] 5139 2-9-0 0........................ WilliamBuick 11 70
(Charlie Appleby) *prom on outer: rdn and outpcd over 2f out: kpt on to press for modest 3rd fnl f: one pce last 100yds* 5/2[2]
5 3 ½ **Night Colours (IRE)** 2-9-0 0........................ PatCosgrave 8 62
(Simon Crisford) *in tch in midfield but rn green and pushed along: outpcd over 2f out: kpt on to take modest 5th ins fnl f* 20/1
6 4 **Royal Nation** 2-9-0 0........................ HollieDoyle 7 52
(Archie Watson) *led to jst over 2f out: wknd rapidly over 1f out* 25/1
66 7 3 ½ **Divine Connection**[34] 5342 2-9-0 0........................ RobHornby 12 44
(Jonathan Portman) *chsd ldrs on outer: rdn and wknd over 2f out* 66/1
00 8 2 **Prestigious (IRE)**[23] 5732 2-8-7 0........................ KateLeahy(7) 9 40
(Archie Watson) *sn off the pce in last quartet: pushed along over 2f out: nvr any ch but kpt on* 100/1
40 9 nk **Impression**[33] 5387 2-9-0 0........................ GeorgeWood 5 39
(Amy Murphy) *in tch in midfield: rdn 3f out: wknd 2f out* 100/1
10 9 **Nurse Finch (FR)** 2-9-0 0........................ DavidProbert 10 18
(Andrew Balding) *s.i.s: a wl bhd in last quartet* 50/1
0 11 3 ½ **Alsukar**[17] 5992 2-9-0 0........................ MartinDwyer 3
(Dean Ivory) *a wl in rr: bhd fr 1/2-way* 100/1
0 12 32 **Hot News (IRE)**[34] 5342 2-8-13 0 ow2........................(h[1]) GaryMahon(3) 1
(Sylvester Kirk) *taken down early and mounted at post: a in rr: last and tailing off sn after 1/2-way* 100/1

1m 38.93s (-0.87) **Going Correction** +0.05s/f (Slow) **12 Ran SP% 121.8**
Speed ratings (Par 91): **106,100,98,96,93 89,85,83,83,74 70,38**
CSF £8.97 TOTE £6.50: £1.40, £1.02, £3.00; EX 12.20 Trifecta £70.60.
Owner Tweenhills Fillies & Merdian Int **Bred** R Kredel **Trained** Newmarket, Suffolk

FOCUS
An impressive performance from the winner, who pulled clear to win by a good margin. She deserves a crack at something better now. The time was very similar to that recorded by the winner of the 0-80 handicap for 3yos that followed. It's been rated at something like face value around the second and third.

6593 32RED.COM H'CAP (LONDON MILE SERIES QUALIFIER) 1m (P)
6:25 (6:25) (Class 4) (0-80,81) 3-Y-O
£6,469 (£1,925; £962; £481; £300; £300) Stalls Low

Form RPR
261 1 **Image Of The Moon**[14] 6075 3-8-11 **73**........................(p) CierenFallon(5) 3 80
(Shaun Keightley) *trckd ldrs: wnt 2nd over 3f out: shkn up to ld jst over 2f out: clr over 1f out: rdn out* 4/1[3]
1546 2 1 ¼ **City Tour**[20] 5863 3-9-2 **73**........................ RichardKingscote 2 77
(Lydia Richards) *racd in last pair: urged along over 3f out: prog 2f out: rdn to take 2nd jst over 1f out: grad clsd on wnr but nvr able to chal* 33/1
5523 3 2 ¾ **Mums Hope**[30] 5505 3-9-6 **77**........................ OisinMurphy 5 75
(Hughie Morrison) *hld up in last pair: prog over 2f out: rdn to dispute 2nd briefly over 1f out: one pce after* 6/4[1]
6220 4 4 ½ **Fares Poet (IRE)**[16] 6026 3-9-5 **76**........................(h) ShaneKelly 4 63
(Marco Botti) *led 3f: lost pl and outpcd over 2f out: no ch after* 6/1
5140 5 nk **Tipperary Jack (USA)**[14] 6076 3-9-10 **81**........................(v[1]) KierenFox 6 68
(John Best) *t.k.h: swift prog fr rr to join ldr over 6f out: led 5f out: hdd jst over 2f out: sn wknd (jockey said colt ran too free)* 3/1[2]
1100 6 20 **Renegade Master**[65] 4188 3-9-10 **81**........................ PatCosgrave 1 22
(George Baker) *chsd ldr to over 6f out: rdn 1/2-way: sn btn: eased 2f out: t.o* 8/1

1m 38.96s (-0.84) **Going Correction** +0.05s/f (Slow) **6 Ran SP% 113.3**
Speed ratings (Par 102): **106,104,102,97,97 77**
CSF £92.96 TOTE £3.80: £1.30, £9.60; EX 92.80 Trifecta £212.70.
Owner Simon Lockyer & Tim Clarke **Bred** Natton House Thoroughbreds **Trained** Newmarket, Suffolk

FOCUS
A fair handicap, run in a similar time to the preceding novice for 2yo fillies. The second has been rated in keeping with this year's best.

6594 32RED CASINO MAIDEN STKS 7f (P)
6:55 (6:59) (Class 5) 3-Y-O+
£3,881 (£1,155; £577; £288) Stalls Low

Form RPR
04 1 **Bear Force One**[58] 4452 3-9-5 0........................ JasonWatson 3 81
(Roger Teal) *trckd ldrs: shkn up and prog over 2f out: chsd ldr over 1f out: styd on wl to ld last 75yds: readily* 10/1
36- 2 1 ¼ **Normal Norman**[169] 6818 5-9-5 0........................ CierenFallon(5) 12 80
(John Ryan) *hld up in rr: prog on outer 4f out: shkn up over 2f out: hdwy to take 3rd jst over 1f out: styd on to take 2nd last stride* 6/1[3]
30 3 nse **Zahee (IRE)**[25] 5650 4-9-10 0........................ OisinMurphy 14 80
(Saeed bin Suroor) *sn trckd ldr: led over 2f out and sent for home: rdn over 1f out: idled and hdd last 75yds: lost 2nd post (vet said colt lost right-fore shoe)* 7/2[2]
3 4 7 **Khabeerah**[21] 5808 3-9-0 0........................ JimCrowley 7 55
(Roger Varian) *trckd ldrs: rdn and nt qckn over 2f out: sn lft bhd and btn* 1/2[1]
03 5 2 ¼ **Itmakesyouthink**[12] 6177 5-9-10 0........................(h) RichardKingscote 11 56
(Mark Loughnane) *hld up in last trio: stl there over 2f out: pushed along and kpt on steadily after: nvr nrr and signs of promise* 50/1
6- 6 4 ½ **Doubly Beautiful (IRE)**[306] 8606 3-9-5 0........................ PatCosgrave 9 42
(Ed de Giles) *mde most to over 2f out: wknd qckly over 1f out (jockey said gelding ran too free)* 25/1
6-5 7 3 ¼ **Sephira Park**[34] 5336 4-9-5 0........................ GeorgeWood 6 31
(Chris Wall) *nvr beyond midfield: wl outpcd over 2f out: no ch after* 100/1
0 8 1 ¾ **Can I Kick It (IRE)**[25] 5650 3-9-0 0........................ CallumShepherd 2 24
(Stuart Williams) *nvr beyond midfield: shkn up over 2f out: sn lft bhd* 100/1
9 7 **Jane Camille** 3-9-0 0........................ CharlesBishop 5
(Peter Hedger) *towards rr: shkn up and no prog wl over 2f out: wknd* 33/1
60 10 1 **Ewell Spring**[14] 6074 3-9-0 0........................ ShaneKelly 1
(Brett Johnson) *prom tl wknd rapidly over 2f out* 100/1
0 11 2 **Reigning Ice**[32] 5428 3-9-0 0........................ HectorCrouch 10
(Clive Cox) *reluctant to enter stall: a in last trio: bhd fnl 2f* 25/1
00 12 1 **Noverre Dancer (IRE)**[9] 6283 3-9-2 0........................ DarraghKeenan(3) 8
(Nick Littmoden) *hld up in last trio: lost tch over 2f out: sn bhd* 100/1

1m 26.57s (0.57) **Going Correction** +0.05s/f (Slow)
WFA 3 from 4yo+ 5lb **12 Ran SP% 128.8**
Speed ratings (Par 103): **98,96,96,88,85 80,77,75,67,65 63,62**
CSF £71.38 TOTE £16.80: £4.70, £1.80, £2.10; EX 82.00 Trifecta £407.00.
Owner Joe Bear Racing **Bred** S M Ransom **Trained** Lambourn, Berks

FOCUS
With the favourite disappointing and the second-favourite having plenty of use made of him, this didn't take a great deal of winning. It's been rated at something like face value.

6595 100% PROFIT BOOST AT 32REDSPORT.COM FILLIES' H'CAP 1m 3f 219y(P)
7:25 (7:29) (Class 5) (0-70,71) 3-Y-O+
£3,752 (£1,116; £557; £300; £300; £300) Stalls Low

Form RPR
0504 1 **Hermosura**[6] 6367 3-9-5 **65**........................(b[1]) HarryBentley 6 76+
(Ralph Beckett) *mde all and allowed to dictate mod pce to 4f out: drvn over 2f out and sn clr: in n.d over 1f out: pushed out after* 7/1[3]
564 2 3 ¾ **Vibrance**[21] 5810 3-9-7 **67**........................ OisinMurphy 2 74+
(James Fanshawe) *hld up but cl up: urged along wl over 2f out and sn outpcd: prog to take modest 2nd jst ins fnl f: styd on but no ch w wnr* 10/11[1]
0504 3 4 **Sibylline**[35] 5287 3-8-6 **52**........................ LukeMorris 5 51
(David Simcock) *sn trckd wnr: urged along whn pce lifted 4f out: lost 2nd over 2f out: wl outpcd after: kpt on u.p* 33/1
4333 4 nse **Swansdown**[26] 5623 3-9-7 **67**........................(p) RyanMoore 4 66
(William Haggas) *cl up: pushed along to chse wnr over 2f out but sn outpcd: lost 2nd and fdd jst ins fnl f* 11/4[2]
054 5 nk **Storm Eleanor**[12] 6187 3-9-5 **65**........................ CharlieBennett 1 63
(Hughie Morrison) *reluctant to enter stall: hld up in last but in tch: outpcd over 2f out: no ch over 1f out: kpt on to press for 3rd nr fin* 8/1
-134 6 12 **Eesha My Flower (USA)**[54] 4599 3-9-4 **71**..........(p) StefanoCherchi(7) 3 50
(Marco Botti) *racd wd: cl up: outpcd over 2f out: sn wknd and bhd* 14/1

2m 36.53s (2.03) **Going Correction** +0.05s/f (Slow) **6 Ran SP% 112.3**
Speed ratings (Par 100): **95,92,89,89,89 81**
CSF £13.96 TOTE £7.20: £2.20, £1.20; EX 18.10 Trifecta £123.30.
Owner Newsells Park Stud **Bred** Newsells Park Stud **Trained** Kimpton, Hants

FOCUS
This was steadily run early on and developed into a dash up the straight. The winner dominated throughout. The third offers some perspective on the level of the form.

6596 32RED ON THE APP STORE H'CAP (LONDON MIDDLE DISTANCE SERIES QUALIFIER) 1m 2f 219y(P)
7:55 (7:57) (Class 4) (0-85,87) 3-Y-O+
£6,469 (£1,925; £962; £481; £300; £300) Stalls Low

Form RPR
1634 1 **Emirates Knight (IRE)**[18] 5973 3-9-5 **84**........................ DavidEgan 2 92
(Roger Varian) *mde all: rdn over 2f out: jnd wl over 1f out: fought on wl fnl f: jst hld on* 2/1[1]

6133 **2** *nse* **Alma Linda**[12] 6186 3-8-7 **72**.....................(p) LukeMorris 4 79
(Sir Mark Prescott Bt) *t.k.h: mostly chsd wnr: urged along 3f out: lost 2nd 2f out: rallied u.p to go 2nd again ins fnl f: clsd nr fin: jst failed* **13/2**

52-0 **3** *1 1/4* **Kitaabaat**[97] 3027 4-9-11 **87**.....................(h[1]) DylanHogan(5) 8 91
(David Simcock) *hld up in last pair: shkn up over 2f out: prog over 1f out: styd on to take 3rd nr fin: too late* **20/1**

6224 **4** *1/2* **Zzoro (IRE)**[11] 6217 6-9-7 **78**..................... JasonWatson 1 81
(Amanda Perrett) *mostly chsd ldng pair: drvn on inner to take 2nd 2f out: upsides wnr wl over 1f out to jst ins fnl f: fdd last 100yds* **10/3**[3]

023- **5** *1* **Sporting Times**[410] 4951 5-9-11 **82**..................... RyanMoore 7 83
(Ed Dunlop) *trckd ldrs: t.k.h after 3f: shkn up over 2f out: nt qckn and nvr able to threaten: one pce over 1f out* **16/1**

3012 **6** *shd* **The Pinto Kid (FR)**[21] 5811 4-9-8 **86**.....................(t) LorenzoAtzori(7) 6 88+
(James Fanshawe) *hld up in last: stl there 2f out as ldrs gng for home: pushed along over 1f out: running on wl but no ch whn rn out of room last strides (jockey said gelding was denied a clear run in closing stages)* **5/2**[2]

2-00 **7** *7* **Maquisard (FR)**[56] 4505 7-9-8 **84**..................... CierenFallon(5) 3 72
(Michael Madgwick) *t.k.h: hld up in tch: shkn up whn appeared to lost action over 2f out: dropped to last over 1f out and eased (jockey said gelding lost its action)* **25/1**

2m 22.26s (1.26) **Going Correction** +0.05s/f (Slow) **7 Ran SP% 112.8**
WFA 3 from 4yo+ 8lb
Speed ratings (Par 105): **100,99,99,98,97 97,92**
CSF £15.22 CT £195.05 TOTE £3.10: £1.70, £2.00; EX 18.20 Trifecta £152.20.
Owner Ziad A Galadari **Bred** Gerard & Anne Corry **Trained** Newmarket, Suffolk

FOCUS
It paid to be up there, and the two 3yos in the race were hard to split at the line. A minor pb from the winner.

6597 32RED H'CAP (JOCKEY CLUB GRASSROOTS FLAT STAYERS SERIES QUALIFIER) 1m 7f 218y(P)
8:25 (8:25) (Class 4) (0-85,82) 3-Y-O **£6,469** (£1,925; £962; £481; £300) **Stalls** Low

Form RPR

1231 **1** **Blame It On Sally (IRE)**[5] 6405 3-8-10 **71** 6ex.....................(v) LukeMorris 1 81
(Sir Mark Prescott Bt) *mde all: rousted passing stands 10f out: stretched on 4f out: drvn for home over 2f out and sn 3 l clr: ld dwindled fnl f but hld on* **11/4**[2]

4253 **2** *nk* **Johnny Kidd**[32] 5452 3-8-11 **72**..................... OisinMurphy 5 82
(Andrew Balding) *trckd wnr: shkn up and nt qckn over 2f out and sn 3 l down: drvn over 1f out: clsd ins fnl f: jst hld* **13/2**

0202 **3** *4 1/2* **Isabella Brant (FR)**[23] 5735 3-9-2 **77**..................... HarryBentley 4 81
(Ralph Beckett) *hld up in 4th: pushed along 4f out: prog to chse ldng pair 2f out and briefly looked a threat: no imp after* **4/1**[3]

0-13 **4** *3* **Baltic Song (IRE)**[26] 5634 3-9-7 **82**..................... RobertHavlin 3 83
(John Gosden) *trckd ldng pair: shkn up and no rspnse over 2f out: sn dropped to 4th and wl btn after* **9/4**[1]

1232 **5** *6* **Smarter (IRE)**[61] 4339 3-9-7 **82**..................... RyanMoore 2 75
(William Haggas) *hld up in last: urged along 4f out: no prog and btn over 2f out: eased* **4/1**[3]

3m 29.8s (-0.30) **Going Correction** +0.05s/f (Slow) **5 Ran SP% 110.8**
Speed ratings (Par 102): **102,101,99,98,95**
CSF £19.48 TOTE £3.90: £1.60, £2.30; EX 16.30 Trifecta £55.30.
Owner Mr & Mrs John Kelsey-Fry **Bred** John Kelsey-Fry **Trained** Newmarket, Suffolk

FOCUS
The third race in a row in which the winner made all, but once again things got tight towards the finish. It's been rated at something like face value.

6598 BET AT RACINGTV.COM H'CAP 6f (P)
8:55 (8:55) (Class 6) (0-65,67) 3-Y-O
£3,105 (£924; £461; £300; £300; £300) **Stalls** Low

Form RPR

-420 **1** **Chil Chil**[70] 4010 3-9-5 **63**.....................(w) OisinMurphy 7 79+
(Andrew Balding) *trckd ldrs: pushed along and prog 2f out: rdn to ld jst ins fnl f: styd on wl and sn clr* **3/1**[1]

6-01 **2** *2 3/4* **Lordsbridge Boy**[26] 5622 3-8-13 **62**..................... SophieRalston(5) 11 69
(Dean Ivory) *led after 100yds: drvn over 1f out: hdd and one pce jst ins fnl f* **12/1**

3155 **3** *nk* **Awa Bomba**[15] 6058 3-9-5 **63**..................... JoeyHaynes 8 69
(Tony Carroll) *chsd ldr after 2f to over 1f out: one pce fnl f* **13/2**

6631 **4** *1 3/4* **Victory Rose**[61] 4328 3-9-8 **66**..................... AndrewElliott 3 66
(Michael Squance) *hld up in rr: rdn on wd outside 2f out: kpt on over 1f out to take 4th nr fin: n.d* **3/1**[1]

3502 **5** *3/4* **Stallone (IRE)**[17] 5985 3-9-8 **66**.....................(v) KieranShoemark 2 64
(Richard Spencer) *in tch: rdn and tried to cl on inner 2f out: one pce and no hdwy fnl f* **4/1**[2]

600 **6** *hd* **Fly The Nest (IRE)**[23] 5750 3-9-5 **63**.....................(h) DavidProbert 1 60
(Tony Carroll) *fast away but hdd after 100yds: chsd ldng pair after 2f: rdn over 2f out: fdd over 1f out* **16/1**

4662 **7** *1/2* **Ricochet (IRE)**[35] 5306 3-9-9 **67**..................... TomMarquand 6 63
(Tom Ward) *nvr bttr than midfield: u.p and no prog over 2f out: n.d after* **6/1**[3]

0060 **8** *2 1/2* **Grandee Daisy**[45] 4959 3-8-7 **58**..................... GeorgiaDobie(7) 10 46
(Ali Stronge) *outpcd in last 1/2-way: no ch after: kpt on fnl f* **50/1**

0-30 **9** *1/2* **Haze**[50] 4763 3-8-9 **58**..................... ScottMcCullagh(5) 5 44
(Sir Mark Todd) *a in rr: shkn up and no prog over 2f out (jockey said filly jumped awkwardly from the stalls)* **25/1**

66-3 **10** *3 3/4* **Catheadans Fiyah**[19] 5890 3-8-12 **56**..................... GeorgeWood 4 30
(Martin Bosley) *plld hrd early: chsd ldrs: clsd 2f out: wknd qckly over 1f out (jockey said filly ran too free)* **16/1**

1m 12.66s (-0.44) **Going Correction** +0.05s/f (Slow) **10 Ran SP% 122.9**
Speed ratings (Par 98): **104,100,99,97,96 96,95,92,91,86**
CSF £43.96 CT £199.16 TOTE £3.70: £1.70, £3.30, £2.70; EX 41.40 Trifecta £303.90.
Owner King Power Racing Co Ltd **Bred** A S Denniff **Trained** Kingsclere, Hants

FOCUS
A modest sprint but won in cosy fashion.

T/Plt: £180.40 to a £1 stake. Pool: £58,125.94 - 235.09 winning units T/Qpdt: £59.60 to a £1 stake. Pool: £6,735.22 - 83.55 winning units **Jonathan Neesom**

6279 LINGFIELD (L-H)
Wednesday, August 28

OFFICIAL GOING: Good to firm (8.4)
Wind: light to medium, half behind Weather: fine, shower race 6

6599 WATCH SKY SPORTS RACING IN HD H'CAP 1m 3f 133y
2:00 (2:03) (Class 6) (0-60,59) 4-Y-O+
£2,781 (£827; £413; £300; £300; £300) **Stalls** High

Form RPR

3205 **1** **Maroon Bells (IRE)**[29] 5528 4-9-7 **59**..................... JasonWatson 10 70+
(David Menuisier) *hld up in tch in midfield: effrt and hdwy to ld over 2f out: in command and pricking ears over 1f out: kpt on: eased towards fin: v comf* **7/2**[2]

3215 **2** *2 1/2* **It's How We Roll (IRE)**[15] 6042 5-8-10 **51**.....................(p) JaneElliott(3) 5 54
(John Spearing) *dwlt: hld up in rr: effrt over 2f out: hdwy u.p over 1f out: styd on wl ins fnl f: wnt 2nd cl home: no ch w wnr (jockey said gelding was never travelling)* **6/1**[3]

1004 **3** *3/4* **Banta Bay**[13] 6115 5-8-12 **50**..................... JosephineGordon 7 52
(John Best) *t.k.h: hld up in tch in midfield: effrt and edgd lft over 2f out: chsd clr wnr over 1f out: kpt on same pce and no imp ins fnl f: lost 2nd cl home* **14/1**

3005 **4** *2* **General Brook (IRE)**[13] 6104 9-8-10 **55**.....................(p) KateLeahy(7) 8 53
(John O'Shea) *taken down early: s.i.s: stdy hdwy on outer to ld 8f out: rdn and hdd over 2f out: 3rd and no ex 1f out: wknd ins fnl f* **10/1**

-000 **5** *2 1/4* **Lady Of York**[156] 1334 5-9-0 **52**..................... JoeyHaynes 12 47
(Chelsea Banham) *taken down early: t.k.h: chsd ldr after 1f tl 8f out: styd chsng ldrs: effrt over 2f out: unable qck over 1f out: wl hld ins fnl f* **9/1**

1104 **6** *1* **Greenview Paradise (IRE)**[36] 5285 5-9-0 **52**..................... KieranO'Neill 2 45
(Jeremy Scott) *chsd ldr for 1f: in tch in midfield after: effrt wl over 2f out: nvr threatened to get on terms w ldrs: plugged on ins fnl f* **7/1**

2232 **7** *1 1/2* **Mistress Nellie**[41] 5106 4-8-10 **48**..................... HollieDoyle 11 39
(William Stone) *midfield: hdwy to chse ldrs 8f out: rdn and struggling to qckn whn carried lft over 2f out: sn outpcd and wl hld fnl f (vet said filly had lost her left-fore shoe)* **3/1**[1]

0-05 **8** *3/4* **Skylark Lady (IRE)**[25] 5680 6-8-7 **45**.....................(p) LukeMorris 9 34
(Nikki Evans) *racd in last trio: effrt and rdn 3f out: no imp and nvr threatened ldrs* **50/1**

0/00 **9** *1 3/4* **Swift Blade (IRE)**[15] 6046 11-8-9 **54**.....................(b) RhysClutterbuck(7) 1 40
(Gary Moore) *flashing tail leaving stalls: midfield: effrt wl over 2f out: no prog and wl hld over 1f out* **50/1**

0210 **10** *5* **Lady Of Authority**[98] 2970 4-8-10 **55**..................... GeorgiaDobie(7) 4 33
(Richard Phillips) *racd in last trio: effrt over 3f out: no prog and nvr involved* **12/1**

2104 **11** *nk* **Born To Reason (IRE)**[8] 6303 5-8-7 **50**.....................(p) CierenFallon(5) 3 28
(Alexandra Dunn) *led tl 8f out: chsd ldr tl over 2f out: sn outpcd and lost pl over 1f out: wknd (trainer could offer no explanation for the gelding's performance)* **7/1**

2m 28.52s (-5.48) **Going Correction** -0.375s/f (Firm) **11 Ran SP% 123.9**
Speed ratings (Par 101): **103,101,100,99,98 97,96,95,94,91 91**
CSF £26.54 CT £270.39 TOTE £4.00: £1.30, £2.40, £3.50; EX 25.50 Trifecta £219.10.
Owner Christopher Wright & Ms E L Banks **Bred** Stratford Place Stud **Trained** Pulborough, W Sussex

FOCUS
Add 2yds to this middle-distance handicap, in which the form horses came to the fore. They went a quick tempo throughout. Straightforward form in behind the winner.

6600 VISIT ATTHERACES.COM CLAIMING STKS 1m 1f
2:30 (2:30) (Class 6) 3-Y-O **£2,781** (£827; £413; £300; £300) **Stalls** Low

Form RPR

0 **1** **Olaf**[9] 6290 3-8-7 0..................... LiamJones 6 56
(John Bridger) *chsd ldrs and pushed along at times: effrt over 3f out: swtchd rt: chsd ldr and clsng 2f out: kpt on u.p despite bhd struck by ldrs rdrs whip to ld wl ins fnl f: ears pricked and gng away at fin* **50/1**

6410 **2** *1 1/2* **Seafaring Girl (IRE)**[21] 5806 3-8-8 **52**.....................(p) LukeMorris 5 54
(Mark Loughnane) *led: clr 5f out: rdn over 2f out: drvn and reduced ld 2f out: hrd drvn and hrd pressed 1f out: hdd and no ex wl ins fnl f* **8/1**

0000 **3** *1 1/4* **Mustadun**[13] 6101 3-8-13 **65**..................... FrannyNorton 3 57
(Mark Johnston) *chsd ldr: effrt over 2f out: swtchd lft and lost 2nd 2f out: stl cl enough and drvn over 1f out: no ex and plugged on same pce ins fnl f* **11/10**[1]

-550 **4** *2 3/4* **Ample Plenty**[18] 5941 3-8-6 **54**..................... HarryBentley 1 44
(David Simcock) *hld up in last pair: dropped to rr over 3f out: effrt over 2f out: clsd and cl enough over 1f out: no ex and btn ins fnl f* **7/2**[3]

0466 **5** *1/2* **Max Guevara (IRE)**[11] 6202 3-8-13 **58**..................... DavidEgan 4 50
(William Muir) *hld up in rr: swtchd rt and hdwy on outer bnd over 3f out: clsd 2f out: no ex u.p 1f out: wknd ins fnl f* **11/4**[2]

1m 54.27s (-2.63) **Going Correction** -0.375s/f (Firm) **5 Ran SP% 109.6**
Speed ratings (Par 98): **96,94,93,91,90**
CSF £344.35 TOTE £34.00: £11.90, £2.50; EX 135.60 Trifecta £301.60.
Owner M J Evans & T M Jones **Bred** D R Botterill **Trained** Liphook, Hants

FOCUS
Add 2yds to this weak event, run at a solid pace, featuring a good ride in defeat and a shock winner. It's been rated negatively around the second.

6601 HAPPY BIRTHDAY STEVE ELDRIDGE H'CAP 2m 68y
3:00 (3:00) (Class 6) (0-65,65) 4-Y-O+
£2,781 (£827; £413; £300; £300; £300) **Stalls** Centre

Form RPR

-150 **1** **Casa Comigo (IRE)**[18] 5974 4-8-10 **54**..................... KierenFox 3 61
(John Best) *t.k.h early: effrt in 6th over 3f out: swtchd rt over 2f out: awkward hd carriage: hung lft but clsd to chal over 1f out: led jst ins fnl f: kpt on (jockey said gelding hung left-handed)* **5/1**[2]

6045 **2** *1/2* **Lazarus (IRE)**[19] 5891 5-8-3 **47**.....................(t) DavidEgan 11 53
(Amy Murphy) *chsd ldrs: chsd ldr over 4f out: effrt to chal and drvn 2f out: pressed wnr and kpt on u.p fr over 1f out: a hld ins fnl f* **7/2**[1]

-035 **3** *3* **Essgee Nics (IRE)**[49] 4796 6-7-11 **46** oh1.....................(p) RhiainIngram(5) 8 49
(Paul George) *t.k.h: led: rdn and over 2f out: hdd over 1f out: sn swtchd rt and kpt on same pce ins fnl f* **10/1**

-323 **4** *3/4* **Danglydontask**[6] 6366 8-8-5 **49**.....................(b) HayleyTurner 9 51
(Mike Murphy) *s.i.s: styd wd early and stdy hdwy to ld 12f out: rdn over 2f out: hdd over 1f out: sn outpcd and plugged on same pce ins fnl f* **7/2**[1]

The Form Book Flat 2019, Raceform Ltd, Newbury, RG14 5SJ

6505 **5** *nk* **Seventii**[29] 5513 5-8-0 **47** oh1 ow1 .... DarraghKeenan(3) 4 49
(Robert Eddery) *hld up in midfield: pushed along 2f out: hdwy and reminder ins fnl f: kpt on ins fnl f: no threat to wnr* **16/1**

0000 **6** *4 1/2* **Everlasting Sea**[6] 6366 5-8-2 **46** oh1 .... KieranO'Neill 1 42
(Stuart Kittow) *trckd ldrs: effrt over 2f out: sn outpcd and btn over 1f out: wknd ins fnl f* **20/1**

024- **7** *3 1/4* **Ormskirk**[14] 1276 6-8-5 **49** .... (bt) RyanPowell 2 41
(Johnny Farrelly) *midfield: effrt wl over 2f out: no prog and wl hld fnl 2f* **16/1**

011/ **8** *nse* **Hiorne Tower (FR)**[760] 5407 8-9-5 **63** .... HectorCrouch 5 55+
(John Best) *v.s.a: t.k.h: clsd onto rr of field after 2f: effrt over 2f out: nvr trbld ldrs (jockey said gelding was slowly away)* **8/1**

50-0 **9** *3/4* **War Drums**[13] 6105 5-9-2 **65** .... (h) CierenFallon(5) 10 56
(Alexandra Dunn) *mounted in chute: chsd ldr for 3f: chsd ldrs after: rdn over 2f out: sn btn and wknd over 1f out* **7/1**[3]

0205 **10** *8* **Sea's Aria (IRE)**[30] 4777 8-8-2 **46** oh1 .... LukeMorris 7 28
(Mark Hoad) *pushed along leaving stalls: midfield: drvn wl over 2f out: sn btn and no ch fnl 2f* **14/1**

0-00 **11** *3* **Ginger Lacey**[97] 3017 4-8-2 **46** oh1 .... HollieDoyle 13 24
(Harry Dunlop) *swtchd lft sn after s: t.k.h: hld up towards rr: effrt 3f out: sn btn and no ch fnl 2f* **25/1**

6-00 **12** *20* **Duration (IRE)**[27] 5596 4-8-7 **51** .... AdrianMcCarthy 6 5
(J R Jenkins) *a towards rr: rdn wl over 2f out: sn wl bhd: t.o ins fnl f* **25/1**

3m 32.46s (-3.54) **Going Correction** -0.375s/f (Firm) **12** Ran SP% **124.7**
Speed ratings (Par 101): **93,92,91,90,90 88,86,86,86,82 80,70**
CSF £23.51 CT £173.54 TOTE £7.60: £2.00, £1.60, £2.90; EX 27.20 Trifecta £201.30.
Owner Simon Malcolm **Bred** Simon Malcom **Trained** Oad Street, Kent

FOCUS
Add 2yds to this modest staying handicap, run at a decent pace. The front two were clear of the remainder. Limited form, with the winner rated in line with his pre-race best.

6602 ROADMARKING EXCEL SUPPORTING DEMELZA HOUSE (S) STKS 6f
3:30 (3:30) (Class 6) 3-Y-O+
£2,781 (£827; £413; £300; £300; £300) **Stalls** Centre

Form RPR

2424 **1** **More Than Likely**[37] 5251 3-8-12 78 .... ShaneKelly 2 67
(Richard Hughes) *pressed ldr: rdn to ld 1f out: asserted and edgd rt 100yds out: styd on: pushed out* **10/11**[1]

5225 **2** *1 1/4* **Terri Rules (IRE)**[9] 6285 4-8-12 54 .... DarraghKeenan(3) 3 63
(Lee Carter) *stdd s: hld up in rr: effrt and swtchd lft ent fnl f: rdn and r.o fnl 100yds: snatched 2nd last stride* **20/1**

4523 **3** *shd* **Harry Beau**[7] 6329 5-9-2 62 .... (vt) HarryBentley 5 64
(David Evans) *led: rdn ent fnl 2f: hdd 1f out: kpt on same pce ins fnl f: lost 2nd last stride* **11/4**[2]

154 **4** *1 3/4* **Chikoko Trail**[25] 5678 4-9-6 64 .... (vt) HectorCrouch 4 63
(Gary Moore) *trckd ldrs: swtchd lft and effrt over 1f out: no imp and wknd wl ins fnl f* **4/1**[3]

4601 **5** *1 1/2* **Devil Or Angel**[19] 5884 4-8-10 55 .... (p) ThoreHammerHansen(5) 6 53
(Bill Turner) *hld up in tch: swtchd lft over 2f out: chsd ldrs but unable qck u.p ent fnl f: wknd ins fnl f* **16/1**

0-45 **6** *8* **Disruptor (FR)**[11] 6197 3-8-13 62 .... LukeMorris 1 30
(Charlie Wallis) *dwlt: hdwy to chse ldrs after 2f: rdn over 2f out: lost pl over 1f out: wl bhd ins fnl f* **33/1**

1m 8.74s (-2.76) **Going Correction** -0.375s/f (Firm)
WFA 3 from 4yo+ 3lb **6** Ran SP% **112.6**
Speed ratings (Par 101): **103,101,101,98,96 86**
CSF £21.88 TOTE £1.70: £1.10, £7.00; EX 20.60 Trifecta £35.90.The winner was bought in for £10,200.
Owner H Pinniger And Peter Cook **Bred** R F And S D Knipe **Trained** Upper Lambourn, Berks

FOCUS
A smooth success for the favourite. She didn't need to match her recent form to win.

6603 RAHMAN RAVELLI EBF FILLIES' NOVICE MEDIAN AUCTION STKS (PLUS 10 RACE) 7f
4:00 (4:01) (Class 5) 2-Y-O £4,140 (£1,232; £615; £307) **Stalls** Centre

Form RPR

46 **1** **Gypsy Whisper**[22] 5772 2-8-12 0 .... JasonWatson 5 77
(David Menuisier) *chsd ldng trio: effrt to chse ldrs 2f out: sn rdn: ev ch 1f out: led ins fnl f: r.o wl and drew clr fnl 100yds* **11/2**[2]

3 **2** *2 1/2* **Follia**[33] 5381 2-8-12 0 .... DanielMuscutt 2 70
(Marco Botti) *w ldrs tl led 1/2-way: rdn over 1f out: drvn ent fnl f: hdd ins fnl f: nt match pce of wnr fnl 100yds* **4/7**[1]

21 **3** *3 1/4* **Restless Endeavour (IRE)**[7] 6344 2-9-5 0 .... TomMarquand 4 68
(Jamie Osborne) *led tl 1/2-way: rdn 2f out: 3rd and no ex u.p 1f out: wknd ins fnl f* **15/2**

4 *1/2* **High Shine** 2-8-12 0 .... (h[1]) CallumShepherd 3 60
(Michael Bell) *s.i.s: in rr: effrt ent fnl 2f: wl hld in 4th and rn green over 1f out: no imp but kpt on steadily ins fnl f* **14/1**

5 *8* **Summer Valley** 2-8-12 0 .... HectorCrouch 6 39
(Gary Moore) *in tch: effrt over 2f out: sn struggling and wl btn over 1f out* **25/1**

6 *7* **Irish Tweed** 2-8-12 0 .... DavidProbert 1 20
(Andrew Balding) *t.k.h: sn w ldrs: stmbld and lost pl qckly over 2f out: rn green and hung lft 2f out: wl bhd ins fnl f (jockey said filly ran too free in the early stages, stumbled and hung left-handed)* **6/1**[3]

1m 21.34s (-2.96) **Going Correction** -0.375s/f (Firm) **6** Ran SP% **115.6**
Speed ratings (Par 91): **101,98,94,93,84 76**
CSF £9.50 TOTE £5.20: £2.00, £1.10; EX 11.40 Trifecta £31.30.
Owner Gail Brown Racing (A) **Bred** Alvediston Stud & Partners **Trained** Pulborough, W Sussex

FOCUS
Not a bad little novice in truth and the field came over to the stands' rail despite the stalls being in the centre. The runner-up had shown major promise on his debut and the third is a previous winner, so the form looks useful enough. The level is a bit fluid.

6604 SKY SPORTS RACING ON VIRGIN 535 NURSERY H'CAP 7f
4:30 (4:30) (Class 6) (0-60,59) 2-Y-O
£2,781 (£827; £413; £300; £300; £300) **Stalls** Centre

Form RPR

055 **1** **Lets Go Lucky**[16] 6028 2-9-6 **58** .... (h) HarryBentley 2 63
(David Evans) *taken down early: racd in centre quartet: in tch in rr: effrt to chal 2f out: rdn to ld jst over 1f out: styd on ins fnl f: rdn out* **2/1**[1]

000 **2** *1 1/4* **Indra Dawn (FR)**[16] 6029 2-8-10 **48** .... (p[1]) AdamMcNamara 5 50
(Archie Watson) *racd in nr side trio: chsd ldrs: effrt wl over 2f out: ev ch 2f out: chsd wnr and kpt on same pce ins fnl f (jockey said gelding ran green in the closing stages)* **6/1**[3]

060 **3** *3* **Ohnotanotherone**[33] 5374 2-8-7 **45** .... (p[1]) KieranO'Neill 3 39
(Stuart Kittow) *racd in centre quartet: overall ldr: rdn over 2f out: hdd jst over 1f out: no ex and wknd wl ins fnl f* **16/1**

0660 **4** *nse* **Now I'm A Believer**[14] 6071 2-8-7 **45** .... FrannyNorton 4 38
(Mick Channon) *racd in centre quartet: chsd ldrs: effrt and ev ch 2f out: no ex 1f out: wknd ins fnl f* **6/1**[3]

4605 **5** *1/2* **Mr Kodi (IRE)**[18] 5958 2-9-7 **59** .... (v[1]) JasonWatson 6 51
(David Evans) *racd in nr side trio: chsd ldrs tl lost pl 1/2-way: rdn 3f out: swtchd lft over 1f out: plugged on ins fnl f: no threat to ldrs* **9/4**[2]

0030 **6** *1 1/4* **Ask Siri (IRE)**[18] 5958 2-8-8 **46** .... LiamJones 7 35
(John Bridger) *racd in nr side trio: chsd ldrs: rdn over 2f out: outpcd and btn over 1f out: wknd ins fnl f* **12/1**

565 **7** *1 1/2* **Halfacrown (IRE)**[4] 6435 2-9-0 **52** .... (t[1]) CallumShepherd 1 37
(Jamie Osborne) *racd in centre quartet: in tch: effrt and pressing ldrs ent fnl 2f: outpcd and btn over 1f out: wknd ins fnl f* **10/1**

1m 23.24s (-1.06) **Going Correction** -0.375s/f (Firm) **7** Ran SP% **115.3**
Speed ratings (Par 92): **91,89,86,86,85 84,82**
CSF £14.86 TOTE £2.40: £1.90, £2.30; EX 14.90 Trifecta £93.60.
Owner R S Brookhouse **Bred** R S Brookhouse **Trained** Pandy, Monmouths

FOCUS
A particularly weak nursery in which it proved beneficial to race out in the centre of the track, most unusually for this venue. The fourth has been rated near her best.

6605 WITHEFORD EQUINE BARRIER TRIALS AT LINGFIELD H'CAP 6f
5:00 (5:00) (Class 6) (0-65,65) 3-Y-O+
£2,781 (£827; £413; £300; £300; £300) **Stalls** Centre

Form RPR

1503 **1** **Napping**[19] 5883 6-8-10 **58** .... SeanKirrane(7) 7 66
(Amy Murphy) *stdd s: racd keenly and sn chsd ldrs: effrt to chal jst over 2f out: rdn to ld jst over 1f out: in command and styd on wl ins fnl f* **5/1**[3]

0345 **2** *2* **Flying Sakhee**[13] 6120 6-8-6 **47** .... (p) KieranO'Neill 11 49
(John Bridger) *in tch in rr: swtchd lft and effrt ent fnl 2f: styd on wl u.p ins fnl f: wnt 2nd towards fin: no threat to wnr* **13/2**

0402 **3** *1/2* **Islay Mist**[15] 6052 3-8-1 **48** .... (tp) DarraghKeenan(3) 5 49
(Lee Carter) *in tch in midfield: rdn and hdwy to chse ldrs over 1f out: drvn to chse wnr ins fnl f: no imp and lost 2nd towards fin* **14/1**

6010 **4** *1 1/4* **Olaudah**[15] 6048 5-8-12 **53** .... JasonWatson 6 50
(Henry Candy) *taken down early: led: rdn ent fnl 2f: drvn and hdd jst over 1f out: wknd wl ins fnl f* **7/2**[1]

0543 **5** *3/4* **Roundabout Magic (IRE)**[15] 6048 5-9-8 **63** .... NickyMackay 10 58
(Simon Dow) *hld up in tch: effrt to chse ldrs over 1f out: no ex u.p 150yds out: wknd wl ins fnl f* **8/1**

3520 **6** *hd* **Brockey Rise (IRE)**[26] 5632 4-9-6 **61** .... (b) HarryBentley 4 55
(David Evans) *in tch in last trio: u.p over 2f out: kpt on ins fnl f: no threat to ldrs* **9/2**[2]

-456 **7** *nk* **Kath's Lustre**[41] 5107 4-9-9 **64** .... (b) ShaneKelly 8 57
(Richard Hughes) *chsd ldr tl jst over 2f out: unable qck u.p over 1f out: wknd ins fnl f* **10/1**

0000 **8** *3/4* **Bernie's Boy**[13] 6132 6-9-3 **65** .... (p) GraceMcEntee(7) 1 56
(Phil McEntee) *hld up in tch: pushed along wl over 1f out: no imp and kpt on same pce ins fnl f* **20/1**

000 **9** *6* **Lacan (IRE)**[15] 6058 8-8-11 **59** .... SaraDelFabbro(7) 2 32
(Michael Bell) *s.i.s: a towards rr: wknd over 1f out* **10/1**

0614 **10** *1/2* **Knockout Blow**[19] 5883 4-9-1 **56** .... (p) HectorCrouch 9 27
(John E Long) *in tch in midfield: unable qck u.p over 1f out: wknd ins fnl f* **8/1**

1m 9.27s (-2.23) **Going Correction** -0.375s/f (Firm)
WFA 3 from 4yo+ 3lb **10** Ran SP% **122.2**
Speed ratings (Par 101): **99,96,95,94,93 92,92,91,83,82**
CSF £39.56 CT £450.42 TOTE £5.50: £2.10, £2.40, £4.00; EX 40.10 Trifecta £958.00.
Owner Eclipse Sports Racing Club **Bred** Aiden Murphy **Trained** Newmarket, Suffolk

FOCUS
A few in-form contenders in an otherwise modest handicap. Once again it proved best to steer clear of the rail. The second, third and fourth help set the level.
T/Plt: £1,115.10 to a £1 stake. Pool: £55,939.43 - 36.62 winning units T/Qpdt: £8.10 to a £1 stake. Pool: £5,978.99 - 545.07 winning units **Steve Payne**

6570 MUSSELBURGH (R-H)
Wednesday, August 28

OFFICIAL GOING: Good to soft (good in places; 8.0)
Wind: Fresh, across Weather: Fine, dry

6606 FRENCH DUNCAN BIBBY FACTORS BRITISH STALLION STUDS EBF MAIDEN STKS (PLUS 10 RACE) 7f 33y
2:10 (2:15) (Class 4) 2-Y-O £4,592 (£1,366; £683; £341) **Stalls** Low

Form RPR

3 **1** **Cognac (IRE)**[24] 5704 2-9-5 0 .... JoeFanning 9 85
(Mark Johnston) *mde all: rdn and hrd pressed whn edgd lft over 1f out: styd on strly to draw clr ins fnl f* **5/2**[2]

33 **2** *2 1/2* **Embolden (IRE)**[20] 5845 2-9-5 0 .... TonyHamilton 1 79
(Richard Fahey) *trckd wnr to 1/2-way: outpcd and edgd rt over 2f out: rallied and chsd (clr) wnr ins fnl f: r.o* **5/1**[3]

4232 **3** *1/2* **Imperial Gloriana (IRE)**[11] 6221 2-9-0 81 .... BenCurtis 5 73
(David O'Meara) *trckd ldrs: wnt 2nd 1/2-way: effrt and ev ch over 1f out: one pce and lost 2nd ins fnl f* **5/6**[1]

4 *5* **Le Chiffre** 2-9-5 0 .... DavidNolan 6 65+
(David O'Meara) *dwlt: sn in tch: rn green and pushed along 1/2-way: effrt over 2f out: no imp fr over 1f out* **14/1**

0 **5** *1 3/4* **Get Boosting**[7] 6336 2-9-5 0 .... ShaneGray 12 61
(Keith Dalgleish) *s.i.s: hld up: pushed along over 2f out: hdwy over 1f out: nvr rchd ldrs* **50/1**

56 **6** *4* **Romînintheglomin (IRE)**[32] 5460 2-8-11 0 .... RowanScott(3) 11 46
(Andrew Hughes, Ire) *in tch: rdn over 2f out: wknd wl over 1f out* **80/1**

7 *7* **Krystal Crown (IRE)** 2-9-0 0 .... TadhgO'Shea 8 28
(Andrew Hughes, Ire) *sn towards rr: drvn along over 2f out: nvr on terms* **22/1**

0 **8** *1 3/4* **Fluttershy**[18] 5961 2-8-7 0 .... LauraPearson(7) 4 24
(John Ryan) *s.s: bhd and a outpcd* **50/1**

04 **9** *3/4* **Summer Heights**[19] 5900 2-9-0 0 .... PaddyMathers 7 22
(Jim Goldie) *dwlt: hld up: struggling 3f out: sn btn* **66/1**

6 **10** *1 1/4* **Garnock Valley**[30] 5485 2-9-0 0 .... JamieGormley 10 19
(R Mike Smith) *dwlt: a struggling in rr* **66/1**

The Form Book Flat 2019, Raceform Ltd, Newbury, RG14 5SJ

11 *10* **Klara Spirit (IRE)** 2-9-0 0 .... AndrewMullen 2
(R Mike Smith) *s.v.s: nvr on terms* 66/1

1m 30.46s (1.46) **Going Correction** +0.30s/f (Good) **11** Ran SP% **120.4**
Speed ratings (Par 96): **103,100,99,93,91 87,79,77,76,75 63**
CSF £15.42 TOTE £3.50: £1.30, £1.20, £1.10; EX 14.50 Trifecta £23.00.
Owner China Horse Club/Ballylinch Stud **Bred** Irish National Stud **Trained** Middleham Moor, N Yorks

FOCUS
Despite the big field, only three really made much appeal to punters judged on the betting and they pulled away from the remainder late on. The race appeared to be run at a quick pace. It's been rated around the second for now.

6607 DOROTHEA HAWTHORNE MEMORIAL H'CAP 5f 1y
2:40 (2:45) (Class 4) (0-85,85) 3-Y-0+
£5,692 (£1,694; £846; £423; £300; £300) **Stalls High**

Form				RPR
0044	1		**Holmeswood**[40] 5119 5-9-6 **83** .... (p) TomEaves 12	91+
			(Julie Camacho) *mde all against stands' rail: pushed along over 1f out: r.o wl fnl f* 5/1[2]	
0030	2	½	**East Street Revue**[38] 5217 6-8-9 **72** .... (b) DavidAllan 11	78
			(Tim Easterby) *in tch against stands' rail: rdn 2f out: hdwy to chse wnr wl ins fnl f: r.o* 4/1[1]	
0541	3	¾	**Economic Crisis (IRE)**[19] 5904 10-8-3 **66** oh2 .... NathanEvans 10	70
			(Alan Berry) *bhd: shkn up whn nt clr run over 2f out to over 1f out: gd hdwy fnl f: tk 3rd last stride* 22/1	
1506	4	shd	**Dapper Man (IRE)**[11] 6208 5-9-8 **85** .... LewisEdmunds 7	88
			(Roger Fell) *pressed ldr: effrt and ev ch over 1f out: one pce wl ins fnl f* 13/2[3]	
0003	5	1	**He'Zanarab (IRE)**[18] 5936 3-9-1 **80** .... PaddyMathers 3	80
			(Jim Goldie) *bhd: rdn along 1/2-way: gd hdwy fnl f: r.o* 28/1	
1002	6	2	**Zig Zag Zyggy (IRE)**[40] 5119 4-9-7 **84** .... TadhgO'Shea 6	76
			(Andrew Hughes, Ire) *bhd and sn outpcd: hdwy on wd outside over 1f out: no further imp ins fnl f* 11/1	
5045	7	¾	**Nicki's Angel (IRE)**[18] 5972 3-8-7 **75** .... (v[1]) SeanDavis(3) 4	65
			(Richard Fahey) *blkd s and sn outpcd: drvn along 1/2-way: sme late hdwy: nvr rchd ldrs* 14/1	
0046	8	¾	**Royal Brave (IRE)**[11] 6227 8-9-6 **83** .... RoystonFfrench 2	70
			(Rebecca Bastiman) *hld up on outside: drvn along over 2f out: no imp fr over 1f out* 7/1	
2110	9	hd	**Lathom**[47] 4894 6-9-7 **84** .... BenRobinson 9	70
			(Paul Midgley) *trckd ldrs: rdn over 2f out: wknd over 1f out* 4/1[1]	
3322	10	2 ¼	**Diamonique**[14] 6070 3-8-8 **73** .... (p[1]) ShaneGray 8	51
			(Keith Dalgleish) *prom: rdn over 2f out: wknd over 1f out* 10/1	

1m 0.67s (0.97) **Going Correction** +0.30s/f (Good) **10** Ran SP% **114.4**
WFA 3 from 4yo+ 2lb
Speed ratings (Par 105): **104,103,102,101,100 97,95,94,94,90**
CSF £24.79 CT £331.59 TOTE £5.80: £1.40, £2.30, £6.30; EX 25.10 Trifecta £540.10.
Owner David W Armstrong **Bred** Highfield Farm Llp **Trained** Norton, N Yorks

FOCUS
It paid to race prominently in this fair sprint handicap, plus be close to the stands' rail.

6608 CATHERINE AND CHARLOTTE ROACHE H'CAP 5f 1y
3:10 (3:14) (Class 6) (0-65,67) 3-Y-0
£3,105 (£924; £461; £300; £300; £300) **Stalls High**

Form				RPR
0655	1		**Northern Society (IRE)**[19] 5904 3-8-13 **57** .... ShaneGray 7	65
			(Keith Dalgleish) *hld up bhd ldng gp: stdy hdwy gng wl over 1f out: shkn up to ld ins fnl f: kpt on strly* 5/1[2]	
3236	2	1 ¾	**Amazing Alba**[9] 6277 3-9-2 **60** .... (h) KevinStott 5	62
			(Alistair Whillans) *prom: rdn along 2f out: n.m.r and swtchd lft ins fnl f: sn chsng wnr: kpt on: nt pce to chal* 11/2[3]	
0321	3	1 ¼	**The Grey Zebedee**[9] 6277 3-9-3 **61** 6ex .... (b) DuranFentiman 1	58
			(Tim Easterby) *trckd ldrs: effrt and wnt 2nd over 1f out: ev ch briefly ins fnl f: kpt on same pce towards fin* 5/1[2]	
65	4	nk	**Jordan Electrics**[19] 5901 3-9-9 **67** .... (h) BenRobinson 2	63
			(Linda Perratt) *w ldr: led over 3f out: rdn 2f out: hdd ins fnl f: no ex* 11/1	
564	5	½	**Gleniffer**[11] 6206 3-9-7 **65** .... JamieGormley 9	59
			(Jim Goldie) *bhd and sn outpcd: hdwy over 1f out: kpt on fnl f: nt pce to chal* 6/1	
5220	6	nk	**Kaafy (IRE)**[17] 5985 3-9-6 **64** .... SamJames 8	57+
			(Grant Tuer) *bhd: effrt whn nt clr run over 1f out: kpt on fnl f: nvr able to chal (jockey said colt was denied a clear run approaching the final furlong)* 4/1[1]	
2140	7	6	**Montalvan (IRE)**[14] 6070 3-9-7 **65** .... (p) BenCurtis 4	37
			(Roger Fell) *led to over 3f out: rdn and wknd over 1f out: lost hind shoe (vet said gelding spread its left hind shoe and lost its right hind shoe)* 11/1	
040	8	6	**Shall We Begin (IRE)**[33] 5393 3-8-4 **48** .... NathanEvans 3	
			(Michael Easterby) *hld up on outside: drvn and struggling over 2f out: sn btn* 9/1	
260-	9	8	**Laoise (USA)**[308] 8541 3-8-9 **53** .... AndrewMullen 6	
			(Linda Perratt) *fly-jmpd and lost many l s: a wl bhd: eased whn no ch fnl f (jockey said filly reared as the stalls opened and then hung both ways)* 40/1	

1m 1.47s (1.77) **Going Correction** +0.30s/f (Good) **9** Ran SP% **112.1**
Speed ratings (Par 98): **97,94,92,91,90 90,80,71,58**
CSF £31.32 CT £142.85 TOTE £7.60: £1.70, £2.00, £1.70; EX 34.30 Trifecta £244.30.
Owner John Kelly, John McNeill & Alan Johnston **Bred** La Estatua Partnership **Trained** Carluke, S Lanarks

FOCUS
Not overly strong form.

6609 EBF STALLIONS WINNERS FILLIES' H'CAP 7f 33y
3:40 (3:41) (Class 4) (0-80,82) 3-Y-0+
£7,309 (£2,175; £1,087; £543; £300; £300) **Stalls Low**

Form				RPR
6053	1		**Maggies Angel (IRE)**[18] 5971 4-9-9 **74** .... (p[1]) SeanDavis(3) 9	81
			(Richard Fahey) *early ldr: cl up: regained ld over 2f out: drvn and kpt on wl fnl f* 11/2[3]	
336	2	1 ¼	**Harvest Day**[48] 4831 4-9-9 **71** .... (t) NathanEvans 7	75
			(Michael Easterby) *t.k.h early: in tch: effrt on outside and chsd wnr over 1f out: kpt on ins fnl f: nt pce to chal* 10/1	
5410	3	nk	**Gometra Ginty (IRE)**[19] 5903 3-9-7 **74** .... ShaneGray 3	75
			(Keith Dalgleish) *trckd ldrs: pushed along over 2f out: effrt and rdn over 1f out: r.o same pce ins fnl f* 9/2[2]	
-506	4	1	**Evolutionary (IRE)**[12] 6176 3-8-13 **66** .... JamieGormley 2	64
			(Iain Jardine) *hld up: pushed along over 2f out: edgd lft and carried hd high over 1f out: one pce fnl f* 14/1	
0412	5	2 ¼	**Firsteen**[20] 5852 3-8-7 **60** .... CamHardie 4	53
			(Alistair Whillans) *s.i.s: sn pushed along in rr: effrt over 2f out: no imp over 1f out* 13/2	
1421	6	2 ¼	**Caustic Love (IRE)**[22] 5790 3-10-1 **82** .... JoeFanning 6	69
			(Keith Dalgleish) *s.i.s: sn prom: rdn over 2f out: wknd over 1f out* 15/8[1]	
4520	7	1 ½	**Oriental Lilly**[19] 5903 5-9-2 **71** .... CoreyMadden(7) 1	56
			(Jim Goldie) *s.i.s: bhd: drvn and struggling over 2f out: sn btn* 20/1	
1146	8	hd	**Beryl The Petal (IRE)**[23] 5724 3-10-1 **82** .... (v) DavidNolan 5	67
			(David O'Meara) *sn led: rdn and hdd over 2f out: wknd over 1f out* 10/1	

1m 30.44s (1.44) **Going Correction** +0.30s/f (Good) **8** Ran SP% **111.3**
WFA 3 from 4yo+ 5lb
Speed ratings (Par 102): **103,101,101,100,97 94,93,93**
CSF £54.92 CT £260.89 TOTE £4.30: £1.70, £3.40, £1.60; EX 57.00 Trifecta £604.70.
Owner P D Smith Holdings Ltd **Bred** Grangemore Stud **Trained** Musley Bank, N Yorks

FOCUS
This doesn't look like strong form for the level, with the winner gaining a first success since her racecourse debut in 2017. The second has been rated in line with this year's best.

6610 AIUA H'CAP 1m 208y
4:10 (4:14) (Class 6) (0-65,66) 3-Y-0
£3,105 (£924; £461; £300; £300; £300) **Stalls Low**

Form				RPR
6323	1		**Catch My Breath**[12] 6164 3-9-7 **63** .... (p) DavidAllan 6	69+
			(John Ryan) *slowly away: hld up: pushed along over 2f out: effrt on outside over 1f out: led ins fnl f: r.o* 6/4[1]	
3206	2	½	**Jazz Hands (IRE)**[13] 6130 3-8-7 **52** .... SeanDavis(3) 10	56
			(Richard Fahey) *sn chsng ldr: effrt and rdn over 2f out: ev ch ins fnl f: kpt on: hld nr fin* 7/1[3]	
4061	3	1 ¼	**Geography Teacher (IRE)**[92] 3204 3-9-4 **60** .... JamieGormley 5	61
			(R Mike Smith) *cl up: effrt and rdn 2f out: kpt on same pce ins fnl f* 33/1	
5403	4	nk	**Osmosis**[13] 6101 3-9-2 **61** .... ConorMcGovern(3) 4	62
			(Jason Ward) *hld up on ins: hmpd 5f out: effrt whn n.m.r briefly over 1f out: kpt on fnl f: nt pce to chal* 11/4[2]	
0000	5	2 ¾	**Princess Florence (IRE)**[13] 6130 3-8-7 **49** .... CamHardie 3	44
			(John Ryan) *led at ordinary gallop: rdn over 2f out: hdd ins fnl f: sn wknd* 20/1	
0000	6	nk	**Bannockburn (IRE)**[2] 6550 3-8-13 **55** .... ShaneGray 9	49
			(Keith Dalgleish) *dwlt: midfield on outside: hdwy 3f out: rdn and hung rt over 1f out: sn outpcd* 25/1	
0340	7	1 ¼	**Treasured Company (IRE)**[57] 4487 3-8-3 **45** .... (e) NathanEvans 1	37
			(Richard Guest) *t.k.h: hld up on ins: rdn over 2f out: sn n.d: btn over 1f out* 12/1	
5010	8	2 ¾	**Archies Lad**[62] 4280 3-9-4 **60** .... PaddyMathers 7	46
			(R Mike Smith) *t.k.h: hld up in tch: rdn along over 2f out: outpcd whn hmpd over 1f out* 28/1	
6415	9	22	**Twentysixthstreet (IRE)**[40] 5123 3-9-10 **66** .... TadhgO'Shea 8	6
			(Andrew Hughes, Ire) *hld up in midfield: hdwy over 3f out: lost pl and struggling over 2f out: eased whn no ch over 1f out (trainer said colt failed to stay the 1m1f trip on this occasion)* 8/1	

1m 56.74s (3.64) **Going Correction** +0.30s/f (Good) **9** Ran SP% **113.0**
Speed ratings (Par 98): **95,94,93,93,90 90,89,86,67**
CSF £11.56 CT £236.64 TOTE £2.30: £1.10, £1.70, £3.80; EX 10.70 Trifecta £80.80.
Owner Gerry McGladery **Bred** Meon Valley Stud **Trained** Newmarket, Suffolk

FOCUS
Probably okay form for the level, nothing more. The second has been rated to this year's best.

6611 WITHERBYS H'CAP 2m 2f 28y
4:40 (4:43) (Class 6) (0-65,67) 4-Y-0+
£3,105 (£924; £461; £300; £300; £300) **Stalls High**

Form				RPR
6232	1		**Kitty's Cove**[18] 5975 4-8-9 **49** .... (tp) DavidAllan 2	57
			(Tim Easterby) *dwlt: hld up: hdwy on outside 2f out: edgd rt and led ins fnl f: styd on wl* 4/1[2]	
000	2	nk	**Put The Law On You (IRE)**[29] 3686 4-8-5 **45** .... (p) AndrewMullen 7	53
			(Alistair Whillans) *cl up: led wl over 2f out: sn hrd pressed: hdd ins fnl f: rallied: hld nr fin* 28/1	
4563	3	6	**Pammi**[18] 5939 4-8-8 **48** .... PaddyMathers 3	49
			(Jim Goldie) *cl up tl rdn and outpcd over 2f out: rallied fnl f to take 3rd towards fin: no ch w first two* 12/1	
1011	4	nk	**Clearance**[1] 6583 5-9-4 **65** 5ex .... HarryRussell(7) 6	65
			(Iain Jardine) *t.k.h: hld up in tch: stdy hdwy whn nt clr run over 3f out: effrt and edgd rt over 2f out: drvn and outpcd fnl f* 4/6[1]	
04-5	5	½	**Gemologist (IRE)**[109] 721 4-8-7 **47** .... (t) NathanEvans 4	47+
			(Lucinda Russell) *hld up: hdwy on outside and ev ch over 2f out to over 1f out: outpcd fnl f* 14/1	
4045	6	2 ¼	**Elite Icon**[18] 5939 5-8-7 **47** .... (v) CamHardie 1	44
			(Jim Goldie) *hld up in tch: drvn and outpcd over 2f out: sn btn* 16/1	
2261	7	1 ¼	**Hugoigo**[7] 6343 5-8-10 **57** 5ex .... CoreyMadden(7) 10	53
			(Jim Goldie) *hld up: rdn along 3f out: sn no imp: btn fnl 2f* 8/1[3]	
0000	8	31	**Dizoard**[26] 5621 9-8-5 **45** .... JamieGormley 9	3
			(Iain Jardine) *led tl hdd wl over 2f out: sn struggling: eased whn btn fnl f (jockey said mare hung left under pressure)* 50/1	

4m 7.88s **8** Ran SP% **116.7**
CSF £101.80 CT £1241.77 TOTE £4.60: £1.20, £5.10, £2.90; EX 86.30 Trifecta £557.60.
Owner Mickley Stud & Partner **Bred** M B Hawtin **Trained** Great Habton, N Yorks

FOCUS
Two pulled away late on in this moderate staying event. The winner has been rated in line with the best view of last month's course run over shorter.

6612 MR AND MRS SMITH H'CAP 1m 4f 104y
5:10 (5:10) (Class 5) (0-70,69) 3-Y-0
£3,428 (£1,020; £509; £300; £300; £300) **Stalls Low**

Form				RPR
5544	1		**Cuba Ruba**[11] 6232 3-8-9 **57** .... (p) DavidAllan 1	64
			(Tim Easterby) *trckd ldrs: n.m.r and stmbld over 3f out: effrt on outside and led over 1f out: edgd rt: rdn and kpt on wl towards fin* 6/4[1]	
1501	2	hd	**Three Castles**[18] 5937 3-9-1 **63** .... JoeFanning 6	70
			(Keith Dalgleish) *t.k.h: hld up: smooth hdwy to ld over 2f out: rdn and hdd over 1f out: rallied and ev ch fnl f: jst hld* 2/1[2]	
002	3	2 ¼	**Magrevio (IRE)**[44] 4990 3-8-8 **56** .... SamJames 7	59
			(Liam Bailey) *trckd ldrs: wnt 2nd over 2f out to over 1f out: outpcd fnl f* 4/1[3]	

2200 **4** 3½ **Spirit Of Lund (IRE)**[14] 6068 3-9-6 **68**........................ JamieGormley 2 66
(Iain Jardine) *hld up: rdn and outpcd 3f out: rallied wl over 1f out: no imp fnl f* **5/1**

5000 **5** 13 **Sleepdancer (IRE)**[15] 6046 3-8-4 **52**........................(vt[1]) CamHardie 5 30
(John Ryan) *pressed ldr: led over 4f out to over 2f out: sn wknd* **25/1**

0000 **6** 19 **Gloryella**[43] 5028 3-8-2 **50** oh5........................ AndrewMullen 3
(Ruth Carr) *led at modest gallop: hdd over 4f out: wknd over 2f out* **33/1**

2m 48.06s (3.56) **Going Correction** +0.30s/f (Good) **6** Ran SP% **116.8**
Speed ratings (Par 100): **100,99,98,96,87 74**
CSF £5.09 CT £9.17 TOTE £2.50: £2.00, £1.40; EX 5.90 Trifecta £17.40.
Owner Reality Partnerships Xiii **Bred** Theakston Stud **Trained** Great Habton, N Yorks

FOCUS
An ordinary middle-distance handicap for mainly modest performers. Straightforward form rated around the first three.
T/Jkpt: £16,618.00 to a £1 stake. Pool: £93,622.58 - 4 winning units T/Plt: £93.10 to a £1 stake. Pool: £59,628.51 - 467.15 winning units T/Qpdt: £25.50 to a £1 stake. Pool: £4,943.85 - 143.41 winning units **Richard Young**

6613 - 6620a (Foreign Racing) - See Raceform Interactive

6336 CARLISLE (R-H)

Thursday, August 29

OFFICIAL GOING: Good to firm (good in places; 7.9)
Wind: Fresh, half against in over 2f of home straight Weather: Overcast, dry

6621 DAVID ALLEN H'CAP (FOR GENTLEMAN AMATEUR RIDERS) 5f 193y

1:40 (1:42) (Class 6) (0-65,65) 3-Y-O+ **£3,119** (£967; £483; £300; £300) **Stalls** Low

Form RPR

0060 **1** **Naples Bay**[10] 6276 5-10-1 **52**........................ MrEireannCagney(7) 8 59
(Katie Scott) *in tch: pushed along and sltly outpcd 2f out: rallied appr fnl f: kpt on wl to ld cl home (trainer said regarding apparent improvement in form that the gelding may have benefited from being more settled on this occasion)* **12/1**

2123 **2** hd **Ninjago**[16] 6058 9-11-7 **65**........................(v) MrSimonWalker 4 71
(Paul Midgley) *trckd ldrs: rdn to ld ent fnl f: edgd rt u.p: kpt on: hdd and no ex cl home* **11/8[1]**

0504 **3** 4 **Carlovian**[10] 6273 6-10-1 **52**........................(p) MarcusHaigh(7) 5 46
(Mark Walford) *led to over 2f out: rdn and outpcd over 1f out: rallied and chsd (clr) ldng pair wl ins fnl f: no imp* **10/3[2]**

1025 **4** ¾ **Mr Greenlight**[10] 6273 4-11-0 **61**........................ MrWilliamEasterby(3) 9 53
(Tim Easterby) *pressed ldr: led over 2f out tl hdd ent fnl f: sn wknd* **4/1[3]**

2055 **5** 6 **Prince Of Time**[21] 5857 7-9-11 **48**........................ MrAlexChadwick(7) 1 22
(Stella Barclay) *t.k.h: in tch: outpcd over 2f out: btn over 1f out* **5/1**

1m 14.58s (-0.02) **Going Correction** -0.025s/f (Good)
WFA 3 from 4yo+ 3lb **5** Ran SP% **109.5**
Speed ratings (Par 101): **99,98,93,92,84**
CSF £29.01 TOTE £12.40: £5.50, £1.10; EX 37.70 Trifecta £68.30.
Owner Byrne Racing And Partners **Bred** Tirnaskea Stud **Trained** Galashiels, Scottish Borders

FOCUS
The inside rail around new stable and 1m bend was moved out. There was just a routine pace on in this ordinary sprint handicap, confined to male amateur riders.

6622 CARRS GROUP PLC BRITISH EBF NOVICE STKS (PLUS 10 RACE) 5f 193y

2:10 (2:12) (Class 4) 2-Y-O **£6,469** (£1,925; £962; £481) **Stalls** Low

Form RPR

1 **Lampang (IRE)** 2-9-5 0........................ DavidAllan 10 84+
(Tim Easterby) *missed break: rn green in rr: gd hdwy over 1f out: qcknd to ld ins fnl f: pushed out: promising* **7/2[1]**

3 **2** 1 **Panic Room (IRE)**[13] 6167 2-9-5 0........................ CliffordLee 7 78
(Tom Dascombe) *midfield: pushed along over 2f out: rallied over 1f out: drifted lft and chsd wnr ins fnl f: kpt on fin* **6/1[3]**

4 **3** 2 **Stroxx (IRE)**[34] 5396 2-9-5 0........................ DuranFentiman 12 72
(Tim Easterby) *cl up: led over 1f out to ins fnl f: sn outpcd* **28/1**

4 shd **Alben Spirit** 2-9-5 0........................ TonyHamilton 8 72
(Richard Fahey) *t.k.h: w ldr: rdn 2f out: edgd lft and one pce ins fnl f* **7/2[1]**

5 1¼ **King Fan** 2-9-5 0........................ JoeFanning 9 68
(Mark Johnston) *prom on outside: effrt and hdwy over 1f out: outpcd ins fnl f* **10/1**

222 **6** ½ **Alix James**[8] 6337 2-9-5 0........................ JamieGormley 5 67
(Iain Jardine) *trckd ldrs: effrt and rdn over 1f out: one pce whn hmpd ins fnl f* **11/2[2]**

33 **7** nk **Magic Timing**[27] 5615 2-9-5 0........................ ShaneGray 6 65
(Keith Dalgleish) *hld up: pushed along 1/2-way: hdwy and edgd rt over 1f out: kpt on fnl f: no imp* **33/1**

8 3½ **Slingshot** 2-9-0 0........................(h[1]) GrahamLee 13 50
(Bryan Smart) *dwlt: bhd and green: rdn over 2f out: edgd rt and sn btn* **40/1**

9 nse **Brazen Point** 2-9-5 0........................(t[1]) RachelRichardson 2 54
(Tim Easterby) *dwlt: bhd and green: hdwy over 1f out: nvr rchd ldrs* **50/1**

3 **10** 1¼ **Solemn Pledge**[31] 5485 2-9-0 0........................ BenCurtis 3 46
(K R Burke) *led to over 1f out: wknd fnl f* **11/1**

06 **11** 6 **Herbert Pocket**[8] 6336 2-9-5 0........................ JamesSullivan 11 32
(Tim Easterby) *hld up: pushed along over 2f out: sn btn* **80/1**

12 2¼ **Jungle Rock (IRE)** 2-9-5 0........................ PaulMulrennan 4 25
(Iain Jardine) *dwlt: bhd: struggling over 2f out: sn btn* **80/1**

02 **13** 8 **Black Caspian (IRE)**[21] 5845 2-9-5 0........................ TomEaves 1
(Kevin Ryan) *in tch on ins: struggling 1/2-way: btn wl over 1f out (trainer said colt was unsuited by the Good to Firm, Good in places on this occasion and will be campaigned on easier ground in the future)* **11/2[2]**

1m 13.59s (-1.01) **Going Correction** -0.025s/f (Good) **13** Ran SP% **120.2**
Speed ratings (Par 96): **105,103,101,100,99 98,98,93,93,91 83,80,70**
CSF £23.89 TOTE £6.20: £2.40, £1.90, £8.40; EX 31.10 Trifecta £469.40.
Owner King Power Racing Co Ltd **Bred** Rosetown Bloodstock Ltd **Trained** Great Habton, N Yorks

FOCUS
This looks juvenile form to be positive about.

6623 ARMSTRONG WATSON H'CAP 5f 193y

2:40 (2:41) (Class 4) (0-85,85) 3-Y-O **£6,469** (£1,925; £962; £481; £300) **Stalls** Low

Form RPR

3011 **1** **Gale Force Maya**[24] 5724 3-8-13 **77**........................ PaulMulrennan 6 84
(Michael Dods) *trckd ldrs: shkn up to ld over 1f out: edgd lft ins fnl f: rdn out* **3/1[3]**

5325 **2** 1 **Tenax (IRE)**[5] 6451 3-9-2 **85**........................ FayeMcManoman(5) 5 89
(Nigel Tinkler) *hmpd sn after s: hld up in tch: stdy hdwy over 2f out: effrt and pressed wnr over 1f out: one pce ins fnl f* **5/2[2]**

1522 **3** 1¾ **Pendleton**[41] 5126 3-9-4 **82**........................ ConnorBeasley 4 81
(Michael Dods) *w ldr: led 1/2-way to over 1f out: rdn and one pce fnl f* **11/8[1]**

3600 **4** 11 **Look Out Louis**[24] 5724 3-9-4 **82**........................ DavidAllan 7 47
(Tim Easterby) *led to 1/2-way: cl up tl rdn and wknd over 1f out (jockey said gelding ran too free)* **10/1**

11-0 **5** 6 **Antagonize**[132] 1926 3-9-7 **85**........................ GrahamLee 3 32
(Bryan Smart) *in tch: rdn over 2f out: wknd over 1f out* **16/1**

1m 12.32s (-2.28) **Going Correction** -0.025s/f (Good) **5** Ran SP% **110.6**
Speed ratings (Par 102): **114,112,110,95,87**
CSF £10.90 TOTE £3.40: £1.90, £1.50; EX 10.90 Trifecta £15.80.
Owner Frank Lowe **Bred** Mrs J Imray **Trained** Denton, Co Durham

FOCUS
A fair little 3yo sprint handicap, run at a sound pace. The second has been rated near his best.

6624 CUBBY CONSTRUCTION H'CAP (JOCKEY CLUB GRASSROOTS MIDDLE DISTANCE SERIES QUALIFIER) 1m 1f

3:10 (3:11) (Class 5) (0-70,70) 3-Y-O
£4,204 (£1,251; £625; £312; £300; £300) **Stalls** Low

Form RPR

6311 **1** **Kermouster**[18] 5984 3-9-6 **69**........................ SamJames 1 76+
(Grant Tuer) *hld up in tch: smooth hdwy over 1f out: rdn to ld ins fnl f: hld on wl cl home* **2/1[1]**

642 **2** shd **Olympic Conqueror (IRE)**[13] 6169 3-9-5 **68**........................ DanielMuscutt 8 75
(James Fanshawe) *sn cl up on outside: led over 2f out: rdn over 1f out: hdd ins fnl f: rallied: jst hld* **11/4[2]**

-555 **3** 1¾ **Lady Lizzy**[21] 5844 3-9-2 **70**........................(v[1]) HarrisonShaw(5) 6 73
(K R Burke) *hld up: hdwy on outside over 2f out: rdn and hung rt over 1f out: hung lft ins fnl f: kpt on* **2/1[1]**

0600 **4** 3 **Artistic Streak**[14] 6101 3-9-0 **63**........................ GrahamLee 4 60
(Donald McCain) *in tch: hdwy over 2f out: rdn and no ex whn checked ent fnl f* **10/1[3]**

B600 **5** 1½ **Harperelle**[21] 5851 3-8-2 **51** oh6........................ JamesSullivan 2 45
(Alistair Whillans) *led to over 2f out: rdn and wknd over 1f out* **20/1**

6000 **6** 7 **Allsfineandandy (IRE)**[12] 6204 3-8-2 **51** oh6........................ CamHardie 3 31
(Lynn Siddall) *dwlt: hld up: outpcd and hung rt over 2f out: sn btn* **40/1**

040 **7** hd **Lady Muk**[51] 4768 3-8-7 **56**........................(p) RoystonFfrench 7 36
(Steph Hollinshead) *prom: rdn over 3f out: wknd fnl 2f* **33/1**

2m 0.06s (1.06) **Going Correction** -0.025s/f (Good) **7** Ran SP% **112.6**
Speed ratings (Par 100): **94,93,92,89,88 82,81**
CSF £7.51 CT £11.09 TOTE £3.10: £1.50, £1.70; EX 9.10 Trifecta £21.10.
Owner D R Tucker **Bred** D R Tucker **Trained** Birkby, N Yorks

FOCUS
A moderate handicap, run at an average pace. Add 9yds. The third has been rated in line with her latest.

6625 NXT RECRUITMENT NURSERY H'CAP (JOCKEY CLUB GRASSROOTS NURSERY QUALIFIER) 6f 195y

3:40 (3:42) (Class 5) (0-75,75) 2-Y-O
£4,204 (£1,251; £625; £312; £300; £300) **Stalls** Low

Form RPR

602 **1** **Ralphy Boy Two (IRE)**[19] 5934 2-9-1 **69**........................ KevinStott 9 72
(Alistair Whillans) *hld up towards rr: rdn over 2f out: hdwy over 1f out: led ins fnl f: hung lft: kpt on wl* **14/1**

4042 **2** ¾ **We Owen A Dragon**[7] 6372 2-8-5 **62**........................ JaneElliott(3) 10 63
(Tom Dascombe) *t.k.h: pressed ldr: led after 3f: rdn and hung lft over 2f out: hdd ins fnl f: kpt on (jockey said gelding hung left throughout)* **5/2[1]**

0330 **3** shd **Little Ted**[7] 6372 2-8-7 **61**........................ JamesSullivan 3 62
(Tim Easterby) *trckd ldrs: effrt and ch over 1f out: kpt on same pce ins fnl f* **7/1**

3332 **4** ½ **Pentewan**[26] 5668 2-9-7 **75**........................ BenCurtis 5 74
(Phillip Makin) *in tch: rdn over 2f out: effrt and edgd lft over 1f out: kpt on same pce ins fnl f* **7/2[2]**

4603 **5** shd **Sir Havelock (IRE)**[14] 6097 2-8-1 **58** ow1........................ SeanDavis(3) 11 57
(Richard Fahey) *towards rr: drvn and outpcd 3f out: rallied over 1f out: kpt on fnl f: nt pce to chal* **18/1**

506 **6** 1 **Hooroo (IRE)**[15] 6065 2-8-13 **67**........................ CliffordLee 7 64
(K R Burke) *midfield: rdn and outpcd over 2f out: rallied fnl f: nvr rchd ldrs* **10/1**

0000 **7** ½ **My Havana**[22] 5815 2-8-3 **57**........................ AndrewMullen 2 52
(Nigel Tinkler) *bhd: drvn along 3f out: edgd lft 2f out: sme late hdwy: nvr rchd ldrs (jockey said gelding missed the break)* **33/1**

0600 **8** shd **River Of Kings (IRE)**[23] 5789 2-8-8 **62**........................ ShaneGray 8 57
(Keith Dalgleish) *hld up: rdn and outpcd over 2f out: sn btn* **22/1**

0006 **9** ¾ **Northern Grace**[16] 6053 2-8-0 **54** oh3........................ CamHardie 6 47
(Brian Ellison) *trckd ldrs: rdn over 2f out: edgd lft and wknd over 1f out* **50/1**

301 **10** 4½ **Mischief Star**[23] 5764 2-9-7 **75**........................ DanielTudhope 1 56
(David O'Meara) *led 3f: cl up tl rdn and wknd over 1f out (jockey said colt hung left throughout)* **4/1[3]**

1m 28.83s (0.83) **Going Correction** -0.025s/f (Good) **10** Ran SP% **113.6**
Speed ratings (Par 94): **94,93,93,92,91 90,90,89,84**
CSF £47.15 CT £277.71 TOTE £12.00: £3.20, £1.30, £2.60; EX 49.70 Trifecta £326.20.
Owner Frank Lowe **Bred** Ballybrennan Stud Ltd **Trained** Newmill-On-Slitrig, Borders

FOCUS
A run-of-the-mill nursery that saw a bunched finish. Add 7yds. Straightforward limited form.

6626 BAINES WILSON LLP H'CAP 7f 173y

4:10 (4:11) (Class 4) (0-80,80) 3-Y-O+
£6,469 (£1,925; £962; £481; £300; £300) **Stalls** Low

Form RPR

5401 **1** **International Man**[23] 5770 4-9-7 **76**........................(b) SeanDavis(3) 10 84
(Richard Fahey) *trckd ldr: rdn to ld over 1f out: sn drvn along: hld on wl cl home* **6/1**

6304 **2** shd **Zoravan (USA)**[16] 6037 6-8-12 **64**........................(b) JoeFanning 5 72
(Keith Dalgleish) *stdd s: hld up: shkn up and stdy hdwy over 1f out: chsd wnr ins fnl f: r.o: jst hld* **11/2[3]**

0541 **3** 2¼ **Royal Shaheen (FR)**[8] 6341 6-9-5 **71** 5ex........................(v) GrahamLee 9 74
(Alistair Whillans) *led: rdn over 2f out: hdd over 1f out: one pce ins fnl f* **3/1[2]**

6060 **4** nse **Socru (IRE)**[13] 6176 3-8-7 **70**........................(h) GerO'Neill(5) 8 71
(Michael Easterby) *rrd as stall opened: hld up in tch: rdn and outpcd over 2f out: rallied over 1f out: hung rt ins fnl f: r.o* **16/1**

6020 **5** ¾ **The Navigator**[24] 5725 4-9-9 **75**.................. JamesSullivan 6 76
(Dianne Sayer) *hld up: rdn over 2f out: hdwy on outside over 1f out: kpt on fnl f: no imp* **10/1**

6522 **6** 2 **Al Erayg (IRE)**[13] 6179 6-9-11 **77**.................(p) DavidAllan 3 73
(Tim Easterby) *trckd ldrs tl rdn and wknd over 1f out (jockey said gelding was unsuited by the slow early pace)* **15/8**[1]

4462 **7** 2¾ **Newmarket Warrior (IRE)**[22] 5817 8-9-2 **68**...........(p) PaulMulrennan 1 58
(Iain Jardine) *hld up in tch: rdn and outpcd over 2f out: sn btn* **12/1**

1m 39.62s (-0.38) **Going Correction** -0.025s/f (Good) **7 Ran SP% 112.1**
WFA 3 from 4yo+ 6lb
Speed ratings (Par 105): **100,99,97,97,96 94,92**
CSF £36.79 CT £116.74 TOTE £7.70: £3.40, £2.10; EX 43.80 Trifecta £141.50.
Owner P D Smith Holdings Ltd **Bred** Bearstone Stud Ltd **Trained** Musley Bank, N Yorks

FOCUS
Not a bad handicap. Add 7yds. The third has been rated near his best recent form.

6627 KINGMOOR PARK PROPERTIES LTD H'CAP (DIV I) 7f 173y
4:45 (4:46) (Class 6) (0-65,66) 4-Y-0+
£3,234 (£962; £481; £300; £300; £300) **Stalls** Low

Form RPR

6336 **1** **Placebo Effect (IRE)**[15] 6068 4-9-8 **66**..................(p[1]) BenRobinson 10 71
(Ollie Pears) *trckd ldr: led over 2f out: hrd pressed fnl f: hld on wl cl home* **4/1**[1]

5636 **2** hd **Mr Cool Cash**[16] 6036 7-8-1 **46** oh1 ow2...................(t) SeanDavis(3) 14 53
(John Davies) *in tch: rdn over 2f out: hdwy and ev ch ins fnl f: kpt on: jst hld: lost front shoe (vet said gelding lost left front shoe)* **20/1**

440 **3** 1¼ **Golden Guest**[44] 5020 5-9-5 **63**.......................... DanielTudhope 3 65
(Les Eyre) *hld up: rdn over 2f out: hdwy on outside over 1f out: chsd ldng pair ins fnl f: one pce towards fin* **6/1**[3]

4000 **4** 1¼ **Snooker Jim**[16] 6059 4-8-6 **50**.......................(t) RoystonFfrench 15 49
(Steph Hollinshead) *in tch: rdn over 2f out: effrt over 1f out: kpt on same pce fnl f* **11/1**

-300 **5** 1¾ **Ballymount**[20] 5899 4-9-1 **64**.............................(p) GerO'Neill(5) 7 59
(Michael Easterby) *t.k.h: prom: rdn over 2f out: rallied over 1f out: no ex ins fnl f* **9/2**[2]

0404 **6** ½ **Tarnhelm**[10] 6275 4-8-3 **54**.......................... RhonaPindar(7) 2 48
(Wilf Storey) *slowly away: bhd: hdwy on outside and prom whn rdr dropped whip over 2f out: rdn over 1f out: outpcd fnl f* **6/1**[3]

0-00 **7** ¾ **Jazz Magic (IRE)**[79] 3682 4-8-2 **46** oh1..................(p[1]) CamHardie 8 38
(Lynn Siddall) *s.i.s: hld up: rdn along over 3f out: sme late hdwy: nvr rchd ldrs* **40/1**

-050 **8** 1 **Shamaheart (IRE)**[38] 5247 9-9-0 **58**...................(tp) DavidAllan 13 48
(Geoffrey Harker) *s.i.s: hld up: rdn over 2f out: nvr rchd ldrs* **16/1**

2044 **9** 2¼ **Tom's Anna (IRE)**[23] 5787 9-7-13 **46** oh1.................. JaneElliott(3) 1 30
(Sean Regan) *cl up tl rdn and wknd over 1f out* **16/1**

6000 **10** 2 **Alexandrakollontai (IRE)**[9] 6327 9-8-9 **56**........(b) ConnorMurtagh(3) 11 36
(Alistair Whillans) *s.i.s: sn pushed along in rr: struggling over 2f out: sn btn* **9/1**

3002 **11** hd **Muradef**[16] 6036 4-8-3 **47**.......................... JamesSullivan 12 26
(Ruth Carr) *led and sn crossed to ins rail: rdn and hdd over 2f out: wknd over 1f out* **13/2**

400- **12** ½ **Amood (IRE)**[272] 9337 8-9-5 **63**.......................... AndrewElliott 6 41
(Simon West) *hld up: drvn and struggling over 2f out: sn btn: lost front shoe (vet said gelding lost left front shoe)* **28/1**

1m 39.93s (-0.07) **Going Correction** -0.025s/f (Good) **12 Ran SP% 120.8**
Speed ratings (Par 101): **99,98,97,96,94 94,93,92,90,88 87,87**
CSF £89.15 CT £494.02 TOTE £4.50: £2.10, £5.00, £1.80; EX 86.30 Trifecta £1333.40.
Owner Timothy O'Gram, Keith West & Ollie Pears **Bred** Hawaiian Dream Partnership **Trained** Norton, N Yorks

FOCUS
They didn't hang about in this moderate handicap. Add 7yds. The fourth is one of those who offers perspective on the level of the form.

6628 KINGMOOR PARK PROPERTIES LTD H'CAP (DIV II) 7f 173y
5:15 (5:18) (Class 6) (0-65,65) 4-Y-0+
£3,234 (£962; £481; £300; £300; £300) **Stalls** Low

Form RPR

1222 **1** **Betty Grable (IRE)**[23] 5787 5-8-5 **56**.................. RhonaPindar(7) 1 63
(Wilf Storey) *hld up in rr: gd hdwy on outside over 1f out: led ins fnl f: kpt on wl* **7/2**[1]

1634 **2** 1½ **Muatadel**[4] 6496 6-9-7 **65**.......................(v[1]) PaulMulrennan 13 69
(John Wainwright) *midfield: drvn along over 2f out: rallied over 1f out: chsd wnr ins fnl f: r.o* **25/1**

6553 **3** hd **Cameo Star (IRE)**[21] 5852 4-9-2 **63**...................(p) SeanDavis(3) 6 66
(Richard Fahey) *trckd ldrs: drvn along over 2f out: effrt over 1f out: one pce ins fnl f* **10/1**

0011 **4** ½ **Dawn Breaking**[16] 6036 4-9-1 **59**........................(b) PhilDennis 12 61
(Richard Whitaker) *led: rdn 2f out: hdd and no ex ins fnl f* **4/1**[2]

5223 **5** hd **Radjash**[10] 6275 5-8-3 **54**..............................(t) ZakWheatley(7) 15 55
(Declan Carroll) *t.k.h: pressed ldr to over 1f out: drvn and no ex ins fnl f* **13/2**

601 **6** shd **My Valentino (IRE)**[42] 5100 6-8-3 **47**...............(bt) JamesSullivan 8 48
(Dianne Sayer) *dwlt: hld up: pushed along over 2f out: hdwy fnl f: kpt on: nrst fin* **18/1**

03 **7** ¾ **Clary (IRE)**[42] 5100 9-8-2 **46** oh1..........................(h) JamieGormley 10 46
(Alistair Whillans) *hld up: rdn and effrt on outside over 2f out: sme late hdwy: nvr rchd ldrs* **25/1**

3000 **8** shd **Magic City (IRE)**[23] 5770 10-9-0 **63**.................. GerO'Neill(5) 3 62
(Michael Easterby) *dwlt: hld up: hdwy over 2f out: rdn and no imp fr over 1f out: btn fnl f* **8/1**

1230 **9** nse **Cliff Bay (IRE)**[16] 6036 5-8-9 **53**......................(p) ShaneGray 7 52
(Keith Dalgleish) *in tch: rdn over 2f out: hung lft over 1f out: btn fnl f* **11/1**

131 **10** 2¼ **Donnelly's Rainbow (IRE)**[27] 5616 6-9-5 **63**............ DavidAllan 11 59
(Rebecca Bastiman) *hld up: hdwy and swtchd rt over 2f out: drvn and no further imp over 1f out* **6/1**[3]

5000 **11** ½ **Haymarket**[42] 5100 10-7-11 **46** oh1.......................... PaulaMuir(5) 9 39
(R Mike Smith) *prom tl rdn and wknd fr 2f out* **50/1**

0500 **12** 9 **Longville Lilly**[16] 6059 4-7-9 **46** oh1.................. IsobelFrancis(7) 4 18
(Trevor Wall) *midfield: struggling 3f out: btn fnl 2f* **66/1**

3000 **13** 3¼ **Anchises**[30] 5518 4-9-3 **61**.............................(tp) GrahamLee 14 26
(Rebecca Menzies) *midfield: drvn and struggling over 3f out: btn fnl 2f* **28/1**

1m 39.96s (-0.04) **Going Correction** -0.025s/f (Good) **13 Ran SP% 118.2**
Speed ratings (Par 101): **99,97,97,96,96 96,95,95,95,93 92,83,80**
CSF £99.96 CT £834.08 TOTE £4.40: £1.90, £7.30, £3.20; EX 112.50 Trifecta £1188.90.
Owner W Storey **Bred** Tally-Ho Stud **Trained** Muggleswick, Co Durham

■ Stewards' Enquiry : James Sullivan two-day ban; careless riding (Sep 12-13)

FOCUS
This second division of the moderate 1m handicap was run at a frantic pace. Add 7yds. A season's best from the runner-up.
T/Jkpt: Not Won. T/Plt: £290.60 to a £1 stake. Pool: £56,506.11 - 141.90 winning units. T/Qpdt: £63.90 to a £1 stake. Pool: £5,539.85 - 64.09 winning units. **Richard Young**

6435 CHELMSFORD (A.W) (L-H)
Thursday, August 29

OFFICIAL GOING: Polytrack: standard
Wind: light, across Weather: sunny and warm

6629 EAST COAST IPA FILLIES' NOVICE AUCTION STKS (PLUS 10 RACE) 7f (P)
1:30 (1:33) (Class 4) 2-Y-0
£5,822 (£1,732; £865; £432) **Stalls** Low

Form RPR

5422 **1** **Hashtagmetoo (USA)**[4] 6504 2-9-0 70.................. TomMarquand 6 71
(Jamie Osborne) *pressed ldr early: settled bk into midfield after: effrt and n.m.r 2f out: hdwy between rivals and drvn to ld jst ins fnl f: hld on wl fnl 100yds* **5/2**[2]

4254 **2** ½ **Incognito (IRE)**[14] 6118 2-9-0 75.......................... JamesDoyle 5 70
(Mick Channon) *in tch: hdwy to chse ldrs on outer 4f out: effrt over 2f out: drvn and ev ch over 1f out: kpt on wl but a jst hld fnl 100yds* **6/4**[1]

53 **3** 1 **Gladice**[51] 4766 2-8-12 0.......................... ShaneKelly 4 66+
(Marco Botti) *hld up in tch in midfield: nt clr run 2f out tl hdwy between rivals 1f out: kpt on u.p ins fnl f* **8/1**

1032 **4** hd **Space Ace (FR)**[3] 6527 2-9-6 76.....................(p) LukeMorris 7 72
(Archie Watson) *chsd ldrs tl clsd to join ldr over 5f out: rdn ent fnl 2f: drvn to ld over 1f out: hdd jst ins fnl f: no ex and jst outpcd fnl 100yds* **5/1**[3]

5 2½ **Decanter** 2-8-12 0.......................... DavidEgan 2 58
(Sylvester Kirk) *s.i.s: hld up in tch in last pair: effrt and swtchd rt over 1f out: pushed along and kpt on steadily ins fnl f: no threat to ldrs* **25/1**

34 **6** 2½ **Sweet Sixteen (GER)**[36] 5314 2-8-12 0.................. GeorgeWood 1 51
(Amy Murphy) *flashed tail leaving stalls: led: rdn and hdd over 1f out: flashed tail u.p and wknd ins fnl f* **20/1**

0 **7** nk **Goddess Of Fire**[105] 2761 2-8-11 0.................. RobertHavlin 3 49
(Ed Dunlop) *s.i.s: hld up in tch in last pair: effrt over 1f out: no imp: nvr involved* **9/1**

1m 26.3s (-0.90) **Going Correction** -0.20s/f (Stan) **7 Ran SP% 115.0**
Speed ratings (Par 93): **97,96,95,95,92 89,89**
CSF £6.73 TOTE £3.00: £1.50, £1.40; EX 6.60 Trifecta £27.50.
Owner The Other Club **Bred** Springhouse Farm **Trained** Upper Lambourn, Berks

FOCUS
Just a fair race of its type and quite a few still had a chance in the home straight. The winner has been rated to form.

6630 OLD SPECKLED HEN H'CAP 1m (P)
2:00 (2:02) (Class 4) (0-85,87) 3-Y-0+ **£5,530** (£1,645; £822; £411; £300) **Stalls** Low

Form RPR

1513 **1** **Solar Heights (IRE)**[54] 4639 3-9-8 **85**..................(v) JamesDoyle 4 98+
(James Tate) *broke wl: chsd ldrs tl wnt 2nd 3f out: rdn to ld over 1f out: sn in command and r.o strly: easily* **1/2**[1]

5060 **2** 6 **Tough Remedy (IRE)**[25] 5709 4-9-11 **87**.............. AndrewBreslin(5) 1 87
(Keith Dalgleish) *dwlt: in tch in last pair and racd lazily early: reminder over 5f out: rdn 3f out: drvn and outpcd over 2f out: no ch w wnr but plugged on to snatch 2nd towards fin* **6/1**[3]

5001 **3** ¾ **Lothario**[16] 6050 5-9-3 **74**.......................... RobertWinston 2 72
(Dean Ivory) *t.k.h: led: rdn and kicked on jst over 2f out: hdd over 1f out: sn brushed aside and wl btn fnl f: lost 2nd towards fin* **7/2**[2]

1550 **4** 2¾ **Liliofthelamplight (IRE)**[17] 6026 3-8-11 **74**............ FrannyNorton 3 65
(Mark Johnston) *s.i.s: hld up in last pair: effrt u.p over 2f out: sn outpcd and wl btn 4th 1f out* **12/1**

/00- **5** 48 **Initiative (IRE)**[296] 8891 4-9-6 **77**.......................... ShaneKelly 5
(Richard Price) *t.k.h to post: sn chsd ldr on outer: lost 2nd 3f out and hung rt: sn bhd and eased: t.o* **33/1**

1m 37.02s (-2.88) **Going Correction** -0.20s/f (Stan) **5 Ran SP% 113.8**
WFA 3 from 4yo+ 6lb
Speed ratings (Par 105): **106,100,99,96,48**
CSF £4.44 TOTE £1.20: £1.10, £1.90; EX 3.90 Trifecta £9.30.
Owner Saeed Manana **Bred** Norelands Bloodstock & Yarraman Park **Trained** Newmarket, Suffolk

FOCUS
The money came for the market leader and she duly won in comfortable style. It's tricky to pin down the level.

6631 ICE BREAKER PALE ALE H'CAP 6f (P)
2:30 (2:30) (Class 5) (0-75,75) 3-Y-0+
£5,175 (£1,540; £769; £384; £300; £300) **Stalls** Centre

Form RPR

1052 **1** **Desert Fox**[20] 5889 5-9-4 **67**..........................(p[1]) RossaRyan 8 74
(Mike Murphy) *bmpd leaving stalls: hld up in tch in rr: swtchd rt and hdwy over 1f out: drvn and str chal jst ins fnl f: sn led and kpt on wl* **9/2**[2]

3453 **2** nk **Restless Rose**[18] 5990 4-9-11 **74**.......................... JamesDoyle 2 80
(Stuart Williams) *wnt lft leaving stalls: t.k.h: chsd ldrs: effrt on inner over 1f out: drvn and ev ch jst ins fnl f: kpt on wl* **11/4**[1]

4504 **3** shd **Consequences (IRE)**[43] 5040 4-9-12 **75**.................. DavidEgan 1 81
(Ian Williams) *bmpd leaving stalls: hld up in tch: nt clr run and swtchd rt over 1f out: hdwy u.p and ev ch ins fnl f: kpt on wl: burst blood vessel (vet said gelding had bled from the nose)* **6/1**[3]

0066 **4** 1 **Kraka (IRE)**[14] 6132 4-9-6 **69**......................(v) KieranO'Neill 3 72
(Christine Dunnett) *t.k.h: led: rdn over 1f out: hdd ins fnl f: no ex and outpcd towards fin* **7/1**

0420 **5** ½ **Chookie Dunedin**[23] 5770 4-9-6 **69**.................. TomMarquand 6 70
(Keith Dalgleish) *hld up in tch: effrt ent fnl 2f: drvn over 1f out: kpt on ins fnl f: nt enough pce to rch ldrs* **9/2**[2]

0010 **6** nse **Broughtons Flare (IRE)**[62] 4338 3-9-3 **69**............ StevieDonohoe 9 70
(Philip McBride) *hld up in tch: effrt on outer wl over 1f out: kpt on ins fnl f: nt enough pce to rch ldrs* **20/1**

1301 **7** 1½ **Creek Harbour (IRE)**[20] 5889 4-9-2 **70**.............. WilliamCarver(5) 5 67
(Milton Bradley) *taken down early: hld up wl in tch in midfield: nt clr run over 1f out: hdwy betwen rivals 1f out: no imp ins fnl f* **7/1**

002P **8** 3½ **Sir Hector (IRE)**[20] 5889 4-8-12 **61**.......................... LukeMorris 4 47
(Charlie Wallis) *t.k.h: pressed ldr: drvn over 1f out: struggling to qckn and lost pl ent fnl f: wknd ins fnl f* **33/1**

The Form Book Flat 2019, Raceform Ltd, Newbury, RG14 5SJ

3605 **9** 1/2 **Gottardo (IRE)**^{24} 5723 4-9-0 **66**.......................(b) MeganNicholls$^{(3)}$ 7 51
(Ed Dunlop) *t.k.h: hung rt and chsd ldrs on outer: unable qck over 1f out: wknd ins fnl f (jockey said gelding hung right-handed and ran too free)* **11/1**

1m 11.57s (-2.13) **Going Correction** -0.20s/f (Stan)
WFA 3 from 4yo+ 3lb **9** Ran SP% **118.4**
Speed ratings (Par 103): **106,105,105,104,103 103,101,96,96**
CSF £17.78 CT £76.24 TOTE £4.60: £1.80, £1.10, £1.80; EX 17.70.
Owner Rogerson, Lemon, Cooper & Arlotte **Bred** C Rogerson & G Parsons **Trained** Westoning, Beds

FOCUS
This fair handicap didn't appear to be run at an overly strong early place, with plenty taking a keen hold. The second has been rated in line with her recent turf form.

6632 GREENE KING IPA CONDITIONS STKS (PLUS 10 RACE) 7f (P)
3:00 (3:01) (Class 2) 2-Y-O **£12,450** (£3,728; £1,864; £932) **Stalls** Low

Form RPR
51 **1** **Surf Dancer (IRE)**^{18} 5980 2-9-7 0.......................... JamesDoyle 2 88+
(William Haggas) *chsd ldng pair: effrt and swtchd rt over 1f out: rdn and qckn to ld 1f out: rn green and wnt lft ins fnl f: r.o and a doing enough fnl 100yds* **4/7**^{1}

1025 **2** 1/2 **Light Angel**^{19} 5962 2-9-7 92.......................... RobertHavlin 1 87
(John Gosden) *wnt rt leaving stalls: led: jinked rt 4f out: rdn wl over 1f out: hdd 1f out: kpt on same pce u.p ins fnl f (vet said colt lost its right-fore shoe)* **11/4**^{2}

3 1 1/2 **State Crown (IRE)** 2-9-0 0.......................... WilliamBuick 3 76+
(Charlie Appleby) *s.i.s: rn green: in tch in rr: effrt over 2f out: edgd lft over 1f out: swtchd rt and reminder ins fnl f: no threat to ldrs but gng on fin* **5/1**^{3}

0331 **4** 1 1/2 **Banmi (IRE)**^{13} 6146 2-9-2 72.......................... TomMarquand 4 74
(Mohamed Moubarak) *chsd ldr: c wd and effrt wl over 1f out: lost 2nd and no ex u.p ent fnl f: wknd fnl 100yds* **25/1**

1m 26.7s (-0.50) **Going Correction** -0.20s/f (Stan) **4** Ran SP% **110.8**
Speed ratings (Par 100): **94,93,91,90**
CSF £2.55 TOTE £1.30; EX 2.30 Trifecta £4.60.
Owner China Horse Club/Ballylinch Stud **Bred** Skymarc Farm & Qatar Bloodstock Limited **Trained** Newmarket, Suffolk

FOCUS
A decent small-field event, with the runner-up appearing to run somewhere close to his best. He rates the benchmark. It's hard to pin the level.

6633 OLD GOLDEN HEN FILLIES' NOVICE STKS 1m 5f 66y(P)
3:30 (3:30) (Class 3) 3-Y-O+ **£9,703** (£2,887; £1,443) **Stalls** Low

Form RPR
34 **1** **Fly The Flag**^{38} 5254 3-9-0 0.......................... RobertHavlin 1 80
(John Gosden) *sn led and mde rest and dictated stdy gallop: rdn and qcknd whn pressed over 2f out: edgd rt and bmpd ins fnl f: hld on wl* **7/4**^{2}

0-36 **2** 3/4 **Royal Family (FR)**^{22} 5810 3-9-0 70.......................(t^{1}) GeorgeWood 2 79
(Amy Murphy) *led: sn hdd and hld up in 3rd: pidn whn gallop qcknd over 2f out: swtchd lft over 1f out: kpt on wl u.p to go 2nd towards fin* **16/1**^{3}

-230 **3** 1/2 **King Power**^{67} 4171 3-9-0 84.......................... JamesDoyle 3 78
(Andrew Balding) *trckd wnr after 1f: rdn and effrt to press wnr over 2f out: stl pressing wnr but struggling to get past whn edgd lft and bmpd ins fnl f: kpt on same pce and lost 2nd towards fin* **4/9**^{1}

2m 54.42s (0.82) **Going Correction** -0.20s/f (Stan) **3** Ran SP% **111.5**
Speed ratings (Par 104): **89,88,88**
CSF £11.98 TOTE £2.50; EX 13.40 Trifecta £11.50.
Owner Denford Stud **Bred** Denford Stud Ltd **Trained** Newmarket, Suffolk

FOCUS
The two market leaders were in the first two throughout, and the leader just kept on going. The winner has been rated to her mark for now.

6634 GREENE KING FREE TRADE H'CAP 1m 6f (P)
4:00 (4:00) (Class 4) (0-80,78) 3-Y-O+ **£5,822** (£1,732; £865; £432; £300) **Stalls** Low

Form RPR
1550 **1** **El Borracho (IRE)**^{10} 6291 4-9-3 74.......................(h) LeviWilliams$^{(7)}$ 5 80
(Simon Dow) *stdd s: t.k.h: hld up in tch in rr: nt clr run over 2f out: sn swtchd rt and effrt to press ldrs 2f out: edgd lft and sltly impeded 1f out: rdn to ld ins fnl f: styd on wl (trainer said regarding apparent improvement in from that the gelding benefitted from the flat galloping track and the step up in trip from 1m3 1/2f to 1m6f)* **16/1**

1032 **2** 1 **Houlton**^{27} 5631 4-9-7 78.......................(tp) StefanoCherchi$^{(7)}$ 2 83
(Marco Botti) *trckd ldrs: effrt over 2f out: swtchd lft and clsd to press ldrs over 1f out: chsd wnr but no imp wl ins fnl f* **5/2**^{2}

1156 **3** 1 1/4 **Mister Chiang**^{12} 6232 3-9-1 75.......................(b) FrannyNorton 3 78
(Mark Johnston) *w ldr tl led after over 1f out: rdn and drifted rt bnd wl over 1f out: sn drvn and hrd pressed: hdd ins fnl f: one pce fnl 100yds* **7/4**^{1}

0610 **4** 10 **Early Summer (IRE)**^{29} 5540 4-9-13 77.......................... JamesDoyle 1 67
(Hughie Morrison) *led for over 1f: chsd ldr: rdn over 2f out: lost pl over 1f out: sn btn and wknd* **3/1**^{3}

-540 **5** 5 **Done Deal (IRE)**^{27} 5625 4-9-8 72.......................... LukeMorris 4 56
(Sir Mark Prescott Bt) *stdd s: t.k.h: hld up wl in tch: effrt u.p wl over 2f out: sn outpcd and btn: bhd over 1f out* **9/2**

2m 57.53s (-5.67) **Going Correction** -0.20s/f (Stan)
WFA 3 from 4yo 10lb **5** Ran SP% **114.0**
Speed ratings (Par 105): **108,107,106,101,98**
CSF £56.77 TOTE £49.90: £5.30, £1.60; EX 80.00 Trifecta £235.30.
Owner Robert Moss **Bred** Christopher Maye **Trained** Epsom, Surrey

FOCUS
An ordinary staying event won by a gelding who'd run moderately on his previous start and wasn't proven at the distance. The second and third suggest the form isn't worth rating any higher.

6635 BOOK TICKETS AT CHELMSFORDCITYRACECOURSE.COM H'CAP (DIV I) 1m 2f (P)
4:30 (4:32) (Class 6) (0-60,61) 3-Y-O+
£3,105 (£924; £461; £300; £300; £300) **Stalls** Low

Form RPR
0001 **1** **Warning Light**^{26} 5652 4-9-2 48.......................(tp) JosephineGordon 9 58+
(Shaun Keightley) *mde virtually all: rdn over 2f out: hung rt but asserting over 1f out: styd on strly and clr ins fnl f: readily* **3/1**^{2}

-044 **2** 4 **Reddiac (IRE)**^{21} 5866 3-9-5 58.......................(p^{1}) RobertHavlin 7 61
(Ed Dunlop) *hld up in tch in midfield: effrt over 2f out: hung lft over 1f out: chsd clr wnr ins fnl f: no imp* **12/1**

0612 **3** nk **Shifting Gold (IRE)**^{26} 5680 3-9-8 61.......................... DavidEgan 10 64
(William Knight) *swtchd lft after s: hld up in last pair: effrt on outer bnd 2f out: kpt on ins fnl f: no threat to wnr* **5/1**^{3}

0603 **4** 1 3/4 **Tronador (IRE)**^{19} 5946 3-9-7 60.......................(b^{1}) ShaneKelly 1 60
(David Lanigan) *awkward leaving stalls and rousted along early and reminder: hld up in last pair and travelling bttr after 2f: effrt ent fnl 2f: hung lft over 1f out: racing awkwardly swtchd rt and no imp ins fnl f (jockey said gelding was slowly away and reluctant to race in the early stages)* **11/4**^{1}

0000 **5** 1 **Reformed Character (IRE)**^{13} 6152 3-7-13 45.......(b) MorganCole$^{(7)}$ 8 43
(Lydia Pearce) *chsd ldrs tl wnt 2nd after 2f: hung rt and wd bnd over 3f out: pressing wnr and gng bk lft over 2f out: no ex over 1f out: lost 2nd and wknd ins fnl f (jockey said colt hung right-handed into the bend)* **50/1**

506 **6** 4 **Lope Athena**^{37} 5268 3-9-4 57.......................... RossaRyan 5 47
(Stuart Williams) *in tch in midfield: effrt and rdn to chse ldrs over 2f out tl lost pl over 1f out: wknd fnl f* **5/1**^{3}

0504 **7** 2 1/2 **Asensio**^{10} 6279 3-9-6 59.......................(t) TomMarquand 3 44
(Mohamed Moubarak) *in tch in midfield: effrt wl over 2f out: sn struggling and lost pl: wl hld over 1f out* **5/1**^{3}

4046 **8** 14 **Carvelas (IRE)**^{31} 5499 10-9-12 58.......................... NickyMackay 2 16
(J R Jenkins) *chsd wnr for 2f: chsd ldng pair after tl rdn and lost pl over 2f out: wl bhd ins fnl f (jockey said gelding ran flat)* **14/1**

2m 6.32s (-2.28) **Going Correction** -0.20s/f (Stan)
WFA 3 from 4yo+ 7lb **8** Ran SP% **118.0**
Speed ratings (Par 101): **101,97,97,96,95 92,90,78**
CSF £39.52 CT £177.65 TOTE £3.50: £1.30, £2.90, £2.00; EX 35.20 Trifecta £171.30.
Owner Simon Lockyer & Tim Clarke **Bred** Mr & Mrs J Davis & P Mitchell B'Stock **Trained** Newmarket, Suffolk

FOCUS
The first division of a moderate handicap in which the winner made pretty much all. The winner has been rated back near her best.

6636 BOOK TICKETS AT CHELMSFORDCITYRACECOURSE.COM H'CAP (DIV II) 1m 2f (P)
5:00 (5:02) (Class 6) (0-60,61) 3-Y-O+
£3,105 (£924; £461; £300; £300; £300) **Stalls** Low

Form RPR
0600 **1** **Petite Malle (USA)**^{14} 6130 3-9-5 58.......................... GeorgeWood 5 66+
(James Fanshawe) *dwlt and squeezed for room leaving stalls: hld up in tch towards rr: effrt over 2f out: hdwy and swtchd rt over 1f out: pressing ldr whn intimidated and wnt rt 1f out: sustained chal to ld last strides* **3/1**^{1}

6060 **2** hd **Thunderoad**^{17} 6022 3-9-5 58.......................... ShaneKelly 6 66+
(Tony Carroll) *hld up in tch: smooth hdwy on outer over 2f out: rdn to ld over 1f out: hung rt 1f out: drvn and kpt on ins fnl f: hdd last strides* **4/1**^{2}

60-0 **3** 3 1/4 **Duke Of Dunabar**^{119} 2341 3-9-0 53.......................(w) RossaRyan 2 54
(Roger Teal) *hld up in tch in midfield on inner: swtchd out and wnt between rivals to chse ldr briefly over 1f out: 3rd and one pce ins fnl f* **9/2**^{3}

-006 **4** 4 **Duke Of Yorkie (IRE)**^{22} 5797 3-8-6 45.......................... JimmyQuinn 8 39
(Adam West) *hld up in tch towards rr: pushed along and hdwy on outer to chse ldrs 5f out: rdn and unable qck over 2f out: wl hld and plugged on same pce fr over 1f out (vet said gelding lost its left fore shoe)* **16/1**

2020 **5** nk **Hard Toffee (IRE)**^{91} 3276 8-9-5 58.......................... GeorgeRooke$^{(7)}$ 7 50
(Louise Allan) *stdd s: hld up in tch in last trio: effrt over 2f out: no imp over 1f out: wl hld and plugged on same pce ins fnl f* **5/1**

004 **6** 1 1/4 **Astral Girl**^{43} 5048 3-9-8 61.......................... TomMarquand 1 52
(Hughie Morrison) *t.k.h early: trckd ldrs on inner: swtchd out rt and effrt to chse ldr over 2f out tl over 1f out: sn outpcd and wknd ins fnl f* **7/1**

0606 **7** 1 3/4 **Eagle Queen**^{24} 5744 3-9-7 60.......................(p^{1}) JosephineGordon 4 48
(Andrew Balding) *wl in tch in midfield: lost pl u.p over 3f out: bhd and hrd drvn 2f out: plugged on but no ch after* **6/1**

040 **7** dht **Bricklebrit**^{37} 5268 3-9-2 55.......................... JFEgan 10 43
(Rae Guest) *hld up in tch in last trio: effrt wl over 1f out: no prog: nvr involved* **25/1**

5541 **9** nk **Smith (IRE)**^{52} 4735 3-9-4 57.......................(v) LukeMorris 3 44
(Lydia Richards) *chsd ldrs: u.p over 2f out: unable qck and lost pl over 1f out: wknd ins fnl f* **14/1**

0000 **10** 1 1/2 **Milistorm**^{43} 5054 3-8-6 45.......................... EoinWalsh 11 29
(Michael Blanshard) *t.k.h: chsd ldr tl lost pl u.p over 2f out: wknd over 1f out* **50/1**

0060 **11** 1 **Lynchpin (IRE)**^{10} 6279 3-9-4 57.......................(b) AdrianMcCarthy 9 39
(Lydia Pearce) *t.k.h: led: rdn over 2f out: hdd and bmpd over 1f out: sn wknd* **33/1**

2m 6.39s (-2.21) **Going Correction** -0.20s/f (Stan)
WFA 3 from 8yo 7lb **11** Ran SP% **127.9**
Speed ratings (Par 101): **100,99,97,94,93 92,91,91,91,89 89**
CSF £16.23 CT £57.36 TOTE £3.30: £1.40, £1.90, £2.10; EX 19.20 Trifecta £127.70.
Owner Dr J P Ryan **Bred** John Ryan **Trained** Newmarket, Suffolk
■ Stewards' Enquiry : Shane Kelly two-day ban; careless riding (Sep 12-13)

FOCUS
The second division of this moderate handicap was run in an almost identical time to the first. The second has been rated within 6lb of this year's best.
T/Plt: £51.70 to a £1 stake. Pool: £25,428.57 - 491.78 winning units. T/Qpdt: £23.60 to a £1 stake. Pool: £2,300.58 - 97.19 winning units. **Steve Payne**

6394 FFOS LAS (L-H)
Thursday, August 29

OFFICIAL GOING: Good (9.1)
Wind: breezy, getting stronger Weather: cloudy, sunny intervals

6637 KP TYRES NURSERY H'CAP 6f
1:20 (1:22) (Class 5) (0-70,72) 2-Y-O
£3,428 (£1,020; £509; £300; £300; £300) **Stalls** Centre

Form RPR
343 **1** **Endless Joy**^{17} 6028 2-9-6 72.......................... OisinMurphy 5 78
(Archie Watson) *mde all: shkn up in 1/2 l ld 1f out: pushed along fnl f: r.o wl* **5/2**^{2}

353 **2** 1 **Jump The Gun (IRE)**^{28} 5591 2-9-5 71.......................... CallumShepherd 6 74
(Jamie Osborne) *slowly away: hld up: tk clsr order 1/2-way: trckd ldrs 2f out: plld out to chal 1 1/2f out: 1/2 l 2nd 1f out: rdn fnl f: r.o but nt pce of wnr* **11/4**^{3}

422 **3** 4 1/2 **Dana Forever (IRE)**[17] 6028 2-9-6 **72**........................ RichardKingscote 2 62
(Tom Dascombe) *prom: pushed along in 2nd 2f out: drvn and dropped to 3rd over 1f out: rdn fnl f: one pce* **15/8**[1]
6163 **4** *nk* **Isobar Wind (IRE)**[16] 6041 2-9-4 **70**........................(h[1]) JasonWatson 7 59
(David Evans) *trckd ldrs: drvn 2f out: rdn over 1f out: one pce* **10/1**
3414 **5** *nk* **Twice As Likely**[48] 4861 2-9-0 **69**........................ FinleyMarsh(3) 1 57
(Richard Hughes) *mid-div: drvn 2f out: rdn in 4th 1f out: one pce fnl f* **7/1**
1250 **6** 4 **Lili Wen Fach (IRE)**[23] 5777 2-9-2 **68**........................ KieranShoemark 3 44
(David Evans) *hld up: last 1/2-way: drvn and effrt over 2f out: rdn and wknd over 1f out* **20/1**
3300 **7** 3 1/2 **Daddies Diva**[16] 6053 2-9-4 **70**........................ CharlieBennett 4 35
(Rod Millman) *trckd ldrs: pushed along and lost pl 1/2-way: last 2f out: reminder and lost tch over 1f out* **33/1**

1m 11.46s (0.56) **Going Correction** -0.125s/f (Firm) **7** Ran SP% **119.3**
Speed ratings (Par 94): **91,89,83,83,82 77,72**
CSF £10.54 TOTE £3.00: £1.60, £2.90; EX 10.90 Trifecta £39.50.
Owner Clipper Logistics **Bred** Whitsbury Manor Stud And Mrs M E Slade **Trained** Upper Lambourn, W Berks

FOCUS
The official going was given as good (GoingStick 9.1). The rail was moved out on the bend, adding 21yds to races 4, 5 and 7 and 35yds to race 6. The pace was steady in this fair nursery, so the first pair deserve credit for pulling so readily clear in the closing stages and will remain of interest. They tacked across to the stands' rail early but it didn't have much bearing on the result. The second's debut form could be rated this high.

6638 WEATHERBYS RACING BANK H'CAP 6f
1:50 (1:51) (Class 5) (0-70,69) 3-Y-O
£3,428 (£1,020; £509; £300; £300; £300) **Stalls** Centre

Form RPR
0311 **1** **Gilt Edge**[6] 6397 3-8-13 **66** 6ex........................ RhiainIngram(5) 4 72+
(Christopher Mason) *trckd ldrs: tk clsr order 1/2-way: pushed into ld 2f out: drvn in 1/2 l ld 1f out: rdn fnl f: hld on wl* **11/10**[1]
1560 **2** 1/2 **Elzaam's Dream (IRE)**[19] 5957 3-8-5 **53**........................(h) RaulDaSilva 6 57
(Ronald Harris) *hld up: pushed along and hdwy to chal 2f out: rdn in 1/2 l 2nd 1f out: r.o fnl f: a jst hld* **4/1**[2]
0043 **3** 2 **Soldier's Son**[23] 5786 3-8-11 **66**........................ EmmaTaff(7) 1 64
(Henry Candy) *led: narrow ld 1/2-way: hdd 2f out: sn rdn: one pce fnl f* **11/2**
5002 **4** 1/2 **Cotubanama**[36] 5308 3-9-2 **69**........................ ScottMcCullagh(5) 5 66
(Mick Channon) *hld up: pushed along 2f out: rdn in 4th over 1f out: one pce fnl f* **8/1**
3000 **5** 1 1/2 **Grandstand (IRE)**[8] 6329 3-8-7 **55**........................ HollieDoyle 7 47
(Richard Price) *mid-div: rdn and lost pl over 2f out: one pce fnl 2f* **18/1**
350- **6** 2 3/4 **Assembly Of Truth (IRE)**[60] 3-9-4 **66**........................ OisinMurphy 2 50
(David Evans) *prom: drvn and lost pl over 2f out: reminder and wknd over 1f out* **9/2**[3]
0000 **7** 12 **Andies Armies**[13] 6181 3-7-13 **45** oh5........................(p) NoelGarbutt(3) 3
(Lisa Williamson) *slowly away: a bhd (jockey said gelding was reluctant to jump from the stalls)* **40/1**

1m 11.17s (0.27) **Going Correction** -0.125s/f (Firm) **7** Ran SP% **120.0**
Speed ratings (Par 100): **93,92,89,89,87 83,67**
CSF £6.38 TOTE £1.90: £1.40, £3.00; EX 7.30 Trifecta £29.80.
Owner S Bishop And C Mason **Bred** Christopher & Annabelle Mason **Trained** Caewent, Monmouthshire

FOCUS
This was more truly run than the nursery, making for a level playing field and a result that can be relied upon. The second has been rated back to her best.

6639 MR AND MRS DAVENPORT 1ST ANNIVERSARY H'CAP 5f
2:20 (2:22) (Class 6) (0-65,61) 3-Y-O+
£2,781 (£827; £413; £300; £300; £300) **Stalls** Centre

Form RPR
0435 **1** **Brandy Station (IRE)**[19] 5952 4-9-3 **59**........................(p[1]) GavinAshton(7) 4 70
(Lisa Williamson) *mde all: 2 l ld 2f out: reminder in 2 1/2 l ld 1f out: pushed further clr fnl f: comf* **10/3**[3]
2023 **2** 4 **Spot Lite**[7] 6365 4-9-7 **56**........................(p) OisinMurphy 2 53
(Rod Millman) *hld up: pushed along 2f out: rdn into 2nd ent fnl f: kpt on: nvr nr wnr* **3/1**[2]
-321 **3** 1 **Tawaafoq**[8] 6329 5-9-9 **61** 5ex........................(h) FinleyMarsh(3) 5 54
(Adrian Wintle) *hld up: pushed along in last 2f out: rdn over 1f out: r.o fnl f: tk 3rd last 50yds* **2/1**[1]
5206 **4** *hd* **Brockey Rise (IRE)**[1] 6605 4-9-12 **61**........................(b) KieranShoemark 6 53
(David Evans) *hld up: drvn 2f out: sn rdn: 5th 1f out: kpt on into 4th fnl f* **5/1**
6025 **5** 1 **Celerity (IRE)**[13] 6168 5-8-8 **46**........................(p) NoelGarbutt(3) 3 35
(Lisa Williamson) *chsd ldr: drvn 2f out: lost pl over 1f out: wknd fnl f* **16/1**
1131 **6** *shd* **Aquadabra (IRE)**[10] 6285 4-9-11 **60** 5ex........................ CallumShepherd 1 48
(Christopher Mason) *restless in stalls: mid-div: pushed along and hdwy over 1f out: wknd and dropped to last fnl f* **6/1**

58.29s (-0.71) **Going Correction** -0.125s/f (Firm) **6** Ran SP% **118.2**
Speed ratings (Par 101): **100,93,92,91,90 89**
CSF £14.66 TOTE £3.40: £1.50, £2.10; EX 15.30 Trifecta £56.10.
Owner A V Wilding (chester) Ltd **Bred** Seamus Finucane **Trained** Taporley, Wrexham

FOCUS
The field split into two groups, which may have disadvantaged the pair that raced on the stands' rail, but it didn't affect the result so far as the easy winner was concerned. He was simply too speedy for his rivals on the day. The winner has been rated as repeating last year's winning figure.

6640 WEATHERBYS VAT SERVICES MAIDEN STKS 7f 80y(R)
2:50 (2:53) (Class 5) 2-Y-O £3,428 (£1,020; £509; £254) **Stalls** Centre

Form RPR
2 **1** **It's Good To Laugh (IRE)**[35] 5345 2-9-5 0........................ HectorCrouch 8 79
(Clive Cox) *prom: pushed along in cl 2nd 2f out: rdn ent fnl f: led 150yds out: sn drifted lft u.p: asserted last 50yds* **8/13**[1]
2 1 1/4 **Black Comedy (FR)** 2-9-5 0........................ SeanLevey 5 76
(Richard Hannon) *led: pushed along in narrow ld 2f out: drvn ent fnl f: rdn and hdd 150yds out: sn carried lft by wnr: kpt on but hld last 50yds* **12/1**[3]
3 1/2 **Raatea** 2-9-5 0........................ MartinDwyer 1 75
(Marcus Tregoning) *t.k.h: chsd ldrs: pushed along 2f out: drvn over 1f out: kpt on fnl f* **20/1**
4 3/4 **Modmin (IRE)** 2-9-5 0........................ DaneO'Neill 12 73+
(Marcus Tregoning) *mid-div: pushed along and hdwy over 2f out: rdn in 4th over 1f out: r.o fnl f (vet said colt lost his right fore shoe)* **16/1**

0 **5** 5 **Abadie**[102] 2869 2-9-5 0........................(w) HollieDoyle 6 60
(Archie Watson) *t.k.h: chsd ldrs: rdn and lost grnd 2f out: no ex fnl f: along* **12/1**[3]
6 **6** *hd* **Mira Star (IRE)**[26] 5684 2-9-0 0........................ JasonWatson 4 55
(Ed Vaughan) *chsd ldrs: drvn over 2f out: reminder over 1f out: no ex fnl f* **5/1**[2]
00 **7** 4 **Staycee**[45] 4992 2-9-0 0........................ CharlieBennett 7 45
(Rod Millman) *hld up: rdn 2f out: no imp* **66/1**
60 **8** 1 3/4 **Big Boris (IRE)**[6] 6395 2-9-5 0........................ KieranShoemark 13 45
(David Evans) *hld up: pushed along 2f out: no imp* **66/1**
9 3 1/4 **Alargedram (IRE)** 2-9-5 0........................ TomQueally 3 37+
(Alan King) *hld up: pushed along and effrt 2f out: sn no ex* **16/1**
10 3 1/4 **Given (IRE)** 2-8-9 0........................ RachealKneller(5) 9 24
(Debbie Hughes) *chsd ldrs on outer: lost pl 3f out: sn drvn and wknd* **66/1**
0 **11** 7 **Mr Jack Daniels**[66] 4184 2-9-5 0........................ RaulDaSilva 2 12
(John Spearing) *t.k.h: mid-div: drvn over 2f out: dropped away over 1f out* **100/1**
00 **12** 9 **John Leo's Son (IRE)**[6] 6395 2-9-0 0........................(t[1]) RhiainIngram(5) 11
(David Evans) *hld up: pushed along and lost tch over 2f out* **100/1**

1m 34.26s (1.16) **Going Correction** -0.125s/f (Firm) **12** Ran SP% **117.0**
Speed ratings (Par 94): **88,86,86,85,79 79,74,72,68,65 57,46**
CSF £8.13 TOTE £1.30: £1.02, £3.70, £6.40; EX 8.40 Trifecta £78.50.
Owner Paul & Clare Rooney **Bred** Shane Molan **Trained** Lambourn, Berks

■ Vulcan was withdrawn. Price at time of withdrawal 4/1. Rule 4 applies to all bets - deduction 20p in the £.

FOCUS
Add 21yds. The hot favourite led home a trio of well-bred newcomers in a race that might prove to be above average, the Hamdan Al Maktoum-owned pair in third and fourth producing particularly eye-catching displays. The pace was modest to start with but picked up around the halfway mark. The winner has been rated in line with his debut.

6641 WEATHERBYS RACING BANK FOREIGN EXCHANGE NOVICE STKS 1m 3f 209y(R)
3:20 (3:26) (Class 5) 3-Y-O+ £3,428 (£1,020; £509; £254) **Stalls** Low

Form RPR
6-1 **1** **Trueshan (FR)**[27] 5634 3-9-9 0........................ HollieDoyle 3 99
(Alan King) *trckd ldrs: pushed along and hdwy over 2f out: led 1 1/2f out: rdn clr fnl f: comf* **9/2**[3]
2423 **2** 2 3/4 **Caravan Of Hope (IRE)**[12] 6211 3-9-2 **81**........................ JackMitchell 5 88
(Hugo Palmer) *kicked by rival in stalls: bked out and checked bef clred to r: prom: pushed into ld over 2f out: rdn and hdd 1 1/2f out: no ex fnl f (colt was kicked by Just Champion in the starting stalls. Having been examined by the vet the colt was deemed fit to race)* **9/4**[2]
0-2 **3** 8 **Alignak**[105] 2769 3-9-2 0........................ OisinMurphy 1 75
(Sir Michael Stoute) *led: pushed along 3f out: rdn and hdd over 2f out: sn wknd* **4/7**[1]
4 **4** 22 **Ruby Wine**[24] 5748 3-8-11 0........................ GeorgeDowning 7 35
(Jeremy Scott) *hld up: drvn 3f out: rdn and lost tch over 2f out* **20/1**
55 **5** 1 **Pensee**[33] 5421 3-8-11 0........................ JasonWatson 6 33
(Roger Charlton) *hld up on outer: drvn 4f out: lost tch over 2f out* **10/1**
P5 **6** 19 **Hurry Kane**[16] 6043 3-8-11 0........................ RhiainIngram(5) 2
(Paul George) *trckd ldrs: lost pl bef 1/2-way: drvn and wknd over 3f out* **40/1**
00 **7** 29 **Binmar's Sexy Lexy (CAN)**[10] 6290 3-8-11 0........................ CallumShepherd 8
(Stuart Kittow) *a in rr: drvn and lost tch 4f out: sn heavily eased* **80/1**

2m 31.18s (-9.02) **Going Correction** -0.125s/f (Firm) course record **7** Ran SP% **130.1**
Speed ratings (Par 103): **116,114,108,94,93 80,61**
CSF £17.45 TOTE £6.10: £2.00, £1.40; EX 28.20 Trifecta £40.80.
Owner Barbury Lions 5 **Bred** Didier Blot **Trained** Barbury Castle, Wilts

■ Just Champion was withdrawn. Price at time of withdrawal 100/1. Rule 4 does not apply.

FOCUS
Add 21yds. The favourite was disappointing, leaving this for an upwardly-mobile gelding to comfortably wear down a solid, yet exposed rival. The rest were beaten a long way. The ratings could be 4lb out either way.

6642 WEATHERBYS TBA H'CAP 1m 6f (R)
3:50 (3:52) (Class 5) (0-75,73) 3-Y-O+
£3,428 (£1,020; £509; £300; £300; £300) **Stalls** Low

Form RPR
0331 **1** **Tavus (IRE)**[23] 5778 3-8-11 **65**........................ JasonWatson 4 73+
(Roger Charlton) *prom early: sn settled in mid-div: pushed along and hdwy over 2f out: drvn to ld ent fnl 2f: rdn over 1f out: asserted fnl f: on top nr fin (jockey said gelding hung right-handed under pressure)* **4/9**[1]
5134 **2** 1 1/2 **Victoriano (IRE)**[6] 6419 3-9-5 **73**........................(b) OisinMurphy 5 77
(Archie Watson) *trckd ldrs: 2nd 4f out: drvn and jinked lft over 2f out: sn rdn: styd on fnl f: no threat to wnr* **3/1**[2]
5520 **3** 3/4 **Arthur Pendragon (IRE)**[17] 6030 3-9-4 **72**........................(bt) MartinDwyer 2 75
(Brian Meehan) *trckd ldrs: hdwy to ld after 3f: pushed along in narrow ld 3f out: drvn 2f out: sn hdd and rdn: kpt on fnl f* **20/1**
203 **4** 1/2 **Marengo**[14] 6104 8-9-12 **70**........................(b) KieranShoemark 3 70
(Bernard Llewellyn) *hld up: pushed along over 3f out: drvn and hdwy over 2f out: cl up whn rdn over 1f out: no ex fnl f: lost shoe (vet said gelding lost his right hind shoe)* **20/1**
414 **5** *hd* **Nabhan**[12] 6218 7-9-9 **72**........................(tp) ScottMcCullagh(5) 8 72
(Bernard Llewellyn) *hld up: pushed along and hdwy over 2f out: rdn to chal over 1f out: no ex fnl f: lost shoe (vet said gelding lost his right fore shoe)* **16/1**
5334 **6** 3 **Panatos (FR)**[12] 6200 4-8-11 **62**........................ LukeCatton(7) 1 58
(Alexandra Dunn) *led: hdd after 3f: trckd ldr whn hdd: 3rd 4f out: pushed along and lost pl over 2f out: rdn and wknd over 1f out* **14/1**[3]
044 **7** 9 **Persepone**[34] 5384 3-8-11 **65**........................ JackMitchell 6 52
(Hugo Palmer) *hld up on outer: drvn and dropped to last over 2f out: sn rdn and lost tch: eased fnl f* **16/1**

3m 4.37s (-4.23) **Going Correction** -0.125s/f (Firm)
WFA 3 from 4yo+ 10lb **7** Ran SP% **122.2**
Speed ratings (Par 103): **107,106,105,105,105 103,98**
CSF £2.42 CT £9.84 TOTE £1.60: £1.10, £2.00; EX 3.00 Trifecta £19.90.
Owner Tony Bloom **Bred** Gillian, Lady Howard De Walden **Trained** Beckhampton, Wilts

FOCUS
Add 35yds. The pace was a bit stop-start but the result wasn't affected, the only improving sort in the field comfortably on top in the end having worked hard to get to the front. The second and third help set the level.

6643 3A'S LEISURE SUPER SITE NANTYCI H'CAP 1m (R)
4:20 (4:23) (Class 6) (0-60,60) 3-Y-0+
£2,781 (£827; £413; £300; £300; £300) Stalls Centre

Form RPR
0-05 1 **Basilisk (USA)**98 3019 3-9-3 58 JasonWatson 11 63+
(Roger Charlton) *disp ld: hdd over 2f out: disp ld 1 1/2f out: drvn 1f out: rdn and drifted lft ins fnl f: led 100yds out: r.o (jockey said gelding hung left-handed under pressure)* 9/2[2]
0421 2 ½ **All Right**21 5867 3-9-2 57 DaneO'Neill 1 61+
(Henry Candy) *trckd ldrs: hdwy and cl up 2f out: rdn to dispute ld 1 1/2f out: hdd 100yds out: no ex* 7/2[1]
3034 3 ½ **Accomplice**8 6334 5-9-6 55 CharlieBennett 16 59
(Michael Blanshard) *hld up: pushed along and hdwy over 2f out: rdn over 1f out: r.o wl into 3rd fnl f: nvr nrr* 11/1
0236 4 shd **Mabo**8 6334 4-9-2 51 (b) KieranShoemark 5 55
(Grace Harris) *hld up: pushed along 2f out: rdn and hdwy over 1f out: r.o wl fnl f: tk 4th nr fin* 14/1
5432 5 ½ **Sea Tea Dea**36 5293 5-8-8 46 FinleyMarsh(3) 4 49
(Adrian Wintle) *mid-div: drvn 2f out: rdn 1f out: kpt on fnl f* 11/1
0001 6 ½ **Set Point Charlie (IRE)**7 6361 3-9-5 60 6ex (t) TomQueally 7 60
(Seamus Durack) *hld up: pushed along 2f out: rdn and hdwy ent fnl f: r.o: nvr nrr* 5/1[3]
5450 7 shd **Edge (IRE)**8 6334 8-9-0 54 (b) ScottMcCullagh(5) 10 55
(Bernard Llewellyn) *hld up in last: hdwy over 2f out: rdn over 1f out: r.o fnl f (jockey said gelding hung left-handed in the straight)* 10/1
2030 8 ¾ **Lonicera**37 5284 3-9-4 59 DavidProbert 6 58
(Henry Candy) *disp ld: led on own 2f out: drvn and hdd 1 1/2f out: sn rdn: wknd fnl f* 8/1
/004 9 ½ **Lovely Acclamation (IRE)**36 5293 5-8-6 46 ow1 (p) RachealKneller(5) 8 44
(Debbie Hughes) *chsd ldrs: drvn 2f out: rdn and wknd over 1f out* 20/1
004 10 1¾ **Elena Osorio (IRE)**13 6169 3-9-2 57 LiamKeniry 14 50
(David Elsworth) *hld up: drvn in rr over 2f out: rdn over 1f out: mod hdwy fnl f* 12/1
0045 11 ½ **Bakht A Rawan (IRE)**14 6123 7-9-3 59 GeorgiaDobie(7) 13 52
(Roger Teal) *hld up: rdn and wknd over 2f out* 18/1
0315 12 1¼ **Lippy Lady (IRE)**14 6117 3-8-9 55 (h) RhiainIngram(5) 12 44
(Paul George) *t.k.h: mid-div: rdn and lost pl over 1f out: wknd and eased fnl f* 10/1
000 13 9 **Medici Moon**8 6334 5-9-0 49 (h[1]) HollieDoyle 3 19
(Richard Price) *hld up: reminder over 3f out: sn rdn and wknd* 16/1
4550 14 1¼ **Warrior Display (IRE)**29 5548 3-9-0 58 (v[1]) WilliamCox(3) 9 24
(Bernard Llewellyn) *mid-div: rdn and wknd 3f out* 33/1

1m 40.44s (-2.46) **Going Correction** -0.125s/f (Firm)
WFA 3 from 4yo+ 6lb **14 Ran SP% 136.2**
Speed ratings (Par 101): **107,106,106,105,105 104,104,104,103,101 101,100,91,89**
CSF £23.61 CT £184.81 TOTE £5.20: £2.50, £1.70, £4.10; EX 37.20 Trifecta £213.70.
Owner K Abdullah **Bred** Juddmonte Farms Inc **Trained** Beckhampton, Wilts
FOCUS
Add 21 yds. They went a good gallop from the outset so, although there were a handful of late closers, the prominently ridden front two look full value for their performances and are the pair to take from the race, which was competitive for the grade. The fourth and fifth help give some perspective on the level of the form.
T/Plt: £38.90 to a £1 stake. Pool: £48,625.07 - 911.83 winning units. T/Qpdt: £9.20 to a £1 stake. Pool: £4,612.75 - 367.11 winning units. **Keith McHugh**

6644 - 6645a (Foreign Racing) - See Raceform Interactive

5994 TIPPERARY (L-H)
Thursday, August 29
OFFICIAL GOING: Round course - good to yielding ; sprint course - good

6646a COOLMORE STUD FAIRY BRIDGE STKS (GROUP 3) (F&M) 7f 110y
5:55 (5:56) 3-Y-0+
£34,549 (£11,126; £5,270; £2,342; £1,171; £585)

RPR
1 **Waitingfortheday (IRE)**5 6480 4-9-5 97 (p) DonnachaO'Brien 11 104+
(Joseph Patrick O'Brien, Ire) *hld up towards rr early: tk clsr order and disp 5th bef 1/2-way: rdn into 4th over 1f out and r.o wl u.p nr side ins fnl f to ld cl home* 6/1[3]
2 ½ **Skitter Scatter (USA)**116 2443 3-9-0 114 RonanWhelan 7 102
(John M Oxx, Ire) *led briefly early tl sn hdd and settled bhd ldrs: disp 5th bef 1/2-way: prog after 1/2-way: impr to chal over 1f out: rdn to ld briefly wl ins fnl f tl hdd cl home* 5/2[1]
3 ½ **Hells Babe**17 6014 6-9-5 94 LewisEdmunds 6 101
(Michael Appleby) *pushed along to sn ld: extended advantage after 1f: reduced ld bef 1/2-way: rdn and pressed clly 1 1/2f out: hdd wl ins fnl f and hld in 3rd cl home* 16/1
4 2 **I Remember You (IRE)**14 6137 3-9-0 97 WayneLordan 4 96
(A P O'Brien, Ire) *chsd ldrs: clsr in 2nd bef 1/2-way: rdn 1 1/2f out and no ex u.p ins fnl f where dropped to 4th* 25/1
5 nk **Wisdom Mind (IRE)**5 6480 4-9-5 95 (t) GaryHalpin 1 95
(Joseph Patrick O'Brien, Ire) *towards rr and pushed along briefly early: hdwy over 2f out to chse ldrs: rdn in 5th far side ins fnl f and no ex u.p clsng stages* 25/1
6 nk **Rionach**5 6480 4-9-5 99 (h) LeighRoche 2 95+
(M D O'Callaghan, Ire) *chsd ldrs early: 7th bef 1/2-way: drvn and n.m.r briefly under 2f out: impeded sltly over 1f out: kpt on clsng stages: nvr trbld ldrs* 16/1
7 nk **Dan's Dream**20 5916 4-9-5 102 WJLee 3 94
(Mick Channon) *chsd ldrs: 4th bef 1/2-way: pushed along bhd ldrs under 2f out: rdn over 1f out and no imp on ldrs: one pce ins fnl f* 11/4[2]
8 nk **Titanium Sky (IRE)**28 5598 3-9-0 96 OisinOrr 9 93
(D K Weld, Ire) *w.w in rr: pushed along out wd into st where n.m.r briefly: sme hdwy 1f out: r.o u.p ins fnl f: nvr nrr* 6/1[3]
9 ½ **Blizzard**27 5608 4-9-5 98 HarryBentley 8 92
(Ralph Beckett) *mid-div: pushed along over 2f out where n.m.r briefly: no ex u.p 1 1/2f out: one pce after* 9/1
10 2½ **Iiex Excelsa (IRE)**77 3786 4-9-5 90 (p) ChrisHayes 12 86
(J A Stack, Ire) *mid-div early: tk clsr order in 3rd bef 1/2-way: gng wl into st: drvn and wknd qckly 1 1/2f out* 66/1
11 3½ **Morpho Blue (IRE)**34 5369 3-9-0 89 (p) TomMadden 13 77
(Mrs John Harrington, Ire) *hld up in rr of mid-div: drvn out wd into st and sn wknd* 33/1
12 ¾ **Fire Fly (IRE)**5 6480 3-9-0 99 (h) SeamieHeffernan 5 75
(A P O'Brien, Ire) *dwlt sltly and in rr briefly: sn settled in rr of mid-div after 1f where short of room and checked sltly: sn dropped to rr: drvn under 2f out where tk clsr order: nt clr run over 1f out: sn eased (jockey said that his mount suffered bad interference in the straight and was pulled up)* 16/1

1m 35.17s
WFA 3 from 4yo+ 5lb **12 Ran SP% 123.6**
CSF £21.62 TOTE £6.90: £2.30, £1.10, £6.40; DF 31.30 Trifecta £194.10.
Owner J Dollard **Bred** James Fennelly **Trained** Owning Hill, Co Kilkenny
FOCUS
A real feather in the cap of Joseph O'Brien, who has done a marvellous job with this four-year-old.

6647a (Foreign Racing) - See Raceform Interactive

6648a ABERGWAUN STKS (LISTED RACE) 5f
6:55 (7:01) 3-Y-0+
£23,918 (£7,702; £3,648; £1,621; £810; £405)

RPR
1 **Nitro Boost (IRE)**36 5325 3-9-0 98 WJLee 9 97
(W McCreery, Ire) *cl up nr side gp: effrt over 1f out: r.o wl to ld ins fnl f: all out cl home where strly pressed: jst hld on (trainer stated that the drop back to 5f and the advantageous stand side draw both contributed to the improvement in form; trainer said that his charge pulled a right fore shoe during the race)* 8/1
2 nse **Rapid Reaction (IRE)**36 5325 4-9-2 88 AndrewSlattery 12 97
(J F Grogan, Ire) *hld up nr side gp: 11th 1/2-way: rdn and hdwy over 1f out: r.o wl ins fnl f where flashed tail to strly press wnr cl home: jst failed* 16/1
3 1½ **Urban Beat (IRE)**76 3818 4-9-10 101 ShaneFoley 11 100
(J P Murtagh, Ire) *w.w towards rr nr side: gp: 10th 1/2-way: prog u.p over 1f out: no imp on wnr in 3rd nr fin: kpt on same pce* 3/1[1]
4 ½ **Deia Glory**33 5471 3-9-0 93 WayneLordan 8 90
(Michael Dods) *prom nr side gp: disp 4th bef 1/2-way: effrt over 1f out: no imp on ldrs in 4th wl ins fnl f: kpt on same pce* 20/1
5 ½ **Gold Filigree (IRE)**25 5705 4-9-2 96 SeamieHeffernan 6 88+
(Richard Hughes) *led and disp far side gp: drvn and hdd after 1/2-way: no ex u.p bhd ldrs ins fnl f: one pce clsngs stages* 10/1
6 ½ **Hit The Bid**173 1111 5-9-7 110 (t) ChrisHayes 1 91+
(D J Bunyan, Ire) *led and disp far side gp early: cl 3rd bef 1/2-way: drvn and led narrowly after 1/2-way: hdd u.p ins fnl f and wknd nr fin* 10/1
7 nk **Chessman (IRE)**40 5205 5-9-7 101 (t) OisinOrr 10 90
(Richard John O'Brien, Ire) *w.w nr side gp early: last bef 1/2-way: rdn after 1/2-way and sme hdwy u.p 1f out: kpt on in 7th nr fin: nvr on terms* 7/1[3]
8 ½ **Ardhoomey (IRE)**40 5205 7-9-7 100 (t) ColinKeane 3 88+
(G M Lyons, Ire) *chsd ldrs far side: pushed along after 1/2-way: rdn briefly ins fnl f and no ex nr fin where dropped to 8th* 7/1[3]
9 1½ **Mistress Of Venice**18 5996 4-9-2 75 (b) NGMcCullagh 5 78+
(K J Condon, Ire) *s.i.s and pushed along briefly early: tk clsr order down centre in 9th bef 1/2-way: pushed along after 1/2-way and no imp u.p over 1f out: one pce after* 40/1
10 3½ **Julia's Magic (IRE)**54 4676 4-9-2 88 GaryCarroll 2 65+
(Mrs Denise Foster, Ire) *cl up far side early: pushed along disputing 4th bef 1/2-way: no ex and wknd 1 1/2f out* 28/1
11 ¾ **Jungle Jane (IRE)**519 1436 3-9-0 0 LeighRoche 7 63+
(W McCreery, Ire) *cl up far side and disp ld briefly bef 1/2-way: pushed along and hdd after 1/2-way: wknd 1 1/2f out* 25/1
12 8½ **Hathiq (IRE)**18 5996 5-9-7 96 (t) RoryCleary 4 37+
(Denis Gerard Hogan, Ire) *w.w far side gp: pushed along in 8th at 1/2-way and wknd fr under 2f out* 4/1[2]

57.77s (-1.23)
WFA 3 from 4yo+ 2lb **12 Ran SP% 119.7** CSF £122.98 TOTE £9.20: £2.60, £5.00, £1.50; DF 178.20 Trifecta £746.80.
Owner Imperial Crown Syndicate **Bred** Philip & Orla Hore **Trained** Rathbride, Co Kildare **FOCUS**
A high draw was obviously a help, with the first four home emerging from stalls 9, 12 11 and 8. The winner is a solid filly who showed her ability against her elders. The second, fourth and ninth potentially limit the level of the form.

6649a-6650a (Foreign Racing) - See Raceform Interactive

4011 LE LION-D'ANGERS (R-H)
Thursday, August 29
OFFICIAL GOING: Turf: good to soft

6651a HANDICAP DU LION D'ANGERS - PRIX DE L'ASSELCO (H'CAP) (4YO+ FILLIES & MARES) (TURF) 1m 2f
12:50 4-Y-0+
£23,423 (£8,900; £6,558; £3,747; £1,873; £1,405)

RPR
1 **Lanana (FR)**17 4-9-6 0 EddyHardouin 11 88
(Robert Collet, France) 184/10
2 1 **Plantlove (FR)**17 4-8-10 0 HugoJourniac 7 76
(M Nigge, France) 9/1
3 2 **L'Indomptable (FR)**14 4-9-4 0 AnthonyCrastus 2 80
(C Escuder, France) 13/1
4 ¾ **Flor De Seda (FR)**17 6031 4-8-2 0 HugoBesnier 16 63
(Jo Hughes, France) *tacked over fr wd draw to ld after 1f: urged along over 2f out: rdn over 1f out: drvn and hdd ins fnl f: no ex fnl 75yds* 61/1
5 ¾ **Creativity (FR)**28 4-8-9 0 RonanThomas 6 69
(J E Hammond, France) 9/1
6 1½ **Blue Hills (FR)**17 5-8-7 0 MaximeGuyon 4 64
(J Reynier, France) 17/5[1]
7 1½ **Cazaline (FR)**122 2226 4-8-11 0 TonyPiccone 9 65
(M Delaplace, France) 21/1
8 ½ **Montina (FR)**17 6031 5-8-5 0 (p) MlleCoraliePacaut 14 58
(Werner Glanz, Germany) 43/5[3]

9 2 **Pop Song**[12] 4-9-7 0 JulienGuillochon 5 70
(H-A Pantall, France) *urged along leaving stalls: settled towards the rr of midfield: pushed along and wd into st: rdn over 1f out: kpt on one pce ins fnl f* **13/1**

10 6 ½ **Vespera (IRE)**[31] 4-9-0 0 (b) Pierre-CharlesBoudot 3 51
(F-H Graffard, France) **68/10**[2]

11 1 **Haya Of Fortune (FR)**[54] 4680 5-9-3 0 TheoBachelot 15 52
(N Leenders, France) **21/1**

12 4 **Lawanda (IRE)**[9] 4-8-10 0 AntoineWerle 13 37
(T Lemer, France) **25/1**

13 4 **Octeville (IRE)**[166] 4-9-3 0 AlexandreRoussel 1 37
(C Lotoux, France) **13/1**

14 11 **Marobob**[12] 5-8-3 0 (p) DelphineSantiago 12 2
(R Le Dren Doleuze, France) **29/1**

F **La Poutanesca (IRE)**[77] 5-9-0 0 AlexisBadel 8
(D Smaga, France) **9/1**

2m 9.33s **15 Ran SP% 120.4**
PARI-MUTUEL (all including 1 euro stake): WIN 19.40; PLACE 6.50, 3.50, 4.50; DF 81.50.
Owner Ballantines Racing Stud Ltd **Bred** Aleyrion Bloodstock **Trained** Chantilly, France

6652a PRIX PAUL SAULOU (CONDITIONS) (3YO) (TURF) 1m 2f

2:35 3-Y-O

£13,513 (£5,135; £3,783; £2,162; £1,081; £810)

RPR

1 **Top Max (FR)**[56] 3-9-0 0 ow1 Pierre-CharlesBoudot 6 90
(H-A Pantall, France) **11/5**[2]

2 nk **Emma Point (USA)**[60] 4424 3-8-9 0 AlexandreRoussel 7 84
(Edouard Monfort, France) **10/1**

3 4 **Frame (FR)**[56] 3-8-6 0 AurelienLemaitre 2 73
(C Lotoux, France) **23/1**

4 2 **Leroy Leroy**[41] 5121 3-8-13 0 (p) TonyPiccone 4 76
(Richard Hannon) *wl into stride: led: urged along over 2f out: rdn 1 1/2f out: drvn and hdd 1f out: no ex ins fnl f* **9/5**[1]

5 1 ¾ **Sparkle In His Eye**[34] 5407 3-8-13 0 MaximeGuyon 3 73
(Mme Pia Brandt, France) **18/5**[3]

6 10 **Marrakech Express (FR)**[27] 3-8-13 0 (p) FabriceVeron 1 53
(Laurent Loisel, France) **76/10**

7 4 **Matricienne (FR)**[24] 3-8-9 0 AnthonyCrastus 5 41
(M Delaplace, France) **14/1**

2m 11.02s **7 Ran SP% 120.3**
PARI-MUTUEL (all including 1 euro stake): WIN 3.20; PLACE 2.30, 4.30; SF 17.30.
Owner Patrice Nicolet **Bred** Ecurie Haras De Quetieville **Trained** France

5668

HAMILTON (R-H)

Friday, August 30

OFFICIAL GOING: Good to soft changing to heavy after race 1 (4.55)
Wind: Light, across Weather: Overcast, persistent rain

6653 LADBROKES PLAY 1-2-FREE NURSERY H'CAP 6f 6y

4:55 (4:58) (Class 5) (0-75,77) 2-Y-O

£4,140 (£1,232; £615; £400; £400; £400) **Stalls Centre**

Form RPR

442 1 **Dutch Decoy**[30] 5553 2-9-7 **75** (p[1]) PaulHanagan 8 78
(Richard Fahey) *dwlt: bhd and outpcd: plenty to do over 2f out: gd hdwy over 1f out: sustained run to ld cl home* **11/2**[2]

334 2 shd **Kayewhykelly (IRE)**[22] 5856 2-8-10 **64** (h[1]) JasonHart 5 67
(Julie Camacho) *trckd ldr: rdn over 2f out: led ins fnl f: kpt on: hdd cl home* **17/2**

4041 3 1 ¼ **What A Business (IRE)**[17] 6053 2-9-3 **71** BenCurtis 3 70
(Roger Fell) *led: rdn over 1f out: hdd ins fnl f: one pce* **5/1**[1]

4143 4 1 ¼ **Havana Dawn**[8] 6369 2-9-2 **70** PaulMulrennan 11 65
(Phillip Makin) *prom: effrt and drvn along 2f out: kpt on same pce ins fnl f* **10/1**

3526 5 1 **Danny Ocean (IRE)**[24] 5777 2-9-0 **68** PJMcDonald 7 60
(K R Burke) *midfield: drvn and outpcd 1/2-way: rallied fnl f: nrst fin* **13/2**[3]

2350 6 hd **Oso Rapido (IRE)**[48] 4938 2-9-7 **75** DavidNolan 9 67
(David O'Meara) *hld up bhd ldng gp: rdn over 2f out: hung rt and no imp over 1f out* **13/2**[3]

3426 7 hd **Kilham**[21] 5913 2-9-2 **70** TomEaves 2 61
(Declan Carroll) *dwlt: hld up: effrt over 2f out: no further imp over 1f out* **10/1**

0512 8 ½ **Singe Anglais (IRE)**[24] 5789 2-8-8 **67** FayeMcManoman(5) 12 57
(Nigel Tinkler) *sn pushed along in rr: short-lived effrt 2f out: sn no imp (jockey said gelding hung right throughout)* **7/1**

2005 9 1 ¼ **Clay Regazzoni**[32] 5485 2-9-9 **77** JoeFanning 6 63
(Keith Dalgleish) *dwlt: bhd: effrt on outside over 2f out: wknd over 1f out* **12/1**

003 10 3 **Trevie Fountain**[20] 5934 2-9-1 **69** BarryMcHugh 4 46
(Richard Fahey) *chsd ldrs: drvn and outpcd over 2f out: sn btn* **16/1**

5042 11 3 **Bob's Oss (IRE)**[11] 6272 2-8-5 **59** NathanEvans 1 27
(Alan Berry) *prom: lost pl 1/2-way: sn struggling* **25/1**

1m 16.28s (3.58) **Going Correction** +0.625s/f (Yiel) **11 Ran SP% 117.3**
Speed ratings (Par 94): **101,100,99,97,96 95,95,95,93,89 85**
CSF £51.62 CT £254.92 TOTE £4.50: £2.00, £2.70, £1.90; EX 60.30 Trifecta £499.40.
Owner Cheveley Park Stud **Bred** Bumble Bloodstock & Cheveley Park Stud **Trained** Musley Bank, N Yorks

FOCUS
After rain during the day the going had changed to good to soft before the first, but with the rain continuing it was changed to heavy after this race and obviously was beforehand. Race distance 5yds further than advertised. An open and decent-looking 0-75 nursery to start things and a winner from the clouds. The first two have been rated as improving on their nursery debuts.

6654 WHYSETTLE IT NETWORKS NOVICE STKS 1m 68y

5:25 (5:28) (Class 5) 2-Y-O **£4,140** (£1,232; £615; £307) **Stalls Low**

Form RPR

4 1 **Grand Rock (IRE)**[57] 4550 2-9-2 0 BenCurtis 7 82+
(William Haggas) *s.i.s: hld up in tch: stdy hdwy over 3f out: rdn and led appr fnl f: pushed out: comf* **7/2**[2]

21 2 3 ½ **Flylikeaneagle (IRE)**[16] 6065 2-9-9 0 JoeFanning 2 81+
(Mark Johnston) *led and sn clr w one other: rdn: carried hd high and hdd appr fnl f: sn hung lft and no ex* **5/4**[1]

01 3 6 **Ten Thousand Stars**[14] 6161 2-9-1 0 BarryMcHugh 3 60+
(Adrian Nicholls) *w ldr to over 2f out: rdn and outpcd wl over 1f out* **8/1**

3 4 1 **Oh Mary Oh Mary**[24] 5764 2-8-11 0 NathanEvans 1 54
(Michael Easterby) *s.i.s: hld up: hdwy over 3f out: rdn and no imp fnl 2f* **9/2**[3]

30 5 3 ½ **Lawaa (FR)**[27] 5665 2-9-2 0 PaulHanagan 4 51
(Richard Fahey) *chsd clr ldng pair to over 3f out: rdn and outpcd over 2f out: sn btn* **9/1**

06 6 8 **Max's Voice (IRE)**[20] 5956 2-9-2 0 PJMcDonald 6 33
(David Loughnane) *in tch: drvn and outpcd over 3f out: sn btn* **28/1**

7 nk **Twin Paradox** 2-9-2 0 JasonHart 5 33
(John Quinn) *slowly away: bhd: struggling over 3f out: sn btn* **20/1**

1m 53.15s (4.75) **Going Correction** +0.625s/f (Yiel) **7 Ran SP% 114.2**
Speed ratings (Par 94): **101,97,91,90,87 79,78**
CSF £8.25 TOTE £4.60: £2.00, £1.30; EX 10.80 Trifecta £47.70.
Owner Hussain Alabbas Lootah **Bred** Peter & Hugh McCutcheon **Trained** Newmarket, Suffolk

FOCUS
Race distance 5yds further than advertised. An interesting novice in the now heavy ground and William Haggas made it 3-6 with 2yos here. The winner has been rated as building on his debut.

6655 STEWART MILNE HOMES H'CAP 1m 68y

5:55 (5:58) (Class 6) (0-55,54) 3-Y-O+

£3,493 (£1,039; £519; £400; £400; £400) **Stalls Low**

Form RPR

6304 1 **Remmy D (IRE)**[20] 5937 4-9-5 **54** (b) PaddyMathers 5 61
(Jim Goldie) *sn pressing ldr: led over 3f out: rdn and drifted lft ins fnl f: jst hld on* **8/1**

6503 2 nse **Star Of Valour (IRE)**[23] 5817 4-9-5 **54** PaulMulrennan 10 61
(Lynn Siddall) *hld up: hdwy over 2f out: chsd wnr ins fnl f: kpt on: jst hld* **13/2**

2131 3 2 ¼ **Retirement Beckons**[20] 5933 4-9-4 **53** (h) BenRobinson 4 55
(Linda Perratt) *s.i.s: hld up in tch: stdy hdwy and chsd wnr 2f out: rdn and sn hung rt: lost 2nd and outpcd ins fnl f* **4/1**[3]

2223 4 3 ½ **Be Bold**[3] 6572 7-9-4 **53** (b) JoeFanning 2 47
(Rebecca Bastiman) *prom: rdn over 2f out: wknd over 1f out* **5/2**[1]

1112 5 5 **Kodimoor (IRE)**[11] 6276 6-9-4 **53** (p) DougieCostello 9 36
(Mark Walford) *led to over 3f out: pressed wnr to 2f out: sn wknd* **10/1**

6660 6 4 **Gilmer (IRE)**[39] 5237 8-9-2 **51** TomEaves 3 25
(Stef Keniry) *hld up: drvn and outpcd 3f out: n.d after* **22/1**

4015 7 nk **Sumner Beach**[15] 6102 5-9-5 **54** BenCurtis 6 28
(Brian Ellison) *s.i.s: bhd: struggling over 3f out: n.d after* **7/2**[2]

0002 8 6 **Crazy Tornado (IRE)**[21] 5899 6-9-2 **51** (h) ShaneGray 8 12
(Keith Dalgleish) *chsd ldrs: rdn over 3f out: wknd over 2f out* **16/1**

1m 53.47s (5.07) **Going Correction** +0.625s/f (Yiel) **8 Ran SP% 114.6**
Speed ratings (Par 101): **99,98,96,93,88 84,83,77**
CSF £58.68 CT £241.53 TOTE £11.70: £2.50, £2.00, £1.60; EX 81.90 Trifecta £572.50.
Owner Whitestonecliffe Racing Partnership **Bred** J F Tuthill **Trained** Uplawmoor, E Renfrews

FOCUS
Race distance 5yds further than advertised. An open looking 1m handicap and not many got into it. The first two have been rated in line with their best 2019 turf form.

6656 EBF STALLIONS SCOTTISH PREMIER SERIES FILLIES' H'CAP 1m 1f 35y

6:25 (6:25) (Class 3) (0-90,85) 3-Y-O+ **£12,566** (£3,844; £1,980; £1,048) **Stalls Low**

Form RPR

6502 1 **Sarvi**[13] 5937 4-8-8 **66** (p) JamieGormley 2 75
(Jim Goldie) *led and clr 3f: pushed along and drew clr fr over 1f out: unchal* **9/2**[3]

0631 2 5 **Set In Stone (IRE)**[42] 5117 5-9-2 **74** TadhgO'Shea 1 74
(Andrew Hughes, Ire) *chsd (clr) wnr 3f: prom: effrt and regained 2nd over 2f out: rdn and no imp fr over 1f out* **3/1**[2]

0005 3 1 ¼ **Summer Daydream (IRE)**[22] 5846 3-9-6 **85** JoeFanning 5 82
(Keith Dalgleish) *prom: hdwy to chse wnr after 3f: drvn and outpcd over 2f out: tk modest 3rd ins fnl f: no imp* **9/2**[3]

1302 4 nk **Never Be Enough**[13] 5218 4-9-12 **84** TomEaves 6 80
(Keith Dalgleish) *stdd in last pl: smooth hdwy to dispute 2nd pl over 2f out: rdn and outpcd over 1f out: no ex fnl f* **6/5**[1]

R-0R R **Duck Egg Blue (IRE)**[12] 4109 5-8-9 **72** FayeMcManoman(5) 4
(Liam Bailey) *ref to r* **14/1**

2m 9.65s (10.65) **Going Correction** +0.625s/f (Yiel) **5 Ran SP% 113.5**
WFA 3 from 4yo+ 7lb
Speed ratings (Par 104): **77,72,71,71,**
CSF £18.57 TOTE £5.60: £2.30, £1.60; EX 21.50 Trifecta £42.50.
Owner James Fyffe & Scott Fyffe **Bred** Saleh Al Homaizi & Imad Al Sagar **Trained** Uplawmoor, E Renfrews
■ Koduro (9-1) was withdrawn. Rule 4 applies to all bets struck prior to withdrawal, but not to SP bets. Deduction - 10p in the pound. New market formed.

FOCUS
Race distance increased by 5yds. A race reduced to four late on and a gritty winner defied all challengers. The winner has been rated in line with her best previous form.

6657 LADBROKES LANARK SILVER BELL H'CAP 1m 4f 15y

6:55 (6:58) (Class 3) (0-95,95) 3-Y-O+

£22,410 (£6,710; £3,355; £1,677; £838; £421) **Stalls High**

Form RPR

10-6 1 **Elysian Flame**[23] 5818 3-8-0 **80** oh2 NathanEvans 8 92+
(Michael Easterby) *hld up: gd hdwy over 2f out: led over 1f out: clr whn pricked ears ins fnl f: readily* **9/1**

6213 2 3 ½ **Dark Lochnagar (USA)**[26] 5706 3-8-7 **87** ShaneGray 6 93
(Keith Dalgleish) *led: rdn and qcknd over 2f out: hdd over 1f out: kpt on u.p ins fnl f* **7/1**

2620 3 nk **Jabbaar**[12] 6255 6-9-2 **87** JamieGormley 4 92
(Iain Jardine) *hld up: hdwy over 2f out: disp 2nd pl ins fnl f: kpt on same pce nr fin* **16/1**

1321 4 1 ¼ **Sapa Inca (IRE)**[20] 5931 3-8-10 **90** JoeFanning 12 93
(Mark Johnston) *hld up: hdwy on outside and prom after 3f: effrt and chsd ldr over 2f out to wl over 1f out: one pce fnl f* **11/2**[3]

0605 5 5 **Multellie**[12] 6255 7-8-5 **76** PaulHanagan 5 72
(Tim Easterby) *in tch: rdn and outpcd over 2f out: kpt on fnl f: no imp* **20/1**

2224 6 2 **Lariat**[34] 5417 3-8-9 **89** PJMcDonald 13 82
(Andrew Balding) *t.k.h: chsd ldr to over 2f out: sn drvn and outpcd: btn over 1f out* **5/1**[2]

4010 7 2 ¾ **Borodin (IRE)**[32] 5489 4-9-7 **95** ConnorMurtagh(3) 14 84
(Richard Fahey) *midfield: drvn and outpcd over 2f out: n.d after* **20/1**

The Form Book Flat 2019, Raceform Ltd, Newbury, RG14 5SJ

351 **8** *2* **Beyond The Clouds**[25] 5742 6-8-13 **84**............................ TomEaves 7 70
(Kevin Ryan) *hld up in midfield on outside: stdy hdwy over 3f out: rdn over 2f out: sn wknd* **4/1**[1]

3-04 **9** *1* **Archi's Affaire**[23] 5818 5-9-3 **88**............................ PaulMulrennan 9 72
(Michael Dods) *t.k.h: hld up in tch: drvn over 2f out: sn wknd* **11/1**

321 **10** *7* **Paths Of Glory**[29] 5578 4-8-8 **79**............................(t[1]) BenCurtis 10 53
(Hugo Palmer) *dwlt: hld up: drvn and struggling over 3f out: sn btn* **9/1**

0052 **11** *½* **Theglasgowwarrior**[20] 5928 5-9-5 **90**............................ BenRobinson 1 63
(Jim Goldie) *hld up: rdn over 3f out: hung rt and wknd over 2f out* **14/1**

200 **12** *½* **My Reward**[9] 6355 7-9-3 **88**............................ DavidNolan 2 60
(Tim Easterby) *prom tl rdn and wknd over 2f out* **28/1**

0-00 **13** *65* **Temple Church (IRE)**[41] 5183 5-9-8 **93**............................ DougieCostello 11
(Hughie Morrison) *hld up towards rr: struggling over 3f out: lost tch fnl 2f: t.o (jockey said gelding stopped quickly 3f out)* **22/1**

2m 45.61s (7.01) **Going Correction** +0.625s/f (Yiel)
WFA 3 from 4yo+ 9lb **13 Ran SP% 122.8**
Speed ratings (Par 107): **101,98,98,97,94 92,91,89,89,84 84,83,40**
CSF £68.78 CT £1015.35 TOTE £11.30: £3.80, £3.10, £4.90; EX 101.00 Trifecta £1190.70.
Owner J Blackburn & Imperial Racing P'Ship **Bred** Ed's Stud Ltd **Trained** Sheriff Hutton, N Yorks

FOCUS
Race distance 5yds further than advertised. The feature contest went the way of a three-year-old for the first time in four years. The form might be a bit better than rated.

6658 LADBROKES ACCA BOOSTY H'CAP 1m 4f 15y
7:25 (7:28) (Class 5) (0-75,75) 4-Y-O+
£4,140 (£1,232; £615; £400; £400; £400)

Form RPR

3215 **1** **Donnachies Girl (IRE)**[22] 5855 6-8-5 **59** ow1............ PaulHanagan 10 66
(Alistair Whillans) *trckd ldrs: rdn and sltly outpcd over 2f out: rallied over 1f out: led ins fnl f: hld on wl cl home* **5/1**[3]

6042 **2** *nse* **Carbon Dating (IRE)**[42] 5122 7-9-2 **70**............................ TadhgO'Shea 7 77
(Andrew Hughes, Ire) *hld up: smooth hdwy over 2f out: effrt and rdn over 1f out: pressed wnr ins fnl f: kpt on: jst hld* **9/1**

4541 **3** *1¼* **Corton Lad**[28] 5621 9-8-13 **67**............................(tp) ShaneGray 3 72
(Keith Dalgleish) *led: rdn over 3f out: hdd ins fnl f: kpt on same pce towards fin* **16/1**

0000 **4** *1¼* **Employer (IRE)**[39] 5240 4-9-6 **74**............................ PaulMulrennan 6 77
(Jim Goldie) *hld up: stdy hdwy whn n.m.r briefly over 2f out: effrt over 1f out: one pce ins fnl f* **12/1**

3000 **5** *¾* **Dragon Mountain**[34] 5423 4-9-3 **71**............................ JoeFanning 9 73
(Keith Dalgleish) *in tch: stdy hdwy over 2f out: sn pushed along: effrt over 1f out: no ex ins fnl f* **20/1**

0421 **6** *8* **Deinonychus**[17] 6059 8-8-10 **64**............................(p) PJMcDonald 4 54
(Michael Appleby) *chsd ldr to over 2f out: drvn and wknd over 1f out* **7/2**[1]

5231 **7** *3* **Flood Defence (IRE)**[17] 6038 5-8-12 **66**............................ JamieGormley 11 52
(Iain Jardine) *hld up: rdn along over 2f out: sn no imp: btn over 1f out (jockey said mare stopped quickly)* **9/2**[2]

0635 **8** *7* **Zabeel Star (IRE)**[20] 5970 7-9-6 **74**............................(p) BenCurtis 5 49
(Karen McLintock) *hld up towards rr: drvn and outpcd over 2f out: sn btn* **7/1**

1063 **9** *2* **Auxiliary**[17] 6038 6-8-9 **70**............................(p) JonathanFisher[(7)] 8 42
(Liam Bailey) *hld up: drvn along and struggling over 3f out: nvr on terms* **10/1**

0140 **10** *21* **Spirit Of Sarwan (IRE)**[9] 6341 5-8-11 **65**............................(p) JasonHart 1 6
(Stef Keniry) *in tch: rdn and struggling over 3f out: sn btn: t.o* **28/1**

0500 **11** *25* **Shrewd**[22] 5849 9-9-7 **75**............................ TomEaves 2
(Iain Jardine) *bhd: lost tch fnl 4f: t.o* **12/1**

2m 47.0s (8.40) **Going Correction** +0.625s/f (Yiel) **11 Ran SP% 118.1**
Speed ratings (Par 103): **97,96,96,95,94 89,87,82,81,67 50**
CSF £49.85 CT £676.38 TOTE £6.00: £2.10, £3.00, £2.80; EX 48.10 Trifecta £992.70.
Owner Mrs Karen Spark **Bred** Darley **Trained** Newmill-On-Slitrig, Borders

FOCUS
Race distance 5yds further than advertised. An open middle-distance handicap which was started by flag as the stalls could not get on the course. The third has been rated near his recent form.

6659 PATERSONS OF GREENOAKHILL H'CAP 5f 7y
8:00 (8:02) (Class 6) (0-65,64) 3-Y-O+
£3,493 (£1,039; £519; £400; £400; £400) **Stalls** Centre

Form RPR

1000 **1** **Groundworker (IRE)**[38] 5276 8-8-11 **51**............................ BarryMcHugh 11 62
(Paul Midgley) *trckd ldrs: led on bit wl over 1f out: rdn clr fnl f: readily* **25/1**

2554 **2** *3¼* **Popping Corks (IRE)**[9] 6338 3-8-9 **51**............................ JamieGormley 15 50
(Linda Perratt) *bhd: drvn along 1/2-way: hdwy over 1f out: chsd (clr) wnr ins fnl f: r.o (jockey said filly hung right in the final furlong)* **20/1**

3602 **3** *2¼* **Burmese Blazer (IRE)**[21] 5904 4-9-5 **59**............................(h) BenRobinson 10 50
(Jim Goldie) *awkward s: bhd and pushed along: hdwy to chse wnr over 1f out to ins fnl f: sn no ex (jockey said gelding missed the break)* **9/1**

-004 **4** *2¼* **Swiss Connection**[16] 6070 3-9-6 **62**............................(h) PaulMulrennan 13 45
(Bryan Smart) *hld up: effrt whn nt clr run over 2f out: rdn over 1f out: kpt on fnl f: nrst fin* **12/1**

0221 **5** *shd* **One Boy (IRE)**[14] 6168 8-9-0 **54**............................ JasonHart 14 37
(Paul Midgley) *in tch: smooth hdwy 1/2-way: effrt and rdn over 1f out: wknd ins fnl f* **13/2**[3]

4231 **6** *1¾* **Piazon**[32] 5491 8-9-8 **62**............................(be) NathanEvans 6 38
(Julia Brooke) *led tl hdd wl over 1f out: sn wknd* **4/1**[1]

0514 **7** *1¼* **I'll Be Good**[11] 6277 10-8-5 **52**............................ ZakWheatley[(7)] 9 24
(Alan Berry) *prom tl rdn and wknd over 1f out* **11/1**

403 **8** *¾* **Astrophysics**[20] 5952 7-9-1 **55**............................(p) PJMcDonald 3 24
(Lynn Siddall) *in tch: drvn along over 2f out: hung rt and wknd over 1f out* **12/1**

5646 **9** *1* **Everkyllachy (IRE)**[20] 5972 5-9-6 **60**............................(b) ShaneGray 5 26
(Karen McLintock) *dwlt: bhd: drvn along over 2f out: nvr on terms* **17/2**

4605 **10** *4½* **Rockley Point**[24] 5765 6-8-6 **49**............................(b) ConnorMurtagh[(3)] 8
(Katie Scott) *sn drvn along in rr: no imp fr 1/2-way* **12/1**

0030 **11** *3¼* **Guardia Svizzera (IRE)**[15] 6099 5-9-9 **63**............................(p[1]) BenCurtis 12
(Roger Fell) *cl up tl rdn and wknd fr 2f out* **5/1**[2]

4043 **12** *½* **Tadaany (IRE)**[17] 6057 7-8-11 **51**............................(p) TomEaves 2
(Ruth Carr) *midfield: drvn along over 2f out: sn wknd (jockey said gelding hung right throughout)* **17/2**

1m 2.3s (1.90) **Going Correction** +0.625s/f (Yiel)
WFA 3 from 4yo+ 2lb **12 Ran SP% 121.1**
Speed ratings (Par 101): **109,103,100,96,96 93,91,90,88,81 76,75**
CSF £461.03 CT £4845.49 TOTE £29.60: £7.60, £3.60, £3.30; EX 494.90.
Owner Blackburn Family **Bred** Knockainey Stud **Trained** Westow, N Yorks

FOCUS
Lots of course winners battling for this 5f contest with the high numbers seemingly favoured. The second has been rated near her recent form.
T/Plt: £347.10 to a £1 stake. Pool: £42,024.45 - 88.37 winning units. T/Qpdt: £69.90 to a £1 stake. Pool: £5,040.51 - 53.3 winning units. **Richard Young**

5851 NEWCASTLE (A.W) (L-H)
Friday, August 30

OFFICIAL GOING: Tapeta: standard to slow
Wind: strong largely against Weather: overcast

6660 PERCY HEDLEY H'CAP 2m 56y (Tp)
5:45 (5:46) (Class 6) (0-60,61) 3-Y-O
£2,781 (£827; £413; £400; £400; £400) **Stalls** Low

Form RPR

4320 **1** **Myklachi (FR)**[21] 5915 3-9-10 **61**............................ DanielTudhope 7 69+
(David O'Meara) *in tch: bit short of room over 2f out: pushed along to chse ldr whn short of room again appr fnl f: sn swtchd rt: styd on wl to ld towards fin: shade cosily* **4/1**[2]

046 **2** *½* **Nataleena (IRE)**[27] 5690 3-9-4 **55**............................ AndrewMullen 2 61
(Ben Haslam) *hld up: rdn and hdwy on outer 2f out: led 1f out: styd on but hdd towards fin* **7/1**[3]

5006 **3** *2¼* **Beaufort (IRE)**[14] 6180 3-9-7 **58**............................ ConnorBeasley 3 62
(Michael Dods) *hld up: racd quite keenly: hdwy 3f out: rdn to ld 2f out: hdd 1f out: no ex fnl 110yds* **9/4**[1]

6644 **4** *nk* **Tabou Beach Boy**[19] 5987 3-8-12 **52**............................(p[1]) RowanScott[(3)] 4 55
(Oliver Greenall) *led at stdy pce: rdn along 3f out: hdd 2f out: plugged on (vet said gelding lost its right-fore shoe)* **9/4**[1]

00-0 **5** *5* **Archie's Sister**[25] 5742 3-8-8 **45**............................(t) AndrewElliott 1 42
(Philip Kirby) *s.i.s: sn trckd ldr: rdn over 2f out: wknd fnl f* **25/1**

-005 **6** *5* **Gordalan**[34] 5425 3-9-5 **56**............................ RobertHavlin 5 47
(Philip Kirby) *prom: rdn over 2f out: wknd over 1f out* **15/2**

3m 52.56s (17.56) **Going Correction** +0.35s/f (Slow) **6 Ran SP% 109.6**
Speed ratings (Par 98): **70,69,68,68,65 63**
CSF £29.11 TOTE £3.50: £2.60, £3.70; EX 22.70 Trifecta £67.10.
Owner Middleham Park Racing XCVII **Bred** Pierre Cadec **Trained** Upper Helmsley, N Yorks

FOCUS
A modest 3yo staying handicap. Despite a slow gallop and 3f sprint finish, the third-favourite still came through to win a shade cosily from towards the rear on the standard to slow Tapeta, possibly helped by being sheltered from the reported headwind in the home straight.

6661 SKY SPORTS RACING ON SKY CHANNEL 415 FILLIES' H'CAP 1m 4f 98y (Tp)
6:15 (6:16) (Class 4) (0-85,83) 3-Y-O+ **£5,207** (£1,549; £774; £400) **Stalls** High

Form RPR

011 **1** **Monica Sheriff**[17] 6043 3-9-5 **83**............................ DanielTudhope 4 89+
(William Haggas) *trckd ldr: pushed into ld 2f out: pressed 1f out: sn rdn: styd on wl and in command fnl 75yds* **1/2**[1]

4634 **2** *1¼* **First Dance (IRE)**[33] 5474 5-8-9 **64** oh1............................ GrahamLee 2 68
(Tom Tate) *hld up: hdwy and trckd ldr 2f out: rdn to chal 1f out: styd on same pce fnl 110yds* **15/2**[3]

-333 **3** *¾* **Albanita**[10] 6323 3-8-12 **76**............................(v[1]) LukeMorris 1 79
(Sir Mark Prescott Bt) *in tch: trckd ldr on bit 2f out: rdn along to chal 1f out: drvn and one pce ins fnl f* **3/1**[2]

15P- **4** *12* **Belisa (IRE)**[364] 6740 5-9-11 **83**............................ JaneElliott[(3)] 3 67
(Ivan Furtado) *led: rdn along and hdd 2f out: sn wknd* **16/1**

2m 44.82s (3.72) **Going Correction** +0.35s/f (Slow)
WFA 3 from 5yo 9lb **4 Ran SP% 109.3**
Speed ratings (Par 102): **101,100,99,91**
CSF £4.90 TOTE £1.40; EX 4.20 Trifecta £7.50.
Owner Duke Of Devonshire **Bred** The Duke Of Devonshire **Trained** Newmarket, Suffolk

FOCUS
A decent middle-distance fillies' handicap. The odds-on favourite came clear late despite an unhelpfully tactical gallop. Muddling form.

6662 DELI FRESH UK NOVICE STKS 1m 2f 42y (Tp)
6:45 (6:48) (Class 5) 3-Y-O+ **£3,428** (£1,020; £509; £254) **Stalls** High

Form RPR

32-2 **1** **Wise Ruler**[27] 5656 3-9-3 80............................ JackMitchell 1 88+
(Simon Crisford) *trckd ldr: led wl over 3f out: pushed along over 1f out: rdn jst ins fnl f: sn in command: pushed out towards fin* **7/4**[2]

-335 **2** *2¾* **Entrusting**[86] 3471 3-9-3 82............................ DanielTudhope 4 83
(James Fanshawe) *hld up in tch: hdwy and trckd ldr gng wl over 2f out: pushed along over 1f out: drvn ent fnl f: one pce and sn hld in 2nd* **5/4**[1]

2-2 **3** *1¼* **Pianissimo**[139] 1756 3-9-3 0............................(p[1]) RobertHavlin 2 81
(John Gosden) *hld up in tch: hdwy and trckd ldr on inner over 2f out: sn rdn: drvn over 1f out: one pce* **3/1**[3]

2046 **4** *5* **Fly Lightly**[55] 4663 3-9-3 75............................(p[1]) LukeMorris 6 72
(Robert Cowell) *trckd ldr: rdn along over 3f out: wknd over 1f out* **22/1**

5 *28* **Spy Fi**[35] 5-9-5 0............................ GrahamLee 5 15
(John Norton) *led: rdn along and hdd wl over 3f out: sn wknd* **150/1**

2m 12.8s (2.40) **Going Correction** +0.35s/f (Slow)
WFA 3 from 5yo 7lb **5 Ran SP% 110.8**
Speed ratings (Par 103): **104,101,100,96,74**
CSF £4.35 TOTE £2.60: £1.40, £1.20; EX 4.70 Trifecta £6.70.
Owner Sheikh Mohammed Obaid Al Maktoum **Bred** Sheikh Mohammed Obaid Al Maktoum **Trained** Newmarket, Suffolk

FOCUS
A fairly decent novice contest, and another modest gallop, but that didn't stop the second-favourite displaying his clear superiority in the home straight. It's been rated at face value, with the third close to form.

6663 CENTRAL EMPLOYMENT H'CAP 1m 2f 42y (Tp)
7:15 (7:17) (Class 6) (0-65,65) 4-Y-O+
£2,781 (£827; £413; £400; £400; £400) **Stalls** High

Form RPR

1502 **1** **Home Before Dusk**[9] 6341 4-9-6 **64**............................(p) DanielTudhope 10 72
(Keith Dalgleish) *trckd ldrs: pushed into ld 2f out: sn strly pressed: rdn and hdd narrowly ins fnl f: drvn and kpt on wl to ld again towards fin* **6/4**[1]

1436 **2** *nk* **Kilbaha Lady (IRE)**[55] 4627 5-9-0 **61**............................ RowanScott[(3)] 13 68
(Nigel Tinkler) *in tch: smooth hdwy over 2f out: rdn to chal over 1f out: edgd ahd ins fnl f: kpt on but hdd towards fin* **6/1**[2]

0340 **3** 2 **Ad Libitum**[14] 6180 4-9-5 **63**....(p) KevinStott 6 67
(Roger Fell) *hld up in midfield: hdwy on outer over 2f out: rdn to go 3rd ent fnl f: kpt on wl* **8/1**

0-36 **4** 4 1/2 **Cottingham**[172] 1145 4-8-0 **47**.... JaneElliott(3) 3 43
(Kevin Frost) *trckd ldrs: rdn along 2f out: outpcd fr over 1f out* **25/1**

5002 **5** 1 1/2 **Kodi Koh (IRE)**[5] 6499 4-8-2 **46**.... LukeMorris 2 39
(Simon West) *midfield: rdn along 2f out: one pce nvr threatened* **9/1**

0500 **6** 2 1/2 **Thawry**[63] 4333 4-9-6 **64**.... CamHardie 9 53
(Antony Brittain) *led for 2f: trckd ldr: rdn over 2f out: wknd appr fnl f* **14/1**

333 **7** 1/2 **Ishebayorgrey (IRE)**[48] 4916 7-9-3 **61**....(h) GrahamLee 5 49
(Iain Jardine) *racd keenly in midfield: rdn over 2f out: no imp (jockey said gelding ran too free)* **7/1**[3]

6060 **8** nse **Irish Minister (USA)**[30] 5560 4-9-0 **58**.... AndrewElliott 1 46
(David Thompson) *hld up: rdn over 2f out: nvr threatened* **16/1**

06-0 **9** 1 **Bromance**[22] 5851 6-8-2 **46** oh1....(p) AndrewMullen 12 32
(Peter Niven) *led after 2f out: rdn 3f out: hdd 2f out: wknd appr fnl f* **25/1**

050 **10** 4 **Lucy's Law (IRE)**[17] 6059 5-8-12 **56**.... JamesSullivan 11 35
(Tom Tate) *slowly away: a towards rr (jockey said mare missed the break)* **14/1**

0-00 **11** 1 **Bigdabog**[14] 6180 4-7-11 **46** oh1.... PaulaMuir(5) 7 23
(Stella Barclay) *trckd ldrs: rdn along over 3f out: wknd over 2f out* **50/1**

40-0 **12** 4 **New Rhythm**[30] 5554 4-7-10 **47** oh1 ow1.... IzzyClifton(7) 4 17
(Alistair Whillans) *a towards rr* **50/1**

5500 **13** 9 **Prosecute (FR)**[17] 6036 6-7-9 **46** oh1.... OwenPayton(7) 14
(Sean Regan) *v.s.a: a in rr (jockey said gelding missed the break)* **66/1**

2m 14.48s (4.08) **Going Correction** +0.35s/f (Slow) **13 Ran SP% 120.2**
Speed ratings (Par 101): **97,96,95,91,90 88,87,87,87,83 83,79,72**
CSF £9.72 CT £57.63 TOTE £2.10: £1.10, £2.40, £2.70; EX 14.10 Trifecta £61.10.
Owner G R Leckie **Bred** G L S Partnership **Trained** Carluke, S Lanarks

FOCUS
A modest handicap. The favourite's winning time was approaching two seconds slower than the previous C&D novice contest from off another modest gallop. A marginal step forward from the second on her previous AW form.

6664 BRITISH EBF MATCHBOOK FUTURE STAYERS NOVICE STKS (PLUS 10 RACE) (SIRE AND DAM RESTRICTED RACE) 7f 14y (Tp)
7:45 (7:47) (Class 4) 2-Y-O **£9,056** (£2,695; £1,346; £673) **Stalls** Centre

Form RPR

1 **Cape Palace** 2-9-5 0.... RobertHavlin 4 91+
(John Gosden) *dwlt sltly: sn trckd ldr: led over 1f out: qckn clr pushed out: impressive* **4/11**[1]

5 **2** 8 **King Carney**[22] 5848 2-9-5 0.... StevieDonohoe 2 70
(Charlie Fellowes) *led: rdn and hdd over 1f out: one pce and sn no ch w wnr* **6/1**[2]

3 3 3/4 **Ambassador (IRE)** 2-9-5 0.... KevinStott 5 60
(Richard Fahey) *dwlt: hld up: hdwy and in tch over 3f out: rdn over 2f out: kpt on to go modest 3rd ins fnl f* **8/1**[3]

4 **4** hd **Philosophical**[27] 5655 2-9-5 0.... JackGarritty 7 60
(Jedd O'Keeffe) *hld up in tch: rdn along over 2f out: no imp* **12/1**

5 **5** 1/2 **Sir Charles Punch**[16] 6065 2-9-5 0.... GrahamLee 3 58
(James Given) *trckd ldrs: rdn over 2f out: wknd fnl f* **33/1**

00 **6** 7 **Fast Track Flyer (IRE)**[16] 6065 2-9-0 0.... CamHardie 1 35
(Brian Ellison) *midfield: rdn along over 3f out: wknd and bhd 2f out* **100/1**

60 **7** shd **America First (IRE)**[22] 5848 2-9-5 0.... ConnorBeasley 6 40
(Michael Dods) *hld up: rdn over 2f out: wknd over 1f out* **33/1**

1m 28.5s (2.30) **Going Correction** +0.35s/f (Slow) **7 Ran SP% 113.3**
Speed ratings (Par 96): **100,90,86,86,85 77,77**
CSF £2.98 TOTE £1.20: £1.10, £2.30; EX 3.60 Trifecta £10.70.
Owner Sheikh Hamdan bin Mohammed Al Maktoum **Bred** Scuderia Blueberry SRL **Trained** Newmarket, Suffolk

FOCUS
The odds-on favourite ran out an impressive winner of this novice from off a modest initial gallop.

6665 ELMER'S GREAT NORTH PARADE H'CAP 7f 14y (Tp)
8:15 (8:16) (Class 5) (0-70,71) 4-Y-O+
£3,428 (£1,020; £509; £400; £400; £400) **Stalls** Centre

Form RPR

0010 **1** **Insurplus (IRE)**[6] 6461 6-9-3 **65**.... DanielTudhope 3 71
(Jim Goldie) *hld up: pushed along and hdwy over 1f out: squeezed through gap to chal ins fnl f: drvn into narrow ld 75yds out: all out (trainer could offer no explanation for the gelding's improved form)* **9/1**

-545 **2** shd **Rock Boy Grey (IRE)**[15] 6116 4-9-1 **63**.... StevieDonohoe 11 69
(Mark Loughnane) *midfield: racd keenly: rdn to chse ldr over 1f out: chal strly fnl 110yds: kpt on* **12/1**

0150 **3** nk **Beverley Bullet**[9] 6341 6-8-9 **60**....(v1) RowanScott(3) 4 65
(Lawrence Mullaney) *midfield: rdn along and hdwy 3f out: led over 1f out: briefly 2 l clr: hdd 75yds out: kpt on same pce* **13/2**[3]

0260 **4** 3 1/4 **Duke Cosimo**[18] 6027 9-8-9 **57**.... PhilDennis 1 54
(Michael Herrington) *hld up in midfield: rdn along over 2f out: hdwy over 1f out: one pce in 4th ins fnl f* **16/1**

-032 **5** 3 1/4 **Black Friday**[17] 6037 4-9-9 **71**....(p) LukeMorris 2 60
(Karen McLintock) *trckd ldrs: racd quite keenly: rdn over 2f out: outpcd and btn over 1f out* **7/2**[1]

0565 **6** 1 3/4 **Kentuckyconnection (USA)**[31] 5517 6-9-4 **66**.... GrahamLee 9 50
(Bryan Smart) *midfield on inner: persistently short of room wl over 1f out tl 1f out: no ch after: swtchd lft and kpt on ins fnl f (jockey said gelding was continually denied a clear run from 2f out until 1f out)* **9/2**[2]

4033 **7** 1/2 **Dandy Highwayman (IRE)**[45] 5020 5-9-0 **62**....(tp) CamHardie 7 45
(Ollie Pears) *trckd ldrs: rdn over 2f out: already lost pl and btn whn short of room over 1f out* **12/1**

3556 **8** nk **Bobby Joe Leg**[14] 6174 5-9-1 **63**....(b) JackGarritty 5 45
(Ruth Carr) *trckd ldrs: rdn over 2f out: wknd over 1f out* **16/1**

0300 **9** hd **Mudawwan (IRE)**[13] 6204 5-8-12 **63**....(b) JaneElliott(3) 6 45
(James Bethell) *pressed ldr: led over 2f out: sn rdn: hdd over 1f out: wknd fnl f* **13/2**[3]

1002 **10** 7 **Smugglers Creek (IRE)**[28] 5616 5-9-7 **69**....(p) AndrewMullen 8 33
(Iain Jardine) *led narrowly: rdn along and hdd over 2f out: wknd over 1f out* **8/1**

646- **11** 2 3/4 **Impulsive Force (IRE)**[468] 2845 4-9-5 **67**.... JamesSullivan 10 25
(Ruth Carr) *s.i.s: a in rr* **33/1**

1m 28.03s (1.83) **Going Correction** +0.35s/f (Slow) **11 Ran SP% 118.3**
Speed ratings (Par 103): **103,102,102,98,95 93,92,92,91,83 80**
CSF £112.57 CT £768.58 TOTE £11.10: £2.90, £4.20, £2.20; EX 173.50 Trifecta £1678.70.
Owner D Renton & J Goldie **Bred** Patrick J Monahan **Trained** Uplawmoor, E Renfrews

FOCUS
An ordinary handicap. Jockey Danny Tudhope registered his fourth win on the card and his mount's winning time was marginally quicker than the previous C&D juvenile novice contest. Straightforward, limited form.

6666 NEWCASTLE STAMPEDE OBSTACLE MUD RUN H'CAP 7f 14y (Tp)
8:45 (8:47) (Class 6) (0-55,55) 3-Y-O+
£2,781 (£827; £413; £400; £400; £400) **Stalls** Centre

Form RPR

0052 **1** **Sophia Maria**[11] 6275 3-8-13 **55**....(p) JaneElliott(3) 10 61
(James Bethell) *trckd ldrs: rdn to ld over 1f out: drvn ins fnl f: hld on towards fin* **13/2**[3]

0402 **2** hd **Im Dapper Too**[34] 5438 8-9-4 **52**....(b) SamJames 13 59
(John Davies) *midfield: pushed along over 2f out: drvn ins fnl f: r.o wl fnl 110yds: gaining at fin* **5/1**[1]

0305 **3** 1 1/4 **With Approval (IRE)**[23] 5803 7-9-1 **52**....(b1) GemmaTutty(3) 5 56
(Karen Tutty) *led: rdn 2f out: hdd appr fnl f: remained chalng tl no ex towards fin* **14/1**

6656 **4** 3/4 **Fard**[11] 6275 4-9-0 **53**.... PaulaMuir(5) 12 55
(Roger Fell) *trckd ldrs: rdn over 1f out: one pce fnl f* **10/1**

3244 **5** 1 1/2 **The Bull (IRE)**[22] 5857 4-9-6 **54**....(p) AndrewMullen 1 52
(Ben Haslam) *hld up: rdn and kpt on fnl f: nrst fin* **7/1**

/503 **6** 1/2 **Ningaloo (GER)**[12] 6259 5-9-7 **55**.... PhilDennis 9 52
(Rebecca Bastiman) *dwlt: hld up: rdn and sme hdwy over 1f out: one pce ins fnl f* **7/1**

5050 **7** 3/4 **Eldelbar (SPA)**[11] 6276 5-9-6 **54**....(h) ConnorBeasley 8 49
(Geoffrey Harker) *hld up: smooth hdwy 2f out: rdn over 1f out: wknd ins fnl f* **16/1**

0006 **7** dht **Proceeding**[34] 5438 4-9-2 **50**.... KevinStott 2 45
(Tracy Waggott) *hld up: rdn 2f out: kpt on fnl f: nvr threatened* **13/2**[3]

3501 **9** 3 1/4 **Three C's (IRE)**[17] 6051 5-9-2 **50**....(p) LukeMorris 14 37
(George Boughey) *in tch: rdn over 2f out: wknd over 1f out (jockey said gelding was unsuited by the wide draw and unable to get cover)* **6/1**[2]

640 **10** 1/2 **Searanger (USA)**[11] 6275 6-8-12 **49**.... RowanScott(3) 6 34
(Rebecca Menzies) *prom: rdn over 2f out: wknd over 1f out* **18/1**

20-P **11** 1 1/4 **Roca Magica**[55] 4642 3-9-2 **55**.... RobertHavlin 4 35
(Ed Dunlop) *midfield: rdn along 2f out: drvn and wknd fnl f* **50/1**

5000 **12** 6 **Tommycole**[17] 6050 4-9-1 **49**.... RachelRichardson 11 16
(Olly Williams) *dwlt: sn midfield: rdn over 3f out: wknd 2f out* **66/1**

0465 **13** 5 **Heart In Havana**[30] 5552 3-9-1 **54**....(t) CamHardie 7 6
(Michael Easterby) *midfield: rdn over 2f out: wknd over 1f out* **16/1**

1m 27.55s (1.35) **Going Correction** +0.35s/f (Slow)
WFA 3 from 4yo+ 5lb **13 Ran SP% 118.9**
Speed ratings (Par 101): **106,105,104,103,101 101,100,100,96,96 94,87,82**
CSF £38.72 CT £461.05 TOTE £7.30: £2.60, £1.80, £4.10; EX 45.40 Trifecta £818.00.
Owner Clarendon Thoroughbred Racing **Bred** Whitsbury Manor Stud **Trained** Middleham Moor, N Yorks

■ Stewards' Enquiry : Jane Elliott two-day ban; misuse of whip (Sep 9, 15)

FOCUS
A moderate handicap, but the truest-run contest on the card, and one of the joint-third favourites produced the best comparative winning time of the night.
T/Plt: £44.60 to a £1 stake. Pool: £47,457.70 - 776.3 winning units. T/Qpdt: £8.10 to a £1 stake. Pool: £5,056.45 - 460.74 winning units. **Andrew Sheret**

5858 SANDOWN (R-H)
Friday, August 30

OFFICIAL GOING: Good to firm (good in places; 7.4)
Wind: Moderate, against Weather: Fine, warm

6667 BETWAY NURSERY H'CAP (JOCKEY CLUB GRASSROOTS NURSERY QUALIFIER) 5f 10y
2:10 (2:10) (Class 5) (0-75,77) 2-Y-O **£4,528** (£1,347; £673; £336; £300) **Stalls** Low

Form RPR

3605 **1** **Port Winston (IRE)**[16] 6073 2-9-6 **72**....(h1) DavidProbert 3 74
(Alan King) *hld up in last: plld out wd and prog wl over 1f out: rdn to ld jst ins fnl f: kpt on wl* **8/1**

6001 **2** 1/2 **Queenoftheclyde (IRE)**[14] 6182 2-8-6 **58**.... DavidEgan 6 58
(K R Burke) *unfurnished; reluctant to go to post: chsd ldng pair: pushed along 1/2-way: rdn to press ldng pair 1f out: kpt on u.p to take 2nd nr fin* **11/2**

262 **3** nk **Seraphinite (IRE)**[19] 5988 2-9-11 **77**.... AdamKirby 1 76
(Jamie Osborne) *chsd clr ldr: clsd 2f out: rdn to ld over 1f out: hdd jst ins fnl f: kpt on same pce and lost 2nd nr fin* **6/4**[1]

6634 **4** 2 3/4 **Queen Aya**[14] 6158 2-9-0 **66**.... LiamKeniry 5 55
(Ed Walker) *leggy; mostly in 4th: pushed along over 1f out: rdn and no imp on ldrs fnl f* **5/1**[3]

2545 **5** 9 **Swinley (IRE)**[14] 6158 2-9-7 **73**....(b1) AndreaAtzeni 7 30
(Richard Hughes) *looked wl; blasted off in front and sn clr: hdd & wknd rapidly over 1f out: t.o (jockey said gelding stopped quickly)* **3/1**[2]

1m 2.98s (1.68) **Going Correction** +0.075s/f (Good) **5 Ran SP% 108.2**
Speed ratings (Par 94): **89,88,87,83,68**
CSF £45.56 TOTE £9.40: £4.00, £3.40; EX 51.70 Trifecta £152.20.
Owner Jamie Magee, Henry Ponsonby & Alan King **Bred** P McEnery & B McEnery **Trained** Barbury Castle, Wilts

FOCUS
Swinley went out much too hard in his first-time blinkers and set the race up for the closers. The first two have been rated as improving slightly.

6668 BETWAY H'CAP 5f 10y
2:40 (2:41) (Class 5) (0-75,75) 3-Y-O+
£5,175 (£1,540; £769; £384; £300; £300) **Stalls** Low

Form RPR

3465 **1** **Our Oystercatcher**[21] 5889 5-9-2 **68**.... HectorCrouch 9 78
(Mark Pattinson) *mde all fr wd draw: stretched on wl over 1f out: drvn fnl f: ld dwindled last 100yds but a holding on* **9/2**[3]

3023 **2** 3/4 **Gnaad (IRE)**[16] 6080 5-9-9 **75**.... DavidEgan 6 82
(Alan Bailey) *looked wl; hld up in last pair: plld out and prog wl over 1f out: drvn to chse wnr jst ins fnl f: clsd last 100yds: a hld (jockey said gelding stumbled over the road crossing)* **4/1**[2]

1242 **3** 2 1/4 **Delagate This Lord**[13] 6203 5-9-9 **75**.... DavidProbert 5 74
(Michael Attwater) *hld up in last pair: prog over 1f out: drvn and kpt on same pce to take 3rd ins fnl f (jockey said gelding was momentarily short of room approaching the final furlong)* **4/1**[2]

5232 **4** 1 ¼ **Secretfact**[9] 6332 6-9-9 75 .... JimmyQuinn 7 70
(Malcolm Saunders) *broke wl but sltly awkwardly: hld up in midfield: prog to chse wnr over 1f out: sn rdn and nt qckn: lost 2nd and fdd jst ins fnl f* **8/1**

11-0 **5** 1 ½ **Irene May (IRE)**[25] 5736 3-9-7 75 .... JasonWatson 4 64
(Sylvester Kirk) *chsd ldrs: rdn 2f out: sn lost pl: no ch fnl f* **20/1**

5313 **6** ¾ **Indian Raj**[11] 6288 5-9-9 75 ....(t) AndreaAtzeni 1 62
(Stuart Williams) *racd against rail: chsd wnr: rdn 2f out: lost 2nd and wknd over 1f out* **3/1**[1]

1345 **7** 1 ¼ **Spanish Star (IRE)**[10] 6301 4-9-8 74 .... LiamKeniry 2 56
(Patrick Chamings) *chsd ldrs: rdn and lost pl 2f out: sn wknd* **11/1**

-606 **8** ½ **Elizabeth Bennet (IRE)**[39] 5251 4-9-8 74 ....(v[1]) AdamKirby 8 54
(Robert Cowell) *chsd ldng pair: rdn 2f out: sn wknd* **20/1**

1m 0.71s (-0.59) **Going Correction** +0.075s/f (Good)
WFA 3 from 4yo+ 2lb 8 Ran SP% **112.2**
Speed ratings (Par 103): **107,105,102,100,97 96,94,93**
CSF £21.91 CT £76.68 TOTE £4.30: £1.60, £1.50, £1.60; EX 19.50 Trifecta £78.30.
Owner Mrs F A Veasey & G B Partnership **Bred** Mrs F A Veasey **Trained** Epsom, Surrey

■ Kodiac Express was withdrawn. Price at times of withdrawal 20-1. Rule 4 does not apply

FOCUS
Plenty of drama in this sprint handicap as Kodiac Express reared over backwards as the stalls opened. The first two home had finished second in reverse order in a similar race in September last year. The winner has been rated back towards his best.

6669 BETWAY BRITISH EBF MAIDEN STKS (PLUS 10 RACE) 7f
3:15 (3:18) (Class 4) 2-Y-O £4,787 (£1,424; £711; £355) **Stalls Low**

Form RPR

1 **Palace Pier** 2-9-5 0 .... FrankieDettori 8 90+
(John Gosden) *athletic; str; looked wl; led 1f: trckd ldng pair: pushed into the ld over 1f out: qckly drew clr: taking debut* **11/8**[1]

2 3 ¾ **Mascat** 2-9-5 0 .... HarryBentley 3 77
(Ralph Beckett) *str; hld up in midfield: pushed along and prog wl over 1f out: rdn and styd on fnl f to take 2nd last stride* **33/1**

3 *shd* **Finest Sound (IRE)** 2-9-5 0 .... DaneO'Neill 14 77
(Simon Crisford) *str; scope; bit bkward; slowly away: sn in midfield: pushed along and prog 2f out: rdn and styd on to chse clr wnr 75yds out: no imp and lost 2nd last stride* **33/1**

6 **4** 1 ¼ **Into Faith (FR)**[36] 5331 2-9-5 0 .... JasonWatson 13 73
(David Menuisier) *str; trckd ldr after 1f: pushed into the ld jst over 2f out: hdd and one pce over 1f out (jockey said colt ran too freely in the early stages and hung right-handed under pressure)* **25/1**

2 **5** *shd* **Discovery Island**[14] 6163 2-9-5 0 .... WilliamBuick 9 73
(Charlie Appleby) *str; looked wl; led after 1f: pushed along and hdd jst over 2f out: outpcd over 1f out* **2/1**[2]

6 1 ¼ **Lord Campari (IRE)** 2-9-5 0 .... AndreaAtzeni 1 70
(Roger Varian) *unfurnished; scope; looked wl; t.k.h early: trckd ldrs: pushed along 2f out: sn outpcd and btn* **11/2**[3]

7 1 ¼ **My Frankel** 2-9-5 0 .... LouisSteward 6 67
(Sir Michael Stoute) *str; hld up in rr: pushed along on inner fnl 2f: n.d but kpt on steadily: nt disgracd* **14/1**

8 ½ **Mars Landing (IRE)** 2-9-5 0 .... KieranShoemark 7 65
(Sir Michael Stoute) *workmanlike; bit bkward; slowly away: mostly in last trio: effrt on wd outside 2f out: hanging and green after and little prog* **33/1**

9 *shd* **Fruition** 2-9-5 0 .... JamesDoyle 2 65
(William Haggas) *tall; trckd ldng trio: shkn up jst over 2f out: steadily wknd over 1f out* **20/1**

0 **10** 3 ½ **Mon Choix**[65] 4252 2-9-5 0 .... DavidProbert 5 56
(Andrew Balding) *ly; hld up in last trio: trying to make prog whn hmpd 2f out and snatched up: nt rcvr and no ch after* **33/1**

11 1 **Willy Nilly (IRE)** 2-9-5 0 .... AdamKirby 4 53
(Clive Cox) *workmanlike; a in last trio: pushed along and no prog over 2f out* **20/1**

12 2 ¼ **Bonus** 2-9-5 0 .... GeraldMosse 11 48
(Jim Boyle) *leggy; wl in tch tl wknd 2f out* **66/1**

1m 30.36s (1.06) **Going Correction** +0.075s/f (Good) 12 Ran SP% **124.1**
Speed ratings (Par 96): **96,91,91,90,90 88,87,86,86,82 81,78**
CSF £64.60 TOTE £2.40: £1.10, £9.60, £8.50; EX 63.10 Trifecta £639.40.
Owner Sheikh Hamdan bin Mohammed Al Maktoum **Bred** Highclere Stud And Floors Farming **Trained** Newmarket, Suffolk

■ Stewards' Enquiry : Louis Steward three-day ban: interference & careless riding (Sep 13, 15-16)

FOCUS
Add 14yds. This looked an above-average maiden on paper and it was hard not to be impressed by the performance of the well backed winner. The race has been rated on the positive side.

6670 PLAY 4 TO SCORE AT BETWAY H'CAP 1m
3:50 (3:50) (Class 3) (0-90,90) 3-Y-O £9,337 (£2,796; £1,398; £699; £349) **Stalls Low**

Form RPR

2313 **1** **Lyndon B (IRE)**[30] 5546 3-9-7 90 ....(v) JamesDoyle 5 99
(George Scott) *looked wl; hld up in last: prog to chse ldr over 1f out: hrd rdn to chal fnl f: sustained effrt to ld narrowly but decisively nr fin* **2/1**[1]

-114 **2** *nk* **Marhaban (IRE)**[136] 1835 3-9-5 88 .... WilliamBuick 4 96
(Charlie Appleby) *looked wl; pushed along early: sn trckd ldrs: wnt 2nd 3f out and shkn up to ld 2f out: drvn and pressed fnl f: r.o but hdd and hld nr fin* **4/1**[3]

0411 **3** 4 **Gin Palace**[14] 6155 3-9-1 84 .... CharlesBishop 6 83
(Eve Johnson Houghton) *t.k.h: pressed ldr: led after 3f: shkn up and hdd 2f out: outpcd over 1f out* **7/2**[2]

2161 **4** 3 **Be More**[34] 5422 3-9-1 84 .... DavidProbert 3 76
(Andrew Balding) *chsd ldrs: cl up over 2f out: sn rdn and nt qckn: fdd over 1f out* **9/2**

41-1 **5** 19 **Reeth (IRE)**[238] 55 3-9-2 85 ....(b) AndreaAtzeni 2 34
(John Gosden) *looked wl; led 3f: w ldr to over 3f out: wknd rapidly: t.o (jockey said colt stopped quickly)* **5/1**

1m 43.6s (0.30) **Going Correction** +0.075s/f (Good) 5 Ran SP% **110.4**
Speed ratings (Par 104): **101,100,96,93,74**
CSF £10.21 TOTE £2.20: £1.50, £1.80; EX 8.20 Trifecta £16.80.
Owner W J and T C O Gredley **Bred** Yeomanstown Stud **Trained** Newmarket, Suffolk

FOCUS
Add 14yds. A good quality 3yo handicap and the form looks strong with the first two pulling clear.

6671 BETWAY LIVE CASINO H'CAP 1m 1f 209y
4:25 (4:25) (Class 4) (0-80,81) 3-Y-O
£7,115 (£2,117; £1,058; £529; £300; £300) **Stalls Low**

Form RPR

5263 **1** **Skyman**[14] 6160 3-9-2 73 .... JasonWatson 3 83+
(Roger Charlton) *trckd ldng pair: nudging match w rival whn angling for room 3f out: clsd 2f out: shkn up to ld over 1f out: styd on and wl in command fnl f* **7/2**[2]

0242 **2** 1 ¾ **Craneur**[16] 6083 3-8-8 65 .... DavidEgan 5 71
(Harry Dunlop) *looked wl; trckd ldr: led 3f out: rdn and hdd over 1f out: one pce* **9/1**

4112 **3** ½ **Dargel (IRE)**[16] 6075 3-9-7 78 .... AdamKirby 4 83
(Clive Cox) *hld up in last pair: effrt on outer over 2f out: hanging rt after: drvn to press for 2nd fnl f: nt go past runner-up nr fin (jockey said colt hung right-handed)* **7/2**[2]

5646 **4** 2 ½ **Athmad (IRE)**[24] 5776 3-9-10 81 .... JamesDoyle 2 81
(Brian Meehan) *hld up in last pair: shkn up 2f out: yet to make prog whn carried rt over 1f out: n.d after* **6/1**[3]

0511 **5** 4 **The Corporal (IRE)**[15] 6129 3-9-10 81 .... WilliamBuick 6 73
(Chris Wall) *hld up in 4th: shkn up and nudging match w rival 3f out: rdn and racd awkwardly over 2f out: impeded and carried rt over 1f out: wknd* **7/4**[1]

0323 **6** 3 **Steeve**[16] 6083 3-9-1 72 ....(p) HectorCrouch 1 59
(Rod Millman) *led to 3f out: sn btn: wkng whn hmpd over 1f out* **14/1**

2m 10.23s (0.03) **Going Correction** +0.075s/f (Good) 6 Ran SP% **111.8**
Speed ratings (Par 102): **102,100,100,98,95 92**
CSF £32.37 TOTE £4.50: £1.90, £4.10; EX 31.00 Trifecta £130.40.
Owner Paul Inglett And Simon De Zoete **Bred** Miss K J Keir **Trained** Beckhampton, Wilts

FOCUS
Add 14yds. This was a little messy but there was no doubting the supremacy of the cosy winner. It's been rated at face value around the second and third.

6672 BETWAY HEED YOUR HUNCH FILLIES' H'CAP 1m 1f 209y
5:00 (5:00) (Class 5) (0-75,77) 3-Y-O+
£5,175 (£1,540; £769; £384; £300; £300) **Stalls Low**

Form RPR

5531 **1** **Geetanjali (IRE)**[5] 6512 4-9-13 77 ....(v) CameronNoble(3) 6 89+
(Michael Bell) *hld up in last: smooth prog on outer over 2f out: led over 1f out: nudged along and wl in command after* **4/1**[2]

011 **2** 1 ½ **Geranium**[7] 6412 4-9-9 70 5ex .... DaneO'Neill 5 77
(Hughie Morrison) *trckd ldng trio: trying to cl but under pressed whn wnr breezed past over 1f out: styd on to take 2nd ins fnl f but no ch* **10/11**[1]

0-12 **3** 1 ¾ **Seascape (IRE)**[30] 5549 3-9-1 69 .... DavidProbert 3 74
(Henry Candy) *trckd ldr: upsides 3f out: shkn up to ld 2f out: hdd and one pce over 1f out* **5/1**[3]

1534 **4** 3 ½ **Kvetuschka**[19] 5982 3-9-8 76 .... JasonWatson 1 74
(Peter Chapple-Hyam) *led: jnd 3f out: drvn and hdd 2f out: wknd over 1f out* **16/1**

3410 **5** 5 **Beguiling Charm (IRE)**[15] 6129 3-9-5 73 .... LiamKeniry 7 62
(Ed Walker) *broke wl but restrained into 5th: pushed along and lft bhd 2f out: rdn and wknd over 1f out* **9/1**

6-15 **6** 1 ¾ **Mulan (IRE)**[69] 4119 3-9-7 75 .... KieranShoemark 2 60
(Sir Michael Stoute) *chsd ldng pair: rdn over 2f out: racd awkwardly and wknd wl over 1f out* **11/1**

2m 10.01s (-0.19) **Going Correction** +0.075s/f (Good)
WFA 3 from 4yo 7lb 6 Ran SP% **113.3**
Speed ratings (Par 100): **103,101,100,97,93 92**
CSF £8.22 TOTE £4.50: £2.70, £1.10; EX 7.00 Trifecta £32.20.
Owner Hugo Merry **Bred** G S K International **Trained** Newmarket, Suffolk

FOCUS
Add 14yds. With all bar one of these having won at least once in their last two starts, this looked a decent fillies-only handicap. It's been rated around the winner and third.
T/Plt: £276.30 to a £1 stake. Pool: £65,911.70 - 174.08 winning units. T/Qpdt: £30.20 to a £1 stake. Pool: £6,280.51 - 153.84 winning units. **Jonathan Neesom**

6174 THIRSK (L-H)
Friday, August 30

OFFICIAL GOING: Good (good to soft in places)
Wind: Virtually nil Weather: Cloudy

6673 BILL COX MEMORIAL NOVICE AUCTION STKS 7f 218y
2:00 (2:01) (Class 5) 2-Y-O £3,881 (£1,155; £577; £288) **Stalls Centre**

Form RPR

022 **1** **Overpriced Mixer**[10] 6314 2-9-5 0 .... CallumShepherd 4 73
(Jamie Osborne) *mde all: pushed along over 2f out: rdn wl over 1f out: strly pressed and drvn ins fnl f: edgd rt and kpt on wl towards fin* **7/4**[1]

4 **2** ¾ **Strawman (IRE)**[16] 6065 2-9-5 0 .... ConnorBeasley 9 71
(Adrian Nicholls) *trckd ldng pair: effrt on outer and cl up over 2f out: rdn to chal wl over 1f out: drvn and ev ch ins fnl f: no ex towards fin* **5/2**[2]

3 2 **Urban Hero (IRE)** 2-9-5 0 .... DanielTudhope 3 68+
(Archie Watson) *hld up: hdwy wl over 2f out: rdn to chse ldrs over 1f out: kpt on wl fnl f* **7/2**[3]

3001 **4** 1 **Our Dave**[11] 6271 2-9-5 53 ....(v) KevinStott 8 65
(John Quinn) *trckd wnr: cl up 1/2-way: rdn along wl over 2f out: drvn and ev ch wl over 1f out: wknd ent fnl f* **18/1**

5 1 **East End Girl** 2-9-0 0 .... GrahamLee 5 58
(Lucy Wadham) *trckd ldrs: effrt 3f out: sn pushed along: rdn 2f out: drvn over 1f out: no imp fnl f* **16/1**

60 **6** *shd* **Glen Esk**[14] 6161 2-9-5 0 .... PatCosgrave 2 62
(Chris Wall) *dwlt and in rr: sme hdwy over 2f out: sn rdn along and n.d* **9/1**

0 **7** 21 **Top Attraction**[22] 5856 2-9-5 0 .... MichaelStainton 1 16
(Chris Fairhurst) *trckd ldng pair on inner: pushed along 1/2-way: rdn 3f out: sn wknd* **66/1**

8 *shd* **Jervaulx** 2-9-5 0 .... AndrewElliott 7 16
(James Bethell) *a in rr: outpcd and bhd fnl 2f* **25/1**

1m 44.43s (2.73) **Going Correction** +0.075s/f (Good) 8 Ran SP% **113.6**
Speed ratings (Par 94): **89,88,86,85,84 84,63,63**
CSF £6.16 TOTE £2.50: £1.10, £1.30, £1.50; EX 6.40 Trifecta £18.10.
Owner The 10 For 10 Partnership **Bred** Glebe Farm Stud **Trained** Upper Lambourn, Berks

FOCUS
Rail movements added 20yds to races over 7f and 1m, and 30yds to the 2m event. A fairly ordinary novice auction stakes. The first two and sixth help set the level for now.

6674 LADIES' DAY @THIRSKRACES SATURDAY 7TH SEPTEMBER BOOK NOW H'CAP — 2m 13y

2:30 (2:31) (Class 5) (0-70,72) 3-Y-0+

£4,398 (£1,309; £654; £327; £300; £300) Stalls Centre

Form | | | | RPR
1221 **1** **Maid In Manhattan (IRE)**[18] 6016 5-9-3 **64**..........(h) HarrisonShaw(5) 4 75
(Rebecca Menzies) *hld up towards rr: stdy hdwy over 6f out: trckd ldrs 4f out: led over 2f out and sn pushed clr: readily* **7/4**[1]

6532 **2** *5* **Diodorus (IRE)**[18] 6016 5-10-1 **71**....................(p) CliffordLee 7 74
(Karen McLintock) *hld up: hdwy 6f out: trckd ldrs 4f out: hdwy 3f out: chsd wnr and rdn wl over 1f out: drvn and no imp fnl f* **13/2**

0-05 **3** *1 ½* **Orsino (IRE)**[25] 5739 5-9-13 **69**.................... CamHardie 8 70
(Seb Spencer) *hld up in rr: hdwy over 3f out: chsd ldrs 2f out: sn rdn: drvn and kpt on same pce fnl f* **20/1**

4235 **4** *10* **Bullion Boss (IRE)**[27] 5654 3-9-2 **70**..................(p) ConnorBeasley 9 61
(Michael Dods) *prom: cl up after 4f: pushed along over 3f out: rdn wl over 2f out: sn drvn and wknd* **3/1**[2]

-226 **5** *9* **Divin Bere (FR)**[90] 3334 6-9-12 **68**....................(tp w) DavidAllan 3 46
(Iain Jardine) *prom: pushed along 4f out: rdn along 3f out: sn wknd* **9/2**[3]

0005 **6** *14* **Bill Cody (IRE)**[17] 6055 4-9-7 **63**.................... GrahamLee 5 25
(Julie Camacho) *led: pushed along 4f out: rdn 3f out: hdd and drvn over 2f out: sn wknd* **20/1**

06/0 **7** *9* **Zamoyski**[17] 6055 9-9-12 **68**....................(p) KevinStott 6 19
(Steve Gollings) *reminders s: chsd ldrs: reminders 7f out: rdn along and lost pl* **50/1**

152- **8** *25* **Brotherly Company (IRE)**[72] 1292 7-10-0 **70**.................... JackGarritty 1
(Joanne Foster) *trckd ldrs: pushed along over 5f out: rdn and wknd over 4f out: sn bhd (jockey said gelding ran flat)* **25/1**

544 **9** *14* **Point Taken (IRE)**[22] 5849 5-10-2 **72**....................(p) AndrewMullen 2
(Micky Hammond) *chsd ldrs: rdn along 6f out: wknd over 4f out: sn bhd (jockey said gelding stopped quickly; vet said a post-race examination revealed the gelding was lame left hind and that an endoscopic examination revealed that he had bled)* **16/1**

3m 31.52s (-2.08) **Going Correction** +0.075s/f (Good) **9** Ran SP% **114.1**
WFA 3 from 4yo+ 12lb
Speed ratings (Par 103): **108,105,104,99,95 88,83,71,64**
CSF £12.76 CT £166.46 TOTE £2.20: £1.10, £1.90, £6.30; EX 13.20 Trifecta £122.10.
Owner Stoneleigh Racing **Bred** John Breslin **Trained** Mordon, Durham

FOCUS
Add 30yds. This modest staying handicap appeared to be run at a decent gallop, and they finished strung out behind an easy winner. A clear pb from the winner.

6675 BRITISH EBF FILLIES' NOVICE STKS (PLUS 10 RACE) — 7f 218y

3:05 (3:06) (Class 4) 2-Y-O £6,469 (£1,925; £962; £481) Stalls Centre

Form | | | | RPR
1 **Divina Gloria (FR)** 2-9-0 0.................... KevinStott 8 77+
(Kevin Ryan) *green and swtchd lft s: sn pushed along in rr: hdwy on wd outside 3f out: rdn to ld appr fnl f: sn rdn and edgd lft: kpt on wl* **4/1**[2]

64 **2** *1* **Golden Lips (IRE)**[66] 4223 2-9-0 0.................... DavidAllan 2 75
(Harry Dunlop) *led 2f: cl up: chal over 3f out: rdn to ld 2f out: sn drvn: hdd ent fnl f: kpt on* **20/1**

03 **3** *1* **Expensive Dirham**[25] 5732 2-9-0 0.................... FrannyNorton 3 73
(Mark Johnston) *trckd ldrs: hdwy 3f out: rdn along: sltly outpcd and hung lft to rail wl over 1f out: kpt on u.p fnl f* **6/1**

241 **4** *1 ¾* **Reclaim Victory (IRE)**[21] 5895 2-8-10 72.................... HarryRussell(7) 6 72
(Brian Ellison) *in tch: hdwy 3f out: chsd ldrs 2f out: sn rdn: kpt on same pce appr fnl f* **11/2**

04 **5** *nk* **Fast And Free**[36] 5342 2-9-0 0.................... DanielTudhope 4 68
(William Haggas) *trckd ldrs: hdwy over 3f out: cl up over 2f out: sn rdn and ev ch: wknd over 1f out* **2/1**[1]

03 **6** *11* **Good Reason**[13] 6205 2-9-0 0.................... TomQueally 1 44
(Saeed bin Suroor) *trckd ldrs on inner: led after 1f: pushed along 3f out: sn rdn and hdd over 2f out: sn wknd* **12/1**

000 **7** *9* **Miss Chilli**[37] 5295 2-8-9 49.................... GerO'Neill(5) 7 24
(Michael Easterby) *chsd ldrs on inner: rdn along 3f out: sn wknd* **100/1**

8 *4* **Eventful** 2-9-0 0.................... PatCosgrave 5 16
(Hugo Palmer) *green and slowly away: a in rr (jockey said filly was restless in the stalls and missed the break)* **5/1**[3]

1m 42.92s (1.22) **Going Correction** +0.075s/f (Good) **8** Ran SP% **113.1**
Speed ratings (Par 93): **96,95,94,92,91 80,71,67**
CSF £74.53 TOTE £4.50: £1.60, £4.90, £2.00; EX 63.50 Trifecta £627.20.
Owner Sheikh Mohammed Obaid Al Maktoum **Bred** S A R L Ecurie Jean Louis Bouchard **Trained** Hambleton, N Yorks

FOCUS
Add 20yds. A nice performance from the winner in a time 1.51sec faster than the earlier novice auction race.

6676 THEAKSTON LEGENDARY ALES BEST BITTER H'CAP — 6f

3:40 (3:46) (Class 3) (0-95,94) 3-Y-0+ £12,938 (£3,850; £1,924; £962) Stalls Centre

Form | | | | RPR
1-1 **1** **Bielsa (IRE)**[104] 2823 4-9-3 **87**.................... KevinStott 5 97
(Kevin Ryan) *trckd ldrs: hdwy to ld 2f out: rdn appr fnl f: hld on wl towards fin* **9/2**[1]

516 **2** *hd* **Lahore (USA)**[13] 6229 5-9-9 **93**.................... GrahamLee 9 102
(Phillip Makin) *trckd ldrs centre: hdwy wl over 1f out: rdn to chal ins fnl f: sn drvn and ev ch: no ex nr fin* **12/1**

3040 **3** *2 ½* **Golden Apollo**[20] 5971 5-9-4 **88**....................(t[1]) DavidAllan 10 90
(Tim Easterby) *chsd ldrs centre: rdn along and sltly outpcd wl over 1f out: kpt on u.p fnl f* **7/1**[3]

4443 **4** *hd* **The Armed Man**[27] 5691 6-8-7 **82**.................... PaulaMuir(5) 3 83
(Chris Fairhurst) *prom centre: cl up 1/2-way: rdn along wl over 1f out: kpt on same pce fnl f* **16/1**

2454 **5** *½* **Tommy Taylor (USA)**[34] 5453 5-9-1 **85**.................... JosephineGordon 4 84
(Kevin Ryan) *in tch centre: hdwy 2f out: sn rdn: kpt on fnl f* **12/1**

2224 **6** *½* **Muscika**[13] 6229 5-9-3 **92**....................(v) HarrisonShaw(5) 11 90
(David O'Meara) *cl up centre: disp ld 1/2-way: rdn along wl over 1f out: grad wknd appr fnl f* **11/2**[2]

2340 **7** *nse* **Roundhay Park**[13] 6208 4-8-10 **83**.................... RowanScott(3) 16 81
(Nigel Tinkler) *racd nr stands' rail: in tch: hdwy 2f out: rdn to chse ldrs over 1f out: sn drvn and no imp* **11/1**

0500 **8** *½* **Flying Pursuit**[13] 6227 6-9-3 **87**....................(t[1]) RachelRichardson 13 83
(Tim Easterby) *racd nr stands' rail: chsd ldrs: rdn along 2f out: drvn over 1f out: kpt on same pce* **25/1**

4333 **9** *1* **Mark's Choice (IRE)**[13] 6227 3-8-9 **82**.................... JamesSullivan 6 75
(Ruth Carr) *towards rr centre tl styd on fnl 2f: n.d* **16/1**

2003 **10** *nk* **Jawwaal**[34] 5454 4-9-5 **89**.................... AndrewMullen 17 81
(Michael Dods) *racd towards stands' side: hld up: sme hdwy 2f out: sn rdn and n.d* **9/1**

2653 **11** *¾* **Wentworth Falls**[58] 4521 7-9-8 **92**....................(v[1]) SamJames 15 82
(Geoffrey Harker) *hld up in rr: hdwy 2f out: sn rdn and n.d* **16/1**

5210 **12** *½* **Zumurud (IRE)**[13] 6220 4-9-0 **84**.................... PhilDennis 14 73
(Rebecca Bastiman) *racd towards stands' rail: in tch: rdn along 2f out: sn wknd* **22/1**

-100 **13** *hd* **Get The Rhythm**[27] 5661 3-8-8 **81**.................... CamHardie 7 69
(Richard Fahey) *dwlt: a towards rr* **25/1**

060- **14** *4* **Rapid Applause**[307] 8632 7-8-12 **87**.................... GerO'Neill(5) 2 63
(Michael Easterby) *chsd ldrs centre: rdn along 2f out: sn wknd* **50/1**

0020 **15** *3 ¼* **Captain Colby (USA)**[14] 6162 7-9-0 **84**.................... PatCosgrave 8 50
(Paul Midgley) *racd centre: led: rdn along and hdd 2f out: sn drvn and wknd* **28/1**

200- **16** *3 ¼* **Al Qahwa (IRE)**[315] 8370 6-9-10 **94**....................(p) DanielTudhope 12 51
(David O'Meara) *towards rr: rdn along over 2f out: sn outpcd* **11/1**

1m 9.65s (-3.15) **Going Correction** +0.075s/f (Good)
WFA 3 from 4yo+ 3lb **16** Ran SP% **123.2**
Speed ratings (Par 107): **115,114,111,111,110 109,109,109,107,107 106,105,105,100,95 91**
CSF £55.23 CT £387.57 TOTE £4.60: £1.30, £3.00, £1.70, £3.80; EX 71.00 Trifecta £574.40.
Owner Highbank Stud **Bred** Highbank Stud **Trained** Hambleton, N Yorks

FOCUS
A warm sprint handicap. They split into two groups at first, the larger one with ten runners down the middle providing the first six home. The time was 0.85sec inside the standard. The second has been rated a length better than when winning at Ripon earlier in the month.

6677 ANDERSON BARROWCLIFF CHARTERED ACCOUNTANTS H'CAP — 7f

4:15 (4:18) (Class 4) (0-85,83) 3-Y-0+

£6,986 (£2,079; £1,038; £519; £300; £300) Stalls Centre

Form | | | | RPR
4002 **1** **Queen's Sargent (FR)**[27] 5692 4-9-6 **78**.................... JosephineGordon 9 86
(Kevin Ryan) *hld up in rr: hdwy on wd outside over 2f out: rdn and str run over 1f out: styd on to ld last 100yds* **4/1**[1]

4214 **2** *½* **Global Spirit**[37] 5303 4-9-4 **76**....................(p) CamHardie 4 83
(Roger Fell) *hld up towards rr: hdwy over 2f out: chsd ldrs over 1f out: sn rdn: styd on wl fnl f (jockey said gelding anticipated the start and missed the break)* **9/1**

0652 **3** *½* **Saluti (IRE)**[12] 6261 5-9-4 **76**.................... GrahamLee 11 82
(Paul Midgley) *in tch: hdwy 2f out: rdn to chse ldng pair ent fnl f: sn drvn and kpt on wl towards fin* **5/1**[2]

0010 **4** *¾* **Start Time (IRE)**[14] 6179 6-9-2 **74**.................... KevinStott 1 78
(Paul Midgley) *t.k.h: led 2f: cl up: led again 2f out: rdn jst over 1f out: drvn ins fnl f: hdd last 100yds: no ex* **8/1**[3]

3450 **5** *1 ½* **Absolutio (FR)**[25] 5749 3-9-4 **81**....................(h) CliffordLee 14 79
(K R Burke) *prom on wd outside: led after 2f: rdn along over 2f out: hdd: cl up and drvn over 1f out: rallied and ev ch ent fnl f: grad wknd* **8/1**[3]

0216 **6** *1 ¼* **Highly Sprung (IRE)**[23] 5821 6-8-12 **75**.................... HarrisonShaw(5) 2 72
(Les Eyre) *in tch: hdwy over 2f out: rdn along to chse ldrs over 1f out: kpt on same pce fnl f* **20/1**

0404 **7** *1 ½* **Florenza**[14] 6179 6-9-7 **79**.................... TomQueally 10 73
(Chris Fairhurst) *prom: pushed along 3f out: rdn over 2f out: sn wknd* **11/1**

\- **8** *nk* **Jewel Maker (IRE)**[67] 4199 4-9-4 **76**.................... DavidAllan 5 68
(Tim Easterby) *trckd ldrs: pushed along over 2f out: sn rdn and wknd over 1f out* **12/1**

1-10 **9** *nk* **Dutch Pursuit (IRE)**[46] 4980 3-9-2 **79**.................... PhilDennis 12 69
(Michael Dods) *awkward s: a towards rr (jockey said gelding missed the break and was slowly away as a result)* **33/1**

4064 **10** *¾* **Tadaawol**[18] 6014 6-9-7 **79**....................(p) LewisEdmunds 8 69
(Roger Fell) *chsd ldrs: rdn along over 2f out: sn drvn and wknd* **25/1**

1333 **11** *½* **Magical Effect (IRE)**[12] 6260 7-9-6 **78**.................... JackGarritty 6 66
(Ruth Carr) *hld up: a towards rr* **12/1**

000- **12** *2 ¼* **La Rav (IRE)**[326] 8044 5-9-6 **83**....................(h[1]) GerO'Neill(5) 13 66
(Michael Easterby) *chsd ldrs on outer: pushed along 3f out: rdn wl over 2f out: sn drvn and grad wknd* **25/1**

2/5- **13** *4* **Tamkeen**[487] 2213 4-9-5 **77**.................... JamesSullivan 7 50
(Ruth Carr) *awkward s: a in rr* **40/1**

0304 **14** *2 ¼* **John Kirkup**[27] 5692 4-9-3 **75**....................(p) PatCosgrave 3 42
(Michael Dods) *a towards rr* **17/2**

1m 27.96s (0.36) **Going Correction** +0.075s/f (Good)
WFA 3 from 4yo+ 5lb **14** Ran SP% **121.0**
Speed ratings (Par 105): **100,99,98,98,96 94,93,92,92,91 91,88,83,81**
CSF £37.35 CT £192.91 TOTE £4.30: £1.70, £2.40, £1.60; EX 31.00 Trifecta £94.30.
Owner Dave Stone **Bred** Pierre Paul Richou **Trained** Hambleton, N Yorks

FOCUS
Add 20yds. Just fair handicap form. The first two came from off the pace. Straightforward form, with the second, third and fourth dictating the level.

6678 HENRY ROBIN KIBERD 20 YEAR CELEBRATION H'CAP (DIV I) — 7f 218y

4:45 (4:46) (Class 5) (0-70,71) 3-Y-O

£4,398 (£1,309; £654; £327; £300; £300) Stalls Centre

Form | | | | RPR
6300 **1** **Gunnison**[15] 6101 3-8-3 **51**....................(p[1]) CamHardie 12 57
(Richard Fahey) *mde all: pushed clr over 2f out: rdn wl over 1f out: drvn ins fnl f: jst hld on* **16/1**

6563 **2** *shd* **Rudy Lewis (IRE)**[16] 6081 3-9-9 **71**.................... StevieDonohoe 11 78+
(Charlie Fellowes) *towards rr: hdwy over 2f out: in tch and rdn wl over 1f out: nt clr run and swtchd rt ent fnl f: fin strly: jst failed* **4/1**[1]

2051 **3** *shd* **Purgatory**[15] 6130 3-9-1 **63**....................(b) PatCosgrave 1 70
(Chris Wall) *trckd ldrs: pushed along and sltly outpcd wl over 1f out: rdn and hdwy whn nt clr run ent fnl f: sn drvn and kpt on wl towards fin* **9/2**[2]

6440 **4** *½* **Jem Scuttle (USA)**[52] 4767 3-9-0 **62**....................(t) KevinStott 4 66
(Declan Carroll) *trckd ldrs: hdwy over 2f out: sn rdn and ev ch over 1f out: drvn and kpt on same pce fnl f* **6/1**[3]

5632 **5** *2 ¼* **Beautiful Gesture**[20] 5941 3-9-5 **67**.................... CliffordLee 5 67
(K R Burke) *cl up: rdn along over 2f out: ev ch over 1f out: sn drvn and grad wknd* **6/1**[3]

The Form Book Flat 2019, Raceform Ltd, Newbury, RG14 5SJ

0-60 **6** *nk* **Schnapps**[95] 3154 3-8-9 **57**.................................. JamesSullivan 9 56
(Jedd O'Keeffe) *hld up towards rr: hdwy over 2f out: rdn wl over 1f out: kpt on fnl f* **25/1**

-003 **7** *shd* **Charlie's Boy (IRE)**[23] 5816 3-8-8 **56**.................................. PhilDennis 8 55
(Michael Dods) *cl up: rdn along 3f out: wknd over 2f out* **6/1**[3]

6065 **8** *nk* **Mac Ailey**[17] 6036 3-8-9 **57**.................................. RachelRichardson 6 55
(Tim Easterby) *a towards rr* **11/1**

5630 **9** *1 3/4* **Fox Kasper (IRE)**[147] 1568 3-9-7 **69**.................................. DavidAllan 10 63
(Tim Easterby) *a in rr* **14/1**

5056 **10** *3/4* **My Boy Lewis (IRE)**[9] 6342 3-9-4 **66**..........................(p) LewisEdmunds 7 59
(Roger Fell) *chsd ldrs: pushed along over 3f out: rdn wl over 2f out: sn wknd* **22/1**

-000 **11** *hd* **Laura Louise (IRE)**[92] 3271 3-7-9 **49** oh1.......................... IzzyClifton(7) 2 42
(Nigel Tinkler) *dwlt: in tch on inner: rdn along 3f out: sn wknd* **50/1**

0-00 **12** *4* **Good Looker (IRE)**[103] 2871 3-8-2 **50**.................................. FrannyNorton 3 33
(Tony Coyle) *a towards rr* **40/1**

1m 43.47s (1.77) **Going Correction** +0.075s/f (Good) **12** Ran SP% **114.5**
Speed ratings (Par 100): **94,93,93,93,91 90,90,90,88,87 87,83**
CSF £73.83 CT £347.83 TOTE £17.80: £5.00, £2.30, £1.50; EX 96.90 Trifecta £554.40.
Owner A B Phipps **Bred** A B Phipps **Trained** Musley Bank, N Yorks
■ Stewards' Enquiry : Stevie Donohoe two-day ban: interference & careless riding (Sep 13, 15)

FOCUS
Add 20yds. A very tight finish to this modest handicap, which was the slower division by 1.14sec. The principals have been rated near their pre-race marks.

6679 HENRY ROBIN KIBERD 20 YEAR CELEBRATION H'CAP (DIV II) 7f 218y
5:15 (5:15) (Class 5) (0-70,70) 3-Y-O
£4,398 (£1,309; £654; £327; £300; £300) **Stalls** Centre

Form RPR

5103 **1** **Mecca's Gift (IRE)**[9] 6342 3-9-7 **70**..........................(b) CliffordLee 1 76
(Michael Dods) *trckd ldrs: hdwy 2f out: rdn over 1f out: chsd ldr ins fnl f: sn drvn and kpt on wl to ld nr fin* **14/1**

4230 **2** *1/2* **Dreamseller (IRE)**[15] 6101 3-8-4 **53**.................................. PhilDennis 3 58
(Tim Easterby) *trckd ldrs: hdwy 3f out: led wl over 1f out: sn rdn: drvn ins fnl f: hdd nr fin* **6/1**[3]

4123 **3** *1 3/4* **The Big House (IRE)**[24] 5771 3-8-6 **60**.................. HarrisonShaw(5) 2 61
(Adrian Nicholls) *trckd ldrs: effrt on inner over 2f out: swtchd rt and rdn wl over 1f out: drvn and kpt on same pce fnl f* **3/1**[1]

5500 **4** *2 1/2* **House Deposit**[14] 6176 3-8-8 **57**..........................(p[1]) LewisEdmunds 5 53
(Roger Fell) *trckd ldr: cl up 3f out: rdn and led briefly over 2f out: drvn and hdd wl over 1f out: grad wknd* **33/1**

0044 **5** *hd* **Uncle Norman (FR)**[14] 6176 3-8-2 **51**..................(b) RachelRichardson 9 46
(Tim Easterby) *hld up in rr: hdwy on outer over 2f out: rdn wl over 1f out: kpt on fnl f* **16/1**

-511 **6** *3/4* **My Ukulele (IRE)**[27] 5695 3-9-5 **68**.................................. DavidAllan 8 61
(John Quinn) *hld up towards rr: pushed along 3f out: rdn over 2f out: drvn wl over 1f out: n.d* **3/1**[1]

0305 **7** *nse* **Abie's Hollow**[14] 6176 3-8-13 **62**.................................. KevinStott 6 55
(Tony Coyle) *dwlt: a in rr* **11/1**

-601 **8** *shd* **Castle Quarter (IRE)**[22] 5852 3-9-2 **65**..........................(p) CamHardie 11 58
(Seb Spencer) *in tch: pushed along 3f out: rdn over 2f out: drvn wl over 1f out: n.d* **16/1**

3502 **9** *1 3/4* **Alfa Dawn (IRE)**[15] 6101 3-9-4 **67**.................................. SamJames 4 56
(Phillip Makin) *led: rdn along 3f out: hdd wl over 2f out: sn wknd* **11/2**[2]

-060 **10** *nse* **Dragons Will Rise (IRE)**[37] 5299 3-8-2 **50** oh1.......... FrannyNorton 10 40
(Micky Hammond) *a in rr* **16/1**

1m 42.33s (0.63) **Going Correction** +0.075s/f (Good) **10** Ran SP% **115.3**
Speed ratings (Par 100): **99,98,96,94,94 93,93,93,91,91**
CSF £94.55 CT £282.52 TOTE £14.50: £3.60, £1.80, £2.10; EX 106.60 Trifecta £467.30.
Owner D J Metcalfe & M Dods **Bred** Doc Bloodstock **Trained** Denton, Co Durham

FOCUS
Add 20yds. The quicker division by 1.14sec. Low draws dominated this time. The second has been rated back to his best and the third near his mark.

6680 AJA NOVICE FLAT AMATEUR RIDERS' H'CAP 6f
5:45 (5:46) (Class 6) (0-65,67) 3-Y-O+
£3,277 (£1,016; £507; £300; £300; £300) **Stalls** Centre

Form RPR

6055 **1** **Buccaneers Vault (IRE)**[3] 6581 7-10-13 **67**...... MrEireannCagney(5) 15 75
(Paul Midgley) *racd towards stands' side: in tch: hdwy wl over 1f out: rdn to ld ins fnl f: kpt on wl* **7/1**[3]

1232 **2** *3/4* **B Fifty Two (IRE)**[11] 6273 10-10-13 **62**..........(tp) MissSarahBowen 12 68
(Marjorie Fife) *in tch centre: hdwy 2f out: rdn over 1f out: kpt on u.p fnl f* **9/1**

4202 **3** *nk* **Cardaw Lily (IRE)**[17] 6058 4-9-11 **46**.................... MissShannonWatts 7 51
(Ruth Carr) *led centre: rdn along wl over 1f out: hdd ins fnl f: kpt on same pce towards fin* **9/1**

003 **4** *1 1/2* **Mansfield**[30] 5558 6-10-8 **57**.................................. SophieSmith 4 57
(Stella Barclay) *in tch centre: hdwy over 2f out: rdn to chse ldrs and ch over 1f out: kpt on same pce* **13/2**[2]

1304 **5** *shd* **Space War**[14] 6174 12-10-2 **56**..........................(t) MissMaisieSharp(5) 5 56
(Michael Easterby) *trckd ldrs centre: effrt 2f out: sn rdn and kpt on same pce* **20/1**

3400 **6** *1 1/2* **Kenny The Captain (IRE)**[8] 6373 8-10-13 **62**........ MissJessicaGillam 1 58
(Tim Easterby) *trckd ldrs on inner: pushed along 2f out: sn rdn and one pce fnl f* **9/1**

0213 **7** *hd* **Sfumato**[28] 5632 5-11-0 **63**.................................. MissAntoniaPeck 2 58
(Adrian Nicholls) *chsd ldrs centre: rdn over 1f out: grad wknd fnl f* **6/1**[1]

6000 **8** *hd* **Mitchum**[14] 6174 10-9-10 **45**.................................. MissAmyCollier 8 39
(Ron Barr) *towards rr centre: rdn along wl over 2f out: n.d* **33/1**

2656 **9** *1 3/4* **Rickyroadboy**[42] 5157 4-10-6 **60**.................................. MarcusHaigh(5) 13 49
(Mark Walford) *cl up centre: rdn along 2f out: sn wknd* **22/1**

3050 **10** *1/2* **Aghast**[19] 5985 3-10-1 **58**.................................. MrBenBromley(5) 14 46
(Kevin Ryan) *cl up centre: rdn along 2f out: sn wknd* **16/1**

3061 **11** *nse* **Winklemann (IRE)**[37] 5302 7-10-13 **62**..........(p) MissImogenMathias 11 49
(John Flint) *awkward and dwlt: a in rr (jockey said gelding was slowly away and outpaced thereafter)* **17/2**

2064 **12** *3/4* **Shortbackandsides (IRE)**[16] 6066 4-10-13 **62**.. MissCharlotteCrane 10 47
(Tim Easterby) *a in rr* **14/1**

2200 **13** *hd* **Ventura Secret (IRE)**[25] 5723 5-10-0 **54**..........(tp) MissChloeDods(5) 9 39
(Michael Dods) *midfield centre: rdn along over 2f out: sn wknd* **11/1**

3000 **14** *1 1/2* **Exchequer (IRE)**[42] 5144 8-10-7 **61**..........(t[1]) MrHenryNewcombe(5) 3 41
(Richard Guest) *s.i.s: a in rr (vet said gelding lost its left hind shoe)* **20/1**

0000 **15** *3/4* **Shawwaslucky**[7] 6389 3-9-2 **45**.................................. MissMintyBloss(5) 6 23
(Derek Shaw) *racd centre: towards rr: rdn along bef 1/2-way: sn outpcd* **66/1**

1m 12.35s (-0.45) **Going Correction** +0.075s/f (Good)
WFA 3 from 4yo+ 3lb **15** Ran SP% **119.8**
Speed ratings (Par 101): **106,105,104,102,102 100,100,99,97,96 96,95,95,93,92**
CSF £63.09 CT £591.60 TOTE £9.40: £3.10, £2.70, £2.30; EX 82.90 Trifecta £224.10.
Owner Sheila Bradley And P T Midgley **Bred** Kilfrush Stud **Trained** Westow, N Yorks

FOCUS
A very modest sprint for amateurs.
T/Jkpt: Not Won. T/Plt: £61.20 to a £1 stake. Pool: £66,088.79 - 788.29 winning units. T/Qpdt: £29.10 to a £1 stake. Pool: £5,868.20 - 149.07 winning units. **Joe Rowntree**

6181 WOLVERHAMPTON (A.W) (L-H)
Friday, August 30

OFFICIAL GOING: Tapeta: standard
Wind: Light behind Weather: Fine

6681 FOLLOW @PTS_ACADEMY FOR TRAINING SOLUTIONS AMATEUR RIDERS' H'CAP 1m 5f 219y (Tp)
4:30 (4:30) (Class 6) (0-65,66) 3-Y-O+
£2,682 (£832; £415; £400; £400; £400) **Stalls** Low

Form RPR

5021 **1** **Percy Prosecco**[11] 6278 4-11-2 **66** 5ex............ MissBrodieHampson 10 72
(Archie Watson) *hld up: hdwy over 3f out: swtchd rt over 2f out: led over 1f out: rdn and hung lft ins fnl f: styd on* **5/2**[1]

3364 **2** *2* **Yasir (USA)**[17] 6046 11-10-2 **52**.......................... MissSerenaBrotherton 7 55
(Sophie Leech) *s.i.s: hld up: hdwy over 6f out: chsd ldr over 3f out: rdn and swtchd lft over 1f out: swtchd rt ins fnl f: styd on* **10/1**

1536 **3** *2 1/4* **Highway Robbery**[27] 5648 3-8-9 **48**..........................(p) MrSamFeilden(7) 1 50
(Julia Feilden) *led early: led again over 12f out: rdn: edgd lft and hdd over 1f out: no ex ins fnl f* **10/1**

6020 **4** *1 1/4* **Earthly (USA)**[71] 4036 5-9-10 **51**..........(tp) MissJessicaLlewellyn(5) 2 49
(Bernard Llewellyn) *chsd ldrs: shkn up over 2f out: styd on same pce fnl f* **16/1**

4210 **5** *1 3/4* **Fern Owl**[8] 5631 7-10-5 **58**..........................(e) MissAliceHaynes(3) 3 54
(John Butler) *mid-div: lost pl over 8f out: hdwy over 2f out: r.o: nt rch ldrs* **6/1**[3]

2060 **6** *6* **Ebqaa (IRE)**[34] 5423 5-11-0 **64**..........................(p) MrAlexEdwards 9 52
(James Unett) *chsd ldrs: lost pl over 8f out: hdwy over 5f out: rdn over 2f out: sn wknd* **9/1**

6005 **7** *hd* **Uncle Bernie (IRE)**[44] 5053 9-10-0 **57**..........(p) MrSeanHawkins(7) 4 45+
(Sarah Hollinshead) *s.s: nvr nrr (jockey said gelding was slowly away)* **33/1**

4446 **8** *3 1/2* **Geomatrician (FR)**[20] 5954 3-9-12 **65**......(v[1]) MissClaudiaMetaireau(7) 8 50
(Andrew Balding) *hld up in tch: racd keenly: lost pl over 8f out: swtchd rt over 5f out: effrt on outer and hung rt over 2f out: n.d* **8/1**

0000 **9** *1 1/2* **Punkawallah**[66] 4216 5-10-5 **62**..........................(tp w) MrTambyWelch(7) 12 43
(Alexandra Dunn) *prom: sn lost pl rdn over 3f out: sn wknd* **33/1**

4004 **10** *1 3/4* **Sellingallthetime (IRE)**[23] 5802 8-9-2 **45**..........(p) MrCiaranJones(7) 6 23
(Mark Usher) *hld up: hdwy on outer over 8f out: wknd over 2f out* **22/1**

0124 **11** *13* **Tour De Paris (IRE)**[122] 2239 4-10-9 **64**..........(v) MrWilliamThirlby(5) 5 25
(Alan King) *chsd ldrs: wnt 2nd over 6f out tl over 3f out: rdn and wknd over 2f out* **3/1**[2]

40-0 **12** *35* **Angel Of The North (IRE)**[14] 6173 4-9-7 **50**......(v) MrFinbarMulrine(7) 11
(Robin Dickin) *sn led: hdd over 12f out: remained w ldr tl over 6f out: wknd over 4f out* **50/1**

3m 5.06s (4.06) **Going Correction** +0.05s/f (Slow)
WFA 3 from 4yo+ 10lb **12** Ran SP% **125.2**
Speed ratings (Par 101): **90,88,87,86,85 82,82,80,79,78 71,51**
CSF £29.67 CT £228.36 TOTE £3.20: £1.60, £3.00, £4.00; EX 21.90 Trifecta £128.70.
Owner The Real Quiz **Bred** Clive Dennett **Trained** Upper Lambourn, W Berks

FOCUS
A moderate affair.

6682 FOR TRAINING AND APPRENTICESHIPS VISIT PTSTRAININGACADEMY.COM H'CAP 6f 20y (Tp)
5:05 (5:07) (Class 6) (0-55,55) 3-Y-O+
£2,781 (£827; £413; £400; £400; £400) **Stalls** Low

Form RPR

3640 **1** **Kinglami**[16] 6084 10-9-7 **55**..........................(b) RossaRyan 7 61
(John O'Shea) *chsd ldrs: rdn to ld and hung lft ins fnl f: styd on (trainer said regarding apparent improvement in form that the gelding appreciated the drop in class and the drop in trip from 7f to 6f)* **10/1**

1060 **2** *1* **Brogans Bay (IRE)**[11] 6285 4-9-7 **55**.................................. JFEgan 5 58
(Simon Dow) *led: rdn over 1f out: hdd ins fnl f: styd on same pce* **16/1**

0010 **3** *1/2* **Classy Cailin (IRE)**[11] 6284 4-9-4 **52**..........................(e[1]) ShaneKelly 2 54
(Pam Sly) *hld up: plld hrd: rdn over 1f out: r.o ins fnl f: nt rch ldrs (jockey said filly missed the break)* **7/1**

6040 **4** *3/4* **Alba Del Sole (IRE)**[65] 4248 4-9-7 **55**.................. RichardKingscote 1 54
(Charlie Wallis) *sn chsng ldr: lost 2nd 1/2-way: rdn over 1f out: styd on same pce ins fnl f* **6/1**

0040 **5** *nk* **Peachey Carnehan**[14] 6174 5-9-6 **54**..........................(v) CharlieBennett 13 52
(Michael Mullineaux) *s.i.s: rdn and r.o ins fnl f: nt rch ldrs* **17/2**

3666 **6** *shd* **Santafiora**[11] 6273 5-9-5 **53**.................................. RobHornby 9 51
(Julie Camacho) *sn chsng ldrs: wnt 2nd 1/2-way tl rdn over 1f out: styd on same pce ins fnl f* **5/1**[3]

0200 **7** *1/2* **Just An Idea (IRE)**[14] 6174 5-9-0 **53**..........(b) RhiainIngram(5) 10 50
(Roger Ingram) *hld up: rdn on outer over 2f out: styd on ins fnl f: nt trble ldrs* **20/1**

6640 **8** *3/4* **Always Amazing**[42] 5147 5-9-4 **52**.................................. TomMarquand 6 46
(Robyn Brisland) *s.i.s: hdwy nt clr run and swtchd lft over 1f out: no ex wl ins fnl f* **3/1**[1]

0060 **9** *1/2* **Royal Connoisseur (IRE)**[79] 3716 8-8-13 **50**.................. SeanDavis(3) 3 43
(Richard Fahey) *prom: sn lost pl: n.d after* **14/1**

506 **10** *1 1/4* **Mystical Moon (IRE)**[21] 5889 4-8-12 **51**.................. CierenFallon(5) 4 40
(David C Griffiths) *prom: lost pl over 5f out: hdwy over 1f out: wknd ins fnl f (jockey said filly was never travelling)* **9/2**[2]

1m 14.57s (0.07) **Going Correction** +0.05s/f (Slow) **10** Ran SP% **123.6**
Speed ratings (Par 101): **101,99,99,98,97 97,96,95,95,93**
CSF £165.96 CT £1238.41 TOTE £12.20: £3.20, £4.40, £2.90; EX 167.60 Trifecta £3483.50.
Owner Pete Smith & Phil Hart Racing **Bred** Cheveley Park Stud Ltd **Trained** Elton, Gloucs

The Form Book Flat 2019, Raceform Ltd, Newbury, RG14 5SJ

FOCUS
Just an ordinary sprint handicap. The second limits the level.

6683 PTS TRAINING ACADEMY, NO MADNESS TRAINING NURSERY H'CAP 6f 20y (Tp)
5:35 (5:38) (Class 6) (0-60,60) 2-Y-O

£2,781 (£827; £413; £400; £400; £400) Stalls Low

Form				RPR
3322	1		**Two Hearts**[4] 6539 2-8-10 49 ... RossaRyan 1	55
			(Grant Tuer) *chsd ldrs: shkn up to ld over 1f out: rdn and edgd lft ins fnl f: all out* 7/4[1]	
0004	2	nse	**Port Noir**[16] 6071 2-8-8 47 ... (t) JohnFahy 5	53
			(Grace Harris) *prom: sn lost pl: hdwy and nt clr run over 1f out: sn rdn: r.o* 12/1	
6452	3	1 1/2	**Red Jasper**[10] 6313 2-9-6 59 ... LiamJones 4	60
			(Michael Appleby) *pushed along to chse ldrs: rdn: carried hd high and hung lft fr over 1f out: nt run on (jockey said gelding hung left-handed throughout)* 3/1[2]	
0503	4	1 1/2	**Street Life**[17] 6032 2-9-3 59 ... (b) SeanDavis(3) 2	56
			(Richard Fahey) *s.i.s: sn pushed along in rr: hdwy over 2f out: rdn: nt clr run and swtchd rt over 1f out: styd on* 14/1	
0350	5	2 1/4	**Javea Magic (IRE)**[46] 4985 2-9-4 57 ... (p) RichardKingscote 8	47
			(Tom Dascombe) *led: rdn and hdd over 1f out: no ex wl ins fnl f* 9/1[3]	
665	6	hd	**Treaty Of Dingle**[25] 5729 2-9-7 60 ... CharlieBennett 7	50
			(Hughie Morrison) *chsd ldrs: lost pl over 4f out: hdwy u.p over 1f out: styd on same pce ins fnl f* 20/1	
6643	7	1 3/4	**Positive Light (IRE)**[10] 6313 2-9-7 60 ... RyanTate 6	44
			(Sir Mark Prescott Bt) *s.i.s: sn pushed along in rr: nvr nrr* 11/1	
6306	8	1/2	**Ice Skate**[17] 6032 2-8-11 50 ... DuranFentiman 3	33
			(Tim Easterby) *chsd ldr tl led over 1f out: sn rdn and hdd: wknd wl ins fnl f* 10/1	
506	9	9	**Sombra De Mollys**[27] 5689 2-9-2 55 ... RobHornby 9	11
			(Brian Ellison) *s.i.s: rdn and flashed tail over 1f out: n.d* 33/1	
3443	10	8	**Ma Boy Harris (IRE)**[14] 6182 2-9-4 60 ... MeganNicholls(3)	13
			(Phillip Makin) *chsd ldrs: shkn up and hung rt over 2f out: wknd over 1f out (jockey said colt hung right-handed throughout)* 12/1	
454	11	7	**Royal Lightning**[81] 3652 2-9-6 59 ... (p[1]) CallumShepherd 11	
			(James Given) *chsd ldrs: pushed along and lost pl over 3f out: wknd over 2f out (jockey said filly hung badly right-handed throughout)* 33/1	

1m 15.41s (0.91) **Going Correction** +0.05s/f (Slow) **11 Ran SP% 121.5**
Speed ratings (Par 92): **95,94,92,90,87 87,85,84,72,62 52**
CSF £25.40 CT £62.28 TOTE £2.20: £1.20, £3.30, £1.40; EX 25.30 Trifecta £126.30.
Owner James Ortega Bloodstock Ltd **Bred** James Ortega Bloodstock Ltd **Trained** Birkby, N Yorks

FOCUS
A tight finish to this ordinary nursery. The winner has been rated close to his Ripon selling form.

6684 AL THE GAS 1953 NOVICE AUCTION STKS 7f 36y (Tp)
6:05 (6:07) (Class 6) 2-Y-O £2,781 (£827; £413; £206) Stalls High

Form				RPR
42	1		**Berkshire Savvy**[19] 5992 2-9-5 0 ... RobHornby 2	77
			(Andrew Balding) *a.p: chsd ldr over 2f out: rdn and carried hd high over 1f out: styd on u.p to ld nr fin* 4/5[1]	
3	2	1/2	**Take Me To The Sky**[14] 6161 2-9-5 0 ... ShaneKelly 1	76
			(Ed Dunlop) *led: rdn over 1f out: hdd nr fin* 2/1[2]	
	3	2 1/4	**Silver Samurai** 2-9-5 0 ... DanielMuscutt 3	70
			(Marco Botti) *s.i.s: hdwy over 2f out: rdn over 1f out: styd on same pce fnl f* 8/1[3]	
5	4	4 1/2	**Gweedore**[10] 6314 2-9-5 0 ... RossaRyan 5	59
			(Jason Ward) *trckd ldrs: racd keenly: rdn over 2f out: wknd ins fnl f* 28/1	
	5	2	**Doctor Nuno** 2-9-5 0 ... RichardKingscote 7	55
			(Mark Loughnane) *s.s: in rr: sme hdwy over 1f out: wknd fnl f* 10/1	
	6	5	**Cafe Milano** 2-9-5 0 ... TomMarquand 6	42
			(Simon Dow) *hld up: a in rr: rdn 1/2-way: wknd wl over 1f out* 20/1	
0	7	25	**Casablanca Kid (IRE)**[8] 6368 2-9-5 0 ... JFEgan 4	
			(Denis Quinn) *chsd ldr tl rdn over 2f out: wknd and eased over 1f out* 50/1	

1m 29.68s (0.88) **Going Correction** +0.05s/f (Slow) **7 Ran SP% 119.3**
Speed ratings (Par 92): **97,96,93,88,86 80,52**
CSF £2.76 TOTE £1.80: £1.10, £1.30; EX 3.00 Trifecta £9.40.
Owner Berkshire Parts & Panels Ltd **Bred** J M Duggan & T P Duggan **Trained** Kingsclere, Hants

FOCUS
No more than a fair novice.

6685 THINK APPRENTICESHIPS - THINK PTS H'CAP 5f 21y (Tp)
6:35 (6:35) (Class 6) (0-65,64) 3-Y-O+

£2,781 (£827; £413; £400; £400; £400) Stalls Low

Form				RPR
5144	1		**Precious Plum**[57] 4563 5-9-4 60 ... (p w) RobertWinston 7	67
			(Charlie Wallis) *mde all: shkn up and edgd rt over 1f out: rdn out* 4/1[2]	
0225	2	1 1/4	**Fairy Fast (IRE)**[14] 6183 3-9-6 64 ... (p) TomMarquand 6	67
			(George Boughey) *rrd s: hld up: hdwy over 1f out: r.o (jockey said filly was slowly away)* 5/1[3]	
3305	3	1/2	**Fareeq**[17] 6048 5-9-6 62 ... (bt) RichardKingscote 2	63
			(Charlie Wallis) *chsd ldrs: rdn and edgd rt over 1f out: styd on (jockey said gelding hung right-handed)* 8/1	
0014	4	nk	**Come On Dave (IRE)**[17] 6048 10-9-4 63 ... (b) DarraghKeenan(3) 8	63
			(John Butler) *chsd wnr after 1f tl rdn and edgd rt over 1f out: no ex wl ins fnl f* 15/2	
5050	5	1 1/4	**Hanati (IRE)**[3] 6575 3-9-2 60 ... RobHornby 9	55
			(Brian Ellison) *s.i.s: hdwy on outer over 3f out: rdn 1/2-way: styd on same pce fnl f* 20/1	
5051	6	1 1/4	**Lysander Belle (IRE)**[14] 6181 3-9-5 63 ... ShaneKelly 11	54
			(Sophie Leech) *chsd ldrs: lost pl over 3f out: pushed along on outer 1/2-way: n.d after* 15/2	
6-03	7	1	**Packington Lane**[52] 4757 3-9-6 64 ... DuranFentiman 3	51
			(Tim Easterby) *wnt rt s: sn prom: rdn over 1f out: no ex fnl f (jockey said gelding jumped right-handed when leaving the stalls)* 12/1	
1063	8	4 1/2	**My Town Chicago (USA)**[58] 4494 4-9-5 61 ... (t[1]) RossaRyan 1	32
			(Kevin Frost) *s.i.s: hld up: hdwy over 1f out: wknd ins fnl f (jockey said gelding was slowly away and was never travelling)* 2/1[1]	
-300	9	10	**Alban's Dream**[14] 6168 3-8-11 60 ... AndrewBreslin(5) 5	
			(Robert Eddery) *hood removed late: a in rr: eased fnl f (jockey said that the blindfold became caught on the cheekpieces and required two attempts to remove; jockey said filly reared when leaving the stalls and moved poorly)* 22/1	
0110	R		**Red Invader (IRE)**[114] 2527 9-9-3 64 ... DylanHogan(5) 4	
			(John Butler) *ref to r (jockey said that in his view the horse had become fractious of its own accord just prior to the start and subsequently refused to race)* 14/1	

1m 2.08s (0.18) **Going Correction** +0.05s/f (Slow) **10 Ran SP% 128.1**
WFA 3 from 4yo+ 2lb
Speed ratings (Par 101): **100,98,97,96,94 92,91,83,67,**
CSF £27.20 CT £165.43 TOTE £5.80: £2.00, £1.50, £2.90; EX 34.20 Trifecta £158.90.
Owner Mrs Julia Hughes **Bred** Mrs J V Hughes **Trained** Ardleigh, Essex

FOCUS
As is often the case round here over the minimum trip, the pace held up.

6686 MATT AND CHARLIE'S ANGELS H'CAP 1m 1f 104y (Tp)
7:05 (7:05) (Class 4) (0-80,81) 3-Y-O+

£5,207 (£1,549; £774; £400; £400; £400) Stalls Low

Form				RPR
4005	1		**Kaser (IRE)**[13] 6210 4-9-4 75 ... ThomasGreatrex(5) 5	83
			(David Loughnane) *s.i.s: hld up: hdwy over 2f out: rdn and r.o to ld nr fin* 11/1	
1342	2	hd	**Cape Victory (IRE)**[18] 6026 3-9-7 80 ... CallumShepherd 8	88
			(James Tate) *chsd ldrs: shkn up to go 2nd over 2f out: rdn over 1f out: styd on to ld wl ins fnl f: hdd nr fin* 5/2[1]	
-022	3	1 1/2	**Scheme**[11] 6280 3-8-12 71 ... (v[1]) RyanTate 1	76
			(Sir Mark Prescott Bt) *led: shkn up 3f out: rdn 2f out: hdd ins fnl f: no ex nr fin* 5/2[1]	
1110	4	2 3/4	**Scofflaw**[20] 5948 5-10-1 81 ... (v) RobertWinston 6	81
			(David Evans) *broke wl: sn stdd and lost pl: hld up: nt clr run over 2f out: hdwy: nt clr run and swtchd rt over 1f out: rdn and edgd lft ins fnl f: nt rch ldrs (jockey said gelding was denied a clear run briefly when turning into the home straight)* 8/1	
6315	5	4	**The Throstles**[15] 6129 4-10-0 80 ... RossaRyan 7	72
			(Kevin Frost) *sn pushed along and prom: lost grnd on ldrs over 6f out: shkn up on outer over 2f out: n.d after* 8/1	
0363	6	2	**Dragons Tail (IRE)**[18] 6026 4-10-1 81 ... (p) RichardKingscote 4	69
			(Tom Dascombe) *chsd ldrs: rdn over 2f out: wknd fnl f* 9/2[2]	
5641	7	14	**Delph Crescent (IRE)**[13] 6210 4-9-6 75 ... (v) SeanDavis(3) 2	37
			(Richard Fahey) *chsd ldr tl rdn over 2f out: sn wknd: edgd lft and eased over 1f out* 5/1[3]	
0006	8	15	**Cohesion**[14] 6151 6-9-4 75 ... PoppyBridgwater(5) 3	8
			(David Bridgwater) *s.i.s: outpcd (jockey said gelding was slowly away and never travelling)* 20/1	

1m 58.31s (-2.49) **Going Correction** +0.05s/f (Slow) **8 Ran SP% 127.3**
WFA 3 from 4yo+ 7lb
Speed ratings (Par 105): **110,109,108,106,102 100,88,74**
CSF £43.36 CT £97.52 TOTE £14.80: £4.20, £1.60, £1.10; EX 63.90 Trifecta £299.10.
Owner Lowe, Lewis And Hoyland **Bred** Irish National Stud **Trained** Tern Hill, Shropshire

FOCUS
There was a disputed early pace and the field was soon strung out. The winner benefited from the leaders going off too quick and has been rated back to his best.

6687 JOYCE AND SMITH 4 WORLD DOMINATION NOVICE MEDIAN AUCTION STKS 1m 4f 51y (Tp)
7:35 (7:35) (Class 5) 3-4-Y-O £3,428 (£1,020; £509; £254) Stalls Low

Form				RPR
2343	1		**Monsieur Lambrays**[24] 5778 3-9-2 72 ... (b) TomMarquand 7	76
			(Tom Clover) *hld up: hdwy to chse ldr over 8f out: led over 2f out: rdn over 1f out: styd on* 5/2[2]	
0-22	2	3/4	**Mojave**[9] 6345 3-8-11 0 ... ThomasGreatrex(5) 3	75
			(Roger Charlton) *led 1f: chsd ldrs: wnt 2nd over 2f out: rdn over 1f out: styd on* 4/5[1]	
5522	3	2 3/4	**Sweet Celebration (IRE)**[51] 4804 3-8-4 72 ... StefanoCherchi(7) 1	65
			(Marco Botti) *chsd ldrs: lost pl over 8f out: hmpd over 2f out: nt clr run and swtchd rt over 1f out: r.o: nt rch ldrs* 4/1[3]	
5	4	2 1/4	**Wadacre Galoubet**[11] 6274 3-9-2 0 ... RichardKingscote 5	67
			(Mark Johnston) *prom: lost pl over 8f out: hdwy on outer over 2f out: styd on same pce fnl f* 10/1	
64	5	1 1/4	**Allocated (IRE)**[9] 6345 3-8-13 0 ... DarraghKeenan(3) 4	65
			(John Butler) *hld up: shkn up over 2f out: nt trble ldrs* 20/1	
	6	2	**Zero To Hero (IRE)**[140] 4-8-13 0 ... Pierre-LouisJamin(7) 8	56
			(Archie Watson) *chsd ldr over 10f out tl over 8f out: remained handy: nt clr run and swtchd rt over 2f out: sn edgd lft: wknd fnl f* 14/1	
	7	16	**Indisposed** 3-9-2 0 ... AntonioFresu 2	36
			(Mrs Ilka Gansera-Leveque) *s.i.s: hld up: racd keenly: nt clr run over 2f out: sn wknd (jockey said gelding ran too freely)* 33/1	
04-	8	30	**Spectaculis**[141] 7275 4-9-8 0 ... (p[1]) TimClark(3) 6	
			(Denis Quinn) *pushed along to ld at stdy pce after 1f: shkn up and hdd over 2f out: wkng whn hmpd sn after* 66/1	

2m 42.6s (1.80) **Going Correction** +0.05s/f (Slow) **8 Ran SP% 129.1**
WFA 3 from 4yo 9lb
Speed ratings (Par 103): **96,95,93,92,91 90,79,59**
CSF £5.54 TOTE £3.60: £1.10, £1.10, £1.60; EX 5.90 Trifecta £13.80.
Owner Exors The Late J T Habershon-Butcher **Bred** Glebe Stud **Trained** Newmarket, Suffolk

FOCUS
This was steadily run and the front two in the market had it between them in the sprint off the home turn. The winner has been rated to his best.
T/Plt: £68.10 to a £1 stake. Pool: £49,087.35 - 525.5 winning units. T/Qpdt: £3.20 to a £1 stake. Pool: £6,624.39 - 1497.63 winning units. **Colin Roberts**

6688 - (Foreign Racing) - See Raceform Interactive

6426
CURRAGH (R-H)
Friday, August 30

OFFICIAL GOING: Straight course - good to yielding; round course - good

6689a FLAME OF TARA IRISH EBF STKS (GROUP 3) (FILLIES) 1m
4:50 (4:51) 2-Y-O

£42,522 (£13,693; £6,486; £2,882; £1,441; £720)

				RPR
	1		**Cayenne Pepper (IRE)**[57] 4577 2-9-0 0 ... ShaneFoley 4	109+
			(Mrs John Harrington, Ire) *mde all: narrow advantage 3f out: stl gng wl over 2f out: rdn 1f out where pressed briefly and styd on wl to assert ins fnl f: comf* 6/4[1]	

2 2 1/2 **So Wonderful (USA)**[7] 6429 2-9-0 101 .... RyanMoore 7 103
(A P O'Brien, Ire) *hld up bhd ldrs: 4th 1/2-way: tk clsr order in 3rd over 3f out: sn pushed along and impr into 2nd over 1f out where rdn and pressed wnr briefly: no imp wl ins fnl f* **7/2**[3]

3 2 3/4 **A New Dawn (IRE)**[63] 4352 2-9-0 88 .... WayneLordan 6 97
(Joseph Patrick O'Brien, Ire) *w.w in rr: last at 1/2-way: pushed along and tk clsr order in 4th over 2f out: sn rdn and kpt on u.p into 3rd wl ins fnl f where no imp on ldrs: nvr on terms* **12/1**

4 3 1/2 **Brook On Fifth (IRE)**[14] 6188 2-9-0 0 .... DonnachaO'Brien 5 89
(Joseph Patrick O'Brien, Ire) *trckd ldr: cl 2nd 3f out: drvn in 2nd 2f out and no imp on wnr u.p over 1f out where dropped to 3rd: wknd* **2/1**[2]

5 4 1/2 **Azila (FR)**[31] 5533 2-9-0 0 ....(p[1]) OisinOrr 1 79
(D K Weld, Ire) *chsd ldrs: disp 3rd after 3f: 4th 3f out: drvn over 2f out and sn no ex in 5th: wknd* **16/1**

6 25 **Lougher (IRE)**[19] 5997 2-9-0 80 .... RobbieColgan 2 24
(Richard John O'Brien, Ire) *dwlt sltly: chsd ldrs early: disp 3rd after 3f: 5th 1/2-way: rdn and wknd 3f out: eased over 1f out* **25/1**

1m 39.39s (-1.21) **Going Correction** +0.05s/f (Good) 6 Ran SP% **113.0**
Speed ratings: **108,105,102,99,94 69**
CSF £7.30 TOTE £2.10: £1.02, £1.60; DF 6.80 Trifecta £35.50.
Owner Jon S Kelly **Bred** G H S Bloodstock & J C Bloodstock **Trained** Moone, Co Kildare

FOCUS
An impressive performance from the winner, a filly of real quality.

6690a ROUND TOWER STKS (GROUP 3) 6f
5:20 (5:20) 2-Y-O £31,891 (£10,270; £4,864; £2,162; £1,081; £540) Stalls Centre

RPR

1 **Lope Y Fernandez (IRE)**[31] 5520 2-9-3 0 .... RyanMoore 2 108
(A P O'Brien, Ire) *chsd ldrs: 4th 1/2-way: hdwy gng wl over 2f out and led far side 1 1/2f out: sn rdn and extended advantage: kpt on wl ins fnl f* **11/8**[1]

2 1 1/2 **Guildsman (FR)**[29] 5584 2-9-3 105 .... OisinMurphy 9 104
(Archie Watson) *hooded to load: dwlt and towards rr early: sn settled in rr of mid-div: 8th fr 1/2-way: stl gng wl under 2f out where nt clr run briefly: swtchd lft 1f out and r.o wl to snatch 2nd on line: nrst fin* **5/1**[2]

3 shd **Fort Myers (USA)**[62] 4413 2-9-3 103 .... DonnachaO'Brien 5 103
(A P O'Brien, Ire) *broke wl to ld: narrow advantage at 1/2-way: drvn under 2f out and sn hdd: no imp on wnr u.p in 2nd ins fnl f: denied 2nd on line* **6/1**[3]

4 1/2 **Zarzyni (IRE)**[36] 5362 2-9-3 0 .... RonanWhelan 10 102
(M Halford, Ire) *chsd ldrs: 6th 1/2-way: rdn and prog nr side over 1f out: no imp on wnr u.p in 3rd wl ins fnl f: dropped to 4th cl home* **16/1**

5 nk **Ventura Lightning (FR)**[13] 6228 2-9-3 0 .... TonyHamilton 12 101
(Richard Fahey) *in rr of mid-div early: 11th 1/2-way: n.m.r briefly over 2f out: sn pushed along and hdwy nr side 1f out where rdn: r.o into 5th ins fnl f: nvr trbld ldrs* **14/1**

6 1 1/2 **Brunelle (IRE)**[43] 5108 2-9-0 0 .... ColinKeane 7 93
(G M Lyons, Ire) *cl up bhd ldr: cl 2nd at 1/2-way: pushed along bhd ldrs 2f out and no ex u.p over 1f out: one pce ins fnl f where dropped to 6th* **12/1**

7 1 1/4 **Prince Of Naples (IRE)**[25] 5752 2-9-3 83 ....(t[1]) RobbieColgan 6 93
(Ms Sheila Lavery, Ire) *chsd ldrs: racd keenly early: 5th 1/2-way: n.m.r briefly 1 1/2f out and sn swtchd rt: no imp on ldrs ins fnl f where nt clr run briefly and swtchd lft: kpt on again cl home* **33/1**

8 hd **Mount Fuji (IRE)**[21] 5922 2-9-3 96 .... WayneLordan 14 92
(A P O'Brien, Ire) *s.i.s and pushed along in rr early: tk clsr order after 1f: 7th fr 1/2-way: pushed along nr side 2f out and sn dropped to rr: sltly impeded and swtchd rt over 1f out: sn rdn and kpt on again ins fnl f* **16/1**

9 nse **Cool Vixen (IRE)**[40] 5221 2-9-0 88 .... ShaneFoley 4 89
(Mrs John Harrington, Ire) *w.w: last after 1f: niggled along briefly at 1/2-way: tk clsr order and swtchd rt over 2f out: sn pushed along and impr to chse ldrs briefly 1f out: no ex u.p and wknd far side ins fnl f* **20/1**

10 2 **Air Force Jet**[14] 6190 2-9-3 99 .... ShaneCrosse 8 86
(Joseph Patrick O'Brien, Ire) *cl up bhd ldr: cl 3rd at 1/2-way: rdn under 2f out and sn no ex: wknd fr over 1f out* **33/1**

11 1 **Arranmore**[13] 6233 2-9-3 0 .... KevinManning 3 83
(J S Bolger, Ire) *hooded to load: hld up: disp 9th at 1/2-way: sme hdwy far side over 2f out to chse ldrs: sn rdn and no ex 1 1/2f out: wknd 1f out* **7/1**

12 5 1/2 **Back To Brussels (IRE)**[70] 4048 2-9-0 87 .... ChrisHayes 1 63
(J A Stack, Ire) *hld up towards rr: disp 9th at 1/2-way: tk clsr order briefly far side after 1/2-way: pushed along under 2f out and sn wknd: eased 1f out* **25/1**

1m 12.76s (-1.44) **Going Correction** +0.05s/f (Good) 12 Ran SP% **126.2**
Speed ratings: **111,109,108,108,107 105,104,103,103,101 99,92**
CSF £8.27 TOTE £1.90: £1.02, £2.40, £1.60; DF 9.10 Trifecta £23.20.
Owner Derrick Smith & Mrs John Magnier & Michael Tabor **Bred** S F Bloodstock LLC **Trained** Cashel, Co Tipperary

FOCUS
A taking performance and indeed an informative one from the winner. The race has been rated slightly cautiously around the second and third.

6691a (Foreign Racing) - See Raceform Interactive

6692a SNOW FAIRY FILLIES STKS (GROUP 3) 1m 1f
6:20 (6:25) 3-Y-O+ £34,549 (£11,126; £5,270; £2,342; £1,171; £585)

RPR

1 **Goddess (USA)**[16] 6090 3-9-0 104 .... RyanMoore 3 103+
(A P O'Brien, Ire) *settled in rr of mid-div: 8th 1/2-way: tk clsr order on inner fr 3f out: pushed along over 2f out and swtchd lft: prog between horses to dispute ld ent fnl f: led ins fnl f and styd on strly cl home* **4/1**[1]

2 1/2 **Credenza (IRE)**[13] 6239 3-9-0 92 .... WayneLordan 8 101
(A P O'Brien, Ire) *sn led: hdd over 2f out and sn rdn: kpt on wl u.p to dispute ld again ent fnl f: hdd by wnr ins fnl f and no ex cl home* **33/1**

3 1 1/4 **Trethias**[41] 5208 3-9-0 105 .... ShaneFoley 7 98
(Mrs John Harrington, Ire) *mid-div: prog after 2f on outer to chse ldrs: 3rd 1/2-way: rdn in 3rd 2f out and dropped to 4th ent fnl f: kpt on same pce to regain 3rd ins fnl f but hld* **4/1**[1]

4 1 **Fresnel**[16] 6090 3-9-0 98 .... GaryHalpin 9 96+
(Jack W Davison, Ire) *chsd ldrs: 4th 1/2-way: pushed along over 2f out and nt qckn w principals but kpt on wl u.p to go 4th cl home* **16/1**[3]

5 nk **Simply Beautiful (IRE)**[13] 6239 3-9-0 99 .... DonnachaO'Brien 11 96
(A P O'Brien, Ire) *mid-div: 6th 1/2-way: pushed along 3f out and sn no ex u.p in 5th: kpt on same pce* **8/1**[2]

6 shd **Harriet's Force (IRE)**[15] 6139 3-9-0 83 .... WJLee 10 95
(Keith Henry Clarke, Ire) *mid-div: prog to trck ldr in 2nd after 2f: pushed along to ld over 2f out: kpt on wl u.p but hdd ent fnl f and no ex: wknd* **66/1**

7 1 1/4 **Solage**[143] 1672 3-9-0 0 .... KevinManning 1 93
(J S Bolger, Ire) *cl up: sn settled bhd ldrs: 5th 1/2-way: pushed along over 2f out and short of room briefly: sn no ex* **4/1**[1]

8 hd **Viadera**[44] 5075 3-9-0 101 .... ColinKeane 6 92+
(G M Lyons, Ire) *hld up towards rr: 9th 1/2-way: rdn over 2f out but sn no imp u.p* **4/1**[1]

9 1/2 **Mia Maria (IRE)**[41] 5210 3-9-0 0 .... OisinOrr 2 91
(D K Weld, Ire) *mid-div: 7th 1/2-way: bit short of room 4f out: rdn over 2f out and sn no ex u.p: kpt on same pce* **8/1**[2]

10 1/2 **Snapraeceps (IRE)**[6] 6480 3-9-0 92 .... ShaneCrosse 12 90
(Joseph Patrick O'Brien, Ire) *in rr: 11th 1/2-way: rdn on outer over 2f out but sn no ex and one pce: nvr in contention* **50/1**

11 3/4 **Dean Street Doll (IRE)**[65] 4263 3-9-0 101 ....(t[1]) RobbieColgan 5 89
(Richard John O'Brien, Ire) *hld up towards rr: 10th 1/2-way: rdn over 2f out but sn no imp and wknd* **20/1**

12 5 1/2 **Annie Fior (IRE)**[16] 6090 5-9-7 98 .... AdamFarragher 4 77
(B A Murphy, Ire) *slowly away: in rr: rdn in rr over 2f out and sn no imp: nvr in contention* **50/1**

1m 53.18s (-2.42) **Going Correction** +0.05s/f (Good)
WFA 3 from 5yo 7lb 12 Ran SP% **121.2**
Speed ratings: **112,111,110,109,109 109,108,107,107,107 106,101**
CSF £165.53 TOTE £2.80: £1.40, £9.90, £1.70; DF 65.40 Trifecta £577.50.
Owner Mrs John Magnier & John G Sikura **Bred** Orpendale & Chelston **Trained** Cashel, Co Tipperary

FOCUS
The winner has been a bit of a slow burner but she finally looks to be getting there and she could well step up again in grade.

6693a TOTE IRISH CAMBRIDGESHIRE (PREMIER H'CAP) 1m
6:50 (6:59) 3-Y-O+
£53,153 (£17,117; £8,108; £3,603; £1,801; £900)

RPR

1 **Jassaar**[31] 5535 4-8-8 **91** .... AndrewSlattery(5) 24 101+
(D K Weld, Ire) *hld up in tch nr side: disp 8th at 1/2-way: pushed along and hdwy under 2f out: sn rdn and r.o wl to ld down centre wl ins fnl f: readily* **10/1**

2 3/4 **Current Option (IRE)**[13] 6237 3-7-13 **88** oh1 .... NathanCrosse(5) 9 93
(Adrian McGuinness, Ire) *chsd ldrs: 4th 1/2-way: gng wl bhd ldrs after 1/2-way: prog between horses to ld under 2f out: sn rdn far side and hdd u.p wl ins fnl f: kpt on wl wout matching wnr* **12/1**

3 hd **Numerian (IRE)**[31] 5535 3-8-13 **97** .... DonnachaO'Brien 4 102
(Joseph Patrick O'Brien, Ire) *chsd ldrs early: disp 8th at 1/2-way: drvn over 2f out and sn swtchd rt: hdwy u.p over 1f out: wnt 3rd far side ins fnl f and kpt on wl: nvr on terms* **6/1**[1]

4 3/4 **Ice Cold In Alex (IRE)**[41] 5205 5-8-6 **84** ....(t) NGMcCullagh 2 88
(K J Condon, Ire) *in rr of mid-div: hdwy far side 2f out to chse ldrs over 1f out where rdn: wnt 4th u.p ins fnl f and kpt on wl: nvr on terms* **12/1**

5 2 **Turnberry Isle (IRE)**[15] 6137 3-9-2 **100** .... RyanMoore 11 99
(A P O'Brien, Ire) *in rr of mid-div: n.m.r briefly 2f out: sme hdwy over 1f out: r.o* **12/1**

6 1/2 **Saltonstall**[26] 5711 5-8-9 **94** ....(tp) GavinRyan(7) 6 93+
(Adrian McGuinness, Ire) *in rr of mid-div: stl gng wl 2f out: nt clr run and swtchd rt 1f out: r.o ins fnl f where n.m.r briefly: nrst fin* **12/1**

7 shd **Yuften**[29] 5597 8-8-5 **90** .... JMSheridan(7) 15 88
(Denis Gerard Hogan, Ire) *chsd ldrs: 6th 1/2-way: rdn 2f out and no imp on ldrs u.p 1f out: one pce fnl f* **16/1**

8 nk **Quizical (IRE)**[26] 5711 4-9-0 **92** .... RobbieColgan 10 90
(Ms Sheila Lavery, Ire) *prom: cl 2nd after 3f: rdn bhd ldr over 2f out and sn no ex between horses: wknd 1 1/2f out* **20/1**

9 hd **Sirjack Thomas (IRE)**[23] 5833 4-8-11 **89** .... DeclanMcDonogh 21 86+
(Adrian McGuinness, Ire) *hld up towards rr: swtchd rt over 2f out stl gng wl: nt clr run briefly over 1f out: sn rdn and r.o nr side ins fnl f: nrst fin* **33/1**

10 1 **Lethal Power (IRE)**[21] 5925 4-8-9 **87** ow1 ....(b) GaryHalpin 5 82
(Joseph G Murphy, Ire) *sn led: narrow advantage after 3f: rdn over 2f out and sn hdd: wknd u.p bhd ldrs far side 1f out* **25/1**

11 nse **Zap**[30] 5546 4-8-10 **88** ....(v) TonyHamilton 19 83
(Richard Fahey) *in rr of mid-div: pushed along nr side after 1/2-way and no imp 2f out: rdn 1 1/2f out and kpt on u.p ins fnl f: nvr nrr* **20/1**

12 hd **Hortzadar**[13] 6231 4-9-4 **96** .... OisinOrr 14 90
(David O'Meara) *chsd ldrs: 5th 1/2-way: effrt nr side almost on terms 2f out: no ex u.p bhd ldrs ent fnl f: wknd* **20/1**

13 1 **Cosmic Horizon (IRE)**[11] 6297 3-8-8 **92** ....(bt[1]) WayneLordan 17 83
(Joseph Patrick O'Brien, Ire) *hld up in tch: disp 8th at 1/2-way: rdn over 2f out and no imp on ldrs: sn wknd* **22/1**

14 nk **Katiymann (IRE)**[26] 5711 7-8-11 **89** ....(t) RonanWhelan 16 80
(M Halford, Ire) *hld up towards rr: stl gng wl over 2f out: sn pushed along and sme hdwy far side over 1f out: rdn and kpt on one pce ins fnl f* **33/1**

15 3/4 **Equitant**[6] 6479 4-8-0 **88** .... MikeySheehy(10) 26 78
(Joseph Patrick O'Brien, Ire) *chsd ldrs: 7th 1/2-way: rdn and wknd 2f out* **20/1**

16 shd **Madam Seamstress (IRE)**[16] 6088 3-8-9 **93** .... RoryCleary 22 81
(J S Bolger, Ire) *dismntd bef s: dwlt and towards rr early: sme hdwy nr side after 1/2-way: no ex u.p 2f out: one pce after* **50/1**

17 hd **Kattani (IRE)**[64] 4312 3-8-4 **88** oh2 .... ChrisHayes 7 76
(D K Weld, Ire) *hld up towards rr: pushed along over 2f out and sme hdwy far side 1 1/2f out: rdn ent fnl f and kpt on nr fin* **8/1**[3]

18 nse **Aussie Valentine (IRE)**[6] 6479 8-8-6 **87** ....(tp) TomMadden(3) 3 76
(Adrian McGuinness, Ire) *cl up tl sn settled bhd ldrs: pushed along in 3rd after 1/2-way and no ex u.p over 2f out: wknd* **33/1**

19 nk **On A Session (USA)**[26] 5711 3-8-12 **96** .... WJLee 12 83
(Aidan F Fogarty, Ire) *hld up in tch: disp 8th at 1/2-way: drvn over 2f out and sn checked sltly: rdn and no ex 1 1/2f out: wknd and eased ins fnl f* **11/1**

20 shd **Innamorare (IRE)**[15] 6139 4-8-5 **83** ....(v) ConorHoban 18 71
(Gavin Cromwell, Ire) *mid-div: drvn 3f out and no ex whn swtchd rt 2f out: wknd over 1f out where short of room and checked: short of room again ins fnl f: eased nr fin* **25/1**

21 1 3/4 **Psychedelic Funk**[110] 2660 5-9-12 **104** .... ColinKeane 13 88
(G M Lyons, Ire) *in rr of mid-div: n.m.r briefly over 2f out: sn pushed along towards rr and no imp ent fnl f: one pce under hands and heels ins fnl f: eased nr fin* **33/1**

22 1 1/4 **Mokhalad**16 6088 6-8-8 **86**...............................(t) OisinMurphy 23 67
(Damian Joseph English, Ire) *dwlt: towards rr: drvn over 2f out and sn swtchd rt: rdn and no imp over 1f out: nvr a factor* **40/1**

23 8 1/2 **Solar Wave (IRE)**21 5925 4-8-13 **91**............................ KevinManning 8 52
(J S Bolger, Ire) *in rr of mid-div best: pushed along after 1/2-way and no imp far side 2f out: wknd and eased ins fnl f* **50/1**

24 nk **Wee Jim (IRE)**31 5535 3-8-4 **88** oh2............................ KillianLeonard 20 48
(Luke Comer, Ire) *mid-div: pushed along after 1/2-way and wknd to rr over 2f out* **66/1**

25 3 **Onlyhuman (IRE)**6 6480 6-9-4 **96**............................ ShaneFoley 1 50
(Mrs John Harrington, Ire) *mid-div: pushed along after 1/2-way and no ex far side over 1f out where rdn: wknd and eased ins fnl f (jockey said that his mount never let himself down on the ground)* **7/1**2

1m 37.74s (-2.86) **Going Correction** +0.05s/f (Good) **25** Ran SP% **142.7**
WFA 3 from 4yo+ 6lb
Speed ratings: **116,115,115,114,112 111,111,111,111,110 110,109,108,108,107 107,107,107,107,107 105,104,95,95,**
CSF £114.17 CT £830.54 TOTE £10.30: £2.80, £6.10, £2.60, £2.30; DF 294.60 Trifecta £2327.80.
Owner Hamdan Al Maktoum **Bred** Shadwell Estate Company Limited **Trained** Curragh, Co Kildare

FOCUS
A good finish to this ultra competitive handicap as the winner asserted late. It's been rated around the balance of the placed horses.

6694 - 6695a (Foreign Racing) - See Raceform Interactive

6496
BEVERLEY (R-H)
Saturday, August 31

OFFICIAL GOING: Good (7.9)
Wind: Strong across Weather: Heavy cloud and showers

6696 WILLIAM HILL SILVER CUP H'CAP 1m 1f 207y
2:05 (2:05) (Class 2) (0-105,102) 3-Y-O
£32,370 (£9,692; £4,846; £2,423; £1,211; £608) **Stalls** Low

Form RPR

1305 1 **Good Birthday (IRE)**50 4882 3-9-0 **95**............................ BenCurtis 1 103+
(Andrew Balding) *dwlt: hld up towards rr: hdwy over 2f out: trckd ldrs over 1f out: effrt and squeezed through on inner ent fnl f: sn rdn: led last 75yds* **11/4**2

3102 2 1/2 **Desert Icon (FR)**21 5966 3-9-0 **95**............................ DanielTudhope 6 101
(William Haggas) *trckd ldng pair: hdwy and cl up 2f out: rdn to take slt ld ent fnl f: sn drvn: hdd and no ex last 75yds* **15/8**1

2-00 3 hd **Three Comets (GER)**31 5541 3-8-11 **92**............................(b1) JackMitchell 5 97
(Roger Varian) *hld up in rr: hdwy on outer 2f out: rdn along on outer over 1f out: styd on wl fnl f* **9/1**

5415 4 1/2 **Victory Command (IRE)**7 6475 3-9-5 **100**............................ ConnorBeasley 2 104
(Mark Johnston) *led 2f: trckd ldr: hdwy and cl up over 2f out: rdn wl over 1f out and sn slt ld: drvn and hdd ent fnl f: kpt on* **9/2**

0406 5 3 3/4 **Dark Vision (IRE)**8 6425 3-9-7 **102**............................(b) JoeFanning 3 98
(Mark Johnston) *t.k.h: trckd ldr: led after 2f and sn clr: pushed along 3f out: sn jnd and rdn: hdd wl over 1f out: wkng whn n.m.r and hmpd on inner: eased after* **7/2**3

1166 6 17 **Arctic Fox**28 5687 3-8-6 **87**............................ PaddyMathers 4 49
(Richard Fahey) *chsd ldrs: rdn along over 2f out: sn wknd* **25/1**

2m 3.24s (-2.46) **Going Correction** +0.025s/f (Good) **6** Ran SP% **115.7**
Speed ratings (Par 106): **110,109,109,109,106 92**
CSF £8.72 TOTE £4.00: £1.80, £1.60; EX 10.50 Trifecta £47.50.
Owner King Power Racing Co Ltd **Bred** Ecurie Normandie Pur Sang **Trained** Kingsclere, Hants

FOCUS
All distances as advertised. After riding in the opener Connor Beasley and Joe Fanning called the ground good, while winning rider Ben Curtis said: 'It's good/good to soft ground.' This was a decent 3yo handicap and there was no hanging about thanks to Dark Vision.

6697 IRISH EBF FILLIES' NOVICE STKS (PLUS 10 RACE) 7f 96y
2:40 (2:40) (Class 4) 2-Y-O
£6,162 (£1,845; £922; £461; £230; £115) **Stalls** Low

Form RPR

2 1 **Freyja (IRE)**16 6118 2-9-0 0............................ JoeFanning 2 84
(Mark Johnston) *trckd ldng pair on inner: hdwy 2f out: rdn to chse ldr over 1f out: swtchd lft and drvn jst ins fnl f: styd on gamely to ld nr line* **11/10**1

6 2 hd **Afraid Of Nothing**25 5774 2-9-0 0............................ DanielTudhope 6 84
(Ralph Beckett) *led: pushed along 2f out: rdn and clr over 1f out: drvn ins fnl f: hdd and no ex nr line* **9/2**2

00 3 6 **Violette Szabo (IRE)**17 6064 2-8-9 0............................ FayeMcManoman(5) 3 69
(Nigel Tinkler) *dwlt and bhd: stdy hdwy on inner over 2f out: in tch and rdn along over 1f out: styd on fnl f* **100/1**

25 4 nk **Fraternity (IRE)**42 5170 2-9-0 0............................ PaddyMathers 4 68
(Richard Fahey) *trckd ldrs: hdwy 3f out: rdn along 2f out: drvn over 1f out: kpt on same pce* **7/2**2

4 5 2 **High Flying Bird (FR)**22 5895 2-9-0 0............................ BenCurtis 7 63
(Tom Dascombe) *chsd ldr: rdn along over 2f out: drvn wl over 1f out: sn wknd* **6/1**

6 2 3/4 **Al Jawhra (IRE)** 2-9-0 0............................ DavidAllan 8 56
(Tim Easterby) *dwlt: green and bhd tl styd on fnl 2f (jockey said filly missed the break)* **25/1**

54 7 4 1/2 **My Dandy Doc (IRE)**31 5553 2-9-0 0............................ PaulMulrennan 5 45
(John Quinn) *in tch: hdwy to chse ldrs 3f out: rdn along over 2f out: sn wknd* **25/1**

05 8 3/4 **Phantom Bride (IRE)**14 6226 2-8-9 0............................ HarrisonShaw(5) 1 44
(K R Burke) *in tch: hdwy to chse ldrs 3f out: sn rdn and wknd (jockey said filly hung left-handed throughout)* **12/1**

1m 32.36s (-0.24) **Going Correction** +0.025s/f (Good) **8** Ran SP% **118.7**
Speed ratings (Par 93): **102,101,94,94,92 89,84,83**
CSF £6.71 TOTE £1.80: £1.10, £2.00, £12.30; EX 6.70 Trifecta £290.00.
Owner Mrs A G Kavanagh **Bred** C O P Hanbury **Trained** Middleham Moor, N Yorks

FOCUS
Not a bad 2yo fillies' novice.

6698 WILLIAM HILL BEVERLEY BULLET SPRINT STKS (LISTED RACE) 5f
3:15 (3:16) (Class 1) 3-Y-O+
£36,861 (£13,975; £6,994; £3,484; £1,748; £877) **Stalls** Low

Form RPR

0016 1 **Judicial (IRE)**29 5611 7-9-2 101............................ JoeFanning 3 108
(Julie Camacho) *t.k.h: trckd ldrs: hdwy over 1f out: rdn to ld narrowly ent fnl f: sn drvn and kpt on strly* **13/2**3

2011 2 3/4 **Queens Gift (IRE)**47 4986 4-8-12 91 ow1............................(p) PaulMulrennan 1 101
(Michael Dods) *trckd ldrs on inner: hdwy and squeezed through to chal ent fnl f: sn rdn and ev ch kpt on* **12/1**

4304 3 shd **Fairy Falcon**18 6056 4-8-11 86............................(b1) DanielTudhope 5 100
(Bryan Smart) *towards rr and sltly hmpd after 100yds: hld up on inner: swtchd lft wl over 1f out: rdn and str run on outer appr fnl f: fin strly* **25/1**

1313 4 3/4 **Danzeno**21 5927 8-9-2 106............................ AlistairRawlinson 9 102
(Michael Appleby) *cl up on outer: pushed along over 1f out: sn rdn and ev ch ent fnl f: sn drvn and kpt on same pce* **6/1**2

0421 5 3/4 **Tis Marvellous**49 4896 5-9-2 111............................(t) BenCurtis 2 100+
(Clive Cox) *hld up in tch on inner: hdwy 2f out: effrt and nt clr run over 1f out and again ent fnl f: sn rdn and kpt on (jockey said gelding was denied a clear run approaching the final furlong)* **2/1**1

6300 6 1 1/4 **Ornate**8 6423 6-9-2 103............................ PhilDennis 4 95
(David C Griffiths) *narrow ld: rdn along over 1f out: drvn and hdd ent fnl f: grad wknd* **6/1**2

2105 7 1/2 **Copper Knight (IRE)**8 6423 5-9-5 106............................(t) DavidAllan 8 96
(Tim Easterby) *cl up: disp ld 2f out: sn rdn: drvn ent fnl f: wknd* **10/1**

3050 8 1/2 **Tarboosh**10 6351 6-9-2 102............................ GrahamLee 6 91
(Paul Midgley) *trckd ldrs: effrt wl over 1f out: sn rdn and no imp (jockey said gelding hung left-handed throughout)* **6/1**2

0150 9 3/4 **Corinthia Knight (IRE)**15 6149 4-9-2 102............................ AdamMcNamara 10 89
(Archie Watson) *in tch on outer: rdn along wl over 1f out: sn drvn and n.d* **50/1**

1-66 10 1 **Intense Romance (IRE)**84 3587 5-8-11 102............................ ConnorBeasley 7 80
(Michael Dods) *a towards rr* **22/1**

1m 1.53s (-1.37) **Going Correction** +0.025s/f (Good) **10** Ran SP% **116.5**
Speed ratings (Par 111): **111,109,109,108,107 105,104,103,102,100**
CSF £78.99 TOTE £8.30: £2.00, £3.10, £5.10; EX 98.50 Trifecta £1264.50.
Owner Elite Racing Club **Bred** Elite Racing Club **Trained** Norton, N Yorks

FOCUS
A solid edition of this Listed sprint. It was run at a frantic pace and the far side was the place to be.

6699 CONSTANT SECURITY H'CAP 5f
3:50 (3:52) (Class 5) (0-75,77) 3-Y-O+
£5,922 (£1,772; £886; £443; £300; £300) **Stalls** Low

Form RPR

2113 1 **Four Wheel Drive**10 6339 3-9-10 **77**............................(p) GrahamLee 9 88
(David Brown) *trckd ldrs: hdwy 2f out: chsd ldr over 1f out: sn rdn to chal: led ins fnl f: kpt on strly* **12/1**

1000 2 1 1/2 **Desert Ace (IRE)**16 6099 8-9-2 **67**............................ PaulMulrennan 12 73+
(Paul Midgley) *rrd s and slowly away: in rr and sn swtchd rt: t.k.h 1/2-way: hdwy and nt clr run over 1f out and again ent fnl f: squeezed through ins fnl 100yds: fin wl (jockey said gelding reared when leaving the stalls and was denied a clear run approaching 1f out)* **40/1**

4032 3 hd **Sheepscar Lad (IRE)**16 6099 5-9-0 **70**............................ FayeMcManoman(5) 4 75
(Nigel Tinkler) *chsd ldrs: rdn and hdwy over 1f out: drvn ins fnl f: kpt on* **4/1**1

2054 4 1/2 **Bowson Fred**15 6178 7-9-7 **72**............................(t) NathanEvans 1 75+
(Michael Easterby) *v awkward s and slowly away: bhd and detached 1/2-way: hdwy over 1f out: swtchd markedly lft arnd field and str run on outer ins fnl f: fin wl (jockey said gelding missed the break and was denied a clear run approaching 1f out)* **6/1**2

3021 5 1/2 **Archimedes (IRE)**6 6503 6-8-13 **64** 5ex............................(vt) DavidAllan 15 65
(David C Griffiths) *sn prom: cl up 1/2-way: rdn to ld 1 1/2f out: drvn and hdd ins fnl f: kpt on same pce* **20/1**

3410 6 shd **Red Pike (IRE)**15 6178 8-9-5 **75**............................ HarrisonShaw(5) 6 76
(Bryan Smart) *trckd ldrs: hdwy wl over 1f out: rdn and n.m.r ent fnl f: kpt on same pce* **12/1**

2051 7 1/2 **Atyaaf**16 6099 4-8-5 **56**............................ PaddyMathers 2 55
(Derek Shaw) *bmpd s: hld up: hdwy 2f out: rdn to chse ldrs and n.m.r ent fnl f: kpt on* **8/1**3

60 8 shd **Excessable**7 6455 6-9-7 **72**............................(p1) RachelRichardson 5 71
(Tim Easterby) *prom: rdn wl over 1f out: drvn appr fnl f: sn wknd* **8/1**3

4040 9 3/4 **Shepherd's Purse**14 6227 7-8-12 **63**............................ JamieGormley 10 59
(Ruth Carr) *towards rr: hdwy 2f out: sn rdn and n.m.r over 1f out: kpt on fnl f (jockey said gelding was denied a clear run approaching 1f out)* **18/1**

4306 10 nk **Van Gerwen**13 6260 6-9-3 **68**............................ LewisEdmunds 13 63
(Les Eyre) *dwlt and in rr: effrt and sme hdwy on outer over 2f out: sn rdn and n.d* **40/1**

0016 11 1 **Moonlit Sands (IRE)**16 6099 4-8-7 **58**............................(tp) BenRobinson 3 49
(Brian Ellison) *in tch on inner: rdn along wl over 1f out: sn drvn and n.m.r: grad wknd (jockey said filly was denied a clear run 1 2/f out)* **16/1**

0402 12 nk **Stoney Lane**10 6339 4-9-8 **73**............................(p) PhilDennis 11 63
(Richard Whitaker) *in tch: rdn along 2f out: sn drvn and wknd over 1f out* **6/1**2

4334 13 3/4 **Tobeeornottobee**20 5985 3-8-2 **62**............................ JessicaAnderson(7) 8 50
(Declan Carroll) *a towards rr* **16/1**

0344 14 1 **Bashiba (IRE)**26 5750 8-8-5 **63**............................(t) IzzyClifton(7) 14 47
(Nigel Tinkler) *in tch: rdn along 2f out: sn drvn and wknd over 1f out* **25/1**

5630 15 5 **Billy Dylan (IRE)**24 5819 4-9-10 **75**............................(v) DanielTudhope 7 41
(David O'Meara) *led: rdn along 2f out: hdd 1 1/2f out: sn wknd* **16/1**

1m 3.29s (0.39) **Going Correction** +0.025s/f (Good) **15** Ran SP% **122.6**
WFA 3 from 4yo+ 2lb
Speed ratings (Par 103): **97,94,94,93,92 92,91,91,90,89 88,87,86,85,77**
CSF £442.49 CT £2303.95 TOTE £14.40: £3.80, £15.20, £2.00; EX 886.00 Trifecta £3789.20.
Owner Bratwa **Bred** A C M Spalding **Trained** Averham Park, Notts

The Form Book Flat 2019, Raceform Ltd, Newbury, RG14 5SJ

FOCUS
This was competitive for the class. Again, a low draw proved an advantage.

6700 EDUCARE OF BEVERLEY H'CAP 7f 96y
4:25 (4:25) (Class 4) (0-80,81) 3-Y-O+
£7,719 (£2,311; £1,155; £577; £300; £300) Stalls Low

Form RPR
0036 1 **Calder Prince (IRE)**[24] 5820 6-9-10 77..............(p[1]) AlistairRawlinson 7 85
(Tom Dascombe) *trckd ldrs: hdwy 2f out: rdn to chal over 1f out: drvn to ld ins fnl f: kpt on wl towards fin* **18/1**
0134 2 ¾ **Twin Appeal (IRE)**[7] 6461 8-9-5 75.............. GemmaTutty(3) 6 81
(Karen Tutty) *hld up towards rr: hdwy on outer wl over 1f out: chsd ldrs and rdn ent fnl f: fin wl* **15/2**
2313 3 ½ **Pickett's Charge**[14] 6201 6-9-4 71..............(t[1]) BenRobinson 2 76
(Brian Ellison) *trckd ldng pair: pushed along 2f out: rdn over 1f out: drvn and kpt on fnl f (jockey said gelding hung right-handed)* **8/1**
3114 4 ½ **Ollivander (IRE)**[19] 6015 3-9-3 75..............(v) DanielTudhope 5 76
(David O'Meara) *trckd ldr: hdwy and cl up 2f out: rdn to ld wl over 1f out: drvn and hdd ins fnl f: kpt on same pce* **10/1**
3215 5 1 ¼ **Northernpowerhouse**[22] 5903 3-9-3 75..............(p) GrahamLee 3 76+
(Bryan Smart) *trckd ldrs on inner: hdwy 2f out: effrt and nt clr run jst over 1f out: swtchd lft and rdn ins fnl f: swtchd rt and kpt on wl towards fin (jockey said colt was denied a clear run on a couple of occasions)* **13/2**[3]
2520 6 ¾ **Candelisa (IRE)**[21] 5948 6-9-12 79..............(t) PhilDennis 10 77
(David Loughnane) *hld up in tch: hdwy over 2f out: rdn to chse ldrs over 1f out: sn drvn and no imp* **10/1**
3214 7 2 **Sezim**[17] 6081 3-9-9 81.............. JackMitchell 8 72
(Roger Varian) *dwlt: a towards rr (trainer could offer no explanation for the performance shown)* **3/1**[1]
0111 8 1 ½ **Red Seeker**[14] 6204 4-9-1 73..............(t) DannyRedmond(5) 9 62
(Tim Easterby) *dwlt: a towards rr* **6/1**[2]
4155 9 1 ½ **Ramesses**[19] 6015 3-9-2 74.............. PaddyMathers 1 57
(Richard Fahey) *dwlt: rapid hdwy on inner and sn led: rdn along 2f out: hdd 1 1/2f out: sn drvn and wknd* **7/1**
-600 10 hd **Armed (IRE)**[21] 5970 4-9-4 71.............. PaulMulrennan 4 56
(Phillip Makin) *trckd ldrs: effrt over 2f out: sn rdn and wknd* **16/1**
1m 32.0s (-0.60) **Going Correction** +0.025s/f (Good)
WFA 3 from 4yo+ 5lb **10 Ran SP% 117.3**
Speed ratings (Par 105): **104,103,102,102,100 99,97,95,94,93**
CSF £147.45 CT £1205.87 TOTE £22.60: £5.40, £2.40, £2.10; EX 153.00 Trifecta £973.90.
Owner Peter Birbeck **Bred** Michael Pitt **Trained** Malpas, Cheshire
FOCUS
This modest handicap was run at a fair enough pace.

6701 BEVERLEY ANNUAL BADGEHOLDERS NOVICE STKS 7f 96y
5:00 (5:01) (Class 4) 3-Y-O+ £5,433 (£1,617; £808; £404) Stalls Low

Form RPR
3-1 1 **Montatham**[15] 6177 3-9-9 0.............. DaneO'Neill 3 86+
(William Haggas) *trckd ldng pair: hdwy over 2f out: sn chal: rdn to ld jst over 1f out: edgd rt ins fnl f: kpt on wl* **30/100**[1]
0 2 1 ¾ **Serenading**[17] 6074 3-8-11 0.............. JoeFanning 5 67
(James Fanshawe) *trckd ldrs: hdwy over 2f out: rdn over 1f out: kpt on wl fnl f* **14/1**
3 ½ **Karisoke** 3-9-2 0.............. JackMitchell 7 71
(Simon Crisford) *wnt lft s: sn chsng ldr: hdwy over 2f out: rdn to chal wl over 1f out: ev ch ent fnl f: sn drvn and kpt on same pce* **5/1**[2]
4 4 1 ½ **Angel Lane (FR)**[63] 4405 3-8-7 0 ow1.............. HarrisonShaw(5) 1 63
(K R Burke) *led: rdn along over 2f out: sn jnd: drvn wl over 1f out: hdd jst over 1f out: kpt on same pce* **12/1**[3]
05 5 6 **Cheerful**[13] 6259 3-8-11 0.............. PhilDennis 6 46
(Philip McBride) *in tch: rdn along to chse ldrs 2f out: sn drvn and one pce* **20/1**
3-4 6 2 ¾ **Sils Maria**[235] 128 3-8-11 0..............(h[1] w) ConnorBeasley 2 38
(Ann Duffield) *chsd ldrs: rdn along 3f out: sn wknd* **33/1**
06 7 1 ¼ **Rent's Dew (IRE)**[15] 6177 3-9-2 0.............. DavidAllan 4 40
(Tim Easterby) *a in rr* **25/1**
1m 32.93s (0.33) **Going Correction** +0.025s/f (Good) **7 Ran SP% 119.5**
Speed ratings (Par 105): **99,97,96,94,87 84,83**
CSF £6.87 TOTE £1.10: £1.10, £4.50; EX 6.60 Trifecta £15.80.
Owner Hamdan Al Maktoum **Bred** Worksop Manor Stud **Trained** Newmarket, Suffolk
FOCUS
No strength in to depth here.

6702 FUTURE STARS APPRENTICE H'CAP 1m 1f 207y
5:35 (5:36) (Class 6) (0-60,62) 3-Y-O
£4,140 (£1,232; £615; £307; £300; £300) Stalls Low

Form RPR
6452 1 **Gylo (IRE)**[24] 5814 3-9-6 62..............(v) HarrisonShaw(3) 1 70
(David O'Meara) *led 1f: trckd ldng pair: hdwy on inner 2f out: nt clr run over 1f out: swtchd lft and rdn ent fnl f: styd on wl to ld last 100yds* **6/4**[1]
0133 2 1 ¼ **Hammy End (IRE)**[16] 6128 3-9-1 59..............(h) Pierre-LouisJamin(5) 7 65
(William Muir) *trckd ldrs: hdwy over 2f out: rdn to chal over 1f out: led jst over 1f out: drvn ins fnl f: hdd last 100yds: kpt on same pce* **7/2**[2]
6060 3 2 ¼ **Necoleta**[12] 6279 3-8-0 46 oh1.............. ElinorJones(7) 4 47
(Sylvester Kirk) *hld up in rr: hdwy on inner 2f out: nt clr run over 1f out: squeezed through ins fnl f: sn rdn and kpt on* **22/1**
0304 4 1 ½ **Minnelli**[16] 6128 3-9-9 62.............. PhilDennis 3 61
(Philip McBride) *cl up: led after 1f: pushed along over 2f out: jnd and rdn wl over 1f out: drvn and hdd appr fnl f: grad wknd* **7/1**[3]
0-00 5 3 ½ **Waterproof**[19] 6030 3-8-5 51.............. GavinAshton(7) 6 43
(Shaun Keightley) *hld up in rr: hdwy on outer to chse ldrs over 2f out: rdn along wl over 1f out: sn wknd* **10/1**
2104 6 ½ **Neileta**[25] 5792 3-9-4 60..............(p) DannyRedmond(3) 2 51
(Tim Easterby) *prom: trckd ldr 1/2-way: effrt and cl up 2f out: sn rdn and hld whn n.m.r and hmpd over 1f out: sn wknd* **7/2**[2]
2m 6.17s (0.47) **Going Correction** +0.025s/f (Good) **6 Ran SP% 110.4**
Speed ratings (Par 98): **99,98,96,95,92 91**
CSF £6.69 TOTE £1.90: £1.60, £1.70; EX 6.00 Trifecta £51.10.
Owner Gallop Racing **Bred** R & R Bloodstock **Trained** Upper Helmsley, N Yorks
FOCUS
An ordinary 3yo handicap, confined to apprentice riders.
T/Plt: £170.40 to a £1 stake. Pool: £69,641.75 - 298.18 winning units T/Qpdt: £80.70 to a £1 stake. Pool: £5,097.17 - 46.69 winning units **Joe Rowntree**

6629 CHELMSFORD (A.W) (L-H)
Saturday, August 31

OFFICIAL GOING: Polytrack: standard
Wind: medium, across Weather: overcast

6703 GREENE KING APPRENTICE H'CAP 7f (P)
5:40 (5:42) (Class 6) (0-65,67) 3-Y-O+
£3,105 (£924; £461; £400; £400; £400) Stalls Low

Form RPR
0020 1 **Blessed To Empress (IRE)**[16] 6116 4-9-7 61..........(v) SeanKirrane(3) 3 68
(Amy Murphy) *dwlt and rousted along leaving stalls: midfield: swtchd rt and effrt 2f out: hdwy u.p to ld ins fnl f: styd on strly and drew away towards fin* **10/1**
2124 2 2 **Sonnet Rose (IRE)**[24] 5828 5-9-11 62..............(bt) SebastianWoods 1 64+
(Conrad Allen) *led for over 1f: trckd ldrs after and travelled strly: led over 1f out and shkn up: rdn and hdd ins fnl f: no ex and outpcd towards fin* **7/2**[2]
4222 3 2 ¼ **Gregorian Girl**[25] 5786 3-9-7 63.............. CierenFallon 8 57
(Dean Ivory) *last trio: effrt on outer over 2f out: chsd clr ldng pair and wandered jst ins fnl f: kpt on but nvr a threat to ldrs* **5/1**[3]
6550 4 3 ½ **Pearl Spectre (USA)**[7] 6441 8-9-9 60..............(v) SeamusCronin 4 46
(Phil McEntee) *pressed ldr: rdn and ev ch over 2f out tl no ex ent fnl f: wknd ins fnl f* **7/1**
05-0 5 nk **Poetic Legacy (IRE)**[13] 6259 3-8-4 46.............. AndrewBreslin 7 29
(Mark Johnston) *s.i.s: detached in last and nvr travelling: swtchd rt 1f out: kpt on to pass btn horses ins fnl f: n.d* **10/1**
6006 6 nk **Barton Mills**[25] 5770 4-10-2 67.............. GerO'Neill 2 51
(Michael Easterby) *t.k.h: w ldr tl led over 5f out: hung rt bnd over 2f out: hdd over 1f out: wknd ins fnl f (jockey said gelding hung off the bend)* **13/8**[1]
0055 7 ¾ **Alfie's Angel (IRE)**[9] 6363 5-8-5 45.............. WilliamCarver(3) 5 27
(Milton Bradley) *hld up in last trio: effrt on inner ent fnl 2f: no imp u.p over 1f out: wknd ins fnl f* **16/1**
6000 8 4 **Tintern Spirit (IRE)**[9] 6361 3-7-12 45.............. ElishaWhittington(5) 6 15
(Milton Bradley) *midfield: rdn over 2f out: struggling and lost pl over 1f out: bhd ins fnl f* **66/1**
1m 24.63s (-2.57) **Going Correction** -0.375s/f (Stan)
WFA 3 from 4yo+ 5lb **8 Ran SP% 115.0**
Speed ratings (Par 101): **99,96,94,90,89 89,88,84**
CSF £45.27 CT £200.35 TOTE £10.30: £2.90, £1.20, £1.50; EX 47.50 Trifecta £163.70.
Owner D De Souza **Bred** Liam Butler & Churchtown House Stud **Trained** Newmarket, Suffolk
FOCUS
Mainly exposed performers in a modest handicap. The gallop was fair and the runner-up is a good guide to the worth of the form.

6704 DONE BROTHERS EBF NOVICE MEDIAN AUCTION STKS 6f (P)
6:15 (6:16) (Class 5) 2-Y-O £4,204 (£1,251; £625; £312) Stalls Centre

Form RPR
21 1 **Fuwayrit (IRE)**[21] 5934 2-9-9 0.............. FrankieDettori 2 87+
(Mark Johnston) *mde all: rdn and fnd ex over 1f out: in command and r.o wl ins fnl f: eased towards fin: comf* **11/8**[1]
54 2 2 ¼ **Music Therapist (IRE)**[11] 6300 2-9-2 0.............. DanielMuscutt 5 73
(George Scott) *restless in stalls: chsd wnr: hung lft u.p and unable to match pce of wnr over 1f out: kpt on same pce ins fnl f (jockey said gelding hung left-handed under pressure)* **16/1**
150 3 1 ¼ **Emten (IRE)**[42] 5185 2-9-4 91.............. DougieCostello 6 72
(Jamie Osborne) *stdd and dropped in after s: hld up towards rr: effrt and wd bnd wl over 1f out: sn rdn: hdwy to chse ldng pair ins fnl f: kpt on but nvr a threat* **5/2**[2]
4 2 **Kohoof** 2-8-11 0.............. JimCrowley 3 59
(William Haggas) *dwlt: sn rcvrd and in tch in midfield: effrt ent fnl f: unable qck over 1f out: 3rd and no imp 1f out: wknd ins fnl f* **9/2**[3]
5 1 **Vintage Polly (IRE)** 2-8-11 0.............. RossaRyan 4 56
(Hugo Palmer) *dwlt: in tch towards rr and rn green: effrt ent fnl 2f: swtchd rt over 1f out: swtchd lft ins fnl f: kpt on towards fin: no threat to ldrs* **16/1**
06 6 nse **Master Rocco (IRE)**[21] 5940 2-9-2 0.............. JFEgan 1 60
(Jane Chapple-Hyam) *chsd ldrs on inner tl outpcd u.p over 1f out: wknd ins fnl f* **33/1**
05 7 1 **Kayat**[23] 5856 2-9-2 0.............. LouisSteward 8 57
(David Simcock) *t.k.h: chsd ldrs on outer after 2f: rdn and ev ch ent fnl 2f: unable qck and outpcd over 1f out: wknd ins fnl f (jockey said colt ran too keen)* **20/1**
8 2 ¼ **Nibras Wish (IRE)** 2-9-2 0.............. JasonWatson 7 51
(Ismail Mohammed) *t.k.h: in tch on outer: dropped to rr over 3f out and sn rdn: n.d after* **12/1**
1m 12.05s (-1.65) **Going Correction** -0.375s/f (Stan) **8 Ran SP% 116.0**
Speed ratings (Par 94): **96,93,91,88,87 87,85,82**
CSF £26.97 TOTE £2.00: £1.10, £2.80, £1.30; EX 17.10 Trifecta £50.90.
Owner H E Sherida Al-Kaabi **Bred** Charel Bloodstock **Trained** Middleham Moor, N Yorks
FOCUS
Not much in the way of strength in depth and a race in which the uneasy market leader was allowed to do his own thing in front. Those held up were at a disadvantage.

6705 TOTEPOOL NURSERY H'CAP 6f (P)
6:45 (6:45) (Class 3) (0-95,87) 2-Y-O £9,703 (£2,887; £1,443; £721) Stalls Centre

Form RPR
221 1 **X Force (IRE)**[39] 5280 2-9-0 80.............. OisinMurphy 3 83+
(Archie Watson) *t.k.h: chsd ldrs tl settled bk and hld up in tch after 2f: swtchd rt and effrt over 1f out: hdwy u.p to ld 100yds out: r.o wl* **7/2**[3]
1155 2 1 **Hard Nut (IRE)**[10] 6356 2-9-5 85.............. RyanMoore 5 85
(Richard Hannon) *chsd ldr: effrt ent fnl 2f: drvn over 1f out: kpt on same pce ins fnl f* **2/1**[1]
1102 3 nse **Eton College (IRE)**[14] 6228 2-9-7 87.............. WilliamBuick 6 87
(Mark Johnston) *dwlt: in tch: hdwy to chse ldrs 4f out: unable qck u.p over 1f out: rallied and kpt on fnl 100yds* **7/1**
5641 4 nk **Champagne Supanova (IRE)**[8] 6387 2-8-7 73..........(v) JasonWatson 2 72
(Richard Spencer) *led: rdn 2f out: drvn and edgd rt 1f out: hdd 100yds out: one pce after and lost 2 pls towards fin* **7/1**
2002 5 2 **Taste The Nectar (USA)**[6] 6515 2-8-3 69..............(p) JamesSullivan 4 62
(Robert Cowell) *hld up in tch in rr: effrt on outer over 1f out: no imp and eased towards fin* **12/1**

3133 **6** 6 **Making History (IRE)**[19] 6020 2-9-0 **85** .... CierenFallon(5) 1 60
(Saeed bin Suroor) *restless in stalls: chsd ldrs: effrt on inner ent fnl 2f: unable qck and btn 1f out: wknd and eased towards fin* **9/4**[2]

1m 11.39s (-2.31) **Going Correction** -0.375s/f (Stan) **6** Ran **SP% 119.0**
Speed ratings (Par 98): **100,98,98,98,95 87**
CSF £11.81 TOTE £4.90: £1.80, £1.70; EX 15.40 Trifecta £61.70.
Owner Qatar Racing Limited & David Redvers **Bred** Maurice Burns **Trained** Upper Lambourn, W Berks

FOCUS
Several useful sorts in a reasonable nursery but an ordinary gallop only picked up on the approach to the home turn and this bare form may not be entirely reliable.

6706 BETFRED CHELMSFORD CITY CUP (HERITAGE H'CAP) 7f (P)

7:15 (7:18) (Class 2) (0-105,104) 3-Y-O+

£62,250 (£18,640; £9,320; £4,660; £2,330; £1,170) **Stalls** Low

Form RPR

5605 **1** **War Glory (IRE)**[21] 5930 6-9-1 **95** .... SeanLevey 14 103
(Richard Hannon) *hld up in midfield: nt clr run over 1f out: swtchd lft and hdwy jst ins fnl f: str run u.p fnl 100yds to ld last stride* **25/1**

1560 **2** *shd* **Documenting**[35] 5413 6-9-9 **103** .... RossaRyan 6 110
(Kevin Frost) *chsd ldrs: effrt to chal over 1f out: drvn to ld ins fnl f: kpt on wl u.p: hdd last stride* **25/1**

4210 **3** *nse* **Charles Molson**[31] 5546 8-9-1 **95** .... DanielMuscutt 11 102
(Patrick Chamings) *hld up in tch in midfield: effrt over 1f out: hdwy and edgd out rt jst ins fnl f: drvn and ev ch wl ins fnl f: kpt on wl* **33/1**

1022 **4** 1 ½ **Vale Of Kent (IRE)**[9] 6376 4-9-10 **104** .... FrankieDettori 10 107
(Mark Johnston) *sn led and grad crossed towards inner: rdn over 1f out: drvn and hdd ins fnl f: no ex and outpcd wl ins fnl f* **5/1**[2]

0164 **5** ½ **Firmament**[9] 6376 7-9-0 **99** ....(p) CierenFallon(5) 7 101
(David O'Meara) *led for almost 1f: chsd ldr: effrt wl over 1f out: sn drvn: no ex and outpcd wl ins fnl f* **20/1**

-603 **6** *nk* **Blue Mist**[35] 5413 4-9-2 **96** ....(t) JasonWatson 5 97
(Roger Charlton) *hld up in midfield: effrt over 1f out: pushed lft jst ins fnl f: kpt on fnl 100yds: nt rch ldrs* **9/2**[1]

-101 **7** *nk* **Habub (USA)**[21] 5945 4-9-3 **97** .... JimCrowley 8 97
(Owen Burrows) *t.k.h: chsd ldrs: effrt on inner to press ldrs over 1f out: no ex and outpcd wl ins fnl f* **5/1**[2]

3345 **8** *nse* **Admirality**[35] 5413 5-9-0 **94** ....(h) BenCurtis 3 94
(Roger Fell) *wl in tch in midfield: swtchd rt and effrt jst over 1f out: kpt on ins fnl f: nt enough pce to rch ldrs* **7/1**[3]

0440 **9** 1 ¼ **Intisaab**[35] 5413 8-9-5 **99** ....(t[1]) OisinMurphy 16 95
(David O'Meara) *swtchd lft after s: hld up in last quintet: effrt over 1f out: swtchd rt 1f out: kpt on ins fnl f: nvr trbld ldrs* **25/1**

-011 **10** *nse* **Beauty Filly**[49] 4905 4-9-8 **102** .... WilliamBuick 1 98+
(William Haggas) *hld up in tch in midfield: effrt over 1f out: edgd lft and drvn ins fnl f: no imp and wknd wl ins fnl f: eased towards fin* **7/1**[3]

1560 **11** *hd* **Keyser Soze (IRE)**[49] 4921 5-9-10 **104** .... AdamKirby 15 100+
(Richard Spencer) *v.s.a: hld up in rr: effrt over 1f out: sme hdwy but stl only midfield whn nt clr run ins fnl f: kpt on but nvr able to cl: eased towards fin (jockey said gelding was denied a clear run in the final furlong)* **14/1**

1060 **12** *hd* **Gulliver**[14] 6229 5-9-4 **98** ....(tp) LouisSteward 12 93
(David O'Meara) *hld up in last quintet: effrt over 1f out: kpt on fnl 100yds: nvr trbld ldrs* **33/1**

2400 **13** ¾ **Reputation (IRE)**[14] 6229 6-9-0 **94** .... JamesSullivan 9 87
(Ruth Carr) *wl in tch in midfield: effrt over 1f out: struggling to qckn whn impeded 1f out: no imp after* **50/1**

3344 **14** ¾ **Cliffs Of Capri**[7] 6445 5-9-0 **94** ....(p) DougieCostello 4 85
(Jamie Osborne) *sn rdn and nvr travelling wl towards rr: kpt on fnl f but nvr involved* **16/1**

2600 **15** 5 **Cenotaph (USA)**[70] 4095 7-9-10 **104** ....(p[1]) RyanMoore 2 82
(Simon Crisford) *t.k.h: chsd ldrs early: wl in tch in midfield: effrt over 1f out: sn btn: bhd ins fnl f (trainer's rep could offer no explanation for the performance shown)* **5/1**[2]

1m 22.85s (-4.35) **Going Correction** -0.375s/f (Stan) **15** Ran **SP% 129.9**
Speed ratings (Par 109): **109,108,108,107,106 106,105,105,104,104 104,103,103,102,96**
CSF £551.06 CT £19019.19 TOTE £40.20: £9.70, £11.40, £14.20; EX 1638.30 Trifecta £2079.60.
Owner Mohamed Saeed Al Shahi **Bred** Pier House Stud **Trained** East Everleigh, Wilts

FOCUS
A competitive handicap in which a reasonable gallop steadied to a degree after a couple of furlongs but this form should prove reliable.

6707 BETFRED CONDITIONS STKS (PLUS 10 RACE) 1m (P)

7:45 (7:46) (Class 2) 2-Y-O **£16,172** (£4,812; £2,405) **Stalls** Low

Form RPR

4211 **1** **King's Caper**[14] 6226 2-9-4 88 .... FrankieDettori 4 95
(Mark Johnston) *led tl over 6f out: styd pressing ldr tl pushed into ld again 2f out: rdn and forged ahd whn edgd lft 1f out: styd on wl* **11/8**[2]

165 **2** 1 ¾ **Wild Thunder (IRE)**[15] 6163 2-9-2 87 .... RyanMoore 3 89
(Richard Hannon) *chsd rivals and niggled along: drvn over 2f out: nt clr run and hmpd 1f out: swtchd rt and chsd wnr ins fnl f: styd on* **5/1**[3]

4132 **3** 3 ¼ **Saqqara King (USA)**[14] 6251 2-9-2 0 ....(p) WilliamBuick 1 84
(Charlie Appleby) *chsd wnr and pushed along early: hdwy to ld over 6f out: hdd 2f out: sn rdn: unable qck and edgd lft ent fnl f: lost 2nd and wknd ins fnl f* **1/1**[1]

1m 37.6s (-2.30) **Going Correction** -0.375s/f (Stan) **3** Ran **SP% 108.8**
Speed ratings (Par 100): **96,94,91**
CSF £6.63 TOTE £2.00; EX 6.40 Trifecta £5.70.
Owner Kingsley Park 13 **Bred** Highclere Stud **Trained** Middleham Moor, N Yorks

FOCUS
A bit of a disappointing turnout for the money on offer but the winner is a likeable and progressive sort who is sure to win more races. The gallop was fair.

6708 BETSI GOLDEN MILE NOVICE STKS (PLUS 10 RACE) 1m (P)

8:15 (8:16) (Class 4) 2-Y-O **£6,469** (£1,925; £962; £481) **Stalls** Low

Form RPR

6 **1** **Vindicate**[22] 5908 2-9-5 0 .... RyanMoore 4 78
(Sir Michael Stoute) *hld up in tch in last trio: effrt on outer over 2f out: drvn and clsd to chal 1f out: edgd lft and led ins fnl f: hld on wl u.p* **9/4**[1]

2 *nk* **Live Your Dream (IRE)** 2-9-5 0 .... OisinMurphy 6 77
(Saeed bin Suroor) *dwlt: steadily rcvrd and chsd ldr after 2f: effrt to chal over 1f out: sustained chal and ev ch whn edgd lft ins fnl f: kpt on wl: jst hld* **6/1**

4 **3** ¾ **Sun Cuisine (USA)**[24] 5823 2-9-5 0 ....(b[1]) WilliamBuick 3 76
(Charlie Appleby) *dwlt and niggled along early: in tch in rr: effrt and swtchd rt bnd 2f out: hdwy 1f out: kpt on wl ins fnl f* **4/1**[3]

4 ½ **Trumpet Man** 2-9-5 0 .... AdamKirby 1 74
(Mark Johnston) *dwlt: in tch in midfield: clsd and nt clr run whn swtchd rt over 1f out: sn chalng: rdn to ld 1f out: bmpd and hdd ins fnl f: jst outpcd towards fin* **6/1**

4 **5** 1 ½ **More Than A Prince**[14] 6219 2-9-5 0 .... SeanLevey 2 71
(Richard Hannon) *hld up in tch in last pair: clsd and nt clr run over 1f out: swtchd rt and kpt on but no threat to ldrs* **10/1**

05 **6** 1 **Optio**[25] 5775 2-9-5 0 .... JasonWatson 8 69
(Brian Meehan) *broke fast: led for over 1f out: chsd ldrs after: effrt ent fnl 2f: drvn over 1f out: sn btn and wknd ins fnl f* **20/1**

6 **7** *nk* **Deverell**[101] 2973 2-9-5 0 .... FrankieDettori 9 68
(John Gosden) *dwlt: steadily rcvrd to ld over 6f out: drvn and hrd pressed over 1f out: hdd 1f out: no ex and wknd fnl 100yds* **7/2**[2]

0 **8** 16 **Werewolf**[8] 6395 2-9-5 0 .... GeorgeWood 5 31
(Archie Watson) *chsd ldrs tl lost pl u.p over 1f out: wl bhd ins fnl f* **25/1**

1m 38.47s (-1.43) **Going Correction** -0.375s/f (Stan) **8** Ran **SP% 119.3**
Speed ratings (Par 96): **92,91,90,90,88 87,87,71**
CSF £17.27 TOTE £2.60: £1.20, £1.70, £1.70; EX 16.10 Trifecta £85.40.
Owner The Queen **Bred** The Queen **Trained** Newmarket, Suffolk

FOCUS
A fair novice event but an ordinary gallop to the home turn saw several finish in a bit of a heap.

6709 CHELMSFORD CITY RACECOURSE FILLIES' H'CAP 1m 2f (P)

8:45 (8:45) (Class 3) (0-95,94) 3-Y-O+ **£9,703** (£2,887; £1,443; £721) **Stalls** Low

Form RPR

422 **1** **Gallic**[40] 5253 3-8-12 **85** .... OisinMurphy 5 92
(Ed Walker) *chsd ldr after 2f: effrt and ev ch over 2f out: led over 1f out: drvn and hld on wl ins fnl f* **9/4**[2]

1314 **2** *shd* **Maid For Life**[21] 5949 3-9-7 **94** ....(h) GeorgeWood 3 101+
(Charlie Fellowes) *t.k.h: hld up in tch in rr: clsd and swtchd rt over 1f out: sn swtchd bk lft and drvn to press ldrs 1f out: str chal ins fnl f: kpt on wl: jst hld* **9/2**

2321 **3** 2 ½ **Shrewdness**[15] 6186 3-8-3 **81** .... CierenFallon(5) 1 83
(William Haggas) *t.k.h: chsd ldrs: effrt and swtchd rt 2f out: chsd wnr over 1f out tl 1f out: wl hld and kpt on same pce fnl 100yds* **2/1**[1]

2114 **4** 4 ½ **Birdcage Walk**[15] 6172 3-8-12 **85** ....(h) RyanMoore 4 79
(Hugo Palmer) *hld up wl in tch: effrt over 2f out: no ex u.p 1f out: wknd ins fnl f* **7/2**[3]

0655 **5** 9 **Plait**[26] 5735 4-9-2 **85** .... CameronNoble(3) 2 60
(Michael Bell) *t.k.h: led: rdn and hrd pressed ent fnl 2f: hdd over 1f out: bhd and eased wl ins fnl f* **10/1**

2m 3.04s (-5.56) **Going Correction** -0.375s/f (Stan) **5** Ran **SP% 113.6**
WFA 3 from 4yo 7lb
Speed ratings (Par 104): **107,106,104,101,94**
CSF £12.84 TOTE £2.90: £1.70, £2.60; EX 11.70 Trifecta £22.40.
Owner Exors Of The Late Lady Rothschild **Bred** Kincorth Investments Inc **Trained** Upper Lambourn, Berks

FOCUS
A reasonable handicap but a steady gallop to the home turn means this form isn't totally reliable.
T/Plt: £1,133.20 to a £1 stake. Pool: £39,378.71 - 34.75 winning units T/Qpdt: £298.00 to a £1 stake. Pool: £4,307.50 - 14.45 winning units **Steve Payne**

5703 CHESTER (L-H)

Saturday, August 31

OFFICIAL GOING: Good (good to soft in places; 7.3)
Wind: fairly strong, largely across Weather: Sunshine and cloud

6710 MBNA / BRITISH STALLION STUDS EBF NOVICE STKS (PLUS 10 RACE) 7f 1y

1:35 (1:35) (Class 4) 2-Y-O **£5,851** (£1,752; £876; £438; £219) **Stalls** Low

Form RPR

44 **1** **Berkshire Rocco (FR)**[28] 5665 2-9-2 0 .... RobHornby 2 84+
(Andrew Balding) *prom: rdn along over 2f out: led 1f out: kpt on* **2/1**[1]

31 **2** 1 **Breathalyze (FR)**[27] 5704 2-9-8 0 .... RichardKingscote 5 87
(Tom Dascombe) *trckd ldrs: rdn 2f out: wnt 2nd fnl 110yds: kpt on but nvr getting to wnr* **2/1**[1]

35 **3** 2 ½ **No Show (IRE)**[23] 5845 2-9-2 0 .... AndreaAtzeni 1 75
(Richard Hannon) *led: rdn 2f out: hdd 1f out: no ex* **13/2**[3]

4 **4** 2 **Creativity**[35] 5456 2-8-11 0 .... TonyHamilton 3 65
(Richard Fahey) *trckd ldrs on inner: pushed along over 2f out: rdn over 1f out: one pce* **16/1**

42 **5** 5 **Dirty Dancer (FR)**[28] 5684 2-8-11 0 .... HarryBentley 4 52
(Ralph Beckett) *dwlt sltly: hld up in tch: pushed along over 2f out: rdn over 1f out: sn wknd* **5/2**[2]

1m 30.4s (2.90) **Going Correction** +0.20s/f (Good) **5** Ran **SP% 114.5**
Speed ratings (Par 96): **91,89,87,84,79**
CSF £6.64 TOTE £2.80: £1.10, £1.30; EX 6.90 Trifecta £21.10.
Owner Berkshire Parts & Panels Ltd **Bred** Seserve S A G L **Trained** Kingsclere, Hants

FOCUS
The going was good, good so soft in places. The rail was moved out between 3yds and 9 yards from inside. Add 24yds. An above-average 2yo novice and a promising winner.

6711 SPORTPESA H'CAP 7f 127y

2:10 (2:11) (Class 2) 3-Y-O+

£28,012 (£8,388; £4,194; £2,097; £1,048; £526) **Stalls** Low

Form RPR

6250 **1** **Oh This Is Us (IRE)**[7] 6445 6-9-10 **105** .... AndreaAtzeni 6 114+
(Richard Hannon) *hld up: pushed along and hdwy on outer over 1f out: drvn to chse ldr ent fnl f: r.o wl: led towards fin* **5/2**[1]

4005 **2** ½ **Alemaratalyoum (IRE)**[21] 5965 5-8-8 **89** ....(p[1]) ShaneGray 8 96
(Stuart Williams) *in tch: gd hdwy on outer 3f out to ld 2f out: rdn 2 l clr appr fnl f: drvn ins fnl f: one pce and hdd towards fin* **33/1**

0214 **3** ½ **Barristan The Bold**[21] 5963 3-8-8 **95** .... RichardKingscote 9 100
(Tom Dascombe) *midfield: pushed along and sme hdwy whn bit tight for room appr fnl f: rdn and kpt on wl fnl 110yds: wnt 3rd towards fin* **5/1**[2]

1252 **4** ½ **Sir Busker (IRE)**[21] 5953 3-8-2 **89** ....(v) JimmyQuinn 3 93
(William Knight) *midfield: racd keenly: rdn and hdwy on outer to chse ldr over 1f out: hung lft and one pce fnl 110yds: lost 3rd towards fin (jockey said gelding hung left-handed in the home straight)* **12/1**

0511 **5** 1 1/4 **Humble Gratitude**[15] 6166 4-8-6 **87**...............................(p) CamHardie 11 89
(Ian Williams) *hld up in rr: rdn and kpt on fnl f: nrst fin* **16/1**

4104 **6** 1 1/2 **Penwortham (IRE)**[27] 5708 6-8-3 **84**........................... DuranFentiman 2 82+
(Richard Fahey) *stdd s: racd keenly in tch: short of room wl over 1f out tl ins fnl f: no ch after but kpt on (jockey said gelding ran freely early on and was denied a clear run entering the home straight)* **16/1**

-300 **7** 1 **Aljady (FR)**[31] 5546 4-8-11 **92**......................................(p[1]) TonyHamilton 4 88
(Richard Fahey) *trckd ldrs: rdn along over 2f out: sn outpcd and lost pl: btn appr fnl f (vet reported gelding lost its right fore shoe)* **13/2**[3]

3100 **8** hd **Hero Hero (IRE)**[21] 5932 3-8-5 **92**................................. MartinDwyer 10 87
(Andrew Balding) *prom on outer racing keenly: led over 5f out: rdn and hdd 2f out: wknd fnl f* **9/1**

4100 **9** 1 1/4 **Gabrial The Wire**[14] 6222 3-8-0 **90**.............................. SeanDavis(3) 7 82
(Richard Fahey) *hld up: rdn 2f out: nvr threatened* **22/1**

0102 **10** 3/4 **Arcanada (IRE)**[20] 5991 6-8-2 **86**..................................(p) JaneElliott(3) 1 77
(Tom Dascombe) *trckd ldrs: lost pl over 2f out: wknd fnl f (jockey said gelding was denied a clear run entering the home straight)* **8/1**

0000 **11** hd **Lake Volta (IRE)**[7] 6445 4-9-1 **96**............................... FrannyNorton 5 87
(Mark Johnston) *led: hdd over 5f out: remained prom: rdn over 2f out: wknd appr fnl f (trainer's rep could offer no explanation for the gelding's performance)* **5/1**[2]

1m 35.02s (-0.68) **Going Correction** +0.20s/f (Good)
WFA 3 from 4yo+ 6lb **11** Ran SP% **123.1**
Speed ratings (Par 109): **109,108,108,107,106 104,103,103,102,101 101**
CSF £106.35 CT £407.29 TOTE £2.70: £1.40, £8.40, £1.60; EX 76.80 Trifecta £486.70.
Owner Team Wallop **Bred** Herbertstown House Stud **Trained** East Everleigh, Wilts

FOCUS
Add 24yds. Competitive stuff and a repeat of last year's success for the winner, who did well to score after being trapped out wide.

6712 SPORTPESA CHESTER STKS (LISTED RACE) 1m 6f 87y
2:45 (2:45) (Class 1) 3-Y-O+

£20,982 (£7,955; £3,981; £1,983; £995; £499) **Stalls** Low

Form RPR

5320 **1** **Vivid Diamond (IRE)**[21] 5931 3-8-2 92.............. FrannyNorton 3 106
(Mark Johnston) *trckd ldrs on inner: gng wl but short of room over 3f out: forced way though gap over 2f out: led 2f out: rdn clr over 1f out* **7/1**

0260 **2** 5 **Persian Moon (IRE)**[8] 6420 3-8-7 97........................... JasonHart 4 104
(Mark Johnston) *led: rdn along over 2f out: hdd 2f out: styd on same pce and sn hld in 2nd* **5/1**[3]

-623 **3** 4 **Outbox**[22] 5909 4-9-3 105..(p) AndreaAtzeni 2 96
(Simon Crisford) *sn prom on outer: pushed along and lost pl sltly 5f out: rdn and chsng ldr towards outer whn bdly blkd over 2f out: no ch after and plugged on in 3rd (trainer's rep could offer no explanation for the performance shown other than that the gelding suffered slight interference in running)* **11/8**[1]

4026 **4** 5 **Mackaar (IRE)**[43] 5121 3-8-7 94...................................(b[1]) HarryBentley 1 91
(Roger Varian) *hld up: rdn along over 4f out: sn btn* **16/1**

5 6 **Stivers (ARG)**[231] 6-9-3 105.................................... ChrisHayes 5 81
(D K Weld, Ire) *hld up: rdn and hdwy on wd outside 3f out: sltly hmpd over 2f out: sn wknd* **5/1**[3]

1102 **6** 12 **Tribal Craft**[16] 6124 3-8-3 91 ow1.............................. MartinDwyer 6 62+
(Andrew Balding) *trckd ldrs: racd keenly: wnt prom but hung rt on bnd over 5f out: rdn along and chsng ldr whn bdly hmpd over 2f out: no ch after and eased (jockey said filly hung right-handed)* **9/2**[2]

3m 10.73s (0.93) **Going Correction** +0.20s/f (Good)
WFA 3 from 4yo+ 10lb **6** Ran SP% **112.0**
Speed ratings (Par 111): **105,102,99,97,93 86**
CSF £40.34 TOTE £8.90: £5.00, £1.90; EX 36.50 Trifecta £110.60.
Owner Markus Graff **Bred** Markus Graff **Trained** Middleham Moor, N Yorks

FOCUS
Add 48yds. Not the strongest of Listed contests, but a 1-2 for Mark Johnston and a winner who seemed to improve markedly for the step up in distance.

6713 SPORTPESA / EBF FILLIES' CONDITIONS STKS (PLUS 10 RACE) 6f 17y
3:20 (3:21) (Class 2) 2-Y-O

£12,450 (£3,728; £1,864; £932; £466; £234) **Stalls** Low

Form RPR

1 **Al Rasmah (IRE)** 2-8-9 0.. TonyHamilton 2 85+
(Richard Fahey) *hld up in tch: pushed along over 2f out: hdwy and chsd ldrs appr fnl f: led 75yds out: pushed out* **12/1**

1310 **2** 1 **Know No Limits (IRE)**[28] 5683 2-8-12 87............... RichardKingscote 5 85
(Tom Dascombe) *led narrowly: rdn 2f out: drvn fnl f: hdd 75yds out: no ex* **5/4**[1]

6165 **3** hd **Glamorous Anna**[15] 6157 2-8-12 85............................ MitchGodwin 3 84
(Christopher Mason) *chsd ldrs: rdn over 2f out: drvn over 1f out: swtchd lft ins fnl f: kpt on same pce* **15/2**[3]

1231 **4** 4 **Dream Kart (IRE)**[27] 5703 2-8-12 90........................... FrannyNorton 6 72
(Mark Johnston) *pressed ldr on outer: pushed along 2f out: drvn 1f out: wknd ins fnl f* **13/8**[2]

2105 **5** 8 **Infinite Grace**[12] 6272 2-8-12 78.................................. CamHardie 1 48
(David O'Meara) *chsd ldrs: rdn and outpcd 3f out: wknd over 1f out* **10/1**

5 **6** 24 **Unauthorised Act (IRE)**[35] 5418 2-8-13 ow1................... TomEaves 4
(Alan Berry) *s.i.s: sn t.o* **50/1**

1m 16.89s (1.39) **Going Correction** +0.20s/f (Good) **6** Ran SP% **113.0**
Speed ratings (Par 97): **98,96,96,91,80 48**
CSF £28.18 TOTE £7.90: £3.10, £1.10; EX 32.00 Trifecta £150.70.
Owner Sheikh Juma Dalmook Al Maktoum **Bred** Castle Estates **Trained** Musley Bank, N Yorks

FOCUS
Add 24yds. Not many runners, but a competitive conditions race. The winner was making her debut and could turn out to be useful.

6714 ESL GROUP H'CAP 5f 110y
3:55 (3:57) (Class 2) (0-100,101) 3-Y-O+

£11,827 (£3,541; £1,770; £885; £442; £222) **Stalls** Low

Form RPR

1000 **1** **Powerallied (IRE)**[21] 5951 6-8-10 **83**.......................... BarryMcHugh 9 91
(Richard Fahey) *trckd ldrs: rdn to chse ldr over 1f out: chal strly ins fnl f: led post (trainer said, regarding the improved form shown, the gelding appreciated the return to chester)* **20/1**

0000 **2** nse **Bossipop**[10] 6339 6-8-9 **82**..(b) CamHardie 5 90
(Tim Easterby) *prom: led over 2f out: sn rdn: strly pressed ins fnl f: kpt on but hdd post* **20/1**

5210 **3** 1 **Angel Alexander (IRE)**[27] 5705 3-9-11 **101**............. RichardKingscote 7 106
(Tom Dascombe) *chsd ldrs: rdn over 1f out: kpt on* **7/2**[1]

6443 **4** 1 **Seen The Lyte (IRE)**[23] 5846 4-8-5 **81**........................(h) RowanScott(3) 6 82
(Nigel Tinkler) *dwlt: sn midfield: rdn over 1f out: kpt on ins fnl f* **25/1**

4005 **5** 1/2 **Diamond Dougal (IRE)**[8] 6396 4-8-13 **86**..................... FrannyNorton 10 86+
(Mick Channon) *hld up: pushed along over 2f out: sme hdwy on outer appr fnl f: drvn and kpt on wl* **12/1**

0001 **6** 3/4 **Growl**[14] 6227 7-9-8 **95**... TonyHamilton 3 92
(Richard Fahey) *dwlt sltly: sn pushed along in midfield on inner: bit outpcd 3f out: sme hdwy and n.m.r appr fnl f: drvn ins fnl f: kpt on: nvr involved* **7/2**[1]

0105 **7** 1/2 **Machree (IRE)**[29] 5617 4-8-13 **86**.................................. JimmyQuinn 4 82
(Declan Carroll) *sltly awkward s: hld up: pushed along over 1f out: rdn and kpt on ins fnl f: nvr threatened (jockey said filly was slowly away)* **25/1**

0020 **8** shd **Gabrial The Saint (IRE)**[28] 5661 4-9-2 **89**..................... JackGarritty 1 84
(Richard Fahey) *trckd ldrs on inner: n.m.r and shuffled bk sltly 2f out: rdn and no ex fnl f* **7/2**[1]

0620 **9** 1 3/4 **Abel Handy (IRE)**[35] 5420 4-9-2 **89**................................. TomEaves 2 79
(Declan Carroll) *led: hdd over 2f out: sn rdn: wknd fnl f* **11/2**[2]

0003 **10** 3/4 **Brian The Snail (IRE)**[4] 6581 5-8-9 **85**........................ SeanDavis(3) 8 72
(Richard Fahey) *dwlt: a towards rr* **7/1**[3]

1652 **11** 1/2 **Peggie Sue**[18] 6056 4-8-6 **84**.. TobyEley(5) 11 69
(Adam West) *s.i.s and swtchd lft to inner: a in rr (jockey said filly was never travelling)* **14/1**

1m 7.78s (-1.22) **Going Correction** +0.20s/f (Good)
WFA 3 from 4yo+ 2lb **11** Ran SP% **126.1**
Speed ratings (Par 109): **112,111,110,109,108 107,106,106,104,103 102**
CSF £371.50 CT £1744.78 TOTE £28.40: £7.50, £6.40, £1.50; EX 250.40 Trifecta £1284.40.
Owner Dr Marwan Koukash **Bred** John R Jeffers **Trained** Musley Bank, N Yorks

FOCUS
Add 22yds. No prisoners taken in this sprint handicap which produced a thrilling finish. The winner's last six wins have all been achieved at this unique venue.

6715 1539 H'CAP 5f 15y
4:30 (4:30) (Class 4) (0-80,80) 3-Y-O

£6,080 (£1,809; £904; £452; £300; £300) **Stalls** Low

Form RPR

2443 **1** **Fairy Stories**[28] 5660 3-8-3 **65**...................................... SeanDavis(3) 3 76
(Richard Fahey) *midfield: rdn and hdwy to chse ldrs over 1f out: drvn and kpt on to ld nr fin* **3/1**[1]

6512 **2** hd **Wild Edric**[39] 5281 3-9-7 **80**.................................. RichardKingscote 5 90
(Tom Dascombe) *prom: rdn to chal strly over 1f out: drvn to ld narrowly over 1f out: kpt on but hdd nr fin* **4/1**[3]

2624 **3** 2 1/2 **Vee Man Ten**[21] 5952 3-9-1 **74**......................................(h) FrannyNorton 4 75
(Ivan Furtado) *led: hdd over 3f out: led again over 1f out: sn rdn: hdd ins fnl f: sn no ex* **7/2**[2]

2153 **4** 4 **Ginvincible**[25] 5791 3-8-6 **65**.. ShaneGray 1 52
(James Given) *midfield on inner: rdn over 1f out: no imp* **7/1**

3105 **5** nk **Exalted Angel (FR)**[25] 5791 3-9-5 **78**............................ CliffordLee 2 64
(K R Burke) *slowly away: hld up: rdn and sme hdwy 2f out: drvn appr fnl f and no further imp (jockey said gelding was slowly away)* **6/1**

5646 **6** 2 1/2 **True Hero**[15] 6148 3-9-1 **77**...................................... RowanScott(3) 8 54
(Nigel Tinkler) *hld up: rdn over 2f out: nvr threatened* **14/1**

062 **7** 3 1/4 **Three Card Trick**[53] 4757 3-9-2 **75**.................................. TomEaves 7 40
(Kevin Ryan) *dwlt: hld up: sn pushed along: outpcd and bhd fnl 2f* **12/1**

120 **8** 19 **The Defiant**[45] 5042 3-8-11 **70**.................................. BarryMcHugh 6
(Paul Midgley) *prom on outer: led 3f out: hdd over 1f out: wknd qckly and eased* **8/1**

1m 2.42s (0.32) **Going Correction** +0.20s/f (Good) **8** Ran SP% **119.5**
Speed ratings (Par 102): **105,104,100,94,93 89,84,54**
CSF £16.04 CT £44.36 TOTE £2.90: £1.10, £1.70, £1.70; EX 15.10 Trifecta £45.50.
Owner Richard Fahey Ebor Racing Club Ltd **Bred** Mrs Sheila Oakes **Trained** Musley Bank, N Yorks

FOCUS
Add 20yds. Another sprint which featured a close finish. The front two pulled nicely clear.

6716 MKM BUILDING SUPPLIES (CHESTER) H'CAP 1m 7f 196y
5:05 (5:09) (Class 4) (0-85,82) 3-Y-O+

£6,080 (£1,809; £904; £452; £300; £300) **Stalls** Low

Form RPR

6210 **1** **Overhaugh Street**[23] 5840 6-9-2 **70**.................................. ShaneGray 6 77
(Ed de Giles) *prom: led over 2f out: sn rdn: drvn fnl f: pressed fnl 75yds: hld on wl (trainer could offer no explanation for the apparent improved form shown)* **16/1**

1413 **2** nk **So Near So Farhh**[16] 6105 4-8-11 **70**.................... ScottMcCullagh(5) 7 76
(Mick Channon) *squeezed out jst after s: hld up in rr: pushed along over 4f out: rdn and gd hdwy on outer 2f out: wnt 2nd jst ins fnl f: chal fnl 75yds: kpt on* **8/1**[3]

1322 **3** 1 1/2 **Celestial Force (IRE)**[10] 6340 4-10-0 **82**........................... CliffordLee 2 86
(Tom Dascombe) *led: rdn along over 3f out: hdd over 2f out: remained chsng ldr: bit short of room on inner over 1f out: styd on ins fnl f (jockey said gelding was denied a clear run approaching the furlong marker)* **7/4**[1]

5225 **4** nk **Gabrial The One (IRE)**[27] 5706 3-8-10 **79**..................... SeanDavis(3) 9 82
(Richard Fahey) *midfield: rdn along 3f out: swtchd rt over 1f out: briefly hung lft: styd on fnl f (jockey said gelding hung left-handed)* **8/1**[3]

1520 **5** nse **Lord Lamington**[33] 5487 3-9-1 **81**................................. FrannyNorton 8 84
(Mark Johnston) *trckd ldrs: rdn along over 2f out: styd on same pce (jockey said gelding was denied a clear run inside the final furlong and had to take a precautionary check off the heels of so near so farhh and so was unable to ride out to the line)* **12/1**

4230 **6** 1 1/2 **Bailarico (IRE)**[31] 5540 6-9-9 **77**......................................(b) JimmyQuinn 1 79
(Warren Greatrex) *s.i.s and briefly rdn along: hld up: hdwy on outer over 4f out: rdn to chse ldrs over 2f out: no ex ins fnl f* **8/1**[3]

2314 **7** 4 **Nafaayes (IRE)**[22] 5897 5-8-9 **66**.................................. JaneElliott(3) 3 63
(Jean-Rene Auvray) *hld up: rdn over 3f out: sn btn* **8/1**[3]

2135 **8** 12 **Angel Gabrial (IRE)**[22] 5897 10-8-10 **64**....................(p) BarryMcHugh 5 46
(Patrick Morris) *midfield: rdn along over 3f: sn lost pl and dropped towards rr: wknd and bhd fnl 2f* **10/1**

0002 **9** 20 **Heart Of Soul (IRE)**[27] 5709 4-9-9 **77**..................(p) RichardKingscote 4 35
(Ian Williams) *trckd ldrs: rdn over 3f out: wknd over 2f out: eased (trainer said gelding was unsuited by the good, good to soft going which in their opinion was tacky ground)* **9/2**[2]

3m 33.95s (2.05) **Going Correction** +0.20s/f (Good)
WFA 3 from 4yo+ 12lb **9** Ran SP% **121.7**
Speed ratings (Par 105): **102,101,101,100,100 100,98,92,82**
CSF £143.97 CT £344.07 TOTE £24.50: £4.70, £2.80, £1.30; EX 215.00 Trifecta £595.90.
Owner Sharron & Robert Colvin **Bred** World Racing Network **Trained** Ledbury, H'fords

The Form Book Flat 2019, Raceform Ltd, Newbury, RG14 5SJ

FOCUS
Add 48yds. A decent staying handicap in which there were plenty in with a chance in the home straight. The winner travelled best and showed determination to hang on.
T/Plt: £90.20 to a £1 stake. Pool: £75,079.13 - 607.08 winning units T/Qpdt: £35.40 to a £1 stake. Pool: £4,746.52 - 99.0 winning units **Andrew Sheret**

6599 **LINGFIELD** (L-H)
Saturday, August 31

OFFICIAL GOING: Polytrack: standard
Wind: slight head wind Weather: overcast, chance of showers

6717 LEANNE SQUIRES TWENTY PLUS TWENTY APPRENTICE H'CAP (RACING EXCELLENCE TRAINING SERIES) 1m 1y(P)
4:20 (4:21) (Class 5) (0-70,72) 4-Y-O+
£3,428 (£1,020; £509; £400; £400; £400) **Stalls** High

Form RPR
5263 **1** **Savitar (IRE)**[16] 6121 4-8-10 **58**........................ LukeCatton(5) 2 68
(Jim Boyle) *racd in midfield on inner: hdwy to chse ldrs 2f out: rdn to ld jst ins fnl f: styd on wl* **3/1**[1]
1612 **2** 1 3/4 **Imperial Act**[8] 6414 4-9-3 **65**........................ MariePerrault(5) 6 71
(Andrew Balding) *s.i.s and racd in last: making hdwy whn forced v wd off home bnd 2f out: rdn and kpt on wl to take clr 2nd ins fnl f* **4/1**[2]
6045 **3** 2 **Noble Peace**[24] 5820 6-9-7 **64**........................(b) GeorgiaDobie 4 65
(Lydia Pearce) *pushed along to ld for 2f then trckd ldr: pushed along to chse ldr over 2f out: sn rdn and no imp over 1f out: plugged on fnl f* **8/1**[3]
5000 **4** 1 **Letsbe Avenue (IRE)**[7] 6469 4-9-10 **67**........................(b[1]) MarkCrehan 8 66
(Richard Hannon) *chsd ldr tl led after 2f out: rdn along and hdd over 1f out: wknd fnl f* **4/1**[2]
0600 **5** 3/4 **Nezar (IRE)**[19] 6026 8-9-10 **72**........................ LukeBacon(5) 7 69
(Dean Ivory) *chsd ldr: rdn along to ld over 1f out: sn hdd by wnr ins fnl f: no ex and wknd clsng stages* **11/1**
1306 **6** 3 3/4 **Gainsay**[44] 5087 4-9-10 **67**........................ TylerSaunders 5 56
(Jonathan Portman) *hld up: pushed along and wd off home bnd 2f out: sn rdn and no imp fnl f* **4/1**[2]
2000 **7** 4 **Subliminal**[11] 6317 4-8-13 **61**........................(b) LeviWilliams(5) 1 41
(Simon Dow) *hld up: rdn and outpcd 2f out: a in rr* **10/1**

1m 37.13s (-1.07) **Going Correction** -0.05s/f (Stan) 7 Ran SP% 113.5
Speed ratings (Par 103): **103,101,99,98,97 93,89**
CSF £14.92 CT £84.71 TOTE £3.30: £1.60, £2.30; EX 12.40 Trifecta £45.10.
Owner Harry Wigan **Bred** Cahermorris Stables Ltd **Trained** Epsom, Surrey

FOCUS
An ordinary handicap for apprentice riders.

6718 QUEENIE O'REILLY, GET ME TO HEAVEN / EBF NOVICE MEDIAN AUCTION STKS 1m 1y(P)
4:55 (5:01) (Class 5) 2-Y-O
£4,140 (£1,232; £615; £307) **Stalls** High

Form RPR
0 **1** **Spantik**[23] 5856 2-9-2 0........................ DavidEgan 3 73+
(Archie Watson) *broke wl and mde all: shkn up w 1 l ld 2f out: rdn and kpt on wl fnl f: a doing enough* **8/1**
4 **2** 2 **North Point**[17] 6079 2-9-2 0........................ RobertWinston 8 68
(David Elsworth) *racd in midfield on outer: hdwy into 3rd 3f out: wnt 2nd and rdn to chse wnr 2f out: drvn and no imp on wnr fnl f* **5/1**[3]
51 **3** nk **Lucander (IRE)**[20] 5992 2-9-8 0........................ PatDobbs 6 74+
(Ralph Beckett) *racd in midfield: pushed along in 5th 2f out: rdn and kpt on wl ins fnl f* **4/1**[2]
55 **4** 1 1/4 **Webuyanyhorse**[15] 6161 2-8-9 0........................ EllieMacKenzie(7) 2 65
(Jamie Osborne) *trckd wnr on inner: pushed along and outpcd by wnr 2f out: kpt on one pce fnl f* **8/1**
026 **5** 2 3/4 **Bermuda Schwartz**[36] 5374 2-9-2 78........................ ShaneKelly 5 59
(Richard Hughes) *in rr of midfield: hdwy u.p 2f out: kpt on fnl f* **7/1**
6 hd **Rachmaninov (USA)** 2-9-2 0........................ PatCosgrave 4 58+
(Hugo Palmer) *midfield on inner: pushed along and no hdwy over 2f out: sn rdn and no imp fnl f* **9/4**[1]
7 1/2 **Licorice** 2-9-2 0........................ LukeMorris 10 57
(Archie Watson) *trckd wnr: pushed along over 2f out: rdn and outpcd over 1f out: one pce after* **11/1**
8 3 **Thank The Irish (IRE)** 2-9-2 0........................ FergusSweeney 9 50+
(Jamie Osborne) *hld up: pushed along in rr over 2f out: kpt on one pce* **25/1**
9 3/4 **Curtiz** 2-9-2 0........................ CharlieBennett 1 48
(Hughie Morrison) *hld up on inner: rdn in rr 2f out: nvr on terms* **33/1**
10 9 **Chamade** 2-8-11 0........................ JosephineGordon 12 23
(Ralph Beckett) *midfield on outer: rdn 5f out: drvn and lost pl over 2f out: sn bhd* **25/1**
11 1 1/4 **Majestyk Fire (IRE)** 2-9-2 0........................(t[1]) TomQueally 11 25
(David Flood) *dwlt bdly racd in last: green at times: rdn in rr over 2f out: nvr on terms* **50/1**

1m 39.31s (1.11) **Going Correction** -0.05s/f (Stan) 11 Ran SP% 123.1
Speed ratings (Par 94): **92,90,89,88,85 85,85,82,81,72 71**
CSF £48.46 TOTE £10.10: £2.70, £2.60, £1.80; EX 62.80 Trifecta £227.30.
Owner Nurlan Bizakov **Bred** Hesmonds Stud Ltd **Trained** Upper Lambourn, W Berks

FOCUS
This was steadily run and developed into a bit of a dash.

6719 SAM HOLLIDAY AND ALAN JONES NOVICE AUCTION STKS 6f 1y(P)
5:30 (5:34) (Class 6) 2-Y-O
£2,781 (£827; £413; £206) **Stalls** Low

Form RPR
6 **1** **Miss Thoughtful**[7] 6442 2-8-13 0........................ PatCosgrave 10 65
(Jamie Osborne) *wl in tch in 4th: gng wl whn carried v wd by rival off home bnd 2f out: sn rdn and picked up really wl ld fnl 50yds: did wl to win* **4/1**[3]
3 **2** nk **Simply Silca (IRE)**[26] 5729 2-9-2 0........................ ShaneKelly 2 68
(Richard Hughes) *trckd ldr on inner: pushed into ld whn ldr blew bnd 2f out: sn rdn w 1 l ld 1f out: kpt on but hdd by wnr fnl 50yds* **8/1**
3352 **3** 1/2 **Ossco**[16] 6113 2-8-10 69........................ MarcoGhiani(7) 7 67
(Mohamed Moubarak) *hld up on inner: hdwy into midfield gng wl over 2f out: rdn and rapid hdwy over 1f out: kpt on wl: nt rch ldng pair (jockey said gelding suffered interference at the start)* **5/2**[1]
4 1 **Great Aim (IRE)** 2-9-3 0........................ DavidEgan 6 64
(James Tate) *trckd ldr: carried wd by ldr off home bnd 2f out: rdn to chse ldr over 1f out: kpt on* **3/1**[2]
5 1 3/4 **Wa'ad** 2-8-12 0........................ CharlesBishop 11 54+
(Denis Coakley) *racd in midfield: keen at times: hdwy under hands and heels 2f out: swtchd lft over 1f out: kpt on wl fnl f under hand riding* **14/1**
66 **6** 3/4 **Koovers (IRE)**[23] 5838 2-9-3 0........................(e[1]) LukeMorris 1 57
(Gay Kelleway) *midfield on inner: rdn along and no imp 2f out: kpt on one pce fnl f* **33/1**
7 1 1/4 **Oasis Song** 2-9-2 0........................ CharlieBennett 9 52
(Hughie Morrison) *midfield: pushed along and outpcd 2f out: one pce fnl f (jockey said filly jumped left-handed leaving the stalls and then hung right handed)* **10/1**
00 **8** nk **Village Rock (IRE)**[86] 3491 2-9-5 0........................ PatDobbs 5 54
(Richard Hughes) *pushed into ld early: rdn along and rn wd off home bnd 2f out: immediately hdd & wknd fr over 1f out* **33/1**
0 **9** 1 1/2 **Lisbeth Salander (IRE)**[17] 6079 2-9-0 0........................ RobertWinston 3 44
(Richard Spencer) *in rr of midfield on inner: rdn along and no imp over 1f out: one pce fnl f* **16/1**
0 **10** 1 **Stopnsearch**[38] 5314 2-9-4 0........................ TomQueally 4 45
(Brett Johnson) *in rr on outer: rdn and outpcd 2f out: a bhd* **14/1**
11 nk **Heleta** 2-8-8 0........................ DarraghKeenan(3) 8 37
(Peter Hedger) *hld up: outpcd in rr 2f out: n.d* **33/1**
06 **12** 1 1/4 **Goodman Square**[22] 5907 2-8-11 0........................(p) JosephineGordon 12 34
(Mark Usher) *hld up: a in rr* **50/1**

1m 13.3s (1.40) **Going Correction** -0.05s/f (Stan) 12 Ran SP% 123.8
Speed ratings (Par 92): **88,87,86,85,83 82,80,80,78,76 76,74**
CSF £36.88 TOTE £5.70: £1.90, £2.10, £1.20; EX 30.20 Trifecta £86.20.
Owner The Q Party **Bred** Moyns Park Estate And Stud Ltd **Trained** Upper Lambourn, Berks

FOCUS
Just a fair novice.

6720 LIN PURVEY BIRTHDAY CELEBRATION H'CAP 1m 7f 169y(P)
6:00 (6:05) (Class 5) (0-70,72) 3-Y-O+
£3,428 (£1,020; £509; £400; £400; £400) **Stalls** Low

Form RPR
4032 **1** **Cogital**[8] 6419 4-9-12 **66**........................(h) PatDobbs 9 75+
(Amanda Perrett) *settled in midfield: hdwy between rivals into 4th over 3f out: hdwy to ld on outer wl over 2f out: sn rdn and kicked 5 l clr 1f out: drvn and reduced margin fnl f: jst hld on* **5/2**[1]
-2P0 **2** nk **Continuum**[52] 4791 10-9-9 **63**........................(v) TomQueally 3 69
(Peter Hedger) *dwlt and racd in last: rdn in rr 2f out: drvn and styd on wl fnl f: nt rch wnr* **25/1**
4410 **3** 1 1/2 **Colwood**[51] 4825 5-9-11 **68**........................(p) DarraghKeenan(3) 5 72
(Robert Eddery) *trckd ldr: rdn along and readily outpcd by wnr over 2f out: kpt on again fnl f* **7/1**
-105 **4** 3/4 **Break The Rules**[29] 5623 3-9-2 **68**........................ EoinWalsh 1 71
(Martin Smith) *racd in midfield: pushed along and no imp 3f out: rdn 2f out: kpt on fnl f (jockey said filly ran in snatches)* **18/1**
5335 **5** nk **Gavlar**[24] 5812 8-10-4 **72**........................(v) DavidEgan 7 75
(William Knight) *led: rdn along and hdd by wnr wl over 2f out: drvn and lost 3 pls fnl f* **9/2**[3]
0005 **6** 3 1/4 **Yvette**[23] 5851 3-8-6 **58**........................(p[1]) LukeMorris 6 59+
(Sir Mark Prescott Bt) *trckd ldr: rdn along and outpcd by wnr over 2f out: drvn and one pce over 1f out: wknd clsng stages* **11/4**[2]
2215 **7** 44 **Tin Fandango**[123] 2239 4-9-13 **67**........................(p) JosephineGordon 8 13
(Mark Usher) *hld up: niggled along 5f out: rdn and detached 2f out: eased fnl f (jockey said gelding was never travelling)* **10/1**
003 **8** 36 **Lucy Lou (IRE)**[18] 6043 3-9-3 **69**........................ RobertWinston 2
(Charles Hills) *midfield on outer: rdn and lost pl 5f out: sn detached (jockey said filly hung left-handed from halfway)* **7/1**

3m 20.59s (-5.11) **Going Correction** -0.05s/f (Stan)
WFA 3 from 4yo+ 12lb 8 Ran SP% 116.6
Speed ratings (Par 103): **110,109,109,108,108 106,84,66**
CSF £64.10 CT £396.29 TOTE £3.20: £1.20, £7.40, £2.30; EX 78.20 Trifecta £252.00.
Owner John Connolly & Odile Griffith **Bred** Meon Valley Stud **Trained** Pulborough, W Sussex

FOCUS
A tight finish in the end but the winner was value for an easier win.

6721 BRITISH EBF PREMIER FILLIES' H'CAP 1m 1y(P)
6:30 (6:32) (Class 3) (0-95,92) 3-Y-O+
£12,450 (£3,728; £1,864; £932; £466; £234) **Stalls** High

Form RPR
01-0 **1** **Dubai Blue (USA)**[108] 2745 3-9-2 **88**........................ JosephineGordon 2 103+
(Saeed bin Suroor) *settled in rr: effrt to chse ldrs 2f out: rdn on outer and rapid hdwy to ld 1f out: sn clr: easily* **8/1**
2053 **2** 3 1/4 **Hateya (IRE)**[8] 6406 4-9-12 **92**........................ PatCosgrave 4 97+
(Jim Boyle) *midfield: bmpd along on inner 2f out: nowhere to go on inner and swtchd rt to outer over 1f out: rdn and styd on wl fnl f: nvr able to chal* **6/1**[3]
-100 **3** 1/2 **Lady Madison (IRE)**[50] 4865 3-9-0 **86**........................ ShaneKelly 7 89
(Richard Hughes) *chsd ldr and racd freely: effrt to chse ldr 2f out: rdn and readily outpcd by wnr 1f out: kpt on* **25/1**
0-22 **4** 1 1/4 **Nkosikazi**[51] 4851 4-9-10 **90**........................ TomMarquand 3 91
(William Haggas) *trckd ldr: rdn and no imp 2f out: sn drvn and one pce fnl f* **7/2**[2]
-321 **5** 1/2 **Scentasia**[24] 5827 3-9-1 **87**........................ NickyMackay 6 86
(John Gosden) *dwlt and racd in last: hdwy into midfield on outer 5f out: rdn and no imp 2f out: one pce fnl f* **6/4**[1]
1100 **6** 2 3/4 **Invitational**[21] 5944 3-9-4 **90**........................ DavidEgan 8 83
(Roger Varian) *led: rdn along and hdd by wnr 1f out: wknd fnl f* **8/1**
5021 **7** nk **Visionara**[16] 6111 3-8-9 **81**........................ LukeMorris 5 73
(Simon Crisford) *racd in midfield: pushed along to chse ldr 2f out: sn rdn and no imp over 1f out: wknd fnl f* **6/1**[3]
0100 **8** 1 1/4 **Daddies Girl (IRE)**[21] 5944 4-9-6 **89**........................ FinleyMarsh(3) 1 79
(Rod Millman) *in rr: racd awkwardly and lost grnd after 2f: rdn and detached 1/2-way: nvr on terms (jockey said filly moved poorly)* **16/1**

1m 34.99s (-3.21) **Going Correction** -0.05s/f (Stan)
WFA 3 from 4yo 6lb 8 Ran SP% 122.7
Speed ratings (Par 104): **114,110,110,109,108 105,105,104**
CSF £59.05 CT £1181.52 TOTE £9.30: £2.20, £2.30, £5.80; EX 68.90 Trifecta £2011.30.
Owner Godolphin **Bred** Godolphin **Trained** Newmarket, Suffolk

FOCUS
This was well run and the first two closed from off the pace.

6722 REBECCA AND MICHAEL H'CAP 1m 4f (P)
7:00 (7:06) (Class 5) (0-75,75) 3-Y-O

£3,428 (£1,020; £509; £400; £400; £400) **Stalls** Low

Form RPR
03-5 **1** **Sea Battle (FR)**[80] 3741 3-8-5 **62** DarraghKeenan(3) 1 69
(Jane Chapple-Hyam) *led for 2f then trckd ldr: clsd on ldr gng wl 2f out: rdn along to ld 1f out: drvn and kpt on wl fnl f (trainer's rep said, regarding the improved form shown, the gelding appreciated the return to the all-weather)* **12/1**

1214 **2** 1 ¼ **Dreamweaver (IRE)**[23] 5861 3-9-7 **75** LiamKeniry 6 80
(Ed Walker) *hld up: effrt on outer over 2f out: rdn and hung in lft bhd wnr over 1f out: kpt on wl clsng stages* **11/8**[1]

3020 **3** 1 ¼ **Bolt N Brown**[70] 4110 3-8-11 **65** (t) LukeMorris 7 68
(Gay Kelleway) *led after 2f at stdy pce: effrt to qckn tempo 2f out: rdn and hdd by wnr 1f out: no ex* **20/1**

2106 **4** 1 **Edmond Dantes (IRE)**[25] 5779 3-9-3 **71** DavidEgan 4 72
(David Menuisier) *settled in midfield: lost pl over 3f out: rdn on inner and wnt 4th 2f out: no further imp fnl f* **5/1**[2]

4112 **5** 3 ¾ **Oliver Hardy**[21] 5954 3-8-12 **73** (t) MarcoGhiani(7) 2 68
(Paul Cole) *racd in midfield: hdwy into 2nd 4f out: rdn and lost pl 2f out: wknd sn after* **7/1**[3]

0466 **6** 4 **Allocator (FR)**[7] 6463 3-8-13 **67** PatDobbs 5 56
(Richard Hannon) *racd keenly in last: effrt to cl on outer over 2f out: rdn to chse ldr 2f out: outpcd over 1f out: wknd fnl f* **10/1**

2m 32.55s (-0.45) **Going Correction** -0.05s/f (Stan) **6** Ran SP% **92.8**
Speed ratings (Par 100): **99,98,97,96,94 91**
CSF £19.47 TOTE £12.20: £4.10, £1.30; EX 28.50 Trifecta £225.90.
Owner Mrs B V Sangster & B V Sangster **Bred** Ben Sangster **Trained** Dalham, Suffolk
■ Dame Freya Stark was withdrawn. Price at time of withdrawal 3/1. Rule 4 applies to all bets - deduction 25p in the pound

FOCUS
There was a false start and Dame Freya Stark was withdrawn after bursting out of the stalls. On the second try, the gallop was a steady one and it turned into a bit of a sprint.

6723 ASTON GROUP H'CAP 1m 2f (P)
7:30 (7:34) (Class 6) (0-55,57) 3-Y-O+

£2,781 (£827; £413; £400; £400; £400) **Stalls** Low

Form RPR
5402 **1** **Fame N Fortune**[12] 6279 3-9-0 **55** (b) CharlesBishop 13 61
(Joseph Tuite) *racd in midfield: effrt to chse ldrs over 2f out: rdn and picked up wl over 1f out: drvn and styd on v strly to ld post* **6/1**[3]

-600 **2** nse **Golden Deal (IRE)**[66] 4232 4-8-12 **46** oh1 LukeMorris 8 51
(Richard Phillips) *prom in 4th: pushed along to chse ldr 2f out: rdn to ld 1f out: drvn fnl f: hdd post* **28/1**

5021 **3** nk **Voice Of A Leader (IRE)**[18] 6049 8-9-5 **53** JoeyHaynes 1 57
(Chelsea Banham) *racd in midfield: effrt to chse ldrs 2f out: rdn over 1f out: kpt on wl fnl f* **5/1**[2]

0001 **4** ½ **Quemonda**[12] 6279 3-9-2 **57** PatDobbs 5 61
(Ken Cunningham-Brown) *trckd ldr: clsd travelling strly over 1f out: short of room and nowhere to go 1f out: rdn once in clr fnl 100yds and unable qck* **7/4**[1]

4002 **5** 1 ¾ **Cat Royale (IRE)**[18] 6049 6-9-1 **49** (b) DannyBrock 7 49
(John Butler) *chsd ldr: rdn to ld 2f out: drvn and hdd by wnr 1f out: no ex* **10/1**

0304 **6** 1 **Gerry The Glover (IRE)**[28] 5675 7-9-7 **55** (v) TomMarquand 3 53
(Lee Carter) *in rr of midfield: rdn and no imp 2f out: sme late hdwy fnl f* **16/1**

2500 **7** hd **Nicky Baby (IRE)**[18] 6049 5-8-8 **47** (b) SophieRalston(5) 6 45
(Dean Ivory) *led: rdn along and hdd 2f out: wknd fnl f* **16/1**

0502 **8** nk **Heatherdown (IRE)**[16] 6117 3-8-13 **54** (v) RobertWinston 4 52
(Ian Williams) *racd in midfield: effrt on inner 2f out: sn rdn and no imp over 1f out: one pce fnl f* **7/1**

5000 **9** 2 ¼ **Luxford**[18] 6049 5-8-12 **46** oh1 (v) ShaneKelly 9 39
(Gary Moore) *hld up: effrt into midfield 2f out: rdn and no imp 1f out: one pce fnl f* **33/1**

054 **10** 1 ¼ **Mousquetaire (FR)**[47] 5004 3-8-11 **52** (h) DavidEgan 2 44
(David Menuisier) *in rr of midfield: rdn and outpcd 2f out: nvr on terms* **14/1**

00-0 **11** shd **Brilliant Riposte**[38] 5310 4-8-6 **47** MichaelPitt(7) 14 37
(Denis Coakley) *hld up: pushed along and dropped to last over 2f out: a in rr* **40/1**

0-00 **12** 1 ½ **Rainbow Spirit**[85] 3528 3-9-0 **55** LiamKeniry 11 44
(Ed Dunlop) *hld up: a in rr* **22/1**

0-50 **13** 6 **Milldean Felix (IRE)**[12] 6279 3-8-9 **50** (v) EoinWalsh 10 27
(Suzi Best) *hld up: a in rr (jockey said gelding ran too free)* **50/1**

0325 **14** 4 ½ **Nabvutika (IRE)**[52] 4794 3-8-12 **53** TomQueally 12 22
(John Butler) *midfield on outer: rdn along and lost pl 2f out: sn bhd* **16/1**

2m 7.4s (0.80) **Going Correction** -0.05s/f (Stan)
WFA 3 from 4yo+ 7lb **14** Ran SP% **128.4**
Speed ratings (Par 101): **94,93,93,93,91 91,90,90,88,87 87,86,81,78**
CSF £180.03 CT £928.82 TOTE £6.50: £2.30, £9.30, £2.20; EX 284.10 Trifecta £1223.20.
Owner Fame N Fortune Syndicate **Bred** L Perry, C Black, J Ball & P Aspell **Trained** Lambourn, Berks

FOCUS
They went a fairly steady gallop here, and there was a tight finish.
T/Plt: £149.90 to a £1 stake. Pool: £39,547.47 - 192.59 winning units T/Qpdt: £26.10 to a £1 stake. Pool: £6,549.90 - 185.07 winning units **Mark Grantham**

6667 SANDOWN (R-H)
Saturday, August 31

OFFICIAL GOING: Good to firm (watered; 7.5)
Wind: Moderate, against Weather: Fine but cloudy becoming overcast, light rain after race 5

6724 PLAY 4 TO SCORE AT BETWAY H'CAP 5f 10y
1:50 (1:50) (Class 3) (0-95,96) 3-Y-O+

£12,450 (£3,728; £1,864; £932; £466; £234) **Stalls** Low

Form RPR
0050 **1** **Justanotherbottle (IRE)**[10] 6351 5-9-9 **95** WilliamBuick 11 102
(Declan Carroll) *fast away: mde all: drvn and hrd pressed fnl f: hld on wl* **4/1**[1]

4063 **2** shd **Tinto**[8] 6413 3-9-0 **88** JasonWatson 13 95
(Amanda Perrett) *hld up in rr: rdn and prog on wd outside 2f out: chsd wnr over 1f out: str chal ins fnl f: jst denied* **10/1**

4502 **3** 1 **Embour (IRE)**[8] 6404 4-9-10 **96** RyanMoore 6 99
(Richard Hannon) *t.k.h: sltly impeded after s: hld up in rr: threaded through fr 2f out: drvn to press ldng pair ins fnl f: nt qckn last 75yds* **4/1**[1]

0402 **4** nk **Saaheq**[14] 6208 5-9-2 **88** DavidEgan 9 90+
(Michael Appleby) *hld up in rr: nt clr run wl over 1f out tl swtchd lft fnl f: r.o and clsd on ldrs nr fin (jockey said gelding was denied a clear run)* **8/1**[3]

4045 **5** nk **Jumira Bridge**[15] 6149 5-9-4 **90** (t[1]) OisinMurphy 3 91+
(Robert Cowell) *taken down early: hld up in last: gng strly whn nt clr run wl over 1f out tl jst ins fnl f: r.o wl nr fin but no ch of catching ldrs by then (jockey said gelding was denied a clear run)* **8/1**[3]

6214 **6** 1 **Daschas**[36] 5371 5-8-4 **83** (t) MarcoGhiani(7) 8 81
(Stuart Williams) *in tch in midfield: rdn and prog over 1f out: kpt on fnl f but nt pce of others* **9/1**

4030 **7** 2 ½ **Spoof**[73] 3993 4-9-4 **90** (h) KieranShoemark 7 79
(Charles Hills) *taken down early: sltly impeded after s: in tch: rdn to press for 2nd pl over 1f out: carried hd high and nt qckn: fdd fnl f* **20/1**

0005 **8** ½ **Gracious John (IRE)**[10] 6339 6-8-5 **84** AngusVilliers(7) 5 71
(Ian Williams) *t.k.h: prom: rdn over 2f out: wknd qckly fnl f* **14/1**

1113 **9** ½ **Only Spoofing (IRE)**[22] 5888 5-9-1 **87** KieranO'Neill 1 72+
(Jedd O'Keeffe) *taken down early: s.s: towards rr: nt clr run on inner over 1f out: no ch whn bdly hmpd ins fnl f (jockey said gelding was denied a clear run)* **7/1**[2]

0-3P **10** nk **Heartwarming**[70] 4101 3-9-4 **92** AdamKirby 12 76
(Clive Cox) *taken down early: chsd wnr to over 1f out: wkng whn short of room ins fnl f* **16/1**

0015 **11** 6 **Mountain Peak**[36] 5371 4-9-2 **88** LiamKeniry 4 50
(Ed Walker) *prom: pushed along 1/2-way: n.m.r 2f out: wknd qckly over 1f out* **12/1**

1m 0.38s (-0.92) **Going Correction** 0.0s/f (Good)
WFA 3 from 4yo+ 2lb **11** Ran SP% **118.8**
Speed ratings (Par 107): **107,106,105,104,104 102,98,97,97,96 87**
CSF £45.70 CT £175.65 TOTE £4.30: £1.70, £3.30, £1.80; EX 35.00 Trifecta £155.40.
Owner Steve Ryan & M J Tedham **Bred** John O'Connor **Trained** Malton, N Yorks
■ Stewards' Enquiry : William Buick three-day ban: careless riding (15-17 Sep)

FOCUS
All distances as advertised. A well contested and good quality sprint handicap. Plenty of these found trouble in-running.

6725 BETWAY HEED YOUR HUNCH H'CAP 1m 1f 209y
2:25 (2:26) (Class 2) 3-Y-O+

£28,012 (£8,388; £4,194; £2,097; £1,048; £526) **Stalls** Low

Form RPR
2336 **1** **Hyanna**[21] 5929 4-8-3 **90** GeorgiaDobie(7) 3 100
(Eve Johnson Houghton) *hld up in midfield: pushed along over 2f out: prog over 1f out nudged by rival but chsd ldr fnl f: styd on stoutly to ld nr fin* **10/1**

1001 **2** nk **Migration (IRE)**[23] 5861 3-8-7 **94** JasonWatson 6 103+
(David Menuisier) *hld up in last: rdn and swift prog on outer over 2f out to ld over 1f out: drvn fnl f: worn down nr fin* **9/4**[1]

0022 **3** 2 **Solid Stone (IRE)**[6] 6516 3-8-7 **94** DavidEgan 5 99
(Sir Michael Stoute) *trckd ldng pair: pushed along over 2f out: nt qckn wl over 1f out: styd on to take 3rd ins fnl f: nt pce to chal* **4/1**[3]

111 **4** ¾ **Country**[21] 5973 3-8-6 **93** (p) LiamJones 1 97+
(William Haggas) *hld up and sn in last pair: pushed along over 2f out: nvr any prog tl styd on wl last 150yds: nrst fin* **7/2**[2]

5003 **5** ¾ **Mordin (IRE)**[28] 5657 5-9-3 **104** (p) MarcoGhiani(7) 4 106
(Simon Crisford) *trckd ldrs: rdn and nt qckn 2f out: n.d after but styd on again ins fnl f* **11/2**

1334 **6** 1 **Mr Top Hat**[15] 6166 4-8-9 **89** OisinMurphy 9 89
(David Evans) *led: hrd pressed 2f out: hdd and fdd over 1f out* **20/1**

5-02 **7** hd **Mutaabeq (IRE)**[24] 5796 4-8-10 **90** JimCrowley 8 90
(Marcus Tregoning) *t.k.h: trckd ldrs on outer: clsd to chal and upsides over 1f out: wknd fnl f* **20/1**

4053 **8** 3 ½ **Ventura Knight (IRE)**[7] 6475 4-9-1 **95** (b) RyanMoore 7 88
(Mark Johnston) *trckd ldr: chal 2f out: upsides over 1f out: losing pl whn impeded sn after: wknd* **10/1**

1661 **9** 1 **My Boy Sepoy**[23] 5858 4-8-2 **82** LukeMorris 2 73
(Stuart Williams) *a in rr: rdn and no prog over 2f out: nvr a factor* **33/1**

2m 6.5s (-3.70) **Going Correction** 0.0s/f (Good)
WFA 3 from 4yo+ 7lb **9** Ran SP% **119.0**
Speed ratings (Par 109): **112,111,110,109,108 108,108,105,104**
CSF £33.14 CT £109.77 TOTE £12.40: £2.50, £1.30, £1.70; EX 42.80 Trifecta £171.50.
Owner G C Vibert **Bred** Al-Baha Bloodstock **Trained** Blewbury, Oxon

FOCUS
Three progressive 3yo headed the market for this warm-looking handicap. They went a stop/start pace and the runner-up looks worth upgrading, given he started his effort from last.

6726 BETWAY ATALANTA STKS (GROUP 3) (F&M) 1m
3:00 (3:01) (Class 1) 3-Y-O+

£39,697 (£15,050; £7,532; £3,752; £1,883; £945) **Stalls** Low

Form RPR
120 **1** **Lavender's Blue (IRE)**[92] 3316 3-8-12 **99** JimCrowley 1 108+
(Amanda Perrett) *trckd ldng pair: trapped bhd them fr over 2f out tl squeezed through 1f out: sn led and pushed clr: decisively* **12/1**

4311 **2** 1 ½ **Duneflower (IRE)**[36] 5369 3-8-12 105 FrankieDettori 4 103
(John Gosden) *sltly awkward s: sn chsd ldng trio: clsd 2f out: rdn to ld briefly 1f out: outpcd by wnr sn after: kpt on* **3/1**[2]

-402 **3** nk **Look Around**[36] 5369 3-8-12 103 OisinMurphy 7 102
(Andrew Balding) *hld up in midfield: rdn and clsd on ldrs over 1f out: nt pce to chal fnl f but styd on wl last 100yds to take 3rd fnl strides* **12/1**

2320 **4** hd **Solar Gold (IRE)**[29] 5608 4-9-4 97 TomMarquand 5 103
(William Haggas) *trckd ldr: chal 2f out: upsides 1f out: outpcd ins fnl f: lost 3rd last strides* **8/1**[3]

1-60 **5** 1 ¼ **Sh Boom**[92] 3316 3-8-12 87 TomQueally 6 99
(Peter Chapple-Hyam) *hld up in midfield: gng wl enough whn waiting for a gap 2f out: shkn up and nt qckn over 1f out: kpt on same pce after* **50/1**

2414 **6** 2 **Exhort**[34] 5475 4-9-4 100 PaulHanagan 9 95
(Richard Fahey) *hld up in last pair: shkn up 2f out: no real prog and nvr a factor* **20/1**

1133 **7** 1 **Jubiloso**[29] 5608 3-8-12 110 RyanMoore 3 92
(Sir Michael Stoute) *led: rdn and jnd 2f out: hdd and sltly impeded 1f out: wknd qckly (trainer's rep could offer no explanation for the performance shown)* **4/5**[1]

3052 **8** 5 **Red Starlight**[21] 5949 4-9-4 98 WilliamBuick 8 82
(Richard Hannon) *hld up in last pair: rdn and no prog 2f out: wknd over 1f out* **12/1**

1m 42.16s (-1.14) **Going Correction** 0.0s/f (Good)
WFA 3 from 4yo 6lb **8** Ran SP% **121.5**
Speed ratings (Par 113): **105,103,103,103,101 99,98,93**
CSF £51.14 TOTE £16.60: £3.40, £1.30, £3.10; EX 64.00 Trifecta £397.90.
Owner Benny Andersson **Bred** Chess Racing **Trained** Pulborough, W Sussex
■ Brassica was withdrawn. Price at time of withdrawal 66-1. Rule 4 does not apply

FOCUS
This looked a good opportunity for the odds-on favourite, who was upwards of 5lb clear on ratings, but she ran disappointingly and trailed in seventh behind the strong travelling winner.

6727 BETWAY SOLARIO STKS (GROUP 3) 7f
3:35 (3:37) (Class 1) 2-Y-O

£28,355 (£10,750; £5,380; £2,680; £1,345; £675) **Stalls** Low

Form RPR

12 **1** **Positive**[32] 5520 2-9-1 0 AdamKirby 6 108
(Clive Cox) *hld up off the pce in 4th: prog over 2f out: rdn to ld over 1f out: drvn and jnd last 100yds: fnd jst enough to hold on* **4/5**[1]

1 **2** nse **Kameko (USA)**[37] 5345 2-9-1 0 OisinMurphy 7 108
(Andrew Balding) *trckd clr ldng pair: shkn up 2f out: stl looked green and lost pl over 1f out: rallied strly fnl f: jnd wnr last 100yds: jst denied* **14/1**

21 **3** 1 **Al Suhail**[16] 6127 2-9-1 0 (h) WilliamBuick 5 105
(Charlie Appleby) *hld up off the pce in last: prog over 2f out: chsd wnr fnl f and looked a real threat: nt qckn and dropped to 3rd last 140yds* **7/4**[2]

311 **4** 5 **Hector Loza**[16] 6112 2-9-1 85 NickyMackay 4 92
(Simon Dow) *t.k.h: trckd clr ldr: clsd to ld wl over 1f out: sn hdd & wknd* **33/1**

01 **5** 1 ½ **Eshaasy**[24] 5809 2-9-1 0 JimCrowley 1 88
(John Gosden) *hld up off the pce in 5th: shkn up over 2f out: no prog and wl btn over 1f out (jockey said colt hung right-handed)* **10/1**[3]

6310 **6** 13 **Full Verse (IRE)**[30] 5587 2-9-1 90 BrettDoyle 3 55
(Charlie Appleby) *led: set scorching pce and had field strung out: hdd wl over 1f out: wknd rapidly and t.o* **50/1**

1m 27.88s (-1.42) **Going Correction** 0.0s/f (Good) **6** Ran SP% **112.6**
Speed ratings (Par 104): **108,107,106,101,99 84**
CSF £14.06 TOTE £1.60: £1.10, £4.40; EX 11.10 Trifecta £18.30.
Owner A D Spence **Bred** Cheveley Park Stud Ltd **Trained** Lambourn, Berks

FOCUS
A fascinating edition of this Group 3 feature, which has an impressive recent roll of honour. The pacemaker ensured a strong pace and the first three home look really promising.

6728 BETWAY NURSERY H'CAP (JOCKEY CLUB GRASSROOTS NURSERY QUALIFIER) 7f
4:10 (4:10) (Class 4) (0-85,81) 2-Y-O

£6,469 (£1,925; £962; £481; £300; £300) **Stalls** Low

Form RPR

642 **1** **Imperial Empire**[16] 6127 2-9-1 75 WilliamBuick 5 78
(Charlie Appleby) *chsd ldrs: shkn up 2f out: clsd u.p to take 2nd fnl f: drvn ahd last 80yds: jst hld on* **5/2**[1]

233 **2** shd **Forbidden Land (IRE)**[30] 5577 2-9-4 78 RyanMoore 1 81
(Richard Hannon) *t.k.h early: hld up in midfield: rdn 2f out: prog jst over 1f out: styd on to take 2nd last 50yds and clsd on wnr: jst failed* **5/1**[3]

3354 **3** 1 **Swinley Forest (IRE)**[15] 6161 2-9-2 76 (p[1]) OisinMurphy 4 76
(Brian Meehan) *led: stl gng strly 2f out: shkn up over 1f out: kpt on but hdd by two rivals last 80yds* **6/1**

513 **4** nk **Silver Mission (IRE)**[31] 5550 2-9-2 76 PaulHanagan 3 76
(Richard Fahey) *t.k.h early: hld up towards rr: rdn 2f out: nt qckn over 1f out: styd on ins fnl f but nvr able to chal* **8/1**

1240 **5** 1 ¼ **Sir Arthur Dayne (IRE)**[9] 6375 2-9-5 79 (v) TomMarquand 8 75
(Mick Channon) *hld up in last pair: pushed along 3f out: rdn and sme prog 2f out: chsd ldrs 1f out: one pce after* **7/1**

0011 **6** 1 ¼ **Mac McCarthy (IRE)**[8] 6394 2-8-13 76 FinleyMarsh(3) 2 69
(Richard Hughes) *trckd ldr 1f: styd prom: lost pl over 1f out: steadily fdd* **12/1**

331 **7** 1 ½ **Moolhim (FR)**[21] 5940 2-9-7 81 AdamKirby 6 70
(Simon Crisford) *trckd ldr after 1f: stl gng wl 2f out: rdn over 1f out: lost 2nd and wknd qckly fnl f* **7/2**[2]

1263 **8** 1 ¼ **Constanzia**[9] 6372 2-8-7 67 KieranO'Neill 7 53
(Jamie Osborne) *dwlt: hld up: a in last: shkn up 2f out: no prog* **20/1**

1m 29.86s (0.56) **Going Correction** 0.0s/f (Good) **8** Ran SP% **117.8**
Speed ratings (Par 96): **96,95,94,94,92 91,89,88**
CSF £15.88 CT £69.24 TOTE £2.80: £1.20, £2.10, £2.10; EX 19.40 Trifecta £79.90.
Owner Godolphin **Bred** Godolphin **Trained** Newmarket, Suffolk

FOCUS
Some potential improvers were on show here in a competitive looking nursery.

6729 BETWAY LIVE CASINO H'CAP 1m
4:45 (4:47) (Class 4) (0-85,85) 3-Y-O+

£6,469 (£1,925; £962; £481; £300; £300) **Stalls** Low

Form RPR

2215 **1** **Siglo Six**[15] 6166 3-9-4 83 (h) KieranShoemark 9 92+
(Hugo Palmer) *hld up in last trio: rdn and prog on wd outside 2f out: drvn to ld last 150yds: kpt on wl* **14/1**

0526 **2** ½ **Delicate Kiss**[7] 6469 5-8-12 71 (b) LiamJones 7 78
(John Bridger) *dwlt: hld up in last trio: rdn 2f out: prog on wd outside fnl f: styd on to take 2nd nr fin: jst too late* **14/1**

4213 **3** 1 ¼ **Eligible (IRE)**[12] 6282 3-9-3 82 AdamKirby 12 85
(Clive Cox) *restless stalls: t.k.h: hld up in midfield and trapped wd to 1/2-way: rdn and prog on outer 2f out: led 1f out: sn hdd and lost 2nd nr fin* **3/1**[1]

2254 **4** nk **Ginger Fox**[21] 5947 3-8-6 78 (p) AngusVilliers(7) 4 80
(Ian Williams) *t.k.h: prom: rdn to chse ldr over 1f out and sn chalng: nt qckn fnl f: kpt on same pce nr fin* **5/1**[3]

2430 **5** shd **Baba Ghanouj (IRE)**[15] 6155 3-9-3 82 OisinMurphy 3 84
(Ed Walker) *trckd ldrs: pushed along 2f out: clsd and tried to chal jst over 1f out: nt qckn fnl f: kpt on nr fin* **4/1**[2]

1424 **6** 1 ½ **Silkstone (IRE)**[20] 5984 3-9-1 80 LiamKeniry 5 80
(Pam Sly) *hld up in midfield: urged along and tried to make prog on inner 2f out: no hdwy 1f out: wl hld after* **12/1**

0162 **7** shd **Mountain Rescue (IRE)**[23] 5862 7-9-12 85 (p) TomMarquand 8 85
(Michael Attwater) *led: kicked 2 l clr on inner 2f out: hdd & wknd 1f out* **8/1**

4-00 **8** nse **Destroyer**[7] 6460 6-8-11 70 PaulHanagan 1 69
(Tom Tate) *rousted early then t.k.h: trckd ldr to over 1f out: wknd* **25/1**

551P **9** hd **Biotic**[43] 5136 8-8-11 73 FinleyMarsh(3) 11 72
(Rod Millman) *slowly away: hld up in last: rdn over 2f out: stl last ins fnl f: styd on wl last 100yds* **12/1**

5036 **10** 2 ¼ **Mr Tyrrell (IRE)**[15] 6155 5-9-11 84 SeanLevey 10 78
(Richard Hannon) *hld up in midfield: rdn 2f out: no prog over 1f out: wknd fnl f* **10/1**

1643 **11** 1 **Poetic Force (IRE)**[24] 5804 5-9-6 79 (t) GeorgeDowning 2 70
(Tony Carroll) *prom: rdn 2f out: nt qckn over 1f out: wknd fnl f* **14/1**

1m 42.5s (-0.80) **Going Correction** 0.0s/f (Good)
WFA 3 from 5yo+ 6lb **11** Ran SP% **121.1**
Speed ratings (Par 105): **104,103,102,101,101 100,100,100,100,97 96**
CSF £200.37 CT £765.72 TOTE £18.00: £5.10, £4.10, £1.70; EX 214.40 Trifecta £1163.20.
Owner John Livock & Nat Lacy **Bred** W Hennessey **Trained** Newmarket, Suffolk

FOCUS
They set off quickly in this and it suited those that were held up off the pace. It was a busy finish the lead changing hands several times in the final 2f.

6730 BETWAY CASINO H'CAP 1m 1f 209y
5:20 (5:20) (Class 4) (0-85,87) 3-Y-O+

£6,469 (£1,925; £962; £481; £300; £300) **Stalls** Low

Form RPR

410 **1** **Dubai Instinct**[105] 2828 3-9-0 85 AngusVilliers(7) 3 92
(Brian Meehan) *t.k.h: trckd ldr: led over 2f out: rdn over 1f out: kpt on wl and a holding off chalrs* **5/2**[2]

1564 **2** ½ **Simoon (IRE)**[51] 4837 5-9-10 81 KieranShoemark 5 87
(Andrew Balding) *racd wd: hld up: shkn up 2f out: clsd on ldrs over 1f out: drvn to chse wnr last 100yds: styd on but a hld* **7/2**[3]

-624 **3** 2 **Cheer The Title (IRE)**[21] 5970 4-9-8 79 PaulHanagan 2 81
(Tom Clover) *slowly away: t.k.h: hld up in last: shkn up and prog 2f out: chsd wnr 1f out and tried to chal: nt qckn and lost 2nd last 100yds: fdd nr fin* **9/2**

1-06 **4** 2 ½ **Thorn**[20] 5984 3-8-7 71 (h) KieranO'Neill 6 69
(Peter Hiatt) *plld hrd early: trckd ldng pair: chal and w wnr over 2f out to over 1f out: lost 2nd and wknd fnl f (jockey said gelding stumbled turning for home)* **25/1**

5 8 **Chef De Troupe (FR)**[14] 6-9-9 80 LiamKeniry 1 61
(Dr Richard Newland) *sn led: hdd & wknd over 2f out* **10/1**

5025 **6** 1 ¼ **Loch Ness Monster (IRE)**[21] 5973 3-9-4 87 (p) TheodoreLadd(5) 4 67
(Michael Appleby) *t.k.h: sn hld up in 5th: pushed along and struggling wl over 2f out: sn no ch (jockey said gelding ran too free)* **2/1**[1]

2m 11.75s (1.55) **Going Correction** 0.0s/f (Good)
WFA 3 from 4yo+ 7lb **6** Ran SP% **115.2**
Speed ratings (Par 105): **93,92,91,89,82 81**
CSF £12.11 TOTE £3.00: £1.70, £2.80; EX 12.00 Trifecta £41.80.
Owner Araam **Bred** Car Colston Hall Stud **Trained** Manton, Wilts

FOCUS
They went very steadily here and the first two finished clear.
T/Jkpt: Not Won. T/Plt: £105.30 to a £1 stake. Pool: £138,189.49 - 957.43 winning units T/Qpdt: £26.70 to a £1 stake. Pool: £12,193.18 - 336.85 winning units **Jonathan Neesom**

6681 WOLVERHAMPTON (A.W) (L-H)
Saturday, August 31

OFFICIAL GOING: Tapeta: standard
Wind: Fresh behind Weather: Fine

6731 FOLLOW US ON FACEBOOK @DESKSTOR H'CAP 1m 142y (Tp)
2:20 (2:21) (Class 6) (0-60,60) 3-Y-O+

£3,428 (£1,020; £509; £300; £300; £300) **Stalls** Low

Form RPR

4406 **1** **French Twist**[11] 6317 3-8-13 59 (p[1]) ThomasGreatrex(5) 5 65
(David Loughnane) *sn chsng ldr: rdn to ld over 1f out: styd on* **15/2**

0060 **2** 1 **I Think So (IRE)**[18] 6059 4-9-7 55 (b[1]) PJMcDonald 4 59
(David Loughnane) *sn led: rdn and hdd over 1f out: styd on same pce towards fin* **12/1**

4406 **3** hd **Sea Shack**[16] 6117 5-8-11 50 (tp) ThoreHammerHansen(5) 1 53
(Julia Feilden) *led early: chsd ldrs: rdn over 1f out: r.o* **11/2**[2]

005 **4** 4 ½ **Knightfall**[16] 6119 3-9-3 58 DanielMuscutt 9 52
(David Lanigan) *sn prom: rdn over 2f out: styd on same pce fnl f* **2/1**[1]

6350 **5** 3 **Mister Musicmaster**[10] 6334 10-9-4 55 WilliamCox(3) 12 43
(Ron Hodges) *chsd ldrs: stdd and lost pl over 7f out: rdn over 2f out: n.d after* **20/1**

-000 **6** ½ **Mr Spirit (IRE)**[21] 5946 3-8-9 57 (b) StefanoCherchi(7) 3 44
(Marco Botti) *s.i.s: hld up: shkn up over 1f out: nvr on terms* **18/1**

004 **7** 1 ¾ **Steal The Scene (IRE)**[11] 6327 7-9-5 56 (tp) MeganNicholls(3) 13 39
(Kevin Frost) *s.s: hld up: rdn and edgd lft over 1f out: nvr nrr (jockey said gelding was slowly away)* **8/1**

-042 **8** ½ **Show The Money**[70] 4131 4-9-11 59 TrevorWhelan 7 41
(Ivan Furtado) *wnt rt s: hld up: hdwy over 2f out: rdn over 1f out: wknd ins fnl f (vet reported gelding lost its right fore shoe)* **6/1**[3]

2050 **9** ½ **Lord Murphy (IRE)**[28] 5675 6-9-5 53 (t) AndrewMullen 10 34
(Mark Loughnane) *s.i.s: hld up: nvr on terms* **14/1**

-000 **10** 3/4 **Dyagilev**[24] 5816 4-9-10 **58**...(p) RoystonFfrench 8 37
(Lydia Pearce) *s.i.s and hmpd s: rdn over 3f out: n.d* **25/1**

5060 **11** 5 **Arrowzone**[33] 5497 8-9-11 **59**... CallumShepherd 6 28
(Katy Price) *prom: rdn over 3f out: wknd over 1f out* **16/1**

0000 **12** 20 **Axel Jacklin**[91] 3354 3-9-2 **57**... JoeyHaynes 11
(Chelsea Banham) *sn pushed along in rr: wknd over 3f out* **20/1**

1m 49.25s (-0.85) **Going Correction** -0.10s/f (Stan)
WFA 3 from 4yo+ 7lb 12 Ran SP% **124.8**
Speed ratings (Par 101): **99,98,97,93,91 90,89,88,88,87 83,65**
CSF £96.34 CT £418.18 TOTE £8.20: £2.90, £4.20, £1.70; EX 106.10 Trifecta £704.50.
Owner Miss Sarah Hoyland **Bred** Godolphin **Trained** Tern Hill, Shropshire
■ Stewards' Enquiry : Trevor Whelan two-day ban: careless riding (Sep 15-16)

FOCUS
Bang average form, even for this grade and very little got into it in truth. The front three, who all raced on or near the speed, came clear in the straight.

6732 VISIT DESKSTOR.CO.UK FOR YOUR BUSINESS FURNITURE MAIDEN STKS 1m 1f 104y (Tp)
2:55 (2:56) (Class 5) 3-Y-O+ **£4,528** (£1,347; £673; £336) **Stalls** Low

Form RPR

4-25 **1** **Casanova**[109] 2713 3-9-5 85... RobertHavlin 12 94+
(John Gosden) *racd keenly in 2nd tl led wl over 6f out: clr over 2f out: eased nr fin* **5/4**[1]

2 4 1/2 **Great Esteem (IRE)** 3-9-5 0... PJMcDonald 10 83+
(Charlie Appleby) *s.i.s: hdwy over 3f out: edgd lft over 1f out: styd on to go 2nd wl ins fnl f: no ch w wnr* **7/4**[2]

2 **3** 2 1/4 **All Yours (FR)**[30] 5578 8-9-9 0... MeganNicholls(3) 11 78
(Sean Curran) *chsd ldrs: shkn up to chse wnr over 2f out: edgd lft and styd on same pce fr over 1f out: lost 2nd wl ins fnl f* **8/1**

4 12 **Exmoor Beast** 3-8-12 0... AledBeech(7) 2 53
(Peter Charalambous) *hld up: sme hdwy and hung rt over 2f out: nvr on terms* **66/1**

4-0 **5** nk **Reaction Time**[13] 6259 4-9-12 0... CallumShepherd 9 52
(Saeed bin Suroor) *led at stdy pce early: hdd wl over 6f out: chsd wnr tl rdn over 2f out: wknd over 1f out* **9/2**[3]

00 **6** 3 3/4 **Capla Huntress**[12] 6290 3-9-0 0... GeorgeWood 1 39
(Chris Wall) *s.i.s: a in rr* **100/1**

0 **7** 3 **Ho Whole Dream (IRE)**[154] 1417 3-9-5 0... SamJames 5 38
(Michael Easterby) *prom: rdn over 4f out: wknd over 3f out* **50/1**

0 **8** 1 1/2 **Inteldream**[30] 5592 3-8-12 0... StefanoCherchi(7) 7 35
(Marco Botti) *prom: nt clr run and lost pl after 1f: n.d after* **33/1**

40 **9** 16 **Viking Prince (IRE)**[12] 6290 3-8-12 0... RPWalsh(7) 8 1
(Ian Williams) *s.i.s: a in rr* **100/1**

10 1/2 **Gms Princess** 3-9-0 0... JoeyHaynes 4
(Sarah Hollinshead) *s.i.s: a in rr* **100/1**

11 3/4 **Alwisaam (IRE)** 3-9-5 0...(h[1]) RoystonFfrench 6
(Ed Dunlop) *s.i.s: rn green and a in rr* **20/1**

12 9 **Lethal Look** 3-9-2 0... GabrieleMalune(3) 13
(Sarah Hollinshead) *s.i.s: sn prom: rdn and wknd over 2f out (jockey said gelding stopped quickly)* **100/1**

1m 57.74s (-3.06) **Going Correction** -0.10s/f (Stan)
WFA 3 from 4yo+ 7lb 12 Ran SP% **125.2**
Speed ratings (Par 103): **109,105,103,92,92 88,86,84,70,70 69,61**
CSF £3.76 TOTE £2.10: £1.10, £1.10, £1.90; EX 4.80 Trifecta £17.00.
Owner HRH Princess Haya Of Jordan **Bred** Godolphin **Trained** Newmarket, Suffolk

FOCUS
Not much depth to this maiden but the third is a 121-rated hurdler who looks capable of winning on the level and the wiinner is clearly quite smart. The front three came a long way clear.

6733 DESKSTOR SUPPLIES CSCM IT SOLUTIONS CLAIMING STKS 1m 1f 104y (Tp)
3:30 (3:30) (Class 5) 3-Y-O+
£4,398 (£1,309; £654; £327; £300; £300) **Stalls** Low

Form RPR

6030 **1** **Ruby Gates (IRE)**[72] 4028 6-9-0 69... DylanHogan(5) 4 66+
(John Butler) *led: hdd over 6f out: remained handy: nt clr run wl over 1f out: rdn to ld ins fnl f: r.o* **5/1**[3]

4046 **2** 1 **Undercolours (IRE)**[26] 5730 3-8-12 67... StefanoCherchi(7) 9 69
(Marco Botti) *chsd ldr: led over 6f out: hdd over 4f out: remained handy: rdn and ev ch ins fnl f: edgd rt: styd on same pce towards fin* **14/1**

3010 **3** 1/2 **Anif (IRE)**[26] 5725 5-9-2 72... ThomasGreatrex(5) 3 63
(Michael Herrington) *s.i.s: hld up: hdwy on outer 5f out: chsd ldr over 3f out: led over 2f out: rdn and hdd ins fnl f: styd on same pce (jockey said gelding was slowly away)* **10/11**[1]

00-0 **4** 3/4 **Seven Clans (IRE)**[66] 4249 7-9-6 79...(b) BrendanPowell 1 61
(Neil Mulholland) *hld up in tch: rdn over 1f out: nt clr run ins fnl f: styd on* **9/1**

1000 **5** nse **Shovel It On (IRE)**[24] 5802 4-8-12 47...(bt) RaulDaSilva 6 53
(Steve Flook) *chsd ldrs: rdn over 2f out: kpt on* **22/1**

426 **6** 3/4 **Baladio (IRE)**[18] 6034 3-8-9 75... ConnorMurtagh(3) 7 58
(Richard Fahey) *prom: lost pl over 7f out: rdn over 2f out: hung rt over 1f out: styd on ins fnl f* **3/1**[2]

7 3 1/2 **By Rail**[17] 5-9-3 65...(h) RhiainIngram(5) 10 55
(Nick Littmoden) *s.i.s: racd keenly: hdwy over 7f out: rdn on outer over 2f out: no ex fr over 1f out* **14/1**

3400 **8** 3 1/2 **Final Attack (IRE)**[137] 1841 8-8-13 50...(p) GabrieleMalune(3) 5 42
(Sarah Hollinshead) *s.i.s: nvr on terms* **20/1**

6606 **9** 4 1/2 **Misty Breese (IRE)**[18] 6049 4-8-8 42... NoelGarbutt(3) 8 28
(Sarah Hollinshead) *chsd ldrs: led over 4f out: rdn and hdd over 2f out: wknd over 1f out (jockey said filly ran too free)* **50/1**

5-00 **10** 10 **General Patton**[11] 6327 5-8-12 37...(p) RoystonFfrench 2 10
(Lydia Pearce) *prom: lost pl after 1f: rdn and wknd over 2f out* **80/1**

2m 2.42s (1.62) **Going Correction** -0.10s/f (Stan)
WFA 3 from 4yo+ 7lb 10 Ran SP% **129.7**
Speed ratings (Par 103): **88,87,86,86,85 85,82,79,75,66**
CSF £76.08 TOTE £7.80: £2.00, £3.10, £1.10; EX 66.40 Trifecta £161.90.There was no bid for the winner
Owner Dave James **Bred** Max Morris **Trained** Newmarket, Suffolk

FOCUS
Quite a competitive claimer won by an inconsistent mare. Difficult form to evaluate.

6734 AVOID BACK PAIN BUY DESKSTOR CHAIRS SILK SERIES LADY RIDERS' H'CAP (PRO-AM LADY RIDERS' RACE) 1m 142y (Tp)
4:05 (4:06) (Class 4) (0-80,80) 3-Y-O+ £5,692 (£1,694; £846; £423; £300; £15) **Stalls** Low

3423 **1** **Noble Prospector (IRE)**[21] 5973 3-9-9 78... MeganNicholls(3) 8 85
(Richard Fahey) *hld up in tch: shkn up over 3f out: rdn to ld wl ins fnl f: jst hld on (vet reported gelding lost its left fore shoe)* **11/4**[2]

0245 **2** shd **Robero**[15] 6164 7-9-7 73...(e) GraceMcEntee(7) 10 79
(Gay Kelleway) *chsd ldrs on outer: led over 1f out: rdn and hdd wl ins fnl f: styd on* **15/2**

3240 **3** 3 1/2 **Brandy Spirit**[26] 5741 3-9-3 74...(h) MissJoannaMason(5) 4 72
(Michael Easterby) *hdwy 7f out: rdn over 2f out: nt clr run 1f out: styd on* **9/2**[3]

-361 **4** nk **Regal Director (IRE)**[7] 6456 4-10-2 80... MissBrodieHampson(5) 6 77
(Archie Watson) *chsd ldr over 7f out tl led 3f out: rdn and hdd over 1f out: no ex ins fnl f* **11/8**[1]

0010 **5** 1 1/4 **Alfa McGuire (IRE)**[15] 6179 4-9-12 76... PoppyBridgwater(5) 1 70
(Phillip Makin) *led: hdd 3f out: rdn and edgd rt 1f out: wknd ins fnl f* **12/1**

1006 **6** 2 3/4 **Stringybark Creek**[9] 6370 5-9-12 78... MissMichelleMullineaux(7) 7 66
(David Loughnane) *s.i.s: hld up: sme hdwy over 1f out: nvr on terms* **16/1**

4060 **7** 3/4 **Burguillos**[15] 6164 6-9-2 68...(t) MissAliceHaynes(7) 3 54
(John Butler) *awkward s: nvr on terms* **28/1**

1441 **8** 1/2 **Inner Circle (IRE)**[17] 6066 5-9-9 73...(p) RhiainIngram(5) 9 58
(Mark Loughnane) *hld up: rdn on outer over 2f out: n.d* **12/1**

0000 **9** 4 **Any Smile (IRE)**[52] 4807 3-8-9 61 oh1... ShelleyBirkett 5 37
(Julia Feilden) *prom 6f (jockey said filly was never travelling)* **33/1**

0-00 **10** 7 **Sinfonietta (FR)**[18] 6050 7-8-13 65...(p[1]) KateLeahy(7) 2 25
(Sophie Leech) *s.i.s: n.d* **66/1**

1m 48.31s (-1.79) **Going Correction** -0.10s/f (Stan)
WFA 3 from 4yo+ 7lb 10 Ran SP% **127.9**
Speed ratings (Par 105): **103,102,99,99,98 95,95,94,91,85**
CSF £26.36 CT £99.54 TOTE £4.00: £1.90, £2.20, £1.60; EX 21.60 Trifecta £103.60.
Owner Mr And Mrs J D Cotton **Bred** Allevamento Ficomontanino Srl **Trained** Musley Bank, N Yorks
■ Stewards' Enquiry : Poppy Bridgwater two-day ban: misuse of the whip (Sep 15-16)

FOCUS
Not many in-form contenders in here but the winner has run a series of good races in defeat and deserved this first success.

6735 PREMIER SUPPLIERS OF BUSINESS FURNITURE DESKSTOR.CO.UK H'CAP 5f 21y (Tp)
4:40 (4:41) (Class 3) (0-95,94) 3-Y-O **£14,231** (£4,235; £2,116; £1,058) **Stalls** Low

Form RPR

2304 **1** **Rocket Action**[32] 5530 3-8-12 85...(t) CallumShepherd 1 93+
(Robert Cowell) *hld up: hdwy: nt clr run and swtchd lft over 1f out: rdn to ld ins fnl f: r.o wl* **7/2**[2]

2043 **2** 1 1/4 **Scale Force**[15] 6183 3-7-13 75 oh5...(v) WilliamCox(3) 7 78
(Gay Kelleway) *prom: lost pl over 3f out: rdn over 1f out: r.o ins fnl f: wnt 2nd post* **20/1**

0032 **3** nk **Prince Of Rome (IRE)**[28] 5649 3-9-1 88...(tp) StevieDonohoe 6 89
(Richard Hughes) *hdwy over 3f out: rdn over 1f out: styd on* **4/1**[3]

1142 **4** nk **Wise Words**[46] 5014 3-9-7 94... PJMcDonald 3 94
(James Tate) *chsd ldrs: shkn up and hmpd over 1f out: styd on same pce wl ins fnl f* **9/4**[1]

4313 **5** hd **Enchanted Linda**[37] 5356 3-8-1 79... ThoreHammerHansen(5) 5 79
(Michael Herrington) *s.i.s: pushed along in rr: r.o ins fnl f: nvr nrr* **7/1**

3 **6** 1 **Broken Spear**[77] 3844 3-9-6 93...(p) AndrewMullen 2 89
(Tony Coyle) *w ldr tl rdn to ld over 1f out: hdd and no ex ins fnl f* **12/1**

1402 **7** 1 **Probability (IRE)**[15] 6148 3-8-8 88... KateLeahy(7) 4 80
(Archie Watson) *led over 3f: no ex ins fnl f* **7/2**[2]

1m 0.53s (-1.37) **Going Correction** -0.10s/f (Stan) 7 Ran SP% **120.2**
Speed ratings (Par 104): **106,104,103,103,102 101,99**
CSF £68.17 TOTE £5.40: £3.30, £9.60; EX 72.20 Trifecta £432.90.
Owner Robert Ng **Bred** Robert Ng **Trained** Six Mile Bottom, Cambs

FOCUS
A tight contest won in quite stylish fashion by a horse with potential now.

6736 BRING YOUR BRAND TO LIFE @DESKSTOR H'CAP 1m 4f 51y (Tp)
5:15 (5:16) (Class 4) (0-80,79) 3-Y-O+
£5,692 (£1,694; £846; £423; £300; £300) **Stalls** Low

Form RPR

3512 **1** **Chicago Doll**[29] 5623 3-8-13 76... ThoreHammerHansen(5) 8 87+
(Alan King) *pushed along early in rr: shkn up over 6f out: hdwy on outer over 2f out: led over 1f out: sn rdn: edgd rt ins fnl f: styd on wl: eased nr fin* **7/2**[2]

-013 **2** 1 1/4 **Stagehand**[42] 5198 3-9-6 78... CallumShepherd 1 86
(Charles Hills) *hld up: hdwy on outer over 1f out: rdn to chse wnr ins fnl f: styd on* **5/1**[3]

3105 **3** 5 **Quintada**[14] 6230 3-9-7 79... AndrewMullen 4 79
(Mark Johnston) *prom: chsd ldr over 9f out tl over 6f out: remained handy: rdn over 2f out: styd on same pce fr over 1f out* **12/1**

000 **4** 2 1/2 **Glan Y Gors (IRE)**[27] 4913 7-9-4 74...(p) AledBeech(7) 3 69
(David Thompson) *hld up in tch: chsd ldr over 6f out tl led wl over 1f out: sn rdn and hdd: edgd lft and wknd wl ins fnl f* **16/1**

0514 **5** 1 1/4 **State Of Affair (USA)**[37] 5347 3-9-6 78... PJMcDonald 9 72
(Ed Walker) *led over 10f out: rdn and hdd wl over 1f out: wknd ins fnl f* **11/8**[1]

1056 **6** 2 **Lost History (IRE)**[24] 5811 6-9-8 71... RyanTate 7 61
(John Spearing) *prom: rdn over 2f out: wknd fnl f* **10/1**

1354 **7** 8 **Dutch Uncle**[23] 5858 7-9-9 75...(p) MeganNicholls(3) 5 52
(Tom Clover) *s.i.s: hld up: shkn up over 2f out: nvr on terms* **12/1**

0004 **8** 3/4 **Ice Canyon**[27] 5706 5-9-2 65...(h) StevieDonohoe 2 41
(Kevin Frost) *chsd ldrs: rdn over 2f out: wknd over 1f out* **20/1**

4606 **9** 8 **Raven's Raft (IRE)**[9] 6371 4-8-3 59... LauraCoughlan(7) 6 22
(David Loughnane) *sn led: racd keenly: hdd over 10f out: remained handy: rdn over 3f out: sn wknd* **16/1**

2m 36.53s (-4.27) **Going Correction** -0.10s/f (Stan)
WFA 3 from 4yo+ 9lb 9 Ran SP% **122.0**
Speed ratings (Par 105): **110,109,105,104,103 102,96,96,90**
CSF £22.87 CT £195.41 TOTE £4.10: £1.60, £1.70, £3.40; EX 20.90 Trifecta £205.20.
Owner Hunscote Stud Limited **Bred** Bredon Hill Bloodstock Ltd **Trained** Barbury Castle, Wilts

FOCUS
One or two unexposed sorts in what looked a reasonable race for the grade. The front two both fall into that category and they came clear.

6737 BEST SHOWS IN WOLVERHAMPTON VISIT GRANDTHEATRE.CO.UK H'CAP — 6f 20y (Tp)
5:50 (5:54) (Class 6) (0-55,56) 3-Y-O
£3,428 (£1,020; £509; £300; £300; £300) **Stalls** Low

Form				RPR
6353	1		**Miss Gargar**15 6181 3-9-7 **55**.....(v) RobertHavlin 8 *(Harry Dunlop) chsd ldrs: pushed along 1/2-way: rdn to ld ins fnl f: r.o* **5/1**3	60
3040	2	3/4	**Senorita Grande (IRE)**28 5659 3-9-7 **55**.....(v) AndrewMullen 6 *(John Quinn) hld up: hdwy u.p over 1f out: r.o* **8/1**	58
024	3	1/2	**Maid Millie**15 6181 3-9-8 **56**.....(v) PJMcDonald 4 *(Robert Cowell) pushed along and hdwy over 4f out: rdn over 1f out: r.o* **5/2**1	57
04R0	4	hd	**Knockabout Queen**12 6285 3-9-5 **53**..... KierenFox 5 *(Tony Carroll) prom: pushed along 1/2-way: rdn and nt clr run ins fnl f: styd on (jockey said filly was denied a clear run 2f out)* **18/1**	54
0606	5	1	**Brother Bentley**15 6181 3-9-4 **52**.....(p) RaulDaSilva 3 *(Ronald Harris) sn chsng ldr: led over 2f out: rdn over 1f out: hdd ins fnl f: no ex towards fin* **12/1**	50
6-	6	1/2	**Frow (IRE)**38 5322 3-8-9 **46** oh1.....(p1) WilliamCox(3) 10 *(Des Donovan, Ire) led early: chsd ldrs: rdn over 2f out: styd on same pce ins fnl f* **22/1**	42
6640	7	hd	**Lincoln Red**15 6174 3-9-4 **55**..... ConnorMurtagh(3) 12 *(Olly Williams) sn pushed along in rr: hung rt and r.o ins fnl f: nvr nrr (jockey said gelding hung right in the home straight)* **16/1**	51
0560	8	1 1/4	**Salmon Fishing (IRE)**16 6130 3-9-8 **56**.....(p1) StevieDonohoe 7 *(Mohamed Moubarak) s.i.s: sn pushed along in rr: shkn up and hung lft over 1f out: nt rch ldrs* **6/1**	48
4600	9	nk	**Kadiz (IRE)**56 4642 3-8-13 **52**.....(p) RhiainIngram(5) 1 *(Paul George) hld up: hdwy over 1f out: no ex ins fnl f* **12/1**	43
0046	10	10	**Twilighting**16 6107 3-9-0 **48**..... CallumShepherd 2 *(Henry Candy) sn led: hdd over 2f out: wknd ins fnl f (jockey said filly lost its action)* **7/2**2	9
3306	11	2 1/2	**Chop Chop (IRE)**30 5582 3-9-2 **53**.....(bt) MeganNicholls(3) 11 *(Brian Barr) sn prom on outer: racd keenly: shkn up over 2f out: wknd and eased over 1f out (jockey said filly hung right. trainer's rep said filly had a breathing problem)* **20/1**	6

1m 14.57s (0.07) **Going Correction** -0.10s/f (Stan) **11 Ran SP% 128.5**
Speed ratings (Par 98): **95,94,93,93,91 91,90,89,88,75 72**
CSF £49.42 CT £128.87 TOTE £6.80: £2.00, £2.70, £1.50; EX 45.80 Trifecta £126.40.
Owner British Racing Club **Bred** Hungerford Park Stud **Trained** Lambourn, Berks

FOCUS
Modest form but they went a good gallop and the winner was never far off the speed.
T/Plt: £150.90 to a £1 stake. Pool: £48,327.32 - 233.70 winning units T/Qpdt: £40.30 to a £1 stake. Pool: £3,519.97 - 64.51 winning units **Colin Roberts**

6738 - 6745a (Foreign Racing) - See Raceform Interactive

6519
BADEN-BADEN (L-H)
Saturday, August 31

OFFICIAL GOING: Turf: good

6746a WACKENHUT MERCEDES-BENZ-PREIS ZUKUNFTSRENNEN (GROUP 3) (2YO) (TURF) — 7f
2:15 2-Y-O
£28,828 (£10,810; £5,405; £2,702; £1,801)

			RPR
1		**Alson (GER)**22 2-9-0 0..... FilipMinarik 5 *(Jean-Pierre Carvalho, Germany) racd keenly: hld up towards rr: plenty to do 1/2-way: hdwy over 2f out: str run to ld last 100yds: sn asserted* **39/10**2	105
2	2	**Well Of Wisdom**34 5481 2-9-2 0..... JamesDoyle 2 *(Charlie Appleby) prom on inner: 5 l 3rd and pushed along 2 1/2f out: sn clsd to ld ent fnl 2f: hdd narrowly 1 1/2f out: styd on u.p fnl f: regained 2nd but nt match wnr* **11/10**1	102
3	1/2	**Above (FR)**15 6184 2-9-0 0..... HollieDoyle 1 *(Archie Watson) chsd ldr on inner: cl 2nd whn ld changed ent fnl 2f: sn drvn and kpt on to ld 1 1/2f out: one pce u.p fnl f and lost two pls* **136/10**	99
4	3/4	**Virginia Joy (GER)**27 2-8-10 0..... AdriedeVries 6 *(J Hirschberger, Germany) midfield on inner: tk clsr order 2f out: styd on u.p to chse ldrs appr fnl f: one pce after* **151/10**	93
5	2 3/4	**Get Set (IRE)**20 6002 2-9-0 0.....(b) AntoineHamelin 4 *(Matthieu Palussiere, France) led outside rival: sn clr: led field towards stands' side st: hdd ent fnl 2f: grad dropped away fnl 1 1/2f* **37/1**	90
6	1 1/2	**Fearless King**34 2-9-0 0..... GeraldMosse 3 *(Frau S Steinberg, Germany) outpcd in rr: rdn and short-lived effrt 2 1/2f out: wknd ins fnl 1 1/2f* **58/10**3	86
7	nk	**Mangkhut (FR)**31 2-9-0 0..... LukasDelozier 9 *(Henk Grewe, Germany) chsd ldrs: rdn and drifted lft wl over 1f out: continued to edge towards ins: one pce u.p* **96/10**	85
8	1 3/4	**Game And Set**15 6159 2-8-10 0..... DavidProbert 7 *(Andrew Balding) prom on outer: rdn and nt qckn 2f out: dropped away appr fnl f* **33/1**	76
9	3	**Nona (GER)**34 2-8-10 0..... BauyrzhanMurzabayev 8 *(Mario Hofer, Germany) towards rr: rdn and no imp 2f out: wl hld fnl 1 1/2f* **222/10**	69
10	3 3/4	**Vallee Des Fleurs (GER)**62 2-8-10 0..... AndraschStarke 10 *(J Hirschberger, Germany) midfield on outer: rdn and no imp 2f out: wl hld fnl 1 1/2f* **269/10**	59

1m 25.07s (1.17) **10 Ran SP% 118.7**
PARI-MUTUEL (all including 1 euro stake): WIN 4.90 PLACE 1.60, 1.30, 2.20; SF 10.30.
Owner Gestut Schlenderhan **Bred** Gestut Schlenderhan **Trained** Germany

6747a T. VON ZASTROW STUTENPREIS (GROUP 2) (3YO+ FILLIES & MARES) (TURF) — 1m 4f
4:10 3-Y-O+
£36,036 (£13,963; £7,207; £3,603; £2,252)

			RPR
1		**Amorella (IRE)**27 5719 4-9-5 0..... MartinSeidl 1 *(Markus Klug, Germany) settled in midfield on inner: c towards stands' side w rest of field into home st: tk clsr order over 2f out: styd on to ld ins fnl 1 1/2f: r.o u.p* **125/10**	106+
2	2 1/4	**Durance (GER)**27 5720 3-8-10 0.....(p) AndraschStarke 5 *(P Schiergen, Germany) hld up towards rr: hdwy 3f out: drvn to ld over 2f out: hdd ins fnl 1 1/2f: styd on u.p: no ex fnl 75yds* **11/5**1	104
3	3	**Shailene (IRE)**28 5662 4-9-5 0..... DavidProbert 2 *(Andrew Balding) settled in fnl trio: clsd 2f out: styng on u.p in 4th whn sltly impeded ins fnl f: nt rch front pair* **41/10**3	98+
4	1 1/2	**Stex (IRE)**20 3-8-10 0..... BauyrzhanMurzabayev 4 *(R Dzubasz, Germany) chsd ldr on inner: outpcd by ldrs 1 1/2f out: drifted rt and slt impeded rival ent fnl f: one pce u.p* **29/1**	97
5	2	**Satomi (GER)**27 5720 3-8-10 0..... MaximPecheur 6 *(Markus Klug, Germany) plld hrd: restrained in midfield: rdn and no imp 2f out: kpt on at same pce u.p* **31/10**2	93
6	2 1/2	**Atlanta (GER)**37 6-9-5 0..... RenePiechulek 8 *(Dr A Bolte, Germany) chsd ldrs: outpcd wl over 1 1/2f out: sn btn* **42/1**	88
7	3/4	**Quantum Joy (GER)**48 3-8-10 0..... AdriedeVries 7 *(Lennart Hammer-Hansen, Germany) sn led: hdd 4f out but remained cl up: rdn but nt go w ldrs over 1 1/2f out: lft bhd appr fnl f* **269/10**	88
8	3 1/4	**Sword Peinture (GER)**34 5483 4-9-5 0..... FilipMinarik 3 *(Andreas Suborics, Germany) t.k.h: chsd ldrs: rdn to hold pl wl over 2f out: wknd ins fnl 1 1/2f* **173/10**	82
9	1/2	**Apadanah (GER)**27 5720 3-8-10 0..... AntoineHamelin 9 *(Waldemar Hickst, Germany) slowly away and adrift in last: rcvrd into fnl trio after 2f: rushed up to press ldr 1/2-way: led 4f out: hdd over 2f out: sn wknd u.p* **9/1**	82
10	22	**In Memory (IRE)**48 3-8-10 0..... MarcoCasamento 10 *(S Richter, Germany) w.w in fnl pair: last after 2f: lost tch wl over 2f out: t.o* **8/1**	47

2m 33.26s (-0.20) **10 Ran SP% 118.5**
WFA 3 from 4yo+ 9lb
PARI-MUTUEL (all including 1 euro stake): WIN 13.50 PLACE 3.20, 1.70, 2.30; SF 44.70.
Owner TINK Racing **Bred** Gestut Hof Ittlingen **Trained** Germany

6748 - 6753a (Foreign Racing) - See Raceform Interactive

6299
BRIGHTON (L-H)
Sunday, September 1

OFFICIAL GOING: Good to firm (7.9)
Wind: slight tail wind in straight Weather: Warm and overcast

6754 SUSAN CATT BIRTHDAY CELEBRATION H'CAP — 5f 60y
2:00 (2:00) (Class 6) (0-65,65) 3-Y-O
£2,781 (£827; £413; £400; £400; £400) **Stalls** Centre

Form				RPR
5322	1		**Urban Highway (IRE)**23 5878 3-9-4 **62**..... TomMarquand 8 *(Tony Carroll) hld up: effrt to cl on outer 2f out: rdn and gd hdwy to ld 1f out: kpt on strly* **7/2**2	69
2262	2	1 3/4	**Thegreyvtrain**5 6562 3-9-4 **62**..... OisinMurphy 4 *(Ronald Harris) trckd ldr: rdn along to ld over 1f out: drvn and sn hdd by wnr 1f out: kpt on* **2/1**1	63
4432	3	shd	**Zaula**5 6561 3-8-3 **47**..... DavidEgan 3 *(Mick Channon) racd in midfield: rdn and outpcd 2f out: kpt on wl clsng stages: no threat to wnr* **9/1**	48
463	4	1	**Pink Iceburg (IRE)**12 6299 3-9-0 **65**..... RhysClutterbuck(7) 1 *(Peter Crate) pushed along to trck ldr on inner: no imp on ldr 2f out: rdn between rivals 1f out: no ex* **7/2**2	64
0422	5	3/4	**Starchant**20 6023 3-8-7 **51**..... KieranO'Neill 5 *(John Bridger) prom on outer: rdn and a no imp over 1f out: kpt on one pce fnl f* **9/2**3	45
0-06	6	shd	**Illegitimate Gains**31 5575 3-8-2 **46** oh1.....(tp) RaulDaSilva 6 *(Adam West) hld up: pushed along in last 2f out: mde sme late hdwy fnl f* **40/1**	40
0000	7	3 3/4	**Not So Shy**20 6024 3-7-9 **46** oh1..... ElishaWhittington(7) 7 *(Lisa Williamson) restless in stalls: midfield: rdn along and outpcd over 1f out: wknd fnl f* **66/1**	27
0005	8	1	**Solesmes**9 6397 3-8-3 **47** oh1 ow1.....(b) MartinDwyer 2 *(Tony Newcombe) led: rdn along and hung lft whn hdd over 1f out: sn eased whn short of room 1f out (jockey said filly hung left-handed)* **20/1**	33

1m 3.15s (0.15) **Going Correction** -0.05s/f (Good) **8 Ran SP% 114.7**
Speed ratings (Par 99): **96,93,93,91,90 90,84,82**
CSF £10.81 CT £56.78 TOTE £4.90: £1.20, £1.02, £2.70; EX 11.20 Trifecta £43.10.
Owner Millen & Partner **Bred** J F Tuthill **Trained** Cropthorne, Worcs

FOCUS
All distances as advertised. A moderate 3yo sprint handicap, rated around the runner-up.

6755 HOLCOMBE MAIDEN AUCTION STKS — 5f 60y
2:30 (2:30) (Class 6) 2-Y-O
£2,781 (£827; £413) **Stalls** Centre

Form				RPR
424	1		**Spanish Angel (IRE)**36 5418 2-9-5 **81**..... OisinMurphy 1 *(Andrew Balding) settled in last: gd hdwy to go 2nd over 1f out: sn rdn and qckly asserted 1f out: rdn out* **4/6**1	78
62	2	2 3/4	**Newyorkstateofmind**76 3942 2-9-5 0..... MartinDwyer 3 *(William Muir) trckd ldr: pushed along to ld over 1f out: sn hdd by wnr 1f out: pushed out* **6/4**2	68
	3	11	**Freshwater Cliffs** 2-9-5 0..... DavidEgan 2 *(Richard Hughes) led: rdn along and hdd over 1f out: wknd fnl f* **9/1**3	30

1m 3.66s (0.66) **Going Correction** -0.05s/f (Good) **3 Ran SP% 110.0**
Speed ratings (Par 93): **92,87,70**
CSF £2.05 TOTE £1.60; EX 2.00 Trifecta £1.40.
Owner J Maldonado **Bred** Elaine Chivers **Trained** Kingsclere, Hants

FOCUS
A modest little 2yo maiden.

6756 CHANDLERS BRIGHTON MINI H'CAP — 5f 215y
3:00 (3:00) (Class 4) (0-85,86) 3-Y-O+ **£5,207** (£1,549; £774; £400; £400) **Stalls** Centre

Form — RPR
3626 1 **Red Alert**[6] 6525 5-9-10 **81**....................(p) TomMarquand 1 88
(Tony Carroll) *hld up: pushed along in last over 2f out: rdn and no immediate imp over 1f out: drvn and styd on strly fnl f to ld cl home (trainer said, regards apparent improvement in form, gelding appreciated a return to Brighton and coming from off a strong pace)* **8/1**
4312 2 ¾ **Chatham House**[15] 6220 3-9-13 **86**....................SeanLevey 6 91
(Richard Hannon) *midfield: t.k.h: effrt to chse ldr over 1f out: sn rdn 1f out: kpt on but nt gng pce of wnr clsng stages* **11/8**[1]
6131 3 ½ **Cent Flying**[16] 6162 4-8-13 **70**....................(t) MartinDwyer 5 73
(William Muir) *trckd ldr: rdn along to ld over 1f out: drvn and lost 2 pls fnl 50yds* **11/4**[2]
6616 4 *nk* **Enthaar**[12] 6301 4-9-1 **72**....................(tp) JasonWatson 2 74
(Stuart Williams) *prom on inner: rdn to chse ldr over 1f out: kpt on one pce fnl f* **15/2**
3216 5 1 ½ **Alicia Darcy (IRE)**[6] 6533 3-8-11 **77**....................(b) KateLeahy(7) 3 74
(Archie Watson) *hld up: rdn and outpcd 2f out: swtchd lft to far rail over 1f out: kpt on one pce* **7/1**[3]
5564 5 *dht* **Michaels Choice**[15] 6197 3-8-10 **69**....................(b[1]) OisinMurphy 4 66
(William Jarvis) *led: rdn and hdd over 1f out: wknd fnl f (jockey said gelding was slowly away)* **11/1**

1m 10.42s (-0.68) **Going Correction** -0.05s/f (Good)
WFA 3 from 4yo+ 2lb **6 Ran SP% 112.5**
Speed ratings (Par 105): **102,101,100,99,97 97**
WIN: 9.30 Red Alert; PL: 1.10 Chatham House 3.00 Red Alert; EX: 26.80; CSF: 19.70 CSF £19.70 TOTE £9.30: £3.00, £1.10; EX 26.80 Trifecta £78.20.
Owner A A Byrne **Bred** Miss Jacqueline Goodearl **Trained** Cropthorne, Worcs

FOCUS
There was a bunched finish to this feature handicap, but it's sound enough form.

6757 NEW BMW X5 NOVICE STKS (PLUS 10 RACE) — 6f 210y
3:30 (3:30) (Class 4) 2-Y-O **£4,463** (£1,328; £663; £331) **Stalls** Centre

Form — RPR
034 1 **Ziggle Pops**[16] 6154 2-9-5 75....................SeanLevey 1 77+
(Richard Hannon) *mde all: shkn up over 1f out: readily drew clr fnl f: comf* **1/1**[1]
2 5 **Herodotus (IRE)** 2-9-5 0....................OisinMurphy 3 62
(Andrew Balding) *trckd wnr: pushed along to chse wnr 2f out: kpt on one pce fnl f* **3/1**[2]
0 3 ½ **Anglo Saxon (IRE)**[51] 4886 2-9-5 0....................StevieDonohoe 4 60+
(Charlie Fellowes) *racd in last: rdn and outpcd 2f out: kpt on nicely fnl f: should do bttr* **9/1**
63 4 *shd* **Striding Edge (IRE)**[38] 5339 2-9-5 0....................FrannyNorton 2 60
(Mark Johnston) *trckd wnr: rdn to chse wnr 2f out: one pce fnl f* **10/3**[3]

1m 23.24s (-0.56) **Going Correction** -0.05s/f (Good) **4 Ran SP% 108.1**
Speed ratings (Par 97): **101,95,94,94**
CSF £4.23 TOTE £1.60; EX 4.50 Trifecta £11.90.
Owner Sullivan B'Stock/ Merriebelle Irish Farm **Bred** St Albans Bloodstock Ltd **Trained** East Everleigh, Wilts

FOCUS
This wasn't a bad 2yo novice contest.

6758 NEW BMW 3 SERIES H'CAP — 7f 211y
4:00 (4:00) (Class 6) (0-55,61) 3-Y-O+
£2,781 (£827; £413; £400; £400; £400) **Stalls** Low

Form — RPR
4104 1 **Harlequin Rose (IRE)**[12] 6305 5-8-11 **49**....................(v) CierenFallon(5) 8 56
(Patrick Chamings) *hld up: effrt into midfield 2f out: rdn and gd hdwy over 1f out: led ins fnl f: won gng away* **11/2**[3]
0050 2 1 ½ **Limerick Lord (IRE)**[25] 5806 7-8-8 **48**....................(p) SeanKirrane(7) 5 52
(Julia Feilden) *in tch in 3rd: pushed along and hdwy to ld over 1f out: rdn and hdd by wnr ins fnl f: no ex* **14/1**
2501 3 1 ½ **Joyful Dream (IRE)**[25] 5806 5-9-5 **52**....................(b) OisinMurphy 10 52
(John Butler) *hld up: effrt on outer to cl on ldrs over 2f out: rdn and minor hdwy over 1f out: kpt on fnl f* **5/2**[1]
3641 4 ¾ **Imbucato**[24] 5837 5-9-7 **54**....................(p) TomMarquand 6 52
(Tony Carroll) *midfield: rdn and outpcd over 2f out: sn drvn and kpt on one pce fnl f* **4/1**[2]
5361 5 2 ¾ **Cristal Pallas Cat (IRE)**[24] 5842 4-8-10 **48**....................RhiainIngram(5) 2 40
(Roger Ingram) *trckd ldr: rdn and outpcd over 1f out: wknd fnl f* **8/1**
0000 6 *hd* **Dalness Express**[8] 6462 6-8-5 **45**....................(tp) Pierre-LouisJamin(7) 1 37
(Archie Watson) *led: rdn along and hdd over 1f out: wknd once btn ins fnl f* **12/1**
6-01 7 2 ¾ **African Showgirl**[6] 6555 6-8-10 **50** 5ex....................GeorgiaDobie(7) 4 35
(Eve Johnson Houghton) *racd in midfield: rdn and no imp 2f out: briefly short of room and carried lft 1f out: no ex* **9/1**
0013 8 10 **Good Luck Charm**[12] 6305 10-10-0 **61**....................(b) HectorCrouch 9 23
(Gary Moore) *racd in midfield: gd hdwy on inner 2f out: rdn over 1f out: wknd fnl f (jockey said gelding moved poorly throughout)* **7/1**
-034 P **Highcastle (IRE)**[52] 4818 4-8-5 **45**....................(b) GavinAshton(7) 7
(Lisa Williamson) *s.i.s: sn completely t.o and p.u* **33/1**

1m 35.34s (-1.56) **Going Correction** -0.05s/f (Good) **9 Ran SP% 114.9**
Speed ratings (Par 101): **105,103,102,101,98 98,95,85,**
CSF £77.84 CT £239.75 TOTE £4.40: £1.60, £3.80, £1.40; EX 63.40 Trifecta £290.40.
Owner G E Bassett & P R Chamings **Bred** Langton Stud **Trained** Baughurst, Hants

FOCUS
A moderate handicap featuring plenty of course regulars.

6759 NEW BMW 8 SERIES/EBF FILLIES' H'CAP — 1m 1f 207y
4:30 (4:30) (Class 4) (0-80,82) 3-Y-O+ **£5,072** (£1,518; £759) **Stalls** High

Form — RPR
0200 1 **Quick**[18] 6081 3-9-7 **78**....................TomMarquand 3 83
(Richard Hannon) *trckd ldr: pushed along and briefly outpcd over 2f out: rdn and clsd on ldr 1f out: responded wl to press to ld cl home (trainers' rep said, regarding the apparent improvement in form, that filly benefitted from the step up in trip)* **15/2**[2]
2112 2 ½ **The Jean Genie**[13] 6289 5-10-3 **82**....................HollieDoyle 2 86
(William Stone) *led: shkn up w 3 l ld 2f out: rdn and reduced advantage 1f out: kpt on but hdd by wnr clsng stages* **11/10**[1]
011 3 10 **Cafe Sydney (IRE)**[23] 5880 3-7-8 **58**....................ElishaWhittington(7) 4 43
(Tony Carroll) *hld up off pce in last: rdn and readily outpcd by ldng pair 2f out: nvr on terms (jockey said filly was never travelling; trainer said filly ran flat)* **11/10**[1]

2m 3.41s (-1.59) **Going Correction** -0.05s/f (Good)
WFA 3 from 4yo+ 6lb **3 Ran SP% 107.0**
Speed ratings (Par 102): **104,103,95**
CSF £15.36 TOTE £5.30; EX 11.90 Trifecta £7.00.
Owner Mrs J Wood **Bred** Brightwalton Bloodstock Ltd **Trained** East Everleigh, Wilts

FOCUS
Despite just the three runners there was no hanging around in this fair little fillies' handicap.

6760 CHANDLERS BRIGHTON BMW AMATEUR RIDERS' H'CAP — 1m 1f 207y
5:00 (5:00) (Class 6) (0-65,67) 3-Y-O+
£2,682 (£832; £415; £400; £400; £400) **Stalls** High

Form — RPR
5246 1 **Light Of Air (FR)**[16] 6173 6-10-7 **59**....................(b) MissKatyBrooks(7) 2 65
(Gary Moore) *cl up in 3rd: pushed along and stdy prog to chse ldr over 1f out: rdn and led ins fnl f: all out (trainers' representative could offer no explanation for the apparent improvement in form)* **8/1**
2212 2 *nse* **Luna Magic**[7] 6507 5-11-8 **67**....................MissBrodieHampson 5 73
(Archie Watson) *led: shkn up 2f out: sn rdn and strly pressed by wnr over 1f out: hdd by wnr ins fnl f: rallied cl home* **7/4**[1]
0561 3 1 ½ **Brother In Arms (IRE)**[7] 6507 5-10-5 **50** 5ex....................MrAlexEdwards 7 53
(Tony Carroll) *dwlt sltly and racd in rr: rdn to chse ldrs over 1f out: kpt on fnl f: nrst fin* **7/1**
6403 4 *hd* **Noble Account**[24] 5841 3-10-13 **64**....................MrSimonWalker 6 68
(Julia Feilden) *trckd ldr: rdn along and no hdwy over 1f out: kpt on one pce fnl f* **7/2**[3]
0405 5 *nse* **Windsorlot (IRE)**[12] 6324 6-9-11 **45**....................(b) MissSarahBowen(3) 1 47
(Tony Carroll) *s.i.s: in rr of midfield: rdn along to chse ldr over 1f out: kpt on one pce fnl f* **10/1**
0-00 6 10 **Angel Of The North (IRE)**[2] 6681 4-9-12 **50**....................(v) MrFinbarMulrine(7) 3 33
(Robin Dickin) *hld up: outpcd over 2f out: a in rr* **33/1**
0602 7 ½ **Circle Of Stars (IRE)**[12] 6304 3-11-0 **65**....................MissJoannaMason 4 48
(Charlie Fellowes) *midfield: rdn and outpcd over 2f out: wknd fnl f (jockey said gelding was unsuited by the slow pace of the race)* **3/1**[2]

2m 7.91s (2.91) **Going Correction** -0.05s/f (Good)
WFA 3 from 4yo+ 6lb **7 Ran SP% 119.2**
Speed ratings (Par 101): **86,85,84,84,84 76,76**
CSF £23.84 TOTE £11.30: £5.10, £1.50; EX 28.80 Trifecta £187.40.
Owner G L Moore **Bred** Rabbah Bloodstock Limited **Trained** Lower Beeding, W Sussex
■ Stewards' Enquiry : Mr Alex Edwards £290 fine; using Mobile phone outside of the phone zone

FOCUS
This ordinary handicap, confined to amateur riders, was run at an uneven pace. Straightforward form.
T/Plt: £180.10 to a £1 stake. Pool: £83,808.53 - 339.52 winning units T/Qpdt: £81.00 to a £1 stake. Pool: £4,750.75 - 43.37 winning units **Mark Grantham**

6761 - 6768a (Foreign Racing) - See Raceform Interactive

6746 BADEN-BADEN (L-H)
Sunday, September 1

OFFICIAL GOING: Turf: good

6769a STADT BADEN-BADEN/VIERERWETTE (LISTED RACE) (3YO+ FILLIES & MARES) (TURF) — 7f
2:15 3-Y-O+ **£12,612** (£5,855; £2,702; £1,351)

RPR
1 **Wasmya (FR)**[74] 3-8-9 0....................Jean-BernardEyquem 1 106
(F-H Graffard, France) **59/10**
2 3 ½ **Miss Celestial (IRE)**[14] 6257 3-8-9 0....................(p) LukeMorris 4 96
(Sir Mark Prescott Bt) *prom on inner: styng on whn hmpd and swtchd ins under 2f out: sn rcvrd to chal 1f out: readily outpcd by wnr last 150yds* **23/5**[2]
3 ½ **Wishfully (IRE)**[24] 3-8-9 0....................WilliamBuick 14 95
(H-A Pantall, France) *w.w towards rr on inner: hdwy 2f out: styd on u.p to go 3rd ins fnl f: nt pce to chal* **41/10**[1]
4 ½ **Ghislaine**[92] 3-8-9 0....................BauyrzhanMurzabayev 3 94
(A Wohler, Germany) **154/10**
5 4 ¼ **Heavenly Holly (IRE)**[39] 5325 4-8-13 0....................JackMitchell 10 84
(Hugo Palmer) *prom on outer: drvn to press ldrs over 2f out: sn rdn and nt qckn: one pce fnl f* **26/5**[3]
6 *shd* **Peace Of Paris (GER)**[14] 6270 3-8-9 0....................MartinSeidl 2 82
(Markus Klug, Germany) **229/10**
7 ½ **Be My Best (GER)**[83] 5-8-13 0....................AdriedeVries 6 83
(T Potters, Germany) **246/10**
8 ¾ **Do It In Rio (FR)**[357] 5-8-13 0....................(p) FilipMinarik 15 81
(Tamara Richter, Austria) **28/1**
9 ¾ **Yanling (FR)**[44] 5168 5-8-13 0....................AntoineHamelin 7 79
(Matthieu Palussiere, France) **113/10**
10 4 ¾ **Adelante (FR)**[29] 5666 3-8-9 0....................DavidProbert 11 64
(George Baker) *towards rr: rdn and effrt on stands' rail 2f out: sn no further imp: wl hld fnl f* **153/10**
11 1 ¾ **My Snowdrop (IRE)**[98] 4-8-13 0....................AlexanderPietsch 9 61
(Claudia Erni, Switzerland) **45/1**
12 4 ¼ **Valrose (FR)**[359] 3-8-9 0....................MaximPecheur 8 48
(Claudia Erni, Switzerland) **165/10**
13 *nk* **Power Zone (IRE)**[37] 3-8-9 0....................EduardoPedroza 5 47
(A Wohler, Germany) **16/1**
14 6 ½ **Caesara**[14] 6270 4-8-13 0....................MichaelCadeddu 13 31
(Jean-Pierre Carvalho, Germany) **20/1**

1m 25.17s (1.27)
WFA 3 from 4yo+ 4lb **14 Ran SP% 118.5**
PARI-MUTUEL (all including 1 euro stake): WIN 6.90 PLACE: 2.10, 1.60, 1.70, 2.40; SF: 28.10.
Owner Al Shaqab Racing **Bred** Al Shaqab Racing **Trained** France

6770a **86TH OETTINGEN-RENNEN (GROUP 2) (3YO+) (TURF)** **1m**
2:55 3-Y-0+ **£36,036** (£13,963; £7,207; £3,603; £2,252)

RPR

1 **Vintager**[77] 3906 4-9-2 0 WilliamBuick 3 110+
(Charlie Appleby) *chsd clr ldr on inner: drvn to chal over 2f out: sustained run to ld appr fnl f: forged clr but drifted rt onto stands' rail: edgd bk ins late on: hld late chal* **4/5**[1]

2 *nk* **Nica (GER)**[42] 5230 4-8-13 0 RenePiechulek 7 106+
(Dr A Bolte, Germany) *chsd clr ldr on outer: drvn to ld narrowly over 2f out: hdd appr fnl f: rallied u.p: clsng on wnr last 100yds: jst hld* **9/2**[2]

3 *3* **Wonnemond (GER)**[21] 6-9-2 0 BayarsaikhanGanbat 1 102
(S Smrczek, Germany) *cl up in main gp: sltly outpcd and scrubbed along 2f out: styd on u.p fnl f: tk 3rd cl home: nt trble front pair* **67/10**[3]

4 *shd* **Ninario (GER)**[33] 4-9-2 0 MarcoCasamento 6 102
(Waldemar Hickst, Germany) *towards rr on inner: clsd fr 2 1/2f out: styd on u.p fr 1 1/2f out: chsd ldrs into fnl f: effrt flattened out late on: lost 3rd cl home* **177/10**

5 *2 1/2* **Crossing The Line**[22] 5944 4-8-13 0 DavidProbert 4 93
(Andrew Balding) *in rr: tk clsr order over 2f out: kpt on u.p: nvr able to get in contention* **15/2**

6 *8 1/2* **Palace Prince (GER)**[42] 5230 7-9-2 0 (p) FilipMinarik 8 76
(Jean-Pierre Carvalho, Germany) *cl up in main gp: chsd ldrs into st over 2f out: sn rdn and btn* **44/5**

7 *33* **Zargun (GER)**[7] 6519 4-9-2 0 (b) LukasDelozier 2 1
(Henk Grewe, Germany) *led: sn clr: c bk to field fr 3f out: hdd over 2f out: wknd qckly* **159/10**

1m 38.39s (-0.72) **7 Ran SP% 120.0**
PARI-MUTUEL (all including 1 euro stake): WIN 1.80 PLACE: 1.20, 1.30, 1.50; SF: 5.20.
Owner Godolphin **Bred** Thurso Bloodstock Ltd **Trained** Newmarket, Suffolk

6771a **147TH LONGINES GROSSER PREIS VON BADEN (GROUP 1) (3YO+) (TURF)** **1m 4f**
4:10 3-Y-0+ **£135,135** (£54,054; £22,522; £13,513)

RPR

1 **Ghaiyyath (IRE)**[126] 2168 4-9-6 0 WilliamBuick 7 128
(Charlie Appleby) *cl up tl led after abt 3f: kicked clr fr over 2f out and wnt towards stands' side: r.o strly: eased last 75yds: impressive* **23/10**[2]

2 *14* **Donjah (GER)**[28] 5720 3-8-9 0 LukasDelozier 8 104
(Henk Grewe, Germany) *towards rr on outer: rdn to chal for pls over 2f out: styd on u.p to take 2nd ins fnl f: nvr anywhere nr wnr* **19/1**

3 *4 1/4* **Laccario (GER)**[56] 4707 3-8-13 0 EduardoPedroza 1 101
(A Wohler, Germany) *prom on outer: scrubbed along over 2f out to join battle for pls: kpt on u.p: nvr trbld ldrs* **9/5**[1]

4 *4 1/2* **Colomano**[28] 5719 5-9-6 0 MaximPecheur 6 92
(Markus Klug, Germany) *led for abt 3f then chsd ldr: rdn and outpcd fr 2 1/2f out: plugged on at same pce* **34/1**

5 *2* **Accon (GER)**[28] 5719 3-8-13 0 JiriPalik 5 90
(Markus Klug, Germany) *midfield: rdn and no imp on ldr fr 2 1/2f out: tried to chal for pls ins fnl 2f: sn wknd* **164/10**

6 *4* **Akribie (GER)**[28] 5720 3-8-9 0 MartinSeidl 9 80
(Markus Klug, Germany) *towards rr on inner: drvn along 2 1/2f out: nvr in contention* **26/1**

7 *6 1/2* **Amiro (GER)**[56] 4707 3-8-13 0 (b) AlexanderPietsch 2 74
(M Figge, Germany) *chsd ldr on inner: rdn and wknd fr over 2f out* **42/1**

8 *28* **Ashrun (FR)**[28] 5718 3-8-13 0 OlivierPeslier 3 29
(A Wohler, Germany) *hld up in rr: pushed along to try and stay in tch 4f out: wknd and eased fr 2 1/2f out* **53/10**

9 *1/2* **Communique (IRE)**[21] 6007 4-9-6 0 JoeFanning 4 26
(Mark Johnston) *midfield on outer: pushed along to hold pl wl over 3f out: lost tch and eased fnl 2 1/2f* **49/10**[3]

2m 30.08s (-3.38)
WFA 3 from 4yo+ 8lb **9 Ran SP% 118.5**
PARI-MUTUEL (all including 1 euro stake): WIN 3.30 PLACE: 1.60, 3.10, 1.40; SF: 42.00.
Owner Godolphin **Bred** Springbank Way Stud **Trained** Newmarket, Suffolk

6772 - (Foreign Racing) - See Raceform Interactive

5115

LONGCHAMP (R-H)

Sunday, September 1

OFFICIAL GOING: Turf: good

6773a **PRIX DE LUTECE (GROUP 3) (3YO) (GRANDE COURSE) (TURF)** **1m 7f**
1:00 3-Y-0 **£36,036** (£14,414; £10,810; £7,207; £3,603)

RPR

1 **Moonlight Spirit (IRE)**[74] 3984 3-9-0 0 JamesDoyle 5 109+
(Charlie Appleby) *cl up on outer: led after 1f: mde rest: kicked for home wl over 2f out: styd on strly: unchal* **7/10**[1]

2 *4 1/2* **Think Of Me (GER)**[31] 3-8-8 0 MaximeGuyon 6 99+
(F-H Graffard, France) *plld hrd: hld up in fnl pair: stmbld after 3f: pushed along but no imp 3f out: styd on over 1f out: wnt 2nd ins fnl f: no ch w wnr* **56/10**

3 *4* **Homer (IRE)**[31] 3-8-11 0 StephanePasquier 1 96
(A Fabre, France) *led: hdd after 1f: chsd new ldr on inner: nt qckn whn asked wl over 2f out: kpt on same pce: wkng ins fnl f but hld on for 3rd* **39/10**[3]

4 *1/2* **Salmana (FR)**[18] 3-8-8 0 MlleMickaelleMichel 4 92
(Laura Lemiere, France) *settled in fnl pair: outpcd and drvn wl over 2f out: styd on late: nvr trbld ldrs* **19/1**

5 *dist* **In Favour**[28] 5717 3-8-11 0 VincentCheminaud 2
(A Fabre, France) *trckd ldr on outer: drvn 2 1/2f out but unable qck: wknd u.p 1 1/2f out: heavily eased* **19/5**[2]

3m 14.76s (-1.24) **5 Ran SP% 120.2**
PARI-MUTUEL (all including 1 euro stake): WIN 1.70; PLACE 1.10, 1.90; SF 7.80.
Owner Godolphin **Bred** Godolphin **Trained** Newmarket, Suffolk

6774a **PRIX DE LA CASCADE (MAIDEN) (UNRACED 2YO FILLIES) (MOYENNE COURSE) (TURF)** **1m**
1:35 2-Y-0 **£12,162** (£4,864; £3,648; £2,432; £1,216)

RPR

1 **Glengowan (IRE)** 2-9-0 0 TonyPiccone 3 80
(Paul Cole) *mde all: pushed along over 3f out: sn rdn: kpt on wl ins fnl f: hld on gamely* **9/1**

2 *snk* **Mille Fois Merci (IRE)** 2-9-0 0 Pierre-CharlesBoudot 8 80+
(A Fabre, France) *towards rr on inner: rdn 2 1/2f out: r.o wl to go 2nd ins fnl f: nt quite rch wnr* **6/4**[1]

3 *hd* **Allucination** 2-9-0 0 ThierryThulliez 4 79
(C Laffon-Parias, France) **74/10**

4 *hd* **Solsticia (IRE)** 2-9-0 0 MaximeGuyon 5 79+
(A Fabre, France) **5/1**[3]

5 *1 1/4* **Layla (FR)** 2-9-0 0 TheoBachelot 9 76
(Mme Pia Brandt, France) **26/1**

6 *1* **Silver Cristal (USA)** 2-8-8 0 AugustinMadamet[(6)] 2 74
(F-H Graffard, France) **22/1**

7 *nse* **Aquitaine (IRE)** 2-9-0 0 CristianDemuro 6 73
(P Bary, France) **18/1**

8 *1/2* **Adabeyaat** 2-9-0 0 ChristopheSoumillon 7 72
(J-C Rouget, France) *chsd ldr on outer: wnt 4th 5f out: rdn 2f out: no imp and wknd ins fnl f* **41/10**[2]

9 *1 3/4* **Twelve Bros (IRE)** 2-9-0 0 MickaelBarzalona 1 68
(Mme Pia Brandt, France) **12/1**

1m 42.49s (4.09) **9 Ran SP% 119.2**
PARI-MUTUEL (all including 1 euro stake): WIN 10.10; PLACE 2.50, 1.30, 1.90; DF 11.60.
Owner Mrs Fitri Hay **Bred** Mrs Fitri Hay **Trained** Whatcombe, Oxon

6775a **PRIX DE LIANCOURT (LISTED RACE) (3YO FILLIES) (GRANDE COURSE) (TURF)** **1m 2f 110y**
2:50 3-Y-0 **£24,774** (£9,909; £7,432; £4,954; £2,477)

RPR

1 **Soudania**[30] 3-8-11 0 AurelienLemaitre 7 104
(F Head, France) **47/10**

2 *1 1/4* **Queen (FR)**[25] 3-8-11 TheoBachelot 4 101+
(Mme Pia Brandt, France) **9/1**

3 *shd* **Sweet Promise**[16] 6187 3-8-11 0 MickaelBarzalona 8 101
(James Fanshawe) *hld up in rr: slt hdwy on inner over 3f out: rdn 1 1/2f out and r.o to go 2nd: nt match wnr: dropped to 3rd cl home* **5/1**

4 *3/4* **Romanciere (IRE)**[36] 5470 3-8-11 0 MaximeGuyon 3 100
(A Fabre, France) **14/5**[1]

5 *3/4* **All Grace (FR)**[36] 5470 3-8-11 0 VincentCheminaud 5 98
(A Fabre, France) **12/1**

6 *3 1/2* **Sand Share**[18] 6082 3-8-11 0 ChristopheSoumillon 1 92
(Ralph Beckett) *chsd ldrs on outer: rdn over 2f out: no imp and wknd ins fnl f* **23/5**[3]

7 *8* **Glance**[37] 5397 3-8-11 0 HarryBentley 6 76
(Ralph Beckett) *trckd ldng pair: impr to go 2nd jst past 1/2-way: rdn over 2 1/2f out: kpt on one pce: fdd* **19/5**[2]

8 *12* **Blissful Beauty (FR)**[31] 3-8-11 0 StephanePasquier 2 54
(Gavin Hernon, France) **34/1**

2m 9.18s (-1.02) **8 Ran SP% 119.8**
PARI-MUTUEL (all including 1 euro stake): WIN 5.70; PLACE 2.30, 2.90, 2.70; DF 23.10.
Owner Wertheimer & Frere **Bred** Wertheimer & Frere **Trained** France

6776a **PRIX DE FONTENOY (MAIDEN) (UNRACED 2YO COLTS & GELDINGS) (MOYENNE COURSE) (TURF)** **1m**
3:25 2-Y-0 **£12,162** (£4,864; £3,648; £2,432; £1,216)

RPR

1 **Victor Ludorum** 2-9-2 0 MickaelBarzalona 10 90+
(A Fabre, France) *mid-div on outer: pushed along 3f out: hdwy 2f out: sn led: extended under hands and heels ride ins fnl f: comf* **7/2**[1]

2 *3 1/2* **Twist (FR)** 2-9-2 0 MaximeGuyon 1 80
(C Laffon-Parias, France) **22/5**[2]

3 *1 3/4* **Mkfancy (FR)** 2-9-2 0 TheoBachelot 7 76
(Mme Pia Brandt, France) **13/1**

4 *1 1/4* **Shut Down (FR)** 2-9-2 0 IoritzMendizabal 4 73
(Mario Hofer, Germany) **15/1**

5 *1 1/4* **Musical Mast (USA)** 2-9-2 0 Pierre-CharlesBoudot 6 70
(P Bary, France) **7/2**[1]

6 *hd* **Falcata** 2-9-2 0 AurelienLemaitre 8 70
(Jo Hughes, France) *mid-div on inner: short of room whn rdn over 2f out: one pce: nvr able to chal* **24/1**

7 *3/4* **Lauenen (FR)** 2-9-2 0 CristianDemuro 11 68
(J-C Rouget, France) **54/10**[3]

8 *5 1/2* **Grand Shang (IRE)** 2-9-2 0 StephanePasquier 3 55
(Gianluca Bietolini, France) **12/1**

9 *1 1/4* **Cellini (ITY)** 2-9-2 0 ChristopheSoumillon 9 52
(G Botti, France) **44/5**

10 *4 1/2* **Arel Nova (FR)** 2-8-10 0 MathieuPelletan[(6)] 2 42
(M Delcher Sanchez, France) **53/1**

11 *hd* **Giant Steps (IRE)** 2-8-10 0 HugoBesnier[(6)] 5 42
(Jo Hughes, France) *hld up in rr: rdn ins fnl 3f: nvr involved* **26/1**

1m 41.88s (3.48) **11 Ran SP% 119.4**
PARI-MUTUEL (all including 1 euro stake): WIN 4.50; PLACE 1.90, 1.90, 3.50; DF 7.30.
Owner Godolphin SNC **Bred** Godolphin **Trained** Chantilly, France

6777a **PRIX LA ROCHETTE (GROUP 3) (2YO) (NEW COURSE: 2ND POST) (TURF)** **7f**
4:10 2-Y-0 **£36,036** (£14,414; £10,810; £7,207; £3,603)

RPR

1 **Kenway (FR)**[29] 2-9-0 0 TheoBachelot 7 107
(F Rossi, France) *w.w in rr: hdwy 1 1/2f out: str run fnl f: led last strides* **37/10**[3]

2 *snk* **Wooded (IRE)**[19] 2-9-0 0 Pierre-CharlesBoudot 2 107
(F-H Graffard, France) *racd keenly: restrained in 3rd: drvn to chse ldr ent fnl f: sustained chal to ld 75yds out: hdd last strides* **6/1**

3 *1/2* **Sujet Libre (FR)**[23] 2-9-0 0 ChristopheSoumillon 4 105
(J-C Rouget, France) *chsd ldr: rdn to ld appr fnl f: styd on u.p: hdd last 75yds: no ex* **14/5**[2]

4 3 **Les Hogues (IRE)**[33] 5539 2-8-10 0 CristianDemuro 3 93
(J-C Rouget, France) *midfield on inner: pushed along 1 1/2f out: kpt on but unable qck: nvr threatened ldrs* 19/10[1]
5 ½ **Femina (IRE)**[21] 2-8-10 0 MaximeGuyon 6 92
(C Laffon-Parias, France) *towards rr: rdn and sme mod late prog: n.d* 9/1
6 3 **Venantimi (FR)**[25] 2-9-0 0 (p) FranckBlondel 8 88
(B De Montzey, France) *a.p on outer: outpcd and drvn over 1 1/2f out: dropped away appr fnl f* 34/1
7 ¾ **Big Reaction**[25] 2-8-10 0 MickaelBarzalona 5 82
(X Thomas-Demeaulte, France) *racd in fnl trio: drvn ins fnl 2f but no imp: wl hld over 1f out* 13/1
8 snk **Patzefredo (FR)**[15] 6251 2-9-0 0 (p) EddyHardouin 1 85
(F Rossi, France) *drvn into ld: sn clr: pushed along over 1 1/2f out: hdd appr fnl f: wknd qckly* 26/1

1m 20.35s (-0.35) **8 Ran SP% 120.1**
PARI-MUTUEL (all including 1 euro stake): WIN 4.70; PLACE 1.90, 2.00, 1.80; DF 14.20.
Owner Le Haras De La Gousserie **Bred** Guy Pariente Holding **Trained** France

6778a- 6788a (Foreign Racing) - See Raceform Interactive

EVREUX
Friday, August 30

OFFICIAL GOING: Turf: good

6789a PRIX ALEXANDRA ROSA (CLAIMER) (LADY AMATEUR RIDERS) (3YO) (TURF) 1m 1f
2:30 3-Y-O **£5,405** (£2,162; £1,621; £1,081; £540)

RPR

1 **Double Or Quits (GER)**[17] 3-9-5 0 MlleMeganePeslier(5) 3 86
(M Nigge, France) 7/5[1]
2 4½ **Wyomia Jasmin (FR)**[50] 3-9-1 0 MissMelaniePlat 7 67
(Waldemar Hickst, Germany) 16/5[2]
3 3 **Hazienda (IRE)**[17] 6063 3-9-2 0 ow1 MlleMarieRollando 10 62
(T Castanheira, France) 83/10
4 8 **Melissa (FR)**[231] 183 3-9-1 0 MlleBarbaraGuenet 5 44
(Ivan Furtado) *trckd ldr: pushed along 2f out: rdn w limited rspnse over 1f out: wknd ins fnl f* 26/1
5 2½ **Punkie (FR)**[140] 3-9-8 0 MlleDelphineGarcia-Dubois 8 46
(Laura Lemiere, France) 10/1
6 ¾ **Money Back (FR)**[37] 5329 3-8-10 0 (b) MlleCamilleCollet-Vidal(5) 11 37
(F Vermeulen, France) 77/10
7 2½ **Ah Pass**[91] 3-8-10 0 (p) MlleMaelleLeLevreur(5) 6 32
(S Gouyette, France) 55/1
8 1 **Bayni Baynak (FR)** 3-9-4 0 MlleTracyMenuet 4 33
(Elias Mikhalides, France) 89/1
9 nk **Vadrouilleur (FR)**[7] 3-9-3 0 MlleRomaneCarronDeLaCarri(4) 1 35
(J Phelippon, France) 76/10[3]
10 3 **Stade Velodrome (FR)**[178] 1028 3-9-6 0 (b[1]) MlleMelanieBourgeais(5) 2 33
(J Bourgeais, France) 23/1

1m 49.9s **10 Ran SP% 119.2**
PARI-MUTUEL (all including 1 euro stake): WIN 2.40; PLACE 1.40, 1.50, 1.80; DF 3.70.
Owner Gerard Augustin-Normand **Bred** Hubert Jacob **Trained** France

4416 CHANTILLY (R-H)
Saturday, August 31

OFFICIAL GOING: Turf: good to soft changing to good after race 1 (11.15)

6790a PRIX DE LA PORTE DE MEAUX (CLAIMER) (4YO+) (TURF) 1m 4f
1:17 4-Y-0+ **£8,558** (£3,423; £2,567; £1,711; £855)

RPR

1 **Sensazione Poy**[123] 2264 4-9-3 0 ow1 RosarioMangione 3 77
(G Botti, France) 51/10[3]
2 nk **Top By Cocooning (FR)**[46] 5035 6-9-2 0 ow1 AlexisLarue 2 76
(J-P Gauvin, France) 36/5
3 hd **My Lord And Master (IRE)**[49] 4935 4-9-2 0 ow1 GeorgiaCox(3) 4 79
(William Haggas) *in rr: moved up qckly after 2f to press ldr on outer: scrubbed along 2f out but no imp on ldr: styd on u.p fnl f but nvr able to chal* 19/10[1]
4 snk **Nabunga (FR)**[80] 7-9-5 0 ow1 (p) MarcNobili 5 78
(J Phelippon, France) 48/10[2]
5 snk **Cutty Pie (IRE)**[70] 5-9-2 0 ow1 (p) FrankPanicucci 8 75
(F Rossi, France) 48/10[2]
6 1¼ **Aztec Warrior (GER)**[62] 4-9-5 0 ow1 (b[1]) HugoBesnier 7 76
(Jean-Pierre Carvalho, Germany) 56/10
7 5 **Discotheque (FR)** 4-8-9 0 ow1 MlleLauraGrosso(3) 6 61
(A Junk, France) 60/1
8 ¾ **Notre Same (GER)**[86] 8-8-13 0 ow2 BenjaminMarie 9 61
(Stephanie Gachelin, France) 57/1
9 4½ **Peaceful City (FR)**[48] 4-9-4 0 ow1 FlavioTafuri 1 59
(M Boutin, France) 30/1

2m 33.52s (2.52) **9 Ran SP% 119.3**
PARI-MUTUEL (all including 1 euro stake): WIN 6.10; PLACE 2.00, 2.10, 1.60; DF 20.50.
Owner Giulio Spozio **Bred** Scuderia Blueberry SRL **Trained** France

FOCUS
This was slowly run and turned into a dash. They finished in a heap.

6791a PRIX D'ARENBERG (GROUP 3) (2YO) (TURF) 5f
1:52 2-Y-0 **£36,036** (£14,414; £10,810; £7,207; £3,603)

RPR

1 **Al Raya**[15] 6157 2-8-11 0 ow1 Pierre-CharlesBoudot 4 104
(Simon Crisford) *mde all: kicked clr wl over 1f out: styd on u.p fnl f: hld on gamely despite drifting rt fnl 125yds* 39/10[3]
2 ¾ **Divine Spirit**[50] 4883 2-8-11 0 ow1 MickaelBarzalona 2 102
(Charlie Appleby) *hld up towards rr: hdwy u.p 1 1/2f out: styd on fnl f to cl on wnr but nvr able to chal* 59/10
3 1¼ **Flaming Princess (IRE)**[21] 5976 2-8-13 0 ow3 ChristopheSoumillon 6 99
(Richard Fahey) *chsd ldng pair: nowhere to go and swtchd outside w 1 1/2f to run: styd on u.p: nt pce to get on terms* 3/1[1]
4 nk **Jolie (FR)**[34] 5481 2-8-11 0 ow1 CristianDemuro 8 96
(Andrea Marcialis, France) *w.w towards rr on outer: hdwy to chse ldrs more than 1 1/2f out: one pce u.p fnl f* 16/5[2]
5 snk **Lady Galore (IRE)**[44] 5116 2-8-11 0 ow1 JulienAuge 1 95
(C Ferland, France) *w.w in rr: drvn but no imp ins fnl 2f: styd on fnl f: nvr trbld ldrs* 67/10
6 snk **Master McGrath (IRE)**[23] 5859 2-9-1 0 ow1 (p) KevinStott 3 99
(Kevin Ryan) *midfield: drvn but no qckn over 1 1/2f out: angled towards outer 1f out: kpt on but n.d* 9/1
7 ¾ **Hand On My Heart**[31] 5542 2-8-11 0 ow1 HectorCrouch 5 92
(Clive Cox) *pressed ldr on outer: rdn and no prog 1 1/2f out: dropped away fnl f* 19/1
8 1¼ **Queen's Order**[13] 6254 2-8-11 0 ow1 StephanePasquier 7 88
(Kevin Ryan) *in tch on outer: pressed ldrs 1/2-way: wknd fnl f* 11/1

58.47s (0.17) **8 Ran SP% 120.0**
PARI-MUTUEL (all including 1 euro stake): WIN 4.90; PLACE 1.60, 1.90, 1.40; DF 8.60.
Owner H H SH Nasser Bin Hamad Al Khalifa **Bred** Ed's Stud Ltd **Trained** Newmarket, Suffolk

6754 BRIGHTON (L-H)
Monday, September 2

OFFICIAL GOING: Good to firm (good in places, 8.3)
Wind: Virtually nil Weather: warm and sunny

6792 SUMMERTIMELIVE.CO.UK CLASSIC IBIZA 7 SEPT NURSERY H'CAP 5f 215y
2:00 (2:00) (Class 5) (0-70,71) 2-Y-O **£3,428** (£1,020; £509; £300) **Stalls** Centre

Form RPR

6415 1 **War Of Clans (IRE)**[20] 6053 2-8-13 **63** HarrisonShaw(3) 3 67
(K R Burke) *trckd ldr: shkn up to ld 2f out: sn rdn w 1 l ld 1f out: kpt on wl* 9/4[2]
0540 2 1½ **King's View (IRE)**[27] 5781 2-9-7 **68** RichardKingscote 2 67
(Richard Hannon) *settled in 3rd: effrt on inner to chse wnr 2f out: rdn and no imp 1f out: kpt on* 9/4[2]
2532 3 1½ **Enjoy The Moment**[14] 6271 2-9-1 **62** DavidEgan 4 56
(Mick Channon) *hld up: rdn and outpcd by wnr 2f out: kpt on one pce ins fnl f (jockey said filly became unbalanced coming down the hill)* 6/1[3]
3513 4 1¼ **Fashion Free**[18] 6113 2-9-10 **71** (p[1]) HollieDoyle 1 61
(Archie Watson) *led: rdn along and hdd by wnr 2f out: grad wknd fr 1f out* 2/1[1]

1m 11.71s (0.61) **Going Correction** -0.10s/f (Good) **4 Ran SP% 109.2**
Speed ratings (Par 95): **91,89,87,85**
CSF £7.60 TOTE £3.10; EX 8.30 Trifecta £21.00.
Owner Ontoawinner 14 & Mrs E Burke **Bred** M Phelan **Trained** Middleham Moor, N Yorks

FOCUS
The bends were moved out 3yds from 4f - 2f poles, adding 3yds to every race. This modest little nursery proved tactical. The second has been rated roughly in line with her pre-race best.

6793 EBF MAIDEN FILLIES' STKS (PLUS 10 RACE) 5f 215y
2:30 (2:32) (Class 5) 2-Y-O **£3,428** (£1,020; £509; £254) **Stalls** Centre

Form RPR

6 1 **Belle Anglaise**[22] 5988 2-9-0 0 RichardKingscote 2 79+
(Stuart Williams) *settled wl in midfield: hdwy to chse ldr 2f out: sn rdn appr fnl f: styd on wl to ld cl home despite bumping rival* 9/2[2]
422 2 nk **Daily Times**[53] 4849 2-9-0 79 RobertHavlin 1 78+
(John Gosden) *led: shkn up w 1 l ld over 1f out: rdn whn strly pressed by wnr fnl f: bmpd and hdd by wnr cl home* 4/11[1]
4 3 5 **Indyzeb (IRE)**[11] 6364 2-9-0 0 HollieDoyle 6 59
(Seamus Mullins) *racd in midfield on outer: swtchd lft and rdn over 1f out: kpt on for remote 3rd* 33/1
3 4 3½ **Baracca Rocks**[32] 5590 2-8-11 0 HarrisonShaw(3) 7 48
(K R Burke) *hld up: rdn and outpcd 2 out: nvr on terms* 14/1
0 5 3½ **Trouser The Cash (IRE)**[140] 1821 2-9-0 0 GeorgeWood 8 37
(Amy Murphy) *hld up: rdn along in rr over 2f out: nvr on terms* 22/1
6 2¾ **Diamonds And Rust** 2-9-0 0 LukeMorris 4 28
(Bill Turner) *in rr of midfield: outpcd 1/2-way: sn bhd* 66/1
40 P **Queen Salamah (IRE)**[28] 5745 2-9-0 0 DanielMuscutt 3
(Richard Spencer) *trckd ldr: rdn to chse ldr 2f out: lost action and p.u qckly fnl f* 10/1[3]

1m 10.28s (-0.82) **Going Correction** -0.10s/f (Good) **7 Ran SP% 116.0**
Speed ratings (Par 92): **101,100,93,89,84 80,**
CSF £6.65 TOTE £7.30: £2.30, £1.10; EX 7.60 Trifecta £72.00.
Owner Graf Stauffenberg **Bred** Howard Barton Stud **Trained** Newmarket, Suffolk

FOCUS
The first pair came clear in this ordinary fillies' maiden, with the centre of the home straight preferred. Add 3yds.

6794 IAN CARNABY (S) H'CAP 5f 215y
3:00 (3:04) (Class 6) (0-60,58) 3-Y-O+
£2,781 (£827; £413; £300; £300; £300) **Stalls** Centre

Form RPR

4R04 1 **Knockabout Queen**[2] 6737 3-9-0 **53** KierenFox 5 61
(Tony Carroll) *settled wl in midfield: hdwy on outer to chse ldr 2f out: rdn and qcknd up wl to ld 1f out: styd on strly* 4/1[2]
000 2 3 **Congress Place (IRE)**[10] 6389 3-8-13 **52** (p[1]) AlistairRawlinson 4 50
(Michael Appleby) *trckd ldr: rdn to chse ldr over 1f out: kpt on fnl f but unable to match wnr* 10/1
5015 3 ¾ **Red Tycoon (IRE)**[12] 6329 7-9-4 **58** (b) FinleyMarsh(3) 2 54
(Ken Cunningham-Brown) *slowly away: racd midfield: hdwy on inner to ld briefly over 1f out: hdd and outpcd by wnr 1f out (jockey said gelding was slowly away)* 10/3[1]
1224 4 1¾ **Monarch Maid**[13] 6321 8-8-9 **53** ElishaWhittington(7) 11 43
(Peter Hiatt) *trckd ldr: rdn upsides and ev ch over 1f out: wknd clsng stages* 5/1
0511 5 3½ **Nervous Nerys (IRE)**[24] 5878 3-8-3 **49** AmeliaGlass(7) 9 28
(Alex Hales) *racd in midfield: rdn along and no imp over 2f out: kpt on one pce fnl f* 9/2[3]
4260 6 ¾ **Waneen (IRE)**[18] 6126 6-8-9 **46** DavidEgan 3 23
(John Butler) *hld up: effrt on inner over 2f out: rdn and no imp over 1f out: one pce after* 7/1
3420 7 1¼ **Red Snapper**[41] 5264 4-8-8 **45** (p) HollieDoyle 6 18
(William Stone) *led: rdn along and hdd over 1f out: wknd fnl f* 8/1

00-6 **8** ½ **Regal Miss**61 4500 7-8-1 45 GeorgeRooke(7) 10 16
(Patrick Chamings) *hld up: outpcd 1/2-way: a in rr* **40/1**

0604 **9** 2½ **Willa's Wish (IRE)**22 5981 3-8-3 45 (b1) DarraghKeenan(3) 7 8
(Tony Carroll) *hld up: a in rr* **33/1**

1m 9.57s (-1.53) **Going Correction** -0.10s/f (Good)
WFA 3 from 4yo+ 2lb **9** Ran SP% **116.0**
Speed ratings (Par 101): **106,102,101,98,94 93,91,90,87**
CSF £43.63 CT £147.71 TOTE £4.50: £1.70, £2.70, £1.40; EX 53.50 Trifecta £246.70.There was no bid for the winner.
Owner Jason Tucker **Bred** Mike Channon Bloodstock Ltd **Trained** Cropthorne, Worcs

FOCUS
This well-established selling handicap was run at a sound pace and again the far side was shunned. Add 3yds.

6795 DAVE WOOD 60TH BIRTHDAY H'CAP 6f 210y
3:30 (3:33) (Class 5) (0-70,69) 4-Y-0+
£3,428 (£1,020; £509; £300; £300; £300) **Stalls** Centre

Form RPR

0030 **1** **Pour La Victoire (IRE)**13 6301 9-9-7 69 (b) HollieDoyle 5 78
(Tony Carroll) *dwlt and racd in last: clsd on ldrs gng wl over 2f out: hdwy on outer 2f out: rdn and qcknd up to ld 1f out: kpt on wl (jockey said gelding hung left-handed)* **5/2**1

0345 **2** 1½ **Bint Dandy (IRE)**8 6518 8-9-7 69 (b) DavidEgan 3 73
(Charlie Wallis) *racd in midfield: rdn and gd hdwy to ld briefly over 1f out: hdd by wnr and outpcd clsng stages* **12/1**

0423 **3** nse **De Little Engine (IRE)**18 6116 5-9-0 67 (p) CierenFallon(5) 4 71
(Alexandra Dunn) *midfield: effrt to chse ldr over 2f out: swtchd lft and rdn on inner over 1f out: kpt on fnl f* **10/3**3

1356 **4** 2¼ **Fieldsman (USA)**10 6414 7-9-6 68 GeorgeDowning 1 65
(Tony Carroll) *led: rdn along and hdd 2f out: kpt on one pce fr 1f out* **13/2**

0201 **5** 4 **Blessed To Empress (IRE)**2 6703 4-8-13 61 (v) JackMitchell 6 45
(Amy Murphy) *midfield on outer: clsd gng wl on outer 2f out: sn rdn and fnd little: wknd clsng stages* **3/1**2

4222 **6** hd **Seprani**10 6401 5-9-7 69 GeorgeWood 2 52
(Amy Murphy) *trckd ldr: led gng wl 2f out: sn rdn and hdd over 1f out: wknd fnl f* **5/1**

1m 22.84s (-0.96) **Going Correction** -0.10s/f (Good) **6** Ran SP% **114.3**
Speed ratings (Par 103): **101,99,99,96,92 91**
CSF £31.92 TOTE £3.60: £1.70, £4.90; EX 27.80 Trifecta £124.60.
Owner Curry House Corner and Partner **Bred** L Fox **Trained** Cropthorne, Worcs

FOCUS
There was a fair pace on in this tight handicap. Add 3yds. The winner has been rated to this year's form, while the third helps set the level.

6796 SUSSEX ART FAIRS (EAST) 12 OCT H'CAP 1m 3f 198y
4:00 (4:01) (Class 6) (0-65,65) 4-Y-0+
£2,781 (£827; £413; £300; £300; £300) **Stalls** High

Form RPR

1003 **1** **Kirtling**13 6303 8-8-12 56 (t) JackMitchell 6 62
(Andi Brown) *dwlt sltly and racd in rr: clsd gng wl over 2f out: shkn up to ld over 1f out: sn in command and rdn out* **5/1**3

000 **2** 1¼ **Sea Of Mystery (IRE)**24 5891 6-9-2 60 (t) AlistairRawlinson 7 64
(Michael Appleby) *midfield on outer: hdwy on outer over 2f out despite hanging rt: rdn to chse wnr over 1f out: kpt on but no match wnr fnl f* **12/1**

0163 **3** 2¼ **Contingency Fee**6 6556 4-8-8 59 (p) GraceMcEntee(7) 8 59
(Phil McEntee) *led after 2f out: pushed along w clr 5 l ld over 3f out: hung lft and rt over 2f out: sn hdd by wnr over 1f out: no ex* **10/1**

5341 **4** 3 **Esspeegee**13 6303 6-9-4 65 (v) DarraghKeenan(3) 2 60
(Alan Bailey) *led for 2f then trckd ldr: effrt to chse ldr over 2f out: rdn and one pce over 1f out: plugged on* **1/1**1

0620 **5** 5 **Roy Rocket (FR)**13 6303 9-8-11 55 JFEgan 1 42
(John Berry) *hld up: hdwy into midfield over 2f out: rdn and no imp fnl f* **11/1**

6465 **6** 4½ **Beer With The Boys**9 6448 4-9-5 63 DavidEgan 4 43
(Mick Channon) *midfield: wnt 2nd 6f out: rdn to chse clr ldr 3f out: no imp over 1f out: wknd clsng stages* **9/2**2

0060 **7** 17 **Brockagh Cailin**26 5795 4-8-11 55 LiamKeniry 3 7
(J S Moore) *racd in rr: rdn and dropped to last 3f out: sn bhd* **33/1**

2m 32.92s (-3.08) **Going Correction** -0.10s/f (Good) **7** Ran SP% **112.9**
Speed ratings (Par 101): **106,105,103,101,98 95,84**
CSF £58.28 CT £572.26 TOTE £6.80: £3.00, £5.00; EX 56.70 Trifecta £317.80.
Owner Faith Hope And Charity **Bred** L P R Partnership **Trained** Newmarket, Suffolk

FOCUS
Not a bad handicap for the class. Add 3yds. Routine form, with the winner rated to his best over recent years.

6797 SKY SPORTS RACING ON SKY 415 NOVICE STKS 5f 60y
4:30 (4:30) (Class 5) 3-Y-0+ **£3,428** (£1,020; £509) **Stalls** Centre

Form RPR

3 **1** **Hassaad**114 2623 3-9-0 0 HollieDoyle 4 74+
(Archie Watson) *wnt rt s and racd in last: smooth hdwy over 2f out: shkn up to ld over 1f out: readily drew clr fnl f: easily* **1/6**1

55-2 **2** 9 **Katherine Place**14 6285 4-9-1 48 (t) RyanTate 3 42
(Bill Turner) *trckd ldr: pushed along to ld over 2f out: rdn and easily hdd by wnr over 1f out: one pce after* **11/2**2

0-30 **3** 16 **Abuja (IRE)**23 5957 3-9-0 51 (h) LiamKeniry 2
(Michael Madgwick) *walked to post early: led: rdn and hdd over 2f out: sn bhd* **16/1**3

1m 2.81s (-0.19) **Going Correction** -0.10s/f (Good)
WFA 3 from 4yo 1lb **3** Ran SP% **107.0**
Speed ratings (Par 103): **97,82,57**
CSF £1.49 TOTE £1.10; EX 1.30 Trifecta £1.20.
Owner Boadicea Bloodstock **Bred** Shadwell Estate Company Limited **Trained** Upper Lambourn, W Berks

FOCUS
A desperately weak little novice event. Add 3yds.

6798 STREAMLINE TAXIS 202020 APPRENTICE H'CAP 5f 60y
5:05 (5:05) (Class 5) (0-75,74) 4-Y-0+ **£3,428** (£1,020; £509; £300; £300) **Stalls** Centre

Form RPR

3053 **1** **Wiley Post**25 5843 6-9-6 74 (b) ElishaWhittington(6) 2 83
(Tony Carroll) *hld up: hdwy between rivals over 2f out: effrt to chse ldr over 1f out: rdn to ld wl ins fnl f: kpt on wl* **2/1**2

5002 **2** 1½ **Tan**7 6547 5-9-3 65 MarkCrehan 4 69
(Michael Appleby) *wnt to post early: led: rdn along w short ld over 1f out: drvn and hdd by wnr wl ins fnl f: jst hld on for 2nd* **5/2**3

6331 **3** nk **Three Little Birds**26 5793 4-9-11 73 GeorgiaDobie 1 76
(Sylvester Kirk) *hld up: rdn to chse ldr on inner over 1f out: kpt on wl ins fnl f: nt rch wnr* **6/4**1

0515 **4** 2¾ **Haveoneyerself (IRE)**6 6562 4-8-10 63 (p) MorganCole(5) 3 56
(John Butler) *trckd ldr: rdn and outpcd 2f out: wknd fnl f* **14/1**

0000 **5** 6 **Bernie's Boy**5 6605 6-8-11 65 (p) GraceMcEntee(6) 5 37
(Phil McEntee) *trckd ldr: rdn and outpcd 1/2-way: sn bhd* **16/1**

1m 2.27s (-0.73) **Going Correction** -0.10s/f (Good) **5** Ran SP% **114.5**
Speed ratings (Par 103): **101,98,98,93,84**
CSF £7.77 TOTE £2.50: £1.40, £1.30; EX 8.00 Trifecta £14.10.
Owner Lady Whent **Bred** Lady Whent **Trained** Cropthorne, Worcs

FOCUS
A modest sprint handicap for apprentice riders. Add 3yds. The winner has been rated close to his best.
T/Plt: £231.30 to a £1 stake. Pool: £59,631.64 - 188.18 winning units T/Qpdt: £67.70 to a £1 stake. Pool: £5,927.52 - 64.76 winning units **Mark Grantham**

6525 CHEPSTOW (L-H)
Monday, September 2

OFFICIAL GOING: Good to firm (good in places) changing to good after race 1 (1.45)
Wind: Moderate, against Weather: Sunny spells

6799 IRISH THOROUGHBRED MARKETING NURSERY H'CAP 5f 16y
1:45 (1:47) (Class 6) (0-60,60) 2-Y-0
£3,428 (£1,020; £509; £300; £300; £300) **Stalls** Centre

Form RPR

2022 **1** **Prissy Missy (IRE)**6 6557 2-8-13 57 ThomasGreatrex(5) 6 61
(David Loughnane) *midfield: rdn after 2f: hdwy over 1f out: drvn and r.o fnl f: led towards fin* **5/2**1

002 **2** nk **Blue Venture**20 6047 2-9-0 53 JohnFahy 8 56
(Tony Carroll) *racd keenly: led: rdn over 1f out: ducked rt ins fnl f: sn edgd lft: hdd towards fin* **7/1**

544 **3** ¾ **Carmel**24 5887 2-9-6 59 (p1) OisinMurphy 7 59
(Archie Watson) *a.p: drvn wl over 1f out: kpt on* **10/3**2

650 **4** 3¼ **Full Spectrum (IRE)**14 6287 2-9-4 60 (p) MeganNicholls(3) 5 48
(Paul George) *s.i.s: midfield on outer: drvn and clsd over 1f out: sn hung lft: kpt on same pce fnl f (jockey said filly hung left-handed)* **12/1**

440 **5** nk **Tilly Tamworth**42 5250 2-9-7 60 RobHornby 1 47
(Rod Millman) *prom: rdn over 2f out: wknd ins fnl f* **10/1**

3266 **6** ½ **Beignet (IRE)**17 6182 2-9-7 60 RossaRyan 10 45
(Richard Hannon) *chsd ldrs: rdn 2f out: wknd fnl f* **4/1**3

0060 **7** ½ **Red Cinderella**32 5576 2-8-1 47 AngusVilliers(7) 2 31
(David Evans) *chsd ldrs: rdn 1/2-way: outpcd and btn appr fnl f* **16/1**

0330 **8** ¾ **Jane Victoria**23 5958 2-9-1 54 RaulDaSilva 4 35
(Adam West) *t.k.h towards rr: rdn 1/2-way: styd on fnl f but nvr a threat* **28/1**

0550 **9** 6 **Good Times Too**39 5340 2-9-4 57 CharlesBishop 9 16
(Mick Channon) *s.i.s: towards rr: drvn 2f out: sn wknd* **20/1**

000 **10** ¾ **Lethal Sensation**22 5988 2-8-11 50 (b1) MartinDwyer 11 7
(Paul Webber) *in rr: pushed along over 3f out: drvn and wknd over 1f out* **25/1**

59.93s (0.53) **Going Correction** -0.10s/f (Good) **10** Ran SP% **118.9**
Speed ratings (Par 93): **91,90,89,84,83 82,82,80,71,70**
CSF £20.56 CT £60.31 TOTE £3.20: £1.40, £2.50, £1.40; EX 18.60 Trifecta £76.30.
Owner Stonegrave Thoroughbreds **Bred** Manister House Stud **Trained** Tern Hill, Shropshire

FOCUS
The going was officially good to firm, good in places. Ten maidens (nine fillies and one gelding) lined up for this moderate nursery and half the field were making their handicap debut. The pace was good and as is often the case here, the runners came towards the stands' side.

6800 DEREK BURRIDGE RACING, SPORTS AND CORPORATE TROPHIES FILLIES' NOVICE STKS (PLUS 10 RACE) 5f 16y
2:15 (2:17) (Class 5) 2-Y-0 **£3,428** (£1,020; £509; £254) **Stalls** Centre

Form RPR

20 **1** **Band Practice (IRE)**18 6096 2-9-0 0 OisinMurphy 7 77+
(Archie Watson) *prom: wnt 2nd over 3f out: rdn to ld over 1f out: r.o* **11/4**2

4404 **2** 2¾ **Chasanda**87 3530 2-9-0 74 (h1) AngusVilliers(7) 9 74
(David Evans) *wnt to post early: trckd ldr tl led over 3f out: rdn and hdd over 1f out: outpcd by wnr fnl f* **14/1**

423 **3** 2¼ **Allez Sophia (IRE)**40 5317 2-9-0 74 CharlesBishop 4 59
(Eve Johnson Houghton) *trckd ldrs: rdn 2f out: hld in 3rd whn unbalanced ent fnl f: kpt on same pce* **11/10**1

40 **4** 3½ **Liscahann**25 5859 2-9-0 0 RobHornby 3 46
(Seamus Mullins) *led over 1f: sn bk in 3rd: rdn 1/2-way: wknd appr fnl f* **10/1**

3 **5** 7 **Just May**26 5794 2-9-0 0 HectorCrouch 1 21
(Clive Cox) *rdn over 3f out: a towards rr* **4/1**3

0 **6** 6 **Erika**14 6287 2-9-0 0 RossaRyan 5
(Neil Mulholland) *chsd ldrs tl rdn and outpcd 1/2-way: wknd over 1f out* **33/1**

0 **7** 13 **Handful Of Gold (IRE)**12 6330 2-9-0 0 JohnFahy 2
(Kevin Bishop) *sn wl bhd* **100/1**

58.48s (-0.92) **Going Correction** -0.10s/f (Good) **7** Ran SP% **114.0**
Speed ratings (Par 92): **103,98,95,89,78 68,47**
CSF £38.52 TOTE £3.60: £1.90, £5.70; EX 21.90 Trifecta £59.70.
Owner Clipper Logistics **Bred** Fergus Cousins **Trained** Upper Lambourn, W Berks

FOCUS
The going was changed to good before this race, an ordinary fillies' novice in which the market got it wrong. The runners stayed more towards the centre this time and the time was 1.45sec quicker than the nursery.

6801 EVAFRAME - ALUMINIUM AND UPVC WINDOW/DOOR SPECIALISTS H'CAP 7f 16y
2:45 (2:46) (Class 5) (0-75,75) 3-Y-O

£3,428 (£1,020; £509; £300; £300; £300) Stalls Centre

Form RPR
2500 1 **Molaaheth**[31] 5622 3-8-13 **67**.....................(t) RossaRyan 4 74
(Alexandra Dunn) *hld up in last: hdwy 2f out: swtchd lft and shkn up over 1f out: drvn to ld ins fnl f: kpt on* **12/1**
4055 2 ½ **Plumette**[22] 5985 3-8-7 **66**........ ThomasGreatrex(5) 1 71
(David Loughnane) *hld up wl in tch: clsd 3f out: led jst over 2f out: drvn ent fnl f: sn hdd and unable qck* **9/2[3]**
5556 3 2¾ **Jungle Juice (IRE)**[10] 6418 3-9-2 **75**........ ScottMcCullagh(5) 5 72
(Mick Channon) *led 2f: remained prom tl rdn and lost pl 2f out: rallied fnl f: wnt 3rd nr fin* **9/2[3]**
1603 4 ½ **Kwela**[18] 6111 3-9-7 **75**.....................(p) CharlesBishop 3 71
(Eve Johnson Houghton) *hld up: clsd to chal over 2f out: drvn and outpcd by ldng pair over 1f out: lost 3rd nr fin* **7/2[2]**
-660 5 2½ **Indomitable (IRE)**[58] 4669 3-9-7 **75**........ OisinMurphy 2 64
(Andrew Balding) *prom: drvn and ev ch over 2f out: wknd fnl f* **6/4[1]**
520 6 3¼ **J'Ouvert (IRE)**[195] 795 3-8-3 **64**........ AngusVilliers(7) 6 44
(David Evans) *t.k.h: prom: led after 2f tl rdn and hdd jst over 2f out: losing pl whn rdr dropped rein over 1f out: wknd (jockey said filly ran too keen)* **18/1**

1m 22.76s (-1.14) **Going Correction** -0.10s/f (Good) **6** Ran SP% **111.5**
Speed ratings (Par 101): **102,101,98,97,94 91**
CSF £62.53 TOTE £13.90: £5.20, £2.80; EX 66.20 Trifecta £278.80.
Owner West Buckland Bloodstock Ltd **Bred** Clare Lloyd & Nell Kent **Trained** West Buckland, Somerset

FOCUS
An ordinary 3yo handicap and again they came up the centre. The winner has been rated back to his best, and the second to her earlier C&D win.

6802 SALUTEM - YOUR APPRENTICE TRAINING PARTNER NOVICE STKS 7f 16y
3:15 (3:15) (Class 5) 3-Y-O+ £3,428 (£1,020; £509; £254) Stalls Centre

Form RPR
52-2 1 **Alrajaa**[18] 6119 3-9-5 82........ JimCrowley 4 84+
(John Gosden) *wnt to post early: trckd ldrs: led gng wl over 2f out: pushed clr over 1f out: eased towards fin* **2/13[1]**
2 9 **Edraak (IRE)** 3-9-5 0........ DaneO'Neill 5 60+
(Owen Burrows) *wnt rt leaving stalls: in rr: hdwy 3f out: shkn up and wnt 2nd over 1f out: no ch w easy wnr* **10/3[2]**
0 3 6 **Plum Duff**[212] 554 3-9-0 0........ CharlesBishop 1 39
(Michael Blanshard) *t.k.h: cl up: led over 3f out tl drvn and hdd over 2f out: lost 2nd over 1f out: hanging rt and wl btn after (jockey said filly hung right-handed)* **66/1**
00U 4 nk **Four Feet (IRE)**[18] 6119 3-8-12 0........ EmmaTaff(7) 2 43
(Henry Candy) *chsd ldrs: rdn 1/2-way: outpcd in last over 2f out: kpt on to press for modest 3rd ins fnl f* **20/1[3]**
0 5 16 **Auntie June**[18] 6119 3-9-0 0........ CallumShepherd 3
(Roy Brotherton) *led tl hdd over 3f out: sn drvn: wknd over 1f out* **66/1**

1m 23.22s (-0.68) **Going Correction** -0.10s/f (Good) **5** Ran SP% **117.5**
Speed ratings (Par 103): **99,88,81,81,63**
CSF £1.27 TOTE £1.10: £1.10, £1.20; EX 1.50 Trifecta £6.20.
Owner Hamdan Al Maktoum **Bred** Shadwell Estate Company Limited **Trained** Newmarket, Suffolk

FOCUS
A distinctly uncompetitive novice. A token rating around the winner has been given.

6803 ACORN PROPERTY GROUP H'CAP 7f 16y
3:45 (3:45) (Class 4) (0-85,87) 3-Y-O+

£5,207 (£1,549; £774; £387; £300; £300) Stalls Centre

Form RPR
0563 1 **Bungee Jump (IRE)**[7] 6525 4-9-10 **85**........ RossaRyan 4 94
(Grace Harris) *mde all: drvn over 1f out: sn hrd pressed: kpt on gamely fnl f* **9/1**
2246 2 ¾ **Sir Roderic (IRE)**[16] 6201 6-8-11 **72**..........(v) OisinMurphy 2 79
(Rod Millman) *chsd wnr virtually thrght: rdn wl over 1f out: sn ev ch: kpt on: jst hld fnl f* **6/1[3]**
5214 3 3½ **Graphite Storm**[16] 6214 5-9-11 **86**........ HectorCrouch 6 84
(Clive Cox) *hld up: rdn and impr to chse ldrs over 2f out: wknd ins fnl f: jst hld 3rd* **5/2[2]**
6140 4 hd **Ragstone View (IRE)**[27] 5776 4-8-12 **73**..........(h) CharlesBishop 3 70
(Rod Millman) *dwlt: in rr: hdwy 3f out: drvn over 1f out: kpt on same pce: pressed for 3rd cl home* **9/1**
2540 5 ½ **Waqt (IRE)**[10] 6414 5-8-7 **71** oh1..........(p) SeanDavis(3) 7 67
(Alexandra Dunn) *hld up in bhd ldrs: rdn and sltly outpcd 2f out: drvn and edgd rt over 1f out: styd on same pce* **25/1**
2321 6 1 **Aluqair (IRE)**[18] 6119 3-9-4 **83**..........(h) JimCrowley 5 74
(Simon Crisford) *wnt to post early: trckd ldrs: drvn over 2f out: wknd fnl f (jockey said gelding was outpaced throughout)* **6/4[1]**
0310 7 10 **I Am A Dreamer**[9] 6440 3-9-8 **87**..........(v) FrannyNorton 1 51
(Mark Johnston) *chsd ldrs: rdn 1/2-way: wknd over 2f out (jockey said colt was never travelling)* **11/1**

1m 22.21s (-1.69) **Going Correction** -0.10s/f (Good)
WFA 3 from 4yo+ 4lb **7** Ran SP% **115.0**
Speed ratings (Par 105): **105,104,100,99,99 98,86**
CSF £61.41 TOTE £8.70: £2.40, £3.10; EX 46.30 Trifecta £151.50.
Owner Ronald Davies & Mrs Candida Davies **Bred** Roundhill Stud **Trained** Shirenewton, Monmouthshire

FOCUS
A fair handicap run at a good pace, but few got into it and the front pair held those positions throughout. The winner has been rated in line with the better view of her form.

6804 BMC BUCKET MANUFACTURING H'CAP 1m 2f
4:15 (4:15) (Class 5) (0-75,77) 4-Y-O+ £3,428 (£1,020; £509; £300; £300) Stalls Low

Form RPR
1002 1 **Freckles**[17] 6160 4-8-12 **66**..........(h) OisinMurphy 5 75
(Marcus Tregoning) *t.k.h: hld up in last pair: hdwy 4f out: wnt 2nd 4f out: sn rdn: led over 1f out: drvn out* **8/11[1]**
5106 2 1½ **Arctic Sea**[22] 5993 5-9-3 **71**........ RossaRyan 1 76
(Paul Cole) *s.i.s: sn trcking ldr: rdn and lost 2nd 3f out: styd on u.p: wnt 2nd again ins fnl f but hld by wnr* **4/1[2]**
635 3 1½ **Essenaitch (IRE)**[28] 5747 6-8-0 **61** oh1........ AngusVilliers(7) 4 63
(David Evans) *t.k.h: led: drvn 2f out: hdd over 1f out: no ex and lost 2nd ins fnl f (jockey said gelding ran too keen)* **11/2[3]**
5130 4 12 **Gendarme (IRE)**[12] 6331 4-9-4 **75**..........(v[1]) SeanDavis(3) 3 53
(Alexandra Dunn) *hld up in last pair: rdn over 3f out: nt run on: wknd over 1f out* **14/1**
50/4 5 34 **Banish (USA)**[26] 5796 6-9-9 **77**..........(t) CharlesBishop 6
(Tom George) *chsd ldng pair: rdn 4f out: wknd over 1f out: eased ins fnl f: t.o (jockey said gelding was never travelling. Vet said gelding had an irregular heartbeat)* **8/1**

2m 5.61s (-7.19) **Going Correction** -0.10s/f (Good) **5** Ran SP% **111.1**
Speed ratings (Par 103): **105,103,102,93,65**
CSF £4.02 TOTE £1.80: £1.10, £1.70; EX 3.50 Trifecta £8.80.
Owner John & Heather Raw **Bred** Heather Raw **Trained** Whitsbury, Hants

FOCUS
A modest handicap. The second and third have been rated close to their recent form.

6805 COUNTY MARQUEES APPRENTICE H'CAP 1m 4f
4:45 (4:45) (Class 6) (0-65,66) 3-Y-O

£2,781 (£827; £413; £300; £300; £300) Stalls Low

Form RPR
2210 1 **Bug Boy (IRE)**[21] 6022 3-9-7 **66**..........(p) RhiainIngram(3) 5 73
(Paul George) *hld up in last pair: hdwy over 3f out: rdn to ld 2f out: styd on wl* **4/1[2]**
5004 2 3¼ **Mr Nice Guy (IRE)**[16] 6202 3-8-12 **57**........ PoppyBridgwater(3) 1 59
(Sylvester Kirk) *hld up in last pair: rdn 4f out: sme hdwy 2f out: no further imp tl styd on fnl f: wnt 2nd cl home (jockey said gelding hung left-handed)* **7/2[1]**
0544 3 shd **Twenty Years On**[26] 5798 3-9-2 **63**..........(p) AngusVilliers(5) 2 65
(Richard Hughes) *t.k.h: trckd ldrs: rdn over 3f out: sn sltly outpcd: styd on to dispute 2nd ins fnl f* **5/1[3]**
0340 4 ¾ **Four Mile Bridge (IRE)**[14] 6279 3-8-12 **57**........ ThomasGreatrex(5) 4 57
(Mark Usher) *hld up: hdwy 3f out: rdn and ev ch 2f out: one pce fnl f: lost 2 pls towards fin* **8/1**
4563 5 4½ **Ocean Reach**[11] 6367 3-7-11 **46**........ IsobelFrancis(7) 3 39
(Richard Price) *prom: rdn over 2f out: outpcd by ldrs over 1f out: wkng whn sltly hmpd ins fnl f (jockey said filly hung right-handed and ran in snatches)* **5/1[3]**
506 6 2½ **Magic Act (IRE)**[14] 6274 3-8-5 **50**........ AndrewBreslin(3) 7 39
(Mark Johnston) *led narrowly: drvn and hdd 2f out: wknd fnl f* **7/1**
2360 7 10 **Bonneville (IRE)**[78] 3888 3-8-1 **50**..........(b) OliverSearle(7) 8 23
(Rod Millman) *t.k.h: w ldr tl rdn and wknd over 2f out* **11/1**
6605 8 20 **Keith**[78] 3888 3-8-6 **48**..........(w) SeanDavis 6
(Rod Millman) *midfield: rdn 4f out and sn dropped to rr: t.o* **9/1**

2m 34.59s (-5.71) **Going Correction** -0.10s/f (Good) **8** Ran SP% **117.5**
Speed ratings (Par 99): **96,93,93,93,90 88,81,68**
CSF £19.02 CT £71.75 TOTE £4.30: £1.50, £1.30, £1.90; EX 21.90 Trifecta £105.00.
Owner A Coutts And K George **Bred** Windflower Overseas **Trained** Crediton, Devon
■ Stewards' Enquiry : Poppy Bridgwater seven-day ban; misuse of whip (Sept 17-23)

FOCUS
A moderate 3yo apprentice handicap. The first two home came from the last two places turning in, which suggests the leaders may have gone off too quick. Straightforward form in behind the winner.
T/Plt: £147.30 to a £1 stake. Pool: £59,252.90 - 293.64 winning units T/Qpdt: £21.20 to a £1 stake. Pool: £5,236.16 - 185.78 winning units **Richard Lowther**

6463 WINDSOR (R-H)
Monday, September 2

OFFICIAL GOING: Good to firm (7.7)
Wind: Fresh, behind Weather: Cloudy

6806 ZUPERMANN AUTOMOTIVE H'CAP 6f 12y
4:25 (4:28) (Class 5) (0-75,73) 3-Y-O+

£3,428 (£1,020; £509; £300; £300; £300) Stalls Centre

Form RPR
4201 1 **Chil Chil**[5] 6598 3-9-3 **69** 6ex........ JamesDoyle 2 88+
(Andrew Balding) *hld up in last pair: prog bef 1/2-way: carried lft 2f out but pushed into the ld over 1f out: sn drew clr* **4/11[1]**
0005 2 4½ **Porto Ferro (IRE)**[47] 5050 5-8-7 **57**..........(t) KieranO'Neill 5 58
(John Bridger) *chsd ldr: led over 2f out but sn hung lft: hdd over 1f out: no ch w wnr but hld on for 2nd* **10/1[3]**
3433 3 ½ **Mr Buttons (IRE)**[19] 6070 3-9-4 **73**..........(p) CameronNoble(3) 7 72
(Linda Stubbs) *pushed along in last and struggling bef 1/2-way: rdn and kpt on fr 2f out: pressed for modest 2nd nr fin* **7/1[2]**
-235 4 2¼ **Shake Me Handy**[40] 5292 4-9-3 **70**........ WilliamCox(3) 6 62
(Roger Teal) *chsd ldrs: rdn and in tch 2f out: wknd over 1f out (vet said gelding bled from nose)* **11/1**
0440 5 5 **Caledonian Gold**[9] 6462 6-8-0 **57** oh12..........(v[1]) GavinAshton(7) 3 38
(Lisa Williamson) *taken down early: pushed along to ld: hung lft fr 1/2-way: hdd & wknd over 2f out: eased fnl f* **50/1**
515 6 1¼ **Good Answer**[30] 5660 3-9-4 **70**..........(p[1]) PatDobbs 4 42
(Robert Cowell) *reluctant to enter stalls: chsd ldrs to 1/2-way: sn wknd* **14/1**

1m 10.0s (-2.10) **Going Correction** -0.10s/f (Good)
WFA 3 from 4yo+ 2lb **6** Ran SP% **111.9**
Speed ratings (Par 103): **110,104,103,100,93 92**
CSF £5.00 TOTE £1.30: £1.10, £3.10; EX 4.80 Trifecta £12.90.
Owner King Power Racing Co Ltd **Bred** A S Denniff **Trained** Kingsclere, Hants

FOCUS
A modest and fairly uncompetitive sprint that was won in dominant style by the favourite. The second has been rated to this year's form.

6807 BRITISH STALLION STUDS EBF NOVICE STKS (PLUS 10 RACE) 6f 12y
4:55 (4:59) (Class 4) 2-Y-O £4,851 (£1,443; £721; £360) Stalls Centre

Form RPR
1 **Dance Fever (IRE)** 2-9-5 0........ AdamKirby 10 80+
(Clive Cox) *slowly away and rn green early: wl bhd in last pair: pushed along and gd prog on outer after 1/2-way: rdn to ld ins fnl f: styd on wl* **9/2[3]**

323 **2** 1¼ **We're Reunited (IRE)**[10] 6395 2-9-5 76................ DavidProbert 5 74
(Ronald Harris) *w ldng pair: narrow ld 2f out: drvn wl over 1f out: hdd and no ex ins fnl f* **11/4**[2]

44 **3** ½ **Phuket Power (IRE)**[9] 6464 2-9-5 0........................ RichardKingscote 7 73
(Tom Dascombe) *chsd ldrs: shkn up over 2f out: nt qckn over 1f out: kpt on to take 3rd ins fnl f* **2/1**[1]

55 **4** ½ **Kassab**[47] 5059 2-9-5 0.. ShaneKelly 4 71
(Peter Chapple-Hyam) *trckd ldrs: gng strly whn waiting for a gap jst over 2f out: drvn and nt qckn over 1f out: kpt on one pce after* **11/1**

0223 **5** ¾ **Cotai Again (IRE)**[10] 6403 2-9-5 78.................... KieranShoemark 3 69
(Charles Hills) *disp ld to 2f out: fdd fnl f* **13/2**

50 **6** 1¾ **Burniston Rocks**[38] 5381 2-9-5 0................................ StevieDonohoe 8 64
(Ed Vaughan) *outpcd and pushed along after 2f: tried to cl on ldrs 2f out: shkn up and one pce after* **18/1**

0 **7** *nk* **Bad Company**[60] 4544 2-9-5 0.................................... CharlieBennett 12 63
(Jim Boyle) *outpcd and pushed along after 2f: tried to cl on ldrs 2f out: fdd over 1f out* **50/1**

0 **8** 2¾ **Gift Of Youth**[14] 6287 2-9-5 0...................................... RobertHavlin 11 54
(Amanda Perrett) *disp ld to 2f out: losing pl whn squeezed out jst ins fnl f: wknd* **50/1**

0 **9** ½ **Ivadream**[19] 6078 2-9-5 0.. JasonWatson 1 53
(Roger Charlton) *chsd ldrs: rdn and wknd 2f out* **10/1**

50 **10** 3½ **Numinous (IRE)**[54] 4798 2-9-5 0.................................... TomMarquand 9 42
(Henry Candy) *outpcd and a struggling* **50/1**

1m 12.26s (0.16) **Going Correction** -0.10s/f (Good) **10 Ran SP% 120.1**
Speed ratings (Par 97): **94,92,91,91,90 87,87,83,82,78**
CSF £17.78 TOTE £5.70: £2.30, £1.30, £1.10; EX 20.30 Trifecta £59.40.

Owner Kennet Valley Thoroughbreds VIII **Bred** Silk Fan Syndicate **Trained** Lambourn, Berks

FOCUS
No hanging around here and the winner came from well off the pace. Ordinary juvenile form. It's been rated as straightforward form in behind the winner.

6808 WINDSOR'S GREATEST SHOW FIREWORKS EXTRAVAGANZA NURSERY H'CAP 1m 31y

5:30 (5:30) (Class 5) (0-75,76) 2-Y-O

£3,428 (£1,020; £509; £300; £300; £300) **Stalls** Low

Form RPR

2134 **1** **Incinerator**[10] 6416 2-10-0 76..........................(t) JamesDoyle 2 81+
(Hugo Palmer) *mde all: hanging lft bnd 5f out: rdn over 1f out: sn clr: comf* **6/4**[1]

0050 **2** 4 **Kentucky Hardboot (IRE)**[10] 6394 2-8-13 61...........(p[1]) GeraldMosse 1 58
(Mick Channon) *dwlt: hld up in last pair: pushed along over 3f out: rdn and prog over 2f out: kpt on to take 2nd fnl f: no ch w wnr* **16/1**

0403 **3** 1 **Max's Thunder (IRE)**[24] 5907 2-9-3 65......................... JamieSpencer 3 59
(David Simcock) *cl up: rdn to chse wnr 3f out: no imp and btn over 1f out: one pce and lost 2nd fnl f* **5/2**[2]

0541 **4** ½ **Lethal Talent**[19] 6071 2-9-0 69................................ TylerSaunders(7) 4 61
(Jonathan Portman) *t.k.h early: cl up: racd wd in st: pushed along over 3f out: nvr able to threaten wnr* **5/1**[3]

046 **5** *nk* **Slavonic Dance (IRE)**[10] 6395 2-9-3 65....................(b[1]) HarryBentley 5 57
(Ralph Beckett) *mostly chsd wnr to 3f out: rdn and one pce after* **10/1**

4606 **6** 1¼ **Pitcher**[10] 6416 2-9-4 66.. SeanLevey 6 55
(Richard Hannon) *hld up in last pair: shkn up over 3f out: no prog and btn 2f out* **7/1**

1m 42.78s (-1.72) **Going Correction** -0.10s/f (Good) **6 Ran SP% 112.7**
Speed ratings (Par 95): **104,100,99,98,98 96**
CSF £25.95 TOTE £2.10: £1.10, £5.10; EX 18.00 Trifecta £62.50.

Owner V I Araci **Bred** V I Araci **Trained** Newmarket, Suffolk

FOCUS
A modest nursery dominated by the favourite, who made all. It's been rated around the second.

6809 JON AND SONYA ANNIVERSARY H'CAP 5f 21y

6:00 (6:01) (Class 4) (0-80,82) 3-Y-O+

£5,207 (£1,549; £774; £387; £300; £300) **Stalls** Centre

Form RPR

2601 **1** **Harry Hurricane**[14] 6288 7-9-4 82.......................(p) CierenFallon(5) 1 88
(George Baker) *wl away: mde virtually all: racd against nr side rail: drvn over 1f out: kpt on* **4/1**[3]

-350 **2** *nk* **Excellent George**[35] 5503 7-8-12 78.......................(t) MarcoGhiani(7) 10 83
(Stuart Williams) *racd alone towards far side: nt on terms w main gp to 1/2-way: drvn and clsd fr 2f out: styd on fnl f: jst failed* **12/1**

3006 **3** *nk* **Line Of Reason (IRE)**[12] 6332 9-9-9 82.......................... HarryBentley 2 86
(Paul Midgley) *dwlt: pushed along in rr: prog fr 1/2-way: chsd wnr in main gp wl over 1f out: kpt on but nvr quite able to chal* **7/2**[2]

6160 **4** *nk* **Benny And The Jets (IRE)**[53] 4847 3-9-7 81................. RobHornby 8 84
(Sylvester Kirk) *towards rr: prog 1/2-way: rdn and kpt on same pce over 1f out* **12/1**

3050 **5** ¾ **Waseem Faris (IRE)**[19] 6080 10-9-7 80............................ PatDobbs 11 80
(Ken Cunningham-Brown) *hld up in last: rdn over 1f out against nr side rail: styd on fnl f: nrst fin but n.d* **28/1**

3531 **6** 1¼ **Maid Of Spirit (IRE)**[19] 6080 4-9-4 77............................ AdamKirby 6 73
(Clive Cox) *w ldrs 1f: trckd after: rdn to cl 2f out: fdd fnl f* **10/3**[1]

535 **7** ½ **Foxy Forever (IRE)**[9] 6455 9-9-7 80.......................(bt) FrannyNorton 5 74
(Michael Wigham) *a towards rr: shkn up and no prog 2f out* **8/1**

54 **8** 3¾ **Just Glamorous (IRE)**[19] 6080 6-9-3 79.................... CameronNoble(3) 9 59
(Grace Harris) *w ldrs on outer: racd centre fr 2f out and wknd* **9/1**

0012 **P** **Look Surprised**[14] 6288 6-8-8 70................................ WilliamCox(3) 4
(Roger Teal) *w wnr to wl over 1f out: wkng qckly whn lost action after: p.u ins fnl f* **13/2**

58.87s (-1.23) **Going Correction** -0.10s/f (Good) **9 Ran SP% 118.6**
WFA 3 from 4yo+ 1lb
Speed ratings (Par 105): **105,104,104,103,102 100,99,93,**
CSF £52.24 CT £187.35 TOTE £3.70: £1.60, £2.90, £1.70; EX 46.20 Trifecta £268.30.

Owner Dare To Dream Racing **Bred** Selwood Bloodstock, Hoskins & Lowry **Trained** Chiddingfold, Surrey

FOCUS
A fair sprint and little between the first two who raced wide apart, with the runner-up racing far side on his own.

6810 VISIT ATTHERACES.COM H'CAP 1m 2f

6:30 (6:31) (Class 5) (0-70,68) 3-Y-O

£3,428 (£1,020; £509; £300; £300; £300) **Stalls** Low

Form RPR

0022 **1** **Verify**[18] 6128 3-9-5 66.. JamieSpencer 3 76+
(Ed Walker) *hld up in midfield: stl gng strly over 2f out: clsd to chal over 1f out: rdn to ld jst ins fnl f: drew clr last 75yds* **5/4**[1]

-053 **2** 1¾ **Slade King (IRE)**[13] 6304 3-9-7 68................................ TomQueally 11 74
(Gary Moore) *trckd ldr: rdn over 2f out: led over 1f out: hdd jst ins fnl f: styd on but outpcd last 75yds* **14/1**

0045 **3** 2¼ **Toybox**[33] 5561 3-9-3 64......................................(p[1]) RobHornby 4 66
(Jonathan Portman) *trckd ldng pair: waiting for a gap over 2f out: rdn over 1f out: kpt on one pce fnl f* **11/1**

-203 **4** *nk* **No Dress Rehearsal**[45] 5156 3-9-7 68........................(h[1]) AdamKirby 10 69
(Michael Easterby) *trckd ldng trio: shkn up and nt qckn over 2f out: kpt on over 1f out but nvr a real threat* **5/1**[2]

1462 **5** ½ **Elsie Violet (IRE)**[17] 6173 3-9-1 62...........................(p) AndreaAtzeni 7 62
(Robert Eddery) *led: rdn over 2f out: hdd over 1f out: fdd fnl f* **8/1**[3]

5530 **6** ¾ **Society Guest (IRE)**[19] 6083 3-9-7 68............................ GeraldMosse 8 66
(Mick Channon) *hld up in last trio: effrt on wd outside wl over 2f out: rdn and kpt on one pce: n.d* **11/1**

006 **7** 1 **Your Thoughts (FR)**[17] 6187 3-8-11 58............................ FrannyNorton 2 54
(Paul Webber) *t.k.h: hld up in last trio: stl there whn rdn 2f out: passed wkng rivals after: n.d* **25/1**

5530 **8** ¾ **Glory**[19] 6083 3-9-5 66.. TomMarquand 1 61
(Richard Hannon) *slowly away: pushed along to rcvr and sn chsd ldrs: rdn over 3f out: styd chsng tl wknd jst over 1f out* **11/1**

4150 **8** *dht* **Lieutenant Conde**[55] 4769 3-9-2 63.......................(t[1] w) CharlieBennett 6 58
(Hughie Morrison) *nvr beyond midfield: shkn up 3f out: no prog 2f out: nvr a factor* **25/1**

650 **10** 2 **So Strictly**[26] 5808 3-8-13 60..(t[1]) SeanLevey 5 51
(Paul Cole) *hld up in last trio: rdn over 2f out: no real prog* **16/1**

400 **11** 2 **Wall Of Sapphire (IRE)**[26] 5807 3-9-1 62.......................(e[1]) ShaneKelly 9 49
(Mark Loughnane) *lost midfield pl after 3f: rdn in rr 3f out: sn btn* **40/1**

5054 **12** 1 **Sea Of Marengo (IRE)**[18] 6123 3-9-0 61........................(p) LukeMorris 12 46
(Grace Harris) *t.k.h: racd on outer in midfield: pushed along 3f out: wknd wl over 1f out* **33/1**

2m 7.71s (-1.29) **Going Correction** -0.10s/f (Good) **12 Ran SP% 122.8**
Speed ratings (Par 101): **101,99,97,97,97 96,95,95,95,93 91,91**
CSF £21.58 CT £150.86 TOTE £2.00: £1.10, £3.60, £3.00; EX 22.60 Trifecta £119.80.

Owner S Stuckey **Bred** Stuart Stuckey **Trained** Upper Lambourn, Berks

FOCUS
A modest 3yo handicap won in ready style by the favourite. The prominent racers fared best, so the winner needs his effort upgrading. The second has been rated back to his best, and the third close to form.

6811 VISIT A L INSPIRED ON FACEBOOK NOVICE STKS 1m 3f 99y

7:00 (7:05) (Class 5) 3-Y-O+ **£3,428** (£1,020; £509; £254) **Stalls** Low

Form RPR

66 **1** **Riverfront (FR)**[23] 5955 3-9-2 0...................................... DavidProbert 8 78
(Andrew Balding) *in tch: pushed along and prog 3f out: rdn to chse ldr over 1f out: styd on to ld ins fnl f* **8/1**

33 **2** ½ **Knockacullion (USA)**[13] 6316 3-9-2 0............................ ShaneKelly 6 77
(Richard Hughes) *mde most: shkn up and pressed 3f out: drvn over 1f out: hdd and no ex ins fnl f* **5/2**[2]

0 **3** ¾ **Torbellino**[14] 6290 3-8-11 0.. KierenFox 4 71
(John Best) *hld up in rr: rdn and prog on outer over 2f out: chsd ldng pair ins fnl f: hung lft after but kpt on* **33/1**

53 **4** 4 **Lumination**[147] 1652 3-9-2 0.. RobHornby 10 69
(Martyn Meade) *trckd ldr after 3f: shkn up to chal 3f out: nt qckn and lost 2nd over 1f out: wknd* **11/8**[1]

30 **5** 1¾ **Waterfall**[26] 5810 3-8-6 0.. CierenFallon(5) 2 61?
(Lucy Wadham) *sn in midfield: rdn wl over 2f out: plugged on one pce and n.d (jockey said filly jumped awkwardly from stalls)* **14/1**

26 **6** 3¼ **Heavenly Tale (IRE)**[171] 1221 3-8-11 0............................ HarryBentley 11 55
(Ralph Beckett) *chsd ldr 3f: styd prom tl wknd u.p 2f out* **4/1**[3]

50 **7** 2¼ **Gibraltarian (IRE)**[14] 6290 3-8-11 0............................ CharlieBennett 7 52
(Jim Boyle) *hld up towards rr: pushed along and no prog over 2f out: nvr in it* **33/1**

06 **8** 12 **Aspiring Diva**[17] 6169 3-8-12 1 ow1............................ GeraldMosse 3 32
(Mohamed Moubarak) *a in rr: rdn and no prog over 2f out: wknd and eased over 1f out* **40/1**

9 99 **Scarlett Sun** 3-9-2 0.. TomQueally 1
(George Margarson) *slowly away: sn t.o: btn wl over a f* **20/1**

10 99 **Chicago Socks** 9-9-6 0.. FinleyMarsh(3) 5
(William de Best-Turner) *reluctant to enter stalls: rel to r: pottered arnd in own time: btn nrly half a m* **100/1**

2m 28.46s (-1.24) **Going Correction** -0.10s/f (Good)
WFA 3 from 9yo 7lb **10 Ran SP% 122.5**
Speed ratings (Par 103): **100,99,99,96,94 92,90,82,10,**
CSF £28.85 TOTE £11.00: £2.40, £1.20, £10.30; EX 35.60 Trifecta £960.60.

Owner L Register & Partner **Bred** S C Thousand Dreams **Trained** Kingsclere, Hants

FOCUS
An ordinary novice run at a steady gallop. Muddling form. The second has been rated to his AW latest for now.

6812 SKY SPORTS RACING ON SKY 415 H'CAP 1m 3f 99y

7:30 (7:31) (Class 5) (0-75,76) 3-Y-O+

£3,428 (£1,020; £509; £300; £300; £300) **Stalls** Low

Form RPR

5001 **1** **Culture (FR)**[21] 6022 3-9-2 76.................................(p) CierenFallon(5) 3 87
(George Baker) *trckd ldr: led over 3f out: rdn wl over 1f out: jnd ins fnl f: urged along and hld on wl* **11/8**[1]

5032 **2** *shd* **Dubious Affair (IRE)**[19] 6069 3-9-1 70...................... RichardKingscote 2 80
(Sir Michael Stoute) *trckd ldng pair to 4f out: sn pushed along: renewed effrt to chse wnr wl over 1f out: drvn to chal and upsides ins fnl f: jst hld last strides* **2/1**[2]

2452 **3** 4½ **Carp Kid (IRE)**[12] 6331 4-9-8 73.................................(p) FinleyMarsh(3) 6 73
(John Flint) *led at mod pce: hdd and nt qckn over 3f out: one pce fnl 2f and no ch w ldng pair* **9/2**[3]

The Form Book Flat 2019, Raceform Ltd, Newbury, RG14 5SJ

0454 **4** 1 1/4 **Bartholomew J (IRE)**[13] 6323 5-9-6 **68**.......................(p) DavidProbert 5 66
(Lydia Pearce) *in tch: effrt to chse wnr 3f out: rdn and wknd wl over 1f out* **25/1**

4015 **5** 3/4 **Tiar Na Nog (IRE)**[64] 4425 7-9-10 **72**............................ CharlesBishop 4 69
(Denis Coakley) *hld up in tch: effrt on outer 3f out: rdn and no prog 2f out: wknd over 1f out* **9/1**

011- **6** 7 **Roundhead**[263] 6095 4-9-12 **74**.......................................(w) JamieSpencer 1 59
(Richard Phillips) *dwlt: hld up in last: outpcd whn pce lifted over 3f out: detached and no ch after* **20/1**

2m 30.23s (0.53) **Going Correction** -0.10s/f (Good)
WFA 3 from 4yo+ 7lb **6 Ran SP% 112.2**
Speed ratings (Par 103): **94,93,90,89,89 84**
CSF £4.35 TOTE £2.10: £1.30, £1.30; EX 4.90 Trifecta £10.40.
Owner Highclere Thoroughbred Racing - Dream On **Bred** S C E A Haras Du Ma & Elise Drouet **Trained** Chiddingfold, Surrey

FOCUS
This played out as the market suggested and the 3yo pair dominated. The gallop was a slow one.
T/Jkpt: £3,335.60 to a £1 stake. Pool: £18,792.40 - 4 winning units T/Plt: £27.90 to a £1 stake. Pool: £72,640.24 - 1899.22 winning units T/Qpdt: £15.80 to a £1 stake. Pool: £9,852.89 - 458.70 winning units **Jonathan Neesom**

6813 - 6819a (Foreign Racing) - See Raceform Interactive

6750 CRAON (R-H)
Monday, September 2

OFFICIAL GOING: Turf: good

6820a PRIX DIRICKX - 11TH ETAPE DU DEFI DU GALOP - (LISTED RACE) (3YO+) (TURF) 1m 4f
2:00 3-Y-O+ £27,027 (£10,810; £8,108; £5,405; £2,702)

RPR

1 **Just Sherry (IRE)**[36] 4-9-0 0.............................. Pierre-CharlesBoudot 4 97
(Edouard Monfort, France) **18/5**[3]

2 3/4 **Good Question (FR)**[48] 5036 4-9-7 0............................ MaximeGuyon 7 102
(C Escuder, France) **11/5**[1]

3 hd **Apollo Flight (FR)**[24] 5926 4-9-3 0................................. DamienBoche 5 98
(L Gadbin, France) **13/1**

4 2 **Brokeback Mountain (FR)**[35] 4-9-3 0.......................... TheoBachelot 3 95
(Y Barberot, France) **14/5**[2]

5 hd **Caravagio (FR)**[90] 6-9-3 0.. MathieuAndrouin 6 94
(Alain Couetil, France) **16/1**

6 3/4 **Dance Legend**[35] 5510 4-9-0 0.................................... IoritzMendizabal 1 90
(Rae Guest) *settled midfield: rowed along over 2f out: rdn over 1f out: drvn and wknd ins fnl f* **22/1**

7 6 **Viridorix**[38] 4-9-3 0...(b[1]) MlleCoraliePacaut 8 84
(J-C Rouget, France) **25/1**

8 3/4 **Solmina (FR)**[48] 5036 7-9-0 0.. AnthonyCrastus 2 79
(J-L Dubord, France) **42/10**

2m 30.03s **8 Ran SP% 119.8**
PARI-MUTUEL (all including 1 euro stake): WIN 4.60; PLACE 1.70, 1.30, 2.70; DF 7.80.
Owner Franck Raoul **Bred** R Roberts **Trained** France

6821 - (Foreign Racing) - See Raceform Interactive

6585 CATTERICK (L-H)
Tuesday, September 3

OFFICIAL GOING: Good to firm (good in places) changing to good after race 2 (2.30)
Wind: Moderate, across in straight of over 2f Weather: Overcast

6822 FOLLOW @CATTERICKRACES NOVICE AUCTION STKS 5f
2:00 (2:01) (Class 5) 2-Y-O £4,140 (£1,232; £615; £307) **Stalls Low**

Form RPR

5144 **1** **Auckland Lodge (IRE)**[21] 6032 2-9-2 73.................. HarrisonShaw(3) 3 75
(Ben Haslam) *mde all: rdn 2f out: asserted and r.o gamely towards fin* **6/1**[3]

0023 **2** 1 1/4 **Flight Of Thunder (IRE)**[32] 5618 2-8-5 56................. RhonaPindar(7) 4 64
(Kevin Ryan) *pressed wnr: rdn 2f out whn chalng: styd on same pce towards fin* **16/1**

3 **3** 1 **Lady Nectar (IRE)**[16] 6254 2-8-12 0............................ PaulMulrennan 5 60
(Ann Duffield) *chsd ldrs: rdn and cl up 2f out: unable qck over 1f out: kpt on same pce ins fnl f* **7/1**

5240 **4** hd **Spygate**[12] 6375 2-9-3 74.. DanielTudhope 7 64
(Richard Fahey) *chsd ldrs: rdn 2f out: kpt on ins fnl f: nt pce to chal front two* **9/2**[2]

4 **5** 2 3/4 **Breguet Boy (IRE)**[6] 6585 2-9-3 0.................................. ShaneGray 2 54
(Keith Dalgleish) *in tch: rdn 1/2-way: sn outpcd: kpt on one pce ins fnl f: nvr able to trble ldrs* **8/1**

532 **6** 2 3/4 **Arriba Arriba (IRE)**[16] 6254 2-9-3 74............................. GrahamLee 8 44
(Rebecca Menzies) *chsd ldrs: rdn 1/2-way: sn outpcd: edgd rt u.p over 1f out: n.d after* **6/1**[3]

021 **7** 3/4 **Vintage Times**[28] 5788 2-9-5 75.................................. DavidAllan 10 44
(Tim Easterby) *in tch on outer: effrt 2f out: wknd ins fnl f (trainer's rep could offer no explanation regarding the filly's performance)* **5/2**[1]

8 1 1/2 **Deevious Beau** 2-9-3 0... BenCurtis 1 36
(David Barron) *pushed along whn outpcd and bhd: nvr a threat* **25/1**

0 **9** 11 **Inver Silver**[24] 5968 2-8-12 0...................................... JamesSullivan 6
(Ollie Pears) *sn pushed along: outpcd after 2f: nvr a threat* **100/1**

10 2 3/4 **Lezardrieux** 2-9-3 0.. SamJames 9
(Grant Tuer) *missed break: a outpcd and wl bhd* **33/1**

58.94s (-1.56) **Going Correction** -0.10s/f (Good) **10 Ran SP% 112.6**
Speed ratings (Par 95): **108,106,104,104,99 95,94,91,74,69**
CSF £90.76 TOTE £8.00: £2.40, £4.30, £1.60; EX 81.80 Trifecta £456.80.
Owner The Auckland Lodge Partnership **Bred** R Galway **Trained** Middleham Moor, N Yorks

FOCUS
The selectively watered ground was given as good to firm, good in places (GoingStick 8.2), but they were kicking the top off and, after riding in the opener, Harrison Shaw and Jimmy Sullivan called the ground good, while Paul Mulrennan and Sam James reckoned it was just on the easy side of good. The rail was dolled out and yards added to race distances beyond 5f. An ordinary novice. The second has been rated as improving slightly.

6823 DINE AND VIEW AT CATTERICK RACES NOVICE STKS 7f 6y
2:30 (2:30) (Class 5) 3-Y-O+ £4,140 (£1,232; £615; £307) **Stalls Low**

Form RPR

3203 **1** **Morning Duel (IRE)**[7] 6582 3-9-10 75.......................(t) DanielTudhope 7 76
(David O'Meara) *chsd ldr: rdn to ld 2f out: strly pressed wl ins fnl f: jst hld on* **11/8**[1]

4 **2** nse **Modakhar (IRE)**[89] 3510 3-9-10 0................................... BenCurtis 6 75
(K R Burke) *in tch: effrt 2f out: chsd wnr for press over 1f out: stl green: str chal wl ins fnl f: r.o towards fin: jst failed* **11/2**[3]

32 **3** 2 **Sloane Garden**[15] 6283 3-9-5 0...................................... DavidAllan 3 65
(James Tate) *hld up: rdn and hdwy 2f out: chsd ldrs for press over 1f out: styd on ins fnl f: one pce towards fin* **5/2**[2]

0004 **4** 7 **Al Suil Eile (FR)**[17] 6204 3-9-10 68................................. JasonHart 2 51
(John Quinn) *chsd ldrs: rdn over 2f out: wknd over 1f out* **6/1**

3 **5** 4 **Blistering Barney (IRE)**[47] 5098 3-9-10 0..................(t) AndrewElliott 5 40
(Christopher Kellett) *hld up: pushed along 3f out: sn outpcd: nvr a threat* **16/1**

6 hd **Anyonecanbeastar (IRE)**[442] 3952 3-9-5 0........................ JoeFanning 4 35
(Mark Johnston) *racd keenly: led: rdn and hdd 2f out: wkng whn edgd rt jst over 1f out* **20/1**

1m 26.17s (-1.23) **Going Correction** -0.10s/f (Good)
WFA 3 from 4yo 4lb **6 Ran SP% 111.0**
Speed ratings (Par 103): **103,102,100,92,88 87**
CSF £9.25 TOTE £2.20: £1.30, £2.80; EX 8.30 Trifecta £13.70.
Owner Clipper Logistics **Bred** Southacre Bloodstock **Trained** Upper Helmsley, N Yorks

FOCUS
Add 15yds. The going was changed to good all round after this race. A modest heat in which the favourite scraped home. The winner has been rated close to form.

6824 WATCH RACING TV NOW CLAIMING STKS 1m 7f 189y
3:05 (3:06) (Class 6) 4-Y-O+ £3,105 (£924; £461; £300; £300; £300) **Stalls Low**

Form RPR

5636 **1** **Gemini**[16] 6256 4-9-4 63...(p[1]) JasonHart 2 68
(John Quinn) *handy: dropped in to chse ldrs after 3f: reminder 1/2-way: pushed along and impr to ld over 5f out: kicked on over 2f out: styd on gamely ins fnl f* **9/4**[2]

0665 **2** 2 3/4 **Valkenburg**[16] 6256 4-9-5 63..(p) JoeFanning 4 66
(William Bethell) *prom: chsd ldr after 5f tl over 5f out: rdn over 4f out: outpcd 3f out: rallied to take 2nd 2f out: nvr quite able to get to wnr: eased whn one pce fnl 50yds* **4/6**[1]

0446 **3** 12 **Demophon**[12] 6366 5-8-9 44.. GrahamLee 6 41
(Steve Flook) *led: hdd over 5f out: rdn 3f out: lost 2nd 2f out: edgd rt over 1f out: wknd fnl f* **15/2**[3]

0500 **4** 6 **Bold Statement (IRE)**[8] 6545 4-8-13 49.......................... CamHardie 1 38
(Alan Berry) *prom: rdn and outpcd over 4f out: wknd 2f out* **50/1**

0300 **5** 7 **Royal Liberty**[19] 6098 4-8-11 47................................... SamJames 5 27
(Geoffrey Harker) *hld up: rdn and outpcd over 4f out: nvr a threat* **28/1**

0 **6** 23 **Fast And Friendly (IRE)**[34] 5555 5-8-6 0............... ConnorMurtagh(3) 3
(Barry Murtagh) *hld up: drvn 5f out: lft bhd over 4f out* **66/1**

3m 34.17s (-1.83) **Going Correction** -0.10s/f (Good) **6 Ran SP% 109.4**
Speed ratings (Par 101): **100,98,92,89,86 74**
CSF £3.87 TOTE £3.70: £1.60, £1.10; EX 4.30 Trifecta £8.80.
Owner Fulbeck Horse Syndicate Ltd **Bred** Windmill Farm Partnership **Trained** Settrington, N Yorks

FOCUS
Add 30yds. A match really, and Jason Hart made the decisive move in the back straight, taking the favourite out of his comfort zone. It's been rated as straightforward form.

6825 EVERY RACE LIVE ON RACING TV FILLIES' H'CAP 7f 6y
3:35 (3:35) (Class 4) (0-80,80) 4-Y-O+ £6,080 (£1,809; £904; £452; £300; £300) **Stalls Low**

Form RPR

6310 **1** **Rux Ruxx (IRE)**[12] 6379 4-9-7 **80**................................(p) DavidAllan 2 87
(Tim Easterby) *in tch: rdn over 2f out: effrt to take 2nd over 1f out: led jst ins fnl f: kpt on wl towards fin* **2/1**[1]

6625 **2** 3/4 **Rose Marmara**[6] 6591 6-8-5 **67**.............................(tp) ConnorMurtagh(3) 1 72
(Brian Rothwell) *led: rdn over 2f out: hdd jst ins fnl f: hld towards fin* **17/2**

/0-3 **3** nk **Kindly**[54] 4822 6-9-0 **78**... GerO'Neill(5) 4 82
(Michael Easterby) *hld up: rdn over 2f out: angled out and hdwy over 1f out: styd on ins fnl f: gng on at fin: nt pce of wnr* **7/1**

-450 **4** 1/2 **Arabian Jazz (IRE)**[17] 6201 4-9-1 **74**................................(h) CliffordLee 3 77
(Michael Bell) *chsd ldrs: rdn over 2f out: kpt on u.p ins fnl f: nt pce to chal* **5/1**[3]

2066 **5** 1 3/4 **Eponina (IRE)**[22] 6025 5-8-0 **64** ow2.......................... TheodoreLadd(5) 5 62
(Michael Appleby) *racd keenly: chsd ldr: rdn and ev ch 2f out: lost 2nd over 1f out: no ex fnl 110yds* **3/1**[2]

0152 **6** 2 1/4 **Strawberryandcream**[10] 6461 4-8-5 **64**............................ PaulHanagan 6 56
(James Bethell) *s.i.s: in rr: rdn 2f out: nvr able to trble ldrs: eased whn btn towards fin* **11/2**

1m 26.07s (-1.33) **Going Correction** -0.10s/f (Good) **6 Ran SP% 113.4**
Speed ratings (Par 102): **103,102,101,101,99 96**
CSF £19.69 TOTE £3.20: £1.90, £3.40; EX 18.90 Trifecta £107.70.
Owner King Power Racing Co Ltd **Bred** Yeomanstown Stud **Trained** Great Habton, N Yorks

FOCUS
Add 15yds. A fairly competitive fillies' handicap. It's been rated around the second to this year's form.

6826 RACINGTV.COM VETERANS' H'CAP 5f 212y
4:10 (4:10) (Class 5) (0-75,77) 6-Y-O+ £4,787 (£1,424; £711; £355; £300; £300) **Stalls Low**

Form RPR

2322 **1** **B Fifty Two (IRE)**[4] 6680 10-8-5 **62**.......................(tp) JaneElliott(3) 7 70
(Marjorie Fife) *midfield: rdn over 2f out: hdwy over 1f out: led narrowly ins fnl f: kpt on wl* **11/2**[2]

0020 **2** nk **Alsvinder**[31] 5691 6-9-7 **75**...(p[1]) KevinStott 3 82
(Philip Kirby) *led: rdn over 2f out: edgd rt and hdd narrowly ins fnl f: kpt on: hld cl home* **16/1**

3066 **3** 2 1/2 **Gin In The Inn (IRE)**[29] 5740 6-9-6 **77**........................ SeanDavis(3) 5 76
(Richard Fahey) *chsd ldrs: effrt 2f out: hung lft ins fnl f: kpt on u.p: no imp on front pair fnl 100yds* **8/1**

3540 **4** 1 **Indian Pursuit (IRE)**[6] 6591 6-8-9 **63**........................(v) JasonHart 6 59
(John Quinn) *prom: rdn and ev ch over 1f out: no ex fnl 100yds* **13/2**[3]

4561 **5** nse **Final Frontier (IRE)**[12] 6373 6-9-0 **68**........................ JackGarritty 4 64
(Ruth Carr) *wnt to post early: hld up: rdn over 2f out: hdwy over 1f out: lugged lft and r.o ins fnl f: gng on at fin: nt rch ldrs (jockey said gelding was slowly into stride which prevented him gaining the desired prominent position)* **9/4**[1]

4260 **6** hd **Zylan (IRE)**[8] 6549 7-9-3 **71**........................(p) BenCurtis 1 66
(Roger Fell) *midfield: rdn over 2f out: hdwy on inner over 1f out: n.m.r briefly ins fnl f: one pce* **7/1**

4300 **7** 1 1/4 **Extrasolar**[6] 6590 9-8-7 **61** oh4........................(t) AndrewMullen 2 52
(Geoffrey Harker) *in rr: pushed along over 3f out: sme hdwy over 1f out: kpt on ins fnl f: nt pce to trble ldrs* **22/1**

3303 **8** 1 1/4 **Highland Acclaim (IRE)**[7] 6567 8-9-6 **74**........................(p[1]) DavidNolan 10 61
(David O'Meara) *hld up: rdn 2f out: sme hdwy over 1f out: nvr threatened ldrs: wknd ins fnl f* **8/1**

1030 **9** hd **Orion's Bow**[17] 6227 8-9-8 **76**........................(tp) DavidAllan 8 62
(Tim Easterby) *prom: rdn and ev ch over 1f out but unable qck: wknd fnl 100yds* **11/1**

5000 **10** 6 **Adam's Ale**[13] 6339 10-8-8 **65**........................(p) ConnorMurtagh(3) 9 32
(Marjorie Fife) *wnt to post early: in tch: rdn over 2f out: wknd over 1f out (jockey said gelding stopped quickly)* **40/1**

1m 13.13s (-0.47) **Going Correction** -0.10s/f (Good) **10 Ran SP% 115.2**
Speed ratings: **99,98,95,93,93 93,91,90,90,82**
CSF £87.85 CT £700.60 TOTE £6.00: £1.50, £4.90, £2.20; EX 93.80 Trifecta £847.90.
Owner Fat Badger Racing **Bred** Mull Enterprises Ltd **Trained** Stillington, N Yorks

FOCUS
Add 15yds. A veterans' sprint won by one of the two oldest runners in the line-up. The second has been rated to his best for his current yard.

6827 2019 CATTERICK TWELVE FURLONG SERIES H'CAP (DIV I) 1m 4f 13y
4:40 (4:40) (Class 6) (0-60,62) 3-Y-O+
£3,105 (£924; £461; £300; £300; £300) **Stalls** Centre

Form RPR

4521 **1** **Gylo (IRE)**[3] 6702 3-9-8 **62**........................ DanielTudhope 4 69
(David O'Meara) *in tch: effrt over 2f out: led wl over 1f out: kpt on wl* **8/13**[1]

2532 **2** 3/4 **Jan De Heem**[15] 6278 9-9-3 **52**........................(v) ConnorMurtagh(3) 3 57
(Tina Jackson) *s.i.s: hld up: rdn over 3f out: hdwy over 2f out: styd on towards fin (jockey said gelding was slowly away)* **17/2**[3]

4134 **3** hd **Remember Rocky**[13] 6341 10-9-11 **62**........................(b) PaulaMuir(5) 10 67
(Lucy Normile) *midfield: hdwy after 5f: chsd ldrs: rdn and sltly outpcd 2f out: rallied wl ins fnl f: styd on towards fin* **14/1**

6522 **4** 1 3/4 **Dew Pond**[18] 6180 7-9-12 **58**........................(bt) DavidAllan 9 60
(Tim Easterby) *hld up: hdwy over 4f out: rdn to chse ldrs over 2f out: one pce fnl 75yds (vet said gelding lost right-fore shoe)* **5/1**[2]

0135 **5** 1/2 **Nearly There**[24] 5974 6-9-6 **55**........................(t) SeanDavis(3) 1 56
(Wilf Storey) *racd keenly: midfield: rdn and outpcd over 3f out: hdwy over 1f out: keeping on whn checked ins fnl f: eased whn no imp towards fin* **14/1**

6-60 **6** 1 **Mr Sundowner (USA)**[15] 6275 7-9-3 **56**........................(t) RhonaPindar(7) 7 55
(Michael Herrington) *racd keenly: prom: led over 5f out: rdn 2f out: hdd wl over 1f out: fdd fnl 100yds* **16/1**

0455 **7** 1/2 **Question Of Faith**[29] 5727 8-10-1 **61**........................(p) PaulHanagan 5 60
(Martin Todhunter) *s.v.s: hld up bhd: rdn over 2f out: hdwy over 1f out: nvr able to trble ldrs* **16/1**

0530 **8** nk **Masters Apprentice (IRE)**[145] 1718 4-9-11 **57**........................(p[1]) DougieCostello 2 55
(Mark Walford) *stmbld s: sn rcvrd to ld: hdd over 5f out: chsd ldr: stuck to inner rail ent st: rdn and lost 2nd over 2f out: fdd ins fnl f (jockey said gelding stumbled when leaving stalls)* **25/1**

06 **9** 28 **Shakiah (IRE)**[46] 5156 4-8-13 **45**........................(h) SamJames 6
(Sharon Watt) *wnt to post early: led early: prom: rdn and wknd over 4f out (trainer said filly was found to have bled)* **50/1**

2m 42.6s (2.00) **Going Correction** -0.10s/f (Good)
WFA 3 from 4yo+ 8lb **9 Ran SP% 120.0**
Speed ratings (Par 101): **89,88,88,87,86 86,85,85,67**
CSF £7.32 CT £44.18 TOTE £1.40: £1.10, £1.80, £3.00; EX 7.20 Trifecta £47.30.
Owner Gallop Racing **Bred** R & R Bloodstock **Trained** Upper Helmsley, N Yorks

FOCUS
Add 15yds. They went steady early on and it was the slower of the two divisions by 3.58sec. The winner has been rated as replicating his latest effort.

6828 2019 CATTERICK TWELVE FURLONG SERIES H'CAP (DIV II) 1m 4f 13y
5:10 (5:10) (Class 6) (0-60,61) 3-Y-O+
£3,105 (£924; £461; £300; £300; £300) **Stalls** Centre

Form RPR

330 **1** **Flower Power**[15] 5974 8-9-9 **57**........................(p) JasonHart 2 66
(Tony Coyle) *hld up: rdn over 2f out: hdwy to ld 1f out: styd on wl to draw clr fnl 100yds (trainer said mare benefitted from a return to the course)* **16/1**

0403 **2** 4 **Point Of Honour (IRE)**[19] 6098 4-8-9 **46** oh1........................(p) HarrisonShaw(3) 5 49
(Phillip Makin) *midfield: hdwy over 6f out: rdn to ld over 1f out: sn hdd: nt pce of wnr fnl 100yds (jockey said gelding stumbled when leaving stalls)* **5/1**

6002 **3** hd **Tommy Hallinan (IRE)**[17] 6210 5-9-12 **60**........................ BenRobinson 1 62
(Brian Ellison) *led for 1f: racd keenly: prom: rdn over 2f out: stl there over 1f out: kpt on u.p ins fnl f but nt pce of wnr (jockey said gelding all reasonable and permissible measures to obtain the best possible placing)* **7/2**[2]

3562 **4** 2 1/4 **Spark Of War (IRE)**[28] 5766 4-9-7 **55**........................(b) ShaneGray 7 54
(Keith Dalgleish) *handy: led 2f out: rdn and hdd over 1f out: stl ev ch and edgd lft ent fnl f: no ex fnl 100yds* **4/1**[3]

2221 **5** shd **Betty Grable (IRE)**[5] 6628 5-9-6 **61** 5ex........................ RhonaPindar(7) 6 60
(Wilf Storey) *in rr: pushed along 2f out: hdwy over 1f out: nvr able to trble ldrs* **11/4**[1]

4540 **6** 3 **Iolani (GER)**[13] 6343 7-9-10 **58**........................(tp) PaulMulrennan 3 52
(Dianne Sayer) *sluggish s: sn in tch: drvn over 4f out: outpcd over 2f out: wknd ins fnl f* **7/1**

0005 **7** 1 1/4 **Albert Boy (IRE)**[8] 6550 6-9-0 **55**........................ JonathanFisher(7) 9 47
(Scott Dixon) *led after 1f: rdn and hdd 2f out: wknd 1f out* **14/1**

0100 **8** 2 **Strategic (IRE)**[18] 6180 4-8-12 **46** oh1........................(h) RachelRichardson 8 35
(Eric Alston) *hld up: pushed along over 6f out: nvr a threat* **28/1**

2m 39.02s (-1.58) **Going Correction** -0.10s/f (Good)
WFA 3 from 4yo+ 8lb **8 Ran SP% 114.1**
Speed ratings (Par 101): **101,98,98,96,96 94,93,92**
CSF £93.00 CT £348.84 TOTE £12.00: £2.70, £1.60, £1.50; EX 102.40 Trifecta £574.90.
Owner Ms Margaret Matheson **Bred** Margaret Matheson **Trained** Norton, N Yorks
■ Stewards' Enquiry : Rhona Pindar two-day ban: failed to take all reasonable and permissible measures to obtain the best possible placing (17-18 Sep)

FOCUS
Add 15yds. This was run in a time 3.58sec quicker than the first division, and they finished more strung out. The second helps pin the level.

6829 RACING AGAIN 10TH SEPTEMBER H'CAP 5f
5:40 (5:41) (Class 5) (0-70,66) 4-Y-O+
£4,075 (£1,212; £606; £303; £300; £300) **Stalls** Low

Form RPR

0544 **1** **Landing Night (IRE)**[41] 5298 7-9-7 **66**........................(bt) CliffordLee 1 71
(Rebecca Menzies) *mde all: rdn 2f out: all out towards fin* **4/1**[2]

5413 **2** hd **Economic Crisis (IRE)**[6] 6607 10-9-2 **64**........................ HarrisonShaw(3) 6 68
(Alan Berry) *hld up: rdn over 2f out: swtchd rt and hdwy over 1f out: r.o towards fin* **5/1**[3]

5321 **3** nk **Red Stripes (USA)**[9] 6510 7-8-7 **59** 4ex........................(b) GavinAshton(7) 9 62
(Lisa Williamson) *chsd ldrs on outer: rdn 2f out: styd on towards fin: nt quite pce of wnr* **7/1**

0204 **4** nk **Longroom**[25] 5901 7-9-6 **65**........................(t) PhilDennis 3 67
(Noel Wilson) *w wnr: rdn over 1f out: kpt on ins fnl f: no ex fnl strides (jockey said gelding lost right-hind shoe)* **10/1**

3-60 **5** 1 1/4 **Pavers Pride**[95] 3291 5-9-0 **64**........................(b w) GerO'Neill(5) 2 62
(Noel Wilson) *chsd ldrs: rdn 2f out: kpt on same pce wl ins fnl f* **11/1**

6115 **6** nk **Boudica Bay (IRE)**[18] 6178 4-9-4 **63**........................ GrahamLee 4 60
(Eric Alston) *chsd ldrs: rdn 2f out: no ex fnl 75yds (jockey said filly hung left-handed throughout)* **11/4**[1]

-200 **7** 3 **Kibaar**[115] 2632 7-8-13 **58**........................ JamesSullivan 8 44
(Ruth Carr) *missed break: in rr: rdn and hdwy 2f out: one pce fnl f: nvr able to trble ldrs* **16/1**

0030 **8** 6 **Cuppacoco**[15] 6277 4-8-10 **55**........................ JoeFanning 7 19
(Ann Duffield) *handy: lost pl after 2f: bhd ins fnl f* **10/1**

0304 **9** 2 1/4 **Funkadelic**[63] 4493 4-8-7 **52** oh5........................ AndrewMullen 5 8
(Ben Haslam) *prom: lost pl over 3f out: pushed along 1/2-way: wknd over 1f out* **16/1**

59.19s (-1.31) **Going Correction** -0.10s/f (Good) **9 Ran SP% 114.1**
Speed ratings (Par 103): **106,105,105,104,102 102,97,87,84**
CSF £24.02 CT £135.28 TOTE £5.90: £2.00, £1.80, £2.10; EX 28.10 Trifecta £147.00.
Owner Titanium Racing Club **Bred** Mrs Claire Doyle **Trained** Mordon, Durham

FOCUS
A modest sprint and they finished in a heap. Limited form rated around the first four. Add 15yds.
T/Plt: £53.80 to a £1 stake. Pool: £61,140.66 - 828.17 winning units T/Qpdt: £9.40 to a £1 stake. Pool: £6,693.39 - 525.29 winning units **Darren Owen**

6504 GOODWOOD (R-H)
Tuesday, September 3

OFFICIAL GOING: Good to firm (good in places; watered; 7.7)
Wind: Virtually nil Weather: Overcast

6830 JEB CONSTRUCTION H'CAP 1m 3f 44y
2:15 (2:15) (Class 5) (0-70,70) 4-Y-O+
£5,433 (£1,617; £808; £404; £300; £300) **Stalls** High

Form RPR

2121 **1** **Seaborn (IRE)**[47] 5086 5-9-2 **70**........................ WilliamCarver(5) 3 80
(Patrick Chamings) *looked wl; in tch in 4th: gd hdwy to ld gng wl over 2f out: rdn appr fnl f w short ld: kpt up to work and won gng away* **5/2**[1]

0030 **2** 2 **Galactic Spirit**[15] 6278 4-9-5 **68**........................ RaulDaSilva 8 75
(James Evans) *on toes; dwlt and racd in rr: stdy hdwy into midfield 2f out: sn rdn to chse ldr 1f out: carried hd high and unable to match wnr fnl f (jockey said gelding was slowly away)* **16/1**

4321 **3** 1 1/4 **Broad Appeal**[23] 5993 5-9-0 **70**........................ TylerSaunders(7) 9 74
(Jonathan Portman) *racd in midfield: rdn along to chse wnr 2f out: kpt on one pce fnl f* **11/2**

0112 **4** 1 **Affluence (IRE)**[29] 5744 4-9-4 **67**........................(p) EoinWalsh 4 73+
(Martin Smith) *towards rr of midfield: hdwy whn short of room over 2f out: hmpd by rival over 1f out: rdn once in clr and styd on wl (jockey said gelding was denied a clear run)* **5/1**[3]

-335 **5** hd **Miss Blondell**[20] 6083 6-9-2 **65**........................(p[1]) JasonWatson 6 67
(Marcus Tregoning) *racd in midfield: rdn along to chse wnr 2f out: swtchd rt over 1f out: kpt on fnl f* **7/2**[2]

6-03 **6** 1/2 **Good Impression**[21] 6042 4-8-7 **56** oh3........................(p) DavidEgan 5 58
(Dai Burchell) *hld up: pushed along and no imp on outer over 3f out: rdn over 1f out: kpt on one pce fnl f* **25/1**

-000 **7** 6 **Lyrica's Lion (IRE)**[38] 5425 5-9-2 **65**........................ TrevorWhelan 1 56
(Sheena West) *looked wl; led: shkn up w short ld 3f out: rdn and hdd by wnr over 2f out: wknd fnl f (jockey said gelding stopped quickly. trainer said gelding had a breathing problem)* **9/1**

26-5 **8** nk **Cheeky Rascal (IRE)**[160] 1363 4-9-6 **69**........................(p) TomMarquand 7 60
(Tom Ward) *trckd ldr: rdn along and outpcd by wnr 2f out: wknd fnl f* **22/1**

5436 **9** 1/2 **Miss M (IRE)**[15] 6291 5-9-0 **63**........................ MartinDwyer 10 53
(William Muir) *hld up: rdn in rr over 2f out: nvr on terms* **10/1**

2303 **10** hd **Hidden Depths (IRE)**[23] 6010 4-9-5 **68**........................ ShaneKelly 2 58
(Neil Mulholland) *trckd ldr on inner: pushed along and no imp 2f out: rdn and lost pl over 1f out: wknd fnl f* **20/1**

2m 25.79s (-2.51) **Going Correction** +0.025s/f (Good) **10 Ran SP% 120.8**
Speed ratings (Par 103): **110,108,107,106,106 106,102,101,101,101**
CSF £45.81 CT £210.87 TOTE £3.30: £1.30, £5.40, £2.00; EX 43.40 Trifecta £286.50.
Owner Ian Beach **Bred** Michael Fennessy **Trained** Baughurst, Hants

FOCUS
Times suggested that the ground was nearer good than good to firm. All race distances as advertised. The opener was just a fair handicap. The second has been rated to last month's Newmarket form.

6831 SOUTHERN CRANES AND ACCESS EBF FILLIES' NOVICE STKS (PLUS 10 RACE) 7f
2:45 (2:46) (Class 4) 2-Y-O **£5,498** (£1,636; £817; £408) **Stalls** Low

Form RPR
05 **1** **Dutch Painting**[22] 6019 2-9-0 0 JasonWatson 6 76
(Michael Bell) *leggy; racd in midfield: gd hdwy on outer to ld over 1f out: sn rdn and short ld 1f out: drvn and strly pressed fnl 100yds: all out* **8/1**
2 *shd* **Festival Day** 2-9-0 0 JamesDoyle 1 76+
(Mark Johnston) *quite str; trckd ldr on inner: pushed along and n.m.r 2f out: swtchd lft over 1f out: sn rdn and kpt on strly clsng stages: jst failed* **6/4**[1]
3 **3** *nk* **Call Me Katie (IRE)**[24] 5961 2-9-0 0 RobertHavlin 2 75
(John Gosden) *leggy: athletic; led: rdn along and hdd by wnr over 1f out: sn drvn and responded wl to press fnl f* **5/1**[3]
3 **4** *2 ¾* **Lady Lynetta (IRE)**[28] 5772 2-9-0 0 ShaneKelly 5 68+
(Richard Hughes) *athletic; looked wl; trckd ldr: rdn along and outpcd by wnr over 1f out: one pce ins fnl f* **7/2**[2]
5 *shd* **Nibras Shadow (IRE)** 2-9-0 0 SeanLevey 7 68+
(Ismail Mohammed) *compact: bit bkward; dwlt and racd in last: rdn and no imp on ldrs 2f out: kpt on one pce* **20/1**
0 **6** *3* **Veleta**[39] 5366 2-9-0 0 HollieDoyle 4 60
(Clive Cox) *racd keenly in midfield: rdn and outpcd 2f out: wknd fnl f (jockey said filly ran too free and hung left-handed)* **11/2**

1m 27.97s (1.27) **Going Correction** +0.025s/f (Good) **6 Ran SP% 110.1**
Speed ratings (Par 94): **93,92,92,89,89 85**
CSF £19.81 TOTE £10.10: £3.80, £1.50; EX 26.00 Trifecta £169.90.
Owner R A Green **Bred** Mrs P A Cave & Cheveley Park Stud **Trained** Newmarket, Suffolk

FOCUS
Fairly useful fillies' form. The winner has been rated as progressing slightly, and the third near her revised debut effort.

6832 MATCHBOOK EBF PETER WILLETT FUTURE STAYERS' MAIDEN STKS (PLUS 10 RACE) (SIRE/DAM-RESTRICTED RACE) 1m
3:20 (3:20) (Class 2) 2-Y-O **£15,752** (£4,715; £2,357) **Stalls** Low

Form RPR
022 **1** **Celtic Art (FR)**[11] 6424 2-9-5 91 PJMcDonald 2 82
(Paul Cole) *looked wl; mde all: shkn up 2f out: rdn and immediately hung lft bumping rival over 1f out: continued to drift lft fnl f but a doing enough (jockey said colt hung left handed under pressure)* **1/4**[1]
0 **2** *¾* **Montanari**[73] 4091 2-9-5 0 OisinMurphy 1 80
(Andrew Balding) *athletic; trckd wnr: effrt to chse wnr 2f out: rdn and bmpd by wnr over 1f out: kpt on fnl f: a being hld (jockey said colt hung left handed under pressure)* **11/4**[2]
0 **3** *25* **Margaretha (IRE)**[31] 5676 2-9-0 0 TomMarquand 4 18
(Amy Murphy) *leggy; racd in last: rdn and readily outpcd by ldng pair 2f out: wknd fnl f* **40/1**[3]

1m 40.04s (0.84) **Going Correction** +0.025s/f (Good) **3 Ran SP% 109.1**
Speed ratings (Par 101): **96,95,70**
CSF £1.32 TOTE £1.10; EX 1.20 Trifecta £1.10.
Owner Mrs Fitri Hay **Bred** Peter Anastasiou **Trained** Whatcombe, Oxon

FOCUS
A disappointing turnout for this valuable maiden, which was won by Grade 1 winner Line Of Duty last year, with Group 3 scorer Sir Ron Priestley in fourth. Despite the small field the time was very respectable. It's tricky to pin down the level.

6833 RACEGOERS CLUB FILLIES' NURSERY H'CAP 6f
3:50 (3:50) (Class 2) 2-Y-O **£15,752** (£4,715; £2,357; £1,180; £587) **Stalls** High

Form RPR
514 **1** **Caspian Queen (IRE)**[22] 6019 2-8-5 **78** DavidEgan 5 84
(Richard Hughes) *quite str: looked wl; racd promly in 4th: shkn up to chse ldr 2f out: rdn and led over 1f out: drvn and kpt on wl fnl f* **8/1**
0410 **2** *½* **Graceful Magic**[17] 6221 2-8-9 **82** CharlesBishop 8 86+
(Eve Johnson Houghton) *trckd ldr on rail: gng wl whn denied a clr run over 1f out: swtchd rt and rdn once in clr fnl f: kpt on wl (jockey said filly was denied a clear run)* **7/1**[3]
641 **3** *nk* **Angel Grey (IRE)**[23] 5988 2-8-7 **79** ow1 OisinMurphy 2 83
(Andrew Balding) *hld up: gd hdwy on outer to chse ldrs over 1f out: rdn and ev ch 1f out: one pce clsng stages* **11/4**[2]
0513 **4** *1 ¼* **Rose Of Kildare (IRE)**[13] 6356 2-9-7 **94** JamesDoyle 3 93
(Mark Johnston) *looked wl; midfield on outer: hdwy u.p to ld v briefly over 1f out: sn rdn and hdd by wnr: one pce fnl f* **5/2**[1]
1655 **5** *shd* **Go Well Spicy (IRE)**[17] 6221 2-8-2 **75** HollieDoyle 6 74
(Mick Channon) *sltly on toes; chsd ldr: rdn along and no imp 2f out: kpt on one pce fnl f* **7/1**[3]
3510 **6** *2 ¾* **Ocasio Cortez (IRE)**[18] 6157 2-8-11 **84** (b[1]) SeanLevey 7 75
(Richard Hannon) *led: rdn along and hdd over 1f out: wknd fnl f* **16/1**
4614 **7** *1 ¾* **Miss Villanelle**[17] 6221 2-8-2 **78** ow2 CierenFallon[(5)] 10 66
(Charles Hills) *hld up: rdn and outpcd over 2f out: nvr on terms* **7/1**[3]
1004 **8** *1 ¾* **Diligent Deb (IRE)**[20] 6073 2-8-5 **78** MartinDwyer 4 58
(William Muir) *dwlt and racd in last: a in rr (trainer said, filly spiked a temperature the following day, and is now heavily in season)* **20/1**

1m 11.98s (-0.12) **Going Correction** +0.025s/f (Good) **8 Ran SP% 114.5**
Speed ratings (Par 98): **101,100,99,98,98 94,92,89**
CSF £62.26 CT £194.61 TOTE £8.30: £2.40, £2.10, £1.40; EX 70.60 Trifecta £243.80.
Owner Davood Vakilgilani **Bred** Rabbah Bloodstock Limited **Trained** Upper Lambourn, Berks

FOCUS
A good fillies' nursery in which half the field were daughters of Gutaifan, but not the winner.

6834 ROYAL SUSSEX REGIMENT H'CAP 2m
4:25 (4:25) (Class 2) (0-105,98) 3-Y-O **£12,602** (£3,772; £1,886; £944; £470) **Stalls** Low

Form RPR
0512 **1** **Themaxwecan (IRE)**[10] 6452 3-9-5 **98** JamesDoyle 2 106
(Mark Johnston) *trckd ldr: shkn up to ld over 2f out: sn rdn and asserted 1f out: drvn out fnl f* **1/1**[1]
0-60 **2** *1* **Platitude**[53] 4884 6-9-13 **95** PatDobbs 5 101
(Amanda Perrett) *looked wl; hld up: gd hdwy on outer to chse wnr over 1f out: rdn ins fnl f and kpt on wl: nt rch wnr* **15/2**
3162 **3** *2* **Seinesational**[34] 5540 4-9-3 **85** (v) OisinMurphy 3 89
(William Knight) *settled in midfield: rdn and no imp 2f out: kpt on one pce ins fnl f (jockey said gelding was denied a clear run)* **4/1**[3]
/14- **4** *2* **Smart Champion**[313] 8582 4-8-11 **84** DylanHogan[(5)] 1 85
(David Simcock) *hld up: making hdwy on rail whn denied a clr run 2f out: swtchd lft and rdn over 1f out: kpt on again but all ch gone* **20/1**
4003 **5** *1 ¼* **What A Welcome**[24] 5928 5-10-0 **96** JoeyHaynes 4 96
(Patrick Chamings) *racd in midfield: hdwy on outer to chse wnr 2f out: drvn and no imp over 1f out: wknd fnl f* **3/1**[2]
-000 **6** *20* **Nakeeta**[52] 4899 8-9-11 **93** RobertWinston 6 80
(Linda Jewell) *racd freely and led: rdn along and hdd by wnr over 2f out: sn lost pl and wknd fnl f (jockey said gelding ran too free)* **33/1**

3m 30.63s (-0.27) **Going Correction** +0.025s/f (Good)
WFA 3 from 4yo+ 11lb **6 Ran SP% 114.5**
Speed ratings (Par 109): **101,100,99,98,97 87**
CSF £9.92 TOTE £1.90: £1.20, £3.10; EX 7.90 Trifecta £55.70.
Owner Douglas Livingston **Bred** Niarchos Family **Trained** Middleham Moor, N Yorks

FOCUS
A good staying handicap. The third helps set the level.

6835 SOUTHERN TRAINING FILLIES' H'CAP 6f
5:00 (5:00) (Class 4) (0-80,78) 3-Y-O- **£7,633** (£2,271; £1,135; £567; £300) **Stalls** High

Form RPR
1211 **1** **Rose Hip**[32] 5606 4-9-9 **78** TomMarquand 5 85
(Tony Carroll) *looked wl; racd freely in last: hdwy between rivals to trck ldr 2f out: rdn along to ld against rail ins fnl f: kpt on wl* **5/2**[1]
150 **2** *½* **Chitra**[39] 5372 3-9-7 **78** DavidEgan 1 83
(Daniel Kubler) *led: rdn along and strly pressed by rivals 1f out: battled on wl ins fnl f: nt match wnr clsng stages* **11/2**
6361 **3** *½* **Sweet Pursuit**[17] 6203 5-9-6 **75** OisinMurphy 4 78
(Rod Millman) *hld up: rdn along to chse ldr over 1f out: upsides and ev ch ins fnl f: no ex fin* **4/1**[2]
6645 **4** *5* **Silca Mistress**[10] 6465 4-9-8 **77** HollieDoyle 3 64
(Clive Cox) *trckd ldr: rdn along and outpcd 2f out: wknd fnl f* **5/2**[1]
-016 **5** *¾* **Wotadoll**[13] 6329 5-8-8 **63** MartinDwyer 2 48
(Mike Murphy) *settled in 3rd: rdn and outpcd 2f out: sn bhd* **9/2**[3]

1m 11.99s (-0.11) **Going Correction** +0.025s/f (Good)
WFA 3 from 4yo+ 2lb **5 Ran SP% 110.7**
Speed ratings (Par 102): **101,100,99,93,92**
CSF £16.18 TOTE £2.80: £1.50, £3.00; EX 16.30 Trifecta £42.40.
Owner Lady Whent **Bred** Lady Whent **Trained** Cropthorne, Worcs

FOCUS
Three finished clear in this interesting little fillies' handicap. The third has been rated to her latest effort.

6836 EVERY RACE LIVE ON RACING TV NOVICE STKS 1m 1f 197y
5:35 (5:36) (Class 4) 3-Y-O+ **£5,498** (£1,636; £817; £408) **Stalls** Low

Form RPR
2332 **1** **Cape Cavalli (IRE)**[21] 6043 3-9-2 81 (v[1]) JamesDoyle 9 64+
(Simon Crisford) *hld up: smooth hdwy into 3rd 2f out: gd prog on bit appr fnl f: rdn to ld fnl 110yds: asserted wl cl home* **5/2**[2]
53 **2** *1* **Look Closely**[47] 5103 3-9-2 0 DavidEgan 1 62+
(Roger Varian) *s.i.s but sn rcvrd to r midfield: hdwy to ld gng wl 2f out: sn rdn appr fnl f: hdd by wnr and no ex fnl 110yds* **3/1**[3]
3-1 **3** *4* **Cadre Du Noir (USA)**[73] 4120 3-9-9 0 RobHornby 3 61+
(Martyn Meade) *athletic; looked wl; racd in midfield: rdn along and no imp on outer 2f out: sn drvn and kpt on one pce fnl f: no ch w ldng pair* **1/1**[1]
2405 **4** *¾* **Passing Clouds**[29] 5744 4-9-5 44 GabrieleMalune[(3)] 6 51
(Michael Attwater) *led: rdn along and hdd 2f out: kpt on one pce ins fnl f* **100/1**
04 **5** *2* **Hindaam (USA)**[69] 4258 3-8-11 0 PatDobbs 8 43
(Owen Burrows) *trckd ldr: shkn up to chse ldr 2f out: sn rdn and no imp appr fnl f: one pce after* **18/1**
0 **6** *5* **Master Milliner (IRE)**[109] 2795 3-9-2 0 TomMarquand 4 38
(Emma Lavelle) *quite str: bit bkward; hld up: niggled along 1/2-way: outpcd 3f out: a bhd* **33/1**
0 **7** *5* **Devizes (IRE)**[15] 6290 3-8-13 0 PaddyBradley[(3)] 5 28
(Pat Phelan) *hld up: pushed along 3f out: sn rdn and outpcd 2f out: wknd fnl f* **80/1**
8 *9* **Shattering (IRE)** 3-9-2 0 SeanLevey 2 10
(Paul Cole) *angular; racd in midfield: hdwy u.p to chse ldr 3f out: sn rdn and lost pl over 1f out* **9/1**

2m 7.39s (-1.51) **Going Correction** +0.025s/f (Good)
WFA 3 from 4yo 6lb **8 Ran SP% 124.0**
Speed ratings (Par 105): **107,106,103,102,100 96,92,85**
CSF £11.58 TOTE £3.70: £1.10, £1.30, £1.10; EX 12.50 Trifecta £18.30.
Owner Sheikh Juma Dalmook Al Maktoum **Bred** Ecurie Des Charmes & Ballylinch Stud **Trained** Newmarket, Suffolk

FOCUS
There are doubts over the form of this novice event, with the favourite disappointing and the 44-rated fourth close enough.
T/Plt: £38.30 to a £1 stake. Pool: £76,469.69 - 1,456.11 winning units T/Qpdt: £9.70 to a £1 stake. Pool: £6,098.98 - 462.57 winning units **Mark Grantham**

6592 KEMPTON (A.W) (R-H)
Tuesday, September 3

OFFICIAL GOING: Polytrack: standard to slow (watered)
Wind: Fresh, mostly across (away from stands) Weather: Fine

6837 MATCHBOOK BETTING PODCAST NURSERY H'CAP 6f (P)
5:45 (5:46) (Class 6) (0-60,61) 2-Y-O
£3,105 (£924; £461; £300; £300; £300) **Stalls** Low

Form RPR
646 **1** **Dreamy Rascal (IRE)**[11] 6415 2-9-9 **61** RossaRyan 7 66
(Richard Hannon) *trckd ldng pair: clsd 2f out: shkn up to ld jst over 1f out: sn clr: rdn out* **10/1**
0066 **2** *1 ½* **Sparkling Diamond**[47] 5101 2-9-7 **59** KieranShoemark 3 61
(Philip McBride) *chsd ldrs: effrt on inner 2f out: impeded over 1f out: styd on wl after to take 2nd fnl 75yds: nt rch wnr (jockey said filly was denied a clear run)* **7/1**[3]
0055 **3** *1 ½* **Sir Rodneyredblood**[14] 6313 2-9-1 **53** TomQueally 2 49
(J R Jenkins) *led 100yds: trckd ldr: led again jst over 2f out gng strly: hdd jst over 1f out: fdd* **8/1**

500 4 ½ **Castel Angelo (IRE)**[12] 6368 2-9-6 **58** DaneO'Neill 4 53
(Henry Candy) *dwlt: t.k.h and hld up wl in rr: shkn up and no prog over 2f out: styd on over 1f out: tk 4th nr fin but too late to threaten* **11/8**[1]

0040 5 1 ¾ **Oribi**[18] 6182 2-8-10 **53** CierenFallon(5) 9 42
(William Haggas) *chsd ldrs: urged along and no prog over 2f out: plugged on at one pce over 1f out* **8/1**

0040 6 ½ **Shaun's Delight (IRE)**[24] 5958 2-8-12 **50** (b[1]) RaulDaSilva 10 38
(Ronald Harris) *spd fr wdst draw to ld after 100yds: racd freely: hdd jst over 2f out: hanging bdly over 1f out and btn after (jockey said colt hung right-handed)* **20/1**

5600 7 2 ¼ **Kahpehlo**[19] 6118 2-9-0 **52** LiamJones 8 33
(John Bridger) *rn in snatches: mostly in rr: rdn and no prog over 2f out* **33/1**

660 8 ¾ **Activius (IRE)**[12] 6368 2-9-6 **58** (b[1]) PJMcDonald 1 37
(Brian Meehan) *sn urged along in last pair: nvr gng the pce* **6/1**[2]

0444 9 shd **Grace Plunkett**[14] 6313 2-8-6 **51** (b) SeanKirrane(7) 5 29
(Richard Spencer) *in tch: drvn and no prog over 2f out: sn wknd (jockey said filly was never travelling)* **6/1**[2]

000 10 10 **Gelsmoor Bay**[22] 6029 2-8-7 **45** PaddyMathers 6
(Derek Shaw) *racd v awkwardly and t.o bef 1/2-way (jockey said filly hung left-handed throughout)* **50/1**

1m 14.87s (1.77) **Going Correction** 0.0s/f (Stan) **10** Ran SP% **124.2**
Speed ratings (Par 93): **88,86,84,83,81 80,77,76,76,62**
CSF £81.71 CT £616.82 TOTE £10.70: £3.30, £1.90, £3.30; EX 85.70 Trifecta £661.30.
Owner Charlie & Julia Rosier And Anna Doyle **Bred** Glenville B/S & Dream Ahead Syndicate **Trained** East Everleigh, Wilts

FOCUS
A modest nursery. The winning time was over four seconds above standard.

6838 MATCHBOOK BETTING EXCHANGE NOVICE STKS 6f (P)
6:15 (6:16) (Class 5) 3-Y-O+ **£3,881** (£1,155; £577; £288) **Stalls** Low

Form RPR

41- 1 **Mubakker (USA)**[306] 8783 3-9-9 0 DaneO'Neill 6 101+
(Sir Michael Stoute) *trckd ldr: led 2f out: shkn up and sn clr: kpt up to work tl eased nr fin* **8/15**[1]

3 2 8 **Don't Jump George (IRE)**[106] 2912 4-9-4 0 (t) RossaRyan 3 68
(Shaun Lycett) *cl up in 3rd: rdn to take 2nd over 1f out but wnr already wl clr: no imp after* **5/1**[3]

3 ½ **Imhotep** 3-9-2 0 AdamMcNamara 2 67+
(Roger Charlton) *slowly away: off the pce in last pair: pushed along 1/2-way: prog over 1f out: styd on to take 3rd ins fnl f and clsd on runner-up nr fin* **3/1**[2]

4 2 ¾ **Hellovasinger** 3-9-2 0 ShaneKelly 5 58
(Richard Hughes) *chsd ldng trio but nt on terms: pushed along 2f out: kpt on one pce after and nvr a threat* **22/1**

44 5 4 ½ **Excelinthejungle (IRE)**[17] 6198 3-9-2 0 TomQueally 1 44
(Seamus Durack) *dwlt: t.k.h: hld up off the pce in last pair: pushed along and no prog over 2f out: nvr in it* **33/1**

005 6 nse **More Salutes (IRE)**[24] 5960 4-9-4 43 (p) RobertHavlin 4 43
(Michael Attwater) *led to 2f out: racd awkwardly and wknd qckly* **66/1**

1m 12.37s (-0.73) **Going Correction** 0.0s/f (Stan)
WFA 3 from 4yo 2lb **6** Ran SP% **115.7**
Speed ratings (Par 103): **104,93,92,89,83 82**
CSF £3.98 TOTE £1.40: £1.10, £2.20; EX 4.00 Trifecta £6.00.
Owner Hamdan Al Maktoum **Bred** WinStar Farm LLC **Trained** Newmarket, Suffolk

FOCUS
A decent novice contest. The odds-on favourite won by a wide margin in convincing fashion in a time 2.5 seconds quicker than the opening C&D nursery. Time may show the second has run close to his debut turf run, but he's been rated below that for now.

6839 MATCHBOOK 2% COMMISSION H'CAP 1m (P)
6:45 (6:45) (Class 5) (0-70,70) 4-Y-O+
£3,752 (£1,116; £557; £300; £300; £300) **Stalls** Low

Form RPR

0643 1 **Makambe (IRE)**[14] 6317 4-9-0 **63** (p) JoeyHaynes 11 72
(Chelsea Banham) *hld up towards rr: gd prog on outer 2f out: rdn to chse ldr fnl f: styd on wl to ld nr fin* **7/1**

3201 2 nk **Highfaluting (IRE)**[14] 6317 5-9-6 **69** RyanTate 3 77+
(James Eustace) *trckd ldng trio: clsd 2f out: led over 1f out: drvn fnl f: worn down nr fin* **5/2**[1]

1243 3 ½ **Bollihope**[27] 5820 7-9-3 **66** ConnorBeasley 9 73
(Shaun Keightley) *hld up wl in rr: nt clr run briefly 2f out: gd prog over 1f out: chsd ldng pair ins fnl f: styd on but nvr quite able to chal* **6/1**[3]

2045 4 2 ¼ **Takeonefortheteam**[13] 6334 4-8-11 **60** LiamJones 13 62
(Mark Loughnane) *dropped in fr wdst draw and hld up in last pair: nt clr run 2f out and swtchd to outer: gd prog over 1f out: tk 4th fnl 75yds: styd on but no ch* **16/1**

5-00 5 2 ¼ **Fronsac**[20] 6083 4-9-6 **69** LiamKeniry 10 66
(Daniel Kubler) *taken down early: chsd ldr: rdn to ld 2f out: hdd over 1f out: sn btn* **20/1**

4410 6 1 **Baashiq (IRE)**[18] 6160 5-9-3 **66** (p) DaneO'Neill 7 61
(Peter Hiatt) *n.m.r s: rcvrd on outer into midfield after 2f: rdn to cl on ldrs 2f out: no hdwy 1f out: fdd ins fnl f: eased (jockey said gelding suffered interference when leaving the stalls)* **11/2**[2]

0000 7 ½ **Weloof (FR)**[14] 6317 5-8-11 **63** DarraghKeenan(3) 4 56
(John Butler) *hld up in midfield: gng wl enough 2f out: pushed along over 1f out: pushed along more firmly fnl f: no real prog: capable of bttr* **40/1**

4403 8 shd **Golden Guest**[5] 6627 5-9-0 **63** LewisEdmunds 6 56
(Les Eyre) *n.m.r s: wl in rr: rdn over 2f out: nvr able to make significant prog (jockey said gelding suffered interference when leaving the stalls)* **7/1**

2334 9 3 ¾ **Chloellie**[11] 6408 4-9-6 **69** TomQueally 2 54
(J R Jenkins) *slowly away: mostly in last pair: rdn over 2f out: only limited prog after* **12/1**

003 10 nk **Rifft (IRE)**[19] 6119 4-8-13 **62** RobertHavlin 12 46
(Lydia Richards) *wl in tch: rdn over 2f out: wknd over 1f out* **33/1**

4100 11 3 ½ **Come On Tier (FR)**[21] 6050 4-9-5 **68** (v) KierenFox 8 44
(Lee Carter) *chsd ldrs: rdn over 2f out: ref to r properly and wknd qckly over 1f out* **33/1**

0000 12 2 ½ **Bengali Boys (IRE)**[8] 6547 4-9-7 **70** (b) GeorgeDowning 5 40
(Tony Carroll) *led at str pce and at least 3 l clr: hdd & wknd rapidly 2f out (jockey said gelding hung left out of the stalls)* **33/1**

6206 13 12 **Roof Garden**[55] 4801 4-9-2 **65** RossaRyan 1 7
(Mike Murphy) *chsd ldng pair: rdn over 2f out: wknd rapidly wl over 1f out: t.o* **7/1**

1m 38.92s (-0.88) **Going Correction** 0.0s/f (Stan) **13** Ran SP% **125.3**
Speed ratings (Par 103): **104,103,103,100,98 97,97,97,93,93 89,87,75**
CSF £24.77 CT £122.26 TOTE £9.50: £3.10, £1.50, £2.90; EX 31.10 Trifecta £210.70.
Owner Turloo F Parrett **Bred** Mrs F Hay **Trained** Cowlinge, Suffolk

FOCUS
An ordinary handicap but solid enough form for the grade. The winner has been rated close to last winter's form, with the third helping to set the level.

6840 MATCHBOOK VIP H'CAP 1m (P)
7:15 (7:17) (Class 5) (0-75,76) 3-Y-O
£3,752 (£1,116; £557; £300; £300; £300) **Stalls** Low

Form RPR

5306 1 **In The Cove (IRE)**[17] 6204 3-9-5 **71** (b[1]) RossaRyan 8 78
(Richard Hannon) *hld up in midfield: pushed along and prog 2f out: rdn to chse ldr fnl f: styd on wl and edgd ahd nr fin* **11/1**

223 2 nk **Stormbomber (CAN)**[13] 6350 3-9-2 **68** LiamKeniry 4 74
(Ed Walker) *trckd ldrs: wnt 2nd 2f out gng strly: led over 1f out: drvn fnl f: nt qckn and hdd nr fin* **5/2**[1]

4200 3 1 ½ **Jabalaly (IRE)**[42] 5267 3-9-10 **76** (b[1]) DaneO'Neill 12 79
(Ed Dunlop) *hld up in last trio: gd prog on inner 2f out: tried to chal fnl f: one pce fnl 100yds* **14/1**

3032 4 1 ½ **Ifton**[19] 6130 3-8-10 **62** RobertHavlin 14 62+
(Ruth Carr) *dropped in fr wdst draw and hld up in last: gd prog on outer 2f out: r.o to take 4th ins fnl f: no ch to threaten* **10/1**

4345 5 2 **Crimewave (IRE)**[24] 5959 3-9-6 **72** (t[1]) HarryBentley 10 67
(Tom Clover) *towards rr: urged along wl over 2f out and no prog: in last pair 1f out: styd on after: tk 5th nr fin* **13/2**[2]

1056 6 nk **Madame Tantzy**[29] 5749 3-9-7 **73** CharlesBishop 7 68
(Eve Johnson Houghton) *hld up in last trio: pushed along 2f out: no prog tl styd on fnl f to press for 5th nr fin: nvr in it* **10/1**

3230 7 ½ **Better Than Ever (IRE)**[11] 6393 3-9-1 **67** ShaneKelly 1 61
(Marco Botti) *chsd ldrs: rdn 2f out: no imp jst over 1f out: wknd fnl f* **14/1**

0012 8 1 ¾ **Dutch Story**[11] 6389 3-8-5 **57** (p) MartinDwyer 13 47
(Amanda Perrett) *pressed ldrs: lost pl and rdn 2f out: steadily wknd* **15/2**[3]

3606 9 1 **Powerful Star (IRE)**[13] 6350 3-9-3 **69** DanielMuscutt 5 56
(David Lanigan) *nvr beyond midfield: rdn and no prog over 2f out: fdd fnl f* **25/1**

0401 10 nk **Sharp Talk (IRE)**[11] 6389 3-8-12 **64** JosephineGordon 3 51
(Shaun Keightley) *led: drvn and hdd over 1f out: wknd qckly fnl f* **8/1**

20-0 11 1 ¾ **Sunvisor (IRE)**[99] 3170 3-9-6 **72** PJMcDonald 2 55
(William Muir) *pressed ldrs tl wknd wl over 1f out* **20/1**

0502 12 1 **Indian Sounds (IRE)**[19] 6111 3-9-4 **70** (b) FrannyNorton 11 50
(Mark Johnston) *pressed ldr to 2f out: wknd qckly* **8/1**

1m 39.44s (-0.36) **Going Correction** 0.0s/f (Stan) **12** Ran SP% **124.3**
Speed ratings (Par 101): **101,100,99,97,95 95,95,93,92,92 90,89**
CSF £40.50 CT £417.51 TOTE £12.10: £4.30, £1.30, £5.20; EX 60.90 Trifecta £1875.30.
Owner Owners Group 027 **Bred** John & Jennifer Coleman **Trained** East Everleigh, Wilts

FOCUS
A fair 3yo handicap. The winning time was notably slower than the previous C&D handicap. The second and third have been rated to form.

6841 MATCHBOOK LONDON MILE SERIES QUALIFIER H'CAP 1m (P)
7:45 (7:46) (Class 3) (0-95,95) 3-Y-O+
£9,337 (£2,796; £1,398; £699; £349; £175) **Stalls** Low

Form RPR

16-0 1 **Kasbaan**[117] 2563 4-9-1 **84** AlistairRawlinson 5 92+
(Michael Appleby) *trckd ldng pair: wnt 2nd over 2f out: rdn to chal over 1f out: narrow ld fnl f: hld on wl* **5/1**[3]

0423 2 ½ **Al Jellaby**[13] 6347 4-9-4 **87** DaneO'Neill 8 94
(Clive Cox) *awkward to post: led: kicked on over 2f out: drvn over 1f out: narrowly hdd fnl f: kpt on wl but a jst hld* **5/1**[3]

0554 3 1 ¾ **Name The Wind**[46] 5150 3-9-5 **93** PJMcDonald 7 95
(James Tate) *cl up: rdn to chse ldng pair over 1f out: cl enough ins fnl f: one pce fnl 100yds* **4/1**[2]

6130 4 ½ **Rectory Road**[20] 6076 3-8-8 **85** WilliamCox(3) 3 86
(Andrew Balding) *t.k.h: hld up towards rr: shkn up and no prog over 2f out: hdwy over 1f out: styd on to take 4th ins fnl f* **6/1**

0000 5 3 ¼ **Blown By Wind**[18] 6150 3-9-7 **95** FrannyNorton 10 88
(Mark Johnston) *trapped wd early: chsd ldr to over 2f out: wknd jst over 1f out* **14/1**

3-60 6 2 ¾ **Eljaddaaf (IRE)**[195] 800 8-9-10 **93** (h) JoeyHaynes 4 81
(Dean Ivory) *hld up in last trio: pushed along and sme prog on inner 2f out: no hdwy 1f out: fdd and eased* **33/1**

1360 7 hd **Hammer Gun (USA)**[29] 5741 6-8-11 **80** (v) PaddyMathers 1 68
(Derek Shaw) *mostly in last pair: drvn and no prog over 2f out: passed a few wkng rivals late on* **50/1**

0252 8 1 ¼ **Masked Identity**[14] 6326 4-9-1 **84** (p[1]) ShaneKelly 2 69
(Shaun Keightley) *nvr beyond midfield: shkn up over 2f out: wknd over 1f out* **8/1**

6024 9 2 **Rampant Lion (IRE)**[26] 5863 4-9-1 **84** (b[1]) KieranShoemark 6 64
(William Jarvis) *v.s.a: t.k.h and hld up in last pair: shkn up and no prog over 2f out: btn after (jockey said gelding was slowly away)* **16/1**

4213 10 9 **Mawakib**[66] 4360 3-9-0 **88** DavidEgan 9 46
(Roger Varian) *trapped out wd: chsd ldrs: shkn up over 2f out: sn wknd: t.o (jockey said colt ran too free and hung left-handed)* **3/1**[1]

1m 37.71s (-2.09) **Going Correction** 0.0s/f (Stan)
WFA 3 from 4yo+ 5lb **10** Ran SP% **121.2**
Speed ratings (Par 107): **110,109,107,107,104 101,101,99,97,88**
CSF £31.59 CT £112.50 TOTE £6.40: £2.00, £2.00, £1.80; EX 41.90 Trifecta £160.30.
Owner The Horse Watchers **Bred** Shadwell Estate Company Limited **Trained** Oakham, Rutland

FOCUS
The feature contest was a good handicap. The joint-third favourites fought out a good tussle in the final furlong in a decent comparative time on the night. It's been rated around the second.

6842 MATCHBOOK CASINO H'CAP 1m 3f 219y(P)
8:15 (8:16) (Class 4) (0-85,87) 3-Y-O+
£6,469 (£1,925; £962; £481; £300; £300) **Stalls** Low

Form RPR

102 1 **El Misk**[15] 6290 3-9-6 **87** RobertHavlin 6 98+
(John Gosden) *trckd ldr: chal 2f out: shkn up to ld over 1f out: styd on and steadily drew away ins fnl f* **15/8**[2]

0111 **2** 2 ¼ **Hydroplane (IRE)**[39] 5385 3-8-11 **78**....................(p) RyanTate 2 84
(Sir Mark Prescott Bt) *led: set mod pce to 4f out: sent for home 3f out: drvn and hdd over 1f out: one pce after* **6/4**[1]

2064 **3** nk **Asian Angel (IRE)**[16] 6255 3-9-2 **83**.................... FrannyNorton 4 88
(Mark Johnston) *hld up in 4th: rdn and nt qckn over 2f out: kpt on to take 3rd fnl f: no ch to threaten* **9/2**[3]

220 **4** 1 **Dono Di Dio**[41] 5321 4-9-4 **82**.................... ScottMcCullagh(5) 5 85
(Michael Madgwick) *awkward s: t.k.h: hld up in 5th: rdn and no rspnse over 2f out: one pce and no imp on ldrs after* **14/1**

5-05 **5** 2 ¼ **Thimbleweed**[19] 6124 4-9-11 **84**.................... HarryBentley 3 83
(Ralph Beckett) *trckd ldng pair: nt qckn and outpcd over 2f out: one pce after and lost 3rd fnl f* **11/2**

2240 **6** 18 **Grand Inquisitor**[38] 5436 7-9-11 **84**....................(v) AlistairRawlinson 7 54
(Conor Dore) *t.k.h: hld up in last: wknd qckly 3f out: t.o (jockey said gelding hung left-handed)* **33/1**

2m 34.79s (0.29) **Going Correction** 0.0s/f (Stan)
WFA 3 from 4yo+ 8lb **6** Ran SP% **118.0**
Speed ratings (Par 105): **99,97,97,96,95 83**
CSF £5.47 TOTE £2.30: £1.40, £1.20; EX 5.40 Trifecta £21.50.
Owner Sheikh Mohammed Bin Khalifa Al Maktoum **Bred** Essafinaat Ltd **Trained** Newmarket, Suffolk

FOCUS
A decent middle-distance handicap. The three 3yos finished ahead of their elders in receipt of 8lb weight-for-age allowances, with the second-favourite winning well. It's been rated at face value, with the third and fourth close to form.

6843 MATCHBOOK BEST BETS H'CAP 1m 3f 219y(P)

8:45 (8:47) (Class 6) (0-55,55) 3-Y-0+
£3,105 (£924; £461; £300; £300; £300) **Stalls** Low

Form RPR

360- **1** **Spice War**[385] 6124 4-9-5 **55**.................... ThomasGreatrex(5) 1 63
(Oliver Sherwood) *trckd ldng quartet: impeded on inner 1/2-way: urged along over 3f out: prog on inner 2f out: drvn to ld jst ins fnl f: hld on* **5/1**[3]

2152 **2** nk **It's How We Roll (IRE)**[6] 6599 5-9-1 **51**....................(p) ScottMcCullagh(5) 6 59
(John Spearing) *hld up wl in rr: stl there 3f out but gng conspicuously bttr than most: prog 2f out: drvn and r.o to take 2nd fnl 130yds: clsd on wnr at fin: too much to do* **8/1**

0011 **3** 2 ½ **Warning Light**[5] 6635 4-9-8 **53** 5ex....................(tp) JosephineGordon 4 57
(Shaun Keightley) *t.k.h: trckd ldng trio: rdn over 2f out: hanging fire over 1f out: kpt on fnl f to take 3rd nr fin but too late* **2/1**[1]

0005 **4** ½ **Lady Of York**[6] 6599 5-9-7 **52**.................... JoeyHaynes 7 55
(Chelsea Banham) *t.k.h: trckd ldr after 1f: rdn to chal over 2f out: fnlly led 1f out but immediately hdd and fdd* **12/1**

0054 **5** 2 **General Brook (IRE)**[6] 6599 9-9-10 **55**....................(p) RossaRyan 14 55
(John O'Shea) *led after 1f: drvn over 2f out: hdd & wknd 1f out (jockey said gelding ran too free)* **16/1**

0430 **6** 2 ¼ **Antidote (IRE)**[11] 6400 3-8-13 **55**....................(b[1]) FinleyMarsh(3) 9 52
(Richard Hughes) *wl away: led 1f: trckd ldng pair after: drvn over 2f out: cl enough over 1f out: wknd fnl f* **8/1**

0035 **7** 3 ½ **Bird To Love**[21] 6039 5-9-1 **49**.................... WilliamCox(3) 11 39
(Mark Usher) *hld up but sn in midfield: outpcd wl over 2f out: no imp on ldrs after* **16/1**

0024 **8** nk **Iballisticvin**[48] 5049 6-9-9 **54**....................(v) HarryBentley 13 44
(Gary Moore) *hld up in rr: sme prog into midfield over 3f out: rdn and no hdwy over 2f out: wl btn after* **9/2**[2]

0340 **9** ½ **Ember's Glow**[104] 2975 5-9-7 **52**.................... LiamKeniry 2 41
(Mark Loughnane) *a in midfield: lost tch w ldrs wl over 2f out: no prog after* **18/1**

R600 **10** 1 **Principia**[18] 6153 4-9-5 **50**....................(e[1]) CharlieBennett 12 37
(Adam West) *a towards rr: rdn and wd bnd 3f out: sn no ch* **50/1**

0300 **11** 1 ¼ **Zahraani**[84] 3705 4-9-4 **49**.................... TomQueally 10 34
(J R Jenkins) *a towards rr: lost tch w ldng gp 3f out: no ch after* **66/1**

5-00 **12** 1 ½ **Rahmah (IRE)**[20] 6077 7-9-9 **54**....................(p) TrevorWhelan 3 37
(Geoffrey Deacon) *s.v.s: wl bhd early and a in rr: hrd rdn and no prog over 2f out (jockey said gelding was slowly away)* **50/1**

2060 **13** 2 ½ **Qayed (CAN)**[68] 4287 4-9-2 **47**....................(p) PJMcDonald 8 26
(Kevin Frost) *nvr beyond midfield: rdn 4f out: struggling 3f out: sn no ch* **18/1**

/0-0 **14** 5 **Delannoy**[21] 6055 5-9-6 **51**....................(p) ShaneKelly 5 22
(Neil Mulholland) *s.i.s: nvr gng wl and a wl in rr* **40/1**

2m 33.86s (-0.64) **Going Correction** 0.0s/f (Stan)
WFA 3 from 4yo+ 8lb **14** Ran SP% **128.2**
Speed ratings (Par 101): **102,101,100,99,98 96,94,94,94,93 92,91,89,86**
CSF £47.50 CT £110.38 TOTE £7.00: £2.50, £2.10, £1.40; EX 58.30 Trifecta £192.80.
Owner Apiafi And Black **Bred** Chasemore Farm **Trained** Upper Lambourn, Berks

FOCUS
A moderate middle-distance handicap. The winning time was nearly a second faster than the previous C&D handicap. The third has been rated in line with this year's best.
T/Jkpt: Not Won. T/Plt: £45.20 to a £1 stake. Pool: £65,943.44 - 1,064.21 winning units T/Qpdt: £8.10 to a £1 stake. Pool: £8,949.22 - 817.46 winning units **Jonathan Neesom**

6414 SALISBURY (R-H)

Tuesday, September 3

OFFICIAL GOING: Good to firm (watered; 8.2)
Wind: Light against Weather: Sunny periods

6844 GIFT OF SIGHT H'CAP (FOR LADY AMATEUR RIDERS) 1m

4:50 (4:53) (Class 6) (0-60,62) 3-Y-0+
£2,950 (£915; £457; £300; £300; £300) **Stalls** Low

Form RPR

0000 **1** **Silvington**[14] 6327 4-9-4 **45**....................(p[1]) MissImogenMathias(5) 8 51
(Mark Loughnane) *hld up towards rr: rdn and hdwy fr 2f out: drifted rt whn chalng ent fnl f: led fnl 130yds: r.o (jockey said gelding hung right-handed)* **33/1**

1320 **2** 2 ½ **Duchess Of Avon**[27] 5804 4-10-5 **62**.................... MissKatyBrooks(7) 1 62
(Gary Moore) *settled bhd ldrs: hdwy over 2f out: led over 1f out but hanging lft: hdd fnl 130yds: no ex* **11/4**[1]

3062 **3** ¾ **Lunar Deity**[14] 6327 10-10-0 **57**.................... MissJuliaEngstrom(7) 5 56
(Stuart Williams) *prom: led after 3f: rdn and hdd over 1f out: kpt on same pce fnl f* **11/1**

3001 **4** ¾ **Haraz (IRE)**[11] 6414 6-9-12 **53**.................... MissMeganTrainor(5) 7 50
(Paddy Butler) *led for 3f: trckd ldrs: ev ch 2f out: sn rdn: kpt on same pce fnl f* **16/1**

0530 **5** nk **Air Of York (IRE)**[20] 6084 7-10-4 **61**....................(p) MissArabellaTucker(7) 2 57
(John Flint) *racd keenly: trckd ldrs: rdn over 1f out: sltly hmpd sn after: kpt on same pce* **9/1**

0003 **6** nk **Letmestopyouthere (IRE)**[55] 4807 5-10-2 **52**(p) MissBrodieHampson 4 47
(Archie Watson) *hld up: swtchd lft 3f out: hdwy 2f out: running on jst bhd wnr whn hmpd over 1f out: hld after but kpt on fnl 120yds* **3/1**[2]

545 **7** 5 **Huddle**[29] 5730 3-10-0 **60**.................... SophieSmith(5) 3 43
(William Knight) *trckd ldrs: rdn over 2f out: wknd jst over 1f out* **4/1**[3]

003 **8** 1 ¼ **Clipsham Tiger (IRE)**[27] 5797 3-9-4 **45**....................(p) MissSerenaBrotherton 9 25
(Michael Appleby) *trckd ldrs: rdn over 2f out: wknd over 1f out* **10/1**

0540 **9** 3 **Bayards Cove**[27] 5806 4-9-6 **45**.................... MissSarahBowen(3) 6 19
(Stuart Kittow) *a towards rr* **12/1**

00-0 **10** 47 **Frank's Legacy**[162] 1339 5-9-10 **51**....................(t[1]) MissJessicaLlewellyn(5) 10
(Nikki Evans) *mid-div: struggling in rr 4f out: sn lost tch: t.o* **66/1**

1m 45.66s (2.16) **Going Correction** +0.175s/f (Good)
WFA 3 from 4yo+ 5lb **10** Ran SP% **117.1**
Speed ratings (Par 101): **96,93,92,92,91 91,86,85,82,35**
CSF £123.33 CT £1133.27 TOTE £46.50: £10.40, £1.30, £2.90; EX 264.40 Trifecta £1565.40.
Owner Martin Millichamp **Bred** The Millinsky Partnership **Trained** Rock, Worcs

FOCUS
A bit of a turn-up in this lady riders' handicap, with one of the two complete outsiders coming to the fore late on. The race has been rated a shade negatively.

6845 DON HEWLETT EBF NOVICE STKS (PLUS 10 RACE) (C&G) 6f

5:25 (5:27) (Class 4) 2-Y-0
£4,851 (£1,443; £721; £360) **Stalls** Low

Form RPR

232 **1** **Lost In Time**[15] 6287 2-9-0 82.................... HectorCrouch 10 85+
(Saeed bin Suroor) *racd keenly: a.p: led 2f out: pushed clr: comf* **6/4**[1]

2 3 ½ **Raaeq (IRE)** 2-9-0 0.................... JimCrowley 13 74+
(Brian Meehan) *mid-div: pushed along over 3f out: hdwy whn carried sltly lft wl over 1f out: kpt on nicely ins fnl f: snatched 2nd fnl stride: no ch w wnr* **3/1**[2]

3 shd **River Nymph** 2-9-0 0.................... AdamKirby 7 73
(Clive Cox) *carried lft s: in tch: hdwy over 2f out: sn rdn to chse wnr: kpt on but nt pce to get on terms: lost 2nd fnl stride* **16/1**

6102 **4** 2 **Don't Stop Dancing (IRE)**[12] 6364 2-8-10 85.................... AngusVilliers(7) 4 70
(Ronald Harris) *sn led: rdn whn hdd 2f out: kpt on same pce fnl f* **8/1**[3]

6 **5** 2 ½ **Roman Melody**[20] 6078 2-9-0 0.................... GeraldMosse 14 60+
(David Elsworth) *mid-div: pushed along over 2f out: no imp tl kpt on ins fnl f but nvr gng pce to get involved* **16/1**

2 **6** 2 ¼ **Lost Empire (IRE)**[28] 5775 2-9-0 0....................(b) GeorgeWood 2 53
(Harry Dunlop) *trckd ldrs: rdn over 2f out: edgd lft: sn one pce* **12/1**

7 1 ½ **Blessed (IRE)** 2-9-0 0.................... JasonWatson 9 48+
(Henry Candy) *s.i.s: sn mid-div: rdn over 2f out: little imp* **20/1**

6 **8** 2 **Live In The Moment (IRE)**[33] 5591 2-9-0 0.................... RoystonFfrench 6 42
(Adam West) *wnt lft s: in tch: effrt over 2f out: wknd over 1f out* **100/1**

9 hd **Edebez (IRE)** 2-9-0 0.................... KieranO'Neill 5 42
(Seamus Mullins) *s.i.s: towards rr: hung lft over 1f out: nvr on terms* **80/1**

10 nk **Brenner Pass** 2-8-11 0.................... FinleyMarsh(3) 12 41
(Richard Hughes) *s.i.s: a towards rr (jockey said colt was slowly away)* **33/1**

0 **11** ¾ **Malmesbury Abbey (FR)**[20] 6079 2-9-0 0.................... RichardKingscote 1 39
(Ed Walker) *trckd ldrs: rdn over 2f out: wknd over 1f out (vet reported colt lost its right fore shoe)* **10/1**

12 2 ¼ **All You Wish** 2-9-0 0.................... DavidProbert 8 32
(Andrew Balding) *s.i.s: a towards rr* **16/1**

13 ½ **Party Island (IRE)** 2-8-7 0.................... MichaelPitt(7) 3 30
(Denis Coakley) *s.i.s: a towards rr* **100/1**

60 **14** 20 **Calbuco**[13] 6330 2-9-0 0.................... JackMitchell 11
(Rod Millman) *chsd ldrs early: sn lost pl: bhd fnl 3f: t.o* **100/1**

1m 14.43s (-0.07) **Going Correction** +0.175s/f (Good) **14** Ran SP% **122.4**
Speed ratings (Par 97): **107,102,102,99,96 93,91,88,88,87 86,83,83,56**
CSF £5.49 TOTE £2.10: £1.10, £1.50, £6.20; EX 7.70 Trifecta £94.80.
Owner Godolphin **Bred** Godolphin **Trained** Newmarket, Suffolk

FOCUS
A fair novice won in good style by the favourite.

6846 SIMPSON HILDER ASSOCIATES SUPPORTING GIFT OF SIGHT EBF FILLIES' NOVICE STKS (PLUS 10 RACE) 6f

6:00 (6:02) (Class 4) 2-Y-0
£4,851 (£1,443; £721; £360) **Stalls** Low

Form RPR

22 **1** **Star In The Making**[18] 6159 2-9-0 0.................... AdamKirby 14 86+
(Clive Cox) *mde all: rdn whn strly chal over 1f out: kpt on wl ins fnl f: asserting at fin* **5/6**[1]

2 1 **Areehaa (IRE)** 2-9-0 0.................... JimCrowley 13 83+
(Sir Michael Stoute) *trckd wnr thrght: rdn for str chal over 1f out: kpt on wl fnl f but a being hld* **6/1**[2]

3 7 **Gossip** 2-9-0 0.................... DavidProbert 12 62
(Martyn Meade) *trckd ldrs: rdn 2f out: kpt on but nt pce of front pair fnl f* **8/1**[3]

4 2 ¼ **Jeanie B** 2-9-0 0.................... CallumShepherd 9 55
(Mick Channon) *mid-div: pushed along and hdwy 2f out: wnt 4th jst ins fnl f: kpt on nicely wout ever threatening* **40/1**

5 2 ¾ **Avanzata** 2-9-0 0.................... JasonWatson 3 47
(Henry Candy) *trckd ldrs: rdn over 2f out: no ex ent fnl f* **8/1**[3]

5 **6** nk **Inevitable Outcome (IRE)**[23] 5988 2-9-0 0.................... LouisSteward 4 46
(David Simcock) *hld up: mid-div 2f out: kpt on but nvr gng pce to get on terms fnl f* **20/1**

7 2 **Ikebana** 2-9-0 0.................... JackMitchell 6 40
(Roger Varian) *hld up: rdn over 2f out: kpt on fnl f: nvr trbld ldrs* **11/1**

8 ¾ **Cesifire (IRE)** 2-9-0 0.................... RoystonFfrench 7 38
(Adam West) *towards rr: rdn over 2f out: kpt on fnl f: nvr trbld ldrs* **66/1**

9 ½ **Miss Carla (IRE)** 2-9-0 0.................... NicolaCurrie 11 36
(Jamie Osborne) *s.i.s: towards rr: sme late prog: nvr a threat* **50/1**

05 **10** hd **Magical Force**[50] 4993 2-9-0 0.................... KieranO'Neill 1 36
(Rod Millman) *in tch: rdn over 2f out: wknd ent fnl f* **33/1**

00 **11** nk **Arabian Dream**[15] 6287 2-9-0 0.................... AndreaAtzeni 10 35
(Ralph Beckett) *in tch: rdn over 2f out: wknd over 1f out* **40/1**

12 nk **Upstage (IRE)** 2-9-0 0.................... StevieDonohoe 2 34
(David Simcock) *squeezed up 1st f: mid-div: rdn over 2f out: wknd over 1f out* **20/1**

0 **13** 3 ¼ **Hot Hot Hot**[22] 6019 2-9-0 0.................... EoinWalsh 5 24
(Tony Carroll) *racd keenly: squeezed up 1st f: mid-div: rdn over 2f out: wknd over 1f out (jockey said filly ran too free)* **100/1**

14 8 **Barboukha** 2-9-0 0 .... FergusSweeney 8
(Luke Dace) *racd green: s.i.s: a bhd* **100/1**
1m 14.51s (0.01) **Going Correction** +0.175s/f (Good) 14 Ran SP% **122.2**
Speed ratings (Par 94): **106,104,95,92,88 88,85,84,83,83 83,82,78,67**
CSF £5.37 TOTE £1.60: £1.10, £2.30, £2.70; EX 7.10 Trifecta £25.10.
Owner A D Spence & M B Spence **Bred** Rabbah Bloodstock Limited **Trained** Lambourn, Berks
FOCUS
Two came clear in this novice and the form looks decent.

6847 BRITISH STALLION STUDS EBF CONDITIONS STKS 6f
6:30 (6:30) (Class 3) 3-Y-O+ **£8,733** (£2,598; £1,298; £649) **Stalls** Low

Form RPR
-005 1 **Emaraaty Ana**[79] 3891 3-9-2 104 .... AndreaAtzeni 3 105
(Kevin Ryan) *sn pushed along to ld: edgd rt 2f out: kpt on wl fnl f: rdn out (vet reported colt lost its right fore shoe)* **5/2**[2]
6300 2 1 1/4 **Ice Age (IRE)**[17] 6229 6-8-11 95 .... GeorgiaDobie(7) 1 101
(Eve Johnson Houghton) *pressed wnr: rdn whn nt clrest of runs 2f out: sn swtchd lft: kpt on wl fnl f but a being hld* **9/1**
4006 3 2 1/2 **Foxtrot Lady**[32] 5608 4-8-13 99 .... DavidProbert 2 88
(Andrew Balding) *trckd ldrs: effrt 2f out: kpt on but nt quite pce to chal* **11/10**[1]
5600 4 1/2 **Baron Bolt**[31] 5664 6-9-4 99 ....(p) JimCrowley 4 91
(Paul Cole) *trckd ldng trio: rdn over 2f out: nt pce to chal but kpt on ins fnl f* **8/1**
0025 5 5 **Jack's Point**[24] 5932 3-9-2 94 .... JasonWatson 5 75
(William Muir) *trckd ldng trio: effrt over 2f out: nt pce to chal: wknd fnl f (jockey said gelding stumbled leaving the stalls)* **13/2**[3]
1m 13.05s (-1.45) **Going Correction** +0.175s/f (Good)
WFA 3 from 4yo+ 2lb 5 Ran SP% **110.6**
Speed ratings (Par 107): **116,114,111,110,103**
CSF £22.47 TOTE £3.00: £1.40, £3.40; EX 22.50 Trifecta £37.30.
Owner Sheikh Mohammed Obaid Al Maktoum **Bred** Rabbah Bloodstock Limited **Trained** Hambleton, N Yorks
FOCUS
A useful conditions race that went to the highest-rated. The winner has been rated close to form.

6848 MEACHERS GLOBAL CLASSIC SUPPORTING GIFT OF SIGHT H'CAP 1m 6f 44y
7:00 (7:00) (Class 3) (0-90,92) 4-Y-O+ **£7,762** (£2,310; £1,154; £577) **Stalls** Far side

Form RPR
2-52 1 **Gwafa (IRE)**[24] 5967 8-9-2 85 .... FergusSweeney 91
(Paul Webber) *prom: led after 3f: strly chal fr 3f out: rdn 2f out: hld on v gamely fnl f: all out* **9/2**[3]
6612 2 nk **Horatio Star**[32] 5604 4-8-7 76 ....(p) JasonWatson 81
(Brian Meehan) *led for 3f: trckd wnr: chal 3f out: sn rdn: hung rt u.p but ev ch thrght fnl f: hld cl home (jockey said gelding hung right-handed under pressure)* **7/2**[2]
0-54 3 hd **Quloob**[39] 5368 5-9-7 90 .... HectorCrouch 95
(Gary Moore) *hld up bhd ldrs: rdn over 2f out: nvr stopped but nt clrest of runs whn making hdwy over 1f out: wnt 3rd fnl 120yds: fin strly and only jst hld* **11/4**[1]
3202 4 1 **Singing The Blues (IRE)**[17] 6200 4-8-5 74 .... KieranO'Neill 77
(Rod Millman) *racd keenly: trckd ldrs: rdn wl over 2f out: nt pce to chal but styd on wl fnl f: snatched 4th fnl strides* **11/4**[1]
00/- 5 nk **Rock Steady (IRE)**[57] 8892 6-9-9 92 ....(p) DavidProbert 95
(Alan King) *trckd ldrs: chal briefly 3f out: sn rdn: styd on same pce fnl 2f: lost 3rd fnl 120yds: lost 4th cl home* **14/1**
2460 6 4 1/2 **Ravenous**[26] 5840 8-7-11 71 .... SophieRalston(5) 68
(Luke Dace) *trckd ldrs: chal briefly 3f out: sn hld: wknd fnl f* **14/1**
0340 7 5 **Lord George (IRE)**[137] 1917 6-9-8 91 .... GeorgeWood 81
(James Fanshawe) *hld up bhd ldrs: effrt over 3f out: wknd over 1f out* **14/1**
3m 11.26s (4.66) **Going Correction** +0.175s/f (Good) 7 Ran SP% **113.7**
Speed ratings (Par 107): **93,92,92,92,91 89,86**
CSF £20.34 TOTE £3.70: £1.70, £2.30; EX 22.30 Trifecta £63.70.
Owner Cropredy Lawn Racing **Bred** Kenilworth House Stud **Trained** Mollington, Oxon
■ Stewards' Enquiry : Jason Watson two-day ban: misuse of the whip (Sep 17-18)
FOCUS
Little gallop on early and it resulted in something of a bunched finish. Muddling form. The second has been rated in line with his Bath latest for now.

6849 ST CHRISTOPHER'S CAR SALES BOURNEMOUTH SUPPORTING GIFT OF SIGHT H'CAP 1m 6f 44y
7:30 (7:30) (Class 5) (0-70,69) 3-Y-O+
£3,737 (£1,112; £555; £300; £300; £300) **Stalls** Far side

Form RPR
0650 1 **Giving Back**[25] 5891 5-9-3 58 ....(p[1]) DavidProbert 66
(Alan King) *trckd ldrs: rdn for str chal over 2f out: tk narrow advantage fnl 100yds: hld on: all out* **7/1**
1054 2 hd **Break The Rules**[3] 6720 3-9-4 68 .... EoinWalsh 76
(Martin Smith) *trckd ldr: rdn into narrow advantage over 1f out: hdd fnl 100yds: kpt on w ev ch: jst hld* **3/1**[3]
0004 3 4 **War Eagle (IRE)**[19] 6104 3-9-5 69 ....(p) JimCrowley 71
(Ian Williams) *trckd ldrs: rdn over 3f out: styd on but nt pce to chal: wnt 3rd nring fin* **2/1**[1]
00R6 4 nk **Threediamondrings**[11] 6419 6-8-9 50 oh5 ....(t) KieranO'Neill 52
(Mark Usher) *led: rdn over 2f out: hdd over 1f out: styd on same pce ins fnl f: lost 3rd nring fin* **33/1**
303 5 3 3/4 **Brooklyn Boy**[54] 4843 3-8-8 58 .... JasonWatson 54
(Harry Dunlop) *hld up but in tch: hdwy over 3f out: chal for 4th over 2f out: fdd ins fnl f* **11/4**[2]
264- 6 9 **With Pleasure**[308] 8051 6-10-0 69 .... BrendanPowell 53
(John Flint) *hld up in last pair: rdn wl over 2f out: nvr any imp: wknd ent fnl f* **16/1**
0000 7 7 **Mini Milk**[12] 6367 3-8-10 60 .... RichardKingscote 36
(Jonathan Portman) *hld up in tch: rdn over 3f out: wknd over 2f out* **12/1**
/6 8 2 3/4 **Mountain Rock (IRE)**[20] 2718 7-9-7 62 ....(b[1]) StevieDonohoe 32
(Johnny Farrelly) *hld up in last pair: pushed along over 5f out: wknd 3f out* **33/1**
3m 12.73s (6.13) **Going Correction** +0.175s/f (Good)
WFA 3 from 5yo+ 9lb 8 Ran SP% **117.0**
Speed ratings (Par 103): **89,88,86,86,84 79,75,73**
CSF £29.03 CT £57.36 TOTE £7.20: £1.70, £1.20, £1.20; EX 29.20 Trifecta £100.70.
Owner Pitchall Stud Partnership & Mrs Pat Toye **Bred** Pitchall Stud **Trained** Barbury Castle, Wilts

FOCUS
Two came clear late in this moderate staying handicap. The pace was again steady. Muddling form. The third has been rated close to form for now.
T/Plt: £30.00 to a £1 stake. Pool: £49,756.35 - 1,207.88 winning units T/Qpdt: £10.00 to a £1 stake. Pool: £6,079.86 - 449.73 winning units **Tim Mitchell**

6850a (Foreign Racing) - See Raceform Interactive

6556 BATH (L-H)
Wednesday, September 4

OFFICIAL GOING: Firm (9.0)
Wind: quite strong against Weather: sunny periods

6851 EMPIRE FIGHTING CHANCE H'CAP 5f 10y
2:00 (2:00) (Class 5) (0-75,75) 3-Y-O **£3,428** (£1,020; £509; £300; £300) **Stalls** Centre

Form RPR
1-05 1 **Irene May (IRE)**[5] 6668 3-9-7 75 .... TomMarquand 1 84
(Sylvester Kirk) *chsd ldrs: led ent fnl f: r.o wl: readily* **9/4**[2]
2403 2 4 **Bluebell Time (IRE)**[18] 6197 3-8-4 58 .... KieranO'Neill 2 53
(Malcolm Saunders) *racd keenly: trckd ldr: led 2f out: rdn and hdd ent fnl f: nt pce of wnr* **5/1**[3]
5442 3 3/4 **Lorna Cole (IRE)**[12] 6397 3-9-1 69 ....(b) MartinDwyer 4 61
(William Muir) *trckd ldr: str chal 2f out tl outpcd by wnr ent fnl f: no ex fnl 120yds* **6/4**[1]
-005 4 4 **Country Rose (IRE)**[50] 5014 3-9-0 68 ....(h) RaulDaSilva 5 46
(Ronald Harris) *led: rdn and hdd 2f out: wknd fnl f* **12/1**
3654 5 2 **Ever Rock (IRE)**[16] 6286 3-7-11 58 .... LauraCoughlan(7) 3 29
(J S Moore) *s.i.s: sn outpcd in last: nvr on terms (jockey said filly was slowly away)* **6/1**
1m 2.55s (0.55) **Going Correction** +0.10s/f (Good) 5 Ran SP% **109.4**
Speed ratings (Par 101): **99,92,91,85,81**
CSF £13.15 TOTE £5.40: £3.00, £1.90; EX 11.70 Trifecta £26.80.
Owner Neil Simpson **Bred** Golden Vale Stud **Trained** Upper Lambourn, Berks
FOCUS
Modest 3yo sprint form. A clear pb from the winner, but little depth in behind.

6852 ITEC EBF NOVICE MEDIAN AUCTION STKS 5f 160y
2:30 (2:30) (Class 5) 2-Y-O **£3,752** (£1,116; £557; £278) **Stalls** Centre

Form RPR
222 1 **Laikaparty (IRE)**[15] 6300 2-9-2 84 ....(b[1]) HollieDoyle 1 79
(Archie Watson) *mde all: pushed clr over 1f out: comf* **8/11**[1]
3012 2 2 1/2 **Audio**[23] 6029 2-9-4 78 .... ThoreHammerHansen(5) 5 77
(Richard Hannon) *trckd ldrs: rdn to chse wnr 2f out: kpt on but nt pce to threaten wnr (jockey said gelding hung left-handed under pressure)* **11/2**[3]
0 3 nk **Alfies Watch**[21] 6079 2-9-2 0 .... FergusSweeney 4 69
(John O'Shea) *hld up in tch: hdwy over 1f out: wnt 3rd ent fnl f: no threat to wnr but kpt on nicely under hands and heels* **66/1**
6 4 4 1/2 **Qinwan**[27] 5859 2-9-2 0 .... RobHornby 3 54
(Andrew Balding) *disp ld for over 1f: trckd ldrs: rdn 2f out: wknd ent fnl f* **9/4**[2]
3 5 1 3/4 **Lady Phyllis**[22] 6047 2-8-11 0 .... CharlieBennett 6 43
(Michael Attwater) *trckd wnr after 1f: rdn 2f out: sn hung lft: wknd ent fnl f (jockey said filly hung left-handed)* **25/1**
6 13 **Lady Codee** 2-8-11 0 .... KieranO'Neill 2
(Michael Attwater) *s.i.s: last but in tch: rdn over 2f out: sn wknd* **50/1**
1m 11.01s (-0.09) **Going Correction** +0.10s/f (Good) 6 Ran SP% **111.4**
Speed ratings (Par 95): **104,100,100,94,91 74**
CSF £5.28 TOTE £1.60: £1.10, £2.60; EX 3.60 Trifecta £54.20.
Owner R F H Partnership 1 **Bred** Kildaragh Stud **Trained** Upper Lambourn, W Berks
FOCUS
Ordinary novice form.

6853 PARRYHOLDMECLOSE WEDDING H'CAP (VALUE RATER RACING CLUB BATH SUMMER STAYERS' SERIES QUALIFIER) 1m 5f 11y
3:00 (3:02) (Class 6) (0-60,61) 4-Y-O+
£2,781 (£827; £413; £300; £300; £300) **Stalls** High

Form RPR
5225 1 **Filament Of Gold (USA)**[14] 6333 8-8-13 52 ....(b) KieranO'Neill 9 57
(Roy Brotherton) *hld up bhd: hdwy in centre over 2f out: disputing 2nd whn hung lft u.p ent fnl f: styd on wl to ld fnl 50yds* **4/1**[2]
/050 2 1/2 **Khismet**[9] 6545 6-8-10 52 ....(p) WilliamCox(3) 3 56
(John Flint) *led: rdn over 1f out: styd on but no ex whn hdd fnl 50yds* **14/1**
0664 3 1 1/2 **Lady Natasha (IRE)**[8] 6556 6-8-2 46 oh1 ....(t) SophieRalston(5) 6 49
(James Grassick) *mid-div: hdwy over 2f out: disputing 2nd and styng on w wnr whn hmpd ent fnl f: no ch after but kpt on to go 3rd cl home* **40/1**
0503 4 3/4 **Taurean Dancer (IRE)**[8] 6560 4-9-7 60 .... RossaRyan 2 61
(Roger Teal) *in tch: rdn over 2f out: sltly hmpd whn chsng ldr ent fnl f: styd on same pce (jockey said gelding was never travelling)* **9/2**[3]
0006 5 1/2 **Everlasting Sea**[7] 6601 5-8-0 46 oh1 .... AngusVilliers(7) 12 46
(Stuart Kittow) *s.i.s: in last pair: hdwy over 2f out: sn rdn: disputing cl 5th ent fnl f: kpt on same pce (jockey said mare was unbalanced on the bend)* **14/1**
0550 6 1 3/4 **Sir Fred (IRE)**[36] 5528 4-8-7 46 oh1 .... ShelleyBirkett 11 46
(Julia Feilden) *prom: rdn over 2f out: looking hld in 5th whn squeezed out ent fnl f: no threat after* **10/1**
0660 7 1 **Mood For Mischief**[49] 5053 4-8-4 48 ow2 ....(p) RachealKneller(5) 10 44
(James Bennett) *racd keenly trcking ldrs: rdn over 2f out: wkng whn squeezed up over 1f out* **18/1**
2000 8 hd **Strictly Art (IRE)**[16] 6278 6-8-11 57 .... GavinAshton(7) 8 53
(Alan Bailey) *nvr really travelling towards rr: rdn over 2f out: little imp (jockey said gelding ran too free and suffered interference in running)* **11/2**
5-00 9 1 **Oyster Card**[61] 4594 6-8-0 46 oh1 ....(v) GeorgeRooke(7) 1 40
(Michael Appleby) *trckd ldrs: rdn over 2f out: wknd ent fnl f* **40/1**
32/0 10 3/4 **Kiruna Peak (IRE)**[13] 5795 5-9-1 61 .... KateLeahy(7) 7 54
(Fergal O'Brien) *v awkwardly away: towards rr: swtchd to centre over 2f out: sn rdn: little imp whn hung lft over 1f out* **16/1**
0622 11 3 **Sacred Sprite**[8] 6556 4-9-2 60 .... DylanHogan(5) 4 49
(John Berry) *mid-div: hdwy on outer over 4f out: short-lived effrt in 4th over 2f out: wknd over 1f out (jockey said filly slipped on both bends)* **3/1**[1]
2m 55.84s (3.04) **Going Correction** +0.10s/f (Good) 11 Ran SP% **117.0**
Speed ratings (Par 101): **94,93,92,92,92 90,90,90,89,89 87**
CSF £58.68 CT £1931.40 TOTE £4.70: £1.70, £4.60, £14.90; EX 61.10 Trifecta £761.80.
Owner M A Geobey **Bred** Darley **Trained** Elmley Castle, Worcs

FOCUS
Moderate form, but it was certainly an open little race. The winner has been rated to his best of recent times.

6854 DOUBLETREE BY HILTON EBF FILLIES' H'CAP 1m 3f 137y
3:30 (3:32) (Class 4) (0-80,82) 3-Y-O+ **£6,080** (£1,819; £910; £455; £300) **Stalls** Low

Form RPR
4-53 **1** **Hope Is High**[14] 6333 6-9-1 **67** MeganNicholls(3) 2 72
(John Berry) *trckd ldrs: rdn to chal ent fnl f: sn led: r.o* 5/1[3]
311 **2** *nk* **Geetanjali (IRE)**[5] 6672 4-10-2 **82** 5ex (v) CameronNoble(3) 5 86
(Michael Bell) *travelled wl bhd ldrs: hdwy over 2f out: chal gng best ent fnl f: sn shkn up: drifted lft: r.o* 5/4[1]
-316 **3** 1 1/4 **Maktabba**[24] 5982 3-9-1 **72** DaneO'Neill 1 74
(William Haggas) *led: rdn whn strly pressed over 2f out: hdd jst ins fnl f: no ex* 2/1[2]
4360 **4** *1* **Miss M (IRE)**[1] 6830 5-9-0 **63** MartinDwyer 3 63
(William Muir) *s.i.s: last of the 5: hdwy fr 3f out: rdn over 1f out: ev ch ent fnl f: sn no ex* 9/1
0046 **5** *shd* **Last Enchantment (IRE)**[10] 6511 4-9-6 **69** (t) TomMarquand 4 69
(Neil Mulholland) *trckd ldrs: str chal over 2f out: sn rdn: ev ch ent fnl f: sn no ex* 25/1

2m 32.71s (1.91) **Going Correction** +0.10s/f (Good)
WFA 3 from 4yo+ 8lb **5 Ran SP% 108.3**
Speed ratings (Par 102): **97,96,95,95,95**
CSF £11.42 TOTE £5.80: £2.00, £1.10; EX 12.10 Trifecta £30.50.
Owner Emma Berry & John Berry **Bred** Miss K Rausing **Trained** Newmarket, Suffolk

FOCUS
No great gallop on here and there was near enough five in a line 1f out. Muddling form.

6855 LANCER SCOTT H'CAP 1m 2f 37y
4:00 (4:01) (Class 6) (0-55,55) 4-Y-O+
£2,781 (£827; £413; £300; £300; £300) **Stalls** Low

Form RPR
0000 **1** **About Glory**[65] 4435 5-8-12 **46** oh1 (vt[1]) TomMarquand 13 53
(Iain Jardine) *trckd ldr: rdn to ld 2f out: jnd ins fnl f: kpt on wl: won on nod* 10/1
0200 **2** *shd* **Red Gunner**[14] 6334 5-9-2 **50** RossaRyan 14 57
(Mark Loughnane) *mid-div: hdwy in centre over 2f out: rdn over 1f out: disp ld ins fnl f: kpt on wl: lost on nod* 7/1
3000 **3** 1 3/4 **Merdon Castle (IRE)**[57] 4753 7-8-9 **46** oh1 MeganNicholls(3) 3 49
(Michael Blake) *hld up: hdwy over 2f out: sn rdn: wnt 3rd ins fnl f: styd on* 6/1[3]
2002 **4** *hd* **Frantical**[8] 6560 7-8-7 **48** ElishaWhittington(7) 4 51
(Tony Carroll) *hld up: hdwy on centre fr 2f out: rdn over 1f out: wnt 4th ins fnl f: styd on* 7/2[2]
0002 **5** 2 1/2 **Telekinetic**[28] 5824 4-8-12 **46** ShelleyBirkett 6 44
(Julia Feilden) *led: rdn and hdd 2f out: styd on same pce ins fnl f (trainer's rep said filly was unsuited by the firm going)* 3/1[1]
5040 **6** 3/4 **Lawyersgunsn'money**[39] 5425 4-9-4 **55** (p[1]) WilliamCox(3) 1 52
(Roger Teal) *racd keenly: trckd ldr: rdn over 2f out: sn one pce* 7/1
4500 **7** *4* **Puzzle Cache**[8] 6560 5-8-12 **46** oh1 (b) CharlieBennett 7 35
(Rod Millman) *trckd ldrs: rdn over 2f out: wknd over 1f out (jockey said mare ran too free)* 25/1
-006 **8** 1 1/4 **Mamnoon (IRE)**[56] 4771 6-8-12 **46** oh1 (p[1]) KieranO'Neill 8 33
(Roy Brotherton) *mid-div: rdn over 2f out: nvr threatened: wknd ent fnl f* 18/1
4200 **9** *nk* **Diamond Reflection (IRE)**[13] 4460 7-8-9 **50** (tp) AngusVilliers(7) 5 36
(Alexandra Dunn) *s.i.s: a towards rr (trainer said gelding had a breathing problem)* 25/1
001 **10** *nk* **Valentine Mist (IRE)**[8] 6560 7-8-10 **49** 4ex SophieRalston(5) 12 35
(James Grassick) *mid-div: rdn over 2f out: little imp: wknd ent fnl f* 14/1
0/00 **11** *26* **My Bubba**[13] 6363 7-8-12 **46** oh1 EoinWalsh 2
(Malcolm Saunders) *s.i.s: towards rr: struggling over 4f out: wknd over 2f out: t.o* 50/1

2m 9.97s (-1.13) **Going Correction** +0.10s/f (Good) **11 Ran SP% 117.2**
Speed ratings (Par 101): **108,107,106,106,104 103,100,99,99,99 78**
CSF £76.56 CT £462.65 TOTE £9.50: £2.90, £2.10, £3.10; EX 92.00 Trifecta £885.20.
Owner I J Jardine **Bred** T Cummins **Trained** Carrutherstown, D'fries & G'way
■ Khaan was withdrawn. Price at time of withdrawal 11/4. Rule 4 applies to all bets struck prior to withdrawal, but not to SP bets. Deduction - 25p in the £. New market formed.

FOCUS
Lowly handicap form. The second has been rated near this year's best.

6856 BRISTOL WATER FILLIES' H'CAP 1m
4:30 (4:30) (Class 5) (0-75,75) 3-Y-O+ **£3,428** (£1,020; £509; £300) **Stalls** Low

Form RPR
431 **1** **Amorously (IRE)**[13] 6362 3-9-7 **75** PatDobbs 1 81
(Richard Hannon) *trckd ldr: chal travelling best over 2f out: led narrowly over 1f out: rdn clr ent fnl f: comf* 4/6[1]
3134 **2** 1 3/4 **Glamorous Crescent**[40] 5377 3-8-4 **58** JimmyQuinn 5 59
(Grace Harris) *led: jnd over 2f out: sn rdn: narrowly hdd over 1f out: kpt on gamely but nt pce of wnr fnl f* 4/1[2]
60- **3** 1 1/4 **City Of Love**[66] 3-9-7 **75** DanielMuscutt 4 73
(David Lanigan) *trckd ldrs: rdn over 2f out: kpt on but nt pce to chal (jockey said filly hung left-handed under pressure)* 11/2[3]
4041 **4** *nk* **Diamond Shower (IRE)**[9] 6526 3-8-4 **65** SeanKirrane(7) 3 62
(John Flint) *trckd ldrs: rdn over 2f out: kpt on but nt pce to chal* 7/1

1m 42.64s (0.94) **Going Correction** +0.10s/f (Good)
WFA 3 from 5yo 5lb **4 Ran SP% 107.9**
Speed ratings (Par 100): **99,97,96,95**
CSF £3.60 TOTE £1.60; EX 3.10 Trifecta £6.40.
Owner Ali Bahbahani **Bred** Haras Don Alberto **Trained** East Everleigh, Wilts

FOCUS
Just the four of them and it proved straightforward for the favourite. The pace was a steady one. It's been rated around the second.

6857 EMPIRE FIGHTING CHANCE WINNERS APPRENTICE H'CAP (RACING EXCELLENCE SERIES) (SUMMER SPRINT QUAL) 5f 160y
5:00 (5:00) (Class 5) (0-70,67) 3-Y-O+
£3,428 (£1,020; £509; £300; £300; £300) **Stalls** Centre

Form RPR
0330 **1** **Devils Roc**[16] 6286 3-9-7 **66** TylerSaunders 2 75
(Jonathan Portman) *trckd ldr: rdn over 2f out: led ent fnl f: r.o wl: comf* 7/2[3]
3506 **2** 3 1/4 **Leo Minor (USA)**[11] 6455 5-9-7 **67** AngusVilliers(3) 3 65
(Robert Cowell) *trckd ldrs: rdn 2f out: kpt on to go 2nd fnl 120yds: no threat to wnr* 3/1[2]
0401 **3** *1* **It Must Be Faith**[121] 2503 9-9-9 **66** MarkCrehan 4 61
(Michael Appleby) *led: 2 l up over 2f out: rdn over 1f out: hdd ent fnl f: sn hld: no ex fnl 120yds* 12/1
2632 **4** *1* **Lalania**[20] 6132 4-9-7 **67** MarcoGhiani(3) 5 59
(Stuart Williams) *trckd ldrs: rdn wl over 1f out: kpt on but nt pce to get on terms* 11/10[1]
0250 **5** *8* **Jaganory (IRE)**[14] 6329 7-8-11 **54** (v) ScottMcCullagh 6 19
(Christopher Mason) *chsd ldrs: rdn wl over 2f out: wknd over 1f out* 12/1
5004 **6** *9* **Yet Another (IRE)**[9] 6526 4-8-5 **53** oh8 (b) KeelanBaker(5) 1
(Grace Harris) *s.i.s: a outpcd: nvr on terms (jockey said gelding was never travelling)* 66/1

1m 11.17s (0.07) **Going Correction** +0.10s/f (Good)
WFA 3 from 4yo+ 2lb **6 Ran SP% 111.7**
Speed ratings (Par 103): **103,98,97,96,85 73**
CSF £14.21 TOTE £4.20: £1.90, £2.00; EX 14.80 Trifecta £82.80.
Owner Roc Steady Partnership **Bred** Petches Farm Ltd **Trained** Upper Lambourn, Berks

FOCUS
Modest sprinting form. The winner has been rated in line with her earlier form.
T/Plt: £213.80 to a £1 stake. Pool: £59,401.97 - 202.81 winning units T/Qpdt: £45.20 to a £1 stake. Pool: £6,375.11 - 104.25 winning units **Tim Mitchell**

6703 CHELMSFORD (A.W) (L-H)
Wednesday, September 4

OFFICIAL GOING: Polytrack: standard
Wind: medium, across Weather: fine

6858 BET AT TOTESPORT.COM MEDIAN AUCTION MAIDEN STKS (PLUS 10 RACE) 7f (P)
5:45 (5:47) (Class 4) 2-Y-O **£5,433** (£1,617; £808; £404) **Stalls** Low

Form RPR
1 **Cobber Kain** 2-9-5 0 FrankieDettori 6 82+
(John Gosden) *sn led and mde rest: rdn over 1f out: r.o wl ins fnl f* 11/4[2]
0 **2** *1* **Strait Of Hormuz (IRE)**[88] 3601 2-9-5 0 DavidProbert 10 79
(Andrew Balding) *w wnr: effrt over 1f out: kpt on wl ins fnl f: a hld* 8/1
3 **3** 3 3/4 **Wailea Nights (IRE)**[32] 5676 2-9-0 0 HarryBentley 1 65
(Marco Botti) *chsd ldrs: effrt u.p over 1f out: unable qck and btn ins fnl f: wknd fnl 75yds* 5/1[3]
00 **4** 1 1/2 **Locked N' Loaded**[12] 6402 2-9-5 0 SeanLevey 2 66
(Richard Hannon) *midfield: effrt ent fnl 2f: kpt on to go 4th ins fnl f: no threat to ldrs* 20/1
64 **5** 1 1/2 **Selecto**[29] 5774 2-9-5 0 JasonWatson 8 62
(Roger Charlton) *pushed along leaving stalls: in tch in midfield: effrt over 2f out: unable qck u.p and hung lft over 1f out: wknd ins fnl f (jockey said colt hung left-handed in str)* 6/1
52 **6** 3/4 **Rocket Dancer**[13] 6368 2-9-5 0 OisinMurphy 11 60
(Sylvester Kirk) *chsd ldrs on outer: effrt over 2f out: unable qck over 1f out: wknd ins fnl f* 9/4[1]
0 **7** *nk* **Thank The Irish (IRE)**[4] 6718 2-9-5 0 NicolaCurrie 4 59+
(Jamie Osborne) *awkward leaving stalls and slowly away: a towards rr: sme late hdwy: nvr trbld ldrs (jockey said colt reared as stalls opened)* 25/1
00 **8** *6* **Grimsthorpe Castle**[12] 6395 2-9-5 0 LiamKeniry 7 44+
(Ed Walker) *in rr of main gp: shkn up over 1f out: sn btn and wknd ins fnl f* 50/1
9 3/4 **Goddess Of Rome (IRE)** 2-9-0 0 JackMitchell 9 37
(Simon Crisford) *dwlt: in tch: effrt over 2f out: outpcd and rn green over 1f out: no ch after* 12/1
10 *nk* **Lenny The Lion** 2-8-12 0 MorganCole(7) 3 41
(Lydia Pearce) *dwlt: a outpcd in rr* 100/1
11 *16* **Kates Star** 2-9-0 0 AdrianMcCarthy 5
(Christine Dunnett) *in tch in midfield early: steadily lost pl and bhd 3f out: lost tch over 1f out* 100/1

1m 24.79s (-2.41) **Going Correction** -0.275s/f (Stan) **11 Ran SP% 119.7**
Speed ratings (Par 97): **102,100,96,94,93 92,91,85,84,83 65**
CSF £24.53 TOTE £3.50: £1.10, £2.60, £1.70; EX 19.10 Trifecta £145.90.
Owner Ms Rachel D S Hood **Bred** Ms Rachel Hood **Trained** Newmarket, Suffolk

FOCUS
The winner controlled the gallop up front and nothing came from off the pace. The opening level is a bit fluid.

6859 TOTEPOOL CASHBACK CLUB AT TOTESPORT.COM H'CAP 5f (P)
6:15 (6:15) (Class 3) (0-95,95) 3-Y-O **£9,703** (£2,887; £1,443) **Stalls** Low

Form RPR
1241 **1** **Furious**[19] 6148 3-9-5 **93** OisinMurphy 3 103
(David Simcock) *dropped in bhd and hld up in tch: edgd rt out and effrt between rivals over 1f out: rdn to ld ins fnl f: r.o wl and gng away at fin (vet said filly lost right-hind shoe)* 4/7[1]
0000 **2** 1 1/4 **Street Parade**[11] 6476 3-9-7 **95** (t) JasonWatson 2 100
(Stuart Williams) *edgd lft leaving stalls: led for almost 1f: rdn and unable qck over 1f out: swtchd lft and kpt on same pce ins fnl f* 4/1[3]
123 **3** *nk* **Pink Flamingo**[15] 6301 3-8-3 **82** CierenFallon(5) 1 86
(Michael Attwater) *t.k.h: w ldr tl led after almost 1f: rdn 2f out: hdd ins fnl f: kpt on same pce after* 3/1[2]

58.65s (-1.55) **Going Correction** -0.275s/f (Stan) **3 Ran SP% 108.7**
Speed ratings (Par 105): **101,99,98**
CSF £3.13 TOTE £1.40; EX 2.70 Trifecta £2.60.
Owner Qatar Racing Ltd & Kin Hung Kei **Bred** Sir Nicholas & Lady Nugent **Trained** Newmarket, Suffolk

FOCUS
A cosy enough success for the improving winner. The race has been rated at face value for now, with the third to form.

6860 EXTRA PLACES AT TOTESPORT.COM (S) H'CAP 1m 2f (P)
6:45 (6:47) (Class 6) (0-60,62) 3-Y-O+
£3,105 (£924; £461; £300; £300; £300) **Stalls** Low

Form RPR
3532 **1** **Fair Power (IRE)**[19] 6152 5-9-7 **56** (p) OisinMurphy 13 63
(John Butler) *t.k.h: chsd ldrs tl wnt 2nd 7f out: rdn and ev ch 2f out: led 100yds out: styd on* 7/4[1]

0066 **2** *¾* **Dawn Treader (IRE)**[30] 5747 3-9-7 **62**........................ SeanLevey 14 69
(Richard Hannon) *prom tl led jst over 8f out: rdn ent fnl 2f: drvn over 1f out: hdd 100yds out: kpt on same pce after* **6/1**[2]

0065 **3** *2 ¾* **Midnight Mood**[19] 6153 6-9-4 **53**........................ CallumShepherd 2 53
(Dominic Ffrench Davis) *hld up in tch in midfield: effrt over 2f out: swtchd rt and drvn over 1f out: chsd clr ldng pair 1f out: no imp* **6/1**[2]

5265 **4** *nk* **Sharp Operator**[19] 6152 6-9-3 **52**........................(h) RichardKingscote 8 53
(Charlie Wallis) *awkward as stalls opened: hld up in tch in midfield: hmpd over 7f out: clsd over 2f out: effrt over 1f out: disputing 3rd ins fnl f: kpt on but no threat to ldrs* **6/1**[2]

0606 **5** *6* **King Of Naples**[10] 6502 6-9-6 **55**........................(h) JackGarritty 9 43
(Ruth Carr) *t.k.h: chsd ldrs: rdn and unable qck over 1f out: wknd ins fnl f* **14/1**

0000 **6** *1* **Squire**[11] 6456 8-9-2 **54**........................(tp) JaneElliott(3) 15 40
(Marjorie Fife) *in tch in midfield: pushed rt over 7f out: effrt over 2f out: unable qck and btn over 1f out: wknd ins fnl f* **20/1**

0000 **7** *1 ½* **Right About Now (IRE)**[15] 6324 5-9-10 **59**........................(p) RobertWinston 6 43
(Charlie Wallis) *t.k.h: chsd ldr early: styd chsng ldrs: effrt over 2f out: unable qck over 1f out: wknd fnl f* **25/1**

3600 **8** *nk* **Flying Moon (GER)**[23] 6030 3-9-0 **55**........................ NicolaCurrie 3 39
(Jonathan Portman) *hld up towards rr: effrt over 2f out: stl plenty to do whn hmpd wl over 1f out: kpt on but no threat to ldrs* **12/1**[3]

0005 **9** *1 ¾* **Reformed Character (IRE)**[6] 6635 3-7-11 **45**........................(b) MorganCole(7) 1 26
(Lydia Pearce) *hld up in tch in midfield: unable qck u.p and btn over 1f out: wknd fnl f* **25/1**

0000 **10** *½* **Roser Moter (IRE)**[20] 6098 4-8-5 **45**........................(v[1]) TheodoreLadd(5) 4 24
(Michael Appleby) *t.k.h: hld up towards rr: effrt over 2f out: stl plenty to do whn hmpd wl over 1f out: no ch after* **33/1**

000 **11** *1 ¼* **Interrogator (IRE)**[46] 5193 3-8-5 **46**........................(t[1]) JoeyHaynes 5 23
(Alan Bailey) *stdd s: hld up in rr: effrt over 2f out: no imp whn hmpd wl over 1f out: no ch after* **20/1**

0600 **12** *6* **Lynchpin (IRE)**[6] 6636 3-8-8 **54**........................(b) CierenFallon(5) 7 20
(Lydia Pearce) *hld up in midfield: stmbld over 7f out: swtchd to outer 6f out: rdn and struggling 3f out wl btn over 1f out: wknd* **20/1**

6400 **13** *21* **Perfect Soldier (IRE)**[33] 5633 5-8-12 **47**........................(p) JosephineGordon 11
(Shaun Keightley) *s.i.s: nvr travelling wl and a bhd: lost tch over 1f: t.o* **16/1**

-000 **14** *9* **Midoura**[44] 5249 3-8-9 **50**........................ DavidProbert 12
(Laura Mongan) *led for almost 2f: steadily lost pl: dropping out whn rdr looked down and eased wl over 1f out: t.o (jockey said filly lost action; post-race examination failed to reveal any abnormalities)* **50/1**

-000 **15** *1 ½* **Poet Pete (IRE)**[13] 6361 3-8-4 **45**........................(p[1]) LiamJones 10
(Mark Usher) *midfield: rdn over 3f out: lost pl and bhd over 1f out: t.o* **50/1**

2m 5.63s (-2.97) **Going Correction** -0.275s/f (Stan)
WFA 3 from 4yo+ 6lb **15** Ran SP% **128.3**
Speed ratings (Par 101): **100,99,97,96,92 91,90,89,88,88 87,82,65,58,57**
CSF £11.07 CT £57.48 TOTE £2.50: £1.10, £1.80, £2.00; EX 14.30 Trifecta £44.00.The winner was sold to John Holmes for £7000.
Owner Dave James **Bred** Pitrizzia Partnership **Trained** Newmarket, Suffolk

FOCUS
They went steady early and few got into this, the two up front having a good battle up the straight. The winner has been rated to the best of this year's form.

6861 IRISH LOTTO AT TOTESPORT.COM H'CAP 1m 2f (P)

7:15 (7:15) (Class 2) (0-105,102) 3-Y-O+ **£12,938** (£3,850; £1,924; £962) **Stalls** Low

Form RPR

4243 **1** **Desert Fire (IRE)**[9] 6536 4-9-12 **102**........................(p) OisinMurphy 3 113
(Saeed bin Suroor) *chsd ldrs: effrt jst over 2f out: chal towards inner over 1f out: led 100yds out: r.o wl* **7/2**[2]

1-1 **2** *nk* **Dubai Warrior**[28] 5808 3-9-2 **98**........................ FrankieDettori 6 108
(John Gosden) *hld up in last pair: t.k.h and hdwy to chse ldr 8f out: effrt and ev ch ent fnl 2f: drvn to ld over 1f out: hdd 100yds out: kpt on wl but a hld after* **2/5**[1]

2002 **3** *5* **The Trader (IRE)**[9] 6541 3-8-8 **90**........................ PJMcDonald 4 90
(Mark Johnston) *led: rdn ent fnl 2f: drvn and hdd over 1f out: no ex and wknd ins fnl f* **5/1**[3]

6000 **4** *¾* **Original Choice (IRE)**[25] 5930 5-9-9 **99**........................(v[1]) JamesDoyle 1 98
(Nick Littmoden) *hld up in tch in last pair: rdn ent fnl 2f: unable qck and btn whn hung lft 1f out: one pce after* **25/1**

052- **5** *4* **Glen Shiel**[290] 9150 5-9-12 **102**........................ HollieDoyle 5 93
(Archie Watson) *chsd ldr for 2f: in tch after: unable qck u.p over 1f out: wknd ins fnl f* **25/1**

0000 **6** *3 ¼* **Glendevon (USA)**[19] 6150 4-8-12 **88**........................(h) ShaneKelly 2 72
(Richard Hughes) *stdd s: hld up in tch in rr: effrt ent fnl 2f: sn u.p and outpcd: wl btn fnl f* **40/1**

2m 3.09s (-5.51) **Going Correction** -0.275s/f (Stan)
WFA 3 from 4yo+ 6lb **6** Ran SP% **120.4**
Speed ratings (Par 109): **111,110,106,106,102 100**
CSF £5.75 TOTE £3.50: £1.40, £1.10; EX 6.50 Trifecta £18.80.
Owner Godolphin **Bred** Godolphin **Trained** Newmarket, Suffolk

FOCUS
An interesting handicap, and the big two in the market had a good battle up the straight, pulling clear of the rest. They have been given credit for beating the third, who arrived off a pb and ran well on his only other start here.

6862 BET IN PLAY AT TOTESPORT.COM NOVICE STKS 1m (P)

7:45 (7:46) (Class 4) 3-Y-O+ **£6,469** (£1,925; £962; £481) **Stalls** Low

Form RPR

31 **1** **Nazeef**[69] 4298 3-9-4 0........................ JimCrowley 5 91+
(John Gosden) *dwlt: sn rcvrd to chse ldr: led over 1f out: sn pushed along and qcknd clr: v easily* **1/4**[1]

4 **2** *2 ¾* **Qatar Queen (IRE)**[28] 5808 3-8-11 0........................ OisinMurphy 1 75+
(James Fanshawe) *t.k.h: trckd ldrs: effrt over 2f out: chsd clr wnr 1f out: no imp* **3/1**[2]

45 **3** *8* **Harbour City (USA)**[21] 6074 3-8-11 0........................ PJMcDonald 4 57
(James Tate) *led tl rdn and hdd over 1f out: sn outpcd and lost btn 2nd 1f out: wknd* **20/1**[3]

54 **4** *2 ½* **Loveheart**[7] 6587 3-8-4 0........................ JoeBradnam(7) 2 51
(Michael Bell) *stdd after s: hld up in rr: effrt over 2f out: sn struggling and outpcd over 1f out: wknd* **33/1**

1m 37.28s (-2.62) **Going Correction** -0.275s/f (Stan) **4** Ran SP% **112.7**
Speed ratings (Par 105): **102,99,91,88**
CSF £1.48 TOTE £1.40; EX 1.60 Trifecta £2.30.
Owner Hamdan Al Maktoum **Bred** Shadwell Estate Company Limited **Trained** Newmarket, Suffolk

FOCUS
The early gallop wasn't strong but they still finished well strung out behind the hot favourite. The third has been rated close to her debut run.

6863 DOUBLE DELIGHT HAT-TRICK HEAVEN AT TOTESPORT.COM H'CAP 1m (P)

8:15 (8:16) (Class 4) (0-85,84) 4-Y-O+
£5,692 (£1,694; £846; £423; £300; £300) **Stalls** Low

Form RPR

0333 **1** **Lawmaking**[43] 5267 6-9-5 **82**........................(p w) LiamKeniry 1 89
(Michael Scudamore) *taken down early: pushed along leaving stalls: in tch in midfield: clsd to trck ldrs over 2f out: swtchd out rt and effrt over 1f out: drvn to ld ins fnl f: r.o wl* **11/4**[1]

0060 **2** *1 ¾* **Banksea**[11] 6460 6-9-4 **84**........................(h) ConnorMurtagh(3) 5 87
(Marjorie Fife) *taken down early: in tch in midfield: effrt and hdwy over 1f out: drvn and ev ch 1f out: kpt on same pce wl ins fnl f* **50/1**

2006 **3** *nk* **Azzeccagarbugli (IRE)**[12] 6391 6-9-5 **82**........................(p) JosephineGordon 9 84
(Mike Murphy) *pushed along leaving stalls: chsd ldr after over 1f tl led 4f out: rdn ent fnl 2f: drvn over 1f out: hdd ins fnl f: no ex and one pce wl ins fnl f* **16/1**

0620 **4** *nk* **Harbour Vision**[18] 6220 4-8-11 **74**........................(v) OisinMurphy 10 76
(Derek Shaw) *dropped in bhd after s: hld up in rr: effrt on inner over 1f out: kpt on u.p ins fnl f* **8/1**

0520 **5** *½* **Blame Culture (USA)**[25] 5945 4-9-4 **81**........................ TomQueally 8 81
(George Margarson) *t.k.h: hld up in tch in last trio: effrt on outer over 1f out: kpt on u.p and edgd lft ins fnl f: nt enough pce to rch wnr* **14/1**

6304 **6** *nk* **Rogue**[18] 6201 4-9-3 **80**........................(p[1]) RossaRyan 2 80
(Alexandra Dunn) *led tl 4f out: styd w ldr: drvn and unable qck over 1f out: wknd ins fnl f* **8/1**

3202 **7** *¾* **Zeyzoun (FR)**[11] 6440 5-9-2 **79**........................(h) JamesDoyle 11 77
(Chris Wall) *chsd ldrs: effrt wl over 1f out: stl pressing ldrs but struggling to qckn whn short of room: snatched up and struck by rivals whip jst ins fnl f: swtchd lft and one pce after* **3/1**[2]

2-32 **8** *1 ¾* **Dourado (IRE)**[100] 3149 5-9-5 **82**........................ DavidProbert 4 76
(Patrick Chamings) *hld up in tch in midfield: effrt over 1f out: drvn and no imp ins fnl f* **7/1**[3]

26-3 **9** *nse* **Tadleel**[15] 6318 4-9-7 **84**........................ JimCrowley 6 78
(Ed Dunlop) *in tch in midfield: unable qck over 1f out: wl hld and one pce ins fnl f* **10/1**

1664 **10** *2 ¾* **Pheidippides**[22] 6050 4-8-12 **75**........................(b) JackMitchell 7 63
(Tom Clover) *w ldr early: rdn over 2f out: lost pl over 1f out: bhd ins fnl f* **12/1**

3250 **11** *3* **Glory Of Paris (IRE)**[147] 1694 5-9-5 **82**........................ LiamJones 3 63
(Michael Appleby) *taken down early: restless in stalls: sn in rr: nvr involved* **16/1**

1m 36.51s (-3.39) **Going Correction** -0.275s/f (Stan) **11** Ran SP% **123.6**
Speed ratings (Par 105): **105,103,102,102,102 101,101,99,99,96 93**
CSF £145.75 CT £1966.81 TOTE £4.00: £1.50, £35.00, £5.30; EX 161.00 Trifecta £1304.70.
Owner Marchwood Aggregates **Bred** Juddmonte Farms Ltd **Trained** Bromsash, H'fords

FOCUS
This was a well-run handicap. The winner has been rated back to last year's form.

6864 CELEBRATE AUGUST'S HERO PAUL BURDER H'CAP 2m (P)

8:45 (8:45) (Class 6) (0-60,66) 3-Y-O+ **£3,105** (£924; £461; £300; £300) **Stalls** Low

Form RPR

6221 **1** **Kensington Art**[7] 6586 3-9-4 **66** 6ex........................(p) ConnorMurtagh(3) 4 72
(Richard Fahey) *dwlt: in tch: effrt on outer to press ldrs ent fnl 2f: drvn and ev ch over 1f out: led ins fnl f: styd on and forged ahd towards fin* **9/4**[2]

6544 **2** *1* **Volcanique (IRE)**[13] 6366 3-7-12 **46**........................(b) JaneElliott(3) 3 51
(Sir Mark Prescott Bt) *led: rdn ent fnl 3f: hdd and rdr dropped rein ent fnl f: drvn and kpt on same pce ins fnl f* **7/1**

2541 **3** *nk* **Barca (USA)**[26] 5891 5-9-12 **60**........................ JimCrowley 2 63
(Marcus Tregoning) *pressed ldr: ev ch and rdn ent fnl 2f: drvn and led ent fnl f: hdd ins fnl f: no ex fnl 50yds* **5/4**[1]

0050 **4** *1 ¼* **Doune Castle**[20] 6104 3-8-9 **54**........................(v[1]) OisinMurphy 1 57
(Andrew Balding) *chsd ldrs: effrt wl over 2f out: nt clrest of runs and swtchd rt 1f out: kpt on ins fnl f* **5/1**[3]

3121 **5** *31* **Thahab Ifraj (IRE)**[9] 6552 6-9-7 **55** 5ex........................ DavidProbert 5 19
(Alexandra Dunn) *in tch in rr: rdn 5f out: lost tch over 1f out: eased: t.o (jockey said gelding hung left-handed and was never travelling)* **10/1**

3m 26.35s (-3.65) **Going Correction** -0.275s/f (Stan)
WFA 3 from 5yo+ 11lb **5** Ran SP% **113.5**
Speed ratings (Par 101): **98,97,97,96,81**
CSF £17.58 TOTE £3.10: £1.50, £3.00; EX 16.80 Trifecta £22.60.
Owner Mrs H Steel **Bred** Mrs H Steel **Trained** Musley Bank, N Yorks

FOCUS
This was a well-contested staying handicap. The winner has been rated close to his Catterick figure.
T/Plt: £16.70 to a £1 stake. Pool: £53,747.69 - 3,211.64 winning units T/Qpdt: £5.00 to a £1 stake. Pool: £6,963.03 - 1,380.70 winning units **Steve Payne**

6865 - 6872a (Foreign Racing) - See Raceform Interactive

4947 MAISONS-LAFFITTE (R-H)

Wednesday, September 4

OFFICIAL GOING: Turf: good

6873a PRIX DE FONTENAY (CLAIMER) (2YO) (TURF) 5f 110y

11:25 2-Y-O **£8,558** (£3,423; £2,567; £1,711; £855)

RPR

1 **Spinning Mist**[11] 6485 2-8-11 0........................(b) CristianDemuro 7 69
(Andrea Marcialis, France) **57/10**

2 *nk* **Skip The Queue (IRE)**[11] 6485 2-8-5 0........................(b) MlleMarieVelon(6) 8 68
(Matthieu Palussiere, France) **27/10**[2]

3 *2* **Galadine (FR)**[18] 2-9-1 0........................ AurelienLemaitre 3 65
(F Head, France) **7/2**[3]

4 *¾* **Panthera Tigris**[11] 6485 2-8-5 0........................ MlleCoraliePacaut(3) 1 56
(Jo Hughes, France) *wl into stride: disp ld early: settled in 3rd: pushed along over 2f out: kpt on same pce fnl f* **20/1**

5 *hd* **Muzy (FR)**[24] 6002 2-9-0 0........................ HugoBesnier(5) 6 66
(Andrea Marcialis, France) **5/2**[1]

6 *3 ½* **Jayadeeva (FR)**[11] 6485 2-9-2 0........................ MaximeGuyon 5 52
(A Giorgi, Italy) **10/1**

7 1 1/4 **Aggression (ITY)**[15] 2-8-13 0 .... MlleMickaelleMichel(3) 4 48
(G Botti, France) 11/1
8 9 **La Maruca (IRE)**[30] 2-8-11 0 .... MickaelBarzalona 2 13
(F Rossi, France) 19/1
1m 4.62s (-2.68) **8 Ran SP% 119.9**
PARI-MUTUEL (all including 1 euro stake): WIN 6.70; PLACE 1.60, 1.40, 1.40; DF 7.90.
Owner Montgomery Motto **Bred** Newsells Park Stud **Trained** France

6874a PRIX DE BONNIERES-SUR-SEINE (CLAIMER) (3YO) (TURF) 1m
12:25 3-Y-O **£8,558** (£3,423; £2,567; £1,711; £855)

RPR
1 **Highest Mountain (FR)**[138] 1909 3-9-1 0 .... FranckForesi 4 69
(Joseph Tuite) *led early: settled to trck ldrs: pushed along to chal over 2f out: rdn to ld 1 1/2f out: drvn and kpt on strly ins fnl f* **22/5**
2 2 **Similaire (FR)**[8] 3-8-11 0 .... MllePerrineCheyer(4) 5 64
(Gianluca Bietolini, France) **33/10**[2]
3 1 3/4 **Royal Gunner (ITY)**[22] 3-8-11 0 ....(p) PierreBazire 3 56
(G Botti, France) **7/2**[3]
4 1 1/4 **Madame Vitesse (FR)**[13] 3-8-11 0 .... RichardJuteau 2 54
(P Monfort, France) **11/2**
5 1 **Made To Order (FR)**[85] 3712 3-8-8 0 .... RosarioMangione 6 48
(E J O'Neill, France) **12/5**[1]
6 7 **Simon's Smile (FR)**[77] 4005 3-8-11 0 .... MlleAudeDuporte(4) 1 39
(Mme G Rarick, France) **15/1**
7 20 **Kenzohope (FR)**[12] 3-8-11 0 ....(b) ArnaudMuste 7
(C Boutin, France) **21/1**
1m 41.24s (-1.06) **7 Ran SP% 119.6**
PARI-MUTUEL (all including 1 euro stake): WIN 5.40; PLACE 2.50, 2.00; SF 18.40.
Owner Matt & Lauren Morgan **Bred** G B Partnership **Trained** Lambourn, Berks

6875 - (Foreign Racing) - See Raceform Interactive

6653 HAMILTON (R-H)
Wednesday, September 4
6876 Meeting Abandoned - Waterlogging

6858 CHELMSFORD (A.W) (L-H)
Thursday, September 5
OFFICIAL GOING: Polytrack: standard
Wind: Light, half against Weather: Fine

6883 BET TOTEPLACEPOT AT TOTESPORT.COM NOVICE AUCTION STKS (PLUS 10 RACE) 6f (P)
5:40 (5:42) (Class 4) 2-Y-O **£6,080** (£1,809; £904; £452) **Stalls** Centre

Form RPR
325 1 **Second Love (IRE)**[22] 6064 2-8-10 71 .... CliffordLee 5 82+
(K R Burke) *chsd ldrs: effrt and hdwy towards inner over 1f out: led 1f out: sn asserted but rn green and hung bdly rt: r.o wl: readily* **2/1**[1]
22 2 4 1/2 **River Cam**[28] 5856 2-8-10 0 .... CallumShepherd 7 69
(James Tate) *chsd ldr: effrt over 2f out: ev ch ent fnl f: jst getting outpcd whn impeded jst ins fnl f: no ch w wnr and plugged on same pce after* **5/2**[2]
30 3 1 1/4 **Never In Red (IRE)**[37] 5514 2-8-10 0 .... KieranO'Neill 6 65
(Robyn Brisland) *midfield: effrt over 2f out: 4th and drvn over 1f out: no ch w wnr but kpt on ins fnl f* **14/1**
64 4 3/4 **Pettinger**[12] 6442 2-8-9 0 .... JFEgan 1 62
(Charles Hills) *midfield: effrt over 2f out: swtchd lft and kpt on ins fnl f: no ch w wnr* **4/1**[3]
6313 5 1/2 **Too Hard To Hold (IRE)**[20] 6147 2-9-5 70 .... FrannyNorton 8 70+
(Mark Johnston) *led: clr over 3f out: rdn and hrd pressed over 1f out: hdd 1f out: sn wknd* **6/1**
50 6 7 **William Thomas (IRE)**[12] 6449 2-8-8 0 .... DarraghKeenan(3) 3 41
(Robert Eddery) *dwlt: a towards rr: nvr involved* **33/1**
00 7 1 3/4 **Goddess Of Fire**[7] 6629 2-8-6 0 .... JosephineGordon 2 31
(Ed Dunlop) *dwlt: a towards rr: rousted along 5f out: nvr involved* **25/1**
0346 8 3 3/4 **Zain Storm (FR)**[21] 6113 2-9-2 67 .... RoystonFfrench 4 30
(John Butler) *midfield: rdn over 2f out: sn struggling: wknd and wl bhd ins fnl f* **16/1**
1m 11.14s (-2.56) **Going Correction** -0.35s/f (Stan) 2y crse rec **8 Ran SP% 115.5**
Speed ratings (Par 97): **103,97,95,94,93 84,82,77**
CSF £7.26 TOTE £2.60: £1.60, £1.60, £4.20; EX 7.10 Trifecta £53.60.
Owner Mrs T Burns **Bred** Newhall Properties Ltd **Trained** Middleham Moor, N Yorks

FOCUS
Standard Polytrack. An easy but errant winner of this fair event. The form has been rated at face value, with the winner credited with significant progress.

6884 BET TOTEEXACTA AT TOTESPORT.COM NURSERY H'CAP 1m (P)
6:10 (6:13) (Class 6) (0-60,60) 2-Y-O
£3,105 (£924; £461; £300; £300; £300) **Stalls** Low

Form RPR
0221 1 **Luna Wish**[12] 6435 2-9-5 58 .... JimmyQuinn 6 63+
(George Margarson) *t.k.h: chsd ldrs tl wnt 2nd 4f out: led ent fnl 2f: rdn over 1f out: drvn and styd on ins fnl f* **7/4**[1]
5004 2 1 1/4 **Chateau Peapod**[27] 5907 2-8-13 52 .... BrettDoyle 10 54
(Lydia Pearce) *chsd ldr tl 4f out: effrt and cl enough in 3rd over 2f out: chsd wnr 1f out: kpt on but a hld* **33/1**
035 3 1 3/4 **Rochford (IRE)**[44] 5265 2-9-6 59 .... JFEgan 8 57+
(Henry Spiller) *dwlt: swtchd lft after s: towards rr: effrt and swtchd rt over 2f out: chsd ldng trio jst over 1f out: styd on to go 3rd ins fnl f: nvr getting to ldrs* **12/1**
6060 4 3 **Interrupted Dream**[9] 6571 2-8-12 58 .... AidenSmithies(7) 7 49
(Mark Johnston) *led tl rdn and hdd ent fnl 2f: 3rd and no ex 1f out: wknd ins fnl f* **33/1**
0602 5 2 1/4 **Inflamed**[12] 6435 2-9-2 55 .... LiamKeniry 9 41+
(Ed Walker) *dwlt and bustled along leaving stalls: swtchd lft and towards rr: effrt over 2f out: wd bnd 2f out: sme late hdwy: nvr trbld ldrs* **9/2**[3]
0400 6 3 1/2 **Clandestine Affair (IRE)**[13] 6394 2-9-7 60 .... CallumShepherd 5 38
(Jamie Osborne) *midfield: rdn over 3f out: outpcd over 2f out: wl btn and hung lft over 1f out: wknd fnl f* **7/1**

0405 7 2 1/4 **Buy Nice Not Twice (IRE)**[13] 6394 2-9-0 53 .... RossaRyan 3 26
(Richard Hannon) *off the pce in last quartet: effrt over 2f out: drvn wl over 1f out: no imp and wl btn whn swtchd lft ins fnl f* **4/1**[2]
6004 8 1 1/4 **Grimbold**[17] 6271 2-9-3 59 ....(b) HarrisonShaw(3) 4 29
(K R Burke) *dwlt: nvr travelling wl and a towards rr: nvr involved* **16/1**
0000 9 7 **Must Dream**[21] 6097 2-8-12 51 .... NathanEvans 1 5
(Seb Spencer) *in tch in midfield: u.p and outpcd in 4th over 2f out: no ch after: wknd fnl f* **10/1**
060 10 nk **Little Lulu (IRE)**[22] 6072 2-8-9 48 ....(p[1]) FrannyNorton 2
(Archie Watson) *chsd ldrs tl lost pl over 2f out: sn wl btn: wknd* **25/1**
1m 38.44s (-1.46) **Going Correction** -0.35s/f (Stan) **10 Ran SP% 119.4**
Speed ratings (Par 93): **93,91,90,87,84 81,79,77,70,70**
CSF £78.53 CT £552.94 TOTE £2.40: £1.10, £19.40, £4.30; EX 104.50 Trifecta £1248.90.
Owner F Butler **Bred** E Cantillon **Trained** Newmarket, Suffolk

FOCUS
Not many got into this low-grade nursery. The second has been rated to her best.

6885 BET TOTEQUADPOT AT TOTESPORT.COM CLASSIFIED STKS 1m (P)
6:40 (6:43) (Class 6) 3-Y-O+
£3,105 (£924; £461; £300; £300; £300) **Stalls** Low

Form RPR
0323 1 **Parknacilla (IRE)**[21] 6131 3-8-11 49 ....(p) PoppyBridgwater(5) 6 56
(Henry Spiller) *midfield: short of room and sltly impeded 5f out: nt clr run over 2f out: swtchd lft over 1f out: rdn to chse clr ldr 1f out: kpt on u.p to ld cl home* **6/1**
6043 2 1/2 **Red Skye Delight (IRE)**[12] 6441 3-9-2 50 .... KieranO'Neill 7 55
(Luke McJannet) *taken down early: led: rdn and kicked clr jst over 2f out: hung rt and racd awkwardly fnl f: hdd cl home* **8/1**
000 3 1 3/4 **Pearl Jam**[22] 6074 3-9-2 47 .... GeorgeWood 8 51
(James Fanshawe) *hld up in last quintet: effrt over 2f out: hdwy over 1f out: swtchd lft 1f out: styd on to go 3rd 100yds out: styd on but nvr getting to ldrs* **8/1**
060 4 2 1/2 **Opera Kiss (IRE)**[28] 5857 3-9-2 33 .... PhilDennis 2 45
(Lawrence Mullaney) *wl in tch in midfield: effrt u.p to chse ldrs over 2f out: outpcd over 1f out: kpt on same pce ins fnl f* **66/1**
5606 5 2 3/4 **Tellovoi (IRE)**[9] 6572 11-9-7 47 ....(p) PhilipPrince 3 40
(Richard Guest) *taken down early: t.k.h: wl in tch in midfield: stmbld 5f out: drvn over 2f out: unable qck and outpcd over 1f out: wl hld and kpt on same pce fnl f* **25/1**
0000 6 3/4 **Emojie**[69] 4349 5-9-2 47 .... RayDawson(5) 15 38
(Jane Chapple-Hyam) *in tch in midfield: swtchd rt and effrt u.p 2f out: no prog: wl hld and kpt on same pce fnl f* **25/1**
0324 7 1/2 **Poetic Motion**[26] 5957 3-9-2 49 .... CharlieBennett 1 36
(Jim Boyle) *chsd ldr: effrt over 2f out: wnt 2nd briefly but wnr gone clr over 1f out: wknd ins fnl f* **4/1**[2]
5000 8 1 3/4 **Nicky Baby (IRE)**[5] 6723 5-9-2 47 ....(v[1]) SophieRalston(5) 12 33
(Dean Ivory) *in tch in midfield: swtchd rt to outer 5f out: unable qck and outpcd bnd 2f out: no ch after* **5/1**[3]
0040 9 hd **Miss Communicate**[37] 5526 3-9-2 50 .... EoinWalsh 5 31
(Lydia Pearce) *rousted along leaving stalls: racd in last trio: nt clr run over 2f out: effrt u.p over 1f out: no imp: nvr involved* **66/1**
10 1 **Force Of Cashen (IRE)**[77] 4044 3-9-2 49 .... DaneO'Neill 9 29
(Tom Gretton) *dwlt and short of room leaving stalls: racd in last quartet: rdn over 2f out: nvr threatened to get on terms w ldrs: wl btn fnl f* **3/1**[1]
0-00 11 3 **Argent Bleu**[105] 3006 4-9-2 40 .... RhiainIngram(5) 4 23
(Roger Ingram) *sn in rr: rdn over 3f out: nvr involved* **66/1**
0400 12 shd **Jailbreak (IRE)**[65] 4485 3-9-2 47 .... JosephineGordon 13 22
(Conrad Allen) *wl in tch in midfield: rdn over 2f out: lost pl and btn over 1f out: wknd fnl f* **16/1**
000 13 2 1/2 **Keep On Laughing (IRE)**[16] 6316 4-9-2 40 ....(t) DylanHogan(5) 16 17
(John Butler) *chsd ldr: rdn and outpcd over 2f out: lost 2nd over 1f out: sn wknd* **33/1**
0004 14 12 **Cuban Spirit**[21] 6117 4-9-4 50 .... DarraghKeenan(3) 11
(Lee Carter) *wnt lft leaving stalls: t.k.h: in tch in midfield: impeded 5f out: lost pl over 2f out: wl bhd fnl f* **12/1**
000 15 6 **Doncaster Star**[68] 4367 4-9-7 30 ....(t) TrevorWhelan 10
(Ivan Furtado) *short of room leaving stalls: a towards rr: nvr involved* **66/1**
1m 37.61s (-2.29) **Going Correction** -0.35s/f (Stan)
WFA 3 from 4yo+ 5lb **15 Ran SP% 128.4**
Speed ratings (Par 101): **97,96,94,92,89 88,88,86,86,85 82,82,79,67,61**
CSF £54.54 TOTE £5.70: £1.90, £2.30, £2.70; EX 44.80 Trifecta £359.00.
Owner Charles & Fiona Spiller **Bred** M Downey & Kildaragh Stud **Trained** Newmarket, Suffolk

FOCUS
A very modest event that was dominated by fillies. The winner has been rated to her best.

6886 BET TOTETRIFECTA AT TOTESPORT.COM H'CAP 1m 2f (P)
7:10 (7:10) (Class 4) (0-80,82) 3-Y-O+ **£5,692** (£1,694; £846; £423; £300) **Stalls** Low

Form RPR
312 1 **Muhaarar's Nephew**[29] 5808 3-9-7 78 .... DaneO'Neill 3 88+
(Owen Burrows) *t.k.h early: trckd ldng pair: edgd out rt and chal between rivals over 1f out: drvn and in command ins fnl f: styd on* **11/8**[1]
352 2 3/4 **Michele Strogoff**[13] 6390 6-9-12 82 .... TheodoreLadd(5) 1 87
(Michael Appleby) *taken down early: led: rdn jst over 2f out: drvn and hdd 1f out: kpt on but a hld ins fnl f* **11/4**[2]
3-22 3 1 1/2 **Maximum Effect**[20] 6187 3-9-6 77 .... KieranO'Neill 5 79
(John Gosden) *wnt rt leaving stalls: sn rcvrd to chse ldr: effrt over 2f out: 3rd and unable qck 1f out: kpt on same pce ins fnl f* **3/1**[3]
1005 4 15 **My Dear Friend**[20] 6186 3-9-4 75 ....(b) HarryBentley 4 48
(Ralph Beckett) *t.k.h early: hld up in tch in last pair: rdn over 2f out: sn outpcd and btn: wknd over 1f out* **8/1**
0530 5 2 **Eddie Cochran (IRE)**[57] 4788 3-9-1 72 .... RossaRyan 2 41
(Richard Hannon) *hld up in tch in rr: effrt and outpcd over 2f out: sn wl btn and wknd over 1f out* **25/1**
2m 4.14s (-4.46) **Going Correction** -0.35s/f (Stan)
WFA 3 from 6yo 6lb **5 Ran SP% 108.7**
Speed ratings (Par 105): **103,102,101,89,87**
CSF £5.26 TOTE £1.90: £1.30, £1.60; EX 4.80 Trifecta £11.10.
Owner Hadi Al-Tajir **Bred** Shadwell Estate Company Limited **Trained** Lambourn, Berks

FOCUS
Fairly useful handicap form, the first three finishing a long way clear. It's been rated around the second.

6887 BET TOTESWINGER AT TOTESPORT.COM NOVICE STKS 1m 2f (P)
7:40 (7:43) (Class 4) 3-Y-O+ £6,080 (£1,809; £904; £452) Stalls Low

Form RPR
22 **1** **Battle of Paradise (USA)**[197] 804 3-9-2 0 .... RyanTate 1 73+
(Sir Mark Prescott Bt) *mde all: rdn wl over 1f out: styd on wl and in command ins fnl f* **4/6[1]**
5 **2** 1 3/4 **Junooh (IRE)**[141] 1852 3-9-2 0 .... DaneO'Neill 5 69+
(Sir Michael Stoute) *wnt rt leaving stalls: sn rcvrd to chse wnr: effrt over 2f out: drvn and kpt on same pce ins fnl f* **15/8[2]**
3 3 3/4 **Overbeck (IRE)** 4-9-8 0 .... JoeyHaynes 4 61
(Dean Ivory) *in tch in midfield: effrt in cl 4th and switche rt over 2f out: unable qck 1f out: edgd lft and outpcd ins fnl f: wnt 3rd cl home* **16/1**
0 **4** nk **Sea It My Way (IRE)**[17] 6290 3-9-2 0 .... GeorgeWood 3 61
(James Fanshawe) *chsd ldng pair: effrt on inner over 2f out: unable qck over 1f out: wknd wl ins fnl f and lost 3rd cl home* **14/1[3]**
0 **5** 1/2 **Honey Lane (IRE)**[33] 5656 3-8-11 0 .... CharlesBishop 7 55
(William Jarvis) *in tch in last trio: pushed along ent fnl 3f: swtchd rt and kpt on steadily ins fnl f: no threat to ldng pair* **50/1**
6 3 **Byron Green (IRE)**[509] 7-9-5 0 .... DarraghKeenan(3) 6 53
(Thomas Gallagher) *dwlt and impeded leaving stalls: t.k.h early: hld up in rr: pushed along and outpcd over 2f out: wl hld and kpt on same pce fr over 1f out* **66/1**
00 **7** 5 **Star Guide (GER)**[17] 6290 3-8-11 0 ....(h) ThomasGreatrex(5) 2 44
(David Menuisier) *hld up in last trio: rdn over 3f out: bhd and wl btn over 1f out* **25/1**

2m 5.09s (-3.51) **Going Correction** -0.35s/f (Stan)
WFA 3 from 4yo+ 6lb 7 Ran SP% **114.6**
Speed ratings (Par 105): **100,98,95,95,94 92,88**
CSF £2.11 TOTE £1.40: £1.10, £1.10; EX 2.00 Trifecta £12.90.
Owner Charles C Walker-Osborne House III **Bred** Neil Jones **Trained** Newmarket, Suffolk
FOCUS
The market told the story in this fair novice stakes, which lacked depth. Muddling form.

6888 BET TOTESCOOP6 AT TOTESPORT.COM H'CAP 1m 6f (P)
8:10 (8:14) (Class 4) (0-85,85) 3-Y-O+
£5,692 (£1,694; £846; £423; £300; £300) Stalls Low

Form RPR
1545 **1** **Brasca**[20] 6171 3-9-0 **80** .... HarryBentley 4 95+
(Ralph Beckett) *hld up in tch in rr: clsd and nt clr run 2f out: gap opened and cruised into ld ent fnl f: wnt clr on bridle: v easily* **11/4[1]**
5205 **2** 6 **Lord Lamington**[5] 6716 3-9-1 **81** .... FrannyNorton 5 83
(Mark Johnston) *hld up in wl in tch: effrt and nt clrest of runs 3f out: gap opened and effrt to chal 2f out: nt match pce of wnr 1f out: wl hld 2nd and plugged on same pce fnl f* **7/2[3]**
0123 **3** 1 1/4 **Wanaasah**[13] 6392 3-8-6 **77** ....(h) ThomasGreatrex(5) 3 77
(David Loughnane) *led: rdn jst over 2f out: hdd ent fnl f: immediately brushed aside by wnr: wl hld 3rd and plugged on same pce fnl f* **3/1[2]**
1653 **4** 2 **Cosmic Landscape**[153] 1566 4-9-2 **73** .... CharlesBishop 2 68
(William Jarvis) *t.k.h: hld up in tch in midfield: nt clrest of runs on inner over 2f out: drvn and unable qck over 1f out: wl hld and plugged on same pce fnl f* **7/1**
6032 **5** 1 **Jukebox Jive (FR)**[21] 6100 5-10-0 **85** ....(t) DougieCostello 7 79
(Jamie Osborne) *chsd ldrs on outer: rdn over 3f out: outpcd and btn over 1f out* **7/1**
2636 **6** 4 1/2 **Thaqaffa (IRE)**[14] 5625 6-8-13 **77** ....(p[1]) SeanKirrane(7) 6 65
(Amy Murphy) *taken down early: chsd ldr tl 2f out: lost pl over 1f out: wknd fnl f* **12/1**

2m 55.61s (-7.59) **Going Correction** -0.35s/f (Stan) course record
WFA 3 from 4yo+ 9lb 6 Ran SP% **106.6**
Speed ratings (Par 105): **107,103,102,101,101 98**
CSF £11.25 TOTE £3.60: £1.50, £1.80; EX 12.00 Trifecta £45.00.
Owner Frank Brady & Brian Scanlon **Bred** Mrs C R Philipson & Lofts Hall Stud **Trained** Kimpton, Hants
■ Amource was withdrawn, price at time of withdrawal 6/1. Rule 4 applies to all bets struck prior to withdrawal, but not to SP bets. Deduction of 10p in the pound. New market formed.
FOCUS
One-way traffic in this decent staying handicap. The second and third have been rated close to their recent runs.

6889 BOOK TICKETS ONLINE AT CHELMSFORDCITYRACECOURSE.COM H'CAP 6f (P)
8:40 (8:42) (Class 6) (0-55,55) 3-Y-O+
£3,105 (£924; £461; £300; £300; £300) Stalls Centre

Form RPR
0402 **1** **Senorita Grande (IRE)**[5] 6737 3-9-5 **55** ....(v) JasonHart 7 62+
(John Quinn) *hld up in tch in midfield: clsd and nt clr run over 1f out: sn swtchd rt and hdwy: rdn to ld ins fnl f: r.o wl* **9/2[1]**
3243 **2** 1 **Prince Rock (IRE)**[17] 6284 4-8-12 **46** ....(h) NickyMackay 4 50
(Simon Dow) *t.k.h: hld up in midfield: swtchd rt and effrt over 1f out: hdwy u.p ins fnl f: kpt on wl to go 2nd towards fin* **9/2[1]**
3650 **3** 1/2 **Englishman**[13] 6401 9-9-7 **55** ....(p) PhilipPrince 8 58
(Milton Bradley) *chsd ldrs: effrt u.p over 1f out: clsd to press ldrs 1f out: drvn and kpt on ins fnl f* **20/1**
2212 **4** 1/2 **Tarseekh**[17] 6284 6-9-7 **55** ....(b) FrannyNorton 12 56
(Charlie Wallis) *w ldrs: drvn to ld over 1f out: sn edgd lft: hdd and one pce ins fnl f* **9/2[1]**
2252 **5** 1/2 **Terri Rules (IRE)**[8] 6602 4-9-3 **54** .... DarraghKeenan(3) 11 54
(Lee Carter) *in tch in midfield: effrt on outer 2f out: kpt on u.p ins fnl f: nt rch ldrs* **16/1**
0031 **6** nk **Kellington Kitty (USA)**[19] 6199 4-9-5 **53** ....(p) RossaRyan 2 52
(Mike Murphy) *hld up in tch in midfield: nt clr run over 1f out: swtchd rt 1f out: sme prog but nt clr run again towards fin: unable to chal* **6/1[2]**
3505 **7** nk **Wild Flower (IRE)**[27] 5883 7-8-10 **47** ....(v[1]) MeganNicholls(3) 10 45
(Luke McJannet) *w ldr tl rdn to ld narrowly ent fnl 2f: carried lft 1f out: no ex and wknd ins fnl f* **33/1**
0435 **8** 3/4 **Quick Recovery**[17] 6284 4-9-4 **52** ....(b) CharlieBennett 6 47
(Jim Boyle) *short of room leaving stalls: hld up in tch in last quartet: effrt over 1f out: kpt on u.p and edging rt ins fnl f: nvr trbld ldrs* **7/1[3]**
4633 **9** nse **Tigerinmytank**[26] 5960 3-8-10 **46** oh1 .... RoystonFfrench 1 41
(John Holt) *chsd ldrs: effrt ent fnl 2f: pressing ldrs whn carried lft 1f out: wknd ins fnl f* **20/1**
500 **10** 2 **Manzoni**[106] 2976 3-9-1 **51** .... KieranO'Neill 5 40
(Mohamed Moubarak) *wnt rt and stdd after s: hld up in rr: effrt over 1f out: edging lft but kpt on u.p ins fnl f: nvr trbld ldrs* **20/1**
5033 **11** 1 1/4 **Swell Song**[16] 6321 3-9-0 **50** ....(p) JosephineGordon 9 36
(Robert Cowell) *led tl ent fnl 2f: stl pressing ldrs but struggling to qckn whn short of room jst ins fnl f: sn wknd* **16/1**
060 **12** shd **Mystical Moon (IRE)**[6] 6682 4-9-3 **51** .... PhilDennis 3 36
(David C Griffiths) *hld up in tch in midfield: effrt on inner over 1f out: chsng ldrs whn nt clr run 1f out: swtchd rt ins fnl f: no ch after* **8/1**
0035 **13** 5 **Good Business (IRE)**[21] 6126 5-9-5 **53** ....(b) HarryBentley 14 23
(Henry Spiller) *a bhd: nvr involved* **20/1**

1m 11.0s (-2.70) **Going Correction** -0.35s/f (Stan)
WFA 3 from 4yo+ 2lb 13 Ran SP% **126.2**
Speed ratings (Par 101): **104,102,102,101,100 100,99,98,98,96 94,94,87**
CSF £23.15 CT £386.41 TOTE £4.80: £1.90, £2.00, £4.90; EX 27.00 Trifecta £537.40.
Owner Zen Racing **Bred** Tally-Ho Stud **Trained** Settrington, N Yorks
FOCUS
Very modest sprinting form. The second has been rated to his latest.
T/Plt: £14.10 to a £1 stake. Pool: £61,024.37 - 3,149.07 winning units T/Qpdt: £6.20 to a £1 stake. Pool: £7,265.53 - 866.98 winning units **Steve Payne**

5947 HAYDOCK (L-H)
Thursday, September 5

OFFICIAL GOING: Soft (good to soft in places) changing to soft after race 2 (2.20)
Wind: Moderate, against in straight of over 4f Weather: Cloudy

6890 RACING TV MAIDEN STKS (PLUS 10 RACE) 1m 3f 140y
1:50 (1:50) (Class 4) 3-Y-O £6,469 (£1,925; £962; £481) Stalls Centre

Form RPR
52 **1** **Arabist**[19] 6216 3-9-5 0 .... FrankieDettori 6 77+
(John Gosden) *chsd ldr: moved upsides over 3f out: rdn to ld over 2f out: kpt on gamely ins fnl f* **8/15[1]**
333 **2** 1 **Swift Wing**[75] 4104 3-9-5 79 ....(b) RobertHavlin 7 76
(John Gosden) *hld up: hdwy to chse front pair ent fnl 3f: sn rdn: styd on ins fnl f: clsd towards fin to take 2nd post: nt trble wnr* **4/1[3]**
32 **3** nse **Noble Music (GER)**[23] 6034 3-9-0 0 .... RichardKingscote 1 71+
(Ralph Beckett) *led: pressed over 3f out: rdn and hdd over 2f out: edgd lft u.p over 1f out: continued to chal: kpt on same pce fnl f 75yds: lost 2nd post* **7/2[2]**
65 **4** 2 3/4 **Casting Spells**[79] 3974 3-9-0 0 .... PJMcDonald 3 66
(Tom Dascombe) *hld up: rdn and outpcd 3f out: kpt on ins fnl f but n.d* **33/1**
4 **5** 1 1/2 **Gabriel Oak**[75] 4104 3-9-5 0 .... PaulMulrennan 4 69?
(Donald McCain) *chsd ldrs: drvn over 3f out: outpcd over 2f out: plugged on whn n.d ins fnl f* **66/1**
04 **6** 4 **Detonation**[17] 6274 3-9-5 0 .... RaulDaSilva 2 62?
(Shaun Harris) *trckd ldrs: pushed along 5f out: rdn and wknd over 3f out* **150/1**
7 90 **Sydney Express** 3-9-5 0 .... JackMitchell 5
(Ismail Mohammed) *in rr: rn green: pushed along over 5f out: eased whn lost tch over 3f out: t.o (jockey said colt ran green)* **25/1**

2m 37.39s (4.09) **Going Correction** +0.45s/f (Yiel) 7 Ran SP% **116.4**
Speed ratings (Par 103): **104,103,103,101,100 97,37**
CSF £3.23 TOTE £1.20: £1.10, £2.40; EX 3.10 Trifecta £3.80.
Owner Denford Stud **Bred** Denford Stud Ltd **Trained** Newmarket, Suffolk
FOCUS
All races on Inner Home Straight. Add 6yds. The ground looked pretty testing and looked to be riding as described. A useful maiden dominated by the market leaders.

6891 BRITISH STALLION STUDS EBF NOVICE STKS (PLUS 10 RACE) (C&G) 6f
2:20 (2:22) (Class 4) 2-Y-O £6,469 (£1,925; £962; £481) Stalls Centre

Form RPR
1 **Duesenberg (IRE)** 2-9-0 0 .... TonyHamilton 6 78
(Richard Fahey) *in tch: pushed along over 2f out: r.o ins fnl f: led fnl 60yds: kpt on cl home and hld on wl* **25/1**
5 **2** hd **Hartswood**[15] 6337 2-9-0 0 .... PaddyMathers 10 77
(Richard Fahey) *in rr: hdwy over 1f out: nt clr run briefly ins fnl f: str run fnl 100yds: jst hld (jockey said colt denied clear run on several occasions ins fnl f)* **12/1**
5 **3** nk **Jamais Assez (USA)**[75] 4098 2-9-0 0 .... BenCurtis 5 76
(K R Burke) *racd keenly: prom: led 2f out: rdn ins fnl f: hdd fnl 60yds: no ex fnl strides and lost anther pl* **15/2[3]**
4 3/4 **Oakenshield (IRE)** 2-9-0 0 .... KevinStott 2 74
(Kevin Ryan) *a.p: rdn over 2f out: styd on u.p ins fnl f: one pce towards fin* **11/2[2]**
5 1 **Moosmee (IRE)** 2-9-0 0 .... PJMcDonald 4 71
(William Haggas) *trckd ldrs: rdn over 1f out: unable qck ins fnl f: kpt on same pce fnl 75yds* **9/1**
0 **6** 3/4 **Jerbourg**[15] 6337 2-9-0 0 .... DavidAllan 7 69
(Tim Easterby) *hld up: rdn and hdwy over 1f out: kpt on u.p ins fnl f: one pce fnl 75yds: nvr able to chal* **20/1**
1 **7** 1 3/4 **Danyah (IRE)**[20] 6167 2-9-6 0 .... JimCrowley 3 69
(Owen Burrows) *led: hdd 2f out: rdn over 1f out: fdd ins fnl f* **8/11[1]**
8 3 **Tom Collins** 2-9-0 0 .... RichardKingscote 1 54
(David Elsworth) *dwlt: towards rr and rn green: wl outpcd over 1f out: nvr a threat* **20/1**
9 1/2 **Siberian Night (IRE)** 2-9-0 0 .... KieranShoemark 8 53
(Ed Walker) *in tch: rdn and wknd over 1f out* **25/1**
10 5 **Due A Win** 2-9-0 0 .... GrahamLee 9 38
(Bryan Smart) *towards rr: nvr bttr than midfield: pushed along over 2f out: wknd over 1f out* **50/1**

1m 17.18s (3.28) **Going Correction** +0.45s/f (Yiel) 10 Ran SP% **121.9**
Speed ratings (Par 97): **96,95,95,94,93 92,89,85,85,78**
CSF £283.21 TOTE £38.70: £13.00, £4.60, £4.00; EX 246.50 Trifecta £2485.50.
Owner Aidan J Ryan **Bred** Bridgetown Stud & Trickledown Stud **Trained** Musley Bank, N Yorks

FOCUS
The ground was changed to soft all over following this novice. A bit of a bunched finish to this novice and the odds-on favourite flopped. The jury is out on the value of the form.

6892 BRITISH EBF NOVICE STKS (PLUS 10 RACE) (C&G) 7f 212y
2:50 (2:51) (Class 4) 2-Y-0 £6,469 (£1,925; £962; £481) Stalls Low

Form RPR

32 **1** **Panic Room (IRE)**[7] 6622 2-9-0 0 ....(p[1]) PJMcDonald 3 81
(Tom Dascombe) *w ldr: led after 2f: mde rest: rdn and edgd rt over 1f out: styd on wl to draw clr ins fnl f* **5/2**[2]

2 *3 ¼* **Tombolo (FR)** 2-9-0 0 .... ConnorBeasley 1 73
(Michael Dods) *hld up: rdn over 2f out: hdwy over 1f out: kpt on to chse wnr wl ins fnl f: no imp* **16/1**

3 *nk* **Grand Bazaar** 2-9-0 0 .... FrankieDettori 2 73+
(John Gosden) *trckd ldrs: rdn over 2f out: no imp over 1f out: edgd rt ins fnl f: kpt on towards fin* **4/6**[1]

4 **4** *1 ¼* **Caledonian Crusade (IRE)**[20] 6163 2-9-0 0 .... JamieSpencer 7 70
(David Simcock) *prom: pushed along and ev ch over 2f out: checked over 1f out: unable to go w wnr and hung lft sn after: lost 2nd wl ins fnl f: no ex fnl 75yds* **10/1**[3]

0 **5** *2 ½* **Make Me Laugh (IRE)**[28] 5848 2-9-0 0 .... TonyHamilton 4 65+
(Richard Fahey) *hld up: rdn over 2f out: stl green: rdn and edgd lft over 1f out: checked sn after: nvr able to get involved* **20/1**

44 **6** *8* **Trumpets Call (IRE)**[14] 6368 2-9-0 0 .... BenCurtis 8 47
(David Loughnane) *racd keenly: led for 2f: remained prom: rdn over 2f out: sn wknd* **14/1**

7 *2* **Peerless Percy (IRE)** 2-9-0 0 .... PaulMulrennan 6 43
(Michael Dods) *trckd ldrs: rdn and lost pl over 3f out: wknd wl over 1f out* **20/1**

0 **8** *1 ½* **Temper Trap**[28] 5845 2-9-0 0 .... DavidAllan 5 39
(Tim Easterby) *in rr: pushed along and outpcd over 3f out: lft bhd over 1f out* **50/1**

1m 46.27s (3.57) **Going Correction** +0.45s/f (Yiel) **8 Ran SP% 121.7**
Speed ratings (Par 97): **100,96,96,95,92 84,82,81**
CSF £41.57 TOTE £3.20: £1.10, £3.30, £1.10; EX 40.30 Trifecta £73.20.
Owner John Dance **Bred** Michael Lyons **Trained** Malpas, Cheshire

FOCUS
Add 6yds. Ordinary novice form.

6893 BRITISH EBF PREMIER FILLIES' H'CAP 1m 2f 42y
3:20 (3:20) (Class 2) (0-100,98) 3-Y-O+ **£18,675** (£5,592; £2,796; £1,398) **Stalls** Centre

Form RPR

212 **1** **Illumined (IRE)**[29] 5810 3-8-7 85 .... RobertHavlin 1 97+
(John Gosden) *mde all: rdn ins fnl f: styd on wl* **4/5**[1]

4412 **2** *2* **Specialise**[61] 4640 3-8-9 87 .... JackMitchell 5 93
(Roger Varian) *prom: effrt 2f out: chsd wnr jst over 1f out: no imp ins fnl f* **13/8**[2]

3603 **3** *2 ½* **Amber Spark (IRE)**[10] 6541 3-8-2 80 .... PaddyMathers 4 81
(Richard Fahey) *in rr: effrt and hdwy 2f out: unable qck u.p over 1f out: kpt on same pce ins fnl f* **10/1**[3]

0520 **4** *½* **Katiesheidinlisa**[21] 6124 3-8-2 83 ....(p) JaneElliott(3) 3 83
(Tom Dascombe) *prom: pushed along over 2f out: lost pl u.p over 1f out: one pce ins fnl f* **14/1**

2m 26.54s (15.74) **Going Correction** +0.45s/f (Yiel)
WFA 3 from 4yo 6lb **4 Ran SP% 109.4**
Speed ratings (Par 96): **55,53,51,51**
CSF £2.39 TOTE £1.50; EX 2.10 Trifecta £3.00.
Owner George Strawbridge **Bred** Forenaghts Stud & Tinnakill Bloodstock **Trained** Newmarket, Suffolk

FOCUS
Add 28yds. No gallop on here and the favourite made all for a ready win. The second has been rated to form and the third to her latest.

6894 GORDON LORD BYRON EBF CONDITIONS STKS 6f 212y
3:50 (3:50) (Class 3) 3-Y-O+ £9,056 (£2,695; £1,346; £673) Stalls Low

Form RPR

2116 **1** **Qaysar (FR)**[14] 6376 4-9-5 100 .... PJMcDonald 3 109
(Richard Hannon) *in tch: effrt to take 2nd 2f out: led over 1f out: kpt on ins fnl f* **5/2**[1]

-650 **2** *nk* **Dubai Dominion**[75] 4092 3-8-11 98 ....(b) JamieSpencer 5 102
(Ed Vaughan) *in tch: lost pl over 2f out: effrt over 1f out: angled rt ins fnl f: r.o to take 2nd towards fin: clsd on wnr* **5/1**

5000 **3** *1 ¼* **Vanbrugh (USA)**[33] 5664 4-9-1 104 .... KieranShoemark 4 101
(Charles Hills) *hld up in rr: hdwy gng wl 2f out: rdn to chal over 1f out: stl ev ch ins fnl f: no ex and lost 2nd towards fin* **9/2**[3]

0/1- **4** *nk* **Mizaah (IRE)**[345] 7647 6-9-1 99 ....(t) JimCrowley 6 100+
(Owen Burrows) *chsd ldr tl over 3f out: rdn and outpcd over 2f out: n.m.r briefly wl ins fnl f: kpt on towards fin* **6/1**

3436 **5** *½* **Gordon Lord Byron (IRE)**[12] 6472 11-9-1 106 .... FrankieDettori 2 99
(T Hogan, Ire) *chsd ldrs: wnt 2nd over 3f out tl rdn 2f out: lost pl over 1f out: kpt on towards fin* **3/1**[2]

0601 **6** *1* **Three Saints Bay (IRE)**[27] 5916 4-9-1 99 .... DavidNolan 1 96
(David O'Meara) *led: rdn and hdd over 1f out: stl there ins fnl f: wknd fnl 75yds* **15/2**

1m 30.7s (1.40) **Going Correction** +0.45s/f (Yiel)
WFA 3 from 4yo+ 4lb **6 Ran SP% 114.5**
Speed ratings (Par 107): **110,109,108,107,107 106**
CSF £15.71 TOTE £3.30: £1.50, £2.70; EX 15.00 Trifecta £65.40.
Owner Al Shaqab Racing **Bred** S N C Scuderia Waldeck **Trained** East Everleigh, Wilts

FOCUS
Add 6yds. A useful conditions race in which the winning favourite put up a smart effort to concede weight all round. The winner's Newmarket form has been franked and he's been rated in line with that.

6895 JOIN RACING TV NOW H'CAP 1m 3f 140y
4:20 (4:20) (Class 2) (0-105,102) 3-Y-O+**£14,231** (£4,235; £2,116; £1,058) Stalls Centre

Form RPR

2035 **1** **Epaulement (IRE)**[13] 6420 4-10-0 102 .... RichardKingscote 4 113
(Tom Dascombe) *mde all: rdn over 1f out: fnd plenty: styd on wl to draw clr fnl 110yds* **2/1**[2]

1203 **2** *4 ½* **Sinjaari (IRE)**[35] 5583 3-9-1 97 .... PJMcDonald 2 101
(William Haggas) *chsd ldrs: wnt 2nd over 3f out: rdn and tried to chal over 1f out: one pce and no ch w wnr fnl 110yds* **7/4**[1]

2-01 **3** *3* **Spanish Archer (FR)**[33] 5657 4-9-10 98 ....(h) DanielMuscutt 7 97
(James Fanshawe) *hld up: rdn to improve and chse front two over 2f out: one pce over 1f out: nvr able to chal (jockey said gelding slipped when leaving stalls)* **5/1**[3]

124 **4** *6* **Dragons Voice**[27] 5902 5-8-12 86 .... JamieSpencer 5 75
(David Menuisier) *stdd s: hld up in rr: drvn and outpcd over 4f out: plugged on fnl f: nvr a threat* **8/1**

3346 **5** *¾* **Mr Top Hat**[5] 6725 4-8-10 89 .... CierenFallon(5) 3 76
(David Evans) *chsd wnr tl over 3f out: rdn and outpcd over 2f out: wknd wl over 1f out (jockey said gelding hung right-handed in hme str)* **12/1**

542 **6** *1* **Autumn War (IRE)**[47] 5174 4-8-12 86 .... KieranShoemark 1 72
(Charles Hills) *chsd ldrs: rdn and outpcd over 2f out: wknd wl over 1f out* **10/1**

2m 35.43s (2.13) **Going Correction** +0.45s/f (Yiel)
WFA 3 from 4yo+ 8lb **6 Ran SP% 114.3**
Speed ratings (Par 109): **110,107,105,101,100 99**
CSF £6.09 TOTE £3.50: £1.50, £1.60; EX 7.50 Trifecta £25.40.
Owner Deva Racing Epaulette Partnership **Bred** Mrs Vanessa Hutch **Trained** Malpas, Cheshire

FOCUS
Add 6yds. A useful handicap and the right horses came to the fore. Another pb from the winner.

6896 RACINGTV.COM H'CAP (FOR GENTLEMAN AMATEUR RIDERS) 1m 3f 140y
4:55 (4:55) (Class 5) (0-70,71) 4-Y-0+
£4,679 (£1,451; £725; £363; £300; £300) Stalls Centre

Form RPR

6/0- **1** **Lightly Squeeze**[253] 1329 5-11-9 71 ....(h) MrMichaelLegg 3 82
(Harry Fry) *hld up in rr: hdwy over 3f out: led over 2f out: styd on wl to draw clr fnl 100yds* **4/1**[3]

15 **2** *4* **Mauricio (IRE)**[17] 6278 5-11-7 69 .... MrAlexEdwards 2 73
(Dr Richard Newland) *hld up: rdn over 4f out: hdwy over 2f out: chsd wnr over 1f out: edgd lft ins fnl f: no imp* **11/2**

4216 **3** *3* **Deinonychus**[6] 6658 8-11-2 64 ....(p) MrSimonWalker 5 63
(Michael Appleby) *hld up: hdwy over 7f out: rdn to ld briefly wl over 2f out: one pce fr over 1f out* **11/4**[1]

3524 **4** *3* **War Brigade (FR)**[20] 6156 5-11-2 69 ....(vt[1]) MrNathanSeery(5) 6 64
(Ian Williams) *handy: rdn and lost pl over 3f out: outpcd after: edgd lft over 1f out: plugged on whn n.d fnl f* **4/1**[3]

0-00 **5** *1* **Born To Please**[23] 6042 5-10-0 55 oh5 .... MrCiaranJones(7) 7 48
(Mark Usher) *prom: led after 1f: rdn over 3f out: hdd wl over 2f out: hld whn edgd lft u.p over 1f out: wknd ins fnl f* **33/1**

6004 **6** *2 ¾* **Brancaster (IRE)**[10] 6535 5-10-11 64 .... MrGeorgeEddery(5) 4 52
(David Elsworth) *led for 1f: remained prom: rdn and ch wl over 2f out: wknd over 1f out* **3/1**[2]

5004 **7** *36* **Bold Statement (IRE)**[2] 6824 4-10-2 55 oh6 .... MrEireannCagney(5) 1
(Alan Berry) *trckd ldrs tl rdn and wknd 5f out: t.o fnl 2f* **66/1**

2m 39.37s (6.07) **Going Correction** +0.45s/f (Yiel) **7 Ran SP% 111.5**
Speed ratings (Par 103): **97,94,92,90,89 87,63**
CSF £24.59 CT £67.32 TOTE £3.90: £1.90, £3.30; EX 26.70 Trifecta £40.00.
Owner J Davies, G Brown & P Govier **Bred** Highbury Stud Ltd **Trained** Seaborough, Dorset

FOCUS
Add 6yds. A modest amateur riders' handicap won in good style. The leaders perhaps got racing too soon. The winner has been rated back to his 3yo form, and the second to form.
T/Plt: £108.90 to a £1 stake. Pool: £54,035.15 - 362.21 winning units T/Qpdt: £6.00 to a £1 stake. Pool: £4,941.20 - 607.92 winning units **Darren Owen**

6717 LINGFIELD (L-H)
Thursday, September 5

OFFICIAL GOING: Good to firm changing to good to firm (firm in places) after race 2 (4.45)
Wind: Moderate, mostly against Weather: Fine

6897 IDRIS MORGAN MEMORIAL APPRENTICE H'CAP 7f
4:15 (4:17) (Class 6) (0-52,57) 3-Y-0+
£2,781 (£827; £413; £300; £300; £300) Stalls Centre

Form RPR

4003 **1** **Hi Ho Silver**[16] 6327 5-9-1 49 .... SebastianWoods(3) 16 61+
(Chris Wall) *hld up in midfield: rdn and swtchd to r against nr side rail over 1f out: qckly clsd on ldrs: led ins fnl f: sn clr* **5/1**[1]

2631 **2** *4* **Muhallab (IRE)**[9] 6575 3-9-8 57 6ex .... SeanDavis 5 57
(Adrian Nicholls) *disp ld: stl gng strly over 2f out: rdn to ld over 1f out: hdd and outpcd ins fnl f* **13/2**[2]

0023 **3** *1* **Arctic Flower (IRE)**[22] 6084 6-9-2 50 .... RhiainIngram(3) 18 49
(John Bridger) *wl away: disp ld to over 1f out: one pce after: jst hld on for 3rd (jockey said mare hung left-handed)* **13/2**[2]

3452 **4** *nk* **Flying Sakhee**[8] 6605 6-9-2 47 ....(p) MitchGodwin 7 45
(John Bridger) *dwlt: wl in rr: rdn wl over 2f out: prog over 1f out: styd on ins fnl f and nrly snatched 3rd* **16/1**

0000 **5** *1* **Ascot Dreamer**[28] 5857 3-9-0 52 ....(p) AndrewBreslin(3) 1 46
(David Brown) *in tch in midfield: rdn over 2f out: kpt on same pce and n.d* **25/1**

4325 **6** *shd* **Sea Tea Dea**[7] 6643 5-9-1 46 .... FinleyMarsh 3 41
(Adrian Wintle) *in tch in midfield: clsd on ldrs 2f out: rdn and one pce after: nvr able to chal (jockey said mare hung right-handed in fnl f)* **7/1**[3]

0006 **7** *shd* **Dalness Express**[4] 6758 6-8-10 46 oh1 ....(tp) Pierre-LouisJamin(5) 15 41
(Archie Watson) *s.i.s: sn pressed ldrs: rdn over 2f out: stl in 3rd over 1f out: fdd* **15/2**

6006 **8** *½* **Reshaan (IRE)**[14] 6363 4-8-12 46 ....(p) TheodoreLadd(3) 10 40
(Alexandra Dunn) *hld up wl in rr: swtchd lft 2f out and rdn: kpt on over 1f out: nvr nrr (jockey said gelding hung right-handed)* **25/1**

05 **9** *¾* **Ubla (IRE)**[75] 4115 6-9-2 52 ....(p) TobyEley(5) 13 44
(Gay Kelleway) *pressed ldrs: rdn over 2f out and lost pl sn after: kpt on u.p fnl f but n.d (jockey said gelding hung both ways)* **22/1**

6005 **10** *1 ¼* **Tavener**[12] 6462 7-8-12 50 ....(t) ZakWheatley(7) 17 39
(Declan Carroll) *chsd ldrs: lost pl 3f out: sn u.p: one pce and nvr able to cl after* **12/1**

0-00 **11** *nk* **Aiguillette**[111] 2790 3-8-13 48 ....(w) PaddyBradley 11 34
(Gary Moore) *nvr beyond midfield: shkn up and no prog over 2f out: wl btn over 1f out* **20/1**

0-10 **12** *1* **Miss Recycled**[58] 4753 4-9-1 49 .... SeamusCronin(3) 9 34
(Michael Madgwick) *wl in rr: rdn and effrt on outer over 2f out: sn no prog* **25/1**

020 **13** *½* **Little Miss Kodi (IRE)**[21] 6131 6-9-1 51 ....(t) SeanKirrane(5) 8 35
(Mark Loughnane) *pressed ldrs to over 2f out: wknd wl over 1f out* **10/1**

0020 **14** 1/2 **Sugar Plum Fairy**29 5806 4-9-1 46 oh1 .... MeganNicholls 12 29
(Tony Carroll) *a in rr: rdn and no prog over 2f out* **25/1**

060 **15** 4 **Tilsworth Diamond**22 6074 4-9-1 46 .... GabrieleMalune 2 18
(Mike Murphy) *mostly in last and nvr a factor* **66/1**

0212 **16** 1 1/4 **Lady Morpheus**29 5806 3-8-10 52 .... LouisGaroghan(7) 14 19
(Gary Moore) *s.i.s: swtchd after s and only one to r against nr side rail thrght: sn prom: wknd wl over 2f out (trainer said, regarding poor performance, filly was unsuited by racing without cover. he further added a post-race endoscopic examination revealed filly had mucus in trachea)* **7/1**3

000- **17** 3 **W G Grace (IRE)**317 8494 4-9-3 51 .... (w) ThomasGreatrex(3) 4 12
(Tim McCarthy) *pressed ldrs tl wknd rapidly 2f out* **50/1**

1m 22.58s (-1.72) **Going Correction** -0.225s/f (Firm) 17 Ran SP% **130.7**
WFA 3 from 4yo+ 4lb
Speed ratings (Par 101): **100,95,94,93,92 92,92,92,91,89 89,88,87,87,82 81,77**
CSF £34.77 CT £233.07 TOTE £5.90: £1.60, £1.90, £2.20, £3.70; EX 41.30 Trifecta £188.70.
Owner Mrs P Toye & Partner **Bred** Mrs P J Toye **Trained** Newmarket, Suffolk

FOCUS
The rail was dolled in down the hill adding 2yds to each round-course race. Most of the apprentice riders initially shunned the near-side rail in this moderate opening handicap. The winner has been rated near his best previous form.

6898 CONSOLIDATED TIMBER HOLDINGS LTD H'CAP 7f
4:45 (4:45) (Class 5) (0-75,75) 3-Y-O+
£3,428 (£1,020; £509; £300; £300; £300) **Stalls** Centre

Form RPR

514 **1** **The Groove**24 6027 6-8-10 66 .... ThomasGreatrex(5) 8 73
(David Evans) *hld up in last: swtchd fr rail to outer 1/2-way: prog over 2f out: rdn to ld jst over 1f out: styd on* **15/2**3

6006 **2** 1 **First Link (USA)**36 5565 4-8-10 61 oh2 .... NicolaCurrie 7 65
(Jean-Rene Auvray) *s.s: sn in tch in rr: clsd on ldrs over 2f out: shkn up to ld over 1f out: fnd little and sn hdd: chsd wnr after but wl hld* **11/1**

P-00 **3** hd **Danecase**56 4844 6-9-2 70 .... (tp) SeanDavis(3) 2 74+
(David Dennis) *pressed ldr 2f: trckd ldrs after: nt clr run wl over 1f out: swtchd to rail and drvn fnl f: styd on and nrly snatched 2nd* **25/1**

4630 **4** 3/4 **Mr Wagyu (IRE)**18 6261 4-9-2 67 .... (v) JasonHart 1 69
(John Quinn) *led and sn crossed to nr side rail: hdd and shkn up over 2f out: drvn and stl upsides over 1f out: one pce after* **12/1**

/20- **5** 3/4 **Revolutionary Man (IRE)**481 2652 4-9-7 75 ....(tp) MeganNicholls(3) 4 75
(Mark Loughnane) *t.k.h: trckd ldrs: rdn 2f out: rt there over 1f out: nt qckn* **25/1**

5113 **6** 1 1/2 **Fighting Temeraire (IRE)**34 5626 6-9-9 74 .... MartinDwyer 6 70
(Dean Ivory) *plld hrd early: pressed ldr after 2f: led over 2f out: sn rdn: hdd & wknd over 1f out (jockey said gelding ran too free)* **11/10**1

0321 **7** nse **Zoraya (FR)**25 5981 4-9-6 71 .... RobertWinston 3 70
(Pam Sly) *w ldng pair after 2f: rdn over 2f out: losing pl and btn whn hmpd over 1f out (jockey said filly was denied a clear run; trainer said filly was unsuited by the ground on this occasion, which was subsequently changed to good to firm, firm in places, and would prefer an easier surface)* **9/4**2

1m 23.19s (-1.11) **Going Correction** -0.225s/f (Firm) 7 Ran SP% **113.9**
Speed ratings (Par 103): **97,95,95,94,93 92,92**
CSF £81.32 CT £1930.97 TOTE £9.40: £3.70, £4.90; EX 69.20 Trifecta £855.80.
Owner Dave & Emma Evans **Bred** Cheveley Park Stud Ltd **Trained** Pandy, Monmouths

FOCUS
This time the riders came straight over to the stands' rail. The winner has been rated in line with his best, and the second to her best turf form.

6899 INJURED JOCKEYS FUND/EBF NOVICE STKS 4f 217y
5:20 (5:21) (Class 5) 2-Y-O
£3,428 (£1,020; £509; £254) **Stalls** Centre

Form RPR

3222 **1** **Poets Dance**9 6577 2-8-11 79 .... PatCosgrave 7 76
(Rae Guest) *trckd ldrs against nr side rail: plld out over 1f out: shkn up to ld ins fnl f: sn in command* **5/4**1

012 **2** 1 1/4 **Cool Sphere (USA)**20 6147 2-9-6 81 .... SeanDavis(3) 8 83
(Robert Cowell) *led and racd against nr side rail: rdn over 1f out: hdd ins fnl f: styd on but readily hld* **9/2**3

2 **3** 4 1/2 **On Tick (IRE)**25 5994 2-9-2 0 .... MartinDwyer 6 60
(Miss Katy Brown, Ire) *pressed ldr to over 1f out: edgd lft and fdd but stl clr in 3rd pl* **10/1**

2150 **4** 1 1/4 **Illusionist (GER)**63 4580 2-9-9 96 .... (b) AdamMcNamara 3 62
(Archie Watson) *pressed ldr to over 1f out: wknd fnl f* **7/2**2

5 **5** 1 1/2 **Barking Mad**15 6330 2-9-2 0 .... HectorCrouch 5 50
(David Evans) *dwlt: outpcd and bhd: nvr a factor but kpt on steadily fr over 1f out* **11/1**

6 7 **Hooray Henry** 2-8-11 0 .... (w) ThomasGreatrex(5) 9 25
(Henry Candy) *dwlt: outpcd and a bhd* **14/1**

7 3/4 **Falacho (IRE)** 2-8-11 0 .... JasonHart 2 17
(David Loughnane) *spd in centre to 1/2-way: wknd 2f out: eased (jockey said filly hung left-handed)* **33/1**

05 **8** 7 **Billesdon**27 5879 2-8-11 0 .... SeamusCronin(5) 1
(Michael Madgwick) *outpcd and a bhd: t.o* **100/1**

57.29s (-1.41) **Going Correction** -0.225s/f (Firm) 8 Ran SP% **112.9**
Speed ratings (Par 95): **102,100,92,90,88 77,76,64**
CSF £6.90 TOTE £2.10: £1.10, £1.40, £2.10; EX 7.30 Trifecta £34.50.
Owner Mrs J E Wallsgrove **Bred** Joyce Wallsgrove **Trained** Newmarket, Suffolk
■ Rathagan was withdrawn, price at time of withdrawal 16/1. Rule 4 does not apply.

FOCUS
The stands' rail was again the place to be in this uncompetitive novice event. The second has been rated in line with his best.

6900 SKY SPORTS RACING ON SKY 415 NURSERY H'CAP 4f 217y
5:50 (5:51) (Class 5) (0-75,74) 2-Y-O
£3,428 (£1,020; £509; £300) **Stalls** Centre

Form RPR

0300 **1** **Manolith**23 6032 2-9-3 70 .... RobbieDowney 5 72
(David O'Meara) *dwlt: outpcd and bhd in last: sed to cl over 1f out: drvn to take 2nd jst ins fnl f: led fnl 50yds: hung lft after* **13/2**

5215 **2** 1/2 **Dandizette (IRE)**12 6436 2-9-4 74 .... SeanDavis(3) 1 74
(Adrian Nicholls) *chsd ldr: led wl over 1f out: sn drvn: hdd fnl 50yds: hld whn carried lft after (jockey said filly hung left-handed and that his saddle slipped)* **10/3**3

423 **3** 1 1/2 **Microscopic (IRE)**24 6011 2-8-11 64 .... PatCosgrave 3 59
(David Simcock) *chsd ldng pair: rdn to take 2nd briefly 1f out: one pce fnl f* **5/2**2

4042 **4** 2 **Chasanda**3 6800 2-9-0 74 .... (h) AngusVilliers(7) 4 61
(David Evans) *led and racd against rail: rdn and hdd wl over 1f out: wknd fnl f* **9/4**1

58.03s (-0.67) **Going Correction** -0.225s/f (Firm) 4 Ran SP% **95.8**
Speed ratings (Par 95): **96,95,92,89**
CSF £19.92 TOTE £6.70; EX 22.50 Trifecta £39.00.
Owner York Thoroughbred Racing **Bred** Selwood Bloodstock Ltd & R S Hoskins **Trained** Upper Helmsley, N Yorks
■ Crime Of Passion was withdrawn, price at time of withdrawal 11/2. Rule 4 applies to all bets. Deduction of 15p in the pound.

FOCUS
A modest little nursery, run at a strong pace. Straightforward form rated around the second.

6901 FOLLOW AT THE RACES ON TWITTER H'CAP 2m 68y
6:20 (6:20) (Class 5) (0-75,73) 3-Y-O+
£3,428 (£1,020; £509; £300; £300; £300) **Stalls** Centre

Form RPR

5134 **1** **Anyonecanhaveitall**12 6459 3-9-4 73 .... JasonHart 6 80
(Mark Johnston) *trckd ldr: led over 3f out: drvn over 2f out: kpt on and steadily u.p after* **5/4**1

5555 **2** 1 3/4 **October Storm**26 5967 6-10-0 72 .... DavidEgan 1 77
(Mick Channon) *trckd ldng pair: rdn to chse wnr over 2f out: nt qckn and no imp over 1f out: one pce* **9/2**3

5000 **3** 1 3/4 **The Way You Dance (IRE)**93 2400 7-9-6 64 .... SeanLevey 2 67
(Michael Attwater) *trckd ldrs: pushed along over 3f out: drvn to dispute 2nd 2f out: nt qckn over 1f out: wknd fnl 100yds and eased nr fin* **25/1**

-341 **4** nk **Cotton Club (IRE)**9 6556 8-9-3 68 .... MarcoGhiani(7) 3 71
(George Boughey) *hld up in last pair: shkn up 3f out: tk 4th 2f out: no imp on ldrs after: kpt on nr fin* **11/4**2

1303 **5** 6 **Age Of Wisdom (IRE)**12 6448 6-9-12 70 .... (p) HectorCrouch 4 65
(Gary Moore) *slow to get gng: hld up in last pair: rdn wl over 2f out: no imp on ldrs after: wknd fnl f* **13/2**

2054 **6** 11 **Fayetta**13 6405 3-8-9 67 .... (b) CameronNoble(3) 5 51
(David Loughnane) *led to over 3f out: wknd qckly over 2f out: eased* **11/1**

3m 33.19s (-2.81) **Going Correction** -0.225s/f (Firm) 6 Ran SP% **114.8**
WFA 3 from 6yo+ 11lb
Speed ratings (Par 103): **98,97,96,96,93 87**
CSF £7.66 TOTE £1.80: £1.10, £1.80; EX 7.90 Trifecta £96.90.
Owner Garrett J Freyne **Bred** Newtown Stud And T J Pabst **Trained** Middleham Moor, N Yorks

FOCUS
Add 2yds. They went a fair enough pace in this ordinary staying handicap. Muddling form, but the second has been rated close to his recent best and the third to his turf best for now.

6902 SKY SPORTS RACING ON VIRGIN 535 FILLIES' H'CAP 1m 2f
6:50 (6:50) (Class 3) (0-90,87) 3-Y-O **£7,246** (£2,168; £1,084; £542; £270) **Stalls** Low

Form RPR

1220 **1** **Nearooz**36 5545 3-9-7 87 .... DavidEgan 5 94+
(Roger Varian) *trckd ldng pair: clsd to ld over 2f out: rdn to assert over 1f out: edgd rt but styd on wl after* **9/4**2

4231 **2** 1 1/2 **Lady Mascara**16 6304 3-8-9 75 .... TomMarquand 3 78+
(James Fanshawe) *dwlt: in tch: cl up whn hung rt 4f out: rdn over 2f out: hanging rt after: nvr able to chal but styd on fnl f to take 2nd last stride (jockey said filly hung right-handed under pressure)* **2/1**1

3-53 **3** nse **Dubai Discovery (USA)**20 6187 3-8-7 76 ....(p1) GabrieleMalune(3) 4 79
(Saeed bin Suroor) *trckd ldr: chal over 2f out: nt qckn and hld over 1f out: lost 2nd last stride* **6/1**

3130 **4** 3 1/4 **Venusta (IRE)**14 6370 3-8-4 70 .... NicolaCurrie 2 67
(Mick Channon) *dwlt: a in last pair: pushed along and detached 4f out: plugged on to take modest 4th ins fnl f* **20/1**

-323 **5** 3 3/4 **Hallalulu**63 4549 3-9-0 80 .... JasonHart 1 69
(Mark Johnston) *led: shkn up and hdd over 2f out: immediately btn: lost modest 4th ins fnl f (trainer rep could offer no explanation for filly's performance; post-race examination failed to reveal any abnormalities)* **11/4**3

2m 6.92s (-5.28) **Going Correction** -0.225s/f (Firm) 5 Ran SP% **109.8**
Speed ratings (Par 102): **112,110,110,108,105**
CSF £7.12 TOTE £2.90: £2.00, £1.40; EX 6.90 Trifecta £26.20.
Owner Sheikh Ahmed Al Maktoum **Bred** Godolphin **Trained** Newmarket, Suffolk

FOCUS
Add 2yds. A fair little 3yo fillies' handicap, run at a routine sort of pace. The winner has been rated in line with her Chester form, and the second to form.

6903 WITHEFORD EQUINE BARRIER TRIALS AT LINGFIELD PARK MAIDEN STKS 1m 3f 133y
7:20 (7:20) (Class 5) 3-Y-O+
£3,428 (£1,020; £509; £254) **Stalls** High

Form RPR

32 **1** **Midnights' Gift**21 6114 3-9-0 0 .... TomMarquand 1 81
(Alan King) *trckd ldr: shkn up to chal over 2f out: racd awkwardly after but tk narrow ld over 1f out: kpt on fnl f* **5/2**2

5353 **2** 3/4 **High Commissioner (IRE)**19 6216 3-9-5 82 .... SeanLevey 4 84
(Paul Cole) *led: shkn up whn pressed over 2f out: hdd and nt qckn over 1f out: a jst hld fnl f* **2/7**1

55 **3** 13 **Parisian Affair**15 6345 4-9-8 0 .... FergusSweeney 7 57
(Neil King) *hld up in last pair: detached 4f out: kpt on steadily to take remote 3rd wl over 1f out: nvr in it* **33/1**

00 **4** 3 1/2 **Angels Chant**26 5955 3-9-0 0 .... (t) PatCosgrave 6 52
(Jim Boyle) *s.i.s: hld up in last pair: detached 4f out: tk remote 4th fnl f: nvr in it (jockey said filly hung left-handed. trainer rep said filly would prefer a flatter track)* **33/1**

46 **5** 1/2 **Sible Hedingham**15 6345 3-9-0 0 .... DavidEgan 5 51
(James Eustace) *chsd ldng pair: outpcd 3f out: edgd rt 2f out: fdd over 1f out (jockey said filly became unbalanced approx 2f out)* **18/1**3

0/0 **6** 8 **UAE Soldier (USA)**223 419 4-9-6 0 .... (h1) GeorgeRooke(7) 2 42
(Paddy Butler) *chsd ldng pair: rdn over 2f out: wknd over 1f out (jockey said gelding hung badly left-handed 3f out)* **100/1**

2m 31.1s (-2.90) **Going Correction** -0.225s/f (Firm) 6 Ran SP% **118.5**
WFA 3 from 4yo 8lb
Speed ratings (Par 103): **100,99,90,88,88 82**
CSF £3.81 TOTE £3.60: £1.20, £1.10; EX 5.00 Trifecta £15.10.
Owner Pitchall Stud Partnership **Bred** Pitchall Stud **Trained** Barbury Castle, Wilts

FOCUS
Add 2yds. The two market leaders dominated this ordinary maiden. The first two have been rated close to form.
T/Plt: £2,098.40 to a £1 stake. Pool: £49,729.48 - 17.3 winning units T/Qpdt: £73.20 to a £1 stake. Pool: £8,368.13 - 84.55 winning units **Jonathan Neesom**

6844 SALISBURY (R-H)

Thursday, September 5

OFFICIAL GOING: Good (good to soft in places; 7.6)

Wind: Light half against Weather: Overcast

6904 SHADWELL RACING EXCELLENCE APPRENTICE H'CAP (WHIPS SHALL BE CARRIED BUT NOT USED) 1m

2:10 (2:12) (Class 5) (0-70,71) 3-Y-O+

£4,398 (£1,309; £654; £327; £300; £300) **Stalls** Low

Form RPR

5004 **1** **Thechildren'strust (IRE)**[22] 6083 4-9-7 **70**........... RhysClutterbuck(5) 2 80
(Gary Moore) *racd keenly trcking ldrs: prom over 4f out: led over 1f out: pushed clr: readily* **4/1**[1]

4325 **2** 2 ¾ **Flying Dragon (FR)**[10] 6540 3-9-7 **70**........................(h[1]) LukeCatton 7 73+
(Richard Hannon) *mid-div tl lost pl 4f out: stl plenty to do u.p over 1f out: hdwy ent fnl f: r.o wl: wnt 2nd towards fin* **12/1**

6122 **3** ¾ **The Lords Walk**[21] 6121 6-9-4 **67**........................(b) GeorgeRooke(5) 10 69
(Bill Turner) *hld up towards rr: pushed along and stdy prog fr over 2f out: kpt on but nt pce to get on terms: wnt 3rd nring fin* **4/1**[1]

0211 **4** nse **Bounty Pursuit**[14] 6363 7-9-12 **70**........................ MarcoGhiani 4 72
(Michael Blake) *hld up: swtchd lft 2f out: hdwy over 1f out: kpt on ins fnl f but nvr gng pce to get on terms: wnt 4th cl home* **7/1**[2]

123 **5** nk **Amor Fati (IRE)**[13] 6414 4-9-13 **71**........................ AngusVilliers 5 72
(David Evans) *s.i.s: mid-div: hdwy over 2f out: wnt 3rd ent fnl f: kpt on but no ex whn losing 2 pls cl home (jockey said gelding was never travelling)* **17/2**[3]

6122 **6** ½ **Imperial Act**[5] 6717 4-9-2 **65**........................ MariePerrault(5) 8 65
(Andrew Balding) *prom: led over 4f out: hdd over 1f out: kpt on tl no ex nring fin* **4/1**[1]

0003 **7** 3 ½ **Mrs Benson (IRE)**[21] 6123 4-8-12 **56** oh4........................ KateLeahy 11 48
(Michael Blanshard) *s.i.s: nvr bttr than mid-div (jockey said filly jumped awkwardly from stalls)* **33/1**

0525 **8** 2 ¼ **Chetan**[21] 6121 7-9-1 **59**........................ ElishaWhittington 12 46
(Tony Carroll) *uns rdr gng to s: prom tl lost pl 4f out: no threat after* **20/1**

3062 **9** nk **Sir Plato (IRE)**[15] 6334 5-9-4 **67**........................(v) OliverSearle(5) 1 53
(Rod Millman) *led for 2f: prom tl wknd over 1f out* **9/1**

0060 **10** 1 ¾ **Dancing Jo**[21] 6123 3-8-10 **64**........................ GeorgeBass(5) 3 45
(Mick Channon) *nvr bttr than mid-div* **20/1**

3555 **11** 2 ½ **Miss Elsa**[43] 5315 3-9-0 **63**........................(p) GeorgiaDobie 6 38
(Eve Johnson Houghton) *trckd ldrs: effrt over 2f out: wknd over 1f out* **28/1**

3060 **12** 21 **Tally's Son**[23] 6045 5-8-7 **56** oh9........................(p) KeelanBaker(5) 9
(Grace Harris) *s.i.s: a towards rr (jockey said gelding reared as stalls opened)* **66/1**

1m 45.09s (1.59) **Going Correction** +0.225s/f (Good)
WFA 3 from 4yo+ 5lb **12 Ran SP% 118.1**
Speed ratings (Par 103): **101,98,97,97,97 96,93,90,90,88 86,65**
CSF £51.53 CT £209.43 TOTE £4.40: £1.70, £3.30, £2.40; EX 51.00 Trifecta £254.30.
Owner Ashley Head **Bred** N Bradley **Trained** Lower Beeding, W Sussex

FOCUS
The rail was erected up the straight course up to 14ft off the permanent far-side rail to rail off ground used on Tuesday. The opener saw a gamble on the Gary Moore runner, and it came off in good style.

6905 IRISH THOROUGHBRED MARKETING NOVICE STKS (PLUS 10 RACE) 1m

2:40 (2:42) (Class 4) 2-Y-O **£4,851** (£1,443; £721; £360) **Stalls** Low

Form RPR

1 **Kenzai Warrior (USA)** 2-9-5 0........................ JasonWatson 6 85+
(Roger Teal) *mde all: rdn whn strly chal 2f out: kpt on gamely ins fnl f: enough in hand and a holding on fnl 100yds* **16/1**

2 nk **Max Vega (IRE)** 2-9-5 0........................ HarryBentley 4 84+
(Ralph Beckett) *trckd ldrs: rdn 2f out: kpt on to go 2nd fnl 120yds: clsng wl on wnr at fin but nvr quite getting there* **18/1**

062 **3** 2 ¼ **Mambo Nights (IRE)**[20] 6154 2-9-5 **87**........................ SeanLevey 9 79
(Richard Hannon) *prom: rdn and ev ch fr 2f out: kpt on same pce ins fnl f* **3/1**[3]

3 **4** ½ **Shandoz**[20] 6163 2-9-5 0........................ DavidEgan 10 78
(Roger Varian) *mid-div: pushed along over 2f out: hdwy over 1f out: kpt on ins fnl f: wnt 4th towards fin but nt pce to threaten* **2/1**[1]

2 **5** 1 **Sea Trout Reach (IRE)**[33] 5655 2-9-5 0........................ JamesDoyle 8 76
(William Haggas) *trckd ldrs: rdn over 2f out: one pce fnl f* **11/4**[2]

6 shd **Khalifa Sat (IRE)** 2-9-5 0........................ OisinMurphy 2 75+
(Andrew Balding) *s.i.s: towards rr: stdy prog fr 2f out: kpt on nicely fnl f but nt gng pce to get on terms (jockey said colt was slowly away)* **14/1**

7 ¾ **Damage Control** 2-9-5 0........................ WilliamBuick 5 74
(Andrew Balding) *s.i.s: towards rr: rdn over 2f out: kpt on fnl f but nvr threatening to get involved: n.d* **16/1**

8 1 ½ **Summeronsevenhills (USA)** 2-9-5 0........................ ShaneKelly 7 70
(Richard Hughes) *dwlt: towards rr: sme prog 2f out: no further imp fnl f* **66/1**

9 7 **Glorious Caesar** 2-9-5 0........................ TomMarquand 3 54
(Ed Walker) *wnt rt s: racd green towards rr: nvr on terms* **33/1**

10 ½ **Sea Voice** 2-9-5 0........................ PatDobbs 1 53
(Richard Hannon) *mid-div: rdn over 2f out: wknd over 1f out* **40/1**

1m 46.59s (3.09) **Going Correction** +0.225s/f (Good) **10 Ran SP% 115.6**
Speed ratings (Par 97): **93,92,90,89,88 88,88,86,79,79**
CSF £260.94 TOTE £19.10: £4.40, £4.50, £1.10; EX 283.80 Trifecta £1085.00.
Owner Mr & Mrs Rae Borras **Bred** John D Gunther **Trained** Lambourn, Berks

FOCUS
This was a three horse market, with the remainder going off 14-1 and longer. However, it was those at longer odds who provided the first two home. The first three to finish were in the first three throughout.

6906 BOB MCCREERY MEMORIAL EBF QUIDHAMPTON MAIDEN FILLIES' STKS (PLUS 10 RACE) 6f 213y

3:10 (3:13) (Class 2) 2-Y-O

£12,450 (£3,728; £1,864; £932; £466; £234) **Stalls** Low

Form RPR

1 **Snow Shower** 2-9-0 0........................ JamesDoyle 8 80+
(Sir Michael Stoute) *hld up towards rr: gd hdwy in centre fr over 2f out: shkn up to ld jst ins fnl f: pushed clr: comf* **16/1**

2 1 ¾ **Alash Orda** 2-9-0 0........................ DavidEgan 5 76+
(Roger Varian) *mid-div: hdwy over 2f out: rdn in 5th over 1f out: kpt on wl ins fnl f: snatched 2nd fnl stride* **4/1**[2]

4 **3** hd **Thanielle (FR)**[26] 5961 2-9-0 0........................ SeanLevey 4 75
(Richard Hannon) *led: rdn 2f out: hdd jst ins fnl f: kpt on but sn hld by wnr: lost 2nd fnl stride* **9/1**

4 ½ **Shuraffa (IRE)** 2-9-0 0........................ WilliamBuick 9 74+
(Charles Hills) *racd keenly: sn prom: rdn and ev ch over 1f out: kpt on same pce fnl f* **8/1**

0 **5** 1 ¾ **Quickstep Lady**[20] 6154 2-9-0 0........................ DavidProbert 3 69
(Andrew Balding) *trckd ldrs: rdn whn nt clr run bhd ldng pair ent fnl f: nt pce to get on terms whn clr ins fnl f* **5/1**[3]

2 **6** 1 **Tadreej**[47] 5170 2-9-0 0........................ OisinMurphy 7 67
(Saeed bin Suroor) *mid-div: rdn 2f out: sn one pce* **15/8**[1]

7 1 ¼ **Aspiration (IRE)** 2-9-0 0........................ RobHornby 11 63
(Martyn Meade) *s.i.s: towards rr: rdn over 2f out: little imp* **14/1**

8 ½ **Madame Peltier (IRE)** 2-9-0 0........................ StevieDonohoe 2 62
(Charlie Fellowes) *s.i.s: towards rr: rdn 2f out: little imp* **25/1**

9 nk **Ascraeus** 2-9-0 0........................ HarryBentley 12 61
(Andrew Balding) *a towards rr* **40/1**

0 **10** 3 ¼ **Acquire**[48] 5132 2-9-0 0........................(h[1]) TomMarquand 6 53
(Richard Hannon) *trckd ldrs: rdn over 2f out: wknd over 1f out* **66/1**

45 **11** 6 **Itmusthavebeenlove (IRE)**[16] 6322 2-9-0 0........................ DanielTudhope 10 37
(Michael Bell) *hld up: hdwy over 2f out: wknd over 1f out* **25/1**

12 nk **Best Address (USA)** 2-9-0 0........................ JasonWatson 1 36
(Amanda Perrett) *a towards rr* **25/1**

1m 30.02s (1.32) **Going Correction** +0.225s/f (Good) **12 Ran SP% 120.6**
Speed ratings (Par 98): **101,99,98,98,96 95,93,93,92,89 82,81**
CSF £76.83 TOTE £13.10: £3.40, £1.70, £2.90; EX 94.20 Trifecta £460.60.
Owner K Abdullah **Bred** Juddmonte Farms Ltd **Trained** Newmarket, Suffolk

FOCUS
Some decent types have landed the maiden in the past decade, so the winner might be a pattern-class performer. The early pace seemed fairly strong. It will take time for the true worth of the form to become clear.

6907 SHADWELL DICK POOLE FILLIES' STKS (GROUP 3) 6f

3:40 (3:41) (Class 1) 2-Y-O

£25,519 (£9,675; £4,842; £2,412; £1,210; £607) **Stalls** Low

Form RPR

1432 **1** **Dark Lady**[12] 6444 2-9-0 **98**........................ PatDobbs 5 105
(Richard Hannon) *trckd ldrs: nt clrest of runs 2f out: chal ent fnl f: sn rdn to take narrow advantage: hld on* **13/2**[3]

1 **2** shd **Millisle (IRE)**[20] 6190 2-9-0 **103**........................ ShaneFoley 1 105
(Mrs John Harrington, Ire) *led: rdn over 1f out: narrowly hdd ins fnl f: kpt on v gamely: jst hld* **9/2**[2]

116 **3** 4 ½ **Summer Romance (IRE)**[40] 5411 2-9-0 **106**........................ WilliamBuick 6 91
(Charlie Appleby) *mid-div: hdwy over 2f out: sn rdn: ch over 1f out: kpt on but nt pce of front pair fnl f* **6/4**[1]

1 **4** ¾ **Final Option**[31] 5737 2-9-0 0........................ TomMarquand 2 89
(William Muir) *s.i.s: towards rr: rdn and stdy prog fr over 2f out: kpt on to go 4th ins fnl f: nt pce to get on terms* **18/1**

614 **5** 1 **Jouska**[20] 6157 2-9-0 **90**........................ JasonWatson 8 86
(Henry Candy) *racd keenly: hld up: hdwy over 3f out: rdn w ch 2f out: sn one pce* **20/1**

1503 **6** 1 ¾ **Good Vibes**[14] 6374 2-9-0 **103**........................ HarryBentley 9 81
(David Evans) *stdd s: racd keenly in rr: hdwy whn nt best of runs over 2f out: sn rdn: nt pce to get involved* **8/1**

1032 **7** 5 **Dr Simpson (FR)**[12] 6474 2-9-0 **94**........................ DavidProbert 3 66
(Tom Dascombe) *disp ld tl rdn over 2f out: wknd over 1f out* **33/1**

1 **8** ¾ **Dear Power (IRE)**[33] 5646 2-9-0 0........................ OisinMurphy 10 63
(Roger Varian) *hld up towards rr: effrt whn swtchd lft over 2f out: nvr threatened: wknd over 1f out* **17/2**

0526 **9** 5 **Kemble (IRE)**[12] 6474 2-9-0 **93**........................ SeanLevey 4 48
(Richard Hannon) *trckd ldrs: rdn over 2f out: sn wknd* **50/1**

10 **10** 5 **So Sharp**[40] 5411 2-9-0 0........................ JamesDoyle 7 33
(Archie Watson) *mid-div: effrt over 2f out: wknd qckly (trainer rep said filly was unsuited by the ground, which was officially described as Good, Good to Soft in places, and would prefer a faster surface)* **12/1**

1m 14.84s (0.34) **Going Correction** +0.225s/f (Good) **10 Ran SP% 115.8**
Speed ratings (Par 102): **106,105,99,98,97 95,88,87,80,74**
CSF £34.92 TOTE £8.20: £2.70, £2.10, £1.10; EX 33.40 Trifecta £99.00.
Owner Cheveley Park Stud **Bred** Cheveley Park Stud Ltd **Trained** East Everleigh, Wilts

FOCUS
This looked a competitive running of this Group 3 but two pulled well clear of the remainder. That pair did their racing along the far rail.

6908 EUROPEAN BLOODSTOCK NEWS EBF "LOCHSONG" FILLIES' H'CAP 6f

4:10 (4:10) (Class 2) (0-100,92) 3-Y-O+

£14,940 (£4,473; £2,236; £1,118; £559; £280) **Stalls** Low

Form RPR

0330 **1** **Belated Breath**[19] 6229 4-9-10 **90**........................ OisinMurphy 2 99
(Hughie Morrison) *trckd ldrs: rdn to take narrow advantage over 1f out: kpt on ins fnl f: asserting nring fin* **2/1**[1]

0636 **2** ½ **Goodnight Girl (IRE)**[28] 5846 4-9-10 **90**........................ RobHornby 8 97
(Jonathan Portman) *prom: rdn for str chal fr 2f out: ev ch ins fnl f: no ex cl home* **14/1**

3033 **3** hd **Lady Dancealot (IRE)**[16] 6319 4-9-2 **82**........................ GeraldMosse 3 89+
(David Elsworth) *chsd ldrs: nt clr run whn travelling wl enough over 1f out: cl 3rd but nt clr run again jst ins fnl f: kpt on whn squeezing through gap fnl 60yds: nvr able to mount chal* **4/1**[2]

1112 **4** 1 **Betsey Trotter (IRE)**[9] 6581 4-9-7 **87**........................(p) DanielTudhope 1 90
(David O'Meara) *in tch: hdwy over 2f out: rdn and ev ch over 1f out: edgd rt ins fnl f: kpt on but no ex towards fin* **5/1**[3]

5113 **5** 1 **Show Stealer**[13] 6404 6-9-12 **92**........................(p) WilliamBuick 7 92
(Rae Guest) *hld up in last pair: hdwy travelling wl enough whn nt clr run jst over 1f out: nt clr run disputing cl 3rd and bmpd fnl 60yds: nvr able to mount chal (jockey said mare was denied a clear run)* **6/1**

4000 **6** 8 **Aim Power (IRE)**[19] 6220 3-8-9 **82**........................ ThoreHammerHansen(5) 4 56
(Richard Hannon) *s.i.s: in last pair: rdn 3f out: nt pce to get involved (jockey said filly was slowly away and never travelling)* **11/1**

202 **7** *nk* **Puds**[20] 6149 4-9-10 **90**.. ShaneKelly 6 63
(Richard Hughes) *led: rdn and hdd over 1f out: sn wknd (jockey said filly ran too freely)* **7/1**

1m 15.06s (0.56) **Going Correction** +0.225s/f (Good) **7** Ran SP% **111.8**
WFA 3 from 4yo+ 2lb
Speed ratings (Par 96): **105,104,104,102,101 90,90**
CSF £30.01 CT £100.80 TOTE £2.60: £1.70, £6.90; EX 24.30 Trifecta £79.60.
Owner Lady Blyth **Bred** Lemington Grange Stud **Trained** East Ilsley, Berks

FOCUS
An open sprint handicap run at a good gallop, which saw a messy finish. The second has been rated to form.

6909 LESTER BRUNT WEALTH MANAGEMENT H'CAP 1m 1f 201y
4:40 (4:40) (Class 4) (0-85,87) 3-Y-0+
£5,692 (£1,694; £846; £423; £300; £300) **Stalls** Low

Form RPR
5222 **1** **Starfighter**[12] 6463 3-8-11 **75**.. OisinMurphy 5 85+
(Ed Walker) *trckd ldrs: chal 2f out: sn rdn to ld: kpt on wl fnl f* **9/4**[1]

6222 **2** *2* **You're Hired**[12] 6447 6-9-10 **87**........................(p) ScottMcCullagh(5) 1 92
(Amanda Perrett) *trckd ldr: hmpd on bnd over 6f out: rdn over 2f out: kpt on ins fnl f: wnt 2nd nring fin* **9/2**[3]

-613 **3** *¾* **Light Up Our Stars (IRE)**[61] 4671 3-9-5 **83**........................ PatDobbs 4 87
(Richard Hughes) *led: rdn and hdd over 1f out: kpt on tl no ex fnl 120yds: lost 2nd nring fin* **7/1**

4343 **4** *nk* **Rotherwick (IRE)**[12] 6447 7-9-12 **84**........................(t) DavidProbert 2 87
(Paul Cole) *hld up bhd ldrs: hdwy over 3f out: sn rdn: nt pce to chal but kpt on ins fnl f* **17/2**

2332 **5** *8* **Alhaazm**[21] 6129 3-9-2 **80**..(vt[1]) JamesDoyle 6 67
(Sir Michael Stoute) *trckd ldrs: rdn over 2f out: wknd over 1f out* **4/1**[2]

00-1 **6** *1* **Blistering Bob**[22] 6083 4-9-4 **79**........................(h) WilliamCox(3) 3 64
(Roger Teal) *trckd ldrs: hmpd and hit rails on bnd over 6f out: nvr really travelling after: wknd over 1f out* **4/1**[2]

2m 10.79s (0.29) **Going Correction** +0.225s/f (Good) **6** Ran SP% **112.0**
WFA 3 from 4yo+ 6lb
Speed ratings (Par 105): **107,105,104,104,98 97**
CSF £12.54 TOTE £2.70: £1.30, £3.00; EX 12.90 Trifecta £38.80.
Owner Laurence Bellman **Bred** Miss K Rausing **Trained** Upper Lambourn, Berks

FOCUS
Probably solid enough form for the level. It's been rated around the second to his recent form.
T/Jkpt: Not Won. T/Plt: £142.10 to a £1 stake. Pool: £67,474.78 - 346.48 winning units T/Qpdt: £23.70 to a £1 stake. Pool: £6,013.48 - 187.34 winning units **Tim Mitchell**

6773 LONGCHAMP (R-H)
Thursday, September 5

OFFICIAL GOING: Turf: good

6910a PRIX DE LA COCHERE - FONDS EUROPEEN DE L'ELEVAGE (LISTED RACE) (3YO+ FILLIES & MARES) (TURF) 1m
5:05 3-Y-0+
£23,423 (£9,369; £7,027; £4,684; £2,342)

RPR
1 **Madeleine Must (FR)**[62] 4621 3-8-9 0.................... StephanePasquier 4 102
(H-A Pantall, France) **11/1**

2 *1 ¼* **Richmond Avenue (IRE)**[35] 4-9-0 0........................ MickaelBarzalona 3 100
(A Fabre, France) *settled in rr of midfield: effrt 2f out: hung rt over 1f out: rdn along and hdwy fnl f: wnt 2nd fnl strides: nt pce of wnr fnl 110yds* **57/10**[3]

3 *shd* **Imperial Charm**[68] 4416 3-9-0 0........................ AndreaAtzeni 5 104
(Simon Crisford) *led 1f: trckd ldr: tk clsr order turning in: drvn along to ld under 2f out: pressed and rdn along over 1f out: kpt on wl u.p: hdd 50yds out: lost 2nd fnl strides* **1/1**[1]

4 *¾* **Matematica (GER)**[21] 6142 3-8-9 0........................ MaximeGuyon 6 97
(C Laffon-Parias, France) **29/10**[2]

5 *1 ¼* **Aviatress (IRE)**[62] 4621 3-8-9 0........................ VincentCheminaud 1 94
(A De Royer-Dupre, France) **14/1**

6 *3* **Savaanah (IRE)**[37] 5525 4-9-0 0....................(b[1]) ChristopheSoumillon 7 88
(Roger Charlton) *led after 1f: shkn up and hdd under 2f out: dropped towards rr ins fnl f: eased cl home* **66/10**

7 *2* **Vivianite (IRE)**[58] 4758 4-9-0 0........................(p) HollieDoyle 2 84
(Archie Watson) *midfield: effrt 2f out: nt qckn and lost position appr fnl f: wl hld* **40/1**

1m 39.22s (0.82) **7** Ran SP% **121.2**
WFA 3 from 4yo 5lb
PARI-MUTUEL (all including 1 euro stake): WIN 12.60; PLACE 5.40, 3.70; SF 67.40.
Owner Guy Heald **Bred** G Heald **Trained** France

5927 ASCOT (R-H)
Friday, September 6

OFFICIAL GOING: Good to firm (rnd 7.6, str 8.6)
Wind: Half against, fresh, moderating through afternoon Weather: Overcast becoming brighter

6911 ITALIAN TOURIST BOARD BRITISH EBF NOVICE AUCTION STKS (PLUS 10 RACE) 6f
1:55 (1:56) (Class 4) 2-Y-0
£6,727 (£2,002; £1,000; £500) **Stalls** High

Form RPR
22 **1** **Cosmic Power (IRE)**[14] 6415 2-9-5 0........................ CharlesBishop 15 80
(Eve Johnson Houghton) *chsd ldrs nr side: pushed along fr 1/2-way: effrt u.p over 1f out: styd on wl fnl f to ld last strides* **6/1**[2]

4 **2** *hd* **Amarillo Star (IRE)**[118] 2610 2-9-5 0........................ StevieDonohoe 8 79
(Charlie Fellowes) *trckd ldng pair in centre: led gp and overall ldr over 1f out: drvn fnl f: kpt on but hdd last strides* **10/1**

43 **3** *1* **Klopp Of The Kop (IRE)**[15] 6375 2-9-5 0........................ AdamKirby 17 76
(Clive Cox) *chsd nr side ldrs: on terms whn led gp over 1f out to ins fnl f: one pce last 100yds* **11/8**[1]

4 *¾* **Qasbaz (IRE)** 2-9-5 0.. NicolaCurrie 2 74
(Jamie Osborne) *hld up in last pair in centre: prog on wd outside over 2f out: clsd on ldrs 1f out: one pce ins fnl f* **28/1**

5 *¾* **Bengal Bay** 2-9-5 0.. RyanMoore 1 72+
(William Haggas) *dwlt: towards rr in centre: prog 2f out: shkn up and styd on same pce fnl f: shaped wl* **7/1**[3]

0 **6** *shd* **Rapidash**[14] 6415 2-9-0 0.. RossaRyan 14 66
(Richard Hannon) *hld up in midfield nr side: gng strly over 2f out: nt clr run briefly sn after: shkn up and clsd over 1f out: styd on same pce fnl f* **50/1**

7 *1* **Queen Of Silca** 2-9-0 0.. CallumShepherd 11 63+
(Mick Channon) *impeded s: in tch nr side: shkn up 2f out: kpt on same pce and nvr able to chal* **20/1**

8 *¾* **Paycheck** 2-9-0 0.. PatCosgrave 10 61
(David Simcock) *awkward and wnt lft s: towards rr nr side: pushed along and kpt on one pce fnl f* **25/1**

5 **9** *½* **Mrs Merton**[13] 6442 2-9-0 0.. OisinMurphy 4 59
(William Knight) *chsd ldrs in centre: clsd on outer to chal 2f out: fdd fnl f* **12/1**

10 *1 ¾* **Sacred Legacy (IRE)** 2-9-5 0........................(h[1]) TomQueally 5 59
(Ronald Harris) *dwlt: hld up in last in centre: pushed along and kpt on one pce fnl 2f: nvr nrr* **66/1**

11 *2* **Cupid's Beau** 2-9-5 0.. DavidEgan 16 53
(David Loughnane) *racd against nr side rail: overall ldr to over 1f out: wknd* **14/1**

4 **12** *2 ¾* **Capla Spirit**[23] 6064 2-9-5 0........................(t) ShaneKelly 9 45
(Gay Kelleway) *chsd nr side ldrs to 1/2-way: sn wknd* **16/1**

13 *½* **Evaporust (IRE)** 2-9-2 0.. WilliamCox(3) 12 43
(Mark Usher) *a struggling in rr (jockey said gelding ran greenly)* **100/1**

5 **14** *1* **Visibility (IRE)**[41] 5439 2-9-5 0.. RobHornby 3 40
(Martyn Meade) *trckd ldr in centre: led gp over 2f out to wl over 1f out: edgd lft and wknd qckly* **12/1**

026 **15** *3* **Jim 'N' Tomic (IRE)**[57] 4839 2-9-5 79........................(p[1] w) KieranO'Neill 13 31
(Dominic Ffrench Davis) *dwlt: sn chsd nr side ldr: wknd qckly 2f out* **20/1**

56 **16** *7* **Merchants Breath**[11] 6548 2-9-5 0........................ JosephineGordon 7 10
(Shaun Keightley) *taken down early: racd freely: led centre gp to over 2f out: wknd rapidly: t.o (jockey said colt ran too freely)* **100/1**

1m 16.36s (2.66) **Going Correction** +0.325s/f (Good) **16** Ran SP% **128.2**
Speed ratings (Par 97): **95,94,93,92,91 91,89,88,88,85 83,79,78,77,73 64**
CSF £63.43 TOTE £6.70: £2.00, £2.90, £1.20; EX 73.90 Trifecta £187.20.
Owner Mcnamee Hewitt Harding Rice **Bred** Epona Bloodstock Ltd **Trained** Blewbury, Oxon

FOCUS
The rail on the round course was 3yds in from the 1m4f start, increasing to 9yds in at the bend entering the home straight. The rail then ended in a cutaway in the home straight. This fair 2yo event saw a split opinion as to the best of the going. The first pair made their efforts down the centre. Steps forward from the first two, with the third a length or so off his York form.

6912 CHARBONNEL ET WALKER BRITISH EBF MAIDEN STKS (PLUS 10 RACE) (SIRE AND DAM RESTRICTED RACE) 7f
2:30 (2:31) (Class 3) 2-Y-0
£10,350 (£3,080; £1,539; £769) **Stalls** High

Form RPR
1 **Enemy** 2-9-5 0.. OisinMurphy 1 86
(John Gosden) *dwlt: sn wl in tch: prog to trck ldng pair wl over 1f out: tk 2nd jst ins fnl f: pushed along and r.o wl to ld narrowly but decisively last 50yds* **10/3**[2]

2 **2** *nk* **Law Of Peace**[71] 4282 2-9-5 0.. WilliamBuick 7 85
(Charlie Appleby) *led: shkn up whn jnd 2f out: rdn and pressed by wnr fnl f: r.o but hdd and clrly hld last 75yds* **1/1**[1]

3 *4* **Crystal Pegasus** 2-9-5 0.. RyanMoore 9 75+
(Sir Michael Stoute) *in tch: pushed along and outpcd over 2f out: styd on over 1f out to take 3rd last 50yds* **14/1**

05 **4** *1* **Honore Daumier (IRE)**[21] 6154 2-9-5 0........................ CharlesBishop 8 73
(Henry Candy) *pressed ldr: chal and upsides 2f out: rdn over 1f out: lost 2nd jst ins fnl f and fdd* **50/1**

5 *1 ½* **Talap** 2-9-5 0.. DavidEgan 5 69
(Roger Varian) *trckd ldrs: shkn up 2f out: steadily wknd over 1f out* **8/1**[3]

6 *hd* **Count Of Amazonia (IRE)** 2-9-5 0........................ AndreaAtzeni 4 68
(Richard Hannon) *in tch: pushed along wl over 2f out: sn outpcd: kpt on same pce fnl f* **12/1**

7 *1* **Establish** 2-9-5 0.. AdamKirby 6 66
(Roger Varian) *s.v.s: mostly in last: lft bhd over 2f out: pushed along and kpt on steadily over 1f out (jockey said colt was slowly away)* **8/1**[3]

8 *3 ¼* **Grinling (IRE)** 2-9-5 0..(h[1]) RossaRyan 3 58
(Richard Hannon) *sn pushed along to stay in tch: wknd 2f out* **33/1**

9 *½* **Old Friend (FR)** 2-9-5 0.. JamieSpencer 10 56
(Ed Walker) *dwlt: a in last pair: wknd 2f out* **33/1**

10 *1 ¼* **By Jove** 2-9-5 0.. CallumShepherd 2 53
(Michael Bell) *pressed ldr to 2f out: wknd qckly* **50/1**

1m 30.8s (3.30) **Going Correction** +0.325s/f (Good) **10** Ran SP% **119.5**
Speed ratings (Par 99): **94,93,89,87,86 86,84,81,80,79**
CSF £7.04 TOTE £4.50: £1.50, £1.10, £2.80; EX 8.50 Trifecta £40.70.
Owner Qatar Racing Ltd & Lady O'Reilly **Bred** Ecurie Des Monceaux & Skymarc Farm Inc **Trained** Newmarket, Suffolk

FOCUS
They headed down the middle and this is 2yo form to be positive about.

6913 GARDEN FOR ALL SEASONS H'CAP 7f
3:05 (3:08) (Class 4) (0-85,87) 3-Y-0
£6,727 (£2,002; £1,000; £500; £300; £300) **Stalls** High

Form RPR
-300 **1** **Riviera Nights**[90] 3599 3-9-9 **87**........................(w) WilliamBuick 4 97+
(Richard Hannon) *hld up towards rr: shkn up over 2f out: rdn and prog to ld jst over 1f out: styd on wl* **13/2**[3]

1450 **2** *1 ½* **Archaeology**[14] 6425 3-9-3 **81**.. JamieSpencer 8 87
(Jedd O'Keeffe) *restrained s: hld up in 9th: shkn up and prog over 1f out: rdn to chse wnr ins fnl f: styd on but nvr able to chal* **7/2**[1]

0165 **3** *1* **Clara Peeters**[23] 6081 3-9-6 **84**.. RyanMoore 2 88
(Gary Moore) *wl in tch: clsd to chal 2f out: disp ld briefly over 1f out: one pce fnl f* **7/1**

6516 **4** *nse* **Golden Force**[29] 5862 3-9-1 **79**.. AdamKirby 10 83
(Clive Cox) *t.k.h early: prom: rdn over 2f out and hanging rt: disp ld briefly over 1f out: one pce fnl f* **9/1**

4303 **5** *2* **Uncle Jerry**[13] 6440 3-8-12 **76**........................(p) OisinMurphy 1 75
(Mohamed Moubarak) *in tch: rdn 2f out: one pce after and nvr able to threaten* **20/1**

2121 **6** *nk* **Shawaaheq (IRE)**[18] 6282 3-9-1 **79**.. JimCrowley 6 77
(Ed Dunlop) *prom: rdn to chal 2f out: n.m.r wl over 1f out: steadily fdd* **13/2**[3]

1031 **7** 3/4 **Jaleel**[23] 6076 3-9-7 **85**....(b) AndreaAtzeni 7 82
(Roger Varian) *hld up towards rr: shkn up 2f out: no prog over 1f out: kpt on one pce fnl f* **9/2**[2]

0-03 **8** 1 3/4 **Invasion Day (IRE)**[12] 6501 3-9-4 **82**....(p) JamesDoyle 9 75
(David O'Meara) *v awkward s and lost many l: mostly in last: shkn up wl over 1f out: nvr able to make much prog (jockey said gelding was very slowly away)* **16/1**

3611 **9** 1 1/2 **Eye Of The Water (IRE)**[18] 6286 3-9-4 **82**.... FrankieDettori 5 71
(Ronald Harris) *led to wl over 1f out: sn wknd qckly* **7/1**

1055 **10** 2 **After John**[20] 6225 3-9-2 **80**.... CallumShepherd 3 64
(Mick Channon) *prom: rdn to ld briefly wl over 1f out: sn wknd qckly* **16/1**

1m 28.15s (0.65) **Going Correction** +0.325s/f (Good) **10** Ran SP% **118.6**
Speed ratings (Par 103): **109,107,106,106,103 103,102,100,98,96**
CSF £30.06 CT £171.51 TOTE £8.20: £2.40, £1.50, £2.30; EX 34.00 Trifecta £219.00.
Owner Imad Alsagar **Bred** Saleh Al Homaizi & Imad Al Sagar **Trained** East Everleigh, Wilts

FOCUS
This fair 3yo handicap was run at an average pace and the main action developed nearer the stands' side. The winner was basically back to his best.

6914 CHAPEL DOWN CLASSIFIED STKS — 1m (S)
3:40 (3:41) (Class 3) 3-Y-O+ — **£9,703** (£2,887; £1,443; £721) **Stalls** High

Form — RPR

120 **1** **Ebury**[140] 1926 3-8-12 90.... RobHornby 3 100+
(Martyn Meade) *hld up in 5th: rdn and prog on outer 2f out: led jst over 1f out: styd on wl* **15/2**

2000 **2** 3/4 **Tulfarris**[34] 5693 3-8-12 90.... StevieDonohoe 4 97
(Charlie Fellowes) *hld up in last: shkn up and prog on outer over 1f out: rdn to chse wnr ins fnl f: styd on but too late to chal* **11/2**[3]

3630 **3** 2 3/4 **Trolius (IRE)**[190] 956 3-8-12 90....(p) WilliamBuick 6 91
(Simon Crisford) *dwlt: trckd ldng pair to 3f out: lost pl and rdn over 1f out: styd on again ins fnl f to take 3rd nr fin* **7/1**

0220 **4** 1 1/4 **Wafy (IRE)**[15] 6376 4-9-3 89.... JimCrowley 2 89
(Charles Hills) *trckd ldng pair: rdn to chal 2f out: led briefly over 1f out: wknd ins fnl f* **15/8**[1]

2320 **5** 1 1/4 **Warning Fire**[15] 6379 3-8-12 87.... FrankieDettori 5 85
(Mark Johnston) *racd freely: led: rdn and hdd over 1f out: wknd* **13/2**

5533 **6** 1 1/2 **Enigmatic (IRE)**[21] 6166 5-8-12 88.... CierenFallon(5) 1 82
(Alan Bailey) *trckd ldr: rdn over 2f out: sn lost pl and wknd over 1f out (trainer's rep could offer no explanation for the poor form shown other than he may have been unsuited by good to firm ground)* **3/1**[2]

1m 41.82s (0.42) **Going Correction** +0.325s/f (Good)
WFA 3 from 4yo+ 5lb **6** Ran SP% **112.8**
Speed ratings (Par 107): **110,109,106,105,104 102**
CSF £46.90 TOTE £8.20: £3.30, £2.80; EX 55.50 Trifecta £279.90.
Owner Chelsea Thoroughbreds - M P R **Bred** Miss K Rausing **Trained** Manton, Wilts

FOCUS
This good-quality classified event was run at a routine pace. Sound form, with the unexposed winner improving.

6915 LEXICON BRACKNELL H'CAP — 1m (S)
4:10 (4:13) (Class 2) (0-105,101) 3-Y-O+
£18,675 (£5,592; £2,796; £1,398; £699; £351) **Stalls** High

Form — RPR

4201 **1** **Bless Him (IRE)**[12] 6516 5-9-6 **97** 5ex....(h) JamieSpencer 5 110+
(David Simcock) *stdd s: hld up in last: smooth prog 2f out: cruised into the ld last 100yds: easily* **4/1**[3]

1-10 **2** 1/2 **Lord North (IRE)**[106] 3026 3-9-2 **98**.... RobertHavlin 6 107
(John Gosden) *trckd ldng pair: rdn to ld over 1f out: hdd last 100yds: styd on but no match for wnr* **9/4**[1]

1303 **3** 2 1/4 **Dubai Legacy (USA)**[27] 5963 3-8-11 **98**.... CierenFallon(5) 1 102
(Saeed bin Suroor) *w ldr at mod pce to 1/2-way: led over 2f out: drvn and hdd over 1f out: one pce* **4/1**[3]

1450 **4** 3 1/4 **Chiefofchiefs**[146] 1753 6-9-7 **98**....(p) JamesDoyle 7 95
(Charlie Fellowes) *hld up in 6th: rdn and prog 2f out: keeping on in 4th but hld whn no room and snatched up 150yds out: wknd* **16/1**

443 **5** nk **Seniority**[14] 6391 5-9-10 **101**.... RyanMoore 4 98
(William Haggas) *hld up in 5th: shkn up over 2f out: no prog and nvr a factor* **3/1**[2]

0023 **6** 1 1/4 **Zhui Feng (IRE)**[13] 6445 6-9-7 **98**.... JimCrowley 3 92
(Amanda Perrett) *mde most: mod pce to 1/2-way: hdd over 2f out: shkn up and no rspnse: wknd* **8/1**

112- **7** 6 **Don't Give Up**[554] 980 5-9-8 **99**.... OisinMurphy 2 79
(Tony Newcombe) *chsd ldng pair: lost pl u.p over 2f out: wknd* **33/1**

1m 41.98s (0.58) **Going Correction** +0.325s/f (Good)
WFA 3 from 5yo+ 5lb **7** Ran SP% **115.7**
Speed ratings (Par 109): **110,109,107,104,103 102,96**
CSF £13.80 TOTE £4.60: £2.20, £2.10; EX 14.40 Trifecta £56.80.
Owner Tony Perkins & Partners **Bred** Knocklong House Stud **Trained** Newmarket, Suffolk
■ Stewards' Enquiry : Robert Havlin caution: careless riding

FOCUS
A classy handicap. The field came stands' side early and they went just an average pace. The winner backed up his Yarmouth win.

6916 SODEXO H'CAP — 6f
4:40 (4:47) (Class 4) (0-85,87) 3-Y-O+
£6,727 (£2,002; £1,000; £500; £300; £300) **Stalls** High

Form — RPR

2264 **1** **Equitation**[13] 6455 5-9-2 **87**....(t) MarcoGhiani(7) 17 98
(Stuart Williams) *hld up in rr: prog on nr side of gp 2f: shkn up to ld jst over 1f out: clr ins fnl f: readily* **7/1**[3]

6022 **2** 2 1/2 **Iconic Knight (IRE)**[13] 6465 4-9-0 **78**.... AndreaAtzeni 15 81
(Ed Walker) *racd towards nr side of gp: led to over 1f out: styd on again fnl f to take 2nd nr fin: no ch w wnr* **7/1**[3]

1232 **3** nk **Whelans Way (IRE)**[69] 4368 3-9-0 **80**.... JamesDoyle 13 82
(Roger Teal) *hld up in rr: rdn 2f out: styd wl fnl f nrest to stands' rail to take 3rd last strides* **5/1**[2]

1313 **4** nk **Cent Flying**[5] 6756 4-8-7 **71** oh1....(t) DavidEgan 12 72
(William Muir) *pressed ldrs: led over 1f out towards centre of gp: sn hdd and kpt on same pce after* **16/1**

2455 **5** hd **Miracle Of Medinah**[17] 6318 8-9-0 **85**.... EllieMacKenzie(7) 10 85
(Mark Usher) *hld up in rr: rdn 2f out: prog towards nr side of gp over 1f out: styd on fnl f and nrly grabbed a pl* **20/1**

3300 **6** 1/2 **Normandy Barriere (IRE)**[21] 6162 7-9-6 **84**....(p) WilliamBuick 16 83
(Nigel Tinkler) *prom on nr side of gp: rdn 2f out: one pce over 1f out* **7/1**[3]

1035 **7** 2 3/4 **Shorter Skirt**[16] 6346 3-8-5 **78**....(p) GeorgiaDobie(7) 4 68
(Eve Johnson Houghton) *dwlt: hld up in tch towards outer of gp: shkn up and sme prog over 1f out: no ch but did best of those on that part of gp* **20/1**

063 **8** 1/2 **Doc Sportello (IRE)**[22] 6109 7-8-8 **72**.... BrettDoyle 8 60
(Tony Carroll) *uns rdr on way to post: in tch in centre of gp: rdn 2f out: no real hdwy over 1f out (trainer's rep said, regarding why gelding was running here at Ascot on going described as good to firm, having declared the gelding a non-runner at Brighton on 9 August 2019 on ground with the same official description, that in the trainer's opinion, t* **33/1**

2044 **9** hd **Big Lachie**[20] 6203 5-8-8 **72**.... LiamJones 11 60
(Mark Loughnane) *dwlt: swtchd to outer of gp: prog and prom 1/2-way: wknd over 1f out* **25/1**

0342 **10** 1 1/4 **Lady Of Aran (IRE)**[16] 6350 4-8-10 **74**.... StevieDonohoe 9 58+
(Charlie Fellowes) *n.m.r s: hld up in rr and racd towards outer of gp: trying to make prog whn nt clr run over 1f out: no hdwy fnl f and eased (jockey said filly was denied a clear run)* **10/1**

0011 **11** 1 3/4 **Mr Orange (IRE)**[30] 5821 6-9-1 **79**....(p) OisinMurphy 6 57
(Paul Midgley) *chsd ldrs in centre of gp: rdn over 2f out: steadily wknd* **16/1**

61-1 **12** shd **Total Commitment (IRE)**[14] 6413 3-8-13 **79**.... RyanMoore 14 57
(Roger Charlton) *chsd ldrs in centre of gp: rdn 2f out: wknd over 1f out* **9/2**[1]

0412 **13** 1 **A Sure Welcome**[11] 6525 5-9-2 **80**....(p) RyanTate 1 55
(John Spearing) *dwlt: hld up on outer of gp: effrt 1/2-way: wknd over 1f out (trainer said, regarding performance, gelding was drawn on wrong side)* **20/1**

6504 **14** 3/4 **Lightning Charlie**[17] 6301 7-8-4 **73**.... CierenFallon(5) 2 45
(Amanda Perrett) *prom on outer of gp: wknd wl over 1f out* **16/1**

454 **15** 4 **Equiano Springs**[10] 6581 5-9-2 **80**.... JamesSullivan 5 39
(Tom Tate) *taken down early: t.k.h: hld up: plld way through to be prom towards outer of gp after 2f: wknd qckly over 2f out (jockey said gelding ran too freely and was denied a clear run)* **10/1**

3100 **16** 1/2 **In The Red (IRE)**[16] 6347 6-8-13 **77**....(p) EoinWalsh 7 35
(Martin Smith) *racd in centre of gp: w ldr to 2f out: wknd rapidly (vet said gelding lost shoe)* **50/1**

1m 14.05s (0.35) **Going Correction** +0.325s/f (Good)
WFA 3 from 4yo+ 2lb **16** Ran SP% **131.2**
Speed ratings (Par 105): **110,106,106,105,105 104,101,100,100,98 96,96,94,93,88 87**
CSF £54.46 CT £228.35 TOTE £8.20: £2.10, £1.90, £1.60, £4.50; EX 65.40 Trifecta £318.40.
Owner A Lyons & T W Morley **Bred** Newsells Park Stud **Trained** Newmarket, Suffolk

FOCUS
A high draw proved crucial in this fair sprint handicap. Solid form, the winner recording a clear pb helped by his rider's claim.

6917 VICTORIA RACING CLUB H'CAP — 1m 3f 211y
5:15 (5:16) (Class 3) (0-95,94) 3-Y-O+ — **£9,703** (£2,887; £1,443; £721) **Stalls** Low

Form — RPR

-005 **1** **Francis Xavier (IRE)**[34] 5657 5-9-11 **93**.... RossaRyan 7 101
(Kevin Frost) *mde all: rdn wl over 1f out: kpt on wl fnl f: hld on nr fin* **12/1**

-051 **2** nk **Protected Guest**[12] 6513 4-9-12 **94** 5ex.... TomQueally 4 101
(George Margarson) *stdd s: hld up in last: pushed along and prog on inner over 1f out: tk 2nd last 150yds: cajoled along w no recrse to whip and clsd on wnr: jst hld* **14/1**

3065 **3** 1 3/4 **Kaloor**[72] 4256 3-9-2 **92**.... DavidEgan 1 96
(Brian Meehan) *trckd ldng pair: rdn over 2f out: nt qckn over 1f out: one pce fnl f* **8/1**[3]

1-50 **4** 1/2 **Kosciuszko (IRE)**[37] 5541 3-8-12 **88**.... FrankieDettori 8 91
(John Gosden) *trckd wnr: rdn wl over 2f out: no imp over 1f out: lost 2nd and one pce last 150yds* **6/4**[1]

2123 **5** 1/2 **Durrell**[29] 5861 3-8-11 **87**.... DanielMuscutt 5 90
(James Fanshawe) *hld up in 6th: rdn wl over 2f out: one pce and no real imp over 1f out* **5/2**[2]

2004 **6** 1/2 **Koeman**[27] 5929 5-9-12 **94**.... JFEgan 3 96
(Mick Channon) *trckd ldng trio: rdn over 2f out: nt qckn over 1f out: fdd ins fnl f* **9/1**

043 **7** 1/2 **Breath Caught**[13] 6452 4-9-9 **91**.... StevieDonohoe 2 92
(David Simcock) *hld up in 5th: shkn up jst over 2f out: no rspnse over 1f out: wl hld fnl f* **9/1**

2m 36.85s (4.25) **Going Correction** +0.325s/f (Good)
WFA 3 from 4yo+ 8lb **7** Ran SP% **114.0**
Speed ratings (Par 107): **98,97,96,96,95 95,95**
CSF £153.62 CT £1421.55 TOTE £11.00: £4.70, £4.20; EX 101.20 Trifecta £1309.10.
Owner Curzon House Partnership **Bred** Rockhart Trading Ltd **Trained** Newcastle-under-Lyme, Staffs

FOCUS
Few landed a serious blow in this decent handicap. The winner is rated back to his best. Add 16yds.
T/Jkpt: Not Won. T/Plt: £48.50 to a £1 stake. Pool: £102,176.34 - 1,534.81 winning units T/Qpdt: £46.60 to a £1 stake. Pool: £9,697.83 - 153.76 winning units **Jonathan Neesom**

6890 HAYDOCK (L-H)
Friday, September 6

OFFICIAL GOING: Soft (6.3)
Wind: moderate, against in straight Weather: Cloudy

6918 BRITISH EBF FILLIES' NOVICE STKS (PLUS 10 RACE) — 7f 212y
1:45 (1:46) (Class 5) 2-Y-O — **£4,851** (£1,443; £721; £360) **Stalls** Low

Form — RPR

1 **Heart Reef (FR)** 2-9-0 0.... TomMarquand 6 78+
(Ralph Beckett) *racd on outer and prom: effrt to ld 1f out: rn green: asserted fnl 100yds: kpt on wl and pushed out towards fin* **9/4**[1]

05 **2** 1 1/2 **Rainbow Jet (IRE)**[28] 5895 2-9-0 0.... JimmyQuinn 2 75
(John Mackie) *trckd ldrs: rdn and unable qck over 1f out: styd on u.p fnl 100yds: tk 2nd post: nt pce to trble wnr* **50/1**

23 **3** nse **Tulip Fields**[36] 5588 2-9-0 0.... FrannyNorton 1 75
(Mark Johnston) *sn led: rdn over 1f out: sn hdd: outpcd by wnr ins fnl f: kpt on same pce: lost 2nd post* **9/4**[1]

126 **4** 1 1/2 **Ursulina (IRE)**[43] 5346 2-9-7 88....(p[1]) RichardKingscote 3 79
(Tom Dascombe) *broke wl: led early: prom: rdn and unable qck over 1f out: kpt on same pce ins fnl f* **10/3**[2]

65 **5** *1 ½* **Sun Crystal (IRE)**[42] 5387 2-9-0 0 TonyHamilton 4 68
(Richard Fahey) *racd keenly: in tch: rdn over 2f out: angled out over 1f out: one pce fnl f* **22/1**

6 *6* **Dusty Dream** 2-9-0 0 DanielTudhope 7 55
(William Haggas) *hld up in rr: rdn over 2f out: nvr able to threaten and outpcd fnl f* **7/2**[3]

1m 46.43s (3.73) **Going Correction** +0.45s/f (Yiel) **6** Ran SP% **113.1**
Speed ratings (Par 92): **99,97,97,95,94 88**
CSF £81.19 TOTE £3.00: £1.40, £9.90; EX 93.40 Trifecta £525.10.
Owner Qatar Racing Limited **Bred** S A R L Lemzar Et Al **Trained** Kimpton, Hants

FOCUS
Inner home straight in use. The going was given as soft (GoingStick 6.3) and there was a headwind in the straight. Add 6yds. They finished fairly close up in this fillies' novice, but there was a lot to like about the way the winner settled matters.

6919 BRITISH STALLION STUDS EBF FILLIES' NOVICE STKS (PLUS 10 RACE) 6f
2:20 (2:21) (Class 5) 2-Y-O £4,851 (£1,443; £721; £360) **Stalls** Centre

Form RPR

1 **Brookside Banner (IRE)** 2-9-0 0 RichardKingscote 10 79+
(Tom Dascombe) *missed break: hld up: hdwy over 3f out: hung lft fr 2f out: led 1f out and continued to hang: r.o ins fnl f* **8/1**

2 *1* **Whatabird (IRE)** 2-9-0 0 TonyHamilton 2 76+
(Richard Fahey) *hld up in rr: hdwy over 1f out: r.o ins fnl f: fin wl: nt quite rch wnr* **16/1**

3 *nk* **Esprit Rose (IRE)** 2-9-0 0 TomMarquand 5 75
(Roger Varian) *missed break: midfield: effrt and hdwy whn carried lft over 1f out: cl up ent fnl f: nt pce of wnr after: styd on towards fin* **5/1**[2]

3 **4** *¾* **Poet's Lady**[21] 6175 2-9-0 0 GrahamLee 4 73
(David Barron) *midfield: hdwy 2f out: rdn to chse ldrs over 1f out: carried lft ins fnl f: kpt on towards fin* **6/1**

5 *1* **Magical Moment (FR)** 2-9-0 0 TomEaves 11 70
(Kevin Ryan) *dwlt: sn prom: led over 2f out: hdd 1f out and edgd lft: no ex fnl 75yds* **12/1**

24 **6** *2* **Hidden Spell (IRE)**[79] 3997 2-9-0 0 DanielTudhope 12 64
(K R Burke) *w ldr: rdn and unable qck whn sltly checked over 1f out: one pce ins fnl f* **5/1**[2]

7 *1* **Pushover** 2-9-0 0 DavidAllan 8 61
(Steph Hollinshead) *dwlt: midfield: pushed along and lost pl 2f out: n.d after* **66/1**

3 **8** *shd* **Pretty In Grey**[26] 5988 2-9-0 0 JasonWatson 9 61
(Marco Botti) *handy: lost pl after 2f: kpt on but n.d ins fnl f* **9/2**[1]

6 **9** *nk* **Jaaneh**[12] 6514 2-9-0 0 DaneO'Neill 7 60
(William Haggas) *in tch: rdn and unable qck over 1f out: one pce ins fnl f* **11/2**[3]

10 *1* **Colouring** 2-9-0 0 LiamKeniry 1 57
(Ed Walker) *racd keenly: green: in rr: rdn over 1f out: nvr got involved* **33/1**

000 **11** *1 ¼* **Hands Down (IRE)**[13] 6457 2-9-0 0 PaulMulrennan 3 53
(Nigel Tinkler) *hld up: rdn over 1f out: nvr able to trble ldrs* **100/1**

022 **12** *¾* **Strawberry Hind (IRE)**[13] 6442 2-9-0 74 GeraldMosse 6 51
(Mick Channon) *led: pushed along and hdd over 2f out: wknd over 1f out (trainer rep could offer no explanation for filly's poor performance other than she stopped quickly; post-race examination failed to reveal any abnormalities)* **7/1**

1m 17.27s (3.37) **Going Correction** +0.45s/f (Yiel) **12** Ran SP% **123.8**
Speed ratings (Par 92): **95,93,93,92,90 88,86,86,86,85 83,82**
CSF £133.32 TOTE £9.00: £2.90, £5.50, £1.90; EX 196.60 Trifecta £2688.80.
Owner Seamus Burns **Bred** Stilvi Compania Financiera Sa **Trained** Malpas, Cheshire

FOCUS
There were one or two in the line-up who had already shown a fair level of form, but newcomers filled the first three places.

6920 RACING TV OPTIONAL CLAIMING H'CAP 6f
2:55 (2:57) (Class 2) 4-Y-O+ £19,407 (£5,775; £2,886; £1,443) **Stalls** Centre

Form RPR

0-20 **1** **Alaadel**[20] 6227 6-8-12 89 (t) GeraldMosse 9 99
(Stuart Williams) *hld up: swtchd lft and hdwy over 2f out: r.o to ld fnl 110yds: in command after* **7/1**

-200 **2** *1 ½* **Ptarmigan Ridge**[89] 3632 5-8-1 85 AngusVilliers[(7)] 2 90
(Richard Hughes) *hld up: rdn over 2f out: hdwy over 1f out: styd on to take 2nd towards fin: nt pce to trble wnr (jockey said gelding was never travelling)* **7/1**

0002 **3** *nk* **Hyperfocus (IRE)**[20] 6227 5-9-3 94 (p) DavidAllan 14 98
(Tim Easterby) *led: rdn over 1f out: hdd fnl 110yds: kpt on same pce towards fin* **7/2**[1]

2U13 **4** *2 ¼* **Royal Residence**[14] 6396 4-9-0 91 TomMarquand 8 88
(James Tate) *hld up: rdn over 2f out: hdwy 1f out: styd on ins fnl f: nt pce to trble front three* **15/2**

4052 **5** *1 ½* **Youkan (IRE)**[82] 3893 4-8-5 82 JimmyQuinn 1 74
(Stuart Kittow) *hld up: hdwy 2f out: rdn to chse ldrs over 1f out: one pce ins fnl f* **16/1**

6023 **6** *¾* **Danzan (IRE)**[81] 3945 4-8-10 87 DavidProbert 12 77
(Andrew Balding) *prom: rdn 2f out: nt pce of ldrs over 1f out: no ex ins fnl f* **9/2**[2]

6160 **7** *¾* **Tawny Port**[20] 6227 5-8-8 85 JasonWatson 10 72+
(Stuart Williams) *midfield: rdn and lost pl 2f out: nt clr run over 1f out: kpt on fnl 150yds whn no ch (jockey said gelding was denied a clear run inside fnl 2f)* **11/1**

0504 **8** *½* **Desert Doctor (IRE)**[27] 5942 4-8-13 90 LiamKeniry 6 76
(Ed Walker) *chsd ldrs: rdn over 2f out: lost pl over 1f out: no imp after* **16/1**

-460 **9** *1 ¼* **Ice Lord (IRE)**[14] 6404 7-8-13 90 RichardKingscote 15 72
(Chris Wall) *hld up: hdwy 1/2-way: rdn over 1f out: no imp* **12/1**

6061 **10** *1 ¼* **Unabated (IRE)**[27] 5942 5-8-3 85 ow2 (t) RayDawson[(5)] 4 63
(Jane Chapple-Hyam) *prom: rdn over 2f out: wknd over 1f out (trainer rep said, regarding poor performance, gelding was unsuited by the Soft ground on this occasion and would prefer a quicker surface)* **5/1**[3]

3006 **11** *½* **Harome (IRE)**[11] 6534 5-8-7 89 BenSanderson[(5)] 11 65
(Roger Fell) *racd keenly: trckd ldrs: rdn 2f out: wknd ent fnl f* **33/1**

1m 15.3s (1.40) **Going Correction** +0.45s/f (Yiel) **11** Ran SP% **124.6**
Speed ratings (Par 109): **108,106,105,102,100 99,98,97,96,94 93**
CSF £58.87 CT £210.20 TOTE £8.40: £2.70, £1.90, £1.90; EX 67.50 Trifecta £401.70.
Owner T W Morley **Bred** Cheveley Park Stud Ltd **Trained** Newmarket, Suffolk

FOCUS
A competitive sprint and the first two came from the back of the field. A pb from the winner with the third helping with the standard.

6921 RACINGTV.COM H'CAP 5f
3:30 (3:31) (Class 4) (0-85,86) 3-Y-O+
£6,469 (£1,925; £962; £481; £300; £300) **Stalls** Centre

Form RPR

2600 **1** **Came From The Dark (IRE)**[20] 6220 3-9-2 80 GeraldMosse 10 97
(Ed Walker) *hld up in midfield: hdwy over 2f out: led over 1f out: r.o wl to draw clr ins fnl f: comf* **9/2**[2]

1060 **2** *3 ¾* **Tomily (IRE)**[20] 6227 5-9-9 86 (p[1]) DanielTudhope 3 89
(David O'Meara) *hld up in rr: rdn and hdwy over 1f out: styd on to take 2nd towards fin: nt trble wnr* **12/1**

1100 **3** *¾* **Lathom**[9] 6607 6-9-7 84 TomEaves 11 84
(Paul Midgley) *hld up: rdn and hdwy over 1f out: sn wnt 2nd: unable to go w wnr ins fnl f: lost 2nd towards fin* **16/1**

6204 **4** *1 ½* **Bellevarde (IRE)**[26] 5989 5-8-10 73 TomMarquand 2 68
(Richard Price) *midfield: rdn 2f out: sn outpcd: hdwy ins fnl f: kpt on: nvr able to chal* **25/1**

6631 **5** *1* **Marietta Robusti (IRE)**[28] 5892 4-8-0 70 oh1 AngusVilliers[(7)] 6 61
(Stella Barclay) *in tch: rdn 2f out: no ex ins fnl f* **16/1**

-046 **6** *hd* **Airglow (IRE)**[11] 6549 4-8-12 80 (h) GerO'Neill[(5)] 9 71
(Michael Easterby) *racd keenly: prom: rdn over 1f out: kpt on same pce ins fnl f* **8/1**

-506 **7** *½* **Major Pusey**[92] 3509 7-8-9 72 (p[1]) JoeyHaynes 4 61
(John Gallagher) *hld up: rdn over 2f out: hdwy over 1f out: one pce ins fnl f* **8/1**

6105 **8** *nse* **Cool Spirit**[34] 5670 4-9-2 79 BarryMcHugh 1 68
(Richard Fahey) *wnt to post early: midfield: rdn over 1f out: no imp* **12/1**

1013 **9** *nk* **Show Palace**[21] 6178 6-8-13 76 (p) GrahamLee 7 64
(Jennie Candlish) *led: rdn and hdd over 1f out: no ex ins fnl f (trainer was informed gelding could not run until day after passing a stalls test)* **12/1**

5122 **10** *1 ¼* **Wild Edric**[6] 6715 3-9-2 80 (p[1]) RichardKingscote 5 63
(Tom Dascombe) *prom: rdn over 1f out: sn wknd (trainer said, regarding poor performance, race had come too soon for gelding following its previous run six days later)* **11/4**[1]

2012 **11** *½* **Somewhere Secret**[22] 6110 5-8-7 70 (p) JasonWatson 8 51
(Michael Mullineaux) *prom: rdn over 2f out: wknd wl over 1f out (trainer could offer no explanation for gelding's poor performance)* **5/1**[3]

1m 1.82s (1.42) **Going Correction** +0.45s/f (Yiel)
WFA 3 from 4yo+ 1lb **11** Ran SP% **122.4**
Speed ratings (Par 105): **106,100,98,96,94 94,93,93,93,91 90**
CSF £60.24 CT £827.91 TOTE £5.50: £2.10, £4.10, £5.70; EX 65.20 Trifecta £701.60.
Owner P K Siu **Bred** Yeomanstown Stud & Doc Bloodstock **Trained** Upper Lambourn, Berks

FOCUS
Another sprint in which it was an advantage to be ridden with patience. A clear pb from the winner, who could have been rated higher at face value.

6922 INTRODUCING RACING TV H'CAP 6f 212y
4:00 (4:01) (Class 3) (0-90,90) 3-Y-O+
£8,715 (£2,609; £1,304; £652; £326; £163) **Stalls** Low

Form RPR

-200 **1** **Young Fire (FR)**[13] 6460 4-9-7 86 DanielTudhope 11 95+
(David O'Meara) *hld up: hdwy over 1f out: r.o to ld briefly fnl 110yds: sn jnd: gamely fnd ex fnl strides* **16/1**

104 **2** *shd* **Molls Memory**[14] 6396 4-9-4 83 TomMarquand 4 91
(Ed Walker) *in tch: rdn over 2f out: big effrt ins fnl f: r.o to draw level fnl 100yds: hld fnl strides* **5/1**[2]

5660 **3** *1* **Whitefountainfairy (IRE)**[15] 6379 4-9-5 84 DavidProbert 3 89
(Andrew Balding) *midfield: rdn 2f out: hdwy ent fnl f: effrt to try and chal: styd on but nt pce of front pair towards fin* **10/1**

0052 **4** *nk* **Alemaratalyoum (IRE)**[6] 6711 5-9-10 89 (p) JasonWatson 9 94
(Stuart Williams) *chsd ldrs: rdn to ld over 1f out: hdd fnl 110yds: no ex towards fin* **9/4**[1]

2020 **5** *nk* **Presidential (IRE)**[13] 6445 5-9-2 86 (p) BenSanderson[(5)] 2 90+
(Roger Fell) *hld up in midfield: lost pl over 3f out: swtchd rt over 1f out: hdwy ins fnl f: styd on towards fin: nt quite pce to rch ldrs* **11/1**

5003 **6** *1 ¼* **Get Knotted (IRE)**[41] 5453 7-9-9 88 (p) PaulMulrennan 8 91+
(Michael Dods) *hld up: hdwy whn nt clr run fr over 1f out: styd on fnl 150yds: nvr able to rch ldrs (jockey said gelding was continually denied a clear run for some distance inside fnl f)* **7/1**[3]

325 **7** *½* **Lincoln Park**[26] 5983 3-9-7 90 FrannyNorton 5 87
(Michael Appleby) *led: rdn and hdd over 1f out: fdd fnl 100yds* **9/1**

4200 **8** *½* **King Of Tonga (IRE)**[14] 6425 3-9-4 87 DavidNolan 7 83
(David O'Meara) *midfield: hdwy over 2f out: cl up: rdn over 1f out: no ex fnl 100yds* **12/1**

6602 **9** *½* **Parys Mountain (IRE)**[9] 6588 5-8-12 77 (t) DavidAllan 6 74
(Tim Easterby) *chsd ldr tl rdn over 2f out: unable qck over 1f out: wknd fnl 150yds* **10/1**

-100 **9** *dht* **Jackstar (IRE)**[125] 2412 3-9-5 88 RichardKingscote 10 83
(Tom Dascombe) *hld up: hdwy over 3f out: rdn to chse ldrs 2f out: no ex fnl 100yds* **14/1**

5450 **11** *1* **Right Action**[34] 5692 5-9-2 81 TonyHamilton 1 75
(Richard Fahey) *chsd ldrs: rdn whn n.m.r on inner over 1f out: lost pl: fdd ins fnl f* **16/1**

1m 30.17s (0.87) **Going Correction** +0.45s/f (Yiel)
WFA 3 from 4yo+ 4lb **11** Ran SP% **122.6**
Speed ratings (Par 107): **113,112,111,111,111 109,109,108,107,107 106**
CSF £98.19 CT £881.14 TOTE £18.90: £5.70, £1.40, £3.10; EX 122.20 Trifecta £1192.00.
Owner Evan M Sutherland **Bred** Cyril Morange **Trained** Upper Helmsley, N Yorks

FOCUS
Add 6yds. Again it was an advantage to be played late. The winner is rated back to his French form.

6923 WATCH RACING TV NOW H'CAP 1m 2f 42y
4:30 (4:31) (Class 3) (0-95,96) 3-Y-O+
£8,715 (£2,609; £1,304; £652; £326; £163) **Stalls** Centre

Form RPR

5204 **1** **Ayutthaya (IRE)**[20] 6231 4-9-2 84 TomEaves 7 93
(Kevin Ryan) *midfield: hdwy over 3f out: led jst over 1f out: drvn out and r.o ins fnl f* **7/1**[3]

3151 **2** 1 1/4 **Qarasu (IRE)**[20] 6211 3-9-6 **94**.......... JasonWatson 1 101+
(Roger Charlton) *hld up: hdwy 4f out: rdn over 2f out: styd on ins fnl f: tk 2nd fnl 75yds: nt rch wnr (jockey said colt was denied a clear run approximately 1 1/2f out)* **11/10**[1]

3163 **3** 1 1/2 **Ocala**[20] 6217 4-9-4 **86**.......... DavidProbert 9 90
(Andrew Balding) *midfield: hdwy 7f out: chsd ldr over 6f out: chalng 2f out: sn rdn: nt pce of wnr ins fnl f: kpt on same pce fnl 100yds* **9/2**[2]

-000 **4** 3/4 **Hot Team (IRE)**[78] 4016 3-9-4 **92**..........(p) TomMarquand 6 94
(Hugo Palmer) *led: rdn whn pressed over 1f out: sn hdd: stl there ins fnl f: no ex fnl 75yds* **16/1**

1160 **5** 1 1/4 **Anythingtoday (IRE)**[14] 6420 5-10-0 **96**..........(p) DanielTudhope 2 96
(David O'Meara) *hld up in rr: rdn and hdwy whn angled out over 1f out: kpt on ins fnl f: no imp fnl 100yds* **12/1**

3306 **6** 2 1/4 **Lunar Jet**[27] 5950 5-9-11 **93**.......... JimmyQuinn 8 88
(John Mackie) *hld up: rdn over 2f out: sme hdwy over 1f out: one pce ins fnl f* **14/1**

-050 **7** 1 3/4 **Awake My Soul (IRE)**[34] 5657 10-9-7 **89**.......... GrahamLee 4 81
(Tom Tate) *chsd ldr tl over 6f out: remained prom: rdn over 2f out: sn wknd* **20/1**

0100 **8** *shd* **Finniston Farm**[41] 5437 4-9-12 **94**..........(p) RichardKingscote 5 85
(Tom Dascombe) *racd keenly: hld up: rdn over 2f out: nvr able to threaten* **12/1**

3-30 **9** 14 **Sawwaah**[83] 3857 4-9-11 **93**.......... DaneO'Neill 3 56
(Owen Burrows) *chsd ldrs: rdn 3f out: wknd jst over 2f out: eased whn wl btn over 1f out (jockey said gelding didn't travel from half way)* **14/1**

2m 15.59s (4.79) **Going Correction** +0.45s/f (Yiel)
WFA 3 from 4yo+ 6lb **9** Ran SP% **117.7**
Speed ratings (Par 107): **98,97,95,95,94 92,91,90,79**
CSF £15.38 CT £40.39 TOTE £6.20: £1.60, £1.10, £1.70; EX 17.30 Trifecta £79.10.
Owner JCG Chua & CK Ong 1 **Bred** Pipe View Stud **Trained** Hambleton, N Yorks

FOCUS
Add 28yds. Once again it proved an advantage to be held up off the pace. The winner is rated to this year's form.

6924 WATCH IRISH RACING ON RACING TV H'CAP (JOCKEY CLUB GRASSROOTS STAYERS' SERIES QUALIFIER) 1m 6f
5:05 (5:07) (Class 4) (0-80,80) 3-Y-O+
£6,469 (£1,925; £962; £481; £300; £300) **Stalls** Low

Form RPR

-566 **1** **Ginistrelli (IRE)**[14] 6411 3-9-2 **77**.......... TomMarquand 7 84
(Ed Walker) *hld up in rr: rdn and no imp over 2f out: plld out ins fnl f: str run fnl 75yds: led towards fin (trainer said, regarding improvement in form, gelding appreciated step up in trip to 1m6f, whilst also appreciating the softer ground on this occasion)* **12/1**

5652 **2** *nk* **Landa Beach (IRE)**[20] 6218 3-9-5 **80**..........(p) DavidProbert 1 86
(Andrew Balding) *chsd ldrs: rdn over 2f out: unable qck over 1f out: styd on wl fnl 100yds to mount str chal: no match for wnr fnl strides* **6/1**

4161 **3** *hd* **Theatro (IRE)**[31] 5792 3-9-3 **78**.......... GrahamLee 6 84
(Jedd O'Keeffe) *chsd ldr: upsides over 3f out: led over 2f out: kpt on ins fnl f: hdd towards fin and lost anther pl* **3/1**[2]

2211 **4** 1/2 **Kensington Art**[2] 6864 3-8-11 **72** 12ex..........(p) TonyHamilton 5 77
(Richard Fahey) *led: jnd over 3f out: rdn and hdd over 2f out: stl ev ch ins fnl f: kpt on u.p: nt pce of ldrs towards fin* **15/2**

2211 **5** 1/2 **Maid In Manhattan (IRE)**[7] 6674 5-9-0 **69** 5ex......(h) HarrisonShaw(3) 8 73
(Rebecca Menzies) *wnt to post early: sluggish s: hld up: hdwy over 2f out: rdn whn chsng ldrs over 1f out: ev ch ins fnl f: no ex towards fin* **7/4**[1]

5161 **6** *nk* **Follow Intello (IRE)**[48] 5179 4-9-10 **76**.......... DanielTudhope 2 81
(Chris Wall) *chsd ldrs: rdn 3f out: kpt on ins fnl f: nt quite pce of ldrs: nt clr run towards fin* **9/2**[3]

0/0 **7** 15 **Lady Camelot (IRE)**[29] 5849 4-9-7 **80**.......... NickBarratt-Atkin(7) 3 61
(Philip Kirby) *hld up in midfield: rdn over 2f out: sn wknd* **50/1**

3m 13.11s (8.51) **Going Correction** +0.45s/f (Yiel)
WFA 3 from 4yo+ 9lb **7** Ran SP% **115.2**
Speed ratings (Par 105): **93,92,92,92,92 91,83**
CSF £81.47 CT £274.67 TOTE £12.50: £5.00, £2.50; EX 63.60 Trifecta £556.10.
Owner Bjorn Nielsen & Eastwind Racing Ltd **Bred** Guaranda Syndicate **Trained** Upper Lambourn, Berks

FOCUS
Add 6yds. The complexion of the race changed dramatically in the closing stages as the winner, having looked held, got up late in a bunched finish. It's hard to know how literally to take this.
T/Plt: £1,474.50 to a £1 stake. Pool: £66,154.75 - 32.75 winning units T/Qpdt: £44.10 to a £1 stake. Pool: £9,707.98 - 162.86 winning units **Darren Owen**

6837 KEMPTON (A.W) (R-H)
Friday, September 6

OFFICIAL GOING: Polytrack: standard to slow
Wind: Light against Weather: Overcast

6925 32RED.COM APPRENTICE H'CAP 1m (P)
5:40 (5:40) (Class 4) (0-80,80) 3-Y-O+
£6,469 (£1,925; £962; £481; £400; £400) **Stalls** Low

Form RPR

4501 **1** **Kheros**[21] 6160 3-9-1 **77**..........(p) Pierre-LouisJamin(3) 4 91
(Archie Watson) *mde all: rdn and edgd rt over 1f out: sn clr* **9/4**[1]

0110 **2** 6 **Fortune And Glory (USA)**[34] 5667 6-9-6 **74**.......... ScottMcCullagh 1 75
(Joseph Tuite) *trckd ldrs: chsd wnr 2f out: sn rdn: styd on same pce fnl f* **9/4**[1]

4304 **3** 1 1/2 **Shyron**[136] 2006 8-9-6 **74**.......... ThoreHammerHansen 8 72
(Lee Carter) *hld up in tch: rdn over 1f out: styd on same pce fnl f* **40/1**

3500 **4** 1 1/4 **Leader Writer (FR)**[16] 6347 7-9-4 **79**.......... CameronIles(7) 2 74+
(David Elsworth) *s.s: pushed along early in rr: hdwy over 1f out: sn rdn: no ex ins fnl f (jockey said horse was slowly away)* **7/1**[3]

0503 **5** 1/2 **Isomer (USA)**[29] 5858 5-9-8 **79**..........(h) WilliamCarver(3) 3 73+
(Andrew Balding) *s.s: sn pushed along in rr: swtchd lft over 2f out: rdn over 1f out: styd on ins fnl f: nvr nrr (jockey said gelding was slowly away)* **11/4**[2]

0640 **6** 6 **Spencers Son (IRE)**[30] 5813 3-8-10 **72**..........(t[1]) SeanKirrane(3) 5 51
(Richard Spencer) *chsd ldrs: chsd wnr 3f out tl 2f out: rdn and wknd over 1f out* **12/1**

50-0 **7** 9 **Abel Tasman**[232] 272 5-9-4 **75**.......... TobyEley(3) 7 34
(Roy Brotherton) *chsd wnr 5f: rdn and wknd wl over 1f out* **100/1**

1m 38.62s (-1.18) **Going Correction** +0.025s/f (Slow)
WFA 3 from 4yo+ 5lb **7** Ran SP% **111.8**
Speed ratings (Par 105): **106,100,98,97,96 90,81**
CSF £7.19 CT £140.46 TOTE £3.10: £1.40, £1.10; EX 9.20 Trifecta £99.60.
Owner W J A Nash & Partner **Bred** Whitwell Bloodstock **Trained** Upper Lambourn, W Berks

FOCUS
The well-backed favourite put in a dominant display to complete a double in this apprentice handicap. The form could be rated a but better at face value.

6926 32RED ON THE APP STORE/BRITISH STALLION STUDS EBF NOVICE STKS (PLUS 10 RACE) 1m (P)
6:10 (6:11) (Class 4) 2-Y-O
£5,822 (£1,732; £865; £432) **Stalls** Low

Form RPR

1 **Acquitted (IRE)** 2-9-5 0.......... JamesDoyle 10 78+
(Hugo Palmer) *broke wl enough: sn lost pl: shkn up and swtchd lft 2f out: hdwy to ld and edgd rt over 1f out: r.o: comf* **10/1**

2 1 1/4 **Byzantine Empire** 2-9-5 0.......... RobertHavlin 4 74+
(John Gosden) *s.s: hdwy over 1f out: r.o to go 2nd wl ins fnl f (jockey said colt was slowly away)* **3/1**[2]

3 *hd* **Stanford (IRE)** 2-9-5 0.......... RobHornby 7 74+
(Andrew Balding) *s.i.s: in rr: shkn up and hdwy over 1f out: r.o* **33/1**

54 **4** 1 3/4 **Vulcan (IRE)**[72] 4252 2-9-5 0.......... JimCrowley 6 70
(Harry Dunlop) *hdwy on outer to ld over 5f out: rdn and hdd over 1f out: styd on same pce ins fnl f* **9/1**[3]

0 **5** *shd* **Looktothelight (USA)**[90] 3601 2-9-5 0.......... NicolaCurrie 11 69
(Jamie Osborne) *s.i.s: rcvrd to ld 7f out: hdd over 5f out: chsd ldr: rdn over 1f out: styd on same pce ins fnl f* **50/1**

0 **6** 1 1/2 **Duke Of Condicote**[34] 5655 2-9-5 0.......... GeorgeWood 8 66
(Alan King) *prom: lost pl over 5f out: rdn and outpcd over 2f out: styd on ins fnl f* **80/1**

5 **7** *shd* **Tafish (IRE)**[14] 6395 2-9-5 0.......... ShaneKelly 3 66+
(Richard Hughes) *s.i.s: hld up: hdwy over 1f out: nt clr run and lost pl sn after: kpt on ins fnl f* **9/1**[3]

0 **8** 3 3/4 **Cabot Cliffs (IRE)**[14] 6424 2-9-5 0.......... RyanMoore 1 57
(Charles Hills) *chsd ldrs: rdn over 1f out: wknd ins fnl f* **14/1**

52 **9** 5 **Stars In The Sky**[20] 6205 2-9-0 0.......... OisinMurphy 5 41
(William Haggas) *led 1f: chsd ldrs: nt clr run and swtchd lft over 4f out: rdn over 2f out: wknd over 1f out (trainer's rep could offer no explanation for the filly's performance)* **11/10**[1]

64 **10** 1 1/2 **Jack Ruby (IRE)**[24] 6040 2-9-5 0.......... SeanLevey 9 42
(Richard Hannon) *chsd ldrs: rdn over 2f out: wknd over 1f out* **50/1**

1m 39.57s (-0.23) **Going Correction** +0.025s/f (Slow) **10** Ran SP% **116.5**
Speed ratings (Par 97): **102,100,100,98,98 97,97,93,88,86**
CSF £39.70 TOTE £9.40: £2.50, £1.50, £5.10; EX 39.70 Trifecta £289.00.
Owner John Livock & Nat Lacy **Bred** Lannister Holdings **Trained** Newmarket, Suffolk

FOCUS
The leading form contender was disappointing and newcomers filled the first three places in this novice event.

6927 32RED CASINO/BRITISH STALLION STUDS EBF NOVICE STKS (PLUS 10 RACE) 7f (P)
6:40 (6:43) (Class 4) 2-Y-O
£5,822 (£1,732; £865; £432) **Stalls** Low

Form RPR

222 **1** **Riot (IRE)**[37] 5563 2-9-5 **87**.......... OisinMurphy 4 81
(John Gosden) *chsd ldr: shkn up to ld ins fnl f: styd on* **5/6**[1]

4 **2** *nk* **Jean Baptiste (IRE)**[29] 5860 2-9-5 0.......... RyanMoore 2 80
(Sir Michael Stoute) *led at stdy pce: shkn up and qcknd over 2f out: rdn and hdd ins fnl f: styd on* **5/1**[3]

3 3/4 **Karibana (IRE)** 2-9-5 0.......... ShaneKelly 9 78+
(Richard Hughes) *hld up in tch: shkn up over 1f out: r.o* **50/1**

2 **4** 1 1/4 **Hot Summer**[14] 6409 2-9-5 0.......... SeanLevey 3 75
(Richard Hannon) *prom: racd keenly: rdn over 1f out: styd on same pce ins fnl f* **2/1**[2]

5 *shd* **Turn On The Charm (FR)** 2-9-5 0.......... GeorgeWood 10 75
(James Fanshawe) *sn prom on outer: shkn up over 1f out: styd on same pce ins fnl f* **12/1**

6 6 **Son Of Red (IRE)** 2-9-5 0.......... TomQueally 11 59+
(Alan King) *s.i.s: hld up: nt clr run over 2f out: shkn up and outpcd over 1f out* **33/1**

6 **7** 1 1/4 **Opine (IRE)**[17] 6314 2-9-5 0.......... CallumShepherd 5 56
(Michael Bell) *hld up: shkn up and outpcd fr over 2f out* **66/1**

00 **8** 2 **Tigerten**[26] 5992 2-9-5 0.......... CharlesBishop 7 51
(Joseph Tuite) *hld up on outer: shkn up over 2f out: hung rt and wknd over 1f out* **100/1**

P0P0 **9** 4 **Austin Taetious**[21] 6185 2-9-0 0.......... TobyEley(5) 1 40
(Adam West) *s.i.s: sn chsng ldrs: rdn over 2f out: wknd over 1f out* **200/1**

1m 29.09s (3.09) **Going Correction** +0.025s/f (Slow) **9** Ran SP% **120.1**
Speed ratings (Par 97): **83,82,81,80,80 73,71,69,65**
CSF £6.14 TOTE £1.60: £1.10, £1.50, £7.80; EX 6.00 Trifecta £88.90.
Owner Qatar Racing Limited **Bred** Mountarmstrong Stud **Trained** Newmarket, Suffolk

FOCUS
The pace was steady and there was a tight finish but the hot favourite came out on top in this novice.

6928 LONGINES IRISH CHAMPIONS WEEKEND EBF "CONFINED" FILLIES' NOVICE STKS (PLUS 10 RACE) 7f (P)
7:10 (7:15) (Class 3) 2-Y-O
£12,291 (£3,657; £1,827; £913) **Stalls** Low

Form RPR

1 **White Moonlight (USA)** 2-9-0 0.......... OisinMurphy 9 76
(Saeed bin Suroor) *s.i.s: sn prom: shkn up over 1f out: r.o to ld post* **9/4**[1]

24 **2** *shd* **Breath Of Joy**[21] 6159 2-9-0 0.......... HarryBentley 8 76
(Amy Murphy) *sn led: hdd over 5f out: chsd ldrs: rdn to ld over 1f out: hdd post (jockey said filly hung left-handed under pressure)* **12/1**

3 *nk* **Donnybrook (IRE)** 2-9-0 0..........(h[1]) RobertHavlin 7 75+
(John Gosden) *stdd s: hld up: plld hrd: hdwy on outer over 1f out: r.o* **11/2**[3]

4 1 3/4 **Sorrel (IRE)** 2-9-0 0.......... RyanMoore 2 70+
(Sir Michael Stoute) *chsd ldrs: shkn up and outpcd over 2f out: rallied over 1f out: swtchd rt ins fnl f: r.o* **7/2**[2]

5 *hd* **Rakassah (IRE)** 2-9-0 0.......... ShaneKelly 10 70
(Richard Hughes) *s.i.s: sn prom: chsd ldr 5f out: led 2f out: rdn and hdd over 1f out: styd on same pce ins fnl f* **66/1**

53 **6** 1/2 **Charming Spirit (IRE)**[12] 6514 2-9-0 0 AndreaAtzeni 11 69
(Roger Varian) *chsd ldrs: led over 5f out: rdn and hdd 2f out: styd on same pce ins fnl f* 8/1

7 1 1/2 **Heliaebel** 2-9-0 0 StevieDonohoe 3 65+
(Charlie Fellowes) *s.i.s: hld up: hdwy over 1f out: nt trble ldrs* 40/1

8 1 1/4 **Pax Britannica (IRE)** 2-9-0 0 CallumShepherd 5 61+
(David Simcock) *s.i.s: hld up: shkn up over 2f out: nt trble ldrs* 40/1

9 3/4 **Via Veritas (USA)** 2-9-0 0 JamieSpencer 4 59
(Michael Bell) *chsd ldrs: lost pl 5f out: shkn up and hung rt fr over 1f out: n.d after* 6/1

0 **10** 1 1/4 **Angels Tread**[32] 5733 2-9-0 0 SeanLevey 6 56
(David Simcock) *hld up: shkn up over 2f out: nvr on terms* 16/1

1m 27.32s (1.32) **Going Correction** +0.025s/f (Slow) 10 Ran SP% 113.7
Speed ratings (Par 96): **93,92,92,90,90 89,88,86,85,84**
CSF £30.14 TOTE £2.70: £1.90, £3.60, £1.70; EX 34.50 Trifecta £199.40.
Owner Godolphin **Bred** Godolphin **Trained** Newmarket, Suffolk
■ Lady De Vega was withdrawn. Price at time of withdrawal 25-1. Rule 4 does not apply

FOCUS
The went a fair pace and there was an exciting finish in this fillies' novice event.

6929 32RED H'CAP 1m 7f 218y(P)
7:40 (7:41) (Class 3) (0-90,91) 3-Y-O+ £9,337 (£2,796; £1,398; £699) Stalls Low

Form RPR

1113 **1** **Land Of Oz**[13] 6471 3-9-3 84 RyanTate 3 93+
(Sir Mark Prescott Bt) *hld up: hdwy over 5f out: shkn up to chse ldr over 1f out: led wl ins fnl f: idled towards fin* 2/5[1]

4320 **2** 1/2 **Cristal Spirit**[37] 5540 4-9-1 71 (p) PatCosgrave 1 77
(George Baker) *chsd ldr: rdn over 2f out: lost 2nd over 1f out: r.o to go 2nd again nr fin* 11/2[2]

3043 **3** nk **Petrastar**[30] 5812 4-9-8 78 (h) JamesDoyle 2 83
(Clive Cox) *led: shkn up and qcknd over 2f out: rdn and edgd lft over 1f out: hdd wl ins fnl f* 6/1[3]

5-40 **4** 3 1/2 **Alfredo (IRE)**[27] 5928 7-10-7 91 (tp) TomQueally 4 91
(Seamus Durack) *chsd ldrs: lost pl over 5f out: sn pushed along: rallied over 1f out: no ex ins fnl f* 16/1

3m 30.57s (0.47) **Going Correction** +0.025s/f (Slow) 4 Ran SP% 107.0
WFA 3 from 4yo+ 11lb
Speed ratings (Par 107): **99,98,98,96**
CSF £2.91 TOTE £1.30; EX 2.70 Trifecta £2.00.
Owner John Brown & Megan Dennis **Bred** Stetchworth & Middle Park Studs Ltd **Trained** Newmarket, Suffolk

FOCUS
They went a stop-start gallop but the hot favourite scored with some authority from off the pace. The form is taken at face value around the second and third, but isn't the most solid.

6930 RACINGTV.COM H'CAP (JOCKEY CLUB GRASSROOTS SPRINT SERIES QUALIFIER) 6f (P)
8:10 (8:10) (Class 5) (0-75,77) 3-Y-O £3,752 (£1,116; £557; £400; £400; £400) Stalls Low

Form RPR

1400 **1** **Revolutionise (IRE)**[20] 6220 3-9-7 75 AndreaAtzeni 9 86
(Roger Varian) *s.i.s: hld up: hdwy over 1f out: r.o to ld wl ins fnl f: comf (trainer's rep said regarding apparent improvement in form that the gelding benefitted from a patient ride and settling better as well a drop-in grade from Class 4 to Class 5)* 11/2[2]

2156 **2** 1 1/4 **Gold At Midnight**[21] 6162 3-9-2 77 MarcoGhiani(7) 2 84
(William Stone) *hld up: hdwy 2f out: rdn and ev ch wl ins fnl f: styd on same pce* 17/2

2011 **3** nk **Chil Chil**[4] 6806 3-9-7 75 12ex OisinMurphy 8 81
(Andrew Balding) *hld up: hdwy over 1f out: rdn and ev ch wl ins fnl f: styd on same pce* 5/6[1]

5543 **4** hd **Motagally**[22] 6108 3-9-7 75 (b[1]) JimCrowley 6 80
(Charles Hills) *s.i.s: hld up: hdwy 2f out: led over 1f out: rdn and hdd wl ins fnl f* 8/1

-012 **5** 3 3/4 **Lordsbridge Boy**[9] 6598 3-8-3 62 SophieRalston(5) 5 55
(Dean Ivory) *led: plld hrd: shkn up over 2f out: hdd over 1f out: wknd wl ins fnl f* 7/1[3]

3655 **6** nk **Porcelain Girl (IRE)**[26] 5989 3-9-3 71 (v[1]) CallumShepherd 3 63
(Michael Bell) *s.i.s: sn prom: rdn over 1f out: no ex fnl f* 12/1

226- **7** 2 1/2 **On Route**[345] 7666 3-8-9 63 RyanTate 7 47
(Sir Mark Prescott Bt) *racd keenly in 2nd tl rdn over 1f out: wknd ins fnl f* 40/1

0433 **8** 3/4 **Soldier's Son**[8] 6638 3-8-5 66 EmmaTaff(7) 4 48
(Henry Candy) *s.i.s: nvr on terms* 20/1

5556 **9** 3/4 **Solar Park (IRE)**[18] 6288 3-9-2 70 RobertHavlin 1 49
(Michael Attwater) *trckd ldrs: rdn over 1f out: wknd fnl f* 33/1

0106 **10** shd **Mendoza (IRE)**[22] 6111 3-9-6 74 PatCosgrave 12 53
(James Eustace) *s.i.s: sn chsng ldrs on outer: rdn over 2f out: wknd over 1f out* 33/1

1m 11.66s (-1.44) **Going Correction** +0.025s/f (Slow) 10 Ran SP% 124.9
Speed ratings (Par 101): **110,108,107,107,102 102,98,97,96,96**
CSF £52.82 CT £80.43 TOTE £7.20: £2.10, £2.10, £1.10; EX 48.80 Trifecta £137.90.
Owner A D Spence **Bred** Ballylinch Stud **Trained** Newmarket, Suffolk

FOCUS
They went a good pace and the winner came from some way back in this handicap. The runner-up is perhaps the key to the form.

6931 100% PROFIT BOOST AT 32REDSPORT.COM H'CAP 1m 3f 219y(P)
8:40 (8:41) (Class 5) (0-75,74) 3-Y-O+ £3,752 (£1,116; £557; £400; £400; £400) Stalls Low

Form RPR

1332 **1** **Alma Linda**[9] 6596 3-9-2 72 (p) RyanTate 1 81
(Sir Mark Prescott Bt) *mde all: rdn over 1f out: styd on wl* 9/4[2]

034 **2** 2 1/2 **Dobrianka**[18] 6290 3-9-2 72 HarryBentley 2 77
(Ralph Beckett) *prom: chsd wnr over 4f out: rdn and ev ch over 1f out: no ex ins fnl f* 7/4[1]

1141 **3** shd **Sir Prize**[17] 6320 4-9-12 74 RobertWinston 5 78
(Dean Ivory) *hld up: hdwy over 2f out: rdn over 1f out: styd on same pce fnl f* 3/1[3]

3105 **4** 2 3/4 **Spirit Of Angel (IRE)**[14] 6393 3-8-8 64 (p) AndreaAtzeni 8 64
(Marcus Tregoning) *hld up: rdn over 2f out: styd on fr over 1f out: nt rch ldrs* 20/1

3442 **5** 2 **Water's Edge (IRE)**[21] 6165 3-9-4 74 PatCosgrave 3 70
(George Baker) *prom: rdn over 2f out: wknd fnl f* 7/1

4006 **6** 7 **Nordic Flight**[17] 6324 4-8-12 60 oh3 (b) ShaneKelly 7 45
(James Eustace) *hld up: rdn over 2f out: wknd over 1f out* 40/1

2440 **7** 35 **Moayadd (USA)**[41] 5452 7-9-10 72 OisinMurphy 6 1
(Neil Mulholland) *sn chsng wnr: lost 2nd over 4f out: rdn over 2f out: sn wknd* 20/1

0000 **8** 39 **Mr Minerals**[25] 6026 5-9-3 65 (p) RossaRyan 4
(Alexandra Dunn) *s.i.s: hld up: rdn over 3f out: wknd over 2f out (vet said gelding had bled from the nose)* 33/1

2m 32.56s (-1.94) **Going Correction** +0.025s/f (Slow) 8 Ran SP% 119.5
WFA 3 from 4yo+ 8lb
Speed ratings (Par 103): **107,105,105,103,102 97,74,48**
CSF £6.66 CT £11.64 TOTE £3.10: £1.10, £1.90, £1.60; EX 7.40 Trifecta £21.70.
Owner Miss K Rausing **Bred** Miss K Rausing **Trained** Newmarket, Suffolk

FOCUS
The winner made all to beat her main market rivals in this middle-distance handicap. The form's rated around the third and fourth.
T/Plt: £14.80 to a £1 stake. Pool: £67,543.84 - 3,329.97 winning units T/Qpdt: £2.70 to a £1 stake. Pool: £7,402.49 - 1,982.77 winning units **Colin Roberts**

6606 MUSSELBURGH (R-H)
Friday, September 6

OFFICIAL GOING: Good to firm (good in places; 8.2)
Wind: Fresh, against in races over 5f and in approximately 4f of home straight in races on the round cours Weather: Overcast, dry

6932 DONALDSON TIMBER ENGINEERING H'CAP 5f 1y
4:25 (4:26) (Class 5) (0-75,75) 3-Y-O+ £3,428 (£1,020; £509; £400; £400; £400) Stalls High

Form RPR

3440 **1** **Bashiba (IRE)**[6] 6699 8-8-6 63 (t) RowanScott(3) 7 69
(Nigel Tinkler) *hld up: stdy hdwy and angled rt over 1f out: led ins fnl f: kpt on wl cl home (trainer's rep said regarding apparent improvement in form that the gelding may have appreciated the better ground on this occasion)* 10/3[2]

0002 **2** nk **Desert Ace (IRE)**[6] 6699 8-8-13 67 KevinStott 4 72
(Paul Midgley) *t.k.h: trckd ldrs: rdn and ev ch ins fnl f: kpt on: hld cl home* 7/2[3]

5645 **3** nk **Gleniffer**[9] 6608 3-8-3 65 CoreyMadden(7) 2 69
(Jim Goldie) *hld up: hdwy on outside over 1f out: rdn and cl up ins fnl f: edgd rt and no ex towards fin* 12/1

600 **4** 1 **Excessable**[6] 6699 6-9-4 72 (t[1]) RachelRichardson 6 72+
(Tim Easterby) *trckd ldrs: effrt whn nt clr run over 1f out to ins fnl f: kpt on fin (jockey said gelding was denied a clear run appr 1f out)* 3/1[1]

0122 **5** 3 **Super Julius**[27] 5936 5-9-7 75 (p) BenCurtis 1 65
(S Donohoe, Ire) *trckd ldr: led and rdn over 1f out: hdd ins fnl f: sn btn (jockey said gelding ran too free)* 9/2

654 **6** 1 3/4 **Jordan Electrics**[9] 6608 3-8-9 67 (h) SeanDavis(3) 5 50
(Linda Perratt) *led to over 1f out: sn rdn and wknd* 6/1

59.94s (0.24) **Going Correction** 0.0s/f (Good) 6 Ran SP% 110.5
WFA 3 from 5yo+ 1lb
Speed ratings (Par 103): **98,97,97,95,90 87**
CSF £14.77 TOTE £5.90: £2.80, £2.00; EX 16.30 Trifecta £79.80.
Owner M Webb **Bred** John T Heffernan & Grainne Dooley **Trained** Langton, N Yorks
■ Stewards' Enquiry : Sean Davis £140 fine; not left sufficient time to travel from Newcastle

FOCUS
The going was good to firm, good in places with all race distances as advertised. A low-key and tight-looking sprint handicap. Modest form.

6933 CALA HOMES (EAST) LTD H'CAP 1m 5f 216y
5:00 (5:00) (Class 5) (0-70,72) 4-Y-O+ £3,428 (£1,020; £509; £400; £400; £400) Stalls Low

Form RPR

5240 **1** **Battle Of Marathon (USA)**[10] 6573 7-9-9 72 BenCurtis 1 81
(John Ryan) *hld up in tch: smooth hdwy to ld over 2f out: rdn and clr over 1f out: kpt on strly: eased towards fin* 12/1

2320 **2** 5 **Remember The Days (IRE)**[19] 6256 5-9-5 71 SeanDavis(3) 6 73
(Jedd O'Keeffe) *in tch: hdwy over 4f out: effrt on outside and chsd (clr) wnr over 1f out: no imp fnl f* 11/1

4-55 **3** nk **Gemologist (IRE)**[9] 6611 4-8-0 54 oh4 ow3 (t) FayeMcManoman(5) 10 56
(Lucinda Russell) *hld up: rdn and hdwy over 2f out: disp 2nd pl over 1f out: one pce fnl f* 14/1

5546 **4** 1/2 **Tor**[32] 5743 5-9-7 70 JamieGormley 5 71
(Iain Jardine) *hld up: stdy hdwy on outside over 3f out: rdn over 2f out: one pce fr over 1f out* 12/5[2]

0003 **5** 1/2 **Kaizer**[45] 5277 4-7-13 55 IzzyClifton(7) 9 56
(Alistair Whillans) *pressed ldr: led briefly over 2f out: drvn and one pce fr over 1f out* 85/40[1]

5633 **6** 3 1/4 **Pammi**[9] 6611 4-8-2 51 oh3 (p) PaddyMathers 8 47
(Jim Goldie) *rrd s: hld up: hdwy and in tch over 3f out: wknd over 1f out* 14/1

5413 **7** 8 **Corton Lad**[7] 6658 9-9-4 67 (tp) ShaneGray 7 52
(Keith Dalgleish) *led at decent gallop: rdn and hdd over 2f out: sn wknd* 7/1[3]

0413 **8** 2 **Stormin Tom (IRE)**[9] 6586 7-9-5 68 DuranFentiman 2 50
(Tim Easterby) *w ldrs 2f: cl up: rdn over 3f out: wknd over 2f out* 9/1

0000 **9** 99 **Enemy Of The State (IRE)**[8] 4515 5-7-11 51 oh6(p) AndrewBreslin(5) 3
(R Mike Smith) *bhd and sn detached: lost tch bef 1/2-way: t.o* 66/1

3m 0.84s (-3.06) **Going Correction** 0.0s/f (Good) 9 Ran SP% 114.8
Speed ratings (Par 103): **108,105,104,104,104 102,97,96,40**
CSF £134.06 CT £1862.20 TOTE £15.10: £2.50, £2.90, £4.00; EX 85.90 Trifecta £1104.10.
Owner Gerry McGladery **Bred** Galleria Bloodstock & Rhinestone B/Stock **Trained** Newmarket, Suffolk

FOCUS
A competitive staying handicap, though a lot came into it out of form and the suicidal battle for the lead did for at least two of them. Dodgy form.

6934 BRITISH STALLION STUDS EBF NOVICE AUCTION STKS 7f 33y
5:30 (5:31) (Class 5) 2-Y-O £3,557 (£1,058; £529; £264) Stalls Low

Form RPR

22 **1** **Yoshimi (IRE)**[23] 6065 2-8-13 0 SeanDavis(3) 3 76
(Richard Fahey) *trckd ldrs: effrt whn n.m.r over 2f out: rdn to over 1f out: rdn and led ins fnl f: kpt on wl* 8/11[1]

05 **2** ½ **Get Boosting**[9] 6606 2-9-2 0 ShaneGray 6 75
(Keith Dalgleish) *cl up: led over 2f out to ins fnl f: one pce towards fin* **14/1**

3 **3** 3½ **Handlebars (IRE)**[10] 6570 2-8-11 0 JasonHart 5 61
(Keith Dalgleish) *led at ordinary gallop: rdn and hdd over 2f out: rallied: outpcd over 1f out* **11/4[2]**

54 **4** 1¼ **Um Elnadim (FR)**[18] 6281 2-8-11 0 JoeFanning 4 57
(Mark Johnston) *s.i.s: t.k.h: hld up in tch: effrt on outside over 2f out: wknd fnl f* **13/2[3]**

5 33 **Ami Li Bert (IRE)** 2-9-5 0 AlistairRawlinson 1
(Michael Appleby) *slowly away: sn t.o* **22/1**

1m 29.47s (0.47) **Going Correction** 0.0s/f (Good) **5 Ran SP% 108.9**
Speed ratings (Par 95): **97,96,92,91,53**
CSF £11.67 TOTE £1.50: £1.10, £4.90; EX 8.60 Trifecta £16.30.
Owner Mrs Lauren Hart & Partner **Bred** Ammerland Verwaltung Gmbh & Co Kg **Trained** Musley Bank, N Yorks

FOCUS
Another race where the pace looked inconsistent, but the best horse got there in the end.

6935 ST ANDREWS TIMBER AND BUILDING SUPPLIES H'CAP 7f 33y
6:00 (6:01) (Class 4) (0-80,80) 3-Y-O+

£5,692 (£1,694; £846; £423; £400; £400) **Stalls** Low

Form RPR

5646 **1** **Glengarry**[28] 5903 6-9-8 **77** JoeFanning 1 85
(Keith Dalgleish) *s.i.s: hld up in tch: smooth hdwy to ld over 1f out: sn rdn: kpt on wl fnl f* **5/1[3]**

-021 **2** 1 **Six Strings**[9] 6591 5-9-10 **79** 5ex AlistairRawlinson 2 87+
(Michael Appleby) *t.k.h: trckd ldrs: effrt whn nt clr run fr over 2f out to ent fnl f: effrt and chsd wnr last 100yds: kpt on fin (jockey said gelding was continually denied a clear run in the final 2 1/2f)* **7/4[1]**

203 **3** ¾ **Be Kool (IRE)**[45] 5283 6-9-8 **77** (p) BenRobinson 5 80
(Brian Ellison) *trckd ldr: led over 2f out to over 1f out: chsd wnr to last 100yds: one pce (jockey said gelding hung right)* **10/1**

1154 **4** shd **Defence Treaty (IRE)**[27] 5971 3-9-3 **79** (p) SeanDavis(3) 3 80
(Richard Fahey) *prom: effrt over 2f out: rdn and edgd rt over 1f out: kpt on same pce ins fnl f* **17/2**

5124 **5** ½ **Battle Of Waterloo (IRE)**[14] 6410 3-9-7 **80** BenCurtis 7 79
(John Ryan) *slowly away: hld up: rdn and effrt on outside 2f out: kpt on same pce fnl f* **7/1**

310 **6** 1¼ **Donnelly's Rainbow (IRE)**[8] 6628 6-8-7 **65** oh2 RowanScott(3) 6 63
(Rebecca Bastiman) *hld up: effrt whn no room fr over 2f out to ins fnl f: sn angled lft and no imp (jockey said gelding was denied a clear run from 2½f out)* **10/1**

5453 **7** hd **Howzer Black (IRE)**[25] 6015 3-9-6 **79** (p) ShaneGray 8 74
(Keith Dalgleish) *hld up in tch: n.m.r over 2f out to over 1f out: rdn and no imp fnl f* **18/1**

2532 **8** 3½ **How Bizarre**[10] 6573 4-9-3 **72** KevinStott 4 60
(Liam Bailey) *led to over 2f out: rallied: wknd fnl f (jockey said gelding ran flat)* **9/2[2]**

1m 28.25s (-0.75) **Going Correction** 0.0s/f (Good)
WFA 3 from 4yo+ 4lb **8 Ran SP% 117.7**
Speed ratings (Par 105): **104,102,102,101,101 99,99,95**
CSF £14.65 CT £86.18 TOTE £4.60: £1.60, £1.70, £2.40; EX 22.50 Trifecta £155.00.
Owner Mrs Janis Macpherson **Bred** Laundry Cottage Stud Farm **Trained** Carluke, S Lanarks

FOCUS
A decent Class 4 and a gamble landed though the runner-up was desperately unlucky. The form's rated around the third and fourth.

6936 JOIN RACINGTV NOW H'CAP 5f 1y
6:30 (6:32) (Class 6) (0-60,64) 3-Y-O+

£2,781 (£827; £413; £400; £400; £400) **Stalls** High

Form RPR

0215 **1** **Archimedes (IRE)**[6] 6699 6-9-12 **64** 5ex (vt) AlistairRawlinson 6 72
(David C Griffiths) *mde all: rdn over 1f out: r.o wl fnl f* **7/1**

0004 **2** 1¼ **Super Florence (IRE)**[10] 6574 4-9-1 **53** (h) JamieGormley 3 57
(Iain Jardine) *in tch: effrt and rdn over 1f out: chsd wnr ins fnl f: one pce towards fin (jockey said filly anticipated the start and as a result was slowly away)* **16/1**

0001 **3** nk **Thornaby Princess**[10] 6574 8-8-11 **49** 4ex (p) JasonHart 4 51
(Jason Ward) *trckd ldrs: effrt and wnt 2nd over 1f out to ins fnl f: kpt on same pce* **22/1**

6551 **4** 1 **Northern Society (IRE)**[9] 6608 3-9-10 **63** 6ex ShaneGray 12 62
(Keith Dalgleish) *in tch: effrt and pushed along over 1f out: kpt on ins fnl f: nt pce to chal* **5/1[2]**

/24- **5** 2½ **Blastofmagic**[90] 3608 5-9-3 **55** (tp) BenCurtis 2 45
(Adrian Brendan Joyce, Ire) *plld hrd in midfield: smooth hdwy over 2f out: rdn over 1f out: sn no ex* **8/1**

6023 **6** hd **Burmese Blazer (IRE)**[7] 6659 4-9-7 **59** (h) BenRobinson 7 48
(Jim Goldie) *wnt lft s: bhd: rdn and hdwy over 1f out: kpt on ins fnl f: nvr able to chal (jockey said gelding missed the break)* **4/1[1]**

3-00 **7** nse **Little Miss Lola**[66] 4493 5-8-4 **47** PaulaMuir(5) 13 36
(Lynn Siddall) *bhd: effrt and edgd rt over 1f out: kpt on fnl f: no imp* **40/1**

60-0 **8** 1 **Laoise (USA)**[9] 6608 3-8-11 **53** SeanDavis(3) 10 38
(Linda Perratt) *midfield: drvn along 2f out: no imp fnl f* **80/1**

5542 **9** 1¼ **Popping Corks (IRE)**[7] 6659 3-8-7 **49** ConnorMurtagh(3) 8 30
(Linda Perratt) *hmpd s: bhd: effrt and rdn on outside over 1f out: no further imp fnl f (jockey said filly suffered interference on leaving the stalls)* **16/1**

2362 **10** nk **Amazing Alba**[9] 6608 3-9-6 **59** (h) KevinStott 5 39
(Alistair Whillans) *pressed wnr to over 1f out: wknd fnl f* **6/1[3]**

020- **11** 1¼ **Griffin Street**[330] 8131 6-8-3 **46** AndrewBreslin(5) 11 21
(Alistair Whillans) *rrd as stall opened: bhd: drvn and shortlived effrt over 1f out: sn btn (jockey said gelding reared as the stalls opened)* **50/1**

0062 **12** 7 **Corton Lass**[10] 6574 4-8-7 **45** JoeFanning 1
(Keith Dalgleish) *bhd on outside: rdn over 2f out: wknd over 1f out* **18/1**

1m 0.38s (0.68) **Going Correction** 0.0s/f (Good)
WFA 3 from 4yo+ 1lb **12 Ran SP% 101.6**
Speed ratings (Par 101): **94,92,91,89,85 85,85,83,81,81 79,68**
CSF £75.13 CT £1208.23 TOTE £6.90: £2.30, £3.80, £5.20; EX 96.50 Trifecta £1135.00.
Owner Ladies And The Tramps **Bred** Paddy Twomey & Irish National Stud **Trained** Bawtry, S Yorks
■ Jeffrey Harris was withdrawn. Price at time of withdrawal 4-1jf. Rule 4 \n\x\x applies to all bets - deduction 20p in the poun

FOCUS
A fairly open-looking sprint handicap but the favourite was withdrawn late and a pillar-to-post victory.

6937 KEYLINE CIVILS SPECIALISTS H'CAP 1m 2y
7:00 (7:00) (Class 6) (0-65,65) 3-Y-O+

£3,428 (£1,020; £509; £400; £400; £400) **Stalls** Low

Form RPR

0060 **1** **Lagenda**[74] 4195 6-9-2 **55** JasonHart 2 61
(Liam Bailey) *trckd ldrs: swtchd lft and led over 1f out: hrd pressed ins fnl f: jst hld on (trainer could offer no explanation for the improved form, other than the gelding may have benefited from a 74 day break)* **18/1**

5045 **2** nse **Zeshov (IRE)**[10] 6573 8-9-12 **65** (p) RobbieDowney 10 72
(Rebecca Bastiman) *s.i.s: hld up: hdwy whn nt clr run briefly over 2f out: effrt and prom whn checked over 1f out: pressed wnr ins fnl f: kpt on: jst hld* **12/1**

6342 **3** ¾ **Muatadel**[8] 6628 6-9-12 **65** (v) KevinStott 1 69
(John Wainwright) *s.i.s: hld up in midfield: effrt over 2f out: kpt on ins fnl f: nt rch first two* **16/1**

0001 **4** ¾ **Echo Of Lightning**[10] 6572 9-9-11 **64** 4ex (p) BenCurtis 3 66
(Roger Fell) *led: rdn and hdd over 1f out: kpt on same pce fnl f* **7/2[1]**

3200 **5** 1 **Chinese Spirit (IRE)**[16] 6341 5-9-6 **62** RowanScott(3) 4 62
(Linda Perratt) *s.i.s: sn midfield: rdn over 2f out: kpt on fnl f: nt pce to chal* **13/2[2]**

1233 **6** ½ **The Big House (IRE)**[7] 6679 3-8-13 **60** SeanDavis(3) 5 58
(Adrian Nicholls) *cl up: effrt and ev ch briefly wl over 1f out: sn edgd lft: outpcd fnl f* **7/2[1]**

0100 **7** 1 **Archies Lad**[9] 6610 3-9-2 **60** PaddyMathers 9 56
(R Mike Smith) *s.i.s: bhd: rdn 3f out: hdwy over 1f out: nvr able to chal* **50/1**

0600 **8** hd **Gworn**[16] 6341 9-8-11 **55** (b) PaulaMuir(5) 6 51
(R Mike Smith) *hld up: rdn along over 2f out: sme late hdwy: nvr rchd ldrs* **14/1**

0020 **9** hd **Crazy Tornado (IRE)**[7] 6655 6-8-12 **51** (h) ConnorBeasley 13 47
(Keith Dalgleish) *midfield: drvn and outpcd over 2f out: n.d after* **20/1**

1313 **10** 2½ **Retirement Beckons**[7] 6655 4-9-0 **53** (h) BenRobinson 11 44
(Linda Perratt) *hld up: effrt whn nt clr run briefly over 2f out: rdn over 1f out: sn btn (jockey said gelding hung left throughout)* **7/1[3]**

2166 **11** 2 **Allux Boy (IRE)**[26] 5899 5-9-3 **61** (p) FayeMcManoman(5) 14 46
(Nigel Tinkler) *hld up: shortlived effrt on outside over 2f out: btn over 1f out* **10/1**

6005 **12** 4½ **Pumaflor (IRE)**[17] 6327 7-8-11 **50** (p) AndrewElliott 7 25
(Philip Kirby) *in tch: drvn and outpcd over 2f out: sn btn* **28/1**

0613 **13** 2½ **Geography Teacher (IRE)**[9] 6610 3-9-2 **60** (p) ShaneGray 12 28
(R Mike Smith) *hld up in tch on outside: rdn over 2f out: wknd wl over 1f out* **28/1**

3260 **14** 16 **Blank Canvas**[10] 6575 3-9-1 **59** JoeFanning 8 +
(Keith Dalgleish) *plld hrd: hld up in midfield on outside: struggling over 2f out: btn and eased over 1f out* **25/1**

1m 39.96s (-0.04) **Going Correction** 0.0s/f (Good)
WFA 3 from 4yo+ 5lb **14 Ran SP% 122.3**
Speed ratings (Par 101): **100,99,99,98,97 96,95,95,95,93 91,86,84,68**
CSF £209.20 CT £3600.75 TOTE £29.90: £7.40, £2.90, £4.10; EX 355.80 Trifecta £1865.70.
Owner Oakfield Racing **Bred** Joyce Wallsgrove **Trained** Middleham, N Yorks
■ Stewards' Enquiry : Robbie Downey two-day ban; misuse of whip (Sep 20-21)

FOCUS
An interesting mile handicap with another winner returning to form.

6938 EVERY RACE LIVE ON RACINGTV H'CAP 1m 4f 104y
7:30 (7:30) (Class 6) (0-65,63) 3-Y-O

£3,105 (£924; £461; £400; £400; £400) **Stalls** Low

Form RPR

0604 **1** **Iron Mike**[16] 6342 3-9-4 **60** (b[1]) ConnorBeasley 6 68
(Keith Dalgleish) *t.k.h: sn led: mde rest: rdn and clr fnl f: kpt on wl: unchal* **10/3[2]**

4433 **2** 2½ **Fantastic Ms Fox**[9] 6589 3-9-4 **63** ConnorMurtagh(3) 2 67
(Richard Fahey) *hld up: effrt whn nt clr run and angled lft over 2f out: chsd (clr) wnr over 1f out: kpt on: nt pce to chal* **9/2[3]**

3505 **3** 3¼ **Royal Countess**[50] 5096 3-7-12 **45** PaulaMuir(5) 4 44
(Lucy Normile) *in tch: drvn and outpcd 3f out: rallied and disp 2nd pl over 1f out: outpcd fnl f* **18/1**

5441 **4** 1¼ **Cuba Ruba**[9] 6612 3-9-7 **63** 6ex (p) DuranFentiman 3 60
(Tim Easterby) *t.k.h: chsd wnr to over 1f out: sn outpcd: btn ins fnl f* **11/2**

023 **5** 1¼ **Magrevio (IRE)**[9] 6612 3-9-0 **56** (p[1]) BenCurtis 7 51
(Liam Bailey) *chsd ldrs: rdn along over 2f out: wknd fnl f* **11/2**

5012 **6** 1¼ **Three Castles**[9] 6612 3-9-7 **63** JoeFanning 1 56+
(Keith Dalgleish) *t.k.h: hld up in tch: stdy hdwy over 2f out: pushed along whn n.m.r and outpcd over 1f out: btn fnl f* **5/2[1]**

001 **7** nse **Lizzie Loch**[53] 4983 3-8-8 **57** IzzyClifton(7) 5 50
(Alistair Whillans) *anticipated s and dwlt: t.k.h in rr: pushed along and outpcd over 2f out: drifted lft and kpt on fnl f: nvr on terms (jockey said filly anticipated the start and hit its head on the gates and as a result was slow away)* **10/1**

2m 43.04s (-1.46) **Going Correction** 0.0s/f (Good) **7 Ran SP% 115.0**
Speed ratings (Par 99): **104,102,100,99,98 97,97**
CSF £18.87 TOTE £4.10: £2.90, £2.60; EX 21.20 Trifecta £173.20.
Owner Weldspec Glasgow Limited **Bred** Clarendon Farm **Trained** Carluke, S Lanarks

FOCUS
Yet another oddly run race where the doubtful stayer appeared to pull too hard yet kept on strongly.
T/Plt: £1,774.70 to a £1 stake. Pool: £41,329.69 - 17 winning units T/Qpdt: £67.70 to a £1 stake. Pool: £6,554.33 - 71.58 winning units **Richard Young**

The Form Book Flat 2019, Raceform Ltd, Newbury, RG14 5SJ

6660 NEWCASTLE (A.W) (L-H)

Friday, September 6

OFFICIAL GOING: Tapeta: standard to slow

Wind: Fresh against

6939 ESH CONSTRUCTION LTD H'CAP — 1m 4f 98y (Tp)

1:30 (1:30) (Class 6) (0-65,66) 4-Y-O+

£2,781 (£827; £413; £300; £300; £300) **Stalls** High

Form — RPR

3403 **1** **Ad Libitum**[7] 6663 4-9-6 **63**.................(p) BenCurtis 10 69+
(Roger Fell) *trckd ldrs: hdwy 4f out: led 2f out: jnd and rdn over 1f out: drvn ins fnl f: kpt on wl towards fin* **9/5**[1]

3532 **2** ½ **Croeso Cymraeg**[23] 6077 5-9-7 **64**.................(h) RaulDaSilva 2 69
(James Evans) *hld up towards rr: stdy hdwy on inner over 4f out: swtchd rt wl over 2f out: chal on bit 1 1/2f out: rdn ent fnl f: sn drvn and ev ch tl no ex last 75yds* **9/4**[2]

4405 **3** ¾ **Majestic Stone (IRE)**[24] 6059 5-8-7 **50** oh2.................CliffordLee 3 54
(Julie Camacho) *dwlt and in rr: hdwy 4f out: chsd ldrs 2f out: rdn wl over 1f out: styd on wl fnl f* **4/1**[3]

14-4 **4** ¾ **Lyford (IRE)**[28] 5905 4-8-12 **55**.................(p[1]) PJMcDonald 4 58
(Alistair Whillans) *trckd ldrs: hdwy 4f out: cl up over 2f out: sn pushed along: rdn wl over 1f out: kpt on same pce u.p fnl f* **7/1**

0 **5** nk **Smart Lass (IRE)**[55] 4914 4-8-7 **50** oh5.................(p) JamieGormley 8 53
(Iain Jardine) *chsd ldr: rdn along and cl up over 2f out: drvn and sltly outpcd over 1f out: kpt on u.p ins fnl f* **40/1**

0005 **6** 1 **Accessor (IRE)**[22] 6115 4-8-12 **55**.................JoeFanning 11 56
(Michael Wigham) *stdd s and hld up in rr: hdwy 4f out: chsd ldrs on outer and rdn along 2f out: drvn and kpt on fnl f* **11/1**

000- **7** 1¾ **Crushed (IRE)**[308] 8113 5-9-7 **64**.................(t[1]) DougieCostello 9 62
(Mark Walford) *chsd ldrs: pushed along over 3f out: rdn over 2f out: drvn over 1f out: sn one pce* **66/1**

0-04 **8** 4 **Chant (IRE)**[38] 5513 9-9-5 **62**.................RoystonFfrench 7 54
(Ann Duffield) *led: pushed along over 3f out: rdn and hdd 2f out: grad wknd* **25/1**

0/60 **9** 35 **Abouttimeyoutoldme**[45] 5277 5-8-2 **50** oh5.................AndrewBreslin(5) 1
(Alistair Whillans) *chsd ldrs: pushed along 1/2-way: sn lost pl and bhd* **150/1**

2m 43.93s (2.83) **Going Correction** +0.625s/f (Slow) 9 Ran SP% **115.8**
Speed ratings (Par 101): **105,104,104,103,103 102,101,98,75**
CSF £5.95 CT £13.39 TOTE £2.60: £1.30, £1.80, £1.10; EX 7.20 Trifecta £18.90.
Owner The Roses Partnership & R G Fell **Bred** Rabbah Bloodstock Limited **Trained** Nawton, N Yorks
■ Stewards' Enquiry : Raul Da Silva two-day ban: used whip incorrect place (Sep 20-21)

FOCUS
The going was standard to slow.\n\x\x Stalls - straight course, centre; 1m2f/1m4f, outside; 2m, inside.\\n\x\x An ordinary handicap which saw the fancied horses dominate the finish. The winner was very determined. He's rated in line with this year's better form.

6940 MOTT MACDONALD BENTLEY H'CAP — 1m 2f 42y (Tp)

2:05 (2:05) (Class 5) (0-75,75) 3-Y-O+

£3,428 (£1,020; £509; £300; £300; £300) **Stalls** High

Form — RPR

5423 **1** **Skerryvore**[34] 5654 3-9-2 **73**.................HollieDoyle 13 81+
(James Fanshawe) *prom: trckd ldr 3f out: effrt 2f out: led 1 1/2f out: sn rdn: drvn and kpt on strly fnl f* **3/1**[1]

3305 **2** ¾ **Algaffaal (USA)**[13] 6460 4-9-10 **75**.................(p) BenRobinson 9 80
(Brian Ellison) *in tch: hdwy over 3f out: trckd ldrs over 2f out: rdn over 1f out: chsd wnr and drvn ins fnl f: no imp towards fin* **4/1**[3]

6516 **3** ½ **Debbonair (IRE)**[25] 6022 3-8-9 **66**.................(b) JackMitchell 7 70
(Hugo Palmer) *trckd ldrs: hdwy 3f out: rdn along wl over 1f out: drvn and kpt on fnl f* **8/1**

2345 **4** nk **Lightning Attack**[19] 6258 3-9-3 **74**.................(p) JackGarritty 14 77
(Richard Fahey) *hld up towards rr: hdwy on outer 3f out: pushed along 2f out: rdn over 1f out: chsd ldrs: kpt on ins fnl f* **12/1**

355 **5** ½ **Flash Point (IRE)**[24] 6034 3-8-13 **70**.................CamHardie 8 72
(Tracy Waggott) *led: pushed along over 2f out: sn rdn and qckn d (jockey said gelding hung right-handed under pressure)* **25/1**

5021 **6** ½ **Home Before Dusk**[7] 6663 4-9-6 **71** 5ex.................(p) JoeFanning 4 72+
(Keith Dalgleish) *t.k.h: hld up in rr on inner: effrt 3f out: sn swtchd rt to outer and rdn wl over 1f out: kpt on fnl f: n.d* **7/2**[2]

00-0 **7** 1 **Major Snugfit**[97] 2096 3-8-9 **66**.................(w) NathanEvans 2 65
(Michael Easterby) *trckd ldr: pushed along over 3f out: rdn wl over 2f out: drvn wl over 1f out: kpt on one pce* **28/1**

-306 **8** ¾ **Snowdon**[18] 6280 4-9-8 **73**.................(p) AndrewMullen 12 71
(Michael Dods) *t.k.h: trckd ldrs on outer: hdwy 3f out: rdn along to chse ldrs over 2f out: drvn wl over 1f out: sn one pce* **40/1**

0200 **9** nk **Elixsoft (IRE)**[48] 5178 4-9-8 **73**.................(p) PhilDennis 3 70
(Roger Fell) *t.k.h: hld up towards rr: sme hdwy on inner over 3f out: rdn along over 2f out: n.d* **33/1**

3000 **10** 1½ **Najashee (IRE)**[16] 6341 5-8-9 **65**.................(v) PaulaMuir(5) 5 59
(Roger Fell) *dwlt: a in rr* **14/1**

0560 **11** nk **Rashdan (FR)**[13] 6460 4-9-8 **73**.................JamieGormley 10 66
(Iain Jardine) *a towards rr* **8/1**

-400 **12** 1½ **Coup De Gold (IRE)**[31] 5792 3-8-3 **67**.................AledBeech(7) 11 58
(David Thompson) *a towards rr* **100/1**

2m 16.81s (6.41) **Going Correction** +0.625s/f (Slow)
WFA 3 from 4yo+ 6lb 12 Ran SP% **117.5**
Speed ratings (Par 103): **99,98,98,97,97 96,96,95,95,94 93,92**
CSF £14.08 CT £87.39 TOTE £3.10: £1.60, £1.30, £3.60; EX 13.30 Trifecta £73.90.
Owner Dr Catherine Wills **Bred** St Clare Hall Stud **Trained** Newmarket, Suffolk
■ Briardale was withdrawn. Price at time of withdrawal 20-1. Rule 4 does not apply.

FOCUS
Ordinary fare. They did not seem to go much of a gallop with the result that there were plenty pulling for their heads. The winner benefited from being ridden close to the pace. The form's rated around the third, fourth and sixth.

6941 FASTFLOW PIPELINE SERVICES LTD NOVICE STKS — 1m 5y (Tp)

2:40 (2:41) (Class 5) 3-Y-O+ **£3,428** (£1,020; £509; £254) **Stalls** Centre

Form — RPR

3 **1** **Shauyra (IRE)**[18] 6290 3-9-0 0.................PaulHanagan 6 78+
(William Haggas) *trckd ldrs: swtchd lft and hdwy to chal over 1f out: shkn up to ld ent fnl f and sn hung rt: sn qcknd clr: readily* **1/3**[1]

503 **2** 4 **Mr Carpenter (IRE)**[17] 6315 3-9-5 80.................PJMcDonald 2 75
(David Lanigan) *prom: cl up 1/2-way: led 2 1/2f out: jnd and rdn over 1f out: hdd ent fnl f: sn swtchd lft: kpt on: no ch w wnr* **9/4**[2]

3 3¼ **Ideal Destiny** 3-9-0 0.................CliffordLee 7 62
(Karen Tutty) *cl up: pushed along over 2f out: rdn wl over 1f out: wknd appr fnl f* **33/1**[3]

4 ¾ **Battle Commander** 3-9-5 0.................JackMitchell 1 65
(Olly Williams) *dwlt and green in rr: hdwy 2f out: rdn and kpt on wl fnl f* **66/1**

5 16 **Kuredu** 3-8-12 0.................VictorSantos(7) 3 28
(Julie Camacho) *green: slowly away and a outpcd in rr* **33/1**[3]

6 **6** nse **Its Toytown**[34] 5669 3-8-12 0.................AledBeech(7) 4 28
(R Mike Smith) *hmpd s: a towards rr: outpcd and bhd fnl 2f* **100/1**

0 **7** 6 **Alltami (IRE)**[69] 4358 3-9-5 0.................RoystonFfrench 5 14
(Steph Hollinshead) *wnt lft s: led: pushed along 3f out: rdn and hdd 2 1/2f out: sn wknd* **100/1**

1m 45.26s (6.66) **Going Correction** +0.625s/f (Slow) 7 Ran SP% **115.1**
Speed ratings (Par 103): **91,87,83,83,67 66,60**
CSF £1.39 TOTE £1.10: £1.10, £1.40; EX 1.50 Trifecta £4.90.
Owner Somerville Lodge Limited **Bred** Airlie Stud **Trained** Newmarket, Suffolk

FOCUS
A weak novice which, as expected, provided easy pickings for the hot favourite. The form's probably held back by the third and fourth.

6942 GOWLAND & DAWSON LTD "BLAYDON RACES" NURSERY H'CAP — 1m 5y (Tp)

3:15 (3:15) (Class 2) 2-Y-O **£14,006** (£4,194; £2,097; £1,048; £524) **Stalls** Centre

Form — RPR

3311 **1** **Gallaside (FR)**[31] 5781 2-9-7 **84**.................HollieDoyle 2 87
(Archie Watson) *slt ld: pushed along wl over 1f out: sn jnd and rdn: edgd rt ins fnl f: sn hdd narrowly: drvn and rallied gamely to ld nr line* **10/11**[1]

6351 **2** hd **Bravo Faisal (IRE)**[29] 5853 2-9-1 **78**.................PaulHanagan 5 81
(Richard Fahey) *trckd ldrs: hdwy over 2f out: cl up wl over 1f out: sn rdn and ev ch whn bmpd ins fnl f: sn drvn: n.m.r and kpt on wl towards fin: fin dead-heat 2nd: awrdd 2nd outrt* **6/1**[3]

4113 **3** dht **Rich Belief**[21] 6184 2-9-3 **83**.................JaneElliott(3) 6 86
(James Bethell) *hld up in rr: hdwy on wd outside wl over 1f out: rdn to chal ent fnl f: sn slt ld and edgd lft: kpt on: hdd and no ex nr line: fin dead-heat 2nd: disqualified and plcd 3rd* **7/1**

0431 **4** 5 **Arthur's Court (IRE)**[25] 6020 2-9-3 **80**.................JackMitchell 3 72
(Hugo Palmer) *trckd ldng pair: effrt and pushed along over 2f out: sn rdn and wknd over 1f out* **11/4**[2]

513 **5** 3 **Anniemation (IRE)**[26] 5992 2-9-0 **77**.................JackGarritty 4 62
(Stella Barclay) *cl up: pushed along over 2f out: sn rdn and wknd* **20/1**

1m 44.45s (5.85) **Going Correction** +0.625s/f (Slow) 5 Ran SP% **110.6**
Speed ratings (Par 101): **95,94,94,89,86**
WIN: 1.90 Gallaside; PL: 1.60 Gallaside 2.00 Bravo Faisal; EX: 9.30; CSF: 6.99 CSF £6.99 TOTE £1.90: £1.60, £2.00; EX 9.30 Trifecta £21.30.
Owner Apple Tree Stud **Bred** Safsaf Canarias Srl & Mme Felix Miranda-Suarez **Trained** Upper Lambourn, W Berks

FOCUS
A valuable nursery which produced a three-way thrust to the line. The winner completed his hat-trick in tenacious fashion and the form's rated around the third.

6943 NORTHUMBRIAN WATER GROUP/EBF NOVICE STKS (PLUS 10 RACE) — 6f (Tp)

3:50 (3:52) (Class 4) 2-Y-O **£4,787** (£1,424; £711; £355) **Stalls** Centre

Form — RPR

01 **1** **Ascension**[23] 6078 2-9-8 0.................JackMitchell 11 83+
(Roger Varian) *prom: led after 2f: rdn clr jst ins fnl f: readily* **2/7**[1]

2 1½ **Gravity Force** 2-9-2 0.................CliffordLee 10 73+
(K R Burke) *towards rr and sn pushed along: rdn along 1/2-way: hdwy u.p over 1f out: styd on wl fnl f* **12/1**

3 2½ **Art Power (IRE)** 2-9-2 0.................PhilDennis 14 65+
(Tim Easterby) *trckd ldng pair: hdwy and cl up over 2f out: rdn and ev ch over 1f out: drvn ent fnl f: kpt on same pce* **17/2**[2]

60 **4** ½ **Aysar (IRE)**[35] 5624 2-9-2 0.................HollieDoyle 7 64
(Ed Dunlop) *in tch: hdwy over 2f out: rdn along wl over 1f out: sn edgd lft and kpt on fnl f (jockey said colt hung left-handed under pressure)* **18/1**

5 nk **Noble Dawn (GER)** 2-8-11 0.................DougieCostello 2 58
(Ivan Furtado) *towards rr: hdwy over 2f out: sn rdn and kpt on fnl f* **25/1**

6 1½ **Full House** 2-9-2 0.................SamJames 12 58
(John Davies) *chsd ldrs: rdn along over 2f out: sn drvn and wknd* **66/1**

0 **7** ¾ **Captain Corelli (IRE)**[29] 5845 2-9-2 0.................CamHardie 6 56
(Julie Camacho) *midfield: hdwy and in tch over 2f out: sn rdn along and no imp* **80/1**

0 **8** ¾ **Jems Bond**[16] 6337 2-9-2 0.................NathanEvans 5 54
(Alan Brown) *towards rr: hdwy on outer 1/2-way: rdn along 2f out: wknd over 1f out* **150/1**

0 **9** 2 **Panist (IRE)**[46] 5234 2-9-2 0.................PJMcDonald 9 48
(Mark Johnston) *led 2f: prom: rdn along wl over 2f out: sn wknd* **10/1**[3]

0 **10** 1 **Somekindasuperstar**[16] 6336 2-8-11 0.................RoystonFfrench 13 40
(Paul Collins) *a in rr* **150/1**

0 **11** ½ **Apples Acre (IRE)**[95] 3419 2-8-11 0.................AndrewMullen 8 38
(Ben Haslam) *midfield: rdn along over 2f out: n.d* **33/1**

0 **12** 7 **Max L (IRE)**[9] 6585 2-9-2 0.................PaulHanagan 1 22
(Alistair Whillans) *dwlt: a in rr* **66/1**

13 2¼ **Ochre Riu (IRE)** 2-9-2 0.................LewisEdmunds 3 15
(Ivan Furtado) *dwlt: a in rr* **50/1**

14 8 **El Jefe (IRE)** 2-9-2 0.................JackGarritty 4
(Brian Ellison) *green: sn outpcd and a bhd (jockey said gelding ran green)* **40/1**

1m 15.7s (3.20) **Going Correction** +0.625s/f (Slow) 14 Ran SP% **127.1**
Speed ratings (Par 97): **103,101,97,97,96 94,93,92,89,88 87,78,75,64**
CSF £5.43 TOTE £1.30: £1.10, £2.10, £2.20; EX 6.40 Trifecta £23.40.
Owner Highclere T'Bred Racing - Benedict Allen **Bred** Highclere Stud & Partners **Trained** Newmarket, Suffolk

FOCUS
A run-of-the-mill novice, but the winner may prove above average and several of the newcomers shaped with promise. Those down the field will govern the form in time.

6944 TURNER & TOWNSEND LTD NOVICE STKS — 5f (Tp)

4:20 (4:24) (Class 5) 3-Y-O+ **£3,428** (£1,020; £509; £254) **Stalls** Centre

Form — RPR

0-3 **1** **Buniann (IRE)**[20] 6206 3-9-5 0.................PaulHanagan 6 72
(Paul Midgley) *trckd ldrs: hdwy wl over 1f out: rdn to chal appr fnl f: sn drvn: led last 75yds: kpt on wl* **6/1**[3]

022 **2** *nk* **Marvel**[20] 6206 3-9-5 68.. CamHardie 8 71
(Julie Camacho) *trckd ldrs: hdwy over 2f out: led wl over 1f out: jnd and rdn jst over 1f out: drvn ins fnl f: hdd and no ex last 75yds* **9/1**

5200 **3** *3 ¼* **Kyllachy Warrior (IRE)**[76] 4128 3-9-5 71......................(w) PhilDennis 3 59
(Lawrence Mullaney) *hld up in rr: hdwy 2f out: rdn over 1f out: chsd ldng pair ins fnl f: no imp* **4/1**[2]

0000 **4** *2 ¼* **Rangefield Express (IRE)**[28] 5914 3-9-5 50.................(b) SamJames 4 51
(Geoffrey Harker) *led: pushed along and hdd over 2f out: sn rdn: kpt on u.p fnl f* **80/1**

3 **5** *½* **Bithiah (IRE)**[10] 6561 3-9-0 0..(t[1]) JackMitchell 5 44
(Ismail Mohammed) *cl up: led over 2f out: rdn and hdd wl over 1f out: sn drvn and wknd fnl f* **22/1**

3420 **6** *3* **Dream Of Honour (IRE)**[21] 6176 3-9-5 68................(bt) NathanEvans 1 38
(Tim Easterby) *chsd ldrs: rdn along over 2f out: sn drvn and outpcd* **6/1**[3]

7 *3 ¾* **Critical Voltage (IRE)** 3-9-5 0.............................. PJMcDonald 2 25
(Richard Fahey) *dwlt: sn chsng ldrs: pushed along 3f out: edgd lft 1/2-way: rdn and hung bdly lft to far rails 2f out: sn bhd (jockey said colt hung left-handed)* **5/4**[1]

4 **8** *1* **Eloquent Style (IRE)**[27] 5969 3-9-5 0.....................(p[1]) DougieCostello 7 21
(Ivan Furtado) *dwlt: sn chsng ldrs: rdn along over 2f out: sn wknd and bhd (jockey said colt was slowly away)* **12/1**

1m 1.57s (2.07) **Going Correction** +0.625s/f (Slow) 8 Ran SP% **116.3**
Speed ratings (Par 103): **108,107,102,98,97 93,87,85**
CSF £58.88 TOTE £6.00: £1.60, £2.50, £1.60; EX 60.90 Trifecta £472.90.
Owner Carl Chapman & Partner **Bred** Shadwell Estate Company Limited **Trained** Westow, N Yorks

FOCUS
Not the strongest of novice contests, but the first two should have a future in sprint handicaps. The runner-up is rated to form, with the winner progressing.

6945 WATERAID H'CAP 7f 14y (Tp)
4:55 (4:58) (Class 6) (0-60,60) 3-Y-O+

£2,781 (£827; £413; £300; £300; £300) **Stalls** Centre

Form RPR

2003 **1** **Ghathanfar (IRE)**[18] 6276 3-8-13 **56**................................... CamHardie 10 65+
(Tracy Waggott) *trckd ldr: cl up 1/2-way: led over 2f out: rdn clr wl over 1f out: kpt on strly* **9/1**

4125 **2** *3* **Firsteen**[9] 6609 3-9-3 **60**.. PaulHanagan 11 62
(Alistair Whillans) *hld up: hdwy over 2f out: rdn over 1f out: drvn ins fnl f: kpt on to take 2nd nr line (jockey said filly was denied a clear run 1 1/2f out)* **4/1**[2]

3-34 **3** *hd* **Midnight In Havana**[127] 2337 3-9-1 **58**...................... RoystonFfrench 3 59
(Bryan Smart) *trckd ldrs: pushed along 2f out: rdn to chse wnr over 1f out: drvn ins fnl f: kpt on same pce* **8/1**

2445 **4** *1 ¼* **The Bull (IRE)**[7] 6666 4-9-1 **54**................................(p) AndrewMullen 8 54
(Ben Haslam) *hld up towards rr: pushed along 2f out: swtchd rt and rdn: over 1f out: kpt on wl fnl f (jockey said gelding was denied a clear run 1 1/2f out)* **11/2**[3]

00-1 **5** *nk* **Scandinavian Lady (IRE)**[224] 406 3-9-1 **58**.............. DougieCostello 12 55
(Ivan Furtado) *trckd ldrs: rdn along 2f out: drvn over 1f out: grad wknd* **25/1**

0060 **6** *½* **Gunmaker (IRE)**[15] 6373 5-8-8 **54**............................... AledBeech[(7)] 5 52
(Ruth Carr) *dwlt and towards rr: hdwy 2f out: sn rdn and kpt on fnl f* **11/1**

3000 **7** *½* **Extrasolar**[3] 6826 9-9-4 **57**...(t) CliffordLee 9 54
(Geoffrey Harker) *chsd ldrs: rdn along over 2f out: sn drvn and wknd* **50/1**

004 **8** *1 ¾* **A Hundred Echoes**[18] 6283 3-9-0 **57**..........................(p[1]) JackMitchell 2 47
(Roger Varian) *dwlt and towards rr: hdwy 1/2-way: rdn along and in tch: over 2f out: sn wknd* **14/1**

4042 **9** *nk* **Barbarosa (IRE)**[11] 6540 3-9-1 **58**................................... PhilDennis 4 48
(Michael Herrington) *hld up: hdwy 3f out: n.m.r and rdn 2f out: sn btn* **11/4**[1]

-000 **10** *3 ½* **Crimson Skies (IRE)**[16] 6341 4-9-4 **57**........................ SamJames 13 40
(John Davies) *led: rdn along and hdd wl over 2f out: sn drvn and wknd* **50/1**

5605 **11** *nk* **No More Regrets (IRE)**[21] 6181 3-8-10 **60**.................. ZakWheatley[(7)] 6 40
(Patrick Morris) *hld up towards rr: effrt and sme hdwy 3f out: rdn along over 2f out: sn wknd* **25/1**

0040 **12** *5* **Dirchill (IRE)**[70] 4335 5-9-7 **60**...............................(b) NathanEvans 14 30
(David Thompson) *trckd ldrs: hdwy over 2f out: rdn wl over 1f out: sn drvn and wknd* **20/1**

3000 **13** *2 ½* **Paradise Papers**[21] 6176 3-9-3 **60**............................ PJMcDonald 1 21
(David Barron) *chsd ldrs: rdn along on outer over 2f out: sn wknd* **22/1**

1m 30.09s (3.89) **Going Correction** +0.625s/f (Slow)
WFA 3 from 4yo+ 4lb 13 Ran SP% **118.9**
Speed ratings (Par 101): **102,98,98,96,96 96,95,93,93,89 88,83,80**
CSF £41.04 CT £314.76 TOTE £9.90: £2.90, £1.60, £2.80; EX 55.20 Trifecta £509.70.
Owner W J Laws **Bred** Shadwell Estate Company Limited **Trained** Spennymoor, Co Durham

FOCUS
An open-looking handicap, but it was won in decisive fashion by an AW debutant who showed improved form.

T/Plt: £6.80 to a £1 stake. Pool: £50,705.37 - 5,422.12 winning units T/Qpdt: £3.50 to a £1 stake. Pool: £4,188.68 - 872.60 winning units **Joe Rowntree**

6946 - 6947a (Foreign Racing) - See Raceform Interactive

6911 ASCOT (R-H)
Saturday, September 7

OFFICIAL GOING: Good to firm (rnd 7.9, str 8.5)
Wind: Moderate, across Weather: Fine but cloudy

6948 ITALIAN TOURIST BOARD BRITISH EBF NOVICE STKS (PLUS 10 RACE) 7f
1:35 (1:36) (Class 4) 2-Y-O **£6,727** (£2,002; £1,000; £500) **Stalls** High

Form RPR

1 **Cherokee Trail (USA)** 2-9-5 0.................................... KieranO'Neill 2 80+
(John Gosden) *quite str: sltly on toes; plld hrd: pressed ldng pair: rdn to ld over 1f out and rn green: styd on wl fnl f* **7/2**[2]

60 **2** *¾* **What An Angel**[50] 5131 2-9-5 0.................................... DaneO'Neill 5 78
(Richard Hannon) *looked wl; pressed ldr: rdn to chal wl over 1f out: chsd wnr after: styd on but a hld fnl f* **25/1**

3 *½* **Zegalo (IRE)** 2-9-5 0.. CharlieBennett 9 77+
(Roger Varian) *quite tall: ly: looked wl; chsd ldrs: shkn up and outpcd 2f out: styd on wl fnl f: tk 3rd last 100yds and clsd nr fin* **16/1**

4 *2* **Hlaitan** 2-9-5 0.. JasonWatson 7 72+
(Hugo Palmer) *quite str; dwlt: hld up in last pair: shkn up 2f out: prog over 1f out: rdn and kpt on to take 4th nr fin* **8/1**

6433 **5** *nk* **Ropey Guest**[17] 6352 2-9-5 99.................................... TomQueally 8 71
(George Margarson) *led: rdn 2f out: hdd over 1f out: fdd fnl f (trainer said colt was unsuited by making the running on this occasion)* **5/4**[1]

6 *1* **Macho Boy (IRE)** 2-9-5 0.. MartinDwyer 4 68
(Brian Meehan) *workmanlike; in tch towards rr: urged along over 2f out: one pce and no real prog* **16/1**

05 **7** *shd* **Ruby Power (IRE)**[24] 6079 2-9-0 0................................ RossaRyan 10 63
(Richard Hannon) *t.k.h: trckd ldrs: shkn up 2f out: sn outpcd: no real hdwy fnl f* **40/1**

8 *1 ¼* **Thrill Seeker (IRE)** 2-9-5 0...................................... TomMarquand 1 65
(William Haggas) *str: gd-bodied: bit bkwrd; s.s: a in last: shkn up and no prog 2f out* **4/1**[3]

1m 29.28s (1.78) **Going Correction** +0.15s/f (Good) 8 Ran SP% **115.8**
Speed ratings (Par 97): **95,94,93,91,90 89,89,88**
CSF £81.80 TOTE £3.80: £1.50, £3.50, £4.70; EX 79.00 Trifecta £1047.10.
Owner M Tabor, D Smith & Mrs J Magnier **Bred** Orpendale, Chelston & Wynatt **Trained** Newmarket, Suffolk

FOCUS
A good juvenile novice contest on paper, won in 2015 by subsequent Group 2 German 2000 Guineas winner Knife Edge. It turned into a sprint though and the overall strength of the form is questionable.

6949 ROYAL FORESTERS BRITISH EBF FILLIES' NOVICE STKS (PLUS 10 RACE) 7f 213y(R)
2:10 (2:10) (Class 4) 2-Y-O **£6,727** (£2,002; £1,000; £500) **Stalls** Low

Form RPR

3 **1** **Pocket Square**[18] 6322 2-9-0 0.................................... JasonWatson 3 83+
(Roger Charlton) *athletic: looked wl; trckd ldng pair: wnt 2nd over 2f out: clsd qckly to ld over 1f out: shkn up and drew clr: comf* **9/4**[2]

033 **2** *3 ¼* **Expensive Dirham**[8] 6675 2-9-0 74.............................. DaneO'Neill 8 76
(Mark Johnston) *quite str; led fr wdst draw: set mod pce tl kicked on over 2f out: hdd over 1f out: one pce over 1f out: hld on for 2nd* **8/1**

3 *¾* **Red Line Alexander (IRE)** 2-9-0 0............................ TomMarquand 1 74+
(Simon Crisford) *leggy: athletic: sltly on toes; slowly away: hld up in last pair: prog 2f out: styd on fnl f to take 3rd nr fin* **11/2**[3]

4 *shd* **Anastarsia (IRE)** 2-9-0 0.. WilliamBuick 2 74+
(John Gosden) *leggy: athletic; hld up in 5th: rdn whn pce lifted over 2f out: chsd clr ldng pair over 1f out: kpt on but lost 3rd nr fin* **6/4**[1]

5 *¾* **Bharani Star (GER)** 2-9-0 0...................................... JFEgan 7 72+
(Peter Chapple-Hyam) *str: sltly on toes: looked wl; trapped out wd: in tch: rdn and prog 2f out: styd on to press for a pl nr fin* **14/1**

6 *7* **Kavadi** 2-9-0 0.. RobHornby 5 57
(Hughie Morrison) *unfurnished; chsd ldng trio to 2f out: wknd* **33/1**

7 *1 ¼* **So Special** 2-9-0 0.. KieranShoemark 6 54
(William Muir) *chsd ldr to over 2f out: wknd wl over 1f out* **25/1**

8 *1 ½* **Al Gaiya (FR)** 2-9-0 0.. RossaRyan 4 51
(Richard Hannon) *quite tall: ly: bit bkwrd; a in last pair: struggling 3f out: sn no ch* **20/1**

1m 44.44s (3.84) **Going Correction** +0.15s/f (Good) 8 Ran SP% **115.5**
Speed ratings (Par 94): **86,82,82,81,81 74,72,71**
CSF £20.10 TOTE £2.60: £1.20, £1.90, £1.60; EX 16.70 Trifecta £85.70.
Owner K Abdullah **Bred** Juddmonte Farms Ltd **Trained** Beckhampton, Wilts

FOCUS
Add 10yds. A decent juvenile fillies' novice contest won in 2017 by subsequent Group 3 Nell Gwyn winner Soliloquy. The winning time was modest from off a slow gallop, but the second-favourite progressed nicely to win well. Improved form from the winner, with the runner-up the key.

6950 CUNARD H'CAP 7f
2:45 (2:47) (Class 2) 3-Y-O+

£49,800 (£11,184; £3,728; £1,864; £936) **Stalls** High

Form RPR

0021 **1** **Salute The Soldier (GER)**[14] 6445 4-9-1 **101**.................. AdamKirby 2 109
(Clive Cox) *mde all: 2 l clr and rdn over 1f out: edgd lft after: hotly pressed nr fin: jst hld on* **10/1**

462 **2** *nk* **Tabarrak (IRE)**[14] 6445 6-9-10 **110**.............................. RossaRyan 9 117
(Richard Hannon) *looked wl; trckd ldrs: rdn to chse wnr over 1f out: styd on fnl f: clsd nr fin: jst hld* **8/1**[3]

0642 **2** *dht* **Ripp Orf (IRE)**[21] 6214 5-8-8 **94**..............................(t) JasonWatson 15 101+
(David Elsworth) *hld up wl in rr: rdn 2f out: no real prog over 1f out: styd on v strly fnl f: jst too late* **7/2**[1]

2135 **4** *nk* **Escobar (IRE)**[14] 6470 5-9-4 **104**............................(t) RobbieDowney 12 110
(David O'Meara) *sweating; hld up in midfield: rdn 2f out: prog over 1f out: styd on ins fnl f: jst hld* **10/1**

3401 **5** *½* **Spanish City**[13] 6517 6-8-4 **97**.............................(p[1]) MarcoGhiani[(7)] 3 102
(Roger Varian) *looked wl; trckd wnr: rdn 2f out: lost 2nd over 1f out: kpt on same pce fnl f* **7/1**[2]

0005 **6** *1* **Another Batt (IRE)**[15] 6391 4-8-2 **95**........................ AngusVilliers[(7)] 1 97
(Richard Hughes) *awkward s: t.k.h and sn chsd ldrs: rdn 2f out: kpt on same pce and nvr able to chal* **16/1**

2006 **7** *½* **Kimifive (IRE)**[14] 6445 4-8-5 **91**.................................... JimmyQuinn 16 92
(Joseph Tuite) *wl in tch in midfield: rdn and prog to chse ldrs over 1f out: one pce fnl f* **16/1**

4400 **8** *shd* **Arbalet (IRE)**[16] 6376 4-8-9 **95**...............................(bt[1]) JFEgan 13 96
(Hugo Palmer) *t.k.h: pressed ldrs: rdn and jst sing to lose pl whn impeded over 1f out: kpt on same pce fnl f (jockey said colt suffered interference in running)* **10/1**

0100 **9** *hd* **Blackheath**[16] 6376 4-8-2 **91** ow2............................ MeganNicholls[(3)] 14 91
(Ed Walker) *dwlt: wl in rr: rdn and no prog 2f out: styd on ins fnl f but nvr able to threaten (vet said gelding lost it's left fore shoe)* **12/1**

0001 **10** *hd* **Pogo (IRE)**[15] 6425 3-9-1 **105**.................................. KieranShoemark 10 102
(Charles Hills) *chsd ldrs: rdn 2f out: one pce and no imp over 1f out* **20/1**

05 **11** *¾* **Sanaadh**[14] 6445 6-8-6 **92**...(t) NickyMackay 7 89
(Michael Wigham) *looked wl; chsd ldrs: rdn and nt qckn over 1f out: one pce and no imp after* **12/1**

0013 **12** *nse* **Rum Runner**[21] 6207 4-8-2 **88**..................................... MartinDwyer 11 85
(Richard Hannon) *looked wl; s.s: hld up in last pair: rdn and prog over 1f out: kpt on but nvr enough pce to threaten* **20/1**

3261 **13** *1 ½* **Breanski**[21] 6207 5-8-1 **87**.. RoystonFfrench 4 80
(Jedd O'Keeffe) *hld up wl in rr: rdn 2f out: stl last 1f out: styd on fnl 150yds: n.d* **20/1**

0221 **14** *1* **Ventura Ocean (IRE)**[35] 5685 3-8-4 **94**........................ KieranO'Neill 17 83
(Richard Fahey) *prom: rdn and nt qckn 2f out: wkng whn squeezed out ins fnl f* **14/1**

042 **15** *hd* **Shady McCoy (USA)**[42] 5416 9-8-0 **89**.................... DarraghKeenan[(3)] 6 79
(Ian Williams) *hld up wl in rr: shkn up and no prog 2f out: wknd over 1f out* **33/1**

4303 **16** ½ **Fanaar (IRE)**[15] 6425 3-8-13 **103**....................................(bt) DaneO'Neill 5 90
(William Haggas) *hld up in rr: rdn and no prog 2f out: n.d after* **12/1**
1m 27.02s (-0.48) **Going Correction** +0.15s/f (Good)
WFA 3 from 4yo+ 4lb **16** Ran SP% **131.8**
Speed ratings (Par 109): **108,107,107,107,106 105,105,104,104,104 103,103,101,100,100 99**
WIN: 11.30 Salute The Soldier; PL: 2.10 Tabarrak, 2.60 Escobar, 1.40 Ripp Orf, 2.80 Salute The Soldier; EX: STS/T 55.20, STS/RO 33.10; CSF: STS/T 45.12, STS/RO 23.00; TC: STS/T 181.60, STS/RO 163.55; TF: STS/T 331.20, STS/RO 280.90;.
Owner Mr & Mrs P Hargreaves & A D Spence **Bred** A Spence **Trained** Lambourn, Berks

FOCUS
A good quality handicap. The race developed centrally in one big group and the favourite got going just too late towards the stands' side of the pack. The winner confirmed form with the runner-up.

6951 RITZ CLUB BRITISH EBF PREMIER FILLIES' H'CAP 1m (S)
3:20 (3:20) (Class 2) (0-100,96) 3-Y-O+ **£19,407** (£5,775; £2,886; £1,443) **Stalls** High

Form RPR
1-31 **1** **She's Got You**[77] 4119 3-8-11 **86**.............................. KieranO'Neill 6 95+
(John Gosden) *sltly on toes; trckd ldr: rdn to ld over 1f out: styd on wl fnl f* **11/4**[1]
5-63 **2** 1¼ **Canton Queen (IRE)**[14] 6451 3-9-1 **90**.............................. TomQueally 7 96
(Richard Hannon) *looked wl; hld up in 4th: stl gng easily whn clsd on ldrs over 1f out: chsd wnr fnl f and sn drvn: fnd little and readily hld* **16/1**
24 **3** ¾ **Salayel**[16] 6379 3-9-3 **92**.............................. KieranShoemark 2 96
(Roger Varian) *looked wl; t.k.h: trckd ldng pair: rdn 2f out: edgd rt fr over 1f out: styd on same pce* **7/2**[2]
1062 **4** ½ **Desirous**[29] 5910 3-8-13 **88**.............................. RossaRyan 4 91
(Ralph Beckett) *looked wl; racd freely: led: rdn and hdd over 1f out: fdd fnl f* **5/1**[3]
03 **5** nk **Lush Life (IRE)**[22] 6151 4-9-8 **92**..............................(p[1]) WilliamBuick 3 95
(Jamie Osborne) *dwlt: hld up in last: rdn and tried to cl on ldrs 2f out: nt qckn over 1f out: one pce after* **11/2**
1116 **6** 4½ **Mubtasimah**[16] 6379 3-9-6 **95**.............................. TomMarquand 1 87
(William Haggas) *hld up in 5th: rdn and no prog 2f out: wknd over 1f out (jockey said filly stopped quickly)* **11/4**[1]
1m 40.94s (-0.46) **Going Correction** +0.15s/f (Good)
WFA 3 from 4yo 5lb **6** Ran SP% **113.5**
Speed ratings (Par 96): **108,106,106,105,105 100**
CSF £43.60 TOTE £3.20: £1.90, £5.20; EX 35.70 Trifecta £180.20.
Owner John Gunther & Tanya Gunther **Bred** John Gunther **Trained** Newmarket, Suffolk

FOCUS
A good fillies' handicap. One of the joint-favourites showed a good winning mentality, improving once again.

6952 LAVAZZA STKS (HERITAGE H'CAP) 1m 3f 211y
3:55 (4:01) (Class 2) 3-Y-O
£62,250 (£18,640; £9,320; £4,660; £2,330; £1,170) **Stalls** Low

Form RPR
5132 **1** **Apparate**[56] 4924 3-8-8 **89**.............................. RossaRyan 2 97
(Roger Varian) *looked wl; hld up in midfield: prog over 2f out: rdn to dispute ld over 1f out: got battle w runner-up after: jst prevailed* **8/1**
2602 **2** shd **Persian Moon (IRE)**[7] 6712 3-9-4 **99**.............................. AdamKirby 14 106
(Mark Johnston) *trckd ldrs: prog to dispute ld over 1f out: drvn and w wnr after in gd battle: jst denied* **7/1**
2132 **3** 2 **Never Do Nothing (IRE)**[28] 5931 3-8-10 **91**.............................. RobHornby 7 95
(Andrew Balding) *reluctant to enter stalls: dwlt and needed early rousting: racd in last trio tl prog 2f out: styd on over 1f out to take 3rd last 100yds* **13/2**[3]
1454 **4** ½ **Travel On**[17] 6349 3-8-12 **93**..............................(p) KieranO'Neill 11 96
(John Gosden) *sweating; trckd ldr after 3f: rdn to chal 2f out: hld whn short of room briefly over 1f out: fdd* **16/1**
6631 **5** nse **I'll Have Another (IRE)**[21] 6223 3-9-3 **98**.............................. BenCurtis 13 101
(Mark Johnston) *looked wl; led after 1f: rdn and hdd over 1f out: fdd ins fnl f: lost 4th last stride* **16/1**
2031 **6** nk **Rhythmic Intent (IRE)**[21] 6216 3-8-3 **84**.............................. JFEgan 4 86+
(Stuart Williams) *looked wl; hld up in last trio: rdn over 2f out: swtchd rt over 1f out: kpt on but nvr enough pce to rch ldrs* **12/1**
0611 **7** 1½ **Baasem (USA)**[35] 5654 3-8-11 **92**.............................. DaneO'Neill 9 92
(Owen Burrows) *sweating; on toes; nvr bttr than midfield: rdn and no prog over 2f out: n.d after* **11/2**[2]
2225 **7** dht **Holy Kingdom (IRE)**[21] 6224 3-8-1 **85** ow3.......... DarraghKeenan(3) 10 85
(Tom Clover) *t.k.h: racd wd: trckd ldrs: lost grnd bnd 3f out and sn in rr: one pce and n.d after (jockey said colt hung left-handed)* **9/1**
211 **9** ½ **Cirque Royal**[176] 1221 3-9-1 **96**.............................. WilliamBuick 6 95
(Charlie Appleby) *ly: athletic; hld up in midfield: rdn over 2f out: nt qckn over 1f out: no prog after* **5/2**[1]
3155 **10** ½ **Zuba**[17] 6349 3-8-0 **81** oh1.............................. JimmyQuinn 3 79
(Amanda Perrett) *led 1f: styd prom: rdn to try to chal 2f out: fdd over 1f out* **25/1**
2400 **11** ¾ **Cap Francais**[37] 5585 3-9-5 **100**.............................. TomMarquand 8 97
(Ed Walker) *hld up in last trio: rdn 3f out: tried to make prog u.p 2f out: one pce after* **9/1**
2m 33.24s (0.64) **Going Correction** +0.15s/f (Good) **11** Ran SP% **124.2**
Speed ratings (Par 107): **103,102,101,101,101 101,100,100,99,99 98**
CSF £66.76 CT £397.53 TOTE £11.40: £2.90, £2.50, £2.00; EX 81.00 Trifecta £488.90.
Owner Sheikh Mohammed Obaid Al Maktoum **Bred** Sheikh Mohammed Obaid Al Maktoum **Trained** Newmarket, Suffolk

FOCUS
Add 16yds. A good middle-distance 3yo handicap. The first two home came slightly clear and it paid to race relatively prominently from off an, at best, even gallop. The runner-up looks the key to the form.

6953 FEVER-TREE H'CAP 6f
4:30 (4:38) (Class 2) (0-105,102) 3-Y-O+
£18,675 (£5,592; £2,796; £1,398; £699; £351) **Stalls** High

Form RPR
3-15 **1** **Swindler**[42] 5442 3-8-12 **90**.............................. LouisSteward 9 104+
(Ed Walker) *looked wl; ref to go to post tl dismntd and led: hld up in midfield: prog over 1f out: swept into the ld 100yds out: hung lft after: won w plenty in hand* **10/3**[1]
1311 **2** ¾ **Alkaraama (USA)**[46] 5266 3-9-2 **94**.............................. DaneO'Neill 14 102
(Sir Michael Stoute) *quite str: sweating; chsd ldrs: rdn 2f out: clsd 1f out: chal ins fnl f: styd on but outpcd nr fin* **7/2**[2]
2224 **3** hd **Open Wide (USA)**[15] 6404 5-9-2 **97**..............................(b) ScottMcCullagh(5) 8 104
(Amanda Perrett) *hld up wl in rr: prog jst over 1f out: squeezed through fnl f and r.o to press ldrs: nt quite pce of wnr nr fin* **6/1**[3]
0403 **4** ½ **Golden Apollo**[8] 6676 5-8-11 **87**..............................(tp) MartinDwyer 2 93
(Tim Easterby) *w ldrs: led 1/2-way: rdn and hdd last 100yds: hmpd and fdd sn after* **10/1**
0622 **5** nse **Count Otto (IRE)**[11] 6565 4-9-0 **90**..............................(h) KieranShoemark 15 96
(Amanda Perrett) *hld up in rr: rdn 2f out: prog over 1f out: chal ins fnl f: outpcd nr fin* **25/1**
0006 **6** 2¼ **Glenamoy Lad**[15] 6404 5-9-1 **91**..............................(t) RossaRyan 13 89
(Michael Wigham) *looked wl; t.k.h: hld up wl in rr: rdn 2f out: sme prog jst over 1f out: one pce ins fnl f* **20/1**
1330 **7** ½ **Dream Today (IRE)**[191] 960 4-9-5 **95**.............................. DougieCostello 5 92
(Jamie Osborne) *cl up bhd ldrs: rdn and no imp over 1f out: fdd ins fnl f* **33/1**
6010 **8** hd **Stone Of Destiny**[17] 6351 4-9-8 **98**.............................. RobHornby 11 94
(Andrew Balding) *trckd ldrs: stl gng strly 2f out: rdn and nt qckn over 1f out: one pce after* **18/1**
1-41 **9** 2 **Lethal Lunch**[18] 6318 4-9-3 **93**.............................. AdamKirby 6 83+
(Clive Cox) *looked wl; hld up wl in rr: shkn up and trying to make prog whn squeezed for room jst over 1f out: no hdwy after* **15/2**
3055 **10** hd **Walk On Walter (IRE)**[46] 5266 4-9-3 **93**..............................(h) JFEgan 10 84
(Jonathan Portman) *w ldrs: rdn over 2f out: wknd over 1f out* **33/1**
3021 **11** shd **Mokaatil**[11] 6565 4-8-5 **88**..............................(p) AngusVilliers(7) 3 77
(Ian Williams) *t.k.h: trckd ldrs: rdn 2f out: wknd over 1f out* **33/1**
0010 **12** 2¼ **Major Partnership (IRE)**[161] 1440 4-9-12 **102**.......... CallumShepherd 7 88
(Saeed bin Suroor) *looked wl; led to 1/2-way: styd w ldrs tl wknd qckly jst over 1f out: no ch whn hmpd nr fin* **14/1**
006 **13** ¾ **Fille De Reve**[14] 6453 4-9-0 **90**.............................. KieranO'Neill 12 69
(Ed Walker) *hld up in last trio: rdn over 2f out: sn btn: hmpd nr fin* **14/1**
1411 **U** **Magical Ride**[28] 5959 4-8-7 **90**.............................. SeanKirrane(7) 4
(Richard Spencer) *sltly on toes; w ldrs: chal over 1f out: 6th and hld whn hmpd: stmbld and uns rdr 50yds out* **11/1**
1m 12.63s (-1.07) **Going Correction** +0.15s/f (Good)
WFA 3 from 4yo+ 2lb **14** Ran SP% **124.8**
Speed ratings (Par 109): **113,112,111,111,111 108,107,107,104,104 104,101,100,**
CSF £14.49 CT £69.94 TOTE £3.50: £1.80, £1.80, £1.80; EX 20.70 Trifecta £74.50.
Owner B E Nielsen **Bred** Bjorn Nielsen **Trained** Upper Lambourn, Berks
■ Stewards' Enquiry : Louis Steward eight-day ban; careless riding (Sept 21-28)

FOCUS
A good sprint handicap. The temperamental winning favourite caused a dangerous incident in behind in the closing stages. He hung left while asserting his clear superiority in the best comparative time on the card. Solid form, rated around the fourth and fifth.

6954 FORTNUM & MASON H'CAP 5f
5:05 (5:12) (Class 3) (0-90,90) 3-Y-O+ **£9,703** (£2,887; £1,443; £721) **Stalls** High

Form RPR
2112 **1** **Texting**[24] 6080 3-8-5 **79**.............................. SeamusCronin(5) 16 87+
(Mohamed Moubarak) *trckd ldng pair: rdn to chal over 1f out: drvn ahd last 120yds: styd on* **11/4**[1]
0015 **2** ½ **Blue De Vega (GER)**[12] 6534 6-9-7 **89**..............................(tp) RossaRyan 11 95
(Robert Cowell) *trckd ldrs: rdn over 1f out: prog nr side of gp fnl f: r.o to take 2nd nr fin* **11/1**
6530 **3** nk **Concierge (IRE)**[15] 6413 3-9-2 **88**..............................(v[1]) MeganNicholls(3) 15 93
(George Scott) *hld up towards rr: shkn up over 1f out: gd prog nr side of gp fnl f: styd on to take 3rd last strides* **16/1**
0114 **4** ½ **Thegreatestshowman**[11] 6565 3-8-10 **86**.............................. SeanKirrane(7) 10 89+
(Amy Murphy) *taken down early: hld up in rr: effrt on outer of gp over 1f out: styd on wl fnl f: nrst fin* **14/1**
1123 **5** nse **Heritage**[17] 6332 3-9-6 **89**..............................(p) AdamKirby 9 92
(Clive Cox) *looked wl; w ldr: led after 2f: drvn over 1f out: hdd and one pce last 120yds: lost pls nr fin* **7/1**[2]
603 **6** nk **Zamjar**[91] 3597 5-9-0 **82**.............................. CallumShepherd 2 84
(Robert Cowell) *dwlt: hld up towards rr: prog towards outer of gp over 1f out: styd on fnl f: nvr able to chal* **40/1**
0232 **7** hd **Gnaad (IRE)**[8] 6668 5-8-5 **76**.............................. DarraghKeenan(3) 5 77
(Alan Bailey) *rrd s but broke on terms: trckd ldrs: rdn over 1f out: styd on same pce fnl f and nvr able to chal* **8/1**[3]
5011 **8** nk **Grandfather Tom**[27] 5990 4-8-6 **81**.............................. AngusVilliers(7) 1 81
(Robert Cowell) *led 2f: pressed ldr: rdn wl over 1f out: one pce and lost pls ins fnl f* **20/1**
0150 **9** hd **Mountain Peak**[7] 6724 4-9-5 **87**.............................. RobHornby 14 86
(Ed Walker) *looked wl; dwlt: hld up wl in rr: rdn and struggling wl over 1f out: kpt on fnl f: nvr nrr* **7/1**[2]
3336 **10** ½ **Wedding Date**[14] 6476 3-9-0 **88**.............................. ThoreHammerHansen(5) 4 86
(Richard Hannon) *hld up in midfield: shkn up over 1f out: kpt on same pce and no threat* **10/1**
0100 **11** shd **Royal Birth**[28] 5942 8-8-12 **87**..............................(t) MarcoGhiani(7) 13 84
(Stuart Williams) *dwlt: t.k.h: hld up wl in rr: rdn and no prog over 1f out: styd on ins fnl f: nvr nrr but n.d* **14/1**
0340 **12** 1¾ **Moonraker**[40] 5504 7-8-13 **81**.............................. AlistairRawlinson 3 72
(Michael Appleby) *taken down early: sn chsd ldrs: rdn and wknd over 1f out* **25/1**
0000 **13** 1¼ **Koditime (IRE)**[12] 6534 4-9-2 **84**..............................(p) DaneO'Neill 12 70
(Clive Cox) *t.k.h: hld up in rr: no prog over 1f out: wknd fnl f* **12/1**
0510 **14** 2¾ **Amplify (IRE)**[14] 6476 3-9-7 **90**.............................. MartinDwyer 7 66
(Brian Meehan) *looked wl; nvr on terms w ldrs: wknd qckly over 1f out* **16/1**
4103 **15** 3 **Secretinthepark**[14] 6455 9-8-9 **77**..............................(b) KieranO'Neill 6 43
(Michael Mullineaux) *propped and rrd s: lost many l and a wl bhd in last* **14/1**
59.83s (-0.87) **Going Correction** +0.15s/f (Good)
WFA 3 from 4yo+ 1lb **15** Ran SP% **130.7**
Speed ratings (Par 107): **112,111,110,109,109 109,109,108,108,107 107,104,102,98,93**
CSF £36.10 CT £444.98 TOTE £3.40: £1.90, £3.60, £6.10; EX 46.40 Trifecta £584.70.
Owner M Moubarak **Bred** Laundry Cottage Stud Farm **Trained** Newmarket, Suffolk
■ Stewards' Enquiry : Megan Nicholls £290 fine; using mobile phone outside of phone zone
Seamus Cronin two-day ban; misuse of whip (Sept 21-22)

FOCUS
A decent sprint handicap. The favourite gamely held on in a typically busy finish centrally. The form's rated around the runner-up.
T/Plt: £230.20 to a £1 stake. Pool: £128,650.96 - 407.80 winning units T/Qpdt: £22.60 to a £1 stake. Pool: £14,231.43 - 464.51 winning units **Jonathan Neesom**

6918 HAYDOCK (L-H)

Saturday, September 7

OFFICIAL GOING: Soft (6.5)

Wind: Almost nil Weather: Fine

6955 BETTER ODDS ON THE BETFAIR EXCHANGE H'CAP 1m 6f

1:50 (1:51) (Class 2) 3-Y-O

£62,250 (£18,640; £9,320; £4,660; £2,330; £1,170) **Stalls** Low

Form RPR

1155 **1** **Ranch Hand**[58] 4845 3-9-1 **94** OisinMurphy 2 104
(Andrew Balding) *in tch: rdn over 2f out: led over 1f out: styd on wl fnl 100yds* **14/1**

6-11 **2** **2** **Trueshan (FR)**[9] 6641 3-8-12 **91** AndreaAtzeni 9 98
(Alan King) *hld up in midfield: c wd ent st over 4f out: rdn and hdwy over 2f out: styd on to chse wnr ins fnl f: no imp fnl 100yds* **8/1**

0-61 **3** ½ **Elysian Flame**[8] 6657 3-8-9 **88** NathanEvans 4 94
(Michael Easterby) *unruly bef r: hld up: c wd ent st over 4f out: rdn over 3f out: hdwy over 2f out: ch 1f out: kpt on u.p ins fnl f but no imp on wnr (vet said gelding lost it's right fore shoe)* **9/1**

1111 **4** hd **Moon King (FR)**[56] 4906 3-8-11 **90** HarryBentley 11 96+
(Ralph Beckett) *trckd ldrs: c wd ent st over 4f out: rdn over 2f out: ch 1f out: kpt on u.p ins fnl f: nt pce of wnr* **9/2[2]**

2155 **5** 2 ¼ **Mondain**[28] 5943 3-8-9 **88** FrannyNorton 10 91
(Mark Johnston) *led: hdd after 2f and j. road: remained prom: rdn to regain ld on far rail over 2f out: hdd over 1f out: kpt on same pce ins fnl f* **40/1**

2421 **6** nk **Laafy (USA)**[22] 6171 3-8-10 **89** (v) RichardKingscote 5 92+
(Sir Michael Stoute) *prom: c wd ent st over 4f out: rdn over 3f out: one pce over 1f out* **6/1[3]**

6212 **7** 3 **Zoffee**[19] 6291 3-8-3 **85** JaneElliott(3) 6 83
(Tom Dascombe) *hld up in rr: c wd ent st over 4f out: rdn over 3f out: chsd ldrs over 2f out: wl there tl no ex and no imp fnl 150yds* **16/1**

0115 **8** 2 **Jackamundo (FR)**[40] 5489 3-8-2 **81** CamHardie 1 77
(Declan Carroll) *midfield: rdn over 3f out: plugged on fnl 2f: nvr able to trble ldrs* **22/1**

4111 **9** ½ **Calculation**[14] 6437 3-8-12 **91** (v) RyanMoore 7 86
(Sir Michael Stoute) *hld up: hdwy after 6f: sn handy: rdn over 3f out: wknd over 1f out* **7/1**

2112 **10** nk **First In Line**[14] 6471 3-9-7 **100** FrankieDettori 12 94
(John Gosden) *s.i.s: sn prom: led after 2f: c wd ent st over 4f out: rdn and hdd over 2f out: wknd over 1f out (trainers' rep said colt was unsuited by the ground on this occasion)* **3/1[1]**

-431 **11** hd **Alemagna**[13] 6509 3-8-4 **83** ow1 NicolaCurrie 3 77
(David Simcock) *hld up: pushed along over 3f out: no imp* **9/1**

431 **12** 22 **Gabrials Boy**[12] 6544 3-8-3 **85** SeanDavis(3) 8 48
(Richard Fahey) *in tch: rdn over 3f out: sn wknd* **50/1**

3m 6.04s (1.44) **Going Correction** +0.25s/f (Good) **12 Ran SP% 122.4**
Speed ratings (Par 107): **105,103,103,103,102 102,100,99,98,98 98,86**
CSF £123.76 CT £1085.42 TOTE £19.40: £5.00, £2.80, £3.40; EX 156.60 Trifecta £1562.30.
Owner Kingsclere Racing Club **Bred** Kingsclere Stud **Trained** Kingsclere, Hants

FOCUS
A dry day, and not as windy as it was on the first two days of the meeting. All races used the stands' side home straight. Add 24yds to races over 1m6f, and add 13yds to the mile races. After riding in the opener Andrea Atzeni and Richard Kingscote called the ground soft and Nathan Evans said: "It's a little bit tacky." This opener was a terrific 3yo handicap, contested by a number of progressive young stayers. They didn't appear to go a great gallop and the time was 12sec outside standard, but nearly a second quicker than the older stayers took in the Old Borough Cup. There was a difference of opinion between the jockeys turning in and the field fanned out across the track, with the three who raced nearest the stands' side perhaps compromised slightly.

6956 BET IN PLAY ON THE BETFAIR EXCHANGE SUPERIOR MILE STKS (GROUP 3) 1m 37y

2:25 (2:25) (Class 1) 3-Y-O+

£35,727 (£13,545; £6,778; £3,376; £1,694; £850) **Stalls** Low

Form RPR

0304 **1** **Great Scot**[23] 6122 3-8-12 107 RichardKingscote 4 115
(Tom Dascombe) *racd keenly: mde all: rdn over 1f out: r.o wl to draw clr ins fnl f: gd ride* **7/2[2]**

1502 **2** 3 ¾ **Matterhorn (IRE)**[14] 6467 4-9-3 111 FrannyNorton 5 107
(Mark Johnston) *chsd wnr: rdn over 2f out: kpt on same pce u.p and no imp fnl f* **9/2[3]**

-431 **3** ½ **Raising Sand**[42] 5413 7-9-3 109 NicolaCurrie 6 106
(Jamie Osborne) *hld up in rr: pushed along over 2f out: hdwy 1f out: styd on fnl 100yds: nvr able to threaten wnr* **5/1**

2510 **4** ¾ **Walkinthesand (IRE)**[37] 5583 3-8-12 108 RyanMoore 7 104
(Richard Hannon) *chsd ldrs: pushed along 3f out: unable to go pce of ldrs over 2f out: hung lft and one pce ins fnl f* **9/2[3]**

10-4 **5** 4 ½ **Here Comes When (IRE)**[107] 3025 9-9-3 109 (h) OisinMurphy 3 94
(Andrew Balding) *s.i.s: chsd ldrs: rdn over 2f out: wknd over 1f out* **8/1**

1200 **6** 1 ½ **Sharja Bridge**[81] 3948 5-9-3 113 AndreaAtzeni 8 91
(Roger Varian) *stdd s: racd keenly: hld up: hdwy over 2f out: rdn over 1f out: no imp ins fnl f: wknd fnl 150yds (trainers' rep could offer no explanation for the poor performance)* **11/4[1]**

1m 44.09s (-0.81) **Going Correction** +0.25s/f (Good)
WFA 3 from 4yo+ 5lb **6 Ran SP% 113.0**
Speed ratings (Par 113): **114,110,109,109,104 103**
CSF £19.55 TOTE £4.10: £2.20, £1.70; EX 17.70 Trifecta £74.30.
Owner Empire State Racing Partnership **Bred** Clyne, Mound, Thompson **Trained** Malpas, Cheshire

FOCUS
Add 13yds. Fair Group 3 form, the race going to one of the two 3yos in the field. The race could be rated better at face value, but there are some doubts. All six stayed on the inside in the straight this time.

6957 READ RYAN MOORE EXCLUSIVELY AT BETFAIR.COM ASCENDANT STKS (LISTED RACE) 1m 37y

3:00 (3:01) (Class 1) 2-Y-O

£14,461 (£5,482; £2,743; £1,366; £685; £344) **Stalls** Low

Form RPR

14 **1** **Pyledriver**[21] 6212 2-9-2 0 PJMcDonald 8 103
(William Muir) *hld up in rr: hdwy 3f out: led over 1f out: edgd lft ins fnl f: styd on wl* **14/1**

1 **2** 1 ¼ **Sound Of Cannons**[22] 6163 2-9-2 0 OisinMurphy 6 100
(Brian Meehan) *chsd ldrs: prom 5f out: led 2f out: rdn and hdd over 1f out: kpt on u.p ins fnl f: hld towards fin* **11/2[3]**

01 **3** 1 ¼ **Tammani**[38] 5563 2-9-2 0 JamesDoyle 3 98
(William Haggas) *s.i.s: hld up: angled out and hdwy over 1f out: styd on ins fnl f: nvr able to trble front two* **5/2[1]**

2162 **4** 1 ¾ **Subjectivist**[15] 6417 2-9-2 98 FrannyNorton 5 94
(Mark Johnston) *chsd ldrs: rdn over 2f out: outpcd over 1f out: styd on fnl 100yds* **13/2**

1412 **5** nk **Sesame Birah (IRE)**[21] 6212 2-8-11 95 RyanMoore 7 88
(Richard Hannon) *hld up: hdwy over 3f out: chsd ldrs over 2f out: kpt on same pce ins fnl f* **7/1**

21 **6** nk **He's A Keeper (IRE)**[29] 5894 2-9-2 0 RichardKingscote 2 92
(Tom Dascombe) *in tch: rdn and outpcd over 2f out: kpt on for press towards fin* **7/2[2]**

0252 **7** 1 ¼ **Light Angel**[9] 6632 2-9-2 92 FrankieDettori 4 90
(John Gosden) *led: rdn over 2f out: sn hdd: unable to go w ldrs 1f out: wknd ins fnl f* **8/1**

153 **8** 6 **Shared Belief (IRE)**[21] 6251 2-9-2 0 DanielTudhope 1 76
(Archie Watson) *prom: rdn and lost pl 2f out: wknd wl over 1f out* **14/1**

1m 45.37s (0.47) **Going Correction** +0.25s/f (Good) **8 Ran SP% 116.5**
Speed ratings (Par 103): **107,105,104,102,102 102,100,94**
CSF £90.01 TOTE £14.80: £3.70, £1.90, £1.20; EX 102.90 Trifecta £559.90.
Owner Knox & Wells Limited And R W Devlin **Bred** Knox & Wells Limited & R Devlin **Trained** Lambourn, Berks

FOCUS
Add 13yds. A decent edition of this event. The best previous winner is Havana Gold (2012), with Chriselliam and Dee Ex Bee among those who were beaten in it. The field raced on the inside in the straight and the form makes sense as rated.

6958 BETFAIR EXCHANGE OLD BOROUGH CUP H'CAP 1m 6f

3:35 (3:38) (Class 2) (0-105,102) 3-Y-O **£64,690** (£19,250; £9,620; £4,810) **Stalls** Low

Form RPR

3001 **1** **Time To Study (FR)**[24] 6095 5-8-10 **93** (p) CierenFallon(5) 5 105
(Ian Williams) *broke wl: chsd clr ldr: rdn over 3f out: clsd to ld over 1f out: hdd narrowly fnl 110yds: rallied gamely to regain ld towards fin* **7/1[3]**

3211 **2** nk **Alright Sunshine (IRE)**[29] 5902 4-9-1 **93** DanielTudhope 15 104
(Keith Dalgleish) *bmpd s: hld up in rr: rdn and hdwy over 2f out: hung lft over 1f out bef moved into 2nd: styd on to ld narrowly fnl 110yds and continued to hang: hdd and hld towards fin (jockey said gelding hung left-handed travelling up the home straight)* **5/2[1]**

3000 **3** 4 **Reshoun (FR)**[28] 5929 5-9-1 **93** (p) JimCrowley 13 98
(Ian Williams) *midfield: rdn and hdwy over 3f out: kpt on u.p ins fnl f: no imp on front two* **8/1**

4150 **4** 1 ½ **Charles Kingsley**[17] 6355 4-9-7 **99** FrannyNorton 12 102
(Mark Johnston) *hld up: rdn over 2f out: hdwy over 1f out: styd on ins fnl f: nt rch ldrs* **16/1**

14-1 **5** ½ **Garbanzo (IRE)**[31] 5811 5-8-12 **90** LiamKeniry 1 92
(Ed Walker) *chsd ldrs: rdn over 3f out: kpt on u.p ins fnl f: nvr able to chal* **14/1**

040 **6** 2 ½ **Blakeney Point**[17] 6355 6-9-6 **98** (bt) JamesDoyle 17 97
(Roger Charlton) *chsd ldrs: rdn over 3f out: no imp 1f out: no ex fnl 100yds* **9/1**

0442 **7** hd **Not So Sleepy**[22] 6171 7-9-2 **94** (t) PJMcDonald 9 92
(Hughie Morrison) *midfield: rdn 3f out: kpt on for press fnl f: nvr able to trble ldrs* **10/1**

14/1 **8** shd **Rainbow Dreamer**[206] 704 6-9-1 **93** (v) OisinMurphy 3 91
(Alan King) *midfield: rdn over 3f out: kpt on one pce fnl 2f* **20/1**

111- **9** hd **Arrowtown**[329] 8197 7-8-13 **91** (h) NathanEvans 8 89
(Michael Easterby) *chsd ldrs: rdn over 3f out: kpt on same pce fnl 2f* **33/1**

2000 **10** 1 ½ **My Reward**[8] 6657 7-8-8 **86** CamHardie 10 82
(Tim Easterby) *midfield: rdn 3f out: nvr got involved* **33/1**

1030 **11** ½ **Crystal King**[43] 5368 4-9-1 **93** (v[1]) RichardKingscote 7 88
(Sir Michael Stoute) *sn led: clr after 3f: abt 20 l clr 4f out: rdn over 2f out: hdd over 1f out: wknd ins fnl f* **12/1**

0050 **12** 15 **Restorer**[15] 6420 7-8-13 **91** AndreaAtzeni 14 65
(Ian Williams) *bmpd s: hld up in rr: rdn over 3f out: nvr a threat* **25/1**

305/ **13** 2 ½ **Putting Green**[39] 6679 7-8-12 **90** (p) WJLee 16 61
(Neil Mulholland) *chsd ldrs: rdn over 4f out: wknd over 1f out* **50/1**

50-0 **14** 2 ¼ **Clever Cookie**[17] 6355 11-9-2 **94** (p) RobertWinston 6 62
(Peter Niven) *midfield tl rdn and wknd over 2f out: eased whn wl btn over 1f out* **25/1**

2022 **15** 18 **Corelli (USA)**[15] 6420 4-9-10 **102** (t) FrankieDettori 2 44
(John Gosden) *hld up: struggling over 2f out: eased whn wl btn over 1f out (trainers' rep said gelding was unsuited by the ground on this occasion)* **11/2[2]**

0004 **P** **Melting Dew**[17] 6355 5-8-13 **91** (p) RyanMoore 11
(Sir Michael Stoute) *hld up: reminders 8f out: p.u 6f out: bled fr the nose (vet said gelding bled from the nose)* **14/1**

3m 6.99s (2.39) **Going Correction** +0.25s/f (Good) **16 Ran SP% 133.9**
Speed ratings (Par 109): **103,102,100,99,99 97,97,97,97,96 96,87,86,85,74**
CSF £25.30 CT £158.27 TOTE £8.70: £2.10, £1.10, £2.40, £3.80; EX 30.40 Trifecta £182.80.
Owner K Sohi **Bred** E A R L Haras Du Quesnay **Trained** Portway, Worcs

FOCUS
Add 24yds. A competitive and classy staying event, but a strange race in which Crystal King went a long way clear before he was swallowed up by the pack. Not many got into it. The time was 0.95sec slower than the opening handicap for 3yos, and the winner is rated in line with his best form from the past year, helped by his rider's claim.

6959 BETFAIR SPRINT CUP STKS (GROUP 1) (BRITISH CHAMPIONS SERIES) 6f

4:10 (4:16) (Class 1) 3-Y-O+

£170,130 (£64,500; £32,280; £16,080; £8,070; £4,050) **Stalls** Centre

Form RPR

-413 **1** **Hello Youmzain (FR)**[78] 4050 3-9-1 114 JamesDoyle 6 121
(Kevin Ryan) *mde all: rdn over 1f out: edgd lft ins fnl f: kpt on wl towards fin* **9/2[1]**

-360 **2** ½ **The Tin Man**[49] 5184 7-9-3 114 OisinMurphy 3 119
(James Fanshawe) *stmbld s: hld up: rdn and hdwy over 1f out: chsd wnr fnl 150yds: r.o and clsd towards fin (jockey said gelding stumbled leaving the stalls)* **7/1[2]**

2112 **3** 2 **Waldpfad (GER)**[13] 6519 5-9-3 112 AndreaAtzeni 11 113
(D Moser, Germany) *hld up: rdn over 2f out: hdwy over 1f out: r.o ins fnl f: gng on at fin: nt rch front two* **9/1[3]**

0102 **4** *hd* **Brando**[34] 5716 7-9-3 116 TomEaves 5 112
(Kevin Ryan) *hld up: rdn and hdwy over 1f out: chsd ldrs ins fnl f: styd on u.p ins fnl f: no imp fnl 75yds: b.b.v (vet said gelding bled from the nose)* 7/1[2]

1010 **5** *nk* **Invincible Army (IRE)**[34] 5716 4-9-3 114 (p[1]) PJMcDonald 1 111
(James Tate) *chsd wnr: rdn over 1f out: unable qck ins fnl f: lost 2nd fnl 150yds: kpt on same pce towards fin* 14/1

6530 **6** *nk* **Fairyland (IRE)**[15] 6423 3-8-12 110 RyanMoore 10 107
(A P O'Brien, Ire) *midfield: hdwy over 2f out: rdn to chse ldrs over 1f out: kpt on ins fnl f: nt pce to chal* 16/1

2301 **7** *1 1/2* **Major Jumbo**[34] 5705 5-9-3 108 KevinStott 9 106
(Kevin Ryan) *prom: rdn over 2f out: unable qck u.p over 1f out: one pce ins fnl f* 25/1

1120 **8** *hd* **Dream Of Dreams (IRE)**[56] 4923 5-9-3 119 DanielTudhope 4 105
(Sir Michael Stoute) *bmpd s: hld up: effrt whn carried lft over 1f out: styd on ins fnl f: nt pce to trble ldrs* 9/2[1]

0503 **9** *1* **So Perfect (USA)**[15] 6423 3-8-12 108 WayneLordan 13 99
(A P O'Brien, Ire) *chsd ldrs: pushed along over 2f out: rdn over 1f out: outpcd after* 16/1

-512 **10** *2* **Forever In Dreams (IRE)**[78] 4050 3-8-12 112 WJLee 7 92
(Aidan F Fogarty, Ire) *in tch: pushed along over 2f out: edgd lft u.p over 1f out and wknd* 11/1

1021 **11** *2 1/4* **Khaadem (IRE)**[35] 5664 3-9-1 116 JimCrowley 12 88
(Charles Hills) *midfield: rdn over 1f out: wknd fnl f (trainer could offer no explanation for the poor performance)* 9/2[1]

1m 12.79s (-1.11) **Going Correction** +0.25s/f (Good) **11 Ran SP% 120.2**
WFA 3 from 4yo+ 2lb
Speed ratings (Par 117): **117,116,113,113,113 112,110,110,109,106 103**
CSF £36.63 CT £282.28 TOTE £5.60: £2.10, £3.10, £2.70; EX 38.30 Trifecta £317.60.
Owner Jaber Abdullah **Bred** Rabbah Bloodstock Limited **Trained** Hambleton, N Yorks

FOCUS
A very open renewal of this Group 1, but one lacking in star quality with Advertise (bad scope) and Ten Sovereigns (ground) both ruled out after being declared. The time in soft ground was only 2.59sec outside the standard and the form is rated up to scratch for the race. Hello Youmzain is the fifth 3yo to win it in the last six years.

6960 BETFAIR EXCHANGE BE FRIENDLY H'CAP 5f
4:45 (4:46) (Class 2) (0-105,100) 3-Y-O+ **£22,641** (£6,737; £3,367; £1,683) **Stalls** Centre

Form RPR

4135 **1** **Maygold**[20] 6257 4-9-2 90 LiamKeniry 6 103+
(Ed Walker) *dwlt: hld up in last pl: swtchd rt and gd hdwy to ld 1f out: sn clr and drifted lft: r.o wl* 4/1[2]

2203 **2** *2 1/4* **Arecibo (FR)**[17] 6351 4-9-12 100 (v) DanielTudhope 8 105
(David O'Meara) *t.k.h: prom: drvn along over 1f out: hdwy to chse wnr ins fnl f: kpt on: nt pce to chal* 4/1[2]

2040 **3** *1/2* **She Can Boogie (IRE)**[14] 6476 3-9-1 90 RichardKingscote 2 93
(Tom Dascombe) *cl up: drvn and ev ch 1f out: one pce fnl 100yds* 6/1[3]

3160 **4** *hd* **Camacho Chief (IRE)**[17] 6351 4-9-10 98 (p) ConnorBeasley 7 100
(Michael Dods) *hld up in tch: smooth hdwy 2f out: drvn and ev ch briefly 1f out: edgd lft and one pce ins fnl f* 5/2[1]

2000 **5** *1 3/4* **Foolaad**[17] 6351 8-9-6 94 (t) RobertWinston 9 90
(Roy Bowring) *wnt rt s: sn cl up: drvn along 2f out: wknd ins fnl f (jockey said gelding was crowded for room in the closing stages)* 11/1

660 **6** *1 1/2* **Intense Romance (IRE)**[7] 6698 5-9-12 100 (p[1]) CallumRodriguez 5 91
(Michael Dods) *led: rdn 2f out: hdd 1f out: sn wknd* 9/1

0001 **7** *1 1/2* **Powerallied (IRE)**[7] 6714 6-8-9 86 SeanDavis(3) 1 71
(Richard Fahey) *in tch: hdwy over 2f out: hung lft and wknd over 1f out* 20/1

36 **8** *3/4* **Broken Spear**[7] 6735 3-9-1 90 (p) KevinStott 3 73
(Tony Coyle) *in tch: drvn along 1/2-way: wknd over 1f out* 7/1

1m 0.82s (0.42) **Going Correction** +0.25s/f (Good) **8 Ran SP% 118.5**
WFA 3 from 4yo+ 1lb
Speed ratings (Par 109): **106,102,101,101,98 96,93,92**
CSF £21.24 CT £96.96 TOTE £5.50: £1.80, £1.50, £2.10; EX 26.80 Trifecta £147.30.
Owner Farleigh Racing **Bred** Farleigh Court Racing Partnership **Trained** Upper Lambourn, Berks

FOCUS
This lacked the depth you'd generally associate with a sprint handicap at this level, though it did feature last year's winner, Intense Romance. They went a good pace and the winner picked up impressively from last. The form's rated at face value.

6961 BETFAIR EACH WAY EDGE H'CAP 1m 37y
5:20 (5:20) (Class 4) (0-80,82) 3-Y-O+ **£13,196** (£3,927; £1,962; £981; £300; £300) **Stalls** Low

Form RPR

640 **1** **Time For A Toot (IRE)**[86] 3763 4-9-10 80 JimCrowley 7 93
(Charles Hills) *hld up: gng wl whn nt clr run over 2f out: effrt and rdn over 1f out: led ins fnl f: sn clr: comf* 14/1

4221 **2** *2* **Barossa Red (IRE)**[28] 5947 3-9-7 82 OisinMurphy 16 89+
(Andrew Balding) *hld up in tch: smooth hdwy to ld over 2f out: rdn and hdd ins fnl f: nt pce of wnr* 2/1[1]

4560 **3** *1 1/2* **Brother McGonagall**[28] 5970 5-9-3 78 DannyRedmond(5) 17 83
(Tim Easterby) *prom: hdwy to chse ldr fr 2f out to ins fnl f: one pce last 100yds* 25/1

2225 **4** *3/4* **Polyphony (IRE)**[22] 6170 4-9-3 73 (h) AndrewMullen 9 76
(John Mackie) *t.k.h: hld up in midfield: hdwy on outside over 2f out: sn rdn: kpt on same pce fnl f* 12/1

1062 **5** *nk* **Greek Hero**[27] 5984 3-9-3 78 DanielTudhope 5 80
(Declan Carroll) *hld up: stdy hdwy and shkn up over 2f out: effrt and rdn over 1f out: one pce fnl f* 11/2[2]

0031 **6** *hd* **This Girl**[30] 5844 4-9-7 77 RichardKingscote 11 79
(Tom Dascombe) *hld up in midfield: hdwy and prom over 2f out: rdn and one pce appr fnl f* 15/2[3]

0030 **7** *2 3/4* **Axe Axelrod (USA)**[54] 4982 3-8-5 66 (p) JamieGormley 6 61
(Michael Dods) *led to over 2f out: rallied: wknd ins fnl f* 28/1

003 **8** *1/2* **Dancin Boy**[28] 5970 3-9-5 80 TomEaves 12 74
(Michael Dods) *hld up: rdn over 2f out: kpt on fnl f: nvr able to chal* 20/1

2653 **9** *1 1/4* **Zip**[22] 6179 3-8-10 74 (v[1]) SeanDavis(3) 3 65
(Richard Fahey) *t.k.h: hld up in midfield: hdwy and prom over 2f out: rdn and edgd lft over 1f out: wknd ins fnl f* 12/1

4204 **10** *3/4* **Storm Ahead (IRE)**[16] 6370 6-9-6 76 (b) PJMcDonald 1 66
(Tim Easterby) *hld up on ins: hdwy over 2f out: rdn and wknd over 1f out* 16/1

0025 **11** *2* **Merweb (IRE)**[21] 6201 4-8-11 70 JaneElliott(3) 2 55
(Heather Main) *trckd ldrs: drvn along over 2f out: wknd over 1f out* 14/1

-006 **12** *1* **London Protocol (FR)**[83] 3880 6-9-4 74 (b) CamHardie 13 57
(John Mackie) *hld up: rdn and hdwy on outside over 2f out: wknd over 1f out* 40/1

0360 **13** *1 1/4* **Vive La Difference (IRE)**[33] 5726 5-9-1 71 DuranFentiman 10 51
(Tim Easterby) *s.i.s: hld up: effrt and drvn on outside over 2f out: sn wknd* 20/1

3054 **14** *1 1/4* **Tronada**[19] 6282 3-8-6 67 LiamJones 8 43
(Alan King) *slowly away: hld up: hdwy over 2f out: rdn and wknd over 1f out* 25/1

-010 **15** *1 1/4* **Amjaady (USA)**[63] 4671 3-9-1 79 HarrisonShaw(3) 4 52
(David O'Meara) *hld up in midfield on ins: drvn along over 2f out: wknd over 1f out* 12/1

1362 **16** *nk* **Salam Zayed**[11] 6582 3-8-12 73 KevinStott 15 46
(Richard Fahey) *pressed ldr to over 2f out: drvn and wknd over 1f out* 14/1

1114 **17** *13* **Street Poet (IRE)**[26] 6026 6-9-4 74 PhilDennis 14 18
(Michael Herrington) *t.k.h early: trckd ldrs: lost pl over 2f out: lost tch and eased ins fnl f* 25/1

1m 45.42s (0.52) **Going Correction** +0.25s/f (Good) **17 Ran SP% 136.4**
WFA 3 from 4yo+ 5lb
Speed ratings (Par 105): **107,105,103,102,102 102,99,99,97,97 95,94,92,91,90 89,76**
CSF £42.90 CT £806.38 TOTE £15.00: £3.40, £1.10, £8.40, £2.70; EX 55.00 Trifecta £758.40.
Owner P Winkworth **Bred** Lynch Bages & Camas Park Stud **Trained** Lambourn, Berks

FOCUS
Add 13yds. This was much more than competitive than the market suggested. The form's rated around the third to his recent best.
T/Jkpt: Not Won. T/Plt: £477.30 to a £1 stake. Pool: £144,677.79 - 221.25 winning units T/Qpdt: £16.10 to a £1 stake. Pool: £14,120.43 - 647.06 winning units **Darren Owen**

6925 KEMPTON (A.W) (R-H)
Saturday, September 7

OFFICIAL GOING: Polytrack: standard to slow
Wind: Fresh against Weather: Cloudy

6962 SUN RACING SEPTEMBER STKS (GROUP 3) 1m 3f 219y(P)
2:05 (2:06) (Class 1) 3-Y-O+
£39,697 (£15,050; £7,532; £3,752; £1,883; £945) **Stalls** Low

Form RPR

11-4 **1** **Royal Line**[64] 4612 5-9-5 111 RobertHavlin 8 114
(John Gosden) *chsd ldrs: shkn up over 2f out: r.o to ld wl ins fnl f* 6/1[2]

1600 **2** *1 1/4* **Mootasadir**[70] 4382 4-9-5 110 BenCurtis 10 112
(Hugo Palmer) *chsd ldr over 10f out: led over 2f out: hdd over 1f out: rallied to ld ins fnl f: sn hdd: styd on same pce towards fin* 7/1[3]

4050 **3** *1/2* **Prince Of Arran**[14] 6473 6-9-5 108 StevieDonohoe 3 111
(Charlie Fellowes) *hld up: hdwy over 8f out: rdn over 1f out: styd on* 9/1

3114 **4** *shd* **Sun Maiden**[37] 5586 4-9-5 106 LouisSteward 5 111
(Sir Michael Stoute) *prom: n.m.r and lost pl wl over 9f out: shkn up over 2f out: r.o ins fnl f* 10/1

1000 **5** *1/2* **Mountain Hunter (USA)**[39] 5519 5-9-5 105 HectorCrouch 1 110
(Saeed bin Suroor) *prom: rdn over 1f out: no ex wl ins fnl f* 14/1

5644 **6** *hd* **Rasima**[43] 5397 4-9-2 96 (p) JackMitchell 4 107
(Roger Varian) *hld up: shkn up over 2f out: r.o ins fnl f: nt rch ldrs* 100/1

110- **7** *hd* **Best Solution (IRE)**[305] 8911 5-9-5 121 PatCosgrave 9 110
(Saeed bin Suroor) *prom: shkn up over 2f out: nt clr run over 1f out: kpt on* 13/8[1]

1/P4 **8** *3/4* **Gibbs Hill (GER)**[15] 6420 6-9-5 105 JoeFanning 11 108
(Roger Varian) *hld up: hdwy on outer to ld and edgd rt over 1f out: rdn and hdd ins fnl f: no ex* 8/1

4015 **9** *2 1/4* **Pivoine (IRE)**[27] 6001 5-9-5 110 (b) DavidProbert 12 105
(Andrew Balding) *chsd ldrs: rdn over 1f out: no ex ins fnl f* 20/1

0300 **10** *1* **Thundering Blue (USA)**[17] 6354 6-9-5 112 SeanLevey 7 103
(David Menuisier) *s.i.s: hld up: rdn and hung rt ins fnl f: nt trble ldrs* 20/1

-150 **11** *2 1/2* **Worth Waiting**[20] 6265 4-9-7 108 ShaneKelly 6 101
(David Lanigan) *hld up: sme hdwy over 1f out: wknd ins fnl f (jockey said filly hung right-handed)* 33/1

1321 **12** *4* **Tamreer**[15] 6420 4-9-2 92 (h) HollieDoyle 2 90
(Roger Fell) *sn led: rdn and hdd over 2f out: wknd over 1f out* 40/1

2m 31.55s (-2.95) **Going Correction** 0.0s/f (Stan) **12 Ran SP% 117.6**
Speed ratings (Par 113): **109,108,107,107,107 107,107,106,105,104 102,100**
CSF £44.43 TOTE £7.10: £3.10, £2.30, £1.50; EX 44.30 Trifecta £292.20.
Owner HH Sheikha Al Jalila Racing **Bred** Darley **Trained** Newmarket, Suffolk

FOCUS
First run in 1979, the September Stakes has been won by some smart performers, including Shernazar, subsequent Melbourne Cup winner Jeune, Mutamam (twice), Dubai World Cup hero Prince Bishop (twice) Jack Hobbs and dual Arc heroine Enable.\n\x\x Although there was not such quality on show this time, the 14th running on Polytrack provided another decent renewal, but fears that there was no guaranteed pace in the race came to fruition, and it turned into something of a sprint, so the worth of the form is open to argument. It was run 2.25 secs slower than standard.

6963 SUN RACING AVAILABLE IN APP STORE NURSERY H'CAP (JOCKEY CLUB GRASSROOTS NURSERY QUALIFIER) 7f (P)
2:40 (2:43) (Class 4) (0-85,86) 2-Y-O
£6,469 (£1,925; £962; £481; £300; £300) **Stalls** Low

Form RPR

0020 **1** **Cheat (IRE)**[16] 6375 2-9-1 77 HollieDoyle 2 79
(Richard Hannon) *chsd ldrs: hmpd and lost pl over 5f out: hdwy over 1f out: rdn to ld wl ins fnl f: r.o (trainers' rep said, regards apparent improvement in form, colt benefitted from a slightly longer break on this occasion)* 9/2[3]

520 **2** *nk* **Onassis (IRE)**[26] 6019 2-8-10 72 DavidProbert 1 73
(Charlie Fellowes) *hld up: hdwy over 1f out: nt clr run and swtchd lft ins fnl f: r.o wl: fin 3rd: plcd 2nd* 4/1[2]

3230 **3** *hd* **Born To Destroy**[17] 6356 2-9-3 79 StevieDonohoe 6 80
(Richard Spencer) *sn led: hdd over 5f out: chsd ldr tl rdn to ld over 1f out: edgd rt and hdd wl ins fnl f: r.o: fin 2nd: plcd 3rd* 7/1

3530 **4** *1 1/2* **Top Buck (IRE)**[16] 6375 2-9-0 76 BenCurtis 5 73
(Brian Meehan) *hld up: rdn over 2f out: r.o ins fnl f: nt rch ldrs* 12/1

153 **5** *nse* **Old News**[14] 6464 2-9-10 86 ShaneKelly 7 83
(Richard Hughes) *racd keenly and sn prom on outer: rdn and hung rt fr over 1f out: styd on same pce ins fnl f* 8/1

551 **6** *shd* **Punchbowl Flyer (IRE)**[18] 6300 2-8-12 **74**.................. CharlesBishop 3 70+
(Eve Johnson Houghton) *sn pushed along in rr: shkn up over 2f out: r.o ins fnl f: nt rch ldrs* **7/2**[1]

3203 **7** *nk* **Written Broadcast (IRE)**[19] 6287 2-9-2 **78**.................. SeanLevey 4 74
(Richard Hannon) *sn prom: rdn over 1f out: styd on same pce ins fnl f* **5/1**

2430 **8** *2* **Xcelente**[37] 5587 2-9-7 **83**.................. JoeFanning 8 75
(Mark Johnston) *led over 5f out: rdn and hdd over 1f out: no ex ins fnl f* **14/1**

1m 26.24s (0.24) **Going Correction** 0.0s/f (Stan) **8** Ran SP% **115.0**
Speed ratings (Par 97): **98,97,97,95,95 95,95,92**
CSF £23.01 CT £124.49 TOTE £5.40: £2.00, £1.60; EX 29.10 Trifecta £141.20.
Owner Mrs J K Powell **Bred** Mr & Mrs John Banahan **Trained** East Everleigh, Wilts

FOCUS
Not the strongest race of its type, but a competitive nursery nonetheless. There was not much between the first three after a sluggish pace, which was 2.49 secs slower than standard, and due to the compressed finish it has to rate as pretty ordinary form.

6964 SUN RACING "LONDON MILE" H'CAP (SERIES FINAL) 1m (P)
3:15 (3:16) (Class 2) 3-Y-O+
£43,575 (£13,048; £6,524; £3,262; £1,631; £819) **Stalls** Low

Form RPR

6-01 **1** **Kasbaan**[4] 6841 4-9-7 **89** 5ex.................. AlistairRawlinson 10 101+
(Michael Appleby) *sn prom: led wl over 1f out: shkn up ins fnl f: styd on: comf* **11/4**[1]

4551 **2** *1 ½* **Kuwait Currency (USA)**[17] 6347 3-9-7 **94**..................(t) SeanLevey 6 101
(Richard Hannon) *hld up in tch: racd keenly: rdn over 2f out: chsd wnr ins fnl f: styd on* **5/1**[3]

3116 **3** *1* **Motawaj**[28] 5963 3-9-10 **97**.................. JackMitchell 1 102
(Roger Varian) *trckd ldrs: racd keenly: rdn over 1f out: styd on same pce towards fin* **4/1**[2]

3335 **4** *1 ¼* **Freerolling**[17] 6347 4-9-3 **85**.................. DavidProbert 11 88
(Charlie Fellowes) *broke wl: sn lost pl: rdn over 2f out: r.o ins fnl f: nt rch ldrs* **9/1**

3050 **5** *¾* **Family Fortunes**[17] 6347 5-8-12 **85**.................. ScottMcCullagh(5) 5 86
(Michael Madgwick) *hld up: hdwy over 1f out: styd on: nt trble ldrs* **22/1**

4213 **6** *½* **Arigato**[13] 6516 4-8-12 **80**..................(p) JosephineGordon 3 80
(William Jarvis) *chsd ldr: wnt upsides over 6f out: rdn over 2f out: ev ch wl over 1f out: no ex wl ins fnl f* **25/1**

3116 **7** *2 ¾* **Mayfair Spirit (IRE)**[28] 5948 3-8-8 **81**..................(t) StevieDonohoe 4 74
(Charlie Fellowes) *s.i.s: hld up: rdn over 2f out: nt trble ldrs* **16/1**

1100 **8** *nk* **Gossiping**[14] 6445 7-9-1 **88**.................. ThomasGreatrex(5) 2 81
(Gary Moore) *led early: chsd ldrs: rdn over 1f out: wknd ins fnl f* **13/2**

5204 **9** *4* **Felix The Poet**[17] 6347 3-9-1 **88**..................(b) HollieDoyle 9 71
(Archie Watson) *sn led: rdn and hdd wl over 1f out: wknd fnl f* **16/1**

1023 **10** *3 ½* **Directory**[66] 4506 4-8-11 **79**.................. RyanTate 8 55
(James Eustace) *s.s: nvr on terms (jockey said gelding was slowly away)* **33/1**

-105 **11** *½* **King's Slipper**[73] 4255 4-9-8 **90**.................. HectorCrouch 7 65
(Clive Cox) *broke wl: sn lost pl: rdn and hung rt over 2f out: sn wknd (trainers' rep could offer no explanation for the poor performance)* **9/1**

1m 37.31s (-2.49) **Going Correction** 0.0s/f (Stan)
WFA 3 from 4yo+ 5lb **11** Ran SP% **119.6**
Speed ratings (Par 109): **112,110,109,108,107 107,104,103,99,96 95**
CSF £16.25 CT £56.65 TOTE £3.50: £1.70, £1.90, £2.00; EX 18.40 Trifecta £90.00.
Owner The Horse Watchers **Bred** Shadwell Estate Company Limited **Trained** Oakham, Rutland

FOCUS
A typically competitive London Mile Final and although it attracted the smallest field in over a decade, several had taken each other on throughout the year. This has been a good race for 4yos and the winner was the tenth from this age group to score since its first running in 2006. The pace was solid and so is the form.

6965 FOLLOW SUN RACING ON TWITTER NURSERY H'CAP 1m (P)
3:50 (3:53) (Class 4) (0-85,86) 2-Y-O **£6,469** (£1,925; £962; £481; £300) **Stalls** Low

Form RPR

2012 **1** **Dramatic Sands (IRE)**[26] 6020 2-9-5 **80**.................. HollieDoyle 1 84
(Archie Watson) *mde all: rdn and hung lft fr over 1f out: styd on (jockey said colt hung left-handed)* **4/1**[2]

6231 **2** *nk* **Hexagon (IRE)**[25] 6040 2-9-2 **82**.................. ThomasGreatrex(5) 5 85
(Roger Charlton) *sn pushed along and bhd: rdn over 2f out: r.o to go 2nd ins fnl f: nt quite get there* **11/2**[3]

3432 **3** *1 ¼* **Always Fearless (IRE)**[15] 6416 2-9-1 **76**.................. SeanLevey 3 76
(Richard Hannon) *chsd ldrs: rdn over 1f out: styd on same pce wl ins fnl f (jockey said colt hung left-handed)* **12/1**

425 **4** *1 ¼* **African Swift (USA)**[15] 6424 2-9-1 **76**.................. JoeFanning 2 73
(Mark Johnston) *chsd ldr: rdn and ev ch 1f out: sn edgd lft: no ex wl ins fnl f* **13/2**

431 **5** *¾* **Dubai Souq (IRE)**[22] 6185 2-9-11 **86**.................. PatCosgrave 4 81
(Saeed bin Suroor) *hld up in tch: rdn over 1f out: no ex ins fnl f* **4/5**[1]

1m 39.45s (-0.35) **Going Correction** 0.0s/f (Stan) **5** Ran SP% **112.0**
Speed ratings (Par 97): **101,100,99,98,97**
CSF £24.78 TOTE £6.50: £2.50, £2.20; EX 25.70 Trifecta £86.20.
Owner Hambleton Racing XLV & Partner **Bred** Tullamaine Castle Stud And Partners **Trained** Upper Lambourn, W Berks

■ Stewards' Enquiry : Hollie Doyle two-day ban; misuse of whip (Sept 21-22)

FOCUS
A useful looking handicap and a small field, which meant the pace was modest and the time was understandably 2.14 secs slower than the previous mile. The form can't be rated much higher with the form compressed.

6966 SUN RACING SIRENIA STKS (GROUP 3) 6f (P)
4:25 (4:28) (Class 1) 2-Y-O
£34,026 (£12,900; £6,456; £3,216; £1,614; £810) **Stalls** Low

Form RPR

113 **1** **Streamline**[14] 6474 2-9-1 **99**..................(h) HectorCrouch 6 101
(Clive Cox) *a.p: chsd ldr over 2f out: rdn to ld wl ins fnl f: styd on* **9/2**[3]

1413 **2** *1* **Oh Purple Reign (IRE)**[12] 6542 2-9-1 **97**.................. SeanLevey 2 98
(Richard Hannon) *wnt lft s: hld up: shkn up over 2f out: r.o ins fnl f: wnt 2nd nr fin: nt rch wnr* **11/4**[2]

11 **3** *nk* **Huraiz (IRE)**[14] 6449 2-9-1 **90**.................. JoeFanning 7 97
(Mark Johnston) *racd keenly in 2nd tl led over 2f out: rdn and hdd wl ins fnl f: styd on same pce* **9/1**

1 **4** *1 ½* **Melodic Charm (IRE)**[26] 6028 2-8-12 **0**.................. DavidProbert 3 90
(James Tate) *hmpd s: hld up: swtchd lft over 2f out: hdwy over 1f out: sn rdn: styd on same pce wl ins fnl f* **14/1**

1423 **5** *2 ¼* **Sun Power (FR)**[21] 6212 2-9-1 **102**.................. JackMitchell 1 86
(Richard Hannon) *trckd ldrs: racd keenly: rdn over 1f out: no ex ins fnl f* **15/8**[1]

41 **6** *nk* **Lexington Rebel (FR)**[16] 6364 2-9-1 **0**.................. HollieDoyle 4 85
(Richard Hannon) *s.i.s: outpcd (jockey said colt was outpaced throughout)* **16/1**

4326 **7** *¾* **Aroha (IRE)**[20] 6264 2-8-12 **101**.................. JasonWatson 5 80
(Brian Meehan) *sn led: hdd over 2f out: wknd ins fnl f* **8/1**

1m 11.94s (-1.16) **Going Correction** 0.0s/f (Stan) **7** Ran SP% **113.3**
Speed ratings (Par 105): **107,105,105,103,100 99,98**
CSF £16.95 TOTE £4.60: £2.00, £2.30; EX 18.30 Trifecta £77.20.
Owner Mainline Racing **Bred** Whitsbury Manor Stud **Trained** Lambourn, Berks

FOCUS
Some useful juveniles have landed this in recent years, with Hooray (2010) and The Last Lion (2016) going on to win the Cheveley Park and Middle Park respectively, and last year's winner Kessar subsequently taking the Group 2 Mill Reef at Newbury. This looked an ordinary renewal for the grade, although the pace was genuine enough. Streamline is the type to do better again.

6967 VISIT SUNRACING.CO.UK FOR TOP BOOKMAKER OFFERS H'CAP (JOCKEY CLUB GRASSROOTS SERIES QUALIFIER) 1m 2f 219y(P)
5:00 (5:03) (Class 4) (0-80,82) 3£6,469 (£1,925; £962; £481; £300; £3015) **Stalls** Low

3132 **1** **Sendeed (IRE)**[27] 5984 3-9-8 **81**..................(p) JasonWatson 2 88
(Saeed bin Suroor) *mde all: set stdy pce tl qcknd over 2f out: pushed out: comf* **10/3**[2]

3521 **2** *¾* **Inclyne**[17] 6345 3-9-5 **78**.................. DavidProbert 11 84
(Andrew Balding) *chsd wnr after 1f: rdn over 1f out: r.o* **6/1**[3]

4044 **3** *nk* **Noble Gift**[31] 5811 9-9-12 **78**.................. KierenFox 1 83
(William Knight) *chsd ldrs: rdn over 2f out: r.o* **8/1**

4312 **4** *¾* **Ritchie Valens (IRE)**[21] 6217 3-9-9 **82**.................. SeanLevey 7 86+
(Richard Hannon) *hld up in tch: racd keenly: outpcd over 2f out: r.o ins fnl f* **6/1**[3]

0-51 **5** *¾* **Sandyman**[28] 5955 3-9-3 **79**.................. MitchGodwin(3) 4 82
(Paul Cole) *chsd ldrs: rdn over 2f out: sn outpcd: styd on ins fnl f* **20/1**

1525 **6** *¾* **Pour Me A Drink**[21] 6217 3-9-6 **79**.................. HectorCrouch 6 81
(Clive Cox) *hld up: racd keenly: r.o ins fnl f: nvr nrr (jockey said gelding ran too free)* **11/4**[1]

4566 **7** *½* **Wimpole Hall**[13] 6512 6-9-10 **76**..................(b) JosephineGordon 5 76
(William Jarvis) *s.i.s: hld up: racd keenly: r.o ins fnl f: nvr nrr* **25/1**

5460 **8** *3 ¼* **Noble Behest**[23] 6105 5-9-1 **67**..................(p) GeorgeDowning 10 62
(Ian Williams) *hld up: shkn up over 2f out: nvr on terms* **66/1**

-623 **9** *½* **Junderstand**[37] 5594 4-9-10 **76**.................. HollieDoyle 8 70
(Alan King) *hld up: rdn over 1f out: n.d* **7/1**

0044 **10** *2* **Showboating (IRE)**[24] 6068 11-9-11 **77**..................(p) LewisEdmunds 3 68
(John Balding) *hld up in tch: rdn over 2f out: wknd fnl f* **50/1**

6306 **11** *nse* **C Note (IRE)**[21] 6217 6-9-4 **77**..................(bt) StefanoCherchi(7) 9 68
(Heather Main) *s.s: a in rr (jockey said gelding was slowly away)* **25/1**

2m 22.3s (1.30) **Going Correction** 0.0s/f (Stan)
WFA 3 from 4yo+ 7lb **11** Ran SP% **117.8**
Speed ratings (Par 105): **98,97,97,96,96 95,95,92,92,91 91**
CSF £22.25 CT £149.85 TOTE £4.40: £2.40, £2.10, £2.40; EX 28.20 Trifecta £169.20.
Owner Godolphin **Bred** Godolphin **Trained** Newmarket, Suffolk

FOCUS
Six of the previous nine winners of this competitive handicap had gone to a 4yo, although four progressive 3yos headed the market and two of those came to the fore in a race that few got into. Ordinary form for the grade.

6968 VISIT SUNRACING.CO.UK FOR TOP TIPS H'CAP 7f (P)
5:35 (5:39) (Class 4) (0-85,85) 3-Y-O+
£6,469 (£1,925; £962; £481; £300; £300) **Stalls** Low

Form RPR

6102 **1** **Delilah Park**[24] 6076 5-9-2 **77**.................. JackMitchell 8 86
(Chris Wall) *chsd ldrs: rdn over 1f out: edgd lft wl ins fnl f: jst hld on* **9/2**[1]

2602 **2** *shd* **Atletico (IRE)**[13] 6518 7-9-1 **76**.................. JasonWatson 3 84
(David Evans) *prom: rdn over 1f out: ev ch ins fnl f: styd on (jockey said gelding hung left-handed)* **14/1**

2524 **3** *1 ¾* **Quick Breath**[18] 6318 4-9-3 **83**.................. ThomasGreatrex(5) 6 86
(Jonathan Portman) *pushed along early in rr: hdwy and hung rt fr over 1f out: styng on same pce whn nt clr run wl ins fnl f* **10/1**

3054 **4** *¾* **Martineo**[22] 6162 4-9-3 **78**.................. SeanLevey 4 79
(John Butler) *hld up: hdwy over 1f out: styd on* **9/1**

-261 **5** *¾* **Envisaging (IRE)**[30] 5870 5-9-0 **82**..................(t) LorenzoAtzori(7) 9 81
(James Fanshawe) *s.i.s: hld up: hung rt and r.o ins fnl f: nt clr run towards fin: nt trble ldrs* **9/1**

1526 **6** *1 ½* **Fabulist**[24] 6081 3-9-5 **84**.................. RobertHavlin 7 77
(John Gosden) *led 1f: chsd ldrs: rdn over 1f out: styd on same pce fnl f* **11/2**[3]

4361 **7** *shd* **Key Player**[11] 6567 4-9-10 **85**..................(p) CharlesBishop 5 80
(Eve Johnson Houghton) *led 6f out: rdn and hdd over 2f out: wknd wl ins fnl f* **8/1**

3-P3 **8** *1* **Brigham Young**[24] 6076 4-9-2 **77**.................. HectorCrouch 11 69
(Ed Walker) *chsd ldr over 5f out: led over 2f out: rdn and hdd over 1f out: wknd ins fnl f* **5/1**[2]

200 **9** *¾* **The Establishment**[17] 6350 4-8-10 **71** oh3..................(h) JoeyHaynes 2 61
(John Butler) *hld up: nvr on terms* **50/1**

-320 **10** *3* **Johnny Reb**[89] 3661 3-8-11 **76**..................(t[1]) StevieDonohoe 1 56
(Charlie Fellowes) *hld up in tch: rdn over 1f out: wknd fnl f* **5/1**[2]

1220 **11** *4* **Rock Of Estonia (IRE)**[70] 4365 4-9-3 **78**.................. ShaneKelly 10 49
(Michael Squance) *a in rr* **33/1**

1m 25.04s (-0.96) **Going Correction** 0.0s/f (Stan)
WFA 3 from 4yo+ 4lb **11** Ran SP% **118.7**
Speed ratings (Par 105): **105,104,102,102,101 99,99,98,97,93 89**
CSF £68.94 CT £616.80 TOTE £5.40: £1.60, £4.10, £2.80; EX 75.20 Trifecta £749.30.
Owner Mr & Mrs De & J Cash And P Turner **Bred** Derra Park Stud **Trained** Newmarket, Suffolk

FOCUS
A tight finish to a fair handicap and the pace was solid. The third looks the best guide.
T/Plt: £119.10 to a £1 stake. Pool: £58,765.62 - 359.91 winning units T/Qpdt: £14.20 to a £1 stake. Pool: £4,926.07 - 255.51 winning units **Colin Roberts**

6673 THIRSK (L-H)

Saturday, September 7

OFFICIAL GOING: Good (good to firm in places)

Wind: light across Weather: overcast

6969 CLIFF STUD REARING WINNERS NURSERY H'CAP 7f 218y

1:55 (1:55) (Class 5) (0-75,74) 2-Y-O

£5,692 (£1,694; £846; £423; £300; £300) **Stalls** Low

Form RPR

0553 1 **International Lion**[32] 5781 2-8-7 **60**........................(p) PaddyMathers 8 64
(Richard Fahey) *slowly away and rdn along in rr early: rdn and hdwy on wd outside over 2f out: led narrowly appr fnl f: drvn out* **10/1**

0050 2 nk **Clay Regazzoni**[8] 6653 2-9-1 **73**........................ BenSanderson(5) 4 76
(Keith Dalgleish) *hld up: rdn and hdwy on outer over 2f out: chal strly appr fnl f: kpt on* **12/1**

6011 3 1 3/4 **Walkonby**[15] 6416 2-9-0 **67**........................ GrahamLee 10 66
(Mick Channon) *trckd ldrs: rdn to chal strly over 1f out: one pce ins fnl f* **4/1**[1]

353 4 1/2 **Topkapi Star**[49] 5170 2-9-7 **74**........................ PaulHanagan 12 72
(Roger Varian) *midfield: rdn over 2f out: chsd ldrs over 1f out: hung lft: styd on ins fnl f* **13/2**

0231 5 2 **Out Of Breath**[11] 6571 2-9-4 **71**........................ SamJames 1 65
(Grant Tuer) *led: pushed along and hdd over 3f out: rdn 2f out: remained chalng tl no ex ins fnl f* **5/1**[2]

5213 6 1 1/4 **G For Gabrial (IRE)**[11] 6579 2-9-3 **70**........................ TonyHamilton 5 61
(Richard Fahey) *midfield: pushed along and outpcd 3f out: rdn 2f out: plugged on ins fnl f* **6/1**[3]

5202 7 nk **Fast Deal**[11] 6579 2-9-5 **72**........................ DavidAllan 6 62
(Tim Easterby) *pressed ldr: led 3f out: rdn 2f out: hdd appr fnl f: wknd ins fnl f* **9/1**

401 8 shd **Magna Moralia (IRE)**[13] 6497 2-9-7 **74**........................ JasonHart 9 64
(John Quinn) *nvr bttr than midfield* **8/1**

0601 9 1/2 **Bankawi**[45] 5296 2-8-2 **55**........................ JamesSullivan 11 45
(Michael Easterby) *hld up: rdn and sme hdwy whn short of room over 1f out tl ins fnl f: no ch after (jockey said filly was denied a clear run approaching the final furlong)* **25/1**

0343 10 3 3/4 **Harswell Approach (IRE)**[21] 6226 2-9-1 **68**........................ PaulMulrennan 3 49
(Liam Bailey) *s.i.s: pushed along to sn chse ldrs: rdn over 2f out: wknd over 1f out (vet said gelding finished lame left fore)* **16/1**

005 11 18 **The Works (IRE)**[53] 5017 2-8-0 **45** oh8........................ JamieGormley 2
(Declan Carroll) *trckd ldrs: lost pl 3f out: wknd and bhd fnl 2f* **66/1**

0401 12 2 3/4 **Lady Erimus**[29] 5912 2-8-8 **61**........................ ShaneGray 7
(Kevin Ryan) *a in rr (jockey said filly was never travelling)* **16/1**

1m 39.31s (-2.39) **Going Correction** -0.20s/f (Firm) **12 Ran SP% 119.3**

Speed ratings (Par 95): **103,102,100,100,98 97,96,96,96,92 74,71**

CSF £125.08 CT £573.85 TOTE £13.20: £3.40, £4.40, £1.90; EX 135.40 Trifecta £924.20.

Owner P D Smith Holdings Ltd **Bred** James Ortega Bloodstock Ltd **Trained** Musley Bank, N Yorks

FOCUS

A wide-open nursery run at what looked a reasonable enough gallop. The winner came from well off the pace and the second was just about back to his earlier form.

6970 JENNY ROBERTS MILLINERY - EBF NOVICE STKS (PLUS 10 RACE) (DIV I) 7f

2:30 (2:32) (Class 4) 2-Y-O

£6,225 (£1,864; £932; £466; £233; £117) **Stalls** Low

Form RPR

1 **Melody King (IRE)** 2-9-5 **0**........................ JasonHart 11 74+
(John Quinn) *prom: pushed along 2f out: led 1f out: rdn out ins fnl f* **10/3**[2]

4 2 3/4 **Le Chiffre**[10] 6606 2-9-5 **0**........................ DavidNolan 4 72
(David O'Meara) *trckd ldrs: pushed along over 2f out: rdn and kpt on fnl f: wnt 2nd nr fin* **9/2**[3]

46 3 nk **Robert Guiscard (IRE)**[21] 6219 2-9-5 **0**........................ AndrewElliott 9 71
(Mark Johnston) *led: pushed along over 2f out: rdn and hdd 1f out: one pce and lost 2nd nr fin* **7/1**

60 4 hd **Araka Li (IRE)**[58] 4826 2-9-5 **0**........................ DavidAllan 3 70+
(Tim Easterby) *dwlt: hld up: pushed along over 2f out: rdn and hdwy on outside appr fnl f: kpt on* **33/1**

4 5 1/2 **Borsdane Wood**[21] 6228 2-9-5 **0**........................ CliffordLee 8 69
(K R Burke) *midfield on outer: rdn over 2f out: edgd lft: hdwy appr fnl f: kpt on* **9/1**

56 6 2 **Cold Light Of Day**[22] 6175 2-9-0 **0**........................ PaulMulrennan 7 59+
(Michael Dods) *midfield: pushed along over 2f out: styd on same pce: nvr threatened* **5/1**

7 1/2 **Quercus (IRE)** 2-9-5 **0**........................ JackGarritty 2 63
(Ann Duffield) *trckd ldrs: pushed along over 2f out: wknd ins fnl f* **40/1**

8 2 3/4 **Helmoona** 2-9-5 **0**........................ JamesSullivan 6 56
(Karen Tutty) *hld up: pushed along over 2f out: nvr threatened* **33/1**

55 9 nk **Internationaltiger**[16] 6368 2-9-5 **0**........................ PaulHanagan 5 55
(Richard Fahey) *midfield: pushed along over 2f out: rdn over 1f out: wknd fnl f* **3/1**[1]

10 2 3/4 **Poco Contante** 2-9-0 **0**........................ BenRobinson 10 43
(David Thompson) *slowly away: a in rr* **66/1**

0 11 26 **New Man**[22] 6175 2-9-5 **0**........................ RachelRichardson 1
(Tim Easterby) *hld up: pushed along 4f out: wknd and bhd over 2f out* **50/1**

1m 28.19s (0.59) **Going Correction** -0.20s/f (Firm) **11 Ran SP% 117.2**

Speed ratings (Par 97): **88,87,86,86,86 83,83,80,79,76 46**

CSF £18.04 TOTE £3.40: £1.90, £1.70, £2.40; EX 20.30 Trifecta £101.00.

Owner Phoenix Thoroughbred Limited **Bred** David C Egan **Trained** Settrington, N Yorks

FOCUS

Probably no more than a reasonable novice event but the well-bred winner has stacks of scope and could easily be smart.

6971 JENNY ROBERTS MILLINERY - EBF NOVICE STKS (PLUS 10 RACE) (DIV II) 7f

3:05 (3:08) (Class 4) 2-Y-O

£6,225 (£1,864; £932; £466; £233; £117) **Stalls** Low

Form RPR

62 1 **Plymouth Rock (IRE)**[37] 5591 2-9-5 **0**........................ JasonHart 4 78+
(John Quinn) *trckd ldr: rdn 2f out: drvn to chal ins fnl f: kpt on to ld towards fin* **11/4**[2]

2 nk **El Naseri (IRE)** 2-9-5 **0**........................ PaulMulrennan 9 77+
(Michael Dods) *s.i.s: hld up: angled rt to outer 2f out: pushed along and gd hdwy appr fnl f: kpt on wl: wnt 2nd post* **20/1**

442 3 nk **Hello Baileys**[36] 5624 2-9-5 **77**........................ CliffordLee 5 76
(Mark Johnston) *led: rdn over 1f out: drvn and strly pressed ins fnl f: hdd towards fin: lost 2nd post* **2/1**[1]

2 4 1 **Manzo Duro (IRE)**[21] 6226 2-9-5 **0**........................ DavidNolan 1 73
(David O'Meara) *dwlt: midfield: pushed along and hdwy to chse ldrs over 1f out: kpt on same pce ins fnl f* **7/2**[3]

32 5 nk **Viceregent**[25] 6035 2-9-5 **0**........................ TonyHamilton 2 73
(Richard Fahey) *trckd ldr: racd keenly: rdn 2f out: kpt on same pce fnl f* **9/1**

6 1 **Top Flight Cool** 2-9-5 **0**........................ DavidAllan 8 70
(Tim Easterby) *hld up: pushed along and hdwy 2f: kpt on ins fnl f: short of room towards fin* **40/1**

7 8 **Just Call Me Ella** 2-9-0 **0**........................ BenRobinson 3 44
(Rebecca Menzies) *in tch: pushed along over 2f out: wknd over 1f out* **33/1**

8 nk **Saracen Spirit** 2-9-5 **0**........................ GrahamLee 6 48
(Mick Channon) *in tch: pushed along over 2f out: wknd over 1f out* **16/1**

9 8 **Onedin (IRE)** 2-9-5 **0**........................ ShaneGray 7 28
(Kevin Ryan) *s.i.s: a towards rr* **16/1**

10 3/4 **Heyday** 2-9-0 **0**........................ PaulHanagan 10 21
(Richard Fahey) *midfield: pushed along 4f out: sn outpcd: wknd and bhd over 2f out* **18/1**

1m 28.36s (0.76) **Going Correction** -0.20s/f (Firm) **10 Ran SP% 119.4**

Speed ratings (Par 97): **87,86,86,85,84 83,74,74,65,64**

CSF £60.19 TOTE £3.00: £1.10, £6.20, £1.10; EX 77.20 Trifecta £256.60.

Owner Tabor,Smith,Magnier & Shanahan **Bred** Peter Jones **Trained** Settrington, N Yorks

FOCUS

Another reasonable novice but not many got into this from off the pace. The winning time was marginally slower than the first division but a slightly positive view has been taken of the form.

6972 BARKERS OF NORTHALLERTON H'CAP 6f

3:40 (3:42) (Class 4) (0-80,82) 4-Y-O+

£8,927 (£2,656; £1,327; £663; £300; £300) **Stalls** Centre

Form RPR

0302 1 **East Street Revue**[10] 6607 6-9-2 **74**........................(b) DavidAllan 8 82
(Tim Easterby) *led centre gp: rdn over 2f out: drvn into overall ld over 1f out: kpt on wl* **9/1**

6035 2 3/4 **Lucky Lucky Man (IRE)**[21] 6227 4-9-5 **77**........................ DavidNolan 13 83
(Richard Fahey) *midfield centre: rdn and hdwy over 1f out: kpt on wl: 2nd of 11 in gp* **10/1**

3050 3 nk **Paddy Power (IRE)**[21] 6227 6-9-7 **79**........................ TonyHamilton 6 84
(Richard Fahey) *dwlt: hld up centre: pushed along and hdwy appr fnl f: kpt on wl: 3rd of 11 in gp* **9/1**

0-33 4 shd **Kindly**[4] 6825 6-9-6 **78**........................ JamesSullivan 9 82
(Michael Easterby) *trckd ldrs centre: rdn over 2f out: kpt on same pce fnl f: 4th of 11 in gp* **9/2**[1]

5200 5 1/2 **Oriental Lilly**[10] 6609 5-8-11 **69**........................(p) PaddyMathers 5 72
(Jim Goldie) *dwlt: sn midfield centre: rdn over 2f out: kpt on: 5th of 11 in gp* **33/1**

5231 6 1 **Case Key**[21] 6220 6-8-13 **71**........................(b) CliffordLee 10 71
(Michael Appleby) *prom in centre: rdn over 2f out: no ex fnl 110yds: 6th of 11 in gp* **8/1**[3]

-205 7 1 1/4 **Final Go**[87] 3722 4-9-0 **72**........................ SamJames 12 68
(Grant Tuer) *trckd ldrs centre: rdn over 2f out: outplcd and btn 1f out: 7th of 11 in gp* **25/1**

033 8 hd **Mostahel**[14] 6461 5-8-11 **69**........................ GrahamLee 2 64
(Paul Midgley) *chsd ldrs centre: rdn over 2f out: wknd ins fnl f: 8th off 11 in gp* **12/1**

1325 9 nk **Musharrif**[29] 5911 7-9-0 **79**........................(t) ZakWheatley(7) 17 73
(Declan Carroll) *midfield stands' side: rdn over 2f out: kpt on: nvr threatened: 1st of 5 in gp* **12/1**

0-00 10 1/2 **Rolladice**[101] 3221 4-8-7 **70**........................(w) GerO'Neill(5) 1 62
(Michael Easterby) *hld up on outside of centre gp: nvr threatened: 9th of 11 in gp* **25/1**

6210 11 nse **Our Little Pony**[16] 6379 4-9-2 **79**........................ FayeMcManoman(5) 15 71
(Lawrence Mullaney) *hld up stands' side: rdn 2f out: kpt on ins fnl f: nvr threatened: 2nd of 5 in gp* **6/1**[2]

0046 12 1 3/4 **Upstaging**[11] 6581 7-9-0 **72**........................(b) JackGarritty 3 59
(Noel Wilson) *dwlt: hld up centre: bit short of room over 1f out and swtchd lft: nvr threatened: 10th of 11 in gp* **25/1**

0626 13 3 **Lucky Beggar (IRE)**[10] 6591 9-8-7 **65**........................ PaulHanagan 18 42
(David C Griffiths) *chsd ldr stands' side: rdn over 2f out: wknd over 1f out: 3rd of 5 in gp* **16/1**

4100 14 nse **Stewardess (IRE)**[21] 6220 4-8-9 **70**........................ ConnorMurtagh(3) 4 47
(Richard Fahey) *racd centre: a towards rr: last of 11 in gp* **40/1**

0560 15 5 **Arcavallo (IRE)**[41] 5476 4-9-2 **74**........................(b[1]) PaulMulrennan 16 35
(Michael Dods) *led stands' side gp and overall ldr: rdn and hdd over 1f out: wknd: 4th of 5 in gp* **20/1**

35/1 16 50 **Society Prince (IRE)**[18] 6325 4-9-0 **72**........................ GeorgeWood 14
(James Fanshawe) *slowly away: hld up in rr stands' side: rdn over 2f out: sn btn: eased (jockey said gelding was never travelling)* **9/1**

1m 11.36s (-1.44) **Going Correction** -0.20s/f (Firm) **16 Ran SP% 125.6**

Speed ratings (Par 105): **101,100,99,99,98 97,95,95,95,94 94,92,88,88,81 14**

CSF £90.54 CT £855.02 TOTE £10.10: £2.30, £2.40, £2.40, £1.60; EX 117.80 Trifecta £638.10.

Owner S A Heley & Partner **Bred** Habton Farms & Mr A Heley **Trained** Great Habton, N Yorks

FOCUS

A wide open handicap in which they split into two groups initially before converging middle to stands' side. The winner was always front rank down the middle and he and the second have been rated to this year's form.

6973 BRITISH STALLION STUDS EBF H'CAP 7f 218y

4:15 (4:19) (Class 3) (0-95,94) 3-Y-O £12,450 (£3,728; £1,864; £932) **Stalls** Low

Form RPR

1306 1 **Irreverent**[12] 6543 3-9-0 **87**........................ PaulHanagan 4 94
(Richard Fahey) *trckd ldr: jnd ldr gng wl 2f out: pushed into ld appr fnl f: rdn out ins fnl f: comf* **8/11**[1]

4615 2 1 1/2 **Smile A Mile (IRE)**[13] 6516 3-9-7 **94**........................ JasonHart 1 97
(Mark Johnston) *trckd ldr: rdn along and bit outpcd over 2f out: kpt on ins fnl f: wnt 2nd towards fin* **3/1**[2]

5610 3 1/2 **I'lletyougonow**[16] 6362 3-8-2 **74**........................(p) JamesSullivan 2 76
(Mick Channon) *led: rdn along and jnd 2f out: hdd appr fnl f: drvn and one pce ins fnl f: lost 2nd towards fin* **11/2**[3]

The Form Book Flat 2019, Raceform Ltd, Newbury, RG14 5SJ

055 **4** 2 ¼ **Jupiter Road**[12] 6541 3-7-11 **77**......................................(tp) IzzyClifton(7) 6 73?
(Nigel Tinkler) *hld up in tch: pushed along over 2f out: hdwy and briefly chsd ldr over 1f out: wknd ins fnl f* **9/1**

1m 38.01s (-3.69) **Going Correction** -0.20s/f (Firm) 4 Ran SP% **108.3**
Speed ratings (Par 105): **110,108,108,105**
CSF £3.16 TOTE £1.40; EX 3.10 Trifecta £6.00.
Owner Mr & Mrs N Wrigley **Bred** Mr & Mrs N Wrigley **Trained** Musley Bank, N Yorks

FOCUS
Only four runners but they went what appeared an even enough gallop and that suited the winner who is normally held up in his races. Quite weak form for the grade.

6974 PERSONAL TOUCHES FILLIES' H'CAP 7f
4:50 (4:51) (Class 3) (0-90,90) 3-Y-0+
£12,450 (£3,728; £1,864; £932; £466; £234) **Stalls** Low

Form RPR
5301 **1** **Excellent Times**[16] 6379 4-9-9 **87**............................ DavidAllan 5 97
(Tim Easterby) *hld up: pushed along and hdwy on outer 2f out: rdn to ld ins fnl f: kpt on wl* **3/1**[1]

0510 **2** 1 ¾ **Pattie**[14] 6445 5-9-11 **89**............................ GrahamLee 4 94
(Mick Channon) *midfield: pushed along over 2f out: rdn and hdwy to chse ldrs appr fnl f: kpt on* **15/2**

0361 **3** 1 ¼ **Astrologer**[15] 6408 3-9-8 **90**............................ DavidNolan 8 90
(David O'Meara) *pressed ldr: pushed into ld wl over 1f out: sn rdn: hdd ins fnl f: no ex* **7/2**[2]

-000 **4** *nk* **Dance Diva**[16] 6379 4-9-9 **87**............................ PaulHanagan 9 88
(Richard Fahey) *midfield on outer: pushed along and hdwy to chse ldrs 2f out: rdn over 1f out: no ex ins fnl f* **5/1**[3]

4040 **5** *nk* **Florenza**[8] 6677 6-8-13 **77**............................ AndrewElliott 3 77
(Chris Fairhurst) *led narrowly: rdn and hdd wl over 1f out: no ex ins fnl f* **16/1**

0000 **6** 1 **Starlight Romance (IRE)**[16] 6379 5-9-5 **83**.................. TonyHamilton 7 80
(Richard Fahey) *chsd ldrs: rdn along 2f out: outpcd and btn 1f out* **14/1**

4010 **7** *nse* **Kylie Rules**[16] 6379 4-9-8 **86**............................ JamesSullivan 6 83
(Ruth Carr) *stdd s: hld up in rr: rdn over 2f out: minor late hdwy: nvr threatened* **7/1**

116- **8** 2 ¼ **Zip Along (IRE)**[352] 7465 4-9-9 **90**.................. ConnorMurtagh(3) 2 81
(Richard Fahey) *hld up: pushed along over 2f out: nvr threatened* **20/1**

434 **9** *hd* **Material Girl**[22] 6170 3-8-5 **73**..................(p) GeorgeWood 1 62
(Richard Spencer) *in tch: rdn over 2f out: wknd over 1f out* **9/1**

1m 24.55s (-3.05) **Going Correction** -0.20s/f (Firm)
WFA 3 from 4yo+ 4lb 9 Ran SP% **115.5**
Speed ratings (Par 104): **109,107,105,105,104 103,103,101,100**
CSF £26.01 CT £82.28 TOTE £3.70: £1.50, £2.10, £1.50; EX 25.50 Trifecta £66.80.
Owner Times Of Wigan **Bred** Times Of Wigan Ltd **Trained** Great Habton, N Yorks

FOCUS
A competitive heat on paper and they went a strong gallop, dragging the hold-up horses into contention in the straight. The standard's set around the runner-up.

6975 CALVERTS CARPETS HAMBLETON CUP H'CAP 1m 4f 8y
5:25 (5:25) (Class 3) (0-90,90) 3-Y-0+ **£12,938** (£3,850; £1,924; £962) **Stalls** High

Form RPR
1310 **1** **Where's Jeff**[35] 5694 4-9-5 **81**............................ JamesSullivan 9 88
(Michael Easterby) *midfield: pushed along over 3f out: rdn and hdwy to chse ldrs 2f out: drvn into narrow ld appr fnl f: kpt on* **15/2**

5236 **2** ½ **Claire Underwood (IRE)**[17] 6355 4-9-10 **86**............... TonyHamilton 4 92
(Richard Fahey) *prom: led over 2f out: rdn over 2f out: hdd appr fnl f: drvn and kpt on* **9/2**[2]

0004 **3** ½ **Employer (IRE)**[8] 6658 4-8-10 **72**............................ PaddyMathers 5 77
(Jim Goldie) *midfield: rdn and hdwy on outer 2f out: drvn to chal strly over 1f out: kpt on same pce ins fnl f* **12/1**

-155 **4** *nk* **Stonific (IRE)**[24] 6067 6-9-6 **82**............................ DavidNolan 1 86
(David O'Meara) *hld up: rdn and hdwy over 1f out: kpt on ins fnl f* **14/1**

00-0 **5** 1 ½ **Star Archer**[14] 6475 5-9-8 **89**............................ GerO'Neill(5) 11 91
(Michael Easterby) *trckd ldrs: pushed along 2f out: rdn and one pce ins fnl f* **50/1**

5456 **6** ½ **Billy No Mates (IRE)**[28] 5973 3-8-10 **80**.................. GrahamLee 3 82
(Michael Dods) *midfield: pushed along over 2f out: rdn over 1f out: keeping on whn short of room jst ins fnl f: no ch after* **8/1**

2142 **7** ¾ **Rowland Ward**[49] 5201 3-9-1 **85**..................(b[1]) HarryBentley 7 86
(Ralph Beckett) *trckd ldrs: rdn along 3f out: drvn to chal 2f out: wknd ins fnl f* **7/4**[1]

5414 **7** *dht* **Trinity Star (IRE)**[25] 6038 8-8-10 **72**..................(v) CliffordLee 8 72
(Karen McLintock) *hld up: pushed along and hung lft over 1f out: kpt on ins fnl f: nvr threatened* **16/1**

5005 **9** 6 **Aiya (IRE)**[11] 6580 4-9-0 **76**..................(h) DavidAllan 10 66
(Tim Easterby) *led: rdn and hdd over 2f out: wknd over 1f out* **6/1**[3]

0460 **10** 2 ¼ **Dance King**[12] 6535 9-8-12 **74**..................(tp) JasonHart 2 61
(Tim Easterby) *hld up: rdn over 2f out: sn wknd* **25/1**

500- **11** 4 ½ **Cape Cova (IRE)**[505] 1955 6-10-0 **90**.................. PaulMulrennan 6 70
(Marjorie Fife) *dwlt: a in rr (jockey said gelding ran too free)* **66/1**

2m 34.59s (-5.41) **Going Correction** -0.20s/f (Firm)
WFA 3 from 4yo+ 8lb 11 Ran SP% **119.2**
Speed ratings (Par 107): **110,109,109,109,108 107,107,107,103,101 98**
WIN: 9.80 Where's Jeff; PL: 1.80 Claire Underwood 2.70 Where's Jeff 3.80 Employer; EX: 33.90; CSF: 41.41; TC: 409.54; TF: 742.00 CSF £41.41 CT £409.54 TOTE £9.80: £2.70, £1.80, £3.80; EX 33.90 Trifecta £742.00.
Owner A G Pollock, Golden Ratio & J Sissons **Bred** Lucky 5 Partnership & Stittenham Racing **Trained** Sheriff Hutton, N Yorks

FOCUS
A really competitive middle-distance handicap, but very ordinary for the grade. The time was modest but the form't taken at face value.

6976 MEDIA DISPLAYS LED SCREEN HIRE H'CAP 5f
5:55 (5:56) (Class 4) (0-85,85) 3-Y-0
£8,927 (£2,656; £1,327; £663; £300; £300) **Stalls** Centre

Form RPR
1131 **1** **Four Wheel Drive**[7] 6699 3-9-5 **83**..................(p) GrahamLee 1 94
(David Brown) *chsd ldr: pushed along to chal over 1f out: rdn to ld jst ins fnl f: sn edgd lft: hld on towards fin* **9/2**[3]

0-10 **2** *hd* **Count D'orsay (IRE)**[14] 6476 3-9-2 **80**.................. DavidAllan 5 90
(Tim Easterby) *midfield: pushed along over 2f out: rdn over 1f out: hdwy and chsd ldr ins fnl f: edgd lft: kpt on to chal towards fin* **9/2**[3]

-040 **3** ½ **Triggered (IRE)**[84] 3865 3-9-7 **85**............................ PaulHanagan 4 93
(Ed Walker) *dwlt: outpcd in rr tl hdwy appr fnl f: hung lft ins fnl f: drvn and r.o wl fnl 110yds: nrst fin (jockey said colt hung left in the final furlong)* **7/2**[2]

6466 **4** 1 ½ **True Hero**[7] 6715 3-8-7 **74**............................ RowanScott(3) 3 77
(Nigel Tinkler) *led narrowly: hdd 3f out: chsd ldr: rdn over 1f out: one pce ins fnl f* **12/1**

3252 **5** 1 ¼ **Tenax (IRE)**[9] 6623 3-9-2 **85**..................(p[1]) FayeMcManoman(5) 2 83
(Nigel Tinkler) *hld up: pushed along over 1f out: rdn ins fnl f: kpt on towards fin: nvr threatened* **5/2**[1]

1200 **6** *hd* **The Defiant**[7] 6715 3-8-7 **71** oh2............................ BenRobinson 6 69
(Paul Midgley) *racd keenly: pressed ldr: led over 3f out: rdn over 1f out: hdd jst ins fnl f: sn wknd (jockey said gelding ran too free)* **16/1**

1541 **7** 3 ½ **Melrose Way**[35] 5660 3-8-7 **71** oh2............................ JamesSullivan 7 56
(Paul Midgley) *midfield: pushed along over 3f out: rdn over 2f out: wknd fnl f (vet said filly finished lame left hind)* **15/2**

58.04s (-1.36) **Going Correction** -0.20s/f (Firm) 7 Ran SP% **112.5**
Speed ratings (Par 103): **102,101,100,98,96 96,90**
CSF £24.01 TOTE £4.20: £2.70, £2.20; EX 22.60 Trifecta £89.50.
Owner Bratwa **Bred** A C M Spalding **Trained** Averham Park, Notts

FOCUS
This sprint handicap was run at a generous early gallop, but those outpaced or in rear struggled to get involved. Another small pb from the winner.
T/Plt: £34.40 to a £1 stake. Pool: £48,113.75 - 1,019.62 winning units T/Qpdt: £6.20 to a £1 stake. Pool: £3,776.24 - 444.45 winning units **Andrew Sheret**

6731 WOLVERHAMPTON (A.W) (L-H)
Saturday, September 7

OFFICIAL GOING: Tapeta: standard
Wind: light breeze, against in home straight Weather: sunny intervals, quite mild

6977 COMPARE BOOKMAKER SITES AT BONUSCODEBETS.CO.UK APPRENTICE H'CAP 1m 142y (Tp)
5:30 (5:30) (Class 6) (0-65,62) 4-Y-0+
£2,781 (£827; £413; £400; £400; £400) **Stalls** Low

Form RPR
05-5 **1** **Pact Of Steel**[99] 3325 4-8-5 **49**..................(t) WilliamCarver(3) 7 56
(Ivan Furtado) *chsd ldrs: tk clsr order 3f out: pushed into ld 1 1/2f out: rdn over 1f out: r.o wl fnl f* **4/1**[2]

31 **2** 1 **Enzo (IRE)**[36] 5633 4-9-7 **62**............................ DylanHogan 5 67
(John Butler) *mid-div: pushed along and hdwy 2f out: rdn and wnt 2nd 1f out: kpt on fnl f* **6/4**[1]

054 **3** ½ **Vipin (FR)**[23] 6119 4-9-5 **60**............................ CierenFallon 1 64
(William Muir) *hld up: drvn 2f out: chsd ldrs and briefly nt clr run over 1f out: rdn fnl f: r.o: secured 3rd last stride* **7/1**[3]

0000 **4** *shd* **Ebbisham (IRE)**[54] 5003 6-8-11 **55**..................(v) TobyEley(3) 4 59
(John Mackie) *hld up: drvn 2f out: rdn and effrt over 1f out: r.o fnl f: jst denied for 3rd (jockey said gelding hung left-handed throughout)* **15/2**

0602 **5** 2 ¼ **I Think So (IRE)**[7] 6731 4-8-12 **56**..................(b) LauraCoughlan(3) 10 55
(David Loughnane) *led: drvn and hdd 1 1/2f out: sn rdn: wknd fnl f* **7/1**[3]

2364 **6** 1 ¾ **Mabo**[9] 6643 4-8-9 **50**..................(b) AndrewBreslin 9 45
(Grace Harris) *prom: drvn and lost pl over 2f out: sn rdn: wknd over 1f out* **14/1**

2050 **7** 4 ½ **Enmeshing**[23] 6104 6-9-3 **58**............................ SebastianWoods 6 44
(Alexandra Dunn) *hld up on outer: drvn over 2f out: sn rdn and wknd* **9/1**

5000 **8** 1 ½ **Longville Lilly**[9] 6628 4-8-0 **45** oh3..................(b[1]) IsobelFrancis(7) 3 31
(Trevor Wall) *t.k.h: hld up in rr: detached fr pack 3f out: rdn over 2f out: no imp (jockey said filly ran too freely)* **100/1**

0600 **9** 2 ¾ **Arrowzone**[7] 6731 8-8-12 **56**..................(b) AledBeech(3) 2 33
(Katy Price) *t.k.h: trckd ldrs: rdn and wknd over 2f out* **33/1**

1m 49.9s (-0.20) **Going Correction** -0.10s/f (Stan) 9 Ran SP% **117.4**
Speed ratings (Par 101): **96,95,94,94,92 91,87,85,83**
CSF £10.56 CT £40.90 TOTE £4.80: £1.70, £1.10, £2.30; EX 14.50 Trifecta £56.50.
Owner Daniel Macauliffe & Anoj Don **Bred** Brightwalton Bloodstock Ltd **Trained** Wiseton, Nottinghamshire

FOCUS
A moderate handicap. The winner can go in again and the second is rated to his latest form.

6978 FOLLOW US ON TWITTER @WOLVESRACES CLAIMING STKS 7f 36y (Tp)
6:00 (6:00) (Class 5) 3-Y-0+
£3,428 (£1,020; £509; £400; £400; £400) **Stalls** High

Form RPR
5303 **1** **Love Dreams (IRE)**[13] 6517 5-9-4 93..................(p) FrannyNorton 4 75+
(Mark Johnston) *mde all: pushed along in narrow ld 2f out: drvn into 1/2 l ld 1f out: strly pressed wl ins fnl f: rdn and hld on wl* **4/6**[1]

4121 **2** *nk* **Tukhoom (IRE)**[13] 6496 6-9-7 83..................(b) CierenFallon(5) 1 82+
(David O'Meara) *chsd ldrs: drvn 2f out: rdn in 3rd ent fnl f: wnt 2nd 1/2f out: kpt on wl: jst hld* **9/4**[2]

0-60 **3** 5 **Global Humor (USA)**[30] 5852 4-9-0 63.................. BarryMcHugh 5 58+
(Tristan Davidson) *prom: cl 2nd 2f out: drvn in 1/2 l 2nd 1f out: rdn and wknd fnl f: lost 2nd 1/2f out* **12/1**

U140 **4** *shd* **Gold Hunter (IRE)**[30] 5839 9-9-0 69..................(tp) RaulDaSilva 7 58+
(Steve Flook) *chsd ldrs: drvn in 4th 2f out: rdn over 1f out: one pce fnl f* **40/1**

4026 **5** *nk* **Imperial State**[71] 4319 6-9-3 75..................(v) NathanEvans 3 60+
(Michael Easterby) *hld up: drvn 1 1/2f out: rdn over 1f out: one pce fnl f* **17/2**[3]

0050 **6** 2 ¾ **De Latour**[19] 6275 3-8-10 43............................ RoystonFfrench 6 48
(Jason Ward) *t.k.h: hld up: drvn over 1f out: dropped away fnl f (jockey said gelding ran too freely)* **100/1**

1m 27.64s (-1.16) **Going Correction** -0.10s/f (Stan)
WFA 3 from 4yo+ 4lb 6 Ran SP% **112.4**
Speed ratings (Par 103): **102,101,95,95,95 92**
CSF £2.38 TOTE £1.60: £1.10, £1.40; EX 2.80 Trifecta £7.50.Love Dreams was claimed by Mr J. A. Osborne for £10,000. Global Humor was claimed by Mr J. S. Goldie for £6,000.
Owner Crone Stud Farms Ltd **Bred** John O'Connor **Trained** Middleham Moor, N Yorks

FOCUS
The favourite had to work for this. The sixth governs the merit of the form.

6979 HOTEL & CONFERENCING AT WOLVERHAMPTON EBF NOVICE STKS 5f 21y (Tp)
6:30 (6:33) (Class 5) 2-Y-O £3,428 (£1,020; £509; £254) Stalls Low

Form RPR
300 **1** **Moon Of Love (IRE)**[16] 6374 2-8-11 81.....................(h[1]) BarryMcHugh 6 80
(Richard Fahey) *chsd ldr: drvn 2f out: rdn in 1/2 l 2nd 1f out: r.o wl fnl f: led last 50yds* 11/8[1]

4000 **2** ½ **Electric Ladyland (IRE)**[38] 5544 2-9-8 85...........(b[1]) AdamMcNamara 7 89
(Archie Watson) *led: rdn 1 1/2f out: 1/2 l ld 1f out: hdd last 50yds: no ex* 6/4[2]

66 **3** 9 **Glamorous Force**[57] 4871 2-9-2 0.............................. FrannyNorton 3 51
(Ronald Harris) *hld up: coming together w rival after 1 1/2f: hdwy into 3rd 3f out: drvn 2f out: rdn and no ex fr 1 1/2f out* 16/1

4 2 ¼ **Knock Knock (IRE)** 2-9-2 0.............................. DanielMuscutt 5 43
(Sylvester Kirk) *slowly away: bhd: drvn into 4th 2f out: reminder 1f out: no ex fnl f* 5/1[3]

500 **5** 7 **Maisie Ellie (IRE)**[89] 3660 2-8-6 64.............................. RhiainIngram(5) 4 13
(Paul George) *hld up: coming together w rival after 1 1/2f and sn dropped to last: no ch after* 28/1

6 3 ½ **Orange Justice** 2-8-8 0.............................. CameronNoble(3) 1
(David Loughnane) *threw jockey on way to s: chsd ldrs: slt stmbld after 2f: sn pushed along and lost pl: eased and dropped to last 1f out: lost shoe (vet said filly lost her right-hind shoe)* 20/1

1m 1.22s (-0.68) **Going Correction** -0.10s/f (Stan) 6 Ran SP% **112.9**
Speed ratings (Par 95): **101,100,85,82,71 65**
CSF £3.77 TOTE £2.20: £1.10, £1.30; EX 3.60 Trifecta £22.20.
Owner The Cool Silk Partnership **Bred** Canice Farrell **Trained** Musley Bank, N Yorks

FOCUS
This was run at a good gallop and the big two in the market dominated throughout. The form's best rated around the second.

6980 SKY SPORTS RACING SKY 415 NURSERY H'CAP 6f 20y (Tp)
7:00 (7:01) (Class 5) (0-75,75) 2-Y-O £3,428 (£1,020; £509; £400; £400; £400) Stalls Low

Form RPR
443 **1** **Stone Soldier**[32] 5780 2-9-3 71.............................. BarryMcHugh 4 81+
(James Given) *chsd ldr: pushed along in 1/2 l 2nd 2f out: drvn to ld 1 1/2f out: rdn clr ent fnl f: r.o wl: comf* 14/1

5040 **2** 2 **Zingaro Boy (IRE)**[16] 6372 2-8-12 71.............................. CierenFallon(5) 9 73
(Hugo Palmer) *hld up on outer: drvn and hdwy over 1f out: sn rdn: r.o into 2nd fnl f: nvr nr wnr (jockey said colt hung right-handed)* 7/1

3532 **3** 1 ¼ **Jump The Gun (IRE)**[9] 6637 2-9-5 73.............................. NicolaCurrie 3 71
(Jamie Osborne) *slowly away: bhd: drvn and hdwy on inner over 1f out: reminders and r.o steadily into 3rd fnl f (jockey said colt suffered interference one furlong after the start)* 7/2[2]

323 **4** 1 ¼ **Baltic State (IRE)**[29] 5913 2-9-6 74.............................. BenCurtis 2 70
(Kevin Ryan) *mid-div: drvn in 4th 2f out: rdn 1 1/2f out: nt clr run ins fnl f: sn in clr: one pce* 11/4[1]

3665 **5** ½ **Bezzas Lad (IRE)**[25] 6032 2-9-0 68.............................(b) SamJames 8 61
(Phillip Makin) *led: pushed along in 1/2 l ld 2f out: rdn and hdd 1 1/2f out: wknd fnl f* 33/1

6 **6** 1 **Kocasandra (IRE)**[35] 5698 2-9-7 75.............................. AdamMcNamara 10 65
(Archie Watson) *slowly away: bhd: pushed along 2f out: rdn and hdwy over 1f out: hmpd ins fnl f: no ch after and eased (jockey said filly suffered interference inside the final furlong)* 20/1

4440 **7** ½ **Zuckerberg (IRE)**[15] 6424 2-9-2 70.............................. TomMarquand 5 59
(Ivan Furtado) *chsd ldr: rdn 2f out: wknd over 1f out* 6/1[3]

366 **8** nk **You're My Rock**[32] 5780 2-9-2 73.............................. SeanDavis(3) 6 61
(Richard Fahey) *hld up: drvn 2f out: rdn 1f out: no imp* 16/1

4421 **9** 1 ½ **Aryaaf (IRE)**[11] 6557 2-9-5 73.............................. FrannyNorton 7 56
(Simon Crisford) *mid-div: drvn over 2f out: dropped away over 1f out* 6/1[3]

043 **10** 66 **Najm**[30] 5856 2-9-2 70.............................(p[1]) RyanTate 1
(Sir Mark Prescott Bt) *bhd and rdr sn lost stirrups: c home in own time (jockey said colt hung badly left-handed coming out of the stalls, causing his saddle to slip)* 10/1

1m 13.59s (-0.91) **Going Correction** -0.10s/f (Stan) 10 Ran SP% **119.3**
Speed ratings (Par 95): **102,99,97,96,95 94,93,92,90,2**
CSF £110.98 CT £435.98 TOTE £15.90: £4.20, £2.60, £1.70; EX 129.90 Trifecta £472.00.
Owner The Cool Silk Partnership **Bred** Laundry Cottage Stud Farm **Trained** Willoughton, Lincs

FOCUS
A competitive nursery and it should throw up a winner or two. The winner took a notable step forward.

6981 SUSAN BOX MEMORIAL H'CAP 1m 4f 51y (Tp)
7:30 (7:30) (Class 3) (0-90,92) 3-Y-O+ £7,246 (£2,168; £1,084; £542; £270) Stalls Low

Form RPR
0351 **1** **Cantiniere (USA)**[19] 6280 4-9-4 85.............................(p) GabrieleMalune(3) 2 94
(Saeed bin Suroor) *trckd ldr: pushed into ld over 2f out: sn drvn: rdn and drifted lft to rail over 1f out: kpt on wl fnl f* 4/1[2]

2201 **2** ½ **Deal A Dollar**[17] 6349 3-9-1 87.............................(bt) DanielTudhope 5 95+
(Sir Michael Stoute) *led: drvn and hdd over 2f out: n.m.r 2f out: swtchd over 1f out: rdn fnl f: r.o* 6/4[1]

-115 **3** 3 ¼ **Flaming Marvel (IRE)**[154] 1596 5-9-12 90.............................. TomMarquand 7 93+
(James Fanshawe) *hld up: drvn in 5th 2f out: rdn over 1f out: kpt on fnl f: tk 3rd nr fin* 9/2[3]

0232 **4** nk **Lexington Empire**[22] 6151 4-10-0 92.............................(b) DanielMuscutt 3 94
(David Lanigan) *mid-div on outer: drvn into 3rd over 2f out: rdn fnl f: no ex: lost 3rd nr fin (jockey said gelding hung left-handed inside the final three furlongs)* 5/1

1650 **5** ¾ **Super Kid**[34] 5706 7-8-12 76.............................(tp) ConnorBeasley 4 77
(Tim Easterby) *hld up: drvn over 2f out: sn rdn: no imp* 33/1

0534 **6** hd **Grandee (IRE)**[28] 5928 5-9-10 88.............................. BenCurtis 1 89
(Roger Fell) *trckd ldrs: drvn and lost pl over 2f out: rdn over 1f out: no ex* 11/2

2m 41.29s (0.49) **Going Correction** -0.10s/f (Stan) 6 Ran SP% **113.2**
WFA 3 from 4yo+ 8lb
Speed ratings (Par 107): **94,93,91,91,90 90**
CSF £10.64 TOTE £4.30: £2.80, £1.60; EX 13.00 Trifecta £50.60.
Owner Godolphin **Bred** Ranjan Racing Inc **Trained** Newmarket, Suffolk
■ Stewards' Enquiry : Gabriele Malune caution; careless riding

FOCUS
A tactical affair which developed into a dash from the home turn. The first two were unexposed and the winner ran a pb with the rider's claim.

6982 SEPTEMBER 21ST - 90'S NIGHT CLASSIFIED STKS 1m 4f 51y (Tp)
8:00 (8:00) (Class 6) 3-Y-O+ £2,781 (£827; £413; £400; £400; £400) Stalls Low

Form RPR
0142 **1** **Blyton Lass**[13] 6502 4-9-7 50.............................. BarryMcHugh 4 56
(James Given) *mid-div: pushed along and hdwy 2f out: drvn to chal over 1f out: rdn to ld ent fnl f: r.o wl* 7/1

0530 **2** 1 ¼ **Cheng Gong**[27] 5987 3-8-13 46.............................. FrannyNorton 6 55
(Tom Clover) *mid-div: hdwy over 2f out: pushed into ld 2f out: drvn and hdd ent fnl f: no ex* 15/2

00-3 **3** hd **Lady Shanawell (IRE)**[12] 5855 3-8-13 50.............................. AndrewMullen 7 55
(Ben Haslam) *hld up: pushed along 2f out: rdn and hdwy into 3rd over 1f out: kpt on fnl f* 7/2[2]

0033 **4** 2 ½ **Tamok (IRE)**[12] 6531 3-8-13 47.............................(v) TomMarquand 10 51
(Michael Bell) *hld up: drvn 3f out: rdn and hdwy over 1f out: tk 4th ent fnl f: one pce* 4/1[3]

0452 **5** 6 **Lazarus (IRE)**[10] 6601 5-9-4 49.............................(tp) SeanDavis(3) 5 40
(Amy Murphy) *trckd ldrs: lost pl 1 1/2f out: rdn over 1f out: sn no ex and eased* 10/1

0-42 **6** 4 ½ **Aussie Breeze**[16] 6367 3-8-13 50.............................. RoystonFfrench 3 34
(Tom George) *prom: drvn in 3rd 2f out: sn rdn and wknd* 7/1

5201 **7** 10 **Melabi (IRE)**[13] 6502 6-9-7 49.............................. CamHardie 8 17
(Stella Barclay) *hld up on outer: drvn 3f out: wknd 2f out* 20/1

0425 **8** 11 **Goodwood Sonnet (IRE)**[21] 6202 3-8-13 50.............................(v) DanielTudhope 1
(William Knight) *led: drvn over 2f out: hdd 2f out: sn wknd and eased (trainers' rep said gelding failed to stay the trip. Vet said gelding displayed a prolonged recovery)* 3/1[1]

006 **9** 39 **Olivia On Green**[68] 4439 3-8-13 5.............................(vp[1]) PhilDennis 9
(Ronald Thompson) *mid-div: rdn and lost pl 4f out: sn dropped to last and lost tch* 80/1

2m 37.93s (-2.87) **Going Correction** -0.10s/f (Stan) 9 Ran SP% **119.1**
WFA 3 from 4yo+ 8lb
Speed ratings (Par 101): **105,104,104,102,98 95,88,81,55**
CSF £60.19 TOTE £7.90: £2.60, £2.80, £1.10; EX 68.00 Trifecta £191.10.
Owner Andy Clarke **Bred** Mrs V J Lovelace **Trained** Willoughton, Lincs

FOCUS
Plenty of pace on here and it suited those ridden with a bit of patience. Straightforward, limited form.

6983 GRAND THEATRE, WOLVERHAMPTON H'CAP 1m 142y (Tp)
8:30 (8:32) (Class 6) (0-55,55) 3-Y-O £2,781 (£827; £413; £400; £400; £400) Stalls Low

Form RPR
2302 **1** **Dreamseller (IRE)**[8] 6679 3-9-6 54.............................(p[1]) PhilDennis 4 62
(Tim Easterby) *hld up: pushed along and hdwy 2f out: led 1f out: rdn clr fnl f* 9/4[1]

4450 **2** 1 ½ **Tails I Win (CAN)**[11] 6578 3-9-4 52.............................. BenCurtis 12 57
(Roger Fell) *hld up: pushed along and hdwy 1 1/2f out: rdn 1f out: r.o into 2nd wl ins fnl f: no threat to wnr* 6/1[3]

3001 **3** 1 ½ **Gunnison**[8] 6678 3-9-3 54.............................(p) SeanDavis(3) 7 56
(Richard Fahey) *t.k.h: prom: drvn in 2nd 2f out: led 1 1/2f out: rdn and hdd 1f out: no ex and lost 2nd ins fnl f* 9/2[2]

6222 **4** 1 ¼ **Chakrii (IRE)**[22] 6153 3-8-13 52.............................(p) DylanHogan(5) 13 51
(Henry Spiller) *bhd: drvn in last over 2f out: rdn over 1f out: kpt on into 4th fnl f: nvr nrr (jockey said gelding was never travelling. Trainers' rep said gelding missed the break)* 8/1

002 **5** ½ **Key Choice**[58] 4818 3-9-7 55.............................. RachelRichardson 10 53
(Eric Alston) *led: drvn in 1 l ld 2f out: hdd 1 1/2f out: rdn and wknd fnl f* 10/1

-660 **6** nk **Transpennine Gold**[29] 5915 3-9-6 54.............................(p[1]) ConnorBeasley 2 51
(Michael Dods) *chsd ldrs: drvn 2f out: sn rdn: no ex* 14/1

-000 **7** 1 ¾ **Dream Model (IRE)**[16] 6361 3-9-2 50.............................(p[1]) AndrewMullen 9 44
(Mark Loughnane) *prom: rdn 2f out: wknd over 1f out* 50/1

5340 **8** nk **Approve The Dream (IRE)**[23] 6130 3-9-6 54.............................. ShelleyBirkett 5 49
(Julia Feilden) *hld up: pushed along 1 1/2f out: nt clr run over 1f out: no ex and eased fnl f (jockey said gelding was restless in the stalls and was also denied a clear run continuously inside the final furlong)* 8/1

3430 **9** hd **Global Acclamation**[23] 6131 3-9-6 54.............................(p) TomMarquand 6 47
(Ed Dunlop) *hld up: drvn 2f out: rdn over 1f out: no imp* 9/1

0060 **10** 1 ¼ **Swiper (IRE)**[16] 6361 3-9-6 54.............................(p) RossaRyan 3 44
(John O'Shea) *chsd ldrs: drvn 2f out: racd wd and lost pl 1 1/2f out: sn rdn and wknd* 11/1

1m 49.74s (-0.36) **Going Correction** -0.10s/f (Stan) 10 Ran SP% **121.5**
Speed ratings (Par 99): **97,95,94,93,92 92,90,90,90,89**
CSF £16.69 CT £60.11 TOTE £3.00: £1.50, £1.90, £1.60; EX 22.10 Trifecta £89.40.
Owner Ryedale Partners No 2 **Bred** Michael O'Mahony **Trained** Great Habton, N Yorks

FOCUS
Just an ordinary handicap, with a minor pb from the winner.
T/Plt: £19.40 to a £1 stake. Pool: £66,133.88 - 2,482.86 winning units T/Qpdt: £17.10 to a £1 stake. Pool: £8,889.27 - 383.16 winning units **Keith McHugh**

6984 - 6985a (Foreign Racing) - See Raceform Interactive

4939
NAVAN (L-H)
Saturday, September 7

OFFICIAL GOING: Good to firm (good in places)

6986a TROYTOWN BAR H'CAP 5f
2:55 (2:56) 3-Y-O+ £13,288 (£4,279; £2,027; £900; £450; £225)

RPR
1 **Cityman**[27] 5996 3-8-5 85.............................(b) AndrewSlattery(5) 7 98+
(Andrew Slattery, Ire) *sn led: rdn w narrow advantage over 1f out and kpt on wl u.p to assert clsng stages* 8/1

2 1 ¾ **Only Spoofing (IRE)**[7] 6724 5-8-13 87.............................. RonanWhelan 6 94
(Jedd O'Keeffe) *cl up: drvn in cl 2nd under 2f out and kpt on wl u.p ins fnl f wout matching wnr: a hld* 7/2[1]

3 1 **Blue Uluru (IRE)**[373] 6731 4-9-4 102.............................. JohnShinnick(10) 11 105
(G M Lyons, Ire) *hld up in tch: rdn into 3rd nr side ins fnl f where no imp on wnr: kpt on wl* 12/1

The Form Book Flat 2019, Raceform Ltd, Newbury, RG14 5SJ

4 nk **Primo Uomo (IRE)**[85] 3818 7-9-13 **101** NGMcCullagh 9 103
(Gerard O'Leary, Ire) *hld up in tch: stl gng wl after 1/2-way: rdn over 1f out and kpt on u.p into 4th wl ins fnl f: nvr trbld ldrs* **9/1**

5 hd **Miss Jabeam (IRE)**[8] 6691 3-8-5 **80** ChrisHayes 13 81
(Aidan Anthony Howard, Ire) *w.w towards rr nr side: pushed along after 1/2-way and r.o wl u.p ins fnl f into nvr threatening 5th cl home: nrst fin* **9/2**[2]

6 1 1/4 **Abstraction (IRE)**[6] 6766 9-8-8 **82** ow1 ShaneFoley 3 79
(Miss Natalia Lupini, Ire) *cl up far side: rdn almost on terms over 1f out and sn no ex* **7/1**

7 1/2 **Aspen Belle (IRE)**[6] 6766 6-8-4 **78** oh1 (t) KillianLeonard 12 73
(Patrick Martin, Ire) *sltly awkward s: towards rr: pushed along in 10th after 1/2-way: kpt on ins fnl f: nvr nrr* **13/2**[3]

8 nk **Hathiq (IRE)**[9] 6648 5-9-0 **95** (t) JMSheridan(7) 5 89
(Denis Gerard Hogan, Ire) *hld up in tch: tk clsr order under 2f out: sn rdn bhd ldrs and no ex u.p far side ins fnl f: one pce clsng stages* **8/1**

9 shd **True Blue Moon (IRE)**[6] 6766 4-8-5 **86** (tp) AlanPersse(7) 1 79
(Joseph Patrick O'Brien, Ire) *chsd ldrs far side: rdn under 2f out and sn no ex: wknd ins fnl f* **20/1**

10 1/2 **Dash D'or (IRE)**[8] 6691 6-7-8 **78** oh7 MikeySheehy(10) 2 70
(Kieran P Cotter, Ire) *dwlt: sn settled bhd ldrs far side: no imp ins fnl f where short of room and checked sltly: wknd and eased nr fin* **16/1**

11 hd **Never Back Down (IRE)**[8] 6691 4-8-9 **83** RoryCleary 8 74
(Adrian McGuinness, Ire) *dwlt: in rr: rdn 1 1/2f out and no imp ins fnl f: kpt on one pce: nvr a factor* **33/1**

12 1 1/4 **Plough Boy (IRE)**[30] 5873 8-8-4 **78** oh3 JoeDoyle 4 64
(Garvan Donnelly, Ire) *chsd ldrs: rdn and no ex 1 1/2f out: sn wknd* **25/1**

59.41s (-7.39)
WFA 3 from 4yo+ 1lb **12 Ran SP% 123.6**
CSF £36.87 CT £349.42 TOTE £9.20: £2.60, £1.30, £3.30; DF 45.50 Trifecta £360.40.
Owner Michael G Quinlan **Bred** Springcombe Park Stud **Trained** Thurles, Co Tipperary

FOCUS
This was competitive with last year's winner \bOnly Spoofing\p back for a repeat.

6987 - 6991a (Foreign Racing) - See Raceform Interactive

1411 FONTAINEBLEAU
Saturday, September 7

OFFICIAL GOING: Turf: good to soft

6992a GRAND PRIX DE FONTAINEBLEAU - FONDS EUROPEEN DE L'ELEVAGE (LISTED RACE) (4YO+ FILLIES & MARES) 1m 2f
4:17 4-Y-0+ **£21,621** (£8,648; £6,486; £4,324; £2,162)

RPR

1 **Tosen Gift (IRE)**[110] 3138 4-9-0 0 FabriceVeron 2 102
(S Kobayashi, France) **48/10**[3]

2 1 1/2 **Lanana (FR)**[9] 6651 4-9-0 0 EddyHardouin 10 99
(Robert Collet, France) **4/1**[1]

3 hd **Queen Of Time**[24] 6082 5-9-0 0 (p) MaximeGuyon 7 99
(Henry Candy) *racd mostly in 2nd on outer: rdn to chal 2f out: r.o wl u.p* **43/10**[2]

4 1/2 **Zillione Sun (FR)**[40] 4-9-0 0 MickaelBerto 5 98
(Mme P Butel & J-L Beaunez, France) **15/1**

5 shd **Ficelle Du Houley (FR)**[14] 4-9-0 0 JeromeCabre 12 97
(Y Barberot, France) **12/1**

6 3/4 **Bubble And Squeak**[29] 5926 4-9-0 0 TheoBachelot 1 96
(Sylvester Kirk) *mostly racd in 3rd on inner: pushed along 2f out: sn rdn and hdd 1f out: kpt on u.p* **11/1**

7 hd **Palmyre (FR)**[48] 5229 4-9-0 0 CristianDemuro 4 96
(H-F Devin, France) **11/1**

8 1 1/4 **Park Bloom (IRE)**[67] 4-9-0 0 (p) MickaelBarzalona 9 93
(H-F Devin, France) **12/1**

9 3 1/2 **Abiona (GER)**[30] 4-9-0 0 RenePiechulek 8 86
(Frau S Steinberg, Germany) **15/1**

10 3 **Fira (FR)**[20] 6263 4-9-0 0 GregoryBenoist 3 80
(S Dehez, France) **76/10**

11 7 **Time Change**[24] 6082 4-9-0 0 Pierre-CharlesBoudot 11 66
(Ralph Beckett) *a in last: rdn along 2f out: one pce and no prog* **12/1**

1m 59.42s **11 Ran SP% 120.0**
PARI-MUTUEL (all including 1 euro stake): WIN 5.80; PLACE 1.80, 1.80, 1.90; DF 11.90.
Owner Takaya Shimakawa **Bred** Kildaragh Stud **Trained** France

4681 BELMONT PARK (L-H)
Saturday, September 7

OFFICIAL GOING: Dirt: fast; turf: good

6993a JOCKEY CLUB OAKS INVITATIONAL STKS (CONDITIONS) (3YO FILLIES) (INNER TURF) (TURF) 1m 3f (T)
10:15 3-Y-0

£314,960 (£110,236; £59,055; £41,338; £23,622; £17,716)

RPR

1 **Edisa (USA)**[42] 5470 3-8-9 0 FlavienPrat 1 108
(A De Royer-Dupre, France) *hld up towards rr: hdwy fr 2 1/2f out: hung rt ent st: rdn ins fnl 2f: styd on wl to ld 50yds out: rdn out* **8/5**[1]

2 3/4 **Wonderment (IRE)**[27] 6003 3-8-9 0 StephanePasquier 6 106
(N Clement, France) *dwlt: sn rcvrd: racd in midfield: in tch whn rdn 2f out: drvn and styd on fr over 1f out: led narrowly 100yds out: hdd 50yds out: kpt on* **83/10**

3 1 1/4 **Dyna Passer (USA)**[41] 3-8-9 0 JoseLezcano 7 104
(Thomas Albertrani, U.S.A) *chsd ldr: rdn and kpt on wl fr 2f out: nt quite able to chal* **23/1**

4 hd **Romantic Pursuit (USA)**[41] 3-8-9 0 LuisSaez 2 104
(Kiaran McLaughlin, U.S.A) *led: rdn 2f out: drvn over 1f out: hdd 100yds out: sn no ex* **92/10**

5 3 3/4 **Love So Deep (JPN)**[20] 6263 3-8-9 0 JamieSpencer 5 97
(Jane Chapple-Hyam) *in tch: trckd ldrs 4f out: rdn 3f out: outpcd ins fnl 2f: wknd ins fnl f* **42/10**[2]

6 1 **Lady Prancealot (IRE)**[20] 6268 3-8-9 0 JosephTalamo 3 95
(Richard Baltas, U.S.A) *hld up in rr: rdn 2f out: wd into st: kpt on steadily: n.d* **11/2**[3]

7 6 3/4 **Art Of Almost (USA)**[27] 3-8-9 0 JavierCastellano 8 83
(Roger L Attfield, Canada) *towards rr of midfield: rdn ins fnl 3f: pushed wd ent st: wknd 1 1/2f out* **31/5**

8 8 1/2 **Desert Ride (CAN)**[28] 3-8-9 0 JohnRVelazquez 4 68
(Neil J Howard, U.S.A) *in tch: rdn and lost pl 3f out: sn struggling* **111/10**

2m 17.02s (1.97) **8 Ran SP% 120.0**
PARI-MUTUEL (all including 2 unit stake): WIN 5.20; PLACE (1-2) 3.90, 7.80; SHOW (1-2-3) 3.10, 5.70, 7.70; SF 33.40.
Owner H H Aga Khan **Bred** H H The Aga Khan Studs Sc **Trained** Chantilly, France

FOCUS
A new race, part of the NYRA's Turf Triple series. Concrete Rose, who won the first two legs, was sidelined.

6994a JOCKEY CLUB DERBY INVITATIONAL STKS (CONDITIONS) (3YO) (MAIN TURF) (TURF) 1m 4f
10:47 3-Y-0

£421,259 (£145,669; £78,740; £51,181; £31,496; £23,622)

RPR

1 **Spanish Mission (USA)**[37] 5585 3-8-10 0 JamieSpencer 9 108
(David Simcock) *hld up in rr: rdn and hdwy fr under 2f out: drvn over 1f out: hrd drvn ins fnl f: styd on wl to ld last stride* **21/10**[1]

2 nse **Pedro Cara (FR)**[50] 5167 3-8-10 0 TonyPiccone 4 108
(M Delcher Sanchez, France) *towards rr of midfield: hdwy on outside fr over 2f out: rdn under 2f out: drvn over 1f out: led under 1f out: kpt on wl: hdd last stride* **38/1**

3 3 1/2 **San Huberto (IRE)**[34] 5717 3-8-10 0 FlavienPrat 5 102
(F Chappet, France) *in tch in midfield: rdn and lost pl over 2f out: styd on fnl f: tk 3rd cl home: no ch w front pair* **191/10**

4 3/4 **A Thread Of Blue (USA)**[34] 5721 3-8-10 0 LuisSaez 1 101
(Kiaran McLaughlin, U.S.A) *led: rdn clr under 2f out: drvn over 1f out: hdd under 1f out: wknd fnl 100yds* **31/10**[3]

5 3/4 **Henley's Joy (USA)**[34] 5721 3-8-10 0 (b) JoseLezcano 3 100
(Michael J Maker, U.S.A) *trckd ldrs: rdn to chse ldr over 2f out: wknd over 1f out* **63/10**

6 3/4 **Current (USA)**[20] 3-8-10 0 JuniorAlvarado 2 99
(Todd Pletcher, U.S.A) *chsd ldr: dropped to midfield 1/2-way: dropped towards rr and rdn 2 1/2f out: rallied on inner under 2f out: sn one pce* **37/1**

7 3/4 **Kadar (USA)**[34] 5721 3-8-10 0 (b) ManuelFranco 7 98
(Michael J Maker, U.S.A) *towards rr of midfield on outside: rdn and outpcd over 2f out: sn no imp* **28/1**

8 2 1/4 **Digital Age (IRE)**[34] 5721 3-8-10 0 JavierCastellano 8 94
(Chad C Brown, U.S.A) *midfield: hdwy to trck ldrs 1/2-way: rdn over 2f out: wknd under 2f out* **5/2**[2]

9 8 **Tone Broke (CAN)**[21] 3-8-10 0 JohnRVelazquez 6 81
(Steven Asmussen, U.S.A) *in tch: chsd ldr 5f out: rdn and outpcd 2 1/2f out: wknd 2f out* **121/10**

2m 27.58s (-1.00) **9 Ran SP% 120.2**
PARI-MUTUEL (all including 2 unit stake): WIN 6.20; PLACE (1-2) 4.60, 25.80; SHOW (1-2-3) 3.50, 11.40, 7.30; SF 115.50.
Owner Honorable Earle Mack & Team Valor LLC **Bred** St Elias Stables LLC **Trained** Newmarket, Suffolk

6995 - 6996a (Foreign Racing) - See Raceform Interactive

6470 YORK (L-H)
Sunday, September 8

OFFICIAL GOING: Good (good to firm in places; 6.9)
Wind: Light against Weather: Fine & dry

6997 JUDITH MARSHALL MEMORIAL BRITISH EBF NOVICE STKS (PLUS 10 RACE) 5f 89y
1:50 (1:51) (Class 3) 2-Y-O **£9,703** (£2,887; £1,443; £721) **Stalls High**

Form RPR

234 1 **Clan Royale**[23] 6167 2-9-4 87 (b1) AndreaAtzeni 9 82
(Roger Varian) *slt ld: rdn along wl over 1f out: jnd ent fnl f: sn drvn and edgd lft: hld on wl towards fin* **7/2**[2]

6 2 nk **Unifier**[100] 3290 2-9-4 0 PaulMulrennan 4 81
(Michael Dods) *dwlt and t.k.h towards rr: hdwy 1/2-way: rdn to chal jst over 1f out: ev ch ins fnl f: drvn and no ex towards fin (vet said colt lost its right fore shoe)* **66/1**

4 3 2 **Alben Spirit**[10] 6622 2-9-4 0 TonyHamilton 2 74
(Richard Fahey) *trckd ldrs: hdwy on outer 2f out: sn rdn and ev ch over 1f out: drvn and kpt on same pce ins fnl f* **9/4**[1]

4325 4 2 3/4 **No Mercy**[23] 6167 2-9-4 78 BenCurtis 3 64+
(K R Burke) *prom: cl up and rdn whn rdr dropped whip over 1f out: kpt on same pce fnl f* **5/1**[3]

4 5 nk **Sam's Call**[44] 5388 2-9-4 0 NathanEvans 10 63
(Michael Easterby) *in tch: rdn along 2f out: styd on fnl f* **12/1**

33 6 1/2 **Lady Nectar (IRE)**[5] 6822 2-8-13 0 FrannyNorton 1 57
(Ann Duffield) *cl up: rdn along wl over 1f out: drvn and wknd appr fnl f* **16/1**

5322 7 1/2 **Leapers Wood**[18] 6336 2-9-4 81 CallumRodriguez 6 60
(Michael Dods) *awkward s: sn trcking ldrs: rdn along 2f out: wknd over 1f out* **7/2**[2]

8 2 1/2 **Willing To Please** 2-8-13 0 HarryBentley 8 46
(David Barron) *t.k.h: towards rr: hdwy to chse ldrs 1/2-way: rdn along 2f out: sn wknd* **25/1**

10 9 nk **Ishvara**[23] 6157 2-9-5 0 RichardKingscote 5 51
(Robert Cowell) *cl up: rdn along over 2f out: drvn over 1f out: grad wknd* **16/1**

0 10 3 1/2 **Northern Celt (IRE)**[64] 4624 2-9-4 0 DavidAllan 7 38
(Tim Easterby) *dwlt: a in rr* **50/1**

1m 4.91s (1.31) **Going Correction** +0.10s/f (Good) **10 Ran SP% 118.6**
Speed ratings (Par 99): **93,92,89,84,84 83,82,78,78,72**
CSF £219.41 TOTE £4.30: £1.50, £14.50, £1.20; EX 327.40 Trifecta £2195.80.
Owner Sheikh Mohammed Obaid Al Maktoum **Bred** Oceanic Bstk, Puerari, Oti, H De St Pair **Trained** Newmarket, Suffolk

FOCUS
The going was good, good to firm in places (GoingStick: 6.9). The rail was moved out 6m from its innermost, providing fresh ground from the 9f point to the entrance to home straight
Amended race distances - races 2, 5 and 7 add 22yds Stalls: 5f89yds - stands side; 6f and 1m4f - centre; remainder - inside
A fair novice which saw the winner react positively to first-time blinkers.

6998 HANSON SPRINGS H'CAP — 1m 2f 56y

2:20 (2:21) (Class 3) (0-90,91) 3-Y-O+ £9,703 (£2,887; £1,443; £721) Stalls Low

Form RPR

1600 1 **Coolagh Forest (IRE)**16 6425 3-9-5 90 .... PaulHanagan 9 101
(Richard Fahey) mde all: jnd and rdn 2f out: drvn ent fnl f: kpt on strly towards fin **12/1**

5160 2 2 1/4 **Poet's Dawn**15 6475 4-9-4 83 .... DavidAllan 6 88
(Tim Easterby) trckd wnr: hdwy and cl up 3f out: chal 2f out: sn rdn: drvn and ev ch ins fnl f: kpt on same pce last 100yds **33/1**

2245 3 3/4 **Addis Ababa (IRE)**62 4730 4-9-6 85 ....(p) DavidNolan 2 89
(David O'Meara) dwlt: sn in tch: hdwy to chse ldrs 3f out: rdn along 2f out: drvn over 1f out: kpt on fnl f **11/1**

0023 4 hd **Give It Some Teddy**15 6460 5-8-12 77 .... DuranFentiman 4 80+
(Tim Easterby) hld up in rr: stdy hdwy on inner 3f out: rdn to chse ldrs 2f out: ev ch over 1f out: sn drvn and kpt on same pce **20/1**

5556 5 1 1/2 **Cote D'Azur**14 6513 6-9-1 80 .... LewisEdmunds 3 80
(Les Eyre) trckd ldrs on inner: hdwy 3f out: chsd ldng pair and rdn along 2f out: drvn over 1f out: wknd fnl f **25/1**

6136 6 2 1/4 **Music Seeker (IRE)**38 5594 5-8-11 83 ....(t) ZakWheatley(7) 7 79
(Declan Carroll) swtchd lft s and hld up towards rr: hdwy into midfield 7f out: pushed along 3f out: rdn over 2f out: kpt on u.p fnl f **25/1**

231 7 1 1/4 **Passion And Glory (IRE)**20 6290 3-9-0 90 .... CierenFallon(5) 11 84
(Saeed bin Suroor) trckd ldrs: effrt on outer over 3f out: rdn along over 2f out: drvn wl over 1f out: sn one pce **2/1**1

2500 8 1 1/2 **Kripke (IRE)**15 6460 4-9-2 81 .... TonyHamilton 17 71
(David Barron) rrd and dwlt s: swtchd lft and hld up in rr: hdwy 3f out: rdn along 2f out: plugged on: n.d **25/1**

3312 9 1 **Archie Perkins (IRE)**25 6067 4-9-3 85 .... RowanScott(3) 8 73
(Nigel Tinkler) trckd ldng pair: rdn along 3f out: wknd over 2f out (vet said gelding lost its right fore shoe) **8/1**3

1311 10 1/2 **Spirorad (IRE)**23 6179 4-9-12 91 .... DanielTudhope 15 78
(David O'Meara) hld up in rr: pushed along and sme hdwy 3f out: rdn over 2f out: n.d **5/1**2

1151 11 1 **Five Helmets (IRE)**14 6500 3-8-6 77 ....(p) JamieGormley 12 63
(Iain Jardine) hld up in rr: hdwy 3f out: rdn along over 2f out: nvr nr ldrs **12/1**

0052 12 1/2 **Fennaan (IRE)**12 6580 4-9-5 84 ....(h) PaulMulrennan 14 68
(Phillip Makin) in tch: rdn 3f out: drvn over 2f out: sn wknd **12/1**

5541 13 nk **Ladies First**43 5458 5-9-0 79 .... NathanEvans 16 63
(Michael Easterby) chsd ldrs: rdn 3f out: sn wknd **14/1**

0142 14 2 3/4 **Alfred Richardson**13 6543 5-9-10 89 .... KevinStott 13 67
(John Davies) a in rr **20/1**

1101 15 1 1/2 **Mr Coco Bean (USA)**39 5556 5-9-1 80 .... GrahamLee 1 55
(David Barron) hld up: a towards rr (trainer's rep could offer no explanation for the gelding's performance) **16/1**

2m 8.53s (-1.77) **Going Correction** +0.10s/f (Good) 15 Ran SP% **129.1**
WFA 3 from 4yo+ 6lb
Speed ratings (Par 107): **111,109,108,108,107 105,104,103,102,102 101,100,100,98,97**
CSF £382.52 CT £4464.49 TOTE £13.90: £4.00, £10.20, £3.80; EX 396.40 Trifecta £3830.60.
Owner Alan Harte **Bred** Leaf Stud **Trained** Musley Bank, N Yorks

FOCUS
Add 22yds. A competitive handicap, but it paid to be up with the pace and very few got into it. A clear pb from the winner.

6999 LNER SUPPORTING CALM GARROWBY STKS (LISTED RACE) — 6f

2:55 (2:55) (Class 1) 3-Y-O+
£28,355 (£10,750; £5,380; £2,680; £1,345; £675) Stalls Centre

Form RPR

5111 1 **Dakota Gold**18 6351 5-9-2 109 .... ConnorBeasley 7 115
(Michael Dods) mde most: rdn wl over 1f out: drvn ins fnl f: kpt on strly **11/8**1

3134 2 1 3/4 **Danzeno**8 6698 8-9-2 105 .... AlistairRawlinson 8 109
(Michael Appleby) trckd ldrs: swtchd lft and hdwy wl over 1f out: rdn to chal ent fnl f: sn drvn and ev ch: kpt on same pce towards fin **8/1**

0002 3 1 3/4 **Marnie James**18 6351 4-9-2 102 .... AndreaAtzeni 1 104
(Jedd O'Keeffe) t.k.h: trckd ldrs: hdwy 2f out: swtchd lft and rdn ent fnl f: kpt on **7/1**3

0221 4 3/4 **Perfection**21 6257 4-9-0 105 ....(v) DanielTudhope 5 99
(David O'Meara) trckd ldrs: effrt over 2f out: rdn along wl over 1f out: drvn and kpt on same pce fnl f **3/1**2

0223 5 nk **Rock On Baileys**15 6453 4-8-11 99 ....(b) RichardKingscote 6 95
(Amy Murphy) towards rr: hdwy 2f out: sn rdn: styd on fnl f: n.d **16/1**

0500 6 5 **Stay Classy (IRE)**17 6379 3-8-9 89 .... HarryBentley 2 79
(Richard Spencer) dwlt: a in rr **33/1**

1666 7 1/2 **Yolo Again (IRE)**21 6257 3-8-9 89 .... BenCurtis 3 78
(Roger Fell) prom early: pushed along bef 1/2-way: rdn and wknd over 2f out **50/1**

0614 8 3/4 **Princes Des Sables**21 6257 3-8-9 96 .... TomEaves 9 75
(Kevin Ryan) racd wd towards stands' side: prom: cl up 1/2-way: rdn along wl over 1f out: sn drvn and wknd **14/1**

0-30 9 2 1/4 **Red Balloons**21 6257 3-8-9 95 .... BarryMcHugh 4 68
(Richard Fahey) hld up: a in rr **16/1**

1m 10.1s (-1.50) **Going Correction** +0.10s/f (Good) 9 Ran SP% **114.0**
WFA 3 from 4yo+ 2lb
Speed ratings (Par 111): **114,111,109,108,107 101,100,99,96**
CSF £13.19 TOTE £2.00: £1.10, £2.50, £2.20; EX 12.80 Trifecta £42.20.
Owner Doug Graham & Ian Davison **Bred** Redgate Bstock & Peter Bottowley Bstock **Trained** Denton, Co Durham

FOCUS
A decent Listed sprint and another dominant display by the progressive winner, who confirmed his recent improved handicap form.

7000 MATCHBOOK EBF FUTURE STAYERS NOVICE STKS (PLUS 10 RACE) (SIRE AND DAM-RESTRICTED RACE) — 7f

3:25 (3:25) (Class 3) 2-Y-O £10,350 (£3,080; £1,539; £769) Stalls Low

Form RPR

13 1 **Wyclif**17 6368 2-9-8 0 .... HarryBentley 6 90+
(Ralph Beckett) dwlt and in rr: hdwy wl over 2 out: trckd ldrs wl over 1f out: sn pushed along to chal: rdn to take slt ld ent fnl f: sn drvn: hld on gamely towards fin **5/2**2

2 nk **Vega Magic (IRE)** 2-9-2 0 .... AndreaAtzeni 1 83+
(Kevin Ryan) led: rdn along 2f out: edgd rt 1 1/2f out: sn jnd: drvn and hdd narrowly ent fnl f: rallied gamely u.p and ev ch tl no ex towards fin **3/1**3

3 5 **Let Her Loose (IRE)** 2-8-11 0 .... PaulHanagan 3 65
(Richard Fahey) t.k.h early: prom: effrt over 2f out: rdn and ev ch over 1f out: kpt on same pce fnl f **8/1**

4 7 **Revestar (IRE)** 2-9-2 0 .... JackMitchell 5 51
(Simon Crisford) a towards rr **9/1**

5 2 1/4 **Dangeroffizz (IRE)** 2-9-2 0 .... RachelRichardson 8 45
(Tim Easterby) a towards rr **25/1**

6 6 2 3/4 **Convict**23 6154 2-9-2 0 .... DanielTudhope 4 37+
(William Haggas) trckd ldng pair whn stmbld bdly path over 5f out: stirrup leather pin c out and rdr lost irons: sn lost pl and bhd (jockey said colt stumbled when travelling over the road crossing approximately 6f out, causing the pin of the stirrup leather to pop out, resulting in him losing his irons for the remainder of the race) **2/1**1

0 7 nk **Hovingham (IRE)**144 1843 2-8-11 0 .... FayeMcManoman(5) 2 36
(Nigel Tinkler) chsd ldrs: rdn along over 2f out: sn wknd **50/1**

8 3 3/4 **More Than Love** 2-9-2 0 .... DavidAllan 7 26+
(Tim Easterby) trckd ldrs: hdwy 3f out: sn cl up: rdn along whn n.m.r and sltly hmpd 1 1/2f out: sn wknd **25/1**

1m 26.12s (1.52) **Going Correction** +0.10s/f (Good) 8 Ran SP% **117.7**
Speed ratings (Par 99): **95,94,88,80,78 75,74,70**
CSF £10.65 TOTE £2.90: £1.20, £1.40, £2.20; EX 10.10 Trifecta £46.60.
Owner Quantum Leap Racing Ix **Bred** Miss K Rausing & Bba 2010 Ltd **Trained** Kimpton, Hants

FOCUS
Quite a valuable novice. The first two pulled clear and look useful.

7001 LITTLE GREEN RASCALS CHILDREN'S NURSERIES H'CAP — 2m 56y

4:00 (4:00) (Class 4) (0-80,79) 3-Y-O+
£9,962 (£2,964; £1,481; £740; £400; £400) Stalls Low

Form RPR

2111 1 **Platform Nineteen (IRE)**24 6100 3-9-3 79 ....(p) CliffordLee 5 90
(Michael Bell) hld up towards rr: stdy hdwy on inner 3f out: chal 2f out: rdn to ld 1 1/2f out: drvn ins fnl f: edgd rt and kpt on wl towards fin **2/1**1

-261 2 3/4 **Forewarning**21 6256 5-9-2 67 .... CamHardie 10 77
(Julia Brooke) hld up towards rr: hdwy on outer 3f out: rdn wl over 1f out: str run to chal jst over 1f out: drvn ent fnl f: ev ch tl no ex last 100yds **8/1**

1132 3 1 **Funny Man**15 6459 3-9-1 77 ....(v1) DanielTudhope 11 86
(David O'Meara) hld up in midfield: hdwy over 4f out: trckd ldrs 3f out: effrt and n.m.r over 1f out: sn swtchd lft and rdn: chsd ldng pair ins fnl f: no imp towards fin **10/3**2

2213 4 7 **Contrebasse**18 6340 4-9-6 71 .... DavidAllan 4 71
(Tim Easterby) trckd clr ldr: tk clsr order 5f out: led 4f out: rdn along wl over 2f out: hdd 1 1/2f out: sn drvn and wknd **6/1**3

3134 5 1 1/2 **Sassie (IRE)**67 4505 4-9-9 79 .... GerO'Neill(5) 3 78
(Michael Easterby) trckd ldrs: hdwy 4f out: effrt 3f out: sn chal and rdn: drvn wl over 1f out: grad wknd **7/1**

54-6 6 2 **Petitioner (IRE)**189 522 5-9-12 77 .... KevinStott 9 73
(John Davies) trckd ldrs: hdwy 5f out: chsd ldrs over 3f out: rdn along over 2f out: sn drvn and wknd **50/1**

0014 7 nse **Ezanak (IRE)**13 6545 6-8-9 58 oh2 .... FrannyNorton 12 56
(John Wainwright) trckd ldrs: pushed along over 4f out: rdn over 3f out: sn wknd **40/1**

2033 8 1 **Echo (IRE)**24 6100 4-9-8 73 ....(v1) JackGarritty 13 68
(Jedd O'Keeffe) trckd clr ldr: tk clsr order 5f out: wd st: cl up and rdn over 3f out: wknd over 2f out **16/1**

2044 9 32 **Shine Baby Shine**25 4983 5-8-13 64 .... JackMitchell 7 21
(Philip Kirby) hld up: a in rr **16/1**

10 10 3 **Trautmann (IRE)**22 4404 5-9-5 70 ....(tp) AlistairRawlinson 2 23
(Rebecca Menzies) dwlt: a in rr **40/1**

3002 11 3/4 **Buyer Beware (IRE)**12 6583 7-8-11 62 ....(v) SamJames 8 14
(Liam Bailey) led and sn clr: pushed along 5f out: rdn and hdd over 4f out: sn wknd **25/1**

034 12 20 **The Resdev Way**33 5769 6-8-11 67 .... PaulaMuir(5) 1
(Philip Kirby) hld up: a in rr (jockey said gelding ran flat) **33/1**

3m 32.39s (-1.51) **Going Correction** +0.10s/f (Good) 12 Ran SP% **119.7**
WFA 3 from 4yo+ 11lb
Speed ratings (Par 105): **107,106,106,102,101 100,100,100,84,82 82,72**
CSF £18.24 CT £53.07 TOTE £2.60: £1.30, £2.30, £1.60; EX 16.10 Trifecta £58.70.
Owner The Royal Ascot Racing Club **Bred** Watership Down Stud **Trained** Newmarket, Suffolk

FOCUS
Add 22yds. A decent staying handicap with the fancied horses to the fore in the closing stages. The form should work out although the race lacked some depth.

7002 COOPERS MARQUEES H'CAP — 6f

4:30 (4:32) (Class 3) (0-95,93) 3-Y-O £9,703 (£2,887; £1,443; £721) Stalls Centre

Form RPR

1313 1 **Roulston Scar (IRE)**15 6476 3-9-1 90 .... MeganNicholls(3) 4 107+
(Kevin Ryan) mde all: rdn clr wl over 1f out: kpt on strly: readily **5/2**1

5223 2 1 1/2 **Pendleton**10 6623 3-8-10 82 ....(p1) CallumRodriguez 3 93
(Michael Dods) trckd ldrs: hdwy 2f out: rdn wl over 1f out: sn chsng wnr: drvn ins fnl f: no imp towards fin **4/1**2

0140 3 4 1/2 **Kinks**22 6222 3-9-7 93 .... AndreaAtzeni 12 90
(Mick Channon) towards rr: hdwy wl over 1f out: sn rdn: kpt on fnl f **10/1**

-400 4 nk **Wasntexpectingthat**32 5821 3-8-5 77 .... PaulHanagan 5 73
(Richard Fahey) towards rr: hdwy 2f out: sn rdn: kpt on fnl f **20/1**

6004 5 2 1/2 **Look Out Louis**10 6623 3-8-8 80 .... CamHardie 7 68
(Tim Easterby) awkward and dwlt s: in rr tl sme late hdwy (jockey said gelding was slowly away) **33/1**

0550 6 1/2 **Yousini**22 6227 3-9-3 89 .... TomEaves 2 75
(Kevin Ryan) prom: chsd wnr 1/2-way: rdn along 2f out: sn drvn and grad wknd **11/1**

4634 7 nk **Princess Power (IRE)**15 6476 3-9-1 87 ....(v) DanielTudhope 6 72
(Nigel Tinkler) a towards rr **9/2**3

1-60 8 3/4 **Jonah Jones (IRE)**16 6425 3-9-5 91 .... RichardKingscote 8 74
(Tom Dascombe) prom: rdn along wl over 2f out: sn drvn and wknd wl over 1f out **8/1**

0035 9 hd **He'Zanarab (IRE)**11 6607 3-8-7 79 .... PaddyMathers 9 61
(Jim Goldie) chsd ldrs: rdn along over 2f out: sn wknd **25/1**

0614 10 20 **The Night Watch**51 5126 3-8-8 85 .... CierenFallon(5) 11
(William Haggas) in tch: rdn along wl over 2f out: sn wknd (jockey said gelding stopped quickly) **7/1**

1m 10.54s (-1.06) **Going Correction** +0.10s/f (Good) 10 Ran SP% **119.3**
Speed ratings (Par 105): **111,109,103,102,99 98,98,97,96,70**
CSF £12.31 CT £88.61 TOTE £3.30: £1.40, £1.70, £2.80; EX 14.00 Trifecta £97.60.
Owner K&J Bloodstock Ltd **Bred** Epona Bloodstock Ltd **Trained** Hambleton, N Yorks

FOCUS
What looked a competitive 3yo sprint handicap was dominated by the winner who looks the type to go on to better things. The first two were clear and the time works out as only 3lb slower than the Listed race.

7003 SHA AND CARAT APPRENTICE H'CAP (A LEG OF THE GO RACING IN YORKSHIRE FUTURE STARS SERIES) 1m 3f 188y
5:00 (5:00) (Class 4) (0-80,82) 4-Y-O+

£9,962 (£2,964; £1,481; £740; £400; £400) **Stalls** Centre

Form RPR

4 **1** **Shamad (IRE)**[9] 6695 5-9-1 **72** OisinOrr 15 79
(Peter Fahey, Ire) *trckd ldng pair: effrt over 2f out: rdn along wl over 1f out: drvn to chal appr fnl f: kpt on wl u.p to ld last 100yds* **7/2**[1]

5042 **2** *nk* **Black Kalanisi (IRE)**[31] 5840 6-9-0 **76** Pierre-LouisJamin(5) 3 82+
(Joseph Tuite) *in tch: pushed along wl over 2f out: sn rdn and sltly outpcd: n.m.r and swtchd rt 1 1/2f out: sn drvn and fin strly* **4/1**[2]

0100 **3** *nk* **Prevent**[20] 6289 4-9-1 **75**(p) CierenFallon(3) 6 81
(Ian Williams) *trckd ldr: hdwy and cl up 3f out: rdn to take slt ld 2f out: drvn over 1f out: hdd last 100yds: no ex towards fin* **20/1**

2442 **4** *nk* **Doctor Cross (IRE)**[21] 6255 5-9-4 **75** ConnorMurtagh 10 80
(Richard Fahey) *trckd ldrs: hdwy over 3f out: rdn along 2f out: drvn and ev ch over 1f out: kpt on same pce u.p ins fnl f* **8/1**

0002 **5** *hd* **Capton**[15] 6456 6-8-9 **73**(p[1]) MarcoGhiani(7) 1 78
(Michael Easterby) *led: pushed along 3f out: sn jnd and rdn: hdd 2f out: cl up and drvn over 1f out: ev ch tl kpt on same pce ins fnl f* **8/1**

2150 **6** *nk* **Bollin Joan**[15] 6456 4-9-0 **71**(p) PhilDennis 7 75
(Tim Easterby) *hld up towards rr: stdy hdwy 3f out: pushed along to chse ldrs 2f out: sn rdn: drvn and kpt on fnl f* **33/1**

4122 **7** *1* **Arabic Culture (USA)**[159] 1508 5-9-6 **77** JaneElliott 9 80
(Grant Tuer) *hld up towards rr: gd hdwy on outer 3f out: chsd ldrs and rdn wl over 1f out: drvn and kpt on same pce fnl f* **16/1**

-305 **8** *1/2* **Needs To Be Seen (FR)**[30] 5902 4-8-13 **70**(p) HarrisonShaw 13 72
(Jim Goldie) *hld up in rr: hdwy wl over 2f out: sn pushed along: rdn wl over 1f out: kpt on fnl f: n.d* **40/1**

3221 **9** *3/4* **Qawamees (IRE)**[32] 5818 4-9-4 **78**(bt) GerO'Neill(3) 2 79
(Michael Easterby) *hld up: stdy hdwy 4f out: trckd ldrs 3f out: effrt over 2f out: sn rdn: drvn over 1f out: grad wknd* **8/1**

0004 **10** *1 1/4* **Glan Y Gors (IRE)**[8] 6736 7-8-10 **72**(b) AledBeech(5) 5 71
(David Thompson) *trckd ldrs on inner: pushed along over 3f out: rdn over 2f out: sn drvn and wknd* **25/1**

0056 **11** *1/2* **Top Notch Tonto (IRE)**[25] 6067 9-9-0 **71**(p) BenRobinson 12 69
(Brian Ellison) *a in rr* **16/1**

0000 **12** *2 1/4* **Desert Ruler**[50] 5201 6-9-4 **75** RowanScott 16 69
(Jedd O'Keeffe) *hld up in rr: sme hdwy on outer over 3f out: rdn along wl over 2f out: sn wknd* **20/1**

0505 **13** *1 1/2* **Framley Garth (IRE)**[69] 4437 7-8-10 **70** PaulaMuir(3) 8 62
(Liam Bailey) *in tch on inner: hdwy 4f out: chsd ldrs 3f out: sn rdn and wknd* **20/1**

1121 **14** *3/4* **Blue Medici**[14] 6511 5-9-4 **75** SeanDavis 11 66
(Mark Loughnane) *trckd ldrs: pushed along over 4f out: rdn wl over 3f out: sn outpcd* **7/1**[3]

2m 34.43s (1.23) **Going Correction** +0.10s/f (Good) **14 Ran SP% 123.3**
Speed ratings (Par 105): **99,98,98,98,98 98,97,97,96,95 95,93,92,92**
Pick Six. Not Won. Pool of 20,136.48 carried forward. Tote Aggregate: 2019: 162,570.00 - 2018: 291,184.00 CSF £15.63 CT £254.50 TOTE £4.50: £1.90, £1.90, £6.00; EX 20.70 Trifecta £329.20.
Owner Direct Bloodstock Limited **Bred** Newtown Anner Stud Farm Ltd **Trained** Monasterevln, Co. Kildare
■ Stewards' Enquiry : Oisin Orr three-day ban; careless riding (Sep 22-24)

FOCUS
Add 22yds. An above-average apprentice handicap which seemed to be run at nothing more than a steady gallop so it was advantageous to be handy. The form's rated around the third and may not be reliable.
T/Jkpt: £2,819.60 to a £1 stake. Pool: £31,771.09 - 8.00 winning units T/Plt: £55.50 to a £1 stake. Pool: £155,424.83 - 2041.52 winning units T/Qpdt: £3.30 to a £1 stake. Pool: £16,120.89 - 3510.70 winning units **Joe Rowntree**

6270 DUSSELDORF (R-H)
Sunday, September 8

OFFICIAL GOING: Turf: good

7004a GROSSER PREIS VON ENGEL & VOLKERS DUSSELDORF - JUNIOREN PREIS (LISTED RACE) (2YO) (TURF) 1m
2:50 2-Y-O **£12,612** (£5,855; £2,702; £1,351)

RPR

1 **Rubaiyat (FR)** 2-9-2 0 LukasDelozier 5 96+
(Henk Grewe, Germany) **19/10**[1]

2 *2 1/4* **Frankel's Storm**[22] 6212 2-9-1 0 AdriedeVries 6 90
(Mark Johnston) *racd alone in centre bef c across to ld field on rail: rdn over 2f out: hdd and no ex ins fnl f* **37/10**[3]

3 *2 1/4* **La La Land (GER)**[39] 2-9-1 0 ClementLecoeuvre 4 85
(Henk Grewe, Germany) **36/5**

4 *1 1/4* **South Africa (GER)** 2-9-2 0 MarcoCasamento 2 83
(Waldemar Hickst, Germany) **14/5**[2]

5 *1/2* **Ancona (IRE)** 2-8-13 0 FilipMinarik 1 79
(Andreas Suborics, Germany) **74/10**

6 *4* **Praetorius (GER)** 2-8-11 0 EduardoPedroza 3 68
(A Wohler, Germany) **69/10**

1m 39.46s (-1.70) **6 Ran SP% 118.8**
PARI-MUTUEL (all including 1 euro stake): WIN 2.9 PLACE: 2.0, 2.6; SF: 10.5.
Owner Darius Racing **Bred** Gestut Karlshof **Trained** Germany

6910 LONGCHAMP (R-H)
Sunday, September 8

OFFICIAL GOING: Turf: good to soft

7005a PRIX DES CHENES (GROUP 3) (2YO COLTS & GELDINGS) (GRANDE COURSE) (TURF) 1m
1:00 2-Y-O **£36,036** (£14,414; £10,810; £7,207; £3,603)

RPR

1 **Ecrivain (FR)**[19] 2-9-2 0 MaximeGuyon 2 109+
(C Laffon-Parias, France) *plld hrd: restrained cl up 3rd on inner: angled out and chal between horses 1 1/2f out: led ins fnl f: r.o: cosily* **41/10**[3]

2 *1* **Hopeful (FR)**[33] 2-9-2 0 ChristopheSoumillon 5 107
(C Laffon-Parias, France) *led: hdd ins fnl f: kpt on for press to hold 2nd* **74/10**

3 *1/2* **Al Dabaran**[43] 5415 2-9-2 0 WilliamBuick 3 106
(Charlie Appleby) *sn trckd ldr on outer: shkn up but nt qckn ins fnl 2f: kpt on fnl f: nt pce to chal* **4/5**[1]

4 *nk* **Happy Bere (FR)**[28] 6002 2-9-2 0 OlivierPeslier 4 105
(A De Watrigant, France) *racd keenly: restrained in 4th on outer: rdn and effrt 1 1/2f out: styd on: nt pce to chal* **13/5**[2]

5 *2* **Troilus (FR)**[11] 2-9-2 0(p) TheoBachelot 1 101
(S Wattel, France) *w.w in rr: clsd 1 1/2f out: sn rdn and no further imp: one pce fnl f* **15/1**

1m 40.97s (2.57) **5 Ran SP% 121.1**
PARI-MUTUEL (all including 1 euro stake): WIN 5.10; PLACE 2.60, 4.30; SF 14.90.
Owner Wertheimer & Frere **Bred** Wertheimer & Frere **Trained** Chantilly, France

7006a PRIX D'AUMALE (GROUP 3) (2YO FILLIES) (GRANDE COURSE) (TURF) 1m
1:35 2-Y-O **£36,036** (£14,414; £10,810; £7,207; £3,603)

RPR

1 **Savarin (JPN)**[33] 2-9-0 0 Pierre-CharlesBoudot 1 100
(A Fabre, France) *racd keenly: hld up bhd ldr on inner: angled out and shkn up to chal 1 1/2f out: sustained run to ld fnl 100yds: drvn out* **7/5**[1]

2 *3/4* **Secret Time (GER)**[52] 2-9-0 0 MickaelBarzalona 2 98
(F Chappet, France) *racd in fnl trio: tk clsr order on inner sn after 1/2-way: drvn to chse ldng pair 1 1/2f out: styd on for press: tk 2nd cl home* **11/1**

3 *shd* **Flighty Lady (IRE)**[24] 2-9-0 0 RyanMoore 4 98
(Gavin Hernon, France) *plld hrd early: restrained bhd ldrs: dropped into fnl trio after 1/2-way: drvn and styd on appr fnl f: tk 3rd cl home* **13/1**

4 *nse* **Alpinista**[15] 6444 2-9-0 0 LukeMorris 5 98
(Sir Mark Prescott Bt) *racd in fnl trio: last and pushed along wl over 2 1/2f out: hrd rdn and hdwy wl over 1f out: missed 3rd on the nod* **69/10**

5 *hd* **Nunzia (FR)**[36] 2-9-0 0 ChristopheSoumillon 7 98
(F Vermeulen, France) *sn led: drvn whn pressed fr 1 1/2f out: rallied gamely: hdd fnl 100yds: dropped to 5th cl home* **5/1**[3]

6 *snk* **Kenlova (FR)**[43] 5469 2-9-0 0 CristianDemuro 3 97
(P Bary, France) *racd keenly: hld up in last: angled off rail and rdn 1 1/2f out: styd on u.p: nvr quite on terms* **54/10**

7 *13* **Warzuzu (IRE)**[37] 2-9-0 0 MaximeGuyon 6 67+
(C Ferland, France) *racd keenly: chsd ldr on outer: 3rd and drvn 2f out: wkng whn sltly impeded wl over 1f out: lost tch and eased* **9/2**[2]

1m 39.18s (0.78) **7 Ran SP% 120.3**
PARI-MUTUEL (all including 1 euro stake): WIN 2.40; PLACE 1.50, 4.10; SF 18.40.
Owner Masaaki Matsushima **Bred** Shadai Farm **Trained** Chantilly, France

7007a PRIX DU MOULIN DE LONGCHAMP (GROUP 1) (3YO+ COLTS, HORSES, FILLIES & MARES) (GRANDE COURSE) (TURF) 1m
2:50 3-Y-O+ **£231,648** (£92,675; £46,337; £23,148; £11,594)

RPR

1 **Circus Maximus (IRE)**[18] 6354 3-8-13 0(b) RyanMoore 6 119
(A P O'Brien, Ire) *chsd ldng pair: drvn to press ldr 1 1/2f out: edgd lft jst mastering ldr whn runner-up led narrowly appr fnl f: dug in gamely u.p and led fnl 120yds continuing to edge lft: r.o* **41/10**[2]

2 *nse* **Romanised (IRE)**[28] 6004 4-9-3 0 WJLee 9 119
(K J Condon, Ire) *settled in midfield on outer: tk clsr order fr 2f out: drvn to ld appr fnl f: hdd fnl 120yds and carried a little lft by wnr: r.o u.p* **16/5**[1]

3 *1* **Line of Duty (IRE)**[28] 6004 3-8-13 0(p) WilliamBuick 2 117+
(Charlie Appleby) *settled towards rr on inner: angled out and hdwy on outer w over 1 1/2f out: rdn and r.o fnl f: nvr quite on terms w front two* **15/2**

4 *1/2* **Olmedo (FR)**[24] 6144 4-9-3 0 CristianDemuro 5 115
(J-C Rouget, France) *racd keenly: hld up in rr: clsd on inner 2f out: styd on u.p fnl f: run flattened out late on* **6/1**

5 *1* **Phoenix Of Spain (IRE)**[39] 5543 3-8-13 0 JamieSpencer 8 113
(Charles Hills) *settled in fnl trio: last 2 1/2f out: swtchd outside and rdn to cl 1 1/2f out: styd on fnl f: nvr nrr* **13/1**

6 *1 1/4* **Shaman (IRE)**[28] 6004 3-8-13 0 MaximeGuyon 3 110
(C Laffon-Parias, France) *s.i.s: racd in fnl trio: nt clrest of runs whn rdn 2f out: sn in clr and styd on: nt pce to trble ldrs and effrt petered out fnl 75yds* **7/1**

7 *1* **Robin Of Navan (FR)**[49] 5230 6-9-3 0(p) ChristopheSoumillon 1 108
(Harry Dunlop) *prom on inner: angled out over 1 1/2f out and n.m.r: kpt on u.p: nt pce to get involved fnl f* **32/1**

8 *snk* **Obligate**[42] 5479 3-8-9 0 Pierre-CharlesBoudot 10 104
(P Bary, France) *racd keenly: led or disp ld on inner: wnt on bef 1/2-way: hrd pressed fr over 1 1/2f out: hdd appr fnl f: sn wknd* **78/10**

9 *1 1/2* **Delaware**[22] 6249 3-8-13 0 VincentCheminaud 4 104
(A Fabre, France) *settled in midfield on inner: rdn and clsd over 1 1/2f out: mot much room appr fnl f: sn outpcd and dropped away* **58/10**[3]

10 *20* **Success Days (IRE)**[28] 6004 7-9-3 0 NGMcCullagh 11 58
(K J Condon, Ire) *led or disp ld on outer: cl up 2nd fr bef 1/2-way: rdn and wknd 1 1/2f out* **83/1**

1m 36.54s (-1.86)
WFA 3 from 4yo+ 5lb **10 Ran SP% 119.4**
PARI-MUTUEL (all including 1 euro stake): WIN 5.10; PLACE 1.90, 1.60, 2.40; DF 8.10.
Owner Flaxman Stables, Mrs Magnier, M Tabor, D Smith **Bred** Flaxman Stables Ireland Ltd **Trained** Cashel, Co Tipperary

FOCUS
With no stand-out star around at the moment over 1m in Europe, this was a competitive contest. The pace was good from the outset but things got tight late on and a stewards inquiry was called. No action was taken but it later emerged that the owner of the second intends on lodging an appeal. The first four are all rated to their marks.

7008a PRIX GLADIATEUR (GROUP 3) (4YO+) (GRANDE COURSE) (TURF) 1m 7f 110y
3:25 4-Y-0+ £36,036 (£14,414; £10,810; £7,207; £3,603)

RPR

1 **Called To The Bar (IRE)**[80] 4015 5-9-4 0 .... MaximeGuyon 2 111+
(Mme Pia Brandt, France) *towards rr: began to cl fr 3 1/2f out: chsd ldr into st: led ins fnl 2f: drvn clr fnl f: wl in command at fin* **1/2**[1]

2 2 **Haky (IRE)**[21] 6266 5-9-0 0 .... RonanThomas 5 104
(J E Hammond, France) *led: sn clr of single-file field: hdd ins fnl 2f: styd on but nt pce of wnr: nvr chal for 2nd* **51/10**[3]

3 2 **Boulevard (IRE)**[13] 4-9-0 0 .... ChristopheSoumillon 6 101
(Charley Rossi, France) *racd keenly: hld up in 3rd: rdn and kpt on fr 2f out: nt pce to trble front two* **39/10**[2]

4 3/4 **Petit Fils (FR)**[98] 3389 4-9-2 0 .... TheoBachelot 1 102
(J-P Gauvin, France) *w.w in rr: clsd fr 2 1/2f out: kpt on u.p: nvr trbld ldrs* **89/10**

5 snk **Line Des Ongrais (FR)**[44] 5409 8-8-10 0 ....(p) MorganDelalande 3 96
(P Chemin & C Herpin, France) *chsd clr ldr: outpcd and rdn over 2f out: styd on again ins fnl f: nvr on terms* **33/1**

6 1 **Palpitator (FR)**[21] 6266 5-9-0 0 .... SebastienMaillot 4 99
(C Bresson, France) *towards rr: mde sme prog 2 1/2f out: rdn and kpt on one pce fnl 1 1/2f* **17/1**

3m 23.42s (1.92) **6 Ran SP% 122.1**
PARI-MUTUEL (all including 1 euro stake): WIN 1.50; PLACE 1.10, 1.50; SF 3.40.
Owner Fair Salinia Ltd & Pia Brandt **Bred** Fair Salinia Ltd **Trained** France

REDON
Sunday, September 8

OFFICIAL GOING: Turf: good

7009a PRIX ROGER ET GAEL DU HALGOUET (CONDITIONS) (4YO+) (TURF) 1m 3f 110y
2:00 4-Y-0+ £2,702 (£1,081; £810; £540; £270)

RPR

1 **Vision Rebelle (FR)**[118] 5-9-7 0 .... AdrienFouassier 7 62
(Adrien Fouassier, France) **13/10**[1]

2 6 1/2 **Wingate**[70] 9-9-6 0 .... FlorentGavilan 3 51
(J Cloerec, France)

3 9 1/2 **La Taniere (FR)**[840] 5-9-1 0 .... RichardJuteau 1 31
(S Gouyette, France)

4 nk **Sun And Polo (FR)**[256] 8-9-7 0 .... MlleClemenceLeGland(4) 2 40
(P Le Gal, France)

5 3/4 **Angelical Eve (IRE)**[44] 5376 5-8-7 0 .... MlleRomaneViolet(3) 5 24
(Dai Williams) *towards rr: rdn and effrt on outer 3f out: sn no imp: kpt on at same pce*

6 1 **Shendail (FR)**[801] 5-8-13 0 .... MlleAxelleNicco(3) 9 29
(Mlle Emmanuelle Barrier, France)

7 3/4 **Shamsoun (FR)**[555] 5-9-1 0 ow1 .... GerardGuillermo 8 26
(G Guillermo, France)

8 1 1/2 **Sweet Fong (FR)**[1452] 7-9-0 0 .... AnthonyBarzalona 6 23
(P Le Gal, France)

9 4 **Selectif**[173] 7-9-0 0 ....(b[1]) JimmyTastayre 4 17
(O Briand, France)

10 dist **Woodlands (FR)**[660] 8-9-0 0 .... HugoMouesan 10
(F Fouquet, France)

PARI-MUTUEL (all including 1 euro stake): WIN 2.20; PLACE 1.30, 2.30, 2.00; DF 6.10.
Owner Stephane Boullais **Bred** L Tillet & Mme L Tillet **Trained** France

SEOUL (L-H)
Sunday, September 8

OFFICIAL GOING: Dirt: muddy

7010a 4TH KEENELAND KOREA SPRINT (LOCAL GRADE 1) (3YO+) (DIRT) 6f
7:05 3-Y-0+ £400,900 (£147,700; £91,433; £35,166; £28,133; £5,064)

RPR

1 **Blue Chipper (USA)**[42] 4-9-0 0 ....(e) YouHyunMyung 13 108
(Kim Young Kwan, Korea) **6/4**[1]

2 1 1/4 **Dia Socks (USA)** 5-9-0 0 ....(e) MoonSeYoung 1 104
(Ji Yong Cheol, Korea) **34/1**

3 nse **Gaon Champ (KOR)** 4-9-0 0 ....(be) LimGiWon 6 104
(An Byung Ki, Korea) **16/1**

4 1 3/4 **Spring Back (USA)** 3-8-11 0 ....(be) ChoiBumHyun 8 97
(An Byung Ki, Korea) **71/1**

5 3/4 **Final Energy (KOR)** 4-9-0 0 ....(e) LimSungSil 2 96
(Kim Jae Sub, Korea) **68/1**

6 3 **Doraonpogyeongseon (USA)**[364] 6-9-0 0 ....(e) ChoiSiDae 4 86
(Min Jang Gi, Korea) **81/1**

7 nk **Global Captain (USA)** 3-8-11 0 ....(be) YooSeung-Wan 9 84
(Jung Ho Ik, Korea) **127/10**

8 1 1/4 **Heartwood (USA)**[260] 5-9-0 0 ....(bt) JohnMcKee 7 81
(James K Chapman, U.S.A) **163/10**

9 4 **Wonder Bolt (USA)**[364] 9-9-0 0 .... ChoHanByeol 16 69
(Ji Yong Cheol, Korea) **170/1**

10 1 **Holy Legal (BRZ)**[855] 6-8-9 0 ....(t) MartinChuan 5 60
(Ignacio Correas IV, U.S.A) **74/10**[3]

11 1 **Today (KOR)**[273] 5-9-0 0 .... LeeHyoSik 10 62
(Kim Young Kwan, Korea) **51/1**

12 2 **Ace Korea (USA)**[206] 729 4-9-0 0 ....(t) FHerholdt 14 56
(Peter Wolsley, Korea) **123/1**

13 hd **Ugly Warrior (NZ)**[88] 3751 5-9-0 0 .... CYHo 12 55
(Y S Tsui, Hong Kong) **5/2**[2]

14 1/2 **Fast Pass (USA)**[71] 6-9-0 0 ....(bt) GerardMelancon 3 54
(Peter R Walder, U.S.A) **17/2**

15 1 1/4 **Bakoel Koffie (IRE)**[119] 2667 5-9-0 0 .... AntonioDavielson 15 50
(M Delcher Sanchez, France) **35/1**

16 4 **Pass The Vino (IRE)**[15] 6476 3-8-11 0 ....(e) DavidEgan 11 36
(Paul D'Arcy) *prom on outer: drvn and nt qckn wl over 2f out: wknd qckly and wandered u.p ins fnl 1 1/2f* **46/1**

1m 11.1s **16 Ran SP% 125.1**
WFA 3 from 4yo+ 2lb
PARI-MUTUEL (all including 1 unit stake): WIN 2.50; PLACE 1.20, 6.60, 2.90; DF 45.00; SF 53.40.

Owner Choi Byeong-Bu **Bred** Diamond A Racing Corp **Trained** Korea
FOCUS
Due to a dispute, Japanese-trained horses were unable to run at this meeting.

7011a 4TH KEENELAND KOREA CUP (LOCAL GRADE 1) (3YO+) (DIRT) 1m 1f
8:15 3-Y-0+ £400,900 (£147,700; £91,433; £35,166; £28,133; £5,570)

RPR

1 **Moonhak Chief (USA)** 4-9-0 0 ....(be) MoonSeYoung 11 113
(Kim Soon Keun, Korea) **57/10**

2 2 1/2 **Cheongdam Dokki (USA)**[273] 5-9-0 0 ....(be) LimGiWon 8 108
(Luigi Riccardi, Korea) **136/10**

3 4 **Ambassadorial (USA)**[23] 6150 5-9-0 0 ....(e) DavidEgan 7 100
(Jane Chapple-Hyam) *sn towards rr: pushed along and clsd into midfield after 1/2-way: rdn and styd on along outer ins fnl 2f: wnt 3rd appr 1f out: no imp on front two fnl f* **71/1**

4 nk **Glorious Artist (IRE)**[95] 3490 5-9-0 0 .... CYHo 1 99
(F C Lor, Hong Kong) **13/5**[2]

5 4 **Dolkong (USA)**[162] 1447 5-9-0 0 .... ParkTaeJong 10 91
(Bae Dae Sun, Korea) **18/5**[3]

6 4 **Harvey Wallbanger (USA)**[127] 3-8-9 0 .... JackGilligan 2 83
(Kenneth McPeek, U.S.A) **44/1**

7 1 3/4 **Baengmunbaekdap (USA)**[42] 4-9-0 0 .... LeeHyoSik 6 79
(Kim Young Kwan, Korea) **52/1**

8 2 1/2 **King Of Glory (USA)**[42] 4-9-0 0 .... YouHyunMyung 4 73
(Peter Wolsley, Korea) **82/1**

9 hd **New Legend (KOR)**[539] 4-9-0 0 .... IoannisPolluis 9 73
(Kim Young Kwan, Korea) **47/1**

10 2 1/2 **Lone Sailor (USA)**[64] 4-9-0 0 ....(t) GerardMelancon 3 68
(Thomas Amoss, U.S.A) **13/10**[1]

11 41 **King Of Ace (USA)** 5-9-0 0 ....(e) FHerholdt 5
(Peter Wolsley, Korea) **142/1**

1m 53.3s **11 Ran SP% 124.3**
WFA 3 from 4yo+ 6lb
PARI-MUTUEL (all including 1 unit stake): WIN 6.70; PLACE 1.60, 2.80, 10.20; DF 20.40; SF 39.90.
Owner Kwon Kyung Ja **Bred** White Fox Farm **Trained** Korea

7012 - 7021a (Foreign Racing) - See Raceform Interactive

6792 **BRIGHTON (L-H)**
Monday, September 9

OFFICIAL GOING: Good to firm (watered; 8.0)
Wind: light, against Weather: overcast

7022 BRIGHTON BUSINESS EXP 3RD OCTOBER FILLIES' H'CAP 5f 215y
1:45 (1:45) (Class 5) (0-70,70) 3-Y-0+ £3,428 (£1,020; £509; £300; £300; £300) Stalls High

Form RPR

3243 1 **Lethal Angel**[17] 6401 4-9-8 **68** ....(p) PatCosgrave 7 75
(Stuart Williams) *chsd ldr: rdn to ld over 1f out: in command and styd on wl ins fnl f* **3/1**[2]

R041 2 1 1/2 **Knockabout Queen**[7] 6794 3-8-11 **59** 6ex .... KierenFox 6 61
(Tony Carroll) *t.k.h early: chsd ldrs: effrt 2f out: kpt on u.p ins fnl f: wnt 2nd cl home: nt enough pce to threaten wnr* **7/2**[3]

0213 3 hd **Foxy Femme**[21] 6286 3-9-6 **68** .... JoeyHaynes 5 69
(John Gallagher) *wl in tch in midfield: effrt over 2f out: chsng ldrs and nt clrest of runs over 1f out: kpt on u.p ins fnl f: nt enough pce to threaten wnr* **5/2**[1]

3452 4 nk **Bint Dandy (IRE)**[7] 6795 8-9-7 **67** ....(b) FrannyNorton 2 67
(Charlie Wallis) *chsd ldrs: effrt over 1f out: drvn and chsd wnr 1f out: kpt on same pce and no imp ins fnl f: lost 2 pls towards fin* **6/1**

2244 5 3/4 **Monarch Maid**[7] 6794 8-8-0 **53** .... ElishaWhittington(7) 3 51
(Peter Hiatt) *led: shkn up over 2f out: rdn and hdd over 1f out: no ex and lost 2nd 1f out: plugged on same pce ins fnl f* **10/1**

2252 6 1 **Fairy Fast (IRE)**[10] 6685 3-8-9 **64** ....(p) MarcoGhiani(7) 8 59
(George Boughey) *stdd s: t.k.h: hld up in last pair: effrt over 1f out: no imp and hld whn hung lft ins fnl f* **10/1**

6060 7 5 **Elizabeth Bennet (IRE)**[10] 6668 4-9-3 **70** ....(h[1]) AngusVilliers(7) 1 49
(Robert Cowell) *hld up in tch in last pair: effrt on inner over 2f out: no imp and btn 1f out: wknd ins fnl f* **16/1**

1m 10.86s (-0.24) **Going Correction** -0.025s/f (Good) **7 Ran SP% 114.1**
WFA 3 from 4yo+ 2lb
Speed ratings (Par 100): **100,98,97,97,96 95,88**
CSF £13.89 CT £28.84 TOTE £3.70: £2.00, £1.80; EX 15.20 Trifecta £54.10.
Owner The Secretly Hopeful Partnership **Bred** Park Farm Racing **Trained** Newmarket, Suffolk
FOCUS
Rails moved out for fresh ground adding 4yds to every race. They went just an ordinary pace in this modest fillies' sprint handicap.

7023 EBF NOVICE STKS 6f 210y
2:15 (2:15) (Class 5) 2-Y-O £3,428 (£1,020; £509; £254) Stalls Centre

Form RPR

1 **Dontaskmeagain (USA)** 2-9-5 0 .... FrannyNorton 4 76+
(Mark Johnston) *mde virtually all: rdn over 1f out: sn asserted but rn green: styd on strly ins fnl f: v readily* **1/1**[1]

00 **2** 4 ½ **Awesome Gary**[16] 6464 2-9-5 0 .... BrettDoyle 1 62
(Tony Carroll) *hld up in tch: swtchd rt and clsd to press ldrs 3f out: hung lft and unable to match pce of wnr over 1f out: wl hld but kpt on for clr 2nd ins fnl f* **33/1**

0 **3** 3 ¼ **Draw Lots (IRE)**[17] 6409 2-9-5 0 .... TomMarquand 5 53
(Brian Meehan) *pressed wnr: rdn ent fnl 2f: outpcd and btn over 1f out: wknd ins fnl f* **7/2**[3]

34 **4** 1 ¼ **Collette (IRE)**[24] 6146 2-9-0 0 .... PatCosgrave 6 45
(Hugo Palmer) *t.k.h: trckd ldrs: effrt over 2f out: outpcd and wl hld whn hung lft over 1f out* **3/1**[2]

5 3 ¼ **Party Popper** 2-9-5 0 .... StevieDonohoe 2 41
(David Simcock) *s.i.s: in rr: outpcd and rdn ent fnl 2f: no ch after* **7/1**

0 **6** *nk* **Am I Dreaming (IRE)**[14] 6532 2-9-0 0 .... RaulDaSilva 3 35
(Adam West) *chsd ldrs: outpcd and rdn over 2f out: bhd over 1f out* **66/1**

1m 24.49s (0.69) **Going Correction** -0.025s/f (Good) **6** Ran SP% **114.2**
Speed ratings (Par 95): **95,89,86,84,81 80**
CSF £36.77 TOTE £1.80: £1.20, £6.70; EX 23.50 Trifecta £57.70.
Owner Crone Stud Farms Ltd **Bred** Gainesway Thoroughbreds Ltd **Trained** Middleham Moor, N Yorks

FOCUS
This 2yo novice event was another slowly run affair. Add 4yds.

7024 BRIGHTON PALACE PIER GALLOPERS H'CAP 6f 210y
2:45 (2:45) (Class 6) (0-60,62) 3-Y-O+

£2,781 (£827; £413; £300; £300; £300) **Stalls** Centre

Form RPR

5013 **1** **Joyful Dream (IRE)**[8] 6758 5-8-10 **52** ....(b) DarraghKeenan(3) 12 62
(John Butler) *hld up in tch in midfield: hdwy and rdn to ld over 1f out: hung lft but in command ins fnl f: pushed out* **11/2**[3]

0122 **2** 2 **Miss Icon**[14] 6529 5-9-3 **61** .... WilliamCarver(5) 14 66
(Patrick Chamings) *hld up towards rr: effrt and hdwy ent fnl 2f: chsd wnr 1f out: kpt on but no imp* **6/4**[1]

52 **3** 1 **Silverturnstogold**[20] 6305 4-9-7 **60** .... TomMarquand 16 62
(Tony Carroll) *stdd s: hld up towards rr: effrt ent fnl 2f: styd on strly ins fnl f: nt rch ldrs* **4/1**[2]

664 **4** *shd* **Penarth Pier (IRE)**[17] 6389 3-8-13 **56** .... HollieDoyle 9 56
(Christine Dunnett) *hld up in tch in midfield: effrt 2f out: swtchd rt ent fnl f: styd on wl ins fnl f: nt rch ldrs* **10/1**

5065 **5** *nse* **Paddy's Pursuit (IRE)**[13] 6569 3-8-8 **56** .... ThomasGreatrex(5) 3 56
(David Loughnane) *hld up in tch in midfield: effrt over 2f out: chsd ldrs but unable qck u.p over 1f out: kpt on same pce ins fnl f: lost 2 pls cl home* **10/1**

0005 **6** 1 ¾ **Stoneyford Lane (IRE)**[27] 6051 5-8-7 **46** ....(b) RoystonFfrench 15 43
(Steph Hollinshead) *dwlt: hld up in rr: effrt wl over 2f out: styd on wl u.p ins fnl f: nvr trbld ldrs* **20/1**

4006 **7** ½ **Soaring Spirits (IRE)**[27] 6058 9-8-11 **55** ....(b) SophieRalston(5) 7 51+
(Dean Ivory) *chsd ldrs: wnt 2nd 4f out tl led over 2f out: rdn and hdd over 1f out: no ex and wknd ins fnl f* **16/1**

0000 **8** 1 ½ **Jagerbond**[15] 6502 3-8-3 **46** oh1 ....(b) RyanPowell 4 36
(Andrew Crook) *s.i.s: in rr: effrt over 2f out: sme hdwy and hung lft 1f out: nvr trbld ldrs* **40/1**

00-4 **9** 1 ¼ **Penwood (FR)**[20] 6302 4-9-1 **54** .... CharlesBishop 10 42+
(Joseph Tuite) *chsd ldrs: ev ch and drvn over 2f out: no ex and outpcd over 1f out: wknd ins fnl f* **20/1**

0-00 **10** 7 **Formally**[21] 6283 3-8-3 **46** .... RaulDaSilva 5 13
(Tony Carroll) *in tch in midfield: effrt over 2f out: sn struggling: bhd over 1f out* **50/1**

4053 **11** *nk* **Yfenni (IRE)**[30] 5957 3-8-3 **46** oh1 .... LukeMorris 8 13
(Milton Bradley) *midfield: unable qck u.p over 2f out: lost pl and wl btn whn hung lft over 1f out* **33/1**

0000 **12** 1 **Tintern Spirit (IRE)**[9] 6703 3-7-12 **46** oh1 .... RhiainIngram(5) 6 10+
(Milton Bradley) *chsd ldr tl 4f out: steadily lost pl: bhd 1f out* **100/1**

4360 **13** *hd* **Cookupastorm (IRE)**[27] 6048 3-8-12 **62** .... JacobClark(7) 1 25+
(Martin Smith) *led tl over 2f out: steadily lost pl: wknd and bhd ins fnl f* **33/1**

6540 **14** 2 **Rivas Rob Roy**[104] 3187 4-8-11 **50** .... HectorCrouch 2 10
(John Gallagher) *in tch in midfield: lost pl and bhd whn hung lft over 1f out* **14/1**

1m 23.61s (-0.19) **Going Correction** -0.025s/f (Good) **14** Ran SP% **126.9**
WFA 3 from 4yo+ 4lb
Speed ratings (Par 101): **100,97,96,96,96 94,93,92,90,82 82,81,80,78**
CSF £13.98 CT £40.24 TOTE £6.80: £2.20, £1.60, £1.10; EX 15.40 Trifecta £41.70.
Owner Gerry Dolan **Bred** Malih Al Basti **Trained** Newmarket, Suffolk

FOCUS
This moderate handicap was run at a fair enough pace and the winner has been rated close to her best. Add 4yds.

7025 SUSSEX ART FAIRS (EAST) 12 OCTOBER H'CAP 1m 3f 198y
3:20 (3:20) (Class 6) (0-60,60) 3-Y-O

£2,781 (£827; £413; £300; £300; £300) **Stalls** High

Form RPR

000- **1** **Atalanta Breeze**[312] 8771 3-9-0 **53** ....(p[1]) KieranShoemark 7 59+
(Marcus Tregoning) *in tch in midfield: swtchd rt and effrt 3f out: chsd ldrs over 1f out: styd on to ld ins fnl f: rn green and pricking ears in front: kpt on: pushed out* **12/1**

-003 **2** ½ **Royal Dancer**[15] 6511 3-8-13 **52** .... TomMarquand 6 57
(Sylvester Kirk) *chsd ldrs: effrt over 2f out: sn ev ch: led over 1f out: hdd ins fnl f: kpt on but a hld towards fin* **8/1**

0536 **3** 1 ¼ **Ramatuelle**[21] 6279 3-8-7 **46** oh1 ....(b[1]) LukeMorris 9 49
(Sir Mark Prescott Bt) *chsd ldr tl rdn to ld over 2f out: hung lft and hdd over 1f out: stl hanging and one pce 3rd ins fnl f* **5/1**[2]

3062 **4** 6 **New Expo (IRE)**[31] 5880 3-8-7 **46** oh1 ....(p[1]) HollieDoyle 8 39
(Julia Feilden) *led: hdd and rdn over 2f out: outpcd and wl hld 4th 1f out: wknd ins fnl f* **7/1**[3]

230 **5** 1 ¼ **Miss Green Dream**[25] 6128 3-8-7 **46** .... ShelleyBirkett 1 37
(Julia Feilden) *hld up in last pair: effrt over 2f out: nvr threatened to get on terms w ldrs: wl hld fnl f* **16/1**

6421 **6** *nk* **Sandy Steve**[24] 6152 3-9-7 **60** .... PatCosgrave 3 51
(Stuart Williams) *hld up in tch in midfield: effrt wl over 2f out: nvr threatened to get on terms and wl hld whn flashed tail u.p 1f out: wknd* **5/6**[1]

0243 **7** 2 ¾ **Risk Mitigation (USA)**[18] 6361 3-8-12 **51** .... JFEgan 5 38
(David Evans) *midfield: u.p over 2f out: sn struggling and wl btn whn edgd rt over 1f out: wknd fnl f* **9/1**

600 **8** 5 **Mystical Jadeite**[26] 6075 3-8-11 **50** .... JohnFahy 2 29
(Grace Harris) *stdd s: t.k.h: hld up in rr: effrt over 2f out: sn btn* **50/1**

2m 36.0s **Going Correction** -0.025s/f (Good) **8** Ran SP% **120.4**
Speed ratings (Par 99): **99,98,97,93,93 92,90,87**
CSF £107.78 CT £553.17 TOTE £18.00: £3.70, £2.40, £1.60; EX 181.90 Trifecta £1168.50.
Owner Miss S Sharp **Bred** Whatton Manor Stud **Trained** Whitsbury, Hants

FOCUS
This weak 3yo handicap was run at an ordinary pace. The winner has been rated as improving. Add 4yds.

7026 ANTIQUES VINTAGE & COLLECTABLES FAIR 20 OCTOBER H'CAP 1m 1f 207y
3:50 (3:54) (Class 5) (0-75,77) 4-Y-O+

£3,428 (£1,020; £509; £300; £300; £300) **Stalls** High

Form RPR

5023 **1** **Escape The City**[37] 5686 4-9-2 **70** .... HollieDoyle 8 78
(Hughie Morrison) *chsd ldrs: effrt over 2f out: chsd ldrs and drvn over 1f out: styd on to ld ins fnl f: rdn out* **4/1**[2]

0021 **2** ¾ **Freckles**[7] 6804 4-9-3 **71** 5ex ....(h) KieranShoemark 4 78
(Marcus Tregoning) *t.k.h: hld up in last trio: effrt jst over 2f out: clsd to chse ldrs 1f out: chsd wnr ins fnl f: styd on but nvr getting to wnr* **11/2**

3-61 **3** 1 ¾ **Long Call**[32] 5841 6-9-2 **70** .... TomMarquand 9 73
(Tony Carroll) *s.i.s: hld up in rr: effrt and swtchd rt jst over 2f out: hdwy u.p over 1f out: clsng whn hung lft ins fnl f: kpt on to go 3rd nr fin: nvr threatened ldrs* **9/4**[1]

1403 **4** ½ **King Of The Sand (IRE)**[21] 6291 4-9-7 **75** .... RobertWinston 1 77
(Gary Moore) *t.k.h: led: rdn over 2f out: hdd 2f out: kpt on and stl pressing ldrs tl no ex and wknd wl ins fnl f* **15/2**

500- **5** ¾ **Maiden Voyage (FR)**[104] 4-9-9 **77** .... AdamMcNamara 2 78
(Archie Watson) *chsd ldr: hmpd over 6f out: effrt and rdn to ld narrowly 2f out: hdd ins fnl f: no ex and wknd wl ins fnl f* **9/2**[3]

3105 **6** 7 **Ashazuri**[14] 6535 5-9-1 **74** ....(h) ThomasGreatrex(5) 3 61
(Jonathan Portman) *in tch in midfield: effrt 3f out: unable qck u.p and btn over 1f out: wknd fnl f* **16/1**

3014 **7** 2 ½ **Trailboss (IRE)**[33] 5825 4-9-3 **71** ....(b) StevieDonohoe 6 53
(Ed Vaughan) *restless in stalls: s.i.s: hld up in last pair: effrt over 2f out: no imp and wl hld over 1f out: wknd fnl f* **10/1**

6016 **8** 5 **Go Fox**[16] 6439 4-9-2 **70** .... PatCosgrave 7 42
(Tom Clover) *chsd ldrs: effrt over 2f out: unable qck and sn lost pl: wknd and bhd ins fnl f* **14/1**

2m 2.97s (-2.03) **Going Correction** -0.025s/f (Good) **8** Ran SP% **117.7**
Speed ratings (Par 103): **107,106,105,104,104 98,96,92**
CSF £27.10 CT £61.32 TOTE £4.40: £1.50, £1.90, £1.10; EX 22.40 Trifecta £81.40.
Owner MNC Racing **Bred** Melksham Craic **Trained** East Ilsley, Berks

FOCUS
This modest handicap was run at a sound early pace. The winner has been rated in line with this year's form. Add 4yds.

7027 SKY SPORTS RACING ON SKY 415 H'CAP 7f 211y
4:20 (4:24) (Class 6) (0-60,62) 3-Y-O

£2,781 (£827; £413; £300; £300; £300) **Stalls** Centre

Form RPR

1206 **1** **Kennocha (IRE)**[16] 6441 3-9-3 **56** ....(t[1]) TomMarquand 4 62
(Amy Murphy) *led: sn hdd and chsd ldrs: effrt to ld again over 1f out: kpt on wl u.p ins fnl f: all out* **12/1**

0650 **2** *hd* **Rosamour (IRE)**[18] 6363 3-9-0 **60** ....(b) GeorgeRooke(7) 3 66
(Richard Hughes) *t.k.h: hld up in tch in midfield: effrt over 2f out: str chal u.p over 1f out: sustained effrt fnl f: jst hld* **11/2**[3]

5-05 **3** *hd* **Poetic Legacy (IRE)**[9] 6703 3-8-7 **46** oh1 .... FrannyNorton 6 51
(Mark Johnston) *midfield: effrt over 2f out: hdwy to chse ldrs and wnt lft ins fnl f: ev ch wl ins fnl f: kpt on* **15/2**

6000 **4** 1 ¼ **Keep It Country Tv**[27] 6049 3-8-10 **49** .... JFEgan 13 51
(Pat Phelan) *in tch in midfield: effrt over 2f out: chsd ldrs and edgd lft ent fnl f: kpt on* **14/1**

0245 **5** ½ **Tattenhams**[20] 6304 3-8-9 **48** .... RaulDaSilva 7 49
(Adam West) *t.k.h: hld up in tch: effrt and hdwy over 1f out: kpt on same pce u.p ins fnl f* **5/1**[2]

0625 **6** ¾ **Reconnaissance**[25] 6130 3-9-6 **59** ....(bt) LukeMorris 14 58
(Tom Clover) *styd wd early: chsd ldrs: effrt over 2f out: unable qck u.p over 1f out: wknd ins fnl f* **5/1**[2]

040 **7** 4 **Moon Artist (FR)**[13] 6569 3-8-2 **46** oh1 .... RhiainIngram(5) 1 36
(Michael Blanshard) *in tch in midfield on outer: effrt wl over 2f out: hdwy 2f out: no imp over 1f out: wknd ins fnl f* **33/1**

0602 **8** 1 **Thunderoad**[11] 6636 3-9-9 **62** .... GeorgeDowning 12 50
(Tony Carroll) *hld up in rr: c stands' side and effrt over 2f out: nvr threatened to get on terms but plugged on ins fnl f* **9/2**[1]

0545 **9** 3 ½ **Forthwith**[18] 6361 3-8-7 **46** oh1 .... BrettDoyle 10 26
(Tony Carroll) *t.k.h: sn led: rdn and hdd over 2f out: hung lft and lost pl over 1f out: wl btn and eased ins fnl f* **9/1**

-400 **10** *shd* **Pinkie Pie (IRE)**[34] 5784 3-8-7 **46** oh1 .... RyanPowell 2 26
(Andrew Crook) *hld up in rr: effrt 2f out: n.d* **66/1**

4223 **11** 2 ¼ **Tarrzan (IRE)**[32] 5837 3-8-13 **52** .... LiamJones 8 26
(John Gallagher) *taken down early: t.k.h: chsd ldrs tl wnt 2nd over 4f out: rdn to ld over 2f out: hdd over 1f out: sn wknd* **12/1**

-605 **12** 11 **Lolita Pulido (IRE)**[13] 6558 3-9-7 **60** ....(t[1]) CharlesBishop 9 9
(Eve Johnson Houghton) *a in rr: lost tch over 1f out* **25/1**

1m 36.8s (-0.10) **Going Correction** -0.025s/f (Good) **12** Ran SP% **119.0**
Speed ratings (Par 99): **99,98,98,97,96 96,92,91,87,87 85,74**
CSF £76.02 CT £540.30 TOTE £13.10: £3.60, £1.80, £2.90; EX 96.50 Trifecta £765.80.
Owner Dale, Knight, Darlington & Robson **Bred** R & T Bloodstock **Trained** Newmarket, Suffolk

FOCUS
This moderate 3yo handicap was wide open and the winner has been rated in line with her better AW figures. Add 4yds.

7028 CYCLE TO THE RACES 16 SEPTEMBER APPRENTICE H'CAP 7f 211y
4:50 (4:52) (Class 6) (0-60,62) 4-Y-O+

£2,781 (£827; £413; £300; £300; £300) **Stalls** Centre

Form RPR

4000 **1** **Barrsbrook**[25] 6121 5-9-3 **60** ....(vt) LouisGaroghan(7) 11 69
(Gary Moore) *dwlt: wnt lft and hmpd leaving stalls: in rr: shkn up and c towards stands' side 3f out: hdwy to chse ldrs over 1f out: hung lft and led jst ins fnl f: sn in command: pushed out* **20/1**

4552 **2** 2 **Duke Of North (IRE)**[13] 6568 7-8-9 **52** ....(p) IsobelFrancis(7) 9 56
(Jim Boyle) *t.k.h: hld up in tch: c wd and effrt over 2f out: hung lft over 1f out: kpt on ins fnl f: wnt 2nd wl ins fnl f: no imp* **9/1**

2654 **3** *nk* **Sharp Operator**[5] 6860 6-8-9 **52**...(h) MarcoGhiani(7) 5 56
(Charlie Wallis) *hld up: sn rcvrd and in tch in midfield: chsd ldrs 4f out: effrt jst over 2f out: ev ch u.p 1f out: kpt on same pce and lost 2nd wl ins fnl f* **9/4**[1]

1041 **4** *hd* **Harlequin Rose (IRE)**[8] 6758 5-8-13 **54** 5ex...(v) WilliamCarver(5) 2 57
(Patrick Chamings) *hld up in tch towards rr: effrt over 2f out: swtchd rt over 1f out: kpt on u.p ins fnl f: nt rch ldrs* **7/2**[2]

0502 **5** *1 ¼* **Limerick Lord (IRE)**[8] 6758 7-8-7 **48**...(p) SeanKirrane(5) 8 48
(Julia Feilden) *chsd ldr: effrt over 2f out: rdn to ld 2f out: hdd jst ins fnl f: no ex and wknd towards fin* **4/1**[3]

3615 **6** *hd* **Cristal Pallas Cat (IRE)**[8] 6758 4-8-9 **48**... RhiainIngram(3) 3 48
(Roger Ingram) *taken down early: led: rdn and hdd 2f out: kpt on and stl ev ch 1f out: no ex and wknd towards fin* **8/1**

0000 **7** *3* **Solveig's Song**[33] 5803 7-8-10 **46**...(p) MeganNicholls 6 39
(Steve Woodman) *chsd ldrs: effrt over 2f out: unable qck: hung rt and outpcd over 1f out: wknd ins fnl f* **16/1**

254 **8** *2 ¼* **Kodiline (IRE)**[27] 6045 5-9-5 **62**... AngusVilliers(7) 4 50
(David Evans) *t.k.h: chsd ldrs for 3f: styd wl in tch in midfield: lost pl over 1f out: wl btn and eased wl ins fnl f* **8/1**

2400 **9** *2* **Coachella (IRE)**[32] 5867 5-8-10 **51**...(b) TobyEley(5) 10 34
(Ed de Giles) *s.i.s: hld up in tch in rr: no hdwy u.p and btn over 1f out: wknd ins fnl f* **20/1**

00 **10** *hd* **Paco Dawn**[42] 5498 5-8-3 **46** oh1... ElishaWhittington(7) 1 29
(Tony Carroll) *in tch in midfield: unable qck and lost pl over 1f out: wknd ins fnl f* **50/1**

1m 36.85s (-0.05) **Going Correction** -0.025s/f (Good) **10 Ran SP% 122.6**
Speed ratings (Par 101): **99,97,96,96,95 95,92,89,87,87**
CSF £193.89 CT £590.10 TOTE £17.60: £4.40, £3.00, £1.30; EX 202.20 Trifecta £1542.10.
Owner G A Jackman **Bred** Mrs J A Gawthorpe **Trained** Lower Beeding, W Sussex

FOCUS
An ordinary handicap for apprentice riders which saw changing fortunes in the final furlong. The winner has been rated in line with this year's best/last year's course form. Add 4yds.
T/Jkpt: Not Won. T/Plt: £137.20 to a £1 stake. Pool: £71,003.29 - 377.59 winning units T/Qpdt: £28.70 to a £1 stake. Pool: £7,456.80 - 192.05 winning units **Steve Payne**

6977 WOLVERHAMPTON (A.W) (L-H)

Monday, September 9

OFFICIAL GOING: Tapeta: standard
Wind: Light behind Weather: Overcast

7029 COMPARE BOOKMAKER SITES AT BONUSCODEBETS.CO.UK FILLIES' NURSERY H'CAP 6f 20y (Tp)

5:30 (5:32) (Class 5) (0-70,71) 2-Y-O

£3,428 (£1,020; £509; £400; £400; £400) **Stalls Low**

Form RPR

3515 **1** **My Motivate Girl (IRE)**[25] 6113 2-9-3 **66**...(b) OisinMurphy 2 69
(Archie Watson) *hld up: hdwy over 2f out: rdn over 1f out: r.o to ld wl ins fnl f* **9/2**[2]

1220 **2** *½* **Calippo (IRE)**[13] 6584 2-9-1 **71**...(p) Pierre-LouisJamin(7) 6 73
(Archie Watson) *sn led: rdn over 1f out: hdd wl ins fnl f* **8/1**

4145 **3** *1 ½* **Twice As Likely**[11] 6637 2-9-4 **67**... ShaneKelly 3 64
(Richard Hughes) *trckd ldrs: wnt 2nd over 2f out: rdn over 1f out: styd on same pce ins fnl f* **8/1**

254 **4** *shd* **Fair Pass (IRE)**[28] 6028 2-9-0 **70**... StefanoCherchi(7) 9 67
(Marco Botti) *hld up: hdwy over 1f out: r.o: nt rch ldrs* **4/1**[1]

2044 **5** *1 ¼* **Doncaster Rosa**[25] 6097 2-9-7 **70**... JasonHart 4 63
(Ivan Furtado) *prom: shkn up and outpcd over 2f out: styd on u.p ins fnl f* **14/1**

2440 **6** *1* **Chromium**[17] 6394 2-9-1 **64**...(p) DavidProbert 10 54
(Mark Usher) *pushed along early in rr: hdwy u.p over 1f out: sn hung rt: no ex ins fnl f (jockey said filly hung right-handed in the straight)* **25/1**

030 **7** *½* **Angels Faces (IRE)**[19] 6337 2-9-3 **66**... SamJames 8 54
(Grant Tuer) *sn chsng ldr: lost 2nd over 2f out: styd on same pce fr over 1f out (jockey said saddle slipped when leaving the stalls)* **6/1**[3]

405 **8** *¾* **Lady Celia**[34] 5788 2-8-11 **63**... SeanDavis(3) 7 49
(Richard Fahey) *s.i.s: in rr: rdn over 2f out: r.o ins fnl f: nvr nrr* **20/1**

3323 **9** *shd* **She Looks Like Fun**[55] 5026 2-9-3 **69**... HarrisonShaw(3) 12 55
(K R Burke) *led early: chsd ldrs on outer: shkn up over 2f out: no ex fr over 1f out (jockey said filly hung right-handed throughout)* **14/1**

13 **10** *hd* **Crime Of Passion (IRE)**[16] 6436 2-9-4 **67**... NicolaCurrie 5 52
(Jamie Osborne) *hld up: rdn over 1f out: nvr on terms* **8/1**

1434 **11** *1 ¼* **Havana Dawn**[10] 6653 2-9-6 **69**...(p[1]) PaulMulrennan 11 51
(Phillip Makin) *prom on outer: rdn over 2f out: wknd over 1f out* **8/1**

560 **12** *½* **Midnight Mimosa (IRE)**[25] 6096 2-8-0 **49**...(b[1]) DuranFentiman 1 29
(Tim Easterby) *s.i.s: a in rr* **25/1**

1m 14.62s (0.12) **Going Correction** -0.10s/f (Stan) **12 Ran SP% 122.7**
Speed ratings (Par 92): **95,94,92,92,90 89,88,87,87,87 85,84**
CSF £40.94 CT £284.03 TOTE £4.20: £1.70, £2.80, £3.40; EX 40.30 Trifecta £299.20.
Owner L Dickinson **Bred** Mrs Andrea Ryan **Trained** Upper Lambourn, W Berks
■ Stewards' Enquiry : Harrison Shaw one-day ban; failure to ride from draw (Sept 23)

FOCUS
A one-two for Archie Watson and both runners rate as improvers.

7030 GRAND THEATRE WOLVERHAMPTON MAIDEN STKS 6f 20y (Tp)

6:00 (6:02) (Class 5) 2-Y-O **£3,428** (£1,020; £509; £254) **Stalls Low**

Form RPR

1 **Desert Safari (IRE)** 2-9-5 0... OisinMurphy 4 78+
(Mark Johnston) *sn chsng ldrs: rdn to ld and edgd rt ins fnl f: r.o* **5/6**[1]

2 **2** *1 ½* **Say It Simple**[25] 6096 2-9-0 0... TonyHamilton 6 68
(Richard Fahey) *chsd ldrs: rdn over 1f out: styd on to go 2nd wl ins fnl f* **3/1**[2]

60 **3** *1 ¼* **Sir Oliver (IRE)**[51] 5186 2-9-5 0... ShaneKelly 1 69+
(Richard Hughes) *hld up: swtchd rt and hdwy over 1f out: r.o to go 3rd post: nt rch ldrs (jockey said, regarding the running and riding, he said he no specific instructions, however he hoped to be handy from stall 1 but was also conscious of getting the colt to relax. He added that the colt settled a little further back than intended after j* **6/1**[3]

6 **4** *nk* **Diamonds And Rust**[7] 6793 2-9-0 0... RyanTate 9 63
(Bill Turner) *led: rdn and edgd lft over 1f out: edgd rt and hdd ins fnl f: no ex towards fin* **100/1**

5 *nk* **Dutch Harbor** 2-9-5 0... DavidProbert 11 67
(Sir Mark Todd) *chsd ldr: rdn over 1f out: lost 2nd ins fnl f: styd on same pce* **28/1**

6 **6** *¾* **Wilfy**[21] 6287 2-9-5 0... LiamKeniry 7 65
(Sylvester Kirk) *hld up: plld hrd: hdwy over 2f out: rdn and hung lft over 1f out: swtchd lft ins fnl f: styd on* **7/1**

55 **7** *3 ½* **Bryn Du**[21] 6287 2-9-0 0... CierenFallon(5) 12 55
(William Haggas) *broke wl enough: sn lost pl: n.d after* **12/1**

60 **8** *2 ¼* **Cappella Fella (IRE)**[14] 6528 2-9-5 0... RobHornby 2 48
(Sarah Hollinshead) *prom: shkn up and wknd over 1f out* **100/1**

9 *1* **Cadeo** 2-8-12 0...(h[1]) StefanoCherchi(7) 5 45
(Marco Botti) *s.i.s: nvr on terms* **25/1**

50 **10** *6* **Fedora Fits**[18] 6368 2-9-0 0... AndrewMullen 13 22
(Mark Loughnane) *s.i.s: nvr on terms* **100/1**

11 *3 ½* **Crowded Express** 2-9-5 0... KieranO'Neill 3 16
(Stuart Kittow) *s.i.s: pushed along early in rr: n.d* **66/1**

1m 14.65s (0.15) **Going Correction** -0.10s/f (Stan) **11 Ran SP% 125.8**
Speed ratings (Par 95): **95,93,91,90,90 89,84,81,80,72 67**
CSF £3.73 TOTE £1.90: £1.10, £1.30, £1.60; EX 5.60 Trifecta £17.40.
Owner Sheikh Hamdan bin Mohammed Al Maktoum **Bred** Godolphin **Trained** Middleham Moor, N Yorks
■ Stewards' Enquiry : Ryan Tate one-day ban; failure to ride from draw (Sept 23)

FOCUS
They went quite steady early on in this maiden. The second/third help set a fluid initial level.

7031 VISIT THE BLACK COUNTRY MAIDEN AUCTION FILLIES' STKS (PLUS 10 RACE) 7f 36y (Tp)

6:30 (6:30) (Class 5) 2-Y-O **£3,428** (£1,020; £509; £254) **Stalls High**

Form RPR

533 **1** **Gladice**[11] 6629 2-8-6 **67**... CierenFallon(5) 4 68
(Marco Botti) *mde all: pushed clr 2f out: rdn and edgd rt ins fnl f: styd on (jockey said filly hung right-handed and ran green in the straight)* **15/8**[2]

2 *1 ½* **Secret Acquisition** 2-9-0 0... KieranO'Neill 2 67
(Daniel Kubler) *w wnr 1f: remained handy: shkn up to go 2nd again over 2f out: rdn and edgd rt over 1f out: styd on* **12/1**

5 **3** *nse* **Decanter**[11] 6629 2-8-11 0... BenCurtis 3 64
(Sylvester Kirk) *hld up: rdn over 1f out: r.o ins fnl f: nt rch ldrs* **10/1**

6 **4** *1 ¾* **Um Aljadeela (IRE)**[16] 6457 2-8-11 0... ShaneGray 6 60
(Kevin Ryan) *chsd ldrs: shkn up and outpcd over 2f out: styd on ins fnl f (jockey said filly hung right-handed throughout)* **5/4**[1]

0 **5** *2* **Chiarodiluna**[17] 6407 2-9-0 0... RobHornby 5 58
(Philip McBride) *hld up: rdn ins fnl f: nvr on terms* **33/1**

0 **6** *hd* **She's A Unicorn**[31] 5895 2-8-5 0... SeanDavis(3) 1 52
(Tom Dascombe) *sn pushed along in rr: reminder over 5f out: nvr on terms* **33/1**

3 **7** *1 ½* **Looks Good (IRE)**[24] 6146 2-9-0 0... ShaneKelly 7 54
(Richard Hughes) *s.i.s: hdwy to chse ldr over 5f out: pushed along 1/2-way: rdn and lost 2nd over 2f out: wknd fnl f* **6/1**[3]

1m 29.01s (0.21) **Going Correction** -0.10s/f (Stan) **7 Ran SP% 116.2**
Speed ratings (Par 92): **94,92,92,90,87 87,86**
CSF £24.98 TOTE £2.80: £1.40, £6.10; EX 27.00 Trifecta £80.10.
Owner Imad Alsagar **Bred** Saleh Al Homaizi & Imad Al Sagar **Trained** Newmarket, Suffolk

FOCUS
Just a modest fillies' maiden.

7032 LIKE WOLVERHAMPTON RACECOURSE ON FACEBOOK FILLIES' NOVICE MEDIAN AUCTION STKS 7f 36y (Tp)

7:00 (7:01) (Class 6) 3-5-Y-O **£2,781** (£827; £413; £206) **Stalls High**

Form RPR

0-4 **1** **Havana Jane**[26] 6074 4-9-1 0... OisinMurphy 6 64
(Andrew Balding) *mde virtually all: rdn over 1f out: edgd rt ins fnl f: styd on* **1/1**[1]

5 **2** *1 ¼* **Siena Mia**[30] 5969 4-8-8 0... NickBarratt-Atkin(7) 4 61
(Philip Kirby) *s.i.s: sn prom: rdn and swtchd lft over 1f out: styd on* **33/1**

2402 **3** *nk* **Casarubina (IRE)**[24] 6181 3-8-11 **60**... PJMcDonald 5 58
(Nick Littmoden) *chsd ldrs: rdn over 1f out: styd on* **3/1**[2]

4 *1* **Festina** 3-8-11 0... RyanTate 1 56+
(Sir Mark Prescott Bt) *s.i.s: hld up: hdwy over 1f out: r.o: nt rch ldrs* **14/1**

3 **5** *½* **Capla Berry**[20] 6325 3-8-11 0... BenCurtis 10 55
(Rae Guest) *s.i.s: hld up on outer: styd on fr over 1f out: nt trble ldrs* **6/1**[3]

00 **6** *nse* **Maryellen**[51] 5193 3-8-11 0... JoeyHaynes 2 54
(Alan Bailey) *s.i.s: hld up: hdwy over 1f out: nt rch ldrs* **66/1**

5000 **7** *2 ¼* **Supreme Dream**[24] 6181 3-8-11 **41**...(b[1]) CharlieBennett 9 49
(Shaun Harris) *chsd ldr over 5f out: rdn over 1f out: no ex ins fnl f* **100/1**

6605 **8** *1 ½* **Nutopia**[54] 5041 4-9-1 **44**... CamHardie 8 47
(Antony Brittain) *rrd s: hld up: hdwy over 1f out: wknd ins fnl f (jockey said filly was slowly away)* **25/1**

045 **9** *nk* **Disey's Edge**[23] 6198 3-8-8 **42**... WilliamCox(3) 3 44
(Christopher Mason) *wnt lft s: sn chsng ldrs: rdn over 1f out: wknd ins fnl f (jockey said filly jumped left-handed)* **66/1**

3400 **10** *6* **Olivia R (IRE)**[37] 5659 3-8-11 **59**... RobbieDowney 11 30
(David Barron) *s.i.s: shkn up over 2f out: nvr on terms* **7/1**

03 **11** *17* **Bluetta**[14] 6551 3-8-11 0... AndrewMullen 7
(Robyn Brisland) *racd keenly: sn prom: hung rt over 2f out: wknd wl over 1f out: b.b.v (vet said filly bled from the nose)* **40/1**

1m 29.25s (0.45) **Going Correction** -0.10s/f (Stan) **11 Ran SP% 121.7**
WFA 3 from 4yo 4lb
Speed ratings (Par 98): **93,91,91,90,89 89,86,85,84,77 58**
CSF £53.57 TOTE £1.60: £1.10, £11.10, £1.20; EX 38.30 Trifecta £232.70.
Owner Farleigh Racing **Bred** Farleigh Court Racing Partnership **Trained** Kingsclere, Hants

FOCUS
The winner didn't need to improve to take this weak race.

7033 WOLVERHAMPTON-RACECOURSE.CO.UK H'CAP 2m 120y (Tp)

7:30 (7:30) (Class 4) (0-80,81) 4-Y-O+

£5,207 (£1,549; £580; £400; £400) **Stalls Low**

Form RPR

1432 **1** **Champarisi**[22] 6256 4-9-5 **77**... SamJames 8 86
(Grant Tuer) *hld up: hdwy over 2f out: styd on u.p to ld wl ins fnl f* **9/2**[2]

0322 **2** *hd* **Houlton**[11] 6634 4-9-0 **79**...(tp) StefanoCherchi(7) 5 87
(Marco Botti) *a.p: chsd ldr over 2f out: led over 1f out: rdn and hdd wl ins fnl f* **9/2**[2]

211 **3** *3* **Charlie D (USA)**[14] 6530 4-9-9 **81**...(tp) RichardKingscote 6 85
(Tom Dascombe) *chsd ldr tl led over 3f out: rdn and hdd over 1f out: no ex ins fnl f* **13/8**[1]

-450 **3** *dht* **Trouble And Strife (IRE)**[47] 5321 4-9-7 **79**...(b[1]) RyanTate 3 83
(Sir Mark Prescott Bt) *hld up: hdwy over 1f out: rdn and hung lft ins fnl f: styd on* **8/1**

4022 **5** *2 1/4* **Norab (GER)**[18] 6366 8-8-4 62..............................(b) JimmyQuinn 1 64
(Bernard Llewellyn) *pushed along to chse ldrs: edgd lft over 2f out: rdn over 1f out: nt clr run: swtchd lft and no ex ins fnl f* **16/1**

5136 **6** *4 1/2* **Jumping Cats**[33] 5812 4-9-6 78..............................(p) JackMitchell 7 74
(Chris Wall) *hld up: rdn over 1f out: nt trble ldrs* **11/2[3]**

5261 **7** *1 1/4* **Arty Campbell (IRE)**[18] 6366 9-9-0 72..............................(p) DavidProbert 2 67
(Bernard Llewellyn) *hld up: nt clr run over 2f out: rdn over 1f out: wknd ins fnl f* **20/1**

-340 **8** *49* **Joycetick (FR)**[22] 5271 5-8-2 63..............................(t) SeanDavis(3) 4
(Nick Littmoden) *led: hdd over 3f out: hmpd and wknd over 2f out: eased (jockey said gelding stopped quickly)* **25/1**

3m 36.03s (-3.27) **Going Correction** -0.10s/f (Stan) **8** Ran SP% **115.4**
Speed ratings (Par 105): **103,102,101,101,100 98,97,74**
WIN: 4.90 Champarisi; PL: 0.50 Charlie D 1.30 Trouble And Strife 1.40 Houlton 1.90 Champarisi; EX: 27.30; CSF: 25.30; TC: 78.52 22.91; TF: 34.10 77.10 CSF £25.30 CT £22.91 TOTE £4.90: £1.90, £1.40, £0.50; EX 27.30 Trifecta £34.10.
Owner Allerton Racing & G Tuer **Bred** Faisal Meshrf Alqahtani **Trained** Birkby, N Yorks

FOCUS
A solidly run staying handicap.

7034 SKY SPORTS RACING SKY 415 CLAIMING STKS 1m 4f 51y (Tp)
8:00 (8:00) (Class 6) 3-4-Y-O

£2,781 (£827; £413; £400; £400; £400) **Stalls Low**

Form RPR

3433 **1** **Hooflepuff (IRE)**[26] 6077 3-9-0 54..............................(p) GeorgeWood 5 66+
(James Fanshawe) *chsd ldr: shkn up over 2f out: led over 1f out: r.o wl* **9/4[2]**

2365 **2** *4 1/2* **Vampish**[23] 6223 4-9-3 72..............................(p[1]) OisinMurphy 2 52
(Philip McBride) *led: shkn up and hdd over 1f out: no ex ins fnl f* **4/7[1]**

0005 **3** *nk* **Shovel It On (IRE)**[9] 6733 4-8-11 50..............................(bt) CierenFallon(5) 4 51
(Steve Flook) *hld up: hdwy over 3f out: styd on same pce fnl f* **20/1**

5006 **4** *3/4* **Thawry**[10] 6663 4-9-10 62.............................. CamHardie 3 58
(Antony Brittain) *stmbld s: hld up: hdwy over 1f out: nt rch ldrs (jockey said gelding stumbled leaving the stalls)* **12/1[3]**

6060 **5** *9* **Misty Breese (IRE)**[9] 6733 4-8-10 40.............................. NoelGarbutt(3) 6 32
(Sarah Hollinshead) *s.i.s: hld up: nvr on terms* **125/1**

54-0 **6** *13* **Rusper's Gift (IRE)**[20] 6317 3-8-13 65.............................. DougieCostello 1 21
(Jamie Osborne) *prom: rdn over 3f out: wknd over 1f out* **18/1**

0000 **7** *9* **Roser Moter (IRE)**[5] 6860 4-8-8 44..............................(p) SeanDavis(3) 8
(Michael Appleby) *chsd ldrs tl rdn and wknd over 2f out (jockey said filly hung right-handed)* **66/1**

2m 39.46s (-1.34) **Going Correction** -0.10s/f (Stan)
WFA 3 from 4yo 8lb **7** Ran SP% **114.4**
Speed ratings (Par 101): **100,97,96,96,90 81,75**
CSF £3.84 TOTE £2.80: £1.70, £1.10; EX 4.20 Trifecta £21.40.Hooflepuff was claimed by Mr Brian Ellison for £10000
Owner The Cool Silk Partnership **Bred** Old Carhue Stud **Trained** Newmarket, Suffolk

FOCUS
This rates a pb from the winner.

7035 STAY AT THE WOLVERHAMPTON HOLIDAY INN MEDIAN AUCTION MAIDEN STKS 1m 4f 51y (Tp)
8:30 (8:30) (Class 6) 3-4-Y-O **£2,781** (£827; £413; £206) **Stalls Low**

Form RPR

00 **1** **Inteldream**[9] 6732 3-8-12 0.............................. StefanoCherchi(7) 7 68
(Marco Botti) *stdd s: hld up: nt clr run over 2f out: hdwy over 1f out: r.o to ld nr fin (trainer said, regards apparent improvement in form, gelding appreciated the step up in trip)* **66/1**

54 **2** *1/2* **Wadacre Galoubet**[10] 6687 3-9-5 0.............................. RichardKingscote 3 67
(Mark Johnston) *chsd ldrs: led 3f out: rdn over 1f out: edgd rt ins fnl f: hdd nr fin* **13/2[3]**

4360 **3** *2* **Star Talent (IRE)**[28] 6030 3-9-5 62..............................(e[1]) ShaneKelly 1 64
(Gay Kelleway) *hld up in tch: chsd ldr and hung lft fr 2f out: sn rdn and ev ch: nt run on* **11/1**

4 *2* **Badessa** 3-9-0 0.............................. OisinMurphy 2 56
(Andrew Balding) *s.i.s: hld up: pushed along over 3f out: styd on fr over 1f out: nt trble ldrs* **7/2[2]**

0 **5** *4* **Gustave Aitch (FR)**[147] 1824 3-9-5 0.............................. LiamKeniry 5 54
(Sophie Leech) *hld up: rdn over 1f out: nvr on terms* **40/1**

6 **6** *3/4* **Zero To Hero (IRE)**[10] 6687 4-9-1 0.............................. Pierre-LouisJamin(7) 4 47
(Archie Watson) *chsd ldrs: rdn over 2f out: wknd fnl f* **25/1**

3 **7** *2 1/2* **Court Order**[24] 6169 3-9-5 0.............................. PJMcDonald 10 49
(James Tate) *s.s: hld up: hdwy on outer over 4f out: rdn over 2f out: wknd fnl f (trainers rep could offer no explanation for the poor performance)* **4/6[1]**

0-5 **8** *9* **Mrs Ivy**[150] 1738 3-9-0 0.............................. RobHornby 9 30
(Ralph Beckett) *chsd ldr tl led over 3f out: sn hdd: wknd over 1f out* **10/1**

064 **9** *nk* **Ozark**[78] 4143 3-9-0 45.............................. AndrewMullen 6 29
(Jennie Candlish) *hld up: wknd over 2f out* **66/1**

P56 **10** *7* **Hurry Kane**[11] 6641 3-9-5 0..............................(p[1]) CharlieBennett 8 23
(Paul George) *led: hdd over 3f out: wknd wl over 1f out* **50/1**

2m 39.5s (-1.30) **Going Correction** -0.10s/f (Stan)
WFA 3 from 4yo 8lb **10** Ran SP% **124.2**
Speed ratings (Par 101): **100,99,98,97,94 93,92,86,85,81**
CSF £466.84 TOTE £70.60: £20.40, £2.50, £2.00; EX 188.70 Trifecta £2240.30.
Owner Fabfive **Bred** Ed's Stud Ltd **Trained** Newmarket, Suffolk

FOCUS
A well-run maiden. They finished slowly and that gave the winner the chance to close from off the pace. The second and third help set the level.
T/Plt: £8.80 to a £1 stake. Pool: £85,237.92 - 6,998.56 winning units T/Qpdt: £3.20 to a £1 stake. Pool: £10,266.80 - 2,365.49 winning units **Colin Roberts**

7036 - 7037a (Foreign Racing) - See Raceform Interactive

3378 LISTOWEL (L-H)
Monday, September 9

OFFICIAL GOING: Soft (soft to heavy in places)

7038a EDMUND & JOSIE WHELAN MEMORIAL LISTOWEL STKS (LISTED RACE) 1m 1f
3:25 (3:27) 3-Y-0+

£26,576 (£8,558; £4,054; £1,801; £900; £450)

RPR

1 **Lancaster House (IRE)**[11] 6649 3-9-3 0.............................. DonnachaO'Brien 17 107+
(A P O'Brien, Ire) *sn chsd ldrs: 4th 1/2-way: gng wl in 2nd over 2f out: rdn in 2nd 1 1/2f out and led 1f out: styd on wl under hands and heels to assert ins fnl f: easily* **7/4[1]**

2 *2 3/4* **Wargrave (IRE)**[39] 5583 3-9-3 100.............................. ChrisHayes 5 101
(J A Stack, Ire) *led tl sn jnd and disp ld: narrow advantage at 1/2-way: 2 l clr over 2f out: rdn and strly pressed 1 1/2f out: hdd 1f out and no imp on easy wnr ins fnl f: kpt on wl* **14/1**

3 *2 1/2* **Winiata (IRE)**[7] 6817 3-8-12 88.............................. NGMcCullagh 9 91+
(J P Murtagh, Ire) *sn settled in mid-div: hdwy on outer 2f out where rdn: no imp on ldrs u.p in 4th ent fnl f: kpt on u.p into nvr threatening 3rd cl home* **8/1[3]**

4 *nk* **Come September (IRE)**[16] 6479 3-8-12 89.............................. RonanWhelan 10 90
(Gavin Cromwell, Ire) *hld up in tch: tk clsr order in 5th at 1/2-way: pushed along into 3rd fr 2f out: sn rdn and no imp on ldrs u.p in 3rd: no ex wl ins fnl f and dropped to 4th cl home* **33/1**

5 *1 3/4* **Riven Light (IRE)**[39] 3953 7-9-9 109.............................. KevinManning 16 92
(W P Mullins, Ire) *mid-div: pushed along over 2f out and sme late hdwy: no imp on ldrs in 6th over 1f out: rdn into 5th wl ins fnl f and kpt on nr fin: nvr trbld ldrs* **3/1[2]**

6 *1/2* **Warnaq (IRE)**[123] 2560 5-9-4 91.............................. ColinKeane 11 86
(Matthew J Smith, Ire) *sn disp ld: cl 2nd at 1/2-way: drvn in 3rd 2f out and sn no ex in 4th: wknd fr over 1f out* **12/1**

7 *1 3/4* **Shelir (IRE)**[16] 6480 3-9-6 98.............................. OisinOrr 4 90
(D K Weld, Ire) *mid-div: 6th 1/2-way: rdn in 5th over 2f out and sn no ex: dropped to 7th over 1f out: one pce after* **16/1**

8 *2 1/2* **Insignia Of Rank (IRE)**[16] 6480 4-9-12 99.............................. GaryCarroll 15 85
(Joseph G Murphy, Ire) *in rr of mid-div early: pushed along towards rr over 3f out: sme hdwy under 2f out: kpt on one pce in 8th ins fnl f: nvr trbld ldrs* **16/1**

9 *1 1/4* **Still Standing (IRE)**[149] 1777 4-9-12 104.............................. ShaneFoley 13 82
(Mrs John Harrington, Ire) *hld up towards rr: swtchd rt under 2f out and sme late hdwy* **10/1**

10 *nk* **Memyselfandmoi (IRE)**[11] 6649 3-8-12 84.............................. DeclanMcDonogh 6 73
(W McCreery, Ire) *chsd ldrs early: dropped to 7th fr 1/2-way: drvn over 2f out and no imp into st: one pce after* **50/1**

11 *1 1/4* **Tipitena**[26] 6090 4-9-4 101.............................. WJLee 12 71
(W McCreery, Ire) *settled in rr early: sme hdwy on outer 3f out: pushed along in 11th bef st and no ex in 8th over 1f out: wknd and eased* **10/1**

12 *4 3/4* **Drombeg Dream (IRE)**[16] 6480 4-9-4 95.............................. RobbieColgan 8 61
(Augustine Leahy, Ire) *hooded to load: mid-div: pushed along over 2f out and sn wknd qckly* **20/1**

13 *4 3/4* **Manjeer (IRE)**[23] 6235 3-9-3 90..............................(b[1]) RossCoakley 2 56
(John M Oxx, Ire) *cl up early tl sn settled bhd ldrs: 3rd 1/2-way: drvn bhd ldrs 3f out and sn wknd* **33/1**

14 *2 1/2* **On The Go Again (IRE)**[16] 6480 6-9-9 97..............................(t) ConorHoban 14 51
(Michael Mulvany, Ire) *hld up towards rr: pushed along under 3f out and sn no imp struggling in rr bef st: wknd* **33/1**

1m 58.47s
WFA 3 from 4yo+ 6lb **14** Ran SP% **132.3**
CSF £31.65 TOTE £2.50: £1.40, £4.00, £2.50; DF 39.40 Trifecta £250.80.
Owner Michael Tabor & Derrick Smith & Mrs John Magnier **Bred** Barronstown Stud **Trained** Cashel, Co Tipperary

FOCUS
This was a proper test for the winner, and he passed it convincingly even if some of his higher rated opponents were not at their best.

7039 - 7042a (Foreign Racing) - See Raceform Interactive

6790 CHANTILLY (R-H)
Monday, September 9

OFFICIAL GOING: Polytrack: standard; turf: good to soft

7043a PRIX DE SAINT-FIRMIN (MAIDEN) (2YO COLTS & GELDINGS) (TURF) 6f
1:25 2-Y-0 **£12,162** (£4,864; £3,648; £2,432; £1,216)

RPR

1 **Dayyan (FR)** 2-9-2 0.............................. MaximPecheur 4 81+
(U Schwinn, Germany) **139/10**

2 *1 3/4* **Be My Day (FR)**[19] 2-9-2 0.............................. ChristopheSoumillon 6 76
(F Chappet, France) **51/10[2]**

3 *2 1/2* **Hernan**[27] 2-9-2 0.............................. MickaelBarzalona 3 68
(Andrea Marcialis, France) **4/5[1]**

4 *shd* **Fighting Don (FR)**[16] 6449 2-9-2 0.............................. TonyPiccone 1 68
(Harry Dunlop) *urged along leaving stalls: sn led: pushed along 2f out: rdn and hdd over 1f out: drvn and kpt on same pce fnl f* **11/2[3]**

5 *1 1/2* **Happy Chrisnat (FR)**[16] 6485 2-9-2 0..............................(p) AntoineHamelin 8 64
(C Plisson, France) **47/1**

6 *3/4* **Tacio** 2-8-6.............................. JenteMarien(5) 7 56
(C Laffon-Parias, France) **13/1**

6 *dht* **Published (IRE)** 2-8-11.............................. FabriceVeron 5 56
(E J O'Neill, France) **20/1**

8 *6* **Hook (FR)** 2-9-2 0.............................. TheoBachelot 2 43
(A Giorgi, Italy) **87/10**

9 *dist* **Bene Bene (FR)**[154] 1657 2-9-2 0.............................. SebastienMaillot 9
(M Boutin, France) **56/1**

1m 13.93s (2.53) **9** Ran SP% **120.1**
PARI-MUTUEL (all including 1 euro stake): WIN 14.90; PLACE 1.90, 1.50, 1.10; DF 30.50.
Owner Stall De Luxe **Bred** Mlle L Kneip & P Perroud **Trained** Germany

7044a PRIX DE VINEUIL (MAIDEN) (2YO FILLIES) (TURF) 6f
2:00 2-Y-O £12,162 (£4,864; £3,648; £2,432; £1,216)

RPR
1 **Minuty (FR)**[25] 2-9-2 0 AurelienLemaitre 10 82+
(F Head, France) 5/1[3]
2 2 **Zaccapa (FR)**[25] 2-9-2 0 StephanePasquier 7 76
(F Chappet, France) 23/10[1]
3 1 **Be Ahead**[23] 2-9-2 0 Pierre-CharlesBoudot 2 73
(E J O'Neill, France) 12/5[2]
4 2 1/2 **Wanaway (FR)**[17] 2-9-2 0 ChristopheSoumillon 3 66
(P Bary, France) 57/10
5 2 **Spring Street (FR)**[19] 2-8-13 0 MlleAlisonMassin(3) 9 60
(S Wattel, France) 13/1
6 3 **Piccata (FR)**[19] 2-9-2 0 LudovicBoisseau 5 51
(T Van Den Troost, Belgium) 88/1
7 nk **Mienvee Flyer**[87] 3817 2-8-10 0 AugustinMadamet(6) 6 50
(F-H Graffard, France) 14/1
8 3 **Good Of Saints**[23] 2-8-13 0 ThomasTrullier(3) 4 41
(C Lerner, France) 9/1
9 dist **Melrose (IRE)** 2-8-11 0 VincentCheminaud 1
(Henry Spiller) *slowly away: pushed along in rr early: nvr a factor and eased over 1f out* 25/1

1m 11.51s (0.11) 9 Ran SP% 120.1
PARI-MUTUEL (all including 1 euro stake): WIN 6.00; PLACE 1.60, 1.30, 1.30; DF 7.80.
Owner Mme Frederic Head **Bred** F Head **Trained** France

7045 - (Foreign Racing) - See Raceform Interactive

6822 CATTERICK (L-H)
Tuesday, September 10

OFFICIAL GOING: Good to firm (watered; 8.7)
Wind: light half behind Weather: Fine

7046 IRISH STALLION FARMS EBF NOVICE MEDIAN AUCTION STKS 5f 212y
1:55 (1:57) (Class 5) 2-Y-O £4,140 (£1,232; £615; £307) Stalls Low

Form RPR
326 1 **Arriba Arriba (IRE)**[7] 6822 2-9-3 74 GrahamLee 5 72
(Rebecca Menzies) *mde all: pushed along over 2f out: rdn over 1f out: kpt on* 7/1
0321 2 1 1/4 **Kendred Soul (IRE)**[27] 6064 2-9-5 71 JackGarritty 8 70
(Jedd O'Keeffe) *trckd ldrs: drvn to chse ldr over 1f out: kpt on same pce* 7/2[3]
3 nk **Seas Of Elzaam (IRE)** 2-9-3 0 DanielTudhope 11 67+
(David O'Meara) *in tch: rdn and hdwy on outer to chse ldr 1f out: kpt on same pce: edgd rt nr fin* 3/1[1]
45 4 3/4 **Breguet Boy (IRE)**[7] 6822 2-9-3 0 ShaneGray 9 65
(Keith Dalgleish) *in tch on inner: rdn over 1f out: kpt on* 14/1
5 hd **Pretty Lady (IRE)** 2-8-12 0 JoeFanning 2 60
(Mark Johnston) *trckd ldrs: pushed along over 2f out: rdn to chse ldr over 1f out: no ex ins fnl f* 10/3[2]
6 1 3/4 **Wadi Al Salaam (IRE)** 2-9-3 0 DuranFentiman 1 59
(Tim Easterby) *dwlt sltly: hld up in midfield: pushed along and hdwy over 2f out: kpt on ins fnl f* 33/1
0 7 5 **Jungle Rock (IRE)**[12] 6622 2-8-12 0 FayeMcManoman(5) 10 44
(Iain Jardine) *nvr bttr than midfield* 50/1
00 8 1 **Youarefullofchat**[32] 5895 2-8-12 0 KieranO'Neill 7 36
(Robyn Brisland) *prom: rdn over 2f out: wknd over 1f out* 200/1
0 9 1 1/2 **Lezardrieux**[7] 6822 2-9-3 0 SamJames 3 37
(Grant Tuer) *dwlt: hld up: nvr threatened* 100/1
10 5 **Queen Of Rock (IRE)** 2-8-12 0 AndrewElliott 6 17
(Philip Kirby) *dwlt: a in rr* 50/1
006 11 1 1/2 **Pull Harder Con**[25] 6167 2-9-3 58 PaulMulrennan 12 17
(Robyn Brisland) *a in rr* 33/1

1m 15.2s (1.60) **Going Correction** +0.075s/f (Good) 11 Ran SP% 100.8
Speed ratings (Par 95): **92,90,89,88,88 86,79,78,76,69 67**
CSF £22.55 TOTE £6.70: £1.80, £1.60, £1.10; EX 18.90 Trifecta £87.10.
Owner The Racing Brothers **Bred** Niall McGrady **Trained** Mordon, Durham
■ Hong Kong Harry was withdrawn. Price at time of withdrawal 5-1. Rule 4 applies to all bets - deduction 15p in the pound.

FOCUS
The going was given as good to firm (GoingStick 8.7). Add 15yds. Just a fair novice. The winner rates near his pre-race level.

7047 RACING TV CLUB DAY HERE TODAY H'CAP 5f
2:30 (2:33) (Class 6) (0-65,65) 3-Y-O £3,105 (£924; £461; £300; £300; £300) Stalls Low

Form RPR
2215 1 **Fox Hill**[28] 6033 3-9-0 58 JasonHart 4 65
(Eric Alston) *mde all: narrow ld tl pushed clr appr fnl f: kpt on wl* 15/8[1]
2206 2 1 3/4 **Kaafy (IRE)**[13] 6608 3-9-6 64 SamJames 10 65
(Grant Tuer) *s.i.s: hld up: pushed along and hdwy over 1f out: rdn to go 2nd ins fnl f: kpt on wl but no threat to wnr* 7/1[3]
3213 3 2 **The Grey Zebedee**[13] 6608 3-9-2 60 (b) DuranFentiman 11 54
(Tim Easterby) *chsd ldrs towards outer: rdn 2f out: kpt on same pce* 6/1[2]
3340 4 1/2 **Tobeornottobee**[10] 6699 3-8-9 60 JessicaAnderson(7) 3 52
(Declan Carroll) *chsd ldrs: rdn and edgd lft over 1f out: one pce ins fnl f* 10/1
0312 5 2 1/4 **Society Star**[24] 6197 3-9-7 65 CamHardie 2 49
(Robert Cowell) *chsd ldrs: rdn 2f out: no ex fnl f* 15/2
0401 6 nk **Jill Rose**[32] 5914 3-9-5 63 (b) PhilDennis 8 46
(Richard Whitaker) *pressed ldr: rdn 2f out: wknd appr fnl f* 9/1
400 7 6 **Shall We Begin (IRE)**[13] 6608 3-8-2 46 NathanEvans 7 7
(Michael Easterby) *dwlt: a towards rr* 28/1
5046 8 1 3/4 **Frosted Lass**[38] 5660 3-8-10 54 BenCurtis 6 9
(David Barron) *a towards rr* 12/1

59.18s (-1.32) **Going Correction** -0.225s/f (Firm) 8 Ran SP% 103.6
Speed ratings (Par 99): **101,98,95,94,90 90,80,77**
CSF £12.20 CT £46.31 TOTE £2.20: £1.10, £3.20, £1.50; EX 12.80 Trifecta £57.80.
Owner Whitehills Racing Syndicate **Bred** Itchen Valley Stud **Trained** Longton, Lancs
■ Tick Tock Croc was withdrawn. Price at time of withdrawal 9-1. Rule 4 applies to all bets - deduction 10p in the pound

FOCUS
A moderate handicap. The main action was up the middle in the straight.

7048 2019 CATTERICK TWELVE FURLONG SERIES H'CAP (QUALIFIER) 1m 4f 13y
3:00 (3:01) (Class 6) (0-65,72) 3-Y-O+ £3,105 (£924; £461; £300; £300; £300) Stalls Centre

Form RPR
5211 1 **Gylo (IRE)**[7] 6827 3-9-13 72 6ex DanielTudhope 5 77
(David O'Meara) *prom: rdn into narrow ld wl over 1f out: drvn fnl f: hld on wl* 11/4[2]
1343 2 1/2 **Remember Rocky**[7] 6827 10-9-6 62 (b) PaulaMuir(5) 11 65
(Lucy Normile) *in tch: hdwy and trckd ldrs over 6f out: rdn to chal strly over 1f out: kpt on* 10/1
301 3 3/4 **Flower Power**[7] 6828 8-9-10 61 4ex (p) JasonHart 9 63
(Tony Coyle) *dwlt and briefly rdn along early: hld up: rdn and hdwy on outer over 2f out: chsd ldr ent fnl f: styd on* 5/2[1]
6-00 4 hd **Straitouttacompton**[125] 2529 3-9-5 64 (t[1]) DougieCostello 1 67
(Ivan Furtado) *midfield on inner: bmpd along in bhd horses over 3f out: swtchd rt to outer 2f out: rdn and sn hdwy: styd on wl fnl f* 33/1
1355 5 1 3/4 **Nearly There**[7] 6827 6-9-1 55 (t) SeanDavis(3) 6 54
(Wilf Storey) *led: rdn over 2f out: hdd wl over 1f out: no ex ins fnl f* 14/1
044 6 2 1/4 **Millie The Minx (IRE)**[35] 5766 5-8-10 47 (p) JamesSullivan 7 42
(Dianne Sayer) *trckd ldrs: rdn over 2f out: edgd lft over 1f out: wknd ins fnl f (trainer said mare was scoped and found to have an epiglottic entrapment)* 10/1
00-5 7 3/4 **Call Me Madam**[16] 6499 4-8-9 49 JaneElliott(3) 15 43
(James Bethell) *prom: rdn over 2f out: outpcd and btn over 1f out* 25/1
0-5 8 nk **Lady Kyria (FR)**[28] 6038 5-9-7 65 NickBarratt-Atkin(7) 3 59
(Philip Kirby) *hld up: rdn over 2f out: sme late hdwy: nvr involved* 50/1
4230 9 nk **Menin Gate (IRE)**[15] 6531 3-9-0 59 (p) TonyHamilton 10 53
(Richard Fahey) *racd keenly in midfield: rdn over 2f out: no imp* 7/1[3]
5354 10 1 1/4 **Hayward Field (IRE)**[41] 5555 6-8-10 47 (e) PhilDennis 12 38
(Noel Wilson) *midfield: rdn over 2f out: wknd over 1f out* 33/1
-606 11 1 1/4 **Mr Sundowner (USA)**[7] 6827 7-8-12 56 (t) RhonaPindar(7) 13 45
(Michael Herrington) *hld up: gd hdwy on outside over 3f out: sn trckd ldrs: rdn over 2f out: wknd appr fnl f* 20/1
060 12 2 **Rent's Dew (IRE)**[10] 6701 3-8-8 53 DuranFentiman 2 40
(Tim Easterby) *hld up: nvr threatened* 20/1
0000 13 5 **Khitaamy (IRE)**[12] 5558 5-8-9 46 oh1 (tp) TomEaves 4 24
(Tina Jackson) *in tch on inner: racd quite keenly: rdn along over 2f out: sn wknd* 80/1
0304 14 3 1/2 **Fillydelphia (IRE)**[29] 6012 8-8-9 46 oh1 (p) RachelRichardson 14 18
(Liam Bailey) *s.i.s: hld up: hdwy into midfield over 7f out: rdn over 2f out: wknd over 1f out* 66/1
4650 15 53 **Heart In Havana**[11] 6666 3-8-5 50 (t) NathanEvans 8
(Michael Easterby) *midfield: lost pl over 5f out: bhd fnl 4f and eased* 33/1

2m 40.23s (-0.37) **Going Correction** +0.075s/f (Good) 15 Ran SP% 119.5
WFA 3 from 4yo+ 8lb
Speed ratings (Par 101): **104,103,103,103,101 100,99,99,99,98 97,96,93,90,55**
CSF £26.22 CT £78.56 TOTE £4.00: £1.30, £2.40, £1.30; EX 25.60 Trifecta £54.30.
Owner Gallop Racing **Bred** R & R Bloodstock **Trained** Upper Helmsley, N Yorks

FOCUS
Add 15yds. It was an advantage to be handy and the winner progressed again.

7049 GET SO MUCH MORE WITH RACING TV H'CAP 7f 6y
3:30 (3:32) (Class 4) (0-80,82) 3-Y-O £6,080 (£1,809; £904; £452; £300; £300) Stalls Low

Form RPR
6234 1 **Woodside Wonder**[13] 6591 3-9-0 73 (v) CallumRodriguez 1 79
(Keith Dalgleish) *chsd ldrs: rdn along wl over 2f out: drvn over 1f out: chal ent fnl f: kpt on to ld towards fin* 7/2[1]
5346 2 nk **Self Assessment (IRE)**[31] 5947 3-8-13 72 BenCurtis 6 77
(K R Burke) *led narrowly: rdn over 2f out: drvn fnl f: kpt on but hdd towards fin* 6/1[3]
3125 3 hd **Friendly Advice (IRE)**[45] 5422 3-9-4 77 (p) JoeFanning 3 81
(Keith Dalgleish) *midfield: rdn along and hdwy on outer 2f out: edgd lft ins fnl f but chal strly 110yds out: one pce towards fin* 4/1[2]
0053 4 1 1/4 **Absolute Dream (IRE)**[19] 6373 3-8-10 69 TonyHamilton 7 70
(Richard Fahey) *hld up: rdn over 2f out: kpt on ins fnl f: nrst fin* 15/2
6300 5 nk **Fox Kasper (IRE)**[11] 6678 3-8-9 68 RachelRichardson 4 68
(Tim Easterby) *midfield towards inner: rdn over 2f out: kpt on fnl f: nvr trbld ldrs (jockey said gelding was denied a clear run app 1/2f out)* 33/1
1460 6 1 1/2 **Beryl The Petal (IRE)**[13] 6609 3-9-7 80 (v) DanielTudhope 2 76
(David O'Meara) *hld up: rdn along 2f out: nvr threatened* 6/1[3]
3455 7 nk **Reeves**[31] 5953 3-9-9 82 (v[1]) LukeMorris 5 77
(Robert Cowell) *chsd ldrs: rdn along wl over 2f out: drvn and hung lft over 1f out: bit outpcd whn hmpd ent fnl f: no ex* 7/2[1]
0400 8 1/2 **Shining Armor**[39] 5617 3-9-4 80 DarraghKeenan(3) 8 74
(John Ryan) *pressed ldr: racd keenly: rdn 2f out: wknd ins fnl f* 20/1

1m 26.94s (-0.46) **Going Correction** +0.075s/f (Good) 8 Ran SP% 112.5
Speed ratings (Par 103): **105,104,104,103,102 100,100,100**
CSF £23.94 CT £85.94 TOTE £4.10: £1.80, £1.60, £1.50; EX 23.60 Trifecta £130.00.
Owner Middleham Park Racing XIV **Bred** Theakston Stud **Trained** Carluke, S Lanarks

FOCUS
Add 15yds. This was a competitive heat and it could be a little better than rated.

7050 RACINGTV.COM H'CAP (DIV I) 5f 212y
4:00 (4:00) (Class 6) (0-65,68) 3-Y-O+ £3,105 (£924; £461; £300; £300; £300) Stalls Low

Form RPR
5043 1 **Carlovian**[12] 6621 6-8-9 50 (v) JasonHart 7 56
(Mark Walford) *mde all: rdn over 2f out: edgd rt ins fnl f: kpt on wl* 8/1[3]
0500 2 1 3/4 **Eldelbar (SPA)**[11] 6666 5-8-10 51 (h) SamJames 8 52
(Geoffrey Harker) *midfield: hdwy whn short of room 2f out: sn pushed along: n.m.r again 1f out: swtchd lft: kpt on wl: wnt 2nd post* 8/1[3]
3221 3 shd **B Fifty Two (IRE)**[7] 6826 10-9-10 68 4ex (tp) JaneElliott(3) 3 68
(Marjorie Fife) *chsd ldr: rdn over 2f out: kpt on same pce* 11/2[2]
1400 4 nk **Montalvan (IRE)**[13] 6608 3-9-7 64 (p) BenCurtis 11 63
(Roger Fell) *midfield on outer: hdwy over 2f out: rdn to chse ldr over 1f out: swtchd lft ins fnl f: one pce towards fin* 18/1
016 5 hd **Pinarella (FR)**[33] 5854 3-9-5 65 (p[1]) HarrisonShaw(3) 10 64
(Ben Haslam) *in tch: rdn over 2f out: kpt on ins fnl f* 16/1
0066 6 1 3/4 **Barton Mills**[10] 6703 4-9-10 65 NathanEvans 4 58
(Michael Easterby) *chsd ldr: pushed along over 2f out: rdn over 1f out: no ex ins fnl f* 17/2

The Form Book Flat 2019, Raceform Ltd, Newbury, RG14 5SJ

5233 **7** 1/2 **Kodicat (IRE)**[35] 5767 5-9-3 **58**..........(v[1]) KevinStott 1 50
(Kevin Ryan) *chsd ldr: rdn over 2f out: edgd rt 2f out: wknd fnl 75yds* **7/2**[1]

6232 **8** 2 **Burtonwood**[16] 6503 7-9-4 **59**.......... GrahamLee 2 45
(Julie Camacho) *midfield: rdn over 2f out: no imp* **11/2**[2]

0200 **9** 3 1/4 **Deeds Not Words (IRE)**[17] 6462 8-9-1 **56**..........(v) RoystonFfrench 5 31
(Tracy Waggott) *hld up: rdn over 2f out: nvr threatened* **28/1**

0604 **10** 8 **Beechwood Izzy (IRE)**[15] 6547 3-9-3 **60**.......... JoeFanning 9 11
(Keith Dalgleish) *a in rr: eased over 1f out (jockey said filly was never travelling)* **17/2**

6305 **11** 1 **Shaleela's Dream**[42] 5526 3-8-9 **57**.......... RayDawson(5) 12 5
(Jane Chapple-Hyam) *hld up: rdn over 2f out: minor hdwy whn checked sltly over 1f out: sn wknd: eased ins fnl f* **12/1**

0-00 **12** 9 **Bobby's Charm (USA)**[47] 5330 4-9-5 **60**..........(b) LukeMorris 6
(Scott Dixon) *dwlt: a in rr: eased over 1f out* **66/1**

1m 14.21s (0.61) **Going Correction** +0.075s/f (Good)
WFA 3 from 4yo+ 2lb **12 Ran SP% 120.0**
Speed ratings (Par 101): **98,95,95,95,94 92,91,89,84,74 72,60**
CSF £71.59 CT £393.08 TOTE £9.00: £3.10, £2.70, £1.50; EX 64.50 Trifecta £375.60.
Owner Profit Pony Racing **Bred** Bradmill Meats Ltd **Trained** Sherriff Hutton, N Yorks

FOCUS
Add 15yds. An all-the-way winner in a similar time to the second division.

7051 RACINGTV.COM H'CAP (DIV II) 5f 212y
4:35 (4:36) (Class 6) (0-65,65) 3-Y-O+
£3,105 (£924; £461; £300; £300; £300) **Stalls** Low

Form RPR

2130 **1** **Sfumato**[11] 6680 5-9-8 **63**.......... ConnorBeasley 1 70
(Adrian Nicholls) *chsd ldrs: rdn to chal strly appr fnl f: kpt on: led nr fin* **9/4**[1]

6252 **2** hd **Rose Marmara**[7] 6825 6-9-10 **65**..........(tp) CamHardie 7 71
(Brian Rothwell) *chsd ldrs: rdn over 2f out: chal strly appr fnl f: led narrowly ins fnl f: drvn fnl 50yds: one pce and hdd nr fin* **4/1**[3]

034 **3** 3/4 **Mansfield**[11] 6680 6-9-2 **57**.......... JackGarritty 12 61
(Stella Barclay) *dwlt sltly: sn midfield: rdn along over 1f out: drvn and kpt on wl fnl f* **15/2**

4310 **4** 2 1/4 **Liam's Lass (IRE)**[89] 3780 3-9-0 **60**.......... WilliamCox(3) 2 57
(Pam Sly) *midfield: rdn over 2f out: kpt on fnl f* **14/1**

0040 **5** shd **Groupie**[13] 6590 5-8-12 **53**.......... GrahamLee 6 50
(Tom Tate) *midfield: rdn 2f out: kpt on fnl f* **14/1**

5404 **6** shd **Indian Pursuit (IRE)**[7] 6826 6-9-7 **62**..........(v) JasonHart 8 58
(John Quinn) *chsd ldrs on outer: rdn over 2f out: no ex ins fnl f* **7/2**[2]

-000 **7** 1 1/2 **Dixieland (IRE)**[32] 5914 3-9-0 **57**.......... DanielTudhope 9 49
(Marjorie Fife) *hld up: pushed along over 2f out: rdn over 1f out: nvr threatened* **33/1**

1-00 **8** 1/2 **Mambila (FR)**[26] 6099 5-9-9 **64**.......... SamJames 4 54
(Geoffrey Harker) *prom: rdn over 2f out: outpcd and btn over 1f out* **16/1**

0254 **9** 1/2 **Mr Greenlight**[12] 6621 4-9-4 **59**..........(p[1]) DuranFentiman 3 48
(Tim Easterby) *led: rdn 2f out: hdd ins fnl f: wknd (jockey said gelding stumbled on the bend; vet said gelding had lost its left-fore shoe)* **12/1**

0160 **10** 1 **Oriental Splendour (IRE)**[16] 6503 7-8-9 **50**..........(b) JamesSullivan 5 36
(Ruth Carr) *dwlt: hld up: rdn 2f out: nvr threatened* **40/1**

1000 **11** 1 3/4 **Point Of Woods**[22] 6273 6-9-4 **59**..........(tp) JamieGormley 11 39
(Tina Jackson) *a towards rr (jockey said gelding was never travelling)* **28/1**

0000 **U** **Astraea**[16] 6503 4-8-9 **50**.......... NathanEvans 10
(Michael Easterby) *rrd and uns rdr s* **40/1**

1m 14.27s (0.67) **Going Correction** +0.075s/f (Good)
WFA 3 from 4yo+ 2lb **12 Ran SP% 122.9**
Speed ratings (Par 101): **98,97,96,93,93 93,91,90,90,88 86,**
CSF £11.17 CT £60.39 TOTE £3.00: £1.10, £1.70, £3.50; EX 12.70 Trifecta £77.50.
Owner J A Rattigan **Bred** Juddmonte Farms Ltd **Trained** Sessay, N Yorks

FOCUS
Add 15yds. This was run in a similar time to the first leg.

7052 EVERY RACE LIVE ON RACING TV H'CAP 5f
5:10 (5:12) (Class 6) (0-65,62) 4-Y-O+
£3,105 (£924; £461; £300; £300; £300) **Stalls** Low

Form RPR

033 **1** **Fiery Breath**[29] 6018 4-8-10 **54**..........(h) DarraghKeenan(3) 6 61
(Robert Eddery) *hld up in midfield: pushed along and hdwy on outer over 1f out: kpt on to ld fnl 25yds: shade cosily* **4/1**[1]

6500 **2** 1/2 **Paco Escostar**[22] 6277 4-8-6 **47**..........(v) CamHardie 12 52
(Julie Camacho) *squeezed out sltly s: sn midfield: hdwy and chsd ldrs over 2f out: rdn along to ld 1f out: edgd rt: kpt on but hdd 25yds out* **8/1**

0450 **3** 3/4 **Young Tiger**[26] 6099 6-8-8 **49**..........(h) JamesSullivan 2 52
(Tom Tate) *stdd s: hld up in rr: racd keenly: pushed along and hdwy over 1f out: kpt on fnl f* **6/1**[2]

0661 **4** nk **Crosse Fire**[15] 6549 7-8-11 **52**..........(b) LukeMorris 11 53
(Scott Dixon) *prom: rdn over 2f out: drvn and chal strly 1f out: one pce ins fnl f* **8/1**

200 **5** 2 1/4 **Pearl Noir**[56] 5018 9-8-12 **53**..........(b) KieranO'Neill 8 46
(Scott Dixon) *led: rdn over 2f out: hdd 1f out: sn wknd* **28/1**

3510 **6** 1/2 **Seamster**[13] 6590 12-8-12 **58**..........(t) ThomasGreatrex(5) 4 50
(David Loughnane) *dwlt: swtchd rt to outer: hld up: rdn over 2f out: nvr threatened* **12/1**

6063 **7** 3/4 **Trulove**[22] 6277 6-8-4 **45**..........(p) JamieGormley 13 34
(John David Riches) *chsd ldrs: rdn over 2f out: wknd over 1f out* **25/1**

4-1 **8** 1 **Rego Park Lady (IRE)**[24] 6234 4-9-5 **60**..........(p) GrahamLee 3 45
(Adrian Murray, Ire) *hld up: rdn 2f out: nvr threatened* **6/1**[2]

0205 **9** nk **Mightaswellsmile**[13] 6590 5-7-13 **45**.......... PaulaMuir(5) 5 29
(Ron Barr) *a towards rr* **8/1**

2316 **10** 3 **Piazon**[11] 6659 8-9-7 **62**..........(be) NathanEvans 14 35
(Julia Brooke) *chsd ldrs: rdn over 2f out: wknd fnl f* **15/2**[3]

5140 **11** 1/2 **I'll Be Good**[11] 6659 10-8-7 **51**.......... HarrisonShaw(3) 9 23
(Alan Berry) *midfield: rdn over 2f out: wknd* **16/1**

0-00 **12** 3 3/4 **Red Hot Fusion (IRE)**[25] 6174 5-8-4 **45**.......... DuranFentiman 10 3
(Alan Berry) *a in rr* **125/1**

59.53s (-0.97) **Going Correction** -0.225s/f (Firm) **12 Ran SP% 115.3**
Speed ratings (Par 101): **98,97,96,95,91 91,89,88,87,83 82,76**
CSF £34.25 CT £192.40 TOTE £4.10: £1.40, £2.90, £2.30; EX 36.80 Trifecta £246.10.
Owner Edwin S Phillips **Bred** S Clarke, G Parsons & A Wideson **Trained** Newmarket, Suffolk

FOCUS
A moderate sprint handicap run at a good gallop.

7053 RACING AGAIN SATURDAY 21ST SEPTEMBER AMATEUR RIDERS' H'CAP 1m 5f 192y
5:45 (5:45) (Class 5) (0-75,77) 4-Y-O+
£3,930 (£1,219; £609; £304; £300; £300) **Stalls** Low

Form RPR

5322 **1** **Jan De Heem**[7] 6827 9-9-11 **55** oh1 ow2..........(v) MissEmmaTodd 2 63
(Tina Jackson) *trckd ldrs: chal gng wl over 2f out: led appr fnl f: sn pushed along: rdn out towards fin* **8/1**

3360 **2** 1 **Duke Of Yorkshire**[22] 6278 9-9-11 **55**..........(p) MissEmilyEasterby 3 61
(Tim Easterby) *led narrowly: rdn along over 2f out: hdd appr fnl f: styd on but a hld* **20/1**

2064 **3** 3 1/2 **St Andrews (IRE)**[23] 6256 6-9-6 **53**..........(v) MissSarahBowen(3) 12 54
(Gillian Boanas) *hld up: rdn along and hdwy over 1f out: styd on wl: wnt 3rd towards fin* **11/2**[2]

4550 **4** 1 3/4 **Question Of Faith**[7] 6827 8-9-12 **61**.......... MrEireannCagney(5) 1 60
(Martin Todhunter) *in tch on inner: trckd ldrs over 3f out: rdn over 2f out: one pce in 3rd fr over 1f out: lost 3rd towards fin* **12/1**

21-4 **5** nk **Chebsey Beau**[36] 5739 9-11-0 **72**.......... MrSimonWalker 5 70
(John Quinn) *in tch: pushed along and outpcd over 3f out: plugged on fnl 2f* **11/4**[1]

1235 **6** 1 3/4 **Thorntoun Care**[17] 6456 8-10-5 **68**.......... MissAmyCollier(5) 13 64
(Karen Tutty) *hld up: pushed along 3f out: sme hdwy 2f out: styd on: nvr threatened* **14/1**

0063 **7** shd **Restive (IRE)**[24] 6218 6-10-4 **62**..........(t) MissSerenaBrotherton 7 58
(Michael Appleby) *hld up: hdwy and n.m.r over 1f out: styd on ins fnl f: nrst fin (vet revealed the gelding to be slightly lame on its left-hind; jockey said regarding running and riding that her instructions were to get the gelding settled in a handy position behind the leaders, but the gelding was slowly away. Adding the she wanted* **13/2**[3]

0255 **8** 1 1/4 **French Mix (USA)**[16] 6511 5-11-2 **77**.......... MissHannahWelch(3) 4 71
(Alexandra Dunn) *midfield: smooth hdwy over 2f out: rdn and no imp* **14/1**

25-0 **9** 1 **Compatriot (IRE)**[24] 5290 5-10-0 **65**..........(p) MissRosieHowarth(7) 11 57
(Roger Fell) *pressed ldr: rdn over 2f out: wknd over 1f out* **50/1**

0440 **10** 3/4 **Country'N'Western (FR)**[30] 5993 7-10-4 **67**.......... MrGeorgeEddery(5) 10 58
(Robert Eddery) *hld up: nvr threatened* **14/1**

6406 **11** 1/2 **Tapis Libre**[22] 6278 11-10-8 **66**..........(t[1]) MissJoannaMason 6 57
(Jacqueline Coward) *midfield on outer: rdn along over 3f out: wknd over 1f out* **16/1**

3153 **12** 3 1/2 **Be Perfect (USA)**[22] 6278 10-10-7 **70**.......... MissEmilyBullock(5) 9 56
(Ruth Carr) *midfield: rdn over 2f out: wknd over 1f out* **8/1**

0-60 **13** 1 1/2 **Kyoto Star (FR)**[206] 754 5-10-7 **70**..........(p) MissCharlotteCrane(5) 14 54
(Tim Easterby) *trckd ldrs: pushed along and hung lft over 2f out: wknd over 1f out* **50/1**

53/0 **14** 1 1/4 **Sigurd (GER)**[11] 99 7-9-2 **53** oh8.......... MissDawnHenry(7) 8 35
(Joanne Foster) *a in rr* **100/1**

3m 5.93s (-1.67) **Going Correction** +0.075s/f (Good) **14 Ran SP% 120.9**
Speed ratings (Par 103): **107,106,104,103,103 102,102,101,100,100 100,98,97,96**
CSF £164.29 CT £964.85 TOTE £10.10: £2.90, £4.80, £2.40; EX 114.20 Trifecta £695.30.
Owner H L Thompson & D Tucker **Bred** Larksborough Stud Limited **Trained** Liverton, Cleveland

FOCUS
Add 15yds. An ordinary amateur riders' event. The early gallop was steady and it didn't pay to be too far off the pace. The winner rates to his best in the last two years.
T/Jkpt: Not won. T/Plt: £18.10 to a £1 stake. Pool: £64,487.27 - 2,586.79 winning units T/Qpdt: £9.60 to a £1 stake. Pool: £5,988.74 - 457.59 winning units **Andrew Sheret**

6368 LEICESTER (R-H)
Tuesday, September 10

OFFICIAL GOING: Good to firm (good in places; watered; 8.3)
Wind: Light behind Weather: Overcast

7054 DALE & HALL & HICKMAN ASSOCIATES EBF FILLIES' NOVICE STKS (PLUS 10 RACE) 7f
2:20 (2:21) (Class 4) 2-Y-O
£6,080 (£1,809; £904; £452) **Stalls** High

Form RPR

32 **1** **Amber Island (IRE)**[21] 6322 2-9-0 0.......... WilliamBuick 3 78+
(Charlie Appleby) *mde all: rdn over 1f out: edgd rt ins fnl f: styd on* **2/1**[2]

45 **2** 1 1/2 **High Flying Bird (FR)**[10] 6697 2-9-0 0.......... RichardKingscote 2 74
(Tom Dascombe) *w wnr 1f: settled in 2nd after: rdn over 1f out: styd on same pce wl ins fnl f* **25/1**

3 1/2 **Princess Bride** 2-9-0 0.......... OisinMurphy 7 73
(Saeed bin Suroor) *chsd ldrs: rdn over 1f out: styd on* **6/1**[3]

3 **4** nse **Woodhouse**[25] 6159 2-9-0 0.......... RyanMoore 6 73
(Sir Michael Stoute) *trckd ldrs: shkn up over 2f out: rdn over 1f out: styd on* **5/4**[1]

5 1 1/4 **Sunset Kiss** 2-9-0 0.......... CallumShepherd 5 69+
(Michael Bell) *hld up: shkn up over 2f out: r.o ins fnl f: nt rch ldrs* **50/1**

6 nk **Hessa** 2-9-0 0.......... JamieSpencer 8 69+
(K R Burke) *s.i.s: hld up: shkn up and hdwy over 1f out: r.o: nrst fin* **50/1**

7 1 **Fleet Street** 2-9-0 0.......... RobertHavlin 1 66
(John Gosden) *s.i.s: hdwy 1/2-way: rdn over 1f out: no ex ins fnl f* **14/1**

8 6 **Turaath** 2-9-0 0.......... JimCrowley 4 50
(Charles Hills) *s.i.s: hld up: shkn up and swtchd lft over 1f out: sn wknd* **12/1**

9 1 1/2 **Lyrical** 2-9-0 0.......... PJMcDonald 10 47
(Ed Dunlop) *s.i.s: sn pushed along and a in rr* **66/1**

10 2 **Chosen Star** 2-9-0 0.......... SeanLevey 9 41
(Michael Bell) *hld up: pushed along 1/2-way: wknd over 1f out* **25/1**

1m 24.46s (-1.24) **Going Correction** -0.15s/f (Firm) **10 Ran SP% 119.5**
Speed ratings (Par 94): **101,99,98,98,97 96,95,88,87,84**
CSF £58.11 TOTE £3.00: £1.40, £6.60, £1.30; EX 44.00 Trifecta £213.00.
Owner Godolphin **Bred** Godolphin **Trained** Newmarket, Suffolk

FOCUS
A fair novice, little got involved with it paying to sit prominently. They raced centre-field.

7055 DENNIS HAMMILL MEMORIAL EBF NOVICE STKS (PLUS 10 RACE) (C&G) 7f
2:50 (2:51) (Class 4) 2-Y-O
£6,469 (£1,925; £962; £481) **Stalls** High

Form

1 **Amaan** 2-9-0 0.......... DaneO'Neill 1 79+
(Simon Crisford) *chsd ldrs: led 2f out: rdn out* **20/1**

2 **2** *1 ½* **Black Comedy (FR)**[12] 6640 2-9-0 0 SeanLevey 7 75
(Richard Hannon) *chsd ldrs: led 4f out: hdd 2f out: sn rdn: styd on same pce ins fnl f* **7/2**[2]

3 *¾* **Global Esteem (IRE)** 2-9-0 0 (h¹) ShaneKelly 11 73
(Gay Kelleway) *s.i.s: plld hrd and sn prom: led over 5f out: hdd 4f out: rdn over 1f out: styd on* **25/1**

4 *½* **Bottom Bay** 2-9-0 0 CallumShepherd 2 72
(Michael Bell) *hld up: hdwy 1/2-way: shkn up over 2f out: rdn and edgd lft ins fnl f: styd on same pce ins fnl f (vet said colt lost its right fore shoe)* **33/1**

6 **5** *nse* **Diyari (IRE)**[25] 6163 2-9-0 0 JimCrowley 4 72
(John Gosden) *prom: pushed along 1/2-way: styd on same pce ins fnl f* **4/1**[3]

6 *3 ¼* **Saeer (IRE)** 2-9-0 0 RyanMoore 6 63+
(Sir Michael Stoute) *s.s: pushed along 1/2-way: styd on ins fnl f: nvr nrr* **8/1**

7 *1 ¼* **Court Of Appeal (IRE)** 2-9-0 0 PJMcDonald 10 60
(James Tate) *chsd ldrs: pushed along over 2f out: wknd over 1f out* **15/2**

8 *¾* **Warning Shot (IRE)** 2-9-0 0 JasonWatson 8 58
(Saeed bin Suroor) *plld hrd: sn led: hdd over 5f out: remained handy: rdn and hung rt over 1f out: wknd ins fnl f (jockey said colt ran too freely)* **13/8**[1]

00 **9** *7* **Itoldyoutobackit (IRE)**[27] 6078 2-9-0 0 LiamKeniry 3 40
(Jonjo O'Neill) *s.s: a in rr* **100/1**

1m 24.75s (-0.95) **Going Correction** -0.15s/f (Firm) **9** Ran SP% **115.7**
Speed ratings (Par 97): **99,97,96,95,95 92,90,89,81**
CSF £86.90 TOTE £17.90: £4.10, £1.70, £6.40; EX 99.40 Trifecta £2336.80.
Owner Hamdan Al Maktoum **Bred** Shadwell Estate Company Limited **Trained** Newmarket, Suffolk

FOCUS
Similar to the first race, they raced centre-field and little got involved from off the pace.

7056 LOWESBY (S) STKS 7f
3:20 (3:20) (Class 5) 2-Y-O
£3,752 (£1,116; £557; £300; £300; £300) **Stalls** High

Form RPR
0566 **1** **Twittering (IRE)**[18] 6387 2-9-0 63 (b¹) NicolaCurrie 4 62
(Jamie Osborne) *trckd ldrs: shkn up over 2f out: led over 1f out: sn rdn: edgd lft ins fnl f: styd on* **14/1**

6045 **2** *2 ¼* **The Ginger Bullet**[15] 6539 2-9-0 55 BarryMcHugh 7 56
(Richard Fahey) *hld up: hdwy over 2f out: rdn over 1f out: chsd wnr ins fnl f: styd on* **5/1**[3]

6544 **3** *2 ¼* **Timon (IRE)**[14] 6563 2-9-0 52 (p) CallumShepherd 5 50
(Mick Channon) *w ldrs: rdn and ev ch over 1f out: no ex ins fnl f* **16/1**

6256 **4** *1 ½* **Percy Green (IRE)**[14] 6571 2-9-0 60 CliffordLee 1 46
(K R Burke) *hld up: hdwy 2f out: rdn over 1f out: no ex fnl f* **7/2**[2]

1634 **5** *4 ½* **Isobar Wind (IRE)**[12] 6637 2-9-4 68 (h) OisinMurphy 8 39
(David Evans) *chsd ldrs: rdn over 2f out: hmpd and wknd over 1f out (trainer could offer no explanation for the gelding's performance)* **6/4**[1]

4003 **6** *2 ½* **Sparkling Breeze**[15] 6539 2-9-0 62 (p) AndrewMullen 6 28
(Michael Dods) *chsd ldrs: pushed along 1/2-way: hmpd and wknd over 1f out* **15/2**

0050 **7** *2 ¼* **Samsar (IRE)**[15] 6539 2-8-7 42 LauraCoughlan(7) 2 22
(Adrian Nicholls) *led: rdn and hdd over 1f out: sn edgd lft and wknd* **50/1**

06 **8** *4 ½* **Sooty's Return (IRE)**[66] 4652 2-9-0 0 TrevorWhelan 3 11
(J S Moore) *s.i.s: in rr and pushed along 1/2-way: wknd over 2f out* **100/1**

3566 **9** *4* **Speed Dating (FR)**[14] 6563 2-8-9 62 CierenFallon(5) 10
(Derek Shaw) *chsd ldrs: rdn 1/2-way: wknd over 2f out* **8/1**

5040 **10** *1 ¾* **Butterfly Pose (IRE)**[14] 6584 2-8-9 0 JFEgan 9
(J S Moore) *hld up: rdn over 2f out: wknd sn after (jockey said filly stopped quickly; vet said that the filly lost its right hind shoe)* **28/1**

1m 24.77s (-0.93) **Going Correction** -0.15s/f (Firm) **10** Ran SP% **120.7**
Speed ratings (Par 95): **99,96,93,92,87 84,81,76,71,69**
CSF £84.87 TOTE £16.00: £4.00, £1.40, £3.80; EX 97.20 Trifecta £1886.10.The winner was bought in for £5,200.
Owner J A Osborne **Bred** Troy Cullen **Trained** Upper Lambourn, Berks
■ Stewards' Enquiry : Laura Coughlan two-day ban; careless riding (Sep 24-25)

FOCUS
Moderate selling form, they finished quite well strung out. The action unfolded down the centre once more.

7057 WELCOMM COMMUNICATIONS AND TECHNOLOGY SOLUTIONS H'CAP 1m 3f 179y
3:50 (3:50) (Class 4) (0-80,79) 3-Y-O+ £5,789 (£1,722; £860) **Stalls** Low

Form RPR
-621 **1** **Fantastic Blue**[17] 6463 3-9-6 79 PatCosgrave 1 85
(Ismail Mohammed) *s.s: sn prom: chsd ldr 5f out: rdn over 3f out: styd on u.p to ld post* **2/5**[1]

3332 **2** *nse* **Dante's View (IRE)**[13] 6589 3-9-5 78 RyanMoore 5 84
(Sir Michael Stoute) *led: shkn up and qcknd over 3f out: rdn over 1f out: hdd post* **11/4**[2]

5432 **3** *2 ¼* **Sempre Presto (IRE)**[19] 6371 4-8-13 67 ConnorMurtagh(3) 4 69
(Richard Fahey) *chsd ldr 7f: remained handy: rdn over 2f out: nt clr run and swtchd lft over 1f out: edgd rt ins fnl f: no imp* **17/2**[3]

2m 34.42s (-0.58) **Going Correction** -0.15s/f (Firm)
WFA 3 from 4yo 8lb **3** Ran SP% **108.6**
Speed ratings (Par 105): **95,94,93**
CSF £1.85 TOTE £1.40; EX 1.90 Trifecta £1.70.
Owner Nabil Mourad **Bred** Whitwell Bloodstock **Trained** Newmarket, Suffolk

FOCUS
An ordinary small-field handicap, just a nose separated the two 3yos at the line. The winner didn't have to match the level of his Windsor success but still a pb from the second.

7058 EBF STALLIONS PRESTWOLD CONDITIONS STKS 5f
4:20 (4:20) (Class 3) 3-Y-O+ £9,451 (£2,829; £1,414) **Stalls** High

Form RPR
1424 **1** **Wise Words**[10] 6735 3-8-10 94 PJMcDonald 2 95
(James Tate) *stdd s: hld up: hdwy over 1f out: shkn up to ld ins fnl f: rdn out* **7/4**[2]

1500 **2** *nk* **Corinthia Knight (IRE)**[10] 6698 4-9-2 100 HollieDoyle 1 99
(Archie Watson) *awkward s: sn chsng ldr: rdn over 1f out: r.o* **6/5**[1]

6100 **3** *½* **Free Love**[17] 6476 3-8-5 88 CierenFallon(5) 3 92
(Michael Appleby) *led at stdy pce: qcknd 2f out: shkn up and edgd rt fr over 1f out: hdd ins fnl f: styd on* **11/4**[3]

1m 2.68s (0.88) **Going Correction** -0.15s/f (Firm)
WFA 3 from 4yo+ 1lb **3** Ran SP% **108.5**
Speed ratings (Par 107): **87,86,85**
CSF £4.22 TOTE £2.60; EX 5.00 Trifecta £3.00.
Owner Sheikh Rashid Dalmook Al Maktoum **Bred** Ropsley Bloodstock Llp **Trained** Newmarket, Suffolk

FOCUS
Little in it between the three of them at the weights and they duly finished within just over 1/2l of each other.

7059 MICK CONNOLLY MEMORIAL H'CAP 7f
4:55 (4:55) (Class 3) (0-95,91) 3-Y-O+ £8,086 (£2,406; £1,202; £601) **Stalls** High

Form RPR
3122 **1** **Chatham House**[9] 6756 3-9-2 86 SeanLevey 5 91+
(Richard Hannon) *chsd ldrs: rdn to ld ins fnl f: edgd rt: styd on* **5/2**[2]

1100 **2** *1* **Firmdecisions (IRE)**[39] 5626 9-9-1 84 RowanScott(3) 1 88
(Nigel Tinkler) *hld up: hdwy over 1f out: sn rdn: styd on same pce towards fin* **14/1**

1516 **3** *nse* **Swift Approval (IRE)**[14] 6567 7-9-2 82 JimCrowley 6 86
(Stuart Williams) *led: rdn over 1f out: hdd ins fnl f: edgd rt: styd on same pce towards fin* **13/2**

0212 **4** *1* **Six Strings**[4] 6935 5-9-2 82 AlistairRawlinson 2 83
(Michael Appleby) *s.s: plld hrd: hdwy over 4f out: chsd ldr over 2f out tl over 1f out: hung rt and styd on same pce ins fnl f (jockey said gelding missed the break and ran too freely)* **6/4**[1]

0356 **5** *4 ½* **Breath Of Air**[18] 6396 3-9-4 88 KieranShoemark 3 75
(Charles Hills) *chsd ldr over 4f: rdn over 1f out: wknd ins fnl f* **7/2**[3]

1m 23.72s (-1.98) **Going Correction** -0.15s/f (Firm)
WFA 3 from 5yo+ 4lb **5** Ran SP% **110.8**
Speed ratings (Par 107): **105,103,103,102,97**
CSF £30.41 TOTE £3.10: £1.70, £5.60; EX 31.90 Trifecta £79.10.
Owner Denford Stud **Bred** Denford Stud Ltd **Trained** East Everleigh, Wilts

FOCUS
A tight handicap, there wasn't much between the five of them approaching the last furlong. A bit muddling, but it has been rated around the front-running third.

7060 SWAN APPRENTICE H'CAP 1m 2f
5:25 (5:25) (Class 6) (0-65,65) 4-Y-O+
£2,846 (£847; £423; £300; £300; £300) **Stalls** Low

Form RPR
0002 **1** **Sea Of Mystery (IRE)**[8] 6796 6-9-4 60 (t) MarkCrehan(3) 2 68
(Michael Appleby) *chsd ldrs: wnt 2nd over 1f out: rdn to ld wl ins fnl f: styd on* **3/1**[1]

0006 **2** *¾* **Orange Suit (IRE)**[61] 4817 4-9-9 65 (b¹ w) MarcoGhiani(3) 4 72
(Ed de Giles) *sn led: rdn over 1f out: hdd wl ins fnl f* **7/2**[2]

0636 **3** *2 ½* **Bhodi (IRE)**[24] 6210 4-9-4 60 TobyEley(3) 7 62+
(Kevin Frost) *hld up: pushed along over 3f out: hdwy over 1f out: swtchd rt ins fnl f: r.o: nt rch ldrs* **16/1**

0120 **4** *½* **Cosmic Ray**[118] 2738 7-9-3 56 (h) GabrieleMalune 8 57
(Les Eyre) *led early: chsd ldr tl rdn over 1f out: no ex ins fnl f* **8/1**

5111 **5** *½* **Compass Point**[152] 1710 4-9-10 63 SeamusCronin 1 63
(Robyn Brisland) *prom: swtchd rt over 3f out: rdn over 2f out: styd on same pce ins fnl f* **12/1**

3530 **6** *nk* **Takiah**[21] 6327 4-8-5 51 oh5 (p) GeorgeRooke(7) 5 51
(Peter Hiatt) *hld up: hdwy over 2f out: rdn over 1f out: no ex ins fnl f* **16/1**

0040 **7** *5* **Mac O'Polo (IRE)**[26] 6098 5-8-9 51 (p) EllaMcCain(3) 3 41
(Donald McCain) *hld up: hdwy and nt clr run over 3f out: rdn over 1f out: wknd ins fnl f* **33/1**

200 **8** *4 ½* **Le Maharajah (FR)**[25] 6160 4-9-12 65 CameronNoble 9 46
(Tom Clover) *prom: rdn over 2f out: wknd over 1f out* **8/1**

6040 **9** *2 ½* **Guvenor's Choice (IRE)**[20] 6341 4-9-8 61 (t) MeganNicholls 12 38
(Marjorie Fife) *hld up in tch: pushed along and lost pl over 3f out: n.d after* **11/1**

0600 **10** *¾* **Brockagh Cailin**[8] 6796 4-8-13 55 (v¹) LauraCoughlan(3) 11 30
(J S Moore) *hld up: rn wd over 4f out: nvr on terms* **50/1**

004 **11** *1 ¼* **Tobacco Road (IRE)**[43] 5499 9-8-5 51 (t) IsobelFrancis(7) 10 24
(Mark Pattinson) *s.i.s: a in rr (jockey said gelding was slowly away and never travelling)* **14/1**

0215 **12** *13* **Destinys Rock**[33] 5850 4-9-11 64 (p) CierenFallon 6 12
(Mark Loughnane) *s.i.s: hld up: shkn up over 3f out: sn wknd* **11/2**[3]

2m 6.04s (-3.16) **Going Correction** -0.15s/f (Firm) **12** Ran SP% **124.2**
Speed ratings (Par 101): **106,105,103,103,102 102,98,94,92,92 91,80**
CSF £13.95 CT £151.39 TOTE £3.30: £1.20, £1.70, £5.50; EX 17.40 Trifecta £199.50.
Owner Frank McAleavy **Bred** Sunderland Holdings Inc **Trained** Oakham, Rutland
■ Stewards' Enquiry : Mark Crehan seven-day ban; misuse of whip (Sep 24-30)

FOCUS
The market leaders came to the fore in this modest handicap.
T/Plt: £715.50 to a £1 stake. Pool: £51,071.08 - 52.10 winning units T/Qpdt: £78.40 to a £1 stake. Pool: £3,644.38 - 34.36 winning units **Colin Roberts**

CHATEAUBRIANT (L-H)
Tuesday, September 10
OFFICIAL GOING: Turf: good to soft

7061a PRIX DE LA FEDERATION (MAIDEN) (3YO) (TURF) 1m 1f 165y
11:55 3-Y-O £7,207 (£2,882; £2,162; £1,441; £720)

RPR
1 **A Fine Romance (FR)**[92] 3-8-13 0 TheoBachelot 10 68
(Mme Pia Brandt, France) **19/10**[1]

2 *nse* **Ephemeral (IRE)** 3-8-13 0 SebastienMaillot 5 68
(N Clement, France) **74/10**

3 *nk* **Gloria Bere (FR)**[31] 3-8-13 0 ChristopherGrosbois 11 67
(J Boisnard, France) **11/1**

4 *2* **Kenwina (FR)**[120] 3-8-3 0 AugustinMadamet(5) 6 58
(P Bary, France) **13/1**

5 *hd* **Melba Rose**[19] 3-8-8 0 JulienGuillochon 12 58
(H-A Pantall, France) *shifted lft leaving stalls: sn rcvrd to trck ldrs: urged along 2f out: rdn and ev ch over 1f out: no ex ins fnl f* **47/10**[2]

6 2 **Star At Midnight**[406] 5603 3-8-8 0 MickaelBerto 9 53
(Jo Hughes, France) *settled in 2nd: pushed along 2f out: rdn w limited rspnse over 1f out: kpt on same pce fnl f* **47/1**
7 nk **Diva Morita (FR)**[19] 3-8-4 0 MlleCeciliaPoirier(9) 3 58
(J Boisnard, France) **49/10**[3]
8 1 **Danseur D'Argent (FR)**[28] 6062 3-8-7 0 HugoBesnier(6) 2 56
(Jo Hughes, France) *hld up towards rr: rowed along over 2f out: rdn and no imp over 1f out: nvr able to chal* **13/1**
9 2 **Valentino (FR)**[151] 1741 3-8-11 0 ClementLecoeuvre 1 50
(Alex Fracas, France) **10/1**
10 4 ½ **Darkange (FR)**[14] 3-8-3 0 QuentinPerrette(5) 7 37
(J-P Sauvage, France) **26/1**
11 1 ¾ **Reine De Lune (FR)**[62] 3-8-3 0 DamienGibelloSacco(5) 4 33
(S Morineau, France) **62/1**
2m 4.66s **11** Ran SP% **120.0**
PARI-MUTUEL (all including 1 euro stake): WIN 2.90; PLACE 1.30, 2.10, 2.60; DF 9.50.
Owner Fair Salinia Limited **Bred** Fair Salinia Ltd **Trained** France

7062a PRIX JOSEPH SEVERE (CONDITIONS) (4YO+) (TURF) 1m 1f 165y
12:25 4-Y-O+

£9,909 (£3,765; £2,774; £1,585; £792; £594)

RPR
1 **Caffe Macchiato (IRE)**[58] 4-8-11 0 (b) TheoBachelot 1 70
(Mme Pia Brandt, France) **23/5**[3]
2 2 **Flor De Seda (FR)**[12] 6651 4-8-3 0 HugoBesnier(5) 3 63
(Jo Hughes, France) *sn prom: trckd ldr: hdwy to chal over 2f out: rdn to ld over 1f out: drvn ins fnl f: hdd fnl 75yds* **11/1**
3 1 ¾ **Octeville (IRE)**[12] 6651 4-9-5 0 AlexandreRoussel 2 70
(C Lotoux, France) **42/10**[2]
4 3 **Duchess Of Danzig (GER)**[43] 5510 4-9-1 0 CyrilleStefan 7 60
(H-F Devin, France) **56/10**
5 2 **Red Onion**[26] 6145 5-9-6 0 ClementCadel 9 61
(Gaspar Vaz, Spain) **15/1**
6 3 **Wooden (FR)**[17] 4-8-6 0 QuentinPerrette(5) 6 45
(M Nigge, France) **17/10**[1]
7 4 **For Ever Fun (FR)**[42] 4-8-9 0 DamienBoche(8) 8 43
(L Gadbin, France) **23/1**
8 3 ½ **Pimpinehorse (FR)**[499] 4-8-11 0 JeffersonSmith 4
(M Drean, France) **69/1**
9 ½ **Eos Quercus (IRE)**[846] 7-8-4 0 MaximilienJustum(7) 5
(N Leenders, France) **9/1**
2m 3.4s **9** Ran SP% **119.5**
PARI-MUTUEL (all including 1 euro stake): WIN 5.60; PLACE 2.10, 3.40, 1.70; DF 18.00.
Owner Andrew Black **Bred** Rathasker Stud **Trained** France

6621 CARLISLE (R-H)
Wednesday, September 11

OFFICIAL GOING: Good to soft (7.1)
Wind: Fairly strong, half against in over 2f of home straight Weather: Overcast

7063 BRITISH EBF FILLIES' NOVICE STKS (PLUS 10 RACE) 5f 193y
1:40 (1:43) (Class 5) 2-Y-O **£4,172** (£1,241; £620; £310) **Stalls Low**

Form RPR
6 1 **Stormy Girl (IRE)**[58] 4993 2-8-9 ThomasGreatrex(5) 6 84
(David Loughnane) *mde all: pushed clr fr 2f out: readily* **25/1**
53 2 5 **Hostelry**[47] 5388 2-9-0 0 ConnorBeasley 1 68
(Michael Dods) *prom: rdn and outpcd 2f out: rallied fnl f: wnt 2nd cl home: no ch w wnr* **2/1**[1]
3 3 ½ **Dandy's Angel (IRE)**[21] 6336 2-8-11 0 SeanDavis(3) 3 66
(John Wainwright) *chsd wnr: rdn 2f out: one pce fnl f: lost 2nd cl home* **9/1**
4 3 ¾ **Quick Recap (IRE)** 2-9-0 0 FrannyNorton 4 54
(Tom Dascombe) *dwlt: bhd and green: hdwy whn nt clr run over 1f out: kpt on fnl f: improve (jockey said filly was denied a clear run approaching 2f out and again approaching the final furlong)* **7/2**[3]
2 5 3 **Sendacard**[33] 5913 2-9-0 0 TonyHamilton 11 45
(Richard Fahey) *chsd ldrs: rdn 2f out: wknd fnl f* **5/2**[2]
0 6 ¾ **Pearl Of India**[16] 6548 2-9-0 0 AndrewMullen 7 42
(Robyn Brisland) *prom: rdn along 1/2-way: wknd over 1f out* **66/1**
7 nk **Niamh's Starlight (IRE)** 2-9-0 0 GrahamLee 2 41
(Bryan Smart) *hld up in midfield on ins: pushed along over 2f out: sn no imp* **20/1**
34 8 4 **Baracca Rocks**[9] 6793 2-9-0 0 BenCurtis 9 29
(K R Burke) *hld up: drvn along over 2f out: sn n.d: btn over 1f out* **20/1**
9 nk **Granny Grey (IRE)** 2-9-0 0 RobbieDowney 10 28
(David Barron) *hld up on outside: struggling over 2f out: sn btn* **66/1**
10 5 **Elfrida Beetle** 2-9-0 0 DuranFentiman 8 12
(Tim Easterby) *s.i.s: bhd: rdn over 2f out: sn wknd* **50/1**
0 11 2 ¼ **Rosa P**[18] 6457 2-8-9 0 TobyEley(5) 12 4
(Steph Hollinshead) *hld up: rdn along 1/2-way: sn wknd (jockey said filly ran green)* **125/1**
12 4 ½ **Mereside Blue** 2-9-0 0 TomEaves 5
(David Barron) *s.i.s: bhd: struggling 1/2-way: btn fnl 2f* **40/1**
1m 14.82s (0.22) **Going Correction** +0.25s/f (Good) **12** Ran SP% **115.7**
Speed ratings (Par 92): **108,101,100,95,91 90,90,84,84,77 74,68**
CSF £70.58 TOTE £35.40: £6.00, £1.10, £2.30; EX 97.90 Trifecta £421.90.
Owner Stonegrave Thoroughbreds **Bred** Rosetown Bloodstock & E McEvoy **Trained** Tern Hill, Shropshire

FOCUS
They raced on the far side on ground which had eased to good to soft from good, overnight and during the morning. An ordinary juvenile fillies' novice contest, rated as straightforward form around the runner-up.

7064 RACINGTV.COM NURSERY H'CAP (JOCKEY CLUB GRASSROOTS NURSERY QUALIFIER) 5f 193y
2:15 (2:16) (Class 5) (0-75,74) 2-Y-O

£4,204 (£1,251; £625; £312; £300; £300) **Stalls Low**

Form RPR
5120 1 **Singe Anglais (IRE)**[12] 6653 2-8-8 **66** FayeMcManoman(5) 11 71
(Nigel Tinkler) *hld up: effrt and plld out over 1f out: hdwy to ld ins fnl f: drifted rt: hld on wl cl home* **5/1**[1]
330 2 shd **Magic Timing**[13] 6622 2-9-2 **69** (b[1]) JoeFanning 4 73
(Keith Dalgleish) *dwlt: hld up: nt clr run over 2f out to over 1f out: hdwy and ev ch last 100yds: carried rt: kpt on: jst hld* **5/1**[1]
5265 3 1 ¾ **Danny Ocean (IRE)**[12] 6653 2-8-10 **66** (p[1]) HarrisonShaw(3) 2 65
(K R Burke) *hld up on ins: rdn over 2f out: hdwy to ld over 1f out to ins fnl f: kpt on same pce* **5/1**[1]
3442 4 2 **Paddy Elliott (IRE)**[18] 6457 2-9-4 **71** BenRobinson 1 64+
(Brian Ellison) *slt ld to over 1f out: drvn and outpcd ins fnl f* **6/1**[2]
6246 5 2 **Star Of St James (GER)**[47] 5390 2-9-1 **71** SeanDavis(3) 5 58
(Richard Fahey) *wnt rt s: hld up bhd ldng gp: pushed along over 2f out: no imp fr over 1f out* **12/1**
0241 6 4 ½ **Nat Love (IRE)**[16] 6532 2-9-7 **74** GrahamLee 9 48
(Mick Channon) *cl up on outside: pushed along over 2f out: ev ch whn hung rt fr over 1f out: wknd fnl f (jockey said gelding hung both ways)* **6/1**[2]
0040 7 1 ½ **Newsical**[38] 5703 2-8-10 **63** AndrewMullen 3 32
(Mark Walford) *trckd ldrs: rdn over 2f out: wknd over 1f out* **40/1**
6021 8 1 ¼ **Ralphy Boy Two (IRE)**[13] 6625 2-9-5 **72** KevinStott 12 37
(Alistair Whillans) *hld up: effrt on outside over 2f out: no imp fr over 1f out (jockey said gelding ran flat)* **13/2**[3]
3126 9 1 ½ **Rose Bandit (IRE)**[39] 5668 2-9-5 **72** ShaneGray 6 33
(Stef Keniry) *w ldr to over 2f out: drvn along whn hmpd over 1f out: sn wknd* **28/1**
4366 10 3 ¼ **Woven Quality (IRE)**[23] 6272 2-8-11 **71** EllaMcCain(7) 10 22
(Donald McCain) *hld up in midfield on outside: effrt over 2f out: wknd over 1f out* **22/1**
1400 11 3 ½ **Gold Venture (IRE)**[23] 6272 2-8-9 **62** BenCurtis 7 3
(Philip Kirby) *in tch tl rdn and wknd over 1f out* **50/1**
604 12 ½ **Wade's Magic**[18] 6457 2-9-1 **68** JamesSullivan 8 7
(Tim Easterby) *sn pushed along in rr: effrt whn n.m.r over 2f out and over 1f out: sn wknd (jockey said gelding was denied a clear run inside the final 2 furlongs and again approaching the final furlong)* **18/1**
1m 15.68s (1.08) **Going Correction** +0.25s/f (Good) **12** Ran SP% **117.1**
Speed ratings (Par 95): **102,101,99,96,94 88,86,84,82,78 73,72**
CSF £27.94 CT £133.80 TOTE £6.90: £2.30, £2.30, £2.00; EX 36.20 Trifecta £208.20.
Owner Geoff Maidment & John Raybould **Bred** Knocktartan House Stud **Trained** Langton, N Yorks

FOCUS
A fair nursery. The market had this race spot on and one of the co-favourites won narrowly in a time nearly a second slower than the previous C&D juvenile fillies' novice contest.

7065 ANDERSONS "DENTON HOLME" H'CAP (DIV I) 5f 193y
2:50 (2:52) (Class 5) (0-70,69) 3-Y-O+

£4,204 (£1,251; £625; £312; £300; £300) **Stalls Low**

Form RPR
0562 1 **Autumn Flight (IRE)**[21] 6338 3-9-0 **62** (b) PJMcDonald 9 72
(Tim Easterby) *mde all: clr over 2f out: edgd rt ins fnl f: r.o wl: unchal* **4/1**[2]
6030 2 1 ½ **Avenue Of Stars**[35] 5821 6-9-3 **63** (v) ConnorBeasley 12 68+
(Karen McLintock) *s.s: bhd: rdn along 1/2-way: hdwy on wd outside over 1f out: chsd wnr ins fnl f: r.o: nt pce to chal (jockey said gelding anticipated the start and hit its head on the stalls, resulting in the gelding missing the break)* **8/1**
4006 3 1 ¼ **Kenny The Captain (IRE)**[12] 6680 8-8-11 **57** RachelRichardson 3 58
(Tim Easterby) *trckd ldrs: effrt and wnt 2nd over 1f out to ins fnl f: one pce* **13/2**
0601 4 3 ¼ **Naples Bay**[13] 6621 5-8-6 **55** SeanDavis(3) 6 46
(Katie Scott) *hld up on outside: rdn over 2f out: kpt on fnl f: nt pce to chal* **11/1**
2353 5 1 ¾ **Amazing Grazing (IRE)**[14] 6591 5-9-6 **66** (p) RobbieDowney 11 51
(Rebecca Bastiman) *midfield: rdn over 2f out: sn outpcd: rallied fnl f: nvr rchd ldrs* **7/2**[1]
5025 6 1 **Patrick (IRE)**[26] 6174 7-8-10 **56** BarryMcHugh 4 38
(Paul Midgley) *in tch: effrt and drvn along 2f out: wknd ins fnl f* **6/1**[3]
0510 7 1 ½ **Hawk In The Sky**[36] 5791 3-9-6 **68** PhilDennis 10 45
(Richard Whitaker) *midfield on outside: rdn along over 2f out: edgd rt and wknd over 1f out* **33/1**
6560 8 ½ **Rickyroadboy**[12] 6680 4-8-12 **58** AndrewMullen 7 34
(Mark Walford) *chsd ldrs: wnt 2nd over 2f out to over 1f out: wknd ins fnl f* **18/1**
0024 9 ¾ **Cotubanama**[13] 6638 3-9-1 **68** ScottMcCullagh(5) 2 41
(Mick Channon) *dwlt: bhd and outpcd: nvr rchd ldrs* **22/1**
1400 10 1 ½ **Luzum (IRE)**[35] 5821 4-9-2 **67** (b[1]) GerO'Neill(5) 8 35
(Michael Easterby) *prom: wnt 2nd over 2f out to over 1f out: wknd fnl f* **15/2**
0034 11 11 **Jacksonfire**[27] 6107 7-8-4 **53** oh7 (p) JaneElliott(3) 1
(Michael Mullineaux) *sn pushed along towards rr on ins: struggling 1/2-way: nvr on terms* **66/1**
23-5 12 10 **Quickly Does It**[16] 6551 3-9-7 **69** BenRobinson 5
(Brian Ellison) *bhd: drvn and struggling 1/2-way: nvr on terms (jockey said filly lost its action 2f out)* **28/1**
1m 15.38s (0.78) **Going Correction** +0.25s/f (Good)
WFA 3 from 4yo+ 2lb **12** Ran SP% **118.5**
Speed ratings (Par 103): **104,102,100,96,93 92,90,89,88,86 72,58**
CSF £34.75 CT £209.21 TOTE £4.70: £1.80, £3.00, £2.30; EX 39.30 Trifecta £189.20.
Owner Ambrose Turnbull & Partner **Bred** Troy Cullen **Trained** Great Habton, N Yorks

FOCUS
The first division of an ordinary sprint handicap. The winner rates close to his 2yo form.

7066 ANDERSONS "DENTON HOLME" H'CAP (DIV II) 5f 193y
3:25 (3:25) (Class 5) (0-70,69) 3-Y-O+

£4,204 (£1,251; £625; £312; £300; £300) **Stalls Low**

Form RPR
6300 1 **I Know How (IRE)**[29] 6058 4-8-12 **58** (b[1]) KevinStott 2 69
(Julie Camacho) *cl up: led 1/2-way: rdn and hung rt over 1f out: kpt on wl fnl f* **15/2**
3640 2 1 ¾ **Suitcase 'N' Taxi**[27] 6099 5-8-10 **56** DuranFentiman 7 61
(Tim Easterby) *led to 1/2-way: chsd wnr: rdn 2f out: kpt on fnl f* **12/1**
55 3 nk **Round The Island**[54] 5157 6-8-8 **54** BenCurtis 9 58
(Richard Whitaker) *hld up: rdn and hdwy 2f out: kpt on ins fnl f* **4/1**[1]
0110 4 ¾ **Hic Bibi**[111] 3014 4-9-1 **66** ThomasGreatrex(5) 1 68
(David Loughnane) *prom: effrt and rdn over 1f out: kpt on same pce ins fnl f* **11/1**
1232 5 ¾ **Ninjago**[13] 6621 9-9-7 **67** (v) PaulMulrennan 10 66
(Paul Midgley) *in tch: smooth hdwy over 2f out: cl up and rdn over 1f out: no ex ins fnl f* **11/2**[3]

0400 **6** 3/4 **Shepherd's Purse**[11] 6699 7-9-2 **62** .... JamesSullivan 6 59
(Ruth Carr) *dwlt: hld up: rdn over 2f out: kpt on fnl f: nvr able to chal* **9/1**

6442 **7** 1 1/4 **Penny Pot Lane**[24] 6260 6-9-6 **66** .... (p) LewisEdmunds 11 59
(Richard Whitaker) *hld up on outside: rdn over 2f out: no imp over 1f out* **9/2**[2]

4060 **8** 6 **Newstead Abbey**[25] 6204 9-8-11 **57** .... (p) TomEaves 8 31
(Rebecca Bastiman) *t.k.h early: hld up: rdn over 2f out: n.d* **50/1**

0-03 **9** 5 **Flint Said No**[34] 5847 3-9-7 **69** .... GrahamLee 5 27
(Bryan Smart) *t.k.h: hld up: effrt over 2f out: wknd over 1f out (jockey said gelding anticipated the start and hit its head on the stalls, resulting in the gelding missing the break)* **8/1**

0011 **10** 3/4 **Night Law**[23] 6273 5-8-10 **56** .... (b) PhilDennis 3 11
(Katie Scott) *cl up tl rdn and wknd wl over 1f out (trainer could offer no explanation for the mare's performance)* **7/1**

1m 16.09s (1.49) **Going Correction** +0.25s/f (Good)
WFA 3 from 4yo+ 2lb **10 Ran SP% 116.9**
Speed ratings (Par 103): **100,97,97,96,95 94,92,84,77,76**
CSF £93.65 CT £422.04 TOTE £8.50: £3.20, £3.00, £1.90; EX 101.10 Trifecta £736.80.
Owner Judy & Richard Peck & Partner **Bred** Miss Sarah Thompson **Trained** Norton, N Yorks

FOCUS
The second division of an ordinary sprint handicap. This has been rated around the runner-up to this's year form.

7067 BRITISH STALLION STUDS EBF MAIDEN STKS (PLUS 10 RACE) 7f 173y
3:55 (3:56) (Class 4) 2-Y-O £6,727 (£2,002; £1,000; £500) Stalls Low

Form RPR

42 **1** **Strawman (IRE)**[12] 6673 2-9-5 0 .... ConnorBeasley 13 80
(Adrian Nicholls) *mde all: rdn and drifted lft fr 2f out: styd on wl fnl f* **5/2**[2]

2 1 1/2 **Bentley Wood** 2-9-5 0 .... TomEaves 10 77
(Mick Channon) *chsd wnr: effrt and ev ch over 1f out: kpt on same pce last 100yds* **22/1**

3 6 **Stag Horn** 2-9-5 0 .... PaulMulrennan 4 64
(Archie Watson) *prom: effrt and pushed along over 2f out: kpt on fr over 1f out: nvr rchd ldrs* **6/4**[1]

4 shd **Notation (IRE)** 2-9-0 0 .... FrannyNorton 7 58+
(Mark Johnston) *slowly away: bhd: hdwy over 2f out: kpt on fnl f: nrst fin* **8/1**[3]

5 1 3/4 **Black Star Dancing (USA)** 2-9-5 0 .... JoeFanning 12 59
(Keith Dalgleish) *t.k.h early in midfield: outpcd 3f out: rallied over 1f out: no imp* **8/1**[3]

6 1/2 **Three Dragons** 2-9-5 0 .... AndrewMullen 6 58
(Ben Haslam) *hld up: pushed along over 2f out: hdwy over 1f out: nvr rchd ldrs* **80/1**

0 **7** 1 **Lady Latte (IRE)**[31] 5988 2-8-7 0 .... RhonaPindar(7) 8 51
(K R Burke) *chsd ldrs: rdn over 2f out: wknd over 1f out* **20/1**

8 7 **La Trinidad** 2-9-5 0 .... BenCurtis 11 41
(Roger Fell) *s.i.s: bhd: pushed along 3f out: nvr on terms* **33/1**

9 1 1/2 **Copperlight (IRE)** 2-9-5 0 .... GrahamLee 14 37
(Ben Haslam) *hld up: rdn over 2f out: sn btn* **40/1**

06 **10** 3/4 **Roman's Empress (IRE)**[85] 3954 2-8-9 0 .... ThomasGreatrex(5) 9 31
(David Loughnane) *cl up tl rdn and wknd fr 2f out* **25/1**

60 **11** 5 **Noble Bertie (USA)**[28] 6065 2-9-5 0 .... DuranFentiman 3 25
(Tim Easterby) *hld up: drvn and struggling over 2f out: sn btn* **66/1**

12 1 1/2 **Brasingamanbellamy** 2-9-5 0 .... JackGarritty 1 21
(Jedd O'Keeffe) *s.i.s: bhd: rdn over 3f out: nvr on terms* **20/1**

13 3 1/4 **Titanium Grey** 2-9-5 0 .... PJMcDonald 15 14
(Jedd O'Keeffe) *s.i.s: a bhd* **18/1**

3 **14** 3 **Holmgarth (FR)**[29] 6035 2-9-5 0 .... AndrewElliott 2 8
(Philip Kirby) *midfield: rdn over 4f out: wknd over 2f out* **100/1**

1m 43.22s (3.22) **Going Correction** +0.25s/f (Good) **14 Ran SP% 122.9**
Speed ratings (Par 97): **93,91,85,85,83 83,82,75,73,72 67,66,63,60**
CSF £64.70 TOTE £3.50: £1.60, £3.20, £1.60; EX 55.60 Trifecta £175.30.
Owner The Strawman Partnership **Bred** Thomas Downey **Trained** Sessay, N Yorks

FOCUS
An ordinary juvenile maiden won on debut in 2016 by the subsequent Group 3 Sagaro Stakes runner-up Time To Study.

7068 SANDRA AND TED ROBERTS MEMORIAL H'CAP 7f 173y
4:30 (4:30) (Class 3) (0-90,90) 3-Y-O+ £9,703 (£2,887; £1,443; £721) Stalls Low

Form RPR

0112 **1** **Alotabottle**[26] 6176 3-8-4 **78** .... SeanDavis(3) 6 89+
(Kevin Ryan) *in tch: rdn and hdwy over 2f out: led over 1f out: drew clr ins fnl f* **4/1**[2]

2121 **2** 2 3/4 **Harvey Dent**[55] 5095 3-9-4 **89** .... PaulMulrennan 7 94+
(Archie Watson) *led: rdn and hdd over 1f out: no ex ins fnl f* **7/2**[1]

1103 **3** 2 1/4 **Global Gift (FR)**[24] 6258 3-9-5 **90** .... (h) TomEaves 4 90
(Ed Dunlop) *hld up: rdn over 2f out: hdwy to chse clr ldng pair ins fnl f: no imp* **12/1**

0024 **4** 1/2 **Fuente**[14] 6588 3-8-9 **80** .... JoeFanning 2 79
(Keith Dalgleish) *t.k.h: in tch: rdn along over 2f out: one pce fnl f* **9/1**

1530 **5** 1 1/4 **Rousayan (IRE)**[16] 6543 8-9-10 **90** .... (h) BenCurtis 9 87
(Roger Fell) *s.i.s: hld up: pushed along over 2f out: no imp fr over 1f out* **16/1**

2314 **6** hd **Mikmak**[16] 6543 6-9-6 **86** .... (p) JackGarritty 8 82
(Tim Easterby) *hld up: rdn and effrt over 2f out: outpcd fr over 1f out* **5/1**[3]

5211 **7** 3 1/2 **Redarna**[37] 5726 5-9-8 **88** .... (p) JamesSullivan 1 76
(Dianne Sayer) *pressed ldr: drvn along and c stands' side over 2f out: wknd over 1f out* **4/1**[2]

3424 **8** 9 **Nubough (IRE)**[18] 6451 3-8-12 **83** .... JamieGormley 3 50
(Iain Jardine) *chsd ldrs: drvn along over 2f out: sn lost pl and struggling* **8/1**

1m 40.88s (0.88) **Going Correction** +0.25s/f (Good) **8 Ran SP% 113.6**
WFA 3 from 5yo+ 5lb
Speed ratings (Par 107): **105,102,100,99,98 98,94,85**
CSF £18.15 CT £151.33 TOTE £5.10: £2.00, £1.80, £3.50; EX 19.70 Trifecta £124.40.
Owner Gordon Bulloch & Steve Ryan **Bred** Saxtead Livestock Ltd **Trained** Hambleton, N Yorks

FOCUS
The feature contest was a decent handicap. One of the prominent runners searched for some fresh ground towards the near rail for the first time on the card. The winner improved again, with the third/fourth rated close to form.

7069 RACING TV H'CAP (JOCKEY CLUB GRASSROOTS MIDDLE DISTANCE SERIES QUALIFIER) 7f 173y
5:05 (5:06) (Class 5) (0-75,75) 3-Y-O+ £4,204 (£1,251; £625; £312; £300; £300) Stalls Low

Form RPR

0205 **1** **The Navigator**[13] 6626 4-9-8 **73** .... JamesSullivan 8 82
(Dianne Sayer) *hld up: stdy hdwy and prom over 1f out: shkn up to ld ins fnl f: comf* **14/1**

4533 **2** 1 **Equidae**[32] 5933 4-9-0 **65** .... (t) TomEaves 9 72
(Iain Jardine) *led: rdn along 2f out: hdd ins fnl f: kpt on same pce towards fin* **10/1**

425 **3** 1 1/4 **Puerto Banus**[74] 4358 3-9-1 **71** .... PJMcDonald 6 74
(Ian Williams) *hld up: effrt over 2f out: chsd ldrs ins fnl f: kpt on fin* **4/1**[1]

3042 **4** nk **Zoravan (USA)**[13] 6626 6-9-1 **66** .... (b) JoeFanning 5 69
(Keith Dalgleish) *hld up: hdwy on outside 2f out: rdn and one pce ins fnl f* **6/1**[3]

5413 **5** 1 1/2 **Royal Shaheen (FR)**[13] 6626 6-9-6 **71** .... (v) GrahamLee 7 71
(Alistair Whillans) *hld up in midfield: effrt over 2f out: no imp over 1f out* **13/2**

2262 **6** nse **First Response**[17] 6500 4-9-10 **75** .... TonyHamilton 13 75
(Linda Stubbs) *cl up: rdn over 2f out: outpcd appr fnl f* **11/2**[2]

3005 **7** 1/2 **Ballymount**[13] 6627 4-8-11 **62** .... (b[1]) PaulMulrennan 3 61
(Michael Easterby) *hld up in tch: outpcd over 2f out: rallied over 1f out: sn no imp* **12/1**

4230 **8** 3 1/2 **Moxy Mares**[26] 6164 4-9-5 **75** .... (p) ThomasGreatrex(5) 10 66
(Mark Loughnane) *prom: rdn over 2f out: wknd over 1f out* **10/1**

5064 **9** nk **Evolutionary (IRE)**[14] 6609 3-8-8 **64** .... (h[1]) JamieGormley 2 53
(Iain Jardine) *in tch: rdn and carried hd high over 1f out: sn wknd* **20/1**

54-0 **10** 1 1/4 **Mrs Hoo (IRE)**[164] 1462 3-8-13 **72** .... SeanDavis(3) 1 58
(Richard Fahey) *trckd ldrs tl rdn and wknd fr 3f out* **33/1**

3464 **11** hd **Ghayyar (IRE)**[15] 6573 5-9-3 **68** .... (tp) RachelRichardson 4 55
(Tim Easterby) *hld up: effrt and rdn over 2f out: hung rt and wknd over 1f out* **8/1**

1005 **12** 3 **Zodiakos (IRE)**[17] 6496 6-9-5 **70** .... (p) BenCurtis 11 50
(Roger Fell) *slowly away: hld up on outside: struggling over 2f out: sn btn (jockey said gelding was slowly away)* **28/1**

520/ **13** 1 1/4 **Dance Of Fire**[43] 8315 7-9-4 **69** .... (b[1]) LucyAlexander 12 46
(N W Alexander) *hld up in tch: lost pl over 2f out: sn struggling* **80/1**

1m 42.52s (2.52) **Going Correction** +0.25s/f (Good)
WFA 3 from 4yo+ 5lb **13 Ran SP% 119.0**
Speed ratings (Par 103): **97,96,94,94,92 92,92,88,88,87 87,84,82**
CSF £141.58 CT £673.81 TOTE £16.00: £4.50, £2.80, £1.80; EX 158.20 Trifecta £1270.30.
Owner G H Bell **Bred** Sir Robert Ogden **Trained** Hackthorpe, Cumbria

FOCUS
A fair handicap. The conclusion of the race developed towards the near rail. This has been rated around the first two.

7070 JOIN RACING TV NOW H'CAP 1m 6f 32y
5:35 (5:35) (Class 6) (0-65,64) 3-Y-O+ £3,234 (£962; £481; £300; £300; £300) Stalls Low

Form RPR

1225 **1** **Well Funded (IRE)**[18] 6459 3-9-3 **63** .... JaneElliott(3) 6 73+
(James Bethell) *hld up in midfield: smooth hdwy to ld 3f out: rdn clr fr 2f out: easily* **10/3**[1]

002 **2** 5 **Put The Law On You (IRE)**[14] 6611 4-9-0 **48** .... (p) AndrewMullen 1 50
(Alistair Whillans) *hld up in tch: pushed along over 4f out: hdwy 2f out: chsd (clr) wnr ins fnl f: r.o* **6/1**

0056 **3** nk **Bill Cody (IRE)**[12] 6674 4-9-12 **60** .... KevinStott 4 61
(Julie Camacho) *prom: effrt and chsd wnr over 2f out to ins fnl f: one pce* **16/1**

0456 **4** 2 1/4 **Elite Icon**[14] 6611 5-8-10 **47** .... (v) HarrisonShaw(3) 9 45
(Jim Goldie) *hld up: pushed along over 4f out: hdwy 2f out: kpt on fnl f: nvr able to chal* **14/1**

2321 **5** 3 **Kitty's Cove**[14] 6611 4-9-5 **53** .... (tp) DuranFentiman 12 47
(Tim Easterby) *slowly away: hld up: hdwy 3f out: rdn and no further imp over 1f out* **11/2**[3]

4504 **6** 1 1/2 **Motahassen (IRE)**[29] 6055 5-9-0 **55** .... (t) ZakWheatley(7) 10 47
(Declan Carroll) *hld up: rdn and hdwy 3f out: no imp fr 2f out* **20/1**

6336 **7** hd **Pammi**[5] 6933 4-8-13 **47** .... (b) PaddyMathers 7 39
(Jim Goldie) *t.k.h: led to 1/2-way: cl up tl rdn and wknd wl over 1f out* **12/1**

55-6 **8** 9 **Something Brewing (FR)**[9] 100 5-9-9 **57** .... (p) PaulMulrennan 2 37
(Iain Jardine) *hld up: rdn along over 3f out: struggling fnl 2f* **22/1**

013 **9** 3 1/4 **Flower Power**[1] 7048 8-9-10 **61** 4ex .... (p) SeanDavis(3) 11 37+
(Tony Coyle) *hld up on outside: stdy hdwy over 4f out: sn rdn: wknd over 2f out* **4/1**[2]

050 **10** 1 1/4 **Ezzrah**[39] 5656 3-9-2 **59** .... (p[1]) GrahamLee 8 36
(Mark Walford) *cl up tl lost pl 3f out: sn struggling* **25/1**

0/02 **11** 10 **Frightened Rabbit (USA)**[21] 6343 7-9-0 **48** .... JamesSullivan 3 10
(Dianne Sayer) *pressed ldr: led 1/2-way to 3f out: sn rdn and wknd (jockey said gelding ran flat)* **8/1**

3m 13.53s (1.93) **Going Correction** +0.25s/f (Good)
WFA 3 from 4yo+ 9lb **11 Ran SP% 117.1**
Speed ratings (Par 101): **104,101,100,99,97 97,97,91,90,89 83**
CSF £22.49 CT £281.57 TOTE £4.30: £1.80, £2.30, £4.30; EX 25.00 Trifecta £273.80.
Owner Clarendon Thoroughbred Racing **Bred** Irish National Stud **Trained** Middleham Moor, N Yorks

FOCUS
A modest staying handicap. This rates a pb from the winner, with the second and fourth helping to pin the level.

T/Jkpt: Not won. T/Plt: £84.20 to a £1 stake. Pool: £59,999.60. 519.75 winning units. T/Qpdt: £20.10 to a £1 stake. Pool: £5,743.28. 210.86 winning units. **Richard Young**

6204 DONCASTER (L-H)

Wednesday, September 11

OFFICIAL GOING: Good to firm (7.9)

Wind: Fresh, against Weather: Fine & dry

7071 BRITISH STALLION STUDS EBF CONDITIONS STKS (PLUS 10 RACE) 6f 2y

1:50 (1:52) (Class 2) 2-Y-O **£11,205** (£3,355; £1,677) **Stalls** High

Form RPR

1 **1** **Lazuli (IRE)**[40] 5624 2-8-13 0................ WilliamBuick 3 97+
(Charlie Appleby) *t.k.h early: trckd ldr: hdwy and cl up 2f out: qcknd to ld jst over 1f out: edgd rt ins fnl f: idled and pushed along tenderly: jst hld on* **4/11**[1]

0260 **2** *nse* **Misty Grey (IRE)**[19] 6422 2-8-13 99................ RyanMoore 2 97
(Mark Johnston) *led: jnd 2f out and sn pushed along: rdn and hdd jst over 1f out: 1 l down and drvn ins fnl f: rallied wl and ev ch towards fin: jst hld* **7/2**[2]

1 **3** *2 ¼* **Brad The Brief**[21] 6330 2-8-11 0................ RichardKingscote 4 88
(Tom Dascombe) *t.k.h early: trckd ldng pair: pushed along over 2f out: rdn wl over 1f out: kpt on same pce (jockey said colt ran greenly)* **8/1**[3]

1m 13.54s (0.84) **Going Correction** +0.125s/f (Good) **3** Ran SP% **106.6**

Speed ratings (Par 101): **99,98,95**

CSF £1.91 TOTE £1.30; EX 1.60 Trifecta £2.00.

Owner Godolphin **Bred** Godolphin **Trained** Newmarket, Suffolk

FOCUS

The round course was railed out from the 1m2f point until the round track joined the straight. Hard to know what to make of this form due to the tactical nature of the race, plus two were having just their second starts following a win, but it's potentially smart form.

7072 PEPSI MAX NURSERY H'CAP 7f 6y

2:25 (2:26) (Class 2) 2-Y-O **£11,644** (£3,465; £1,731; £865) **Stalls** High

Form RPR

3512 **1** **Bravo Faisal (IRE)**[5] 6942 2-8-7 **78**................ PaulHanagan 5 84
(Richard Fahey) *hld up in rr: swtchd lft to outer and gd hdwy over 2f out: rdn to chal over 1f out: drvn to ld ins fnl f: edgd rt and kpt on wl towards fin* **10/1**

1311 **2** *½* **Hariboux**[18] 6450 2-9-7 **92**................(h) JackMitchell 3 97
(Hugo Palmer) *trckd ldrs: hdwy over 2f out: rdn to chal over 1f out: ev ch ent fnl f: sn drvn: edgd rt and kpt on towards fin* **10/3**[1]

1010 **3** *1 ¼* **Iffraaz (IRE)**[19] 6422 2-9-5 **90**................ FrankieDettori 1 92
(Mark Johnston) *trckd ldng pair: pushed along to chal 2f out: rdn to take slt ld over 1f out: drvn and hdd ins fnl f: kpt on same pce* **9/2**

3101 **4** *1 ¾* **Owney Madden**[21] 6356 2-9-4 **89**................ RobHornby 2 86
(Martyn Meade) *led: pushed along 2f out: sn rdn and hdd narrowly over 1f out: drvn and kpt on same pce fnl f* **4/1**[3]

021 **5** *1 ¼* **Modern British Art (IRE)**[35] 5794 2-8-11 **82**................ JasonWatson 7 76
(Michael Bell) *chsd ldrs: rdn along 2f out: drvn over 1f out: grad wknd (jockey said colt ran too freely and hung left-handed under pressure)* **10/1**

210 **6** *¾* **Ethic**[21] 6352 2-9-1 **86**................ JamesDoyle 4 78
(William Haggas) *t.k.h: in tch: pushed along over 2f out: sn rdn and sltly outpcd: plugged on fnl f* **7/2**[2]

1050 **7** *½* **Hurstwood**[21] 6356 2-9-1 **86**................ DavidAllan 10 77
(Tim Easterby) *chsd ldr: hdwy and cl up over 2f out: rdn wl over 1f out: wknd appr fnl f* **16/1**

3324 **8** *6* **Pentewan**[13] 6625 2-8-4 **75**................(b) JimmyQuinn 6 51
(Phillip Makin) *t.k.h: a towards rr* **20/1**

2414 **9** *5* **Reclaim Victory (IRE)**[12] 6675 2-8-1 **72**................ CamHardie 9 36
(Brian Ellison) *dwlt: a in rr* **20/1**

1m 27.01s (0.61) **Going Correction** +0.125s/f (Good) **9** Ran SP% **117.1**

Speed ratings (Par 101): **101,100,99,97,95 94,94,87,81**

CSF £44.02 CT £172.78 TOTE £8.30: £2.40, £1.50, £1.90; EX 39.90 Trifecta £123.90.

Owner Sheikh Abdullah Almalek Alsabah **Bred** Lynn Lodge Stud **Trained** Musley Bank, N Yorks

FOCUS

This fair nursery looked wide open and it rates slightly improved form from the winner. They kept stands' side.

7073 DC TRAINING AND DEVELOPMENT SERVICES SCARBROUGH STKS (LISTED RACE) 5f 3y

3:00 (3:01) (Class 1) 2-Y-O+

£22,684 (£8,600; £4,304; £2,144; £1,076; £540) **Stalls** High

Form RPR

4206 **1** **Equilateral**[52] 5222 4-9-11 108................ RyanMoore 5 102+
(Charles Hills) *trckd ldrs: hdwy wl over 1f out: rdn to chal ent fnl f: drvn and kpt on wl to ld cl home* **9/4**[2]

0112 **2** *hd* **Queens Gift (IRE)**[11] 6698 4-9-6 99................(p) CallumRodriguez 1 96
(Michael Dods) *trckd ldrs: hdwy on outer wl over 1f out: rdn to chal 1f out: drvn to ld ins fnl f: hdd and no ex cl home* **8/1**

4002 **3** *1 ¼* **Duke Of Firenze**[16] 6534 10-9-11 91................ DavidAllan 2 96
(David C Griffiths) *hld up in rr: swtchd lft to outer and hdwy wl over 1f out: sn rdn: str run ent fnl f: sn drvn and kpt on* **40/1**

4215 **4** *1 ¼* **Tis Marvellous**[11] 6698 5-9-11 111................(t) AdamKirby 3 92
(Clive Cox) *trckd ldr: effrt wl over 1f out and sn pushed along: sn rdn to chal: drvn to take slt ld ent fnl f: sn hdd and kpt on same pce* **2/1**[1]

1250 **5** *nk* **El Astronaute (IRE)**[19] 6423 6-10-0 108................ JasonHart 6 93
(John Quinn) *led: pushed along and jnd wl over 1f out: drvn and hdd narrowly ent fnl f: kpt on same pce* **3/1**[3]

2003 **6** *2 ½* **Dark Shot**[16] 6549 6-9-11 85................(p) KieranO'Neill 4 81
(Scott Dixon) *stdd s and keen early: hld up in rr: pushed along over 2f out: sn rdn and n.d* **50/1**

1110 **7** *1 ¾* **Archer's Dream (IRE)**[61] 4891 3-9-8 98................ GeorgeWood 7 73
(James Fanshawe) *trckd ldrs: pushed along 2f out: sn rdn and outpcd wl over 1f out* **8/1**

59.23s (-0.37) **Going Correction** +0.125s/f (Good)

WFA 3 from 4yo+ 1lb **7** Ran SP% **115.7**

Speed ratings: **107,106,104,102,102 98,95**

CSF £20.97 TOTE £2.80: £1.60, £4.00; EX 17.60 Trifecta £309.40.

Owner K Abdullah **Bred** Juddmonte Farms Ltd **Trained** Lambourn, Berks

FOCUS

The third dictates the level, running to best since June last year. This could be up to 8lb better at face value but it's hard to see the third running to that level.

7074 MONDIALISTE LEGER LEGENDS CLASSIFIED STKS 1m (S)

3:35 (3:43) (Class 5) 3-Y-O+

£6,727 (£2,002; £1,000; £500; £300; £300) **Stalls** Centre

Form RPR

2622 **1** **Dubai Acclaim (IRE)**[20] 6370 4-11-5 69................(p[1]) SammyJoBell 7 77
(Richard Fahey) *hld up in rr: stdy hdwy 3f out: swtchd rt and effrt 2f out: rdn to ld jst over 1f out: drvn ins fnl f: hld on wl* **5/1**[2]

3600 **2** *shd* **Hammer Gun (USA)**[8] 6841 6-11-5 69................(v) NoelFehily 6 78+
(Derek Shaw) *hld up towards rr: smooth hdwy wl over 2f out: trckd ldrs whn nt clr run jst over 1f out: sn swtchd rt and rdn: fin strly: jst failed (jockey said gelding was denied a clear run)* **4/1**[1]

3252 **3** *¾* **Flying Dragon (FR)**[6] 6904 3-11-0 69................(h) AdrianNicholls 8 74
(Richard Hannon) *trckd ldrs: hdwy and cl up 2f out: rdn and ev ch over 1f out: drvn and kpt on fnl f* **5/1**[2]

4362 **4** *2 ¼* **Kilbaha Lady (IRE)**[12] 6663 5-11-5 69................ KierenFallon 2 70
(Nigel Tinkler) *hld up in tch: hdwy wl over 2f out: rdn to chse ldrs over 1f out: drvn and kpt on same pce fnl f* **6/1**[3]

103 **5** *1 ¾* **Ascot Week (USA)**[42] 5560 5-11-5 70................(v) TimmyMurphy 1 66
(John Quinn) *hld up towards rr: hdwy wl over 2f out: rdn wl over 1f out: kpt on fnl f* **20/1**

5235 **6** *½* **Kannapolis (IRE)**[20] 6370 4-11-5 70................(b[1]) BarryKeniry 16 65
(Michael Easterby) *cl up: rdn along 2f out: drvn over 1f out: grad wknd* **9/1**

-000 **7** *¾* **Destroyer**[11] 6729 6-11-5 67................ ColinBolger 12 63
(Tom Tate) *led: rdn along over 2f out: drvn and hdd over 1f out: sn edgd rt and wknd* **33/1**

2412 **8** *2 ¼* **One To Go**[17] 6501 3-11-0 68................(p) BrianHarding 13 57
(Tim Easterby) *chsd ldrs: rdn along 2f out: sn drvn and grad wknd* **13/2**

0123 **9** *4* **Whatwouldyouknow (IRE)**[15] 6573 4-11-5 69................ DerekMcGaffin 3 49
(Richard Guest) *in tch: hdwy wl over 2f out: rdn along wl over 1f out: sn wknd* **16/1**

6621 **10** *¾* **Valley Of Fire**[18] 6461 7-11-5 69................(p) AndrewThornton 17 47
(Les Eyre) *hld up towards rr: effrt and sme hdwy over 2f out: n.d* **20/1**

4330 **11** *nk* **Poet's Pride**[18] 6461 4-11-5 68................ CharliePoste 11 46
(David Barron) *hld up: a towards rr* **20/1**

5054 **12** *¾* **Sands Chorus**[15] 6580 7-11-5 70................(p) VictoriaSmith 10 45
(Scott Dixon) *cl up: rdn along 3f out: sn wknd* **33/1**

3361 **13** *3* **Placebo Effect (IRE)**[13] 6627 4-11-5 67................(p) OlliePears 5 38
(Ollie Pears) *prom: cl up 3f out: rdn along over 2f out: wknd wl over 1f out* **25/1**

0440 **14** *6* **Dream Walker (FR)**[28] 6066 10-11-5 68................ JamieMackay 4 24
(Brian Ellison) *a in rr* **50/1**

3403 **15** *4 ½* **Windsor Cross (IRE)**[27] 6129 4-11-5 70................ LukeHarvey 14 14
(Richard Fahey) *midfield: pushed along over 3f out: sn outpcd and bhd* **14/1**

1660 **16** *2 ¼* **Allux Boy (IRE)**[5] 6937 5-11-5 61................(p) GaryBardwell 15 8
(Nigel Tinkler) *t.k.h: hld up towards rr: hdwy into midfield 3f out: rdn along over 2f out: sn wknd* **66/1**

1m 39.09s (-1.11) **Going Correction** +0.125s/f (Good)

WFA 3 from 4yo+ 5lb **16** Ran SP% **131.0**

Speed ratings (Par 103): **110,109,109,106,105 104,103,101,97,96 96,95,92,86,82 80**

CSF £24.61 TOTE £5.90: £2.20, £2.80, £2.60; EX 36.30 Trifecta £195.50.

Owner S & G Clayton **Bred** Rathbarry Stud & Abbeylands Farm **Trained** Musley Bank, N Yorks

FOCUS

Another competitive edition of this unique classified event. Straightforward form, rated around the first three.

7075 BRITISH EBF PREMIER FILLIES' H'CAP 1m 3f 197y

4:10 (4:10) (Class 2) (0-100,98) 3-Y-O+ **£18,675** (£5,592; £2,796; £1,398) **Stalls** Low

Form RPR

6134 **1** **Maybe Today**[121] 2680 4-9-4 **88**................(p) WilliamBuick 4 96
(Simon Crisford) *trckd ldr: hdwy 3f out: pushed along over 2f out: rdn to chal over 1f out: led ent fnl f: kpt on wl* **4/1**

113 **2** *1 ¾* **Litigious**[27] 6124 3-8-13 **91**................ FrankieDettori 1 96
(John Gosden) *led: pushed along and qcknd wl over 2f out: rdn and jnd over 1f out: hdd ent fnl f: sn drvn and kpt on same pce* **6/4**[1]

6220 **3** *1 ¾* **Makawee (IRE)**[21] 6355 4-9-8 **92**................ DanielTudhope 2 94
(David O'Meara) *hld up in rr: hdwy over 2f out: rdn along wl over 1f out: drvn and no imp fnl f* **11/4**[2]

3-24 **4** *hd* **Asoof**[209] 728 4-9-9 **98**................(h) CierenFallon(5) 3 100
(Saeed bin Suroor) *trckd ldng pair: hdwy over 2f out: rdn along wl over 1f out: sn drvn and btn over 1f out* **7/2**[3]

2m 32.1s (-4.50) **Going Correction** -0.20s/f (Firm)

WFA 3 from 4yo 8lb **4** Ran SP% **108.9**

Speed ratings (Par 96): **107,105,104,104**

CSF £10.43 TOTE £6.20; EX 13.60 Trifecta £25.40.

Owner Sheikh Juma Dalmook Al Maktoum **Bred** R Cantoni **Trained** Newmarket, Suffolk

FOCUS

Add 9yds, making the official distance 1m3f 206yds. Not much changed throughout the early stages and the first two home were in the first two throughout.

7076 WILLIAM HILL LEADING RACECOURSE BOOKMAKER CONDITIONS STKS 1m 2f 43y

4:45 (4:45) (Class 2) 3-Y-O+

£12,450 (£3,728; £1,864; £932; £466; £234) **Stalls** High

Form RPR

143- **1** **Fox Tal**[319] 8663 3-8-10 105................ OisinMurphy 2 114+
(Andrew Balding) *hld up in rr: hdwy on inner 2f out: swtchd rt and rdn ent fnl f: qcknd wl to ld last 100yds: sn clr* **16/1**

15-6 **2** *2* **Elwazir**[111] 3025 4-9-2 105................(h[1]) JimCrowley 4 109
(Owen Burrows) *led: pushed along and qcknd wl over 2f out: rdn wl over 1f out: drvn ins fnl f: hdd last 100yds: kpt on same pce* **9/1**

5104 **3** *¾* **Walkinthesand (IRE)**[4] 6956 3-9-0 108................ RyanMoore 1 112
(Richard Hannon) *trckd ldng pair on inner: pushed along wl over 2f out: rdn to chse ldr over 1f out: drvn and ev ch ent fnl f: kpt on same pce* **4/1**[3]

2405 **4** *1* **Big Country (IRE)**[18] 6466 6-9-2 106................(p) AlistairRawlinson 6 106
(Michael Appleby) *hld up in rr: hdwy on outer wl over 2f out: rdn to chse ldrs over 1f out: ev ch appr fnl f: sn drvn and kpt on same pce* **33/1**

-420 **5** *2 ¾* **Willie John**[85] 3953 4-9-2 106................ AndreaAtzeni 5 100
(Roger Varian) *trckd ldrs: hdwy 3f out: rdn along 2f out: drvn over 1f out: sn wknd* **5/2**[2]

02-5 **6** 7 **Loxley (IRE)**[186] 1115 4-9-2 112........................ WilliamBuick 3 86
(Charlie Appleby) *trckd ldr: pushed along over 2f out: sn rdn and wknd wl over 1f out (jockey said gelding stopped quickly)* **6/5**[1]

2m 8.42s (-3.88) **Going Correction** -0.20s/f (Firm) **6 Ran SP% 112.8**
WFA 3 from 4yo+ 6lb
Speed ratings (Par 109): **107,105,104,104,101 96**
CSF £139.94 TOTE £10.90: £3.70, £3.70; EX 81.10 Trifecta £289.60.
Owner King Power Racing Co Ltd **Bred** Rabbah Bloodstock Limited **Trained** Kingsclere, Hants

FOCUS
Although there were just six runners, this classy conditions race proved a true test. The winner rates an improver, rated around the front-running second. Add 9yds.

7077 PARKES BROS ROOFING CONTRACTORS H'CAP 5f 3y
5:20 (5:23) (Class 4) (0-85,87) 3-Y-O+
£6,727 (£2,002; £1,000; £500; £300; £300) **Stalls High**

Form RPR
4204 **1** **Dark Shadow (IRE)**[16] 6525 3-9-7 **84**........................(b[1]) AdamKirby 13 95
(Clive Cox) *towards rr: hdwy 2f out: chsd ldrs towards centre and swtchd rt ent fnl f: sn rdn: kpt on strly to ld last 100yds* **20/1**
0063 **2** 1 ¼ **Line Of Reason (IRE)**[9] 6809 9-9-6 **82**........................ OisinMurphy 15 89
(Paul Midgley) *trckd ldrs towards centre: hdwy 2f out: rdn to ld ent fnl f and sn edgd rt: sn drvn: hdd and no ex last 100yds* **8/1**[3]
2066 **3** 1 **Manshood (IRE)**[21] 6339 6-9-4 **80**........................(b) CallumRodriguez 9 83
(Paul Midgley) *bdly hmpd s and bhd centre: hdwy wl over 1f out: n.m.r and swtchd lft 1f out: sn rdn and kpt on wl towards fin (vet said gelding lost its right fore shoe)* **25/1**
3400 **4** nk **Roundhay Park**[12] 6676 4-9-0 **81**........................ CierenFallon(5) 10 83+
(Nigel Tinkler) *bdly hmpd s and bhd centre: hdwy 2f out: rdn over 1f out: styd on fnl f* **3/1**[1]
3330 **5** 1 **Mark's Choice (IRE)**[12] 6676 3-9-4 **81**........................ SamJames 19 79
(Ruth Carr) *racd towards stands' side: trckd ldrs: hdwy and cl up over 1f out: sn rdn and ev ch ent fnl f: sn drvn and kpt on same pce* **16/1**
2251 **6** hd **Afandem (IRE)**[29] 6057 5-8-12 **74**........................(p) DavidAllan 12 72
(Tim Easterby) *racd centre: chsd ldrs centre: rdn along over 1f out: kpt on fnl f* **20/1**
1200 **7** nk **Nibras Again**[18] 6455 5-9-0 **79**........................ ConnorMurtagh(3) 4 76
(Paul Midgley) *racd centre: cl up: ev ch wl over 1f out: sn rdn: wknd fnl f* **25/1**
0544 **8** ¾ **Bowson Fred**[11] 6699 7-8-10 **72**........................ NathanEvans 18 66
(Michael Easterby) *racd nr stands' rail: cl up: led 3f out: rdn over 1f out: drvn and hdd ent fnl f: grad wknd* **10/1**
6200 **9** nse **Abel Handy (IRE)**[11] 6714 4-9-11 **87**........................(t[1]) JamesDoyle 20 81
(Declan Carroll) *racd nr stands' rail: led: hdd 3f out: cl up: rdn wl over 1f out: grad wknd* **8/1**[3]
222 **10** ½ **War Whisper (IRE)**[18] 6455 6-9-7 **83**........................ PaulHanagan 17 75
(Paul Midgley) *racd nr stands' rail: chsd ldrs: rdn along wl over 1f out: grad wknd* **10/1**
1030 **11** hd **Secretinthepark**[4] 6954 9-9-1 **77**........................(b) RichardKingscote 7 68
(Michael Mullineaux) *hmpd s: sn in midfield: hdwy to chse ldrs centre 2f out: sn rdn and wknd over 1f out* **20/1**
2146 **12** 1 **Daschas**[11] 6724 5-8-13 **82**........................(t) MarcoGhiani(7) 6 70
(Stuart Williams) *prom centre: cl up 2f out: sn rdn and wknd over 1f out* **7/1**[2]
2201 **13** nse **Han Solo Berger (IRE)**[18] 6455 4-8-13 **75**........................(p) TomQueally 11 62
(Chris Wall) *wnt bdly lft s: a in rr* **9/1**
6320 **14** 1 **Samovar**[16] 6549 4-8-11 **73**........................(b) KieranO'Neill 16 57
(Scott Dixon) *chsd ldrs towards stands' side: rdn along 2f out: sn wknd* **40/1**
4050 **15** ½ **Pipers Note**[15] 6581 9-9-4 **80**........................(p[1]) DavidNolan 1 62
(Ruth Carr) *racd centre: a towards rr* **25/1**
006 **16** ½ **Pea Shooter**[21] 6335 10-8-7 **69** oh2........................(b) CamHardie 5 49
(Brian Ellison) *racd ldrs centre: rdn along wl over 1f out: sn wknd* **50/1**
2151 **17** ¾ **Archimedes (IRE)**[5] 6936 6-8-7 **69** 5ex........................(vt) DavidEgan 8 46
(David C Griffiths) *bdly hmpd s: a in rr* **25/1**
5404 **18** ¾ **Normal Equilibrium**[30] 6017 9-8-7 **69** oh12........................(p) JasonHart 14 44
(Ivan Furtado) *racd centre: cl up: ev ch 2f out: sn rdn and wknd qckly* **66/1**

59.33s (-0.27) **Going Correction** +0.125s/f (Good) **18 Ran SP% 129.3**
WFA 3 from 4yo+ 1lb
Speed ratings (Par 105): **107,105,103,102,101 101,100,99,99,98 98,96,96,94,94 93,92,90**
CSF £164.26 CT £4059.87 TOTE £26.50: £4.80, £2.50, £5.70, £1.60; EX 270.90 Trifecta £2553.00.
Owner J Goddard **Bred** Redpender Stud Ltd **Trained** Lambourn, Berks

FOCUS
The early part of the race suggested those on the stands' side might have the advantage, but the action unfolded down the middle inside the final furlong. This rates a clear pb from the winner.
T/Plt: £1,549.30 to a £1 stake. Pool: £97,569.53. 45.97 winning units. T/Qpdt: £460.00 to a £1 stake. Pool: £7,336.34. 11.80 winning units. **Joe Rowntree**

6962 KEMPTON (A.W) (R-H)
Wednesday, September 11

OFFICIAL GOING: Polytrack: standard to slow
Wind: Moderate, across (away from stands) Weather: Fine but cloudy

7078 100% PROFIT BOOST AT 32REDSPORT.COM CLASSIFIED CLAIMING STKS 6f (P)
5:30 (5:30) (Class 5) 3-Y-O+
£3,752 (£1,116; £557; £400; £400; £400) **Stalls Low**

Form RPR
3300 **1** **Dream Catching (IRE)**[15] 6567 4-9-0 74........................ WilliamCarver(5) 1 74+
(Andrew Balding) *trckd ldng pair: pushed into ld over 1f out: 2 l ahd fnl f: drvn after: jst hld on* **11/8**[1]
225 **2** shd **Swiss Pride (IRE)**[16] 6533 3-9-0 75........................ AngusVilliers(7) 4 78
(Richard Hughes) *cl up: pushed along 1/2-way: rdn and nt qckn 2f out: styd on to take 2nd jst ins fnl f: clsd on wnr last 100yds: jst hld* **11/4**[2]
6034 **3** ¾ **Kwela**[9] 6801 3-9-0 75........................ GeorgiaDobie(7) 3 75
(Eve Johnson Houghton) *sat off the pce in 5th: clsd over 2f out: rdn and tried to mount an effrt on inner over 1f out: tk 3rd ins fnl f: styd on but nvr able to chal (jockey said filly was slowly away)* **11/2**[3]
3010 **4** 1 ¼ **Creek Harbour (IRE)**[13] 6631 4-8-4 70........................ StefanoCherchi(7) 6 60
(Milton Bradley) *pressed ldr: rdn to chal over 1f out: chsd wnr to jst ins fnl f: wknd* **7/1**

4200 **5** 4 ½ **George Dryden (IRE)**[21] 6335 7-8-5 70........................(t[1]) LukeMorris 5 40
(George Boughey) *led to over 1f out: sn wknd* **10/1**
0216 **6** 7 **Majorette**[27] 6120 5-9-1 63........................ TrevorWhelan 2 29
(Brian Barr) *v awkward s: a last and mostly bhd: wknd over 2f out: t.o* **25/1**

1m 12.46s (-0.64) **Going Correction** +0.025s/f (Slow) **6 Ran SP% 109.6**
WFA 3 from 4yo+ 2lb
Speed ratings (Par 103): **105,104,103,102,96 86**
CSF £5.01 TOTE £1.90: £1.20, £1.80; EX 6.00 Trifecta £12.00.
Owner M Payton & A M Balding **Bred** Mount Coote Stud And Anthony Warrender **Trained** Kingsclere, Hants

FOCUS
The winner took this with a bit more in hand than the margin suggests.

7079 WISE BETTING AT RACINGTV.COM NURSERY H'CAP 7f (P)
6:00 (6:01) (Class 6) (0-65,66) 2-Y-O
£3,105 (£924; £461; £400; £400; £400) **Stalls Low**

Form RPR
005 **1** **Pitchcombe**[92] 3694 2-9-5 **63**........................(p[1]) HectorCrouch 12 72+
(Clive Cox) *mde virtually all: pushed along and drew clr wl over 1f out: comf* **6/1**[3]
0662 **2** 3 **Sparkling Diamond**[8] 6837 2-9-1 **59**........................ KieranShoemark 13 60
(Philip McBride) *in tch in midfield: rdn and prog 2f out: tk 2nd jst ins fnl f: kpt on but no ch w wnr* **16/1**
6003 **3** ¾ **Souter Johnnie (IRE)**[33] 5886 2-9-5 **63**........................ ShaneKelly 5 62
(Richard Hughes) *trckd ldrs: shkn up and nt qckn jst over 2f out: prog over 1f out: styd on to take 3rd wl ins fnl f* **7/2**[1]
400 **4** hd **Cece Ceylon**[36] 5772 2-9-4 **62**........................(b[1]) HarryBentley 6 61
(Ralph Beckett) *dwlt: wl in rr: pushed along wl over 2f out: sed to stay on over 1f out: fin wl and nrly snatched 3rd* **8/1**
040 **5** ½ **You Don't Own Me (IRE)**[31] 5988 2-8-10 **54**........................ CharlesBishop 3 51
(Joseph Tuite) *prom: rdn to chse wnr over 1f out: no imp and lost 2nd jst ins fnl f: fdd* **9/1**
2630 **6** nk **Constanzia**[11] 6728 2-9-8 **66**........................ NicolaCurrie 4 62
(Jamie Osborne) *t.k.h: hld up towards rr: nt clr run briefly over 2f out: pushed along and prog over 1f out: kpt on same pce ins fnl f* **5/1**[2]
023 **7** 2 ¾ **Hiconic**[23] 6281 2-9-5 **63**........................ LukeMorris 8 52
(Alex Hales) *s.i.s: sn in midfield: effrt on inner 2f out and sn drvn: no imp on ldrs fnl f* **20/1**
4066 **8** 2 ¼ **Leave Em Alone (IRE)**[40] 5630 2-8-13 **57**........................ JFEgan 1 40
(David Evans) *wl in rr: nt clr run briefly over 2f out: rdn and modest prog over 1f out: sn no hdwy (jockey said filly hung badly right-handed)* **33/1**
600 **9** 2 ½ **Jazz Style (IRE)**[49] 5294 2-8-12 **56**........................ RobertHavlin 7 33
(David Brown) *chsd wnr to over 1f out: wknd qckly (vet said gelding had been struck into on its left hind)* **25/1**
6053 **10** 1 ¼ **Champagne Highlife (GER)**[35] 5800 2-9-0 **65**........ GeorgiaDobie(7) 11 39
(Eve Johnson Houghton) *t.k.h: trapped out wd early: pressed ldrs to 2f out: wknd* **12/1**
0053 **11** 2 ¾ **Speed Merchant (IRE)**[19] 6394 2-8-12 **63**........................(b[1]) AngusVilliers(7) 9 30
(Brian Meehan) *chsd ldrs to over 2f out: wknd* **12/1**
006 **12** ½ **Party Potential (USA)**[36] 5775 2-9-1 **59**........................ TomMarquand 10 24
(Alan King) *sn pushed along and nvr gng the pce in rr (jockey said gelding was never travelling)* **14/1**
4003 **13** 2 ½ **Krishmaya (IRE)**[15] 6563 2-8-3 **47**........................ RaulDaSilva 14 6
(Adam West) *rel to r and lft 20 l: tk fierce hold and ct up at bk of field after 2f: wd in st and sn btn (jockey said filly was slowly away)* **40/1**
506 **14** 18 **Pink Tulip**[28] 6072 2-9-2 **60**........................ StevieDonohoe 2
(David Simcock) *dwlt: a in last pair: t.o* **20/1**

1m 27.44s (1.44) **Going Correction** +0.025s/f (Slow) **14 Ran SP% 121.0**
Speed ratings (Par 93): **92,88,87,87,86 86,83,80,78,76 73,72,70,49**
CSF £91.14 CT £402.23 TOTE £7.40: £3.10, £4.40, £1.50; EX 82.10 Trifecta £395.90.
Owner Alan G Craddock **Bred** Alan Craddock **Trained** Lambourn, Berks

FOCUS
This looked a fairly open nursery but the all-the-way winner was never really threatened, showing improved form.

7080 32RED CASINO H'CAP 7f (P)
6:30 (6:31) (Class 5) (0-70,70) 3-Y-O+
£3,752 (£1,116; £557; £400; £400; £400) **Stalls Low**

Form RPR
0430 **1** **Gavi Di Gavi (IRE)**[25] 6204 4-8-10 **56**........................ NicolaCurrie 11 65+
(Alan King) *s.s: hld up in last: stl there 3f out: gd prog on inner and clr run through fr 2f out: rdn and r.o to ld last 100yds: won gng away* **7/1**[3]
6204 **2** 1 ¼ **Little Palaver**[21] 6335 7-9-3 **70**........................(p) ImogenCarter(7) 12 75
(Clive Cox) *t.k.h: hld up but prog arnd rivals fr 4f out: led 2f out and stl gng strly: hdd and nt qckn last 100yds* **16/1**
0321 **3** ½ **Mochalov**[27] 6116 4-8-13 **62**........................ DarraghKeenan(3) 8 66
(Jane Chapple-Hyam) *hld up wl in tch: stl gng strly whn asked to make prog over 2f out: chsd ldrs over 1f out but rdn and nt qckn fnl f: styd on to take 3rd nr fin* **3/1**[1]
4064 **4** nk **Jack Berry House**[34] 5847 3-9-4 **68**........................(t) JamieSpencer 9 69
(George Boughey) *wl in tch: rdn 2f out: styd on over 1f out: nvr quite rchd ldrs but kpt on (vet said gelding lost its right hind shoe)* **9/1**
000 **5** hd **Walkman (IRE)**[76] 4297 3-9-6 **70**........................ ShaneKelly 2 70
(Tim Pinfield) *led to 2f out: styd pressing ldrs: one pce fnl f* **16/1**
4226 **6** ¾ **Roman Spinner**[22] 6326 4-9-5 **70**........................(t) SebastianWoods(5) 14 62
(Rae Guest) *trapped wd: mostly in midfield: lost grnd bnd 3f out: rdn and prog over 1f out: no hdwy fnl f* **4/1**[2]
602 **7** 3 ¼ **Turn To Rock (IRE)**[195] 943 3-9-3 **67**........................ LiamKeniry 5 59
(Ed Walker) *chsd ldrs: rdn 2f out: no imp 1f out: fdd ins fnl f* **12/1**
1-00 **8** 2 **Declamation (IRE)**[16] 6547 9-8-9 **60**........................ DylanHogan(5) 1 46
(John Butler) *s.i.s: wl in rr: rdn and no real prog over 2f out* **40/1**
-060 **9** nk **Albishr (IRE)**[29] 6050 4-9-5 **65**........................(p) TomMarquand 10 50
(Simon Dow) *chsd ldr to jst over 2f out: wknd* **20/1**
0000 **10** 1 ½ **Inaam (IRE)**[16] 6547 6-9-8 **68**........................(h) JoeyHaynes 6 49
(John Butler) *t.k.h: hld up wl in rr: no prog over 2f out or whn shkn up over 1f out (jockey said gelding ran too free in the early stages)* **33/1**
653 **11** ¾ **Tulloona**[48] 5352 3-9-4 **68**........................(p[1]) LukeMorris 4 45
(Tom Clover) *nvr beyond midfield: rdn and no prog over 2f out* **9/1**
0003 **12** 7 **Viola Park**[56] 5051 5-8-10 **56**........................(p) DavidProbert 13 16
(Ronald Harris) *prom 4f: wknd qckly over 2f out* **11/1**

The Form Book Flat 2019, Raceform Ltd, Newbury, RG14 5SJ

4-00 **13** *16* **Intricate**[23] 6286 3-8-13 **63**.............................(v[1]) HectorCrouch 7
(Clive Cox) *hld up wl in rr: hanging bdly whn shkn up over 2f out: sn eased (jockey said filly hung badly right-handed in the straight)* **25/1**
1m 26.13s (0.13) **Going Correction** +0.025s/f (Slow)
WFA 3 from 4yo+ 4lb 13 Ran SP% **119.3**
Speed ratings (Par 103): **100,98,98,97,97 92,93,90,90,88 87,79,61**
CSF £108.10 CT £411.30 TOTE £9.20: £2.90, £4.60, £1.20; EX 139.00 Trifecta £538.90.
Owner L Field, N Farrell, B Cognet & King **Bred** Killarkin Stud **Trained** Barbury Castle, Wilts
FOCUS
A modest heat but there was a gamble landed.

7081 32RED.COM BREEDERS BACKING RACING EBF FILLIES' NOVICE STKS 1m 3f 219y(P)
7:00 (7:01) (Class 4) 3-Y-0+ **£6,469** (£1,925; £962; £481) **Stalls** Low

Form RPR
22 **1** **Strelka**[18] 6438 3-8-11 0............................. HarryBentley 6 71+
(Ralph Beckett) *trckd ldng pair: pushed into ld 2f out: sn clr: easily* **1/4[1]**
6- **2** *4 1/2* **Persuer**[323] 8511 3-8-11 0............................. JamieSpencer 2 64+
(David Simcock) *stdd s: hld up in last pair: prog and swtchd lft over 2f out: pushed into 2nd over 1f out but wnr already clr: styd on but no imp* **4/1[2]**
-362 **3** *3 3/4* **Royal Family (FR)**[13] 6633 3-8-11 78.............................(t) GeorgeWood 1 58
(Amy Murphy) *trckd ldrs: rdn over 2f out: chal for 2nd over 1f out: outpce by ldng pair after* **11/2[3]**
4442 **4** *2* **Elegant Love**[17] 6505 3-8-11 64............................. JFEgan 3 55
(David Evans) *led 4f: w ldr: led over 3f out to 2f out: sn lft bhd* **8/1**
6000 **5** *1 1/4* **Miss Pollyanna (IRE)**[35] 5803 3-8-11 45.............................(h[1]) RobertHavlin 4 53?
(Roger Ingram) *stdd s: hld up in midfield: effrt over 2f out: outpcd wl over 1f out* **66/1**
0 **6** *19* **Tops No**[29] 6043 4-9-5 0............................. CharlesBishop 5 22
(William Muir) *mostly in last pair: prog arnd rivals bnd 4f out: wknd qckly wl over 2f out: t.o* **66/1**
0000 **7** *4* **Another Approach (FR)**[25] 6202 3-8-11 48.............................(p) NicolaCurrie 7 16
(Amanda Perrett) *t.k.h: w ldr: led after 4f to over 3f out: wknd rapidly over 2f out: t.o (jockey said filly ran too free and stopped quickly)* **40/1**
0-06 **8** *3 3/4* **De Beau Tant**[29] 6043 4-9-5 38............................. CharlieBennett 8 9
(Dai Burchell) *a towards rr: rdn and wknd wl over 2f out: t.o* **150/1**
2m 33.36s (-1.14) **Going Correction** +0.025s/f (Slow)
WFA 3 from 4yo 8lb 8 Ran SP% **132.6**
Speed ratings (Par 102): **104,101,98,97,96 83,81,78**
CSF £2.62 TOTE £1.10: £1.02, £1.40, £1.40; EX 2.70 Trifecta £6.20.
Owner K Abdullah **Bred** Juddmonte Farms Ltd **Trained** Kimpton, Hants
FOCUS
A weak novice, so easy pickings for the odds-on favourite.

7082 32RED H'CAP 1m 7f 218y(P)
7:30 (7:30) (Class 4) (0-80,80) 3-Y-0 **£6,469** (£1,925; £962; £481; £400) **Stalls** Low

Form RPR
5211 **1** **Trouble Shooter (IRE)**[20] 6367 3-8-2 61.............................(v) JosephineGordon 6 68
(Shaun Keightley) *plld hrd early: hld up in last: pushed along 5f out: detached and drvn 3f out: no rspnse tl sed to run on wl over 1f out: clsd qckly after: led 120yds out: sn in command* **7/1**
1364 **2** *1* **Great Bear**[19] 6411 3-9-7 80.............................(p) AdamMcNamara 1 86
(Roger Charlton) *t.k.h: led 7f: trckd ldr: rdn to ld over 2f out: hdd and no ex last 120yds* **3/1[2]**
3614 **3** *4 1/2* **Young Merlin (IRE)**[27] 6125 3-9-2 75.............................(p) JasonWatson 4 75
(Roger Charlton) *hld up in 4th: cl up fr 6f out: pushed along over 3f out: drvn and fnd little over 2f out: tk 3rd ins fnl f* **7/2[3]**
1421 **4** *nk* **Manton Warrior (IRE)**[19] 6392 3-9-0 73.............................(t) StevieDonohoe 2 73
(Charlie Fellowes) *tk fierce hold: mostly in 3rd: drvn over 2f out: nt qckn and hld over 1f out* **9/4[1]**
1630 **5** *3/4* **Buriram (IRE)**[39] 5694 3-9-7 80............................. HarryBentley 3 79
(Ralph Beckett) *tk fierce hold: pressed ldr: led after 7f: rdn and hdd over 2f out: wknd jst over 1f out* **9/2**
3m 31.93s (1.83) **Going Correction** +0.025s/f (Slow) 5 Ran SP% **108.7**
Speed ratings (Par 103): **96,95,93,93,92**
CSF £26.85 TOTE £4.80: £3.50, £1.30; EX 29.30 Trifecta £65.60.
Owner Simon Lockyer **Bred** Kildaragh Stud & M Downey **Trained** Newmarket, Suffolk
FOCUS
A messy, tactical race, and it was the outsider of the party who benefited.

7083 32RED ON THE APP STORE H'CAP 1m 2f 219y(P)
8:00 (8:03) (Class 5) (0-70,70) 3-Y-0+ **£3,752** (£1,116; £557; £400; £400; £400) **Stalls** Low

Form RPR
5635 **1** **Topology**[17] 6507 6-9-0 58............................. CharlesBishop 14 66
(Joseph Tuite) *hld up in last pair: nt clr run wl over 2f out: gd prog between rivals wl over 1f out: sustained effrt to ld last 100yds: pushed out* **16/1**
0 **2** *1/2* **By Rail**[11] 6733 5-9-4 62.............................(b[1]) CallumShepherd 3 69
(Nick Littmoden) *trckd ldrs: rdn over 2f out: prog to ld over 1f out: hdd last 100yds: kpt on but hld nr fin* **33/1**
-066 **3** *1 1/4* **Settle Petal**[26] 6160 5-9-3 64............................. PaddyBradley(3) 4 69
(Pat Phelan) *trckd ldrs: rdn to try to chal on outer over 1f out: styd on same pce fnl f* **16/1**
4255 **4** *3/4* **Kingdom Of Dubai (FR)**[18] 6439 3-9-1 66.............................(b) JackMitchell 10 70
(Roger Varian) *hld up in midfield: lost pl 3f out and in rr over 2f out: rdn and prog over 1f out: kpt on fnl f but nvr able to chal* **7/2[1]**
6436 **5** *3/4* **Gallatin**[21] 6331 3-9-5 70............................. DavidProbert 12 72
(Andrew Balding) *slowly away: in rr: prog over 3f out: rdn and hdwy to chal over 1f out: nt qckn and sn hld (jockey said filly was slowly away)* **8/1**
5530 **6** *nk* **Manfadh (IRE)**[38] 5709 4-9-8 66............................. RossaRyan 13 68
(Kevin Frost) *trapped wd: trckd ldrs: rdn and cl enough wl over 1f out: one pce after* **14/1**
5300 **7** *1/2* **Glory**[9] 6810 3-9-1 66............................. TomMarquand 6 67
(Richard Hannon) *hld up in last pair: drvn and prog on inner 2f out: one pce and no further hdwy fnl f* **9/1**
0626 **8** *1* **Perfect Refuge**[23] 6289 4-9-11 69............................. HectorCrouch 1 68
(Clive Cox) *trckd ldng pair: pushed into ld over 2f out: rdn and fnd nil wl over 1f out: sn hdd and btn* **5/1[2]**
0600 **9** *1 1/4* **Love Your Work (IRE)**[19] 6393 3-9-5 70............................. RoystonFfrench 5 67
(Adam West) *t.k.h: hld up towards rr: shkn up over 2f out: prog jst over 1f out: one pce and no hdwy fnl f* **25/1**
3000 **10** *shd* **Paco's Prince**[18] 6439 4-9-3 68............................. AledBeech(7) 8 65
(Nick Littmoden) *t.k.h: hld up towards rr: drvn and wl in rr over 2f out: plugged on but no ch* **16/1**
-040 **11** *2 3/4* **Give Him Time**[94] 3633 8-9-12 70............................. LiamKeniry 7 62
(Nick Gifford) *dwlt: t.k.h: hld up wl in rr: prog towards inner over 2f out: chsd ldrs over 1f out: sn wknd tamely* **11/1**
4552 **12** *2 3/4* **Militry Decoration (IRE)**[29] 6059 4-9-3 61............................. LukeMorris 9 49
(Dr Jon Scargill) *a towards rr: u.p and no prog over 2f out* **15/2[3]**
00 **13** *4 1/2* **Pilot Wings (IRE)**[96] 3547 4-9-7 65.............................(p[1]) KieranShoemark 2 45
(David Dennis) *led at fair pce: hdd over 2f out: sn wknd qckly* **14/1**
13-0 **14** *6* **Zarrar (IRE)**[22] 6320 4-9-6 64.............................(t[1]) FergusSweeney 11 34
(Camilla Poulton) *trckd ldr to 3f out: wknd rapidly over 2f out: t.o* **50/1**
2m 21.18s (0.18) **Going Correction** +0.025s/f (Slow)
WFA 3 from 4yo+ 7lb 14 Ran SP% **119.8**
Speed ratings (Par 103): **103,102,101,101,100 100,100,99,98,98 96,94,91,86**
CSF £469.93 CT £8278.96 TOTE £19.70: £5.40, £9.40, £4.60; EX 763.30 Trifecta £2496.10.
Owner The Singleton Park Partnership 2 **Bred** North Farm Stud **Trained** Lambourn, Berks
FOCUS
An ordinary handicap.

7084 WISE BETTING RACINGTV.COM H'CAP 1m (P)
8:30 (8:32) (Class 6) (0-65,65) 3-Y-0+ **£3,105** (£924; £461; £400; £400; £400) **Stalls** Low

Form RPR
0513 **1** **Purgatory**[12] 6678 3-9-5 65.............................(b) PatCosgrave 9 71
(Chris Wall) *trckd ldrs: clsd 2f out: rdn to ld over 1f out: jnd and bdly bmpd 150yds out: jst hld on* **5/2[1]**
1150 **2** *nse* **Mitigator**[26] 6164 3-8-12 65.............................(b) MorganCole(7) 3 71
(Lydia Pearce) *hld up towards rr: prog on inner 2f out: urged along to take 2nd fnl f: hung bdly lft: cannoned into wnr 150yds out and stmbld bdly: rcvrd and w wnr after: nudged along and jst failed* **12/1**
0004 **3** *2 1/4* **Letsbe Avenue (IRE)**[11] 6717 4-9-5 65.....(b) ThoreHammerHansen(5) 8 67
(Richard Hannon) *hld up in midfield: prog on outer over 2f out: rdn to chal over 1f out: nt qckn and hld ins fnl f (jockey said gelding was slowly away)* **9/2[2]**
66-0 **4** *3/4* **Professor**[22] 6317 9-9-5 60.............................(p) KierenFox 7 60+
(William Knight) *s.v.s: sn in tch in last pair: rdn and no prog wl over 2f out: styd on over 1f out to take 4th nr fin (jockey said gelding was slowly away)* **33/1**
0655 **5** *3/4* **Kodiac Lass (IRE)**[32] 5941 3-9-5 65.............................(p) HarryBentley 5 62
(Marco Botti) *t.k.h: disp ld 2f: styd cl up: nt qckn and lost pl 2f out: effrt again jst over 1f out: one pce* **11/2[3]**
0600 **6** *1 3/4* **Dancing Jo**[6] 6904 3-9-4 64.............................(p[1]) CallumShepherd 6 57
(Mick Channon) *wl in rr: rdn over 2f out: sme prog over 1f out: kpt on but nvr a threat* **11/1**
4500 **7** *1/2* **Bond Angel**[20] 6362 4-9-2 64............................. AngusVilliers(7) 4 57
(David Evans) *dwlt: hld up in last trio: rdn and no prog wl over 2f out: kpt on fnl f: no ch* **16/1**
2000 **8** *2* **Winterkoenigin**[32] 5941 3-9-3 63.............................(b[1]) DanielMuscutt 10 50
(David Lanigan) *nvr bttr than midfield: rdn and struggling towards rr over 2f out: n.d after* **16/1**
5500 **9** *3/4* **Arlecchino's Leap**[35] 5807 7-9-5 60.............................(p) FergusSweeney 2 47
(Mark Usher) *chsd ldrs: rdn over 2f out: no prog over 1f out: wl hld after* **16/1**
6-04 **10** *1/2* **Is It Off (IRE)**[50] 5284 4-9-6 61............................. LiamKeniry 12 47
(Sean Curran) *disp ld 2f: styd cl up: led over 2f out to over 1f out: wknd* **16/1**
0000 **11** *nse* **Vixen (IRE)**[22] 6317 5-9-9 64.............................(h) TomMarquand 13 49
(Emma Lavelle) *racd v wd early: led after 2f: hdd over 2f out: wknd tamely over 1f out* **14/1**
612 **12** *1 1/2* **Fantasy Justifier (IRE)**[20] 6363 8-9-2 57.............................(p) DavidProbert 1 39
(Ronald Harris) *restrained after s and hld up in last trio: rdn and no prog over 2f out* **16/1**
1m 39.44s (-0.36) **Going Correction** +0.025s/f (Slow)
WFA 3 from 4yo+ 5lb 12 Ran SP% **117.2**
Speed ratings (Par 101): **102,101,99,98,98 96,95,93,93,92 92,91**
CSF £33.82 CT £132.54 TOTE £2.80: £1.40, £3.70, £1.90; EX 37.60 Trifecta £200.10.
Owner Des Thurlby **Bred** Des Thurlby **Trained** Newmarket, Suffolk
■ Stewards' Enquiry : Morgan Cole six-day ban: interference & careless riding (Sep 25-30)
FOCUS
An eventful finish to this routine handicap and the winner found slight improvement.
T/Plt: £209.40 to a £1 stake. Pool: £71,014.63. 247.46 winning units. T/Qpdt: £127.80 to a £1 stake. Pool: £10,777.53. 62.36 winning units. **Jonathan Neesom**

LAYTOWN
Wednesday, September 11
OFFICIAL GOING: Beach: standard

7085a BOHAN HYLAND & ASSOCIATES H'CAP 6f
4:00 (4:02) (50-75,75) 4-Y-0+ **£6,122** (£1,978; £942; £424; £217; £113)

RPR
1 **Plough Boy (IRE)**[4] 6986 8-10-9 75............................. ShaneCrosse(5) 4 83
(Garvan Donnelly, Ire) *cl up tl sn led narrowly: jnd bef 1/2-way: regained narrow advantage over 1f out and rdn: kpt on wl clsngs stages where strly pressed* **7/1**
2 *nk* **Shore Step (IRE)**[19] 6432 9-10-4 68............................. ShaneBKelly(3) 11 75
(J P Murtagh, Ire) *cl up: rdn in 3rd 1 1/2f out and r.o u.p into 2nd wl ins fnl f and strly pressed wnr nr fin: jst hld* **9/2[2]**
3 *1 1/2* **Aleef (IRE)**[47] 5402 6-11-0 75.............................(t) EmmetMcNamara 2 77
(K J Condon, Ire) *led briefly tl sn jnd and hdd: disp ld bef 1/2-way: rdn and hdd narrowly far side over 1f out: no ex wl ins fnl f where dropped to 3rd* **6/1**
4 *1/2* **Dapper Power (IRE)**[47] 5402 5-10-8 69............................. DeclanMcDonogh 3 70
(Edward Lynam, Ire) *chsd ldrs: rdn in 4th 1 1/2f out and no imp on wnr wl ins fnl f: kpt on same pce: b.b.vs (vet said the gelding was found to have blood on its nostrils as a result of exercise induced pulmonary haemorrhage)* **5/2[1]**
5 *nk* **Nigg Bay (IRE)**[25] 6203 5-10-7 73............................. RickyDoyle(5) 12 73
(J F Levins, Ire) *hooded to load: dwlt: towards rr: hdwy 2f out: rdn in 7th 1 1/2f out and r.o into nvr threatening 5th ins fnl fin: nrst fin* **10/1**

6 2 1/4 **It's All A Joke (IRE)**[10] 6766 4-10-12 **73**.......................... ColinKeane 1 65
(Adrian McGuinness, Ire) *chsd ldrs early tl dropped to mid-div after 1f: tk clsr order fr bef 1/2-way: rdn in 5th under 2f out and no imp on ldrs in 6th ins fnl f: kpt on one pce* **10/1**

7 3/4 **The Right Choice (IRE)**[39] 5677 4-10-7 **68**....................... PBBeggy 5 58
(Jamie Osborne) *chsd ldrs: drvn fr bef 1/2-way and no imp on ldrs u.p in 6th under 2f out: one pce fnl f* **12/1**

8 2 1/2 **Faraasah (IRE)**[277] 9462 4-10-11 **72**........................ DougieCostello 9 54
(Jamie Osborne) *dwlt: sn chsd ldrs and disp 5th briefly after 2f: no imp on ldrs after 1/2-way: wknd* **14/1**

9 1 **Sevenleft (IRE)**[12] 6691 6-10-8 **74**.......................(t) ChrisTimmons(5) 8 53
(Ms Sheila Lavery, Ire) *in tch early: no imp towards rr fr bef 1/2-way: one pce after* **5/1**[3]

10 3 1/4 **Room To Roam (IRE)**[13] 9040 5-10-13 **74**...................... RossCoakley 7 42
(Peter Fahey, Ire) *in rr and pushed along early: rdn and no imp after 1/2-way: eased ins fnl f: nvr a factor* **16/1**

1m 11.42s **10 Ran SP% 128.6**
CSF £42.82 CT £214.76 TOTE £11.00: £2.50, £1.90, £2.10; DF 46.00 Trifecta £366.70.
Owner Mrs J P Duffy **Bred** J P Keappock **Trained** Garristown, Co Dublin

FOCUS
This was quite a competitive affair for the 45-75 grade. The first three home were always front rank.

7086a FOLLOW @MELBOURNE10RACING ON INSTAGRAM H'CAP 6f
4:35 (4:36) (45-65,65) 4-Y-0+

£5,590 (£1,806; £860; £387; £198; £104)

RPR

1 **Tyrconnell (IRE)**[56] 5068 5-10-2 **58**......................... ShaneCrosse(5) 1 70
(Sarah Lynam, Ire) *mid-div early: swtchd rt after 1/2-way and pushed along: hdwy nr side under 2f out: rdn to chal on terms over 1f out and led narrowly ins fnl f: styd on wl to assert clsng stages* **9/4**[1]

2 1 1/2 **My Good Brother (IRE)**[14] 6618 10-10-8 **59**.................. ColinKeane 5 66
(T G McCourt, Ire) *chsd ldrs: clsr in 3rd after 1f: effrt nr side under 2f out and disp ld briefly tl hdd narrowly ins fnl f: no imp on wnr in 2nd wl ins fnl f* **5/1**

3 1/2 **Pillar**[14] 6618 6-9-10 **47**.. DeclanMcDonogh 3 53
(Adrian McGuinness, Ire) *led briefly tl sn hdd and settled bhd ldrs after 1f: disp ld bef 1/2-way: drvn and led under 2f out: jnd over 1f out and sn hdd: no imp on wnr in 3rd wl ins fnl f* **10/1**

4 2 3/4 **Caesar's Comet (IRE)**[14] 6616 5-10-13 **64**.......................... DGHogan 7 61
(Denis Gerard Hogan, Ire) *dwlt sltly: mid-div early tl tk clsr order bhd ldrs bef 1/2-way: n.m.r fr after 1/2-way: rdn in 5th over 1f out and sn no imp on ldrs: kpt on into nvr threatening 4th fnl stride* **4/1**[2]

5 hd **Monumental Man**[32] 5959 10-11-0 **65**......................... DougieCostello 4 61
(Jamie Osborne) *cl up and sn disp ld briefly tl hdd after 1f: disp ld at 1/2-way: hdd under 2f out and no ex bhd ldrs in 4th over 1f out: one pce after: denied 4th fnl stride* **9/1**

6 1 1/4 **Bellick**[25] 6234 4-10-1 **52**.. RossCoakley 11 44
(John C McConnell, Ire) *mid-div: pushed along fr 1/2-way: sn rdn and no imp on ldrs u.p in 6th over 1f out: kpt on one pce* **9/2**[3]

7 6 1/2 **Carpet Time (IRE)**[60] 4942 4-10-0 **54**.................... ConorMaxwell(3) 9 25
(Leanne Breen, Ire) *trckd ldrs tl impr to ld after 1f: pushed along and jnd bef 1/2-way: hdd after 1/2-way and wknd u.p under 2f out* **25/1**

8 1 **Baile An Roba (IRE)**[102] 3363 6-9-8 **45**..................... MarkGallagher 8 13
(Kieran P Cotter, Ire) *towards rr: pushed along and tk clsr order far side bef 1/2-way: rdn in 6th after 1/2-way and no ex u.p 1 1/2f out: sn wknd* **33/1**

9 2 **Mimic's Memory**[14] 6616 5-9-6 **46**.......................... TomMadden(3) 12 8
(T G McCourt, Ire) *hld up in 8th: niggled along bef 1/2-way and sn lost pl: no imp u.p in rr under 2f out: kpt on one pce ins fnl f: nvr a factor* **10/1**

10 1 1/4 **Texas Radio (IRE)**[10] 6765 6-9-1 **45**.................... DMSimmonson(7) 10
(John James Feane, Ire) *sddled slipped jst after s and rdr lost irons: pushed along after in rr and wnt 9th at 1/2-way: no imp 1 1/2f out: eased ins fnl f: dropped to rr: nvr a factor (jockey said he lost his irons soon after the start)* **16/1**

1m 10.59s **10 Ran SP% 126.5**
CSF £15.10 CT £98.23 TOTE £3.10: £1.10, £1.80, £1.70; DF 11.10 Trifecta £109.30.
Owner Edward Lynam **Bred** J Hanly, T Stewart & A Stroud **Trained** Dunshaughlin, Co. Meath

FOCUS
This was an emphatic success for the favourite who obviously relishes this slick surface.

7087a GILNA'S COTTAGE INN PRIDE OF PLACE MAIDEN 7f
5:10 (5:10) 4-Y-0+

£6,655 (£2,150; £1,024; £461; £236; £123)

RPR

1 **Loose Chippings (IRE)**[27] 6098 5-9-12 53............ GabrieleMalune(5) 2 58
(Ivan Furtado) *led and disp early tl settled bhd ldrs after 1f: tk clsr order and disp ld bef 1/2-way and sn led: jnd 2f out: sn rdn on terms and led again 1f out: kpt on wl u.p ins fnl f* **7/1**[3]

2 1/2 **Perfect Beauty**[10] 6764 4-9-9 66.............................. ShaneBKelly(3) 9 52
(J P Murtagh, Ire) *cl up bhd ldrs and sn disp ld: hdd narrowly after 1/2-way: rdn bhd ldrs under 2f out and ev ch almost on terms ent fnl f: kpt on wl wout matching wnr clsng stages* **7/1**[3]

3 3/4 **Approbare (IRE)**[271] 9542 7-10-3 53............................. ColinKeane 6 55
(Ross O'Sullivan, Ire) *cl up bhd ldrs early tl dropped to 8th after 2f: hdwy after 1/2-way to chal on terms 2f out: edgd sltly lft u.p over 1f out and sn hdd: no ex in 3rd wl ins fnl f* **14/1**

4 1 **Myth Creation (USA)**[37] 5758 4-9-7 69...............(t) ShaneCrosse(5) 7 47
(Joseph Patrick O'Brien, Ire) *dwlt sltly: mid-div: rdn in 5th under 2f out and clsd u.p into 4th ins fnl f where no imp on ldrs: kpt on* **11/8**[1]

5 1 1/4 **House Call (IRE)**[34] 5872 4-9-12 51.................... DeclanMcDonogh 5 44
(Gordon Elliott, Ire) *w.w in rr early: hdwy far side fr bef 1/2-way to chse ldrs: rdn almost on terms over 2f out: impeded on inner over 1f out and sn no ex: wknd into 5th ins fnl f (jockey said filly checked in the final furlong)* **10/1**

6 5 **Kashid (USA)**[47] 5405 4-10-3 51............................... NiallPMadden 12 35
(J J Lambe, Ire) *mid-div: tk clsr order bhd ldrs nr side after 2f: drvn after 1/2-way and outpcd briefly: no imp on ldrs u.p in 6th over 1f out: one pce fnl f* **25/1**

7 2 1/2 **Drummer**[14] 6613 4-10-3 0... DGHogan 10 29
(Denis Gerard Hogan, Ire) *mid-div early: drvn and no imp after 1/2-way: n.m.r fr over 2f out: 9th 1 1/2f out: kpt on under hands and heels between horses ins fnl f* **16/1**

8 hd **Cloak Of Darkness (IRE)**[37] 6172 4-10-0 0............. TomMadden(3) 11 28
(Paul Nolan, Ire) *dwlt sltly: sn cltsd ldrs early: pushed along and outpcd after 1/2-way: no imp in rr over 1f out: kpt on one pce ins fnl f* **14/1**

9 1/2 **Ambient (IRE)**[68] 4607 4-10-3 75............................. DougieCostello 1 27
(Jamie Osborne) *hld up towards rr early: pushed along bef 1/2-way and sme hdwy far side over 2f out: rdn and no ex in 6th 1 1/2f out: wknd ins fnl f* **3/1**[2]

10 8 1/2 **Broadway Queen (IRE)**[51] 5262 4-9-12 0...................... PBBeggy 8
(Luke W Comer, Ire) *led and disp early: rdn fr 1/2-way and sn hdd u.p: wknd fr over 2f out where bmpd sltly: eased ins fnl f* **50/1**

1m 23.89s **10 Ran SP% 126.2**
CSF £60.11 TOTE £8.90: £2.80, £2.80, £4.30; DF 66.60 Trifecta £1410.90.
Owner The Giggle Factor Partnership **Bred** Limestone And Tara Studs **Trained** Wiseton, Nottinghamshire

FOCUS
Once again it paid to race close to the pace. The winner was rated 16lb inferior to the favourite and was giving her 5lb as well, which probably left punters scratching thier heads.

7088a SCOTCH HALL SHOPPING CENTRE CLAIMING RACE 7f
5:40 (5:42) 4-Y-0+

£5,590 (£1,806; £860; £387; £198; £104)

RPR

1 **Sir Ottoman (FR)**[39] 5678 6-9-12 65..................... GabrieleMalune(5) 10 73+
(Ivan Furtado) *chsd ldrs: rdn under 3f out and gd hdwy nr side to ld under 2f out: extended advantage over 1f out where in command and styd on strly: eased cl home: easily* **8/1**

2 5 **Hee Haw (IRE)**[47] 5401 5-10-3 55..................................... ColinKeane 5 60
(Adrian McGuinness, Ire) *w.w: 8th bef 1/2-way: prog after 1/2-way to chse ldrs: rdn between horses 1 1/2f out and no imp on easy wnr in 2nd ent fnl f: kpt on same pce* **2/1**[1]

3 1 1/2 **Al Batal**[49] 5322 6-10-3 53.......................................(t) RossCoakley 3 55
(John C McConnell, Ire) *loaded wout rdr: cl up: pushed along bhd ldrs under 3f out and no imp on easy wnr u.p in 3rd ent fnl f: kpt on same pce* **16/1**

4 3/4 **Ticks The Boxes (IRE)**[16] 6546 7-10-0 57..................... ShaneBKelly(3) 7 53
(Brian Ellison) *chsd ldrs: pushed along after 1/2-way and u.p disputing 5th under 2f out: wnt 4th 1f out where no imp on easy wnr: kpt on same pce* **11/4**[2]

5 2 **Pari Passu (IRE)**[18] 5872 6-10-3 50................................. PBBeggy 1 48
(Peter Fahey, Ire) *cl up far side: 3rd bef 1/2-way: rdn and disp ld over 2f out tl sn hdd: wknd u.p 1 1/2f out* **16/1**

6 3/4 **Grove Hill (IRE)**[7] 6865 6-10-3 60..................(t) EmmetMcNamara 8 46+
(Michael Mulvany, Ire) *w.w: pushed along in rr bef 1/2-way: rdn in 9th under 2f out and sme late hdwy fr over 1f out into nvr threatening 6th: nvr trbld ldrs* **10/1**

7 3 1/4 **Marylebone**[27] 6134 6-9-12 45................................ ShaneCrosse(5) 6 37
(Joseph Patrick O'Brien, Ire) *dwlt sltly: mid-div: rdn in 6th bef 1/2-way and no imp in 8th under 2f out: kpt on one pce ins fnl f: eased nr fin* **12/1**

8 1 1/4 **Poetic Light**[14] 6615 4-10-0 56..................................... TomMadden(3) 9 34
(Adrian McGuinness, Ire) *mid-div: 7th bef 1/2-way: rdn and no ex over 2f out: one pce after: eased nr fin: b.b.vs (jockey said gelding burst a blood vessel)* **20/1**

9 3 3/4 **Rippling Waters (FR)**[180] 1216 5-10-3 61..................... DougieCostello 2 24
(Jamie Osborne) *led narrowly: pushed along and jnd over 2f out: sn hdd & wknd qckly 1 1/2f out: eased ins fnl f* **7/1**[3]

10 hd **Monsieur Jimmy**[36] 5787 7-10-3 64........................ DeclanMcDonogh 13 23
(Brian Ellison) *a bhd: 9th bef 1/2-way: rdn and no imp in rr 1 1/2f out: eased ins fnl f* **8/1**

1m 23.61s **10 Ran SP% 128.0**
CSF £26.88 TOTE £10.40: £2.60, £1.20, £8.30; DF 41.90 Trifecta £286.70.
Owner Carl Hodgson **Bred** Madame Marie-Therese Mimouni **Trained** Wiseton, Nottinghamshire

FOCUS
A quickfire double for Ivan Furtado and Gabriele Malune. You would seldom see an easier winner on the beach.

7089a O'NEILLS SPORTS (Q.R.) H'CAP 7f
6:10 (6:11) (50-80,80) 4-Y-0+

£6,655 (£2,150; £1,024; £461; £236; £123)

RPR

1 **Royal Admiral (IRE)**[14] 6620 5-11-1 **66**..................... MrMJO'Hare(3) 2 75
(Adrian McGuinness, Ire) *cl up tl sn disp ld: narrow advantage at 1/2-way: rdn and strly pressed far side under 2f out: kpt on wl u.p to assert wl ins fnl f* **16/1**

2 2 1/4 **War Hero (IRE)**[39] 5699 4-11-12 **74**..........................(t) MrBO'Neill 12 77
(Adrian McGuinness, Ire) *chsd ldrs: gng wl nr side after 1/2-way: impr into 2nd fr 2f out: sn rdn and strly pressed wnr: no imp on wnr wl ins fnl f: kpt on wl* **4/1**[2]

3 2 1/2 **Ken's Sam's (IRE)**[14] 6618 6-10-9 **62**..................... MrNMcParlan(5) 13 58
(Adrian McGuinness, Ire) *mid-div: gng wl after 1/2-way and tk clsr order: rdn 2f out and sn wnt 3rd: no imp on ldrs u.p in 3rd ins fnl f: kpt on same pce* **12/1**

4 1 **Alfirak**[236] 305 5-11-0 **65**... MrDGLavery(3) 3 59
(Damian Joseph English, Ire) *s.i.s and awkward s: in rr: tk clsr order fr 1/2-way: pushed along bhd ldrs over 2f out: sn rdn and u.p disputing 4th over 1f out: no imp on ldrs in 4th ins fnl f: kpt on one pce* **12/1**

5 1 3/4 **Koybig (IRE)**[41] 5597 7-11-11 **76**........................ MrFinianMaguire(3) 11 65
(David Marnane, Ire) *chsd ldrs: rdn under 3f out and u.p disputing 4th over 1f out: no imp on ldrs in 5th ins fnl f: kpt on one pce* **8/1**

6 1 1/4 **Lappet (IRE)**[7] 6865 4-10-7 **60**................................. MrHDDunne(5) 1 45
(Gavin Cromwell, Ire) *sltly awkward s: cl up far side: pushed along disputing 2nd after 1/2-way and no ex over 2f out where n.m.r on inner briefly: sn lost tch: kpt on one pce in 6th ins fnl f* **10/1**

7 2 1/4 **Geological (IRE)**[34] 5873 7-12-4 **80**............................. MrJJCodd 4 59
(Damian Joseph English, Ire) *led and disp: pushed along disputing cl 2nd fr 1/2-way and wknd fr over 2f out* **4/1**[2]

8 1 **Blacklooks (IRE)**[12] 6694 4-11-4 **69**........................ MrTHamilton(3) 6 46
(Joseph Patrick O'Brien, Ire) *hld up in rr of mid-div: drvn and no imp 3f out: u.p in 8th under 2f out: kpt on one pce: nvr a factor* **5/2**[1]

9 3 **Able Jack**[107] 3147 6-11-8 **75**................................ MrRDeegan(5) 8 44
(P J F Murphy, Ire) *got upset in stalls and dislodged rdr briefly bef s: towards rr: pushed along bef 1/2-way and lost tch fr 3f out: nvr a factor* **33/1**

10 3/4 **Florencio**180 1213 6-12-3 79 MsLO'Neill 10 46
(Jamie Osborne) *got upset in stalls: in rr of mid-div early: pushed along bef 1/2-way and sn dropped to rr: no imp and lost tch after 1/2-way: nvr a factor* 11/2[3]
1m 24.56s 10 Ran SP% 128.4
CSF £87.08 CT £856.30 TOTE £24.70: £5.20, £1.90, £4.10; DF 131.90 Trifecta £1689.90.
Owner Shamrock Thoroughbreds **Bred** Michael Downey & Roalso Ltd **Trained** Lusk, Co Dublin
■ Stewards' Enquiry : Mr N McParlan three-day ban: used whip with excessive frequency (tba)

FOCUS
A 1-2-3 for trainer Adrian McGuinness.

7090a HIBERNIA STEEL (Q.R.) RACE 7f
6:40 (6:40) 4-Y-0+ **£7,986** (£2,581; £1,229; £554; £283)

RPR

1 **Confident Kid**77 4260 6-11-4 46 MrTHamilton(3) 1 61
(Adrian McGuinness, Ire) *prom early tl sn settled bhd ldrs: disp 3rd after 2f: tk clsr order far side after 1/2-way: gng wl in cl 2nd 2f out: rdn to ld over 1f out: sn extended ld: strly pressed u.p nr fin: hld on wl* 7/1

2 1/2 **Twenty Minutes**26 6195 4-12-0 78 (t) MrJJCodd 2 67+
(Damian Joseph English, Ire) *hld up bhd ldrs: last at 1/2-way: tk clsr order and swtchd rt in 4th over 2f out: wnt 3rd 1 1/2f out: r.o wl u.p into 2nd wl ins fnl f and strly pressed wnr nr fin: hld* 2/1[2]

3 1 1/4 **Commander Han (FR)**46 5434 4-12-0 81 MsLO'Neill 3 64
(Jamie Osborne) *sn led and racd keenly early: narrow advantage at 1/2-way: rdn and hdd over 1f out: u.p in 2nd whn j. shadow ins fnl f and sn lost pl: no ex in 3rd nr fin (jockey said gelding went to jump and lost its action about a furlong from the finish)* 11/10[1]

4 5 1/2 **Reverberation**28 6092 4-11-11 60 MrDGLavery(3) 4 49
(J J Lambe, Ire) *cl up bhd ldr: cl 2nd at 1/2-way: drvn under 3f out and sn lost pl: no ex u.p in 4th 1 1/2f out: wknd* 6/1[3]

5 2 3/4 **Barbie O'Conor**11 6744 4-10-11 38 MrRDeegan(5) 5 29
(Donal Kinsella, Ire) *hld up bhd ldrs: tk clsr order and disp 3rd after 2f: drvn under 3f out and wknd to rr u.p over 2f out* 25/1

1m 25.49s 5 Ran SP% 111.6
Tote Aggs - 2018: 121,618; 2019: 105,406 CSF £21.65 TOTE £7.60: £2.40, £1.40; DF 25.80 Trifecta £75.90.
Owner Confident Kid Syndicate **Bred** D J And Mrs Deer **Trained** Lusk, Co Dublin

FOCUS
A shock result on ratings but having been a general 40-1 shot (as big as 50-1 in a place) earlier, this didn't appear to come as a surprise to his supporters.
T/Jkpt: Not won. T/Plt: @1,051.20. Pool: @18,907.52. **Brian Fleming**

7091a - 7102a (Foreign Racing) - See Raceform Interactive

6883 CHELMSFORD (A.W) (L-H)
Thursday, September 12

OFFICIAL GOING: Polytrack: standard
Wind: Light across Weather: Sunny spells

7103 BET AT TOTESPORT.COM NOVICE STKS (PLUS 10 RACE) 6f (P)
5:20 (5:22) (Class 4) 2-Y-0 **£6,080** (£1,809; £904; £452) **Stalls** Centre

Form RPR

105 1 **Last Surprise (IRE)**75 4398 2-9-5 85 PatCosgrave 5 82+
(Simon Crisford) *chsd ldr: rdn over 1f out: r.o to ld wl ins fnl f* 7/4[1]

46 2 1 1/4 **Shoot To Kill (IRE)**48 5367 2-9-4 0 DanielMuscutt 1 77
(George Scott) *led: rdn over 1f out: hdd and unable qck wl ins fnl f* 7/2[3]

5 3 1 3/4 **Bill The Butcher (IRE)**19 6464 2-9-4 0 AdamKirby 7 72
(Richard Spencer) *chsd ldrs: reminder over 3f out: outpcd over 2f out: rdn over 1f out: rallied and hung lft ins fnl f: r.o (jockey said colt hung left-handed from 3f out)* 9/4[2]

6 4 1 **Dubai Romance (IRE)**113 2968 2-8-13 0 CallumShepherd 4 64
(Saeed bin Suroor) *chsd ldrs: rdn over 1f out: no ex ins fnl f* 7/1

5 7 **San Juan (IRE)** 2-9-4 0 NickyMackay 3 48
(Shaun Keightley) *s.i.s: sme hdwy over 1f out: wknd ins fnl f* 12/1

6 6 **Red's Rocket** 2-8-13 0 NicolaCurrie 6 25
(Laura Mongan) *s.s: outpcd (jockey said filly was outpaced early stages)* 66/1

00 7 2 1/4 **Casablanca Kid (IRE)**13 6684 2-8-13 0 DylanHogan(5) 2 23
(Denis Quinn) *broke wl enough: sn lost pl: rdn 1/2-way: wknd 2f out* 66/1

1m 11.77s (-1.93) **Going Correction** -0.20s/f (Stan) 7 Ran SP% 112.5
Speed ratings (Par 97): **104,102,100,98,89 81,78**
CSF £8.01 TOTE £2.10: £1.20, £2.10; EX 6.80 Trifecta £16.20.
Owner Sheikh Rashid Dalmook Al Maktoum **Bred** Mr & Mrs C Booth & Mrs S Cammidge **Trained** Newmarket, Suffolk

FOCUS
A fairly decent juvenile novice contest. The favourite got well on top under strong driving in the final 150 yards.

7104 DAVID BRIFFAUT NOVICE AUCTION STKS (PLUS 10 RACE) 7f (P)
5:50 (5:53) (Class 4) 2-Y-0 **£6,080** (£1,809; £904; £452) **Stalls** Low

Form RPR

10 1 **Love Destiny**21 6375 2-9-8 0 AdamKirby 3 81
(Mark Johnston) *a.p: chsd ldr over 2f out: rdn and edgd rt over 1f out: led ins fnl f: edgd lft: drvn out* 6/4[1]

3 2 1/2 **Silver Samurai**13 6684 2-9-0 0 GeorgeWood 9 72
(Marco Botti) *plld hrd and prom: rdn and nt clr run over 1f out: r.o* 4/1[2]

4154 3 1 1/4 **Mitty's Smile (IRE)**21 6369 2-9-1 72 (p1) AdamMcNamara 10 69
(Archie Watson) *sn led: rdn and hung rt wl over 1f out: hdd ins fnl f: styd on same pce towards fin* 8/1[3]

0 4 3 3/4 **Ventura Star (IRE)**27 6161 2-9-1 0 DanielMuscutt 1 60+
(David Lanigan) *prom: outpcd over 2f out: rallied over 1f out: styd on same pce ins fnl f* 4/1[2]

61 5 4 1/2 **Miss Thoughtful**12 6719 2-9-1 0 NicolaCurrie 8 48
(Jamie Osborne) *hld up: styd on fr over 1f out: nt trble ldrs* 8/1[3]

60 6 hd **Disarming (IRE)**27 6161 2-8-5 0 DarraghKeenan(3) 7 40
(Dr Jon Scargill) *hld up: styd on fr over 1f out: nvr on terms* 33/1

0 7 2 **Oasis Song**12 6719 2-8-9 0 PJMcDonald 2 36
(Hughie Morrison) *prom: rdn over 2f out: hung lft and wknd over 1f out* 16/1

00 8 3 1/4 **Lisbeth Salander (IRE)**12 6719 2-8-9 0 CallumShepherd 4 28
(Richard Spencer) *s.i.s: hld up: n.d (jockey said filly did not face the kickback on this occasion)* 50/1

0 9 22 **One Alc (FR)**33 5956 2-9-2 0 PatCosgrave 5
(Dean Ivory) *s.i.s: hdwy to chse ldr over 4f out tl rdn over 2f out: wknd over 1f out* 33/1

P **Typhoon Lily (IRE)** 2-8-8 0 FinleyMarsh(3) 6
(Richard Hughes) *s.s: outpcd: p.u over 1f out (jockey said filly ran green and was outpaced throughout)* 25/1

1m 26.53s (-0.67) **Going Correction** -0.20s/f (Stan) 10 Ran SP% 119.8
Speed ratings (Par 97): **95,94,93,88,83 83,81,77,52,**
CSF £7.47 TOTE £2.00: £1.10, £1.40, £2.10; EX 8.10 Trifecta £33.70.
Owner M Doyle **Bred** Cheveley Park Stud Ltd **Trained** Middleham Moor, N Yorks

FOCUS
An ordinary juvenile novice auction contest. The favourite won gamely in a comparatively modest time.

7105 EXTRA PLACES AT TOTESPORT.COM H'CAP 6f (P)
6:20 (6:20) (Class 5) (0-70,72) 3-Y-0
£5,110 (£1,520; £759; £400; £400; £400) **Stalls** Centre

Form RPR

0023 1 **Across The Sea**57 5056 3-9-9 72 (v) PJMcDonald 9 81+
(James Tate) *sn led: hdd over 3f out: led again over 2f out: rdn and hung lft fr over 1f out: r.o* 9/4[1]

6431 2 2 1/4 **Invincible Larne (IRE)**36 5826 3-9-7 70 (v) PatCosgrave 8 70
(Mick Quinn) *pushed along to join wnr: led over 3f out tl over 2f out: rdn over 1f out: styd on same pce ins fnl f* 5/1[3]

0243 3 nk **Maid Millie**12 6737 3-8-0 56 (p) AngusVilliers(7) 5 55
(Robert Cowell) *s.i.s: pushed along in rr: hdwy over 1f out: rdn to go 3rd: nt clr run and swtchd rt ins fnl f: r.o* 9/2[2]

065R 4 1 1/4 **Greybychoice (IRE)**73 4454 3-8-10 62 DarraghKeenan(3) 7 57
(Nick Littmoden) *s.i.s: hld up: hdwy over 1f out: sn rdn: styng on same pce whn nt clr run wl ins fnl f* 10/1

3002 5 1/2 **Sepahi**35 5869 3-8-8 62 (p) DylanHogan(5) 4 55
(Henry Spiller) *s.i.s: pushed along in rr: nt clr run and hmpd over 1f out: nt trble ldrs* 12/1

0600 6 3/4 **Painted Dream**24 6286 3-8-6 62 MorganCole(7) 1 53
(George Margarson) *sn pushed along in rr: sme hdwy over 1f out: no ex fnl f* 5/1[3]

0500 7 8 **Such Promise**24 6284 3-7-9 51 oh1 (v) IsobelFrancis(7) 6 16
(Mike Murphy) *chsd ldrs: rdn over 2f out: sn hung rt: wknd over 1f out (jockey said gelding hung right-handed throughout)* 16/1

004 8 12 **Lovin (USA)**35 5854 3-9-9 72 (vt) AdamKirby 2
(David O'Meara) *chsd ldrs: rdn over 2f out: wknd over 1f out: eased* 8/1

1m 11.59s (-2.11) **Going Correction** -0.20s/f (Stan) 8 Ran SP% 116.1
Speed ratings (Par 101): **106,103,102,100,100 99,88,72**
CSF £13.89 CT £46.88 TOTE £2.60: £1.10, £2.00, £1.70; EX 16.50 Trifecta £37.80.
Owner Saeed Manana **Bred** Rabbah Bloodstock Limited **Trained** Newmarket, Suffolk

FOCUS
An ordinary 3yo handicap. The favourite got on top of a duel for the lead and bravely found more for an eased-down victory in the final furlong.

7106 IRISH LOTTO AT TOTESPORT.COM H'CAP 1m (P)
6:50 (6:51) (Class 2) (0-105,102) 3-Y-0+ **£12,938** (£3,850; £1,924; £962) **Stalls** Low

Form RPR

2101 1 **Maamora (IRE)**43 5564 3-9-0 95 DavidEgan 8 102
(Simon Crisford) *sn led: shkn up and qcknd over 2f out: rdn and edgd rt over 1f out: styd on* 5/1[3]

6251 2 3/4 **Bedouin's Story**47 5453 4-9-11 101 (p) HectorCrouch 3 107
(Saeed bin Suroor) *hld up: shkn up and hdwy on outer over 1f out: rdn and edgd lft ins fnl f: r.o* 9/2[2]

140- 3 1 **Commander Cole**355 7532 5-9-12 102 PatCosgrave 2 106
(Saeed bin Suroor) *hld up: hdwy over 1f out: r.o* 5/1[3]

6421 4 shd **Ibraz**17 6543 4-9-9 99 DaneO'Neill 6 102
(Roger Varian) *prom: rdn to chse wnr over 1f out tl ins fnl f: styd on same pce* 4/1[1]

4401 5 1 **Universal Gleam**19 6460 4-9-1 91 CallumRodriguez 4 92
(Keith Dalgleish) *hld up: rdn over 1f out: styd on ins fnl f: nt trble ldrs* 12/1

2206 6 3/4 **Qaroun**27 6150 4-9-1 91 LouisSteward 1 90
(Sir Michael Stoute) *hld up in tch: rdn over 1f out: styd on same pce ins fnl f* 10/1

0053 7 3/4 **Akvavera**39 5708 4-8-12 88 HarryBentley 7 86
(Ralph Beckett) *s.i.s: hdwy to chse wnr over 6f out: racd keenly: rdn and lost 2nd over 1f out: no ex ins fnl f* 16/1

5131 8 1 1/2 **Solar Heights (IRE)**14 6630 3-8-13 94 (v) PJMcDonald 5 87
(James Tate) *prom: rdn over 1f out: wknd ins fnl f* 4/1[1]

1m 36.27s (-3.63) **Going Correction** -0.20s/f (Stan)
WFA 3 from 4yo+ 5lb 8 Ran SP% 114.2
Speed ratings (Par 109): **110,109,108,108,107 106,105,104**
CSF £27.62 CT £118.29 TOTE £5.80: £1.80, £1.60, £1.80; EX 31.40 Trifecta £187.80.
Owner Sheikh Ahmed Al Maktoum **Bred** Godolphin **Trained** Newmarket, Suffolk

FOCUS
The feature contest was a good handicap; sound-looking form.

7107 BET IN PLAY AT TOTESPORT.COM H'CAP 5f (P)
7:20 (7:21) (Class 3) (0-95,97) 3-Y-0+ **£9,703** (£2,887; £1,443; £721) **Stalls** Low

Form RPR

1000 1 **Royal Birth**5 6954 8-9-4 97 (t) MarcoGhiani(7) 5 105
(Stuart Williams) *plld hrd in 2nd tl led and hung rt over 3f out: rdn over 1f out: r.o* 8/1

650 2 nk **Lord Riddiford (IRE)**22 6351 4-9-3 89 JasonHart 2 96
(John Quinn) *led: hdd over 3f out: remained w wnr: rdn and ev ch fr over 1f out: r.o* 11/8[1]

5111 3 1/2 **Harry's Bar**34 5888 4-9-5 91 GeorgeWood 4 96+
(James Fanshawe) *s.i.s: hld up: racd keenly: shkn up over 1f out: rdn and r.o ins fnl f: nt rch ldrs* 6/4[2]

35-5 4 nse **Sparkalot**23 6319 5-8-5 84 LeviWilliams(7) 3 89
(Simon Dow) *s.i.s: hld up: hdwy over 1f out: styd on* 7/1[3]

2000 5 hd **Encore D'Or**27 6149 7-9-10 96 PJMcDonald 1 100
(Robert Cowell) *chsd ldrs: nt clr run and swtchd rt over 1f out: styd on* 8/1

58.5s (-1.70) **Going Correction** -0.20s/f (Stan)
WFA 3 from 4yo+ 1lb 5 Ran SP% 116.8
Speed ratings (Par 107): **105,104,103,103,103**
CSF £20.89 TOTE £11.90: £3.60, £1.20; EX 22.50 Trifecta £80.00.
Owner The Morley Family **Bred** Old Mill Stud & S Williams & J Parry **Trained** Newmarket, Suffolk

The Form Book Flat 2019, Raceform Ltd, Newbury, RG14 5SJ

FOCUS
A good sprint handicap. The five horses finished within about a length of each other in a busy finish.

7108 TOTEPOOL CASHBACK CLUB AT TOTESPORT.COM H'CAP 1m 5f 66y(P)
7:50 (7:50) (Class 4) (0-80,86) 3-Y-O **£5,757** (£1,713; £856) **Stalls** Low

Form RPR
5242 **1** **Australis (IRE)**[26] 6224 3-9-2 **76**..........(b) DavidEgan 3 85
(Roger Varian) *mde virtually all: shkn up over 5f out: rdn over 3f out: styd on u.p (vet said gelding lost its right fore shoe)* **3/1**[2]
5451 **2** *1 1/2* **Brasca**[7] 6888 3-9-12 **86** 6ex.......... HarryBentley 2 93
(Ralph Beckett) *trckd wnr: shkn up over 2f out: rdn and hung lft fr over 1f out: styd on same pce ins fnl f (jockey said gelding hung left-handed)* **4/9**[1]
422 **3** *3* **Withoutdestination**[40] 5654 3-8-11 **78**..........(b) StefanoCherchi(7) 1 80
(Marco Botti) *s.i.s: hld up: shkn up over 4f out: outpcd fr over 2f out* **5/1**[3]
2m 51.28s (-2.32) **Going Correction** -0.20s/f (Stan) **3** Ran SP% **110.9**
Speed ratings (Par 103): **99,98,96**
CSF £5.12 TOTE £4.40; EX 5.00 Trifecta £4.40.
Owner Biddestone Racing Xx **Bred** Lynchbages Edgeridge Ltd & Glenvale Stud **Trained** Newmarket, Suffolk

FOCUS
A fair little 3yo staying handicap. They went a tactical gallop and the order never changed. This rates a pb from the winner.

7109 DOUBLE DELIGHT HAT-TRICK HEAVEN AT TOTESPORT.COM H'CAP 1m 5f 66y(P)
8:20 (8:20) (Class 5) (0-70,72) 4-Y-O+ **£5,110** (£1,520; £759; £400; £400) **Stalls** Low

Form RPR
040 **1** **Conkering Hero (IRE)**[22] 6333 5-9-7 **68**..........(b) CharlesBishop 1 77
(Joseph Tuite) *mde all: rdn and edgd rt over 1f out: styd on wl: comf* **5/2**[1]
4334 **2** *4 1/2* **Brittanic (IRE)**[18] 6512 5-9-1 **67**.......... DylanHogan(5) 6 68
(David Simcock) *s.i.s: hld up: rdn over 2f out: styd on u.p to go 2nd ins fnl f: no ch w wnr* **5/2**[1]
3045 **3** *1 3/4* **Sauchiehall Street (IRE)**[56] 5106 4-9-11 **72**..........(p) CallumShepherd 5 71
(Noel Williams) *chsd wnr tl rdn over 2f out: no ex ins fnl f* **11/4**[2]
5450 **4** *shd* **Sir Gnet (IRE)**[44] 5528 5-9-0 **61**..........(h) DanielMuscutt 3 59
(Ed Dunlop) *chsd ldrs: wnt 2nd over 2f out: sn rdn: no ex ins fnl f* **7/2**[3]
0460 **5** *25* **Carvelas (IRE)**[14] 6635 10-8-10 **57**.......... NickyMackay 4 18
(J R Jenkins) *s.i.s: hld up: rdn over 3f out: outpcd fr over 2f out: eased over 1f out* **12/1**
2m 52.24s (-1.36) **Going Correction** -0.20s/f (Stan) **5** Ran SP% **113.7**
Speed ratings (Par 103): **96,93,92,92,76**
CSF £9.43 TOTE £3.50: £1.70, £1.80; EX 8.90 Trifecta £26.70.
Owner C R Lambourne, M Forbes, D Losse **Bred** J Hutchinson **Trained** Lambourn, Berks

FOCUS
An ordinary staying handicap. One of the joint-favourites decisively made all in a time about a second slower than the previous C&D handicap.
T/Plt: £44.80 to a £1 stake. Pool: £58,084.34 - 945.73 winning units T/Qpdt: £20.20 to a £1 stake. Pool: £8,215.10 - 300.88 winning units **Colin Roberts**

6799 CHEPSTOW (L-H)
Thursday, September 12

OFFICIAL GOING: Good to soft (good in places; 6.3)
Wind: Blustery and quite strong, mainly across Weather: Sunny spells

7110 BETUK.COM NURSERY H'CAP 5f 16y
1:50 (1:51) (Class 6) (0-60,60) 2-Y-O
£2,781 (£827; £413; £300; £300; £300) **Stalls** Centre

Form RPR
3640 **1** **Lara Silvia**[30] 6032 2-9-7 **60**.......... RossaRyan 4 64
(Iain Jardine) *mde all: drvn and jnd over 1f out: hld on wl towards fin (trainer said, regarding the improved form shown, the filly seemed better suited by today's ground (good to soft, good in places))* **9/2**[3]
4530 **2** *nk* **Santorini Sal**[29] 6071 2-8-12 **54**.......... MitchGodwin(3) 8 57
(John Bridger) *midfield: drvn over 1f out: only 4th ent fnl f: r.o to go 2nd nr fin: jst hld* **3/1**[2]
0022 **3** *3/4* **Blue Venture**[10] 6799 2-9-0 **53**.......... JohnFahy 10 53
(Tony Carroll) *sn prom: pushed along 2f out: ev ch over 1f out: drvn ins fnl f: no ex and lost 2nd fnl 50yds* **11/8**[1]
0406 **4** *nk* **Shaun's Delight (IRE)**[9] 6837 2-8-11 **50**..........(b) DavidProbert 1 49
(Ronald Harris) *prom: rdn over 2f out: hung rt over 1f out: kpt on* **10/1**
506 **5** *2 3/4* **Mumsbirthdaygirl (IRE)**[122] 2694 2-8-8 **47** ow2.......... EoinWalsh 9 36
(Mark Loughnane) *in rr: drvn and sme hdwy over 1f out: hung lft and no imp fnl f* **25/1**
060 **6** *1 1/4* **Goodman Square**[12] 6719 2-7-13 **45**.......... IsobelFrancis(7) 7 30
(Mark Usher) *in rr: rdn and outpcd 1/2-way: sn hung lft: r.o fnl f (jockey said filly hung badly left-handed throughout)* **50/1**
050 **7** *2* **Mayflower Lady (IRE)**[28] 6106 2-8-6 **45**..........(b[1]) RaulDaSilva 6 23
(Ronald Harris) *rdn over 2f out: a towards rr* **33/1**
0600 **8** *1 1/2* **Red Cinderella**[10] 6799 2-8-8 **47**.......... LiamJones 5 19
(David Evans) *midfield: pushed along over 3f out: drvn over 1f out: wknd ins fnl f* **20/1**
0553 **9** *3 1/4* **Sir Rodneyredblood**[9] 6837 2-9-0 **53**.......... TomQueally 3 13
(J R Jenkins) *t.k.h: prom: lost pl over 2f out: rdn and wknd over 1f out* **8/1**
1m 1.97s (2.57) **Going Correction** +0.275s/f (Good) **9** Ran SP% **119.0**
Speed ratings (Par 93): **90,89,88,87,83 81,78,75,70**
CSF £18.32 CT £28.28 TOTE £5.00: £1.40, £2.10, £1.10; EX 16.70 Trifecta £52.90.
Owner Mrs Lesley-Anne Drummond **Bred** Russell Drummond **Trained** Carrutherstown, D'fries & G'way

FOCUS
There was a tight four-way finish down the centre to this moderate nursery. The winner rates to her pre-race mark.

7111 BETUK.COM YOUR HOME FOR ONLINE BETTING NURSERY H'CAP 1m 14y
2:25 (2:27) (Class 6) (0-60,60) 2-Y-O
£2,781 (£827; £413; £300; £300; £300) **Stalls** Centre

Form RPR
6604 **1** **Now I'm A Believer**[15] 6604 2-8-6 **45**.......... KieranO'Neill 6 49
(Mick Channon) *a.p: rdn over 2f out: led 1f out: sn drvn: hung rt nr fin: hld on gamely* **14/1**
006 **2** *shd* **Today Power (IRE)**[16] 6564 2-9-6 **59**.......... RossaRyan 12 63
(Richard Hannon) *midfield: rdn over 2f out: drvn over 1f out: styd on wl fnl f: jst failed* **9/2**[1]
600 **3** *nk* **Big Boris (IRE)**[14] 6640 2-9-2 **55**.......... RobertHavlin 10 58
(David Evans) *hld up: rdn and hdwy over 2f out: swtchd rt and drvn ins fnl f: styd on wl towards fin: jst hld* **7/1**[2]
4050 **4** *5* **Buy Nice Not Twice (IRE)**[7] 6884 2-8-9 **53**.. ThoreHammerHansen(5) 1 46
(Richard Hannon) *midfield: drvn over 2f out: styng on but no threat whn edgd rt and snatched up ins fnl f (jockey said filly hung right-handed inside the final furlong)* **9/2**[1]
0604 **5** *1/2* **Interrupted Dream**[7] 6884 2-8-11 **57**.......... AidenSmithies(7) 3 48
(Mark Johnston) *led: drvn 2f out: hdd 1f out: wknd* **9/1**
066 **6** *4* **Max's Voice (IRE)**[13] 6654 2-9-2 **60**..........(b[1]) ThomasGreatrex(5) 8 42
(David Loughnane) *chsd ldrs: rdn 2f out: wknd fnl f* **9/2**[1]
0603 **7** *shd* **Ohnotanotherone**[15] 6604 2-8-3 **45**..........(p) WilliamCox(3) 2 27
(Stuart Kittow) *t.k.h: prom: drvn 2f out: wknd appr fnl f* **33/1**
0364 **8** *9* **Boston Girl (IRE)**[34] 5912 2-9-0 **53**..........(p[1]) DavidProbert 7 15
(Ed Dunlop) *midfield: rdn over 3f out: wknd 2f out* **16/1**
000 **9** *1* **Camacho Man (IRE)**[59] 4992 2-9-4 **57**.......... TomQueally 9 17
(Jennie Candlish) *drvn over 3f out: a towards rr* **8/1**[3]
6600 **10** *1/2* **Activius (IRE)**[9] 6837 2-9-5 **58**..........(b) RobHornby 5 17
(Brian Meehan) *chsd ldrs over 2f: sn pushed along and lost pl: bhd fnl 3f* **20/1**
0000 **11** *14* **Lightning Bug (IRE)**[34] 5886 2-8-3 **47**.......... RhiainIngram(5) 13
(Suzy Smith) *in rr: rdn 3f out: wknd 2f out* **25/1**
060 **12** *12* **Order Of Merritt (IRE)**[17] 6548 2-8-6 **45**..........(b[1]) LukeMorris 11
(Sir Mark Prescott Bt) *t.k.h: hld up: rdn over 3f out: wknd over 2f out* **8/1**[3]
1m 39.64s (3.64) **Going Correction** +0.275s/f (Good) **12** Ran SP% **123.4**
Speed ratings (Par 93): **92,91,91,86,86 82,82,73,72,71 57,45**
CSF £77.45 CT £504.07 TOTE £16.60: £4.40, £1.70, £1.70; EX 106.30 Trifecta £1029.50.
Owner T P Radford **Bred** Ferdlant Stud Ltd **Trained** West Ilsley, Berks

FOCUS
The principals came well clear in this ordinary nursery and the winner rates an improver.

7112 KIER CONSTRUCTION H'CAP 5f 16y
3:00 (3:00) (Class 5) (0-70,71) 3-Y-O+
£3,428 (£1,020; £509; £300; £300; £300) **Stalls** Centre

Form RPR
0062 **1** **Atty's Edge**[21] 6365 3-8-1 **53** oh2.......... RhiainIngram(5) 13 64
(Christopher Mason) *s.s: in rr: rdn over 3f out: hdwy 2f out: drvn over 1f out: r.o wl to ld towards fin* **11/2**[3]
4311 **2** *1/2* **Kodiak Attack (IRE)**[26] 6197 3-9-8 **71**.......... RobHornby 5 78
(Sylvester Kirk) *led: rdn 2f out: drvn and edgd lft ins fnl f: hdd towards fin* **8/1**
3213 **3** *1 3/4* **Red Stripes (USA)**[9] 6829 7-8-2 **57**..........(b) GavinAshton(7) 3 58
(Lisa Williamson) *prom: rdn wl over 1f out: unable qck ins fnl f* **11/2**[3]
3505 **4** *hd* **Pettochside**[24] 6288 10-9-2 **64**.......... RossaRyan 9 64
(John Bridger) *midfield: rdn 2f out: r.o wl fnl f* **4/1**[2]
5161 **5** *1 3/4* **Secret Potion**[21] 6365 5-9-7 **69**.......... DavidProbert 11 63
(Ronald Harris) *towards rr: rdn 1/2-way: drvn over 1f out: r.o fnl f: nt rch ldrs (jockey said gelding was never travelling)* **10/3**[1]
1100 **6** *hd* **Perfect Charm**[16] 6562 3-8-12 **68**..........(b) KateLeahy(7) 2 61
(Archie Watson) *prom: rdn 2f out: hung lft appr fnl f: no threat after* **22/1**
4032 **7** *1 3/4* **Bluebell Time (IRE)**[8] 6851 3-8-9 **58**.......... KieranO'Neill 7 45
(Malcolm Saunders) *wnt rt leaving stalls: chsd ldrs: rdn 1/2-way: fdd fnl f* **11/1**
0300 **8** *1/2* **David's Beauty (IRE)**[32] 5986 6-8-9 **57**..........(b) LukeMorris 1 42
(Brian Baugh) *racd on far rail: prom: rdn 2f out: losing pl whn sltly hmpd appr fnl f* **16/1**
4500 **9** *hd* **Test Valley (IRE)**[21] 6363 4-8-8 **55** oh1 ow1.......... JohnFahy 8 40
(Tracey Barfoot-Saunt) *sltly hmpd leaving stalls: in rr: bhd and pushed along 1/2-way: rdn and r.o past btn rivals fnl f* **16/1**
5560 **10** *3/4* **Silverrica (IRE)**[41] 5607 9-8-11 **59**.......... EoinWalsh 12 41
(Malcolm Saunders) *racd on stands' rail: chsd ldrs: rdn over 2f out: wknd over 1f out* **33/1**
010 **11** *1 1/2* **Compton Poppy**[21] 6365 5-8-12 **60**..........(b) GeorgeDowning 10 36
(Tony Carroll) *midfield: rdn over 2f out: wknd over 1f out (trainer said mare was not suited by the good to soft, good in places going and would prefer a quicker surface)* **16/1**
2253 **12** *3/4* **Edged Out**[36] 5793 9-8-4 **53** oh2.......... WilliamCox(3) 4 29
(Christopher Mason) *trckd ldrs: rdn 2f out: wknd qckly fnl f* **16/1**
0060 **13** *10* **Swendab (IRE)**[28] 6107 11-8-7 **45** oh10..........(b) LiamJones 6
(John O'Shea) *sn towards rr and chsd along: wl bhd fnl 2f* **66/1**
1m 0.44s (1.04) **Going Correction** +0.275s/f (Good)
WFA 3 from 4yo+ 1lb **13** Ran SP% **125.6**
Speed ratings (Par 103): **102,101,98,98,95 94,92,91,91,89 87,86,70**
CSF £51.16 CT £269.96 TOTE £6.90: £3.50, £2.60, £2.00; EX 62.70 Trifecta £236.60.
Owner International Plywood (Importers) Ltd **Bred** Christopher & Annabelle Mason **Trained** Caewent, Monmouthshire

FOCUS
The main action developed down the middle in this run-of-the-mill sprint handicap and the first two rate as improving.

7113 BAA BREWING EBF NOVICE STKS 7f 16y
3:35 (3:37) (Class 5) 2-Y-O **£3,428** (£1,020; £509; £254) **Stalls** Centre

Form RPR
0 **1** **Sea Voice**[7] 6905 2-9-0 0.......... ThoreHammerHansen(5) 4 75
(Richard Hannon) *a.p: led wl over 2f out: sn rdn: drvn ent fnl f: r.o strly fnl 110yds* **25/1**
0 **2** *2* **General Joe (IRE)**[36] 5809 2-9-2 0.......... WilliamCox(3) 3 70
(Clive Cox) *midfield: hdwy 3f out: drvn 2f out: ev ch 1f out: hung rt ins fnl f: outpcd by wnr fnl 110yds (jockey said gelding hung right-handed inside the final 1/2f)* **20/1**
53 **3** *nk* **Sky Vega (IRE)**[36] 5801 2-9-5 0.......... RossaRyan 1 69
(Richard Hannon) *hld up in tch: hdwy over 2f out: rdn and hung rt over 1f out: kpt on same pce fnl f (jockey said colt hung right-handed when under pressure inside the final 1 1/2f)* **5/4**[1]
65 **4** *1 1/2* **Ocho Grande (IRE)**[20] 6415 2-9-5 0.......... TomQueally 8 66
(Eve Johnson Houghton) *hld up: shkn up and hdwy 3f out: drvn over 1f out: unable qck fnl f: hld in 4th whn n.m.r nr fin* **11/1**
6 **5** *2 1/2* **Maximilius (GER)**[28] 6106 2-9-5 0.......... RobHornby 5 59
(Ralph Beckett) *cl up tl pushed along and lost pl 1/2-way: rdn 2f out: sme late hdwy* **5/1**[3]
6 *3/4* **Blairlogie** 2-9-5 0.......... KieranO'Neill 6 57
(Mick Channon) *chsd ldrs: stmbld and lost grnd 1/2-way: sn rdn: no threat fr over 1f out* **9/1**

32 **7** 3/4 **Magic Twist (USA)**[42] 5572 2-9-0 0 LukeMorris 9 51
(Mark Johnston) *prom: rdn 3f out: sn ev ch: drvn and wknd appr fnl f* **3/1**[2]
8 2 3/4 **The Fitzpiers Lion (IRE)** 2-9-5 0 RaulDaSilva 2 49
(Ronald Harris) *s.s: in rr and early reminder: rdn 1/2-way: hdwy on outer over 2f out: wknd over 1f out* **50/1**
9 17 **Viking Honour (IRE)** 2-9-5 0 GeorgeDowning 10 6
(Joseph Tuite) *hld up: hdwy 1/2-way: rdn over 2f out: sn wknd* **50/1**
10 1/2 **I'm Watching You** 2-9-5 0 DavidProbert 7 5
(Ronald Harris) *led tl rdn and hdd wl over 2f out: wknd over 1f out* **33/1**
0 **11** 10 **Leo's Luckyman**[68] 4652 2-9-5 0 LiamJones 11
(David Flood) *missed break: racd keenly and sn chsng ldrs: rdn 3f out: sn wknd* **50/1**

1m 26.75s (2.85) **Going Correction** +0.275s/f (Good) **11** Ran SP% **121.9**
Speed ratings (Par 95): **94,91,91,89,86 85,85,81,62,61 50**
CSF £423.69 TOTE £35.40: £8.10, £6.50, £1.10; EX 954.00 Trifecta £3505.50.
Owner Promenade Bloodstock Limited **Bred** Promenade Bloodstock Limited **Trained** East Everleigh, Wilts

FOCUS
The centre was again favoured in this modest novice event.

7114 PLAY SLOTS AT BETUK.COM NOVICE STKS 7f 16y
4:05 (4:08) (Class 5) 3-Y-O+ **£3,428** (£1,020; £509; £254) **Stalls** Centre

Form RPR
1 **1** **Severnaya (IRE)**[195] 971 3-9-5 0 RobertHavlin 5 88+
(John Gosden) *s.i.s: t.k.h and sn prom: led wl over 2f out: shkn up over 1f out: sn clr: in command whn drvn ins fnl f* **1/2**[1]
2 4 1/2 **Snow Ocean (IRE)**[49] 5363 3-9-3 68 (h[1]) EoinWalsh 3 70
(David Evans) *hld up: rdn 3f out: hdwy 2f out: styd on to go 2nd ins fnl f: no threat to wnr (jockey said gelding was slowly away)* **6/1**[3]
0-2 **3** 4 1/2 **A Place To Dream**[26] 6198 3-9-3 0 RossaRyan 2 58
(Mike Murphy) *t.k.h early: in rr: shkn up 3f out: kpt on steadily fnl 2f: wnt modest 3rd ins fnl f (jockey said gelding was never travelling)* **12/1**
45 **4** 3 **Sally Hope**[27] 6169 3-8-7 0 ThomasGreatrex(5) 8 45
(John Gallagher) *midfield: rdn and no ch fr 1/2-way: modest late prog: wnt 4th last strides* **20/1**
0- **5** hd **Maerchengarten**[276] 9485 3-8-7 0 ThoreHammerHansen(5) 7 44
(Ed de Giles) *led: rdn over 3f out: hdd wl over 2f out: outpcd by wnr over 1f out: lost 2nd and wknd ins fnl f* **66/1**
6 9 **Wherewithal** 3-9-3 0 RobHornby 1 25
(Ralph Beckett) *chsd ldrs: rdn over 3f out: sn outpcd: wknd over 1f out* **3/1**[2]
3 **7** 4 1/2 **Alameery**[24] 6283 3-9-3 0 DavidProbert 4 13
(Ed Dunlop) *t.k.h: prom: rdn over 2f out: sn outpcd by ldng pair: wknd and lost 3rd over 1f out* **9/1**
0- **8** 7 **Star Command (IRE)**[345] 7875 3-8-5 0 MichaelPitt(7) 6
(Denis Coakley) *midfield: rdn after 3f: sn struggling in rr* **80/1**
9 2 3/4 **Dansepo** 3-9-3 0 TomQueally 9
(Adam West) *s.s: a bhd* **66/1**

1m 25.44s (1.54) **Going Correction** +0.275s/f (Good) **9** Ran SP% **132.6**
Speed ratings (Par 103): **102,96,91,88,88 77,72,64,61**
CSF £5.65 TOTE £1.30: £1.10, £1.80, £2.60; EX 7.30 Trifecta £43.90.
Owner HH Sheikha Al Jalila Racing **Bred** Godolphin **Trained** Newmarket, Suffolk

FOCUS
An uncompetitive 3yo novice event, rated around the runner-up to this year's form.

7115 SPORTS BETTING AT BETUK.COM H'CAP 6f 16y
4:40 (4:41) (Class 4) (0-80,79) 3-Y-O+
£5,207 (£1,549; £774; £387; £300; £300) **Stalls** Centre

Form RPR
4454 **1** **Young John (IRE)**[23] 6326 6-9-1 73 RossaRyan 1 85
(Mike Murphy) *racd alone far side: cl up: rdn to ld 2f out: drvn appr fnl f: r.o strly* **2/1**[1]
5010 **2** 4 1/2 **Handytalk (IRE)**[34] 5882 6-9-0 79 (v) OliverSearle(7) 2 77
(Rod Millman) *t.k.h: led: rdn over 2f out: sn hdd: kpt on but no ch w wnr fnl f* **10/1**
0432 **3** 1 1/4 **Smokey Lane (IRE)**[28] 6109 5-8-6 69 ThomasGreatrex(5) 5 63
(David Evans) *awkward s and slowly away: in rr: hdwy 1/2-way: rdn to go 3rd 2f out: sn drvn: kpt on but nvr any threat to wnr (jockey said gelding was slowly away)* **10/3**[2]
6401 **4** 5 **Kinglami**[13] 6682 10-8-7 60 oh5 (b) LukeMorris 7 43
(John O'Shea) *in tch: rdn over 2f out: sn outpcd by ldrs: wnt modest 4th nr fin* **14/1**
3111 **5** 1/2 **Gilt Edge**[14] 6638 3-8-8 73 RhiainIngram(5) 6 49
(Christopher Mason) *in rr: pushed along after 2f: clsd 1/2-way: drvn over 2f out: wknd appr fnl f: lost modest 4th nr fin* **5/1**[3]
1-26 **6** 3 **Angel Mead**[22] 6346 3-9-5 79 RobHornby 3 45
(Joseph Tuite) *chsd ldrs: rdn over 2f out: sn btn: wknd fnl f* **6/1**
2165 **7** 4 **Alicia Darcy (IRE)**[11] 6756 3-8-10 77 (b) KateLeahy(7) 4 31
(Archie Watson) *chsd ldrs: rdn and lost pl over 2f out: wknd over 1f out (jockey said filly ran flat)* **10/1**

1m 11.86s (0.36) **Going Correction** +0.275s/f (Good)
WFA 3 from 5yo+ 2lb **7** Ran SP% **112.2**
Speed ratings (Par 105): **108,102,100,93,93 89,83**
CSF £22.03 TOTE £2.60: £1.70, £1.70; EX 19.20 Trifecta £67.30.
Owner Murphy, Cooper & East **Bred** Carpet Lady Partnership **Trained** Westoning, Beds

FOCUS
The far side proved the place to be in this modest sprint handicap. The winner rates to his best in the last two years.

7116 PLAY ROULETTE AT BETUK.COM H'CAP 1m 4f
5:10 (5:11) (Class 6) (0-65,67) 3-Y-O+
£2,781 (£827; £413; £300; £300; £300) **Stalls** Low

Form RPR
4630 **1** **Paddy The Chef (IRE)**[23] 6303 4-9-7 64 (p) ThoreHammerHansen(5) 12 77
(Ian Williams) *trckd ldrs: led over 2f out: rdn clr over 1f out: styd on strly: eased towards fin (trainer could offer no explanation for the gelding's improved form)* **9/1**
0545 **2** 2 3/4 **General Brook (IRE)**[9] 6843 9-9-2 54 (p) RossaRyan 8 58
(John O'Shea) *wnt to post early: in 2nd almost thrght: rdn over 2f out: kpt on but no ch w wnr fr over 1f out* **11/1**
2101 **3** 1 1/4 **Bug Boy (IRE)**[10] 6805 3-9-1 66 (p) RhiainIngram(5) 3 69
(Paul George) *s.s: in rr: rdn and hdwy on outer over 2f out: styd on to go 3rd ins fnl f: nvr any threat to easy wnr (jockey said gelding was slowly away)* **13/8**[1]
35 **4** 2 1/2 **Born To Frolic (IRE)**[48] 5378 4-8-11 54 RachealKneller(5) 14 52
(Debbie Hughes) *chsd ldrs: rdn over 2f out: styd on same pce* **11/2**[2]
5532 **5** 1 1/4 **Chinese Alphabet**[30] 6042 3-9-3 63 (p) LukeMorris 2 61
(William Knight) *chsd ldrs: rdn over 3f out: drvn over 2f out: one pce after: disputing hld 3rd 1f out* **7/1**[3]
0104 **6** 1/2 **Neff (GER)**[50] 5316 4-9-10 62 BrendanPowell 6 58
(Gary Moore) *towards rr: hdwy on inner 3f out: rdn and outpcd by ldrs over 2f out: styd on fnl f* **9/1**
0364 **7** 1/2 **Helian (IRE)**[34] 5898 3-9-7 67 DavidProbert 10 63
(Ed Dunlop) *midfield: rdn over 3f out: kpt on to dispute 3rd 1f out: sn wknd* **7/1**[3]
06-0 **8** 1 1/4 **Bostonian**[20] 6419 9-9-6 58 (t) RyanPowell 4 51
(Shaun Lycett) *racd keenly: led: rdn and hdd over 2f out: lost 3rd over 1f out: grad wknd* **50/1**
6353 **9** 3/4 **Essenaitch (IRE)**[10] 6804 6-9-3 60 ThomasGreatrex(5) 7 52
(David Evans) *hld up: hdwy 4f out: rdn 3f out: wknd 2f out* **14/1**
1333 **10** 3/4 **Magic Shuffle (IRE)**[34] 5880 3-9-4 64 TrevorWhelan 11 56
(Barry Brennan) *in tch towards rr: rdn over 3f out: wknd over 1f out (jockey said gelding hung right-handed)* **28/1**
4534 **11** 1/2 **Searching (IRE)**[12] 3940 7-10-0 66 (p) TomQueally 5 56
(Grace Harris) *rdn over 3f out: a in rr* **25/1**

2m 38.11s (-2.19) **Going Correction** -0.15s/f (Firm)
WFA 3 from 4yo+ 8lb **11** Ran SP% **122.7**
Speed ratings (Par 101): **101,99,98,96,95 95,95,94,93,93 93**
CSF £106.25 CT £245.92 TOTE £11.40: £2.80, £2.50, £1.10; EX 109.30 Trifecta £411.60.
Owner Mr & Mrs H Parmar **Bred** Holborn Trust Co **Trained** Portway, Worcs
■ Boutan was withdrawn, price at time of withdrawal 20/1. Rule 4 does not apply.

FOCUS
They were soon strung out in this moderate handicap.
T/Plt: £40.70 to a £1 stake. Pool: £54,526.51 - 976.18 winning units T/Qpdt: £11.00 to a £1 stake. Pool: £6,280.20 - 420.00 winning units **Richard Lowther**

7071 DONCASTER (L-H)
Thursday, September 12

OFFICIAL GOING: Good to firm (watered; 8.1)
Wind: Moderate against; fresh after race 2

7117 BRITISH STALLION STUDS EBF "CARRIE RED" FILLIES' NURSERY H'CAP 6f 111y
2:10 (2:12) (Class 2) 2-Y-O **£31,505** (£9,430; £4,715; £2,360; £1,175) **Stalls** Centre

Form RPR
4102 **1** **Graceful Magic**[9] 6833 2-8-11 82 CharlesBishop 10 89
(Eve Johnson Houghton) *hld up towards rr: hdwy over 2f out: chsd ldrs and n.m.r over 1f out: rdn ent fnl f: styd on wl to ld fnl 50yds: drvn and hld on wl nr fin* **5/1**[1]
324 **2** shd **Stylistique**[19] 6444 2-9-9 94 DavidEgan 7 101
(Roger Varian) *hld up towards rr: hdwy wl over 2f out: effrt whn sltly hmpd and swtchd rt over 1f out: rdn to ld jst ins fnl f: sn drvn: edgd lft and hld fnl 50yds: kpt on gamely towards fin (jockey said filly suffered interference approximately 1 1/2f out)* **5/1**[1]
1424 **3** hd **Rosadora (IRE)**[40] 5683 2-8-11 82 HarryBentley 14 88
(Ralph Beckett) *dwlt and towards rr: hdwy on outer 2f out: rdn to chse ldrs over 1f out: drvn and kpt on wl fnl f* **8/1**[3]
103 **4** 1/2 **Special Secret**[31] 6019 2-8-8 79 RyanMoore 12 84
(Eve Johnson Houghton) *trckd ldrs and plld hrd early: sn restrained and towards rr: hdwy 2f out: rdn over 1f out: kpt on wl fnl f (vet said filly lost its right fore shoe)* **9/1**
4041 **5** nk **Galadriel**[28] 6096 2-8-7 78 AndreaAtzeni 13 82+
(Kevin Ryan) *prom: effrt wl over 1f out and sn cl up: rdn to take slt ld 1f out: sn hdd and drvn: kpt on same pce fnl 100yds* **13/2**[2]
012 **6** 1 1/2 **Company Minx (IRE)**[31] 6019 2-8-9 80 HectorCrouch 8 80+
(Clive Cox) *led in centre: hdd 3f out: cl up: rdn to ld again over 1f out: drvn and hdd 1f out: grad wknd* **9/1**
2116 **7** nk **Keep Busy (IRE)**[17] 6542 2-8-7 78 JasonHart 9 77
(John Quinn) *hld up towards rr: effrt over 2f out and sn pushed along: rdn wl over 1f out: kpt on fnl f* **18/1**
2401 **8** 3/4 **Insania**[21] 6369 2-8-12 83 CliffordLee 6 80
(K R Burke) *hld up in tch: hdwy 2f out: rdn to chse ldrs over 1f out: sn drvn and wknd fnl f* **11/1**
351 **9** 1/2 **Red Treble**[16] 6570 2-8-6 77 (h) CamHardie 15 73
(Rebecca Menzies) *racd towards stands' side: cl up: led 3f out: rdn and wandered over 1f out: sn hdd & wknd* **22/1**
2542 **10** 1 1/2 **Incognito (IRE)**[14] 6629 2-8-3 74 HollieDoyle 4 66
(Mick Channon) *hld up: hdwy over 2f out: rdn and cl up on outer wl over 1f out: sn drvn and wknd (jockey said filly hung right-handed under pressure)* **12/1**
211 **11** 1 1/2 **Nirodha (IRE)**[19] 6458 2-8-5 79 SeanDavis(3) 3 67
(Amy Murphy) *chsd ldrs: rdn along wl over 2f out: sn wknd* **20/1**
0025 **12** 3/4 **Taste The Nectar (USA)**[12] 6705 2-7-11 71 (p) JaneElliott(3) 5 57
(Robert Cowell) *hld up: a towards rr (jockey said filly was denied a clear run approaching 2f out)* **40/1**
103 **13** 6 **Ultra Violet**[16] 6577 2-9-4 89 OisinMurphy 11 58
(Ed Vaughan) *t.k.h: chsd ldrs: rdn along over 2f out: sn wknd* **12/1**

1m 20.36s (0.76) **Going Correction** +0.10s/f (Good) **13** Ran SP% **118.3**
Speed ratings (Par 101): **99,98,98,98,97 96,95,94,94,92 90,89,83**
CSF £27.31 CT £206.45 TOTE £4.80: £1.90, £2.10, £2.90; EX 26.40 Trifecta £196.50.
Owner The Kimber Family **Bred** Dr Scott Kimber **Trained** Blewbury, Oxon

FOCUS
Racing centre-field, before several of the runners edged stands' side in the final 2f, they went pretty steady in this fair fillies' nursery, but into a headwind, so the closers still came to the fore.

7118 DFS PARK HILL STKS (GROUP 2) (F&M) 1m 6f 115y
2:40 (2:42) (Class 1) 3-Y-O+
£56,710 (£21,500; £10,760; £5,360; £2,690; £1,350) **Stalls** Low

Form RPR
1211 **1** **Enbihaar (IRE)**[40] 5663 4-9-8 113 JimCrowley 8 114+
(John Gosden) *wnt rt s: hld up in rr: stdy hdwy 4f out: trckd ldrs over 2f out: chal over 1f out: rdn to take narrow ld ent fnl f: sn drvn: kpt on wl (jockey said filly slipped on the bend turning into the home straight)* **6/5**[1]
6353 **2** shd **Delphinia (IRE)**[26] 6239 3-8-9 104 RyanMoore 7 110
(A P O'Brien, Ire) *hld up towards rr: hdwy over 4f out: trckd ldrs over 2f out: rdn to chal over 1f out: cl up ent fnl f: sn drvn and ev ch tl no ex nr fin* **15/2**[3]

3201 **3** 2 3/4 **Vivid Diamond (IRE)**[12] 6712 3-8-9 100 FrannyNorton 2 106
(Mark Johnston) *trckd ldr: hdwy to ld over 3f out: rdn along 2f out: drvn and jnd over 1f out: hdd ent fnl f: kpt on same pce* **12/1**

1304 **4** 2 **South Sea Pearl (IRE)**[21] 6377 3-8-9 101 SeamieHeffernan 5 103
(A P O'Brien, Ire) *hld up in rr: hdwy on outer over 3f out: pushed along over 2f out: rdn to case ldrs over 1f out: sn drvn and no imp* **20/1**

4212 **5** 4 **Star Terms**[32] 6003 3-8-9 99 AndreaAtzeni 6 98
(Richard Hannon) *trckd ldrs: pushed along and hdwy over 3f out: rdn over 2f out: drvn wl over 1f out: sn one pce* **12/1**

-211 **6** 5 **Dame Malliot**[25] 6263 3-8-12 110 FrankieDettori 4 94
(Ed Vaughan) *hld up towards rr: effrt and sme hdwy 4f out: rdn along 3f out: n.d (jockey said filly ran flat; trainer said filly may have been feeling the effects of a hard race on heavy going on its previous run)* **9/4**[2]

4112 **7** 1 3/4 **Oydis**[26] 6223 3-8-9 92 HarryBentley 1 89
(Ralph Beckett) *chsd ldng pair: rdn along over 3f out: sn wknd* **33/1**

1660 **8** 7 **Peach Tree (IRE)**[25] 6263 3-8-9 100 WayneLordan 3 79
(A P O'Brien, Ire) *led: pushed along 3f out: rdn and hdd over 3f out: sn wknd* **33/1**

3m 2.79s (-8.81) **Going Correction** +0.15s/f (Good)
WFA 3 from 4yo 10lb **8** Ran SP% **114.0**
Speed ratings (Par 115): **116,115,114,113,111 108,107,103**
CSF £10.84 CT £70.64 TOTE £2.00: £1.10, £1.80, £2.70; EX 13.30 Trifecta £64.60.

Owner Hamdan Al Maktoum **Bred** Haras Du Mezeray **Trained** Newmarket, Suffolk

FOCUS
Add 9yds. Not a strong race edition of the race, but it was run at a good gallop, courtesy of Ballydoyle pacemaker Peach Tree. The winner didn't quite match her last-time-out Goodwood form.

7119 WEATHERBYS RACING BANK £300,000 2-Y-O STKS 6f 111y
3:15 (3:20) (Class 2) 2-Y-O

£147,540 (£59,040; £29,520; £14,730; £7,380; £7,380) **Stalls** Centre

Form RPR

2 **1** **King's Lynn**[19] 6464 2-8-9 0 OisinMurphy 1 92+
(Andrew Balding) *in tch: hdwy over 2f out: rdn to ld ent fnl f: drvn and kpt on wl towards fin* **12/1**

143 **2** 1/2 **Repartee (IRE)**[20] 6422 2-9-2 101 AndreaAtzeni 3 98
(Kevin Ryan) *hld up in rr: hdwy 1/2-way: swtchd lft and effrt 2f out: rdn to chse ldrs over 1f out: drvn and kpt on strly fnl f* **5/1**[2]

5123 **3** shd **Toro Strike (USA)**[42] 5587 2-8-9 90 TonyHamilton 12 91
(Richard Fahey) *trckd ldrs: cl up over 2f out: rdn to ld 1 1/2f out: hdd ent fnl f: sn drvn and kpt on wl towards fin* **22/1**

42 **4** 1/2 **Manigordo (USA)**[61] 4897 2-9-0 0 PatDobbs 6 94+
(Richard Hannon) *hld up towards rr: hdwy over 2f out: n.m.r over 1f out: sn rdn: styd on wl fnl f* **14/1**

6505 **5** 1 1/2 **King Neptune (USA)**[27] 6190 2-9-2 96 WayneLordan 11 92
(A P O'Brien, Ire) *midfield: hdwy wl over 1f out: rdn and chsd ldrs ent fnl f: kpt on* **33/1**

66 **6** nk **Pistoletto (USA)**[20] 6422 2-9-2 98 SeamieHeffernan 2 91
(A P O'Brien, Ire) *trckd ldrs: hdwy over 2f out: rdn and ev ch over 1f out: sn drvn: kpt on same pce (jockey said colt jumped a sheet of paper approximately a furlong out)* **20/1**

522 **7** 2 **Harpocrates (IRE)**[22] 6352 2-9-2 105 (b) RyanMoore 9 86
(A P O'Brien, Ire) *dwlt and towards rr: swtchd lft to inner and hdwy over 2f out: rdn wl over 1f out: styd on fnl f: nrst fin (jockey said colt reared as the stalls opened)* **4/1**[1]

213 **8** nse **Glasvegas (IRE)**[85] 3988 2-8-6 99 DavidEgan 4 76
(Keith Dalgleish) *in tch: hdwy to chse ldrs over 2f out: rdn along wl over 1f out: drvn and kpt on same pce fr over 1f out* **7/1**[3]

0341 **9** nk **Ziggle Pops**[11] 6757 2-9-2 75 SeanLevey 17 85
(Richard Hannon) *towards rr: hdwy wl over 1f out: sn rdn: kpt on fnl f* **50/1**

2 **10** shd **Unforgetable (IRE)**[49] 5361 2-8-11 97 FrankieDettori 10 80+
(Joseph Patrick O'Brien, Ire) *cl up centre: led over 2f out: sn rdn: hdd 1 1/2f out: sn drvn and grad wknd* **8/1**

2232 **11** shd **Electrical Storm**[19] 6449 2-9-2 86 DanielTudhope 15 84
(Saeed bin Suroor) *racd towards stands' side: chsd ldrs: rdn along over 2f out: sn drvn and wknd over 1f out* **12/1**

0302 **12** 1 1/4 **Rayong**[21] 6375 2-8-9 97 BenCurtis 7 79+
(K R Burke) *towards rr: hdwy 2f out: rdn over 1f out: styng on whn n.m.r ins fnl f: eased* **14/1**

1141 **13** 1 **War Storm**[18] 6515 2-8-9 88 (p) HollieDoyle 5 71+
(Archie Watson) *cl up centre: rdn along over 2f out: sn wknd* **33/1**

223 **14** 1/2 **Great Ambassador**[40] 5665 2-9-2 86 HarryBentley 16 77+
(Ralph Beckett) *racd towards stands' side: hld up: hdwy and in tch 1/2-way: sn chsng ldrs: rdn along 2f out: sn wknd* **12/1**

1541 **15** 8 **Indian Creak (IRE)**[20] 6403 2-8-12 86 WilliamBuick 20 51+
(Mick Channon) *racd towards stands' side: chsd ldrs: rdn along over 2f out: sn wknd* **66/1**

4203 **16** shd **When Comes Here (IRE)**[21] 6364 2-8-9 78 (b[1]) FrannyNorton 14 48
(Andrew Balding) *a towards rr* **100/1**

52 **17** 1 **Skontonovski**[20] 6395 2-8-6 0 MartinDwyer 19 42+
(Richard Spencer) *t.k.h: hld up: a towards rr* **33/1**

32 **18** nse **Soaring Star (IRE)**[27] 6175 2-9-2 0 KevinStott 22 52+
(Kevin Ryan) *racd towards stands' side: a towards rr* **40/1**

015 **19** 3 **D Day (IRE)**[22] 6344 2-8-9 85 TomMarquand 13 36
(Richard Hannon) *chsd ldrs centre: rdn along wl over 2f out: sn wknd* **100/1**

3543 **20** 1 1/2 **Swinley Forest (IRE)**[12] 6728 2-8-9 76 (p) JasonHart 8 32+
(Brian Meehan) *led centre: rdn along and hdd over 2f out: sn wknd (jockey said colt hung right-handed throughout)* **100/1**

1m 18.81s (-0.79) **Going Correction** +0.10s/f (Good) **20** Ran SP% **123.5**
Speed ratings (Par 101): **108,107,107,106,105 104,102,102,102,101 101,100,99,98,89 89,88,88,84,83**
CSF £64.26 TOTE £11.10: £3.80, £2.20, £7.10; EX 100.20 Trifecta £4196.00.

Owner The Queen **Bred** The Queen **Trained** Kingsclere, Hants

FOCUS
An open and interesting race, and the winner improved plenty. The time was slower than standard, but appreciably quicker than the opening nursery run over the same trip. The winner was another one for first-season sire sensation Cable Bay.

7120 WILLIAM HILL MAY HILL STKS (GROUP 2) (FILLIES) 1m (S)
3:45 (3:51) (Class 1) 2-Y-O

£39,697 (£15,050; £7,532; £3,752; £1,883; £945) **Stalls** Centre

Form RPR

1 **1** **Powerful Breeze**[20] 6407 2-9-0 0 JamesDoyle 1 106+
(Hugo Palmer) *hld up towards rr: swtchd lft to inner and hdwy wl over 2f out: led wl over 1f out: sn rdn: edgd rt ent fnl f: sn drvn and kpt on* **6/1**[2]

411 **2** 1 **Boomer**[19] 6444 2-9-0 99 RichardKingscote 2 104
(Tom Dascombe) *trckd ldng pair: hdwy and cl up over 2f out: sn disputing ld: rdn and ev ch over 1f out: drvn and kpt on fnl f* **8/1**

21 **3** nk **Alpen Rose (IRE)**[26] 6205 2-9-0 0 WilliamBuick 9 103
(Charlie Appleby) *hld up in rr: hdwy on outer over 2f out: sn chsng ldrs: rdn and ev ch over 1f out: drvn and kpt on fnl f* **10/1**

341 **4** 1/2 **Run Wild (GER)**[15] 6592 2-9-0 93 OisinMurphy 3 102
(John Gosden) *t.k.h: trckd ldrs: pushed along and sltly outpcd over 2f out: hdwy wl over 1f out: sn rdn: kpt on fnl f* **7/1**[3]

315 **5** 1 1/2 **Ananya**[33] 5964 2-9-0 92 BrettDoyle 4 99
(Peter Chapple-Hyam) *chsd ldrs: rdn along wl over 1f out: kpt on same pce* **18/1**

1 **6** nk **Cloak Of Spirits (IRE)**[48] 5366 2-9-0 0 AndreaAtzeni 8 98
(Richard Hannon) *cl up: disp ld 2f out: rdn and ev ch over 1f out: drvn and wknd ent fnl f (jockey said filly hung right-handed)* **6/4**[1]

7 3 **Passion (IRE)**[11] 6761 2-9-0 0 RyanMoore 5 95
(A P O'Brien, Ire) *hld up in tch: hdwy over 2f out: rdn along wl over 1f out: sn drvn and wknd (jockey said filly was denied a clear run approaching the final furlong)* **9/1**

151 **8** 2 1/4 **West End Girl**[33] 5964 2-9-0 101 FrannyNorton 7 87
(Mark Johnston) *led: pushed along 3f out: jnd and rdn 2f out: sn hdd & wknd (trainer said he was unable to confirm whether the filly had performed poorly due to lack of experience)* **8/1**

1 **9** 4 **Anna Of Sussex (IRE)**[35] 5838 2-9-0 0 TomMarquand 6 78
(Sylvester Kirk) *a in rr* **100/1**

1m 39.31s (-0.89) **Going Correction** +0.10s/f (Good) **9** Ran SP% **114.4**
Speed ratings (Par 104): **108,107,106,106,104 104,101,99,95**
CSF £52.45 CT £472.26 TOTE £6.20: £1.80, £2.00, £3.20; EX 53.10 Trifecta £293.80.

Owner Dr Ali Ridha **Bred** Rabbah Bloodstock Limited **Trained** Newmarket, Suffolk

FOCUS
This rates a modest renewal. They raced centre-field and the pace was steady.

7121 SILK SERIES LADY RIDERS' H'CAP (PRO-AM LADY RIDERS' RACE) 6f 2y
4:20 (4:22) (Class 3) (0-90,89) 3-Y-O+ **£12,938** (£3,850; £1,924; £962) **Stalls** Centre

Form RPR

6523 **1** **Saluti (IRE)**[13] 6677 5-9-7 **78** GeorgiaCox(3) 1 86
(Paul Midgley) *trckd ldrs centre: hdwy 2f out: rdn to ld appr fnl f: drvn and kpt on wl towards fin* **9/1**

4314 **2** nk **Athollblair Boy (IRE)**[57] 5058 6-9-7 **82** IzzyClifton(7) 11 89
(Nigel Tinkler) *dwlt and towards rr centre: hdwy 1/2-way: rdn along to chse ldrs over 1f out: kpt on strly fnl f (jockey said gelding became upset in the stalls and as a result was slowly away)* **12/1**

2142 **3** 1/2 **Hart Stopper**[27] 6162 5-9-12 **83** (t) MeganNicholls(3) 8 88
(Stuart Williams) *hld up in rr centre: hdwy over 2f out: swtchd lft to inner and rdn over 1f out: styd on strly fnl f* **10/1**

0600 **4** 3/4 **Von Blucher (IRE)**[40] 5692 6-9-1 **76** (p) MissJessicaBedi(7) 2 79
(Rebecca Menzies) *prom: cl up 2f out: sn rdn and ev ch over 1f out: drvn and kpt on same pce fnl f* **14/1**

0020 **5** shd **Savalas (IRE)**[47] 5454 4-10-6 **88** (v[1]) JosephineGordon 3 91
(Kevin Ryan) *racd centre: led: rdn along wl over 1f out: drvn and hdd appr fnl f: grad wknd* **12/1**

2231 **6** shd **Lucky Louie**[42] 5579 6-9-3 **78** (p) EllieMacKenzie(7) 13 80
(Roger Teal) *racd centre: in rr: hdwy 2f out: swtchd lft and rdn wl over 1f out: kpt on wl fnl f: nrst fin (jockey said gelding hung left-handed throughout)* **13/2**[2]

3030 **7** 1 1/2 **Tommy G**[26] 6208 6-9-2 **77** MissShannonWatts(7) 17 75+
(Jim Goldie) *awkward s: stdd and swtchd lft to centre: in rr: hdwy 2f out: n.m.r and swtchd rt towards stands' side over 1f out: sn rdn and kpt on fnl f (jockey said gelding was denied a clear run)* **20/1**

0602 **8** nk **Tomily (IRE)**[6] 6921 5-10-1 **86** (p) JaneElliott(3) 6 83
(David O'Meara) *racd centre: hld up in tch: hdwy 2f out: sn rdn and n.d* **10/1**

6210 **9** 1/2 **Mujassam**[16] 6567 7-9-2 **75** (b) MissBeckySmith(5) 5 70
(Sophie Leech) *chsd ldrs centre: rdn along 2f out: sn drvn and wknd* **33/1**

3006 **10** hd **Normandy Barriere (IRE)**[6] 6916 7-9-11 **84** (p) FayeMcManoman(5) 15 78
(Nigel Tinkler) *hld up in centre: effrt and sme hdwy 2f out: sn rdn and n.d* **15/2**[3]

6260 **11** 1/2 **Lucky Beggar (IRE)**[5] 6972 9-9-2 **65** oh5 RachelRichardson 7 63
(David C Griffiths) *prom centre: rdn along over 2f out: sn wknd (jockey said gelding suffered interference approximately 1 1/2f out)* **50/1**

2106 **12** 1 **Poyle Vinnie**[16] 6565 9-10-0 **89** MissEmilyBullock(7) 10 79
(Ruth Carr) *t.k.h: chsd ldrs centre: rdn along 2f out: sn wknd* **20/1**

66-6 **13** nk **Tangled (IRE)**[19] 6460 4-9-13 **84** GemmaTutty(3) 16 73
(Karen Tutty) *racd towards stands' side: towards rr: rdn along and sme hdwy over 2f out: sn wknd* **12/1**

0035 **14** 1 **Nick Vedder**[23] 6326 5-8-10 **71** (b) RhonaPindar(7) 4 56
(Robyn Brisland) *dwlt: a towards rr* **28/1**

4434 **15** nk **The Armed Man**[13] 6676 6-9-8 **81** PaulaMuir(5) 14 65
(Chris Fairhurst) *racd towards stands' side: in tch: hdwy over 2f out* **10/1**

112 **16** 32 **Drummond Warrior (IRE)**[20] 6413 3-10-3 **87** HollieDoyle 12
(Pam Sly) *racd centre: a in rr: bhd and eased fnl 2f (jockey said gelding lost its action 2f out; vet said gelding finished stiff behind)* **9/2**[1]

1m 13.08s (0.38) **Going Correction** +0.10s/f (Good)
WFA 3 from 4yo+ 2lb **16** Ran SP% **128.2**
Speed ratings (Par 107): **101,100,99,98,98 98,96,96,95,95 94,93,92,91,91 48**
CSF £111.32 CT £1169.92 TOTE £9.70: £2.60, £3.20, £2.20, £4.30; EX 171.90 Trifecta £3570.40.

Owner R Bradley & M Hammond **Bred** J Hanly **Trained** Westow, N Yorks

FOCUS
A useful and open-looking sprint that produced a thrilling finish.

7122 MAGNERS ROSE H'CAP 1m 2f 43y
4:55 (4:55) (Class 2) (0-105,98) 3-Y-0+
£15,562 (£4,660; £2,330; £1,165; £582; £292) Stalls High

Form RPR
1101 1 **Davydenko**33 5963 3-9-7 98 RyanMoore 1 108+
(Sir Michael Stoute) *set stdy pce: jnd and pushed along 3f out: rdn 2f out: edgd rt ent fnl f: kpt on strly* 11/10[1]
0104 2 1 ½ **Certain Lad**18 6513 3-9-7 98 BenCurtis 8 105
(Mick Channon) *trckd ldrs: hdwy 3f out: cl up and rdn along 2f out: drvn over 1f out: kpt on same pce fnl f (jockey said gelding hung left-handed inside the final 2f)* 7/1[3]
2114 3 1 **Nicholas T**33 5930 7-9-11 96 BenRobinson 4 101
(Jim Goldie) *in tch: hdwy on inner 3f out: rdn along 2f out: sn cl up: drvn over 1f out: kpt on same pce (jockey said gelding ran too freely)* 14/1
0000 4 nse **Waarif (IRE)**21 6376 6-9-10 95 DanielTudhope 2 100
(David O'Meara) *trckd ldrs: hdwy and cl up 3f out: chal over 2f out: sn rdn: drvn over 1f out: grad wknd* 11/1
040 5 4 ½ **First Sitting**44 5519 8-9-10 95 JamesDoyle 7 91
(Chris Wall) *hld up in rr: sme hdwy 3f out: rdn along over 2f out: n.d* 9/1
010 6 nk **Desert Wind (IRE)**62 4884 4-9-13 98 StevieDonohoe 6 93
(Ed Vaughan) *hld up in rr: hdwy on outer 4f out: chsd ldng pair 3f out: rdn along over 2f out: sn wknd* 15/2
5044 7 2 **Leroy Leroy**14 6652 3-8-13 90 (p) HollieDoyle 5 81
(Richard Hannon) *t.k.h: hld up towards rr: pushed along wl over 2f out: sn rdn: carried hd high and wknd* 6/1[2]
2m 15.67s (3.37) **Going Correction** +0.15s/f (Good)
WFA 3 from 4yo+ 6lb 7 Ran SP% **111.2**
Speed ratings (Par 109): **92,90,90,89,86 86,84**
CSF £8.72 CT £64.68 TOTE £1.70: £1.20, £3.30; EX 8.60 Trifecta £56.00.
Owner Cheveley Park Stud **Bred** Cheveley Park Stud Ltd **Trained** Newmarket, Suffolk
FOCUS
Add 9yds. No surprise to see the 3yos dominate this handicap. They went a dawdling gallop and the winner made all, so hardly solid form.

7123 DFS H'CAP 7f 6y
5:30 (5:30) (Class 2) (0-100,97) 3-Y-0 £12,450 (£3,728; £1,864; £932) Stalls Centre

Form RPR
2111 1 **Mutamaasik**26 6225 3-9-7 97 JimCrowley 1 107
(Roger Varian) *trckd ldr: hdwy to chal over 2f out: led wl over 1f out: jnd and rdn ent fnl f: sn hdd: rallied wl to ld again nr fin* 5/6[1]
-003 2 shd **The Great Heir (FR)**33 5953 3-8-10 86 ShaneGray 5 95
(Kevin Ryan) *trckd ldng pair: hdwy over 2f out: cl up over 1f out: rdn to ld narrowly ins fnl f: sn drvn: hdd and no ex nr fin* 13/2
4502 3 6 **Archaeology**6 6913 3-8-2 81 SeanDavis(3) 6 74
(Jedd O'Keeffe) *hld up in rr: hdwy over 2f out: rdn to chse ldng pair over 1f out: sn drvn and no imp* 3/1[2]
6-00 4 2 ¾ **Dutch Treat**19 6445 3-9-0 90 OisinMurphy 2 76
(Andrew Balding) *led: pushed along and jnd over 2f out: sn rdn: hdd wl over 1f out: wknd* 6/1[3]
1m 26.79s (0.39) **Going Correction** +0.10s/f (Good) 4 Ran SP% **107.2**
Speed ratings (Par 107): **101,100,94,90**
CSF £6.35 TOTE £1.60; EX 5.60 Trifecta £8.80.
Owner Hamdan Al Maktoum **Bred** Shadwell Estate Company Limited **Trained** Newmarket, Suffolk
FOCUS
An interesting and very useful handicap despite the lack of runners and the front two, who finished clear, rate as improvers.
T/Jkpt: Not Won. T/Plt: £160.30 to a £1 stake. Pool: £166,761.36 - 759.27 winning units T/Qpdt: £45.00 to a £1 stake. Pool: £13,399.45 - 220.21 winning units **Joe Rowntree**

6563 EPSOM (L-H)
Thursday, September 12
OFFICIAL GOING: Good (good to firm in places; watered; 6.3)
Wind: Light, across Weather: Fine

7124 BRITISH STALLION STUDS EBF NOVICE MEDIAN AUCTION STKS (PLUS 10 RACE) 7f 3y
1:40 (1:42) (Class 4) 2-Y-0 £4,787 (£1,424; £711; £355) Stalls Low

Form RPR
62 1 **Afraid Of Nothing**12 6697 2-9-0 0 JasonWatson 6 74+
(Ralph Beckett) *mde all: readily wnt clr over 2f out: in n.d after: v easily* 2/7[1]
0 2 6 **Moondance**42 5588 2-9-0 0 LiamKeniry 4 59+
(Gary Moore) *stdd short of room and flashed tail leaving stalls: hld up in last pair: effrt over 2f out: hdwy to chse clr wnr over 1f out: no imp but kpt on for clr 2nd* 66/1
05 3 3 **Pure Purfection (IRE)**17 6532 2-9-0 0 CharlieBennett 2 51
(Jim Boyle) *chsd wnr for over 1f: effrt over 2f out: no ch to wnr and wl hld 3rd fr over 1f out* 50/1
0 4 hd **Compensate**21 6368 2-9-0 0 WilliamCarver(5) 1 55
(Andrew Balding) *hld up in last pair: effrt 2f out: no imp and hung lft 2f out: swtchd rt and kpt on ins fnl f: no ch w wnr* 12/1[3]
5 5 1 ½ **Buto**28 6106 2-8-12 0 GeorgiaDobie(7) 7 52
(Eve Johnson Houghton) *hld up in midfield: effrt over 2f out: no prog and sn outpcd: wl btn over 1f out* 5/1[2]
0 6 1 ¾ **Scallywagtail (IRE)**23 6300 2-9-5 0 KieranShoemark 3 47
(Gary Moore) *hld up in midfield: effrt towards inner over 2f out: sn outpcd and wl btn over 1f out (jockey said colt was unsuited by the undulating track)* 40/1
0 7 13 **Bonus**13 6669 2-9-5 0 PatCosgrave 5 13
(Jim Boyle) *racd freely: chsd wnr after over 1f out: upsides wnr 5f out tl shkn up 3f out: sn outpcd and wl btn whn lost 2nd over 1f out: bhd and eased ins fnl f (jockey said colt was unsuited by the undulating track)* 16/1
1m 24.76s (1.36) **Going Correction** +0.10s/f (Good) 7 Ran SP% **113.9**
Speed ratings (Par 97): **96,89,85,85,83 81,66**
CSF £37.54 TOTE £1.20: £1.10, £21.80; EX 34.70 Trifecta £139.20.
Owner Qatar Racing Limited **Bred** The Lady Dragon Partnership **Trained** Kimpton, Hants
FOCUS
The rail was moved out in search of fresh ground. Add 20 yards. An uncompetitive juvenile contest.

7125 BACK TO THE 80S NYE PARTY H'CAP 1m 113y
2:15 (2:18) (Class 5) (0-75,77) 4-Y-0+
£4,528 (£1,347; £673; £336; £300; £300) Stalls Low

Form RPR
2361 1 **Kingston Kurrajong**19 6469 6-9-10 77 JasonWatson 1 84
(William Knight) *hld up in tch in midfield: effrt and swtchd rt over 2f out: drvn and clsd to chal over 1f out: led 150yds out: kpt on and a gng to hold on* 7/2[2]
0-00 2 nk **Bombastic (IRE)**79 4226 4-9-2 69 PatCosgrave 8 75+
(Ed de Giles) *stdd and dropped in bhd after s: hld up in rr: effrt and stl plenty to do ent fnl 2f: clsd over 1f out: str run ins fnl f: wnt 2nd cl home: nvr quite getting to wnr* 11/1
-300 3 ½ **Balmoral Castle**70 4561 10-8-11 71 TylerSaunders(7) 3 76
(Jonathan Portman) *chsd ldrs early: sn settled bk and in tch in midfield: effrt over 2f out: clsd over 1f out: chsd ldrs and styd on wl ins fnl f: nvr quite getting to wnr* 25/1
0041 4 nk **Thechildren'strust (IRE)**7 6904 4-9-3 70 KieranShoemark 5 74
(Gary Moore) *taken down early: led: shkn up ent fnl 3f: hrd pressed and u.p over 1f out: hdd ins fnl f: kpt on same pce after: lost 2 pls towards fin* 6/4[1]
-000 5 2 ¼ **Sing Out Loud (IRE)**24 6289 4-9-2 74 ScottMcCullagh(5) 11 73
(Michael Madgwick) *midfield: rdn and outpcd over 2f out: rallied and styd on ins fnl f: no threat to ldrs* 16/1
2631 6 2 ½ **Savitar (IRE)**12 6717 4-8-10 63 CharlieBennett 4 57
(Jim Boyle) *hld up in tch in midfield: effrt over 2f out: no imp: wl hld but plugged on ins fnl f* 8/1
406 7 1 ½ **Kenstone (FR)**96 3575 6-9-0 74 (p) AngusVilliers(7) 10 64
(Adrian Wintle) *t.k.h: chsd ldrs tl wnt 2nd 4f out tl no ex u.p: lost 2nd and hung lft over 1f out: wknd ins fnl f* 16/1
3113 8 2 **La Sioux (IRE)**63 4828 5-9-1 68 BarryMcHugh 2 53
(Richard Fahey) *chsd ldr tl 4f out: no ex u.p 2f out: wknd fnl f (jockey said mare was unsuited by the undulating track)* 7/1[3]
00 9 7 **Rakematiz**38 5747 5-9-2 69 DanielMuscutt 6 38
(Brett Johnson) *in tch in midfield: outpcd u.p over 2f out: wknd over 1f out* 20/1
6-12 10 8 **Canford's Joy (IRE)**38 5760 4-9-0 72 CierenFallon(5) 9 23
(Alexandra Dunn) *hld up in last pair: nvr involved* 14/1
1m 47.15s (0.75) **Going Correction** +0.10s/f (Good) 10 Ran SP% **121.2**
Speed ratings (Par 103): **100,99,99,97 94,93,91,85,78**
CSF £43.77 CT £878.45 TOTE £4.20: £1.50, £3.10, £6.00; EX 50.20 Trifecta £728.20.
Owner Canisbay Bloodstock **Bred** Kingston Park Studs Pty Ltd **Trained** Angmering, W Sussex
FOCUS
Add 28 yards. A fair handicap and the winner rates to his best since spring 2017.

7126 "GROW YOUR BUSINESS" H'CAP 1m 2f 17y
2:50 (2:50) (Class 5) (0-75,75) 3-Y-0
£4,528 (£1,347; £673; £336; £300; £300) Stalls Low

Form RPR
3212 1 **Knowing**23 6323 3-9-7 75 GeorgeWood 2 83+
(James Fanshawe) *trckd ldrs: swtchd out rt and clsd over 2f out: rdn to chal 2f out: led over 1f out: intimidated: edgd lft and hdd ins fnl f: rallied gamely towards fin: led again last stride* 11/4[2]
6031 2 shd **Sootability (IRE)**22 6342 3-9-0 68 BarryMcHugh 5 75
(Richard Fahey) *hld up in tch in last pair: effrt over 2f out: hdwy and chalng u.p over 1f out: led and edgd lft ins fnl f: hdd last stride* 3/1[3]
-601 3 4 ½ **The Dancing Poet**20 6393 3-9-3 71 (p) KieranShoemark 1 75+
(Ed Vaughan) *chsd ldr tl led over 3f out: sn rdn: hdd over 1f out: stl pressing ldrs but one pces whn squeezed for room and hmpd ins fnl f: nt rcvr and coasted home towards fin* 10/1
6221 4 3 ¼ **Isle Of Wolves**16 6568 3-9-2 70 PatCosgrave 6 62
(Jim Boyle) *hld up wl in tch in midfield: effrt over 2f out: drvn to press ldrs 2f out: sn outpcd: wknd fnl f* 9/4[1]
256 5 7 **Gazton**25 6259 3-9-5 73 (h) DougieCostello 3 51
(Ivan Furtado) *taken down early: sn pushed into ld: hdd and rdn over 3f out: outpcd u.p 2f out: wl btn over 1f out* 25/1
0036 6 ½ **Guildhall**27 6165 3-9-5 73 (b) JasonWatson 4 50
(Ralph Beckett) *hld up in last pair: effrt and drifted rt over 2f out: sn outpcd and no ch over 1f out (jockey said gelding suffered from post-race ataxia)* 5/1
2m 9.15s (-0.85) **Going Correction** +0.10s/f (Good) 6 Ran SP% **112.0**
Speed ratings (Par 101): **107,106,103,100,95 94**
CSF £11.36 TOTE £3.10: £1.80, £2.00; EX 13.10 Trifecta £56.70.
Owner Gary Marney **Bred** Mr & Mrs G Marney **Trained** Newmarket, Suffolk
■ Stewards' Enquiry : Barry McHugh two-day ban: careless riding (26-27 Sep)
FOCUS
Add 28 yards. Four of the six runners had recent winning form, so it's wise to suggest this is fair form for the grade. The first two pulled clear and the winner progressed again.

7127 JUMP JOCKEYS' DERBY H'CAP 1m 4f 6y
3:25 (3:26) (Class 4) (0-85,83) 4-Y-0+
£7,762 (£2,310; £1,154; £577; £300; £300) Stalls Centre

Form RPR
1162 1 **Berrahri (IRE)**19 6448 8-11-9 82 JoeyHaynes 3 89
(John Best) *mde all: rdn over 3f out: 2 l clr over 1f out: kpt on and pushed out wl ins fnl f: eased cl home* 11/2
1444 2 1 **Rydan (IRE)**19 6448 8-11-4 77 (v) JoshuaMoore 2 82
(Gary Moore) *in tch in midfield: clsd and n.m.r over 2f out: drvn over 1f out: chsd wnr ins fnl f: kpt on but nvr enough pce to get on terms* 12/1
2361 3 1 **C'Est No Mour (GER)**17 6535 6-11-6 79 (v) LeightonAspell 5 82
(Peter Hedger) *s.i.s: hld up in rr: clsd on inner over 2f out: swtchd out rt and chsd wnr over 1f out: kpt on but no real imp: lost 2nd ins fnl f* 11/4[2]
6410 4 3 **Delph Crescent (IRE)**13 6686 4-11-2 75 (v) BrianHughes 6 74
(Richard Fahey) *hld up in tch in last pair: clsd to press ldrs but edgd lft down camber 2f out: effrt over 1f out: unable qck u.p and wknd ins fnl f* 9/1
3003 5 4 **Mandalayan (IRE)**27 6156 4-11-10 83 HarryBannister 1 75
(Jonathan Portman) *chsd ldrs: effrt to chse wnr over 2f out tl over 1f out: sn outpcd and wknd ins fnl f* 4/1[3]
2312 6 6 **Allegiant (USA)**17 6535 4-11-9 82 JackQuinlan 7 65
(Stuart Williams) *chsd wnr tl over 8f out: lost pl u.p ent fnl 2f: sn wknd and bhd ins fnl f (trainer's rep said gelding ran flat)* 9/4[1]

1304 7 16 **Gendarme (IRE)**[10] 6804 4-11-2 **75**....................(b) AdamWedge 4 32
(Alexandra Dunn) *chsd ldrs: wnt 2nd over 8f out tl over 2f out: sn lost pl and bhd* **28/1**

2m 42.42s (1.62) **Going Correction** +0.10s/f (Good) 7 Ran SP% **114.0**
Speed ratings (Par 105): **98,97,96,94,92 88,77**
CSF £64.96 TOTE £5.40: £2.20, £5.00; EX 62.70 Trifecta £230.30.
Owner White Turf Racing UK **Bred** Kilnamoragh Stud **Trained** Oad Street, Kent

FOCUS
Add 28 yards. Many of these had shown a liking for this track in the past.

7128 KOVARA KLASSIC H'CAP 7f 3y
3:55 (3:55) (Class 4) (0-80,82) 3-Y-0+
£7,762 (£2,310; £1,154; £577; £300; £300) **Stalls** Low

Form RPR
3032 1 **Casement (IRE)**[35] 5863 5-8-13 **78**.................... MarkCrehan(7) 1 86
(Michael Appleby) *mounted in the chute and taken down early: mde all: pushed along over 2f out: rdn ins fnl f: a jst holding on* **9/2**[1]
655 2 hd **Buckingham (IRE)**[19] 6440 3-8-12 **81**.................... GeorgiaDobie(7) 7 86
(Eve Johnson Houghton) *hld up in last trio: hdwy u.p over 1f out: str run ins fnl f: wnt 2nd towards fin: nt quite rch wnr* **11/1**
3133 3 1 **Luis Vaz De Torres (IRE)**[15] 6588 7-9-7 **79**.................... BarryMcHugh 8 83
(Richard Fahey) *t.k.h: chsd ldng trio: effrt to chse wnr 2f out: edgd u.p ins fnl f: kpt on but nvr quite getting on terms: lost 2nd towards fin* **11/2**[3]
116 4 3 1/4 **Big Storm Coming**[47] 5416 9-9-5 **82**.................... CierenFallon(5) 5 78
(John Quinn) *led: sn hdd and chsd wnr: edgd rt u.p and lost 2nd 2f out: no ex and wknd ins fnl f* **5/1**[2]
0021 5 1 1/2 **Indian Viceroy**[22] 6350 3-9-2 **78**.................... JasonWatson 6 67
(Hughie Morrison) *sn niggled along in midfield: no imp u.p over 1f out: kpt on same pce ins fnl f* **9/2**[1]
6430 6 3 1/2 **Poetic Force (IRE)**[12] 6729 5-9-6 **78**....................(t) JoeyHaynes 3 60
(Tony Carroll) *s.i.s: a towards rr: nvr involved (ran without its left hind shoe)* **5/1**[2]
2100 7 2 1/4 **Itizzit**[43] 5545 3-9-3 **79**.................... CharlieBennett 2 53
(Hughie Morrison) *chsd ldrs: effrt ent fnl 2f: unable qck u.p and btn over 1f out: sn wknd* **12/1**
0250 8 1 3/4 **Mamillius**[16] 6567 6-9-2 **79**.................... ScottMcCullagh(5) 4 50
(George Baker) *v.s.a: a towards rr (jockey said gelding was very slowly away)* **7/1**

1m 23.46s (0.06) **Going Correction** +0.10s/f (Good)
WFA 3 from 5yo+ 4lb 8 Ran SP% **113.6**
Speed ratings (Par 105): **103,102,101,97,96 92,89,87**
CSF £52.50 CT £278.08 TOTE £4.10: £1.50, £4.30, £2.00; EX 66.00 Trifecta £282.80.
Owner On The Case Partnership **Bred** Mrs Clodagh McStay **Trained** Oakham, Rutland

FOCUS
Add 20 yards. A competitive handicap and a small pb from the front-running winner.

7129 NEWTON WOOD H'CAP 1m 113y
4:30 (4:31) (Class 5) (0-75,77) 3-Y-0
£4,528 (£1,347; £673; £336; £300; £300) **Stalls** Low

Form RPR
2113 1 **Bring Us Paradise**[33] 5947 3-8-12 **71**.................... CierenFallon(5) 8 86+
(Tony Carroll) *hld up in tch in midfield: effrt and hdwy to ld jst over 2f out: sn clr and in command over 1f out: heavily eased towards fin: v easily* **15/8**[1]
-064 2 4 1/2 **Thorn**[12] 6730 3-9-0 **68**....................(h) LiamKeniry 7 70
(Peter Hiatt) *hld up in tch in midfield: effrt over 2f out: rdn to chse clr wnr jst over 1f out: kpt on for clr 2nd: no ch w wnr* **14/1**
6345 3 4 **Memphis Bleek**[33] 5937 3-9-2 **75**....................(b[1]) WilliamCarver(5) 1 68
(Ivan Furtado) *in tch in midfield: effrt to chse ldrs and swtchd lft 2f out: sn outpcd and no ch w wnr: kpt on same pce after* **4/1**[2]
1504 4 3/4 **Black Medick**[16] 6567 3-9-2 **70**.................... JasonWatson 2 61
(Laura Mongan) *chsd ldrs: effrt and led briefly over 2f out: unable to match pce of wnr in 2nd out: lost 2nd ent fnl f: wknd* **8/1**
6-20 5 nk **Ambersand (IRE)**[75] 4358 3-8-12 **66**.................... BarryMcHugh 3 56
(Richard Fahey) *hld up in rr: effrt and hung lft over 2f out: nvr threatened to get on terms: stl hanging and wl hld ins fnl f (trainer's rep said filly was unsuited by the undulating track)* **14/1**
5230 6 1 3/4 **Welcoming (FR)**[33] 5970 3-9-9 **77**.................... JoeFanning 6 63
(Mark Johnston) *chsd ldr: effrt and ev ch briefly over 2f out: sn outpcd and wl hld over 1f out: wknd ins fnl f* **9/2**[3]
6123 7 1 3/4 **Conspiritor**[16] 6558 3-9-3 **71**.................... KieranShoemark 4 53
(Charles Hills) *hld up in tch in last trio: effrt and hung lft over 2f out: no prog and wl btn whn nt clr run and hmpd ins fnl f (trainer's rep said gelding was unsuited by the undulating track)* **15/2**
00 8 10 **Gennaro (IRE)**[33] 5975 3-8-4 **61** oh1....................(t) GabrieleMalune(3) 5 20
(Ivan Furtado) *taken down early: led tl rdn and hdd over 2f out: sn dropped out and wl bhd ins fnl f (jockey said gelding stopped quickly)* **20/1**

1m 45.59s (-0.81) **Going Correction** +0.10s/f (Good) 8 Ran SP% **113.9**
Speed ratings (Par 101): **107,103,99,98,98 96,95,86**
CSF £30.51 CT £95.74 TOTE £2.40: £1.10, £4.80, £1.30; EX 29.30 Trifecta £139.90.
Owner D Boocock **Bred** Boocock Trading Ltd **Trained** Cropthorne, Worcs

FOCUS
Add 28 yards. This handicap was turned into a procession by the heavily punted favourite who posted a clear pb.

7130 SPECTACULAR CHRISTMAS PARTIES AT EPSOM DOWNS H'CAP 6f 3y
5:05 (5:05) (Class 5) (0-75,74) 3-Y-0+
£4,528 (£1,347; £673; £336; £300; £300) **Stalls** High

Form RPR
3134 1 **Cent Flying**[6] 6916 4-9-4 **70**....................(t) JasonWatson 8 78
(William Muir) *hld up in last trio: effrt over 2f out: hdwy u.p over 1f out: led wl ins fnl f: r.o wl* **7/2**[1]
4532 2 1/2 **Restless Rose**[14] 6631 4-9-8 **74**.................... JoeFanning 6 80
(Stuart Williams) *chsd ldrs: effrt over 2f out: clsd u.p over 1f out: ev ch ins fnl f: kpt on wl but jst hld cl home* **4/1**[2]
0531 3 1/2 **Wiley Post**[10] 6798 6-9-3 **74**....................(b) ScottMcCullagh(5) 3 79
(Tony Carroll) *hld up in last trio: short of room and hmpd over 4f out: effrt 2f out: str run u.p ins fnl f: wnt 3rd last stride: nt quite rch ldrs* **9/2**[3]
3030 4 nk **Highland Acclaim (IRE)**[9] 6826 8-9-7 **73**....................(p) KieranShoemark 9 77
(David O'Meara) *led: rdn 2f out: kpt on wl u.p: hdd and no ex wl ins fnl f* **6/1**

0024 5 3/4 **Swanton Blue (IRE)**[36] 5799 6-8-6 **63**.................... TobyEley(5) 7 64
(Ed de Giles) *midfield: effrt jst over 2f out: hung lft over 1f out: swtchd rt and kpt on towards fin: nvr getting to ldrs (jockey said gelding hung left-handed)* **12/1**
3635 6 1/2 **Perfect Symphony (IRE)**[36] 5799 5-8-9 **61**.................... CharlieBennett 1 61
(Mark Pattinson) *chsd ldr for over 1f out: effrt to chse ldr again over 2f out tl ins fnl f: no ex and wknd towards fin* **16/1**
6051 7 1/2 **The Lamplighter (FR)**[20] 6401 4-9-0 **71**....................(tp) CierenFallon(5) 4 76+
(George Baker) *hld up in tch in midfield: effrt ent fnl 2f: carried lft and clsd over 1f out: chsd ldrs whn nt clr run ins fnl f: nowhere to go and forced to ease wl ins fnl f (jockey said gelding was denied a clear run for a sustained period)* **5/1**
3450 8 8 **Spanish Star (IRE)**[13] 6668 4-9-6 **72**.................... LiamKeniry 2 45
(Patrick Chamings) *hld up in last trio: short of room and hmpd over 4f out: shkn up 2f out: sn outpcd and wl btn fnl f (jockey said gelding ran too free)* **14/1**
0152 9 8 **Zac Brown (IRE)**[18] 6510 8-9-6 **72**....................(t) BarryMcHugh 5 19
(Charlie Wallis) *hood off sltly late: chsd ldrs tl 2nd over 4f out tl over 2f out: sn dropped out: wl bhd ins fnl f (jockey was slow to remove blindfold)* **14/1**

1m 9.94s (0.04) **Going Correction** +0.10s/f (Good) 9 Ran SP% **118.3**
Speed ratings (Par 103): **103,102,101,101,100 99,98,88,77**
CSF £18.04 CT £65.00 TOTE £4.30: £1.30, £1.60, £1.90; EX 19.90 Trifecta £125.30.
Owner Clarke, Edginton, Niven **Bred** Frank Brady **Trained** Lambourn, Berks
■ Stewards' Enquiry : Jason Watson two-day ban: used whip above permitted level (Sep 26-27)

FOCUS
Add 12 yards. This looked competitive beforehand and the first five finished in a bit of a heap.
T/Plt: £262.90 to a £1 stake. Pool: £45,286.30 - 125.72 winning units T/Qpdt: £49.80 to a £1 stake. Pool: £4,614.41 - 68.44 winning units **Steve Payne**

7131 - 7135a (Foreign Racing) - See Raceform Interactive

7005
LONGCHAMP (R-H)
Thursday, September 12

OFFICIAL GOING: Turf: good

7136a PRIX VICTORIA BEACHCOMBER RESORT & SPA (CLAIMER) (4YO+) (NEW COURSE: 2ND POST) (TURF) 7f
3:35 4-Y-0+ **£8,558** (£3,423; £2,567; £1,711; £855)

RPR
1 **Zock (FR)**[20] 5-9-1 0....................(b) MaximeGuyon 5 79
(F Rossi, France) **19/5**[2]
2 3 **Mister Magic (IRE)**[18] 4-9-4 0.................... StephanePasquier 6 74
(Gianluca Bietolini, France) **9/1**
3 3/4 **Cloud Dancer (FR)**[20] 4-8-11 0.................... IoritzMendizabal 14 65
(Mario Hofer, Germany) **14/1**
4 1 1/4 **Constantino (IRE)**[28] 6-9-2 0....................(p) ChristopheSoumillon 13 67
(F Vermeulen, France) **11/5**[1]
5 shd **O'Goshi (FR)**[224] 5-9-1 0.................... ClementGuitraud(5) 12 70
(J Boisnard, France) **18/1**
6 3/4 **Kensai (FR)**[16] 5-8-11 0....................(p) FabriceVeron 4 59
(Laurent Loisel, France) **20/1**
7 snk **Daimyo**[124] 4-9-4 0.................... Pierre-CharlesBoudot 8 66
(F Vermeulen, France) **9/1**
8 3/4 **Lefortovo (FR)**[39] 5715 6-9-1 0.................... MlleCoraliePacaut(3) 11 64
(Jo Hughes, France) *settled in midfield: pushed along over 2f out: rdn w limited rspnse over 1f out: no ex ins fnl f* **39/1**
9 hd **Overdose D'Oroux (FR)**[492] 4-9-1 0.................... TheoBachelot 3 60
(Carmen Bocskai, Germany) **23/1**
10 hd **Inseo (FR)**[16] 8-9-1 0....................(p) HugoJourniac 1 60
(M Boutin, France) **31/1**
11 2 1/2 **Gourel (FR)**[49] 5-9-4 0.................... EddyHardouin 2 56
(Mme M Bollack-Badel, France) **61/10**[3]
12 2 1/2 **Bibi Voice (FR)**[115] 4-8-5 0.................... MlleMickaelleMichel(3) 9 39
(N Caullery, France) **27/1**
13 2 **Copper Baked (FR)**[211] 5-8-6 0.................... MlleSophieTison(9) 10 41
(L Rovisse, France) **25/1**
14 1 1/2 **Parinacota (FR)**[416] 5-8-8 0....................(b) StephaneBreux 7 30
(Stephanie Gachelin, France) **119/1**

1m 21.79s (1.09) 14 Ran SP% **120.9**
PARI-MUTUEL (all including 1 euro stake): WIN 4.80; PLACE 2.40, 3.50, 3.50; DF 20.70.
Owner Mme Janina Burger **Bred** Jean-Claude Seroul **Trained** France

7137a PRIX DES TOURELLES - FONDS EUROPEEN DE L'ELEVAGE (LISTED RACE) (3YO+ FILLIES & MARES) (GRANDE CRS) 1m 4f
4:05 3-Y-0+ **£23,423** (£9,369; £7,027; £4,684; £2,342)

RPR
1 **Muette**[27] 3-8-10 0.................... MaximeGuyon 2 99
(A Fabre, France) **49/10**[2]
2 snk **Golden Box (USA)**[32] 6003 3-8-11 0 ow1.......... ChristopheSoumillon 8 100
(A De Royer-Dupre, France) **11/10**[1]
3 3/4 **Marouche (FR)**[45] 4-9-4 0.................... MickaelBerto 10 96
(A De Royer-Dupre, France) **19/1**
4 hd **River On The Hills (FR)**[45] 5510 5-9-4 0.................... GregoryBenoist 1 96
(Mme Pia Brandt, France) **12/1**
5 1 1/4 **Blue Gardenia (IRE)**[19] 6446 3-8-10 0....................(p) MickaelBarzalona 3 95
(David O'Meara) *midfield early: rowed along and hdwy 2f out: rdn over 1f out: kpt on same pce fnl f* **5/1**[3]
6 nse **Eleni (FR)**[32] 4-9-4.................... TheoBachelot 9 94
(Waldemar Hickst, Germany) **18/1**
7 snk **Mannaal (IRE)**[28] 6124 3-8-10 0.................... StephanePasquier 5 95
(Simon Crisford) *trckd ldr on outer: pushed along to chal 2f out: rdn and limited rspnse over 1f out: no ex ins fnl f* **54/10**
8 3 1/2 **Manorah (IRE)**[24] 6280 3-8-10 0.................... JackMitchell 4 89
(Roger Varian) *settled bhd ldr in 3rd: rdn along 2f out: drvn and wknd over 1f out: eased ins fnl f* **24/1**

2m 35.01s (4.61)
WFA 3 from 4yo+ 8lb 8 Ran SP% **118.8**
PARI-MUTUEL (all including 1 euro stake): WIN 5.90; PLACE 1.60, 1.20, 2.50; DF 5.40.
Owner Wertheimer & Frere **Bred** Wertheimer & Frere **Trained** Chantilly, France

7138a PRIX DU PAVILLON DES ANGLAIS (H'CAP) (3YO) (MOYENNE COURSE) (TURF) 1m
5:05 3-Y-O £8,108 (£3,243; £2,432; £1,621; £810)

RPR

1 **Millie Lily (IRE)**27 3-9-3 0 MickaelBarzalona 8 72
(R Le Gal, France) 42/10[2]
2 hd **Come Say Hi (FR)**30 3-9-4 0 (p) HugoJourniac 11 72
(M Nigge, France) 14/1
3 2 **Mister Charlie (FR)**23 3-9-5 0 MickaelBerto 12 69
(A Le Duff, France) 16/1
4 3/4 **Soho Vicky (IRE)**41 3-9-5 0 JulienGuillochon 2 67
(H-A Pantall, France) 73/10
5 1 1/4 **Baylagan (FR)**12 3-8-13 0 MlleAudeDuporte(6) 7 64
(Mme G Rarick, France) 39/10[1]
6 2 **Jojo (IRE)**30 6063 3-9-3 0 MlleCoraliePacaut(3) 6 61
(Jo Hughes, France) *wl into stride: led: jnd 4f out: rdn along 2f out: drvn w limited rspnse over 1f out: wknd ins fnl f* 14/1
7 snk **Luce Des Aigles (FR)**23 3-8-11 0 MlleFriedaValleSkar(7) 9 58
(Mme C Barande-Barbe, France) 10/1
8 1 3/4 **Mazeltof (FR)**12 3-9-1 0 RonanThomas 10 51
(J Phelippon, France) 10/1
9 nk **La Mirada (FR)**12 3-8-8 0 (p) EddyHardouin 4 43
(Mlle V Dissaux, France) 37/1
10 hd **Lady Walli (FR)**49 3-9-4 0 StephanePasquier 1 53
(Gianluca Bietolini, France) 9/1
11 1 1/4 **Mr Bold (FR)**36 3-9-3 0 FabriceVeron 3 49
(O Trigodet, France) 61/10[3]
12 4 **Montfiquet (FR)**44 5538 3-9-5 0 SylvainRuis 5 42
(N Caullery, France) 23/1

1m 42.53s (4.13) **12 Ran SP% 120.0**
PARI-MUTUEL (all including 1 euro stake): WIN 5.20; PLACE 2.20, 4.60, 5.50; DF 43.20.
Owner Daniel Dumoulin **Bred** G.B. Partnership **Trained** France

6710 CHESTER (L-H)
Friday, September 13

OFFICIAL GOING: Good (good to soft in places; 7.3)
Wind: light across Weather: sunny

7139 CHESTER BET SUPPORTING BRITISH STALLIONS EBF NOVICE STKS (PLUS 10 RACE) (C&G) 7f 127y
1:50 (1:52) (Class 4) 2-Y-O £5,851 (£1,752; £876; £438) Stalls Low

Form RPR

312 1 **Breathalyze (FR)**13 6710 2-9-6 88 RichardKingscote 3 87
(Tom Dascombe) *trckd ldr: pushed along over 2f out: drvn ins fnl f: kpt on to ld nr fin* 7/4[2]
31 2 nk **Cognac (IRE)**16 6606 2-9-6 0 FrannyNorton 1 86
(Mark Johnston) *led: pushed along over 1f out: rdn and 2 l up 1f out: drvn and reduced advantage fnl 50yds: hdd nr fin* 1/1[1]
2132 3 3 3/4 **The New Marwan**40 5704 2-9-6 81 PaulHanagan 4 77
(Richard Fahey) *dwlt sltly: hld up in tch: rdn 2f out: no imp in 3rd fnl f* 7/1[3]
05 4 1/2 **Wild Hero (IRE)**43 5572 2-9-0 0 DavidProbert 2 70
(Andrew Balding) *trckd ldr on inner: rdn and bit outpcd 2f out: dropped to 4th fnl f* 9/1

1m 33.59s (-2.11) **Going Correction** -0.15s/f (Firm) **4 Ran SP% 108.9**
Speed ratings (Par 97): **104,103,99,99**
CSF £3.92 TOTE £2.50; EX 3.40 Trifecta £3.70.
Owner More Turf Racing **Bred** Bloodstock Agency Ltd **Trained** Malpas, Cheshire

FOCUS
Drying ground, and the opener was run in a time only 2.39sec slower than standard. All race distances as advertised. The first three in this decent novice stakes met in a similar event over 7f here a month ago.

7140 MBNA NURSERY H'CAP 7f 1y
2:25 (2:26) (Class 4) (0-85,86) 2-Y-O £6,080 (£1,809; £904; £452; £300; £300) Stalls Low

Form RPR

631 1 **Powertrain (IRE)**27 6219 2-9-7 81 BenCurtis 1 86+
(Hugo Palmer) *trckd ldrs on inner: pushed along and short of room over 1f out tl jst ins fnl f: rdn and kpt on wl: led 25yds out: shade cosily* 5/4[1]
3102 2 nk **Know No Limits (IRE)**13 6713 2-9-12 86 RichardKingscote 3 87
(Tom Dascombe) *led: rdn and pressed over 1f out: drvn ins fnl f: kpt on but hdd 25yds out* 3/1[2]
3010 3 nk **Mischief Star**15 6625 2-9-0 74 ShaneGray 4 74
(David O'Meara) *prom: rdn 2f out: chal whn bmpd sltly by rival appr fnl f: kpt on* 20/1
3303 4 4 1/2 **Little Ted**15 6625 2-8-2 62 (b[1]) JamesSullivan 11 51+
(Tim Easterby) *hld up: rdn along 2f out: kpt on fnl f: wnt modest 4th post: nvr trbld ldrs* 20/1
4252 5 shd **Lexi The One (IRE)**20 6458 2-8-10 70 PaulHanagan 6 58
(Richard Fahey) *chsd ldrs: rdn along over 2f out: wknd ins fnl f: lost 4th post* 12/1
1340 6 2 3/4 **Ambyfaeirvine (IRE)**22 6372 2-8-10 70 (b[1]) JasonHart 2 51
(Ivan Furtado) *midfield on inner: rdn along over 2f out: drvn over 1f out: no imp* 9/1
332 7 nk **Embolden (IRE)**16 6606 2-9-6 80 (v[1]) TonyHamilton 9 60+
(Richard Fahey) *hld up: minor late hdwy: nvr involved* 13/2[3]
0422 8 1 1/4 **We Owen A Dragon**15 6625 2-8-8 68 (p[1]) FrannyNorton 10 45
(Tom Dascombe) *midfield: rdn over 2f out: wknd ins fnl f* 14/1
2005 9 7 **Iva Reflection (IRE)**62 4938 2-9-1 78 (p) JaneElliott(3) 7 37+
(Tom Dascombe) *dwlt and swtchd lft to rail: a in rr* 16/1
0420 10 1/2 **Bob's Oss (IRE)**14 6653 2-8-1 61 CamHardie 5 19+
(Alan Berry) *hld up in midfield: rdn along 3f out: sn wknd* 50/1

1m 26.59s (-0.91) **Going Correction** -0.15s/f (Firm) **10 Ran SP% 124.5**
Speed ratings (Par 97): **99,98,98,93,93 89,89,88,80,79**
CSF £5.22 CT £53.74 TOTE £1.90: £1.10, £1.10, £5.10; EX 6.90 Trifecta £67.30.
Owner Isa Salman **Bred** Coolmore **Trained** Newmarket, Suffolk

FOCUS
Not many got into this nursery, in which the first three, all drawn low, finished clear.

7141 DEEPBRIDGE CAPITAL H'CAP 1m 2f 70y
3:00 (3:01) (Class 4) (0-85,81) 3-Y-O £6,080 (£1,809; £904; £452; £300; £300) Stalls High

Form RPR

4231 1 **Noble Prospector (IRE)**13 6734 3-9-4 81 MeganNicholls(3) 3 92+
(Richard Fahey) *hld up in tch on inner: swtchd rt to outer over 1f out: pushed along and qcknd up wl to ld ins fnl f: kpt on wl pushed out: comf* 2/1[1]
031 2 2 **Torochica**55 5193 3-9-5 79 KierenFox 1 85
(John Best) *trckd ldrs on inner: rdn along over 1f out: swtchd rt and briefly bit tight for room appr fnl f: styd on to go 2nd fnl 75yds (jockey said filly was denied a clear run approaching the home turn; vet said filly had lost its right-hind shoe)* 9/4[2]
164 3 nk **Trinity Lake**41 5690 3-9-5 79 DavidNolan 5 84
(Declan Carroll) *in tch: rdn along to chse ldrs 2f out: kpt on fnl f* 8/1
-240 4 1 1/4 **Top Power (FR)**42 5614 3-9-6 80 DavidProbert 7 82
(Andrew Balding) *prom: racd quite keenly: rdn along to chal strly 2f out: no ex ins fnl f* 8/1
1234 5 3/4 **Conundrum**16 6589 3-9-2 76 JackGarritty 2 77
(Jedd O'Keeffe) *led: rdn and strly pressed 2f out: hdd ins fnl f: no ex* 7/2[3]
5264 6 6 **Madeeh**18 6541 3-8-10 77 (t) NickBarratt-Atkin(7) 6 66
(Philip Kirby) *hld up in tch: rdn over 2f out: wknd over 1f out* 25/1
400 7 13 **Viking Prince (IRE)**13 6732 3-8-2 62 oh3 PaddyMathers 4 25
(Ian Williams) *s.i.s: rcvrd to sn chse ldrs on outer: rdn over 2f out: wknd over 1f out* 33/1
0000 8 10 **Hilbre Lake (USA)**19 6505 3-7-9 62 oh17 GavinAshton(7) 8 5
(Lisa Williamson) *hld up: racd keenly: wknd and bhd fnl 2f* 125/1

2m 12.82s (-1.48) **Going Correction** -0.15s/f (Firm) **8 Ran SP% 116.1**
Speed ratings (Par 103): **99,97,97,96,95 90,80,72**
CSF £6.82 CT £28.03 TOTE £2.60: £1.50, £1.10, £2.10; EX 7.00 Trifecta £31.60.
Owner Mr And Mrs J D Cotton **Bred** Allevamento Ficomontanino Srl **Trained** Musley Bank, N Yorks

FOCUS
Not a strong race for the grade, this was run at what looked an ordinary gallop. The second confirmed her novice form, while the fourth has been rated close to form.

7142 ESL GROUP H'CAP 7f 1y
3:30 (3:33) (Class 3) (0-90,91) 3-Y-O+ £7,470 (£2,236; £1,118; £559; £279; £140) Stalls Low

Form RPR

0605 1 **Sir Maximilian (IRE)**21 6404 10-9-12 91 BenCurtis 3 101
(Ian Williams) *trckd ldrs: pushed along 3f out: rdn over 1f out: kpt on to ld 50yds out: pushed out* 8/1
0200 2 3/4 **Gabrial The Saint (IRE)**13 6714 4-9-8 87 PaulHanagan 5 94
(Richard Fahey) *half-rrd s but sn prom: rdn 2f out: drvn to ld ins fnl f: hdd 50yds out: one pce* 6/1[2]
2410 3 hd **Revich (IRE)**44 5546 3-9-2 88 MeganNicholls(3) 4 92+
(Richard Spencer) *hld up in midfield: pushed along over 2f out: swtchd rt to outer over 1f out: rdn and kpt on wl* 8/1
1020 4 1 1/4 **Arcanada (IRE)**13 6711 6-9-7 86 (p) RichardKingscote 2 89
(Tom Dascombe) *led: rdn 2f out: hdd ins fnl f: sn no ex* 9/2[1]
1046 5 1 3/4 **Penwortham (IRE)**13 6711 6-9-4 83 TonyHamilton 9 81
(Richard Fahey) *midfield on inner: rdn along 2f out: drvn appr fnl f: kpt on* 7/1[3]
6603 6 1 **Whitefountainfairy (IRE)**7 6922 4-9-5 84 DavidProbert 12 80
(Andrew Balding) *dwlt and swtchd lft to rail: hld up: rdn along 2f out: angled rt over 1f out: kpt on fnl f (trainer said filly missed the break)* 7/1[3]
4016 7 3/4 **Moraawed**20 6451 3-9-8 91 CharlieBennett 10 83
(Roger Varian) *hld up in rr: pushed along over 2f out: rdn over 1f out: swtchd rt ins fnl f: kpt on: nrst fin* 14/1
3636 8 hd **Dragons Tail (IRE)**14 6686 4-8-12 80 (p) JaneElliott(3) 6 73
(Tom Dascombe) *midfield: rdn over 2f out: no imp* 14/1
4011 9 1 3/4 **International Man**15 6626 4-8-11 79 (b) SeanDavis(3) 1 67
(Richard Fahey) *trckd ldrs on inner: rdn over 2f out: wknd ins fnl f (vet said a post-race examination revealed the gelding to be lame on its left-hind)* 6/1[2]
0304 10 2 1/2 **Scottish Summit (IRE)**20 6460 6-9-0 79 SamJames 11 61
(Geoffrey Harker) *trckd ldrs on outer: rdn over 2f out: wknd fnl f (starter reported that the gelding was reluctant to enter the stalls; trainer was informed that the gelding could not run until the day after passing a stalls test)* 25/1
5206 11 1 1/4 **Candelisa (IRE)**13 6700 6-8-9 79 (t) ThomasGreatrex(5) 13 57
(David Loughnane) *hld up in midfield on outer: sn rdn along: wknd 2f out (jockey said gelding was never travelling)* 16/1
-255 12 1/2 **Wufud**28 6155 4-9-3 82 (t) KieranShoemark 8 59
(Charles Hills) *hld up in midfield: rdn over 2f out: wknd over 1f out* 12/1

1m 25.38s (-2.12) **Going Correction** -0.15s/f (Firm)
WFA 3 from 4yo+ 4lb **12 Ran SP% 124.7**
Speed ratings (Par 107): **106,105,104,103,101 100,99,99,97,94 92,92**
CSF £58.49 CT £410.58 TOTE £9.30: £2.70, £2.30, £3.10; EX 57.40 Trifecta £384.90.
Owner Paul Wildes **Bred** Holborn Trust Co **Trained** Portway, Worcs

FOCUS
Decent handicap form. The first four home all came from the lowest five stalls. The winner has been rated back to the level of his Doncaster win in May, with the race rated around the second.

7143 HOMESERVE NOVICE STKS 1m 2f 70y
4:05 (4:05) (Class 4) 3-Y-O+ £5,851 (£1,752; £876; £438; £219; £109) Stalls High

Form RPR

34 1 **Invictus Spirit**42 5634 3-9-1 0 FrannyNorton 6 93+
(Sir Michael Stoute) *trckd ldrs: pushed along whn hmpd over 2f out: briefly outpcd: rdn and hdwy appr fnl f: led 110yds out: styd on wl: wnt wrong after line* 3/1[3]
62 2 2 1/2 **Mayne (IRE)**24 6316 3-9-1 0 DavidProbert 1 83
(Andrew Balding) *led: pressed tl 5f out: rdn over 2f out: drvn appr fnl f: hdd 110yds out: no ex* 5/2[2]
- 3 6 **Plantadream** 4-9-7 0 KierenFox 5 70
(John Best) *dwlt: hld up in tch: rdn along and hdwy on outside 3f out: chal briefly 2f out: wknd appr fnl f (jockey said gelding hung both ways and raced greenly throughout)* 50/1

323 **4** ½ **Two Bids**[39] 5742 3-9-1 80................................ PaulHanagan 2 70
(William Haggas) *pressed ldr: racd keenly: dropped bk to trck ldr 5f out: rdn along whn briefly short of room on inner over 1f out: wknd fnl f (jockey said colt hung left-handed inside the final 3f)* **1/1**[1]

00 **5** 3¼ **Ho Whole Dream (IRE)**[13] 6732 3-8-10 0................ GerO'Neill(5) 4 64?
(Michael Easterby) *hld up in rr: minor late hdwy: nvr a threat* **100/1**

3 **6** 18 **Diaboleo (FR)**[134] 3-9-1 0.............................. RichardKingscote 3 28
(Ian Williams) *hld up in tch: rdn along over 3f out: sn wknd* **12/1**

2m 10.99s (-3.31) **Going Correction** -0.15s/f (Firm) **6** Ran SP% **114.2**
WFA 3 from 4yo 6lb
Speed ratings (Par 105): **107,105,100,99,97 82**
CSF £11.24 TOTE £3.50: £1.20, £1.90; EX 12.90 Trifecta £125.90.
Owner The Queen **Bred** The Queen **Trained** Newmarket, Suffolk

FOCUS
There was an unfortunate aftermath to this decent novice event, which saw a contested lead until halfway. Muddling form, but the second has been rated close to his latest for now.

7144 DIB CONNECT H'CAP — 1m 4f 63y
4:40 (4:40) (Class 3) (0-95,92) 3-Y-O+ **£7,470** (£2,236; £1,118; £559) **Stalls** Low

Form RPR

1311 **1** **Hereby (IRE)**[26] 6255 3-8-7 79............................ PaulHanagan 1 91+
(Ralph Beckett) *mde all: pushed clr fr over 1f out: easily* **1/1**[1]

2254 **2** 4 **Gabrial The One (IRE)**[13] 6716 3-8-4 79................ SeanDavis(3) 2 83
(Richard Fahey) *trckd ldr: rdn over 2f out: outpcd in 2nd over 1f out: plugged on ins fnl f* **7/2**[3]

0421 **3** 1¼ **Gossip Column (IRE)**[30] 6067 4-9-11 89.................... BenCurtis 3 91
(Ian Williams) *trckd ldr: rdn over 2f out: outpcd and btn over 1f out* **2/1**[2]

6505 **4** ½ **Super Kid**[6] 6981 7-8-12 76..................................(tp) JasonHart 4 77
(Tim Easterby) *hld up in tch: rdn over 2f out: no imp* **12/1**

2m 37.9s (-4.30) **Going Correction** -0.15s/f (Firm) **4** Ran SP% **113.2**
WFA 3 from 4yo+ 8lb
Speed ratings (Par 107): **108,105,104,104**
CSF £5.16 TOTE £1.70; EX 3.70 Trifecta £6.50.
Owner J H Richmond-Watson **Bred** Lawn Stud **Trained** Kimpton, Hants

FOCUS
Just a small field, but fairly useful fillies' form. It's been rated at face value, with the second and third to form.

7145 HORSERADISH H'CAP (FOR GENTLEMAN AMATEUR RIDERS) — 7f 127y
5:15 (5:18) (Class 4) (0-80,80) 3-Y-O+
£5,864 (£1,818; £908; £454; £300; £300) **Stalls** Low

Form RPR

6020 **1** **Parys Mountain (IRE)**[7] 6922 5-11-4 77..............(t) MrWilliamEasterby 3 85
(Tim Easterby) *midfield: pushed along and hdwy 2f out: rdn to chse ldr ins fnl f: kpt on to ld fnl 50yds* **5/1**[3]

0361 **2** 1½ **Calder Prince (IRE)**[13] 6700 6-11-7 80..............(p) MrSimonWalker 8 84
(Tom Dascombe) *led narrowly: rdn over 1f out: drvn and hdd 50yds out: no ex* **4/1**[2]

4046 **3** 1 **Confrontational (IRE)**[28] 6179 5-10-10 74.........(p) MrRyanHolmes(5) 12 76
(Jennie Candlish) *pressed ldr: rdn and sltly outpcd in 2nd over 1f out: kpt on same pce in 3rd ins fnl f* **17/2**

0066 **4** ¾ **Stringybark Creek**[13] 6734 5-10-10 76............... MrBradleyRoberts(7) 13 76
(David Loughnane) *chsd ldrs: rdn over 2f out: drvn over 1f out: kpt on* **16/1**

0265 **5** ½ **Imperial State**[6] 6978 6-10-11 75........................(v) MrMatthewEnnis(5) 6 73
(Michael Easterby) *dwlt: hld up: racd quite keenly: rdn and hdwy over 1f out: kpt on fnl f* **12/1**

-000 **6** 6 **Quixote (GER)**[95] 3649 9-10-11 70..........................(t) MrAlexEdwards 2 53
(James Unett) *midfield: rdn over 2f out: wknd over 1f out* **33/1**

3620 **7** 1½ **Salam Zayed**[6] 6961 3-10-4 73............................ MrEireannCagney(5) 1 52
(Richard Fahey) *trckd ldrs on inner: rdn over 2f out: wknd over 1f out* **7/2**[1]

0405 **8** ½ **Peachey Carnehan**[14] 6682 5-9-9 61 oh8.........(v) MrPatrickBarlow(7) 9 39
(Michael Mullineaux) *hld up on outer: rdn over 2f out: sn btn* **66/1**

0044 **9** 1¾ **Baltic Prince (IRE)**[36] 5839 9-10-9 75.................. MrNiallReynolds(7) 5 49
(Tony Carroll) *midfield on outer: rdn 3f out: wknd over 1f out* **14/1**

1000 **10** nk **Mister Music**[22] 6370 10-10-4 70.................... MrGrahamGilbertson(7) 10 43
(Tony Carroll) *slowly away: hld up in rr: nvr threatened* **33/1**

4560 **11** ½ **Pacino**[40] 5708 3-10-11 75.. MrJamesKing 14 46
(Richard Fahey) *trckd ldrs: rdn over 2f out: sn wknd* **25/1**

000 **12** 1½ **Intense Style (IRE)**[37] 5816 7-10-5 64...................... MrJamesHarding 4 32
(Les Eyre) *hld up in midfield: rdn over 2f out: sn wknd* **8/1**

60-0 **13** 8 **Thermal (IRE)**[185] 1166 3-9-11 66.................... DrMishaVoikhansky(5) 11 13
(Ian Williams) *awkward and wnt lft s: hmpd after 1f: a in rr (jockey said filly anticipated the start and hit the gates which caused him to be slowly away)* **33/1**

3305 **14** 6 **Bell Heather (IRE)**[40] 5709 6-10-6 65..................(p) MrPatrickMillman 7
(Patrick Morris) *bucked and unrideable leaving s: a t.o* **7/1**

1m 35.26s (-0.44) **Going Correction** -0.15s/f (Firm) **14** Ran SP% **127.4**
WFA 3 from 5yo+ 5lb
Speed ratings (Par 105): **96,94,93,92,92 86,84,84,82,82 81,80,72,66**
CSF £25.79 CT £180.81 TOTE £5.20: £1.70, £1.80, £3.20; EX 26.30 Trifecta £191.00.
Owner Reality Partnerships Xii **Bred** Yeomanstown Stud **Trained** Great Habton, N Yorks

FOCUS
A fair handicap for amateurs, and another race in which prominent racers did well. The winner has been rated in line with this year's form.
T/Plt: £54.70 to a £1 stake. Pool: £66,011.23 - 880.14 winning units T/Qpdt: £19.80 to a £1 stake. Pool: £5,826.64 - 217.72 winning units **Andrew Sheret**

7117

DONCASTER (L-H)
Friday, September 13

OFFICIAL GOING: Good to firm (watered; 8.1)
Wind: Moderate half against Weather: Fine and dry

7146 JAPAN RACING ASSOCIATION SCEPTRE STKS (GROUP 3) (F&M) — 7f 6y
2:10 (2:12) (Class 1) 3-Y-O+
£34,026 (£12,900; £6,456; £3,216; £1,614; £810) **Stalls** Centre

Form RPR

1015 **1** **Breathtaking Look**[22] 6379 4-9-2 92............................ JimCrowley 12 105
(Stuart Williams) *mde all: rdn and qcknd clr wl over 1f out: kpt on strly* **20/1**

-204 **2** 1 **Preening**[49] 5369 4-9-2 99.. WilliamBuick 5 102
(James Fanshawe) *hld up towards rr: hdwy wl over 2f out and sn pushed along: rdn over 1f out: chsd wnr ins fnl f: sn drvn and kpt on* **14/1**

0600 **3** ½ **Mot Juste (USA)**[19] 6508 3-8-12 101............................ AndreaAtzeni 4 99
(Roger Varian) *dwlt and in rr: hdwy wl over 2f out: swtchd lft and rdn wl over 1f out: styd on wl fnl f* **8/1**

3211 **4** 1 **Posted**[20] 6451 3-8-12 90......................................(h) SeanLevey 8 96+
(Richard Hannon) *hld up and bhd: hdwy jst over 2f out: sn rdn: kpt on wl fnl f* **18/1**

0063 **5** ½ **Foxtrot Lady**[10] 6847 4-9-2 99.................................... OisinMurphy 13 97
(Andrew Balding) *chsd ldrs: rdn along and sltly outpcd 2f out: kpt on u.p fnl f* **16/1**

-011 **6** ½ **Farzeen**[30] 6074 3-8-12 91.. JackMitchell 2 93
(Roger Varian) *t.k.h: in tch: n.m.r and stmbld sltly over 5f out: hdwy 3f out: rdn along to chse ldrs wl over 1f out: sn drvn and btn* **15/2**

-612 **7** ½ **California Love**[34] 5944 3-8-12 97............................ FrankieDettori 3 92
(Richard Spencer) *prom: pushed along wl over 2f out: rdn wl over 1f out: grad wknd appr fnl f* **11/1**

0140 **8** 2 **Sunday Star**[26] 6257 3-8-12 99.................................... JamieSpencer 9 87
(Ed Walker) *in rr: sme hdwy over 2f out: sn rdn and n.d* **33/1**

5324 **9** hd **Di Fede (IRE)**[19] 6508 4-9-2 102.................................. HarryBentley 7 88
(Ralph Beckett) *trckd ldrs: pushed along wl over 2f out: rdn wl over 1f out: sn btn* **7/1**[3]

3204 **10** 2½ **Solar Gold (IRE)**[13] 6726 4-9-2 98............................ DanielTudhope 6 81
(William Haggas) *trckd wnr: pushed along 3f out: rdn over 2f out: sn wknd (trainer's rep could offer no explanation for the filly's performance; jockey said filly stopped quickly)* **9/2**[1]

4300 **11** 2¼ **Angel's Hideaway (IRE)**[19] 6508 3-8-12 105..............(p) PJMcDonald 14 73
(John Gosden) *trckd ldrs: rdn along 2f out: sn wknd* **8/1**

2160 **12** 1 **Servalan (IRE)**[20] 6472 3-8-12 99................................ ShaneFoley 11 70
(Mrs John Harrington, Ire) *chsd ldrs: rdn wl over 2f out: sn wknd* **22/1**

-100 **13** ½ **Pretty Baby (IRE)**[42] 5608 4-9-5 104.............................. RyanMoore 1 74
(William Haggas) *towards rr: rdn along 1/2-way: sn outpcd and bhd (trainer's rep could offer no explanation for the filly's performance; jockey said filly was never travelling)* **11/2**[2]

1m 23.4s (-3.00) **Going Correction** +0.025s/f (Good) **13** Ran SP% **118.2**
WFA 3 from 4yo 4lb
Speed ratings (Par 113): **115,113,113,112,111 111,110,108,107,105 102,101,100**
CSF £268.02 TOTE £23.70: £6.50, £4.00, £3.20; EX 295.00 Trifecta £3314.70.
Owner J W Parry **Bred** Ellis Stud And Bellow Hill Stud **Trained** Newmarket, Suffolk

FOCUS
The third day of the St Leger festival and clerk of the course Roderick Duncan said: "The track walks exactly like yesterday. We put 3mm of irrigation on last night and there is no sign of any rain."\n\x\x A wide-open edition of this fillies' Group 3 and, run at a muddling pace, it saw a surprise result. The second has been rated close to her best.

7147 WILLIAM HILL MALLARD H'CAP — 1m 6f 115y
2:40 (2:41) (Class 2) (0-110,101) 3-Y-O+ **£25,876** (£7,700; £3,848; £1,924) **Stalls** Low

Form RPR

3020 **1** **Sleeping Lion (USA)**[23] 6355 4-9-3 91........................ JamieSpencer 5 99
(James Fanshawe) *hld up in rr: pushed along and hdwy on outer wl over 2f out: rdn to chal wl over 1f out: sn edgd lft and led jst over 1f out: jnd and drvn ins fnl f: kpt on wl towards fin* **4/1**[3]

1504 **2** ¾ **Charles Kingsley**[6] 6958 4-9-11 99.............................. FrankieDettori 3 106
(Mark Johnston) *hld up towards rr: effrt and hdwy whn n.m.r 1 1/2f out: sn swtchd rt and rdn to chal jst ins fnl f: sn drvn and ev ch tl no ex last 50yds* **11/4**[2]

520 **3** 3 **Theglasgowwarrior**[14] 6657 5-9-2 90............................ DanielTudhope 1 93
(Jim Goldie) *trckd ldrs: hdwy on inner 3f out: effrt and nt clr run wl over 1f out: sn swtchd rt and rdn: chsd ldng pair ins fnl f: no imp* **13/2**

1400 **4** ½ **Bartholomeu Dias**[23] 6355 4-9-3 91.............................. RyanMoore 4 93
(Charles Hills) *trckd ldr: hdwy and cl up 3f out: led over 2f out: rdn and hdd jst over 1f out: sn drvn and kpt on same pce* **12/1**

-411 **5** 2¾ **Saroog**[20] 6452 5-9-13 101.. WilliamBuick 6 100
(Simon Crisford) *trckd ldng pair: hdwy and cl up 3f out: rdn along wl over 2f out: sn drvn and btn (jockey said gelding hung left-handed in the home straight)* **2/1**[1]

0420 **6** 2½ **Genetics (FR)**[21] 6420 5-9-4 92.................................... OisinMurphy 2 87
(Andrew Balding) *led: pushed along over 3f out: rdn and hdd over 2f out: sn wknd* **9/1**

3m 3.93s (-7.67) **Going Correction** -0.275s/f (Firm) **6** Ran SP% **111.0**
Speed ratings (Par 109): **109,108,107,106,105 103**
CSF £15.01 TOTE £4.90: £2.20, £1.90; EX 14.60 Trifecta £60.10.
Owner Merry Fox Stud Limited **Bred** Merry Fox Stud Limited **Trained** Newmarket, Suffolk

FOCUS
The smallest field since 2013 for the Mallard but there was an even pace, before they got racing 4f out. It's good, straightforward form.

7148 MAGNERS ROSE DONCASTER CUP STKS (GROUP 2) (BRITISH CHAMPIONS SERIES) — 2m 1f 197y
3:10 (3:10) (Class 1) 3-Y-O+ **£56,710** (£21,500; £10,760; £5,360; £2,690) **Stalls** Low

Form RPR

1111 **1** **Stradivarius (IRE)**[21] 6421 5-9-10 121.......................... FrankieDettori 4 118+
(John Gosden) *led at stdy pce: hdd after 3f: trckd ldng pair: smooth hdwy 3f out: cl up on bit over 1f out: shkn up and qcknd to ld ent fnl f: sn clr* **1/9**[1]

6130 **2** 1¾ **Cleonte (IRE)**[20] 6473 6-9-5 103.................................. OisinMurphy 2 108
(Andrew Balding) *trckd ldng pair tl led after 3f: qcknd pce over 6f out: pushed along 3f out: rdn 2f out: sn jnd: hdd ent fnl f: sn drvn and kpt on: no ch w wnr* **16/1**

0-30 **3** 2½ **Max Dynamite (FR)**[20] 6473 9-9-5 107............................ RyanMoore 3 105
(W P Mullins, Ire) *trckd ldrs: pushed along and hdwy 3f out: rdn to chse ldng pair 2f out: drvn over 1f out: kpt on same pce* **14/1**

3335 **4** 2½ **Barsanti (IRE)**[20] 6473 7-9-5 108...........................(b) AndreaAtzeni 6 103
(Roger Varian) *hld up in rr: pushed along over 5f out: rdn along 4f out: plugged on: nvr a factor* **10/1**[2]

5 11 **Sneaky Getaway (IRE)**[27] 6244 6-9-5 101...................... JamieSpencer 1 90
(Emmet Mullins, Ire) *t.k.h: trckd ldr: pushed along 4f out: rdn 3f out: sn drvn and outpcd* **12/1**[3]

3m 59.28s (4.28) **Going Correction** -0.275s/f (Firm) **5** Ran SP% **119.3**
Speed ratings (Par 115): **79,78,77,76,71**
CSF £4.97 TOTE £1.10: £1.10, £3.60; EX 3.10 Trifecta £9.70.
Owner B E Nielsen **Bred** Bjorn Nielsen **Trained** Newmarket, Suffolk

FOCUS
After the defection of old rival Dee Ex Bee (going) this year's Doncaster Cup was a penalty kick for Stradivarius's bid for the staying Triple Crown. It unsurprisingly proved a tactical affair. The second, who has been rated to his best, is the key to the form.

7149 WAINWRIGHT FLYING CHILDERS STKS (GROUP 2) 5f 3y
3:45 (3:46) (Class 1) 2-Y-O

£39,697 (£15,050; £7,532; £3,752; £1,883; £945) Stalls Centre

Form				RPR
2115	1		**A'Ali (IRE)**[26] 6264 2-9-1 0 ... FrankieDettori 7 (Simon Crisford) *trckd ldr: hdwy to chal over 1f out: rdn ent fnl f: led last 110yds: kpt on wl* **6/4**[2]	112+
2010	2	1	**Dream Shot (IRE)**[20] 6474 2-9-1 96 ... PJMcDonald 4 (James Tate) *hld up in tch: hdwy 2f out: swtchd rt and rdn to chse ldrs over 1f out: drvn and edgd lft ins fnl f: kpt on: tk 2nd on line* **20/1**	105
025	3	nse	**Wheels On Fire (FR)**[44] 5542 2-9-1 101 ... DanielTudhope 6 (Aidan F Fogarty, Ire) *led: rdn along and jnd over 1f out: drvn ins fnl f: hdd last 110yds: kpt on: lost 2nd on line* **12/1**[3]	105
0013	4	1 ¼	**Flaming Princess (IRE)**[13] 6791 2-8-12 99 ... BarryMcHugh 1 (Richard Fahey) *chsd ldng pair: rdn along wl over 1f out: drvn and kpt on same pce fnl f* **14/1**	98
1503	5	2 ¼	**Emten (IRE)**[13] 6704 2-8-12 86 ... NicolaCurrie 2 (Jamie Osborne) *dwlt and bhd: pushed along 1/2-way: rdn 2f out: kpt on fnl f (jockey said filly missed the break)* **66/1**	90
21	6	½	**Alligator Alley**[20] 6474 2-9-1 104 ... DonnachaO'Brien 5 (Joseph Patrick O'Brien, Ire) *awkward s: trckd ldrs: effrt wl over 1f out: sn rdn and btn (jockey said colt became upset in the stalls)* **1/1**[1]	91
10	7	7	**Seize The Time (IRE)**[28] 6157 2-8-12 0 ... RyanMoore 8 (K R Burke) *chsd ldrs rdn along 2f out: sn wknd* **40/1**	63

59.35s (-0.25) **Going Correction** +0.025s/f (Good) 7 Ran SP% **113.1**
Speed ratings (Par 107): **103,101,101,99,95 94,83**
CSF £29.61 CT £266.19 TOTE £2.10: £1.20, £6.40; EX 22.50 Trifecta £122.90.
Owner Shaikh Duaij Al Khalifa **Bred** Tally-Ho Stud **Trained** Newmarket, Suffolk

FOCUS
A race that was in danger of just producing good juvenile sprinters that don't necessarily train on (or not given the opportunity to) until Soldier's Call subsequently placed in three Group 1s after taking the previous year's renewal. The match race the market predicted never materialised, but this year's winner can go on to prove himself at the highest level too. The sectionals suggested it was not a true pace for a 5f race as they went slow early on.

7150 WEATHERBYS GLOBAL STALLIONS APP FLYING SCOTSMAN STKS (LISTED RACE) 7f 6y
4:20 (4:21) (Class 1) 2-Y-O £17,013 (£6,450; £3,228; £1,608; £807) Stalls Centre

Form				RPR
21	1		**Molatham**[21] 6424 2-9-0 0 ... JimCrowley 5 (Roger Varian) *hld up in tch: hdwy on outer 2f out: rdn to ld jst over 1f out: kpt on strly* **1/1**[1]	104+
	2	½	**Wichita (IRE)**[21] 6426 2-9-0 0 ... RyanMoore 2 (A P O'Brien, Ire) *trckd ldng pair: cl up 2f out: rdn and ev ch over 1f out: drvn ins fnl f: edgd rt and kpt on wl towards fin* **11/4**[2]	103+
513	3	¾	**Berlin Tango**[21] 6417 2-9-0 96 ... OisinMurphy 4 (Andrew Balding) *trckd ldr: hdwy and cl up 2f out: rdn to chal over 1f out: ev ch: drvn and edgd rt and kpt on same pce fnl f* **14/1**	101
134	4	nk	**Visinari (FR)**[45] 5520 2-9-0 106 ... FrankieDettori 3 (Mark Johnston) *led: pushed along over 2f out: rdn wl over 1f out: hdd appr fnl f: drvn and hld whn n.m.r towards fin: lost 3rd nr line* **3/1**[3]	100
3111	5	3	**Tomfre**[34] 5962 2-9-0 90 ... HarryBentley 1 (Ralph Beckett) *t.k.h: chsd ldrs: effrt and cl up 2f out: sn rdn and appr fnl f* **14/1**	92

1m 25.35s (-1.05) **Going Correction** +0.025s/f (Good) 5 Ran SP% **115.0**
Speed ratings (Par 103): **107,106,105,105,101**
CSF £4.34 TOTE £1.90: £1.30, £1.40; EX 4.50 Trifecta £19.00.
Owner Hamdan Al Maktoum **Bred** Cheveley Park Stud Ltd **Trained** Newmarket, Suffolk

FOCUS
A 2yo Listed event which often throws up a top-notcher, Frankel being a glaring example in 2010. This year's edition was another tactical affair on the card, with all five runners abreast 2f out, and the bare form should be treated with a little caution.

7151 GARY REID MEMORIAL IRISH EBF MAIDEN STKS (PLUS 10 RACE) (SIRE AND DAM-RESTRICTED RACE) 7f 6y
4:55 (4:57) (Class 3) 2-Y-O £9,703 (£2,887; £1,443; £721) Stalls Centre

Form				RPR
	1		**Raaeb (IRE)** 2-9-5 0 ... JimCrowley 2 (Saeed bin Suroor) *trckd ldr: hdwy and cl up over 2f out: rdn and qcknd to ld over 1f out: kpt on strly* **11/10**[1]	85+
32	2	1 ¼	**Arabian Moon**[31] 6040 2-9-5 0 ... HarryBentley 6 (Ralph Beckett) *led: pushed along and jnd over 2f out: rdn and hdd over 1f out: kpt on u.p fnl f* **8/1**	81
55	3	shd	**Sir Charles Punch**[14] 6664 2-9-5 0 ... GrahamLee 1 (James Given) *hld up: hdwy wl over 1f out: rdn ent fnl f: sn drvn and kpt on wl towards fin* **50/1**	81
3	4	shd	**Maori Knight (IRE)**[56] 5131 2-9-5 0 ... ShaneKelly 3 (Richard Hughes) *hld up in rr: hdwy 3f out: chsd ldrs 2f out: rdn and edgd lft over 1f out: drvn ins fnl f: kpt on* **5/2**[2]	80
5	5	2 ¾	**Talap**[7] 6912 2-9-5 0 ... AndreaAtzeni 4 (Roger Varian) *trckd ldng pair: pushed along 2f out: rdn over 1f out: grad wknd* **7/2**[3]	73

1m 27.64s (1.24) **Going Correction** +0.025s/f (Good) 5 Ran SP% **111.5**
Speed ratings (Par 99): **93,91,91,91,88**
CSF £10.75 TOTE £1.90: £1.20, £2.40; EX 9.10 Trifecta £75.70.
Owner Godolphin **Bred** Shadwell Estate Company Limited **Trained** Newmarket, Suffolk

FOCUS
Restricted to horses whose sire or dam won a race over 1m 4f+, the 2018 edition of this worked out well, with winner Royal Marine going on to win the Group 1 Jean-Luc Lagardere on its subsequent start. This year looked ordinary on paper, but Godolphin took the spoils again with another potentially smart sort. They went slow early, and only got sprinting 3f out.

7152 FOLLOW @WILLHILLRACING ON TWITTER H'CAP 6f 111y
5:30 (5:32) (Class 2) (0-105,100) 3-Y-O+ £12,938 (£3,850; £1,924; £962) Stalls Centre

Form				RPR
-520	1		**Enjazaat**[20] 6453 4-9-8 100 ... JimCrowley 7 (Owen Burrows) *hld up in rr: hdwy over 2f out: chsd ldrs over 1f out: rdn to chal jst ins fnl f: sn drvn and kpt on wl to ld towards fin* **6/1**[3]	108+
0420	2	nk	**Medahim (IRE)**[32] 6014 5-9-4 96 ... SeanLevey 2 (Ivan Furtado) *led: pushed along over 2f out: rdn wl over 1f out: drvn ins fnl f: edgd rt: hdd and no ex towards fin* **9/1**	103
4400	3	1	**Intisaab**[13] 6706 8-9-6 98 ... (tp) DanielTudhope 3 (David O'Meara) *hld up in tch: hdwy over 2f out: rdn wl over 1f out: drvn and kpt on wl fnl f* **9/1**	102
0313	4	shd	**Citron Major**[27] 6229 4-8-9 90 ... (tp) RowanScott(3) 1 (Nigel Tinkler) *trckd ldrs: hdwy 2f out: rdn and ev ch over 1f out: drvn ins fnl f: kpt on same pce* **6/1**[3]	94
2/45	5	1 ¼	**Battered**[205] 800 5-9-5 97 ... HarryBentley 5 (Ralph Beckett) *hld up towards rr: pushed along over 2f out: rdn wl over 1f out: kpt on fnl f* **16/1**	97+
4034	6	½	**Golden Apollo**[6] 6953 5-8-9 87 ... (tp) DavidAllan 8 (Tim Easterby) *trckd ldrs: hdwy over 2f out: rdn wl over 1f out: sn drvn and btn* **5/2**[1]	86
4000	7	3 ¼	**Reputation (IRE)**[13] 6706 6-9-0 92 ... BarryMcHugh 6 (Ruth Carr) *prom: cl up 3f out: rdn along over 2f out: sn drvn and wknd* **10/1**	82
1310	8	nk	**Flavius Titus**[41] 5664 4-9-6 98 ... AndreaAtzeni 4 (Roger Varian) *trckd ldr: cl up 3f out: rdn along over 2f out: sn wknd* **10/3**[2]	87

1m 18.09s (-1.51) **Going Correction** +0.025s/f (Good) 8 Ran SP% **115.2**
Speed ratings (Par 109): **109,108,107,107,105 105,101,101**
CSF £58.31 CT £486.47 TOTE £6.50: £1.70, £3.00, £2.50; EX 63.00 Trifecta £347.30.
Owner Hamdan Al Maktoum **Bred** C J Mills **Trained** Lambourn, Berks

FOCUS
A good-quality sprint handicap. The second has been rated close to his best, with the third and fourth close to form.

7153 COOPERS MARQUEES CLASSIFIED STKS 1m 2f 43y
6:00 (6:00) (Class 3) 3-Y-O+

£9,337 (£2,796; £1,398; £699; £349; £175) Stalls Low

Form				RPR
242	1		**Sandret (IRE)**[21] 6410 3-8-12 85 ... GrahamLee 6 (Ben Haslam) *hld up in rr: hdwy on inner 3f out: swtchd rt wl over 1f out and sn chsng ldrs: rdn to chal ent fnl f: styd on wl to ld fnl 100yds* **7/1**	96+
2451	2	1	**Storting**[26] 6259 3-8-12 85 ... OisinMurphy 1 (Mick Channon) *trckd ldrs: hdwy over 3f out: rdn to ld jst over 1f out: jnd and drvn ent fnl f: hdd last 100yds: no ex* **5/4**[1]	93
1122	3	3 ¾	**The Jean Genie**[12] 6759 5-9-4 82 ... PJMcDonald 2 (William Stone) *led: pushed along wl over 2f out: rdn wl over 1f out: hdd jst over 1f out: kpt on same pce* **14/1**	85
1631	4	1 ¾	**Benadalid**[17] 6580 4-9-4 83 ... DanielTudhope 3 (Chris Fairhurst) *hld up towards rr: hdwy on outer over 3f out: rdn along to chse ldrs 2f out: sn drvn and no imp* **7/2**[2]	82
6133	5	1 ¼	**Light Up Our Stars (IRE)**[8] 6909 3-8-12 83 ... AndreaAtzeni 5 (Richard Hughes) *trckd ldng pair: hdwy to trck ldr 1/2-way: effrt 3f out and sn pushed along: rdn over 2f out: sn drvn and wknd over 1f out* **4/1**[3]	79
0602	6	7	**Banksea**[9] 6863 6-9-1 84 ... (h) ConnorMurtagh(3) 4 (Marjorie Fife) *trckd ldr: pushed along 4f out: rdn along 3f out: sn wknd* **20/1**	65

2m 6.24s (-6.06) **Going Correction** -0.275s/f (Firm)
WFA 3 from 4yo+ 6lb 6 Ran SP% **110.6**
Speed ratings (Par 107): **113,112,109,107,106 101**
CSF £15.84 TOTE £9.00: £3.40, £1.30; EX 23.40 Trifecta £117.70.
Owner Mrs C Barclay & Ben Haslam Racing Synd **Bred** Tally-Ho Stud **Trained** Middleham Moor, N Yorks

FOCUS
Only six runners but the ratings suggested it was a close-knit classified event where they all had a chance. They went an even gallop throughout. 3yos have won 8 out of the last ten renewals, and they filled the first two places here.
T/Jkpt: £3,196.30 to a £1 stake. Pool: £45,018.70 - 10 winning units T/Plt: £116.10 to a £1 stake. Pool: £151,484.84 - 951.67 winning units T/Qpdt: £6.70 to a £1 stake. Pool: £12,478.80 - 1,363.11 winning units **Joe Rowntree**

6904 SALISBURY (R-H)
Friday, September 13

OFFICIAL GOING: Good (good to firm in places; 7.9)
Wind: virtually nil Weather: sunny

7154 T & M GLASS LTD NOVICE MEDIAN AUCTION STKS 1m
4:35 (4:39) (Class 5) 2-Y-O £4,140 (£1,232; £615; £307) Stalls Low

Form				RPR
	1		**Oleksander** 2-9-2 0 ... DavidEgan 9 (Archie Watson) *a.p: str chal fr 3f out: tk narrow advantage over 1f out: kpt on wl fnl f: rdn out* **7/2**[2]	74
01	2	¾	**Luigi Vampa (FR)**[19] 6504 2-9-9 0 ... JoeFanning 2 (David Menuisier) *trckd ldrs: rdn over 2f out: nt pce to chal: kpt on wl to go 2nd fnl 120yds: a being hld* **13/2**	79
42	3	2 ¼	**North Point**[13] 6718 2-9-2 0 ... LiamKeniry 7 (David Elsworth) *led: rdn and hdd over 1f out: kpt on tl no ex fnl 120yds* **5/1**[3]	67
0	4	1 ¾	**Machios**[38] 5774 2-8-13 0 ... WilliamCox(3) 8 (Andrew Balding) *awkwardly away: t.k.h: hld up: sme prog 3f out: sn rdn: nt gng pce to get on terms but kpt on ins fnl f: wnt 4th cl home (jockey said colt ran too freely in the early stages of the race and also ran green)* **16/1**	63+
5	5	nk	**Tantivy**[29] 6112 2-9-2 0 ... FergusSweeney 10 (Richard Hannon) *t.k.h to post: trckd ldrs: edgd rt whn outpcd u.p over 2f out: nvr threatened* **50/1**	62+
4	6	2 ¾	**Red Missile (IRE)**[35] 5908 2-9-2 0 ... TomMarquand 5 (William Haggas) *s.i.s: in last pair: rdn over 2f out: little imp (jockey said colt was slowly away)* **7/4**[1]	56+
00	7	shd	**Thank The Irish (IRE)**[9] 6858 2-9-2 0 ... CallumShepherd 3 (Jamie Osborne) *in tch: rdn over 2f out: nvr threatened: wknd ent fnl f* **50/1**	56
0	8	¾	**Galispeed (FR)**[86] 3990 2-9-2 0 ... HollieDoyle 6 (Archie Watson) *in tch: pushed along over 3f out: sn btn* **20/1**	54
2	9	½	**Her Indoors (IRE)**[25] 6281 2-8-11 0 ... HectorCrouch 1 (Alan King) *dwlt bdly: bhd: carried lft over 2f out: nvr on terms (jockey said filly was also slowly away and was unruly in the stalls)* **8/1**	48+

1m 44.93s (1.43) **Going Correction** +0.025s/f (Good) 9 Ran SP% **114.3**
Speed ratings (Par 95): **93,92,90,88,87 85,85,84,83**
CSF £25.66 TOTE £4.30: £1.40, £1.50, £1.60; EX 28.10 Trifecta £105.20.
Owner Nurlan Bizakov **Bred** Hesmonds Stud Ltd **Trained** Upper Lambourn, W Berks

■ Spring To Mind was withdrawn. Price at time of withdrawal 16-1. Rule 4 does not apply.

FOCUS

A total of 12mm of rain over the preceding four days negated any need to water, and racing took place in pleasant, sunny conditions. The stalls were on the far side for this opening juvenile novice auction stakes, in which only three were ever meaningfully involved. It's been rated as straightforward form, with the second to his Goodwood win.

7155 T & M GLASS LTD NURSERY H'CAP 6f 213y

5:10 (5:11) (Class 5) (0-75,77) 2-Y-O

£3,737 (£1,112; £555; £400; £400; £400) Stalls Low

Form / RPR

4451 **1** **Royal Ambition (IRE)**[29] 6113 2-9-5 **73**............ HectorCrouch 6 76
(Clive Cox) *mde all: rdn over 1f out: jst hld on: all out* **20/1**

444 **2** *nk* **Mellad**[42] 5624 2-9-6 **74**............ CallumShepherd 10 76
(Peter Chapple-Hyam) *mid-div: hdwy over 1f out: sn rdn: r.o wl ins fnl f: jst failed* **11/1**

4502 **3** *1* **Qaaddim (IRE)**[21] 6403 2-9-7 **75**............ DavidEgan 9 75
(Roger Varian) *pushed along leaving stalls: towards rr: hdwy over 3f out: chsd wnr but drifting rt over 1f out: kpt on fnl f: no ex nring fin* **3/1**[1]

361 **4** *2 ½* **Elegant Erin (IRE)**[29] 6118 2-9-9 **77**............ TomMarquand 4 70
(Richard Hannon) *slowly away and hmpd s: towards rr: struggling 3f out: hdwy over 1f out but hanging rt: kpt on same pce fnl f* **4/1**[2]

543 **5** *1* **Masaakin**[21] 6407 2-9-5 **73**............ HollieDoyle 8 64
(Richard Hannon) *racd keenly: sn prom: rdn and ev ch 2f out: wknd ins fnl f* **4/1**[2]

2416 **6** *1* **Nat Love (IRE)**[2] 7064 2-9-1 **74**............ ScottMcCullagh(5) 2 62+
(Mick Channon) *s.i.s: towards rr: making hdwy whn bdly hmpd over 1f out: kpt on ins fnl f but no ch after* **9/2**[3]

050 **7** *nse* **Boasty (IRE)**[20] 6449 2-9-0 **68**............ StevieDonohoe 3 56+
(Charlie Fellowes) *broke wl enough but sn squeezed up and lost pl: mid-div: nt clr run on rails fr 2f out tl swtchd lft ent fnl f: kpt on but nt pce to get on terms* **14/1**

5414 **8** *2* **Lethal Talent**[11] 6808 2-9-1 **69**............ LiamKeniry 1 52
(Jonathan Portman) *trckd ldrs: rdn 2f out: wknd ent fnl f* **20/1**

5402 **9** *1 ¾* **King's View (IRE)**[11] 6792 2-9-0 **68**............ FergusSweeney 7 46
(Richard Hannon) *mid-div: rdn over 2f out: wknd ent fnl f* **33/1**

5423 **10** *11* **Goodwood Rebel (IRE)**[57] 5088 2-9-7 **75**............(b[1]) JoeFanning 5 24+
(Ralph Beckett) *untidily away: racd keenly: trcking ldrs whn bdly squeezed up 1st f: chal 3f out: sn rdn: wkng whn bdly hmpd over 1f out* **14/1**

1m 29.26s (0.56) **Going Correction** +0.025s/f (Good) 10 Ran SP% **117.3**
Speed ratings (Par 95): **97,96,95,92,91 90,90,88,86,73**
CSF £218.86 CT £856.22 TOTE £25.60: £6.00, £2.90, £1.10; EX 166.70 Trifecta £876.80.
Owner J Goddard **Bred** Gus Roche **Trained** Lambourn, Berks

FOCUS

Stalls on far side. A fairly competitive nursery on paper, but a few of these got in each other's way behind an evidently versatile winner.

7156 IRISH STALLION FARMS EBF FILLIES' NURSERY H'CAP 6f

5:40 (5:40) (Class 3) (0-90,86) 2-Y-O £8,086 (£2,406; £1,202; £601) Stalls Low

Form / RPR

2213 **1** **Mild Illusion (IRE)**[27] 6221 2-8-9 **74**............ HollieDoyle 6 85+
(Jonathan Portman) *trckd ldrs: shkn up to ld ent fnl f: r.o wl: readily* **6/4**[1]

0330 **2** *3 ¼* **Companion**[57] 5116 2-9-7 **86**............ JoeFanning 1 87
(Mark Johnston) *stmbld leaving stalls: sn pressing ldr: rdn and ev ch fr 2f out tl ent fnl f: sn tight for room: nt pce of wnr* **6/1**

1653 **3** *1 ¼* **Glamorous Anna**[13] 6713 2-9-3 **85**............ MitchGodwin(3) 2 82
(Christopher Mason) *led: wandered u.p fr 2f out: hdd ent fnl f: no ex fnl 100yds* **11/2**[3]

P621 **4** *hd* **Love Powerful (IRE)**[32] 6019 2-8-10 **75**............ TomMarquand 3 72
(Richard Hannon) *trckd ldrs: rdn 2f out: kpt on fnl f but nt pce to get on terms* **15/8**[2]

3160 **5** *1 ¾* **Bartat**[22] 6369 2-8-1 **66**............ DavidEgan 4 57
(Mick Channon) *s.i.s: last of the 5 but wl in tch: rdn over 2f out: nt pce to get on terms* **16/1**

1m 14.58s (0.08) **Going Correction** +0.025s/f (Good) 5 Ran SP% **110.3**
Speed ratings (Par 96): **100,95,94,93,91**
CSF £10.76 TOTE £2.20: £1.30, £3.00; EX 9.70 Trifecta £28.60.
Owner Old Stoic Racing Club **Bred** Marston Stud **Trained** Upper Lambourn, Berks

FOCUS

Stalls on far side. Maybe not the deepest 0-90, but a taking winner and a fine piece of placement by her handler. It's been rated as straightforward form.

7157 EXCALIBUR COMMUNICATIONS H'CAP 6f

6:10 (6:11) (Class 6) (0-65,66) 3-Y-O

£3,058 (£910; £454; £400; £400; £400) Stalls Low

Form / RPR

2031 **1** **Grisons (FR)**[27] 6198 3-9-1 **62**............ WilliamCox(3) 1 74+
(Clive Cox) *hmpd s: led after 1f: rdn clr over 1f out: comf* **4/1**[2]

4330 **2** *2 ¾* **Soldier's Son**[7] 6930 3-9-0 **65**............ EmmaTaff(7) 8 69
(Henry Candy) *wnt rt s: trckd ldrs: rdn to chse wnr wl over 1f out: kpt on but nvr gng pce to get on terms* **8/1**

6620 **3** *3* **Ricochet (IRE)**[16] 6598 3-9-7 **65**............ TomMarquand 4 60
(Tom Ward) *bmpd leaving stalls: trckd ldrs: rdn to chse wnr over 2f out tl wl over 1f out: kpt on same pce fnl f* **7/1**

3553 **4** *½* **Mrs Worthington (IRE)**[51] 5315 3-9-4 **62**............(p) RobHornby 3 56
(Jonathan Portman) *bmpd leaving stalls: mid-div tl outpcd over 3f out: hdwy over 1f out: kpt on wout threatening fnl f* **13/2**[3]

3301 **5** *shd* **Devils Roc**[9] 6857 3-9-1 **66**............ TylerSaunders(7) 6 59
(Jonathan Portman) *s.i.s and sltly hmpd s: in last pair: rdn over 2f out: no imp tl kpt on ins fnl f: n.d* **6/4**[1]

0-40 **6** *2 ½* **Geneva Spur (USA)**[17] 6569 3-9-3 **61**............ DavidEgan 9 47
(Roger Varian) *mid-div: hdwy 3f out: sn rdn: nt pce to get on terms: wknd ins fnl f (vet said filly lost her left-fore shoe)* **14/1**

5034 **7** *2 ½* **Molly's Game**[51] 5315 3-9-7 **65**............(b[1]) HollieDoyle 5 43
(David Elsworth) *hld up: rdn 2f out: no imp (jockey said filly was slowly away)* **9/1**

6406 **8** *4 ½* **Autumn Splendour (IRE)**[29] 6110 3-9-6 **64**............ PhilipPrince 11 29
(Milton Bradley) *wnt lft s: a towards rr* **66/1**

2600 **9** *2* **Wye Bother (IRE)**[105] 3319 3-8-7 **51** oh6............(t) RaulDaSilva 2 10
(Milton Bradley) *led for 1f: chsd wnr: rdn 3f out: wknd 2f out* **50/1**

1m 14.78s (0.28) **Going Correction** +0.025s/f (Good) 9 Ran SP% **117.1**
Speed ratings (Par 99): **99,95,91,90,90 87,83,77,75**
CSF £36.48 CT £220.93 TOTE £4.10: £1.20, £2.50, £2.30; EX 39.00 Trifecta £183.90.
Owner China Horse Club International Limited **Bred** S A R L Eds Stud Ltd **Trained** Lambourn, Berks

FOCUS

Stalls on far side. Another race on the evening where it paid to be at the front end throughout, and few ever landed a blow. It's been rated with feet on the ground around the second and third.

7158 NIKKI COOMBS BIRTHDAY CELEBRATION "PERSIAN PUNCH" CONDITIONS STKS 1m 6f 44y

6:40 (6:40) (Class 2) 3-Y-O+ £13,382 (£4,660) Stalls Far side

Form / RPR

6140 **1** **Weekender**[20] 6473 5-9-9 **110**............ RobertHavlin 117
(John Gosden) *trckd ldr: chal 3f out: tk narrow advantage 2f out: sn rdn: edgd rt fnl f: styd on: drvn out* **2/1**[2]

6110 **2** *nk* **King's Advice**[20] 6473 5-9-9 **112**............ JoeFanning 116
(Mark Johnston) *led: narrowly hdd 2f out: sn rdn: tight for room but styd on gamely w ev ch thrght fnl f: hld cl home* **8/15**[1]

-602 **R** **Platitude**[10] 6834 6-9-5 **95**............ DavidEgan
(Amanda Perrett) *ref to r: tk no part* **9/1**[3]

3m 19.08s (12.48) **Going Correction** +0.025s/f (Good) 3 Ran SP% **108.6**
Speed ratings (Par 109): **65,64,**
CSF £3.61 TOTE £2.60; EX 3.10 Trifecta £4.50.
Owner K Abdullah **Bred** Juddmonte Farms Ltd **Trained** Newmarket, Suffolk

FOCUS

A flag start as usual for this long-established conditions event. An already numerically disappointing turnout was reduced further by Platitude's refusal to start, but the remaining pair, both last seen well down the field in the Ebor, served up a thriller. The winner has been rated to his best.

7159 CROUCH MEMORIAL BRITISH EBF NOVICE STKS 1m 1f 201y

7:10 (7:11) (Class 4) 3-Y-O+ £5,498 (£1,636; £817; £408) Stalls Low

Form / RPR

1 **Tonyx** 3-8-10 **0**............ LiamKeniry 3 86+
(Ed Walker) *in tch: hdwy over 2f out: led jst over 1f out: sn drifted rt: styd on strly to draw clr: comf* **25/1**

04 **2** *8* **Roving Mission (USA)**[31] 6043 3-8-10 **0**............ RobHornby 10 70
(Ralph Beckett) *prom: led over 2f out: sn rdn: hdd jst over 1f out: styd on same pce fnl f* **8/1**[3]

3 *nk* **Good Tidings (FR)** 3-9-1 **0**............ RobertHavlin 11 74+
(John Gosden) *slowly away: trckd ldrs after 2f: rdn and ev ch 2f out tl jst over 1f out: styd on same pce fnl f* **1/1**[1]

4 **4** *6* **Its Nice Tobe Nice**[170] 1359 3-8-10 **0**............ MartinDwyer 6 57
(William Muir) *mid-div: rdn over 2f out: little imp tl styd on ins fnl f: wnt 4th cl home* **16/1**

202 **5** *shd* **Hawridge Storm (IRE)**[21] 6399 3-9-1 **77**............ DavidEgan 4 62
(Rod Millman) *s.i.s: towards rr: gd hdwy over 4f out to trck ldrs: rdn and ev ch over 2f out: sn hld: fdd fnl f* **4/1**[2]

6 *shd* **The Rocket Park (IRE)**[196] 6-9-7 **0**............ HectorCrouch 5 61
(John Berry) *mid-div: struggling over 3f out: styd on ins fnl f: n.d* **50/1**

6 **7** *2* **Manucci (IRE)**[126] 2566 3-9-1 **0**............ HollieDoyle 2 58
(Amanda Perrett) *mid-div: rdn over 3f out: nvr any imp: fdd ins fnl f* **14/1**

0420 **8** *¾* **Hazm (IRE)**[27] 6211 4-9-7 **80**............ TomMarquand 8 56
(Tim Vaughan) *led tl over 2f out: sn rdn: wknd jst over 1f out* **4/1**[2]

9 *2* **Dereham** 3-9-1 **0**............ RaulDaSilva 9 53
(John Berry) *s.i.s: a towards rr* **100/1**

10 *24* **Mighty Matilda** 3-8-7 **0**............ WilliamCox(3) 1
(Simon Earle) *towards rr: veered lft u.p over 2f out: t.o (jockey said filly ran green)* **66/1**

0-0 **11** *33* **Dark Seraphim (IRE)**[74] 4452 4-9-7 **0**............ CallumShepherd 7
(Charles Hills) *chsd ldrs tl wknd qckly over 3f out: t.o (trainer's rep said gelding had a breathing problem)* **40/1**

2m 8.95s (-1.55) **Going Correction** +0.025s/f (Good)
WFA 3 from 4yo+ 6lb 11 Ran SP% **124.4**
Speed ratings (Par 105): **107,100,100,95,95 95,93,93,91,72 46**
CSF £219.03 TOTE £30.80: £5.40, £2.10, £1.10; EX 331.60 Trifecta £977.10.
Owner Nyx Racing Club **Bred** Springfield Farm Partnership **Trained** Upper Lambourn, Berks

FOCUS

Stalls on inner. An ordinary event, but the winner created a very good impression and came from far further back than any other on the evening. The level is a bit fluid, but the second has been rated a little higher than her latest effort and the fourth close to her debut run for now.

T/Plt: £217.60 to a £1 stake. Pool: £51,806.93 - 173.79 winning units T/Qpdt: £17.00 to a £1 stake. Pool: £8,866.77 - 384.37 winning units **Tim Mitchell**

6724 SANDOWN (R-H)

Friday, September 13

OFFICIAL GOING: Good (good to firm in places)

Wind: Light, half behind Weather: Sunny, warm

7160 BRITISH STALLION STUDS EBF MAIDEN STKS (PLUS 10 RACE) 5f 10y

2:20 (2:24) (Class 4) 2-Y-O £4,787 (£1,424; £711; £355) Stalls Low

Form / RPR

422 **1** **Sand Diego (IRE)**[23] 6330 2-9-5 **76**............ PatDobbs 7 77
(Peter Crate) *s.i.s: hld up in last trio: prog 1/2-way: swtchd sharply lft over 1f out: clsd qckly fnl f to ld last 75yds* **4/1**[2]

2 *¾* **Qaseeda** 2-9-0 **0**............ JamesDoyle 10 69+
(William Haggas) *s.i.s: hld up in last pair: prog over 1f out: rdn and r.o wl fnl f: tk 2nd last strides* **9/1**[3]

22 **3** *nk* **Spreadsheet (IRE)**[58] 5059 2-9-5 **0**............ JasonWatson 2 73
(Roger Varian) *taken down early and steadily to post: reluctant to enter stalls: led after 1f: rdn over 2f out: crossed to rail over 1f out: hrd drvn and floundered fnl f: hdd last 75yds and lost 2nd fnl strides (jockey said colt hung left-handed and then hung right-handed under pressure)* **2/5**[1]

03 **4** *½* **Many A Star (IRE)**[20] 6449 2-9-5 **0**............ TomQueally 1 71
(James Given) *led 1f: chsd ldr: sltly impeded over 1f out: clsd ins fnl f but lost 2 pls last 100yds (jockey said colt suffered interference in running)* **14/1**

033 **5** *½* **Lin Chong**[26] 6262 2-9-5 **0**............(t[1]) LukeMorris 8 70
(Paul Cole) *chsd ldrs: rdn to go 3rd 1/2-way to 1f out: nvr able to chal but styd on fnl f* **16/1**

0 **6** *3 ¼* **Brenner Pass**[10] 6845 2-9-5 **0**............ AdamKirby 3 58+
(Richard Hughes) *dwlt: hld up in last pair: nudged along and styd on steadily over 1f out: signs of promise (jockey said colt was slowly away)* **66/1**

06 **7** *½* **Rapidash**[7] 6911 2-9-0 **0**............ RossaRyan 6 51
(Richard Hannon) *chsd ldrs: rdn to dispute 3rd briefly over 1f out: wknd fnl f* **10/1**

6 **8** 3 ½ **Hooray Henry**[8] 6899 2-9-5 0 CharlesBishop 5 44
(Henry Candy) *taken down early: chsd ldng pair to 1/2-way: wknd* **33/1**
0 **9** 2 ½ **Marzipan**[33] 5988 2-9-0 0 RobHornby 4 30
(Jonathan Portman) *spd 2f: sn wknd* **100/1**
00 **10** 1 ½ **Woodsmokehill**[30] 6078 2-9-0 0 RobertHavlin 9 24
(Rod Millman) *a towards rr: bhd fnl f* **100/1**
1m 1.32s (0.02) **Going Correction** +0.10s/f (Good) **10** Ran SP% **129.5**
Speed ratings (Par 97): **103,101,101,100,99 94,93,88,84,81**
CSF £43.96 TOTE £6.10: £1.30, £2.30, £1.10; EX 53.90 Trifecta £96.40.
Owner Peter Crate **Bred** P Delaney **Trained** Newdigate, Surrey
FOCUS
A decent juvenile maiden sprint. The odds-on favourite got tired in the closing stages after decisively winning a battle for the lead. Straightforward form.

7161 CHRISTMAS PARTIES AT SANDOWN PARK H'CAP 5f 10y
2:50 (2:54) (Class 5) (0-75,76) 3-Y-O+
£4,528 (£1,347; £673; £336; £300; £300) **Stalls** Low

Form RPR
3241 **1** **Union Rose**[23] 6335 7-9-8 **76** (v) RaulDaSilva 8 85
(Ronald Harris) *trckd ldrs: prog on outer 2f out: rdn to ld 1f out: styd on wl* **9/1**
4651 **2** 1 ½ **Our Oystercatcher**[14] 6668 5-9-4 **72** LukeMorris 9 76
(Mark Pattinson) *led: rdn and pressed 2f out: hdd 1f out: no ch w wnr last 100yds but kpt on* **9/4**[1]
4155 **3** ¾ **Rewaayat**[30] 6080 4-9-3 **71** DaneO'Neill 6 72
(Charles Hills) *t.k.h: hld up in last pair: rdn and prog on outer over 1f out: styd on same pce fnl f to take 3rd nr fin* **7/2**[2]
6000 **4** ¾ **Bahamian Sunrise**[79] 4230 7-8-4 **61** (b) DarraghKeenan(3) 7 60
(John Gallagher) *prom: trckd ldr after 2f: rdn to chal 2f out tl lost 2nd 1f out: nt qckn after: lost 3rd nr fin (jockey said gelding hung right-handed)* **16/1**
0351 **5** 1 ¼ **Dr Doro (IRE)**[45] 5532 6-9-2 **73** (v) CierenFallon(3) 5 67
(Ian Williams) *dwlt: in tch in rr: urged along over 1f out: kpt on but nvr gng pce to chal (jockey said mare hung right-handed)* **12/1**
3136 **6** 1 ½ **Indian Raj**[14] 6668 5-9-6 **74** (t) JamesDoyle 2 63
(Stuart Williams) *racd against rail: chsd ldr 2f: sn rdn: lost pl and fdd over 1f out* **7/2**[2]
2404 **7** *nk* **King Robert**[33] 5990 6-9-7 **75** AdamKirby 4 63
(Charlie Wallis) *in tch: rdn and no prog wl over 1f out: fdd after* **13/2**[3]
0165 **8** 1 ¼ **Wotadoll**[10] 6835 5-8-9 **63** MartinDwyer 3 46
(Mike Murphy) *sltly awkward s: in tch and racd against rail: no prog 2f out: fdd over 1f out* **16/1**
1m 0.3s (-1.00) **Going Correction** +0.10s/f (Good) **8** Ran SP% **118.0**
Speed ratings (Par 103): **112,109,108,107,105 102,102,100**
CSF £30.67 CT £87.59 TOTE £10.20: £2.60, £1.30, £1.80; EX 36.00 Trifecta £189.20.
Owner Adrian Evans **Bred** Home Farm **Trained** Earlswood, Monmouths
FOCUS
A fair sprint handicap in which being drawn wide and challenging centrally proved no barrier to success. The winner's time was a second quicker than the previous C&D juvenile contest. The second helps set the level, rated to his C&D latest.

7162 BRITISH STALLION STUDS EBF NOVICE STKS (PLUS 10 RACE) 1m
3:20 (3:22) (Class 4) 2-Y-O **£4,787** (£1,424; £711; £355) **Stalls** Low

Form RPR
1 **1** **Miss Yoda (GER)**[39] 5732 2-9-5 0 RobertHavlin 6 87
(John Gosden) *sn wl in tch: prog 2f out: shkn up over 1f out: styd on wl to ld last 100yds: in command fin* **13/8**[1]
00 **2** 1 ¼ **Dogged**[37] 5809 2-9-4 0 DaneO'Neill 5 83
(David Elsworth) *led: shkn up and hdd wl over 1f out: sn led again: kpt on wl but hdd and outpcd last 100yds* **50/1**
22 **3** ½ **Global Storm (IRE)**[34] 5940 2-9-4 0 JamesDoyle 13 82
(Charlie Appleby) *racd on outer: trckd ldrs: prog over 2f out: rdn to ld wl over 1f out: sn hdd: lost 2nd and kpt on same pce ins fnl f* **2/1**[2]
0 **4** 2 **Campari**[21] 6395 2-9-4 0 JasonWatson 4 78
(Roger Charlton) *trckd ldrs: stl looked green whn shkn up jst over 2f out: kpt on steadily over 1f out: nvr able to chal but shaped wl (jockey said colt hung left-handed under pressure)* **20/1**
5 2 **Cadeau D'Or (FR)** 2-9-4 0 RobHornby 3 73
(Andrew Balding) *chsd ldng pair to over 2f out: shkn up and steadily fdd over 1f out* **25/1**
6 *nk* **Surrey Pride (IRE)** 2-9-4 0 CharlesBishop 9 73+
(Joseph Tuite) *wl in rr: prog 2f out but rn green: styd on fnl f: nt disgracd* **40/1**
45 **7** *nk* **More Than A Prince**[13] 6708 2-9-4 0 RossaRyan 12 72
(Richard Hannon) *in tch in midfield: shkn up 3f out: outpcd over 2f out: kpt on again over 1f out* **16/1**
53 **8** 5 **Impatient**[18] 6528 2-9-4 0 PatDobbs 7 61
(Ralph Beckett) *dwlt: hld up in last: passed a few stragglers fr 2f out: nvr in it: likely to do bttr* **4/1**[3]
9 2 ¼ **Chinese Whisperer (FR)** 2-9-4 0 TomQueally 10 56
(Alan King) *dwlt: a in rr: brief prog over 2f out: no hdwy wl over 1f out* **50/1**
10 ¾ **Cosa Orga (IRE)** 2-9-4 0 MartinDwyer 8 54
(Brian Meehan) *chsd ldr to over 2f out: wknd qckly wl over 1f out* **16/1**
0 **11** 2 ¼ **Arabescato**[28] 6154 2-9-4 0 LukeMorris 11 49
(Richard Spencer) *a towards rr: rdn and struggling 3f out* **66/1**
12 ½ **Jen's Lad (IRE)** 2-9-4 0 JohnFahy 1 48
(Richard Hannon) *nvr beyond midfield: rdn and wknd over 2f out* **50/1**
06 **13** 5 **Dazzling Darren (IRE)**[21] 6402 2-9-4 0 JimmyQuinn 2 37
(Adam West) *a in last trio: wknd over 2f out* **66/1**
1m 44.18s (0.88) **Going Correction** +0.10s/f (Good) **13** Ran SP% **123.1**
Speed ratings (Par 97): **99,97,97,95,93 92,92,87,85,84 82,81,76**
CSF £110.66 TOTE £2.40: £1.10, £12.90, £1.10; EX 121.30 Trifecta £462.40.
Owner Westerberg **Bred** Gestut Etzean **Trained** Newmarket, Suffolk
FOCUS
Add 22yds. A fair juvenile novice contest. The clear favourite took a while to get to grips with the long-time leader but was well on top by the line. The third is among those who help pin the level.

7163 ROGER STACK MEMORIAL H'CAP 1m
3:55 (3:55) (Class 3) (0-95,91) 3-Y-O+
£9,337 (£2,796; £1,398; £699; £349; £175) **Stalls** Low

Form RPR
-251 **1** **Casanova**[13] 6732 3-9-6 **91** RobertHavlin 4 100
(John Gosden) *t.k.h: hld up in 4th: prog 2f out: shkn up to ld jst over 1f out but sn pressed: rdn and styd on wl fnl f* **5/2**[1]
0221 **2** 1 ½ **Pinnata (IRE)**[22] 6370 5-8-7 **80** (t) MarcoGhiani(7) 6 87
(Stuart Williams) *hld up in 5th: pushed along and dropped to last over 2f out: prog jst over 1f out: styd on to take 2nd last 100yds but no imp on wnr after* **11/4**[2]
2151 **3** *nk* **Siglo Six**[13] 6729 3-9-2 **87** (h) JamesDoyle 3 92
(Hugo Palmer) *hld up in last: prog on outer over 2f out: rdn to chal jst over 1f out: nt qckn and sn hld: lost 2nd last 100yds* **5/1**
6111 **4** 1 ¾ **Alfred Boucher**[30] 6081 3-9-3 **88** CharlesBishop 7 89
(Henry Candy) *led: rdn and hdd jst over 1f out: fdd* **7/2**[3]
2060 **5** 1 ¼ **The Emperor Within (FR)**[77] 4342 4-9-10 **90** EoinWalsh 5 89
(Martin Smith) *trckd ldr: shkn up 2f out: lost 2nd over 1f out: fdd* **14/1**
4332 **6** ¾ **House Of Kings (IRE)**[34] 5947 3-9-1 **86** PatDobbs 2 82
(Clive Cox) *t.k.h early: trckd ldng pair to over 1f out: nudged along and steadily lost pl* **8/1**
1m 42.93s (-0.37) **Going Correction** +0.10s/f (Good)
WFA 3 from 4yo+ 5lb **6** Ran SP% **111.9**
Speed ratings (Par 107): **105,103,103,101,100 99**
CSF £9.61 TOTE £3.60: £1.70, £1.40; EX 10.70 Trifecta £39.80.
Owner HRH Princess Haya Of Jordan **Bred** Godolphin **Trained** Newmarket, Suffolk
FOCUS
Add 22yds. A fairly good handicap. The favourite won a shade cosily and his winning time was over a second quicker than the previous C&D juvenile novice contest. The third has been rated to his C&D latest.

7164 SANDOWN PARK OPTIONAL CLAIMING H'CAP 7f
4:30 (4:31) (Class 2) 4-Y-O+
£18,675 (£5,592; £2,796; £1,398; £699; £351) **Stalls** Low

Form RPR
1212 **1** **Tukhoom (IRE)**[6] 6978 6-8-0 **78** (v) AngusVilliers(7) 6 86
(David O'Meara) *t.k.h: trckd ldr after 2f: led over 3f out: shkn up and more than 2 l ahd over 1f out: ld ebbed ins fnl f but nvr really threatened* **9/4**[1]
2106 **2** 1 **Boy In The Bar**[34] 5942 8-8-8 **82** (v) CierenFallon(3) 3 87
(Ian Williams) *hld up in rr: shkn up over 2f out: prog on outer over 1f out: styd on wl fnl f to take 2nd nr fin* **12/1**
0000 **3** *nk* **So Beloved**[22] 6376 9-10-0 **99** (p) AdamKirby 9 103
(David O'Meara) *dwlt: hld up in last: prog wl over 1f out: rdn and styd on wl fnl f to take 3rd last stride* **5/1**[3]
0034 **4** *nse* **Zwayyan**[21] 6391 6-10-0 **99** (b) JamesDoyle 8 103
(Andrew Balding) *hld up in rr: shkn up over 2f out: prog on outer over 1f out: rdn and styd on fnl f to press for 2nd nr fin* **9/2**[2]
1430 **5** ½ **Glenn Coco**[27] 6220 5-8-6 **84** (t) MarcoGhiani(7) 5 87
(Stuart Williams) *hld up in midfield: shkn up 2f out: prog to chse wnr 1f out: kpt on but nvr able to chal and lost several pls nr fin* **11/2**
0516 **6** 2 ¼ **Plunger**[18] 6538 4-8-6 **77** (b) LukeMorris 10 74
(Paul Cole) *led to over 3f out: drvn and lost 2nd 1f out: wknd* **12/1**
0652 **7** ¾ **Haddaf (IRE)**[19] 6517 4-8-9 **80** (t) JasonWatson 2 75
(Stuart Williams) *trckd ldr 2f: styd prom: rdn and lost pl jst over 1f out: wl btn whn short of room ins fnl f (jockey said gelding hung right-handed under pressure)* **11/1**
0063 **8** ½ **Azzeccagarbugli (IRE)**[9] 6863 6-8-5 **79** (p) GabrieleMalune(3) 1 72
(Mike Murphy) *trckd ldrs: pushed along and steadily lost pl fr 2f out* **14/1**
0050 **9** 2 **Above The Rest (IRE)**[40] 5711 8-9-13 **98** (h) PatDobbs 4 86
(David Barron) *hld up in last pair: pushed along and no prog on inner fr 2f out: nvr in it* **25/1**
2462 **10** *nse* **Sir Roderic (IRE)**[11] 6803 6-8-1 **72** (v) JimmyQuinn 7 65
(Rod Millman) *trckd ldrs: lost pl over 1f out: wkng whn twice short of room ins fnl f* **14/1**
1m 29.51s (0.21) **Going Correction** +0.10s/f (Good) **10** Ran SP% **121.9**
Speed ratings (Par 109): **102,100,100,100,99 97,96,95,93,93**
CSF £33.70 CT £133.35 TOTE £2.90: £1.30, £2.80, £1.90; EX 33.70 Trifecta £222.10.Tukhoom was subject to a friendly claim of £13,200
Owner R Bremer **Bred** Kabansk Ltd & Rathbarry Stud **Trained** Upper Helmsley, N Yorks
■ Stewards' Enquiry : Marco Ghiani two-day ban: careless riding (27th & 29th Sep)
FOCUS
Add 22yds. A good claiming handicap. The well-backed favourite broke well and proved dominant in the home straight. The second and third have been rated close to form.

7165 JOIN RACING TV NOW FILLIES' H'CAP 7f
5:05 (5:06) (Class 4) (0-85,76) 3-Y-O+
£6,469 (£1,925; £962; £481; £300; £300) **Stalls** Low

Form RPR
2132 **1** **Crystal Casque**[30] 6085 4-8-11 **70** AngusVilliers(7) 1 78
(Rod Millman) *cl up: trckd ldr over 2f out: pushed into ld wl over 1f out: rdn fnl f: styd on and a fending off rivals* **10/1**
5262 **2** ¾ **Delicate Kiss**[13] 6729 5-9-6 **72** LiamJones 7 78
(John Bridger) *hld up in last: prog on outer wl over 2f out: drvn and cl up over 1f out but nt qckn: styd on ins fnl f to take 2nd last strides* **4/1**[2]
2252 **3** *hd* **Quarry Beach**[21] 6418 3-9-2 **72** JasonWatson 3 75
(Henry Candy) *taken down early: led at gd pce: rdn and hdd wl over 1f out: rallied and w wnr ins fnl f: no ex last 100yds: lost 2nd fnl strides* **11/4**[1]
-156 **4** ¾ **Kitcarina (FR)**[31] 6050 4-9-8 **74** JamesDoyle 2 77
(Andrew Balding) *hld up in last trio: rdn 2f out: sing to stay on whn rn into trble fnl f and nvr able to land a blow (jockey said filly was denied a clear run)* **4/1**[2]
3642 **5** *nk* **Hunni**[21] 6408 4-9-7 **73** LukeMorris 8 76
(Tom Clover) *trckd ldng trio: effrt on outer over 2f out: drvn and cl up over 1f out but nt qckn: one pce fnl f* **7/1**[3]
2113 **6** ½ **Bedtime Bella (IRE)**[23] 6338 3-8-8 **71** (v) MarcoGhiani(7) 4 70
(Michael Appleby) *t.k.h: trckd ldr to over 2f out: lost pl over 1f out and rdn: one pce fnl f* **4/1**[2]
5410 **7** 3 ½ **Chica De La Noche**[24] 6318 5-9-10 **76** (p) AdamKirby 6 68
(Simon Dow) *hld up in last trio: rdn over 2f out: sn in last and struggling* **10/1**
1m 29.64s (0.34) **Going Correction** +0.10s/f (Good)
WFA 3 from 4yo+ 4lb **7** Ran SP% **117.3**
Speed ratings (Par 102): **102,101,100,100,99 99,95**
CSF £51.33 CT £143.04 TOTE £11.90: £3.70, £2.10; EX 29.80 Trifecta £101.00.
Owner The Dirham Partnership **Bred** Mrs J E Laws **Trained** Kentisbeare, Devon

FOCUS
Add 22yds. A fair fillies' handicap. One of the slight outsiders won bravely in a good comparative time for the grade. The second, third and fourth have been rated pretty much to form.

7166 HWFA WILLIAMS H'CAP — 1m 1f 209y
5:35 (5:35) (Class 4) (0-80,84) 3-Y-O+
£6,469 (£1,925; £962; £481; £300; £300) Stalls Low

Form — RPR

2244 **1** **Zzoro (IRE)**[16] 6596 6-9-3 77 ....(t[1]) MarcoGhiani(7) 7 — 86
(Amanda Perrett) *hld up in 4th: clsd over 2f out: led wl over 1f out gng strly: sn put rivals to the sword: rdn out* 9/4[1]

3333 **2** 2 ¾ **Elhafei (USA)**[19] 6512 4-9-4 71 ....(p) AlistairRawlinson 8 — 75
(Michael Appleby) *t.k.h: hld up in last pair: prog 2f out: drvn and kpt on to take 2nd ins fnl f: no ch w wnr* 11/4[3]

6610 **3** 2 **My Boy Sepoy**[13] 6725 4-10-1 82 .... AdamKirby 6 — 82
(Stuart Williams) *led 2f: trckd ldr: led over 2f out but sn rdn: hdd wl over 1f out and no ch w wnr after: lost 2nd ins fnl f* 5/2[2]

3001 **4** 1 ½ **Secret Art (IRE)**[21] 6390 9-9-8 75 .... LukeMorris 1 — 72
(Gary Moore) *trckd ldng pair: rdn and cl up 2f out: sn lft bhd* 8/1

125- **5** 7 **Rollicking (IRE)**[353] 7644 3-9-2 75 .... PatDobbs 2 — 59
(Richard Hannon) *led after 2f to over 2f out: pushed along and wknd over 1f out* 10/1

5-55 **6** 1 ¼ **Swilly Sunset**[19] 6512 6-9-1 71 .... DarraghKeenan(3) 3 — 51
(Anthony Carson) *awkward s: hld up in last: shkn up over 2f out: no rspnse and sn wknd* 11/1

2m 12.93s (2.73) **Going Correction** +0.10s/f (Good) — **6** Ran SP% **114.5**
WFA 3 from 4yo+ 6lb
Speed ratings (Par 105): **93,90,89,88,82 81**
CSF £9.07 CT £15.55 TOTE £2.70: £1.80, £1.80; EX 7.80 Trifecta £21.20.
Owner Mr & Mrs F Cotton, Mr & Mrs P Conway **Bred** Hatta Bloodstock **Trained** Pulborough, W Sussex

FOCUS
Add 22yds. A fairly decent handicap. The favourite won easily in a comparatively slow time from off a modest gallop. The second has been rated close to form.
T/Plt: £30.50 to a £1 stake. Pool: £48,993.28 - 1,170.30 winning units T/Qpdt: £17.70 to a £1 stake. Pool: £4,358.22 - 181.48 winning units **Jonathan Neesom**

7167 - 7171a (Foreign Racing) - See Raceform Interactive

6851 BATH (L-H)
Saturday, September 14

OFFICIAL GOING: Firm (8.7)
Wind: light across Weather: sunny

7172 SDS INTELLISTORM H'CAP — 5f 160y
2:00 (2:03) (Class 6) (0-60,60) 3-Y-O+
£2,781 (£827; £413; £300; £300; £300) Stalls Centre

Form — RPR

0412 **1** **Knockabout Queen**[5] 7022 3-9-5 59 .... DavidEgan 12 — 72
(Tony Carroll) *mid-div: hdwy over 2f out: led over 1f out: sn qcknd readily clr: easily* 3/1[1]

-505 **2** 4 **Wild Dancer**[19] 6529 6-9-3 60 .... WilliamCarver(5) 11 — 60
(Patrick Chamings) *stmbld leaving stalls: towards rr: hdwy whn swtchd lft over 1f out: r.o ins fnl f to go 2nd fnl 120yds: no ch w wnr (jockey said mare stumbled when leaving the stalls)* 7/2[2]

000 **3** nk **Amor Kethley**[77] 4378 3-8-8 55 ....(t w) SeanKirrane(7) 17 — 54
(Amy Murphy) *trckd ldrs: rdn to dispute ld over 2f out tl over 1f out: sn outpcd by wnr: no ex fnl 120yds* 16/1

-040 **4** 2 **Molly Blake**[29] 6181 3-9-4 58 .... LiamKeniry 13 — 50
(Clive Cox) *trckd ldrs: rdn over 2f out: kpt on but nt pce to chal* 10/1

2505 **5** ½ **Jaganory (IRE)**[10] 6857 7-8-7 52 ....(v) AngusVilliers(7) 16 — 42
(Christopher Mason) *in tch: rdn over 1f out: kpt on same pce fnl f* 14/1

1550 **6** ½ **Tilsworth Rose**[30] 6126 5-8-5 48 ....(b) TobyEley(5) 2 — 37
(J R Jenkins) *trckd ldrs: rdn over 2f out: sn one pce (jockey said mare was unsettled in the stalls)* 20/1

0305 **7** 1 ¼ **North Korea (IRE)**[33] 6017 3-8-6 46 oh1 .... RaulDaSilva 14 — 30
(Brian Baugh) *s.i.s: towards rr: hdwy into midfield over 2f out: sn rdn: kpt on same pce fnl f* 50/1

-340 **8** 2 **Amberine**[24] 6329 5-8-10 48 ow2 .... RyanTate 9 — 26
(Malcolm Saunders) *in tch: rdn over 2f out: nt pce to get on terms: hld whn nt clr run over 1f out: wknd fnl f* 14/1

1316 **9** ½ **Aquadabra (IRE)**[16] 6639 4-9-0 57 .... RhiainIngram(5) 10 — 33
(Christopher Mason) *disp ld: rdn and hdd over 1f out: wknd ent fnl f: eased fnl 100yds (jockey said filly stopped quickly)* 12/1

0/00 **10** hd **Picc And Go**[74] 4481 6-8-3 46 oh1 ....(b[1]) RachealKneller(5) 6 — 21
(Debbie Hughes) *racd keenly towards rr: midfield over 2f out: rdn over 1f out: fdd fnl f* 28/1

0006 **11** 4 **Wiff Waff**[20] 6510 4-9-7 59 ....(p[1]) FergusSweeney 15 — 21
(Chris Gordon) *a towards rr* 20/1

0200 **12** 4 **Sugar Plum Fairy**[9] 6897 4-8-8 46 oh1 .... JohnFahy 8
(Tony Carroll) *s.i.s: a towards rr* 10/1

0500 **13** 1 **Vino Rosso (IRE)**[23] 6361 3-8-7 47 .... JimmyQuinn 7
(Michael Blanshard) *s.i.s: a towards rr (jockey said filly was slowly into stride)* 33/1

-066 **14** 2 ¼ **Illegitimate Gains**[13] 6754 3-8-6 46 oh1 ....(tp) RyanPowell 5
(Adam West) *towards rr of midfield: rdn wl over 2f out: sn hung lft: wknd over 1f out (jockey said filly hung left-handed)* 50/1

5000 **15** 13 **Coastal Cyclone**[29] 6174 5-8-8 46 oh1 ....(v) MartinDwyer 3
(Harry Dunlop) *disp ld tl rdn over 2f out: hld whn sltly hmpd over 1f out: sn wknd (fin lame) (jockey said gelding moved poorly; vet said a post-race examination found the gelding to be lame on its left-fore)* 8/1[3]

1m 9.13s (-1.97) **Going Correction** -0.175s/f (Firm) — **15** Ran SP% **123.3**
WFA 3 from 4yo+ 2lb
Speed ratings (Par 101): **106,100,100,97,96 96,94,91,91,91 85,80,79,76,58**
CSF £12.08 CT £152.08 TOTE £3.60: £1.60, £1.70, £6.60; EX 13.30 Trifecta £163.40.
Owner Jason Tucker **Bred** Mike Channon Bloodstock Ltd **Trained** Cropthorne, Worcs

FOCUS
A big field sprint but only a handful came here in any kind of form, foremost of which was Knockabout Queen who is absolutely thriving at the moment. A minor pb from the winner.

7173 SDS SYMBIOTIC NURSERY H'CAP — 1m
2:35 (2:35) (Class 5) (0-75,75) 2-Y-O
£3,428 (£1,020; £509; £300) Stalls Low

Form — RPR

5304 **1** **Top Buck (IRE)**[7] 6963 2-9-7 75 ....(p[1]) LiamKeniry 4 — 79
(Brian Meehan) *pushed along leaving stalls: trckd ldrs: led ent fnl f: r.o wl: rdn out* 13/8[1]

3600 **2** 3 ¾ **Breck's Selection (FR)**[23] 6372 2-8-12 66 .... DavidEgan 1 — 61
(Mark Johnston) *led: rdn whn hdd ent fnl f: kpt on but nt pce of wnr* 5/1

0240 **3** 1 ¾ **Willa**[44] 5587 2-9-4 72 ....(b[1]) FergusSweeney 5 — 63
(Richard Hannon) *trckd ldr tl outpcd over 2f out: hld after but kpt on to regain 3rd towards fin* 4/1[3]

0116 **4** ½ **Mac McCarthy (IRE)**[14] 6728 2-9-4 75 .... FinleyMarsh(3) 2 — 65
(Richard Hughes) *trckd ldrs: rdn in cl 3rd over 1f out: nt quite pce to chal: no ex towards fin* 9/5[2]

1m 39.61s (-2.09) **Going Correction** -0.175s/f (Firm) — **4** Ran SP% **110.5**
Speed ratings (Par 95): **103,99,97,97**
CSF £9.53 TOTE £2.40; EX 10.00 Trifecta £22.30.
Owner Manton Thoroughbreds Iv **Bred** Eimear Mulhern **Trained** Manton, Wilts

FOCUS
Hard to enthuse too much over this form with all the runners having some sort of question to answer. The winner was well backed, however. The winner has been rated back to his best.

7174 SDS/EBF NOVICE AUCTION STKS (PLUS 10 RACE) — 1m
3:10 (3:11) (Class 4) 2-Y-O
£4,787 (£1,424; £711; £355) Stalls Low

Form — RPR

1 **Zabeel Champion** 2-9-2 0 .... DavidEgan 2 — 74+
(Mark Johnston) *sn led: kpt finding whn strly chal fr over 2f out: kpt on wl to assert ins fnl f: pushed out* 9/4[2]

1 **2** 1 **Bronze River**[25] 6314 2-9-2 0 .... WilliamCarver(5) 5 — 77
(Andrew Balding) *trckd ldr: upsides fr over 4f out: rdn for str chal fr over 2f out but sn hung rt: ev ch fnl f: no ex fnl 75yds (jockey said gelding hung right-handed in the home straight)* 8/11[1]

0324 **3** 6 **Space Ace (FR)**[16] 6629 2-9-3 75 ....(p) AdamMcNamara 6 — 59
(Archie Watson) *trckd ldrs: rdn over 2f out: kpt on but nt pce of front pair* 9/2[3]

500 **4** 10 **Numinous (IRE)**[12] 6807 2-9-1 46 .... MartinDwyer 3 — 33
(Henry Candy) *hld up 5th: rdn into 4th over 2f out: wknd over 1f out* 25/1

05 **5** 10 **Unbridled Light (FR)**[19] 6527 2-8-7 0 .... JohnFahy 1 — 1
(Anthony Honeyball) *chsd ldrs tl outpcd over 2f out: wknd over 1f out* 50/1

1m 42.07s (0.37) **Going Correction** -0.175s/f (Firm) — **5** Ran SP% **112.7**
Speed ratings (Par 97): **91,90,84,74,64**
CSF £4.39 TOTE £2.80: £1.20, £1.10; EX 4.00 Trifecta £7.80.
Owner Jaber Abdullah **Bred** Hascombe & Valiant Stud Ltd **Trained** Middleham Moor, N Yorks

FOCUS
No depth to this and very few got into it, but the winner could be above average. The second has been credited with minor improvement.

7175 SDS WATER MANAGEMENT H'CAP — 5f 160y
3:45 (3:45) (Class 3) (0-95,91) 4-Y-O+
£10,893 (£3,262; £1,631; £815; £407; £204) Stalls Centre

Form — RPR

0550 **1** **Walk On Walter (IRE)**[7] 6953 4-9-7 91 ....(h) NicolaCurrie 7 — 99
(Jonathan Portman) *trckd ldr: led after 1f: rdn whn strly pressed over 1f out: jst hld on* 7/2[2]

1500 **2** hd **Mountain Peak**[7] 6954 4-9-2 86 .... LiamKeniry 4 — 93
(Ed Walker) *trckd ldrs: rdn over 1f out: edgd lft ins fnl f: kpt on wl towards fin: jst failed* 13/2

6225 **3** 1 ¾ **Count Otto (IRE)**[7] 6953 4-8-13 90 ....(h) AngusVilliers(7) 1 — 92
(Amanda Perrett) *last pair: hdwy to trck ldrs 3f out: rdn over 1f out: wnt 3rd ins fnl f: kpt on same pce* 5/2[1]

3100 **4** nk **Shamshon (IRE)**[19] 6534 8-8-12 82 .... DavidEgan 3 — 83
(Stuart Williams) *stdd s: in last pair: hdwy over 2f out: rdn w ch ent fnl f: kpt on same pce* 14/1

5243 **5** 1 ¾ **Little Boy Blue**[18] 6565 4-9-6 90 ....(h) RyanTate 5 — 85
(Bill Turner) *led for over 1f: prom: rdn and ev ch over 1f out: hld ent fnl f: no ex fnl 120yds* 5/1

0455 **6** 2 **Jumira Bridge**[14] 6724 5-9-1 90 ....(t) WilliamCarver(5) 2 — 78
(Robert Cowell) *hld up bhd ldrs: effrt over 2f out: wknd fnl f* 9/2[3]

3134 **7** hd **Oeil De Tigre (FR)**[21] 6465 8-8-4 81 .... LauraCoughlan(7) 6 — 69
(Tony Carroll) *s.i.s: in trcking ldrs: rdn and ev ch 2f out: wknd ent fnl f (jockey said gelding was slowly away)* 10/1

1m 8.92s (-2.18) **Going Correction** -0.175s/f (Firm) — **7** Ran SP% **114.7**
Speed ratings (Par 107): **107,106,104,104,101 99,98**
CSF £26.28 TOTE £4.40: £2.40, £5.10; EX 29.60 Trifecta £71.20.
Owner Philip Simpson **Bred** Sandro Garavelli **Trained** Upper Lambourn, Berks

FOCUS
A competitive sprint but it was the sort of race that would throw up a different result every time it's run. Straightforward form rated around the first two.

7176 JOHN HERMAN H'CAP — 1m
4:20 (4:20) (Class 4) (0-85,87) 3-Y-O
£5,207 (£1,549; £774; £387; £300; £300) Stalls Low

Form — RPR

6144 **1** **Sash**[34] 5991 3-9-10 87 .... AdamMcNamara 3 — 95
(Amanda Perrett) *mde all: rdn whn strly chal over 2f out: styd on wl to assert ins fnl f: rdn out* 7/2[2]

-301 **2** ¾ **Tell William**[18] 6558 3-8-10 73 ....(b) MartinDwyer 6 — 79
(Marcus Tregoning) *trckd wnr: upsides over 3f out: rdn for str chal fr 2f out: styd on but hld ins fnl f* 7/2[2]

0222 **3** 2 ½ **Strict Tempo**[24] 6346 3-9-2 84 .... WilliamCarver(5) 2 — 84
(Andrew Balding) *trckd ldrs: rdn 2f out: hung lft fnl f: styd on but nt pce to get on terms* 5/2[1]

4311 **4** 2 ¼ **Amorously (IRE)**[10] 6856 3-9-2 79 .... FergusSweeney 1 — 74
(Richard Hannon) *trckd ldrs: rdn over 2f out: kpt on same pce* 10/1

1-30 **5** nk **Elamirr (IRE)**[64] 4865 3-9-3 80 .... DavidEgan 5 — 74
(Roger Varian) *hld up in tch: rdn over 2f out: styd on but nt pce to get involved* 7/1

4320 **6** *9* **Hold Still (IRE)**[22] 6425 3-9-2 **79** NicolaCurrie 4 53
(William Muir) *s.i.s: nvr really travelling in last: outpcd over 2f out (jockey said colt lost his action coming around the final bend into the home straight)* **9/2**[3]

1m 39.94s (-1.76) **Going Correction** -0.175s/f (Firm) **6** Ran SP% **112.8**
Speed ratings (Par 103): **101,100,97,95,95 86**
CSF £16.19 TOTE £3.40: £1.70, £2.30; EX 15.90 Trifecta £61.80.
Owner K Abdullah **Bred** Juddmonte Farms Ltd **Trained** Pulborough, W Sussex

FOCUS
A competitive race on paper but the pace held up and the front two had it between them from a fair way out. Muddling form which has been rated a bit cautiously.

7177 SDS AQUA-XCHANGE NOVICE STKS 1m 3f 137y
4:55 (4:56) (Class 5) 3-Y-O+ **£3,428** (£1,020; £509) **Stalls** Low

Form RPR

-222 **1** **Mojave**[15] 6687 3-9-2 75 AdamMcNamara 3 78
(Roger Charlton) *trckd ldr: led over 3f out: rdn clr over 2f out: v easily (vet said gelding lost his right fore shoe)* **1/3**[1]

2 *35* **Education** 3-9-2 0 (v[1]) RaulDaSilva 1 20+
(Ismail Mohammed) *slowly away and sn pushed along to chse ldrs: drvn to stay in tch over 5f out: no ch over 2f out: wnt modest 2nd towards fin* **3/1**[2]

66 **3** *1* **Zero To Hero (IRE)**[5] 7035 4-8-12 0 Pierre-LouisJamin(7) 2 13
(Archie Watson) *led tl over 3f out: sn no ch w wnr: wknd over 1f out: lost 2nd towards fin* **9/1**[3]

2m 27.86s (-2.94) **Going Correction** -0.175s/f (Firm)
WFA 3 from 4yo 8lb **3** Ran SP% **110.0**
Speed ratings (Par 103): **102,78,78**
CSF £1.76 TOTE £1.30; EX 1.90 Trifecta £1.40.
Owner K Abdullah **Bred** Juddmonte Farms Ltd **Trained** Beckhampton, Wilts

FOCUS
With the newcomer not offering any sort of challenge, this was effectively a non event and we didn't learn anything from it.

7178 LOVELY LOUISE HUDSON BIRTHDAY H'CAP 5f 10y
5:30 (5:30) (Class 4) (0-80,84) 3-Y-O+
£5,207 (£1,549; £774; £387; £300; £300) **Stalls** Centre

Form RPR

2324 **1** **Secretfact**[15] 6668 6-9-4 **74** (p) JimmyQuinn 5 81
(Malcolm Saunders) *hld up: hdwy ent fnl f: r.o strly: led cl home* **11/4**[1]

233 **2** *shd* **Pink Flamingo**[10] 6859 3-9-10 **81** NicolaCurrie 6 87
(Michael Attwater) *hld up in last pair: hdwy over 1f out: tk narrow advantage jst ins fnl f: r.o: hdd cl home* **11/4**[1]

4241 **3** *1 ¼* **More Than Likely**[17] 6602 3-8-12 **76** AngusVilliers(7) 2 77
(Richard Hughes) *led for 1f: prom: rdn and ev ch ent fnl f: kpt on but nt pce of front pair* **7/2**[2]

0522 **4** *2 ¼* **Glamorous Rocket (IRE)**[25] 6299 4-8-9 **70** RhiainIngram(5) 7 63
(Christopher Mason) *chsd ldrs: led wl over 1f out: hdd jst ins fnl f: fdd fnl 100yds* **13/2**

0250 **5** *3 ½* **Good Luck Fox (IRE)**[44] 5589 3-9-7 **78** FergusSweeney 3 58
(Richard Hannon) *trckd ldrs: rdn and ev ch 2f out: wknd ent fnl f* **9/1**

4013 **6** *¾* **It Must Be Faith**[10] 6857 9-8-9 **65** (p) DavidEgan 1 43
(Michael Appleby) *little slowly away: led after 1f: rdn and hdd wl over 1f out: wknd ent fnl f* **5/1**[3]

1m 0.89s (-1.11) **Going Correction** -0.175s/f (Firm)
WFA 3 from 4yo+ 1lb **6** Ran SP% **115.6**
Speed ratings (Par 105): **101,100,98,95,89 88**
CSF £10.98 TOTE £3.30: £1.90, £1.70; EX 12.10 Trifecta £48.20.
Owner Premier Conservatory Roofs **Bred** M S Saunders & D Collier **Trained** Green Ore, Somerset

FOCUS
A trappy sprint handicap and but it was won by the only previous course winner in the line-up. The first two have been rated pretty much to their best.
T/Plt: £47.40 to a £1 stake. Pool: £38,290.81 - 588.87 winning units T/Qpdt: £12.60 to a £1 stake. Pool: £2,287.03 - 134.08 winning units **Tim Mitchell**

7139 CHESTER (L-H)
Saturday, September 14

OFFICIAL GOING: Good (7.3)
Wind: Light, half behind in straight of over 1f Weather: Sunny

7179 MBNA / EBF STALLIONS NOVICE STKS (PLUS 10 RACE) 6f 17y
1:30 (1:34) (Class 4) 2-Y-O
£7,096 (£2,124; £1,062; £531; £265; £133) **Stalls** Low

Form RPR

6 **1** **Roseina's Voice**[107] 3244 2-8-6 0 ThomasGreatrex(5) 2 80
(David Loughnane) *mde all: rdn 2f out: r.o wl to draw clr ins fnl f* **20/1**

43 **2** *3 ½* **Stroxx (IRE)**[16] 6622 2-9-2 0 DavidAllan 7 74
(Tim Easterby) *dwlt: impr to go prom 4f out: wnt 2nd over 2f out: sn rdn: tried to get to wnr over 1f out: sn no imp and kpt on same pce* **9/2**[3]

31 **3** *1 ¼* **Huboor (IRE)**[74] 4482 2-9-3 0 JoeFanning 3 71
(Mark Johnston) *racd a little worse than midfield: niggled along over 4f out: plld to outer under 2f out: no imp over 1f out: styd on wl towards fin to snatch 3rd fnl stride: nvr nrr* **9/4**[2]

0 **4** *hd* **Seven Emirates (IRE)**[29] 6175 2-9-2 0 AndrewMullen 5 70
(K R Burke) *in tch: pushed along 3f out: effrt 2f out: kpt on u.p ins fnl f: nvr able to get on terms* **8/1**

240 **5** *5* **Lilkian**[29] 6167 2-8-9 67 GavinAshton(7) 6 55
(Shaun Keightley) *chsd wnr tl rdn over 2f out: sn sltly unbalanced: wknd fnl f* **25/1**

6 *1* **Sheung Wan** 2-8-13 0 ConnorMurtagh(3) 1 52
(Richard Fahey) *green in paddock: chsd ldrs: rdn over 2f out: sn lost pl and outpcd: wknd fnl f (jockey said colt hung right-handed in the home straight)* **16/1**

1 **7** *5* **Deb's Delight**[24] 6336 2-9-8 0 PaulHanagan 4 43
(Richard Fahey) *dwlt and n.m.r s: towards rr: pushed along 4f out: nvr able to get on terms (trainer's rep said colt failed to handle the track)* **11/8**[1]

00 **8** *8* **Courtney Rose**[45] 5547 2-8-11 0 LewisEdmunds 8 8
(Ivan Furtado) *dwlt: a bhd: sn pushed along: outpcd 4f out: nvr involved* **150/1**

1m 15.65s (0.15) **Going Correction** -0.075s/f (Good) **8** Ran SP% **117.3**
Speed ratings (Par 97): **96,91,89,89,82 81,74,64**
CSF £108.54 TOTE £21.40: £4.20, £1.30, £1.20; EX 106.70 Trifecta £441.90.
Owner Lancashire Lads 2, Gentech & Hoyland **Bred** Mrs G S Rees **Trained** Tern Hill, Shropshire

FOCUS
The going was good. GoingStick 7.3. The rail between the 6f and 1 1/2f points was moved out by 3yds. Amended race distances: Races 1, 5 and 6 add 13yds; Race 2 add 20yds; Race 3 add 26yds; Race 4 add 10yds; Race 7 add 14yds. Stalls: 1m 2f - outside; all other races - inside. With the two at the head of the market slowly away and never able to land a blow, the way was left clear for the front-running winner to spring a surprise.

7180 SPORTPESA STAND CUP STKS (LISTED RACE) 1m 4f 63y
2:05 (2:05) (Class 1) 3-Y-O+ **£22,116** (£8,385; £4,196; £2,090) **Stalls** Low

Form RPR

4114 **1** **Sextant**[28] 6213 4-9-3 103 LouisSteward 1 111
(Sir Michael Stoute) *chsd ldrs: racd in 2nd pl after nrly 2f: effrt to ld jst over 1f out: r.o ins fnl f: comf* **7/2**[3]

4523 **2** *1* **Manuela De Vega (IRE)**[21] 6446 3-8-4 103 HarryBentley 3 106
(Ralph Beckett) *led: rdn and hdd jst over 1f out: kpt on u.p ins fnl f but a hld* **5/4**[1]

-402 **3** *¾* **Grace And Danger (IRE)**[21] 6466 3-8-4 102 DuranFentiman 2 104
(Andrew Balding) *racd keenly: chsd ldr for nrly 2f: racd in 3rd pl after: rdn over 2f out to go pce: swtchd rt fnl 100yds: kpt on towards fin* **8/1**

-200 **4** *4* **Ben Vrackie**[21] 6473 4-9-3 106 RobertHavlin 5 102
(John Gosden) *hld up in rr: rdn to go pce over 2f out: eased whn wl hld ins fnl 100yds* **2/1**[2]

2m 38.0s (-4.20) **Going Correction** -0.075s/f (Good)
WFA 3 from 4yo 8lb **4** Ran SP% **111.1**
Speed ratings (Par 111): **111,110,109,107**
CSF £8.58 TOTE £4.50; EX 8.50 Trifecta £14.10.
Owner The Queen **Bred** The Queen **Trained** Newmarket, Suffolk

FOCUS
Add 20yds. Four useful types contested this Listed contest, but there didn't seem to be a great deal of early pace. The winner was in the right place to strike and scored nicely. The second has been rated a bit below form, with the third to her Windsor latest.

7181 SPORTPESA H'CAP 1m 6f 87y
2:40 (2:41) (Class 3) (0-95,93) 4-Y-O+
£10,582 (£3,168; £1,584; £792; £396; £198) **Stalls** Low

Form RPR

0223 **1** **Diocletian (IRE)**[32] 6044 4-8-13 **85** DavidProbert 8 100
(Andrew Balding) *stdd s: hld up: hdwy travelling wl over 3f out: swtchd rt over 2f out: c 3 wd ent st: led over 1f out: sn rdn clr and r.o strly: edgd lft ins fnl f: eased cl home* **9/2**[3]

3223 **2** *11* **Celestial Force (IRE)**[14] 6716 4-8-10 **82** (p) RichardKingscote 1 82
(Tom Dascombe) *led: pushed along over 3f out: rdn and jnd over 2f out: hdd over 1f out: no ch w wnr fnl f* **15/8**[1]

0100 **3** *hd* **Mancini**[24] 6355 5-9-7 **93** AlistairRawlinson 4 93
(Jonathan Portman) *chsd ldr: chalng 3f out: sn rdn upsides: kpt on to battle for 2nd ins fnl f whn no ch w wnr* **4/1**[2]

0606 **4** *6* **Manjaam (IRE)**[49] 5443 6-8-11 **83** (p) RobertHavlin 5 74
(Ian Williams) *stdd s: hld up towards rr: rdn 2f out: plugged on fnl f: nvr able to get involved* **12/1**

0000 **5** *1 ½* **My Reward**[7] 6958 7-8-12 **84** DavidAllan 6 73
(Tim Easterby) *chsd ldrs: rdn over 3f out: outpcd over 2f out: n.d after* **9/1**

6203 **6** *1 ¼* **Jabbaar**[15] 6657 6-9-1 **87** JamieGormley 9 74
(Iain Jardine) *dwlt: in rr: pushed along over 5f out: drvn 3f out: nvr a threat (jockey said gelding was never travelling)* **15/2**

-540 **7** *7* **Fun Mac (GER)**[45] 5540 8-9-2 **88** (t) CharlieBennett 7 66
(Hughie Morrison) *dwlt: chsd ldrs: rdn over 4f out: lost pl over 3f out: sn wknd* **7/1**

3m 4.85s (-4.95) **Going Correction** -0.075s/f (Good) **7** Ran SP% **114.9**
Speed ratings (Par 107): **111,104,104,101,100 99,95**
CSF £13.54 CT £35.88 TOTE £5.00: £1.70, £1.50; EX 13.30 Trifecta £66.70.
Owner Richard Wilmot-Smith **Bred** R J C Wilmot-Smith **Trained** Kingsclere, Hants

FOCUS
Add 26yds. A competitive stayers' handicap on paper, but the race was blown apart by the ultra-impressive winner. The form could be a bit better than rated.

7182 STELLAR GROUP NURSERY H'CAP 5f 15y
3:15 (3:18) (Class 3) (0-95,96) 2-Y-O
£11,827 (£3,541; £1,770; £885; £442; £222) **Stalls** Low

Form RPR

1140 **1** **Praxeology (IRE)**[24] 6356 2-9-7 **88** JoeFanning 6 92
(Mark Johnston) *chsd ldrs: rdn over 1f out: led ins fnl f: r.o* **9/2**[2]

423 **2** *¾* **Ainsdale**[24] 6337 2-8-8 **75** AndrewMullen 3 76
(K R Burke) *bmpd early: in tch: effrt to chal 1f out: kpt on ins fnl f: nt quite pce of wnr* **11/2**[3]

424 **3** *nk* **Hot Heels**[33] 6029 2-8-10 **77** RichardKingscote 4 77
(Tom Dascombe) *edgd lft early and bmpd: hld up: pushed along over 2f out: effrt on outer over 1f out: styd on towards fin: nt pce to chal* **9/2**[2]

0210 **4** *1 ¾* **Vintage Times**[11] 6822 2-8-11 **78** DavidAllan 1 72
(Tim Easterby) *led: rdn whn pressed over 1f out: hdd ins fnl f: no ex fnl 100yds* **3/1**[1]

2166 **5** *1 ¾* **Raahy**[23] 6375 2-9-10 **96** (v[1]) SeamusCronin(5) 5 84
(George Scott) *w ldr: rdn and unable qck whn lost 2nd over 1f out: no ex ins fnl f (jockey said gelding ran too free)* **3/1**[1]

034 **6** *9* **Dark Optimist (IRE)**[20] 6515 2-8-10 **77** (t) HarryBentley 2 32
(David Evans) *s.i.s: a outpcd and bhd: nvr on terms (starter reported that the colt was reluctant to enter the stalls; trainer was informed that the colt could not run until the day after passing a stalls test)* **8/1**

1m 1.93s (-0.17) **Going Correction** -0.075s/f (Good) **6** Ran SP% **112.9**
Speed ratings (Par 99): **98,96,96,93,90 76**
CSF £28.77 TOTE £4.80: £2.40, £4.10; EX 30.00 Trifecta £92.90.
Owner Dr J Walker **Bred** Yeomanstown Stud **Trained** Middleham Moor, N Yorks
■ Stewards' Enquiry : Seamus Cronin two-day ban: interference & careless riding (Sep 29-30)

FOCUS
Add 10yds. An above-average nursery run at a fair clip. The winner was had no trouble dropping back from 6f and has been rated as running a pb.

7183 WHITE HORSE H'CAP 6f 17y
3:50 (3:52) (Class 4) (0-85,84) 3-Y-O+
£6,727 (£2,002; £1,000; £500; £300; £300) **Stalls** Low

Form RPR

3100 **1** **Gabrial The Tiger (IRE)**[41] 5708 7-8-7 **72** ConnorMurtagh(3) 8 80
(Richard Fahey) *mde all: rdn over 1f out: kpt on ins fnl f: jst hld on fin (trainer's rep said, regarding the improved form shown, the gelding benefitted from the quicker going and a drop in grade)* **14/1**

1304 **2** *shd* **Gabrial The Devil (IRE)**[35] 5951 4-9-8 **84**.................. PaulHanagan 5 91
(Richard Fahey) *in tch: effrt over 1f out: r.o to take 2nd ins fnl f: pressed wnr towards fin: jst failed* **4/1**[1]

3123 **3** *½* **Baby Steps**[21] 6465 3-8-10 **79**.................. ThomasGreatrex(5) 14 84+
(David Loughnane) *racd on outer: midfield: pushed along 4f out: hdwy over 2f out: r.o ins fnl f: gng on at fin* **10/1**

0304 **4** *¾* **Private Matter**[25] 6319 5-8-11 **73**..................(b) JackMitchell 3 76
(Amy Murphy) *racd keenly: chsd ldrs: rdn over 1f out: kpt on same pce ins fnl f* **9/2**[2]

0612 **5** *1* **Redrosezorro**[17] 6591 5-8-8 **70**..................(h) ShelleyBirkett 2 69
(Eric Alston) *dwlt: in tch: rdn over 1f out: checked whn nt clr run ins fnl f: kpt on: nt pce to chal* **9/2**[2]

0002 **6** *½* **Bossipop**[14] 6714 6-9-8 **84**..................(b) DavidAllan 9 82
(Tim Easterby) *w wnr: rdn and ev ch over 1f out: lost 2nd ins fnl f: no ex fnl 100yds* **7/1**[3]

4434 **7** *shd* **Seen The Lyte (IRE)**[14] 6714 4-9-0 **79**..................(h) RowanScott(3) 4 77
(Nigel Tinkler) *missed break: hld up in midfield: nt clr run on inner 2f out: hdwy over 1f out: styd on towards fin: nt quite rch ldrs* **8/1**

1050 **8** *1¼* **Machree (IRE)**[14] 6714 4-9-8 **84**.................. HarryBentley 12 78
(Declan Carroll) *hld up towards rr: rdn over 1f out: kpt on ins fnl f: nvr able to trble ldrs* **25/1**

0050 **9** *2¼* **Gracious John (IRE)**[14] 6724 6-9-7 **83**.................. RichardKingscote 6 69
(Ian Williams) *hld up: rdn over 1f out: sme hdwy ins fnl f: nvr able to get involved* **8/1**

4050 **10** *nk* **Peachey Carnehan**[1] 7145 5-8-8 **70** oh17..................(v) AndrewMullen 1 55
(Michael Mullineaux) *missed break: bhd: u.p over 1f out: nvr able to get involved* **40/1**

2044 **11** *nk* **Bellevarde (IRE)**[8] 6921 5-8-9 **71**.................. JoeFanning 7 55
(Richard Price) *chsd ldrs: rdn over 1f out: checked whn nt qckning ins fnl f: wknd fnl 100yds* **20/1**

5105 **12** *½* **Pass The Gin**[30] 6108 3-9-3 **81**.................. DavidProbert 13 64
(Andrew Balding) *racd keenly: midfield: rdn ent fnl 2f: carried hd high u.p: wknd over 1f out* **12/1**

560 **13** *6* **Galloway Hills**[38] 5821 4-9-0 **81**..................(p) DylanHogan(5) 10 45
(Phillip Makin) *dwlt: hld up: rdn over 1f out: lft bhd ins fnl f* **25/1**

1m 15.03s (-0.47) **Going Correction** -0.075s/f (Good)
WFA 3 from 4yo+ 2lb **13 Ran SP% 129.4**
Speed ratings (Par 105): **100,99,99,98,96 96,96,94,91,91 90,89,81**
CSF £72.29 CT £636.43 TOTE £25.10: £5.90, £2.40, £3.80; EX 61.10 Trifecta £1183.10.
Owner Dr Marwan Koukash **Bred** Kenneth Heelan **Trained** Musley Bank, N Yorks

FOCUS
Add 13yds. A decent sprint handicap which produced a one-two for the Richard Fahey/Dr Marwan Koukash combination. The second has been rated to his best, and the third as running as well as ever.

7184 COMMONHALL STREET SOCIAL H'CAP 7f 127y
4:25 (4:27) (Class 3) (0-95,94) 3-Y-O+
£10,582 (£3,168; £1,584; £792; £396; £198) **Stalls** Low

Form RPR

1000 **1** **Gabrial The Wire**[14] 6711 3-9-1 **88**.................. PaulHanagan 7 97
(Richard Fahey) *chsd ldrs: rdn over 2f out: led ins fnl f: edgd lft fnl 100yds: r.o wl* **11/2**

5115 **2** *2¼* **Humble Gratitude**[14] 6711 4-9-2 **87**..................(p) CierenFallon(3) 6 92
(Ian Williams) *dwlt: towards rr: pushed along over 3f out: rdn over 2f out: hdwy over 1f out: styd on to take 2nd wl ins fnl f: nt pce of wnr towards fin (jockey said gelding hung left-handed)* **11/4**[1]

6152 **3** *nk* **Smile A Mile (IRE)**[7] 6973 3-9-7 **94**.................. JoeFanning 3 97
(Mark Johnston) *chsd ldr: led 2f out: rdn over 1f out: hdd ins fnl f: carried lft after: styd on same pce fnl 100yds* **5/1**[3]

0631 **4** *2* **Mickey (IRE)**[72] 4552 6-8-13 **84**..................(v) RichardKingscote 2 81
(Tom Dascombe) *led: rdn and hdd 2f out: stl there over 1f out: edgd lft and one pce fnl 100yds* **11/2**

6510 **5** *1¾* **King's Pavilion (IRE)**[35] 5948 6-9-6 **88**.................. RobertHavlin 5 84
(Jason Ward) *hld up: rdn and outpcd 2f out: no imp fnl f* **8/1**

1550 **6** *1¾* **Sha La La La Lee**[41] 5708 4-9-6 **91**..................(p) JaneElliott(3) 4 82
(Tom Dascombe) *missed break: n.m.r on inner early on: in rr: drvn 5f out: outpcd over 2f out: nvr able to get involved (jockey said gelding was slowly away and never travelling)* **8/1**

3210 **7** *nk* **Spirit Warning**[22] 6425 3-9-3 **90**.................. DavidProbert 1 80
(Andrew Balding) *chsd ldrs: rdn over 2f out: wknd over 1f out (jockey said gelding stopped quickly)* **7/2**[2]

1m 34.26s (-1.44) **Going Correction** -0.075s/f (Good)
WFA 3 from 4yo+ 5lb **7 Ran SP% 118.5**
Speed ratings (Par 107): **104,101,101,99,97 95,95**
CSF £22.15 TOTE £8.50: £3.50, £3.30; EX 31.00 Trifecta £183.90.
Owner Dr Marwan Koukash **Bred** S Emmet And Miss R Emmet **Trained** Musley Bank, N Yorks

FOCUS
Add 13yds. Quite a valuable handicap and another one-two for owner Dr Marwan Koukash. It's been rated at face value around the second and third.

7185 THYME PEOPLE H'CAP 1m 2f 70y
5:00 (5:01) (Class 4) (0-80,80) 4-Y-O+
£6,727 (£2,002; £1,000; £500; £300; £300) **Stalls** High

Form RPR

1-30 **1** **Involved**[189] 1096 4-9-1 **74**.................. RichardKingscote 5 83
(Daniel Kubler) *midfield: rdn over 2f out: hdwy over 1f out: led fnl 150yds: sn pressed: kpt on wl and a doing enough towards fin* **16/1**

1104 **2** *¾* **Scofflaw**[15] 6686 5-9-6 **79**..................(v) HarryBentley 10 86
(David Evans) *hld up in midfield: rdn over 2f out: hdwy over 1f out: swtchd rt ins fnl f: chalng fnl 100yds: hld towards fin* **5/1**[2]

0560 **3** *1¾* **Top Notch Tonto (IRE)**[6] 7003 9-8-12 **71**.................. AlistairRawlinson 7 75
(Brian Ellison) *midfield: rdn and hdwy 2f out: styd on ins fnl f: nt rch front two* **14/1**

0165 **4** *¾* **Medalla De Oro**[26] 6289 5-9-6 **79**..................(h) JackMitchell 1 81+
(Tom Clover) *chsd ldr: rdn to ld 2f out: hdd fnl 150yds: no ex towards fin* **5/1**[2]

0533 **5** *¾* **Garden Oasis**[18] 6580 4-9-1 **74**.................. DavidAllan 6 75
(Tim Easterby) *in tch: rdn 2f out: no imp 1f out: one pce fnl 100yds* **10/3**[1]

0051 **6** *½* **Kaser (IRE)**[15] 6686 4-8-9 **73**.................. ThomasGreatrex(5) 3 73
(David Loughnane) *chsd ldrs: rdn over 2f out: unable qck ins fnl f: no ex fnl 100yds* **7/1**[3]

0064 **7** *2* **Central City (IRE)**[26] 6291 4-9-2 **78**..................(p) CierenFallon(3) 14 74
(Ian Williams) *in rr: rdn over 2f out: kpt on ins fnl f: gng on at fin: nvr able to trble ldrs (jockey said gelding was denied a clear run between 5 and 4 furlongs out)* **16/1**

5565 **8** *nk* **Cote D'Azur**[6] 6998 6-9-7 **80**.................. LewisEdmunds 13 75
(Les Eyre) *led: rdn and hdd 2f out: stl there 1f out: wknd fnl 150yds* **8/1**

4163 **9** *nk* **Indomeneo**[29] 6165 4-9-2 **75**.................. PaulHanagan 8 69
(Richard Fahey) *in rr: pushed along 4f out: kpt on ins fnl f: nvr able to trble ldrs* **17/2**

2140 **10** *5* **Bit Of A Quirke**[48] 5474 6-8-13 **72**..................(v) AndrewMullen 4 56
(Mark Walford) *chsd ldrs tl rdn and wknd over 2f out* **12/1**

0-04 **11** *½* **Seven Clans (IRE)**[14] 6733 7-8-12 **71**..................(b) DavidProbert 11 54
(Neil Mulholland) *hld up: rdn 3f out: nvr a threat* **25/1**

10-0 **12** *1½* **Jamih**[92] 3811 4-9-4 **80**.................. RowanScott(3) 9 60
(Tina Jackson) *hld up: pushed along over 2f out: nvr a threat* **33/1**

3/0- **13** *16* **Most Celebrated (IRE)**[348] 7848 6-9-6 **79**.................. BrendanPowell 2 27
(Neil Mulholland) *hld up in midfield tl rdn and wknd 3f out* **20/1**

2m 11.17s (-3.13) **Going Correction** -0.075s/f (Good) **13 Ran SP% 128.2**
Speed ratings (Par 105): **109,108,107,106,105 105,103,103,103,99 98,97,84**
CSF £99.05 CT £1195.96 TOTE £26.70: £6.90, £2.70, £3.80; EX 128.60 Trifecta £2889.10.
Owner Peter Onslow & Gary Middlebrook **Bred** Peter Onslow **Trained** Lambourn, Berks

FOCUS
Add 14yds. A decent handicap won by one of the least exposed runners. The second helps set the level.
T/Plt: £618.70 to a £1 stake. Pool: 64,968.89 - 76.65 winning units T/Qpdt: £44.90 to a £1 stake. Pool: £5,446.72 - 89.71 winning units **Darren Owen**

7103 CHELMSFORD (A.W) (L-H)
Saturday, September 14

OFFICIAL GOING: Polytrack: standard
Wind: virtually nil Weather: sunny and warm

7186 TOTESPORT.COM EBF NOVICE AUCTION STKS (PLUS 10 RACE) 5f (P)
1:35 (1:36) (Class 4) 2-Y-O
£6,727 (£2,002; £1,000; £500) **Stalls** Low

Form RPR

0333 **1** **Colonel Whitehead (IRE)**[28] 6219 2-8-9 71.......... EllieMacKenzie(7) 5 71
(Heather Main) *chsd ldrs: effrt over 2f out: clsd u.p to chse ldr ins fnl f: led wl ins fnl f: styd on strly and sn clr* **7/4**[1]

1 **2** *1½* **Mr Duepearl**[60] 5026 2-9-9 0.................. TomMarquand 1 73
(Robyn Brisland) *chsd ldr: effrt over 2f out: drvn jst over 1f out: kpt on same pce and lost 2nd ins fnl f: styd on but no threat to wnr and regained 2nd last strides* **5/2**[2]

3135 **3** *hd* **Too Hard To Hold (IRE)**[9] 6883 2-9-4 70.................. AndrewBreslin(5) 3 72
(Mark Johnston) *led: clr over 3f out: rdn over 1f out: hdd wl ins fnl f: no ex and sn outpcd: lost 2nd last strides* **3/1**[3]

00 **4** *1½* **Rushcutters Bay**[37] 5856 2-9-2 0.................. PatCosgrave 4 59
(Hugo Palmer) *awkward leaving stalls and s.i.s: in last pair: hdwy on inner 3f out: rdn and kpt on same pce fr over 1f out* **5/1**

3 **5** *4* **Freshwater Cliffs**[13] 6755 2-9-2 0.................. ShaneKelly 6 45
(Richard Hughes) *t.k.h: hld up in rr: 5th and no imp over 1f out: nvr involved* **25/1**

00 **6** *11* **Hell Of A Joker**[150] 1843 2-8-11 0..................(p) RayDawson(5) 2 5
(Bill Turner) *midfield: rdn over 3f out: sn struggling and dropped to rr 3f out: wl bhd and eased ins fnl f* **33/1**

59.36s (-0.84) **Going Correction** -0.30s/f (Stan) **6 Ran SP% 113.4**
Speed ratings (Par 97): **94,91,91,88,82 64**
CSF £6.55 TOTE £2.30: £1.50, £1.50; EX 7.60 Trifecta £15.20.
Owner Andrew Tuck And Wetumpka Racing **Bred** Wood Hall Stud **Trained** Kingston Lisle, Oxon

FOCUS
Not a strong novice sprint, but the pace was solid. Straightforward form, with the winner rated in line with his pre-race mark.

7187 HAVENS HOSPICE H'CAP 6f (P)
2:10 (2:11) (Class 3) (0-95,95) 3-Y-O **£9,703** (£2,887; £1,443; £721) **Stalls** Centre

Form RPR

6332 **1** **Intuitive (IRE)**[53] 5266 3-8-13 **87**.................. TomMarquand 7 101
(James Tate) *wnt rt leaving stalls: hld up in tch: clsd whn nt clr run over 1f out: sn swtchd rt and clsd to chal: led ins fnl f: r.o strly and drew clr: readily* **10/3**[2]

1234 **2** *2½* **Heath Charnock**[24] 6339 3-8-12 **86**.................. CallumRodriguez 6 92
(Michael Dods) *sn led: rdn over 1f out: hdd ins fnl f: no ex and nt match pce of wnr fnl 100yds* **3/1**[1]

2033 **3** *1¼* **Woven**[28] 6222 3-9-5 **93**.................. CallumShepherd 5 95
(David Simcock) *hld up in tch in last trio: effrt: nudged out rt and bmpd over 1f out: hdwy u.p to chse ldng pair 100yds out: no imp after* **5/1**[3]

0323 **4** *1½* **Prince Of Rome (IRE)**[14] 6735 3-9-0 **88**..................(tp) ShaneKelly 1 85
(Richard Hughes) *chsd ldrs: nt clr run over 1f out: swtchd rt jst ins fnl f: sn drvn and kpt on same pce fnl 100yds* **8/1**

5303 **5** *hd* **Concierge (IRE)**[7] 6954 3-8-11 **88**..................(v) MeganNicholls(3) 8 85
(George Scott) *s.i.s: t.k.h: hld up in tch in last trio: effrt whn hung lft and bmpd over 1f out: no imp ins fnl f (jockey said gelding was slowly away)* **8/1**

6000 **6** *hd* **Quiet Endeavour (IRE)**[91] 3865 3-9-0 **88**.................. PatCosgrave 3 84
(George Baker) *rousted along leaving stalls: chsd ldr: rdn and ev ch over 1f out: no ex u.p 1f out: edgd rt u.p and wknd ins fnl f* **16/1**

036 **7** *1¼* **Blonde Warrior (IRE)**[42] 5685 3-9-0 **88**..................(b[1]) SeanLevey 2 80
(Hugo Palmer) *rousted along leaving stalls: sn chsng ldrs: drvn: unable qck: hung lft and then wnt rt over 1f out: lost pl and wknd ins fnl f* **6/1**

0200 **8** *nse* **Junius Brutus (FR)**[21] 6476 3-9-7 **95**.................. AdamKirby 4 87
(Ralph Beckett) *restless in stalls: rrd as stalls opened and slowly away: in tch in rr: effrt and nt clrest of runs jst over 1f out: no imp ins fnl f (jockey said gelding fly leapt leaving the stalls and was denied a clear run inside the final furlong)* **9/1**

1m 10.65s (-3.05) **Going Correction** -0.30s/f (Stan) **8 Ran SP% 117.1**
Speed ratings (Par 105): **108,104,103,101,100 100,98,98**
CSF £14.20 CT £49.23 TOTE £3.80: £1.60, £1.80, £1.90; EX 15.30 Trifecta £49.10.
Owner Sheikh Hamed Dalmook Al Maktoum **Bred** Domenico Fonzo & Maria Teresa Matouani **Trained** Newmarket, Suffolk

FOCUS
A fairly competitive handicap for the grade and run in a good time. It's been rated on the positive side around the second and third.

7188 LUXDECO.COM ELSENHAM H'CAP 7f (P)
2:45 (2:47) (Class 2) (0-105,98) 3-Y-O+
£37,350 (£11,184; £5,592; £2,796; £1,398; £702) **Stalls** Low

Form RPR
-410 **1** **Lethal Lunch**[7] 6953 4-9-5 **93** AdamKirby 6 102
(Clive Cox) *hld up in tch in midfield: clsd nt clr run and swtchd lft over 1f out: nt clr run again and swtchd rt ins fnl f: sn drvn and chal 100yds: r.o wl to ld last strides* **5/1**[3]
1010 **2** *hd* **Habub (USA)**[14] 6706 4-9-9 **97** RossaRyan 3 105
(Owen Burrows) *led tl over 4f out: styd pressing ldr and rdn to ld again ent fnl 2f: edgd rt u.p over 1f out: edgd rt again and hdd wl ins fnl f: kpt on wl u.p towards fin* **4/1**[1]
6051 **3** *nse* **War Glory (IRE)**[14] 6706 6-9-10 **98** SeanLevey 12 106
(Richard Hannon) *stdd s: hld up in tch towards rr: swtchd lft and hdwy over 1f out: drvn to ld 100yds out: edgd lft: hdd and lost 2 pls last strides* **8/1**
1645 **4** *1 ¼* **Firmament**[14] 6706 7-9-10 **98** (p) RobbieDowney 7 103
(David O'Meara) *hld up in tch in midfield: swtchd rt and effrt over 1f out: kpt on u.p ins fnl f* **16/1**
302 **5** *¾* **Busby (IRE)**[25] 6319 4-8-0 **77** ow1 (p) GabrieleMalune(3) 10 80
(Conrad Allen) *chsd ldrs: effrt and nudged rt over 1f out: no ex and one pce ins fnl f* **25/1**
4000 **6** *nk* **Arbalet (IRE)**[7] 6950 4-9-5 **93** (bt) PatCosgrave 1 95
(Hugo Palmer) *chsd ldrs: effrt on inner to press ldrs over 1f out: no ex and outpcd fnl 100yds* **5/1**[3]
0-05 **7** *1* **Piece Of History (IRE)**[28] 6214 4-9-1 **89** CallumShepherd 2 88
(Saeed bin Suroor) *chsd ldrs: effrt and sltly impeded over 1f out: stl chsng ldrs but keeping on same pce whn nt clr run and hmpd ins fnl f: hld after* **9/2**[2]
1602 **8** *shd* **Diocles Of Rome (IRE)**[25] 6318 4-9-0 **88** TomMarquand 8 87
(Ralph Beckett) *hld up in tch towards rr: effrt and drvn over 1f out: keeping on whn nt clr run and swtchd rt ins fnl f: nvr trbld ldrs (jockey said gelding was denied a clear run inside the final furlong)* **10/1**
2661 **9** *shd* **Turn 'n Twirl (USA)**[24] 6346 3-8-8 **89** MeganNicholls(3) 9 86
(Simon Crisford) *hld up in tch towards rr: effrt over 1f out: drvn 1f out: kpt on ins fnl f: nvr trbld ldrs* **14/1**
0000 **10** *¾* **Lake Volta (IRE)**[14] 6711 4-9-2 **95** AndrewBreslin(5) 11 92
(Mark Johnston) *midfield: dropped to rr and rdn over 4f out: sme late hdwy u.p fnl 100yds: no threat to ldrs* **20/1**
-504 **11** *1 ¼* **Breathless Times**[128] 2551 4-9-7 **95** (t[1]) CallumRodriguez 13 88
(Stuart Williams) *hld up in last pair on outer: c wd and effrt over 1f out: nvr involved* **16/1**
2121 **12** *nse* **Sonja Henie (IRE)**[19] 6533 3-8-0 **81** WilliamCox(3) 4 72
(David Loughnane) *w ldr tl led over 4f out: rdn and hdd ent fnl 2f: losing pl whn short of room ins fnl f: wknd* **20/1**
6050 **13** *1 ¾* **Zap**[15] 6693 4-9-0 **88** (v) TonyHamilton 5 76
(Richard Fahey) *midfield: rdn over 2f out: drvn and no imp over 1f out: wknd ins fnl f* **14/1**

1m 22.95s (-4.25) **Going Correction** -0.30s/f (Stan)
WFA 3 from 4yo+ 4lb **13** Ran SP% **130.2**
Speed ratings (Par 109): **112,111,111,110,109 109,107,107,107,106 105,105,103**
CSF £27.04 CT £174.05 TOTE £4.80: £2.30, £1.90, £3.10; EX 28.90 Trifecta £388.50.
Owner The Rat Pack Partnership 2017 **Bred** Horizon Bloodstock Limited **Trained** Lambourn, Berks

FOCUS
A decent handicap for good money and the pace was genuine, giving the form a solid feel. Personal bests from the first two, with the third rated to the better view of his form.

7189 WHAT WOULD JOHNNY DO (WWJD) H'CAP 7f (P)
3:20 (3:22) (Class 5) (0-70,73) 3-Y-O
£5,433 (£1,617; £808; £404; £300; £300) **Stalls** Low

Form RPR
4156 **1** **Hunterwali**[37] 5844 3-9-7 **70** CallumRodriguez 1 77
(Michael Dods) *chsd ldrs: effrt to chal on inner over 1f out: led 1f out: edgd rt and hld on wl ins fnl f* **12/1**
624 **2** *½* **Al Moataz (IRE)**[25] 6316 3-9-2 **72** StefanoCherchi(7) 5 78
(Marco Botti) *chsd ldrs: effrt to chal and cannoned into jst over 1f out: ev ch ins fnl f: edgd rt but kpt on wl: hld wl towards fin (jockey said gelding hung right-handed)* **8/1**[3]
0554 **3** *nk* **Punjab Mail**[20] 6518 3-9-5 **68** SeanLevey 13 73
(Ian Williams) *hld up in tch in midfield: effrt and hdwy u.p 1f out: wnt between horses and chsd ldrs wl ins fnl f: styd on wl towards fin* **7/1**[2]
4050 **4** *1 ¼* **Bullington Boy (FR)**[53] 5270 3-9-0 **68** RayDawson(5) 12 70
(Jane Chapple-Hyam) *dropped in bhd sn after s: effrt and hdwy over 1f out: swtchd rt and hdwy ins fnl f: styd on wl towards fin: no threat to ldrs* **14/1**
4-66 **5** *½* **Alabama Dreaming**[96] 3651 3-9-0 **66** (v[1]) MeganNicholls(3) 7 66
(George Scott) *mounted in the chute and taken down early: chsd ldrs: effrt 2f out: drvn and ev ch 1f out: no ex and outpcd wl ins fnl f* **33/1**
3061 **6** *2* **In The Cove (IRE)**[11] 6840 3-9-10 **73** (b) RossaRyan 6 71+
(Richard Hannon) *hld up in midfield: effrt and swtchd rt over 1f out: clsd to chse ldrs whn squeezed for room and hmpd ins fnl f: nt rcvr and no imp (jockey said colt was denied a clear run)* **4/1**[1]
3544 **7** *nse* **Mykindofsunshine (IRE)**[23] 6373 3-9-7 **70** AdamKirby 3 65
(Clive Cox) *t.k.h: chsd ldr: ev ch and wnt lft u.p jst over 1f out: no ex and outpcd fnl 100yds (jockey said gelding ran too freely)* **4/1**[1]
-450 **8** *1 ½* **Just Later**[46] 5531 3-9-0 **63** (t[1]) TomMarquand 2 54
(Amy Murphy) *hld up wl in tch in midfield: effrt over 1f out: sn swtchd rt and drvn: no imp and wknd ins fnl f* **14/1**
3124 **9** *nse* **Fashionesque (IRE)**[28] 6225 3-9-5 **68** ShaneKelly 11 59
(Rae Guest) *hld up in last pair: pushed rt over 3f out: rdn and sme hdwy on outer over 2f out: no imp over 1f out: wknd ins fnl f* **20/1**
0-6 **10** *nse* **Limit Long**[15] 6691 3-9-9 **72** (t) CallumShepherd 4 62
(D J Bunyan, Ire) *led: rdn and hrd pressed over 1f out: bmpd and hdd 1f out: wknd ins fnl f* **7/1**[2]
0601 **11** *4 ½* **Sirius Slew**[18] 6569 3-9-5 **71** (p) GabrieleMalune(3) 10 49
(Alan Bailey) *stdd after s: t.k.h: hld up towards rr: edgd out rt over 3f out: effrt over 1f out: edgd lft and no hdwy 1f out: nvr involved* **16/1**
0104 **12** *½* **Run After Genesis (IRE)**[68] 4737 3-9-4 **67** DanielMuscutt 8 44
(Brett Johnson) *sn towards rr: bhd 3f out: n.d after* **7/1**[2]

004 **13** *nk* **Royal Sands (FR)**[101] 3464 3-9-7 **70** BarryMcHugh 9 46
(James Given) *stdd s: t.k.h: hld up in rr: effrt 2f out: no imp over 1f out: wl btn and eased ins fnl f (jockey said gelding ran too freely)* **14/1**

1m 25.09s (-2.11) **Going Correction** -0.30s/f (Stan) **13** Ran SP% **129.9**
Speed ratings (Par 101): **100,99,99,97,97 94,94,93,92,92 87,87,86**
CSF £114.00 CT £773.58 TOTE £13.00: £3.80, £3.10, £3.10; EX 133.30 Trifecta £1752.30.
Owner Redgate Bloodstock **Bred** Redgate Bloodstock Ltd **Trained** Denton, Co Durham

FOCUS
An ordinary handicap, though competitive for the grade and it paid to be near the pace. The third has been rated close to his more recent form, and the fourth close to form.

7190 CELEBRATE SEPTEMBER'S HERO AVA CHAPMAN FILLIES' NOVICE STKS 1m (P)
3:55 (4:02) (Class 4) 3-Y-O+
£6,469 (£1,925; £962; £481) **Stalls** Low

Form RPR
1 **Perfect Number** 3-8-11 **0** PatCosgrave 2 71+
(Saeed bin Suroor) *hld up in tch in midfield: hmpd and lost pl over 6f out: swtchd rt and hdwy over 1f out: str run u.p ins fnl f: led wl ins fnl f and gng away at fin* **15/8**[2]
2 **2** *1 ¼* **New Angel**[31] 6074 3-8-11 **0** NickyMackay 6 68+
(John Gosden) *in tch in midfield: clsd to chse ldrs over 2f out: unable qck and rn green over 1f out: styd on ins fnl f: wnt 2nd towards fin* **6/4**[1]
1 **3** *½* **Toronado Queen (IRE)**[17] 6587 3-9-4 **0** TonyHamilton 8 74
(Richard Fahey) *led: bmpd and rdn over 1f out: drvn and kpt on wl tl hdd and no ex wl ins fnl f: lost 2nd towards fin* **6/1**[3]
- **4** *hd* **Almahha** 3-8-11 **0** RossaRyan 3 67
(Owen Burrows) *t.k.h: chsd ldrs: effrt on inner and ev ch u.p over 1f out: kpt on tl no ex and jst outpcd towards fin* **12/1**
02 **5** *nk* **Serenading**[14] 6701 3-8-11 **0** GeorgeWood 11 66
(James Fanshawe) *grad c towards inner fr wd draw: chsd ldr: rdn and ev ch whn edgd lft over 1f out: sustained chal tl no ex and jst outpcd towards fin* **8/1**
0 **6** *3 ¼* **Adashelby (IRE)**[43] 5627 3-8-4 **0** LauraPearson(7) 4 59?
(John Ryan) *dwlt: hld up in tch in rr: effrt over 1f out: rdn 1f out: kpt on ins fnl f: no threat to ldrs* **66/1**
5 **7** *1 ¼* **Calima Calling (IRE)**[17] 6587 3-8-11 **0** TomMarquand 9 56?
(Michael Appleby) *hld up in rr: swtchd rt and effrt wl over 1f out: no imp and kpt on same pce ins fnl f* **50/1**
8 *2* **Limalima (IRE)** 3-8-11 **0** CallumShepherd 1 51
(Stuart Williams) *in tch in midfield: effrt 2f out: unable qck and outpcd over 1f out: wknd ins fnl f* **16/1**
60 **9** *2 ¼* **Chamomile**[38] 5808 3-8-11 **0** RobbieDowney 10 46
(Daniel Kubler) *t.k.h: chsd ldrs: sltly impeded over 6f out: lost pl and bhd over 1f out: wknd fnl f* **33/1**
05- **10** *8* **Indian Sea**[374] 6941 3-8-8 **0** WilliamCox(3) 5 27
(Dr Jon Scargill) *hld up in tch towards rr: hdwy to chse ldrs 4f out: rdn and lost pl over 2f out: bhd fnl f* **66/1**

1m 38.34s (-1.56) **Going Correction** -0.30s/f (Stan) **10** Ran SP% **121.6**
Speed ratings (Par 102): **95,93,93,93,92 89,88,86,84,76**
CSF £5.27 TOTE £2.50: £1.30, £1.20, £1.50; EX 5.40 Trifecta £17.00.
Owner Godolphin **Bred** Godolphin **Trained** Newmarket, Suffolk

FOCUS
A fair fillies' novice event. The gallop was solid and the debutante winner should go on to better things. Muddling form, likely limited by the sixth and seventh. The third has been rated to her Catterick win for now.

7191 FAIRWOOD PARK DEVELOPMENTS H'CAP 1m (P)
4:30 (4:32) (Class 4) (0-85,87) 3-Y-O+
£6,080 (£1,809; £904; £452; £300; £300) **Stalls** Low

Form RPR
6141 **1** **Attainment**[21] 6440 3-9-9 **87** AdamKirby 2 97
(James Tate) *led and dictated gallop: rdn and kicked on over 1f out: clr and styd on wl ins fnl f* **7/4**[1]
5254 **2** *2* **Philamundo (IRE)**[29] 6151 4-9-3 **76** (b) TomMarquand 1 83
(Richard Spencer) *s.i.s: detached in last tl clsd onto rr of field 4f out: swtchd rt and effrt over 1f out: hdwy u.p to chse clr wnr 100yds out: kpt on but nvr a threat* **8/1**
4106 **3** *1 ¼* **Harbour Spirit (FR)**[24] 6347 3-9-6 **84** (p) ShaneKelly 7 87
(Richard Hughes) *mounted in the chute: dropped in bhd after s: hld up in tch: nt clr run over 2f out: effrt 1f out: drvn and kpt on ins fnl f: no threat to wnr* **14/1**
0632 **4** *½* **Glory Awaits (IRE)**[22] 6391 9-9-0 **73** (b) CallumShepherd 8 76
(David Simcock) *hld up in tch in rr of main gp: effrt over 1f out: drvn and kpt on same pce ins fnl f: no threat to wnr* **10/1**
01-4 **5** *nse* **Mostawaa**[25] 6315 3-9-0 **85** EllieMacKenzie(7) 5 87
(Heather Main) *chsd wnr tl 3f out: rdn and struggling to qckn over 2f out: no ch w wnr and kpt on same pce ins fnl f* **6/1**[3]
2500 **6** *1 ¼* **Glory Of Paris (IRE)**[10] 6863 5-9-7 **80** (p[1]) LiamJones 6 80
(Michael Appleby) *taken down early: chsd ldrs tl wnt 2nd 3f out: drvn and unable to match pce of wnr over 1f out: btn whn lost 2nd and wknd fnl 100yds* **33/1**
431 **7** *1 ½* **Motfael (IRE)**[22] 6399 3-9-7 **85** RossaRyan 4 83
(Owen Burrows) *t.k.h: chsd ldrs: rdn and lost pl over 2f out: wl hld over 1f out: wknd ins fnl f (trainer could offer no explanation for the colt's performance)* **9/4**[2]
1400 **8** *hd* **Reggae Runner (FR)**[28] 6231 3-8-13 **82** AndrewBreslin(5) 3 77
(Mark Johnston) *in tch in midfield: effrt ent fnl 2f: no imp u.p over 1f out: wknd ins fnl f* **8/1**

1m 37.16s (-2.74) **Going Correction** -0.30s/f (Stan)
WFA 3 from 4yo+ 5lb **8** Ran SP% **122.3**
Speed ratings (Par 105): **101,99,97,97,97 95,94,94**
CSF £18.38 CT £161.04 TOTE £2.50: £1.10, £2.30, £3.90; EX 17.70 Trifecta £190.40.
Owner Saeed Manana **Bred** Rabbah Bloodstock Limited **Trained** Newmarket, Suffolk

FOCUS
All bar two were rated 82 or above, so plenty of depth to this decent handicap, in which they went no more than a respectable gallop. The winner made all. Another clear pb from the winner, with the second helping to set the level.

7192 FRED DONE H'CAP 1m 5f 66y(P)
5:05 (5:05) (Class 6) (0-65,66) 3-Y-O
£3,234 (£962; £481; £300; £300; £300) **Stalls** Low

Form RPR
3350 **1** **Fragrant Belle**[36] 5898 3-9-7 **65** (h[1]) TomMarquand 8 72
(Ralph Beckett) *hld up in tch towards rr: drvn over 3f out: clsd on outer 2f out: styd on to ld ins fnl f: sn clr* **7/1**

-053 **2** 2 1/2 **Avenue Foch**[33] 6030 3-9-7 **65**........................ DanielMuscutt 2 68
(James Fanshawe) *in tch in midfield: hdwy to chse ldr over 3f out: drvn and ev ch over 1f out: kpt on same pce ins fnl f* **3/1**[2]

0-50 **3** hd **Jeweller**[26] 6290 3-9-4 **62**........................(v[1]) ShaneKelly 6 65
(Sir Michael Stoute) *chsd ldrs tl hdwy to press ldr 7f out: led 4f out: drvn and hrd pressed over 1f out: hdd and no ex ins fnl f: lost 2nd last stride* **6/1**[3]

4132 **4** 1/2 **Robeam (IRE)**[36] 5915 3-8-12 **56**........................(p) TonyHamilton 10 58
(Richard Fahey) *chsd ldr tl 7f out: styd prom: unable qck u.p over 1f out: kpt on same pce ins fnl f* **7/1**

0445 **5** nk **Island Jungle (IRE)**[25] 6320 3-9-6 **64**........................(p) AdamKirby 4 66
(Mark Usher) *hld up in tch: clsd and nt clr run over 2f out: effrt over 1f out: chsd ldrs u.p and swtchd lft 1f out: kpt on same pce ins fnl f* **7/1**

0060 **6** 8 **Cinzento (IRE)**[39] 5784 3-8-4 **48**........................ GeorgeWood 1 38
(Stuart Williams) *in tch towards rr: clsd and effrt over 3f out: unable qck u.p over 1f out: wknd ins fnl f* **10/1**

5541 **7** 2 **Blowing Dixie**[19] 6550 3-8-10 **59**........................ RayDawson(5) 7 46
(Jane Chapple-Hyam) *in tch in midfield: effrt over 3f out: unable qck u.p over 1f out: wknd ins fnl f (trainer said gelding was unsuited by the Polytrack surface here at Chelmsford, and in her opinion, would prefer a slower surface having won at Southwell last time out)* **11/4**[1]

645 **8** 7 **Allocated (IRE)**[15] 6687 3-9-5 **66**........................ DarraghKeenan(3) 3 43
(John Butler) *restless in stalls: hld up in tch in rr: clsd over 3f out: effrt ent fnl 2f: sn no imp and wknd fnl f* **25/1**

0430 **9** 14 **Barb's Prince (IRE)**[35] 5974 3-8-1 **48**........................(b) GabrieleMalune(3) 9 5
(Ian Williams) *led tl 4f out: steadily lost pl and bhd over 1f out* **25/1**

0005 **10** 154 **Sleepdancer (IRE)**[17] 6612 3-8-4 **48**........................ NickyMackay 5
(John Ryan) *racd awkwardly: in tch towards rr: dropped to last and lost tch 3f out: sn eased: t.o (jockey said gelding hung right-handed throughout)* **50/1**

2m 48.93s (-4.67) **Going Correction** -0.30s/f (Stan) **10 Ran SP% 122.2**
Speed ratings (Par 99): **102,100,100,100,99 94,93,89,80,**
CSF £29.30 CT £139.31 TOTE £7.60: £2.10, £1.50, £2.40; EX 41.30 Trifecta £293.50.
Owner Robert Ng **Bred** Robert Ng **Trained** Kimpton, Hants

FOCUS
A modest staying handicap and the winner came from off the ordinary pace. The fourth offers perspective on the level of the form.
T/Plt: £32.30 to a £1 stake. Pool: £29,689.62 - 916.88 winning units T/Qpdt: £19.60 to a £1 stake. Pool: £2,619.87 - 133.12 winning units **Steve Payne**

7146 DONCASTER (L-H)

Saturday, September 14

OFFICIAL GOING: Good to firm (watered; 8.2)
Wind: Moderate half against Weather: Cloudy with sunny periods

7193 WILLIAM HILL PORTLAND H'CAP — 5f 143y
1:50 (1:53) (Class 2) 3-Y-O+
£37,350 (£11,184; £5,592; £2,796; £1,398; £702) **Stalls** Centre

Form RPR

2642 **1** **Oxted**[28] 6222 3-9-4 **105**........................ CierenFallon(3) 14 115
(Roger Teal) *trckd ldrs centre: hdwy 2f out: chal over 1f out: rdn to take narrow ld ins fnl f: drvn out* **14/1**

0006 **2** 1/2 **A Momentofmadness**[24] 6351 6-8-13 **95**........................(h) WilliamBuick 13 103
(Charles Hills) *led centre: rdn along 2f out: sn jnd and drvn over 1f out: hdd ins fnl f: rallied gamely towards fin* **9/1**[2]

1135 **3** nk **Show Stealer**[9] 6908 6-8-7 **92**........................(p) CameronNoble(3) 20 99
(Rae Guest) *racd towards stands' side: in rr: hdwy 2f out: rdn over 1f out: kpt on strly fnl f* **40/1**

2032 **4** nk **Arecibo (FR)**[7] 6960 4-9-4 **100**........................(b) DavidNolan 2 106
(David O'Meara) *sn swtchd to centre and trckd ldrs: hdwy over 1f out: rdn to chal ent fnl f: sn drvn and ev ch: no ex towards fin* **33/1**

6530 **5** nk **Wentworth Falls**[15] 6676 7-8-8 **90**........................(p) SamJames 9 99+
(Geoffrey Harker) *hld up and bhd centre: gd hdwy over 1f out: nt clr run and swtchd markedly rt towards stands' side ins fnl f: rdn and kpt on wl towards fin (jockey said gelding was denied a clear run 2f out)* **14/1**

5023 **6** hd **Embour (IRE)**[14] 6724 4-9-0 **96**........................ PatDobbs 8 100
(Richard Hannon) *in rr centre: hdwy 2f out: sn pushed along: rdn to chse ldrs over 1f out: drvn and kpt on fnl f* **16/1**

2104 **7** 1/2 **Makanah**[24] 6351 4-9-1 **97**........................ KieranO'Neill 1 100
(Julie Camacho) *racd towards far side: trckd ldrs: hdwy gng wl 2f out: rdn to chal and edgd lft towards far rail 1/1/2f out: ev ch tl drvn ins fnl f and grad wknd (jockey said gelding hung left-handed)* **25/1**

2243 **8** hd **Open Wide (USA)**[7] 6953 5-9-2 **98**........................(b) AndreaAtzeni 12 100+
(Amanda Perrett) *dwlt and in rr centre: hdwy 2f out: rdn over 1f out: kpt on wl u.p fnl f (vet said gelding lost its left hind shoe)* **9/1**[2]

2641 **8** dht **Equitation**[8] 6916 5-8-5 **94**........................(t) MarcoGhiani(7) 22 96
(Stuart Williams) *midfield: hdwy wl over 1f out: sn rdn and kpt on fnl f* **12/1**

0501 **10** 2 3/4 **Justanotherbottle (IRE)**[14] 6724 5-9-3 **99**........................ FrankieDettori 21 92
(Declan Carroll) *racd towards stands' side: chsd ldrs: rdn along wl over 1f out: drvn and kpt on same pce fnl f* **10/1**[3]

2246 **11** hd **Muscika**[15] 6676 5-8-9 **91**........................(v) FrannyNorton 4 83
(David O'Meara) *clsd up centre: rdn along wl over 1f out: drvn and wknd appr fnl f* **33/1**

1631 **12** 1 1/2 **Dazzling Dan (IRE)**[28] 6222 3-9-6 **104**........................ RobHornby 11 91
(Pam Sly) *nvr bttr than midfield* **10/1**[3]

5610 **13** nse **Orvar (IRE)**[24] 6351 6-8-10 **92**........................ LeighRoche 18 79
(Paul Midgley) *racd towards stands' side: in tch: pushed along and hdwy 2f out: sn rdn and n.d* **25/1**

004 **14** nk **Muthmir (IRE)**[29] 6149 9-9-4 **100**........................(p) DaneO'Neill 16 86
(William Haggas) *racd towards stands' side: towards rr: sme hdwy 2f out: sn rdn and n.d* **20/1**

1-11 **15** 1 1/4 **Bielsa (IRE)**[15] 6676 4-8-11 **93**........................ KevinStott 17 75
(Kevin Ryan) *racd towards stands' side: in tch: rdn along over 2f out: sn btn (trainer could offer no explanation for the gelding's performance)* **7/2**[1]

335 **16** nk **Watchable**[24] 6351 9-9-1 **97**........................(p) TomQueally 3 78
(David O'Meara) *cl up centre: rdn along 2f out: sn drvn and wknd over 1f out* **50/1**

600 **17** shd **Gunmetal (IRE)**[24] 6351 6-9-3 **99**........................ DonnachaO'Brien 6 80
(David Barron) *racd centre: rdn along over 2f out: sn wknd* **20/1**

0511 **18** 1 **Green Power**[22] 6404 4-9-2 **98**........................ GeraldMosse 19 75
(John Gallagher) *nvr bttr than midfield* **20/1**

3004 **19** 1 **Konchek**[49] 5442 3-9-0 **98**........................(tp) HectorCrouch 5 72
(Clive Cox) *in tch centre: pushed along wl over 2f out: sn rdn and wknd* **25/1**

0023 **20** nk **Marnie James**[6] 6999 4-9-6 **102**........................ JackGarritty 7 75
(Jedd O'Keeffe) *midfield: rdn along over 2f out: sn wknd* **12/1**

1050 **21** 2 1/2 **Copper Knight (IRE)**[14] 6698 5-9-5 **106**........................(t) DannyRedmond(5) 10 71
(Tim Easterby) *chsd ldrs centre: rdn along over 2f out: sn wknd* **33/1**

0000 **22** 22 **Teruntum Star (FR)**[40] 5740 7-8-10 **92**........................ PhilDennis 15
(David C Griffiths) *a towards rr (jockey said gelding lost its action approaching the line)* **80/1**

1m 6.31s (-1.79) **Going Correction** 0.0s/f (Good)
WFA 3 from 4yo+ 2lb **22 Ran SP% 135.3**
Speed ratings (Par 109): **111,110,109,109,109 108,108,107,107,104 104,102,101,101,99 99,99,98,96,96 92,63**
WIN: 16.50 Oxted; PL: 4.30 Oxted 6.50 Arecibo 2.00 A Momentofmadness 11.50 Show Stealer; EX: 211.20; CSF: 123.68; TC: 5048.31; TF: 7461.20 CSF £123.68 CT £5048.31 TOTE £16.50: £4.30, £2.00, £11.50, £6.50; EX 211.20 Trifecta £7461.20.
Owner S Piper, T Hirschfeld & D Fish **Bred** Homecroft Wealth Racing **Trained** Lambourn, Berks

FOCUS
No changes to advertised race distances. After riding in the opener Hector Crouch and Kevin Stott called the ground 'quick' and Kieran O'Neill said: "It's lively enough." A tremendously competitive sprint handicap, and solid form. The pace was centre-to-far side. The third is among those that helps set the level.

7194 HIRD RAIL GROUP PARK STKS (GROUP 2) — 7f 6y
2:25 (2:25) (Class 1) 3-Y-O+ **£61,331** (£23,252; £11,636; £5,796; £2,909) **Stalls** Centre

Form RPR

4145 **1** **Sir Dancealot (IRE)**[21] 6472 5-9-7 114........................ GeraldMosse 2 116
(David Elsworth) *racd centre: trckd ldrs: smooth hdwy over 2f out: sn chsng ldr: rdn to ld over 1f out: clr ins fnl f* **11/4**[2]

0-11 **2** 1 1/2 **Never No More (IRE)**[35] 5979 3-9-0 107........................ DonnachaO'Brien 1 107
(A P O'Brien, Ire) *racd centre: trckd ldng pair: hdwy over 2f out: rdn along wl over 1f out: drvn and kpt on same pce fnl f* **15/2**

0505 **3** 1/2 **Breton Rock (IRE)**[20] 6508 9-9-4 103........................ AndreaAtzeni 5 108
(David Simcock) *racd centre: hld up and bhd: hdwy 2f out: rdn over 1f out: kpt on fnl f* **33/1**

-161 **4** 1 1/2 **Shine So Bright**[21] 6472 3-9-3 115........................ WilliamBuick 4 105
(Andrew Balding) *racd alone towards stands' side: sn led: clr 1/2-way: pushed along 2f out: sn jnd and rdn: hdd over 1f out: wknd ent fnl f* **10/11**[1]

0210 **5** 23 **Azano**[69] 4705 3-9-0 104........................(t) FrankieDettori 3 79
(John Gosden) *racd centre: chsd ldr: rdn along over 2f out: sn lost pl: bhd and eased fr over 1f out (trainer could offer no explanation for the colt's performance)* **5/1**[3]

1m 23.84s (-2.56) **Going Correction** 0.0s/f (Good)
WFA 3 from 5yo+ 4lb **5 Ran SP% 110.4**
Speed ratings (Par 115): **114,112,111,110,83**
CSF £21.49 TOTE £3.80: £1.60, £2.10; EX 24.40 Trifecta £144.80.
Owner C Benham/ D Whitford/ L Quinn/ K Quinn **Bred** Vincent Duignan **Trained** Newmarket, Suffolk

FOCUS
No great depth to this Group 2 and it didn't take a huge amount of winning. All bar the favourite, who raced away from the other four more towards the stands' side, came down the centre and they got racing plenty soon enough. The third has been rated to this year's form.

7195 POMMERY CHAMPAGNE STKS (GROUP 2) (C&G) — 7f 6y
3:00 (3:00) (Class 1) 2-Y-O **£42,532** (£16,125; £8,070; £4,020; £2,017) **Stalls** Centre

Form RPR

1221 **1** **Threat (IRE)**[22] 6422 2-9-3 113........................ PatDobbs 3 115
(Richard Hannon) *t.k.h: hld up in rr: smooth hdwy 2f out and sn cl up: effrt over 1f out: sn chal: rdn to ld ins fnl f: jinked rt and kpt on wl towards fin* **6/5**[1]

1 **2** nk **Royal Crusade**[22] 6409 2-9-0 0........................ WilliamBuick 2 111
(Charlie Appleby) *trckd ldrs: hdwy and cl up 2f out: led wl over 1f out: sn jnd and rdn: hdd ins fnl f: kpt on u.p towards fin* **9/4**[2]

12 **3** 3/4 **Juan Elcano**[63] 4920 2-9-0 0........................ AndreaAtzeni 1 109
(Kevin Ryan) *cl up: led 4f out: rdn along over 2f out: hdd wl over 1f out: drvn and kpt on same pce fnl f* **4/1**[3]

2433 **4** 1/2 **Fort Myers (USA)**[15] 6690 2-9-0 103........................ DonnachaO'Brien 4 108
(A P O'Brien, Ire) *slt ld: hdd 4f out: cl up: rdn along over 2f out: drvn over 1f out: kpt on same pce fnl f* **8/1**

30 **5** 3 1/4 **Royal Dornoch (IRE)**[10] 6868 2-9-0 102........................ PBBeggy 5 100
(A P O'Brien, Ire) *trckd ldng pair: hdwy and cl up 1/2-way: rdn along over 2f out: sn drvn and wknd* **20/1**

1m 25.42s (-0.98) **Going Correction** 0.0s/f (Good) **5 Ran SP% 112.1**
Speed ratings (Par 107): **105,104,103,103,99**
CSF £4.27 TOTE £1.80: £1.30, £1.50; EX 4.30 Trifecta £12.70.
Owner Cheveley Park Stud **Bred** La Lumiere Partnership **Trained** East Everleigh, Wilts

FOCUS
An up-to-scratch edition of this Group 2, if perhaps not at the level of last year's race which saw Too Darn Hot beat Phoenix Of Spain. The time was 1.58sec slower than the older horses in the Park Stakes, the early pace having been slow, and the first four were separated by only a length and a half at the line. The winner confirmed himself as a smart colt. It's been rated as an ordinary renewal.

7196 WILLIAM HILL ST LEGER STKS (GROUP 1) (BRITISH CHAMPIONS SERIES) (C&F) — 1m 6f 115y
3:35 (3:35) (Class 1) 3-Y-O
£396,970 (£150,500; £75,320; £37,520; £18,830; £9,450) **Stalls** Low

Form RPR

1111 **1** **Logician**[24] 6353 3-9-1 115........................ FrankieDettori 4 119+
(John Gosden) *t.k.h: stdd early and hld up towards rr: smooth hdwy 3f out: sn swtchd rt towards stands' side and effrt to ld 2f out: rdn clr jst over 1f out: kpt on strly: readily* **5/6**[1]

0111 **2** 2 1/4 **Sir Ron Priestley**[21] 6446 3-9-1 108........................ FrannyNorton 6 114
(Mark Johnston) *trckd ldrs: hdwy over 3f out: cl up and rdn 2f out: drvn over 1f out: kpt on wl u.p fnl f* **7/1**[3]

3215 **3** hd **Nayef Road (IRE)**[24] 6353 3-9-1 108........................ AndreaAtzeni 3 113
(Mark Johnston) *trckd ldrs: hdwy 4f out: cl up over 2f out: sn rdn: drvn over 1f out: kpt on wl u.p fnl f* **40/1**

154 **4** 3/4 **Sir Dragonet (IRE)**[29] 6192 3-9-1 117........................ DonnachaO'Brien 7 112
(A P O'Brien, Ire) *hld up in rr: hdwy 3f out: trckd ldrs over 2f out: rdn and ev ch wl over 1f out: drvn and kpt on same pce fnl f* **11/4**[2]

2-03 **5** *2* **Il Paradiso (USA)**[22] 6421 3-9-1 115...............................(p) PBBeggy 2 110
(A P O'Brien, Ire) *trckd clr ldr: tk clsr order over 4f out: pushed along to ld jst over 3f out: rdn and hdd 2f out: sn drvn and wknd over 1f out* **8/1**

5161 **6** *1 1/2* **Technician (IRE)**[28] 6213 3-9-1 109.............................. RobHornby 8 108
(Martyn Meade) *a towards rr* **20/1**

3145 **7** *6* **Dashing Willoughby**[46] 5522 3-9-1 113......................... WilliamBuick 5 100
(Andrew Balding) *chsd ldrs: rdn along 3f out: drvn over 2f out: sn wknd* **14/1**

1000 **8** *10* **Western Australia (IRE)**[62] 4963 3-9-1 105..........(p[1]) MichaelHussey 1 86
(A P O'Brien, Ire) *led: clr after 4f: pushed along 4f out: hdd over 3f out: sn wknd* **50/1**

3m 0.27s (-11.33) **Going Correction** -0.25s/f (Firm) course record **8** Ran SP% **120.7**
Speed ratings (Par 115): **120,118,118,118,117 116,113,107**
CSF £8.23 CT £146.33 TOTE £1.60: £1.10, £1.80, £8.60; EX 6.90 Trifecta £110.60.

Owner K Abdullah **Bred** Juddmonte Farms Ltd **Trained** Newmarket, Suffolk

■ Stewards' Enquiry : Franny Norton four-day ban: used whip above the permitted level (Sep 29-30, Oct 1-2)

FOCUS
An average edition of the race (four of the first five scored at least once at handicap level this season) but hard not to be taken with Logician, who retained his unbeaten record and set a new course record in the process. The pace was a good one, courtesy of Ballydoyle pacemaker Western Australia, and they headed centre-field in the straight. It's been rated as a below-par renewal around the second and third.

7197 NAPOLEONS CASINOS & RESTAURANTS NURSERY H'CAP 1m (S)
4:10 (4:12) (Class 2) 2-Y-O **£12,450** (£3,728; £1,864; £932; £466) **Stalls** Centre

Form RPR

513 **1** **Lucander (IRE)**[14] 6718 2-8-12 **79**.............................. RobHornby 1 86+
(Ralph Beckett) *trckd ldrs towards centre: hdwy 2f out: rdn over 1f out: styd on wl fnl f to ld last 75yds* **9/1**

1652 **2** *1/2* **Wild Thunder (IRE)**[14] 6707 2-9-6 **87**.............................. PatDobbs 3 92
(Richard Hannon) *trckd ldng pair: hdwy 2f out: rdn to take narrow ld wl over 1f out: drvn ent fnl f: hdd and no ex last 75yds* **5/1**

310 **3** *1 1/4* **Kingbrook**[24] 6352 2-9-7 **88**.............................. FrannyNorton 2 90
(Mark Johnston) *trckd ldr: hdwy and cl up 2f out: rdn and ev ch over 1f out: drvn ent fnl f: kpt on same pce* **7/4**[1]

332 **4** *hd* **Forbidden Land (IRE)**[14] 6728 2-8-13 **80**.................... AndreaAtzeni 5 82
(Richard Hannon) *sltly hmpd s: hld up in rr: hdwy over 2f out: cl up over 1f out: sn rdn and ev ch ent fnl f: sn drvn and wknd last 100yds* **7/2**[3]

1341 **5** *10* **Incinerator**[12] 6808 2-9-2 **83**..............................(t) WilliamBuick 4 63
(Hugo Palmer) *wnt rt s: t.k.h and led: pushed along 2f out: rdn and hdd wl over 1f out: sn wknd (jockey said colt stopped quickly)* **11/4**[2]

1m 38.48s (-1.72) **Going Correction** 0.0s/f (Good) **5** Ran SP% **111.9**
Speed ratings (Par 101): **108,107,106,106,96**
CSF £50.20 TOTE £11.20: £3.90, £2.40; EX 48.60 Trifecta £136.20.

Owner Mrs M E Slade & B Ohlsson **Bred** John Connolly **Trained** Kimpton, Hants

FOCUS
A decent nursery in which they raced in two mini-groups for much of the way. The early pace was quite strong. It's been rated on the positive side.

7198 P J TOWEY CONSTRUCTION LTD H'CAP 1m (S)
4:45 (4:46) (Class 2) (0-110,104) 3-Y-O+ **£15,562** (£4,660; £2,330) **Stalls** Centre

Form RPR

1161 **1** **Qaysar (FR)**[9] 6894 4-9-10 **104**.............................. PatDobbs 1 110
(Richard Hannon) *trckd ldr: effrt and cl up over 1f out: sn rdn: qcknd to take slt ld ins fnl f: kpt on wl: cleverly* **13/8**[2]

3230 **2** *hd* **Bayroot (IRE)**[42] 5666 3-8-12 **97**.............................. AndreaAtzeni 4 101
(Roger Varian) *led: pushed along and jnd wl over 1f out: sn rdn: drvn and hdd narrowly ins fnl f: kpt on wl u.p to wards fin* **11/8**[1]

0250 **3** *hd* **Baltic Baron (IRE)**[23] 6376 4-9-4 **98**..............................(t[1]) DavidNolan 5 102
(David O'Meara) *trckd ldng pair: hdwy and cl up 2f out: rdn over 1f out: ev ch ins fnl f: sn drvn and kpt on* **5/2**[3]

1m 40.42s (0.22) **Going Correction** 0.0s/f (Good)
WFA 3 from 4yo+ 5lb **3** Ran SP% **108.8**
Speed ratings (Par 109): **98,97,97**
CSF £4.19 TOTE £2.00; EX 3.40 Trifecta £3.40.

Owner Al Shaqab Racing **Bred** S N C Scuderia Waldeck **Trained** East Everleigh, Wilts

FOCUS
Just the three of them remaining, but they were all good-quality handicappers and two heads separated them at the line. They raced centre-field at a steady pace and it turned into a dash. All three have been rated close to their marks.

7199 YATES DRYWALL LTD H'CAP 1m 3f 197y
5:55 (5:55) (Class 2) (0-110,98) 3-Y-O+ **£12,450** (£3,728) **Stalls** Low

Form RPR

2-03 **1** **Kitaabaat**[17] 6596 4-9-4 **87**..............................(h) AndreaAtzeni 1 93
(David Simcock) *trckd ldr: hdwy over 1f out: rdn to chal ins fnl f: kpt on wl to ld nr fin* **6/4**[2]

0023 **2** *nk* **The Trader (IRE)**[10] 6861 3-9-1 **92**.............................. FrannyNorton 2 97
(Mark Johnston) *led: pushed along over 1f out: shkn up ent fnl f: sn rdn: drvn: hdd and no ex towards fin* **1/2**[1]

2m 32.51s (-4.09) **Going Correction** -0.25s/f (Firm)
WFA 3 from 4yo 8lb **2** Ran SP% **106.7**
Speed ratings (Par 109): **103,102**
TOTE £2.00.

Owner Khalifa Dasmal & Partners **Bred** Shadwell Estate Company Limited **Trained** Newmarket, Suffolk

FOCUS
A low-key end to the St Leger meeting, but the two runners produced a good finish. They came down the centre in the straight. Both have been rated pretty much to form.

T/Jkpt: Partly Won. £10,969.70 to a £1 stake. Pool: 15,450.40 - 0.50 winning unit. T/Plt: £684.00 to a £1 stake. Pool: £167,004.01 - 178.22 winning units T/Qpdt: £29.10 to a £1 stake. Pool: £11,676.51 - 296.67 winning units **Joe Rowntree**

6897 LINGFIELD (L-H)
Saturday, September 14

OFFICIAL GOING: Good to firm (good in places; watered; 8.3)
Wind: Almost nil Weather: Sunny, warm

7200 CONGRATULATIONS GEORGE & KRISTY FILLIES' H'CAP 1m 3f 133y
1:10 (1:10) (Class 5) (0-70,70) 3-Y-O+ **£3,428** (£1,020; £509; £300; £300) **Stalls** High

Form RPR

-350 **1** **Maria Magdalena (IRE)**[17] 1351 3-8-11 **65**... ThoreHammerHansen[(5)] 4 68
(Alex Hales) *racd in last: pushed along at times fr 1/2-way: rdn 3f out: clsd on ldrs 2f out: hanging lft but led ins fnl f: kpt on* **5/1**[3]

6640 **2** *3/4* **Teemlucky**[34] 5987 3-8-4 **53**.............................. JosephineGordon 3 55
(Ian Williams) *led or disp ld: shkn up over 3f out: hdd wl over 1f out: kpt on but a hld* **25/1**

2051 **3** *nse* **Maroon Bells (IRE)**[17] 6599 4-9-12 **67**.............................. HollieDoyle 1 69
(David Menuisier) *t.k.h: hld up in 4th: pushed along over 4f out: rdn and prog over 2f out: narrow ld wl over 1f out: hdd and nt qckn ins fnl f: lost 2nd last stride (jockey said filly was never travelling)* **4/5**[1]

0-60 **4** *5* **Gladden (IRE)**[49] 5430 4-8-4 **50** oh5.............................. SophieRalston[(5)] 6 44?
(Lee Carter) *plld hrd: trckd ldrs: shkn up wl over 1f out: hung lft and wknd (jockey said filly hung left-handed throughout)* **66/1**

1313 **5** *2 1/4* **Junoesque**[18] 6566 5-9-9 **67**..............................(p) DarraghKeenan[(3)] 5 57
(John Gallagher) *led or disp ld to over 2f out: wknd u.p wl over 1f out* **9/4**[2]

2m 29.86s (-4.14) **Going Correction** -0.325s/f (Firm)
WFA 3 from 4yo+ 8lb **5** Ran SP% **108.3**
Speed ratings (Par 100): **100,99,99,96,94**
CSF £75.76 TOTE £5.00: £1.70, £5.80; EX 32.40 Trifecta £87.70.

Owner The Problem Solvers **Bred** Golden Vale Stud **Trained** Edgcote, Northamptonshire

FOCUS
Add 4yds. A fair handicap where the 8lb 3yo weight-for-age allowance proved decisive. Dubious form.

7201 BRITISH STALLION STUDS EBF CONDITIONS STKS 1m 3f 133y
1:40 (1:41) (Class 3) 3-Y-O+ **£9,766** (£2,923; £1,461) **Stalls** High

Form RPR

0004 **1** **Original Choice (IRE)**[10] 6861 5-9-3 95..............................(v) HollieDoyle 1 99
(Nick Littmoden) *dwlt: hld up in last: clsd 3f out: rdn to ld wl over 1f out: kpt on wl* **11/4**[3]

0046 **2** *1 1/2* **Koeman**[8] 6917 5-9-3 93.............................. StevieDonohoe 3 97
(Mick Channon) *led at mod pce: rdn over 2f out: hdd wl over 1f out: one pce after* **7/4**[2]

514 **3** *1/2* **Lady Of Shalott**[28] 6223 4-8-12 91..............................(h) KieranShoemark 2 91
(David Simcock) *t.k.h: trckd ldr: rdn to chal over 2f out: nt qckn wl over 1f out: one pce and hld fnl f* **5/4**[1]

2m 32.76s (-1.24) **Going Correction** -0.325s/f (Firm) **3** Ran SP% **107.5**
Speed ratings (Par 107): **91,90,89**
CSF £7.28 TOTE £3.10; EX 6.90 Trifecta £8.00.

Owner A A Goodman **Bred** Ballybrennan Stud **Trained** Newmarket, Suffolk

FOCUS
Add 4yds. With no obvious front-runner in the field this was likely to be a tactical affair and so it proved with the outsider winning the dash to the line. The second has been rated close to his turf best, but this is not solid form.

7202 EMPTY SAFE H'CAP 1m 6f
2:15 (2:20) (Class 6) (0-60,57) 3-Y-O+
£2,781 (£827; £413; £300; £300; £300) **Stalls** Low

Form RPR

4442 **1** **Spring Run**[22] 6400 3-9-3 **55**.............................. CharlesBishop 5 63+
(Jonathan Portman) *dwlt: sn trckd ldng pair: wnt 2nd 1/2-way: shkn up to ld over 2f out: in command over 1f out: readily* **9/2**[1]

5065 **2** *2 1/4* **Hatsaway (IRE)**[18] 6566 8-9-9 **55**..............................(p) PaddyBradley[(3)] 8 58
(Pat Phelan) *wl in tch: trckd ldng trio 1/2-way: rdn to chse wnr 2f out: kpt on but no imp* **14/1**

6455 **3** *3/4* **Ignatius (IRE)**[42] 5648 3-9-1 **53**.............................. KierenFox 13 57
(John Best) *trckd ldr to 1/2-way: styd cl up: rdn over 2f out: kpt on same pce over 1f out* **11/2**[2]

0043 **4** *1 1/2* **Banta Bay**[17] 6599 5-9-7 **50**.............................. JosephineGordon 9 50
(John Best) *racd on outer in midfield: lost pl after 6f: rdn 3f out: prog 2f out: hanging lft but kpt on fnl f: nvr able to chal* **15/2**[3]

5363 **5** *nk* **Highway Robbery**[15] 6681 3-8-5 **48**..............................(p) SophieRalston[(5)] 14 50
(Julia Feilden) *chsd ldrs: outpcd over 3f out: kpt on u.p fnl 2f: nvr able to chal* **8/1**

3006 **6** *2 3/4* **Lady Elysia**[34] 5987 3-9-1 **53**.............................. HollieDoyle 11 51
(Harry Dunlop) *t.k.h: trckd ldrs: rdn over 2f out and no prog: wknd over 1f out* **10/1**

5055 **7** *3/4* **Seventii**[17] 6601 5-8-13 **45**.............................. DarraghKeenan[(3)] 10 40
(Robert Eddery) *hld up wl in rr: rdn and sme prog over 2f out: no hdwy and btn wl over 1f out* **14/1**

1046 **8** *3/4* **Greenview Paradise (IRE)**[17] 6599 5-9-3 **51**....... ScottMcCullagh[(5)] 12 45
(Jeremy Scott) *hld up wl in rr: rdn and prog over 2f out: wknd over 1f out* **14/1**

0/ **9** *nk* **Montys Angel (IRE)**[26] 2598 9-8-13 **45**.............................. MitchGodwin[(3)] 1 39
(John Bridger) *hld up wl in rr: rdn and no significant prog over 2f out* **50/1**

0042 **10** *hd* **Mr Nice Guy (IRE)**[12] 6805 3-9-0 **57**.............................. PoppyBridgwater[(5)] 7 53
(Sylvester Kirk) *nvr really gng: towards rr: dropped to last of main gp and detached 4f out: plugged on over 1f out (jockey said gelding was never travelling and moved poorly)* **11/2**[2]

4600 **11** *7* **Affair**[30] 6115 5-9-6 **49**.............................. StevieDonohoe 6 33
(Hughie Morrison) *led to over 2f out: wknd rapidly* **20/1**

3023 **12** *16* **Beechwood James (FR)**[19] 6552 3-8-10 **53**. ThoreHammerHansen[(5)] 3 19
(Richard Hannon) *in tch in midfield: rdn 5f out: wknd 3f out: eased and t.o (jockey said colt stopped quickly)* **12/1**

606 **13** *74* **Brass (FR)**[21] 6438 3-8-12 **53**.............................. GeorgiaCox[(3)] 4
(Paul Webber) *dwlt: a last: t.o 5f out (jockey said filly was never travelling)* **25/1**

3m 0.86s (-10.34) **Going Correction** -0.325s/f (Firm)
WFA 3 from 5yo+ 9lb **13** Ran SP% **119.2**
Speed ratings (Par 101): **112,110,110,109,109 107,107,106,106,106 102,93,51**
CSF £67.19 CT £359.18 TOTE £5.00: £1.80, £4.60, £1.60; EX 63.00 Trifecta £417.00.

Owner British Racing Club **Bred** The Hon Mrs R Pease **Trained** Upper Lambourn, Berks

FOCUS
Add 4yds. A moderate handicap where it paid to race prominently. The form might be a shade better than rated.

7203 COMPARE BOOKMAKER SITES AT BONUSCODEBETS.CO.UK EBF FILLIES' NOVICE STKS (PLUS 10 RACE) 7f 135y
2:50 (3:08) (Class 4) 2-Y-O £4,463 (£1,328; £663; £331) Stalls Centre

Form				RPR
642	1		**Golden Lips (IRE)**[15] 6675 2-9-0 75 JosephineGordon 9 (Harry Dunlop) *mde all: shkn up and in command wl over 1f out: pushed out fnl f* 3/1[2]	68+
25	2	2 1/4	**Lola Paige (IRE)**[71] 4605 2-8-11 0 GeorgiaCox(3) 2 (William Haggas) *wl in tch: rdn to chse wnr 2f out: one pce and no imp after* 5/2[1]	63
0	3	nk	**Rhyme Scheme (IRE)**[71] 4605 2-8-9 0 ScottMcCullagh(5) 1 (Mick Channon) *mostly in last tl shkn up and prog over 2f out: styd on to take 3rd ins fnl f* 6/1	62
	4	1/2	**My Poem** 2-9-0 0 KieranShoemark 6 (Sir Michael Stoute) *dwlt: rn green but in tch: awkward path 5f out: prog 2f out: styd on fnl f to press for 3rd nr fin (jockey said filly lost its action on the crossing)* 11/2	61
6000	5	1	**Kahpehlo**[11] 6837 2-8-11 50 MitchGodwin(3) 5 (John Bridger) *mostly chsd wnr: rdn 3f out: lost 2nd 2f out: one pce u.p after* 100/1	58
0	6	2 3/4	**Lovers' Gait (IRE)**[42] 5684 2-9-0 0 AdrianMcCarthy 7 (Ed Dunlop) *chsd ldrs: rdn and wknd 2f out* 66/1	52
0	7	3	**Kashmirella (IRE)**[30] 6118 2-9-0 0 CharlesBishop 3 (Eve Johnson Houghton) *a towards rr: rdn and no prog over 2f out* 5/1[3]	44
50	8	3/4	**Poetic Lilly**[58] 5082 2-9-0 0 HollieDoyle 8 (David Menuisier) *t.k.h: prom: disp 2nd fr 3f out to 2f out: wknd qckly* 14/1	43
	9	2 1/2	**Highland Dreamer (IRE)** 2-9-0 0 StevieDonohoe 4 (Charlie Fellowes) *dwlt: a in last pair: wl btn fnl 2f* 14/1	37

1m 32.52s (0.82) **Going Correction** -0.25s/f (Firm) 9 Ran SP% 115.7
Speed ratings (Par 94): **85,82,82,81,80 78,75,74,71**
CSF £10.96 TOTE £3.30: £1.20, £1.80, £1.70; EX 11.30 Trifecta £54.50.
Owner Haven't A Pot & Ballylinch Stud **Bred** Ballylinch Stud **Trained** Lambourn, Berks

FOCUS
A weak looking fillies' novice won under a finely judged front-running ride. It's hard to set the opening level.

7204 INJURED JOCKEYS FUND H'CAP 7f 135y
3:25 (3:43) (Class 5) (0-70,72) 3-Y-O+ £3,428 (£1,020; £509; £300; £300; £300) Stalls Centre

Form				RPR
032	1		**Narak**[17] 6587 3-9-4 67 HollieDoyle 8 (George Scott) *racd against nr side rail: trckd ldr: plld out 2f out: rdn to ld jst over 1f out: styd on wl: readily* 4/1[3]	76+
0031	2	2 1/4	**Fancy Flyer**[32] 6052 3-9-0 70 LukeBacon(7) 2 (Dean Ivory) *t.k.h: led: crossed to nr side rail 1/2-way: shkn up over 2f out: hdd and one pce jst over 1f out* 17/2	72
3400	3	1/2	**Approve The Dream (IRE)**[7] 6983 3-8-0 54 oh1 SophieRalston(5) 1 (Julia Feilden) *rrd s: in tch: rdn on wd outside over 2f out: prog to take 3rd fnl f: kpt on but n.d to wnr* 12/1	55+
-005	4	1	**Fronsac**[11] 6839 4-9-9 67 JosephineGordon 5 (Daniel Kubler) *walked to post: chsd ldrs: rdn over 2f out: one pce over 1f out* 7/2[2]	66
0254	5	hd	**Balata Bay**[22] 6418 3-9-1 71 (b) MarkCrehan(7) 7 (Richard Hannon) *taken to post v steadily: chsd ldrs: rdn over 2f out: one pce over 1f out* 7/2[2]	69
5433	6	2 3/4	**Annexation (FR)**[49] 5431 3-9-0 63 KieranShoemark 3 (Ed Dunlop) *chsd ldrs: drvn over 2f out: no prog on outer over 1f out: wknd fnl f* 11/4[1]	54
00-4	7	8	**Tanqeeb**[136] 2285 3-9-2 72 RPWalsh(7) 6 (Ian Williams) *s.s: mostly in last and detached: pushed along and no prog over 2f out: nvr in it* 25/1	43
-000	8	4 1/2	**Aegean Legend**[42] 5675 4-8-3 54 oh9 (p) GeorgeRooke(7) 4 (John Bridger) *chsd ldrs: rdn and wknd qckly 2f out* 40/1	15

1m 28.94s (-2.76) **Going Correction** -0.25s/f (Firm) 8 Ran SP% 115.6
WFA 3 from 4yo 5lb
Speed ratings (Par 103): **103,100,100,99,99 96,88,83**
CSF £37.91 CT £377.64 TOTE £5.70: £2.80, £2.30, £2.50; EX 27.00 Trifecta £219.70.
Owner R A H Evans **Bred** R A H Evans **Trained** Newmarket, Suffolk

FOCUS
A fair handicap won in nice style by the handicap debutante, the only filly in the race. The third has been rated close to form, with the fourth to his recent effort.

7205 SKY SPORTS RACING ON SKY 415 H'CAP 7f
4:00 (4:12) (Class 4) (0-85,85) 3-Y-O+ £5,207 (£1,549; £774; £387; £300; £300) Stalls Centre

Form				RPR
010	1		**Kachumba**[18] 6567 4-9-1 76 HollieDoyle 7 (Rae Guest) *trckd ldrs: rdn 2f out: clsd jst over 1f out: drvn ahd ins fnl f: hld on wl* 7/1	82
1136	2	hd	**Fighting Temeraire (IRE)**[9] 6898 6-8-13 74 JoeyHaynes 5 (Dean Ivory) *hld up in last: rdn and prog on outer 2f out: drvn to chal ins fnl f: jst hld last nr fin* 4/1[3]	79
13-3	3	1/2	**Reloaded (IRE)**[159] 1646 3-9-6 85 KieranShoemark 6 (George Scott) *trckd ldrs: rdn whn nt clr run briefly 2f out and swtchd lft: no prog tl styd on wl fnl f: tk 3rd last strides and gaining at fin* 5/2[1]	89+
4445	4	nk	**Maksab (IRE)**[18] 6567 4-9-0 80 ScottMcCullagh(5) 3 (Mick Channon) *led and sn crossed to nr side rail: hdd after 2f: pressed ldr tl fnl f: kpt on same pce after* 7/2[2]	83
4504	5	1/2	**Global Tango (IRE)**[21] 6440 4-9-8 83 (v[1]) AdrianMcCarthy 4 (Luke McJannet) *led after 2f: rdn 2f out: hdd & wknd ins fnl f* 16/1	85
1515	6	2 3/4	**Gambon (GER)**[19] 6525 3-9-3 82 CharlesBishop 2 (Eve Johnson Houghton) *t.k.h: trckd ldrs: rdn and cl up 2f out: wknd fnl f* 6/1	75
3100	7	11	**I Am A Dreamer**[12] 6803 3-9-6 85 (v) JosephineGordon 1 (Mark Johnston) *pressed ldrs on outer: rdn over 2f out: sn wknd and eased (vet said colt was lame on its left-hind)* 10/1	48

1m 21.7s (-2.60) **Going Correction** -0.25s/f (Firm) 7 Ran SP% 112.6
WFA 3 from 4yo+ 4lb
Speed ratings (Par 105): **104,103,103,102,102 99,86**
CSF £33.75 TOTE £8.60: £3.30, £1.90; EX 29.90 Trifecta £202.20.
Owner The Bucket List Racing Syndicate **Bred** Brook Stud Bloodstock Ltd **Trained** Newmarket, Suffolk

FOCUS
A useful handicap brought up a treble for Hollie Doyle in a blanket finish. Muddling form, but the second has been rated to his recent form.

7206 WATCH SKY SPORTS RACING IN HD FILLIES' H'CAP 6f
4:35 (4:44) (Class 4) (0-85,79) 3-Y-O+ £5,207 (£1,549; £774; £387; £300) Stalls Centre

Form				RPR
5625	1		**Dizzy G (IRE)**[18] 6565 4-9-2 74 JoeyHaynes 5 (K R Burke) *mde virtually all and racd against nr side rail: jnd and rdn jst over 1f out: kpt on wl last 100yds* 3/1[3]	80
121	2	1/2	**Whisper Aloud**[18] 6561 3-9-4 78 HollieDoyle 1 (Archie Watson) *trckd ldng pair: clsd over 1f out: drvn to chal ins fnl f and w wnr: nt qckn last 100yds* 11/4[2]	82
1502	3	1/2	**Chitra**[11] 6835 3-9-5 79 KieranShoemark 4 (Daniel Kubler) *trckd wnr: rdn to chal over 1f out: nt qckn and lost 2nd ins fnl f: kpt on* 4/1	82
-140	4	4 1/2	**Ascended (IRE)**[44] 5573 3-9-2 79 GeorgiaCox(3) 3 (William Haggas) *a in 4th and nvr really gng the pce: rdn 2f out: wknd over 1f out* 9/1	67
0350	5	1 3/4	**Shorter Skirt**[8] 6916 3-8-10 77 (p) GeorgiaDobie(7) 2 (Eve Johnson Houghton) *v.s.a and lost 8 l: jst abt latched on to field by 1/2-way: no prog 2f out: wknd fnl f (jockey said filly was slowly away)* 9/4[1]	60

1m 8.84s (-2.66) **Going Correction** -0.25s/f (Firm) 5 Ran SP% 112.4
WFA 3 from 4yo 2lb
Speed ratings (Par 102): **107,106,105,99,97**
CSF £11.82 TOTE £4.50: £2.00, £1.60; EX 15.60 Trifecta £32.50.
Owner Mrs Melba Bryce **Bred** Laurence & David Gleeson **Trained** Middleham Moor, N Yorks

FOCUS
A useful fillies' handicap produced a tight finish with the winner having the rail to help her get back up on the line. The winner has been rated to this year's form.
T/Plt: £1,048.50 to a £1 stake. Pool: £39,570.83 - 27.55 winning units T/Qpdt: £26.80 to a £1 stake. Pool: £5,273.46 - 145.28 winning units **Jonathan Neesom**

6932 MUSSELBURGH (R-H)
Saturday, September 14

OFFICIAL GOING: Good to firm (8.9)
Wind: Overcast Weather: Fairly strong, across

7207 JMC HEALTHCARE H'CAP (DIV I) 7f 33y
3:30 (3:31) (Class 6) (0-60,59) 3-Y-O+ £3,105 (£924; £461; £400; £400; £400) Stalls Low

Form				RPR
0601	1		**Lagenda**[8] 6937 6-9-7 58 JasonHart 6 (Liam Bailey) *trckd ldr: effrt 2f out: led ins fnl f: pricked ears: r.o wl* 7/2[1]	65
0/3-	2	1 1/4	**Villa Maria**[96] 3669 4-9-6 57 (b) DougieCostello 5 (S Donohoe, Ire) *sn pushed along to ld: rdn over 2f out: hdd ins fnl f: kpt on same pce* 10/1	61
0401	3	nse	**Lukoutoldmakezebak**[39] 5787 6-8-9 49 (p) HarrisonShaw(3) 2 (David Thompson) *hld up on ins: effrt and angled lft over 1f out: kpt on wl fnl f: nrst fin* 11/2[2]	53
3220	4	1 1/2	**Perfect Swiss**[26] 6275 3-9-0 55 JamesSullivan 1 (Tim Easterby) *s.i.s: hld up: hdwy 2f out: kpt on fnl f: nt pce to chal* 7/2[1]	53+
60	5	hd	**Vivacious Spirit**[56] 5176 3-9-1 59 (p[1]) SeanDavis(3) 11 (Phillip Makin) *chsd ldrs: rdn over 2f out: edgd rt and one pce ins fnl f* 10/1	56
0500	6	shd	**Joyful Star**[79] 4293 9-8-11 48 NathanEvans 8 (Fred Watson) *t.k.h: hld up: rdn over 2f out: kpt on fnl f: nvr able to chal* 25/1	47
5000	7	1	**The Retriever (IRE)**[39] 5768 4-8-10 47 GrahamLee 9 (Micky Hammond) *s.i.s: bhd: rdn over 2f out: kpt on fnl f: no imp* 25/1	43
1340	8	nk	**Forever A Lady (IRE)**[18] 6572 6-9-8 59 ShaneGray 3 (Keith Dalgleish) *hld up in midfield on ins: n.m.r over 2f out: effrt over 1f out: no imp* 12/1	55
034P	9	4	**Leeshaan (IRE)**[26] 6276 4-8-9 46 LukeMorris 4 (Rebecca Bastiman) *chsd ldrs: rdn over 2f out: wknd over 1f out* 9/1	31
3663	10	2 1/4	**God Of Dreams**[18] 6575 3-9-1 56 PaulMulrennan 7 (Iain Jardine) *plld hrd early in midfield: rdn and outpcd over 2f out: sn btn (jockey said gelding ran too free)* 15/2[3]	33
1000	11	4	**Archies Lad**[8] 6937 3-9-2 57 CamHardie 10 (R Mike Smith) *bhd: rdn and struggling over 2f out: sn btn* 25/1	24

1m 28.85s (-0.15) **Going Correction** -0.05s/f (Good) 11 Ran SP% 119.0
WFA 3 from 4yo+ 4lb
Speed ratings (Par 101): **98,96,96,94,94 94,93,92,88,85 81**
CSF £39.49 CT £185.69 TOTE £3.80: £1.60, £2.50, £2.40; EX 34.70 Trifecta £74.80.
Owner Oakfield Racing **Bred** Joyce Wallsgrove **Trained** Middleham, N Yorks

FOCUS
The going was officially good to firm for this run-of-the-mill handicap in which most were exposed sorts. The early pace was ordinary, several pulled hard and the first two on the turn were the first two home. Routine form.

7208 JOIN RACINGTV NOW NURSERY H'CAP 5f 1y
4:05 (4:08) (Class 6) (0-65,62) 2-Y-O £3,105 (£924; £461; £400; £400; £400) Stalls High

Form				RPR
0550	1		**Shepherds Way (IRE)**[39] 5789 2-9-7 62 ConnorBeasley 4 (Michael Dods) *hld up: hdwy on outside 1/2-way: effrt and led over 1f out: rdn and edgd lft ins fnl f: r.o (trainer said, regarding the improved form shown, the filly benefited from the drop in grade)* 5/1[3]	66+
040	2	3/4	**Summer Heights**[17] 6606 2-9-0 55 PaddyMathers 9 (Jim Goldie) *dwlt: bhd and outpcd: swtchd rt and gd hdwy on outside over 1f out: wnt 2nd wl ins fnl f: kpt on* 40/1	56
0364	3	nse	**Maybellene (IRE)**[19] 6539 2-9-7 62 NathanEvans 3 (Alan Berry) *chsd ldrs: effrt and ev ch over 1f out: chsd wnr to wl ins fnl f: kpt on* 22/1	63
400	4	1/2	**Sweet Embrace (IRE)**[30] 6096 2-8-11 52 CamHardie 10 (John Wainwright) *hld up in midfield: nt clr run 1/2-way: effrt and rdn over 1f out: kpt on ins fnl f* 50/1	51
4064	5	nk	**Comeatchoo (IRE)**[29] 6182 2-8-11 52 (b) RachelRichardson 5 (Tim Easterby) *t.k.h: hld up: hdwy to chse ldrs over 1f out: kpt on same pce ins fnl f* 16/1	50
0012	6	2	**Queenoftheclyde (IRE)**[15] 6667 2-9-1 59 HarrisonShaw(3) 8 (K R Burke) *cl up: pushed along whn n.m.r over 1f out: rdn and outpcd fnl f (jockey said filly hung right-handed)* 11/4[1]	50

The Form Book Flat 2019, Raceform Ltd, Newbury, RG14 5SJ

0655 **7** *hd* **Invincible Bertie (IRE)**29 6182 2-9-0 **55**.......................... TomEaves 11 46
(Nigel Tinkler) *hld up: nt clr run over 2f out: effrt and swtchd rt over 1f out: no imp fnl f* **3/1**2

0300 **8** *2 ¾* **She's Easyontheeye (IRE)**26 6272 2-9-7 **62**.......................... JasonHart 6 42
(John Quinn) *led tl rdn and hdd over 1f out: sn wknd* **18/1**

0020 **9** *¾* **Chocoholic**43 5618 2-9-0 **55**..........................(b1) GrahamLee 2 33
(Bryan Smart) *prom: rdn over 2f out: wknd over 1f out (jockey said gelding hung both ways)* **18/1**

553 **10** *1 ¾* **Puerto Sol (IRE)**115 2957 2-9-4 **59**.......................... BenRobinson 1 30
(Brian Ellison) *dwlt and swtchd lft s: sn outpcd and struggling: nvr on terms (jockey said gelding was slowly away)* **10/1**

3060 **11** *2 ½* **Ice Skate**15 6683 2-8-8 **49**..........................(b1) JamesSullivan 7 11
(Tim Easterby) *cl up tl rdn and wknd over 1f out* **11/2**

1m 0.25s (0.55) **Going Correction** -0.05s/f (Good) **11 Ran SP% 118.0**
Speed ratings (Par 93): **93,91,91,90,90 87,86,82,81,78 74**
CSF £193.17 CT £4058.37 TOTE £5.90: £1.90, £5.80, £4.90; EX 903.80 Trifecta £780.70.
Owner D W Armstrong & M J K Dods **Bred** Mountarmstrong Stud **Trained** Denton, Co Durham

FOCUS
This was a low-grade sprint nursery run at a strong gallop in which they bet big prices bar the first five in the market. They went hard up front and the finish was fought out by those more patiently ridden. Limited form.

7209 POMMERY CHAMPAGNE EDINBURGH CUP H'CAP 1m 7f 217y
4:40 (4:42) (Class 3) (0-90,88) 3-Y-O

£24,900 (£7,456; £3,728; £1,864; £932; £468) **Stalls High**

Form RPR

3115 **1** **Just Hubert (IRE)**21 6471 3-9-5 **86**.......................... GrahamLee 5 95
(William Muir) *hld up: stdy hdwy 4f out: rdn to ld over 1f out: kpt on strly fnl f* **3/1**1

1341 **2** *1 ½* **Anyonecanhaveitall**9 6901 3-8-9 **76**.......................... JasonHart 8 83
(Mark Johnston) *pressed ldr: led after 5f: rdn over 2f out: hdd over 1f out: rallied: one pce wl ins fnl f* **4/1**2

1523 **3** *2 ¼* **Agravain**21 6459 3-8-2 **69** oh3.......................... JamesSullivan 6 73
(Tim Easterby) *t.k.h: hld up: smooth hdwy to chse ldrs whn n.m.r briefly over 2f out: rdn over 1f out: one pce fnl f* **20/1**

-222 **4** *2 ¾* **Whiskey And Water**41 4779 3-8-5 **72**..........................(p1) CamHardie 2 73
(Brian Ellison) *prom: rdn along 3f out: kpt on same pce fr over 1f out* **12/1**

2132 **5** *3* **Dark Lochnagar (USA)**15 6657 3-9-7 **88**.......................... ShaneGray 4 85
(Keith Dalgleish) *hld up in midfield on ins: rdn along over 3f out: no imp fr 2f out* **6/1**3

2052 **6** *nk* **Lord Lamington**9 6888 3-9-0 **81**.......................... ConnorBeasley 10 78
(Mark Johnston) *led 5f: cl up: drvn and ev ch over 2f out: wknd over 1f out* **14/1**

3555 **7** *1 ¼* **Flash Point (IRE)**8 6940 3-8-2 **69**.......................... RoystonFfrench 9 64
(Tracy Waggott) *t.k.h: in tch: lost pl after 6f: rdn over 3f out: effrt on outside over 1f out: nvr able to chal* **50/1**

1112 **8** *1* **Hydroplane (IRE)**11 6842 3-8-12 **79**..........................(v1) LukeMorris 3 73
(Sir Mark Prescott Bt) *prom: effrt 3f out: wknd over 1f out (jockey said gelding failed to stay the 2 mile trip)* **4/1**2

1114 **9** *nk* **Champagne Marengo (IRE)**35 5943 3-8-5 **72**........(p) PaddyMathers 1 66
(Ian Williams) *dwlt and wnt rt s: bhd: hdwy on outside over 4f out: hung rt and wknd 2f out* **8/1**

2111 **10** *13* **Euro Implosion (IRE)**17 6589 3-8-5 **75**.......................... SeanDavis(3) 7 53
(Keith Dalgleish) *rrd s: sn midfield on outside: rdn over 4f out: wknd over 2f out (jockey said gelding ran flat)* **16/1**

3m 26.9s (-4.60) **Going Correction** -0.05s/f (Good) **10 Ran SP% 117.4**
Speed ratings (Par 105): **109,108,107,105,104 104,103,102,102,96**
CSF £14.93 CT £203.66 TOTE £3.90: £1.50, £2.10, £5.50; EX 17.90 Trifecta £277.40.
Owner Foursome Thoroughbreds **Bred** Ringfort Stud **Trained** Lambourn, Berks

FOCUS
A well-contested staying handicap for three-year-olds run at a sound gallop. They finished well strung out and the form should prove solid. Sound form which has been rated in line with the race standard.

7210 JMC HEALTHCARE H'CAP (DIV II) 7f 33y
5:15 (5:18) (Class 6) (0-60,59) 3-Y-O+

£3,105 (£924; £461; £400; £400; £400) **Stalls Low**

Form RPR

016 **1** **My Valentino (IRE)**16 6628 6-8-10 **47**..........................(b) JamesSullivan 10 53
(Dianne Sayer) *s.i.s: bhd: pushed along and plenty to do over 2f out: hdwy over 1f out: kpt on strly to ld towards fin* **18/1**

-062 **2** *nk* **Be Proud (IRE)**63 4916 3-8-9 **53**.......................... HarrisonShaw(3) 6 56
(Jim Goldie) *midfield: rdn over 2f out: hdwy and edgd rt over 1f out: kpt on fnl f to take 2nd cl home* **10/1**

0000 **3** *nse* **Exchequer (IRE)**15 6680 8-9-8 **59**..........................(tp) LukeMorris 4 64
(Richard Guest) *t.k.h: cl up: rdn and led over 1f out: rdn: edgd rt and idled ins fnl f: hdd and no ex towards fin* **20/1**

0530 **4** *1 ¾* **Parion**50 5389 3-8-6 **50**.......................... SeanDavis(3) 2 49
(Richard Fahey) *led to over 1f out: kpt on same pce ins fnl f* **9/1**

0160 **5** *½* **Moonlit Sands (IRE)**14 6699 4-9-6 **57**..........................(tp) BenRobinson 5 56
(Brian Ellison) *hld up in midfield: effrt over 2f out: hdwy whn checked over 1f out: kpt on fnl f: nt pce to chal* **25/1**

2604 **6** *nk* **Duke Cosimo**15 6665 9-9-5 **56**.......................... TomEaves 1 54
(Michael Herrington) *hld up on ins: rdn and outpcd over 2f out: kpt on fnl f: nvr rchd ldrs (vet said gelding finished lame right-hind)* **16/1**

2300 **7** *nk* **Cliff Bay (IRE)**16 6628 5-9-0 **51**..........................(b1) GrahamLee 3 49
(Keith Dalgleish) *hld up in midfield: rdn along over 2f out: kpt on fnl f: no imp* **5/1**2

4046 **8** *½* **Tarnhelm**16 6627 4-8-8 **52**.......................... RhonaPindar(7) 8 48
(Wilf Storey) *slowly away: bhd: pushed along 3f out: hdwy on outside over 1f out: nvr rchd ldrs* **10/1**

2000 **9** *4* **Temple Of Wonder (IRE)**32 6036 3-9-0 **55**...........(p) PaulMulrennan 12 39
(Liam Bailey) *pressed ldr: ev ch over 2f out: wknd over 1f out* **33/1**

6312 **10** *10* **Muhallab (IRE)**9 6897 3-9-3 **58**.......................... ConnorBeasley 11 16
(Adrian Nicholls) *chsd ldrs tl rdn and wknd fr 2f out: eased fnl f (jockey said gelding was never travelling)* **15/8**1

6002 **11** *nk* **Robben Rainbow**18 6572 5-9-1 **52**.......................... JasonHart 7 11
(Katie Scott) *in tch on outside: rdn and hung rt over 2f out: wknd over 1f out (trainer could offer no explanation for the gelding's performance)* **6/1**3

1m 28.35s (-0.65) **Going Correction** -0.05s/f (Good)
WFA 3 from 4yo+ 4lb **11 Ran SP% 116.6**
Speed ratings (Par 101): **101,100,100,98,98 97,97,96,92,80 80**
CSF £180.47 CT £3669.48 TOTE £19.00: £4.90, £2.50, £6.00; EX 210.80 Trifecta £3799.70.
Owner Dennis J Coppola & Mrs Dianne Sayer **Bred** Lynch Bages Ltd & Camas Park Stud **Trained** Hackthorpe, Cumbria

FOCUS
The second division of the 46-60 7f handicap but unlike the first division they went a decent gallop and the winner came from last to first. The second is among those that suggest the bare form is little better than rated.

7211 EBF FILLIES' CONDITIONS STKS (PLUS 10 RACE) 5f 1y
5:45 (5:52) (Class 3) 2-Y-O

£8,092 (£2,423; £1,211; £605; £302; £152) **Stalls High**

Form RPR

201 **1** **Band Practice (IRE)**12 6800 2-9-3 **80**.......................... PaulMulrennan 2 86
(Archie Watson) *pressed ldr: led over 2f out: rdn and hrd pressed ins fnl f: kpt on strly towards fin* **4/1**2

2325 **2** *1 ½* **Mighty Spirit (IRE)**21 6474 2-8-12 **93**.......................... CliffordLee 6 76
(Richard Fahey) *t.k.h early: trckd ldrs: wnt 2nd and pushed along over 1f out: ev ch and rdn ins fnl f: one pce towards fin* **2/5**1

30 **3** *6* **Solemn Pledge**16 6622 2-8-9 **0**.......................... HarrisonShaw(3) 8 54
(K R Burke) *prom: drvn along and outpcd 1/2-way: kpt on fnl f to take modest 3rd cl home* **10/1**

3410 **4** *nse* **Ventura Flame (IRE)**24 6356 2-9-3 **82**.......................... JasonHart 3 59
(Keith Dalgleish) *led to over 2f out: rdn and outpcd fr over 1f out: lost 3rd cl home* **9/2**3

60 **5** *¾* **Garnock Valley**17 6606 2-8-12 **0**.......................... PaddyMathers 1 52
(R Mike Smith) *dwlt and wnt rt s: bhd and outpcd: sme late hdwy: nvr on terms* **80/1**

0 **6** *½* **Gina D'Cleaner**165 1499 2-8-12 **0**.......................... ShaneGray 4 50
(Keith Dalgleish) *dwlt: chsd clr ldng quintet: rdn along 1/2-way* **16/1**

56 **7** *17* **Unauthorised Act (IRE)**14 6713 2-8-12 **0**.......................... TomEaves 7
(Alan Berry) *bhd and sn outpcd: lost tch fr 1/2-way* **66/1**

0 **8** *4* **Klara Spirit (IRE)**17 6606 2-8-12 **0**.......................... NathanEvans 5
(R Mike Smith) *dwlt: bhd and outpcd: no ch fr 1/2-way* **66/1**

59.11s (-0.59) **Going Correction** -0.05s/f (Good) **8 Ran SP% 128.8**
Speed ratings (Par 96): **102,99,90,89,88 87,60,54**
CSF £6.82 TOTE £6.00: £1.40, £1.10, £1.90; EX 12.50 Trifecta £38.80.
Owner Clipper Logistics **Bred** Fergus Cousins **Trained** Upper Lambourn, W Berks

FOCUS
A conditions event for juveniles in which few featured and though the first two finished well clear it is hard to ascertain the value of the form.

7212 MAX DAVIS' 21ST BIRTHDAY H'CAP 1m 2y
6:15 (6:18) (Class 4) (0-80,82) 4-Y-O+

£5,692 (£1,694; £846; £423; £400; £400) **Stalls Low**

Form RPR

5603 **1** **Brother McGonagall**7 6961 5-9-5 **78**.......................... JamesSullivan 7 87
(Tim Easterby) *chsd clr ldr: hdwy to ld over 2f out: rdn over 1f out: kpt on fnl f: jst lasted* **8/1**

/440 **2** *shd* **Mustarrid (IRE)**35 5948 5-9-8 **81**.......................... TomEaves 4 89
(Ian Williams) *hld up: rdn and hdwy on outside 2f out: wnt 2nd ins fnl f: kpt on strly: jst failed* **8/1**

-515 **3** *1 ¾* **Grey Spirit (IRE)**57 5130 4-9-9 **82**..........................(p1) LukeMorris 5 86
(Sir Mark Prescott Bt) *prom: drvn along over 2f out: kpt on u.p ins fnl f* **11/2**2

6461 **4** *nk* **Glengarry**8 6935 6-9-9 **82**.......................... ConnorBeasley 10 85
(Keith Dalgleish) *slowly away: hld up: effrt and rdn over 2f out: edgd rt over 1f out: kpt on same pce ins fnl f* **13/2**3

36-2 **5** *nk* **Normal Norman**17 6594 5-9-3 **76**.......................... CamHardie 9 78
(John Ryan) *prom: pushed along over 2f out: hdwy to chse wnr over 1f out to ins fnl f: one pce nr fin* **7/2**1

0452 **6** *1* **Zeshov (IRE)**8 6937 8-8-8 **67**..........................(p) CliffordLee 1 67
(Rebecca Bastiman) *hld up on ins: hdwy and angled lft over 2f out: kpt on same pce ins fnl f* **10/1**

4430 **7** *½* **Glasses Up (USA)**21 6475 4-9-4 **77**..........................(b1) PaulMulrennan 2 77
(R Mike Smith) *s.i.s: hld up: pushed along over 2f out: hdwy over 1f out: keeping on whn n.m.r ins fnl f: no imp (jockey said gelding was denied a clear run on several occasions inside the final two furlongs)* **10/1**

3133 **8** *2* **Pickett's Charge**14 6700 6-8-12 **71**..........................(tp) BenRobinson 11 65
(Brian Ellison) *hld up in midfield: rdn along over 2f out: wknd over 1f out* **16/1**

6201 **9** *nk* **Calvados Spirit**29 6164 6-9-2 **78**.......................... SeanDavis(3) 6 72
(Richard Fahey) *s.i.s: hld up: drvn along over 2f out: no imp fr over 1f out* **10/1**

5320 **10** *1 ½* **How Bizarre**8 6935 4-8-13 **72**..........................(v1) JasonHart 8 62
(Liam Bailey) *t.k.h: led and clr: rdn over 2f out: wknd over 1f out* **14/1**

3512 **11** *7* **Four Kingdoms (IRE)**18 6576 5-9-2 **75**.......................... PaddyMathers 13 49
(R Mike Smith) *midfield on outside: drvn and struggling over 2f out: sn wknd* **20/1**

1m 39.29s (-0.71) **Going Correction** -0.05s/f (Good) **11 Ran SP% 117.7**
Speed ratings (Par 105): **101,100,99,98,98 97,97,95,94,93 86**
CSF £70.67 CT £386.23 TOTE £9.50: £2.60, £3.50, £2.30; EX 80.70 Trifecta £925.50.
Owner Reality Partnerships VI **Bred** J P Coggan **Trained** Great Habton, N Yorks

FOCUS
This was quite a competitive mile handicap with several coming into it in good form. The gallop was strong. The winner has been rated back to the level of his Beverley win in June.

7213 YOUR CONVEYANCER H'CAP 1m 208y
6:45 (6:47) (Class 4) (0-80,82) 3-Y-O

£6,986 (£2,079; £1,038; £519; £400; £400) **Stalls Low**

Form RPR

3422 **1** **Cape Victory (IRE)**15 6686 3-9-10 **82**.......................... PaulMulrennan 6 96
(James Tate) *pressed ldr: led gng wl over 2f out: pushed clr fr over 1f out: readily* **7/2**1

2544 **2** *8* **Ginger Fox**14 6729 3-9-5 **77**..........................(p) JasonHart 8 74
(Ian Williams) *prom: rdn 3f out: rallied and chsd (clr) wnr 1f out: kpt on: no imp* **4/1**2

1142 **3** *1 ¼* **Langholm (IRE)**31 6068 3-8-7 **65**..........................(t) CamHardie 5 60
(Declan Carroll) *led tl rdn and hdd over 2f out: one pce and lost 2nd 1f out* **7/1**3

231 **4** *½* **Northern Lyte**20 6501 3-8-7 **70**..........................(t) FayeMcManoman(5) 4 64
(Nigel Tinkler) *hld up in midfield: effrt and rdn over 2f out: no imp fr over 1f out* **7/1**3

2364 **5** *1* **Highwaygrey**19 6540 3-8-8 **66**.......................... RachelRichardson 10 57
(Tim Easterby) *s.i.s: hld up: effrt on outside 2f out: kpt on same pce fnl f* **20/1**

4103 **6** *1* **Gometra Ginty (IRE)**17 6609 3-9-1 **73**.......................... ShaneGray 2 62
(Keith Dalgleish) *chsd ldrs: effrt and rdn over 2f out: outpcd fr over 1f out* **17/2**

3111 **7** *1 1/2* **Kermouster**[16] 6624 3-9-0 **72**............................ SamJames 12 58
(Grant Tuer) *slowly away: bhd and outpcd: hdwy 2f out: no further imp fnl f (jockey said filly reared as the stalls opened and was slowly away)* **17/2**
3454 **8** *4 1/2* **Lightning Attack**[8] 6940 3-8-12 **73**.....................(p) SeanDavis(3) 1 50
(Richard Fahey) *hld up: rdn and outpcd over 2f out: btn over 1f out* **17/2**
1245 **9** *5* **Battle Of Waterloo (IRE)**[8] 6935 3-9-7 **79**..................(p[1]) LukeMorris 3 45
(John Ryan) *hld up: drvn along over 2f out: sn wknd* **11/1**
0- **10** *6* **Exchequer (FR)**[86] 3-8-11 **69**............................ NathanEvans 11 23
(Lucinda Russell) *hld up: rdn along 1/2-way: wknd over 2f out* **33/1**
0000 **11** *1 1/2* **Liberation Day**[61] 5002 3-8-12 **70**.....................(p) AndrewElliott 7 20
(Philip Kirby) *sn rdn along in rr: struggling fr 1/2-way: nvr on terms* **66/1**
4 **12** *8* **Beethoven's Gal**[27] 6259 3-8-7 **65**............................ PaddyMathers 9
(Richard Fahey) *hld up: rdn and struggling 3f out: lost action and btn 2f out: eased whn no ch fnl f (jockey said filly lost his action 2 furlongs out)* **22/1**

1m 51.0s (-2.10) **Going Correction** -0.05s/f (Good) **12** Ran SP% **120.7**
Speed ratings (Par 103): **107,99,98,98,97 96,95,91,86,81 80,73**
CSF £16.82 CT £95.44 TOTE £4.30: £2.70, £1.80, £1.80; EX 20.50 Trifecta £154.90.
Owner Saeed Manana **Bred** Rabbah Bloodstock Limited **Trained** Newmarket, Suffolk

FOCUS
A well-contested 1m1f handicap and though the gallop was fair few got into it. The race could be rated higher if taken at face value.

7214 LOTHIAN DAF H'CAP 5f 1y
7:15 (7:17) (Class 6) (0-55,54) 3-Y-O+

£3,105 (£924; £461; £400; £400; £400) **Stalls** High

Form RPR
0042 **1** **Super Florence (IRE)**[8] 6936 4-9-3 **53**....................(h) HarrisonShaw(3) 8 60
(Iain Jardine) *in tch: stdy hdwy 2f out: rdn to ld ins fnl f: r.o wl* **10/3**[1]
0013 **2** *1* **Thornaby Princess**[8] 6936 8-9-1 **48**.....................(p) TomEaves 3 51
(Jason Ward) *trckd ldrs: led and rdn over 1f out: hdd ins fnl f: one pce towards fin* **10/1**
3520 **3** *1 1/4* **Arnoul Of Metz**[30] 6126 4-9-4 **54**.....................(p) SeanDavis(3) 12 53
(Henry Spiller) *t.k.h: cl up: rdn and effrt over 1f out: r.o ins fnl f* **10/1**
24-5 **4** *hd* **Blastofmagic**[8] 6936 5-9-7 **54**.....................(tp) GrahamLee 5 52
(Adrian Brendan Joyce, Ire) *hld up in midfield: stdy hdwy and cl up over 1f out: sn rdn: one pce ins fnl f* **6/1**[3]
3040 **5** *hd* **Jessie Allan (IRE)**[21] 6462 8-8-5 **45**............................ CoreyMadden(7) 9 42
(Jim Goldie) *sn bhd: hdwy on outside over 1f out: kpt on fnl f: nvr rchd ldrs* **22/1**
006 **6** *3/4* **Lord Of The Glen**[18] 6574 4-9-2 **49**.....................(v) PaddyMathers 6 44
(Jim Goldie) *hld up: rdn along 2f out: kpt on fnl f: nt pce to chal* **7/1**
5455 **7** *3/4* **Star Cracker (IRE)**[18] 6574 7-8-12 **45**.....................(p) PaulMulrennan 10 38
(Jim Goldie) *midfield: effrt whn nt clr run and swtchd rt over 1f out: kpt on fnl f: no imp* **10/1**
20-0 **8** *1 1/4* **Griffin Street**[8] 6936 6-8-12 **45**.....................(b) RoystonFfrench 13 33
(Alistair Whillans) *slowly away: bhd tl sme late hdwy: nvr rchd ldrs (jockey said gelding was slowly away)* **50/1**
0-3 **9** *hd* **Zeb City (IRE)**[18] 6574 4-8-12 **45**............................ SamJames 11 32
(Mark L Fagan, Ire) *led tl rdn and hdd over 1f out: wknd fnl f* **7/2**[2]
2/ **10** *nk* **Dulcina**[899] 1418 5-9-1 **48**............................ ShaneGray 4 34
(S Donohoe, Ire) *slowly away: bhd: rdn over 2f out: sn no imp: hld whn j. winning line* **33/1**
0620 **11** *1 1/4* **Corton Lass**[8] 6936 4-8-12 **45**............................ JasonHart 14 26
(Keith Dalgleish) *t.k.h: cl up: rdn over 2f out: wknd over 1f out* **16/1**
040 **12** *1* **Spenny's Lass**[18] 6572 4-8-13 **46**.....................(p) LukeMorris 2 24
(John Ryan) *midfield on outside: rdn along 1/2-way: wknd over 1f out* **16/1**
0-00 **13** *nse* **Laoise (USA)**[8] 6936 3-8-13 **47**............................ BenRobinson 1 24
(Linda Perratt) *slowly away: bhd: effrt on outside over 2f out: wknd appr fnl f (jockey said filly stopped quickly)* **40/1**

(0.30) **Going Correction** -0.05s/f (Good)
WFA 3 from 4yo+ 1lb **13** Ran SP% **122.8**
Speed ratings (Par 101): **95,93,91,91,90 89,88,86,86,85 83,81,81**
CSF £37.18 CT £324.68 TOTE £3.60: £2.20, £2.70, £3.40; EX 30.70 Trifecta £213.10.
Owner Top Of The Hill Racing Club **Bred** Tally-Ho Stud **Trained** Carrutherstown, D'fries & G'way

FOCUS
A sprint handicap for horses rated 46-55. Most of the runners were exposed and not easy to win with and the form not likely to be strong.
T/Plt: £968.50 to a £1 stake. Pool: £46,808.13 - 35.28 winning units T/Qpdt: £42.00 to a £1 stake. Pool: £6,767.77 - 119.11 winning units **Richard Young**

6133

LEOPARDSTOWN (L-H)
Saturday, September 14

OFFICIAL GOING: Good (good to firm in places; watered)

7215a BALLYLINCH STUD IRISH EBF INGABELLE STKS (LISTED RACE) (FILLIES) (INNER TRACK) 7f
1:55 (1:57) 2-Y-O

£53,153 (£17,117; £8,108; £3,603; £1,801; £900)

RPR
1 **Blissful (IRE)**[16] 6645 2-9-0 0............................ RyanMoore 6 97
(A P O'Brien, Ire) *sn trckd ldr in 2nd: pushed along over 2f out: nt qckn immediately w runner-up and 2 l down 1f out: kpt on strly u.p ins fnl f to ld on line* **13/2**
2 *nse* **Nurse Barbara (IRE)**[13] 6762 2-9-0 0............................ ColinKeane 4 97
(G M Lyons, Ire) *sn led: rdn 2f out and kicked 2 l clr 1f out: kpt on wl u.p but reduced advantage wl ins fnl f and hdd on line* **7/2**[2]
3 *3/4* **Pronouncement (USA)**[40] 5752 2-9-0 0............................ ChrisHayes 8 95
(J P Murtagh, Ire) *sn mid-div: t.k.h early: sn settled in 5th: wnt 4th 3f out: pushed along in 3rd over 2f out and nt qckn w front pair but kpt on strly u.p to cl deficit all way to line: lame post-r (vet said filly to be lame on her right foreleg post race)* **11/2**
4 *2* **Ha'penny Bridge (IRE)**[85] 4083 2-9-0 78............................ TomMadden 1 89
(Mrs John Harrington, Ire) *hld up towards rr: 7th 1/2-way: pushed along over 2f out and stdy hdwy u.p between horses to go 4th ins fnl f: kpt on wl* **33/1**
5 *1/2* **Punita Arora (IRE)**[7] 6987 2-9-0 98............................ ShaneFoley 2 88
(Mrs John Harrington, Ire) *t.k.h early: hld up in rr: 9th 1/2-way: pushed along over 2f out and stdy hdwy on outer to go 5th u.p cl home: nvr nrr (jockey said filly was slowly away from the starting stalls)* **9/2**[3]
6 *1/2* **Lady Jane Wilde (IRE)**[36] 5919 2-9-0 0............................ NGMcCullagh 7 87
(John M Oxx, Ire) *hld up in mid-div: 6th 1/2-way: rdn 2f out and sn no ex u.p: kpt on same pce* **8/1**
7 *1 1/2* **Raven's Cry (IRE)**[21] 6477 2-9-0 0............................ WJLee 9 83
(P Twomey, Ire) *chsd ldrs on outer: 3rd 1/2-way: pushed along 3f out and lost pl: no imp u.p: grad wknd (jockey said filly missed the break and was outpaced during the race)* **3/1**[1]
8 *3/4* **Camachita (IRE)**[30] 6133 2-9-0 0............................ DeclanMcDonogh 3 81
(J P Murtagh, Ire) *towards rr: 8th 1/2-way: rdn over 2f out but no imp u.p and kpt on same pce* **20/1**
9 *2 1/4* **Sailing South (IRE)**[5] 7036 2-9-0 0............................ KevinManning 5 75
(J S Bolger, Ire) *sn chsd ldrs on inner: 4th 1/2-way: pushed along over 2f out but sn no ex u.p: hmpd sltly whn btn 1f out: eased* **33/1**

1m 29.55s (-0.85) **Going Correction** -0.05s/f (Good) **9** Ran SP% **115.9**
Speed ratings: **102,101,101,98,98 97,95,95,92**
CSF £29.01 TOTE £6.70: £1.70, £1.50, £2.20; DF 28.20 Trifecta £140.90.
Owner Mrs John Magnier & Michael Tabor & Derrick Smith **Bred** Coolmore **Trained** Cashel, Co Tipperary

FOCUS
The winner has found a new level since being upped in trip and will get further again. She only just got there on the line in a race where nothing got involved from the rear. It's been rated as a slightly below-par renewal.

7216a IRISH STALLION FARMS EBF "PETINGO" H'CAP (PREMIER HANDICAP) (INNER TRACK) 1m 4f 180y
2:30 (2:31) 3-Y-O+

£79,729 (£25,675; £12,162; £5,405; £2,702; £1,351)

RPR
1 **Kastasa (IRE)**[22] 6431 3-8-10 **92**............................ AndrewSlattery(5) 18 99+
(D K Weld, Ire) *chsd ldrs: 5th 5f out: rdn over 2f out and hdwy into 3rd under 2f out: styd on strly u.p to ld 75yds out: hld on wl cl home* **6/1**[3]
2 *nk* **Buildmeupbuttercup**[45] 5567 5-9-11 **94**.....................(t) ChrisHayes 15 99
(W P Mullins, Ire) *hld up towards rr: clsr in 10th 5f out: pushed along 2f out and gd prog between horses to go 3rd 1f out: wnt 2nd u.p 50yds out but hld by wnr cl home* **7/2**[1]
3 *3/4* **Trossachs**[31] 6089 3-9-8 **99**.....................(t) KevinManning 16 105
(J S Bolger, Ire) *chsd ldrs: bit keen early: cl 5th 5f out: pushed along over 2f out and led under 2f out: kpt on strly u.p but hdd 75yds out and no ex* **9/1**
4 *1/2* **Edification**[17] 6619 6-8-13 **82**............................ RonanWhelan 2 85+
(Mark Fahey, Ire) *hld up in rr: stl towards rr 3f out: sn pushed along and nt clr run under 2f out: rdn ent fnl f and kpt on v strly between horses to go 4th cl home: nrst fin* **33/1**
5 *1* **Nessun Dorma (IRE)**[314] 8860 6-9-10 **93**............................ ShaneFoley 17 94
(W P Mullins, Ire) *hld up towards rr: pushed along 3f out and gd prog on outer: styd on steadily to go 5th cl home: nrst fin* **8/1**
6 *nk* **Machine Learner**[52] 5321 6-9-4 **87**............................ OisinMurphy 10 88
(Joseph Tuite) *chsd ldrs: dropped to 8th 5f out: pushed along over 2f out and wnt 5th under 2f out: no ex u.p ins fnl f but kpt on wl* **14/1**
7 *3/4* **Act Of God**[15] 6695 4-8-8 **77**.....................(h) NGMcCullagh 14 77
(E J O'Grady, Ire) *in rr of mid-div on outer: pushed along over 3f out and tk clsr order in 8th: kpt on wl but no ex u.p and one pce fr over 1f out* **33/1**
8 *1/2* **Eminence (IRE)**[21] 6471 3-9-7 **98**............................ RyanMoore 6 99
(A P O'Brien, Ire) *chsd ldrs: 3rd 5f out: rdn 2f out but no ex u.p fr over 1f out and grad wknd* **5/1**[2]
9 *3/4* **Share The Honour**[15] 6695 6-8-8 **77**.....................(t) WayneLordan 4 75
(A J Martin, Ire) *in rr of mid-div: 11th 5f out: pushed along 2f out and n.m.r bhd horses: no ex u.p whn in clr fr over 1f out and one pce ins fnl f* **14/1**
10 *1 1/4* **One Cool Poet (IRE)**[42] 5700 7-9-7 **90**.....................(bt) WJLee 1 86
(Matthew J Smith, Ire) *towards rr: 12th 5f out: pushed along on inner 3f out and angled between horses 2f out: sme hdwy u.p but no ex ent fnl f* **12/1**
11 *hd* **Eminent Authority (IRE)**[29] 6191 3-9-7 **98**..........(t) DeclanMcDonogh 9 95
(Joseph Patrick O'Brien, Ire) *hld up in rr: detached and pushed along 4f out: sme late prog u.p but nvr nr to chal* **16/1**
12 *1* **Marlborough Sounds**[21] 6483 4-8-11 **80**............................ KillianLeonard 3 74
(John Joseph Murphy, Ire) *chsd ldrs: pushed along over 4f out and dropped to 8th: sn no imp u.p and one pce* **40/1**
13 *3/4* **Effernock Fizz (IRE)**[16] 6431 4-8-4 **73** oh5............................ MarkGallagher 12 66
(Miss Katy Brown, Ire) *chsd ldrs on outer: 6th 5f out: pushed along 4f out and no ex u.p: wknd* **20/1**
14 *1* **Contrapposto (IRE)**[31] 6089 5-8-5 **81**............................ AlanPersse(7) 11 72
(Mrs A M O'Shea, Ire) *towards rr: rdn over 2f out but no ex u.p and one pce: nvr nr to chal* **22/1**
15 *2 3/4* **Pythion (FR)**[61] 5006 3-9-5 **96**.....................(b[1]) ColinKeane 8 85
(G M Lyons, Ire) *sn led: racd freely early: pushed along over 2f out: hdd under 2f out and sn no ex u.p: wknd* **20/1**
16 *4 1/2* **Coolongolook**[37] 8596 4-9-2 **85**............................ RoryCleary 7 64
(Gordon Elliott, Ire) *in rr of mid-div: rdn 3f out but no ex: nvr nr to chal* **40/1**
17 *1* **Barbados (IRE)**[65] 4845 3-9-12 **103**.....................(p[1]) SeamieHeffernan 13 83
(A P O'Brien, Ire) *sn trckd ldr in 2nd: pushed along 4f out and sn lost pl: grad wknd (jockey said colt was checked when dropping back out of the race)* **11/1**

2m 43.25s
WFA 3 from 4yo+ 8lb **17** Ran SP% **134.2**
CSF £27.51 CT £202.82 TOTE £6.30: £1.70, £1.60, £2.40, £6.60; DF 28.20 Trifecta £181.10.
Owner H H Aga Khan **Bred** His Highness The Aga Khan's Studs S C **Trained** Curragh, Co Kildare

FOCUS
Competitive stuff, as you would expect for the prize-money on offer. The gallop was generous early but settled down after a furlong or two and there were plenty in contention on the home turn. What was most interesting was the fact the first three home were drawn 18, 15 and 16, while six of the first seven home had double-figure draws. The level is set by the second, third, fourth, seventh and eighth.

7217a KPMG CHAMPIONS JUVENILE STKS (GROUP 2) (INNER TRACK) 1m
3:05 (3:07) 2-Y-O

£79,729 (£25,675; £12,162; £5,405; £2,702; £1,351)

RPR
1 **Mogul**[15] 6688 2-9-3 0............................ RyanMoore 7 110+
(A P O'Brien, Ire) *chsd ldrs in 4th: wnt 3rd 1/2-way: pushed along over 2f out and prog to ld 1 1/2f out: kpt on strly u.p ins fnl f* **1/2**[1]

2 1 1/4 **Sinawann (IRE)**[22] 6427 2-9-3 0........................ RonanWhelan 2 107+
(M Halford, Ire) *cl up and disp ld: dropped to cl 4th 1/2-way: pushed along under 2f out and kpt on strly u.p between horses to go 2nd 1f out: no ex ins fnl f and hld* **5/1**[2]
3 1 3/4 **Agitare (IRE)**[10] 6868 2-9-3 0........................ KevinManning 3 104
(J S Bolger, Ire) *chsd ldrs: short of room after 1f and snatched up: t.k.h towards rr in 6th: pushed along in 6th over 2f out and kpt on wl to go 3rd 100yds out but no ex cl home* **14/1**
4 1/2 **Rebel Tale (USA)**[22] 6430 2-9-3 107........................ BenCoen 5 102
(Andrew Slattery, Ire) *settled bhd ldrs 5th 1/2-way: rdn over 2f out and kpt on wl u.p to go 4th 1f out but no ex cl home* **14/1**
5 1 1/4 **Cormorant (IRE)**[37] 5871 2-9-3 0........................ SeamieHeffernan 6 99
(A P O'Brien, Ire) *cl up: led after 1f: pushed along over 2f out but no ex u.p and hdd 1 1/2f out: wknd ins fnl f* **12/1**[3]
6 3/4 **Royal County Down (IRE)**[13] 6763 2-9-3 89..........(p[1]) WayneLordan 1 97
(A P O'Brien, Ire) *rrd sltly after s and dropped to rr: 6th 1/2-way: pushed along over 2f out but sn no imp u.p: one pce* **25/1**
7 2 1/2 **Howling Wolf (IRE)**[58] 5109 2-9-3 0........................ RoryCleary 4 92
(Anthony Mullins, Ire) *cl up: sn trckd ldr in 2nd: rdn over 2f out but sn no ex u.p and wknd* **14/1**

1m 42.59s (-1.21) **Going Correction** -0.05s/f (Good) **7 Ran SP% 114.9**
Speed ratings: **104,102,101,100,99 98,96**
CSF £3.46 TOTE £1.40: £1.02, £2.00; DF 3.40 Trifecta £18.20.
Owner Michael Tabor & Derrick Smith & Mrs John Magnier **Bred** Newsells Park Stud **Trained** Cashel, Co Tipperary

FOCUS
A classy performance from a high class prospect. It's tricky to pin down the level of the form.

7218a PADDY POWER BETTING SHOP STKS (GROUP 3) (INNER TRACK) 1m 4f
3:40 (3:42) 3-Y-0+

£53,153 (£17,117; £8,108; £3,603; £1,801; £900)

RPR

1 **Norway (IRE)**[24] 6353 3-9-1 104........................ SeamieHeffernan 4 109+
(A P O'Brien, Ire) *in rr of mid-div on inner: 6th 1/2-way: pushed along 2f out and gd prog on inner to go 2nd ent fnl f: kpt on wl to ld 100yds out and styd on strly cl home* **7/2**[1]
2 1 1/4 **Buckhurst (IRE)**[29] 6192 3-9-4 113........................ WayneLordan 8 110
(Joseph Patrick O'Brien, Ire) *towards rr: 7th 1/2-way: pushed along on outer 2f out and kpt on wl u.p to go 3rd ent fnl f: hld by wnr but wnt 2nd on line* **7/2**[1]
3 nk **Blenheim Palace (IRE)**[23] 6381 3-9-1 104............ EmmetMcNamara 6 107
(A P O'Brien, Ire) *sn led: pushed along over 2f out and sn wnt 2 l clr: kpt on wl u.p but hdd 100yds out and no ex: dropped to 3rd on line* **20/1**
4 shd **Mount Everest (IRE)**[349] 7818 3-9-1 110........................ RyanMoore 5 107
(A P O'Brien, Ire) *hld up in rr: 8th 1/2-way: pushed along over 2f out and stdy hdwy on outer to go 4th ins fnl f but no ex cl home* **7/1**
5 2 3/4 **Leo De Fury (IRE)**[29] 6192 3-9-1 109........................ ShaneFoley 7 102
(Mrs John Harrington, Ire) *chsd ldrs in 5th whn clipped heels and stmbld after 1 1/2f: wnt 4th 1/2-way: pushed along 3f out and disp 2nd briefly under 2f out: sn no ex u.p and one pce (jockey said colt was tight for room on the first bend and stumbled)* **6/1**[3]
6 1 1/2 **Guaranteed (IRE)**[29] 6192 3-9-1 109........................(t) KevinManning 2 100
(J S Bolger, Ire) *chsd ldrs in 3rd: t.k.h early: pushed along over 2f out and sn disp 2nd: no ex u.p ent fnl f and wknd* **7/1**
7 nk **Broad Street**[37] 5874 4-9-9 106........................ OisinOrr 3 99
(D K Weld, Ire) *chsd ldrs: 5th 1/2-way: pushed along to hold pl over 4f out: no imp u.p over 2f out and wknd* **9/2**[2]
8 1 1/4 **Kelly's Dino (FR)**[21] 6473 6-9-9 110........................(p) BenCurtis 9 97
(K R Burke) *sn trckd ldr in 2nd: pushed along over 2f out but sn no ex u.p and wknd* **8/1**
9 5 1/2 **Stivers (ARG)**[14] 6712 6-9-9 103........................ ChrisHayes 1 88
(D K Weld, Ire) *hld up in rr: 9th 1/2-way: pushed along and no imp 3f out: sn detached: nvr a factor* **33/1**

2m 32.81s (-5.49) **Going Correction** -0.05s/f (Good)
WFA 3 from 4yo+ 8lb **9 Ran SP% 120.7**
Speed ratings: **116,115,114,114,113 112,111,111,107**
CSF £16.45 TOTE £4.50: £1.50, £1.70, £4.70; DF 22.70 Trifecta £211.40.
Owner Derrick Smith & Mrs John Magnier & Michael Tabor **Bred** Southern Bloodstock **Trained** Cashel, Co Tipperary
■ Stewards' Enquiry : Ben Curtis one-day ban: careless riding (tba)

FOCUS
This was a deep Group 3. The entire field were rated 103 or higher. Aidan O'Brien was responsible for the first, third and fourth home. Blenheim Palace ensured this was run at a decent pace throughout. It's been rated around the balance of the first four.

7219a QIPCO IRISH CHAMPION STKS (GROUP 1) (OUTER TRACK) 1m 2f
4:15 (4:16) 3-Y-0+

£641,891 (£213,963; £101,351; £45,045; £22,522; £11,261)

RPR

1 **Magical (IRE)**[23] 6377 4-9-4 122........................ RyanMoore 3 120
(A P O'Brien, Ire) *sn trckd ldr in 2nd: pushed along over 2f out and led 2f out: kicked 2 l clr ent fnl f and styd on strly u.p cl home* **11/10**[1]
2 2 1/4 **Magic Wand (IRE)**[34] 6001 4-9-4 111....................(p) SeamieHeffernan 5 115
(A P O'Brien, Ire) *settled in mid-div: 5th 1/2-way: pushed along in 4th over 2f out and kpt on strly to go 2nd jst ins fnl f: sn no ex and hld by wnr* **20/1**
3 hd **Anthony Van Dyck (IRE)**[49] 5414 3-9-1 118............ WayneLordan 2 119
(A P O'Brien, Ire) *chsd ldrs on inner: 4th 1/2-way: pushed along over 2f out and dropped to 5th briefly: kpt on wl u.p to go 3rd ins fnl f but no imp on wnr* **12/1**
4 1/2 **Deirdre (JPN)**[44] 5586 5-9-4 116........................ OisinMurphy 6 114+
(Mitsuru Hashida, Japan) *hld up towards rr: 7th 1/2-way: gng wl but no room bhd horses in 8th on inner over 2f out: taken to outer ent fnl f and rdn: str run to go 4th cl home: nrst fin* **11/1**
5 1/2 **Headman**[30] 6143 3-9-1 112........................ JasonWatson 7 117
(Roger Charlton) *fly-jmpd at s and sn in rr: pushed along on outer over 2f out and hdwy to go 3rd under 2f out: no ex u.p and dropped to 4th jst ins fnl f: 5th cl home* **11/2**[3]
6 1 1/4 **Madhmoon (IRE)**[30] 6137 3-9-1 117........................ ChrisHayes 4 114
(Kevin Prendergast, Ire) *hld up towards rr: 6th 1/2-way: pushed along over 2f out and sn prog to go 5th: bit short of room jst ins fnl f but no ex u.p and sn one pce* **5/1**[2]
7 2 1/4 **Elarqam**[24] 6354 4-9-7 120........................ JimCrowley 8 109
(Mark Johnston) *sn chsd ldrs in 3rd: rdn over 2f out and wnt 2nd briefly under 2f out but sn no ex u.p and grad wknd* **5/1**[2]
8 1/2 **Hunting Horn (IRE)**[34] 6001 4-9-7 115................(p) EmmetMcNamara 1 108
(A P O'Brien, Ire) *sn led: rdn over 2f out but sn hdd and no ex u.p: wknd* **66/1**

2m 6.49s (-5.21) **Going Correction** -0.05s/f (Good)
WFA 3 from 4yo+ 6lb **8 Ran SP% 118.6**
Speed ratings: **118,116,116,115,115 114,112,112**
CSF £29.37 CT £191.51 TOTE £1.70: £1.02, £4.60, £3.90; DF 21.90 Trifecta £104.80.
Owner Derrick Smith & Mrs John Magnier & Michael Tabor **Bred** Orpendale, Chelston & Wynatt **Trained** Cashel, Co Tipperary

FOCUS
The presence of the Arc bound Enable or the injured Crystal Ocean would have made this a vintage renewal, but their absence could not prevent this from being a decent edition. We had the Derby first and second, progressive sorts like Elarqam and Headman and the Nassau winner who was the first Japanese runner on these shores. The key horse was Magical whose rating of 122 was the best on offer and she was understandably made favourite. As expected, Hunting Horn set the pace but he didn't stray the field out like many expected and just three lengths covered the entire field passing the 2f pole. The second and fifth have been rated to the best view of their form, with the third thereabouts.

7220a CLIPPER LOGISTICS BOOMERANG STKS (GROUP 2) (OUTER TRACK) 1m
4:50 (4:52) 3-Y-0+

£106,306 (£34,234; £16,216; £7,207; £3,603; £1,801)

RPR

1 **Space Traveller**[21] 6470 3-9-3 113........................ WJLee 7 114+
(Richard Fahey) *hld up in rr: 9th 1/2-way: pushed along on outer over 2f out and gd prog to go 3rd ent fnl f: kpt on strly u.p to ld cl home* **13/2**
2 nk **Matterhorn (IRE)**[7] 6956 4-9-8 111........................ OisinMurphy 5 113
(Mark Johnston) *sn chsd ldrs: wnt 2nd after 1f: dropped to 4th briefly over 2f out: sn pushed along and hdwy between horses to ld narrowly ent fnl f: kpt on wl u.p but hdd cl home* **7/2**[2]
3 1 3/4 **Pincheck (IRE)**[30] 6137 5-9-8 106........................ ShaneFoley 2 109
(Mrs John Harrington, Ire) *sn led: pushed along over 2f out: kpt on strly u.p but hdd ent fnl f and no ex in 3rd fnl 150yds* **20/1**
4 1 **Suedois (FR)**[20] 6508 8-9-8 110........................(p) DanielTudhope 6 107
(David O'Meara) *hld up in rr: 8th 1/2-way: pushed along over 2f out and tk clsr order: kpt on wl u.p to go 4th ent fnl f but no ex wl ins fnl f* **4/1**[3]
5 hd **Surrounding (IRE)**[44] 5598 6-9-5 105........................(t) RonanWhelan 1 103
(M Halford, Ire) *cl up: sn settled in 4th on inner: short of room briefly under 3f out: sn pushed along and kpt on wl u.p fr 2f out but no ex* **12/1**
6 1/2 **Coral Beach (IRE)**[43] 5645 3-9-0 99........................ WayneLordan 3 101
(A P O'Brien, Ire) *towards rr: 7th 1/2-way: rdn over 2f out and wnt 6th on inner over 1f out but no ex ins fnl f* **33/1**
7 1 **Lancaster House (IRE)**[5] 7038 3-9-3 109........................ RyanMoore 4 102
(A P O'Brien, Ire) *chsd ldrs: cl 5th 1/2-way: rdn over 2f out and sn no ex u.p: one pce: lame on lft-fore (vet said colt to be lame on his left foreleg post race)* **13/8**[1]
8 3/4 **Turnberry Isle (IRE)**[15] 6693 3-9-3 99..................(p[1]) SeamieHeffernan 9 100
(A P O'Brien, Ire) *mid-div: 6th 1/2-way: prog on outer 3f out to dispute 2nd briefly 2f out: sn rdn and no ex u.p ent fnl f: wknd* **20/1**
9 17 **Ancient Spirit (GER)**[30] 6137 4-9-8 107........................ KevinManning 8 62
(J S Bolger, Ire) *towards rr: t.k.h: hdwy on outer after 2f into 3rd: wnt 2nd 3f out: sn rdn but no ex u.p 2f out and wknd (jockey said colt ran too keen in the early part of this race and tired in the straight)* **25/1**

1m 39.31s (-4.49) **Going Correction** -0.05s/f (Good)
WFA 3 from 4yo+ 5lb **9 Ran SP% 117.7**
Speed ratings: **120,119,117,116,116 116,115,114,97**
CSF £28.53 TOTE £7.30: £1.80, £1.40, £4.20; DF 33.20 Trifecta £301.00.
Owner Clipper Logistics **Bred** El Catorce Partnership **Trained** Musley Bank, N Yorks
■ Stewards' Enquiry : W J Lee eight-day ban: excessive use of the whip (Oct 25-26, 28, 30, Nov 1, 3, 6, 8)

FOCUS
This was quite a poor renewal of this Group 2 and the favourite ran no sort of race either. It was dominated by a British-trained pair. The third, sixth and eighth limit the form.

7221a COOLMORE "FASTNET ROCK" MATRON STKS (GROUP 1) (F&M) (OUTER TRACK) 1m
5:25 (5:25) 3-Y-0+

£186,036 (£59,909; £28,378; £12,612; £6,306; £3,153)

RPR

1 **Iridessa (IRE)**[56] 5208 3-9-0 111........................ WayneLordan 4 114+
(Joseph Patrick O'Brien, Ire) *chsd ldrs: 4th 1/2-way: pushed along over 2f out: sn rdn and kpt on strly u.p to ld 150yds out: shifted lft sltly but hld on wl cl home (trainer said, regarding the improved form shown, the filly dropped back in trip to 1 mile, a distance over which she had previously gained Group 1 success and this was the contributing factor to her improved performance)* **10/1**
2 3/4 **Hermosa (IRE)**[44] 5586 3-9-0 116........................ RyanMoore 6 112
(A P O'Brien, Ire) *sn trckd ldr in 2nd: pushed along over 2f out and led under 2f out: kpt on wl u.p but hdd 150yds out and no ex* **7/2**[2]
3 hd **Just Wonderful (USA)**[44] 5586 3-9-0 110..................(h[1]) OisinMurphy 5 112+
(A P O'Brien, Ire) *hld up in mid-div: 5th 1/2-way: rdn 2f out and wnt 4th ent fnl f: kpt on wl to go 3rd 150yds out and almost snatched 2nd* **12/1**
4 2 **Laurens (FR)**[21] 6472 4-9-5 116........................ PJMcDonald 2 108
(K R Burke) *sn led: pushed along over 2f out: hdd under 2f out and no ex in 3rd ent fnl f: dropped to 4th ins fnl f* **1/1**[1]
5 4 1/2 **I Can Fly**[27] 6265 4-9-5 112........................ SeamieHeffernan 7 98
(A P O'Brien, Ire) *bit slowly away: in rr: 7th 1/2-way: rdn over 2f out and wnt modest 5th ent fnl f: sn one pce and nvr nr to chal* **6/1**[3]
6 4 3/4 **Happen (USA)**[43] 5645 3-9-0 103........................(t) EmmetMcNamara 3 86
(A P O'Brien, Ire) *hld up towards rr: 6th 1/2-way: rdn over 2f out but no imp and one pce* **33/1**
7 11 **Skitter Scatter (USA)**[16] 6646 3-9-0 112........................ RonanWhelan 1 61
(John M Oxx, Ire) *sn chsd ldrs: 3rd 1/2-way: rdn over 2f out but no ex and sn wknd: eased ins fnl f (jockey said filly lost her action two furlongs from the finish)* **14/1**

1m 38.81s (-4.99) **Going Correction** -0.05s/f (Good)
WFA 3 from 4yo 5lb **7 Ran SP% 112.9**
Speed ratings: **122,121,121,119,114 109,98**
CSF £43.60 TOTE £13.80: £4.50, £1.90; DF 57.50 Trifecta £271.80.
Owner Mrs C C Regalado-Gonzalez **Bred** Whisperview Trading Ltd **Trained** Owning Hill, Co Kilkenny

FOCUS
Laurens and Hermosa got racing pretty early and may well have just set it up for the runners in behind. Take nothing away from the winner, Hermosa, who came into this under the radar after a below-par effort in the Irish Oaks but confirmed herself a classy filly on her day. The third helps set the level.

7222a IRISH STALLION FARMS EBF "SOVEREIGN PATH" H'CAP (PREMIER HANDICAP) (OUTER TRACK) 7f
6:00 (6:00) 3-Y-O+

£79,729 (£25,675; £12,162; £5,405; £2,702; £1,351)

RPR

1 **Current Option (IRE)**[15] 6693 3-8-12 **89** RonanWhelan 11 92+
(Adrian McGuinness, Ire) *bmpd s and t.k.h: chsd ldrs on outer: 3rd 1/2-way: gng wl in 2nd over 2f out and pushed along to ld 1 1/2f out: kpt on strly u.p ins fnl f: hld on wl cl home* **11/2**[2]

2 *nk* **Black Magic Woman (IRE)**[21] 6480 3-9-4 **95** GaryHalpin 13 97
(Jack W Davison, Ire) *sn mid-div: 9th 1/2-way: rdn over 2f out and prog on outer to go 2nd ins fnl f: kpt on strly u.p but hld cl home* **20/1**

3 *nk* **Ice Cold In Alex (IRE)**[15] 6693 5-8-12 **85** (t) NGMcCullagh 16 88
(K J Condon, Ire) *hld up in rr of mid-div: 11th 1/2-way: tk clsr order on inner under 3f out: rdn under 2f out and gd prog between horses ins fnl f to go 3rd but hld cl home* **15/2**

4 *3/4* **Bopedro (FR)**[3] 7093 3-9-2 **93** (p) KevinManning 3 92+
(J S Bolger, Ire) *mid-div: 7th 1/2-way: rdn in 8th over 2f out and sn bit short of room bhd horses: kpt on wl again u.p between horses ent fnl f to go 4th cl home* **5/1**[1]

5 *nk* **Admirality**[14] 6706 5-9-6 **93** (h) BenCurtis 17 94
(Roger Fell) *sn mid-div: 10th 1/2-way: rdn on outer over 2f out and styd on steadily to go 5th ins fnl f but no ex cl home* **8/1**

6 *3/4* **Ducky Mallon (IRE)**[3] 7093 8-8-4 **77** oh2 (t) WayneLordan 2 76
(Donal Kinsella, Ire) *chsd ldrs: 5th 1/2-way: rdn over 2f out and kpt on wl to dispute 3rd briefly under 2f out: no ex u.p ins fnl f* **25/1**

7 *3/4* **Crotchet**[21] 6480 4-8-13 **91** (t) ShaneCrosse(5) 14 87
(Joseph Patrick O'Brien, Ire) *in rr of mid-div: 12th 1/2-way: pushed along over 2f out and n.m.r bhd horses under 2f out: gd prog between horses ent fnl f and kpt on wl: nrst fin* **25/1**

8 *nk* **Shawaamekh**[42] 5692 5-9-3 **90** (t) OisinMurphy 8 86
(Declan Carroll) *cl up and sn trckd ldr in 2nd: t.k.h: led 4f out: rdn whn chal over 2f out: hdd 1 1/2f out and no ex: grad wknd* **6/1**[3]

9 *1* **Viadera**[15] 6692 3-9-10 **101** ColinKeane 1 92
(G M Lyons, Ire) *chsd ldrs on inner: 6th 1/2-way: rdn over 2f out and kpt on wl u.p: n.m.r ent fnl f but sn no ex and one pce: eased cl home* **10/1**

10 *nk* **Jassaar**[15] 6693 4-9-6 **98** AndrewSlattery(5) 5 90
(D K Weld, Ire) *mid-div: 8th 1/2-way: pushed along and lost pl under 3f out: kpt on again u.p under 2f out but no imp* **6/1**[3]

11 *hd* **Marshall Jennings (IRE)**[28] 6235 7-9-9 **99** (p[1]) TomMadden(3) 6 91
(Mrs John Harrington, Ire) *chsd ldrs: 4th 1/2-way: rdn in 4th over 2f out but sn no ex u.p and wknd* **33/1**

12 *hd* **Morpho Blue (IRE)**[16] 6646 3-8-6 **88** (v[1]) NathanCrosse(5) 7 77
(Mrs John Harrington, Ire) *in rr: rdn on inner over 2f out and sme hdwy u.p on far side but nvr nr to chal* **33/1**

13 *1* **Mokhalad**[15] 6693 6-8-12 **85** (t) RoryCleary 4 73
(Damian Joseph English, Ire) *sn led: hdd 4f out and dropped to 3rd over 3f out: rdn over 2f out and no ex u.p: wknd* **33/1**

14 *3/4* **Silverkode (IRE)**[15] 6691 5-8-10 **83** (p) GaryCarroll 10 69
(Joseph G Murphy, Ire) *towards rr: rdn over 2f out but no imp u.p: nvr in contention* **8/1**

15 *3/4* **Trading Point (FR)**[3] 7093 5-9-0 **87** DeclanMcDonogh 15 71
(Damian Joseph English, Ire) *sn in rr: rdn over 2f out and sme hdwy on outer u.p but no ex ent fnl f* **25/1**

16 *6 1/2* **Innamorare (IRE)**[15] 6693 4-8-8 **81** (b) ChrisHayes 9 48
(Gavin Cromwell, Ire) *sn in rr: rdn and no imp over 2f out: nvr a factor (jockey said filly caught heels twice in the early part of this race and checked on both occasions)* **20/1**

17 *16* **Klute (IRE)**[77] 4409 3-9-2 **93** (vt[1]) ShaneFoley 12 15
(Mrs John Harrington, Ire) *wnt lft s and bmpd rival: in rr of mid-div: tk a false step under 3f out and snatched up: sn eased to rr (jockey said colt lost his action about two furlongs out and felt lame but returned sound to the unsaddling area)* **33/1**

1m 27.16s (-3.24) **Going Correction** -0.05s/f (Good) **17 Ran SP% 136.5**
WFA 3 from 4yo+ 4lb
Speed ratings: **116,115,115,114,114 113,112,112,110,110 110,110,108,108,107 99,81**
Pick Six: Not Won. Pool of 22,287.74 carried forward to Curragh on Sunday 15th September. Tote Aggregates - 2018: 727,629.00, 2019: 488,907.00 CSF £123.69 CT £855.96 TOTE £6.40: £1.80, £3.90, £2.40, £1.30; DF 271.10 Trifecta £4015.60.
Owner Dooley T'breds & Shamrock T'breds & B T O'Sullivan **Bred** Grangecon Holdings Ltd **Trained** Lusk, Co Dublin

FOCUS
A brilliant performance from the winner who did this the hard way. He was good and tough when he had to be and rates as an improving handicapper. It's been rated around the balance of the second and fifth.
T/Jkpt: @217.00. Pool: @10,000.00 - 32.25 winning units T/Plt: @57.70. Pool: @39,802.57 - 482.05 winning units **Tyrone Molloy**

1908 CHOLET (R-H)
Saturday, September 14

OFFICIAL GOING: Turf: very soft

7223a PRIX JUSSIEU AMBULANCES (CLAIMER) (3YO+) (TURF) 6f 165y
11:45 3-Y-O+ **£5,405** (£2,162; £1,621; £1,081; £540)

RPR

1 **Cloud Eight (IRE)**[39] 4-9-3 0 (p) SoufianeSaadi 5 72
(P Monfort, France) **17/5**[2]

2 *nk* **Karbayane (FR)**[44] 6-9-0 0 ValentinSeguy 6 68
(W Walton, France) **19/5**[3]

3 *2* **Get Even**[73] 4532 4-9-0 0 AlexandreRoussel 4 62
(Jo Hughes, France) *chsd ldrs: c towards stands' side st w 2f out: sn rdn and styd on: nvr quite on terms: effrt evened out fnl 100yds* **9/2**

4 *2* **Ucel (IRE)**[17] 5-8-8 0 (b) QuentinPerrette(6) 8 56
(F Hassine, France) **13/2**

5 *1/2* **Rum Lad**[62] 4959 3-8-11 0 ChristopherGrosbois 7 54
(Jo Hughes, France) *dwlt: racd keenly: hld up in midfield on outer: wnt wd and dropped last first bnd: rdn and clsd down centre of trck 2f out: run flattened out ins fnl f: nvr trbld ldrs* **15/1**

6 *6* **Mark Of Excellence (IRE)**[130] 5-8-5 0 (b) MlleLucieOger(9) 3 37
(L Gadbin, France) **2/1**[1]

7 *10* **Joan Jet (FR)**[71] 4-8-5 0 ClementGuitraud(5) 2 4
(N Milliere, France) **46/1**

8 *dist* **Gocrazyprince (FR)**[450] 6-8-10 0 MlleLinePayet-Burin(4) 1
(Mlle L Payet-Burin, France) **47/1**

1m 22.56s **8 Ran SP% 118.9**
WFA 3 from 4yo+ 4lb
PARI-MUTUEL (all including 1 euro stake): WIN 4.40; PLACE 1.90, 1.80, 1.80; DF 10.50.
Owner Paul Richard **Bred** Kevin Blake **Trained** France

5484 WOODBINE (L-H)
Saturday, September 14

OFFICIAL GOING: Turf: yielding changing to good before 10.42pm race; tapeta: fast

7224a CANADIAN STKS PRESENTED BY THE JAPAN RACING ASSOCIATION (GRADE 2) (3YO+ FILLIES & MARES) (TURF) 1m 1f
9:30 3-Y-O+

£86,206 (£28,735; £15,804; £8,620; £3,448; £1,436)

RPR

1 **Starship Jubilee (USA)**[21] 6491 6-8-7 0 LuisContreras 6 112
(Kevin Attard, Canada) **11/5**[2]

2 *4 1/4* **Magnetic Charm**[50] 5369 3-7-12 0 KazushiKimura 3 100+
(William Haggas) *settled in fnl trio: last but wl in tch w 3 1/2f to run: rdn and hdwy 1 1/2f out: styd on to take 2nd cl home: no ch w wnr* **97/20**[3]

3 *nse* **Competitionofideas (USA)**[35] 5978 4-8-9 0 (b) JoelRosario 5 105
(Chad C Brown, U.S.A) **27/20**[1]

4 *nk* **Holy Helena (CAN)**[77] 5-8-9 0 RafaelManuelHernandez 2 104
(James Jerkens, U.S.A) **21/4**

5 *1 1/2* **Dixie Moon (CAN)**[63] 4-8-4 0 ow1 EuricoRosaDaSilva 4 96
(Catherine Day Phillips, Canada) **33/1**

6 *2 3/4* **Giovanna Blues (USA)**[27] 6-8-5 0 GaryBoulanger 7 91
(Francine A Villeneuve, Canada) **51/1**

7 *1 3/4* **Touriga (BRZ)**[56] 4-8-9 0 TylerGaffalione 1 92
(H Graham Motion, U.S.A) **133/10**

1m 45.84s **7 Ran SP% 118.8**
WFA 3 from 4yo+ 6lb

Owner Blue Heaven Farm LLC **Bred** William P Sorren **Trained** Canada

7225a RICOH WOODBINE MILE STKS (GRADE 1) (3YO+) (TURF) 1m (T)
10:42 3-Y-O+

£413,793 (£114,942; £57,471; £28,735; £11,494; £5,747)

RPR

1 **El Tormenta (CAN)**[21] 4-8-11 0 (b) EuricoRosaDaSilva 1 115
(Gail Cox, Canada) **45/1**

2 *1/2* **Got Stormy (USA)**[35] 5977 4-8-11 0 TylerGaffalione 5 114
(Mark Casse, Canada) **31/20**[1]

3 *nk* **Raging Bull (FR)**[35] 5977 4-8-11 0 (b) JoelRosario 7 112+
(Chad C Brown, U.S.A) **19/5**[2]

4 *1/2* **Lucullan (USA)**[42] 5-8-7 0 LuisSaez 2 109
(Kiaran McLaughlin, U.S.A) **27/4**

5 *1/2* **Synchrony (USA)**[77] 6-8-11 0 FlavienPrat 4 111
(Michael Stidham, U.S.A) **39/10**[3]

6 *2 3/4* **Emmaus (IRE)**[77] 5-8-7 0 ChanningHill 10 101
(Conor Murphy, U.S.A) **78/1**

7 *4 1/2* **Admiralty Pier (USA)**[21] 4-8-7 0 (b) PatrickHusbands 11 90
(Barbara J Minshall, Canada) **116/1**

8 *1/2* **Made You Look (USA)**[35] 5977 5-8-7 0 LuisContreras 9 89
(Chad C Brown, U.S.A) **164/10**

9 *1/2* **Silent Poet (CAN)**[21] 4-8-11 0 GaryBoulanger 3 92
(Nicholas Gonzalez, Canada) **154/10**

10 *1 1/2* **Awesometank**[35] 5978 4-8-4 0 JFEgan 6 82
(William Haggas) **122/10**

11 *7 1/4* **American Guru (USA)**[34] 5-8-7 0 RafaelManuelHernandez 8 68
(Michael J Doyle, Canada) **63/1**

1m 32.6s **11 Ran SP% 118.6**
PARI-MUTUEL (all including 2 unit stake): WIN 91.40; PLACE (1-2) 21.40, 3.90; SHOW (1-2-3) 9.50, 2.80, 2.80; SF 344.70.
Owner Sam-Son Farm **Bred** Sam-Son Farm **Trained** Canada

7226a NORTHERN DANCER TURF STKS (GRADE 1) (3YO+) (TURF) 1m 4f (T)
11:17 3-Y-O+

£103,448 (£34,482; £18,965; £12,413; £3,448; £2,068)

RPR

1 **Old Persian**[34] 6007 4-9-0 0 JamesDoyle 1 115+
(Charlie Appleby) *slowly away: chsd ldng pair: gng wl and smooth hdwy passed 4f out: engaged outside ldr passed 2f out: led appr 1 1/2f out: r.o wl u.p* **13/20**[1]

2 *2 1/2* **Nessy (USA)**[41] 6-8-7 0 (b) LuisSaez 4 104
(Ian R Wilkes, U.S.A) *settled in rr: shkn up over 6f out: rowed along between horses 2f out: drvn nr 1 1/2f out: jst got up for 2nd: nvr trbld wnr* **232/10**

3 *nse* **Focus Group (USA)**[49] 5-8-11 0 (b) JoelRosario 3 108
(Chad C Brown, U.S.A) *settled toward rr: hdwy three wd appr 3f out: rowed along nr 2f out: styd on u.p but missed 2nd* **39/10**[3]

4 *hd* **Tiz A Slam (CAN)**[48] 5484 5-8-11 0 StevenRonaldBahen 6 108
(Roger L Attfield, Canada) *settled in 2nd: gng wl and began to cl fr 6f out: led 3 1/2f out: drvn passed 2f out: hdd appr 1 1/2f out: no ch w wnr: kpt on u.p: lost two pls late on* **29/10**[2]

5 *20* **Sir Sahib (USA)**[48] 5484 4-8-7 0 LuisContreras 5 72
(Kevin Attard, Canada) *midfield: rowed along nr 3f out: drvn 2f out and wknd* **224/10**

6 15 3/4 **Cooler Mike (CAN)**[16] 4-8-7 0................................(b) PatrickHusbands 2 47
(Nicholas Nosowenko, Canada) *sn led wl clr of rest of the field: opened up abt a dozen l on the field nr 1m out: began to tire passed 6f out: hdd 3 1/2f out and t.o* **34/1**

2m 27.78s (-1.82) **6** Ran SP% **117.9**
PARI-MUTUEL (all including 2 unit stake): WIN 3.30; PLACE (1-2) 2.80, 9.60; SHOW (1-2-3) 2.20, 4.70, 2.90; SF 38.00.
Owner Godolphin **Bred** Godolphin **Trained** Newmarket, Suffolk

7172 BATH (L-H)
Sunday, September 15

OFFICIAL GOING: Firm (8.9)
Wind: virtually nil Weather: sunny

7227 VISIT VALUERATER.CO.UK NURSERY H'CAP 5f 10y
2:15 (2:17) (Class 5) (0-75,75) 2-Y-O
£3,816 (£1,135; £567; £400; £400; £400) **Stalls** Centre

Form RPR
33 **1** **Allez Sophia (IRE)**[13] 6800 2-8-13 **74**.......................... GeorgiaDobie(7) 4 79+
(Eve Johnson Houghton) *trckd ldrs: led 2f out: kpt on strly fnl f: readily* **11/4**[2]
0523 **2** 2 **Airbrush (IRE)**[19] 6557 2-9-1 **69**.. PatDobbs 1 67
(Richard Hannon) *trckd ldrs: rdn to chse wnr jst ins fnl f: kpt on but nt pce to chal* **6/1**
1200 **3** 1 1/2 **Mia Diva**[24] 6375 2-9-7 **75**.. BenRobinson 5 67
(John Quinn) *prom: rdn and ev ch 2f out: lost 2nd ent fnl f: kpt on same pce* **6/4**[1]
4405 **4** 3/4 **Tilly Tamworth**[13] 6799 2-8-4 **58**................................ FrannyNorton 6 48
(Rod Millman) *sn pushed along chsng ldrs: rdn 2f out: kpt on but nt pce to threaten* **16/1**
1505 **5** 1 3/4 **Execlusive (IRE)**[19] 6557 2-9-1 **69**..........................(b[1]) AdamMcNamara 2 52
(Archie Watson) *led: rdn and hdd 2f out: fdd ins fnl f* **16/1**
622 **6** 1 **Newyorkstateofmind**[14] 6755 2-9-0 **68**...................... MartinDwyer 3 48
(William Muir) *racd keenly: trckd ldrs: rdn over 2f out: wknd fnl f (jockey said colt ran too free)* **4/1**[3]

1m 1.74s (-0.26) **Going Correction** -0.20s/f (Firm) **6** Ran SP% **112.7**
Speed ratings (Par 95): **94,90,88,87,84 82**
CSF £19.26 TOTE £3.50: £1.80, £3.20; EX 17.20 Trifecta £52.40.
Owner Trevor C Stewart **Bred** T Stewart **Trained** Blewbury, Oxon

FOCUS
A dry run up to a meeting staged on firm ground. A fair event run at a reasonable gallop and, although the well-backed market leader disappointed, this form should prove reliable. The level is a bit fluid.

7228 VISIT SANDSTORM AT VALUERATER.CO.UK NOVICE STKS 1m
2:45 (2:47) (Class 5) 3-Y-O+ **£3,816** (£1,135; £567; £283) **Stalls** Low

Form RPR
21 **1** **New Arrangement**[59] 5098 3-9-7 0.................................. FrannyNorton 3 95
(James Tate) *mde all: shkn up to draw clr over 1f out: v easily* **1/6**[1]
01 **2** 14 **Olaf**[18] 6600 3-8-9 0.. GraceMcEntee(7) 5 56
(George Boughey) *trckd ldrs: rdn to chse wnr over 2f out: sn outpcd* **7/1**[3]
00- **3** 3/4 **Summer Skies**[376] 6898 3-8-11 0...................................(p[1]) MartinDwyer 2 49
(Marcus Tregoning) *disp ld for 3f: trckd wnr tl rdn over 2f out: sn one pce* **4/1**[2]
4 14 **Lilly's Legacy** 3-8-11 0.. JohnFahy 1 16
(Nikki Evans) *trckd ldrs: rdn over 2f out: wknd over 1f out: sn eased* **66/1**
5 3/4 **Kira's Star** 3-8-6 0.. RhiainIngram(5) 4 14
(Richenda Ford) *s.i.s: sn outpcd in detached last: nvr on terms (trainer said filly was unsuited by the going)* **66/1**

1m 39.8s (-1.90) **Going Correction** -0.20s/f (Firm) **5** Ran SP% **121.2**
Speed ratings (Par 103): **101,87,86,72,71**
CSF £3.01 TOTE £1.10: £1.02, £2.20; EX 1.90 Trifecta £2.90.
Owner Saeed Manana **Bred** Rabbah Bloodstock Limited **Trained** Newmarket, Suffolk
■ Stewards' Enquiry : Rhiain Ingram two-day ban: failing to take all reasonable and permissible measures to obtain the best possible placing (Sep 29-30)

FOCUS
A very one-sided novice in which the short-priced market leader didn't have to improve to win by a wide margin. The winner's Hamilton win has been franked by the runner-up since, and he's been rated in line with that.

7229 WINNING POST BOOKMAKERS BRISTOL H'CAP 1m 2f 37y
3:20 (3:20) (Class 5) (0-75,75) 3-Y-O+
£3,816 (£1,135; £567; £400; £400; £400) **Stalls** Low

Form RPR
0062 **1** **Orange Suit (IRE)**[5] 7060 4-8-10 **65**..........................(b) MarcoGhiani(7) 5 73
(Ed de Giles) *trckd ldr: led 2f out: styd on wl and in command fnl f* **7/4**[1]
3355 **2** 1 1/2 **Miss Blondell**[12] 6830 6-8-9 **64**..........................(v[1]) AngusVilliers(7) 7 69
(Marcus Tregoning) *trckd ldrs: pushed along over 2f out: chsd wnr over 1f out: kpt on but nt pce to chal (trainer said mare was unsuited by the going)* **5/1**[3]
3333 **3** 1 3/4 **Albanita**[16] 6661 3-9-7 **75**..(b[1]) RyanTate 4 78
(Sir Mark Prescott Bt) *hld up: pushed along and stdy prog fr over 2f out: wnt 3rd ent fnl f: nt pce to get on terms* **9/4**[2]
2121 **4** 3 1/4 **Princess Way (IRE)**[39] 5795 5-9-2 **69**..........................(v) RhiainIngram(5) 2 64
(Paul George) *racd freely: led tl 2f out: sn rdn: wknd fnl f (jockey said mare ran too free)* **5/1**[3]
5043 **5** 10 **Couldn't Could She**[19] 6568 4-8-10 **63**........................ TobyEley(5) 1 38
(Adam West) *hld up: rdn and hdwy over 2f out: nvr threatened: wknd over 1f out (trainer said filly was unsuited by the going)* **16/1**
4666 **6** 28 **Allocator (FR)**[15] 6722 3-8-3 **62**.................... ThoreHammerHansen(5) 3
(Richard Hannon) *trckd wnr tl failed to handle bnd over 4f out: sn lost pl: wknd over 2f out (jockey said gelding lost its action and became unbalanced app 4f out; vet said gelding was lame and had a wound right fore)* **12/1**

2m 6.62s (-4.48) **Going Correction** -0.20s/f (Firm)
WFA 3 from 4yo+ 6lb **6** Ran SP% **114.0**
Speed ratings (Par 103): **109,107,106,103,95 73**
CSF £11.28 TOTE £2.80: £1.60, £2.60; EX 10.20 Trifecta £31.60.
Owner Tight Lines Partnership **Bred** Barronstown Stud **Trained** Ledbury, H'fords

FOCUS
A modest event in which the gallop was sound throughout. The winner has been rated similar to his latest effort, with the second and third close to form.

7230 BEST FREE TIPS AT VALUERATER.CO.UK SUMMER SPRINT SERIES FINAL H'CAP 5f 160y
3:55 (3:56) (Class 2) 3-Y-O+
£12,450 (£3,728; £1,864; £932; £466; £234) **Stalls** Centre

Form RPR
2423 **1** **Delagate This Lord**[16] 6668 5-9-5 **75**.......................... SeamusCronin(5) 9 83
(Michael Attwater) *t.k.h early: settled bhd ldrs after 1f: rdn to chal over 1f out: led jst ins fnl f: r.o: rdn out* **4/1**[1]
4233 **2** nk **Princely**[19] 6562 4-8-12 **63**.. MartinDwyer 13 70
(Tony Newcombe) *a.p: led over 2f out: sn rdn and strly chal: narrowly hdd jst ins fnl f: kpt on* **25/1**
0440 **3** shd **Big Lachie**[9] 6916 5-9-6 **71**.................................... RichardKingscote 2 78+
(Mark Loughnane) *hld up: hdwy on inner 3f out: rdn over 1f out: wnt 3rd ins fnl f: kpt on wl fnl 100yds* **11/2**[2]
5011 **4** 1 1/4 **Top Boy**[61] 5013 9-9-1 **69**...................................... DarraghKeenan(3) 11 72+
(Tony Carroll) *mid-div: hdwy over 2f out: sn rdn: ch ent fnl f: kpt on same pce* **7/1**
3313 **5** 1 **Three Little Birds**[13] 6798 4-9-3 **73**............................ WilliamCarver(5) 6 72
(Sylvester Kirk) *led for over 1f: prom: rdn and ev ch ent fnl f: no ex fnl 100yds* **11/1**
-111 **6** nk **Bay Watch (IRE)**[43] 5678 5-9-2 **67**................................ JohnFahy 10 65+
(Tracey Barfoot-Saunt) *hld up towards rr: stdy prog fr 2f out: swtchd lft over 1f out: swtchd rt jst ins fnl f: kpt on but nt pce to get on terms* **7/1**
3046 **7** nk **Powerful Dream (IRE)**[50] 5449 6-8-8 **59**...................(p) KieranO'Neill 4 56
(Ronald Harris) *stdd s: in last pair: hdwy over 2f out: sn rdn: chal for 4th ent fnl f: no ex fnl 100yds* **33/1**
3213 **8** 1 1/4 **Tawaafoq**[17] 6639 5-8-0 **58**......................................(h) AngusVilliers(7) 3 51
(Adrian Wintle) *racd keenly in midfield: hdwy 2f out: sn rdn: one pce fnl f* **20/1**
5044 **9** 1 1/4 **Essaka (IRE)**[19] 6562 7-8-8 **64**.................................... SophieRalston(5) 14 53
(Tony Carroll) *hld up towards rr of midfield: rdn over 1f out: little imp* **50/1**
4-P2 **10** 1 3/4 **Catheadans Fury**[25] 6329 5-8-9 **60**..............................(t) GeorgeWood 5 43
(Martin Bosley) *mid-div: hdwy over 2f out: sn rdn: wknd fnl f* **16/1**
4111 **11** 1 **Awsaaf**[19] 6562 4-9-6 **71**...(t) FrannyNorton 12 51
(Michael Wigham) *hld up towards rr: pushed along over 2f out: little imp* **6/1**[3]
3015 **12** 1/2 **Devils Roc**[2] 7157 3-9-5 **72**.. RobHornby 1 50
(Jonathan Portman) *mid-div: hdwy over 2f out: sn rdn: nt pce to get on terms: wknd fnl f* **7/1**
0232 **13** 7 **Spot Lite**[17] 6639 4-7-12 **54**...(p) RhiainIngram(5) 15 9
(Rod Millman) *sn trcking ldrs: rdn over 2f out: wknd over 1f out* **33/1**
3005 **14** hd **Met By Moonlight**[29] 6203 5-9-3 **68**............................ JackMitchell 8 23
(Ron Hodges) *towards rr: hmpd after 1f: rdn over 2f out: wknd over 1f out* **16/1**
0066 **15** 1 3/4 **Coronation Cottage**[39] 5793 5-8-6 **64**........................ MarcoGhiani(7) 7 13
(Malcolm Saunders) *s.i.s: rcvrd to ld after 1f: rdn and hdd over 2f out: sn wknd (jockey said mare was slowly away)* **20/1**

1m 9.56s (-1.54) **Going Correction** -0.20s/f (Firm)
WFA 3 from 4yo+ 2lb **15** Ran SP% **128.5**
Speed ratings (Par 109): **102,101,101,99,98 98,97,96,94,92 90,90,80,80,78**
CSF £120.53 CT £591.94 TOTE £5.10: £2.00, £7.70, £2.10; EX 86.50 Trifecta £580.70.
Owner Mrs M S Teversham **Bred** Mrs Monica Teversham **Trained** Epsom, Surrey
■ Stewards' Enquiry : Seamus Cronin two-day ban: used whip above permitted level (Oct 1-2)
Rhiain Ingram four-day ban: careless riding (1-4 Oct)

FOCUS
A competitive handicap on paper but, although the gallop was sound, those held up were at a bit of a disadvantage. The second has been rated to form.

7231 VALUE RATER RACING CLUB H'CAP (SUMMER STAYING SERIES FINAL) 1m 6f
4:30 (4:31) (Class 2) 3-Y-O+
£12,450 (£3,728; £1,864; £932; £466; £234) **Stalls** High

Form RPR
113 **1** **Charlie D (USA)**[6] 7033 4-9-10 **81**........................(tp) RichardKingscote 14 89
(Tom Dascombe) *trckd ldr: led over 2f out: hld on wl fnl f: rdn out* **10/3**[1]
6103 **2** nk **Sufi**[23] 6419 5-9-2 **73**... PatDobbs 8 80
(Milton Harris) *in tch: hdwy over 2f out: chal over 1f out: rdn and ev ch ins fnl f: hld nring fin* **9/1**
2024 **3** 3 1/4 **Singing The Blues (IRE)**[12] 6848 4-8-9 **73**............. AngusVilliers(7) 10 75
(Rod Millman) *trckd ldrs: rdn over 2f out: styd on but nt pce to chal* **9/2**[2]
1342 **4** 2 3/4 **Victoriano (IRE)**[17] 6642 3-8-8 **74**..........................(b) AdamMcNamara 6 73
(Archie Watson) *mid-div: hdwy to trck ldrs after 5f: rdn over 2f out: styd on same pce fr over 1f out* **11/2**[3]
1402 **5** hd **Rosie Royale (IRE)**[25] 6333 7-8-6 **63**........................... GeorgeWood 2 61
(Roger Teal) *mid-div: rdn wl over 2f out: styd on but nvr gng pce to get on terms* **16/1**
2003 **6** 2 1/2 **The Detainee**[29] 6200 6-8-7 **64**.................................(v) FrannyNorton 4 59
(Neil Mulholland) *awkwardly away: hld up towards rr: rdn 3f out: styd on fnl 2f but nvr gng pce to get involved* **18/1**
-531 **7** 3/4 **Hope Is High**[11] 6854 6-8-11 **71**................................ MeganNicholls(3) 1 65
(John Berry) *mid-div: hdwy 2f out: hung lft u.p ent fnl f: fdd* **9/2**[2]
3414 **8** 3/4 **Cotton Club (IRE)**[10] 6901 8-8-8 **72**..........................(p) MarcoGhiani(7) 12 65
(George Boughey) *trckd ldrs: rdn whn squeezed up 2f out: one pce after* **12/1**
2251 **9** 1 **Filament Of Gold (USA)**[11] 6853 8-8-0 **57** oh3............(b) KieranO'Neill 7 48
(Roy Brotherton) *s.i.s: sn pushed along and detached last: styd on steadily past btn horses fnl 2f: nvr any threat* **25/1**
0502 **10** 1 1/4 **Khismet**[11] 6853 6-8-0 **57** oh5...................................(p) RyanPowell 11 47
(John Flint) *led tl rdn over 2f out: wknd over 1f out (vet said mare finished lame left fore)* **50/1**
6643 **11** 3 3/4 **Lady Natasha (IRE)**[11] 6853 6-7-9 **57** oh12...........(t) SophieRalston(5) 5 41
(James Grassick) *struggling over 4f out: a towards rr* **66/1**
6361 **12** 2 3/4 **Gemini**[12] 6824 4-8-6 **63**..(v[1]) BenRobinson 3 43
(John Quinn) *a towards rr* **12/1**
-015 **13** 9 **Street Jester**[53] 5290 5-8-0 **60** oh7 ow3.......................... DarraghKeenan(3) 9 28
(Robert Stephens) *mid-div: pushed along after 5f: rdn over 3f out: wknd over 1f out* **40/1**

2m 58.97s (-7.13) **Going Correction** -0.20s/f (Firm) course record
WFA 3 from 4yo+ 9lb **13** Ran SP% **121.1**
Speed ratings (Par 109): **112,111,109,108,108 106,106,106,105,104 102,101,95**
CSF £33.93 CT £140.15 TOTE £4.00: £1.60, £2.90, £1.90; EX 33.10 Trifecta £147.10.
Owner D R Passant & T Dascombe **Bred** Rabbah Bloodstock Ltd **Trained** Malpas, Cheshire

The Form Book Flat 2019, Raceform Ltd, Newbury, RG14 5SJ

FOCUS
A fair handicap in which an ordinary gallop picked up on the turn for home. The first two pulled clear in the closing stages and have been rated as running small personal bests.

7232 FRESHERS H'CAP 1m 2f 37y
5:10 (5:12) (Class 6) (0-55,55) 3-Y-O+
£3,169 (£943; £471; £400; £400; £400) **Stalls Low**

Form RPR
0001 **1** **About Glory**[11] 6855 5-9-1 **49**.........................(vt) FrannyNorton 10 56
(Iain Jardine) *in tch: tk clsr order over 4f out: rdn to ld over 1f out: styd on wl* **4/1**[2]
0004 **2** *2* **Dolly McQueen**[30] 6152 3-8-3 **46** oh1..................... DarraghKeenan(3) 1 50
(Anthony Carson) *mid-div: hdwy over 2f out: sn rdn: wnt 2nd ins fnl f: styd on but no threat to wnr (jockey said filly hung right-handed)* **11/1**
3505 **3** *nse* **Mister Musicmaster**[15] 6731 10-9-2 **53**....................... FinleyMarsh(3) 5 56
(Ron Hodges) *hld up towards rr: rdn and hdwy over 1f out: styd on strly fnl f: snatched 3rd cl home* **15/2**
-010 **4** *½* **African Showgirl**[14] 6758 6-8-5 **46** oh1..................... GeorgiaDobie(7) 12 48
(Eve Johnson Houghton) *hld up towards rr: hdwy on outer over 4f out: rdn to chse ldrs over 2f out: disp 2nd ins fnl f: no ex cl home* **14/1**
-500 **5** *½* **Milldean Felix (IRE)**[15] 6723 3-8-7 **47**.........................(b) RyanPowell 7 49
(Suzi Best) *led after 1f: rdn over 2f out: hdd over 1f out: styd on but no ex fnl f* **25/1**
0-03 **6** *¾* **Duke Of Dunabar**[17] 6636 3-8-13 **53**............................. JackMitchell 3 54
(Roger Teal) *mid-div: hdwy 2f out: sn rdn: styd on but nt pce to get on terms* **4/1**[2]
2002 **7** *½* **Red Gunner**[11] 6855 5-9-4 **52**.................................(p) RichardKingscote 11 51
(Mark Loughnane) *hld up towards rr: hdwy on inner 3f out: nt clr run 2f out: rdn whn in the clr ent fnl f: nt pce to get on terms (jockey said gelding was denied a clear run)* **3/1**[1]
6100 **8** *¾* **Rocksette**[19] 6560 5-9-2 **55**..................................(h) TobyEley(5) 6 52
(Adam West) *s.i.s: towards rr: rdn over 2f out: styd on fnl f: n.d (jockey said mare was slowly away)* **33/1**
6340 **9** *1* **Bader**[29] 6202 3-8-13 **53**... PatDobbs 4 50
(Richard Hannon) *trckd ldr tl lost pl over 4f out: midfield whn rdn over 2f out: nvr bk on terms* **7/1**[3]
0060 **10** *3* **Mamnoon (IRE)**[11] 6855 6-8-12 **46** oh1.........................(b) KieranO'Neill 2 36
(Roy Brotherton) *sn chsng ldr: hung rt u.p 2f out: sn wknd* **25/1**
0010 **11** *4* **Valentine Mist (IRE)**[11] 6855 7-8-9 **48**....................... SophieRalston(5) 8 30
(James Grassick) *led for 1f: trckd ldrs: rdn over 2f out: sn wknd (jockey said mare suffered interference inside final furlong)* **33/1**

2m 8.65s (-2.45) **Going Correction** -0.20s/f (Firm) **11 Ran SP% 117.8**
WFA 3 from 4yo+ 6lb
Speed ratings (Par 101): **101,99,99,98,98 97,97,96,96,93 90**
CSF £45.22 CT £316.98 TOTE £4.30: £1.50, £3.40, £2.50; EX 53.00 Trifecta £343.40.
Owner I J Jardine **Bred** T Cummins **Trained** Carrutherstown, D'fries & G'way

FOCUS
A moderate handicap in which the gallop was no more than fair. A couple of these underperformed but the winner is clearly on the upgrade. The second and fourth give some perspective as to the level of the form.

7233 VISIT FOUR FROM THE TOP AT VALUERATER.CO.UK APPRENTICE H'CAP 1m 3f 137y
5:45 (5:48) (Class 5) (0-75,73) 3-Y-O+
£3,816 (£1,135; £567; £400; £400; £400) **Stalls Low**

Form RPR
1062 **1** **Arctic Sea**[13] 6804 5-9-12 **73**.................................. MeganNicholls 4 78
(Paul Cole) *s.i.s: in last pair: hdwy 2f out: chal ent fnl f: styd on wl: led fnl stride (jockey said gelding was slowly away; vet said gelding lost left fore shoe)* **4/1**[2]
4523 **2** *nse* **Carp Kid (IRE)**[13] 6812 4-9-12 **73**..........................(p) FinleyMarsh 1 78
(John Flint) *trckd ldrs: rdn to ld whn drifting rt over 1f out: strly pressed thrght fnl f: hdd fnl stride* **9/4**[1]
4656 **3** *2 ¾* **Beer With The Boys**[13] 6796 4-9-0 **61**....................(v[1]) ScottMcCullagh 3 61
(Mick Channon) *hld up in last pair: rdn over 2f out: hdwy whn swtchd lft jst over 1f out: styd on to go 3rd sn after: nt pce of front pair* **10/1**
0465 **4** *2 ½* **Last Enchantment (IRE)**[11] 6854 4-9-2 **66**..................(t) MarcoGhiani(3) 2 62
(Neil Mulholland) *trckd ldrs: rdn to take narrow advantage 2f out: hdd whn sltly hmpd jst over 1f out: no ex fnl f* **9/1**[3]
6-50 **5** *2* **Cheeky Rascal (IRE)**[12] 6830 4-9-2 **68**....................(v[1]) LukeCatton(5) 7 61
(Tom Ward) *pressed ldr: rdn and ev ch 2f out: disputing cl 2nd whn bdly hmpd jst over 1f out: no threat after (jockey said gelding was denied a clear run)* **16/1**
1420 **6** *2 ¼* **Perfect Grace**[31] 6104 3-8-13 **71**.......................(p) Pierre-LouisJamin(3) 6 61
(Archie Watson) *led: rdn and hdd 2f out: hld whn hmpd over 1f out: fdd fnl f* **4/1**[2]
0023 **7** *8* **Simbirsk**[38] 5850 4-9-4 **70**...................................(p) KateLeahy(5) 5 46
(John O'Shea) *in tch: effrt over 2f out: wknd over 1f out* **4/1**[2]

2m 27.52s (-3.28) **Going Correction** -0.20s/f (Firm) **7 Ran SP% 115.7**
WFA 3 from 4yo+ 8lb
Speed ratings (Par 103): **102,101,100,98,97 95,90**
CSF £13.81 TOTE £5.40: £2.50, £1.80; EX 15.00 Trifecta £107.70.
Owner P F I Cole Ltd **Bred** Waratah Thoroughbreds Pty Ltd **Trained** Whatcombe, Oxon
■ Stewards' Enquiry : Finley Marsh three-day ban: careless riding (29-30 Sep, 1 Oct)
Marco Ghiani two-day ban: used whip above permitted level (30 Sep, 1 Oct)

FOCUS
Exposed performers in an ordinary handicap. A modest gallop only picked up in the last quarter mile. It's been rated a bit cautiously, with the first two close to their recent best.
T/Plt: £66.70 to a £1 stake. Pool: £82,392.04 - 900.75 winning units T/Qpdt: £26.70 to a £1 stake. Pool: £7,442.57 - 206.24 winning units **Tim Mitchell**

6637 FFOS LAS (L-H)
Sunday, September 15

OFFICIAL GOING: Good (good to soft in places; 7.1)
Wind: Moderate headwind Weather: Cloudy

7234 GOMER WILLIAMS SOLICITORS CENTENARY CELEBRATIONS NURSERY H'CAP 6f
2:05 (2:06) (Class 6) (0-60,68) 2-Y-O
£2,781 (£827; £413; £400; £400; £400) **Stalls High**

Form RPR
566 **1** **Romintheglomin (IRE)**[18] 6606 2-8-7 **48**..................... RowanScott(3) 2 53
(Andrew Hughes, Ire) *hld up: hdwy on outer to ld after 2f: drvn wl over 1f out: kpt on wl (regarding the apparent improvement in form, trainer said filly appreciated a drop back in trip to six furlongs from seven furlongs and her first run in a handicap)* **16/1**
000 **2** *1 ¼* **Kitos**[20] 6548 2-8-8 **46**..(b[1]) LukeMorris 8 47
(Sir Mark Prescott Bt) *s.i.s: towards rr: drvn over 3f out: hdwy over 2f out: chsd wnr ent fnl f: styd on* **10/1**
0042 **3** *1* **Port Noir**[16] 6683 2-9-1 **53**...(t) RossaRyan 10 52
(Grace Harris) *racd stands' side: towards rr: hdwy 2f out: nt clr run over 1f out: drvn and r.o wl fnl f* **4/1**[1]
000 **4** *¾* **Village Rock (IRE)**[15] 6719 2-9-2 **54**............................. ShaneKelly 7 50
(Richard Hughes) *chsd ldrs: n.m.r after 2f: rdn 2f out: nt clr run over 1f out: drvn and r.o fnl f (jockey said colt suffered interference in early stages)* **16/1**
560 **5** *1 ¾* **A Go Go**[45] 5577 2-9-2 **54**.. HarryBentley 6 45
(David Evans) *t.k.h: hld up: hdwy 1/2-way: rdn to chse wnr over 2f out: lost 2nd ent fnl f: wknd* **33/1**
6461 **6** *1 ½* **Dreamy Rascal (IRE)**[12] 6837 2-9-9 **68**......................... MarkCrehan(7) 4 54
(Richard Hannon) *t.k.h: trckd ldrs: drvn and nt qckn over 1f out: wknd ins fnl f* **8/1**
065 **7** *1* **Carriage Clock**[22] 6458 2-9-6 **58**.............................. RoystonFfrench 3 41
(Steph Hollinshead) *prom: rdn over 2f out: outpcd over 1f out: grad wknd* **25/1**
5443 **8** *1 ¾* **Carmel**[13] 6799 2-9-7 **59**...(p) TomMarquand 1 37
(Archie Watson) *cl up: led after 1f to 4f out: drvn over 2f out: wknd over 1f out* **6/1**[3]
000 **9** *1* **Bockos Amber (IRE)**[22] 6442 2-9-3 **58**......................... CierenFallon(3) 5 33
(Roger Teal) *prom tl lost pl after 2f: hdwy over 2f out: wknd fnl f (vet said filly had a small cut to inside right fore-limb)* **5/1**[2]
5443 **10** *10* **Timon (IRE)**[5] 7056 2-9-0 **52**..................................(v[1]) CallumShepherd 9
(Mick Channon) *racd stands' side: led 1f: lost pl 1/2-way: rdn 2f out: sn bhd* **4/1**[1]
060 **11** *31* **Candid (IRE)**[66] 4840 2-8-12 **50**.................................. NicolaCurrie 11
(Jonathan Portman) *racd stands' side: a in rr: lost tch 2f out: t.o (jockey said filly hung right-handed throughout; trainer said filly would prefer a quicker surface)* **8/1**

1m 14.63s (3.73) **Going Correction** +0.275s/f (Good) **11 Ran SP% 120.8**
Speed ratings (Par 93): **86,84,83,82,79 77,76,74,72,59 18**
CSF £171.12 CT £788.29 TOTE £26.10: £5.90, £3.50, £1.40; EX 225.90 Trifecta £1676.90.
Owner Thistle Bloodstock Limited **Bred** Barry Judge **Trained** Kells, Co Kilkenny

FOCUS
A modest nursery in which only a handful played a meaningful part. They stayed stands' side. A pb from the second.

7235 3AS LEISURE BIRTHDAY CELEBRATIONS FOR CATHERINE'S 30TH EBF NOVICE STKS 1m (R)
2:35 (2:36) (Class 5) 2-Y-O
£3,428 (£1,020; £509; £254) **Stalls Low**

Form RPR
5 **1** **Night Colours (IRE)**[18] 6592 2-9-0 0................................ DaneO'Neill 2 77+
(Simon Crisford) *s.i.s: sn trcking ldrs: rdn to ld 2f out: drvn and r.o strly fnl f: comf* **7/1**[3]
24 **2** *2 ½* **Hot Summer**[9] 6927 2-9-5 0... SeanLevey 3 75
(Richard Hannon) *a.p: drvn over 1f out: outpcd by wnr fnl f: kpt on* **5/6**[1]
0 **3** *nk* **Fashion Royalty**[23] 6407 2-9-0 0................................... JasonWatson 12 69
(Roger Charlton) *chsd ldrs: rdn over 1f out: sn ev ch: unable qck and disp hld 2nd fnl f* **9/1**
034 **4** *1 ¾* **Protagonist (FR)**[23] 6395 2-9-5 78................................ NicolaCurrie 8 70
(Jamie Osborne) *t.k.h in midfield on outer: rdn and sme hdwy over 2f out: outpcd by ldrs over 1f out: styd on ins fnl f* **9/2**[2]
0 **5** *nk* **Jellystone (IRE)**[37] 5908 2-9-5 0................................... HarryBentley 6 69
(Ralph Beckett) *led: hung rt bnd over 4f out: drvn and hdd 2f out: wknd fnl f (jockey said colt ran green)* **8/1**
6 *3 ½* **Molinari (IRE)** 2-9-5 0.. TomMarquand 10 61+
(William Muir) *hld up: drvn 3f out: hdwy and edgd lft over 1f out: no further imp* **20/1**
7 *1 ½* **Arthalot (IRE)** 2-9-5 0.. LukeMorris 5 58
(Paul George) *midfield: drvn 4f out: wknd over 2f out* **50/1**
8 *nk* **Derek Le Grand** 2-9-5 0... RossaRyan 9 57
(Grace Harris) *towards rr: rdn and sme prog 4f out: wknd over 2f out* **66/1**
45 **9** *½* **Bealach (IRE)**[58] 5131 2-9-5 0..................................... DavidProbert 1 56
(Eve Johnson Houghton) *prom: rdn over 3f out: wknd wl over 1f out* **14/1**
10 *4 ½* **On The Rhine (IRE)** 2-9-2 0.. RowanScott(3) 11 46
(Andrew Hughes, Ire) *a in rr* **40/1**

1m 45.31s (2.41) **Going Correction** +0.275s/f (Good) **10 Ran SP% 123.7**
Speed ratings (Par 95): **98,95,95,93,93 89,88,87,87,82**
CSF £13.82 TOTE £9.00: £2.00, £1.10, £2.80; EX 19.90 Trifecta £121.70.
Owner Hussain Alabbas Lootah **Bred** Grenane House Stud **Trained** Newmarket, Suffolk

FOCUS
Add 31yds. Potentially quite a useful little novice and the winner could easily be above average. The level is a bit fluid.

7236 ISCOED CHAMBER H'CAP 7f 80y(R)
3:10 (3:14) (Class 6) (0-60,61) 3-Y-O+
£2,781 (£827; £413; £400; £400; £400) **Stalls Low**

Form RPR
3646 **1** **Mabo**[8] 6977 4-8-13 **49**..(b) RossaRyan 4 58
(Grace Harris) *chsd ldrs: rdn to ld over 1f out: sn clr: edgd lft and drvn out fnl f* **8/1**
53/2 **2** *1 ¾* **Midnitemudcrabs (IRE)**[62] 4979 6-9-9 **59**.......................(p) LukeMorris 8 64
(John James Feane, Ire) *midfield: shkn up and hdwy over 2f out: drvn over 1f out: sn in 2nd: kpt on same pce fnl f: nt rch wnr* **9/2**[2]

0543 **3** 1 1/4 **Vipin (FR)**[8] 6977 4-9-7 **60** .... GeorgiaCox(3) 9 62
(William Muir) *midfield: lost pl 4f out: drvn on outer wl over 2f out: hdwy over 1f out: styd on to go 3rd nr fin* **6/1**[3]

0313 **4** 1/2 **Jupiter**[20] 6529 4-9-4 **57** ....(v) CierenFallon(3) 14 57
(Alexandra Dunn) *chsd ldrs: drvn 3f out: kpt on same pce fnl 2f: lost 3rd nr fin* **12/1**

0056 **5** nk **Stoneyford Lane (IRE)**[6] 7024 5-8-10 **46** ....(b) RoystonFfrench 7 46
(Steph Hollinshead) *hld up: rdn 3f out: no prog tl styd on wl fnl f: nrst fin* **16/1**

0300 **6** 2 3/4 **Lonicera**[17] 6643 3-9-3 **57** .... DavidProbert 13 48
(Henry Candy) *hld up: hdwy over 3f out: rdn and nt clr run over 2f out: styd on same pce* **10/1**

0 **7** 1 1/2 **Force Of Cashen (IRE)**[10] 6885 3-8-7 **47** ....(b[1]) JasonWatson 2 34
(Tom Gretton) *led narrowly tl hdd 4f out: drvn 3f out: styd prom tl outpcd over 1f out: wknd ins fnl f (jockey said gelding hung left-handed under pressure inside last furlong)* **16/1**

0 **8** 3/4 **Satchville Flyer**[24] 6363 8-9-9 **59** .... HarryBentley 6 46
(David Evans) *hld up: rdn 3f out: hdwy 2f out: edgd lft over 1f out: fdd fnl f* **28/1**

321 **9** 1 **Captain Sedgwick (IRE)**[20] 6529 5-8-8 **51** .... SaraDelFabbro(7) 12 36
(John Spearing) *chsd ldrs: rdn 3f out: wknd 2f out (trainer's rep said mare would prefer a quicker surface)* **3/1**[1]

005- **10** 1/2 **Skating Away (IRE)**[356] 7604 3-8-13 **53** .... LiamKeniry 10 35
(Joseph Tuite) *towards rr: rdn wl over 2f out: edgd lft over 1f out: swtchd rt 1f out: styd on* **50/1**

-400 **11** nse **Outer Space**[25] 6334 8-9-7 **60** ....(p) WilliamCox(3) 5 44
(John Flint) *prom: led 3f out: sn drvn: hdd over 1f out: wknd fnl f (jockey said gelding stopped quickly; vet said gelding lost right fore shoe)* **9/1**

0062 **12** 1 3/4 **First Link (USA)**[10] 6898 4-9-11 **61** .... NicolaCurrie 3 40
(Jean-Rene Auvray) *dwlt: t.k.h in rr: rdn over 2f out: sme prog whn n.m.r on inner over 1f out: wknd* **12/1**

4603 **13** 1 **Mooroverthebridge**[20] 6526 5-9-4 **54** ....(p) ShaneKelly 11 31
(Grace Harris) *w ldr: led 4f out tl drvn and hdd 3f out: wknd over 1f out* **50/1**

1342 **14** 1 3/4 **Glamorous Crescent**[11] 6856 3-9-4 **58** .... JimmyQuinn 1 29
(Grace Harris) *t.k.h in midfield: drvn over 2f out: wknd over 1f out* **20/1**

1m 34.88s (1.78) **Going Correction** +0.275s/f (Good)
WFA 3 from 4yo+ 4lb **14 Ran SP% 127.0**
Speed ratings (Par 101): **100,98,96,96,95 92,90,89,88,88 88,86,85,83**
CSF £44.97 CT £448.00 TOTE £10.40: £3.10, £2.00, £3.60; EX 82.00 Trifecta £1954.10.
Owner Paul & Ann de Weck **Bred** Fernham Farm Ltd **Trained** Shirenewton, Monmouthshire

FOCUS
Add 31yds. A weak handicap in which the the gamble on Captain Sedgwick went astray. Probably not form to place too much faith in. The form could be rated 2lb higher through the second, third and fourth.

7237 GOMER WILLIAMS SOLICITORS CENTENARY CELEBRATIONS FILLIES' H'CAP 1m (R)
3:45 (3:46) (Class 5) (0-70,72) 3-Y-O+
£3,428 (£1,020; £509; £400; £400; £400) **Stalls Low**

Form RPR

5105 **1** **Kyllachys Tale (IRE)**[24] 6362 5-9-1 **62** .... CierenFallon(3) 7 71
(Roger Teal) *cl up: rdn over 2f out: led over 1f out: drvn out* **11/4**[2]

5306 **2** 1 1/4 **Society Guest (IRE)**[13] 6810 3-9-3 **66** .... CallumShepherd 4 71
(Mick Channon) *chsd ldrs: drvn 2f out: wnt 2nd 1f out: kpt on same pce* **8/1**

5206 **3** 1 1/4 **J'Ouvert (IRE)**[13] 6801 3-8-12 **61** ....(h[1]) JasonWatson 8 63
(David Evans) *hld up: rdn over 2f out: hdwy on inner to chse ldrs over 1f out: no imp fnl f* **33/1**

3052 **4** 1 **Madeleine Bond**[24] 6362 5-9-10 **71** .... GeorgiaCox(3) 10 72
(Henry Candy) *midfield: drvn over 2f out: chsd ldrs over 1f out: one pce fnl f* **5/2**[1]

0343 **5** 1 1/2 **Accomplice**[17] 6643 5-8-10 **54** .... CharlieBennett 3 51
(Michael Blanshard) *t.k.h: trckd ldrs: drvn 2f out: wknd fnl f* **7/1**[3]

2-00 **6** 4 1/2 **Perfect Showdance**[108] 3264 3-9-7 **70** .... DavidProbert 6 56
(Clive Cox) *s.i.s: towards rr: rdn over 2f out: no real imp: wknd ins fnl f* **12/1**

000 **7** nk **Paco Dawn**[6] 7028 5-8-7 **45** oh6............ LukeMorris 9 37
(Tony Carroll) *t.k.h: hld up: rdn over 2f out: wknd over 1f out* **50/1**

535 **8** 1/2 **Rapture (FR)**[39] 5808 3-9-9 **72** .... TomMarquand 2 56
(Archie Watson) *led: rdn over 2f out: hdd over 1f out: sn wknd* **11/4**[2]

66-6 **9** 27 **Zalpa (USA)**[88] 3-9-9 **72** .... HarryBentley 5
(David Evans) *towards rr: rdn over 2f out: no rspnse: eased over 1f out: t.o (jockey said filly stopped quickly)* **33/1**

1m 44.89s (1.99) **Going Correction** +0.275s/f (Good)
WFA 3 from 5yo 5lb **9 Ran SP% 121.1**
Speed ratings (Par 100): **101,99,98,97,96 91,91,90,63**
CSF £26.10 CT £616.99 TOTE £3.70: £1.10, £2.20, £10.30; EX 26.90 Trifecta £622.40.
Owner Barry Kitcherside And Darren Waterer **Bred** Old Carhue Stud **Trained** Lambourn, Berks

FOCUS
Add 31yds. Ordinary stuff, even for this grade but they went a reasonable gallop. The second has been rated close to form.

7238 OC DAVIES MG CELEBRATING 50 YEARS/EBF FILLIES' H'CAP 1m 2f (R)
4:20 (4:20) (Class 4) (0-80,79) 3-Y-O+
£5,207 (£1,549; £774; £400; £400; £400) **Stalls Low**

Form RPR

1 **Sarah Jessica (IRE)**[104] 3436 3-8-6 **64** .... NicolaCurrie 5 70
(Gavin Cromwell, Ire) *hld up in last pair: shkn up and hdwy over 2f out: led appr fnl f: rdn out* **4/1**[2]

0014 **2** 1 1/2 **Capriolette (IRE)**[30] 6165 4-9-4 **70** .... LiamKeniry 3 73
(Ed Walker) *trckd ldr: drvn to ld 2f out: hdd appr fnl f: kpt on same pce* **4/1**[2]

3 1 **Triple Nickle (IRE)**[18] 6613 3-8-6 **64** ....(p[1]) JimmyQuinn 6 65
(Bernard Llewellyn) *t.k.h: trckd ldrs: rdn over 2f out: sn ev ch: kpt on same pce fnl f* **16/1**

5341 **4** 3 1/2 **Sincerity**[33] 6039 3-9-2 **74** .... TomMarquand 7 68
(James Fanshawe) *hld up in last pair: rdn and hdwy over 2f out: drvn: outpcd and wandered over 1f out: no imp* **4/5**[1]

065 **5** 1 1/2 **Zest Of Zambia (USA)**[27] 6290 3-8-2 **60** .... LukeMorris 4 51
(Dai Burchell) *trckd ldrs: rdn 3f out: outpcd and btn 2f out* **16/1**

1324 **6** 7 **Tabassor (IRE)**[29] 6209 3-9-7 **79** .... DaneO'Neill 1 67
(Charles Hills) *led tl rdn and hdd 2f out: sn wknd: eased ins fnl f (jockey said filly stopped quickly; trainer's rep said filly had a breathing problem)* **13/2**[3]

2m 13.66s (0.96) **Going Correction** +0.15s/f (Good)
WFA 3 from 4yo 6lb **6 Ran SP% 120.7**
Speed ratings (Par 102): **102,100,100,97,96 90**
CSF £21.87 TOTE £4.70: £1.30, £2.00; EX 27.00 Trifecta £112.60.
Owner I Reilly, M Dunphy, T Liston, D Healy **Bred** Mrs J Norris **Trained** Navan, Co. Meath

FOCUS
Add 31yds. One or two potential improvers in here, including the winner, but the well-backed market leader bombed out which holds the form back. They didn't appear to go very hard up front but the leader dropped right out and the winner came from the back. It's been rated around the second.

7239 JO-JO SMITH MEMORIAL H'CAP 2m (R)
5:00 (5:01) (Class 4) (0-85,86) 3-Y-O+
£5,207 (£1,549; £774; £400; £400; £400) **Stalls Low**

Form RPR

0300 **1** **Blue Laureate**[25] 6355 4-10-1 **86** ....(p[1]) CierenFallon(3) 3 97+
(Ian Williams) *hld up: plenty to do whn rdn over 5f out: chsd ldng pair 4f out: wnt 2nd 2f out: drvn to ld over 1f out: edgd lft and sn clr: eased towards fin* **15/2**

0112 **2** 7 **Nuits St Georges (IRE)**[37] 5897 4-10-0 **82** .... SeanLevey 5 83
(David Menuisier) *wnt rt leaving stalls: prom: trckd ldr after 3f: led 4f out: rdn over 2f out: hdd over 1f out: sn btn but hld clr 2nd* **4/1**[3]

034 **3** 6 **Marengo**[17] 6642 8-9-1 **69** ....(b) ShaneKelly 7 63
(Bernard Llewellyn) *bmpd s: sn chsd along in rr: hdwy to ld over 13f out: drvn over 5f out: hdd 4f out: lost 2nd 2f out: grad wknd* **25/1**

1411 **4** 17 **Cambric**[23] 6419 3-8-13 **78** .... JasonWatson 2 53
(Roger Charlton) *chsd ldrs and in 4th virtually thrght: rdn 5f out: styd on u.p tl wknd 2f out* **5/2**[2]

2342 **5** 3 3/4 **General Zoff**[25] 6348 4-9-2 **70** .... TomMarquand 4 39
(William Muir) *prom: led after 1f tl hdd over 13f out: rdn over 5f out: lost 3rd 4f out: wknd 3f out: t.o* **11/1**

2105 **6** 20 **Goscote**[33] 6044 4-9-4 **72** .... DavidProbert 1 17
(Henry Candy) *led 1f: sn in midfield: rdn 5f out: wknd 4f out: t.o (jockey said filly stopped quickly; vet said filly displayed a prolonged recovery)* **20/1**

0011 **P** **Tigerskin**[23] 6400 3-8-9 **74** ....(bt) HarryBentley 6
(Ralph Beckett) *carried rt leaving stalls: hld up: rdn 7f out: lost tch and virtually p.u 5f out: dismntd 1f out (jockey said gelding stopped quickly; trainer's rep said gelding had a breathing problem)* **11/8**[1]

3m 37.8s (1.10) **Going Correction** +0.15s/f (Good)
WFA 3 from 4yo+ 11lb **7 Ran SP% 119.4**
Speed ratings (Par 105): **103,99,96,88,86 76,**
CSF £39.50 CT £728.84 TOTE £8.40: £4.10, £1.10; EX 43.80 Trifecta £573.00.
Owner A Dale **Bred** Cavendish Bloodstock **Trained** Portway, Worcs

FOCUS
Add 42yds. They finished strung out and the short-priced favourite was the first beat. It's been rated around the winner.

7240 GOMER WILLIAMS SOLICITORS CENTENARY CELEBRATIONS H'CAP 1m 3f 209y(R)
5:35 (5:38) (Class 6) (0-60,60) 3-Y-O+
£2,781 (£827; £413; £400; £400; £400) **Stalls Low**

Form RPR

-036 **1** **Good Impression**[12] 6830 4-9-2 **53** ....(p) CierenFallon(3) 12 60
(Dai Burchell) *hld up: hdwy on outer 1/2-way: rdn to ld wl over 1f out: sn drvn: hrd pressed ins fnl f: jst hld on* **18/1**

0-40 **2** hd **Visor**[39] 5824 4-9-12 **60** ....(h) NicolaCurrie 13 67
(James Fanshawe) *t.k.h in rr: gd hdwy on inner 3f out: drvn over 1f out: sn chsng wnr: ev ch ins fnl f: jst hld* **7/1**

23 **3** 1 1/4 **Just Once**[33] 6039 3-9-2 **58** .... DaneO'Neill 9 64
(Mrs Ilka Gansera-Leveque) *s.s: plld hrd in rr: stdy hdwy 5f out: rdn and swtchd rt wl over 1f out: sn in 3rd: drvn and hung lft ins fnl f: hld towards fin (jockey said filly hung left-handed)* **11/2**[3]

4 3 1/2 **Early Strike (FR)**[60] 5065 3-8-4 **46** oh1............ JimmyQuinn 11 46
(Gavin Cromwell, Ire) *midfield: hdwy to chse ldrs after 4f: rdn 3f out: hung lft 2f out: nt qckn: hld in 4th whn carried lft ins fnl f* **3/1**[2]

6000 **5** 3 3/4 **Flying Moon (GER)**[11] 6860 3-8-8 **50** .... DavidProbert 15 44
(Jonathan Portman) *prom: trckd ldr after 3f: rdn to ld narrowly over 2f out: hdd wl over 1f out: lost 2nd appr fnl f: no ex* **28/1**

600- **6** 1 3/4 **Poucor**[180] 9054 4-9-2 **50** .... CallumShepherd 5 40
(Mick Channon) *prom: rdn and ev ch 2f out: sn one pce: wknd fnl f* **16/1**

0601 **7** 5 **Kasuku**[20] 6531 3-8-9 **51** ....(b) HarryBentley 16 34
(Ralph Beckett) *led: drvn: hung rt and hdd over 2f out: grad wknd* **5/2**[1]

0050 **8** 4 **Famous Dynasty (IRE)**[32] 6077 5-9-5 **53** .... CharlieBennett 10 28
(Michael Blanshard) *s.s: in rr: drvn and sme hdwy 3f out: no ch fnl 2f* **66/1**

0536 **9** 3 3/4 **Purple Jazz (IRE)**[23] 6400 4-9-5 **53** ....(t) RossaRyan 6 22
(Jeremy Scott) *midfield: drvn 3f out: wknd 2f out* **12/1**

000 **10** 2 **Star Guide (GER)**[10] 6887 3-8-8 **55** ....(h) ThomasGreatrex(5) 4 21
(David Menuisier) *towards rr: rdn 5f out: racd alone on stands' rail fnl 4f: grad wknd (jockey said gelding was slowly away and never travelling)* **20/1**

3433 **11** 1/2 **Pike Corner Cross (IRE)**[30] 6153 7-9-3 **51** ....(t[1]) TomMarquand 2 16
(David Evans) *towards rr: rdn over 3f out: wknd over 2f out* **20/1**

0-00 **12** 4 **Mister Fawkes**[30] 6153 3-8-3 **52** .... GeorgeRooke(7) 8 11
(Richard Hughes) *wnt to post early: midfield: drvn over 4f out: wknd wl over 2f out* **50/1**

0005 **13** 6 **Pecorino**[24] 6367 3-9-1 **57** .... ShaneKelly 7 6
(Richard Hughes) *chsd ldrs: rdn 4f out: wknd over 2f out (jockey said gelding stopped quickly)* **16/1**

035 **14** 24 **Brooklyn Boy**[12] 6849 3-9-0 **56** .... LukeMorris 1
(Harry Dunlop) *prom: drvn 4f out: wknd 3f out: t.o (jockey said colt stopped quickly)* **18/1**

0-00 **15** 2 3/4 **Logan's Choice**[54] 5269 4-9-7 **55** .... JasonWatson 14
(Roger Charlton) *chsd ldrs tl lost pl after 4f: drvn 4f out: wknd qckly: t.o (jockey said gelding stopped quickly)* **10/1**

05-0 **16** *76* **Magojiro (USA)**[41] 5757 4-8-13 **47**..............................(v) LiamKeniry 3
(W J Martin, Ire) *midfield: rdn 5f out: wknd qckly: virtually p.u 3f out: t.o (jockey said gelding was never travelling)* **33/1**

2m 40.71s (0.51) **Going Correction** +0.15s/f (Good)
WFA 3 from 4yo+ 8lb **16** Ran SP% **139.9**
Speed ratings (Par 101): **104,103,103,100,98 97,93,91,88,87 86,84,80,64,62 11**
CSF £150.30 CT £826.44 TOTE £22.60: £3.10, £1.70, £1.80, £1.40; EX 176.00 Trifecta £2812.50.
Owner B M G Group **Bred** Juddmonte Farms Ltd **Trained** Briery Hill, Blaenau Gwent

FOCUS
Add 31yds. A weak handicap in which very few came here in any kind of form.
T/Jkpt: Not Won. T/Plt: £618.30 to a £1 stake. Pool: £84,083.41 - 99.26 winning units T/Qpdt: £136.00 to a £1 stake. Pool: £8,275.52 - 45 winning units **Richard Lowther**

6688 CURRAGH (R-H)

Sunday, September 15

OFFICIAL GOING: Straight course - good (good to firm in places); round course - good to firm (good in places)

7241a IRISH STALLION FARMS EBF "BOLD LAD" SPRINT H'CAP (PREMIER HANDICAP) 6f

1:20 (1:22) 3-Y-0+

£79,729 (£25,675; £12,162; £5,405; £2,702; £1,351) **Stalls** Centre

RPR

1 **Buffer Zone**[37] 5923 4-9-6 **99**.............................. ColinKeane 6 110
(G M Lyons, Ire) *chsd ldrs in centre of trck: wnt 2nd 2f out: rdn to ld over 1f out: styd on wl ins fnl f* **11/2**[1]

2 *1 ¾* **Make A Challenge (IRE)**[30] 6195 4-8-6 **92**............(p) JMSheridan(7) 15 97
(Denis Gerard Hogan, Ire) *chsd ldrs in centre gp: travelled wl in 3rd under 2f out: rdn in 2nd appr fnl f: no imp on wnr fnl 100yds: kpt on wl* **11/2**[1]

3 *shd* **Gulliver**[15] 6706 5-9-4 **97**..............................(tp) DanielTudhope 18 102+
(David O'Meara) *racd in mid-div in centre of trck: rdn along 2f out: short of room over 1f out and swtchd lft: plenty to do ent fnl f: styd on strly into 3rd cl home: nrst fin* **9/1**[2]

4 *¾* **Gordon Lord Byron (IRE)**[10] 6894 11-9-12 **105**.............. WJLee 2 107
(T Hogan, Ire) *chsd ldrs far side: clsr in 4th ent fnl f: wnt 3rd fnl 150yds: kpt on same pce: dropped to 4th cl home* **20/1**

5 *½* **Blairmayne (IRE)**[16] 6691 6-8-4 **83** oh1.................. KillianLeonard 3 84
(Miss Natalia Lupini, Ire) *racd in mid-div far side: cl in 7th ent fnl f: kpt on wl into 5th clsng stages: nvr nrr* **14/1**

6 *¾* **Castletownshend (IRE)**[16] 6691 4-7-8 **83** oh11..... MikeySheehy(10) 16 81
(T M Walsh, Ire) *racd in mid-div in centre of trck: prog under 2f out: kpt on wl ins fnl f: nvr nrr* **25/1**

7 *1 ¼* **Venturous (IRE)**[43] 5661 6-8-10 **89**........................ RobbieDowney 1 83
(David Barron) *racd in rr of mid-div on far side: prog on outer over 1f out: briefly wnt 5th ins fnl f: no ex clsng stages* **14/1**

8 *nk* **Ardhoomey (IRE)**[17] 6648 7-9-4 **97**..............................(t) GaryCarroll 4 90
(G M Lyons, Ire) *chsd ldrs far side: wnt 3rd 2f out: nt qckn ent fnl f: no ex fnl 100yds* **16/1**

9 *1 ½* **Twenty Minutes**[4] 7090 4-8-4 **83** oh5..........................(tp) LeighRoche 8 72
(Damian Joseph English, Ire) *racd in rr of mid-div far side: no imp under 2f out: kpt on wl ins fnl f: nvr on terms* **33/1**

10 *nk* **Mary Salome (IRE)**[4] 7093 3-8-4 **85** oh2.................. DavidEgan 21 73
(Madeleine Tylicki, Ire) *chsd ldrs on nr side: rdn and no imp appr fnl f: kpt on same pce* **20/1**

11 *½* **Scorching Heat**[16] 6691 5-8-4 **83**.............................. ConorHoban 12 69
(Adrian McGuinness, Ire) *sn trckd ldrs in centre of trck: 2nd at 1/2-way: rdn and nt qckn 1f out: wknd* **20/1**

12 *shd* **Primo Uomo (IRE)**[8] 6986 7-9-8 **101**.................... NGMcCullagh 13 87
(Gerard O'Leary, Ire) *racd in mid-div: clsr 2f out: no imp ent fnl f: kpt on same pce* **25/1**

13 *nk* **Sirjack Thomas (IRE)**[4] 7093 4-8-9 **88**.................... ShaneFoley 5 73
(Adrian McGuinness, Ire) *racd in mid-div far side: rdn 2f out: kpt on same pce fr over 1f out: nvr on terms* **12/1**

14 *½* **Sunset Nova (IRE)**[4] 7092 3-7-11 **85** oh12.............. AlanPersse(7) 22 68
(Andrew Slattery, Ire) *chsd ldrs on nr side: bit short of room under 2f out and sn swtchd rt: no imp ent fnl f* **50/1**

15 *hd* **That's Not Me (IRE)**[18] 6591 3-7-10 **87** oh15 ow2(p[1]) CharlieO'Dwyer(10) 7 69
(Anthony McCann, Ire) *led centre gp tl hdd over 1f out: wknd fnl f* **66/1**

16 *1 ½* **Master Matt**[29] 6238 3-8-2 **86** oh2 ow1..................(p) SeanDavis(3) 20 64
(Matthew J Smith, Ire) *t.k.h early and sn trckd ldr of nr side gp: nt qckn appr fnl f: sn one pce* **16/1**

17 *hd* **Tresorier**[103] 3457 5-7-13 **83** oh5.................... GabrieleMalune(5) 24 60
(John James Feane, Ire) *racd in mid-div nr side: no imp appr fnl f* **25/1**

18 *hd* **Rhydwyn (IRE)**[29] 6235 3-8-6 **92**..............................(t) BenCoen(5) 25 68
(T Hogan, Ire) *chsd ldrs on nr side: short of room over 2f out and sn no imp: kpt on again clsng stages* **16/1**

19 *¾* **Maarek**[16] 6691 12-8-4 **83** oh6.............................. MarkGallagher 11 57
(Miss Evanna McCutcheon, Ire) *racd towards rr in centre of trck: rdn 2f out: kpt on one pce fnl f: nvr a factor* **50/1**

20 *2* **Alfredo Arcano (IRE)**[16] 6691 5-8-9 **88**..................(t) GaryHalpin 23 56
(David Marnane, Ire) *led nr side gp to 1/2-way: wknd fr under 2f out* **25/1**

21 *nk* **Blyton**[16] 6691 3-8-4 **85** oh6..............................(b) JoeDoyle 17 52
(Luke Comer, Ire) *chsd ldrs in centre of trck to 1/2-way: nt qckn under 2f out: short of room over 1f out and again fnl 100yds: sn eased* **50/1**

22 *2 ¾* **North Wind (IRE)**[57] 5207 3-8-8 **89**........................(t) ChrisHayes 10 47
(Damian Joseph English, Ire) *trckd ldr in centre of trck: 3rd at 1/2-way: wknd qckly under 2f out: eased clsng stages (jockey said colt hung left under pressure)* **33/1**

23 *10* **Miss Jabeam (IRE)**[8] 6986 3-7-13 **85** oh5.............. NathanCrosse(5) 19 11
(Aidan Anthony Howard, Ire) *sn towards rr in centre of trck: detached 1/2-way: eased under 2f out: sddle slipped (jockey said saddle slipped leaving stalls)* **11/1**[3]

24 *21* **Eclipse Storm**[57] 5205 3-8-8 **94**........................ AndrewSlattery(5) 14
(J A Stack, Ire) *bit slowly away: sn outpcd and detached in rr: nvr a factor (jockey said gelding got upset in the starting stalls, jumped out slowly and did not participate thereafter)* **11/1**[3]

1m 10.68s (-3.52) **Going Correction** 0.0s/f (Good)
WFA 3 from 4yo+ 2lb **24** Ran SP% **139.0**
Speed ratings: **117,114,114,113,112 111,110,109,107,107 106,106,106,105,105 103,103,102,101,99 98,95,81,53**
CSF £29.04 CT £295.15 TOTE £6.40: £1.70, £1.80, £2.90, £5.30; DF 41.20 Trifecta £223.50.
Owner Sean Jones/David Spratt/Mrs Lynne Lyons **Bred** Juddmonte Farms Ltd **Trained** Dunsany, Co Meath

FOCUS
Narrowly beaten in the Scurry here in July, the winner showed the required improvement and won well. No particular stalls bias was evident from this.

7242a MOYGLARE "JEWELS" BLANDFORD STKS (GROUP 2) (F&M) 1m 2f

1:55 (1:56) 3-Y-0+

£132,882 (£42,792; £20,270; £9,009; £4,504; £2,252)

RPR

1 **Tarnawa (IRE)**[29] 6239 3-9-0 107.............................. ChrisHayes 7 108
(D K Weld, Ire) *trckd ldrs in 3rd: rdn to ld 2f out: styd on wl ins fnl f: edgd rt ins fnl 150yds: kpt on wl* **3/1**[2]

2 *1 ½* **Goddess (USA)**[16] 6692 3-9-0 104.............................. RyanMoore 8 105
(A P O'Brien, Ire) *hld up towards rr: swtchd towards outer under 2f out in 7th: styd on wl into 3rd ent fnl f: kpt on wl into 2nd cl home: nt rch wnr* **15/8**[1]

3 *½* **Credenza (IRE)**[16] 6692 3-9-0 102.............................. DonnachaO'Brien 3 104
(A P O'Brien, Ire) *trckd early ldr in 2nd and led after 2f: hdd 2f out: kpt on same pce fnl f in 2nd whn squeezed for room on far rails fnl 150yds: dropped to 3rd cl home* **8/1**

4 *1* **Waitingfortheday (IRE)**[17] 6646 4-9-6 100..........(p) DeclanMcDonogh 9 101
(Joseph Patrick O'Brien, Ire) *hld up in rr tl prog on outer over 1f out: styd on wl into 4th fnl 100yds: nvr nrr* **14/1**

5 *1 ¼* **Trethias**[16] 6692 3-9-0 105.............................. ShaneFoley 2 100
(Mrs John Harrington, Ire) *chsd ldrs on inner in 4th: rdn and nt qckn under 2f out: no imp ent fnl f: kpt on same pce* **5/1**[3]

6 *hd* **Nausha**[91] 3905 3-9-0 102.............................. AndreaAtzeni 6 99
(Roger Varian) *racd in mid-div: 5th at 1/2-way: rdn and nt qckn ent fnl f: kpt on same pce* **10/1**

7 *nk* **Lady Wannabe (IRE)**[22] 6480 3-9-0 101.............................. ColinKeane 4 99
(J A Stack, Ire) *led for 2f: trckd ldr in 2nd tl briefly on terms appr 2f out where hdd: nt qckn appr fnl f: wknd* **8/1**

8 *3* **Chablis (IRE)**[56] 5223 3-9-0 97.............................. SeamieHeffernan 5 93
(A P O'Brien, Ire) *racd in rr of mid-div: clsr in 4th 2f out: nt qckn ent fnl f and dropped to rr: nt hrd rdn fnl 100yds* **33/1**

2m 9.41s (-2.09) **Going Correction** +0.05s/f (Good)
WFA 3 from 4yo 6lb **8** Ran SP% **117.4**
Speed ratings: **110,108,108,107,106 106,106,103**
CSF £9.33 TOTE £4.00: £1.40, £1.10, £2.60; DF 7.60 Trifecta £59.50.
Owner H H Aga Khan **Bred** His Highness The Aga Khan's Studs S C **Trained** Curragh, Co Kildare

FOCUS
Chris Hayes kept it simple on the winner and it proved the winning of the race. It's been rated around the balance of the first four.

7243a DERRINSTOWN STUD FLYING FIVE STKS (GROUP 1) 5f

2:25 (2:26) 3-Y-0+

£205,405 (£68,468; £32,432; £14,414; £7,207; £3,603) **Stalls** Centre

RPR

1 **Fairyland (IRE)**[8] 6959 3-9-0 110.............................. RyanMoore 1 112
(A P O'Brien, Ire) *chsd ldrs far side: clsr appr fnl f: led 1f out: strly pressed cl home: hld on wl* **12/1**

2 *shd* **So Perfect (USA)**[8] 6959 3-9-0 108.............................. DonnachaO'Brien 7 112
(A P O'Brien, Ire) *chsd ldrs: rdn under 2f out: wnt 3rd ent fnl f: wnt 2nd fnl 150yds on strly clsng stages to press wnr* **12/1**

3 *1 ½* **Invincible Army (IRE)**[8] 6959 4-9-4 114..............(p) PJMcDonald 9 110
(James Tate) *chsd ldrs: 3rd at 1/2-way: edgd lft ent fnl f: kpt on wl clsng stages to hold 3rd* **12/1**

4 *½* **Soldier's Call**[23] 6423 3-9-3 114.............................. DanielTudhope 3 108
(Archie Watson) *trckd ldr in 2nd: rdn in 5th ent fnl f: kpt on wl into 4th fnl 100yds* **13/2**

5 *¾* **Soffia**[56] 5222 4-9-1 115.............................. DeclanMcDonogh 5 102
(Edward Lynam, Ire) *chsd ldrs: little keen early: pushed along and nt qckn over 1f out whn briefly short of room: kpt on same pce fnl f: burst blood vessel (vet said filly was found to have blood on the nose as a result of exercise induced pulmonary haemorrhage)* **13/8**[1]

6 *½* **Mabs Cross**[23] 6423 5-9-1 0.............................. GeraldMosse 11 100+
(Michael Dods) *bit slowly away: racd in mid-div: pushed along 1/2-way: no imp in rr appr fnl f: kpt on again clsng stages: nvr nrr* **4/1**[2]

7 *nk* **Caspian Prince (IRE)**[25] 6351 10-9-4 100..........(t) AlistairRawlinson 4 102
(Michael Appleby) *broke wl and led tl hdd 1f out: wknd fnl 150yds* **66/1**

8 *hd* **Hit The Bid**[17] 6648 5-9-4 109..............................(t) ChrisHayes 2 102
(D J Bunyan, Ire) *nvr bttr than mid-div towards far side: sme prog 1f out into 6th: no ex fnl 100yds* **14/1**

9 *nk* **Chessman (IRE)**[17] 6648 5-9-4 101..............................(t) WJLee 6 100
(Richard John O'Brien, Ire) *towards rr for most: rdn and no imp appr fnl f: kpt on wl clsng stages: nvr on terms* **50/1**

10 *nk* **Houtzen (AUS)**[44] 5611 5-9-1 109..............................(b) ColinKeane 12 96
(Martyn Meade) *bit slowly away and racd in rr for most: kpt on late: nvr nrr* **5/1**[3]

11 *nk* **True Mason**[29] 6252 3-9-3 95..............................(v) BenCurtis 10 98
(K R Burke) *racd in mid-div: pushed along 2f out: no imp appr fnl f: kpt on one pce* **66/1**

57.88s (-2.52) **Going Correction** +0.05s/f (Good)
WFA 3 from 4yo+ 1lb **11** Ran SP% **122.8**
Speed ratings: **114,113,111,110,109 108,108,107,107,106 106**
CSF £152.52 CT £1816.06 TOTE £11.00: £2.50, £3.60, £2.80; DF 84.60 Trifecta £975.00.
Owner Mrs E M Stockwell & Michael Tabor & Derrick Smith **Bred** Tally-Ho Stud **Trained** Cashel, Co Tipperary

FOCUS
One of those results really as two fillies well held in the best sprints all season filled the first two placings. The winner has been rated back to her 2yo best.

7244a MOYGLARE STUD STKS (GROUP 1) (FILLIES) 7f

3:00 (3:02) 2-Y-0

£205,405 (£68,468; £32,432; £14,414; £7,207; £3,603)

RPR

1 **Love (IRE)**[23] 6429 2-9-0 104.............................. RyanMoore 8 111
(A P O'Brien, Ire) *chsd ldrs disputing 3rd tl rdn into 2nd appr fnl f: led fnl 200yds: styd on wl clsng stages* **6/1**[3]

2 *¾* **Daahyeh**[65] 4883 2-9-0 107.............................. WilliamBuick 9 109
(Roger Varian) *racd in mid-div: clsr over 1f out: wnt 3rd fnl 200yds: styd on wl into 2nd fnl 50yds: nt rch wnr* **13/8**[1]

3 ¾ **So Wonderful (USA)**16 6689 2-9-0 101 SeamieHeffernan 4 107+
(A P O'Brien, Ire) *racd in mid-div: 5th at 1/2-way: clsr to dispute 4th ent fnl f where briefly short of room: kpt on wl into 3rd clsng stages where again n.m.r: nvr nrr (jockey said filly received some interference in the latter stages and was checked back onto the bridle and finished in that manner)* 16/1

4 ½ **Soul Search (IRE)**23 6429 2-9-0 103 ColinKeane 3 106
(G M Lyons, Ire) *trckd ldr in 2nd tl led under 2f out: strly pressed 1f out and sn hdd: kpt on wl tl no ex fnl 50yds in 4th: lost coordination clsng stages (jockey said filly lost her coordination behind and rolled around in the latter stages but finished her race with full coordination)* 9/1

5 shd **Under The Stars (IRE)**24 6374 2-9-0 103 PJMcDonald 5 106
(James Tate) *racd in rr of mid-div: rdn and no imp ent fnl f: styd on again fnl 150yds into 5th: nvr nrr* 9/1

6 ½ **Albigna (IRE)**79 4352 2-9-0 0 ShaneFoley 6 104
(Mrs John Harrington, Ire) *bit keen early and sn chsd ldrs disputing 3rd: pushed along over 2f out: nt qckn appr fnl f in 5th: kpt on same pce (jockey said filly shied away from the winner when being passed by her)* 9/4²

7 hd **Tango (IRE)**23 6429 2-9-0 99 (p¹) DonnachaO'Brien 2 104
(A P O'Brien, Ire) *led tl hdd under 2f out: wknd ins fnl f* 9/1

8 2 ¾ **Precious Moments (IRE)**24 6374 2-9-0 102 (t¹) MichaelHussey 1 97
(A P O'Brien, Ire) *a towards rr: pushed along under 2f out: no imp 1f out: kpt on one pce: nvr a factor* 25/1

9 2 **Assurance (IRE)** 2-9-0 0 KevinManning 7 91
(J S Bolger, Ire) *in rr thrght: detached under 2f out: kpt on ins fnl f: nvr on terms* 40/1

1m 24.28s (-0.72) **Going Correction** 0.0s/f (Good) **9** Ran SP% **125.3**
Speed ratings: **104,103,102,101,101 101,100,97,95**
CSF £17.66 CT £161.90 TOTE £7.30: £1.90, £1.10, £3.90; DF 21.00 Trifecta £232.50.
Owner Michael Tabor & Derrick Smith & Mrs John Magnier **Bred** Coolmore **Trained** Cashel, Co Tipperary

FOCUS
It might have been expected that one or two would prove too good for the winner, it was to her credit that this was not the case. The winner has been rated in line with her Silver Flash Stakes win.

7245a GOFFS VINCENT O'BRIEN NATIONAL STKS (GROUP 1) (ENTIRE COLTS & FILLIES) 7f
3:35 (3:36) 2-Y-O

£205,405 (£68,468; £32,432; £14,414; £7,207; £3,603)

RPR

1 **Pinatubo (IRE)**47 5520 2-9-3 120 WilliamBuick 6 128+
(Charlie Appleby) *settled jst off ldrs in 5th: clsr travelling wl to trck ldrs 3f out and led over 2f out: shkn up and qcknd clr over 1f out: styd on strly: impressive* 1/3¹

2 9 **Armory (IRE)**23 6430 2-9-3 110 RyanMoore 5 105
(A P O'Brien, Ire) *hld up in 6th: pushed along in 4th under 2f out: kpt on into 2nd fnl 150yds: sn no imp on impressive wnr* 10/3²

3 nk **Arizona (IRE)**28 6264 2-9-3 108 DonnachaO'Brien 3 104
(A P O'Brien, Ire) *trckd ldrs in 3rd: 2nd at 1/2-way: rdn 2f out and sn no match for wnr: kpt on same pce tl dropped to 3rd fnl 150yds* 5/1³

4 2 ¼ **Monoski (USA)**25 6356 2-9-3 93 JoeFanning 7 98
(Mark Johnston) *trckd early ldrs on outer in 4th: led 1/2-way tl hdd over 2f out: no ex in 4th ent fnl f: kpt on same pce* 50/1

5 2 ¼ **Iberia (IRE)**23 6430 2-9-3 0 SeamieHeffernan 8 92
(A P O'Brien, Ire) *racd towards rr: pushed along over 2f out: kpt on one pce fnl f: nvr on terms* 20/1

6 hd **Geometrical (IRE)**23 6430 2-9-3 105 KevinManning 2 92
(J S Bolger, Ire) *sn led: hdd 1/2-way: wknd under 2f out* 16/1

7 nk **Roman Turbo (IRE)**23 6430 2-9-3 104 RonanWhelan 4 91
(M Halford, Ire) *racd in rr: pushed along over 2f out: kpt on one pce fr over 1f out: nvr on terms* 16/1

8 7 ½ **Toronto (IRE)**23 6430 2-9-3 96 MichaelHussey 1 71
(A P O'Brien, Ire) *trckd ldrs on inner in 2nd: 4th at 1/2-way: sn pushed along: wknd in rr 2f out* 50/1

1m 21.82s (-3.18) **Going Correction** 0.0s/f (Good) **8** Ran SP% **135.2**
Speed ratings: **116,105,105,102,100 100,99,91**
CSF £2.67 CT £4.00 TOTE £1.20: £1.02, £1.10, £1.20; DF 2.60 Trifecta £3.80.
Owner Godolphin **Bred** Godolphin **Trained** Newmarket, Suffolk

FOCUS
A brilliant winner remains unbeaten in what might just have been the best performance by a juvenile since Arazi.

7246a COMER GROUP INTERNATIONAL IRISH ST. LEGER (GROUP 1) 1m 6f
4:10 (4:11) 3-Y-O+

£308,108 (£102,702; £48,648; £21,621; £10,810; £5,405)

RPR

1 **Search For A Song (IRE)**24 6378 3-8-11 105 ChrisHayes 8 118
(D K Weld, Ire) *racd in rr of mid-div: keen and gd hdwy on outer 1m out and sn led: travelled wl over 2f out and extended ld appr fnl f: styd on strly* 10/1

2 2 ¼ **Kew Gardens (IRE)**107 3314 4-9-9 119 RyanMoore 9 116+
(A P O'Brien, Ire) *racd towards rr: swtchd lft in 8th 3f out: plenty to do on outer in 8th appr fnl f: styd on strly into 2nd cl home: nt trble wnr* 7/2²

3 1 ½ **Southern France (IRE)**30 6191 4-9-9 113 SeamieHeffernan 5 114
(A P O'Brien, Ire) *chsd early ldrs in 3rd: mid-div at 1/2-way: rdn over 2f out: kpt on wl into 2nd fnl 100yds: dropped to 3rd cl home* 9/1

4 hd **Cross Counter**47 5522 4-9-9 118 WilliamBuick 7 114
(Charlie Appleby) *racd in mid-div: t.k.h: pushed along 3f out: no imp under 2f out: kpt on wl ins fnl f into 4th cl home: nvr nrr* 6/4¹

5 shd **Master Of Reality (IRE)**30 6191 4-9-9 118 AndreaAtzeni 3 114
(Joseph Patrick O'Brien, Ire) *led tl hdd over 7f out: rdn in 2nd over 2f out and no imp in 2nd over 1f out: no ex fnl 100yds and wknd clsng stages* 14/1

6 1 ½ **Latrobe (IRE)**38 5874 4-9-9 112 DonnachaO'Brien 2 111
(Joseph Patrick O'Brien, Ire) *trckd ldr in 2nd: 3rd at 1/2-way: rdn over 2f out: no imp appr fnl f: kpt on one pce* 7/1³

7 ¾ **Twilight Payment (IRE)**79 4351 6-9-9 113 (p) KevinManning 4 110
(Joseph Patrick O'Brien, Ire) *chsd ldrs on inner in 4th: rdn over 2f out: no imp appr fnl f: wknd* 14/1

8 1 ½ **Cypress Creek (IRE)**87 4015 4-9-9 103 (b¹) EmmetMcNamara 1 108
(A P O'Brien, Ire) *racd in rr of mid-div: towards rr at 1/2-way: rdn and detached 2f out: kpt on ins fnl f: nvr on terms* 100/1

9 nk **Salouen (IRE)**50 5414 5-9-9 115 JimCrowley 10 108
(Sylvester Kirk) *a towards rr: brief hdwy under 2f out on outer: no imp appr fnl f* 14/1

10 nk **Capri (IRE)**30 6191 5-9-9 111 PBBeggy 6 107
(A P O'Brien, Ire) *racd in mid-div: pushed along on inner over 2f out and clsr: no imp whn short of room appr fnl f: wknd to rr clsng stages* 20/1

3m 3.24s (-4.66) **Going Correction** +0.05s/f (Good)
WFA 3 from 4yo+ 9lb **10** Ran SP% **119.6**
Speed ratings: **115,113,112,112,112 111,111,110,110,110**
CSF £46.20 CT £337.14 TOTE £10.60: £2.40, £1.50, £2.50; DF 59.50 Trifecta £544.50.
Owner Moyglare Stud Farm **Bred** Moyglare Stud Farm Ltd **Trained** Curragh, Co Kildare

FOCUS
Easily a career best performance from the winner and she looks like she has what it takes to get to the top of the staying tree. It's been rated around the balance of the third, sixth, seventh and eighth.

7247a TATTERSALLS IRELAND SUPER AUCTION SALE STKS (PLUS 10 RACE) 6f 63y
5:25 (5:27) 2-Y-O

£132,882 (£51,801; £24,774; £15,765; £9,009; £4,504) **Stalls Centre**

RPR

1 **Stone Circle (IRE)**45 5587 2-9-5 0 AndreaAtzeni 14 94
(Michael Bell) *chsd ldrs in centre of trck: gd hdwy appr fnl f: wnt 4th ins fnl f: pressed ldr in 2nd fnl 100yds: kpt on best to ld cl home* 12/1

2 hd **Maystar (IRE)**20 6548 2-9-3 0 HollieDoyle 4 91
(Archie Watson) *trckd ldr in 2nd of far side gp tl led under 2f out: strly pressed fnl 100yds: hdd cl home* 14/1

3 nk **Hamish Macbeth**23 6415 2-9-3 0 RyanMoore 26 93
(Hugo Palmer) *racd in rr of mid-div on nr side: hdwy over 1f out: wnt 7th ent fnl f: styd on wl into 3rd cl home: nvr nrr* 9/4²

4 ½ **Prince Of Naples (IRE)**16 6690 2-9-3 92 (t) RobbieColgan 17 91
(Ms Sheila Lavery, Ire) *chsd ldrs nr side: clsr travelling wl 2f out: rdn to press ldr in 2nd ent fnl f: no imp in 3rd fnl 100yds: dropped to 4th cl home* 16/1

5 ½ **Milltown Star**35 6002 2-8-13 0 RonanWhelan 23 84+
(Mick Channon) *racd in mid-div nr side: rdn over 2f out: chsd ldrs ent fnl f: styd on wl into 5th cl home: nvr nrr* 8/1³

6 shd **Champers Elysees (IRE)**13 6813 2-8-8 0 ShaneFoley 6 78
(J P Murtagh, Ire) *racd in mid-div far side: rdn clsr to chse ldrs over 1f out: kpt on fnl f: no ex ins fnl 100yds* 12/1

7 1 ½ **Odyssey Girl (IRE)**22 6442 2-8-8 0 DavidEgan 9 74
(Richard Spencer) *led far side gp tl hdd under 2f out: no imp fnl 150yd: wknd* 20/1

8 nse **Red Lark (IRE)**41 5755 2-8-6 0 NGMcCullagh 8 72
(J P Murtagh, Ire) *chsd ldrs far side: clsr in 5th over 1f out: no imp fnl 150yds* 50/1

9 2 ¾ **Commit No Nuisance (IRE)**43 5676 2-8-11 0 ChrisHayes 7 69
(William Knight) *racd towards rr of far side gp: rdn under 2f out: kpt on ins fnl f: nvr on terms* 50/1

10 ½ **Coastal Mist (IRE)**33 6053 2-9-1 0 JasonHart 19 71
(John Quinn) *disp nr side gp to 1/2-way: nt qckn appr fnl f: sn one pce* 33/1

11 hd **Last Opportunity (IRE)**31 6133 2-9-3 0 ColinKeane 10 73
(G M Lyons, Ire) *chsd ldrs far side: rdn 2f out: no imp appr fnl f: kpt on one pce* 7/4¹

12 2 **Western Hero (IRE)**23 6424 2-9-3 0 SamJames 21 67
(Kevin Ryan) *racd in rr of mid-div nr side: pushed along towards rr over 2f out: kpt on ins fnl f: nvr nrr* 25/1

13 ¾ **Sir Dotti (IRE)**18 6614 2-8-13 0 (t) RossCoakley 20 61
(John C McConnell, Ire) *racd towards rr nr side: rdn over 2f out: kpt on fr over 1f out: nvr on terms* 100/1

14 nk **Lexington Warfare (IRE)**40 5764 2-9-3 0 (v¹) SeanDavis 2 64
(Richard Fahey) *racd in mid-div far side: briefly clsr on far rails over 1f out: sn no imp* 50/1

15 nk **Bendy Spirit (IRE)**139 2191 2-8-11 0 (p¹) GaryHalpin 3 57
(Richard Fahey) *racd in mid-div far side: rdn clsr 2f out: no imp 1f out: sn one pce* 33/1

16 hd **Ocasio Cortez (IRE)**12 6833 2-8-10 0 (b) KevinManning 22 56
(Richard Hannon) *chsd ldrs nr side: rdn and no imp over 1f out: sn one pce* 25/1

17 ¾ **Half Nutz (IRE)**15 6740 2-8-11 61 RobbieDowney 13 54
(Ms Sheila Lavery, Ire) *racd in mid-div nr side: clsr in centre of trck 2f out: sn rdn and no imp* 66/1

18 ½ **Windham Belle (IRE)**14 6763 2-8-8 82 NathanCrosse 24 50
(W McCreery, Ire) *a in rr of mid-div nr side: no imp over 1f out* 25/1

19 ½ **Rare Kylla (IRE)**6 7036 2-8-8 0 BenCoen 25 48
(Peter Fahey, Ire) *racd in rr of nr side gp: rdn 2f out: sn no imp* 66/1

20 hd **Strawberry Morn (IRE)**29 6233 2-8-6 0 LeighRoche 11 46
(W McCreery, Ire) *nvr bttr than rr of mid-div: no imp under 2f out* 66/1

21 1 **Simply True (IRE)**15 6741 2-9-1 72 WJLee 1 52
(A Oliver, Ire) *trckd ldrs far side: rdn 2f out: no imp over 1f out: wknd* 50/1

22 6 **Our Patron Saint (IRE)**15 6740 2-8-11 0 ConorMaxwell 5 31
(Sarah Dawson, Ire) *chsd ldrs far side to 1/2-way: no imp towards rr under 2f out: eased clsng stages* 100/1

23 1 ¾ **Tyler Durden (IRE)**22 6457 2-8-13 0 DeclanMcDonogh 15 28
(Richard Spencer) *disp nr side gp to 1/2-way: nt qckn under 2f out: sn wknd: eased clsng stages* 50/1

24 10 **In A Bubble (IRE)**22 6478 2-8-8 60 (p¹) ConorHoban 18
(A Oliver, Ire) *racd in mid-div nr side: rdn 1/2-way: dropped towards rr 2f out: no ex: eased ins fnl f* 100/1

25 1 ¾ **Depardieu**23 6426 2-8-11 0 RoryCleary 16
(M C Grassick, Ire) *racd towards rr nr side: rdn 1/2-way: no imp towards rr under 2f out: eased ins fnl f* 100/1

26 3 ¾ **Upstate New York (IRE)**30 6167 2-9-3 0 (v¹) DanielTudhope 12
(Richard Fahey) *racd in mid-div far side: t.k.h: no imp 2f out: eased over 1f out (jockey said he had difficulty steering colt, possibly caused by the headgear fitted)* 25/1

1m 17.23s (-0.47) **Going Correction** 0.0s/f (Good) **26** Ran SP% **150.4**
Speed ratings: **103,102,102,101,101 100,98,98,95,94 94,91,90,90,89 89,88,87,87,86 85,77,75,61,59 54**
CSF £178.53 TOTE £19.50: £5.30, £5.10, £1.60; DF 265.40 Trifecta £1259.60.
Owner The Fitzrovians 3 **Bred** Stephen Curran **Trained** Newmarket, Suffolk
■ Stewards' Enquiry : Andrea Atzeni caution: careless riding
Hollie Doyle caution: careless riding

FOCUS
A race dominated by the visitors although there were few high-class performers in the race. It's been rated as an up-to-scratch renewal.

7248 - (Foreign Racing) - See Raceform Interactive

4157 **DORTMUND** (R-H)

Sunday, September 15

OFFICIAL GOING: Turf: good

7249a **135TH DEUTSCHES ST LEGER (GROUP 3) (3YO+) (TURF)** **1m 6f**
3:50 3-Y-O+ **£28,828** (£10,810; £5,405; £2,702; £1,801)

RPR

1 **Ispolini**[121] 2807 4-9-6 0........................ JamesDoyle 1 106
(Charlie Appleby) *mid-div on inner: nudged along and swtchd to outer 2 1/2f out: sn rdn: led ent fnl f: hld on in clsng stages* **7/10**[1]

2 *nk* **Djukon**[28] 3-8-11 0........................ AndraschStarke 7 107
(Andreas Suborics, Germany) *hld up towards rr: shkn up 3f out: r.o wl ins fnl f: jst failed* **31/5**[2]

3 *hd* **Moonshiner (GER)**[17] 6-9-6 0........................(p) FilipMinarik 10 105
(Jean-Pierre Carvalho, Germany) *slowly away and racd in fnl pair: effrt and gd hdwy towards inner over 2f out: wnt 2nd ins fnl 1/2f: dropped to 3rd cl home* **40/1**

4 *1 1/4* **Oriental Eagle (GER)**[42] 5719 5-9-6 0........................ RobertHavlin 13 103
(J Hirschberger, Germany) *sn led: rdn to assert over 2f out: hdd 1 1/2f out: no ex ins fnl f* **237/10**

5 *1* **Nacida (GER)**[36] 5-9-3 0........................ StephenHellyn 4 99
(Yasmin Almenrader, Germany) *towards rr: rdn to chal 2 1/2f out: sme prog ins fnl f: nt rch ldrs* **64/1**

6 *1 1/2* **Ernesto (GER)**[17] 4-9-6 0........................ MartinSeidl 12 100
(Markus Klug, Germany) *mid-div on outer: rdn ent st: kpt on: mod prog ins fnl f* **42/1**

7 *3/4* **Accon (GER)**[14] 6771 3-8-11 0........................ JiriPalik 9 101
(Markus Klug, Germany) *chsd ldng pair on outer: pushed along wl over 3f out: sn rdn: lost position and one pce thereafter* **116/10**

8 *1/2* **Power Euro (IRE)**[17] 7-9-6 0........................ LukasDelozier 11 98
(Henk Grewe, Germany) *towards rr: rdn and wdst of all over 2f out: no imp* **96/10**

9 *3* **Sweet Man**[21] 4-9-6 0........................(p) AdriedeVries 5 94
(J Hirschberger, Germany) *mid-div on inner: shkn up 2 1/2f out: no imp* **28/1**

10 *3/4* **Nikkei (GER)**[42] 5719 4-9-6 0........................ DennisSchiergen 2 93
(P Schiergen, Germany) *cl up on inner: asked for effrt 3f out: kpt on one pce: wknd ins fnl f* **41/1**

11 *1 1/2* **Magical Touch**[36] 4-9-3 0........................ JulienGuillochon 6 88
(H-A Pantall, France) *chsd ldr in 2nd: rdn to chal ins fnl 2f: wknd sn after* **44/5**[3]

12 *10* **Abadan**[28] 6263 5-9-3 0........................(p) MirkoSanna 3 74
(Henk Grewe, Germany) *a in rr: nvr involved* **79/1**

13 *10* **Secret Potion (GER)**[24] 6385 3-8-11 0........................(p) ClementLecoeuvre 8 65
(Henk Grewe, Germany) *mid-div: no imp whn rdn over 2f out: sn wknd: eased over 1 1/2f out* **50/1**

2m 57.08s (-8.42) **13 Ran SP% 119.7**
WFA 3 from 4yo+ 9lb
PARI-MUTUEL (all including 1 euro stake): WIN 1.7 PLACE: 1.8, 2.0, 5.8; SF: 9.5.
Owner Godolphin **Bred** Newsells Park Stud **Trained** Newmarket, Suffolk

HANOVER (L-H)

Sunday, September 15

OFFICIAL GOING: Turf: good

7250a **GROSSER PREIS DER BURCKHARDT METALL GLAS GMBH (LISTED RACE) (3YO+ FILLIES & MARES) (TURF)** **1m**
2:25 3-Y-O+ **£12,612** (£5,855; £2,702; £1,351)

RPR

1 **Firebird Song (IRE)**[30] 3-8-9 0........................ SoufianeSaadi 3 97
(H-A Pantall, France) *mid-div on inner: pushed along and hdwy over 2f out: sn rdn and led: moved across to nr side rail fnl f: kpt on wl* **6/4**[1]

2 *2* **Best On Stage (GER)**[18] 3-8-9 0........................(b) MaximPecheur 4 92
(P Schiergen, Germany) **26/5**[3]

3 *nk* **Nayala**[56] 5227 3-8-9 0........................ JozefBojko 7 91
(A Wohler, Germany) **115/10**

4 *1 1/4* **Clear For Take Off**[35] 6006 5-9-3 0........................ WladimirPanov 5 92
(D Moser, Germany) **36/5**

5 *2 1/4* **Global Cloud (GER)**[70] 3-8-9 0........................ BayarsaikhanGanbat 9 83
(R Dzubasz, Germany) **122/10**

6 *hd* **Reaction (GER)**[35] 3-8-9 0........................ RenePiechulek 8 83
(Eva Fabianova, Germany) **161/10**

7 *1* **Cabarita (GER)**[28] 6270 4-9-0 0........................ MarcoCasamento 6 82
(H-J Groschel, Germany) **179/10**

8 *1 1/4* **Epouville (FR)**[112] 4-9-0 0........................(b) AntoineHamelin 10 79
(F Vermeulen, France) **47/10**[2]

9 *8* **Al Nafoorah**[450] 4076 5-9-0 0........................ MichaelCadeddu 2 60
(Michael Wigham) *racd keenly: sn disp ld on outer: rdn appr fnl 2f: no imp and wknd* **166/10**

1m 38.11s **9 Ran SP% 118.3**
WFA 3 from 4yo+ 5lb
PARI-MUTUEL (all including 1 euro stake): WIN 2.5 PLACE: 1.3, 1.8, 2.3; SF: 8.3.
Owner Godolphin SNC **Bred** Godolphin **Trained** France

7136 **LONGCHAMP** (R-H)

Sunday, September 15

OFFICIAL GOING: Turf: good

7251a **QATAR PRIX FOY (GROUP 2) (4YO+) (GRANDE COURSE) (TURF)** **1m 4f**
1:35 4-Y-O+ **£66,756** (£25,765; £12,297; £8,198; £4,099)

RPR

1 **Waldgeist**[50] 5414 5-9-2 0........................ Pierre-CharlesBoudot 2 118+
(A Fabre, France) *trckd ldr: shkn up to chal jst under 2f out: led over 1f out: r.o strly under hands and heels riding ins fnl f: readily* **2/5**[1]

2 *2* **Way To Paris**[63] 4962 6-9-2 0........................ CristianDemuro 4 114
(Andrea Marcialis, France) *in rr: pushed along over 2f out: briefly short of racing room and had to wait for gap 1 1/2f out: drvn ins fnl f: kpt on wl: no ch w wnr* **31/5**[3]

3 *1* **Kiseki (JPN)**[84] 4158 5-9-2 0........................ ChristopheSoumillon 3 112
(Katsuhiko Sumii, Japan) *led: asked to qckn 2f out: sn pressed 1 1/2f out: hdd over 1f out: fdd ins fnl f: no ex* **13/5**[2]

4 *hd* **Silverwave (FR)**[84] 4159 7-9-2 0........................ MaximeGuyon 1 112
(F Vermeulen, France) *settled in 3rd: angled out and pushed along over 2f out: limited rspnse: rdn over 1f out: unable qck: kpt on same pce ins fnl f* **11/1**

2m 27.57s (-2.83) **Going Correction** +0.175s/f (Good) **4 Ran SP% 121.4**
Speed ratings: **116,114,114,113**
PARI-MUTUEL (all including 1 euro stake): WIN 1.40; SF 4.80.
Owner Gestut Ammerland & Newsells Park **Bred** The Waldlerche Partnership **Trained** Chantilly, France

FOCUS
About as uncompetitive as it can get for an Arc trial and the class act of the race won readily. The pace was steady.

7252a **QATAR PRIX VERMEILLE (GROUP 1) (3YO+ FILLIES & MARES) (GRANDE COURSE) (TURF)** **1m 4f**
2:50 3-Y-O+ **£308,864** (£123,567; £61,783; £30,864; £15,459)

RPR

1 **Star Catcher**[57] 5208 3-8-9 0........................ FrankieDettori 1 112+
(John Gosden) *mde all: rdn 2f out: kpt on wl and a doing enough ins fnl f* **11/10**[1]

2 *3/4* **Musis Amica (IRE)**[28] 6265 4-9-3 0........................ MickaelBarzalona 8 110+
(A Fabre, France) *hld up in rr: rdn and angled out wd appr fnl 2f: r.o wl: nt rch wnr fnl f* **12/1**

3 *1* **Ligne D'Or**[28] 6263 4-9-3 0........................ VincentCheminaud 4 108
(A Fabre, France) *towards rr: rdn and n.m.r 2f out: hdwy between horses ins fnl f: wnt 3rd cl home* **48/1**

4 *snk* **Villa Marina**[50] 5470 3-8-9 0........................ OlivierPeslier 7 109
(C Laffon-Parias, France) *towards rr on outer: effrt over 2f out: prog to go 3rd appr fnl f: kpt on wout chalng wnr: dropped to 4th cl home* **20/1**

5 *hd* **Fleeting (IRE)**[36] 5978 3-8-9 0........................ WayneLordan 6 109
(A P O'Brien, Ire) *prom on outer: shkn up to briefly go 2nd appr fnl 2f: wknd ins fnl f* **17/2**

6 *2 1/2* **Channel (IRE)**[45] 5586 3-8-9 0........................ Pierre-CharlesBoudot 3 105
(F-H Graffard, France) *mid-div: rdn and moved across to rail 2f out: no imp* **8/1**

7 *1 1/4* **Anapurna**[107] 3316 3-8-9 0........................ OisinMurphy 2 103
(John Gosden) *promiment on inner: effrt whn nt clr run 2f out: one pce thereafter* **19/5**[2]

8 *1 1/4* **Pink Dogwood (IRE)**[57] 5208 3-8-9 0........................ ChristopheSoumillon 5 101
(A P O'Brien, Ire) *chsd ldr on inner: shkn up and ev ch appr fnl 2f: no imp: wknd* **79/10**[3]

9 *15* **Tamniah (FR)**[35] 6003 3-8-9 0........................ MaximeGuyon 9 77
(A Fabre, France) *trckd ldr on outer: u.p over 3f out: sn gng bkwards ins fnl 2f: eased sn after* **29/1**

2m 27.63s (-2.77) **Going Correction** +0.175s/f (Good)
WFA 3 from 4yo 8lb **9 Ran SP% 119.2**
Speed ratings: **116,115,114,114,114 112,112,111,101**
PARI-MUTUEL (all including 1 euro stake): WIN 2.10; PLACE 1.30, 2.80, 6.00; DF 15.10.
Owner A E Oppenheimer **Bred** Hascombe And Valiant Studs **Trained** Newmarket, Suffolk

FOCUS
Often a top-quality event, it played out predictably with the well-backed favourite dominating from the front.

7253a **QATAR PRIX NIEL (GROUP 2) (3YO) (GRANDE COURSE) (TURF)** **1m 4f**
3:25 3-Y-O **£66,756** (£25,765; £12,297; £8,198; £4,099)

RPR

1 **Sottsass (FR)**[105] 3390 3-9-2 0........................ CristianDemuro 1 120+
(J-C Rouget, France) *racd in 3rd early: sltly outpcd and pushed along 3f out: dropped to rr 2f out: short of racing room whn effrt on inner 1 1/2f out: drvn whn gap opened ins fnl f: picked up wl to ld fnl 75yds* **1/2**[1]

2 *1 1/4* **Mutamakina**[29] 6250 3-8-13 0........................ OlivierPeslier 4 111
(C Laffon-Parias, France) *cl up: pushed along to chse ldr jst under 2f out: rdn over 1f out: pressed ldr jst ins fnl f: kpt on: nt match pce of eventual wnr fnl 75yds* **51/10**[3]

3 *snk* **Mohawk (IRE)**[42] 5721 3-9-2 0........................ WayneLordan 2 114+
(A P O'Brien, Ire) *in rr: pushed along over 2 1/2f out: rdn 1 1/2f out: prog on outer ins fnl f: r.o wl to snatch 3rd cl home* **73/10**

4 *3/4* **Veronesi (FR)**[94] 3789 3-9-2 0........................ HugoJourniac 3 113
(J-C Rouget, France) *led: 6 l clr over 1/2-way: reduced advantage whn asked to qckn 2f out: rdn over 1f out: hrd pressed jst ins fnl f: hdd fnl 75yds: no ex* **17/1**

5 *1 1/2* **Quest The Moon (GER)**[49] 5483 3-9-2 0........................ Pierre-CharlesBoudot 5 110
(Frau S Steinberg, Germany) *racd in fnl pair: sme prog into 3rd bef 1/2-way: asked for effrt jst under 2f out: unable qck w ldrs ins fnl f: kpt on same pce* **7/2**[2]

2m 27.46s (-2.94) **Going Correction** +0.175s/f (Good) **5 Ran SP% 122.9**
Speed ratings: **116,115,115,114,113**
PARI-MUTUEL (all including 1 euro stake): WIN 1.50; PLACE 1.10, 1.20; SF 3.80.
Owner White Birch Farm **Bred** Ecurie Des Monceaux **Trained** Pau, France

FOCUS
A typical trial with little pace on, but the red-hot favourite still proved much the best, asserting late on to win with plenty in hand.

7254a **QATAR PRIX DU PETIT COUVERT (GROUP 3) (3YO+) (SPRINT COURSE) (TURF)** **5f (S)**
4:00 3-Y-O+ **£36,036** (£14,414; £10,810; £7,207; £3,603)

RPR

1 **Glass Slippers**[42] 5714 3-8-9 0........................ TomEaves 8 113
(Kevin Ryan) *s.i.s: outpcd in rr: swtchd to outer and pushed along over 2f out: prog fr 1 1/2f out: r.o strly u.p: led last strides* **149/10**

2 *snk* **Shades Of Blue (IRE)**[28] 6257 3-8-9 0........................ HectorCrouch 9 112
(Clive Cox) *prom: pushed along to dispute ld jst under 2f out: led over 1f out: hrd pressed u.p ins fnl f: hdd last strides* **39/10**[2]

3 *1 1/2* **Gold Vibe (IRE)**[50] 5471 6-9-0 0........................(b) CristianDemuro 11 111
(P Bary, France) *towards rr on outer: pushed along between rivals 2f out: sn rdn: prog to chse ldr over 1f out: kpt on but nt match pce of front pair* **10/1**

4 1 1/2 **Sestilio Jet (FR)**[105] 3388 4-9-3 0.................................... FrankieDettori 7 109
(Andrea Marcialis, France) *midfield: pushed along and effrt 2f out: drvn over 1f out: r.o into clr 4th ins fnl f: nvr gng pce to threaten* **21/10**[1]
5 1 1/4 **Comedia Eria (FR)**[21] 6520 7-8-10 0.................................... MaximeGuyon 6 97
(P Monfort, France) *racd in fnl pair: pushed along between horses jst under 2f out: rdn over 1f out: kpt on ins fnl f but nvr in contention* **24/1**
6 1 **Buonasera (IRE)**[7] 4-9-0 0.................................... MirkoSanna 1 97
(P L Giannotti, Italy) *led on inner: tried to qckn 2f out: hrd pressed u.p 1 1/2f out: hdd over 1f out: grad wknd ins fnl f* **84/1**
7 hd **Stake Acclaim (IRE)**[21] 6520 7-9-0 0.................. Pierre-CharlesBoudot 5 97
(Dean Ivory) *prom: asked to chse ldr 2f out: unable qck and sn struggling: fdd ins fnl f* **5/1**[3]
8 1 1/4 **Forza Capitano (FR)**[83] 4205 4-9-0 0.................. VincentCheminaud 4 92
(H-A Pantall, France) *racd in fnl quartet: sltly hmpd whn pushed along 2f out: no rspnse whn drvn 1 1/2f out: kpt on same pce ins fnl f* **10/1**
9 hd **Poetry**[21] 6520 3-8-9 0.................................... MickaelBarzalona 12 87
(Michael Bell) *midfield on outer: struggling to go pce over 2f out: no imp whn rdn over 1 1/2f out: btn ent fnl f* **10/1**
10 3/4 **Hackney Road**[31] 6-8-10 0..............(p) Jose-LuisBorregoGarcia-Penue 2 85
(Fernando Perez-Gonzalez, Spain) *midfield on inner: outpcd and bustled along over 1/2-way: rdn jst under 2f out: sn btn* **46/1**
11 1 3/4 **Mubaalegh**[35] 6006 5-9-0 0.................................... RonanThomas 10 82
(J E Hammond, France) *cl up early: asked for effrt over 1/2-way: nt qckn and dropped towards rr over 1f out: allowed to fin in own time* **26/1**
12 5 **Samskara (IRE)**[53] 3-8-9 0.................................... OlivierPeslier 3 60
(C Laffon-Parias, France) *slowly away: sn racing in midfield: struggling to go pce over 2 1/2f out: dropped to rr 1 1/2f out: eased ins fnl f* **17/1**

55.77s (-0.53) **Going Correction** +0.175s/f (Good)
WFA 3 from 4yo+ 1lb 12 Ran SP% **119.5**
Speed ratings: **111,110,108,105,103 102,102,100,99,98 95,87**
PARI-MUTUEL (all including 1 euro stake): WIN 15.90; PLACE 3.90, 2.10, 3.00; DF 25.70.
Owner Bearstone Stud Limited **Bred** Bearstone Stud Ltd **Trained** Hambleton, N Yorks

FOCUS
The British runners came to the fore in this Group 3 sprint, a trial for the Prix de l'Abbaye.

7255a QATAR PRIX DU PIN (GROUP 3) (3YO+) (NEW COURSE: 2ND POST) (TURF) 7f
4:35 3-Y-O+ **£36,036** (£14,414; £10,810; £7,207; £3,603)

RPR
1 **City Light (FR)**[44] 5-9-2 0.................................... ChristopheSoumillon 5 117+
(S Wattel, France) *racd a little keenly in midfield: angled out and shkn up over 1f out: readily qcknd up to ld jst ins fnl f: v readily* **5/2**[1]
2 1 1/2 **Graignes (FR)**[35] 6004 3-8-13 0.................................... CristianDemuro 2 112+
(Y Barberot, France) *hld up towards rr on inner: prog between rivals fr 2f out: pushed along to chse eventual wnr over 1f out: kpt on wl into 2nd cl home* **15/2**
3 1/2 **Larchmont Lad (IRE)**[21] 6508 5-9-2 0.................................... CharlesBishop 4 112
(Joseph Tuite) *midfield: pushed along on outer over 2f out: rdn to chal over 1f out: led briefly ent fnl f: sn hdd: lost 2nd cl home* **12/1**
4 nk **Marianafoot (FR)**[73] 4581 4-9-2 0.................................... MickaelBarzalona 9 111
(J Reynier, France) *racd keenly: prom: asked for effrt jst under 2f out: drvn to chal over 1f out: unable qck w ldrs ins fnl f: kpt on same pce clsng stages* **57/10**[2]
5 shd **Momkin (IRE)**[21] 6508 3-8-13 0....................................(b) OisinMurphy 1 110
(Roger Charlton) *midfield on inner: pushed along 2f out: rdn over 1f out: kpt on wl ins fnl f but nvr threatened* **67/10**[3]
6 2 1/2 **Stunning Spirit**[21] 5-9-2 0.................................... AurelienLemaitre 10 104
(F Head, France) *racd in fnl trio: struggling to go pce and pushed along over 2f out: rdn 1 1/2f out: limited rspnse and kpt on same pce ins fnl f: nvr involved* **71/10**
7 snk **Lilly Kafeine (FR)**[21] 5-8-13 0.................................... FrankieDettori 12 101
(A Schutz, France) *s.i.s: in rr: outpcd and pushed along on outer over 2f out: sn rdn: edgd rt u.p: sme modest prog ins fnl f: nvr a factor* **17/1**
8 hd **Bravo Sierra**[42] 5714 3-8-9 0.................................... VincentCheminaud 8 98
(A Fabre, France) *trckd ldr: pushed along to chal jst under 2f out: sn drvn: unable qck w ldrs: one pce clsng stages* **15/1**
9 3 1/2 **Red Torch (FR)**[35] 6006 4-9-2 0.................................... OlivierPeslier 3 94
(H-A Pantall, France) *midfield: short-lived effrt on inner jst under 2f out: no imp and wknd ins fnl f* **39/1**
10 3 1/2 **Tour To Paris (FR)**[22] 4-9-2 0.................................... MaximeGuyon 11 84
(Mme Pia Brandt, France) *led: tried to qckn whn pressed jst under 2f out: hdd over 1f out: sn eased* **69/10**
11 6 **Fas (IRE)**[21] 5-9-2 0....................................(b) TheoBachelot 7 68
(Mme Pia Brandt, France) *a towards rr: effrt jst under 2f out: no imp and eased ins fnl f* **26/1**

1m 18.37s (-2.33) **Going Correction** +0.175s/f (Good)
WFA 3 from 4yo+ 4lb 11 Ran SP% **119.0**
Speed ratings: **115,113,112,112,112 109,109,109,105,101 94**
PARI-MUTUEL (all including 1 euro stake): WIN 3.50; PLACE 1.70, 2.40, 3.70; DF 16.00.
Owner Ecurie Jean-Louis Bouchard **Bred** Sarl Jedburgh Stud & Mme I Corbani **Trained** France

FOCUS
Useful Group 3 form, with the right horses coming to the fore. It's been rated around the balance of the first eight.

7256a - 7266a (Foreign Racing) - See Raceform Interactive

7224 WOODBINE (L-H)
Sunday, September 15

OFFICIAL GOING: Turf: yielding

7267a NATALMA STKS (GRADE 1) (2YO FILLIES) (TURF) 1m (T)
10:49 2-Y-O

£86,206 (£28,735; £15,804; £7,183; £2,873; £1,436)

RPR
1 **Abscond (USA)**[32] 2-8-9 0.................................... IradOrtizJr 7 99
(Eddie Kenneally, U.S.A) *broke wl but rt: pressed ldr: sustained chal fr 2f out: led narrowly 1 1/2f out: sn hdd: rallied gamely: won on the nod* **19/2**
2 nse **Walk In Marrakesh (IRE)**[29] 6248 2-8-9 0.................................... JamieSpencer 1 99
(Mark Johnston) *led: pressed thrght: hdd narrowly 1 1/2f out: sn ralled to regain ld: styd on gamely u.p: hdd post* **19/4**[2]
3 nk **Fair Maiden (USA)**[29] 2-8-9 0.................................... FlavienPrat 3 98
(Eoin Harty, U.S.A) *chsd ldrs: strly rdn to chal ins fnl 1 1/2f: styd on u.p: no ex cl home* **3/5**[1]
4 1 **Diamond Sparkles (USA)**[51] 5387 2-8-9 0.................................... TylerGaffalione 2 96
(Mark Casse, Canada) *s.i.s: settled in rr: rdn and hdwy 2f out: styd on fnl f: nvr quite on terms* **126/10**
5 nse **Secret Stash (IRE)**[74] 4524 2-8-9 0.................................... JohnRVelazquez 6 96
(Mark Casse, Canada) *racd in fnl trio: drvn and styd on last 1 1/2f: nvr able to chal* **97/20**[3]
6 3 3/4 **Saratoga Vision (USA)**[29] 2-8-9 0....................................(b) JeffreylanAlderson 5 87
(Alexander P Patykewich, Canada) *prom: drvn but no imp on front three fr 1 1/2f out: one pce fnl f* **66/1**
7 1 1/4 **Runway Dreamer (USA)**[22] 2-8-9 0.................................... LuisContreras 4 85
(Josie Carroll, Canada) *settled in fnl trio: rdn and short-lived effrt on rail 2f out: wl hld ins fnl 1 1/2f* **26/1**

1m 36.51s 7 Ran SP% **119.1**
PARI-MUTUEL (all including 2 unit stake): WIN 21.00; PLACE (1-2) 6.60, 5.60; SHOW (1-2-3) 2.80, 2.90, 2.10; SF 89.30.
Owner Apogee Bloodstock & Mike Anderson Racing LLC **Bred** Michael Niall **Trained** USA

7022 BRIGHTON (L-H)
Monday, September 16

OFFICIAL GOING: Good to firm (good in places; watered; 7.0)
Wind: virtually nil Weather: overcast, warm

7268 SKY SPORTS RACING ON SKY 415 H'CAP 5f 215y
1:40 (1:40) (Class 4) (0-80,79) 3-Y-O+

£5,207 (£1,549; £774; £387; £300; £300) **Stalls Centre**

Form RPR
5434 1 **Motagally**[10] 6930 3-9-2 **75**....................................(b) JimCrowley 2 86
(Charles Hills) *stdd after s: hld up in rr: clsd and travelling strly 2f out: effrt and rdn to chal 1f out: led ins fnl f: sn clr: comf* **9/4**[1]
0301 2 2 1/4 **Pour La Victoire (IRE)**[14] 6795 9-9-2 **73**....................................(b) HollieDoyle 6 77
(Tony Carroll) *in tch in last pair: effrt over 1f out: hdwy u.p to chse wnr ins fnl f: kpt on for clr 2nd: no threat to wnr* **11/2**
2500 3 3 **Mamillius**[4] 7128 6-9-8 **79**....................................(p) PatCosgrave 4 73
(George Baker) *hld up in tch in midfield: effrt over 2f out: chal and hung lft over 1f out: no ex and wknd ins fnl f (jockey said gelding hung left-handed)* **5/1**[3]
1650 4 2 1/4 **Alicia Darcy (IRE)**[4] 7115 3-8-10 **76**....................................(b) KateLeahy[(7)] 3 63
(Archie Watson) *chsd ldrs tl wnt 2nd 4f out: effrt 2f out: rdn to ld jst over 1f out: hdd ins fnl f: sn wknd* **12/1**
5163 5 1/2 **Harrogate (IRE)**[21] 6534 4-9-7 **78**....................................(b) CharlieBennett 7 64
(Jim Boyle) *led after almost 1f: rdn ent fnl 2f: hdd jst over 1f out: no ex and sn wknd (trainer said, regarding why gelding was running here on going described as Good to Firm, Good in places, having declared the gelding a non-runner at Epsom on 27 August 2019 on ground with the same official description, that having walked the course, in* **6/1**
1000 6 nk **Whataguy**[30] 6227 3-9-2 **78**....................................(p) MeganNicholls[(3)] 5 63
(Paul Nicholls) *broke fast and led for almost 1f: chsd ldrs after: effrt ent fnl 2f: ev ch over 1f out tl no ex jst ins fnl f: wknd* **3/1**[2]
1000 7 9 **In The Red (IRE)**[10] 6916 6-9-4 **75**....................................(p) EoinWalsh 1 31
(Martin Smith) *sn rdn: chsd ldr after almost 1f tl 4f out: lost pl and in rr 2f: bhd and eased ins fnl f* **40/1**

1m 10.36s (-0.74) **Going Correction** -0.05s/f (Good)
WFA 3 from 4yo+ 2lb 7 Ran SP% **112.2**
Speed ratings (Par 105): **102,99,95,92,91 90,78**
CSF £14.49 TOTE £2.70: £1.80, £2.20; EX 13.60 Trifecta £55.20.
Owner Hamdan Al Maktoum **Bred** Whitsbury Manor Stud **Trained** Lambourn, Berks

FOCUS
All distances as advertised. The closers came to the fore in this fair sprint, with the favourite winning quite readily. He's rated in line with his earlier form.

7269 SUSSEX ART FAIRS (EAST) 12 OCTOBER MAIDEN AUCTION STKS 6f 210y
2:10 (2:10) (Class 6) 2-Y-O **£2,781** (£827; £413; £206) **Stalls Centre**

Form RPR
303 1 **Never In Red (IRE)**[11] 6883 2-9-2 69.................................... KieranO'Neill 6 67
(Robyn Brisland) *dwlt: hld up in tch in last pair: effrt over 2f out: swtchd lft and chal u.p over 1f out: led ins fnl f: rn green in front but styd on and in command fnl 75yds* **9/2**[3]
05 2 1 1/2 **Grace Note**[48] 5527 2-8-10 0....................................(b[1]) HollieDoyle 2 57
(Archie Watson) *sn chsng ldr tl led over 2f out: sn rdn: hdd ins fnl f: no ex and one pce after* **16/1**
03 3 4 1/2 **Annie Quickstep (IRE)**[21] 6527 2-8-10 0.................................... RobHornby 1 45
(Jonathan Portman) *led after almost 1f: rdn and hdd over 2f out: no ex ent fnl 1f: wknd ins fnl f* **13/2**
22 4 1/2 **Simply Susan (IRE)**[45] 5602 2-8-11 0.................................... CharlesBishop 3 44
(Eve Johnson Houghton) *in tch: chsd ldrs after 2f: effrt over 2f out: 3rd and no ex u.p 1f out: wknd ins fnl f* **11/4**[2]
4 5 11 **Great Aim (IRE)**[16] 6719 2-9-3 0.................................... TomMarquand 5 21
(James Tate) *broke wl and led for almost 1f: midfield after 2f: effrt over 2f out: sn struggling and wl hld whn hung lft over 1f out: wknd fnl f (trainer rep said, regarding poor performance, colt was unsuited by track and would prefer a less undulating track)* **13/8**[1]
6 14 **Toolmaker** 2-9-4 0.................................... DavidProbert 4
(David Flood) *s.i.s: rn green in rr: rdn and lost tch 3f out: eased ins fnl f* **12/1**

1m 24.21s (0.41) **Going Correction** -0.05s/f (Good) 6 Ran SP% **109.9**
Speed ratings (Par 93): **95,93,88,87,75 59**
CSF £60.68 TOTE £3.90: £1.80, £5.70; EX 52.40 Trifecta £217.70.
Owner Mrs Jo Brisland **Bred** Mrs Amanda McCreery **Trained** Danethorpe, Notts

FOCUS
Very modest juvenile form, with the winner rated to his pre-race mark.

7270 VINTAGE ANTIQUES & COLLECTABLES FAIR 20 OCTOBER APPRENTICE (S) H'CAP 1m 1f 207y
2:40 (2:40) (Class 6) (0-65,65) 3-Y-O+

£2,781 (£827; £413; £300; £300; £300) **Stalls Centre**

Form RPR
5363 1 **Ramatuelle**[7] 7025 3-7-13 **47** ow2....................................(b) GavinAshton[(7)] 1 58
(Sir Mark Prescott Bt) *trckd ldng pair and hugged inner thrght: effrt to ld over 1f out: clr and in command ins fnl f: eased towards fin: easily* **5/2**[1]

1040 **2** *4* **Born To Reason (IRE)**[19] 6599 5-8-9 **48**...(b) ThoreHammerHansen(3) 8 48
(Alexandra Dunn) *sn led: rdn over 2f out: hdd over 1f out: no ch w wnr and kpt on same pce fnl f* **10/1**

0662 **3** *1 3/4* **Dawn Treader (IRE)**[12] 6860 3-9-3 **63**........................ MarkCrehan(5) 6 61
(Richard Hannon) *chsd ldng trio: effrt on centre over 2f out: nvr threatened to get on terms w ldr: wnt wl hld 3rd and kpt on same pce ins fnl f* **9/2[3]**

2060 **4** *3 1/4* **Diviner (IRE)**[20] 6582 3-9-2 **64**........................ AidanRedpath(7) 4 56
(Mark Johnston) *chsd ldr: clsd to join ldr 5f out: 3rd and no ex u.p over 1f out: wknd ins fnl f* **28/1**

0001 **5** *hd* **Barrsbrook**[7] 7028 5-9-8 **65** 5ex........................(vt) LouisGaroghan(7) 2 55
(Gary Moore) *hld up in midfield: effrt and stl plenty to do ent fnl 2f: nvr threatened to get on terms: plugged on and swtchd rt ins fnl f* **7/1**

3306 **6** *8* **Mongolia**[21] 6531 3-8-10 **54**........................(p) TheodoreLadd(3) 7 30
(Michael Appleby) *squeezed for room and hmpd sn after s: hld up in rr: effrt in centre and plenty to do over 2f out: no prog and wl btn over 1f out* **5/1**

4610 **7** *1 1/4* **Creative Talent (IRE)**[22] 6507 7-9-8 **61**........................ CierenFallon(3) 5 34
(Tony Carroll) *v.s.a: t.k.h: clsd on to rr of field after 2f: midfield but nt on terms w ldrs 6f out: hung lft u.p and no prog over 1f out: wknd (jockey said gelding ran too freely and hung left-handed)* **4/1[2]**

3350 **8** *67* **Prerogative (IRE)**[20] 6560 5-8-9 **45**........................(p) MeganNicholls 3
(Tony Carroll) *midfield: dropped to rr 3f out: lost tch over 1f out: virtually p.u ins fnl f: t.o: dismntd sn after fin (jockey said gelding was never travelling; post-race examination failed to reveal any abnormalities)* **14/1**

2m 3.57s (-1.43) **Going Correction** -0.05s/f (Good)
WFA 3 from 5yo+ 5lb **8** Ran **SP% 115.1**
Speed ratings (Par 101): **103,99,98,95,95 89,88,34**
CSF £29.08 CT £107.08 TOTE £3.20: £1.10, £3.30, £1.80; EX 22.10 Trifecta £174.80.The winner was sold to Laura Mongan for £5,500. Diviner was claimed by Archie Watson for £6,000.
Owner Neil Greig **Bred** W N Greig **Trained** Newmarket, Suffolk

FOCUS
Lowly form, little got into it with the pace holding up. They were strung out from quite an early stage. The form's rated with feet on the ground.

7271 VALERIE WHITMARSH H'CAP — 1m 3f 198y
3:10 (3:11) (Class 6) (0-55,54) 3-Y-O+ **£2,781** (£827; £413; £300; £300) **Stalls** High

Form RPR

3005 **1** **King Athelstan (IRE)**[27] 6303 4-9-7 **54**........................(b) HectorCrouch 3 60
(Gary Moore) *hld up in midfield: effrt over 2f out: hdwy over 1f out: chal u.p 1f out: led ins fnl f: r.o wl* **5/2[1]**

1522 **2** *1 1/2* **It's How We Roll (IRE)**[13] 6843 5-9-2 **54**........................(p) ScottMcCullagh(5) 1 58
(John Spearing) *hld up in last trio: clsd and nt clr run over 2f out: swtchd lft and hdwy 2f out: ev ch over 1f out: nt match pce of wnr and one pce ins fnl f* **3/1[2]**

4000 **3** *shd* **Millie May**[34] 6046 5-8-7 **45**........................ ThoreHammerHansen(5) 7 48
(Jimmy Fox) *hld up in tch in midfield: clsd to chse ldrs on inner 5f out: rdn to ld 2f out: hdd and one pce ins fnl f* **12/1**

6305 **4** *1 1/4* **Sweet Nature (IRE)**[20] 6568 4-9-0 **47**........................ NicolaCurrie 8 48
(Laura Mongan) *chsd ldrs tl lost pl 6f out: effrt and swtchd lft jst over 2f out: pressing ldrs and u.p over 1f out: no ex and one pce ins fnl f* **10/1**

5613 **5** *3 1/4* **Brother In Arms (IRE)**[15] 6760 5-9-3 **50**........................ TomMarquand 11 46
(Tony Carroll) *s.i.s: hld up in rr: effrt on outer over 2f out: no imp u.p over 1f out: wknd ins fnl f* **5/1[3]**

4435 **5** *dht* **Winter Snowdrop (IRE)**[24] 6412 3-8-0 **45**........................ SophieRalston(5) 4 42
(Julia Feilden) *chsd ldr tl led over 2f out: hdd 2f out: no ex and lost pl 1f out: wknd ins fnl f* **6/1**

6666 **7** *hd* **Just Right**[75] 4498 4-8-9 **45**........................(p[1]) WilliamCox(3) 6 41
(John Flint) *chsd ldrs: effrt to press ldrs ent fnl 2f: unable qck u.p over 1f out: wknd ins fnl f* **20/1**

4055 **8** *1/2* **Windsorlot (IRE)**[15] 6760 6-8-12 **45**........................ GeorgeDowning 2 40
(Tony Carroll) *s.i.s: hld up in tch in last trio: clsd 5f out: effrt in centre to press ldrs over 2f out: sn edgd lft: unable qck u.p over 1f out: wknd ins fnl f (jockey said gelding was slowly away)* **12/1**

-000 **9** *24* **Oyster Card**[12] 6853 6-8-7 **45**........................(v) TheodoreLadd(5) 9 2
(Michael Appleby) *led tl over 2f out: hung lft and lost pl over 1f out: bhd and eased ins fnl f* **40/1**

0000 **10** *7* **Interrogator (IRE)**[12] 6860 3-8-5 **45**........................(tp) JoeyHaynes 5
(Alan Bailey) *dwlt: sn wl in tch in midfield: effrt u.p over 2f out: unable qck and lost pl over 1f out: bhd and eased ins fnl f* **28/1**

2m 36.96s (0.96) **Going Correction** -0.05s/f (Good)
WFA 3 from 4yo+ 7lb **10** Ran **SP% 119.6**
Speed ratings (Par 101): **94,93,92,92,89 89,89,89,73,68**
CSF £10.09 CT £76.49 TOTE £3.10: £1.20, £1.90, £2.50; EX 9.30 Trifecta £108.60.
Owner Caplin & Sheridan **Bred** M J Rozenbroek **Trained** Lower Beeding, W Sussex

FOCUS
Run at a steady gallop, eight of the runners still held a chance racing past the 2f-marker but ultimately it was the favourite who picked up best. Limited form.

7272 JINGLE & MINGLE CHRISTMAS PARTY NIGHTS H'CAP — 7f 211y
3:40 (3:40) (Class 5) (0-70,72) 3-Y-O+ **£3,428** (£1,020; £509; £300; £300; £300) **Stalls** High

Form RPR

4106 **1** **Baashiq (IRE)**[13] 6839 5-9-6 **66**........................(p) LiamKeniry 4 74
(Peter Hiatt) *mde all and racd keenly: rdn 2f out: drvn over 1f out: styd on wl ins fnl f* **13/2**

05-4 **2** *2* **Turntable**[145] 2034 3-9-4 **68**........................ JackMitchell 3 71+
(Simon Crisford) *stdd after s: racd in last pair: hdwy over 4f out: effrt over 2f out: kpt on ins fnl f: chsd wnr towards fin: nvr getting on terms* **5/2[1]**

6332 **3** *1* **Juanito Chico (IRE)**[20] 6567 5-9-12 **72**........................(p) DavidProbert 1 73
(Michael Attwater) *chsd wnr: effrt ent fnl 2f: drvn over 1f out: kpt on same pce ins fnl f: lost 2nd towards fin* **9/2[3]**

5606 **4** *1 1/4* **Aubretia (IRE)**[20] 6569 3-8-11 **64**........................ CierenFallon(3) 2 62
(Richard Hannon) *midfield: effrt over 2f out: no imp u.p over 1f out: kpt on fnl 100yds: no threat to wnr* **3/1[2]**

5405 **5** *1 1/4* **Waqt (IRE)**[14] 6803 5-9-8 **68**........................(b[1]) RossaRyan 6 63
(Alexandra Dunn) *stmbld leaving stalls: chsd ldrs: effrt over 2f out: unable qck over 1f out: wknd ins fnl f* **7/1**

0026 **6** *2* **Prairie Spy (IRE)**[21] 6540 3-9-7 **71**........................ TomMarquand 5 62
(Mark Johnston) *in tch towards rr: effrt wl over 2f out: no imp u.p over 1f out: wl hld ins fnl f* **12/1**

6310 **7** *19* **Wilson (IRE)**[39] 5839 4-9-5 **65**........................(p) ShelleyBirkett 7 12
(Julia Feilden) *stmbld leaving stalls: a in rr: effrt 3f out: no prog: wl bhd and eased ins fnl f (jockey said gelding stumbled leaving stalls)* **16/1**

1m 35.45s (-1.45) **Going Correction** -0.05s/f (Good)
WFA 3 from 4yo+ 4lb **7** Ran **SP% 111.2**
Speed ratings (Par 103): **105,103,102,100,99 97,78**
CSF £21.82 TOTE £6.70: £3.30, £1.90; EX 27.60 Trifecta £237.90.
Owner Phil Kelly **Bred** Shadwell Estate Company Limited **Trained** Hook Norton, Oxon

FOCUS
Little got into this, with the winner making all. He's rated in line with his Kempton win.

7273 BRIGHTON BUSINESS EXPO 3 OCTOBER H'CAP — 6f 210y
4:10 (4:10) (Class 6) (0-65,67) 3-Y-O+ **£2,781** (£827; £413; £300; £300; £300) **Stalls** Centre

Form RPR

4233 **1** **De Little Engine (IRE)**[14] 6795 5-10-0 **67**........................(p) RossaRyan 7 73
(Alexandra Dunn) *in tch in midfield: effrt over 2f out: drvn and chsd ldrs over 1f out: kpt on u.p to ld wl ins fnl f* **11/4[2]**

0131 **2** *3/4* **Joyful Dream (IRE)**[7] 7024 5-9-1 **57** 5ex........................(b) DarraghKeenan(3) 4 61
(John Butler) *chsd ldrs: effrt on inner over 2f out: pressed ldr over 1f out: ev ch ins fnl f: kpt on but nt quite match pce of wnr towards fin* **15/8[1]**

2230 **3** *nk* **Tarrzan (IRE)**[7] 7027 3-8-7 **52**........................ CierenFallon(3) 5 54
(John Gallagher) *taken down early: led for almost 1f: chsd ldr tl led again 2f out: sn drvn: hdd and no ex wl ins fnl f* **8/1[3]**

6606 **4** *3/4* **Born To Finish (IRE)**[59] 5123 6-9-10 **63**........................ PatCosgrave 8 64
(Ed de Giles) *stdd and awkward leaving stalls: hld up in tch: effrt jst over 2f out: chsd ldrs u.p 1f out: kpt on ins fnl f* **8/1[3]**

0050 **5** *nk* **Field Of Vision (IRE)**[21] 6529 6-8-13 **52**........................(b) NicolaCurrie 6 52
(John Flint) *led after almost 1f: rdn and hdd 2f out: unable qck over 1f out: kpt on same pce ins fnl f* **11/1**

4235 **6** *2 1/2* **Melo Pearl**[39] 5842 3-8-4 **46**........................(v) RaulDaSilva 1 39
(Mrs Ilka Gansera-Leveque) *chsd ldrs early: settled bk into last pair: effrt over 2f out: kpt on but nvr threatened to get on terms* **8/1[3]**

00-0 **7** *2 3/4* **Shoyd**[32] 6116 4-8-9 **55**........................ LukeCatton(7) 2 41
(Richard Hannon) *a towards rr: effrt over 2f out: no imp: nvr involved* **33/1**

0060 **8** *1 3/4* **Soaring Spirits (IRE)**[7] 7024 9-9-2 **55**........................(b) JoeyHaynes 3 38
(Dean Ivory) *midfield: effrt ent fnl 2f: unable qck and btn 1f out: wknd ins fnl f (trainer rep said gelding was unsuited by Good to Firm, Good in places ground, and would prefer a slower surface)* **17/2**

1m 24.04s (0.24) **Going Correction** -0.05s/f (Good)
WFA 3 from 4yo+ 3lb **8** Ran **SP% 116.6**
Speed ratings (Par 101): **96,95,94,93,93 90,87,85**
CSF £8.52 CT £35.39 TOTE £3.50: £1.50, £1.40, £3.10; EX 8.70 Trifecta £39.10.
Owner Golden Equinox Racing & Team Dunn **Bred** Glenvale Stud **Trained** West Buckland, Somerset

FOCUS
Moderate handicap form, although the right horses came to the fore. Straightforward form.

7274 BRIGHTON LIONS FIREWORK NIGHT NOVEMBER 3RD H'CAP — 5f 60y
4:40 (4:40) (Class 6) (0-65,66) 3-Y-O+ **£2,781** (£827; £413; £300; £300; £300) **Stalls** Centre

Form RPR

533 **1** **Toni's A Star**[36] 5986 7-9-3 **59**........................ TomMarquand 4 64
(Tony Carroll) *mde all: rdn wl over 1f out: kpt on wl u.p and a doing enough ins fnl f* **5/1[3]**

5154 **2** *1 1/4* **Haveoneyerself (IRE)**[14] 6798 4-9-2 **61**........................(p) DarraghKeenan(3) 7 62
(John Butler) *chsd wnr: effrt and drvn over 1f out: kpt on same pce ins fnl f* **14/1**

06U6 **3** *1* **Arzaak (IRE)**[20] 6562 5-9-8 **64**........................(b) PatCosgrave 1 61
(Charlie Wallis) *chsd ldrs: effrt towards inner ent fnl 2f: kpt on same pce u.p ins fnl f* **12/1**

4333 **4** *1 3/4* **Threefeetfromgold (IRE)**[20] 6569 3-9-2 **66**........................ JacobClark(7) 2 57
(Martin Smith) *dwlt: hld up in tch in rr: effrt towards inner over 2f out: hdwy over 1f out: chsd ldrs and kpt on same pce ins fnl f* **7/2[2]**

2321 **5** *3/4* **Big Time Maybe (IRE)**[27] 6299 4-9-4 **63**........................(p) CierenFallon(3) 8 51
(Michael Attwater) *in tch in midfield on outer: effrt over 2f out: hung lft: rdr dropped whip and kpt on same pce ins fnl f* **9/4[1]**

6542 **6** *4 1/2* **Hellovaqueen**[21] 6526 4-8-9 **58**........................(b) GeorgeRooke(7) 3 30
(Richard Hughes) *wl in tch in midfield: effrt over 2f out: unable qck over 1f out: wknd ins fnl f* **7/1**

2024 **7** *3 1/2* **Ghepardo**[27] 6299 4-9-6 **62**........................ DavidProbert 5 21
(Patrick Chamings) *dwlt: hld up in last pair: swtchd rt and effrt over 2f out: no prog and wl hld fnl f (jockey said filly was upset in stalls and slowly away)* **7/1**

6140 **8** *1 1/2* **Knockout Blow**[19] 6605 4-9-0 **56**........................(v) HectorCrouch 6 10
(John E Long) *dwlt: in tch in midfield: effrt u.p over 2f out: lost pl and bhd 1f out: wknd ins fnl f* **14/1**

1m 2.19s (-0.81) **Going Correction** -0.05s/f (Good)
WFA 3 from 4yo+ 1lb **8** Ran **SP% 115.7**
Speed ratings (Par 101): **104,102,100,97,96 89,83,81**
CSF £70.93 CT £802.49 TOTE £5.40: £2.00, £3.30, £2.70; EX 66.60 Trifecta £669.30.
Owner A Star Recruitment Ltd **Bred** Paul Green **Trained** Cropthorne, Worcs

FOCUS
Modest sprint form and another all-the-way winner. Very limited form, rated around the front trio.
T/Plt: £78.00 to a £1 stake. Pool: £55,142.08 - 515,57 winning units T/Qpdt: £6.40 to a £1 stake.
Pool: £7,357.93 - 842.05 winning units **Steve Payne**

7078 KEMPTON (A.W) (R-H)
Monday, September 16

OFFICIAL GOING: Polytrack: standard to slow (watered)
Wind: Light, half against Weather: Overcast, drizzly

7275 100% PROFIT BOOST AT 32REDSPORT.COM NURSERY H'CAP — 7f (P)
4:55 (4:56) (Class 6) (0-60,58) 2-Y-O **£3,105** (£924; £461; £400; £400; £400) **Stalls** Low

Form RPR

6045 **1** **Interrupted Dream**[4] 7111 2-8-12 **56**........................ AidenSmithies(7) 7 60
(Mark Johnston) *mde all: pushed along 2f out: edgd lft after but wl in command and nvr seriously chal* **7/1**

5004 **2** *1 1/2* **Castel Angelo (IRE)**[13] 6837 2-9-7 **58**........................ CharlesBishop 10 58
(Henry Candy) *wnt sltly lft s: t.k.h: hld up in last quartet: shkn up over 2f out: rdn and prog over 1f out: styd on fnl f to take 2nd last 75yds: nvr pce to threaten wnr* **11/4[1]**

The Form Book Flat 2019, Raceform Ltd, Newbury, RG14 5SJ

4440 **3** ½ **Grace Plunkett**[13] 6837 2-8-12 **49**............................(b) KieranShoemark 5 48
(Richard Spencer) *hld up towards rr: rdn and prog wl over 1f out: kpt on to dispute 2nd ins fnl f: no threat to wnr* **25/1**

650 **4** *1* **Dandy Dancer**[58] 5186 2-9-3 **54**................................. ShaneKelly 8 50
(Richard Hughes) *hld up in 6th: gng strly over 2f out: shkn up and prog wl over 1f out: disp 2nd fnl f: one pce last 100yds* **20/1**

6656 **5** ½ **Treaty Of Dingle**[17] 6683 2-9-7 **58**................................. HollieDoyle 3 53
(Hughie Morrison) *trckd ldrs: rdn and prog to dispute 2nd over 1f out: one pce fnl f* **4/1**[2]

006 **6** ½ **Star Of St Louis (FR)**[61] 5059 2-8-13 **50**........................ KieranO'Neill 9 44
(Denis Quinn) *mostly chsd wnr to jst over 1f out: steadily fdd ins fnl f* **66/1**

0660 **7** 4½ **Leave Em Alone (IRE)**[5] 7079 2-9-6 **57**......................(h[1]) HarryBentley 11 39
(David Evans) *awkward s and sltly impeded: mostly in last pair: rdn and no prog over 2f out: plugged on over 1f out* **14/1**

000 **8** *nk* **Comvida (IRE)**[49] 5501 2-8-9 **46**................................(p) JosephineGordon 1 27
(Hugo Palmer) *in tch in midfield but sn pushed along: rdn over 2f out: wknd over 1f out* **9/2**[3]

0050 **9** *nk* **The Works (IRE)**[9] 6969 2-8-8 **45**.. DavidEgan 2 26
(Declan Carroll) *trckd ldng pair: dispute 2nd 2f out: wknd over 1f out* **16/1**

666 **10** 2¼ **Koovers (IRE)**[16] 6719 2-9-6 **57**..(b[1]) LukeMorris 6 32
(Gay Kelleway) *t.k.h: trckd ldng trio: hrd rdn over 2f out: wknd over 1f out* **25/1**

550 **11** *6* **Parker's Boy**[33] 6079 2-9-6 **57**.. GeraldMosse 4 16
(Brian Barr) *t.k.h: hld up in last quartet: no prog over 2f out: sn wknd* **14/1**

000 **12** 3½ **Farewell Kiss (IRE)**[22] 6514 2-9-6 **57**.................(v[1]) CallumShepherd 12 7
(Michael Bell) *slowly away and wnt lft s fr wdst draw: a in last pair: nvr a factor* **25/1**

1m 26.87s (0.87) **Going Correction** -0.075s/f (Stan) **12** Ran SP% **114.4**
Speed ratings (Par 93): **92,90,89,88,88 87,82,81,81,79 72,68**
CSF £23.78 CT £461.46 TOTE £6.10: £2.40, £1.60, £5.80; EX 20.90 Trifecta £242.70.
Owner John Farley And Gay Kelleway **Bred** Bjorn Nielsen **Trained** Middleham Moor, N Yorks

FOCUS
A low-grade nursery to open proceedings with the winner providing apprentice Aiden Smithies with a first career success. Limited form.

7276 32RED.COM NOVICE AUCTION STKS 6f (P)

5:30 (5:33) (Class 5) 2-Y-O £3,881 (£1,155; £577; £288) Stalls Low

Form RPR

03 **1** **Progressive Rating**[24] 6415 2-9-3 0................................ OisinMurphy 1 88+
(William Knight) *mde all: shkn up and drew wl clr over 1f out: unchal* **8/11**[1]

2 *7* **River Sprite** 2-8-12 0.. KieranShoemark 4 62
(Daniel Kubler) *w ldrs: wnt 2nd jst over 2f out: no ch w wnr after but kpt on steadily* **16/1**

3 3¾ **Royal Charmer** 2-8-10 0.. EllieMacKenzie[(7)] 8 56
(Mark Usher) *off the pce in midfield: prog over 2f out: tk v modest 3rd ins fnl f: no imp on ldng pair after* **66/1**

4 *hd* **Thunderdome (FR)** 2-9-3 0.. LukeMorris 2 55
(Gay Kelleway) *plld hrd early: w ldrs: outpcd and rdn over 2f out: kpt on again nr fin* **20/1**

34 **5** 1¼ **Spiritofthenorth (FR)**[46] 5591 2-9-3 0..................... JosephineGordon 6 51
(Kevin Ryan) *sn shoved along and off the pce: nvr a factor but kpt on fnl f* **11/4**[2]

0354 **6** *nk* **The Blue Bower (IRE)**[24] 6415 2-8-12 65........................ HollieDoyle 9 46
(Suzy Smith) *stdd s: sn wl off the pce in last pair: rdn over 2f out: kpt on over 1f out but nvr a factor (jockey said filly was never travelling)* **16/1**

7 *hd* **Rockin' N Raven** 2-9-3 0.. RobHornby 3 50
(Sylvester Kirk) *sn wl off the pce in rr: sme prog over 2f out but nvr a threat: no hdwy fnl f* **12/1**[3]

0 **8** *hd* **Heleta**[16] 6719 2-8-12 0.. CharlesBishop 5 44
(Peter Hedger) *t.k.h: hld up and sn off the pce: no ch fnl 2f* **100/1**

56 **9** *nse* **Fair Sabra**[28] 6281 2-8-12 0.. GeraldMosse 10 44
(David Elsworth) *sn wl off the pce in rr: nvr a factor: plugged on late* **33/1**

1453 **10** ¾ **Twice As Likely**[7] 7029 2-9-5 67..(b[1]) ShaneKelly 11 49
(Richard Hughes) *w ldrs: outpcd 2f out: stl in modest 3rd 1f out: wknd and eased* **12/1**[3]

1m 12.29s (-0.81) **Going Correction** -0.075s/f (Stan) **10** Ran SP% **121.9**
Speed ratings (Par 95): **102,92,87,87,85 85,85,84,84,83**
CSF £16.74 TOTE £1.50: £1.02, £3.80, £23.90; EX 15.10 Trifecta £569.20.
Owner Progressive Racing & A Hetherton **Bred** Peter Winkworth **Trained** Angmering, W Sussex
■ Stopnsearch was withdrawn. Price at time of withdrawal 66/1. Rule 4 does not apply.

FOCUS
Not much depth to this novice auction and the winner proved to be in a different league to his rivals. A few down the field may anchor the form to this sort of level.

7277 BET AT RACINGTV.COM NURSERY H'CAP 1m (P)

6:00 (6:05) (Class 6) (0-65,66) 2-Y-O

£3,105 (£924; £461; £400; £400; £400) Stalls Low

Form RPR

6025 **1** **Inflamed**[11] 6884 2-8-11 **55**.. OisinMurphy 7 60
(Ed Walker) *pressed ldrs: pushed along 3f out: prog and rdn to ld over 1f out but immediately jnd: drvn and kpt on wl fnl f* **4/1**[1]

606 **2** ½ **Glen Esk**[17] 6673 2-9-4 **62**.. JackMitchell 10 66
(Chris Wall) *t.k.h: hld up in midfield: prog on outer over 3f out: clsd on ldrs 2f out gng wl: chal and w wnr over 1f out: sn drvn and edgd rt: nt qckn last 150yds* **4/1**[1]

0052 **3** 2¾ **Jungle Book (GER)**[24] 6394 2-9-1 **66**........................ TylerSaunders[(7)] 3 64
(Jonathan Portman) *tried to ld but forced to chse ldrs: rdn and prog over 2f out: tk cl 3rd over 1f out then sltly impeded: nt qckn and wl hld fnl f: jst hld on for 3rd* **4/1**[1]

303 **4** *nse* **Moorland Spirit (IRE)**[21] 6532 2-9-6 **64**........................(b) HollieDoyle 2 62
(Archie Watson) *chsd ldrs: shkn up 3f out: prog on inner over 1f out: kpt on fnl f and nrly snatched 3rd* **9/1**[2]

0424 **5** 4½ **Lexington Quest (IRE)**[24] 6394 2-9-5 **63**........................ PatDobbs 6 51
(Richard Hannon) *wl in rr: pushed along in 8th and nt on terms 2f out: shkn up and passed wkng rivals nr fin: nvr in it (jockey said gelding was slowly away)* **14/1**

660 **6** *nk* **Divine Connection**[19] 6592 2-9-7 **65**........................ RobHornby 12 52
(Jonathan Portman) *sn trckd ldr: chal and upsides over 2f out to over 1f out: wknd* **16/1**

5003 **7** *hd* **Broughtons Compass**[23] 6435 2-8-2 **46**........................(p[1]) LukeMorris 8 33
(Mark Hoad) *led 150yds: chsd ldrs after: rdn and cl up whn squeezed for room over 1f out: no ch after* **25/1**

660 **8** 1¼ **Secret Passion**[42] 5733 2-9-7 **65**........................ AdamMcNamara 9 49
(Archie Watson) *won contested battle for ld after 150yds: jnd over 2f out: hdd & wknd over 1f out* **33/1**

0465 **9** 1¾ **Slavonic Dance (IRE)**[14] 6808 2-9-4 **62**........................(b) HarryBentley 4 42
(Ralph Beckett) *racd in midfield but sn pushed along: nvr able to pose a threat* **10/1**[3]

0500 **10** 1¼ **Son Of Prancealot (IRE)**[24] 6394 2-9-1 **59**....................(t) TomQueally 5 36
(David Evans) *s.i.s: impeded and snatched up after 150yds: a wl in rr after (jockey said gelding clipped heels shortly after start)* **50/1**

544 **11** *18* **Um Elnadim (FR)**[10] 6934 2-9-6 **64**........................ FrannyNorton 1
(Mark Johnston) *sltly impeded after 150yds: a wl in rr: bhd and eased fnl f: t.o (jockey said filly jumped right-handed leaving stalls)* **16/1**

0502 **12** *4* **Kentucky Hardboot (IRE)**[14] 6808 2-9-1 **59**........................(p) GeraldMosse 13
(Mick Channon) *trapped out wd: nvr beyond midfield: wknd 3f out: eased 2f out: t.o* **12/1**

1m 39.71s (-0.09) **Going Correction** -0.075s/f (Stan) **12** Ran SP% **114.0**
Speed ratings (Par 93): **97,96,93,93,89 88,88,87,85,84 66,62**
CSF £16.85 CT £67.76 TOTE £4.50: £1.50, £1.80, £2.40; EX 20.70 Trifecta £84.90.
Owner P K Siu **Bred** Theakston Stud **Trained** Upper Lambourn, Berks

FOCUS
The market principals came to the fore in this low-grade nursery. The front pair pulled clear and are worth following.

7278 32RED CASINO MEDIAN AUCTION MAIDEN STKS 1m (P)

6:30 (6:34) (Class 5) 3-5-Y-O £3,881 (£1,155; £577; £288) Stalls Low

Form RPR

2353 **1** **Jack D'Or**[23] 6469 3-9-5 73.. OisinMurphy 3 78
(Ed Walker) *trckd ldrs: wnt 2nd wl over 1f out: sn drvn: grad clsd after: led last 50yds* **8/11**[1]

-206 **2** ½ **Characteristic (IRE)**[31] 6186 3-9-5 73........................(v[1]) JackMitchell 6 77
(Tom Clover) *led: sent for home over 2f out: drvn and styd on fr over 1f out but worn down last 50yds* **4/1**[2]

56 **3** *6* **Uzincso**[27] 6315 3-9-5 0.. DanielMuscutt 9 63+
(John Butler) *hld up and sn fnd himself in last: stdy prog over 3f out: kpt on encouragingly fnl 2f: tk 3rd last strides: likely to do bttr* **40/1**

3-26 **4** ½ **Burning Topic (GER)**[37] 5969 3-9-0 70........................ ShaneKelly 8 57
(David Lanigan) *pressed wnr: rdn and outpcd over 2f out: lost 2nd wl over 1f out: steadily fdd and lost 3rd last strides* **12/1**

5 1½ **Never To Forget** 4-9-6 0.. DarraghKeenan[(3)] 4 59
(John Butler) *hld up towards rr: stdy prog fr 1/2-way: rchd modest 4th over 1f out: no hdwy after: nt disgracd* **40/1**

3630 **6** *1* **Pamper**[30] 6204 3-9-0 68..(v[1]) HarryBentley 5 51
(James Fanshawe) *towards rr: urged along fr 1/2-way: sme prog over 2f out: plugged on but nvr a threat* **6/1**[3]

06 **7** *9* **Master Milliner (IRE)**[13] 6836 3-9-5 0........................ RobHornby 7 36
(Emma Lavelle) *urged along early: swtchd to wd outside and prog to press ldng pair after 3f: wknd over 3f out* **66/1**

0 **8** ½ **Miss Ditsy (IRE)**[32] 6119 3-9-0 0........................ RobertHavlin 2 29
(Michael Attwater) *dwlt: a towards rr: lft bhd fr 3f out* **150/1**

6 **9** 3¾ **Forgotten Girl**[27] 6325 3-9-0 0........................ AdrianMcCarthy 11 21
(Christine Dunnett) *wl in rr: last and struggling over 3f out (jockey said filly hung left-handed on bnd)* **200/1**

0 **10** 1¼ **Jane Camille**[19] 6594 3-9-0 0........................ CharlesBishop 10 18
(Peter Hedger) *nvr beyond midfield: outpcd 3f out: sn wknd* **125/1**

32 **11** *10* **Don't Jump George (IRE)**[13] 6838 4-9-9 0........................(t) RossaRyan 12
(Shaun Lycett) *prom tl wknd rapidly 3f out: t.o (jockey said gelding lost its action; vet said gelding had superficial wound to right-hind)* **9/1**

005 **12** *11* **Little Lady Luck**[20] 6559 3-8-11 0........................(h[1]) WilliamCox[(3)] 1
(Mark Usher) *chsd ldrs to 1/2-way: wknd qckly: t.o* **200/1**

1m 39.09s (-0.71) **Going Correction** -0.075s/f (Stan)
WFA 3 from 4yo 4lb **12** Ran SP% **118.7**
Speed ratings (Par 103): **100,99,93,93,91 90,81,81,77,76 66,55**
CSF £3.80 TOTE £1.40: £1.02, £1.40, £9.40; EX 4.30 Trifecta £55.00.
Owner Ebury Racing 2 **Bred** Star Pointe Ltd **Trained** Upper Lambourn, Berks

FOCUS
A modest maiden, the first two home both BHA-rated 73, but a good finish and there were some interesting performances in behind. It's unlikely the first two improved.

7279 32RED H'CAP 1m 3f 219y(P)

7:00 (7:01) (Class 4) (0-80,79) 3-Y-O

£6,469 (£1,925; £962; £481; £400; £400) Stalls Low

Form RPR

436 **1** **Imperium (IRE)**[67] 4842 3-8-12 **70**........................ AdamMcNamara 7 76+
(Roger Charlton) *s.i.s: detached in last and nt gng: latched on to gp by 1/2-way but stl needed pushing: prog jst over 2f out: rdn and clsd fnl f: styd on stoutly to ld post* **10/1**

3321 **2** *shd* **Alma Linda**[10] 6931 3-9-6 **78**........................(p) LukeMorris 3 84
(Sir Mark Prescott Bt) *trckd ldng pair: urged and cajoled along to take 2nd over 1f out: grad clsd to ld 100yds out: hdd post* **9/4**[1]

024 **3** ½ **Grey D'Ars (FR)**[23] 6454 3-9-7 **79**........................ HollieDoyle 4 84
(Nick Littmoden) *t.k.h: w ldr after 2f tl led over 2f out: drvn over 1f out: hdd and one pce last 100yds* **5/1**[3]

2106 **4** ¾ **Sashenka (GER)**[30] 6211 3-9-0 **72**........................ LiamKeniry 5 76
(Sylvester Kirk) *hld up in 5th: effrt on inner over 2f out: tk 3rd over 1f out and cl enough: one pce fnl f* **9/1**

1003 **5** *4* **Robert L'Echelle (IRE)**[61] 5055 3-9-2 **74**........................ RobertHavlin 8 71
(Hughie Morrison) *mostly in 6th: dropped to last and struggling over 2f out: wl btn after but kpt on fnl f* **15/2**

5041 **6** *1* **Hermosura**[19] 6595 3-9-0 **72**........................(b) HarryBentley 1 68
(Ralph Beckett) *led: jnd after 2f: rdn and hdd over 2f out: steadily wknd over 1f out* **6/1**

-533 **7** 1½ **Dubai Discovery (USA)**[11] 6902 3-9-4 **76**........................(p) OisinMurphy 6 69
(Saeed bin Suroor) *trckd ldng trio: shkn up over 2f out: sn lost pl: dropped away over 1f out* **9/2**[2]

2m 32.23s (-2.27) **Going Correction** -0.075s/f (Stan) **7** Ran SP% **110.8**
Speed ratings (Par 103): **104,103,103,103,100 99,98**
CSF £30.82 CT £121.85 TOTE £8.10: £3.60, £1.80; EX 30.10 Trifecta £176.30.
Owner Weston Brook Farm & Bromfield **Bred** Southern Bloodstock **Trained** Beckhampton, Wilts

The Form Book Flat 2019, Raceform Ltd, Newbury, RG14 5SJ

FOCUS
A middle-distance handicap run at a steady pace produced a remarkable performance from the winner, who could develop into a useful handicapper. The form's rated around the third.

7280 RACING TV H'CAP 1m 3f 219y(P)
7:30 (7:33) (Class 6) (0-60,59) 3-Y-O
£3,105 (£924; £461; £400; £400; £400) Stalls Low

Form RPR
1432 1 **Celtic Classic (IRE)**[21] 6531 3-9-2 **54**..............................(b) RossaRyan 1 62
(Paul Cole) *prom: trckd ldr 5f out: disp ld on inner over 2f out: drvn ahd over 1f out: edgd lft after but kpt on wl (jockey said gelding hung left-handed)* **3/1**[1]
-005 2 1 1/4 **Waterproof**[16] 6702 3-8-9 **47**..............................(p[1]) JosephineGordon 2 53
(Shaun Keightley) *led: jnd by wnr over 2f out and clr of rest: hdd over 1f out: edgd lft but kpt on* **28/1**
0456 3 3 1/4 **Homesick Boy (IRE)**[32] 6128 3-9-2 **54**..............................(v[1]) RobertHavlin 11 55
(Ed Dunlop) *slowly away: wl in rr: gd prog on inner jst over 2f out: styd on to take 3rd fnl f: no threat to ldng pair* **16/1**
006 4 3/4 **Capla Huntress**[16] 6732 3-9-3 **55**.............................. GeorgeWood 10 55
(Chris Wall) *hld up wl in rr: prog 3f out: chsd ldng pair briefly over 1f out: kpt on same pce after* **16/1**
-440 5 shd **Percy's Prince**[63] 4998 3-8-13 **51**.............................. LukeMorris 3 50
(Sir Mark Prescott Bt) *racd in midfield: u.p 5f out: dropped to rr over 2f out: styd on again over 1f out: gng on at fin but nt v qckly* **7/2**[2]
2663 6 1 1/4 **Sea Art**[24] 6405 3-9-7 **59**..............................(v) OisinMurphy 7 56
(William Knight) *slowly away: sn in midfield: rdn over 2f out: one pce and no imp on ldrs over 1f out* **15/2**[3]
6060 7 1 3/4 **Eagle Queen**[18] 6636 3-9-5 **57**.............................. DavidProbert 6 52
(Andrew Balding) *hld up in rr: shkn up 3f out: no real prog tl kpt on one pce over 1f out: n.d* **16/1**
504 8 shd **Lady Navarra (IRE)**[25] 6371 3-9-5 **57**..............................(e[1]) ShaneKelly 8 51
(Gay Kelleway) *t.k.h: prom: chsd ldng pair over 2f out to over 1f out: wknd* **28/1**
0-04 9 1/2 **Maykir**[70] 4735 3-8-8 **46**.............................. AdrianMcCarthy 14 40
(J R Jenkins) *hld up and sn in last: swtchd to inner and briefly threatened to make prog 2f out: no real hdwy over 1f out* **100/1**
-030 10 1 1/2 **Garrison Law**[41] 5784 3-9-6 **58**.............................. HarryBentley 9 49
(David Simcock) *slowly away: wl in rr: effrt and sme prog over 2f out: wknd fnl f* **8/1**
500 11 hd **Savoy Brown**[28] 6279 3-8-10 **48**.............................. KierenFox 12 39
(Michael Attwater) *nvr beyond midfield: wknd over 1f out* **33/1**
0606 12 2 3/4 **Champ Ayr**[27] 6320 3-9-6 **58**.............................. KieranShoemark 13 45
(David Menuisier) *slowly away: rapid rcvry fr wd draw to press ldr to 5f out: lost 3rd and wknd qckly over 2f out* **25/1**
6332 13 4 1/2 **Dolly Dupree**[21] 6550 3-9-3 **55**.............................. HollieDoyle 4 34
(Paul D'Arcy) *a in rr: struggling over 3f out* **8/1**
6400 14 28 **Lucky Lou (IRE)**[21] 6531 3-9-3 **55**..............................(h) DanielMuscutt 5
(Patrick Chamings) *slowly away: sn in midfield: wknd rapidly over 2f out: t.o (jockey said filly stopped quickly, post-race examination failed to reveal any abnormalities)* **40/1**

2m 34.03s (-0.47) **Going Correction** -0.075s/f (Stan) 14 Ran SP% **116.0**
Speed ratings (Par 99): **98,97,95,94,94 93,92,92,92,91 90,89,86,67**
CSF £98.79 CT £1161.89 TOTE £3.90: £1.30, £5.80, £6.00; EX 91.30 Trifecta £1323.20.
Owner P F I Cole Ltd **Bred** Gerard Corry & Cristian Healy **Trained** Whatcombe, Oxon

FOCUS
A weak race and although the front two pulled clear, it's not form to take a positive view of.

7281 32RED ON THE APP STORE H'CAP (DIV I) 7f (P)
8:00 (8:03) (Class 6) (0-55,55) 3-Y-O+
£3,105 (£924; £461; £400; £400; £400) Stalls Low

Form RPR
050 1 **Ubla (IRE)**[11] 6897 6-9-7 **55**..............................(e) LukeMorris 12 63
(Gay Kelleway) *plld hrd early: hld up in last quartet: cajoled along and prog 2f out: burst through jst over 1f out: led last 150yds and sn drvn clr* **14/1**
4524 2 2 1/2 **Flying Sakhee**[11] 6897 6-8-13 **47**..............................(p) KieranO'Neill 8 49
(John Bridger) *hld up in last quartet: swtchd to outer over 2f out: rdn and prog over 1f out: styd on fnl f to take 2nd last strides* **25/1**
0026 3 1/2 **Rock In Society (IRE)**[21] 6546 4-9-2 **53**..............(b) DarraghKeenan(3) 10 53
(John Butler) *racd freely: led: rdn over 1f out: hdd and outpcd last 150yds: lost 2nd last strides* **15/2**
0004 4 3/4 **Impressionable**[39] 5869 3-9-2 **53**..............................(t[1]) HollieDoyle 13 50
(William Muir) *hld up in last pair: stl in last trio jst over 1f out: fin strly last 150yds to take 4th fnl strides* **20/1**
2432 5 nk **Prince Rock (IRE)**[11] 6889 4-8-6 **47**..............................(h) LeviWilliams(7) 7 44
(Simon Dow) *t.k.h: pressed ldrs on outer: rdn and nt qckn 2f out: one pce after and lost pls ins fnl f* **8/1**
4063 6 1/2 **Sea Shack**[16] 6731 5-8-12 **51**..............................(tp) ScottMcCullagh(5) 1 47
(Julia Feilden) *cl up on inner: rdn 2f out: nt qckn over 1f out: one pce after* **11/2**[1]
5010 7 nk **Three C's (IRE)**[17] 6666 5-9-2 **50**..............................(p) PatCosgrave 14 45
(George Boughey) *nvr bttr than midfield on outer: rdn 3f out: lost pl 2f out: kpt on one pce fnl f* **8/1**
020 8 shd **Secret Treaties**[32] 6130 3-9-1 **52**.............................. EoinWalsh 6 46
(Christine Dunnett) *mostly chsd ldr to jst over 1f out: fdd fnl f* **33/1**
0500 9 1/2 **Holy Tiber (IRE)**[23] 6441 4-9-6 **54**.............................. JoeyHaynes 2 48
(Chelsea Banham) *s.i.s: hld up but sn in midfield: lost pl 2f out: nvr on terms after: kpt on nr fin but nvr really in it* **13/2**[3]
5300 10 nk **Bidding War**[32] 6131 4-9-3 **51**.............................. AlistairRawlinson 4 44
(Michael Appleby) *hld up towards rr: rdn 2f out: one pce and nvr much prog* **8/1**
50 11 3/4 **Es Que Magic (IRE)**[40] 5799 3-9-1 **52**..............................(b[1]) DavidProbert 5 42
(Alex Hales) *trckd ldrs: rdn and nt qckn over 2f out: steadily lost pl over 1f out* **6/1**[2]
0000 12 3/4 **Dyagilev**[16] 6731 4-9-6 **54**..............................(b) AdrianMcCarthy 11 43
(Lydia Pearce) *dwlt: a in last quartet: rdn and no prog over 2f out* **33/1**
000 13 3/4 **Picket Line**[35] 6018 7-9-7 **55**..............................(b) LiamKeniry 3 42
(Geoffrey Deacon) *nvr beyond midfield: rdn over 2f out: wknd over 1f out* **28/1**
0600 14 2 1/2 **Mystical Moon (IRE)**[11] 6889 4-9-1 **49**.............................. NicolaCurrie 9 30
(David C Griffiths) *sn in rr: dropped to last and btn 3f out* **25/1**

1m 26.05s (0.05) **Going Correction** -0.075s/f (Stan)
WFA 3 from 4yo+ 3lb 14 Ran SP% **116.6**
Speed ratings (Par 101): **96,93,92,91,91 90,90,90,89,89 88,87,86,84**
CSF £329.92 CT £2795.58 TOTE £19.90: £6.50, £2.00, £2.20; EX 329.40 Trifecta £4082.70.
Owner Strictly Fun Racing Club **Bred** Tenuta Genzianella **Trained** Exning, Suffolk

FOCUS
A low-grade handicap but the winner took full advantage of the drop in class. The first two home came from well off the pace but the third had made the running. The winner is rated to his best form of the last 18 months.

7282 32RED ON THE APP STORE H'CAP (DIV II) 7f (P)
8:30 (8:31) (Class 6) (0-55,55) 3-Y-O+
£3,105 (£924; £461; £400; £400; £400) Stalls Low

Form RPR
2520 1 **Cauthen (IRE)**[26] 6329 3-9-4 **55**.............................. PatDobbs 10 61
(Milton Harris) *prog fr midfield 1/2-way to trck ldrs over 2f out: wnt 2nd over 1f out: rdn and steadily clsd on clr ldr to ld last 75yds* **9/1**
0050 2 1/2 **Tavener**[11] 6897 7-9-2 **50**..............................(t) CallumShepherd 2 56
(Declan Carroll) *led: stretched for home over 2f out: 4 l ahd over 1f out: tired fnl f: hdd last 75yds* **7/1**[3]
0000 3 1 1/4 **Masai Spirit**[60] 5080 3-9-1 **52**.............................. DavidProbert 1 53
(Philip McBride) *chsd ldrs: rdn to dispute 2nd 2f out: nt qckn over 1f out: kpt on fnl f but nvr able to chal* **25/1**
0-P0 4 1 3/4 **Roca Magica**[17] 6666 3-9-1 **52**.............................. RobertHavlin 6 49
(Ed Dunlop) *stdd s: hld up in rr: sme prog over 2f out gng strly: urged along over 1f out: styd on but nvr rchd chalng position* **33/1**
0003 5 hd **Independence Day (IRE)**[32] 6126 6-9-6 **54**.............................. JoeyHaynes 14 51
(Chelsea Banham) *wl in rr fr wdst draw: rdn over 2f out: prog over 1f out: styd on fnl f and nrly snatched 4th* **11/2**[2]
0631 6 2 3/4 **Brigand**[73] 4589 4-9-6 **54**.............................. OisinMurphy 3 44
(John Butler) *prom: chsd clr ldr over 2f out to over 1f out: wknd* **7/4**[1]
U000 7 2 **Indian Affair**[25] 6363 9-8-13 **47**..............................(tp) PhilipPrince 5 32
(Milton Bradley) *nvr beyond midfield: rdn and btn 2f out* **40/1**
0555 8 1 1/2 **Prince Of Time**[18] 6621 7-8-9 **46**.............................. DarraghKeenan(3) 8 27
(Stella Barclay) *trapped wd: chsd ldrs: steadily wknd over 2f out* **20/1**
020 9 hd **Master Poet**[25] 6363 4-9-5 **53**..............................(p) HectorCrouch 9 34
(Gary Moore) *chsd ldr to over 2f out: wknd* **12/1**
066P 10 3 1/2 **Caesonia**[34] 6052 3-9-2 **53**.............................. KieranShoemark 13 24
(Charles Hills) *a wl in rr: shkn up and no prog over 2f out* **33/1**
000/ 11 2 1/4 **True Colors**[654] 9034 5-9-0 **51**.............................. PaddyBradley(3) 7 17
(Mark Pattinson) *mostly in last: struggling wl over 2f out (jockey said gelding was outpaced)* **40/1**
4056 12 2 1/4 **Kafoo**[45] 5633 6-9-0 **48**.............................. AlistairRawlinson 4 8
(Michael Appleby) *nvr bttr than midfield: lost pl and struggling 1/2-way: wl btn over 2f out (jockey said gelding was never travelling)* **7/1**[3]
0233 13 5 **Arctic Flower (IRE)**[11] 6897 6-9-2 **50**.............................. KieranO'Neill 12
(John Bridger) *t.k.h: prom to 1/2-way: sn wknd qckly* **12/1**

1m 25.76s (-0.24) **Going Correction** -0.075s/f (Stan)
WFA 3 from 4yo+ 3lb 13 Ran SP% **121.5**
Speed ratings (Par 101): **98,97,96,94,93 90,88,86,86,82 79,77,71**
CSF £66.55 CT £1574.32 TOTE £9.60: £4.60, £2.10, £3.90; EX 100.30 Trifecta £2965.50.
Owner David Henery And Lee Turland **Bred** Robert Norton **Trained** Warminster, Wiltshire

FOCUS
This looked the more interesting of the two divisions and the form should prove reliable. The runner-up set a solid pace.
T/Plt: £13.90 to a £1 stake. Pool: £60,330.14 - 3,163.09 winning units T/Qpdt: £7.90 to a £1 stake. Pool: £10,494.75 - 978.08 winning units **Jonathan Neesom**

6969 THIRSK (L-H)
Monday, September 16

OFFICIAL GOING: Good to firm (good in places)
Wind: Almost nil Weather: Sunny

7283 VISIT SRI LANKA NURSERY H'CAP (DIV I) 6f
2:00 (2:00) (Class 6) (0-65,65) 2-Y-O
£3,737 (£1,112; £555; £300; £300; £300) Stalls Centre

Form RPR
050 1 **Idoapologise**[31] 6175 2-9-2 **60**..............................(h) PJMcDonald 7 67+
(James Bethell) *hld up: hdwy 1/2-way: rdn over 1f out: led ent fnl f: sn edgd lft: r.o wl: readily* **5/2**[1]
000 2 2 **Rebel Redemption**[52] 5388 2-9-2 **60**..............................(p[1]) JasonHart 4 61
(John Quinn) *w ldr: rdn to ld over 1f out: hdd ent fnl f: nt pce of wnr fnl 100yds* **15/2**[3]
4430 3 3/4 **Ma Boy Harris (IRE)**[17] 6683 2-9-1 **59**..............................(p[1]) BenCurtis 8 58
(Phillip Makin) *racd keenly: trckd ldrs: rdn and unable qck 1f out: kpt on towards fin* **10/1**
4523 4 1/2 **Red Jasper**[17] 6683 2-9-7 **65**..............................(p[1]) LiamJones 2 62
(Michael Appleby) *racd keenly: in tch: rdn over 2f out: chalng over 1f out: styd on same pce ins fnl f* **15/2**[3]
6525 5 1 1/4 **It's Not My Fault (IRE)**[32] 6097 2-8-10 **54**.............................. KevinStott 10 48
(Paul Midgley) *led: rdn over 2f out: hdd over 1f out: stl there u.p ent fnl f: no ex fnl 75yds* **11/1**
6660 6 3/4 **Secret Identity**[41] 5789 2-9-5 **63**.............................. JackGarritty 1 54
(Jedd O'Keeffe) *hld up: rdn 2f out: hdwy over 1f out: styd on ins fnl f: nt able to trble ldrs* **10/1**
0605 7 3 1/4 **Baileys Prayer (FR)**[20] 6571 2-8-1 **48**..............................(v[1]) SeanDavis(3) 5 30
(Richard Fahey) *towards rr: sn pushed along: drvn in midfield 1/2-way: no imp over 1f out: one pce* **16/1**
6305 8 nk **Schumli**[28] 6271 2-9-0 **58**.............................. CamHardie 3 39
(David O'Meara) *midfield: rdn over 2f out: no imp and outpcd over 1f out* **50/1**
0000 9 1 1/2 **Bosun's Chair**[69] 4756 2-8-7 **51**..............................(b[1]) DuranFentiman 9 27
(Tim Easterby) *s.i.s: hld up in midfield: rdn over 2f out: wknd over 1f out* **40/1**
4540 10 1 1/4 **Royal Lightning**[17] 6683 2-8-13 **57**.............................. TomEaves 11 29
(James Given) *chsd ldrs: pushed along 1/2-way: rdn over 2f out: hung lft whn wknd wl over 1f out* **33/1**
5063 11 6 **Wots The Wifi Code**[30] 6228 2-9-4 **62**.............................. PaulHanagan 6 16
(Tony Coyle) *midfield: rdn over 2f out: sn wknd: bhd fnl f (trainer said gelding was unsuited by Good To Firm, Good in places ground)* **10/3**[2]

1m 11.53s (-1.27) **Going Correction** -0.375s/f (Firm) 11 Ran SP% **114.9**
Speed ratings (Par 93): **93,90,89,88,87 86,81,81,79,77 69**
CSF £20.88 CT £159.50 TOTE £3.00: £1.30, £2.60, £2.50; EX 21.30 Trifecta £144.00.
Owner Clarendon Thoroughbred Racing **Bred** The Shiba Partnership **Trained** Middleham Moor, N Yorks

FOCUS
Some light drizzle overnight but the official going was changed from good, good to firm in places to good to firm, good in places a few hours before racing. A trappy first division of the nursery to open proceedings but it turned into a lively betting heat, dominated by the Bethell runner, who duly rewarded his supporters. They came up the middle and the pace was fairly even, with the time confirming that the ground was getting quicker all the time. The form of this race makes sense.

7284 VISIT SRI LANKA NURSERY H'CAP (DIV II) 6f
2:30 (2:30) (Class 6) (0-65,64) 2-Y-O

£3,737 (£1,112; £555; £300; £300; £300) **Stalls Centre**

Form RPR

4034 **1** **Craigburn**[38] 5885 2-9-3 **60**.....(p[1]) BenCurtis 1 63
(Tom Clover) *racd keenly: hld up in midfield: rdn and hdwy over 1f out: led narrowly wl ins fnl f: sn jinked lft: all out (trainer said, regarding improved form, gelding benefited from the application of cheekpieces and a return to turf)* **11/1**

500 **2** *shd* **Holloa**[110] 3220 2-9-3 **60**..... DavidAllan 3 63
(Tim Easterby) *led: rdn over 1f out: hdd narrowly wl ins fnl f: rallied towards fin: jst hld* **17/2**

0221 **3** *nk* **Prissy Missy (IRE)**[14] 6799 2-8-13 **61**..... ThomasGreatrex(5) 4 63
(David Loughnane) *trckd ldrs gng wl: nt clr run over 2f out: swtchd rt ent fnl 2f: rdn whn chsng ldrs fnl f: r.o towards fin: nt quite pce of front two* **7/2[1]**

0045 **4** *1 ¾* **Geepower (IRE)**[20] 6563 2-8-12 **55**.....(b) BenRobinson 10 52
(Brian Ellison) *hmpd s: prom: rdn over 1f out: unable qck ins fnl f: styd on same pce fnl 100yds* **12/1**

056 **5** *nk* **Maurice Dancer**[29] 6254 2-9-7 **64**..... PaulMulrennan 8 60
(Julie Camacho) *bmpd and carried lft s: hld up in rr: rdn and hdwy over 1f out: hung lft ins fnl f: kpt on: nvr able to chal* **6/1**

4400 **6** *½* **King Lenox**[26] 6337 2-9-2 **62**..... RowanScott(3) 7 56
(Nigel Tinkler) *carried lft s: hld up: pushed along over 2f out: hdwy over 1f out: kpt on ins fnl f: nvr able to trble ldrs* **4/1[2]**

0040 **7** *5* **Mr Gus (IRE)**[41] 5789 2-8-7 **53**.....(p[1]) SeanDavis(3) 2 32
(Richard Fahey) *prom: drvn and lost pl over 2f out: wknd 1f out: eased whn wl btn fnl 75yds* **5/1[3]**

6005 **8** *1 ¾* **Tiltilys Rock (IRE)**[30] 6228 2-8-4 **47**..... CamHardie 9 22
(Andrew Crook) *bmpd s: in tch: pushed along over 2f out: sn sltly hmpd: lost pl ent fnl 2f: n.d after* **25/1**

0450 **9** *shd* **Yorkshire Grey (IRE)**[27] 6313 2-9-1 **58**.....(p[1]) JoeFanning 11 32
(Ann Duffield) *wnt to post early: wnt lft s: racd keenly: in tch: rdn and wknd wl over 1f out* **11/1**

1m 11.58s (-1.22) **Going Correction** -0.375s/f (Firm) **9 Ran SP% 111.9**
Speed ratings (Par 93): **93,92,92,90,89 89,82,80,79**
CSF £96.20 CT £393.24 TOTE £11.20: £3.20, £2.30, £1.50; EX 103.60 Trifecta £531.60.
Owner The Craigburn Partnership **Bred** Whatton Manor Stud **Trained** Newmarket, Suffolk

FOCUS
This second division of the nursery was run in a near identical time to the opener, and the principals came clear. Ordinary form.

7285 THIRSK RACECOURSE LICENSED FOR WEDDING CEREMONIES NOVICE AUCTION STKS 7f
3:00 (3:02) (Class 6) 2-Y-O **£3,166** (£942; £470; £235) **Stalls Low**

Form RPR

52 **1** **Hartswood**[11] 6891 2-9-2 0..... SeanDavis(3) 12 75+
(Richard Fahey) *midfield: hdwy 3f out: rdn 2f out: led over 1f out: drvn out and r.o ins fnl f: in command towards fin* **11/8[1]**

3 **2** *1 ½* **Challet (IRE)**[23] 6457 2-9-5 0..... CallumRodriguez 8 71
(Michael Dods) *plld hrd: prom on outer: rdn to chal 2f out: kpt on u.p: nt pce of wnr towards fin (jockey said trainer ran too free)* **5/2[2]**

54 **3** *1 ½* **King's Charisma (IRE)**[48] 5512 2-9-5 0..... DavidNolan 9 67
(David O'Meara) *trckd ldrs: rdn 2f out: styd on towards fin: nt pce to chal* **16/1**

06 **4** *nk* **Clifftop Heaven**[25] 6368 2-9-5 0..... DougieCostello 1 66
(Mark Walford) *led: rdn and hdd over 1f out: kpt on u.p ins fnl f but nt pce of ldrs* **33/1**

4 **5** *3* **Kuwaity**[21] 6532 2-9-0 0..... SeamusCronin(5) 5 58
(Mohamed Moubarak) *trckd ldrs: rdn over 1f out: one pce and no imp fnl f* **11/1**

0 **6** *nk* **Quercus (IRE)**[9] 6970 2-9-5 0..... JoeFanning 6 57
(Ann Duffield) *chsd ldr tl rdn ent fnl 2f: edgd rt u.p ent fnl f: no ex fnl 100yds* **28/1**

7 *1* **Fansurper (IRE)** 2-9-5 0..... BenCurtis 3 54
(Roger Fell) *s.i.s: towards rr: rdn and hdwy over 2f out: one pce ins fnl f: nvr able to rch ldrs* **40/1**

6 **8** *nk* **Top Flight Cool**[9] 6971 2-9-5 0..... DavidAllan 11 54
(Tim Easterby) *midfield: hdwy 2f out: rdn to chse ldrs over 1f out: no ex ins fnl f* **7/1[3]**

9 *nk* **Starbo (IRE)** 2-9-5 0..... JasonHart 4 53
(John Quinn) *s.i.s: midfield: rdn over 3f out: wknd over 2f out* **11/1**

10 *shd* **Fiannoglaigh (IRE)** 2-9-0 0..... CamHardie 13 48
(Rebecca Menzies) *wnt rt s: towards rr: pushed along 5f out: rdn over 2f out: nvr able to get on terms w ldrs* **66/1**

11 *1* **War Defender** 2-9-5 0..... RachelRichardson 10 50
(Tim Easterby) *missed break: bhd and detached for 3f: rdn over 2f out: nvr a threat* **50/1**

12 *15* **Class Clown (IRE)** 2-9-5 0.....(b[1]) RobbieDowney 2 9
(David Barron) *hld up: rdn 3f out: outpcd after: lft bhd fnl f* **50/1**

1m 26.8s (-0.80) **Going Correction** -0.375s/f (Firm) **12 Ran SP% 120.0**
Speed ratings (Par 93): **89,87,85,85,81 81,80,79,79,79 78,61**
CSF £4.49 TOTE £2.30: £1.10, £1.30, £4.10; EX 6.50 Trifecta £47.70.
Owner Percy / Green Racing 2 **Bred** D Lancaster-Smith & Moreton Manor Stud **Trained** Musley Bank, N Yorks

FOCUS
They didn't hang around in this modest 2yo novice event. There's a slight doubt over the worth of the form.

7286 SRI LANKA AWAITS YOU (S) H'CAP 6f
3:30 (3:33) (Class 6) (0-65,67) 3-6-Y-O

£3,737 (£1,112; £555; £300; £300; £300) **Stalls Centre**

Form RPR

6564 **1** **Fard**[17] 6666 4-8-4 **52**..... PaulaMuir(5) 17 60
(Roger Fell) *racd off the pce: pushed along and hdwy 1/2-way: hung lft ent fnl f: led fnl 130yds: r.o* **9/1**

2526 **2** *1 ¼* **Fairy Fast (IRE)**[7] 7022 3-9-5 **64**.....(p) PJMcDonald 12 68
(George Boughey) *prom: led after 2f: rdn over 1f out: hdd fnl 130yds: kpt on: nt pce of wnr towards fin* **14/1**

0300 **3** *½* **Guardia Svizzera (IRE)**[17] 6659 5-9-4 **61**.....(h) BenCurtis 6 64
(Roger Fell) *chsd ldrs: effrt to chal over 1f out: kpt on u.p: hld towards fin (trainer said gelding hung right-handed)* **18/1**

0400 **4** *1 ¼* **Racquet**[31] 6174 6-8-3 **46** oh1.....(b) JamesSullivan 4 45
(Ruth Carr) *hld up in midfield: rdn and hdwy over 2f out: styd on ins fnl f: nvr able to chal* **33/1**

0330 **5** *½* **Dandy Highwayman (IRE)**[17] 6665 5-9-3 **60**.....(tp) BenRobinson 20 58
(Ollie Pears) *prom: rdn and hung lft over 1f out: unable qck: styd on same pce fnl 100yds* **7/1[1]**

0060 **6** *1 ½* **Optimickstickhill**[21] 6547 4-8-0 **50** ow2.....(b) RhonaPindar(7) 2 43
(Scott Dixon) *chsd ldrs: pushed along over 2f out: styd on same pce ins fnl f* **25/1**

046 **7** *nk* **Roaring Rory**[39] 5857 6-8-5 **48**..... CamHardie 5 40
(Ollie Pears) *missed break: bhd: rdn and hdwy over 2f out: styd on ins fnl f: nvr able to trble ldrs (jockey said gelding was slowly away)* **18/1**

3060 **8** *nk* **Van Gerwen**[16] 6699 6-9-8 **65**..... DanielTudhope 1 56
(Les Eyre) *prom: rdn over 1f out: unable qck: no ex fnl 100yds* **15/2[2]**

-030 **9** *1* **Packington Lane**[17] 6685 3-9-1 **60**.....(p) DavidAllan 15 48
(Tim Easterby) *chsd ldrs: rdn over 2f out: one pce ins fnl f* **33/1**

0460 **10** *shd* **Frosted Lass**[6] 7047 3-8-9 **54**..... PhilDennis 14 42
(David Barron) *midfield: rdn and hdwy 1/2-way: one pce ins fnl f* **33/1**

0054 **11** *nk* **Cupid's Arrow (IRE)**[34] 6058 5-8-8 **51**..... JamieGormley 7 38
(Ruth Carr) *wnt to post early: led for 2f: remained prom: rdn over 2f out: fdd fnl 150yds* **10/1**

5660 **12** *nk* **Fort Benton (IRE)**[146] 2016 3-8-10 **55**.....(w) RobbieDowney 3 41
(David Barron) *stdd s: in rr: pushed along 1/2-way: kpt on ins fnl f: nvr got involved* **33/1**

3336 **13** *1* **Cooperess**[21] 6529 6-8-0 **46**.....(p) JaneElliott(3) 8 29
(Adrian Wintle) *midfield: rdn over 2f out: no imp over 1f out: no ex fnl 150yds* **16/1**

2064 **14** *¾* **Brockey Rise (IRE)**[18] 6639 4-9-2 **59**.....(b) StevieDonohoe 16 40
(David Evans) *hld up: rdn 1/2-way: no imp (jockey said gelding was never travelling)* **12/1**

4046 **15** *2 ¾* **Indian Pursuit (IRE)**[6] 7051 6-9-4 **61**.....(v) JasonHart 18 34
(John Quinn) *chsd ldrs: rdn over 2f out: n.m.r and hmpd whn hld jst over 1f out: wknd ins fnl f* **8/1[3]**

0005 **16** *1 ¾* **Ascot Dreamer**[11] 6897 3-8-1 **51**.....(h[1]) AndrewBreslin(5) 19 18
(David Brown) *chsd ldrs: rdn over 2f out: sn wknd* **18/1**

0050 **17** *2* **La Cumparsita (IRE)**[39] 5852 5-8-3 **46**..... JoeFanning 9 7
(Tristan Davidson) *in tch: lost pl 1/2-way: outpcd after* **7/1[1]**

2360 **18** *7* **My Girl Maisie (IRE)**[108] 3304 5-8-3 **46** oh1.....(e) AndrewMullen 10
(Richard Guest) *wnt to post early: hld up: pushed along and bhd 1/2-way: nvr a threat* **50/1**

1035 **19** *6* **Metal Exchange**[63] 4977 3-9-5 **67**..... ConnorMurtagh(3) 11
(Marjorie Fife) *midfield: rdn and wknd 1/2-way* **50/1**

1m 10.7s (-2.10) **Going Correction** -0.375s/f (Firm)
WFA 3 from 4yo+ 2lb **19 Ran SP% 122.5**
Speed ratings: **99,97,96,95,94 92,91,91,90,90 89,89,87,86,83 80,78,68,60**
CSF £119.63 CT £2277.21 TOTE £10.80: £2.90, £3.30, £4.30, £6.70; EX 137.30 Trifecta £1398.10.There was no bid for the winner. Fairy Fast was subject to a friendly claim. Van Gerwen was claimed by Paul Midgley for £6000.
Owner Northern Marking Ltd & Partners **Bred** Lofts Hall Stud & B Sangster **Trained** Nawton, N Yorks

FOCUS
This was a decent winning time for the class. The second and third set a fairly straightforward level.

7287 BRITISH EBF FILLIES' NOVICE STKS 1m 4f 8y
4:00 (4:00) (Class 4) 3-Y-O+ **£7,439** (£2,213; £1,106; £553) **Stalls High**

Form RPR

31 **1** **Ahorsewithnoname**[28] 6274 4-10-0 0..... BenRobinson 6 81+
(Brian Ellison) *prom: rdn over 2f out: led over 1f out: r.o ins fnl f* **8/11[1]**

6-25 **2** *1* **Tranquil Storm (IRE)**[78] 5009 4-9-7 67..... TomEaves 4 72
(Kevin Ryan) *hld up: impr to ld after over 1f: rdn over 2f out: hdd over 1f out: kpt on ins fnl f but hld* **20/1**

2034 **3** *3* **No Dress Rehearsal**[14] 6810 3-9-0 67.....(h) PaulMulrennan 2 67
(Michael Easterby) *hld up: impr to trck ldrs after 4f: rdn to go pce over 3f: chsd front two 2f out: no imp fnl f* **12/1[3]**

5642 **4** *4* **Vibrance**[19] 6595 3-9-0 67..... DanielTudhope 3 64
(James Fanshawe) *prom: rdn to go pce over 2f out: one pce over 1f out: eased whn wl btn fnl 75yds* **7/4[2]**

0 **5** *30* **Strictly Legal (IRE)**[19] 6587 3-8-9 0..... RobJFitzpatrick(5) 5 14
(David O'Meara) *plld hrd early: led for over 1f: hld up after: rdn: outpcd and edgd rt over 2f out: eased and lost tch over 1f out* **80/1**

00/ **6** *47* **Arabellas Fortune**[761] 6057 4-9-7 0..... ShaneGray 1
(Stef Keniry) *in rr: nvr really travelling: lost tch over 4f out: t.o* **100/1**

2m 34.53s (-5.47) **Going Correction** -0.375s/f (Firm)
WFA 3 from 4yo 7lb **6 Ran SP% 108.9**
Speed ratings (Par 102): **103,102,100,97,77 46**
CSF £15.24 TOTE £1.70: £1.10, £3.60; EX 9.60 Trifecta £21.00.
Owner D J Burke & P Alderson **Bred** Whitley Stud **Trained** Norton, N Yorks

FOCUS
An uncompetitive novice for fillies and the runner-up puts the form into perspective. The winner had a straightforward task.

7288 THIRSK RACECOURSE CONFERENCE & EVENTS CENTRE FILLIES' H'CAP 7f 218y
4:30 (4:32) (Class 5) (0-75,75) 3-Y-O+

£4,398 (£1,309; £654; £327; £300; £300) **Stalls Low**

Form RPR

3362 **1** **Harvest Day**[19] 6609 4-9-6 **71**.....(t) NathanEvans 8 78
(Michael Easterby) *hld up: pushed along and hdwy over 2f out: led over 1f out: rdn out* **4/1[1]**

0665 **2** *½* **Eponina (IRE)**[13] 6825 5-8-10 **61**..... LewisEdmunds 10 67
(Michael Appleby) *chsd ldrs: led over 2f out: rdn and hdd over 1f out: kpt on u.p ins fnl f but hld* **8/1**

323 **3** *1* **Sloane Garden**[13] 6823 3-9-3 **72**..... PJMcDonald 3 76
(James Tate) *rrd s: chsd ldrs: rdn over 2f out: tried to chal over 1f out: kpt on u.p ins fnl f: no ex nr fin* **15/2**

0405 **4** *1 ¼* **Florenza**[9] 6974 6-9-10 **75**..... AndrewElliott 9 76
(Chris Fairhurst) *midfield: rdn and hdwy over 2f out: hung lft whn chsng ldrs over 1f out: no imp ins fnl f* **6/1[3]**

5553 **5** *1 ¼* **Lady Lizzy**[18] 6624 3-9-0 **69**..............................(v) CliffordLee 5 67
(K R Burke) *led: drvn and hdd over 2f out: unable to go w ldrs over 1f out: no ex ins fnl f* **13/2**

5064 **6** *½* **Love Explodes**[20] 6559 3-9-5 **74**.............................. StevieDonohoe 7 71
(Ed Vaughan) *midfield: rdn and outpcd over 2f out: kpt on ins fnl f: nvr able to trble ldrs* **20/1**

2000 **7** *1* **Elixsoft (IRE)**[10] 6940 4-8-11 **62**..............................(p) BenCurtis 6 57
(Roger Fell) *hld up: rdn over 2f out: kpt on ins fnl f: no imp* **12/1**

0000 **8** *2 ¼* **Alexandrakollontai (IRE)**[18] 6627 9-8-5 **56** oh2.............. JamesSullivan 4 45
(Alistair Whillans) *in rr: rdn 4f out: nvr a threat* **33/1**

5020 **9** *1 ¼* **Alfa Dawn (IRE)**[17] 6679 3-8-12 **67**.............................. SamJames 2 53
(Phillip Makin) *chsd ldrs: rdn over 2f out: wknd over 1f out* **8/1**

0203 **10** *5* **Ideal Candy (IRE)**[22] 6500 4-9-2 **70**..............................(h) GemmaTutty(3) 11 45
(Karen Tutty) *wnt to post early: rrd s: midfield: lost pl over 3f out: wl bhd over 1f out (jockey said filly was slowly away and never travelling thereafter)* **5/1**[2]

1m 37.06s (-4.64) **Going Correction** -0.375s/f (Firm)
WFA 3 from 4yo+ 4lb **10** Ran SP% **113.7**
Speed ratings (Par 100): **108,107,106,105,104 103,102,100,99,94**
CSF £35.16 CT £233.28 TOTE £4.00: £1.90, £2.50, £2.70; EX 38.40 Trifecta £343.60.
Owner Mrs C E Mason & Partner **Bred** Howard Barton Stud **Trained** Sheriff Hutton, N Yorks

FOCUS
This modest handicap was run at a sound pace. Ordinary if competitive fillies' form.

7289 CHESTNUT ROOM AT THIRSK RACECOURSE IDEAL PARTY VENUE H'CAP 7f

5:00 (5:01) (Class 5) (0-75,76) 4-Y-O+

£4,398 (£1,309; £654; £327; £300; £300) **Stalls** Low

Form RPR

1342 **1** **Twin Appeal (IRE)**[16] 6700 8-9-5 **76**.............................. GemmaTutty(3) 9 84
(Karen Tutty) *midfield: hdwy 2f out: rdn over 1f out: led fnl 175yds: kpt on wl towards fin* **6/1**[3]

0050 **2** *½* **Deansgate (IRE)**[23] 6461 6-8-9 **66**.............................. HarrisonShaw(3) 6 73
(Julie Camacho) *wnt to post early: hld up: rdn over 2f out: hdwy over 1f out: r.o ins fnl f: pressed wnr towards fin* **12/1**

2606 **3** *1* **Zylan (IRE)**[13] 6826 7-9-1 **69**..............................(p) BenCurtis 5 73
(Roger Fell) *midfield: rdn over 2f out: hdwy over 1f out: r.o ins fnl f: run flattened out cl home: nt quite pce of front two* **16/1**

3555 **4** *nse* **Esprit De Corps**[23] 6461 5-9-3 **71**.............................. DanielTudhope 16 75
(David Barron) *midfield: rdn and hdwy over 2f out: chalng ins fnl f: styd on same pce towards fin* **5/1**[2]

3040 **5** *1 ¾* **John Kirkup**[17] 6677 4-9-6 **74**..............................(p) ConnorBeasley 13 73
(Michael Dods) *chsd ldrs: rdn to ld over 1f out: hdd fnl 175yds: no ex towards fin* **12/1**

1301 **6** *shd* **Sfumato**[6] 7051 5-8-11 **68** 5ex.............................. SeanDavis(3) 3 67
(Adrian Nicholls) *midfield: rdn over 2f out: hdwy over 1f out: styd on ins fnl f: nt pce to chal* **12/1**

0105 **7** *nk* **Alfa McGuire (IRE)**[16] 6734 4-9-7 **75**..............................(p) SamJames 8 73
(Phillip Makin) *chsd ldr: rdn to ld over 2f out: hdd over 1f out: stl there ins fnl f: styd on same pce fnl 100yds* **20/1**

0020 **8** *½* **Smugglers Creek (IRE)**[17] 6665 5-9-0 **68**..............................(p) PaulMulrennan 1 65
(Iain Jardine) *chsd ldrs: rdn over 2f out: unable qck over 1f out: kpt on same pce ins fnl f* **33/1**

1110 **9** *½* **Red Seeker**[16] 6700 4-9-0 **73**..............................(t) DannyRedmond(5) 12 68
(Tim Easterby) *chsd ldrs: rdn over 2f out: one pce fnl f* **12/1**

5600 **10** *shd* **Arcavallo (IRE)**[9] 6972 4-9-2 **70**.............................. CallumRodriguez 14 65
(Michael Dods) *hld up: pushed along 4f out: rdn over 2f out: kpt on u.p ins fnl f: nvr able to trble ldrs* **16/1**

-136 **11** *¾* **Aliento**[45] 5616 4-8-10 **64**.............................. TomEaves 10 57
(Michael Dods) *hld up: rdn over 2f out: hdwy over 1f out to chse ldrs: one pce ins fnl f* **6/1**[3]

4040 **12** *½* **Uncle Charlie (IRE)**[68] 4785 5-8-6 **60**..............................(w) JoeFanning 4 52
(Ann Duffield) *midfield: rdn over 2f out: losing pl whn n.m.r over 1f out: sn swtchd rt: n.d after* **7/1**

3400 **13** *¾* **Highlight Reel (IRE)**[80] 4322 4-9-3 **71**.............................. PhilDennis 2 61
(Rebecca Bastiman) *stdd s: hld up: rdn over 2f out: kpt on steadily ins fnl f: nvr a threat* **18/1**

0200 **14** *3* **Billy Wedge**[28] 6275 4-8-2 **56** oh5.............................. RoystonFfrench 11 38
(Tracy Waggott) *hld up: rdn over 2f out: no bttr than midfield: wknd over 1f out* **20/1**

0104 **15** *7* **Start Time (IRE)**[17] 6677 6-9-6 **74**.............................. KevinStott 7 37
(Paul Midgley) *led: rdn and hdd over 2f out: wknd over 1f out (trainer said, regarding poor performance, gelding was unsuited by being unable to dominate on this occasion)* **4/1**[1]

1m 24.15s (-3.45) **Going Correction** -0.375s/f (Firm) **15** Ran SP% **138.0**
Speed ratings (Par 103): **104,103,102,102,100 100,99,99,98,98 97,97,96,92,84**
CSF £85.60 CT £1158.54 TOTE £7.30: £2.40, £4.50, £5.40; EX 156.20 Trifecta £979.90.
Owner Mrs Mary Winetroube & Thoroughbred Homes **Bred** Glashare House Stud **Trained** Osmotherley, N Yorks

FOCUS
This competitive handicap was run to suit the closers. The winner's best since this time last year.

7290 LAST RACE @THIRSKRACES 2019 H'CAP 1m 4f 8y

5:35 (5:36) (Class 6) (0-60,62) 3-Y-O

£4,075 (£1,212; £606; £303; £300; £300) **Stalls** Low

Form RPR

0006 **1** **Feebi**[35] 6030 3-8-2 **45** oh1.............................. PaulaMuir(5) 2 53
(Chris Fairhurst) *hld up in rr: rdn over 3f out: hdwy over 2f out: styd on to ld ins fnl f: pushed out and in command towards fin (trainer said, regarding improved form shown, filly benefited from the stronger pace today and a return to turf were noted)* **14/1**

1332 **2** *1 ¼* **Hammy End (IRE)**[16] 6702 3-9-7 **60**..............................(h) DanielTudhope 11 65
(William Muir) *midfield: hdwy 4f out: rdn to ld 2f out: hdd ins fnl f: kpt on u.p: hld towards fin* **5/2**[1]

0030 **3** *1 ½* **Half Bolly**[24] 6400 3-9-2 **55**.............................. JasonHart 7 58
(Mark Walford) *prom: rdn to ld over 2f out: sn hdd: stl ev ch 1f out: styd on same pce fnl 100yds* **6/1**[2]

6063 **4** *nk* **Alpasu (IRE)**[35] 6012 3-9-9 **62**.............................. ConnorBeasley 4 64
(Adrian Nicholls) *chsd ldrs: rdn over 3f out: outpcd over 2f out: kpt on ins fnl f: nvr able to chal* **12/1**

5024 **5** *1* **Smashing Lass (IRE)**[20] 6578 3-8-7 **46**..............................(p) BenRobinson 8 47
(Ollie Pears) *swtchd lft s: midfield: lost pl 4f out: outpcd after: styd on ins fnl f: nt rch ldrs (jockey said filly lost her action on hme bnd)* **16/1**

2031 **6** *½* **Brutalab**[22] 6499 3-9-4 **57**..............................(p) DavidAllan 5 57
(Tim Easterby) *racd keenly: sn led: rdn and hdd over 2f out: stl there u.p over 1f out whn hung rt: wknd fnl 100yds (jockey said gelding hung right-handed)* **5/2**[1]

5040 **7** *½* **Asensio**[18] 6635 3-8-13 **57**..............................(t) SeamusCronin(5) 1 56
(Mohamed Moubarak) *hld up in rr: rdn over 2f out: hdwy u.p over 1f out: one pce fnl 75yds* **16/1**

00 **8** *1* **Holy Hymn (IRE)**[91] 3938 3-9-5 **58**..............................(t) BenCurtis 9 55
(Kevin Frost) *hld up: rdn 5f out: hdwy u.p over 2f out: hung lft over 1f out: nt get to ldrs: no ex fnl 100yds (jockey said gelding hung left in hme straight)* **20/1**

1046 **9** *9* **Neileta**[16] 6702 3-9-6 **59**..............................(p) DuranFentiman 10 42
(Tim Easterby) *chsd ldrs: pushed along 5f out: rdn over 3f out: wknd over 2f out* **10/1**[3]

0000 **10** *26* **Laura Louise (IRE)**[17] 6678 3-8-2 **46**.............................. FayeMcManoman(5) 3
(Nigel Tinkler) *midfield: hdwy to chse ldrs after 3f: rdn and wknd over 3f out: t.o* **33/1**

2m 35.47s (-4.53) **Going Correction** -0.375s/f (Firm) **10** Ran SP% **114.3**
Speed ratings (Par 99): **100,99,98,97,97 96,96,95,89,72**
CSF £48.16 CT £239.24 TOTE £17.70: £4.00, £1.40, £2.10; EX 78.70 Trifecta £416.90.
Owner Allan Davies **Bred** J Wigan & London Thoroughbred Services **Trained** Middleham, N Yorks

FOCUS
This weak 3yo handicap was run at an average pace.
T/Jkpt: Not won. T/Plt: £163.20 to a £1 stake. Pool: £55,107.64 - 246.41 winning units T/Qpdt: £22.60 to a £1 stake. Pool: £6,698.29 - 219.28 winning units **Darren Owen**

6873 MAISONS-LAFFITTE (R-H)

Monday, September 16

OFFICIAL GOING: Turf: good

7291a PRIX AD ALTIORA (CONDITIONS) (3YO) (TURF) 1m 4f

1:25 3-Y-O **£11,261** (£4,504; £3,378; £2,252; £1,126)

RPR

1 **Youmna (FR)**[72] 3-9-2 0.............................. Pierre-CharlesBoudot 9 84
(H-A Pantall, France) **3/1**[2]

2 *2 ½* **Guardian Fay (IRE)**[38] 3-8-13 0.............................. MaximeGuyon 4 77
(Jean-Pierre Carvalho, Germany) **11/5**[1]

3 *shd* **Sermandakfi (FR)**[31] 3-8-13 0.............................. FabriceVeron 11 77
(F Monnier, France) **26/1**

4 *¾* **Deacon**[275] 3-8-11 0..............................(b[1]) AurelienLemaitre 10 74
(F Head, France) **9/1**

5 *snk* **Sister Midnight (IRE)**[72] 3-8-13 0.............................. StephanePasquier 6 75
(P Bary, France) **4/1**[3]

6 *2 ½* **Armen Basc (FR)** 3-8-11 0.............................. GregoryBenoist 2 69
(A Junk, France) **25/1**

7 *8* **Dakharo (FR)** 3-8-11 0.............................. CyrilleStefan 5 57
(C E Cayeux, France) **60/1**

8 *1 ¼* **Robin Du Bois (FR)** 3-9-2 0..............................(p) ClementLecoeuvre 8 60
(Carmen Bocskai, Germany) **24/1**

9 *1 ¼* **Sameer (FR)**[80] 3-9-2 0.............................. TheoBachelot 7 58
(Ian Williams) *dwlt: in rr early: impr into midfield over 3f out: rdn along over 2f out: drvn over 1f out: no imp fnl f* **79/10**

10 *7* **Silverstrand (IRE)**[21] 3-8-11 0..............................(b) MickaelBarzalona 3 41
(H-F Devin, France) *racd in rr of midfield on inner: shuffled bk to last 5f out: rdn and no imp fnl 3f: nvr involved* **10/1**

2m 32.1s (152.10) **10** Ran SP% **119.8**
PARI-MUTUEL (all including 1 euro stake): WIN 4.00; PLACE 1.60, 1.40, 4.20; DF 7.10.
Owner H H Sheikh Abdulla Bin Khalifa Al Thani **Bred** Scea Du Haras De Victot **Trained** France

7292a PRIX ECLIPSE (GROUP 3) (2YO) (TURF) 6f

2:00 2-Y-O **£36,036** (£14,414; £10,810; £7,207; £3,603)

RPR

1 **Devil (IRE)**[29] 6264 2-8-11 0.............................. MaximeGuyon 1 105+
(F Head, France) *hld up in rr: urged along 2f out: rdn to chal over 1f out: drvn to ld ins fnl f: kpt on strly* **2/1**[1]

2 *½* **Nina Bailarina**[38] 5906 2-8-8 0.............................. OisinMurphy 2 101+
(Ed Walker) *sn led: jnd and disp ld after 2f: pushed along 2f out: rdn and chal over 1f out: hdd ins fnl f: kpt on* **2/1**[1]

3 *7* **Golden Boy (FR)**[29] 6262 2-8-11 0.............................. TheoBachelot 5 83
(S Wattel, France) *prom early: jnd ldr after 2f: rdn and outpcd over 1f out: styd on same pce fnl f* **16/5**[2]

4 *snk* **Jolie (FR)**[16] 6791 2-8-8 0.............................. MaximPecheur 4 79
(Andrea Marcialis, France) *t.k.h early: settled to trck ldrs: rdn along 2f out: drvn w limited rspnse over 1f out: no ex ins fnl f* **81/10**

5 *½* **Abama (FR)**[16] 2-8-8 0.............................. StephanePasquier 3 78
(Y Barberot, France) *settled in 3rd: rowed along over 2f out: rdn over 1f out: wknd ins fnl f* **49/10**[3]

1m 10.26s (-3.14) **5** Ran SP% **118.4**
PARI-MUTUEL (all including 1 euro stake): WIN 3.00; PLACE 1.50, 1.60; SF 7.70.
Owner Wertheimer & Frere **Bred** Wertheimer & Frere **Trained** France

FOCUS
This lacked depth and the form is rated a shade cautiously.

7293a LA COUPE DE MAISONS-LAFFITTE (GROUP 3) (3YO+) (TURF) 1m 2f (S)

3:10 3-Y-O+ **£36,036** (£14,414; £10,810; £7,207; £3,603)

RPR

1 **Villa Rosa (FR)**[22] 6522 4-8-13 0.............................. MickaelBarzalona 5 108
(H-F Devin, France) *mde virtually all: qcknd up over 2f out: rdn 1 1/2f out: styd on strly ins fnl f: a doing enough* **17/5**[3]

2 *¾* **Intellogent (IRE)**[36] 6001 4-9-2 0..............................(p) CristianDemuro 2 110
(F Chappet, France) *hld up in last pair: pushed along and prog fr over 2f out: rdn to chse ldr 1 1/2f out: kpt on ins fnl f: nt quite pce to chal* **23/10**[2]

3 *½* **Trais Fluors**[32] 6144 5-9-2 0.............................. Pierre-CharlesBoudot 1 109
(A Fabre, France) *settled in 3rd: asked for effrt over 2f out: drvn bhd wnr 1 1/2f out: kpt on but nvr pce to chal* **7/10**[1]

4 *3* **Monde Chat Luna (JPN)**[50] 8-9-2 0.............................. MlleMickaelleMichel 4 103
(Hiroo Shimizu, France) *cl up: unable qck w ldr whn pushed along over 2f out: sn lost position and u.p: grad wknd fr over 1f out* **22/1**

5 *2* **Magical Dreamer (IRE)**[50] 5479 5-8-13 0.............................. PierreBazire 3 97
(E J O'Neill, France) *hld up in rr: struggling to go pce over 2 1/2f out: edgd rt whn pushed along 2f out: btn ent fnl f: kpt on same pce* **15/1**

2m 5.09s (2.69) **5** Ran SP% **122.5**
PARI-MUTUEL (all including 1 euro stake): WIN 4.40; PLACE 2.60, 1.60; SF 15.10.

Owner Mme Henri Devin **Bred** Mme H Devin **Trained** France
FOCUS
This wasn't truly run and the fourth and fifth may be flattered.

7110 CHEPSTOW (L-H)

Tuesday, September 17

OFFICIAL GOING: Good (good to soft in places; 7.2)
Wind: Moderate, mainly behind Weather: Fine

7294 CAROLYN PERCHARD 60TH CELEBRATION H'CAP — 1m 4f

2:20 (2:20) (Class 4) (0-85,83) 4-Y-O+

£5,207 (£1,549; £774; £387; £300; £300) **Stalls** Low

Form / RPR

3210 **1** **Paths Of Glory**[18] 6657 4-9-2 **78**.....(t) OisinMurphy 2 91+
(Hugo Palmer) *hld up: hdwy to trck ldrs 7f out: rdn to ld narrowly 2f out: r.o strly to assert fnl 110yds (trainer rep said, regarding improved form shown, gelding had appreciated the better ground, which was officially described as Good, Good to soft in places on this occasion)* **2/1**[1]

110- **2** *2 ½* **Astromachia**[340] 8164 4-9-7 **83**.....(w) PatDobbs 8 92
(Amanda Perrett) *chsd ldrs: chal 2f out: sn rdn: ev ch tl no ex and outpcd by wnr fnl 110yds* **7/1**[3]

3434 **3** *4* **Rotherwick (IRE)**[12] 6909 7-9-6 **82**.....(t) DavidProbert 3 85
(Paul Cole) *hld up: rdn and hdwy on outer over 2f out: wnt 3rd 1f out: no imp on ldng pair* **15/2**

4145 **4** *¾* **Nabhan**[19] 6642 7-8-6 **71**.....(tp) WilliamCox(3) 4 73
(Bernard Llewellyn) *hld up: rdn over 2f out: sme prog over 1f out: sn outpcd by ldrs* **20/1**

2014 **5** *½* **Ascot Day (FR)**[23] 6511 5-8-10 **72**.....(p) HarryBentley 5 73
(Bernard Llewellyn) *s.s: sn t.k.h in midfield: rdn 3f out: kpt on same pce* **7/1**[3]

1003 **6** *1* **Prevent**[9] 7003 4-8-10 **75**.....(p) CierenFallon(3) 1 74
(Ian Williams) *t.k.h: cl up: led after 2f: rdn and hdd 2f out: sn outpcd by ldng pair: lost 3rd 1f out: wknd (jockey said gelding ran too freely)* **9/1**

00-5 **7** *2* **Maiden Voyage (FR)**[8] 7026 4-9-1 **77**.....HollieDoyle 9 73
(Archie Watson) *trckd ldng pair: lost pl 7f out: nt clr run 3f out: sn drvn: styng on but no ch w ldrs whn hmpd ins fnl f (jockey said filly was denied clear run)* **3/1**[2]

6026 **8** *¾* **Never Surrender (IRE)**[24] 6448 5-9-2 **78**.....KieranShoemark 7 73
(Charles Hills) *led 2f: rdn over 3f out and sn lost 2nd: wknd over 2f out (jockey said gelding hung left-handed)* **14/1**

6056 **9** *2* **Winged Spur (IRE)**[31] 6224 4-9-2 **78**.....FrannyNorton 6 70
(Mark Johnston) *midfield: n.m.r on inner and lost pl over 3f out: btn 2f out* **25/1**

2m 33.73s (-6.57) **Going Correction** -0.625s/f (Hard) **9 Ran SP% 120.4**
Speed ratings (Par 105): **96,94,91,91,90 90,88,88,87**
CSF £17.70 CT £91.32 TOTE £2.90: £1.40, £2.40, £1.80; EX 18.60 Trifecta £118.00.
Owner China Horse Club International Limited **Bred** Dayton Investments Ltd **Trained** Newmarket, Suffolk
FOCUS
An ordinary handicap run at a steady enough pace, although two progressive types pulled clear. The form's rated slightly positively.

7295 PETE SMITH CAR SALES (S) STKS — 1m 2f

2:50 (2:53) (Class 6) 3-Y-O

£2,781 (£827; £413; £300; £300; £300) **Stalls** Low

Form / RPR

4424 **1** **Elegant Love**[6] 7081 3-8-9 64.....HarryBentley 7 66+
(David Evans) *trckd ldr: led 3f out: rdn 2f out: sn clr: eased towards fin* **1/1**[1]

5550 **2** *1* **Miss Elsa**[12] 6904 3-8-2 60.....GeorgiaDobie(7) 4 61+
(Eve Johnson Houghton) *hld up: stl last 4f out: hdwy on outer over 2f out: rdn to go 2nd appr fnl f: r.o wl: clsd on eased wnr towards fin: too much to do* **7/1**[3]

3600 **3** *7* **Bonneville (IRE)**[15] 6805 3-9-0 48.....(b) OisinMurphy 3 53
(Rod Millman) *trckd ldrs: rdn 3f out: one pce fnl 2f* **10/1**

3150 **4** *½* **Lippy Lady (IRE)**[19] 6643 3-8-7 54.....(h) RhiainIngram(5) 9 50
(Paul George) *wnt to post early: t.k.h in rr: hdwy on outer 5f out: wnt 2nd and rdn wl over 2f out: outpcd by wnr over 1f out: sn lost 2nd: no ex* **10/1**

5 *½* **Quare Lucky (IRE)**[54] 5363 3-8-9 43.....(b) KieranO'Neill 1 46
(Peter Fahey, Ire) *chsd ldrs: drvn 3f out: sn btn* **10/1**

0-66 **6** *2 ½* **Lord Howard (IRE)**[23] 6505 3-9-0 46.....(p[1]) DavidProbert 8 46
(Mick Channon) *midfield: rdn over 3f out: sn outpcd and no ch* **20/1**

0003 **7** *3 ¾* **Mustadun**[20] 6600 3-9-3 63.....FrannyNorton 5 42
(Mark Johnston) *rdn 3f out: a towards rr* **13/2**[2]

1006 **8** *4 ½* **Renegade Master**[20] 6593 3-9-3 77.....(p[1]) CierenFallon(3) 6 36
(George Baker) *hld up towards rr: drvn over 3f out: sme hdwy over 2f out: wknd over 1f out* **8/1**

4- **9** *19* **Olwen's Dream (IRE)**[195] 1046 3-8-6 48.....WilliamCox(3) 2
(Jimmy Frost) *led tl rdn and hdd 3f out: wkng whn hmpd jst over 2f out* **66/1**

2m 4.75s (-8.05) **Going Correction** -0.625s/f (Hard) **9 Ran SP% 120.5**
Speed ratings (Par 99): **107,106,100,100,99 97,94,91,76**
CSF £9.20 TOTE £1.80: £1.10, £1.80, £2.80; EX 9.10 Trifecta £62.60.The winner was bought in for £7,200.
Owner Wayne Clifford **Bred** Mrs S Clifford **Trained** Pandy, Monmouths
FOCUS
The front pair came clear in this seller, the favourite having the luxury of being eased despite the strong finish of the runner-up.

7296 JOHN LEWIN NURSERY H'CAP — 6f 16y

3:20 (3:24) (Class 5) (0-70,72) 2-Y-O

£3,428 (£1,020; £509; £300; £300; £300) **Stalls** Centre

Form / RPR

542 **1** **Music Therapist (IRE)**[17] 6704 2-9-10 **71**.....HarryBentley 8 73+
(George Scott) *t.k.h: sn prom: rdn to dispute ld 2f out: kpt on u.p to assert fnl 75yds* **11/8**[1]

644 **2** *¾* **Broken Rifle**[61] 5082 2-9-11 **72**.....(p[1]) SeanLevey 5 72
(Ivan Furtado) *plld hrd: prom: disp ld after 2f: drvn and lost lft cheekpiece 2f out: kpt on and ev ch tl hld fnl 75yds (gelding lost left cheekpiece ins 2f marker)* **9/4**[2]

2506 **3** *1 ½* **Lili Wen Fach (IRE)**[19] 6637 2-9-3 **64**.....(v[1]) OisinMurphy 2 59
(David Evans) *led: jnd after 2f: rdn and hdd 2f out: stl ev ch tl no ex fnl 110yds (jockey said filly changed its lead legs on several occasions ins fnl 1 1/2f)* **5/1**[3]

6506 **4** *2 ½* **Falconidae (IRE)**[27] 6330 2-9-6 **67**.....PatDobbs 3 55
(Richard Hannon) *wnt to post early: chsd ldng trio: drvn and outpcd over 2f out: no ch after* **14/1**

600 **5** *1* **Calbuco**[14] 6845 2-8-3 **57**.....AngusVilliers(7) 4 42
(Rod Millman) *prom tl lost pl and rdn over 4f out: outpcd in last pair fr 1/2-way* **33/1**

1460 **6** *¾* **Shani**[21] 6563 2-9-0 **61**.....KieranO'Neill 9 44
(John Bridger) *hld up: rdn over 3f out: sn outpcd: hung lft over 1f out* **18/1**

1m 11.18s (-0.32) **Going Correction** -0.375s/f (Firm) **6 Ran SP% 104.4**
Speed ratings (Par 95): **87,86,84,80,79 78**
CSF £3.97 CT £6.90 TOTE £1.90: £1.30, £1.40; EX 4.00 Trifecta £8.10.
Owner Mr Chris Wright, Ms Emma Banks & Partners **Bred** Hyde Park Stud **Trained** Newmarket, Suffolk
■ Burniston Rocks was withdrawn. Price at time of withdrawal 8/1. Rule 4 applies to all bets - deduction 10p in the pound
FOCUS
The right horses came to the fore in this modest nursery. They raced centre-field.

7297 CHEPSTOW PLANT INTERNATIONAL EBF FILLIES' NOVICE STKS (PLUS 10 RACE) — 7f 16y

3:50 (3:50) (Class 5) 2-Y-O

£3,428 (£1,020; £509; £254) **Stalls** Centre

Form / RPR

2 **1** **Festival Day**[14] 6831 2-9-0 0.....FrannyNorton 2 86+
(Mark Johnston) *mde all: shkn up over 1f out: sn qcknd clr: r.o strly* **4/6**[1]

43 **2** *6* **Anfield Girl (IRE)**[74] 4605 2-9-0 0.....RichardKingscote 4 68
(Tom Dascombe) *hld up and rn green at times: rdn over 2f out: impr to go modest 2nd appr fnl f: no ch w easy wnr* **7/2**[2]

361 **3** *1 ¾* **Gert Lush (IRE)**[22] 6527 2-9-4 68.....OisinMurphy 1 68
(Roger Teal) *s.i.s: sn chsng ldrs: pushed along and btn over 1f out: rdn to go modest 3rd ins fnl f* **9/1**

6 **4** *½* **Royal Nation**[20] 6592 2-9-0 0.....HollieDoyle 5 63
(Archie Watson) *trckd wnr: rdn over 2f out: hung lft and outpcd over 1f out: sn lost 2nd: fdd* **7/1**[3]

35 **5** *½* **Kodiellen (IRE)**[32] 6159 2-9-0 0.....RossaRyan 3 61
(Richard Hannon) *t.k.h: trckd ldrs tl rdn and lost pl over 2f out: no ch after* **14/1**

0 **6** *9* **Power Packed**[57] 5250 2-9-0 0.....DavidProbert 6 38
(Henry Candy) *hld up in last: drvn 3f out: sn outpcd* **66/1**

1m 20.48s (-3.42) **Going Correction** -0.375s/f (Firm) 2y crse rec **6 Ran SP% 112.9**
Speed ratings (Par 92): **104,97,95,94,94 83**
CSF £3.34 TOTE £1.50: £1.10, £2.50; EX 3.50 Trifecta £9.70.
Owner Sheikh Hamdan bin Mohammed Al Maktoum **Bred** Godolphin **Trained** Middleham Moor, N Yorks
FOCUS
One-way traffic in this novice, with the impressive winner breaking the juvenile track record. They again raced down the centre.

7298 LINDA AND LUCY TONGE FILLIES' NOVICE STKS — 7f 16y

4:20 (4:22) (Class 5) 3-Y-O+

£3,428 (£1,020; £509; £254) **Stalls** Centre

Form / RPR

4004 **1** **Daryana**[26] 6362 3-8-7 67.....GeorgiaDobie(7) 5 58
(Eve Johnson Houghton) *s.s: sltly detached in last: clsd 3f out: hdwy 2f out: sn drvn: wnt 2nd appr fnl f: kpt on to ld nr fin* **10/11**[1]

60- **2** *nk* **Mac Jetes**[363] 7414 3-8-9 0.....ThomasGreatrex(5) 3 57
(David Loughnane) *cl up: rdn to ld over 2f out: kpt on u.p: hdd nr fin* **25/1**

4326 **3** *2* **Gleeful**[81] 4335 3-9-0 69.....HarryBentley 1 51
(David O'Meara) *hld up in tch on outer: drvn to chse ldr 2f out: lost 2nd appr fnl f: kpt on same pce* **7/4**[2]

4 *1 ½* **Sagittarian Wind**[43] 5758 3-9-0 0.....HollieDoyle 2 47
(Archie Watson) *hld up in tch: rdn and sme prog over 1f out: no imp fnl f but kpt on steadily* **14/1**

0450 **5** *1 ¼* **Disey's Edge**[8] 7032 3-8-11 42.....(p[1]) WilliamCox(3) 6 44
(Christopher Mason) *led tl drvn and hdd over 2f out: fdd fnl f* **66/1**

0P **6** *3* **Theban Air**[190] 1142 3-8-11 0.....CierenFallon(3) 4 36
(Lucy Wadham) *hld up: tk clsr order after 2f: shkn up and outpcd over 2f out: reminder appr fnl f: no imp* **8/1**[3]

03 **7** *2 ½* **Plum Duff**[15] 6802 3-9-0 0.....DavidProbert 7 29
(Michael Blanshard) *cl up: rdn over 2f out: wknd over 1f out* **40/1**

1m 21.49s (-2.41) **Going Correction** -0.375s/f (Firm) **7 Ran SP% 114.3**
Speed ratings (Par 100): **98,97,95,93,92 88,85**
CSF £27.74 TOTE £1.50: £1.10, £11.30; EX 23.70 Trifecta £53.20.
Owner Lionel Godfrey & Peter Wollaston **Bred** Rabbah Bloodstock Limited **Trained** Blewbury, Oxon
FOCUS
Very modest novice form, limited by the fifth. They raced down the centre.

7299 IDC CONVEYORS BELT AND ROLLER TRACK H'CAP — 7f 16y

4:50 (4:51) (Class 5) (0-70,70) 3-Y-O+

£3,428 (£1,020; £509; £300; £300; £300) **Stalls** Centre

Form / RPR

2114 **1** **Bounty Pursuit**[12] 6904 7-9-4 **70**.....MeganNicholls(3) 12 80
(Michael Blake) *midfield: rdn 2f out: r.o to ld ins fnl f: sn in command* **13/2**[3]

2133 **2** *1 ½* **Foxy Femme**[8] 7022 3-9-2 **68**.....JoeyHaynes 1 73
(John Gallagher) *hld up towards rr: rdn 3f out: hdwy on outer over 2f out: wnt 2nd ins fnl f: nt pce of wnr* **11/1**

-003 **3** *1 ¼* **Danecase**[12] 6898 6-9-4 **70**.....(tp) CierenFallon(3) 4 73
(David Dennis) *led: rdn over 2f out: hdd over 1f out: kpt on* **16/1**

5-0 **4** *nk* **Canford Art (IRE)**[87] 4135 4-8-13 **62**.....KieranO'Neill 10 64
(Peter Fahey, Ire) *prom: drvn to ld wl over 1f out: hdd ins fnl f: no ex fnl 100yds* **5/4**[1]

141 **5** *¾* **The Groove**[12] 6898 6-8-12 **68**.....AngusVilliers(7) 5 68
(David Evans) *rdr dropped whip leaving stall: plld hrd early: chsd ldrs: rdn 2f out: kpt on (jockey said gelding dropped his whip leaving stalls)* **10/1**

0552 **6** *nk* **Plumette**[15] 6801 3-8-11 **68**.....ThomasGreatrex(5) 6 66
(David Loughnane) *hld up: effrt over 2f out: nt clr run over 1f out: drvn and r.o fnl f* **7/1**

1404 **7** *¾* **Gold Hunter (IRE)**[10] 6978 9-9-4 **67**.....(tp) RaulDaSilva 11 64
(Steve Flook) *sed awkwardly: towards rr: rdn 3f out: styd on fnl 2f but nvr any threat* **20/1**

The Form Book Flat 2019, Raceform Ltd, Newbury, RG14 5SJ

2046 **8** *nk* **Dreaming Of Paris**[70] 4751 5-9-2 **65**....(v[1]) LiamKeniry 8 61
(Patrick Chamings) *sn trcking ldr: rdn and ev ch 2f out: wknd appr fnl f* **33/1**

4323 **9** *3/4* **Smokey Lane (IRE)**[5] 7115 5-9-6 **69**....(b) HarryBentley 7 63
(David Evans) *midfield: rdn over 2f out: outpcd by ldrs and btn over 1f out* **11/2**[2]

120 **10** *3* **Fantasy Justifier (IRE)**[6] 7084 8-8-8 **57**....(p) DavidProbert 2 43
(Ronald Harris) *hld up: hdwy 1/2-way: rdn 2f out: hung lft over 1f out: wknd fnl f* **16/1**

035 **11** *6* **Itmakesyouthink**[20] 6594 5-8-12 **61**....(h) RichardKingscote 3 31
(Mark Loughnane) *prom: rdn over 2f out: wknd wl over 1f out (trainer said gelding was unsuited by track and would prefer a less undulating surface)* **20/1**

00-5 **12** *nk* **Initiative (IRE)**[19] 6630 4-9-7 **70**....(h) StevieDonohoe 9 39
(Richard Price) *wnt to post early: s.i.s: in rr: rdn and lost tch over 2f out* **50/1**

1m 20.53s (-3.37) **Going Correction** -0.375s/f (Firm)
WFA 3 from 4yo+ 3lb **12** Ran SP% **129.3**
Speed ratings (Par 103): **104,102,100,100,99 99,98,98,97,93 86,86**
CSF £79.55 CT £1149.25 TOTE £6.70: £1.80, £3.50, £5.20; EX 86.00 Trifecta £872.10.
Owner Racing For A Cause **Bred** Cecil And Miss Alison Wiggins **Trained** Trowbridge, Wilts

FOCUS
A modest handicap, they raced down the centre once more and the pace was steady. Straightforward form.

7300 COMPARE BOOKMAKER SITES AT BONUSCODEBETS.CO.UK H'CAP 2m

5:20 (5:20) (Class 6) (0-65,64) 3-Y-O+
£2,781 (£827; £413; £300; £300; £300) **Stalls** Low

Form RPR

6501 **1** **Giving Back**[14] 6849 5-9-13 **62**....(v[1]) DavidProbert 2 68
(Alan King) *chsd ldrs: impr to ld wl over 2f out: drvn over 1f out: styd on u.p* **8/1**

0505 **2** *1/2* **Tribal Commander**[29] 6291 3-8-13 **61**.... CierenFallon(3) 6 68
(Ian Williams) *midfield: hdwy on outer to chse wnr over 2f out: drvn over 1f out: kpt on: no ex fnl 100yds* **5/1**[3]

0225 **3** *1 1/4* **Norab (GER)**[8] 7033 8-9-13 **62**....(b) StevieDonohoe 3 66
(Bernard Llewellyn) *led 2f: remained in cl 2nd: drvn to ld 3f out: sn hdd and bk in 3rd: nt clr run and swtchd rt ins fnl f: styd on (jockey said gelding hung left-handed)* **8/1**

0424 **4** *1* **King Christophe (IRE)**[10] 6988 7-9-9 **58**....(b) LiamKeniry 1 61
(Peter Fahey, Ire) *chsd ldrs: drvn 3f out: kpt on same pce fnl 2f* **9/1**

036 **5** *1/2* **Cochise**[22] 6290 3-9-0 **64**.... ThomasGreatrex(5) 4 68
(Roger Charlton) *midfield: rdn over 4f out: sn outpcd and lost pl: styd on fnl f* **4/1**[2]

0003 **6** *4 1/2* **The Way You Dance (IRE)**[12] 6901 7-10-0 **63**.... SeanLevey 10 60
(Michael Attwater) *hld up: rdn 4f out: styd on fnl 2f: nvr able to chal* **16/1**

553 **7** *hd* **Parisian Affair**[12] 6903 4-9-11 **60**.... FergusSweeney 9 56
(Neil King) *hld up: rdn and sme hdwy over 3f out: btn over 1f out* **50/1**

5 **8** *1 1/4* **Give Battle (IRE)**[24] 6483 7-9-5 **54**....(p) RobHornby 8 49
(C Byrnes, Ire) *chsd along early: sn trcking ldrs: rdn over 3f out: wknd over 1f out* **7/4**[1]

6060 **9** *2 3/4* **Raven's Raft (IRE)**[17] 6736 4-9-7 **56**.... RichardKingscote 11 48
(David Loughnane) *hld up: rdn 3f out: no hdwy* **33/1**

/0-0 **10** *5* **Late Shipment**[137] 2359 8-9-11 **60**....(p) TrevorWhelan 12 46
(Nikki Evans) *hld up: rdn 4f out: sn wknd (trainer said gelding was unsuited by the ground, which was officially described as Good, Good to Soft in places on this occasion but had dried throughout the day, and the gelding would prefer an easier surface)* **66/1**

036 **11** *1 1/2* **Sweetest Smile (IRE)**[47] 5596 4-8-8 **46**....(b) JaneElliott(3) 7 30
(Ed de Giles) *t.k.h: prom: led after 2f: drvn and hdd 3f out: sn wknd* **14/1**

3m 31.38s (-10.72) **Going Correction** -0.625s/f (Hard)
WFA 3 from 4yo+ 10lb **11** Ran SP% **124.2**
Speed ratings (Par 101): **101,100,100,99,99 97,97,96,95,92 91**
CSF £50.25 CT £343.04 TOTE £5.60: £2.40, £1.60, £3.70; EX 42.90 Trifecta £777.00.
Owner Pitchall Stud Partnership & Mrs Pat Toye **Bred** Pitchall Stud **Trained** Barbury Castle, Wilts
■ Stewards' Enquiry : Rob Hornby two-day ban: careless riding (Oct 1, 2)

FOCUS
Moderate staying form.
T/Jkpt: £603.10 to a £1 stake. Pool: £20,506.70 - 34 winning units T/Plt: £26.80 to a £1 stake. Pool: £54,419.49 - 1477.59 winning units T/Qpdt: £8.50 to a £1 stake. Pool: £4,774.83 - 415.38 winning units **Richard Lowther**

6939 NEWCASTLE (A.W) (L-H)
Tuesday, September 17

OFFICIAL GOING: Tapeta: standard
Wind: Breezy, half behind on the straight course and in over 3f of home straight in races on the round cou Weather: Fine, dry

7301 GOREBOOT H'CAP 1m 4f 98y (Tp)

5:30 (5:31) (Class 5) (0-75,76) 3-Y-O+
£3,428 (£1,020; £509; £400; £400; £400) **Stalls** High

Form RPR

2142 **1** **Dreamweaver (IRE)**[17] 6722 3-9-6 **75**.... HectorCrouch 2 84+
(Ed Walker) *dwlt: hld up in tch: stdy hdwy over 2f out: angled rt and led over 1f out: edgd lft ins fnl f: pushed out: comf* **6/4**[1]

4031 **2** *1 3/4* **Ad Libitum**[11] 6939 4-9-4 **66**....(p) BenCurtis 8 71+
(Roger Fell) *pressed ldr: led gng wl over 2f out: rdn and hdd over 1f out: rallied: one pce last 100tds* **8/1**[3]

2256 **3** *nk* **Royal Flag**[27] 6340 9-8-13 **61**.... BenRobinson 7 65
(Brian Ellison) *led at ordinary gallop: rdn and hdd over 2f out: rallied: kpt on same pce ins fnl f* **50/1**

142 **4** *nk* **Granite City Doc**[43] 5725 6-8-13 **66**.... PaulaMuir(5) 3 70
(Lucy Normile) *hld up in tch: stdy hdwy on outside to chse ldrs over 1f out: rdn and one pce ins fnl f* **11/1**

6342 **5** *1 1/4* **First Dance (IRE)**[18] 6661 5-9-2 **64**.... GrahamLee 5 66
(Tom Tate) *missed break: hld up: shkn up and hdwy wl over 1f out: kpt on fnl f: nvr rchd ldrs* **8/1**[3]

2403 **6** *nk* **Brandy Spirit**[17] 6734 3-9-4 **73**....(h) NathanEvans 4 76
(Michael Easterby) *hld up on ins: hdwy and prom over 2f out: rdn and edgd lft over 1f out: sn outpcd* **6/1**[2]

0005 **7** *nk* **Dragon Mountain**[18] 6658 4-9-7 **69**.... JoeFanning 9 70
(Keith Dalgleish) *hld up in rr: effrt and hung lft over 2f out: no imp fr over 1f out* **6/1**[2]

0040 **8** *8* **Glan Y Gors (IRE)**[9] 7003 7-9-10 **72**....(p) CliffordLee 6 60
(David Thompson) *t.k.h: trckd ldrs: pushed along over 2f out: wknd over 1f out* **8/1**[3]

-023 **9** *3/4* **Iconic Belle**[80] 4363 5-9-7 **76**.... NickBarratt-Atkin(7) 1 63
(Philip Kirby) *trckd ldrs tl rdn and wknd fr 2f out* **100/1**

2m 41.44s (0.34) **Going Correction** +0.10s/f (Slow)
WFA 3 from 4yo+ 7lb **9** Ran SP% **113.2**
Speed ratings (Par 103): **102,100,100,100,99 99,99,93,93**
CSF £13.95 CT £406.44 TOTE £2.10: £1.20, £1.70, £7.90; EX 14.20 Trifecta £148.30.
Owner Mrs Olivia Hoare **Bred** Mrs Olivia Hoare **Trained** Upper Lambourn, Berks

FOCUS
A fair middle-distance handicap. The favourite won well from just off a modest pace in a time nearly six seconds slower than standard. The race is rated around the runner-up and the fourth.

7302 RSM H'CAP 1m 4f 98y (Tp)

6:00 (6:01) (Class 3) (0-90,90) 3-Y-O
£8,086 (£2,406; £1,202; £601) **Stalls** High

Form RPR

2012 **1** **Deal A Dollar**[10] 6981 3-9-7 **90**....(bt) JimCrowley 5 100+
(Sir Michael Stoute) *dwlt: hld up in last pl: hdwy on outside to ld over 1f out: rdn out fnl f* **5/4**[1]

5612 **2** *1 3/4* **Natty Night**[75] 4559 3-8-6 **75**.... MartinDwyer 2 82
(William Muir) *led: rdn and hrd pressed over 2f out: hdd over 1f out: rallied: one pce fnl 100yds* **11/2**[3]

2-21 **3** *1* **Wise Ruler**[18] 6662 3-9-3 **86**.... JackMitchell 1 92
(Simon Crisford) *t.k.h: trckd ldrs: hdwy to chal over 2f out: edgd rt over 1f out: edgd lft and no ex ins fnl f* **2/1**[2]

-132 **4** *7* **Proton (IRE)**[31] 6209 3-8-12 **81**.... PaulMulrennan 4 75
(Jedd O'Keeffe) *in tch: rdn and hung lft over 2f out: wknd over 1f out* **20/1**

2416 **5** *23* **Battle Of Wills (IRE)**[32] 6156 3-9-6 **89**....(p) PJMcDonald 3 46
(James Tate) *trckd ldrs: rdn and struggling over 2f out: sn wknd* **9/1**

2m 37.97s (-3.13) **Going Correction** +0.10s/f (Slow) **5** Ran SP% **107.9**
Speed ratings (Par 105): **114,112,112,107,92**
CSF £8.13 TOTE £1.90: £1.40, £2.30; EX 8.00 Trifecta £15.30.
Owner Saeed Suhail **Bred** Rabbah Bloodstock Limited **Trained** Newmarket, Suffolk

FOCUS
The feature contest was a fairly good middle-distance 3yo handicap and, from off a much more respectable gallop, the favourite won well centrally in a notably quicker time than the previous C&D contest. The winner progressed again.

7303 MUCKLE GALLOWGATE GALLOP MEDIAN AUCTION MAIDEN STKS 7f 14y (Tp)

6:30 (6:32) (Class 6) 3-5-Y-O
£2,781 (£827; £413; £206) **Stalls** Centre

Form RPR

0 **1** **Fortamour (IRE)**[113] 3157 3-9-6 0.... GrahamLee 6 73+
(Ben Haslam) *hld up: smooth hdwy over 2f out: shkn up to ld ins fnl f: sn clr: readily* **9/4**[1]

54 **2** *2 1/2* **Clifton**[85] 4196 3-9-6 0.... NathanEvans 5 65
(Michael Easterby) *t.k.h early: cl up: rdn over 2f out: led over 1f out to ins fnl f: kpt on same pce* **5/2**[2]

35 **3** *3/4* **Blistering Barney (IRE)**[14] 6823 3-9-6 0.... AndrewElliott 3 63
(Christopher Kellett) *led: rdn over 2f out: hdd over 1f out: rallied: one pce ins fnl f* **25/1**

4 **4** *4* **Festina**[8] 7032 3-9-1 0.... LukeMorris 2 48
(Sir Mark Prescott Bt) *t.k.h: in tch: rdn along over 2f out: wknd over 1f out* **7/2**[3]

2 **5** *hd* **Ravenscar (IRE)**[38] 5969 3-9-1 0.... SamJames 1 48
(Grant Tuer) *chsd ldrs: rdn along over 2f out: wknd fnl f* **5/2**[2]

0-00 **6** *10* **Hey Jazzy Lady (IRE)**[24] 6462 3-8-10 45.... PaulaMuir(5) 7 23
(Andrew Crook) *t.k.h: hld up: struggling over 2f out: sn btn* **100/1**

- **7** *1* **Arthur Shelby** 3-9-6 0.... PhilDennis 8 25
(David C Griffiths) *hld up: rdn and outpcd over 2f out: sn btn* **28/1**

-600 **8** *3* **Mithayel Style (FR)**[48] 5558 3-9-1 48.... CliffordLee 4 13
(David Thompson) *in tch: rdn over 2f out: sn wknd* **150/1**

66 **9** *17* **Its Toytown**[11] 6941 3-9-6 0....(p[1]) PJMcDonald 9
(R Mike Smith) *prom: rdn over 3f out: wknd over 2f out: t.o* **100/1**

1m 27.07s (0.87) **Going Correction** +0.10s/f (Slow) **9** Ran SP% **120.1**
Speed ratings (Par 101): **99,96,95,90,90 79,77,74,55**
CSF £8.52 TOTE £3.20: £1.20, £1.30, £5.50; EX 9.00 Trifecta £82.00.
Owner Mrs C Barclay & P Wood **Bred** D Ryan, D S Ryan & R A Williams **Trained** Middleham Moor, N Yorks

FOCUS
An ordinary, effectively 3yo, maiden. The significant money for the favourite proved spot on, who won going away in decent fashion from off an, at best, even gallop.

7304 ONTRAC SOFTWARE EBF MAIDEN FILLIES' STKS (PLUS 10 RACE) 7f 14y (Tp)

7:00 (7:02) (Class 5) 2-Y-O
£3,428 (£1,020; £509; £254) **Stalls** Centre

Form RPR

04 **1** **Lasting Legacy**[27] 6336 2-9-0 0.... MichaelStainton 8 80+
(Chris Fairhurst) *cl up: led 2f out: rdn and clr whn edgd lft ins fnl f: kpt on strly* **50/1**

2 *3 1/4* **Finery** 2-9-0 0.... BenCurtis 4 71
(K R Burke) *t.k.h: prom: rdn and green 2f out: rallied and chsd (clr) wnr ins fnl f: kpt on* **5/2**[2]

2 **3** *1/2* **Faakhirah (IRE)**[23] 6514 2-9-0 0.... JimCrowley 6 70
(Saeed bin Suroor) *t.k.h: led at modest gallop: hdd and rdn 2f out: no ex and lost 2nd ins fnl f* **4/7**[1]

05 **4** *1 1/4* **Parikarma (IRE)**[25] 6407 2-9-0 0.... RobertHavlin 2 67
(Ed Dunlop) *hld up: pushed along and effrt over 1f out: edgd lft: sn no imp* **18/1**

66 **5** *nk* **Clegane**[36] 6019 2-9-0 0.... HectorCrouch 7 66
(Ed Walker) *cl up: effrt and rdn over 2f out: outpcd fnl f* **3/1**[3]

0 **6** *2 1/4* **Exotic Escape**[45] 5684 2-9-0 0.... DanielMuscutt 3 61
(David Lanigan) *hld up: pushed along and shortlived effrt wl over 1f out: sn btn (vet said filly lost left-fore shoe)* **125/1**

7 *2* **Escalade (IRE)** 2-9-0 0.... LukeMorris 5 56
(Sir Mark Prescott Bt) *s.i.s: hld up: rdn over 2f out: nvr rchd ldrs* **40/1**

0 **8** *7* **Jamaal Danehill**[40] 5856 2-9-0 0.... ShaneGray 1 38
(Kevin Ryan) *unruly bef s: prom tl rdn and wknd over 2f out* **66/1**

0 **9** *1/2* **Just Call Me Ella**[10] 6971 2-9-0 0.... CamHardie 9 37
(Rebecca Menzies) *hld up in tch: rdn over 2f out: sn wknd* **125/1**

1m 27.47s (1.27) **Going Correction** +0.10s/f (Slow) **9** Ran SP% **130.0**
Speed ratings (Par 92): **96,92,91,90,89 87,85,77,76**
CSF £193.80 TOTE £36.10: £11.10, £1.30, £1.02; EX 293.10 Trifecta £1010.70.

Owner Exors Of The Late Mrs L Peacock **Bred** Mrs R D Peacock **Trained** Middleham, N Yorks

FOCUS

A fair juvenile fillies' maiden. An outsider won going away in decent fashion in a time slightly slower than the previous C&D 3yo maiden.

7305 NUTSHELL APPS H'CAP 1m 5y (Tp)

7:30 (7:30) (Class 5) (0-75,75) 3-Y-0+

£3,428 (£1,020; £509; £400; £400; £400) **Stalls** Centre

Form RPR

1000 **1** **Tum Tum**[38] 5970 4-9-9 **74**....................(p[1]) TomEaves 3 81
(Michael Herrington) *mde all: set stdy gallop: rdn and qcknd clr wl over 1f out: dwindling advantage last 100yds: jst lasted* **33/1**

0216 **2** *nse* **Home Before Dusk**[11] 6940 4-9-4 **69**....................(p) DanielTudhope 1 76+
(Keith Dalgleish) *hld up: hdwy and rdn over 1f out: chsd (clr) wnr last 100yds: kpt on strly: jst failed* **4/1**[1]

3102 **3** *1½* **Toro Dorado**[28] 6317 3-9-0 **69**.................... RobertHavlin 14 72
(Ed Dunlop) *hld up: rdn and hdwy over 1f out: kpt on fnl f: no imp towards fin* **13/2**[3]

6000 **4** *½* **Armed (IRE)**[17] 6700 4-9-2 **67**.................... PaulMulrennan 10 69+
(Phillip Makin) *t.k.h: hld up: nt clr run over 2f out: effrt and pushed along over 1f out: kpt on wl fnl f: nrst fin* **18/1**

0101 **5** *nk* **Insurplus (IRE)**[18] 6665 6-9-3 **68**.................... PaddyMathers 5 70
(Jim Goldie) *hld up: pushed along over 2f out: hdwy over 1f out: kpt on fnl f: no imp* **28/1**

4620 **6** *nse* **Newmarket Warrior (IRE)**[19] 6626 8-8-13 **67**.......(p) HarrisonShaw(3) 2 68
(Iain Jardine) *hld up: rdn and hdwy over 1f out: kpt on fnl f: no imp* **25/1**

1006 **7** *½* **Fitzrovia**[42] 5782 4-9-1 **66**.................... BarryMcHugh 4 66
(Ed de Giles) *t.k.h: cl up: chsd wnr over 2f out to last 100yds: sn btn* **22/1**

5533 **8** *2¼* **Cameo Star (IRE)**[19] 6628 4-8-8 **62**....................(p) SeanDavis(3) 13 57
(Richard Fahey) *in tch: effrt and drvn along over 2f out: outpcd fnl f* **10/1**

344 **9** *1¼* **Fiery Mission (USA)**[35] 6034 3-9-3 **72**....................(t) JimCrowley 12 64
(Sir Michael Stoute) *midfield: rdn and outpcd over 2f out: sn n.d* **9/2**[2]

6000 **10** *nse* **Ghayadh**[24] 6469 4-9-10 **75**....................(h) PJMcDonald 6 67
(George Boughey) *midfield: outpcd over 2f out: sn wknd* **10/1**

1330 **10** *dht* **Pickett's Charge**[3] 7212 6-9-6 **71**....................(p) BenRobinson 7 63
(Brian Ellison) *t.k.h: prom: lost pl 2f out: sn struggling* **13/2**[3]

3650 **12** *1¾* **Roller**[21] 6582 6-9-4 **69**....................(p) AndrewMullen 11 57
(Mark Loughnane) *rrd s: bhd: pushed along over 2f out: nvr on terms* **25/1**

5656 **13** *3¼* **Kentuckyconnection (USA)**[18] 6665 6-9-1 **66**.................... GrahamLee 8 47
(Bryan Smart) *midfield: drvn and struggling over 2f out: sn btn* **12/1**

1m 40.22s (1.62) **Going Correction** +0.10s/f (Slow)
WFA 3 from 4yo+ 4lb **13 Ran SP% 114.4**
Speed ratings (Par 103): **95,94,93,92,92 92,92,89,88,88 88,86,83**
CSF £147.41 CT £1022.95 TOTE £36.60: £11.10, £2.00, £2.30; EX 207.50 Trifecta £2499.40.

Owner Mrs H Lloyd-Herrington **Bred** Jeremy Green And Sons **Trained** Cold Kirby, N Yorks

FOCUS

A fair handicap. An outsider desperately clung on towards the centre in a photo-finish from off his own modest gallop. The level looks pretty ordinary.

7306 MAX RECYCLE NURSERY H'CAP 7f 14y (Tp)

8:00 (8:02) (Class 6) (0-60,60) 2-Y-O

£2,781 (£827; £413; £400; £400; £400) **Stalls** Centre

Form RPR

3660 **1** **Constitutional (IRE)**[35] 6032 2-9-4 **60**.................... HarrisonShaw(3) 7 62
(K R Burke) *cl up in centre of gp: rdn to ld over 1f out: hld on wl fnl f (trainer said, regarding the apparent improvement in form, the gelding benefited from the step up in trip and appreciated the removal of headgear)* **33/1**

0353 **2** *¾* **Rochford (IRE)**[12] 6884 2-9-7 **60**....................(p[1]) JFEgan 13 60
(Henry Spiller) *hld up in midfield on nr side of gp: hdwy and ev ch briefly wl over 1f out: kpt on ins fnl f* **7/2**[1]

6000 **3** *shd* **River Of Kings (IRE)**[19] 6625 2-9-6 **59**....................(h[1]) JoeFanning 12 59
(Keith Dalgleish) *unruly in stalls and missed break: hld up on far side of gp: hdwy over 1f out: r.o ins fnl f: nrst fin (jockey said gelding was slowly away)* **11/2**[3]

4044 **4** *hd* **Red Maharani**[25] 6387 2-9-5 **58**.................... BarryMcHugh 9 57
(James Given) *hld up in centre of gp: rdn and hdwy over 1f out: kpt on ins fnl f: nrst fin* **12/1**

0002 **5** *nse* **Indra Dawn (FR)**[20] 6604 2-8-11 **50**....................(b[1]) AdamMcNamara 3 49
(Archie Watson) *cl up towards far side of gp: rdn and outpcd 2f out: rallied ins fnl f: r.o* **15/2**

0000 **6** *nk* **My Havana**[19] 6625 2-9-2 **55**....................(p[1]) AndrewMullen 6 54
(Nigel Tinkler) *s.i.s: hld up on far side of gp: rdn along and hdwy over 1f out: kpt on fnl f: nrst fin* **10/1**

6550 **7** *1½* **Callipygian**[22] 6539 2-9-5 **58**....................(t) TomEaves 5 53
(James Given) *led in centre of gp: rdn and hdd over 1f out: wknd last 100yds* **40/1**

0506 **8** *nk* **The Trendy Man (IRE)**[33] 6097 2-8-11 **50**....................(p) ShaneGray 8 44
(David O'Meara) *cl up towards centre of gp: drvn and ch briefly wl over 1f out: wknd ins fnl f* **18/1**

000 **9** *1* **Inductive**[48] 5553 2-9-3 **56**.................... CallumRodriguez 14 48
(Michael Dods) *hld up on nr side of gp: effrt and pushed along 2f out: no further imp fnl f* **5/1**[2]

500 **10** *hd* **Imperial Eagle (IRE)**[34] 6064 2-9-2 **55**.................... PhilDennis 10 46
(Lawrence Mullaney) *hld up in centre of gp: drvn along over 2f out: no imp over 1f out* **22/1**

060 **11** *nk* **Congratulate**[77] 4486 2-9-1 **54**.................... JamesSullivan 2 44
(Tim Easterby) *t.k.h: in tch on far side of gp tl rdn and wknd over 1f out* **50/1**

0014 **12** *1¼* **Our Dave**[18] 6673 2-9-7 **60**....................(v) JasonHart 11 47
(John Quinn) *prom on nr side of gp: rdn and wknd over 1f out* **15/2**

006 **13** *hd* **Fast Track Flyer (IRE)**[18] 6664 2-9-2 **55**.................... BenRobinson 1 42
(Brian Ellison) *cl up on far side of gp tl rdn and wknd 2f out* **28/1**

1m 28.74s (2.54) **Going Correction** +0.10s/f (Slow) **13 Ran SP% 115.0**
Speed ratings (Par 93): **89,88,88,87,87 87,85,85,84,83 83,82,81**
CSF £136.03 CT £777.25 TOTE £31.60: £8.60, £1.50, £1.90; EX 131.40 Trifecta £3293.30.

Owner Owners For Owners & Mrs E Burke **Bred** Tally-Ho Stud **Trained** Middleham Moor, N Yorks

FOCUS

A modest nursery. Another outsider won gamely in a busy finish and his winning time was over a second slower than the earlier C&D juvenile fillies' maiden.

7307 GAINFORD GROUP H'CAP 5f (Tp)

8:30 (8:33) (Class 6) (0-60,60) 3-Y-O+

£2,781 (£827; £413; £400; £400; £400) **Stalls** Centre

Form RPR

0-00 **1** **Gleaming Arch**[61] 5094 5-9-3 **55**.................... KevinStott 14 62
(Fred Watson) *hld up on nr side of gp: rdn and hdwy over 1f out: led and edgd lft ins fnl f: r.o wl* **12/1**

0044 **2** *nk* **Swiss Connection**[18] 6659 3-9-7 **60**....................(h) GrahamLee 6 66
(Bryan Smart) *t.k.h: cl up in centre of gp: led over 2f out to ins fnl f: kpt on: hld nr fin* **7/1**[2]

203 **3** *½* **Gorgeous General**[22] 6547 4-9-6 **58**....................(b[1]) PhilDennis 4 62
(Lawrence Mullaney) *cl up on far side of gp: effrt and ev ch over 1f out to ins fnl f: no ex towards fin* **9/1**[3]

0622 **4** *½* **Be Proud (IRE)**[3] 7210 3-9-0 **53**.................... DanielTudhope 13 59+
(Jim Goldie) *hld up in midfield on nr side of gp: rdn and hdwy whn n.m.r appr fnl f: hmpd and snatched up last 150yds: kpt on wl towards fin: unlucky* **9/4**[1]

1031 **5** *hd* **Someone Exciting**[20] 6590 6-8-9 **50**.................... HarrisonShaw(3) 8 52
(David Thompson) *hld up in centre of gp: effrt and hdwy wl over 1f out: kpt on ins fnl f* **14/1**

26-0 **6** *¾* **On Route**[11] 6930 3-9-7 **60**....................(p) LukeMorris 3 59
(Sir Mark Prescott Bt) *in tch in centre of gp: rdn along over 2f out: effrt and drvn over 1f out: one pce ins fnl f* **16/1**

0001 **7** *1¼* **Groundworker (IRE)**[18] 6659 8-9-6 **58**.................... BarryMcHugh 12 52
(Paul Midgley) *cl up on nr side of gp: effrt and ev ch briefly over 1f out: no ex ins fnl f* **22/1**

2133 **8** *hd* **The Grey Zebedee**[7] 7047 3-9-7 **60**....................(b) DuranFentiman 1 54
(Tim Easterby) *prom on far side of gp tl rdn and no ex fr over 1f out* **18/1**

5003 **9** *¾* **Alqaab**[24] 6462 4-9-1 **53**....................(h) JackGarritty 10 44
(Ruth Carr) *dwlt: hld up in centre of gp: pushed along and hdwy over 1f out: no imp fnl f* **9/1**[3]

6460 **10** *½* **Everkyllachy (IRE)**[18] 6659 5-9-3 **58**.................... SeanDavis(3) 5 47
(Karen McLintock) *hld up on far side of gp: drvn and outpcd 2f out: n.d after* **22/1**

2000 **11** *¾* **Kibaar**[14] 6829 7-9-4 **56**.................... JamesSullivan 7 42
(Ruth Carr) *hld up: shortlived effrt in centre of gp over 1f out: sn btn* **40/1**

2000 **12** *hd* **Deeds Not Words (IRE)**[7] 7050 8-9-4 **56**....................(p) JasonHart 9 42
(Tracy Waggott) *led on nr side of gp: hdd over 2f out: wknd over 1f out* **28/1**

0505 **13** *4* **Hanati (IRE)**[18] 6685 3-9-3 **56**.................... BenRobinson 11 27
(Brian Ellison) *bhd in centre of gp: drvn along bef 1/2-way: sn struggling (jockey said filly was slowly and never travelling)* **50/1**

59.36s (-0.14) **Going Correction** +0.10s/f (Slow)
WFA 3 from 4yo+ 1lb **13 Ran SP% 105.3**
Speed ratings (Par 101): **105,104,103,102,102 101,99,99,97,97 95,95,89**
CSF £73.04 CT £660.79 TOTE £16.20: £4.70, £2.10, £2.90; EX 100.90 Trifecta £674.80.

Owner F Watson **Bred** F Watson **Trained** Sedgefield, Co Durham

■ Arnold was withdrawn. Price at time of withdrawal 10/1. Rule 4 applies to all bets - deduction 5p in the pound

■ Stewards' Enquiry : Kevin Stott six-day ban: careless riding (1-5 & 7 Oct)

FOCUS

A modest handicap. The latterly wayward winner came home powerfully towards the stands' rail in a good comparative time.

T/Plt: £32.70 to a £1 stake. Pool: £66,672.00 - 1485.71 winning units T/Qpdt: £12.90 to a £1 stake. Pool: £8,186.14 - 468.19 winning units **Richard Young**

6456 REDCAR (L-H)

Tuesday, September 17

OFFICIAL GOING: Good to firm (watered; 8.7)

Wind: light against Weather: Sunny

7308 JOIN RACING TV NOW NOVICE AUCTION STKS 5f

2:00 (2:01) (Class 5) 2-Y-O **£4,043** (£1,203; £601; £300) **Stalls** Centre

Form RPR

1 **Modular Magic** 2-9-3 0.................... JoeFanning 2 71+
(David Barron) *trckd ldrs: led over 1f out: kpt on pushed out: shade cosily* **17/2**

2 *½* **Rebel Soldier Boy** 2-9-5 0.................... DanielTudhope 4 71+
(David O'Meara) *hld up in tch: rdn and hdwy over 1f out: drvn to chse wnr ins fnl f: kpt on* **4/1**[3]

222 **3** *2¾* **River Cam**[12] 6883 2-9-0 73.................... PJMcDonald 5 56
(James Tate) *prom: rdn along 2f out: drvn and no ex ins fnl f* **2/1**[1]

4 *hd* **Lincoln Gamble** 2-9-1 0.................... PaulHanagan 6 57
(Richard Fahey) *dwlt sltly: hld up in tch: rdn along 2f out: kpt on fnl f* **7/2**[2]

00 **5** *2¼* **Lezardrieux**[7] 7046 2-9-1 0.................... SamJames 1 48
(Grant Tuer) *hld up: pushed along over 2f out: sme hdwy over 1f out: one pce fnl 110yds* **100/1**

006 **6** *¾* **Norton Lad**[20] 6585 2-9-1 46.................... DavidAllan 9 46
(Tim Easterby) *led: rdn and hdd over 1f out: sn outpcd and btn* **100/1**

0232 **7** *2½* **Flight Of Thunder (IRE)**[14] 6822 2-8-9 62.................... TheodoreLadd(5) 8 40
(Kevin Ryan) *dwlt: sn chsd ldrs: rdn over 2f out: wknd over 1f out* **7/2**[2]

4 **8** *½* **Queens Road (IRE)**[165] 1556 2-8-7 0.................... SeanDavis(3) 3 30
(Bill Turner) *chsd ldrs tl hung lft and wknd appr fnl f* **20/1**

05 **9** *7* **Petite Steps (IRE)**[37] 5994 2-8-3 0.................... SiobhanRutledge(7) 7 5
(Miss Katy Brown, Ire) *slowly away and wnt lft s: a in rr* **100/1**

59.01s (0.51) **Going Correction** -0.025s/f (Good) **9 Ran SP% 116.0**
Speed ratings (Par 95): **94,93,88,88,84 83,79,78,67**
CSF £42.04 TOTE £10.40: £2.60, £1.20, £1.10; EX 51.70 Trifecta £206.70.

Owner P McKenna, L O Kane & Partner **Bred** Ncf & Harrowgate Bloodstock Ltd **Trained** Maunby, N Yorks

FOCUS
The ground, given as good to firm (GoingStick 8.7), had been watered but looked in good nick and wasn't loose on top. A modest novice, and a couple of newcomers finished clear. The fifth/sixth and the time give perspective.

7309 MARKET CROSS JEWELLERS NURSERY H'CAP 7f
2:30 (2:30) (Class 5) (0-75,76) 2-Y-O
£3,500 (£1,041; £520; £300; £300; £300) Stalls Centre

Form RPR
3506 1 **Oso Rapido (IRE)**18 6653 2-9-6 73 .... DanielTudhope 8 75
(David O'Meara) *hld up: hdwy on outer over 2f out: rdn to chal appr fnl f: hung lft but kpt on to ld fnl 75yds* **3/1**2
2506 2 ½ **Kilig**39 5896 2-8-7 60 .... (bt1) PhilDennis 1 61
(Tim Easterby) *led: rdn over 2f out: hdd over 1f out: kpt on ins fnl f* **50/1**
6363 3 ¾ **Rusalka (IRE)**21 6571 2-8-3 56 .... (t1) DuranFentiman 7 55
(Tim Easterby) *hld up: rdn and gd hdwy over 2f out: drvn to ld narrowly over 1f out: hdd 75yds out: no ex* **20/1**
0542 4 2 **Light The Fuse (IRE)**21 6563 2-9-4 74 .... (p1) HarrisonShaw(3) 3 68
(K R Burke) *chsd ldrs: rdn along 3f out: no ex fnl 110yds (jockey said colt hung left-handed under pressure)* **11/2**
3360 5 2¼ **Don't Joke**54 5340 2-9-1 68 .... PJMcDonald 6 56
(Mark Johnston) *chsd ldrs: rdn over 2f out: outpcd and btn over 1f out* **28/1**
3232 6 3½ **Lord Of The Alps (IRE)**33 6097 2-9-9 76 .... JoeFanning 4 55
(Mark Johnston) *prom: rdn over 2f out: wknd over 1f out* **2/1**1
013 7 hd **Ten Thousand Stars**18 6654 2-9-3 70 .... BarryMcHugh 2 48+
(Adrian Nicholls) *in tch: rdn over 2f out: wknd over 1f out* **4/1**3
5034 8 6 **Street Life**18 6683 2-8-6 59 .... (b) PaulHanagan 5 21
(Richard Fahey) *midfield: rdn over 2f out: wknd over 1f out* **10/1**
1m 25.15s (-0.25) **Going Correction** -0.025s/f (Good) 8 Ran SP% **113.0**
Speed ratings (Par 95): **100,99,98,96,93 89,89,82**
CSF £138.23 CT £2540.73 TOTE £3.70: £1.50, £11.60, £3.50; EX 155.60 Trifecta £1162.40.
Owner Kevin Bailey & Gabriel Chrysanthou **Bred** George Kent **Trained** Upper Helmsley, N Yorks

FOCUS
An ordinary nursery with the winner rated to his mark.

7310 WEATHERBYS RACING BANK APPRENTICE H'CAP 7f
3:00 (3:01) (Class 4) (0-80,82) 3-Y-O+
£5,692 (£1,694; £846; £423; £300; £300) Stalls Centre

Form RPR
2005 1 **Oriental Lilly**10 6972 5-8-2 68 .... (p) CoreyMadden(7) 4 76
(Jim Goldie) *dwlt: hld up: rdn and hdwy 2f out: chal appr fnl f: led ins fnl f: kpt on* **11/1**
3142 2 ¾ **Athollblair Boy (IRE)**5 7121 6-9-2 82 .... IzzyClifton(7) 2 88
(Nigel Tinkler) *slowly away: hld up: hdwy 2f out: sn chsd ldrs: short of room 1f out and sn swtchd lft: rdn and kpt on but nt rch wnr* **11/8**1
0640 3 1½ **Tadaawol**18 6677 6-9-4 77 .... (p) PaulaMuir 6 79
(Roger Fell) *dwlt: hld up in tch: sn pushed along: hdwy over 2f out: chal wl over 1f out: led appr fnl f: hdd ins fnl f: one pce fnl 110yds* **4/1**2
5020 4 5 **Indian Sounds (IRE)**14 6840 3-8-7 69 .... (b) AndrewBreslin 7 56
(Mark Johnston) *pressed ldr: led over 3f out: rdn and edgd rt 2f out: hdd appr fnl f: wknd ins fnl f* **28/1**
6045 5 2 **Daafr (IRE)**37 5984 3-8-11 76 .... (p) KieranSchofield(3) 5 58
(Antony Brittain) *chsd ldrs: rdn over 2f out: wknd fnl f* **28/1**
3061 6 1½ **So Macho (IRE)**28 6302 4-8-7 66 oh2 .... BenSanderson 1 45
(Grant Tuer) *chsd ldrs: rdn over 2f out: wknd fnl f* **6/1**3
-0 7 shd **Jewel Maker (IRE)**18 6677 4-9-0 73 .... DannyRedmond 8 52
(Tim Easterby) *prom: rdn over 2f out: wknd over 1f out* **16/1**
4206 8 2½ **Saisons D'Or (IRE)**20 6588 4-9-0 80 .... OwenPayton(7) 3 52
(Jedd O'Keeffe) *led narrowly: racd keenly: hdd over 3f out: sn rdn along: wknd over 1f out* **15/2**
1m 24.3s (-1.10) **Going Correction** -0.025s/f (Good)
WFA 3 from 4yo+ 3lb 8 Ran SP% **109.3**
Speed ratings (Par 105): **105,104,102,96,94 92,92,89**
CSF £24.28 CT £66.23 TOTE £11.40: £1.90, £1.10, £1.40; EX 33.00 Trifecta £92.40.
Owner Johnnie Delta Racing **Bred** Johnnie Delta Racing **Trained** Uplawmoor, E Renfrews

FOCUS
The early lead was disputed and the race was run to suit those held up. The winner is rated in line with this year's turf form.

7311 WEATHERBYS RACING BANK FOREIGN EXCHANGE H'CAP 5f 217y
3:30 (3:31) (Class 5) (0-75,77) 3-Y-O+
£3,500 (£1,041; £520; £300; £300; £300) Stalls Centre

Form RPR
0551 1 **Buccaneers Vault (IRE)**18 6680 7-9-5 71 .... KevinStott 1 81
(Paul Midgley) *dwlt: hld up: pushed along over 3f out: rdn and hdwy over 1f out: drvn to chse ldr ins fnl f: led 75yds out: kpt on wl* **7/2**1
1123 2 1¾ **Golden Parade**22 6533 3-9-7 75 .... (p) DavidAllan 9 79
(Tim Easterby) *led: rdn 2f out: edgd rt appr fnl f: hdd 75yds out: no ex (jockey said gelding hung right-handed)* **7/2**1
6304 3 nk **Mr Wagyu (IRE)**12 6898 4-9-0 66 .... (v) JasonHart 5 69
(John Quinn) *prom: rdn over 2f out: drvn over 1f out: kpt on same pce* **8/1**
3330 4 nse **Magical Effect (IRE)**18 6677 7-9-11 77 .... (p1) JamieGormley 4 80
(Ruth Carr) *in tch: rdn over 2f out: drvn over 1f out: kpt on ins fnl f* **7/1**3
2046 5 ¾ **Mutabaahy (IRE)**26 6373 4-8-13 65 .... CamHardie 7 66
(Antony Brittain) *dwlt: sn chsd ldrs: rdn over 2f out: no ex ins fnl f* **8/1**
0000 6 3½ **Almurr (IRE)**20 6591 3-8-13 70 .... SeanDavis(3) 2 60
(Phillip Makin) *dwlt: hld up: rdn over 2f out: nvr a threat* **50/1**
0000 7 shd **Black Isle Boy (IRE)**80 4365 5-9-6 72 .... (w) DanielTudhope 3 61
(David C Griffiths) *chsd ldrs: rdn along and lost pl over 2f out: sn btn* **11/1**
0031 8 7 **Gullane One (IRE)**21 6581 4-9-1 67 .... (p) RachelRichardson 8 34
(Tim Easterby) *chsd ldrs: rdn over 2f out: wknd over 1f out (jockey said gelding slipped leaving stalls and was unable to gain a prominent position)* **11/1**
2330 9 2¼ **Kolossus**27 6338 3-9-0 68 .... ConnorBeasley 6 28
(Michael Dods) *trckd ldrs: rdn over 2f out: wknd over 1f out* **9/2**2
1m 11.67s (-0.13) **Going Correction** -0.025s/f (Good)
WFA 3 from 4yo+ 2lb 9 Ran SP% **116.0**
Speed ratings (Par 103): **103,100,100,100,99 94,94,85,82**
CSF £15.62 CT £91.41 TOTE £3.80: £1.50, £1.40, £2.20; EX 20.90 Trifecta £98.50.
Owner Sheila Bradley And P T Midgley **Bred** Kilfrush Stud **Trained** Westow, N Yorks

FOCUS
A pretty open handicap. The winner backed up his latest form.

7312 RACING TV STRAIGHT MILE SERIES H'CAP (RACING UK STRAIGHT MILE SERIES QUALIFIER) 7f 219y
4:00 (4:00) (Class 4) (0-85,86) 3-Y-O+
£5,692 (£1,694; £846; £423; £300; £300) Stalls Centre

Form RPR
0234 1 **Give It Some Teddy**9 6998 5-9-3 77 .... DuranFentiman 6 86
(Tim Easterby) *hld up in midfield: hdwy 2f out: led appr fnl f: rdn and kpt on wl* **10/3**1
2152 2 1½ **Star Shield**24 6460 4-9-10 84 .... DavidNolan 3 90
(David O'Meara) *midfield: pushed along and hdwy to chal appr fnl f: drvn and kpt on* **10/3**1
1544 3 nk **Defence Treaty (IRE)**11 6935 3-9-1 79 .... (p) DanielTudhope 2 84
(Richard Fahey) *chsd ldrs: pushed along over 3f out: drvn over 1f out: kpt on ins fnl f* **5/1**2
2610 4 nk **Breanski**10 6950 5-9-12 86 .... JackGarritty 10 91
(Jedd O'Keeffe) *hld up: pushed along and hdwy over 1f out: swtchd rt jst ins fnl f: rdn and kpt on* **16/1**
5010 5 1½ **Wind In My Sails**45 5667 7-9-8 82 .... BarryMcHugh 5 83
(Ed de Giles) *trckd ldrs: rdn along over 2f out: bit outpcd over 1f out: kpt on ins fnl f* **33/1**
0006 6 shd **Hayadh**31 6231 6-9-12 86 .... PhilDennis 4 87
(Rebecca Bastiman) *prom: rdn into narrow ld over 1f out: hdd appr fnl f: no ex* **16/1**
2306 7 ¾ **Dawaaleeb (USA)**21 6580 5-9-12 86 .... (v) LewisEdmunds 7 85
(Les Eyre) *prom: rdn over 2f out: no ex fnl f* **12/1**3
120P 8 1¾ **Rey Loopy (IRE)**82 4292 5-8-13 73 .... PaulMulrennan 9 68
(Ben Haslam) *hld up: pushed along over 2f out: nvr threatened* **16/1**
2110 9 2½ **Irv (IRE)**25 6425 3-9-7 85 .... JamesSullivan 8 74
(Micky Hammond) *dwlt: a towards rr* **16/1**
0321 10 8 **Casement (IRE)**5 7128 5-9-4 83 5ex .... TheodoreLadd(5) 1 54
(Michael Appleby) *led: rdn over 2f out: hdd over 1f out: sn wknd: eased (jockey said gelding stopped quickly; post-race examination failed to reveal any abnormalities)* **5/1**2
1m 36.14s (-0.46) **Going Correction** -0.025s/f (Good)
WFA 3 from 4yo+ 4lb 10 Ran SP% **113.7**
Speed ratings (Par 105): **101,99,99,98,97 97,96,94,92,84**
CSF £13.40 CT £53.32 TOTE £4.00: £1.30, £1.80, £1.50; EX 16.10 Trifecta £48.40.
Owner Lee Bond **Bred** Usk Valley Stud **Trained** Great Habton, N Yorks

FOCUS
A soundly run affair won by a course specialist. Solid form.

7313 EVERY RACE LIVE ON RACING TV NOVICE STKS 5f 217y
4:30 (4:35) (Class 5) 3-Y-O+ £4,204 (£1,251; £625; £312) Stalls Centre

Form RPR
52 1 **Call Me Ginger**209 806 3-9-5 0 .... DanielTudhope 2 81+
(Jim Goldie) *trckd ldr: pushed along briefly over 2f out: led gng wl over 1f out: pushed clr ins fnl f: comf* **2/1**2
0324 2 2¾ **Desert Land (IRE)**50 5494 3-9-5 73 .... PaulHanagan 3 72
(David Simcock) *led: rdn along over 2f out: hung lft and hdd over 1f out: one pce and no ch w wnr fnl f* **8/11**1
0 3 nk **Critical Voltage (IRE)**11 6944 3-9-5 0 .... TonyHamilton 1 71
(Richard Fahey) *hld up: pushed along and bit outpcd 2f out: rdn and hung lft over 1f out: kpt on ins fnl f* **5/1**3
6-5 4 20 **Danzena**54 5357 4-8-11 0 .... TheodoreLadd(5) 5 28
(Michael Appleby) *trckd ldr: racd keenly: pushed over 2f out: wknd and eased* **20/1**
1m 12.02s (0.22) **Going Correction** -0.025s/f (Good)
WFA 3 from 4yo 2lb 4 Ran SP% **112.7**
Speed ratings (Par 103): **101,97,96,70**
CSF £4.07 TOTE £2.90; EX 4.40 Trifecta £6.40.
Owner Johnnie Delta Racing **Bred** Jim Goldie **Trained** Uplawmoor, E Renfrews
■ Look Who It Isnae was withdrawn. Price at time of withdrawal 150/1. Rule 4 does not apply

FOCUS
A nice performance from the winner on his return from an absence. The winner did not need to match his AW form.

7314 RACINGTV.COM H'CAP 1m 5f 218y
5:00 (5:01) (Class 6) (0-60,60) 3-Y-O+
£3,500 (£1,041; £520; £300; £300; £300) Stalls Low

Form RPR
3021 1 **The Fiddler**38 5974 4-9-9 55 .... PaulHanagan 7 62+
(Chris Wall) *midfield: hdwy 3f out: pushed into ld over 1f out: rdn out ins fnl f* **7/4**1
5004 2 ½ **Reassurance**34 6069 4-9-12 58 .... (b1) DavidAllan 5 63
(Tim Easterby) *led narrowly: hdd 11f out but remained cl up: rdn to ld again over 2f out: hdd over 1f out: styd on but a hld* **7/1**
3221 3 1½ **Jan De Heem**7 7053 9-9-7 56 4ex .... (v) RowanScott(3) 12 59
(Tina Jackson) *hld up: hdwy on outer 2f out: rdn to chse ldrs over 1f out: styd on ins fnl f* **6/1**3
0056 4 2¾ **Miss Ranger (IRE)**22 6550 7-9-4 50 .... (p) JasonHart 8 49
(Roger Fell) *hld up: racd keenly: rdn and sme hdwy over 2f out: plugged on in modest 4th ins fnl f* **28/1**
0006 5 2¼ **Bogardus (IRE)**39 5905 8-9-6 52 .... DavidNolan 3 48
(Liam Bailey) *trckd ldrs: rdn 3f out: outpcd and btn over 1f out* **22/1**
5300 6 hd **Masters Apprentice (IRE)**14 6827 4-9-10 56 .... (p) DougieCostello 9 52
(Mark Walford) *prom: led 11f out: rdn and hdd over 2f out: outpcd and btn over 1f out* **33/1**
0-05 7 shd **Archie's Sister**18 6660 3-8-5 46 oh1 .... (t) CamHardie 1 43
(Philip Kirby) *midfield: rdn over 2f out: no imp* **66/1**
0543 8 hd **Lincoln Tale (IRE)**26 6371 3-9-6 60 .... DanielTudhope 4 60
(David O'Meara) *hld up: rdn along over 2f out: sn no prog* **5/2**2
0565 9 1½ **Seaborough (IRE)**24 6180 4-9-6 55 .... (p) HarrisonShaw(3) 10 48
(David Thompson) *hld up: racd keenly: minor hdwy on inner over 1f out: wknd ins fnl f (jockey said gelding ran too free)* **11/1**
005 10 3¼ **Midnight Warrior**20 6586 9-8-13 46 oh1 .... (t) JamesSullivan 11 34
(Ron Barr) *trckd ldrs: rdn over 3f out: wknd over 1f out* **50/1**
3m 4.4s (-2.60) **Going Correction** -0.025s/f (Good)
WFA 3 from 4yo+ 8lb 10 Ran SP% **114.2**
Speed ratings (Par 101): **106,105,104,103,102 101,101,101,100,99**
CSF £13.56 CT £60.07 TOTE £2.80: £1.20, £2.00, £1.50; EX 14.60 Trifecta £86.10.
Owner The Equema Partnership **Bred** Genesis Green Stud Ltd **Trained** Newmarket, Suffolk

FOCUS
A cosy follow-up win for the favourite. There's likely to be more to come from him.

T/Plt: £77.80 to a £1 stake. Pool: £49,976.16 - 468.56 winning units T/Qpdt: £6.40 to a £1 stake. Pool: £5,634.57 - 648.17 winning units **Andrew Sheret**

6512 YARMOUTH (L-H)

Tuesday, September 17

OFFICIAL GOING: Good (7.0)
Wind: light, half behind Weather: fine

7315 EAGLE BREWERY NURSERY H'CAP — 7f 3y

2:10 (2:10) (Class 5) (0-70,70) 2-Y-O

£3,428 (£1,020; £509; £300; £300; £300) **Stalls Centre**

Form — RPR

2260 1 **Blausee (IRE)**[31] 6221 2-9-5 **68**...................... TomMarquand 7 74
(Philip McBride) *hld up in tch in last pair: effrt and hdwy jst over 2f out: drvn to chse ldrs over 1f out: chal ins fnl f: led fnl 75yds: styd on* **7/2**[2]

2564 2 1 **Percy Green (IRE)**[7] 7056 2-8-11 **60**...................(p[1]) GeraldMosse 3 63
(K R Burke) *in tch in midfield: effrt to chse ldrs over 2f out: rdn to ld wl over 1f out: hdd and one pce fnl 75yds* **5/1**

6013 3 3 ¼ **Foad**[25] 6387 2-9-2 **65**...................... DaneO'Neill 5 60+
(Ed Dunlop) *in tch in midfield: swtchd rt and effrt jst over 2f out: chsd ldrs and no imp over 1f out: chsd clr ldng pair and kpt on same pce ins fnl f* **7/2**[2]

2211 4 2 ¼ **Luna Wish**[12] 6884 2-9-4 **67**...................... JimmyQuinn 1 56
(George Margarson) *pressed ldr and racd away fr rivals tl 1/2-way: rdn and ev ch over 2f out tl no ex ent fnl f: wknd ins fnl f* **4/1**[3]

634 5 nk **Striding Edge (IRE)**[16] 6757 2-9-7 **70**...................... AndreaAtzeni 4 58
(Mark Johnston) *led: rdn over 2f out: hdd wl over 1f out: sn outpcd and wknd ins fnl f (vet said colt lost right fore shoe)* **10/3**[1]

060 6 1 ½ **Dark Side Division**[69] 4802 2-8-7 **56**...................(p[1]) DavidEgan 6 40
(John Ryan) *chsd ldrs: rdn over 2f out: sn struggling and lost pl over 1f out: wknd ins fnl f (vet said gelding lost left hind shoe)* **20/1**

000 7 5 **Goddess Of Fire**[12] 6883 2-8-4 **53**...................(b[1]) JosephineGordon 2 24
(Ed Dunlop) *dwlt and niggled along early: in tch in last pair: hdwy into midfield 4f out: rdn and lost pl 3f out: bhd over 1f out* **25/1**

1m 23.41s (-1.69) **Going Correction** -0.175s/f (Firm) **7 Ran SP% 112.8**
Speed ratings (Par 95): **102,100,97,94,94 92,86**
CSF £20.59 CT £63.92 TOTE £4.70: £2.40, £2.20; EX 19.10 Trifecta £93.40.
Owner Maelor Racing **Bred** Robert Allcock **Trained** Newmarket, Suffolk

FOCUS
This run-of-the-mill nursery was run at a solid pace down the centre and two pulled clear.

7316 BRITISH STALLION STUDS EBF NOVICE STKS (PLUS 10 RACE) — 6f 3y

2:40 (2:43) (Class 4) 2-Y-O £6,727 (£2,002; £1,000; £500) **Stalls Centre**

Form — RPR

3 1 **Tiger Crusade (FR)**[33] 6127 2-9-2 0...................... JamieSpencer 8 79+
(David Simcock) *hld up in tch in midfield: effrt and swtchd rt wl over 1f out: hanging and racing awkwardly over 1f out: rdn hands and heels and clsd to chal ins fnl f: r.o and led towards fin* **11/8**[1]

4 2 ½ **One Night Stand**[24] 6449 2-9-2 0...................... AdrianMcCarthy 4 78
(William Jarvis) *stdd after s: t.k.h: chsd ldrs tl trckd ldr over 2f out: rdn and drvn to chal over 1f out: kpt on but nt quite match pce of wnr towards fin* **8/1**

2156 3 ½ **Buhturi (IRE)**[27] 6356 2-9-8 87...................... DaneO'Neill 5 82
(Charles Hills) *nt that wl away: sn rcvrd to ld: rdn 2f out: sn hrd pressed and drvn: hdd and no ex towards fin* **13/8**[2]

0 4 3 ¾ **Abbaleka**[22] 6548 2-9-2 0...................... AlistairRawlinson 3 65
(Michael Appleby) *in tch in midfield: effrt to chse ldrs 2f out: edgd lft and unable qck over 1f out: wknd ins fnl f* **33/1**

5 3 ¼ **Aberffraw** 2-9-2 0...................... JamesDoyle 6 55
(William Haggas) *rn green in last trio: effrt ent fnl 2f: 5th and no imp over 1f out: wknd ins fnl f* **6/1**[3]

6 7 **Theheartneverlies** 2-9-2 0...................... RyanTate 7 34
(Sir Mark Prescott Bt) *dwlt: rn green in rr: wknd over 1f out* **16/1**

7 2 ½ **Uncle Sid** 2-9-2 0...................... CallumShepherd 2 27
(William Jarvis) *rn green in last trio: wknd over 1f out* **33/1**

0 8 16 **Dark Side Prince**[97] 3739 2-8-13 0...................... DarraghKeenan[(3)] 1
(Charlie Wallis) *chsd ldr tl over 2f out: sn lost pl: t.o ins fnl f* **100/1**

1m 11.29s (-1.31) **Going Correction** -0.175s/f (Firm) **8 Ran SP% 118.4**
Speed ratings (Par 97): **101,100,99,94,90 81,77,56**
CSF £13.93 TOTE £2.30: £1.10, £2.10, £1.10; EX 12.70 Trifecta £30.20.
Owner Sun Bloodstock Sarl & Qatar Racing Ltd **Bred** Dominique Ades-Hazan & Lily Ades **Trained** Newmarket, Suffolk

FOCUS
The principals came clear in this 2yo novice event and it's fair form for the class.

7317 DAN HAGUE, YARMOUTH'S NUMBER 1 BOOKMAKER H'CAP — 1m 3f 104y

3:10 (3:10) (Class 2) (0-100,93) 3-Y-O £12,450 (£3,728; £1,864) **Stalls Low**

Form — RPR

310 1 **Universal Order**[24] 6471 3-9-2 **88**...................... JamieSpencer 1 96+
(David Simcock) *stdd s: hld up in 3rd: cruised upsides rivals on bridle 3f out: briefly shkn up and qcknd to ld 100yds out: sn clr: v easily* **5/2**[2]

1021 2 2 ¼ **El Misk**[14] 6842 3-9-7 **93**...................... FrankieDettori 2 96
(John Gosden) *trckd ldr: effrt and rdn to chal ent fnl 3f: led 2f out but pressed by cruising wnr: hdd 100yds out: immediately outpcd* **5/6**[1]

-003 3 4 ½ **Three Comets (GER)**[17] 6696 3-9-7 **93**...................(b) AndreaAtzeni 3 89
(Roger Varian) *wnt rt leaving stalls: led: rdn and hrd pressed 3f out: hdd 2f out: no ex over 1f out: wknd ins fnl f* **3/1**[3]

2m 27.07s (-0.73) **Going Correction** -0.175s/f (Firm) **3 Ran SP% 108.1**
Speed ratings (Par 107): **95,93,90**
CSF £5.05 TOTE £3.20; EX 4.90 Trifecta £3.00.
Owner Abdulla Al Mansoori **Bred** Rabbah Bloodstock Limited **Trained** Newmarket, Suffolk

FOCUS
This was a game of cat and mouse until the dash for home developed 3f out. The form's best rated around the runner-up.

7318 LA CONTINENTAL CAFE OF GREAT YARMOUTH H'CAP — 1m 3f 104y

3:40 (3:41) (Class 6) (0-60,60) 3-Y-O+

£2,781 (£827; £413; £300; £300; £300) **Stalls Low**

Form — RPR

3044 1 **Minnelli**[17] 6702 3-9-6 **60**...................... TomMarquand 11 67
(Philip McBride) *hld up in tch in midfield: nt clr run and swtchd rt over 2f out: hdwy to chse ldrs ins fnl f: styd on strly u.p to ld last stride* **12/1**

0021 2 shd **Sea Of Mystery (IRE)**[7] 7060 6-9-5 **60**...................(t) MarkCrehan[(7)] 2 66+
(Michael Appleby) *hld up wl in tch in midfield: clsd and nt clr run 2f out: swtchd rt and effrt to chse ldrs over 1f out: styd on to ld cl home hdd last stride* **15/8**[1]

3215 3 ½ **No Thanks**[33] 6128 3-9-6 **60**...................... CallumShepherd 3 66
(William Jarvis) *chsd ldrs: clsd to press ldr ent fnl 2f: rdn to ld 1f out: drvn ins fnl f: hdd and lost 2 pls cl home* **8/1**[3]

3323 4 1 ¼ **Percy Toplis**[28] 6324 5-8-13 **47**...................(b) EoinWalsh 4 50
(Christine Dunnett) *in tch in midfield: effrt wl over 2f out: chsd ldrs and kpt on u.p ins fnl f: nvr quite enough pce to chal* **14/1**

2560 5 shd **Movie Star (GER)**[28] 6324 4-9-12 **60**...................(t[1]) JamieSpencer 6 63
(Amy Murphy) *stdd s: hld up in last pair: swtchd lft and clsd 2f out: hdwy and pushed lft over 1f out: kpt on u.p ins fnl f: nvr getting to ldrs* **9/1**

0045 6 nk **Incredible Dream (IRE)**[41] 5824 6-8-11 **50**.........(tp) WilliamCarver[(5)] 16 52
(Conrad Allen) *chsd ldrs tl rdn to ld 2f out: hdd 1f out: no ex and outpcd wl ins fnl f* **12/1**

0031 7 ½ **Kirtling**[15] 6796 8-9-8 **59**...................(t) DarraghKeenan[(3)] 15 61
(Andi Brown) *stdd s: hld up in last pair: hdwy over 3f out: chsd ldrs and rdn over 1f out: kpt on same pce ins fnl f* **12/1**

2320 8 2 ¼ **Mistress Nellie**[20] 6599 4-8-7 **48**...................... MarcoGhiani[(7)] 14 46
(William Stone) *in tch in midfield: shuffled bk towards rr and nt clr run 3f out: drvn over 1f out: swtchd rt 1f out: kpt on u.p: no threat to ldrs* **8/1**[3]

4605 9 hd **Carvelas (IRE)**[5] 7109 10-9-0 **48**...................... ShaneKelly 8 46
(J R Jenkins) *hld up in last quartet: clsd on inner 3f out: nt clr run and swtchd rt over 1f out: kpt on same pce and no imp ins fnl f* **66/1**

1633 10 1 ½ **Contingency Fee**[15] 6796 4-9-3 **58**...................(p) GraceMcEntee[(7)] 12 53
(Phil McEntee) *prom tl led after over 1f: rdn and hdd 2f out: no ex over 1f out: wknd ins fnl f* **25/1**

-335 11 ½ **Konigin**[26] 6371 4-9-12 **60**...................(p) DaneO'Neill 9 54
(John Berry) *hld up in last quartet: effrt over 2f out: kpt on u.p but nvr involved* **15/2**[2]

0-20 12 1 ¾ **Lily Ash (IRE)**[28] 6324 6-9-7 **55**...................... JosephineGordon 5 47
(Mike Murphy) *wl in tch: effrt over 2f out: struggling to qckn whn short of room and hmpd over 1f out: wknd ins fnl f* **20/1**

0000 13 3 **Right About Now (IRE)**[13] 6860 5-9-8 **56**...................(p) DavidEgan 1 43
(Charlie Wallis) *sn led: hdd after over 1f out: chsd ldrs after tl lost pl u.p over 1f out: wknd ins fnl f (vet said gelding lost left fore shoe)* **33/1**

5420 14 1 ¼ **Zappiness (USA)**[29] 6279 3-9-3 **57**...................... TomQueally 7 43
(Peter Chapple-Hyam) *hld up in tch in midfield: swtchd rt over 3f out: swtchd rt and effrt over 2f out: no prog and wl hld over 1f out: wknd ins fnl f* **33/1**

0-00 15 9 **Sexy Secret**[49] 5528 8-9-1 **49**...................(p) AdrianMcCarthy 13 19
(Lydia Pearce) *prom early: grad lost pl: struggling u.p over 3f out: bhd fnl f* **66/1**

2m 29.56s (1.76) **Going Correction** -0.175s/f (Firm)
WFA 3 from 4yo+ 6lb **15 Ran SP% 126.0**
Speed ratings (Par 101): **86,85,85,84,84 84,84,82,82,81 80,79,77,76,69**
CSF £34.06 CT £207.77 TOTE £15.20: £4.00, £1.30, £2.80; EX 54.20 Trifecta £338.60.
Owner PMRacing **Bred** Jeremy Green & Sons & Mr P Bickmore **Trained** Newmarket, Suffolk
■ Stewards' Enquiry : Mark Crehan two-day ban: careless riding (Oct 1, 2)

FOCUS
This looked more competitive than the market suggested.

7319 MOULTON NURSERIES OF ACLE NOVICE STKS — 6f 3y

4:10 (4:15) (Class 5) 3-Y-O+ £3,428 (£1,020; £509; £254) **Stalls Centre**

Form — RPR

5 1 **Futuristic (IRE)**[31] 6206 3-9-5 0...................... CallumShepherd 4 77
(James Tate) *dwlt: in tch: effrt and hdwy u.p 2f out: clsd to chse ldrs and swtchd lft 1f out: led ins fnl f: r.o wl* **9/2**[2]

00-3 2 1 ¾ **Spirited Guest**[190] 1139 3-9-5 68...................... TomQueally 7 71
(George Margarson) *w ldr tl led ent fnl 2f: drvn over 1f out: hdd and one pce ins fnl f* **10/1**

3 3 1 ¼ **Imhotep**[14] 6838 3-9-5 0...................... JamesDoyle 5 67
(Roger Charlton) *in tch in midfield: effrt over 2f out: sn drvn and chsd ldrs 2f out: chsd ldr but unable qck over 1f out: 3rd and one pce ins fnl f* **8/11**[1]

0 4 4 ½ **Breath Of Spring (IRE)**[45] 5650 3-8-12 0...........(b[1]) StefanoCherchi[(7)] 2 53
(Marco Botti) *sn towards rr: struggling and rdn 1/2-way: hdwy 1f out: styd on to pass btn horses ins fnl f: no threat to ldrs* **9/1**[3]

4 5 1 ¼ **Wings Of Dubai (IRE)**[25] 6399 3-9-0 0...................... TomMarquand 8 44
(Ismail Mohammed) *w ldrs: rdn over 2f out: outpcd and edgd lft over 1f out: wknd ins fnl f* **14/1**

046 6 ¾ **George Thomas**[68] 4827 3-9-5 65...................... PatCosgrave 3 46
(Mick Quinn) *led tl ent fnl 2f: no ex and lost pl over 1f out: wknd ins fnl f* **12/1**

0065 7 nse **Diamond Cara**[28] 6325 3-8-7 29...................(v[1]) MarcoGhiani[(7)] 1 41
(Stuart Williams) *broke wl: sn restrained and chsd ldrs: effrt jst over 2f out: no ex u.p over 1f out: wknd ins fnl f* **100/1**

4 8 2 ¾ **Hellovasinger**[14] 6838 3-9-5 0...................... ShaneKelly 6 37
(Richard Hughes) *stdd s: t.k.h: hld up in tch in last pair: effrt jst over 2f out: sn struggling and hung lft: wknd over 1f out* **14/1**

00 9 5 **Can I Kick It (IRE)**[20] 6594 3-9-0 0...................... DavidEgan 9 16
(Stuart Williams) *restless in stalls and s.i.s: a towards rr (jockey said filly was restless in stalls and jumped awkwardly)* **80/1**

1m 10.4s (-2.20) **Going Correction** -0.175s/f (Firm) **9 Ran SP% 118.4**
Speed ratings (Par 103): **107,104,103,97,95 94,94,90,83**
CSF £49.92 TOTE £5.60: £1.70, £2.20, £1.10; EX 56.10 Trifecta £134.40.
Owner Saeed Manana **Bred** Rabbah Bloodstock Limited **Trained** Newmarket, Suffolk

FOCUS
The principals were clear at the finish in this interesting 3yo novice sprint. The winner improved from his debut.

7320 GROSVENOR CASINO OF GREAT YARMOUTH H'CAP — 6f 3y

4:40 (4:41) (Class 5) (0-70,71) 3-Y-O+

£3,428 (£1,020; £509; £300; £300; £300) **Stalls Centre**

Form — RPR

3213 1 **Global Hope (IRE)**[23] 6518 4-9-4 **65**...................(tp) ShaneKelly 7 70
(Gay Kelleway) *stdd and dropped in bhd after s: hld up in tch in rr: clsd and swtchd rt over 1f out: rdn and hdwy 1f out: qcknd u.p to ld 50yds out: sn in command* **3/1**[2]

6314 2 1 ¼ **Victory Rose**[20] 6598 3-9-0 **66**...................... DarraghKeenan[(3)] 6 67
(Michael Squance) *hld up wl in tch: effrt 2f out: drvn to chal 1f out: edgd lft ins fnl f: unable to match pce of wnr fnl 50yds* **11/4**[1]

4312 3 nk **Invincible Larne (IRE)**[5] 7105 3-9-7 **70**...................... PatCosgrave 1 70
(Mick Quinn) *led: rdn ent fnl 2f: drvn over 1f out: hdd and one pce fnl 50yds* **3/1**[2]

0420 **4** *2* **Phoenix Star (IRE)**[32] 6183 3-8-9 **65**.................. MarcoGhiani(7) 3 59
(Stuart Williams) *t.k.h: chsd ldrs tl wnt 2nd after over 1f: rdn 2f out: no ex u.p 1f out: wknd ins fnl f* **7/2**[3]

0001 **5** *1 ½* **Dark Side Dream**[28] 6321 7-9-1 **62**..........................(p) JosephineGordon 2 54
(Charlie Wallis) *chsd ldr for over 1f out: effrt jst over 2f out: no ex u.p 1f out: btn ins fnl f and eased towards fin (jockey said gelding lost its action; post-race examination revealed gelding was slightly lame right hind)* **10/1**

2040 **6** *8* **Alliseeisnibras (IRE)**[29] 6286 3-9-4 **67**.................. TomMarquand 5 30
(Ismail Mohammed) *wl in tch: effrt over 2f out: no ex u.p ent fnl f: sn wknd (jockey said filly stopped quickly; post-race examination failed to reveal any abnormalities)* **11/1**

1m 10.7s (-1.90) **Going Correction** -0.175s/f (Firm)
WFA 3 from 4yo+ 2lb **6** Ran SP% **116.3**
Speed ratings (Par 103): **105,103,102,100,98 87**
CSF £12.26 TOTE £3.90: £2.00, £1.80; EX 13.00 Trifecta £38.50.
Owner M Walker, N Scandrett, G Kelleway **Bred** Airlie Stud & Mrs S M Rogers **Trained** Exning, Suffolk

FOCUS
This competitive little sprint handicap saw a tight finish, but the winner is value for further. The form's rated around the centre.

7321 INJURED JOCKEYS' FUND H'CAP 5f 42y
5:10 (5:11) (Class 4) (0-85,84) 3-Y-O+
£5,207 (£1,549; £774; £387; £300; £300) **Stalls** Centre

Form RPR

2010 **1** **Han Solo Berger (IRE)**[6] 7077 4-8-12 **75**..................(p) TomQueally 4 82
(Chris Wall) *hld up in last pair: clsd 1/2-way: effrt over 1f out: ev ch 1f out: drvn to ld ins fnl f: hld on wl towards fin* **13/8**[1]

3502 **2** *hd* **Excellent George**[15] 6809 7-8-9 **79**..................(t) MarcoGhiani(7) 6 85
(Stuart Williams) *c to r nr stands' rail: chsd ldrs: clsd 1/2-way: chsd ldr 2f out: ev ch and hung lft 1f out: kpt on wl u.p* **9/2**[3]

350 **3** *1* **Foxy Forever (IRE)**[15] 6809 9-9-2 **79**..................(bt) JamieSpencer 1 81
(Michael Wigham) *hld up in midfield: clsd 1/2-way: trckd ldrs over 1f out: effrt and ev ch 1f out: no ex and outpcd wl ins fnl f* **6/1**

2601 **4** *1 ¼* **Merry Banter**[22] 6534 5-9-7 **84**.................. PatCosgrave 2 82
(Paul Midgley) *taken down early: led and sn clr: rdn over 1f out: drvn and hrd pressed 1f out: hdd ins fnl f: wknd towards fin* **7/2**[2]

2316 **5** *2* **Case Key**[10] 6972 6-8-8 **71**..................(b) JimmyQuinn 3 62
(Michael Appleby) *squeezed for room and hmpd sn after s: in rr: effrt over 1f out: no imp and wl hld ins fnl f* **15/2**

3400 **6** *shd* **Moonraker**[10] 6954 7-9-2 **79**..................(t[1]) AlistairRawlinson 5 69
(Michael Appleby) *taken down early: chsd ldr tl 2f out: sn u.p and outpcd: wknd ins fnl f* **9/1**

1m 0.05s (-1.85) **Going Correction** -0.175s/f (Firm) **6** Ran SP% **114.5**
Speed ratings (Par 105): **107,106,105,103,99 99**
CSF £9.60 TOTE £2.40: £1.40, £2.90; EX 10.50 Trifecta £47.10.
Owner Mrs B Berresford **Bred** Irish National Stud **Trained** Newmarket, Suffolk

FOCUS
This feature sprint handicap rates as ordinary form for the grade.
T/Plt: £27.00 to a £1 stake. Pool: £58,216.68 - 1572.47 winning units T/Qpdt: £10.60 to a £1 stake. Pool: £4,603.80 - 318.41 winning units **Steve Payne**

7322 - 7328a (Foreign Racing) - See Raceform Interactive

6696
BEVERLEY (R-H)
Wednesday, September 18

OFFICIAL GOING: Good to firm (watered; 7.9)
Wind: Moderate against

7329 SKIRLAUGH CLAIMING STKS 5f
2:00 (2:00) (Class 6) 2-Y-O
£3,105 (£924; £461; £300; £300; £300) **Stalls** Low

Form RPR

6011 **1** **Queens Blade**[23] 6539 2-8-10 **66**..................(b) DuranFentiman 3 55
(Tim Easterby) *awkward s: trckd ldrs: rdn along wl over 1f out: sn swtchd lft to outer and chal: slt ld jst ins fnl f: sn drvn and hld on wl towards fin* **3/1**[3]

0645 **2** *shd* **Comeatchoo (IRE)**[4] 7208 2-8-12 **52**..................(b) DavidAllan 1 57
(Tim Easterby) *trckd ldrs: hdwy over 2f out: rdn over 1f out: chal ent fnl f: sn drvn and ev ch: no ex nr fin* **7/1**

3230 **3** *2 ¾* **She Looks Like Fun**[9] 7029 2-8-13 **69**..................(p[1]) CliffordLee 4 48
(K R Burke) *led 1f: cl up: rdn to take slt ld jst over 1f out: sn edgd rt: drvn and hdd jst ins fnl f: wknd fnl 100yds* **11/4**[2]

2202 **4** *1 ¾* **Calippo (IRE)**[9] 7029 2-8-4 **71**..................(b[1]) Pierre-LouisJamin(7) 6 39
(Archie Watson) *cl up on outer: led after 1f: rdn along wl over 1f out: drvn and hdd appr fnl f: n.m.r and grad wknd* **5/4**[1]

6060 **5** *1 ¾* **South Light (IRE)**[39] 5968 2-8-1 **48**..................(t) KieranSchofield(5) 2 28
(Antony Brittain) *dwlt and towards rr: hdwy over 2f out: rdn wl over 1f out: sn drvn and wknd* **40/1**

0006 **6** *3 ½* **Teasel's Rock (IRE)**[23] 6539 2-8-5 **36**..................(p) RachelRichardson 5 15
(Tim Easterby) *prom: rdn along bef 1/2-way: sn lost pl and bhd* **50/1**

1m 3.69s (0.79) **Going Correction** -0.05s/f (Good) **6** Ran SP% **113.0**
Speed ratings (Par 93): **91,90,86,83,80 75**
CSF £23.65 TOTE £3.70: £1.80, £2.50; EX 19.30 Trifecta £47.30.
Owner HP Racing Queens Blade & Partner **Bred** Mrs J McMahon & Mickley Stud **Trained** Great Habton, N Yorks

FOCUS
Two pulled clear late on in this modest claiming event.

7330 WEEL EBF FILLIES' NOVICE STKS (PLUS 10 RACE) 7f 96y
2:30 (2:32) (Class 5) 2-Y-O
£4,140 (£1,232; £615; £307) **Stalls** Low

Form RPR

21 **1** **Freyja (IRE)**[18] 6697 2-9-7 **0**.................. JoeFanning 1 81
(Mark Johnston) *mde all: pushed clr 2f out: easily* **1/12**[1]

0 **2** *4* **Eventful**[19] 6675 2-9-0 **0**.................. BenCurtis 3 61+
(Hugo Palmer) *awkward s: green and hld up in tch: hdwy to chse wnr wl over 2f out: rdn along wl over 1f out: keeping on but no ch w wnr whn rdr dropped rein ent fnl f* **12/1**[2]

3 *3 ¾* **Samille (IRE)** 2-9-0 **0**.................. KevinStott 4 51
(Amy Murphy) *chsd wnr: cl up 1/2-way: pushed along 3f out: rdn over 2f out: sn wknd* **25/1**

6 **4** *2 ½* **Al Jawhra (IRE)**[18] 6697 2-9-0 **0**.................. DavidAllan 2 44
(Tim Easterby) *dwlt and towards rr: sme hdwy 1/2-way: rdn along wl over 2f out: sn outpcd* **16/1**[3]

1m 32.25s (-0.35) **Going Correction** -0.05s/f (Good) **4** Ran SP% **109.8**
Speed ratings (Par 92): **100,95,91,88**
CSF £2.17 TOTE £1.10; EX 2.40 Trifecta £6.50.
Owner Mrs A G Kavanagh **Bred** C O P Hanbury **Trained** Middleham Moor, N Yorks

FOCUS
Not a great deal changed in the early part of this contest, and the favourite won without having a hard time.

7331 BEVERLEY ANNUAL BADGEHOLDERS EBF NOVICE AUCTION STKS 7f 96y
3:05 (3:05) (Class 5) 2-Y-O
£4,140 (£1,232; £615) **Stalls** Low

Form RPR

212 **1** **Flylikeaneagle (IRE)**[19] 6654 2-9-9 **85**.................. JoeFanning 2 86
(Mark Johnston) *mde all: pushed clr 2f out: readily* **2/7**[1]

0323 **2** *3 ¼* **Bertie's Princess (IRE)**[25] 6458 2-8-8 **68**.................. RowanScott(3) 3 64
(Nigel Tinkler) *trckd wnr: pushed along wl over 2f out: sn rdn: drvn over 1f out: kpt on: no imp* **4/1**[2]

0 **3** *2 ¼* **Liberty Filly**[44] 5733 2-8-11 **0**.................. AdamMcNamara 1 58
(Roger Charlton) *dwlt: rn green in rr: effrt and sme hdwy wl over 2f out: sn rdn along: kpt on same pce (jockey said filly ran green)* **9/1**[3]

1m 35.01s (2.41) **Going Correction** -0.05s/f (Good) **3** Ran SP% **107.8**
Speed ratings (Par 95): **84,80,77**
CSF £1.80 TOTE £1.10; EX 1.60 Trifecta £1.20.
Owner Barbara & Alick Richmond Racing **Bred** Corduff Stud **Trained** Middleham Moor, N Yorks

FOCUS
All very straightforward for the market leader.

7332 CHRIS AND SARAH BURROWS H'CAP 1m 4f 23y
3:35 (3:35) (Class 4) (0-85,82) 3-Y-O+
£6,474 (£1,938; £969; £484) **Stalls** Low

Form RPR

0410 **1** **Regal Mirage (IRE)**[35] 6067 5-9-6 **74**.................. DavidAllan 4 79
(Tim Easterby) *hld up in rr: hdwy over 2f out: rdn over 1f out: sn chal: drvn ins fnl f: kpt on wl to ld nr line* **9/4**[2]

1510 **2** *shd* **Five Helmets (IRE)**[10] 6998 3-9-2 **77**.................. JamieGormley 3 81
(Iain Jardine) *sn led tl jinked at path and hdd over 10f out: trckd ldng pair: pushed along and hdwy 3f out: sn cl up: rdn to take slt ld 2f out: drvn and edgd rt ent fnl f: kpt on wl: hdd nr line* **6/5**[1]

6066 **3** *7* **Cape Islay (FR)**[22] 6576 3-9-7 **82**.................. JoeFanning 5 75
(Mark Johnston) *cl up: pushed along 3f out: sn slt ld: rdn and hdd narrowly 2f out: drvn and hld whn n.m.r jst ins fnl f: sn wknd* **7/2**[3]

1504 **4** *6* **Zihaam**[34] 6100 5-8-7 **66**..................(p) BenSanderson(5) 2 49
(Roger Fell) *prom: reminders early: slt ld over 2f out: pushed along 4f out: rdn 3f out: sn hdd: drvn over 2f out: sn btn* **8/1**

2m 36.95s (-1.85) **Going Correction** -0.05s/f (Good)
WFA 3 from 5yo 7lb **4** Ran SP% **109.6**
Speed ratings (Par 105): **104,103,99,95**
CSF £5.45 TOTE £2.60; EX 5.10 Trifecta £8.20.
Owner Ryedale Partners No 7 **Bred** Norelands, Lofts Hall & A Gold **Trained** Great Habton, N Yorks

FOCUS
As could be expected in a small field, all the action happened in the final couple of furlongs. A modest event, the first pair rated to form.

7333 HANNAH ALI RACECOURSE PHOTOGRAPHY EBF NOVICE STKS 5f
4:10 (4:11) (Class 5) 2-Y-O
£4,140 (£1,232; £615; £307) **Stalls** Low

Form RPR

1 **Magical Journey (IRE)** 2-8-11 **0**.................. PJMcDonald 10 74
(James Tate) *hld up in rr and sn swtchd rt: in tch: swtchd to inner and hdwy 2f out: chsd ldrs and squeezed through on inner ent fnl f: sn rdn to chal: led fnl 75yds: kpt on wl* **5/1**[2]

01 **2** *1 ¼* **Reassure**[33] 6147 2-9-4 **0**.................. DanielTudhope 4 76
(William Haggas) *qckly away and led: rdn along over 1f out: drvn and edgd lft ins fnl f: hdd fnl 75yds: kpt on same pce* **11/4**[1]

62 **3** *1 ¼* **Astrozone**[21] 6585 2-8-11 **0**.................. GrahamLee 2 66
(Bryan Smart) *trckd ldrs: effrt and n.m.r wl over 1f out: swtchd rt and nt clr run ent fnl f: sn rdn and kpt on wl towards fin* **8/1**

04 **4** *½* **Araifjan**[40] 5913 2-9-2 **0**.................. TonyHamilton 1 68
(Richard Fahey) *trckd ldr on inner: hdwy 2f out: rdn and ev ch over 1f out: drvn ent fnl f: kpt on same pce* **10/1**

0 **5** *2* **Triple Spear**[23] 6548 2-8-11 **0**.................. TheodoreLadd(5) 3 61
(Michael Appleby) *towards rr: pushed along 1/2-way: rdn 2f out: kpt on fnl f (jockey said gelding fly leapt the stalls)* **66/1**

0244 **6** *nk* **Exclusively**[30] 6272 2-9-4 **82**..................(p) HollieDoyle 7 61
(Archie Watson) *cl up: rdn along 2f out: drvn over 1f out: grad wknd* **6/1**[3]

0 **7** *½* **Cupid's Beau**[12] 6911 2-8-11 **0**.................. ThomasGreatrex(5) 9 58
(David Loughnane) *prom on outer: rdn along wl over 1f out: sn drvn and wknd* **12/1**

0 **8** *¾* **Deevious Beau**[15] 6822 2-9-2 **0**.................. RobbieDowney 5 55
(David Barron) *a towards rr* **66/1**

9 *2 ¼* **Only Alone (IRE)** 2-8-11 **0**.................. PaulMulrennan 6 42
(Jedd O'Keeffe) *towards rr and hmpd sn after s: a bhd* **25/1**

10 **10** *14* **Wonderwork (IRE)**[25] 6474 2-9-9 **0**..................(h[1]) BenCurtis 8 3
(K R Burke) *awkward s and dwlt: plld hrd and sn in tch: rdn and lost pl 2f out: sn bhd and eased (jockey said colt ran too free)* **11/4**[1]

1m 2.45s (-0.45) **Going Correction** -0.05s/f (Good) **10** Ran SP% **119.0**
Speed ratings (Par 95): **101,99,97,96,93 92,91,90,86,64**
CSF £19.42 TOTE £5.60: £2.00, £1.70, £2.10; EX 20.40 Trifecta £133.30.
Owner Saeed Manana **Bred** Camas Park, Lynch Bages & Summerhill **Trained** Newmarket, Suffolk

FOCUS
This looked a decent contest and the winner could be above average.

7334 WESTWOOD H'CAP 5f
4:40 (4:40) (Class 5) (0-75,70) 3-Y-O+
£4,032 (£1,207; £603; £302; £300; £300) **Stalls** Low

Form RPR

0022 **1** **Desert Ace (IRE)**[12] 6932 8-9-6 **68**.................. KevinStott 4 76
(Paul Midgley) *trckd ldrs whn squeezed out and towards rr after 1f: swtchd to inner and hdwy wl over 1f out: chsd ldr and swtchd lft ins fnl f: sn rdn to chal: kpt on to ld fnl 50yds* **11/2**

1510 **2** *1* **Archimedes (IRE)**[7] 7077 6-9-7 **69**..................(vt) DavidAllan 1 73
(David C Griffiths) *led: rdn over 1f out: drvn and jnd ins fnl f: hdd and no ex fnl 50yds* **7/2**[2]

0323 **3** ½ **Sheepscar Lad (IRE)**[18] 6699 5-9-3 **70**.............. FayeMcManoman(5) 2 72
(Nigel Tinkler) *trckd ldrs: effrt over 1f out: sn rdn: kpt on fnl f (jockey said gelding hung left-handed throughout)* **11/8**[1]

6004 **4** 3 **Excessable**[12] 6932 6-9-8 **70**..........................(tp) RachelRichardson 6 61
(Tim Easterby) *chsd ldrs: rdn along over 1f out: sn drvn and kpt on same pce* **6/1**

0066 **5** 2 ¾ **Qaaraat**[38] 5986 4-8-13 **61**..(p) CamHardie 5 43
(Antony Brittain) *chsd ldrs: rdn along wl over 1f out: sn drvn and wknd appr fnl f* **14/1**

0022 **6** 4 ½ **Tan**[16] 6798 5-8-12 **65**.. TheodoreLadd(5) 7 30
(Michael Appleby) *rrd and wnt lft s: hdwy and cl up after 1f: rdn along wl over 1f out: sn drvn and wknd* **5/1**[3]

1m 2.07s (-0.83) **Going Correction** -0.05s/f (Good) **6** Ran SP% **117.3**
Speed ratings (Par 103): **104,102,101,96,92 85**
CSF £26.11 TOTE £6.50: £3.40, £2.40; EX 18.40 Trifecta £74.90.
Owner M Hammond, Mad For Fun & Partners **Bred** Kildaragh Stud **Trained** Westow, N Yorks

FOCUS
This was effectively a 0-70, with the top weights 5lb below the ceiling rating for the contest. The form is rated around the runner-up.

7335 RACING AGAIN NEXT TUESDAY APPRENTICE CLASSIFIED STKS (RACING EXCELLENCE TRAINING SERIES) (DIV I) 1m 100y

5:10 (5:11) (Class 6) 3-Y-O+

£3,105 (£924; £461; £300; £300; £300) **Stalls** Low

Form RPR

-003 **1** **Dependable (GER)**[29] 6302 4-9-4 55.............................. TylerSaunders 5 58+
(Charles Hills) *trckd ldng pair: swtchd lft to outer and hdwy over 2f out: rdn to ld over 1f out: drvn and edgd rt ins fnl f: styd on* **9/2**[2]

0030 **2** ½ **Clipsham Tiger (IRE)**[15] 6844 3-8-9 44...............(h[1]) GeorgeRooke(5) 11 57
(Michael Appleby) *towards rr: hdwy 3f out: rdn along to chse ldrs 2f out: ev ch over 1f out: sn drvn and kpt on* **25/1**

6003 **3** 1 ¾ **Corked (IRE)**[34] 6102 6-9-4 48.. AledBeech 3 53
(Alistair Whillans) *towards rr: hdwy 3f out: swtchd rt to inner and chsd ldrs whn n.m.r over 1f out: sn rdn: drvn and n.m.r ins fnl f: kpt on towards fin* **3/1**[1]

5503 **4** ½ **Klipperty Klopp**[56] 5304 3-9-0 55.............................. KieranSchofield 4 52
(Antony Brittain) *trckd ldrs: hdwy and cl up 3f out: rdn to ld 2f out: sn drvn and hdd over 1f out: kpt on same pce* **6/1**

0025 **5** 1 ¾ **Kodi Koh (IRE)**[19] 6663 4-8-11 47.............................. OwenPayton(7) 7 49
(Simon West) *rrd and dwlt s: in rr: hdwy 3f out: rdn along 2f out: swtchd rt and kpt on fnl f (jockey said filly jumped awkwardly from the stalls)* **6/1**

6030 **6** 1 ½ **Henrietta's Dream**[35] 6066 5-9-4 44...........................(p) MarkCrehan 1 45
(Robyn Brisland) *chsd ldrs: rdn along wl over 2f out: sn drvn and wknd* **12/1**

0020 **7** 1 ¼ **Hippeia (IRE)**[30] 6276 4-9-4 55.............................(v) Pierre-LouisJamin 10 43
(Lawrence Mullaney) *led: pushed along 3f out: rdn over 2f out: sn rdn and hdd over 1f out: grad wknd* **5/1**[3]

0000 **8** 2 ¼ **Supreme Dream**[9] 7032 3-8-9 41.............................. ZakWheatley(5) 8 38
(Shaun Harris) *t.k.h: chsd ldrs: rdn along 3f out: sn wknd* **33/1**

05 **9** 3 ¾ **Phenakite**[22] 6578 3-9-0 50.. TobyEley 6 30
(Ollie Pears) *stmbld and dwlt s: a in rr (jockey said gelding was never travelling)* **8/1**

100 **10** 6 **Bob's Girl**[24] 6499 4-9-1 47...................................(b) AmeliaGlass(3) 9 18
(Michael Mullineaux) *prom: cl up 1/2-way: rdn along 3f out: sn drvn and wknd* **16/1**

1m 46.13s (-0.27) **Going Correction** -0.05s/f (Good)
WFA 3 from 4yo+ 4lb **10** Ran SP% **119.9**
Speed ratings (Par 101): **99,98,96,96,94 93,91,89,85,79**
CSF £111.30 TOTE £5.00: £1.50, £5.60, £1.70; EX 168.10 Trifecta £368.00.
Owner Windmill Racing **Bred** Gestut Rottgen **Trained** Lambourn, Berks

FOCUS
The first division of a moderate contest was marginally quicker than the second.

7336 RACING AGAIN NEXT TUESDAY APPRENTICE CLASSIFIED STKS (RACING EXCELLENCE TRAINING SERIES) (DIV II) 1m 100y

5:40 (5:41) (Class 6) 3-Y-O+

£3,105 (£924; £461; £300; £300; £300) **Stalls** Low

Form RPR

6301 **1** **Amity Island**[22] 6578 4-9-4 52.. TobyEley 2 53+
(Ollie Pears) *reminders s and in rr: hdwy 3f out: chsd ldrs over 1f out: sn rdn and chal ent fnl f: kpt on wl to ld fnl 100yds* **6/4**[1]

4065 **2** 2 **Elysee Star**[54] 5392 4-8-13 47.............................. ZakWheatley(5) 6 49
(Mark Walford) *hld up towards rr: hdwy 3f out: chsd ldrs on outer wl over 1f out: rdn to ld appr fnl f: sn jnd and drvn: hdd and kpt on same pce fnl 100yds* **5/2**[2]

0006 **3** 2 **Lisnamoyle Lady (IRE)**[53] 5430 4-8-11 40...............(bt) JacobClark(7) 10 45
(Martin Smith) *dwlt: sn prom: chsd ldr 1/2-way: rdn along over 2f out: drvn wl over 1f out: kpt on same pce* **40/1**

0400 **4** 1 ½ **Grey Berry (IRE)**[24] 6502 3-9-0 51.........................(b) Pierre-LouisJamin 8 41
(Tim Easterby) *led: rdn along over 2f out: drvn wl over 1f out: hdd appr fnl f: wknd* **5/1**[3]

5536 **5** 1 ½ **Foxy Rebel**[61] 5151 5-9-4 43.. EllaMcCain 7 38
(Ruth Carr) *prom: rdn along wl over 2f out: drvn wl over 1f out: sn one pce* **9/1**

0604 **6** 2 **Opera Kiss (IRE)**[13] 6885 3-9-0 42.............................. LauraCoughlan 4 34
(Lawrence Mullaney) *in tch: hdwy on inner to chse ldrs 3f out: rdn over 2f out: sn wknd* **14/1**

6005 **7** ¾ **Harperelle**[20] 6624 3-9-0 43..(p) AledBeech 9 33
(Alistair Whillans) *chsd ldrs: rdn along wl over 2f out: sn wknd* **15/2**

1m 46.51s (0.11) **Going Correction** -0.05s/f (Good)
WFA 3 from 4yo+ 4lb **7** Ran SP% **116.1**
Speed ratings (Par 101): **97,95,93,91,90 88,87**
CSF £5.61 TOTE £2.40: £1.40, £1.90; EX 7.30 Trifecta £115.10.
Owner Ollie Pears & Ownaracehorse Ltd **Bred** Red House Stud **Trained** Norton, N Yorks

■ Stewards' Enquiry : Jacob Clark two-day ban: used whip without giving mount time to respond (2-3 Oct)

FOCUS
The two market leaders dominated the final stages.
T/Plt: £82.10 to a £1 stake. Pool: £36,873.86 - 327.47 winning units T/Qpdt: £24.10 to a £1 stake. Pool: £3,121.83 - 95.49 winning units **Joe Rowntree**

7160 SANDOWN (R-H)

Wednesday, September 18

OFFICIAL GOING: Good (good to firm in places; watered; 7.1)
Wind: Light, behind Weather: Sunny, warm

7337 COUNTRYSIDE DAY NOVEMBER 10 H'CAP (JOCKEY CLUB GRASSROOTS SPRINT SERIES QUALIFIER) 5f 10y

1:50 (1:51) (Class 5) (0-75,80) 3-Y-O+

£4,528 (£1,347; £673; £336; £300; £300) **Stalls** High

Form RPR

6164 **1** **Enthaar**[17] 6756 4-9-6 **72**..(tp) JasonWatson 3 80
(Stuart Williams) *chsd ldrs: rdn and prog on outer 2f out: led jst over 1f out: drvn out as ld dwindled nr fin (jockey said gelding hung right-handed under pressure)* **10/1**

630 **2** ½ **Doc Sportello (IRE)**[12] 6916 7-9-4 **70**...............................(p) BrettDoyle 11 76+
(Tony Carroll) *s.i.s: racd in last trio: rdn and prog on outer wl over 1f out: str run to take 2nd fnl 75yds: clsd on wnr nr fin* **8/1**[3]

036 **3** 1 ½ **Joegogo (IRE)**[35] 6080 4-9-0 **73**..............................(v[1]) AngusVilliers(7) 9 74
(David Evans) *prom: chsd ldr 3f out to over 1f out: kpt on same pce fnl f* **14/1**

5645 **4** *nk* **Michaels Choice**[17] 6756 3-9-0 **67**............................(b) KieranShoemark 6 67
(William Jarvis) *led and racd against rail: rdn 2f out: hdd jst over 1f out: one pce* **20/1**

2320 **5** *shd* **Gnaad (IRE)**[11] 6954 5-9-10 **76**.. OisinMurphy 7 75+
(Alan Bailey) *scratchy to post: awkward s and slowest away: racd in last trio: rdn and prog wl over 1f out: styd on wl fnl f but nvr quite pce to chal (jockey said gelding was slowly away)* **9/4**[1]

2411 **6** 1 ½ **Union Rose**[5] 7161 7-10-0 **80** 4ex..............................(v) RaulDaSilva 5 76+
(Ronald Harris) *chsd ldr 1f: trckd ldrs after: pushed along whn sltly impeded over 1f out: one pce and hld whn hmpd ins fnl f (jockey said gelding was denied a clear run)* **3/1**[2]

5062 **7** *shd* **Leo Minor (USA)**[14] 6857 5-8-12 **67**..............................(t[1]) CierenFallon(3) 1 65+
(Robert Cowell) *trckd ldrs against rail: pushed along whn n.m.r over 1f out: rdn and styng on in dispute of 3rd whn nowhere to go ins fnl f and lost all ch (jockey said gelding was denied a clear run)* **9/1**

0052 **8** ½ **Porto Ferro (IRE)**[16] 6806 5-8-2 **59** oh3.....................(t) RhiainIngram(5) 8 51
(John Bridger) *towards rr: rdn 2f out: one pce and n.d to ldrs* **25/1**

6020 **9** ¾ **Madrinho (IRE)**[32] 6203 6-9-5 **71**...................................... GeorgeDowning 4 60
(Tony Carroll) *s.i.s: racd in last trio and sn pushed along: rdn and no prog over 1f out: kpt on one pce after* **20/1**

2015 **10** 4 ½ **Major Blue**[55] 5356 3-9-7 **74**..(b) AdamKirby 2 47
(James Eustace) *chsd ldrs: rdn 2f out: lost pl over 1f out: wknd rapidly fnl f (jockey said gelding lost its action inside the final furlong; vet said gelding had lost its left fore shoe)* **10/1**

4634 **11** 19 **Pink Iceburg (IRE)**[17] 6754 3-8-10 **63**..........................(b[1]) ShaneKelly 10
(Peter Crate) *free to post: chsd ldr 4f out to 3f out: wknd rapidly: t.o* **20/1**

1m 0.17s (-1.13) **Going Correction** +0.10s/f (Good)
WFA 3 from 4yo+ 1lb **11** Ran SP% **119.9**
Speed ratings (Par 103): **113,112,109,109,109 106,106,105,104,97 67**
CSF £83.67 CT £1161.54 TOTE £11.50: £2.90, £2.60, £3.90; EX 135.00 Trifecta £1531.60.
Owner B Piper & D Cobill **Bred** Abbey Farm Stud **Trained** Newmarket, Suffolk

■ Stewards' Enquiry : Cieren Fallon one-day ban: failing to take all reasonable and permissible measures to obtain the best possible placing (Sep 22)

Shane Kelly two-day ban: interference & careless riding (Oct 2-3)

FOCUS
All distances as advertised. Ordinary sprint form. The winner is rated to his best.

7338 BRITISH STALLION STUDS EBF NOVICE STKS (PLUS 10 RACE) 1m

2:20 (2:23) (Class 4) 2-Y-O £4,787 (£1,424; £711; £355) **Stalls** Low

Form RPR

1 **Via De Vega (FR)** 2-9-5 0.. OisinMurphy 4 84+
(Andrew Balding) *difficult to load into stall: sn in midfield: shkn up in 6th over 2f out and rn green: prog over 1f out but stl 6 l bhd ldr fnl f: storming run fnl 150yds to ld fnl stride* **14/1**

3 **2** *hd* **Never Alone**[26] 6409 2-9-5 0.. WilliamBuick 1 84
(Charlie Appleby) *led: jnd after 3f: shkn up over 2f out: asserted wl over 1f out and rdn 3 l clr ins fnl f: styd on but hdd post* **7/2**[2]

3 **3** 3 **Finest Sound (IRE)**[19] 6669 2-9-5 0.............................. AndreaAtzeni 11 77
(Simon Crisford) *trckd ldr after 1f: chal and upsides over 2f out: rdn and btn over 1f out: lost 2nd and fdd fnl 75yds* **11/2**[3]

26 **4** ½ **Heaven Forfend**[88] 4091 2-9-5 0.. RyanMoore 8 75+
(Sir Michael Stoute) *trckd ldr 1f: styd prom: shkn up over 2f out: outpcd over 1f out: one pce and lost 3rd ins fnl f* **7/2**[2]

5 4 **Gold Desert** 2-9-5 0.. PatDobbs 2 66
(Richard Hannon) *prom: shkn up over 2f out: steadily wknd over 1f out* **50/1**

602 **6** 3 ¼ **What An Angel**[11] 6948 2-9-5 81.. SeanLevey 7 59
(Richard Hannon) *t.k.h: cl up tl wknd 2f out* **16/1**

0 **7** 3 ¼ **Willy Nilly (IRE)**[19] 6669 2-9-5 0.. AdamKirby 9 51
(Clive Cox) *a off the pce and towards rr: no prog fnl 2f* **33/1**

8 1 ¼ **Fear Naught** 2-9-5 0.. NicolaCurrie 5 48
(George Baker) *a towards rr: pushed along 3f out: no ch fnl 2f* **100/1**

2 **9** *nk* **Byzantine Empire**[12] 6926 2-9-5 0.. FrankieDettori 6 48
(John Gosden) *slowly away: racd in last quartet: pushed along and no prog 3f out: nvr a factor (jockey said colt ran green)* **6/4**[1]

10 1 ½ **Arthurian Fable (IRE)** 2-9-5 0.. MartinDwyer 10 44
(Brian Meehan) *a wl in rr: pushed along and struggling over 3f out* **66/1**

11 2 ½ **Adonis Blue (IRE)** 2-9-5 0.. JasonWatson 12 39
(Roger Charlton) *slowly away: a in last pair and wl bhd* **66/1**

0 **12** 4 ½ **Thunder Flash**[25] 6464 2-9-5 0.. KieranShoemark 3 28
(Ed Walker) *chsd ldrs tl wknd rapidly jst over 2f out (jockey said colt became unbalanced from approximately 3f out)* **66/1**

1m 43.9s (0.60) **Going Correction** +0.10s/f (Good) 2y crse rec **12** Ran SP% **122.7**
Speed ratings (Par 97): **101,100,97,97,93 90,86,85,85,83 81,76**
CSF £64.20 TOTE £20.20: £4.20, £1.40, £1.80; EX 96.30 Trifecta £512.20.
Owner Pdr Properties **Bred** S C E A Haras De Saint Pair **Trained** Kingsclere, Hants

The Form Book Flat 2019, Raceform Ltd, Newbury, RG14 5SJ

FOCUS
Bit of a turn up in this novice, with the winner making up loads of ground in the last furlong to chase down the front-runners. The pace was an ordinary one.

7339 MAX PATEL WEALTH MANAGER OF CHOICE NOVICE STKS (PLUS 10 RACE) 7f
2:55 (2:56) (Class 3) 2-Y-O **£7,762** (£2,310; £1,154; £577) **Stalls** Low

Form RPR

1 **1** **Palace Pier**[19] 6669 2-9-8 0 FrankieDettori 3 96+
(John Gosden) *mde all: pushed along 2f out: reminder over 1f out: lened clr fnl f: eased fnl 75yds* **1/8**[1]

0 **2** 4 1/2 **Mars Landing (IRE)**[19] 6669 2-9-2 0 RyanMoore 2 77
(Sir Michael Stoute) *cl up: chsd wnr over 2f out: rdn and spirited effrt over 1f out: lft bhd fnl f but clr of rest* **4/1**[2]

3 5 **Southern Dancer** 2-9-2 0 OisinMurphy 4 63
(Brian Meehan) *chsd wnr to over 2f out: easily lft bhd over 1f out: jst clung on for 3rd* **20/1**

0 **4** shd **Junkanoo**[46] 5665 2-9-2 0 LiamKeniry 7 63
(Gary Moore) *hld up in last of main gp: shkn up 2f out: styd on steadily over 1f out: nrly snatched 3rd* **20/1**

5 2 1/2 **Balzac** 2-9-2 0 KieranShoemark 5 56
(Ed Walker) *chsd ldrs: outpcd over 2f out: no ch over 1f out (jockey said colt hung right-handed)* **17/2**[3]

0 **6** 3/4 **Summeronsevenhills (USA)**[13] 6905 2-9-2 0 ShaneKelly 1 54
(Richard Hughes) *a towards rr: pushed along 1/2-way: outpcd over 2f out and no ch after* **33/1**

0 **7** 1 3/4 **Marion's Boy (IRE)**[33] 6154 2-9-2 0 JasonWatson 6 50
(Roger Teal) *chsd ldrs on outer: outpcd over 2f out: wknd over 1f out* **14/1**

8 32 **Tremor (IRE)** 2-9-2 0 NicolaCurrie 8
(Alan King) *slowly away: sn t.o (jockey said gelding was slowly away and hung left-handed)* **33/1**

1m 29.81s (0.51) **Going Correction** +0.10s/f (Good) **8 Ran SP% 141.5**
Speed ratings (Par 99): **101,95,90,90,87 86,84,47**
CSF £2.06 TOTE £1.10: £1.02, £1.30, £4.00; EX 2.40 Trifecta £17.10.
Owner Sheikh Hamdan bin Mohammed Al Maktoum **Bred** Highclere Stud And Floors Farming **Trained** Newmarket, Suffolk

FOCUS
Little depth to this novice and the only two who mattered in the market dominated.

7340 CHASEMORE FARM FORTUNE STKS (LISTED RACE) 1m
3:25 (3:25) (Class 1) 3-Y-O+ **£22,684** (£8,600; £4,304; £2,144; £1,076; £540) **Stalls** Low

Form RPR

2-12 **1** **King Of Change**[137] 2411 3-9-0 115 SeanLevey 1 114+
(Richard Hannon) *wl in tch: clsd on ldrs 2f out: pushed into ld jst over 1f out: edgd lft and drvn ins fnl f: styd on wl fnl 100yds* **11/4**[2]

5242 **2** 1 1/4 **Turgenev**[25] 6443 3-9-0 112 (p) FrankieDettori 3 110
(John Gosden) *stdd s: hld up in last: pushed along and prog 2f out: rdn and swtchd rt ins fnl f: chsd wnr fnl 100yds: styd on but no imp* **7/4**[1]

5-15 **3** 1 1/2 **Silver Line (IRE)**[27] 6376 5-9-4 106 OisinMurphy 5 107
(Saeed bin Suroor) *trckd ldr after 2f: led jst over 2f out: rdn and hdd jst over 1f out: one pce fnl f* **11/2**

135- **4** 1 1/2 **Prince Eiji**[329] 8563 3-9-0 104 AndreaAtzeni 4 103
(Roger Varian) *t.k.h: led 1f: trckd ldrs after: shkn up and waiting for room 2f out: rdn and clsd on ldrs briefly 1f out: fdd fnl 75yds* **12/1**

-420 **5** 1 3/4 **Wootton (FR)**[172] 1445 4-9-4 112 WilliamBuick 6 99
(Charlie Appleby) *led after 1f: rdn and hdd jst over 2f out: fdd over 1f out* **4/1**[3]

6 3/4 **Last Winter (SAF)**[599] 6-9-4 116 RyanMoore 2 97
(Sir Michael Stoute) *t.k.h: hld up in last pair: pushed along 2f out: one pce and no prog* **12/1**

1m 42.6s (-0.70) **Going Correction** +0.10s/f (Good)
WFA 3 from 4yo+ 4lb **6 Ran SP% 113.8**
Speed ratings (Par 111): **107,105,104,102,101 100**
CSF £8.19 TOTE £3.60: £1.80, £1.50; EX 7.60 Trifecta £25.50.
Owner Ali Abdulla Saeed **Bred** Rabbah Bloodstock Limited **Trained** East Everleigh, Wilts

FOCUS
A solid Listed race and the two classy 3yos came to the fore.

7341 STELRAD RADIATOR GROUP FILLIES' H'CAP 1m
4:00 (4:00) (Class 4) (0-85,84) 3-Y-O **£6,469** (£1,925; £962; £481; £300; £300) **Stalls** Low

Form RPR

6331 **1** **Magical Rhythms (USA)**[29] 6316 3-9-6 83 FrankieDettori 7 89+
(John Gosden) *hld up in last trio: rdn 2f out: prog on outer jst over 1f out: edgd lft but clsd on ldr fnl f: r.o to ld last strides (jockey said filly hung right-handed on the run to the line)* **5/2**[1]

4-51 **2** nk **Lady Bowthorpe**[30] 6283 3-9-1 78 KieranShoemark 6 83
(William Jarvis) *t.k.h: trckd ldng pair: rdn 2f out: clsd fnl f: one of three in line 50yds out: jst outpcd whn crowded last strides* **6/1**

1653 **3** hd **Clara Peeters**[12] 6913 3-9-7 84 RyanMoore 4 89
(Gary Moore) *trckd ldng pair: rdn to ld wl over 1f out: drvn fnl f: hdd last strides and n.m.r fin* **6/1**

4241 **4** 2 **Alandalos**[22] 6559 3-8-12 75 DaneO'Neill 2 75
(Charles Hills) *trckd ldr: rdn jst over 2f out and edgd lft: nt qckn wl over 1f out: one pce after* **9/1**

6103 **5** nse **I'lletyougonow**[11] 6973 3-8-10 73 (p) OisinMurphy 1 73
(Mick Channon) *led: rdn and hdd wl over 1f out: chsd ldr tl ins fnl f: fdd nr fin* **14/1**

222 **6** 3 **Loving Glance**[29] 6315 3-9-7 84 AndreaAtzeni 5 77
(Martyn Meade) *hld up in last: pushed along 3f out: no prog whn rdn 2f out* **7/2**[2]

1102 **7** 4 1/2 **Al Messila**[30] 6282 3-9-5 82 PatDobbs 3 65
(Richard Hannon) *hld up in last trio: shkn up and no prog over 2f out: wknd over 1f out* **9/2**[3]

1m 43.23s (-0.07) **Going Correction** +0.10s/f (Good) **7 Ran SP% 114.2**
Speed ratings (Par 100): **104,103,103,101,101 98,93**
CSF £17.88 TOTE £3.10: £1.70, £3.00; EX 17.90 Trifecta £109.70.
Owner Prince A A Faisal **Bred** Nawara Stud Company Ltd **Trained** Newmarket, Suffolk

FOCUS
A fair fillies' handicap run at an okay gallop, it produced something of a bunched finish. The form's rated around the third.

7342 CHRISTMAS PARTIES AT SANDOWN PARK H'CAP (JOCKEY CLUB GRASSROOTS FLAT MIDDLE DISTANCE SERIES QUAL) 1m 1f 209y
4:35 (4:35) (Class 4) (0-85,87) 3-Y-O **£6,469** (£1,925; £962; £481; £300; £300) **Stalls** Low

Form RPR

-223 **1** **Sucellus**[118] 3011 3-9-10 87 (w) FrankieDettori 4 96+
(John Gosden) *hld up in last trio: prog on outer over 2f out: trckd ldr over 1f out gng easily: cajoled along to take narrow ld ins fnl f: jst hld on* **10/3**[3]

3321 **2** shd **Cape Cavalli (IRE)**[15] 6836 3-9-4 81 (v) WilliamBuick 8 89+
(Simon Crisford) *dwlt: hld up in last: stl there and pushed along 2f out: prog over 1f out: rdn and r.o fnl f to take 2nd nr fin and clsd on wnr: jst too late* **5/2**[1]

0532 **3** 3/4 **Slade King (IRE)**[16] 6810 3-8-7 70 JasonWatson 5 76
(Gary Moore) *trckd ldr 4f: pushed along 4f out: responded wl and clsd to ld 2f out: sn drvn: narrowly hdd ins fnl f: kpt on wl but lost 2nd nr fin* **16/1**

3125 **4** 3/4 **Marronnier (IRE)**[41] 5861 3-9-9 86 (t) OisinMurphy 6 91
(Stuart Williams) *hld up in last trio: trckd ldrs gng strly over 2f out and waiting for a gap: rdn to chse ldng pair over 1f out: nt qckn and hld ins fnl f* **7/2**

3312 **5** 1 **Just The Man (FR)**[41] 5861 3-9-9 86 AdamKirby 3 89+
(Clive Cox) *trckd ldrs: trapped on inner over 2f out: dropped bk to last briefly over 1f out: rdn and styd on fnl f but no ch to threaten (jockey said colt was denied a clear run)* **3/1**[2]

2403 **6** 6 **Sophosc (IRE)**[26] 6390 3-9-7 84 CharlesBishop 1 75
(Joseph Tuite) *broke wl: t.k.h: led: shkn up and hdd 2f out: wknd over 1f out* **20/1**

4142 **7** 1 1/2 **Bint Soghaan**[25] 6454 3-9-6 83 DaneO'Neill 7 71
(Richard Hannon) *dwlt: pushed along to rcvr: chsd ldr after 4f to jst over 2f out: wknd tamely over 1f out* **14/1**

2m 10.94s (0.74) **Going Correction** +0.10s/f (Good) **7 Ran SP% 116.2**
Speed ratings (Par 103): **101,100,100,99,98 94,92**
CSF £12.52 CT £114.73 TOTE £4.30: £2.20, £1.90; EX 13.50 Trifecta £84.40.
Owner A E Oppenheimer **Bred** Hascombe And Valiant Studs **Trained** Newmarket, Suffolk

FOCUS
A useful 3yo handicap that was run at a steady gallop. The third limits the form, but it should prove better in time.

7343 SEASON FINALE FILLIES' H'CAP (DIV I) 1m 1f 209y
5:05 (5:08) (Class 5) (0-70,72) 3-Y-O+ **£4,528** (£1,347; £673; £336; £300; £300) **Stalls** Low

Form RPR

0142 **1** **Colony Queen**[50] 5518 3-9-5 67 AdamKirby 1 75
(Steve Gollings) *trckd ldng pair: rdn and lost pl 2f out and others wnt for home: drvn and styd on 1f out: burst between rivals to ld fnl 75yds* **10/1**

2622 **2** 3/4 **Delicate Kiss**[5] 7165 5-10-1 72 LiamJones 9 78
(John Bridger) *t.k.h and restrained in last trio: swift prog on outer over 2f out: led over 1f out: hrd pressed after: hdd and nt qckn fnl 75yds* **10/3**[2]

0244 **3** shd **Scenesetter (IRE)**[26] 6412 3-9-1 63 (p) AndreaAtzeni 2 69
(Marco Botti) *trckd ldr: chal over 2f out: upsides after tl nt qckn fnl 75yds* **6/1**[3]

6123 **4** 3/4 **Shifting Gold (IRE)**[20] 6635 3-8-13 61 JasonWatson 5 65
(William Knight) *hld up in midfield: rdn 2f out: prog over 1f out: kpt on fnl f to take 4th last strides: nt pce to chal* **8/1**

0113 **5** nk **Cafe Sydney (IRE)**[17] 6759 3-8-10 58 BrettDoyle 7 62
(Tony Carroll) *hld up in last: swift prog on outer over 2f out to chal over 1f out: stl pressing ins fnl f: fdd and lost pls nr fin* **20/1**

-302 **6** 1/2 **Shufoog**[48] 5344 6-9-2 66 EllieMacKenzie(7) 8 69
(Mark Usher) *hld up and sn in last: rdn 2f out: sme prog over 1f out: kpt on steadily fnl f and nvr nrr* **14/1**

-530 **7** 3 1/2 **Arctic Spirit**[80] 4424 3-9-7 69 (h) OisinMurphy 10 65
(Ed Dunlop) *nvr bttr than midfield: rdn and no prog 2f out: dropped to rr and btn over 1f out* **12/1**

0453 **8** 1 1/2 **Toybox**[16] 6810 3-9-1 63 (p) RobHornby 3 56
(Jonathan Portman) *led: pressed over 2f out: rdn and hdd over 1f out: wknd fnl f* **10/1**

-100 **9** 2 1/2 **Miss Recycled**[13] 6897 4-8-4 50 oh1 JaneElliott(3) 4 38
(Michael Madgwick) *plld hrd: chsd ldrs tl wknd 2f out* **50/1**

-123 **10** nse **Seascape (IRE)**[19] 6672 3-9-7 69 CharlesBishop 6 57
(Henry Candy) *trckd ldrs: shkn up over 2f out: lost pl wl over 1f out: sn wknd (trainer's rep could offer no explanation for the filly's performance)* **2/1**[1]

2m 12.23s (2.03) **Going Correction** +0.10s/f (Good)
WFA 3 from 4yo+ 5lb **10 Ran SP% 121.1**
Speed ratings (Par 100): **95,94,94,93,93 93,90,89,87,87**
CSF £45.12 CT £226.42 TOTE £8.90: £2.50, £1.70, £1.90; EX 38.80 Trifecta £206.00.
Owner David & Ros Chapman **Bred** Mrs J A Cornwell **Trained** Scamblesby, Lincs

FOCUS
The first leg of a modest handicap, and ordinary form for the track and grade.

7344 SEASON FINALE FILLIES' H'CAP (DIV II) 1m 1f 209y
5:35 (5:38) (Class 5) (0-70,71) 3-Y-O+ **£4,528** (£1,347; £673; £336; £300; £300) **Stalls** Low

Form RPR

2 **1** **Mina Vagante**[26] 6412 3-9-5 71 CierenFallon(3) 6 79
(Hugo Palmer) *wl in tch: shkn up and clsd to ld 2f out: rdn over 1f out: styd on wl and in command fnl f* **9/4**[1]

3143 **2** 1 3/4 **Angel's Whisper (IRE)**[23] 6538 4-9-12 70 OisinMurphy 9 75
(Amy Murphy) *trckd ldng pair: moved up to chal gng strly over 2f out: wnr wnt past sn after: rdn wl over 1f out: nt qckn and a wl hld fnl f* **9/4**[1]

1304 **3** nk **Venusta (IRE)**[13] 6902 3-9-6 69 PatDobbs 4 73
(Mick Channon) *hld up in midfield: gng strly over 2f out: shkn up and nt qckn wl over 1f out: styd on fnl f to take 3rd fnl 100yds: nvr nrr* **14/1**

5220 **4** 1 1/2 **Uncertain Smile (IRE)**[32] 6202 3-8-9 61 (h) WilliamCox(3) 3 62
(Clive Cox) *led: rdn and hdd 2f out: one pce over 1f out (jockey said filly stumbled on the bend)* **11/1**

0055 **5** 1 **Guroor**[37] 6030 3-9-0 63 (p1) AndreaAtzeni 8 62
(Marco Botti) *mostly chsd ldr to over 2f out: outpcd u.p over 1f out: one pce after* **7/1**[3]

0060 **6** 3 3/4 **Your Thoughts (FR)**[16] 6810 3-8-7 56 MartinDwyer 1 47
(Paul Webber) *t.k.h: trckd ldng pair tl wknd wl over 1f out* **20/1**

6001 **7** *1* **Petite Malle (USA)**[20] 6636 3-9-0 **63** .... NicolaCurrie 7 52
(James Fanshawe) *a towards rr: rdn and struggling over 2f out: sn btn (jockey said filly was never travelling)* **5/1**[2]

5300 **8** *3 ¾* **Narjes**[23] 6538 5-9-6 **64** .... CharlesBishop 2 46
(Laura Mongan) *free to post: s.s: plld hrd in last pair: prog on wd outside and in tch over 2f out: wknd wl over 1f out: eased (jockey said mare ran too freely)* **33/1**

2235 **9** *2 ¾* **Falcon Cliffs (IRE)**[200] 991 5-9-3 **61** .... GeorgeDowning 5 37
(Tony Carroll) *dwlt: hld up and sn in last: shkn up and no prog over 2f out: sn no ch* **25/1**

2m 11.31s (1.11) **Going Correction** +0.10s/f (Good)
WFA 3 from 4yo+ 5lb **9** Ran SP% **117.3**
Speed ratings (Par 100): **99,97,97,96,95 92,91,88,86**
CSF £6.86 CT £55.52 TOTE £3.00: £1.20, £1.20, £3.00; EX 9.30 Trifecta £90.10.
Owner V I Araci **Bred** V I Araci **Trained** Newmarket, Suffolk

FOCUS
This looked the stronger of the two divisions and the time was almost a second quicker. The form's rated around the first two.
T/Plt: £190.80 to a £1 stake. Pool: £66,173.99 - 253.14 winning units T/Qpdt: £4.70 to a £1 stake. Pool: £6,834.96 - 1,059.88 winning units **Jonathan Neesom**

7315 YARMOUTH (L-H)
Wednesday, September 18

OFFICIAL GOING: Good to firm (good in places; 6.9)
Wind: Light, behind Weather: Sunny

7345 YOUNGS LONDON ORIGINAL FILLIES' H'CAP 6f 3y
1:40 (1:41) (Class 5) (0-75,75) 3-Y-O+
£3,428 (£1,020; £509; £300; £300; £300) **Stalls** Centre

Form RPR

5322 **1** **Restless Rose**[6] 7130 4-9-4 **74** .... MarcoGhiani(7) 2 82
(Stuart Williams) *chsd ldrs tl wnt 2nd after 1f: shkn up over 1f out: pushed into ld ent fnl f: r.o wl* **7/4**[1]

2014 **2** *1 ¼* **Great Shout (IRE)**[23] 6533 3-9-6 **71** ....(t) GeorgeWood 1 75
(Amy Murphy) *stdd leaving stalls: t.k.h: hld up in tch: effrt and hdwy over 1f out: chsd wnr 1f out: kpt on u.p but a hld ins fnl f* **9/2**[3]

5563 **3** *¾* **Jungle Juice (IRE)**[16] 6801 3-9-4 **74** .... ScottMcCullagh(5) 4 76
(Mick Channon) *chsd ldr for 1f: styd chsng ldrs: effrt over 1f out: kpt on same pce u.p ins fnl f* **14/1**

2415 **4** *1 ½* **Dubai Elegance**[42] 5828 5-8-4 **56** ....(p) NoelGarbutt(3) 3 53
(Derek Shaw) *taken down early: hld up in last pair: effrt over 1f out: sme hdwy u.p 1f out: kpt on same pce ins fnl f* **16/1**

0420 **5** *1* **Excelled (IRE)**[34] 6111 3-9-10 **75** .... TomMarquand 6 69
(James Fanshawe) *taken down early: stdd s: hld up in tch in last pair: nt clrest of runs over 1f out: swtchd lft 1f out: kpt on same pce and no threat to ldrs ins fnl f* **11/2**

6324 **6** *1 ½* **Lalania**[14] 6857 4-9-3 **66** .... JimCrowley 8 55
(Stuart Williams) *led: rdn 2f out: hdd ent fnl f: no ex and wknd ins fnl f (vet said filly lost right hind shoe)* **4/1**[2]

2104 **7** *2 ¾* **Princess Keira (IRE)**[55] 5352 4-9-0 **63** .... PatCosgrave 7 43
(Mick Quinn) *hld up wl in tch in midfield: nt clr run and shuffled bk over 1f out: bhd and no hdwy ins fnl f: eased towards fin* **9/1**

1m 10.29s (-2.31) **Going Correction** -0.30s/f (Firm)
WFA 3 from 4yo+ 2lb **7** Ran SP% **112.5**
Speed ratings (Par 100): **103,101,100,98,97 95,91**
CSF £9.47 CT £79.06 TOTE £2.40: £1.30, £2.30; EX 9.50 Trifecta £58.70.
Owner Happy Valley Racing & Breeding Limited **Bred** M E Broughton **Trained** Newmarket, Suffolk

FOCUS
The elected to race on the near side and went just an ordinary pace in this modest sprint handicap for fillies. The winner didn't need to find much on her recent form, aided by her jockey's claim.

7346 BRITISH STALLION STUDS EBF MAIDEN STKS (PLUS 10 RACE) 7f 3y
2:10 (2:13) (Class 4) 2-Y-O **£4,851** (£1,443; £721; £360) **Stalls** Centre

Form RPR

3 **1** **Maqtal (USA)**[55] 5331 2-9-5 0 .... JimCrowley 3 75
(Roger Varian) *pressed ldr tl 4f out: styd prom: rdn over 2f out: drvn over 1f out: kpt on u.p to ld 100yds out: rdn out* **6/4**[1]

2 **2** *½* **Zafeer (JPN)**[42] 5823 2-9-5 0 .... DavidEgan 6 74
(Marco Botti) *chsd ldrs tl pressed ldr 4f out: effrt and ev ch ent fnl f: kpt on wl u.p: one pce towards fin* **5/1**[3]

3 *hd* **Kinsman** 2-9-5 0 .... JamesDoyle 7 73
(William Haggas) *in tch in midfield: effrt and rdn 2f out: nt clr run and swtchd rt over 1f out: hdwy ins fnl f: styd on strly fnl 100yds: nt quite rch ldrs* **3/1**[2]

03 **4** *hd* **Anglo Saxson (IRE)**[17] 6757 2-9-5 0 .... StevieDonohoe 11 73
(Charlie Fellowes) *led: rdn over 2f out: drvn and kpt on wl over 1f out: hdd 100yds out: no ex and lost two pls last strides* **28/1**

5 *hd* **Frankly Mr Shankly (GER)** 2-9-2 0 ....(h[1]) CameronNoble(3) 4 72
(Michael Bell) *taken down early: t.k.h: hld up in tch in midfield: effrt ent fnl 2f: hdwy and drvn to press ldrs 1f out: kpt on ins fnl f: one pce towards fin* **33/1**

0 **6** *2 ½* **Nibras Wish (IRE)**[18] 6704 2-9-5 0 .... TomMarquand 2 66
(Ismail Mohammed) *stdd after s: hld up in last trio: effrt and reminder 2f out: kpt on same pce ins fnl f: nvr threatened ldrs* **33/1**

7 *½* **Shoot The Moon (IRE)** 2-9-5 0 .... AdrianMcCarthy 9 64
(William Jarvis) *uns rdr in the paddock: stdd s: t.k.h: hld up in midfield: hdwy to press ldrs 4f out: rdn jst over 2f out: edgd lft and unable qck over 1f out: wknd ins fnl f* **33/1**

8 *1 ¼* **Sefton Warrior** 2-9-5 0 .... HarryBentley 1 61
(Richard Spencer) *stdd and swtchd rt after the s: hld up in rr: effrt and sme hdwy ent fnl 2f: no imp and one pce fnl f* **9/1**

9 *2* **Gigi's Beach** 2-9-5 0 .... JackMitchell 5 56
(Hugo Palmer) *chsd ldrs early: sn settled and in tch in midfield: effrt over 2f out: unable qck and lost pl over 1f out: wknd ins fnl f* **10/1**

10 *7* **Flying Standard (IRE)** 2-9-5 0 .... GeorgeWood 10 38
(Chris Wall) *t.k.h: midfield: rdn over 3f out: struggling over 2f out: bhd over 1f out: wknd fnl f* **33/1**

0 **11** *2 ¼* **By Jove**[12] 6912 2-9-5 0 .... CallumShepherd 8 32
(Michael Bell) *taken down early: stdd s: hld up in rr: rdn wl over 2f out: sn struggling: bhd ins fnl f* **50/1**

0 **12** *1* **Kates Star**[14] 6858 2-9-0 0 .... EoinWalsh 12 24
(Christine Dunnett) *chsd ldrs early: losing pl and rdn 3f out: sn struggling and lost pl: bhd ins fnl f* **200/1**

1m 23.93s (-1.17) **Going Correction** -0.30s/f (Firm) **12** Ran SP% **118.4**
Speed ratings (Par 97): **94,93,93,92,92 89,89,87,85,77 75,73**
CSF £8.70 TOTE £2.10: £1.10, £1.30, £1.40; EX 8.30 Trifecta £26.60.
Owner Hamdan Al Maktoum **Bred** Shadwell Farm LLC **Trained** Newmarket, Suffolk

FOCUS
It paid to be handy in this interesting novice event and there was a blanket finish.

7347 EBF STALLIONS JOHN MUSKER FILLIES' STKS (LISTED RACE) 1m 2f 23y
2:45 (2:45) (Class 1) 3-Y-O+
£28,110 (£10,700; £5,355; £2,670; £1,340; £675) **Stalls** Low

Form RPR

3011 **1** **Fanny Logan (IRE)**[35] 6082 3-9-0 106 ....(h) RobertHavlin 16 106+
(John Gosden) *hld up in midfield: smooth hdwy 2f out: shkn up to ld over 1f out: reminder and r.o strly ins fnl f: v readily* **6/5**[1]

4111 **2** *3* **Bighearted**[74] 4626 3-8-11 91 .... CameronNoble 11 97
(Michael Bell) *chsd ldr: rdn to ld 2f out: hdd over 1f out: nt match pce of wnr but kpt on to hold 2nd* **20/1**

416- **3** *1* **Brassica (IRE)**[353] 7813 3-8-11 83 .... LukeMorris 3 95
(Sir Mark Prescott Bt) *wl in tch in midfield: effrt over 2f out: chsd ldrs and drvn over 1f out: kpt on ins fnl f: no ch w wnr* **33/1**

-130 **4** *¾* **Naqaawa (IRE)**[27] 6378 4-9-2 93 .... JamesDoyle 7 93
(William Haggas) *chsd ldrs: effrt over 2f out: unable qck u.p over 1f out: kpt on same pce and no ch w wnr ins fnl f* **12/1**

60 **5** *½* **Cnoc An Oir (IRE)**[35] 6090 3-8-11 90 ....(h) TomMarquand 4 92
(Joseph Patrick O'Brien, Ire) *hld up in tch in midfield: effrt over 2f out: nt clr run and swtchd rt over 1f out: kpt on u.p ins fnl f: no ch w wnr* **33/1**

2150 **6** *shd* **Time Change**[11] 6992 4-9-2 85 .... HarryBentley 2 92
(Ralph Beckett) *hld up in midfield: short of room and hmpd after 2f: clsd and swtchd rt over 2f out: unable qck u.p over 1f out: kpt on same pce ins fnl f* **50/1**

-206 **7** *1 ¾* **Tauteke**[27] 6378 3-8-11 90 .... DavidEgan 5 89
(Roger Varian) *t.k.h: chsd ldrs: rdn to chse ldr 2f out tl 3rd and unable qck over 1f out: wknd ins fnl f* **10/1**

3142 **8** *hd* **Maid For Life**[18] 6709 3-8-11 96 ....(h) GeorgeWood 13 88
(Charlie Fellowes) *stdd s: hld up in tch in midfield: effrt jst over 2f out: unable qck and no imp over 1f out: wknd ins fnl f* **12/1**

2512 **9** *1 ¼* **Norma**[26] 6398 3-8-11 85 .... JackMitchell 12 86
(James Fanshawe) *hld up in tch in midfield: effrt over 2f out: no imp and btn over 1f out: wknd ins fnl f* **25/1**

3151 **10** *nk* **Moll Davis (IRE)**[32] 6209 3-8-11 94 .... JamieSpencer 14 85
(George Scott) *hld up in midfield: swtchd rt 3f out: effrt over 2f out: no imp over 1f out and nvr getting on terms w ldrs: kpt on same pce fnl f* **6/1**[2]

4251 **11** *¾* **Inference**[25] 6438 3-8-11 88 .... NickyMackay 9 84
(John Gosden) *led tl rdn and hdd 2f out: no ex u.p and wknd ins fnl f* **8/1**[3]

221 **12** *nse* **Gallic**[18] 6709 3-8-11 88 .... HectorCrouch 8 83
(Ed Walker) *chsd ldrs: rdn over 3f out: sn struggling and lost pl over 1f out: wknd fnl f* **20/1**

-605 **13** *½* **Sh Boom**[18] 6726 3-8-11 95 .... TomQueally 10 82
(Peter Chapple-Hyam) *stdd s: hld up towards rr: nvr involved* **16/1**

400 **14** *½* **Snapraeceps (IRE)**[19] 6692 3-8-11 92 .... GeraldMosse 15 81
(Joseph Patrick O'Brien, Ire) *stdd s: t.k.h: hld up towards rr: effrt wl over 2f out: no prog u.p and nvr involved* **40/1**

2 **15** *17* **Brown Honey**[22] 6559 3-8-11 0 .... PatCosgrave 6 47
(Ismail Mohammed) *a towards rr: lost tch over 2f out* **66/1**

2m 4.17s (-4.63) **Going Correction** -0.30s/f (Firm)
WFA 3 from 4yo 5lb **15** Ran SP% **126.4**
Speed ratings (Par 108): **106,103,102,102,101 101,100,100,99,98 98,98,97,97,83**
CSF £35.55 TOTE £1.90: £1.10, £5.30, £12.10; EX 25.10 Trifecta £1967.50.
Owner HH Sheikha Al Jalila Racing **Bred** Godolphin **Trained** Newmarket, Suffolk

FOCUS
A mixed bag of fillies in this Listed event and it was run at a muddling pace. The winner didn't quite have to match her previous best. The sixth is the doubt over the form.

7348 DANNY & PEGGY WRIGHT MEMORIAL H'CAP 5f 42y
3:15 (3:15) (Class 2) (0-100,91) 3-Y-**£12,602** (£3,772; £1,886; £944; £470) **Stalls** Centre

Form RPR

1460 **1** **Daschas**[7] 7077 5-8-8 **82** ....(t) MarcoGhiani(7) 3 91
(Stuart Williams) *hld up in tch towards rr: swtchd lft and clsd over 2f out: effrt to chse ldr over 1f out: rdn to ld 100yds out: r.o wl* **7/2**[1]

0441 **2** *¾* **Holmeswood**[21] 6607 5-9-6 **87** ....(p) TomEaves 5 93
(Julie Camacho) *led: rdn over 1f out: drvn and hdd 100yds out: kpt on same pce after* **4/1**[2]

1144 **3** *2* **Thegreatestshowman**[11] 6954 3-8-10 **85** .... SeanKirrane(7) 9 84+
(Amy Murphy) *taken down early: sltly awkward leaving stalls: hld up in tch in midfield: effrt over 1f out: hdwy u.p to chse ldrs 1f out: kpt on but no imp ins fnl f* **11/2**[3]

4024 **4** *½* **Saaheq**[18] 6724 5-9-7 **88** .... AlistairRawlinson 4 85
(Michael Appleby) *wl in tch in midfield: effrt over 1f out: rdn and kpt on same pce ins fnl f* **7/2**[1]

0152 **5** *1 ½* **Blue De Vega (GER)**[11] 6954 6-9-9 **90** ....(tp) RossaRyan 2 82
(Robert Cowell) *hld up in tch: effrt and clsd over 1f out: no prog u.p 1f out: wknd ins fnl f* **7/1**

-3P0 **6** *nk* **Heartwarming**[18] 6724 3-9-7 **89** ....(h[1]) HectorCrouch 8 80
(Clive Cox) *chsd ldr tl unable qck u.p and lost pl over 1f out: wknd ins fnl f* **20/1**

0632 **7** *¾* **Line Of Reason (IRE)**[7] 7077 9-9-1 **82** .... LukeMorris 6 70
(Paul Midgley) *hld up in tch: effrt wl over 1f out: no prog u.p over 1f out: wl hld ins fnl f* **11/2**[3]

036 **8** *½* **Zamjar**[11] 6954 5-8-13 **80** .... DavidEgan 1 66
(Robert Cowell) *chsd ldrs: rdn ent fnl 2f: unable qck u.p over 1f out: wknd ins fnl f* **14/1**

59.16s (-2.74) **Going Correction** -0.30s/f (Firm) course record
WFA 3 from 5yo+ 1lb **8** Ran SP% **119.1**
Speed ratings (Par 109): **109,107,104,103,101 100,99,98**
CSF £18.57 CT £77.50 TOTE £4.60: £1.90, £1.70, £2.20; EX 20.90 Trifecta £128.00.
Owner T W Morley **Bred** Juddmonte Farms Ltd **Trained** Newmarket, Suffolk

FOCUS
This good-quality sprint handicap was run at a fair enough pace down the middle. It saw a new course record, and a pb from the winner.

7349 PARKLANDS LEISURE HOLIDAY DISTRIBUTORS H'CAP 1m 3y
3:45 (3:48) (Class 3) (0-90,90) 3-Y-O **£7,876** (£2,357; £1,178; £590; £293) **Stalls** Centre

Form RPR
3215 1 **Scentasia**[18] 6721 3-9-4 87 ... RobertHavlin 3 101+
(John Gosden) *mde all: rdn over 1f out: styd on strly and drew clr fnl f: v readily* **7/4**[1]

21-5 2 4 1/2 **Khuzaam (USA)**[123] 2833 3-9-6 89 ...(w) DavidEgan 4 93
(Roger Varian) *hld up in tch: effrt jst over 2f out: hdwy to chse wnr ent fnl f: sn brushed aside and kpt on same pce ins fnl f* **9/4**[2]

3-11 3 1 1/4 **Montatham**[18] 6701 3-9-7 90 ... JimCrowley 6 91
(William Haggas) *chsd ldrs: effrt jst over 2f out: unable qck u.p over 1f out: no ch w wnr and kpt on same pce ins fnl f* **3/1**[3]

5142 4 3/4 **Canal Rocks**[33] 6155 3-8-13 82 ... DavidProbert 1 81
(Henry Candy) *chsd wnr: rdn jst over 2f out: unable qck u.p over 1f out: lost 2nd ent fnl f: wknd* **8/1**

4060 5 2 1/2 **Chairmanoftheboard (IRE)**[126] 2746 3-9-7 90 ... GeraldMosse 5 84
(Mick Channon) *hld up in rr: effrt over 2f out: no prog u.p and wl hld over 1f out: eased wl ins fnl f* **18/1**

1m 34.42s (-3.78) **Going Correction** -0.30s/f (Firm) 5 Ran SP% **108.5**
Speed ratings (Par 105): **106,101,100,99,97**
CSF £5.78 TOTE £2.50: £1.30, £1.40; EX 5.70 Trifecta £13.80.
Owner Sheikh Juma Dalmook Al Maktoum **Bred** Godolphin **Trained** Newmarket, Suffolk

FOCUS
A tidy little 3yo handicap. They went steady early on and the winner dictated. The level of the form is a bit fluid with the 2-3 unexposed.

7350 SEA DEER H'CAP 1m 3y
4:20 (4:23) (Class 4) (0-85,83) 3-Y-O+
£5,207 (£1,549; £774; £387; £300; £300) **Stalls** Centre

Form RPR
3212 1 **Rock The Cradle (IRE)**[25] 6468 3-9-3 80 ... JamieSpencer 1 93+
(Ed Vaughan) *stdd and dropped in bhd after s: hld up in tch in rr: clsd to trck ldrs and travelling strly over 1f out: gap opened and led ins fnl f: shkn up qcknd clr: easily* **7/2**[2]

055 2 1 3/4 **Mainsail Atlantic (USA)**[37] 6026 4-9-5 78 ...(p) TomMarquand 2 82
(James Fanshawe) *chsd ldrs: effrt and ev ch jst over 2f out: led 1f out and sn edgd rt: hdd ins fnl f: nt match pce of wnr and one pce fnl 100yds* **7/1**[3]

0-13 3 1 **Lady Dauphin (IRE)**[22] 6559 3-8-12 75 ... StevieDonohoe 4 77
(Charlie Fellowes) *chsd ldrs: effrt over 1f out: kpt on same pce u.p ins fnl f* **9/1**

054 4 1 1/2 **Balgair**[24] 6516 5-9-10 83 ...(h) LukeMorris 5 81
(Tom Clover) *stdd s: t.k.h: hld up in tch in last pair: effrt over 2f out: sn swtchd rt: no ch w wnr whn nt clr run ins fnl f: swtchd rt and kpt on cl home* **9/1**

6-30 5 shd **Tadleel**[14] 6863 4-9-10 83 ...(p) JimCrowley 3 81
(Ed Dunlop) *chsd ldrs: effrt and pressed ldng pair jst over 2f out: no ex ins fnl f: wknd towards fin* **20/1**

0300 6 hd **Jackpot Royale**[32] 6217 4-9-7 80 ... GeraldMosse 6 78
(Michael Appleby) *in tch in midfield: rdn over 2f out: struggling to qckn whn nt clr run 1f out: wl hld ins fnl f* **25/1**

2212 7 nk **Pinnata (IRE)**[5] 7163 5-9-0 80 ...(t) MarcoGhiani(7) 7 77
(Stuart Williams) *led: rdn ent fnl 2f: hdd 1f out: no ex and wknd ins fnl f* **10/11**[1]

1m 34.96s (-3.24) **Going Correction** -0.30s/f (Firm)
WFA 3 from 4yo+ 4lb 7 Ran SP% **115.7**
Speed ratings (Par 105): **104,102,101,99,99 99,99**
CSF £28.40 TOTE £3.60: £1.80, £2.40; EX 24.50 Trifecta £109.50.
Owner Moroney, Singh & Partner **Bred** D Bourke **Trained** Newmarket, Suffolk

FOCUS
This fair handicap was run at a routine pace towards the near side. The winner did it well but there was no great depth to the race.

7351 DENNIS BARRETT JOLLY BOYS OUTING H'CAP 6f 3y
4:50 (4:52) (Class 4) (0-85,86) 3-Y-O
£5,207 (£1,549; £774; £387; £300; £300) **Stalls** Centre

Form RPR
0126 1 **Majaalis (FR)**[26] 6413 3-9-10 86 ...(p1) JimCrowley 6 99+
(William Haggas) *s.i.s: in rr: clsd and swtchd lft 2f out: pressing ldrs and cruising 1f out: shkn up to ld ins fnl f: sn asserted and pushed out* **11/4**[1]

1562 2 1 1/4 **Gold At Midnight**[12] 6930 3-8-9 78 ... MarcoGhiani(7) 2 82
(William Stone) *chsd ldrs early but sn struggling to go pce: dropped to last pair 4f out and sn pushed along: clsd u.p over 1f out: kpt on to go 2nd towards fin: no threat to wnr* **9/2**

3120 3 1 1/4 **Tin Hat (IRE)**[25] 6465 3-8-13 82 ...(p) GeorgiaDobie(7) 1 82
(Eve Johnson Houghton) *chsd ldr: effrt 2f out: drvn and ev ch over 1f out: led jst ins fnl f: sn hdd and no ex* **9/1**

2431 4 1/2 **Queen Of Burgundy**[29] 6326 3-9-3 79 ... GeraldMosse 5 77
(Christine Dunnett) *led: rdn jst over 2f out: drvn over 1f out: hdd jst ins fnl f: no ex and one pce after* **10/3**[2]

4000 5 nse **Alfie Solomons (IRE)**[25] 6476 3-9-4 80 ...(vt) LukeMorris 3 78
(Richard Spencer) *short of room leaving stalls: chsd ldng trio 4f out: effrt over 2f out: drvn over 1f out: kpt on same pce ins fnl f* **15/2**

5164 6 2 3/4 **Golden Force**[12] 6913 3-9-3 79 ...(p1) HectorCrouch 4 68
(Clive Cox) *taken down early: chsd ldrs: effrt 2f out: no ex u.p ent fnl f: wknd ins fnl f* **7/2**[3]

1m 9.98s (-2.62) **Going Correction** -0.30s/f (Firm) 6 Ran SP% **111.9**
Speed ratings (Par 103): **105,103,101,101,100 97**
CSF £15.22 TOTE £2.80: £1.50, £2.30; EX 12.40 Trifecta £77.40.
Owner Hamdan Al Maktoum **Bred** Jean-Philippe Dubois **Trained** Newmarket, Suffolk

FOCUS
This fair little 3yo sprint handicap had a tight look about it, but the winner was in a different league. The pace was strong.
T/Jkpt: £800.00 to a £1 stake. Pool: £10,000.00 - 12.5 winning units T/Plt: £29.10 to a £1 stake. Pool: £67,424.44 - 1,689.48 winning units T/Qpdt: £14.30 to a £1 stake. Pool: £6,139.55 - 316.09 winning units **Steve Payne**

7352 - 7359a (Foreign Racing) - See Raceform Interactive

7171 SAINT-CLOUD (L-H)
Wednesday, September 18

OFFICIAL GOING: Turf: good

7360a PRIX CORONATION (LISTED RACE) (3YO FILLIES) (TURF) 1m
3:27 3-Y-O **£24,774** (£9,909; £7,432; £4,954; £2,477)

RPR
1 **Alzire (FR)**[53] 5470 3-8-11 0 ... ChristopheSoumillon 4 105
(J-C Rouget, France) **79/10**

2 2 **Audarya (FR)**[26] 6406 3-8-11 0 ... DanielMuscutt 8 101
(James Fanshawe) *settled midfield: waiting for gap to appear over 2f out: rdn once clr to chse clr ldr over 1f out: kpt on strly ins fnl f: nrest at fin* **18/1**

3 1 1/4 **Grace Spirit**[34] 6142 3-8-11 0 ... AntoineHamelin 2 98
(A De Royer-Dupre, France) **49/1**

4 1/2 **Nuala (FR)**[65] 5008 3-8-11 0 ... Pierre-CharlesBoudot 6 97
(A Fabre, France) **7/2**[1]

5 3 **Testa (IRE)**[29] 3-8-11 0 ... TheoBachelot 11 90
(S Wattel, France) **12/1**

6 1 **Ya Hala (IRE)**[319] 8836 3-8-11 0 ... MickaelBarzalona 1 88
(Charlie Appleby) *disp ld early: settled to trck ldr: rowed along over 2f out: rdn and limited rspnse over 1f out: no ex ins fnl f* **18/1**

7 1 **Turea**[41] 3-8-11 0 ... AurelienLemaitre 9 85
(F Head, France) **17/1**

8 1/2 **Simplicity (FR)**[59] 5227 3-8-11 0 ...(b) MaximeGuyon 5 84
(F Chappet, France) **16/1**

9 3/4 **Paramount (FR)**[32] 6249 3-8-11 0 ... JulienAuge 3 82
(C Ferland, France) **59/10**[3]

10 1 1/2 **Noor Sahara (IRE)**[34] 6142 3-9-2 0 ... StephanePasquier 7 84
(F Chappet, France) **6/1**

11 3/4 **Bowled Over (IRE)**[104] 3-8-11 0 ... RonanThomas 10 77
(F-H Graffard, France) **48/10**[2]

12 2 1/2 **Justfirstlady (IRE)**[37] 3-8-11 0 ... CristianDemuro 12 72
(J-C Rouget, France) **11/1**

1m 39.34s (-8.16) 12 Ran SP% **119.5**
PARI-MUTUEL (all including 1 euro stake): WIN 8.90; PLACE 3.40, 6.00, 11.70; DF 78.10.
Owner Haras Voltaire **Bred** Haras D'Etreham & Pencarrow Stud Ltd **Trained** Pau, France

5933 AYR (L-H)
Thursday, September 19

OFFICIAL GOING: Good (good to soft in places; 7.5)
Wind: Light, half against in sprints and in over 3f of home straight in races on the round course Weather: Fine, dry

7361 EBF NOVICE STKS (PLUS 10 RACE) 1m
1:30 (1:32) (Class 4) 2-Y-O
£6,474 (£1,938; £969; £484; £242; £121) **Stalls** Low

Form RPR
515 1 **Morisco (IRE)**[29] 6352 2-9-5 93 ... RichardKingscote 3 84+
(Tom Dascombe) *sn trcking ldrs: chal over 2f out: shkn up to ld over 1f out: pushed out fnl f: comf* **1/1**[1]

4 2 1 1/4 **Arch Moon**[33] 6226 2-9-2 0 ... CallumRodriguez 8 78+
(Michael Dods) *trckd ldrs: pushed along over 2f out: rallied and pressed wnr over 1f out: one pce ins fnl f* **6/1**[2]

3 4 **Salamanca School (FR)** 2-9-2 0 ... JoeFanning 9 69
(Mark Johnston) *t.k.h: hld up bhd ldng gp: effrt on outside over 2f out: sn edgd lft: chsd clr ldng pair ins fnl f: kpt on: no imp* **9/1**

3 4 1 1/4 **Ambassador (IRE)**[20] 6664 2-9-2 0 ... PaddyMathers 7 67
(Richard Fahey) *in tch: rdn along over 2f out: rallied over 1f out: no imp fnl f* **20/1**

5 nk **Will Sommers** 2-9-2 0 ... TomEaves 5 66+
(Kevin Ryan) *missed break: hld up: pushed along over 3f out: kpt on fr over 1f out: nvr rchd ldrs* **8/1**[3]

54 6 nk **Gweedore**[20] 6684 2-9-2 0 ... BenCurtis 2 65
(Jason Ward) *led: jnd over 2f out: rdn and hdd over 1f out: wknd ins fnl f* **66/1**

5 7 1 1/4 **Black Star Dancing (USA)**[8] 7067 2-9-2 0 ... DanielTudhope 4 63
(Keith Dalgleish) *pressed ldr to 3f out: rdn and wknd over 1f out* **12/1**

0 8 nk **Handsome Yank (USA)**[114] 3194 2-9-2 0 ... TrevorWhelan 12 62
(Ivan Furtado) *midfield: pushed along over 3f out: edgd lft and wknd over 1f out* **100/1**

33 9 nse **Handlebars (IRE)**[13] 6934 2-8-11 0 ... ShaneGray 11 57
(Keith Dalgleish) *s.i.s: hld up: shortlived effrt over 2f out: sn no imp* **33/1**

0 10 1 3/4 **Twin Paradox**[20] 6654 2-9-2 0 ... JasonHart 10 58
(John Quinn) *plld hrd: hld up: rdn over 2f out: nvr rchd ldrs* **50/1**

11 1/2 **Bouncing Bobby (IRE)** 2-9-2 0 ... KevinStott 1 57
(Michael Dods) *s.i.s: sn in tch: rdn over 2f out: wknd over 1f out* **33/1**

12 3/4 **Dreaming Blue** 2-9-2 0 ... TonyHamilton 6 55
(Richard Fahey) *t.k.h: hld up: pushed along over 2f out: sn btn* **12/1**

1m 43.79s (0.99) **Going Correction** +0.10s/f (Good) 12 Ran SP% **115.9**
Speed ratings (Par 97): **99,97,93,92,92 91,90,90,90,88 88,87**
CSF £6.23 TOTE £1.70: £1.10, £1.60, £2.90; EX 6.90 Trifecta £38.60.
Owner Mrs Caroline Ingram **Bred** Kildaragh Stud **Trained** Malpas, Cheshire

FOCUS
The home bend was out 8yds for this first day of the Gold Cup meeting, thus adding 24yds to all bar the penultimate race. After riding in the opening race Callum Rodriguez called the ground 'good' and Richard Kingscote said: "It's a bit dead, on the slow side of good." This wasn't a bad novice event and the market leaders came clear. The sixth is likely to prove the key to the level.

7362 CALA HOMES H'CAP 7f 50y
2:00 (2:02) (Class 4) (0-85,85) 3-Y-O+
£6,727 (£2,002; £1,000; £500; £300; £300) **Stalls** High

Form RPR
2060 1 **Markazi (FR)**[40] 5948 5-9-7 84 ...(v) DanielTudhope 1 95
(David O'Meara) *mde all: rdn over 1f out: kpt on strly ins fnl f: unchal* **9/1**

5341 2 2 1/2 **Sparklealot (IRE)**[22] 6588 3-9-5 85 ...(p) TrevorWhelan 8 89
(Ivan Furtado) *chsd wnr thrght: rdn over 2f out: edgd lft over 1f out: one pce fnl f* **17/2**

4545 **3** *nk* **Tommy Taylor (USA)**[20] 6676 5-9-6 **83**.......... TomEaves 10 87+
(Kevin Ryan) *hld up towards rr: rdn along over 2f out: hdwy over 1f out: chsd ldng pair wl ins fnl f: kpt on* **11/1**

4514 **4** *½* **Monsieur Noir**[27] 6413 3-9-3 **83**.......... DavidEgan 3 84
(Roger Varian) *hld up in tch: stdy hdwy to chse clr ldng pair over 2f out: rdn over 1f out: no ex and lost 3rd wl ins fnl f* **7/1**[3]

2000 **5** *½* **King Of Tonga (IRE)**[13] 6922 3-9-5 **85**.......... DavidNolan 9 85
(David O'Meara) *in tch: drvn along over 2f out: kpt on same pce fr over 1f out* **10/1**

1000 **6** *¾* **Jackstar (IRE)**[13] 6922 3-9-5 **85**.......... RichardKingscote 14 83+
(Tom Dascombe) *t.k.h early: hld up: rdn over 2f out: kpt on fnl f: nvr able to chal* **16/1**

4500 **7** *½* **Right Action**[13] 6922 5-8-13 **79**.......... ConnorMurtagh(3) 13 77
(Richard Fahey) *prom: drvn along over 2f out: outpcd over 1f out* **20/1**

0021 **8** *1 ¼* **Queen's Sargent (FR)**[20] 6677 4-9-5 **82**.......... ShaneGray 5 77
(Kevin Ryan) *hld up: rdn along over 2f out: kpt on fnl f: nvr able to chal* **9/1**

4614 **9** *½* **Glengarry**[5] 7212 6-9-5 **82**.......... JoeFanning 4 75
(Keith Dalgleish) *s.i.s: hld up on ins: pushed along over 2f out: no imp over 1f out* **15/2**

0531 **10** *½* **Maggies Angel (IRE)**[22] 6609 4-9-1 **78**..........(p) PaulHanagan 2 70
(Richard Fahey) *t.k.h: chsd clr ldng pair to over 2f out: drvn and outpcd fr over 1f out* **6/1**[1]

0006 **11** *1 ¼* **Starlight Romance (IRE)**[12] 6974 5-9-3 **80**..........(v[1]) TonyHamilton 12 69
(Richard Fahey) *slowly away: bhd: rdn and edgd lft over 2f out: sn wknd* **28/1**

0350 **12** *4 ½* **He'Zanarab (IRE)**[11] 7002 3-8-10 **79**..........(h) HarrisonShaw(3) 6 55
(Jim Goldie) *fly-jmpd s: bhd: drvn along over 2f out: nvr on terms* **50/1**

0201 **13** *4 ½* **Parys Mountain (IRE)**[6] 7145 5-9-5 **82** 5ex..........(t) DavidAllan 11 47
(Tim Easterby) *hld up: rdn and struggling over 2f out: sn btn (trainer said, regarding poor performance, gelding was never travelling. post-race examination failed to reveal any abnormalities)* **13/2**[2]

00-0 **14** *1 ½* **La Rav (IRE)**[20] 6677 5-9-2 **79**..........(h) JamesSullivan 7 40
(Michael Easterby) *dwlt: t.k.h: hld up: rdn and struggling over 2f out: sn btn (jockey said gelding flyleapt stalls and missed break)* **50/1**

1m 31.16s (-1.34) **Going Correction** +0.10s/f (Good)
WFA 3 from 4yo+ 3lb **14 Ran SP% 117.8**
Speed ratings (Par 105): **111,108,107,107,106 105,105,103,103,102 101,96,90,89**
CSF £78.86 CT £874.05 TOTE £9.50: £3.20, £3.20, £3.30; EX 85.80 Trifecta £592.60.
Owner Thoroughbred British Racing **Bred** S C H H The Aga Khan's Studs **Trained** Upper Helmsley, N Yorks

FOCUS
Add 24yds. This had looked a really open handicap, but little got into it with the first two holding there positions throughout. The winner set a decent clip.

7363 JIMMY LAWRIE MEMORIAL H'CAP (DIV I) 1m
2:30 (2:32) (Class 5) (0-75,75) 3-Y-O+
£4,463 (£1,328; £663; £331; £300; £300) **Stalls** Low

Form RPR

106 **1** **Donnelly's Rainbow (IRE)**[13] 6935 6-8-12 **63**.......... JamieGormley 10 71
(Rebecca Bastiman) *hld up in midfield: effrt and rdn over 1f out: led ins fnl f: r.o* **12/1**

0424 **2** *1* **Zoravan (USA)**[8] 7069 6-9-1 **66**..........(b) JoeFanning 5 72
(Keith Dalgleish) *s.i.s: hld up: stdy hdwy whn nt clr run fr over 1f out tl swtchd lft wl ins fnl f: tk 2nd cl home (jockey said gelding was denied a clear run in fnl f)* **8/1**

2040 **3** *nk* **Storm Ahead (IRE)**[12] 6961 6-9-10 **75**..........(b) DavidAllan 13 80
(Tim Easterby) *hld up: effrt and gd hdwy on outside 2f out: wnt 2nd ins fnl f tl no ex cl home* **9/1**

0330 **4** *shd* **Carey Street (IRE)**[29] 6341 3-8-10 **65**.......... JasonHart 8 70
(John Quinn) *pressed ldr: led over 2f out to ins fnl f: kpt on same pce towards fin* **7/1**[3]

0036 **5** *1* **Make Me**[26] 6461 4-8-11 **62**.......... PaulHanagan 1 65
(Tim Easterby) *trckd ldrs: effrt and rdn over 1f out: ev ch briefly ins fnl f: sn no ex* **4/1**[1]

-520 **6** *1 ¼* **Agar's Plough**[80] 4446 4-9-3 **68**.......... JamesSullivan 7 68
(Michael Easterby) *t.k.h: in tch: drvn along over 2f out: one pce fr over 1f out* **16/1**

6500 **7** *2 ½* **Mustaqbal (IRE)**[45] 5726 7-9-5 **70**..........(p) CallumRodriguez 3 64
(Michael Dods) *hld up in tch: effrt and rdn 2f out: wknd ins fnl f* **16/1**

4540 **8** *½* **Lightning Attack**[5] 7213 3-9-4 **73**..........(p) TonyHamilton 2 66
(Richard Fahey) *led to over 2f out: rallied: wknd ins fnl f* **15/2**

35-0 **9** *nse* **Elusive Heights (IRE)**[34] 6179 6-9-5 **70**.......... DavidEgan 9 63
(Roger Fell) *hld up in midfield: stdy hdwy over 2f out: drvn and outpcd fr over 1f out: btn fnl f* **11/1**

310 **10** *2 ½* **Mount Ararat (IRE)**[40] 5948 4-9-10 **75**.......... BenCurtis 6 62
(K R Burke) *cl up: rdn over 2f out: wknd over 1f out* **5/1**[2]

0000 **11** *¾* **My Amigo**[52] 5490 6-8-13 **67**..........(t) JaneElliott(3) 4 52
(Marjorie Fife) *t.k.h: hld up: drvn and outpcd over 2f out: sn btn* **40/1**

4000 **12** *8* **Tagur (IRE)**[43] 5817 5-8-6 **64**..........(p) HarriettLees(7) 11 31
(Kevin Ryan) *slowly away: bhd and outpcd: nvr on terms* **50/1**

1m 42.59s (-0.21) **Going Correction** +0.10s/f (Good)
WFA 3 from 4yo+ 4lb **12 Ran SP% 114.2**
Speed ratings (Par 103): **105,104,103,103,102 101,98,98,98,95 95,87**
CSF £100.93 CT £922.07 TOTE £13.60: £4.30, £2.10, £3.50; EX 87.60 Trifecta £550.70.
Owner Rebecca Bastiman Racing 1 **Bred** Airlie Stud **Trained** Cowthorpe, N Yorks

FOCUS
Another wide-open looking handicap and it saw a tight finish. Add 24yds.

7364 WESTERN HOUSE H'CAP (DIV II) 1m
3:00 (3:02) (Class 5) (0-75,79) 3-Y-O+
£4,463 (£1,328; £663; £331; £300; £300) **Stalls** Low

Form RPR

246 **1** **Bardo Contiguo (IRE)**[89] 4121 3-9-1 **70**.......... DavidEgan 10 78+
(Roger Varian) *t.k.h early: hld up: effrt whn nt clr run over 2f out and over 1f out: swtchd to outside and sustained run fnl f to ld cl home* **6/1**

035 **2** *hd* **Ascot Week (USA)**[8] 7074 5-9-5 **70**..........(v) JasonHart 14 77
(John Quinn) *hld up: pushed along over 2f out: hdwy over 1f out: hung lft and led briefly wl ins fnl f: jst hld* **14/1**

2005 **3** *½* **Chinese Spirit (IRE)**[13] 6937 5-8-7 **61** oh1.......... HarrisonShaw(3) 8 66
(Linda Perratt) *hld up on ins: stdy hdwy over 2f out: led and veered rt over 1f out: hdd and no ex wl ins fnl f* **14/1**

0043 **4** *nk* **Employer (IRE)**[12] 6975 4-9-7 **72**.......... PaddyMathers 5 77
(Jim Goldie) *hld up in midfield: nt clr run over 2f out to over 1f out: rallied and ch whn carried lft and blkd ins fnl f: r.o* **10/1**

0240 **5** *nk* **Rampant Lion (IRE)**[16] 6841 4-9-10 **75**..........(p) JoeFanning 3 79
(William Jarvis) *dwlt: hld up in midfield on ins: nt clr run over 2f out to appr fnl f: sn chsng ldrs: kpt on: hld nr fin (jockey said gelding was denied a clear run approx 1f out)* **6/1**[1]

5340 **6** *1* **Coviglia (IRE)**[35] 6102 5-8-13 **64**.......... JamesSullivan 4 66+
(Jacqueline Coward) *t.k.h: in tch: nt clr run over 2f out to over 1f out: sn rdn: kpt on ins fnl f: nt pce to chal (jockey said gelding was denied a clear run 1 1/2f out)* **18/1**

3600 **7** *¾* **Vive La Difference (IRE)**[12] 6961 5-9-3 **68**..........(b[1]) DavidAllan 2 68
(Tim Easterby) *s.i.s: hld up: nt clr run over 2f out to over 1f out: sn rdn: keeping on whn nt clr run last 100yds: nt rcvr (jockey said gelding was continually denied a clear run from 2f out)* **13/2**[2]

2041 **8** *nk* **Ventura Royal (IRE)**[23] 6573 4-9-2 **67**..........(h) DanielTudhope 12 71+
(David O'Meara) *prom: effrt and chsd ldr over 1f out: cl 5th but no ex whn hmpd and snatched up ins fnl f* **8/1**[3]

36-0 **9** *1 ¾* **Silver Dust (IRE)**[170] 1504 3-9-4 **73**.......... PaulHanagan 7 68
(Richard Fahey) *hld up towards rr: rdn and edgd lft over 1f out: rallied: outpcd ins fnl f* **33/1**

2341 **10** *1* **Woodside Wonder**[9] 7049 3-9-10 **79** 6ex..........(v) CallumRodriguez 1 72
(Keith Dalgleish) *chsd ldrs: rdn over 2f out: wknd appr fnl f* **18/1**

231- **11** *3 ½* **Mischief Managed (IRE)**[335] 8388 5-9-5 **70**..........(e) DavidNolan 11 55
(Tim Easterby) *dwlt: hld up: nt clr run over 2f out to over 1f out: sn rdn and wknd* **9/1**

5332 **12** *1 ¾* **Equidae**[8] 7069 4-9-0 **65**..........(t) TomEaves 6 53+
(Iain Jardine) *led: rdn and hdd whn checked over 1f out: sn wknd (jockey said colt suffered interference approaching fnl f)* **6/1**[1]

1000 **13** *½* **Pudding Chare (IRE)**[40] 5933 5-8-12 **63**..........(t) BenCurtis 13 43
(R Mike Smith) *chsd ldr to over 2f out: rdn and wknd over 1f out* **28/1**

0014 **14** *7* **Roaring Forties (IRE)**[40] 5938 6-8-10 **61**..........(p) JamieGormley 9 25
(Rebecca Bastiman) *cl up: drvn over 2f out: wknd over 1f out* **50/1**

1m 43.6s (0.80) **Going Correction** +0.10s/f (Good)
WFA 3 from 4yo+ 4lb **14 Ran SP% 118.6**
Speed ratings (Par 103): **100,99,99,99,98 97,96,96,94,93 90,88,88,81**
CSF £86.72 CT £1161.78 TOTE £4.80: £1.80, £3.70, £4.30; EX 101.20 Trifecta £1964.60.
Owner Sheikh Mohammed Obaid Al Maktoum **Bred** John O'Connor **Trained** Newmarket, Suffolk
■ Stewards' Enquiry : Jason Hart six-day ban: careless riding (Oct 3-5, 7-9)

FOCUS
Add 24yds. 6-1 the field for this open and competitive handicap, they didn't go overly fast and there was a bunched, messy finish.

7365 WILLIAM HILL DOONSIDE CUP STKS (LISTED RACE) 1m 2f
3:30 (3:30) (Class 1) 3-Y-O+
£36,861 (£13,975; £6,994; £3,484; £1,748; £877) **Stalls** Low

Form RPR

226 **1** **Encapsulation (IRE)**[55] 5397 3-8-7 **102**.......... BenCurtis 6 105
(Andrew Balding) *prom: hdwy to ld over 1f out: rdn: edgd lft and r.o strly fnl f* **9/2**[3]

0301 **2** *1* **What's The Story**[28] 6376 5-9-3 **108**..........(p) JoeFanning 4 107
(Keith Dalgleish) *t.k.h: hld up in tch: hdwy over 1f out: effrt whn n.m.r briefly ins fnl f: wnt 2nd last 75yds: kpt on* **15/8**[1]

4054 **3** *½* **Big Country (IRE)**[8] 7076 6-9-3 **106**..........(p) AlistairRawlinson 5 106
(Michael Appleby) *pressed ldr: led over 2f out to over 1f out: chsd wnr to last 75yds: one pce* **7/1**

4146 **4** *1* **Exhort**[19] 6726 4-9-1 **99**.......... PaulHanagan 7 102
(Richard Fahey) *s.i.s: hld up in last pl: effrt on outside wl over 1f out: kpt on fnl f: nt pce to chal* **11/1**

2000 **5** *hd* **Iconic Choice**[82] 4416 3-8-7 **100**.......... RichardKingscote 1 100
(Tom Dascombe) *trckd ldrs: rdn over 2f out: one pce fr over 1f out* **8/1**

2166 **6** *1 ¼* **Forest Ranger (IRE)**[26] 6470 5-9-10 **111**.......... TonyHamilton 2 108
(Richard Fahey) *led at ordinary gallop: rdn and hdd over 2f out: outpcd fr over 1f out* **3/1**[2]

2m 11.99s (-0.41) **Going Correction** +0.10s/f (Good)
WFA 3 from 4yo+ 5lb **6 Ran SP% 109.9**
Speed ratings (Par 111): **105,104,103,103,102 101**
CSF £12.82 TOTE £4.70: £2.20, £1.30; EX 15.70 Trifecta £56.20.
Owner Mrs Barbara M Keller **Bred** D J Maher **Trained** Kingsclere, Hants

FOCUS
A fair edition of this Listed prize. Add 24yds.

7366 BRITISH STALLION STUDS SCOTTISH PREMIER SERIES EBF FILLIES' H'CAP 1m 2f
4:00 (4:02) (Class 4) (0-85,82) 3-Y-O+
£8,345 (£2,483; £1,240; £620; £300; £300) **Stalls** Low

Form RPR

312 **1** **Eva Maria**[32] 6259 3-9-7 **82**.......... PaulHanagan 13 95+
(Richard Fahey) *hld up: hdwy on outside 2f out: rdn: edgd lft and led ins fnl f: kpt on strly* **9/4**[1]

5410 **2** *1* **Ladies First**[11] 6998 5-9-9 **79**.......... BenCurtis 12 89
(Michael Easterby) *cl up: led over 2f out: rdn over 1f out: hdd ins fnl f: sn one pce* **7/2**[2]

5034 **3** *1 ¾* **Fannie By Gaslight**[25] 6509 4-9-0 **70**.......... DavidEgan 2 77
(Mick Channon) *trckd ldrs: effrt and drvn along 2f out: kpt on same pce ins fnl f* **11/1**

1506 **4** *1* **Bollin Joan**[11] 7003 4-9-1 **71**..........(p) DavidAllan 9 76
(Tim Easterby) *t.k.h: hld up: effrt whn nt clr run over 2f out to over 1f out: sn prom: kpt on same pce ins fnl f (jockey said filly was denied a run continuously from 2f out)* **8/1**

5021 **5** *3 ¼* **Sarvi**[20] 6656 4-9-2 **72**..........(p) DanielTudhope 5 70
(Jim Goldie) *t.k.h: hld up in midfield on outside: rdn over 2f out: effrt whn checked over 1f out: kpt on fnl f: nt pce to chal* **7/1**[3]

1665 **6** *1 ¼* **Maulesden May (IRE)**[23] 6576 6-9-2 **72**.......... CallumRodriguez 14 68
(Keith Dalgleish) *s.i.s: hld up: pushed along over 2f out: kpt on fnl f: nvr rchd ldrs (jockey said mare was slowly away)* **16/1**

2310 **7** *hd* **Flood Defence (IRE)**[20] 6658 5-8-9 **65**.......... JamieGormley 3 60
(Iain Jardine) *midfield: n.m.r briefly over 2f out and over 1f out: sn rdn and outpcd* **16/1**

6033 **8** *½* **Amber Spark (IRE)**[14] 6893 3-9-4 **79**.......... TonyHamilton 1 74
(Richard Fahey) *hld up in tch: hdwy and cl up over 2f out: wknd over 1f out* **16/1**

4040 **9** *2* **Double Reflection**[25] 6512 4-9-3 **73**.......... MichaelStainton 6 63
(K R Burke) *missed break: hld up: effrt and drvn on outside over 2f out: sn no imp (jockey said filly was slowly away)* **20/1**

1660 **10** *1* **La Voix Magique**[40] 5947 3-9-4 **79**.......... JasonHart 8 68
(Steph Hollinshead) *t.k.h: in tch: rdn over 2f out: wknd over 1f out (jockey said filly ran too free)* **40/1**

The Form Book Flat 2019, Raceform Ltd, Newbury, RG14 5SJ

0053 **11** 4 ½ **Summer Daydream (IRE)**[20] 6656 3-9-7 **82** JoeFanning 4 62
(Keith Dalgleish) *led to over 2f out: wknd wl over 1f out* **14/1**

514- **12** ½ **Koduro (IRE)**[420] 5392 3-9-4 **82** HarrisonShaw(3) 11 61
(K R Burke) *prom: rdn and lost pl over 2f out: sn struggling* **50/1**

2m 12.83s (0.43) **Going Correction** +0.10s/f (Good)
WFA 3 from 4yo+ 5lb **12 Ran SP% 118.4**
Speed ratings (Par 102): **102,101,99,99,96 95,95,94,93,92 88,88**
CSF £9.34 CT £71.75 TOTE £3.10: £1.50, £1.80, £2.30; EX 12.20 Trifecta £109.50.
Owner W J and T C O Gredley **Bred** Stetchworth & Middle Park Studs Ltd **Trained** Musley Bank, N Yorks

FOCUS
Add 24yds. A fair fillies' handicap, they went just an ordinary gallop.

7367 BRANDINGHUB SIGNS & PRINT AYRSHIRE H'CAP 5f
4:30 (4:42) (Class 5) (0-70,70) 3-Y-O+
£4,463 (£1,328; £663; £331; £300; £300) **Stalls** Centre

Form RPR

0540 **1** **Militia**[29] 6339 4-9-5 **65** PaulHanagan 8 75
(Richard Fahey) *prom towards far side: pushed along over 1f out: led 110yds out: rdn out* **7/1**[2]

2540 **2** 1 ¼ **Mr Greenlight**[9] 7051 4-8-13 **59** (p) BenCurtis 3 64
(Tim Easterby) *prom far side: rdn along to ld over 1f out: drvn and hdd 110yds out: one pce* **12/1**

1104 **3** *shd* **Gamesome (FR)**[37] 6057 8-9-6 **69** ConnorMurtagh(3) 18 74
(Paul Midgley) *racd stands' side: hld up: hdwy and chsd ldr 1/2-way: rdn appr fnl f: kpt on wl* **20/1**

2006 **4** 2 **The Defiant**[12] 6976 3-9-7 **68** KevinStott 20 65
(Paul Midgley) *racd against stands' rail and led: rdn over 2f out: drvn and hdd over 1f out: no ex ins fnl f* **20/1**

2142 **5** ¾ **Orange Blossom**[24] 6533 3-9-9 **70** BarryMcHugh 5 65
(Richard Fahey) *chsd ldrs far side: rdn over 2f out: one pce* **9/2**[1]

4041 **6** *hd* **Dream House**[34] 6183 3-9-4 **65** (b) DavidAllan 1 59
(Tim Easterby) *hld up far side: hdwy 2f out: rdn over 1f out: kpt on same pce fnl f* **16/1**

4550 **7** *nse* **Star Cracker (IRE)**[5] 7214 7-8-5 **51** oh6 (p) PaddyMathers 19 45
(Jim Goldie) *in tch stands' side: sn pushed along: rdn and outpcd 1/2-way: kpt on ins fnl f but no threat* **33/1**

-605 **8** *shd* **Pavers Pride**[16] 6829 5-9-3 **63** (b) JasonHart 14 56+
(Noel Wilson) *dwlt: hld up centre: rdn 2f out: kpt on ins fnl f: nvr threatened* **12/1**

4132 **9** *nk* **Economic Crisis (IRE)**[16] 6829 10-9-6 **66** JamieGormley 6 58
(Alan Berry) *hld up: far side: rdn 2f out: kpt on ins fnl f: nvr a threat* **20/1**

0236 **10** *nk* **Burmese Blazer (IRE)**[13] 6936 4-8-9 **58** (h) HarrisonShaw(3) 2 49
(Jim Goldie) *hld up far side: rdn and kpt on fnl f: nvr involved* **17/2**[3]

5441 **11** 1 ¾ **Landing Night (IRE)**[16] 6829 7-9-8 **68** (bt) AlistairRawlinson 10 53
(Rebecca Menzies) *chsd ldrs far side: rdn over 2f out: wknd ins fnl f (jockey said gelding hung left final 2f)* **16/1**

0405 **12** *nse* **Jessie Allan (IRE)**[5] 7214 8-7-13 **52** oh6 ow1 CoreyMadden(7) 13 37
(Jim Goldie) *hld up in centre: nvr threatened* **28/1**

2213 **13** *nk* **B Fifty Two (IRE)**[9] 7050 10-9-2 **65** (vt) JaneElliott(3) 9 49
(Marjorie Fife) *chsd ldrs far side: rdn over 2f out: wknd fnl f* **16/1**

-006 **14** 1 **Arogo**[52] 5486 3-8-10 **57** TomEaves 16 37
(Kevin Ryan) *racd centre: a towards rr* **12/1**

0040 **15** ½ **Our Place In Loule**[68] 4911 6-9-6 **66** (p w) DavidNolan 17 44
(Noel Wilson) *midfield in centre: rdn 2f out: wknd ins fnl f* **50/1**

2600 **16** 2 ½ **Blank Canvas**[13] 6937 3-8-8 **55** (b[1]) JoeFanning 4 24
(Keith Dalgleish) *racd far side: a towards rr* **25/1**

6200 **17** 3 **Corton Lass**[5] 7214 4-8-5 **51** oh6 (v[1]) ShaneGray 15 10
(Keith Dalgleish) *racd centre: chsd ldrs: rdn 2f out: wknd appr fnl f: eased* **50/1**

59.79s (-0.21) **Going Correction** +0.10s/f (Good)
WFA 3 from 4yo+ 1lb **17 Ran SP% 110.4**
Speed ratings (Par 103): **105,103,102,99,98 98,98,97,97,96 94,94,93,91,91 87,82**
CSF £59.10 CT £1037.57 TOTE £7.30: £2.40, £3.20, £4.00, £4.60; EX 75.40 Trifecta £1369.70.
Owner Middleham Park Racing Cxvi & Partner **Bred** Jnp Bloodstock Ltd **Trained** Musley Bank, N Yorks

FOCUS
This moderate sprint handicap was delayed 12mins due to Rolladice breaking loose from the stalls, which then saw gambled-on Chookie Dunedin get scratched. There appeared no real bias with the draw.

7368 S.T. ANDREW PLANT HIRE H'CAP 1m 5f 26y
5:00 (5:11) (Class 5) (0-70,70) 3-Y-O+
£4,463 (£1,328; £663; £331; £300; £300) **Stalls** Low

Form RPR

0-45 **1** **Dreams And Visions (IRE)**[47] 5656 3-9-4 **67** JamesSullivan 3 76
(Michael Easterby) *reluctant to enter stalls: t.k.h: in tch: hdwy on outside to press ldr over 2f out: rdn and edgd lft over 1f out: led ins fnl f: styd on wl* **10/1**

6041 **2** ¾ **Iron Mike**[13] 6938 3-9-4 **67** (b) JoeFanning 17 75
(Keith Dalgleish) *racd wd early: prom: hdwy on outside to ld over 2f out: rdn and edgd lft over 1f out: hdd ins fnl f: one pce towards fin* **9/2**[2]

00-0 **3** 1 **Qasr**[105] 3500 5-9-9 **65** CallumRodriguez 9 71
(Keith Dalgleish) *led: rdn and hdd over 2f out: rallied: kpt on same pce fnl f* **50/1**

-114 **4** 2 ¾ **True Romance (IRE)**[34] 6180 5-9-6 **62** KevinStott 10 64
(Julia Brooke) *trckd ldrs: effrt and rdn over 2f out: no ex appr fnl f* **4/1**[1]

3432 **5** 1 ½ **Remember Rocky**[9] 7048 10-9-3 **62** (b) ConnorMurtagh(3) 1 62
(Lucy Normile) *in tch: rdn and outpcd 2f out: rallied ins fnl f: kpt on* **22/1**

4323 **6** ½ **Sempre Presto (IRE)**[9] 7057 4-9-11 **67** PaulHanagan 6 66
(Richard Fahey) *hld up in midfield: rdn 3f out: kpt on fr 2f out: nt pce to chal* **14/1**

1223 **7** 2 **Firewater**[29] 6341 3-9-5 **68** (p) TonyHamilton 15 64
(Richard Fahey) *hld up towards rr: drvn and effrt 3f out: no imp fr 2f out* **12/1**

2-23 **8** *nk* **Sbraase**[42] 5876 8-9-13 **69** OisinOrr 7 64
(Noel C Kelly, Ire) *hld up on outside: hdwy into midfield after 6f: rdn and outpcd 2f out: sme late hdwy: no imp* **14/1**

4130 **9** 1 ½ **Corton Lad**[13] 6933 9-9-11 **67** (tp) ShaneGray 13 60
(Keith Dalgleish) *cl up: drvn along over 2f out: wknd over 1f out* **40/1**

3340 **10** 1 **Sioux Frontier (IRE)**[68] 4913 4-9-13 **69** JamieGormley 8 61
(Iain Jardine) *hld up on ins: pushed along over 2f out: nvr able to chal* **20/1**

3050 **11** 2 **Needs To Be Seen (FR)**[11] 7003 4-9-11 **70** (p) HarrisonShaw(3) 16 59
(Jim Goldie) *s.i.s: bhd: drvn over 3f out: nvr on terms* **18/1**

5224 **12** 2 **Dew Pond**[16] 6827 7-9-2 **58** (bt) DavidAllan 4 44
(Tim Easterby) *hld up: drvn along 3f out: sn btn* **16/1**

5000 **13** 5 **Shrewd**[20] 6658 9-10-0 **70** (p) TomEaves 11 48
(Iain Jardine) *midfield on outside: rdn whn checked over 2f out: sn wknd* **11/2**[3]

3201 **14** 2 ½ **Myklachi (FR)**[20] 6660 3-9-2 **65** DanielTudhope 5 41
(David O'Meara) *hld up in midfield: drvn along over 2f out: sn btn* **10/1**

100 **15** ½ **Trautmann (IRE)**[11] 7001 5-10-0 **70** (tp) AlistairRawlinson 2 44
(Rebecca Menzies) *slowly away: bhd: rdn 3f out: sn struggling* **40/1**

2m 54.76s (0.36) **Going Correction** +0.10s/f (Good)
WFA 3 from 4yo+ 7lb **15 Ran SP% 119.9**
Speed ratings (Par 103): **102,101,100,99,98 98,96,96,95,95 93,92,89,87,87**
CSF £50.96 CT £2180.94 TOTE £11.60: £3.80, £1.60, £14.90; EX 74.20 Trifecta £1989.00.
Owner Imperial Racing, J Blackburn & P Scott **Bred** Sir E J Loder **Trained** Sheriff Hutton, N Yorks

FOCUS
Add 24yds. Modest handicap form.
T/Jkpt: Not won. T/Plt: £154.10 to a £1 stake. Pool: £51,813.50 - 245.38 winning units T/Qpdt: £26.40 to a £1 stake. Pool: £6,320.83 - 176.93 winning units **Richard Young\andrew Sheret**

7186 CHELMSFORD (A.W) (L-H)
Thursday, September 19

OFFICIAL GOING: Polytrack: standard
Wind: light, half against Weather: fine

7369 CONTOUR ROOFING "THE CONTOUR WAY" NURSERY H'CAP 5f (P)
4:55 (4:55) (Class 4) (0-85,84) 2-Y-O **£5,822** (£1,732; £865; £432; £400) **Stalls** Low

Form RPR

0122 **1** **Audio**[15] 6852 2-8-10 **78** (t) ThoreHammerHansen(5) 5 81
(Richard Hannon) *trckd ldrs tl wnt 2nd over 2f out: effrt and hung lft whn reminders 1f out: swtchd rt and kpt on to press wnr ins fnl f: kpt on wl to ld cl home* **5/1**[3]

110 **2** ½ **He's A Laddie (IRE)**[26] 6474 2-9-7 **84** HollieDoyle 1 85
(Archie Watson) *wnt rt leaving stalls: sn led: rdn over 1f out: drvn and hrd pressed ins fnl f: hdd and no ex cl home* **10/11**[1]

002 **3** *nse* **Dazzling Des (IRE)**[26] 6436 2-9-4 **81** JasonWatson 3 82
(David O'Meara) *in tch: swtchd rt and effrt over 1f out: edgd rt and ev ch ins fnl f: kpt on unable qck cl hone (jockey said gelding hung right-handed)* **4/1**[2]

6414 **4** ½ **Champagne Supanova (IRE)**[19] 6705 2-8-6 **72** (v) MeganNicholls(3) 6 71
(Richard Spencer) *hld up in tch in rr: effrt on outer over 2f out: hung lft briefly jst ins fnl f: kpt on u.p fnl 100yds: nt quite rch ldrs (jockey said gelding lugged left-handed)* **6/1**

233 **5** ¾ **Microscopic (IRE)**[14] 6900 2-7-9 **63** oh1 RhiainIngram(5) 2 59
(David Simcock) *chsd ldr tl over 2f out: outpcd u.p over 1f out: rallied and swtchd rt ins fnl f: kpt on but no threat to ldrs* **12/1**

59.97s (-0.23) **Going Correction** -0.175s/f (Stan) **5 Ran SP% 111.0**
Speed ratings (Par 97): **94,93,93,92,91**
CSF £10.24 TOTE £5.60: £2.10, £1.30; EX 10.90 Trifecta £32.30.
Owner Highclere T'Bred Racing-Hilton-Barber 1 **Bred** D A Bloodstock **Trained** East Everleigh, Wilts

FOCUS
The long-time leader was closed down late and they finished in a heap. Straightforward form.

7370 BIDWELLS GOLDEN TRIANGLE H'CAP 1m 6f (P)
5:30 (5:30) (Class 5) (0-75,77) 3-Y-O+
£5,110 (£1,520; £759; £400; £400; £400) **Stalls** Low

Form RPR

401 **1** **Conkering Hero (IRE)**[7] 7109 5-9-13 **73** 5ex (b) CharlesBishop 3 80
(Joseph Tuite) *racd keenly: led and dictated stdy gallop tl hdd 9f out: chsd ldng pair after tl effrt to chse ldr over 2f out: kpt on u.p to ld wl ins fnl f* **8/1**

3311 **2** 1 ¾ **Tavus (IRE)**[21] 6642 3-9-2 **70** JasonWatson 6 74
(Roger Charlton) *chsd ldr tl led over 2f out: sn rdn: drvn over 1f out: hdd and one pce wl ins fnl f* **15/8**[2]

4214 **3** 1 **Manton Warrior (IRE)**[8] 7082 3-9-5 **73** (t) PJMcDonald 2 76+
(Charlie Fellowes) *hld up in rr: effrt over 3f out: clsd u.p over 1f out: chsd ldng pair ins fnl f: styd on but nvr getting on terms w ldrs* **7/4**[1]

5501 **4** 4 **El Borracho (IRE)**[21] 6634 4-9-10 **77** (h) LeviWilliams(7) 5 74
(Simon Dow) *t.k.h: hld up in midfield: swtchd rt and effrt to chse ldrs 2f out: no imp: 4th and wknd ins fnl f* **8/1**

1244 **5** 13 **Tigray (USA)**[106] 3474 3-9-5 **73** AdamKirby 1 54
(Michael Appleby) *broke fast: sn restrained and hld up in last pair: effrt over 3f out: struggling and outpcd 2f out: wl bhd ins fnl f* **7/1**[3]

6204 **6** 4 ½ **Baydar**[29] 6348 6-9-11 **71** (v) DanielMuscutt 4 44
(Ivan Furtado) *trckd ldng pair: swtchd rt and hdwy to ld 9f out: rdn and hdd over 2f out: sn struggling and outpcd: wl bhd ins fnl f (jockey said gelding stopped quickly)* **20/1**

3m 2.22s (-0.98) **Going Correction** -0.175s/f (Stan)
WFA 3 from 4yo+ 8lb **6 Ran SP% 110.6**
Speed ratings (Par 103): **95,94,93,91,83 81**
CSF £22.81 TOTE £7.60: £3.40, £1.80; EX 27.80 Trifecta £60.50.
Owner C R Lambourne, M Forbes, D Losse **Bred** J Hutchinson **Trained** Lambourn, Berks

FOCUS
They went steady early on but the gallop picked up heading out on the final circuit.

7371 MOVING MADE EASY CLASSIFIED STKS 6f (P)
6:00 (6:02) (Class 6) 3-Y-O+
£3,105 (£924; £461; £400; £400; £400) **Stalls** Centre

Form RPR

000 **1** **Resurrected (IRE)**[76] 4582 3-9-0 **30** (t) DannyBrock 2 53
(Philip McBride) *chsd ldrs tl wnt 2nd 3f out: drvn to ld over 1f out: kpt on u.p ins fnl f: a gng to hold on (trainer said, regarding improvement in form, that the filly had benefited from drop in trip to 6f and the yard were in better form at present)* **10/1**[3]

4325 **2** ½ **Prince Rock (IRE)**[3] 7281 4-9-2 **47** (h) AdamKirby 4 52
(Simon Dow) *midfield: nt clr run over 2f out: effrt 2f out: swtchd lft and hdwy u.p over 1f out: chsng ldrs and nt clr run 1f out: swtchd rt and hdwy to chse wnr wl ins fnl f: styd on* **11/8**[1]

406 **3** 1 ½ **Royal Mezyan (IRE)**[35] 6126 8-9-2 **50** LouisSteward 9 47
(Henry Spiller) *hld up in last quintet: effrt on outer over 1f out: kpt on u.p ins fnl f: snatched 3rd last stride* **10/1**[3]

6400 **4** *nk* **Always Amazing**[20] 6682 5-9-2 49 ....(b[1]) TomMarquand 1 46
(Robyn Brisland) *chsd ldr tl 1/2-way: rdn over 2f out: swtchd rt and drvn over 1f out: keeping on same pce whn squeezed for room ins fnl f: lost 3rd last strides* **10/3**[2]

6000 **5** *1/2* **Mystical Moon (IRE)**[3] 7281 4-9-2 49 ....(vt) JasonWatson 3 44
(David C Griffiths) *in tch in midfield: clsd to chse ldrs and rdn 2f out: unable qck u.p 1f out: no ex and outpcd wl ins fnl f* **10/1**[3]

-000 **6** *1 1/4* **Aiguillette**[14] 6897 3-9-0 46 .... HarryBentley 13 40
(Gary Moore) *led: drvn and hdd over 1f out: no ex and wknd ins fnl f* **25/1**

0000 **7** *1* **Keep On Laughing (IRE)**[14] 6885 4-9-2 38 ....(t) JoeyHaynes 14 37
(John Butler) *midfield on outer: clsd to chse ldrs and rdn ent fnl 2f: no ex 1f out: wknd ins fnl f* **50/1**

4023 **8** *1 1/4* **Islay Mist**[22] 6605 3-8-11 47 ....(tp) DarraghKeenan(3) 5 34
(Lee Carter) *dwlt: hld up in midfield: hdwy on outer to chse ldrs over 2f out: unable qck over 1f out: wknd ins fnl f* **16/1**

0002 **9** *3/4* **Quduraat**[42] 5864 3-9-0 49 ....(h[1]) PJMcDonald 11 31
(Michael Appleby) *free to post: off the pce towards rr: effrt over 1f out: kpt on ins fnl f: nvr trbld ldrs* **20/1**

4323 **10** *nk* **Zaula**[18] 6754 3-9-0 47 .... HollieDoyle 10 30
(Mick Channon) *dwlt and hmpd leaving stalls: off the pce in rr: effrt over 1f out: plugged on ins fnl f: nvr trbld ldrs (jockey said filly was never travelling)* **12/1**

005- **11** *1 1/2* **Badger Berry**[308] 9066 3-9-0 49 ....(e[1]) RobHornby 6 26
(Nick Littmoden) *a towards rr: hung rt over 1f out: nvr involved* **25/1**

5506 **12** *3/4* **Tilsworth Rose**[5] 7172 5-8-11 48 ....(b) TobyEley(5) 12 24
(J R Jenkins) *stdd and swtchd lft leaving stalls: a bhd: nvr involved* **25/1**

600 **13** *3* **Ewell Spring**[22] 6594 3-8-9 32 .... RayDawson(5) 8 15
(Brett Johnson) *midfield: unable qck over 1f out: wknd ins fnl f* **66/1**

1m 12.82s (-0.88) **Going Correction** -0.175s/f (Stan)
WFA 3 from 4yo+ 2lb **13** Ran SP% **125.8**
Speed ratings (Par 101): **98,97,95,94,94 92,91,89,88,88 86,85,81**
CSF £23.75 TOTE £10.60: £3.50, £1.40, £2.30; EX 35.10 Trifecta £508.80.
Owner Miss Charlie McPhillips **Bred** P Moyles **Trained** Newmarket, Suffolk
■ Stewards' Enquiry : Danny Brock £140 fine - used a modified whip

FOCUS
A low-grade affair, but notable for the winner being well backed. Straightforward form in behind the winner.

7372 TOTAL PROTECTION "SERVICE WITHOUT COMPROMISE" H'CAP 6f (P)
6:30 (6:34) (Class 2) (0-100,93) 3-Y-0+ **£12,938** (£3,850; £1,924; £962) **Stalls** Centre

Form RPR

5040 **1** **Desert Doctor (IRE)**[13] 6920 4-9-11 **92** .... TomMarquand 7 99
(Ed Walker) *in tch in midfield: effrt over 1f out: hdwy 1f out: kpt on wl ins fnl f: led cl home: jst hld on* **7/1**

1110 **2** *nse* **Shimmering Dawn (IRE)**[57] 5325 3-9-6 **89** .... PJMcDonald 11 96+
(James Tate) *stdd and dropped in bhd after s: hld up in tch in rr: effrt on outer over 1f out: str run u.p ins fnl f: chal towards fin: jst failed* **4/1**[2]

0524 **3** *hd* **Alemaratalyoum (IRE)**[13] 6922 5-9-9 **90** ....(p) SeanLevey 10 96
(Stuart Williams) *t.k.h: chsd ldr over 4f out tl rdn to ld over 1f out: kpt on wl u.p: tl hdd and no ex cl home* **13/2**[3]

0610 **4** *3/4* **Unabated (IRE)**[13] 6920 5-9-2 **88** ....(t) RayDawson(5) 1 92
(Jane Chapple-Hyam) *trckd ldrs: effrt to chse ldr over 1f out: drvn ent fnl f: kpt on but nvr quite getting on terms w ldr: lost 2 pls towards fin* **7/1**

3300 **5** *3/4* **Dream Today (IRE)**[12] 6953 4-9-12 **93** .... DougieCostello 6 94+
(Jamie Osborne) *hld up in last trio: clsd on inner over 1f out: nt clrest of runs and swtchd rt ins fnl f: kpt on wl fnl 100yds: nt rch ldrs* **14/1**

-350 **6** *1* **Almufti**[70] 4847 3-9-7 **90** ....(t[1] w) JamesDoyle 5 91+
(Hugo Palmer) *hld up in tch in midfield: swtchd lft and effrt over 1f out: drvn to chse ldrs 1f out: no ex ins fnl f: wknd towards fin* **3/1**[1]

5045 **7** *1/2* **Global Tango (IRE)**[5] 7205 4-9-2 **83** ....(v) JackMitchell 8 79
(Luke McJannet) *hld up towards rr: nt clrest of runs wl over 1f out: sn rdn: kpt on ins fnl f: nvr threatened ldrs* **10/1**

0-50 **8** *3/4* **Mythmaker**[29] 6351 7-9-12 **93** .... RoystonFfrench 4 87
(Bryan Smart) *led for almost 1f: chsd ldr tl over 4f out: styd chsng ldrs tl unable qck u.p over 1f out: wknd ins fnl f* **25/1**

-606 **9** *1/2* **Eljaddaaf (IRE)**[16] 6841 8-9-5 **91** ....(h) SophieRalston(5) 3 83
(Dean Ivory) *t.k.h: hld up in last trio: n.m.r and impeded bnd 2f out: effrt over 1f out: sn rdn and no hdwy: nvr involved (jockey said gelding suffered interference rounding home bend)* **14/1**

146- **10** *11* **Restive Spirit**[287] 9429 4-9-12 **93** .... JasonWatson 9 50
(Charlie Wallis) *led after almost 1f: rdn and hdd over 1f out: sn dropped out: bhd and eased wl ins fnl f* **50/1**

1m 11.48s (-2.22) **Going Correction** -0.175s/f (Stan)
WFA 3 from 4yo+ 2lb **10** Ran SP% **111.6**
Speed ratings (Par 109): **107,106,106,105,104 103,102,101,101,86**
CSF £32.10 CT £165.74 TOTE £7.00: £2.20, £1.80, £1.90; EX 47.10 Trifecta £200.20.
Owner Mrs Fitri Hay **Bred** Skeaghmore Hill **Trained** Upper Lambourn, Berks

FOCUS
A decent handicap and a tight finish.

7373 SEABRO SCAFFOLDING "NOT AFRAID OF HEIGHTS" NOVICE STKS 1m (P)
7:00 (7:03) (Class 4) 3-Y-0+ **£6,080** (£1,809; £904; £452) **Stalls** Low

Form RPR

61- **1** **Dubai Icon**[337] 8327 3-9-9 0 .... OisinMurphy 6 91+
(Saeed bin Suroor) *chsd ldrs tl wnt 2nd 5f out: rdn to ld over 1f out: hung lft but in command ins fnl f: r.o: quite comf* **6/4**[1]

0 **2** *2 3/4* **Extrodinair**[87] 4189 4-9-1 0 .... RayDawson(5) 1 74+
(Jane Chapple-Hyam) *chsd ldr for 3f: styd chsng ldrs: effrt over 1f out: 3rd whn squeezed for room and hmpd jst ins fnl f: swtchd rt and rallied ins fnl f: chsd wnr towards fin: no imp* **66/1**

3 *3/4* **It Had To Be You** 3-9-2 0 .... JamesDoyle 3 71
(William Haggas) *midfield tl chsd ldrs 5f out: effrt and unable qck over 1f out: no threat to wnr but kpt on ins fnl f* **11/4**[2]

3 **4** *1* **Karisoke**[19] 6701 3-9-2 0 .... JackMitchell 8 69
(Simon Crisford) *led: rdn and hdd over 1f out: struggling to qckn and hung lft 1f out: kpt on same pce and lost 2 pls ins fnl f* **12/1**

12- **5** *2 1/4* **Equal Sum**[274] 9607 3-9-4 0 .... SeanLevey 4 66
(Richard Hannon) *restless in stalls: s.i.s: t.k.h: hld up towards rr: hdwy 4f out: effrt and hung lft over 1f out: no imp and plugged on same pce fnl f* **8/1**

6 **6** *3/4* **Dr Jekyll (IRE)**[149] 2023 3-9-2 0 .... HarryBentley 10 62+
(David Simcock) *s.i.s: hld up in rr: effrt over 1f out: kpt on ins fnl f: nvr trbld ldrs* **9/2**[3]

7 *1* **Anything For You** 3-8-11 0 .... RobHornby 5 54
(Jonathan Portman) *midfield tl dropped towards rr over 2f out: no imp over 1f out: wl hld fnl f* **50/1**

0-0 **8** *1 1/2* **Martin King**[197] 1034 3-9-2 0 ....(w) AdamKirby 2 56
(Clive Cox) *chsd ldrs for 3f: midfield after: no imp and wl hld whn wnt rt ent fnl f: kpt on same pce ins fnl f* **50/1**

0 **9** *1 3/4* **Shattering (IRE)**[16] 6836 3-9-2 0 .... PJMcDonald 7 52
(Paul Cole) *stdd after s: hld up towards rr: nvr involved* **50/1**

10 *3/4* **Detective** 3-9-2 0 .... LouisSteward 9 50
(Sir Michael Stoute) *s.i.s: rn green and a in rr: nvr involved* **16/1**

1m 38.02s (-1.88) **Going Correction** -0.175s/f (Stan)
WFA 3 from 4yo 4lb **10** Ran SP% **116.9**
Speed ratings (Par 105): **102,99,98,97,95 94,93,92,90,89**
CSF £132.04 TOTE £2.10: £1.30, £55.30, £1.20; EX 111.80 Trifecta £811.30.
Owner Godolphin **Bred** Godolphin **Trained** Newmarket, Suffolk

FOCUS
It paid to be handy here, the first four racing in the first four positions throughout.

7374 SICURO "CAUGHT ON CAMERA" H'CAP 1m (P)
7:30 (7:32) (Class 6) (0-55,55) 3-Y-0+
£3,105 (£924; £461; £400; £400; £400) **Stalls** Low

Form RPR

3231 **1** **Parknacilla (IRE)**[14] 6885 3-8-12 **52** ....(p) CierenFallon(3) 2 58
(Henry Spiller) *hld up towards rr: swtchd rt and hdwy on outer over 2f out: chsd ldr and hung lft ent fnl f: styd on strly to ld ins fnl f: sn in command and r.o wl* **5/2**[1]

450 **2** *1 1/4* **Seaquinn**[30] 6327 4-8-12 **45** .... KierenFox 6 48
(John Best) *hld up in tch in midfield: swtchd rt and effrt over 1f out: edgd lft but styd on wl ins fnl f: wnt 2nd last strides: nvr getting to wnr* **12/1**

0006 **3** *nk* **Squire**[15] 6860 8-9-2 **52** ....(tp) MeganNicholls(3) 3 54
(Marjorie Fife) *s.i.s: hld up in tch in midfield: hdwy to chse ldrs over 1f out: kpt on to go 2nd wl ins fnl f: no imp and lost 2nd last strides (jockey said gelding was slowly away)* **14/1**

060 **4** *1 1/4* **Obsession For Gold (IRE)**[26] 6441 3-8-13 **50** ....(t) BrettDoyle 14 50
(Mrs Ilka Gansera-Leveque) *t.k.h: led for over 1f: chsd ldr tl led again 3f out: rdn and kicked clr 2f out: drvn over 1f out: hdd ins fnl f: no ex and wknd* **33/1**

3256 **5** *1 1/2* **Sea Tea Dea**[14] 6897 5-8-12 **45** ....(t) HollieDoyle 5 42
(Adrian Wintle) *hld up in tch in midfield: nt clr run on inner over 2f out: swtchd rt and effrt over 1f out: kpt on same pce u.p ins fnl f* **14/1**

3435 **6** *1/2* **Accomplice**[4] 7237 5-9-7 **54** ....(p[1]) CharlesBishop 4 49
(Michael Blanshard) *t.k.h: hld up towards rr: hdwy on inner over 1f out: kpt on same pce and no imp u.p ins fnl f (jockey said mare was denied clear run rounding home turn)* **8/1**[3]

0004 **7** *1* **Herringswell (FR)**[35] 6131 4-8-5 **45** .... GeorgiaDobie(7) 7 38
(Henry Spiller) *in tch in midfield: pushed along over 3f out: clsd and rdn ent fnl 2f: unable qck u.p over 1f out: wknd ins fnl f* **33/1**

5-51 **8** *1/2* **Pact Of Steel**[12] 6977 4-9-2 **54** ....(t) WilliamCarver(5) 8 46
(Ivan Furtado) *chsd ldrs: unable qck u.p over 1f out: losing pl whn swtchd rt ins fnl f: sn wknd* **4/1**[2]

0436 **9** *2* **Agent Of Fortune**[30] 6327 4-9-7 **54** ....(v[1]) AdamKirby 11 41
(Christine Dunnett) *dwlt: midfield: effrt ent fnl 2f: drvn and no imp over 1f out: wl hld ins fnl f* **8/1**[3]

5050 **10** *1/2* **Dukes Meadow**[79] 4473 8-8-7 **45** .... RhiainIngram(5) 1 31
(Roger Ingram) *chsd ldrs: chsd ldr 2f out: no imp and lost 2nd ent fnl f: wknd fnl 150yds* **50/1**

055 **11** *hd* **Cheerful**[19] 6701 3-8-13 **55** .... RayDawson(5) 13 40
(Philip McBride) *stdd after s: hld up in rr: wd bnd 2f out: nudged along over 1f out: edgd lft and kpt on ins fnl f: nvr trbld ldrs (vet reported filly finished lame on left fore)* **16/1**

00U4 **12** *1 1/2* **Four Feet (IRE)**[17] 6802 3-8-6 **50** .... EmmaTaff(7) 15 32
(Henry Candy) *s.i.s: sn swtchd lft: bhd: effrt over 1f out: kpt on ins fnl f: nvr involved* **33/1**

0053 **13** *4* **London Pride**[35] 6117 3-9-0 **51** ....(p) RobHornby 10 24
(Jonathan Portman) *chsd ldrs tl unable qck and lost pl over 1f out: wknd ins fnl f* **16/1**

0000 **14** *1 1/2* **Irish Times**[47] 5652 4-9-5 **52** .... PJMcDonald 9 21
(Henry Spiller) *hld up towards rr: pushed along over 1f out: no prog: nvr involved* **12/1**

6065 **15** *1 1/4* **Tellovoi (IRE)**[14] 6885 11-8-13 **46** ....(p) PhilipPrince 12 12
(Richard Guest) *taken down early: chsd ldr tl led over 6f out: hdd 3f out: lost pl 2f out: wkng whn short of room over 1f out: bhd ins fnl f* **33/1**

1m 37.81s (-2.09) **Going Correction** -0.175s/f (Stan)
WFA 3 from 4yo+ 4lb **15** Ran SP% **125.0**
Speed ratings (Par 101): **103,101,101,100,98 98,97,96,94,94 94,92,88,87,85**
CSF £33.88 CT £373.19 TOTE £3.10: £1.60, £4.10, £3.00; EX 41.10 Trifecta £340.90.
Owner Charles & Fiona Spiller **Bred** M Downey & Kildaragh Stud **Trained** Newmarket, Suffolk
■ Stewards' Enquiry : Brett Doyle two-day ban: using whip above permitted level (Oct 3-4)
Ray Dawson £140 fine: failed to report reason for poor performance

FOCUS
A moderate affair. Limited form, rated around the runner-up.

7375 REDROW "A BETTER WAY TO LIVE" H'CAP (DIV I) 1m 2f (P)
8:00 (8:03) (Class 6) (0-60,62) 3-Y-0+
£3,105 (£924; £461; £400; £400; £400) **Stalls** Low

Form RPR

-053 **1** **Poetic Legacy (IRE)**[10] 7027 3-8-5 **45** .... RoystonFfrench 8 57
(Mark Johnston) *chsd ldr tl rdn to ld wl over 1f out: clr and in command whn edgd lft ins fnl f: styd on strly* **6/1**[3]

4021 **2** *3 1/2* **Fame N Fortune**[19] 6723 3-9-4 **58** ....(b) CharlesBishop 11 64
(Joseph Tuite) *chsd ldrs: effrt over 1f out: chsd clr wnr jst ins fnl f: kpt on for clr 2nd but no imp on wnr* **3/1**[2]

3404 **3** *4 1/2* **Cash N Carrie (IRE)**[150] 2004 5-8-10 **45** .... PJMcDonald 2 41
(Michael Appleby) *led: rdn over 2f out: hdd wl over 1f and unable qck: lost btn 2nd jst ins fnl f: wknd* **33/1**

3404 **4** *nk* **Four Mile Bridge (IRE)**[17] 6805 3-9-2 **56** .... JasonWatson 10 52
(Mark Usher) *midfield: effrt but outpcd u.p over 2f out: no ch but plugged on ins fnl f* **6/1**[3]

5000 **5** *nk* **Presence Process**[36] 6077 5-9-5 **57** .... PaddyBradley(3) 9 52
(Pat Phelan) *chsd ldrs: rdn over 2f out: unable qck and btn whn hung lft over 1f out: wknd ins fnl f* **16/1**

2224 **6** *1 3/4* **Chakrii (IRE)**[12] 6983 3-8-12 **52** ....(p) OisinMurphy 4 45
(Henry Spiller) *midfield: 5th and drvn over 2f out: sn outpcd and no ch w wnr over 1f out* **5/2**[1]

3006 **7** *1* **Foxrush Take Time (FR)**[25] 6499 4-8-10 **45**...........(e) JFEgan 6 35
(Richard Guest) *taken down early: midfield: outpcd and drvn over 2f out: no threat to ldrs after and wl btn over 1f out* **14/1**

1000 **8** *½* **Rocksette**[4] 7232 5-9-1 **55**...........(p[1]) TobyEley(5) 1 44
(Adam West) *hld up in midfield: effrt and plenty to do over 2f out: swtchd lft and u.p over 1f out: no prog and nvr involved* **20/1**

064 **9** *1 ¾* **Ahfad**[37] 6049 4-8-10 **45**...........(b) HarryBentley 7 30
(Gary Moore) *s.i.s: effrt u.p and plenty to do over 1f out: no real prog: nvr involved* **10/1**

400- **10** *nk* **Sunshine Coast**[295] 9293 4-9-10 **59**........... DougieCostello 5 44
(Jamie Osborne) *a towards rr: rdn over 3f out: no imp and nvr involved* **25/1**

4665 **11** *2* **Max Guevara (IRE)**[22] 6600 3-9-3 **57**........... TomMarquand 13 39
(William Muir) *hld up in rr: outpcd over 2f out: no ch after* **25/1**

3250 **12** *hd* **Nabvutika (IRE)**[19] 6723 3-8-9 **52**........... DarraghKeenan(3) 3 34
(John Butler) *midfield: outpcd over 2f out: no imp u.p and wl btn over 1f out* **20/1**

13 *13* **Mia Vittoria**[109] 3-9-8 **62**........... JackMitchell 12 19
(Amy Murphy) *t.k.h: hld up towards rr: bhd fnl 2f: eased ins fnl f* **33/1**

2m 4.31s (-4.29) **Going Correction** -0.175s/f (Stan)
WFA 3 from 4yo+ 5lb **13 Ran SP% 126.9**
Speed ratings (Par 101): **110,107,103,103,103 101,100,100,99,98 97,97,86**
CSF £23.59 CT £573.94 TOTE £6.50: £1.90, £1.80, £10.20; EX 25.40 Trifecta £226.10.
Owner Clipper Logistics **Bred** Azienda Agricola Mariano **Trained** Middleham Moor, N Yorks

FOCUS
They went fairly steady and the first three raced in the first four places throughout. Improved form from the winner.

7376 REDROW "A BETTER WAY TO LIVE" H'CAP (DIV II) 1m 2f (P)
8:30 (8:32) (Class 6) (0-60,62) 3-Y-0+
£3,105 (£924; £461; £400; £400; £400) **Stalls** Low

Form RPR

5321 **1** **Fair Power (IRE)**[15] 6860 5-9-10 **59**........... OisinMurphy 13 66
(John Butler) *midfield: hdwy to chse ldr 7f out: rdn to ld wl over 1f out: rdn clr 1f out: r.o wl* **11/8**[1]

4104 **2** *1 ½* **Billie Beane**[40] 5941 4-9-1 **53**........... DarraghKeenan(3) 7 57
(Dr Jon Scargill) *led for over 1f: chsd ldr tl 7f out: styd trcking ldrs: effrt to chse wnr over 1f out: kpt on but no imp ins fnl f* **14/1**

0442 **3** *1 ¼* **Reddiac (IRE)**[21] 6635 3-9-4 **58**...........(p) JasonWatson 4 61
(Ed Dunlop) *t.k.h: hld up towards rr: nt clr run and swtchd rt over 1f out: edgd lft but styd on ins fnl f: nvr getting to wnr (jockey said gelding hung left-handed)* **8/1**[2]

4205 **4** *1 ½* **Picture Poet (IRE)**[58] 5284 3-8-12 **57**........... RayDawson(5) 1 57
(Henry Spiller) *hld up in tch in midfield: nt clr run and swtchd rt over 1f out: hdwy u.p 1f out: kpt on same pce ins fnl f* **8/1**[2]

5020 **5** *1 ½* **Heatherdown (IRE)**[19] 6723 3-8-11 **54**...........(v) CierenFallon(3) 8 51
(Ian Williams) *chsd ldrs: drvn and struggling to qckn and edgd lft over 1f out: no threat to wnr and kpt on same pce ins fnl f* **8/1**[2]

0000 **6** *½* **Luxford**[19] 6723 5-8-10 **45**...........(v) HarryBentley 3 40
(Gary Moore) *hld up in tch in midfield: effrt over 1f out: sn drvn and no imp ins fnl f: wknd towards fin* **10/1**

4640 **7** *½* **Buzz Lightyere**[23] 6560 6-9-1 **53**...........(v) MeganNicholls(3) 12 47
(Patrick Chamings) *s.i.s and rousted along early: hld up in rr: swtchd rt and effrt over 1f out: kpt on ins fnl f: nvr trbld ldrs (jockey said gelding was slowly away)* **25/1**

-000 **8** *1 ½* **Argent Bleu**[14] 6885 4-8-10 **45**........... JackMitchell 6 36
(Roger Ingram) *chsd ldrs: rdn ent fnl 3f: edgd rt and no ex u.p over 1f out: wknd ins fnl f* **66/1**

400 **9** *3 ¼* **Moon Artist (FR)**[10] 7027 3-8-0 **45**........... RhiainIngram(5) 5 31
(Michael Blanshard) *in tch in midfield: lost pl u.p over 1f out: wknd ins fnl f (jockey said filly hung right-handed)* **50/1**

0603 **10** *½* **Grasmere (IRE)**[37] 6049 4-8-12 **47**...........(t) BrettDoyle 2 31
(Alan Bailey) *wnt rt and bmpd leaving stalls: rousted along early: hld up towards rr: nt clrest of runs on inner over 2f out: effrt and sme hdwy over 1f out: no imp 1f out and wknd ins fnl f* **20/1**

0205 **11** *1 ¾* **Hard Toffee (IRE)**[21] 6636 8-9-8 **57**........... AdamKirby 11 38
(Louise Allan) *s.i.s: rousted along and early reminders: clsd on to rr of field and travelling bttr after 3f: effrt 2f out: no prog: sn btn and bhd ins fnl f* **9/1**[3]

453 **12** *3 ½* **Harbour City (USA)**[15] 6862 3-9-8 **62**........... PJMcDonald 9 37
(James Tate) *t.k.h: chsd ldrs tl led after over 1f: rdn and hdd wl over 1f out: sn btn and fdd ins fnl f* **8/1**[2]

2m 5.0s (-3.60) **Going Correction** -0.175s/f (Stan) **12 Ran SP% 124.4**
WFA 3 from 4yo+ 5lb
Speed ratings (Par 101): **107,105,104,103,102 102,101,100,97,97 96,93**
CSF £24.23 CT £128.86 TOTE £2.00: £1.10, £3.00, £2.80; EX 28.90 Trifecta £326.40.
Owner N N Holmes **Bred** Pitrizzia Partnership **Trained** Newmarket, Suffolk

FOCUS
The slower of the two divisions by 0.69sec. The winner was still on a good mark on the best of last year's form.
T/Plt: £36.90 to a £1 stake. Pool: £29,031.60 - 785.06 winning units T/Qpdt: £14.70 to a £1 stake. Pool: £4,615.06 - 312.77 winning units **Steve Payne**

6254 PONTEFRACT (L-H)
Thursday, September 19

OFFICIAL GOING: Good to firm (good in places; watered; 8.0)
Wind: Virtually nil Weather: Fine & dry

7377 NAPOLEONS CASINO BRADFORD MEDIAN AUCTION MAIDEN STKS 5f 3y
2:10 (2:12) (Class 5) 2-Y-O
£3,881 (£1,155; £577; £288) **Stalls** Low

Form RPR

4 **1** **Jeanie B**[16] 6846 2-9-0 **0**........... FrannyNorton 6 74
(Mick Channon) *mde all: rdn wl over 1f out: kpt on strly fnl f* **7/2**[2]

2 *2 ½* **Spirit Of The Sky** 2-8-11 **0**........... SeanDavis(3) 5 65
(Richard Fahey) *t.k.h: trckd ldrs on inner: n.m.r wl over 1f out: sn swtchd rt and rdn: chsd wnr ins fnl f: sn drvn and no imp* **5/1**[3]

246 **3** *nk* **Hidden Spell (IRE)**[13] 6919 2-9-0 **73**........... CliffordLee 7 64
(K R Burke) *chsd wnr: rdn along 2f out: sltly hmpd over 1f out: kpt on same pce fnl f* **9/1**

0 **4** *¾* **Joshua R (IRE)**[26] 6457 2-9-5 **0**........... ConnorBeasley 1 66
(David Barron) *in tch: hdwy on inner 2f out: rdn over 1f out: kpt on fnl f* **7/2**[2]

2342 **5** *shd* **Mecca's Hot Steps**[37] 6032 2-9-0 **70**........... PaulMulrennan 3 61
(Michael Dods) *t.k.h and n.m.r after 1f: sn trcking ldrs: hdwy on outer 2f out: rdn over 1f out: drvn and kpt on same pce fnl f* **5/2**[1]

3 **6** *2 ¼* **Seas Of Elzaam (IRE)**[9] 7046 2-9-5 **0**........... RobbieDowney 9 58
(David O'Meara) *dwlt: sn in tch: pushed along over 2f out: rdn wl over 1f out: sn no imp* **11/1**

0 **7** *2 ¾* **Apache Bay**[142] 2248 2-9-0 **0**........... GrahamLee 8 43
(John Quinn) *in tch whn n.m.r after 1f: towards rr after* **33/1**

00 **8** *2 ¼* **Sassy Lassy (IRE)**[129] 2694 2-8-9 **0**........... ThomasGreatrex(5) 2 35
(David Loughnane) *a towards rr (jockey said filly was slowly away)* **40/1**

6 **9** *1 ½* **Orange Justice**[12] 6979 2-9-0 **0**........... PhilDennis 10 29
(David Loughnane) *towards rr: effrt and sme hdwy on wd outside 2f out: sn rdn along and n.d (jockey said filly hung right off bnd)* **100/1**

10 *18* **Belle Voci** 2-9-0 **0**........... JackGarritty 4
(Stella Barclay) *dwlt: a in rr* **50/1**

1m 2.96s (-0.94) **Going Correction** -0.225s/f (Firm) **10 Ran SP% 116.3**
Speed ratings (Par 95): **98,94,93,92,92 88,84,80,78,49**
CSF £20.97 TOTE £4.60: £1.30, £1.90, £2.30; EX 31.60 Trifecta £166.80.
Owner Bastian Family **Bred** E & R Bastian **Trained** West Ilsley, Berks

FOCUS
This looked to have a bit of depth to it, so the form could well be sound in the short term.

7378 MATTY BOWN H'CAP 1m 6y
2:40 (2:41) (Class 4) (0-80,76) 3-Y-0+
£5,336 (£1,588; £793; £396; £300; £300) **Stalls** Low

Form RPR

6002 **1** **Hammer Gun (USA)**[8] 7074 6-9-3 **69**...........(v) FrannyNorton 1 75
(Derek Shaw) *hld up in rr: hdwy over 2f out: sn swtchd rt to outer and pushed along over 1f out: rdn and styd on wl fnl f to ld nr fin* **11/8**[1]

3212 **2** *hd* **Data Protection**[24] 6538 4-9-10 **76**...........(t) LewisEdmunds 8 81
(William Muir) *trckd ldng pair on inner: hdwy 2f out: swtchd rt and rdn to chal over 1f out: drvn to take slt ld ins fnl f: hdd and no ex nr fin* **5/1**[3]

0000 **3** *¾* **Destroyer**[8] 7074 6-9-1 **67**........... AndrewMullen 5 70
(Tom Tate) *cl up: led after 1f: rdn along 2f out: drvn and hdd narrowly ins fnl f: kpt on wl u.p towards fin* **7/1**

5606 **4** *1* **International Law**[38] 6026 5-9-2 **68**........... CamHardie 4 70+
(Antony Brittain) *trckd ldrs: pushed along 2f out: rdn over 1f out: drvn and kpt on same pce fnl f (jockey said gelding was denied a run in closing stages)* **20/1**

2626 **5** *¾* **First Response**[8] 7069 4-9-9 **75**........... PhilDennis 3 74
(Linda Stubbs) *trckd ldrs on inner: effrt 2f out: pushed along over 1f out: n.m.r and rdn ins fnl f: kpt on same pce* **9/2**[2]

235 **6** *8* **Amor Fati (IRE)**[14] 6904 4-8-13 **70**........... ThomasGreatrex(5) 2 51
(David Evans) *hld up in rr: hdwy on wd outside whn pushed wd home turn: sn rdn and n.d* **13/2**

0000 **7** *1 ½* **New Look (FR)**[23] 6582 4-9-1 **67**...........(b) RachelRichardson 6 44
(Tim Easterby) *hld up towards rr: hdwy over 2f out: sltly hmpd and edgd rt home turn: sn btn* **33/1**

140 **8** *hd* **Miss Sheridan (IRE)**[42] 5844 5-9-5 **71**........... NathanEvans 7 48
(Michael Easterby) *led 1f: trckd ldr: rdn along over 2f out: drvn and wknd wl over 1f out* **18/1**

1m 42.63s (-3.27) **Going Correction** -0.225s/f (Firm) **8 Ran SP% 115.8**
Speed ratings (Par 105): **107,106,106,105,104 96,94,94**
CSF £8.67 CT £35.97 TOTE £2.20: £1.10, £1.40, £2.30; EX 9.80 Trifecta £56.30.
Owner A Flint **Bred** Her Majesty The Queen **Trained** Sproxton, Leics

FOCUS
A fair event, run at a respectable pace early on.

7379 PONTEFRACT & DISTRICT GOLF CLUB LTD H'CAP 1m 2f 5y
3:10 (3:10) (Class 4) (0-85,80) 3-Y-0+
£5,336 (£1,588; £793; £396; £300; £300) **Stalls** Low

Form RPR

0050 **1** **Aiya (IRE)**[12] 6975 4-9-3 **73**...........(h) CamHardie 4 80
(Tim Easterby) *sn led: pushed along over 2f out: rdn and hdd narrowly over 1f out: drvn and led again ins fnl f: hld on gamely* **14/1**

2211 **2** *shd* **Anna Bunina (FR)**[33] 6230 3-9-4 **79**........... JackGarritty 8 86+
(Jedd O'Keeffe) *trckd ldrs on outer: hdwy wl over 1f out: rdn to chal ins fnl f: sn drvn: kpt on wl towards fin: jst hld* **11/2**[3]

4300 **3** *¾* **Glasses Up (USA)**[5] 7212 4-9-7 **77**........... RossaRyan 1 82
(R Mike Smith) *trckd ldng pair: hdwy over 2f out: rdn to chal over 1f out: drvn and ev ch ins fnl f: kpt on same pce towards fin* **15/8**[1]

4125 **4** *1* **Billy Roberts (IRE)**[53] 5474 6-9-0 **70**........... ConnorBeasley 6 73
(Richard Whitaker) *cl up: rdn to take slt ld over 1f out: drvn and hdd ins fnl f: kpt on same pce* **7/1**

2545 **5** *nse* **Fraser Island (IRE)**[30] 6323 3-9-0 **75**...........(v[1]) FrannyNorton 7 78
(Mark Johnston) *hld up in tch: effrt over 2f out: rdn along wl over 1f out: kpt on u.p fnl f* **8/1**

-340 **6** *1 ½* **Sheberghan (IRE)**[164] 1644 4-9-10 **80**........... AdrianMcCarthy 5 80
(Ed Dunlop) *trckd ldrs on inner: pushed along over 2f out: rdn wl over 1f out: sn drvn and grad wknd* **33/1**

33 **7** *2 ¾* **Railport Dolly**[33] 6230 4-9-4 **74**...........(h) GrahamLee 2 68
(David Barron) *hld up: a towards rr* **5/2**[2]

100 **8** *¾* **Briardale (IRE)**[61] 5198 7-9-1 **71**...........(p) PaulMulrennan 3 64
(James Bethell) *dwlt: hld up: a in rr (jockey said gelding was slowly away)* **25/1**

2m 10.19s (-4.81) **Going Correction** -0.225s/f (Firm)
WFA 3 from 4yo+ 5lb **8 Ran SP% 115.8**
Speed ratings (Par 105): **110,109,109,108,108 107,105,104**
CSF £89.52 CT £213.74 TOTE £13.10: £3.40, £1.50, £1.10; EX 116.40 Trifecta £438.20.
Owner King Power Racing Co Ltd **Bred** Lynch Bages & Camas Park Stud **Trained** Great Habton, N Yorks
■ Stewards' Enquiry : Jack Garritty two-day ban: used whip above permitted level (Oct 3-4)

FOCUS
They didn't go that quickly throughout the early stages, so this developed into a sprint off the home bend.

7380 ELKINGTON STUD SUPPORTS RACING TO SCHOOL EBF PREMIER FILLIES' H'CAP 6f
3:40 (3:41) (Class 2) (0-100,88) 3-Y-0+
£18,675 (£5,592; £2,796; £1,398; £699; £351) **Stalls** Low

Form RPR

3420 **1** **Lady Of Aran (IRE)**[13] 6916 4-8-12 **74**........... StevieDonohoe 9 87+
(Charlie Fellowes) *dwlt: hld up in rr: hdwy and swtchd rt 2f out: rdn over 1f out: str run ent fnl f: led last 100yds* **8/1**

0111 **2** *1* **Gale Force Maya**[21] 6623 3-9-4 **82**.............................. PaulMulrennan 8 92+
(Michael Dods) *hld up in tch: smooth hdwy on outer over 2f out: led jst over 1f out: sn rdn and edgd lft: drvn ins fnl f: hdd last 100yds* **7/2**[2]

1124 **3** *3 ¾* **Betsey Trotter (IRE)**[14] 6908 4-9-6 **87**...............(p) ScottMcCullagh(5) 3 85
(David O'Meara) *trckd ldrs: pushed along over 2f out: rdn wl over 1f out: kpt on fnl f* **8/1**

-334 **4** *hd* **Kindly**[12] 6972 6-9-2 **78**.....................................(v) NathanEvans 6 75
(Michael Easterby) *chsd ldrs on outer: hdwy 3f out: cl up 2f out: rdn and ev ch over 1f out: drvn ent fnl f: kpt on same pce* **7/1**

6504 **5** *hd* **Alicia Darcy (IRE)**[3] 7268 3-8-12 **76**........................(b) AdamMcNamara 7 73
(Archie Watson) *dwlt and in rr: hdwy on wd outside wl over 1f out: sn rdn: kpt on fnl f* **40/1**

16-0 **6** *1 ½* **Zip Along (IRE)**[12] 6974 4-9-12 **88**...................................... JackGarritty 1 80
(Richard Fahey) *trckd ldrs on inner: pushed along 2f out: n.m.r and rdn over 1f out: n.d* **9/2**[3]

1210 **7** *2 ¼* **Sonja Henie (IRE)**[5] 7188 3-8-12 **81**........................ ThomasGreatrex(5) 5 66
(David Loughnane) *prom: cl up 1/2-way: rdn to take narrow ld wl over 1f out: hdd appr fnl f: sn wknd (jockey said filly ran flat)* **5/2**[1]

8 *3 ½* **Dragons Call (IRE)**[57] 5328 3-9-4 **82**................................ GrahamLee 4 56
(John James Feane, Ire) *led: rdn along wl over 2f out: drvn and hdd wl over 1f out: sn wknd* **10/1**

3135 **9** *1 ¼* **Enchanted Linda**[19] 6735 3-9-1 **79**.................................... PhilDennis 2 49
(Michael Herrington) *t.k.h: trckd ldrs: effrt over 2f out: sn rdn and wknd wl over 1f out* **20/1**

1m 14.75s (-2.35) **Going Correction** -0.225s/f (Firm)
WFA 3 from 4yo+ 2lb 9 Ran SP% **120.0**
Speed ratings (Par 96): **106,104,99,99,99 97,94,89,87**
CSF £37.66 CT £240.27 TOTE £8.00: £2.70, £1.70, £2.80; EX 52.20 Trifecta £303.10.
Owner Bengough, Fellowes, Horsford And Soiza **Bred** Mountarmstrong Stud **Trained** Newmarket, Suffolk

FOCUS
A lot changed in the final stages of this race, with the winner pouncing late.

7381 MADAM LILIBET H'CAP 2m 1f 27y
4:10 (4:10) (Class 5) (0-75,70) 3-Y-O+ **£3,881** (£1,155; £577; £300) **Stalls** Low

Form RPR

53-1 **1** **Rubenesque (IRE)**[148] 1815 7-10-0 **70**...............................(t) PhilDennis 2 77
(Tristan Davidson) *set decent pce: pushed along over 2f out: rdn jst over 1f out: drvn ins fnl f: kpt on wl towards fin* **6/1**[3]

2612 **2** *nk* **Forewarning**[11] 7001 5-9-11 **67**... CamHardie 4 73
(Julia Brooke) *trckd wnr: effrt 2f out: rdn along over 1f out: drvn to chal ins fnl f: sn drvn and ev ch: no ex towards fin* **8/13**[1]

0113 **3** *2 ½* **Stormin Norman**[32] 6256 4-9-8 **64**...................................... GrahamLee 5 67
(Micky Hammond) *hld up in rr: pushed along 5f out: rdn over 2f out: drvn wl over 1f out: kpt on same pce* **7/2**[2]

3215 **4** *6* **Kitty's Cove**[8] 7070 4-8-11 **53**.......................................(tp) DuranFentiman 3 50
(Tim Easterby) *trckd ldng pair: hdwy to chse wnr 5f out: rdn along 3f out: drvn wl over 1f out: sn wknd* **9/1**

3m 52.61s (3.41) **Going Correction** -0.225s/f (Firm) 4 Ran SP% **108.4**
Speed ratings (Par 103): **83,82,81,78**
CSF £10.51 TOTE £5.60; EX 12.60 Trifecta £15.90.
Owner Toby Noble And Andy Bell **Bred** John Joseph Murphy **Trained** Irthington, Cumbria

FOCUS
A good ride from the front was enough to land this marathon contest.

7382 PAUL HARRATT MAIDEN STKS 1m 4f 5y
4:40 (4:43) (Class 3) 3-Y-O+ **£9,337** (£2,796; £1,398; £699; £349) **Stalls** Low

Form RPR

4-25 **1** **Ballylemon (IRE)**[125] 2796 3-9-2 80.............................. FinleyMarsh(3) 2 88+
(Richard Hughes) *set stdy pce: pushed along 2f out: rdn clr wl over 1f out: kpt on strly* **6/4**[1]

2-23 **2** *3 ¾* **Pianissimo**[20] 6662 3-9-5 82................................(b[1]) FrannyNorton 1 80
(John Gosden) *trckd ldng pair: hdwy to chse wnr wl over 1f out: sn rdn: carried hd high and no imp* **6/4**[1]

3 *10* **Rory And Me (FR)**[46] 4-9-12 0.. GrahamLee 5 63
(Micky Hammond) *trckd ldrs: pushed along over 2f out: sn rdn and plugged on for mod 3rd* **16/1**[3]

06- **4** *2 ½* **The Accountant**[29] 668 4-9-12 0.................................(v) RossaRyan 4 59
(Amy Murphy) *trckd wnr: cl up 1/2-way: rdn along 3f out: drvn and outpcd fnl 2f (jockey said gelding hung left-handed)* **33/1**

5 *13* **Isocrates (USA)** 3-9-5 0...(v[1]) PaulMulrennan 3 39
(Simon Crisford) *dwlt: a in rr: outpcd and bhd fr over 2f out* **7/2**[2]

2m 38.03s (-3.07) **Going Correction** -0.225s/f (Firm)
WFA 3 from 4yo 7lb 5 Ran SP% **111.0**
Speed ratings (Par 107): **101,98,91,90,81**
CSF £3.99 TOTE £2.80: £1.30, £1.10; EX 4.40 Trifecta £19.50.
Owner Graham Doyle & Hazel Lawrence **Bred** Frank Hutchinson **Trained** Upper Lambourn, Berks

FOCUS
Just three of the five were given any chance by punters, but only one mattered in the home straight.

7383 LIKE RACING TV ON FACEBOOK APPRENTICE H'CAP 6f
5:10 (5:10) (Class 5) (0-70,72) 3-Y-O+ **£3,881** (£1,155; £577; £300; £300; £300) **Stalls** Low

Form RPR

53 **1** **Round The Island**[8] 7066 6-8-10 **56** oh2...................(p) RowanScott 3 64
(Richard Whitaker) *hld up in tch: hdwy 2f out: chsd ldrs over 1f out: rdn to ld ent fnl f: sn drvn and wandered: kpt on wl towards fin* **4/1**[3]

6022 **2** *hd* **Atletico (IRE)**[12] 6968 7-9-8 **68**...................................... FinleyMarsh 8 75
(David Evans) *hld up in rr: hdwy 2f out: chsd ldrs over 1f out: rdn to chal ins fnl f: ev ch: sn drvn and no ex towards fin* **10/3**[1]

1136 **3** *2 ¼* **Bedtime Bella (IRE)**[6] 7165 3-9-2 **71**.................(v) GeorgeRooke(7) 5 71
(Michael Appleby) *hld up: hdwy 2f out: rdn to chse ldrs over 1f out: drvn and kpt on same pce fnl f* **4/1**[3]

4420 **4** *2* **Penny Pot Lane**[8] 7066 6-9-6 **66**..........................(p) SebastianWoods 2 59
(Richard Whitaker) *trckd ldng pair: hdwy over 2f out: rdn to take narrow ld over 1f out: hdd and drvn ent fnl f: sn wknd* **7/2**[2]

1104 **5** *6* **Hic Bibi**[8] 7066 4-9-6 **66**.. ThomasGreatrex 6 40
(David Loughnane) *chsd ldrs: rdn along 2f out: sn drvn and wknd over 1f out* **9/1**

6300 **6** *2* **Billy Dylan (IRE)**[19] 6699 4-9-12 **72**......................(p) ScottMcCullagh 4 40
(David O'Meara) *cl up: led wl over 2f out: sn rdn: drvn and hdd over 1f out: wknd* **25/1**

0600 **7** *nse* **Bugler Bob (IRE)**[71] 4781 3-9-7 **69**................................ DannyRedmond 7 37
(John Quinn) *a towards rr* **33/1**

0014 **8** *3 ½* **Echo Of Lightning**[13] 6937 9-9-6 **66**..............................(p) PaulaMuir 1 22
(Roger Fell) *led: hdd wl over 2f out: sn rdn and wknd wl over 1f out* **7/1**

1m 15.04s (-2.06) **Going Correction** -0.225s/f (Firm)
WFA 3 from 4yo+ 2lb 8 Ran SP% **114.6**
Speed ratings (Par 103): **104,103,100,98,90 87,87,82**
CSF £17.81 CT £56.15 TOTE £4.80: £1.50, £1.60, £1.70; EX 19.30 Trifecta £63.90.
Owner Nice Day Out Partnership **Bred** R Dollar, T Adams & G F Pemberton **Trained** Scarcroft, W Yorks

FOCUS
They went a good pace in the early stages of the contest, with the two that went on ending up well beaten.
T/Plt: £71.20 to a £1 stake. Pool: £48,817.25 - 500.32 winning units T/Qpdt: £19.90 to a £1 stake. Pool: £3,796.84 - 140.84 winning units **Joe Rowntree**

6546 SOUTHWELL (L-H)
Thursday, September 19

OFFICIAL GOING: Fibresand: standard
Wind: Light across Weather: Fine

7384 HALL-FAST INDUSTRIAL SUPPLIES LTD H'CAP 7f 14y(F)
5:15 (5:20) (Class 6) (0-60,60) 3-Y-O+ **£2,781** (£827; £413; £400; £400; £400) **Stalls** Low

Form RPR

0001 **1** **Break The Silence**[24] 6546 5-8-6 **51**...................(b) JonathanFisher(7) 12 60
(Scott Dixon) *s.i.s: hdwy 5f out: rdn to ld over 2f out: styd on* **9/2**[2]

0002 **2** *1 ¼* **Mister Freeze (IRE)**[24] 6546 5-8-13 **51**......................(vt) DavidProbert 7 57
(Patrick Chamings) *sn pushed along in rr: hdwy u.p over 1f out: chsd wnr ins fnl f: styd on same pce nr fin* **5/1**[3]

3050 **3** *1 ½* **Abie's Hollow**[20] 6679 3-9-5 **60**.................................... BenRobinson 11 61
(Tony Coyle) *hld up: nt clr run 5f out: pushed along 1/2-way: hdwy over 1f out: sn rdn and hung lft: no ex wl ins fnl f (jockey said gelding hung left-handed in straight)* **9/1**

6400 **4** *¾* **Searanger (USA)**[20] 6666 6-8-9 **47**...........................(vt[1]) CliffordLee 1 47
(Rebecca Menzies) *s.s and rel to r: bhd: r.o ins fnl f: nrst fin (jockey said gelding was slowly away)* **20/1**

5605 **5** *1 ¼* **Essenza (IRE)**[36] 6070 3-9-2 **60**.................................. SeanDavis(3) 4 56
(Richard Fahey) *chsd ldr: rdn and ev ch over 2f out: wknd wl ins fnl f* **12/1**

0005 **6** *½* **The Thorny Rose**[41] 5914 3-8-10 **51**.............................. AndrewMullen 9 45
(Michael Dods) *s.i.s: hdwy over 4f out: rdn 1/2-way: sn outpcd: rallied over 1f out: no ex ins fnl f* **20/1**

5100 **7** *3* **Bee Machine (IRE)**[24] 6546 4-8-9 **54**.....................(bt[1]) ZakWheatley(7) 14 42
(Declan Carroll) *chsd ldrs: rdn 1/2-way: wknd over 1f out* **16/1**

4/0 **8** *¾* **Caso Do Lago (IRE)**[24] 6547 8-8-10 **55**..................(p[1]) MarkCrehan(7) 8 41
(Robyn Brisland) *chsd ldrs: lost pl over 5f out: n.d after* **40/1**

1024 **9** *1 ¾* **Fly True**[24] 6546 6-9-8 **60**... NickyMackay 5 41
(Ivan Furtado) *s.i.s: hld up: pushed along 1/2-way: nvr on terms* **13/2**

3500 **10** *1* **Secret Glance**[28] 6363 7-8-8 **46** oh1................................ NicolaCurrie 13 24
(Adrian Wintle) *chsd ldrs: rdn 1/2-way: sn lost pl* **20/1**

4200 **11** *4* **Filbert Street**[24] 6546 4-8-7 **50**.............................(b[1]) TheodoreLadd(5) 2 18
(Michael Appleby) *sn led: hdd over 2f out: wknd over 1f out (jockey said gelding stopped quickly, vet reported gelding finished stiff)* **5/2**[1]

0060 **12** *9* **Dalness Express**[14] 6897 6-8-8 **46** oh1............................(bt) LukeMorris 6
(Archie Watson) *sn drvn along in rr: hdwy over 4f out: wknd over 2f out* **20/1**

260 **13** *1 ½* **Billiebrookedit (IRE)**[31] 6275 4-8-8 **46** oh1...................... JosephineGordon 10
(Kevin Frost) *in rr and pushed along over 5f out: bhd fr 1/2-way* **16/1**

1m 30.08s (-0.22) **Going Correction** -0.075s/f (Stan)
WFA 3 from 4yo+ 3lb 13 Ran SP% **127.7**
Speed ratings (Par 101): **98,96,94,94,92 92,88,87,85,84 80,69,68**
CSF £26.97 CT £205.60 TOTE £5.40: £1.90, £1.70, £4.30; EX 26.90 Trifecta £260.10.
Owner Winning Connections Racing **Bred** Richard Moses Bloodstock **Trained** Babworth, Notts

FOCUS
Extremely modest stuff. They went quickly enough here and that suited those ridden from off the pace. The winner got closer towards his better 2018 form.

7385 SKY SPORTS RACING ON SKY 415 H'CAP 1m 13y(F)
5:45 (5:53) (Class 6) (0-60,58) 3-Y-O+ **£2,781** (£827; £413; £400; £400; £400) **Stalls** Low

Form RPR

0005 **1** **Muqarred (USA)**[31] 6276 7-9-4 **57**.........................(b) GemmaTutty(3) 6 70
(Karen Tutty) *sn chsng ldrs: led over 2f out: rdn clr fr over 1f out* **7/1**[3]

1664 **2** *5* **Khaan**[23] 6560 4-8-11 **54**.. MarkCrehan(7) 14 56
(Michael Appleby) *s.i.s: hdwy on outer 1/2-way: chsd wnr over 1f out: sn rdn and hung lft: no ex fnl f* **2/1**[1]

3600 **3** *1 ¼* **Atalanta Queen**[24] 6546 4-8-6 **49**...........................(b) SeanKirrane(7) 9 48
(Robyn Brisland) *sn pushed along in rr: hdwy u.p and edgd rt over 1f out: nt rch ldrs* **12/1**

0013 **4** *5* **Gunnison**[12] 6983 3-8-11 **54**...(p) SeanDavis(3) 5 41
(Richard Fahey) *prom: drvn along over 4f out: swtchd rt over 3f out: wknd fnl f* **12/1**

00-6 **5** *2 ½* **Shouranour (IRE)**[23] 6582 9-9-8 **58**..................................(b) LukeMorris 13 39
(Peter Niven) *sn led: rdn and hdd over 2f out: wknd over 1f out* **28/1**

3500 **6** *1 ½* **Sooqaan**[64] 5051 8-9-0 **55**....................................(p) KieranSchofield(5) 11 33
(Antony Brittain) *sn chsng ldr: rdn and ev ch over 2f out: wknd over 1f out (jockey said gelding hung left-handed)* **20/1**

0000 **7** *1 ¼* **Dream Model (IRE)**[12] 6983 3-8-7 **47**...........................(p) AndrewMullen 7 22
(Mark Loughnane) *s.i.s: hld up: nvr on terms* **50/1**

0150 **8** *5* **Sumner Beach**[20] 6655 5-9-3 **53**...................................... BenRobinson 2 17
(Brian Ellison) *s.s: sn pushed along in rr: nvr nrr (jockey said gelding was slowly away and never travelling)* **10/1**

4212 **9** *6* **All Right**[21] 6643 3-9-4 **58**.. DavidProbert 10 8
(Henry Candy) *chsd ldrs: rdn over 3f out: wknd 2f out: eased fnl f (trainers rep said filly was unsuited by fibresand on this occasion)* **6/1**[2]

435 **10** *12* **Port Soif**[63] 4349 5-9-0 **50**..(p) KieranO'Neill 4
(Scott Dixon) *pushed along to chse ldrs: rdn 1/2-way: wknd over 2f out (trainer could offer no explanation for poor performance other than mare was never travelling, vet reported mare finished stiff)* **6/1**[2]

-052 **11** *5* **Willett**[28] 6361 3-8-5 **48**...(v) WilliamCox(3) 3
(Sarah Hollinshead) *hood removed late: s.i.s: sn pushed along and a in rr (jockey said gelding did not face the kickback on this occasion)* **33/1**

1m 43.52s (-0.18) **Going Correction** -0.075s/f (Stan)
WFA 3 from 4yo+ 4lb 11 Ran SP% **112.0**
Speed ratings (Par 101): **97,92,90,85,83 81,80,75,69,57 52**
CSF £17.27 CT £112.99 TOTE £7.70: £2.00, £1.40, £3.80; EX 24.90 Trifecta £178.50.

Owner Thoroughbred Homes Ltd **Bred** Shadwell Farm LLC **Trained** Osmotherley, N Yorks

FOCUS

A run-of-the-mill low-grade handicap. The winner was thrown in on early-season form.

7386 SKY SPORTS RACING ON VIRGIN 535 MEDIAN AUCTION MAIDEN STKS — 6f 16y(F)

6:15 (6:21) (Class 6) 2-Y-O — **£2,781** (£827; £413; £206) **Stalls** Low

Form	Pos	Dist	Horse / Trainer / Comment	Jockey	RPR
5323	1		**Jump The Gun (IRE)**[12] 6980 2-9-5 73 (Jamie Osborne) *chsd ldrs: led over 2f out: rdn clr and hung lft fnl f* **8/11**[1]	NicolaCurrie 9	79
64	2	7	**Qinwan**[15] 6852 2-9-5 0 (Andrew Balding) *racd keenly in 2nd tl led wl over 3f out: hdd over 2f out: no ex fnl over 1f out* **11/4**[2]	DavidProbert 4	58
454	3	hd	**Dancing Leopard (IRE)**[23] 6570 2-9-0 65 (v[1]) (K R Burke) *sn pushed along and prom: rdn over 3f out: edgd lft and no ex fr over 1f out* **15/2**	CliffordLee 6	52
	4	9	**Evora Knights** 2-9-5 0 (Michael Easterby) *s.i.s: sn prom: rdn over 2f out: wknd over 1f out* **20/1**	NathanEvans 3	30
	5	2 1/4	**Belle Rousse** 2-9-0 0 (Sir Mark Prescott Bt) *dwlt: outpcd* **18/1**	RyanTate 5	19+
0	6	3 1/4	**American Dreamer**[44] 5780 2-9-5 0 (Jamie Osborne) *led: hdd wl over 3f out: wknd over 1f out: bhd whn hmpd ins fnl f (jockey said colt hung right-handed in the straight)* **33/1**	CallumShepherd 2	14
	7	1/2	**Cliffs Of Freedom (IRE)**[19] 6740 2-9-5 0 (Kevin Thomas Coleman, Ire) *s.i.s: sn pushed along in rr: rdn and wkng whn hung lft fr over 2f out (trainer said, regarding poor performance, that the colt was unsuited by the fibresand surface on this occasion)* **9/2**[3]	KieranO'Neill 8	12

1m 16.57s (0.07) **Going Correction** -0.075s/f (Stan) — 7 Ran SP% **127.5**

Speed ratings (Par 93): **96,86,86,74,71 67,66**

CSF £3.68 TOTE £1.60: £1.10, £1.90; EX 3.70 Trifecta £12.10.

Owner Ballylinch Stud And Partner **Bred** Ballylinch Stud **Trained** Upper Lambourn, Berks

■ Capla Cubiste was withdrawn. Price at time of withdrawal 18-1. Rule 4\n\x\x does not apply

FOCUS

This was desperately weak and the odds-on favourite ran out a bloodless winner. The level of the form is a bit guessy.

7387 FOLLOW AT THE RACES ON TWITTER H'CAP — 4f 214y(F)

6:45 (6:48) (Class 4) (0-80,81) 3-Y-O+ — **£5,207** (£1,549; £774; £400; £400; £400) **Stalls** Centre

Form	Pos	Dist	Horse / Trainer / Comment	Jockey	RPR
6614	1		**Crosse Fire**[9] 7052 7-9-7 80 (b) (Scott Dixon) *led early: chsd ldrs and sn pushed along: hrd rdn fr over 1f out: r.o to ld wl ins fnl f* **8/1**	LukeMorris 10	87
0564	2	nse	**Miningggold**[61] 5181 6-8-10 69 (p) (Michael Dods) *hdwy 3f out: rdn and edgd lft over 1f out: ev ch wl ins fnl f: r.o* **14/1**	AndrewMullen 12	76
2050	3	1	**Honey Gg**[68] 4911 4-8-0 66 oh3 (Declan Carroll) *sn w ldr: led 1/2-way: rdn over 1f out: hdd wl ins fnl f* **12/1**	ZakWheatley(7) 8	69
1430	4	1 1/2	**Jack The Truth (IRE)**[26] 6455 5-9-2 80 (George Scott) *prom: outpcd over 3f out: rallied over 1f out: styd on* **9/2**[2]	SeamusCronin(5) 5	78+
5502	5	nk	**Wrenthorpe**[37] 6057 4-9-1 74 (Bryan Smart) *chsd ldrs: hung lft over 3f out: rdn over 1f out: styd on same pce ins fnl f* **9/2**[2]	GrahamLee 3	71
0560	6	hd	**Sandridge Lad (IRE)**[26] 6455 3-8-13 73 (John Ryan) *hld up: outpcd over 3f out: rdn and r.o ins fnl f: nt rch ldrs* **20/1**	StevieDonohoe 11	69
0031	7	1/2	**Requited (IRE)**[37] 6048 3-8-7 67 (Hughie Morrison) *chsd ldrs: outpcd over 3f out: rdn over 1f out: styd on* **4/1**[1]	CharlieBennett 2	61+
1650	8	nk	**Little Legs**[26] 6476 3-9-7 81 (Brian Ellison) *chsd ldrs: rdn over 1f out: no ex ins fnl f* **8/1**	BenRobinson 1	74
1300	9	1 3/4	**Timetodock**[36] 6070 3-8-10 70 (b) (Tim Easterby) *s.i.s and stmbld s: outpcd: nvr nrr (jockey said gelding stumbled when leaving stalls)* **14/1**	PhilDennis 4	57
004	10	1	**Warrior's Valley**[24] 6549 4-8-12 71 (tp) (David C Griffiths) *sn led: hdd 1/2-way: wknd fnl f* **15/2**[3]	JosephineGordon 9	54
3200	11	4 1/2	**Samovar**[8] 7077 4-9-0 73 (b) (Scott Dixon) *s.i.s: outpcd* **8/1**	KieranO'Neill 6	40

59.09s (-0.61) **Going Correction** -0.075s/f (Stan)

WFA 3 from 4yo+ 1lb — 11 Ran SP% **127.2**

Speed ratings (Par 105): **101,100,99,96,96 96,95,94,92,90 83**

CSF £123.65 CT £1368.38 TOTE £8.10: £2.40, £2.90, £5.00; EX 65.60 Trifecta £947.60.

Owner Paul J Dixon, K Brennan & Darren Lucas **Bred** Dr A Gillespie **Trained** Babworth, Notts

FOCUS

This was competitive and looks strong form form for the level on the surface. Crosse Fire finished best and made it 13 course wins. This is his best form since his early 2016 peak.

7388 SOUTHWELL GOLF CLUB MAIDEN STKS — 7f 14y(F)

7:15 (7:17) (Class 5) 2-Y-O — **£3,428** (£1,020; £509; £254) **Stalls** Low

Form	Pos	Dist	Horse / Trainer / Comment	Jockey	RPR
45	1		**Borsdane Wood**[12] 6970 2-9-5 0 (K R Burke) *led: hdd over 4f out: led again 1/2-way: rdn clr fnl f* **9/2**[2]	CliffordLee 8	80
5	2	4	**Tinnahalla (IRE)**[50] 5563 2-9-5 0 (Jamie Osborne) *plld hrd and prom: shkn up 1/2-way: rdn over 1f out: styd on same pce: wnt 2nd wl ins fnl f* **9/4**[1]	NicolaCurrie 7	70
44	3	1 3/4	**Creativity**[19] 6710 2-8-11 0 (Richard Fahey) *prom: rdn to chse wnr over 1f out tl no ex ins fnl f* **11/2**[3]	SeanDavis(3) 2	60
	4	4 1/2	**Stittenham Wood** 2-9-5 0 (Michael Easterby) *sn chsng wnr: led over 4f out: hdd 1/2-way: rdn: hung lft and lost 2nd over 1f out: wknd ins fnl f* **11/2**[3]	NathanEvans 10	53
5	5	6	**Ami Li Bert (IRE)**[13] 6934 2-8-12 0 (Michael Appleby) *s.i.s: bhd whn hung rt over 5f out: nvr nrr* **33/1**	MarkCrehan(7) 6	38+
	6	1/2	**Revolver (IRE)** 2-9-5 0 (Sir Mark Prescott Bt) *chsd ldrs: pushed along 1/2-way: wknd over 2f out* **9/1**	LukeMorris 9	36
	7	4 1/2	**Overwrite (IRE)** 2-9-5 0 (Mark Johnston) *s.i.s: hdwy 1/2-way: rdn and hung lft fr over 2f out: wknd over 1f out* **9/2**[2]	FrannyNorton 1	25
	8	1/2	**Anno Lucis (IRE)** 2-9-5 0 (Sir Mark Prescott Bt) *s.i.s: outpcd* **16/1**	RyanTate 3	23
34	9	2 1/2	**Oh Mary Oh Mary**[20] 6654 2-9-0 0 (Michael Easterby) *s.i.s: sn outpcd* **7/1**	GrahamLee 4	12
0	10	4 1/2	**El Jefe (IRE)**[13] 6943 2-9-5 0 (Brian Ellison) *s.s: outpcd (jockey said gelding ran green)* **50/1**	BenRobinson 5	

1m 29.76s (-0.54) **Going Correction** -0.075s/f (Stan) — 10 Ran SP% **131.2**

Speed ratings (Par 95): **100,95,93,88,81 80,75,75,72,67**

CSF £17.17 TOTE £5.60: £1.80, £1.60, £1.60; EX 13.10 Trifecta £76.20.

Owner David W Armstrong **Bred** Highfield Farm Llp **Trained** Middleham Moor, N Yorks

FOCUS

Very few figured in this likely ordinary maiden, though the winner is clearly on the upgrade.

7389 WINTER FLOODLIT RACING AT SOUTHWELL RACECOURSE H'CAP — 6f 16y(F)

7:45 (7:47) (Class 6) (0-60,58) 3-Y-O+ — **£2,781** (£827; £413; £400; £400; £400) **Stalls** Low

Form	Pos	Dist	Horse / Trainer / Comment	Jockey	RPR
405	1		**Queen Of Kalahari**[24] 6546 4-8-12 48 (p) (Les Eyre) *chsd ldrs: led over 4f out: rdn clr fnl f: eased nr fin* **11/2**[3]	LewisEdmunds 12	65+
6504	2	5	**Catapult**[26] 6441 4-8-9 45 (p) (Shaun Keightley) *w ldrs: led 5f out to over 4f out: chsd wnr: rdn over 1f out: no ex fnl f* **3/1**[1]	JosephineGordon 11	47
0440	3	1/2	**Tease Maid**[48] 5620 3-9-6 58 (John Quinn) *chsd ldrs: rdn over 2f out: no ex fnl f* **7/1**	PaulMulrennan 6	59
3045	4	nk	**Space War**[20] 6680 12-9-5 55 (t) (Michael Easterby) *s.i.s: hdwy over 3f out: rdn over 1f out: styd on* **4/1**[2]	NathanEvans 10	55
060	5	5	**Reshaan (IRE)**[14] 6897 4-8-9 45 (p) (Alexandra Dunn) *s.i.s: hdwy on outer over 3f out: rdn over 2f out: wknd fnl f* **8/1**	FrannyNorton 14	30
140	6	2	**Billyoakes (IRE)**[50] 5559 7-9-6 56 (p) (Ollie Pears) *sn pushed along in rr: nvr nrr* **14/1**	BenRobinson 8	35
0126	7	1	**Grimsdyke**[26] 6462 3-9-0 52 (Tim Easterby) *s.i.s and stmbld s: pushed along over 4f out: nvr on terms (jockey said gelding stumbled leaving stalls)* **4/1**[2]	DuranFentiman 7	28
2005	8	1 1/4	**Pearl Noir**[9] 7052 9-8-9 45 (b) (Scott Dixon) *prom: drvn along over 3f out: wknd over 2f out* **20/1**	LukeMorris 3	17
0000	9	4 1/2	**Mitchum**[20] 6680 10-8-2 45 (Ron Barr) *prom: lost pl 5f out: n.d after* **33/1**	AledBeech(7) 2	3
0000	10	hd	**Bevsboy (IRE)**[37] 6036 5-8-9 45 (p[1]) (Lynn Siddall) *chsd ldrs: lost pl after 1f: n.d after* **40/1**	CamHardie 4	3
50/0	11	15	**Mysterious Look**[34] 6168 6-9-2 55 (Sarah Hollinshead) *led 1f: chsd ldrs: rdn and wknd over 2f out (jockey said mare stopped quickly)* **50/1**	WilliamCox(3) 9	

1m 15.01s (-1.49) **Going Correction** -0.075s/f (Stan)

WFA 3 from 4yo+ 2lb — 11 Ran SP% **122.8**

Speed ratings (Par 101): **106,99,98,98,91 88,87,85,79,79 59**

CSF £21.84 CT £109.26 TOTE £7.50: £2.30, £1.50, £2.20; EX 21.90 Trifecta £104.50.

Owner Les Eyre Racing Partnership I **Bred** Minster Stud **Trained** Catwick, N Yorks

■ Mad Endeavour was withdrawn. Price at time of withdrawal 14-1. Rule 4 applies to all bets - deduction 5p in the pound.

FOCUS

This low-grade handicap was taken apart from the front by the speedy Queen Of Kalahari, who matched her 2018 level.

7390 8TH NOVEMBER 30TH ANNIVERSARY DINNER H'CAP — 1m 6f 21y(F)

8:15 (8:16) (Class 6) (0-55,54) 3-Y-O+ — **£2,781** (£827; £413; £400; £400; £400) **Stalls** Low

Form	Pos	Dist	Horse / Trainer / Comment	Jockey	RPR
6035	1		**Land Of Winter (FR)**[41] 5915 3-8-11 51 (Rae Guest) *hld up: hdwy on outer over 6f out: led on bit over 2f out: shkn up and wnt readily clr fr over 1f out* **7/2**[2]	PaulMulrennan 6	64+
005	2	11	**Postie**[91] 4022 3-8-9 49 (James Eustace) *led 1f: chsd ldrs: led over 3f out: hdd over 2f out: no ex fr over 1f out* **12/1**	RyanTate 5	48
0402	3	3 1/2	**Thornton Le Clay**[24] 6552 3-8-9 49 (Michael Easterby) *s.i.s and stmbld s: hdwy 10f out: rdn and ev ch over 2f out: no ex fr over 1f out* **11/4**[1]	NathanEvans 13	42
5442	4	15	**Volcanique (IRE)**[15] 6864 3-8-6 46 (b) (Sir Mark Prescott Bt) *drvn along almost thrght: wnt prom 12f out: led over 4f out: hdd over 3f out: wknd 2f out* **5/1**[3]	LukeMorris 9	20
0504	5	25	**Doune Castle**[15] 6864 3-8-12 52 (v) (Andrew Balding) *hld up: rdn and wknd over 4f out* **7/2**[2]	DavidProbert 12	
0	6	1 1/2	**Foresee (GER)**[35] 6104 6-9-8 54 (Tony Carroll) *prom over 9f (jockey said gelding stopped quickly)* **8/1**	GeorgeDowning 8	
0350	7	3	**Bird To Love**[16] 6843 5-8-9 48 (Mark Usher) *sn prom: chsd ldr 10f out tl led over 7f out: hdd over 4f out: wknd over 3f out* **14/1**	EllieMacKenzie(7) 11	
032-	8	1 3/4	**Sincerely Resdev**[264] 9750 4-9-2 48 (p) (Philip Kirby) *chsd ldrs: lost pl 6f out: wknd over 4f out* **12/1**	AndrewElliott 2	
0605	9	1/2	**Misty Breese (IRE)**[10] 7034 4-8-10 45 (Sarah Hollinshead) *hld up: rdn and wknd over 4f out* **50/1**	NoelGarbutt(3) 7	
5523	10	17	**Guaracha**[37] 6046 8-8-13 45 (v) (Alexandra Dunn) *prom: lost pl after 1f: in rr and rdn 8f out: sn swtchd rt: wknd over 6f out (jockey said gelding did not face kickback on this occasion)* **20/1**	FrannyNorton 4	
300-	11	56	**Red Douglas**[388] 6632 5-8-13 45 (p) (Scott Dixon) *s.i.s: rcvrd to ld after 1f: hdd over 7f out: rdn and wknd over 5f out (vet reported gelding bled from nose)* **33/1**	KieranO'Neill 10	

3m 6.38s (-1.92) **Going Correction** -0.075s/f (Stan)

WFA 3 from 4yo+ 8lb — 11 Ran SP% **130.6**

Speed ratings (Par 101): **102,95,93,85,70 70,68,67,67,57 25**

CSF £50.04 CT £140.28 TOTE £5.10: £1.50, £6.10, £1.30; EX 69.80 Trifecta £322.70.

Owner Paul Smith & Rae Guest **Bred** Claydons Bloodstock Ltd **Trained** Newmarket, Suffolk

FOCUS

An impressive winner in an otherwise poor staying handicap and it has to rate a pb from him. They came home at long intervals.

T/Plt: £79.20 to a £1 stake. Pool: £58,991.12 - 543.05 winning units T/Qpdt: £14.40 to a £1 stake. Pool: £7,792.37 - 400.41 winning units **Colin Roberts**

[7345] YARMOUTH (L-H)

Thursday, September 19

OFFICIAL GOING: Good to firm (watered; 7.1)

Wind: virtually nil Weather: Warm and sunny

7391 KEN LINDSAY MEMORIAL NURSERY H'CAP — 6f 3y

1:50 (1:53) (Class 4) (0-80,82) 2-Y-O

£4,347 (£1,301; £650; £325; £300; £300) **Stalls** Centre

Form RPR

5451 1 **Gobi Sunset**[89] 4098 2-9-7 **80** .... OisinMurphy 2 83
(Mark Johnston) *mde all: shkn up w short ld 2f out: sn rdn and responded wl to press 1f out: kpt on wl fnl f* **5/2**[1]

3462 2 1 **Dark Silver (IRE)**[34] 6184 2-9-0 **73** .... AndreaAtzeni 3 73
(Ed Walker) *trckd wnr: pushed along to chse wnr 2f out: drvn and kpt on wl ins fnl f: a hld by wnr* **9/2**[2]

554 3 1 1/4 **Kassab**[17] 6807 2-9-0 **73** .... (b[1]) JamesDoyle 8 69
(Peter Chapple-Hyam) *hld up: hdwy into midfield over 2f out: rdn to chse ldrs over 1f out: kpt on fnl f* **7/1**

6033 4 hd **Little Brown Trout**[25] 6515 2-8-7 **73** .... MarcoGhiani(7) 7 69
(William Stone) *prom and racd freely: rdn along and ev ch over 1f out: kpt on one pce fnl f* **25/1**

5516 5 nk **Punchbowl Flyer (IRE)**[12] 6963 2-9-1 **74** .... (p[1]) CharlesBishop 9 69
(Eve Johnson Houghton) *in tch in midfield: rdn and no imp over 2f out: drvn and hung lft 1f out: kpt on (jockey said colt hung left)* **6/1**[3]

5360 6 2 **Outtake**[28] 6372 2-8-7 **66** .... HarryBentley 4 55
(Richard Hannon) *midfield: rdn along and no prog over 2f out: one pce ins fnl f* **40/1**

042 7 1/2 **Order Of St John**[44] 5780 2-8-10 **72** .... CierenFallon(3) 10 59
(John Ryan) *midfield: rdn and no imp over 2f out: kpt gng at same pce fnl f* **7/1**

0215 8 1 3/4 **Modern British Art (IRE)**[8] 7072 2-9-9 **82** .... JamieSpencer 5 64
(Michael Bell) *hld up: effrt to cl over 2f out: rdn and no imp over 1f out: n.d (jockey said colt hung left throughout)* **13/2**

3150 9 1 3/4 **Fantom Force (IRE)**[27] 6416 2-9-3 **76** .... SeanLevey 6 53
(Richard Hannon) *trckd ldr: rdn and outpcd 2f out: wknd fnl f* **22/1**

6051 10 6 **Port Winston (IRE)**[20] 6667 2-9-2 **75** .... (h) JimCrowley 1 34
(Alan King) *hld up: rdn along and fnd little 2f out: wknd fnl f* **16/1**

1m 11.41s (-1.19) **Going Correction** -0.175s/f (Firm) **10** Ran SP% **115.9**
Speed ratings (Par 97): **100,98,97,96,96 93,93,90,88,80**
CSF £13.03 CT £70.65 TOTE £2.80: £1.30, £1.70, £2.00; EX 13.50 Trifecta £89.80.
Owner N Browne,I Boyce, S Frosell & S Richards **Bred** Lordship Stud **Trained** Middleham Moor, N Yorks

FOCUS
A fair nursery. The favourite made all centrally in convincing fashion. His Ayr form could be rated this high.

7392 BRITISH STALLION STUDS EBF NOVICE STKS (PLUS 10 RACE) — 1m 3y

2:20 (2:20) (Class 4) 2-Y-O **£4,851** (£1,443; £721; £360) **Stalls** Centre

Form RPR

23 1 **Ursa Minor (IRE)**[54] 5439 2-9-5 0 .... RobertHavlin 1 80
(John Gosden) *mde all and travelled wl: shkn up over 1f out: rdn ins fnl f and asserted wl fnl stages* **11/10**[1]

4 2 1 1/4 **Hlaitan**[12] 6948 2-9-5 0 .... JamesDoyle 6 77
(Hugo Palmer) *midfield: rdn and no immediate imp 2f out: drvn to chse wnr 1f out: kpt on* **10/1**

2 3 nk **Live Your Dream (IRE)**[19] 6708 2-9-5 0 .... OisinMurphy 2 76
(Saeed bin Suroor) *trckd wnr: pushed along 2f out: rdn and ev ch 1f out: kpt on* **5/2**[2]

4 1 1/2 **Carlos Felix (IRE)** 2-9-5 0 .... JamieSpencer 3 73
(David Simcock) *hld up: smooth prog on to heels of ldrs 2f out: rdn over 1f out: one pce fnl f* **6/1**[3]

5 5 1 **Robert Walpole**[27] 6409 2-9-5 0 .... HarryBentley 9 71
(George Scott) *hld up: rdn along and one pce over 1f out: kpt on fnl f* **12/1**

6 6 nse **Count Of Amazonia (IRE)**[13] 6912 2-9-5 0 .... AndreaAtzeni 7 71
(Richard Hannon) *trckd wnr: rdn along and outpcd 2f out: drvn and briefly hung lft ins fnl f: one pce after* **20/1**

7 39 **Valletta Sunset** 2-9-5 0 .... ShelleyBirkett 4
(Julia Feilden) *racd towards rr: lost grnd and detached 1/2-way: sn bhd* **100/1**

1m 37.68s (-0.52) **Going Correction** -0.175s/f (Firm) **7** Ran SP% **113.0**
Speed ratings (Par 97): **95,93,93,91,90 90,51**
CSF £13.35 TOTE £1.90: £1.20, £3.40; EX 9.90 Trifecta £28.50.
Owner Godolphin **Bred** Airlie Stud **Trained** Newmarket, Suffolk

FOCUS
A fair juvenile novice contest, won by subsequent 1m2f Listed winner Gabr in 2017. The favourite picked up well off his own modest gallop in the final furlong. The form makes sense rated around the winner and third.

7393 BRITISH EBF FILLIES' NOVICE STKS (PLUS 10 RACE) — 6f 3y

2:50 (2:51) (Class 4) 2-Y-O **£4,463** (£1,328; £663; £331) **Stalls** Centre

Form RPR

1 **Jamaheery (IRE)** 2-9-0 0 .... JimCrowley 12 84+
(Richard Hannon) *midfield: smooth hdwy to chal over 1f out: shkn up to ld and qckly asserted over 1f out: pushed out fnl f* **8/1**

3 2 2 3/4 **Esprit Rose (IRE)**[13] 6919 2-9-0 0 .... AndreaAtzeni 10 75
(Roger Varian) *midfield: pushed along to chse wnr over 1f out: sn rdn and kpt on wl fnl f* **13/8**[1]

26 3 shd **Thread Of Silver**[27] 6407 2-9-0 0 .... (h) WilliamBuick 6 75
(Charlie Appleby) *led: rdn along and hdd by wnr over 1f out: kpt on wl fnl f: lost 2nd fnl strides* **7/2**[2]

5 4 1 1/2 **Vintage Polly (IRE)**[19] 6704 2-9-0 0 .... JamesDoyle 7 71
(Hugo Palmer) *racd in midfield: pushed along and outpcd 2f out: rdn and kpt on one pce ins fnl f* **16/1**

33 5 1/2 **Call Me Katie (IRE)**[16] 6831 2-9-0 0 .... RobertHavlin 5 69
(John Gosden) *settled in midfield: rdn along and no imp 2f out: kpt on one pce fnl f* **6/1**

30 6 1 **Pretty In Grey**[13] 6919 2-9-0 0 .... ShaneKelly 11 66+
(Marco Botti) *hld up: hdwy into midfield u.p 2f out: sn rdn and kpt on wl clsng stages but n.d* **22/1**

7 nk **Purple Power** 2-9-0 0 .... PatCosgrave 8 65
(Mick Quinn) *hld up and racd freely: hdwy into midfield 3f out: rdn and no imp over 1f out: kpt on one pce* **66/1**

0 8 1 1/2 **Upstage (IRE)**[16] 6846 2-8-9 0 .... DylanHogan(5) 9 61
(David Simcock) *trckd ldr: rdn along and lost pl 2f out: wknd 1f out* **80/1**

0 9 1 1/4 **Queen Of Silca**[13] 6911 2-9-0 0 .... OisinMurphy 1 57
(Mick Channon) *trckd ldr: rdn along and lost pl over 1f out: wknd fnl f* **11/2**[3]

10 3/4 **Amicia** 2-9-0 0 .... DanielMuscutt 2 55
(Marco Botti) *hld up: rdn and rn green over 2f out: hung lft u.p over 1f out: nvr on terms* **40/1**

11 1/2 **Greek Oasis** 2-9-0 0 .... JackMitchell 4 53
(Chris Wall) *hld up: rdn and no imp 2f out: nvr on terms* **50/1**

05 12 14 **Sea Willow**[34] 6146 2-9-0 0 .... DaneO'Neill 3 11
(Henry Spiller) *in rr of midfield: rdn and fnd little 2f out: eased fnl f* **100/1**

1m 10.94s (-1.66) **Going Correction** -0.175s/f (Firm) **12** Ran SP% **119.4**
Speed ratings (Par 94): **104,100,100,98,97 96,95,93,92,91 90,71**
CSF £21.03 TOTE £9.20: £3.00, £1.10, £1.50; EX 29.60 Trifecta £135.40.
Owner Hamdan Al Maktoum **Bred** Rabbah Bloodstock Limited **Trained** East Everleigh, Wilts

FOCUS
A fairly decent juvenile fillies' novice, won on debut in 2018 by subsequent Grade 1 Del Mar Oaks runner-up and Sandown Listed winner Hidden Message. Another debutante impressed on this occasion. The level of the form will take time to settle.

7394 DAN HAGUE - BETTING ON THE RAILS H'CAP — 1m 6f 17y

3:20 (3:23) (Class 2) (0-100,97) 3-Y-O£12,602 (£3,772; £1,886; £944; £470) **Stalls** High

Form RPR

3046 1 **Summer Moon**[56] 5347 3-9-0 **91** .... RyanMoore 1 100
(Mark Johnston) *mde all: pushed along 3f out: rdn and strly pressed over 1f out: drvn and kpt on strly fnl f (trainer could offer no explanation for colt's improved performance)* **9/4**[2]

0512 2 1 1/4 **Protected Guest**[13] 6917 4-10-0 **97** .... TomQueally 5 104
(George Margarson) *hld up: smooth hdwy on to heels of ldrs 2f out: wnt 2nd on bit over 1f out: rdn and fnd little fnl f* **7/1**[3]

0-46 3 1 1/4 **Eynhallow**[27] 6420 5-9-12 **95** .... WilliamBuick 6 100
(Charlie Appleby) *trckd wnr: rdn along to chse wnr over 1f out: outpcd 1f out: kpt on* **15/8**[1]

5321 4 shd **Past Master**[26] 6448 6-8-13 **82** .... DaneO'Neill 4 87
(Henry Candy) *midfield: rdn and no imp over 2f out: drvn and kpt on one pce fnl f* **7/1**[3]

4060 5 1 1/4 **Hermoso Mundo (SAF)**[27] 6420 7-9-9 **92** .... OisinMurphy 3 95
(Hughie Morrison) *prom and racd keenly at times: rdn and lost pl 2f out: plugged on fnl f* **12/1**

1153 6 nk **Flaming Marvel (IRE)**[12] 6981 5-9-7 **90** .... TomMarquand 8 93
(James Fanshawe) *hld up in last: drvn along in rr over 2f out: r.o one pce clsng stages* **14/1**

430 7 1 1/2 **Breath Caught**[13] 6917 4-9-7 **90** .... JamieSpencer 7 91
(David Simcock) *hld up: hdwy on bit over 3f out: rdn and no further imp 2f out: wknd fnl f* **8/1**

000 8 24 **Great Hall**[33] 6224 9-8-9 **78** oh1 .... MartinDwyer 2 45
(Mick Quinn) *midfield: rdn and lost pl 3f out: sn bhd* **50/1**

3m 1.63s (-3.07) **Going Correction** -0.175s/f (Firm)
WFA 3 from 4yo+ 8lb **8** Ran SP% **118.0**
Speed ratings (Par 109): **101,100,99,99,98 98,97,84**
CSF £19.27 CT £34.99 TOTE £3.20: £1.40, £2.10, £1.10; EX 18.00 Trifecta £46.80.
Owner The Originals **Bred** Miss K Rausing **Trained** Middleham Moor, N Yorks

FOCUS
The feature contest was a good staying handicap. There was a gamble on the second-favourite, a 3yo in a good race for that age-group, and he gamely made full use of his 8lb weight-for-age allowance from the front.

7395 BRITISH EBF PREMIER FILLIES' H'CAP — 1m 3f 104y

3:50 (3:50) (Class 4) (0-80,81) 3-Y-O+

£8,927 (£2,656; £1,327; £663; £300; £300) **Stalls** Low

Form RPR

4321 1 **Oh It's Saucepot**[33] 6224 5-9-12 **80** .... JackMitchell 2 91
(Chris Wall) *prom: clsd gng wl over 2f out: shkn up to ld over 1f out: qcknd clr 1f out: pushed out* **15/8**[1]

3301 2 4 **Miss Latin (IRE)**[33] 6200 4-9-4 **77** .... DylanHogan(5) 1 81
(David Simcock) *hld up in last pair: hdwy u.p over 2f out: rdn and wnt 2nd over 1f out: kpt on fnl f: no ch w wnr* **20/1**

0-63 3 shd **Honfleur (IRE)**[35] 6114 3-8-10 **70** .... RyanMoore 4 74
(Sir Michael Stoute) *j. awkwardly: sn rcvrd to ld for 3f then trckd ldr tl 3f out: rdn and outpcd over 2f out: rallied wl u.p fnl f* **5/1**[2]

5312 4 1 1/4 **Lightening Dance**[25] 6511 5-9-9 **77** .... (b) JimCrowley 6 79
(Amanda Perrett) *hld up: hdwy u.p 2f out: rdn and styd on one pce fnl f* **7/1**[3]

4305 5 1 3/4 **Baba Ghanouj (IRE)**[19] 6729 3-9-7 **81** .... OisinMurphy 5 80
(Ed Walker) *hld up: pushed along and hdwy 2f out: sn rdn and no further imp fr 1f out* **5/1**[2]

2341 6 3 1/2 **Potters Lady Jane**[30] 6323 7-9-4 **72** .... (p) JamieSpencer 3 65
(Lucy Wadham) *midfield: rdn along and outpcd 2f out: one pce fnl f (vet said mare lost right hind shoe)* **7/1**[3]

3462 7 14 **Quicksand (IRE)**[25] 6509 4-9-10 **78** .... JamesDoyle 7 48
(Hughie Morrison) *prom on outer then led after 3f: rdn along and hdd by wnr wl over 1f out: wknd fnl f (jockey said filly stopped quickly)* **5/1**[2]

2m 23.57s (-4.23) **Going Correction** -0.175s/f (Firm)
WFA 3 from 4yo+ 6lb **7** Ran SP% **114.5**
Speed ratings (Par 102): **108,105,105,104,102 100,90**
CSF £42.42 TOTE £2.70: £1.60, £10.40; EX 34.70 Trifecta £167.90.
Owner The Eight Of Diamonds **Bred** Mrs C J Walker **Trained** Newmarket, Suffolk

FOCUS
A fair middle-distance fillies' handicap. The clear favourite won decisively in a good comparative time.

7396 YOUNGS CITYSCAPE H'CAP — 1m 2f 23y

4:20 (4:20) (Class 3) (0-90,91) 3-Y-O-£7,876 (£2,357; £1,178; £590; £293) **Stalls** Low

Form RPR

2133 1 **Harrovian**[25] 6506 3-9-6 **91** .... (b[1]) RobertHavlin 1 102
(John Gosden) *settled wl in midfield: clsd gng best whn short of room over 1f: rdn through gap on rail to ld ins fnl f: qcknd up wl* **2/1**[1]

0064 2 1 1/4 **Pactolus (IRE)**[24] 6537 8-8-12 **78** .... (t) OisinMurphy 3 84
(Stuart Williams) *midfield: shkn up to cl on outer 2f out: rdn and ev ch 1f out: nt pce of wnr fnl 100yds* **10/1**[3]

5115 3 1 1/4 **The Corporal (IRE)**[20] 6671 3-8-10 **81** .... WilliamBuick 2 85
(Chris Wall) *led: rdn and strly pressed over 1f out drifted off rail and hdd by wnr ins fnl f: no ex* **9/4**[2]

321 **4** 2 1/4 **Cardano (USA)**[26] 6454 3-9-3 **88**...(p) RyanMoore 4 86
(Ian Williams) *trckd ldr tl over 2f out: rdn and outpcd 2f out: kpt on one pce fnl f* **9/4**[2]

1300 **5** 2 **El Ghazwani (IRE)**[78] 4504 4-9-10 **90**...(t) JimCrowley 6 85
(Hugo Palmer) *hld up: rdn and no imp on outer 2f out: one pce fnl f* **10/1**[3]

2m 7.05s (-1.75) **Going Correction** -0.175s/f (Firm) **5** Ran SP% **113.1**
WFA 3 from 4yo+ 5lb
Speed ratings (Par 107): **100,99,98,96,94**
CSF £20.89 TOTE £2.70: £1.50, £4.70; EX 17.60 Trifecta £64.70.
Owner HH Sheikh Zayed bin Mohammed Racing **Bred** Miss K Rausing **Trained** Newmarket, Suffolk

FOCUS
A decent handicap. They went a modest gallop and the favourite was lucky that the third-horse home moved slightly off the far rail for the sprint for home.

7397 INTU CHAPELFIELD SHOPPING CENTRE H'CAP 6f 3y
4:50 (4:50) (Class 3) (0-95,95) 3-Y-O+ **£7,876** (£2,357; £1,178; £590; £293) **Stalls** Centre

Form RPR

0632 **1** **Tinto**[19] 6724 3-8-13 **91**... MarcoGhiani(7) 6 101+
(Amanda Perrett) *hld up: smooth hdwy on outer over 1f out: rdn to ld ins fnl f: r.o wl* **9/2**[2]

5030 **2** 1 3/4 **Swiss Knight**[26] 6465 4-8-9 **78**...(t[1]) GeorgeWood 3 82
(Stuart Williams) *prom: hdwy to cl over 1f out: rdn and outpcd by wnr ins fnl f: no ex* **14/1**

1403 **3** nk **Kinks**[11] 7002 3-9-8 **93**... AndreaAtzeni 2 96
(Mick Channon) *midfield: hdwy u.p over 1f out: rdn and ev ch 1f out: unable to match wnr clsng stages* **5/1**[3]

0111 **4** 3/4 **Yimou (IRE)**[26] 6465 4-9-3 **86**... MartinDwyer 1 87
(Dean Ivory) *led: rdn along and reduced ld over 1f out: drvn and hdd ins fnl f: no ex* **5/4**[1]

3002 **5** 3/4 **Ice Age (IRE)**[16] 6847 6-9-5 **95**... GeorgiaDobie(7) 5 93
(Eve Johnson Houghton) *chsd ldr tl 2f out: rdn and outpcd over 1f out: wknd fnl f* **13/2**

6055 **6** 1 3/4 **Polybius**[40] 5942 8-9-2 **85**... JamieSpencer 4 81
(David Simcock) *restrained in last: swtchd lft and rdn to chal over 1f out: unable to sustain effrt and wknd fnl f* **7/1**

1m 10.2s (-2.40) **Going Correction** -0.175s/f (Firm) **6** Ran SP% **111.8**
WFA 3 from 4yo+ 2lb
Speed ratings (Par 107): **109,106,106,105,104 101**
CSF £56.97 TOTE £5.40: £2.00, £6.00; EX 49.00 Trifecta £223.30.
Owner D James, S Jenkins & M Quigley **Bred** Llety Farms **Trained** Pulborough, W Sussex

FOCUS
A decent sprint handicap. The second-favourite swooped to conquer towards the near side in the second best comparative time on the day.
T/Plt: £18.30 to a £1 stake. Pool: £67,123.70 - 2665.23 winning units T/Qpdt: £10.10 to a £1 stake. Pool: £6,964.43 - 508.57 winning units **Mark Grantham**

7361 AYR (L-H)
Friday, September 20

OFFICIAL GOING: Good (good to soft in places; 7.5)
Wind: Breezy, half behind in sprints and in over 3f of home straight in races on the round course Weather: Sunny, hot

7398 AL MAKTOUM COLLEGE, DUNDEE/BRITISH STALLION STUDS EBF NOVICE STKS (PLUS 10 RACE) 7f 50y
1:40 (1:41) (Class 4) 2-Y-O **£6,727** (£2,002; £1,000; £500) **Stalls** High

Form RPR

2 **1** **Gravity Force**[14] 6943 2-9-2 0... CliffordLee 8 78
(K R Burke) *prom on outside: rdn and edgd rt over 2f out: edgd lft and hdwy to ld over 1f out: drvn and kpt on wl fnl f* **8/1**

2 **2** 1/2 **El Naseri (IRE)**[13] 6971 2-9-2 0... PaulMulrennan 1 77
(Michael Dods) *t.k.h: prom: nt clr run over 2f out: effrt over 1f out: pressed wnr ins fnl f: r.o* **9/2**[2]

1 **3** nse **Melody King (IRE)**[13] 6970 2-9-8 0... JasonHart 2 83+
(John Quinn) *t.k.h: hld up: effrt on outside whn blkd over 1f out: kpt on wl fnl f: nrst fin* **13/2**

4 1/2 **Celestial Bliss** 2-9-2 0... KevinStott 7 76+
(Kevin Ryan) *dwlt: hld up bhd ldng gp: effrt and pushed along over 1f out: kpt on ins fnl f* **20/1**

1 **5** 1/2 **Duesenberg (IRE)**[15] 6891 2-9-5 0... SeanDavis(3) 3 80
(Richard Fahey) *led: rdn and hdd over 1f out: pressed wnr to ins fnl f: no ex* **6/1**[3]

5 **6** 3/4 **Cassy O (IRE)**[30] 6336 2-9-2 0... DavidAllan 9 73
(Tim Easterby) *cl up on outside: effrt and ev ch over 1f out: one pce whn n.m.r last 100yds* **50/1**

7 1 1/2 **Got The T Shirt** 2-9-2 0... PJMcDonald 10 69
(Keith Dalgleish) *s.i.s: hld up: rdn over 2f out: hdwy fnl f: nrst fin* **28/1**

6 **8** 2 1/2 **Gift Of Kings**[28] 6424 2-9-2 0... DanielTudhope 4 63+
(Kevin Ryan) *in tch: rdn over 2f out: edgd rt over 1f out: sn wknd* **6/4**[1]

052 **9** 2 3/4 **Get Boosting**[14] 6934 2-9-2 **76**... ShaneGray 6 56
(Keith Dalgleish) *t.k.h: pressed ldr: rdn and ev ch over 1f out: wknd fnl f* **20/1**

10 1/2 **Double D's** 2-9-2 0... CallumRodriguez 5 54
(Michael Dods) *s.i.s: t.k.h in rr: pushed along and outpcd 3f out: nvr on terms* **20/1**

1m 31.97s (-0.53) **Going Correction** -0.25s/f (Firm) **10** Ran SP% **116.6**
Speed ratings (Par 97): **93,92,92,91,91 90,88,85,82,82**
CSF £40.41 TOTE £9.20: £2.00, £1.50, £2.10; EX 37.60 Trifecta £189.50.
Owner Bearstone Stud Limited **Bred** Bearstone Stud **Trained** Middleham Moor, N Yorks

FOCUS
It was dry overnight but the going was described the same as the previous day, being good, good to soft in places (GoingStick 7.5). After riding in the opener Kevin Stott said: "It's good ground," Jason Hart said: "It's the same as yesterday" and Paul Mulrennan said: "It's a bit dead." The rail on the home bend was out 8yds. Add 12yds. They finished in a bit of a heap in this novice, and it's hard to rate the form that highly.

7399 SHADWELL STALLIONS NURSERY H'CAP 6f
2:10 (2:14) (Class 2) 2-Y-O **£15,562** (£4,660; £2,330; £1,165; £582; £292) **Stalls** Centre

Form RPR

3144 **1** **Aberama Gold**[48] 5668 2-8-8 **76**... ShaneGray 8 80
(Keith Dalgleish) *in tch in main centre gp: effrt and rdn over 1f out: hdwy to ld ins fnl f: kpt on wl towards fin* **20/1**

0413 **2** 1/2 **What A Business (IRE)**[21] 6653 2-7-13 **72**... PaulaMuir(5) 7 75
(Roger Fell) *cl up in main centre gp: led 2f out: drvn and hdd ins fnl f: kpt on: hld nr fin* **12/1**

2220 **3** nk **Asmund (IRE)**[49] 5612 2-8-10 **78**... BenCurtis 2 80
(K R Burke) *cl up in far side quartet: rdn and led that gp over 1f out: kpt on fnl f: hld towards fin* **8/1**[3]

1160 **4** 1 **Keep Busy (IRE)**[8] 7117 2-8-10 **78**... JasonHart 9 77
(John Quinn) *prom: effrt and rdn 2f out: kpt on ins fnl f* **16/1**

4421 **5** 2 **Dutch Decoy**[21] 6653 2-8-13 **81**...(v[1]) PaulHanagan 3 74
(Richard Fahey) *hld up in tch in far side quartet: effrt and rdn 2f out: kpt on fnl f: no imp* **8/1**[3]

4155 **6** 2 1/2 **One Bite (IRE)**[25] 6548 2-8-7 **75**... JamesSullivan 6 60
(Keith Dalgleish) *dwlt: bhd in main centre gp: rdn and hdwy over 1f out: kpt on fnl f: no imp* **40/1**

1014 **7** 3/4 **Owney Madden**[9] 7072 2-9-7 **89**... PaulMulrennan 14 72
(Martyn Meade) *plld hrd to post: dwlt: t.k.h: hld up in midfield in main centre gp: rdn and outpcd 2f out: r.o ins fnl f: nt gng pce to chal (jockey said colt ran too free)* **13/2**[2]

1352 **8** nk **Tom Tulliver**[26] 6498 2-8-13 **81**... DanielTudhope 11 63
(Declan Carroll) *cl up in main centre gp: ev ch over 2f out to wl over 1f out: outpcd fnl f* **14/1**

0320 **9** nk **Barbarella (IRE)**[29] 6375 2-8-8 **76**... SamJames 12 57
(Kevin Ryan) *led main centre gp to 2f out: drvn and outpcd fnl f* **18/1**

226 **10** 3/4 **Alix James**[22] 6622 2-8-10 **78**... GrahamLee 13 57
(Iain Jardine) *t.k.h: in tch in main centre gp: rdn over 2f out: outpcd over 1f out* **12/1**

2142 **11** hd **One Hart (IRE)**[37] 6073 2-9-1 **83**... JoeFanning 1 61
(Mark Johnston) *led far side quartet to over 1f out: sn rdn and wknd* **9/1**

0500 **12** nse **Hurstwood**[9] 7072 2-9-4 **86**...(b[1]) DavidAllan 16 64
(Tim Easterby) *racd alone stands' rail: cl up tl rdn and wknd over 1f out* **16/1**

210 **13** 1/2 **Byline**[28] 6422 2-9-5 **87**... TomEaves 4 64
(Kevin Ryan) *dwlt: in tch in far side quartet: drvn along over 2f out: wknd over 1f out* **5/1**[1]

015 **14** 1 1/2 **Big City**[73] 4750 2-8-9 **77**... HollieDoyle 5 49
(Roger Fell) *dwlt: hld up in main centre gp: drvn along over 2f out: nvr rchd ldrs* **40/1**

401 **15** 1 3/4 **Rapid Russo**[39] 6011 2-8-9 **77**... KevinStott 17 44
(Michael Dods) *t.k.h: hld up in main centre gp: rdn along and outpcd over 2f out: btn over 1f out* **14/1**

0253 **16** 1/2 **Ellenor Gray (IRE)**[23] 6585 2-8-0 **71** ow3... SeanDavis(3) 19 36
(Richard Fahey) *bhd in main centre gp: struggling over 2f out: sn btn* **50/1**

110 **17** 12 **Malvern**[30] 6356 2-9-3 **85**... RossaRyan 10 14
(Richard Hannon) *midfield in main centre gp: drvn along and struggling over 2f out: lost tch over 1f out (jockey said colt hung right throughout)* **16/1**

1m 12.1s (-1.00) **Going Correction** -0.25s/f (Firm) **17** Ran SP% **125.5**
Speed ratings (Par 101): **96,95,94,93,90 87,86,86,85,84 84,84,83,81,79 78,62**
CSF £242.75 CT £2106.23 TOTE £22.20: £5.20, £3.20, £2.80, £4.40; EX 253.80 Trifecta £2399.50.
Owner Weldspec Glasgow Limited **Bred** Mrs J McMahon **Trained** Carluke, S Lanarks

FOCUS
A hugely competitive and good quality nursery, if not strong for the grade. They raced in three groups, the main bulk of runners coming down the centre.

7400 SHADWELL STUD/EBF STALLIONS HARRY ROSEBERY STKS (LISTED RACE) 5f
2:40 (2:44) (Class 1) 2-Y-O
£22,684 (£8,600; £4,304; £2,144; £1,076; £540) **Stalls** Centre

Form RPR

4 **1** **Piece Of Paradise (IRE)**[29] 6375 2-8-12 0...(bt) ChrisHayes 11 98
(J A Stack, Ire) *hld up: stdy hdwy over 2f out: rdn to ld ins fnl f: kpt on wl cl home* **16/1**

2 1 **Lady Penelope (IRE)**[20] 6738 2-8-12 0...(t) JasonHart 6 94
(Joseph Patrick O'Brien, Ire) *in tch: effrt and rdn over 1f out: wnt 2nd last 30yds: kpt on* **3/1**[1]

1R0 **3** 1/2 **Ickworth (IRE)**[84] 4352 2-9-1 **97**... BenCurtis 8 96
(W McCreery, Ire) *dwlt: hld up in midfield: stdy hdwy over 2f out: effrt and ev ch briefly ins fnl f: sn pressing wnr: lost 2nd and no ex last 30yds* **17/2**

0320 **4** nk **Dr Simpson (FR)**[15] 6907 2-8-12 **94**... RichardKingscote 12 92
(Tom Dascombe) *in tch: rdn along 2f out: kpt on ins fnl f: nt pce to chal* **10/1**

0302 **5** nk **Isabeau (IRE)**[35] 6190 2-8-12 **101**...(b) LeighRoche 13 90
(M D O'Callaghan, Ire) *hld up: rdn along 2f out: kpt on fnl f: nvr able to chal* **7/2**[2]

0220 **6** nk **Dylan De Vega**[27] 6474 2-9-3 **92**... TonyHamilton 7 94
(Richard Fahey) *w ldr: led over 1f out to ins fnl f: no ex* **14/1**

4104 **7** 2 1/4 **Ventura Flame (IRE)**[6] 7211 2-8-12 **82**... CallumRodriguez 1 81
(Keith Dalgleish) *in tch: effrt and drvn along wl over 1f out: sn no imp* **25/1**

2314 **8** hd **Dream Kart (IRE)**[20] 6713 2-8-12 **90**... JoeFanning 5 81
(Mark Johnston) *wnt lft s: hld up: effrt and pushed along 2f out: sn no imp* **18/1**

4046 **9** hd **American Lady (IRE)**[35] 6157 2-8-12 **85**... ShaneKelly 9 80
(J A Stack, Ire) *prom: rdn and lost pl 2f out: n.d after* **40/1**

2230 **10** nse **Show Me Show Me**[29] 6375 2-9-3 **101**... PaddyMathers 4 85+
(Richard Fahey) *blkd s: bhd: rdn over 2f out: nvr rchd ldrs (jockey said colt suffered interference leaving the stalls)* **6/1**[3]

5631 **11** 1 1/2 **She Can Dance**[27] 6436 2-8-12 **85**... SamJames 3 74
(Kevin Ryan) *bhd: struggling over 2f out: nvr on terms* **18/1**

210 **12** 5 **Queen's Order**[20] 6791 2-8-12 0... DanielTudhope 10 56
(Kevin Ryan) *led tl edgd lft and hdd over 1f out: wknd qckly fnl f (jockey said filly weakened quickly)* **9/1**

57.79s (-2.21) **Going Correction** -0.25s/f (Firm) **12** Ran SP% **120.5**
Speed ratings (Par 103): **107,105,104,104,103 103,99,99,98,98 96,88**
CSF £64.68 TOTE £16.80: £4.50, £1.70, £3.00; EX 90.40 Trifecta £948.20.
Owner M O'Flynn, Mrs J Magnier, Mrs P Shanahan **Bred** Rockfield Farm **Trained** Golden, Co. Tipperary

FOCUS
An average Listed race, if not slightly below par for the grade, and Irish horses filled the first three places.

7401 AL MAKTOUM CUP ARRAN SCOTTISH FILLIES' SPRINT STKS (LISTED RACE) 5f 110y
3:15 (3:19) (Class 1) 3-Y-0+
£28,355 (£10,750; £5,380; £2,680; £1,345; £675) Stalls Centre

Form RPR
124 1 **Lady In France**[88] 4205 3-8-12 94 BenCurtis 1 104
(K R Burke) *cl up on far side of gp: rdn to ld over 1f out: kpt on wl fnl f* 12/1
3411 2 ½ **Que Amoro (IRE)**[27] 6476 3-8-12 98 (p) PaulMulrennan 2 101
(Michael Dods) *led on far side of gp: rdn and hdd over 1f out: rallied fnl f: hld nr fin* 5/1[3]
0345 3 ½ **Gold Filigree (IRE)**[22] 6648 4-9-0 96 (p[1]) ShaneKelly 6 99
(Richard Hughes) *cl up in centre of gp: rdn and edgd lft 2f out: one pce ins fnl f* 28/1
111 4 ¾ **Last Empire**[41] 5951 3-8-12 91 DanielTudhope 8 96
(Kevin Ryan) *hld up on far side of gp: effrt and rdn 2f out: kpt on ins fnl f* 11/2
22 5 1 **Woody Creek**[42] 5923 3-8-12 102 ChrisHayes 9 93+
(J A Stack, Ire) *hld up on nr side of gp: plenty to do whn nt clr run over 2f out to over 1f out: gd hdwy fnl f: fin wl (jockey said filly was denied a clear run from 2½f out to 1f out)* 4/1[1]
1511 6 nk **Dandy's Beano (IRE)**[41] 5936 4-9-0 85 (h) KevinStott 15 92
(Kevin Ryan) *cl up on nr side of gp: rdn over 2f out: edgd lft and no ex over 1f out* 80/1
0565 7 1¼ **Heavenly Holly (IRE)**[19] 6769 4-9-0 95 (t[1]) JoeFanning 12 87
(Hugo Palmer) *in tch in centre of gp: rdn over 2f out: no imp over 1f out* 10/1
4330 8 ½ **Reticent Angel (IRE)**[75] 4703 3-8-12 91 (p) PaulHanagan 18 85
(Clive Cox) *slowly away: bhd on nr side of gp: effrt and rdn over 2f out: edgd lft and no imp over 1f out* 66/1
1-35 9 ½ **Red Impression**[125] 2826 3-8-12 94 (w) AdamMcNamara 11 84
(Roger Charlton) *dwlt: hld up in centre of gp: effrt and pushed along over 2f out: no imp over 1f out* 9/2[2]
4141 10 shd **Raincall**[36] 6120 4-9-0 74 JamesSullivan 16 83
(Henry Candy) *bhd on nr side of gp: rdn and edgd lft over 1f out: nvr able to chal* 50/1
3043 11 nk **Fairy Falcon**[20] 6698 4-9-0 99 (b) GrahamLee 3 82
(Bryan Smart) *midfield on far side of gp: rdn over 2f out: sn no imp: btn fnl f* 20/1
6564 12 1¾ **Deia Glory**[22] 6648 3-8-12 93 CallumRodriguez 19 76
(Michael Dods) *midfield in centre of gp: drvn over 2f out: wknd over 1f out* 25/1
3100 13 ¾ **Fool For You (IRE)**[30] 6351 4-9-0 89 PJMcDonald 10 73
(Richard Fahey) *hld up in centre of gp: shortlived effrt over 2f out: sn btn* 20/1
-400 14 1¾ **Signora Cabello (IRE)**[94] 3950 3-8-12 106 (b) JasonHart 13 67
(John Quinn) *dwlt: bhd in centre of gp: drvn along over 2f out: btn over 1f out* 16/1
4214 15 1 **Inspired Thought (IRE)**[40] 6006 3-8-12 91 (p) HollieDoyle 7 63
(Archie Watson) *midfield in centre of gp: drvn along over 2f out: wknd over 1f out* 28/1
4020 16 3 **Probability (IRE)**[20] 6735 3-8-12 88 RichardKingscote 20 52
(Archie Watson) *midfield on nr side of gp: rdn along and outpcd over 2f out: sn btn* 33/1

1m 3.77s (-2.73) **Going Correction** -0.25s/f (Firm)
WFA 3 from 4yo 1lb 16 Ran SP% 120.8
Speed ratings (Par 108): **108,107,106,105,104 103,102,101,100,100 100,98,97,94,93 89**
CSF £63.02 TOTE £13.20: £3.90, £2.30, £7.90; EX 78.30 Trifecta £1895.30.
Owner Clipper Logistics **Bred** Whitsbury Manor Stud **Trained** Middleham Moor, N Yorks

FOCUS
Just the second ever running of this Listed sprint and it attracted a competitive field. However, with just two of the runners rated in excess of 100, it was limited in terms of quality. Improvement from the unexposed winner. The low drawn horses dominated.

7402 WILLIAM HILL AYR BRONZE CUP H'CAP 6f
3:45 (3:51) (Class 2) 3-Y-0+
£18,675 (£5,592; £2,796; £1,398; £699; £351) Stalls Centre

Form RPR
2021 1 **Music Society (IRE)**[30] 6339 4-9-8 81 5ex PaulMulrennan 9 90+
(Tim Easterby) *hld up in tch in far side gp: smooth hdwy over 1f out: led ins fnl f: kpt on strly: 1st of 14 in gp* 20/1
2166 2 1¼ **Highly Sprung (IRE)**[21] 6677 6-9-2 75 LewisEdmunds 13 80
(Les Eyre) *hld up in far side gp: rdn over 2f out: kpt on wl fnl f to take 2nd last stride: 2nd of 14 in gp* 40/1
6251 3 nse **Dizzy G (IRE)**[6] 7206 4-9-7 80 5ex CliffordLee 7 85
(K R Burke) *mde most in far side gp tl hdd ins fnl f: no ex and lost 2nd last stride: 3rd of 14 in gp* 22/1
0460 4 hd **Upstaging**[13] 6972 7-9-2 75 (p) RossaRyan 12 79
(Noel Wilson) *hld up in midfield far side gp: drvn along over 2f out: r.o ins fnl f: 4th of 14 in gp* 66/1
2232 5 nk **Pendleton**[12] 7002 3-9-7 82 (p) CallumRodriguez 25 85+
(Michael Dods) *chsd stands' side ldrs: hdwy to ld that gp over 1f out: sn rdn and drifted lft: kpt on ins fnl f: 1st of 10 in gp* 10/3[1]
0503 6 ½ **Paddy Power (IRE)**[13] 6972 6-9-6 79 TonyHamilton 15 81
(Richard Fahey) *hld up far side gp: rdn along over 2f out: r.o fnl f: nrst fin: 5th of 14 in gp* 22/1
4403 7 nk **Big Lachie**[5] 7230 5-8-13 72 RichardKingscote 16 73+
(Mark Loughnane) *hld up in stands' side gp: effrt and rdn 2f out: kpt on fnl f: 2nd of 10 in gp* 10/1[3]
303 8 ½ **Captain Jameson (IRE)**[41] 5951 4-9-9 82 JasonHart 8 81
(John Quinn) *prom far side gp: rdn over 2f out: kpt on same pce fnl f: 6th of 14 in gp* 16/1
1253 9 shd **Friendly Advice (IRE)**[10] 7049 3-9-2 77 (p) KevinStott 14 76
(Keith Dalgleish) *hld up far side gp: drvn along over 2f out: kpt on fnl f: nt rch ldrs: 7th of 14 in gp* 18/1
0006 10 ½ **Dark Defender**[54] 5476 6-9-10 83 (b) JoeFanning 23 80+
(Rebecca Bastiman) *hld up stands' side gp: rdn along 2f out: kpt on fnl f: 3rd of 10 in gp* 40/1
-040 11 shd **Big Les (IRE)**[24] 6581 4-9-9 82 PJMcDonald 3 79
(Karen McLintock) *w ldrs in far side gp to over 1f out: no ex fnl f: 8th of 14 in gp* 28/1
2511 12 shd **Inexes**[33] 6260 7-9-3 76 5ex (p) TomEaves 2 73
(Ivan Furtado) *dwlt: hld up far side: rdn and effrt over 1f out: sn no imp: 9th of 14 in gp* 25/1
0300 13 hd **Tommy G**[8] 7121 6-9-4 77 DanielTudhope 20 73+
(Jim Goldie) *cl up nr side: rdn and carried lft over 1f out: sn one pce: 4th of 10 in gp* 7/1[2]
3220 14 ¾ **Diamonique**[23] 6607 3-8-12 73 ShaneGray 4 66
(Keith Dalgleish) *hld up in tch: effrt and drvn along 2f out: outpcd fnl f: 10th of 14 in gp* 66/1
3500 15 ¾ **He'Zanarab (IRE)**[1] 7362 3-9-5 80 PaddyMathers 5 71
(Jim Goldie) *wnt rt s: w far side ldrs to 2f out: rdn and wknd fnl f: 11th of 14 in gp* 50/1
1000 16 ½ **Get The Rhythm**[21] 6676 3-9-6 81 BarryMcHugh 11 70
(Richard Fahey) *hld up far side: drvn along over 2f out: nvr rchd ldrs: 12th of 14 in gp* 25/1
0352 17 ½ **Lucky Lucky Man (IRE)**[13] 6972 4-9-5 78 DavidNolan 19 66+
(Richard Fahey) *prom stands' side: drvn along over 2f out: no imp over 1f out: 5th of 10 in gp* 11/1
6040 18 nk **Shallow Hal**[97] 3865 3-9-10 85 (v) BenCurtis 24 72+
(K R Burke) *led stands' side gp to over 1f out: rdn and wknd ins fnl f: 6th of 10 in gp* 10/1[3]
2131 19 ½ **Global Hope (IRE)**[3] 7320 4-8-12 71 5ex (tp) ShaneKelly 1 56
(Gay Kelleway) *hld up far side: drvn along over 2f out: nvr on terms: 13th of 14 in gp* 10/1[3]
0051 20 hd **Oriental Lilly**[3] 7310 5-8-5 71 (p) CoreyMadden(7) 17 56+
(Jim Goldie) *hld up: pushed along 2f out: sn n.d: 7th of 10 in gp* 18/1
4530 21 1¼ **Howzer Black (IRE)**[14] 6935 3-8-13 79 (p) BenSanderson(5) 18 60+
(Keith Dalgleish) *dwlt: hld up in tch stands' side gp: rdn over 2f out: wknd over 1f out: 8th of 10 in gp* 40/1
0466 22 ½ **Airglow (IRE)**[14] 6921 4-9-7 80 (h) NathanEvans 6 59
(Michael Easterby) *awkward s: sn prom far side tl rdn and wknd 2f out: last of 14 in gp* 40/1
0045 23 3 **Look Out Louis**[12] 7002 3-9-7 82 DavidAllan 22 51+
(Tim Easterby) *dwlt: hld up stands' side gp: rdn over 2f out: no imp over 1f out: 9th of 10 in gp (jockey said gelding ran too free)* 33/1
4004 24 2¼ **Wasntexpectingthat**[12] 7002 3-9-2 77 PaulHanagan 21 39+
(Richard Fahey) *hld up stands' side: drvn along over 2f out: wknd over 1f out: last of 10 in gp* 25/1

1m 10.47s (-2.63) **Going Correction** -0.25s/f (Firm)
WFA 3 from 4yo+ 2lb 24 Ran SP% 133.7
Speed ratings (Par 109): **107,105,105,105,104 103,103,102,102,102 101,101,101,100,99 98,98,97,97,96 95,94,90,87**
CSF £661.60 CT £16277.50 TOTE £22.70: £5.20, £10.80, £4.50, £16.10; EX 1056.50 Trifecta £2409.10.
Owner Richard Taylor & Philip Hebdon **Bred** Pier House Stud **Trained** Great Habton, N Yorks

FOCUS
They split into two groups, the largest, containing 14 horses, racing more towards the far side, and it was from that bunch that the first four emerged. The winner could yet get back to his 2yo level.

7403 BAM PROPERTIES LTD H'CAP 2m 1f 105y
4:20 (4:22) (Class 3) (0-95,97) 4-Y-0+ £10,350 (£3,080; £1,539; £769) Stalls Low

Form RPR
2112 1 **Alright Sunshine (IRE)**[13] 6958 4-9-13 97 JoeFanning 3 107+
(Keith Dalgleish) *hld up: smooth hdwy 3f out: trckd ldr 2f out: led ins fnl f: hung lft: rdn out* 7/4[1]
203 2 1½ **Theglasgowwarrior**[7] 7147 5-9-6 90 DanielTudhope 1 95
(Jim Goldie) *prom: led 3f out: sn rdn: drvn over 1f out: hdd ins fnl f: styng on same pce and hld whn hmpd 50yds out* 13/2[3]
1345 3 ¾ **Sassie (IRE)**[12] 7001 4-8-9 79 KevinStott 8 83
(Michael Easterby) *hld up in rr: rdn and hdwy on outer over 2f out: styd on ins fnl f: wnt 3rd towards fin* 11/1
1623 4 nk **Seinesational**[17] 6834 4-9-1 85 (v) HollieDoyle 5 89+
(William Knight) *trckd ldrs: rdn over 2f out: styd on same pce: lost 3rd towards fin* 9/1
2210 5 3½ **Qawamees (IRE)**[12] 7003 4-8-8 78 (bt) JamesSullivan 4 78
(Michael Easterby) *in tch: racd keenly: rdn along 2f out: drvn and no ex ins fnl f* 40/1
640- 6 1½ **Project Bluebook (FR)**[48] 7284 6-8-7 77 (p) JasonHart 6 75
(John Quinn) *midfield: rdn over 2f out: no imp* 4/1[2]
2362 7 1 **Claire Underwood (IRE)**[13] 6975 4-9-3 87 TonyHamilton 9 84
(Richard Fahey) *led: rdn along and hdd 3f out: wknd 2f out* 7/1
11-0 8 ½ **Arrowtown**[13] 6958 7-9-7 91 (h) NathanEvans 2 88
(Michael Easterby) *midfield: rdn over 2f out: sn outpcd and btn* 14/1
4132 9 4 **So Near So Farhh**[20] 6716 4-8-2 72 PaddyMathers 7 64
(Mick Channon) *hld up: hdwy and trckd ldrs 6f out: rdn over 3f out: wknd 2f out* 18/1

3m 51.9s (-9.60) **Going Correction** -0.25s/f (Firm) 9 Ran SP% 114.9
Speed ratings (Par 107): **112,111,110,110,109 108,107,107,105**
CSF £13.44 CT £95.97 TOTE £2.40: £1.20, £2.00, £3.30; EX 14.00 Trifecta £74.50.
Owner Paul & Clare Rooney **Bred** Peter & Hugh McCutcheon **Trained** Carluke, S Lanarks
■ Stewards' Enquiry : Joe Fanning two-day ban: interference & careless riding (tba)

FOCUS
Add 12yds. A decent staying handicap, which appeared to revolve around Old Borough Cup runner-up Alright Sunshine. They went fairly steadily before quickening off the home turn. The form's rated around the second, third and fourth.

7404 H&V COMMISSIONING SERVICES LTD H'CAP (DIV I) 1m
4:55 (5:01) (Class 5) (0-70,72) 3-Y-0
£4,787 (£1,424; £711; £355; £300; £300) Stalls Low

Form RPR
5116 1 **My Ukulele (IRE)**[21] 6679 3-9-4 67 JasonHart 11 75+
(John Quinn) *stdd in rr: effrt whn n.m.r over 2f out: effrt and angled rt over 1f out: hdwy to ld wl ins fnl f: r.o* 11/1
2523 2 ¾ **Flying Dragon (FR)**[9] 7074 3-9-7 70 (h) RossaRyan 3 76
(Richard Hannon) *hld up in midfield: effrt over 2f out: kpt on fnl f to take 2nd nr fin* 9/2[2]
3021 3 ½ **Dreamseller (IRE)**[13] 6983 3-8-11 60 (p) DavidAllan 13 65
(Tim Easterby) *t.k.h early: trckd ldrs: led gng wl over 2f out: rdn over 1f out: hdd wl ins fnl f: lost 2nd cl home* 6/1[3]
0312 4 2¼ **Sootability (IRE)**[8] 7126 3-9-5 68 PaulHanagan 7 68
(Richard Fahey) *prom: effrt and drvn along over 2f out: kpt on same pce fnl f* 5/2[1]
6630 5 1¼ **God Of Dreams**[6] 7207 3-8-7 56 (h[1]) JoeFanning 8 53
(Iain Jardine) *hld up on outside: hdwy over 2f out: drvn and outpcd fnl f* 25/1

2004 **6** *hd* **Spirit Of Lund (IRE)**[23] 6612 3-9-3 **66**........................ PaulMulrennan 12 62
(Iain Jardine) *s.i.s: hld up in detached last: pushed along and effrt over 1f out: kpt on fnl f: nvr nrr* **33/1**

0126 **7** *1* **Three Castles**[14] 6938 3-9-2 **65**........................ DanielTudhope 2 59
(Keith Dalgleish) *hld up towards rr: stdy hdwy whn nt clr run over 2f out: effrt whn nt clr run over 1f out: sn rdn and no imp* **17/2**

-205 **8** *shd* **Mardle**[38] 6037 3-9-9 **72**........................ CliffordLee 10 66
(K R Burke) *hld up: rdn over 2f out: hdwy and edgd lft over 1f out: sn no imp: btn ins fnl f* **20/1**

0030 **9** *3/4* **Charlie's Boy (IRE)**[21] 6678 3-8-7 **56** oh1........................ HollieDoyle 5 48
(Michael Dods) *pressed ldr: drvn along and ev ch over 2f out: wknd over 1f out* **17/2**

4404 **10** *1 1/2* **Jem Scuttle (USA)**[21] 6678 3-9-0 **63**........................(t) DavidNolan 1 52
(Declan Carroll) *prom: drvn along over 2f out: wknd over 1f out* **17/2**

1405 **11** *1 1/2* **Lethal Laura**[24] 6575 3-8-2 **56** oh6........................ KieranSchofield(5) 9 41
(R Mike Smith) *hld up in midfield: drvn along over 2f out: wknd over 1f out* **50/1**

-036 **12** *1* **Uh Oh Chongo**[44] 5814 3-8-12 **61**........................ NathanEvans 14 44
(Michael Easterby) *led to over 2f out: rdn and wknd over 1f out* **50/1**

3020 **13** *2 1/2* **Dark Poet**[36] 6101 3-8-8 **57**........................ JamesSullivan 6 34
(Ruth Carr) *hld up: rdn and outpcd over 2f out: sn btn* **33/1**

1m 40.6s (-2.20) **Going Correction** -0.25s/f (Firm) **13** Ran SP% **119.4**
Speed ratings (Par 101): **101,100,99,97,96 96,95,94,94,92 91,90,87**
CSF £56.00 CT £343.07 TOTE £12.10: £3.30, £1.80, £2.30; EX 60.60 Trifecta £337.70.
Owner Andrew W Robson **Bred** Andrew W Robson **Trained** Settrington, N Yorks
■ Geography Teacher was withdrawn. Price at time of withdrawal 50-1. Rule 4 does not apply

FOCUS
Add 12yds. A modest handicap but the first three finished nicely clear. The form's rated around the runner-up.

7405 H&V COMMISSIONING SERVICES LTD H'CAP (DIV II) 1m
5:30 (5:31) (Class 5) (0-70,70) 3-Y-O

£4,787 (£1,424; £711; £355; £300; £300) **Stalls** Low

Form RPR

3302 **1** **Power Player**[30] 6342 3-9-5 **68**........................ BenCurtis 2 75+
(K R Burke) *t.k.h: trckd ldrs: hdwy to ld 2f out: sn hrd pressed: hld on gamely fnl f* **5/1**[1]

6224 **2** *nk* **Be Proud (IRE)**[3] 7307 3-8-7 **56** oh3........................ PaddyMathers 4 62
(Jim Goldie) *hld up: hdwy 2f out: rdn to chal ins fnl f: kpt on: hld cl home* **5/1**[1]

1502 **3** *3/4* **Mitigator**[9] 7084 3-8-11 **65**........................(b) RayDawson(5) 9 69
(Lydia Pearce) *midfield on outside: hdwy to dispute ld over 1f out to last 100yds: kpt on same pce towards fin* **6/1**[2]

553 **4** *1 1/4* **Grazeon Roy**[41] 5969 3-9-7 **70**........................ JasonHart 3 71
(John Quinn) *trckd ldrs: effrt and rdn 2f out: kpt on same pce fnl f* **15/2**

0650 **5** *hd* **Mac Ailey**[21] 6678 3-8-7 **56** oh1........................ JamesSullivan 7 57
(Tim Easterby) *hld up: rdn and effrt over 1f out: kpt on ins fnl f: nt pce to chal* **7/1**[3]

0-40 **6** *hd* **George Ridsdale**[145] 2152 3-8-7 **56**........................ NathanEvans 13 57+
(Michael Easterby) *t.k.h: hld up: effrt whn angled rt and n.m.r over 1f out: kpt on fnl f: no imp (jockey said gelding was denied a clear run from 3f out to approaching the final furlong)* **22/1**

6203 **7** *1 3/4* **Smeaton (IRE)**[25] 6540 3-8-12 **61**........................ ShaneKelly 11 57
(Roger Fell) *s.i.s: hld up: hdwy into midfield after 3f: rdn 2f out: fdd ins fnl f* **7/1**[3]

605 **8** *1 3/4* **Vivacious Spirit**[6] 7207 3-8-10 **59**........................(p) TonyHamilton 10 51
(Phillip Makin) *w ldr: rdn and ev ch over 2f out: wknd ins fnl f* **12/1**

0000 **9** *shd* **Archies Lad**[6] 7207 3-8-8 **57**........................ PaulHanagan 5 49
(R Mike Smith) *hld up: effrt whn n.m.r over 1f out and ent fnl f: n.d* **28/1**

6040 **10** *6* **Beechwood Izzy (IRE)**[10] 7050 3-8-11 **60**........................(h[1]) JoeFanning 12 38
(Keith Dalgleish) *hld up: rdn along on outside over 2f out: wknd over 1f out: eased whn btn ins fnl f* **28/1**

0640 **11** *2 1/2* **Evolutionary (IRE)**[9] 7069 3-9-1 **64**........................ PaulMulrennan 1 36
(Iain Jardine) *led to 2f out: sn rdn and wknd* **18/1**

0403 **12** *8* **Ride The Monkey (IRE)**[24] 6578 3-9-7 **70**........................ CallumRodriguez 6 24
(Michael Dods) *t.k.h: prom: lost pl over 2f out: sn struggling* **10/1**

1m 40.48s (-2.32) **Going Correction** -0.25s/f (Firm) **12** Ran SP% **117.7**
Speed ratings (Par 101): **101,100,99,98,98 98,96,94,94,88 86,78**
CSF £28.12 CT £154.43 TOTE £5.30: £2.30, £1.70, £2.30; EX 29.20 Trifecta £151.10.
Owner Khalifa Dasmal **Bred** Carmel Stud **Trained** Middleham Moor, N Yorks
■ Stewards' Enquiry : Nathan Evans two-day ban: careless riding (tba)

FOCUS
Add 12yds. This wasn't particularly inspiring but it was every bit as competitive as the first division. It was marginally the quicker of the two races.
T/Jkpt: Not Won. T/Plt: £9,276.70 to a £1 stake. Pool: £95,308.86 - 7.5 winning units T/Qpdt: £405.50 to a £1 stake. Pool: £11,317.48 - 20.65 winning units **Richard Young & Andrew Sheret**

6211 NEWBURY (L-H)
Friday, September 20

OFFICIAL GOING: Good (good to firm in places; watered; 6.8)
Wind: Fresh, behind on straight course Weather: Sunny, warm

7406 BRITISH STALLION STUDS EBF MAIDEN STKS (PLUS 10 RACE) (DIV I) 6f
1:15 (1:20) (Class 4) 2-Y-O

£6,145 (£1,828; £913; £456) **Stalls** Centre

Form RPR

1 **Theotherside (IRE)** 2-9-0 0........................ PatDobbs 3 77+
(Richard Hannon) *quite str; mde all: stl gng easily over 1f out: pushed along and stretched clr fnl f: comf* **33/1**

2 *1 1/2* **King Ragnar** 2-9-5 0........................ AndreaAtzeni 7 77+
(Roger Varian) *athletic; dwlt: rn green in rr and pushed along: sme prog over 2f out: sed to run on over 1f out: fin wl to take 2nd last strides (jockey said colt was denied a clear run from 1 1/2f out)* **5/2**[1]

65 **3** *1/2* **Roman Melody**[17] 6845 2-9-5 0........................ GeraldMosse 4 76
(David Elsworth) *quite str; looked wl; sn pushed along towards rr: prog on far side of gp 2f out but hanging lft: rdn to chse wnr jst ins fnl f: no imp and lost 2nd last strides* **7/1**[3]

4 *3/4* **Nugget** 2-9-5 0........................ SeanLevey 1 73
(Richard Hannon) *compact; w wnr to over 1f out: lost 2nd and one pce jst ins fnl f* **7/1**[3]

66 **5** *3/4* **Wilfy**[11] 7030 2-9-5 0........................ LiamKeniry 2 71
(Sylvester Kirk) *unfurnished; dwlt: trckd ldrs: rdn and cl up over 1f out: nt qckn and hld fnl f* **33/1**

6 *2 1/4* **Albert Edward (IRE)** 2-9-5 0........................ OisinMurphy 11 64+
(Brian Meehan) *compact; towards rr: pushed along 2f out: nvr on terms but kpt on steadily fnl f* **16/1**

7 *nk* **Vandad (IRE)** 2-9-5 0........................ RyanMoore 15 63
(Richard Hughes) *compact; dwlt: in rr and racd towards nr side of gp: pushed along and kpt on fnl 2f: nvr nrr* **9/1**

4 **8** *nk* **Populaire (FR)**[45] 5772 2-9-0 0........................ JimCrowley 6 57
(Amanda Perrett) *athletic; t.k.h: trckd ldrs: reminder over 1f out: wknd fnl f* **10/3**[2]

00 **9** *3/4* **Ivadream**[18] 6807 2-9-5 0........................ JasonWatson 10 60
(Roger Charlton) *quite str; t.k.h: w ldng pair to 2f out: wknd over 1f out* **66/1**

5 **10** *3 1/4* **Doctor Nuno**[21] 6684 2-9-5 0........................ TomMarquand 14 50
(Mark Loughnane) *unfurnished; racd on nr side of gp: spd to 1/2-way: steadily wknd 2f out (vet said colt lost its right hind shoe)* **80/1**

00 **11** *3 1/2* **Malmesbury Abbey (FR)**[17] 6845 2-9-5 0........................ HectorCrouch 12 40
(Ed Walker) *quite str; prom 4f: wknd* **66/1**

3 **12** *1/2* **Tommy Rock (IRE)**[30] 6330 2-9-5 0........................ AdamKirby 13 38
(Clive Cox) *compact; chsd ldrs: rdn and wknd wl over 1f out* **7/1**[3]

13 *10* **Jungle Capers (IRE)** 2-9-5 0........................ CallumShepherd 9 8
(Mick Channon) *leggy; slowly away: a in rr: bhd fnl 2f: t.o* **80/1**

14 *1 1/4* **Lady Sarah** 2-9-0 0........................ BrettDoyle 5
(Tony Carroll) *workmanlike; slowly away: a bhd: t.o* **100/1**

15 *4 1/2* **Vintage Port (IRE)** 2-9-5 0........................ DavidProbert 8
(Tony Carroll) *leggy; dwlt: a bhd: t.o* **100/1**

1m 12.5s (-0.70) **Going Correction** -0.25s/f (Firm) **15** Ran SP% **118.3**
Speed ratings (Par 97): **94,92,91,90,89 86,85,85,84,80 75,74,61,59,53**
CSF £111.81 TOTE £41.40: £9.00, £1.80, £2.30; EX 194.30 Trifecta £1401.20.
Owner Excel Racing **Bred** Kevin Lyons **Trained** East Everleigh, Wilts

FOCUS
Rail movements added 15yds to races 3 and 8. After winning the first Pat Dobbs called it "proper good ground." There was a tailwind on the day. This looked a fairly ordinary maiden, but the big-priced winner did it well. Most of the principals raced on the far side of the group. It was the slower division by 1.21sec.

7407 BRITISH STALLION STUDS EBF MAIDEN STKS (PLUS 10 RACE) (DIV II) 6f
1:50 (1:52) (Class 4) 2-Y-O

£6,145 (£1,828; £913; £456) **Stalls** Centre

Form RPR

32 **1** **Smokey Bear (IRE)**[53] 5501 2-9-5 0........................ JasonWatson 12 85
(Roger Charlton) *athletic; w ldr: shkn up to ld over 1f out: rdn and styd on wl fnl f* **9/4**[1]

3 **2** *1 1/4* **River Nymph**[17] 6845 2-9-5 0........................ AdamKirby 11 82
(Clive Cox) *tall; looked wl; mde most: rdn and hdd over 1f out: styd on but readily hld last 100yds* **7/2**[2]

03 **3** *3 1/4* **Gleeds Girl**[31] 6300 2-9-0 0........................ TomMarquand 9 67
(Mick Channon) *compact; chsd ldrs: rdn and outpcd over 1f out: kpt on to take 3rd nr fin* **25/1**

60 **4** *hd* **Live In The Moment (IRE)**[17] 6845 2-9-5 0........................ RobertHavlin 14 71
(Adam West) *workmanlike; trckd ldrs: stl gng strly 2f out: shkn up to chse ldng pair jst over 1f out but outpcd by them: one pce after and lost 3rd nr fin* **150/1**

5 *3 1/2* **Abnaa** 2-9-5 0........................ JimCrowley 3 60+
(Brian Meehan) *quite str; w ldrs: pushed along 2f out: steadily fdd over 1f out* **7/1**

23 **6** *shd* **Harlequin**[37] 6079 2-9-5 0........................ OisinMurphy 6 60
(William Knight) *unfurnished; w ldrs: rdn 2f out: hanging and nt qckn over 1f out: fdd (jockey said colt hung left-handed under pressure; vet said colt was struck into on its right hind)* **4/1**[3]

0 **7** *3 1/4* **Party Island (IRE)**[17] 6845 2-8-12 0........................ MichaelPitt(7) 15 50+
(Denis Coakley) *quite str; dwlt: towards rr and stl looked green: nvr on terms and outpcd fr 2f out* **150/1**

8 *3* **Bruisa** 2-9-0 0........................ SeanLevey 2 36
(Richard Hannon) *str; difficult to load into stalls: towards rr: outpcd 2f out: no real hdwy after* **12/1**

6 **9** *2 1/4* **Shadow Glen**[88] 4184 2-9-5 0........................ CharlesBishop 1 35
(Eve Johnson Houghton) *athletic; chsd ldrs: rdn and wknd 2f out* **9/1**

10 *9* **Midnight Welcome** 2-9-0 0........................ JoeyHaynes 7 3
(Patrick Chamings) *leggy; dwlt: a bhd: t.o* **80/1**

00 **11** *2 1/4* **Hot Hot Hot**[17] 6846 2-9-0 0........................ BrettDoyle 4
(Tony Carroll) *leggy; in tch tl wknd rapidly 2f out: t.o* **150/1**

12 *2* **Priest (IRE)** 2-9-5 0........................ RobHornby 5
(Martyn Meade) *compact; slowly away: rn v green and a bhd: t.o* **16/1**

0 **13** *1/2* **Viking Honour (IRE)**[8] 7113 2-9-5 0........................ LiamKeniry 10
(Joseph Tuite) *leggy; dwlt: a bhd: t.o (vet said gelding lost its left and right hind shoes)* **100/1**

1m 11.29s (-1.91) **Going Correction** -0.25s/f (Firm) **13** Ran SP% **117.1**
Speed ratings (Par 97): **102,100,96,95,91 90,86,82,79,67 64,61,61**
CSF £9.58 TOTE £2.30: £1.30, £1.50, £4.00; EX 10.60 Trifecta £103.00.
Owner De Zoete, Inglett & Jones **Bred** Corduff Stud **Trained** Beckhampton, Wilts

FOCUS
Just fair maiden form, but the quicker division by 1.21sec. This time, high numbers prevailed, and again the principals raced prominently.

7408 DUBAI DUTY FREE H'CAP (96PLUS RACE) 1m 4f
2:20 (2:20) (Class 2) (0-110,100) 3-Y-O+**£16,172** (£4,812; £2,405; £1,202) **Stalls** Low

Form RPR

1533 **1** **Shailene (IRE)**[20] 6747 4-9-11 **99**........................ OisinMurphy 3 105
(Andrew Balding) *looked wl; trckd ldrs: pushed along 2f out: brought between rivals fnl f: cajoled along and r.o to ld last 50yds* **7/2**[2]

1120 **2** *1/2* **Soto Sizzler**[52] 5519 4-9-8 **96**........................ JimCrowley 1 101
(William Knight) *led: rdn and pressed 2f out: kpt on wl but hdd and outpcd last 50yds* **13/8**[1]

2040 **3** *1/2* **Scarlet Dragon**[28] 6420 6-9-12 **100**........................(h) TomMarquand 6 104
(Alan King) *hld up in 4th: rdn over 2f out: clsd to chse ldr wl over 1f out and sn chalng: lost 2nd ins fnl f: kpt on* **6/1**

0406 **4** *6* **Blakeney Point**[13] 6958 6-9-8 **96**........................(t[1]) JasonWatson 5 93
(Roger Charlton) *chsd ldr: urged along 3f out: lost 2nd wl over 1f out but stl cl up: wknd qckly and eased ins fnl f* **5/1**

1026 **5** *18* **Almost Midnight**[42] 5909 3-9-3 **98**........................ AndreaAtzeni 4 65
(David Simcock) *a last: pushed along 5f out: wknd over 2f out: t.o (jockey said colt stopped quickly)* **9/2**[3]

2m 33.27s (-4.73) **Going Correction** -0.25s/f (Firm)
WFA 3 from 4yo+ 7lb **5** Ran SP% **109.5**
Speed ratings (Par 109): **105,104,104,100,88**
CSF £9.53 TOTE £3.40: £1.60, £1.60; EX 9.60 Trifecta £28.00.
Owner George Strawbridge **Bred** George Strawbridge **Trained** Kingsclere, Hants

FOCUS
Add 15yds. A classy small-field handicap, run at what appeared to be a reasonable gallop. The winner and third are rated close to their Goodwood form.

7409 DUBAI DUTY FREE NURSERY H'CAP 7f (S)
2:55 (2:56) (Class 3) (0-90,86) 2-Y-O

£6,225 (£1,864; £932; £466; £233; £117) **Stalls Centre**

Form RPR

2600 **1** **Separate**[30] 6356 2-9-2 **81**..............................(b) JamesDoyle 10 87
(Richard Hannon) *hld up in last: prog on nr side over 2f out: rdn to ld over 1f out: edgd rt u.p but styd on wl fnl f* **12/1**

5410 **2** *2* **Indian Creak (IRE)**[8] 7119 2-9-7 **86**.............................. PatDobbs 9 87
(Mick Channon) *hld up in tch: shkn up 2f out: prog nr side over 1f out: rdn and styd on to take 2nd last 100yds: no imp on wnr* **20/1**

0051 **3** *3/4* **Pitchcombe**[9] 7079 2-8-1 **69** 6ex..............................(p) WilliamCox(3) 2 68
(Clive Cox) *looked wl; sltly on toes; led: rdn 2f out: hdd over 1f out: outpcd but kpt on wl (jockey said gelding hung right-handed)* **12/1**

461 **4** *1 1/2* **Gypsy Whisper**[23] 6603 2-8-13 **78**.............................. JasonWatson 11 73
(David Menuisier) *trckd ldrs: rdn over 2f out: chal and upsides wl over 1f out: nt qckn and wknd fnl f (jockey said filly hung left and right-handed)* **12/1**

3120 **5** *1* **St Ives**[29] 6375 2-9-0 **79**.............................. GeraldMosse 1 71
(William Haggas) *in tch: prog far side of gp jst over 2f out: rdn and tried to cl over 1f out: edgd rt and wknd fnl f* **5/1[2]**

522 **6** *nk* **Dark Kris (IRE)**[81] 4456 2-8-13 **78**.............................. RyanMoore 7 70
(Richard Hughes) *hld up towards rr but wl in tch: lost pl over 2f out and dropped to last: effrt over 1f out: n.d but kpt on* **14/1**

0201 **7** *3 1/4* **Cheat (IRE)**[13] 6963 2-9-2 **81**.............................. OisinMurphy 6 64
(Richard Hannon) *on toes; trckd ldrs: stl gng strly over 2f out: shkn up and wknd wl over 1f out* **10/1**

11 **8** *nk* **Macho Time (IRE)**[51] 5553 2-9-7 **86**.............................. SeanLevey 8 68+
(K R Burke) *quite str; looked wl; mostly pressed ldr to 2f out: wknd (jockey said colt stopped quickly; vet said colt was struck into on its right fore)* **7/2[1]**

221 **9** *nse* **Cosmic Power (IRE)**[14] 6911 2-9-2 **81**.............................. CharlesBishop 3 63
(Eve Johnson Houghton) *in tch towards rr: no prog 2f out: wknd over 1f out* **6/1[3]**

2030 **10** *12* **Written Broadcast (IRE)**[13] 6963 2-8-11 **76**.............................. AndreaAtzeni 5 27
(Richard Hannon) *looked wl; trckd ldrs: urged along 3f out: wknd 2f out: t.o (jockey said colt stopped quickly)* **17/2**

142 **11** *1 1/4* **Dancinginthewoods**[84] 4324 2-9-3 **82**.............................. JoeyHaynes 4 30
(Dean Ivory) *cl up tl wknd over 2f out: t.o (jockey said colt was never travelling)* **7/1**

1m 25.2s (-1.80) **Going Correction** -0.25s/f (Firm) **11 Ran SP% 119.8**
Speed ratings (Par 99): **100,97,96,95,94 93,89,89,89,75 74**
CSF £231.54 CT £2977.59 TOTE £14.10: £3.60, £5.70, £4.20; EX 264.80 Trifecta £2487.20.
Owner Martin Hughes & Mark Murphy **Bred** Guy Bloodstock Ltd **Trained** East Everleigh, Wilts

FOCUS
Decent nursery form. Three of the first four were drawn high and the winner is rated back to her best.

7410 HAYNES, HANSON & CLARK CONDITIONS STKS (PLUS 10 RACE) (C&G) 1m (S)
3:25 (3:28) (Class 2) 2-Y-O

£9,960 (£2,982; £1,491; £745; £372; £187) **Stalls Centre**

Form RPR

41 **1** **Tritonic**[28] 6395 2-8-12 0.............................. OisinMurphy 9 93
(Alan King) *quite tall; ly; trckd ldrs: shkn up to ld wl over 1f out: styd on wl fnl f* **12/1**

14 **2** *1 1/2* **Man Of The Night (FR)**[28] 6417 2-9-1 0.............................. RyanMoore 2 93
(Richard Hannon) *quite str; pressed ldr: chal 2f out: drvn to chse wnr over 1f out: kpt on but no imp* **11/2[2]**

1 **3** *1 1/4* **Cape Palace**[21] 6664 2-9-1 0.............................. FrankieDettori 4 91
(John Gosden) *athletic; hld up in tch: effrt on outer of gp over 2f out: nt qckn wl over 1f out: styd on to take 3rd jst ins fnl f: nt pce to threaten (jockey said colt ran too freely)* **1/2[1]**

1 **4** *1 1/4* **Acquitted (IRE)**[14] 6926 2-9-1 0.............................. JamesDoyle 1 87
(Hugo Palmer) *quite str; dwlt: in tch: swtchd rt and rdn over 2f out: kpt on one pce and nvr able to chal* **6/1[3]**

5 *shd* **Code Of Conduct** 2-8-12 0.............................. JasonWatson 8 84+
(Roger Charlton) *unfurnished; coltish; slowly away: in tch: rn green and dropped to last over 2f out: styd on fr jst over 1f out: gng on at fin (jockey said colt ran greenly)* **33/1**

3 **6** *hd* **Raatea**[22] 6640 2-8-12 0.............................. JimCrowley 6 84
(Marcus Tregoning) *unfurnished; t.k.h: pressed ldng pair: rdn and steadily wknd over 1f out* **16/1**

552 **7** *hd* **Dyami (FR)**[28] 6433 2-8-12 0.............................. CierenFallon 3 83
(George Baker) *str; led: rdn and hdd wl over 1f out: wknd fnl f* **20/1**

21 **8** *1 1/2* **It's Good To Laugh (IRE)**[22] 6640 2-8-12 0.............................. HectorCrouch 7 80
(Clive Cox) *mostly in last but in tch: rdn over 2f out: no prog and wl btn over 1f out: one pce after* **10/1**

1m 38.45s (-1.45) **Going Correction** -0.25s/f (Firm) 2y crse rec **8 Ran SP% 126.7**
Speed ratings (Par 101): **97,95,94,93,92 92,92,91**
CSF £84.16 TOTE £17.80: £3.00, £1.60, £1.10; EX 115.70 Trifecta £310.70.
Owner Mcneill Family & Ian Dale **Bred** Miss K Rausing **Trained** Barbury Castle, Wilts

FOCUS
This long-established race hasn't been won by any stars in recent years, but horses of the calibre of Dashing Willoughby, Beat Le Bon and Nayef Road were all beaten in it last year. The winner took a big step forward.

7411 DUBAI DUTY FREE CUP STKS (LISTED RACE) 7f (S)
3:55 (3:58) (Class 1) 3-Y-O+

£20,982 (£7,955; £3,981; £1,983; £995; £499) **Stalls Centre**

Form RPR

622 **1** **Tabarrak (IRE)**[13] 6950 6-9-2 112.............................. JimCrowley 3 104+
(Richard Hannon) *trckd ldrs: shkn up to ld over 1f out: rdn out and in command fnl f* **8/11[1]**

5504 **2** *3/4* **Sir Thomas Gresham (IRE)**[27] 6453 4-9-2 99..............(t) MartinDwyer 9 102
(Tim Pinfield) *wl in tch: prog nr side of gp over 2f out: drvn over 1f out: styd on to chse wnr ins fnl f: a wl hld* **20/1**

0211 **3** *1 1/2* **Salute The Soldier (GER)**[13] 6950 4-9-2 104.............................. AdamKirby 4 98
(Clive Cox) *looked wl; trckd ldr: led 2f out to over 1f out: one pce fnl f and jst hld on for 3rd* **4/1[2]**

160 **4** *nk* **I Could Do Better (IRE)**[27] 6453 3-8-13 94..............(h[1]) AndreaAtzeni 2 96
(Ian Williams) *hld up in last: shkn up 3f out: sme prog over 1f out but hanging and racd awkwardly: hrd rdn and styd on fnl f: nrly snatched 3rd* **14/1**

5231 **5** *nse* **Dirty Rascal (IRE)**[51] 5546 3-8-13 92..............(b) TomMarquand 8 95
(Tom Ward) *looked wl; trckd ldrs: drvn and nt qckn 2f out: styd on again fnl f to press for 3rd nr fin* **20/1**

0003 **6** *4 1/2* **Vanbrugh (USA)**[15] 6894 4-9-2 103.............................. KieranShoemark 5 84
(Charles Hills) *t.k.h: hld up in tch: shkn up and no prog 2f out: sn wknd* **8/1[3]**

0520 **7** *1* **Red Starlight**[20] 6726 4-8-11 98.............................. PatDobbs 7 76
(Richard Hannon) *trckd ldrs: rdn 2f out: wknd jst over 1f out* **9/1**

060 **8** *60* **Fille De Reve**[13] 6953 4-8-11 87.............................. OisinMurphy 1
(Ed Walker) *racd freely: led to 2f out: wknd rapidly and eased: t.o (jockey said filly lost its action)* **25/1**

1m 24.36s (-2.64) **Going Correction** -0.25s/f (Firm)
WFA 3 from 4yo+ 3lb **8 Ran SP% 119.1**
Speed ratings (Par 111): **105,104,102,102,102 96,95,27**
CSF £22.62 TOTE £1.60: £1.10, £5.30, £1.40; EX 19.70 Trifecta £56.20.
Owner Hamdan Al Maktoum **Bred** Rathbarry Stud & F & N Woods **Trained** East Everleigh, Wilts

FOCUS
Not the strongest of Listed races. The likes of the fourth and fifth determine the form's level.

7412 DUBAI DUTY FREE FULL OF SURPRISES BRITISH EBF FILLIES' CONDITIONS STKS (PLUS 10 RACE) 7f (S)
4:30 (4:31) (Class 2) 2-Y-O

£10,271 (£3,075; £1,537; £768; £384; £193) **Stalls Centre**

Form RPR

1 **1** **Quadrilateral**[35] 6154 2-9-1 0.............................. JasonWatson 7 101+
(Roger Charlton) *str; looked wl; hld up in last: smooth prog to ld wl over 1f out: drew rt away and pushed out firmly: impressive* **7/4[2]**

51 **2** *9* **Kalsara**[37] 6072 2-8-12 0.............................. OisinMurphy 4 75
(Andrew Balding) *quite str; t.k.h: trckd ldr: chal 2f out: distant view of wnr over 1f out but clung on for 2nd* **11/1**

1 **3** *shd* **Melnikova**[46] 5733 2-9-1 0.............................. RyanMoore 2 78+
(Sir Michael Stoute) *athletic; looked wl; led: rdn and hdd wl over 1f out: no ch w wnr but plugged on to dispute distant 2nd nr fin* **5/4[1]**

210 **4** *shd* **Nasaiym (USA)**[29] 6374 2-9-1 90.............................. TomMarquand 5 77
(James Tate) *hld up in tch: rdn over 2f out: kpt on over 1f out to press for distant 2nd nr fin* **6/1[3]**

16 **5** *3/4* **Dalanijujo (IRE)**[41] 5964 2-8-12 0.............................. DavidProbert 6 73
(Mick Channon) *leggy; trckd ldrs: drvn 2f out: kpt on to press for a pl fnl f* **20/1**

10 **6** *19* **Anna Of Sussex (IRE)**[8] 7120 2-8-12 0.............................. AndreaAtzeni 1 23
(Sylvester Kirk) *unfurnished; prom tl wknd rapidly over 2f out: t.o* **33/1**

7 *1 3/4* **Alezan** 2-8-12 0.............................. CharlesBishop 3 19
(Eve Johnson Houghton) *unfurnished; dwlt: plld hrd and v green: in tch to over 2f out: wknd rapidly: t.o (jockey said filly ran too freely)* **33/1**

1m 24.32s (-2.68) **Going Correction** -0.25s/f (Firm) **7 Ran SP% 114.1**
Speed ratings (Par 98): **105,94,94,94,93 71,69**
CSF £20.07 TOTE £2.20: £1.50, £3.40; EX 13.60 Trifecta £33.80.
Owner K Abdullah **Bred** Juddmonte Farms Ltd **Trained** Beckhampton, Wilts

FOCUS
The John Gosden pair Nathra and Dabyah, who won this in 2016 and 2017, both went on to be Group 1-placed. This edition probably lacked depth, but it produced an impressive winner who's Group-race bound. The time was fractionally quicker than that of the older-horse Listed race.

7413 T T TENTS H'CAP 1m 2f
5:05 (5:06) (Class 4) (0-85,84) 3-Y-O+

£5,207 (£1,549; £774; £387; £300; £300) **Stalls Low**

Form RPR

3352 **1** **Entrusting**[21] 6662 3-9-3 **82**.............................. RyanMoore 10 93
(James Fanshawe) *hld up in 8th off str pce: prog 3f out: rdn to cl on ldrs 2f out: chal over 1f out: led ins fnl f: drvn out* **9/2[3]**

5256 **2** *1/2* **Pour Me A Drink**[13] 6967 3-8-13 **78**.............................. HectorCrouch 4 88
(Clive Cox) *looked wl; pressed ldrs at str pce: led over 3f out: drvn 2f out: kpt on wl but hdd and hld ins fnl f* **4/1[2]**

5462 **3** *6* **City Tour**[23] 6593 3-8-10 **75**.............................. RobertHavlin 5 73
(Lydia Richards) *dwlt: hld up in last trio off str pce: prog wl over 2f out: rdn and kpt on over 1f out to take 3rd fnl stride* **40/1**

0650 **4** *nse* **He's Amazing (IRE)**[30] 6347 4-9-3 **77**.............................. TomMarquand 1 74+
(Ed Walker) *rousted s to go prom: pressed ldr at str pce: urged along over 3f out: outpcd over 1f out: fdd and lost 3rd last stride* **7/1**

0000 **5** *1* **George Of Hearts (FR)**[86] 4255 4-9-5 **82**..............(t[1]) CierenFallon(3) 8 77
(George Baker) *hld up in midfield: prog 3f out: rdn to chal 2f out: btn over 1f out: wknd (vet said gelding lost its left fore shoe)* **16/1**

2221 **6** *2 1/4* **Starfighter**[15] 6909 3-9-1 **80**.............................. OisinMurphy 11 71
(Ed Walker) *looked wl; restless stalls: hld up in last trio: shkn up and no real prog 3f out: plugged on over 1f out: no ch (jockey said gelding banged its head in the stalls)* **9/4[1]**

0-02 **7** *4 1/2* **Mystic Meg**[101] 3698 4-9-8 **82**..............(h) JasonWatson 6 63
(Hughie Morrison) *t.k.h: pressed ldrs at str pce tl wknd jst over 2f out (jockey said filly ran too freely)* **10/1**

6103 **8** *4 1/2* **My Boy Sepoy**[7] 7166 4-9-8 **82**.............................. AdamKirby 9 54
(Stuart Williams) *hld up in tch: lost pl and struggling wl over 2f out: sn wknd* **16/1**

6410 **9** *6* **Regular Income (IRE)**[86] 4241 4-9-7 **81**.............................. JimmyQuinn 7 41
(Adam West) *hld up in last: no prog 3f out: wl bhd fnl 2f* **33/1**

-006 **10** *12* **Nayel (IRE)**[126] 2800 7-9-10 **84**..............(p) PatDobbs 2 20
(Richard Hannon) *racd freely: led at str pce but pressed: hdd & wknd over 3f out: t.o* **25/1**

2422 **11** *3 1/2* **Craneur**[21] 6671 3-8-5 **70** oh4..............(p[1]) NicolaCurrie 3
(Harry Dunlop) *prom early: steadily lost pl: toiling in rr wl over 3f out: t.o (trainer said gelding did not face the first-time cheek-pieces)* **14/1**

2m 5.12s (-4.58) **Going Correction** -0.25s/f (Firm)
WFA 3 from 4yo+ 5lb **11 Ran SP% 118.2**
Speed ratings (Par 105): **108,107,102,102,101 100,96,92,88,78 75**
CSF £22.59 CT £644.26 TOTE £5.00: £1.90, £1.70, £9.30; EX 22.00 Trifecta £1021.40.
Owner Ben CM Wong **Bred** Newsells Park Stud **Trained** Newmarket, Suffolk

FOCUS
Add 15yds. This fair handicap was run at a decent gallop. The first two, both sons of Nathaniel, finished clear. A clear pb from the winner.
T/Plt: £38.50 to a £1 stake. Pool: £60,608.37 - 1,146.58 winning units T/Qpdt: £10.80 to a £1 stake. Pool: £6,238.40 - 424.58 winning units **Jonathan Neesom**

[7301] NEWCASTLE (A.W) (L-H)

Friday, September 20

OFFICIAL GOING: Tapeta: standard changing to standard to slow after race 1 (5.15)

Wind: light, largely across Weather: fine

7414 FLAME H'CAP 2m 56y (Tp)

5:15 (5:17) (Class 4) (0-85,87) 3-Y-O+ **£5,207** (£1,549; £774; £400) **Stalls** Low

Form RPR

3412 **1** **Anyonecanhaveitall**[6] 7209 3-9-0 **76** FrannyNorton 3 85
(Mark Johnston) *trckd ldr: drvn over 2f out: led over 1f out: styd on wl to draw clr ins fnl f* **11/10**[1]

2311 **2** *4* **Blame It On Sally (IRE)**[23] 6597 3-9-0 **76** (v) LukeMorris 1 80
(Sir Mark Prescott Bt) *led: rdn 3f out: drvn and hdd over 1f out: sn one pce* **7/4**[2]

5346 **3** *nk* **Grandee (IRE)**[13] 6981 5-10-6 **86** DavidEgan 4 89
(Roger Fell) *hld up in tch: pushed along and hdwy over 3f out: rdn over 2f out: sn one pce* **4/1**[3]

00-0 **4** *52* **Cape Cova (IRE)**[13] 6975 6-10-7 **87** DougieCostello 2 26
(Marjorie Fife) *in tch: rdn over 4f out: sn wknd: eased* **40/1**

3m 30.98s (-4.02) **Going Correction** -0.05s/f (Stan)
WFA 3 from 5yo+ 10lb **4 Ran SP% 106.4**
Speed ratings (Par 105): **108,106,105,79**
CSF £3.20 TOTE £1.80; EX 3.80 Trifecta £3.40.
Owner Garrett J Freyne **Bred** Newtown Stud And T J Pabst **Trained** Middleham Moor, N Yorks

FOCUS
The feature contest was a decent little staying handicap. The favourite won well off a modest gallop and the two 3yos finished first and second in receipt of 10lb weight-for-age allowances. The winner is rated in line with a better view of his Musselburgh run. The going was changed to standard to slow from standard after this race.

7415 SHIREMOOR PRESS H'CAP 1m 4f 98y (Tp)

5:50 (5:50) (Class 6) (0-60,62) 3-Y-O+
£2,781 (£827; £413; £400; £400; £400) **Stalls** High

Form RPR

0063 **1** **Beaufort (IRE)**[21] 6660 3-9-5 **57** ConnorBeasley 4 65
(Michael Dods) *hld up: angled rt to outer and hdwy 3f out: pushed along to chse ldrs over 1f out: led 110yds out: drvn out* **7/1**

05 **2** *hd* **Smart Lass (IRE)**[14] 6939 4-9-2 **47** (p) JamieGormley 6 54
(Iain Jardine) *prom: rdn to ld over 2f out: sn strly pressed: hdd 110yds out: styd on* **20/1**

5021 **3** *½* **Sulafaat (IRE)**[25] 6545 4-9-1 **53** (p) RussellHarris(7) 10 59
(Rebecca Menzies) *midfield: hdwy on outside 4f out: rdn to chal strly wl over 1f out: no ex towards fin* **12/1**

4331 **4** *3 ¼* **Hooflepuff (IRE)**[11] 7034 3-9-8 **60** 6ex (p) BenRobinson 7 62
(Brian Ellison) *trckd ldrs: rdn over 3f out: kpt on same pce* **3/1**[1]

4053 **5** *1* **Majestic Stone (IRE)**[14] 6939 5-9-1 **49** HarrisonShaw(3) 8 49
(Julie Camacho) *slowly away: hld up: rdn along and sme hdwy 2f out: styd on same pce (jockey said gelding was slowly away)* **4/1**[2]

6004 **6** *3 ¾* **Raashdy (IRE)**[10] 5001 6-9-7 **52** LukeMorris 1 46
(Sam England) *midfield: rdn over 3f out: wknd over 1f out* **5/1**[3]

0462 **7** *½* **Nataleena (IRE)**[21] 6660 3-9-4 **56** AndrewMullen 3 50
(Ben Haslam) *trckd ldrs: bit tight for room over 3f out: sn rdn: wknd over 1f out* **11/2**

0064 **8** *1 ¼* **Thawry**[11] 7034 4-10-3 **62** CamHardie 2 53
(Antony Brittain) *hld up: nvr threatened* **20/1**

4000 **9** *nk* **Love Rat**[99] 3769 4-9-10 **62** (p) JonathanFisher(7) 9 53
(Scott Dixon) *chsd ldrs: hdwy and led over 5f out: rdn and hdd over 2f out: sn wknd* **40/1**

4-44 **10** *34* **Lyford (IRE)**[14] 6939 4-9-6 **54** (v[1]) RowanScott(3) 5
(Alistair Whillans) *led: hdd over 5f out: rdn over 3f out: sn wknd: eased (trainer's rep could offer no explanation for the gelding's performance)* **11/1**

2m 39.23s (-1.87) **Going Correction** -0.05s/f (Stan)
WFA 3 from 4yo+ 7lb **10 Ran SP% 117.5**
Speed ratings (Par 101): **104,103,103,101,100 98,97,97,96,74**
CSF £138.16 CT £1652.37 TOTE £7.90: £2.40, £5.00, £3.20; EX 122.30 Trifecta £1583.80.
Owner Peter Appleton & M J K Dods **Bred** Garryard Stables **Trained** Denton, Co Durham
■ Stewards' Enquiry : Connor Beasley two-day ban; misuse of whip (Oct 4,7)

FOCUS
A modest middle-distance handicap. One of the three 3yos tanked into contention in receipt of his 7lb weight-for-age allowance. He found enough to narrowly defeat two older fillies close home and is rated to this year's best.

7416 AZURE MAIDEN AUCTION STKS 1m 5y (Tp)

6:20 (6:20) (Class 5) 2-Y-O **£3,428** (£1,020; £509; £254) **Stalls** Centre

Form RPR

03 **1** **Island Storm (IRE)**[31] 6314 2-9-5 **0** LukeMorris 2 73
(Heather Main) *pressed ldr: pushed along to ld over 1f out: sn edgd rt: rdn out ins fnl f* **3/1**[2]

3 **2** *1* **Urban Hero (IRE)**[21] 6673 2-9-5 **0** DavidEgan 4 71
(Archie Watson) *led narrowly: rdn and hdd over 1f out: styd on same pce* **5/4**[1]

5 **3** *1 ¾* **First Impression (IRE)**[26] 6497 2-9-5 **0** BenRobinson 5 67
(John Quinn) *prom: drvn and one pce in 3rd fr over 1f out* **6/1**

0 **4** *½* **Take That**[26] 6497 2-9-2 **0** SeanDavis(3) 6 66
(Richard Fahey) *hld up in tch: pushed along over 3f out: rdn appr fnl f: styd on wl towards fin* **25/1**

4 **5** *1 ¾* **Reggino (FR)**[26] 6497 2-9-5 **0** JackGarritty 1 62
(Jedd O'Keeffe) *trckd ldrs: racd keenly: rdn 2f out: wknd ins fnl f* **9/2**[3]

0 **6** *¾* **Copperlight (IRE)**[9] 7067 2-9-5 **0** AndrewMullen 3 60
(Ben Haslam) *dwlt: hld up in tch: pushed along 3f out: rdn over 1f out: sn btn* **28/1**

1m 41.32s (2.72) **Going Correction** -0.05s/f (Stan) **6 Ran SP% 109.2**
Speed ratings (Par 95): **84,83,81,80,79 78**
CSF £6.74 TOTE £2.80: £1.50, £1.20; EX 7.60 Trifecta £26.50.
Owner Donald Kerr & Wetumpka Racing **Bred** Roy W Tector **Trained** Kingston Lisle, Oxon

FOCUS
An ordinary juvenile maiden auction contest and the winning time was comparatively slow. Not form to place too much faith in.

7417 BAXI 800 WITH 10 YEAR WARRANTY NOVICE STKS 5f (Tp)

6:50 (6:50) (Class 5) 3-Y-O+ **£3,428** (£1,020; £509; £254) **Stalls** Centre

Form RPR

34-3 **1** **Lucky Charm**[28] 6388 3-9-0 **70** GeorgeWood 3 71
(Chris Wall) *mde all: pushed along over 1f out: 3 l clr ins fnl f: rdn out w reduced advantage towards fin* **7/2**[2]

0222 **2** *½* **Marvel**[14] 6944 3-9-2 **68** HarrisonShaw(3) 4 74+
(Julie Camacho) *racd in 4th: arnd 4 l bhd ldr (and eventual wnr): pushed along over 2f out: hdwy over 1f out: hung lft ent fnl f: wnt 2nd ins fnl f but stl 3 l down: rdn and kpt on wl* **4/9**[1]

35 **3** *4 ½* **Bithiah (IRE)**[14] 6944 3-9-0 **0** (h[1]) JackMitchell 2 53
(Ismail Mohammed) *rrd s: hld up: rdn and hdwy over 1f out: kpt on to go modest 3rd fnl 75yds* **16/1**[3]

0004 **4** *2* **Rangefield Express (IRE)**[14] 6944 3-9-5 **50** (b) AndrewMullen 1 51
(Geoffrey Harker) *prom: rdn 2f out: wknd ins fnl f* **33/1**

3 **5** *3 ¾* **Moudallal**[39] 6013 3-9-0 **0** LukeMorris 6 32
(Robert Cowell) *s.i.s: hld up: rdn over 2f out: nvr threatened* **20/1**

6 **6** *1 ½* **Anyonecanbeastar (IRE)**[17] 6823 3-9-0 **0** FrannyNorton 5 27
(Mark Johnston) *prom: rdn over 2f out: wknd appr fnl f* **16/1**[3]

58.96s (-0.54) **Going Correction** -0.05s/f (Stan) **6 Ran SP% 110.9**
Speed ratings (Par 103): **102,101,94,90,84 82**
CSF £5.27 TOTE £4.50: £1.80, £1.10; EX 7.10 Trifecta £22.00.
Owner Lady Juliet Tadgell **Bred** Lady Juliet Tadgell **Trained** Newmarket, Suffolk

FOCUS
An ordinary, effectively 3yo, novice sprint contest. The second-favourite grabbed a good early advantage over the strong market leader and gamely made all in a decent comparative time. She set the standard on her 2yo best.

7418 INTERGAS BOILER H'CAP 7f 14y (Tp)

7:20 (7:21) (Class 5) (0-70,70) 3-Y-O+
£3,428 (£1,020; £509; £400; £400; £400) **Stalls** Centre

Form RPR

0031 **1** **Blindingly (GER)**[42] 5918 4-9-7 **70** (p) HarrisonShaw(3) 8 78
(Ben Haslam) *prom in centre: racd keenly: led over 2f out: drvn over 1f out: pressed ins fnl f: hld on wl* **5/1**[2]

0010 **2** *nk* **Al Ozzdi**[101] 3704 4-9-2 **62** (w) DavidEgan 14 69
(Roger Fell) *racd stands' side: hld up: pushed along and hdwy over 2f out: drvn to chse ldr over 1f out: chal ins fnl f: kpt on* **11/1**

6010 **3** *hd* **Castle Quarter (IRE)**[21] 6679 3-9-1 **64** (p) BenRobinson 1 69
(Seb Spencer) *midfield in centre: rdn over 2f out: drvn and hdwy to chse ldr over 1f out: chal 110yds out: kpt on* **10/1**

5452 **4** *¾* **Rock Boy Grey (IRE)**[21] 6665 4-9-5 **65** StevieDonohoe 3 69
(Mark Loughnane) *dwlt: hld up in centre: rdn and hdwy over 1f out: sn chsd ldrs: kpt on ins fnl f* **9/2**[1]

330 **5** *¾* **Mostahel**[13] 6972 5-9-8 **68** GrahamLee 6 70
(Paul Midgley) *trckd ldrs centre: rdn along 2f out: no ex fnl 110yds* **7/1**[3]

0325 **6** *1 ¼* **Black Friday**[21] 6665 4-9-10 **70** (p) ConnorBeasley 12 69
(Karen McLintock) *racd stands' side: midfield overall: rdn over 2f out: edgd lft and kpt on fnl f* **9/2**[1]

0534 **7** *¾* **Absolute Dream (IRE)**[10] 7049 3-9-3 **69** SeanDavis(3) 4 65
(Richard Fahey) *in tch towards far side of centre gp: pushed along over 2f out: rdn over 1f out: no ex ins fnl f* **16/1**

0306 **8** *1 ¾* **Fair Alibi**[41] 5951 3-9-5 **68** FrannyNorton 2 59
(Tom Tate) *hld up towards far side of centre gp: rdn along 2f out: nvr threatened* **14/1**

2543 **9** *¾* **Lucky Lodge**[39] 6027 9-9-9 **69** (b) CamHardie 13 59
(Antony Brittain) *racd stands' side: trckd ldrs overall: rdn over 2f out: wknd over 1f out* **25/1**

005 **10** *2 ½* **Evie Speed (IRE)**[72] 4781 3-9-5 **68** JackGarritty 7 50
(Jedd O'Keeffe) *racd centre and led: rdn along and hdd over 2f out: sn drvn: wknd fnl f* **40/1**

5560 **11** *hd* **Bobby Joe Leg**[21] 6665 5-9-1 **61** (b) AndrewMullen 9 44
(Ruth Carr) *s.i.s: hld up in centre: nvr threatened* **50/1**

0000 **12** *¾* **False Id**[76] 4657 6-9-3 **63** (b) PhilDennis 10 43
(Fred Watson) *slowly away: racd centre: a in rr* **66/1**

5011 **13** *7* **Chaplin Bay (IRE)**[32] 6275 7-9-8 **68** JamieGormley 11 30
(Ruth Carr) *midfield in centre: rdn over 2f out: wknd (trainer's rep could offer no explanation for the gelding's performance)* **12/1**

0334 **14** *hd* **Supaulette (IRE)**[33] 6260 4-9-5 **65** (bt) DuranFentiman 5 26
(Tim Easterby) *midfield in centre: racd quite keenly: rdn 2f out: wknd over 1f out (vet said filly was found to be lame on its right fore)* **28/1**

1m 25.96s (-0.24) **Going Correction** -0.05s/f (Stan)
WFA 3 from 4yo+ 3lb **14 Ran SP% 116.4**
Speed ratings (Par 103): **99,98,98,97,96 95,94,92,91,88 88,87,79,79**
CSF £54.34 CT £545.53 TOTE £6.20: £2.40, £3.60, £3.70; EX 73.30 Trifecta £759.40.
Owner Mrs C Barclay **Bred** Gestut Westerberg **Trained** Middleham Moor, N Yorks

FOCUS
An ordinary handicap, but sound form. The third-favourite came through to gamely dominate the main group centrally while the narrow runner-up came home well towards the near rail from a separate group of three.

7419 2019 SARA'S HOPE FOUNDATION NURSERY H'CAP 6f (Tp)

7:50 (7:52) (Class 5) (0-75,76) 2-Y-O
£3,428 (£1,020; £509; £400; £400; £400) **Stalls** Centre

Form RPR

0430 **1** **Najm**[13] 6980 2-9-2 **70** (b[1]) LukeMorris 7 75
(Sir Mark Prescott Bt) *mde all: rdn 2f out: drvn fnl f: kpt on wl* **16/1**

2653 **2** *¾* **Danny Ocean (IRE)**[9] 7064 2-8-9 **66** (p) HarrisonShaw(3) 10 69
(K R Burke) *hld up in rr: pushed along and hdwy over 1f out: rdn to chse ldr ins fnl f: kpt on wl* **4/1**[3]

3240 **3** *1 ¾* **Pentewan**[9] 7072 2-9-4 **75** (b) RowanScott(3) 3 73
(Phillip Makin) *hld up: drvn and hdwy over 1f out: kpt on to go 3rd towards fin* **16/1**

3342 **4** *hd* **Kayewhykelly (IRE)**[21] 6653 2-9-0 **68** (h) GrahamLee 2 65
(Julie Camacho) *trckd ldrs: rdn 2f out: kpt on same pce fnl f* **8/1**

463 **5** *nk* **Robert Guiscard (IRE)**[13] 6970 2-9-3 **71** FrannyNorton 1 67
(Mark Johnston) *prom: rdn over 2f out: edgd lft over 1f out: drvn and one pce ins fnl f* **11/1**

66 **6** *¾* **Kocasandra (IRE)**[13] 6980 2-9-2 **75** SeamusCronin(5) 8 69
(Archie Watson) *trckd ldrs: rdn 2f out: drvn appr fnl f: wknd fnl 50yds* **8/1**

644 **7** 3/4 **Pettinger**15 6883 2-8-12 **66**.......... StevieDonohoe 9 58
(Charles Hills) *hld up: rdn and sme hdwy over 1f out: no further imp* **25/1**

0030 **8** 3/4 **Trevie Fountain**21 6653 2-8-11 **68**.......... SeanDavis(3) 5 58
(Richard Fahey) *midfield: rdn along and outpcd over 2f out: no threat after* **50/1**

0402 **9** 2 1/2 **Zingaro Boy (IRE)**13 6980 2-9-6 **74**.......... JackMitchell 4 56
(Hugo Palmer) *trckd ldrs: racd keenly: rdn 2f out: wknd ins fnl f (trainer's rep said colt behaved in a coltish manner at the start and ran too freely)* **10/3**1

443 **10** 2 3/4 **Phuket Power (IRE)**18 6807 2-9-8 **76**..........(p1) DavidEgan 6 50+
(Tom Dascombe) *wnt rt and stmbld s: hld up: racd keenly: rdn 2f out: sn wknd (jockey said colt stumbled shortly after the start; vet said colt suffered an over-reach to its left-fore)* **7/2**2

1m 12.42s (-0.08) **Going Correction** -0.05s/f (Stan) **10** Ran SP% **113.4**
Speed ratings (Par 95): **98,97,94,94,94 93,92,91,87,84**
CSF £76.96 CT £1078.03 TOTE £19.40: £5.30, £2.10, £5.00; EX 90.80 Trifecta £604.00.
Owner Malih L Al Basti **Bred** Malih L Al Basti **Trained** Newmarket, Suffolk

FOCUS
A fair nursery. One of the relative outsiders made all bravely in a fair time towards the stands' rail.

7420 POPPYS DELIGHT H'CAP 6f (Tp)
8:20 (8:22) (Class 6) (0-55,57) 3-Y-O+
£2,781 (£827; £413; £400; £400; £400) **Stalls** Centre

Form RPR

5641 **1** **Fard**4 7286 4-9-6 **57** 5ex.......... PaulaMuir(5) 10 66+
(Roger Fell) *dwlt: hld up in rr and sn pushed along: swtchd lft towards outer over 2f out: rdn and sn gd hdwy: led ins fnl f: kpt on wl to draw clr* **13/8**1

000 **2** 2 3/4 **Breathoffreshair**43 5857 5-9-2 **48**..........(bt1) FrannyNorton 12 49
(Richard Guest) *hld up in rr: rdn over 2f out: hrd drvn over 1f out: swtchd lft and r.o ins fnl f: wnt 2nd post* **20/1**

0000 **3** nse **Extrasolar**14 6945 9-9-7 **53**..........(t) ConnorBeasley 3 54
(Geoffrey Harker) *trckd ldrs: rdn 2f out: drvn to chal strly appr fnl f: one pce ins fnl f: lost 2nd post* **22/1**

6050 **4** nk **Rockley Point**21 6659 6-9-5 **51**..........(b) PhilDennis 2 51
(Katie Scott) *led: rdn over 2f out: drvn and strly pressed appr fnl f: hdd ins fnl f: one pce* **25/1**

5600 **5** nk **Salmon Fishing (IRE)**20 6737 3-9-1 **54**..........(p) SeamusCronin(5) 6 53
(Mohamed Moubarak) *hld up: rdn over 2f out: kpt on ins fnl f* **12/1**

0430 **6** hd **Tadaany (IRE)**21 6659 7-9-4 **50**..........(v) JackGarritty 4 49
(Ruth Carr) *midfield: rdn along and sme hdwy 2f out: drvn appr fnl f: kpt on same pce* **14/1**

/600 **7** 3/4 **One Last Hug**162 1722 4-9-2 **48**.......... BenRobinson 8 44
(Jim Goldie) *hld up: rdn 2f out: kpt on ins fnl f: nvr threatened* **22/1**

0316 **8** hd **Kellington Kitty (USA)**15 6889 4-9-7 **53**..........(p) LukeMorris 13 49
(Mike Murphy) *hld up: rdn over 2f out: kpt on ins fnl f: nvr threatened* **14/1**

0405 **9** hd **Groupie**10 7051 5-9-7 **53**.......... GrahamLee 11 48
(Tom Tate) *midfield: pushed along over 2f out: rdn over 1f out: no imp* **9/1**3

0040 **10** hd **A Hundred Echoes**14 6945 3-9-6 **54**..........(b1) DavidEgan 1 49
(Roger Varian) *prom: rdn 2f out: wknd ins fnl f* **16/1**

4010 **11** 1 1/2 **Ingleby Molly (IRE)**32 6276 4-9-3 **52**..........(h) HarrisonShaw(3) 9 42
(Jason Ward) *prom: rdn over 2f out: wknd ins fnl f* **7/1**2

200 **12** 3 1/4 **Little Miss Kodi (IRE)**15 6897 6-9-4 **50**..........(t) AndrewMullen 14 30
(Mark Loughnane) *midfield: rdn over 2f out: wknd over 1f out* **33/1**

2600 **13** 4 **Viking Way (IRE)**45 5767 4-9-3 **49**..........(b) JackMitchell 7 17
(Olly Williams) *trckd ldrs: rdn over 2f out: wknd over 1f out* **9/1**3

1m 12.24s (-0.26) **Going Correction** -0.05s/f (Stan)
WFA 3 from 4yo+ 2lb **13** Ran SP% **117.7**
Speed ratings (Par 101): **99,95,95,94,94 94,93,92,92,92 90,86,80**
CSF £43.52 CT £561.91 TOTE £2.60: £1.30, £5.50, £4.70; EX 50.40 Trifecta £741.90.
Owner Northern Marking Ltd & Partners **Bred** Lofts Hall Stud & B Sangster **Trained** Nawton, N Yorks

FOCUS
A moderate sprint handicap. The clear favourite's winning time was marginally quicker than the previous C&D nursery, and it's just about his best effort of the year.
T/Plt: £501.40 to a £1 stake. Pool: £61,014.00 - 88.82 winning units T/Qpdt: £24.50 to a £1 stake. Pool: £10,672.20 - winning units **Andrew Sheret**

7421 - 7428a (Foreign Racing) - See Raceform Interactive

7398 AYR (L-H)
Saturday, September 21

OFFICIAL GOING: Good (7.7)
Wind: Breezy, half behind up the straight Weather: Sunny, hot

7429 MILLAR CALLAGHAN ENGINEERING 20TH ANNIVERSARY EBF NURSERY H'CAP 1m
1:25 (1:26) (Class 2) 2-Y-O
£12,450 (£3,728; £1,864; £932; £466; £234) **Stalls** Low

Form RPR

512 **1** **Tell Me All**37 6112 2-9-7 **83**.......... ColinKeane 10 88
(Sir Mark Prescott Bt) *t.k.h: pressed ldr: led 3f out: rdn wl over 1f out: hld on wl cl home* **9/4**1

221 **2** shd **Yoshimi (IRE)**15 6934 2-9-3 **79**.......... PaulHanagan 2 84
(Richard Fahey) *t.k.h: trckd ldrs: effrt and wnt 2nd over 1f out: kpt on wl fnl f: jst hld* **8/1**

2405 **3** 3 **Sir Arthur Dayne (IRE)**21 6728 2-9-1 **77**..........(v) OisinMurphy 9 75
(Mick Channon) *hld up: rdn over 2f out: hdwy over 1f out: kpt on wl fnl f to take 3rd cl home (jockey said colt suffered interference 1 1/2f out)* **14/1**

556 **4** 1/2 **Bye Bye Euro (IRE)**35 6226 2-8-2 **64** oh1 ow2.......... JoeFanning 6 61
(Keith Dalgleish) *chsd ldrs: drvn along over 2f out: one pce fnl f: lost 3rd cl home* **50/1**

5531 **5** 2 **International Lion**14 6969 2-8-3 **65**..........(p) PaddyMathers 1 57
(Richard Fahey) *dwlt: hld up: rdn over 2f out: kpt on fnl f: nvr able to chal* **10/1**

621 **6** hd **Atheeb**44 5848 2-9-6 **82**.......... ColmO'Donoghue 5 74
(Sir Michael Stoute) *in tch on ins: rdn over 2f out: edgd rt and one pce over 1f out* **11/2**3

621 **7** nk **Plymouth Rock (IRE)**14 6971 2-9-3 **79**.......... JasonHart 7 70
(John Quinn) *t.k.h: hld up in tch: rdn over 2f out: outpcd whn checked over 1f out: sn n.d* **4/1**2

325 **8** 1 **Viceregent**14 6971 2-8-12 **74**.......... TonyHamilton 3 63
(Richard Fahey) *led to 3f out: rdn and wknd over 1f out* **22/1**

3041 **9** hd **Top Buck (IRE)**7 7173 2-9-3 **79**..........(p) BenCurtis 4 67
(Brian Meehan) *midfield: lost pl over 3f out: sn rdn: n.d after* **11/1**

0502 **10** 2 3/4 **Clay Regazzoni**14 6969 2-9-1 **77**.......... DanielTudhope 8 59
(Keith Dalgleish) *hld up: rdn along over 2f out: sn no imp: btn over 1f out* **9/1**

1m 39.84s (-2.96) **Going Correction** -0.35s/f (Firm) **10** Ran SP% **117.7**
Speed ratings (Par 101): **100,99,96,96,94 94,93,92,92,89**
CSF £21.29 CT £212.76 TOTE £2.60: £1.40, £2.10, £3.70; EX 20.30 Trifecta £197.50.
Owner Cheveley Park Stud **Bred** Cheveley Park Stud Ltd **Trained** Newmarket, Suffolk

FOCUS
All race distances as advertised. The final day of the Gold Cup meeting and after riding in the opener Oisin Murphy said: "It's good ground, maybe a bit slower in places," Joe Fanning said: "It's quicker than yesterday" and Paul Hanagan said: "It's dried out from yesterday but it's nice, safe good ground."\n\x\x This was a fair nursery and the first pair drew clear in a bobbing finish. They both took a step forward.

7430 WILLIAM HILL FOUNDATION:UNITING AGAINST DEMENTIA H'CAP 1m
2:00 (2:00) (Class 2) (0-105,101) 3-Y-O+
£18,675 (£5,592; £2,796; £1,398; £699; £351) **Stalls** Low

Form RPR

0004 **1** **Waarif (IRE)**9 7122 6-9-6 **95**.......... DanielTudhope 9 103
(David O'Meara) *trckd ldrs: led over 2f out: rdn over 1f out: edgd rt ins fnl f: r.o wl* **11/2**3

2253 **2** 1/2 **Kynren (IRE)**30 6376 5-9-12 **101**.......... PJMcDonald 3 108
(David Barron) *in tch: rdn 3f out: hdwy over 1f out: chsd wnr ins fnl f: edgd rt: kpt on: hld nr fin* **7/4**1

0100 **3** nk **Kylie Rules**14 6974 4-8-10 **85**.......... TomEaves 7 91
(Ruth Carr) *stdd in last pl: hdwy on outside over 2f out: chsd wnr over 1f out to ins fnl f: one pce* **28/1**

3061 **4** 2 **Irreverent**14 6973 3-8-11 **90**..........(p1) PaulHanagan 11 92
(Richard Fahey) *trckd ldr: ev ch over 2f out to over 1f out: no ex ins fnl f* **5/1**2

1420 **5** 2 1/2 **Alfred Richardson**13 6998 5-9-0 **89**..........(b) KevinStott 8 85
(John Davies) *dwlt: hld up towards rr: rdn over 2f out: hdwy over 1f out: kpt on fnl f: nvr able to chal* **12/1**

0240 **6** 1 **Byron's Choice**63 5173 4-9-2 **91**.......... CallumRodriguez 10 85
(Michael Dods) *hld up: rdn along 3f out: effrt u.p over 1f out: no imp fnl f* **10/1**

1240 **7** 2 **Club Wexford (IRE)**30 6376 8-9-4 **93**.......... BenCurtis 4 82
(Roger Fell) *led to 2f out: sn rdn and wknd* **11/1**

-502 **8** 6 **Gulf Of Poets**93 4035 7-9-3 **92**.......... NathanEvans 1 67
(Michael Easterby) *prom: rdn and lost pl over 2f out: sn struggling* **22/1**

536 **9** 2 1/4 **Boston George (IRE)**29 6425 3-8-5 **87**..........(p1) SeanDavis(3) 2 57
(Keith Dalgleish) *s.i.s: in tch on ins: drvn and struggling over 2f out: sn btn: lost front shoe (vet said colt lost its left fore shoe)* **9/1**

1523 **10** 23 **Smile A Mile (IRE)**7 7184 3-9-1 **94**.......... JoeFanning 12 11
(Mark Johnston) *t.k.h: prom on outside: lost pl 3f out: sn struggling: eased whn no ch fr 2f out (trainer's rep could offer no explanation for the poor form shown)* **12/1**

1m 37.62s (-5.18) **Going Correction** -0.35s/f (Firm)
WFA 3 from 4yo+ 4lb **10** Ran SP% **119.0**
Speed ratings (Par 109): **111,110,110,108,105 104,102,96,94,71**
CSF £15.83 CT £254.91 TOTE £6.00: £1.90, £1.20, £6.40; EX 16.80 Trifecta £297.60.
Owner Middleham Park Racing XLIX **Bred** Joseph Stewart Investments **Trained** Upper Helmsley, N Yorks

FOCUS
This decent handicap was run at a sound pace and the principals fought it out down the centre. Straightforward form.

7431 WILLIAM HILL AYR SILVER CUP H'CAP 6f
2:40 (2:42) (Class 2) 3-Y-O+
£37,350 (£11,184; £5,592; £2,796; £1,398; £702) **Stalls** Centre

Form RPR

0346 **1** **Golden Apollo**8 7152 5-9-4 **88**..........(tp) DavidAllan 5 97
(Tim Easterby) *midfield on far side of gp: effrt and edgd lft over 1f out: led ins fnl f: kpt on strly* **12/1**

2002 **2** nk **Gabrial The Saint (IRE)**8 7142 4-9-5 **89**.......... PaulHanagan 2 97
(Richard Fahey) *led on far side of gp: rdn over 1f out: hdd ins fnl f: rallied: hld towards fin* **20/1**

0036 **3** 1 **Get Knotted (IRE)**15 6922 7-9-4 **88**..........(p) CallumRodriguez 20 93
(Michael Dods) *hld up in midfield on nr side of gp: stdy hdwy over 2f out: effrt and rdn over 1f out: chsd ldng pair ins fnl f: r.o* **14/1**

1353 **4** nk **Show Stealer**7 7193 6-9-8 **92**..........(p) RichardKingscote 23 96+
(Rae Guest) *hld up: rdn and gd hdwy over 1f out: kpt on fnl f: nrst fin* **12/1**1

5000 **5** 1 1/2 **Flying Pursuit**22 6676 6-9-3 **87**..........(t1) RachelRichardson 6 86
(Tim Easterby) *cl up on far side of gp: rdn over 2f out: no ex ins fnl f* **25/1**

4505 **6** 1/2 **Admirality**7 7222 5-9-10 **94**.......... BenCurtis 15 91
(Roger Fell) *hld up in centre: effrt and swtchd to far side of gp 2f out: sn prom: rdn and no ex fnl f* **11/2**2

3112 **7** hd **Alkaraama (USA)**14 6953 3-9-8 **94**.......... ColmO'Donoghue 12 91
(Sir Michael Stoute) *in tch in centre of gp: effrt and rdn over 1f out: one pce whn checked ins fnl f* **5/1**1

2460 **8** nse **Muscika**7 7193 5-9-8 **92**.......... DavidNolan 19 89
(David O'Meara) *midfield in centre of gp: pushed along 1/2-way: hdwy over 1f out: kpt on: nrst fin* **20/1**

60-0 **9** nk **Rapid Applause**22 6676 7-9-3 **87**.......... NathanEvans 16 83
(Michael Easterby) *reluctant to enter stalls: bhd in centre of gp: rdn over 2f out: kpt on fnl f: nvr rchd ldrs* **80/1**

020 **10** 1 **Venturous (IRE)**6 7241 6-9-5 **89**.......... RobbieDowney 4 81
(David Barron) *midfield on far side of gp: pushed along and effrt 2f out: no imp fnl f* **14/1**

5162 **11** nk **Lahore (USA)**22 6676 5-9-9 **93**.......... PaulMulrennan 25 85
(Phillip Makin) *hld up on nr side of gp: effrt and rdn over 1f out: sn n.d* **9/1**3

0023 **12** 3/4 **Hyperfocus (IRE)**15 6920 5-9-10 **94**..........(p) JasonHart 11 83
(Tim Easterby) *cl up in centre of gp tl rdn and wknd over 1f out: lost front shoe (vet said colt lost it's left front shoes)* **25/1**

3111 **13** nse **Major Valentine**26 6525 7-9-1 **92** 5ex.......... KateLeahy(7) 22 81
(John O'Shea) *racd alone towards stands' side: prom: outpcd 2f out: n.d after* **33/1**

0030 **13** dht **Jawwaal**22 6676 4-9-2 **89**..........(p) SeanDavis(3) 18 78
(Michael Dods) *t.k.h: cl up in centre of gp: rdn and edgd lft over 1f out: wknd ins fnl f* **22/1**

1000 **15** ½ **Rathbone**[28] 6476 3-9-6 **92** .... TomEaves 21 79
(Kevin Ryan) *hld up on nr side of gp: effrt and drvn over 2f out: sn no imp* **40/1**

3134 **16** ¾ **Citron Major**[8] 7152 4-9-3 **90** .... (tp) RowanScott(3) 17 75
(Nigel Tinkler) *dwlt: bhd in centre of gp: rdn over 2f out: no imp fr over 1f out* **16/1**

0205 **17** ½ **Savalas (IRE)**[9] 7121 4-9-4 **88** .... KevinStott 24 71
(Kevin Ryan) *dwlt: hld up on nr side of gp: rdn over 2f out: wl able to chal* **25/1**

2000 **18** ½ **Magical Wish (IRE)**[42] 5932 3-9-9 **95** .... RossaRyan 14 77
(Richard Hannon) *in tch on nr side of gp tl rdn and wknd over 1f out* **25/1**

U134 **19** ½ **Royal Residence**[15] 6920 4-9-7 **91** .... PJMcDonald 1 71
(James Tate) *in tch on far side of gp: rdn over 2f out: wknd over 1f out: lost front shoe (vet said colt lost it's left front shoes)* **14/1**

0066 **20** 2 ¾ **Glenamoy Lad**[14] 6953 5-9-9 **93** .... (t) JoeFanning 13 64
(Michael Wigham) *dwlt: bhd in centre of gp: pushed along over 2f out: sn btn* **18/1**

5506 **21** *nk* **Yousini**[13] 7002 3-9-3 **89** .... (v[1]) TonyHamilton 3 59
(Kevin Ryan) *in tch on far side of gp tl rdn and wknd over 1f out* **33/1**

3020 **22** 2 ½ **James Watt (IRE)**[28] 6476 3-8-13 **85** .... ColinKeane 10 47
(Michael Bell) *hld up on far side of gp: drvn along over 2f out: sn btn* **50/1**

3250 **23** ¾ **Lincoln Park**[15] 6922 3-9-4 **90** .... OisinMurphy 7 50
(Michael Appleby) *prom in centre of gp: lost pl 2f out: sn struggling* **20/1**

-300 **24** ½ **Red Balloons**[13] 6999 3-9-9 **95** .... DanielTudhope 8 53
(Richard Fahey) *midfield in centre of gp: n.m.r briefly over 2f out: rdn and wknd over 1f out* **20/1**

1m 9.63s (-3.47) **Going Correction** -0.35s/f (Firm)
WFA 3 from 4yo+ 2lb **24** Ran SP% **138.9**
Speed ratings (Par 109): **109,108,107,106,104 104,103,103,103,102 101,100,100,100,100 99,98,97,97,93 92,89,88,87**
WIN: 14.40 Golden Apollo; PL: 2.40 Show Stealer 5.30 Gabrial The Saint 3.90 Get Knotted 3.20 Golden Apollo; EX: 286.50; CSF: 243.18; TC: 3485.23; TF: 3801.40 CSF £243.18 CT £3485.23 TOTE £14.40: £3.20, £5.30, £3.90, £2.40; EX 286.50 Trifecta £3801.40.
Owner David Scott & Partner **Bred** Cheveley Park Stud Ltd **Trained** Great Habton, N Yorks
■ Stewards' Enquiry : Callum Rodriguez two-day ban; careless riding (Oct 7-8)

FOCUS
Although consolation for those not getting into the feature, the Silver Cup is a fair prize in its own right, and this year's edition was fiercely competitive. All bar \bMajor Valentine\p raced nearer the far side and so low numbers held a definite advantage. The form is rated around the first two.

7432 WILLIAM HILL FIRTH OF CLYDE STKS (GROUP 3) (FOR THE AYRSHIRE AGRICULTURAL CHALLENGE CUP) (FILLIES) 6f

3:15 (3:18) (Class 1) 2-Y-O

£36,861 (£13,975; £6,994; £3,484; £1,748; £877) **Stalls** Centre

Form RPR

5134 **1** **Rose Of Kildare (IRE)**[18] 6833 2-9-0 94 .... JoeFanning 9 100
(Mark Johnston) *prom: rdn along 2f out: drvn appr fnl f: led 110yds out: kpt on* **8/1**

1021 **2** ½ **Graceful Magic**[9] 7117 2-9-0 86 .... RichardKingscote 2 99
(Eve Johnson Houghton) *hld up: pushed along over 2f out: rdn appr fnl f: kpt on wl fnl f: wnt 2nd towards fin* **5/1**[3]

3431 **3** ½ **Endless Joy**[23] 6637 2-9-0 78 .... DanielTudhope 10 97
(Archie Watson) *led narrowly after 1f: rdn over 2f out: drvn over 1f out: hdd 110yds out: one pce* **20/1**

4141 **4** 1 ½ **Orlaith (IRE)**[36] 6157 2-9-0 100 .... PaulMulrennan 4 93
(Iain Jardine) *hld up: pushed along and hdwy over 2f out: chsd ldrs appr fnl f: rdn and kpt on same pce ins fnl f* **6/1**

14 **5** *shd* **Final Option**[16] 6907 2-9-0 0 .... BenCurtis 7 92
(William Muir) *in tch: pushed along 2f out: rdn appr fnl f: kpt on same pce* **11/2**

1042 **6** 1 ¼ **Lambeth Walk**[26] 6542 2-9-0 96 .... OisinMurphy 1 88
(Archie Watson) *led for 1f: chsd ldrs: rdn along over 2f out: drvn over 1f out: wknd fnl 110yds* **4/1**[1]

41 **7** 1 ¾ **Piece Of Paradise (IRE)**[1] 7400 2-9-0 0 .... (bt) PaulHanagan 6 83
(J A Stack, Ire) *hld up in tch: racd keenly: rdn over 1f out: wknd ins fnl f* **9/2**[2]

1 **8** 2 ¾ **Al Rasmah (IRE)**[21] 6713 2-9-0 0 .... TonyHamilton 3 75
(Richard Fahey) *hld up: rdn along over 2f out: sn btn* **7/1**

1 **9** 1 ¼ **Aleneva (IRE)**[107] 3506 2-9-0 0 .... PJMcDonald 8 71
(Richard Fahey) *trckd ldrs: rdn 2f out: wknd fnl f* **16/1**

1m 10.76s (-2.34) **Going Correction** -0.35s/f (Firm) **9** Ran SP% **118.8**
Speed ratings (Par 102): **101,100,99,97,97 95,93,89,88**
CSF £49.12 TOTE £8.20: £2.30, £2.10, £4.70; EX 47.60 Trifecta £639.10.
Owner Kingsley Park 14 **Bred** Wansdyke Farms Ltd **Trained** Middleham Moor, N Yorks

FOCUS
An open race as the betting suggested, but probably a below-par renewal. The winner stepped forward again.

7433 WILLIAM HILL AYR GOLD CUP (HERITAGE H'CAP) 6f

3:50 (3:53) (Class 2) 3-Y-O+

£124,500 (£37,280; £18,640; £9,320; £4,660; £2,340) **Stalls** Centre

Form RPR

2103 **1** **Angel Alexander (IRE)**[21] 6714 3-8-13 **101** .... RichardKingscote 24 111
(Tom Dascombe) *chsd stands' side ldrs: rdn to ld that gp over 1f out: hung lft and kpt on strly to take overall ld towards fin: 1st of 6 in gp* **28/1**

0016 **2** ½ **Growl**[21] 6714 7-8-9 **95** .... TonyHamilton 18 103
(Richard Fahey) *in tch far side gp: effrt and rdn over 1f out: led ins fnl f: kpt on: hdd towards fin: 1st of 18 in gp* **28/1**

6003 **3** ½ **Gulliver**[6] 7241 5-8-12 **98** .... (tp) JasonHart 9 104
(David O'Meara) *in tch far side: effrt and rdn over 1f out: ev ch ins fnl f: kpt on: hld nr fin: 2nd of 18 in gp* **8/1**[2]

342 **4** ¾ **Summerghand (IRE)**[35] 6229 5-9-2 **102** .... DavidNolan 13 106
(David O'Meara) *hld up far side: rdn and hdwy over 1f out: kpt on fnl f: nrst fin: 3rd of 18 in gp* **11/1**

0236 **5** *hd* **Embour (IRE)**[7] 7193 4-8-9 **95** .... PaddyMathers 16 98
(Richard Hannon) *hld up in midfield on far side: effrt and hdwy over 1f out: kpt on ins fnl f: no further imp towards fin: 4th of 18 in gp* **20/1**

1234 **6** *nk* **Louie De Palma**[71] 4866 7-8-9 **95** .... HectorCrouch 10 97
(Clive Cox) *cl up far side: led that gp over 2f out to ins fnl f: no ex towards fin: 5th of 18 in gp* **20/1**

1000 **7** *hd* **Soldier's Minute**[49] 5664 4-8-10 **96** .... (h[1]) JoeFanning 3 98
(Keith Dalgleish) *dwlt: bhd far side: hdwy and edgd rt over 1f out: kpt on ins fnl f: nvr able to chal: 6th of 18 in gp* **18/1**

0324 **8** ½ **Arecibo (FR)**[7] 7193 4-8-12 **98** .... (v) DanielTudhope 17 98
(David O'Meara) *dwlt: hld up far side: rdn and effrt over 1f out: kpt on same pce ins fnl f: 7th of 18 in gp* **10/1**[3]

000 **9** *nk* **Gunmetal (IRE)**[7] 7193 6-9-1 **101** .... (b[1]) OisinMurphy 23 100
(David Barron) *chsd stands' side ldrs: drvn along over 2f out: wnt 2nd that gp ins fnl f: no imp: 2nd of 6 in gp* **20/1**

1305 **10** *nse* **Staxton**[35] 6229 4-8-12 **98** .... (p) DavidAllan 4 97
(Tim Easterby) *prom far side: rdn and hung lft over 2f out: rallied over 1f out: one pce ins fnl f: 8th of 18 in gp* **16/1**

060 **11** *nk* **Merhoob (IRE)**[48] 5705 7-8-13 **99** .... BenCurtis 12 97
(John Ryan) *dwlt: bhd far side: rdn and hdwy over 1f out: no imp fnl f: 9th of 18 in gp* **66/1**

4003 **12** *nse* **Intisaab**[8] 7152 8-8-6 **99** .... (tp) AngusVilliers(7) 7 97
(David O'Meara) *dwlt: hld up far side: rdn along over 2f out: kpt on fnl f: nvr rchd ldrs: 10th of 18 in gp* **14/1**

0010 **13** *hd* **Good Effort (IRE)**[28] 6453 4-8-12 **98** .... PaulMulrennan 15 95
(Ismail Mohammed) *in tch far side: effrt and cl up over 1f out: no ex ins fnl f: 11th of 18 in gp* **33/1**

3010 **14** ½ **Major Jumbo**[14] 6959 5-9-8 **108** .... TomEaves 20 104
(Kevin Ryan) *led stands' side gp to over 1f out: no ex ins fnl f: 3rd of 6 in gp* **16/1**

-001 **15** ¾ **Cold Stare (IRE)**[105] 3589 4-8-12 **98** .... (t w) RobbieDowney 11 91
(David O'Meara) *midfield far side: rdn whn checked briefly over 1f out: sn no imp: 12th of 18 in gp* **40/1**

5020 **16** ¾ **Hey Jonesy (IRE)**[56] 5413 4-9-3 **103** .... (v[1]) KevinStott 8 94
(Kevin Ryan) *cl up far side: drvn along over 2f out: wknd fnl f: lost front shoe: 13th of 18 in gp* **10/1**[3]

-251 **17** 1 ½ **Buffer Zone**[6] 7241 4-9-4 **104** 5ex .... ColinKeane 21 90
(G M Lyons, Ire) *hld up in tch stands' side gp: effrt and edgd lft 2f out: wknd fnl f: 4th of 6 in gp (trainer said gelding ran flat and that the race may have come to soon for the gelding having run only 6 days previous)* **10/3**[1]

0100 **18** *hd* **Stone Of Destiny**[14] 6953 4-8-13 **99** .... PJMcDonald 22 84
(Andrew Balding) *dwlt: hld up stands' side: stdy hdwy over 2f out: rdn over 1f out: sn wknd: 5th of 6 in gp* **33/1**

0000 **19** *nk* **George Bowen (IRE)**[35] 6229 7-8-10 **96** .... (v) PaulHanagan 19 80
(Richard Fahey) *hld up far side: drvn over 2f out: sn no imp: btn over 1f out: 14th of 18 in gp* **33/1**

6600 **20** *nse* **Mr Lupton (IRE)**[28] 6472 6-9-7 **110** .... SeanDavis(3) 1 94
(Richard Fahey) *bhd far side: drvn along 1/2-way: nvr on terms: 15th of 18 in gp* **20/1**

0556 **21** *shd* **Barbill (IRE)**[42] 5932 3-8-9 **97** .... NathanEvans 6 81
(Mick Channon) *towards rr far side: drvn along over 3f out: sn no imp: btn over 1f out: 16th of 18 in gp* **25/1**

00-0 **22** 1 ½ **Bacchus**[91] 4095 5-9-6 **106** .... (p) ColmO'Donoghue 25 85
(Brian Meehan) *prom stands' side: lost pl over 2f out: sn struggling: last of 6 in gp* **33/1**

5010 **23** ½ **Justanotherbottle (IRE)**[7] 7193 5-8-8 **101** 5ex .... ZakWheatley(7) 2 79
(Declan Carroll) *t.k.h: led far side to over 2f out: wknd over 1f out: 17th of 18 in gp* **25/1**

4320 **24** 1 ½ **Laugh A Minute**[64] 5120 4-9-3 **103** .... (b[1]) RossaRyan 5 76
(Roger Varian) *hld up far side: drvn over 2f out: edgd rt and wknd over 1f out: last of 18 in gp* **12/1**

1m 9.26s (-3.84) **Going Correction** -0.35s/f (Firm)
WFA 3 from 4yo+ 2lb **24** Ran SP% **141.4**
Speed ratings (Par 109): **111,110,109,108,108 108,107,107,106,106 106,106,105,105,104 103,101,100,100,100 100,98,97,95**
CSF £679.13 CT £6800.69 TOTE £32.70: £7.40, £5.80, £2.50, £3.00; EX 1234.60 Trifecta £22078.40.
Owner Birbeck Mound Trowbridge & Owen **Bred** Mountarmstrong Stud **Trained** Malpas, Cheshire

FOCUS
Half a dozen kept stands' side in this cracking edition of the Ayr Gold Cup, with the rest heading more far side early. There was a blanket finish, with the main action developed down the middle, and it's rock-solid form. The runner-up is the best guide.

7434 WILLIAM HILL LEADING RACECOURSE BOOKMAKER H'CAP (FOR THE KILKERRAN CUP) 1m 2f

4:25 (4:26) (Class 2) (0-100,98) 3-Y-O+

£15,562 (£4,660; £2,330; £1,165; £582; £292) **Stalls** Low

Form RPR

1042 **1** **Certain Lad**[9] 7122 3-9-7 **98** .... BenCurtis 9 106
(Mick Channon) *hld up: smooth hdwy over 2f out: rdn to ld appr fnl f: drvn out: hld on towards fin* **11/4**[1]

1143 **2** *nk* **Nicholas T**[9] 7122 7-9-10 **96** .... BenRobinson 1 103
(Jim Goldie) *hld up in rr: swtchd rt to wd outside over 2f out: sn hdwy: drvn to chse ldr appr fnl f: kpt on wl* **15/2**

1605 **3** 1 ½ **Anythingtoday (IRE)**[15] 6923 5-9-9 **95** .... (v[1]) DanielTudhope 2 99
(David O'Meara) *hld up: hdwy and gng wl in bhd horses 2f out: angled rt to outer over 1f out: pushed along to sn chse ldr: drvn and kpt on same pce ins fnl f* **11/1**

0050 **4** ¾ **Society Red**[28] 6475 5-9-0 **86** .... PaulHanagan 4 89
(Richard Fahey) *midfield: rdn along 2f out: hung lft but styd on ins fnl f* **11/2**[2]

50-4 **5** *shd* **Another Touch**[70] 4935 6-9-8 **94** .... TonyHamilton 8 96
(Richard Fahey) *trckd ldrs: led 2f out: sn rdn along: hdd appr fnl f: wknd fnl 110yds* **11/2**[2]

4015 **6** 4 **Universal Gleam**[9] 7106 4-9-2 **91** .... SeanDavis(3) 6 85
(Keith Dalgleish) *midfield: hdwy 3f out: rdn to chal briefly 2f out: wknd fnl f* **16/1**

1602 **7** ½ **Poet's Dawn**[13] 6998 4-8-12 **84** .... DavidAllan 3 77
(Tim Easterby) *trckd ldrs: rdn along over 2f out: wknd fnl f* **15/2**

0232 **8** 2 ¼ **The Trader (IRE)**[7] 7199 3-9-1 **92** .... JoeFanning 7 81
(Mark Johnston) *prom: rdn into narrow ld over 2f out: sn hdd: wknd appr fnl f* **7/1**[3]

0100 **9** ¾ **Borodin (IRE)**[22] 6657 4-9-8 **94** .... (p) PaddyMathers 5 81
(Richard Fahey) *sn led: racd keenly: rdn and hdd over 2f out: wknd over 1f out* **12/1**

0-05 **10** 2 ¼ **Star Archer**[14] 6975 5-9-2 **88** .... NathanEvans 10 71
(Michael Easterby) *hld up in midfield on outer: rdn along 3f out: wknd over 1f out* **25/1**

2m 7.53s (-4.87) **Going Correction** -0.35s/f (Firm)
WFA 3 from 4yo+ 5lb **10** Ran SP% **119.2**
Speed ratings (Par 109): **105,104,103,102,102 99,99,97,96,95**
CSF £24.41 CT £201.07 TOTE £3.40: £1.60, £2.40, £3.80; EX 26.30 Trifecta £194.70.
Owner C R Hirst **Bred** Barry Walters **Trained** West Ilsley, Berks

FOCUS
An competitive race for useful handicappers, run at what appeared to be an even tempo. The winner backed up his improved latest form.

7435 MICROTECH GROUP H'CAP 7f 50y
4:55 (4:57) (Class 3) (0-95,94) 3-Y-O+ £9,703 (£2,887; £1,443; £721) Stalls High

Form RPR

310 **1** **Wise Counsel**[42] 5953 3-9-3 **91** .... DanielTudhope 12 99
(Clive Cox) *hld up in tch: smooth hdwy to ld over 2f out: rdn over 1f out: hld on wl fnl f* **7/1**

2110 **2** *nk* **Redarna**[10] 7068 5-9-3 **88** ....(p) TomEaves 13 96
(Dianne Sayer) *hld up on outside: hdwy and ev ch over 2f out: rdn over 1f out: kpt on fnl f: hld nr fin* **11/1**

3435 **3** *3/4* **Raydiance**[42] 5971 4-9-7 **92** .... BenCurtis 4 98
(K R Burke) *prom: hdwy to chal over 2f out: kpt on same pce last 100yds* **11/2**[3]

5300 **4** *3/4* **Howzer Black (IRE)**[1] 7402 3-7-13 **78** .... AndrewBreslin(5) 8 82+
(Keith Dalgleish) *hld up: effrt and edgd lft 2f out: kpt on same pce ins fnl f* **18/1**

3000 **5** *3/4* **Aljady (FR)**[21] 6711 4-9-5 **90** ....(v[1]) TonyHamilton 5 92
(Richard Fahey) *t.k.h: cl up: effrt and ev ch over 2f out: drvn and outpcd over 1f out* **5/1**[2]

2210 **6** *1 1/4* **Ventura Ocean (IRE)**[14] 6950 3-9-3 **94** .... SeanDavis(3) 1 92
(Richard Fahey) *hld up in tch: rdn over 2f out: outpcd over 1f out* **14/1**

7 *nse* **Giga White (IRE)**[52] 5568 3-8-11 **85** .... ColinKeane 7 83
(G M Lyons, Ire) *hld up: rdn and effrt over 2f out: hung lft over 1f out: kpt on: nvr able to chal* **9/2**[1]

5102 **8** *1 1/4* **Pattie**[14] 6974 5-9-5 **90** .... JoeFanning 6 86
(Mick Channon) *s.i.s: hld up: pushed along over 2f out: no imp fr over 1f out* **11/2**[3]

-551 **9** *3/4* **Wahoo**[42] 5971 4-9-3 **88** .... PaulMulrennan 2 82
(Michael Dods) *trckd ldrs: rdn over 2f out: wknd over 1f out* **11/2**[3]

-000 **10** *2 1/2* **Drogon (IRE)**[42] 5947 3-8-8 **82** .... PaulHanagan 9 68
(Jackie Stephen) *t.k.h: hld up in midfield: rdn along over 2f out: sn wknd* **25/1**

2-0 **11** *7* **Nordic Fire**[35] 6207 3-8-13 **87** .... RobbieDowney 11 55
(David O'Meara) *led to over 2f out: wknd over 1f out* **33/1**

1m 28.38s (-4.12) **Going Correction** -0.35s/f (Firm)
WFA 3 from 4yo+ 3lb 11 Ran SP% **120.6**
Speed ratings (Par 107): **109,108,107,106,106 104,104,103,102,99 91**
CSF £83.68 CT £470.13 TOTE £8.80: £3.00, £3.30, £2.20; EX 82.40 Trifecta £589.30.
Owner Clipper Logistics **Bred** South Acre Bloodstock **Trained** Lambourn, Berks

FOCUS
This was competitive and it saw a tight finish down the centre. Sound form, the second and third helping with the standard.

7436 JORDAN ELECTRICS LTD H'CAP 1m 5f 26y
5:30 (5:32) (Class 3) (0-90,87) 3-Y-O+ £11,644 (£3,465; £1,731; £865) Stalls Low

Form RPR

41 **1** **Shamad (IRE)**[13] 7003 5-8-13 **75** .... SeanDavis(3) 4 84
(Peter Fahey, Ire) *hld up in tch: rdn to ld 2f out: edgd lft and sn hrd pressed: hld on gamely ins fnl f* **6/1**[3]

0434 **2** *shd* **Employer (IRE)**[2] 7364 4-8-13 **72** .... DanielTudhope 7 81
(Jim Goldie) *hld up in midfield: smooth hdwy over 2f out: edgd lft and disp ld fr over 1f out: kpt on wl fnl f: jst hld* **9/2**[2]

2401 **3** *nk* **Battle Of Marathon (USA)**[15] 6933 7-9-4 **77** .... BenCurtis 8 85
(John Ryan) *hld up in midfield: hdwy over 2f out: effrt and chsd ldng pair 1f out: kpt on wl: jst hld* **18/1**

6125 **4** *7* **Beechwood Jude (FR)**[31] 6340 3-8-3 **74** ....(p[1]) AndrewBreslin(5) 13 74
(Keith Dalgleish) *hld up on ins: rdn along and hdwy over 2f out: kpt on fnl f: no imp* **22/1**

4424 **5** *3* **Doctor Cross (IRE)**[13] 7003 5-9-2 **75** .... PaulHanagan 14 68
(Richard Fahey) *prom: rdn along 3f out: outpcd over 1f out: n.d after* **15/2**

1325 **6** *nk* **Dark Lochnagar (USA)**[7] 7209 3-9-7 **87** .... JoeFanning 9 82
(Keith Dalgleish) *led tl rdn and hdd 2f out: wknd fnl f* **9/2**[2]

0553 **7** *nk* **Mistiroc**[26] 6535 8-10-0 **87** ....(v) JasonHart 11 79
(John Quinn) *cl up: rdn and edgd lft over 2f out: wknd over 1f out* **11/1**

0642 **8** *1* **Mordred (IRE)**[40] 6021 3-9-6 **86** .... RossaRyan 6 79
(Richard Hannon) *midfield: rdn and effrt over 2f out: hung lft and wknd over 1f out* **7/1**

3510 **9** *1 1/4* **Beyond The Clouds**[22] 6657 6-9-11 **84** .... TomEaves 3 73
(Kevin Ryan) *cl up: rdn over 2f out: wknd over 1f out* **4/1**[1]

5051 **10** *shd* **Mutamaded (IRE)**[25] 6576 6-9-13 **86** .... PaulMulrennan 15 75
(Ruth Carr) *t.k.h early: hld up: rdn and outpcd wl over 2f out: sn btn* **20/1**

11 *4 1/2* **Manzil (IRE)**[455] 4150 4-9-10 **83** ....(w) NathanEvans 10 65
(Michael Easterby) *hld up: reminder after 5f: drvn and struggling 3f out: sn btn* **33/1**

/20- **12** *nk* **Astute Boy (IRE)**[12] 3705 5-9-1 **74** ....(t) CallumRodriguez 12 55
(R Mike Smith) *s.i.s: hld up: rdn along and struggling over 2f out: sn btn* **50/1**

5120 **13** *1 1/4* **Four Kingdoms (IRE)**[7] 7212 5-9-2 **75** .... JackGarritty 5 55
(R Mike Smith) *prom tl rdn and wknd fr 2f out* **28/1**

650- **14** *hd* **Royal Reserve**[22] 8188 6-9-7 **87** ....(p) ZakWheatley(7) 16 66
(Lucinda Russell) *slowly away: t.k.h in rr: struggling 3f out: sn btn* **33/1**

2m 49.72s (-4.68) **Going Correction** -0.35s/f (Firm)
WFA 3 from 4yo+ 7lb 14 Ran SP% **128.9**
Speed ratings (Par 107): **100,99,99,95,93 93,93,92,91,91 89,88,88,87**
CSF £33.03 CT £485.54 TOTE £7.00: £2.80, £2.00, £5.20; EX 57.30 Trifecta £1010.20.
Owner Direct Bloodstock Limited **Bred** Newtown Anner Stud Farm Ltd **Trained** Monasterevln, Co. Kildare

■ Stewards' Enquiry : Sean Davis two-day ban; misuse of whip (Oct 7-8)

FOCUS
A difficult-looking finale saw a really tight finish, with three coming away from the remainder. Another pb from the winner, helped by his jockey's claim.

T/Jkpt: Not Won T/Plt: £600.60 to a £1 stake. Pool: £153,962.61 - 187.12 winning units T/Qpdt: £175.40 to a £1 stake. Pool: £18,128.66 - 76.45 winning units **Richard Young & Andrew Sheret**

7046 CATTERICK (L-H)
Saturday, September 21

OFFICIAL GOING: Good to firm (watered; 8.9)
Wind: Moderate behind Weather: Fine and dry

7437 BRITISH STALLION STUDS EBF NOVICE STKS 5f 212y
1:50 (1:50) (Class 5) 2-Y-O £4,140 (£1,232; £615; £307) Stalls Low

Form RPR

01 **1** **Romantic Vision (IRE)**[24] 6585 2-9-6 0 .... SamJames 6 83+
(Kevin Ryan) *wnt lft s: mde all: rdn clr jst over 1f out: kpt on strly* **9/1**

0 **2** *2* **Great Image (IRE)**[29] 6409 2-8-13 0 .... GabrieleMalune(3) 8 73
(Saeed bin Suroor) *trckd ldrs: hdwy 3f out: rdn along 2f out: kpt on to chse wnr ins fnl f: no imp* **11/4**[3]

2220 **3** *1/2* **Sermon (IRE)**[30] 6375 2-8-13 80 ....(p) JaneElliott(3) 1 71
(Tom Dascombe) *dwlt and in rr: hdwy 1/2-way: rdn along 2f out: chsd ldrs and edgd lft appr fnl f: kpt on (jockey said gelding was slowly away)* **7/4**[1]

00 **4** *2 1/4* **Panist (IRE)**[15] 6943 2-9-2 0 .... FrannyNorton 7 64
(Mark Johnston) *trckd wnr: cl up wl over 2f out: sn rdn: drvn and edgd lft over 1f out: grad wknd* **25/1**

41 **5** *1* **Dick Datchery (IRE)**[61] 5234 2-9-6 0 ....(t) HarrisonShaw(3) 5 68+
(David O'Meara) *n.m.r s: trckd ldrs: pushed along 1/2-way: rdn over 2f out: sn drvn and kpt on one pce* **9/4**[2]

6 **6** *1/2* **Wadi Al Salaam (IRE)**[11] 7046 2-9-2 0 .... DuranFentiman 2 59
(Tim Easterby) *towards rr: pushed along wl over 2f out: swtchd rt and rdn wl over 1f out: kpt on fnl f* **25/1**

00 **7** *6* **Bal Mal (FR)**[31] 6336 2-9-2 0 .... DougieCostello 3 40
(John Quinn) *trckd wnr on inner: rdn along wl over 2f out: sn drvn and wknd* **80/1**

00 **8** *1 3/4* **Apples Acre (IRE)**[15] 6943 2-8-11 0 .... AndrewMullen 4 29
(Ben Haslam) *hmpd s: a in rr* **100/1**

03 **9** *8* **Draw Lots (IRE)**[12] 7023 2-9-2 0 ....(p[1]) GrahamLee 9
(Brian Meehan) *in tch on outer: effrt and chsd ldrs over 3f out: rdn along wl over 2f out: wknd qckly and sn bhd* **33/1**

1m 13.46s (-0.14) **Going Correction** -0.30s/f (Firm) 9 Ran SP% **116.7**
Speed ratings (Par 95): **88,85,84,81,80 79,71,69,58**
CSF £33.24 TOTE £6.20: £1.70, £1.10, £1.40; EX 37.10 Trifecta £187.90.
Owner Roger Peel & Clipper Logistics **Bred** Messrs J , R & J Hyland **Trained** Hambleton, N Yorks

FOCUS
A fair-looking juvenile novice in which one of the previous winners turned over better fancied rivals. Run of the mill form.

7438 LINDSAY BAIRD "SLAMANNAN MAN" BIG 50 NURSERY H'CAP 7f 6y
2:25 (2:27) (Class 4) (0-85,87) 2-Y-O
£5,692 (£1,694; £846; £423; £300; £300) Stalls Low

Form RPR

665 **1** **Kuwait Shield**[46] 5764 2-8-13 **68** .... BarryMcHugh 3 73+
(Richard Fahey) *disp ld early: trckd ldng pair on inner: hdwy over 2f out: swtchd rt and rdn to chal over 1f out: slt ld appr fnl f: sn rdn and kpt on strly towards fin* **11/2**[3]

1023 **2** *2* **Eton College (IRE)**[21] 6705 2-10-4 **87** .... FrannyNorton 6 87
(Mark Johnston) *chsd ldng pair: led after 1f: pushed along 2f out: sn jnd and rdn: hdd appr fnl f: sn drvn and kpt on same pce* **5/4**[1]

3510 **3** *shd* **Red Treble**[9] 7117 2-9-7 **76** ....(h) CamHardie 1 75
(Rebecca Menzies) *in tch: pushed along and sltly outpcd 3f out: rdn over 2f out: styd on strly fnl f* **11/2**[3]

3034 **4** *2 1/4* **Little Ted**[8] 7140 2-8-6 **61** ....(b) JamesSullivan 5 55
(Tim Easterby) *trckd ldrs: hdwy on outer and cl up 2f out: sn rdn and edgd lft: drvn and hld whn j. shadow and wknd ins fnl f* **7/2**[2]

056 **5** *4* **Optio**[21] 6708 2-9-4 **73** .... GrahamLee 2 55
(Brian Meehan) *a in rr* **10/1**

0445 **6** *10* **Doncaster Rosa**[12] 7029 2-9-0 **69** ....(p[1]) DougieCostello 7 24
(Ivan Furtado) *disp ld early: chsd ldr on outer: rdn along over 2f out: sn wknd* **28/1**

1m 25.93s (-1.47) **Going Correction** -0.30s/f (Firm) 6 Ran SP% **110.0**
Speed ratings (Par 97): **96,93,93,91,86 75**
CSF £12.36 TOTE £5.90: £2.20, £1.10; EX 14.80 Trifecta £69.20.
Owner Sheikh Abdullah Almalek Alsabah **Bred** Carmel Stud **Trained** Musley Bank, N Yorks

FOCUS
A competitive looking nursery handicap and they seemed to go a good gallop from the start. The winner found a few lengths on his previous form.

7439 CONGRATULATIONS ON YOUR WEDDING CALLUM SHARP H'CAP 1m 5f 192y
3:00 (3:00) (Class 4) (0-80,80) 3-Y-O+
£6,080 (£1,809; £904; £452; £300; £300) Stalls Low

Form RPR

4321 **1** **Champarisi**[12] 7033 4-10-0 **80** .... SamJames 8 89+
(Grant Tuer) *hld up towards rr: hdwy over 5f out: chsd ldrs 3f out: rdn along wl over 1f out: styd on strly fnl f to ld towards fin* **4/1**[3]

1563 **2** *1 1/4* **Mister Chiang**[23] 6634 3-9-1 **75** ....(v[1]) FrannyNorton 2 82
(Mark Johnston) *led: pushed along over 2f out: rdn clr over 1f out: drvn ins fnl f: hdd and no ex towards fin* **11/4**[1]

4503 **3** *4 1/2* **Trouble And Strife (IRE)**[12] 7033 4-9-12 **78** ....(b) RyanTate 1 79
(Sir Mark Prescott Bt) *trckd ldng pair: pushed along 3f out: rdn over 2f out: drvn wl over 1f out: kpt on same pce* **4/1**[3]

4130 **4** *1 3/4* **Stormin Tom (IRE)**[15] 6933 7-9-2 **68** .... DuranFentiman 7 66
(Tim Easterby) *rn in snatched: cl up: pushed along 1/2-way: rdn over 3f out: drvn 2f out: sn one pce* **22/1**

1530 **5** *6* **Be Perfect (USA)**[11] 7053 10-9-3 **69** .... JamesSullivan 4 59
(Ruth Carr) *in tch: pushed along 5f out: effrt over 3f out: sn rdn along and n.d* **25/1**

2040 **6** *6* **L'Un Deux Trois (IRE)**[46] 5778 3-8-8 **68** ....(v[1]) CliffordLee 3 49
(Michael Bell) *trckd ldng pair: pushed along 4f out: rdn wl over 2f out: sn drvn and wknd* **7/2**[2]

-001 **7** *2* **Near Kettering**[23] 6180 5-9-0 **66** ....(t) CamHardie 6 45
(Sam England) *hld up: a in rr (trainer could offer no explanation for the gelding's performance)* **13/2**

-600 **8** *1* **Kyoto Star (FR)**[11] 7053 5-9-2 **68** .... PhilDennis 5 45
(Tim Easterby) *a in rr* **33/1**

2m 58.94s (-8.66) **Going Correction** -0.30s/f (Firm)
WFA 3 from 4yo+ 8lb 8 Ran SP% **113.4**
Speed ratings (Par 105): **112,111,108,107,104 100,99,99**
CSF £14.92 CT £45.42 TOTE £4.30: £1.90, £1.20, £1.30; EX 15.00 Trifecta £49.90.

Owner Allerton Racing & G Tuer **Bred** Faisal Meshrf Alqahtani **Trained** Birkby, N Yorks

FOCUS

Add 6yds. This decent staying handicap, featuring a couple of previous winners, was run at a sound gallop, but the winner was the only one to come from off the pace. The winner continues to improve.

7440 BOOK NOW FOR SATURDAY 19TH OCTOBER NURSERY H'CAP 5f

3:35 (3:36) (Class 5) (0-75,75) 2-Y-O

£4,075 (£1,212; £606; £303; £300; £300) **Stalls** Low

Form					RPR
1441	**1**		**Auckland Lodge (IRE)**[18] 6822 2-9-3 **74** HarrisonShaw(3) 4 (Ben Haslam) *sn led: jnd and rdn wl over 1f out: drvn ins fnl f: kpt on wl towards fin* **11/8**[1]		78
3643	**2**	¾	**Maybellene (IRE)**[7] 7208 2-8-8 **62** CamHardie 1 (Alan Berry) *dwlt: in tch on inner: hdwy 1/2-way: rdn to chse ldng pair and n.m.r wl over 1f out: sn swtchd rt: drvn ins fnl f: kpt on wl towards fin* **20/1**		63
5264	**3**	shd	**Point Of Order**[28] 6436 2-9-6 **74** AndrewMullen 3 (Archie Watson) *chsd wnr: hdwy and cl up 1/2-way: rdn to chal wl over 1f out: drvn and ev ch ins fnl f: no ex towards fin* **9/1**		75
3000	**4**	3 ¼	**She's Easyontheeye (IRE)**[7] 7208 2-8-4 **58** DuranFentiman 6 (John Quinn) *chsd ldrs: rdn along 2f out: sn drvn and kpt on same pce* **33/1**		47
6521	**5**	nk	**Balancing Act (IRE)**[43] 5913 2-9-7 **75** GrahamLee 5 (Jedd O'Keeffe) *n.m.r s: sn outpcd and bhd: rdn along 1/2-way: hdwy on wd outside over 1f out: styd on wl fnl f* **3/1**[2]		63
2152	**6**	2 ½	**Dandizette (IRE)**[16] 6900 2-9-0 **75** LauraCoughlan(7) 8 (Adrian Nicholls) *prom on outer: cl up 1/2-way: rdn along 2f out: sn drvn and grad wknd* **6/1**[3]		54
6452	**7**	½	**Comeatchoo (IRE)**[3] 7329 2-8-0 **54** oh3 (b) JamesSullivan 7 (Tim Easterby) *chsd ldrs: rdn along 2f out: sn drvn and wknd* **6/1**[3]		31

58.43s (-2.07) **Going Correction** -0.30s/f (Firm) **7 Ran SP% 113.4**

Speed ratings (Par 95): **104,102,102,97,96 92,92**

CSF £31.15 CT £183.83 TOTE £2.60: £1.50, £6.40; EX 26.20 Trifecta £106.50.

Owner The Auckland Lodge Partnership **Bred** R Galway **Trained** Middleham Moor, N Yorks

FOCUS

Another competitive nursery over the minimum trip this time and it paid to be close to the pace. It's rated around the second.

7441 CONSTANT SECURITY H'CAP (CATTERICK TWELVE FURLONG SERIES FINAL) 1m 4f 13y

4:10 (4:11) (Class 2) 3-Y-O+

£12,450 (£3,728; £1,864; £932; £466; £234) **Stalls** Centre

Form					RPR
5064	**1**		**Bollin Joan**[2] 7366 4-9-0 **71** (p) DannyRedmond(5) 2 (Tim Easterby) *trckd ldrs on inner: hdwy over 2f out: chsd ldr and swtchd rt over 1f out: sn rdn to chal: drvn to ld ins fnl f: kpt on wl* **15/2**		79
2215	**2**	1 ½	**Betty Grable (IRE)**[18] 6828 5-8-0 **59** RhonaPindar(7) 13 (Wilf Storey) *trckd ldr: led 3f out: rdn along 2f out: jnd over 1f out: sn drvn: hdd ins fnl f: no ex towards fin* **14/1**		65
4332	**3**	1	**Fantastic Ms Fox**[15] 6938 3-8-4 **63** FrannyNorton 6 (Richard Fahey) *in tch on inner: hdwy over 2f out: rdn over 1f out: chsd ldng pair and drvn ins fnl f: kpt on* **4/1**[1]		67
0023	**4**	1 ¼	**Tommy Hallinan (IRE)**[18] 6828 5-8-3 **60** (bt[1]) KieranSchofield(5) 10 (Brian Ellison) *led: pushed along and hdd 3f out: cl up and rdn: over 2f out: drvn wl over 1f out: kpt on same pce fnl f* **9/1**		62
2213	**5**	1 ¾	**Jan De Heem**[4] 7314 9-8-7 **59** (v) JamesSullivan 9 (Tina Jackson) *hld up and bhd: hdwy over 2f out: rdn along and n.m.r wl over 1f out: swtchd rt to outer and drvn: styd on wl fnl f: nvr nr ldrs* **12/1**		58
-004	**6**	1 ½	**Straitouttacompton**[11] 7048 3-8-3 **65** (t) GabrieleMalune(3) 3 (Ivan Furtado) *chsd ldrs: rdn along 3f out: drvn 2f out: grad wknd fr over 1f out* **6/1**[3]		62
1110	**7**	nse	**Euro Implosion (IRE)**[7] 7209 3-9-2 **75** GrahamLee 8 (Keith Dalgleish) *hld up: hdwy on outer over 4f out: rdn along to chse ldrs over 2f out: sn drvn and no imp* **6/1**[3]		72
0-50	**8**	1 ½	**Lady Kyria (FR)**[11] 7048 5-8-3 **62** NickBarratt-Atkin(7) 1 (Philip Kirby) *hld up towards rr: pushed along and hdwy wl over 2f out: in tch and rdn wl over 1f out: n.d* **66/1**		56
0130	**9**	hd	**Flower Power**[10] 7070 8-8-11 **63** DougieCostello 7 (Tony Coyle) *towards rr: reminders after 3f: nvr a factor* **25/1**		57
6060	**10**	2	**Mr Sundowner (USA)**[11] 7048 7-8-1 **53** ow1 (t) AndrewMullen 5 (Michael Herrington) *trckd ldrs: pushed along 3f out: rdn over 2f out: sn drvn and wknd* **16/1**		44
2111	**11**	1 ¾	**Gylo (IRE)**[11] 7048 3-9-0 **76** HarrisonShaw(3) 12 (David O'Meara) *hld up towards rr: hdwy 3f out: in tch and rdn along on outer over 2f out: sn drvn and btn (jockey said was slowly away and unable to gain a desired prominent position)* **5/1**[2]		64
1333	**12**	1 ¼	**Ingleby Hollow**[16] 5743 7-9-10 **76** (t) CamHardie 4 (David O'Meara) *a in rr* **14/1**		62
2240	**13**	4 ½	**Dew Pond**[2] 7368 7-8-6 **58** (bt) DuranFentiman 11 (Tim Easterby) *awkward s and rdr lost iron: a bhd (jockey said gelding stumbled badly leaving the stalls which resulted in him loosing and iron and being very slowly away)* **33/1**		37

2m 34.72s (-5.88) **Going Correction** -0.30s/f (Firm) **13 Ran SP% 122.2**

WFA 3 from 4yo+ 7lb

Speed ratings (Par 109): **107,106,105,104,103 102,102,101,101,99 98,97,94**

CSF £108.95 CT £488.22 TOTE £10.80: £3.10, £4.40, £1.80; EX 97.10 Trifecta £290.80.

Owner N Arton, P Hebdon, R Taylor & Prtnr **Bred** Habton Farms **Trained** Great Habton, N Yorks

FOCUS

Add 6yds. The feature contest and competitive, but not that strong a race for the grade, and once again it paid to race close to the leaders. The winner is rated better than ever.

7442 PENNINE BREWING CO. NOVICE STKS 7f 6y

4:45 (4:46) (Class 5) 3-Y-O+ **£4,140** (£1,232; £615) **Stalls** Low

Form					RPR
6622	**1**		**Mogsy (IRE)**[36] 6177 3-8-13 **85** JaneElliott(3) 3 (Tom Dascombe) *mde all: rdn clr over 2f out: easily* **4/9**[1]		83
6	**2**	9	**Thornaby Spirit (IRE)**[58] 5336 4-9-2 **0** HarrisonShaw(3) 1 (Jason Ward) *s.i.s and bhd: hdwy 3f out: rdn along over 2f out: kpt on u.p to take modest 2nd ins fnl f* **33/1**[3]		60?
42-0	**3**	3 ½	**Tilghman (IRE)**[129] 2736 4-9-5 **78** CamHardie 2 (David O'Meara) *t.k.h: chsd wnr: rdn along wl over 2f out: sn outpcd: lost modest 2nd ins fnl f* **15/8**[2]		50

1m 25.58s (-1.82) **Going Correction** -0.30s/f (Firm)

WFA 3 from 4yo 3lb **3 Ran SP% 107.0**

Speed ratings (Par 103): **98,87,83**

CSF £8.30 TOTE £1.30; EX 6.50 Trifecta £7.20.

Owner Satchell Moran Solicitors **Bred** Michael McGlynn **Trained** Malpas, Cheshire

FOCUS

An uncompetitive novice stakes that was run 0.35 secs faster than the earlier nursery. It provided stallion Dandy Man with a third winner at the course on the afternoon. The winner is rated to form.

7443 RACING AGAIN 8TH OCTOBER H'CAP (DIV I) 7f 6y

5:20 (5:20) (Class 6) (0-60,61) 3-Y-O+

£3,105 (£924; £461; £300; £300; £300) **Stalls** Low

Form					RPR
5660	**1**		**Christmas Night**[53] 5517 4-8-12 **53** (w) HarrisonShaw(3) 3 (Ollie Pears) *trckd ldrs on inner: hdwy over 2f out: swtchd rt and rdn to chal over 1f out: led ent fnl f: drvn out* **5/1**[2]		61
6402	**2**	1	**Suitcase 'N' Taxi**[10] 7066 5-9-4 **56** DuranFentiman 2 (Tim Easterby) *led: rdn along 2f out: jnd drvn over 1f out: hdd ent fnl f: no ex last 100yds* **8/1**		61
343	**3**	1 ¾	**Mansfield**[11] 7051 6-9-5 **57** CamHardie 7 (Stella Barclay) *hld up towards rr: hdwy over 2f out: rdn wl over 1f out: kpt on wl fnl f* **7/1**[3]		58
0-15	**4**	nk	**Scandinavian Lady (IRE)**[15] 6945 3-9-0 **58** GabrieleMalune(3) 11 (Ivan Furtado) *chsd ldr: cl up on outer 3f out: rdn over 2f out: drvn and edgd rt over 1f out: kpt on same pce* **20/1**		57
5002	**5**	1 ¼	**Eldelbar (SPA)**[11] 7050 5-8-13 **51** (h) SamJames 10 (Geoffrey Harker) *chsd ldrs: edgd rt: wd st and lost pl: sn rdn: hdwy over 1f out: kpt on fnl f* **4/1**[1]		48
0403	**6**	¾	**Vallarta (IRE)**[24] 6590 9-8-8 **46** oh1 JamesSullivan 12 (Ruth Carr) *hld up towards rr: hdwy on inner 3f out: rdn along and chsd ldrs 2f out: sn drvn and no imp* **22/1**		41+
0003	**7**	hd	**Exchequer (IRE)**[7] 7210 8-9-8 **60** (tp) DougieCostello 4 (Richard Guest) *chsd ldng pair: rdn along over 2f out: wknd over 1f out* **10/1**		54
0020	**8**	½	**Robben Rainbow**[7] 7210 5-8-13 **51** PhilDennis 13 (Katie Scott) *towards rr: hdwy over 2f out: sn swtchd lft and rdn: n.d* **16/1**		44
4013	**9**	2	**Lukoutoldmakezebak**[7] 7207 6-8-13 **51** (p) JamieGormley 14 (David Thompson) *a towards rr* **16/1**		39
4102	**10**	½	**Seafaring Girl (IRE)**[24] 6600 3-8-11 **52** (p) AndrewMullen 5 (Mark Loughnane) *in tch: rdn along over 2f out: sn wknd* **33/1**		38
0460	**11**	½	**Tarnhelm**[7] 7210 4-8-6 **51** RhonaPindar(7) 9 (Wilf Storey) *dwlt and in rr: wd st and bhd* **7/1**[3]		36
330	**12**	2 ½	**Ishebayorgrey (IRE)**[22] 6663 7-9-9 **61** GrahamLee 1 (Iain Jardine) *towards rr: hdwy to chse ldrs over 3f out: rdn along 2f out: sn drvn and wknd* **7/1**[3]		40
4063	**13**	2	**Lady Lavinia**[40] 6024 3-8-7 **48** BarryMcHugh 8 (Michael Easterby) *in tch: rdn along wl over 2f out: sn wknd* **16/1**		21

1m 25.03s (-2.37) **Going Correction** -0.30s/f (Firm)

WFA 3 from 4yo+ 3lb **13 Ran SP% 124.1**

Speed ratings (Par 101): **101,99,97,97,96 95,95,94,92,91 91,88,85**

CSF £45.57 CT £289.89 TOTE £5.10: £2.30, £3.50, £2.40; EX 80.60 Trifecta £320.80.

Owner Ownaracehorse Ltd & Ollie Pears **Bred** Worksop Manor Stud **Trained** Norton, N Yorks

FOCUS

The first division of this low-grade handicap was run just over half a second faster than the preceding contest. Again it paid to race close to the speed. Straightforward enough form.

7444 RACING AGAIN 8TH OCTOBER H'CAP (DIV II) 7f 6y

5:50 (5:50) (Class 6) (0-60,60) 3-Y-O+

£3,105 (£924; £461; £300; £300; £300) **Stalls** Low

Form					RPR
2336	**1**		**The Big House (IRE)**[15] 6937 3-9-3 **58** AndrewMullen 14 (Adrian Nicholls) *prom: cl up 4f out: led 3f out: rdn along 2f out: hdd 1f out: drvn and rallied gamely ins fnl f to ld again last 75yds* **5/1**[3]		64
0521	**2**	nk	**Sophia Maria**[22] 6666 3-9-0 **58** (p) JaneElliott(3) 2 (James Bethell) *trckd ldrs: hdwy over 3f out: chal 2f out: rdn to take narrow ld 1f out: sn drvn: hdd and no ex last 75yds* **10/3**[1]		63
0400	**3**	1	**Uncle Charlie (IRE)**[5] 7289 5-9-8 **60** FrannyNorton 4 (Ann Duffield) *trckd ldrs: hdwy wl over 2f out: chal over 1f out: sn rdn and ev ch ent fnl f: drvn and no ex last 75yds* **7/2**[2]		63
0154	**4**	1 ½	**Sharrabang**[25] 6575 3-8-13 **54** CamHardie 13 (Stella Barclay) *led: pushed along and hdd 3f out: rdn 2f out: drvn over 1f out: grad wknd* **12/1**		52
-343	**5**	2 ¾	**Midnight In Havana**[15] 6945 3-9-3 **58** GrahamLee 7 (Bryan Smart) *chsd ldrs: lost pl and towards rr after 2f: hdwy 2f out: sn rdn and kpt on fnl f* **5/1**[3]		49
0005	**6**	1 ¼	**Rebel State (IRE)**[46] 5787 6-8-7 **52** (p) OwenPayton(7) 8 (Jedd O'Keeffe) *in rr: pushed along and hdwy on inner 2f out: rdn over 1f out: kpt on same pce* **16/1**		41+
0500	**7**	1 ¾	**Here's Rocco (IRE)**[68] 4979 3-8-11 **52** JamesSullivan 1 (John Quinn) *chsd ldrs: hdwy 3f out: rdn along 2f out: sn drvn and wknd* **20/1**		35
0000	**8**	3 ¼	**Lord Rob**[46] 5766 8-8-8 **46** oh1 JamieGormley 10 (David Thompson) *dwlt: a in rr (jockey said gelding was slowly away)* **40/1**		21
1125	**9**	¾	**Kodimoor (IRE)**[22] 6655 6-9-0 **52** (p) DougieCostello 5 (Mark Walford) *in tch on outer: rdn along 3f out: sn outpcd* **7/1**		25
6024	**10**	¾	**Isabella Ruby**[24] 6590 4-8-8 **46** oh1 (p) AndrewElliott 3 (Lisa Williamson) *t.k.h: chsd ldrs: rdn along wl over 2f out: sn drvn and wknd (jockey said filly stumbled shortly after the start)* **33/1**		17
100	**11**	43	**Magical Molly Joe**[101] 3716 5-8-13 **51** (h) PhilDennis 6 (David Barron) *a towards rr (vet said mare bled from the nose)* **25/1**		

1m 25.01s (-2.39) **Going Correction** -0.30s/f (Firm) **11 Ran SP% 118.7**

WFA 3 from 4yo+ 3lb

Speed ratings (Par 101): **101,100,99,97,94 93,91,87,86,85 36**

CSF £21.31 CT £68.04 TOTE £5.10: £2.10, £1.80, £1.90; EX 24.90 Trifecta £67.60.

Owner Dave Stone **Bred** Peter Molony **Trained** Sessay, N Yorks

FOCUS

The second division of this low-grade handicap was run fractionally faster than the first leg in the best time of the four races over the trip on the day.

T/Plt: £19.10 to a £1 stake. Pool: £40,964.38 - 1,562.63 winning units T/Qpdt: £7.60 to a £1 stake. Pool: £2,546.14 - 245.66 winning units **Joe Rowntree**

[7369] **CHELMSFORD (A.W)** (L-H)
Saturday, September 21

OFFICIAL GOING: Polytrack: standard
Wind: Virtually nil Weather: Warm and sunny

7445 BET TOTEPLACEPOT AT TOTESPORT.COM NOVICE STKS (PLUS 10 RACE) 7f (P)
1:40 (1:42) (Class 4) 2-Y-O £6,469 (£1,925; £962; £481) Stalls Low

Form RPR
1 **Seasony (IRE)** 2-9-2 0 JamesDoyle 2 80+
(Mark Johnston) *mde all: shkn up w 1 l ld 2f out: rdn and kpt on wl fnl f: a doing enough* 6/5[1]
416 2 ½ **Lexington Rebel (FR)**[14] 6966 2-9-3 90 ThoreHammerHansen(5) 5 85
(Richard Hannon) *hld up: hdwy on outer 2f out: rdn and grad clsd on wnr 1f out: kpt on but a hld by wnr* 6/4[2]
3 nk **Animal Instinct** 2-8-9 0 GavinAshton(7) 1 78
(Sir Mark Prescott Bt) *hld up in last: hdwy between rivals over 1f out: kpt on wl fnl f wout threatening: should improve* 20/1
05 4 3 ¾ **Abadie**[23] 6640 2-9-2 0 HollieDoyle 4 68
(Archie Watson) *trckd wnr: rdn and outpcd 2f out: wknd fnl f* 6/1[3]
5 4 **Pinatar (IRE)** 2-9-2 0 KierenFox 3 58
(John Best) *dwlt sltly: sn rcvrd to r midfield: pushed along 3f out: rdn and lost pl over 1f out: sn bhd (jockey said colt ran green)* 14/1
1m 26.2s (-1.00) **Going Correction** -0.20s/f (Stan) 5 Ran SP% 111.2
Speed ratings (Par 97): **97,96,96,91,87**
CSF £3.32 TOTE £2.00: £1.30, £1.20; EX 3.10.
Owner Hussain Alabbas Lootah **Bred** Ballygallon Stud Ltd **Trained** Middleham Moor, N Yorks
FOCUS
A decent little juvenile novice contest. The favourite won well from the front and the runner-up's rated to his mark.

7446 BET TOTEEXACTA AT TOTESPORT.COM H'CAP (DIV I) 6f (P)
2:15 (2:16) (Class 6) (0-65,65) 3-Y-O+
£3,493 (£1,039; £519; £300; £300; £300) Stalls Centre

Form RPR
4245 1 **Miss Liberty Belle (AUS)**[29] 6389 3-8-10 56 DavidProbert 2 62
(William Jarvis) *hld up: gd hdwy between rivals into midfield 2f out: rdn and hung lft to rail 1f out: forced gap between rivals 100yds out and qcknd up wl to ld post* 9/2[2]
4021 2 shd **Senorita Grande (IRE)**[16] 6889 3-9-0 60 (v) SeanLevey 5 66
(John Quinn) *racd in midfield: effrt on outer 2f out: rdn to chse ldrs over 1f out: kpt on wl fnl f: jst failed* 7/2[1]
5535 3 nk **Poeta Brasileiro (IRE)**[27] 6503 4-8-12 61 (t[1]) ThoreHammerHansen(5) 3 66
(David Brown) *led: pushed along w short ld 2f out: rdn and strly pressed 1f out: kpt on wl but lost 2 pls fnl strides* 7/2[1]
5031 4 nk **Napping**[24] 6605 6-8-13 64 SeanKirrane(7) 6 68
(Amy Murphy) *trckd ldr: rdn upsides and ev ch 1f out: kpt on fnl f* 14/1
0153 5 4 **Red Tycoon (IRE)**[19] 6794 7-9-0 58 (b) LiamKeniry 4 50
(Patrick Chamings) *dwlt sltly: towards rr of midfield: hdwy 2f out: rdn and outpcd over 1f out: one pce fnl f* 10/1
5631 6 6 **Aquarius (IRE)**[43] 5890 3-8-12 58 LiamJones 1 32
(Michael Appleby) *wnt to post early: racd lazily in midfield: pushed along 3f out: rdn and no imp over 1f out: nvr travelling (jockey said filly was also never travelling)* 5/1[3]
3053 7 2 **Fareeq**[22] 6685 5-9-3 61 (bt) TomMarquand 8 29
(Charlie Wallis) *hld up: pushed along on outer 3f out: rdn and no hdwy 2f out: nvr on terms* 20/1
0005 8 2 ¾ **Bernie's Boy**[19] 6798 6-9-2 60 (p) NicolaCurrie 9 20
(Phil McEntee) *hld up: rdn and detached 3f out: nvr on terms (jockey said gelding was never travelling early)* 33/1
4145 9 3 ¾ **Evening Attire**[30] 6373 8-9-6 64 HollieDoyle 10 12
(William Stone) *pushed along to be prom on outer: rdn and lost pl 2f out: wknd fnl f (vet said gelding bled from the nose)* 5/1[3]
1m 11.69s (-2.01) **Going Correction** -0.20s/f (Stan)
WFA 3 from 4yo+ 2lb 9 Ran SP% 119.4
Speed ratings (Par 101): **105,104,104,104,98 90,88,84,79**
CSF £21.46 CT £62.46 TOTE £5.20: £1.70, £1.50, £1.60; EX 24.40 Trifecta £100.30.
Owner Kevin Hickman **Bred** Independent Stallions Pty Ltd **Trained** Newmarket, Suffolk
FOCUS
The first division of a modest handicap. The third-favourite squeezed through late to win an exciting race in a good time for the grade. Limited, straightforward form.

7447 BET TOTEEXACTA AT TOTESPORT.COM H'CAP (DIV II) 6f (P)
2:50 (2:51) (Class 6) (0-65,65) 3-Y-O+
£3,493 (£1,039; £519; £300; £300; £300) Stalls Centre

Form RPR
003 1 **Amor Kethley**[7] 7172 3-8-7 60 (tp) SeanKirrane(7) 8 67
(Amy Murphy) *dwlt but sn rcvrd to r in midfield: smooth hdwy 2f out: rdn and clsd wl to ld ins fnl f: pushed out* 8/1
02P0 2 1 ¼ **Sir Hector (IRE)**[23] 6631 4-8-13 57 DanielMuscutt 5 60
(Charlie Wallis) *prom in 3rd: swtchd rt and rdn to chse ldrs over 1f out: kpt on wl but unable to match wnr fnl f* 20/1
6050 3 shd **Gottardo (IRE)**[23] 6631 4-9-6 64 JamesDoyle 1 69+
(Ed Dunlop) *racd in midfield: hdwy u.p 2f out: swtchd rt and rdn 1f out: kpt on wl fnl f* 3/1[1]
0104 4 1 ¼ **Olaudah**[24] 6605 5-9-3 61 DavidProbert 6 60
(Henry Candy) *led: rdn and strly pressed by rival over 1f out: drvn and hdd by wnr ins fnl f: no ex* 8/1
5 ½ **Split Down South**[58] 5363 3-9-0 60 JosephineGordon 2 58
(Phil McEntee) *hld up: rdn along and outpcd over 1f out: kpt on one pce fnl f* 7/1
5623 6 ¾ **La Fortuna**[31] 6335 6-9-2 65 (t) RayDawson(5) 10 60
(Charlie Wallis) *hld up: hdwy u.p over 1f out: kpt on one pce fnl f* 8/1
6503 7 nse **Englishman**[16] 6889 9-8-11 55 (p) PhilipPrince 7 50
(Milton Bradley) *trckd ldr: rdn almost upsides and ev ch over 1f out: wknd and lost pl fnl f* 10/1
0023 8 ½ **Crackin Dream (IRE)**[58] 5358 3-9-4 64 (b) LiamKeniry 4 58
(Clive Cox) *hld up: rdn and no imp on outer 2f out: kpt on one pce fnl f* 5/1[2]
6203 9 1 ½ **Ricochet (IRE)**[8] 7157 3-9-3 63 (p[1]) TomMarquand 9 52
(Tom Ward) *settled in tch: rdn and carried hd awkwardly over 1f out: sn wknd (jockey said gelding hung left-handed throughout)* 6/1[3]
240 10 1 ¾ **Valley Belle (IRE)**[82] 4457 3-8-2 55 GraceMcEntee(7) 3 39
(Phil McEntee) *midfield: rdn along and briefly short of room over 1f out: nt rcvr (trainer was informed that the filly could not run until the day after passing a stalls test)* 16/1
1m 12.03s (-1.67) **Going Correction** -0.20s/f (Stan)
WFA 3 from 4yo+ 2lb 10 Ran SP% 121.5
Speed ratings (Par 101): **103,101,101,99,98 97,97,97,95,92**
CSF £159.68 CT £606.65 TOTE £8.80: £3.00, £9.30; EX 169.60 Trifecta £993.50.
Owner D De Souza **Bred** Whitsbury Manor Stud **Trained** Newmarket, Suffolk
FOCUS
The second division of a modest handicap and the winning time was slightly slower.

7448 BET TOTEQUADPOT AT TOTESPORT.COM H'CAP 7f (P)
3:25 (3:25) (Class 2) (0-105,105) 3-Y-O+ £12,938 (£3,850; £1,924; £962) Stalls Low

Form RPR
0513 1 **War Glory (IRE)**[7] 7188 6-9-7 100 SeanLevey 5 108
(Richard Hannon) *hld up: gd hdwy 2f out: swtchd rt and rdn 1f out: styd on strly to ld wl ins fnl f* 3/1[1]
5602 2 1 **Documenting**[21] 6706 6-9-12 105 JamesDoyle 4 110
(Kevin Frost) *in tch in 3rd: effrt on outer 2f out: sn rdn to ld 1f out: drvn and hdd by wnr ins fnl f: no ex* 4/1[2]
0255 3 hd **Jack's Point**[18] 6847 3-8-11 93 (p[1]) HollieDoyle 1 96
(William Muir) *led: rdn along and hdd 2f out: kpt on one pce ins fnl f* 12/1
2103 4 ½ **Charles Molson**[21] 6706 8-9-4 97 DanielMuscutt 3 100
(Patrick Chamings) *midfield on inner: rdn and no imp over 1f out: drifted lft u.p 1f out: kpt on* 7/1[3]
0333 5 ¾ **Woven**[7] 7187 3-8-10 92 StevieDonohoe 7 92
(David Simcock) *hld up: c wdst of all of home bnd 2f out: sn rdn and no imp over 1f out: sme late hdwy fnl f* 10/1
/1-4 6 shd **Mizaah (IRE)**[16] 6894 6-9-6 99 (t) DavidProbert 8 100+
(Owen Burrows) *rrd as stalls opened and broke slowly: rcvrd and quick hdwy to trck ldr after 2f: rdn and lost pl over 1f out: wknd fnl f (jockey said gelding reared when leaving the stalls)* 4/1[2]
5543 7 hd **Name The Wind**[18] 6841 3-8-10 92 TomMarquand 6 91
(James Tate) *towards rr of midfield: rdn along and outpcd 2f out: drvn and no imp 1f out: plugged on* 4/1[2]
1m 24.82s (-2.38) **Going Correction** -0.20s/f (Stan)
WFA 3 from 4yo+ 3lb 7 Ran SP% 114.3
Speed ratings (Par 109): **105,103,103,103,102 102,101**
CSF £15.15 CT £123.10 TOTE £3.10: £2.30, £2.20; EX 10.10 Trifecta £104.20.
Owner Mohamed Saeed Al Shahi **Bred** Pier House Stud **Trained** East Everleigh, Wilts
FOCUS
The feature contest was a good quality handicap. The favourite's winning time was comparatively modest for the grade but he won well. He confirmed last month's form with the second and third.

7449 BET TOTETRIFECTA AT TOTESPORT.COM H'CAP 5f (P)
4:00 (4:02) (Class 2) (0-105,100) 3-Y-O £12,938 (£3,850; £1,924; £962) Stalls Low

Form RPR
1100 1 **Leodis Dream (IRE)**[98] 3855 3-9-7 100 DavidProbert 2 109
(David O'Meara) *mde all: shkn up w 1 l ld over 1f out: sn rdn and kpt on wl fnl f: a doing enough* 6/1
3041 2 1 **Rocket Action**[21] 6735 3-8-12 91 (t) TomMarquand 3 96
(Robert Cowell) *in tch in 4th: gd hdwy to chse wnr over 1f out: rdn and kpt on wl fnl f: nvr getting to wnr* 11/4[1]
1235 3 1 ¾ **Heritage**[14] 6954 3-8-9 88 (p) LiamKeniry 4 87
(Clive Cox) *settled in 3rd: wnt 2nd 3f out: rdn and outpcd over 1f out: one pce fnl f* 4/1[3]
2411 4 1 **Furious**[17] 6859 3-9-5 98 StevieDonohoe 5 94
(David Simcock) *hld up: c wd off home bnd 2f out: sn rdn and no imp over 1f out: one pce fnl f* 3/1[2]
-244 5 ½ **Deputise**[117] 3166 3-9-7 100 JamesDoyle 1 94
(William Haggas) *trckd ldr to 3f out: settled in 3rd: rdn along and no imp over 1f out: wknd fnl f* 3/1[2]
58.59s (-1.61) **Going Correction** -0.20s/f (Stan) 5 Ran SP% 111.0
Speed ratings (Par 107): **104,102,99,98,97**
CSF £22.61 TOTE £6.80: £2.90, £1.90; EX 20.90 Trifecta £59.70.
Owner Andrew Kendall-Jones I **Bred** R & M Bloodstock **Trained** Upper Helmsley, N Yorks
FOCUS
A good 3yo sprint handicap. The relative outsider of the quintet made all in game fashion in the best comparative time on the card. He resumed his early-season progress.

7450 BET TOTESWINGER AT TOTESPORT.COM H'CAP 1m 5f 66y(P)
4:35 (4:36) (Class 6) (0-65,66) 3-Y-O
£3,105 (£924; £461; £300; £300; £300) Stalls Low

Form RPR
-433 1 **Waterfront (IRE)**[28] 6439 3-9-7 65 JackMitchell 3 72
(Simon Crisford) *in tch: effrt to trck ldr 6f out: pushed along 3f out: rdn to ld 2f out: drvn and responded wl to press 1f out: kpt on wl* 2/1[2]
0056 2 1 ¼ **Fountain Of Life**[49] 5653 3-8-3 51 ow1 (b[1]) ThoreHammerHansen(5) 5 57
(Philip McBride) *hld up: c wdst of all off home bnd 2f out: sn rdn and wnt 2nd 1f out: kpt on: nt rch wnr* 6/1
5043 3 1 ½ **Sibylline**[24] 6595 3-8-6 50 LiamJones 2 53
(David Simcock) *in tch: niggled along 4f out: rdn along and no imp over 1f out: kpt on one pce fnl f* 16/1
542 4 ½ **Wadacre Galoubet**[12] 7035 3-9-8 66 JamesDoyle 8 68
(Mark Johnston) *hld up: rapid hdwy on outer to go 3rd 5f out: rdn and no further imp 2f out: plugged on fnl f* 5/1[3]
0-00 5 ¾ **Miss Swift**[26] 6531 3-8-2 46 oh1 RaulDaSilva 1 47
(Marcus Tregoning) *led for 1f then remained handy: rdn along on inner and outpcd over 1f out: kpt on one pce fnl f* 33/1
2305 6 ¾ **Miss Green Dream**[12] 7025 3-8-2 46 oh1 HollieDoyle 6 46
(Julia Feilden) *racd in midfield: effrt on outer 2f out: rdn and no imp over 1f out: no further hdwy (jockey said filly lugged left-handed in the home straight)* 20/1
0600 7 ¾ **Blue Beirut (IRE)**[61] 5249 3-8-5 49 KieranO'Neill 7 48
(William Muir) *racd in rr of midfield: pushed along on inner 3f out: sn rdn and no hdwy 2f out: plugged on* 33/1
3-51 8 1 **Sea Battle (FR)**[21] 6722 3-9-4 65 TimClark(3) 4 62
(Jane Chapple-Hyam) *restless in stalls: pushed along to ld after 1f out: rdn along and hdd 2f out: wknd over 1f out (trainer said that the gelding may have failed to stay 1m5f having been ridden more prominently on this occasion)* 6/4[1]
2m 50.62s (-2.98) **Going Correction** -0.20s/f (Stan) 8 Ran SP% 120.8
Speed ratings (Par 99): **101,100,99,99,98 98,97,97**
CSF £15.20 CT £152.53 TOTE £2.50: £1.10, £1.40, £2.20; EX 15.70 Trifecta £73.30.
Owner Abdulla Belhabb **Bred** Rabbah Bloodstock Limited **Trained** Newmarket, Suffolk

FOCUS
A modest 3yo staying handicap. The second-favourite won convincingly, once on the lead at the top of the home straight, from just off a modest gallop. The bare form feels sensible.

7451 BET TOTESCOOP6 AT TOTESPORT.COM EBF FILLIES' NOVICE STKS 1m 2f (P)
5:05 (5:08) (Class 4) 3-Y-O+ £6,727 (£2,002; £1,000) Stalls Low

Form RPR
5 1 **Lenya**[64] 5141 3-8-11 0 KieranO'Neill 5 74
(John Gosden) *mde all: rn v green at times: shkn up 2f out and hung rt multiple times: stened up and rdn over 1f out: kpt on wl (jockey said filly ran green)* 15/8[2]
6- 2 1 1/4 **Malika I Jahan (FR)**[344] 8151 3-8-11 0 DanielMuscutt 4 71
(David Lanigan) *trckd ldr: pushed along and carried rt by wnr off home bnd: sn rdn and bmpd by wnr over 1f out: kpt on fnl f* 2/1[3]
6-2 3 1 1/2 **Persuer**[10] 7081 3-8-11 0 StevieDonohoe 1 68
(David Simcock) *dwlt and racd in last: effrt to take clsr order on outer over 2f out: pushed along and carried rt by rivals off home bnd: sn swtchd lft and rdn over 1f out: no ex* 11/8[1]
2m 8.36s (-0.24) **Going Correction** -0.20s/f (Stan) 3 Ran SP% 110.2
Speed ratings (Par 102): **92,91,89**
CSF £5.66 TOTE £2.20; EX 5.50 Trifecta £6.10.
Owner George Strawbridge **Bred** George Strawbridge **Trained** Newmarket, Suffolk
■ Stewards' Enquiry : Kieran O'Neill two-day ban; careless riding (Oct 7-8)

FOCUS
A fair little 3yo fillies' novice contest. The second-favourite won well from the front off her own gradually increasing tempo. She has obvious potential to do better.

7452 BOOK TICKETS ONLINE AT CHELMSFORDCITYRACECOURSE.COM H'CAP 1m 2f (P)
5:40 (5:42) (Class 5) (0-75,76) 3-Y-O+ £5,433 (£1,617; £808; £404; £300; £300) Stalls Low

Form RPR
0012 1 **Junior Rip (IRE)**[29] 6393 3-9-1 71 (p[1]) SeanLevey 3 79
(Roger Charlton) *trckd ldr: pushed along to ld 2f out: sn drvn and responded generously to press ins fnl f: hld on gamely* 5/1[2]
3330 2 shd **Power Of States (IRE)**[35] 6217 3-9-6 76 (bt[1]) JamesDoyle 1 83
(Hugo Palmer) *in tch on rail: gd hdwy on to heels of ldrs 2f out: rdn and clsd on wnr 1f out: kpt on wl: jst failed* 11/4[1]
6422 3 3/4 **Olympic Conqueror (IRE)**[23] 6624 3-9-0 70 DanielMuscutt 8 75
(James Fanshawe) *prom in 3rd: rdn along and ev ch 1f out: kpt on wl fnl f but nt match front pair* 8/1
2622 4 1/2 **Queen Constantine (GER)**[41] 5982 3-9-5 75 DavidProbert 5 79
(William Jarvis) *racd in midfield: hdwy into 4th over 1f out: sn rdn and kpt on fnl f (jockey said filly ran too freely)* 6/1[3]
3164 5 4 1/2 **Stormingin (IRE)**[36] 6160 6-9-10 75 LiamKeniry 6 69
(Gary Moore) *in rr of midfield: hdwy u.p 2f out: sn rdn and kpt on one pce ins fnl f* 10/1
4415 6 2 **Melgate Majeure**[38] 6068 3-8-7 63 HollieDoyle 4 54
(Michael Easterby) *racd in midfield: rdn along and no prog 3f out: sn outpcd: plugged on fnl f* 5/1[2]
5632 7 1 1/2 **Rudy Lewis (IRE)**[22] 6678 3-9-4 74 StevieDonohoe 9 62
(Charlie Fellowes) *hld up: rdn along in rr 2f out: no imp over 1f out: one pce (jockey said gelding ran too freely)* 7/1
4446 8 2 1/4 **Molly Mai**[37] 6101 3-8-2 63 ThoreHammerHansen(5) 2 47
(Philip McBride) *hld up: rdn along in rr 3f out: nvr on terms* 12/1
5504 9 4 **Liliofthelamplight (IRE)**[23] 6630 3-9-2 72 JackMitchell 7 48
(Mark Johnston) *led at a stdy pce: rdn along and hdd by wnr 2f out: sn wknd* 20/1
540 10 22 **Foxes Flyer (IRE)**[88] 4225 3-8-10 66 KieranO'Neill 10
(Luke McJannet) *bmpd leaving stalls and racd in last: a bhd* 33/1
2m 4.41s (-4.19) **Going Correction** -0.20s/f (Stan) 10 Ran SP% 122.4
WFA 3 from 6yo 5lb
Speed ratings (Par 103): **108,107,107,106,103 101,100,98,95,77**
CSF £20.20 CT £112.94 TOTE £5.80: £2.10, £1.70, £2.80; EX 26.50 Trifecta £184.20.
Owner Nick Bradley Racing 19 & Sohi **Bred** Pigeon Park Stud **Trained** Beckhampton, Wilts

FOCUS
A fair handicap. One of the joint-second favourites won gamely in a good comparative time for the grade, nearly four seconds quicker than the previous C&D fillies' novice contest. The form makes sense.
T/Plt: £89.50 to a £1 stake. Pool: £33,960.45 - 276.80 winning units T/Qpdt: £69.70 to a £1 stake. Pool: £2,220.39 - 23.56 winning units **Mark Grantham**

7406 NEWBURY (L-H)
Saturday, September 21

OFFICIAL GOING: Good to firm (good in places; 6.9)
Wind: Quite strong at times, behind Weather: Bright and warm

7453 SIS FAMILY FUN DAY EBF NOVICE STKS (PLUS 10 RACE) (DIV I) 7f (S)
1:10 (1:14) (Class 4) 2-Y-O £5,207 (£1,549; £774; £387) Stalls Centre

Form RPR
1 1 **Cherokee Trail (USA)**[14] 6948 2-9-8 0 RyanMoore 8 91
(John Gosden) *led: rdn whn strly chal over 1f out: kpt on wl ins fnl f: asserting towards fin* 8/13[1]
2 1 **Imrahor** 2-9-2 0 KieranShoemark 1 82+
(Hugo Palmer) *athletic; bit bkward; prom: rdn for str chal over 1f out: ev ch ins fnl f: drifted lft fnl 140yds: hld towards fin (jockey said colt ran greenly)* 12/1
3 5 **Hukum (IRE)** 2-9-2 0 JimCrowley 2 69
(Owen Burrows) *quite tall; bit bkward; trckd ldrs: rdn wl over 1f out: sn chsng ldng pair: nt pce to get on terms* 6/1[3]
4 2 1/4 **Evening Sun** 2-9-2 0 JasonWatson 9 64+
(Roger Charlton) *quite str; rn green: wnt bdly rt and slowly away: last but in tch: hdwy over 1f out: wnt 4th ent fnl f: kpt on (jockey said colt ran greenly)* 12/1
5 4 1/2 **On The Right Track** 2-9-2 0 (w) JoeyHaynes 7 52
(Mark Usher) *unfurnished; prom: rdn and ev ch over 2f out: wknd ent fnl f* 66/1
5 6 hd **Millionaire Waltz**[156] 1887 2-9-2 0 AndreaAtzeni 6 51
(Paul Cole) *compact; sweating; sltly on toes; trckd ldrs: rdn and ev ch over 2f out: wknd ent fnl f* 11/2[2]
7 1 **Tahitian Prince (FR)** 2-9-2 0 RobertHavlin 5 49
(Richard Hannon) *athletic; chsd ldrs: rdn over 2f out: wknd over 1f out* 14/1
8 4 1/2 **Island Nation (IRE)** 2-8-9 0 EllieMacKenzie(7) 3 37
(Heather Main) *compact; bit bkward; s.i.s: towards rr: rdn over 2f out: sn wknd* 50/1
6 9 3/4 **Blairlogie**[9] 7113 2-9-2 0 CallumShepherd 4 35
(Mick Channon) *compact; a towards rr* 40/1
1m 25.51s (-1.49) **Going Correction** -0.225s/f (Firm) 9 Ran SP% 119.5
Speed ratings (Par 97): **99,97,92,89,84 84,83,77,77**
CSF £10.43 TOTE £1.50: £1.10, £2.80, £1.90; EX 9.00 Trifecta £42.10.
Owner M Tabor, D Smith & Mrs J Magnier **Bred** Orpendale, Chelston & Wynatt **Trained** Newmarket, Suffolk

FOCUS
Jamie Spencer said on the ground: "It's a bit dead in places, but generally good." The first leg of a decent juvenile novice, they raced down the centre and the front two pulled clear. A step forward from the winner.

7454 DUBAI INTERNATIONAL AIRPORT WORLD TROPHY STKS (GROUP 3) 5f 34y
1:45 (1:45) (Class 1) 3-Y-O+ £34,026 (£12,900; £6,456; £3,216; £1,614; £810) Stalls Centre

Form RPR
5-10 1 **Maid In India (IRE)**[91] 4101 5-8-12 100 JamieSpencer 2 110
(Eric Alston) *trckd ldrs: rdn to ld ins fnl f: kpt on wl: drvn out* 12/1
1111 2 1/2 **Dakota Gold**[13] 6999 5-9-1 110 ConnorBeasley 7 111
(Michael Dods) *looked wl; prom: hrd rdn over 1f out: pressed wnr ins fnl f: kpt on gamely but a being jst hld* 15/8[1]
2060 3 2 **Hit The Bid**[6] 7243 5-9-1 109 (t) AntonioFresu 3 104+
(D J Bunyan, Ire) *prom: led over 2f out: rdn and hdd ins fnl f: no ex fnl 100yds* 15/2
1036 4 3/4 **Keystroke**[27] 6520 7-9-4 109 (t) AdamKirby 5 104
(Stuart Williams) *hld up: hdwy 2f out: sn rdn: chal for hld 4th ent fnl f: kpt on same pce* 11/1
0161 5 1 1/4 **Judicial (IRE)**[21] 6698 7-9-1 107 JimCrowley 6 97
(Julie Camacho) *trckd ldrs: rdn in 4th over 1f out: nt pce to get on terms: fdd fnl 100yds* 13/2[3]
2061 6 2 **Equilateral**[10] 7073 4-9-1 108 RyanMoore 8 90
(Charles Hills) *hld up in tch: effrt over 1f out: nt pce to get on terms: fdd ins fnl f* 7/2[2]
41-3 7 1 1/4 **Blue Uluru (IRE)**[14] 6986 4-8-12 102 AndreaAtzeni 4 82
(G M Lyons, Ire) *chsd ldrs: rdn 2f out: wknd ent fnl f* 11/1
3006 8 2 3/4 **Ornate**[21] 6698 6-9-1 103 JasonWatson 1 75
(David C Griffiths) *led tl over 2f out: sn rdn: wknd over 1f out (jockey said gelding ran flat)* 14/1
59.31s (-2.19) **Going Correction** -0.225s/f (Firm) 8 Ran SP% 113.1
Speed ratings (Par 113): **108,107,104,102,100 97,95,91**
CSF £34.22 TOTE £12.60: £3.20, £1.10, £2.30; EX 38.10 Trifecta £200.20.
Owner Con Harrington **Bred** C F Harrington **Trained** Longton, Lancs

FOCUS
This was a good race for the level, with the market principals all in decent form. The pace looked strong from the outset. The winner is rated back to form.

7455 DUBAI DUTY FREE LEGACY CUP STKS (GROUP 3) (FORMERLY THE ARC TRIAL) 1m 3f
2:20 (2:20) (Class 1) 3-Y-O+ £34,026 (£12,900; £6,456; £3,216; £1,614) Stalls Low

Form RPR
0311 1 **Desert Encounter (IRE)**[28] 6467 7-9-6 115 (h) JamieSpencer 2 116+
(David Simcock) *hld up: smooth hdwy 2f out: chal jst over 1f out: nudged into ld ins fnl f: readily* 9/4[2]
0150 2 1 **Pivoine (IRE)**[14] 6962 5-9-3 110 (b) RobHornby 4 110
(Andrew Balding) *trckd ldrs: pushed along 2f out: cl 4th whn nt clr run jst over 1f out: sn swtchd rt: rdn and r.o wl ins fnl f: wnt 2nd towards fin* 14/1
1622 3 1/2 **Pondus**[42] 5950 3-8-11 107 RyanMoore 1 110
(James Fanshawe) *looked wl; trckd ldr: disp ld over 2f out: sn rdn: narrowly hdd over 1f out: kpt on ins fnl f* 7/4[1]
561 4 hd **Waldstern**[42] 5966 3-8-11 105 (v) RobertHavlin 3 109
(John Gosden) *trckd ldrs: disp ld over 2f out: rdn into narrow advantage over 1f out: hdd jst ins fnl f: kpt on but no ex* 4/1[3]
0264 5 26 **Wadilsafa**[42] 5950 4-9-3 109 JimCrowley 5 67
(Owen Burrows) *led tl rdn over 2f out: sn wknd (jockey said colt stopped quickly; trainer reported that the colt had a breathing problem)* 11/2
2m 18.34s (-4.86) **Going Correction** -0.225s/f (Firm)
WFA 3 from 4yo+ 6lb 5 Ran SP% 109.2
Speed ratings (Par 113): **108,107,106,106,87**
CSF £27.15 TOTE £2.70: £1.40, £3.70; EX 21.80 Trifecta £46.70.
Owner Abdulla Al Mansoori **Bred** Tally-Ho Stud **Trained** Newmarket, Suffolk

FOCUS
Distance increased by 4yds. No great depth to this Group 3, it was run at an ordinary gallop and produced a bunched finish. The winner scored with a bit in hand, though. The form is rated around the third and fourth.

7456 DUBAI DUTY FREE MILL REEF STKS (GROUP 2) 6f
2:55 (2:55) (Class 1) 2-Y-O £42,532 (£16,125; £8,070; £4,020; £2,017; £1,012) Stalls Centre

Form RPR
1 1 **Pierre Lapin (IRE)**[120] 3047 2-9-1 0 AndreaAtzeni 6 111+
(Roger Varian) *tall; ly; racd keenly: trckd ldrs: shkn up 2f out: led jst ins fnl f: kpt on wl to assert fnl 120yds: readily* 9/4[1]
116 2 1 1/2 **Mystery Power (IRE)**[53] 5520 2-9-4 111 RyanMoore 5 109
(Richard Hannon) *prom: rdn 2f out: nt quite pce of wnr but kpt on wl towards fin* 9/4[1]
1013 3 1/2 **Shadn (IRE)**[28] 6444 2-8-12 99 JimCrowley 3 102
(Andrew Balding) *hld up: swtchd rt over 2f out: hdwy over 1f out: sn rdn to chal for 2nd: kpt on same pce fnl 140yds* 8/1[3]
410 4 3/4 **Royal Commando (IRE)**[51] 5584 2-9-1 95 KieranShoemark 7 102
(Charles Hills) *looked wl; trckd ldrs: rdn 2f out: kpt on same pce fnl f* 14/1
114 5 1 1/4 **Malotru**[29] 6422 2-9-1 0 GeraldMosse 1 99+
(Marco Botti) *looked wl; trckd ldr: rdn to ld 2f out: sn hung lft: hdd jst ins fnl f: fdd fnl 120yds (jockey said colt hung left-handed)* 11/2[2]
160 6 3 1/4 **Firepower (FR)**[93] 4012 2-9-1 90 (h[1]) AdamKirby 2 89
(Clive Cox) *led: rdn and hdd 2f out: wknd ins fnl f* 25/1
41 7 nk **Mr Kiki (IRE)**[44] 5865 2-9-1 0 JasonWatson 4 88
(Michael Bell) *wnt lft s: chsd ldrs: rdn over 2f out: wknd fnl f (jockey said colt boiled over in the preliminaries)* 11/1

The Form Book Flat 2019, Raceform Ltd, Newbury, RG14 5SJ

41 **8** *7* **Impressor (IRE)**[38] 6079 2-9-1 0 MartinDwyer 8 67
(Marcus Tregoning) *prom: rdn 2f out: sn wknd (trainer said colt was unsuited by the going, which was officially described as Good to Firm, Good in places on this occasion, and in his opinion was loose on top)* **10/1**

1m 10.9s (-2.30) **Going Correction** -0.225s/f (Firm) 8 Ran SP% **116.0**
Speed ratings (Par 107): **106,104,103,102,100 96,95,86**
CSF £7.03 CT £32.78 TOTE £2.70: £1.40, £1.20, £2.30; EX 7.70 Trifecta £28.90.
Owner Sheikh Mohammed Obaid Al Maktoum **Bred** Cbs Bloodstock **Trained** Newmarket, Suffolk

FOCUS
It can't be said this was strong Group 2 form, but the winner got well on top late. The third looks the best guide. The raced centre-field.

7457 DUBAI DUTY FREE H'CAP 1m 2f
3:30 (3:30) (Class 2) (0-105,105) 3-Y-0+
£43,575 (£13,048; £6,524; £3,262; £1,631; £819) **Stalls** Low

Form RPR
1413 **1** **Caradoc (IRE)**[29] 6420 4-9-0 **95** RyanMoore 4 104
(Ed Walker) *mid-div: hdwy over 2f out: rdn to dispute 2nd over 1f out: str run ins fnl f: led cl home* **5/1**[2]
1412 **2** *½* **Great Example**[27] 6506 3-8-10 **96** (p[1]) CallumShepherd 1 104
(Saeed bin Suroor) *looked wl; mid-div: hdwy to ld 2f out: sn rdn: styd on: ct cl home* **10/1**
/P40 **3** *shd* **Gibbs Hill (GER)**[14] 6962 6-9-10 **105** AndreaAtzeni 13 113
(Roger Varian) *s.i.s: in last pair: swtchd to centre over 3f out: hdwy fr 2f out: rdn over 1f out: styd on strly w wnr ins fnl f: nrly snatched 2nd* **12/1**
2222 **4** *2 ¼* **You're Hired**[16] 6909 6-8-6 **87** (p) MartinDwyer 2 91
(Amanda Perrett) *trckd ldrs: chal over 2f out: sn rdn: styd on same pce fnl f* **33/1**
0012 **5** *nk* **Migration (IRE)**[21] 6725 3-8-8 **94** JasonWatson 11 98+
(David Menuisier) *hld up towards rr: hdwy whn nt clr run and swtchd rt jst over 2f out: sn rdn: styd on wl fnl f but nvr gng pce to rch ldrs (jockey said colt was denied a clear run)* **10/1**
3361 **6** *1 ¾* **Hyanna**[21] 6725 4-8-7 **95** 5ex GeorgiaDobie(7) 6 94
(Eve Johnson Houghton) *trckd ldrs: rdn over 2f out: one pce fnl f* **20/1**
6233 **7** *3 ½* **Oasis Prince**[27] 6513 3-8-10 **96** JamieSpencer 9 89
(Mark Johnston) *s.i.s: towards rr: sme prog over 2f out: sn rdn: no further imp fnl f* **33/1**
3400 **8** *1* **Exec Chef (IRE)**[53] 5519 4-8-13 **94** PatCosgrave 12 84
(Jim Boyle) *mid-div: effrt wl over 2f out: nt pce to threaten: fdd fnl f* **12/1**
4154 **9** *¾* **Victory Command (IRE)**[21] 6696 3-9-0 **100** ConnorBeasley 8 90
(Mark Johnston) *mid-div: rdn over 2f out: nvr any imp* **33/1**
062 **10** *hd* **Johnny Drama (IRE)**[28] 6475 4-9-2 **97** RobHornby 5 86
(Andrew Balding) *looked wl; trckd ldrs: rdn over 2f out: wknd over 1f out* **11/1**
1411 **11** *½* **Forest Of Dean**[28] 6475 3-9-5 **105** 5ex RobertHavlin 7 94
(John Gosden) *mid-div: rdn over 2f out: nvr any imp: wknd fnl f (jockey said colt ran too freely)* **13/8**[1]
3354 **12** *nk* **Freerolling**[14] 6964 4-8-4 **85** CharlieBennett 3 72
(Charlie Fellowes) *racd keenly: led tl rdn 2f out: wknd ent fnl f* **50/1**
2214 **13** *7* **Rise Hall**[28] 6475 4-9-4 **99** (b) JimCrowley 10 72
(Martyn Meade) *trckd ldr: chal over 4f out: rdn over 2f out: wknd over 1f out (jockey said gelding stopped quickly; trainer's rep reported that the gelding had a breathing problem)* **8/1**[3]

2m 5.02s (-4.68) **Going Correction** -0.225s/f (Firm)
WFA 3 from 4yo+ 5lb 13 Ran SP% **123.3**
Speed ratings (Par 109): **109,108,108,106,106 105,102,101,100,100 100,100,94**
CSF £53.10 CT £585.51 TOTE £5.50: £1.90, £2.70, £4.90; EX 45.60 Trifecta £558.70.
Owner P K Siu **Bred** P & B Bloodstock **Trained** Upper Lambourn, Berks

FOCUS
Add 4yds. A competitive handicap, in which a few at the head of the pack early on were taking keen holds. the first three were all on good marks and the fourth helps with the standard.

7458 SIS FAMILY FUN DAY EBF NOVICE STKS (PLUS 10 RACE) (DIV II) 7f (S)
4:05 (4:07) (Class 4) 2-Y-0 **£5,207** (£1,549; £774; £387) **Stalls** Centre

Form RPR
2 **1** **Raaeq (IRE)**[18] 6845 2-9-5 0 JimCrowley 4 88+
(Brian Meehan) *quite str; looked wl; mde all: rdn whn strly chal over 1f out: kpt on wl fnl f: all out* **11/8**[1]
0 **2** *½* **Establish**[15] 6912 2-9-5 0 AndreaAtzeni 2 87+
(Roger Varian) *compact; prom: rdn for str chal over 1f out: ev ch thrght fnl f: hld cl home* **11/2**[3]
3 *3 ¼* **Declared Interest** 2-9-0 0 HarryBentley 3 73+
(Ralph Beckett) *quite str; looked wl; s.i.s: sn trcking ldrs: rdn over 1f out: kpt on but nt pce of front pair fnl f* **12/1**
4 *2 ¾* **Haqeeqy (IRE)** 2-9-5 0 RobertHavlin 5 71+
(John Gosden) *compact; hld up: pushed along over 2f out: hdwy ent fnl f: kpt on but nt pce to get on terms* **9/2**[2]
10 **5** *3 ¾* **Sovereign Beauty (IRE)**[72] 4840 2-9-3 0 AdamKirby 9 59
(Clive Cox) *leggy; in tch: effrt 2f out: wnt hld 4th jst over 1f out: fdd fnl 120yds* **16/1**
20 **6** *2 ¼* **Smuggler**[49] 5665 2-9-5 0 MartinDwyer 6 56
(Marcus Tregoning) *compact; racd keenly trcking ldrs: rdn 2f out: wknd jst over 1f out* **8/1**
7 *¾* **Juan Les Pins** 2-9-5 0 PatCosgrave 1 54+
(Ed Walker) *unfurnished; scope; bit bkward; racd keenly in tch: effrt 2f out: nt pce to threaten: wknd fnl f (jockey said colt ran too freely)* **25/1**
8 *2 ¾* **Maurimo** 2-9-0 0 JasonWatson 8 41
(Roger Charlton) *athletic; hld up: rdn 2f out: nvr threatened: wknd fnl f* **10/1**
9 *5* **Jadeer (IRE)** 2-9-5 0 GeraldMosse 7 33
(Mick Channon) *athletic; racd keenly in last pair: wknd over 1f out (jockey said colt ran greenly and the bit slipped through the colt's mouth)* **33/1**

1m 24.89s (-2.11) **Going Correction** -0.225s/f (Firm) 9 Ran SP% **116.2**
Speed ratings (Par 97): **103,102,98,95,91 88,87,84,79**
CSF £9.20 TOTE £2.20: £1.10, £1.90, £3.60; EX 9.80 Trifecta £75.80.
Owner Hamdan Al Maktoum **Bred** Shadwell Estate Company Limited **Trained** Manton, Wilts

FOCUS
Leg two of what was a useful juvenile novice and the time was 0.62secs quicker than the first division. The form is rated in line with the race averages.

7459 DUBAI DUTY FREE FINEST SURPRISE H'CAP 1m 4f
4:40 (4:40) (Class 3) (0-95,95) 3-Y-0+ **£7,439** (£2,213; £1,106; £553) **Stalls** Low

Form RPR
0462 **1** **Koeman**[7] 7201 5-9-10 **93** GeraldMosse 6 100
(Mick Channon) *trckd ldrs: pushed along over 3f out: rdn over 1f out: led fnl 140yds: styd on wl* **9/1**
-504 **2** *½* **Kosciuszko (IRE)**[15] 6917 3-8-11 **87** RobertHavlin 4 93
(John Gosden) *looked wl; trckd ldr: led over 2f out: sn rdn: hdd fnl 140yds: styd on same pce* **5/1**
0035 **3** *hd* **What A Welcome**[18] 6834 5-9-12 **95** JoeyHaynes 3 101
(Patrick Chamings) *hld up: hdwy over 2f out: sn rdn: styd on ins fnl f: clsng on wnr at fin* **7/2**[2]
2246 **4** *2 ¾* **Lariat**[22] 6657 3-8-12 **88** MartinDwyer 1 89
(Andrew Balding) *led: rdn and hdd over 2f out: lost 2nd ent fnl f: styd on same pce* **4/1**[3]
6211 **5** *2 ¼* **Fantastic Blue**[11] 7057 3-8-6 **82** (p[1]) HarryBentley 2 80
(Ismail Mohammed) *trckd ldrs: rdn over 2f out: sn one pce* **11/4**[1]
0653 **6** *½* **Kaloor**[15] 6917 3-9-2 **92** JimCrowley 5 89
(Brian Meehan) *hld up: hdwy over 3f out: effrt over 2f out: wknd ent fnl f* **5/1**

2m 34.88s (-3.12) **Going Correction** -0.225s/f (Firm)
WFA 3 from 5yo 7lb 6 Ran SP% **112.2**
Speed ratings (Par 107): **101,100,100,98,97 96**
CSF £51.66 TOTE £10.20: £4.00, £2.40; EX 67.70 Trifecta £271.50.
Owner Peter Taplin & Susan Bunney **Bred** B V Sangster **Trained** West Ilsley, Berks

FOCUS
Distance increased by 4yds. Just the six of them but good handicap form, rated around the two older horses. The pace was steady enough.

7460 HEATHERWOLD STUD H'CAP 7f (S)
5:15 (5:15) (Class 4) (0-80,79) 3-Y-0
£5,207 (£1,549; £774; £387; £300; £300) **Stalls** Centre

Form RPR
041 **1** **Bear Force One**[24] 6594 3-9-7 **79** JasonWatson 8 95
(Roger Teal) *looked wl; mde all: rdn clr over 1f out: drifted rt fnl f: comf* **13/2**
2523 **2** *5* **Quarry Beach**[8] 7165 3-9-0 **72** KieranShoemark 2 74
(Henry Candy) *mid-div: hdwy 2f out: sn rdn: styd on to go 2nd ins fnl f: no ch w wnr* **13/2**
3062 **3** *1* **Society Guest (IRE)**[6] 7237 3-8-8 **66** (p[1]) NicolaCurrie 3 65
(Mick Channon) *mid-div: hdwy over 2f out: rdn in 3rd over 1f out: kpt on same pce fnl f* **12/1**
3420 **4** *1* **Majestic Mac**[45] 5804 3-9-5 **77** (t[1]) AndreaAtzeni 7 74
(Hughie Morrison) *looked wl; s.i.s: towards rr: hdwy 2f out: sn rdn: kpt on into 4th jst ins fnl f: nt pce to get on terms* **3/1**[1]
2222 **5** *1 ¾* **Voltaic**[56] 5428 3-9-0 **72** JimCrowley 9 64
(Paul Cole) *racd alone on stands' side: trckd ldrs: drifted lft u.p whn chsng wnr over 1f out: fdd ins fnl f* **11/2**[2]
0324 **6** *1 ¼* **Ifton**[18] 6840 3-8-4 **62** MartinDwyer 5 51
(Ruth Carr) *wnt rt s: hld up: rdn over 1f out: nvr threatened: wknd fnl f* **6/1**[3]
5425 **7** *½* **Oloroso (IRE)**[28] 6468 3-9-1 **73** RobHornby 6 60
(Andrew Balding) *trckd ldrs: rdn over 2f out: drifted lft over 1f out: sn wknd* **7/1**
0241 **8** *1 ¼* **Song Of The Isles (IRE)**[29] 6418 3-8-9 **74** EllieMacKenzie(7) 4 58
(Heather Main) *trckd ldrs: rdn over 2f out: sn wknd* **8/1**
0-00 **9** *1* **Sunvisor (IRE)**[18] 6840 3-8-10 **68** RobertHavlin 1 49
(William Muir) *prom: rdn over 2f out: wknd over 1f out* **33/1**

1m 23.43s (-3.57) **Going Correction** -0.225s/f (Firm) 9 Ran SP% **115.6**
Speed ratings (Par 103): **111,105,104,103,101 99,99,97,96**
CSF £48.25 CT £499.49 TOTE £6.10: £2.20, £2.10, £3.70; EX 50.40 Trifecta £610.70.
Owner Joe Bear Racing **Bred** S M Ransom **Trained** Lambourn, Berks

FOCUS
The lightly raced winner took this in fine style, but a lot of his rivals were exposed maidens. The form is taken at face value.
T/Plt: £31.90 to a £1 stake. Pool: £90,646.32 - 2,068.93 winning units T/Qpdt: £17.30 to a £1 stake. Pool: £6,913.05 - 295.31 winning units **Tim Mitchell**

6449 NEWMARKET (R-H)
Saturday, September 21

OFFICIAL GOING: Good to firm (watered; 7.3)
Wind: medium to fresh, against Weather: sunny and warm

7461 HEATH COURT HOTEL BESTWESTERN.CO.UK BRITISH EBF FILLIES' NOVICE STKS (PLUS 10 RACE) 1m
2:10 (2:12) (Class 4) 2-Y-0 **£5,175** (£1,540; £769; £384) **Stalls** High

Form RPR
2 **1** **Queen Daenerys (IRE)**[57] 5366 2-9-0 0 WilliamBuick 7 86+
(Roger Varian) *trckd ldrs tl effrt to chse ldr ent fnl 2f: sn swtchd rt and drvn to chal over 1f out: sustained effrt to ld ins fnl f: styd on gamely* **5/4**[1]
21 **2** *nk* **Wasaayef (IRE)**[64] 5139 2-9-6 0 DaneO'Neill 1 91+
(John Gosden) *led: rdn ent fnl 2f: sn edgd lft and drvn whn hrd pressed over 1f out: hdd ins fnl f: kpt on gamely but hld towards fin* **11/8**[2]
3 *3 ½* **Golden Pass** 2-9-0 0 JackMitchell 2 77+
(Hugo Palmer) *dwlt and wnt rt leaving stalls: hld up in tch in rr: clsd and nt clrest of runs over 2f out: effrt to chse ldrs wl over 1f out: unable qck 1f out: kpt on same pce* **5/1**[3]
5 **4** *4 ½* **Bharani Star (GER)**[14] 6949 2-9-0 0 JFEgan 4 67
(Peter Chapple-Hyam) *in tch in midfield: clsd to chse ldrs over 3f out: sn rdn: no ex and outpcd wl over 1f out: wl hld and plugged on same pce fnl f* **10/1**
5 *1 ½* **Corazonada (IRE)** 2-9-0 0 DavidEgan 8 64
(Ismail Mohammed) *in tch in midfield: rdn and outpcd over 2f out: wl hld and plugged on same pce fr over 1f out* **33/1**
0 **6** *1 ¾* **Al Gaiya (FR)**[14] 6949 2-9-0 0 PatDobbs 6 60
(Richard Hannon) *chsd ldr tl ent fnl 2f: sn outpcd and wandered wl over 1f out: wl btn fnl f* **50/1**

06 **7** *4* **Loco Dempsey (FR)**[35] 6205 2-9-0 0 SamHitchcott 9 51
(Richard Hannon) *chsd ldrs: rdn 3f out: sn struggling and lost pl: wl btn over 1f out: wknd* **50/1**

8 *30* **Theydon Louboutin** 2-9-0 0 AdrianMcCarthy 5
(Peter Charalambous) *v.s.a and rn green: a in rr: rdn over 3f out: sn struggling and lost tch: t.o (jockey said filly ran green)* **100/1**

9 *12* **Theydon Bagel** 2-8-7 0 AledBeech(7) 3
(Peter Charalambous) *dwlt and rn green early: in tch in rr: last and struggling 1/2-way: sn lost tch: t.o (jockey said filly ran green)* **100/1**

1m 40.7s (2.30) **Going Correction** +0.30s/f (Good) **9** Ran SP% **121.2**
Speed ratings (Par 94): **100,99,96,91,90 88,84,54,42**
CSF £3.44 TOTE £2.10: £1.10, £1.10, £1.60; EX 3.20 Trifecta £6.70.
Owner H H SH Nasser Bin Hamad Al Khalifa **Bred** Coolmore **Trained** Newmarket, Suffolk

FOCUS
Far-side course used. Stalls stands' side except 1m4f and 1m6f: far side. Good to firm ground, 7.3 on the stick.\n A couple with plenty of potential and an interesting newcomer for this 1m novice.

7462 HEATH COURT HOTEL CHRISTMAS H'CAP 7f
2:45 (2:45) (Class 4) (0-85,89) 3-Y-O+
£6,469 (£1,925; £962; £481; £300; £300) **Stalls High**

Form RPR
0043 **1** **Sir Titan**[32] 6326 5-8-11 **78** CierenFallon(3) 3 88
(Tony Carroll) *sn led and mde rest: rdn 2f out: styd on strly and a doing enough ins fnl f* **11/2**[3]

3216 **2** *1 3/4* **Aluqair (IRE)**[19] 6803 3-9-1 **82** WilliamBuick 1 86
(Simon Crisford) *t.k.h: trckd ldrs tl chsd wnr 3f out: sn rdn: kpt on same pce and no imp ins fnl f* **3/1**[1]

1221 **3** *hd* **Chatham House**[11] 7059 3-9-8 **89** PatDobbs 2 92
(Richard Hannon) *stdd s: hld up in tch in last pair: clsd to chse ldrs 2f out: sn rdn: kpt on same pce ins fnl f* **3/1**[1]

4305 **4** *1/2* **Glenn Coco**[8] 7164 5-8-12 **83** (t) MarcoGhiani(7) 4 86
(Stuart Williams) *led: sn hdd and chsd wnr tl 3f out: styd prom: rdn ent fnl 2f: unable qck and kpt on same pce ins fnl f* **3/1**[1]

2143 **5** *3 1/4* **Graphite Storm**[19] 6803 5-9-7 **85** DaneO'Neill 6 79
(Clive Cox) *t.k.h: hld up in tch in last pair: clsd over 2f out: nt clr run briefly wl over 1f out: sn rdn and no imp: wl hld fnl f (jockey said gelding was denied a clear run approaching 1 1/2f out)* **5/1**[2]

2465 **6** *1 1/2* **Elysium Dream**[77] 4662 4-8-11 **75** SamHitchcott 5 65
(Richard Hannon) *chsd ldrs: rdn and outpcd jst over 2f out: wl hld and plugged on same pce fnl f* **25/1**

0565 **7** *5* **Greek Kodiac (IRE)**[37] 6132 3-8-4 **69** oh2 LukeMorris 7 47
(Mick Quinn) *dwlt: wl in tch in midfield: effrt 3f out: sn struggling and bhd whn edgd rt over 1f out: eased ins fnl f* **25/1**

1m 26.71s (1.31) **Going Correction** +0.30s/f (Good)
WFA 3 from 4yo+ 3lb **7** Ran SP% **114.7**
Speed ratings (Par 105): **104,102,101,101,97 95,90**
CSF £22.50 TOTE £7.70: £2.90, £2.30; EX 31.20 Trifecta £68.40.
Owner Wedgewood Estates **Bred** Mrs Liza Judd **Trained** Cropthorne, Worcs

FOCUS
Plenty of good recent form on offer in this 7f class 4 handicap, and the rail looked the place to be. The winner built on his recent runs, with the next pair running as well as ever.

7463 HEATH COURT DINING CLUB FILLIES' H'CAP 1m
3:20 (3:20) (Class 3) (0-95,93) 3-Y-O+ **£9,056** (£2,695; £1,346; £673) **Stalls High**

Form RPR
311 **1** **Nazeef**[17] 6862 3-9-8 **93** DaneO'Neill 2 106+
(John Gosden) *stdd s: hld up in tch in centre: clsd and travelling strly over 2f out: pushed along to ld over 1f out: edgd lft and sn asserted: r.o strly: v readily: impressive* **6/4**[1]

243 **2** *6* **Salayel**[14] 6951 3-9-7 **92** DavidEgan 3 91
(Roger Varian) *hld up in tch and racd nr stands' rail: swtchd rt and clsd ent fnl 3f: rdn to ld 2f out: sn hdd and outpcd: wl btn fnl f* **7/4**[2]

1515 **3** *4 1/2* **Saikung (IRE)**[36] 6160 3-8-9 **80** WilliamBuick 1 68
(Charles Hills) *led and racd in centre: rdn and hdd 2f out: sn outpcd and wl btn 3rd over 1f out: wknd* **6/1**

3613 **4** *7* **Astrologer**[14] 6974 3-9-5 **90** PatDobbs 4 61
(David O'Meara) *pressed ldr and racd nr stands' rail: rdn and lost pl over 2f out: wl btn over 1f out: wknd (jockey said filly ran too free; trainer said filly was unsuited by being unable to dominate on this occasion)* **5/1**[3]

1m 38.7s (0.30) **Going Correction** +0.30s/f (Good) **4** Ran SP% **107.3**
Speed ratings (Par 104): **110,104,99,92**
CSF £4.37 TOTE £1.90; EX 4.00 Trifecta £10.10.
Owner Hamdan Al Maktoum **Bred** Shadwell Estate Company Limited **Trained** Newmarket, Suffolk

FOCUS
A small-field fillies' handicap, but they were all in form and the winner was impressive.

7464 HEATH COURT HOTEL CESAREWITCH TRIAL H'CAP 2m 2f
3:55 (4:02) (Class 2) (0-105,100) 3-Y-O+
£31,125 (£9,320; £4,660; £2,330; £1,165; £585) **Stalls Low**

Form RPR
1131 **1** **Land Of Oz**[15] 6929 3-8-0 **87** LukeMorris 4 99+
(Sir Mark Prescott Bt) *stdd s: t.k.h: hld up in last pair: stdy prog 6f out: led and travelling strly over 2f out: asserted and edgd rt u.p over 1f out: styd on and a in command ins fnl f: rdn out* **11/10**[1]

14-4 **2** *1 1/2* **Smart Champion**[18] 6834 4-8-8 **84** (h[1]) AdrianMcCarthy 1 91
(David Simcock) *stdd s: hld up in tch in last pair: effrt 3f out: drvn and hdwy to chse wnr jst over 1f out: kpt on but a hld ins fnl f* **16/1**

3001 **3** *2 1/4* **Blue Laureate**[6] 7239 4-8-12 **91** 5ex (v[1]) CierenFallon(3) 8 96
(Ian Williams) *hld up in tch in midfield: clsd to chse ldrs 3f out: nt clrest of runs over 2f out: swtchd lft and effrt wl over 1f out: 3rd and kpt on same pce ins fnl f* **4/1**[3]

0-36 **4** *1 3/4* **Champagne Champ**[144] 2254 7-8-2 **78** (t) DavidEgan 2 81
(Rod Millman) *in tch in midfield: effrt 3f out: hdwy u.p 2f out: no ex and unable qck over 1f out: kpt on same pce ins fnl f* **16/1**

5042 **5** *6* **Charles Kingsley**[8] 7147 4-9-10 **100** WilliamBuick 7 96
(Mark Johnston) *pressed ldr tl led after 4f: rdn and hdd over 2f out: no ex u.p: lost 2nd and btn over 1f out: wknd ins fnl f: eased towards fin* **7/2**[2]

1366 **6** *2 1/4* **Jumping Cats**[12] 7033 4-8-0 **76** (p) JimmyQuinn 5 70
(Chris Wall) *in tch in midfield: dropped to last pair 8f out: rdn and outpcd 3f out: n.d after* **33/1**

6312 **7** *hd* **Graceful Lady**[26] 6530 6-8-2 **81** DarraghKeenan(3) 3 74
(Robert Eddery) *t.k.h: chsd ldrs tl wnt 2nd 7f out: ev ch briefly and rdn over 2f out: sn outpcd and btn over 1f out: wknd* **11/1**

0506 **8** *30* **Aircraft Carrier (IRE)**[28] 6452 4-9-2 **92** (p) TomQueally 6 52
(John Ryan) *led for 4f: chsd ldr tl 7f out: rdn and dropped to rr 4f out: wl bhd and eased ins fnl f: t.o* **25/1**

3m 57.53s (2.03) **Going Correction** +0.30s/f (Good)
WFA 3 from 4yo+ 11lb **8** Ran SP% **116.7**
Speed ratings (Par 109): **107,106,105,104,101 100,100,87**
CSF £23.13 CT £57.23 TOTE £1.90: £1.10, £4.20, £1.50; EX 17.00 Trifecta £55.00.
Owner John Brown & Megan Dennis **Bred** Stetchworth & Middle Park Studs Ltd **Trained** Newmarket, Suffolk

FOCUS
The Cesarewitch trial had a very progressive winner, but he almost certainly won't get in the big race despite his very progressive profile. He doesn't win by far and is hard to pin down.

7465 HEATH COURT HOTEL AMATEUR RIDERS' CAMBRIDGESHIRE (H'CAP) 1m 1f
4:30 (4:33) (Class 3) (0-90,80) 3-Y-O+ **£12,478** (£3,870; £1,934; £968) **Stalls High**

Form RPR
-613 **1** **Long Call**[12] 7026 6-10-4 **70** MissSarahBowen 5 82
(Tony Carroll) *stdd s: hld up in tch in rr: clsd on outer to press ldrs 2f out: rdn to ld and edgd lft over 1f out: clr and r.o strly ins fnl f: readily* **5/1**[3]

112 **2** *4* **Geranium**[22] 6672 4-10-8 **74** MissSerenaBrotherton 4 77
(Hughie Morrison) *chsd ldrs: pushed along 3f out: nt clrest of runs: effrt and shifted rt over 1f out: kpt on same pce ins fnl f: wnt 2nd on post* **7/2**[1]

2554 **3** *nse* **Global Art**[33] 6289 4-11-0 **80** SophieSmith 7 83
(Ed Dunlop) *wl in tch in midfield: clsd to chse ldrs and nt clr run over 2f out: effrt over 1f out: kpt on to chse clr wnr wl ins fnl f: no imp: lost 2nd on post* **16/1**

5442 **4** *1/2* **Ginger Fox**[7] 7213 3-10-6 **77** (v) MissABO'Connor 3 80
(Ian Williams) *t.k.h: w ldr tl led over 3f out: rdn ent fnl 2f: hdd and unable qck over 1f out: kpt on same pce and lost 2 pls wl ins fnl f* **4/1**[2]

51P0 **5** *2* **Biotic**[21] 6729 8-10-6 **72** MissJoannaMason 8 70
(Rod Millman) *stdd after s: t.k.h: hld up in tch in last pair: clsd and nt clr run over 2f out: effrt over 1f out: kpt on same pce and no imp ins fnl f (jockey said gelding was denied a clear run from 2f out)* **16/1**

2131 **6** *1 1/4* **First Flight (IRE)**[40] 6012 8-10-7 **73** MissBeckySmith 2 68
(Brian Ellison) *dwlt: in tch in last trio: clsd and nt clr run over 2f out: swtchd lft and rdn over 1f out: no imp and plugged on same pce ins fnl f* **7/1**

3614 **7** *1 3/4* **Regal Director (IRE)**[21] 6734 4-11-0 **80** MissBrodieHampson 1 71
(Archie Watson) *wl in tch in midfield: clsd and ev ch 3f out: struggling to qckn u.p whn short of room: hmpd and swtchd rt over 1f out: no ex and wknd fnl f* **4/1**[2]

3236 **8** *1* **Steeve**[22] 6671 3-10-0 **71** (b[1]) MrPatrickMillman 6 61
(Rod Millman) *led tl over 3f out: sn u.p and lost pl over 2f out: bhd ins fnl f* **8/1**

1m 53.57s (2.47) **Going Correction** +0.30s/f (Good)
WFA 3 from 4yo+ 5lb **8** Ran SP% **114.3**
Speed ratings (Par 107): **101,97,97,96,95 94,92,91**
CSF £22.82 CT £258.39 TOTE £7.10: £1.90, £1.60, £4.50; EX 30.10 Trifecta £250.30.
Owner A A Byrne **Bred** Rabbah Bloodstock Limited **Trained** Cropthorne, Worcs

FOCUS
A tight amateur rider's race but a clearcut winner, who posted a pb under an improving jockey.

7466 PARK REGIS KRIS KIN HOTEL DUBAI BRITISH EBF FILLIES' H'CAP 1m 4f
5:00 (5:05) (Class 3) (0-90,89) 3-Y-O+ **£9,703** (£2,887; £1,443; £721) **Stalls Low**

Form RPR
1053 **1** **Quintada**[21] 6736 3-8-10 **78** JFEgan 3 84
(Mark Johnston) *trckd ldr tl rdn to ld 3f out: drvn over 2f out: forged ahd wl over 1f out: styd on wl ins fnl f* **5/2**[2]

0526 **2** *2* **Point In Time (IRE)**[47] 5735 4-9-1 **76** DaneO'Neill 4 79
(Mark Usher) *stdd and dropped in bhd after s: hld up last: effrt over 2f out: drvn over 1f out: styd on to chse wnr wl ins fnl f: no imp after* **5/1**[3]

-050 **3** *3/4* **Garrel Glen**[92] 4052 3-9-7 **89** TomQueally 1 91
(James Eustace) *stdd s: t.k.h: hld up in 3rd: effrt and clsd over 2f out: chsd wnr jst over 1f out: no imp and kpt on same pce ins fnl f: lost 2nd wl ins fnl f* **7/1**

0132 **4** *4* **Stagehand**[21] 6736 3-8-12 **80** PatDobbs 2 75
(Charles Hills) *t.k.h: led tl hdd 3f out: rdn ent fnl 2f: no ex and lost 2nd over 1f out: wknd ins fnl f (trainer's rep said that the filly was unsuited by the Good to Firm going on this occasion, which in their opinion was riding quicker than described, would prefer an easier surface)* **10/11**[1]

2m 36.1s (3.60) **Going Correction** +0.30s/f (Good)
WFA 3 from 4yo 7lb **4** Ran SP% **110.1**
Speed ratings (Par 104): **100,98,98,95**
CSF £13.70 TOTE £2.70; EX 13.40 Trifecta £38.90.
Owner Miss K Rausing **Bred** R Cantoni **Trained** Middleham Moor, N Yorks

FOCUS
A small field and some very different profiles clashing. The form isn't entirely solid.

7467 HEATH COURT HOTEL H'CAP 6f
5:35 (5:35) (Class 4) (0-85,85) 3-Y-O+
£6,469 (£1,925; £962; £481; £300; £300) **Stalls High**

Form RPR
4540 **1** **Equiano Springs**[15] 6916 5-9-1 **79** TomQueally 1 86
(Tom Tate) *restless in stalls: trckd ldrs and travelled strly: clsd and upsides 2f out: rdn over 1f out: led jst ins fnl f: hld on wl* **7/1**

0333 **2** *nk* **Lady Dancealot (IRE)**[16] 6908 4-9-4 **82** DaneO'Neill 6 88
(David Elsworth) *hld up in tch in last trio: clsd and nt clr run ent fnl 2f: gap opened and edgd out rt over 1f out: clsd and ev ch u.p ins fnl f: r.o wl: jst hld* **2/1**[1]

1341 **3** *nk* **Cent Flying**[9] 7130 4-8-6 **73** (t) GeorgiaCox(3) 5 78
(William Muir) *restless in stalls: short of room sn after s: hld up in tch in last trio: effrt and hdwy over 2f out: ev ch u.p ins fnl f: kpt on wl: no ex cl home* **7/1**

1245 **4** *shd* **Suzi's Connoisseur**[36] 6162 8-8-12 **76** (b) JFEgan 2 81
(Jane Chapple-Hyam) *wnt lft leaving stalls: chsd ldrs: nt clrest of runs and swtchd lft over 1f out: kpt on wl u.p ins fnl f* **16/1**

0313 **5** *hd* **Spirit Of May**[51] 5581 3-8-7 **78** SeamusCronin(5) 9 82
(Roger Teal) *w ldr: rdn and led over 1f out: hdd jst ins fnl f: no ex and jst outpcd wl ins fnl f* **11/2**[3]

1002 **6** *1 1/4* **Firmdecisions (IRE)**[11] 7059 9-9-1 **84** FayeMcManoman(5) 7 84
(Nigel Tinkler) *hld up in tch in rr: clsd and nt clr run over 2f out: swtchd lft over 1f out: swtchd bk rt and hdwy ins fnl f: styd on: nvr getting to ldrs* **14/1**

000 **7** ½ **Erissimus Maximus (FR)**[84] 4369 5-9-0 **85**................ SeanKirrane(7) 8 83
(Amy Murphy) *led: rdn ent fnl 2f: hdd over 1f out: no ex and wknd wl ins fnl f* **16/1**

6520 **8** 2¾ **Haddaf (IRE)**[8] 7164 4-8-7 **78**.....................................(t¹) MarcoGhiani(7) 4 68
(Stuart Williams) *bmpd leaving stalls: in tch in midfield: effrt 2f out: unable qck over 1f out: wknd ins fnl f* **5/1**[2]

0200 **9** 5 **Captain Colby (USA)**[22] 6676 7-9-3 **81**........................... PatDobbs 10 55
(Paul Midgley) *w ldrs tl settled bk into midfield after over 1f: effrt ent fnl f: sn struggling: bhd and struggling ins fnl f* **10/1**

1m 12.71s (0.81) **Going Correction** +0.30s/f (Good)
WFA 3 from 4yo+ 2lb **9** Ran SP% **117.9**
Speed ratings (Par 105): **106,105,105,105,104 103,102,98,92**
CSF £21.87 CT £105.66 TOTE £7.40: £2.40, £1.20, £2.60; EX 25.30 Trifecta £121.90.
Owner T T Racing **Bred** Paddock Space **Trained** Tadcaster, N Yorks
■ Stewards' Enquiry : J F Egan 13-day ban; careless riding (Oct 5,7-18)

FOCUS
A thrilling sprint handicap to end things and the favourite got beat again. Ordinary form.
T/Plt: £122.90 to a £1 stake. Pool: £54,730.74 - 325.04 winning units T/Qpdt: £32.80 to a £1 stake. Pool: £3,782.44 - 85.21 winning units **Steve Payne**

7029 WOLVERHAMPTON (A.W) (L-H)

Saturday, September 21

OFFICIAL GOING: Tapeta: standard
Wind: Light across Weather: Fine

7468 FARLEY & JONES RECRUITMENT CLASSIFIED STKS 5f 21y (Tp)

5:25 (5:30) (Class 6) 3-Y-O+

£2,781 (£827; £413; £400; £400; £400) **Stalls** Low

Form RPR

0536 **1** **One One Seven (IRE)**[41] 5985 3-8-11 49...................... WilliamCox(3) 7 56
(Antony Brittain) *s.i.s: hld up: hdwy over 1f out: rdn to ld wl ins fnl f: r.o* **4/1**[2]

0330 **2** 1¼ **Swell Song**[16] 6889 3-9-0 49...(p) ShaneGray 2 52
(Robert Cowell) *chsd ldrs: wnt 2nd 2f out: led 1f out: rdn and hdd wl ins fnl f* **3/1**[1]

0132 **3** 1¼ **Thornaby Princess**[7] 7214 8-9-1 49.............................(p) ShaneKelly 3 47
(Jason Ward) *pushed along and prom: rdn over 1f out: styd on same pce wl ins fnl f* **5/1**

0000 **4** ½ **Raffle King (IRE)**[78] 4586 5-8-12 46....................(v¹) ConnorMurtagh(3) 1 45
(Julia Brooke) *stmbld s: hld up in tch: nt clr run 4f out: rdn: hung lft and nt clr run over 1f out: swtchd rt: no ex wl ins fnl f* **4/1**[2]

5-22 **5** 1¼ **Katherine Place**[19] 6797 4-9-1 48..........................(t) AdamMcNamara 4 41
(Bill Turner) *hld up: hdwy u.p over 1f out: nt rch ldrs* **9/2**[3]

6 1½ **Dandy Pearl (IRE)**[17] 6865 3-9-0 42...........................(p¹) GaryHalpin 11 35
(Denis Gerard Hogan, Ire) *s.i.s: outpcd: swtchd rt over 1f out: sn rdn and hung lft: nt trble ldrs* **33/1**

0005 **7** nk **Scarlet Red**[98] 3836 4-9-1 50..(p¹) EoinWalsh 6 34
(Malcolm Saunders) *sn led: rdn 2f out: hdd 1f out: wknd wl ins fnl f* **20/1**

06 **8** 1¾ **Mysusy (IRE)**[45] 5822 3-9-0 48....................................(b) GeorgeWood 10 28
(Robert Cowell) *chsd ldrs: shkn up over 1f out: wknd ins fnl f* **16/1**

2000 **9** 8 **Dodgy Bob**[47] 5723 6-8-8 48...(v) AmeliaGlass(7) 9 +
(Michael Mullineaux) *hood stl on after the stalls had opened: a wl bhd (jockey said that the hood got stuck on the bridle and took several attempts to remove)* **14/1**

030- **10** ½ **Mocead Cappall**[390] 6634 4-9-1 47.............................. RoystonFfrench 8
(John Holt) *chsd ldr 3f: sn wkng whn n.m.r over 1f out* **33/1**

1m 1.63s (-0.27) **Going Correction** -0.10s/f (Stan)
WFA 3 from 4yo+ 1lb **10** Ran SP% **123.0**
Speed ratings (Par 101): **98,96,94,93,91 88,88,85,72,71**
CSF £17.13 TOTE £4.80: £1.80, £1.70, £1.70; EX 20.20 Trifecta £104.60.
Owner John And Tony Jarvis And Partner **Bred** Lynch Bages, Camas Park & Summerhill B/S **Trained** Warthill, N Yorks

FOCUS
A moderate classified event. The second and third are among those that set the level.

7469 COMPARE BOOKMAKER SITES AT BONUSCODEBETS.CO.UK (S) STKS 6f 20y (Tp)

5:55 (5:56) (Class 6) 2-Y-O

£2,781 (£827; £413; £400; £400; £400) **Stalls** Low

Form RPR

4406 **1** **Chromium**[12] 7029 2-8-9 62.......................................(v¹) JosephineGordon 6 60
(Mark Usher) *sn outpcd: pushed along and hdwy on outer over 2f out: sn edgd lft: rdn ins fnl f: stvd on to ld nr fin* **7/1**

6655 **2** hd **Bezzas Lad (IRE)**[14] 6980 2-9-0 66..............................(b) ShaneGray 5 64
(Phillip Makin) *sn led: hdd over 3f out: led again over 2f out: rdn over 1f out: hdd nr fin* **9/2**[2]

0 **3** 1¾ **Amazon Princess**[143] 2275 2-8-9 0.......................(b¹) AdamMcNamara 11 54
(Archie Watson) *chsd ldrs: rdn over 1f out: styd on same pce ins fnl f* **16/1**

0036 **4** 1¼ **Sparkling Breeze**[11] 7056 2-9-0 59..........................(p) ConnorBeasley 2 55
(Michael Dods) *sn pushed along in rr: hdwy u.p over 1f out: nt rch ldrs* **6/1**

340 **5** nse **Baracca Rocks**[10] 7063 2-8-9 54.............................(v¹) LewisEdmunds 8 50
(K R Burke) *chsd ldrs: rdn over 1f out: edgd lft and no ex ins fnl f* **22/1**

3400 **6** 1½ **Mr Fudge**[42] 5968 2-8-11 68................................... ConnorMurtagh(3) 4 51
(Richard Fahey) *prom: nt clr run over 2f out: rdn over 1f out: no ex ins fnl f (jockey said gelding was denied a clear run app the 2f marker)* **5/1**[3]

3505 **7** 5 **Javea Magic (IRE)**[22] 6683 2-8-11 55...................(v¹) CameronNoble(3) 1 36
(Tom Dascombe) *sn w ldr: led over 3f out tl over 2f out: wknd ins fnl f* **9/1**

0634 **8** 2¾ **Amnaa**[42] 5968 2-8-8 66.. StefanoCherchi(7) 7 29
(Marco Botti) *s.i.s: sn outpcd (jockey said filly was slowly away)* **9/4**[1]

9 8 **Don'tstophimnow (IRE)** 2-9-0 0............................... TrevorWhelan 9 4
(J S Moore) *dwlt: outpcd* **50/1**

10 1¾ **Worthamonkey** 2-8-9 0... DylanHogan(5) 10
(Denis Quinn) *hdwy over 4f out: rdn whn hmpd over 2f out: sn wknd* **50/1**

054 **11** 2¼ **Is She The One**[142] 2331 2-8-6 50................................(p¹) NoelGarbutt(3) 3
(Denis Quinn) *prom: lost pl after 1f: n.d after* **50/1**

1m 15.01s (0.51) **Going Correction** -0.10s/f (Stan) **11** Ran SP% **118.5**
Speed ratings (Par 93): **92,91,89,87,87 85,79,75,64,62 59**
CSF £37.94 TOTE £8.20: £2.50, £2.00, £3.60; EX 45.70 Trifecta £843.70.There was no bid for the winner. Bezzas Lad was claimed by Mr A. W. Carroll for £6,300. Amazon Princess was claimed by Mr A. G. Newcombe for £6,300.
Owner Rowdown Racing Partnership **Bred** John M Troy **Trained** Upper Lambourn, Berks

FOCUS
A modest seller. The first two were notable class droppers.

7470 FOLLOW US ON FACEBOOK FARLEY&JONES RECRUITMENT LTD H'CAP 6f 20y (Tp)

6:20 (6:21) (Class 5) (0-75,77) 3-Y-O+

£3,428 (£1,020; £509; £400; £400; £400) **Stalls** Low

Form RPR

2014 **1** **Holdenhurst**[59] 5289 4-8-8 **62**... EoinWalsh 8 69
(Bill Turner) *led early: chsd ldr: shkn up to ld over 1f out: hrd rdn ins fnl f: jst hld on* **40/1**

01-6 **2** nk **Evasive Power (USA)**[20] 6766 3-9-4 **74**.........................(p¹) GaryHalpin 7 80
(Denis Gerard Hogan, Ire) *s.i.s: pushed along in rr: rdn over 1f out: r.o wl ins fnl f: wnt 2nd towards fin: nt quite rch wnr* **11/4**[2]

5043 **3** ¾ **Consequences (IRE)**[23] 6631 4-9-7 **75**...................... ConnorBeasley 6 79
(Ian Williams) *broke wl: lost pl after 1f: hdwy over 1f out: sn rdn: r.o* **6/1**[3]

5645 **4** 2 **Tathmeen (IRE)**[34] 6260 4-9-1 **72**............................... WilliamCox(3) 10 70
(Antony Brittain) *hld up in tch on outer: rdn and hung lft over 1f out: no ex ins fnl f* **12/1**

303 **5** 1¾ **Zahee (IRE)**[24] 6594 4-9-8 **76**................................ JosephineGordon 11 69
(Saeed bin Suroor) *racd freely: sn led: swtchd lft over 5f out: rdn: hung lft and hdd over 1f out: wknd ins fnl f (jockey said colt hung left-handed inside the final furlong)* **2/1**[1]

-P30 **6** ½ **Brigham Young**[14] 6968 4-9-9 **77**.................................... ShaneKelly 4 68
(Ed Walker) *chsd ldrs: pushed along over 3f out: sn lost pl* **11/4**[2]

530 **7** 5 **Laubali**[42] 5972 4-9-7 **75**...(p) ShaneGray 3 51
(David O'Meara) *s.i.s: hld up: nt clr run over 2f out: n.d* **20/1**

4405 **8** 1 **Caledonian Gold**[19] 6806 6-8-0 **61** oh16...................... GavinAshton(7) 2 34
(Lisa Williamson) *prom tl wknd over 1f out* **100/1**

1m 13.68s (-0.82) **Going Correction** -0.10s/f (Stan)
WFA 3 from 4yo+ 2lb **8** Ran SP% **116.8**
Speed ratings (Par 103): **101,100,99,96,94 93,87,85**
CSF £149.77 CT £788.98 TOTE £25.90: £5.80, £1.10, £1.80; EX 422.60 Trifecta £2779.30.
Owner Ansells Of Watford **Bred** Southill Stud **Trained** Sigwells, Somerset

FOCUS
A fair handicap in which the favourite couldn't maintain a strong pace.

7471 MARY & FRED DIAMOND WEDDING ANNIVERSARY FILLIES' H'CAP 7f 36y (Tp)

6:50 (6:53) (Class 4) (0-85,86) 3-Y-O+

£5,207 (£1,549; £774; £400; £400; £400) **Stalls** High

Form RPR

3205 **1** **Warning Fire**[15] 6914 3-9-12 **86**... OisinMurphy 3 93
(Mark Johnston) *edgd lft s: chsd ldrs: swtchd rt over 1f out: sn edgd lft: rdn and r.o to ld wl ins fnl f* **5/2**[1]

2002 **2** 1½ **Turanga Leela**[40] 6025 5-8-11 **73**...............................(b) TobyEley(5) 6 77
(John Mackie) *w ldr tl led 2f out: sn rdn: hdd wl ins fnl f (jockey said mare hung left-handed on the run to the line)* **12/1**

0210 **3** hd **Visionara**[21] 6721 3-9-3 **80**.. MeganNicholls(3) 2 82
(Simon Crisford) *s.i.s and hmpd s: hld up: hdwy over 1f out: nt clr run sn after: rdn ins fnl f: r.o (jockey said filly suffered interference upon leaving the stalls)* **3/1**[2]

611 **4** nk **Image Of The Moon**[24] 6593 3-9-2 **79**.....................(t¹) CierenFallon(3) 5 81
(Shaun Keightley) *s.i.s: hdwy over 5f out: shkn up over 2f out: nt clr run and lost pl over 1f out: swtchd rt 1f out: r.o wl* **3/1**[2]

-115 **5** 4½ **Made Of Honour (IRE)**[217] 756 5-9-12 **83**.....................(p) DavidEgan 4 74
(David Loughnane) *s.i.s: in rr: rdn over 1f out: edgd lft: nvr on terms* **12/1**

330 **6** ½ **Praxidice**[42] 5953 3-8-12 **72**.. CliffordLee 7 60
(K R Burke) *w ldrs tl pushed along on outer over 2f out: styd on same pce fr over 1f out* **5/1**[3]

4504 **7** 3½ **Arabian Jazz (IRE)**[18] 6825 4-8-13 **73**....................(h) CameronNoble(3) 1 53
(Michael Bell) *led: hdd 2f out: sn rdn: wknd ins fnl f* **20/1**

1m 27.41s (-1.39) **Going Correction** -0.10s/f (Stan)
WFA 3 from 4yo+ 3lb **7** Ran SP% **115.4**
Speed ratings (Par 102): **103,101,101,100,95 95,91**
CSF £33.34 TOTE £3.30: £1.60, £5.00; EX 32.90 Trifecta £134.00.
Owner Sheikh Hamdan bin Mohammed Al Maktoum **Bred** Godolphin **Trained** Middleham Moor, N Yorks

FOCUS
A useful fillies' handicap and the form should work out. The winner was back to her Goodwood level.

7472 JC CYBER SECURITY SERVICES LTD H'CAP 7f 36y (Tp)

7:20 (7:23) (Class 6) (0-65,65) 3-Y-O

£2,781 (£827; £413; £400; £400; £400) **Stalls** High

Form RPR

2604 **1** **Redemptive**[56] 5431 3-9-4 **62**... LukeMorris 3 68
(John Butler) *chsd ldrs: rdn to ld over 1f out: edgd rt ins fnl f: styd on u.p* **12/1**

4010 **2** ¾ **Sharp Talk (IRE)**[18] 6840 3-9-5 **63**........................ JosephineGordon 5 67
(Shaun Keightley) *hld up: swtchd rt over 1f out: rdn and r.o to go 2nd wl ins fnl f: nt rch wnr* **5/1**[2]

3104 **3** ¾ **Liam's Lass (IRE)**[11] 7051 3-9-1 **59**.................................... ShaneKelly 8 61
(Pam Sly) *hld up: hdwy over 2f out: rdn over 1f out: styd on* **11/1**

2061 **4** nk **Kennocha (IRE)**[12] 7027 3-9-1 **59**.............................(tp) TomMarquand 7 61
(Amy Murphy) *chsd ldr tl led over 2f out: rdn and hdd over 1f out: no ex wl ins fnl f* **13/2**[3]

0300 **5** ¾ **Axe Axelrod (USA)**[14] 6961 3-9-6 **64**....................(p) ConnorBeasley 6 64
(Michael Dods) *chsd ldrs: rdn over 2f out: styd on same pce ins fnl f* **6/4**[1]

6 **6** 2 **Ariette Du Rue (USA)**[162] 1742 3-9-7 **65**.................... OisinMurphy 11 60
(Ed Vaughan) *hld up: swtchd rt over 1f out: sn rdn: r.o ins fnl f: nvr nrr (jockey said filly was never travelling)* **7/1**

0100 **7** 1 **Rita's Folly**[29] 6389 3-8-10 **57**.................................... DarraghKeenan(3) 2 49
(Anthony Carson) *prom: nt clr run fr over 2f out tl over 1f out: sn rdn: styd on same pce fnl f* **25/1**

653 **8** 1 **Friday Fizz (IRE)**[24] 6587 3-8-12 **59**........................(p¹) CierenFallon(3) 4 49
(Mark Loughnane) *hld up: rdn over 1f out: nt trble ldrs (jockey said filly ran too freely)* **14/1**

-305 **9** ½ **Vikivaki (USA)**[106] 3535 3-9-1 **62**.............................. CameronNoble(3) 12 51
(David Loughnane) *prom on outer: rdn over 2f out: wknd ins fnl f* **33/1**

1000 **10** 1 **Murqaab**[30] 6373 3-9-4 **62**...(b) LewisEdmunds 10 48
(John Balding) *s.i.s: hld up: nvr on terms* **40/1**

-406 **11** nk **Geneva Spur (USA)**[8] 7157 3-9-1 **59**.................................. DavidEgan 9 45
(Roger Varian) *hld up: hdwy over 1f out: wknd ins fnl f* **16/1**

3050 12 16 **Gabriela Laura**[49] 5677 3-9-4 **65**.............................. WilliamCox(3) 1 11
(Alexandra Dunn) *led: hdd over 2f out: rdn and wknd over 1f out* **50/1**

1m 28.27s (-0.53) **Going Correction** -0.10s/f (Stan) **12** Ran SP% **122.3**
Speed ratings (Par 99): **99,98,97,96,96 93,92,91,90,89 89,71**
CSF £71.44 CT £713.80 TOTE £11.20: £3.30, £1.80, £3.00; EX 92.10 Trifecta £682.60.
Owner Miss M Bishop-Peck **Bred** Kevin Quinn **Trained** Newmarket, Suffolk

FOCUS
This was a tight five-way finish in this ordinary 3yo sprint handicap.

7473 PROTECT YOUR BUSINESS ASSETS VISIT JC-CYBERSECURITY.CO.UK EBF NOVICE STKS (PLUS 10 RACE) 1m 142y (Tp)
7:50 (7:51) (Class 4) 2-Y-O **£4,851** (£1,443; £721; £360) **Stalls** Low

Form RPR
34 **1** **Shandoz**[16] 6905 2-9-5 0.............................. DavidEgan 3 80
(Roger Varian) *s.i.s: hld up: hdwy and nt clr run over 2f out: rdn over 1f out: r.o to ld nr fin* **9/4**[1]
4 **2** *hd* **Trumpet Man**[21] 6708 2-9-5 0.............................. OisinMurphy 6 80
(Mark Johnston) *sn chsng ldr: led over 2f out: rdn over 1f out: hdd and rdr dropped rein nr fin* **4/1**[2]
2420 **3** *shd* **Sword Beach (IRE)**[30] 6375 2-9-5 84.............................. TomMarquand 2 79
(Eve Johnson Houghton) *chsd ldrs: shkn up and swtchd rt over 1f out: rdn and edgd lft ins fnl f: r.o* **15/2**[3]
0 **4** *5* **Alargedram (IRE)**[23] 6640 2-9-2 0.............................. MeganNicholls(3) 7 69
(Alan King) *s.i.s: hld up: shkn up and swtchd rt over 2f out: r.o ins fnl f: nt trble ldrs* **25/1**
4 **5** *2 1/2* **Falcon Claws (USA)**[42] 5940 2-9-5 0.............................. ShaneKelly 5 64
(Marco Botti) *sn led: rdn and hdd over 2f out: hung lft over 1f out: wknd fnl f* **33/1**
4 **6** *4* **Ben Lilly (IRE)**[37] 6112 2-9-5 0.............................. HarryBentley 4 55
(Ralph Beckett) *led early: chsd ldrs: rdn over 2f out: hung lft and wknd over 1f out* **20/1**
7 *3 3/4* **Lismore (IRE)** 2-9-0 0.............................. LukeMorris 9 42
(Sir Mark Prescott Bt) *s.i.s: rn green and a in rr (did not enter the Parade Ring due to difficulty with the girth when saddling the filly)* **50/1**
5 **8** *18* **Isolde (IRE)**[42] 5956 2-9-0 0.............................. GeorgeWood 8 5
(Amy Murphy) *chsd ldrs tl rdn and wknd over 2f out (jockey said filly ran green)* **66/1**

1m 49.32s (-0.78) **Going Correction** -0.10s/f (Stan) **8** Ran SP% **77.5**
Speed ratings (Par 97): **99,98,98,94,92 88,85,69**
CSF £3.94 TOTE £2.30: £1.10, £1.10, £1.40; EX 5.10 Trifecta £16.30.
Owner Nurlan Bizakov **Bred** Hesmonds Stud Ltd **Trained** Newmarket, Suffolk
■ Ya Hayati was withdrawn. Price at time of withdrawal 11/10F. Rule 4 applies to all bets - deduction 45p in the pound

FOCUS
The principals dominated this modest novice event, which changed complexion after the late withdrawal of the market leader. The level of the form will take time to settle.

7474 RATINGTHERACES.COM BEST HORSE RACING RATINGS H'CAP 1m 4f 51y (Tp)
8:20 (8:20) (Class 6) (0-65,65) 3-Y-O+ **£2,781** (£827; £413; £400; £400; £400) **Stalls** Low

Form RPR
2150 **1** **Gold Arch**[32] 6320 3-9-7 **65**.............................. (b) ShaneKelly 8 74+
(David Lanigan) *s.i.s: hdwy on outer over 9f out: chsd ldr over 7f out: led 2f out: hung lft over 1f out: rdn clr and edgd rt ins fnl f* **3/1**[1]
3633 **2** *2* **Forbidden Dance**[38] 6069 3-9-7 **65**.............................. (b[1]) OisinMurphy 4 71
(Hughie Morrison) *chsd ldrs: rdn and hung lft over 1f out: styd on* **5/1**[3]
6020 **3** *1 3/4* **Circle Of Stars (IRE)**[20] 6760 3-9-0 **65**.............................. AledBeech(7) 6 68
(Charlie Fellowes) *hld up in tch: rdn over 1f out: styd on u.p* **14/1**
0113 **4** *2* **Warning Light**[18] 6843 4-9-4 **55**.............................. (tp) JosephineGordon 12 54
(Shaun Keightley) *led over 10f out: hdd 2f out: sn rdn: no ex ins fnl f* **5/1**[3]
0650 **5** *3/4* **Delta Bravo (IRE)**[38] 6094 3-8-7 **51**.............................. DavidEgan 1 50
(J S Moore) *hld up: nt clr run over 2f out: hdwy u.p over 1f out: nt trble ldrs* **50/1**
0050 **6** *shd* **Ballymount**[10] 7069 4-9-6 **60**.............................. CierenFallon(3) 7 57
(Michael Easterby) *hld up: hdwy on outer over 3f out: rdn over 2f out: nt trble ldrs (jockey said gelding was never travelling,)* **4/1**[2]
3642 **7** *nk* **Yasir (USA)**[22] 6681 11-9-2 **53**.............................. LukeMorris 10 50
(Sophie Leech) *s.i.s: r.o ins fnl f: nvr nrr* **10/1**
0012 **8** *1 1/4* **Genuine Approval (IRE)**[60] 5285 6-9-7 **61**.............................. DarraghKeenan(3) 9 56
(John Butler) *chsd ldrs: lost pl over 8f out: n.d after* **7/1**
5505 **9** *3 1/2* **Tarbeyah (IRE)**[36] 6187 4-9-10 **61**.............................. (t) CliffordLee 5 50
(Kevin Frost) *chsd ldrs: rdn over 2f out: wknd fnl f* **16/1**
0000 **10** *3* **Punkawallah**[22] 6681 5-9-5 **59**.............................. (tp) WilliamCox(3) 2 44
(Alexandra Dunn) *led: hdd over 10f out: chsd ldrs: nt clr run over 2f out: rdn and wknd over 1f out* **25/1**
650 **11** *5* **Rubensian**[31] 2233 6-9-12 **63**.............................. (bt[1]) HarryBentley 3 40
(David Dennis) *hld up: rdn over 2f out: a in rr* **28/1**
0-63 **12** *28* **Jackblack**[92] 2502 7-9-4 **60**.............................. (p[1]) TobyEley(5) 11
(Nikki Evans) *hld up: plld hrd: rdn over 4f out: wknd over 3f out (jockey said gelding ran too freely)* **66/1**

2m 39.01s (-1.79) **Going Correction** -0.10s/f (Stan) **12** Ran SP% **123.2**
WFA 3 from 4yo+ 7lb
Speed ratings (Par 101): **101,99,98,97,96 96,96,95,93,91 87,69**
CSF £18.27 CT £189.79 TOTE £4.20: £1.80, £2.10, £3.50; EX 22.00 Trifecta £163.70.
Owner Middleham Park, Ventura, Delaney & Black **Bred** Trinity Park Stud **Trained** Newmarket, Suffolk

FOCUS
A modest middle-distance handicap. Straightforward form in behind the winner.
T/Plt: £143.90 to a £1 stake. Pool: £74,120.20 - 375.92 winning units T/Qpdt: £38.30 to a £1 stake. Pool: £9,797.77 - 189.13 winning units **Colin Roberts**

7475 - (Foreign Racing) - See Raceform Interactive

6820 CRAON (R-H)
Saturday, September 21

OFFICIAL GOING: Turf: good to soft

7476a PRIX JM BOULAY SON VIDEO - PRIX DU MAINE (MAIDEN) (3YO) (TURF) 1m 4f
4:30 3-Y-O **£6,306** (£2,522; £1,891; £1,261; £630)

RPR
1 **Foligno (FR)**[156] 3-9-2 0.............................. AlexandreRoussel 7 70
(E Libaud, France) **73/10**[1]
2 *1 1/2* **Grazano (FR)** 3-8-11 0.............................. MathieuAndrouin 11 63
(Alain Couetil, France)
3 *6* **Testiange (FR)** 3-8-8 0.............................. DamienBoche(3) 3 53
(P Monfort, France)
4 *2* **Pedrozzo (FR)** 3-9-2 0.............................. ChristopherGrosbois 6 55
(E Leenders, France)
5 *hd* **High River (FR)** 3-8-11 0.............................. WilliamsSaraiva 10 49
(N Paysan, France)
6 *5* **Orchidees (FR)**[30] 3-8-8 0.............................. YoannBarille 4 38
(N Leenders, France)
7 *15* **Star At Midnight**[11] 7061 3-8-5 0.............................. MlleCoraliePacaut(3) 1 14
(Jo Hughes, France) *chsd ldr: began to labour and rdn ins fnl 2f: sn wknd*
8 *6* **Speed Lady (FR)**[7] 3-8-4 0.............................. (b) MlleCeciliaPoirier(9) 9 10
(C Lecrivain, France)
9 *1 1/2* **Barenne (FR)** 3-8-4 0.............................. (p) MaximilienJustum(7) 2 5
(N Leenders, France)
10 *5* **Nickorette (FR)** 3-8-10 0 ow2.............................. ThibaultSpeicher 5
(A Kahn, France)
11 *15* **Fantasy In March (FR)** 3-8-8 0.............................. AnthonyBernard 8
(S Renaud, France)

2m 35.69s **11** Ran SP% **12.0**
PARI-MUTUEL (all including 1 euro stake): WIN 8.30; PLACE 2.30, 1.80, 2.00; DF 8.90.
Owner Ecurie Prunier **Bred** P Lamy, S Lamy & Mme M Lamy **Trained** France

7251 LONGCHAMP (R-H)
Saturday, September 21

OFFICIAL GOING: Turf: good

7477a PRIX BERTRAND DE TARRAGON (GROUP 3) (3YO+ FILLIES & MARES) (MOYENNE COURSE) (TURF) 1m 1f
2:50 3-Y-O+ **£36,036** (£14,414; £10,810; £7,207; £3,603)

RPR
1 **Silva (IRE)**[37] 6142 3-8-11 0.............................. TheoBachelot 5 110
(Mme Pia Brandt, France) *mde all: led: drvn clr wl over 1f out: styd on strly: won easing down* **93/10**
2 *2* **Duneflower (IRE)**[21] 6726 3-8-11 0.............................. FrankieDettori 4 106
(John Gosden) *a.p: scrubbed along over 3f out: no immediate imp: styd on ins fnl 1 1/2f: secured 2nd fnl 100yds: nt rch wnr* **3/5**[1]
3 *snk* **Spirit Of Nelson (IRE)**[34] 6265 4-9-2 0.............................. CristianDemuro 3 105
(J Reynier, France) *hld up in midfield on inner: chsd ldng pair fr 1/2-way: rdn and tk 2nd ins fnl 1 1/2f: styd on same pce: dropped to 3rd last 100yds* **49/10**[2]
4 *2 1/2* **Dariyza (FR)**[25] 3-8-11 0.............................. ChristopheSoumillon 8 101
(A De Royer-Dupre, France) *dwlt: w.w in fnl pair: began to take clsr order over 2 1/2f out: no further imp fr 1 1/2f out: tk 4th late on* **68/10**[3]
5 *shd* **Mythic (FR)**[37] 3-8-11 0.............................. StephanePasquier 1 101
(A De Royer-Dupre, France) *trckd ldr: pushed along appr 2f out: sn rdn and no imp: outpcd by ldrs fr wl over 1f out* **12/1**
6 *3* **All Grace (FR)**[20] 6775 3-8-11 0.............................. VincentCheminaud 6 95
(A Fabre, France) *midfield on outer: dropped into fnl pair 1/2-way: no hdwy whn asked 2f out: nvr in contention* **19/1**
7 *2 1/2* **Folie De Louise (FR)**[24] 5-9-2 0.............................. OlivierPeslier 7 89
(Carmen Bocskai, Germany) *settled in rr: scrubbed along over 2f out but mde no prog: wl hld last 1 1/2f* **18/1**

1m 54.65s (3.05) **7** Ran SP% **119.9**
WFA 3 from 4yo+ 5lb
PARI-MUTUEL (all including 1 euro stake): WIN 10.30; PLACE 1.20, 1.10, 1.10; DF 6.50.
Owner Zalim Bifov **Bred** Zalim Bifov **Trained** France

7478a PRIX DU PRINCE D'ORANGE (GROUP 3) (3YO) (GRANDE COURSE) (TURF) 1m 2f
4:00 3-Y-O **£36,036** (£14,414; £10,810; £7,207; £3,603)

RPR
1 **Soudania**[20] 6775 3-9-0 0 ow1.............................. AurelienLemaitre 3 110+
(F Head, France) *led: hdd after 1 1/2f and chsd new ldr on inner: eased into ld 2f out: sn clr: easily* **5/2**[2]
2 *3* **Queen (FR)**[20] 6775 3-9-0 0 ow1.............................. TheoBachelot 8 103
(Mme Pia Brandt, France) *w.w in fnl trio on outer: hdwy 1 1/2f out: styd on to go 2nd last 70yds: no ch w wnr* **13/1**
3 *3/4* **Goya Senora (FR)**[41] 6005 3-9-3 0 ow1.............................. CristianDemuro 2 105
(Y Barberot, France) *midfield on inner: clsd more than 1 1/2f out: chsd clr ldr w more than 1f to run: kpt on at same pce: lost 2nd last 70yds* **15/1**
4 *nk* **Winterfuchs (GER)**[103] 3674 3-9-3 0 ow1.............................. OlivierPeslier 5 104
(Carmen Bocskai, Germany) *midfield on outer: drvn and no imp ins fnl 2 1/2f: dropped to fnl 1 1/2f out: styd on ins fnl f: nrly snatched 3rd* **17/2**
5 *1 3/4* **Alwaab (FR)**[41] 6005 3-9-3 0 ow1.............................. VincentCheminaud 7 101
(A Fabre, France) *settled in rr: pushed along and tried to cl ins fnl 2f: sme prog under 1 1/2f out: effrt petered out fnl 75yds* **73/10**
6 *2* **Argyron (IRE)**[100] 3789 3-9-3 0 ow1.............................. Pierre-CharlesBoudot 1 97
(A Fabre, France) *settled in fnl trio on inner: pushed along and effrt 1 1/2f out: no further imp ins fnl f* **23/1**
7 *2* **Dubai Warrior**[17] 6861 3-9-3 0 ow1.............................. FrankieDettori 6 93
(John Gosden) *wnt rt s and bmpd rival: led after 1 1/2f: drvn for home over 2 1/2f out: hdd w 2f to run: wknd appr fnl f* **8/5**[1]
8 *3* **Dave (FR)**[35] 6249 3-9-3 0 ow1.............................. MickaelBarzalona 4 88
(Mme Pia Brandt, France) *chsd ldr on outer: rdn and outpcd ins fnl 1 1/2f: dropped away fnl f* **69/10**[3]

2m 5.13s (1.13) **8** Ran SP% **119.8**
PARI-MUTUEL (all including 1 euro stake): WIN 3.50; PLACE 1.60, 2.90, 2.90; DF 12.70.
Owner Wertheimer & Frere **Bred** Wertheimer & Frere **Trained** France

FOCUS
The two fillies finished 1-2.

PARX (L-H)
Saturday, September 21

OFFICIAL GOING: Dirt: fast

7479a COTILLION STKS (GRADE 1) (3YO FILLIES) (MAIN TRACK) (DIRT) 1m 110y(D)
10:14 3-Y-O

£472,440 (£157,480; £78,740; £47,244; £31,496; £11,811)

RPR

1 **Street Band (USA)**[35] 6253 3-8-10 0.....................(b) SophieDoyle 3 113
(J Larry Jones, U.S.A) *hld up in rr: gd hdwy fr 1/2-way: chsd ldrs on outside whn rdn 2f out: led 1f out: kpt on wl and drew clr fnl f* **77/10**

2 2 1/4 **Guarana (USA)**[62] 5231 3-8-12 0..................... JoseLOrtiz 8 110
(Chad C Brown, U.S.A) *in tch: pressed ldr 3f out: rdn to ld 2f out: drvn 1 1/2f out: hdd 1f out: kpt on same pce* **11/10**[1]

3 3 3/4 **Horologist (USA)**[35] 3-8-10 0.....................(b) LuisSaez 6 100
(John Mazza, U.S.A) *in tch in midfield: rdn to chse ldrs over 2f out: outpcd by front pair fnl f: kpt on* **216/10**

4 3 1/4 **Bellafina (USA)**[49] 5701 3-8-12 0.....................(b) FlavienPrat 10 95
(Simon Callaghan, U.S.A) *chsd ldr after 2f: led 3 1/2f out: rdn over 2f out: hdd 2f out: sn drvn: wknd over 1f out* **67/10**

5 2 1/2 **Sweet Sami D (USA)**[35] 3-8-5 0.....................(b) PacoLopez 9 82
(Patrick B McBurney, U.S.A) *midfield: rdn and no imp fr 3f out* **99/1**

6 2 1/2 **Serengeti Empress (USA)**[49] 5701 3-8-12 0..................... IradOrtizJr 1 84
(Thomas Amoss, U.S.A) *led: hdd after 2f: trckd ldrs: rdn 2f out: wknd 1 1/2f out* **16/5**[2]

7 1/2 **Jaywalk (USA)**[35] 3-8-10 0.....................(b) JoelRosario 11 81
(John C Servis, U.S.A) *led after 2f: hdd 3 1/2f out: lost pl 2 1/2f out: sn btn* **57/10**[3]

8 3/4 **Afleet Destiny (USA)**[19] 3-8-8 0 ow3.....................(b) AnthonySalgado 2 77
(Uriah St Lewis, U.S.A) *a towards rr* **176/1**

9 4 3/4 **Jeltrin (USA)**[19] 3-8-10 0..................... LeonelReyes 4 68
(Alexis Delgado, U.S.A) *towards rr of midfield: rdn and no imp fr 2 1/2f out* **35/1**

10 10 **She Makes Me Smile (USA)**[19] 3-8-5 0..................... WesleyTorres 7 41
(Trevor Gallimore, U.S.A) *a in rr* **140/1**

11 7 **Collegeville Girl (USA)**[21] 3-8-5 0..................... AngelCastillo 5 26
(Richard Vega, U.S.A) *a in rr* **159/1**

1m 44.2s **11** Ran SP% **120.9**
PARI-MUTUEL (all including 2 unit stake): WIN 17.40; PLACE (1-2) 5.40, 2.80; SHOW (1-2-3) 4.40, 2.40, 5.00; SF 48.40.
Owner Ray Francis, Cindy Jones Et Al **Bred** Larry Jones, Cindy Jones & Ray Francis **Trained** USA

7480a PENNSYLVANIA DERBY (GRADE 1) (3YO) (MAIN TRACK) (DIRT) 1m 1f (D)
10:48 3-Y-O

£472,440 (£157,480; £78,740; £47,244; £31,496; £11,811)

RPR

1 **Math Wizard (USA)**[49] 3-8-6 0 ow1..................... IradOrtizJr 1 109
(Saffie A Joseph Jr, U.S.A) *hld up: shkn up and stdy hdwy fr under 3f out: rdn 2f out: wd into st: drvn and styd on wl fnl f: led cl home* **31/1**

2 nk **Mr. Money (USA)**[49] 3-8-10 0..................... GabrielSaez 6 112
(W Bret Calhoun, U.S.A) *led: rdn 1 1/2f out: drvn ins fnl f: kpt on wl: hdd cl home* **17/10**[2]

3 1 **War Of Will (USA)**[56] 3-8-12 0..................... TylerGaffalione 4 112
(Mark Casse, Canada) *chsd ldr: rdn 2 1/2f out: drvn 1 1/2f out: kpt on fnl f: nt quite able to chal* **33/10**[3]

4 nse **Improbable (USA)**[26] 3-8-7 0.....................(b) MikeESmith 2 107
(Bob Baffert, U.S.A) *restless in stalls: s.i.s: in rr early: grad rcvrd: in tch at 1/2-way: rdn to chse ldr on inner 1 1/2f out: pressed ldr ins fnl f: no ex fnl 100yds* **6/5**[1]

5 nk **Spun To Run (USA)**[19] 3-8-10 0.....................(b) PacoLopez 5 109
(Juan Carlos Guerrero, U.S.A) *restless in stalls: trckd ldrs: rdn under 2f out: hung rt on turn into st: kpt on* **74/10**

6 25 **Shanghai Superfly (USA)**[14] 3-8-5 0.....................(b) FrankiePennington 3 49
(Marcos Zulueta, U.S.A) *towards rr: lost tch 3f out: t.o* **90/1**

1m 50.94s **6** Ran SP% **121.9**
PARI-MUTUEL (all including 2 unit stake): WIN 64.20; PLACE (1-2) 12.00, 3.60; SHOW (1-2-3) 4.80, 2.60, 4.00; SF 196.00.
Owner John Fanelli, Collamele Vitelli Stables LLC Et Al **Bred** Lucky Seven Stable **Trained** North America

7481a - 7485a (Foreign Racing) - See Raceform Interactive

6653 HAMILTON (R-H)
Sunday, September 22

OFFICIAL GOING: Soft (good to soft in places)
Wind: Light, across Weather: overcast, showers

7486 FRASER TOOL HIRE, TOOL & PLANT SPECIALISTS H'CAP 6f 6y
2:00 (2:01) (Class 5) (0-70,71) 3-Y-O

£5,433 (£1,617; £808; £404; £400; £400) Stalls Centre

Form RPR

4150 1 **Twentysixthstreet (IRE)**[25] 6610 3-9-4 66.....................(b[1]) RowanScott(3) 4 77
(Andrew Hughes, Ire) *prom in chsng gp: hdwy to chse wnr over 1f out: kpt on wl fnl f to ld cl home* **16/1**

5621 2 nse **Autumn Flight (IRE)**[11] 7065 3-9-7 66.....................(b) DavidAllan 1 76
(Tim Easterby) *plld hrd: led and sn clr: rdn and dwindling advantage over 1f out: edgd lft and kpt on fnl f: hdd cl home* **5/2**[1]

2151 3 2 3/4 **Fox Hill**[12] 7047 3-9-5 64..................... JasonHart 9 65+
(Eric Alston) *dwlt: bhd and pushed along: hdwy and edgd rt over 1f out: chsd clr ldng pair ins fnl f: r.o* **7/2**[2]

2062 4 1/2 **Kaafy (IRE)**[12] 7047 3-9-5 64..................... SamJames 12 64
(Grant Tuer) *hld up: rdn and hdwy over 1f out: chsd clr ldng pair briefly ins fnl f: one pce* **8/1**

64 5 4 **Double Martini (IRE)**[27] 6551 3-9-12 71..................... BenCurtis 7 58
(Roger Fell) *t.k.h early: prom: rdn and outpcd 2f out: n.d after* **25/1**

2300 6 1/2 **Josiebond**[44] 5914 3-8-6 51..................... JamieGormley 3 36
(Rebecca Bastiman) *in tch: rdn and outpcd over 2f out: sn btn* **16/1**

600 7 3/4 **Inner Charm**[35] 6259 3-9-1 60.....................(h) KevinStott 5 43
(Kevin Ryan) *chsd clr ldr: drvn along over 2f out: edgd rt and wknd over 1f out* **28/1**

8 2 3/4 **Fugacious (IRE)**[36] 6238 3-9-1 63.....................(p[1]) HarrisonShaw(3) 2 37
(John James Feane, Ire) *in tch: drvn and outpcd bef 1/2-way: btn fnl 2f* **9/2**[3]

0046 9 1/2 **Spotton (IRE)**[26] 6575 3-8-3 48 oh1 ow1.....................(b[1]) PaddyMathers 8 20
(Rebecca Bastiman) *prom: rdn along over 2f out: sn wknd* **25/1**

10 7 **Anythingyouwantobe**[15] 6985 3-8-7 55.....................(h) SeanDavis(3) 6 5
(W P Browne, Ire) *bhd and sn outpcd: no ch fr 1/2-way: lost front shoe (vet said filly lost right fore shoe)* **7/1**

1m 14.52s (1.82) **Going Correction** +0.475s/f (Yiel) **10** Ran SP% **115.5**
Speed ratings (Par 101): **106,105,102,101,96 95,94,90,90,80**
CSF £54.47 CT £181.85 TOTE £18.40: £4.30, £1.10, £1.40; EX 60.20 Trifecta £298.50.
Owner Thistle Bloodstock Limited **Bred** Springbank Way Stud **Trained** Kells, Co Kilkenny
■ Stewards' Enquiry : Rowan Scott seven-day ban: used whip with excessive frequency (7-13 Oct)

FOCUS
The loop rail was out 5yds, adding approximately 13yds to races 3, 4, 5, 6, 7 & 8.\n\x\x The first pair came clear in this ordinary 3yo sprint handicap. The race is rated around the second, who's back in top form.

7487 BARBARA ANN LETHAM & SON JONATHAN MEMORIAL H'CAP (DIV I) 5f 7y
2:30 (2:31) (Class 6) (0-60,61) 3-Y-O+

£3,493 (£1,039; £519; £400; £400; £400) Stalls Centre

Form RPR

5420 1 **Popping Corks (IRE)**[16] 6936 3-8-10 48..................... BenRobinson 9 56
(Linda Perratt) *cl up: rdn and edgd rt over 1f out: led ent fnl f: kpt on wl* **7/1**

3003 2 1 1/2 **Guardia Svizzera (IRE)**[6] 7286 5-9-10 61.....................(h) BenCurtis 7 64
(Roger Fell) *cl up in centre: rdn 2f out: wnt 2nd ins fnl f: kpt on: nt pce to chal* **9/5**[1]

5260 3 hd **Bronze Beau**[26] 6574 12-9-5 56.....................(tp) ShaneGray 10 58
(Linda Stubbs) *led against stands' rail: rdn and hdd ent fnl f: kpt on same pce towards fin* **22/1**

4-10 4 1 1/2 **Rego Park Lady (IRE)**[12] 7052 4-9-8 59.....................(p) JamesSullivan 4 55
(Adrian Murray, Ire) *hld up in tch: effrt and rdn over 1f out: one pce ins fnl f* **7/2**[2]

2215 5 1/2 **One Boy (IRE)**[23] 6659 8-9-1 52..................... GrahamLee 1 47
(Paul Midgley) *t.k.h early: sn stdd in rr: effrt over 1f out: kpt on fnl f: nt pce to chal* **11/2**[3]

6 nk **Realtin Fantasy (IRE)**[22] 6739 3-8-10 51..................... SeanDavis(3) 6 45
(W P Browne, Ire) *in tch: drvn along over 2f out: kpt on fnl f: no imp* **14/1**

5500 7 2 1/2 **Star Cracker (IRE)**[3] 7367 7-8-8 45.....................(p) PaddyMathers 5 30
(Jim Goldie) *in tch: drvn and outpcd 1/2-way: sn btn* **13/2**

6500 8 3 **Milabella**[55] 5486 3-8-2 45..................... PaulaMuir(5) 8 19
(R Mike Smith) *in tch: drvn along over 2f out: sn wknd* **50/1**

4000 9 15 **Raise A Billion**[26] 6574 8-8-5 45..................... ConnorMurtagh(3) 2
(Alan Berry) *bhd and outpcd: struggling fr 1/2-way: t.o* **50/1**

1m 2.3s (1.90) **Going Correction** +0.475s/f (Yiel)
WFA 3 from 4yo+ 1lb **9** Ran SP% **114.1**
Speed ratings (Par 101): **103,100,100,97,97 96,92,87,63**
CSF £19.52 CT £260.73 TOTE £7.90: £2.10, £1.30, £4.60; EX 26.80 Trifecta £241.60.
Owner B Jordan **Bred** Grangemore Stud **Trained** East Kilbride, S Lanarks

FOCUS
Few landed a blow in this weak sprint handicap, with the main action coming down the centre. The winner rates near her turf best.

7488 BARBARA ANN LETHAM & SON JONATHAN MEMORIAL H'CAP (DIV II) 5f 7y
3:00 (3:00) (Class 6) (0-60,60) 3-Y-O+

£3,493 (£1,039; £519; £400; £400; £400) Stalls Centre

Form RPR

0630 1 **Trulove**[12] 7052 6-8-8 46 oh1.....................(p) JamieGormley 8 54
(John David Riches) *hld up in tch: hung rt and hdwy to press ldr over 1f out: led ins fnl f: r.o wl* **16/1**

0440 2 1/2 **Lydiate Lady**[64] 5181 7-9-6 58..................... JasonHart 3 64
(Eric Alston) *led: rdn over 1f out: hdd ins fnl f: rallied: one pce last 50yds* **7/2**[2]

3000 3 2 3/4 **David's Beauty (IRE)**[10] 7112 6-9-3 55.....................(b) PaulMulrennan 7 51
(Brian Baugh) *prom: effrt and chsd ldng pair over 1f out: edgd rt and one pce ins fnl f* **17/2**

0400 4 1/2 **Quanah (IRE)**[80] 4563 3-9-4 57..................... PhilDennis 2 52
(Liam Bailey) *dwlt: hld up in midfield: rdn and outpcd 2f out: r.o ins fnl f* **20/1**

0460 5 hd **Jeffrey Harris**[26] 6574 4-9-0 52..................... DanielTudhope 1 46
(Jim Goldie) *hld up: effrt and rdn 2f out: no imp ins fnl f* **15/8**[1]

1400 6 3/4 **I'll Be Good**[12] 7052 10-8-8 49..................... ConnorMurtagh(3) 5 40
(Alan Berry) *chsd ldrs: rdn and outpcd wl over 1f out: n.d after* **10/1**

5300 7 1 1/4 **Classic Pursuit**[48] 5722 8-9-8 60.....................(v) SamJames 4 47
(Marjorie Fife) *pressed ldr: rdn over 2f out: wknd over 1f out* **11/1**

0-00 8 6 **Griffin Street**[8] 7214 6-8-3 46 oh1.....................(b) AndrewBreslin(5) 9 11
(Alistair Whillans) *dwlt: bhd and outpcd: struggling fr 1/2-way* **33/1**

9 1 1/2 **Cozy Sky (USA)**[20] 6815 3-8-7 46 oh1..................... JoeFanning 6 6
(Gordon Elliott, Ire) *bhd: drvn along 1/2-way: sn btn* **6/1**[3]

1m 2.29s (1.89) **Going Correction** +0.475s/f (Yiel)
WFA 3 from 4yo+ 1lb **9** Ran SP% **112.8**
Speed ratings (Par 101): **103,102,97,97,96 95,93,83,81**
CSF £69.75 CT £519.12 TOTE £13.50: £3.40, £1.60, £2.30; EX 82.70 Trifecta £298.00.
Owner J R Racing **Bred** Mrs L Wohlers **Trained** Pilling, Lancashire

FOCUS
The second division of the weak 5f handicap was run at a frantic pace. The first two were clear but the form is rated cautiously.

7489 TOP CAT WINDOW BLINDS "HOPES N DREAMS" (S) STKS 1m 1f 35y
3:30 (3:30) (Class 4) 3-5-Y-O

£6,727 (£2,002; £1,000; £500; £400; £400) Stalls Low

Form RPR

6312 1 **Set In Stone (IRE)**[23] 6656 5-8-6 74..................... RowanScott(3) 2 59+
(Andrew Hughes, Ire) *mde all at modest gallop: rdn 2f out: hld on wl fnl f* **5/2**[1]

601- **2** *nk* **Firlinfeu**[20] 6819 4-8-11 67................................ HarrisonShaw(3) 3 63+
(John James Feane, Ire) *in tch: rdn 3f out: rallied over 1f out: chsd wnr ins fnl f: kpt on fin* **9/2**

6550 **3** *2 1/4* **Redgrave (IRE)**[49] 5709 5-9-0 73................................ CharlesBishop 4 59+
(Joseph Tuite) *t.k.h: hld up in tch: hdwy whn nt clr run over 1f out to ins fnl f: kpt on towards fin (jockey said gelding was denied a clear run 2f out and again app final furlong)* **4/1**[3]

224- **4** *1/2* **The Last Emperor**[70] 4311 4-9-0 82..............................(t) DanielTudhope 6 58
(Emmet Mullins, Ire) *sn trcking ldr: effrt and drvn along 2f out: lost 2nd and outpcd ins fnl f* **11/4**[2]

1630 **5** *1 1/4* **Indomeneo**[8] 7185 4-9-2 74................................ SeanDavis(3) 1 60
(Richard Fahey) *trckd ldrs: rdn along and disp 2nd pl over 1f out to ins fnl f: sn no ex* **8/1**

0000 **6** *4 1/2* **Archies Lad**[2] 7405 3-9-0 53................................ DavidAllan 7 52
(R Mike Smith) *t.k.h: hld up: drvn and outpcd over 2f out: n.d after* **50/1**

0-00 **7** *shd* **New Rhythm**[23] 6663 4-8-9 38................................ JamesSullivan 11 41
(Alistair Whillans) *dwlt: hld up: stdy hdwy 1/2-way: drvn and outpcd over 2f out: n.d after* **100/1**

4030 **8** *hd* **Windsor Cross (IRE)**[11] 7074 4-9-0 68................................ TonyHamilton 10 46
(Richard Fahey) *hld up in last pl: drvn and struggling over 3f out: nvr rchd ldrs* **20/1**

5600 **9** *shd* **Rashdan (FR)**[16] 6940 4-9-0 71................................ JamieGormley 9 46
(Iain Jardine) *hld up: rdn and struggling 3f out: sn btn* **16/1**

6500 **10** *1 1/4* **Can Can Sixty Two**[32] 6343 4-8-4 58................................ KieranSchofield(5) 5 38
(R Mike Smith) *hld up: rdn along and outpcd over 2f out: sn btn* **50/1**

2m 5.78s (6.78) **Going Correction** +0.475s/f (Yiel)
WFA 3 from 4yo+ 5lb **10 Ran SP% 120.1**
Speed ratings (Par 105): **88,87,85,85,84 80,80,79,79,78**
CSF £14.40 TOTE £3.70: £1.50, £1.60, £1.50; EX 17.80 Trifecta £68.00.The winner was bought in for £12,000. Firlinfeu was claimed by Jim Goldie for £10,000. The Last Emperor was claimed by David Haddrell for £10,000.
Owner Thistle Bloodstock Limited **Bred** Thistle Bloodstock Limited **Trained** Kells, Co Kilkenny
■ Stewards' Enquiry : Harrison Shaw two-day ban: used whip above permitted level (7-8 Oct)

FOCUS
It paid to be handy in this valuable seller. The likes of the seventh give perspective. Add 13yds.

7490 APEX TRAFFIC MANAGEMENT NOVICE STKS 1m 68y
4:00 (4:00) (Class 5) 3-Y-O+
£4,787 (£1,424; £711) **Stalls Low**

Form RPR

42 **1** **Modakhar (IRE)**[19] 6823 3-9-2 0................................ BenCurtis 2 83
(K R Burke) *trckd ldr to 4f out: cl up: smooth hdwy to ld over 2f out: pushed along over 1f out: drew clr w ears pricked fnl f: comf* **5/4**[2]

21 **2** *3 3/4* **Roman Stone (USA)**[40] 6034 3-9-9 0................................ JoeFanning 1 81
(Keith Dalgleish) *led at ordinary gallop: rdn and hdd over 2f out: rallied: outpcd fr over 1f out* **10/11**[1]

3 *3 1/2* **Bashful Boy (IRE)**[31] 6381 3-8-13 0................................ HarrisonShaw(3) 3 66
(John James Feane, Ire) *t.k.h: trckd ldrs: hdwy into 2nd pl 4f out: rdn over 2f out: hung rt and wknd over 1f out* **7/1**[3]

1m 51.63s (3.23) **Going Correction** +0.475s/f (Yiel) **3 Ran SP% 109.3**
Speed ratings (Par 103): **102,98,94**
CSF £2.84 TOTE £2.10; EX 2.90 Trifecta £2.40.
Owner Carl Waters & Mrs E Burke **Bred** John Hutchinson **Trained** Middleham Moor, N Yorks

FOCUS
Not surprisingly this interesting little 3yo novice event proved tactical. The winner built on his latest form. Add 13yds.

7491 SODEXO FILLIES' H'CAP 1m 68y
4:30 (4:30) (Class 4) (0-80,82) 3-Y-O+
£8,345 (£2,483; £1,240; £620; £400; £400) **Stalls Low**

Form RPR

2306 **1** **Welcoming (FR)**[10] 7129 3-9-7 74................................ JoeFanning 5 83
(Mark Johnston) *mde all: shkn up over 2f out: clr fnl f: unchal (trainer's rep could offer no explanation for the apparent improvement in form)* **9/1**

0215 **2** *2 1/4* **Sarvi**[3] 7366 4-9-9 72................................(p) DanielTudhope 1 76
(Jim Goldie) *s.i.s: hld up in tch: hdwy on outside to chse wnr 3f out: sn rdn: kpt on fnl f: nt pce to chal* **11/4**[1]

2425 **3** *nk* **Iconic Code**[32] 6341 4-9-0 63................................ ShaneGray 7 66
(Keith Dalgleish) *hld up: effrt and rdn 2f out: kpt on fnl f: tk 3rd cl home* **12/1**

4153 **4** *nk* **Dream World (IRE)**[30] 6408 4-9-3 73................................ MarkCrehan(7) 2 76
(Michael Appleby) *trckd ldrs: rdn and outpcd over 2f out: edgd lft: rallied and disp 2nd pl over 1f out to wl ins fnl f: lost 3rd cl home* **8/1**

52 **5** *1 1/4* **Lady Alavesa**[36] 6230 4-9-1 64................................(p) PhilDennis 9 64
(Michael Herrington) *stdd s: hld up: stdy hdwy over 2f out: rdn over 1f out: no further imp fnl f* **13/2**

1036 **6** *3 3/4* **Gometra Ginty (IRE)**[8] 7213 3-9-5 72................................ GrahamLee 4 63
(Keith Dalgleish) *hld up towards rr: drvn and outpcd over 2f out: n.d after* **9/1**

1110 **7** *5* **Kermouster**[8] 7213 3-9-5 72................................ SamJames 3 52
(Grant Tuer) *chsd ldrs: outpcd whn n.m.r and lost pl over 2f out: sn struggling* **5/1**[3]

4216 **8** *12* **Caustic Love (IRE)**[25] 6609 3-10-1 82................................ CallumRodriguez 6 34
(Keith Dalgleish) *chsd wnr to 3f out: rdn and wknd fr 2f out* **9/2**[2]

0500 **9** *1 1/2* **Just Heather (IRE)**[28] 6499 5-8-7 56 oh11................................(p) CamHardie 8 5
(John Wainwright) *bhd and nvr gng wl: lost tch 3f out: nvr on terms* **80/1**

1m 50.58s (2.18) **Going Correction** +0.475s/f (Yiel)
WFA 3 from 4yo+ 4lb **9 Ran SP% 114.9**
Speed ratings (Par 102): **108,105,105,105,103 100,95,83,81**
CSF £33.84 CT £304.47 TOTE £7.90: £2.80, £1.60, £3.40; EX 45.60 Trifecta £639.90.
Owner Tactful Finance Limited **Bred** Hugues Rousseau **Trained** Middleham Moor, N Yorks
■ Stewards' Enquiry : Mark Crehan two-day ban: careless riding

FOCUS
This feature handicap proved a decent test. The winner returned to form with the ground the key. Add 13yds.

7492 SODEXO H'CAP 1m 4f 15y
5:00 (5:00) (Class 6) (0-60,60) 4-Y-O+
£3,816 (£1,135; £567; £400; £400; £400) **Stalls High**

Form RPR

1 **Chica Buena (IRE)**[239] 7585 4-8-10 49................................ GrahamLee 1 59+
(Keith Dalgleish) *in tch: shkn up 3f out: hdwy to ld over 1f out: drew clr w ears pricked fnl f: readily* **1/2**[1]

/020 **2** *2 1/4* **Frightened Rabbit (USA)**[11] 7070 7-8-9 48................................ JamesSullivan 4 52
(Dianne Sayer) *hld up in midfield: rdn over 2f out: hdwy to chse (clr) wnr ins fnl f: r.o* **20/1**

5452 **3** *3/4* **General Brook (IRE)**[10] 7116 9-9-2 55................................(p) RossaRyan 2 58
(John O'Shea) *chsd ldr: hdwy to ld over 2f out: hdd over 1f out: one pce and lost 2nd ins fnl f* **10/1**[3]

0035 **4** *1/2* **Kaizer**[16] 6933 4-9-1 54................................ AndrewMullen 7 56
(Alistair Whillans) *t.k.h early: chsd ldrs: effrt and drvn along over 2f out: one pce fr over 1f out* **6/1**[2]

2- **5** *2 1/4* **Viscount Wilson**[6] 9677 4-9-0 56................................(bt) SeanDavis(3) 5 55
(Gordon Elliott, Ire) *hld up in midfield on ins: drvn along and outpcd over 3f out: rallied over 1f out: kpt on: nvr rchd ldrs* **20/1**

3360 **6** *1 1/2* **Pammi**[11] 7070 4-8-0 46 oh1................................(p) CoreyMadden(7) 11 43
(Jim Goldie) *led: rdn and hdd over 2f out: rallied: wknd over 1f out* **12/1**

0-00 **7** *1 3/4* **Princess Nearco (IRE)**[18] 5277 5-8-11 50................................ PhilDennis 8 44
(Liam Bailey) *missed break: hld up: drvn along 3f out: no imp fnl 2f* **25/1**

5040 **8** *shd* **Doon Star**[43] 5933 4-8-7 46................................ PaddyMathers 6 40
(Jim Goldie) *t.k.h: hld up towards rr: hdwy over 2f out: rdn and fdd over 1f out* **25/1**

0140 **9** *6* **Ezanak (IRE)**[14] 7001 6-9-2 58................................ HarrisonShaw(3) 9 43
(John Wainwright) *hld up: drvn and outpcd over 3f out: nvr on terms* **20/1**

6000 **10** *1 1/4* **Gworn**[16] 6937 9-9-0 53................................ BenCurtis 12 36
(R Mike Smith) *t.k.h early: hld up: rdn and struggling over 2f out: sn wknd: lost front shoe (vet said gelding lost left front shoe)* **25/1**

6656 **11** *6* **Airplane (IRE)**[54] 5513 4-9-4 57................................ TomEaves 10 31
(Paul Collins) *hld up in midfield on outside: drvn over 3f out: wknd over 2f out* **33/1**

2m 44.44s (5.84) **Going Correction** +0.475s/f (Yiel) **11 Ran SP% 126.5**
Speed ratings (Par 101): **99,97,97,96,95 94,93,92,88,88 84**
CSF £19.16 CT £71.34 TOTE £1.60: £1.10, £3.10, £3.20; EX 17.70 Trifecta £106.90.
Owner Straightline Bloodstock **Bred** John Foley **Trained** Carluke, S Lanarks

FOCUS
The ground played a big part in this moderate handicap. The second and third help the opening level. Add 13yds.

7493 RACING TV HD ON SKY 426 H'CAP 1m 4f 15y
5:30 (5:33) (Class 5) (0-75,80) 3-Y-O
£5,433 (£1,617; £808; £404; £400; £400) **Stalls High**

Form RPR

0-54 **1** **Art Of Diplomacy**[27] 6544 3-9-0 65................................ NathanEvans 5 73
(Michael Easterby) *trckd ldr 3f: cl up: drvn along over 3f out: swtchd lft: rallied and bmpd runner-up over 1f out: led ins fnl f: styd on wl (regarding the apparent improvement in form, trainer said gelding may have benefited from the step up in trip and the softer ground on this occasion)* **10/1**

1323 **2** *1 1/2* **Funny Man**[14] 7001 3-10-1 80................................(v) DanielTudhope 4 86
(David O'Meara) *hld up in tch: effrt over 2f out: bmpd over 1f out: rallied and chsd wnr ins fnl f: kpt on* **15/8**[1]

6601 **3** *1 3/4* **George Mallory**[44] 5898 3-9-3 68................................ TomEaves 8 71
(Kevin Ryan) *led: rdn and hrd pressed fr 3f out: hdd ins fnl f: one pce* **4/1**[3]

0201 **4** *hd* **Soloist (IRE)**[45] 5855 3-9-7 72................................(b) JoeFanning 3 75
(Keith Dalgleish) *prom: wnt 2nd after 3f: effrt and ev ch fr 3f out to ins fnl f: one pce last 100yds* **9/1**

4414 **5** *8* **Cuba Ruba**[16] 6938 3-8-9 60................................(p) DavidAllan 2 50
(Tim Easterby) *in tch: drvn and outpcd over 2f out: wknd fr over 1f out* **5/2**[2]

0010 **6** *2* **Lizzie Loch**[16] 6938 3-8-6 57................................ AndrewMullen 1 44
(Alistair Whillans) *hld up: drvn along: effrt over 3f out: wknd fr 2f out* **20/1**

7 *nk* **Pour Sioux (IRE)**[22] 6742 3-8-4 58................................ SeanDavis(3) 6 44
(Gordon Elliott, Ire) *hld up in tch: effrt on outside over 3f out: wknd 2f out* **25/1**

8 *11* **Karasheni (IRE)**[77] 4701 3-9-7 72................................ PaulMulrennan 7 41
(Iain Jardine) *dwlt: hld up: struggling over 3f out: sn lost tch* **14/1**

2m 46.0s (7.40) **Going Correction** +0.475s/f (Yiel) **8 Ran SP% 117.7**
Speed ratings (Par 101): **94,93,91,91,86 85,84,77**
CSF £30.13 CT £91.51 TOTE £11.70: £3.20, £1.10, £1.80; EX 42.80 Trifecta £340.00.
Owner Imperial Racing, J Blackburn & P Scott **Bred** G E Amey **Trained** Sheriff Hutton, N Yorks

FOCUS
Not a bad 3yo handicap for the class. The first four were clear. Add 13yds.
T/Jkpt: Not won. T/Plt: £117.30 to a £1 stake. Pool of £92,075.01 - 572.85 winning units T/Qpdt: £36.30 to a £1 stake. Pool of £7,306.69 - 148.63 winning units **Richard Young**

3902 BRO PARK (L-H)
Sunday, September 22

OFFICIAL GOING: Turf: good; dirt: fast

7494a TATTERSALLS NICKES MINNESLOPNING (LISTED RACE) (3YO+) (DIRT) 1m
2:00 3-Y-O+
£44,286 (£13,286; £7,085; £3,542; £2,657)

RPR

1 **Duca Di Como (IRE)**[28] 6523 4-9-4 0................................ ElioneChaves 1 103
(Cathrine Erichsen, Norway) **37/20**[1]

2 *5* **Wonnemond (GER)**[21] 6770 6-9-4 0................................ BayarsaikhanGanbat 4 91
(S Smrczek, Germany) **17/4**[3]

3 *nk* **Red Hot Chili (SWE)**[53] 6-9-4 0................................(p) MartinRodriguez 3 90
(Patrick Wahl, Sweden) **123/10**

4 *1 1/2* **Victor Kalejs (USA)**[28] 6524 5-9-4 0................................(p) Per-AndersGraberg 2 87
(Roy Arne Kvisla, Sweden) **12/1**

5 *2 1/2* **Plata O Plomo (USA)**[15] 5-9-4 0................................(b) CarlosLopez 6 81
(Susanne Berneklint, Sweden) **51/20**[2]

6 *2 1/2* **Kashgar (SWE)**[70] 5-9-4 0................................(p) ManuelMartinez 9 76
(Roy Arne Kvisla, Sweden) **35/1**

7 *6* **Another Batt (IRE)**[15] 6950 4-9-4 0................................ ShaneKelly 5 62
(Richard Hughes) *sn prom: pushed along over 3f out: sn outpcd by ldr and rdn along 2f out: wknd fnl 2f* **244/10**

8 *nk* **Cabanac**[1057] 6-9-4 0................................ RafaeldeOliveira 7 61
(Bent Olsen, Denmark) **62/1**

9 *9* **Hills And Dales (IRE)**[15] 7-9-4 0................................ ShaneKarlsson 10 40
(Hans-Inge Larsen, Sweden) **37/1**

10 *1 1/2* **Christmas (IRE)**[43] 3-9-0 0................................(p) OliverWilson 8 37
(Flemming Velin, Denmark) **99/10**

1m 36.8s
WFA 3 from 4yo+ 4lb **10 Ran SP% 117.6**

Owner Stall Como **Bred** Crone Stud Farms Ltd **Trained** Norway

The Form Book Flat 2019, Raceform Ltd, Newbury, RG14 5SJ

7495a CHAMPAGNE TAITTINGER SVEALANDLOPNING (CONDITIONS) (2YO) (TURF) 7f
2:25 2-Y-O £26,572 (£8,857; £4,428; £2,657; £1,771)

RPR
1 Old News[15] 6963 2-9-4 ....(p) ShaneKelly 12 86
(Richard Hughes) *settled in midfield: effrt over 2f out: hdwy to ld 1f out: drvn out and a doing enough fnl f* 15/2[3]
2 nk Silent Night (SWE)[32] 2-9-1 0.... CarlosLopez 1 82
(Patrick Wahl, Sweden) 43/20[1]
3 3 1/2 Acapello (IRE) 2-9-4 0.... RafaeldeOliveira 5 76
(Bent Olsen, Denmark) 269/10
4 nk Nordic (GER)[17] 2-9-4 0.... DaleSwift 4 75
(Wido Neuroth, Norway) 106/10
5 nse Outragusandangerus (USA)[49] 2-9-4 0.... Per-AndersGraberg 10 75
(Roy Arne Kvisla, Sweden) 182/10
6 1 Couleur Cafe (IRE) 2-9-1 0.... Jan-ErikNeuroth 2 70
(Wido Neuroth, Norway) 74/10[2]
7 hd Youonlyliveonce (FR)[18] 2-9-4 0.... OliverWilson 8 72
(Lars Kelp, Sweden) 106/10
8 1 1/2 Allhallowtide (IRE)[32] 2-9-1 0.... KaiaSofieIngolfsland 14 65
(Claes Bjorling, Sweden) 35/1
9 nse Grey Flash (USA)[49] 2-9-4 0.... FredrikJanetzky 15 68
(Bent Olsen, Denmark) 58/1
10 1/2 Debbie Dawn (IRE) 2-9-1 0.... ManuelMartinez 3 64
(Cathrine Erichsen, Norway) 26/1
11 1/2 Chinese Emperor 2-9-4 0.... RobertHavlin 7 65
(Lars Kelp, Sweden) 41/1
12 1/2 Monsieur Vic (FR) 2-9-4 0.... ShaneKarlsson 6 64
(Jessica Long, Sweden) 109/10
13 1/2 Mitty's Smile (IRE)[10] 7104 2-9-1 ....(p) LukeMorris 9 60
(Archie Watson) *led: drvn along whn pressed 3f out: hdd 2f out: sn wknd: wl hld fnl f* 31/1
14 1 Hypochondriac[32] 2-9-1 0.... RebeccaColldin 13 57
(Claes Bjorling, Sweden) 45/1
15 1/2 Gulfstream Tiger (USA) 2-9-4 0.... ElioneChaves 11 59
(Francisco Castro, Sweden) 74/10[2]

1m 24.7s 15 Ran SP% 117.6

Owner The Queens **Bred** Biddestone Stud Ltd **Trained** Upper Lambourn, Berks

7496a LANWADES STUD STKS (LISTED RACE) (3YO+ FILLIES & MARES) (TURF) 1m
2:50 3-Y-O+ £44,286 (£13,286; £7,085; £3,542; £2,657)

RPR
1 Appelina (DEN)[28] 6524 6-9-4 0.... Jan-ErikNeuroth 7 100
(Wido Neuroth, Norway) 4/6[1]
2 1/2 Maamora (IRE)[10] 7106 3-9-0.... DavidEgan 5 99
(Simon Crisford) *sn cl up: led 2 1/2f out: hdd 2f out: rdn along and led again 1 1/2f out: hdd 75yds out: no ex* 7/2[2]
3 1/2 Hateya (IRE)[22] 6721 4-9-4.... ShaneKelly 8 98
(Jim Boyle) *in tch towards rr: drvn along 2f out: styd on u.p fnl f: nt clr run 1/2f out: swtchd rt and drvn out* 166/10
4 1/2 Gypsy Spirit[35] 6270 3-9-0.... PJMcDonald 4 97
(Tom Clover) *trckd ldrs: effrt 2f out: sn pressed ldrs: outpcd fnl 110yds* 26/1
5 1 Sea Race (IRE) 3-9-0 0.... ElioneChaves 2 94
(Paul Fitzsimons, Sweden) 205/10
6 1 1/2 High As A Kite (FR)[85] 4419 5-9-4 0.... ManuelMartinez 6 91
(Jan Bjordal, Norway) 215/10
7 nk Seaside Song[52] 5-9-4 0.... CarlosLopez 1 90
(Cathrine Erichsen, Norway) 33/4[3]
8 nk Unwanted Beauty (IRE)[303] 9227 3-9-0 0.... Per-AndersGraberg 3 89
(Annike Bye Hansen, Norway) 152/10

1m 38.1s
WFA 3 from 4yo+ 4lb 8 Ran SP% 117.7

Owner Stall Perlen **Bred** Stutteri Hjortebo **Trained** Norway

7497a CLARION SIGN BRO PARK SPRINT CHAMPIONSHIP (LISTED RACE) (3YO+) (TURF) 6f
3:40 3-Y-O+ £44,286 (£13,286; £7,085; £3,542; £2,657)

RPR
1 Corinthia Knight (IRE)[12] 7058 4-9-4 0.... LukeMorris 5 100
(Archie Watson) *chsd ldrs: effrt over 2f out: rdn in 2nd 1f out: grad clsd on ldr: led fnl 50yds* 71/10
2 nk Ambiance (IRE)[32] 8-9-4 0.... Per-AndersGraberg 8 99
(Roy Arne Kvisla, Sweden) 103/20[2]
3 nse Puds[17] 6908 4-9-1 0.... ShaneKelly 12 96
(Richard Hughes) *settled in midfield: angled out and drvn along under 2f out: wnt 3rd and rdn along 1f out: styd on but nt quite getting there: clst fin* 174/10
4 1 1/2 Captain America (SWE)[28] 6523 9-9-4 0....(b) CarlosLopez 11 94
(Annike Bye Hansen, Norway) 11/2[3]
5 1/2 Sarookh (USA)[28] 6523 4-9-4 0.... ShaneKarlsson 13 93
(Jessica Long, Sweden) 227/10
6 hd Backcountry[28] 6523 7-9-4 0....(b) FredrikJanetzky 14 92
(Annette Stjernstrand, Sweden) 64/1
7 1 Dardenne (NOR)[53] 5-9-4 0.... DaleSwift 2 89
(Wido Neuroth, Norway) 79/10
8 1/2 Xtara (IRE)[32] 3-9-2 0....(b) ElioneChaves 3 87
(Dina Danekilde, Sweden) 25/1
9 nk Sandtastic (FR)[382] 5-9-4 0.... JosefinLandgren 6 86
(Bettina Andersen, Denmark) 129/10
10 1/2 Nipozzano (IRE)[105] 3-9-2 0.... NikolajStott 4 85
(Marc Stott, Denmark) 26/1
11 1 Prime Red (DEN)[364] 7589 6-9-4 0.... AnnieNilssonLindahl 1 81
(Birgitte Nielsen, Denmark) 42/1
12 nse Brian Ryan[28] 6523 4-9-4 0.... Jan-ErikNeuroth 10 81
(Wido Neuroth, Norway) 43/20[1]
13 1 1/2 Monza (IRE)[98] 4-9-1 0....(p) ManuelGMartinez 7 73
(Bent Olsen, Denmark) 36/1

1m 10.4s
WFA 3 from 4yo+ 2lb 13 Ran SP% 117.9

Owner Ontoawinner & Partner **Bred** Tally-Ho Stud **Trained** Upper Lambourn, W Berks

7498a STOCKHOLM CUP INTERNATIONAL (GROUP 3) (3YO+) (TURF) 1m 4f
4:10 3-Y-O+ £88,573 (£31,000; £15,057; £10,628; £5,314)

RPR
1 Square De Luynes (FR)[28] 6524 4-9-4 0.... RobertHavlin 11 111
(Niels Petersen, Norway) *led after 1f: gng wl in front 3f out: clr and drvn along 2f out: r.o wl: impressive* 8/15[1]
2 7 Freestyler (SWE)[1026] 5-9-4 0.... ShaneKarlsson 4 100
(Jessica Long, Sweden) *in rr of midfield: hdwy w plenty to do 3f out: rdn along to chse ldr 1 1/2f out: kpt on same pce: no ch w easy wnr* 123/10[3]
3 nk Master Bloom (SWE)[43] 4-9-4 0.... CarlosLopez 2 99
(Cathrine Erichsen, Norway) *led 100yds: settled in midfield: hdwy 3f out: rdn along to chse clr ldr under 2f out: kpt on for 3rd: rdn out* 151/10
4 1 Learn By Heart[28] 6524 4-9-4 0.... RafaeldeOliveira 10 98
(Bent Olsen, Denmark) *in rr of midfield: drvn along and hdwy 3f out: kpt on into 4th but nvr a threat* 51/1
5 1 1/2 Suspicious Mind (DEN)[43] 6-9-4 0.... ElioneChaves 8 95
(Nina Lensvik, Sweden) *sn settled in 4th: tk clsr order 3f out: outpcd by ldr over 2f out: rdn along and lost position under 2f out: kpt on* 216/10
6 nk King David (DEN)[38] 6144 4-9-4 0.... OliverWilson 12 95
(Marc Stott, Denmark) *towards rr: effrt and hdwy between runners fr 2f out: kpt on same pce fnl f* 166/10
7 4 Amazing Red (IRE)[38] 6145 6-9-4.... PJMcDonald 7 88
(Ed Dunlop) *settled in midfield: pushed along and hdwy 3f out: rdn along and one pce fnl 2f: nvr on terms* 196/10
8 1 1/2 Crowned Eagle[29] 6466 5-9-4 0....(p) LukeMorris 6 86
(Marco Botti) *sn settled in 2nd: drvn along 3f out: outpcd by ldr and rdn over 2f out: wknd wl over 1f out: plugged on* 69/10[2]
9 nk Quarterback (GER)[28] 6524 7-9-4....(p) SandroDePaiva 1 86
(Yvonne Durant, Norway) *midfield: lost position 3f out: hld fnl 2f* 70/1
10 1/2 Giuseppe Piazzi (IRE)[43] 7-9-4 0....(p) MartinRodriguez 9 85
(Flemming Velin, Denmark) *towards rr: pushed along to stay in tch over 3f out: plugged on: nvr a factor* 54/1
11 3 Bokan (FR)[85] 4419 7-9-4 0.... Jan-ErikNeuroth 3 80
(Wido Neuroth, Norway) *led after 100yds: hdd after 1f: settled in 5th: effrt 3f out: wknd fnl 2f* 63/1
12 6 Gold Tyranny (DEN)[43] 5-9-4 0.... Per-AndersGraberg 5 70
(Lennart Reuterskiold Jr, Sweden) *cl up 1f: settled bhd ldrs: pushed along and lost position over 3f out: wl hld fnl 2f* 188/10

2m 26.8s 12 Ran SP% 118.3

Owner Stall Power Girls **Bred** Jacques Beres **Trained** Norway

3674 COLOGNE (R-H)
Sunday, September 22

OFFICIAL GOING: Turf: good

7499a PREIS DES CASINO BADEN-BADEN - KOLNER STUTENPREIS (LISTED RACE) (3YO+) (TURF) 1m 1f 55y
2:05 3-Y-O+ £12,612 (£5,855; £2,702; £1,351)

RPR
1 Wish You Well (GER)[25] 3-8-13 0.... EduardoPedroza 12 97
(Jean-Pierre Carvalho, Germany) 83/10
2 shd Mythica (IRE)[49] 5720 3-8-10 0.... FilipMinarik 2 94
(Jean-Pierre Carvalho, Germany) 26/5[2]
3 hd Wishfully (IRE)[21] 6769 3-8-10 0.... MickaelBarzalona 3 93
(H-A Pantall, France) *mid-div on inner: shkn up ins fnl 3f: hdwy to go 4th 2f out: r.o ins fnl f: nvr nrr* 7/5[1]
4 hd Freedom Rising (GER)[25] 3-8-10 0.... AdriedeVries 8 93
(Yasmin Almenrader, Germany) 31/1
5 4 Park Bloom (IRE)[15] 6992 4-9-2 0....(p) CyrilleStefan 11 85
(H-F Devin, France) 233/10
6 1 3/4 Viva Gloria (GER)[25] 4-9-2 0.... AndraschStarke 10 81
(J Hirschberger, Germany) 63/10[3]
7 1/2 Nareia (GER)[1045] 7927 5-9-2 0.... RenePiechulek 13 80
(Frau Erika Mader, Germany) 46/1
8 hd Amatriciana (FR)[25] 3-8-10 0.... AntoineCoutier 1 79
(Carina Fey, France) 42/1
9 shd Liberty London (GER)[35] 3-8-10 0.... MarcoCasamento 7 79
(H-J Groschel, Germany) 222/10
10 hd Bubble And Squeak[15] 6992 4-9-2 0.... JasonWatson 6 79
(Sylvester Kirk) *mid-div in centre: rdn over 3f out: no imp and wknd* 115/10
11 3/4 Baccara Rose (GER)[25] 4-9-2 0.... NicolPolli 4 77
(S Smrczek, Germany) 17/1
12 5 1/2 Vadivina (IRE)[310] 3-8-10 0.... LukasDelozier 9 66
(F Vermeulen, France) 125/10

1m 52.17s
WFA 3 from 4yo+ 5lb 12 Ran SP% 119.2
PARI-MUTUEL (all including 1 euro stake): WIN 9.30 PLACE: 1.70, 1,50, 1.30; SF: 30.90.
Owner Gestut Hony-Hof **Bred** Gestut Hony-Hof **Trained** Germany

7500a 57TH PREIS VON EUROPA (GROUP 1) (3YO+) (TURF) 1m 4f
4:10 3-Y-O+ £90,090 (£27,027; £13,513; £6,306; £2,702)

RPR
1 Aspetar (FR)[84] 4430 4-9-6 0.... JasonWatson 5 115+
(Roger Charlton) *prom and a little keen early: sn settled in 3rd: pushed along and hdwy ins fnl 3f: drvn along to ld 1 1/2f out: r.o wl* 36/5
2 2 1/2 Amorella (IRE)[22] 6747 4-9-3 0.... MartinSeidl 7 108
(Markus Klug, Germany) *towards rr: tk clsr order and drvn along 3f out: styd on wl to go 2nd cl home: nvr trbld wnr* 195/10
3 1/2 Donjah (GER)[21] 6771 3-8-10 0.... LukasDelozier 1 108
(Henk Grewe, Germany) *led 1f: sn trckd ldr: shkn up to ld 2f out: sn pressed and hdd 1 1/2f out: no ex: lost 2nd cl home* 17/10[1]

4 4 **Colomano**[21] 6771 5-9-6 0 AndraschStarke 10 104
(Markus Klug, Germany) *towards rr: effrt 3f out: styd on wl: nvr on terms w ldrs* **25/1**

5 6 **Best Solution (IRE)**[15] 6962 5-9-6 0 PatCosgrave 3 94
(Saeed bin Suroor) *sn settled towards rr: pushed along 4f out: drvn along w plenty to do 3f out: kpt on: nvr on terms* **27/10**[2]

6 2 1/2 **Royal Youmzain (FR)**[29] 6487 4-9-6 0 BauyrzhanMurzabayev 6 90
(A Wohler, Germany) *led after 1f: hdd after 2f: led again after 3f tl hdd 2f out: rdn along and wknd fnl 2f* **13/1**

7 9 **Weltstar (GER)**[35] 4-9-6 MaximPecheur 4 76
(Markus Klug, Germany) *midfield: effrt over 3f out: wl hld and eased fnl 1 1/2f* **105/10**

8 7 **Communique (IRE)**[21] 6771 4-9-6 WilliamBuick 2 64
(Mark Johnston) *midfield: pushed along over 3f out: no imp and sn rdn: eased whn wl btn 2f out* **6/1**[3]

9 53 **Bristano**[49] 5719 3-9-0 0 FilipMinarik 8
(M G Mintchev, Germany) *led after 2f: hdd after 3f: settled in midfield: pushed along and lost position wl over 3f out: wl hld fnl 3f* **26/1**

2m 26.0s (-6.90) 9 Ran SP% 118.8
WFA 3 from 4yo+ 7lb
PARI-MUTUEL (all including 1 euro stake): WIN 8.20 PLACE: 2.60, 2.90, 1.40; SF: 187.30.
Owner H H Sheikh Mohammed Bin Khalifa Al Thani **Bred** Hh Sheikh Mohammed Bin Khalifa Al Thani **Trained** Beckhampton, Wilts

LANDIVISIAU
Sunday, September 22

OFFICIAL GOING: Turf: good to soft

7501a PRIX FRANCOIS CORBEL (CONDITIONS) (5YO+) (TURF) 1m 2f 165y
4:00 5-Y-0+ £4,279 (£1,711; £1,283; £855; £427)

RPR

1 **Bokra Fil Mishmish (FR)**[387] 5-9-1 0 GerardGuillermo 3 61
(G Guillermo, France) **47/1**[1]

2 3/4 **History Dream (FR)**[163] 8-9-4 0 MlleAlexandraLeLay(9) 5 72
(B Audouin, France)

3 3 1/2 **Savoyard (IRE)**[506] 6-8-5 0 MlleCeciliaPoirier(9) 12 52
(J Boisnard, France)

4 10 **Sulal Nair (FR)**[28] 6-9-1 0 BenjaminMarie(5) 10 38
(X-L Le Stang, France)

5 1/4 **Notnowcedric (FR)**[1556] 8-9-0 0 SebastienMartino 4 31
(B Le Regent, France)

6 1 **Bohemian Rapsody (FR)**[55] 9-9-6 0 JulienGuillochon 8 35
(E D'Andigne, France)

7 10 **Rock Of Glenstal**[1710] 189 9-8-8 0 HugoMouesan(6) 6 9
(S Gouyette, France)

8 5 1/2 **La Taniere (FR)**[14] 7009 5-8-10 0 ChloeGendron(9) 2 3
(S Gouyette, France)

9 12 **Dub Steps (FR)**[213] 5-8-13 0 EnzoBonnet 1
(F Guillossou, France)

10 3 1/2 **Selectif**[14] 7009 7-8-5 0 MlleSophieChuette(9) 11
(O Briand, France)

11 dist **Spaliburg Rosetgri (FR)**[104] 8-9-1 0 DamienGibelloSacco(5) 9
(F Fouquet, France)

12 17 **Angelical Eve (IRE)**[14] 7009 5-8-13 0 MorganDelalande 7
(Dai Williams) *towards rr on outer: niggled along whn began to lose grnd in bk st: sn bhd: eased home*

12 Ran SP% 2.1

Owner Gerard Guillermo **Bred** J-L Valerien-Perrin **Trained** France

4432 SAN SIRO (R-H)
Sunday, September 22

OFFICIAL GOING: Turf: good

7502a PREMIO DEL PIAZZALE MEMORIAL ENRICO CAMICI (GROUP 3) (3YO+) (GRANDE COURSE) (TURF) 1m 110y
3:10 3-Y-0+ £29,279 (£12,882; £7,027; £3,513)

RPR

1 **Anda Muchacho (IRE)**[105] 3643 5-9-2 0 AntonioFresu 6 110
(Nicolo Simondi, Italy) *prom on outer: rdn to chal 1 1/2f out: led ent fnl f: hld on gamely whn pressed by rival cl home* **17/20**[1]

2 nk **Mission Boy**[21] 3-8-9 0 CarloFiocchi 3 108
(A Botti, Italy) *towards rr on outer: pushed along 2 1/2f out: sn rdn: r.o wl ins fnl f: unable to reel in wnr* **37/20**[2]

3 2 1/4 **Time To Choose**[84] 4432 6-9-0 0 FabioBranca 2 102
(A Botti, Italy) *w.w in rr: rdn to improve 2f out: mde late hdwy past a couple of btn rivals late on* **47/10**

4 1 1/2 **Presley (ITY)**[91] 4173 6-9-0 0 DarioVargiu 4 99
(A Botti, Italy) *trckd ldr: shkn up whn ev ch 1 1/2f out: sn no imp: dropped to 4th in clsng stages* **91/20**[3]

5 3 1/2 **Siberius (ITY)** 3-8-9 0 SilvanoMulas 5 92
(Cristiano Davide Fais, Italy) *mid-div on inner: rdn 2f out: no initial imp on ldrs bef r.o late to go 5th ins fnl 110yds* **52/1**

6 1 3/4 **Greg Pass (IRE)**[127] 7-9-0 0 WalterGambarota 1 87
(Nicolo Simondi, Italy) *led: rdn to assert 2f out: hdd ent fnl f: sn no ex and wknd* **17/20**[1]

7 1 **Sun Devil (ITY)**[679] 5-9-0 0 (t) FedericoBossa 7 85
(Diego Dettori, Italy) *towards rr: u.p and pushed along wl over 3f out: n.d* **25/1**

1m 39.9s (-9.60) 7 Ran SP% 184.5
WFA 3 from 5yo+ 4lb
PARI-MUTUEL (all including 1 euro stake): WIN 1.86; PLACE 1.22, 1.34; DF 2.42.
Owner Scuderia Incolinx & Diego Romeo **Bred** Thomas Hassett **Trained** Italy

7503a PREMIO ELENA E SERGIO CUMANI (GROUP 3) (3YO+ FILLIES & MARES) (GRANDE COURSE) (TURF) 1m
3:50 3-Y-0+ £31,531 (£13,873; £7,567; £3,783)

RPR

1 **Style Presa (FR)**[28] 4-9-0 0 CristianDemuro 4 106
(Rod Collet, France) *trckd ldr: rdn and swtchd to outer 2f out: sn led: r.o wl to draw clr ins fnl f: comf* **40/95**[1]

2 2 1/2 **Stone Tornado**[38] 6142 3-8-9 0 (t) JulienAuge 7 99
(C Ferland, France) *w.w in rr: rdn to improve 2f out: r.o to make eyecatching hdwy on outer: wnt 2nd ins fnl 110yds: unable to reduce deficit to wnr* **195/10**

3 1 **Musa D'Oriente**[21] 8-9-0 0 (t) LucaManiezzi 5 98
(M Gonnelli, Italy) *led: rdn to assert ent fnl 2f: hdd appr fnl f: no ex and dropped to 3rd cl home* **19/2**

4 1 **Party Goer (IRE)**[21] 4-9-0 0 (tp) DarioVargiu 9 96
(Endo Botti, Italy) *racd towards rr on inner: short of room whn swtchd off rail 2f out: rdn sn after: no imp ins fnl f* **13/1**

5 shd **Binti Al Nar (GER)**[85] 4-9-0 0 (b) CarloFiocchi 10 95
(P Schiergen, Germany) *racd in fnl trio: asked for effrt 2 1/2f out: kpt on for sme late prog ins fnl f* **25/4**[3]

6 2 1/2 **Lamaire (IRE)**[91] 4171 3-9-0 0 FabioBranca 3 94
(Riccardo Santini, Italy) *mid-div on outer: shkn up ent fnl 2f: kpt on one pce: eased towards fin* **91/20**[2]

7 1 1/4 **Greach (IRE)**[119] 3-8-9 0 (t) MarioSanna 6 86
(Diego Dettori, Italy) *towards rr: rdn appr 2f out: no imp: n.d* **26/1**

8 1 3/4 **Cima Fire (FR)**[91] 4171 3-8-9 0 (t) SilvanoMulas 1 82
(Grizzetti Galoppo SRL, Italy) *cl up on inner: no imp whn rdn over 1f out: wknd ins fnl f* **40/1**

9 2 1/2 **Intense Battle (IRE)**[21] 3-8-9 0 DarioDiTocco 2 76
(Marco Gasparini, Italy) *chsd ldrs between horses: rdn to chal over 2f out: no imp: wknd* **139/10**

10 6 **Verde E Rosa (IRE)**[147] 2161 3-8-9 0 AntonioFresu 8 62
(Nicolo Simondi, Italy) *prom on outer: pushed along 3f out: squeezed out sltly appr fnl f: n.d afterwards* **189/10**

1m 34.0s (-8.10) 10 Ran SP% 141.6
WFA 3 from 4yo+ 4lb
PARI-MUTUEL (all including 1 euro stake): WIN 1.43; PLACE 1.06, 1.80, 1.50; DF 16.52.
Owner Ecurie D'Haspel **Bred** Haras D'Haspel **Trained** France

7504a PREMIO FEDERICO TESIO (GROUP 2) (3YO+) (GRANDE COURSE) (TURF) 1m 3f
4:25 3-Y-0+ £63,063 (£27,747; £15,135; £7,567)

RPR

1 **Chestnut Honey (IRE)**[84] 3-8-7 0 FabioBranca 5 109
(A Botti, Italy) *w.w towards rr: asked to improve 3f out: r.o to go 2nd appr fnl f: styd on to ld 110yds out: a doing enough* **68/10**

2 snk **Royal Julius (IRE)**[38] 6144 6-8-13 0 CristianDemuro 1 107
(J Reynier, France) *chsd ldng pair: reduced deficit over 3f out: rdn ent fnl 2f: led 1 1/2f out: kpt on tl no ex and hdd ins fnl 110yds* **4/6**[1]

3 3 1/2 **Sword Peinture (GER)**[22] 6747 4-8-9 0 AndreaMezzatesta 2 97
(Andreas Suborics, Germany) *hld up in rr: rdn to chal 2f out: r.o to go 3rd appr fnl f: unable to make an imp on ldng pair* **139/10**

4 10 **Trita Sass (IRE)**[126] 2887 3-8-7 0 (t) DarioVargiu 3 84
(A Botti, Italy) *trckd ldr: shkn up over 2f out: no imp and sn in rr ent fnl f: kpt on to pass tired rival late on* **48/10**[3]

5 4 **Akribie (GER)**[21] 6771 3-8-6 0 AndreasHelfenbein 4 76
(Markus Klug, Germany) *led: hdd 1 1/2f out: no ex and wknd ins fnl f* **39/20**[2]

2m 12.6s (-6.00) 5 Ran SP% 130.7
WFA 3 from 4yo+ 6lb
PARI-MUTUEL (all including 1 euro stake): WIN 7.82; PLACE 2.45, 1.26; DF 20.20.
Owner Scuderia Effevi SRL **Bred** Camogue Stud Ltd **Trained** Italy

5286 COMPIEGNE (L-H)
Tuesday, September 17

OFFICIAL GOING: Turf: good to soft

7505a PRIX DE L'IMPERATRICE EUGENIE (H'CAP) (3YO+ FILLIES & MARES) (TURF) 1m 1f
5:30 3-Y-0+ £12,612 (£4,792; £3,531; £2,018; £1,009; £756)

RPR

1 **Sri Prada (FR)**[24] 5-9-0 0 AurelienLemaitre 2 70
(G Doleuze, France) **81/10**

2 nse **Heads Together**[65] 4-9-2 0 (p) AtsuyaNishimura 11 71
(S Kobayashi, France) **19/1**

3 hd **Midgrey (IRE)**[21] 4-9-2 0 (p) MlleAlisonMassin(3) 5 74
(F-X Belvisi, France) **10/1**

4 1 **Magic Song (FR)**[36] 6031 5-9-1 0 TonyPiccone 4 68
(S Kobayashi, France) **10/1**

5 nse **Peaceful City (FR)**[17] 6790 4-8-9 0 MlleCoraliePacaut(4) 8 66
(M Boutin, France) **37/1**

6 1 1/2 **Espionne (FR)**[61] 4-8-7 0 MaximeGuyon 12 57
(H De Nicolay, France) **56/10**[2]

7 snk **Freiheit (IRE)**[96] 4-9-2 0 ThomasTrullier(2) 9 67
(N Clement, France) **16/1**

8 1 1/4 **Flor De Seda (FR)**[7] 7062 4-8-10 0 HugoBesnier(4) 3 61
(Jo Hughes, France) *midfield: pushed along between rivals jst under 2f out: limited rspnse: hdwy over 1f out: kpt on same pce: n.d* **59/10**[3]

9 2 1/2 **Kenava (FR)**[43] 3-9-6 0 TheoBachelot 6 67
(J-P Gauvin, France) **12/1**

10 1 1/4 **Dream Night (FR)**[54] 3-9-1 0 Pierre-CharlesBoudot 10 60
(H-A Pantall, France) **9/1**

11 1/2 **Ophelia's Dream**[24] 3-9-2 0 MickaelBarzalona 7 60
(H-A Pantall, France) *t.k.h: midfield: prog to r promly over 1/2-way: short-lived effrt jst under 2f out: sn lost position and wknd ins fnl f* **5/2**[1]

12 ¾ **April Angel (FR)**[128] 5-8-3 0 ow3 ... RosarioMangione 1 39
(P Capelle, France) **53/1**

1m 48.41s
WFA 3 from 4yo+ 5lb **12** Ran SP% **120.4**
PARI-MUTUEL (all including 1 euro stake): WIN 9.10; PLACE 3.10, 6.00, 3.90; DF 94.30.
Owner Mlle Claire Stephenson **Bred** S.C.E.A. Des Prairies & B Jeffroy **Trained** France

[7486] HAMILTON (R-H)
Monday, September 23

OFFICIAL GOING: Soft (6.5)
Wind: Breezy, half behind in sprints and in over 4f of home straight in races on the round course Weather: Sunny spells

7506 LANARKSHIRE CHAMBER OF COMMERCE EBF NOVICE STKS (PLUS 10 RACE) 6f 6y
2:00 (2:01) (Class 4) 2-Y-O **£5,433** (£1,617; £808; £404) **Stalls** Centre

Form RPR
2130 **1** **Glasvegas (IRE)**[11] 7119 2-9-8 98 ... CallumRodriguez 2 82
(Keith Dalgleish) *chsd ldr: rdn over 2f out: led over 1f out: kpt on wl fnl f* **1/6**[1]
2 1¾ **Leoch** 2-9-2 0 ... KevinStott 3 71
(Kevin Ryan) *t.k.h: led: rdn and hdd over 1f out: rallied: one pce ins fnl f* **5/1**[2]
00 **3** 5 **Jungle Rock (IRE)**[13] 7046 2-8-11 0 ... FayeMcManoman(5) 10 56
(Iain Jardine) *t.k.h: prom: rdn and outpcd over 2f out: rallied over 1f out: kpt on fnl f: nt pce to chal* **50/1**
605 **4** nk **Garnock Valley**[9] 7211 2-8-11 56 ... PaddyMathers 4 50
(R Mike Smith) *hld up in tch: rdn along and effrt over 2f out: no imp fr over 1f out* **50/1**
0 **5** 3¾ **Krystal Crown (IRE)**[26] 6606 2-8-8 0 ... RowanScott(3) 1 39
(Andrew Hughes, Ire) *hld up in tch: rdn over 2f out: wknd over 1f out* **18/1**
6 ½ **Funky Dunky (IRE)** 2-9-2 0 ... ShaneGray 6 42+
(Keith Dalgleish) *slowly away: rn green and detached: sme hdwy over 1f out: nvr rchd ldrs* **20/1**
6 **7** ½ **Full House**[17] 6943 2-9-2 0 ... SamJames 8 41
(John Davies) *hld up in tch: rdn over 2f out: sn wknd* **16/1**
8 ¾ **The Tripple T (IRE)** 2-9-2 0 ... PaulMulrennan 5 39
(Andrew Hughes, Ire) *bhd and outpcd: nvr on terms* **12/1**[3]
00 **9** 10 **Klara Spirit (IRE)**[9] 7211 2-8-11 0 ... JamesSullivan 7 4
(R Mike Smith) *dwlt: bhd and sn struggling: no ch fr 1/2-way* **100/1**

1m 14.41s (1.71) **Going Correction** +0.325s/f (Good) **9** Ran SP% **130.9**
Speed ratings (Par 97): **101,98,92,91,86 85,85,84,70**
CSF £2.22 TOTE £1.10: £1.02, £1.30, £12.90; EX 2.50 Trifecta £49.30.
Owner Weldspec Glasgow Limited **Bred** Gigginstown House Stud **Trained** Carluke, S Lanarks
FOCUS
An uncompetitive novice, the red-hot favourite ran out just a workmanlike winner.

7507 RANDSTAD RECRUITMENT AND PAYSTREAM H'CAP 6f 6y
2:30 (2:31) (Class 6) (0-65,64) 4-Y-O+
£3,493 (£1,039; £519; £300; £300; £300) **Stalls** Centre

Form RPR
0640 **1** **Shortbackandsides (IRE)**[24] 6680 4-9-3 60 ... (p) JamesSullivan 9 72
(Tim Easterby) *in tch: drvn along over 2f out: hdwy to ld ins fnl f: rdn clr (trainer could offer no explanation for the apparent improvement in form)* **6/1**[3]
2330 **2** 3¾ **Kodicat (IRE)**[13] 7050 5-9-0 57 ... (p) KevinStott 5 58
(Kevin Ryan) *w ldrs: led over 1f out to ins fnl f: nt pce of wnr* **15/2**
3400 **3** nk **Forever A Lady (IRE)**[9] 7207 6-9-1 58 ... JoeFanning 11 58
(Keith Dalgleish) *hld up: pushed along 1/2-way: hdwy over 1f out: kpt on fnl f: nrst fin* **11/1**
0032 **4** 1¼ **Guardia Svizzera (IRE)**[1] 7487 5-8-13 61 ... (h) PaulaMuir(5) 4 57
(Roger Fell) *t.k.h early: w ldrs to over 2f out: drvn and one pce fr over 1f out* **5/1**[2]
2600 **5** nk **Lucky Beggar (IRE)**[11] 7121 9-9-6 63 ... DavidAllan 6 58
(David C Griffiths) *w ldrs to over 2f out: sn rdn: no ex fr over 1f out* **15/2**
0431 **6** 1 **Carlovian**[13] 7050 6-8-11 54 ... (v) AndrewMullen 3 46
(Mark Walford) *disp ld to over 1f out: rdn and btn fnl f* **12/1**
0302 **7** 1 **Avenue Of Stars**[12] 7065 6-9-6 63 ... (v) ConnorBeasley 7 52
(Karen McLintock) *dwlt: bhd and sn drvn along: hdwy over 1f out: nvr rchd ldrs (jockey said gelding missed the break)* **3/1**[1]
0600 **8** ¾ **Newstead Abbey**[12] 7066 9-8-11 54 ... (p) JamieGormley 8 41
(Rebecca Bastiman) *hld up: drvn along over 2f out: no imp fr over 1f out* **40/1**
6014 **9** ¾ **Naples Bay**[12] 7065 5-8-11 54 ... PhilDennis 12 39
(Katie Scott) *slt ld to over 1f out: sn rdn and wknd* **18/1**
0415 **10** 4 **Fumbo Jumbo (IRE)**[51] 5659 6-9-0 64 ... EllieMacKenzie(7) 2 37
(Rebecca Bastiman) *in tch: drvn and outpcd over 2f out: btn over 1f out* **14/1**
6606 **11** 27 **Gilmer (IRE)**[24] 6655 8-8-3 49 ... (b) SeanDavis(3) 10
(Stef Keniry) *dwlt: bhd: lost tch after 2f: eased whn no ch fr 1/2-way (jockey said gelding was never travelling)* **22/1**

1m 14.04s (1.34) **Going Correction** +0.325s/f (Good) **11** Ran SP% **114.2**
Speed ratings (Par 101): **104,99,98,96,96 95,93,92,91,86 50**
CSF £48.99 CT £490.79 TOTE £7.10: £2.40, £2.60, £2.90; EX 45.50 Trifecta £538.60.
Owner Habton Farms **Bred** Thomas Jones **Trained** Great Habton, N Yorks
FOCUS
Lowly sprint form. The winner has been rated back to last year's best.

7508 ALEX FERGUSSON MEMORIAL H'CAP (DIV I) 1m 68y
3:05 (3:05) (Class 6) (0-55,55) 4-Y-O+
£3,493 (£1,039; £519; £300; £300; £300) **Stalls** Low

Form RPR
0161 **1** **My Valentino (IRE)**[9] 7210 6-9-2 50 ... (b) JamesSullivan 1 59
(Dianne Sayer) *hld up: hdwy over 2f out: led and edgd rt over 1f out: sn hrd pressed: hld on wl towards fin* **15/2**
3500 **2** hd **Gamesters Icon**[72] 4914 4-9-7 55 ... (t[1]) KevinStott 9 64
(Oliver Greenall) *chsd clr ldr: rdn to ld briefly wl over 1f out: edgd lft and ev ch thrght fnl f: jst hld* **11/2**[3]
2234 **3** 5 **Be Bold**[24] 6655 7-9-4 52 ... (b) DavidAllan 2 50
(Rebecca Bastiman) *t.k.h: cl up in chsng gp: effrt and rdn over 2f out: kpt on same pce fr over 1f out* **9/2**[2]
0600 **4** ½ **Rosarno (IRE)**[123] 3007 5-9-3 51 ... (p[1]) JoeyHaynes 6 48
(Chelsea Banham) *s.i.s: hld up: hdwy and edgd lft over 2f out: rdn and no imp over 1f out* **11/4**[1]
-050 **5** ½ **The Brora Pobbles**[54] 5560 4-9-0 48 ow2 ... PaulMulrennan 3 44
(Alistair Whillans) *hld up on ins: pushed along and effrt over 2f out: no imp fr over 1f out* **25/1**
6362 **6** 4½ **Mr Cool Cash**[25] 6627 7-9-0 48 ... (t) SamJames 5 34
(John Davies) *in tch: pushed along and outpcd whn checked over 2f out: sn wknd* **13/2**
0200 **7** 3¾ **Crazy Tornado (IRE)**[17] 6937 6-9-1 49 ... (h) CallumRodriguez 4 27+
(Keith Dalgleish) *t.k.h: led: clr after 2f to over 2f out: rdn and hdd wl over 1f out: sn btn* **10/1**
0024 **8** ½ **Poyle George Two**[67] 5100 4-8-12 49 ... RowanScott(3) 8 26
(John Hodge) *hld up: drvn and struggling over 2f out: sn btn* **8/1**
0-00 **9** 7 **Dose**[39] 6102 6-9-6 54 ... PaulHanagan 10 15
(Richard Fahey) *t.k.h: chsd ldrs: rdn and lost pl over 2f out: sn btn* **18/1**

1m 49.58s (1.18) **Going Correction** +0.325s/f (Good) **9** Ran SP% **114.6**
Speed ratings (Par 101): **107,106,101,101,100 96,92,92,85**
CSF £47.97 CT £209.50 TOTE £8.80: £1.80, £2.40, £1.70; EX 62.10 Trifecta £397.10.
Owner Dennis J Coppola & Mrs Dianne Sayer **Bred** Lynch Bages Ltd & Camas Park Stud **Trained** Hackthorpe, Cumbria
FOCUS
Add 8yds. The first leg of a lowly handicap. It's been rated slightly negatively.

7509 ALEX FERGUSSON MEMORIAL H'CAP (DIV II) 1m 68y
3:40 (3:41) (Class 6) (0-55,54) 4-Y-O+
£3,493 (£1,039; £519; £300; £300; £300) **Stalls** Low

Form RPR
5 **1** **House Call (IRE)**[12] 7087 4-9-1 51 ... SeanDavis(3) 1 57
(Gordon Elliott, Ire) *hld up: effrt on outside over 2f out: kpt on wl fnl f to ld towards fin* **13/2**
3130 **2** ¾ **Retirement Beckons**[17] 6937 4-9-5 52 ... (h) BenRobinson 7 56
(Linda Perratt) *hld up in tch: hdwy to chal 2f out: kpt on fnl f: pressed wnr towards fin* **5/1**[3]
0004 **3** nk **Snooker Jim**[25] 6627 4-9-1 48 ... (t) DavidAllan 2 52
(Steph Hollinshead) *t.k.h: trckd ldrs: led gng wl over 2f out: sn hrd pressed and rdn: edgd lft ins fnl f: hdd and no ex towards fin (jockey said gelding hung left)* **4/1**[2]
3000 **4** 1½ **Cliff Bay (IRE)**[9] 7210 5-9-2 49 ... (b) CallumRodriguez 3 49
(Keith Dalgleish) *t.k.h: prom: swtchd lft and effrt over 2f out: edgd lft over 1f out: one pce fnl f* **5/2**[1]
0200 **5** nk **French Flyer (IRE)**[41] 6036 4-9-0 47 ... LewisEdmunds 8 47
(Rebecca Bastiman) *led to over 2f out: drvn and outpcd over 1f out* **11/1**
5624 **6** 1¼ **Spark Of War (IRE)**[20] 6828 4-9-7 54 ... (b) ShaneGray 6 51
(Keith Dalgleish) *t.k.h early: in tch: rdn over 2f out: wknd over 1f out* **5/1**[3]
350 **7** 2½ **Midnight Vixen**[58] 5438 5-9-6 53 ... (p) AndrewMullen 5 44
(Ben Haslam) *slowly away: hld up: drvn and struggling 3f out: sme late hdwy: nvr on terms* **22/1**
060 **8** 1¼ **The Mekon**[29] 6502 4-9-3 50 ... ConnorBeasley 9 39
(Noel Wilson) *t.k.h: chsd ldr to over 2f out: sn struggling: btn over 1f out (trainer said gelding stopped quickly and scoped dirty)* **20/1**

1m 51.57s (3.17) **Going Correction** +0.325s/f (Good) **8** Ran SP% **112.7**
Speed ratings (Par 101): **97,96,95,94,94 92,90,89**
CSF £37.64 CT £146.44 TOTE £6.10: £1.90, £1.50, £1.70; EX 38.60 Trifecta £150.10.
Owner Money For Jam Syndicate **Bred** Mr & Mrs Francis & Teresa Killen **Trained** Longwood, Co Meath
FOCUS
Add 8yds. This ended up being a touch more competitive than the first leg. The closers came to the fore. Strightforward form.

7510 ALLIED IRISH BANK VETERANS' H'CAP 1m 4f 15y
4:10 (4:11) (Class 4) (0-80,82) 6-Y-O+
£8,345 (£2,483; £1,240; £620; £300; £300) **Stalls** High

Form RPR
6055 **1** **Multellie**[24] 6657 7-9-3 74 ... DavidAllan 7 82
(Tim Easterby) *led to over 2f out: sn rdn: rallied and regained ld ins fnl f: rdn out* **4/1**[2]
636- **2** 1¼ **River Icon**[30] 8375 7-9-7 78 ... (p) PaulMulrennan 1 84
(Iain Jardine) *prom: drvn along 3f out: rallied over 1f out: pressed wnr ins fnl f: kpt on: hld towards fin* **20/1**
0422 **3** 2 **Carbon Dating (IRE)**[24] 6658 7-8-12 72 ... RowanScott(3) 9 75+
(Andrew Hughes, Ire) *hld up: gd hdwy on outside to ld over 3f out: rdn and hdd ins fnl f: one pce* **11/2**[3]
1300 **4** ½ **Corton Lad**[4] 7368 9-8-7 69 ow2 ... (tp) BenSanderson(5) 4 71
(Keith Dalgleish) *sn chsng ldr: drvn along over 2f out: rallied: one pce fnl f* **12/1**
1554 **5** 8 **Stonific (IRE)**[16] 6975 6-9-11 82 ... DavidNolan 2 71
(David O'Meara) *s.i.s: hld up: stdy hdwy over 3f out: rdn and effrt over 2f out: wknd over 1f out* **7/1**
0025 **6** nse **Capton**[15] 7003 6-9-2 73 ... (p) NathanEvans 8 62
(Michael Easterby) *prom: lost pl over 2f out: sn btn* **12/1**
0422 **7** 2 **Black Kalanisi (IRE)**[15] 7003 6-9-7 78 ... CharlesBishop 5 64
(Joseph Tuite) *hld up: hdwy and prom on outside over 3f out: wknd wl over 1f out (jockey said gelding was unsuited by the soft ground)* **5/2**[1]
6656 **8** ½ **Maulesden May (IRE)**[4] 7366 6-9-1 72 ... CallumRodriguez 3 57
(Keith Dalgleish) *hld up: rdn and outpcd over 2f out: sn btn* **25/1**
2151 **9** ½ **Donnachies Girl (IRE)**[24] 6658 6-8-7 64 oh2 ... PaulHanagan 6 48
(Alistair Whillans) *in tch: effrt and cl up over 3f out: rdn and wknd over 1f out (jockey said mare was unsuited by the soft ground)* **13/2**

2m 42.23s (3.63) **Going Correction** +0.325s/f (Good) **9** Ran SP% **113.8**
Speed ratings: **100,99,97,97,92 92,90,90,90**
CSF £77.24 CT £439.40 TOTE £4.50: £1.50, £5.30, £2.00; EX 56.10 Trifecta £399.40.
Owner David Scott & Partner **Bred** Habton Farms **Trained** Great Habton, N Yorks
FOCUS
Add 8yds. A fair handicap. The second has been rated to her best.

7511 OVERTON FARM H'CAP 5f 7y
4:45 (4:46) (Class 5) (0-75,73) 3-Y-O+
£5,433 (£1,617; £808; £404; £300; £300) **Stalls** Centre

Form RPR
4431 **1** **Fairy Stories**[23] 6715 3-9-3 71 ... SeanDavis(3) 4 82+
(Richard Fahey) *hld up: rdn and gd hdwy to ld over 1f out: drvn out fnl f* **6/1**[3]

1501 2 3/4 **Twentysixthstreet (IRE)**[1] 7486 3-9-4 72 6ex..........(b) RowanScott(3) 6 79
(Andrew Hughes, Ire) *hld up in tch: hdwy to chse wnr over 1f out: rdn and r.o fnl f* **13/2**

2360 3 2 1/4 **Burmese Blazer (IRE)**[4] 7367 4-8-8 58..................(p[1]) PaddyMathers 8 57
(Jim Goldie) *w ldr: led 1/2-way to over 1f out: kpt on same pce ins fnl f* **7/1**

0063 4 nse **Kenny The Captain (IRE)**[12] 7065 8-8-6 56.......... RachelRichardson 9 55
(Tim Easterby) *prom: drvn along 1/2-way: kpt on ins fnl f* **4/1**[1]

6315 5 nk **Marietta Robusti (IRE)**[17] 6921 4-9-5 69.......................... JackGarritty 5 67
(Stella Barclay) *trckd ldrs: effrt and rdn over 1f out: no ex ins fnl f* **16/1**

0604 6 1/2 **Prestbury Park (USA)**[39] 6099 4-9-1 65.............................. KevinStott 1 61
(Paul Midgley) *dwlt: hld up: hdwy on outside over 2f out: effrt and cl up over 1f out: no ex ins fnl f* **5/1**[2]

2130 7 5 **B Fifty Two (IRE)**[4] 7367 10-9-0 67...............................(t) JaneElliott(3) 2 45
(Marjorie Fife) *towards rr: drvn and outpcd 1/2-way: btn over 1f out* **9/1**

2200 8 shd **Diamonique**[3] 7402 3-9-8 73.. ShaneGray 7 50
(Keith Dalgleish) *hld up: rdn along 2f out: edgd lft and sn wknd* **9/1**

5600 9 1 3/4 **Rickyroadboy**[12] 7065 4-8-5 55..............................(v[1]) AndrewMullen 10 26
(Mark Walford) *led to 1/2-way: rdn and wknd over 1f out* **11/1**

0400 10 1/2 **Our Place In Loule**[4] 7367 6-9-2 66.........................(b) ConnorBeasley 3 35
(Noel Wilson) *hld up bhd ldng gp: outpcd over 2f out: btn whn hung rt over 1f out* **33/1**

1m 0.77s (0.37) **Going Correction** +0.325s/f (Good)
WFA 3 from 4yo+ 1lb 10 Ran SP% 113.9
Speed ratings (Par 103): **110,108,105,105,104 103,95,95,92,92**
CSF £43.66 CT £278.01 TOTE £5.10: £2.00, £2.40, £2.50; EX 47.60 Trifecta £287.40.
Owner Richard Fahey Ebor Racing Club Ltd **Bred** Mrs Sheila Oakes **Trained** Musley Bank, N Yorks

FOCUS
A modest sprint, but it was certainly open. The second has been rated in line with the better view of his win the previous day.

7512 "JOIN THE CHAMBER" H'CAP 1m 68y
5:15 (5:16) (Class 5) (0-75,75) 3-Y-O
£5,433 (£1,617; £808; £404; £300; £300) **Stalls Low**

Form RPR

0403 1 **Kingson (IRE)**[37] 6209 3-8-13 67.............................. PaulHanagan 6 76
(Richard Fahey) *s.i.s: hld up in tch: pushed along 3f out: hdwy over 1f out: led wl ins fnl f: kpt on wl* **9/2**[3]

3410 2 hd **Woodside Wonder**[4] 7364 3-9-7 75.......................(v) CallumRodriguez 3 83
(Keith Dalgleish) *t.k.h: trckd ldrs: rdn over 2f out: hdwy to ld 1f out: edgd lft: hdd wl ins fnl f: kpt on* **5/1**

4120 3 3 3/4 **One To Go**[12] 7074 3-9-0 68..(p) DavidAllan 9 67
(Tim Easterby) *prom: rdn over 2f out: kpt on same pce fr over 1f out* **10/3**[1]

2534 4 nk **Creek Island (IRE)**[38] 6164 3-9-2 70.............................. JoeFanning 4 69
(Mark Johnston) *t.k.h: led at modest gallop: rdn over 2f out: hdd 1f out: sn outpcd* **7/2**[2]

1031 5 3 1/4 **Mecca's Gift (IRE)**[24] 6679 3-9-5 73.......................(b) ConnorBeasley 7 64
(Michael Dods) *t.k.h early: trckd ldr: ev ch over 2f out to over 1f out: wknd ins fnl f* **5/1**

5050 6 1 **Darwina**[27] 6575 3-8-2 56 oh6..................................(h) JamesSullivan 2 45
(Alistair Whillans) *hld up in last pl: drvn along over 2f out: sn wknd* **40/1**

2403 7 nk **Double Honour**[28] 6544 3-9-7 75..................................(p) PJMcDonald 1 63
(James Bethell) *s.i.s: hld up in tch: struggling 3f out: sn btn* **15/2**

1m 51.0s (2.60) **Going Correction** +0.325s/f (Good) 7 Ran SP% 111.0
Speed ratings (Par 101): **100,99,96,95,92 91,91**
CSF £25.33 CT £79.89 TOTE £5.60: £2.10, £2.50; EX 27.40 Trifecta £130.00.
Owner Mr & Mrs P Ashton & Partner **Bred** Godolphin **Trained** Musley Bank, N Yorks

FOCUS
Add 8yds. Modest 3yo form, with the pace a steady one. A turf pb from the second, with the winner rated something like his debut form.

7513 RACING TV HD ON SKY 426 APPRENTICE H'CAP 1m 1f 35y
5:50 (5:50) (Class 5) (0-70,71) 4-Y-O+
£5,433 (£1,617; £808; £404; £300; £300) **Stalls Low**

Form RPR

1400 1 **Spirit Of Sarwan (IRE)**[24] 6658 5-9-1 64.........................(v) JaneElliott 6 71
(Stef Keniry) *s.i.s: hld up: rdn and swtchd lft over 2f out: sustained run to ld ins fnl f: r.o wl (regarding the apparent improvement in form, trainer said gelding may have benefitted from a drop back in trip)* **25/1**

1424 2 1 **Granite City Doc**[6] 7301 6-9-3 66.............................. PaulaMuir 2 71
(Lucy Normile) *prom: effrt and chsd clr ldr over 2f out to ins fnl f: kpt on wl to press wnr towards fin* **9/2**[1]

3041 3 1/2 **Remmy D (IRE)**[24] 6655 4-7-13 58 ow1..................(b) CoreyMadden(10) 4 62+
(Jim Goldie) *led 2f: w ldr: regained ld over 3f out: sn clr: rdn 2f out: wknd and hdd ins fnl f: lost 2nd cl home* **5/1**[2]

5032 4 1 1/4 **Star Of Valour (IRE)**[24] 6655 4-8-7 56.......................... ConnorMurtagh 9 57
(Lynn Siddall) *hld up in midfield: hdwy to dispute 2nd pl over 2f out to ins fnl f: sn no ex* **5/1**[2]

5036 5 shd **Ningaloo (GER)**[24] 6666 5-8-9 58.............................. RowanScott 13 59
(Rebecca Bastiman) *bhd: rdn over 2f out: kpt on wl fnl f: nrst fin* **20/1**

0515 6 1/2 **Zealous (IRE)**[28] 6545 6-8-6 62...........................(p) IzzyClifton(7) 5 62
(Alistair Whillans) *midfield: pushed along over 2f out: kpt on fnl f: nt pce to chal* **6/1**[3]

1414 7 1 **Dutch Coed**[29] 6500 7-8-11 65.............................. AidenBlakemore(5) 1 63
(Nigel Tinkler) *bhd: rdn over 3f out: kpt on fnl f: n.d* **9/1**

-062 8 6 **Knightly Spirit**[27] 6578 4-8-12 61.............................. BenRobinson 11 46
(Iain Jardine) *hld up: rdn along over 3f out: no imp fr 2f out* **16/1**

5000 9 1 1/4 **Can Can Sixty Two**[1] 7489 4-8-6 58.......................... KieranSchofield(3) 8 41
(R Mike Smith) *t.k.h early: trckd ldrs: rdn over 3f out: wknd fr 2f out* **33/1**

-050 10 20 **Parole (IRE)**[33] 6341 7-8-13 65...........................(t) DannyRedmond(3) 10 6
(Tim Easterby) *hld up towards rr: struggling over 3f out: sn lost tch: t.o* **28/1**

0050 11 3/4 **Dragon Mountain**[6] 7301 4-9-6 69.............................. SeanDavis 7 8
(Keith Dalgleish) *in tch tl rdn and wknd over 2f out: t.o* **12/1**

3651 12 3 1/2 **Pioneering (IRE)**[45] 5899 5-9-4 70.......................(p) BenSanderson(3) 14 2
(Roger Fell) *t.k.h: w ldr: led after 2f to over 3f out: sn wknd: t.o (jockey said gelding failed to get cover in early stages and as a result ran too free)* **7/1**

2m 2.47s (3.47) **Going Correction** +0.325s/f (Good) 12 Ran SP% 116.9
Speed ratings (Par 103): **97,96,95,94,94 94,93,87,86,68 68,65**
CSF £128.03 CT £671.60 TOTE £22.10: £6.20, £1.30, £1.90; EX 199.30 Trifecta £2163.90.
Owner Mrs Stef Keniry **Bred** John Fallon **Trained** Middleham, N Yorks
■ Stewards' Enquiry : Jane Elliott four-day ban: used whip above permitted level (7-10 Oct)

FOCUS
Add 8yds. A wide-open apprentice handicap and it went to one of the complete outsiders. The second has been rated to his best.
T/Jkpt: Part won. £11,833.50 to a £1 stake - 0.5 winning units. T/Plt: £80.60 to a £1 stake. Pool: £54,959.34 - 497.56 winning units T/Qpdt: £21.90 to a £1 stake. Pool: £6,191.92 - 208.40 winning units **Richard Young**

7275 KEMPTON (A.W) (R-H)
Monday, September 23

OFFICIAL GOING: Polytrack: standard to slow (watered)
Wind: Moderate, half behind Weather: Overcast, drizzle/rain

7514 32RED ON THE APP STORE H'CAP 6f (P)
5:25 (5:25) (Class 5) (0-75,75) 3-Y-O
£3,752 (£1,116; £557; £400; £400; £400) **Stalls Low**

Form RPR

0343 1 **Kwela**[12] 7078 3-8-12 73...(p) GeorgiaDobie(7) 4 80
(Eve Johnson Houghton) *awkward s: in tch towards rr: prog on inner to chse ldng pair 2f out: rdn to cl fnl f: led last 75yds: styd on* **6/1**[3]

4333 2 1 **Mr Buttons (IRE)**[21] 6806 3-8-13 70..........................(p) CameronNoble(3) 1 74
(Linda Stubbs) *chsd ldrs: wnt 2nd sn after 1/2-way: rdn to cl over 1f out: chal and upsides 75yds out: nt qckn* **10/1**

2252 3 3/4 **Swiss Pride (IRE)**[12] 7078 3-9-0 75.......................... AngusVilliers(7) 9 77+
(Richard Hughes) *racd freely: led: drew at least 2 l clr over 1f out: wknd and hdd last 75yds* **5/1**[2]

6026 4 1 1/4 **Turn To Rock (IRE)**[12] 7080 3-8-11 65.......................... OisinMurphy 5 63
(Ed Walker) *in tch: outpcd over 2f out: styd on over 1f out: nvr nrr but n.d* **7/1**

5045 5 3/4 **Alicia Darcy (IRE)**[4] 7380 3-9-7 75..............................(b) HollieDoyle 6 70
(Archie Watson) *dwlt: pushed along early and racd in last pair: rdn and outpcd whn impeded 2f out: styd on fr over 1f out: nrst fin* **9/1**

5633 6 5 **Jungle Juice (IRE)**[5] 7345 3-9-1 74.......................... ScottMcCullagh(5) 8 53
(Mick Channon) *mostly in last pair: outpcd over 2f out: brief prog over 1f out: sn no hdwy* **12/1**

-005 7 7 **Almokhtaar (USA)**[91] 4179 3-8-9 63..........................(b[1]) JamieSpencer 2 20
(Kevin Ryan) *taken down early: mostly chsd ldr to sn after 1/2-way: wknd qckly: t.o (trainers' rep said gelding was unsuited by the drop in trip and would prefer going back up to a mile)* **7/2**[1]

0312 8 1 **Fancy Flyer**[9] 7204 3-8-9 70.. LukeBacon(7) 7 24
(Dean Ivory) *t.k.h: spd on outer to 1/2-way: wknd: t.o* **7/1**

4423 9 2 3/4 **Lorna Cole (IRE)**[19] 6851 3-9-1 69..............................(b) MartinDwyer 3 14
(William Muir) *pressed ldrs: disp 2nd pl 1/2-way to jst over 2f out: wknd rapidly: t.o* **10/1**

1m 12.6s (-0.50) **Going Correction** +0.075s/f (Slow) 9 Ran SP% 114.0
Speed ratings (Par 101): **106,104,103,102,101 94,85,83,80**
CSF £63.12 CT £322.77 TOTE £6.40: £1.50, £3.10, £1.50; EX 56.80 Trifecta £300.40.
Owner Mr & Mrs James Blyth Currie **Bred** Exors Of The Late Sir Eric Parker **Trained** Blewbury, Oxon

FOCUS
They went a solid gallop in this fair handicap. The winner has been rated back to her best, the second in line with his recent form, and the third close to his best.

7515 32RED CASINO FILLIES' NOVICE AUCTION STKS (PLUS 10 RACE) 1m (P)
6:00 (6:06) (Class 5) 2-Y-O
£3,881 (£1,155; £577; £288) **Stalls Low**

Form RPR

32 1 **Rosardo Senorita**[27] 6570 2-9-0 0.............................. PatCosgrave 2 77
(Rae Guest) *chsd ldrs: rdn and prog 3f out: drvn to ld wl over 1f out: styd on wl and clr fnl f* **5/1**[3]

2 2 5 **Secret Acquisition**[14] 7031 2-9-0 0.............................. DavidEgan 12 65
(Daniel Kubler) *prom but trapped wd: chsd ldr after 3f: rdn to ld wl over 2f out: hdd wl over 1f out and sn no ch w wnr: wknd fnl f but hld on for 2nd* **8/1**

53 3 1/2 **Single (IRE)**[29] 6504 2-9-0 0..................................(h) OisinMurphy 8 66+
(Mick Channon) *broke on terms but lost pl bdly and sn struggling in rr: rdn 3f out: prog on outer wl over 1f out: r.o to take 3rd last 50yds* **9/4**[1]

4 1 1/4 **Stony Look (IRE)** 2-8-11 0.. WilliamCox(3) 7 61
(Andrew Balding) *dwlt but sn wl in tch: rdn over 2f out: prog to chse clr ldng pair jst over 1f out: plugged on but no imp and lost 3rd last 50yds* **25/1**

5 1 1/2 **Untouchable Beauty** 2-9-0 0.. JamesDoyle 11 58
(Hugo Palmer) *slowest away: in tch towards rr: rdn and prog over 2f out: rchd 4th briefly fnl f but nvr any ch* **4/1**[2]

6306 6 1 **Constanzia**[12] 7079 2-9-7 65.. NicolaCurrie 10 62
(Jamie Osborne) *broke on terms but restrained into last: sme prog and shkn up over 1f out: no imp on ldrs and nvr in it* **25/1**

0 7 nk **Russian Rumour (IRE)**[39] 6118 2-9-0 0.......................... RobHornby 9 55
(Jonathan Portman) *s.i.s: wl in rr: rdn 3f out: kpt on over 1f out: nvr nrr* **20/1**

53 8 3/4 **Decanter**[14] 7031 2-9-0 0.. JasonWatson 3 53
(Sylvester Kirk) *chsd ldrs: rdn over 2f out: sn outpcd: wknd over 1f out* **11/1**

9 2 1/2 **Dancing Girl (FR)** 2-9-0 0.. LukeMorris 5 47+
(Harry Dunlop) *fractious bef ent stalls: chsd ldrs: urged along 1/2-way: wknd wl over 1f out (trainer said filly broke one of it's teeth in the stalls)* **50/1**

5 10 1 1/2 **East End Girl**[24] 6673 2-9-0 0.. DavidProbert 6 44
(Lucy Wadham) *led after 2f to wl over 2f out: wknd rapidly wl over 1f out* **12/1**

0 11 2 3/4 **Goddess Of Rome (IRE)**[19] 6858 2-9-0 0.......................... JackMitchell 1 37
(Simon Crisford) *led 2f: styd prom: drvn over 2f out: wknd rapidly* **14/1**

12 5 **Agreeable (IRE)** 2-9-0 0.. MartinDwyer 4 26
(Conrad Allen) *a in rr: wknd over 2f out: t.o* **66/1**

1m 42.71s (2.91) **Going Correction** +0.075s/f (Slow) 12 Ran SP% 117.1
Speed ratings (Par 92): **88,83,82,81,79 78,78,77,75,73 70,65**
CSF £41.37 TOTE £5.90: £1.90, £2.50, £1.50; EX 45.80 Trifecta £163.90.
Owner Top Hat And Tails **Bred** J W Haydon **Trained** Newmarket, Suffolk

The Form Book Flat 2019, Raceform Ltd, Newbury, RG14 5SJ

FOCUS
An ordinary novice. It's been rated a shade cautiously.

7516 BET AT RACINGTV.COM NURSERY H'CAP 1m (P)
6:30 (6:36) (Class 6) (0-60,62) 2-Y-O

£3,105 (£924; £461; £400; £400; £400) Stalls Low

Form RPR

060 1 **Hermano Bello (FR)**[32] 6368 2-9-6 58....................(b[1]) TomMarquand 13 62
(Richard Hannon) *pushed up fr rr to go prom after 2f: nvr appeared to be gng that wl and scrubbed along fr 1/2-way: chal on outer 2f out: hrd rdn and w ldr jst over 1f out: narrow ld last 100yds: urged along and kpt on* **8/1**

4403 2 hd **Grace Plunkett**[7] 7275 2-8-11 49....................(b) LukeMorris 14 53
(Richard Spencer) *towards rr: rdn and prog on outer wl over 2f out: clsd to chal and w ldng pair fnl f: nt qckn last 100yds* **14/1**

606 3 hd **Disarming (IRE)**[11] 7104 2-9-2 54.................... HollieDoyle 8 57
(Dr Jon Scargill) *chsd ldrs: rdn and prog on outer over 2f out: drvn into narrow ld jst over 1f out: hdd and hld last 100yds* **16/1**

400 4 4 **Impression**[26] 6592 2-9-6 58....................(p[1]) DavidProbert 9 52
(Amy Murphy) *trckd ldrs: rdn to chal 2f out: nt qckn over 1f out: fdd fnl f* **10/1**

000 5 1 **Lafontaine (FR)**[90] 4222 2-8-12 50.................... JasonWatson 6 42
(Sylvester Kirk) *wl in tch: rdn and cl up 2f out: outpcd over 1f out: no imp on ldrs after (jockey said filly hung badly left-handed)* **16/1**

0042 6 1 3/4 **Chateau Peapod**[18] 6884 2-9-4 56.................... BrettDoyle 10 44
(Lydia Pearce) *alternated ld: stl disputing towards inner over 1f out: wknd* **9/1**

065 7 3/4 **Pearl Beach**[37] 6205 2-9-5 57.................... DavidEgan 3 43
(William Knight) *dwlt: wl in rr: lft bhd over 2f out: rdn to take modest 8th over 1f out: kpt on fnl f* **14/1**

6041 8 hd **Now I'm A Believer**[11] 7111 2-8-11 49.................... KieranO'Neill 7 34
(Mick Channon) *alternated ld: stl disputing over 1f out towards inner: wknd* **15/2[3]**

6504 9 4 **Dandy Dancer**[7] 7275 2-9-2 54.................... ShaneKelly 4 30
(Richard Hughes) *t.k.h: trckd ldrs: cl up wl over 1f out: wknd qckly* **11/2[2]**

5000 10 6 **Swiss Bond**[60] 5340 2-9-7 59.................... LiamKeniry 1 21
(J S Moore) *nvr on terms w ldrs: wknd over 2f out: t.o* **50/1**

000 11 nk **Grimsthorpe Castle**[19] 6858 2-9-4 56.................... OisinMurphy 2 18
(Ed Walker) *a towards rr: rdn and no prog over 2f out: t.o* **2/1[1]**

0P00 12 1 **Austin Taetious**[17] 6927 2-8-7 45.................... RyanPowell 12 4
(Adam West) *a bhd: struggling 1/2-way: t.o* **50/1**

060 13 9 **Sooty's Return (IRE)**[13] 7056 2-8-4 45....................(p[1]) WilliamCox(3) 11
(J S Moore) *chsd ldrs on outer to 1/2-way: wknd rapidly: t.o* **50/1**

1m 42.15s (2.35) **Going Correction** +0.075s/f (Slow) 13 Ran SP% 121.7
Speed ratings (Par 93): **91,90,90,86,85 83,83,82,78,72 72,71,62**
CSF £116.19 CT £1804.12 TOTE £8.70: £2.90, £2.40, £5.10; EX 103.70 Trifecta £1697.80.
Owner Justin Dowley & Michael Pescod **Bred** Remi Boucret **Trained** East Everleigh, Wilts
■ Today Power (3-1) was withdrawn. Rule 4 applies to all bets struck prior to withdrawal, but not to SP bets. Deduction - 25p in the pound. New market formed.

FOCUS
The first three finished nicely clear in this nursery. A minor pb from the second.

7517 32RED H'CAP 1m (P)
7:00 (7:03) (Class 3) (0-90,90) 3-Y-O+

£9,337 (£2,796; £1,398; £699; £349; £175) Stalls Low

Form RPR

2524 1 **Sir Busker (IRE)**[23] 6711 3-9-4 89.................... JamieSpencer 1 98
(William Knight) *hld up in last pair: prog on inner jst over 2f out: cajoled along furiously to chal fnl f: edgd lft but styd on to ld nr fin* **17/2**

5110 2 nk **Edaraat**[31] 6425 3-9-4 89.................... JimCrowley 7 97
(Roger Varian) *hld up in 6th: clsd on ldrs 2f out: rdn to ld jst ins fnl f: edgd lft after: hdd and nt qckn nr fin* **11/4[1]**

3-13 3 1 **Cadre Du Noir (USA)**[20] 6836 3-9-2 87.................... OisinMurphy 2 92
(Martyn Meade) *dwlt and awkward s: sn rcvrd to chse ldng pair: rdn wl over 2f out: clsd to chal and disp ld jst over 1f out to jst ins fnl f: one pce last 100yds* **9/2[3]**

1652 4 hd **Pesto**[33] 6347 3-9-5 90.................... JamesDoyle 6 95
(Richard Hannon) *chsd ldrs on outer: struggling to hold pl and pushed along 1/2-way: drvn in rr 2f out: rallied fnl f: styd on to press for 3rd nr fin* **4/1[2]**

3331 5 1 1/2 **Lawmaking**[19] 6863 6-9-5 86....................(p) LiamKeniry 4 88
(Michael Scudamore) *trckd ldrs: cl up and rdn over 1f out: nt qckn and fdd ins fnl f* **6/1**

022 6 nk **Donncha (IRE)**[37] 6231 8-9-7 88.................... TomMarquand 5 89
(Seb Spencer) *dwlt: mostly in last pair: rdn over 3f out: struggling over 2f out: kpt on fnl f: nvr nrr* **18/1**

5243 7 1 1/4 **Quick Breath**[16] 6968 4-8-11 83.................... TylerSaunders(5) 3 81
(Jonathan Portman) *trckd ldr: rdn to chal 2f out: disp ld briefly jst over 1f out: wknd ins fnl f* **16/1**

-001 8 2 **Surrey Hope (USA)**[28] 6538 5-9-5 86.................... JasonWatson 8 79
(Hughie Morrison) *led: rdn 2f out: hdd & wknd jst over 1f out* **8/1**

1m 39.45s (-0.35) **Going Correction** +0.075s/f (Slow)
WFA 3 from 4yo+ 4lb 8 Ran SP% 111.9
Speed ratings (Par 107): **104,103,102,102,101 100,99,97**
CSF £30.79 CT £118.92 TOTE £8.50: £2.60, £1.40, £1.80; EX 30.90 Trifecta £194.70.
Owner Kennet Valley Thoroughbreds XI Racing **Bred** Ms Ann Foley **Trained** Angmering, W Sussex

FOCUS
A good handicap in which those held up proved favoured. A clear pb from the winner, with the fourth rated to his solid latest.

7518 32RED.COM NOVICE STKS 1m 2f 219y(P)
7:30 (7:33) (Class 4) 3-Y-O+ £6,469 (£1,925; £962; £481) Stalls Low

Form RPR

0-23 1 **Alignak**[25] 6641 3-9-2 85.................... OisinMurphy 9 84+
(Sir Michael Stoute) *trckd ldng trio: led wl over 2f out and sent for home: rdn clr over 1f out: in n.d after* **6/4[1]**

323 2 4 1/2 **Noble Music (GER)**[18] 6890 3-8-11 77.................... HarryBentley 6 71
(Ralph Beckett) *hld up in 8th: prog on inner over 3f out: rdn and styd on to chse wnr over 1f out: no imp after* **10/3[3]**

06-3 3 nk **Omnivega (FR)**[48] 5783 3-9-2 79....................(h[1]) JamieSpencer 7 75+
(David Simcock) *stdd s: hld up in last: pushed along and prog over 2f out but ldrs already gone: drvn and styd on strly over 1f out: clsd on runner-up nr fin: far too late* **3/1[2]**

4054 4 10 **Passing Clouds**[20] 6836 4-9-8 46.................... KierenFox 5 57
(Michael Attwater) *led at decent pce: kicked on over 3f out: hdd wl over 2f out: wknd qckly over 1f out* **50/1**

645- 5 nk **Master Of The Moon**[387] 6808 4-9-8 68.................... PatCosgrave 1 57
(Ismail Mohammed) *wl in tch: shkn up and outpcd over 2f out: n.d after: wknd fnl f* **16/1**

44- 6 1 1/2 **Mantovani (FR)**[267] 3159 4-9-8 0....................(w) ShaneKelly 2 54
(Harry Fry) *trckd ldng pair: wnt 2nd 4f out to 3f out: sn rdn: wknd wl over 1f out* **8/1**

04 7 2 3/4 **Sea It My Way (IRE)**[18] 6887 3-9-2 0.................... GeorgeWood 4 51
(James Fanshawe) *in tch in midfield: outpcd whn effrt over 2f out: no hdwy over 1f out: wknd sn after* **16/1**

00- 8 9 **Que Quieres (USA)**[285] 9499 3-9-2 0.................... NickyMackay 3 35
(Simon Dow) *a in rr and nudged along after 4f: nvr a factor: t.o* **100/1**

000 9 1 **Prime Approach (IRE)**[94] 4066 3-9-2 0....................(v) DavidProbert 10 34
(Brett Johnson) *a wl in rr: t.o* **150/1**

44 10 17 **Ruby Wine**[25] 6641 3-8-11 0.................... KieranO'Neill 11
(Jeremy Scott) *trapped wd: chsd ldrs tl wknd rapidly 4f out: t.o* **100/1**

11 69 **Disciple (IRE)**[347] 5-9-8 0.................... TomMarquand 8
(Amy Murphy) *chsd ldr to 4f out: wknd v rapidly and sn wl t.o* **33/1**

2m 19.99s (-1.01) **Going Correction** +0.075s/f (Slow)
WFA 3 from 4yo+ 6lb 11 Ran SP% 118.5
Speed ratings (Par 105): **109,105,105,98,98 96,94,88,87,75 25**
CSF £6.63 TOTE £2.30: £1.10, £1.40, £1.20; EX 7.50 Trifecta £19.90.
Owner Orchard Bloodstock Ltd **Bred** Miss K Rausing **Trained** Newmarket, Suffolk

FOCUS
The first three pulled well clear and the winner bounced back to form with a comfortable success. The second has been rated to her latest.

7519 100% PROFIT BOOST AT 32REDSPORT.COM H'CAP 7f (P)
8:00 (8:01) (Class 5) (0-75,75) 3-Y-O+

£3,752 (£1,116; £557; £400; £400; £400) Stalls Low

Form RPR

2003 1 **Jabalaly (IRE)**[20] 6840 3-9-4 75....................(b) JimCrowley 12 88
(Ed Dunlop) *dwlt: hld up off the pce in last trio: prog gng strly jst over 2f out: clsd over 1f out: rdn to ld jst ins fnl f: styd on wl and in command last 100yds* **8/1[3]**

2012 2 1 **Highfaluting (IRE)**[20] 6839 5-9-3 71.................... GeraldMosse 1 82
(James Eustace) *trckd ldrs: shkn up over 2f out: clsd over 1f out to chal fnl f: styd on but outpcd last 100yds* **11/8[1]**

3035 3 3 **Uncle Jerry**[17] 6913 3-8-12 74.................... SeamusCronin(5) 8 76
(Mohamed Moubarak) *trckd ldng pair: rdn to ld 2f out: hdd and one pce jst ins fnl f* **14/1**

0564 4 2 1/2 **Kamikaze Lord (USA)**[33] 6350 3-9-1 72....................(t) RobertHavlin 7 67
(John Butler) *chsd ldrs: rdn and no prog over 2f out: outpcd over 1f out: kpt on to take 4th nr fin* **5/1[2]**

4230 5 1/2 **Eula Varner**[38] 6170 5-9-7 75.................... DavidProbert 3 70
(Henry Candy) *in tch on inner: effrt 2f out: no prog over 1f out: btn after* **12/1**

6242 6 hd **Al Moataz (IRE)**[9] 7189 3-8-10 74.................... StefanoCherchi(7) 6 67
(Marco Botti) *t.k.h: pressed ldr: upsides 2f out: wknd over 1f out (jockey said gelding hung right-handed early in the home straight)* **9/1**

6064 7 1 3/4 **Born To Finish (IRE)**[7] 7273 6-9-4 72....................(p) PatCosgrave 9 62
(Ed de Giles) *awkward s: off the pce in last trio: rdn over 2f out: kpt on one pce over 1f out: nvr on terms* **33/1**

6454 8 2 1/2 **Silca Mistress**[20] 6835 4-9-7 75.................... AdamKirby 2 58
(Clive Cox) *led to 2f out: wknd qckly over 1f out* **14/1**

623 9 1 1/2 **Midas Girl (FR)**[40] 6074 3-8-10 67.................... OisinMurphy 10 45
(Ed Walker) *a in rr: rdn and no prog over 2f out* **12/1**

000 10 4 **The Establishment**[16] 6968 4-8-10 67....................(h) DarraghKeenan(3) 4 35
(John Butler) *s.s: mostly in last: nvr a factor* **50/1**

1100 11 19 **Astrospeed (IRE)**[33] 6350 4-9-2 70....................(h) GeorgeWood 5
(James Fanshawe) *plld hrd: chsd ldrs to 3f out: wknd rapidly: t.o (jockey said gelding ran too freely)* **16/1**

1m 25.61s (-0.39) **Going Correction** +0.075s/f (Slow)
WFA 3 from 4yo+ 3lb 11 Ran SP% 119.4
Speed ratings (Par 103): **105,103,100,97,97 96,94,91,90,85 63**
CSF £19.58 CT £163.82 TOTE £9.90: £3.00, £1.20, £4.10; EX 35.50 Trifecta £174.20.
Owner Hamdan Al Maktoum **Bred** Rathbarry Stud & Abbeylands Farm **Trained** Newmarket, Suffolk

FOCUS
Dropping back to seven proved key for the winner. A clear pb from the winner, and another pb from the second.

7520 WISE BETTING AT RACINGTV.COM H'CAP 1m 7f 218y(P)
8:30 (8:35) (Class 6) (0-65,66) 3-Y-O

£3,105 (£924; £461; £400; £400; £400) Stalls Low

Form RPR

4405 1 **Percy's Prince**[7] 7280 3-8-8 51....................(p[1]) LukeMorris 8 58
(Sir Mark Prescott Bt) *trckd ldr after 2f: hrd rdn to ld 2f out: plodded on in front: hrd pressed whn hung lft and bmpd rival nr fin: hld on* **11/2[3]**

0206 2 nk **Nordano (GER)**[98] 3931 3-9-6 63.................... FergusSweeney 9 70
(Neil King) *rn in snatches towards rr: rdn 4f out: prog 2f out: styd on to take 2nd ins fnl f and clsd on ldr: chalng whn bmpd nr fin: nt rcvr* **11/1**

4553 3 4 1/2 **Ignatius (IRE)**[9] 7202 3-8-10 53.................... KierenFox 2 54
(John Best) *led after 2f: rdn and hdd 2f out: wknd fnl f* **5/1[2]**

0365 4 1 **Cochise**[6] 7300 3-9-7 64....................(b[1]) JasonWatson 5 64
(Roger Charlton) *t.k.h: cl up: trckd ldng pair 5f out: rdn over 3f out: nt qckn over 2f out and wl hld after (jockey said gelding hung right-handed)* **5/2[1]**

0624 5 2 1/2 **New Expo (IRE)**[14] 7025 3-8-2 45.................... HollieDoyle 1 42
(Julia Feilden) *led 2f: trckd ldng pair to 5f out: sn rdn: styd in tch tl fdd fnl 2f* **16/1**

-040 6 12 **Maykir**[7] 7280 3-8-3 46.................... AdrianMcCarthy 4 29
(J R Jenkins) *dwlt: hld up in last: rdn over 3f out: no prog over 2f out and sn wknd* **66/1**

0000 7 17 **Angel Black (IRE)**[180] 1353 3-8-4 47.................... JosephineGordon 11 9
(Shaun Keightley) *racd wd: chsd ldrs: dropped to last and rdn 5f out: t.o* **66/1**

0406 8 nk **Riverina**[41] 6046 3-8-5 48....................(b[1]) GeorgeWood 7 10
(Harry Dunlop) *t.k.h: trckd ldrs: stl gng strly 4f out: rdn and wknd qckly 3f out: t.o (jockey said filly stopped quickly)* **25/1**

The Form Book Flat 2019, Raceform Ltd, Newbury, RG14 5SJ

305 9 11 **Waterfall**[21] 6811 3-9-5 **62**.......................... DavidProbert 3 11
(Lucy Wadham) *reluctant to enter stalls: t.k.h: hld up in last pair: stl gng wl 4f out: rdn and wknd rapidly 3f out: t.o* **25/1**

3m 32.52s (2.42) **Going Correction** +0.075s/f (Slow) 9 Ran SP% **85.5**
Speed ratings (Par 99): **96,95,93,93,91 85,77,77,71**
CSF £30.70 CT £110.47 TOTE £4.80: £1.60, £2.90, £1.40; EX 44.30 Trifecta £134.10.
Owner W F Charnley Helen Jones & Chris Jenkins **Bred** Chris Jenkins **Trained** Newmarket, Suffolk
■ Whistler Bowl was withdrawn. Price at time of withdrawal 2/1f. Rule 4 applies to all bets - deduction 30p in the pound
■ Stewards' Enquiry : Luke Morris caution; careless riding
Fergus Sweeney two-day ban; misuse of whip (Oct 7-8)

FOCUS
A moderate staying handicap. The second helps set the level.
T/Plt: £95.10 to a £1 stake. Pool: £67,179.30 - 515.24 winning units T/Qpdt: £29.80 to a £1 stake. Pool: £11,914.16 - 295.13 winning units **Jonathan Neesom**

7054 **LEICESTER** (R-H)
Monday, September 23

OFFICIAL GOING: Good to firm (good in places, watered, 7.6)
Wind: Fresh behind Weather: Cloudy turning to rain after race 6

7521 BRITISH STALLION STUDS EBF KEGWORTH NOVICE STKS (PLUS 10 RACE) 7f
1:50 (1:53) (Class 3) 2-Y-O £6,469 (£1,925; £962; £481) Stalls High

Form RPR
1 **Highest Ground (IRE)** 2-9-5 0.......................... RyanMoore 11 86+
(Sir Michael Stoute) *s.s: pushed along and bhd whn swtchd rt over 5f out: hdwy over 2f out: led wl over 1f out: r.o wl* **3/1**[2]
6 2 2 ¾ **Macho Boy (IRE)**[16] 6948 2-9-5 0.......................... JasonWatson 8 76
(Brian Meehan) *chsd ldrs: rdn and edgd rt over 1f out: r.o to go 2nd nr fin* **33/1**
3 nk **Well Prepared** 2-9-5 0.......................... PatDobbs 4 76
(Richard Hannon) *led: hdd wl over 1f out: styd on same pce ins fnl f* **40/1**
22 4 2 **Law Of Peace**[17] 6912 2-9-5 0.......................... WilliamBuick 1 70
(Charlie Appleby) *chsd ldrs: rdn over 1f out: hung lft and styd on same pce ins fnl f* **8/15**[1]
6 5 hd **Dulas (IRE)**[73] 4886 2-9-5 0.......................... KieranShoemark 10 70+
(Charles Hills) *hld up: plld hrd: hdwy and hung rt fr over 1f out: nt rch ldrs (jockey said colt ran too free)* **9/2**[3]
446 6 1 ½ **Trumpets Call (IRE)**[18] 6892 2-9-0 72.......................... ThomasGreatrex(5) 3 66
(David Loughnane) *prom: chsd ldr over 5f out: rdn and ev ch wl over 1f out: no ex ins fnl f* **50/1**
7 2 ¼ **Zambezi Magic** 2-9-5 0.......................... (h[1]) HectorCrouch 6 60
(Clive Cox) *dwlt: in rr and pushed along over 4f out: styd on fr over 1f out: nt trble ldrs* **50/1**
5 8 1 ¾ **Tiger Zone (IRE)**[46] 5860 2-9-5 0.......................... LiamKeniry 2 56
(Clive Cox) *hld up: hdwy over 2f out: rdn and wknd over 1f out* **100/1**
6 9 ½ **Son Of Red (IRE)**[17] 6927 2-9-5 0.......................... TomQueally 9 54
(Alan King) *hld up: shkn up over 2f out: wknd over 1f out* **100/1**
10 4 **Real Poet (IRE)** 2-9-5 0.......................... DavidProbert 5 44
(Sir Michael Stoute) *prom: rdn over 2f out: wknd over 1f out* **40/1**
11 nk **Mostaqel (IRE)** 2-9-5 0.......................... JimCrowley 7 43
(Richard Hannon) *w ldr tl over 5f out: remained handy tl wknd over 1f out* **25/1**

1m 23.33s (-2.37) **Going Correction** -0.35s/f (Firm) 2y crse rec 11 Ran SP% **126.0**
Speed ratings (Par 99): **99,95,95,93,93 91,88,86,86,81 81**
CSF £96.28 TOTE £5.30: £1.80, £5.60, £11.70; EX 90.40 Trifecta £1499.10.
Owner Niarchos Family **Bred** Niarchos Family **Trained** Newmarket, Suffolk

FOCUS
This interesting novice event produced a fair winning time.

7522 ASTON FLAMVILLE FILLIES' NURSERY H'CAP 6f
2:20 (2:21) (Class 5) (0-75,75) 2-Y-O £3,493 (£1,039; £519; £300; £300; £300) Stalls High

Form RPR
005 1 **Clever Candy**[29] 6514 2-8-6 **60**.......................... HarryBentley 10 67+
(Michael Bell) *hld up in tch: rdn over 1f out: led ins fnl f: styd on wl* **16/1**
5321 2 1 ¾ **Come On Girl**[34] 6313 2-8-8 **62**.......................... RaulDaSilva 8 62
(Tony Carroll) *led: plld hrd: rdn and edgd lft over 1f out: edgd rt and hdd ins fnl f: styd on same pce* **20/1**
3633 3 nk **Rusalka (IRE)**[6] 7309 2-8-2 **56**.......................... (t) DuranFentiman 1 55
(Tim Easterby) *hld up: hdwy over 2f out: rdn and ev ch over 1f out: styd on same pce ins fnl f* **6/1**
536 4 ½ **Charming Spirit (IRE)**[17] 6928 2-9-7 **75**.......................... AndreaAtzeni 5 73
(Roger Varian) *prom: lost pl over 4f out: hdwy u.p over 1f out: r.o* **10/3**[1]
6555 5 ¾ **Go Well Spicy (IRE)**[20] 6833 2-9-6 **74**.......................... CallumShepherd 4 69
(Mick Channon) *chsd ldrs: wnt 2nd over 2f out: rdn and ev ch over 1f out: no ex ins fnl f* **4/1**[2]
6164 6 ¾ **Ebony Adams**[32] 6372 2-8-12 **66**.......................... JasonWatson 7 59
(Brian Meehan) *prom: rdn over 2f out: no ex fnl f* **9/1**
5405 7 1 ¼ **Bella Brazil (IRE)**[32] 6372 2-8-13 **67**.......................... (b[1]) TomEaves 6 56
(David Barron) *s.i.s: hld up: rdn over 2f out: hung rt fr over 1f out: nt trble ldrs* **12/1**
2213 8 3 **Prissy Missy (IRE)**[7] 7284 2-8-7 **61**.......................... DavidProbert 11 41
(David Loughnane) *chsd ldr tl shkn up over 2f out: rdn over 1f out: wknd ins fnl f* **9/1**
5005 9 7 **Maisie Ellie (IRE)**[16] 6979 2-8-6 **60**.......................... (t[1]) JFEgan 3 19
(Paul George) *s.i.s: sn pushed along in rr: rdn over 2f out: sn wknd* **100/1**
050 10 4 **Ruby Power (IRE)**[16] 6948 2-8-13 **67**.......................... RyanMoore 2 14
(Richard Hannon) *chsd ldrs: rdn over 2f out: wknd over 1f out: eased fnl f* **5/1**[3]

1m 11.14s (-0.96) **Going Correction** -0.35s/f (Firm) 2y crse rec 10 Ran SP% **113.4**
Speed ratings (Par 92): **92,89,89,88,87 86,84,80,71,66**
CSF £286.46 CT £2182.22 TOTE £20.50: £5.10, £4.30, £1.80; EX 429.30 Trifecta £1071.80.
Owner C Philipps T Redman & T Trotter **Bred** Mr & Mrs Oliver S Tait **Trained** Newmarket, Suffolk

FOCUS
Not a bad fillies' nursery. The second and third have been rated to their best.

7523 JOIN RACING TV NOW (S) STKS 7f
2:55 (2:55) (Class 5) 3-Y-O £3,493 (£1,039; £519; £300; £300; £300) Stalls High

Form RPR
0044 1 **Al Suil Eile (FR)**[20] 6823 3-9-0 67.......................... JasonHart 10 67
(John Quinn) *chsd ldrs: rdn to ld 1f out: edgd rt: styd on* **4/1**
-003 2 1 ¾ **Jean Valjean**[40] 6085 3-8-7 66.......................... (h) SeanKirrane(7) 5 62
(Richard Spencer) *trckd ldrs: plld hrd: rdn and ev ch 1f out: styd on same pce wl ins fnl f* **11/4**[1]
2545 3 1 **Balata Bay**[9] 7204 3-9-4 70.......................... (b) JohnFahy 11 64
(Richard Hannon) *hld up: hdwy over 2f out: rdn over 1f out: styd on to go 3rd post* **7/2**[3]
4121 4 nk **Knockabout Queen**[9] 7172 3-9-3 68.......................... KierenFox 4 62+
(Tony Carroll) *led: racd keenly: rdn and hdd 1f out: no ex wl ins fnl f (jockey said filly ran too free)* **10/3**[2]
5 1 ½ **The Grey Goat (IRE)** 3-9-0 0.......................... AdrianMcCarthy 9 55
(Peter Charalambous) *s.i.s: outpcd: swtchd lft over 2f out: sn rdn: r.o ins fnl f: nvr nrr (jockey said gelding ran green)* **66/1**
5004 6 nk **House Deposit**[24] 6679 3-9-4 55.......................... (p) BenCurtis 7 58
(Roger Fell) *hld up: plld hrd: hdwy over 2f out: rdn over 1f out: styd on* **7/1**
0240 7 5 **Harbour Times (IRE)**[27] 6569 3-8-4 46.......................... TheodoreLadd(5) 2 36
(Patrick Chamings) *hld up: hdwy over 2f out: rdn and wknd over 1f out* **14/1**
000 8 5 **Secret Magic (IRE)**[42] 6024 3-8-10 44 ow1.......................... EoinWalsh 6 24
(Mark Loughnane) *prom: sn pushed along: lost pl over 4f out: wknd over 2f out* **100/1**
0000 9 11 **Society Sweetheart (IRE)**[47] 5797 3-8-9 43.......................... JFEgan 1
(J S Moore) *chsd ldrs: rdn 1/2-way: wknd over 2f out* **80/1**

1m 22.87s (-2.83) **Going Correction** -0.35s/f (Firm) 9 Ran SP% **114.9**
Speed ratings (Par 101): **102,100,98,98,96 96,90,85,72**
CSF £15.36 TOTE £5.70: £2.10, £1.20, £1.50; EX 17.70 Trifecta £55.60.The winner was bought in for £8000. Balata Bay was claimed by Mr D McCain Jnr for £7000. House Deposit was claimed by Mr Declan Carroll for £7000.
Owner Harmon, Bruton & Partner **Bred** Thierry De La Heronniere & Jedburgh Stud **Trained** Settrington, N Yorks

FOCUS
Typically moderate form for the class. It's been rated a shade cautiously around the principals.

7524 RACING TV H'CAP 5f
3:25 (3:25) (Class 3) (0-95,90) 3-Y-O **£7,876** (£2,357; £1,178; £590; £293) Stalls High

Form RPR
1004 1 **Shamshon (IRE)**[9] 7175 8-8-5 **81**.......................... MarcoGhiani(7) 8 89
(Stuart Williams) *hld up: pushed along 1/2-way: rdn: edgd rt and r.o ins fnl f: led post* **6/1**
332 2 nk **Pink Flamingo**[9] 7178 3-8-10 **83**.......................... CierenFallon(3) 1 90
(Michael Attwater) *chsd ldrs: led 2f out: rdn ins fnl f: hdd post* **5/1**[3]
0300 3 ½ **Spoof**[23] 6724 4-9-4 **87**.......................... (h) KieranShoemark 5 92
(Charles Hills) *s.i.s: hld up: hdwy over 1f out: r.o* **9/1**
1003 4 ½ **Free Love**[13] 7058 3-8-13 **88**.......................... TheodoreLadd(5) 7 91
(Michael Appleby) *chsd ldrs: pushed along 1/2-way: rdn and edgd rt over 1f out: styd on* **11/1**
1604 5 shd **Benny And The Jets (IRE)**[21] 6809 3-8-11 **81**.......................... TomMarquand 2 84
(Sylvester Kirk) *chsd ldrs: rdn and ev ch over 1d out: styd on same pce ins fnl f* **7/2**[2]
1311 6 1 ½ **Four Wheel Drive**[16] 6976 3-9-3 **87**.......................... (p) GrahamLee 6 85
(David Brown) *w ldr 1/2-way: sn rdn: edgd rt and styd on same pce ins fnl f* **8/1**
502 7 5 **Lord Riddiford (IRE)**[11] 7107 4-9-7 **90**.......................... JasonHart 3 70
(John Quinn) *racd freely: led 3f: sn rdn: wknd fnl f (trainers rep could offer no explanation for the poor performance)* **2/1**[1]

58.1s (-3.70) **Going Correction** -0.35s/f (Firm) 7 Ran SP% **116.0**
WFA 3 from 4yo+ 1lb
Speed ratings (Par 107): **107,106,105,104,104 102,94**
CSF £36.58 CT £269.68 TOTE £5.90: £1.90, £2.30; EX 25.90 Trifecta £218.30.
Owner T W Morley & Regents Racing **Bred** Stonethorn Stud Farms Ltd **Trained** Newmarket, Suffolk

FOCUS
There was a blanket finish to this fair sprint handicap, but it rates as sound form. The winner has has been rated in line with this year's form, and the second in line with her better form.

7525 BREEDERS BACKING RACING EBF NOVICE STKS 1m 3f 179y
4:00 (4:00) (Class 4) 3-Y-O+ £5,433 (£1,617; £808; £404) Stalls Low

Form RPR
532 1 **Look Closely**[20] 6836 3-9-2 78.......................... AndreaAtzeni 5 91
(Roger Varian) *chsd ldr tl led over 2f out: shkn up and edgd rt over 1f out: sn drvn clr* **4/1**[2]
2 2 6 **Great Esteem (IRE)**[23] 6732 3-9-2 0.......................... WilliamBuick 2 81
(Charlie Appleby) *chsd ldrs: shkn up over 3f out: chsd wnr over 1f out: sn outpcd* **1/2**[1]
41 3 3 ¼ **Monaafasah (IRE)**[89] 4234 3-9-4 0.......................... JimCrowley 1 78
(Marcus Tregoning) *led at stdy pce tl qcknd over 3f out: hdd over 2f out: wknd fnl f* **5/1**[3]
12 4 9 **Mankayan (IRE)**[66] 5153 3-9-9 0.......................... (p[1]) StevieDonohoe 8 69
(Charlie Fellowes) *prom: rdn over 3f out: wknd over 2f out* **16/1**
5 20 **Social City** 3-9-2 0.......................... TomQueally 6 30
(Tony Carroll) *s.i.s: rn green and a in rr: wknd over 3f out* **100/1**
6 12 **Smart Samba (IRE)** 3-9-2 0.......................... GeorgeWood 4 10
(Chris Wall) *rn green in rr: rdn and wknd over 3f out (jockey said gelding ran green)* **66/1**

2m 35.08s (0.08) **Going Correction** -0.35s/f (Firm) 6 Ran SP% **111.7**
Speed ratings (Par 105): **85,81,78,72,59 51**
CSF £6.33 TOTE £3.50: £1.30, £1.30; EX 9.80 Trifecta £15.20.
Owner Sheikh Mohammed Obaid Al Maktoum **Bred** Sun Kingdom Pty Ltd **Trained** Newmarket, Suffolk

The Form Book Flat 2019, Raceform Ltd, Newbury, RG14 5SJ

FOCUS
They went steadily yet still finished strung out in this fair-looking novice contest. The second has been rated close to his debut form.

7526 HIGHFIELDS FILLIES' H'CAP — 1m 53y
4:30 (4:32) (Class 5) (0-70,72) 3-Y-O+
£3,493 (£1,039; £519; £300; £300; £300) **Stalls** Low

Form — RPR

4504 **1** **The Stalking Moon (IRE)**[35] 6276 5-8-12 **58**..........(p[1]) CierenFallon(3) 2 — 67
(Adrian Nicholls) *chsd ldrs: led over 1f out: rdn out* — **7/1**[3]

6-03 **2** 1 ½ **Nantucket (IRE)**[77] 4738 3-9-8 **69**.......................... RyanMoore 7 — 74
(Sir Michael Stoute) *hld up in tch: shkn up over 2f out: rdn to go 2nd and edgd rt wl ins fnl f: nt rch wnr* — **11/2**[2]

2340 **3** 1 ½ **Elena**[32] 6362 3-9-1 **62**.......................... KieranShoemark 12 — 64
(Charles Hills) *led: hdd over 6f out: chsd ldr: rdn over 2f out: led over 1f out: sn hdd: styd on same pce ins fnl f* — **20/1**

2254 **4** ¾ **Polyphony (IRE)**[16] 6961 4-10-1 **72**..........(h) JasonHart 9 — 72
(John Mackie) *hld up: hdwy on outer over 3f out: shkn up over 2f out: rdn and hung rt fr over 1f out: styd on* — **10/11**[1]

0000 **5** 1 ½ **Elixsoft (IRE)**[7] 7288 4-9-5 **62**..........(p) BenCurtis 5 — 59
(Roger Fell) *hld up: rdn over 1f out: r.o ins fnl f: nt rch ldrs* — **11/1**

4625 **6** ½ **Elsie Violet (IRE)**[21] 6810 3-8-11 **61**..........(b[1]) DarraghKeenan(3) 8 — 57
(Robert Eddery) *chsd ldr tl led over 6f out: rdn and hdd over 1f out: wknd wl ins fnl f* — **16/1**

5624 **7** 1 ¼ **Beatbybeatbybeat**[108] 3547 6-9-9 **66**..........(v) CamHardie 4 — 59
(Antony Brittain) *hld up: rdn over 1f out: styd on: nt trble ldrs* — **33/1**

5306 **8** 1 ¾ **Takiah**[13] 7060 4-8-0 **50** oh4..........(p) GeorgeRooke(7) 3 — 39
(Peter Hiatt) *hld up: hdwy over 3f out: sn rdn: wknd ins fnl f* — **20/1**

200 **9** ½ **Club Tropicana**[38] 6160 4-9-5 **69**..........(t) SeanKirrane(7) 1 — 57
(Richard Spencer) *s.i.s: sn pushed along to chse ldrs: rdn over 2f out: wknd ins fnl f* — **11/1**

0000 **10** 2 ¾ **Alexandrakollontai (IRE)**[7] 7288 9-8-11 **54**.......... GrahamLee 6 — 35
(Alistair Whillans) *s.i.s: rdn over 3f out: a in rr* — **33/1**

0000 **11** 11 **Plissken**[59] 5380 3-8-3 **55**.......... SophieRalston(5) 10 — 11
(Richard Price) *prom: rn wd and lost pl over 5f out: wknd over 3f out* — **100/1**

1m 43.4s (-2.90) **Going Correction** -0.35s/f (Firm)
WFA 3 from 4yo+ 4lb — **11** Ran SP% **119.2**
Speed ratings (Par 100): **100,98,97,96,94 94,93,91,90,88 77**
CSF £43.20 CT £758.28 TOTE £7.20: £1.90, £1.80, £5.10; EX 55.50 Trifecta £650.20.
Owner Lycett Racing 100 Club **Bred** Norman Orminston **Trained** Sessay, N Yorks
■ Lucky Turn was withdrawn. Price at time of withdrawal 33/1. Rule 4 does not apply

FOCUS
There was a solid pace on in this modest fillies' handicap. The third has been rated close to form.

7527 RACING EXCELLENCE "HANDS AND HEELS" APPRENTICE SERIES H'CAP (RACING EXCELLENCE SERIES) — 7f
5:05 (5:05) (Class 6) (0-65,66) 3-Y-O+
£2,846 (£847; £423; £300; £300; £300) **Stalls** High

Form — RPR

0500 **1** **Peachey Carnehan**[9] 7183 5-8-12 **53**..........(v) AmeliaGlass 9 — 60
(Michael Mullineaux) *prom: racd keenly: shkn up over 1f out: r.o to ld and edgd lft wl ins fnl f* — **20/1**

3404 **2** 1 ¼ **Tobeeornottobee**[13] 7047 3-8-9 **58**.......... JessicaAnderson(5) 12 — 61
(Declan Carroll) *racd keenly: prom: led over 2f out: shkn up over 1f out: edgd rt and hdd wl ins fnl f* — **12/1**

5534 **3** ½ **Puchita (IRE)**[55] 5517 4-8-7 **51** oh6..........(p) ZakWheatley(3) 6 — 53
(Antony Brittain) *chsd ldrs: ev ch fr over 2f out: shkn up over 1f out: styng on same pce whn nt clr run nr fin* — **14/1**

1222 **4** 1 ¾ **Miss Icon**[14] 7024 5-9-4 **62**.......... GeorgeRooke(3) 14 — 60
(Patrick Chamings) *hld up in tch: shkn up and edgd rt fr over 1f out: styd on* — **7/2**[2]

0240 **5** 4 ½ **Cotubanama**[12] 7065 3-9-5 **66**..........(p[1]) GeorgeBass(3) 4 — 51
(Mick Channon) *edgd lft s: hld up: hdwy over 2f out: shkn up over 1f out: no ex fnl f* — **25/1**

5504 **6** ½ **Pearl Spectre (USA)**[23] 6703 8-8-13 **54**..........(p) GraceMcEntee 7 — 39
(Phil McEntee) *led over 4f: wknd fnl f* — **16/1**

0002 **7** 1 ½ **Garth Rockett**[39] 6131 5-9-1 **56**..........(tp) SeanKirrane 2 — 37
(Mike Murphy) *hld up: hdwy over 2f out: sn pushed along: wknd fnl f* **4/1**[3]

0006 **8** nk **Quixote (GER)**[10] 7145 9-9-10 **65**..........(t) LukeCatton 15 — 45
(James Unett) *s.s: outpcd: nvr nrr (jockey said horse was slowly away and hung badly right-handed)* — **22/1**

6534 **9** ¾ **Espresso Freddo (IRE)**[29] 6507 5-9-3 **58**..........(p) GavinAshton 10 — 36
(Robert Stephens) *hld up: racd keenly: hdwy over 2f out: wknd over 1f out* — **8/1**

0031 **10** 2 ¾ **Hi Ho Silver**[18] 6897 5-8-11 **57**.......... PamDuCrocq(5) 5 — 28
(Chris Wall) *s.i.s and hmpd s: nvr on terms (trainer said gelding suffered interference leaving the stalls and was unsuited by racing in rear)* **10/3**[1]

6124 **11** ¾ **Misu Pete**[40] 6085 7-9-7 **65**..........(p) IsobelFrancis(3) 3 — 34
(Mark Usher) *chsd ldrs to 1/2-way* — **12/1**

0001 **12** 1 ¾ **Silvington**[20] 6844 4-8-5 **51** oh2..........(p) MolliePhillips(5) 1 — 16
(Mark Loughnane) *sn pushed along and a in rr* — **25/1**

0000 **13** 8 **Hellofagame**[39] 6107 4-8-10 **51** oh6.......... KateLeahy 11
(Richard Price) *hld up in tch: plld hrd: wknd 1/2-way* — **100/1**

1m 22.92s (-2.78) **Going Correction** -0.35s/f (Firm)
WFA 3 from 4yo+ 3lb — **13** Ran SP% **122.1**
Speed ratings (Par 101): **101,99,99,97,91 91,89,89,88,85 84,82,73**
CSF £234.55 CT £3470.87 TOTE £27.00: £5.60, £4.00, £2.60; EX 401.40 Trifecta £2327.70.
Owner Keith Jones **Bred** J M Duggan & The Late T Duggan **Trained** Alpraham, Cheshire

FOCUS
A competitive race of its type. It's been rated as straightforward form.
T/Plt: £564.20 to a £1 stake. Pool: £49,854.85 - 64.50 winning units T/Qpdt: £11.80 to a £1 stake. Pool: £6,878.22 - 428.77 winning units **Colin Roberts**

7528 - 7531a (Foreign Racing) - See Raceform Interactive

5065 FAIRYHOUSE (R-H)
Monday, September 23

OFFICIAL GOING: Good (good to yielding in places) changing to yielding after race 1 (3.00) changing to yielding to soft after race 4 (4.40)

7532a BALLYHANE BLENHEIM STKS (LISTED RACE) — 6f
5:10 (5:11) 2-Y-O — **£26,576** (£8,558; £4,054; £1,801; £900)

RPR

1 **Sir Boris (IRE)**[28] 6542 2-9-3 90.......... DeclanMcDonogh 6 — 108
(Tom Dascombe) *broke wl to ld: over 1 l clr at 1/2-way: pushed along nr side 2f out and hdd 1 1/2f out: sn rdn and kpt on wl u.p to regain advantage wl ins fnl f* — **14/1**

2 1 ½ **Soul Search (IRE)**[8] 7244 2-8-12 105.......... ColinKeane 7 — 98
(G M Lyons, Ire) *trckd ldrs in 3rd: tk clsr order in 2nd over 2f out: impr to ld nr side 1 1/2f out: sn rdn and strly pressed: hdd u.p wl ins fnl f: no ex cl home* — **5/4**[1]

3 4 ½ **Zarzyni (IRE)**[24] 6690 2-9-3 102.......... RonanWhelan 1 — 90
(M Halford, Ire) *trckd ldrs: pushed along in 2nd bef 1/2-way: lost pl over 2f out: swtchd rt in 3rd nr side under 2f out and rdn: no imp on ldrs u.p in 3rd ins fnl f: kpt on one pce* — **3/1**[3]

4 3 **Pistoletto (USA)**[11] 7119 2-9-3 98.......... DonnachaO'Brien 5 — 81
(A P O'Brien, Ire) *hld up in rr: pushed along over 2f out and no imp on ldrs over 1f out where rdn briefly: kpt on one pce in 4th wl ins fnl f* **9/4**[2]

5 ½ **Real Appeal (GER)**[38] 6190 2-9-6 0..........(b) ShaneFoley 3 — 82
(J S Bolger, Ire) *w.w in 4th: pushed along into st: rdn over 2f out and no imp on ldrs down centre: one pce after and dropped to rr wl ins fnl f* **16/1**

1m 17.18s (4.68) — **5** Ran SP% **112.8**
CSF £33.24 TOTE £7.90: £3.90, £1.30; DF 23.90 Trifecta £93.90.
Owner Mr & Mrs R Scott **Bred** Parks Farm Stud **Trained** Malpas, Cheshire

FOCUS
A tough performance from the winner and his attitude won the day.

7533 - 7535a (Foreign Racing) - See Raceform Interactive

7476 CRAON (R-H)
Monday, September 23

OFFICIAL GOING: Turf: soft

7536a PRIX DE LA COMMUNAUTE DE COMMUNES DU PAYS DE CRAON (H'CAP) (4YO+) (TURF) — 1m 7f
12:50 4-Y-O+
£23,423 (£8,900; £6,558; £3,747; £1,873; £1,405)

RPR

1 **Angelo Dream (FR)**[337] 6-8-5 **0**.......... JulienGuillochon 6 — 76
(Mlle B Dahm, France) — **245/10**

2 1 **Menuetto**[35] 4-9-0 **0**.......... MickaelBarzalona 7 — 84
(H-A Pantall, France) *prom: prog to ld over 3f out: asked to qckn 2f out: chal u.p ins fnl f: hdd fnl 50yds: drvn out* — **9/1**[3]

3 1 ½ **Smart Whip (FR)**[35] 8-9-6 **0**.......... AlexandreRoussel 9 — 88
(C Lotoux, France) — **38/1**

4 snk **Karlstad (FR)**[29] 6521 4-9-3 **0**.......... CristianDemuro 4 — 85
(Mme Pia Brandt, France) — **14/5**[1]

5 1 **Alacovia (FR)**[35] 5-8-11 **0**..........(p) TonyPiccone 8 — 78
(S Cerulis, France) — **9/1**[3]

6 nk **Sancho (FR)**[56] 5-8-6 **0**.......... AurelienLemaitre 11 — 72
(M Delcher Sanchez, France) — **19/1**

7 1 **Elysian Star (FR)**[29] 6521 5-8-7 **0**.......... JeromeClaudic 14 — 72
(B Moreno-Navarro, France) — **51/1**

8 1 ½ **Magical Forest (IRE)**[29] 6521 5-9-2 **0**.......... TheoBachelot 5 — 79
(H Blume, Germany) — **12/1**

9 1 **King Nonantais (FR)**[35] 7-8-7 **0**.......... AlexandreChesneau 13 — 69
(Andreas Suborics, Germany) — **24/1**

10 1 **Carnageo (FR)**[29] 6521 6-8-8 **0**..........(b) FabriceVeron 10 — 69
(P Monfort, France) — **15/1**

11 ½ **Shepton Joa (FR)**[75] 6-8-8 **0**..........(p) GuillaumeTrolleyDePrevaux 15 — 68
(N Paysan, France) — **19/1**

12 6 **Artificier (USA)**[35] 7-8-7 **0**.......... MlleMarylineEon 2 — 60
(Alain Couetil, France) — **42/10**[2]

13 nk **Nardo (FR)**[134] 9-9-5 **0**..........(b) ChristopherGrosbois 3 — 72
(F Foucher, France) — **13/1**

14 5 **Culmination**[29] 6521 7-9-5 **0**.......... AntoineHamelin 16 — 66
(Jo Hughes, France) *prom: struggling to go pce and pushed along over 3f out: sn lost position: grad wknd fr over 2f out* — **24/1**

15 6 **L'Ami Pierrot**[35] 4-8-10 **0**..........(b[1]) EddyHardouin 12 — 50
(Matthieu Palussiere, France) — **37/1**

16 8 **Gonzalo**[69] 5035 6-9-0 **0**..........(p) MlleCoraliePacaut 1 — 44
(N Bellanger, France) — **24/1**

3m 23.07s — **16** Ran SP% **119.7**
PARI-MUTUEL (all including 1 euro stake): WIN 25.50; PLACE 8.40, 4.10, 10.90; DF 98.10.
Owner Mlle Blandine Dahm **Bred** Mlle M Baconnet & G Morosini **Trained** France

7537 - (Foreign Racing) - See Raceform Interactive

7329 BEVERLEY (R-H)
Tuesday, September 24

OFFICIAL GOING: Soft
Wind: light across Weather: Heavy cloud and rain

7538 BEVERLEY ANNUAL BADGEHOLDERS NOVICE AUCTION STKS — 5f
2:00 (2:01) (Class 5) 2-Y-O — **£4,140** (£1,232; £615; £307) **Stalls** Low

Form — RPR

53 **1** **Able Kane**[105] 3694 2-9-5 0.......... PaulMulrennan 5 — 71
(Rod Millman) *mde most: rdn and edgd lft over 1f out: drvn and kpt on wl fnl f* — **9/2**[2]

2 **2** ¾ **Rebel Soldier Boy**[7] 7308 2-9-5 0.......... DavidNolan 1 — 68+
(David O'Meara) *cl up on inner and sn pushed along: rdn 2f out: ev ch: drvn and kpt on fnl f* — **10/11**[1]

3036 **3** *1 3/4* **Dancinginthesand (IRE)**[71] 4985 2-9-5 57 .... GrahamLee 4 62
(Bryan Smart) *cl up: rdn and ev ch over 1f out: sn drvn and kpt on same pce* **20/1**

40 **4** *hd* **Capla Spirit**[18] 6911 2-9-5 0 .... JasonHart 6 61
(Gay Kelleway) *chsd ldrs: pushed along over 2f out: rdn wl over 1f out: kpt on same pce* **5/1[3]**

00 **5** *3 1/4* **Deevious Beau**[6] 7333 2-9-5 0 .... RobbieDowney 9 50+
(David Barron) *in rr: pushed along 1/2-way: rdn wl over 1f out: kpt on fnl f (jockey said gelding stumbled shortly after the start)* **50/1**

0 **6** *1 1/2* **Bella Figlia**[41] 6064 2-9-0 0 .... BenRobinson 7 39
(Ollie Pears) *towards rr: pushed along 1/2-way: sn rdn: kpt on fnl f* **33/1**

0000 **7** *1* **Bosun's Chair**[8] 7283 2-9-5 51 ....(b) DavidAllan 2 41
(Tim Easterby) *chsd ldrs: rdn along 2f out: sn outpcd* **66/1**

8 *1 3/4* **Secret Diary** 2-9-0 0 .... DanielTudhope 8 29
(Declan Carroll) *a towards rr* **8/1**

4 **9** *12* **Knock Knock (IRE)**[17] 6979 2-9-5 0 .... BenCurtis 3
(Sylvester Kirk) *dwlt: a in rr* **12/1**

1m 4.16s (1.26) **Going Correction** +0.325s/f (Good) **9** Ran SP% **117.2**
Speed ratings (Par 95): **102,100,98,97,92 90,88,85,66**
CSF £8.90 TOTE £5.20: £1.60, £1.10, £4.20; EX 11.70 Trifecta £62.70.
Owner T H Chadney **Bred** Tom Chadney & Peter Green **Trained** Kentisbeare, Devon

FOCUS
A dreary day and the going was downgraded from good to soft all over prior to the opener. The first four dominated this modest 2yo novice event and it looked hard work late on. It's been rated cautiously.

7539 RACING TO SCHOOL EBFSTALLIONS.COM NOVICE STKS 7f 96y
2:30 (2:30) (Class 5) 2-Y-O **£4,140** (£1,232; £615; £307) **Stalls Low**

Form RPR

1 **1** **Dontaskmeagain (USA)**[15] 7023 2-9-9 0 .... JoeFanning 5 89+
(Mark Johnston) *mde all: c wd to centre off home turn: rdn along 2f out: clr ent fnl f: kpt on strly* **7/2[2]**

3 **2** *2 1/2* **Zegalo (IRE)**[17] 6948 2-9-2 0 .... AndreaAtzeni 9 76+
(Roger Varian) *trckd ldrs: effrt 2f out: sn rdn along and sltly outpcd: hdwy to chse wnr jst ins fnl f: kpt on: no imp* **8/11[1]**

553 **3** *2* **Sir Charles Punch**[11] 7151 2-9-2 77 .... GrahamLee 1 71
(James Given) *chsd ldng pair: rdn along and hdwy over 2f out: cl up wl over 1f out: sn drvn and kpt on same pce* **9/1[3]**

5 **4** *1 3/4* **Rakassah (IRE)**[18] 6928 2-8-11 0 .... ShaneKelly 8 62
(Richard Hughes) *trckd wnr: hdwy on outer and cl up over 2f out: rdn along wl over 1f out: drvn appr fnl f: grad wknd* **12/1**

0 **5** *5* **La Trinidad**[13] 7067 2-9-2 0 .... BenCurtis 2 54
(Roger Fell) *dwlt and rr whn n.m.r bnd over 4f out: hdwy 3f out: rdn along 2f out: kpt on fnl f* **50/1**

3232 **6** *2* **Bertie's Princess (IRE)**[6] 7331 2-8-8 68 .... RowanScott(3) 7 45
(Nigel Tinkler) *chsd ldrs: rdn along over 2f out: drvn wl over 1f out: sn wknd* **12/1**

05 **7** *4 1/2* **Make Me Laugh (IRE)**[19] 6892 2-9-2 0 .... PaulHanagan 4 39
(Richard Fahey) *towards rr whn hung lft bnd over 4f out: sn outpcd and bhd* **10/1**

00 **8** *16* **Hovingham (IRE)**[16] 7000 2-8-11 0 .... FayeMcManoman(5) 6
(Nigel Tinkler) *a in rr: outpcd and bhd fnl 3f* **100/1**

1m 35.61s (3.01) **Going Correction** +0.325s/f (Good) **8** Ran SP% **117.6**
Speed ratings (Par 95): **95,92,89,87,82 79,74,56**
CSF £6.57 TOTE £4.10: £1.80, £1.10, £1.70; EX 7.20 Trifecta £29.10.
Owner Crone Stud Farms Ltd **Bred** Gainesway Thoroughbreds Ltd **Trained** Middleham Moor, N Yorks

FOCUS
Again the centre was favoured from 2f out in this interesting novice contest and the third sets a fair level.

7540 PIPE AND GLASS @ BEVERLEY RACECOURSE H'CAP 7f 96y
3:05 (3:05) (Class 5) (0-75,80) 3-Y-O+
£4,032 (£1,207; £603; £302; £300; £300) **Stalls Low**

Form RPR

6221 **1** **Dubai Acclaim (IRE)**[13] 7074 4-9-1 72 ....(p) SeanDavis(3) 2 79
(Richard Fahey) *in tch: hdwy 2f out: rdn over 1f out: chal ins fnl f: styd on wl to ld last 75yds* **4/1[1]**

1144 **2** *1/2* **Ollivander (IRE)**[24] 6700 3-9-3 74 ....(v) DanielTudhope 5 79
(David O'Meara) *led: c wd towards stands' side and pushed along over 2f out: rdn wl over 1f out: drvn ent fnl f: hdd and no ex last 75yds* **6/1**

6210 **3** *1* **Valley Of Fire**[13] 7074 7-9-1 69 ....(p) LewisEdmunds 9 72
(Les Eyre) *trckd ldrs: pushed along 2f out: sn rdn and sltly outpcd: drvn and styd on wl fnl f* **10/1**

1150 **4** *3/4* **Keepup Kevin**[35] 6326 5-9-6 74 .... ShaneKelly 3 75
(Pam Sly) *trckd ldr: wd to stands' rail over 2f out: rdn along and ev ch whn nt clr run over 1f out: sn drvn and kpt on same pce* **5/1[2]**

3421 **5** *3/4* **Twin Appeal (IRE)**[8] 7289 8-9-9 80 4ex .... GemmaTutty(3) 12 80
(Karen Tutty) *wnt lft s and in rr: hdwy over 2f out: rdn wl over 1f out: styd on fnl f* **5/1[2]**

6063 **6** *1/2* **Zylan (IRE)**[8] 7289 7-9-1 69 ....(p) BenCurtis 11 67
(Roger Fell) *chsd ldrs: hdwy and wd towards stands' rail over 2f out: rdn and nt clr run over 1f out: sn swtchd rt and drvn: kpt on same pce* **16/1**

0664 **7** *1/2* **Stringybark Creek**[11] 7145 5-9-7 75 .... JasonHart 8 72
(David Loughnane) *trckd ldng pair: hdwy and wd towards stands' rail over 2f out: rdn and ev ch 1 1/2f out: sn drvn and wknd ent fnl f* **11/2[3]**

6432 **8** *2* **Coolagh Magic**[61] 5335 3-9-5 76 .... NathanEvans 6 67
(Seb Spencer) *hld up: a towards rr* **33/1**

3005 **9** *3/4* **Fox Kasper (IRE)**[14] 7049 3-8-9 66 .... DavidAllan 14 55
(Tim Easterby) *carried lft s: a towards rr* **25/1**

0140 **10** *3 1/2* **Roaring Forties (IRE)**[5] 7364 6-8-7 61 ....(b) JoeFanning 4 42
(Rebecca Bastiman) *hld up in midfield effrt and sme hdwy 3f out: rdn along over 2f out: sn wknd* **10/1**

3360 **11** *3* **Ventura Gold (IRE)**[31] 6456 4-9-5 73 .... PJMcDonald 10 46
(Steve Gollings) *hld up in midfield: hdwy to chse ldrs 3f out: rdn along over 2f out: sn wknd (vet said gelding lost its right-fore shoe)* **16/1**

1m 35.5s (2.90) **Going Correction** +0.325s/f (Good)
WFA 3 from 4yo+ 3lb **11** Ran SP% **119.7**
Speed ratings (Par 103): **96,95,94,93,92 92,91,89,88,84 80**
CSF £28.39 CT £232.25 TOTE £4.60: £1.70, £2.00, £5.10; EX 32.00 Trifecta £382.60.
Owner S & G Clayton **Bred** Rathbarry Stud & Abbeylands Farm **Trained** Musley Bank, N Yorks

FOCUS
This competitive handicap was run at a solid pace and the main action developed near side in the home straight.

7541 EDDIE AND VIOLET SMITH CONDITIONS STKS 5f
3:35 (3:36) (Class 2) 3-Y-O+ **£12,450** (£3,728; £1,864; £932; £466) **Stalls Low**

Form RPR

0500 **1** **Tarboosh**[24] 6698 6-9-0 101 .... KevinStott 4 95+
(Paul Midgley) *dwlt: hld up in rr: smooth hdwy on bit 2f out: chal over 1f out: shkn up and qcknd to ld ins fnl f* **6/5[1]**

0036 **2** *1 1/2* **Dark Shot**[13] 7073 6-9-0 85 ....(p) BenCurtis 2 90
(Scott Dixon) *set stdy pce: pushed along and qcknd wl over 1f out: sn rdn: hdd and drvn ins fnl f: kpt on* **7/1[3]**

6-61 **3** *3 1/4* **Kyllang Rock (IRE)**[42] 6056 5-9-3 105 .... DanielTudhope 7 81
(James Tate) *plld hrd: trckd ldr 2f: chsd ldng pair 2f out: rdn over 1f out: kpt on same pce (jockey said gelding ran too free; bet said that the gelding lost its right-fore shoe)* **15/8[2]**

0023 **4** *1/2* **Duke Of Firenze**[13] 7073 10-9-5 91 .... DavidAllan 3 82
(David C Griffiths) *trckd ldrs on inner: hdwy and cl up over 1f out: effrt ins fnl f: n.d* **8/1**

0-00 **5** *1/2* **Rapid Applause**[3] 7431 7-9-0 85 .... NathanEvans 6 75
(Michael Easterby) *t.k.h: chsd ldng pair: hdwy and cl up 3f out: rdn along to chal 2f out: drvn over 1f out: kpt on same pce (jockey said gelding was restless in the stalls)* **11/1**

1m 5.84s (2.94) **Going Correction** +0.80s/f (Soft)
WFA 3 from 5yo+ 1lb **5** Ran SP% **112.2**
Speed ratings (Par 109): **108,105,100,99,98**
CSF £10.29 TOTE £2.10: £1.50, £2.40; EX 8.40 Trifecta £24.20.
Owner The Guys & Dolls & Sandfield Racing **Bred** Landmark Racing Limited **Trained** Westow, N Yorks

FOCUS
This classy conditions sprint was run at anything but 5f pace and it's form to treat with some caution.

7542 SEASON FINALE H'CAP 1m 100y
4:10 (4:10) (Class 5) (0-70,72) 3-Y-O+
£4,032 (£1,207; £603; £302; £300; £300) **Stalls Low**

Form RPR

0410 **1** **Ventura Royal (IRE)**[5] 7364 4-9-7 67 ....(h) DanielTudhope 10 81
(David O'Meara) *swtchd lft s: t.k.h and racd wd early: sn cl up: led over 5f out: wd st to stands' rail over 2f out: rdn clr over 1f out: styd on* **10/3[1]**

4034 **2** *5* **Osmosis**[27] 6610 3-8-11 61 .... JasonHart 12 64
(Jason Ward) *led: hdd over 5f out: rdn along and wd st towards stands' side: chsd ldrs: rdn and lost pl 2f out: drvn over 1f out: kpt on fnl f: no ch w wnr* **5/1[3]**

3026 **3** *1* **Straight Ash (IRE)**[28] 6573 4-9-0 63 .... HarrisonShaw(3) 14 64
(Ollie Pears) *hld up in rr: hdwy towards stands' side 2f out: rdn wl over 1f out: drvn appr fnl f: kpt on* **8/1**

2300 **4** *1 1/2* **John Clare (IRE)**[85] 4440 3-9-6 70 .... ShaneKelly 13 68
(Pam Sly) *trckd ldrs on outer: wd st to stands' side: sn chsng wnr: rdn along 2f out: drvn over 1f out: sn wknd* **12/1**

3610 **5** *1/2* **Placebo Effect (IRE)**[13] 7074 4-9-7 67 ....(p) BenRobinson 8 64
(Ollie Pears) *trckd ldng pair: pushed along over 2f out: rdn wl over 1f out: sn drvn and grad wknd* **5/1[3]**

0440 **6** *1 3/4* **Showboating (IRE)**[17] 6967 11-9-2 62 ....(p) LewisEdmunds 1 55
(John Balding) *hld up: a towards rr* **11/1**

0554 **7** *hd* **Hackle Setter (USA)**[29] 6538 3-9-6 70 .... BenCurtis 6 63
(Sylvester Kirk) *trckd ldrs on inner: rdn along over 2f out: sn wknd* **4/1[2]**

6200 **8** *23* **Salam Zayed**[11] 7145 3-9-8 72 .... PaulHanagan 2 16
(Richard Fahey) *hld up towards rr: effrt and sme hdwy 3f out: rdn along over 2f out: sn wknd* **7/1**

1m 51.37s (4.97) **Going Correction** +0.80s/f (Soft)
WFA 3 from 4yo+ 4lb **8** Ran SP% **116.0**
Speed ratings (Par 103): **107,102,101,99,99 97,97,74**
CSF £20.53 CT £123.21 TOTE £4.40: £1.90, £1.70, £2.30; EX 18.80 Trifecta £100.60.
Owner Middleham Park Racing CXVII **Bred** Rabbah Bloodstock Limited **Trained** Upper Helmsley, N Yorks

FOCUS
There was a fair pace on in this modest handicap and once again the stands' side was the place to be.

7543 RFM EQUINEPHOTOS NOVICE STKS 1m 1f 207y
4:40 (4:41) (Class 5) 3-Y-O+ **£5,433** (£1,617; £808; £404) **Stalls Low**

Form RPR

52 **1** **Junooh (IRE)**[19] 6887 3-9-5 0 .... DaneO'Neill 1 79
(Sir Michael Stoute) *mde all: wd st to stands' rail: rdn clr wl over 1f out: easily* **4/7[1]**

2 *6* **Cathedral Street (IRE)** 3-9-5 0 .... JasonHart 3 67
(Mark Johnston) *trckd ldr: cl up over 3f out: rdn along 2f out: sn drvn and plugged on: no ch w wnr* **4/1[3]**

3 *6* **Zane Daddy (USA)**[86] 3-9-5 0 .... JoeFanning 2 58
(Mark Johnston) *trckd ldng pair: hdwy 3f out: rdn along 2f out: sn drvn and outpcd* **5/2[2]**

4 *15* **Montelimar**[182] 4-9-0 0 .... AndrewBreslin(5) 4 19
(Andrew Crook) *a in rr: outpcd and bhd fnl 3f* **100/1**

2m 12.72s (7.02) **Going Correction** +0.80s/f (Soft)
WFA 3 from 4yo 5lb **4** Ran SP% **113.2**
Speed ratings (Par 103): **103,98,93,81**
CSF £3.62 TOTE £1.50; EX 3.50 Trifecta £4.60.
Owner Hamdan Al Maktoum **Bred** Shadwell Estate Company Limited **Trained** Newmarket, Suffolk

FOCUS
This interesting little novice event proved tactical.

7544 BRIAN AND JASON MERRINGTON MEMORIAL AMATEUR RIDERS' H'CAP (DIV I) 1m 1f 207y
5:15 (5:16) (Class 6) (0-65,67) 3-Y-O+
£2,994 (£928; £464; £300; £300; £300) **Stalls Low**

Form RPR

2356 **1** **Thorntoun Care**[14] 7053 8-10-13 67 ....(p) MissAmyCollier(5) 2 74
(Karen Tutty) *outpcd and in rr early: stdy hdwy over 3f out: chsd ldrs 2f out: rdn to ld and edgd lft jst over 1f out: drvn and hung lft to stands' rail ins fnl f: kpt on* **11/2[2]**

4055 **2** 1 ½ **Bollin Ted**34 6343 5-11-0 63..............(p) MissEmilyEasterby 4 67
(Tim Easterby) *trckd ldrs: hdwy 3f out: led 2f out: sn rdn: hdd and sltly hmpd jst over 1f out: ev ch ins fnl f: sn swtchd rt and drvn: kpt on same pce* **6/1**3

0652 **3** 2 ¾ **Elysee Star**6 7336 4-9-12 47..............(p) MissEmmaTodd 8 46
(Mark Walford) *in tch: hdwy 3f out: rdn along 2f out: drvn over 1f out: kpt on same pce fnl f* **14/1**

6340 **4** 2 **Dark Devil (IRE)**28 6573 6-10-8 62..............(p) MrEireannCagney(5) 5 57
(Richard Fahey) *hld up towards rr: hdwy over 3f out: rdn along on inner to chse ldrs wl over 1f out: ev ch appr fnl f: sn drvn and one pce* **8/1**

0063 **5** 1 ¼ **Star Ascending (IRE)**30 6499 7-10-3 57..........(p) MrRyanHolmes(5) 14 50+
(Jennie Candlish) *t.k.h: cl up: led over 3f out: rdn along over 2f out: sn hdd: grad wknd fr over 1f out* **20/1**

0031 **6** 1 **Maldonado (FR)**35 6305 5-10-10 59..............(p) MissJoannaMason 7 50+
(Michael Easterby) *t.k.h: chsd ldrs: cl up over 7f out: led 5f out: rdn along and hdd over 3f out: grad wknd fnl 2f* **7/1**

0220 **7** 3 **Greengage (IRE)**47 5851 4-9-13 55.......... MissRachelHuskisson(7) 12 41
(Tristan Davidson) *dwlt and in rr: hdwy wl over 2f out: sn rdn and plugged on: nvr rch ldrs* **8/1**

2600 **8** *nk* **Bigbadboy (IRE)**30 6502 6-9-10 45.............. MissAlysonDeniel 1 30
(Clive Mulhall) *chsd ldrs: rdn along wl over 2f out: sn wknd* **10/1**

3011 **9** 1 ¼ **Amity Island**6 7336 4-10-0 52.............. MissSarahBowen(3) 6 35
(Ollie Pears) *towards rr: rdn along over 3f out: n.d (trainer said that the gelding didn't stay the 1m2f on rain softened ground)* **4/1**1

5603 **10** 4 ½ **Barney Bullet (IRE)**29 6545 4-9-3 45..............(e) MissPaigeHopper(7) 9 20
(Noel Wilson) *a in rr* **33/1**

11 38 **Irregardless (IRE)**81 4619 3-9-5 45..........(b1) MissSerenaBrotherton 10 +
(Donal Kinsella, Ire) *sn led: hdd over 5f out: prom: rdn along 3f out: sn wknd* **16/1**

5061 **12** 1 ½ **The Rutland Rebel (IRE)**48 5814 3-10-12 66....... MrPatrickMillman 11
(Micky Hammond) *chsd ldrs: lost pl over 4f out: sn bhd (trainer had no explanation for the gelding performance other than he was unsuited by the lack of pace in the early stages)* **9/1**

2m 13.67s (7.97) **Going Correction** +0.875s/f (Soft)
WFA 3 from 4yo+ 5lb **12 Ran SP% 123.7**
Speed ratings (Par 101): **103,101,99,98,97 96,93,93,92,88 58,57**
CSF £40.39 CT £453.43 TOTE £7.00: £2.60, £2.00, £4.80; EX 31.90 Trifecta £1017.50.
Owner Irvine Lynch & Thoroughbred Homes Ltd **Bred** W M Johnstone **Trained** Osmotherley, N Yorks

FOCUS
The first, and quicker, division of this very moderate handicap for amateur riders. The leaders went fast. Straightforward form, with the winner rated to this year's better form and the second near his mark.

7545 BRIAN AND JASON MERRINGTON MEMORIAL AMATEUR RIDERS' H'CAP (DIV II) 1m 1f 207y

5:45 (5:45) (Class 6) (0-65,65) 3-Y-0+
£2,994 (£928; £464; £300; £300; £300) **Stalls Low**

Form RPR

0316 **1** **Brutalab**8 7290 3-10-1 57..............(p) MrWilliamEasterby 8 62
(Tim Easterby) *prom: trckd ldr over 5f out: cl up over 3f out: wd st towards stands' side and led over 2f out: rdn and edgd lft to stands' rail wl over 1f out: drvn ent fnl f: jst hld on* **11/4**1

6640 **2** *shd* **Abushamah (IRE)**28 6582 8-10-5 61.............. MissEmilyBullock(5) 12 65
(Ruth Carr) *trckd ldrs: hdwy and wd st: rdn to chse wnr whn n.m.r and swtchd rt jst over 1f out: sn chal and ev ch ins fnl f: drvn and edgd rt towards fin: jst hld* **15/2**

4446 **3** 1 ¼ **Quoteline Direct**31 6456 6-10-9 60..............(h) MissBeckySmith 13 62
(Micky Hammond) *hld up towards rr: hdwy 4f out: in tch and rdn along 2f out: chsd ldrs and drvn over 1f out: kpt on fnl f* **8/1**

0-00 **4** *nk* **Major Snugfit**18 6940 3-10-8 64..............(h1) MissJoannaMason 11 66
(Michael Easterby) *hld up towards rr: hdwy 4f out: in tch and rdn along 2f out: sn drvn: styd on appr fnl f* **11/2**2

0600 **5** *nk* **Burguillos**24 6734 6-10-11 65..............(tp1) MissAliceHaynes(3) 10 65
(John Butler) *in tch: hdwy over 3f out: rdn along to chse ldng pair wl over 1f out: drvn and ch appr fnl f: kpt on same pce* **9/1**

0005 **6** 1 ½ **Dutch Artist (IRE)**39 6173 7-9-5 49 ow2......... MissBelindaJohnson(7) 5 47
(Nigel Tinkler) *dwlt: a in rr* **20/1**

1204 **7** 1 ½ **Cosmic Ray**14 7060 7-10-5 56..............(h) MrJamesHarding 6 51
(Les Eyre) *cl up: led 7f out: rdn along over 3f out: hdd wl over 2f out: sn wknd* **6/1**3

5-00 **8** 6 **Compatriot (IRE)**14 7053 5-10-4 62..............(p) MissRosieHowarth(7) 3 46
(Roger Fell) *a towards rr* **14/1**

-006 **9** 3 **Angel Of The North (IRE)**13 6760 4-9-4 48......(v) MrFinbarMulrine(7) 7 26
(Robin Dickin) *in tch: rdn along 4f out: wknd 3f out* **50/1**

0361 **10** *hd* **Rosy Ryan (IRE)**40 6103 9-10-0 51.............. MissEmmaTodd 4 29
(Tina Jackson) *led: hdd 7f out: chsd ldrs: rdn along 3f out: drvn and wknd over 2f out (trainer said that the mare didn't stay the 1m2f on the rain softened ground)* **6/1**3

0-00 **11** 33 **Monzino (USA)**39 6173 11-9-2 46 oh1.............. MissMintyBloss(7) 9
(Michael Chapman) *dwlt: a in rr: t.o fnl 3f* **100/1**

2m 14.42s (8.72) **Going Correction** +0.875s/f (Soft)
WFA 3 from 4yo+ 5lb **11 Ran SP% 117.9**
Speed ratings (Par 101): **100,99,98,98,98 97,96,91,88,88 62**
CSF £23.56 CT £149.53 TOTE £3.70: £1.20, £2.80, £2.40; EX 22.40 Trifecta £140.70.
Owner Ontoawinner 10 **Bred** D R Tucker **Trained** Great Habton, N Yorks
■ Stewards' Enquiry : Mr William Easterby two-day ban; misuse of whip (Oct 8,14)

FOCUS
As in the first division, the leaders went off rather fast. The time was 0.75sec slower. Limited form.
T/Plt: £9.70 to a £1 stake. Pool: £54,927.43 - 4,122.62 winning units. T/Qpdt: £10.40 to a £1 stake. Pool: £4,139.35 - 292.27 winning units. **Joe Rowntree**

7445 CHELMSFORD (A.W) (L-H)

Tuesday, September 24

OFFICIAL GOING: Polytrack: standard
Wind: light, half behind Weather: showers

7546 BET AT TOTESPORT.COM NOVICE STKS (PLUS 10 RACE) 5f (P)

4:50 (4:53) (Class 4) 2-Y-O £6,080 (£1,809; £904; £452) **Stalls Low**

Form RPR

0002 **1** **Electric Ladyland (IRE)**17 6979 2-9-8 87..............(b) LukeMorris 6 92
(Archie Watson) *w ldr tl led over 2f out: rdn over 1f out: styd on strly and drew clr ins fnl f* **7/2**2

1665 **2** 3 ¼ **Raahy**10 7182 2-9-9 94.............. HarryBentley 4 81
(George Scott) *led tl over 2f out: sn rdn: no ex and outpcd ins fnl f* **1/1**1

0 **3** 1 ¼ **Catechism**49 5772 2-8-11 0.............. KieranShoemark 3 65
(Richard Spencer) *chsd ldng trio but nt on terms w ldng pair: effrt ent fnl 2f: swtchd rt over 1f out: kpt on ins fnl f: nvr getting to ldrs* **9/1**

35 **4** 1 ¾ **Lady Phyllis**20 6852 2-8-6 0.............. SeamusCronin(5) 1 58+
(Michael Attwater) *stdd s: hld up off the pce in last pair: shkn up over 1f out: hdwy 1f out: swtchd rt and kpt on wl ins fnl f: nvr trbld ldrs* **20/1**

5 2 ¼ **Rathagan** 2-8-13 0.............. FinleyMarsh(3) 8 55
(Richard Hughes) *dwlt and hmpd leaving stalls: midfield: 5th and no imp over 1f out: wl hld and plugged on same pce fnl f* **14/1**

0 **6** *nse* **Falacho (IRE)**19 6899 2-8-6 0.............. ThomasGreatrex(5) 7 50
(David Loughnane) *chsd ldng pair: rdn and no imp over 2f out: wknd ins fnl f* **50/1**

7 6 **Tiger Balm** 2-8-11 0.............. JackMitchell 5 28
(George Boughey) *s.i.s: a in rr: nvr involved (jockey said filly was slowly away)* **25/1**

5 **8** ¾ **Magical Moment (FR)**18 6919 2-8-11 0.............. JamieSpencer 9 26
(Kevin Ryan) *stdd and wnt rt leaving stalls: in rr of main gp but off the pce: effrt over 2f out: no hdwy and wl btn whn eased fnl f* **4/1**3

00 **9** 8 **Dark Side Prince**7 7316 2-8-11 0.............. RayDawson(5) 10 2
(Charlie Wallis) *hung rt and wd: midfield: struggling over 2f out: wl bhd ins fnl f* **100/1**

58.75s (-1.45) **Going Correction** -0.175s/f (Stan) **9 Ran SP% 120.4**
Speed ratings (Par 97): **104,98,96,94,90 90,80,79,66**
CSF £7.53 TOTE £4.40: £1.20, £1.10, £1.20; EX 9.30 Trifecta £34.60.
Owner Miss Emily Asprey & Christopher Wright **Bred** Rathasker Stud **Trained** Upper Lambourn, W Berks

FOCUS
A fairly good juvenile novice sprint contest. Those behind the first two will likely govern the level.

7547 TOTEPOOL CASHBACK CLUB AT TOTESPORT.COM FILLIES' NOVICE MEDIAN AUCTION STKS (PLUS 10 RACE) 7f (P)

5:25 (5:27) (Class 4) 2-Y-O £6,080 (£1,809; £904; £452) **Stalls Low**

Form RPR

61 **1** **Belle Anglaise**22 6793 2-9-0 0.............. MarcoGhiani(7) 3 81
(Stuart Williams) *broke wl: restrained and in tch in midfield: shifted rt after 1f: effrt and hdwy over 1f out: chal ins fnl f: r.o wl to ld towards fin* **5/2**1

2 ½ **Cranberry** 2-9-0 0.............. DavidEgan 2 73+
(Richard Hughes) *midfield: pushed rt after 1f: effrt ent fnl 2f: swtchd rt jst over 1f out: r.o v strly ins fnl f: wnt 2nd cl home: nt quite rch wnr* **10/1**

0 **3** ½ **Paycheck**18 6911 2-9-0 0.............. JamieSpencer 7 73
(David Simcock) *w ldr early: chsd ldng trio after 1f: effrt and hdwy over 1f out: rdn to ld 1f out: hdd: edgd lft and lost 2 pls cl home* **6/1**

5420 **4** 1 **Incognito (IRE)**12 7117 2-9-0 72..............(p1) GeraldMosse 10 69
(Mick Channon) *flashing tail leaving stalls: led after almost 1f: rdn over 1f out: drvn and hdd 1f out: no ex and kpt on same pce ins fnl f* **7/2**2

0 **5** 2 ¾ **Mums The Law**31 6449 2-9-0 0.............. JFEgan 11 62
(Jane Chapple-Hyam) *restless in stalls: chsd ldr after 1f out: rdn and struggling to qckn over 2f out: losing pl and shifted rt ent fnl f: wknd ins fnl f* **33/1**

2420 **6** ½ **Feelinlikeasomeone**31 6442 2-9-0 73.............. FrannyNorton 8 61
(Mark Johnston) *led for almost 1f: chsd ldrs: effrt ent 2f out: no ex u.p 1f out: wknd ins fnl f* **10/1**

7 ½ **Taamer** 2-9-0 0.............. JimCrowley 1 59
(Charles Hills) *in tch in midfield: effrt over 1f out: no imp and wknd ins fnl f* **9/2**3

8 ½ **Sky Lake (GER)** 2-9-0 0.............. HarryBentley 6 58
(Marco Botti) *in tch in last trio: hdwy on outer over 2f out: unable qck over 1f out: wknd ins fnl f* **20/1**

9 1 ½ **Taima** 2-9-0 0.............. LukeMorris 9 54
(Sir Mark Prescott Bt) *rousted along leaving stalls: bmpd after 1f: nvr bttr than midfield: rdn and lost pl over 1f out: wl hld and plugged on same pce fnl f* **25/1**

6 **10** *nse* **Lady Codee**20 6852 2-8-9 0.............. SeamusCronin(5) 4 54
(Michael Attwater) *s.i.s: effrt and wd bnd ent fnl 2f: kpt on but nvr involved* **50/1**

11 1 ¾ **Bright Spells (IRE)** 2-9-0 0.............. NicolaCurrie 5 49
(Jamie Osborne) *rn green in rr: effrt on inner over 1f out: nvr involved* **20/1**

1m 26.77s (-0.43) **Going Correction** -0.175s/f (Stan) **11 Ran SP% 119.7**
Speed ratings (Par 94): **95,94,93,92,89 89,88,87,86,86 84**
CSF £27.21 TOTE £2.90: £1.30, £3.40, £2.00; EX 33.20 Trifecta £198.10.
Owner Graf Stauffenberg **Bred** Howard Barton Stud **Trained** Newmarket, Suffolk
■ Stewards' Enquiry : Marco Ghiani two-day ban; careless riding (Oct 8-9)

FOCUS
A fair juvenile fillies' novice auction maiden contest. It's likely the form is no better than rated.

7548 EXTRA PLACES AT TOTESPORT.COM NURSERY H'CAP 1m (P)

6:00 (6:02) (Class 5) (0-75,76) 2-Y-O
£5,175 (£1,540; £769; £400; £400; £400) **Stalls Low**

Form RPR

663 **1** **Oslo**32 6402 2-9-7 75..............(v1) JimCrowley 4 78
(Sir Michael Stoute) *t.k.h: hld up in tch towards rr: effrt and hdwy over 1f out: led ins fnl f: r.o strly* **3/1**2

350 **2** 1 **London Calling (IRE)**33 6372 2-9-0 68.............. KieranShoemark 8 69
(Richard Spencer) *t.k.h: hld up in tch in rr: effrt and hdwy on outer over 1f out: pressed ldrs ins fnl f: chsd wnr and kpt on fnl 100yds* **25/1**

3411 **3** 1 ½ **Lady Red Moon**38 6221 2-9-1 76.............. StefanoCherchi(7) 5 74
(Marco Botti) *t.k.h: hld up in tch in midfield: effrt over 1f out: pressing ldrs whn struck on nose by rivals whip 1f out: kpt on same pce ins fnl f* **7/1**3

4254 **4** 1 **African Swift (USA)**17 6965 2-9-7 75.............. FrannyNorton 10 70
(Mark Johnston) *led and grad crossed to inner: rdn ent fnl 2f: drvn and edgd rt over 1f out: hdd ins fnl f: no ex and wknd towards fin* **8/1**

450 **5** *hd* **More Than A Prince**11 7162 2-9-7 75.............. PatDobbs 3 70
(Richard Hannon) *chsd ldrs: wnt 2nd 5f out: rdn ent fnl 2f: ev ch and drvn whn carried rt over 1f out: no ex ins fnl f: wknd towards fin* **8/1**

554 **6** 1 ¾ **Webuyanyhorse**24 6718 2-9-5 73.............. NicolaCurrie 6 64
(Jamie Osborne) *t.k.h: pressed ldr tl 5f out: styd chsng ldrs: effrt on inner over 1f out: unable qck 1f out and wknd ins fnl f (vet said gelding lost its right hind shoe)* **8/1**

004 **7** ¾ **Locked N' Loaded**20 6858 2-9-2 70.............. RossaRyan 9 63+
(Richard Hannon) *t.k.h: hld up in tch in rr: swtchd rt ent fnl 2f: continually denied a run fr over 1f out tl ins fnl f: any ch had gone and wl hld after (jockey said colt was denied a clear run and hung left-handed throughout)* **14/1**

3314 **8** 3/4 **Banmi (IRE)**[26] 6632 2-8-13 **72**............................... SeamusCronin(5) 2 59
(Mohamed Moubarak) *chsd ldrs: effrt over 1f out: unable qck u.p and wknd ins fnl f* **16/1**

2114 **9** 2 1/4 **Luna Wish**[7] 7315 2-8-6 **67**............................... MarcoGhiani(7) 1 53+
(George Margarson) *t.k.h: wl in tch in midfield on inner: short of room 5f out: effrt on inner over 1f out: no imp and wknd ins fnl f (jockey said filly ran too freely)* **9/4**[1]

000 **10** 1/2 **Thank The Irish (IRE)**[11] 7154 2-9-0 **68**............................... DougieCostello 7 49
(Jamie Osborne) *in tch in midfield on outer: hdwy and effrt to chse ldrs over 2f out: unable qck over 1f out: wknd ins fnl f* **50/1**

1m 39.74s (-0.16) **Going Correction** -0.175s/f (Stan) **10** Ran SP% **120.0**
Speed ratings (Par 95): **93,92,90,89,89 87,86,86,83,83**
CSF £76.74 CT £499.25 TOTE £3.30: £1.70, £7.70, £2.20; EX 80.00 Trifecta £531.60.
Owner K Abdullah **Bred** Juddmonte Farms Ltd **Trained** Newmarket, Suffolk

FOCUS
A fair nursery. It's been rated as ordinary form.

7549 IRISH LOTTO AT TOTESPORT.COM H'CAP (DIV I) 1m (P)

6:30 (6:34) (Class 6) (0-55,55) 3-Y-O+

£3,105 (£924; £461; £400; £400; £400) **Stalls** Low

Form RPR

0003 **1** **Masai Spirit**[8] 7282 3-9-1 **52**............................... KieranShoemark 4 59
(Philip McBride) *chsd ldrs: rdn and outpcd over 2f out: swtchd rt and rallied u.p over 1f out: styd on to ld wl ins fnl f: gng away at fin* **6/1**[3]

0006 **2** 1 1/4 **Emojie**[19] 6885 5-8-8 **46**...............................(b[1]) RayDawson(5) 7 50
(Jane Chapple-Hyam) *led: rdn and kicked clr w rival over 2f out: kpt on wl u.p tl hdd and no ex wl ins fnl f* **12/1**

644 **3** 3/4 **Penarth Pier (IRE)**[15] 7024 3-9-4 **55**............................... HollieDoyle 5 57
(Christine Dunnett) *pushed along leaving stalls and sn chsd ldr: rdn and kicked clr w ldr over 2f out: ev ch over 1f out tl no ex and outpcd wl ins fnl f* **9/2**[1]

4500 **4** 2 1/2 **Edge (IRE)**[26] 6643 8-9-5 **52**...............................(b) StevieDonohoe 9 49
(Bernard Llewellyn) *hld up in tch: hdwy and swtchd rt ent fnl 2f: drifted rt and drvn over 1f out: kpt on ins fnl f: nvr trbld ldrs* **5/1**[2]

2002 **5** 1 **Red Cossack (CAN)**[116] 3304 8-9-0 **47**...............................(b) LukeBacon(7) 8 48
(Dean Ivory) *awkward leaving stalls and slowly away: t.k.h: hld up in rr: effrt on inner jst over 1f out: kpt on ins fnl f: nvr trbld ldrs (jockey said gelding fly leapt leaving the stalls)* **8/1**

0100 **6** nk **Three C's (IRE)**[8] 7281 5-9-3 **50**...............................(p) PatCosgrave 6 44
(George Boughey) *t.k.h: chsd ldrs: rdn and outpcd over 2f out: drvn over 1f out: nvr getting bk on terms and kpt on same pce ins fnl f* **6/1**[3]

0000 **7** 1 1/2 **Roser Moter (IRE)**[15] 7034 4-8-7 **45**...............................(t[1]) KevinLundie(5) 1 35
(Michael Appleby) *in tch in midfield: outpcd u.p over 1f out: no threat to ldrs and kpt on same pce ins fnl f* **50/1**

0655 **8** 2 3/4 **Paddy's Pursuit (IRE)**[15] 7024 3-8-13 **55**............... ThomasGreatrex(5) 3 39
(David Loughnane) *hld up in tch towards rr: rdn over 3f out: outpcd over 2f out: no threat to ldrs after: plugged on ins fnl f* **9/2**[1]

-430 **9** 10 **Dreamingofdiamonds (IRE)**[39] 6152 3-9-0 **51**.......... DanielMuscutt 10 12
(David Lanigan) *stdd after s: hld up in last pair: outpcd over 2f out: no ch fnl 2f* **28/1**

400 **10** 1 3/4 **Treasured Company (IRE)**[27] 6610 3-8-8 **45**..........(e[1]) FrannyNorton 2 2
(Richard Guest) *taken down early: t.k.h: hld up in midfield: rdn and struggling over 2f out: wknd and bhd fnl f* **8/1**

0414 **11** nse **Harlequin Rose (IRE)**[15] 7028 5-9-4 **54**..................... CierenFallon(3) 11 11
(Patrick Chamings) *in tch towards rr and wd: rdn over 3f out: sn struggling and bhd over 1f out* **12/1**

1m 38.71s (-1.19) **Going Correction** -0.175s/f (Stan) **11** Ran SP% **124.6**
WFA 3 from 4yo+ 4lb
Speed ratings (Par 101): **98,96,96,93,92 92,90,87,77,76 76**
CSF £80.64 CT £364.41 TOTE £7.50: £2.30, £2.90, £2.10; EX 104.30 Trifecta £628.90.
Owner Mrs Jacqui Barrs & P J McBride **Bred** Steve Lock **Trained** Newmarket, Suffolk

FOCUS
The first division of a moderate handicap. The joint-fourth favourite's winning time was about a second quicker than the previous C&D nursery and the second division of this contest. The third, fifth and seventh highlight the limitations of the form.

7550 IRISH LOTTO AT TOTESPORT.COM H'CAP (DIV II) 1m (P)

7:00 (7:03) (Class 6) (0-55,55) 3-Y-O+

£3,105 (£924; £461; £400; £400; £400) **Stalls** Low

Form RPR

6543 **1** **Sharp Operator**[15] 7028 6-9-4 **51**...............................(h) DavidEgan 2 58
(Charlie Wallis) *hld up in tch in midfield: nt clr run ent fnl 2f: hdwy between rivals 1f out: chsd ldr 100yds out: styd on to ld cl home* **4/1**[2]

0432 **2** 1/2 **Red Skye Delight (IRE)**[19] 6885 3-9-0 **51**............... KieranO'Neill 10 56
(Luke McJannet) *taken down early: led: rdn over 1f out: kpt on but drifted rt ins fnl f: hdd cl home* **9/2**[3]

0650 **3** 1 1/4 **Tellovoi (IRE)**[5] 7374 11-8-13 **46**...............................(p) PhilipPrince 8 48
(Richard Guest) *taken down early: stdd s: hld up in rr: effrt on inner over 1f out: styd on wl ins fnl f to snatch 3rd last stride: nvr getting to ldrs* **20/1**

0600 **4** shd **Sittin Handy (IRE)**[32] 6389 3-8-3 **45**...............................(p) SophieRalston(5) 6 47
(Dean Ivory) *chsd ldrs: drvn to chse ldr over 1f out: kpt on same pce and lost 2 pls ins fnl f* **50/1**

0003 **5** 1/2 **Merdon Castle (IRE)**[20] 6855 7-8-10 **46**............... MeganNicholls(3) 4 47
(Michael Blake) *hld up in tch towards rr: effrt and swtchd lft over 1f out: kpt on ins fnl f: nvr getting to ldrs* **5/1**

1300 **6** 1 **Quick Monet (IRE)**[29] 6546 6-9-0 **47**............................... RaulDaSilva 1 45
(Shaun Harris) *chsd ldr: effrt ent fnl 2f: lost 2nd over 1f out: no ex and wknd fnl 100yds* **6/1**

0213 **7** 1 **Voice Of A Leader (IRE)**[24] 6723 8-9-7 **54**............... JoeyHaynes 3 50
(Chelsea Banham) *hld up wl in tch in midfield: unable qck u.p over 1f out: kpt on same pce ins fnl f* **7/2**[1]

0063 **8** 1/2 **Squire**[5] 7374 8-9-5 **52**...............................(tp) LukeMorris 7 47
(Marjorie Fife) *dwlt: t.k.h: hld up in tch towards rr: effrt over 1f out: drvn 1f out: one pce and no imp* **7/1**

-000 **9** 7 **Sesame (IRE)**[34] 6342 3-9-4 **55**............................... AlistairRawlinson 5 34
(Michael Appleby) *mounted in the chute: restless in stalls: dwlt and swtchd lft after s: hld up in rr: effrt over 2f out: rdn over 1f out: sn btn and wknd* **20/1**

0000 **10** 22 **Another Approach (FR)**[13] 7081 3-8-8 **45**............... NicolaCurrie 11
(Amanda Perrett) *midfield on outer: lost pl and bhd over 2f out: lost tch over 1f out (jockey said filly stopped quickly)* **14/1**

1m 39.74s (-0.16) **Going Correction** -0.175s/f (Stan) **10** Ran SP% **122.0**
WFA 3 from 6yo+ 4lb
Speed ratings (Par 101): **93,92,91,91,90 89,88,88,81,59**
CSF £23.04 CT £336.30 TOTE £4.40: £1.70, £1.80, £9.40; EX 24.90 Trifecta £268.00.
Owner Lee Brooks **Bred** Bumble Bloodstock & Mrs S Nicholls **Trained** Ardleigh, Essex

FOCUS
The second division of a moderate handicap. The second-favourite's winning time was about a second slower. Modest form, rated around the winner.

7551 BET IN PLAY AT TOTESPORT.COM H'CAP 7f (P)

7:30 (7:32) (Class 3) (0-90,90) 3-Y-O+ **£9,703** (£2,887; £1,443; £721) **Stalls** Low

Form RPR

4/1- **1** **Alfarqad (USA)**[362] 7692 4-9-0 **83**............................... JimCrowley 2 91
(Owen Burrows) *chsd ldr: effrt and upsides over 1f out: drvn to ld 100yds out: styd on wl* **3/1**[2]

3522 **2** nk **Michele Strogoff**[19] 6886 6-8-9 **83**............................... TheodoreLadd(5) 3 90
(Michael Appleby) *led: rdn 2f out: hrd pressed and drvn over 1f out: hdd 100yds out: kpt on wl but a hld after* **8/1**

5243 **3** 1 3/4 **Alemaratalyoum (IRE)**[5] 7372 5-9-7 **90**...............................(p) JamieSpencer 5 92
(Stuart Williams) *hld up in tch in midfield: swtchd rt and effrt over 1f out: kpt on u.p ins fnl f: nvr getting to ldrs* **2/1**[1]

0310 **4** nk **Jaleel**[18] 6913 3-8-13 **85**...............................(b) JackMitchell 4 85+
(Roger Varian) *hld up in tch in rr: effrt whn nt clr run and hmpd over 1f out: sn swtchd lft and hdwy: kpt on ins fnl f: nvr getting to ldrs* **7/1**

411 **5** 1 3/4 **Aljari**[32] 6388 3-9-4 **90**............................... LukeMorris 7 86
(Marco Botti) *in tch in last trio: effrt over 2f out: c towards centre and rdn wl over 1f out: edgd rt 150yds out: kpt on but nvr threatened ldrs* **8/1**

5006 **6** 1/2 **Glory Of Paris (IRE)**[10] 7191 5-8-10 **79**............................... LiamJones 6 74
(Michael Appleby) *taken down early: chsd ldng trio: effrt over 2f out: drvn over 1f out: no ex and wknd fnl 100yds* **25/1**

214- **7** 7 **Madkhal (USA)**[326] 8804 3-9-4 **90**............................... PatCosgrave 1 65
(Saeed bin Suroor) *chsd ldng pair: effrt on inner over 1f out: unable qck and btn 1f out: wknd ins fnl f* **5/1**[3]

5200 **8** 7 **Florencio**[13] 7089 6-9-1 **84**...............................(p) DougieCostello 8 42
(Jamie Osborne) *hood removed late: hld up in tch in last trio: effrt ent fnl 2f: sn struggling and wknd over 1f out (jockey said he was slow to remove the blindfold)* **50/1**

1m 24.09s (-3.11) **Going Correction** -0.175s/f (Stan) **8** Ran SP% **115.5**
WFA 3 from 4yo+ 3lb
Speed ratings (Par 107): **110,109,107,107,105 104,96,88**
CSF £27.44 CT £58.17 TOTE £3.40: £1.50, £1.80, £1.30; EX 27.10 Trifecta £102.50.
Owner Hamdan Al Maktoum **Bred** Three Chimneys Farm Llc **Trained** Lambourn, Berks

FOCUS
The feature contest was a decent handicap. The second-favourite won well in a good comparative time. A step forward from the winner, with the second a better guide to the level than the third and fourth.

7552 DOUBLE DELIGHT HAT-TRICK HEAVEN AT TOTESPORT.COM H'CAP 6f (P)

8:00 (8:00) (Class 5) (0-70,72) 3-Y-O+

£5,175 (£1,540; £769; £400; £400; £400) **Stalls** Centre

Form RPR

4110 **1** **Fantastic Flyer**[43] 6025 4-9-7 **70**...............................(p) JoeyHaynes 8 80
(Dean Ivory) *wl in tch: clsd to trck ldrs over 2f out: effrt to chal and edgd lft 1f out: led ins fnl f: r.o wl* **10/1**

0311 **2** 1/2 **Grisons (FR)**[11] 7157 3-9-2 **70**............................... WilliamCox(3) 4 78
(Clive Cox) *taken down early: awkward leaving stalls: wl in tch in midfield on inner: effrt and ev ch jst over 1f out: kpt on wl: hld towards fin (jockey said colt fly leapt leaving the stalls)* **4/1**[2]

0620 **3** 2 **Three Card Trick**[24] 6715 3-9-7 **72**...............................(p[1]) JamieSpencer 9 74
(Kevin Ryan) *led: rdn and drifted rt wl over 1f out: edgd lft u.p 1f out: hdd ins fnl f: no ex and one pce wl ins fnl f* **16/1**

0521 **4** 1/2 **Desert Fox**[26] 6631 5-9-5 **68**............................... RossaRyan 5 68+
(Mike Murphy) *hld up in rr: nt clr run: swtchd lft and effrt over 1f out: swtchd rt and styd on u.p ins fnl f: nt rch ldrs* **2/1**[1]

0664 **5** shd **Kraka (IRE)**[26] 6631 4-9-5 **68**...............................(v) KieranO'Neill 10 68
(Christine Dunnett) *t.k.h: pressed ldr: rdn over 1f out: struggling to qckn and sltly impeded jst ins fnl f: wknd ins fnl f* **12/1**

1540 **6** hd **Real Estate (IRE)**[75] 4835 4-9-5 **68**...............................(p) CallumShepherd 6 71+
(Michael Attwater) *hld up in tch in midfield: clsd to chse ldrs whn squeezed for room and hmpd jst ins fnl f: swtchd rt 100yds out: kpt on towards fin: no threat to ldrs (jockey said gelding was denied a clear run)* **14/1**

0104 **7** 1/2 **Creek Harbour (IRE)**[13] 7078 4-9-1 **69**............................... WilliamCarver(5) 1 66
(Milton Bradley) *pressed ldr on inner: drvn over 1f out: bmpd jst ins fnl f: unable qck and wknd ins fnl f* **8/1**[3]

-003 **8** 1 **Kingsley Klarion (IRE)**[53] 5629 6-8-4 **56** oh1.......... DarraghKeenan(3) 7 50+
(John Butler) *hld up in tch in last trio: clsd over 1f out: nt clr run: hmpd and swtchd lft jst ins fnl f: kpt on but no threat to ldrs (jockey said gelding was denied a clear run)* **14/1**

0000 **9** 3 1/2 **Black Isle Boy (IRE)**[7] 7311 5-9-9 **72**............................... HarryBentley 2 66+
(David C Griffiths) *chsd ldrs: effrt over 1f out: nt clr run and hmpd jst ins fnl f: n.d after: eased towards fin* **8/1**[3]

0051 **10** nse **Dahik (IRE)**[31] 6462 4-8-13 **62**...............................(b) CamHardie 11 45
(Michael Easterby) *chsd ldrs on outer: unable qck u.p over 1f out: wknd ins fnl f* **14/1**

10-0 **11** 4 **Faraasah (IRE)**[13] 7085 4-9-7 **70**............................... DougieCostello 12 40
(Jamie Osborne) *hld up in last trio: effrt and hung rt wl over 1f out: sn btn and bhd ins fnl f (jockey said gelding hung right-handed)* **40/1**

1m 11.52s (-2.18) **Going Correction** -0.175s/f (Stan) **11** Ran SP% **120.7**
WFA 3 from 4yo+ 2lb
Speed ratings (Par 103): **107,106,103,103,102 102,101,100,95,95 90**
CSF £51.14 CT £664.09 TOTE £10.80: £3.30, £1.80, £3.60; EX 48.20 Trifecta £660.30.
Owner Mrs L A Ivory **Bred** Gracelands Stud **Trained** Radlett, Herts
■ Wotadoll was withdrawn. Price at time of withdrawal 25/1. Rule 4 does not apply.

FOCUS
An ordinary handicap. A 4yo won well from towards the head of the handicap in a good comparative time for the grade. There was plenty of trouble on the inside in the final furlong. Sound form.

7553 BOOK YOUR CHRISTMAS PARTY HERE H'CAP 1m 6f (P)

8:30 (8:30) (Class 6) (0-65,66) 3-Y-O+

£3,105 (£924; £461; £400; £400; £400) **Stalls** Low

Form RPR

60-1 **1** **Spice War**[21] 6843 4-9-8 **59**............................... ThomasGreatrex(5) 3 66+
(Oliver Sherwood) *mde all: rdn over 2f out: styd on wl and in command ins fnl f* **11/10**[1]

0032 **2** 2 1/2 **Royal Dancer**[15] 7025 3-8-12 **52**............................... LukeMorris 2 57
(Sylvester Kirk) *chsd wnr for 3f: chsd ldrs tl effrt to chse wnr again ent fnl 2f: hrd drvn over 1f out: kpt on same pce ins fnl f* **12/1**

The Form Book Flat 2019, Raceform Ltd, Newbury, RG14 5SJ

5413 **3** 3/4 **Barca (USA)**[20] 6864 5-10-0 **60** JimCrowley 4 63
(Marcus Tregoning) *chsd ldrs: chsd wnr 3f out tl over 2f out: kpt on same pce u.p fr over 1f out* **7/4**[2]
3342 **4** 4 1/2 **Brittanic (IRE)**[12] 7109 5-10-1 **66** (p) DylanHogan(5) 5 63
(David Simcock) *hld up in tch in midfield: effrt over 2f out: sn outpcd: wl hld and plugged on same pce fr over 1f out* **8/1**[3]
3020 **5** 3/4 **Das Kapital**[60] 5378 4-9-3 **49** (p) JFEgan 6 45
(John Berry) *stdd s: t.k.h: hld up in last pair: effrt over 2f out: sn outpcd: wl hld and plugged on same pce fr over 1f out* **25/1**
0204 **6** 9 **Earthly (USA)**[25] 6681 5-9-4 **50** (tp) StevieDonohoe 8 33
(Bernard Llewellyn) *t.k.h: hld up in tch in midfield: rdn and outpcd over 2f out: sn btn and wl hld over 1f out* **12/1**
0040 **7** 12 **Tobacco Road (IRE)**[14] 7060 9-9-3 **49** (t) CharlieBennett 7 16
(Mark Pattinson) *stdd s: t.k.h: hld up in rr: rdn over 3f out: lost tch over 2f out* **33/1**

3m 1.24s (-1.96) **Going Correction** -0.175s/f (Stan)
WFA 3 from 4yo+ 8lb **7** Ran SP% **117.3**
Speed ratings (Par 101): **98,96,96,93,93 88,81**
CSF £16.98 CT £23.56 TOTE £1.60: £1.20, £3.70; EX 13.30 Trifecta £43.60.
Owner Apiafi And Black **Bred** Chasemore Farm **Trained** Upper Lambourn, Berks

FOCUS
A modest staying handicap. The favourite won convincingly off his own tactically increasing tempo.
T/Jkpt: Not Won. T/Plt: £45.70 to a £1 stake. Pool: £43,424.98 - 949.71 winning units. T/Qpdt: £16.20 to a £1 stake. Pool: £7,418.49 - 455.18 winning units. **Steve Payne**

7200 LINGFIELD (L-H)
Tuesday, September 24

OFFICIAL GOING: Polytrack: standard
Wind: Fresh, mostly behind Weather: Fine but cloudy

7554 FOLLOW AT THE RACES ON TWITTER H'CAP 1m 1y(P)
1:50 (1:52) (Class 5) (0-75,75) 3-Y-O+
£3,428 (£1,020; £509; £300; £300; £300) **Stalls** High

Form RPR
0626 **1** **Pytilia (USA)**[86] 4424 3-9-3 **75** OisinMurphy 12 84
(Richard Hughes) *prom on outer: chsd ldr 5f out: rdn to ld over 1f out: drvn out* **9/2**[2]
2204 **2** 1 1/4 **Fares Poet (IRE)**[27] 6593 3-9-0 **75** (h) CierenFallon(3) 9 81
(Marco Botti) *hld up bhd ldrs: effrt over 2f out: drvn to chse wnr fnl f: no imp after* **8/1**
-002 **3** 1/2 **Bombastic (IRE)**[12] 7125 4-9-3 **71** PatCosgrave 3 76
(Ed de Giles) *stdd s: hld up in last pair: prog on outer 3f out: rdn 2f out: kpt on to take 3rd nr fin* **6/1**
4440 **4** 3/4 **Oneovdem**[88] 4320 5-9-2 **75** TheodoreLadd(5) 10 78
(Tim Pinfield) *won battle for ld fr wd draw: rdn 2f out: hdd over 1f out: fdd ins fnl f* **16/1**
3060 **5** 1/2 **Here's Two**[38] 6201 6-9-2 **70** DavidProbert 8 72
(Ron Hodges) *hld up towards rr: stl there 2f out: prog on outer over 1f out: styd on but too late to threaten* **28/1**
0223 **6** 1/2 **Scheme**[25] 6686 3-9-3 **75** (v) LukeMorris 4 76
(Sir Mark Prescott Bt) *prom: rdn over 2f out: hanging and nt qckn over 1f out: btn after* **10/3**[1]
-254 **7** hd **Carnival Rose**[48] 5813 3-9-2 **74** GeorgeWood 11 74
(James Fanshawe) *hld up in last trio: stl there but gng wl enough 2f out: pushed along on inner over 1f out: limited prog and nvr in it* **17/2**
6640 **8** 1 **Pheidippides**[20] 6863 4-9-6 **74** (b) JackMitchell 6 72
(Tom Clover) *wl in tch in midfield: rdn and nt qckn over 1f out: no prog after (vet said gelding lost it's left-fore shoe)* **8/1**
0250 **9** 1 **Merweb (IRE)**[17] 6961 4-9-2 **73** JaneElliott(3) 7 69
(Heather Main) *chsd ldr 3f: rdn 3f out: wknd over 1f out* **5/1**[3]
1205 **10** 1 **Mr Mac**[169] 1655 5-9-2 **70** (p) TomMarquand 1 63
(Peter Hedger) *stdd s: hld up in last: rdn and no prog 2f out* **20/1**

1m 36.36s (-1.84) **Going Correction** -0.275s/f (Stan)
WFA 3 from 4yo+ 4lb **10** Ran SP% **119.1**
Speed ratings (Par 103): **98,96,96,95,95 94,94,93,92,91**
CSF £41.37 CT £225.72 TOTE £5.80: £3.30, £2.60, £2.20; EX 39.70 Trifecta £379.40.
Owner K Dhunjibhoy & Z Dhunjibhoy **Bred** Mike Pietrangelo **Trained** Upper Lambourn, Berks
■ Stewards' Enquiry : Oisin Murphy £140 fine; unapproved whip

FOCUS
The early fractions were fast but there was a tailwind in the straight and the pace did not collapse.

7555 EVIE WALLAGE WISH TREE MAIDEN AUCTION STKS 1m 1y(P)
2:20 (2:22) (Class 5) 2-Y-O **£3,428** (£765; £254) **Stalls** High

Form RPR
4 **1** **Revestar (IRE)**[16] 7000 2-9-3 0 JackMitchell 7 78
(Simon Crisford) *trckd ldr after 2f: rdn to chal over 2f out: led over 1f out: hrd pressed fnl f: kpt on nr fin* **9/4**[1]
35 **2** 1 **Inca Man (FR)**[32] 6433 2-8-11 0 RossaRyan 2 70+
(Paul Cole) *chsd ldrs: rdn over 2f out and sn outpcd: styd on over 1f out: fin wl* **9/2**[2]
2 dht **Princesse Animale** 2-8-6 0 CharlieBennett 5 65
(Pat Phelan) *trckd ldrs: wnt 3rd 3f out: chal on inner over 1f out: upsides fnl f: no ex last 75yds* **33/1**
4 1 3/4 **Aquascape (IRE)** 2-9-1 0 RobertHavlin 11 72
(Harry Dunlop) *led: rdn and hdd over 1f out: short of room sn after: one pce* **33/1**
5 1 1/2 **Summer Palace (USA)** 2-9-2 0 JamieSpencer 6 68+
(Alan King) *towards rr: pushed along and prog over 2f out: chsd ldng quartet fnl f: kpt on steadily* **9/2**[2]
6 3 1/2 **Indigo Times (IRE)** 2-9-2 0 CallumShepherd 9 59
(David Simcock) *dwlt: wl in rr: pushed along over 2f out: prog over 1f out: tk 6th fnl f but no hdwy after (jockey said gelding ran green)* **40/1**
7 1 1/2 **Total Perfection (IRE)** 2-9-2 0 OisinMurphy 8 56
(Richard Hannon) *t.k.h: trckd ldrs: lost pl over 2f out: fdd over 1f out* **8/1**
8 hd **Nicks Not Wonder** 2-9-3 0 NicolaCurrie 1 57
(Jamie Osborne) *stdd s: hld up in last: pushed along 2f out: kpt on steadily after: nvr in it (jockey said colt hung left-handed in the straight)* **16/1**
9 hd **Filo's Flyer (IRE)** 2-8-11 0 HollieDoyle 12 50
(Archie Watson) *t.k.h: trckd ldr 2f: prom tl wknd over 1f out* **9/1**
04 **10** 2 **Ventura Star (IRE)**[12] 7104 2-9-1 0 DanielMuscutt 3 50
(David Lanigan) *nvr beyond midfield: struggling over 2f out: wknd* **13/2**[3]
11 **10** **Bee Able (USA)** 2-8-12 0 RobHornby 4 24
(Ralph Beckett) *s.i.s: a wl in rr: t.o* **10/1**
12 **3** **Alizes (FR)** 2-8-11 1 ow1 MitchGodwin(3) 10 19
(Harry Dunlop) *prom on outer to 1/2-way: wknd qckly: t.o* **50/1**

1m 37.09s (-1.11) **Going Correction** -0.275s/f (Stan) **12** Ran SP% **126.8**
Speed ratings (Par 95): **94,93,93,91,89 86,84,84,84,82 72,69**
WIN: 3.30 Revestar; PL: 1.30 Revestar, 2.60 Inca Man, 15.80 Princesse Animale; EX: R/IM 7.10 R/PA 121.90; CSF: R/PA 50.46, R/IM 6.38; TF: R/IM/PA 306.70, R/PA/IM 1011.70.
Owner Stanley Lodge **Bred** Tullpark Ltd **Trained** Newmarket, Suffolk

FOCUS
A fair maiden, and it paid to be up with the pace.

7556 OILFIELD INSURANCE AGENCIES BRITISH EBF NURSERY H'CAP 5f 6y(P)
2:55 (2:56) (Class 5) (0-70,70) 2-Y-O
£4,787 (£1,424; £711; £355; £300; £300) **Stalls** High

Form RPR
532 **1** **Augustus Caesar (USA)**[29] 6548 2-9-7 **70** AdamKirby 1 77
(David O'Meara) *mde all: drvn to assert over 1f out: pressed again last 75yds: a holding on* **11/10**[1]
6226 **2** nk **Newyorkstateofmind**[9] 7227 2-9-5 **68** MartinDwyer 2 74
(William Muir) *pressed wnr: rdn and nt qckn over 1f out: styd on again ins fnl f: a jst hld* **10/1**
5024 **3** 3 **Royal Council (IRE)**[42] 6041 2-9-7 **70** TomMarquand 6 65
(James Tate) *mostly in last trio: rdn 2f out: prog over 1f out: styd on to take 3rd nr fin* **4/1**[2]
3503 **4** nk **Dynamighty**[43] 6029 2-9-4 **67** KieranShoemark 4 61
(Richard Spencer) *dwlt sltly but chsd ldrs: drvn to dispute 3rd over 2f out: one pce over 1f out* **16/1**
2405 **5** 1/2 **Lilkian**[10] 7179 2-9-1 **64** JosephineGordon 3 56
(Shaun Keightley) *hld up: short of room and snatched up after 100yds: mostly in last after: nudged along and stylish hdwy fnl f: nvr in it* **10/1**
5232 **6** shd **Airbrush (IRE)**[9] 7227 2-9-6 **69** OisinMurphy 8 61
(Richard Hannon) *dwlt sltly: in rr: effrt over 2f out: one pce and no prog over 1f out* **6/1**[3]
6344 **7** nk **Queen Aya**[25] 6667 2-9-1 **64** PatCosgrave 5 55
(Ed Walker) *chsd ldrs: rdn to dispute 3rd over 2f out: fdd over 1f out* **9/1**
4606 **8** 2 **Shani**[7] 7296 2-8-12 **61** (p[1]) KieranO'Neill 7 44
(John Bridger) *trapped wd and lost grnd 4f out: wd again bnd 2f out and btn* **33/1**
020 **9** 4 **Force Of Impact (IRE)**[34] 6330 2-9-2 **65** JFEgan 9 34
(Paul George) *trapped wdst of all and lost grnd 4f out: wd bnd 2f out and wknd (vet said colt was lame on it's left-fore leg)* **25/1**

57.59s (-1.21) **Going Correction** -0.275s/f (Stan) 2y crse rec **9** Ran SP% **122.8**
Speed ratings (Par 95): **98,97,92,92,91 91,90,87,81**
CSF £15.13 CT £38.23 TOTE £2.20: £1.30, £2.00, £1.50; EX 14.40 Trifecta £49.70.
Owner Lamont Racing **Bred** China Horse Club International Limited **Trained** Upper Helmsley, N Yorks

FOCUS
The pace held up here, the two up front dominating throughout. The winner's latest second at Southwell could be better than rated.

7557 SKY SPORTS RACING ON SKY 415 H'CAP 5f 6y(P)
3:25 (3:26) (Class 6) (0-60,59) 3-Y-O+
£2,781 (£827; £413; £300; £300; £300) **Stalls** High

Form RPR
6015 **1** **Devil Or Angel**[27] 6602 4-8-13 **55** (p) ThoreHammerHansen(5) 5 63
(Bill Turner) *pressed ldr: rdn to chal over 1f out: kpt on wl to ld nr fin* **10/1**
0602 **2** nk **Brogans Bay (IRE)**[25] 6682 4-9-4 **55** OisinMurphy 3 62
(Simon Dow) *led: drvn over 1f out: kpt on but worn down nr fin* **11/4**[1]
0404 **3** 3 1/4 **Molly Blake**[10] 7172 3-9-4 **56** AdamKirby 2 51
(Clive Cox) *dwlt: rousted to rcvr and chsd ldng pair on inner 1/2-way: rdn and no imp over 1f out* **11/4**[1]
3060 **4** nk **Awake In Asia**[36] 6285 3-9-0 **52** (p) PatCosgrave 7 46
(Charlie Wallis) *chsd ldrs: rdn over 1f out: one pce and no imp* **20/1**
0034 **5** nk **Flowing Clarets**[30] 6510 6-8-10 **47** LiamJones 6 40
(John Bridger) *restrained after s and swtchd to inner: mostly in midfield: rdn and kpt on same pce over 1f out* **12/1**
0-40 **6** nk **Penwood (FR)**[15] 7024 4-8-13 **50** RobHornby 10 42
(Joseph Tuite) *racd on outer: pressed ldng pair to 1/2-way: steadily lost pl fnl 2f* **12/1**
531 **7** 1/2 **Miss Gargar**[24] 6737 3-9-7 **59** (v) RobertHavlin 9 50
(Harry Dunlop) *hld up in rr fr wd draw: pushed along and only modest prog fnl f: nvr in it (jockey said filly was denied a clear run)* **7/1**[2]
4225 **8** 1/2 **Starchant**[23] 6754 3-8-11 **49** KieranO'Neill 8 37
(John Bridger) *dwlt: racd wdst of all: lost grnd bnd 2f out and in rr: one pce after* **8/1**[3]
0054 **9** 6 **Sandfrankskipsgo**[36] 6285 10-9-2 **53** TomQueally 4 20
(Peter Crate) *dwlt: hld up in last pair: nvr a factor* **9/1**
0-60 **10** 3/4 **Staffa (IRE)**[82] 4556 6-9-0 **51** CharlesBishop 1 15
(Denis Coakley) *s.i.s: a in rr: no ch over 1f out* **20/1**

57.66s (-1.14) **Going Correction** -0.275s/f (Stan)
WFA 3 from 4yo+ 1lb **10** Ran SP% **120.9**
Speed ratings (Par 101): **98,97,92,91,91 90,90,89,79,78**
CSF £39.16 CT £98.67 TOTE £11.50: £3.20, £1.50, £1.30; EX 49.10 Trifecta £201.70.
Owner Mrs Tracy Turner **Bred** Lady Whent **Trained** Sigwells, Somerset

FOCUS
As in the nursery that preceded it, this handicap was fought out by the two leaders, who drew clear of the rest. Small personal bests from the first two.

7558 OILFIELD OFFSHORE UNDERWRITING H'CAP 1m 7f 169y(P)
4:00 (4:00) (Class 6) (0-65,67) 4-Y-O+
£2,781 (£827; £413; £300; £300; £300) **Stalls** Low

Form RPR
1501 **1** **Casa Comigo (IRE)**[27] 6601 4-9-0 **58** KierenFox 3 68+
(John Best) *hld up in tch: clsd on ldrs gng strly 3f out: rdn to ld over 1f out: sn clr: comf* **2/1**[1]
2P02 **2** 5 **Continuum**[24] 6720 10-9-7 **65** (v) TomQueally 10 69
(Peter Hedger) *rel to r and lft 15 l: ct up after 6f: prog 3f out: rdn and hung fire 2f out: r.o over 1f out to take 2nd nr fin (jockey said gelding was slowly away)* **7/1**
0434 **3** 1/2 **Banta Bay**[10] 7202 5-8-5 **49** JosephineGordon 11 52
(John Best) *trckd ldrs: urged along over 2f out: prog on inner to chse wnr fnl f: no imp and lost 2nd nr fin* **7/1**

5011 **4** ½ **Giving Back**[7] 7300 5-9-9 **67** 5ex..............................(v) DavidProbert 2 70
(Alan King) *hld up in rr: prog 4f out: cruised through on inner to ld over 2f out: drvn wl over 1f out: sn hdd and fnd nil* **11/4**[2]

0564 **5** 7 **Dancing Lilly**[32] 6400 4-8-5 **49**.................................. MartinDwyer 8 43
(Debbie Hughes) *hanging rt most of way: trckd ldr: chal and upsides over 2f out: wknd over 1f out (jockey said filly hung right-handed)* **11/2**[3]

5506 **6** 2¼ **Sir Fred (IRE)**[20] 6853 4-8-2 **46** oh1............................ HollieDoyle 5 38
(Julia Feilden) *prom: lost pl after 4f: struggling in rr 5f out: tried to rally over 2f out: no threat over 1f out (jockey said gelding ran in snatches)* **16/1**

3234 **7** 1½ **Danglydontask**[27] 6601 8-8-3 **47**..............................(b) KieranO'Neill 4 37
(Mike Murphy) *led to over 2f out: sn wknd* **12/1**

00-5 **8** ¾ **Bazooka (IRE)**[37] 4661 8-8-11 **62**..........................(bt[1]) EllieMacKenzie(7) 6 51
(David Flood) *hld up: prog on outer 5f out: rdn and wknd over 2f out* **25/1**

4525 **9** 20 **Lazarus (IRE)**[17] 6982 5-8-5 **49**..............................(tp) GeorgeWood 7 14
(Amy Murphy) *nvr beyond midfield: rdn 4f out: wknd 3f out: t.o (jockey said gelding stopped quickly)* **12/1**

0/0 **10** 12 **Montys Angel (IRE)**[10] 7202 9-7-11 **46** oh1.............. RhiainIngram(5) 1
(John Bridger) *trckd ldrs tl rdn and lost pl 5f out: sn struggling in last: t.o (jockey said mare stopped quickly)* **50/1**

3m 19.92s (-5.78) **Going Correction** -0.275s/f (Stan) **10** Ran SP% **127.5**
Speed ratings (Par 101): **103,100,100,100,96 95,94,94,84,78**
CSF £18.97 CT £90.77 TOTE £3.40: £1.20, £2.00, £2.20; EX 22.90 Trifecta £118.00.
Owner Simon Malcolm **Bred** Simon Malcom **Trained** Oad Street, Kent

FOCUS
A well-run staying handicap. The winner has threatened to rate this high.

7559 VISIT ATTHERACES.COM NOVICE STKS 1m 2f (P)
4:30 (4:37) (Class 5) 3-Y-O+ **£3,428** (£1,020; £509; £254) **Stalls** Low

Form RPR

3 **1** **Good Tidings (FR)**[11] 7159 3-9-2 0.............................. RobertHavlin 6 84
(John Gosden) *trckd ldr after 3f: led over 2f out: shkn up and edgd rt fr over 1f out: styd on wl* **10/11**[1]

2 2½ **Nsnas (IRE)** 3-9-2 0.. OisinMurphy 7 79
(Saeed bin Suroor) *sn trckd ldrs: wnt 3rd 3f out: effrt to chse wnr fnl f and briefly looked a threat: pushed along and no imp after* **7/4**[2]

24 **3** 5 **Final Orders**[50] 5742 3-9-2 0..................................(p[1]) RyanPowell 1 69
(Simon Crisford) *led to over 2f out: fdd fnl f* **9/2**[3]

4 **4** 2½ **Exmoor Beast**[24] 6732 3-8-9 0............................ AledBeech(7) 2 64
(Peter Charalambous) *trckd ldr 3f: styd cl up: urged along and outpcd 3f out: nt on terms after* **33/1**

64- **5** nk **Chicago Guy**[430] 5209 3-9-2 0................................ DavidProbert 5 63
(Alan King) *hld up in last pair: outpcd and pushed along over 3f out: wl off the pce 2f out: kpt on steadily fnl f (vet said gelding was lame on it's right-fore)* **50/1**

3 **6** 40 **Overbeck (IRE)**[19] 6887 4-9-7 0................................ JoeyHaynes 4
(Dean Ivory) *reluctant to come on to the crse: reluctant to enter stalls: in tch to 4f out: sn wknd: t.o* **25/1**

2m 2.82s (-3.78) **Going Correction** -0.275s/f (Stan)
WFA 3 from 4yo 5lb **6** Ran SP% **115.7**
Speed ratings (Par 103): **104,102,98,96,95 63**
CSF £2.86 TOTE £1.60: £1.10, £1.40; EX 3.40 Trifecta £6.50.
Owner HH Sheikh Zayed bin Mohammed Racing **Bred** David Powell **Trained** Newmarket, Suffolk
■ Flashdanza was withdrawn. Price at time of withdrawal 100/1. Rule 4 does not apply.

FOCUS
This went as the market predicted.

7560 WATCH SKY SPORTS RACING IN HD H'CAP 1m 2f (P)
5:05 (5:06) (Class 5) (0-70,69) 3-Y-O+ **£3,428** (£1,020; £509; £300; £300; £300) **Stalls** Low

Form RPR

0031 **1** **Contrast (IRE)**[35] 6324 5-9-6 **66**..............................(b) CamHardie 9 74
(Michael Easterby) *dwlt: hld up wl in rr: gng easily but stl there 3f out: prog over 2f out: urged along and clsd qckly on ldrs over 1f out: r.o to ld last 75yds* **9/1**

1214 **2** nk **Kendergarten Kop (IRE)**[35] 6317 4-9-8 **68**.................... DavidProbert 2 75
(David Flood) *hld up in midfield: gng easily 3f out: prog over 2f out: rdn and hanging over 1f out: clsd to chal last 100yds: jst outpcd* **7/1**[3]

2232 **3** ½ **Stormbomber (CAN)**[21] 6840 3-9-4 **69**........................ OisinMurphy 12 75
(Ed Walker) *prom in chsng gp: wnt 2nd over 2f out: clsd to ld 1f out: drvn fnl f: hdd and no ex last 75yds* **6/4**[1]

6530 **4** 1 **Tangramm**[31] 6439 7-9-8 **68**..(p) RyanTate 5 72
(Dean Ivory) *hld up towards rr: prog on outer over 2f out: clsd on ldrs w others over 1f out: ch 100yds out: no ex* **16/1**

0035 **5** 1 **Sweet Charity**[29] 6538 4-9-8 **68**.............................. CharlesBishop 7 70
(Denis Coakley) *hld up in midfield: prog over 2f out: clsd w others over 1f out: one pce ins fnl f* **8/1**

0620 **6** 2¼ **Noble Fox**[31] 6469 3-9-3 **68**..(p) AdamKirby 3 66
(Clive Cox) *hld up in rr: rdn and prog over 2f out: nt pce to cl on ldrs over 1f out: plugged on* **10/1**

0453 **7** nk **Noble Peace**[24] 6717 6-9-2 **62**..............................(b) RobertHavlin 13 59
(Lydia Pearce) *prom: led after 3f and sn clr: 6 l up over 2f out: hdd & wknd 1f out* **25/1**

0301 **8** 3 **Ruby Gates (IRE)**[24] 6733 6-9-6 **69**...................... DarraghKeenan(3) 6 60
(John Butler) *cl up in chsng gp: drvn on inner 2f out: tried to cl over 1f out but no imp fnl f* **20/1**

0663 **9** 1½ **Settle Petal**[13] 7083 5-9-1 **64**.................................. PaddyBradley(3) 1 52
(Pat Phelan) *prom in chsng gp: chsd clr ldr over 3f out to over 2f out: wknd (jockey said mare ran flat)* **12/1**

4-06 **10** 6 **Top Top (IRE)**[108] 3604 3-9-3 **68**................................ TomMarquand 10 44
(Sir Michael Stoute) *s.s: a in rr: rdn and no prog over 2f out* **11/2**[2]

3000 **11** nk **Narjes**[6] 7344 5-9-2 **67**...(h) RhiainIngram(5) 11 42
(Laura Mongan) *s.s: a in rr: rdn and no prog over 2f out: bhd after* **33/1**

6/30 **12** 12 **Onomatopoeia**[82] 4547 5-9-5 **65**................................... KierenFox 14 16
(Camilla Poulton) *t.k.h: hld up in midfield: rdn and wknd over 2f out: t.o* **66/1**

5305 **13** 14 **Eddie Cochran (IRE)**[19] 6886 3-8-12 **68**....... ThoreHammerHansen(5) 8
(Richard Hannon) *led 3f: chsd ldr: rdn 1/2-way: wknd over 3f out: eased and t.o* **33/1**

006- **14** 36 **Finisher (USA)**[313] 9082 4-9-1 **64**................................. TimClark(3) 4
(Mark Gillard) *s.s: a last and nvr gng: t.o (jockey said gelding was never travelling)* **66/1**

2m 3.12s (-3.48) **Going Correction** -0.275s/f (Stan)
WFA 3 from 4yo+ 5lb **14** Ran SP% **129.1**
Speed ratings (Par 103): **102,101,101,100,99 97,97,95,94,89 89,79,68,39**
CSF £71.78 CT £151.76 TOTE £10.20: £2.80, £1.80, £1.20; EX 75.10 Trifecta £248.70.
Owner A Saha Racing **Bred** Lynn Lodge Stud **Trained** Sheriff Hutton, N Yorks

FOCUS
This was run at a strong pace and the finish was fought out mainly by hold-up horses.
T/Plt: £18.30 to a £1 stake. Pool: £64,779.65 - 2,571.71 winning units. T/Qpdt: £3.70 to a £1 stake. Pool: £7,962.52 - 1,591.48 winning units. **Jonathan Neesom**

6992 FONTAINEBLEAU
Tuesday, September 24

OFFICIAL GOING: Turf: soft

7561a PRIX DE LA SOCIETE DES COURSES DE RAMBOUILLET (CLAIMER) (3YO) (TURF) 1m
2:00 3-Y-O **£8,558** (£3,423; £2,567; £1,711; £855)

RPR

1 **Synchrone (FR)**[203] 1028 3-8-6 0............................ MlleMarieVelon(9) 1 72
(J-P Gauvin, France) **48/10**[3]

2 1¼ **Vida Pura (FR)**[94] 3-8-4 0.............................. AugustinMadamet(7) 10 65
(A Fabre, France) **14/5**[1]

3 ¾ **Jaayiz (IRE)**[16] 3-9-2 0..(b) ThomasTrullier(3) 8 71
(P Monfort, France) **22/5**[2]

4 1¼ **Great Gunnar** 3-8-8 0.. AlexandreChesneau(3) 9 60
(Vaclav Luka Jr, Czech Republic) **19/1**

5 snk **Sarati (FR)**[61] 3-8-5 0.. MlleLeaBails(6) 7 60
(M Maillard, France) **53/10**

6 8 **Faux Pas**[123] 3-8-4 0...(b) BenjaminMarie(7) 11 41
(F Head, France) **19/1**

7 shd **Think Love (IRE)**[272] 3-8-3 0.............................. MlleAmbreMolins(8) 6 41
(J Parize, France) **78/10**

8 ¾ **Life's A Breeze (IRE)**[124] 3-8-9 0....................... MlleFriedaValleSkar(9) 4 46
(R Le Gal, France) **11/1**

9 hd **Melissa (FR)**[25] 6789 3-8-3 0.. HugoBesnier(5) 2 36
(Ivan Furtado) *midfield: struggling to go pce and pushed along over 2 1/2f out: sn rdn: no imp and wl btn ent fnl f: eased clsng stages* **41/1**

10 dist **Jukov (FR)**[12] 3-8-7 0...(b) ClementGuitraud(8) 3
(Y Barberot, France) **10/1**

1m 43.26s **10** Ran SP% **119.1**
PARI-MUTUEL (all including 1 euro stake): WIN 5.80; PLACE 1.70, 1.50, 1.70; DF 12.00.
Owner Ecurie JP Bonardel, Boualem Mekki Et Al **Bred** T De La Heronniere **Trained** France

6830 GOODWOOD (R-H)
Wednesday, September 25

OFFICIAL GOING: Soft (heavy in places; 5.1) changing to heavy (soft in places) after race 1 (2.00)
Wind: minor cross wind Weather: showers, heavy at times

7562 HEINEKEN 0.0% FUTURE STAYERS' EBF MAIDEN STKS (PLUS 10 RACE) 1m 1f 197y
2:00 (2:00) (Class 2) 2-Y-O **£9,451** (£2,829; £1,414; £708; £352) **Stalls** Low

Form RPR

6 **1** **Khalifa Sat (IRE)**[20] 6905 2-9-5 0.............................. JamieSpencer 10 80+
(Andrew Balding) *unfurnished: scope; prom on outer: clsd on ldrs gng wl 2f out: c over to stands' rail and rdn to ld over 1f out: kpt up to work fnl f: styd on* **7/4**[1]

55 **2** 1½ **Tantivy**[12] 7154 2-9-5 0.. SeanLevey 9 77
(Richard Hannon) *tall; trckd ldr: effrt to ld 2f out: sn rdn and hdd by wnr over 1f out: kpt on clsng stages* **40/1**

3 **3** ½ **Stag Horn**[14] 7067 2-9-5 0... HollieDoyle 5 76
(Archie Watson) *workmanlike; in tch: pushed along to maintain position in 4th over 2f out: swtchd rt and rdn over 1f out: drvn to go 3rd 1f out: kpt on* **13/2**

63 **4** nk **Herman Hesse**[48] 5860 2-9-5 0....................................... RobertHavlin 2 75
(John Gosden) *str: looked wl; racd in midfield: pushed along to chse ldrs 2f out: sn rdn and minor hdwy 1f out: kpt on* **5/2**[2]

06 **5** 1½ **Duke Of Condicote**[19] 6926 2-9-5 0............................ DavidProbert 4 73+
(Alan King) *athletic; hld up: pushed along in rr 3f out: mde gd stdy hdwy under mostly hands and heels ins fnl f: nrst fin* **20/1**

6 1¾ **Bondi Sands (IRE)** 2-9-5 0... JoeFanning 6 69
(Mark Johnston) *athletic; dwlt sltly but sn rcvrd: in tch: pushed along 3f out: rdn and outpcd 2f out: plugged on fnl f* **12/1**

55 **7** 8 **Buto**[13] 7124 2-9-5 0... CharlesBishop 7 54
(Eve Johnson Houghton) *hld up: rdn and no prog 3f out: nvr on terms* **66/1**

3 **8** 5 **Merryweather**[43] 6054 2-9-0 0... HarryBentley 8 40
(Ralph Beckett) *leggy; led: rdn along and hdd 2f out: wknd qckly fnl f (trainer said filly had tied-up post-race)* **6/1**[3]

054 **9** ¾ **Selsey Sizzler**[33] 6402 2-9-5 66............................ Pierre-LouisJamin 3 43
(William Knight) *compact; j. awkwardly racd in rr: a in last pair: t.o* **33/1**

0 **10** 7 **Jen's Lad (IRE)**[12] 7162 2-9-5 0................................ TomMarquand 1 30
(Richard Hannon) *racd in midfield: rdn and outpcd 3f out: sn t.o* **66/1**

2m 19.04s (10.14) **Going Correction** +1.05s/f (Soft) **10** Ran SP% **113.4**
Speed ratings (Par 101): **101,99,99,99,97 96,90,86,85,79**
CSF £86.98 TOTE £2.70: £1.30, £9.00, £1.60; EX 96.70 Trifecta £422.00.
Owner Ahmad Al Shaikh **Bred** Declan Phelan & Irish National Stud **Trained** Kingsclere, Hants

FOCUS
The ground was changed to heavy, soft in places following this opener. A decent juvenile maiden, there wasn't much pace on and they headed centre to stands' side in the straight. It's hard to pin down the level.

7563 OLD MOUT OPTIONAL CLAIMING H'CAP 1m
2:30 (2:33) (Class 2) 4-Y-O+ **£18,903** (£5,658; £2,829; £1,416; £705) **Stalls** Centre

Form RPR

2433 **1** **Alemaratalyoum (IRE)**[1] 7551 5-9-4 **90**...........................(t) SeanLevey 5 103
(Stuart Williams) *racd in midfield: smooth hdwy on heels of ldrs 2f out: led on bit over 1f out: rdn to extend advantage ins fnl f: drew clr* **5/2**[1]

52-5 **2** 4 **Glen Shiel**[21] 6861 5-10-0 **100**...................................... HollieDoyle 12 105
(Archie Watson) *prom in 3rd: clsd to ld 3f out: rdn along and hdd by wnr over 1f out: kpt on fnl f for clr 2nd* **12/1**

1620 **3** 1½ **Mountain Rescue (IRE)**[25] 6729 7-8-7 **79**.................(p) DavidProbert 7 80
(Michael Attwater) *looked wl; trckd ldr tl 3f out: rdn and outpcd 2f out: kpt on u.p ins fnl f* **10/1**

420 **4** *1 1/4* **Shady McCoy (USA)**[18] 6950 9-8-13 **88**...................... CierenFallon(3) 9 87
(Ian Williams) *looked wl; dwlt sltly and racd in rr: hdwy on outer u.p over 2f out: rdn and outpcd over 1f out: one pce after* **10/1**

2121 **5** *nk* **Tukhoom (IRE)**[12] 7164 6-7-13 **78**..........................(v) AngusVilliers(7) 10 76
(David O'Meara) *racd in midfield: pushed along amongst rivals over 2f out: sn rdn and one pce over 1f out: plugged on* **4/1**[2]

-020 **6** *4 1/2* **Mutaabeq (IRE)**[25] 6725 4-9-4 **90**........................ JimCrowley 3 79
(Marcus Tregoning) *looked wl; in tch in midfield: hdwy to chse ldrs over 2f out: rdn and qckly btn over 1f out: no ex* **9/2**[3]

3031 **7** *1 1/4* **Love Dreams (IRE)**[18] 6978 5-8-13 **85**........................(p) NicolaCurrie 11 71
(Jamie Osborne) *prom on outer: rdn and lost pl 3f out: sn outpcd: wknd over 1f out* **10/1**

0000 **8** *10* **Taurean Star (IRE)**[90] 4299 6-8-0 **75** ow2............ DarraghKeenan(3) 4 40
(Luke Dace) *hld up: remained on outer 3f out: rdn and hung bdly rt to far rail 2f out: t.o* **33/1**

3610 **9** *5* **Key Player**[18] 6968 4-8-13 **85**..(p) CharlesBishop 1 40
(Eve Johnson Houghton) *led tl 3f out: rdn along and lost pl over 2f out: wknd fnl f (jockey said gelding was unsuited by the ground, which was officially described as Heavy, Soft in places on this occasion)* **10/1**

1m 47.13s (7.93) **Going Correction** +1.05s/f (Soft) **9** Ran SP% **113.8**
Speed ratings (Par 109): **102,98,96,95,94 90,89,79,74**
CSF £33.74 CT £256.91 TOTE £3.30: £1.20, £3.50, £3.10; EX 34.70 Trifecta £204.90.Tukhoom was subject to a friendly claim.
Owner Mrs J Morley **Bred** Ammerland Verwaltung Gmbh & Co Kg **Trained** Newmarket, Suffolk

FOCUS
Add 16yds. A useful claiming handicap, nearly all the runners headed towards the stands' rail in the straight. The winner has been rated back to the level of last autumn's heavy ground win at Haydock.

7564 BIRRA MORETTI H'CAP 6f
3:05 (3:07) (Class 4) (0-85,86) 3-Y-O+
£5,433 (£1,617; £808; £404; £300; £300) **Stalls** High

Form RPR

6216 **1** **Atalanta's Boy**[41] 6109 4-8-10 **75**.........................(h) ThomasGreatrex(5) 8 89+
(David Menuisier) *looked wl; mde all: shkn up w a 2 l ld over 1f out: sn rdn fnl f and a in command* **7/2**[1]

3613 **2** *2 1/4* **Sweet Pursuit**[22] 6835 5-8-12 **75**.................................... FinleyMarsh(3) 9 80
(Rod Millman) *hld up: hdwy u.p against stands' rail over 1f out: swtchd rt and rdn fnl f: wnt 2nd clsng stages (jockey said mare jumped awkwardly)* **8/1**

0550 **3** *1 1/4* **After John**[19] 6913 3-9-1 **77**.. CallumShepherd 3 78
(Mick Channon) *hld up: swtchd lft amongst rivals and rdn 2f out: hdwy to chse ldr in 2nd over 1f out: kpt on but lost 2nd clsng stages* **11/2**[3]

0030 **4** *3 1/2* **Quench Dolly**[67] 5180 5-9-1 **78**.................................. CierenFallon(3) 7 69
(John Gallagher) *prom in 3rd: rdn along to go 2nd briefly 2f out: sn outpcd and wknd fnl f* **12/1**

4231 **5** *3 1/4* **Delagate This Lord**[10] 7230 5-9-1 **80** 5ex................. SeamusCronin(5) 5 61
(Michael Attwater) *towards rr of midfield: effrt to cl on ldrs 2f out: rdn and no imp over 1f out: one pce after* **6/1**

3044 **6** *1 1/2* **Private Matter**[11] 7183 5-8-12 **72**.................................(b) DavidProbert 10 49
(Amy Murphy) *trckd ldr tl 2f out: rdn and lost pl over 1f out: wknd fnl f* **9/1**

0006 **7** *1 3/4* **Quiet Endeavour (IRE)**[11] 7187 3-9-10 **86**.................... PatCosgrave 4 57
(George Baker) *midfield: rdn along and no imp 2f out: one pce fnl f: n.d* **16/1**

3413 **8** *5* **Cent Flying**[4] 7467 4-8-13 **73**..(t) MartinDwyer 2 29
(William Muir) *midfield on outer: rdn and outpcd over 2f out: sn lost pl over 1f out (trainer's rep said gelding was unsuited by the ground, which was officially described as Heavy, Soft in places)* **13/2**

0525 **9** *3 1/2* **Youkan (IRE)**[19] 6920 4-9-7 **81**.. RobHornby 6 27
(Stuart Kittow) *dwlt sltly but sn rcvrd into midfield: rdn and lost pl 2f out: wknd fnl f (jockey said gelding ran flat)* **5/1**[2]

1m 16.42s (4.32) **Going Correction** +1.05s/f (Soft)
WFA 3 from 4yo+ 2lb **9** Ran SP% **116.6**
Speed ratings (Par 105): **110,107,105,100,96 94,92,85,80**
CSF £32.35 CT £152.93 TOTE £3.80: £1.50, £2.30, £2.30; EX 35.00 Trifecta £252.30.
Owner Mrs Monica Josefina Borton & Partner **Bred** Monica Martinez-Trumm **Trained** Pulborough, W Sussex

FOCUS
A fair sprint. The second has been rated in line with her recent form.

7565 BRITISH STALLION STUDS EBF FOUNDATION STKS (LISTED RACE) 1m 1f 197y
3:40 (3:40) (Class 1) 3-Y-O+
£25,519 (£9,675; £4,842; £2,412; £1,210; £607) **Stalls** Low

Form RPR

42-3 **1** **Air Pilot**[192] 1244 10-9-2 114.. HarryBentley 2 112
(Ralph Beckett) *settled in midfield: hdwy to chse ldrs 2f out: rdn and gd hdwy on outer to ld ins fnl f: won gng away* **9/2**[3]

1512 **2** *1 1/4* **Qarasu (IRE)**[19] 6923 3-8-11 96.. JasonWatson 6 109
(Roger Charlton) *t.k.h to post: hld up and a little lazy at times: effrt to chse ldrs 2f out and hung sltly lft: rdn and bmpd by rival 1f out: kpt on wl to go 2nd fnl strides* **9/4**[1]

2121 **3** *nk* **Illumined (IRE)**[20] 6893 3-8-6 91.................................. KieranO'Neill 5 103+
(John Gosden) *looked wl; hld up in tch: briefly dropped to last 4f out: gd hdwy to cl on ldr 2f out: rdn to ld over 1f out and sn hung bdly rt bumping rival: continued to drift rt fnl f and lost 2nd fnl strides (jockey said filly hung right-handed)* **9/2**[3]

2610 **4** *3 1/4* **Getchagetchagetcha**[97] 4013 3-8-11 101.......................... HectorCrouch 7 102
(Clive Cox) *prom on outer: rdn along and dropped to last 3f out: hung rt u.p 2f out: kpt on fnl f* **14/1**

5-62 **5** *1* **Elwazir**[14] 7076 4-9-2 105...(h) JimCrowley 1 103+
(Owen Burrows) *looked wl; led after 1f: rdn along w short ld 2f out: hdd and wkng whn bdly hmpd over 1f out: nt rcvr* **7/2**[2]

2466 **6** *nk* **Nyaleti (IRE)**[32] 6443 4-8-11 105...................................... JoeFanning 8 94
(Mark Johnston) *led for 1f then trckd ldr: rdn whn short of room and lost pl 2f out: wknd fnl f* **5/1**

2m 16.59s (7.69) **Going Correction** +1.05s/f (Soft)
WFA 3 from 4yo+ 5lb **6** Ran SP% **112.7**
Speed ratings (Par 111): **111,110,109,107,106 106**
CSF £15.18 TOTE £4.90: £2.10, £1.80; EX 16.60 Trifecta £62.70.
Owner Lady Cobham **Bred** Lady Cobham **Trained** Kimpton, Hants
■ Stewards' Enquiry : Jason Watson two-day ban; careless riding (Oct 9-10); four-day ban; misuse of whip (Oct 13-16)
Kieran O'Neill two-day ban; careless riding (Oct 9-10)

FOCUS
Solid form for the level, with a pair of progressive 3yos bested by a classy veteran. The pace was a steady one and they headed centre to stands' side in the straight. The winner has been rated close to last year's form, but the level is a bit fluid.

7566 THOROUGHBRED BREEDERS ASSOCIATION FILLIES' H'CAP 1m 6f
4:10 (4:10) (Class 2) (0-105,98) 3-Y-O+
£28,012 (£8,388; £4,194; £2,097; £1,048; £526) **Stalls** Low

Form RPR

0111 **1** **Monica Sheriff**[26] 6661 3-8-10 **87**.................................. TomMarquand 6 106
(William Haggas) *looked wl; trckd ldr: cruised into ld on bit 2f out: shkn up and shot clr over 1f out: pushed out fnl f: v impressive* **7/2**[3]

6315 **2** *20* **I'll Have Another (IRE)**[18] 6952 3-9-7 **98**............................ JoeFanning 2 91
(Mark Johnston) *looked wl; led: shkn up w short ld 3f out: sn rdn and readily brushed aside by wnr over 1f out: battled on fnl f for a v remote 2nd* **8/1**

5040 **3** *1 1/2* **Lorelina**[46] 5928 6-9-6 **92**.. WilliamCox(3) 3 81
(Andrew Balding) *hld up in last pair: rdn along and outpcd 3f out: drvn and mde sme minor hdwy passed btn rivals fnl f* **10/1**

204 **4** *1* **Dono Di Dio**[22] 6842 4-8-9 **81**....................................(b[1]) CierenFallon(3) 1 69
(Michael Madgwick) *prom: rdn along and readily outpcd 2f out: plugged on one pce fnl f* **20/1**

3101 **5** *4 1/2* **Nette Rousse (GER)**[45] 5982 3-8-8 **85**........................ HarryBentley 7 69
(Ralph Beckett) *midfield: pushed along and no imp 2f out: rdn and no rspnse over 1f out: wknd fnl f* **9/4**[2]

1132 **6** *10* **Litigious**[14] 7075 3-9-0 **91**... RobertHavlin 5 62
(John Gosden) *hld up: smooth hdwy to chse ldrs 2f out: rdn along and fnd little over 1f out: wknd fnl f (trainer's rep said filly may not have stayed the 1m6f trip)* **2/1**[1]

3m 15.85s (12.15) **Going Correction** +1.05s/f (Soft)
WFA 3 from 4yo+ 8lb **6** Ran SP% **111.3**
Speed ratings (Par 96): **107,95,94,94,91 85**
CSF £29.32 TOTE £3.80: £1.80, £2.70; EX 22.30 Trifecta £67.20.
Owner Duke Of Devonshire **Bred** The Duke Of Devonshire **Trained** Newmarket, Suffolk

FOCUS
A couple of the key players failed to fire in this fillies' handicap, with the 1m6f test on heavy ground perhaps being too much for some, but it certainly wasn't an issue for the impressive winner. They came centre-field in the straight. The level is hard to pin down.

7567 ORCHARD THIEVES H'CAP 1m 1f 11y
4:45 (4:45) (Class 4) (0-85,85) 4-Y-O+
£5,433 (£1,617; £808; £404; £300; £300) **Stalls** Low

Form RPR

5642 **1** **Simoon (IRE)**[25] 6730 5-9-4 **82**..............................(p[1]) JasonWatson 7 91+
(Andrew Balding) *trckd ldr: clsd gng wl over 2f out: shkn up to ld 2f out: rdn and sn in command 1f out: rdn out* **5/4**[1]

6555 **2** *2* **Plait**[25] 6709 4-9-1 **82**.. CameronNoble(3) 2 85
(Michael Bell) *prom in 3rd: effrt to chse ldrs over 2f out: making minor hdwy to go 2nd ins fnl f whn rdr lost whip fnl 100yds: kpt on under hands and heels* **17/2**

1120 **3** *hd* **Los Camachos (IRE)**[40] 6155 4-8-13 **77**........................ HectorCrouch 8 79
(John Gallagher) *led tl rdn along: hdd and readily outpcd by wnr 2f out: sn drvn and battled on wl fnl f: lost 2nd fnl 100yds* **9/1**

0505 **4** *1/2* **Family Fortunes**[18] 6964 5-9-1 **84**........................ ScottMcCullagh(5) 10 85
(Michael Madgwick) *looked wl; in rr of midfield: pushed along to cl over 2f out: rdn and v briefly short of room 1f out: kpt on* **8/1**[3]

300- **5** *1* **Keswick**[272] 9723 5-8-11 **82**..................................(t w) AngusVilliers(7) 6 81
(Heather Main) *settled in 4th: effrt to chse ldrs 2f out: sn rdn and one pce 1f out: plugged on* **12/1**

365- **6** *3 3/4* **Beat The Judge (IRE)**[157] 6884 4-8-0 **71** oh3.......... LouisGaroghan(7) 5 62
(Gary Moore) *hld up: brief effrt to cl u.p 2f out: sn outpcd and n.d* **4/1**[2]

7 *1* **Touchthesoul (ITY)**[129] 4-9-4 **82**.................................... GeorgeWood 3 71
(Gary Moore) *in rr of midfield: rdn along and little rspnse over 2f out: sn bhd* **8/1**[3]

2m 5.88s (8.48) **Going Correction** +1.05s/f (Soft) **7** Ran SP% **114.9**
Speed ratings (Par 105): **104,102,102,101,100 97,96**
CSF £13.07 CT £68.34 TOTE £2.10: £1.30, £4.30; EX 13.20 Trifecta £70.40.
Owner Lord Blyth **Bred** Lemington Grange Stud **Trained** Kingsclere, Hants

FOCUS
Add 16yds. Little got into this ordinary handicap. It's been rated cautiously.

7568 HEINEKEN UK APPRENTICE H'CAP 5f
5:20 (5:20) (Class 5) (0-75,77) 3-Y-O+
£3,493 (£1,039; £519; £300; £300; £300) **Stalls** High

Form RPR

5054 **1** **Pettochside**[13] 7112 10-8-7 **63**.. TobyEley(3) 2 73+
(John Bridger) *squeezed for room leaving stalls and carried rt sn after: hld up and given time to rcvr: hdwy to cl on ldrs 2f out: rdn to chal 1f out: styd on wl to ld fnl 100yds: excellent ride (jockey said gelding was short of room shortly after leaving the stalls)* **10/3**[2]

3112 **2** *1 3/4* **Kodiak Attack (IRE)**[13] 7112 3-8-13 **74**........................ ElinorJones(7) 6 78
(Sylvester Kirk) *prom: pushed along to chse ldr 2f out: led over 1f out: drvn and hdd by wnr fnl 100yds: no ex* **7/1**

4053 **3** *1 1/4* **Firenze Rosa (IRE)**[31] 6510 4-8-4 **60** oh15...................... AledBeech(3) 1 60
(John Bridger) *led: rdn along and hdd over 1f out: kpt on one pce fnl f* **25/1**

6225 **4** *nk* **Valentino Sunrise**[34] 6365 3-8-6 **60**................................ TheodoreLadd 4 58
(Mick Channon) *bmpd s and snatched up briefly: hdwy on outer 2f out: rdn and hung rt over 1f out: one pce fnl f* **11/2**[3]

0621 **5** *1* **Atty's Edge**[13] 7112 3-8-1 **60**.................................... AngusVilliers(5) 10 55
(Christopher Mason) *racd promly: rdn along and lost pl 2f out: plugged on fnl f* **3/1**[1]

3001 **6** *shd* **Dream Catching (IRE)**[14] 7078 4-9-4 **74**........................ WilliamCarver(3) 7 68
(Andrew Balding) *hld up: hdwy over 2f out: rdn along and no further imp over 1f out: one pce fnl f (jockey said gelding was slowly away)* **8/1**

2413 **7** *1/2* **More Than Likely**[11] 7178 3-9-0 **75**................................ TylerHeard(7) 13 68
(Richard Hughes) *midfield: hdwy whn briefly short of room 2f out: pushed along and short of racing room again over 1f out: sn swtchd rt: nvr able to chal (jockey said filly was denied a clear run)* **12/1**

5060 **8** *1 3/4* **Major Pusey**[19] 6921 7-9-2 **69**.................................(p) ThomasGreatrex 12 55
(John Gallagher) *in tch: rdn along and outpcd 2f out: wkng whn hmpd 1f out: nt rcvr (jockey said gelding was denied a clear run)* **6/1**

The Form Book Flat 2019, Raceform Ltd, Newbury, RG14 5SJ

1006 **9** *5* **Perfect Charm**[13] 7112 3-8-13 **67**......(b) SeamusCronin 8 35
(Archie Watson) *chsd ldr tl 2f out: rdn along and lost pl over 1f out: sn bhd* **25/1**

1m 2.76s (4.66) **Going Correction** +1.05s/f (Soft)
WFA 3 from 4yo+ 1lb **9** Ran SP% **116.7**
Speed ratings (Par 103): **104,101,99,98,97 96,96,93,85**
CSF £27.33 CT £490.23 TOTE £4.80: £1.50, £2.30, £6.00; EX 30.40 Trifecta £785.60.
Owner P Cook **Bred** New Hall Stud **Trained** Liphook, Hants
■ Stewards' Enquiry : Angus Villiers two-day ban; careless riding (Oct 9-10)

FOCUS
An open-looking apprentice sprint. The third is the key to the form, but she's been rated similar to last year's C&D win on heavy ground for now. The second has been rated to his latest.
T/Jkpt: £3,622.30 to a £1 stake. Pool: £17,856.72. 3.5 winning units. T/Plt: £115.20 to a £1 stake. Pool: £71,330.33. 451.76 winning units. T/Qpdt: £20.20 to a £1 stake. Pool: £6,932.23. 253.66 winning units. **Mark Grantham**

7514 KEMPTON (A.W) (R-H)
Wednesday, September 25

OFFICIAL GOING: Polytrack: standard to slow
Wind: Fresh, across (away from stands) Weather: Fine

7569 32RED ON THE APP STORE NOVICE MEDIAN AUCTION STKS (DIV I) 6f (P)
5:00 (5:03) (Class 5) 2-Y-O **£3,881** (£1,155; £577; £288) **Stalls** Low

Form RPR
1 **1** **Desert Safari (IRE)**[16] 7030 2-9-9 0......RyanMoore 10 95+
(Mark Johnston) *mde all: stretched on 2f out: clr fnl f: pushed out firmly* **6/5**[1]

4 **2** *4 ½* **Qasbaz (IRE)**[19] 6911 2-9-2 0......NicolaCurrie 7 74
(Jamie Osborne) *chsd ldrs: pushed along over 2f out: tk 2nd over 1f out: shkn up and no imp on wnr (vet said colt lost it's left fore shoe)* **11/4**[2]

0 **3** *½* **Sterling Stamp (IRE)**[93] 4184 2-9-2 0......SeanLevey 9 73
(Paul Cole) *chsd ldrs: pushed along over 2f out: kpt on over 1f out: edgd lft fnl f but tk 3rd last 100yds (jockey said colt hung left-handed)* **8/1**

3 **4** *1 ¾* **Autumn Trail**[56] 5547 2-8-11 0......JFEgan 3 62
(Rae Guest) *t.k.h: hld up in midfield: pushed along and prog 2f out: ch of a pl fnl f: one pce* **7/1**[3]

33 **5** *3 ½* **Wailea Nights (IRE)**[21] 6858 2-8-11 0......ShaneKelly 8 52
(Marco Botti) *chsd wnr to over 1f out: wknd* **12/1**

6 *1 ¾* **Twelve Diamonds (IRE)** 2-8-11 0......DaneO'Neill 1 47
(Charles Hills) *nvr beyond midfield: pushed along and outpcd 2f out: no hdwy after* **20/1**

56 **7** *¾* **Inevitable Outcome (IRE)**[22] 6846 2-8-6 0......DylanHogan(5) 2 44
(David Simcock) *stdd s: hld up in last pair: pushed along over 2f out: limited prog and nvr in it* **20/1**

35 **8** *shd* **Just May**[23] 6800 2-8-11 0......LiamKeniry 5 44
(Clive Cox) *dwlt: hld up in last trio: shkn up and outpcd 2f out: no ch after* **25/1**

00 **9** *10* **Lady Florence (IRE)**[35] 6330 2-8-11 0......(p[1]) EoinWalsh 4 14
(Malcolm Saunders) *t.k.h: racd wd: prom tl wknd rapidly over 2f out: t.o (jockey said filly ran too freely)* **66/1**

06 **10** *1* **Hootenanny (IRE)**[36] 6300 2-9-2 0......CharlieBennett 6 16
(Adam West) *a in last trio: wknd sn after 1/2-way: t.o* **66/1**

1m 13.52s (0.42) **Going Correction** +0.075s/f (Slow) **10** Ran SP% **119.8**
Speed ratings (Par 95): **100,94,93,91,86 84,83,82,69,68**
CSF £4.31 TOTE £1.90: £1.10, £1.20, £2.90; EX 5.30 Trifecta £31.40.
Owner Sheikh Hamdan bin Mohammed Al Maktoum **Bred** Godolphin **Trained** Middleham Moor, N Yorks

FOCUS
The favourite defied a late drift to make it 2-2 in the first division of an ordinary median auction. It's been rated at face value in behind the winner.

7570 32RED ON THE APP STORE NOVICE MEDIAN AUCTION STKS (DIV II) 6f (P)
5:30 (5:31) (Class 5) 2-Y-O **£3,881** (£1,155; £577; £288) **Stalls** Low

Form RPR
1 **1** **Dance Fever (IRE)**[23] 6807 2-9-9 0......AdamKirby 3 87+
(Clive Cox) *led: shkn up and narrowly hdd 2f out: drvn over 1f out: led again jst ins fnl f: edgd lft but kpt on* **5/6**[1]

2 *½* **Pepper Bay** 2-8-11 0......HollieDoyle 5 74+
(Archie Watson) *pressed wnr: pushed into narrow ld 2f out: rdn: hung lft and hdd jst ins fnl f: kpt on after but jst hld* **2/1**[2]

03 **3** *3 ¾* **Alfies Watch**[21] 6852 2-9-2 0......RossaRyan 9 67
(John O'Shea) *in tch: outpcd over 2f out: shkn up to take 3rd over 1f out: no imp on clr ldng pair* **12/1**

00 **4** *1 ¼* **Gift Of Youth**[23] 6807 2-9-2 0......(p[1]) KieranShoemark 8 64
(Amanda Perrett) *in tch: outpcd over 2f out: plugged on to take 4th jst over 1f out* **50/1**

5 **5** *1 ½* **San Juan (IRE)**[13] 7103 2-9-2 0......JosephineGordon 4 59
(Shaun Keightley) *dwlt: hld up in rr: outpcd over 2f out: nudged along and kpt on steadily* **25/1**

00 **6** *nk* **Bad Company**[23] 6807 2-9-2 0......CharlieBennett 2 58
(Jim Boyle) *chsd ldng pair to over 1f out: steadily wknd* **22/1**

02 **7** *2 ½* **Moondance**[13] 7124 2-8-11 0......RyanMoore 1 46
(Gary Moore) *dwlt: hld up in rr: nudged along and no prog 2f out* **8/1**[3]

00 **8** *2 ½* **Upstage (IRE)**[6] 7393 2-8-6 0......DylanHogan(5) 6 38
(David Simcock) *awkward s: t.k.h: hld up in rr: wknd 2f out* **25/1**

9 *22* **Scorpio's Dream** 2-9-2 0......EoinWalsh 7
(Charlie Wallis) *s.v.s: nrly ct up at bk of field 1/2-way: sn wknd: t.o (jockey said gelding was slowly away and ran green)* **66/1**

1m 14.12s (1.02) **Going Correction** +0.075s/f (Slow) **9** Ran SP% **122.2**
Speed ratings (Par 95): **96,95,90,88,86 86,82,79,50**
CSF £2.70 TOTE £1.60: £1.10, £1.10, £2.40; EX 3.30 Trifecta £13.40.
Owner Kennet Valley Thoroughbreds VIII **Bred** Silk Fan Syndicate **Trained** Lambourn, Berks

FOCUS
This may have been slightly weaker than the opening division and it was 0.6 seconds slower. Another winning favourite scoring under a penalty.

7571 32RED.COM NOVICE STKS (PLUS 10 RACE) 7f (P)
6:00 (6:01) (Class 4) 2-Y-O **£5,822** (£1,732; £865; £432) **Stalls** Low

Form RPR
0 **1** **All You Wish**[22] 6845 2-9-5......DavidProbert 9 83+
(Andrew Balding) *mde virtually all: hrd pressed on both sides over 1f out: fought on wl and hld on nr fin (vet said colt lost his right-hind shoe)* **33/1**

42 **2** *nk* **Jean Baptiste (IRE)**[19] 6927 2-9-5 0......RyanMoore 10 82
(Sir Michael Stoute) *mostly trckd wnr: rdn to chal over 1f out: upsides after tl nt qckn nr fin* **9/4**[2]

2 **3** *2* **End Zone**[48] 5848 2-9-5 0......OisinMurphy 6 77
(David Simcock) *coltish paddock: impeded s but sn trckd ldng pair: rdn to chal over 1f out and upsides: nt qckn and hld last 150yds* **10/11**[1]

5 **4** *8* **Pinatar (IRE)**[4] 7445 2-9-5 0......KierenFox 8 56
(John Best) *t.k.h: in tch: outpcd over 2f out: kpt on to take remote 4th nr fin* **33/1**

5 *½* **Jumaira Bay (FR)** 2-9-5 0......AndreaAtzeni 13 55+
(Roger Varian) *slowly away and sltly impeded s: sn in midfield: outpcd but sme prog over 2f out: tk remote 4th fnl f tl nr fin* **12/1**

6 *shd* **Mackelly (IRE)** 2-9-5 0......ShaneKelly 14 54
(Richard Hughes) *mostly chsd ldng trio: outpcd over 2f out and no ch after: lost remote 4th fnl f* **50/1**

7 *2* **Ahdab (IRE)** 2-9-5 0......JimCrowley 3 49+
(Ed Dunlop) *v s.i.s: rn green in last early: sme prog over 2f out: n.d but kpt on* **9/1**[3]

8 *1 ¾* **Diamond Cottage** 2-9-0 0......EoinWalsh 7 40
(Malcolm Saunders) *wnt rt s: prom in chsng gp tl wknd over 1f out* **50/1**

0 **9** *½* **Kings Creek (IRE)**[58] 5493 2-9-5 0......(w) TomQueally 11 43
(Alan King) *dwlt: wl in rr: nvr a factor: kpt on over 1f out* **40/1**

10 *3 ½* **Baltic Wolve** 2-9-5 0......KieranO'Neill 4 34
(John Gosden) *rn green and sn pushed along: a bhd* **9/1**[3]

00 **11** *12* **Power Of Love**[97] 4030 2-9-5 0......PatCosgrave 2
(George Baker) *towards rr: wknd over 2f out: t.o* **100/1**

12 *3* **San Bernardo** 2-9-5 0......(h[1]) JosephineGordon 12
(Shaun Keightley) *plld hrd in midfield: dropped to rr after 3f: wknd 3f out: t.o (jockey said colt ran too freely)* **66/1**

1m 27.46s (1.46) **Going Correction** +0.075s/f (Slow) **12** Ran SP% **125.6**
Speed ratings (Par 97): **94,93,91,82,81 81,79,77,76,72 58,55**
CSF £111.55 TOTE £36.20: £6.00, £1.40, £1.02; EX 139.00 Trifecta £249.30.
Owner M M Stables **Bred** W & R Barnett Ltd **Trained** Kingsclere, Hants

FOCUS
A fair novice with the first three, who occupied those positions throughout, pulling well clear. It's been rated around the second and third.

7572 100% PROFIT BOOST AT 32REDSPORT.COM NOVICE STKS 1m (P)
6:30 (6:31) (Class 4) 3-Y-O+ **£5,822** (£1,732; £865; £432) **Stalls** Low

Form RPR
0- **1** **The Gill Brothers**[362] 7736 3-9-5 0......(t) SeanLevey 9 85
(Stuart Williams) *dwlt: t.k.h: hld up in last pair: pushed along over 2f out: gd prog over 1f out: shkn up and swept into the ld 60yds out* **33/1**

3 **2** *1 ¼* **Informed Front (USA)**[118] 3277 3-9-5 0......(t) RobertHavlin 8 82
(John Gosden) *hld up disputing 5th: wd bnd 3f out: shkn up over 2f out: picked up and prog over 1f out: shkn up to ld ins fnl f: hdd and outpcd last 60yds* **4/9**[1]

06 **3** *1 ¼* **Squelch**[89] 4341 3-9-0 0......DavidProbert 1 74
(Rae Guest) *hld up disputing 5th: pushed along and stdy prog 2f out: nt pce to chal but styd on to take 3rd ins fnl f* **16/1**

3 **4** *2 ¾* **Big Daddy Kane**[145] 2375 3-9-5 0......DanielMuscutt 4 72
(Marco Botti) *led: shkn up 2f out: hdd & wknd ins fnl f* **9/2**[2]

5 *2 ¼* **Early Riser (IRE)** 3-9-0 0......TomMarquand 6 62
(James Tate) *dwlt: hld up in last pair: urged along and no prog over 2f out: kpt on fnl f* **5/1**[3]

6 **6** *1* **Wherewithal**[13] 7114 3-9-5 0......HarryBentley 5 65
(Ralph Beckett) *trckd ldr: shkn up to chal 2f out: btn over 1f out: wknd qckly fnl f* **10/1**

06 **7** *4 ½* **Adashelby (IRE)**[11] 7190 3-9-0 0......KieranO'Neill 2 49
(John Ryan) *chsd ldng pair to jst over 2f out: wknd qckly* **50/1**

0 **8** *2 ¼* **Dansepo**[13] 7114 3-9-5 0......CharlieBennett 7 48
(Adam West) *chsd ldng pair to wl over 2f out: wknd qckly* **100/1**

1m 40.43s (0.63) **Going Correction** +0.075s/f (Slow) **8** Ran SP% **125.0**
Speed ratings (Par 105): **99,97,96,93,91 90,86,83**
CSF £53.39 TOTE £29.80: £5.40, £1.02, £5.90; EX 85.30 Trifecta £564.90.
Owner The Gill Brothers **Bred** P A & M J Reditt & Catridge Stud **Trained** Newmarket, Suffolk

FOCUS
A strange novice, they didn't seem to go that quick early, but the winner came from last-to-first, causing a turn up in the process. It's been rated at face value, with the second and third close to their previous runs, and fourth close to form.

7573 RASHER & MAUREEN FRITH MEMORIAL H'CAP 1m (P)
7:00 (7:01) (Class 6) (0-65,65) 3-Y-O
£3,105 (£924; £461; £400; £400; £400) **Stalls** Low

Form RPR
2223 **1** **Gregorian Girl**[25] 6703 3-9-5 **63**......MartinDwyer 11 72
(Dean Ivory) *trckd ldrs: prog 2f out: rdn to ld over 1f out: edgd rt but kpt on wl fnl f* **10/1**

1666 **2** *1* **Comeonfeeltheforce (IRE)**[42] 6075 3-9-2 **65**(t) ThoreHammerHansen(5) 9 72
(Lee Carter) *trckd ldrs: prog 2f out: rdn to chal over 1f out: chsd wnr after: nt qckn and hld fnl f* **14/1**

0046 **3** *3* **Astral Girl**[27] 6636 3-9-1 **59**......OisinMurphy 13 59
(Hughie Morrison) *towards rr: rdn and prog 2f out: styd on fnl f to take 3rd nr fin* **14/1**

3330 **4** *nk* **Magic Shuffle (IRE)**[13] 7116 3-9-5 **63**......AdamKirby 2 62
(Barry Brennan) *chsd ldng pair: urged along at times fr 1/2-way: drvn and tried to chal over 1f out: one pce after* **8/1**[3]

6440 **5** *½* **Padura Brave**[37] 6279 3-9-1 **59**......(v) JosephineGordon 1 57+
(Mark Usher) *hmpd by loose horse after 1f and dropped to rr: t.k.h after: virtually last over 2f out: drvn and prog over 1f out: kpt on and nrst fin* **10/1**

-051 **6** *nse* **Basilisk (USA)**[27] 6643 3-9-3 **61**......JasonWatson 5 59
(Roger Charlton) *pushed up to ld: tried to kick for home over 2f out: hdd and nt qckn over 1f out: fdd* **11/8**[1]

6502 **7** *5* **Rosamour (IRE)**[16] 7027 3-8-11 **62**......(b) GeorgeRooke(7) 6 48
(Richard Hughes) *chsd ldng pair: disp 2nd briefly 2f out: wknd over 1f out* **10/1**

026- **8** *5* **Havana Sunset**[342] 8351 3-9-4 **62**......RossaRyan 12 37
(Mike Murphy) *dropped in fr wd draw and hld up in last trio: rdn 3f out: no real prog* **33/1**

6555 **9** *4 ½* **Kodiac Lass (IRE)**[14] 7084 3-8-13 **64**......(p) StefanoCherchi(7) 8 28
(Marco Botti) *w ldr to jst over 2f out: wknd qckly* **9/1**

06-0 **10** *¾* **The Great Phoenix**[54] 5622 3-9-7 **65**......ShaneKelly 10 28
(Gay Kelleway) *wl in tch: rdn and fnd nil over 2f out: sn btn* **33/1**

000 11 2 **Mystical Jadeite**16 7025 3-8-0 47 (p1) WilliamCox(3) 3 5
(Grace Harris) *dwlt: rousted to rcvr but stl a towards rr: wknd 2f out* 40/1
0030 12 1 1/2 **Moneta**44 6018 3-8-10 54 DavidProbert 7 9
(Ronald Harris) *hld up in last pair: no prog over 2f out* 25/1
6006 U **Dancing Jo**14 7084 3-9-3 61 (p) AndreaAtzeni 4
(Mick Channon) *pitched and uns rdr s* 7/1[2]
1m 40.27s (0.47) **Going Correction** +0.075s/f (Slow) **13 Ran SP% 128.5**
Speed ratings (Par 99): **100,99,96,95,95 95,90,85,80,79 77,76,**
CSF £147.74 CT £1276.29 TOTE £10.00: £2.50, £3.60, £2.80; EX 180.60 Trifecta £1096.80.
Owner Skipsey, Franks & Roper And A Chapman **Bred** Shortgrove Manor Stud **Trained** Radlett, Herts
FOCUS
A true pace to this modest handicap.

7574 32RED CASINO H'CAP (LONDON MIDDLE DISTANCE SERIES QUALIFIER) 1m 2f 219y(P)
7:30 (7:31) (Class 3) (0-95,95) 3-Y-O £9,337 (£2,796; £1,398; £699; £349) Stalls Low

Form RPR
4112 1 **Faylaq**74 4901 3-9-7 95 JimCrowley 5 110+
(William Haggas) *hld up in 4th: prog 2f out and cruised into ld over 1f out: pushed out fnl f: v readily* 5/4[1]
1106 2 1 1/4 **Babbo's Boy (IRE)**74 4924 3-9-1 89 (w) JasonWatson 4 98
(Michael Bell) *dwlt: hld up in last: pushed along and looked to be hanging over 2f out: prog over 1f out: chsd wnr fnl f: no threat but r.o wl and clr of rest* 12/1
6341 3 6 **Emirates Knight (IRE)**28 6596 3-9-0 88 AndreaAtzeni 3 87
(Roger Varian) *led: rdn and jnd over 2f out: hdd over 1f out: wl outpcd after* 3/1[3]
321 4 3/4 **Midnights' Gift**20 6903 3-8-6 80 HollieDoyle 2 78
(Alan King) *trckd ldr after 3f: rdn to chal and upsides over 2f out tl wnr cruised by over 1f out: wl outpcd after* 14/1
1235 5 1 3/4 **Durrell**19 6917 3-8-12 86 DanielMuscutt 1 81
(James Fanshawe) *trckd ldr 3f: styd cl up in 3rd: drvn 2f out: sn wl btn: wknd fnl f* 5/2[2]
2m 20.91s (-0.09) **Going Correction** +0.075s/f (Slow) **5 Ran SP% 112.4**
Speed ratings (Par 105): **106,105,100,100,98**
CSF £16.66 TOTE £2.10: £1.10, £5.00; EX 16.70 Trifecta £31.60.
Owner Hamdan Al Maktoum **Bred** Teruya Yoshida **Trained** Newmarket, Suffolk
FOCUS
The small field 3yo feature race was taken apart by the impressive winner. The second has been rated in line with the better view of his Leicester win.

7575 32RED H'CAP 1m 3f 219y(P)
8:00 (8:00) (Class 4) (0-80,80) 3-Y-O+ £6,469 (£1,925; £962; £481; £400; £400) Stalls Low

Form RPR
23 1 **All Yours (FR)**25 6732 8-9-10 78 JamesDoyle 5 87+
(Sean Curran) *chsd ldrs: pushed along over 3f out: drvn and prog to ld jst over 2f out: looked in command fnl f: jst lasted* 11/4[1]
1413 2 nse **Sir Prize**19 6931 4-9-7 75 RobertHavlin 4 83
(Dean Ivory) *hld up in last trio: urged along wl over 2f out: prog over 1f out: chsd wnr last 100yds: clsd qckly nr fin: jst failed* 3/1[2]
1032 3 1 3/4 **Sufi**10 7231 5-9-5 73 (t1) PatDobbs 10 78
(Milton Harris) *trckd ldr after 2f: rdn to chal and upsides 2f out: chsd wnr after: one pce and lost 2nd last 100yds* 8/1
1211 4 nk **Seaborn (IRE)**22 6830 5-9-3 76 WilliamCarver(5) 3 81
(Patrick Chamings) *t.k.h: trckd ldr 2f: styd cl up: rdn and outpcd jst over 2f out: styd on again fnl f and nrly snatched 3rd* 10/1
05 5 2 1/4 **Unit Of Assessment (IRE)**54 5625 5-9-12 80 (vt) AdamKirby 8 81
(William Knight) *prom: rdn to chal and upsides 2f out: nt qckn over 1f out: wknd ins fnl f* 9/1
3555 6 3 1/4 **Running Cloud (IRE)**49 5811 4-9-7 75 (v) TomMarquand 1 71
(Alan King) *hld up in last: rdn and no real prog over 2f out: wl btn after* 6/1[3]
0123 7 3/4 **Argus (IRE)**102 3861 7-9-9 77 RossaRyan 6 72
(Alexandra Dunn) *led: stretched on over 3f out: hdd jst over 2f out: sn wknd* 11/1
012- 8 5 **Nelson River**194 8054 4-9-3 71 GeorgeDowning 2 58
(Tony Carroll) *hld up in last trio: rdn and no prog wl over 2f out: wl btn after* 7/1
140 9 8 **Cafe Espresso**41 6129 3-9-1 76 JoeyHaynes 9 51
(Chelsea Banham) *in tch: rdn over 3f out: wknd over 2f out: t.o* 33/1
010R P **Buckland Boy (IRE)**39 6224 4-9-4 72 (b1) StevieDonohoe 7
(Charlie Fellowes) *virtually ref to r: p.u after 2f* 8/1
2m 33.79s (-0.71) **Going Correction** +0.075s/f (Slow)
WFA 3 from 4yo+ 7lb **10 Ran SP% 131.0**
Speed ratings (Par 105): **105,104,103,103,102 99,99,96,90,**
CSF £12.83 CT £65.12 TOTE £3.70: £1.80, £1.50, £2.70; EX 14.60 Trifecta £131.10.
Owner Power Geneva Ltd **Bred** S C A La Perrigne **Trained** Upper Lambourn, Berks
FOCUS
A fair race, with most of these having some angle which gave them a chance. The third and fourth give the form a solid look.

7576 WISE BETTING AT RACINGTV.COM H'CAP 6f (P)
8:30 (8:32) (Class 6) (0-60,60) 3-Y-O+ £3,105 (£924; £461; £400; £400; £400) Stalls Low

Form RPR
2312 1 **Magicinthemaking (USA)**32 6441 5-9-2 58 HollieDoyle 9 65
(John E Long) *hld up in last of main gp: gd prog on outer 2f out: rdn to ld jst over 1f out: styd on wl* 7/2[1]
0630 2 1 **My Town Chicago (USA)**26 6685 4-8-13 60 ThoreHammerHansen(5) 3 64
(Kevin Frost) *led: rdn 2f out: hdd jst over 1f out and sn dropped to 3rd: kpt on wl to take 2nd last strides* 10/1
6356 3 nk **Perfect Symphony (IRE)**13 7130 5-9-4 60 CharlieBennett 6 63
(Mark Pattinson) *pressed ldr: chal and upsides over 1f out: chsd new ldr (and wnr) after: no imp and lost 3rd last strides* 11/2[2]
6-06 4 shd **On Route**8 7307 3-9-2 60 (v1) RyanTate 12 63
(Sir Mark Prescott Bt) *dwlt: hld up in last trio and swtchd to inner: shkn up and sme prog 2f out: rdn and r.o fnl f: nrly grabbed a pl* 7/1
4006 5 1 **Shepherd's Purse**14 7066 7-9-4 60 TomMarquand 4 60
(Ruth Carr) *blindfold off late and dwlt: chsd ldrs: rdn and tried to cl on inner fr 2f out: one pce fnl f (jockey said blindfold got stuck in the noseband and took two attempts to remove it)* 6/1[3]
1300 6 2 3/4 **Rajman**69 5092 3-9-2 60 (h) HarryBentley 8 52
(Tom Clover) *hld up in rr: rdn and no prog 2f out: kpt on fnl f* 14/1
4014 7 hd **Kinglami**13 7115 10-9-2 58 (p) RossaRyan 1 49
(John O'Shea) *trckd ldng pair: rdn and cl up wl over 1f out: steadily wknd* 13/2
0660 8 1 1/2 **Miaella**32 6441 4-9-2 58 (p1) JoeyHaynes 10 44
(Chelsea Banham) *pressed ldrs on outer: rdn over 2f out: wknd over 1f out* 12/1
0245 9 1/2 **Swanton Blue (IRE)**13 7130 6-9-4 60 PatCosgrave 11 45
(Ed de Giles) *hld up in rr: shkn up and no prog 2f out* 10/1
4023 10 5 **Casarubina (IRE)**16 7032 3-9-2 60 CallumShepherd 2 30
(Nick Littmoden) *chsd ldrs: rdn over 2f out: wknd jst over 1f out: eased last 100yds (vet said filly was lame in behind)* 8/1
0005 11 27 **The Lacemaker**36 6299 5-9-3 59 (p) JFEgan 7 +
(Milton Harris) *blindfold off v late and c out of stall nrly 20 l bhd: a t.o (jockey said mare reared her head as he attempted to remove the blindfold so therefore it took a second attempt to remove it)* 25/1
1m 13.09s (-0.01) **Going Correction** +0.075s/f (Slow)
WFA 3 from 4yo+ 2lb **11 Ran SP% 125.2**
Speed ratings (Par 101): **103,101,101,101,99 96,95,93,93,86 50**
CSF £42.74 CT £201.11 TOTE £3.20: £1.30, £4.10, £2.00; EX 49.80 Trifecta £297.80.
Owner Martin J Gibbs & R D John **Bred** Janice Woods **Trained** Brighton, East Sussex
FOCUS
Almost a classified event, with just 2lb covering the entire field in a competitive, albeit very moderate, handicap.
T/Plt: £16.40 to a £1 stake. Pool: £51,529.95. 2,288.35 winning units. T/Qpdt: £12.10 to a £1 stake. Pool: £5,554.87. 338.86 winning units. **Jonathan Neesom**

7414 NEWCASTLE (A.W) (L-H)
Wednesday, September 25

OFFICIAL GOING: Tapeta: standard
Wind: Virtually nil Weather: Cloudy

7577 DESIGNS.UK.NET H'CAP 1m 4f 98y (Tp)
5:15 (5:15) (Class 4) (0-85,83) 3-Y-O+ £5,207 (£1,549; £774; £400; £400; £400) Stalls High

Form RPR
4526 1 **Lopes Dancer (IRE)**137 2636 7-9-2 73 BenRobinson 2 80
(Brian Ellison) *led 3f: trckd ldr: led again 2f out: sn rdn: jnd and drvn over 1f out: kpt on wl towards fin* 18/1
0643 2 3/4 **Asian Angel (IRE)**22 6842 3-9-5 83 FrannyNorton 5 89
(Mark Johnston) *trckd ldrs: hdwy 4f out: pushed along 3f out: sn rdn and sltly outpcd: styd on u.p fnl f* 5/2[2]
3104 3 1/2 **Autretot (FR)**60 5436 4-9-11 82 DanielTudhope 3 87
(David O'Meara) *hld up in rr: smooth hdwy over 3f out: cl up 2f out: chal on bit over 1f out: rdn and ev ch ent fnl f: sn drvn and kpt on same pce* 2/1[1]
3322 4 1 1/2 **Dante's View (IRE)**15 7057 3-9-2 80 RichardKingscote 7 83
(Sir Michael Stoute) *cl up: led after 3f: rdn over 2f out: sn hdd and drvn: wknd wl over 1f out* 2/1[1]
1040 5 3/4 **Royal Cosmic**74 4913 5-8-12 72 SeanDavis(3) 4 74
(Richard Fahey) *trckd ldrs: pushed along 3f out: rdn along 2f out: sn drvn and plugged on one pce (vet said mare had a wound on it's left hind foot)* 22/1
0000 6 7 **Desert Ruler**17 7003 6-9-12 83 JackGarritty 1 73
(Jedd O'Keeffe) *hld up: a towards rr* 16/1[3]
2m 42.83s (1.73) **Going Correction** +0.10s/f (Slow)
WFA 3 from 4yo+ 7lb **6 Ran SP% 110.7**
Speed ratings (Par 105): **98,97,97,96,95 91**
CSF £61.00 TOTE £9.70: £6.00, £1.50; EX 25.00 Trifecta £102.50.
Owner W A Bethell **Bred** Carol Burke & Lope De Vega Syndicate **Trained** Norton, N Yorks
FOCUS
A competitive opener, won by a course specialist. They didn't go awfully quick throughout and it paid to sit handy. The form makes sense, with the winner rated close to his best, and the second close to form.

7578 DESIGNS SIGNAGE H'CAP 1m 2f 42y (Tp)
5:45 (5:46) (Class 6) (0-55,55) 3-Y-O+ £2,781 (£827; £413; £400; £400; £400) Stalls High

Form RPR
0033 1 **Corked (IRE)**7 7335 6-9-5 52 PJMcDonald 14 61
(Alistair Whillans) *stdd s and hld up in rr: swtchd rt and hdwy 2f out: str run fr over 1f out: rdn and styd on wl fnl f to ld last 75yds* 14/1
0531 2 1 1/4 **Poetic Legacy (IRE)**6 7375 3-9-2 54 6ex DanielTudhope 11 62
(Mark Johnston) *racd wd early: cl up: effrt to ld 2f out: rdn ent fnl f: hdd and drvn last 75yds: kpt on same pce* 1/1[1]
4032 3 3/4 **Point Of Honour (IRE)**22 6828 4-8-13 46 (p) PaulMulrennan 3 51
(Phillip Makin) *trckd ldrs: hdwy over 2f out: rdn over 1f out: drvn and kpt on fnl f* 7/1[3]
0011 4 nk **About Glory**10 7232 5-9-7 54 5ex (vt) DavidAllan 8 59
(Iain Jardine) *prom: hdwy over 3f out: cl up over 2f out: rdn and ev ch over 1f out: drvn and kpt on same pce fnl f* 6/1[2]
0255 5 3/4 **Kodi Koh (IRE)**7 7335 4-8-11 47 RowanScott(3) 1 51
(Simon West) *trckd ldrs: hdwy 3f out: cl up wl over 1f out: sn rdn and ev ch: drvn and wknd fnl f (jockey said filly hung right-handed under pressure)* 18/1
0256 6 1 **Ritchie Star (IRE)**47 5915 3-9-3 55 AndrewMullen 9 58
(Ben Haslam) *midfield: effrt and hdwy 3f out: rdn along wl over 1f out: sn drvn and n.d* 14/1
2010 7 1/2 **Melabi (IRE)**18 6982 6-9-2 49 JackGarritty 12 50
(Stella Barclay) *hld up towards rr: effrt 3f out: rdn along over 2f out: n.d* 66/1
4502 8 1 1/2 **Tails I Win (CAN)**18 6983 3-9-1 53 (h) BenCurtis 7 52
(Roger Fell) *t.k.h: nvr bttr than midfield (jockey said filly ran too free)* 12/1
0-03 9 1 **My Renaissance**15 5851 9-9-4 54 (bt) JaneElliott(3) 10 50
(Sam England) *hld up towards rr: hdwy on inner 3f out: chsd ldrs and rdn along wl over 1f out: grad wknd* 100/1
-364 10 2 1/4 **Cottingham**26 6663 4-8-13 46 LukeMorris 4 38
(Kevin Frost) *chsd ldrs: rdn along wl over 2f out: drvn wl over 1f out: sn wknd* 20/1
5502 11 nk **Silk Mill Blue**56 5555 5-9-3 50 PhilDennis 13 42
(Richard Whitaker) *a towards rr* 33/1
500 12 1 3/4 **Lucy's Law (IRE)**26 6663 5-9-7 54 (p1) DavidNolan 2 43
(Tom Tate) *a towards rr* 33/1

The Form Book Flat 2019, Raceform Ltd, Newbury, RG14 5SJ

0005 13 2¾ **Laqab (IRE)**[49] 5817 6-9-4 **51**........................ PaddyMathers 5 35
(Derek Shaw) *s.i.s: a in rr (jockey said gelding was slowly away)* **33/1**

3-46 14 10 **Sils Maria**[25] 6701 3-8-13 **51**........................(h) ConnorBeasley 6 18
(Ann Duffield) *led: pushed along over 3f out: sn rdn: hdd 2f out and wknd qckly* **125/1**

2m 10.91s (0.51) **Going Correction** +0.10s/f (Slow)
WFA 3 from 4yo+ 5lb **14 Ran SP% 119.9**
Speed ratings (Par 101): **102,101,100,100,99 98,98,97,96,94 94,92,90,82**
CSF £27.13 CT £119.53 TOTE £16.90: £3.70, £1.10, £2.50; EX 38.50 Trifecta £244.50.
Owner Shmelt For Gold **Bred** Lisieux Stud **Trained** Newmill-On-Slitrig, Borders

FOCUS
A low grade handicap, with a muddling gallop, and a surprise winner from well off the pace.

7579 DESIGNS SIGNAGE EBF NOVICE STKS 1m 5y (Tp)
6:15 (6:19) (Class 5) 2-Y-O £3,752 (£1,116; £557; £278) **Stalls Centre**

Form RPR

4 1 **Anastarsia (IRE)**[18] 6949 2-9-0 0........................ PJMcDonald 2 79+
(John Gosden) *mde all: pushed along 2f out: rdn over 1f out: strly chal and drvn ins fnl f: kpt on strly* **3/1**[3]

3 2 1½ **Crystal Pegasus**[19] 6912 2-9-5 0........................ RichardKingscote 6 81
(Sir Michael Stoute) *trckd ldng pair: hdwy to chse wnr wl over 1f out: sn rdn: chal ent fnl f: ev ch tl drvn and kpt on same pce last 100yds* **5/6**[1]

0 3 7 **Genesius (IRE)**[57] 5512 2-9-5 0........................ PaulMulrennan 7 67
(Julie Camacho) *trckd ldrs: hdwy 2f out: sn rdn: kpt on one pce fnl f* **125/1**

4 2 **Despoina (IRE)** 2-9-0 0........................ GrahamLee 4 56
(Jedd O'Keeffe) *green and towards rr: hdwy 2f out: sn rdn along and kpt on fnl f* **40/1**

5 nk **Imperial Square (IRE)** 2-9-5 0........................ DanielTudhope 5 61
(Mark Johnston) *cl up: pushed along 2f out: sn rdn and wknd* **11/4**[2]

0 6 16 **Anno Lucis (IRE)**[6] 7388 2-9-5 0........................ LukeMorris 8 25
(Sir Mark Prescott Bt) *towards rr: pushed along 3f out: sn rdn and outpcd fnl 2f* **150/1**

0 7 8 **Helmoona**[18] 6970 2-9-5 0........................ JamesSullivan 3 8
(Karen Tutty) *t.k.h: chsd ldrs: rdn along bef 1/2-way: sn outpcd and bhd* **100/1**

1m 40.02s (1.42) **Going Correction** +0.10s/f (Slow) **7 Ran SP% 111.1**
Speed ratings (Par 95): **96,94,87,85,85 69,61**
CSF £5.60 TOTE £4.10: £1.60, £1.10; EX 6.60 Trifecta £105.30.
Owner M J & L A Taylor **Bred** Elysian Bloodstock Ltd **Trained** Newmarket, Suffolk

FOCUS
An interesting novice stakes, with the front two pulling well clear, indicating they may be well above average.

7580 EQUINE PRODUCTS EBF FILLIES' NOVICE STKS (PLUS 10 RACE) 6f (Tp)
6:45 (6:51) (Class 5) 2-Y-O £3,752 (£1,116; £557; £278) **Stalls Centre**

Form RPR

31 1 **Jovial**[31] 6514 2-9-7 0........................ RichardKingscote 8 76+
(Sir Michael Stoute) *prom: cl up 1/2-way: chal 2f out: slt ld 1 1/2f out: rdn ins fnl f: kpt on strly* **2/5**[1]

2 1 **Zezenia (IRE)** 2-9-0 0........................ DavidEgan 9 66+
(Roger Varian) *t.k.h: led: jnd 2f out and sn pushed along rdn and hdd narrowly 1 1/2f out: ev ch tl kpt on same pce ins fnl f* **4/1**[2]

00 3 2½ **Somekindasuperstar**[19] 6943 2-9-0 0........................ DavidAllan 11 59
(Paul Collins) *trckd ldrs: hdwy 2f out: rdn along wl over 1f out: kpt on u.p fnl f* **250/1**

4 nk **Grace And Virtue (IRE)** 2-9-0 0........................ TonyHamilton 10 58+
(Richard Fahey) *trckd ldrs: hdwy wl over 1f out: sn rdn and kpt on fnl f* **14/1**

5 ½ **Momentum** 2-9-0 0........................ CamHardie 12 56
(Antony Brittain) *trckd ldrs: effrt over 2f out: sn rdn: kpt on same pce fr over 1f out* **150/1**

6 nk **Rock Of Fame** 2-9-0 0........................ JackMitchell 2 55+
(Roger Varian) *green and towards rr: pushed along and hdwy wl over 1f out: swtchd rt to stands' rail ent fnl f: fin wl* **25/1**

7 ½ **Bound For Heaven** 2-9-0 0........................ PJMcDonald 7 54
(K R Burke) *cl up: rdn along over 2f out: wknd wl over 1f out* **16/1**

3 8 1 **Excel And Succeed (IRE)**[41] 6096 2-9-0 0........................ PaulMulrennan 3 51
(Michael Dods) *t.k.h: chsd ldrs: rdn along over 2f out: grad wknd* **9/1**[3]

9 1½ **Sea Ewe** 2-9-0 0........................ JamesSullivan 1 46
(Alistair Whillans) *green: a towards rr* **150/1**

10 nse **Global Orchid (IRE)** 2-9-0 0........................ GeraldMosse 6 46
(Tom Dascombe) *dwlt: a in rr* **28/1**

0 11 nk **Elfrida Beetle**[14] 7063 2-9-0 0........................ DuranFentiman 5 45
(Tim Easterby) *midfield: pushed along 1/2-way: wknd over 2f out* **250/1**

1m 15.04s (2.54) **Going Correction** +0.10s/f (Slow) **11 Ran SP% 123.4**
Speed ratings (Par 92): **87,85,82,81,81 80,80,78,76,76 76**
CSF £2.52 TOTE £1.30: £1.02, £1.60, £25.40; EX 3.20 Trifecta £195.80.
Owner K Abdullah **Bred** Juddmonte Farms Ltd **Trained** Newmarket, Suffolk

FOCUS
A straight forward success for the well-backed favourite. It paid to race prominent.

7581 SKY SPORTS RACING ON VIRGIN CHANNEL 535 H'CAP 1m 5y (Tp)
7:15 (7:18) (Class 6) (0-60,60) 3-Y-O+ £2,781 (£827; £413; £400; £400; £400) **Stalls Centre**

Form RPR

5202 1 **Colonel Slade (IRE)**[63] 5304 3-9-2 **58**........................(t w) BenCurtis 1 65
(Phillip Makin) *mde all: rdn wl over 1f out: strly pressed and drvn ins fnl f: kpt on gamely towards fin* **6/1**[3]

2003 2 ½ **Traveller (FR)**[60] 5438 5-9-4 **56**........................(tp) CamHardie 8 62
(Antony Brittain) *trckd ldrs: hdwy 2f out: sn rdn to chal: drvn to dispute ld and ev ch ins fnl f: no ex towards fin* **11/2**[2]

1-03 3 nk **Troop**[50] 5787 4-8-13 **51**........................ FrannyNorton 12 56
(Ann Duffield) *trckd ldng pair: hdwy 3f out: rdn along over to chse wnr wl 1f out: drvn ent fnl f: kpt on towards fin* **15/2**

300 4 1¾ **Blazing Dreams (IRE)**[48] 5852 3-9-4 **60**........................(p) AndrewMullen 7 61
(Ben Haslam) *in tch: pushed along and sltly outpcd over 2f out: sn rdn: styd on to chse ldrs ent fnl f: sn drvn and no imp* **5/1**[1]

2062 5 2¼ **Jazz Hands (IRE)**[28] 6610 3-8-8 **53**........................ SeanDavis(3) 10 49
(Richard Fahey) *hld up towards rr: hdwy over 2f out: rdn wl over 1f out: kpt on fnl f* **14/1**

0065 6 1¾ **Hitman**[37] 6275 6-9-6 **58**........................ LewisEdmunds 13 51
(Rebecca Bastiman) *hld up in rr: hdwy 2f out: rdn to chse ldrs jst over 1f out: kpt on fnl f (vet said gelding lost it's right-hind shoe)* **20/1**

0020 7 shd **Bold Show**[30] 6529 3-9-0 **56**........................(v) TonyHamilton 6 48
(Richard Fahey) *towards rr: pushed along and hdwy 2f out: rdn over 1f out: kpt on fnl f* **20/1**

0445 8 1¼ **Uncle Norman (FR)**[26] 6679 3-8-8 **50**........................(b) DuranFentiman 5 40
(Tim Easterby) *dwlt and towards rr: hdwy and in tch 3f out: rdn along over 2f out: n.d* **10/1**

000- 9 1¼ **Mamdood (IRE)**[396] 6538 5-8-13 **54**........................ HarrisonShaw(3) 4 41
(Stef Keniry) *chsd ldrs: rdn along over 2f out: sn wknd* **12/1**

-606 10 ¾ **Schnapps**[26] 6678 3-8-13 **55**........................ JackGarritty 3 40
(Jedd O'Keeffe) *trckd ldrs: pushed along 3f out: rdn over 2f out: sn wknd* **14/1**

0461 11 nk **Top Offer**[36] 6327 10-8-11 **49**........................(p) DavidEgan 14 34
(Patrick Morris) *a towards rr* **10/1**

00-0 12 1¾ **Amood (IRE)**[27] 6627 8-9-8 **60**........................ AndrewElliott 2 41
(Simon West) *chsd wnr: rdn along over 3f out: sn wknd* **40/1**

3050 13 26 **Clovenstone**[74] 4915 3-9-3 **59**........................ GrahamLee 9
(Alistair Whillans) *midfield: pushed along over 5f out: rdn along wl over 3f out: sn wknd (jockey said gelding hung right-handed throughout)* **28/1**

-056 14 1 **Bouclier (IRE)**[149] 2215 9-9-7 **59**........................ LukeMorris 11
(James Unett) *a towards rr* **33/1**

1m 38.03s (-0.57) **Going Correction** +0.10s/f (Slow)
WFA 3 from 4yo+ 4lb **14 Ran SP% 115.7**
Speed ratings (Par 101): **106,105,105,103,101 99,99,98,96,96 95,94,68,67**
CSF £34.49 CT £258.78 TOTE £5.30: £2.30, £2.10, £2.70; EX 25.00 Trifecta £111.10.
Owner P J Makin **Bred** Kellsgrange Stud & T & J Hurley **Trained** Easingwold, N Yorks

FOCUS
Another race where it paid to sit handy. A thrilling, protracted battle for this weak handicap. A minor pb from the third.

7582 SKY SPORTS RACING ON SKY 415 NURSERY H'CAP 7f 14y (Tp)
7:45 (7:52) (Class 6) (0-65,67) 2-Y-O £2,781 (£827; £413; £400; £400; £400) **Stalls Centre**

Form RPR

000 1 **Kyllwind**[67] 5185 2-9-9 **67**........................ DanielTudhope 11 72+
(Martyn Meade) *trckd ldrs: smooth hdwy 2f out: effrt and qcknd to ld ent fnl f: readily* **4/1**[2]

6035 2 1 **Sir Havelock (IRE)**[27] 6625 2-8-13 **57**........................(p[1]) TonyHamilton 9 59
(Richard Fahey) *towards rr: hdwy over 2f out: rdn over 1f out: styd on wl fnl f* **22/1**

4220 3 nk **We Owen A Dragon**[12] 7140 2-9-7 **65**........................(p) RichardKingscote 3 66
(Tom Dascombe) *trckd ldrs: hdwy and cl up over 2f out: rdn to ld 1 1/2f out: hdd ent fnl f: sn drvn and kpt on same pce* **7/2**[1]

5062 4 nse **Kilig**[8] 7309 2-9-2 **60**........................(bt) DavidAllan 12 61
(Tim Easterby) *racd nr stands' rail: led: pushed along 2f out: rdn over 1f out: hdd ent fnl f: sn drvn and kpt on* **10/1**

0000 5 ½ **Inductive**[8] 7306 2-8-12 **56**........................ CallumRodriguez 1 55
(Michael Dods) *trckd ldrs in centre: hdwy 2f out: rdn over 1f out: drvn and kpt on fnl f* **18/1**

0006 6 1¼ **My Havana**[8] 7306 2-8-11 **55**........................(p) AndrewMullen 13 51
(Nigel Tinkler) *hld up in rr: hdwy 2f out: rdn over 1f out: drvn and kpt on fnl f* **18/1**

6601 7 nk **Constitutional (IRE)**[8] 7306 2-9-5 **66** 6ex........................ HarrisonShaw(3) 4 62
(K R Burke) *trckd ldrs centre: hdwy 2f out: rdn over 1f out: drvn ent fnl f: kpt on same pce* **9/1**

450 7 dht **Don Ramiro (IRE)**[72] 4984 2-9-6 **64**........................ TomEaves 6 60
(Kevin Ryan) *midfield: effrt over 2f out: sn rdn along and no imp over 1f out* **7/1**[3]

0003 9 1¼ **River Of Kings (IRE)**[8] 7306 2-9-0 **58**........................(h) ShaneGray 7 50
(Keith Dalgleish) *a towards rr* **15/2**

0500 10 2¼ **The Works (IRE)**[9] 7275 2-8-1 **45**........................ CamHardie 10 32
(Declan Carroll) *cl up: rdn along over 2f out: sn drvn and wknd* **80/1**

0452 11 nk **The Ginger Bullet**[15] 7056 2-8-11 **58**........................ SeanDavis(3) 5 44
(Richard Fahey) *cl up: rdn along over 2f out: sn drvn and wknd* **18/1**

0000 12 13 **Gelsmoor Bay**[22] 6837 2-8-2 **46** ow1........................ PaddyMathers 2
(Derek Shaw) *prom centre: rdn along over 3f out: sn wknd* **150/1**

0002 R **Kitos**[10] 7234 2-8-2 **46**........................(b) LukeMorris 8
(Sir Mark Prescott Bt) *ref to r* **16/1**

1m 27.02s (0.82) **Going Correction** +0.10s/f (Slow) **13 Ran SP% 113.5**
Speed ratings (Par 93): **99,97,97,97,96 95,95,95,93,91 90,75,**
WIN: 4.30 Kyllwind; PL: 2.20 Kyllwind 1.10 We Owen A Dragon 6.30 Sir Havelock; EX: 72.70; CSF: 88.34; TC: 345.94; TF: 293.40 CSF £88.34 CT £345.94 TOTE £4.30: £2.20, £6.30, £1.10; EX 72.70 Trifecta £293.40.
Owner Nick Bradley Racing - Mm45 **Bred** Hungerford Park Stud **Trained** Manton, Wilts

FOCUS
A nursery with improving types and a cosy winner. Limited form.

7583 PHOBIA HALLOWEEN EVENT AT NEWCASTLE RACECOURSE FILLIES' H'CAP 7f 14y (Tp)
8:15 (8:19) (Class 5) (0-75,74) 3-Y-O+ £3,428 (£1,020; £509; £400; £400; £400) **Stalls Centre**

Form RPR

522 1 **Critical Time**[53] 5690 3-9-7 **74**........................ DanielTudhope 9 81+
(William Haggas) *racd nr stands' rail: led: rdn along and hdd narrowly over 1f out: drvn ins fnl f: rallied gamely to ld on line* **11/4**[1]

0005 2 nse **Elixsoft (IRE)**[2] 7526 4-9-8 **72**........................(p) BenCurtis 2 80
(Roger Fell) *trckd ldrs on outer: hdwy and cl up 2f out: rdn to take narrow ld over 1f out: drvn and edgd rt ins fnl f: hdd on line* **9/1**

4463 3 1¾ **Regal Banner**[34] 6362 3-9-5 **72**........................(b[1]) DavidEgan 4 74
(Roger Varian) *cl up: pushed along over 2f out: rdn wl over 1f out: drvn and kpt on same pce fnl f* **4/1**[2]

2245 4 ½ **Nooshin**[56] 5565 3-9-7 **74**........................(t[1]) JackMitchell 6 75
(Amy Murphy) *t.k.h: trckd ldrs: hdwy 2f out: rdn to chse ldng pair over 1f out: drvn and kpt on fnl f* **8/1**

0300 5 1¼ **Verdigris (IRE)**[32] 6461 4-8-13 **63**........................ TomEaves 3 62
(Ruth Carr) *hld up in rr: hdwy 2f out: rdn over 1f out: kpt on same pce fnl f* **12/1**

0510 6 ½ **Oriental Lilly**[5] 7402 5-8-11 **68**........................(p) CoreyMadden(7) 8 65
(Jim Goldie) *hld up in rr tl styd on fr wl over 1f out: n.d* **15/2**

1360 7 1¾ **Aliento**[9] 7289 4-9-0 **64**........................ CallumRodriguez 5 56
(Michael Dods) *prom: cl up 1/2-way: rdn along wl over 2f out: grad wknd* **6/1**[3]

1252 8 1 **Firsteen**[19] 6945 3-8-7 **60**........................ AndrewMullen 1 49
(Alistair Whillans) *dwlt: t.k.h and sn chsng ldrs: rdn along wl over 2f out: sn wknd* **15/2**

000 9 3 **Jo's Girl (IRE)**68 5117 4-8-5 **58** HarrisonShaw(3) 7 40
(Micky Hammond) *a towards rr* **33/1**
1m 26.85s (0.65) **Going Correction** +0.10s/f (Slow)
WFA 3 from 4yo+ 3lb **9 Ran SP% 116.2**
Speed ratings (Par 100): **100,99,97,97,95 95,93,92,88**
CSF £28.67 CT £99.53 TOTE £2.50: £1.90, £3.10, £1.70; EX 31.00 Trifecta £74.50.
Owner Mr & Mrs R Scott **Bred** Mr & Mrs R & P Scott **Trained** Newmarket, Suffolk
FOCUS
A moderate handicap. Two groups merged to the stands' side after 2f and a head-bob finish. The second has been rated to her best.
T/Plt: £22.40 to a £1 stake. Pool: £55,884.35. 1,821.03 winning units. T/Qpdt: £5.60 to a £1 stake. Pool: £8,408.94. 1,101.89 winning units. **Joe Rowntree**

7308 REDCAR (L-H)
Wednesday, September 25

OFFICIAL GOING: Good (good to soft in places)
Wind: virtually nil Weather: overcast

7584 BEST FLAT RACES LIVE ON RACING TV NURSERY H'CAP 5f 217y
12:15 (12:17) (Class 6) (0-60,61) 2-Y-O
£3,500 (£1,041; £520; £300; £300; £300) **Stalls Centre**

Form RPR
303 1 **Solemn Pledge**11 7211 2-9-5 **61** HarrisonShaw(3) 2 69+
(K R Burke) *midfield: pushed along and hdwy over 2f out: chal over 1f out: sn edgd rt: rdn to ld ins fnl f: kpt on* **5/1**
3221 2 3/4 **Two Hearts**26 6683 2-9-4 **57** SamJames 5 63
(Grant Tuer) *prom: rdn into narrow ld over 1f out: bmpd sltly and hdd ins fnl f: kpt on but hld in 2nd fnl 110yds* **10/3**2
5530 3 3 1/4 **Puerto Sol (IRE)**11 7208 2-9-4 **57** BenRobinson 6 53
(Brian Ellison) *dwlt sltly: midfield: sn pushed along: rdn over 2f out: kpt on ins fnl f: wnt 3rd towards fin* **33/1**
0002 4 hd **Rebel Redemption**9 7283 2-9-7 **60** (p) JasonHart 10 56
(John Quinn) *trckd ldrs: rdn 2f out: kpt on same pce ins fnl f* **3/1**1
5065 5 nk **Mumsbirthdaygirl (IRE)**13 7110 2-8-6 **45** AndrewMullen 3 40
(Mark Loughnane) *hld up: rdn and hdwy over 1f out: kpt on ins fnl f* **66/1**
640 6 hd **Pearl Stream**36 6313 2-9-6 **59** CallumRodriguez 9 53
(Michael Dods) *midfield: rdn over 2f out: styd on ins fnl f* **12/1**
5660 7 1 **Speed Dating (FR)**15 7056 2-9-3 **59** (v1) NoelGarbutt(3) 4 50
(Derek Shaw) *hld up: sn pushed along: nvr threatened* **28/1**
0400 8 hd **Newsical**14 7064 2-9-7 **60** DougieCostello 1 51+
(Mark Walford) *slowly away and in rr: sme late hdwy: nvr a threat (jockey said gelding was slowly away)* **14/1**
0600 9 1 1/2 **Order Of Merritt (IRE)**13 7111 2-8-6 **45** (b) LukeMorris 8 31
(Sir Mark Prescott Bt) *led: rdn over 2f out: hdd over 1f out: wknd fnl f* **40/1**
5002 10 2 **Holloa**9 7284 2-9-7 **60** DavidAllan 11 40
(Tim Easterby) *trckd ldrs towards outer: rdn 2f out: wknd ins fnl f (trainer's rep could offer no explanation for the filly's performance)* **9/2**3
5255 11 5 **It's Not My Fault (IRE)**9 7283 2-9-1 **54** KevinStott 7 19
(Paul Midgley) *chsd ldrs: rdn over 2f out: wknd appr fnl f* **8/1**
4004 12 1 1/4 **Sweet Embrace (IRE)**11 7208 2-8-12 **51** TomEaves 12 12
(John Wainwright) *hld up: rdn 2f out: sn wknd* **50/1**
1m 12.41s (0.61) **Going Correction** +0.025s/f (Good) **12 Ran SP% 120.7**
Speed ratings (Par 93): **96,95,90,90,90 89,88,88,86,83 76,75**
CSF £21.71 CT £509.97 TOTE £6.50: £2.20, £1.40, £10.70; EX 21.00 Trifecta £379.50.
Owner Pau-Perth Partnership & Mrs E Burke **Bred** Highclere Stud & Jake Warren Ltd **Trained** Middleham Moor, N Yorks
FOCUS
They went a routine pace in this moderate nursery and two came nicely clear. The winning time was indicative of some cut underfoot. Straightforward form.

7585 WILLIAM HILL LEADING RACECOURSE BOOKMAKER NURSERY H'CAP 7f 219y
12:45 (12:46) (Class 5) (0-70,71) 2-Y-O
£3,737 (£1,112; £555; £300; £300; £300) **Stalls Centre**

Form RPR
454 1 **Breguet Boy (IRE)**15 7046 2-9-5 **67** CallumRodriguez 5 71
(Keith Dalgleish) *trckd ldrs: pushed along and bit short of room over 1f out: angled rt and in clr appr fnl f: rdn and styd on wl: led 50yds out* **11/2**3
2315 2 1 **Out Of Breath**18 6969 2-9-9 **71** SamJames 2 73
(Grant Tuer) *prom: led over 2f out: sn pushed along: rdn and pressed appr fnl f: styd on but hdd fnl 50yds* **4/1**1
566 3 nk **Cold Light Of Day**18 6970 2-9-2 **64** PaulMulrennan 1 65
(Michael Dods) *dwlt: sn midfield: racd quite keenly: pushed along 3f out: hdwy and chsd ldrs 2f out: rdn to chal appr fnl f: styd on same pce* **6/1**
0606 4 2 1/4 **Carriesmatic**31 6497 2-8-9 **57** JasonHart 4 53
(David Barron) *dwlt: hld up: rdn and hdwy over 1f out: styd on to go 4th ins fnl f* **18/1**
2136 5 3 **G For Gabrial (IRE)**18 6969 2-9-7 **69** PaulHanagan 9 58
(Richard Fahey) *trckd ldrs: rdn 2f out: wknd ins fnl f* **5/1**2
5060 6 shd **The Trendy Man (IRE)**8 7306 2-8-2 **50** (p) AndrewMullen 6 39
(David O'Meara) *prom: rdn over 2f out: outpcd over 1f out: wknd ins fnl f* **66/1**
060 7 2 3/4 **Roman's Empress (IRE)**14 7067 2-8-9 **57** DavidEgan 3 39
(David Loughnane) *sn led: rdn and hdd over 2f out: wknd appr fnl f* **25/1**
604 8 1/2 **Araka Li (IRE)**18 6970 2-9-9 **71** DavidAllan 7 52
(Tim Easterby) *hld up: racd keenly: pushed along over 2f out: sn btn (jockey said colt ran too free)* **8/1**
213 9 1 **Restless Endeavour (IRE)**28 6603 2-9-9 **71** DougieCostello 8 50
(Jamie Osborne) *midfield: rdn over 2f out: wknd fnl f* **20/1**
655 10 nk **Sun Crystal (IRE)**19 6918 2-9-6 **68** TonyHamilton 12 46
(Richard Fahey) *hld up: nvr threatened* **16/1**
0632 11 3/4 **Susie Javea**47 5912 2-8-1 **49** CamHardie 11 26
(Ollie Pears) *hld up in midfield: rdn over 2f out: wknd over 1f out (jockey said filly hung left-handed from 1/2f out)* **28/1**
550 12 hd **Bryn Du**16 7030 2-9-0 **62** DanielTudhope 10 38
(William Haggas) *hld up: pushed along over 2f out: sme hdwy 2f out: briefly short of room over 1f out: sn rdn: wknd ins fnl f* **5/1**2
5020 13 11 **Kentucky Hardboot (IRE)**9 7277 2-8-11 **59** (v1) FrannyNorton 14 10
(Mick Channon) *midfield: rdn over 2f out: wknd over 1f out* **33/1**
1m 39.28s (2.68) **Going Correction** +0.025s/f (Good) **13 Ran SP% 121.8**
Speed ratings (Par 95): **87,86,85,83,80 80,77,77,76,75 75,74,63**
CSF £26.69 CT £126.94 TOTE £9.90: £2.80, £2.00, £2.10; EX 35.50 Trifecta £249.20.
Owner Raymond McNeill **Bred** Kevin F O'Donnell & Miriam O'Donnell **Trained** Carluke, S Lanarks
FOCUS
The principals dominated the finish of this run-of-the-mill nursery. Ordinary form.

7586 BRITISH EBF FUTURE STAYERS MAIDEN STKS (PLUS 10 RACE) (A MATCHBOOK EBF SIRE & DAM RESTRICTED RACE) 7f
1:15 (1:15) (Class 4) 2-Y-O
£10,350 (£3,080; £1,539; £769) **Stalls Centre**

Form RPR
66 1 **Convict**17 7000 2-9-5 0 DanielTudhope 4 82+
(William Haggas) *sn trckd ldrs: pushed along to chse ldr 2f out: led 1f out: rdn and styd on wl: eased towards fin* **6/4**1
2 2 1/4 **Bright Eyed Eagle (IRE)** 2-9-5 0 LukeMorris 10 74+
(Ed Walker) *dwlt: hld up: hdwy into midfield over 3f out: sn pushed along: chsd ldrs over 1f out: styd on wl fnl f: wnt 2nd towards fin* **14/1**
55 3 3/4 **Talap**12 7151 2-9-5 0 (p1) DavidEgan 6 72
(Roger Varian) *prom: led 5f out: rdn 2 l clr 2f out: hdd 1f out: sn no ex: lost 2nd towards fin* **7/1**3
2 4 1 **Bentley Wood**14 7067 2-9-5 0 TomEaves 1 69
(Mick Channon) *sn trckd ldrs: rdn over 2f out: drvn over 1f out: kpt on same pce* **15/8**2
5 3 1/4 **Eagle Court (IRE)** 2-9-5 0 DavidNolan 7 61
(David O'Meara) *midfield: racd quite keenly: pushed along over 3f out: kpt on ins fnl f* **33/1**
6 3 **Puckle** 2-9-0 0 DavidAllan 5 48
(Tim Easterby) *prom: rdn over 2f out: wknd appr fnl f* **50/1**
44 7 nk **Philosophical**26 6664 2-9-5 0 GrahamLee 8 52
(Jedd O'Keeffe) *dwlt: hld up: minor late hdwy: nvr threatened* **28/1**
0 8 2 1/4 **Peerless Percy (IRE)**20 6892 2-9-5 0 CallumRodriguez 9 47
(Michael Dods) *hld up in midfield: pushed along and outpcd 3f out: no threat after* **50/1**
9 3 **Rulers Kingdom (IRE)** 2-9-5 0 FrannyNorton 2 39
(Mark Johnston) *led: hdd 5f out: remained prom tl wknd 2f out* **15/2**
5 10 1/2 **Dangeroffizz (IRE)**17 7000 2-9-5 0 RachelRichardson 11 37
(Tim Easterby) *a towards rr* **66/1**
0 11 8 **More Than Love**17 7000 2-9-0 0 (t1) DannyRedmond(5) 3 17
(Tim Easterby) *prom: racd keenly: wknd over 2f out* **66/1**
1m 25.38s (-0.02) **Going Correction** +0.025s/f (Good) **11 Ran SP% 119.0**
Speed ratings (Par 97): **101,98,97,96,92 89,88,86,82,82 73**
CSF £23.46 TOTE £2.80: £1.10, £4.20, £1.90; EX 33.20 Trifecta £130.90.
Owner B Haggas **Bred** J B Haggas **Trained** Newmarket, Suffolk
FOCUS
This wasn't a bad 2yo maiden and they went a fair pace. The opening level is a bit fluid.

7587 FOLLOW @WILLHILLRACING ON TWITTER (S) STKS 7f 219y
1:45 (1:47) (Class 5) 3-Y-O+
£3,737 (£1,112; £555; £300; £300; £300) **Stalls Centre**

Form RPR
033 1 **Be Kool (IRE)**19 6935 6-9-0 **77** (v) BenRobinson 12 60+
(Brian Ellison) *chsd ldrs: rdn along over 2f out: led over 1f out: edgd rt: kpt on wl* **6/4**1
000 2 2 3/4 **Intense Style (IRE)**12 7145 7-9-0 **61** (b) DanielTudhope 6 54
(Les Eyre) *slowly away: hld up: rdn and outpcd in rr 4f out: hdwy over 1f out: wnt 2nd ins fnl f: kpt on* **7/1**3
0500 3 1 3/4 **Shamaheart (IRE)**27 6627 9-9-0 **55** (tp) DavidAllan 11 50
(Geoffrey Harker) *hld up: pushed along over 2f out: sme hdwy appr fnl f: kpt on* **22/1**
3423 4 nk **Muatadel**19 6937 6-9-10 **64** (v) PaulMulrennan 2 59
(John Wainwright) *midfield: rdn over 2f out: kpt on fnl f* **12/1**
0000 5 1 **Lord Rob**4 7444 8-8-11 **42** HarrisonShaw(3) 1 47
(David Thompson) *slowly away: hld up: hdwy into midfield over 3f out: rdn over 2f out: kpt on same pce (jockey said gelding was slowly away)* **100/1**
0060 6 nk **Proceeding**26 6666 4-9-0 **48** (p1) CamHardie 4 46
(Tracy Waggott) *nvr bttr than midfield* **33/1**
0260 7 1/2 **Ambient (IRE)**14 7087 4-9-0 **73** (p) DougieCostello 8 45
(Jamie Osborne) *prom: led over 2f out: sn rdn: hdd over 1f out: wknd ins fnl f (jockey said gelding hung right-handed under pressure)* **8/1**
0200 8 nk **Hippeia (IRE)**7 7335 4-8-9 **55** (v) PhilDennis 7 39
(Lawrence Mullaney) *sn led: rdn and hdd over 2f out: wknd fnl f* **25/1**
1202 9 10 **Thornaby Nash**56 5560 8-9-10 **68** (b) TomEaves 3 31
(Jason Ward) *chsd ldrs: rdn over 2f out: wknd over 1f out* **11/2**2
0000 10 1 **Crimson Skies (IRE)**19 6945 4-8-9 **53** (b1) SamJames 5 14
(John Davies) *midfield: rdn over 3f out: wknd 2f out* **25/1**
6500 11 8 **Roller**8 7305 6-9-0 **69** PaulHanagan 10
(Mark Loughnane) *midfield: rdn over 2f out: wknd (trainer's rep said that gelding was unsuited by the good, good to soft going and would prefer a quicker surface)* **11/2**2
1m 38.64s (2.04) **Going Correction** +0.025s/f (Good) **11 Ran SP% 118.0**
Speed ratings (Par 103): **90,87,85,85,84 83,83,83,73,72 64**
CSF £11.63 TOTE £2.00: £1.10, £3.40, £5.30; EX 14.20 Trifecta £180.80.There was no bid for the winner. Intense Style was claimed by Mr. Denis Quinn for £10,000.
Owner Miss Jessica J Bell **Bred** E Lonergan **Trained** Norton, N Yorks
FOCUS
There was a solid pace on in this moderate seller. The fifth is among those who limits the level.

7588 WILLIAM HILL BETTING TV H'CAP 5f
2:20 (2:21) (Class 5) (0-70,70) 3-Y-O+
£3,737 (£1,112; £555; £300; £300; £300) **Stalls Centre**

Form RPR
330 1 **Hard Solution**54 5620 3-8-13 **63** DanielTudhope 6 73
(David O'Meara) *prom: rdn into narrow ld over 1f out: drvn and kpt on wl in sustained duel w 2nd fnl f (trainer could offer no explanation for the gelding's apparent improved form)* **8/1**
4402 2 nk **Lydiate Lady**3 7488 7-8-9 **58** JasonHart 3 67
(Eric Alston) *prom: rdn to chal strly appr fnl f: kpt on but a jst hld* **3/1**1
3160 3 2 1/2 **Piazon**15 7052 8-8-12 **61** (be) NathanEvans 7 61
(Julia Brooke) *chsd ldrs: rdn over 2f out: kpt on same pce* **20/1**
4030 4 1/2 **Astrophysics**26 6659 7-8-7 **56** oh2 (p) CamHardie 8 54
(Lynn Siddall) *hld up: rdn and hdwy over 1f out: kpt on ins fnl f* **40/1**
5514 5 nk **Northern Society (IRE)**19 6936 3-8-12 **62** ShaneGray 1 59
(Keith Dalgleish) *dwlt: hld up: rdn and sme hdwy appr fnl f: kpt on* **9/1**
5440 6 3/4 **Bowson Fred**14 7077 7-9-2 **70** GerO'Neill(5) 10 64
(Michael Easterby) *dwlt: sn midfield: rdn over 2f out: briefly chsd ldrs on outer over 1f out: no ex ins fnl f* **10/3**2
3000 7 1/2 **Timetodock**6 7387 3-9-6 **70** (b) DavidAllan 9 63
(Tim Easterby) *chsd ldrs: rdn over 2f out: wknd ins fnl f* **16/1**

4100 **8** *1* **Superseded (IRE)**[40] 6183 3-9-4 **68**.................... DavidEgan 2 57
(John Butler) *chsd ldrs: rdn over 2f out: wknd fnl f* **16/1**

060 **9** *½* **Angel Force (IRE)**[102] 3868 4-9-5 **68**....................(w) PhilDennis 5 55
(David C Griffiths) *stmbld s but sn led: rdn and hdd over 1f out: sn wknd* **20/1**

2004 **10** *shd* **Tomahawk Ridge (IRE)**[54] 5603 3-8-11 **61**.................... PJMcDonald 4 48
(John Gallagher) *chsd ldrs: rdn along and outpcd 3f out: wknd ins fnl f* **14/1**

0-31 **11** *1 ¼* **Buniann (IRE)**[19] 6944 3-9-5 **69**.................... KevinStott 12 51
(Paul Midgley) *hld up on outer: rdn 2f out: nvr threatened* **11/2**[3]

4401 **12** *¾* **Bashiba (IRE)**[19] 6932 8-8-13 **65**....................(t) RowanScott(3) 11 45
(Nigel Tinkler) *a towards rr* **14/1**

58.49s (-0.01) **Going Correction** +0.025s/f (Good) **12 Ran SP% 121.6**
WFA 3 from 4yo+ 1lb
Speed ratings (Par 103): **101,100,96,95,95 94,93,91,90,90 88,87**
CSF £32.25 CT £482.06 TOTE £8.20: £2.80, £1.40, £5.40; EX 38.60 Trifecta £612.90.
Owner Rasio Cymru Racing 1 & Partner **Bred** Whitsbury Manor Stud **Trained** Upper Helmsley, N Yorks

FOCUS
The first pair came clear nearer the far side in this modest sprint handicap. The second has been rated as backing up her recent Hamilton effort.

7589 WILLIAM HILL BEST ODDS GUARANTEED H'CAP 1m 2f 1y
2:50 (2:51) (Class 4) (0-85,86) 3-Y-O+
£5,692 (£1,694; £846; £423; £300; £300) **Stalls Low**

Form RPR

3040 **1** **Scottish Summit (IRE)**[12] 7142 6-9-3 **78**.................... SamJames 8 89+
(Geoffrey Harker) *midfield: smooth hdwy over 2f out: chsd ldr appr fnl f: led 110yds out: pushed out (trainer said gelding appreciated the step up in trip to 1m2f)* **25/1**

2453 **2** *½* **Addis Ababa (IRE)**[17] 6998 4-9-10 **85**....................(p) DanielTudhope 7 95
(David O'Meara) *dwlt but sn led: rdn 3 l clr over 2f out: drvn and reduced advantage appr fnl f: hdd 110yds out: one pce* **9/4**[1]

4104 **3** *3 ½* **Delph Crescent (IRE)**[13] 7127 4-9-0 **75**....................(v) PaulHanagan 4 78
(Richard Fahey) *trckd ldrs: racd keenly: rdn over 2f out: kpt on same pce* **16/1**

1010 **4** *¾* **Mr Coco Bean (USA)**[17] 6998 5-9-4 **79**.................... GrahamLee 1 81+
(David Barron) *midfield: short of room on inner and lost pl over 2f out: lot to do after: swtchd rt ins fnl f: kpt on: nrst fin* **14/1**

16-3 **5** *½* **Brassica (IRE)**[7] 7347 3-9-3 **83**.................... LukeMorris 6 85
(Sir Mark Prescott Bt) *prom: racd keenly: pushed along over 3f out: drvn over 1f out: wknd ins fnl f (jockey said filly ran flat)* **9/4**[1]

2223 **6** *hd* **Takumi (IRE)**[33] 6411 3-9-4 **84**.................... DavidEgan 9 85
(Roger Varian) *hld up in rr: rdn over 2f out: kpt on fnl f: nvr threatened* **7/2**[2]

5603 **7** *2* **Top Notch Tonto (IRE)**[11] 7185 9-8-10 **71** oh1.................... BenCurtis 10 67
(Brian Ellison) *hld up: rdn along 3f out: nvr threatened* **16/1**

0-00 **8** *nk* **Jamih**[11] 7185 4-9-1 **76**.................... TomEaves 2 72
(Tina Jackson) *prom: rdn along and outpcd over 2f out: swtchd rt over 1f out: plugging on whn short of room fnl 75yds* **80/1**

165 **9** *1* **Edgar Allan Poe (IRE)**[51] 5725 5-9-1 **76**.................... PhilDennis 5 70
(Rebecca Bastiman) *hld up: pushed along whn bit short of room 2f out: nvr threatened* **50/1**

0500 **10** *¾* **Awake My Soul (IRE)**[19] 6923 10-9-11 **86**.................... JamesSullivan 3 78
(Tom Tate) *trckd ldrs: rdn along 3f out: outpcd and losing pl whn short of room over 1f out: wknd ins fnl f* **12/1**[3]

2m 7.35s (0.45) **Going Correction** +0.025s/f (Good) **10 Ran SP% 116.9**
WFA 3 from 4yo+ 5lb
Speed ratings (Par 105): **99,98,95,95,94 94,93,92,92,91**
CSF £80.93 CT £974.33 TOTE £29.40: £5.60, £1.40, £3.50; EX 102.70 Trifecta £1693.60.
Owner T Banerjee,N Mather,P Downes & G Harker **Bred** Ballymacoll Stud Farm Ltd **Trained** Thirkleby, N Yorks

FOCUS
This feature handicap was run at a searching pace and few landed a blow. The second has been rated to form.

7590 WATCH RACE REPLAYS AT RACINGTV.COM H'CAP (DIV I) 5f 217y
3:25 (3:26) (Class 6) (0-60,65) 3-Y-O+
£3,500 (£1,041; £520; £300; £300; £300) **Stalls Centre**

Form RPR

1260 **1** **Grimsdyke**[6] 7389 3-8-10 **51**.................... DavidAllan 8 61
(Tim Easterby) *prom: rdn along 2f out: drvn to ld 1f out: kpt on wl* **11/4**[1]

0056 **2** *2 ½* **Chickenfortea (IRE)**[37] 6276 5-8-9 **48**.................... TomEaves 1 51
(Eric Alston) *led narrowly: rdn over 2f out: hdd 1f out: one pce and sn no ch w wnr* **11/2**[3]

531 **3** *1 ½* **Round The Island**[6] 7383 6-9-1 **54**....................(p) LewisEdmunds 6 52+
(Richard Whitaker) *dwlt: hld up: pushed along and hdwy over 2f out: rdn to chse ldrs over 1f out: kpt on same pce* **3/1**[2]

4004 **4** *shd* **Quanah (IRE)**[3] 7488 3-9-2 **57**.................... PhilDennis 2 55
(Liam Bailey) *dwlt: sn midfield: rdn over 2f out: kpt on ins fnl f* **16/1**

0540 **5** *1 ¼* **Cupid's Arrow (IRE)**[9] 7286 5-8-12 **51**.................... JamieGormley 10 45+
(Ruth Carr) *pressed ldr: rdn 2f out: wknd ins fnl f* **11/1**

1605 **6** *1 ¼* **Moonlit Sands (IRE)**[11] 7210 4-9-3 **56**....................(tp) BenCurtis 3 46
(Brian Ellison) *chsd ldrs: sn pushed along: outpcd whn edgd rt 2f out: plugged on ins fnl f (jockey said filly hung right-handed throughout)* **8/1**

4004 **7** *1 ¾* **Racquet**[9] 7286 6-8-7 **46** oh1....................(v[1]) JamesSullivan 4 31
(Ruth Carr) *hld up: sme hdwy over 1f out: nvr trbld ldrs* **20/1**

4154 **8** *2 ½* **Dubai Elegance**[7] 7345 5-9-0 **56**....................(p) NoelGarbutt(3) 13 33+
(Derek Shaw) *dwlt: hld up: nvr threatened (jockey said mare was never travelling)* **14/1**

0032 **9** *4 ½* **Tizwotitiz**[32] 6462 3-8-13 **54**....................(h) GrahamLee 9 21
(Steph Hollinshead) *midfield: sn pushed along: short of room 2f out: sn wknd* **16/1**

0340 **10** *shd* **Jacksonfire**[14] 7065 7-8-7 **46**....................(p) NathanEvans 14 10+
(Michael Mullineaux) *a towards rr* **50/1**

0606 **11** *¾* **Optimickstickhill**[9] 7286 4-8-2 **48**....................(b) RhonaPindar(7) 16 9+
(Scott Dixon) *chsd ldrs on wd outside: rdn over 2f out: wknd over 1f out* **33/1**

3036 **12** *3* **Spirit Of Zebedee (IRE)**[28] 6590 6-8-7 **46**....................(v) JasonHart 15 +
(John Quinn) *midfield: rdn over 2f out: wknd over 1f out* **16/1**

3600 **13** *3* **My Girl Maisie (IRE)**[9] 7286 5-8-8 **47** oh1 ow1....................(b[1]) CliffordLee 12 +
(Richard Guest) *a towards rr* **50/1**

1m 10.26s (-1.54) **Going Correction** +0.025s/f (Good) **13 Ran SP% 122.4**
WFA 3 from 4yo+ 2lb
Speed ratings (Par 101): **107,103,101,101,99 98,95,92,86,86 85,81,77**
CSF £17.99 CT £49.41 TOTE £3.40: £1.40, £2.70, £1.40; EX 18.70 Trifecta £80.00.
Owner James Bowers **Bred** J Bowers **Trained** Great Habton, N Yorks

FOCUS
The far side was again the place to be in this ordinary sprint handicap.

7591 WATCH RACE REPLAYS AT RACINGTV.COM H'CAP (DIV II) 5f 217y
3:55 (3:58) (Class 6) (0-60,60) 3-Y-O+
£3,500 (£1,041; £520; £300; £300; £300) **Stalls Centre**

Form RPR

0634 **1** **Kenny The Captain (IRE)**[2] 7511 8-9-3 **56**.................... DavidAllan 2 71
(Tim Easterby) *mde all against far rail: pushed clr over 1f out: eased towards fin* **11/10**[1]

0100 **2** *3 ¼* **Ingleby Molly (IRE)**[5] 7420 4-8-7 **46** oh1....................(h) PaulHanagan 5 48
(Jason Ward) *chsd ldrs: rdn over 2f out: wnt 2nd over 1f out: kpt on but no ch w wnr* **10/1**

0030 **3** *4* **Exchequer (IRE)**[4] 7443 8-9-7 **60**....................(tp) GrahamLee 3 50
(Richard Guest) *prom: rdn over 2f out: outpcd and hld in 3rd over 1f out* **15/2**[3]

0033 **4** *½* **Red Allure**[47] 5893 4-8-9 **48**.................... NathanEvans 6 37
(Michael Mullineaux) *chsd ldrs: rdn over 2f out: outpcd over 1f out: plugged on ins fnl f* **16/1**

1000 **5** *¾* **Alisia R (IRE)**[41] 6126 3-8-4 **48**....................(h) GabrieleMalune(3) 4 35
(Les Eyre) *chsd ldrs: rdn over 2f out: outpcd over 1f out: plugged on ins fnl f* **33/1**

4042 **6** *¾* **Tobeeornottobee**[2] 7527 3-8-10 **58**.................... JessicaAnderson(7) 10 42+
(Declan Carroll) *midfield towards outer: rdn along 3f out: plugged on* **13/2**[2]

1600 **7** *1* **Oriental Splendour (IRE)**[15] 7051 7-8-10 **49**....................(b) TomEaves 13 30+
(Ruth Carr) *hld up: rdn and sme hdwy over 1f out: nvr threatened* **50/1**

6666 **8** *1* **Santafiora**[26] 6682 5-8-11 **50**.................... CallumRodriguez 11 28+
(Julie Camacho) *dwlt: nvr bttr than midfield* **12/1**

0000 **9** *½* **Deeds Not Words (IRE)**[8] 7307 8-9-1 **54**....................(p) CamHardie 12 31+
(Tracy Waggott) *hld up: nvr threatened* **50/1**

0315 **10** *nk* **Someone Exciting**[8] 7307 6-9-1 **57**.................... HarrisonShaw(3) 15 33+
(David Thompson) *hld up on outside: nvr involved* **20/1**

2023 **11** *1 ¼* **Cardaw Lily (IRE)**[26] 6680 4-8-8 **47**.................... JamesSullivan 7 19
(Ruth Carr) *midfield: rdn over 2f out: wknd over 1f out* **9/1**

2050 **12** *1 ¼* **Mightaswellsmile**[15] 7052 5-8-7 **46** oh1.................... JamieGormley 9 14+
(Ron Barr) *midfield on outside: rdn over 2f out: wknd over 1f out* **50/1**

-503 **13** *5* **Ad Vitam (IRE)**[56] 5559 11-8-2 **46** oh1....................(bt) FayeMcManoman(5) 14
(Suzzanne France) *a outpcd in rr (jockey said gelding was never travelling)* **33/1**

1m 10.31s (-1.49) **Going Correction** +0.025s/f (Good) **13 Ran SP% 121.9**
WFA 3 from 4yo+ 2lb
Speed ratings (Par 101): **107,102,97,96,95 94,93,92,91,90 89,87,80**
CSF £12.45 CT £60.81 TOTE £1.90: £1.10, £3.00, £2.80; EX 13.90 Trifecta £67.60.
Owner Reality Partnerships V **Bred** Joe Foley & John Grimes **Trained** Great Habton, N Yorks

FOCUS
Those drawn low were at a big advantage in this second division of the 5f handicap. The winner has been rated back to the best of this year's form.
T/Plt: £93.00 to a £1 stake. Pool: £40,039.12. 314.03 winning units. T/Qpdt: £16.70 to a £1 stake. Pool: £4,677.96. 206.78 winning units. **Andrew Sheret**

7592a - 7600a (Foreign Racing) - See Raceform Interactive

7291 MAISONS-LAFFITTE (R-H)
Wednesday, September 25

OFFICIAL GOING: Turf: good to soft

7601a PRIX D'ACHERES (CLAIMER) (4YO+) (TURF) 6f 110y
11:25 4-Y-O+ £8,558 (£3,423; £2,567; £1,711; £855)

RPR

1 **Noordhout (FR)**[13] 4-8-8 0.................... FranckBlondel 7 74
(R Martens, France) **61/10**

2 *1 ¼* **Mujassam**[13] 7121 7-8-11 0....................(b) ChristopheSoumillon 6 73
(Sophie Leech) *towards rr on outer: asked for effrt over 2 1/2f out: prog fr 2f out: r.o wl u.p ins fnl f: nvr gng pce to chal wnr* **6/1**

3 *1* **Blue Tango (GER)**[9] 4-9-0 0.................... HugoBesnier(5) 4 78
(M Munch, Germany) **83/10**

4 *nk* **Skalleto (FR)**[115] 5-8-9 0.................... MlleMarieVelon(9) 10 77
(J-P Gauvin, France) **42/10**[2]

5 *3* **Smart Move (FR)**[46] 4-8-11 0.................... EddyHardouin 11 61
(D & P Prod'Homme, France) **12/1**

6 *¾* **Ocamonte (IRE)**[414] 5-9-2 0....................(b) MickaelBarzalona 3 64
(X Thomas-Demeaulte, France) **7/2**[1]

7 *2* **Forty Bere (FR)**[368] 4-9-4 0.................... Pierre-CharlesBoudot 5 60
(Robert Collet, France) **16/1**

8 *1* **Lefortovo (FR)**[13] 7136 6-8-11 0.................... MlleCoraliePacaut(4) 8 54
(Jo Hughes, France) *midfield on outer: pushed along over 2 1/2f out: sn rdn: unable qck and grad wknd fr over 1f out: n.d* **18/1**

9 *snk* **North End (FR)**[16] 6-8-11 0....................(b) LukasDelozier 1 50
(F Rossi, France) **51/10**[3]

10 *1* **Le Gitan (FR)**[265] 4-8-13 0.................... ArnaudMuste(5) 2 54
(C Boutin, France) **32/1**

1m 17.05s **10 Ran SP% 118.8**
PARI-MUTUEL (all including 1 euro stake): WIN 7.10; PLACE 2.40, 2.40, 2.90; DF 22.00.
Owner Antoine Bardini **Bred** T Storme **Trained** Chantilly, France

7602a PRIX SARACA (LISTED RACE) (2YO) (TURF) 6f 110y
12:25 2-Y-O £27,027 (£10,810; £8,108; £5,405; £2,702)

RPR

1 **Alocasia**[60] 5469 2-8-13 0.................... Pierre-CharlesBoudot 2 100+
(H-F Devin, France) **11/2**[3]

2 *1* **Jessely (FR)**[43] 2-8-13 0.................... MickaelBarzalona 8 97
(Andrea Marcialis, France) **13/2**

3 *¾* **Ikigai**[57] 5527 2-8-13 0.................... CristianDemuro 7 95
(Mrs Ilka Gansera-Leveque) *prom: pushed along to chse ldr 2 1/2f out: rdn 2f out: unable qck w ldrs ent fnl f: kpt on clsng stages* **15/1**

4 *¾* **Minuty (FR)**[16] 7044 2-8-13 0.................... AurelienLemaitre 4 93
(F Head, France) **79/10**

5 *snk* **Guildsman (FR)**[26] 6690 2-9-2 0.................... OisinMurphy 3 96
(Archie Watson) *cl up early: pushed along in midfield over 2 1/2f out: switch rt and effrt 2f out: unable qck u.p: kpt on same pce ins fnl f* **9/5**[1]

6 *¾* **Lloyd (IRE)**[43] 2-9-2 0....................(p) MaximeGuyon 1 93
(Mlle J Soudan, France) **41/5**

7 1 1/2 **Hector Loza**[25] 6727 2-9-2 0 .... NickyMackay 6 89
(Simon Dow) *racd keenly in rr: outpcd and pushed along jst under 3f out: sn rdn: no imp and kpt on same pce ins fnl f: nvr a factor* **27/1**

8 2 1/2 **Ventura Lightning (FR)**[26] 6690 2-9-2 0 .... ChristopheSoumillon 5 87
(Richard Fahey) *slowly away: a towards rr: asked for effrt over 2 1/2f out: no rspnse: eased whn wl btn ins fnl f* **16/5**[2]

1m 17.82s **8 Ran SP% 120.2**
PARI-MUTUEL (all including 1 euro stake): WIN 6.50; PLACE 2.20, 2.50, 3.90; DF 19.90.
Owner K Abdullah **Bred** Juddmonte Farms **Trained** France

7546 CHELMSFORD (A.W) (L-H)

Thursday, September 26

OFFICIAL GOING: Polytrack: standard
Wind: light, half behind Weather: fine

7603 BET TOTEPLACEPOT AT TOTESPORT.COM AMATEUR RIDERS' H'CAP (DIV I) 7f (P)

4:55 (4:57) (Class 6) (0-60,62) 3-Y-0+

£2,994 (£928; £464; £400; £400; £400) **Stalls** Low

Form RPR

0610 1 **Winklemann (IRE)**[27] 6680 7-11-4 **62** ....(p) MissImogenMathias(5) 3 74
(John Flint) *taken down early: trckd ldrs: effrt to chse ldr over 1f out: rdn and clsd to ld ins fnl f: r.o strly* **9/4**[1]

0036 2 3 1/4 **Letmestopyouthere (IRE)**[23] 6844 5-10-12 **51**(p) MissBrodieHampson 4 55
(Archie Watson) *chsd ldrs: edgd rt over 6f out: hdwy to ld wl over 2f out: rdn clr over 1f out: hdd and nt match pce of wnr ins fnl f* **11/4**[2]

060/ 3 6 **Sixth Of June**[650] 9237 5-10-6 **45** .... MrJamesHarding 5 33
(Simon Earle) *midfield: hmpd and dropped to rr of main gp over 6f out: styd on u.p to pass btn horses ins fnl f: snatched 3rd cl home: no threat to ldrs* **33/1**

0666 4 1/2 **Gulland Rock**[42] 6131 8-9-13 **45** .... MissKerryanneAlexander(7) 7 32
(Anthony Carson) *led tl wl over 2f out: rdn and outpcd over 1f out: wl hld 3rd 1f out: wknd ins fnl f* **20/1**

2000 5 1 3/4 **Just An Idea (IRE)**[27] 6682 5-10-4 **50** ....(b) MissCamillaSwift(7) 8 33
(Roger Ingram) *dwlt: racd wd: hdwy to chse ldrs over 6f out: outpcd: reminder and wnt lft over 1f out: sn btn and wknd ins fnl f* **16/1**

6503 6 2 **Tellovoi (IRE)**[2] 7550 11-10-7 **46** ....(p) MrSimonWalker 6 23
(Richard Guest) *taken down early: w ldr tl over 2f out: outpcd and rdn over 1f out: sn btn and wknd ins fnl f* **7/2**[3]

0014 7 shd **Haraz (IRE)**[23] 6844 6-10-9 **53** .... MissMeganTrainor(5) 9 30
(Paddy Butler) *dwlt: a towards rr of main gp: nvr involved* **25/1**

2455 8 2 1/4 **Your Mothers' Eyes**[49] 5869 3-10-12 **61** ....(p) MissEmmaJack(7) 2 31
(Alan Bailey) *chsd ldrs: rdn and outpcd ent fnl 2f: sn btn and wknd fnl f* **5/1**

6040 9 3 1/2 **Exning Queen (IRE)**[42] 6131 3-9-10 **45** .... MrSamFeilden(7) 1 6
(Julia Feilden) *v.s.a: nvr rcvrd and a bhd (trainer said filly was slowly away)* **16/1**

1m 26.14s (-1.06) **Going Correction** -0.25s/f (Stan)
WFA 3 from 5yo+ 3lb **9 Ran SP% 119.6**
Speed ratings (Par 101): **96,92,85,84,82 80,80,77,73**
CSF £8.75 CT £159.96 TOTE £3.50: £1.60, £1.50, £11.70; EX 10.90 Trifecta £232.20.
Owner Mel Mathias **Bred** Allevamento La Nuova Sbarra **Trained** Kenfig Hill, Bridgend

FOCUS
The first division of two very moderate amateur riders' handicaps. The winner has been rated within 4lb of last year's best.

7604 BET TOTEPLACEPOT AT TOTESPORT.COM AMATEUR RIDERS' H'CAP (DIV II) 7f (P)

5:30 (5:30) (Class 6) (0-60,61) 3-Y-0+

£2,994 (£928; £464; £400; £400; £400) **Stalls** Low

Form RPR

5050 1 **Wild Flower (IRE)**[21] 6889 7-10-3 **46** ....(p) MissBeckySmith 8 52
(Luke McJannet) *led tl 1/2-way: styd upsides ldr: rdn over 1f out: led again 1f out: wnt sltly rt but hld on wl u.p ins fnl f: fin 1st: disqualified and plcd 2nd* **7/1**

0230 2 nk **Islay Mist**[7] 7371 3-9-8 **47** ....(tp) MissSuzannahStevens(7) 5 51
(Lee Carter) *in tch in midfield: wnt 3rd over 2f out: swtchd rt and effrt wl over 1f out: rdn to chal ent fnl f: sustained effrt and sltly impeded ins fnl f but a jst hld: fin 2nd: awrdd r* **9/1**

-350 3 1 3/4 **Caribbean Spring (IRE)**[166] 1766 6-10-9 **57**. MissRosieMargarson(5) 1 58
(George Margarson) *w ldr on inner: led 1/2-way: pushed along over 1f out: hdd 1f out: kpt on same pce ins fnl f* **7/2**[3]

0034 4 1 1/2 **Art Echo**[65] 5282 6-10-11 **61** ....(vt) MissCLGoodwin(7) 4 58
(John Mackie) *in tch in midfield: chsd ldng trio over 1f out: nudged along and kpt on same pce ins fnl f* **11/4**[2]

0502 5 7 **Tavener**[10] 7282 7-10-7 **50** ....(t[1]) MissSerenaBrotherton 9 29
(David C Griffiths) *s.i.s: rcvrd and hdwy to chse ldrs over 6f out: rdn and lost 3rd over 2f out wknd u.p over 1f out (jockey said gelding was slowly away)* **15/8**[1]

0/06 6 20 **UAE Soldier (USA)**[21] 6903 4-9-13 **47** ....(h) MissMichelleBryant(5) 6
(Paddy Butler) *a in rr: outpcd 3f out: wl btn over 1f out* **33/1**

0010 7 3 1/4 **Mime Dance**[87] 4460 8-10-4 **52** .... MrMatthewJohnson(5) 7
(John Butler) *s.i.s: a in last pair: rdn and struggling 3f out: wl btn over 1f out* **14/1**

1m 26.38s (-0.82) **Going Correction** -0.25s/f (Stan)
WFA 3 from 4yo+ 3lb **7 Ran SP% 115.8**
Speed ratings (Par 101): **94,93,91,89,81 59,55**
CSF £70.14 CT £264.74 TOTE £9.50: £3.40, £3.90; EX 42.80 Trifecta £162.40.
Owner Miss Rebecca Dennis **Bred** Peter Harms **Trained** Newmarket, Suffolk
■ Stewards' Enquiry : Miss Becky Smith three-day ban: careless riding (Oct 14, 18, 25)

FOCUS
The second division of this amateur riders' handicap proved the more competitive of the two. There was a twist in the tale as the stewards reversed the placings of the first two. Straightforward form.

7605 BET TOTEEXACTA AT TOTESPORT.COM BRITISH EBF NOVICE MEDIAN AUCTION STKS 7f (P)

6:00 (6:02) (Class 5) 2-Y-0 **£4,204** (£1,251; £625; £312) **Stalls** Low

Form RPR

1 1 **Cobber Kain**[22] 6858 2-9-9 0 .... RobertHavlin 4 82
(John Gosden) *mde all: shkn up over 1f out: rdn and kpt on wl ins fnl f* **1/3**[1]

35 2 2 **Freshwater Cliffs**[12] 7186 2-8-13 0 .... FinleyMarsh(3) 2 70
(Richard Hughes) *t.k.h: chsd wnr tl after over 1f: effrt to chse wnr again wl over 1f out: no ex and btn wl ins fnl f* **16/1**

0 3 1 1/2 **Cadeo**[17] 7030 2-8-9 0 ....(h) StefanoCherchi(7) 7 66
(Marco Botti) *hld up in tch in midfield: effrt to chse ldng trio over 1f out: kpt on to go 3rd 100yds out: nvr getting to ldng pair* **25/1**

4 4 1 **Costello**[54] 5676 2-9-2 0 .... KieranO'Neill 9 63
(Mike Murphy) *dwlt: hdwy to chse wnr and t.k.h after over 1f: rdn ent fnl 2f: lost 2nd wl over 1f out: wknd ins fnl f (jockey said colt ran too free)* **10/1**[3]

5 3 1/4 **Dutugamunu (IRE)** 2-8-13 0 .... MeganNicholls(3) 10 54
(Richard Spencer) *s.i.s: rn green in rr: effrt and rdn ent fnl 2f: edgd lft and sme hdwy over 1f out: kpt on ins fnl f: nvr trbld ldrs* **10/1**[3]

0660 6 3 1/2 **Mungo's Quest (IRE)**[37] 6313 2-9-2 48 .... HectorCrouch 8 45
(Simon Dow) *t.k.h: hld up in tch in midfield: rdn and outpcd ent fnl 2f: wknd ins fnl f* **66/1**

7 3 **Love Not Money** 2-8-4 0 .... AngusVilliers(7) 5 32
(Robert Cowell) *dwlt: hld up in tch: effrt and rdn ent fnl 2f: outpcd and wl hld over 1f out* **16/1**

0 8 5 **Rajan**[122] 3165 2-9-2 0 .... StevieDonohoe 6 23
(Tom Clover) *chsd ldrs early: in tch in midfield: struggling u.p over 2f out: wknd over 1f out* **25/1**

0 9 hd **Licorice**[26] 6718 2-9-2 0 ....(p[1]) HollieDoyle 1 23
(Archie Watson) *dwlt: a in rr: rdn 3f out: sn struggling and wl btn over 1f out (jockey said gelding anticipated the start)* **6/1**[2]

5 10 6 **Belle Rousse**[7] 7386 2-8-11 0 .... RyanTate 3 2
(Sir Mark Prescott Bt) *midfield tl dropped to rr and pushed along after 2f: rdn and struggling 3f out: wl btn over 1f out* **33/1**

1m 26.11s (-1.09) **Going Correction** -0.25s/f (Stan) **10 Ran SP% 131.4**
Speed ratings (Par 95): **96,93,92,90,87 83,79,74,73,66**
CSF £10.35 TOTE £1.10: £1.10, £3.80, £3.90; EX 14.40 Trifecta £133.60.
Owner Ms Rachel D S Hood **Bred** Ms Rachel Hood **Trained** Newmarket, Suffolk

FOCUS
This looked a straightforward task for the odds-on favourite, who ran out a workmanlike winner. It's been rated cautiously.

7606 BET TOTEQUADPOT AT TOTESPORT.COM H'CAP 6f (P)

6:30 (6:34) (Class 7) (0-50,50) 3-Y-0+ **£2,911** (£866; £432; £216) **Stalls** Centre

Form RPR

5-45 1 **Broughton Excels**[32] 6510 4-9-7 **50** .... StevieDonohoe 10 61
(Stuart Williams) *trckd ldrs: swtchd rt and effrt away fr rivals over 1f out: rdn and hdwy to ld ins fnl f: r.o strly* **11/1**

0006 2 2 3/4 **Aiguillette**[7] 7371 3-9-1 **46** .... HectorCrouch 11 49
(Gary Moore) *led after almost 1f: rdn over 1f out: hdd ins fnl f: nt match pce of wnr fnl 100yds* **14/1**

3252 3 1/2 **Prince Rock (IRE)**[7] 7371 4-9-4 **47** ....(p[1]) AdamKirby 1 48
(Simon Dow) *in tch in midfield: effrt ent fnl 2f: drvn over 1f out: kpt on ins fnl f* **7/4**[1]

060 4 hd **Frea**[128] 2926 3-9-1 **46** .... RobertHavlin 8 47
(Harry Dunlop) *hmpd leaving stalls: bhd: nt clr run 2f out: wnt between rivals and hdwy over 1f out: styd on strly ins fnl f: nt rch wnr* **33/1**

2000 5 3/4 **Filbert Street**[7] 7384 4-9-2 **50** ....(b) KevinLundie(5) 9 48
(Michael Appleby) *led over 4f out: rdn over 1f out: hdd ins fnl f: no ex: edgd lft and wknd towards fin* **6/1**[3]

6000 6 2 **Wye Bother (IRE)**[13] 7157 3-8-9 **45** ....(t) WilliamCarver(5) 3 37
(Milton Bradley) *led for almost 1f: chsd ldrs: effrt on inner over 1f out: no ex u.p 1f out: btn whn short of room towards fin* **40/1**

0005 7 hd **Mystical Moon (IRE)**[7] 7371 4-9-6 **49** ....(vt) AlistairRawlinson 2 41
(David C Griffiths) *racd in last trio: effrt and edgd rt over 1f out: kpt on ins fnl f: nvr trbld ldrs* **14/1**

2606 8 1 3/4 **Waneen (IRE)**[24] 6794 6-9-2 **45** .... HollieDoyle 12 32
(John Butler) *chsd ldrs on outer: rdn and losing pl over 2f out: wknd fnl f* **16/1**

0002 9 1 **Breathoffreshair**[6] 7420 5-9-5 **48** ....(bt) RobHornby 6 32
(Richard Guest) *wnt rt leaving stalls: a towards rr: nt clr run over 1f out: nvr involved* **10/1**

4350 10 3/4 **Quick Recovery**[21] 6889 4-9-4 **50** ....(b) CierenFallon(3) 5 31
(Jim Boyle) *in tch in midfield on outer: rdn and struggling over 2f out: edgd lft over 1f out: lost pl and wl btn whn nt clr run 1f out (jockey said filly hung left-handed)* **7/2**[2]

5555 11 6 **Ar Saoirse**[85] 4500 4-9-2 **45** ....(vt) CallumShepherd 4 8
(Clare Hobson) *chsd ldrs early: sn midfield: edgd rt and lost pl over 1f out: fdd ins fnl f* **16/1**

1m 11.57s (-2.13) **Going Correction** -0.25s/f (Stan)
WFA 3 from 4yo+ 2lb **11 Ran SP% 120.8**
Speed ratings (Par 97): **104,100,99,99,98 95,95,93,91,90 82**
CSF £158.92 CT £409.91 TOTE £13.40: £2.70, £6.20, £1.20; EX 312.80 Trifecta £1465.00.
Owner Broughton Thermal Insulation **Bred** Salisbury Bloodstock Ltd **Trained** Newmarket, Suffolk

FOCUS
Extremely moderate stuff, though they went quickly and it likely represents fair form for the level. The winner has been rated in line with last year's AW form.

7607 BET TOTETRIFECTA AT TOTESPORT.COM H'CAP 6f (P)

7:00 (7:00) (Class 4) (0-80,82) 3-Y-0+

£5,530 (£1,645; £822; £411; £400; £400) **Stalls** Centre

Form RPR

4420 1 **With Caution (IRE)**[59] 5503 3-9-5 **79** .... PJMcDonald 1 85
(James Tate) *mde all: rdn and 2 l clr over 1f out: kpt on u.p ins fnl f* **7/2**[3]

5022 2 1 **Excellent George**[9] 7321 7-9-0 **79** ....(t) MarcoGhiani(7) 6 82
(Stuart Williams) *in tch on outer: effrt to chse ldrs 1f out: edgd lft and kpt on ins fnl f: wnt 2nd last strides* **3/1**[2]

0350 3 nk **Nick Vedder**[14] 7121 5-9-10 **82** .... KieranO'Neill 5 84
(Robyn Brisland) *in tch in rr: effrt on inner over 1f out: chsd wnr 1f out: kpt on but nvr quite getting on terms: lost 2nd last strides* **16/1**

2124 4 2 **Six Strings**[16] 7059 5-9-10 **82** .... AlistairRawlinson 2 77
(Michael Appleby) *taken down early: t.k.h: chsd ldrs: n.m.r wl over 1f out: hmpd and swtchd lft 1f out: kpt on same pce ins fnl f (jockey said gelding ran too free)* **11/4**[1]

3200 5 1 1/4 **Johnny Reb**[19] 6968 3-9-0 **74** ....(v[1]) StevieDonohoe 3 65
(Charlie Fellowes) *wnt rt leaving stalls: chsd wnr: edging rt over 1f out: lost 2nd 1f out: wknd ins fnl f* **10/1**

0433 **6** ¾ **Consequences (IRE)**[5] 7470 4-9-0 **75** CierenFallon(3) 4 64
(Ian Williams) *impeded leaving stalls: in tch: hdwy on inner to chse ldrs over 3f out: drvn over 1f out: unable qck and wknd ins fnl f (jockey said gelding was slowly away)* **3/1**[2]

1m 10.99s (-2.71) **Going Correction** -0.25s/f (Stan)
WFA 3 from 4yo+ 2lb **6** Ran SP% **113.9**
Speed ratings (Par 105): **108,106,106,103,101 100**
CSF £14.70 TOTE £4.50: £2.50, £2.00; EX 14.70 Trifecta £108.00.
Owner Saeed Manana **Bred** Ballyphilip Stud **Trained** Newmarket, Suffolk

FOCUS
They appeared to go steadily and the winner dictated from the front.

7608 BET TOTESWINGER AT TOTESPORT.COM FILLIES' H'CAP 1m (P)

7:30 (7:30) (Class 5) (0-75,74) 3-Y-0+ **£5,110** (£1,520; £759; £400; £400) **Stalls** Low

Form RPR
5435 **1** **Zafaranah (USA)**[30] 6582 5-9-12 **74** AdamKirby 1 79
(Pam Sly) *t.k.h: chsd ldr tl over 2f out: styd trcking ldrs: swtchd lft and effrt on inner to ld over 1f out: styd on wl ins fnl f* **2/1**[2]

60-3 **2** nk **City Of Love**[22] 6856 3-9-7 **73** DanielMuscutt 4 77
(David Lanigan) *hld up in tch in last pair: effrt over 1f out: hdwy u.p to press wnr 100yds out: kpt on wl but hld towards fin* **14/1**

2-05 **3** 1¾ **Mary Somerville**[133] 2765 3-9-8 **74** RobertHavlin 2 74
(John Gosden) *dwlt: hld up in tch in last pair: swtchd lft and effrt on inner over 1f out: no imp u.p ins fnl f: eased towards fin* **11/10**[1]

4524 **4** ½ **Bint Dandy (IRE)**[17] 7022 8-9-7 **69** (b) PJMcDonald 3 68
(Charlie Wallis) *broke wl: sn restrained and chsd ldrs: chsd ldr over 2f out: effrt over 1f out: drvn to chse wnr 1f out tl ins fnl f: wknd towards fin* **9/2**[3]

0000 **5** 5 **Any Smile (IRE)**[26] 6734 3-8-5 **57** (p[1]) ShelleyBirkett 5 45
(Julia Feilden) *sn led: rdn and hdd over 1f out: lost pl and wknd ins fnl f* **33/1**

1m 38.03s (-1.87) **Going Correction** -0.25s/f (Stan)
WFA 3 from 5yo+ 4lb **5** Ran SP% **108.7**
Speed ratings (Par 100): **99,98,96,96,91**
CSF £24.34 TOTE £2.90: £1.30, £4.10; EX 23.60 Trifecta £44.40.
Owner Pam's People **Bred** Shadwell Farm LLC **Trained** Thorney, Cambs

FOCUS
An ordinary fillies' only handicap.

7609 BET TOTESCOOP6 AT TOTESPORT.COM H'CAP 1m (P)

8:00 (8:02) (Class 6) (0-65,67) 3-Y-0+
£3,105 (£924; £461; £400; £400; £400) **Stalls** Low

Form RPR
045 **1** **Hindaam (USA)**[23] 6836 3-9-5 **63** JimCrowley 12 69
(Owen Burrows) *trckd ldrs: effrt ent fnl 2f: rdn to chse ldr ent fnl f: r.o wl to ld fnl 50yds* **6/1**[2]

0000 **2** ¾ **My Amigo**[7] 7363 6-9-13 **67** (p) HollieDoyle 9 71
(Marjorie Fife) *pressed ldr tl rdn to ld ent fnl 2f: drvn over 1f out: kpt on u.p tl hdd and one pce fnl 50yds* **25/1**

4631 **3** nk **Zefferino**[36] 6334 5-9-7 **61** (t) GeorgeWood 4 65
(Martin Bosley) *in tch in midfield: effrt ent fnl 2f: edgd out rt and hdwy u.p over 1f out: kpt on wl ins fnl f: nt quite rch ldrs* **12/1**

0455 **4** 1 **Cashel (IRE)**[37] 6317 4-9-6 **60** AlistairRawlinson 5 61
(Michael Appleby) *chsd ldrs: swtchd rt and effrt over 1f out: chsd ldrs and edgd lft ins fnl f: kpt on same pce wl ins fnl f* **5/1**[1]

4336 **5** 1 **Annexation (FR)**[12] 7204 3-9-3 **61** RobertHavlin 11 60
(Ed Dunlop) *swtchd lft after s: hld up in last quartet: effrt and hdwy over 1f out: edgd lft but kpt on wl ins fnl f: nt rch ldrs* **12/1**

3004 **6** hd **Fiction Writer (USA)**[33] 6439 3-9-5 **63** AdamKirby 6 62
(Mark Johnston) *dwlt: sn in tch in midfield: effrt u.p over 1f out: kpt on same pce ins fnl f: swtchd rt towards fin* **8/1**

502 **7** 1½ **Seaquinn**[7] 7374 4-8-10 **50** oh5 KierenFox 7 45
(John Best) *midfield tl dropped towards rr after: swtchd rt and u.p over 1f out: styd on ins fnl f: no ch w ldrs* **8/1**

1115 **8** 2¼ **Compass Point**[16] 7060 4-9-9 **63** KieranO'Neill 3 53
(Robyn Brisland) *led: rdn and hdd ent fnl 2f: edgd rt and unable qck over 1f out: wknd ins fnl f* **6/1**[2]

0514 **9** hd **Clem A**[31] 6529 3-9-4 **65** CierenFallon(3) 1 54
(Alan Bailey) *in tch in midfield: effrt on inner over 1f out: no imp 1f out: wknd ins fnl f* **7/1**[3]

0644 **10** 1¼ **Jack Berry House**[15] 7080 3-9-9 **67** (t) OisinMurphy 10 54
(George Boughey) *in tch in midfield: rdn over 2f out: unable qck and lost pl over 1f out: wknd ins fnl f* **7/1**[3]

0056 **11** 1¾ **Accessor (IRE)**[20] 6939 4-8-12 **52** JimmyQuinn 2 35
(Michael Wigham) *hld up in last quartet: effrt over 1f out: nvr trbld ldrs* **11/1**

544 **12** 11 **Loveheart**[22] 6862 3-9-3 **61** CallumShepherd 14 18
(Michael Bell) *swtchd lft after s: a bhd: eased ins fnl f* **33/1**

1m 37.59s (-2.31) **Going Correction** -0.25s/f (Stan) **12** Ran SP% **123.0**
WFA 3 from 4yo+ 4lb
Speed ratings (Par 101): **101,100,99,98,97 97,96,94,93,92 90,79**
CSF £150.66 CT £1791.14 TOTE £6.80: £2.10, £11.20, £3.10; EX 140.60 Trifecta £1990.90.
Owner Hamdan Al Maktoum **Bred** Shadwell Farm LLC **Trained** Lambourn, Berks

FOCUS
A modest but competitive handicap. The winner overcame a wide draw on this handicap debut and is open to further improvement. The third has been rated in line with his recent best.

7610 BOOK TICKETS AT CHELMSFORDCITYRACECOURSE.COM H'CAP 1m 2f (P)

8:30 (8:30) (Class 4) (0-80,82) 3-Y-0+
£5,530 (£1,645; £822; £411; £400; £400) **Stalls** Low

Form RPR
1160 **1** **Mayfair Spirit (IRE)**[19] 6964 3-9-5 **80** (t) StevieDonohoe 7 88
(Charlie Fellowes) *chsd ldr for over 1f: trckd ldrs after: swtchd rt and effrt wl over 1f out: chal between rivals ins fnl f: led 75yds out: hld on wl* **5/1**[3]

0100 **2** shd **Amjaady (USA)**[19] 6961 3-9-3 **78** AdamKirby 9 85
(David O'Meara) *dwlt: rousted along and early reminder: hdwy to chse ldr after over 1f: effrt and ev ch ent fnl 2f: drvn over 1f out: kpt on u.p: jst hld cl home* **8/1**

1223 **3** ¾ **The Jean Genie**[13] 7153 5-9-12 **82** HollieDoyle 2 87
(William Stone) *led: pressed and rdn ent fnl 2f: kpt on wl u.p: hdd 75yds out: no ex and jst outpcd towards fin* **7/2**[1]

3145 **4** 1¾ **Boutonniere (USA)**[143] 2470 3-9-0 **75** OisinMurphy 8 77
(Andrew Balding) *chsd ldrs: effrt 2f out: drvn ent fnl 2f: kpt on same pce ins fnl f* **6/1**

2433 **5** hd **Bollihope**[23] 6839 7-8-11 **67** RobertHavlin 3 68
(Shaun Keightley) *hld up in tch in last trio: effrt over 1f out: chsd ldrs 1f out: kpt on same pce ins fnl f* **7/2**[1]

2406 **6** 1 **Grand Inquisitor**[23] 6842 7-9-10 **80** (b[1]) AlistairRawlinson 1 79
(Conor Dore) *hld up in tch in midfield: swtchd lft and effrt over 1f out: kpt on same pce fnl 100yds* **20/1**

0516 **7** 1¼ **Kaser (IRE)**[12] 7185 4-9-3 **78** ThomasGreatrex(5) 4 75
(David Loughnane) *hld up in tch in midfield: effrt over 1f out: unable qck: wl hld and kpt on same pce ins fnl f* **4/1**[2]

-556 **8** 11 **Swilly Sunset**[13] 7166 6-8-6 **69** MarcoGhiani(7) 6 44
(Anthony Carson) *hld up in last trio: rdn over 3f out: struggling over 2f out: bhd over 1f out* **20/1**

5400 **9** 21 **Foxes Flyer (IRE)**[5] 7452 3-8-5 **66** (p) KieranO'Neill 5
(Luke McJannet) *s.i.s: a in rr: rdn over 3f out: wl bhd over 1f out* **33/1**

2m 4.19s (-4.41) **Going Correction** -0.25s/f (Stan)
WFA 3 from 4yo+ 5lb **9** Ran SP% **119.0**
Speed ratings (Par 105): **107,106,106,104,104 103,102,94,77**
CSF £44.35 CT £160.08 TOTE £6.30: £2.00, £2.90, £1.60; EX 51.00 Trifecta £200.20.
Owner J Soiza **Bred** Ringfort Stud Ltd **Trained** Newmarket, Suffolk

FOCUS
This looked competitive beforehand and there was little to split the first three home. They went steadily and it paid to race up with the pace.
T/Plt: £104.30 to a £1 stake. Pool: £32,563.81 - 312.04 winning units T/Qpdt: £8.60 to a £1 stake. Pool: £1,492.00 - 594.07 winning units **Steve Payne**

7461 NEWMARKET (R-H)

Thursday, September 26

OFFICIAL GOING: Good (ovr 7.0, stands' 7.0, ctr 6.9, far 7.1)
Wind: breezy Weather: mainly overcast with sunny spells; 19 degrees

7611 HEATH COURT HOTEL BRITISH EBF MAIDEN STKS (PLUS 10 RACE) (C&G) 1m

1:50 (1:51) (Class 4) 2-Y-O **£6,469** (£1,925; £962; £481) **Stalls** High

Form RPR
2 **1** **Mascat**[27] 6669 2-9-0 0 HarryBentley 4 86+
(Ralph Beckett) *trckd ldrs racing freely: taken rt over 2f out: rdn and sustained effrt fr over 1f out: led fnl 100yds: kpt on wl* **6/4**[1]

25 **2** ½ **Discovery Island**[27] 6669 2-9-0 0 WilliamBuick 2 85
(Charlie Appleby) *pressed ldr: rdn over 2f out: led 1f out: hdd and nt qckn fnl 100yds* **9/4**[2]

3 **3** 3¾ **Karibana (IRE)**[20] 6927 2-9-0 0 RyanMoore 5 76
(Richard Hughes) *tall; led: rdn over 2f out: hdd 1f out: one pce and wl hld after* **10/1**

4 7 **Thai Power (IRE)** 2-9-0 0 OisinMurphy 3 60
(Andrew Balding) *str; racd in last pair: rdn and outpcd over 2f out* **5/2**[3]

4 **5** 10 **Sea Of Cool (IRE)**[146] 2362 2-9-0 0 GeraldMosse 1 37
(John Ryan) *unfurnished; racd keenly on outside: pressed ldrs tl rdn over 2f out: sn lft bhd: t.o and eased* **50/1**

1m 38.53s (0.13) **Going Correction** -0.025s/f (Good) **5** Ran SP% **110.4**
Speed ratings (Par 97): **98,97,93,86,76**
CSF £5.21 TOTE £2.30: £1.10, £1.90; EX 5.10 Trifecta £12.70.
Owner Y Nasib **Bred** Coln Valley Stud **Trained** Kimpton, Hants

FOCUS
Far side course. Stalls: stands' side, except 1m4f and 2m: far side. The going was given as good (GoingStick 7.0. Stands' side 7.0; centre 6.9; far side 7.1). Of the previous seven winners of this maiden, five went on to win Group races, namely Telescope, Master The World, Eminent, Ghaiyyath and Kick On, while another, Mustajeer, has this year won a Listed race and the Ebor. There was a smaller field than usual, but the first two pulled nicely clear.

7612 FIRST CALL TRAFFIC MANAGEMENT NURSERY H'CAP 1m

2:25 (2:25) (Class 2) 2-Y-O **£11,644** (£3,465; £1,731; £865) **Stalls** High

Form RPR
002 **1** **Dogged**[13] 7162 2-8-10 **80** TomMarquand 1 85+
(David Elsworth) *unfurnished; sn pressing ldr: rdn to ld wl over 1f out: a holding chalr fnl 100yds* **14/1**

421 **2** ¾ **Cloud Drift**[44] 6054 2-8-8 **78** JasonWatson 2 81
(Michael Bell) *str; t.k.h and cl up on outer: rdn to go 2nd over 1f out: ev ch after but no imp* **10/3**[1]

10U5 **3** 1½ **Milltown Star**[11] 7247 2-9-3 **87** GeraldMosse 5 87
(Mick Channon) *t.k.h towards rr: effrt 2f out: drvn over 1f out: nt qckn fnl f* **7/1**

2520 **4** nk **Light Angel**[19] 6957 2-9-4 **91** CierenFallon(3) 7 90
(John Gosden) *taken down early: t.k.h and prom: rdn and outpcd over 3f out: rallied ins fnl f and kpt on wl wout threatening* **5/1**[3]

421 **5** hd **Berkshire Savvy**[27] 6684 2-8-8 **78** ow1 OisinMurphy 8 77
(Andrew Balding) *unfurnished: looked wl; pressed ldrs: rdn wl over 2f out: btn over 1f out* **4/1**[2]

101 **6** 1½ **Love Destiny**[14] 7104 2-8-12 **82** JoeFanning 6 77
(Mark Johnston) *str: looked wl; led: rdn and hdd wl over 1f out: nt qckn after* **8/1**

634 **7** ¾ **Fantasy Believer (IRE)**[31] 6528 2-8-6 **76** HarryBentley 3 69
(Charles Hills) *workmanlike; last away: pushed along in rr: effrt 1/2-way: pressing ldrs 2f out: sn btn* **8/1**

6026 **8** nse **What An Angel**[8] 7338 2-8-11 **81** RyanMoore 9 79
(Richard Hannon) *a towards rr: btn whn squeezed for room over 1f out: eased cl home (jockey said colt was denied clear run)* **12/1**

4314 **9** hd **Arthur's Court (IRE)**[20] 6942 2-8-10 **80** JackMitchell 4 73
(Hugo Palmer) *pushed along in rr: hdwy on outer 3f out: drvn and fdd over 1f out* **12/1**

1m 38.02s (-0.38) **Going Correction** -0.025s/f (Good) **9** Ran SP% **116.5**
Speed ratings (Par 101): **100,99,97,97,97 95,95,94,94**
CSF £60.99 CT £366.32 TOTE £12.80: £2.70, £1.60, £2.00; EX 85.40 Trifecta £758.90.
Owner David Elsworth & Michael Elliott **Bred** Whitsbury Manor Stud And Mrs M E Slade **Trained** Newmarket, Suffolk

The Form Book Flat 2019, Raceform Ltd, Newbury, RG14 5SJ

FOCUS
A fair sprint in which plenty had some sort of chance inside the final couple of furlongs. The first two home were making their handicap debuts.

7613 BRITISH EBF PREMIER FILLIES' H'CAP 6f
3:00 (3:00) (Class 2) 3-Y-O+
£31,125 (£9,320; £4,660; £2,330; £1,165; £585) Stalls High

Form				RPR
0113	1		**Chil Chil**[20] 6930 3-8-8 78 OisinMurphy 7 (Andrew Balding) towards rr: outpcd 1/2-way: rdn 2f out: v str run on stands' rails fnl f to ld nr fin and dash clr 9/2[2]	89
1112	2	1	**Gale Force Maya**[7] 7380 3-8-12 82 PaulMulrennan 1 (Michael Dods) trckd ldrs: rdn to ld 1f out: ct cl home 4/1[1]	90
3221	3	nk	**Restless Rose**[8] 7345 4-8-5 80 5ex MarcoGhiani(7) 8 (Stuart Williams) looked wl; prom: drvn and ev ch 1f out: nt qckn fnl 100yds 12/1	87
1212	4	½	**Whisper Aloud**[12] 7206 3-8-9 79 HollieDoyle 9 (Archie Watson) looked wl; sn led: drvn and hdd 1f out: no ex cl home (jockey said filly hung right-handed off the bridle from 2f out) 14/1	84
2431	5	1	**Lethal Angel**[17] 7022 4-8-4 72 (p) KieranO'Neill 10 (Stuart Williams) pressed ldrs: rdn over 1f out: n.m.r briefly and nt qckn ins fnl f 20/1	74
-051	6	¾	**Irene May (IRE)**[22] 6851 3-8-12 82 JasonWatson 11 (Sylvester Kirk) towards rr: styng on nicely ins fnl f 28/1	82
6362	7	½	**Goodnight Girl (IRE)**[21] 6908 4-9-8 90 JamesDoyle 12 (Jonathan Portman) w ldr 2f: drvn and btn over 1f out 9/1	88
3301	8	1	**Belated Breath**[21] 6908 4-9-10 92 RyanMoore 6 (Hughie Morrison) prom: drvn over 1f out: wknd ins fnl f 7/1	87
5006	9	¾	**Stay Classy (IRE)**[18] 6999 3-8-10 87 SeanKirrane(7) 3 (Richard Spencer) dwlt: t.k.h: sn chsng ldrs: rdn and btn over 1f out 25/1	80
4201	10	nse	**Lady Of Aran (IRE)**[7] 7380 4-8-11 79 5ex StevieDonohoe 5 (Charlie Fellowes) dwlt: a bhd 6/1	71
3352	11	1 ¼	**Lady Calcaria**[62] 5399 3-8-5 75 DuranFentiman 2 (Tim Easterby) nvr bttr than midfield: rdn and btn wl over 1f out 33/1	63
042	12	hd	**Molls Memory**[20] 6922 4-9-3 85 TomMarquand 4 (Ed Walker) looked wl; sn drvn along: a outpcd (jockey said filly was never travelling) 5/1[3]	73

1m 10.92s (-0.98) **Going Correction** -0.025s/f (Good)
WFA 3 from 4yo 2lb 12 Ran SP% 121.0
Speed ratings (Par 96): **105,103,103,102,101 100,99,98,97,97 95,95**
CSF £22.26 CT £210.95 TOTE £4.40: £1.70, £1.90, £4.10; EX 21.70 Trifecta £303.90.
Owner King Power Racing Co Ltd **Bred** A S Denniff **Trained** Kingsclere, Hants

FOCUS
A competitive fillies' sprint handicap.

7614 TATTERSALLS STKS (REGISTERED AS THE SOMERVILLE TATTERSALL STAKES) (GROUP 3) (C&G) 7f
3:35 (3:35) (Class 1) 2-Y-O
£28,355 (£10,750; £5,380; £2,680; £1,345; £675) Stalls High

Form				RPR
2	1		**Wichita (IRE)**[13] 7150 2-9-0 0 RyanMoore 5 (A P O'Brien, Ire) tall: ly: looked wl; pressed ldr: led gng best over 2f out: sn rdn: wl clr fnl f: v decisive 10/11[1]	117+
16	2	7	**Persuasion (IRE)**[36] 6352 2-9-0 0 JamesDoyle 3 (Charles Hills) looked wl; chsd ldrs: rdn to chse wnr wl over 1f out: nvr nr him: edgd sltly lft ins fnl f 6/1[3]	99
4335	3	1 ¼	**Ropey Guest**[19] 6948 2-9-0 98 TomQueally 7 (George Margarson) racd in last pair: rdn and effrt 2f out: chalng for 3rd whn n.m.r 1f out: sn chsng ldng pair vainly: kpt on gamely (jockey said colt was denied clear run) 20/1	97
3344	4	2 ½	**Monoski (USA)**[11] 7245 2-9-0 93 WilliamBuick 6 (Mark Johnston) taken down early: led and t.k.h: rdn and hdd over 2f out: wkng whn lost 3rd 1f out 10/1	89
424	5	3 ½	**Manigordo (USA)**[14] 7119 2-9-0 98 OisinMurphy 1 (Richard Hannon) str: sweating; prom tl rdn over 2f out: sn btn (trainer said colt ran flat) 9/2[2]	80
4132	6	3	**Oh Purple Reign (IRE)**[19] 6966 2-9-0 102 TomMarquand 2 (Richard Hannon) racd in last pair: struggling u.p 1/2-way (jockey said colt was never travelling) 6/1[3]	72

1m 23.55s (-1.85) **Going Correction** -0.025s/f (Good) 6 Ran SP% 113.0
Speed ratings (Par 105): **109,101,99,96,92 89**
CSF £7.06 TOTE £1.80: £1.10, £2.70; EX 6.60 Trifecta £39.80.
Owner Derrick Smith & Mrs John Magnier & Michael Tabor **Bred** W Maxwell Ervine **Trained** Cashel, Co Tipperary

FOCUS
With Lord Of The Lodge a significant non-runner, this looked at the mercy of the market leader. He didn't disappoint those who backed him, and has been rated as taking a big step forward.

7615 JOCKEY CLUB ROSE BOWL STKS (LISTED RACE) 2m
4:10 (4:12) (Class 1) 3-Y-O+ £22,684 (£8,600; £4,304; £2,144; £1,076) Stalls Low

Form				RPR
0-10	1		**Withhold**[33] 6473 6-9-3 113 (p) JasonWatson 1 (Roger Charlton) looked wl; mde all: rdn 2f out: immediately responded to easily go clr 10/11[1]	111+
0340	2	6	**Austrian School (IRE)**[89] 4382 4-9-3 109 JoeFanning 2 (Mark Johnston) settled in 3rd: pushed along over 3f out: chsd wnr vainly wl over 1f out 6/4[2]	104
602R	3	2 ½	**Platitude**[13] 7158 6-9-3 96 JimCrowley 3 (Amanda Perrett) mounted on crse and taken down early: settled 4th: rdn and brief effrt wl over 2f out: sn no rspnse: wnt mod 3rd 1f out 16/1	101
0-00	4	nk	**Sevenna Star (IRE)**[97] 4053 4-9-3 97 (t) GeraldMosse 4 (John Ryan) racd in last pl: drvn and brief effrt on outer over 2f out: plugged on and sn btn 50/1	100
	5	3 ¼	**Hasanabad (IRE)**[55] 5640 4-9-3 97 RyanMoore 5 (Ian Williams) chsd ldr: rdn over 2f out: lost 2nd wl over 1f out: fdd and eased 8/1[3]	97

3m 25.44s (-3.86) **Going Correction** -0.025s/f (Good) 5 Ran SP% 111.3
Speed ratings (Par 111): **108,105,103,103,101**
CSF £2.56 TOTE £1.90: £1.10, £1.40; EX 2.60 Trifecta £5.90.
Owner Tony Bloom **Bred** Millsec Limited **Trained** Beckhampton, Wilts

FOCUS
This proved a straightforward task for the odds-on favourite.

7616 WEATHERBYS TBA H'CAP 1m 4f
4:45 (4:47) (Class 2) (0-100,98) 3-Y-O+ £12,938 (£3,850; £1,924; £962) Stalls Low

Form				RPR
4211	1		**Dramatic Device**[34] 6411 4-9-2 86 PatCosgrave 5 (Chris Wall) settled towards rr: hdwy in 2nd 2f out: drvn and sustained chal fnl f: waved tail once but r.o gamely to ld cl home 3/1[1]	96
1-50	2	½	**Spirit Ridge**[110] 3600 4-9-6 90 JimCrowley 1 (Amanda Perrett) looked wl; led: drvn 2f out: hrd pressed fnl f: hdd and no ex fnl 50yds 7/2[3]	99
036	3	9	**Buzz (FR)**[54] 5657 5-10-0 98 OisinMurphy 6 (Hughie Morrison) taken down early: a 2nd or 3rd: rdn 2f out: outpcd by ldng pair over 1f out 10/3[2]	93
51-5	4	½	**Persian Sun**[150] 2209 4-8-10 80 (t[1]) PJMcDonald 4 (Stuart Williams) cl up: drvn 2f out: one pce and wl hld in 4th after 11/1	74
0015	5	3 ¼	**Stamford Raffles**[34] 6411 6-8-12 87 RayDawson(5) 3 (Jane Chapple-Hyam) chsd ldrs tl rdn over 2f out: sn wl btn and hung lft (jockey said gelding left-handed) 20/1	76
0041	6	4 ½	**Original Choice (IRE)**[12] 7201 5-9-11 95 (v) JamesDoyle 7 (Nick Littmoden) last mostly: rdn over 3f out: sn struggling: eased cl home 14/1	76
4544	7	34	**Travel On**[19] 6952 3-9-2 93 (b[1]) FrankieDettori 2 (John Gosden) trckd ldrs tl rdn 4f out: fnd nil and qckly lost pl: t.o and heavily eased fnl f (trainers rep could offer no explanation for gelding's performance) 3/1[1]	21

2m 29.36s (-3.14) **Going Correction** -0.025s/f (Good)
WFA 3 from 4yo+ 7lb 7 Ran SP% 115.1
Speed ratings (Par 109): **109,108,102,102,100 97,74**
CSF £14.02 TOTE £3.40: £1.80, £2.90; EX 14.90 Trifecta £38.60.
Owner The Clodhoppers **Bred** Godolphin **Trained** Newmarket, Suffolk

FOCUS
This looked quite a competitive event but two of the field pulled right away in the final stages.

7617 MOLSON COORS H'CAP 1m
5:20 (5:20) (Class 3) (0-95,93) 3-Y-O+ £9,056 (£2,695; £1,346; £673) Stalls High

Form				RPR
1-1	1		**Top Rank (IRE)**[166] 1764 3-8-10 83 PJMcDonald 4 (James Tate) str: looked wl; pressed ldr travelling wl: led wl over 1f out: sn clr: pushed out: readily 10/11[1]	92
1441	2	2 ¾	**Sash**[12] 7176 3-9-5 92 JimCrowley 6 (Amanda Perrett) looked wl; led: drvn and hdd wl over 1f out: no match for wnr after but a holding rest 4/1[2]	95
3202	3	1 ½	**Nicklaus**[41] 6150 4-9-10 93 (h[1]) JamesDoyle 3 (William Haggas) t.k.h chsng ldrs on outer: rdn 2f out: wnt 3rd but outpcd by ldrs 1f out: nvr looked like getting in a blow 13/2[3]	93
3-33	4	1 ½	**Reloaded (IRE)**[12] 7205 3-8-12 85 WilliamBuick 2 (George Scott) racd in last pl: pushed along over 2f out: sn btn: mod 4th ins fnl f 8/1	81
0506	5	1	**Dark Jedi (IRE)**[75] 4934 3-9-0 87 KieranShoemark 5 (Charles Hills) chsd ldrs: rdn over 2f out: sn btn 20/1	81
4113	6	3 ½	**Gin Palace**[27] 6670 3-8-11 84 CharlesBishop 1 (Eve Johnson Houghton) pressed ldng pair: drvn over 2f out: fdd wl over 1f out 9/1	70

1m 36.31s (-2.09) **Going Correction** -0.025s/f (Good)
WFA 3 from 4yo 4lb 6 Ran SP% 111.6
Speed ratings (Par 107): **109,106,104,103,102 98**
CSF £4.73 TOTE £1.80: £1.10, £2.70; EX 4.80 Trifecta £18.80.
Owner Saeed Manana **Bred** Wicklow Bloodstock **Trained** Newmarket, Suffolk

FOCUS
Few got into this and the winner always had his main market rival covered.

7618 NEWMARKET CHALLENGE WHIP H'CAP 1m 2f
5:50 (5:50) (Class 4) (0-85,82) 3-Y-O+ £Stalls High

Form				RPR
-404	1		**Felix**[77] 4830 3-9-3 82 (w) RyanMoore 3 (Sir Michael Stoute) settled trcking ldrs: clsd 2f out: led 1f out: rdn and kpt on wl 9/2[3]	93
2001	2	¾	**Quick**[25] 6759 3-9-1 80 TomMarquand 6 (Richard Hannon) towards rr: drvn 2f out: wnt 2nd ins fnl f: kpt on but wl hld by wnr 8/1	89
433	3	4	**Voice Of Calm**[36] 6345 3-8-2 67 JimmyQuinn 5 (Harry Dunlop) racd freely in 2nd tl led over 3f out: hdd 1f out: wknd 14/1	68
5035	4	3 ½	**Isomer (USA)**[20] 6925 5-9-3 77 OisinMurphy 1 (Andrew Balding) dwlt: rn in snatches: btn wl over 1f out 2/1[1]	70
-055	5	1 ½	**Thimbleweed**[23] 6842 4-9-7 81 HarryBentley 4 (Ralph Beckett) led: drvn and hdd 3f out: struggling over 2f out 5/2[2]	71
5004	6	6	**Leader Writer (FR)**[20] 6925 7-9-3 77 (v[1]) GeraldMosse 2 (David Elsworth) t.k.h: prom: rdn and edgd rt over 1f out: sn wl btn: heavily eased 6/1	55

2m 4.73s (-0.67) **Going Correction** -0.025s/f (Good)
WFA 3 from 4yo+ 5lb 6 Ran SP% 112.2
Speed ratings (Par 105): **101,100,97,94,93 88**
CSF £37.73 TOTE £3.70: £1.90, £3.70; EX 15.10 Trifecta £95.20.
Owner Fittocks Stud **Bred** Fittocks Stud **Trained** Newmarket, Suffolk

FOCUS
Most of these had questions to answer for one reason or another, so this may turn out to be ordinary form.
T/Plt: £22.10 to a £1 stake. Pool: £69,670.10 - 2298.25 winning units T/Qpdt: £5.30 to a £1 stake. Pool: 7,288.18 - 999.85 winning units **Iain Mackenzie**

7377 PONTEFRACT (L-H)
Thursday, September 26

OFFICIAL GOING: Good to soft (6.8)
Wind: virtually nil Weather: cloudy and heavy showers

7619 PROCUREMENTSEMINARS.CO.UK EBF MAIDEN STKS (PLUS 10 RACE) 6f
2:15 (2:16) (Class 4) 2-Y-O £4,528 (£1,347; £673; £336) Stalls Low

Form				RPR
43	1		**Alben Spirit**[18] 6997 2-9-5 0 TonyHamilton 1 (Richard Fahey) trckd ldrs: pushed along to chal on inner over 1f out: briefly short of room ent fnl f: led 110yds out: pushed out 7/4[1]	77+

3254 **2** 1 **Good Earth (IRE)**[55] 5635 2-9-5 77 NicolaCurrie 3 74
(Jamie Osborne) *led: rdn and pressed over 1f out: hdd 110yds out: edgd rt and one pce* **6/1**

3 1 1/2 **Lairig Ghru** 2-9-5 0 GrahamLee 11 70
(Micky Hammond) *prom: rdn 2f out: no ex in 3rd fr appr fnl f* **33/1**

0 **4** 1/2 **Brazen Point**[28] 6622 2-9-5 0 (t) DavidAllan 7 68
(Tim Easterby) *midfield: pushed along over 2f out: kpt on ins fnl f* **3/1**[2]

00 **5** 4 **Captain Corelli (IRE)**[20] 6943 2-9-5 0 CallumRodriguez 2 56
(Julie Camacho) *midfield: rdn along 2f out: no ex ins fnl f* **25/1**

6 nk **Superiority (IRE)** 2-8-7 0 RhonaPindar(7) 8 50
(K R Burke) *hld up: pushed along 2f out: kpt on ins fnl f: nvr a threat* **40/1**

45 **7** shd **Sam's Call**[18] 6997 2-9-5 0 NathanEvans 12 55
(Michael Easterby) *trckd ldrs on outer: rdn over 2f out: wknd over 1f out* **11/1**

0 **8** 6 **Saracen Spirit**[19] 6971 2-9-5 0 DavidEgan 4 37
(Mick Channon) *hld up: pushed along over 2f out: wknd over 1f out* **50/1**

9 2 **Total Distraction** 2-9-5 0 CliffordLee 9 31
(K R Burke) *hld up: sn pushed along: wknd over 1f out* **4/1**[3]

00 **10** 19 **Northern Celt (IRE)**[18] 6997 2-9-5 0 RachelRichardson 10
(Tim Easterby) *dwlt: hld up: hdwy and in tch on outside over 3f out: rdn over 2f out: sn wknd* **100/1**

1m 19.37s (2.27) **Going Correction** +0.20s/f (Good) **10** Ran SP% **116.2**
Speed ratings (Par 97): **92,90,88,88,82 82,82,74,71,46**
CSF £12.39 TOTE £2.20: £1.10, £1.70, £9.50; EX 9.10 Trifecta £105.50.
Owner J K Shannon & M A Scaife **Bred** Llety Farms **Trained** Musley Bank, N Yorks

FOCUS
Ordinary juvenile form. It's been rated a shade cautiously.

7620 IRISH STALLION FARMS EBF FILLIES' NURSERY H'CAP 1m 6y
2:50 (2:50) (Class 4) (0-85,77) 2-Y-O
£6,469 (£1,925; £962; £481; £300; £300) **Stalls** Low

Form RPR
0113 **1** **Walkonby**[19] 6969 2-8-12 68 GrahamLee 1 75
(Mick Channon) *reminders s and in rr: hdwy on outer and tk clsr order over 4f out: cl up over 2f out: rdn to ld wl over 1f out: clr ent fnl f: sn drvn: jst hld on* **2/1**[1]

0332 **2** nk **Expensive Dirham**[19] 6949 2-9-5 75 FrannyNorton 4 81+
(Mark Johnston) *niggled along and rr early: tk clsr order 1/2-way: chsd ldrs whn sltly outpcd over 2f out: hdwy and edgd lft wl over 1f out: plld wd and drvn: styd on strly fnl f* **10/3**[3]

452 **3** 6 **High Flying Bird (FR)**[16] 7054 2-9-5 75 RichardKingscote 2 68
(Tom Dascombe) *set gd pce: rdn along over 2f out: hdd wl over 1f out: kpt on same pce* **3/1**[2]

3534 **4** 6 **Topkapi Star**[19] 6969 2-9-4 74 DavidEgan 6 54
(Roger Varian) *trckd ldng pair: cl up 1/2-way: rdn over 2f out: sn drvn and wknd* **9/2**

2110 **5** 5 **Nirodha (IRE)**[14] 7117 2-9-4 77 (p1) SeanDavis(3) 5 46
(Amy Murphy) *prom: rdn along over 3f out: wknd over 2f out* **20/1**

6034 **6** 8 **Irish Eileen**[102] 3881 2-9-4 74 NathanEvans 3 25
(Michael Easterby) *in tch: pushed along 1/2-way: sn rdn: outpcd and bhd fnl 2f* **16/1**

1m 48.71s (2.81) **Going Correction** +0.20s/f (Good) **6** Ran SP% **110.2**
Speed ratings (Par 94): **93,92,86,80,75 67**
CSF £8.58 TOTE £2.80: £1.60, £1.90; EX 9.50 Trifecta £29.30.
Owner M Channon **Bred** Mike Channon Bloodstock Limited **Trained** West Ilsley, Berks

FOCUS
The front pair pulled clear in this modest nursery. They went a good pace and the runners finished strung out in behind the front pair.

7621 EVERY RACE LIVE ON RACING TV H'CAP 6f
3:25 (3:25) (Class 4) (0-85,87) 3-Y-O+
£5,336 (£1,588; £793; £396; £300; £300) **Stalls** Low

Form RPR
1662 **1** **Highly Sprung (IRE)**[6] 7402 6-9-1 75 LewisEdmunds 8 86
(Les Eyre) *hld up in midfield: hdwy 2f out: chsd ldrs: rdn to ld ent fnl f: kpt on* **7/1**[2]

4541 **2** 2 1/2 **Young John (IRE)**[14] 7115 6-9-5 79 RossaRyan 6 82
(Mike Murphy) *dwlt and swtchd rt s: hld up towards rr: hdwy over 2f out: rdn to chal on outer over 1f out: sn ev ch: drvn and kpt on same pce ins fnl f* **4/1**[1]

5231 **3** 2 **Saluti (IRE)**[14] 7121 5-9-7 81 GrahamLee 13 78
(Paul Midgley) *hmpd s and hld up in rr: hdwy 2f out: rdn and n.m.r over 1f out: kpt on fnl f* **8/1**[3]

3305 **4** 1/2 **Mark's Choice (IRE)**[15] 7077 3-9-4 80 JamesSullivan 9 75
(Ruth Carr) *chsd ldrs: rdn along 2f out: drvn over 1f out: kpt on same pce* **12/1**

6113 **5** shd **Captain Dion**[95] 4148 6-8-7 70 (b) GabrieleMalune(3) 10 65
(Ivan Furtado) *wnt rt s: cl up: led 2f out: rdn and hdd ent fnl f: sn wknd* **14/1**

0110 **6** 1 1/4 **Mr Orange (IRE)**[20] 6916 6-9-2 79 (p) HarrisonShaw(3) 1 70
(Paul Midgley) *outpcd and bhd: rdn along over 2f out: hdwy over 1f out: kpt on fnl f* **7/1**[2]

3304 **7** nk **Magical Effect (IRE)**[9] 7311 7-9-3 77 (p) JamieGormley 3 67
(Ruth Carr) *hld up in midfield: effrt 2f out: sn rdn: n.d* **10/1**

0060 **8** 1 **Normandy Barriere (IRE)**[14] 7121 7-9-2 81 (p) FayeMcManoman(5) 4 68
(Nigel Tinkler) *in rr: sme hdwy on inner 2f out: sn rdn: n.d* **11/1**

1040 **9** 2 1/2 **Start Time (IRE)**[10] 7289 6-9-0 74 KevinStott 7 53
(Paul Midgley) *chsd ldrs: rdn along over 2f out: wknd over 1f out* **12/1**

4020 **10** 4 1/2 **Stoney Lane**[26] 6699 4-8-13 73 (p) PhilDennis 11 37
(Richard Whitaker) *hmpd s: sn chsng ldrs on outer: rdn along over 2f out: sn wknd (jockey said gelding suffered interference leaving stalls)* **11/1**

600 **11** 12 **Galloway Hills**[12] 7183 4-9-2 79 (p) SeanDavis(3) 12 5
(Phillip Makin) *hmpd s: sn prom: rdn along 1/2-way: wknd over 2f out* **40/1**

0663 **12** 13 **Gin In The Inn (IRE)**[23] 6826 6-9-2 76 PaulHanagan 14
(Richard Fahey) *qckly away and swtchd lft to inner: led: rdn along and hdd 2f out: wknd qckly and eased (vet said gelding was lame on right hind)* **8/1**[3]

1m 16.93s (-0.17) **Going Correction** +0.20s/f (Good) **12** Ran SP% **117.5**
WFA 3 from 4yo+ 2lb
Speed ratings (Par 105): **109,105,103,102,102 100,100,98,95,89 73,56**
CSF £34.71 CT £235.50 TOTE £7.00: £2.40, £1.90, £2.80; EX 36.70 Trifecta £199.30.
Owner A Turton & Dr V Webb **Bred** Patrick J Moloney **Trained** Catwick, N Yorks
■ Stewards' Enquiry : Paul Hanagan one-day ban: Failure to ride to their draw (Oct 10)

FOCUS
The closers came to the fore late on in this fair sprint.

7622 SIMON SCROPE DALBY SCREW-DRIVER H'CAP 1m 2f 5y
4:00 (4:00) (Class 3) (0-95,97) 3-Y-O **£9,337** (£2,796; £1,398; £699; £349) **Stalls** Low

Form RPR
2041 **1** **Ayutthaya (IRE)**[20] 6923 4-9-7 88 TomEaves 2 98
(Kevin Ryan) *trckd ldrs: hdwy over 2f out: rdn to ld 1f out: drvn ins fnl f: kpt on wl towards fin* **10/11**[1]

0051 **2** 3/4 **Francis Xavier (IRE)**[20] 6917 5-10-2 97 RossaRyan 4 105
(Kevin Frost) *trckd ldr: cl up 3f out: led over 2f out: jnd and rdn wl over 1f out: hdd 1f out: drvn and ev ch ins fnl f tl no ex last 100yds* **5/2**[2]

5000 **3** 4 **Awake My Soul (IRE)**[1] 7589 10-9-5 86 JamesSullivan 1 86
(Tom Tate) *trckd ldng pair: effrt on inner over 2f out: rdn along wl over 1f out: sn no imp* **6/1**[3]

0440 **4** 9 **Leroy Leroy**[14] 7122 3-8-11 88 (p) TheodoreLadd(5) 5 71
(Richard Hannon) *led: rdn along and hdd over 2f out: sn wknd* **6/1**[3]

100- **5** 7 **Jamil (IRE)**[335] 8596 4-9-2 83 PaulHanagan 3 51
(Tina Jackson) *a in rr: outpcd and bhd fr over 2f out* **20/1**

2m 15.82s (0.82) **Going Correction** +0.20s/f (Good) **5** Ran SP% **114.3**
WFA 3 from 4yo+ 5lb
Speed ratings (Par 107): **104,103,100,93,87**
CSF £3.65 TOTE £1.90: £1.20, £1.50; EX 4.00 Trifecta £10.20.
Owner JCG Chua & CK Ong 1 **Bred** Pipe View Stud **Trained** Hambleton, N Yorks

FOCUS
A useful handicap run at an ordinary gallop. The front two came clear late.

7623 JUMPING RETURNS TO YORKSHIRE NEXT MONTH NOVICE AUCTION STKS (PLUS 10 RACE) 1m 6y
4:35 (4:38) (Class 4) 2-Y-O **£4,528** (£1,347; £673; £336) **Stalls** Low

Form RPR
2 **1** **Max Vega (IRE)**[21] 6905 2-9-4 0 RichardKingscote 7 86+
(Ralph Beckett) *trckd ldrs: smooth hdwy 2f out: led wl over 1f out: rdn clr fnl f* **2/5**[1]

06 **2** 6 **She's A Unicorn**[17] 7031 2-8-7 0 JaneElliott(3) 8 63
(Tom Dascombe) *cl up: rdn over 2f out: drvn over 1f out: kpt on same pce* **50/1**

02 **3** 1 **Green Book (FR)**[44] 6054 2-9-5 0 TomEaves 9 70
(Brian Ellison) *prom: cl up on outer 2f out: sn rdn and ev ch tl drvn and kpt on same pce fnl f* **11/4**[2]

4 3 **Provocation (IRE)** 2-9-5 0 JasonHart 4 63
(Mark Johnston) *led: rdn along over 2f out: drvn and hdd wl over 1f out: wknd* **7/1**[3]

5 5 **Bringitonboris (USA)** 2-9-5 0 CallumRodriguez 1 52
(Keith Dalgleish) *chsd ldrs: rdn over 2f out: sn one pce* **14/1**

0 **6** 3/4 **War Defender**[10] 7285 2-9-4 0 RachelRichardson 5 50
(Tim Easterby) *a towards rr* **50/1**

7 1/2 **Rally Driver** 2-9-1 0 DavidEgan 6 45
(Mick Channon) *a towards rr* **25/1**

1m 47.69s (1.79) **Going Correction** +0.20s/f (Good) **7** Ran SP% **125.0**
Speed ratings (Par 97): **99,93,92,89,84 83,82**
CSF £42.87 TOTE £1.20: £1.20, £11.00; EX 47.10 Trifecta £153.70.
Owner The Pickford Hill Partnership **Bred** Tullpark Ltd **Trained** Kimpton, Hants

FOCUS
One-way traffic in this novice. The level is fluid in behind the winner.

7624 JOIN RACING TV NOW H'CAP 5f 3y
5:05 (5:05) (Class 4) (0-80,82) 3-Y-O+
£5,336 (£1,588; £793; £396; £300; £300) **Stalls** Low

Form RPR
6046 **1** **Prestbury Park (USA)**[3] 7511 4-8-9 65 KevinStott 5 81
(Paul Midgley) *trckd ldng pair: hdwy over 2f out: led wl over 1f out: sn rdn clr: easily* **3/1**[2]

0016 **2** 7 **Hawaam (IRE)**[41] 6178 4-9-12 82 (p) DanielTudhope 6 73
(Roger Fell) *led: rdn along and jnd 2f out: sn hdd and drvn: kpt on same pce* **9/2**

3233 **3** nk **Sheepscar Lad (IRE)**[8] 7334 5-8-9 70 FayeMcManoman(5) 1 60
(Nigel Tinkler) *dwlt and hld up in rr: hdwy towards inner 2f out: rdn to chse ldng pair ent fnl f: sn drvn and no imp* **5/2**[1]

5100 **4** 2 1/4 **Hawk In The Sky**[15] 7065 3-8-8 65 PhilDennis 7 47
(Richard Whitaker) *chsd ldng pair: pushed along on outer and outpcd 2f out: sn rdn and kpt on fnl f* **33/1**

0214 **5** hd **Johnny Cavagin**[50] 5819 10-9-6 76 GrahamLee 2 57
(Paul Midgley) *dwlt and hld up towards rr: hdwy towards inner 2f out: sn rdn: n.d* **7/2**[3]

0606 **6** 1 **Henley**[50] 5819 7-9-1 71 CamHardie 3 48
(Tracy Waggott) *chsd ldrs: rdn along 2f out: sn drvn and btn* **14/1**

0500 **7** 9 **Pipers Note**[15] 7077 9-9-7 77 (p) JackGarritty 8 22
(Ruth Carr) *cl up on outer: rdn and wd st to stands' rai: sn wknd and bhd* **16/1**

0202 **8** 1 1/2 **Alsvinder**[23] 6826 6-9-4 77 (p) SeanDavis(3) 4 17
(Philip Kirby) *hld up towards rr: rdn along 2f out: sn wknd (trainers rep said, regarding performance, that the colt was unsuited by the good to soft going and would prefer a quicker surface)* **20/1**

1m 3.04s (-0.86) **Going Correction** +0.20s/f (Good) **8** Ran SP% **114.2**
WFA 3 from 4yo+ 1lb
Speed ratings (Par 105): **110,98,98,94,94 92,78,76**
CSF £16.92 CT £37.69 TOTE £4.30: £1.70, £1.40, £1.30; EX 19.00 Trifecta £60.90.
Owner R Bradley & M Hammond **Bred** Godolphin **Trained** Westow, N Yorks

FOCUS
An ordinary sprint that was turned into a romp by the winner.

7625 FOLLOW @RACINGTV ON TWITTER APPRENTICE H'CAP 1m 4f 5y
5:40 (5:40) (Class 5) (0-75,76) 3-Y-O+ **£3,881** (£1,155; £577; £300; £300) **Stalls** Low

Form RPR
0024 **1** **Air Force Amy**[37] 6304 3-9-5 69 ScottMcCullagh 7 80
(Mick Channon) *hld up in rr: gd hdwy on outer over 2f out: rdn to ld over 1f out: sn clr: easily* **5/1**[3]

000- **2** 9 **All Points West**[343] 8345 3-9-2 68 (w) GavinAshton(2) 5 65
(Sir Mark Prescott Bt) *t.k.h early: trckd ldng pair: hdwy to ld over 2f out: sn rdn: hdd over 1f out: sn one pce* **6/4**[1]

4600 **3** 1 3/4 **Dance King**[19] 6975 9-10-0 71 (tp) DannyRedmond 2 64
(Tim Easterby) *trckd ldrs: effrt over 2f out: rdn wl over 1f out: sn drvn and kpt on one pce* **5/1**[3]

6336 4 14 **Hermocrates (FR)**[51] 5778 3-9-2 66..............(b) ThoreHammerHansen 6 37
(Richard Hannon) *cl up: rdn along 3f out: wknd over 2f out (jockey said gelding hung left-handed under pressure)* 7/2[2]

0-50 5 28 **Maiden Voyage (FR)**[9] 7294 4-10-5 76..............(p[1]) Pierre-LouisJamin 3 2
(Archie Watson) *led: rdn and hdd over 2f out: sn wknd* 6/1

2m 43.68s (2.58) **Going Correction** +0.20s/f (Good)
WFA 3 from 4yo+ 7lb **5 Ran SP% 109.8**
Speed ratings (Par 103): **99,93,91,82,63**
CSF £12.97 TOTE £4.80: £1.90, £1.50; EX 8.70 Trifecta £37.10.
Owner Stoneham Park Stud **Bred** Norman Court Stud **Trained** West Ilsley, Berks

FOCUS
Modest handicap form and another wide-margin winner on the card.
T/Jkpt: £740.70 to a £1 stake. Pool: £14,084.51 - 13.50 winning units T/Plt: £6.60 to a £1 stake. Pool: £50,426.00 - 5562.38 winning units T/Qpdt: £3.00 to a £1 stake. Pool: £4,528.26 - 1106.73 winning units **Joe Rowntree**

7384 SOUTHWELL (L-H)
Thursday, September 26

OFFICIAL GOING: Fibresand: standard
Wind: Moderate, half behind in straight of over 2f Weather: Showers before racing, turning fine

7626 FOLLOW AT THE RACES ON TWITTER NURSERY H'CAP 1m 13y(F)
5:15 (5:17) (Class 6) (0-60,62) 2-Y-O
£2,781 (£827; £413; £400; £400; £400) Stalls Low

Form RPR

050 1 **Sophar Sogood (IRE)**[35] 6368 2-8-13 50.............. JFEgan 9 58+
(Paul D'Arcy) *in tch: rdn and outpcd over 4f out: rallied 2f out: wnt 2nd 1f out: styd on to ld fnl 100yds: won a shade comf (trainer said, regarding apparent improvement in form, that the gelding appreciated the fast pace on fibresand surface in what he believed to be a weaker race)* 5/1[2]

0451 2 1 ¼ **Interrupted Dream**[10] 7275 2-9-3 61 6ex.............. AidenSmithies(7) 6 66
(Gay Kelleway) *led: rdn wl over 1f out: hdd fnl 100yds: no ex towards fin* 4/1[1]

000 3 7 **Ontheradar (IRE)**[51] 5764 2-8-8 45..............(e[1]) RaulDaSilva 3 34
(Ronald Thompson) *sn drvn to chse ldrs: outpcd over 4f out: styd on u.p fr over 1f out: tk 3rd post: nt trble front two* 33/1

0530 4 shd **Speed Merchant (IRE)**[15] 7079 2-9-11 62.............. LiamKeniry 7 51
(Brian Meehan) *w ldr: pushed along and ev ch 2f out: unable qck bef lost 2nd 1f out: wknd ins fnl f* 11/2[3]

0004 5 ¾ **Village Rock (IRE)**[11] 7234 2-9-3 54.............. ShaneKelly 12 41
(Richard Hughes) *chsd ldrs: drvn over 4f out: outpcd 2f out: wknd over 1f out* 4/1[1]

0025 6 8 **Indra Dawn (FR)**[9] 7306 2-8-13 50..............(b) LukeMorris 1 19+
(Archie Watson) *sn drvn towards rr: swtchd rt over 5f out: no imp on ldrs but plugged on fnl 2f (jockey said gelding was never travelling)* 8/1

000 7 ¾ **Fair Warning**[41] 6161 2-9-0 56.............. DylanHogan(5) 2 23
(Henry Spiller) *midfield on inner: rdn and lost pl 5f out: outpcd after and n.d* 10/1

4010 8 2 ½ **Lady Erimus**[19] 6969 2-9-3 61..............(p[1]) RhysClutterbuck(7) 8 22
(Kevin Ryan) *rdn and bhd thrght: nvr on terms* 11/1

6000 9 4 **Activius (IRE)**[14] 7111 2-9-2 53..............(p[1]) DavidProbert 5 5
(Brian Meehan) *hld up early: rdn and edgd rt after nrly 2f: nvr on terms (jockey said colt was never travelling)* 12/1

040 10 1 ¾ **Thomas Hawk**[35] 6368 2-8-8 45.............. AndrewMullen 10
(Alan Brown) *s.i.s: drvn to r in tch: rdn over 4f out: outpcd over 3f out: wknd 2f out* 20/1

1m 43.0s (-0.70) **Going Correction** -0.30s/f (Stan) **10 Ran SP% 116.0**
Speed ratings (Par 93): **91,89,82,82,81 73,73,70,66,64**
CSF £25.18 CT £611.91 TOTE £6.00: £2.30, £1.80, £10.50; EX 25.60 Trifecta £824.90.
Owner Sandy Seymour **Bred** Ms A R Nugent **Trained** Newmarket, Suffolk

FOCUS
A moderate nursery and plenty were struggling from an early stage. The front two finished clear.

7627 SKY SPORTS RACING ON SKY 415 NOVICE STKS 6f 16y(F)
5:45 (5:49) (Class 5) 2-Y-O £3,428 (£1,020; £509; £254) Stalls Low

Form RPR

4 1 **Royal Context (IRE)**[31] 6548 2-9-5 0.............. ConnorBeasley 11 75+
(Michael Dods) *wnt to post early: chsd ldr: led over 2f out: sn rdn and hdd narrowly: regained ld fnl 175yds: kpt on strly and asserted towards fin (vet said gelding lost right-hind shoe)* 11/8[1]

06 2 2 ¼ **Brenner Pass**[13] 7160 2-9-5 0.............. ShaneKelly 14 68
(Richard Hughes) *s.i.s: sn prom: led gng wl 2f out: rdn over 1f out: hdd fnl 175yds: no ex towards fin (vet said colt lost right-fore shoe)* 11/2[2]

3 3 ½ **Alex Gracie** 2-8-7 0.............. JonathanFisher(7) 2 53+
(Scott Dixon) *pushed along towards rr: styd on fnl 2f: gng on at fin: nvr gng pce of front two* 22/1

4 nse **Sunset Breeze** 2-9-5 0.............. LukeMorris 10 58
(Sir Mark Prescott Bt) *chsd ldrs: drvn over 3f out: kpt on same pce fnl f* 16/1

5 ½ **Bavardages (IRE)** 2-9-5 0.............. FrannyNorton 5 56
(Mark Johnston) *in tch: rdn and outpcd in midfield over 3f out: styd on u.p ins fnl f: nvr able to trble ldrs* 9/1

6 ¾ **Convene (IRE)** 2-9-2 0..............(h[1]) HarrisonShaw(3) 6 54
(K R Burke) *led: rdn and hdd over 2f out: unable to go w ldrs over 1f out: wknd ins fnl f* 6/1[3]

7 hd **Brass Clankers** 2-9-5 0.............. DavidProbert 3 53
(Robyn Brisland) *pushed along and outpcd: styd on u.p fnl f: nvr able to trble ldrs* 25/1

06 8 2 ¾ **Pearl Of India**[15] 7063 2-9-0 0.............. AndrewMullen 12 40
(Robyn Brisland) *s.i.s: in tch: drvn over 3f out: wknd 2f out* 50/1

0060 9 1 ¼ **Pull Harder Con**[16] 7046 2-9-5 56.............. DavidNolan 8 41
(Robyn Brisland) *outpcd and bhd: plugged on fnl f: nvr involved* 25/1

6 10 2 ½ **Sheung Wan**[12] 7179 2-9-2 0.............. ConnorMurtagh(3) 1 34+
(Richard Fahey) *sed awkwardly: bhd: drvn and outpcd over 3f out: nvr on terms (jockey said colt fly leapt leaving the stalls)* 14/1

06 11 2 **American Dreamer**[7] 7386 2-9-5 0.............. NicolaCurrie 9 28
(Jamie Osborne) *a bhd and outpcd* 66/1

0 12 1 **Queen Of Rock (IRE)**[16] 7046 2-9-0 0.............. AndrewElliott 7 20
(Philip Kirby) *hld up: rdn and outpcd over 3f out: nvr on terms* 100/1

64 13 2 **Diamonds And Rust**[17] 7030 2-9-0 0.............. EoinWalsh 4 14
(Bill Turner) *upset in stalls: chsd ldrs: rdn over 3f out: wknd over 2f out* 18/1

1m 15.51s (-0.99) **Going Correction** -0.30s/f (Stan) **13 Ran SP% 116.1**
Speed ratings (Par 95): **94,91,86,86,85 84,84,80,79,75 73,71,69**
CSF £7.52 TOTE £2.10: £1.10, £2.00, £6.60; EX 9.50 Trifecta £113.30.
Owner Geoff & Sandra Turnbull **Bred** Elwick Stud **Trained** Denton, Co Durham
■ Stewards' Enquiry : Shane Kelly two-day ban: careless riding (Oct 10, 13)

FOCUS
An easy win for the market leader who may prove quite useful. The opening level is fluid.

7628 WATCH SKY SPORTS RACING IN HD CLASSIFIED STKS 4f 214y(F)
6:15 (6:18) (Class 6) 3-Y-O+
£2,781 (£827; £413; £400; £400; £400) Stalls Centre

Form RPR

040/ 1 **Eesha Says (IRE)**[652] 9198 4-9-1 50.............. GeorgeDowning 10 56+
(Tony Carroll) *mde all: rdn over 1f out: kpt on wl towards fin* 66/1

000- 2 1 ¼ **Blackcurrent**[365] 7666 3-9-3 50 ow3.............. DavidNolan 3 55
(Alan Brown) *a.p: rdn over 2f out: ev ch 1f out: kpt on ins fnl f: nt pce of wnr towards fin* 50/1

0004 3 1 ¼ **Raffle King (IRE)**[5] 7468 5-8-12 46..............(v) ConnorMurtagh(3) 5 47
(Julia Brooke) *wnt to post early: midfield: rdn over 2f out: hdwy over 1f out: styd on towards fin: nt pce to chal* 9/1

0001 4 ½ **Bluella**[31] 6551 4-9-1 49..............(bt) AndrewMullen 9 45
(Robyn Brisland) *w wnr: rdn and ev ch 1f out: unable qck ins fnl f: no ex fnl 75yds* 15/2[3]

4306 5 hd **Tadaany (IRE)**[6] 7420 7-9-1 50..............(v) JamesSullivan 1 44
(Ruth Carr) *wnt to post early: chsd ldrs: rdn over 2f out: wl there 1f out: no ex fnl 75yds* 3/1[2]

-225 6 hd **Katherine Place**[5] 7468 4-9-1 48..............(t) LukeMorris 14 44
(Bill Turner) *handy: drvn over 2f out: hung lft and outpcd over 1f out: kpt on towards fin* 16/1

042 7 1 **Lyons Lane**[31] 6551 3-9-0 48.............. CallumRodriguez 4 40
(Michael Dods) *in tch: n.m.r and lost pl after 1f: sn pushed along: swtchd lft 2f out: hdwy to chse ldrs over 1f out: one pce ins fnl f: eased whn n.d fnl 50yds* 5/2[1]

6506 8 1 ½ **Atwaar**[118] 3319 3-8-11 45.............. NoelGarbutt(3) 7 35
(Charles Smith) *hld up: rdn over 2f out: sme hdwy u.p over 1f out: one pce fnl 100yds: nvr able to chal* 50/1

0000 9 2 ½ **Furni Factors**[51] 5765 4-9-1 47..............(b) RaulDaSilva 8 26
(Ronald Thompson) *hmpd early: hld up: midfield: rdn over 2f out: outpcd over 1f out* 10/1

3406 10 1 ½ **Sing Bertie (IRE)**[41] 6183 3-8-11 44.............. RowanScott(3) 11 20
(Derek Shaw) *pushed along and outpcd: nvr involved* 20/1

06-0 11 2 ¼ **Savannah Beau**[72] 5018 7-8-8 48.............. JonathanFisher(7) 2 12
(Scott Dixon) *in tch: pushed along over 3f out: outpcd over 2f out: wknd over 1f out* 12/1

5300 12 1 ¼ **Glyder**[51] 5765 5-8-10 43..............(p) TobyEley(5) 12 8
(John Holt) *n rr: sn pushed along: outpcd over 3f out: nvr on terms (jockey said mare did not face the kick back)* 40/1

4003 13 3 **Purely Prosecco**[143] 2300 3-9-0 43.............. PaddyMathers 6
(Derek Shaw) *prom: lost pl qckly 3f out: eased whn wl btn over 1f out (jockey said filly lost action approx 3f out)* 33/1

58.57s (-1.13) **Going Correction** -0.30s/f (Stan)
WFA 3 from 4yo+ 1lb **13 Ran SP% 113.6**
Speed ratings (Par 101): **97,95,93,92,91 91,89,87,83,81 77,75,70**
CSF £1868.40 TOTE £157.90: £25.00, £18.30, £2.70; EX 3736.40.
Owner A W Carroll **Bred** Ringfort Stud **Trained** Cropthorne, Worcs

FOCUS
A shock result to this moderate contest.

7629 VISIT ATTHERACES.COM H'CAP 1m 4f 14y(F)
6:45 (6:45) (Class 5) (0-70,71) 3-Y-O+
£3,428 (£1,020; £509; £400; £400; £400) Stalls Low

Form RPR

5410 1 **Blowing Dixie**[12] 7192 3-8-11 59.............. JFEgan 2 78+
(Jane Chapple-Hyam) *racd keenly: in tch: angled to outer over 2f out: led ent fnl 2f: r.o to draw clr fnl 75yds: eased cl home* 7/2[2]

0351 2 3 ½ **Land Of Winter (FR)**[7] 7390 3-8-9 57 6ex.............. LukeMorris 4 70
(Rae Guest) *pushed along towards rr: hdwy 5f out: prom 4 wd on turn 4f out: rdn to ld over 2f out: hdd ent fnl 2f: edgd lft u.p ins fnl f: eased whn no ex fnl 75yds* 4/5[1]

0212 3 11 **Sea Of Mystery (IRE)**[9] 7318 6-9-5 65..............(t) TheodoreLadd(5) 6 59
(Michael Appleby) *hld up: rdn over 3f out: carried hd to one side and hdwy u.p to take 3rd 1f out: no ch w front two* 12/1

-351 4 2 **Dame Freya Stark**[49] 5866 3-9-9 71.............. FrannyNorton 3 63
(Mark Johnston) *led: hdd 4f out: rallied u.p and ev ch over 2f out: btn over 1f out* 6/1[3]

5-00 5 1 ¾ **Sociologist (FR)**[180] 1418 4-9-3 65..............(p) JonathanFisher(7) 5 53
(Scott Dixon) *sn prom: led 4f out: rdn and hdd over 3f out: wknd over 2f out* 66/1

0545 6 shd **Storm Eleanor**[29] 6595 3-9-1 63.............. CharlieBennett 7 52
(Hughie Morrison) *prom: lost pl but stl gng ok bhd ldrs over 7f out: led over 3f out: rdn and hdd over 2f out: wknd over 1f out* 25/1

3120 7 4 ½ **Cold Harbour**[89] 4370 4-9-6 61..............(t) NicolaCurrie 1 42
(Robyn Brisland) *too str hold: prom: rdn and lost pl over 4f out: no imp after* 14/1

2m 34.93s (-6.07) **Going Correction** -0.30s/f (Stan)
WFA 3 from 4yo+ 7lb **7 Ran SP% 111.8**
Speed ratings (Par 103): **108,105,98,97,95 95,92**
CSF £6.33 TOTE £3.20: £1.90, £1.20; EX 7.80 Trifecta £33.90.
Owner Mohammed Alenezi **Bred** Merry Fox Stud Limited **Trained** Dalham, Suffolk

FOCUS
A modest handicap but a clear-cut winner. The front two finished a long way clear of the third and the time was reasonable.

7630 VISIT SOUTHWELL NOVICE STKS 1m 13y(F)
7:15 (7:17) (Class 5) 3-Y-O+ £3,428 (£1,020; £509; £254) Stalls Low

Form RPR

332 1 **Knockacullion (USA)**[24] 6811 3-9-2 77.............. ShaneKelly 9 92
(Richard Hughes) *prom: led 4f out: kicked clr over 2f out: r.o strly: rdn out* 8/11[1]

44 2 16 **Angel Lane (FR)**[26] 6701 3-8-8 0.............. HarrisonShaw(3) 6 50
(K R Burke) *trckd ldrs: rdn to go pce 3f out: swtchd lft 2f out: wnt 2nd over 1f out: no ch w wnr (jockey said filly hung right-handed)* 6/1[3]

3 5 **End Over End** 3-8-11 0.. AdamMcNamara 3 39
(Archie Watson) *sn pushed along: outpcd after 2f: kpt on u.p fnl 2f: nvr able to trble ldrs* **9/1**

4 3 ½ **Six Til Twelve (IRE)** 3-9-2 0.. PaulMulrennan 2 36
(Robyn Brisland) *racd keenly: in tch: swtchd rt after 2f: rdn to chse wnr over 2f out tl over 1f out but no ch: wknd fnl f* **33/1**

5 2 ¾ **Bobba Tee**[383] 7-9-6 0.. PhilDennis 1 29
(Lawrence Mullaney) *s.i.s: outpcd and bhd: drifted rt after 2f: plugged on fnl f: nvr involved* **50/1**

6 6 1 ¾ **Son Of Beauty (IRE)**[43] 6066 3-9-2 67........................(h[1]) RaulDaSilva 5 25
(Shaun Harris) *ponied to s: broke wl: handy: drvn and lost pl 5f out: n.d after* **33/1**

3 7 4 **Ideal Destiny**[20] 6941 3-8-11 0.. ShaneGray 7
(Karen Tutty) *sn led: hdd 4f out: sn rdn: wknd over 2f out* **22/1**

8 3 ¼ **Classic Design (IRE)** 3-9-2 0.. JackMitchell 8
(Simon Crisford) *in tch on outer: forced wd 5f out: rdn 4f out: sn wknd: eased whn wl btn fnl f* **3/1[2]**

1m 39.87s (-3.83) **Going Correction** -0.30s/f (Stan)
WFA 3 from 7yo 4lb **8 Ran SP% 119.4**
Speed ratings (Par 103): **107,91,86,82,79 78,74,70**
CSF £5.99 TOTE £1.50: £1.10, £1.90, £1.50; EX 6.50 Trifecta £27.00.
Owner Gallagher Bloodstock Limited **Bred** Bettina L Jenney **Trained** Upper Lambourn, Berks

FOCUS
There were never any worries for odds-on backers as the favourite hosed up.

7631 WATCH SKY SPORTS RACING ON VIRGIN 535 H'CAP 2m 102y(F)
7:45 (7:45) (Class 5) (0-75,75) 3-Y-0+
£3,428 (£1,020; £509; £400; £400; £400) **Stalls Low**

Form RPR

5632 1 **Mister Chiang**[5] 7439 3-9-4 75........................(v) FrannyNorton 7 86
(Mark Johnston) *mde all: rdn 2f out: drew clr over 1f out: styd on strly* **1/1[1]**

2445 2 6 **Tigray (USA)**[7] 7370 3-8-11 73........................ TheodoreLadd[(5)] 4 78
(Michael Appleby) *midfield: hdwy 7f out: prom 4f out: rdn 3f out: wnt 2nd ent fnl 2f whn unable to go w wnr: no imp after (jockey said gelding hung left-handed from 4f out)* **8/1[3]**

4103 3 2 ¼ **Colwood**[26] 6720 5-9-4 68........................(b) DarraghKeenan[(3)] 2 69
(Robert Eddery) *midfield: effrt on inner 4f out: rdn to chse ldrs 3f out: kpt on same pce fnl 2f* **7/1[2]**

00-0 4 nk **Pumblechook**[138] 2626 6-9-5 73........................ SeanKirrane[(7)] 9 74
(Amy Murphy) *chsd ldrs: wnt 2nd over 4f out: rdn 3f out: lost 2nd ent fnl 2f: kpt on same pce after* **25/1**

0440 5 2 **Shine Baby Shine**[18] 7001 5-8-9 63........................ NickBarratt-Atkin[(7)] 8 62
(Philip Kirby) *in rr: rdn and hdwy 4f out: sn chsd ldrs: one pce u.p fnl 2f* **12/1**

/060 6 14 **Percy (IRE)**[53] 5706 5-10-0 75........................ PaulMulrennan 5 57
(Frank Bishop) *racd keenly: taken bk after 2f: hld up: rdn 6f out: toiling over 2f out* **12/1**

340 7 6 **The Resdev Way**[18] 7001 6-9-9 75........................ PaulaMuir[(5)] 6 50
(Philip Kirby) *in rr: u.p 5f out: edgd rt over 1f out: nvr involved* **40/1**

3424 8 18 **Victoriano (IRE)**[11] 7231 3-9-3 74........................(b) AdamMcNamara 1 27
(Archie Watson) *chsd ldrs: pushed along and lost pl bef 1/2-way: wknd over 4f out: eased whn wl btn fnl f (jockey said gelding was never travelling)* **12/1**

/062 9 11 **Remember The Man (IRE)**[98] 4019 6-9-9 70........................ LukeMorris 10 10
(Neil King) *chsd wnr: rdn 5f out: lost 2nd over 4f out: wknd over 3f out: eased whn wl btn fnl f (jockey said gelding stopped quickly)* **8/1[3]**

3m 38.54s (-6.96) **Going Correction** -0.30s/f (Stan)
WFA 3 from 5yo+ 10lb **9 Ran SP% 114.1**
Speed ratings (Par 103): **105,102,100,100,99 92,89,80,75**
CSF £9.42 CT £37.56 TOTE £1.90: £1.10, £1.90, £1.30; EX 9.50 Trifecta £34.80.
Owner The Originals **Bred** Miss K Rausing **Trained** Middleham Moor, N Yorks

FOCUS
A fair handicap won, like many of the races on the card, in easy fashion.

7632 SOUTHWELL GOLF CLUB H'CAP 6f 16y(F)
8:15 (8:17) (Class 6) (0-65,67) 3-Y-0+
£2,781 (£827; £413; £400; £400; £400) **Stalls Low**

Form RPR

4051 1 **Queen Of Kalahari**[7] 7389 4-8-12 53 5ex........................(p) LewisEdmunds 5 65+
(Les Eyre) *chsd ldr: rdn to ld over 1f out: kpt on wl* **5/4[1]**

0310 2 1 ¼ **Requited (IRE)**[7] 7387 3-9-10 67........................ CharlieBennett 12 75
(Hughie Morrison) *led: displayed plenty of pce to get over to ins rail: rdn and hdd over 1f out: stl ev ch ins fnl f: hld towards fin* **12/1**

5042 3 2 ¼ **Catapult**[7] 7389 4-8-5 45 oh1........................(p) JosephineGordon 1 48
(Shaun Keightley) *midfield: rdn and hdwy over 2f out: kpt on ins fnl f: no real imp* **8/1[3]**

4016 4 1 **Jill Rose**[16] 7047 3-9-5 62........................(b) PhilDennis 10 61
(Richard Whitaker) *chsd ldrs: rdn over 2f out: outpcd over 1f out: kpt on ins fnl f* **20/1**

1553 5 nse **Awa Bomba**[29] 6598 3-9-6 63........................ JoeyHaynes 11 61
(Tony Carroll) *hld up: pushed along and outpcd over 3f out: swtchd rt over 2f out: hdwy over 1f out: styd on and edgd lft ins fnl f: nt pce to trble ldrs* **4/1[2]**

2500 6 1 **Mr Strutter (IRE)**[33] 6461 5-9-7 62........................ AndrewElliott 14 57
(Ronald Thompson) *midfield: rdn over 3f out: kpt on ins fnl f: nvr involved* **20/1**

0605 7 1 ¼ **Reshaan (IRE)**[7] 7389 4-8-3 48 oh1 ow3....(t[1]) ThoreHammerHansen[(5)] 9 41
(Alexandra Dunn) *s.i.s: outpcd and bhd: styd on u.p on outer fnl f: nvr involved* **25/1**

0500 8 1 **Aghast**[27] 6680 3-9-1 58........................(v[1]) KevinStott 8 47
(Kevin Ryan) *in tch: rdn over 3f out: wknd over 2f out* **18/1**

1346 9 3 ¼ **Bumbledom**[49] 5847 3-9-7 64........................(p) ConnorBeasley 7 43
(Michael Dods) *pushed along to chse ldrs: rdn over 2f out: wknd over 1f out* **16/1**

4000 10 3 ¼ **Luzum (IRE)**[15] 7065 4-9-5 65........................(p) GerO'Neill[(5)] 6 34
(Michael Easterby) *in tch: rdn over 3f out: wknd over 1f out* **16/1**

110R 11 1 ½ **Red Invader (IRE)**[27] 6685 9-9-6 64........................ DarraghKeenan[(3)] 4 29
(John Butler) *racd keenly: hld up: rdn over 1f out: nvr involved* **50/1**

0000' 12 10 **Bengali Boys (IRE)**[23] 6839 4-9-12 67........................ GeorgeDowning 3
(Tony Carroll) *unruly to post: pushed along and nvr bttr than midfield: wknd 3f out: eased whn wl btn over 1f out (jockey said gelding ran freely to post)* **25/1**

1m 14.75s (-1.75) **Going Correction** -0.30s/f (Stan)
WFA 3 from 4yo+ 2lb **12 Ran SP% 119.5**
Speed ratings (Par 101): **99,97,94,93,92 91,89,88,84,79 77,64**
CSF £16.55 CT £94.09 TOTE £2.20: £1.40, £3.30, £2.30; EX 19.30 Trifecta £138.80.
Owner Les Eyre Racing Partnership I **Bred** Minster Stud **Trained** Catwick, N Yorks

FOCUS
Only two mattered here from some way out in this moderate handicap and the result went the way of favourite backers.
T/Plt: £104.30 to a £1 stake. Pool: £32,563.81 - 312.04 winning units T/Qpdt: £8.60 to a £1 stake. Pool: £1,1492.00 - 594.07 winning units **Darren Owen**

7633 - 7634a (Foreign Racing) - See Raceform Interactive

6865

GOWRAN PARK (R-H)
Thursday, September 26

OFFICIAL GOING: Soft

7635a DENNY CORDELL LAVARACK & LANWADES STUD FILLIES STKS (GROUP 3) 1m 1f 100y
2:45 (2:45) 3-Y-0+
£38,536 (£12,409; £5,878; £2,612; £1,306; £653)

RPR

1 **Four White Socks**[68] 5190 4-9-5 0........................ DeclanMcDonogh 7 106
(Joseph Tuite) *sn settled in mid-div: disp 7th at 1/2-way: checked sltly into st: rdn and hdwy nr side 2f out: r.o wl to ld ins fnl f: eased cl home: comf (jockey said filly was checked after turning into straight)* **14/1**

2 3 ½ **Snapraeceps (IRE)**[8] 7347 3-9-0 93........................ ShaneCrosse 14 100
(Joseph Patrick O'Brien, Ire) *hld up towards rr early: gng wl in 6th after 1/2-way: pushed along and hdwy over 2f out: rdn in 2nd under 2f out and no imp on wnr wl ins fnl f: kpt on same pce* **50/1**

3 hd **Tipitena**[17] 7038 4-9-5 101........................ WJLee 8 99
(W McCreery, Ire) *chsd ldrs early: last at 1/2-way: hdwy 2f out to chse ldrs over 1f out where rdn: wnt 3rd ins fnl f where no imp on wnr: kpt on same pce* **12/1**

4 1 ½ **Who's Steph (IRE)**[43] 6090 4-9-8 106........................ ColinKeane 12 99
(G M Lyons, Ire) *sn chsd ldrs on outer and impr to ld narrowly briefly after 2f: sn jnd briefly: narrow ld at 1/2-way: pushed along down centre over 2f out: sn rdn and hdd ins fnl f: wknd nr fin* **7/4[1]**

5 hd **Terzetto (IRE)**[73] 5007 4-9-5 85........................ RonanWhelan 10 96
(M Halford, Ire) *mid-div: rdn and sme hdwy nr side under 2f out: kpt on same pce ins fnl f* **66/1**

6 4 **Solage**[27] 6692 3-9-0 95........................ KevinManning 13 89
(J S Bolger, Ire) *sn chsd ldrs: 3rd 1/2-way: rdn down centre 2f out and sn no ex* **6/1[3]**

7 3 ½ **Dean Street Doll (IRE)**[27] 6692 3-9-0 101........................(t) ChrisHayes 6 82
(Richard John O'Brien, Ire) *mid-div: rdn far side 2f out and no imp on ldrs: one pce after* **25/1**

8 nk **Frosty (IRE)**[35] 6378 3-9-0 100........................ DonnachaO'Brien 2 81
(A P O'Brien, Ire) *mid-div: disp 7th at 1/2-way: pushed along and tk clsr order far side over 2f out: sn rdn in 5th and no ex 1f out: wknd* **5/1[2]**

9 2 **I Remember You (IRE)**[28] 6646 3-9-0 96........................ WayneLordan 9 77
(A P O'Brien, Ire) *hld up towards rr: rdn 2f out and kpt on one pce* **25/1**

10 ½ **Credenza (IRE)**[11] 7242 3-9-0 104........................ SeamieHeffernan 5 76
(A P O'Brien, Ire) *hld up: pushed along towards rr bef st: kpt on one pce far side fnl 2f (vet said filly gave a couple of coughs when examined post-race)* **6/1[3]**

11 5 ½ **Come September (IRE)**[17] 7038 3-9-0 94........................ GaryCarroll 3 65
(Gavin Cromwell, Ire) *cl up early: 5th over 3f out: rdn and wknd over 2f out* **10/1**

12 1 ¼ **Shenanigans (IRE)**[90] 4332 5-9-5 0........................ ShaneFoley 1 62
(Roger Varian) *led briefly early tl sn settled bhd ldrs: 4th 1/2-way: rdn bhd ldrs far side over 2f out and sn wknd (jockey said mare didn't handle ground)* **8/1**

13 1 ¼ **Latoyah Of North (IRE)**[17] 7039 6-9-5 86........................(t) LeighRoche 11 59
(Michael Mulvany, Ire) *in rr early: 9th 1/2-way: pushed along into st and no imp in rr 2f out* **33/1**

14 7 **Satisfy (IRE)**[13] 7170 5-9-5 80........................ DarraghO'Keeffe 4 45
(B A Murphy, Ire) *cl up early: disp ld at times: cl 2nd at 1/2-way: pushed along bhd ldr over 3f out and wknd qckly into st* **66/1**

2m 4.92s (-2.08)
WFA 3 from 4yo+ 5lb **14 Ran SP% 131.7**
CSF £620.22 TOTE £25.30: £5.00, £17.60, £4.00; DF 1728.40.
Owner Mrs R G Hillen **Bred** Meon Valley Stud **Trained** Lambourn, Berks

FOCUS
An impressive performance from the winner, on much more suitable ground than would have been available here the previous Saturday. The third and fifth help set the level.

7636 - 7640a (Foreign Racing) - See Raceform Interactive

LE MANS (R-H)
Thursday, September 26

OFFICIAL GOING: Turf: good

7641a PRIX MONT BLANC (CLAIMER) (2YO) (TURF) 7f
11:25 2-Y-0
£5,855 (£2,342; £1,756; £1,171; £585)

RPR

1 **Moremi (FR)**[16] 2-8-10 0........................(b[1]) ClementMerille[(8)] 4 71
(D Guillemin, France) **17/10[1]**

2 ¾ **My Premier County (FR)**[13] 2-9-2 0........................(b) AntoineHamelin 8 67
(Matthieu Palussiere, France) **58/10[3]**

3 hd **Melrose (IRE)**[17] 7044 2-8-4 0 ow1........................(p) QuentinPerrette[(5)] 1 59
(P De Chevigny, France) **13/1**

4 2 **Panthera Tigris**[22] 6873 2-8-11 0........................ MickaelBerto 9 56
(Jo Hughes, France) *hld up in rr: circled runners to take clsr order over 2f out: rdn over 1f out: kpt on ins fnl f* **41/5**

5 1 ½ **Go Canada (IRE)**[13] 2-8-8 0........................(b) MlleCoraliePacaut[(3)] 5 52
(A Giorgi, Italy) **79/10**

6 2 **Irish Diana** 2-8-8 0........................ DamienBoche[(3)] 7 47
(P Monfort, France) **29/1**

7 1 1/2 **Loupedra (FR)**[56] 2-8-11 0....(p) ChristopherGrosbois 3 43
(J Boisnard, France) **48/10**[2]
8 3/4 **Jayadeeva (FR)**[22] 6873 2-9-2 0....(p) DelphineSantiago(3) 6 49
(Guillaume Courbot, France) **71/10**
9 hd **Dalkelef (FR)**[44] 6060 2-9-1 0.... AlexandreRoussel 2 45
(M Boutin, France) **20/1**
1m 26.58s **9** Ran SP% **118.7**
PARI-MUTUEL (all including 1 euro stake): WIN 2.70; PLACE 1.50, 2.10, 3.80; DF 8.30.
Owner Ecurie Jarlan **Bred** Ecurie Jarlan & M Jarlan **Trained** France

7642a PRIX GROUPAMA (CLAIMER) (3YO) (TURF) 7f
12:25 3-Y-O **£5,855** (£2,342; £1,756; £1,171; £585)

RPR
1 **Zorro Cass (FR)**[12] 3-8-11 0.... AntoineHamelin 9 64
(Matthieu Palussiere, France) **36/5**
2 2 1/2 **Misstic (FR)**[6] 3-8-11 0.... SebastienMartino 10 57
(Edouard Monfort, France) **56/10**
3 3/4 **Madison Vanzales (FR)**[18] 3-8-13 0....(p) MlleCoraliePacaut(3) 12 60
(M Boutin, France) **16/5**[1]
4 1 1/4 **Rum Lad**[12] 7223 3-8-11 0.... ChristopherGrosbois 1 52
(Jo Hughes, France) *dwlt: sn rcvrd to settle in midfield: urged along over 2f out: rdn over 1f out: kpt on u.p ins fnl f* **17/1**
5 3/4 **Will Ness (IRE)**[90] 4357 3-8-8 0.... DelphineSantiago(3) 5 50
(D Allard, France) **53/10**[3]
6 3/4 **Madame Vitesse (FR)**[22] 6874 3-8-13 0....(p) RichardJuteau 11 50
(P Monfort, France) **26/5**[2]
7 shd **Grand Secret (FR)**[27] 3-9-2 0....(b) MlleAlisonMassin(3) 13 56
(M Boutin, France) **21/1**
8 2 **La Belle De Mai (FR)**[12] 3-8-8 0....(b) FabienLefebvre 4 39
(I Endaltsev, Czech Republic) **33/1**
9 3 **Recovery Road (IRE)**[35] 3-8-11 0.... TonyPiccone 3 34
(I Endaltsev, Czech Republic) **13/1**
10 4 **Hamper (FR)**[27] 3-9-5 0.... SoufianeSaadi 6 31
(P Adda, France) **54/1**
11 2 **Deluree (FR)**[69] 5165 3-8-5 0....(b) MlleMickaelleMichel(3) 2 15
(N Caullery, France) **17/1**
12 6 **Charlene Du Champ (FR)**[125] 3066 3-9-1 0.... ClementLecoeuvre 7 6
(Tamara Richter, Austria) **11/1**
1m 25.29s **12** Ran SP% **119.1**
PARI-MUTUEL (all including 1 euro stake): WIN 8.20; PLACE 2.50, 2.00, 1.60; DF 18.40.
Owner Mrs Theresa Marnane **Bred** A Cicenas **Trained** France

6955 HAYDOCK (L-H)
Friday, September 27

OFFICIAL GOING: Heavy (6.0) (racing abandoned after race 3 (3.25) due to waterlogging)
Wind: light behind Weather: rain on and off

7643 JW LEES MPA H'CAP 1m 3f 175y
2:15 (2:15) (Class 5) (0-70,71) 3-Y-O+
£4,851 (£1,443; £721; £360; £300; £300) **Stalls** Centre

Form RPR
3541 1 **Vindolanda**[44] 6069 3-9-6 **71**.... BenCurtis 5 83
(Charles Hills) *trckd ldrs: pushed along to ld over 2f out: rdn over 1f out: drvn out ins fnl f* **4/1**[1]
2424 2 3/4 **Duke Of Alba (IRE)**[126] 3054 4-9-3 **61**.... JoeFanning 4 71
(John Mackie) *hld up: racd quite keenly: swtchd lft and hdwy 4f out: pushed along to chal 2f out: rdn over 1f out: styd on wl but a hld* **9/2**[2]
455- 3 7 **Ormesher**[37] 8054 4-8-11 **62**.... EllaMcCain(7) 1 61
(Donald McCain) *midfield: pushed along and hdwy 3f out: rdn to chal 2f out: sn rdn: wknd ins fnl f (jockey said gelding hung right-handed)* **8/1**
3043 4 nk **Venusta (IRE)**[9] 7344 3-8-13 **69**.... ScottMcCullagh(5) 6 67
(Mick Channon) *slowly away: hld up: plugged on fnl 2f* **12/1**
654 5 12 **Casting Spells**[22] 6890 3-9-5 **70**.... PJMcDonald 7 49
(Tom Dascombe) *prom: led 3f out: rdn and hdd over 2f out: wknd over 1f out* **11/1**
200 6 3/4 **Cormier (IRE)**[37] 6340 3-9-1 **66**.... TomEaves 2 44
(Stef Keniry) *trckd ldrs: rdn along 3f out: wknd 2f out* **7/1**[3]
0-10 7 nk **Bombero (IRE)**[79] 4792 5-9-12 **70**.... BarryMcHugh 11 47
(Ed de Giles) *midfield: rdn 3f out: sn btn* **8/1**
33 8 6 **Just Once**[12] 7240 3-8-7 **58**.... AndrewElliott 9 26
(Mrs Ilka Gansera-Leveque) *slowly away: a towards rr (trainer could offer no explanation for the poor form shown)* **4/1**[1]
4140 9 7 **Trinity Star (IRE)**[20] 6975 8-9-12 **70**....(v) CliffordLee 3 27
(Karen McLintock) *a towards rr* **16/1**
5265 10 6 **Overtrumped**[47] 5982 4-9-1 **59**....(b1) RossaRyan 8 6
(Mike Murphy) *racd keenly and sn led: rdn and hdd 3f out: wknd* **20/1**
2m 48.4s (15.10) **Going Correction** +1.00s/f (Soft)
WFA 3 from 4yo+ 7lb **10** Ran SP% **119.6**
Speed ratings (Par 103): **89,88,83,83,75 75,74,70,66,62**
CSF £22.53 CT £140.22 TOTE £4.90: £2.40, £1.70, £2.70; EX 22.80 Trifecta £179.80.
Owner Mrs Fiona Williams **Bred** Mrs F S Williams **Trained** Lambourn, Berks

FOCUS
All races on stands' side home straight. Add 27yds. An ordinary middle-distance handicap which took place in worsening conditions on heavy ground. They came over to raced towards the stands' rail in the home straight.

7644 VIRGIN BET EBF MAIDEN FILLIES' STKS (PLUS 10 RACE) 6f
2:50 (2:52) (Class 5) 2-Y-O **£4,851** (£1,443; £721; £360) **Stalls** Centre

Form RPR
2 1 **Whatabird (IRE)**[21] 6919 2-9-0 0.... TonyHamilton 10 77
(Richard Fahey) *in tch: racd quite keenly: angled lft to outer and hdwy over 1f out: rdn and sn chsd ldr: narrow ld 50yds out: drvn out* **9/4**[1]
4 2 shd **Quick Recap (IRE)**[16] 7063 2-9-0 0.... RichardKingscote 7 77
(Tom Dascombe) *prom: pushed into ld over 1f out: drvn ins fnl f: hdd 50yds out: kpt on* **5/2**[2]
3 1 **Made For All (FR)** 2-9-0 0.... CliffordLee 2 74
(K R Burke) *in tch on outer: rdn along over 2f out: drvn and hdwy to chse ldr ent fnl f: chal ins fnl f: one pce towards fin* **14/1**
5 4 1 3/4 **Noble Dawn (GER)**[21] 6943 2-9-0 0.... DougieCostello 6 68
(Ivan Furtado) *s.i.s: hld up in tch: racd quite keenly: rdn along and edgd lft to outside over 1f out: drvn and styd on fnl f (jockey said filly was slowly away)* **25/1**
0 5 3 **Ikebana**[24] 6846 2-9-0 0.... JackMitchell 9 59
(Roger Varian) *trckd ldrs: rdn along over 2f out: wknd fnl f* **9/2**[3]
50 6 1/2 **Mrs Merton**[21] 6911 2-9-0 0.... DanielTudhope 5 58
(William Knight) *trckd ldrs: rdn to chal 2f out: wknd ins fnl f* **7/1**
43 7 2 1/2 **Reviette**[44] 6064 2-9-0 0.... TomEaves 8 50
(Kevin Ryan) *led against stands' rail: rdn over 2f out: hdd over 1f out: sn wknd* **8/1**
8 1/2 **Emma Cappelen** 2-9-0 0.... BenCurtis 1 49
(K R Burke) *hld up on outer: rdn over 2f out: wknd over 1f out* **16/1**
0 9 3 1/2 **Pushover**[21] 6919 2-9-0 0.... DavidAllan 3 38
(Steph Hollinshead) *dwlt: hld up: rdn along over 2f out: sn wknd* **40/1**
10 28 **Herring Bay** 2-8-9 0.... TobyEley(5) 4
(John Holt) *hld up: sn pushed along: wknd and bhd 1/2-way (jockey said filly ran greenly)* **80/1**
1m 20.5s (6.60) **Going Correction** +1.00s/f (Soft) **10** Ran SP% **121.2**
Speed ratings (Par 92): **96,95,94,92,88 87,84,83,78,41**
CSF £8.33 TOTE £2.60: £1.20, £1.40, £3.80; EX 11.50 Trifecta £50.40.
Owner Lady Mimi Manton **Bred** Coolmore **Trained** Musley Bank, N Yorks

FOCUS
A fair juvenile fillies' maiden. The rain had relented and they all came over to race slightly away from the stands' rail.

7645 PRICE BOOSTS AT VIRGIN BET EBF MAIDEN STKS (PLUS 10 RACE) (C&G) 6f
3:25 (3:25) (Class 4) 2-Y-O **£6,469** (£1,925; £962; £481) **Stalls** Centre

Form RPR
4 1 **Gifted Ruler**[50] 5845 2-9-0 0.... RichardKingscote 1 80+
(Tom Dascombe) *prom: rdn to ld 1f out: strly pressed fnl 110yds: edgd sltly rt: hld on wl* **4/5**[1]
53 2 nk **Jamais Assez (USA)**[22] 6891 2-9-0 0.... BenCurtis 3 79
(K R Burke) *dwlt: sn trckd ldrs racing keenly: briefly n.m.r over 1f out: pushed along ent fnl f: drvn to chal strly fnl 110yds: kpt on but a jst hld* **6/4**[2]
06 3 5 **Jerbourg**[22] 6891 2-9-0 0.... DavidAllan 2 64
(Tim Easterby) *led narrowly: rdn and hdd 1f out: wknd* **7/1**[3]
00 4 3 3/4 **Jems Bond**[21] 6943 2-9-0 0.... GrahamLee 4 53
(Alan Brown) *trckd ldrs: rdn along over 1f out: wknd ins fnl f* **66/1**
1m 20.28s (6.38) **Going Correction** +1.00s/f (Soft) **4** Ran SP% **109.5**
Speed ratings (Par 97): **97,96,89,84**
CSF £2.31 TOTE £1.60; EX 2.20 Trifecta £2.80.
Owner D R Passant **Bred** Denniff Farms Ltd **Trained** Malpas, Cheshire

FOCUS
A decent little juvenile maiden. The front two in the market fought out a good battle centrally and the winning favourite drifted right onto the runner-up near the line. He deservedly kept the race in the stewards' inquiry.

7646 J W LEES BITTER 1828 NURSERY H'CAP 5f
(4:00) (Class 2) 2-Y-O £

7647 DOWNLOAD THE APP AT VIRGIN BET H'CAP 1m 6f
(4:35) (Class 3) (0-90,) 3-Y-O £

7648 LEE THOMAS CHRISTY MEMORIAL H'CAP 1m 37y
(5:10) (Class 3) (0-90,) 3-Y-O+ £

7649 VIRGINBET.COM HAYDOCK PARK TRAINING SERIES APPRENTICE H'CAP (RACING EXCELLENCE INITIATIVE) 1m 2f 100y
(5:40) (Class 5) (0-75,) 3-Y-O+ £

T/Plt: £4.40 to a £1 stake. Pool: £10,217.88 - 10217.88 winning units T/Qpdt: £1.60 to a £1 stake. Pool: £2,724.55 - 2,724.55 winning units **Andrew Sheret**

7577 NEWCASTLE (A.W) (L-H)
Friday, September 27

OFFICIAL GOING: Tapeta: standard
Wind: Breezy, half against in races on the straight course and in over 3f of home straight in races on the Weather: Overcast, raining

7650 SPORTS BETTING AT BETUK.COM FILLIES' H'CAP 1m 4f 98y (Tp)
5:25 (5:26) (Class 5) (0-70,72) 3-Y-O+
£3,428 (£1,020; £509; £400; £400; £400) **Stalls** High

Form RPR
1064 1 **Sashenka (GER)**[11] 7279 3-9-9 **72**.... LiamKeniry 4 79
(Sylvester Kirk) *trckd ldrs: rdn to ld over 1f out: kpt on wl fnl f* **7/2**[1]
0213 2 1 1/4 **Sulafaat (IRE)**[7] 7415 4-8-5 **54** ow1....(p) RussellHarris(7) 5 59
(Rebecca Menzies) *t.k.h: in tch: stdy hdwy whn nt clr run and swtchd lft 2f out: rdn and chsd wnr ins fnl f: r.o* **4/1**[2]
2014 3 3/4 **Soloist (IRE)**[5] 7493 3-9-9 **72**....(b) PaulMulrennan 6 76
(Keith Dalgleish) *hld up: smooth hdwy on outside over 2f out: rdn and pressed wnr over 1f out to ins fnl f: sn one pce* **4/1**[2]
0203 4 2 1/4 **Bolt N Brown**[27] 6722 3-9-1 **64**....(t) LukeMorris 7 64
(Gay Kelleway) *racd wd early: pressed ldr: rdn over 2f out: outpcd over 1f out* **9/1**
5223 5 1 **Sweet Celebration (IRE)**[28] 6687 3-9-4 **70**.... CierenFallon(3) 3 69
(Marco Botti) *hld up: rdn along 3f out: hdwy against far rail over 1f out: no further imp fnl f* **7/1**
3425 6 4 1/2 **First Dance (IRE)**[10] 7301 5-9-8 **64**.... JamesSullivan 1 55
(Tom Tate) *led: rdn over 2f out: hdd over 1f out: sn wknd* **5/1**[3]
3060 7 1/2 **Snowdon**[21] 6940 4-10-1 **71**....(p) CallumRodriguez 2 62
(Michael Dods) *hld up in tch: rdn and struggling 2f out: sn btn* **10/1**
2m 42.12s (1.02) **Going Correction** +0.125s/f (Slow)
WFA 3 from 4yo+ 7lb **7** Ran SP% **110.5**
Speed ratings (Par 100): **101,100,99,98,97 94,94**
CSF £16.36 TOTE £5.10: £4.00, £2.00; EX 17.10 Trifecta £64.20.
Owner N Pickett **Bred** Stiftung Gestut Fahrhof **Trained** Upper Lambourn, Berks

FOCUS
Muddling form rated around the runner-up.

7651 BET £10 GET £10 AT BETUK.COM APPRENTICE H'CAP 5f (Tp)
6:00 (6:03) (Class 6) (0-60,63) 3-Y-O+

£2,781 (£827; £413; £400; £400; £400) **Stalls** Centre

Form				RPR
2242	1		**Be Proud (IRE)**[7] 7405 3-8-7 **54** CoreyMadden(10) 11 (Jim Goldie) *dwlt and n.m.r s: hld up: gd hdwy to ld over 1f out: rdn clr ins fnl f: readily* **15/8**[1]	65
331	2	4 ½	**Toni's A Star**[11] 7274 7-9-13 **63** 4ex CierenFallon 12 (Tony Carroll) *hld up in tch: effrt and rdn whn checked over 1f out: rallied and chsd (clr) wnr ins fnl f: r.o* **14/1**	61
2033	3	hd	**Gorgeous General**[10] 7307 4-9-3 **58** (v[1]) SeanKirrane(5) 13 (Lawrence Mullaney) *disp ld to over 1f out: sn rdn and checked: kpt on ins fnl f* **5/2**[2]	55
620	4	hd	**Great Suspense**[72] 5057 3-9-11 **62** CameronNoble 10 (David O'Meara) *w ldrs: rdn whn hung rt over 1f out: hung lft and no ex ins fnl f* **11/2**[3]	58
5000	5	1	**Star Cracker (IRE)**[5] 7487 7-8-10 **46** oh1 (p) RowanScott 9 (Jim Goldie) *hld up bhd ldng gp: rdn over 2f out: hdwy over 1f out: nvr rchd ldrs* **12/1**	39
0-03	6	1 ¼	**Sambucca Spirit**[52] 5765 3-8-9 **46** oh1 ConnorMurtagh 4 (Paul Midgley) *disp ld tl rdn and hdd over 1f out: wknd ins fnl f* **11/1**	34
0421	7	2 ½	**Super Florence (IRE)**[13] 7214 4-9-8 **58** (h) HarrisonShaw 8 (Iain Jardine) *in tch: effrt and rdn over 1f out: wknd fnl f* **18/1**	37
00-0	8	1 ½	**Mixed Up Miss (IRE)**[102] 3932 3-8-9 **49** ow1 (b[1]) BenSanderson(3) 3 (Bryan Smart) *sn bdly outpcd and detached: hdwy fnl f: kpt on: nvr rchd ldrs* **100/1**	23
0000	9	2	**Raypeteafterme**[84] 4586 3-8-5 **52** (t) ZakWheatley(10) 5 (Declan Carroll) *fly-jmpd s: hld up bhd ldng gp: rdn over 2f out: wknd over 1f out* **25/1**	19
0300	10	4	**Packington Lane**[11] 7286 3-9-3 **60** (p) DannyRedmond(6) 6 (Tim Easterby) *w ldrs to 1/2-way: rdn and wknd fr 2f out* **33/1**	12
500	11	shd	**Lady Joanna Vassa (IRE)**[31] 6574 6-8-10 **46** oh1 (v) GeorgiaCox 7 (Richard Guest) *bhd: rdn and outpcd over 2f out: sn btn (jockey said mare was briefly tightened for room on leaving the stalls; vet said mare had lost its left front shoe)* **125/1**	
0000	12	nk	**Encoded (IRE)**[66] 5278 6-8-10 **46** JaneElliott 1 (Lynn Siddall) *slowly away: a outpcd and struggling (jockey said mare was slowly away; trainer said mare was found to have a small trickle of blood from both nostrils post-race)* **40/1**	

59.02s (-0.48) **Going Correction** +0.125s/f (Slow)
WFA 3 from 4yo+ 1lb 12 Ran SP% **117.7**
Speed ratings (Par 101): **108,100,100,100,98 96,92,90,86,80 80,79**
CSF £29.36 CT £68.88 TOTE £3.00: £1.40, £3.10, £1.50; EX 29.40 Trifecta £94.40.
Owner Gregg And O Shea **Bred** John Lyons **Trained** Uplawmoor, E Renfrews

FOCUS
This moderate sprint handicap, confined to apprentice riders, was run at a frantic pace and the winner has been rated back towards his best.

7652 DOWNLOAD THE LEO VEGAS ANDROID APP H'CAP 7f 14y (Tp)
6:30 (6:32) (Class 5) (0-70,69) 3-Y-O+

£3,428 (£1,020; £509; £400; £400; £400) **Stalls** Centre

Form				RPR
1015	1		**Insurplus (IRE)**[10] 7305 6-9-9 **68** PaddyMathers 1 (Jim Goldie) *hld up: pushed along 3f out: rdn and hdwy over 1f out: led ins fnl f: kpt on: eased towards fin* **22/1**	77
4242	2	1	**Zoravan (USA)**[8] 7363 6-9-7 **66** (b) CallumRodriguez 5 (Keith Dalgleish) *hld up on outside: hdwy over 2f out: led over 1f out: rdn: edgd lft and hdd ins fnl f: one pce* **7/1**	72
0036	3	1 ¼	**Global Exceed**[73] 5021 4-9-0 **62** (t) GemmaTutty(3) 7 (Karen Tutty) *slowly away: hld up: hdwy over 2f out: effrt whn nt clr run wl over 1f out and appr fnl f: chsd ldng pair last 100yds: kpt on (jockey said that she missed the blindfold on the first attempt)* **25/1**	65+
3005	4	1 ¾	**Axe Axelrod (USA)**[6] 7472 3-9-2 **64** (b[1]) ConnorBeasley 2 (Michael Dods) *t.k.h: cl up: led over 2f out to over 1f out: outpcd fnl f (jockey said gelding hung right in the closing stages)* **5/1**[3]	61
5543	5	¾	**Punjab Mail**[13] 7189 3-9-4 **69** CierenFallon(3) 8 (Ian Williams) *in tch: rdn over 2f out: hdwy to chse ldr over 1f out to ins fnl f: sn outpcd (jockeys aid gelding ran too free)* **11/4**[2]	64
0102	6	1 ¾	**Al Ozzdi**[7] 7418 4-9-3 **62** LukeMorris 6 (Roger Fell) *t.k.h: trckd ldrs: rdn over 2f out: wknd fnl f (jockey said gelding ran flat)* **2/1**[1]	53
1643	7	5	**Primeiro Boy (IRE)**[42] 6176 3-8-13 **64** SeanDavis(3) 3 (Richard Fahey) *t.k.h: led at slow gallop: rdn and hdd over 2f out: wknd over 1f out* **25/1**	41
0060	8	2	**Fitzrovia**[10] 7305 4-9-7 **66** BarryMcHugh 9 (Ed de Giles) *plld hrd: in tch: drvn over 2f out: wknd over 1f out* **10/1**	38
15-0	9	10	**Crash Helmet**[40] 6260 4-9-6 **65** PaulMulrennan 4 (Micky Hammond) *t.k.h: trckd ldrs: lost pl qckly over 2f out: sn struggling* **50/1**	10

1m 30.3s (4.10) **Going Correction** +0.125s/f (Slow)
WFA 3 from 4yo+ 3lb 9 Ran SP% **112.3**
Speed ratings (Par 103): **81,79,78,76,75 73,67,65,54**
CSF £156.78 CT £3868.70 TOTE £25.30: £4.90, £2.20, £4.80; EX 114.30 Trifecta £2217.10.
Owner D Renton & J Goldie **Bred** Patrick J Monahan **Trained** Uplawmoor, E Renfrews

FOCUS
An ordinary handicap but the winner rates better than ever, with the runner-up to form.

7653 PLAY ROULETTE AT BETUK.COM H'CAP 1m 5y (Tp)
7:00 (7:02) (Class 4) (0-80,82) 3-Y-O+

£5,207 (£1,549; £774; £400; £400; £400) **Stalls** Centre

Form				RPR
2420	1		**Jalaad (IRE)**[56] 5626 4-9-12 **81** TomQueally 11 (Saeed bin Suroor) *trckd ldrs: rdn to ld over 1f out: edgd lft ins fnl f: drvn out* **5/1**[1]	90
2162	2	nk	**Home Before Dusk**[10] 7305 4-9-0 **69** (p) CallumRodriguez 4 (Keith Dalgleish) *dwlt: hld up on outside: hdwy over 1f out: chsd wnr ins fnl f: kpt on fin* **5/1**[1]	77
3140	3	¾	**Wild Hope**[36] 6370 3-9-7 **80** KevinStott 3 (Kevin Ryan) *cl up on outside: effrt and pressed wnr over 1f out to ins fnl f: one pce towards fin* **16/1**	86
-030	4	hd	**Invasion Day (IRE)**[21] 6913 3-9-7 **80** (p) DavidNolan 10 (David O'Meara) *t.k.h: hld up: hdwy and rdn over 1f out: kpt on ins fnl f: nrst fin* **28/1**	86+
2140	5	¾	**Sezim**[27] 6700 3-9-4 **80** (b[1]) CierenFallon(3) 5 (Roger Varian) *hld up in midfield: hdwy and prom 2f out: drvn and one pce fnl f* **11/2**[2]	84
1216	6	¾	**Shawaaheq (IRE)**[21] 6913 3-9-6 **79** DaneO'Neill 2 (Ed Dunlop) *hld up in midfield on outside: rdn over 2f out: hdwy over 1f out: kpt on same pce ins fnl f* **14/1**	81
6350	7	1 ¾	**Zabeel Star (IRE)**[28] 6658 7-9-0 **72** (p) HarrisonShaw(3) 9 (Karen McLintock) *missed break: hld up: rdn and outpcd over 2f out: rallied over 1f out: no imp fnl f (jockey said gelding was slowly away)* **16/1**	70
5023	8	½	**Archaeology**[15] 7123 3-9-9 **82** JackGarritty 6 (Jedd O'Keeffe) *hld up: effrt and pushed along 2f out: nvr able to chal (jockey said gelding ran too free)* **9/1**	79
2452	9	1	**Robero**[27] 6734 7-9-6 **75** (e) LukeMorris 7 (Gay Kelleway) *t.k.h in midfield: hdwy to chse ldrs 2f out: rdn and wknd over 1f out* **12/1**	70
5443	10	nk	**Defence Treaty (IRE)**[10] 7312 3-9-3 **79** (p) SeanDavis(3) 8 (Richard Fahey) *t.k.h: trckd ldrs tl rdn and wknd wl over 1f out (vet said gelding had been struck into right hind)* **13/2**[3]	73
4505	11	½	**Absolutio (FR)**[28] 6677 3-9-7 **80** (h) BenCurtis 13 (K R Burke) *t.k.h: led against stands' rail: rdn and hdd over 1f out: sn wknd* **9/1**	73
	12	5	**Western Dawn (IRE)**[106] 3784 3-9-5 **78** PaulMulrennan 12 (Phillip Makin) *midfield: hdwy over 2f out: rdn and wknd over 1f out* **66/1**	60

1m 39.52s (0.92) **Going Correction** +0.125s/f (Slow)
WFA 3 from 4yo+ 4lb 12 Ran SP% **113.1**
Speed ratings (Par 105): **100,99,98,98,98 97,95,95,94,93 93,88**
CSF £27.76 CT £372.72 TOTE £5.00: £1.90, £2.40, £4.90; EX 34.60 Trifecta £406.30.
Owner Godolphin **Bred** Ballinacurra Stud Ltd **Trained** Newmarket, Suffolk

FOCUS
A competitive handicap rated on the positive side.

7654 BETUK.COM H'CAP 7f 14y (Tp)
7:30 (7:31) (Class 6) (0-55,62) 3-Y-O+

£2,781 (£827; £413; £400; £400; £400) **Stalls** Centre

Form				RPR
0130	1		**Lukoutoldmakezebak**[6] 7443 6-9-0 **51** (p) HarrisonShaw(3) 12 (David Thompson) *hld up in midfield: hdwy to ld over 1f out: drvn out fnl f* **11/1**	57
2000	2	¾	**Billy Wedge**[11] 7289 4-9-3 **51** BarryMcHugh 7 (Tracy Waggott) *dwlt: hld up: hdwy 2f out: effrt and chsd wnr ins fnl f: kpt on: hld nr fin* **12/1**	55
4454	3	1	**The Bull (IRE)**[21] 6945 4-9-5 **53** (p) PaulMulrennan 4 (Ben Haslam) *hld up in midfield: hdwy over 2f out: effrt and ev ch over 1f out: kpt on same pce ins fnl f* **13/2**[2]	55
0501	4	¾	**Ubla (IRE)**[11] 7281 6-9-12 **60** 5ex (e) LukeMorris 9 (Gay Kelleway) *midfield: effrt whn n.m.r briefly over 2f out: hdwy over 1f out: drvn and one pce ins fnl f* **12/1**	60
4050	5	¾	**Groupie**[7] 7420 5-9-3 **51** JamesSullivan 8 (Tom Tate) *hld up: rdn over 2f out: hdwy over 1f out: no imp ins fnl f* **14/1**	49
0000	6	1	**Temple Of Wonder (IRE)**[13] 7210 3-9-1 **52** (p) DavidNolan 14 (Liam Bailey) *hld up: rdn and hdwy over 1f out: kpt on ins fnl f: nvr able to chal* **33/1**	46
6005	7	½	**Salmon Fishing (IRE)**[7] 7420 3-8-12 **54** (p) SeamusCronin(5) 10 (Mohamed Moubarak) *hld up: effrt whn nt clr run over 1f out: rdn and kpt on fnl f: nvr rchd ldrs* **8/1**[3]	47
0056	8	½	**Rebel State (IRE)**[6] 7444 6-8-11 **52** (b) OwenPayton(7) 11 (Jedd O'Keeffe) *t.k.h: cl up tl rdn and wknd over 1f out* **12/1**	45
6411	9	1	**Fard**[7] 7420 4-9-9 **62** 10ex PaulaMuir(5) 1 (Roger Fell) *dwlt: hld up on outside: hdwy and prom over 2f out: rdn and wknd fnl f* **9/4**[1]	52+
6400	10	1	**Lincoln Red**[27] 6737 3-9-3 **54** PhilDennis 5 (Olly Williams) *cl up tl rdn and wknd over 1f out* **25/1**	41+
0040	11	¾	**Gun Case**[42] 6174 7-9-6 **54** (p) DougieCostello 2 (Alistair Whillans) *dwlt: hld up on outside: rdn over 2f out: sn no imp: btn over 1f out* **12/1**	40+
2000	12	nse	**Hippeia (IRE)**[2] 7587 4-9-2 **55** (v) DannyRedmond(5) 3 (Lawrence Mullaney) *t.k.h: led tl rdn and hdd over 1f out: sn wknd* **28/1**	41+
4044	13	3 ½	**Relight My Fire**[43] 6102 9-9-1 **49** (b) JasonHart 13 (Tim Easterby) *cl up: drvn along over 2f out: wknd wl over 1f out* **28/1**	26

1m 27.47s (1.27) **Going Correction** +0.125s/f (Slow)
WFA 3 from 4yo+ 3lb 13 Ran SP% **114.7**
Speed ratings (Par 101): **97,96,95,94,93 92,91,91,89,88 87,87,83**
CSF £125.12 CT £958.97 TOTE £10.90: £3.20, £3.90, £2.20; EX 151.20 Trifecta £1553.80.
Owner NE1 Racing Club **Bred** Peter J McMahon **Trained** Bolam, Co Durham

FOCUS
This moderate handicap was run to suit the closers.

7655 HIT THE TARGET AT BETUK.COM NOVICE STKS 6f (Tp)
8:00 (8:03) (Class 5) 3-Y-O+ **£3,428** (£1,020; £509; £254) **Stalls** Centre

Form				RPR
	1		**Brushwork** 3-9-2 0 BenCurtis 2 (Charles Hills) *t.k.h: cl up: effrt and rdn over 1f out: led ins fnl f: kpt on strly* **16/1**	86+
51	2	2 ¾	**Futuristic (IRE)**[10] 7319 3-9-9 0 CallumShepherd 6 (James Tate) *prom: effrt and drvn over 1f out: chsd wnr ins fnl f: r.o* **7/1**[3]	85
1-0	3	1 ½	**Magic J (USA)**[161] 1926 3-9-6 0 CierenFallon(3) 5 (Ed Vaughan) *t.k.h: led: rdn over 1f out: hdd ins fnl f: sn no ex (jockey said colt ran too free)* **11/10**[1]	80
	4	2	**Moment Of Silence (IRE)** 3-8-11 0 TomQueally 8 (Saeed bin Suroor) *prom: rdn over 2f out: one pce fr over 1f out* **5/4**[2]	61
0	5	7	**Global Challenger (IRE)**[39] 6283 3-8-11 0 (v[1]) TobyEley(5) 3 (Gay Kelleway) *dwlt: bhd: rdn and struggling over 2f out: sn btn* **150/1**	44
00	6	1 ½	**Hasili Filly**[114] 3482 3-8-11 0 PaulMulrennan 7 (Lawrence Mullaney) *t.k.h: prom tl rdn and wknd fr 2f out* **200/1**	34
	7	33	**Getonsam**[337] 7-9-4 0 (t[1] w) JasonHart 4 (Tristan Davidson) *s.v.s: sn t.o* **150/1**	

1m 12.18s (-0.32) **Going Correction** +0.125s/f (Slow)
WFA 3 from 7yo 2lb 7 Ran SP% **112.3**
Speed ratings (Par 103): **107,103,101,98,89 87,43**
CSF £111.73 TOTE £12.10: £3.30, £2.20; EX 57.60 Trifecta £146.00.
Owner K Abdullah **Bred** Bearstone Stud Ltd **Trained** Lambourn, Berks

FOCUS
This has been rated around the runner-up.

7656 BETUK.COM YOUR HOME FOR ONLINE BETTING H'CAP 6f (Tp)
8:30 (8:32) (Class 5) (0-75,77) 3-Y-O+
£3,428 (£1,020; £509; £400; £400; £400) **Stalls** Centre

Form RPR
2165 1 **Magical Spirit (IRE)**[63] 5399 3-9-8 77...........(w) KevinStott 7 84
(Kevin Ryan) *t.k.h: mde all at ordinary gallop: rdn over 1f out: edgd lft ins fnl f: hld on wl cl home* **7/2**[2]
2050 2 ½ **Final Go**[20] 6972 4-9-3 70........... SamJames 10 75
(Grant Tuer) *t.k.h: prom: effrt and chsd wnr 1f out: kpt on: hld nr fin* **6/1**
5511 3 ¾ **Buccaneers Vault (IRE)**[10] 7311 7-9-8 75 4ex........... PaulMulrennan 1 78
(Paul Midgley) *hld up in tch: pushed along over 2f out: effrt and rdn over 1f out: one pce ins fnl f* **2/1**[1]
1022 4 ½ **Epeius (IRE)**[92] 4280 6-9-6 73...........(v) AndrewMullen 9 74
(Ben Haslam) *dwlt: hld up: effrt and pushed along 2f out: kpt on ins fnl f: nt pce to chal* **7/1**
0006 5 ¾ **Almurr (IRE)**[10] 7311 3-8-12 70........... SeanDavis(3) 4 69
(Phillip Makin) *pressed ldr to 1f out: rdn: edgd lft and no ex ins fnl f* **33/1**
366 6 6 **Onebaba (IRE)**[111] 3580 3-9-1 73........... CierenFallon(3) 5 52
(Tony Carroll) *dwlt: hld up: pushed along and outpcd over 2f out: sn btn* **5/1**[3]
040/ 7 nk **Fast And Furious (IRE)**[955] 730 6-9-5 75........... JaneElliott(3) 11 53
(James Bethell) *sn pushed along in rr: struggling over 2f out: nvr on terms* **50/1**
1000 8 11 **Stewardess (IRE)**[20] 6972 4-9-1 68........... DavidNolan 6 11
(Richard Fahey) *towards rr: shortlived effrt over 2f out: sn wknd: eased whn btn ins fnl f* **14/1**
1502 9 16 **Raspberry**[50] 5854 3-8-10 68........... ConnorMurtagh(3) 3
(Olly Williams) *hld up in tch: rdn over 2f out: sn struggling: t.o (jockey said filly lost its action)* **40/1**

1m 12.31s (-0.19) **Going Correction** +0.125s/f (Slow)
WFA 3 from 4yo+ 2lb **9** Ran SP% **113.0**
Speed ratings (Par 103): **106,105,104,103,102 94,94,79,58**
CSF £23.83 CT £51.75 TOTE £3.90: £1.50, £1.70, £2.00; EX 22.20 Trifecta £69.70.
Owner Hambleton Racing Ltd XXXII **Bred** S E B/Stock,W J B/Stock& Norrismount **Trained** Hambleton, N Yorks

FOCUS
This wasn't a bad sprint handicap and has been rated around the runner-up to this year's form.
T/Plt: £1,217.20 to a £1 stake. Pool: £74,918.23 - 44.93 winning units T/Qpdt: £158.00 to a £1 stake. Pool: £10,321.10 - 48.33 winning units **Richard Young**

7611 NEWMARKET (R-H)
Friday, September 27

OFFICIAL GOING: Good (ovr 7.5, stands' 7.5, ctr 7.3, far 7.6)
Wind: medium becoming strong across, changing to half behind Weather: blustery showers and bright spells

7657 TASLEET BRITISH EBF ROSEMARY STKS (LISTED RACE) (F&M) 1m
1:50 (1:51) (Class 1) 3-Y-O+
£22,684 (£8,600; £4,304; £2,144; £1,076; £540) **Stalls** Low

Form RPR
2232 1 **Agincourt (IRE)**[36] 6379 4-9-2 94........... RyanMoore 7 102
(David O'Meara) *looked wl; hld up in midfield: swtchd lft ent fnl 2f: rdn and hdwy over 1f out: styd on wl u.p to ld 50yds out: hld on cl home* **12/1**
-311 2 nk **She's Got You**[20] 6951 3-8-12 92........... FrankieDettori 2 101
(John Gosden) *mounted on the crse and taken down early: keen to post: stdd s: hld up in midfield: clsd and pushed along 3f out: rdn to ld over 1f out: hdd 50yds out: kpt on but hld cl home* **13/2**[3]
4-02 3 nse **Richmond Avenue (IRE)**[22] 6910 4-9-2 0........... MickaelBarzalona 12 101
(A Fabre, France) *compact; hld up in midfield: effrt 2f out: hdwy over 1f out: styd on wl ins fnl f: ev ch wl ins fnl f: kpt on wl cl home* **13/2**[3]
2114 4 1 **Posted**[14] 7146 3-8-12 95...........(h) SeanLevey 5 99
(Richard Hannon) *looked wl; taken down early: midfield: n.m.r over 2f out: effrt ent fnl 2f: hung rt and chsd ldrs over 1f out: kpt on same pce u.p ins fnl f* **14/1**
1464 5 ½ **Exhort**[8] 7365 4-9-5 99........... PaulHanagan 9 100+
(Richard Fahey) *s.i.s and pushed along leaving stalls: in rr: effrt and swtchd rt 2f out: hdwy over 1f out: swtchd lft and kpt on wl ins fnl f: nt rch ldrs* **33/1**
0635 6 nse **Foxtrot Lady**[14] 7146 4-9-2 97........... OisinMurphy 10 97
(Andrew Balding) *broke wl but stmbld sltly leaving stalls: chsd main gp ldrs: effrt ent fnl 2f: hdwy over 1f out: kpt on same pce ins fnl f* **16/1**
-433 7 nse **Chaleur**[36] 6379 3-8-12 100........... HarryBentley 4 97
(Ralph Beckett) *looked wl; chsd main gp ldrs: effrt over 2f out: kpt on same pce u.p ins fnl f* **9/2**[2]
6050 8 ½ **Sh Boom**[9] 7347 3-8-12 95...........(b[1]) TomMarquand 11 96
(Peter Chapple-Hyam) *in rr: effrt and n.m.r ent fnl 2f: hdwy over 1f out: hung rt 1f out: kpt on wl ins fnl f: nt rch ldrs* **33/1**
211 9 4 **Lady Lawyer (USA)**[48] 5944 3-8-12 96........... RobertHavlin 13 87
(John Gosden) *sweating; sn led main gp and chsd clr ldr: effrt and clsd to press ldr over 1f out: sn no ex and wknd ins fnl f* **16/1**
2500 10 2 **Clon Coulis (IRE)**[36] 6379 5-9-2 101...........(h) JamieSpencer 8 82
(David Barron) *stdd after s: hld up in rr: clsd over 3f out: n.m.r ent fnl 2f: hdwy u.p over 1f out: no imp whn squeezed for room and hmpd 1f out: wknd ins fnl f* **8/1**
0440 11 10 **Shepherd Market (IRE)**[82] 4706 4-9-2 96........... AdamKirby 6 59
(Clive Cox) *prom in main gp: rdn 3f out: losing pl and squeezed for room over 1f out: wknd ins fnl f* **40/1**
1100 12 1¾ **Maqsad (FR)**[57] 5586 3-9-1 107........... JimCrowley 3 58
(William Haggas) *hld up in midfield: effrt over 2f out: hdwy 2f out: no imp whn sltly impeded over 1f out: wknd ins fnl f (trainer could offer no explanation for the filly's performance)* **9/4**[1]
1003 13 shd **Lady Madison (IRE)**[27] 6721 3-8-12 85........... ShaneKelly 1 55
(Richard Hughes) *led and racd along against far rail: sn clr: hung lft fr 3f out: hdd over 1f out: sn btn and wknd fnl f (trainer said filly hung left-handed)* **66/1**

1m 37.65s (-0.75) **Going Correction** +0.075s/f (Good)
WFA 3 from 4yo+ 4lb **13** Ran SP% **122.7**
Speed ratings (Par 111): **106,105,105,104,104 104,104,103,99,97 87,85,85**
CSF £88.59 TOTE £14.90: £3.50, £2.10, £2.70; EX 104.10 Trifecta £525.40.
Owner Sir Robert Ogden **Bred** Sir Robert Ogden **Trained** Upper Helmsley, N Yorks

FOCUS
Ordinary form for the grade, although it was certainly competitive and there was a bunched finish. They basically ignored clear leader Lady Madison. The first two have been rated as improving.

7658 PRINCESS ROYAL MUHAARAR STKS (GROUP 3) (F&M) 1m 4f
2:25 (2:26) (Class 1) 3-Y-O+
£34,026 (£12,900; £6,456; £3,216; £1,614; £810) **Stalls** Centre

Form RPR
4243 1 **Spirit Of Appin**[36] 6378 4-9-3 102........... MartinDwyer 5 108
(Brian Meehan) *looked wl; led after 1f: mde rest and styd on far rail st: clr: rdn and edgd lft over 1f out: styd on wl and a doing enough ins fnl f* **9/1**
3225 2 1¾ **Simply Beautiful (IRE)**[10] 7326 3-8-10 99........... RyanMoore 3 105
(A P O'Brien, Ire) *hld up in midfield: styd on far rail st: effrt to chse clr wnr over 2f out: drvn over 1f out: kpt on ins fnl f: a hld* **12/1**
312 3 9 **Promissory (IRE)**[34] 6446 3-8-10 103........... FrankieDettori 1 91
(John Gosden) *midfield: c towards centre st: chsd ldng pair and effrt 3f out: chsd clr wnr wl over 2f out: no imp and sn lost 2nd: wl btn and plugged on fnl f (jockey said filly lost its action)* **8/11**[1]
5331 4 3¾ **Shailene (IRE)**[7] 7408 4-9-3 99........... OisinMurphy 2 85
(Andrew Balding) *looked wl; dwlt: hld up in last pair: c towards centre st: effrt 3f out: no imp and wl btn over 1f out: plugged on* **6/1**[2]
3210 5 1½ **Tamreer**[20] 6962 4-9-3 92...........(h) JimCrowley 6 82
(Roger Fell) *led for 1f: chsd wnr after: c towards centre st: rdn and lost 2nd wl over 2f out: sn btn* **25/1**
6446 6 6 **Rasima**[20] 6962 4-9-3 102...........(p) DavidEgan 8 73
(Roger Varian) *stdd and dropped in after s: hld up in last pair: c towards centre st: effrt 3f out: nvr threatened to get on terms: 6th and wl btn whn hung rt over 1f out* **28/1**
2125 7 17 **Star Terms**[15] 7118 3-8-10 99........... AndreaAtzeni 7 46
(Richard Hannon) *looked wl; midfield: c towards centre st: rdn over 3f out: sn btn: t.o fnl f* **7/1**[3]
1304 8 3 **Naqaawa (IRE)**[9] 7347 4-9-3 93........... JamesDoyle 4 41
(William Haggas) *midfield: c towards centre st: effrt over 3f out: sn struggling and wl btn 2f out: t.o fnl f (jockey said filly stopped quickly)* **20/1**
5545 9 25 **Blue Gardenia (IRE)**[15] 7137 3-8-10 97...........(p) JamieSpencer 9
(David O'Meara) *chsd ldrs: c towards centre st: lost pl and dropped to rr 4f out: eased fnl 2f: t.o (jockey said filly hung right-handed)* **25/1**

2m 29.68s (-2.82) **Going Correction** +0.075s/f (Good)
WFA 3 from 4yo 7lb **9** Ran SP% **118.3**
Speed ratings (Par 113): **112,110,104,102,101 97,86,84,67**
CSF £102.74 TOTE £8.40: £2.30, £2.60, £1.10; EX 96.80 Trifecta £359.20.
Owner James Stewart **Bred** Wellsummers Farm **Trained** Manton, Wilts

FOCUS
They finished well strung out in this fillies' Group 3, the first two possibly benefiting from racing close to the far rail.

7659 SHADWELL ROCKFEL STKS (GROUP 2) (FILLIES) 7f
3:00 (3:01) (Class 1) 2-Y-O
£56,710 (£21,500; £10,760; £5,360; £2,690; £1,350) **Stalls** Low

Form RPR
1122 1 **Daahyeh**[12] 7244 2-9-0 107........... WilliamBuick 7 110+
(Roger Varian) *wl in tch in midfield: rdn and hdwy to ld 2f out: edgd rt and forged ahd over 1f out: kpt on gamely u.p ins fnl f* **11/8**[1]
3242 2 ½ **Stylistique**[15] 7117 2-9-0 97........... FrankieDettori 8 109
(Roger Varian) *str; looked wl; stdd s: hld up in rr: effrt and clsd over 2f out: rdn to chse ldng trio over 1f out: kpt on wl ins fnl f: snatched 2nd last stride* **14/1**
16 3 shd **Cloak Of Spirits (IRE)**[15] 7120 2-9-0 0........... AndreaAtzeni 2 108
(Richard Hannon) *chsd ldr: rdn and ev ch 2f out: kpt on wl u.p sustained chal: a jst hld ins fnl f* **4/1**[2]
1145 4 nk **Under The Stars (IRE)**[12] 7244 2-9-0 103........... OisinMurphy 3 108
(James Tate) *looked wl; pressed ldrs: ev ch and rdn ent fnl 2f: drvn and sustained chal ins fnl f: a jst hld* **5/1**[3]
21 5 7 **Hot Touch**[79] 4790 2-9-0 0........... JamesDoyle 5 89
(Hugo Palmer) *leggy; wl in tch in midfield: effrt over 2f out: no hdwy u.p over 1f out: wknd ins fnl f* **28/1**
01 6 ½ **Blissful (IRE)**[13] 7215 2-9-0 0........... RyanMoore 4 88
(A P O'Brien, Ire) *unfurnished; pressed ldrs: rdn and ev ch over 2f tl outpcd and btn over 1f out: wknd ins fnl f* **13/2**
2415 7 ¾ **Alabama Whitman**[62] 5469 2-9-0 95........... AdamKirby 9 86
(Richard Spencer) *bustled along leaving stalls: a in last pair: rdn and struggling over 2f out: wl btn over 1f out* **33/1**
21 8 8 **Festival Day**[10] 7297 2-9-0 0........... FrannyNorton 6 65
(Mark Johnston) *racd freely: led tl rdn and hdd 2f out: sn lost pl: wknd fnl f* **7/1**

1m 24.14s (-1.26) **Going Correction** +0.075s/f (Good) **8** Ran SP% **117.7**
Speed ratings (Par 104): **110,109,109,108,100 100,99,90**
CSF £24.75 CT £67.22 TOTE £2.10: £1.10, £2.90, £1.70; EX 20.70 Trifecta £92.10.
Owner H H SH Nasser Bin Hamad Al Khalifa **Bred** D J And Mrs Deer **Trained** Newmarket, Suffolk

FOCUS
Sound enough form for the grade - it's been rated in line with the race par - and two of the quartet who pulled clear had run well at Group 1 level in Ireland earlier in the month.

7660 SHADWELL JOEL STKS (GROUP 2) 1m
3:35 (3:35) (Class 1) 3-Y-O+
£56,710 (£21,500; £10,760; £5,360; £2,690; £1,350) **Stalls** Low

Form RPR
512- 1 **Benbatl**[335] 8660 5-9-4 123...........(t) OisinMurphy 3 124
(Saeed bin Suroor) *looked wl; mde all and dictated gallop: rdn and qcknd clr over 1f out: r.o strly: v readily* **4/1**[2]
1124 2 5 **King Of Comedy (IRE)**[37] 6354 3-9-0 118........... FrankieDettori 4 113+
(John Gosden) *taken down early: awkward leaving stalls and slowly away: t.k.h: hld up towards rr: hdwy to chse ldrs 5f out: effrt ent fnl 2f: wnt 2nd but wnr gone clr over 1f out: no imp ins fnl f* **6/5**[1]
1201 3 1¼ **Zaaki**[34] 6470 4-9-4 113........... RyanMoore 5 110
(Sir Michael Stoute) *t.k.h: hld up in tch: effrt ent fnl 2f: no ch w wnr but kpt on ins fnl f to go 3rd last strides* **8/1**
11 4 nk **UAE Jewel**[146] 2413 3-9-0 108........... AndreaAtzeni 6 109
(Roger Varian) *looked wl; chsd wnr: effrt over 2f out: unable to match pce of wnr and lost 2nd over 1f out: wl hld ins fnl f: lost 3rd last strides* **4/1**[2]
1043 5 2¼ **Happy Power (IRE)**[34] 6443 3-9-0 115........... JamesDoyle 2 104
(Andrew Balding) *looked wl; t.k.h: chsd ldrs tl 5f out: styd wl in tch: effrt over 2f out: outpcd and btn over 1f out: wknd ins fnl f* **15/2**[3]

The Form Book Flat 2019, Raceform Ltd, Newbury, RG14 5SJ

1650 **6** 3 ¼ **Anna Nerium**33 6508 4-9-1 107 .... TomMarquand 7 93
(Richard Hannon) *hld up in tch in last pair: effrt over 2f out: sn struggling and outpcd over 1f out: wknd ins fnl f* **33/1**

1m 35.6s (-2.80) **Going Correction** +0.075s/f (Good)
WFA 3 from 4yo+ 4lb **6** Ran SP% **111.3**
Speed ratings (Par 115): **117,112,110,110,108 104**
CSF £9.09 TOTE £4.30: £2.20, £1.10; EX 9.50 Trifecta £36.90.
Owner Godolphin **Bred** Darley **Trained** Newmarket, Suffolk

FOCUS
A strong Group 2 and an impressive return to action from the winner, albeit with everything going his way. He has been rated to his best.

7661 DERRINSTOWN IRISH EBF MAIDEN STKS (PLUS 10 RACE) (C&G) 7f
4:10 (4:10) (Class 4) 2-Y-O £6,469 (£1,925; £962; £481) Stalls Low

Form RPR

1 **New World Tapestry (USA)**92 4310 2-9-0 0 .... RyanMoore 1 86
(A P O'Brien, Ire) *str; bmpd leaving stalls: led: rdn ent fnl 2f: hdd and drvn ent fnl f: rallied u.p to ld again ins fnl f: styd on wl* **1/1**[1]

2 ¾ **Colour Image (IRE)** 2-9-0 0 .... OisinMurphy 6 84+
(Saeed bin Suroor) *compact: looked wl; trckd ldrs: clsd to press ldrs 3f out: rdn and led ent fnl f: drvn and hdd ins fnl f: kpt on same pce after* **5/2**[2]

3 3 ½ **Hibernian Warrior (USA)** 2-9-0 0 .... JFEgan 3 75+
(Roger Varian) *str; stdd s: t.k.h: hld up in tch in last trio: hdwy into midfield 1/2-way: effrt 2f out: chsd clr ldng pair jst ins fnl f: kpt on but no threat to ldrs* **9/1**

4 1 ¼ **Society Lion** 2-9-0 0 .... JamesDoyle 8 72+
(Sir Michael Stoute) *tall; ly; stdd s: t.k.h: hld up in last pair: effrt jst over 2f out: no imp and hung lft over 1f out: kpt on same pce ins fnl f (jockey said colt ran green)* **15/2**[3]

00 **5** 1 ½ **Mon Choix**28 6669 2-9-0 0 .... WilliamBuick 2 68
(Andrew Balding) *wnt rt and bmpd wnr leaving stalls: chsd wnr tl no ex u.p and outpcd over 1f out: wknd ins fnl f* **16/1**

6 3 **Buwardy** 2-9-0 0 .... RobertHavlin 7 60+
(John Gosden) *workmanlike: bit bkward; s.i.s: rn green and wnt rt sn after s: in tch in rr: effrt 3f out: no imp and btn 2f out: wknd over 1f out* **8/1**

7 4 **Chairmanic (IRE)** 2-9-0 0 .... TomMarquand 4 50
(Brian Meehan) *leggy; chsd ldrs: effrt ent fnl 2f: no ex u.p and outpcd over 1f out: fdd ins fnl f: lame (vet said colt was lame on its left fore)* **33/1**

05 **8** 6 **Debt Of Honour**35 6402 2-8-7 0 .... JoeBradnam(7) 5 34
(Michael Bell) *workmanlike; midfield tl lost pl 3f out: bhd fnl 2f* **66/1**

1m 25.96s (0.56) **Going Correction** +0.075s/f (Good) **8** Ran SP% **121.8**
Speed ratings (Par 97): **99,98,94,92,91 87,83,76**
CSF £3.98 TOTE £1.80: £1.10, £1.10, £2.30; EX 3.80 Trifecta £18.90.
Owner Tabor/Smith/Mrs Magnier/Flaxman Stables **Bred** Flaxman Holdings Ltd, Orpendale Et Al **Trained** Cashel, Co Tipperary

FOCUS
The two market leaders dominated this useful maiden, which has been rated in line with the race average.

7662 MUKHADRAM GODOLPHIN STKS (LISTED RACE) 1m 4f
4:45 (4:48) (Class 1) 3-Y-O+ £22,684 (£8,600; £4,304; £2,144; £1,076) Stalls Centre

Form RPR

0005 **1** **Mountain Hunter (USA)**20 6962 5-9-5 105 .... OisinMurphy 4 111
(Saeed bin Suroor) *pressed ldr: rdn to ld over 2f out: hdd and carried lft over 1f out: swtchd lft and 2 l down 1f out: rallied as ldr idled ins fnl f: kpt on u.p to ld on post* **11/2**[3]

2-56 **2** nse **Loxley (IRE)**16 7076 4-9-5 110 .... WilliamBuick 5 113+
(Charlie Appleby) *trckd ldrs: clsd to join ldrs jst over 2f out: rdn to ld and edgd rt over 1f out: 2 l clr 1f out: drvn ins fnl f: idling in front 100yds out: worn down and hdd on post* **7/1**

1401 **3** 2 ½ **Weekender**14 7158 5-9-5 112 .... FrankieDettori 3 107+
(John Gosden) *looked wl; led: rdn 3f out: hdd over 2f out: unable qck and outpcd 2f out: kpt on ins fnl f: snatched 3rd last stride* **4/1**[2]

2-4 **4** shd **Mount Everest (IRE)**13 7218 3-8-12 110 .... RyanMoore 2 107
(A P O'Brien, Ire) *athletic; trckd ldrs: clsd to press ldrs 3f out: sn rdn: drvn and unable qck 2f out: 3rd and swtchd lft over 1f out: kpt on same pce ins fnl f: lost 3rd last stride* **10/11**[1]

3511 **5** 1 ¾ **Ojooba**42 6172 3-8-7 95 .... AndreaAtzeni 1 99
(Owen Burrows) *hld up in tch in rr: effrt ent fnl 2f: unable qck u.p over 1f out: wl hld and one pce fnl f* **8/1**

2m 31.22s (-1.28) **Going Correction** +0.075s/f (Good)
WFA 3 from 4yo+ 7lb **5** Ran SP% **111.4**
Speed ratings (Par 111): **107,106,105,105,104**
CSF £39.28 TOTE £6.40: £2.40, £2.60; EX 30.80 Trifecta £128.70.
Owner Godolphin **Bred** Darley **Trained** Newmarket, Suffolk

FOCUS
A muddling Listed race but this rates a length pb from the winner. The second has been rated back to his best (rated as a length winner).

7663 SHADWELL FARM H'CAP (SILVER CAMBRIDGESHIRE) 1m 1f
5:20 (5:20) (Class 2) 3-Y-O+ £31,125 (£9,320; £4,660; £2,330; £1,165; £585) Stalls Low

Form RPR

2122 **1** **Data Protection**8 7378 4-9-10 76 .... (t) JamesDoyle 4 87
(William Muir) *sn led: mde rest and dictated gallop: travelling best and clr 2f out: rdn ent fnl f: r.o strly: easily* **5/2**[1]

0231 **2** 3 ½ **Escape The City**18 7026 4-9-1 74 4ex .... AngusVilliers(7) 2 78
(Hughie Morrison) *chsd ldrs: effrt over 2f out: chsd clr wnr over 1f out: no imp but kpt on for clr 2nd* **11/4**[2]

1316 **3** 3 **First Flight (IRE)**6 7465 8-9-7 73 .... BenRobinson 5 70
(Brian Ellison) *chsd wnr early: settled bk and wl in tch in midfield after: effrt over 2f out: wl hld 3rd and kpt on same pce fnl f* **6/1**[3]

0413 **4** 2 ½ **Cuttin' Edge (IRE)**37 6334 5-9-0 66 .... MartinDwyer 8 58
(William Muir) *hdwy to chse wnr after 1f: rdn over 2f out: unable qck and lost btn 2nd 1f out: wknd ins fnl f* **8/1**

2450 **5** 2 ¾ **Battle Of Waterloo (IRE)**13 7213 3-9-9 80 .... AdamKirby 7 67
(John Ryan) *stdd s: hld up in rr: clsd over 2f out: nt clr run: swtchd lft and effrt over 1f out: sn btn and wknd ins fnl f* **9/1**

0544 **6** 1 ¼ **Sheila's Showcase**62 5450 3-9-4 75 .... DavidEgan 1 60
(Denis Coakley) *chsd ldrs early: wl in tch in midfield tl lost pl u.p 3f out: no ch fnl 2f* **9/1**

3155 **7** shd **The Throstles**28 6686 4-9-6 72 .... AndreaAtzeni 6 55
(Kevin Frost) *stdd s: hld up in tch: hdwy into midfield 4f out: rdn over 2f out: unable qck and btn over 1f out: wknd ins fnl f* **7/1**

1m 51.14s (0.04) **Going Correction** +0.075s/f (Good)
WFA 3 from 4yo+ 5lb **7** Ran SP% **113.1**
Speed ratings (Par 109): **102,98,96,94,91 90,90**
CSF £9.40 CT £35.14 TOTE £2.90: £1.60, £2.00; EX 8.10 Trifecta £24.80.
Owner Muir Racing Partnership - Santa Anita **Bred** Mr & Mrs J Laws **Trained** Lambourn, Berks

FOCUS
A much smaller field than usual, and not for the first time on the card the winner made most next to the far rail. He has been rated back to his best.
T/Jkpt: Not Won. T/Plt: £70.40 to a £1 stake. Pool: £118,945.13 - 1,231.92 winning units T/Qpdt: £15.00 to a £1 stake. Pool: £10,692.19 - 525.24 winning units **Steve Payne**

7664 - 7667a (Foreign Racing) - See Raceform Interactive

7421 DUNDALK (A.W) (L-H)
Friday, September 27

OFFICIAL GOING: Polytrack: standard

7668a MATTHEWS.IE DIAMOND STKS (GROUP 3) 1m 2f 150y(P)
7:15 (7:15) 3-Y-O+
£33,486 (£10,783; £5,108; £1,702; £1,702; £567)

RPR

1 **Blenheim Palace (IRE)**13 7218 3-9-3 109 .... (b) DonnachaO'Brien 6 103+
(A P O'Brien, Ire) *sn led: strly pressed appr fnl f and briefly hdd ins fnl f: rallied wl to ld cl home* **5/1**[2]

2 hd **Numerian (IRE)**12 7248 3-9-3 104 .... DeclanMcDonogh 4 103
(Joseph Patrick O'Brien, Ire) *broke wl and disp early: sn trckd ldrs in 3rd: pushed along to press ldr in 2nd over 1f out: led narrowly ins fnl f: kpt on wl: hdd cl home* **5/1**[2]

3 ½ **Antilles (USA)**12 7248 3-9-3 103 .... WayneLordan 1 102+
(A P O'Brien, Ire) *racd in rr tl prog on inner ent fnl f: styd on wl into 3rd fnl 50yds: nt rch principals* **10/1**[3]

4 ¾ **Fresnel**28 6692 3-9-0 99 .... GaryHalpin 2 98
(Jack W Davison, Ire) *racd in mid-div: pushed along under 2f out: swtchd rt in 4th ent fnl f and bit short of room: rallied wl to dead-heat for 4th on line* **12/1**

4 dht **Massif Central (IRE)**12 7248 5-9-8 101 .... (t[1]) RonanWhelan 7 99+
(M Halford, Ire) *hld up towards rr: clsr to chse ldrs over 1f out: briefly wnt 3rd ent fnl f: no imp ins fnl 100yds: kpt on same pce and jnd for 4th on line* **14/1**

6 1 ¼ **Harriet's Force (IRE)**28 6692 3-9-0 96 .... RobbieColgan 5 95
(Keith Henry Clarke, Ire) *chsd ldrs in 4th: rdn and no imp ent fnl f: kpt on same pce fnl 150yds* **40/1**

7 1 ¾ **Mootasadir**20 6962 4-9-8 109 .... ColinKeane 8 93
(Hugo Palmer) *sn trckd ldr in 2nd: rdn under 2f out: wknd appr fnl f: sn no ex: lame (vet said colt was lame post race)* **4/6**[1]

P **Altair (IRE)**35 6431 3-9-0 90 .... (b[1]) ShaneCrosse 3
(Joseph Patrick O'Brien, Ire) *racd in rr: detached after 2f and sn p.u: fatally injured* **40/1**

2m 12.97s (-2.53) **Going Correction** +0.225s/f (Slow)
WFA 3 from 4yo+ 6lb **8** Ran SP% **121.6**
Speed ratings: **116,115,115,114,114 114,112,**
WIN: 4.90 Blenheim Palace; PL: 1.40 Blenheim Palace, 3.20 Antilles, 1.60 Numerian; EX: 20.40; CSF: 32.24; TC: ; TF: 97.60;.
Owner Mrs John Magnier & Michael Tabor & Derrick Smith **Bred** Liberty Bloodstock **Trained** Cashel, Co Tipperary

FOCUS
The fourth, fifth and sixth set the standard in a tight finish.

7669 - 7672a (Foreign Racing) - See Raceform Interactive

4159 LYON PARILLY (R-H)
Friday, September 27

OFFICIAL GOING: Turf: good to soft

7673a CRITERIUM DE LYON (LISTED RACE) (2YO) (TURF) 1m
1:07 2-Y-O £27,027 (£10,810; £8,108; £5,405; £2,702)

RPR

1 **Chares (GER)**27 2-9-0 0 .... JulienAuge 7 100+
(C Ferland, France) **11/10**[1]

2 nk **Choise Of Raison**18 2-9-0 0 .... FranckBlondel 6 99
(F Rossi, France) **68/10**

3 2 ½ **Magic Attitude**15 2-8-10 0 .... IoritzMendizabal 3 91
(F Chappet, France) **14/1**

4 nk **Shared Belief (IRE)**20 6957 2-9-0 0 .... (p) HollieDoyle 1 93
(Archie Watson) *led: asked to qckn over 2f out: chal 1 1/2f out: sn u.p: hdd over 1f out: grad wknd ins fnl f: no ex* **53/10**[3]

5 2 ½ **Taranta (IRE)**38 2-8-10 0 .... TonyPiccone 4 83
(Mlle J Soudan, France) **9/1**

6 2 ½ **Santurin (FR)**30 2-9-0 0 .... AntoineHamelin 2 82
(Henk Grewe, Germany) **47/10**[2]

7 8 ½ **Big Boss Man (FR)**18 2-9-0 0 .... (b) MarvinGrandin 5 62
(Cedric Rossi, France) **9/1**

1m 40.25s **7** Ran SP% **120.5**
PARI-MUTUEL (all including 1 euro stake): WIN 2.10; PLACE 1.60, 3.60; SF 7.40.
Owner Ecurie Waldeck **Bred** C Walter **Trained** France

7360 SAINT-CLOUD (L-H)
Friday, September 27

OFFICIAL GOING: Turf: very soft

7674a PRIX DE SAINT-FORGET (CLAIMER) (2YO COLTS & GELDINGS) (TURF) 7f
12:50 2-Y-O £10,360 (£4,144; £3,108; £2,072; £1,036)

RPR

1 **Salar Island (ITY)**13 2-9-4 0 .... CristianDemuro 4 87
(Andrea Marcialis, France) **17/10**[1]

2 3 **Licankabur (FR)**[48] 2-8-11 0 VincentCheminaud 3 73
(H-A Pantall, France) **9/1**

3 1/2 **Jangkhe (FR)**[55] 2-9-4 0 StephanePasquier 5 78
(K Borgel, France) **10/1**

4 3/4 **Mister Jingle (FR)**[38] 2-8-13 0 HugoBesnier(5) 7 76
(K Borgel, France) **14/1**

5 1/2 **Kongastet (FR)**[43] 6141 2-9-1 0 (b) TheoBachelot 8 72
(S Wattel, France) **23/5**[3]

6 1/2 **Mucho Macho (FR)**[27] 6750 2-8-9 0 JordanPlateaux(6) 1 71
(Simone Brogi, France) **11/5**[2]

7 12 **Giant Steps (IRE)**[26] 6776 2-9-4 0 AurelienLemaitre 6 44
(Jo Hughes, France) *slowly away: racd in fnl pair: struggling to go pce and nudged along over 1/2-way: rdn 2 1/2f out: no imp and sn wl btn: allowed to fin in own time* **37/1**

8 dist **Goldmembers (FR)**[84] 2-8-8 0 MlleCoraliePacaut(3) 2
(M Boutin, France) **24/1**

1m 31.91s (-0.29) **8** Ran SP% **118.5**
PARI-MUTUEL (all including 1 euro stake): WIN 2.70; PLACE 1.50, 2.60, 2.70; DF 14.10.
Owner Gerard Augustin-Normand & Francesco Loi **Bred** Giovanni Latina **Trained** France

7675a PRIX LOUQSOR (MAIDEN) (2YO COLTS & GELDINGS) (TURF) 1m

2:32 2-Y-O **£12,162** (£4,864; £3,648; £2,432; £1,216)

RPR

1 **Mkfancy (FR)**[26] 6776 2-9-2 0 MaximeGuyon 13 84+
(Mme Pia Brandt, France) **31/10**[2]

2 3 **Firstman (FR)**[35] 6433 2-9-2 0 CristianDemuro 12 75
(J-C Rouget, France) **77/10**

3 2 **Jean Racine (FR)**[45] 2-9-2 0 Pierre-CharlesBoudot 14 71
(H-A Pantall, France) **16/1**

4 hd **Zealandia (FR)** 2-8-11 0 HugoJourniac 7 66+
(M Nigge, France) **57/1**

5 3/4 **Aiguiere D'Argent (FR)** 2-8-10 0 ThomasTrullier(6) 6 69+
(N Clement, France) **21/1**

6 1 1/2 **Brave Shiina (FR)**[107] 2-9-2 0 FabienLefebvre 9 66
(Hiroo Shimizu, France) **65/1**

7 2 1/2 **Farout (IRE)**[38] 2-9-2 0 StephanePasquier 11 60+
(F-H Graffard, France) **20/1**

8 1/2 **Zucesso (FR)**[37] 2-9-2 0 CyrilleStefan 10 59
(S Smrczek, Germany) **80/1**

9 1 **Shoal Of Time (FR)**[38] 2-9-2 0 VincentCheminaud 8 57
(A Fabre, France) *prom: pushed along to chal 2f out: edgd rt u.p: rdn briefly 1 1/2f out: sn struggling and grad fdd fr over 1f out* **19/10**[1]

10 2 **Charlesquint (IRE)**[22] 2-9-2 0 GregoryBenoist 1 52+
(Y Barberot, France) **61/10**[3]

11 2 1/2 **London Memories (FR)**[100] 2-8-13 0 MlleMickaelleMichel(3) 2 47+
(A Spanu, France) **33/1**

12 7 **King Gold (FR)** 2-8-11 0 EddyHardouin 3 27+
(N Caullery, France) **20/1**

13 3/4 **Rock Blanc (FR)**[14] 2-9-2 0 (b[1]) TheoBachelot 4 30+
(R Le Dren Doleuze, France) **36/1**

14 7 **Falcata**[26] 6776 2-9-2 AurelienLemaitre 5 14+
(Jo Hughes, France) *midfield: asked for effrt over 2 1/2f out: limited rspnse: rdn 2f out: no imp and wl btn 1 1/2f out* **18/1**

1m 46.77s (-0.73) **14** Ran SP% **119.8**
PARI-MUTUEL (all including 1 euro stake): WIN 4.10; PLACE 2.00, 2.50, 4.70; DF 13.70.
Owner Abdullah Al Maddah **Bred** Marbat Llc **Trained** France

7676a PRIX DE GARGENVILLE (CLAIMER) (4YO+) (TURF) 1m 4f

4:49 4-Y-O+ **£8,558** (£3,423; £2,567; £1,711; £855)

RPR

1 **Pascasha D'Or (FR)**[19] 5-9-1 0 TheoBachelot 10 76
(S Wattel, France) **5/2**[1]

2 1/2 **Zafiro (FR)**[7] 7-8-9 0 HugoBesnier(6) 1 75
(D De Waele, France) **37/1**

3 snk **Cutty Pie (IRE)**[27] 6790 5-9-1 0 (p) AlexisBadel 9 75
(J Phelippon, France) **10/1**

4 hd **Quevillon (FR)**[43] 5-8-11 0 CristianDemuro 7 71
(S Cerulis, France) **17/2**[3]

5 hd **Pachadargent (FR)**[32] 8-9-0 0 MlleMarieVelon(8) 3 81
(J-P Gauvin, France) **7/2**[2]

6 3/4 **Sudfaa (FR)**[33] 4-8-11 0 JackyNicoleau(6) 6 75
(M Le Forestier, France) **18/1**

7 9 **Bonfire Heart (FR)**[18] 7-8-8 0 DelphineSantiago(3) 5 55
(R Le Gal, France) **19/1**

8 1 **Ventaron (FR)**[39] 8-9-5 0 MlleCoraliePacaut(3) 2 64
(C Boutin, France) **19/1**

9 8 **Miro (GER)** 4-8-6 0 JimmyTastayre(5) 8 40
(M Le Forestier, France) **32/1**

10 dist **My Lord And Master (IRE)**[27] 6790 4-9-4 0 ChristopheSoumillon 4
(William Haggas) *dwlt s: in rr: prog to r promly after 2f: struggling to go pce and pushed along 3f out: no imp and wknd fr 2f out: eased ent fnl f* **5/2**[1]

2m 45.08s (4.68) **10** Ran SP% **119.9**
PARI-MUTUEL (all including 1 euro stake): WIN 3.50; PLACE 2.10, 6.70, 2.90; DF 37.70.
Owner Aubry-Dumand Elevage **Bred** Aubry-Dumand Elevage **Trained** France

7179 CHESTER (L-H)

Saturday, September 28

OFFICIAL GOING: Soft (6.8)
Wind: Moderate, across in straight of over 1f Weather: Sunshine and Showers

7677 BOODLES EBF NOVICE AUCTION STKS (PLUS 10 RACE) 7f 1y

1:35 (1:35) (Class 4) 2-Y-O
£5,851 (£1,752; £876; £438; £219; £109) **Stalls** Low

Form RPR

02 1 **Strait Of Hormuz (IRE)**[24] 6858 2-9-3 0 DavidProbert 7 77
(Andrew Balding) *chsd ldrs: rdn 2f out: wnt 2nd jst over 1f out: styd on to ld ins fnl 100yds: pushed out towards fin* **13/8**[1]

0 2 1 1/2 **Overwrite (IRE)**[9] 7388 2-9-3 0 FrannyNorton 6 73
(Mark Johnston) *led: rdn and tried to slip field over 1f out: sn over 2 l clr: all out ins fnl f: hdd ins fnl 100yds: no ex (jockey said colt lost his action approximately one furlong out)* **16/1**

2525 3 2 1/4 **Lexi The One (IRE)**[15] 7140 2-8-12 67 PaulHanagan 10 63
(Richard Fahey) *midfield: rdn and hdwy over 1f out: styd on to chse front two wl ins fnl f: nvr able to chal* **10/1**

61 4 1 1/4 **Roseina's Voice**[14] 7179 2-9-0 0 ThomasGreatrex(5) 8 67
(David Loughnane) *racd keenly: w ldr: rdn 2f out: unable qck: lost 2nd jst over 1f out: no ex ins fnl f: wknd fnl 100yds* **7/2**[2]

56 5 1 **Murraymint (FR)**[34] 6504 2-9-3 0 SeanLevey 5 62
(Ralph Beckett) *missed break: midfield: rdn over 2f out: kpt on ins fnl f: nvr able to trble ldrs* **10/1**

4060 6 nk **Precision Storm**[36] 6394 2-9-3 62 AndrewMullen 3 61
(Mark Loughnane) *bmpd s: hld up: u.p over 2f out: styd on ins fnl f: nvr able to trble ldrs* **33/1**

7 3 1/2 **Girl From Mars (IRE)** 2-8-12 0 RichardKingscote 1 48
(Tom Dascombe) *s.i.s: bhd: a pushed along: nvr involved* **5/1**[3]

5 8 2 1/4 **Dutch Harbor**[19] 7030 2-9-3 0 AlistairRawlinson 9 47
(Sir Mark Todd) *s.i.s: hld up towards rr: pushed along over 4f out: outpcd over 2f out: nvr on terms* **16/1**

56 9 nk **Cassy O (IRE)**[8] 7398 2-9-3 0 DuranFentiman 2 46
(Tim Easterby) *bmpd s: chsd ldrs: niggled along over 4f out: drvn and lost pl over 2f out: wknd over 1f out* **8/1**

1m 32.73s (5.23) **Going Correction** +0.775s/f (Yiel) **9** Ran SP% **121.0**
Speed ratings (Par 97): **101,99,96,95,94 93,89,87,86**
CSF £33.60 TOTE £2.30: £1.30, £4.20, £2.50; EX 26.20 Trifecta £182.30.
Owner M M Stables **Bred** Epona Bloodstock Ltd **Trained** Kingsclere, Hants

FOCUS
There was 5mm of rain the previous day and the going was given as soft (GoingStick 6.6). The rail was at its innermost configuration and distances were as advertised. A fair novice.

7678 MR & MRS WILSON H'CAP 7f 1y

2:10 (2:11) (Class 4) (0-85,87) 4-Y-O+
£6,080 (£1,809; £904; £452; £300; £300) **Stalls** Low

Form RPR

0463 1 **Confrontational (IRE)**[15] 7145 5-8-10 **74** (p) ShaneGray 2 84
(Jennie Candlish) *wnt to post early: chsd ldrs: rdn to take 2nd jst over 2f out: styd on to ld ins fnl f: hld on wl cl home* **11/2**[2]

6360 2 nk **Dragons Tail (IRE)**[15] 7142 4-8-11 **78** (p) JaneElliott(3) 8 87
(Tom Dascombe) *midfield: hdwy over 2f out: rdn over 1f out: styd on to take 2nd wl ins fnl f: pressed wnr towards fin but hld* **14/1**

0204 3 3 3/4 **Arcanada (IRE)**[15] 7142 6-9-7 **85** (p) RichardKingscote 5 84
(Tom Dascombe) *w ldr: led over 4f out: rdn 2f out: hdd ins fnl f: no ex fnl 100yds* **11/2**[2]

3612 4 2 1/4 **Calder Prince (IRE)**[15] 7145 6-9-2 **80** (p) AlistairRawlinson 13 74
(Tom Dascombe) *chsd ldrs: effrt on outer over 2f out: styd on same pce fnl f: no imp* **20/1**

4004 5 3/4 **Frankelio (FR)**[63] 5416 4-8-10 **74** GrahamLee 4 66
(Micky Hammond) *midfield: nt clr run on inner 2f out: rdn and angled out over 1f out: kpt on ins fnl f: nvr able to trble ldrs* **10/1**

0465 6 1/2 **Penwortham (IRE)**[15] 7142 6-9-4 **82** PaddyMathers 9 72
(Richard Fahey) *hld up: rdn over 1f out: swtchd rt ent fnl f: kpt on: nvr able to trble ldrs* **11/1**

3042 7 nse **Gabrial The Devil (IRE)**[14] 7183 4-9-7 **85** PaulHanagan 11 75
(Richard Fahey) *midfield: pushed along over 2f out: effrt on outer over 1f out: no imp on ldrs (trainer's rep said the gelding was unsuited by the soft going and would prefer a firmer surface)* **7/1**

6-60 8 1 **Tangled (IRE)**[16] 7121 4-9-1 **82** GemmaTutty(3) 7 70
(Karen Tutty) *chsd ldrs: pushed along over 2f out: rdn and outpcd over 1f out: wknd fnl 150yds* **10/1**

6036 9 3 3/4 **Whitefountainfairy (IRE)**[15] 7142 4-9-6 **84** DavidProbert 10 62
(Andrew Balding) *towards rr: rdn over 3f out: nvr involved (jockey said filly was never travelling)* **8/1**

0130 10 1/2 **Rum Runner**[21] 6950 4-9-9 **87** SeanLevey 3 64
(Richard Hannon) *dwlt: bhd: pushed along over 3f out: nvr a threat (trainer's rep said the colt was unsuited by the soft going and would prefer a firmer surface)* **13/2**[3]

1001 11 3/4 **Gabrial The Tiger (IRE)**[14] 7183 7-8-7 **74** SeanDavis(3) 1 49
(Richard Fahey) *wnt to post early: led: hdd over 4f out: rdn and outpcd whn lost 2nd jst over 2f out: wknd ins fnl f* **9/2**[1]

0222 12 19 **Atletico (IRE)**[9] 7383 7-8-7 **71** oh1 LiamJones 12
(David Evans) *towards rr: u.p over 4f out: bhd over 2f out: lost tch over 1f out (jockey said gelding was not suited by the soft going and would prefer a firmer surface)* **25/1**

1m 31.22s (3.72) **Going Correction** +0.775s/f (Yiel) **12** Ran SP% **127.7**
Speed ratings (Par 105): **109,108,104,101,100 100,100,99,94,94 93,71**
CSF £86.83 CT £465.72 TOTE £7.70: £3.10, £5.00, £3.10; EX 114.60 Trifecta £809.50.
Owner Brian Verinder **Bred** Highfort Stud & D McAbhaird **Trained** Basford Green, Staffs

FOCUS
A competitive handicap run at a good pace.

7679 INCOM-CNS GROUP 30TH ANNIVERSARY NURSERY H'CAP 6f 17y

2:45 (2:47) (Class 2) 2-Y-O
£11,827 (£3,541; £1,770; £885; £442; £222) **Stalls** Low

Form RPR

4431 1 **Stone Soldier**[21] 6980 2-8-11 **80** TomEaves 1 85
(James Given) *mde all: rdn over 1f out: sn nrly 3 l clr: all out wl ins fnl f: hld on wl* **7/1**[3]

1604 2 1/2 **Keep Busy (IRE)**[8] 7399 2-8-6 **78** HarrisonShaw(3) 7 81
(John Quinn) *hld up: hdwy 3f out: rdn over 2f out: styd on to take 2nd fnl 150yds: clsd on wnr towards fin* **8/1**

2260 3 3 **Alix James**[8] 7399 2-8-6 **75** PhilDennis 5 69
(Iain Jardine) *prom on outer: rdn to chse ldrs over 2f out: styd on same pce fnl f* **10/1**

1205 4 1/2 **St Ives**[8] 7409 2-8-8 **77** (p[1]) LiamJones 3 70
(William Haggas) *prom: rdn and ev ch 2f out: unable qck over 1f out: lost 2nd fnl 150yds: no ex* **9/2**[2]

2110 5 4 1/2 **Pop Dancer (IRE)**[38] 6356 2-9-7 **90** PaulHanagan 8 69
(Richard Fahey) *rdn and outpcd over 2f out: n.d after* **8/1**

061 6 shd **Winning Streak**[40] 6287 2-9-4 **87** (t) SeanLevey 11 66
(Stuart Williams) *hld up: rdn and outpcd over 2f out: nvr a threat* **20/1**

211 **7** 4 1/2 **Fuwayrit (IRE)**28 6704 2-9-7 **90** FrannyNorton 2 55
(Mark Johnston) *sn prom: pushed along 4f out: rdn 2f out: wknd over 1f out (trainer's rep said the colt suffered interference early in the race)* **11/8**1

3212 **8** 2 1/2 **Kendred Soul (IRE)**18 7046 2-8-3 **72** PaddyMathers 6 30
(Jedd O'Keeffe) *chsd ldrs: pushed along over 3f out: wknd over 1f out* **25/1**

3232 **9** 14 **We're Reunited (IRE)**26 6807 2-8-7 **76** DavidProbert 4
(Ronald Harris) *a pushed along and towards rr: eased whn wl btn over 1f out* **10/1**

4200 **10** 1/2 **Bob's Oss (IRE)**15 7140 2-8-0 **58** oh11 JimmyQuinn 9
(Alan Berry) *a outpcd and bhd: nvr on terms (trainer said the gelding was not suited by the soft going and would prefer a firmer surface)* **100/1**

3221 **11** 1 1/4 **Heer We Go Again**145 2469 2-8-5 **79** RayDawson(5) 12
(David Evans) *hld up: outpcd over 3f out: nvr a threat* **40/1**

1m 20.05s (4.55) **Going Correction** +0.775s/f (Yiel) 11 Ran SP% **125.2**
Speed ratings (Par 101): **100,99,95,94,88 88,82,79,60,59 58**
CSF £63.84 CT £586.00 TOTE £9.00: £2.50, £2.60, £3.00; EX 65.30 Trifecta £528.60.
Owner The Cool Silk Partnership **Bred** Laundry Cottage Stud Farm **Trained** Willoughton, Lincs

FOCUS
Few got a look in the winner controlling the pace.

7680 RAYMOND & KATHLEEN CORBETT MEMORIAL H'CAP 1m 2f 70y
3:20 (3:22) (Class 3) (0-90,89) 3-Y-O+

£8,715 (£2,609; £1,304; £652; £326; £163) **Stalls** High

Form RPR

4213 **1** **Gossip Column (IRE)**15 7144 4-9-5 **89** ThomasGreatrex(5) 4 96
(Ian Williams) *chsd ldrs: rdn and outpcd over 2f out: rallied and swtchd rt ent fnl f: wnt 2nd fnl 150yds: styd on to ld towards fin* **9/2**

0500 **2** 3/4 **Restorer**21 6958 7-9-9 **88** DavidProbert 3 94
(Ian Williams) *s.i.s: hld up: hdwy over 3f out: rdn and looked awkward ent st wl over 1f out: styd on ins fnl f: chalng towards fin but nt quite pce of wnr* **11/4**1

1033 **3** nse **Global Gift (FR)**17 7068 3-9-5 **89** GeraldMosse 1 94
(Ed Dunlop) *broke wl: racd keenly: chsd ldr: rdn 2f out: led over 1f out: edgd lft ins fnl f: hdd and no ex towards fin* **9/2**

0640 **4** 3 1/4 **Central City (IRE)**14 7185 4-8-5 **77** RPWalsh(7) 7 76
(Ian Williams) *sn led: hung rt on bnd wl over 7f out: rdn and hdd over 1f out: stl ev ch u.p whn n.m.r and checked ins fnl f: sn lost pl and no ex: eased* **16/1**

1042 **5** 1 **Scofflaw**14 7185 5-9-2 **81** (v) SeanLevey 6 78
(David Evans) *hld up: rdn over 2f out: kpt on ins fnl f: nvr able to trble ldrs* **4/1**3

-301 **6** 13 **Involved**14 7185 4-9-0 **79** RichardKingscote 5 50
(Daniel Kubler) *hld up in tch: rdn 4f out: wknd over 2f out (trainer's rep said gelding was not suited by the soft going and would prefer a firmer surface)* **7/2**2

2646 **7** 31 **Madeeh**15 7141 3-8-5 **75** oh1 (t) PhilDennis 2
(Philip Kirby) *prom: pushed along wl over 4f out: wknd over 3f out* **33/1**

2m 20.82s (6.52) **Going Correction** +0.775s/f (Yiel)
WFA 3 from 4yo+ 5lb 7 Ran SP% **114.1**
Speed ratings (Par 107): **104,103,103,100,99 89,64**
CSF £17.21 CT £57.86 TOTE £5.10: £2.30, £1.50; EX 16.80 Trifecta £58.60.
Owner Dr Marwan Koukash **Bred** Peter Reynolds & Robert Dore **Trained** Portway, Worcs

FOCUS
This was run at a good gallop and the first two benefited from sitting off the pace in the early stages.

7681 ESL GROUP NOVICE STKS 7f 127y
3:55 (3:58) (Class 4) 3-Y-O+

£5,851 (£1,752; £876; £438; £219; £109) **Stalls** Low

Form RPR

6243 **1** **James Park Woods (IRE)**36 6418 3-9-1 74 (b1) SeanLevey 9 78
(Ralph Beckett) *racd keenly: chsd ldrs: effrt on outer to ld jst over 2f out: clr over 1f out: styd on strly: rdn out* **2/1**2

0650 **2** 10 **Prince Consort (IRE)**32 6578 4-9-5 44 (b) GrahamLee 3 54
(John Wainwright) *in tch: rdn 3f out: rdn and unable to go w ldrs over 2f out: kpt on ins fnl f: tk 2nd fnl 150yds: no ch w wnr* **50/1**

0504 **3** 1 1/4 **Bullington Boy (FR)**14 7189 3-8-10 67 RayDawson(5) 13 51
(Jane Chapple-Hyam) *midfield: rdn 3f out: hdwy over 2f out: kpt on ins fnl f: no ch w wnr: one pce nr fin* **7/1**

0623 **4** shd **Society Guest (IRE)**7 7460 3-8-10 66 (p) FrannyNorton 7 46
(Mick Channon) *racd keenly: w ldr: ev ch 3f out: rdn and unable to go w wnr over 1f out: no ex ins fnl f* **3/1**3

13 **5** 5 **Toronado Queen (IRE)**14 7190 3-9-3 0 PaulHanagan 1 41
(Richard Fahey) *led: pushed along 3f out: hdd jst over 2f out: unable to go w wnr over 1f out: wknd fnl f* **15/8**1

0240 **6** 5 **Isabella Ruby**7 7444 4-8-9 44 (p) ThomasGreatrex(5) 2 22
(Lisa Williamson) *wnt to post early: stdd s: hld up: n.m.r and hmpd on inner over 6f out: pushed along and hdwy over 3f out: drvn and no imp over 2f out: wknd over 1f out* **20/1**

4560 **7** 1 1/4 **Corrida De Toros (IRE)**52 5797 3-9-1 66 (p) ShaneGray 10 24
(Ed de Giles) *towards rr: wnt lft over 6f out: u.p 4f out: nvr involved* **12/1**

0000 **8** 1/2 **Andies Armies**30 6638 3-9-1 38 (p) PhilDennis 6 23
(Lisa Williamson) *sed awkwardly: towards rr: rdn over 3f out: nvr involved* **100/1**

U-0 **9** 13 **Loveatfirstlight (IRE)**165 1838 3-8-10 0 DavidProbert 11
(James Unett) *chsd ldrs: rdn over 3f out: wknd over 2f out* **40/1**

5000 **10** 1 **Just Heather (IRE)**6 7491 5-8-11 40 (v) HarrisonShaw(3) 14
(John Wainwright) *towards rr: niggled along over 4f out: wl outpcd over 2f out* **100/1**

11 19 **Notwhatiam (IRE)**90 9-9-5 0 PaddyMathers 5
(Alan Berry) *missed break and bmpd s: a wl bhd: nvr on terms* **40/1**

0000 **12** 38 **Hilbre Lake (USA)**15 7141 3-9-1 35 JFEgan 4
(Lisa Williamson) *chsd ldrs: pushed along 5f out: wknd over 4f out: eased whn wl btn fnl 3f: t.o* **100/1**

1m 40.58s (4.88) **Going Correction** +0.775s/f (Yiel)
WFA 3 from 4yo+ 4lb 12 Ran SP% **127.9**
Speed ratings (Par 105): **106,96,94,94,89 84,83,82,69,68 49,11**
CSF £116.34 TOTE £3.20: £1.20, £16.80, £2.50; EX 200.80 Trifecta £2541.60.
Owner Quantum Leap Racing Iv **Bred** Hunscote Stud **Trained** Kimpton, Hants
■ Stewards' Enquiry : Sean Levey two-day ban: misuse of the whip (Oct 13-14)

FOCUS
A modest novice won in convincing fashion.

7682 GT RADIAL TYRE FILLIES' H'CAP 1m 2f 70y
4:30 (4:30) (Class 4) (0-80,81) 3-Y-O+

£6,080 (£1,809; £904; £452; £300; £300) **Stalls** High

Form RPR

0343 **1** **Fannie By Gaslight**9 7366 4-9-3 **70** GeraldMosse 1 80
(Mick Channon) *in tch: n.m.r on inner and lost pl after 2f: dropped to midfield: hdwy on inner 3f out: led wl over 2f out: styd on strly ins fnl f: edgd rt: rdn out* **13/8**1

525 **2** 3 1/2 **Lady Alavesa**6 7491 4-8-11 **64** PhilDennis 3 67
(Michael Herrington) *hld up: hdwy on inner 3f out: chsd wnr jst over 2f out: rdn over 1f out: no imp ins fnl f: edgd lft towards fin* **11/2**3

0606 **3** 1 **Ebqaa (IRE)**29 6681 5-8-10 **63** (p) LiamJones 13 64
(James Unett) *in rr: pushed along over 4f out: rdn and hdwy to chse ldrs over 2f out: kpt on ins fnl f: swtchd rt towards fin: nvr able to chal (vet said mare lost her left fore-shoe)* **25/1**

5212 **4** 3/4 **Inclyne**21 6967 3-9-7 **79** DavidProbert 2 79
(Andrew Balding) *chsd ldrs: n.m.r and lost pl after 2f: dropped to midfield: hdwy over 2f out: sn cl up chsng ldrs and nt clr run: rdn and unable qck over 1f out: kpt on same pce ins fnl f* **11/4**2

3050 **5** 10 **Bell Heather (IRE)**15 7145 6-8-12 **65** (p) PaulHanagan 6 45
(Patrick Morris) *led: hdd after 2f: remained prom: rdn over 2f out: sn bmpd sltly: wknd over 1f out* **20/1**

2312 **6** 9 **Lady Mascara**23 6902 3-9-3 **75** DanielMuscutt 4 37
(James Fanshawe) *s.i.s: hld up: rdn and hdwy 2f out: nt get to ldrs: wknd over 1f out (jockey said filly reared as the stalls opened. trainer's rep said the filly was unsuited by the soft going and would prefer a firmer surface)* **7/1**

3 **7** 2 1/4 **Triple Nickle (IRE)**13 7238 3-8-5 **63** (p) JimmyQuinn 10 20
(Bernard Llewellyn) *racd keenly: hld up in midfield: rdn and hdwy over 3f out: sn ev ch briefly: wknd over 2f out* **33/1**

6502 **8** 5 **Cuban Sun**53 5785 3-8-12 **70** TomEaves 8 17
(James Given) *w ldr: led after 2f: rdn and hdd over 2f out: sn forced sltly rt and wknd* **14/1**

5344 **9** 17 **Kvetuschka**29 6672 3-9-2 **74** JFEgan 9
(Peter Chapple-Hyam) *racd keenly: prom: rdn over 2f out: sn wknd: eased whn btn ins fnl f* **16/1**

5204 **10** 14 **Katiesheidinlisa**23 6893 3-9-9 **81** (p) RichardKingscote 5
(Tom Dascombe) *trckd ldrs: pushed along over 4f out: wknd ent fnl 3f: eased whn wl btn over 1f out* **14/1**

2063 **11** 9 **J'Ouvert (IRE)**13 7237 3-8-3 **61** (h) PaddyMathers 11
(David Evans) *hld up: racd keenly wout cover in midfield after 2f: wnt prom over 6f out: rdn 4f out: wknd over 2f out: eased whn wl btn over 1f out* **40/1**

0050 **12** 20 **Piccolo Ramoscello**91 4358 6-8-0 **60** oh15 (p) AledBeech(7) 7
(Lisa Williamson) *hld up: stmbld after nrly 2f: rdn 4f out: lost tch 3f out: t.o* **100/1**

2m 21.44s (7.14) **Going Correction** +0.775s/f (Yiel)
WFA 3 from 4yo+ 5lb 12 Ran SP% **126.8**
Speed ratings (Par 102): **102,99,98,97,89 82,80,76,63,52 44,28**
CSF £11.42 CT £179.41 TOTE £2.10: £1.10, £2.80, £9.40; EX 11.70 Trifecta £221.30.
Owner Aston Bloodstock **Bred** Mike Channon Bloodstock Ltd **Trained** West Ilsley, Berks

FOCUS
A fair fillies' handicap, and they finished quite well strung out in the testing ground.

7683 MBNA H'CAP 1m 6f 87y
5:05 (5:07) (Class 4) (0-80,79) 3-Y-O+

£6,080 (£1,809; £904; £452; £300; £300) **Stalls** Low

Form RPR

2251 **1** **Well Funded (IRE)**17 7070 3-8-8 **69** JaneElliott(3) 12 80+
(James Bethell) *chsd ldr: led 3f out: rdn over 1f out: edgd rt ins fnl f: kpt on wl towards fin* **6/1**3

6305 **2** 1 **Buriram (IRE)**17 7082 3-9-6 **78** SeanLevey 3 87
(Ralph Beckett) *racd keenly: midfield: hdwy over 3f out: chsd wnr over 2f out: styd on and tried to chal ins fnl f: hld cl home* **7/1**

4606 **3** 10 **Ravenous**25 6848 8-9-0 **69** ThomasGreatrex(5) 6 62
(Luke Dace) *missed break: in rr: pushed along over 5f out: hdwy over 4f out: rdn and outpcd over 2f out: kpt on to chse front two over 1f out: no imp fnl f* **14/1**

2542 **4** 3/4 **Gabrial The One (IRE)**15 7144 3-9-7 **79** PaulHanagan 10 73
(Richard Fahey) *hld up: hdwy over 3f out: rdn over 2f out: nvr able to trble ldrs* **7/1**

2101 **5** 5 **Overhaugh Street**28 6716 6-9-9 **73** ShaneGray 8 58
(Ed de Giles) *led: rdn and hdd 3f out wknd over 1f out (trainer's rep said the gelding was not suited by the soft going and would prefer a firmer surface)* **6/1**3

22-2 **6** shd **Wolf Prince (IRE)**40 6274 3-9-4 **76** GeraldMosse 7 63
(Amy Murphy) *midfield: rdn and lost pl over 4f out: plugged on fnl f* **4/1**1

0343 **7** 2 **Marengo**13 7239 8-9-3 **67** (b) JimmyQuinn 5 49
(Bernard Llewellyn) *hld up: rdn over 4f out: sme hdwy over 1f out: plugged on fnl f: nvr able to trble ldrs* **16/1**

000 **8** 5 **Rayna's World (IRE)**40 6278 4-9-5 **69** PhilDennis 9 44
(Philip Kirby) *completely missed break: in rr: rdn over 4f out: plugged on fnl f: nvr involved* **50/1**

406- **9** 1 1/4 **Lucky Lover Boy (IRE)**155 8610 4-9-6 **70** (t) GrahamLee 2 43
(Oliver Greenall) *trckd ldrs: rdn over 4f out: drvn and wknd over 2f out* **11/2**2

4355 **10** 1/2 **Seeusoon (IRE)**108 3729 3-8-11 **69** DavidProbert 4 44
(Andrew Balding) *midfield: rdn over 3f out: btn over 2f out* **9/1**

0145 **11** 3 1/4 **Ascot Day (FR)**11 7294 5-9-7 **71** (p) FrannyNorton 13 39
(Bernard Llewellyn) *in tch: dropped to midfield after 4f: rdn and wknd over 2f out* **20/1**

0020 **12** 10 **Heart Of Soul (IRE)**28 6716 4-9-13 **77** (p) TomEaves 1 31
(Ian Williams) *trckd ldrs: rdn over 2f out: sn wknd* **20/1**

1350 **13** 49 **Angel Gabrial (IRE)**28 6716 10-8-10 **63** (p) SeanDavis(3) 14
(Patrick Morris) *racd keenly: prom: rdn 5f out: wknd over 3f out: eased whn btn over 2f out: t.o* **33/1**

3m 25.0s (15.20) **Going Correction** +0.775s/f (Yiel)
WFA 3 from 4yo+ 8lb 13 Ran SP% **125.9**
Speed ratings (Par 105): **87,86,80,80,77 77,76,73,72,72 70,64,36**
CSF £48.38 CT £584.72 TOTE £6.80: £2.20, £2.30, £4.50; EX 60.70 Trifecta £1071.90.
Owner Clarendon Thoroughbred Racing **Bred** Irish National Stud **Trained** Middleham Moor, N Yorks

FOCUS
The early pace wasn't that strong and the first two finished well clear of the rest in the deteriorating ground.
T/Plt: £239.90 to a £1 stake. Pool: £68,126.86 - 207.27 winning units T/Qpdt: £53.80 to a £1 stake. Pool: £6,480.99 - 88.98 winning units **Darren Owen**

7603 CHELMSFORD (A.W) (L-H)
Saturday, September 28

OFFICIAL GOING: Polytrack: standard
Wind: medium, half behind Weather: overcast

7684 BET AT TOTESPORT.COM H'CAP 7f (P)
5:20 (5:20) (Class 5) (0-70,72) 4-Y-0+
£5,175 (£1,540; £769; £400; £400; £400) **Stalls Low**

Form RPR

1242 1 **Sonnet Rose (IRE)**[28] 6703 5-8-8 **62**....................(bt) WilliamCarver(5) 3 70
(Conrad Allen) *restless in stalls: led for almost 1f: trckd ldrs: effrt over 1f out: rdn to ld 150yds out: styd on wl and hld on cl home* **4/1**[2]

2226 2 *nk* **Seprani**[26] 6795 5-8-11 **67**....................(h) SeanKirrane(7) 8 74
(Amy Murphy) *hld up in tch: nt clr run over 2f out: swtchd rt and effrt wl over 1f out: hdwy u.p and ev ch 100yds out: styd on wl but hld cl home* **12/1**

2521 3 *3/4* **Vincenzo Coccotti (USA)**[35] 6441 7-8-5 **57**....................(p) CierenFallon(3) 9 62
(Patrick Chamings) *restless in stalls: chsd ldrs: effrt over 1f out: drvn and ev ch 1f out: kpt on u.p: no ex and one pce towards fin (jockey said gelding anticipated the start)* **5/1**[3]

3345 4 *hd* **Coverham (IRE)**[38] 6350 5-9-9 **72**.................... RyanTate 10 76
(James Eustace) *urged along leaving stalls: hdwy to ld after almost 1f out: hdd 4f out: chsd ldr tl rdn to ld again ent fnl f: hdd 150yds out: keeping on same pce and btn whn short of room and eased cl home (jockey said gelding suffered interference inside the final half furlong)* **7/1**

3/30 5 *1/2* **I Can (IRE)**[145] 2488 4-9-7 **70**....................(w) JosephineGordon 2 73
(Sir Mark Todd) *t.k.h: hld up in last pair: effrt over 2f out: nt clr run over 1f out: gap opened and hdwy u.p ins fnl f: kpt on wl towards fin: nt rch ldrs* **10/1**

-206 6 *1/2* **Al Reeh (IRE)**[56] 5651 5-9-2 **72**....................(h) StefanoCherchi(7) 5 75
(Marco Botti) *awkward leaving stalls: in rr early: hdwy into midfield after 2f: nt clr run over 1f out: effrt u.p 1f out: chsng ldrs and kpt on same pce fnl 100yds: nt clr run cl home* **7/2**[1]

0625 7 *1/2* **Full Intention**[52] 5821 5-9-5 **68**....................(p) PJMcDonald 1 68
(Lydia Pearce) *hld up in tch in midfield: effrt and nt clr run over 1f out tl ins fnl f: kpt on wl ins fnl f: nvr threatened ldrs (jockey said gelding was denied a clear run)* **5/1**[3]

2060 8 *nk* **Choral Music**[39] 6317 4-8-11 **67**.................... EllieMacKenzie(7) 4 67
(John E Long) *t.k.h: hld up in last pair: effrt over 1f out: edgd lft ins fnl f: kpt on: nvr trbld ldrs* **8/1**

5000 9 *4 1/2* **Holy Tiber (IRE)**[12] 7281 4-8-7 **56** oh4....................(b) JoeyHaynes 7 43
(Chelsea Banham) *taken down early: squeezed for room and hmpd leaving stalls: sn swtchd rt and hdwy to chse ldr after 2f: led 4f out: rdn over 1f out: hdd ent fnl f: wknd fnl 150yds* **33/1**

1m 24.88s (-2.32) **Going Correction** -0.30s/f (Stan) 9 Ran SP% **118.9**
Speed ratings (Par 103): **101,100,99,99,99 98,97,97,92**
CSF £52.40 CT £249.86 TOTE £3.30: £1.60, £4.40, £2.20; EX 72.80 Trifecta £932.90.
Owner John C Davies **Bred** J C Davies **Trained** Newmarket, Suffolk

FOCUS
Mainly exposed performers in an ordinary handicap. The gallop was respectable and this form should prove reliable.

7685 TOTEPOOL CASHBACK CLUB AT TOTESPORT.COM H'CAP 1m 2f (P)
5:50 (5:53) (Class 6) (0-60,63) 3-Y-0+
£3,105 (£924; £461; £400; £400; £400) **Stalls Low**

Form RPR

50 1 **Charlie Arthur (IRE)**[37] 6361 3-9-0 **58**.................... FinleyMarsh(3) 7 66
(Richard Hughes) *wnt rt leaving stalls: rousted along early: chsd ldrs: effrt and drvn over 1f out: led ins fnl f: rn green in front but kpt on: drvn out* **8/1**

0603 2 *1/2* **Necoleta**[28] 6702 3-8-2 **46** oh1.................... WilliamCox(3) 14 53
(Sylvester Kirk) *chsd ldrs: drvn and sltly outpcd ent fnl 2f: rallied u.p to chse wnr 100yds out: kpt on wl* **25/1**

0 3 *1 1/2* **Dreamboat Dave (IRE)**[36] 6393 3-9-1 **56**.................... EoinWalsh 5 60
(Sarah Humphrey) *midfield: effrt u.p over 1f out: clsng and wnt lft 1f out: chsng ldrs and rdr dropped whip ins fnl f: kpt on to go 3rd towards fin: nvr getting to ldrs* **25/1**

3211 4 *1* **Fair Power (IRE)**[9] 7376 5-9-13 **63**.................... PJMcDonald 12 64
(John Butler) *led tl over 8f out: pressed ldr tl led again over 6f out: drvn over 1f out: hdd ins fnl f: no ex and wknd towards fin* **2/1**[1]

4500 5 *hd* **Just Later**[14] 7189 3-9-5 **60**....................(t) GeorgeWood 4 62
(Amy Murphy) *in tch in midfield: effrt and clsd u.p over 1f out: pressing ldrs and drvn 1f out: no ex and wknd wl ins fnl f* **16/1**

6020 6 *nse* **Thunderoad**[19] 7027 3-9-4 **62**.................... CierenFallon(3) 3 64
(Tony Carroll) *hld up in midfield: swtchd rt and effrt over 1f out: edgd lft 1u.p 1f out: kpt on fnl 100yds: nt rch ldrs* **11/4**[2]

0000 7 *3/4* **Dyagilev**[12] 7281 4-9-0 **50**....................(b) AdrianMcCarthy 2 49
(Lydia Pearce) *edgd lft leaving stalls and stdd: hld up in last trio: hdwy over 2f out: clsd u.p 1f out: kpt on ins fnl f: nt rch ldrs* **50/1**

0054 8 *hd* **Lady Of York**[25] 6843 5-9-1 **51**.................... JoeyHaynes 13 50
(Chelsea Banham) *taken down early: w ldr tl led over 8f out: hdd over 6f out but styd pressing ldr: drvn and ev ch over 1f out tl no ex and wknd fnl 100yds* **7/1**

4423 9 *6* **Reddiac (IRE)**[9] 7376 3-9-3 **58**....................(p) RobertHavlin 11 47
(Ed Dunlop) *in tch in midfield: effrt over 2f out: sn outpcd and btn over 1f out: wknd ins fnl f* **6/1**[3]

0300 10 *3* **Garrison Law**[12] 7280 3-9-1 **56**.................... StevieDonohoe 9 39
(David Simcock) *squeezed for room leaving stalls: hld up in midfield: effrt over 2f out: sn outpcd and wl btn over 1f out* **16/1**

6050 11 *nk* **Carvelas (IRE)**[11] 7318 10-9-4 **54**.................... JosephineGordon 8 35
(J R Jenkins) *pushed rt and impeded leaving stalls: swtchd lft and hld up in rr: effrt and plenty to do over 2f out: sn outpcd and wl btn over 1f out* **50/1**

0064 12 *3 1/2* **Duke Of Yorkie (IRE)**[30] 6636 3-8-5 **46** oh1.................... RyanPowell 10 22
(Adam West) *squeezed for room leaving stalls: rousted along early: midfield and stuck wd: rdn over 3f out: outpcd over 2f out: wl btn and edgd lft over 1f out (jockey said gelding was never travelling)* **40/1**

0600 13 *4* **Albishr (IRE)**[17] 7080 4-9-10 **60**.................... HectorCrouch 6 27
(Simon Dow) *hld up in last trio: effrt and plenty to do over 2f out: sn struggling and wl btn whn swtchd rt 1f out* **12/1**

0000 14 *6* **Interrogator (IRE)**[12] 7271 3-8-2 **46** oh1....................(tp) DarraghKeenan(3) 1 3
(Alan Bailey) *edgd rt and bmpd leaving stalls: midfield: losing pl u.p over 2f out: bhd ins fnl f* **80/1**

2m 5.12s (-3.48) **Going Correction** -0.30s/f (Stan)
WFA 3 from 4yo+ 5lb 14 Ran SP% **132.6**
Speed ratings (Par 101): **101,100,99,98,98 98,97,97,92,90 90,87,84,79**
CSF £210.78 CT £4810.35 TOTE £8.80: £2.50, £7.80, £10.20; EX 231.00 Trifecta £4148.30.
Owner L Turland And A Smith **Bred** Rathbarry Stud **Trained** Upper Lambourn, Berks

FOCUS
Not much to dwell on in an ordinary handicap. The gallop was a modest one and those held up never figured.

7686 EXTRA PLACES AT TOTESPORT.COM H'CAP 1m 2f (P)
6:20 (6:25) (Class 2) (0-105,105) 4-Y-0+
£12,450 (£3,728; £1,864; £932; £466; £234) **Stalls Low**

Form RPR

/133 1 **Bin Battuta**[212] 958 5-9-7 **105**....................(p) HectorCrouch 6 114
(Saeed bin Suroor) *chsd ldr for over 1f: styd chsng ldrs: effrt to chal over 1f out: led and hung lft 1f out: kpt on ins fnl f* **4/1**[2]

40-3 2 *nk* **Commander Cole**[16] 7106 5-9-4 **102**.................... PatCosgrave 5 110
(Saeed bin Suroor) *chsd ldrs: effrt and drvn to ld over 1f out: hdd 1f out: carried lft and nudged ins fnl f: kpt on but hld cl home* **4/1**[2]

4046 3 *3 1/4* **Highbrow**[47] 6021 4-8-3 **87**....................(p[1]) MartinDwyer 8 89
(David Simcock) *s.i.s and swtchd lft after s: hld up in last trio: effrt and hdwy u.p over 1f out: no threat to ldng pair but kpt on ins fnl f to go 3rd nr fin* **20/1**

4004 4 *3/4* **Bartholomeu Dias**[15] 7147 4-8-13 **97**.................... PJMcDonald 7 97
(Charles Hills) *pressed ldr over 8f out: rdn to ld wl over 1f out: sn hdd and outpcd in 3rd 1f out: wknd ins fnl f: lost 3rd nr fin (vet reported gelding lost his left-fore shoe)* **12/1**

1050 5 *1* **King's Slipper**[21] 6964 4-8-2 **89**.................... WilliamCox(3) 2 87
(Clive Cox) *stdd s: t.k.h: hld up in rr: effrt and c wd wl over 1f out: edgd lft and kpt on ins fnl f: no threat to ldrs* **25/1**

3005 6 *3/4* **El Ghazwani (IRE)**[9] 7396 4-8-6 **90**....................(t) NicolaCurrie 3 87
(Hugo Palmer) *in tch in midfield: no hdwy u.p over 1f out: wl hld ins fnl f* **20/1**

4300 7 *1 1/2* **Breath Caught**[9] 7394 4-8-9 **93**.................... TomMarquand 1 87
(David Simcock) *hld up in last trio: effrt on inner over 1f out: no imp and wl hld ins fnl f* **14/1**

2141 8 *1 1/4* **Star Of Southwold (FR)**[36] 6391 4-8-7 **96**.................... TheodoreLadd(5) 4 87
(Michael Appleby) *hld up in midfield: effrt on outer over 2f out: unable qck and btn over 1f out: wknd ins fnl f (jockey said gelding stopped quickly)* **9/2**[3]

-105 9 *3 1/2* **Star Of Bengal**[35] 6467 4-9-7 **105**....................(p) RobertHavlin 9 89
(John Gosden) *sn led and crossed to inner: rdn ent fnl 2f: hdd wl over 1f out: sn outpcd u.p and btn: wknd fnl f (jockey said colt stopped quickly)* **9/4**[1]

2m 1.81s (-6.79) **Going Correction** -0.30s/f (Stan) course record 9 Ran SP% **116.7**
Speed ratings (Par 109): **115,114,112,111,110 110,108,107,105**
CSF £19.99 CT £285.59 TOTE £4.30: £1.60, £1.40, £6.00; EX 19.80 Trifecta £237.50.
Owner Godolphin **Bred** Darley **Trained** Newmarket, Suffolk

FOCUS
A good quality handicap and, although a couple of the market leaders underperformed, the first two - both smart types - deserve credit for pulling clear in the closing stages. The gallop was fair.

7687 IRISH LOTTO AT TOTESPORT.COM CONDITIONS STKS 6f (P)
6:50 (6:53) (Class 2) 3-Y-0+ £16,172 (£4,812; £2,405; £1,202) **Stalls Centre**

Form RPR

0001 1 **Royal Birth**[16] 7107 8-9-11 99....................(t) PJMcDonald 1 107
(Stuart Williams) *trckd ldng pair: edgd out rt and effrt over 1f out: clsd to chal ins fnl f: rdn to ld 75yds out: r.o wl* **10/1**

1113 2 *3/4* **Harry's Bar**[16] 7107 4-9-7 91.................... JamieSpencer 3 101
(James Fanshawe) *mounted in the chute: broke wl: restrained and hld up in tch in midfield: effrt over 1f out: drvn and clsd to press ldrs 1f out: wnt 2nd and kpt on same pce fnl 50yds* **7/4**[1]

0460 3 *3/4* **Lancelot Du Lac (ITY)**[42] 6229 9-9-7 104....................(h) MartinDwyer 5 99
(Dean Ivory) *t.k.h: sn pressing ldr tl led over 1f out: sn rdn: drvn and hdd 75yds out: no ex and wknd towards fin* **7/1**

1102 4 *2* **Shimmering Dawn (IRE)**[9] 7372 3-9-0 91.................... TomMarquand 6 87
(James Tate) *stdd s: hld up in last pair: effrt over 2f out: drvn over 1f out: edgd lft and kpt on ins fnl f: nvr trbld ldrs* **9/4**[2]

213 5 *2* **Tropics (USA)**[43] 6149 11-9-11 107....................(h) JoeyHaynes 2 90
(Dean Ivory) *led: rdn ent fnl f: drvn and hdd over 1f out: no ex and wknd ins fnl f* **7/2**[3]

6520 6 *2* **Peggie Sue**[28] 6714 4-9-2 83.................... TobyEley 4 74
(Adam West) *stdd after s: t.k.h: hld up in tch in last pair: effrt ent fnl 2f: no imp u.p over 1f out: wknd ins fnl f (jockey said filly ran too free)* **33/1**

1m 10.61s (-3.09) **Going Correction** -0.30s/f (Stan)
WFA 3 from 4yo+ 2lb 6 Ran SP% **113.9**
Speed ratings (Par 109): **108,107,106,103,100 98**
CSF £28.68 TOTE £11.70: £3.80, £1.50; EX 35.30 Trifecta £108.40.
Owner The Morley Family **Bred** Old Mill Stud & S Williams & J Parry **Trained** Newmarket, Suffolk

FOCUS
A decent conditions event in which an ordinary gallop picked up on the approach to the home turn.

7688 BET IN PLAY AT TOTESPORT.COM H'CAP 1m 6f (P)
7:20 (7:22) (Class 3) (0-90,92) 4-Y-0+ £10,350 (£3,080; £1,539; £769) **Stalls Low**

Form RPR

0126 1 **The Pinto Kid (FR)**[31] 6596 4-9-5 **86**....................(t) TomMarquand 8 95
(James Fanshawe) *hld up in tch in last trio: effrt 2f out: nt clr run and swtchd lft over 1f out: rdn and qcknd to ld jst ins fnl f: sn in command and r.o wl* **5/1**[3]

2P06 2 *1 1/2* **Ulster (IRE)**[50] 5902 4-8-13 **87**.................... KateLeahy(7) 4 94
(Archie Watson) *mde most: rdn over 2f out: drvn 1f out: sn hdd: edgd rt and kpt on same pce ins fnl f* **8/1**

-031 3 *shd* **Kitaabaat**[14] 7199 4-9-7 **88**....................(h) JamieSpencer 5 95
(David Simcock) *stdd s: hld up in tch in rr: effrt and c wd over 1f out: hdwy 1f out: edgd lft and kpt on ins fnl f: no threat to wnr (jockey said gelding hung left-handed in the straight)* **3/1**[1]

1621 4 *1 1/4* **Berrahri (IRE)**[16] 7127 8-9-4 **85**.................... KierenFox 1 90
(John Best) *awkward leaving stalls: sn rcvrd and w ldr: rdn 3f out: stl ev ch and drvn over 1f out tl nt match pce of wnr jst ins fnl f: kpt on same pce after* **10/1**

6064 **5** *nk* **Manjaam (IRE)**[14] 7181 6-9-0 **81**.................................(p) PJMcDonald 6 85
(Ian Williams) *trckd ldrs: effrt: edgd out rt and nt clr run over 1f out: keeping on but nt threatening wnr whn short of room and swtchd lft wl ins fnl f* **8/1**

0236 **6** *1* **Machine Learner**[14] 7216 6-9-6 **87**.................... CharlesBishop 3 90
(Joseph Tuite) *hld up in tch in midfield: swtchd lft and effrt over 1f out: clsd and drvn to chse ldrs 1f out: no ex and wknd ins fnl f* **14/1**

-032 **7** *¾* **Lady Bergamot (FR)**[101] 3995 5-9-7 **88**..................... GeorgeWood 7 90
(James Fanshawe) *trckd ldrs: effrt over 1f out: keeping on but nt threatening wnr whn squeezed for room and hmpd ins fnl f: no imp after* **5/1**[3]

23-5 **8** *nk* **Sporting Times**[31] 6596 5-9-0 **81**.............................. RobertHavlin 2 83
(Ed Dunlop) *hld up in tch in midfield: effrt on inner over 1f out: no imp 1f out: wl hld and kpt on same pce ins fnl f* **14/1**

5310 **9** *2¾* **Hope Is High**[13] 7231 6-8-4 **71**.............................. NicolaCurrie 9 69
(John Berry) *hld up in tch in last trio: effrt on inner over 1f out: no imp: nvr trbld ldrs* **33/1**

-000 **10** *3¼* **Big Challenge (IRE)**[240] 513 5-9-8 **92**.............. CierenFallon(3) 10 85
(Saeed bin Suroor) *chsd ldrs on outer: rdn over 2f out: lost pl and bhd whn wnt lft 1f out: wknd ins fnl f* **9/2**[2]

2m 55.92s (-7.28) **Going Correction** -0.30s/f (Stan) **10** Ran SP% **124.1**
Speed ratings (Par 107): **108,107,107,106,106 105,105,105,103,101**
CSF £47.89 CT £145.06 TOTE £5.80: £1.90, £2.60, £1.50; EX 58.20 Trifecta £313.50.
Owner Fred Archer Racing - Bruce **Bred** Petra Bloodstock Agency Ltd **Trained** Newmarket, Suffolk

FOCUS
A useful handicap in which an ordinary gallop only picked up at the 3f marker and this bare form may not be entirely reliable.

7689 DOUBLE DELIGHT HAT-TRICK HEAVEN AT TOTESPORT NOVICE STKS 1m 5f 66y(P)
7:50 (7:50) (Class 3) 3-Y-O+ **£9,703** (£2,887; £1,443) **Stalls** Low

Form RPR

2250 **1** **Holy Kingdom (IRE)**[21] 6952 3-9-2 82.......................... CierenFallon(3) 3 79
(Tom Clover) *t.k.h: trckd ldr: effrt over 2f out: rdn to ld ent fnl f: r.o wl* **8/13**[1]

3332 **2** *1¼* **Swift Wing**[23] 6890 3-9-5 79.................................(b) RobertHavlin 1 76
(John Gosden) *led: rdn 2f out: drvn and hdd ent fnl f: no ex and outpcd fnl 100yds* **5/4**[2]

6 **3** *4* **King's Counsel**[182] 1419 3-9-5 0.............................. JosephineGordon 2 70?
(Daniel Kubler) *t.k.h: trckd rivals: effrt over 2f out: outpcd and btn 1f out: kpt on same pce ins fnl f* **25/1**[3]

2m 54.45s (0.85) **Going Correction** -0.30s/f (Stan) **3** Ran SP% **110.2**
Speed ratings (Par 107): **85,84,81**
CSF £1.77 TOTE £1.40; EX 1.50 Trifecta £1.60.
Owner The Rogues Gallery Two **Bred** Cliveden Stud Ltd **Trained** Newmarket, Suffolk

FOCUS
A disappointing turnout for the money on offer. A modest gallop only picked up turning for home and the proximity of the third suggests the bare form isn't entirely reliable. The race was run in driving rain.

7690 RACEGOERS CLUB H'CAP 5f (P)
8:20 (8:21) (Class 6) (0-65,67) 4-Y-O+ **£3,105** (£924; £461; £400; £400; £400) **Stalls** Low

Form RPR

2133 **1** **Red Stripes (USA)**[16] 7112 7-8-12 **61**.................(b) SeamusCronin(5) 1 68
(Lisa Williamson) *mde virtually all: drifted rt bnd wl over 1f out: drvn and hld on wl ins fnl f* **6/1**[3]

5353 **2** *¾* **Poeta Brasileiro (IRE)**[7] 7446 4-8-12 **61**....(t) ThoreHammerHansen(5) 3 65
(David Brown) *chsd ldrs: n.m.r ent fnl 2f: effrt over 1f out: pressed wnr jst ins fnl f: kpt on u.p but a hld* **6/4**[1]

0620 **3** *hd* **Leo Minor (USA)**[10] 7337 5-9-2 **67**..................(t) MarcoGhiani(7) 5 71+
(Robert Cowell) *hld up in rr: hdwy over 1f out: drvn to chse ldrs ins fnl f: kpt on* **9/2**[2]

0 **4** *1¼* **Snow Patch (IRE)**[86] 4571 4-9-1 **62**........................ CierenFallon(3) 4 61
(D J Bunyan, Ire) *w wnr: rdn and drifted rt bnd wl over 1f out: no ex u.p 1f out: kpt on same pce ins fnl f (jockey said filly hung right-handed)* **6/1**[3]

1441 **5** *½* **Precious Plum**[29] 6685 5-9-7 **65**..................................(p) DavidEgan 9 62
(Charlie Wallis) *taken down early: hld up in midfield: effrt over 1f out: drvn and kpt on ins fnl f: nvr trbld ldrs* **10/1**

6U63 **6** *¾* **Arzaak (IRE)**[12] 7274 5-9-5 **63**..............................(b) PatCosgrave 10 58
(Charlie Wallis) *towards rr: effrt over 1f out: kpt on ins fnl f: swtchd rt towards fin: nvr trbld ldrs* **16/1**

4560 **7** *½* **Kath's Lustre**[31] 6605 4-8-11 **62**............................(b) GeorgeRooke(7) 7 55
(Richard Hughes) *chsd ldrs: unable qck and lost pl over 1f out: wl hld and one pce ins fnl f* **16/1**

5435 **8** *1¾* **Roundabout Magic (IRE)**[31] 6605 5-9-3 **61**............... NickyMackay 2 49
(Simon Dow) *hld up in tch in midfield: effrt and hdwy on inner over 1f out: no imp u.p and btn 1f out: wknd ins fnl f and eased towards fin* **10/1**

2005 **9** *4* **George Dryden (IRE)**[17] 7078 7-9-9 **67**..................(bt[1]) PJMcDonald 11 39
(George Boughey) *wd thrght: towards rr: sme prog 1/2-way: lost pl and btn over 1f out: bhd ins fnl f* **16/1**

5504 **10** *2* **Camino**[44] 6126 6-8-7 **51** oh6..................................(p) NicolaCurrie 8 16
(Andi Brown) *chsd ldrs: lost pl and btn over 1f out: bhd ins fnl f* **50/1**

58.42s (-1.78) **Going Correction** -0.30s/f (Stan) **10** Ran SP% **124.5**
Speed ratings (Par 101): **102,100,100,98,97 96,95,92,86,83**
CSF £16.49 CT £48.06 TOTE £6.10: £1.70, £1.10, £1.60; EX 16.20 Trifecta £68.70.
Owner E H Jones (paints) Ltd **Bred** Tim Ahearn **Trained** Taporley, Wrexham

FOCUS
Exposed performers in a modest handicap.
T/Plt: £606.50 to a £1 stake. Pool: £61,653.20 - 74.20 winning units T/Qpdt: £17.80 to a £1 stake. Pool: £11,964.99 - 495.52 winning units **Steve Payne**

7657 NEWMARKET (R-H)
Saturday, September 28
OFFICIAL GOING: Good (ovr 7.4, stands' 7.5, ctr 7.1, far 7.5)
Wind: Fresh half-behind Weather: Cloudy

7691 JUDDMONTE ROYAL LODGE STKS (GROUP 2) (C&G) 1m
1:50 (1:50) (Class 1) 2-Y-O
£70,887 (£26,875; £13,450; £6,700; £3,362; £1,687) **Stalls** Centre

Form RPR

305 **1** **Royal Dornoch (IRE)**[14] 7195 2-9-0 102...................... WayneLordan 3 112
(A P O'Brien, Ire) *sn chsng ldr: led wl over 2f out: sn hdd: rdn and edgd rt fr over 1f out: styd on to ld nr fin* **16/1**

12 **2** *nk* **Kameko (USA)**[28] 6727 2-9-0 0............................ OisinMurphy 4 111
(Andrew Balding) *trckd ldrs: led over 2f out: rdn and edgd lft over 1f out: hdd nr fin* **6/5**[1]

05 **3** *1½* **Iberia (IRE)**[13] 7245 2-9-0 98.............................. DonnachaO'Brien 8 108
(A P O'Brien, Ire) *hld up: hdwy over 1f out: sn rdn and edgd rt: styd on: nt rch ldrs* **9/1**

00 **4** *2¼* **Year Of The Tiger (IRE)**[77] 4920 2-9-0 0......................... RyanMoore 7 103
(A P O'Brien, Ire) *hld up: hdwy over 2f out: rdn over 1f out: styd on same pce ins fnl f* **6/1**[3]

12 **5** *1* **Sound Of Cannons**[21] 6957 2-9-0 0........................ FrankieDettori 2 100
(Brian Meehan) *sn led: shkn up and hdd wl over 2f out: no ex ins fnl f* **8/1**

13 **6** *8* **Highland Chief (IRE)**[98] 4091 2-9-0 0........................ PJMcDonald 5 82+
(Paul Cole) *s.i.s: pushed along early in rr: hdwy over 2f out: rdn and wknd over 1f out (trainer's rep could offer no explanation for the colt's performance)* **5/1**[2]

141 **7** *8* **Pyledriver**[21] 6957 2-9-0 102.............................. MartinDwyer 1 64
(William Muir) *chsd ldrs tl rdn and wknd over 2f out (trainer said colt had lost some of its strength having grown throughout the summer)* **8/1**

1m 35.13s (-3.27) **Going Correction** -0.225s/f (Firm) 2y crse rec **7** Ran SP% **114.5**
Speed ratings (Par 107): **107,106,105,102,101 93,85**
CSF £36.09 CT £195.63 TOTE £15.70: £7.10, £1.10; EX 46.40 Trifecta £255.50.
Owner Michael Tabor & Derrick Smith & Mrs John Magnier **Bred** Barronstown Stud **Trained** Cashel, Co Tipperary

FOCUS
There was a tailwind which contributed to some fast times including a juvenile course record in this race. This contest has a chequered history when it comes to producing Classic winners. Frankel in 2010 was the last winner to then land the 2,000 Guineas (third-placed Treasure Beach won the Irish Derby), while Benny The Dip in 1996 was the last Derby winner to win this. It's probable no Classic winner will emerge this time.

7692 JUDDMONTE CHEVELEY PARK STKS (GROUP 1) (FILLIES) 6f
2:25 (2:25) (Class 1) 2-Y-O
£165,355 (£62,689; £31,374; £15,628; £7,843; £3,936) **Stalls** Centre

Form RPR

12 **1** **Millisle (IRE)**[23] 6907 2-9-0 103............................ ShaneFoley 9 116
(Mrs John Harrington, Ire) *broke wl: sn lost pl: pushed along 1/2-way: hdwy over 1f out: rdn: hung rt and r.o to ld wl ins fnl f* **16/1**

1112 **2** *1¾* **Raffle Prize (IRE)**[41] 6264 2-9-0 113...................... FrankieDettori 10 111
(Mark Johnston) *s.i.s: sn chsng ldrs: led over 3f out: rdn over 1f out: edgd lft and hdd wl ins fnl f* **10/11**[1]

11 **3** *½* **Tropbeau**[42] 6248 2-9-0 108.............................. MickaelBarzalona 8 111
(A Fabre, France) *pushed along in rr: hdwy and nt clr run over 1f out: swtchd lft ins fnl f: styng on whn hmpd wl ins fnl f* **9/2**[2]

0660 **4** *2* **Tango (IRE)**[13] 7244 2-9-0 103..................................(b[1]) RyanMoore 3 104
(A P O'Brien, Ire) *sn led: hdd over 3f out: rdn and ev ch over 1f out: no ex ins fnl f* **12/1**

3131 **5** *shd* **Living In The Past (IRE)**[37] 6374 2-9-0 108............. DanielTudhope 11 103
(K R Burke) *w ldrs tl rdn over 1f out: edgd lft and no ex ins fnl f* **12/1**

2 **6** *¾* **Nurse Barbara (IRE)**[14] 7215 2-9-0 0........................ ColinKeane 7 101+
(G M Lyons, Ire) *hld up in tch: rdn whn tk a false step over 1f out: no ex ins fnl f* **20/1**

4321 **7** *hd* **Dark Lady**[23] 6907 2-9-0 104..................................... PatDobbs 4 100
(Richard Hannon) *hld up: hdwy over 2f out: rdn over 1f out: no ex ins fnl f* **16/1**

1 **8** *nk* **Etoile (USA)**[132] 2881 2-9-0 0.............................. DonnachaO'Brien 6 99
(A P O'Brien, Ire) *chsd ldrs: rdn over 1f out: no ex ins fnl f* **8/1**[3]

623 **9** *3½* **Lil Grey (IRE)**[43] 6190 2-9-0 95........................... RobbieColgan 5 89
(Ms Sheila Lavery, Ire) *hld up in tch: rdn over 2f out: wknd over 1f out* **40/1**

3001 **10** *3½* **Moon Of Love (IRE)**[21] 6979 2-9-0 81.........................(h) BarryMcHugh 2 78
(Richard Fahey) *prom: lost pl over 3f out: n.d after* **100/1**

212 **11** *8* **Nina Bailarina**[12] 7292 2-9-0 0............................. OisinMurphy 1 54
(Ed Walker) *led early: chsd ldrs: lost pl over 2f out: sn wknd (jockey said filly ran free to post for a short time)* **25/1**

1m 9.39s (-2.51) **Going Correction** -0.225s/f (Firm) 2y crse rec **11** Ran SP% **120.9**
Speed ratings (Par 106): **107,104,104,101,101 100,99,99,94,90 79**
CSF £31.11 CT £87.93 TOTE £17.90: £4.20, £1.10, £1.80; EX 43.20 Trifecta £205.70.
Owner Stonethorn Stud Farms Limited **Bred** Stonethorn Stud Farms Ltd **Trained** Moone, Co Kildare

FOCUS
The winner, possibly helped by challenging towards the near rail, rates a big improver, with the second, who helped force a solid pace, a little off her best. With a tailwind to help, the time was a course record until Earthlight, closely matched with the runner-up, went 0.08sec quicker in the Middle Park. The action was middle to near side.

7693 JUDDMONTE MIDDLE PARK STKS (GROUP 1) (COLTS) 6f
3:00 (3:01) (Class 1) 2-Y-O
£155,952 (£59,125; £29,590; £14,740; £7,397; £3,712) **Stalls** Centre

Form RPR

11 **1** **Earthlight (IRE)**[41] 6264 2-9-0 119........................ MickaelBarzalona 4 118+
(A Fabre, France) *broke wl enough: sn lost pl: hdwy over 1f out: rdn and r.o to ld wl ins fnl f* **11/4**[1]

1513 **2** *nk* **Golden Horde (IRE)**[41] 6264 2-9-0 113........................ AdamKirby 8 117
(Clive Cox) *chsd ldr tl over 3f out: shkn up to go 2nd again 2f out: rdn to ld 1f out: hdd wl ins fnl f: r.o* **16/1**

3165 **3** *1¾* **Summer Sands**[36] 6422 2-9-0 96.............................. BarryMcHugh 9 112
(Richard Fahey) *chsd ldrs: rdn over 2f out: styd on u.p to go 3rd nr fin* **100/1**

5055 **4** *½* **King Neptune (USA)**[16] 7119 2-9-0 96......................... WayneLordan 1 110
(A P O'Brien, Ire) *led: rdn and hdd 1f out: styd on same pce wl ins fnl f* **66/1**

2211 **5** 3/4 **Threat (IRE)**[14] 7195 2-9-0 114 .... PatDobbs 6 108
(Richard Hannon) *s.i.s: hld up: rdn over 1f out: r.o ins fnl f: nt trble ldrs* **8/1**[3]

231 **6** *shd* **Lope Y Fernandez (IRE)**[29] 6690 2-9-0 107 .... DonnachaO'Brien 5 108
(A P O'Brien, Ire) *hld up: hdwy 2f out: sn rdn: styd on same pce ins fnl f* **9/1**

11 **7** 1 1/4 **Mums Tipple (IRE)**[37] 6375 2-9-0 116 .... OisinMurphy 3 104
(Richard Hannon) *prom: chsd ldr over 3f out tl edgd lft 2f out: no ex ins fnl f (vet reported colt was lame on its left-fore shortly after the race)* **3/1**[2]

22 **8** 1 3/4 **Monarch Of Egypt (USA)**[50] 5922 2-9-0 111 .... RyanMoore 7 99
(A P O'Brien, Ire) *hld up: rdn over 2f out: sn edgd lft: nt trble ldrs* **9/1**

1m 9.31s (-2.59) **Going Correction** -0.225s/f (Firm) 2y crse rec **8 Ran SP% 91.1**
Speed ratings (Par 109): **108,107,105,104,103 103,101,99**
CSF £27.78 CT £1405.09 TOTE £2.50: £1.10, £3.10, £10.10; EX 27.30 Trifecta £596.40.
Owner Godolphin SNC **Bred** Godolphin **Trained** Chantilly, France
■ Siskin was withdrawn. Price at time of withdrawal 3-1. Rule 4 applies to all bets. Deduction - 25p in the pound.

FOCUS
This looked a fantastic race beforehand but unbeaten Phoenix Stakes winner Siskin was withdrawn after being unruly in the stalls and the seventh and eighth-placed finishers were below form. The third and fourth could be used to anchor the level but their runs can be explained to a point and the winner has been rated to the same sort of mark as in the Prix Morny. With a tailwind to help the time was a new course record - 0.08sec quicker than the Cheveley Park. The action was middle to near side.

7694 BET365 CAMBRIDGESHIRE H'CAP (HERITAGE HANDICAP) 1m 1f
3:40 (3:41) (Class 2) 3-Y-0+
£99,600 (£29,824; £14,912; £7,456; £3,728; £1,872) **Stalls** Centre

Form RPR
-102 **1** **Lord North (IRE)**[22] 6915 3-8-10 **98** .... FrankieDettori 29 113+
(John Gosden) *hld up: shkn up and hdwy 2f out: chsd ldr over 1f out: led wl ins fnl f: comf* **9/2**[1]

0250 **2** 3/4 **Beringer**[35] 6475 4-8-9 **97** ....(p) ThoreHammerHansen(5) 15 109
(Alan King) *chsd ldrs: led overall over 3f out: rdn over 1f out: edgd lft and hdd wl ins fnl f* **16/1**

3051 **3** 4 **Good Birthday (IRE)**[28] 6696 3-8-10 **98** .... OisinMurphy 32 103+
(Andrew Balding) *hld up: hdwy and swtchd rt over 1f out: r.o to go 3rd nr fin* **9/1**

0035 **4** 3/4 **Mordin (IRE)**[28] 6725 5-9-0 **104** ....(p) MarcoGhiani(7) 28 106
(Simon Crisford) *prom: chsd ldr over 2f out tl rdn over 1f out: no ex ins fnl f* **12/1**

1003 **5** *shd* **Majestic Dawn (IRE)**[78] 4882 3-8-1 **89** .... DavidEgan 20 92
(Paul Cole) *led gp towards stands' side tl rdn over 2f out: styd on same pce fnl f* **8/1**[3]

4065 **6** 3/4 **Dark Vision (IRE)**[28] 6696 3-8-13 **101** ....(v[1]) WilliamBuick 9 102
(Mark Johnston) *s.i.s: hld up: pushed along 1/2-way: hdwy u.p over 1f out: nt rch ldrs* **20/1**

1020 **7** 1 1/4 **Jazeel (IRE)**[36] 6420 4-9-0 **97** .... JamieSpencer 7 95
(Jedd O'Keeffe) *hld up: swtchd lft over 4f out: styd on fr over 1f out: nt trble ldrs* **14/1**

1355 **8** *shd* **Fifth Position (IRE)**[57] 5609 3-8-12 **100** .... AndreaAtzeni 24 98
(Roger Varian) *hld up: hdwy over 3f out: rdn over 2f out: styd on same pce ins fnl f* **10/1**

0334 **9** *hd* **Alternative Fact**[59] 5564 4-8-5 **88** .... JosephineGordon 6 85
(Ed Dunlop) *hld up: pushed along over 4f out: styd on u.p fr over 1f out: nvr nrr* **50/1**

1100 **10** 1 3/4 **Badenscoth**[49] 5929 5-8-9 **92** .... JoeyHaynes 16 85
(Dean Ivory) *s.i.s: hdwy over 3f out: rdn over 1f out: wknd ins fnl f* **100/1**

2224 **11** 3/4 **You're Hired**[7] 7457 6-8-4 **87** ....(p) MartinDwyer 31 79
(Amanda Perrett) *chsd ldrs: rdn over 2f out: wknd ins fnl f* **33/1**

1432 **12** *nk* **Nicholas T**[7] 7434 7-8-13 **96** .... BenRobinson 34 87
(Jim Goldie) *hld up: hdwy over 3f out: sn rdn: wknd over 1f out* **25/1**

4232 **13** 3/4 **Al Jellaby**[25] 6841 4-8-1 **87** .... WilliamCox(3) 1 77
(Clive Cox) *overall ldr towards centre: hdd over 3f out: rdn over 1f out: wknd ins fnl f* **40/1**

2503 **14** 1/2 **Baltic Baron (IRE)**[14] 7198 4-9-1 **98** ....(t) DanielTudhope 30 86
(David O'Meara) *s.i.s: hld up: rdn over 2f out: n.d* **28/1**

115- **15** 1 1/4 **Dubai Horizon (IRE)**[373] 7450 5-9-7 **107** ....(v) CierenFallon(3) 26 93
(Saeed bin Suroor) *hld up in tch: rdn over 3f out: wknd over 1f out* **25/1**

1000 **16** 1/2 **History Writer (IRE)**[37] 6376 4-8-12 **95** ....(t) PJMcDonald 14 80
(David Menuisier) *chsd ldrs: rdn and hung lft over 2f out: wknd fnl f* **50/1**

1141 **17** 3/4 **Le Don De Vie**[34] 6506 3-8-13 **101** .... RyanMoore 33 85
(Hughie Morrison) *prom: lost pl 1/2-way: n.d after* **15/2**[2]

-150 **18** *nk* **Afaak**[57] 5610 5-9-10 **107** .... JimCrowley 2 90
(Charles Hills) *hld up: hdwy 1/2-way: rdn and hung lft over 1f out: wknd fnl f* **20/1**

4030 **19** 1/2 **Petrus (IRE)**[37] 6376 4-9-2 **99** ....(p) TomMarquand 23 81
(Brian Meehan) *hld up: hdwy over 3f out: rdn and wknd over 1f out* **40/1**

3126 **20** 3/4 **Korcho**[58] 5583 3-8-3 **91** .... NicolaCurrie 22 72
(Hughie Morrison) *prom over 4f* **16/1**

1230 **21** 1/2 **Cockalorum (IRE)**[35] 6475 4-8-6 **89** ow2 ....(b) BenCurtis 3 68
(Roger Fell) *hld up: pushed along 5f out: nvr on terms* **50/1**

5230 **22** 1 **Smile A Mile (IRE)**[7] 7430 3-8-1 **94** .... AndrewBreslin(5) 21 72
(Mark Johnston) *prom: rdn and lost pl over 4f out: n.d after* **100/1**

0236 **23** 1 **Zhui Feng (IRE)**[22] 6915 6-9-1 **98** .... PatDobbs 4 73
(Amanda Perrett) *chsd ldrs: rdn over 2f out: wknd over 1f out* **50/1**

6163 **24** 1 3/4 **Queen Of Time**[21] 6992 5-9-0 **97** ....(p) HarryBentley 5 68
(Henry Candy) *hld up: pushed along 1/2-way: rdn and wknd over 2f out* **50/1**

1000 **25** *nk* **Mulligatawny (IRE)**[32] 6580 6-8-1 **87** ....(p) GabrieleMalune(3) 27 57
(Roger Fell) *chsd ldrs: rdn over 3f out: wknd over 1f out* **100/1**

0-45 **26** *hd* **Another Touch**[7] 7434 6-8-11 **94** .... TonyHamilton 8 64
(Richard Fahey) *hld up: rdn over 3f out: wknd over 2f out* **20/1**

1366 **27** 2 **Music Seeker (IRE)**[20] 6998 5-7-11 **83** ....(t) NoelGarbutt(3) 17 49
(Declan Carroll) *chsd ldrs: rdn over 4f out: wknd over 2f out* **100/1**

131- **28** 3/4 **Little Jo**[330] 8809 5-7-9 **83** ....(p) KieranSchofield(5) 19 47
(Brian Ellison) *hld up: hdwy over 3f out: rdn and wknd over 2f out* **25/1**

30-0 **29** 1 1/4 **Fajjaj (IRE)**[163] 1890 4-9-8 **105** ....(t[1]) JamesDoyle 25 67
(Hugo Palmer) *hld up: rdn and wknd over 3f out (jockey said gelding was never travelling)* **50/1**

1115 **30** 1 1/2 **Chance**[35] 6447 3-8-1 **89** .... RyanPowell 11 48
(Simon Crisford) *hld up in tch: rdn and wknd over 3f out* **33/1**

1m 46.99s (-4.11) **Going Correction** -0.225s/f (Firm) course record
WFA 3 from 4yo+ 5lb **30 Ran SP% 142.0**
Speed ratings (Par 109): **109,108,104,104,104 103,102,102,101,100 99,99,98,98,97 96,96,95,95,94 94,93,92,91,90 90,88,88**
CSF £67.51 CT £673.11 TOTE £5.00: £2.00, £4.50, £3.30, £4.10; EX 109.00 Trifecta £1393.80.

Owner HH Sheikh Zayed bin Mohammed Racing **Bred** Godolphin **Trained** Newmarket, Suffolk

FOCUS
John Gosden's winners of this race tend to go on to better things and that looks likely with his 2019 vintage. The front two finished well clear and this was another course record.

7695 BLANDFORD BLOODSTOCK MAIDEN FILLIES' STKS (PLUS 10 RACE) 7f
4:15 (4:17) (Class 4) 2-Y-O
£6,469 (£1,925; £962; £481) **Stalls** Centre

Form RPR
34 **1** **Lady Lynetta (IRE)**[25] 6831 2-9-0 0 .... ShaneKelly 1 80
(Richard Hughes) *t.k.h: mde virtually all: rdn and edgd lft over 1f out: hld on gamely u.p ins fnl f* **14/1**

6 **2** 1/2 **Baaqy (IRE)**[77] 4918 2-9-0 0 .... JimCrowley 9 80+
(John Gosden) *hld up wl in tch in midfield: clsd to chse ldrs 2f out: nt clr run over 1f out: swtchd rt and hdwy ins fnl f: r.o wl to snatch 2nd last strides: nt quite rch wnr* **5/1**[1]

5 **3** *nk* **Sunset Kiss**[18] 7054 2-9-0 0 .... JamesDoyle 4 78
(Michael Bell) *pressed ldrs: pressed wnr 4f out: rdn and ev ch over 1f out: sustained effrt and kpt on wl ins fnl f: jst hld towards fin: lost 2nd last strides* **5/1**[1]

3 **4** 1 **Princess Bride**[18] 7054 2-9-0 0 .... TomQueally 11 76
(Saeed bin Suroor) *pressed ldrs: cl up in 3rd whn nt clr run and hmpd 1f out: nvr enough room and unable to make any prog ins fnl f (jockey said filly was denied a clear run and had to take a slight check)* **6/1**[2]

5 2 **Evening Spirit** 2-9-0 0 .... HarryBentley 8 70+
(Ralph Beckett) *s.i.s: hld up in midfield: effrt jst over 2f out: pushed rt and hdwy over 1f out: reminder 1f out: r.o wl ins fnl f: nt rch ldrs* **6/1**[2]

6 *hd* **Folk Dance** 2-9-0 0 .... JamieSpencer 2 69+
(David Simcock) *stdd and swtchd lft after s: hld up in tch in midfield: clsd to chse ldrs 2f out: effrt over 1f out: pushed along and unable qck 1f out: wknd wl ins fnl f* **16/1**

0 **7** 3/4 **Love Bracelet (USA)**[54] 5751 2-9-0 0 .... RyanMoore 7 67
(A P O'Brien, Ire) *t.k.h: pressed wnr tl over 4f out: styd chsng ldrs: effrt ent fnl 2f: n.m.r wl over 1f out: no ex 1f out: wknd ins fnl f* **6/1**[2]

8 2 1/2 **Dream Round (IRE)** 2-9-0 0 .... OisinMurphy 14 61
(Andrew Balding) *wl in tch in midfield: clsd to chse ldrs 3f out: effrt ent fnl 2f: unable qck and outpcd over 1f out: wl hld and kpt on same pce ins fnl f* **11/1**

9 2 1/2 **Island Hideaway** 2-9-0 0 .... StevieDonohoe 13 54
(David Lanigan) *midfield: pushed along and edgd sltly rt over 1f out: no imp 1f out: wknd ins fnl f* **33/1**

10 *shd* **Folie D'Amour** 2-9-0 0 .... MartinDwyer 12 54+
(Eve Johnson Houghton) *in tch in last trio: effrt jst over 2f out: nvr threatened to get on terms but kpt on steadily ins fnl f* **50/1**

0 **11** 1 3/4 **Pax Britannica (IRE)**[22] 6928 2-9-0 0 .... PatDobbs 5 50+
(David Simcock) *hld up in tch towards rr: effrt 2f out: no imp and wknd ins fnl f* **33/1**

5 **12** 1 1/4 **Nibras Shadow (IRE)**[25] 6831 2-9-0 0 .... TomMarquand 6 46
(Ismail Mohammed) *in tch in midfield: rdn 3f out: no imp whn nudged rt over 1f out: wknd ins fnl f* **22/1**

13 *nse* **Queen's Favour** 2-9-0 0 .... WilliamBuick 10 46
(Sir Michael Stoute) *racd in last pair: rdn 1/2-way: nvr involved* **8/1**[3]

14 3/4 **Sablet** 2-9-0 0 .... CharlesBishop 3 44
(Eve Johnson Houghton) *a towards rr: rdn 3f out: nvr involved* **50/1**

6 **15** 2 3/4 **Princess Siyouni (IRE)**[49] 5961 2-9-0 0 .... PatCosgrave 15 37
(Mick Quinn) *chsd ldrs: rdn 3f out: struggling u.p and lost pl 2f out: wknd over 1f out* **50/1**

1m 24.57s (-0.83) **Going Correction** -0.225s/f (Firm) **15 Ran SP% 124.3**
Speed ratings (Par 94): **95,94,94,92,90 90,89,86,83,83 81,80,80,79,76**
CSF £80.67 TOTE £14.90: £3.70, £2.00, £2.10; EX 99.10 Trifecta £1007.40.
Owner Khalifa Dasmal **Bred** Castle Paddock Bloodstock Ltd **Trained** Upper Lambourn, Berks

FOCUS
An intriguing maiden - won by Nell Gwyn winner Qabala last year - and there may be a few useful types lurking in here too.

7696 BRITISH STALLION STUDS EBF "JERSEY LILY" FILLIES' NURSERY H'CAP 7f
4:50 (4:51) (Class 2) 2-Y-O
£31,125 (£9,320; £4,660; £2,330; £1,165; £585) **Stalls** Centre

Form RPR
313 **1** **Huboor (IRE)**[14] 7179 2-8-11 **78** .... JimCrowley 2 87+
(Mark Johnston) *racd centre: chsd ldrs: rdn to ld 1f out: edgd lft: styd on: 1sy of 9 in gp* **14/1**

6001 **2** 1/2 **Separate**[8] 7409 2-9-2 **88** ....(b) ThoreHammerHansen(5) 11 95
(Richard Hannon) *racd stands' side: hld up: hdwy over 1f out: sn rdn: r.o to ld that gp wl ins fnl f: nt quite rch wnr: 1st of 6 in gp* **16/1**

1051 **3** 2 **Last Surprise (IRE)**[16] 7103 2-9-4 **85** .... PatCosgrave 15 87
(Simon Crisford) *racd stands' side: chsd ldrs: led that gp over 2f out: rdn over 1f out: hdd wl ins fnl f: 2nd of 6 in gp* **33/1**

5141 **4** 3/4 **Caspian Queen (IRE)**[25] 6833 2-9-2 **83** .... DavidEgan 4 83
(Richard Hughes) *racd centre: chsd ldrs: overall ldr over 1f out: rdn and hdd 1f out: no ex wl ins fnl f: 2nd of 9 in gp* **12/1**

5203 **5** 1 **Onassis (IRE)**[21] 6963 2-8-9 **76** .... JamieSpencer 9 73
(Charlie Fellowes) *racd centre: s.i.s: sn chsng ldrs: overall ldr 3f out: rdn: hung lft and hdd over 1f out: styd on same pce ins fnl f: 3rd of 9 in gp* **12/1**

3614 **6** 1 **Elegant Erin (IRE)**[15] 7155 2-8-10 **77** .... TomMarquand 7 72
(Richard Hannon) *racd centre: hld up in tch: rdn over 2f out: styd on same pce ins fnl f: 4th of 9 in gp* **33/1**

4221 **7** 1 **Hashtagmetoo (USA)**[30] 6629 2-8-6 **73** .... NicolaCurrie 12 65
(Jamie Osborne) *racd stands' side: chsd ldrs: rdn over 2f out: wknd ins fnl f: 3rd of 6 in gp* **33/1**

2131 **8** 1/2 **Mild Illusion (IRE)**[15] 7156 2-9-2 **83** .... OisinMurphy 1 74
(Jonathan Portman) *racd centre: edgd rt s: hld up: hdwy over 2f out: rdn over 1f out: wknd wl ins fnl f: 5th of 9 in gp* **10/1**

4610 **9** 2 3/4 **Picture Frame**[58] 5587 2-9-2 **83** .... HarryBentley 8 67
(Saeed bin Suroor) *led centre 4f: rdn over 1f out: wknd ins fnl f: 6th of 9 in gp* **10/1**

4243 **10** *nk* **Rosadora (IRE)**[16] 7117 2-8-12 **86** .... MarcoGhiani(7) 6 69
(Ralph Beckett) *racd centre: s.i.s: hdwy u.p and hung lft over 1f out: wknd ins fnl f: 7th of 9 in gp* **16/1**

1110 **11** 2 1/2 **Oti Ma Boati**[38] 6356 2-9-0 **81** ....(t[1]) JamesDoyle 3 58
(William Haggas) *racd centre: prom: lost pl 5f out: in rr and rdn whn swtchd lft over 2f out: n.d after: 8th of 9 in gp (trainer's rep could offer no explanation for the performance shown)* **6/1**[2]

1034 12 hd **Special Secret**[16] 7117 2-9-1 **82** .... CharlesBishop 5 58
(Eve Johnson Houghton) *racd centre: hld up: rdn over 2f out: wknd over 1f out: last of 9 in gp* **16/1**

051 13 2 **Dutch Painting**[25] 6831 2-8-12 **79** .... RyanMoore 14 50
(Michael Bell) *racd stands' side: trckd ldrs: rdn over 2f out: wknd over 1f out: 4th of 6 in gp* **16/1**

221 14 hd **Star In The Making**[25] 6846 2-9-4 **85** .... AdamKirby 10 55
(Clive Cox) *racd stands' side: hld up: rdn over 2f out: wknd over 1f out: 5th of 6 in gp (trainer's rep said the filly ran flat)* **9/4**[1]

321 15 19 **Amber Island (IRE)**[18] 7054 2-8-13 **80** .... WilliamBuick 13
(Charlie Appleby) *overall ldr stands' side 4f: hdd that gp over 2f out: wknd over 1f out: last of 6 in gp (jockey said filly stopped quickly)* **13/2**[3]

1m 23.25s (-2.15) **Going Correction** -0.225s/f (Firm) **15 Ran SP% 131.0**
Speed ratings (Par 98): **103,102,100,99,98 97,95,95,92,91 88,88,86,86,64**
CSF £235.05 CT £7252.10 TOTE £9.00: £3.20, £5.20, £12.60; EX 206.10 Trifecta £2654.30.
Owner Hamdan Al Maktoum **Bred** China Horse Club **Trained** Middleham Moor, N Yorks
■ Stewards' Enquiry : Thore Hammer Hansen six-day ban: misuse of the whip (Oct 12-17)

FOCUS
This looked a super-competitive nursery full of potential improvers but some of the more likely types ran below expectations. There were two groups early, one up the middle and the other near side, before they merged with the finish unfolding near side.

7697 NEWMARKET JOURNAL AND VELVET MAGAZINE H'CAP 7f
5:25 (5:26) (Class 2) (0-105,98) 3-Y-O+ **£12,938** (£3,850; £1,924; £962) **Stalls** Centre

Form RPR

3033 1 **Dubai Legacy (USA)**[22] 6915 3-9-6 **97** .... OisinMurphy 12 104
(Saeed bin Suroor) *led stands' side pair tl shkn up and hdd over 1f out: rallied and edgd rt ins fnl f: r.o to ld nr fin: 1st of 2 that side* **9/4**[1]

4015 2 ½ **Spanish City**[21] 6950 6-9-2 **97** .... MarcoGhiani(7) 11 104
(Roger Varian) *trckd ldr on stands' side: tl rdn to ld that pair over 1f out: led overall and edgd rt ins fnl f: hdd nr fin: 2nd of 2 that side* **7/1**

3001 3 nk **Riviera Nights**[22] 6913 3-9-2 **93** .... WilliamBuick 1 98
(Richard Hannon) *racd centre: chsd ldrs: rdn and ev ch fr over 1f out: r.o: 1st of 10 in gp* **13/2**[3]

/455 4 shd **Battered**[15] 7152 5-9-8 **96** .... HarryBentley 8 102
(Ralph Beckett) *racd centre: hld up: racd keenly: hdwy over 2f out: rdn over 1f out: r.o: 2nd of 10 in gp* **10/1**

1142 5 shd **Vitralite (IRE)**[36] 6425 3-9-7 **98** .... BenCurtis 7 103
(K R Burke) *racd centre: hmpd s: sn chsng ldrs: led 1/2-way: hdd over 2f out: rdn to ld again over 1f out: hdd ins fnl f: styd on: 3rd of 10 in gp* **11/2**[2]

6454 6 ½ **Firmament**[14] 7188 7-9-10 **98** ....(p) DanielTudhope 9 102
(David O'Meara) *racd centre: hld up in tch: racd keenly: rdn over 1f out: styd on: 4th of 10 in gp* **12/1**

0500 7 1 **Above The Rest (IRE)**[15] 7164 8-9-7 **95** ....(h) DavidEgan 10 97
(David Barron) *racd centre: hld up: shkn up and nt clr run over 1f out: r.o: nt rch ldrs: 5th of 10 in gp* **33/1**

1000 8 ½ **Blackheath**[21] 6950 4-9-0 **88** .... AndreaAtzeni 4 88
(Ed Walker) *racd centre: hld up: hdwy over 2f out: outpcd over 1f out: rallied ins fnl f: styd on same pce towards fin: 6th of 10 in gp* **7/1**

2253 9 ½ **Count Otto (IRE)**[14] 7175 4-9-1 **89** ....(h) PatDobbs 5 88
(Amanda Perrett) *racd centre: chsd ldrs: rdn and n.m.r over 1f out: styd on same pce ins fnl f: 7th of 10 in gp* **22/1**

5040 10 1½ **Breathless Times**[14] 7188 4-9-0 **88** ....(t) JimCrowley 6 83
(Stuart Williams) *edgd lft s: overall ldr in centre: hdd 1/2-way: led again over 2f out tl rdn and hdd over 1f out: wknd ins fnl f: 8th of 10 in gp* **14/1**

1000 11 1¼ **Gossiping**[21] 6964 7-9-8 **96** .... ShaneKelly 3 87
(Gary Moore) *racd centre: chsd ldrs: rdn over 1f out: wknd fnl f: 9th of 10 in gp* **25/1**

453 12 3 **Model Guest**[80] 4806 3-8-13 **90** .... TomQueally 2 72
(George Margarson) *racd centre: hld up: hdwy over 2f out: wknd over 1f out: last of 10 in gp* **40/1**

1m 24.33s (-1.07) **Going Correction** -0.225s/f (Firm)
WFA 3 from 4yo+ 3lb **12 Ran SP% 121.5**
Speed ratings (Par 109): **97,96,96,95,95 95,94,93,93,91 89,86**
CSF £17.70 CT £94.90 TOTE £3.10: £1.40, £2.50, £2.30; EX 18.10 Trifecta £145.40.
Owner Godolphin **Bred** Godolphin **Trained** Newmarket, Suffolk

FOCUS
Only two of these raced near side (looked quick on this card) throughout and they finished one-two, with the others more towards the middle although the field merged late on.
T/Jkpt: Not won. T/Plt: £156.70 to a £1 stake. Pool: £155,694.02 - 725.21 winning units T/Qpdt: £90.30 to a £1 stake. Pool: £15,000.75 - 122.88 winning units **Colin Roberts**

6577 RIPON (R-H)
Saturday, September 28

OFFICIAL GOING: Good to soft (7.3)
Wind: fresh across Weather: fine

7698 THEAKSTON LEGENDARY ALES EBF NOVICE STKS 6f
1:55 (1:56) (Class 5) 2-Y-O **£3,881** (£1,155; £577; £288) **Stalls** High

Form RPR

1 1 **Lampang (IRE)**[30] 6622 2-9-9 **0** .... DavidAllan 5 95+
(Tim Easterby) *trckd ldr: led gng wl over 1f out: pushed clr ent fnl f: eased towards fin* **10/11**[1]

0 2 5 **Intrinsic Bond**[49] 5968 2-9-2 **0** .... CamHardie 6 69
(Tracy Waggott) *hld up: sn pushed along: swtchd lft 2f out: rdn and hdwy appr fnl f: kpt on: wnt 2nd towards fin* **150/1**

312 3 1 **Be Prepared**[79] 4832 2-9-6 **88** .... JackMitchell 7 70
(Simon Crisford) *dwlt and bmpd s: sn midfield: rdn and hdwy over 1f out: drvn to chse ldr ent fnl f: edgd rt and sn no ex: lost 2nd towards fin* **6/5**[2]

0 4 6 **Fansurper (IRE)**[12] 7285 2-8-11 **0** .... PaulaMuir(5) 1 48+
(Roger Fell) *carried rt s: sn in tch on outer: pushed along 1/2-way: wknd fnl f* **25/1**

06 5 ¾ **Quercus (IRE)**[12] 7285 2-9-2 **0** .... ConnorBeasley 3 46
(Ann Duffield) *led: rdn over 2f out: drvn and hdd over 1f out: wknd fnl f* **18/1**

6 3¾ **Findhorn** 2-9-2 **0** .... KevinStott 2 35+
(Kevin Ryan) *wnt rt s: sn chsd ldr on outer: rdn along over 2f out: wknd over 1f out* **11/2**[3]

7 ½ **Clotherholme (IRE)** 2-9-2 **0** .... PaulMulrennan 9 33
(Ann Duffield) *wnt rt s: chsd ldr: outpcd and lost pl 1/2-way: wknd over 1f out* **40/1**

8 11 **The Last Bow** 2-8-6 **0** .... GerO'Neill(5) 8
(Michael Easterby) *hmpd s: a outpcd and bhd* **33/1**

9 31 **Masham Moor** 2-9-2 **0** .... MichaelStainton 4
(Chris Fairhurst) *chsd ldr: rdn along and lost pl 4f out: wknd and bhd over 2f out* **66/1**

1m 14.49s (1.99) **Going Correction** +0.325s/f (Good) **9 Ran SP% 129.9**
Speed ratings (Par 95): **99,92,91,83,82 77,76,61,20**
CSF £215.12 TOTE £1.80: £1.10, £25.00, £1.10; EX 186.30 Trifecta £536.20.
Owner King Power Racing Co Ltd **Bred** Rosetown Bloodstock Ltd **Trained** Great Habton, N Yorks

FOCUS
All distances as advertised. A decent juvenile novice contest. The favourite won easing down by a pretty wide margin in testing conditions for young horses. His winning time was nearly four seconds outside of standard.

7699 CONSTANT SECURITY NURSERY H'CAP 1m
2:30 (2:30) (Class 4) (0-85,86) 2-Y-O **£4,722** (£1,405; £702; £351) **Stalls** Low

Form RPR

3131 1 **World Title (IRE)**[32] 6579 2-9-7 **85** .... HollieDoyle 4 89
(Archie Watson) *mde all: narrow ld tl rdn and asserted over 1f out: drvn out ins fnl f* **9/4**[2]

0301 2 1 **Gold Souk (IRE)**[32] 6564 2-9-8 **86** .... JoeFanning 1 88
(Mark Johnston) *trckd ldrs: swtchd lft to outer over 2f out: sn rdn along: styd on to go 2nd fnl 110yds* **11/4**[3]

421 3 1 **Strawman (IRE)**[17] 7067 2-9-0 **78** .... ConnorBeasley 5 78
(Adrian Nicholls) *dwlt: sn pressed ldr: rdn over 2f out: drvn and bit outpcd over 1f out: styd on same pce ins fnl f* **6/5**[1]

305 4 7 **Lawaa (FR)**[29] 6654 2-8-7 **71** .... CamHardie 2 56
(Richard Fahey) *trckd ldrs: pushed along over 3f out: rdn over 2f out: hung rt and wknd 2f out* **14/1**

1m 44.5s (3.50) **Going Correction** +0.325s/f (Good) **4 Ran SP% 109.6**
Speed ratings (Par 97): **95,94,93,86**
CSF £8.60 TOTE £2.70; EX 10.10 Trifecta £11.40.
Owner Clipper Logistics **Bred** Oghill House Stud & Joseph M Burke **Trained** Upper Lambourn, W Berks

FOCUS
A decent little nursery. Once again it looked hard work for these young horses and the second-favourite gamely dominated in nearly seven seconds outside of the standard.

7700 NOEL HETHERTON MEMORIAL H'CAP 5f
3:05 (3:06) (Class 4) (0-85,87) 3-Y-O+
£6,663 (£1,982; £990; £495; £300; £300) **Stalls** High

Form RPR

-102 1 **Count D'orsay (IRE)**[21] 6976 3-9-4 **83** .... DavidAllan 7 94
(Tim Easterby) *midfield: pushed along and hdwy to chse ldrs over 1f out: led 100yds out: drvn and kpt on wl* **10/3**[1]

360 2 1¾ **Broken Spear**[21] 6960 3-9-3 **87** ....(v[1]) GeorgiaDobie(5) 6 92
(Tony Coyle) *pressed ldr: rdn 2f out: kpt on same pce fnl f* **11/2**[3]

1550 3 ½ **Canford Bay (IRE)**[56] 5691 5-9-2 **80** .... CamHardie 10 83
(Antony Brittain) *led narrowly: rdn 2f out: hdd 110yds out: no ex* **6/1**

6066 4 ½ **Henley**[2] 7624 7-8-7 **71** .... JoeFanning 3 72
(Tracy Waggott) *prom on outer: rdn 2f out: one pce* **12/1**

5064 5 1 **Dapper Man (IRE)**[31] 6607 5-9-2 **85** .... PaulaMuir(5) 4 83
(Roger Fell) *chsd ldrs: rdn along and outpcd over 1f out: kpt on same pce ins fnl f* **6/1**

6020 6 ¾ **Tomily (IRE)**[16] 7121 5-9-7 **85** ....(p) DavidNolan 2 80
(David O'Meara) *hld up: sn pushed along: rdn and kpt on ins fnl f: nvr a threat* **8/1**

1003 7 2¼ **Lathom**[22] 6921 6-9-5 **83** .... KieranO'Neill 1 70
(Paul Midgley) *hld up: rdn over 2f out: drvn over 1f out: no imp* **5/1**[2]

2000 8 44 **Captain Colby (USA)**[7] 7467 7-9-0 **78** ....(p) KevinStott 9
(Paul Midgley) *v.s.a: effectively tk no part (jockey said the gelding put his head over the side of the stalls just as the starter dropped his flag)* **7/1**

1m 0.21s (0.81) **Going Correction** +0.325s/f (Good)
WFA 3 from 4yo+ 1lb **8 Ran SP% 115.0**
Speed ratings (Par 105): **106,103,102,101,100 98,95,24**
CSF £21.87 CT £104.86 TOTE £3.30: £1.70, £2.30, £1.90; EX 26.30 Trifecta £116.00.
Owner Ambrose Turnbull & John Cruces **Bred** Corrin Stud **Trained** Great Habton, N Yorks

FOCUS
A useful sprint handicap, and the third straight winner on the card by Dandy Man.

7701 RIPON CATHEDRAL CITY OF THE DALES H'CAP 6f
3:35 (3:38) (Class 2) (0-105,107) 3-Y-O+
£15,562 (£4,660; £2,330; £1,165; £582; £292) **Stalls** High

Form RPR

0055 1 **Diamond Dougal (IRE)**[28] 6714 4-8-10 **84** ....(v[1]) KieranO'Neill 1 95
(Mick Channon) *midfield: rdn and hdwy to chse ldrs 2f out: drvn to ld appr fnl f: kpt on wl* **12/1**

000 2 2¼ **Gunmetal (IRE)**[7] 7433 6-9-10 **98** .... JoeFanning 5 102
(David Barron) *dwlt sltly: sn chsd ldr: rdn to ld wl over 1f out: drvn and hdd appr fnl f: one pce* **9/2**[2]

0005 3 nse **Flying Pursuit**[7] 7431 6-8-11 **85** ....(tp) RachelRichardson 4 89+
(Tim Easterby) *dwlt sltly: hld up: sn pushed along: stl lot to do appr fnl f: rdn and kpt on wl: nrst fin* **3/1**[1]

0010 4 1¾ **Cold Stare (IRE)**[7] 7433 4-9-9 **97** ....(t) RobbieDowney 8 95
(David O'Meara) *midfield: pushed along and outpcd 1/2-way: rdn and kpt on ins fnl f* **9/1**

4600 5 ½ **Muscika**[7] 7431 5-9-1 **89** ....(v) CamHardie 6 85
(David O'Meara) *pressed ldr: rdn 2f out: no ex ins fnl f* **6/1**[3]

1340 6 2 **Citron Major**[7] 7431 4-8-12 **89** ....(tp) RowanScott(3) 7 79
(Nigel Tinkler) *dwlt: hld up: sn pushed along: nvr a threat* **6/1**[3]

0026 7 1¼ **Bossipop**[14] 7183 6-8-9 **83** ....(b) DavidAllan 2 69
(Tim Easterby) *led: rdn and hdd wl over 1f out: wknd ins fnl f* **9/1**

6004 8 4½ **Baron Bolt**[25] 6847 6-9-7 **95** ....(b) RossaRyan 9 67
(Paul Cole) *in tch: rdn over 2f out: hung rt and wknd over 1f out* **15/2**

12-2 9 2½ **Muntadab (IRE)**[168] 1763 7-10-0 **107** .... PaulaMuir(5) 3 71
(Roger Fell) *a towards rr* **16/1**

1m 13.87s (1.37) **Going Correction** +0.325s/f (Good) **9 Ran SP% 117.1**
Speed ratings (Par 109): **103,100,99,97,96 94,92,86,83**
CSF £66.17 CT £209.72 TOTE £13.00: £3.50, £1.50, £1.60; EX 95.70 Trifecta £513.50.
Owner Insignia Racing (flag) **Bred** Con Marnane **Trained** West Ilsley, Berks

FOCUS
The feature contest was a good sprint handicap.

7702 MICHAEL RABY MEMORIAL H'CAP — 1m 4f 10y
4:10 (4:14) (Class 4) (0-85,86) 3-Y-0+
£6,663 (£1,982; £990; £495; £300; £300) Stalls Centre

Form					RPR
2331	1		**Tammooz**[40] 6291 3-9-7 **85** ... JackMitchell 9		96+
			(Roger Varian) *midfield: smooth hdwy over 2f out: pushed along to ld appr fnl f: rdn ins fnl f: edgd rt and idled fnl 50yds*	7/2[2]	
1215	2	1 ¼	**Teodora De Vega (IRE)**[43] 6172 3-8-13 **77** ... KevinStott 1		82
			(Ralph Beckett) *dwlt: hld up: rdn and hdwy on outer over 2f out: styd on fnl f: wnt 2nd post*	7/1	
-040	3	hd	**Archi's Affaire**[29] 6657 5-10-1 **86** ... PaulMulrennan 5		90
			(Michael Dods) *trckd ldr: rdn to ld wl over 1f out: hdd appr fnl f: one pce: lost 2nd post*	14/1	
4566	4	hd	**Billy No Mates (IRE)**[21] 6975 3-9-0 **78** ... ConnorBeasley 6		82
			(Michael Dods) *in tch: pushed along over 2f out: edgd rt and bit tight for room over 1f out: drvn and styd on ins fnl f*	6/1	
0551	5	2 ¼	**Multellie**[5] 7510 7-9-7 **78** 4ex ... DavidAllan 8		78
			(Tim Easterby) *led: rdn and hdd wl over 1f out: no ex ins fnl f*	11/4[1]	
0510	6	5	**Mutamaded (IRE)**[7] 7436 6-10-1 **86** ... JamesSullivan 10		78
			(Ruth Carr) *in tch: rdn to chse ldrs 2f out: wknd ins fnl f*	18/1	
3124	7	1 ¾	**Ritchie Valens (IRE)**[21] 6967 3-9-4 **82** ... RossaRyan 2		72
			(Richard Hannon) *midfield on inner: rdn along over 3f out: sn outpcd and btn*	11/2[3]	
5054	8	4	**Super Kid**[15] 7144 7-9-2 **73** ... (tp) CamHardie 3		56
			(Tim Easterby) *hld up: rdn along over 4f out: nvr threatened*	33/1	
3235	9	3 ¾	**Hallalulu**[23] 6902 3-9-1 **79** ... JoeFanning 4		57
			(Mark Johnston) *trckd ldr: rdn over 3f out: wknd over 2f out*	20/1	
304	10	1 ¼	**Appointed**[42] 6230 5-9-4 **75** ... (t) RachelRichardson 7		50
			(Tim Easterby) *a in rr*	22/1	

2m 37.0s (0.70) **Going Correction** +0.325s/f (Good)
WFA 3 from 5yo+ 7lb — 10 Ran SP% **115.0**
Speed ratings (Par 105): **110,109,109,108,107 104,102,100,97,96**
CSF £27.02 CT £303.85 TOTE £4.50: £1.70, £2.30, £4.20; EX 30.40 Trifecta £449.10.
Owner Sheikh Ahmed Al Maktoum **Bred** Bartisan Racing Ltd **Trained** Newmarket, Suffolk

FOCUS
A decent middle-distance handicap.

7703 LLOYD LAND ROVER RIPON APPRENTICE H'CAP — 6f
4:45 (4:48) (Class 5) (0-70,73) 3-Y-0+
£3,752 (£1,116; £557; £300; £300; £300) Stalls High

Form					RPR
4204	1		**Penny Pot Lane**[9] 7383 6-9-5 **65** ... (p) GavinAshton 2		75
			(Richard Whitaker) *hld up in rr: rdn over 2f out: hdwy on outer appr fnl f: led ins fnl f: kpt on wl*	4/1[2]	
1300	2	3 ¼	**B Fifty Two (IRE)**[5] 7511 10-8-13 **66** ... (tp) NickBarratt-Atkin(7) 4		66
			(Marjorie Fife) *chsd ldrs: rdn 2f out: kpt on same pce ins fnl f*	20/1	
0311	3	1	**Blindingly (GER)**[8] 7418 4-9-8 **73** ... (p) GeorgeBass(5) 3		69
			(Ben Haslam) *hld up: drvn over 1f out: kpt on to go 3rd fnl 110yds: wnt 3rd towards fin*	2/1[1]	
0310	4	¾	**Gullane One (IRE)**[11] 7311 4-9-7 **67** ... (p) AidenBlakemore 6		61
			(Tim Easterby) *led narrowly: pushed along 2f out: rdn and along and hdd appr fnl f: wknd fnl 110yds*	15/2	
0465	5	½	**Mutabaahy (IRE)**[11] 7311 4-9-4 **64** ... RussellHarris 7		56
			(Antony Brittain) *prom: rdn to ld appr fnl f: hdd ins fnl f: wknd fnl 110yds*	9/2[3]	
4004	6	¾	**Montalvan (IRE)**[18] 7050 3-8-12 **63** ... (p) ZakWheatley(3) 5		53
			(Roger Fell) *pressed ldr: rdn along 2f out: wknd fnl 110yds*	8/1	
0624	7	6	**Kaafy (IRE)**[6] 7486 3-9-2 **64** ... (p[1]) LukeCatton 1		35
			(Grant Tuer) *hld up: rdn over 2f out: wknd over 1f out*	6/1	

1m 14.55s (2.05) **Going Correction** +0.325s/f (Good)
WFA 3 from 4yo+ 2lb — 7 Ran SP% **113.4**
Speed ratings (Par 103): **99,94,93,92,91 90,82**
CSF £71.27 TOTE £4.10: £2.40, £7.10; EX 52.80 Trifecta £439.40.
Owner A Melville **Bred** Hellwood Stud Farm & G P Clarke **Trained** Scarcroft, W Yorks

FOCUS
An ordinary apprentice riders' handicap.

7704 THANK YOU TO OUR GROUNDSTAFF NOVICE STKS — 1m 4f 10y
5:20 (5:23) (Class 5) 3-Y-0+
£3,881 (£1,155; £577; £288) Stalls Centre

Form					RPR
2023	1		**Isabella Brant (FR)**[31] 6597 3-8-11 76 ... RossaRyan 4		73
			(Ralph Beckett) *trckd ldrs: pushed along 3f out: swtchd lft over 2f out: sn chal: led narrowly over 1f out: drvn all out*	8/13[1]	
3	2	nk	**Rory And Me (FR)**[9] 7382 4-9-9 0 ... (t) PaulMulrennan 5		76
			(Micky Hammond) *trckd ldrs: pushed along to chal 3f out: drvn into narrow ld 2f out: hdd over 1f out: styd on but a jst hld*	10/1	
2255	3	1 ½	**Lady Scatterley (FR)**[34] 6500 3-8-11 67 ... DavidAllan 2		70
			(Tim Easterby) *led narrowly: rdn along 3f out: hdd 2f out: no ex in 3rd fnl f*	3/1[2]	
3/	4	8	**Lough Salt (IRE)**[170] 7629 8-9-9 0 ... ConnorBeasley 6		61
			(Richard Guest) *s.i.s: hld up in tch: pushed along over 3f out: outpcd fnl 2f*	28/1	
	5	8	**Mystic Dragon** 3-8-11 0 ... AndrewElliott 7		44
			(Mrs Ilka Gansera-Leveque) *pressed ldrs: rdn along and lost pl over 3f out: wknd over 2f out*	25/1	
	6	25	**Secret Escape (IRE)**[45] 7-8-11 0 ... EllaMcCain(7) 1		3
			(Donald McCain) *hld up: sn pushed along: wknd and bhd fnl 4f*	7/1[3]	
	7	1 ¼	**Kall To Alms** 3-9-2 0 ... CamHardie 3		7
			(Stef Keniry) *s.i.s: hld up: wnt in snatches: wknd and bhd fnl 4f*	50/1	

2m 39.33s (3.03) **Going Correction** +0.325s/f (Good)
WFA 3 from 4yo+ 7lb — 7 Ran SP% **117.8**
Speed ratings (Par 103): **102,101,100,95,90 73,72**
CSF £8.66 TOTE £1.60: £1.10, £3.10; EX 7.30 Trifecta £14.80.
Owner Merriebelle Irish Farm Limited **Bred** Merriebelle Irish Farm Ltd **Trained** Kimpton, Hants

FOCUS
A ordinary middle-distance novice contest.
T/Plt: £168.60 to a £1 stake. Pool: £56,117.86 - 242.88 winning units T/Qpdt: £47.90 to a £1 stake. Pool: £4,628.93 - 71.42 winning units **Andrew Sheret**

7643 HAYDOCK (L-H)
Saturday, September 28
7705 Meeting Abandoned - Waterlogged

7712 - (Foreign Racing) - See Raceform Interactive

7241 CURRAGH (R-H)
Saturday, September 28

OFFICIAL GOING: Round course - yielding (yielding to soft in places); straight course - soft (yielding to soft in places)

7713a AES RENAISSANCE STKS (GROUP 3) — 6f
2:00 (2:00) 3-Y-0+ £31,891 (£10,270; £4,864; £2,162; £1,081; £540) Stalls Centre

				RPR
1		**Speak In Colours**[35] 6472 4-9-5 111 ... (t) ShaneCrosse 2		111
		(Joseph Patrick O'Brien, Ire) *led briefly early tl sn jnd and hdd: cl 5th at 1/2-way: tk clsr order travelling wl far side 2f out and impr to ld over 1f out: strly pressed briefly ins fnl f where rdn: kpt on wl to assert nr fin*	6/5[1]	
2	1 ¼	**Downforce (IRE)**[43] 6195 7-9-5 96 ... (v) WJLee 6		107
		(W McCreery, Ire) *hld up bhd ldrs: 5th 1/2-way: prog gng wl under 2f out to chal over 1f out where rdn in 2nd: strly pressed wnr briefly ins fnl f: kpt on wl wout matching wnr nr fin*	20/1	
3	2 ¼	**Chessman (IRE)**[13] 7243 5-9-5 101 ... (t) DeclanMcDonogh 1		100
		(Richard John O'Brien, Ire) *hld up in rr: last at 1/2-way: nt clr run briefly gng wl over 2f out and sn swtchd: prog between horses into 3rd jst ins fnl f where rdn: kpt on same pce*	16/1	
4	1 ½	**Gustavus Weston (IRE)**[50] 5923 3-9-6 106 ... GaryCarroll 4		98
		(Joseph G Murphy, Ire) *cl up bhd ldrs: disp ld at 1/2-way: led narrowly gng wl down centre under 2f out: hdd over 1f out and sn no ex u.p in 4th*	5/1[3]	
5	½	**Perfection**[20] 6999 4-9-2 105 ... (v) RonanWhelan 3		90
		(David O'Meara) *cl up bhd ldrs: cl 4th at 1/2-way: sn pushed along and no ex u.p under 2f out: wknd*	9/2[2]	
6	½	**Gordon Lord Byron (IRE)**[13] 7241 11-9-5 105 ... AndrewSlattery 7		92
		(T Hogan, Ire) *sn led and disp nr side: pushed along and hdd after 1/2-way: no ex u.p bhd ldrs 1 1/2f out: wknd*	12/1	
7	1	**Beckford**[50] 5923 4-9-5 101 ... ChrisHayes 5		89
		(Gordon Elliott, Ire) *sn led and disp: pushed along on terms after 1/2-way and hdd u.p under 2f out: sn wknd*	6/1	

1m 15.64s (1.44) **Going Correction** +0.625s/f (Yiel)
WFA 3 from 4yo+ 2lb — 7 Ran SP% **112.9** Speed ratings: **115,113,110,108,107 107,105**
CSF £27.73 TOTE £1.40: £1.02, £10.30; DF 24.10 Trifecta £368.20.
Owner Mrs C C Regalado-Gonzalez **Bred** Scuderia Archi Romani **Trained** Owning Hill, Co Kilkenny

FOCUS
A nice performance from the winner who showed his versatility.

7714a - 7716a (Foreign Racing) - See Raceform Interactive

7717a HOLDEN PLANT RENTALS LOUGHBROWN STKS (GROUP 3) — 2m
4:20 (4:22) 3-Y-0+ £31,891 (£10,270; £4,864; £2,162) Stalls Far side

				RPR
1		**Kastasa (IRE)**[14] 7216 3-8-10 98 ... AndrewSlattery 3		113+
		(D K Weld, Ire) *led briefly early tl sn hdd and settled bhd ldr: mod 2nd at 1/2-way: niggled along under 4f out and tk clsr order bhd ldr into st: led gng best fr 2f out: rdn clr over 1f out and styd on wl: easily*	11/8[2]	
2	7	**Cypress Creek (IRE)**[13] 7246 4-9-9 106 ... (b) PBBeggy 2		107+
		(A P O'Brien, Ire) *hld up bhd ldrs in 3rd: mod 3rd at 1/2-way: niggled along in 3rd over 4f out and no imp on ldrs into st: kpt on u.p into mod 2nd ins fnl f: nt trble easy wnr*	7/1[3]	
3	4 ¾	**Capri (IRE)**[13] 7246 5-9-9 111 ... (b[1]) SeamieHeffernan 4		103
		(A P O'Brien, Ire) *cl up tl sn led: over 3 l clr after 3f: extended ld bef 1/2-way: stl gng wl 4f out: rdn and reduced ld into st: hdd u.p fr 2f out and sn no imp on easy wnr: wknd into mod 3rd*	5/4[1]	
4	14	**Moteo (IRE)**[11] 7326 4-9-6 99 ... RonanWhelan 1		88
		(John M Oxx, Ire) *w.w in rr of quartet: detached bef 1/2-way: pushed along in clsr 4th under 4f out: rdn and no ex over 2f out: sn wknd and eased*	12/1	

3m 42.78s (8.88) **Going Correction** +0.75s/f (Yiel)
WFA 3 from 4yo+ 10lb — 4 Ran SP% **106.7**
Speed ratings: **107,103,101,94**
CSF £9.74 TOTE £1.90; DF 8.90 Trifecta £13.20.
Owner H H Aga Khan **Bred** His Highness The Aga Khan's Studs S C **Trained** Curragh, Co Kildare

FOCUS
The winner bolted up and this rates a clear pb.

7718 - 7723a (Foreign Racing) - See Raceform Interactive

7502 SAN SIRO (R-H)
Saturday, September 28

OFFICIAL GOING: Turf: good

7724a PREMIO COOLMORE (LISTED RACE) (2YO FILLIES) (MEDIA COURSE) (TURF) — 7f 110y
4:45 2-Y-0 £17,567 (£7,729; £4,216; £2,108)

				RPR
1		**Festive Star**[39] 6322 2-8-9 0 ... FabioBranca 9		104+
		(Simon Crisford) *a.p: smooth prog to ld ins fnl 2f: wnt clr over 1f out: easily*	4/5[1]	
2	5	**Ancona (IRE)**[20] 7004 2-8-9 0 ... RenePiechulek 11		90
		(Andreas Suborics, Germany)	43/5	
3	nk	**Norohna (FR)**[54] 5759 2-8-9 0 ... SergioUrru 3		89
		(Nicolo Simondi, Italy)	123/10	
4	2 ½	**Mighty Rock**[13] 2-8-9 0 ... (t) AntonioFresu 10		83
		(Sebastiano Guerrieri, Italy)	30/1	
5	1 ¼	**Frivola** 2-8-9 0 ... DarioVargiu 1		80
		(A Botti, Italy)	48/10[2]	
6	4	**Gladice**[19] 7031 2-8-9 0 ... ClaudioColombi 8		71
		(Marco Botti) *hld up towards rr: moved into midfield 1/2-way: drvn and no further imp 1 1/2f out: one pce u.p*	596/100	

7	3/4	**Catenda** 2-8-9 0 (p) DarioDiTocco 7 (R Rohne, Germany) 58/10[3]	69
8	1 1/2	**Mera Di Breme** 2-8-9 0 (bt) AndreaMezzatesta 2 (R Biondi, Italy) 127/20	65
9	4	**Labelleepoque (IRE)** 2-8-9 0 (t) SilvanoMulas 4 (V Fazio, Italy) 227/10	56
10	dist	**Shiso (IRE)**[46] 6060 2-8-9 0 LucaManiezzi 5 (R Rohne, Germany) 58/10[3]	

1m 29.7s (-5.80) **10 Ran SP% 155.6**
PARI-MUTUEL (all including 1 euro stake): WIN 1.79; PLACE 1.27, 3.07, 2.93; DF 11.88.
Owner Rabbah Racing **Bred** Sun Kingdom Pty Ltd **Trained** Newmarket, Suffolk

7124 EPSOM (L-H)

Sunday, September 29

OFFICIAL GOING: Heavy (soft in places; 4.6)
Wind: strong, across Weather: windy, showers and bright spells

7725 IDF 2020 TICKETS ON SALE TOMORROW NURSERY H'CAP 7f 3y

2:00 (2:00) (Class 4) (0-85,86) 2-Y-O
£6,469 (£1,925; £962; £481; £400; £400) **Stalls Low**

Form				RPR
621	1		**Afraid Of Nothing**[17] 7124 2-9-6 81 OisinMurphy 5 (Ralph Beckett) mde all: rdn over 1f out: styd on wl and asserted ins fnl f: gng away at fin 4/1[2]	87+
2321	2	2 1/4	**Lost In Time**[26] 6845 2-9-11 86 HectorCrouch 3 (Saeed bin Suroor) trckd ldrs: clsd to press wnr over 1f out: sn rdn: no ex and outpcd ins fnl f 8/11[1]	86+
2313	3	1 1/2	**Hubert (IRE)**[46] 6073 2-9-2 77 LukeMorris 2 (Sylvester Kirk) hld up in last pair: nt clr run and swtchd lft over 1f out: chsd ldng pair and kpt on same pce fnl f 16/1	74
5424	4	3 1/2	**Light The Fuse (IRE)**[12] 7309 2-8-12 73 SeanLevey 6 (K R Burke) dwlt: rousted along early: midfield: effrt over 2f out: no imp u.p over 1f out: wknd ins fnl f 12/1	61
4166	5	1	**Nat Love (IRE)**[16] 7155 2-8-13 74 CallumShepherd 4 (Mick Channon) chsd wnr tl over 1f: sn rdn and outpcd: wknd ins fnl f 14/1	59
221	6	1 1/4	**Stoweman**[34] 6528 2-9-7 82 AdamKirby 7 (Clive Cox) chsd ldrs: rdn over 2f out: jst getting outpcd and nudged lft over 1f out: wknd ins fnl f 5/1[3]	64
0065	7	4 1/2	**Barry Magoo**[37] 6403 2-8-0 61 oh2 RaulDaSilva 1 (Adam West) hld up in rr: rdn and hdwy over 2f out: lost pl and btn over 1f out: bhd ins fnl f 40/1	32

1m 27.37s (3.97) **Going Correction** +0.70s/f (Yiel) **7 Ran SP% 117.3**
Speed ratings (Par 97): **105,102,100,96,95 94,89**
CSF £7.59 TOTE £4.40: £2.20, £1.10; EX 8.70 Trifecta £51.60.
Owner Qatar Racing Limited **Bred** The Lady Dragon Partnership **Trained** Kimpton, Hants

FOCUS
No less than 55m of rain had fallen in the previous seven days, including 11mm from 8pm the previous evening to 9am ahead of this afternoon meeting. A blustery day and overcast for the track's season finale. Add 4yds to the distance of this fair nursery, which contained a trio of last-time-out novice winners, and was run at a modest pace, over 7.07secs outside of the standard. They came stands' side.

7726 INVESTEC DERBY "WILD CARD" CONDITIONS STKS (PLUS 10 RACE) 1m 113y

2:30 (2:30) (Class 2) 2-Y-O **£12,450** (£3,728; £1,864) **Stalls Low**

Form				RPR
41	1		**Grand Rock (IRE)**[30] 6654 2-9-2 0 JamesDoyle 1 (William Haggas) chsd ldr: clsd and upsides over 1f out: shkn up to ld ent fnl f: rdn and asserted ins fnl f: eased cl home 5/4[1]	91
51	2	nk	**Night Colours (IRE)**[14] 7235 2-8-11 0 DaneO'Neill 3 (Simon Crisford) hld up in 3rd: effrt over 1f out: kpt on to chse wnr wl ins fnl f: clsng nr fin as wnr eased but a hld 9/4[3]	85
2111	3	1 3/4	**King's Caper**[29] 6707 2-9-7 96 JoeFanning 2 (Mark Johnston) led: jnd and rdn over 1f out: hdd ent fnl f: no ex: lost 2nd and wknd wl ins fnl f 13/8[2]	92

1m 53.34s (6.94) **Going Correction** +0.70s/f (Yiel) **3 Ran SP% 113.3**
Speed ratings (Par 101): **97,96,95**
CSF £4.42 TOTE £2.30; EX 5.50 Trifecta £5.40.
Owner Hussain Alabbas Lootah **Bred** Peter & Hugh McCutcheon **Trained** Newmarket, Suffolk

FOCUS
Add 6yds to the distance of this fascinating conditions event, where a trio of last-time-out winners lined up for a race where the winner receives an entry to the 2020 Derby. Although it is unlikely any of them will be back here in June for the big one, it looked a decent heat, despite the time, which was 11.64secs slower than standard. They again came stands' side.

7727 SEASON FINALE H'CAP 1m 2f 17y

3:05 (3:05) (Class 3) (0-95,95) 3-Y-O+ **£12,450** (£3,728; £1,864; £932; £466) **Stalls Low**

Form				RPR
001	1		**Torcello (IRE)**[43] 6217 5-8-7 81 oh3 MeganNicholls(3) 6 (Shaun Lycett) mde all: pushed along and fnd ex over 1f out: r.o strly and in n.d ins fnl f: pushed out 9/2[3]	94
441	2	6	**Zzoro (IRE)**[16] 7166 6-8-11 82 (t) JasonWatson 3 (Amanda Perrett) chsd wnr for 1f: effrt and drvn to chse wnr again over 1f out: sn outpcd: wl hld and kpt on same pce ins fnl f 11/4[2]	83
2330	3	1/2	**Oasis Prince**[8] 7457 3-9-4 94 JoeFanning 7 (Mark Johnston) chsd wnr after 1f: effrt over 2f out: unable qck and lost 2nd over 1f out: wl hld and kpt on same pce ins fnl f 11/2	95
4000	4	nse	**Exec Chef (IRE)**[8] 7457 4-9-7 92 PatCosgrave 4 (Jim Boyle) hld up in tch in 4th: effrt and swtchd lft over 1f out: no ch w wnr and kpt on same pce ins fnl f 7/4[1]	92
6420	5	13	**Mordred (IRE)**[8] 7436 3-8-9 85 SeanLevey 2 (Richard Hannon) hld up in rr: rdn over 2f out: sn struggling and wl btn fnl 2f 11/2	60

2m 14.54s (4.54) **Going Correction** +0.70s/f (Yiel) **5 Ran SP% 112.0**
WFA 3 from 4yo+ 5lb
Speed ratings (Par 107): **109,104,103,103,93**
CSF £17.30 TOTE £5.00: £2.00, £1.80; EX 15.60 Trifecta £60.70.
Owner Dan Gilbert **Bred** Rathasker Stud **Trained** Leafield, Oxon

FOCUS
Add 6yds to the distance of this decent handicap, which was run at a fair pace for the conditions and paucity of runners. Again, they came stands' side and the winner made all.

7728 KIDS TAKEOVER H'CAP 1m 113y

3:35 (3:35) (Class 3) (0-90,91) 3-Y-O
£9,337 (£2,796; £1,398; £699; £349; £175) **Stalls Low**

Form				RPR
1254	1		**Marronnier (IRE)**[11] 7342 3-9-5 86 (t) SeanLevey 5 (Stuart Williams) hld up in tch in last pair: clsd to press ldr wl over 2f out: rdn to ld over 1f out: styd on and in command ins fnl f 4/1[2]	97
5120	2	2 3/4	**I'm Available (IRE)**[100] 4052 3-9-5 86 OisinMurphy 4 (Andrew Balding) pressed ldr for over 1f: chsd ldrs: swtchd rt and pressed ldr again 5f out: led 4f out: hdd over 1f out: rdn and kpt on same pce fnl f 11/10[1]	91
0004	3	6	**Hot Team (IRE)**[23] 6923 3-9-7 91 (p) CierenFallon(3) 6 (Hugo Palmer) pressed ldr tl led 5f out: hdd 4f out: 3rd and rdn over 2f out: outpcd and wl hld over 1f out: plugged on same pce ins fnl f 7/1	83
3326	4	nk	**House Of Kings (IRE)**[16] 7163 3-9-4 85 (p[1]) AdamKirby 1 (Clive Cox) trckd ldrs: effrt u.p over 2f out: outpcd and hung lft over 1f out: wl hld and plugged on same pce ins fnl f 5/1[3]	77
0624	5	4	**Desirous**[22] 6951 3-9-6 87 HarryBentley 2 (Ralph Beckett) led tl 5f out: rdn over 3f out: outpcd over 2f out: wl btn over 1f out (trainer could offer no explanation for the poor performance) 7/1	70
4425	6	1 1/2	**Water's Edge (IRE)**[23] 6931 3-8-7 74 NicolaCurrie 7 (George Baker) dwlt: a in rr: rdn and no reponse over 2f out (jockey said gelding anticipated the start and was never travelling) 20/1	54

1m 49.6s (3.20) **Going Correction** +0.70s/f (Yiel) **6 Ran SP% 114.0**
Speed ratings (Par 105): **113,110,105,104,101 100**
CSF £9.09 TOTE £5.40: £2.60, £1.20; EX 13.20 Trifecta £46.60.
Owner GG Thoroughbreds III **Bred** Skymarc Farm **Trained** Newmarket, Suffolk

FOCUS
Add 6yds to the distance of this decent handicap, which was competitive for the grade. The first two had it to themselves from 2f out and again they came stands' side.

7729 APPRENTICES' DERBY STKS (A H'CAP) 1m 4f 6y

4:10 (4:10) (Class 4) (0-85,86) 3-Y-O+
£6,469 (£1,925; £962; £481; £400; £400) **Stalls Centre**

Form				RPR
4034	1		**King Of The Sand (IRE)**[20] 7026 4-8-11 74 RhysClutterbuck(7) 6 (Gary Moore) mde all: clr 4f out and unchal after: pushed along over 1f out: kpt on wl: eased towards fin 14/1	84
1120	2	5	**Hydroplane (IRE)**[15] 7209 3-8-9 79 (p) GavinAshton(7) 5 (Sir Mark Prescott Bt) hld up in tch in midfield: hdwy to chse ldrs 5f out: chsd clr wnr 4f out: rdn over 2f out: hung lft over 1f out: wl hld ins fnl f: eased towards fin 3/1[2]	83
1633	3	nk	**Ocala**[23] 6923 4-9-11 86 WilliamCarver(5) 2 (Andrew Balding) hld up in tch in midfield: hdwy to chse ldng pair 4f out: effrt and wnt lft over 2f out: no imp and kpt on same pce ins fnl f 9/4[1]	87
4343	4	15	**Rotherwick (IRE)**[12] 7294 7-9-11 81 (t) HarrisonShaw 7 (Paul Cole) hld up in last pair: lost tch w ldrs 5f out: plugged on st to go modest 4th nr fin: nvr involved 10/1	60
0035	5	1/2	**Mandalayan (IRE)**[17] 7127 4-9-7 82 TylerSaunders(5) 4 (Jonathan Portman) midfield: pushed along to chse ldrs 8f out: struggling over 4f out: styd centre st and wl btn fnl 3f 6/1	60
0011	6	43	**Culture (FR)**[27] 6812 3-9-6 83 (p) CierenFallon 3 (George Baker) chsd wnr for 2f: steadily lost pl: in last trio and rdn 6f out: wl btn and styd centre st: t.o and virtually p.u ins fnl f (trainers rep said gelding was unsuited by the ground and would prefer a quicker surface) 10/1	
1161	7	1/2	**Gas Monkey**[43] 6218 4-9-8 83 (h) SeanKirrane(5) 1 (Julia Feilden) chsd ldrs: wnt 2nd 10f out tl lost 2nd and impeded 4f out: sn struggling and dropped out: t.o and virtually p.u ins fnl f (jockey said gelding was never travelling. Trainer said gelding was unsuited by the ground and would prefer a quicker surface) 9/2[3]	
000	8	39	**Maquisard (FR)**[32] 6596 7-9-11 84 ScottMcCullagh(3) 8 (Michael Madgwick) broke okay but sn dropped to last pair: lost tch 4f out: t.o and eased fnl 2f (jockey said gelding was never travelling) 33/1	

2m 47.36s (6.56) **Going Correction** +0.70s/f (Yiel) **8 Ran SP% 116.0**
WFA 3 from 4yo+ 7lb
Speed ratings (Par 105): **106,102,102,92,92 63,63,37**
CSF £56.80 CT £133.59 TOTE £15.80: £3.60, £1.40, £1.30; EX 77.00 Trifecta £303.60.
Owner Jacobs Construction & J Harley **Bred** R Coffey **Trained** Lower Beeding, W Sussex

FOCUS
Add 6yds to the distance of this competitive apprentices' handicap and this stiff trip took some getting in these testing conditions. They finished well strung out as the leader made all.

7730 BACK TO THE 80'S NYE PARTY NOVICE STKS 1m 2f 17y

4:45 (4:45) (Class 5) 3-Y-O+ **£4,528** (£1,347; £673; £336) **Stalls Low**

Form				RPR
2-	1		**Edinburgh Castle (IRE)**[347] 8311 3-9-2 0 OisinMurphy 7 (Andrew Balding) s.i.s: steadily rcvrd to chse ldrs 1/2-way: effrt to chal over 2f out: rdn to ld jst over 1f out: styd on and drew clr ins fnl f 5/4[1]	81+
60	2	4 1/2	**Manucci (IRE)**[16] 7159 3-9-2 0 KieranShoemark 6 (Amanda Perrett) chsd ldr: rdn and outpcd over 2f out: rn green and over 1f out: no ch w wnr and kpt on same pce ins fnl f: wnt 2nd again last strides 14/1[3]	72
042	3	nk	**Roving Mission (USA)**[16] 7159 3-8-11 70 HarryBentley 4 (Ralph Beckett) pushed along leaving stalls: in tch: trckd ldrs 1/2-way tl rdn to ld over 2f out: hdd jst over 1f out: no ex and wknd ins fnl f: lost 2nd last strides 5/4[1]	66+
00	4	2 1/2	**Shattering (IRE)**[10] 7373 3-9-2 0 SeanLevey 3 (Paul Cole) off the pce in last pair: 5th and no imp over 2f out: no ch w wnr but kpt on steadily ins fnl f 33/1	66
3453	5	1 3/4	**Memphis Bleek**[17] 7129 3-8-13 74 (b) GabrieleMalune(3) 1 (Ivan Furtado) led tl rdn and hdd over 2f out: btn and hung lft over 1f out: wknd ins fnl f (jockey said gelding stopped quickly) 6/1[2]	63
0	6	24	**Dereham**[16] 7159 3-9-2 0 RaulDaSilva 5 (John Berry) sn in rr: losing tch and styd centre over 3f out: t.o 50/1	15

The Form Book Flat 2019, Raceform Ltd, Newbury, RG14 5SJ

7 84 **Big Bang** 6-9-7 0 .... ShelleyBirkett 2
(Julia Feilden) *chsd ldrs tl 7f out: sn bhd and t.o fnl 4f (trainer said gelding was unsuited by the ground and would prefer a quicker surface)* **33/1**

2m 18.4s (8.40) **Going Correction** +0.70s/f (Yiel)
WFA 3 from 6yo 5lb **7** Ran SP% **117.7**
Speed ratings (Par 103): **94,90,90,88,86 67,**
CSF £22.78 TOTE £2.10: £1.30, £4.80; EX 22.10 Trifecta £33.00.
Owner Mrs Fitri Hay **Bred** Roundhill Stud **Trained** Kingsclere, Hants

FOCUS
Add 6yds to the distance of this modest novice. They came stands' side in the testing ground and the winner defied a long lay-off in dogged fashion.

7731 SPECTACULAR CHRISTMAS PARTIES AT EPSOM DOWNS H'CAP 7f 3y
5:15 (5:15) (Class 4) (0-80,82) 3-Y-0+
£6,469 (£1,925; £962; £481; £400; £400) **Stalls** Low

Form RPR
2020 1 **Zeyzoun (FR)**[25] 6863 5-9-7 **79** ....(h) GeorgeWood 5 86
(Chris Wall) *taken down early: pressed ldr tl led and travelling strly 2f out: shkn up over 1f out: rdn and kpt on ins fnl f* **9/4**[1]

5163 2 1 1/4 **Swift Approval (IRE)**[19] 7059 7-9-10 **82** .... SeanLevey 2 86
(Stuart Williams) *led: rdn and hdd 2f out: drvn over 1f out: kpt on u.p but a hld ins fnl f* **5/1**

1105 3 1 **Global Destination (IRE)**[52] 5847 3-8-10 **71** .... RobertHavlin 8 71+
(Ed Dunlop) *stdd after s: hld up in last pair: clsd and nt clr run over 1f out: swtchd ins fnl f: r.o fnl 100yds to go 3rd nr fin: no threat to wnr* **14/1**

-320 4 1/2 **Dourado (IRE)**[25] 6863 5-9-6 **81** .... CierenFallon(3) 6 81
(Patrick Chamings) *in tch in midfield: effrt to chse ldr 2f out: rdn and kpt on same pce fr over 1f out: lost 3rd nr fin* **7/2**[2]

0242 5 3 **Poet's Magic**[33] 6569 3-8-4 **65** oh1 .... NicolaCurrie 7 56
(Jonathan Portman) *restless in stalls and dwlt: pushed along leaving stalls: in tch in midfield: effrt ent fnl 2f: rdn and no imp over 1f out: wl hld ins fnl f (jockey said filly was restless in the stalls and jumped awkwardly)* **10/1**

0564 6 1 **Red Bravo (IRE)**[45] 6111 3-8-11 **72** .... KieranShoemark 1 60
(Charles Hills) *in tch in midfield: swtchd lft 2f out and sn rdn: no imp 1f out: wknd ins fnl f* **8/1**

6-54 7 1/2 **Young Bernie**[92] 4377 4-8-9 **67** .... OisinMurphy 4 55
(Andrew Balding) *stdd s: hld up in rr: clsd ent fnl 2f: rdn and effrt over 1f out: no imp and wknd ins fnl f* **9/2**[3]

2330 8 3/4 **Arctic Flower (IRE)**[13] 7282 6-8-0 **65** oh16 .... GeorgeRooke(7) 3 51
(John Bridger) *chsd ldrs tl 2f: unable qck and hung lft over 1f out: lost pl and wknd ins fnl f* **33/1**

1m 28.2s (4.80) **Going Correction** +0.70s/f (Yiel)
WFA 3 from 4yo+ 3lb **8** Ran SP% **117.6**
Speed ratings (Par 105): **100,98,97,96,93 92,91,90**
CSF £14.38 CT £130.28 TOTE £2.70: £1.10, £2.00, £4.40; EX 11.80 Trifecta £130.70.
Owner Michael Bringloe **Bred** H H The Aga Khan's Studs Et Al **Trained** Newmarket, Suffolk

FOCUS
Add 4yds to the distance. Mot much depth in this handicap with a few out of form, and again it paid to be near the pace and near the stands' rail. Few got into it.
T/Jkpt: £18,926.10 to a £1 stake. Pool: £53,313.20 - 2 winning units T/Plt: £41.20 to a £1 stake. Pool: £82,182.44 - 1454.63 winning units **Steve Payne**

7207 MUSSELBURGH (R-H)
Sunday, September 29

OFFICIAL GOING: Good to soft (soft in places; 7.7)
Wind: Fresh, across

7732 LG PHARMACY LYNN'S LAST GALLOP H'CAP (DIV I) 1m 4f 104y
1:40 (1:40) (Class 6) (0-60,62) 3-Y-0+
£2,911 (£866; £432; £400; £400; £400) **Stalls** Low

Form RPR
052 1 **Smart Lass (IRE)**[9] 7415 4-9-3 **48** .... JamieGormley 6 57
(Iain Jardine) *cl up: led 1/2-way: mde rest: drvn along 2f out: kpt on strly fnl f* **12/1**

5430 2 1 3/4 **Lincoln Tale (IRE)**[12] 7314 3-9-7 **59** .... DanielTudhope 8 66
(David O'Meara) *hld up: hdwy on outside over 2f out: effrt and chsd wnr over 1f out: edgd rt and clsd ins fnl f: one pce fnl 100yds* **9/1**[3]

1 3 3 1/4 **Chica Buena (IRE)**[7] 7492 4-9-9 **54** 5ex .... GrahamLee 3 56
(Keith Dalgleish) *prom: pushed along over 5f out: rallied and chsd wnr 3f out to over 1f out: rdn and no ex fnl f* **2/7**[1]

-553 4 10 **Gemologist (IRE)**[23] 6933 4-9-3 **53** ....(t) FayeMcManoman(5) 2 40
(Lucinda Russell) *hld up: rdn along over 3f out: plugged on fnl f: nvr able to chal* **16/1**

5053 5 3/4 **Royal Countess**[23] 6938 3-8-2 **45** .... PaulaMuir(5) 9 31
(Lucy Normile) *chsd ldrs: rdn over 2f out: edgd rt and wknd over 1f out* **18/1**

/000 6 2 **Circuit**[130] 2963 5-8-7 **45** .... RhonaPindar(7) 7 27
(Wilf Storey) *hld up in tch: rdn along over 3f out: wknd fr 2f out* **40/1**

3252 7 1 **Apache Blaze**[40] 6324 4-10-3 **62** ....(v[1]) PJMcDonald 4 43
(Robyn Brisland) *prom on ins: drvn along over 2f out: wknd wl over 1f out* **8/1**[2]

0060 8 10 **Foxrush Take Time (FR)**[10] 7375 4-9-0 **45** ....(e) ConnorBeasley 1 11
(Richard Guest) *hld up bhd ldng gp: rdn over 4f out: wknd fnl 2f* **25/1**

0050 9 22 **Gremoboy**[82] 4761 3-8-12 **50** ....(p) DavidAllan 10
(Tim Easterby) *led to 1/2-way: pressed wnr to 3f out: sn rdn and wknd: t.o* **28/1**

0040 10 99 **Bold Statement (IRE)**[24] 6896 4-9-0 **45** .... CamHardie 5
(Alan Berry) *bhd and sn rdn along: lost tch 1/2-way: t.o* **100/1**

2m 47.11s (2.61) **Going Correction** +0.275s/f (Good)
WFA 3 from 4yo+ 7lb **10** Ran SP% **128.4**
Speed ratings (Par 101): **102,100,98,92,91 90,89,82,68,2**
CSF £121.60 CT £135.46 TOTE £11.70: £2.50, £2.70, £1.02; EX 118.00 Trifecta £290.60.
Owner I J Jardine **Bred** Ben Browne **Trained** Carrutherstown, D'fries & G'way

FOCUS
The bottom bend was moved out 2yds. Few landed any sort of a blow in this moderate handicap. Add 7yds.

7733 IRISH STALLION FARMS EBF NOVICE STKS (PLUS 10 RACE) 7f 33y
2:10 (2:18) (Class 4) 2-Y-O **£4,592** (£1,366; £683; £341) **Stalls** Low

Form RPR
41 1 **Johan**[50] 5956 2-9-9 0 .... DanielTudhope 3 87+
(William Haggas) *mde all: rdn clr fr 2f out: readily* **8/13**[1]

1 2 6 **Amaysmont**[39] 6337 2-9-6 0 .... SeanDavis(3) 1 71
(Richard Fahey) *t.k.h: prom: hdwy to chse ldr after 2f: effrt and rdn over 2f out: kpt on same pce fr over 1f out* **2/1**[2]

3 shd **Hua Mulan (IRE)** 2-8-11 0 .... CallumRodriguez 4 59
(Keith Dalgleish) *s.i.s: hld up in tch: rdn over 2f out: hdwy over 1f out: kpt on fnl f: no imp* **28/1**

4 1 **Marie's Gem (IRE)** 2-9-2 0 .... PJMcDonald 2 62
(Mark Johnston) *chsd wnr 2f: cl up: rdn over 2f out: no ex fr over 1f out* **9/1**[3]

5 hd **Grandads Best Girl** 2-8-11 0 .... BenRobinson 5 56+
(Linda Perratt) *dwlt: hld up: rdn over 3f out: hdwy over 1f out: no imp fnl f* **33/1**

0 6 7 **Ventura Destiny (FR)**[43] 6226 2-8-11 0 .... ShaneGray 6 38
(Keith Dalgleish) *prom: rdn and outpcd over 3f out: wknd over 2f out* **50/1**

1m 30.7s (1.70) **Going Correction** +0.275s/f (Good) **6** Ran SP% **113.6**
Speed ratings (Par 97): **101,94,94,92,92 84**
CSF £2.09 TOTE £1.50: £1.10, £1.10; EX 2.00 Trifecta £10.60.
Owner Jon and Julia Aisbitt **Bred** Jon And Julia Aisbitt **Trained** Newmarket, Suffolk

FOCUS
There was an 8min delay to this modest little 2yo contest due to officials looking for a loose shoe on the track. Add 7yds.

7734 EVERY RACE LIVE ON RACINGTV NURSERY H'CAP 5f 1y
2:40 (2:45) (Class 6) (0-65,66) 2-Y-O
£2,911 (£866; £432; £400; £400; £400) **Stalls** High

Form RPR
6401 1 **Lara Silvia**[17] 7110 2-9-5 **63** .... DanielTudhope 2 67+
(Iain Jardine) *dwlt: sn rcvrd to ld: rdn and hdd over 1f out: rallied ins fnl f: kpt on gamely to regain ld cl home* **5/2**[1]

5501 2 nk **Shepherds Way (IRE)**[15] 7208 2-9-8 **66** .... ConnorBeasley 5 69
(Michael Dods) *trckd ldrs: hdwy to ld over 1f out: rdn and kpt on fnl f: hdd cl home* **4/1**[2]

063 3 1 1/2 **Not On Your Nellie (IRE)**[57] 5689 2-9-6 **64** .... TomEaves 6 62
(Nigel Tinkler) *dwlt: hld up: rdn and hdwy over 1f out: kpt on ins fnl f: nrst fin* **5/1**[3]

6432 4 hd **Maybellene (IRE)**[8] 7440 2-9-5 **63** .... CamHardie 3 60
(Alan Berry) *t.k.h early: prom: effrt and rdn over 1f out: kpt on same pce ins fnl f* **6/1**

2666 5 3/4 **Beignet (IRE)**[27] 6799 2-9-0 **58** .... BenRobinson 8 53
(Linda Perratt) *early ldr: cl up: effrt whn nt clr run briefly over 1f out: rdn and one pce fnl f* **25/1**

4520 6 2 1/4 **Comeatchoo (IRE)**[8] 7440 2-8-8 **52** ....(b) DuranFentiman 1 38
(Tim Easterby) *t.k.h: cl up: ev ch over 2f out to over 1f out: sn rdn and edgd rt: wknd ins fnl f* **10/1**

0402 7 3/4 **Summer Heights**[15] 7208 2-8-12 **56** .... PaddyMathers 7 39
(Jim Goldie) *bhd and sn pushed along: effrt on outside over 1f out: rdn and no further imp fnl f* **15/2**

4050 8 1/2 **Lady Celia**[20] 7029 2-8-13 **60** .... SeanDavis(3) 9 42
(Richard Fahey) *sn pushed along in rr: drvn and no imp fr 2f out* **11/1**

560 9 5 **Unauthorised Act (IRE)**[15] 7211 2-8-1 **45** .... JamieGormley 4 9
(Alan Berry) *bhd and sn outpcd: struggling 1/2-way: sn btn* **66/1**

1m 1.87s (2.17) **Going Correction** +0.275s/f (Good) **9** Ran SP% **114.1**
Speed ratings (Par 93): **106,105,103,102,101 98,96,96,88**
CSF £12.18 CT £45.45 TOTE £3.60: £1.60, £1.40, £1.60; EX 12.10 Trifecta £54.50.
Owner Mrs Lesley-Anne Drummond **Bred** Russell Drummond **Trained** Carrutherstown, D'fries & G'way

FOCUS
An ordinary nursery. There was a sound pace on and the stands' rail was the place to be.

7735 IRISH STALLION FARMS EBF SCOTTISH PREMIER FILLIES' H'CAP 1m 2y
3:15 (3:15) (Class 3) (0-95,90) 3-Y-O+
£15,562 (£4,660; £2,330; £1,165; £582; £292) **Stalls** Low

Form RPR
0366 1 **Gometra Ginty (IRE)**[7] 7491 3-8-4 **72** ....(p[1]) ShaneGray 8 81
(Keith Dalgleish) *trckd ldr: rdn and led over 1f out: kpt on strly fnl f* **9/1**

161 2 1 1/2 **My Ukulele (IRE)**[9] 7404 3-8-1 **72** .... SeanDavis(3) 5 78+
(John Quinn) *hld up: rdn and effrt on outside over 2f out: hdwy to chse wnr ins fnl f: kpt on (jockey said filly slipped on the bend turning into the home straight)* **25/1**

2051 3 1 1/4 **Warning Fire**[8] 7471 3-9-8 **90** .... PJMcDonald 3 93
(Mark Johnston) *t.k.h: led: rdn and hdd over 1f out: rallied: lost 2nd ins fnl f: one pce* **13/2**

0004 4 1 1/4 **Dance Diva**[22] 6974 4-9-7 **85** ....(v[1]) PaulHanagan 1 85
(Richard Fahey) *trckd ldrs: rdn and edgd lft over 1f out: outpcd fnl f* **9/2**[2]

1003 5 3 3/4 **Kylie Rules**[8] 7430 4-9-7 **85** .... JamesSullivan 7 77
(Ruth Carr) *dwlt: t.k.h: hld up: rdn and outpcd over 2f out: hung rt and no imp fr over 1f out* **4/1**[1]

2152 6 1 **Sarvi**[7] 7491 4-8-8 **72** ....(p) PaddyMathers 6 61
(Jim Goldie) *dwlt: sn drvn along in rr: no imp fr over 2f out* **9/1**

3101 7 hd **Rux Ruxx (IRE)**[26] 6825 4-9-5 **83** ....(p) DavidAllan 4 72
(Tim Easterby) *prom: effrt and rdn over 2f out: wknd over 1f out* **9/2**[2]

0530 8 4 1/2 **Summer Daydream (IRE)**[10] 7366 3-8-11 **79** ....(p) CallumRodriguez 2 57
(Keith Dalgleish) *hld up on ins: drvn and struggling wl over 2f out: sn btn* **11/1**

1m 41.78s (1.78) **Going Correction** +0.275s/f (Good)
WFA 3 from 4yo 4lb **8** Ran SP% **114.7**
Speed ratings (Par 104): **102,100,99,98,94 93,93,88**
CSF £53.47 CT £317.61 TOTE £10.90: £3.20, £2.00, £2.20; EX 66.00 Trifecta £236.60.
Owner Ken McGarrity & Partner **Bred** Tally-Ho Stud **Trained** Carluke, S Lanarks

FOCUS
They went a fair pace in this feature handicap for fillies. Add 7yds.

7736 VIRGIN MEDIA OOMPH H'CAP 5f 1y
3:45 (3:46) (Class 4) (0-80,82) 3-Y-O+
£5,498 (£1,636; £817; £408; £400; £400) **Stalls** High

Form RPR
2516 1 **Afandem (IRE)**[18] 7077 5-9-1 **73** ....(p) NathanEvans 4 84
(Tim Easterby) *prom: smooth hdwy 1/2-way: shkn up to ld over 1f out: rdn clr fnl f: readily* **6/1**[3]

1156 2 4 **Boudica Bay (IRE)**[26] 6829 4-8-4 **62** .... JamesSullivan 6 59
(Eric Alston) *chsd ldr to over 2f out: cl up: effrt and chsd (clr) wnr ins fnl f: kpt on: no imp* **3/1**[2]

0460 **3** 1 1/2 **Royal Brave (IRE)**[32] 6607 8-9-8 **80**............................ DanielTudhope 3 71
(Rebecca Bastiman) *n.m.r s: hld up: effrt whn nt clr run fr 1/2-way to ins fnl f: kpt on to take 3rd cl home: no imp (jockey said gelding was continually denied a clear run in the final two furlongs)* **6/1**[3]

0221 **4** *nk* **Desert Ace (IRE)**[11] 7334 8-9-0 **72**............................ KevinStott 2 62
(Paul Midgley) *sn bhd: rdn and hdwy over 1f out: one pce ins fnl f* **6/1**[3]

1320 **5** 1 1/4 **Economic Crisis (IRE)**[10] 7367 10-8-7 **65**............................ CamHardie 1 51
(Alan Berry) *prom on outside: rdn along 2f out: wknd ins fnl f* **20/1**

6050 **6** 1/2 **Pavers Pride**[10] 7367 5-8-3 **61** oh1............................(b) DuranFentiman 5 45
(Noel Wilson) *dwlt: hld up bhd ldng gp: effrt and rdn over 1f out: wknd ins fnl f* **11/1**

4005 **7** 2 **Lomu (IRE)**[34] 6549 5-9-10 **82**............................(b[1]) CallumRodriguez 7 59
(Keith Dalgleish) *t.k.h: led: rdn and hdd over 1f out: wknd fnl f* **5/2**[1]

1m 0.22s (0.52) **Going Correction** +0.275s/f (Good) **7 Ran SP% 109.5**
Speed ratings (Par 105): **106,99,97,96,94 93,90**
CSF £22.22 TOTE £6.90: £2.60, £2.10; EX 26.90 Trifecta £127.50.
Owner Reality Partnerships Xi **Bred** Rabbah Bloodstock Limited **Trained** Great Habton, N Yorks

FOCUS
The stands' side was again favoured in this modest sprint handicap.

7737 ROYAL SCOTS CLUB H'CAP 5f 1y
4:20 (4:21) (Class 6) (0-55,54) 3-Y-O+
£2,911 (£866; £432; £400; £400; £400) **Stalls High**

Form RPR

0304 **1** **Astrophysics**[4] 7588 7-9-7 **54**............................(p) PaulMulrennan 10 66
(Lynn Siddall) *hld up in tch: smooth hdwy to ld over 1f out: pushed clr ins fnl f: readily* **4/1**[2]

4605 **2** 2 1/4 **Jeffrey Harris**[7] 7488 4-9-5 **52**............................ DanielTudhope 12 56
(Jim Goldie) *dwlt: hld up: shkn up and hdwy over 1f out: rdn and chsd wnr ins fnl f: kpt on: nt pce to chal* **9/4**[1]

2000 **3** 1 1/2 **Corton Lass**[10] 7367 4-8-12 **45**............................ CallumRodriguez 3 44
(Keith Dalgleish) *in tch on outside: effrt and ev ch briefly over 1f out: rdn and one pce ins fnl f* **25/1**

1323 **4** 2 **Thornaby Princess**[8] 7468 8-9-2 **49**............................(p) TomEaves 13 40
(Jason Ward) *midfield: pushed along 2f out: hdwy over 1f out: kpt on fnl f: nt pce to chal* **17/2**

-000 **5** *nse* **Little Miss Lola**[23] 6936 5-8-8 **46**............................ PaulaMuir(5) 6 37
(Lynn Siddall) *towards rr: rdn along 1/2-way: hdwy on outside over 1f out: kpt on fnl f: no imp* **28/1**

2155 **6** 1/2 **One Boy (IRE)**[7] 7487 8-9-5 **52**............................ KevinStott 4 41
(Paul Midgley) *hld up in tch: hdwy and cl up over 1f out: rdn and no ex ins fnl f* **9/2**[3]

000 **7** *hd* **Lady Joanna Vassa (IRE)**[2] 7651 6-8-12 **45**...........(v) ConnorBeasley 1 34
(Richard Guest) *cl up on outside: effrt and led briefly over 1f out: no ex ins fnl f* **33/1**

066 **8** 1/2 **Lord Of The Glen**[15] 7214 4-9-0 **47**............................(v) PaddyMathers 7 34
(Jim Goldie) *sn pushed along in rr: hdwy fnl f: kpt on: nvr able to chal* **17/2**

4-00 **9** 1 1/4 **Kemmeridge Bay**[251] 341 3-8-12 **46**............................ SamJames 9 28
(Grant Tuer) *w ldr to 1/2-way: rdn and wknd fnl f* **25/1**

-000 **10** 2 1/4 **Griffin Street**[7] 7488 6-8-7 **45**............................(b) AndrewBreslin(5) 8 19
(Alistair Whillans) *dwlt: bhd and outpcd: nvr on terms* **40/1**

00 **11** 1 1/2 **Poppy Jag (IRE)**[89] 4481 4-8-12 **45**............................ JasonHart 11 14
(Kevin Frost) *sn drvn along in rr: nvr on terms* **22/1**

6660 **12** 1 1/2 **Kyroc (IRE)**[153] 2197 3-8-12 **46**............................ PhilDennis 14 9
(Susan Corbett) *chsd ldrs: rdn over 2f out: wknd over 1f out* **40/1**

0014 **13** 3/4 **Bluella**[3] 7628 4-9-2 **49**............................(bt) AndrewMullen 5 10
(Robyn Brisland) *led tl rdn and hdd over 1f out: sn wknd* **14/1**

-000 **14** 1 1/2 **Laoise (USA)**[15] 7214 3-8-11 **45**............................ JamesSullivan 2
(Linda Perratt) *s.i.s: bhd: drvn along on outside over 2f out: wknd over 1f out* **50/1**

1m 1.05s (1.35) **Going Correction** +0.275s/f (Good)
WFA 3 from 4yo+ 1lb **14 Ran SP% 121.9**
Speed ratings (Par 101): **100,96,94,90,90 89,89,88,86,83 80,78,77,74**
CSF £12.24 CT £210.52 TOTE £4.00: £1.40, £1.50, £7.60; EX 14.20 Trifecta £293.80.
Owner Jimmy Kay **Bred** Sarah Stoneham **Trained** Colton, N Yorks

FOCUS
Straightforward sprint form for the class.

7738 ROYAL REGIMENT OF SCOTLAND H'CAP 1m 2y
4:55 (4:56) (Class 5) (0-70,72) 3-Y-O+
£3,557 (£1,058; £529; £400; £400; £400) **Stalls Low**

Form RPR

3200 **1** **How Bizarre**[15] 7212 4-9-12 **70**............................ DanielTudhope 8 75
(Liam Bailey) *mde all at modest gallop: rdn and hrd pressed over 1f out: hld on wl fnl f* **7/2**[2]

005 **2** *nk* **Princess Florence (IRE)**[32] 6610 3-8-3 **51** oh4............... CamHardie 5 55
(John Ryan) *trckd ldr: rdn and ev ch over 1f out: kpt on fnl f: hld cl home* **33/1**

061 **3** 3/4 **Donnelly's Rainbow (IRE)**[10] 7363 6-9-9 **67**............... JamieGormley 3 69
(Rebecca Bastiman) *hld up: pushed along over 2f out: hdwy to chse clr ldng pair over 1f out: kpt on fnl f* **7/2**[2]

6000 **4** 1 **Vive La Difference (IRE)**[10] 7364 5-9-10 **68**..................(b) DavidAllan 6 68
(Tim Easterby) *slowly away: t.k.h: hld up: hdwy on outside over 2f out: effrt: edgd rt and disp 3rd pl over 1f out: one pce ins fnl f (jockey said gelding was slowly away)* **2/1**[1]

0000 **5** 6 **Haymarket**[31] 6628 10-8-2 **51** oh6............................ AndrewBreslin(5) 11 37
(R Mike Smith) *hld up: rdn and outpcd over 2f out: no imp fr over 1f out* **50/1**

6011 **6** *nse* **Lagenda**[15] 7207 6-9-6 **64**............................ JasonHart 2 50
(Liam Bailey) *t.k.h: trckd ldrs: rdn over 2f out: wknd over 1f out* **5/1**[3]

0200 **7** 1/2 **Robben Rainbow**[8] 7443 5-8-7 **51** oh1............................ PhilDennis 9 36
(Katie Scott) *t.k.h: in tch: drvn along over 2f out: wknd over 1f out* **22/1**

1130 **8** 2 **La Sioux (IRE)**[17] 7125 5-9-7 **68**............................ SeanDavis(3) 7 48
(Richard Fahey) *fly-jmpd leaving stalls: hld up towards rr: drvn and outpcd 3f out: btn fnl 2f* **16/1**

4255 **9** 2 1/2 **Let Right Be Done**[33] 6572 7-8-7 **51** oh6..................(p) AndrewMullen 1 26
(Linda Perratt) *t.k.h: hld up on ins: drvn over 3f out: wknd over 2f out* **25/1**

1m 43.59s (3.59) **Going Correction** +0.275s/f (Good)
WFA 3 from 4yo+ 4lb **9 Ran SP% 113.4**
Speed ratings (Par 103): **93,92,91,90,84 84,84,82,79**
CSF £112.61 CT £433.01 TOTE £4.20: £1.70, £4.10, £1.50; EX 103.90 Trifecta £639.90.
Owner Harswell Thoroughbred Racing, Fpr Ltd **Bred** Mrs Janis Macpherson **Trained** Middleham, N Yorks

FOCUS
It paid to be handy in this ordinary handicap. Add 7yds.

7739 LG PHARMACY LYNN'S LAST GALLOP H'CAP (DIV II) 1m 4f 104y
5:25 (5:28) (Class 6) (0-60,60) 3-Y-O+
£2,911 (£866; £432; £400; £400; £400) **Stalls Low**

Form RPR

0354 **1** **Kaizer**[7] 7492 4-9-6 **54**............................ AndrewMullen 5 66+
(Alistair Whillans) *chsd ldrs: hdwy to ld over 2f out: rdn clr fnl f* **5/4**[1]

0000 **2** 7 **Gworn**[7] 7492 9-9-5 **53**............................ PJMcDonald 9 55
(R Mike Smith) *hld up in tch: hdwy over 2f out: effrt and chsd wnr over 1f out: no imp fnl f* **11/1**

0400 **3** 1 1/2 **Doon Star**[7] 7492 4-8-12 **46**............................ PaddyMathers 2 45
(Jim Goldie) *led 1f: chsd ldr: regained ld over 3f out: hdd over 2f out: chsd wnr to over 1f out: sn one pce* **7/1**[3]

4060 **4** 10 **So Hi Cardi (FR)**[34] 6552 3-8-6 **52**............................(h) PaulaMuir(5) 4 37
(Roger Fell) *hld up: rdn and outpcd over 5f out: rallied over 1f out: kpt on: no ch w first three* **11/1**

0006 **5** *shd* **Bannockburn (IRE)**[32] 6610 3-8-9 **50**............................(b[1]) ShaneGray 7 35
(Keith Dalgleish) *s.i.s: hdwy to ld after 1f rn wd bnd after 2f and reminders bnd ent bk st: hdd over 3f out: sn outpcd: rallied wl over 1f out: sn no imp* **4/1**[2]

4036 **6** *nk* **Life Knowledge (IRE)**[74] 4274 7-9-3 **51**............................ DanielTudhope 3 35
(Liam Bailey) *hld up in tch: outpcd whn n.m.r briefly over 2f out: n.d after* **8/1**

1000 **7** 8 **Strategic (IRE)**[26] 6828 4-8-12 **46** oh1............................(h) JasonHart 8 18
(Eric Alston) *hld up: drvn and struggling over 3f out: btn fnl 2f (vet said gelding lost it's right fore shoe)* **10/1**

000/ **8** 3/4 **Satis House**[329] 2921 5-8-12 **46** oh1............................(t) PaulMulrennan 6 17
(Susan Corbett) *hld up: rdn and struggling over 3f out: sn btn* **22/1**

2m 48.39s (3.89) **Going Correction** +0.275s/f (Good)
WFA 3 from 4yo+ 7lb **8 Ran SP% 118.2**
Speed ratings (Par 101): **98,93,92,85,85 85,80,79**
CSF £17.65 CT £74.55 TOTE £2.00: £1.10, £3.60, £2.40; EX 18.40 Trifecta £75.90.
Owner Mrs Elizabeth Ferguson **Bred** Mrs James Wigan **Trained** Newmill-On-Slitrig, Borders
■ Stewards' Enquiry : Shane Gray four-day ban; failure to obtain best possible placing (Oct 13-16)

FOCUS
This second division of the moderate 1m4f handicap was run at a solid pace yet it was 4.8secs slower. Add 7yds.
T/Plt: £18.50 to a £1 stake. Pool: £76,312.47 - 3005.07 winning units T/Qpdt: £16.20 to a £1 stake. Pool: £7,127.64 - 324.59 winning units **Richard Young**

7740 - 7741a (Foreign Racing) - See Raceform Interactive

7712

CURRAGH (R-H)
Sunday, September 29

OFFICIAL GOING: Heavy

7742a WELD PARK STKS (GROUP 3) (FILLIES) 7f
2:50 (2:53) 2-Y-O **£35,878** (£11,554; £5,472; £2,432; £1,216; £608)

RPR

1 **New York Girl (IRE)**[28] 6761 2-9-0 0............................ ShaneCrosse 2 105
(Joseph Patrick O'Brien, Ire) *w.w: 8th 1/2-way: n.m.r briefly 2f out where tk clsr order: rdn into 3rd over 1f out and r.o wl ins fnl f to ld fnl strides* **12/1**

2 *nk* **A New Dawn (IRE)**[30] 6689 2-9-0 96............................ WayneLordan 5 104
(Joseph Patrick O'Brien, Ire) *chsd ldrs: disp 4th at 1/2-way: pushed along over 2f out where n.m.r briefly: sn wnt 2nd and rdn: kpt on wl u.p ins fnl f to dispute ld briefly fnl strdes where hdd* **6/1**

3 1/2 **Know It All**[37] 6429 2-9-0 98............................ RonanWhelan 6 103+
(J P Murtagh, Ire) *cl up bhd ldr: cl 2nd at 1/2-way: led travelling wl over 2f out: extended advantage and 2 l clr 1 1/2f out: sn rdn and reduced ld wl ins fnl f where strly pressed: hdd fnl strides and dropped to 3rd* **9/2**[2]

4 4 1/2 **Shehreen (IRE)**[12] 7325 2-9-0 0............................ OisinOrr 1 92
(D K Weld, Ire) *hooded to load: hld up: short of room briefly after 1f: 7th 1/2-way: checked 2f out: hdwy in 8th 1 1/2f out: n.m.r briefly and swtchd rt over 1f out: r.o between horses into nvr threatening 4th* **12/1**

5 1 1/4 **Nope (IRE)**[55] 5752 2-9-0 88............................ TomMadden 9 89+
(Mrs John Harrington, Ire) *rrd and s.i.s: detached in rr: pushed along and no imp stl in rr over 2f out: swtchd lft ins fnl f and r.o wl: nrst fin* **25/1**

6 1 1/4 **Unknown Pleasures (IRE)**[28] 6761 2-9-0 0............................ ShaneFoley 7 86
(Mrs John Harrington, Ire) *chsd ldrs: 3rd 1/2-way: drvn bhd ldrs over 2f out and no ex u.p 1 1/2f out: sn wknd* **5/1**[3]

7 2 3/4 **Love Locket (IRE)**[11] 7353 2-9-0 0............................ DonnachaO'Brien 3 79
(A P O'Brien, Ire) *disp ld early tl sn settled bhd ldrs: disp 4th at 1/2-way: rdn over 2f out where n.m.r briefly and sn wknd: no imp whn short of room again 1f out: eased* **6/1**

8 1 **Tasalka (IRE)**[31] 6645 2-9-0 0............................ ChrisHayes 4 76
(D K Weld, Ire) *sn disp and led after 1f: narrow advantage at 1/2-way: rdn and hdd over 2f out: wknd in 3rd 1 1/2f out: eased (vet said filly sustained a wound to the lateral aspect of her left hind cannon)* **7/2**[1]

9 3/4 **Deidra (IRE)**[11] 7353 2-9-0 0............................ LeighRoche 8 74
(M D O'Callaghan, Ire) *dwlt and settled towards rr: 6th 1/2-way: pushed along and tk clsr order nr side over 2f out: rdn and no ex 1 1/2f out: sn wknd: eased ins fnl f* **7/1**

1m 30.14s (5.14) **Going Correction** +0.80s/f (Soft) **9 Ran SP% 117.4**
Speed ratings: **102,101,101,95,94 93,89,88,87**
CSF £83.34 TOTE £15.20: £3.60, £2.10, £1.50; DF 88.70 Trifecta £656.10.
Owner Mark Dobbin **Bred** P F Kelly & Peter Kelly **Trained** Owning Hill, Co Kilkenny

FOCUS
A race that did not seem to have an outstanding candidate and that was probably borne out by the outcome.

7743a (Foreign Racing) - See Raceform Interactive

7744a BERESFORD STKS (GROUP 2) 1m
4:00 (4:01) 2-Y-O **£58,468** (£18,828; £8,918; £3,963; £1,981)

RPR

1 **Innisfree (IRE)**[62] 5506 2-9-3 0............................ DonnachaO'Brien 3 108+
(A P O'Brien, Ire) *chsd ldr: 4 l bhd in 2nd at 1/2-way: tk clsr order bhd ldr after 1/2-way: travelling wl over 2f out: pushed along to chal 1 1/2f out: rdn over 1f out and sn disp ld: styd on wl to ld narrowly cl home* **4/6**[1]

2 *nk* **Shekhem (IRE)**[18] 7091 2-9-3 91............................ ChrisHayes 2 107
(D K Weld, Ire) *attempted to make all: racd keenly early: 4 l clr bef 1/2-way: reduced ld after 1/2-way: stl gng wl 2f out where pressed: rdn over 1f out and sn jnd: hdd narrowly cl home: kpt on wl* **11/4**[2]

3 3 3/4 **Gold Maze**[37] 6427 2-9-3 0 ShaneFoley 6 99
(Mrs John Harrington, Ire) *chsd ldrs in 3rd: pushed along bhd ldrs into st: rdn in 3rd 1 1/2f out and no ex ins fnl f: kpt on same pce* **9/1**

4 6 1/2 **Camorra (IRE)**[39] 6357 2-9-3 0 ColinKeane 1 85
(G M Lyons, Ire) *got upset in stalls: dwlt: chsd ldrs in 4th: drvn in 4th into st and no imp on ldrs: one pce fnl 2f* **6/1**[3]

5 12 **Silvertown (IRE)**[37] 6427 2-9-3 0 RonanWhelan 7 58
(A Oliver, Ire) *dwlt: in rr thrght: drvn into st and no imp on ldrs: wknd* **50/1**

1m 50.06s (9.46) **Going Correction** +0.80s/f (Soft) **5** Ran SP% **112.9**
Speed ratings: **84,83,79,73,61**
CSF £2.90 TOTE £1.40: £1.02, £1.70; DF 2.80 Trifecta £7.30.
Owner D Smith & Mrs J Magnier & M Tabor & Mrs A M O'Brie **Bred** Whisperview Trading Ltd **Trained** Cashel, Co Tipperary

FOCUS
An interesting clash between two colts with nothing between them and what happens next year is eagerly awaited.

7745 - 7748a (Foreign Racing) - See Raceform Interactive

7004 DUSSELDORF (R-H)
Sunday, September 29

OFFICIAL GOING: Turf: soft

7749a RACEBETS.DE - WINTERKONIGIN-TRIAL (LISTED RACE) (2YO FILLIES) (TURF) 7f 110y
2:55 2-Y-O **£12,612** (£5,855; £2,702; £1,351)

RPR

1 **Romsey**[36] 6444 2-9-2 0 GeraldMosse 4 97
(Hughie Morrison) *cl up 1f: trckd ldr: shkn up in 2nd 2f out: hdwy ins fnl f to ld 110yds out: drvn out* **17/10**[1]

2 3/4 **Sound Machine (GER)**[92] 4417 2-9-2 0 LukasDelozier 6 95
(Mario Hofer, Germany) **9/2**[3]

3 3/4 **Flamingo Girl (GER)**[49] 2-9-2 0 BayarsaikhanGanbat 3 93
(Henk Grewe, Germany) **32/5**

4 2 **Lips Eagle (GER)**[56] 2-8-11 0 AndraschStarke 5 84
(Andreas Suborics, Germany) **11/2**

5 3 1/2 **Sea Of Love (GER)** 2-8-11 0 MaximPecheur 2 76
(Markus Klug, Germany) **9/1**

6 3/4 **Amalita (GER)** 2-8-11 0 FilipMinarik 1 74
(Jean-Pierre Carvalho, Germany) **31/10**[2]

1m 33.36s **6** Ran SP% **118.5**
PARI-MUTUEL (all including 1 euro stake): WIN 2.70; PLACE 2.10, 2.40; SF 11.30.
Owner The End-R-Ways Partnership & Partners **Bred** The Lavington Stud **Trained** East Ilsley, Berks

7750a 99TH GROSSER PREIS DER LANDESHAUPTSTADT DUSSELDORF (GROUP 3) (3YO+) (TURF) 1m 110y
4:10 3-Y-O+ **£28,828** (£10,810; £5,405; £2,702; £1,801)

RPR

1 **Kronprinz (GER)**[70] 5230 4-9-2 0 LukasDelozier 2 105
(P Schiergen, Germany) *settled bhd ldng pair: effrt and qcknd to ld over 1 1/2f out: rdn along over 1f out: r.o strly fnl f* **176/10**

2 4 **Ninario (GER)**[28] 6770 4-9-0 MarcoCasamento 6 94
(Waldemar Hickst, Germany) *in rr of midfield: swtchd lft and rdn along 1 1/2f out: styd on wl fnl f to take 2nd fnl strides* **89/10**

3 nse **Broderie**[70] 5230 4-8-13 0 VincentCheminaud 4 93
(H-A Pantall, France) *midfield: tk clsr order 2f out: rdn along and wnt 2nd over 1f out: sn outpcd by wnr: lost 2nd fnl strides: all out* **33/10**[2]

4 hd **Nica (GER)**[28] 6770 4-8-13 0 RenePiechulek 1 92
(Dr A Bolte, Germany) *led after 1f: drvn along over 2f out: hdd over 1 1/2f out: sn rdn: kpt on same pce* **1/1**[1]

5 2 1/4 **Sun At Work (GER)**[49] 7-9-2 0 MaximPecheur 5 91
(W Haustein, Germany) *led 1f: trckd ldr: rdn along and lost position 2f out: kpt on same pce* **178/10**

6 1 1/2 **Emerita (GER)**[42] 6270 4-8-13 0 AndraschStarke 7 84
(H-J Groschel, Germany) *wnt lft s: settled in last: effrt under 2f out: kpt on: nvr on terms* **36/5**

7 3 **Bella Ragazza**[102] 3986 4-8-10 0 GeraldMosse 8 75
(Hughie Morrison) *carried lft s: towards rr on outer: drvn along to stay in tch over 2f out: plugged on same pce: eased in last cl home* **32/5**[3]

1m 46.55s (-1.03) **7** Ran SP% **119.8**
PARI-MUTUEL (all including 1 euro stake): WIN 18.60 PLACE: 3.90, 2.50, 1.80; SF: 35.20.
Owner Abdulmagid A Alyousfi **Bred** Gestut Etzean **Trained** Germany

7751 - 7753a (Foreign Racing) - See Raceform Interactive

7227 BATH (L-H)
Monday, September 30

OFFICIAL GOING: Good to soft (soft in places; 6.5) changing to soft after race 6 (4.40)
Wind: Fresh half-against Weather: Overcast turning to rain after race 5

7754 HOBBS SHOW BORN AND RAISED IN BRISTOL NURSERY H'CAP 5f 160y
2:00 (2:03) (Class 5) (0-75,75) 2-Y-O
£3,428 (£1,020; £509; £300; £300; £300) **Stalls** Centre

Form RPR

033 1 **Gleeds Girl**[10] 7407 2-9-0 **68** TomMarquand 8 71
(Mick Channon) *a.p: rdn to ld ins fnl f: r.o* **11/2**[3]

604 2 3/4 **Live In The Moment (IRE)**[10] 7407 2-9-5 **73** RobertHavlin 12 74
(Adam West) *chsd ldrs: rdn to ld over 1f out: hdd ins fnl f: styd on* **12/1**

6060 3 nk **Shani**[6] 7556 2-8-4 **58** (p) KieranO'Neill 1 58
(John Bridger) *led: rdn and hdd over 1f out: ev ch ins fnl f: no ex towards fin* **25/1**

350 4 1/2 **Global Agreement**[35] 6528 2-8-12 **66** HollieDoyle 16 64
(Milton Harris) *prom: pushed along and lost pl after 1f: rdn 1/2-way: hdwy on outer over 1f out: r.o* **14/1**

533 5 1 1/2 **Sky Vega (IRE)**[18] 7113 2-9-7 **75** SeanLevey 3 68
(Richard Hannon) *sn pushed along in rr: hdwy 3f out: rdn and hung rt over 2f out: styd on same pce ins fnl f* **5/1**[2]

0554 6 shd **Bowling Russian (IRE)**[38] 6403 2-9-2 **70** PatCosgrave 13 63
(George Baker) *prom: hung lft and lost pl over 4f out: hdwy over 1f out: sn rdn: styd on same pce ins fnl f* **5/1**[2]

004 7 3/4 **Rushcutters Bay**[16] 7186 2-8-6 **60** MartinDwyer 5 51
(Hugo Palmer) *s.i.s: hdwy 3f out: rdn and ev ch wl over 1f out: no ex ins fnl f* **9/1**

666 8 1 1/4 **Kocasandra (IRE)**[10] 7419 2-9-5 **73** (b[1]) AdamMcNamara 7 59
(Archie Watson) *chsd ldr: rdn and ev ch 2f out: wknd wl ins fnl f* **16/1**

4230 9 1 1/2 **Goodwood Rebel (IRE)**[17] 7155 2-9-5 **73** HarryBentley 14 55
(Ralph Beckett) *s.i.s: styd on ins fnl f: nvr nrr* **11/1**

3331 10 shd **Colonel Whitehead (IRE)**[16] 7186 2-8-10 **71** EllieMacKenzie[(7)] 4 52
(Heather Main) *prom: rdn over 1f out: wknd ins fnl f* **7/2**[1]

4020 11 7 **King's View (IRE)**[17] 7155 2-8-8 **67** ThoreHammerHansen[(5)] 2 25
(Richard Hannon) *s.i.s: hdwy 4f out: wknd fnl f* **16/1**

0230 12 22 **Littleton Hall (IRE)**[147] 2476 2-9-5 **73** CallumShepherd 11
(Mick Channon) *sn outpcd: eased over 1f out* **50/1**

404 13 8 **Liscahann**[28] 6800 2-8-9 **66** GeorgiaCox[(3)] 9
(Seamus Mullins) *chsd ldrs: pushed along and lost pl over 3f out: wknd 1/2-way* **33/1**

1m 11.5s (0.40) **Going Correction** +0.10s/f (Good) **13** Ran SP% **124.1**
Speed ratings (Par 95): **101,100,99,98,96 96,95,94,92,92 82,53,42**
CSF £71.87 CT £1600.84 TOTE £5.90: £2.30, £3.60, £9.90; EX 56.70 Trifecta £676.00.
Owner Trojan Way & Partner **Bred** Aston Mullins Stud **Trained** West Ilsley, Berks

FOCUS
A total of 30mm rainfall over the weekend eased the usually quick going to good to soft all over.\n\x\x It paid to be handy in this modest nursery, with the main action developing down the centre. The winning time suggested the going was still lively enough. Limited late-season form.

7755 MATCHBOOK EBF FUTURE STAYERS' NOVICE STKS (PLUS 10 RACE) (SIRE AND DAM RESTRICTED RACE) 1m
2:30 (2:34) (Class 4) 2-Y-O **£9,056** (£2,695; £1,346; £673) **Stalls** Low

Form RPR

6 1 **Surrey Pride (IRE)**[17] 7162 2-9-2 0 CharlesBishop 3 78
(Joseph Tuite) *hdwy over 6f out: chsd ldr over 2f out: rdn to ld 1f out: r.o* **4/1**[3]

2 nk **So I Told You (IRE)** 2-8-8 0 FinleyMarsh[(3)] 5 73+
(Richard Hughes) *prom: nt clr run and lost pl over 2f out: sn swtchd rt: hdwy over 1f out: r.o wl* **20/1**

544 3 1 1/4 **Vulcan (IRE)**[24] 6926 2-9-2 77 (p[1]) JasonWatson 9 75
(Harry Dunlop) *led 7f out: rdn: hung rt and hdd 1f out: no ex towards fin (jockey said colt hung right-handed under pressure)* **14/1**

0 4 2 **Damage Control**[25] 6905 2-9-2 0 DavidProbert 11 71
(Andrew Balding) *chsd ldr over 6f out tl rdn and hung lft over 2f out: styd on same pce ins fnl f (jockey said colt ran green)* **9/4**[1]

5 2 **Midnights Legacy** 2-9-2 0 HollieDoyle 2 66+
(Alan King) *s.i.s: hld up: r.o ins fnl f: nt rch ldrs* **33/1**

5 6 1 **Sea Of Marmoon**[73] 5139 2-8-11 0 DaneO'Neill 6 59
(Mark Johnston) *chsd ldrs: rdn over 1f out: wknd ins fnl f* **25/1**

415 7 nk **Passing Fashion (IRE)**[38] 6417 2-9-5 90 HarryBentley 8 66
(Ralph Beckett) *racd keenly: led 1f: remained handy: shkn up and nt clr run over 2f out: rdn over 1f out: wknd fnl f* **3/1**[2]

24 8 1/2 **Bentley Wood**[5] 7586 2-9-2 0 TomMarquand 1 62
(Mick Channon) *hld up: nt clr run over 5f out: swtchd rt and hdwy over 2f out: rdn over 1f out: hung lft and wknd ins fnl f* **5/1**

0 9 1 1/2 **Derek Le Grand**[15] 7235 2-9-2 0 RossaRyan 4 59
(Grace Harris) *s.i.s: effrt over 2f out: styd on same pce fr over 1f out* **66/1**

0 10 hd **Grinling (IRE)**[24] 6912 2-9-2 0 (h) SeanLevey 7 59
(Richard Hannon) *s.i.s: sn pushed along in rr: nvr on terms* **40/1**

4 11 1 1/4 **High Shine**[33] 6603 2-8-11 0 (h) CallumShepherd 10 51
(Michael Bell) *s.i.s: nvr on terms* **33/1**

6 12 4 1/2 **Molinari (IRE)**[15] 7235 2-9-2 0 MartinDwyer 12 46
(William Muir) *chsd ldrs on outer: rdn over 2f out: wknd over 1f out* **12/1**

06 13 10 **Erika**[28] 6800 2-8-11 0 RobertHavlin 13 19
(Neil Mulholland) *difficult to load: broke wl and plld hrd: sn stdd but remained prom: hung rt over 3f out: wknd over 2f out (jockey said filly hung right-handed)* **100/1**

1m 43.04s (1.34) **Going Correction** +0.10s/f (Good) **13** Ran SP% **126.2**
Speed ratings (Par 97): **97,96,95,93,91 90,90,89,88,87 86,82,72**
CSF £88.61 TOTE £5.00: £1.50, £4.60, £3.30; EX 105.30 Trifecta £1299.60.
Owner Surrey Racing (SP) **Bred** Vimal And Gillian Khosla **Trained** Lambourn, Berks

FOCUS
Not a bad novice event, confined to 2yos whose dam/sire won over 1m2f or further. It proved a solid test. The third has been rated to his best.

7756 EMPIRE FIGHTING CHANCE KEYNSHAM 10K H'CAP 1m 2f 37y
3:05 (3:05) (Class 5) (0-70,70) 3-Y-O+
£3,428 (£1,020; £509; £300; £300; £300) **Stalls** Low

Form RPR

3104 1 **Mandocello (FR)**[38] 6414 3-9-4 **69** CharlieBennett 11 76
(Rod Millman) *hld up: shkn up over 2f out: swtchd lft and hdwy over 1f out: rdn to ld wl ins fnl f: r.o* **8/1**[3]

5163 2 1 1/4 **Debbonair (IRE)**[24] 6940 3-9-1 **66** (b) JackMitchell 7 70
(Hugo Palmer) *prom: rdn over 2f out: styd on same pce wl ins fnl f* **6/1**[2]

-505 3 nk **Cheeky Rascal (IRE)**[15] 7233 4-9-7 **67** (v) TomMarquand 6 70
(Tom Ward) *hld up: rdn over 2f out: hdwy over 1f out: styd on* **28/1**

0330 4 1/2 **Highway One (USA)**[181] 1497 5-9-0 **60** PatCosgrave 4 62
(George Baker) *stall opened fractionally early: led 1f: chsd ldrs: led over 2f out: rdn and hung rt fr over 1f out: hdd and unable qck wl ins fnl f* **16/1**

0010 5 2 **Gloweth**[72] 5178 4-9-3 **63** JasonWatson 13 61
(Stuart Kittow) *prom: lost pl over 8f out: hdwy on outer over 3f out: sn rdn: styd on same pce ins fnl f* **6/1**[2]

0142 6 1/2 **Capriolette (IRE)**[15] 7238 4-9-7 **70** CierenFallon[(3)] 10 67
(Ed Walker) *chsd ldrs: shkn up over 2f out: ev ch over 1f out: hmpd ins fnl f: cl up whn hmpd again and lost all ch wl ins fnl f* **11/4**[1]

4206 7 3/4 **Perfect Grace**[15] 7233 3-9-3 **68** (p) HollieDoyle 1 64
(Archie Watson) *pushed along leaving stalls: led after 1f: rdn and hdd over 2f out: ev ch ins fnl f: wknd towards fin (vet said filly had thumps shortly after the race)* **12/1**

0656 8 1/2 **Uther Pendragon (IRE)**[37] 6447 4-9-10 **70** (p) LiamKeniry 3 65
(J S Moore) *s.i.s: hld up: hdwy over 2f out: rdn over 1f out: wknd ins fnl f* **12/1**

02-0 9 3 **Doctor Jazz (IRE)**[69] 4601 4-9-6 **66** AlistairRawlinson 2 55
(Michael Appleby) *hld up in tch: rdn over 2f out: wknd over 1f out* **20/1**

6260 10 hd **Perfect Refuge**[19] 7083 4-9-8 **68** HectorCrouch 5 57
(Clive Cox) *hld up: nt clr run over 2f out: hmpd over 1f out: n.d* **8/1**[3]

50 11 7 **Less Of That (IRE)**[139] 2714 5-9-4 **64** MartinDwyer 8 39
(Debbie Hughes) *chsd ldrs: lost pl 8f out: hdwy on outer over 2f out: wknd fnl f* **25/1**

6062 **12** *2 3/4* **Ekayburg (FR)**[59] 4287 5-8-13 **62**.........................(t[1] w) FinleyMarsh(3) 12 31
(David Pipe) *s.i.s: hdwy 8f out: chsd ldr over 6f out: ev ch over 2f out: wknd over 1f out (jockey said gelding stopped quickly)* **8/1**[3]

2m 11.9s (0.80) **Going Correction** +0.10s/f (Good) **12** Ran SP% **121.9**
WFA 3 from 4yo+ 5lb
Speed ratings (Par 103): **100,99,98,98,96 96,95,95,92,92 87,85**
CSF £55.69 CT £1306.51 TOTE £9.80: £2.80, £2.10, £7.20; EX 58.90 Trifecta £1503.10.
Owner D J Deer **Bred** Oakgrove Stud **Trained** Kentisbeare, Devon
■ Stewards' Enquiry : Pat Cosgrave three-day ban; careless riding (Oct 14-16)

FOCUS
This open-looking handicap saw changing fortunes inside the final furlong. It's been rated around the second and third.

7757 STARSPORTS.BET H'CAP 5f 10y
3:35 (3:36) (Class 6) (0-65,64) 3-Y-O+

£2,781 (£827; £413; £300; £300; £300) **Stalls** Centre

Form RPR

0460 **1** **Powerful Dream (IRE)**[15] 7230 6-9-3 **57**.....................(p) DavidProbert 14 67
(Ronald Harris) *mid-div: hdwy over 1f out: sn rdn: r.o to ld nr fin* **16/1**

0533 **2** *hd* **Firenze Rosa (IRE)**[5] 7568 4-7-12 **45**............................ AledBeech(7) 2 54
(John Bridger) *chsd ldrs: led 1/2-way: rdn and edgd rt over 1f out: hdd nr fin* **11/2**[2]

0541 **3** *1 3/4* **Pettochside**[5] 7568 10-9-4 **63**.. TobyEley(5) 6 66
(John Bridger) *prom: pushed along over 3f out: sn outpcd: hdwy u.p over 1f out: r.o* **2/1**[1]

4060 **4** *1 1/2* **Autumn Splendour (IRE)**[17] 7157 3-9-4 **59**...............(p) PhilipPrince 3 57
(Milton Bradley) *sn led: hdd 1/2-way: rdn over 1f out: no ex ins fnl f* **50/1**

0403 **5** *hd* **Mayfair Madame**[38] 6397 3-8-13 **54**.............................. JasonWatson 9 51
(Stuart Kittow) *mid-div: rdn over 1f out: r.o ins fnl f: nvr nrr* **14/1**

3215 **6** *1 1/4* **Big Time Maybe (IRE)**[14] 7274 4-9-5 **62**...............(p) CierenFallon(3) 5 54
(Michael Attwater) *mid-div: rdn over 3f out: r.o ins fnl f: nrst fin* **7/1**[3]

0003 **7** *hd* **David's Beauty (IRE)**[8] 7488 6-9-1 **55**.........................(b) RossaRyan 16 47
(Brian Baugh) *chsd ldrs on outer: rdn over 1f out: styd on same pce* **20/1**

0004 **8** *3/4* **Bahamian Sunrise**[17] 7161 7-9-4 **58**.........................(b) HectorCrouch 11 47
(John Gallagher) *led early: chsd ldrs: rdn 1/2-way: wknd wl ins fnl f* **10/1**

2130 **9** *3/4* **Tawaafoq**[15] 7230 5-9-0 **57**..(h) FinleyMarsh(3) 4 43
(Adrian Wintle) *chsd ldrs: rdn over 1f out: nt clr run: swtchd rt and wknd ins fnl f* **14/1**

2332 **10** *hd* **Princely**[15] 7230 4-9-10 **64**.. EoinWalsh 10 50
(Tony Newcombe) *hld up: plld hrd: shkn up over 1f out: nvr nr to chal (jockey said colt ran too free in the early stages and was never travelling. Trainer said colt was unsuited by being held up on this occasion and would benefit from more positive tactics)* **11/2**[2]

04 **11** *1* **The Golden Cue**[45] 6168 4-9-2 **56**................................. KieranO'Neill 15 38
(Steph Hollinshead) *s.i.s: sn chsng ldrs: rdn over 2f out: wknd ins fnl f* **25/1**

0006 **12** *1 1/2* **Who Told Jo Jo (IRE)**[81] 4824 5-9-1 **55**........................ CharlesBishop 7 32
(Joseph Tuite) *hld up: pushed along 1/2-way: n.d* **33/1**

-600 **13** *3/4* **Staffa (IRE)**[6] 7557 6-8-4 **51**..(v[1]) MichaelPitt(7) 13 25
(Denis Coakley) *s.i.s: outpcd* **66/1**

4043 **14** *3 1/4* **Molly Blake**[6] 7557 3-9-1 **56**..(p[1]) LiamKeniry 1 18
(Clive Cox) *edgd lft s: sn in tch: rdn 1/2-way: wknd wl over 1f out* **16/1**

/000 **15** *1 1/2* **Picc And Go**[16] 7172 6-8-5 **45**.......................................(b) MartinDwyer 8 2
(Debbie Hughes) *s.i.s: outpcd* **50/1**

1m 1.9s (-0.10) **Going Correction** +0.10s/f (Good) **15** Ran SP% **127.8**
WFA 3 from 4yo+ 1lb
Speed ratings (Par 101): **104,103,100,98,98 96,95,94,93,93 91,89,87,82,80**
CSF £101.87 CT £269.41 TOTE £16.50: £4.60, £1.60, £1.40; EX 165.40 Trifecta £787.50.
Owner Ridge House Stables Ltd **Bred** Ballyhane Stud **Trained** Earlswood, Monmouths

FOCUS
A moderate sprint handicap in which it again paid to race centrally in the home straight.

7758 EMPIRE FIGHTING CHANCE "TRAINING WITH THE CHAMPIONS" H'CAP 1m
4:10 (4:12) (Class 6) (0-65,64) 3-Y-O+

£2,781 (£827; £413; £300; £300; £300) **Stalls** Low

Form RPR

5340 **1** **Espresso Freddo (IRE)**[7] 7527 5-9-6 **58**.....................(v) DaneO'Neill 7 70
(Robert Stephens) *s.s: bhd: hdwy to ld wl over 1f out: rdn clr: easily (Trainer said, regards apparent improvement in form, gelding was suited by a change of headgear from cheek-pieces to a visor and the ground was also beneficial)* **8/1**[3]

6461 **2** *4* **Mabo**[15] 7236 4-9-2 **54**...(b) RossaRyan 14 56
(Grace Harris) *s.i.s: hdwy 6f out: rdn over 2f out: styd on same pce fnl f* **6/1**[2]

006U **3** *nk* **Dancing Jo**[5] 7573 3-9-5 **61**.....................................(p) CallumShepherd 6 63
(Mick Channon) *chsd ldrs: wnt 2nd over 2f out: sn rdn and ev ch: styd on same pce fnl f* **14/1**

5433 **4** *1/2* **Vipin (FR)**[15] 7236 4-9-5 **60**... GeorgiaCox(3) 10 60
(William Muir) *s.i.s: pushed along in rr: nt clr run over 2f out: styd on fr over 1f out* **6/1**[2]

3010 **5** *2 1/4* **Incentive**[34] 6567 5-9-5 **64**.......................................(p) AngusVilliers(7) 13 59
(Stuart Kittow) *chsd ldrs: rdn over 2f out: sn ev ch: wknd ins fnl f* **20/1**

0450 **6** *1/2* **Bakht A Rawan (IRE)**[32] 6643 7-9-1 **56**.......................... CierenFallon(3) 2 50
(Roger Teal) *s.i.s: pushed along in rr: hdwy u.p over 2f out: wknd ins fnl f* **8/1**[3]

1230 **7** *8* **Confrerie (IRE)**[53] 5842 4-9-9 **61**..................................... PatCosgrave 1 38
(George Baker) *hld up in tch: rdn over 2f out: wknd fnl f* **9/1**

0460 **8** *hd* **Dreaming Of Paris**[13] 7299 5-9-10 **62**.........................(v) LiamKeniry 11 38+
(Patrick Chamings) *led: rdn and hdd wl over 1f out: sn wknd* **20/1**

4-12 **9** *nk* **Scoffsman**[94] 4336 4-9-10 **62**... DanielMuscutt 8 38
(Kevin Frost) *s.i.s: racd keenly and sn prom: shkn up on outer over 2f out: wknd over 1f out (jockey said gelding ran too free)* **6/4**[1]

6000 **10** *15* **Face Like Thunder**[151] 2349 4-9-5 **57**.......................(p[1]) JoeyHaynes 9 +
(John Butler) *prom: racd keenly: jnd ldr over 6f out tl over 4f out: rdn and lost 2nd over 2f out: sn wknd and eased* **25/1**

1m 41.94s (0.24) **Going Correction** +0.10s/f (Good) **10** Ran SP% **120.8**
WFA 3 from 4yo+ 4lb
Speed ratings (Par 101): **102,98,97,97,94 94,86,86,85,70**
CSF £55.78 CT £694.64 TOTE £7.80: £2.30, £2.40, £3.60; EX 64.90 Trifecta £633.50.
Owner Threes Company **Bred** Knocklong House Stud **Trained** Penhow, Newport

FOCUS
Another handicap that saw a messy start and changing fortunes late in the piece. Straightforward form in behind the winner.

7759 FOOT ANSTEY SUPPORTING EMPIRE FIGHTING CHANCE H'CAP 1m 5f 11y
4:40 (4:40) (Class 6) (0-60,58) 3-Y-O+

£2,781 (£827; £413; £300; £300; £300) **Stalls** High

Form RPR

6636 **1** **Sea Art**[14] 7280 3-9-3 **57**...(v) JasonWatson 2 65
(William Knight) *led after 1f: sn hdd: chsd ldr: rdn to ld over 1f out: styd on wl* **9/2**[2]

6235 **2** *1 1/4* **Givepeaceachance**[47] 6077 4-9-7 **54**............................ CharlesBishop 6 58
(Denis Coakley) *pushed along to ld 1f: remained handy: rdn and ev ch fr over 1f out tl no ex nr fin* **8/1**

0500 **3** *3* **Famous Dynasty (IRE)**[15] 7240 5-9-2 **49**............................ DaneO'Neill 1 49
(Michael Blanshard) *chsd ldrs: led 2f out: sn rdn: edgd lft and hdd: no ex wl ins fnl f* **50/1**

4321 **4** *3 1/4* **Celtic Classic (IRE)**[14] 7280 3-9-4 **58**............................(b) RossaRyan 12 55
(Paul Cole) *s.i.s: sn rcvrd to chse ldrs: rdn and nt clr run over 2f out: hung lft and wknd ins fnl f (jockey said gelding hung left-handed)* **7/2**[1]

06 **5** *2 1/4* **Foresee (GER)**[11] 7390 6-9-4 **51**...................................... TomMarquand 9 42
(Tony Carroll) *prom: chsd ldr over 11f out: led over 2f out: sn rdn: edgd rt and hdd: wknd ins fnl f* **11/2**[3]

0430 **6** *3 1/2* **Normandy Blue**[76] 5029 4-9-3 **50**....................................(p) EoinWalsh 7 36
(Luke McJannet) *hld up: pushed along 1/2-way: nvr nrr* **33/1**

0652 **7** *1/2* **Hatsaway (IRE)**[16] 7202 8-9-5 **55**...........................(p) PaddyBradley(3) 10 40
(Pat Phelan) *w ldrs tl over 11f out: remained handy: rdn over 2f out: hung lft and wknd over 1f out (jockey said gelding ran flat)* **9/2**[2]

0361 **8** *3/4* **Good Impression**[15] 7240 4-9-6 **56**..........................(p) CierenFallon(3) 3 40
(Dai Burchell) *bhd 10f out: nvr on terms (jockey said gelding was never travelling)* **8/1**

3462 **9** *1/2* **Butterfield (IRE)**[54] 5802 6-9-3 **50**................................... HollieDoyle 5 34
(Brian Forsey) *hld up: bhd fnl 9f (jockey said gelding was never travelling)* **16/1**

1346 **10** *hd* **Becky Sharp**[40] 6333 4-9-2 **49**.....................................(b) CharlieBennett 13 32
(Jim Boyle) *s.i.s: rcvrd on outer to ld over 11f out: rdn and hdd over 2f out: wknd over 1f out* **14/1**

0-06 **11** *5* **Highway Bess**[47] 6077 4-9-3 **50**.. LiamKeniry 8 26
(Patrick Chamings) *s.i.s: hld up: hdwy over 6f out: rdn and wknd over 2f out: eased* **40/1**

0050 **12** *33* **Zaydanides (FR)**[38] 6400 7-9-7 **54**................................... MartinDwyer 4
(Tim Pinfield) *s.i.s: hld up: racd keenly early: rdn over 3f out: wknd over 2f out: eased over 1f out* **12/1**

006/ **13** *9* **Heezararity**[772] 6175 11-9-1 **53**................................ GeorgiaDobie(5) 11
(David Weston) *prom: lost pl over 11f: wknd over 4f out* **66/1**

2m 55.28s (2.48) **Going Correction** +0.10s/f (Good) **13** Ran SP% **125.3**
WFA 3 from 4yo+ 7lb
Speed ratings (Par 101): **96,95,93,91,90 87,87,87,86,86 83,63,57**
CSF £41.95 CT £1640.68 TOTE £5.50: £2.40, £2.80, £13.30; EX 33.00 Trifecta £2012.20.
Owner G Roddick **Bred** T G Roddick **Trained** Angmering, W Sussex

FOCUS
There was a solid pace on in this ordinary staying handicap.

7760 DOWNLOAD THE STARSPORTS APP NOW APPRENTICE H'CAP (RACING EXCELLENCE HANDS AND HEELS SERIES) 5f 160y
5:10 (5:14) (Class 5) (0-75,74) 3-Y-O+

£3,428 (£1,020; £509; £300; £300; £300) **Stalls** Centre

Form RPR

4500 **1** **Spanish Star (IRE)**[18] 7130 4-9-4 **70**............................ GeorgeRooke(3) 10 78
(Patrick Chamings) *hld up: plld hrd: shkn up and hdwy over 1f out: r.o to ld post* **13/2**[3]

0510 **2** *hd* **The Lamplighter (FR)**[18] 7130 4-9-8 **71**....................(tp) SeanKirrane 3 78
(George Baker) *s.i.s: sn prom: chsd ldr over 3f out: shkn up to ld over 1f out: hdd post* **9/2**[2]

1122 **3** *1/2* **Kodiak Attack (IRE)**[5] 7568 3-9-4 **74**............................ ElinorJones(5) 2 79
(Sylvester Kirk) *sn led: shkn up and hdd over 1f out: styd on same pce towards fin* **2/1**[1]

1116 **4** *1 3/4* **Bay Watch (IRE)**[15] 7230 5-9-1 **67**................................. LukeBacon(3) 5 67
(Tracey Barfoot-Saunt) *pushed along in rr: swtchd wd 1/2-way: r.o ins fnl f: nt rch ldrs* **9/2**[2]

1115 **5** *1* **Gilt Edge**[18] 7115 3-9-5 **73**... IsobelFrancis(3) 8 69
(Christopher Mason) *chsd ldrs: shkn up and ev ch over 1f out: no ex ins fnl f* **9/1**

0040 **6** *2 1/4* **Champion Brogie (IRE)**[43] 6267 3-8-9 **65**....................... OwenLewis(5) 4 54
(J S Moore) *prom: pushed along 1/2-way: wknd ins fnl f* **16/1**

0455 **7** *8* **Alicia Darcy (IRE)**[7] 7514 3-9-9 **74**...............................(b) KateLeahy 9 36
(Archie Watson) *s.i.s: a in rr: wknd over 2f out* **16/1**

0050 **8** *2 3/4* **Met By Moonlight**[15] 7230 5-9-3 **66**................................. GeorgiaDobie 6 19
(Ron Hodges) *sn chsng ldr tl pushed along over 3f out: wknd over 1f out* **7/1**

1m 11.7s (0.60) **Going Correction** +0.10s/f (Good) **8** Ran SP% **117.3**
WFA 3 from 4yo+ 2lb
Speed ratings (Par 103): **100,99,99,96,95 92,81,78**
CSF £36.73 CT £80.77 TOTE £7.00: £2.10, £1.70, £1.20; EX 44.20 Trifecta £194.50.
Owner Shirley Symonds & Fred Camis **Bred** David Webb **Trained** Baughurst, Hants

FOCUS
They spread across the track in this modest sprint handicap, confined to apprentices. The second has been rated as backing up his Goodwood win, with the third to his recent improved form.
T/Jkpt: Not won. T/Plt: £949.70 to a £1 stake. Pool: £65,415.41 - 50.28 winning units T/Qpdt: £118.00 to a £1 stake. Pool: £9,044.56 - 56.70 winning units **Colin Roberts**

7506 HAMILTON (R-H)

Monday, September 30

OFFICIAL GOING: Heavy (5.4)

Wind: Almost nil Weather: Overcast

7761 CHANNEL FINANCE SCOTLAND, FINANCE MADE SIMPLE H'CAP (FOR GENTLEMAN AMATEUR RIDERS) 6f 6y

1:50 (1:53) (Class 6) (0-65,56) 4-Y-O+

£3,369 (£1,044; £522; £300; £300; £300) **Stalls** Centre

Form RPR

4036 **1** **Vallarta (IRE)**[9] 7443 9-10-10 **45**........................ MrWilliamEasterby 1 55+
(Ruth Carr) *cl up on far side of gp: led after 1f: mde rest: clr 2f out: rdn and r.o wl fnl f: unchal* **3/1**[1]

004 **2** *3* **Cosmic Chatter**[55] 5767 9-11-0 **49**........................(p) MrPatrickMillman 3 50
(Ruth Carr) *prom in centre of gp: effrt and chsd wnr over 2f out: rdn over 1f out: sn no imp* **7/2**[2]

5550 **3** *3 1/4* **Prince Of Time**[14] 7282 7-10-3 **45**........................(p) MrConnorWood(7) 7 36
(Stella Barclay) *in tch towards centre of gp: effrt over 2f out: edgd lft over 1f out: sn outpcd* **11/1**

0640 **4** *3* **Minty Jones**[42] 6277 10-10-3 **45**........................(v) MrPatrickBarlow(7) 9 27
(Michael Mullineaux) *racd nr stands' rail: led 1f: chsd wnr: rdn and hung rt over 2f out: wknd over 1f out* **50/1**

6060 **5** *nk* **Gilmer (IRE)**[7] 7507 8-10-9 **49**........................(b) AidanMacdonald(5) 5 30
(Stef Keniry) *s.i.s: bhd and detached on far side of gp: hung rt and hdwy over 1f out: nvr rchd ldrs* **12/1**

3603 **6** *1 1/4* **Burmese Blazer (IRE)**[7] 7511 4-11-7 **56**........................(p) MrJamesHarding 2 34
(Jim Goldie) *dwlt: hld up in tch on far side of gp: effrt over 2f out: wknd over 1f out* **3/1**[1]

0600 **7** *4 1/2* **Royal Connoisseur (IRE)**[31] 6682 8-10-7 **47**..(v) MrEireannCagney(5) 6 11
(Richard Fahey) *prom in centre of gp: pushed along over 2f out: wknd wl over 1f out* **4/1**[3]

0000 **8** *2* **Raise A Billion**[8] 7487 8-10-3 **45**........................ MrLiamHamblett(7) 4 3
(Alan Berry) *prom in centre of gp: lost pl over 2f out: sn struggling* **100/1**

000 **9** *3 1/2* **Red Hot Fusion (IRE)**[20] 7052 5-10-3 **45**........................(t[1]) MrDannyKerr(7) 8
(Alan Berry) *s.i.s: bhd nr stands' rail: struggling 1/2-way: nvr on terms* **100/1**

1m 19.09s (6.39) **Going Correction** +0.725s/f (Yiel) **9** Ran SP% **112.2**

Speed ratings (Par 101): **86,82,77,73,73 71,65,62,58**

CSF £13.15 CT £97.66 TOTE £4.10: £1.40, £1.50, £2.60; EX 15.40 Trifecta £81.10.

Owner D Renton And Mrs R Carr **Bred** Frank O'Meara **Trained** Huby, N Yorks

FOCUS

There had been plenty of rain over the previous week and the going was given as heavy (GoingStick 5.4). They finished well strung out in this amateur riders' event.

7762 BB FOODSERVICE FILLIES' H'CAP 6f 6y

2:20 (2:21) (Class 4) (0-80,79) 3-Y-O+

£8,021 (£2,387; £1,192; £596; £300; £300) **Stalls** Centre

Form RPR

5035 **1** **Conga**[38] 6408 3-9-7 **76**........................ KevinStott 4 85
(Kevin Ryan) *t.k.h early: mde all: rdn and edgd rt over 1f out: hrd pressed fnl f: hld on gamely towards fin* **9/2**[3]

2125 **2** *hd* **Quirky Gertie (IRE)**[42] 6286 3-9-3 **72**........................ AndreaAtzeni 6 80
(Mick Channon) *trckd ldrs: effrt and wnt 2nd 2f out: drvn and disp ld thrght fnl f: hld cl home* **12/5**[2]

5126 **3** *7* **Dancing Rave**[43] 6261 3-9-5 **74**........................ DanielTudhope 5 60
(David O'Meara) *stdd in tch: effrt over 2f out: rdn and chsd clr ldng pair over 1f out: sn no imp* **9/4**[1]

4330 **4** *2 1/4* **Yes You (IRE)**[37] 6461 5-9-5 **72**........................ JamieGormley 1 50
(Iain Jardine) *prom: drvn and outpcd over 2f out: n.d after* **11/2**

1526 **5** *1/2* **Strawberryandcream**[27] 6825 4-8-10 **63**........................ PaulHanagan 7 40
(James Bethell) *dwlt: hld up in last pl: effrt and rdn over 2f out: edgd rt and wknd wl over 1f out* **11/1**

5410 **6** *10* **Melrose Way**[23] 6976 3-9-0 **69**........................ CallumRodriguez 2 14
(Paul Midgley) *pressed wnr to 2f out: sn rdn and wknd* **17/2**

1m 16.57s (3.87) **Going Correction** +0.725s/f (Yiel)

WFA 3 from 4yo+ 2lb **6** Ran SP% **112.6**

Speed ratings (Par 102): **103,102,93,90,89 76**

CSF £15.81 TOTE £4.80: £2.10, £1.40; EX 14.30 Trifecta £50.60.

Owner Guy Reed Racing **Bred** Copgrove Hall Stud **Trained** Hambleton, N Yorks

■ Stewards' Enquiry : Kevin Stott two-day ban; misuse of whip (Oct 14-15)

FOCUS

The first two had a good battle and pulled well clear of the rest.

7763 BB FOODSERVICE 2-Y-O SERIES FINAL (A NURSERY H'CAP) 6f 6y

2:55 (2:56) (Class 2) 2-Y-O

£12,450 (£3,728; £1,864; £932; £466; £234) **Stalls** Centre

Form RPR

4215 **1** **National League (IRE)**[39] 6375 2-8-10 **82**........................ PaulHanagan 6 86
(Richard Fahey) *cl up: rdn to ld over 1f out: hung rt ins fnl f: hld on wl cl home* **2/1**[1]

2404 **2** *hd* **Spygate**[27] 6822 2-7-13 **74** oh1 ow2........................ SeanDavis(3) 5 77
(Richard Fahey) *in tch: rdn over 2f out: rallied over 1f out: chsd wnr last 100yds: kpt on wl cl home: jst hld* **12/1**

3413 **3** *3/4* **Good Night Mr Tom (IRE)**[42] 6272 2-8-12 **84**........................ JasonHart 4 85
(Mark Johnston) *led: rdn and hdd over 1f out: rallied: no ex ins fnl f* **11/2**

0012 **4** *2* **Makyon (IRE)**[52] 5900 2-9-7 **93**........................ JoeFanning 2 88
(Mark Johnston) *t.k.h: cl up: ev ch over 1f out to ins fnl f: edgd rt and no ex last 100yds* **5/2**[2]

1420 **5** *4* **One Hart (IRE)**[10] 7399 2-8-10 **82**........................ AndreaAtzeni 3 65
(Mark Johnston) *in tch: drvn and outpcd over 2f out: n.d after* **7/2**[3]

5661 **6** *hd* **Romintheglomin (IRE)**[15] 7234 2-8-0 **72** oh18........ JamieGormley 1 54
(Andrew Hughes, Ire) *dwlt: sn prom: rdn and outpcd over 2f out: sn btn* **25/1**

1m 17.02s (4.32) **Going Correction** +0.725s/f (Yiel) **6** Ran SP% **111.1**

Speed ratings (Par 101): **100,99,98,96,90 90**

CSF £24.95 TOTE £2.80: £1.30, £5.40; EX 20.10 Trifecta £89.00.

Owner R A Fahey **Bred** Rockhart Trading Ltd **Trained** Musley Bank, N Yorks

FOCUS

A tight little nursery. The second has been rated close to his previous standout run.

7764 EXCEL ENVIRONMENTAL SERVICES, PEST MANAGEMENT SERVICES H'CAP 6f 6y

3:25 (3:27) (Class 6) (0-65,72) 3-Y-O

£3,493 (£1,039; £519; £300; £300; £300) **Stalls** Centre

Form RPR

0044 **1** **Quanah (IRE)**[5] 7590 3-9-4 **57**........................ DanielTudhope 3 64
(Liam Bailey) *trckd ldr: rdn to ld over 1f out: hld on wl fnl f* **10/1**

5610 **2** *1/2* **Ey Up Its Mick**[35] 6546 3-9-7 **60**........................(b) PaulHanagan 5 65
(Tony Coyle) *dwlt: hld up in tch: rdn and outpcd 1/2-way: rallied over 1f out: pressed wnr wl ins fnl f: r.o fin* **12/1**

0503 **3** *3/4* **Abie's Hollow**[11] 7384 3-9-7 **60**........................ KevinStott 7 63
(Tony Coyle) *hld up: shkn up and hdwy over 2f out: chsd ldrs over 1f out: sn drvn: one pce wl ins fnl f* **11/1**

0224 **4** *1/2* **Pearl Of Qatar**[39] 6365 3-9-4 **57**........................ JasonHart 2 58
(Tristan Davidson) *t.k.h: led to over 1f out: drvn and one pce wl ins fnl f* **8/1**[3]

5340 **5** *1 1/2* **Absolute Dream (IRE)**[10] 7418 3-9-11 **67**........................ SeanDavis(3) 4 64
(Richard Fahey) *prom: effrt and drvn along wl over 1f out: kpt on same pce fnl f* **12/1**

2601 **6** *1* **Grimsdyke**[5] 7590 3-9-4 **57** 6ex........................ DavidAllan 6 51
(Tim Easterby) *hld up in tch: stdy hdwy and shkn up over 2f out: drvn over 1f out: no ex ins fnl f* **6/4**[1]

5012 **7** *3 1/4* **Twentysixthstreet (IRE)**[7] 7511 3-10-2 **72** 6ex........(b) RowanScott(3) 8 56
(Andrew Hughes, Ire) *bhd: rdn over 2f out: shortlived effrt on outside over 2f out: edgd rt and wknd over 1f out* **5/2**[2]

0000 **8** *21* **Liberty Diva (IRE)**[68] 5297 3-8-6 **45**........................ NathanEvans 1
(Alan Berry) *trckd ldrs: rdn along over 3f out: wknd over 2f out: eased whn no ch over 1f out* **100/1**

1m 16.9s (4.20) **Going Correction** +0.725s/f (Yiel) **8** Ran SP% **113.5**

Speed ratings (Par 99): **101,100,99,98,96 95,91,63**

CSF £117.73 CT £1348.29 TOTE £9.90: £2.50, £3.10, £2.80; EX 138.90 Trifecta £744.80.

Owner Mrs Ailsa Stirling **Bred** Stonecross Stud **Trained** Middleham, N Yorks

FOCUS

A competitive sprint. The winner has been rated close to his best for his previous yard.

7765 ST ANDREW'S FIRST AID EBF NOVICE STKS (PLUS 10 RACE) 5f 7y

4:00 (4:00) (Class 4) 2-Y-O **£5,433** (£1,617; £808; £404) **Stalls** Centre

Form RPR

1040 **1** **Ventura Flame (IRE)**[10] 7400 2-9-5 80........................ CallumRodriguez 1 81
(Keith Dalgleish) *wnt lft s: mde all: rdn over 1f out: kpt on wl fnl f* **11/4**[3]

41 **2** *1* **Jeanie B**[11] 7377 2-9-2 0........................ DanielTudhope 8 74
(Mick Channon) *chsd wnr thrght: rdn 2f out: edgd rt ins fnl f: one pce fnl 100yds* **5/2**[2]

4 **3** *4 1/2* **Stittenham Wood**[11] 7388 2-9-4 0........................ NathanEvans 9 60
(Michael Easterby) *dwlt: t.k.h and sn prom: rdn over 2f out: outpcd by first two fr over 1f out* **16/1**

6 **4** *2 3/4* **Funky Dunky (IRE)**[7] 7506 2-9-1 0........................ SeanDavis(3) 5 50
(Keith Dalgleish) *blkd s: hld up: rdn and outpcd over 2f out: sme hdwy over 1f out: no imp* **40/1**

4 **5** *1/2* **Oakenshield (IRE)**[25] 6891 2-9-4 0........................ AndreaAtzeni 3 49+
(Kevin Ryan) *wnt lft and blkd s: in tch: drvn and outpcd over 2f out: btn over 1f out* **5/4**[1]

05 **6** *3/4* **Krystal Crown (IRE)**[7] 7506 2-8-10 0........................ RowanScott(3) 7 41
(Andrew Hughes, Ire) *prom: rdn along over 2f out: wknd wl over 1f out* **40/1**

0520 **7** *1* **Get Boosting**[10] 7398 2-9-4 73........................ ShaneGray 2 42
(Keith Dalgleish) *carried rt s: in tch: drvn along over 2f out: wknd over 1f out* **22/1**

1m 3.72s (3.32) **Going Correction** +0.725s/f (Yiel) **7** Ran SP% **114.8**

Speed ratings (Par 97): **102,100,93,88,88 86,85**

CSF £10.09 TOTE £3.80: £2.30, £1.50; EX 10.80 Trifecta £56.80.

Owner Middleham Park Racing Lxxxiii & Partner **Bred** Emmet Mullins **Trained** Carluke, S Lanarks

FOCUS

A fair novice in which the first two finished clear. The race has been rated at face value around them.

7766 MEMBERS OF HAMILTON PARK RACECOURSE H'CAP 5f 7y

4:30 (4:31) (Class 5) (0-70,70) 3-Y-O+

£4,140 (£1,232; £615; £307; £300; £300) **Stalls** Centre

Form RPR

6212 **1** **Autumn Flight (IRE)**[8] 7486 3-9-5 **66**........................(b) DavidAllan 4 82+
(Tim Easterby) *mde all: shkn up and qcknd clr fnl f: eased towards fin: readily* **1/1**[1]

0010 **2** *3 1/2* **Groundworker (IRE)**[13] 7307 8-8-11 **57**........................ BarryMcHugh 1 59
(Paul Midgley) *chsd wnr thrght: rdn along 2f out: one pce fnl f* **5/1**[2]

4006 **3** *1/2* **I'll Be Good**[8] 7488 10-8-0 **51** oh2........................ PaulaMuir(5) 7 51
(Alan Berry) *hld up on outside: rdn and outpcd 2f out: rallied and tk 3rd pl wl ins fnl f: no imp* **20/1**

4201 **4** *nk* **Popping Corks (IRE)**[8] 7487 3-8-4 **54** 6ex........................ HarrisonShaw(3) 6 53
(Linda Perratt) *prom: drvn along and edgd rt over 1f out: no ex ins fnl f (jockey said filly hung right-handed throughout)* **6/1**[3]

0120 **5** *1* **Somewhere Secret**[24] 6921 5-9-10 **70**........................(p) NathanEvans 3 65
(Michael Mullineaux) *dwlt: bhd and outpcd: sme late hdwy: nvr rchd ldrs* **9/1**

3155 **6** *3 3/4* **Marietta Robusti (IRE)**[7] 7511 4-9-9 **69**........................ JackGarritty 5 51
(Stella Barclay) *prom: rdn over 2f out: wknd wl over 1f out* **8/1**

0140 **7** *1 1/4* **Naples Bay**[7] 7507 5-8-8 **54**........................ JasonHart 2 31
(Katie Scott) *dwlt: bhd: outpcd whn hung rt over 2f out: nvr on terms (trainer said gelding was never travelling)* **12/1**

1m 3.69s (3.29) **Going Correction** +0.725s/f (Yiel)

WFA 3 from 4yo+ 1lb **7** Ran SP% **114.5**

Speed ratings (Par 103): **102,96,95,95,93 87,85**

CSF £6.36 TOTE £1.70: £1.30, £2.30; EX 7.50 Trifecta £90.20.

Owner Ambrose Turnbull & Partner **Bred** Troy Cullen **Trained** Great Habton, N Yorks

FOCUS

This proved a straightforward task for the short-priced favourite. The second has been rated close to his win here the previous month.

T/Plt: £333.50 to a £1 stake. Pool: £49,820.27 - 109.05 winning units T/Qpdt: £67.20 to a £1 stake. Pool: £5,718.46 - 62.88 winning units **Richard Young**

7468 WOLVERHAMPTON (A.W) (L-H)

Monday, September 30

OFFICIAL GOING: Tapeta: standard

Wind: negligible Weather: steady rain, quite cool

7767 COMPARE BOOKMAKER SITES AT BONUSCODEBETS.CO.UK NURSERY H'CAP 7f 36y (Tp)

5:25 (5:29) (Class 6) (0-65,65) 2-Y-O

£2,781 (£827; £413; £400; £400; £400) **Stalls** High

Form				RPR
0551	1		**Lets Go Lucky**[33] 6604 2-9-6 **64**.................................(h) BenCurtis 6 (David Evans) *trckd ldrs: pushed along and hdwy on outer 1 1/2f out: led over 1f out: rdn clr fnl f: eased nr fin* **6/1**[3]	74+
0633	2	3 ¾	**Bacchalot (IRE)**[38] 6416 2-9-6 **64**......................... RichardKingscote 3 (Richard Hannon) *chsd ldr: pushed along 1 1/2f out: rdn in 2nd ent fnl f: kpt on: no ch w wnr* **4/1**[1]	64
6622	3	1 ¼	**Sparkling Diamond**[19] 7079 2-9-4 **62**...................... KieranShoemark 5 (Philip McBride) *hld up: drvn and hdwy over 1f out: tk 3rd 1f out: kpt on fnl f* **4/1**[1]	59
0000	4	½	**Camacho Man (IRE)**[18] 7111 2-8-11 **55**........................ PJMcDonald 4 (Jennie Candlish) *hld up: drvn 1 1/2f out: rdn and hdwy ent fnl f: tk 4th 1/2f out: kpt on* **8/1**	50
0426	5	¾	**Chateau Peapod**[7] 7516 2-8-12 **56**.................................. BrettDoyle 1 (Lydia Pearce) *trckd ldrs: drvn 1 1/2f out: briefly nt clr run ins fnl f: one pce* **12/1**	49
4004	6	nk	**Cece Ceylon**[19] 7079 2-9-4 **62**.................................(b) HarryBentley 9 (Ralph Beckett) *slowly away: bhd: hdwy on outer over 2f out: sn rdn: no ex* **7/1**	55
5661	7	nk	**Twittering (IRE)**[20] 7056 2-9-6 **64**................................(b) NicolaCurrie 2 (Jamie Osborne) *led: drvn 1 1/2f out: hdd over 1f out: rdn and wknd fnl f* **8/1**	56
0523	8	½	**Jungle Book (GER)**[14] 7277 2-9-7 **65**.............................. RobHornby 11 (Jonathan Portman) *prom: pushed along in 2nd 2f out: drvn and lost pl over 1f out: rdn and wknd fnl f* **11/2**[2]	56
4000	9	shd	**Gold Venture (IRE)**[19] 7064 2-8-8 **59**.................. NickBarratt-Atkin(7) 7 (Philip Kirby) *hld up: drvn on outer 1 1/2f out: no imp* **50/1**	49
6600	10	½	**Speed Dating (FR)**[5] 7584 2-9-1 **59**............................(v) LewisEdmunds 10 (Derek Shaw) *hld up: drvn over 1f out: sn rdn: no imp* **28/1**	48
4430	11	1 ¾	**Carmel**[15] 7234 2-9-1 **59**..(p) JimmyQuinn 8 (Archie Watson) *awkward leaving stalls: in rr: drvn 1 1/2f out: no imp (jockey said filly fly leapt stalls)* **20/1**	44

1m 28.75s (-0.05) **Going Correction** -0.075s/f (Stan) **11 Ran SP% 122.3**

Speed ratings (Par 93): **97,92,91,90,89 89,89,88,88,87 85**

CSF £30.95 CT £111.17 TOTE £8.00: £2.70, £1.50, £1.50; EX 40.30 Trifecta £179.40.

Owner R S Brookhouse **Bred** R S Brookhouse **Trained** Pandy, Monmouths

FOCUS

An ordinary nursery run in pretty unpleasant conditions, but the winner did it well.

7768 INSIGHT TRAINING AND CONSULTANCY (S) STKS 7f 36y (Tp)

5:50 (5:54) (Class 6) 2-Y-O

£2,781 (£827; £413; £400; £400; £400) **Stalls** High

Form				RPR
6345	1		**Isobar Wind (IRE)**[20] 7056 2-9-5 67.................................(b) BenCurtis 5 (David Evans) *mid-div: hdwy on outer to ld 1/2-way: drvn in 3 l ld 1 1/2f out: rdn in reduced ld ent fnl f: kpt on wl* **5/4**[1]	63
050	2	2 ¼	**Serious Jockin**[37] 6464 2-8-7 44........................... GeorgeBass(7) 7 (Mick Channon) *hld up: drvn and hdwy on outer over 2f out: wnt 3rd 2f out: chsd wnr in 2nd 1 1/2f out: rdn fnl f: kpt on* **14/1**	53
0045	3	1 ½	**Village Rock (IRE)**[4] 7626 2-9-0 53..............................(b[1]) ShaneKelly 1 (Richard Hughes) *t.k.h: led: hdd 1/2-way: rdn in 2nd 2f out: lost 2nd 1 1/2f out: one pce fnl f* **4/1**[2]	49
3050	4	hd	**Schumli**[14] 7283 2-8-9 54... CamHardie 3 (David O'Meara) *chsd ldr: dropped to 3rd 1/2-way: drvn and dropped to 4th 2f out: rdn over 1f out: one pce* **16/1**	44
000	5	1	**Made Guy (USA)**[46] 6141 2-9-0 0...............................(b) SeanLevey 2 (J S Moore) *mid-div: drvn over 2f out: rdn over 1f out: one pce* **18/1**	46
0300	6	1 ½	**Moontide (IRE)**[56] 5759 2-9-0 0.................................. DougieCostello 9 (J S Moore) *mid-div: drvn over 2f out: rdn over 1f out: no imp* **9/1**	42
6340	7	12	**Amnaa**[9] 7469 2-9-0 64..(b[1]) LukeMorris 6 (Marco Botti) *hld up: drvn over 2f out: reminder 1 1/2f out: sn lost tch* **11/2**[3]	12
5000	8	3 ¾	**Imperial Eagle (IRE)**[13] 7306 2-8-9 53..........................(h[1]) PhilDennis 4 (Lawrence Mullaney) *slowly away: nvr a factor (jockey said filly never travelling)* **7/1**	
0	9	13	**Worthamonkey**[9] 7469 2-9-0 0..................................... DannyBrock 8 (Denis Quinn) *prom: drvn and dropped away 3f out* **100/1**	
0	10	17	**Don'tstophimnow (IRE)**[9] 7469 2-9-0 0.......................... JosephineGordon 11 (J S Moore) *slowly away: a bhd* **100/1**	

1m 29.86s (1.06) **Going Correction** -0.075s/f (Stan) **10 Ran SP% 122.1**

Speed ratings (Par 93): **90,87,85,85,84 82,68,64,49,30**

CSF £24.03 TOTE £1.90: £1.10, £4.60, £2.00; EX 30.60 Trifecta £143.20.There was no bid for the winner.

Owner E R Griffiths **Bred** Eric Griffiths **Trained** Pandy, Monmouths

FOCUS

Not much depth to this seller and the favourite proved far too good.

7769 FOLLOW US ON LINKEDIN @THECOMMERCIALFLOORINGCOMPANYLTD NOVICE STKS 6f 20y (Tp)

6:20 (6:20) (Class 5) 2-Y-O

£3,428 (£1,020; £509; £254) **Stalls** Low

Form				RPR
13	1		**Brad The Brief**[19] 7071 2-9-9 0.......................... RichardKingscote 7 (Tom Dascombe) *mid-div: pushed along and hdwy 1 1/2f out: drvn in 2 l 2nd 1f out: rdn fnl f: r.o wl to ld last 50yds: pushed out nr fin* **5/4**[1]	82+
35	2	½	**Vasari (USA)**[53] 5859 2-9-2 0.. LouisSteward 2 (Sir Michael Stoute) *chsd ldr: led 2f out: drvn in 2 l ld 1f out: rdn fnl f: hdd last 50yds: no ex* **9/4**[2]	73
	3	3	**Is That Love (IRE)** 2-9-2 0.. TomEaves 4 (Kevin Ryan) *led: pushed along and hdd 2f out: dropped to 3rd ent fnl f: no ex* **20/1**	64
	4	1	**Streeton (IRE)** 2-9-2 0.. HarryBentley 9 (Ralph Beckett) *hld up: drvn 2f out: plenty to do and reminder on outer 1f out: kpt on steadily into 4th fnl f* **8/1**	61
	5	hd	**Pretty Lady (IRE)**[20] 7046 2-8-11 0.................................. PJMcDonald 6 (Mark Johnston) *mid-div: drvn to chse ldrs 1 1/2f out: no ex fnl f* **9/2**[3]	55
	6	2 ¼	**Kingmans Spirit (IRE)** 2-8-6 0............................ ThomasGreatrex(5) 5 (David Loughnane) *prom on outer: drvn in 3rd 2f out: reminder 1 1/2f out: sn wknd* **22/1**	49
0	7	½	**The Grey Bay (IRE)**[52] 5913 2-9-2 0.............................. PaulMulrennan 8 (Julie Camacho) *t.k.h: hld up: pushed along and effrt 1 1/2f out: sn no ex (jockey said colt ran freely)* **50/1**	52
6	8	1 ¼	**Theheartneverlies**[13] 7316 2-9-2 0.................................. LukeMorris 1 (Sir Mark Prescott Bt) *slowly away: bhd: drvn 2f out: no imp* **50/1**	48
0	9	½	**Heartstar**[49] 6028 2-8-11 0.. CamHardie 3 (John Mackie) *prom: drvn and lost pl 1 1/2f out: dropped away fr 1f out* **125/1**	42

1m 15.24s (0.74) **Going Correction** -0.075s/f (Stan) **9 Ran SP% 118.3**

Speed ratings (Par 95): **92,91,87,86,85 82,82,80,79**

CSF £4.14 TOTE £2.20: £1.10, £1.10, £5.00; EX 5.00 Trifecta £43.80.

Owner Chasemore Farm **Bred** Chasemore Farm **Trained** Malpas, Cheshire

FOCUS

Few could be fancied in this novice, but a stirring finish between the big two in the market. The time and those down the field govern the opening level.

7770 FOLLOW US ON INSTAGRAM @THECOMMERCIALFLOORINGCO H'CAP 6f 20y (Tp)

6:50 (6:53) (Class 6) (0-55,55) 3-Y-O+

£2,781 (£827; £413; £400; £400; £400) **Stalls** Low

Form				RPR
0030	1		**Viola Park**[19] 7080 5-9-5 **55**.................................(p) DavidProbert 12 (Ronald Harris) *trckd ldrs: pushed along and hdwy 1 1/2f out: drvn to ld ent fnl f: sn rdn: r.o wl* **16/1**	60
5361	2	nk	**One One Seven (IRE)**[9] 7468 3-9-2 **54**.............................. CamHardie 5 (Antony Brittain) *hld up: drvn and hdwy over 1f out: rdn fnl f: r.o wl: tk 2nd last stride* **13/2**[3]	58
0460	3	hd	**Roaring Rory**[14] 7286 6-9-4 **54**.................................. LewisEdmunds 4 (Ollie Pears) *hld up: drvn 1 1/2f out: hdwy over 1f out: r.o fnl f: tk 3rd nr fin* **8/1**	58
R451	4	nk	**Dandilion (IRE)**[42] 6284 6-8-11 **52**.................. ThoreHammerHansen(5) 2 (Alex Hales) *hld up: pushed along and hdwy on inner 1 1/2f out: ev ch ent fnl f: sn rdn: one pce* **6/1**[2]	55
406	5	hd	**Billyoakes (IRE)**[11] 7389 7-9-5 **55**.............................(p) BenRobinson 13 (Ollie Pears) *chsd ldr: pushed into ld 2f out: sn drvn: hdd ent fnl f: no ex* **28/1**	57
5001	6	½	**Peachey Carnehan**[7] 7527 5-9-3 **53**..............................(v) HarryBentley 8 (Michael Mullineaux) *hmpd leaving stalls and sn bhd: drvn and hdwy on outer 1 1/2f out: sn rdn: kpt on fnl f: nvr nrr (jockey said gelding was hampered by unseated rider at start)* **9/4**[1]	54+
4530	7	½	**Halle's Harbour**[42] 6286 3-9-3 **55**..................................(v) LukeMorris 3 (Paul George) *mid-div: pushed along 2f out: drvn over 1f out: rdn fnl f: one pce* **20/1**	54
0404	8	½	**Alba Del Sole (IRE)**[31] 6682 4-9-4 **54**...................... RichardKingscote 1 (Charlie Wallis) *trckd ldrs: wknd fnl f (jockey said filly jumped right handed from stalls)* **10/1**	52
0030	9	1 ¾	**Alqaab**[13] 7307 4-9-2 **52**..(h) JamesSullivan 10 (Ruth Carr) *mid-div: drvn 1 1/2f out: rdn and wknd fnl f* **16/1**	44
04-0	10	¾	**Madame Ritz (IRE)**[59] 5629 4-9-5 **55**........................ KieranShoemark 11 (Richard Phillips) *hld up: drvn 1 1/2f out: no imp* **50/1**	45
5025	11	¾	**Tavener**[4] 7604 7-9-2 **52**...(p) PhilDennis 6 (David C Griffiths) *led: drvn and hdd 2f out: rdn and wknd over 1f out* **13/2**[3]	40
00-0	12	40	**Juan Horsepower**[263] 166 5-9-1 **54**................................(p) TimClark(3) 7 (Denis Quinn) *hld up: reminder after 2f: lost tch fr 2f out* **66/1**	
5030	U		**Englishman**[9] 7447 9-9-4 **54**..(p) PJMcDonald 9 (Milton Bradley) *stmbld and uns rdr leaving stalls* **10/1**	

1m 14.04s (-0.46) **Going Correction** -0.075s/f (Stan) **13 Ran SP% 124.4**

WFA 3 from 4yo+ 2lb

Speed ratings (Par 101): **100,99,99,98,98 98,97,96,94,93 92,39,**

CSF £118.17 CT £953.21 TOTE £17.20: £3.60, £1.60, £2.90; EX 161.20 Trifecta £2156.90.

Owner John & Margaret Hatherell & RHS Ltd **Bred** Limestone Stud **Trained** Earlswood, Monmouths

FOCUS

A moderate handicap and a dramatic race with the principals finishing in a heap. It's hard to rate the race much higher than this.

7771 COMMERCIAL FLOORING COMPANY LTD H'CAP 5f 21y (Tp)

7:20 (7:23) (Class 4) (0-85,85) 3-Y-O+

£5,207 (£1,549; £774; £400; £400; £400) **Stalls** Low

Form				RPR
0244	1		**The Daley Express (IRE)**[40] 6332 5-9-7 **85**.................... DavidProbert 3 (Ronald Harris) *mid-div: hdwy and pushed along 1 1/2f out: str run fnl f: led 75yds out: sn clr: cosily (jockey said gelding hung left-handed in str)* **8/1**	93
3503	2	1	**Foxy Forever (IRE)**[13] 7321 9-9-0 **78**.............................(bt) BenCurtis 1 (Michael Wigham) *mid-div: drvn and hdwy 1f out: rdn fnl f: r.o wl: tk 2nd last stride* **9/2**[2]	82
3241	3	shd	**Secretfact**[16] 7178 6-8-13 **77**.. JimmyQuinn 5 (Malcolm Saunders) *hld up: pushed along and hdwy on inner over 1f out: rdn ins fnl f: r.o wl: tk 3rd last stride* **9/1**	81
0343	4	nse	**Acclaim The Nation (IRE)**[44] 6208 6-9-6 **84**.....................(p) TomEaves 7 (Eric Alston) *led: drvn 1 1/2f out: rdn in 1 l ld 1f out: hdd 75yds out: no ex: lost two pls last two strides* **5/2**[1]	88
-400	5	1 ½	**Glory Fighter**[40] 6332 3-8-13 **78**..................................... GeraldMosse 10 (Charles Hills) *prom: drvn in 2nd 2f out: rdn and wknd fnl f* **16/1**	76
2000	6	½	**Nibras Again**[19] 7077 5-8-10 **77**............................. ConnorMurtagh(3) 6 (Paul Midgley) *hld up: drvn on outer 1 1/2f out: sn rdn: kpt on fnl f* **7/1**[3]	74+
5150	7	½	**You're Cool**[52] 5888 7-9-3 **81**..(t) LewisEdmunds 4 (John Balding) *chsd ldrs: drvn in 4th 2f out: rdn over 1f out: wknd fnl f* **16/1**	76
6014	8	½	**Merry Banter**[13] 7321 5-9-6 **84**.. HarryBentley 2 (Paul Midgley) *chsd ldrs: drvn in 3rd 2f out: rdn and wknd over 1f out* **9/1**	77
4040	9	1	**King Robert**[17] 7161 6-9-6 **84**..(v) DavidEgan 11 (Charlie Wallis) *hld up: rdn 1 1/2f out: no imp* **20/1**	73

The Form Book Flat 2019, Raceform Ltd, Newbury, RG14 5SJ

1126 **10** 2 1/2 **Arishka (IRE)**[126] 3159 3-8-8 73 JosephineGordon 9 53
(Daniel Kubler) *jockey dismntd as rival in adjacent stall bec unruly: bked out and reloaded: mid-div on outer: drvn and lost pl 1 1/2f out: sn rdn and dropped away* **50/1**

1m 0.53s (-1.37) **Going Correction** -0.075s/f (Stan)
WFA 3 from 5yo+ 1lb **10** Ran SP% **108.9**
Speed ratings (Par 105): **107,105,105,105,102 101,101,100,98,94**
CSF £37.24 CT £246.91 TOTE £7.70: £2.10, £1.80, £1.90; EX 41.00 Trifecta £301.20.
Owner The W H O Society **Bred** Allevamento Ficomontanino Srl **Trained** Earlswood, Monmouths
■ A Sure Welcome was withdrawn. Price at time of withdrawal 9/1. Rule 4 applies to all bets - deduction 10p in the pound

FOCUS
A fair sprint handicap and they went quick, which suited the winner. The winner has been rated in line with this year's turf form, and the second and third close to their recent form.

7772 GAV LOVES A MIDWEEK BET NOVICE MEDIAN AUCTION STKS 1m 142y (Tp)
7:50 (7:51) (Class 5) 3-5-Y-O £3,428 (£1,020; £509; £254) **Stalls Low**

Form RPR

60-2 **1** **Mac Jetes**[13] 7298 3-8-6 61 ThomasGreatrex(5) 12 70
(David Loughnane) *mid-div: hdwy into 3rd 2f out: sn drvn: wnt into 1 l 2nd 1f out: led over 1/2f out: sn pushed clr* **9/1**

0646 **2** 1 1/2 **Love Explodes**[14] 7288 3-8-11 72 (b[1]) StevieDonohoe 11 67
(Ed Vaughan) *chsd clr ldr: tk clsr order 1/2-way: led 1 1/2f out: rdn in 1 l ld 1f out: hdd over 1/2f out: no ex (jockey said filly hung left-handed throughout)* **5/2**[2]

0 **3** nk **Levanter (FR)**[136] 2790 3-8-11 0 HarryBentley 8 66
(Harry Dunlop) *hld up: pushed along and hdwy 2f out: rdn in 4th over 1f out: kpt on into 3rd fnl f* **8/1**[3]

00 **4** 2 1/2 **Hurricane Ali (IRE)**[104] 3972 3-9-2 0 CamHardie 5 65
(John Mackie) *hld up: drvn and hdwy over 1f out: r.o into 4th fnl f: nrst fin* **10/1**

3-34 **5** 2 3/4 **Kentucky Kingdom (IRE)**[255] 290 3-9-2 73 RaulDaSilva 9 59
(James Evans) *led: sn 5 l clr: reduced ld 1/2-way: rdn and hdd 1 1/2f out: wknd fnl f* **11/1**

60- **6** 9 **George Junior**[362] 7907 3-9-2 0 LiamKeniry 10 38
(Ed Walker) *slowly away: bhd: rdn 1 1/2f out: plugged on past btn horses fnl f* **20/1**

5 **7** hd **Never To Forget**[14] 7278 4-9-4 0 DarraghKeenan(3) 6 37
(John Butler) *chsd ldrs: drvn in 4th 2f out: sn rdn and wknd* **10/1**

40 **8** 2 1/4 **Eloquent Style (IRE)**[24] 6944 3-9-2 0 DougieCostello 4 33
(Ivan Furtado) *mid-div: drvn over 2f out: sn wknd* **33/1**

3-0 **9** 1/2 **Monogamy**[157] 2087 3-8-11 0 (h[1]) RobHornby 1 26
(Martyn Meade) *t.k.h: chsd ldrs: drvn and lost pl over 2f out: sn bhd and eased* **7/4**[1]

4 **10** 17 **Lilly's Legacy**[15] 7228 3-8-11 0 JohnFahy 7
(Nikki Evans) *slowly away: a bhd* **100/1**

P **Bonsai Bay**[57] 4-9-4 0 (w) TimClark(3) 3
(David Evans) *slowly away: bhd: t.o whn p.u 2f out: bled fr nose (vet said gelding had bled from nse and had irregular heartbeat)* **40/1**

1m 49.13s (-0.97) **Going Correction** -0.075s/f (Stan)
WFA 3 from 4yo 5lb **11** Ran SP% **123.7**
Speed ratings (Par 103): **101,99,99,97,94 86,86,84,84,69**
CSF £32.74 TOTE £10.30: £3.00, £1.40, £1.90; EX 46.40 Trifecta £315.50.
Owner Peter Onslow **Bred** Peter Onslow **Trained** Tern Hill, Shropshire
■ Stewards' Enquiry : Stevie Donohoe three-day ban: careless riding (Oct 14-16)

FOCUS
The absence of Fortamour meant this novice took much less winning and it was a strange contest, with the leader going off too quick and the race falling into the lap of the hold-up horses. It's been rated around the second.

7773 DAVE HOWES - A TRUE GENTLEMAN H'CAP 1m 1f 104y (Tp)
8:20 (8:21) (Class 5) (0-75,77) 3-Y-O
£3,428 (£1,020; £509; £400; £400; £400) **Stalls Low**

Form RPR

5026 **1** **Kashagan**[48] 6044 3-9-10 77 (b) PaulMulrennan 12 88
(Archie Watson) *prom: led after 2f: mde rest: pushed along in 2 l ld 1 1/2f out: rdn fnl f: r.o wl* **16/1**

5045 **2** 2 **Blood Eagle (IRE)**[94] 4321 3-9-4 71 DavidProbert 11 78+
(Andrew Balding) *hld up: hdwy on outer over 2f out: pushed into 2nd ent fnl f: sn rdn: kpt on but a hld* **11/2**[2]

6013 **3** 1 1/4 **The Dancing Poet**[18] 7126 3-9-4 71 (p) StevieDonohoe 13 75
(Ed Vaughan) *trckd ldrs: wnt 2nd 1/2-way: drvn 2f out: rdn over 1f out: dropped to 3rd ent fnl f: no ex* **9/1**[3]

3455 **4** 2 **Crimewave (IRE)**[27] 6840 3-9-3 70 (t) LukeMorris 3 70
(Tom Clover) *mid-div: rdn and hdwy over 2f out: chsd ldr 1 1/2f out: wknd fnl f* **9/1**[3]

550 **5** nk **Sea Wings**[54] 5808 3-9-1 68 (b) BenCurtis 5 68
(William Haggas) *mid-div: pushed along to take clsr order over 2f out: rdn in 4th 2f out: no ex fr over 1f out* **5/2**[1]

6344 **6** 1 **Baryshnikov**[55] 5776 3-9-9 76 LiamKeniry 8 73
(Ed Walker) *hld up: rdn over 2f out: kpt on fnl f (jockey said gelding was never travelling)* **5/2**[1]

4340 **7** 1 1/4 **Global Express**[47] 6083 3-9-4 71 GeraldMosse 2 66
(Ed Dunlop) *hld up: drvn over 2f out: sn rdn: no imp: eased fnl f* **16/1**

4135 **8** 2 **Rambaldi (IRE)**[47] 6075 3-9-4 71 (t) ShaneKelly 1 62
(Marco Botti) *mid-div: drvn over 2f out: sn rdn and wknd* **12/1**

-006 **9** 17 **Perfect Showdance**[15] 7237 3-9-9 76 HectorCrouch 7 31
(Clive Cox) *slowly away: bhd: no ch fr 3f out: eased fnl f* **33/1**

466 **10** 15 **Red Derek**[58] 5656 3-8-12 65 CamHardie 4
(Lisa Williamson) *led: hdd after 2f: sn drvn along: wknd 3f out: sn dropped away* **66/1**

0000 **11** 2 1/2 **Liberation Day**[16] 7213 3-8-7 67 (b) NickBarratt-Atkin(7) 6
(Philip Kirby) *hld up: drvn and wknd over 2f out* **100/1**

0266 **12** 9 **Prairie Spy (IRE)**[14] 7272 3-9-7 74 HarryBentley 9
(Mark Johnston) *hld up: rdn and lost tch over 2f out: sn heavily eased* **22/1**

1m 58.11s (-2.69) **Going Correction** -0.075s/f (Stan) **12** Ran SP% **121.8**
Speed ratings (Par 101): **108,106,105,103,103 102,101,99,84,70 68,60**
CSF £102.45 CT £864.54 TOTE £16.30: £4.40, £2.20, £1.50; EX 93.50 Trifecta £389.70.
Owner Nurlan Bizakov **Bred** Hesmonds Stud Ltd **Trained** Upper Lambourn, W Berks

FOCUS
An ordinary 3yo handicap and not many got into it. The third has been rated to form.
T/Plt: £132.70 to a £1 stake. Pool: £84,584.41 - 465.27 winning units T/Qpdt: £61.00 to a £1 stake. Pool: £10,352.54 - 125.54 winning units **Keith McHugh**

7043 CHANTILLY (R-H)
Monday, September 30

OFFICIAL GOING: Turf: soft

7774a PRIX DE CONDE (GROUP 3) (2YO) (TURF) 1m 1f
10:55 2-Y-O £36,036 (£14,414; £10,810; £7,207; £3,603)

RPR

1 **Hopeful (FR)**[22] 7005 2-8-13 0 MaximeGuyon 6 107
(C Laffon-Parias, France) *trckd ldr on outer after 1f: pushed along to chal 2f out: drvn and led narrowly ent fnl f: kpt on strly clsng stages* **2/1**[2]

2 1/2 **Al Dabaran**[22] 7005 2-8-13 0 WilliamBuick 1 106
(Charlie Appleby) *led: asked to qckn whn pressed over 2f out: rdn 1 1/2f out: hdd ent fnl f: kpt on gamely u.p: jst hld on for 2nd* **1/1**[1]

3 hd **The Summit (FR)**[25] 2-8-13 0 Pierre-CharlesBoudot 3 106
(H-A Pantall, France) *wnt lft and impeded rival s: 3rd on inner: gng wl looking for gap to open 2f out: pushed along between rivals ent fnl f: r.o strly: nt quite pce to chal* **14/1**

4 shd **Tammani**[23] 6957 2-8-13 0 JamesDoyle 2 105
(William Haggas) *racd in 4th: pushed along and effrt on outer 2f out: sn rdn: r.o strly ins fnl f: nt quite pce to trble ldrs* **9/1**

5 3 **Wally (IRE)**[38] 6433 2-8-13 0 ChristopheSoumillon 5 99
(J-C Rouget, France) *bmpd s: hld up in rr: pushed along 2f out: unable qck: kpt on same pce under hands and heels riding ins fnl f* **61/10**[3]

6 2 1/2 **Carnival Zain**[31] 2-8-13 0 CristianDemuro 4 94
(E J O'Neill, France) *hmpd s: racd in fnl pair: pushed along over 2f out: limited rspnse: rdn over 1f out: no imp and grad wknd clsng stages* **17/1**

1m 56.94s (5.84) **6** Ran SP% **119.6**
PARI-MUTUEL (all including 1 euro stake): WIN 3.00; PLACE 1.30, 1.10; SF 5.20.
Owner Wertheimer & Frere **Bred** Wertheimer & Frere **Trained** Chantilly, France

FOCUS
A tactical affair.

7775a CRITERIUM DE VITESSE (LISTED RACE) (2YO) (TURF) 5f
1:07 2-Y-O £27,027 (£10,810; £8,108; £5,405; £2,702)

RPR

1 **Band Practice (IRE)**[16] 7211 2-8-9 0 OisinMurphy 8 105
(Archie Watson) *mde virtually all: qcknd up over 2f out: rdn ent fnl f: r.o strly: a doing enough cl home* **7/2**[2]

2 3/4 **Divine Spirit**[30] 6791 2-8-9 0 WilliamBuick 1 102
(Charlie Appleby) *disp 3rd: pushed along to chse ldr over 2f out: rdn in 2nd 1 1/2f out: r.o wl ins fnl f: nt pce to chal* **6/5**[1]

3 6 **Has D'Emra (FR)**[51] 5976 2-8-13 0 (b) MaximeGuyon 7 84
(F Rossi, France) **43/10**[3]

4 nk **Baileys Courage (FR)**[157] 2-8-9 0 AurelienLemaitre 5 79
(J-V Toux, France) **18/1**

5 6 **Lorelei Rock (IRE)**[30] 2-8-9 0 TheoBachelot 4 58
(G Botti, France) *racd in fnl pair: struggling to go pce and pushed along over 2f out: unable qck: wl btn over 1f out: eased clsng stages* **81/10**

6 5 **Kenzydancer (FR)**[8] 2-8-13 0 Pierre-CharlesBoudot 6 44
(P Sogorb, France) **5/1**

1m 1.49s (3.19) **6** Ran SP% **119.5**
PARI-MUTUEL (all including 1 euro stake): WIN 4.50; PLACE 1.40, 1.10; SF 3.60.
Owner Clipper Logistics **Bred** Fergus Cousins **Trained** Upper Lambourn, W Berks

7429 AYR (L-H)
Tuesday, October 1

OFFICIAL GOING: Soft (heavy in places; 6.1)
Wind: Fresh, half behind in sprints and in over 3f of home straight in races on the round course Weather: Cloudy, sunny spells

7776 JOIN RACING TV NOW APPRENTICE H'CAP (PART OF RACING EXCELLENCE APPRENTICE TRAINING INITIATIVE) 1m
1:50 (1:51) (Class 6) (0-65,66) 3-Y-O+
£2,975 (£885; £442; £300; £300; £300) **Stalls Low**

Form RPR

5002 **1** **Gamesters Icon**[8] 7508 4-9-3 55 (tp) AidenBlakemore(3) 11 66
(Oliver Greenall) *prom on outside: rdn and outpcd over 3f out: rallied and edgd lft 2f out: led ins fnl f: pushed out* **4/1**[1]

\- **2** 1 1/2 **Highway To Heaven (IRE)**[5] 7638 4-9-5 54 KieranSchofield 6 62
(T G McCourt, Ire) *hld up: hdwy on outside over 2f out: edgd lft and kpt on fnl f to take 2nd towards fin: nt rch wnr* **7/1**[3]

5041 **3** hd **The Stalking Moon (IRE)**[3] 7526 5-10-0 63 5ex (p) LauraCoughlan 12 71
(Adrian Nicholls) *hld up on ins: gd hdwy over 2f out: led and rdn over 1f out: hdd ins fnl f: one pce and lost 2nd towards fin* **9/1**

0053 **4** 1 3/4 **Chinese Spirit (IRE)**[12] 7364 5-9-12 61 RhonaPindar 3 65
(Linda Perratt) *bhd: plenty to do over 3f out: gd hdwy on outside over 1f out: edgd lft: kpt on fnl f: nrst fin* **9/1**

0043 **5** nk **Snooker Jim**[8] 7509 4-8-13 48 (t) TobyEley 14 51
(Steph Hollinshead) *hld up in midfield: smooth hdwy over 2f out: rdn and cl up over 1f out: no ex ins fnl f* **16/1**

3320 **6** 6 **Equidae**[12] 7364 4-10-3 66 (t) HarryRussell 7 56
(Iain Jardine) *led: rdn over 2f out: hdd over 1f out: sn wknd* **12/1**

6402 **7** 1 1/4 **Abushamah (IRE)**[7] 7545 8-9-9 61 GavinAshton(3) 5 48
(Ruth Carr) *in tch: rdn over 2f out: wknd wl over 1f out* **17/2**

0004 **8** 1/2 **Cliff Bay (IRE)**[8] 7509 5-9-0 49 (b) EllaMcCain 4 35
(Keith Dalgleish) *t.k.h in midfield: hdwy to press ldr 1/2-way to over 2f out: sn lost pl and struggling (jockey said gelding ran too free)* **11/1**

1 **9** nk **Kinch (IRE)**[33] 6647 3-9-7 59 SeanKirrane 2 44
(J F Levins, Ire) *hld up: pushed along 3f out: nvr able to chal* **6/1**[2]

0360 **10** 3/4 **Uh Oh Chongo**[11] 7404 3-9-2 59 ZakWheatley(5) 8 43
(Michael Easterby) *t.k.h in midfield: pushed along over 3f out: wknd over 2f out* **66/1**

0440 **11** 5 **Tom's Anna (IRE)**[33] 6627 9-8-5 45 IzzyClifton(5) 9 18
(Sean Regan) *chsd ldr to 1/2-way: rdn and wknd over 2f out* **40/1**

0506 **12** 1/2 **Darwina**[8] 7512 3-8-9 50 (h) RussellHarris(3) 1 22
(Alistair Whillans) *trckd ldrs: drvn along over 2f out: sn lost pl and struggling* **66/1**

The Form Book Flat 2019, Raceform Ltd, Newbury, RG14 5SJ

0000 **13** 1 3/4 **Pudding Chare (IRE)**[12] 7364 5-9-10 **62**............(t) OliverStammers(3) 10 30
(R Mike Smith) *bhd: struggling over 3f out: nvr on terms* **66/1**

0413 **14** nk **Remmy D (IRE)**[8] 7513 4-9-5 **57**..............................(b) CoreyMadden(3) 13 24
(Jim Goldie) *hld up: rdn over 3f out: wknd fnl 2f (jockey said gelding was never travelling)* **7/1**[3]

1m 49.1s (6.30) **Going Correction** +0.80s/f (Soft) **14 Ran SP% 118.6**
WFA 3 from 4yo+ 3lb
Speed ratings (Par 101): **100,98,98,96,96 90,89,88,88,87 82,81,80,79**
CSF £30.30 CT £243.24 TOTE £3.50: £1.40, £3.00, £3.10; EX 34.00 Trifecta £276.60.
Owner Gamesters Partnership **Bred** D V Williams **Trained** Oldcastle Heath, Cheshire

FOCUS
The going was soft, heavy in places (GoingStick: 6.1) and there was quite a tailwind blowing the runners up the straight. The back straight rail was out 2yds, the home straight far rail out 8yds and the home bend out 4yds, adding 12yds to all races on the round course. A modest apprentice handicap to start and despite the class of contest, a winning time 11.9sec outside standard shows how testing conditions were. The second has been rated to this year's mark.

7777 CHRISTMAS DAY LUNCH AT WESTERN HOUSE HOTEL H'CAP 6f

2:20 (2:22) (Class 5) (0-75,74) 3-Y-O+

£3,622 (£1,078; £538; £300; £300; £300) **Stalls** Centre

Form RPR

0405 **1** **John Kirkup**[15] 7289 4-9-6 **73**..............................(b[1]) ConnorBeasley 5 86
(Michael Dods) *t.k.h: prom: smooth hdwy to ld over 1f out: drvn clr fnl f: eased towards fin* **11/4**[1]

1263 **2** 5 **Dancing Rave**[1] 7762 3-9-6 **74**.............................. DanielTudhope 7 71
(David O'Meara) *hld up in tch: pushed along over 2f out: hdwy to chse wnr over 1f out: hung lft: one pce fnl f* **4/1**[3]

3535 **3** 2 **Amazing Grazing (IRE)**[20] 7065 5-8-12 **65**...................... PhilDennis 2 56
(Rebecca Bastiman) *cl up: drvn along 1/2-way: rallied: one pce fnl f* **11/2**

/4-1 **4** 3/4 **Eleuthera**[71] 5238 7-8-2 **62** ow1..............................(t) SeanKirrane(7) 4 50
(J F Levins, Ire) *t.k.h: led: rdn and hdd over 1f out: no ex fnl f* **7/2**[2]

/00- **5** 2 1/2 **Rattling Jewel**[18] 7168 7-8-12 **70**.............................. GavinRyan(5) 6 50
(J J Lambe, Ire) *cl up: rdn over 2f out: wknd over 1f out* **7/1**

4-11 **6** 9 **Tai Sing Yeh (IRE)**[24] 6985 5-8-9 **65**..............................(t) SeanDavis(3) 3 16
(J F Levins, Ire) *dwlt: hld up: rdn over 2f out: wknd and eased over 1f out* **15/2**

5420 **7** 3 3/4 **Naadirr (IRE)**[34] 6591 8-9-7 **74**..............................(v) TomEaves 8 13
(Kevin Ryan) *blindfold slow to remove and slowly away: hld up: rdn and struggling over 2f out: lost tch over 1f out* **20/1**

1m 15.49s (2.39) **Going Correction** +0.60s/f (Yiel) **7 Ran SP% 113.3**
WFA 3 from 4yo+ 1lb
Speed ratings (Par 103): **112,105,102,101,98 86,81**
CSF £13.70 CT £54.80 TOTE £3.30: £1.90, £2.20; EX 14.10 Trifecta £55.00.
Owner Mrs Suzanne Kirkup & Kevin Kirkup **Bred** W M Lidsey **Trained** Denton, Co Durham

FOCUS
An ordinary sprint handicap, but a gamble landed in emphatic fashion. They raced up the middle. The winner has been rated to his best since his 2yo days.

7778 WATCH ON RACING TV MEDIAN AUCTION MAIDEN STKS 1m

2:50 (2:51) (Class 6) 2-Y-O **£2,975** (£885; £442; £221) **Stalls** Low

Form RPR

53 **1** **First Impression (IRE)**[11] 7416 2-9-5 0.............................. JasonHart 5 77+
(John Quinn) *prom: hdwy over 2f out: led over 1f out: rdn: drifted lft and hrd pressed ins fnl f: styd on wl towards fin* **16/1**

5020 **2** 1 **Clay Regazzoni**[10] 7429 2-9-5 76..............................(h[1]) CallumRodriguez 2 75
(Keith Dalgleish) *dwlt: hld up: hdwy over 2f out: rdn and pressed wnr over 1f out: ev ch ins fnl f: kpt on same pce towards fin* **4/1**[2]

3 **3** 5 **Let Her Loose (IRE)**[23] 7000 2-8-11 0.............................. SeanDavis(3) 1 59
(Richard Fahey) *hld up: pushed along over 3f out: hdwy over 1f out: kpt on fnl f: nt rch first two* **7/1**

4 1 3/4 **Perfect Empire** 2-9-5 0.............................. BenCurtis 7 60
(Mark Johnston) *led: rdn over 2f out: hdd over 1f out: wknd ins fnl f* **20/1**

533 **5** 2 1/4 **Single (IRE)**[8] 7515 2-9-0 0.............................. TomEaves 8 50
(Mick Channon) *prom on outside: hdwy and cl up 3f out: hung lft and outpcd 2f out: sn n.d* **5/1**[3]

0 **6** 1 **The Tripple T (IRE)**[8] 7506 2-9-5 0.............................. PaulMulrennan 4 53
(Andrew Hughes, Ire) *t.k.h: hld up bhd ldng gp: rdn over 2f out: sn no imp: btn over 1f out* **66/1**

24 **7** nse **Manzo Duro (IRE)**[24] 6971 2-9-5 0.............................. DanielTudhope 3 53
(David O'Meara) *chsd ldr to 1/2-way: cl up: rdn over 2f out: wknd wl over 1f out* **6/4**[1]

8 4 **Batalha** 2-9-5 0.............................. JoeFanning 10 44
(Mark Johnston) *hld up on outside: pushed along over 2f out: hung lft and sn no imp: btn over 1f out* **17/2**

0 **9** 5 **On The Rhine (IRE)**[16] 7235 2-9-2 0.............................. RowanScott(3) 6 33
(Andrew Hughes, Ire) *t.k.h: prom: wnt 2nd 1/2-way to over 2f out: sn rdn and wknd* **66/1**

000 **10** 12 **Klara Spirit (IRE)**[8] 7506 2-8-9 0.............................. KieranSchofield(5) 9 2
(R Mike Smith) *bhd: struggling 1/2-way: btn over 2f out* **200/1**

1m 49.51s (6.71) **Going Correction** +0.80s/f (Soft) **10 Ran SP% 113.8**
Speed ratings (Par 93): **98,97,92,90,88 87,86,82,77,65**
CSF £76.17 TOTE £17.90: £3.00, £1.40, £2.10; EX 73.70 Trifecta £386.70.
Owner Blackburn, Fox, McWilliams, & Pendelbury **Bred** John Dwan & Make Believe Syndicate **Trained** Settrington, N Yorks

FOCUS
Add 12yds to race distance. Not the deepest median auction maiden with the first two pulling clear and the runner-up setting the benchmark. The balance of the second's form is probably the best guide to the level.

7779 BOOK YOUR CHRISTMAS PARTY AT AYR RACECOURSE H'CAP (DIV I) 7f 50y

3:20 (3:21) (Class 6) (0-60,62) 3-Y-O+

£2,975 (£885; £442; £300; £300; £300) **Stalls** High

Form RPR

0-03 **1** **Sienna Dream**[52] 5938 4-8-4 **48**..............................(h[1]) AndrewBreslin(5) 4 57
(Alistair Whillans) *hld up: hdwy over 2f out: led and rdn over 1f out: drew clr ins fnl f* **15/2**

1302 **2** 2 1/4 **Retirement Beckons**[8] 7509 4-8-13 **52**..............................(h) BenRobinson 8 55
(Linda Perratt) *hld up: hdwy over 2f out: effrt and ev ch over 1f out: sn rdn and edgd lft: one pce ins fnl f* **3/1**[1]

34P0 **3** 2 1/4 **Leeshaan (IRE)**[17] 7207 4-8-7 **46** oh1.............................. PhilDennis 3 43
(Rebecca Bastiman) *t.k.h: in tch: effrt whn nt clr run over 2f out to wl over 1f out: rdn and kpt on fnl f: nt rch first two* **10/1**

6000 **4** 2 1/4 **One Last Hug**[11] 7420 4-8-7 **46**.............................. PaddyMathers 5 38
(Jim Goldie) *midfield: drvn and outpcd over 3f out: rallied whn n.m.r briefly 2f out: kpt on fnl f to take 4th cl home* **25/1**

0110 **5** nk **Chaplin Bay (IRE)**[11] 7418 7-9-4 **57**.............................. JamesSullivan 2 48
(Ruth Carr) *t.k.h: trckd ldrs: led over 2f out to over 1f out: rdn and wknd ins fnl f* **10/1**

5330 **6** 1 **Cameo Star (IRE)**[14] 7305 4-9-6 **62**..............................(p) SeanDavis(3) 1 51
(Richard Fahey) *pressed ldr: drvn along over 2f out: wknd over 1f out* **9/1**

0- **7** 1/2 **Rince Deireanach (IRE)**[107] 3897 4-8-11 **55**.............................. GavinRyan(5) 12 43
(J J Lambe, Ire) *t.k.h: led to over 2f out: rdn and wknd over 1f out* **12/1**

0565 **8** 1/2 **Stoneyford Lane (IRE)**[16] 7236 5-8-7 **46** oh1..............................(b) JamieGormley 6 32
(Steph Hollinshead) *dwlt: hld up: effrt on outside over 2f out: sn no imp: btn over 1f out* **17/2**

2560 **9** nk **Khazix (IRE)**[24] 6985 4-8-13 **59**.............................. SeanKirrane(7) 11 45
(J F Levins, Ire) *hld up: shkn up over 2f out: sn n.d: btn over 1f out (jockey said gelding hung left-handed in hme str)* **13/2**[3]

6400 **10** 1 **Evolutionary (IRE)**[11] 7405 3-9-6 **61**.............................. PaulMulrennan 13 43
(Iain Jardine) *stdd in rr: t.k.h: pushed along over 2f out: wknd wl over 1f out* **33/1**

-044 **11** 6 **Bea Ryan (IRE)**[56] 5770 4-9-7 **60**.............................. DavidNolan 7 28
(Declan Carroll) *t.k.h: cl up tl rdn and wknd fr 2f out (jockey said filly hung right-handed throughout)* **6/1**[2]

1m 37.61s (5.11) **Going Correction** +0.775s/f (Yiel) **11 Ran SP% 117.6**
WFA 3 from 4yo+ 2lb
Speed ratings (Par 101): **101,98,95,93,92 91,91,90,90,89 82**
CSF £30.19 CT £234.95 TOTE £8.70: £3.00, £1.30, £4.10; EX 33.80 Trifecta £465.70.
Owner A C Whillans **Bred** Howard Barton Stud **Trained** Newmill-On-Slitrig, Borders

FOCUS
Add 12yds to race distance. The first division of a moderate handicap. The winner has been rated back towards her best.

7780 BOOK YOUR CHRISTMAS PARTY AT AYR RACECOURSE H'CAP (DIV II) 7f 50y

3:50 (3:50) (Class 6) (0-60,61) 3-Y-O+

£2,975 (£885; £442; £300; £300; £300) **Stalls** High

Form RPR

0/0- **1** **Stamp Of Authority (IRE)**[34] 6615 7-8-12 **56**..............................(t) KarenKenny(7) 6 62
(T G McCourt, Ire) *t.k.h: led after 1f: mde rest: rdn over 1f out: hld on wl fnl f* **12/1**

4003 **2** nk **Forever A Lady (IRE)**[8] 7507 6-9-7 **58**.............................. JoeFanning 9 63
(Keith Dalgleish) *hld up in midfield: hdwy over 2f out: effrt and chsd wnr over 1f out: kpt on fnl f: hld nr fin* **11/2**[3]

2343 **3** 1 1/2 **Be Bold**[8] 7508 7-9-1 **52**..............................(b) DavidAllan 7 54
(Rebecca Bastiman) *prom: rdn and edgd lft 2f out: sn outpcd: rallied ins fnl f: kpt on to take 3rd cl home* **9/2**[2]

0230 **4** nk **Cardaw Lily (IRE)**[6] 7591 4-8-10 **47**.............................. JamesSullivan 10 48
(Ruth Carr) *trckd ldrs: effrt and rdn 2f out: kpt on same pce ins fnl f* **17/2**

3361 **5** 1 **The Big House (IRE)**[10] 7444 3-9-8 **61**.............................. AndrewMullen 2 58
(Adrian Nicholls) *hld up in midfield: effrt and rdn over 2f out: kpt on same pce fnl f* **9/4**[1]

4050 **6** hd **Jessie Allan (IRE)**[12] 7367 8-8-1 **45**.............................. CoreyMadden(7) 4 43
(Jim Goldie) *hld up on ins: rdn over 2f out: no imp fr over 1f out* **20/1**

4000 **7** 3 **Pinkie Pie (IRE)**[22] 7027 3-8-1 **45**.............................. AndrewBreslin(5) 1 35
(Andrew Crook) *hld up: rdn along 3f out: effrt wl over 1f out: sn no imp* **50/1**

6305 **8** 3/4 **God Of Dreams**[11] 7404 3-9-0 **53**..............................(h) PaulMulrennan 3 41
(Iain Jardine) *t.k.h: in tch: rdn over 2f out: edgd lft and wknd over 1f out* **11/1**

0500 **9** 1/2 **Explain**[56] 5770 7-9-10 **61**..............................(v) TomEaves 11 49
(Ruth Carr) *hld up: rdn along over 2f out: sn n.d: btn over 1f out* **17/2**

0050 **10** 4 **Harperelle**[13] 7336 3-8-6 **45**..............................(p) JamieGormley 12 22
(Alistair Whillans) *hld up in midfield on outside: drvn and outpcd bnd over 3f out: btn fnl 2f* **28/1**

0055 **11** 1/2 **Dark Crystal**[52] 5933 8-8-8 **45**.............................. BenRobinson 13 21
(Linda Perratt) *cl up: rdn over 2f out: wknd wl over 1f out* **20/1**

0500 **12** 16 **Bareed (USA)**[35] 6572 4-8-8 **45**.............................. NathanEvans 5
(Linda Perratt) *sn pushed along in rr: struggling 1/2-way: lost tch fnl 3f* **22/1**

1m 37.89s (5.39) **Going Correction** +0.775s/f (Yiel) **12 Ran SP% 120.7**
WFA 3 from 4yo+ 2lb
Speed ratings (Par 101): **100,99,97,97,96 96,92,91,91,86 86,67**
CSF £72.72 CT £351.44 TOTE £17.00: £4.00, £1.90, £2.20; EX 104.70 Trifecta £354.00.
Owner Mrs P McCourt **Bred** C Farrell **Trained** Stamullen, Co Meath
■ Stewards' Enquiry : Karen Kenny four-day ban: excessive use of whip (Oct 15-18)

FOCUS
Add 12yds to race distance. The winning time was 0.28sec slower than the first division and this was a race in which the pace held up. Straightforward form, with the first two rated to their 2019 best.

7781 LEGENDARY WESTERN HOUSE HOGMANAY BALL H'CAP 7f 50y

4:20 (4:20) (Class 3) (0-90,90) 3-Y-O+ **£7,439** (£2,213; £1,106; £553) **Stalls** High

Form RPR

363 **1** **Get Knotted (IRE)**[10] 7431 7-9-9 **89**..............................(p) CallumRodriguez 1 101+
(Michael Dods) *in tch: effrt whn nt clr run 2f out: rdn and gd hdwy to ld ins fnl f: pushed out: comf* **3/1**[2]

3004 **2** 1 1/4 **Howzer Black (IRE)**[10] 7435 3-8-5 **78**.............................. AndrewBreslin(5) 11 84
(Keith Dalgleish) *hld up: hdwy to press ldr over 1f out: rdn and led briefly ins fnl f: kpt on same pce fnl 50yds* **16/1**

0324 **3** 4 **Kapono**[52] 5953 3-8-10 **78**..............................(p) BenCurtis 12 74
(Roger Fell) *midfield: hdwy on outside to ld 2f out: rdn and hdd ins fnl f: sn outpcd* **9/1**

0-0 **4** 3/4 **Sagittarius Rising (IRE)**[18] 7168 4-8-11 **77**............(t) RobbieDowney 10 72
(John C McConnell, Ire) *t.k.h in midfield: rdn and outpcd over 2f out: rallied and prom over 1f out: no ex ins fnl f* **5/1**[3]

3000 **5** hd **Tommy G**[11] 7402 6-8-2 **75**.............................. CoreyMadden(7) 2 69
(Jim Goldie) *t.k.h: hld up on ins: effrt whn nt clr run 2f out: sn hmpd and outpcd: r.o fnl f: no imp* **10/1**

2001 **6** nk **Young Fire (FR)**[25] 6922 4-9-9 **89**.............................. DanielTudhope 5 82
(David O'Meara) *hld up: hdwy on outside and prom over 1f out: rdn and wknd ins fnl f* **5/2**[1]

0244 **7** 9 **Fuente**[20] 7068 3-8-10 **78**..............................(b[1]) JoeFanning 9 47
(Keith Dalgleish) *plld hrd: chsd ldrs: rdn over 2f out: wknd over 1f out* **9/1**

0040 **8** 2 **Wasntexpectingthat**[11] 7402 3-8-2 **73**.............................. SeanDavis(3) 7 37
(Richard Fahey) *hld up: effrt on outside over 2f out: rdn and wknd over 1f out* **40/1**

4240 **9** ½ **Nubough (IRE)**[20] 7068 3-8-12 **80** .... JamieGormley 8 42
(Iain Jardine) *pressed ldr: ev ch and rdn over 2f out: wknd over 1f out* **14/1**

5300 **10** 4½ **Celebrity Dancer (IRE)**[45] 6207 3-9-1 **83** .... TomEaves 6 34
(Kevin Ryan) *led to over 2f out: sn rdn and wknd* **25/1**

1m 36.4s (3.90) **Going Correction** +0.775s/f (Yiel)
WFA 3 from 4yo+ 2lb **10** Ran **SP% 118.2**
Speed ratings (Par 107): **108,106,102,101,100 100,90,88,87,82**
CSF £51.07 CT £402.32 TOTE £4.00: £1.60, £4.00, £2.60; EX 45.60 Trifecta £336.50.
Owner D Neale **Bred** Rossenarra Bloodstock Limited **Trained** Denton, Co Durham
■ Stewards' Enquiry : Callum Rodriguez eight-day ban: careless riding (Oct 15-19, 21-23)

FOCUS
Add 12yds to race distance. The best race on the card and quite a dramatic contest. The winner has been rated in line with his best form over the past two years, and the second to his best.

7782 WINTER WEDDINGS AT WESTERN HOUSE HOTEL H'CAP 1m 2f
4:50 (4:50) (Class 4) (0-85,85) 3-Y-O+
£5,433 (£1,617; £808; £404; £300; £300) **Stalls** Low

Form RPR

4532 **1** **Addis Ababa (IRE)**[6] 7589 4-9-10 **85** ....(p) DanielTudhope 7 95
(David O'Meara) *trckd ldrs: smooth hdwy to ld over 2f out: drvn and carried hd high over 1f out: hld on wl fnl f* **5/2**[1]

3003 **2** 1½ **Glasses Up (USA)**[12] 7379 4-9-2 **77** .... DavidAllan 13 84
(R Mike Smith) *hld up: hdwy over 3f out: effrt and chsd wnr over 1f out: drvn and one pce ins fnl f* **9/1**[2]

4342 **3** 3¼ **Employer (IRE)**[10] 7436 4-9-0 **75** .... PaddyMathers 3 76
(Jim Goldie) *hld up: smooth hdwy 3f out: effrt and chsng ldrs whn hung lft over 1f out: sn no ex* **9/1**[2]

3431 **4** nk **Fannie By Gaslight**[3] 7682 4-9-0 **75** 5ex................................ TomEaves 12 75
(Mick Channon) *midfield: stdy hdwy 4f out: effrt and rdn over 2f out: one pce fr over 1f out: lost hind shoe (vet said filly lost left-hind shoe)* **5/2**[1]

4065 **5** 1 **Flint Hill**[53] 5898 3-8-6 **71** oh2................................(p) AndrewMullen 10 70
(Michael Dods) *hld up in tch: rdn over 2f out: outpcd and hung lft over 1f out: sn no imp* **40/1**

0412 **6** 4½ **Iron Mike**[12] 7368 3-8-6 **71** oh2................................(b) ShaneGray 9 61
(Keith Dalgleish) *sn led: rdn and hdd over 2f out: wknd wl over 1f out* **10/1**[3]

0334 **7** ½ **Detachment**[45] 6210 6-8-12 **73** .... BenCurtis 6 61
(Roger Fell) *hld up towards rr: rdn along over 2f out: wknd over 1f out* **12/1**

1400 **8** 3½ **Navigate By Stars (IRE)**[20] 7094 3-8-3 **71** ....(p) SeanDavis(3) 2 53
(Gordon Elliott, Ire) *hld up on ins: rdn and struggling over 3f out: nvr on terms* **33/1**

0030 **9** 2 **Dancin Boy**[24] 6961 3-9-0 **79** .... CallumRodriguez 5 57
(Michael Dods) *early ldr: chsd ldr to over 3f out: rdn and wknd over 2f out* **12/1**

6464 **10** 13 **Athmad (IRE)**[32] 6671 3-9-0 **79** ....(b[1]) JasonHart 11 31
(Brian Meehan) *s.i.s: hld up on ins: struggling over 3f out: sn btn* **18/1**

004- **11** 10 **Kilbarchan (GER)**[319] 9106 3-8-13 **78** .... JoeFanning 1 10
(Mark Johnston) *in tch on ins: lost pl 4f out: struggling fnl 3f* **25/1**

2m 20.1s (7.70) **Going Correction** +0.80s/f (Soft)
WFA 3 from 4yo+ 4lb **11** Ran **SP% 116.1**
Speed ratings (Par 105): **101,99,97,96,96 92,92,89,87,77 69**
CSF £25.83 CT £176.11 TOTE £2.70: £1.10, £2.60, £2.80; EX 21.50 Trifecta £123.40.
Owner Sir Robert Ogden **Bred** Sir Robert Ogden **Trained** Upper Helmsley, N Yorks

FOCUS
Add 12yds to race distance. A fair handicap with two dominating the market and one of them proved successful. The winner has been rated in line with his latest, and the second close to this year's form.

7783 YOUR CHRISTMAS BREAK AT WESTERN HOUSE HOTEL H'CAP 1m 2f
5:20 (5:20) (Class 6) (0-65,64) 3-Y-O+
£2,975 (£885; £442; £300; £300; £300) **Stalls** Low

Form RPR

4253 **1** **Iconic Code**[9] 7491 4-9-11 **63** ....(p[1]) JoeFanning 5 70
(Keith Dalgleish) *hld up in midfield: smooth hdwy whn n.m.r briefly over 2f out: rdn and led over 1f out: hld on wl fnl f* **10/3**[1]

0202 **2** nk **Frightened Rabbit (USA)**[9] 7492 7-8-10 **48** .... TomEaves 10 54
(Dianne Sayer) *s.i.s: hld up: swtchd rt and hdwy over 2f out: effrt and pressed wnr over 1f out: kpt on fnl f: hld cl home* **15/2**

1260 **3** ¾ **Three Castles**[11] 7404 3-9-7 **63** .... CallumRodriguez 6 69
(Keith Dalgleish) *hld up: effrt on outside over 2f out: chsng ldrs whn rdn and hung lft over 1f out: hung lft ins fnl f: r.o* **4/1**[2]

0505 **4** 1¾ **The Brora Pobbles**[8] 7508 4-8-3 **46** .... AndrewBreslin(5) 3 48
(Alistair Whillans) *s.i.s: hld up: hdwy over 2f out: kpt on fnl f: nt pce to chal* **25/1**

6000 **5** 5 **Rosin Box (IRE)**[62] 5560 6-8-13 **51** .... JasonHart 11 44
(Tristan Davidson) *hld up: hdwy on outside over 3f out: led over 2f out to over 1f out: sn rdn and wknd* **14/1**

3606 **6** 1¾ **Pammi**[9] 7492 4-8-7 **45** ....(p) PaddyMathers 1 35
(Jim Goldie) *prom: rdn and outpcd 2f out: n.d after* **11/1**

5200 **7** nk **Majeste**[41] 6343 5-9-11 **63** .... DavidAllan 12 52
(Rebecca Bastiman) *trckd ldrs: ev ch over 3f out to over 2f out: rdn and wknd over 1f out* **12/1**

0000 **8** 3½ **Can Can Sixty Two**[8] 7513 4-9-6 **58** .... BenCurtis 4 41
(R Mike Smith) *in tch: rdn along over 2f out: wknd wl over 1f out* **28/1**

-406 **9** 1 **George Ridsdale**[11] 7405 3-8-12 **54** .... NathanEvans 14 36
(Michael Easterby) *led 2f: pressed ldr: regained ld 1/2-way: hdd over 2f out: sn rdn and wknd* **6/1**[3]

51 **10** 1¼ **House Call (IRE)**[8] 7509 4-9-1 **56** 5ex................................ SeanDavis(3) 7 35
(Gordon Elliott, Ire) *midfield: effrt on outside over 2f out: wknd wl over 1f out* **8/1**

0020 **11** 29 **Muraadef**[33] 6627 4-8-7 **45** .... JamesSullivan 9
(Ruth Carr) *t.k.h: cl up: led after 2f: hdd 1/2-way: drvn and wknd over 3f out: t.o (jockey said gelding ran too free)* **20/1**

2m 22.26s (9.86) **Going Correction** +0.80s/f (Soft)
WFA 3 from 4yo+ 4lb **11** Ran **SP% 115.0**
Speed ratings (Par 101): **92,91,91,89,85 84,84,81,80,79 56**
CSF £26.98 CT £102.57 TOTE £3.60: £1.30, £2.80, £1.10; EX 26.70 Trifecta £134.80.
Owner Sir Ian & Ms Catriona Good **Bred** Norman Court Stud **Trained** Carluke, S Lanarks

FOCUS
Add 12yds to race distance. A modest handicap to end with the first four pulling clear, that quartet all coming from well off the pace. Straightforward form, with the winner rated back towards last year's best.
T/Jkpt: Not Won. T/Plt: £285.90 to a £1 stake. Pool: £69,377.67 - 177.10 winning units T/Qpdt: £25.30 to a £1 stake. Pool: £7,131.94 - 208.17 winning units **Richard Young**

[7569] KEMPTON (A.W) (R-H)
Tuesday, October 1

OFFICIAL GOING: Polytrack: standard to slow
Wind: Light, across Weather: Changeable; mostly heavy rain after race 3 (6.10) onwards

7784 BET AT RACINGTV.COM H'CAP 5f (P)
5:10 (5:11) (Class 7) (0-50,50) 3-Y-O+ **£2,587** (£770; £384; £192) **Stalls** Low

Form RPR

2256 **1** **Katherine Place**[5] 7628 4-9-3 **48** ....(t) RyanTate 1 58
(Bill Turner) *mde virtually all fr ins draw: rdn over 1f out: kpt on wl fnl f* **7/2**[1]

460 **2** 1¼ **Twilighting**[31] 6737 3-9-3 **48** .... DavidProbert 6 55
(Henry Candy) *dwlt: chsd ldrs: nipped through on inner to take 2nd 2f out: tried to chal over 1f out: clr of rest but no imp on wnr fnl f* **9/1**

5055 **3** 4 **Jaganory (IRE)**[17] 7172 7-8-12 **50** ....(v) AngusVilliers(7) 10 41+
(Christopher Mason) *pushed along in last pair fr wdst draw: rdn and prog over 1f out: styd on to take modest 3rd ins fnl f: no ch to threaten* **14/1**

-406 **4** 3 **Penwood (FR)**[7] 7557 4-9-5 **50** .... RobHornby 3 30
(Joseph Tuite) *sn urged along in last trio: kpt on to take 4th ins fnl f: no hdwy after* **4/1**[2]

2250 **5** 1½ **Starchant**[7] 7557 3-9-1 **49** ....(p[1]) MitchGodwin(3) 7 25
(John Bridger) *chsd ldrs: wd bnd over 3f out: wd bnd 2f out and lost grnd: no ch after* **12/1**

0206 **6** ½ **Gold Club**[43] 6284 8-9-2 **47** ....(p) SeanLevey 4 20
(Lee Carter) *prom: outpcd 2f out: disp mkodest 3rd 1f out: wknd fnl f (vet said gelding lost it's right hind shoe)* **7/1**

6000 **7** ½ **Kadiz (IRE)**[31] 6737 3-9-5 **50** ....(v[1]) LukeMorris 9 22
(Paul George) *dwlt: pushed along in rr: prog on inner bnd 2f out: drvn to dispute modest 3rd briefly 1f out: wknd* **20/1**

0345 **8** ¾ **Flowing Clarets**[7] 7557 6-9-2 **47** .... LiamJones 2 16
(John Bridger) *prom: chsd ldng pair 2f out but sn outpcd: fnd nil u.p over 1f out: wknd fnl f (jockey said mare hung left-handed)* **8/1**

0050 **9** 3 **Scarlet Red**[10] 7468 4-9-2 **47** ....(p) EoinWalsh 8 5
(Malcolm Saunders) *pressed wnr: wd bnd over 3f out: hung bdly lft bnd 2f out and lost all ch (jockey said filly hung left-handed)* **33/1**

3302 **10** 1¼ **Swell Song**[10] 7468 3-9-5 **50** ....(p) JosephineGordon 5
(Robert Cowell) *wd bnd over 3f out: chsd ldrs to 2f out: wknd (jockey said filly hung left-handed)* **11/2**[3]

1m 0.03s (-0.47) **Going Correction** -0.025s/f (Stan) **10** Ran **SP% 113.3**
Speed ratings (Par 97): **102,100,93,88,86 85,84,83,78,76**
CSF £34.31 CT £397.12 TOTE £5.00: £1.80, £2.70, £4.50; EX 35.00 Trifecta £364.00.
Owner Ansells Of Watford **Bred** The Hon Mrs R Pease **Trained** Sigwells, Somerset

FOCUS
A low-grade opener in which the well-backed favourite rewarded her supporters. It's been rated cautiously.

7785 GET SWITCHED ON WITH MATCHBOOK NURSERY H'CAP 5f (P)
5:40 (5:41) (Class 5) (0-75,77) 2-Y-O
£3,752 (£1,116; £557; £400; £400; £400) **Stalls** Low

Form RPR

2262 **1** **Newyorkstateofmind**[7] 7556 2-8-13 **67** .... MartinDwyer 8 74
(William Muir) *spd fr wd draw to press ldr after 1f: pushed along over 2f out: rdn to ld jst over 1f out: styd on wl* **4/1**[2]

5421 **2** 1¾ **Music Therapist (IRE)**[14] 7296 2-9-9 **77** .... HarryBentley 5 78
(George Scott) *dwlt: wl in rr and off the pce: prog on inner 2f out: chsd clr ldng pair 1f out: kpt on to take 2nd nr fin* **6/1**

5455 **3** nk **Swinley (IRE)**[32] 6667 2-9-3 **71** .... OisinMurphy 7 71
(Richard Hughes) *racd wd in rr and off the pce: v wd bnd over 3f out: rdn 2f out: styd on fnl f to take 3rd last strides* **12/1**

1353 **4** nk **Too Hard To Hold (IRE)**[17] 7186 2-9-4 **72** .... RichardKingscote 1 71
(Mark Johnston) *led fr ins draw: clr w wnr 1/2-way: hdd jst over 1f out: fdd and lost 2 pls nr fin* **9/2**[3]

5064 **5** nse **Falconidae (IRE)**[14] 7296 2-8-10 **64** .... SeanLevey 3 63
(Richard Hannon) *off the pce in midfield: kpt on over 1f out: nrst fin* **20/1**

560 **6** ½ **Fair Sabra**[15] 7276 2-8-5 **59** .... HollieDoyle 9 56
(David Elsworth) *outpcd in last: styd on over 1f out: nrst fin* **50/1**

4622 **7** nse **Dark Silver (IRE)**[12] 7391 2-9-7 **75** .... AndreaAtzeni 4 72
(Ed Walker) *off the pce in rr: rdn over 1f out: kpt on fnl f: nrst fin* **9/4**[1]

2003 **8** 1 **Mia Diva**[16] 7227 2-9-3 **74** .... CierenFallon(3) 6 67
(John Quinn) *chsd ldng pair: rdn and no imp over 2f out: wknd jst over 1f out* **13/2**

0424 **9** hd **Chasanda**[26] 6900 2-9-1 **74** ....(h) RayDawson(5) 2 66
(David Evans) *chsd ldng pair: rdn and no imp over 2f out: lost 3rd and wknd fnl f* **20/1**

1m 0.31s (-0.19) **Going Correction** -0.025s/f (Stan) **9** Ran **SP% 115.7**
Speed ratings (Par 95): **100,97,96,96,96 95,95,93,93**
CSF £27.48 CT £264.63 TOTE £3.60: £1.60, £2.00, £4.00; EX 24.90 Trifecta £240.30.
Owner Purple & Lilac Racing-Spotted Dog P'Ship **Bred** M E Broughton **Trained** Lambourn, Berks

FOCUS
This looked competitive beforehand but in the end the winner came home well on top, the rest of the field finishing in a heap in behind. Straightforward form.

7786 MATCHBOOK BEST VALUE EXCHANGE MAIDEN FILLIES' STKS (PLUS 10 RACE) 5f (P)
6:10 (6:13) (Class 5) 2-Y-O **£3,881** (£1,155; £577; £288) **Stalls** Low

Form RPR

1 **Rosa (IRE)** 2-9-0 0................................ HollieDoyle 2 76+
(Archie Watson) *mde all: rdn over 1f out: in command after: readily* **10/11**[1]

0 **2** 2¼ **Colouring**[25] 6919 2-9-0 0................................ OisinMurphy 1 68
(Ed Walker) *chsd ldng pair tl lft in 2nd over 2f out: rdn and no imp on wnr over 1f out: kpt on* **5/2**[2]

06 **3** 2¾ **Veleta**[28] 6831 2-9-0 0................................ HectorCrouch 5 58
(Clive Cox) *chsd ldrs: lft in 3rd over 2f out: one pce and no imp on ldng pair after* **16/1**

4 ¾ **Urtzi (IRE)** 2-9-0 0................................ LukeMorris 10 55
(Michael Attwater) *nt that wl away fr wdst draw: rcvrd to chse ldrs after 2f: urged along 2f out: no hdwy fnl f* **50/1**

5 nk **Trecco Bay** 2-9-0 0 .... GeraldMosse 3 54+
(David Elsworth) *slowly away: virtually t.o after 1f: latched on to bk of field 1/2-way: carried lft fnl f but kpt on: nrst fin (jockey said filly was slowly away)* **9/1**

6 6 nse **Don'tyouwantmebaby (IRE)**[46] 6159 2-9-0 0 .... KieranShoemark 4 54
(Richard Spencer) *hanging lft and dropped to rr over 3f out: nvr a factor after: hung lft but kpt on fnl f (jockey said filly hung left-handed)* **25/1**

00 7 ¾ **Heleta**[15] 7276 2-9-0 0 .... CharlesBishop 8 51
(Peter Hedger) *nvr on terms in rr: no real hdwy over 1f out* **100/1**

40 8 ½ **Queens Road (IRE)**[14] 7308 2-9-0 0 .... RyanTate 7 50
(Bill Turner) *chsd ldng trio to over 2f out: steadily wknd over 1f out* **40/1**

0 9 3 ¼ **Edge Of The Bay**[50] 6019 2-8-11 0 .... MitchGodwin(3) 6 38
(Christopher Mason) *chsd wnr: hung bdly lft bnd 2f out: dropped to rr and no ch after (jockey said filly hung left-handed)* **100/1**

44 10 2 ¼ **Miss Paxman**[66] 5447 2-9-0 0 .... (b¹) RobHornby 9 30
(Martyn Meade) *reluctant to enter stalls: a wl in rr* **13/2³**

1m 0.75s (0.25) **Going Correction** -0.025s/f (Stan) **10 Ran SP% 120.4**
Speed ratings (Par 92): **97,93,89,87,87 87,86,85,80,76**
CSF £3.32 TOTE £1.70: £1.10, £1.10, £3.00; EX 3.50 Trifecta £19.50.
Owner Saeed Bin Mohammed Al Qassimi **Bred** Michael Mullins **Trained** Upper Lambourn, W Berks

FOCUS
Not an especially strong maiden on the face of it but a taking performance from the winner and there were some promising efforts in behind too.

7787 MATCHBOOK CASINO NOVICE AUCTION STKS 7f (P)
6:40 (6:43) (Class 6) 2-Y-O £3,105 (£924; £461; £230) **Stalls Low**

Form RPR

0221 1 **Overpriced Mixer**[32] 6673 2-9-9 79 .... NicolaCurrie 9 79
(Jamie Osborne) *mde virtually all: shkn up 2f out: hrd pressed ins fnl f: hld on wl (jockey said colt hung left-handed in the final furlong)* **7/4¹**

52 2 hd **Lyricist Voice**[41] 6344 2-9-2 0 .... AndreaAtzeni 11 71
(Marco Botti) *chsd ldrs: shkn up and prog over 1f out: chsd wnr ins fnl f: str chal fnl 100yds: nt qckn nr fin* **2/1²**

3 1 ¼ **Diamond Falls (IRE)** 2-9-2 0 .... KieranShoemark 3 68+
(Amanda Perrett) *wl in rr: pushed along over 2f out: prog and swtchd rt over 1f out: r.o fnl f to take 3rd last strides: nrst fin* **16/1**

032 4 shd **I Had A Dream**[53] 5895 2-8-11 67 .... LukeMorris 6 63
(Tom Clover) *chsd ldng pair: rdn over 2f out: tried to chal over 1f out: one pce ins fnl f* **6/1³**

03 5 nk **Liberty Filly**[13] 7331 2-8-11 0 .... JasonWatson 4 62
(Roger Charlton) *chsd ldrs: shkn up over 2f out: kpt on steadily over 1f out but nvr quite pce to chal: nt disgracd* **9/1**

6 1 ½ **Stealth Command** 2-9-2 0 .... ShaneKelly 10 63
(Murty McGrath) *t.k.h early: trckd wnr: chal over 2f out to over 1f out: wknd fnl f* **66/1**

60 7 4 **Opine (IRE)**[25] 6927 2-9-2 0 .... CallumShepherd 2 53
(Michael Bell) *sltly awkward s: wl in rr: pushed along and no prog over 2f out: passed wkng rivals over 1f out to take modest 7th fnl f: nvr in it* **40/1**

8 1 ¾ **Berkshire Philly** 2-8-11 0 .... RobHornby 1 43
(Andrew Balding) *dwlt: nvr bttr than midfield: rdn and no prog over 2f out* **14/1**

9 1 ¾ **Enchantee (IRE)** 2-8-11 0 .... DavidProbert 5 39
(Sir Mark Todd) *awkward s: a in rr: brief effrt over 2f out: sn no prog (jockey said filly was slowly away)* **33/1**

10 2 ¼ **Centrifuge (IRE)** 2-8-11 0 .... HollieDoyle 8 33
(Michael Blanshard) *rn green and a in last trio: nvr a factor* **50/1**

05 11 1 ¼ **Abenakian (IRE)**[55] 5823 2-8-11 0 .... (b¹) RayDawson(5) 7 35
(Jane Chapple-Hyam) *t.k.h: chsd ldng trio tl wknd qckly over 1f out (jockey said gelding ran green)* **66/1**

0 12 8 **Lenny The Lion**[27] 6858 2-8-9 0 .... MorganCole(7) 12 14
(Lydia Pearce) *hung bdly lft and racd v wd thrght: a bhd (jockey said colt hung badly left-handed throughout)* **100/1**

1m 28.02s (2.02) **Going Correction** -0.025s/f (Stan) **12 Ran SP% 117.8**
Speed ratings (Par 93): **87,86,85,85,84 83,78,76,74,72 70,61**
CSF £5.14 TOTE £2.80: £1.10, £1.20, £3.50; EX 5.80 Trifecta £47.00.
Owner The 10 For 10 Partnership **Bred** Glebe Farm Stud **Trained** Upper Lambourn, Berks
■ Stewards' Enquiry : Jason Watson £290 fine; use of mobile outside of phone zone

FOCUS
A good finish to this novice auction event but probably unwise to get carried away by the bare form. The second and third were the only pair to make up any ground from off the pace. A minor pb from the winner.

7788 MATCHBOOK BETTING PODCAST FILLIES' H'CAP 1m (P)
7:10 (7:11) (Class 4) (0-80,81) 3-Y-O+ £6,469 (£1,925; £962; £481; £400; £400) **Stalls Low**

Form RPR

1321 1 **Crystal Casque**[18] 7165 4-8-12 73 .... AngusVilliers(7) 2 80
(Rod Millman) *hld up in 6th: impeded on inner over 4f out: prog to chse ldr over 2f out: pushed into ld over 1f out: rdn and kpt on fnl f* **6/1³**

2260 2 ¾ **Yusra**[104] 3994 4-9-7 78 .... CierenFallon(3) 3 83
(Marco Botti) *t.k.h: in tch: prog to chse ldng pair wl over 1f out: sn rdn: kpt on fnl f to take 2nd nr fin (jockey said filly hung right-handed and ran too free early on)* **15/2**

5233 3 ½ **Mums Hope**[34] 6593 3-9-5 76 .... (b¹) JasonWatson 4 80
(Hughie Morrison) *mde most: rdn over 2f out: hdd over 1f out: one pce and hld after: lost 2nd nr fin* **3/1²**

12-5 4 3 ¾ **Equal Sum**[12] 7373 3-9-10 81 .... SeanLevey 1 76
(Richard Hannon) *trckd ldng pair: shkn up and nt qckn over 2f out: fdd over 1f out (jockey said filly hung left-handed)* **7/1**

66-0 5 3 ¼ **Al Nafoorah**[16] 7250 5-9-12 80 .... HectorCrouch 5 68
(Michael Wigham) *stdd s: hld up in last: impeded over 4f out: shkn up 2f out: no great prog and nvr in it (jockey said mare suffered interference in running and was then never travelling)* **33/1**

-021 6 3 ¼ **Dubrava**[55] 5813 3-9-7 78 .... AndreaAtzeni 6 58
(Roger Varian) *chsd ldrs: pushed along over 3f out: dropped to last and struggling 2f out: wl btn after (jockey said filly stopped quickly; trainers rep could offer no explanation for the poor performance)* **2/1¹**

0-41 7 nk **Havana Jane**[22] 7032 4-8-12 66 .... OisinMurphy 7 46
(Andrew Balding) *t.k.h: racd wd early: mostly chsd ldr to over 2f out: wknd* **7/1**

1m 39.79s (-0.01) **Going Correction** -0.025s/f (Stan) **7 Ran SP% 112.3**
WFA 3 from 4yo+ 3lb
Speed ratings (Par 102): **99,98,97,94,90 87,87**
CSF £47.17 TOTE £7.80: £3.00, £2.80; EX 43.10 Trifecta £149.90.
Owner The Dirham Partnership **Bred** Mrs J E Laws **Trained** Kentisbeare, Devon

FOCUS
They didn't appear to go too hard early here but the field still finished well strung out. Another pb from the second, with the third rated to form.

7789 MATCHBOOK VIP H'CAP 6f (P)
7:40 (7:41) (Class 4) (0-80,80) 3-Y-O+ £6,469 (£1,925; £962; £481; £400; £400) **Stalls Low**

Form RPR

1-10 1 **Total Commitment (IRE)**[25] 6916 3-9-7 80 .... JasonWatson 3 92
(Roger Charlton) *trckd ldrs: clsd to take 2nd over 2f out: pushed into ld over 1f out: wl in command after: readily (trainers rep said, regards apparent improvement in form, gelding's run at Ascot came too soon and the gelding benefitted from the return to Kempton)* **5/1³**

025 2 1 ¼ **Busby (IRE)**[17] 7188 4-9-3 75 .... (p) MartinDwyer 9 83
(Conrad Allen) *dwlt: sn chsd ldrs: shkn up over 2f out: prog over 1f out: drvn to take 2nd fnl 100yds: nvr able to chal* **7/2²**

4001 3 ½ **Revolutionise (IRE)**[25] 6930 3-9-7 80 .... AndreaAtzeni 10 86+
(Roger Varian) *dwlt: swtchd to r on inner and hld up in last trio: shkn up and prog wl over 1f out: styd on on fnl f to take 3rd nr fin: too late to chal (jockey said gelding hung right-handed)* **15/8¹**

1646 4 ¾ **Golden Force**[13] 7351 3-9-5 78 .... (p) HectorCrouch 4 82
(Clive Cox) *mde most at fast pce to over 1f out: lost 2nd and one pce fnl 100yds* **14/1**

0302 5 ½ **Swiss Knight**[12] 7397 4-9-6 78 .... (t) RichardKingscote 11 80
(Stuart Williams) *towards rr: effrt over 2f out: kpt on over 1f out: nt pce to threaten* **9/1**

3505 6 3 ¾ **Shorter Skirt**[17] 7206 3-9-4 77 .... CharlesBishop 1 67
(Eve Johnson Houghton) *slowly away: wl in rr: rdn 2f out: sme late prog but nvr a threat (jockey said filly was slowly away)* **20/1**

2523 7 1 ½ **Swiss Pride (IRE)**[8] 7514 3-8-9 75 .... (p¹) AngusVilliers(7) 6 61
(Richard Hughes) *w ldng pair at fast pce for 2f: steadily wknd fr 2f out* **15/2**

1640 8 2 ½ **Fuwairt (IRE)**[176] 1644 7-9-1 78 .... ThomasGreatrex(5) 2 56
(David Loughnane) *dwlt and awkward s: mostly in last and nvr a factor (jockey said gelding was slowly away)* **20/1**

2200 9 hd **Rock Of Estonia (IRE)**[24] 6968 4-9-4 76 .... DanielMuscutt 7 53
(Michael Squance) *in tch: effrt on inner 2f out: no prog over 1f out: sn wknd* **80/1**

3153 10 13 **Shining**[94] 4375 3-9-5 78 .... CharlieBennett 5 13
(Jim Boyle) *tk fierce hold: w ldr 2f: lost 2nd and wknd rapidly over 2f out: t.o* **66/1**

1m 12.55s (-0.55) **Going Correction** -0.025s/f (Stan) **10 Ran SP% 114.4**
WFA 3 from 4yo+ 1lb
Speed ratings (Par 105): **102,100,99,98,98 93,91,87,87,70**
CSF £21.57 CT £44.66 TOTE £5.60: £1.70, £1.20, £1.30; EX 23.20 Trifecta £72.70.
Owner Brook Farm Bloodstock **Bred** Watership Down Stud **Trained** Beckhampton, Wilts

FOCUS
A solid, contested pace for this competitive sprint handicap and the winner quickly bounced back from his Ascot disappointment, looking one to keep on the right side of in the process. It's been rated around the second.

7790 MATCHBOOK H'CAP 1m 3f 219y(P)
8:10 (8:11) (Class 6) (0-65,65) 4-Y-O+ £3,105 (£924; £461; £400; £400; £400) **Stalls Low**

Form RPR

6542 1 **Mullarkey**[35] 6566 5-9-1 59 .... KierenFox 6 65
(John Best) *prom: shkn up to ld wl over 1f out: sn hdd: rallied fnl f to ld last strides* **11/2²**

3604 2 nk **Miss M (IRE)**[27] 6854 5-9-3 61 .... MartinDwyer 9 67
(William Muir) *hld up in midfield: prog 3f out: rdn to ld over 1f out: kpt on fnl f but hdd last strides* **10/1**

6563 3 2 ¼ **Beer With The Boys**[16] 7233 4-8-10 59 .... (v) ScottMcCullagh(5) 2 61
(Mick Channon) *chsd ldr 2f: styd v prom: lost pl and shkn up over 2f out: styd on again over 1f out to take 3rd ins fnl f* **10/1**

3030 4 nk **Hidden Depths (IRE)**[28] 6830 4-9-6 64 .... (t¹) ShaneKelly 10 65
(Neil Mulholland) *hld up towards rr: briefly waiting for a gap over 2f out: prog over 1f out: styd on to take 4th ins fnl f: nt pce to chal* **33/1**

02 5 1 ¾ **By Rail**[20] 7083 5-9-6 64 .... (b) CallumShepherd 1 63
(Nick Littmoden) *cl up: rdn over 2f out: nt qckn and outpcd over 1f out: one pce after* **8/1**

2434 6 1 **Agent Gibbs**[66] 5425 7-9-4 62 .... (p) RossaRyan 14 59
(John O'Shea) *trckd ldr after 2f: led 3f out to wl over 1f out: fdd fnl f* **14/1**

3054 7 1 ¼ **Sweet Nature (IRE)**[15] 7271 4-8-12 56 .... LukeMorris 5 51
(Laura Mongan) *awkward s: mostly in last trio: rdn 3f out: kpt on u.p fnl 2f: nvr nrr (jockey said filly jumped awkwardly leaving the stalls)* **33/1**

6351 8 nse **Topology**[20] 7083 6-9-4 62 .... CharlesBishop 8 57
(Joseph Tuite) *towards rr: pushed along 4f out: promising hdwy 2f out to chse ldrs over 1f out: effrt sn fizzled out* **15/2³**

5322 9 1 **Croeso Cymraeg**[25] 6939 5-9-7 65 .... RaulDaSilva 11 58
(James Evans) *stdd s: hld up in last pair: gng strly but stl there 3f out: prog 2f out: shkn up over 1f out: no hdwy after* **5/2¹**

4114 10 ½ **Power Home (IRE)**[162] 1988 5-9-6 64 .... OisinMurphy 12 57
(Denis Coakley) *racd wd: nvr beyond midfield: rdn and lft bhd over 2f out* **14/1**

5030 11 ½ **Dimmesdale**[67] 5378 4-8-8 52 .... LiamJones 13 44
(John O'Shea) *mostly in last pair: drvn in detached last 3f out: plugged on over 1f out* **40/1**

0040 12 5 **Ice Canyon**[31] 6736 5-9-4 62 .... EoinWalsh 7 46
(Kevin Frost) *trckd ldrs: effrt on inner and short of room over 2f out: wknd qckly wl over 1f out* **25/1**

3-00 13 nk **Zarrar (IRE)**[20] 7083 4-9-4 62 .... (bt) RyanTate 4 45
(Camilla Poulton) *a towards rr: rdn 3f out: wknd (jockey said gelding jumped left leaving the stalls)* **40/1**

4654 14 28 **Last Enchantment (IRE)**[16] 7233 4-9-4 65 .... (t) CierenFallon(3) 3 3
(Neil Mulholland) *sn led: false step over 8f out: hdd & wknd rapidly 3f out: eased and t.o (jockey said filly took a false step and was never travelling thereafter)* **25/1**

2m 36.18s (1.68) **Going Correction** -0.025s/f (Stan) **14 Ran SP% 116.8**
Speed ratings (Par 101): **93,92,91,91,89 89,88,88,87,87 87,83,83,64**
CSF £53.05 CT £533.86 TOTE £6.20: £1.60, £3.30, £3.90; EX 58.10 Trifecta £392.30.
Owner Thomson & Partners **Bred** Best Breeding **Trained** Oad Street, Kent

FOCUS
A steady pace for the finale, the winner digging deep to gain a deserved success. Straightforward form rated around the first two.
T/Plt: £60.60 to a £1 stake. Pool: £66,309.48 - 798.59 winning units T/Qpdt: £8.50 to a £1 stake. Pool: £12,905.99 - 1,112.71 winning units **Jonathan Neesom**

7791 - 7793a (Foreign Racing) - See Raceform Interactive

6761
CORK (R-H)
Tuesday, October 1

OFFICIAL GOING: Yielding to soft (soft in places on round course)

7794a NAVIGATION STKS (LISTED RACE) 1m 125y
3:35 (3:36) 3-Y-O+

£23,918 (£7,702; £3,648; £1,621; £810; £405)

RPR

1 **Up Helly Aa (IRE)**[75] 5112 3-9-4 103 .... WJLee 8 106+
(W McCreery, Ire) *racd in mid-div: prog u.p 2f out: chsd ldrs in 3rd ent fnl f: kpt on wl under hands and heels to ld fnl 50yds* **11/4**[1]

2 *nk* **Pincheck (IRE)**[17] 7220 5-9-7 109 .... ShaneFoley 10 104
(Mrs John Harrington, Ire) *sn chsd ldrs in 4th: clsr in 2nd over 2f out: led over 1f out: strly pressed fnl 100yds: hdd fnl 50yds* **9/2**[3]

3 *1 1/4* **Laughifuwant (IRE)**[20] 7093 4-9-7 99 .... ColinKeane 2 101
(Gerard Keane, Ire) *led for 2f: chsd ldrs tl clsr briefly in 2nd appr fnl f: dropped to 3rd ins fnl 150yds: kpt on same pce* **7/2**[2]

4 *1/2* **Amedeo Modigliani (IRE)**[181] 1531 4-9-7 98 ......(t[1]) DonnachaO'Brien 3 100
(A P O'Brien, Ire) *mid-div early: sn towards rr of mid-div: prog far side 2f out to chse ldrs: travelled wl whn briefly short of room appr fnl f in 4th: no imp fnl 150yds where again squeezed for room: kpt on same pce (jockey said colt got no run)* **8/1**

5 *2* **Wisdom Mind (IRE)**[33] 6646 4-9-2 94 ....(t) DeclanMcDonogh 5 91
(Joseph Patrick O'Brien, Ire) *chsd early ldrs on inner: mid-div 1/2-way: rdn and no imp appr fnl f in 7th: kpt on wl into 5th cl home* **25/1**

6 *hd* **Psychedelic Funk**[32] 6693 5-9-7 100 ....(b) GaryCarroll 7 95
(G M Lyons, Ire) *chsd ldrs: rdn in 4th 2f out: no imp ent fnl f: kpt on same pce: dropped to 6th cl home* **14/1**

7 *1 1/4* **Wargrave (IRE)**[22] 7038 3-9-4 103 .... ChrisHayes 14 94
(J A Stack, Ire) *trckd ldrs in 3rd tl led after 2f: hdd over 1f out: wknd fnl f* **7/1**

8 *nk* **Myth Creation (USA)**[8] 7529 4-9-2 77 ....(t) ShaneCrosse 6 87
(Joseph Patrick O'Brien, Ire) *racd towards rr tl prog under 2f out: no imp in 8th ent fnl f: kpt on same pce* **66/1**

9 *3 1/4* **Rionach**[33] 6646 4-9-2 98 ....(h) LeighRoche 1 80
(M D O'Callaghan, Ire) *racd in rr tl rdn and prog on inner under 2f out: wnt 9th ent fnl f: kpt on same pce: nvr on terms* **20/1**

10 *2 1/2* **Drombeg Dream (IRE)**[22] 7038 4-9-2 93 .... RobbieColgan 11 74
(Augustine Leahy, Ire) *racd in rr of mid-div: pushed along over 3f out: no imp 2f out* **50/1**

11 *shd* **Tinandali (IRE)**[75] 5112 3-9-4 102 .... OisinOrr 12 81
(D K Weld, Ire) *racd in mid-div: clsr to chse ldrs after 3f: pushed along over 3f out: no imp under 2f out: sn no ex* **10/1**

12 *1 3/4* **Shekiba (IRE)**[78] 5007 4-9-2 87 ....(b) GaryHalpin 4 70
(Joseph G Murphy, Ire) *a towards rr: rdn 3f out: sn no imp* **50/1**

13 *8* **Allegio (IRE)**[38] 6480 6-9-7 94 .... SeamieHeffernan 9 57
(Denis Gerard Hogan, Ire) *trckd ldr in 2nd tl under 3f out: wknd qckly fr 2f out* **20/1**

1m 52.95s
WFA 3 from 4yo+ 4lb **13 Ran SP% 125.2**
CSF £14.77 TOTE £3.30: £1.50, £1.70, £1.50; DF 14.30 Trifecta £63.30.
Owner Flaxman Stables Ireland Ltd **Bred** Flaxman Stables Ireland Ltd **Trained** Rathbride, Co Kildare

FOCUS
Things got pretty tight between some of these in the closing stages but the well-bred winner confirmed that he is a highly-exciting sort for next season. The second, rated close to his latest, helps set the level.

7795 - 7798a (Foreign Racing) - See Raceform Interactive

7601
MAISONS-LAFFITTE (R-H)
Tuesday, October 1

OFFICIAL GOING: Turf: soft

7799a PRIX DE POISSY (CLAIMER) (2YO) (TURF) 1m 1f
2:35 2-Y-0 £12,162 (£4,864; £3,648; £2,432; £1,216)

RPR

1 **Terre De France (FR)**[11] 2-8-11 0 .... MaximeGuyon 7 78
(F Rossi, France) **17/10**[1]

2 *2 1/2* **Wing Power (IRE)**[19] 2-8-11 0 .... MickaelBerto 4 73
(S Dehez, France) **15/1**

3 *snk* **Saint Romain (FR)**[19] 2-8-13 0 ow2 .... ChristopheSoumillon 1 74
(C Boutin, France) **43/10**[2]

4 *snk* **Miss Roazhon**[52] 2-8-8 0 ....(p) MlleCoraliePacaut[(3)] 3 72
(P Monfort, France) **12/1**

5 *3* **Akyo (FR)**[19] 2-8-11 0 .... TonyPiccone 6 66
(M Boutin, France) **59/10**[3]

6 *1 1/2* **Mira Star (IRE)**[33] 6640 2-8-8 0 .... MickaelBarzalona 9 60
(Ed Vaughan) *dwlt: hld up in rr early: hdwy into midfield over 3f out: rowed along 2f out: rdn w limited rspnse over 1f out: kpt on one pce fnl f* **9/1**

7 *hd* **Headhunter (FR)** 2-8-11 0 .... LukasDelozier 5 63
(Andrea Marcialis, France) **22/1**

8 *1 1/4* **Pink Clover (FR)** 2-8-8 0 ....(p) AlexisBadel 2 57
(M Brasme, France) **68/10**

9 *shd* **Kairos (ITY)**[17] 2-9-1 0 .... CristianDemuro 8 64
(Andrea Marcialis, France) **15/1**

10 *3/4* **Mozzarella (FR)** 2-8-8 0 .... TristanBaron 11 55
(Mlle L Kneip, France) **59/1**

1m 52.52s (-2.18) **10 Ran SP% 119.4**
PARI-MUTUEL (all including 1 euro stake): WIN 2.70; PLACE 1.50, 2.60, 1.80; DF 14.30.
Owner L Haegel & Alexandre Giannotti **Bred** Sunday Horses Club S.L. & M Delcher Sanchez **Trained** France

7800a L'EXPRESS (CLAIMER) (4YO+) (TURF) 4f
4:20 4-Y-0+ £12,162 (£4,864; £3,648; £2,432; £1,216)

RPR

1 **Snoozy Sioux (IRE)**[22] 5-8-8 0 ....(b) FilipMinarik 6 68
(T Van Den Troost, Belgium) **79/10**

2 *1 3/4* **Sant Angelo (GER)**[112] 3715 5-8-8 0 .... ThomasTrullier[(3)] 2 64
(S Smrczek, Germany) **9/2**[2]

3 *snk* **Koutsounakos**[22] 4-8-11 0 ....(p) LukasDelozier 8 63
(Mario Hofer, Germany) **84/10**

4 *hd* **Kerascouet (FR)**[15] 5-8-11 0 .... TonyPiccone 12 63
(J-V Toux, France) **67/10**[3]

5 *1* **Finalize (FR)**[133] 5-8-2 0 .... MlleFriedaValleSkar[(6)] 4 56
(Rosine Bouckhuyt, Belgium) **38/1**

6 *1 1/2* **Imperial Tango (FR)**[22] 5-9-1 0 .... ChristopheSoumillon 7 57
(A Schutz, France) **9/5**[1]

7 *nse* **Zalkaya (FR)**[15] 7-8-2 0 .... MlleLauraGrosso[(6)] 11 49
(N Milliere, France) **29/1**

8 *2 1/2* **Predetermined (IRE)**[37] 6-8-11 0 .... AurelienLemaitre 3 42
(J-V Toux, France) **12/1**

9 *1 1/4* **Cox Bazar (FR)**[52] 5972 5-8-11 0 .... GabrieleMalune 9 37
(Ivan Furtado) *pushed along to dispute ld early: rdn and outpcd over 1f out: wknd ins fnl f* **17/2**

10 *3* **Castle Dream (FR)**[133] 2956 5-8-11 0 .... MickaelBerto 10 25
(Andrew Hollinshead, France) **16/1**

11 *1 1/2* **Never Without You (FR)**[15] 5-8-9 0 .... BenjaminMarie[(6)] 5 23
(P Capelle, France) **81/1**

45.94s **11 Ran SP% 120.0**
PARI-MUTUEL (all including 1 euro stake): WIN 8.90; PLACE 2.10, 2.10, 2.70; DF 30.20.
Owner Mme Nicole Moons **Bred** Mrs Michelle Smith **Trained** Belgium

7801 - 7810a (Foreign Racing) - See Raceform Interactive

7784
KEMPTON (A.W) (R-H)
Wednesday, October 2

OFFICIAL GOING: Polytrack: standard to slow
Wind: Quite fresh, half against Weather: Fine

7811 RACING TV PROFITS RETURNED TO RACING H'CAP (DIV I) 7f (P)
4:35 (4:36) (Class 6) (0-65,67) 3-Y-0+

£3,105 (£924; £461; £400; £400; £400) **Stalls Low**

Form RPR

0230 1 **Crackin Dream (IRE)**[11] 7447 3-9-5 **63** ....(p[1]) AdamKirby 1 70
(Clive Cox) *mde all: rdn 2f out: clr fnl f: drvn out* **11/2**

0020 2 *1 1/2* **Garth Rockett**[9] 7527 5-9-0 **56** ....(tp) LukeMorris 8 60+
(Mike Murphy) *taken down early: dwlt: wl in rr: urged along whn nt clr run 2f out: prog and squeezed between rivals over 1f out: styd on wl to take 2nd last 100yds: clsd on wnr but no ch* **12/1**

6316 3 *1* **Savitar (IRE)**[20] 7125 4-8-13 **62** .... LukeCatton[(7)] 3 64
(Jim Boyle) *hld up in midfield: sme prog over 2f out: shoved along and styd on over 1f out: tk 3rd last 75yds* **2/1**[1]

0204 4 *1 1/4* **Indian Sounds (IRE)**[15] 7310 3-9-9 **67** ....(b) JamesDoyle 12 64
(Mark Johnston) *chsd ldrs: prog over 2f out: disp 2nd over 1f out and looked a possible threat: fdd tamely fnl f* **7/2**[2]

-665 5 *1 1/2* **Alabama Dreaming**[18] 7189 3-9-4 **65** ....(v) MeganNicholls[(3)] 2 58
(George Scott) *trckd ldng pair: chsd wnr over 2f out: no imp over 1f out: wknd fnl f* **9/2**[3]

366 6 *1/2* **Altar Boy**[139] 2773 3-9-1 **66** .... ShariqMohd[(7)] 5 58
(Sylvester Kirk) *mostly in last trio: rdn over 2f out: modest late prog but nvr a factor (vet said colt bled from the nose)* **33/1**

400 7 *shd* **Hollander**[37] 6546 5-8-4 **51** ow1 ....(tp) ThoreHammerHansen[(5)] 10 44
(Alexandra Dunn) *towards rr: rdn wl over 2f out: no prog tl kpt on fnl f: n.d* **25/1**

5000 8 *1/2* **Secret Glance**[13] 7384 7-8-7 **49** oh4 .... HollieDoyle 9 40
(Adrian Wintle) *chsd ldrs on outer: rdn over 2f out: steadily wknd over 1f out* **80/1**

-001 9 *3* **Magwadiri (IRE)**[128] 3158 5-8-13 **60** .... KevinLundie[(5)] 13 44
(Mark Loughnane) *mostly in last trio: rdn and no real prog over 2f out* **40/1**

-000 10 *5* **Sinfonietta (FR)**[32] 6734 7-9-4 **60** .... ShaneKelly 6 31
(Sophie Leech) *chsd wnr to over 2f out: wknd qckly* **80/1**

65R4 11 *9* **Greybychoice (IRE)**[20] 7105 3-8-9 **60** .... AledBeech[(7)] 11 6
(Nick Littmoden) *taken down early: v awkward s and looked reluctant: ct up at bk of field: wknd over 2f out: t.o (jockey said gelding was slowly away)* **16/1**

1m 26.28s (0.28) **Going Correction** +0.025s/f (Slow)
WFA 3 from 4yo+ 2lb **11 Ran SP% 115.6**
Speed ratings (Par 101): **99,97,96,94,93 92,92,91,88,82 72**
CSF £63.67 CT £176.63 TOTE £4.40: £1.50, £2.20, £1.60; EX 41.90 Trifecta £163.90.
Owner Mrs Olive Shaw **Bred** Forenaghts Stud Farm Ltd **Trained** Lambourn, Berks

FOCUS
The track was again riding standard to slow, and the time of the opener was almost 3sec slower than standard, which was 0.38sec quicker than the second division. This lacked obvious progressive types.

7812 RACING TV PROFITS RETURNED TO RACING H'CAP (DIV II) 7f (P)
5:10 (5:11) (Class 6) (0-65,66) 3-Y-0+

£3,105 (£924; £461; £400; £400; £400) **Stalls Low**

Form RPR

3121 1 **Magicinthemaking (USA)**[7] 7576 5-9-5 **63** 5ex .... HollieDoyle 3 69
(John E Long) *t.k.h: hld up in last pair: brought wdst of all in st and gd prog over 1f out: rdn to dispute ld fnl 150yds: edgd ahd nr fin* **7/2**[2]

0264 2 *shd* **Turn To Rock (IRE)**[9] 7514 3-9-5 **65** .... JamieSpencer 1 70
(Ed Walker) *hld up in last quartet: rdn and prog on inner jst over 2f out: chal fnl f: disp ld last 150yds: jst pipped (jockey said gelding became upset in the stalls)* **13/2**[3]

4301 3 *3/4* **Gavi Di Gavi (IRE)**[21] 7080 4-9-3 **61** .... NicolaCurrie 10 65
(Alan King) *c out of stall slowly: hld up in last pair: prog on inner over 2f out: clsd w others over 1f out: styd on same pce fnl f* **15/8**[1]

0054 4 *shd* **Fronsac**[18] 7204 4-9-8 **66** ....(p[1]) JosephineGordon 8 70
(Daniel Kubler) *taken down early: chsd ldrs: rdn to cl w others over 1f out: sn nt qckn: kpt on same pce fnl f* **7/1**

5052 5 *nk* **Wild Dancer**[18] 7172 6-9-2 **60** .... DanielMuscutt 4 63
(Patrick Chamings) *hld up in midfield: prog 2f out: clsd w others over 1f out: kpt on same pce fnl f (jockey said mare hung right-handed inside the final furlong)* **25/1**

3134 6 *1 1/2* **Jupiter**[17] 7236 4-8-9 **56** ....(v) CierenFallon[(3)] 5 55
(Alexandra Dunn) *led: kicked for home over 2f out and 3 l ahd: wilted and hdd last 150yds (jockey said gelding stopped quickly)* **18/1**

2500 7 ½ **Ghazan (IRE)**[48] 6102 4-9-4 62....................(p) LiamKeniry 2 60
(Ivan Furtado) *hld up in last quartet: gng wl enough over 2f out: tried to make prog on inner over 1f out: kpt on one pce and nvr really in it (jockey said gelding was denied a clear run)* **12/1**

5242 8 nk **Flying Sakhee**[16] 7281 6-8-7 51 oh4....................(p) LukeMorris 6 48
(John Bridger) *towards rr: rdn and prog 2f out: lost pl over 1f out: n.d after (jockey said mare suffered interference in the home straight)* **66/1**

1226 9 3 **Imperial Act**[27] 6904 4-9-0 65.................... MariePerrault(7) 9 54
(Andrew Balding) *racd wd: wl in tch: pushed along and lost pl wl over 1f out: wknd* **14/1**

5534 10 3 ¼ **Mrs Worthington (IRE)**[19] 7157 3-9-1 61.................... CharlesBishop 12 41
(Jonathan Portman) *chsd ldr after 1f to over 1f out: losing pl whn hmpd sn after: wknd* **40/1**

0000 11 1 ¾ **Tintern Spirit (IRE)**[23] 7024 3-8-2 51 oh6.................... WilliamCox(3) 7 26
(Milton Bradley) *chsd ldr 1f: styd prom tl wknd wl over 1f out* **150/1**

1m 26.66s (0.66) **Going Correction** +0.025s/f (Slow)
WFA 3 from 4yo+ 2lb **11 Ran SP% 111.6**
Speed ratings (Par 101): **97,96,96,95,95 93,93,92,89,85 83**
CSF £24.27 CT £51.84 TOTE £5.30: £1.60, £1.80, £1.20; EX 18.30 Trifecta £55.20.
Owner Martin J Gibbs & R D John **Bred** Janice Woods **Trained** Brighton, East Sussex
■ Stewards' Enquiry : Daniel Muscutt two-day ban; careless riding (Oct 16-17)

FOCUS
The slower division by 0.38sec. The first three came from the back of the field. A minor pb from the second.

7813 32RED.COM/BRITISH STALLION STUDS EBF FILLIES' NOVICE STKS (PLUS 10 RACE) 6f (P)
5:40 (5:42) (Class 5) 2-Y-0 £3,881 (£1,155; £577; £288) **Stalls Low**

Form RPR

5435 1 **Masaakin**[19] 7155 2-9-0 73.................... JimCrowley 2 77
(Richard Hannon) *chsd ldrs in 5th: shkn up over 2f out: prog over 1f out: chsd ldng pair fnl f: styd on wl to ld last 75yds* **7/2**[3]

100 2 1 **So Sharp**[27] 6907 2-9-7 91.................... OisinMurphy 4 81
(Archie Watson) *led: rdn 2f out: hdd jst over 1f out: rallied and upsides as wnr wnt past 75yds out: kpt on but outpcd* **9/4**[2]

6533 3 ¾ **Glamorous Anna**[19] 7156 2-9-4 83.................... MitchGodwin(3) 12 79
(Christopher Mason) *spd fr wdst draw to chse ldr: rdn 2f out: led jst over 1f out: hdd and no ex last 75yds* **11/1**

4 1 ½ **Spinacia (IRE)** 2-8-9 0.................... GeorgiaDobie(5) 8 67
(Eve Johnson Houghton) *dwlt: racd in 7th and jst in tch: rdn over 2f out: kpt on over 1f out: nvr able to chal* **50/1**

2 5 hd **Qaseeda**[19] 7160 2-9-0 0.................... JamesDoyle 1 67
(William Haggas) *chsd ldng pair: rdn over 2f out: one pce and nvr able to cl* **6/4**[1]

06 6 2 ¾ **Cindy Bear (IRE)**[58] 5737 2-9-0 0.................... HarryBentley 6 58
(Roger Varian) *chsd ldng pair tl steadily wknd wl over 1f out* **12/1**

43 7 hd **Indyzeb (IRE)**[30] 6793 2-9-0 0.................... HollieDoyle 5 58
(Seamus Mullins) *wl off the pce in last trio: rdn over 2f out: nvr a threat but kpt on over 1f out* **100/1**

8 ½ **Lipslikecherries** 2-9-0 0.................... NicolaCurrie 11 56
(Jamie Osborne) *dwlt: wl off the pce in last trio: shkn up over 2f out: nvr a threat but kpt on over 1f out (jockey said filly ran greenly)* **100/1**

9 9 **Little Floozie** 2-9-0 0....................(w) ShaneKelly 9 29
(Brett Johnson) *slowly away: rcvrd to chse ldrs in 6th: wknd qckly over 2f out* **150/1**

10 7 **Perfect Sunset** 2-9-0 0.................... DavidProbert 7 8
(Andrew Balding) *v awkward s and slowly away: rn green in last: a bhd (jockey said filly reared as the stalls opened and hung left-handed)* **33/1**

1m 12.98s (-0.12) **Going Correction** +0.025s/f (Slow) **10 Ran SP% 120.5**
Speed ratings (Par 92): **101,99,98,96,96 92,92,91,79,70**
CSF £11.77 TOTE £5.30: £1.70, £1.30, £2.70; EX 11.90 Trifecta £67.70.
Owner Hamdan Al Maktoum **Bred** Shadwell Estate Company Limited **Trained** East Everleigh, Wilts

FOCUS
A fair novice race in which the leaders appeared to go quite quick.

7814 32RED CASINO EBF NOVICE STKS (PLUS 10 RACE) 1m (P)
6:10 (6:12) (Class 4) 2-Y-0 £5,822 (£1,732; £865; £432) **Stalls Low**

Form RPR

1 **First View (IRE)** 2-9-5 0.................... HectorCrouch 11 75
(Saeed bin Suroor) *trckd ldr to 2f out: sn rdn: rallied wl fnl f to ld nr fin* **7/1**

3 2 ½ **Stanford (IRE)**[26] 6926 2-9-5 0.................... OisinMurphy 8 74
(Andrew Balding) *led at mod pce: rdn and hdd 2f out: rallied to ld ins fnl f: hdd nr fin* **9/2**[3]

3 nk **Lord Neidin** 2-9-5 0.................... DavidProbert 6 73
(Alan King) *trckd ldng pair: clsd to ld 2f out but move nt decisive: drvn over 1f out: hdd ins fnl f: kpt on but hld* **50/1**

05 4 shd **Jellystone (IRE)**[17] 7235 2-9-5 0.................... HarryBentley 13 73
(Ralph Beckett) *trckd ldng pair: rdn and nt qckn 2f out: styd on again fnl f: gng on at fin* **33/1**

42 5 nk **Hlaitan**[13] 7392 2-9-5 0.................... JamesDoyle 2 72
(Hugo Palmer) *trckd ldrs: cl up fr 2f out: nt clr run 1f out and lost momentum: drvn and styd on nr fin (jockey said colt hung left-handed)* **9/4**[1]

6 2 ¾ **Ya Hayati (USA)** 2-9-5 0.................... WilliamBuick 3 66
(Charlie Appleby) *wl in tch: pushed along over 2f out: tk 6th over 1f out but no imp on ldrs after* **5/2**[2]

0 7 nse **Bee Able (USA)**[8] 7555 2-9-0 0.................... JosephineGordon 4 61+
(Ralph Beckett) *towards rr: urged along over 2f out: no prog tl kpt on ins fnl f* **66/1**

54 8 ¾ **Pinatar (IRE)**[7] 7571 2-9-5 0.................... KierenFox 12 64
(John Best) *hld up in last pair: pushed along and prog on inner 2f out: one pce and no imp fnl f* **100/1**

0 9 ½ **Chinese Whisperer (FR)**[19] 7162 2-9-5 0.................... TomQueally 7 63+
(Alan King) *t.k.h: hld up in midfield and trapped wd: shkn up over 2f out: one pce after* **66/1**

10 ½ **Spanish Kiss** 2-9-5 0.................... HollieDoyle 14 62+
(William Knight) *hld up in last fr wdst draw: no prog tl styd on fnl f: fin w a bit of a flourish* **66/1**

0 11 1 **Lismore (IRE)**[11] 7473 2-9-0 0.................... LukeMorris 5 55
(Sir Mark Prescott Bt) *nvr beyond midfield: bmpd along and no prog 2f out* **200/1**

12 shd **Savanna Gold (IRE)** 2-9-5 0.................... KieranShoemark 1 59
(Hugo Palmer) *dwlt: mostly in last quartet: shkn up and one pce fnl 2f (jockey said colt ran greenly)* **22/1**

13 ¾ **Cloud Thunder** 2-9-5 0.................... RichardKingscote 9 58
(Heather Main) *a towards rr: rdn and no prog over 2f out* **66/1**

6 14 3 ¾ **Saeer (IRE)**[22] 7055 2-9-5 0.................... RyanMoore 10 49
(Sir Michael Stoute) *a in last quartet: shkn up and hanging over 2f out: sn btn (trainers rep could offer no explanation for the poor performance)* **7/1**

1m 42.33s (2.53) **Going Correction** +0.025s/f (Slow) **14 Ran SP% 119.2**
Speed ratings (Par 97): **88,87,87,87,86 84,84,83,82,82 81,81,80,76**
CSF £36.73 TOTE £8.60: £2.70, £1.10, £18.10; EX 37.10 Trifecta £2055.90.
Owner Godolphin **Bred** Godolphin **Trained** Newmarket, Suffolk

FOCUS
This didn't appear to be run at a solid gallop and nothing got into it from the rear. The first five finished in a heap. The bare form is unlikely to prove better than rated.

7815 32RED H'CAP 1m (P)
6:40 (6:43) (Class 3) (0-95,97) 3-Y-O+
£9,337 (£2,796; £1,398; £699; £349; £175) **Stalls Low**

Form RPR

5512 1 **Kuwait Currency (USA)**[25] 6964 3-9-10 97....................(t) PatDobbs 4 104+
(Richard Hannon) *trckd ldng pair: wnt 2nd over 2f out: clsd over 1f out: rdn to ld last 100yds: hld on* **11/4**[2]

6311 2 nk **Romola**[40] 6410 3-9-6 93....................(v) RyanMoore 9 99
(Sir Michael Stoute) *trckd ldng trio: rdn to go 3rd jst over 2f out: drvn and kpt on over 1f out: tk 2nd and clsd on wnr nr fin* **9/1**

0530 3 ¾ **Akvavera**[20] 7106 4-9-1 85.................... HarryBentley 1 89
(Ralph Beckett) *racd freely: led: drvn for home over 2f out: hdd and no ex last 100yds (jockey said filly hung left-handed)* **9/1**

-133 4 shd **Cadre Du Noir (USA)**[9] 7517 3-9-0 87....................(b[1]) OisinMurphy 3 91
(Martyn Meade) *s.i.s: hld up in 6th: urged along over 2f out: prog over 1f out: styd on ins fnl f but nvr in time to chal* **5/2**[1]

5305 5 1 ¾ **Rousayan (IRE)**[21] 7068 8-9-4 88....................(h) BenCurtis 2 88
(Roger Fell) *chsd ldrs: rdn over 2f out: no prog and one pce over 1f out* **28/1**

1304 6 1 **Rectory Road**[29] 6841 3-8-8 84.................... WilliamCox(3) 5 82
(Andrew Balding) *t.k.h: hld up in last pair: rdn 2f out: kpt on but nvr enough pce to pose a threat* **5/1**[3]

1411 7 6 **Attainment**[18] 7191 3-9-7 94.................... AdamKirby 10 77
(James Tate) *chsd ldr to over 2f out: sn btn* **6/1**

0-60 8 1 **Golden Wolf (IRE)**[174] 522 5-9-1 85.................... ShaneKelly 6 66
(Tony Carroll) *stdd s: hld up in last pair: looked to be gng wl enough over 2f out: pushed along over 1f out and wknd* **100/1**

1m 38.4s (-1.40) **Going Correction** +0.025s/f (Slow)
WFA 3 from 4yo+ 3lb **8 Ran SP% 144.0**
Speed ratings (Par 107): **108,107,106,106,105 104,98,97**
CSF £25.60 CT £185.34 TOTE £2.80: £1.10, £2.60, £1.70; EX 22.60 Trifecta £152.60.
Owner Sheikh Abdullah Almalek Alsabah **Bred** Kenneth L Ramsey & Sarah K Ramsey **Trained** East Everleigh, Wilts

FOCUS
Useful handicap form. The winner has been rated in line with his 2yo best, with the fourth close to his latest.

7816 100% PROFIT BOOST AT 32REDSPORT.COM H'CAP (LONDON MIDDLE DISTANCE SERIES QUALIFIER) 1m 2f 219y(P)
7:10 (7:11) (Class 4) (0-80,82) 3-Y-O+
£6,469 (£1,925; £962; £481; £400; £400) **Stalls Low**

Form RPR

5145 1 **State Of Affair (USA)**[32] 6736 3-9-7 77.................... JamieSpencer 6 84
(Ed Walker) *mde all: set modest pce to 1/2-way: stretched on 4f out: drvn 3 l clr 2f out: all out but unchal* **6/1**[3]

4623 2 1 **City Tour**[12] 7413 3-9-5 75.................... RichardKingscote 4 80
(Lydia Richards) *hld up towards rr: ct out whn wnr wnt clr jst over 2f out: prog over 1f out: r.o to take 2nd nr fin: too late* **6/1**[3]

5153 3 ½ **Grey Spirit (IRE)**[18] 7212 4-10-3 82....................(p) LukeMorris 11 86
(Sir Mark Prescott Bt) *slowly away: t.k.h and sn trckd ldrs: rdn and prog to chse wnr wl over 1f out: kpt on but edgd rt: nvr able to chal and lost 2nd nr fin* **12/1**

401 4 nk **Champs De Reves**[42] 6331 4-9-4 72.................... MeganNicholls(3) 9 76
(Michael Blake) *hld up in rr: ct out whn wnr wnt clr jst over 2f out: drvn and styd on over 1f out: nrst fin but too late* **12/1**

0302 5 1 **Galactic Spirit**[29] 6830 4-9-5 70.................... FergusSweeney 1 72
(James Evans) *s.v.s: ct up at bk of field after 4f: cajoled along and tried to weave through fr 2f out: nt clr run and nvr able to threaten (jockey said gelding was slowly away and was denied a clear run in the home straight)* **33/1**

0121 6 1 ½ **Junior Rip (IRE)**[11] 7452 3-9-4 74....................(p) JasonWatson 7 73
(Roger Charlton) *trckd wnr to 1/2-way: drvn and nt qckn over 2f out: effrt to dispute 3rd briefly 1f out: fdd (jockey said gelding hung right-handed)* **5/1**[2]

4253 7 nk **Puerto Banus**[21] 7069 3-9-1 71.................... WilliamBuick 3 70
(Ian Williams) *prom: chsd wnr 1/2-way to wl over 1f out: pushed along and wknd fnl f* **7/1**

8 shd **Andaleep (IRE)**[10] 6166 3-9-1 71.................... LiamKeniry 2 69?
(Graeme McPherson) *wl in tch: shkn up over 2f out: briefly disp 2nd wl over 1f out: fdd fnl f* **66/1**

36-3 9 1 ½ **Purdey's Gift**[184] 1484 3-9-4 74.................... OisinMurphy 8 78+
(Andrew Balding) *dwlt: hld up in rr: ct out whn wnr wnt clr jst over 2f out: trying to make prog on inner whn nt clr run and snatched up 1f out (jockey said colt was denied a clear run inside the final furlong)* **9/4**[1]

0312 10 8 **Ad Libitum**[15] 7301 4-9-3 68....................(p) BenCurtis 10 49
(Roger Fell) *racd on outer: prog to dispute 2nd 1/2-way to 3f out: wknd over 2f out* **25/1**

2m 20.82s (-0.18) **Going Correction** +0.025s/f (Slow)
WFA 3 from 4yo+ 5lb **10 Ran SP% 113.7**
Speed ratings (Par 105): **104,103,102,102,101 100,100,100,99,93**
CSF £39.47 CT £413.64 TOTE £6.20: £2.60, £1.50, £3.40; EX 33.80 Trifecta £147.70.
Owner Mrs Fitri Hay **Bred** Forging Oaks Farm Llc **Trained** Upper Lambourn, Berks

FOCUS
Fairly decent handicap form. Muddling form.

7817 32RED ON THE APP STORE H'CAP 1m 2f 219y(P)
7:40 (7:42) (Class 6) (0-60,60) 3-Y-O
£3,105 (£924; £461; £400; £400; £400) **Stalls Low**

Form RPR

4216 1 **Sandy Steve**[23] 7025 3-9-7 60.................... OisinMurphy 10 70
(Stuart Williams) *hld up in last quartet: gd prog on inner 3f out: clsd on ldrs 2f out: led over 1f out: rdn out fnl f* **2/1**[1]

0056 **2** *1 ½* **Yvette**[32] 6720 3-9-4 **57**.....................(p) LukeMorris 3 64
(Sir Mark Prescott Bt) *sltly awkward s but sn trckd ldrs: rdn to cl over 2f out: led v briefly over 1f out: chsd wnr and kpt on but readily hld* **12/1**

0555 **3** *nse* **Guroor**[14] 7344 3-9-0 **60**.....................(p) MarcoGhiani(7) 9 67
(Marco Botti) *trckd ldrs: shkn up to cl 2f out: rdn and nt qckn over 1f out: kpt on to dispute 2nd fnl f: wl hld by wnr* **10/1**

5502 **4** *3 ½* **Miss Elsa**[15] 7295 3-9-1 **59**..................... GeorgiaDobie(5) 13 60
(Eve Johnson Houghton) *hld up in last pair: followed wnr through on inner whn making prog over 2f out: rdn and kpt on same pce over 1f out* **33/1**

4044 **5** *2 ½* **Four Mile Bridge (IRE)**[13] 7375 3-9-1 **54**..................... JasonWatson 1 50
(Mark Usher) *mostly trckd ldr: chal and upsides wl over 1f out: wknd fnl f* **14/1**

040 **6** *2* **Red Secret (CAN)**[60] 5656 3-9-7 **60**..................... DanielMuscutt 12 53
(Ed Dunlop) *dwlt: mostly in last pair and nt gng wl: drvn 4f out: styd on past wkng rivals fnl 2f* **20/1**

2204 **7** *1 ½* **Uncertain Smile (IRE)**[14] 7344 3-9-6 **59**.....................(h) AdamKirby 2 49+
(Clive Cox) *led at str pce: clr 1/2-way: hdd & wknd over 1f out* **10/1**

00-1 **8** *shd* **Atalanta Breeze**[23] 7025 3-9-3 **56**.....................(p) KieranShoemark 8 46
(Marcus Tregoning) *a towards rr on outer: drvn and no prog over 2f out: plugged on* **8/1**[3]

0212 **9** *¾* **Fame N Fortune**[13] 7375 3-9-4 **60**.....................(b) CierenFallon(3) 5 49
(Joseph Tuite) *mostly in midfield: sme prog over 3f out: drvn and no hdwy over 2f out: fdd (jockey said gelding hung right-handed)* **13/2**[2]

0431 **10** *2 ¼* **Ragstone Cowboy (IRE)**[46] 6202 3-9-6 **59**.....................(v) ShaneKelly 11 44
(Gary Moore) *dwlt: sn rchd midfield: rdn and no prog over 2f out: wknd over 1f out (jockey said gelding was slowly away)* **12/1**

6000 **11** *4 ½* **Lynchpin (IRE)**[28] 6860 3-8-6 **50**.....................(b) RayDawson(5) 14 27
(Lydia Pearce) *a wl in rr: rdn and no prog over 2f out* **150/1**

-036 **12** *19* **Duke Of Dunabar**[17] 7232 3-8-12 **51**..................... BenCurtis 4
(Roger Teal) *disp 2nd pl to 3f out: wknd rapidly: t.o* **14/1**

0005 **13** *3 ¾* **Miss Pollyanna (IRE)**[21] 7081 3-9-2 **55**.....................(h) FergusSweeney 6
(Roger Ingram) *a towards rr: wknd rapidly over 2f out: t.o* **80/1**

0400 **14** *3 ½* **Asensio**[16] 7290 3-9-1 **54**.....................(vt[1]) HectorCrouch 7
(Mohamed Moubarak) *pushed up to chse ldrs: wknd qckly 3f out: eased 2f out and t.o* **40/1**

2m 19.34s (-1.66) **Going Correction** +0.025s/f (Slow) **14 Ran SP% 116.7**
Speed ratings (Par 99): **110,108,108,106,104 103,101,101,101,99 96,82,79,77**
CSF £25.31 CT £198.62 TOTE £3.00: £2.00, £3.10, £3.60; EX 32.90 Trifecta £192.80.
Owner J W Parry **Bred** J W Parry **Trained** Newmarket, Suffolk
■ Stewards' Enquiry : Cieren Fallon two-day ban; careless riding (Oct 16-17)

FOCUS
This modest event was run at what appeared to be a sound gallop, and the time was a second and a half quicker than the preceding Class 4 event. A minor pb from the winner.

7818 BET AT RACINGTV.COM H'CAP 1m 7f 218y(P)
8:10 (8:12) (Class 6) (0-60,63) 3-Y-O+
£3,105 (£924; £461; £400; £400; £400) **Stalls** Low

Form RPR

5011 **1** **Casa Comigo (IRE)**[8] 7558 4-10-1 **63** 5ex..................... KierenFox 8 70+
(John Best) *hld up in midfield: nt clr run briefly wl over 2f out: prog sn after: led over 1f out and qckly asserted: rdn out* **13/8**[1]

5045 **2** *1 ½* **Doune Castle**[13] 7390 3-8-8 **51**.....................(v) DavidProbert 10 58
(Andrew Balding) *hld up wl in rr: swtchd lft over 2f out: rdn and prog after: styd on to dispute take 2nd 100yds out but edgd lft after* **16/1**

6420 **3** *shd* **Yasir (USA)**[11] 7474 11-9-4 **52**..................... ShaneKelly 3 57
(Sophie Leech) *slowly away and rousted: mostly in last pair tl prog on wd outside over 2f out: drvn and styd on to dispute 2nd last 100yds: carried lft after* **25/1**

4051 **4** *1 ½* **Percy's Prince**[9] 7520 3-8-12 **55** 6ex.....................(p) LukeMorris 1 60
(Sir Mark Prescott Bt) *trckd ldr: led over 3f out: tried to go for home over 2f out: hdd and one pce over 1f out* **10/3**[2]

324 **5** *1* **Sinndarella (IRE)**[37] 6531 3-8-2 **48**.....................(p[1]) NoelGarbutt(3) 7 52
(Sarah Hollinshead) *hld up in rr: nt clr run briefly wl over 2f out: swtchd lft wl over 1f out and drvn: kpt on but nvr able to threaten* **33/1**

4133 **6** *1 ½* **Barca (USA)**[8] 7553 5-9-12 **60**.....................(v[1]) JimCrowley 2 60
(Marcus Tregoning) *trckd ldng pair: wnt 2nd 3f out: drvn over 2f out and nt qckn: fdd jst over 1f out* **11/2**[3]

4463 **7** *3* **Demophon**[29] 6824 5-8-13 **47** oh1 ow1.....................(t[1]) OisinMurphy 6 44
(Steve Flook) *hld up in midfield: prog over 2f out: rdn and tried to cl on ldrs wl over 1f out: sn wknd* **25/1**

5350 **8** *hd* **Brinkleys Katie**[95] 4400 3-8-6 **49**.....................(v) JosephineGordon 11 47
(Paul George) *plld hrd: hld up in last: stl taking fierce hold after 1/2-way: shkn up on wd outside 2f out: kpt on but n.d (jockey said filly ran too freely)* **100/1**

3500 **9** *3 ½* **Bird To Love**[13] 7390 5-9-0 **48**.....................(p[1]) JasonWatson 12 40
(Mark Usher) *trckd ldrs: rdn over 3f out: stl cl enough over 2f out: sn wknd* **50/1**

5230 **10** *2 ¾* **Guaracha**[13] 7390 8-8-7 **46** oh1.....................(v) ThoreHammerHansen(5) 4 35
(Alexandra Dunn) *trckd ldrs: rdn over 2f out: wknd wl over 1f out* **50/1**

110/ **11** *5* **The Young Master**[158] 656 10-9-6 **54**.....................(p) AdamKirby 13 37
(Neil Mulholland) *rousted early: chsd ldrs on outer: rdn 4f out: wknd over 2f out* **16/1**

435- **12** *1 ¾* **Hattaab**[16] 8144 6-9-4 **52**..................... LiamKeniry 5 33
(Graeme McPherson) *dwlt: wl in rr: rdn 4f out: no prog over 2f out: wknd* **25/1**

4421 **13** *nk* **Spring Run**[18] 7202 3-9-2 **59**..................... CharlesBishop 9 41
(Jonathan Portman) *prom: rdn and stl cl up wl over 2f out: sn wknd qckly* **8/1**

6000 **14** *40* **Daniel Dravot**[83] 4834 3-8-0 **46** oh1..................... WilliamCox(3) 14
(Michael Attwater) *led to over 3f out: wknd rapidly: t.o (jockey said gelding stopped quickly)* **50/1**

3m 31.22s (1.12) **Going Correction** +0.025s/f (Slow)
WFA 3 from 4yo+ 9lb **14 Ran SP% 120.8**
Speed ratings (Par 101): **98,97,97,96,95 95,93,93,91,90 87,87,86,66**
CSF £29.62 CT £504.17 TOTE £2.90: £1.30, £2.40, £5.60; EX 38.90 Trifecta £354.40.
Owner Simon Malcolm **Bred** Simon Malcom **Trained** Oad Street, Kent

FOCUS
Very modest staying form, but a progressive winner. Solid form rated around the second, third and fourth.
T/Jkpt: Not won. T/Plt: £162.90 to a £1 stake. Pool: £55,838.10 - 250.10 winning units. T/Qpdt: £58.00 to a £1 stake. Pool: £6,830.15 - 87.01 winning units. **Jonathan Neesom**

7650 NEWCASTLE (A.W) (L-H)
Wednesday, October 2

OFFICIAL GOING: Tapeta: standard to slow
Wind: Light, half against on the straight course and in over 3f of home straight in race on the round cour

7819 GRANNY ELIZABETH H'CAP 2m 56y (Tp)
5:55 (5:55) (Class 4) (0-85,85) 4-Y-O+
£5,207 (£1,549; £774; £400; £400; £400) **Stalls** Low

Form RPR

3-11 **1** **Rubenesque (IRE)**[13] 7381 7-8-10 **74**.....................(t) JasonHart 2 81+
(Tristan Davidson) *dwlt: sn trcking ldrs: rdn to ld over 2f out: hrd pressed over 1f out: styd on wl fnl f* **10/1**

4140 **2** *1* **Cotton Club (IRE)**[17] 7231 8-9-2 **80**..................... JackMitchell 1 85
(George Boughey) *hld up in tch: hdwy over 2f out: effrt and ev ch over 1f out: edgd rt: kpt on same pce ins fnl f (jockey said gelding hung right-handed in the home straight)* **28/1**

1066 **3** *¾* **Handiwork**[84] 4782 9-9-6 **84**.....................(p) JoeFanning 7 88
(Steve Gollings) *dwlt: t.k.h: hld up: smooth hdwy on outside over 2f out: effrt and ev ch briefly over 1f out: rdn and one pce ins fnl f* **33/1**

4030 **4** *7* **Polish**[63] 5540 4-9-2 **80**.....................(p) ConnorBeasley 4 76
(John Gallagher) *chsd ldr: led gng wl over 3f out: rdn and hdd over 2f out: sn outpcd: n.d after* **8/1**[3]

3463 **5** *9* **Grandee (IRE)**[12] 7414 5-9-7 **85**..................... DanielTudhope 5 80
(Roger Fell) *hld up: rdn and outpcd 3f out: btn over 1f out (trainer could offer no explanation for the poor peformance)* **5/6**[1]

5033 **6** *41* **Trouble And Strife (IRE)**[11] 7439 4-8-13 **77**.....................(b) RyanTate 3 13
(Sir Mark Prescott Bt) *t.k.h: led to over 3f out: rdn and wknd over 2f out: sn lost tch: t.o (jockey said filly stopped quickly; trainers rep said filly ran too freely in the early stages)* **11/4**[2]

3m 36.19s (1.19) **Going Correction** +0.275s/f (Slow) **6 Ran SP% 116.9**
Speed ratings (Par 105): **108,107,107,103,99 78**
CSF £177.52 TOTE £7.10: £3.50, £8.50; EX 80.10 Trifecta £400.40.
Owner Toby Noble And Andy Bell **Bred** John Joseph Murphy **Trained** Irthington, Cumbria

FOCUS
A decent staying event, in which the pace was steady but not slow. The winner has been rated as backing up her latest effort.

7820 VALUED ACCOUNTANCY APPRENTICE H'CAP 7f 14y (Tp)
6:25 (6:25) (Class 5) (0-75,76) 4-Y-O+
£3,428 (£1,020; £509; £400; £400; £400) **Stalls** Centre

Form RPR

6560 **1** **Kentuckyconnection (USA)**[15] 7305 6-9-3 **65**..................... BenSanderson 5 74
(Bryan Smart) *dwlt: hld up: rdn and hdwy over 2f out: led ins fnl f: sn clr (trainers rep could offer no explanation for the apparent improvement in form)* **11/1**

3621 **2** *3 ¾* **Harvest Day**[16] 7288 4-9-12 **74**.....................(t) GerO'Neill 3 73
(Michael Easterby) *dwlt and wnt lft s: sn in tch: smooth hdwy to ld over 1f out: rdn and hdd ins fnl f: kpt on: nt pce of wnr* **3/1**[2]

5430 **3** *2 ¼* **Lucky Lodge**[12] 7418 9-9-2 **67**.....................(v) KieranSchofield(3) 2 60
(Antony Brittain) *in tch: effrt and drvn along over 2f out: kpt on same pce fnl f* **12/1**

6403 **4** *¾* **Tadaawol**[15] 7310 6-10-0 **76**.....................(p) PaulaMuir 7 67
(Roger Fell) *t.k.h: led: rdn and hdd over 1f out: sn one pce* **11/2**[3]

3113 **5** *2* **Blindingly (GER)**[4] 7703 4-9-8 **73**.....................(p) HarryRussell(3) 5 58
(Ben Haslam) *hld up: rdn over 3f out: hdwy over 2f out: outpcd appr fnl f (jockey said gelding ran flat)* **6/4**[1]

0200 **6** *7* **Smugglers Creek (IRE)**[16] 7289 5-9-5 **67**.....................(p) ConnorMurtagh 6 33
(Iain Jardine) *t.k.h: cl up: drvn and outpcd over 2f out: sn btn* **16/1**

6500 **7** *6* **Ower Fly**[35] 6588 6-9-12 **74**..................... JaneElliott 1 24
(Ruth Carr) *cl up: disp ld 4f out to over 2f out: sn wknd* **28/1**

4000 **8** *½* **Staplegrove (IRE)**[95] 4365 4-8-7 **60**..................... StefanoCherchi(5) 8 9
(Stella Barclay) *hld up: rdn and struggling 3f out: btn fnl 2f* **66/1**

1m 27.41s (1.21) **Going Correction** +0.275s/f (Slow) **8 Ran SP% 107.2**
Speed ratings (Par 103): **104,99,97,96,94 86,79,78**
CSF £38.71 CT £347.70 TOTE £11.40: £2.80, £1.50, £2.10; EX 51.90 Trifecta £288.10.
Owner Woodcock Electrical Limited **Bred** Turner Breeders LLC **Trained** Hambleton, N Yorks

FOCUS
The two that were most involved in the finish were patiently ridden behind what appeared to be a strong early pace. The winner has been rated in line with his 6f win here in April.

7821 KENTECHY DERBY NOVICE STKS 1m 5y (Tp)
6:55 (6:56) (Class 5) 2-Y-O
£3,428 (£1,020; £509; £254) **Stalls** Centre

Form RPR

4 **1** **Tsar**[82] 4886 2-9-5 0..................... RobertHavlin 7 78+
(John Gosden) *dwlt: t.k.h: hld up: smooth hdwy over 2f out: led over 1f out: rdn and edgd lft ins fnl f: kpt on wl* **2/7**[1]

2 *½* **Glenties (USA)** 2-9-5 0..................... JoeFanning 1 77+
(Mark Johnston) *trckd ldrs: shkn up and sltly outpcd over 1f out: rallied and chsd wnr ins fnl f: kpt on fin* **28/1**

3 *1* **Emaraty Hero** 2-9-5 0..................... DanielTudhope 8 74
(K R Burke) *trckd ldrs: effrt and ev ch over 1f out: lost 2nd and one pce ins fnl f* **7/1**[2]

0 **4** *4 ½* **Court Of Appeal (IRE)**[22] 7055 2-9-5 0..................... PaulMulrennan 3 64
(James Tate) *led at modest pce: rdn and hdd over 1f out: outpcd fnl f* **10/1**

5 *1 ¾* **Finely Tuned (IRE)** 2-9-5 0..................... JackMitchell 2 60
(Simon Crisford) *dwlt: hld up: rdn and rn green over 2f out: n.d after* **15/2**[3]

06 **6** *8* **Anno Lucis (IRE)**[7] 7579 2-9-5 0..................... RyanTate 6 42
(Sir Mark Prescott Bt) *hld up in midfield: rdn over 2f out: wknd wl over 1f out* **200/1**

50 **7** *1 ¼* **Black Star Dancing (USA)**[13] 7361 2-9-5 0..................... CallumRodriguez 9 39
(Keith Dalgleish) *hld up: pushed along and outpcd over 2f out: sn wknd* **22/1**

04 **8** *nk* **Take That**[12] 7416 2-9-5 0..................... JackGarritty 4 38
(Richard Fahey) *chsd ldrs: drvn and outpcd over 2f out: sn btn* **20/1**

00 **9** *4* **Castashadow**[125] 3245 2-9-5 0..................... DavidNolan 10 29
(Alan Brown) *hld up: rdn along 3f out: sn struggling* **200/1**

10 4 **Roddy Ransom** 2-9-5 0 AndrewMullen 5 20
(Ben Haslam) *hld up: rdn over 3f out: sn btn* **66/1**
1m 42.1s (3.50) **Going Correction** +0.275s/f (Slow) **10** Ran SP% **126.2**
Speed ratings (Par 95): **93,92,91,87,85 77,76,75,71,67**
CSF £23.55 TOTE £1.20: £1.10, £5.00, £1.60; EX 13.50 Trifecta £46.40.
Owner K Abdullah **Bred** Juddmonte Farms Ltd **Trained** Newmarket, Suffolk
FOCUS
The betting told the story of this race, with the market leader proving to be very popular with punters. Three came away from the remainder, with two of those holding Group 1 entries.

7822 ZENCOS ARCHITECTURAL FILLIES' NOVICE STKS 1m 5y (Tp)
7:25 (7:26) (Class 5) 3-Y-0+ £3,428 (£1,020; £509; £254) Stalls Centre

Form RPR
22 1 **New Angel**[18] 7190 3-8-12 0 RobertHavlin 4 75+
(John Gosden) *led: rdn and hdd briefly over 1f out: kpt on strly to draw clr ins fnl f* **2/1**[2]
10 2 3 **Robotique Danseur (FR)**[158] 2102 3-9-5 0 DanielTudhope 2 74
(K R Burke) *cl up: effrt and ev ch over 2f out to over 1f out: kpt on same pce ins fnl f* **16/1**
1 3 ¾ **Perfect Number**[18] 7190 3-9-5 0 PatCosgrave 1 72
(Saeed bin Suroor) *cl up: rdn and led briefly over 1f out: drvn and no ex ins fnl f* **1/1**[1]
4 3¾ **Sailing (GER)** 3-8-12 0 AdamMcNamara 3 56
(Roger Charlton) *dwlt: t.k.h: hld up in tch: rdn and outpcd over 2f out: btn over 1f out* **5/1**[3]
5 3¼ **Kiraleah** 3-8-12 0 DougieCostello 5 48
(Ivan Furtado) *missed break: sn rcvrd and in tch: drvn and struggling over 2f out: sn btn* **150/1**
1m 41.9s (3.30) **Going Correction** +0.275s/f (Slow) **5** Ran SP% **106.5**
Speed ratings (Par 100): **94,91,90,86,83**
CSF £25.56 TOTE £2.60: £1.10, £4.00; EX 21.60 Trifecta £28.00.
Owner George Strawbridge **Bred** George Strawbridge **Trained** Newmarket, Suffolk
FOCUS
They got racing quite a way from home considering the small field size, so this should be reliable form. The level is a bit fluid.

7823 BUILDING SELF BELIEF H'CAP 6f (Tp)
7:55 (7:56) (Class 6) (0-60,60) 3-Y-0+
£2,781 (£827; £413; £400; £400; £400) Stalls Centre

Form RPR
2244 1 **Pearl Of Qatar**[2] 7764 3-9-2 57 PhilDennis 13 68
(Tristan Davidson) *hld up: hdwy to ld over 1f out: rdn clr ins fnl f* **8/1**[3]
305 2 2¾ **Dandy Highwayman (IRE)**[16] 7286 5-9-5 59 (bt[1]) BenRobinson 9 62
(Ollie Pears) *cl up: led over 2f out to over 1f out: rdn and kpt on fnl f: nt pce of wnr (jockey said gelding hung right-handed throughout)* **9/1**
060 3 1¾ **At Your Service**[137] 2846 5-9-5 59 JoeyHaynes 10 57
(Chelsea Banham) *t.k.h: in tch: hdwy to dispute ld over 2f out to over 1f out: rdn and one pce fnl f* **14/1**
5- 4 nk **Iron Ryan (FR)**[80] 4956 7-9-4 58 TomEaves 3 55
(Lee Smyth, Ire) *hld up: stdy hdwy over 2f out: effrt and rdn over 1f out: kpt on ins fnl f: nvr rchd ldrs* **40/1**
2421 5 nk **Be Proud (IRE)**[5] 7651 3-9-2 57 PaddyMathers 14 53
(Jim Goldie) *hld up: rdn over 2f out: hdwy and prom over 1f out: kpt on same pce ins fnl f* **13/8**[1]
0665 6 nk **Qaaraat**[14] 7334 4-9-4 58 (p) CamHardie 7 53
(Antony Brittain) *t.k.h: hld up in midfield: effrt and drvn over 1f out: no imp fnl f (jockey said gelding ran too free)* **22/1**
433 7 ¾ **Mansfield**[11] 7443 6-9-3 57 JackGarritty 6 50+
(Stella Barclay) *plld hrd: hld up in midfield: nt clr run over 2f out to over 1f out: sn rdn and no imp* **14/1**
300 8 ¾ **Ishebayorgrey (IRE)**[11] 7443 7-9-5 59 PaulMulrennan 4 49
(Iain Jardine) *t.k.h: hld up: drvn and outpcd over 2f out: n.d after* **14/1**
5212 9 nk **Sophia Maria**[11] 7444 3-9-2 60 JaneElliott[(3)] 12 49
(James Bethell) *in tch: drvn along over 2f out: outpcd over 1f out: n.d after* **5/1**[2]
40 10 hd **Arnold**[38] 6503 5-9-5 59 (p) FrannyNorton 2 48
(Ann Duffield) *plld hrd: cl up: chal over 3f out to over 2f out: rdn and wknd over 1f out* **22/1**
446- 11 nk **Warrior Goddess**[319] 9125 4-8-13 58 DylanHogan[(5)] 5 46
(John Butler) *hld up: rdn and outpcd over 2f out: nvr on terms* **33/1**
4403 12 2½ **Tease Maid**[13] 7389 3-9-2 57 JasonHart 8 37
(John Quinn) *led to over 2f out: rdn and wknd over 1f out* **18/1**
1m 14.01s (1.51) **Going Correction** +0.275s/f (Slow)
WFA 3 from 4yo+ 1lb **12** Ran SP% **125.7**
Speed ratings (Par 101): **100,96,94,93,93 92,91,90,90,90 89,86**
CSF £72.24 CT £991.97 TOTE £4.30: £3.10, £3.00, £4.80; EX 68.70 Trifecta £1344.60.
Owner Beswick Brothers Bloodstock **Bred** Mrs Julie Anne Martin **Trained** Irthington, Cumbria
FOCUS
They didn't look to go that quickly in the early stages, as plenty of the field were keen under restraint. The winner has been rated back towards her best.

7824 PHIL EADON ALLANCIA H'CAP 5f (Tp)
8:25 (8:28) (Class 6) (0-55,55) 3-Y-0+
£2,781 (£827; £413; £400; £400; £400) Stalls Centre

Form RPR
4503 1 **Young Tiger**[22] 7052 6-9-0 48 (h) AndrewMullen 3 58
(Tom Tate) *dwlt: hld up on far side of gp: hdwy over 1f out: sustained run to ld last 100yds: r.o wl* **16/1**
0300 2 nk **Cuppacoco**[29] 6829 4-9-7 55 (b[1]) FrannyNorton 8 64
(Ann Duffield) *led: rdn and qcknd 2 l clr over 1f out: rdn: edgd lft and hdd last 100yds: rallied: hld cl home* **18/1**
0504 3 3¼ **Rockley Point**[12] 7420 6-9-2 50 (b) PhilDennis 12 47
(Katie Scott) *hld up on nr side of gp: rdn over 2f out: hdwy to chse clr ldng pair ins fnl f: kpt on: no imp* **9/1**
0035 4 1 **Independence Day (IRE)**[16] 7282 6-9-5 53 JoeyHaynes 1 47
(Chelsea Banham) *midfield on far side of gp: hdwy and cl up 2f out: rdn and one pce fnl f* **9/1**
4316 5 hd **Carlovian**[9] 7507 6-9-6 54 (p) DougieCostello 7 47
(Mark Walford) *prom in centre of gp: drvn along 2f out: one pce fnl f* **22/1**
0320 6 1 **Tizwotitiz**[7] 7590 3-9-6 54 (v) JasonHart 11 44
(Steph Hollinshead) *prom on nr side of gp: drvn along 2f out: outpcd fnl f* **22/1**
0044 7 ½ **Rangefield Express (IRE)**[12] 7417 3-9-2 50 (b) SamJames 6 39
(Geoffrey Harker) *hld up on far side of gp: effrt and rdn 2f out: no imp fnl f* **33/1**
0000 8 ¾ **Kibaar**[15] 7307 7-9-5 53 JamesSullivan 5 38
(Ruth Carr) *hld up in centre of gp: shortlived effrt 2f out: sn no imp (vet said gelding lost it's right-hind shoe)* **40/1**
5002 9 1¾ **Paco Escostar**[22] 7052 4-9-0 48 (b[1]) BenRobinson 13 27
(Julie Camacho) *midfield on nr side of gp: hdwy and prom 1/2-way: wknd fnl f (jockey said filly stopped quickly)* **15/2**[3]
5203 10 2 **Arnoul Of Metz**[18] 7214 4-9-0 53 (p) DylanHogan[(5)] 10 24
(Henry Spiller) *prom in centre of gp: drvn over 2f out: wknd over 1f out* **11/1**
3612 11 ¾ **One One Seven (IRE)**[2] 7770 3-9-6 54 CamHardie 9 24
(Antony Brittain) *midfield on nr side of gp: rdn and outpcd 1/2-way: n.d after (jockey said gelding ran flat)* **11/4**[1]
1556 12 1 **One Boy (IRE)**[3] 7737 8-9-4 52 (b) PaulMulrennan 4 17
(Paul Midgley) *racd towards far side of gp: disp ld to 1/2-way: wknd over 1f out* **16/1**
353 13 shd **Bithiah (IRE)**[12] 7417 3-9-3 51 (h) JackMitchell 14 17
(Ismail Mohammed) *dwlt: bhd on nr side of gp: drvn along 1/2-way: nvr on terms* **7/1**[2]
3462 14 6 **Maid From The Mist**[48] 6120 3-9-3 51 ConnorBeasley 2
(John Gallagher) *chsd ldrs on far side of gp: drvn and outpcd 1/2-way: sn struggling* **28/1**
1m 0.3s (0.80) **Going Correction** +0.275s/f (Slow) **14** Ran SP% **113.8**
Speed ratings (Par 101): **104,103,98,96,96 94,94,92,90,86 85,84,83,74**
CSF £244.11 CT £2804.38 TOTE £12.90: £4.20, £4.10, £3.50; EX 209.60 Trifecta £2201.80.
Owner T T Racing **Bred** Mrs J McMahon & Mickley Stud **Trained** Tadcaster, N Yorks
FOCUS
A moderate handicap, in which two came away from the remainder. The second has been rated in line with this year's best.
T/Plt: £1,228.70 to a £1 stake. Pool: £68,404.26 - 40.64 winning units. T/Qpdt: £65.20 to a £1 stake. Pool: £9,227.46 - 104.62 winning units. **Richard Young**

6167 NOTTINGHAM (L-H)
Wednesday, October 2

OFFICIAL GOING: Heavy (soft in places; 5.6)
Wind: Moderate northerly. Weather: Sunny, cool.

7825 ROA REWARDS MEMBER EBF MAIDEN STKS (PLUS 10 RACE) 5f 8y
1:55 (1:58) (Class 4) 2-Y-0 £5,822 (£1,732; £865; £432) Stalls High

Form RPR
2 1 **Spirit Of The Sky**[13] 7377 2-9-0 0 TonyHamilton 3 73+
(Richard Fahey) *led: racd freely: nudged along over 1f out: pushed out hands and heels: r.o wl: comf* **2/1**[2]
5 2 2¼ **Rathagan**[8] 7546 2-9-2 0 FinleyMarsh[(3)] 2 69
(Richard Hughes) *blindfold slow to be removed: s.i.s: rdn over 2f out: sn drvn and unable to rch ldr: kpt on (jockey was slow to remove blindfold and explained that it had become caught on the bridle)* **13/2**
04 3 4 **Abbaleka**[15] 7316 2-9-5 0 AlistairRawlinson 4 55
(Michael Appleby) *trckd ldr: rdn wl over 2f out: one pce fnl 1f* **6/5**[1]
4 1¾ **Baileys Blues (FR)** 2-9-5 0 FrannyNorton 6 48
(Mark Johnston) *prom nrside: wnt 2nd wl over 2f out: rdn wl over 1f out: sn one pce* **11/2**[3]
1m 3.05s (2.85) **Going Correction** +0.50s/f (Yiel) **4** Ran SP% **174.2**
Speed ratings (Par 97): **97,93,87,84**
CSF £12.92 TOTE £2.00; EX 9.30 Trifecta £11.20.
Owner Racegoers Club Owners Group **Bred** Whitsbury Manor Stud **Trained** Musley Bank, N Yorks
FOCUS
The course survived a morning inspection and obviously it was demanding underfoot. The outer track was used. The four-strong field went an average pace down the middle in this ordinary 2yo maiden. It's been rated cautiously. Winning rider Tony Hamilton felt the going description of heavy, soft in places is accurate and said it was hard work. Finley Marsh felt it was soft and Franny Norton described conditions as tough going.

7826 EBF JOIN 8,000 ROA MEMBERS MAIDEN FILLIES' STKS (PLUS 10 RACE) 1m 75y
2:25 (2:28) (Class 4) 2-Y-0 £5,822 (£1,732; £865; £432) Stalls Centre

Form RPR
1 **Dubai Love** 2-9-0 0 OisinMurphy 2 79+
(Saeed bin Suroor) *slowly away: racd keenly: sn trcking ldrs: led wl over 1f out: pushed out: comf* **5/2**[2]
052 2 1¼ **Rainbow Jet (IRE)**[26] 6918 2-9-0 73 JimmyQuinn 9 76
(John Mackie) *racd keenly: trckd ldrs: rdn 2f out: styd on wl fnl 1f* **12/1**
4 3 2¾ **Notation (IRE)**[21] 7067 2-9-0 0 FrannyNorton 8 70
(Mark Johnston) *trckd ldrs: rdn wl over 2f out: styd on fnl 1f* **7/1**[3]
22 4 1 **Craylands**[62] 5588 2-9-0 0 CallumShepherd 4 68
(Michael Bell) *prom: led wl over 2f out: rdn and hdd wl over 1f out: no ex fnl 100yds* **4/5**[1]
0 5 3¼ **Ascraeus**[27] 6906 2-9-0 0 BenCurtis 7 61
(Andrew Balding) *trckd ldrs: rdn 3f out: drvn 2f out: one pce fnl 1f* **14/1**
0 6 3 **Heliaebel**[26] 6928 2-9-0 0 StevieDonohoe 12 54
(Charlie Fellowes) *unsettled in stalls: mid-div: rdn over 3f out: one pce fnl 2f* **25/1**
6 7 3¾ **Kavadi**[25] 6949 2-9-0 0 GeraldMosse 3 46
(Hughie Morrison) *led: rdn and hdd wl over 2f out: sn wknd* **40/1**
8 5 **Wendreda** 2-9-0 0 BrettDoyle 6 35
(Mrs Ilka Gansera-Leveque) *hld up towards rr: rdn 3f out: one pce fnl 2f* **100/1**
9 4½ **Lightning Blue** 2-9-0 0 DavidEgan 11 25
(Mick Channon) *slowly away: hld up toward rr: rdn 3f out: grad wknd* **66/1**
10 1¾ **Volcano Bay** 2-9-0 0 SeanLevey 1 21
(Ismail Mohammed) *dwlt: hld up towards rr: rdn 3f out: sn wknd (jockey said filly was slowly away)* **100/1**
1m 48.42s (1.72) **Going Correction** +0.225s/f (Good) **10** Ran SP% **120.7**
Speed ratings (Par 94): **100,98,96,95,91 88,85,80,75,73**
CSF £32.11 TOTE £3.40: £1.10, £2.30, £1.50; EX 26.30 Trifecta £118.40.
Owner Godolphin **Bred** Petches Farm Ltd **Trained** Newmarket, Suffolk
■ La Foglietta was withdrawn. Price at time of withdrawal 16/1. Rule 4 does not apply.

FOCUS
An interesting 2yo fillies' maiden that represented a thorough test. The runner-up has been rated as backing up her latest effort.

7827 REWARDING OWNERSHIP WITH THE ROA NURSERY H'CAP (THE JOCKEY CLUB GRASSROOTS NURSERY SERIES FINAL) 6f 18y

2:55 (2:58) (Class 3) 2-Y-O £16,172 (£4,812; £2,405; £1,202) Stalls High

Form RPR
6532 1 **Danny Ocean (IRE)**[12] 7419 2-8-7 **69**....................(p) BenCurtis 5 77
(K R Burke) *chsd ldrs: rdn to ld 1f out: sn clr: rdn out* 9/2[1]
0210 2 2 1/4 **Ralphy Boy Two (IRE)**[21] 7064 2-8-9 **71**....................(p[1]) GrahamLee 8 72
(Alistair Whillans) *chsd ldrs: rdn 3f out: hdwy 2f out: styd on wl fnl 1f* 14/1
4132 3 1 **What A Business (IRE)**[12] 7399 2-8-13 **75**.................. PaulHanagan 11 73
(Roger Fell) *prom: rdn 3f out: drvn ent fnl 1f: kpt on tl hdd for 2nd fnl strides* 9/2[1]
1336 4 3 **Making History (IRE)**[32] 6705 2-9-9 **85**.................. CallumShepherd 12 74
(Saeed bin Suroor) *prom nrside: rdn 2f out: sn drvn and one pce fnl 1f* 12/1
4424 5 3/4 **Paddy Elliott (IRE)**[21] 7064 2-8-8 **70**.......................... BenRobinson 13 57
(Brian Ellison) *a towards rr: n.d* 9/1[3]
5234 6 2 1/4 **Red Jasper**[16] 7283 2-8-1 **63**....................(p) JimmyQuinn 9 43
(Michael Appleby) *hld up: rdn 2f out: styd on fr wl over 1f out* 16/1
6040 7 1 1/4 **Wade's Magic**[21] 7064 2-8-3 **65**....................(b[1]) DuranFentiman 6 41
(Tim Easterby) *led: hdd 1f out: wknd fnl 150yds* 33/1
3212 8 2 1/4 **Come On Girl**[9] 7522 2-8-0 **62**.......................... RaulDaSilva 3 32
(Tony Carroll) *slowly away: hdwy to trck ldrs 3f out: rdn 2f out: sn one pce* 12/1
3000 9 1 1/2 **Daddies Diva**[34] 6637 2-8-4 **66**....................(b[1]) DavidEgan 7 31
(Rod Millman) *hld up: asked for effrt 3f out: sn btn* 16/1
4300 10 nse **Xcelente**[25] 6963 2-9-4 **80**.......................... FrannyNorton 2 45
(Mark Johnston) *chsd ldrs far side: rdn 3f out: no imp* 16/1
6260 11 2 3/4 **Streaker**[42] 6356 2-9-0 **76**.......................... TomEaves 10 33
(Kevin Ryan) *prom: travelled wl: rdn wl over 2f out: grad wknd* 12/1
3406 12 4 1/2 **Ambyfaeirvine (IRE)**[19] 7140 2-8-6 **68**....................(p[1]) KieranO'Neill 14 11
(Ivan Furtado) *prom: rdn 3f out: sn wknd* 18/1
4244 13 1 1/4 **Light The Fuse (IRE)**[3] 7725 2-8-11 **73**....................(b[1]) SeanLevey 4 12
(K R Burke) *trckd ldrs: rdn 3f out: no imp* 11/2[2]

1m 16.74s (2.94) **Going Correction** +0.50s/f (Yiel) 13 Ran SP% 117.3
Speed ratings (Par 99): **100,97,95,91,90 87,86,83,81,80 77,71,69**
CSF £67.38 CT £310.88 TOTE £4.70: £2.20, £3.80, £1.40; EX 89.20 Trifecta £734.80.
Owner Ontoawinner, Strecker & Burke **Bred** D Allen & E Barry **Trained** Middleham Moor, N Yorks

FOCUS
A wide-open looking nursery. It paid to be handy down the centre.

7828 MAKE THE MOST OF RACEHORSE OWNERSHIP WITH ROA H'CAP (JOCKEY CLUB GRASSROOTS SPRINT SERIES FINAL) 6f 18y

3:25 (3:30) (Class 3) 3-Y-O+ £15,562 (£4,660; £2,330; £1,165; £582; £292) Stalls High

Form RPR
2122 1 **Fantasy Keeper**[37] 6549 5-9-0 **80**.......................... AngusVilliers(7) 8 90
(Michael Appleby) *trckd ldr: rdn 3f out: drvn wl over 1f out: led fnl 150yds: styd on strly* 4/1[1]
1425 2 1/2 **Orange Blossom**[13] 7367 3-8-10 **70**.......................... BarryMcHugh 10 78
(Richard Fahey) *led: travelled wl: rdn wl over 1f out: hdd fnl 150yds: kpt on* 20/1
5025 3 3/4 **Stallone (IRE)**[35] 6598 3-8-6 **66**....................(v) MartinDwyer 5 72
(Richard Spencer) *hld up towards rr: rdn bef 1/2-way: drvn fnl 1f: styd on* 14/1
6116 4 hd **Ugo Gregory**[42] 6338 3-8-8 **68**.......................... NathanEvans 9 73+
(Tim Easterby) *hld up: rdn 2f out: sn drvn: styd on fnl 1f* 8/1
0604 5 1/2 **Socru (IRE)**[34] 6626 3-8-9 **69**....................(h) JamesSullivan 1 73
(Michael Easterby) *trckd ldrs far side: rdn bef 1/2-way: drvn fnl 1f: styd on same pce* 25/1
600 6 1 **Zapper Cass (FR)**[51] 6027 6-8-4 **68**.......................... TheodoreLadd(5) 2 69
(Michael Appleby) *mid-div: pushed along 1/2-way: one pce fnl 1f* 20/1
5206 7 1/2 **Peggie Sue**[4] 7687 4-9-5 **83**.......................... TobyEley(5) 16 82
(Adam West) *trckd ldrs nrside: pushed along 2f out: kpt on same pce fnl 1f* 20/1
0440 8 nse **Bellevarde (IRE)**[18] 7183 5-8-10 **69**.......................... DavidEgan 7 68
(Richard Price) *Prominent: rdn 2f out: sn drvn and wknd* 33/1
2454 9 nk **Suzi's Connoisseur**[11] 7467 8-9-3 **76**....................(b) JFEgan 3 74
(Jane Chapple-Hyam) *trckd ldrs: hdwy 3f out: drvn wl over 1f out: one pce (vet said gelding lost its right fore shoe)* 12/1
5161 10 3/4 **Afandem (IRE)**[3] 7736 5-9-5 **78** 5ex....................(p) DavidAllan 13 73
(Tim Easterby) *chsd ldrs: rdn bef 1/2-way: hmpd sltly 1f out: nvr able to chal* 6/1[2]
1232 11 1/2 **Golden Parade**[15] 7311 3-9-1 **75**....................(p) CamHardie 17 69
(Tim Easterby) *mid-div nrside: pushed along 4f out: drvn wl over 1f out: one pce* 14/1
3205 12 1 1/4 **Gnaad (IRE)**[14] 7337 5-8-13 **75**.......................... DarraghKeenan(3) 4 65
(Alan Bailey) *restless in stalls: rrd and almost uns rdr leaving stalls: a towards rr (jockey said gelding reared as the stalls opened)* 18/1
0200 13 nse **Madrinho (IRE)**[14] 7337 6-8-10 **69**.......................... GeorgeDowning 6 59
(Tony Carroll) *hld up towards rr: rdn bef 1/2-way: one pce fnl 1f* 20/1
6125 14 1 3/4 **Redrosezorro**[18] 7183 5-8-11 **70**....................(h) PhilDennis 15 54
(Eric Alston) *trckd ldrs nrside: rdn 2f out: drvn wl over 1f out: sn wknd* 14/1
0000 15 nse **Bengali Boys (IRE)**[6] 7632 4-8-8 **67**.......................... RaulDaSilva 12 51
(Tony Carroll) *prom: rdn 2f out: grad wknd* 50/1
6341 16 1 **Kenny The Captain (IRE)**[7] 7591 8-8-1 **60** 4ex......... DuranFentiman 11 41
(Tim Easterby) *prom: rdn wl over 2f out: grad wknd* 7/1[3]
4314 17 17 **Queen Of Burgundy**[14] 7351 3-9-5 **79**.......................... JoeyHaynes 14 5
(Christine Dunnett) *slowly away: a bhd: eased fnl 2f (trainer said filly was unsuited by the ground and would prefer a quicker surface)* 40/1

1m 16.34s (2.54) **Going Correction** +0.50s/f (Yiel)
WFA 3 from 4yo+ 1lb 17 Ran SP% 121.1
Speed ratings (Par 107): **103,102,101,101,100 99,98,98,97,96 96,94,94,92,92 90,68**
CSF £89.81 CT £1041.09 TOTE £4.70: £1.70, £5.30, £3.40, £1.90; EX 95.20 Trifecta £1154.70.
Owner The Fantasy Fellowship B **Bred** Cheveley Park Stud Ltd **Trained** Oakham, Rutland

FOCUS
A highly competitive sprint handicap, as befits a series final. Those drawn centrally were again favoured. A pb from the winner, with the third and fourth helping to set the level.

7829 ROA: A VOICE FOR RACEHORSE OWNERS H'CAP (THE JOCKEY CLUB GRASSROOTS MIDDLE DISTANCE SERIES FINAL) 1m 2f 50y

3:55 (3:56) (Class 3) 3-Y-O+ £15,562 (£4,660; £2,330; £1,165; £582; £292) Stalls Low

Form RPR
2163 1 **Deinonychus**[27] 6896 8-8-0 **64** ow1....................(h) TheodoreLadd(5) 2 76
(Michael Appleby) *mid-div: hdwy far rail wl over 2f out: swtchd to chal ins fnl 1f: led 100yds: r.o wl* 11/2[1]
1321 2 2 1/4 **Sendeed (IRE)**[25] 6967 3-9-8 **85**....................(p) JasonWatson 14 93+
(Saeed bin Suroor) *led: hdd 4f out: rdn to regain ld wl over 1f out: sn clr: hdd and no ex fnl 100yds* 11/2[1]
3660 3 4 1/2 **Music Seeker (IRE)**[4] 7694 5-9-2 **82**....................(t) ZakWheatley(7) 8 81
(Declan Carroll) *trckd ldr: hdwy to ld 4f out: hdd wl over 1f out: kpt on* 15/2[3]
4100 4 1 **Regular Income (IRE)**[12] 7413 4-9-7 **80**....................(b) JimmyQuinn 7 77
(Adam West) *slowly away: hld up in rr: rdn 3f out: drvn wl over 1f out: styd on (jockey said gelding was slowly away)* 10/1
2230 5 hd **Firewater**[13] 7368 3-8-1 **67**....................(p) SeanDavis(3) 12 63
(Richard Fahey) *hld up: rdn 3f out: drvn 1f out: styd on* 12/1
3645 6 hd **Highwaygrey**[18] 7213 3-8-2 **65**.......................... DuranFentiman 10 61+
(Tim Easterby) *rrd in stalls: hld up: hdwy on outside wl over 2f out: rdn 1f out: one pce* 22/1
0530 7 2 1/4 **Ghalib (IRE)**[62] 5594 7-9-4 **77**.......................... PhilDennis 6 68
(Rebecca Bastiman) *trckd ldr: rdn wl over 2f out: sn one pce* 25/1
3404 8 1 3/4 **Dark Devil (IRE)**[8] 7544 6-8-3 **62**....................(p) CamHardie 5 50
(Richard Fahey) *hld up: rdn wl over 1f out: no imp* 18/1
1503 9 1 **Beverley Bullet**[33] 6665 6-8-4 **63**....................(p) DavidEgan 11 49
(Lawrence Mullaney) *hld up towards rr: rdn 3f out: one pce* 11/1
0621 10 2 3/4 **Orange Suit (IRE)**[17] 7229 4-8-10 **69**....................(b) BarryMcHugh 15 49
(Ed de Giles) *trckd ldr: travelled wl: rdn wl over 2f out: sn wknd* 16/1
3060 11 1 1/2 **C Note (IRE)**[25] 6967 6-9-2 **75**.......................... TomMarquand 13 52
(Heather Main) *hld up towards rr: rdn 4f out: sn wknd* 10/1
4135 12 3 **Royal Shaheen (FR)**[21] 7069 6-8-11 **70**....................(v) GrahamLee 4 41
(Alistair Whillans) *hld up towards rr: rdn and wknd 4f out: n.d* 12/1
3126 13 1 3/4 **Allegiant (USA)**[20] 7127 4-9-8 **81**.......................... RossaRyan 3 49
(Stuart Williams) *hld up in tch: effrt wl over 3f out: grad wknd* 6/1[2]
4-00 14 6 **Mrs Hoo (IRE)**[21] 7069 3-8-7 **70**.......................... PaulHanagan 16 27
(Richard Fahey) *hld up: rdn 3f out: sn btn* 66/1

2m 14.25s (0.85) **Going Correction** +0.225s/f (Good)
WFA 3 from 4yo+ 4lb 14 Ran SP% 129.1
Speed ratings (Par 107): **105,103,99,98,98 98,96,95,94,92 91,88,87,82**
CSF £33.68 CT £232.17 TOTE £5.60: £2.40, £1.90, £3.30; EX 45.70 Trifecta £498.30.
Owner I R Hatton **Bred** Howdale Bloodstock Ltd **Trained** Oakham, Rutland

FOCUS
Another wide-open and competitive handicap. It proved hard to make up ground from off the pace. The winner has been rated back to his 2017 form, with the third close to his recent best.

7830 BENEFITS FOR ROA MEMBERS AT ROA.CO.UK H'CAP (JC GRASSROOTS STAYERS DISTANCE SERIES FINAL) 1m 6f

4:25 (4:26) (Class 3) 3-Y-O+ £15,562 (£4,660; £2,330; £1,165; £582; £292) Stalls Low

Form RPR
2115 1 **Maid In Manhattan (IRE)**[26] 6924 5-8-11 **74**.......(h) HarrisonShaw(3) 13 83+
(Rebecca Menzies) *hld up towards rr: hdwy 3f out: led wl over 1f out: pushed out fnl 1f: kpt on gamely* 13/2[3]
2232 2 3/4 **Celestial Force (IRE)**[18] 7181 4-9-8 **82**....................(p) CliffordLee 7 89
(Tom Dascombe) *Led: hdd wl over 1f out: sn drvn: kpt on but a hld* 9/2[1]
2325 3 1 1/2 **Smarter (IRE)**[35] 6597 3-8-13 **80**....................(b) MartinDwyer 2 85
(William Haggas) *hld up in rr: sn rdn: outpcd 3f out: swtchd rt and hdwy wl over 1f out: styd on wl* 14/1
2134 4 1/2 **Contrebasse**[24] 7001 4-8-10 **70**....................(p[1]) DavidAllan 1 74
(Tim Easterby) *mid-div: rdn wl over 2f out: styd on fnl 1f (jockey said gelding was denied a clear run approaching the final furlong)* 15/2
3453 5 shd **Sassie (IRE)**[12] 7403 4-9-5 **79**.......................... NathanEvans 11 83
(Michael Easterby) *hld up: hdwy 4f out: rdn to chal wl over 1f out: one pce fnl 1f* 13/2[3]
2114 6 7 **Kensington Art**[26] 6924 3-8-2 **72**....................(p) SeanDavis(3) 12 66
(Richard Fahey) *trckd ldr: rdn 3f out: one pce fnl 2f* 14/1
6/63 7 2 3/4 **Be My Sea (IRE)**[50] 6055 8-8-11 **71**.......................... GeorgeDowning 8 61
(Tony Carroll) *trckd ldr: rdn wl over 3f out: one pce* 50/1
0243 8 1/2 **Singing The Blues (IRE)**[17] 7231 4-8-5 **72**.......................... AngusVilliers(7) 16 62
(Rod Millman) *Tracked ldr: rdn 3f out: one pce* 13/2[3]
2563 9 nk **Royal Flag**[15] 7301 9-8-2 **62**.......................... DavidEgan 6 51
(Brian Ellison) *mid-div: pushed along early: drvn wl over 4f out: grad wknd (jockey said gelding was never travelling)* 25/1
5046 10 4 **Motahassen (IRE)**[21] 7070 5-8-0 **60** oh6....................(t) JamesSullivan 15 43
(Declan Carroll) *hld up: rdn 3f out: n.d* 40/1
1616 11 1 1/4 **Follow Intello (IRE)**[26] 6924 4-9-2 **76**.......................... GeraldMosse 4 58
(Chris Wall) *trckd ldr: drvn 3f out: grad wknd (trainer could offer no explanation for the poor peformance)* 5/1[2]
0420 12 1/2 **Dagueneau (IRE)**[102] 4112 4-9-1 **75**....................(p w) GrahamLee 14 56
(Emma Lavelle) *mid-div: rdn wl over 3f out: sn wknd* 33/1
6001 13 16 **Eye Of The Storm (IRE)**[50] 6055 9-8-13 **73**............ AlistairRawlinson 9 32
(Conor Dore) *mid-div: rdn 5f out: sn wknd* 20/1

3m 7.01s (0.61) **Going Correction** +0.225s/f (Good)
WFA 3 from 4yo+ 7lb 13 Ran SP% 123.2
Speed ratings (Par 107): **107,106,105,105,105 101,99,99,99,97 96,96,86**
CSF £32.63 CT £398.05 TOTE £5.60: £2.70, £1.70, £3.60; EX 34.90 Trifecta £824.00.
Owner Stoneleigh Racing **Bred** John Breslin **Trained** Mordon, Durham

FOCUS
They went a solid pace in this fair staying handicap and it proved hard work. The fourth and fifth help set the level.

7831 ROA OWNERS JACKPOT H'CAP 5f 8y

4:55 (4:56) (Class 5) (0-75,77) 3-Y-O+ £3,881 (£1,155; £577; £300; £300; £300) Stalls High

Form RPR
5025 1 **Wrenthorpe**[13] 7387 4-9-7 **73**.......................... GrahamLee 8 83
(Bryan Smart) *led: travelled wl: plld clr over 1f out: rdn out: comf* 9/4[1]

1103 **2** 2 3/4 **Aperitif**[48] 6120 3-8-13 **68**........ CameronNoble(3) 3 69
(Michael Bell) *s.i.s: chsd ldrs: rdn 3f out: hdwy wl over 1f out: sn rdn: kpt on but no ch w wnr* **10/3**[2]

1615 **3** 3/4 **Secret Potion**[20] 7112 5-9-3 **69**........ RaulDaSilva 4 66
(Ronald Harris) *hld up: rdn 3f out: hdwy ent fnl 1f: no ex fnl 100yds* **7/1**

5402 **4** 3 3/4 **Mr Greenlight**[13] 7367 4-8-8 **60**........(p) DuranFentiman 10 44
(Tim Easterby) *trckd ldr: rdn 2f out: one pce fnl 1f* **15/2**

0503 **5** 5 **Honey Gg**[13] 7387 4-8-6 **65**........(b) ZakWheatley(7) 1 31
(Declan Carroll) *prom: rdn wl 3f out: drvn 2f out: no imp (jockey said filly attempted to duck at the same time as the start was effected)* **5/1**[3]

4420 **6** 4 1/2 **King Crimson**[42] 6335 7-9-2 **71**........ DarraghKeenan(3) 6 21
(John Butler) *trckd ldr: rdn and wknd fnl 2f* **33/1**

40 **7** 3 1/4 **Just Glamorous (IRE)**[30] 6809 6-9-10 **76**........ RossaRyan 9 14
(Grace Harris) *swtchd to r alone on stands' rail on leaving stalls: prom: rdn 2f out: grad wknd (vet said gelding bled from the nose)* **6/1**

1m 1.83s (1.63) **Going Correction** +0.50s/f (Yiel) **7 Ran SP% 147.3**
Speed ratings (Par 103): **107,102,101,95,87 80,75**
CSF £9.43 CT £42.43 TOTE £2.90: £1.80, £1.90; EX 11.90 Trifecta £55.80.
Owner Dan Maltby Bloodstock Ltd & B Smart **Bred** C J Mills **Trained** Hambleton, N Yorks
■ Stewards' Enquiry : Rossa Ryan one-day ban; failure to ride from draw (Oct 16)

FOCUS
The going played a huge part in this modest sprint handicap. The form could be better than rated.
T/Plt: £125.20 to a £1 stake. Pool: £59,562.02 - 347.13 winning units. T/Qpdt: £9.90 to a £1 stake. Pool: £8,284.51 - 619.06 winning units. **Jonathan Doidge**

7684 CHELMSFORD (A.W) (L-H)
Thursday, October 3

OFFICIAL GOING: Polytrack: standard
Wind: light, half behind Weather: overcast

7832 BET TOTEPLACEPOT AT TOTESPORT.COM EBF FILLIES' NOVICE STKS (PLUS 10 RACE) 7f (P)
5:30 (5:32) (Class 4) 2-Y-O **£6,080** (£1,809; £904; £452) **Stalls** Low

Form RPR

26 **1** **Tadreej**[28] 6906 2-9-0 0........ JimCrowley 1 80
(Saeed bin Suroor) *trckd ldrs: swtchd rt and effrt to chse ldr over 1f out: rdn to chal 1f out: kpt on wl to ld fnl 50yds* **5/2**[2]

2 nk **Rideson** 2-9-0 0........ AndreaAtzeni 3 79+
(Roger Varian) *s.i.s: sn rcvrd and in tch in midfield: effrt 2f out: rdn and hdwy to chse ldng pair ins fnl f: styd on wl to go 2nd last strides: nt quite rch wnr* **2/1**[1]

42 **3** hd **Predictable Tully (IRE)**[58] 5772 2-9-0 0........ HectorCrouch 6 79
(Clive Cox) *led: rdn over 1f out: sn edgd lft and hrd pressed 1f out: kpt on u.p tl hdd and one pce fnl 50yds: lost 2nd last strides* **9/2**[3]

4 **4** 1 1/4 **My Poem**[19] 7203 2-9-0 0........ OisinMurphy 8 75
(Sir Michael Stoute) *chsd ldrs: effrt ent fnl 2f: edgd out rt over 1f out: kpt on same pce u.p ins fnl f* **8/1**

335 **5** 1/2 **Call Me Katie (IRE)**[14] 7393 2-9-0 78........ RobertHavlin 2 74
(John Gosden) *chsd ldr: rdn 2f out: lost 2nd over 1f out and unable qck u.p 1f out: one pce ins fnl f* **10/1**

6 4 **Kepala** 2-9-0 0........(h1) CharlesBishop 5 64
(Eve Johnson Houghton) *midfield: effrt in 6th 2f out: kpt on steadily ins fnl f: nvr threatened ldrs* **25/1**

0 **7** 2 **Madame Peltier (IRE)**[28] 6906 2-9-0 0........ JamieSpencer 9 59+
(Charlie Fellowes) *restless in stalls: s.i.s: hld up towards rr: sme prog into midfield and edgd out rt over 1f out: no imp fnl f* **25/1**

0 **8** 2 1/2 **Escalade (IRE)**[16] 7304 2-9-0 0........ RyanTate 4 52
(Sir Mark Prescott Bt) *midfield: lost pl and struggling on outer over 2f out: v wd bnd 2f out and wl hld after* **50/1**

06 **9** hd **Exotic Escape**[16] 7304 2-9-0 0........ DanielMuscutt 10 52
(David Lanigan) *hld up towards rr: nt clr run and swtchd rt 2f out: no imp after: nvr involved* **50/1**

00 **10** 1 1/2 **Queen Of Silca**[14] 7393 2-9-0 0........ NicolaCurrie 11 48
(Mick Channon) *t.k.h: hld up in rr: outpcd over 2f out: nvr involved (jockey said filly hung right-handed throughout)* **33/1**

11 3 3/4 **Ramsha (IRE)** 2-9-0 0........ FrannyNorton 7 38
(Mark Johnston) *midfield: rdn over 3f out: struggling and outpcd over 2f out: bhd fnl f* **20/1**

1m 27.04s (-0.16) **Going Correction** -0.175s/f (Stan) **11 Ran SP% 148.2**
Speed ratings (Par 94): **93,92,92,91,90 85,83,80,80,78 74**
CSF £7.40 TOTE £2.30: £1.40, £1.30, £1.50; EX 10.10 Trifecta £26.30.
Owner Godolphin **Bred** Shadwell Estate Company Limited **Trained** Newmarket, Suffolk

FOCUS
A fair juvenile fillies' novice contest. The front of the market dominated but the favourite missed a costly beat at the start here on debut.

7833 BET TOTEEXACTA AT TOTESPORT.COM NURSERY H'CAP 6f (P)
6:00 (6:02) (Class 6) (0-60,60) 2-Y-O **£3,105** (£924; £461; £400; £400; £400) **Stalls** Centre

Form RPR

050 **1** **Last Date**[46] 6254 2-9-1 **54**........ DougieCostello 9 59
(Ivan Furtado) *hld up in midfield: nt clrest of runs 2f out tl hdwy ent fnl f: chsd ldr jst ins fnl f: styd on wl u.p to ld cl home* **40/1**

2212 **2** 1/2 **Two Hearts**[8] 7584 2-9-4 **57**........ SamJames 8 61
(Grant Tuer) *wl in tch in midfield: effrt to press ldrs over 1f out: rdn to ld 1f out: hdd and no ex cl home* **1/1**[1]

224 **3** 2 **Simply Susan (IRE)**[17] 7269 2-9-5 **58**........ CharlesBishop 14 56
(Eve Johnson Houghton) *midfield on outer: effrt over 2f out: swtchd rt and drvn over 1f out: kpt on wl ins fnl f: nt rch ldrs* **10/1**[3]

0066 **4** nse **Star Of St Louis (FR)**[17] 7275 2-8-9 **48**........ KieranO'Neill 12 45
(Denis Quinn) *hld up in rr of main gp: effrt over 1f out: swtchd rt and u.p ent fnl f: styd on strly ins fnl f: nt rch ldrs* **20/1**

000 **5** shd **Jochi Khan (USA)**[72] 5265 2-8-9 **48** ow1........ RobertHavlin 2 46
(Mohamed Moubarak) *hld up in tch in rr of main gp: nt clr run 2f out: swtchd rt over 1f out: hdwy and styd on wl ins fnl f (jockey said gelding was denied a clear run)* **10/1**[3]

600 **6** 1 1/4 **Jungle Boogaloo (IRE)**[66] 5500 2-8-12 **58**........(h1) MarcoGhiani(7) 5 51
(Andi Brown) *taken down early: dwlt and impeded leaving stalls: detached in last: effrt over 1f out: swtchd rt and hdwy 1f out: styd on strly ins fnl f: nvr trbld ldrs* **14/1**

4000 **7** 3/4 **Il Maestro (IRE)**[58] 5789 2-9-7 **60**........ AndreaAtzeni 3 52
(John Quinn) *stmbld leaving stalls: wl in tch in midfield: nt clrest of runs and swtchd rt 2f out: drvn and clsd to press ldrs over 1f out: no ex and wknd ins fnl f (jockey said gelding stumbled leaving the stalls)* **5/1**[2]

0040 **8** 1/2 **Sweet Embrace (IRE)**[8] 7584 2-8-9 **51**........ RowanScott(3) 6 41
(John Wainwright) *pressed ldr: rdn to ld over 1f out: hdd 1f out: no ex and wknd ins fnl f* **33/1**

5530 **9** nk **Sir Rodneyredblood**[21] 7110 2-8-13 **52**........ AdrianMcCarthy 11 41
(J R Jenkins) *t.k.h: chsd ldrs on outer: unable qck u.p over 1f out: wknd ins fnl f* **25/1**

000 **10** 2 3/4 **Red Hottie**[39] 6514 2-8-1 **45**........ TheodoreLadd(5) 10 25
(Michael Appleby) *chsd ldrs tl unable qck u.p over 1f out: wknd ins fnl f* **14/1**

000 **11** nse **Lisbeth Salander (IRE)**[21] 7104 2-8-6 **45**........ HayleyTurner 1 25
(Richard Spencer) *hld up in tch in midfield: clsd to chse ldrs and nt clrest of runs over 1f out: sn rdn and fnd little: wknd ins fnl f* **14/1**

606 **12** 2 **Goodman Square**[21] 7110 2-8-6 **45**........ NicolaCurrie 7 19
(Mark Usher) *a off the pce in last pair: nvr involved (jockey said filly hung left-handed throughout)* **50/1**

000 **13** 4 **Sassy Lassy (IRE)**[14] 7377 2-8-3 **45**........(p1) DarraghKeenan(3) 4 7
(David Loughnane) *led: drvn and hdd over 1f out: sn outpcd: wknd ins fnl f* **20/1**

1m 14.45s (0.75) **Going Correction** -0.175s/f (Stan) **13 Ran SP% 125.6**
Speed ratings (Par 93): **88,87,84,84,84 82,81,81,80,77 77,74,69**
CSF £80.40 CT £514.23 TOTE £70.60: £16.50, £1.10, £2.60; EX 157.20 Trifecta £899.30.
Owner Eamon Spain **Bred** Eamon Patrick Spain **Trained** Wiseton, Nottinghamshire

FOCUS
A modest nursery.

7834 WEATHERBYS STALLION BOOK EBF MAIDEN STKS (PLUS 10 RACE) 1m 2f (P)
6:30 (6:30) (Class 4) 2-Y-O **£6,080** (£1,809; £904; £452) **Stalls** Low

Form RPR

53 **1** **Baptism (IRE)**[37] 6564 2-9-5 0........(p1) RobertHavlin 3 80
(John Gosden) *mde all: rdn 2f out: styd on wl u.p and in command ins fnl f* **4/1**[2]

52 **2** 1 3/4 **South Coast (USA)**[37] 6564 2-9-0 0........ OisinMurphy 6 72
(Saeed bin Suroor) *chsd wnr thrght: effrt over 1f out: edgd lft u.p and kpt on same pce ins fnl f* **5/4**[1]

6 **3** 4 **Bondi Sands (IRE)**[8] 7562 2-9-5 0........ FrannyNorton 2 69
(Mark Johnston) *bustled along leaving stalls: chsd ldng pair: rdn over 3f out: outpcd by ldng pair over 1f out: wl hld and plugged on same pce after* **4/1**[2]

45 **4** 7 **Falcon Claws (USA)**[12] 7473 2-9-5 0........ AndreaAtzeni 4 56
(Marco Botti) *hld up in last pair: effrt in 4th but outpcd by ldng pair over 2f out: wl hld after: eased towards fin* **25/1**

44 **5** 4 **Caledonian Crusade (IRE)**[28] 6892 2-9-5 0........ JamieSpencer 5 48
(David Simcock) *stdd s: hld up in tch in rr: outpcd and shkn up over 2f out: wl btn over 1f out: eased towards fin* **9/2**[3]

6 4 **Douglas Fir (IRE)** 2-9-5 0........ JimCrowley 1 41
(Mark Johnston) *rn green and sn rdn in midfield: struggling and outpcd over 2f out: wl btn over 1f out* **14/1**

2m 6.87s (-1.73) **Going Correction** -0.175s/f (Stan) **6 Ran SP% 113.1**
Speed ratings (Par 97): **99,97,94,88,85 82**
CSF £9.62 TOTE £4.10: £1.70, £1.30; EX 8.40 Trifecta £33.20.
Owner Cheveley Park Stud **Bred** Tullpark Ltd **Trained** Newmarket, Suffolk

FOCUS
An ordinary staying juvenile maiden.

7835 BET TOTEQUADPOT AT TOTESPORT.COM FILLIES' H'CAP 1m 2f (P)
7:00 (7:02) (Class 5) (0-70,72) 3-Y-O+ **£5,110** (£1,520; £759; £400; £400; £400) **Stalls** Low

Form RPR

44-0 **1** **Lucky Turn (IRE)**[132] 3050 3-9-5 **67**........ HayleyTurner 10 78+
(Michael Bell) *swtchd lft after s: in rr: effrt on outer over 1f out: hdwy to chal and hung lft u.p 1f out: sn led and r.o strly* **25/1**

4365 **2** 3 **Gallatin**[22] 7083 3-9-7 **69**........ OisinMurphy 6 74
(Andrew Balding) *awkward leaving stalls: in tch in midfield: impeded wl over 7f out: effrt and chsng ldrs whn squeezed for room 1f out: rallied and styd on fnl 100yds to snatch 2nd last strides: no threat to wnr* **5/1**[3]

3624 **3** nk **Kilbaha Lady (IRE)**[22] 7074 5-9-4 **65**........ RowanScott(3) 7 69
(Nigel Tinkler) *hld up in rr: stdy hdwy on outer 4f out: rdn and ev ch wl over 1f out: 2nd but unable to match pce of wnr jst ins fnl f: kpt on same pce and lost 2nd last strides* **12/1**

0241 **4** nk **Air Force Amy**[7] 7625 3-9-2 **69**........ ScottMcCullagh(5) 3 73
(Mick Channon) *hld up in tch in midfield: nt clrest of runs on inner over 2f out: clsd and nt clr run jst ins fnl f: swtchd lft and r.o ins fnl f: no threat to wnr* **4/1**[1]

1432 **5** nk **Angel's Whisper (IRE)**[15] 7344 4-9-6 **71**........ MarcoGhiani(7) 2 74
(Amy Murphy) *chsd ldr: sltly impeded and edgd lft wl over 7f out: nt clr run and lost 2nd over 2f out: swtchd rt and chal 2f out: drvn to ld over 1f out: hdd jst ins fnl f: no ex and one pce after* **6/1**

0010 **6** 1 1/4 **Petite Malle (USA)**[15] 7344 3-9-1 **63**........ GeorgeWood 9 64
(James Fanshawe) *hld up in tch towards rr: effrt over 2f out: clsd 1f out: kpt on ins fnl f: no threat to wnr* **14/1**

3334 **7** 3/4 **Swansdown**[36] 6595 3-9-0 **65**........ CierenFallon(3) 1 64
(William Haggas) *chsd ldrs tl impeded wl over 7f out: in tch in midfield after: nt clr run on inner over 1f out: effrt 1f out: no imp and sn btn: wknd ins fnl f* **5/1**[3]

4344 **8** 3 **Reasoned (IRE)**[89] 4642 3-8-13 **61**........ RyanTate 11 54
(James Eustace) *in tch in midfield: effrt and unable qck over 1f out: lost pl and wl hld ins fnl f* **33/1**

4241 **9** 1 **Perfecimperfection (IRE)**[40] 6439 3-9-2 **71**........ StefanoCherchi(7) 8 62
(Marco Botti) *t.k.h: chsd ldrs wl over 7f out: pressed ldr and rdn ent fnl 2f: no ex u.p 1f out: wknd ins fnl f* **9/2**[2]

5300 **10** 2 **Arctic Spirit**[15] 7343 3-9-5 **67**........(p1) RobertHavlin 4 54
(Ed Dunlop) *hld up in last trio: nt clr run and swtchd rt 1f out: nvr involved* **33/1**

4101 **11** 10 **Ventura Royal (IRE)**[9] 7542 4-10-0 **72** 5ex........(h) JamieSpencer 5 39
(David O'Meara) *taken down early: led: edgd lft wl over 7f out: stdd gallop 1/2-way: rdn ent fnl 2f: drvn and hdd over 1f out: sn lost pl: bhd and eased ins fnl f* **8/1**

2m 6.19s (-2.41) **Going Correction** -0.175s/f (Stan) **11 Ran SP% 121.0**
WFA 3 from 4yo+ 4lb
Speed ratings (Par 100): **102,99,99,99,98 97,97,94,94,92 84**
CSF £147.96 CT £1609.32 TOTE £86.50: £15.50, £1.80, £3.50; EX 388.20 Trifecta £1484.20.
Owner Mrs I Corbani **Bred** Rockhart Trading Ltd **Trained** Newmarket, Suffolk

The Form Book Flat 2019, Raceform Ltd, Newbury, RG14 5SJ

FOCUS
The winner rates a big improver, with the second and third close to form.

7836 BET TOTETRIFECTA AT TOTESPORT.COM H'CAP 1m (P)
7:30 (7:32) (Class 4) (0-85,87) 3-Y-0+
£5,530 (£1,645; £822; £411; £400; £400) **Stalls** Low

Form RPR
2-21 **1** **Alrajaa**[31] 6802 3-9-3 **82** JimCrowley 7 97+
(John Gosden) *v.s.a and styd wd early: off the pce in rr of main gp: clsd 1/2-way: effrt and swtchd rt bnd 2f out: rdn: hdwy to ld and edgd lft 1f out: r.o strly: readily* **7/4[1]**
2223 **2** *3 ½* **Strict Tempo**[19] 7176 3-9-4 **83** OisinMurphy 1 87
(Andrew Balding) *hld up off the pce in rr of main gp: clsd 1/2-way: swtchd rt and effrt wl over 1f out: styd on u.p ins fnl f: wnt 2nd cl home: no ch w wnr* **11/2[3]**
0205 **3** *nk* **Balladeer**[39] 6501 3-8-11 **76** HayleyTurner 2 79
(Michael Bell) *midfield: clsd and in tch 1/2-way: edgd out rt and drvn over 1f out: kpt on u.p to press for 2nd towards fin: no ch w wnr* **20/1**
2162 **4** *1* **Aluqair (IRE)**[12] 7462 3-9-3 **82** PatCosgrave 5 83
(Simon Crisford) *chsd ldrs: clsd 1/2-way: swtchd lft and effrt on inner over 1f out: ev ch briefly 1f out: nt match pce of wnr sn and hld in 2nd 100yds out: lost 2 pls cl home* **8/1**
5222 **5** *2* **Michele Strogoff**[9] 7551 6-9-2 **83** TheodoreLadd(5) 3 79+
(Michael Appleby) *taken down early: led: rdn ent fnl 2f: hdd 1f out: no ex and wknd ins fnl f* **7/2[2]**
3206 **6** *¾* **Hold Still (IRE)**[19] 7176 3-8-13 **78** NicolaCurrie 4 73
(William Muir) *v.s.a: nt travelling and sn detached in last: clsd u.p over 2f out: kpt on ins fnl f: nvr trbld ldrs (jockey said colt was outpaced early)* **14/1**
552 **7** *2 ¼* **Buckingham (IRE)**[21] 7128 3-9-4 **83** CharlesBishop 6 73
(Eve Johnson Houghton) *hld up in midfield: clsd 1/2-way: effrt over 1f out: unable qck and sn btn: wknd ins fnl f* **14/1**
6003 **8** *nse* **Commander Han (FR)**[22] 7090 4-9-4 **80** (p) DougieCostello 8 69
(Jamie Osborne) *pressed ldr: rdn and ev ch over 1f out: nt qckn u.p and wknd ins fnl f* **20/1**
2040 **9** *7* **Felix The Poet**[26] 6964 3-9-8 **87** (b) HollieDoyle 9 60
(Archie Watson) *chsd ldrs: clsd 1/2-way: rdn over 2f out: lost pl over 1f out: bhd ins fnl f* **9/1**

1m 37.86s (-2.04) **Going Correction** -0.175s/f (Stan)
WFA 3 from 4yo+ 3lb **9** Ran SP% **117.9**
Speed ratings (Par 105): **103,99,99,98,96 95,93,93,86**
CSF £11.99 CT £138.72 TOTE £2.30: £1.20, £2.10, £4.70; EX 15.10 Trifecta £121.80.
Owner Hamdan Al Maktoum **Bred** Shadwell Estate Company Limited **Trained** Newmarket, Suffolk

FOCUS
The feature contest was a decent handicap.

7837 BET TOTESWINGER AT TOTESPORT.COM H'CAP 6f (P)
8:00 (8:02) (Class 5) (0-70,72) 3-Y-0+
£5,175 (£1,540; £769; £400; £400; £400) **Stalls** Centre

Form RPR
0030 **1** **Kingsley Klarion (IRE)**[9] 7552 6-8-5 **55** DarraghKeenan(3) 10 69
(John Butler) *pressed ldr early: settled bk and wl in tch in midfield: effrt over 1f out: rdn and hdwy to ld 1f out: r.o strly: readily* **7/1**
5214 **2** *3 ¼* **Desert Fox**[9] 7552 5-9-7 **68** (p) RossaRyan 1 71
(Mike Murphy) *hld up in tch in midfield: clsd and edgd out lft and nt clr run over 1f out: swtchd rt 1f out: r.o ins fnl f to snatch 2nd last strides: no ch w wnr* **11/4[1]**
0503 **3** *hd* **Gottardo (IRE)**[12] 7447 4-9-3 **64** HollieDoyle 2 67
(Ed Dunlop) *t.k.h: hld up in last trio: effrt and c wd bnd 2f out: styd on wl u.p ins fnl f: no ch w wnr* **8/1**
4315 **4** *hd* **Lethal Angel**[7] 7613 4-9-11 **72** (p) JimCrowley 12 74
(Stuart Williams) *wnt rt leaving stalls: sn pressing ldr and t.k.h: rdn and ev ch over 1f out: unable to match pce of wnr 1f out: wl hld and one pce fnl 100yds: lost 2 pls cl home* **4/1[2]**
2P02 **5** *1* **Sir Hector (IRE)**[12] 7447 4-8-10 **57** LukeMorris 8 56
(Charlie Wallis) *led: hdd ent fnl 2f: sn rdn and stl ev ch tl unable to match pce of wnr 1f out: wl hld and one pce ins fnl f* **25/1**
5406 **6** *1 ¼* **Real Estate (IRE)**[9] 7552 4-9-7 **68** (p) CallumShepherd 5 63
(Michael Attwater) *wnt rt leaving stalls: hld up in tch in midfield: effrt over 1f out: unable qck and kpt on same pce ins fnl f* **11/2[3]**
4204 **7** *¾* **Phoenix Star (IRE)**[16] 7320 3-8-8 **63** (t[1]) MarcoGhiani(7) 4 55
(Stuart Williams) *hld up in last pair: effrt over 1f out: kpt on ins fnl f: nvr trbld ldrs* **9/1**
30 **8** *shd* **Dreamboat Annie**[211] 1038 4-8-8 **55** NicolaCurrie 6 47
(Mark Usher) *dwlt and hmpd leaving stalls: in rr: effrt on inner over 1f out: swtchd rt 1f out: kpt on ins fnl f: nvr involved (jockey said filly was slowly away)* **50/1**
0304 **9** *2 ½* **Highland Acclaim (IRE)**[21] 7130 8-9-11 **72** (p) JamieSpencer 3 56
(David O'Meara) *led early: chsd ldrs: nt clr run over 1f out: btn and eased ins fnl f (trainers rep could offer no explanation for the poor peformance)* **6/1**
0150 **10** *1 ¾* **Major Blue**[15] 7337 3-9-7 **72** (b) CierenFallon(3) 7 50
(James Eustace) *in tch in midfield: hdwy on outer and rdn to ld 2f out: drvn over 1f out: hdd 1f out: sn wknd* **20/1**

1m 12.15s (-1.55) **Going Correction** -0.175s/f (Stan)
WFA 3 from 4yo+ 1lb **10** Ran SP% **133.0**
Speed ratings (Par 103): **103,98,98,98,96 95,94,94,90,88**
CSF £27.02 CT £166.39 TOTE £6.80: £3.00, £1.20, £2.30; EX 39.90 Trifecta £308.70.
Owner Madeira Racing **Bred** Pier House Stud & Martinstown **Trained** Newmarket, Suffolk

FOCUS
A fair sprint handicap.

7838 BET TOTESCOOP6 AT TOTESPORT.COM H'CAP 6f (P)
8:30 (8:32) (Class 7) (0-50,55) 3-Y-0+ **£2,911** (£866; £432; £216) **Stalls** Centre

Form RPR
0423 **1** **Catapult**[7] 7632 4-9-2 **45** (p) JosephineGordon 10 52
(Shaun Keightley) *hld up in tch in last quartet: hdwy over 1f out: swtchd rt 1f out: r.o strly u.p to ld last strides* **7/1[3]**
-451 **2** *hd* **Broughton Excels**[7] 7606 4-9-12 **55** 5ex StevieDonohoe 1 61
(Stuart Williams) *hld up in tch in midfield: swtchd lft and effrt over 1f out: sn rdn and qcknd to ld jst over 1f out: kpt on u.p: hdd last strides* **5/4[1]**
604 **3** *1* **Obsession For Gold (IRE)**[14] 7374 3-9-5 **49** (t) BrettDoyle 3 52
(Mrs Ilka Gansera-Leveque) *squeezed for room and hmpd leaving stalls: in tch in midfield: swtchd lft and effrt on inner over 1f out: chsd ldr 1f out: kpt on same pce ins fnl f: lost 2nd towards fin* **5/1[2]**
0034 **4** *1* **Storm Lightning**[39] 6503 10-9-2 **45** EoinWalsh 7 45
(Kevin Frost) *chsd ldrs: effrt over 1f out: kpt on same pce u.p ins fnl f* **25/1**
5060 **5** *1 ¼* **Atwaar**[7] 7628 3-8-12 **45** NoelGarbutt(3) 11 42
(Charles Smith) *stdd s: hld up in rr: hdwy over 1f out: swtchd lft and kpt on wl ins fnl f: nvr trbld ldrs* **50/1**
5000 **6** *½* **Manzoni**[28] 6889 3-9-5 **49** KieranO'Neill 2 44
(Mohamed Moubarak) *sn prom and t.k.h: effrt to chal and rdn over 1f out: unable qck 1f out: wknd ins fnl f* **8/1**
604 **7** *2* **Frea**[7] 7606 3-9-2 **46** RobertHavlin 6 35
(Harry Dunlop) *in tch in midfield: effrt and wd over 1f out: edgd lft u.p and no imp 1f out: wknd ins fnl f* **7/1[3]**
6060 **8** *1 ¼* **Waneen (IRE)**[7] 7606 6-9-2 **45** HollieDoyle 12 30
(John Butler) *sn towards rr: swtchd rt and effrt over 1f out: nvr trbld ldrs* **20/1**
0350 **9** *1* **Good Business (IRE)**[28] 6889 5-9-4 **50** (v) CierenFallon(3) 8 32
(Henry Spiller) *stdd s: hld up in rr: sme hdwy ins fnl f: nvr involved* **33/1**
5000 **10** *1 ¼* **Such Promise**[21] 7105 3-9-3 **47** (t[1]) RossaRyan 4 26
(Mike Murphy) *sn led: drifted rt and drvn over 1f out: hdd jst over 1f out: wknd ins fnl f* **20/1**
063 **11** *¾* **Royal Mezyan (IRE)**[14] 7371 8-9-5 **48** LouisSteward 5 24
(Henry Spiller) *hld up in midfield: effrt over 1f out: sn btn and wknd ins fnl f* **12/1**
5550 **12** *4 ½* **Ar Saoirse**[7] 7606 4-9-2 **45** (bt) LukeMorris 14 8
(Clare Hobson) *w ldr: rdn over 2f out: lost pl and btn over 1f out: bhd ins fnl f* **33/1**
0452 **13** *7* **Praxedis**[47] 6199 4-9-4 **47** (v) HayleyTurner 13
(Robert Cowell) *midfield on outer: hdwy to chse ldrs over 2f out: lost pl u.p over 1f out: bhd ins fnl f* **25/1**

1m 12.85s (-0.85) **Going Correction** -0.175s/f (Stan)
WFA 3 from 4yo+ 1lb **13** Ran SP% **131.9**
Speed ratings (Par 97): **98,97,96,95,93 92,90,88,87,85 84,78,69**
CSF £16.28 CT £56.36 TOTE £8.70: £2.10, £1.20, £1.70; EX 24.50 Trifecta £145.90.
Owner Simon Lockyer **Bred** Owen O'Brien **Trained** Newmarket, Suffolk

FOCUS
A moderate sprint handicap, but a thrilling finale, and a fine winning ride by Josephine Gordon.
T/Jkpt: Not won. T/Plt: £24.10 to a £1 stake. Pool: £38,706.20 - 1601.89 winning units T/Qpdt: £18.50 to a £1 stake. Pool: £4,849.70 - 262.09 winning units **Steve Payne**

7554 LINGFIELD (L-H)
Thursday, October 3

OFFICIAL GOING: Polytrack: standard
Wind: Almost nil becoming moderate, behind Weather: Overcast becoming brighter

7839 DOWNLOAD THE STAR SPORTS APP NOW! H'CAP 1m 1y(P)
1:40 (1:41) (Class 5) (0-75,77) 3-Y-0+
£3,428 (£1,020; £509; £300; £300; £300) **Stalls** High

Form RPR
-656 **1** **Bobby Biscuit (USA)**[246] 473 4-9-1 **69** JFEgan 8 75+
(Roger Varian) *s.i.s: hld up and racd wd: urged along wl over 2f out: prog over 1f out: drvn and styd on fnl f to ld last 50yds* **9/4[1]**
6442 **2** *nk* **Recondite (IRE)**[40] 6469 3-9-2 **73** (b[1]) HarryBentley 2 78
(Ralph Beckett) *hld up in last trio: prog on inner over 1f out: squeezed through ins fnl f: styd on to take 2nd last stride: jst too late* **6/1[3]**
-560 **3** *shd* **Deference**[41] 6418 3-8-13 **70** RobertHavlin 4 75
(Amanda Perrett) *hld up in midfield: prog on inner 2f out: drvn to ld narrowly jst ins fnl f: hdd last 50yds: lost 2nd fnl stride* **33/1**
166 **4** *½* **Plunger**[20] 7164 4-9-7 **75** (p[1]) BenCurtis 11 79
(Paul Cole) *t.k.h: pressed ldr: rdn 2f out: led jst over 1f out to jst ins fnl f: one pce last 100yds* **13/2**
6222 **5** *hd* **Delicate Kiss**[15] 7343 5-9-4 **72** KieranO'Neill 5 76
(John Bridger) *trckd ldrs: rdn 2f out: clsd w others to chal ins fnl f: one pce last 100yds* **8/1**
3323 **6** *2* **Juanito Chico (IRE)**[17] 7272 5-9-4 **72** (p) LukeMorris 10 71
(Michael Attwater) *t.k.h: trckd ldrs: rdn and lost pl wl over 1f out: no ch after but kpt on again nr fin* **25/1**
2142 **7** *¾* **Kendergarten Kop (IRE)**[9] 7560 4-9-0 **68** (p) DavidProbert 9 65
(David Flood) *slowly away: hld up in last: shkn up 2f out: no prog tl styd on fnl 150yds (jockey said gelding was slowly away)* **4/1[2]**
3213 **8** *hd* **Mochalov**[22] 7080 4-8-5 **62** DarraghKeenan(3) 6 59
(Jane Chapple-Hyam) *t.k.h: hld up in midfield: rdn and tried to cl on ldrs over 1f out: fdd ins fnl f* **10/1**
1061 **9** *¾* **Baashiq (IRE)**[17] 7272 5-9-3 **71** (p) LiamKeniry 7 66
(Peter Hiatt) *led: rdn and hdd jst over 1f out: wknd* **14/1**
0010 **10** *¾* **Forseti**[57] 5804 3-9-3 **77** (h) CierenFallon(3) 3 70
(Michael Appleby) *t.k.h: racd wd: prog fr midfield 1/2-way: rdn to chse ldng pair 2f out: wknd over 1f out (jockey said gelding ran too free)* **12/1**
25-5 **11** *2 ¼* **Rollicking (IRE)**[20] 7166 3-9-2 **73** SeanLevey 1 61
(Richard Hannon) *dwlt: hld up in last trio: shkn up and no prog over 1f out* **33/1**

1m 35.13s (-3.07) **Going Correction** -0.225s/f (Stan)
WFA 3 from 4yo+ 3lb **11** Ran SP% **122.7**
Speed ratings (Par 103): **106,105,105,105,104 102,102,101,101,100 98**
CSF £16.43 CT £363.45 TOTE £3.20: £1.50, £2.00, £10.60; EX 19.80 Trifecta £396.40.
Owner Damien Brennan **Bred** Flaxman Holdings Limited **Trained** Newmarket, Suffolk

FOCUS
A good-quality handicap and busy finish.

7840 SHARD SOLUTIONS AND ORIGIN NURSERY H'CAP 1m 1y(P)
2:10 (2:12) (Class 4) (0-85,85) 2-Y-0
£4,463 (£1,328; £663; £331; £300; £300) **Stalls** High

Form RPR
5023 **1** **Qaaddim (IRE)**[20] 7155 2-8-13 **77** (p) AndreaAtzeni 8 80
(Roger Varian) *racd wd: in tch in rr: urged along fr 3f out: prog on outer over 1f out: styd on wl fnl f to ld last strides* **11/1**
0513 **2** *nk* **Pitchcombe**[13] 7409 2-8-5 **72** (p) WilliamCox(3) 7 74
(Clive Cox) *t.k.h: trckd ldng pair: rdn over 1f out: narrow ld jst ins fnl f: hdd and jst outpcd last strides (jockey said gelding hung right-handed)* **14/1**
2312 **3** *¾* **Hexagon (IRE)**[26] 6965 2-9-7 **85** JasonWatson 5 86
(Roger Charlton) *pressed ldr: rdn to chal 2f out: upsides 1f out: one pce last 100yds* **7/2[2]**

3415 **4** nk **Incinerator**[19] 7197 2-9-4 **82**..............(t) JamesDoyle 6 82
(Hugo Palmer) *t.k.h: hld up and last after 3f: rdn over 1f out: hanging lft and racing awkwardly: sed to run on fnl f but stl hanging and rn into trble: fin w smething lft (jockey said colt was denied a clear run to the line)* **10/1**

0121 **5** ½ **Dramatic Sands (IRE)**[26] 6965 2-9-6 **84**.............. HollieDoyle 1 83
(Archie Watson) *led: rdn and pressed 2f out: hdd and fdd jst ins fnl f* **9/2**[3]

6421 **6** 1½ **Imperial Empire**[33] 6728 2-9-0 **78**.............. WilliamBuick 4 74
(Charlie Appleby) *wl in tch: cl up bhd ldrs over 1f out: sn rdn and fnd nil: wknd fnl f* **3/1**[1]

530 **7** ½ **Impatient**[20] 7162 2-8-13 **77**.............. HarryBentley 3 72+
(Ralph Beckett) *v s.i.s: sn in tch in last pair: pushed along on inner and nt clr run over 1f out: nvr able to become involved* **6/1**

324 **8** 2¾ **Forbidden Land (IRE)**[19] 7197 2-9-2 **80**.............. SeanLevey 2 68
(Richard Hannon) *chsd ldrs: rdn 2f out: wknd qckly jst over 1f out* **8/1**

1m 35.7s (-2.50) **Going Correction** -0.225s/f (Stan) 2y crse rec **8** Ran SP% **114.9**
Speed ratings (Par 97): **103,102,101,101,101 99,99,96**
CSF £148.85 CT £651.52 TOTE £9.20: £2.30, £4.00, £1.50; EX 140.90 Trifecta £692.20.
Owner Sheikh Ahmed Al Maktoum **Bred** Peter Molony **Trained** Newmarket, Suffolk

FOCUS
A fair nursery and plenty of potential on show.

7841 STARSPORTS.BET MAIDEN STKS — 1m 1y(P)
2:45 (2:47) (Class 5) 3-Y-O+ — £3,428 (£1,020; £509; £254) **Stalls High**

Form — RPR

4 **1** **Reine De Vitesse (FR)**[61] 5650 3-9-0 0.............. JFEgan 7 74+
(Jane Chapple-Hyam) *trckd ldng pair: shkn up to cl on outer 2f out: rdn to ld jst over 1f out: styd on wl: readily* **5/2**[2]

3- **2** 2¼ **Sheriffmuir (USA)**[440] 5169 3-9-5 0..............(p[1]) RobertHavlin 4 74+
(John Gosden) *s.i.s: t.k.h and swiftly rcvrd to ld after 2f: rdn and hdd over 1f out: styd on same pce fnl f* **6/5**[1]

-4 **3** 1½ **Almahha**[19] 7190 3-9-0 0.............. JimCrowley 10 65
(Owen Burrows) *led 2f: trckd ldr: rdn to ld briefly over 1f out: one pce fnl f* **5/1**

33 **4** ½ **Imhotep**[16] 7319 3-9-5 0.............. JasonWatson 3 69
(Roger Charlton) *trckd ldng pair: cl up 2f out: rdn and nt qckn over 1f out: one pce after* **7/2**[3]

5 **5** 1¾ **The Grey Goat (IRE)**[10] 7523 3-9-5 0.............. AdrianMcCarthy 8 65
(Peter Charalambous) *a in 5th: nvr on terms w ldrs but clr of rest fr 3f out: shkn up on inner over 1f out: kpt on steadily* **66/1**

6 5 **Dawry (IRE)** 3-9-5 0.............. LukeMorris 2 53
(Heather Main) *s.i.s: rn green and a bhd in 2nd half of field: rdn 2f out: kpt on to ld that bunch fnl f* **20/1**

7 2 **Fire Island** 3-9-0 0.............. HollieDoyle 9 43
(Tom Ward) *a bhd in 2nd half of field: brief effrt 2f out but no real prog* **50/1**

8 1 **Rockstar Max (GER)** 3-9-5 0.............. DougieCostello 6 46
(Denis Coakley) *a bhd in 2nd half of field: led that bunch over 3f out tl fnl f* **66/1**

5 **9** 4 **Kira's Star**[18] 7228 3-8-11 0.............. WilliamCox(3) 5 31
(Richenda Ford) *a bhd and mostly in last: nvr a factor* **100/1**

0-0 **10** 3¾ **Star Command (IRE)**[21] 7114 3-8-7 0.............. MichaelPitt(7) 1 22
(Denis Coakley) *nvr bttr than 6th: wknd 3f out* **100/1**

1m 35.88s (-2.32) **Going Correction** -0.225s/f (Stan) **10** Ran SP% **124.6**
Speed ratings (Par 103): **102,99,98,97,96 91,89,88,84,80**
CSF £6.28 TOTE £3.70: £1.20, £1.10, £1.50; EX 8.50 Trifecta £26.00.
Owner Johnstone Partnership **Bred** Patrick Roulois **Trained** Dalham, Suffolk

FOCUS
This maiden lacked depth and was dominated by the top two in the market. The winner set the standard and didn't need to match her best.

7842 READ SILVESTRE DE SOUSA'S EXCLUSIVE BLOG STARSPORTSBET.CO.UK EBF NOVICE STKS — 7f 1y(P)
3:15 (3:18) (Class 5) 2-Y-O — £3,428 (£1,020; £509; £254) **Stalls Low**

Form — RPR

2 **1** **Rovaniemi (IRE)**[54] 5956 2-9-2 0.............. JamieSpencer 1 78+
(David Simcock) *trckd ldrs: plld out over 1f out: cajoled along and clsd to ld last 100yds: styd on wl* **1/1**[1]

1 **2** 1¾ **Amaan**[23] 7055 2-9-9 0.............. JimCrowley 5 80
(Simon Crisford) *mde most: rdn wl over 1f out: hdd and outpcd last 100yds* **5/2**[2]

3 1 **Ayr Harbour** 2-9-2 0.............. SeanLevey 11 71
(Richard Hannon) *trckd ldrs: wnt 2nd over 2f out gng strly and sn upsides: shkn up and nt qckn over 1f out: kpt on same pce after* **33/1**

3 **4** ¾ **Transition**[49] 6112 2-9-2 0.............. JasonWatson 6 69+
(Amanda Perrett) *trckd ldrs: lost pl after 3f and in midfield: shkn up 2f out: rdn in 9th over 2f out: styd on wl over 1f out: gaining at fin* **4/1**[3]

5 ¾ **Al Rufaa (FR)** 2-9-2 0.............. RobertHavlin 7 67+
(John Gosden) *t.k.h: hld up towards rr: pushed along and prog 2f out: styd on quite wl fnl f: nrst fin* **12/1**

6 2¼ **Almuerzo Loco (IRE)** 2-9-2 0.............. PatDobbs 13 60
(Richard Hannon) *hld up towards rr: prog on inner over 2f out: chsd ldng trio briefly over 1f out: fdd fnl f* **50/1**

0 **7** 1 **Glencoe Boy (IRE)**[43] 6344 2-8-13 0.............. DarraghKeenan(3) 9 58
(David Flood) *racd wd and hanging rt: w ldr to over 2f out: wd bnd sn after and wknd* **100/1**

02 **8** 1¾ **General Joe (IRE)**[21] 7113 2-9-2 0.............. AdamKirby 14 53
(Clive Cox) *racd wd: prog fr midfield to chse ldrs over 2f out: sn drvn: wknd over 1f out* **10/1**

9 7 **Gaelic Kingdom (IRE)** 2-9-2 0.............. KieranShoemark 10 34
(Charles Hills) *green preliminaries: wl in tch tl wknd qckly 2f out* **50/1**

6 **10** 3¾ **Revolver (IRE)**[14] 7388 2-9-2 0.............. LukeMorris 3 24
(Sir Mark Prescott Bt) *sn pushed along: a wl in rr* **66/1**

0 **11** ¾ **Barboukha**[30] 6846 2-8-11 0.............. GeorgeDowning 8 17
(Luke Dace) *mostly in last and a bhd* **100/1**

00 **12** 2½ **Leo's Luckyman**[21] 7113 2-8-9 0.............. EllieMacKenzie(7) 2 15
(David Flood) *a in rr: wknd over 2f out* **100/1**

1m 23.32s (-1.48) **Going Correction** -0.225s/f (Stan) **12** Ran SP% **128.7**
Speed ratings (Par 95): **99,97,95,95,94 91,90,88,80,76 75,72**
CSF £3.90 TOTE £1.80: £1.10, £1.10, £7.20; EX 4.90 Trifecta £68.90.
Owner Sun Bloodstock Sarl **Bred** Epona Bloodstock Ltd **Trained** Newmarket, Suffolk

FOCUS
This looked an above-average novice on paper and there was a lot to like about the performances of the first two. The second has been rated in line with his debut.

7843 DOWNLOAD THE STAR SPORTS APP NOW! FILLIES' H'CAP — 7f 1y(P)
3:50 (3:50) (Class 5) (0-70,70) 3-Y-O+ — £3,428 (£1,020; £509; £300; £300; £300) **Stalls Low**

Form — RPR

5350 **1** **Rapture (FR)**[18] 7237 3-9-8 **70**.............. HollieDoyle 1 80+
(Archie Watson) *mde all: drvn at least 2 l clr on inner over 1f out: drvn out and a holding on* **8/1**

2262 **2** 1¼ **Seprani**[5] 7684 5-9-0 **67**..............(h) StefanoCherchi(7) 10 74
(Amy Murphy) *racd on outer: in tch in midfield: rdn over 1f out: r.o fnl f u.p: tk 2nd last 50yds: too late to chal* **9/2**[3]

0150 **3** 1 **Devils Roc**[18] 7230 3-9-8 **70**.............. RobHornby 4 73
(Jonathan Portman) *trckd ldng pair: rdn 2f out: chsd wnr ins fnl f: no imp and lost 2nd last 50yds* **20/1**

5244 **4** hd **Bint Dandy (IRE)**[7] 7608 8-9-9 **69**..............(b) BenCurtis 6 73
(Charlie Wallis) *hld up in last pair: stl there 2f out: rdn and prog over 1f out: styd on wl last 150yds: too late* **7/1**

3040 **5** ½ **Javelin**[80] 4994 4-9-10 **70**.............. JamesDoyle 2 72
(William Muir) *trckd ldrs on inner: rdn over 1f out: pressed for a pl fnl f: one pce last 100yds* **11/4**[1]

5044 **6** ¾ **Black Medick**[21] 7129 3-9-7 **69**.............. LukeMorris 8 68
(Laura Mongan) *chsd wnr: rdn to chal 2f out: nt qckn over 1f out: lost 2nd and wknd ins fnl f* **14/1**

-264 **7** 1½ **Burning Topic (GER)**[17] 7278 3-9-6 **68**.............. LiamKeniry 7 63
(David Lanigan) *hld up towards rr: shkn up 2f out: no real prog over 1f out* **11/1**

5526 **8** 2 **Plumette**[16] 7299 3-9-1 **68**..............(p) ThomasGreatrex(5) 12 58
(David Loughnane) *racd wd: chsd ldrs: wd bnd 2f out and wknd* **8/1**

0-00 **9** 1 **Shoyd**[17] 7273 4-8-1 **52**.............. ThoreHammerHansen(5) 9 40
(Richard Hannon) *dropped to last and rdn 4f out: nvr a factor* **33/1**

3210 **10** ½ **Zoraya (FR)**[28] 6898 4-9-10 **70**.............. AdamKirby 3 57
(Pam Sly) *urged along early towards rr: in tch: rdn and no prog over 2f out: fdd* **4/1**[2]

1m 23.56s (-1.24) **Going Correction** -0.225s/f (Stan) **10** Ran SP% **128.2**
WFA 3 from 4yo+ 2lb
Speed ratings (Par 100): **98,96,95,95,94 93,92,89,88,88**
CSF £46.18 CT £730.53 TOTE £7.40: £2.40, £1.90, £5.30; EX 38.70 Trifecta £307.70.
Owner Clipper Logistics **Bred** Dayton Investments Limited **Trained** Upper Lambourn, W Berks

FOCUS
A modest, but competitive fillies' only handicap. The winner stole a march on her rivals off the home bend and posted a pb.

7844 CALL STAR SPORTS ON 08000 521 321 H'CAP — 5f 6y(P)
4:20 (4:21) (Class 6) (0-60,60) 3-Y-O+ — £2,781 (£827; £413; £300; £300; £300) **Stalls High**

Form — RPR

0540 **1** **Sandfrankskipsgo**[9] 7557 10-9-1 **53**.............. PatDobbs 10 58
(Peter Crate) *racd on outer: w ldng pair: pushed into ld over 1f out: hrd pressed last 100yds: hld on wl (trainer said gelding benefitted from jumping well from the stalls and racing prominently on this occasion)* **25/1**

3160 **2** shd **Aquadabra (IRE)**[19] 7172 4-9-5 **57**.............. CallumShepherd 8 62
(Christopher Mason) *trckd ldrs: pushed along to cl over 1f out: str chal ins fnl f: jst hld* **12/1**

2530 **3** nse **Edged Out**[21] 7112 9-8-11 **52**.............. MitchGodwin(3) 5 56
(Christopher Mason) *trckd ldrs: clsd on inner to chal fnl f: jst hld nr fin* **12/1**

6600 **4** 2½ **Miaella**[8] 7576 4-9-6 **58**..............(p) JoeyHaynes 9 53
(Chelsea Banham) *w ldr: narrow ld 2f out to over 1f out: wknd last 100yds* **10/1**

0604 **5** shd **Awake In Asia**[9] 7557 3-9-0 **52**..............(p) JasonWatson 3 48
(Charlie Wallis) *dwlt: towards rr: rdn over 2f out: kpt on fnl f but n.d* **14/1**

0151 **6** ¾ **Devil Or Angel**[9] 7557 4-9-3 **60** 5ex..............(p) ThoreHammerHansen(5) 7 52
(Bill Turner) *dwlt: racd on outer in rr: rdn over 2f out: wd bnd sn after: nvr on terms* **9/2**[3]

-064 **7** ½ **On Route**[8] 7576 3-9-6 **58**..............(v) LukeMorris 2 50
(Sir Mark Prescott Bt) *dwlt: rn in snatches and mostly in last: drvn and one pce over 1f out* **2/1**[1]

5046 **8** ¾ **Ask The Guru**[45] 6285 9-8-7 **45**..............(p) JimmyQuinn 1 33
(Michael Attwater) *sn in last pair: rdn 2f out: no real prog* **25/1**

6022 **9** 2½ **Brogans Bay (IRE)**[9] 7557 4-9-3 **55**.............. AdamKirby 6 34
(Simon Dow) *led on inner to 2f out: wknd over 1f out: eased* **5/2**[2]

57.95s (-0.85) **Going Correction** -0.225s/f (Stan) **9** Ran SP% **122.8**
Speed ratings (Par 101): **97,96,96,92,92 91,90,89,85**
CSF £298.81 CT £3780.77 TOTE £20.40: £2.90, £2.20, £4.70; EX 122.30 Trifecta £1935.00.
Owner Peter Crate **Bred** Peter Crate **Trained** Newdigate, Surrey

FOCUS
Three pulled clear in this very ordinary sprint handicap and fought out a close finish. The three market principals all finished in rear. The second, along with the compressed finish, suggests the form can't be rated much higher.

7845 FIRST FOR INDUSTRY JOBS VISIT STARRECRUITMENT.BET H'CAP — 1m 7f 169y(P)
4:55 (4:55) (Class 5) (0-75,76) 3-Y-O+ — £3,428 (£1,020; £509; £300; £300; £300) **Stalls Low**

Form — RPR

2121 **1** **Road To Paris (IRE)**[43] 6333 3-8-13 **68**..............(p) LukeMorris 6 80+
(Sir Mark Prescott Bt) *pressed ldr gng wl: led 5f out: sent for home over 3f out and sn clr: 5 l up 1f out: drvn and ld dwindled but nvr gng to be ct* **5/1**[3]

4361 **2** 1¾ **Imperium (IRE)**[17] 7279 3-9-5 **74**.............. JasonWatson 11 82+
(Roger Charlton) *hld up wl in rr: lft bhd 3f out: gd prog on inner 2f out: chsd clr wnr jst ins fnl f: fin wl and cutting bk deficit nr fin but too much to do* **11/4**[1]

2143 **3** 2¾ **Manton Warrior (IRE)**[14] 7370 3-9-4 **73**..............(t) StevieDonohoe 2 78+
(Charlie Fellowes) *buried away in midfield: outpcd 3f out: nt clr run briefly 2f out: rdn and prog over 1f out: r.o to take 3rd ins fnl f: nrst fin* **8/1**

2130 **4** 2¼ **Bird For Life**[41] 6400 5-9-1 **68**..............(p) EllieMacKenzie(7) 14 70
(Mark Usher) *hld up in last pair: stl there over 2f out and long way bhd wnr: prog on inner over 1f out: styd on wl to take 4th nr fin: no ch to threaten* **40/1**

The Form Book Flat 2019, Raceform Ltd, Newbury, RG14 5SJ

0321 **5** *nk* **Cogital**33 6720 4-9-9 **69**..........(h) PatDobbs 13 71
(Amanda Perrett) *hld up in last pair: lft bhd 3f out: prog on inner over 2f out: chsd ldrs 1f out but no ch: one pce ins fnl f* **6/1**

2350 **6** *shd* **Falcon Cliffs (IRE)**15 7344 5-8-9 **58**.......... CierenFallon(3) 7 60
(Tony Carroll) *dwlt: sn in midfield: lost pl and outpcd 3f out: rdn and styd on again over 1f out but no ch* **25/1**

3501 **7** *½* **Fragrant Belle**19 7192 3-9-1 **70**..........(h) HarryBentley 12 71
(Ralph Beckett) *hld up wl in rr: outpcd 3f out: effrt and wdst of all bnd 2f out: kpt on but no ch* **4/1**2

011 **8** *¾* **Conkering Hero (IRE)**14 7370 5-10-2 **76**..........(b) RossaRyan 4 76
(Joseph Tuite) *led to 5f out: chsd wnr: outpcd 3f out: lost 2nd and wknd jst ins fnl f* **14/1**

3425 **9** *1* **General Zoff**18 7239 4-9-9 **69**..........(p) JFEgan 3 68
(William Muir) *prom: outpcd 3f out: rdn to chse clr ldng pair over 2f out: wknd fnl f* **12/1**

1240 **10** *1 ¼* **Tour De Paris (IRE)**34 6681 4-8-12 **63**.......(v) ThoreHammerHansen(5) 8 61
(Alan King) *nvr beyond midfield: outpcd 3f out: no hdwy over 1f out* **25/1**

3355 **11** *½* **Gavlar**33 6720 8-9-11 **71**..........(v) CallumShepherd 5 68
(William Knight) *trckd ldrs: outpcd 3f out: no ch after: wknd over 1f out* **20/1**

2150 **12** *2 ¼* **Tin Fandango**33 6720 4-9-7 **67**..........(p) JosephineGordon 9 61
(Mark Usher) *t.k.h: pressed ldrs on outer: outpcd over 3f out: wknd over 2f out (jockey said gelding hung right-handed throughout)* **50/1**

600 **13** *14* **Swordbill**43 6333 4-10-0 **74**..........(p) AdamKirby 1 52
(Ian Williams) *hld up towards rr: rdn 3f out: wknd over 2f out: t.o* **20/1**

0036 **14** *nk* **The Way You Dance (IRE)**16 7300 7-9-2 **69**...... RhysClutterbuck(7) 10 46
(Michael Attwater) *sn in midfield: wknd over 2f out: t.o* **50/1**

3m 21.82s (-3.88) **Going Correction** -0.225s/f (Stan)
WFA 3 from 4yo+ 9lb **14** Ran SP% **126.7**
Speed ratings (Par 103): **100,99,97,96,96 96,96,95,95,94 94,93,86,86**
CSF £18.63 CT £114.43 TOTE £5.60: £2.10, £1.50, £3.30; EX 25.40 Trifecta £191.60.
Owner Jones, Julian, Lee, Royle & Wicks **Bred** Rabbah Bloodstock Limited **Trained** Newmarket, Suffolk

FOCUS
This was steadily run but the first three rate as on the upgrade.
T/Plt: £489.70 to a £1 stake. Pool: £74,331.32 - 110.79 winning units T/Qpdt: £67.30 to a £1 stake. Pool: £9,019.59 - 99.08 winning units **Jonathan Neesom**

7154 SALISBURY (R-H)
Thursday, October 3
7846 Meeting Abandoned - Waterlogged Track

7767 WOLVERHAMPTON (A.W) (L-H)
Thursday, October 3
OFFICIAL GOING: Tapeta: standard
Wind: Light behind Weather: Showers

7853 COMPARE BOOKMAKER SITES AT BONUSCODEBETS.CO.UK NURSERY H'CAP 5f 21y (Tp)
5:10 (5:14) (Class 6) (0-60,60) 2-Y-O
£2,781 (£827; £413; £400; £400; £400) **Stalls** Low

Form RPR

05 **1** **A Go Go**18 7234 2-8-12 **51**.......... CliffordLee 1 54
(David Evans) *led 1f: chsd ldr to 1/2-way: rdn over 1f out: nt clr run and swtchd rt ins fnl f: styd on u.p to ld nr fin* **14/1**

0223 **2** *½* **Blue Venture**21 7110 2-9-3 **56**.......... TomMarquand 8 57
(Tony Carroll) *led 4f out: rdn over 1f out: hdd nr fin* **7/2**2

0004 **3** *½* **She's Easyontheeye (IRE)**12 7440 2-9-1 **54**.......... BenRobinson 3 53
(John Quinn) *chsd ldrs: rdn over 1f out: r.o to go 3rd nr fin* **11/1**

663 **4** *½* **Glamorous Force**26 6979 2-8-12 **51**.......... DuranFentiman 10 49
(Ronald Harris) *sn prom: chsd ldr 1/2-way: rdn over 1f out: styd on same pce wl ins fnl f* **13/2**

126 **5** *¾* **Queenoftheclyde (IRE)**19 7208 2-9-3 **59**.......... HarrisonShaw(3) 9 54+
(K R Burke) *sn pushed along in rr: rdn and hung lft fr over 1f out: r.o ins fnl f: nt rch ldrs* **9/2**3

024 **6** *½* **Call Me Cheers**37 6557 2-9-6 **59**.......... DanielTudhope 2 52
(David Evans) *chsd ldrs: hung rt 1/2-way: sn outpcd: rdn over 1f out: styd on ins fnl f* **11/4**1

6456 **7** *1 ½* **Hollaback Girl**40 6436 2-8-11 **57**..........(p) SeanKirrane(7) 4 45
(Richard Spencer) *s.i.s: hld up: shkn up over 1f out: nt trble ldrs (jockey said filly was slowly into stride and was never travelling in the early stages of the race)* **9/1**

0565 **8** *½* **La Chica Lobo**36 6585 2-9-4 **57**.......... CamHardie 7 43
(Lisa Williamson) *hld up: rdn 1/2-way: n.d* **28/1**

0000 **9** *1 ¾* **Bockos Amber (IRE)**18 7234 2-9-3 **56**.......... JackMitchell 6 36
(Roger Teal) *prom: shkn up and hung rt 1/2-way: wknd fnl f* **8/1**

6660 **10** *1 ¾* **Koovers (IRE)**17 7275 2-8-9 **55**..........(b) AidenSmithies(7) 5 28
(Gay Kelleway) *hld up: shkn up and hung lft over 1f out: nvr on terms* **20/1**

0050 **11** *shd* **Maisie Ellie (IRE)**10 7522 2-9-0 **60**..........(p1) Pierre-LouisJamin(7) 11 33
(Paul George) *s.s: outpcd* **66/1**

1m 1.32s (-0.58) **Going Correction** -0.175s/f (Stan) **11** Ran SP% **126.2**
Speed ratings (Par 93): **97,96,95,94,93 92,90,89,86,83 83**
CSF £66.33 CT £597.33 TOTE £19.70: £4.60, £1.60, £4.00; EX 115.70 Trifecta £797.60.
Owner R Kent **Bred** Mickley Stud **Trained** Pandy, Monmouths

FOCUS
Moderate form here with the market leader never running any sort of race.

7854 FOLLOW AT THE RACES ON TWITTER NOVICE STKS 5f 21y (Tp)
5:45 (5:46) (Class 5) 3-Y-O+ **£3,428** (£1,020; £509; £254) **Stalls** Low

Form RPR

0-32 **1** **Spirited Guest**16 7319 3-9-3 68.......... TomQueally 2 76
(George Margarson) *trckd ldrs: racd keenly: led on bit 1f out: shkn up ins fnl f: r.o: comf* **5/4**1

31 **2** *1 ¼* **Hassaad**31 6797 3-9-5 0.......... AdamMcNamara 3 74
(Archie Watson) *sn led: plld hrd: rdn and hdd 1f out: styd on same pce wl ins fnl f* **11/8**2

3242 **3** *2 ½* **Desert Land (IRE)**16 7313 3-8-12 73..........(p1) DylanHogan(5) 5 63
(David Simcock) *hmpd and lost pl sn after s: hdwy over 1f out: rdn ins fnl f: styd on same pce* **7/2**3

00- **4** *1 ¾* **Miss Gradenko**357 8138 3-8-12 0.......... RichardKingscote 6 51
(Robert Cowell) *prom: shkn up and edgd lft over 1f out: no ex ins fnl f* **50/1**

0-5 **5** *3* **Maerchengarten**21 7114 3-8-9 0.......... JaneElliott(3) 4 40
(Ed de Giles) *chsd ldr: hung rt fr 1/2-way: rdn and lost 2nd over 1f out: wknd fnl f (jockey said filly hung right-handed throughout and did not handle the bend)* **25/1**

1m 0.76s (-1.14) **Going Correction** -0.175s/f (Stan) **5** Ran SP% **116.5**
Speed ratings (Par 103): **102,100,96,93,88**
CSF £3.49 TOTE £2.10: £1.30, £1.10; EX 3.90 Trifecta £5.90.
Owner John Guest Racing **Bred** Crossfields Bloodstock Ltd **Trained** Newmarket, Suffolk

FOCUS
Not a strong race, rated around the front two.

7855 WATCH SKY SPORT RACING IN HD H'CAP 5f 21y (Tp)
6:15 (6:15) (Class 5) (0-70,70) 3-Y-O+
£3,428 (£1,020; £509; £400; £400; £400) **Stalls** Low

Form RPR

0044 **1** **Choosey (IRE)**63 5595 4-8-11 **65**..........(t) GerO'Neill(5) 4 73
(Michael Easterby) *prom: nt clr run and lost pl over 4f out: shkn up and hung lft over 1f out: r.o wl ins fnl f to ld post (trainers rep said, regards apparent improvement in form, gelding appreciated the Tapeta surface)* **14/1**

0461 **2** *nse* **Prestbury Park (USA)**7 7624 4-9-7 **70** 5ex.......... PaulMulrennan 7 80+
(Paul Midgley) *hdwy 1/2-way: nt clr run and swtchd rt over 1f out: rdn and ev ch wl ins fnl f: r.o (jockey said gelding was denied a clear run approximately one furlong out)* **11/8**1

4623 **3** *shd* **Show Me The Bubbly**69 5375 3-9-0 **70**.......... KateLeahy(7) 6 78
(John O'Shea) *sn chsng ldr: rdn to ld and edgd rt ins fnl f: hdd post* **12/1**

4410 **4** *3 ¼* **Landing Night (IRE)**14 7367 7-9-4 **67**..........(bt) CliffordLee 9 63
(Rebecca Menzies) *sn led: rdn over 1f out: hdd ins fnl f: styd on same pce* **10/1**

1040 **5** *¾* **Creek Harbour (IRE)**9 7552 4-9-6 **69**.......... PhilipPrince 11 62
(Milton Bradley) *s.s: outpcd: r.o towards fin: nt rch ldrs (jockey said gelding fly leapt as the stalls opened and was slowly away as a result)* **16/1**

6 *nk* **Heavenly Rainbow (IRE)**31 6814 3-9-5 **68**.......... PhilDennis 5 61
(Michael Herrington) *s.i.s: outpcd: swtchd rt over 1f out: r.o ins fnl f: nt trble ldrs* **15/2**

0136 **7** *hd* **It Must Be Faith**19 7178 9-8-10 **62**..........(p) JaneElliott(3) 3 53
(Michael Appleby) *chsd ldrs: rdn and hung lft fr over 1f out: no ex ins fnl f* **14/1**

5102 **8** *1* **Archimedes (IRE)**15 7334 6-9-6 **69**..........(vt) DavidAllan 2 57
(David C Griffiths) *pushed along to chse ldrs: rdn 1/2-way: no ex fnl f* **7/1**3

0416 **9** *½* **Dream House**14 7367 3-9-2 **65**..........(b) DuranFentiman 1 52
(Tim Easterby) *s.i.s: in rr: hdwy over 1f out: wknd wl ins fnl f* **13/2**2

4351 **10** *1 ½* **Brandy Station (IRE)**35 6639 4-8-10 **66**..........(p) GavinAshton(7) 8 46
(Lisa Williamson) *prom: rdn and hung lft over 1f out: wknd ins fnl f: eased towards fin* **16/1**

1m 0.43s (-1.47) **Going Correction** -0.175s/f (Stan) **10** Ran SP% **128.3**
Speed ratings (Par 103): **104,103,103,98,97 96,96,94,94,91**
CSF £35.12 CT £261.92 TOTE £17.20: £5.30, £1.10, £4.50; EX 50.60 Trifecta £697.90.
Owner K Wreglesworth **Bred** Martin Mulligan **Trained** Sheriff Hutton, N Yorks

FOCUS
A modest handicap but it produced a thrilling three-way finish. The front three finished clear.

7856 VISIT ATTHERACES.COM H'CAP 7f 36y (Tp)
6:45 (6:47) (Class 4) (0-85,85) 3-Y-O+
£5,207 (£1,549; £774; £400; £400; £400) **Stalls** High

Form RPR

0106 **1** **Assimilation (IRE)**44 6318 3-9-0 **80**.......... GeraldMosse 8 90
(Ed Walker) *s.i.s: hdwy over 5f out: shkn up over 2f out: led over 1f out: rdn out* **5/1**2

-334 **2** *1 ¾* **Reloaded (IRE)**7 7617 3-9-5 **85**.......... TomMarquand 9 90
(George Scott) *hld up in tch: lost pl over 5f out: hdwy over 1f out: n.m.r sn after: r.o to go 2nd wl ins fnl f: nt rch wnr* **6/1**3

-305 **3** *nk* **Tadleel**15 7350 4-9-3 **81**..........(b1) DaneO'Neill 10 86
(Ed Dunlop) *hld up: hdwy over 1f out: sn rdn: styd on same pce wl ins fnl f* **12/1**

1140 **4** *hd* **Street Poet (IRE)**26 6961 6-8-10 **74**.......... PhilDennis 7 78
(Michael Herrington) *chsd ldrs: rdn over 1f out: styd on same pce wl ins fnl f (vet said gelding lost it's left fore-shoe)* **9/1**

V4-5 **5** *½* **Barrington (IRE)**266 164 5-9-2 **80**.......... AlistairRawlinson 5 83
(Michael Appleby) *s.i.s: hld up: r.o ins fnl f: nt rch ldrs (jockey said gelding ran too freely)* **33/1**

6314 **6** *¾* **Mickey (IRE)**19 7184 6-9-3 **81**..........(v) RichardKingscote 3 82
(Tom Dascombe) *s.i.s: hld up: shkn up over 1f out: r.o ins fnl f: nt rch ldrs (jockey said gelding was denied a clear run approximately two furlongs out)* **4/1**1

4215 **7** *nk* **Twin Appeal (IRE)**9 7540 8-8-12 **79**.......... GemmaTutty(3) 2 79
(Karen Tutty) *prom: shkn up over 1f out: styd on same pce ins fnl f* **7/1**

5205 **8** *½* **Blame Culture (USA)**29 6863 4-9-2 **80**.......... TomQueally 11 79
(George Margarson) *hld up: plld hrd: hdwy on outer over 2f out: rdn and edgd lft over 1f out: styd on same pce fnl f* **15/2**

4120 **9** *¾* **Lestrade**160 2082 3-8-13 **79**..........(h) DanielTudhope 4 75
(David O'Meara) *s.i.s: hld up: rdn over 1f out: nvr on terms (jockey said gelding was slowly away)* **7/1**

0455 **10** *½* **Daafr (IRE)**16 7310 3-9-0 **80**.......... CamHardie 6 75
(Antony Brittain) *chsd ldr tl over 4f out: remained handy: rdn over 1f out: wknd wl ins fnl f* **25/1**

1155 **11** *1 ¾* **Made Of Honour (IRE)**12 7471 5-9-4 **82**..........(p) DavidEgan 12 73
(David Loughnane) *s.i.s: hdwy over 5f out: jnd ldr over 4f out: rdn and ev ch over 1f out: wknd wl ins fnl f* **33/1**

2000 **12** *1 ¼* **Abel Handy (IRE)**22 7077 4-9-7 **85**..........(t) DavidNolan 1 72
(Declan Carroll) *led: rdn and hdd over 1f out: wknd wl ins fnl f* **12/1**

1m 26.85s (-1.95) **Going Correction** -0.175s/f (Stan)
WFA 3 from 4yo+ 2lb **12** Ran SP% **122.8**
Speed ratings (Par 105): **104,102,101,101,100 100,99,99,98,97 95,94**
CSF £35.88 CT £348.24 TOTE £5.30: £2.00, £2.90, £3.60; EX 47.10 Trifecta £441.60.
Owner Exors Of The Late S F Hui **Bred** Rathbarry Stud **Trained** Upper Lambourn, Berks

FOCUS
This was a useful and open-looking sprint but the winner did this well, posting a clear pb.

7857 COME TO OKTOBERFEST THIS SATURDAY H'CAP — 1m 4f 51y (Tp)
7:15 (7:15) (Class 6) (0-55,55) 3-Y-O+
£2,781 (£827; £413; £400; £400; £400) Stalls Low

Form RPR
0064 1 **Capla Huntress**[17] 7280 3-9-2 54 .... JackMitchell 5 69+
(Chris Wall) *prom: lost pl over 9f out: nt clr run fr over 2f out tl wl over 1f out: hmpd sn after: rdn to ld ins fnl f: r.o wl* 2/1[1]
0114 2 3 ½ **About Glory**[8] 7578 5-9-7 53 .... (vt) TomMarquand 1 59
(Iain Jardine) *chsd ldrs: rdn to ld and hmpd over 1f out: hdd and no ex ins fnl f* 11/2[3]
4000 3 1 ¼ **Final Attack (IRE)**[33] 6733 8-8-13 48 .... (p) GabrieleMalune(3) 6 52
(Sarah Hollinshead) *chsd ldrs: rdn over 2f out: styd on same pce wl ins fnl f* 50/1
0053 4 nk **Shovel It On (IRE)**[24] 7034 4-9-3 49 .... (bt) RaulDaSilva 11 53
(Steve Flook) *hld up: rdn over 1f out: edgd lft and r.o u.p ins fnl f: nrst fin* 25/1
4563 5 shd **Homesick Boy (IRE)**[17] 7280 3-9-2 54 .... (v) DanielTudhope 7 58
(Ed Dunlop) *hld up: hdwy on outer over 3f out: rdn and ev ch over 1f out: no ex ins fnl f* 9/2[2]
3400 6 2 ½ **Ember's Glow**[30] 6843 5-9-4 50 .... AndrewMullen 9 49
(Mark Loughnane) *hld up: pushed along over 6f out: rdn over 1f out: nt trble ldrs* 18/1
000 7 3 **Holy Hymn (IRE)**[17] 7290 3-9-3 55 .... (t[1]) CliffordLee 8 51
(Kevin Frost) *prom: pushed along 1/2-way: rdn over 1f out: wknd fnl f* 16/1
330- 8 ½ **Moans Cross (USA)**[66] 8319 5-9-2 53 .... (v[1]) PoppyBridgwater(5) 4 47
(David Bridgwater) *s.i.s: hld up: racd keenly and hdwy on outer over 9f out: led 8f out: rdn and hdd whn n.m.r over 1f out: wknd ins fnl f* 16/1
0653 9 nse **Midnight Mood**[29] 6860 6-9-6 52 .... GeraldMosse 10 46
(Dominic Ffrench Davis) *chsd ldr over 3f: remained handy: wnt 2nd again over 5f out: led wl over 1f out: sn rdn: hung lft and hdd: wknd ins fnl f* 8/1
354 10 13 **Born To Frolic (IRE)**[21] 7116 4-9-7 53 .... DavidProbert 2 26
(Debbie Hughes) *hld up: drvn along over 4f out: sn wknd (trainer could offer no explanation for the poor performance; jockey said gelding was never travelling)* 7/1
635/ 11 40 **Alpine Peak (USA)**[6] 7670 4-9-6 52 .... RichardKingscote 3
(Miss Natalia Lupini, Ire) *sn led: hdd 8f out: chsd ldr tl over 5f out: rdn over 4f out: wknd over 3f out* 11/1

2m 37.77s (-3.03) **Going Correction** -0.175s/f (Stan) 11 Ran SP% 121.7
WFA 3 from 4yo+ 6lb
Speed ratings (Par 101): **103,100,99,99,99 97,95,95,95,86 60**
CSF £13.37 CT £432.30 TOTE £3.30: £2.30, £1.90, £9.20; EX 14.80 Trifecta £1264.00.
Owner Strawberry Fields Stud **Bred** Strawberry Fields Stud **Trained** Newmarket, Suffolk

FOCUS
Ultimately this was an easy win for the favourite but backers would have been concerned at one stage.

7858 GRAND THEATRE WOLVERHAMPTON H'CAP — 1m 1f 104y (Tp)
7:45 (7:46) (Class 6) (0-65,65) 3-Y-O+
£2,781 (£827; £413; £400; £400; £400) Stalls Low

Form RPR
4433 1 **Canasta**[41] 6393 3-9-2 62 .... JackMitchell 8 71+
(James Fanshawe) *led early: chsd ldr tl led wl over 1f out: rdn and edgd lft ins fnl f: styd on (vet said filly lost her right hind-shoe)* 5/2[1]
2300 2 1 ¾ **Better Than Ever (IRE)**[30] 6840 3-9-4 64 .... TomMarquand 12 70
(Marco Botti) *hld up in tch: rdn over 1f out: chsd wnr: carried hd high and hung lft ins fnl f: nt run on (jockey said gelding hung left-handed under pressure)* 9/1
5306 3 2 ¼ **Manfadh (IRE)**[22] 7083 4-9-8 64 .... PaulMulrennan 2 64
(Kevin Frost) *chsd ldrs: rdn over 1f out: styd on same pce wl ins fnl f* 5/1[2]
000 4 1 **Pilot Wings (IRE)**[22] 7083 4-9-6 62 .... (t[1]) ConnorBeasley 3 60
(David Dennis) *prom: racd keenly: rdn over 1f out: styd on same pce ins fnl f* 20/1
3403 5 ¾ **Elena**[10] 7526 3-9-2 62 .... RichardKingscote 1 60
(Charles Hills) *hld up in tch: rdn over 1f out: styd on same pce fnl f* 7/1[3]
320 6 1 **Celtic Artisan (IRE)**[79] 5025 8-9-9 65 .... (bt) CliffordLee 5 60
(Rebecca Menzies) *sn pushed along to ld: rdn and hdd over 1f out: wknd ins fnl f* 11/1
2604 7 ½ **King Oswald (USA)**[65] 5531 6-9-6 62 .... (tp) DavidProbert 6 56
(James Unett) *hld up: rdn over 1f out: nvr on terms* 12/1
5325 8 hd **Chinese Alphabet**[21] 7116 3-9-2 62 .... (p) DavidEgan 13 56
(William Knight) *hld up: rdn on outer over 2f out: nvr on terms* 5/1[2]
1-00 9 hd **Deleyll**[44] 6317 5-9-6 62 .... LewisEdmunds 4 55
(John Butler) *s.i.s: hld up: shkn up over 1f out: n.d* 11/1
2150 10 nse **Destinys Rock**[23] 7060 4-9-7 63 .... AndrewMullen 11 56
(Mark Loughnane) *s.s: hld up: rdn and hung lft ins fnl f: n.d* 50/1
004 11 5 **Global Rock (FR)**[85] 4806 3-9-4 64 .... GeraldMosse 7 48
(Ed Dunlop) *hld up: drvn along over 3f out: wknd over 1f out* 10/1

1m 58.78s (-2.02) **Going Correction** -0.175s/f (Stan) 11 Ran SP% 157.9
WFA 3 from 4yo+ 4lb
Speed ratings (Par 101): **101,99,97,96,95 95,94,94,94,94 89**
CSF £28.07 CT £111.69 TOTE £2.70: £1.60, £3.30, £2.60; EX 28.50 Trifecta £160.20.
Owner Elite Racing Club **Bred** Eminent Kind Ltd **Trained** Newmarket, Suffolk

FOCUS
A modest handicap where the winner was getting off the mark at the seventh attempt.

7859 WOLVERHAMPTON HOLIDAY INN H'CAP — 1m 142y (Tp)
8:15 (8:15) (Class 6) (0-55,55) 3-Y-O+
£2,781 (£827; £413; £400; £400; £400) Stalls Low

Form RPR
2500 1 **Cwynar**[70] 5344 4-9-6 54 .... DavidProbert 11 62
(Andrew Balding) *a.p: chsd ldr over 3f out: led 2f out: rdn out* 11/1
5312 2 ½ **Poetic Legacy (IRE)**[8] 7578 3-9-2 54 .... DanielTudhope 8 62
(Mark Johnston) *chsd ldrs: rdn to chse wnr over 1f out: edgd lft: styd on* 6/4[1]
4330 3 ¾ **Pike Corner Cross (IRE)**[18] 7240 7-9-2 50 .... (vt[1]) BenCurtis 10 55
(David Evans) *s.i.s: hld up: hdwy on outer 1/2-way: rdn over 1f out: hung lft ins fnl f: r.o* 9/1
0250 4 ½ **Caledonia Laird**[49] 6117 8-9-5 53 .... (e) ConnorBeasley 7 58
(Gay Kelleway) *prom: lost pl over 6f out: hdwy and nt clr run over 1f out: r.o* 25/1
040 5 hd **Steal The Scene (IRE)**[33] 6731 7-9-7 55 .... (tp) CliffordLee 9 59
(Kevin Frost) *s.i.s: hld up: hdwy and nt clr run over 1f out: r.o (jockey said gelding was denied a clear run turning in)* 25/1
6025 6 ½ **I Think So (IRE)**[26] 6977 4-9-2 55 .... (b) ThomasGreatrex(5) 6 58
(David Loughnane) *led over 7f out: hdd over 6f out: chsd ldrs: rdn and hung lft over 1f out: styd on same pce ins fnl f* 12/1
-510 7 1 **Pact Of Steel**[14] 7374 4-9-1 54 .... (t) WilliamCarver(5) 1 55
(Ivan Furtado) *led 1f: chsd ldrs: rdn over 1f out: no ex ins fnl f* 6/1[3]
0600 8 ½ **Mr Sundowner (USA)**[12] 7441 7-9-2 50 .... (t[1]) PhilDennis 3 50
(Michael Herrington) *hld up: rdn over 1f out: r.o ins fnl f: nvr nrr* 20/1
6505 9 2 ½ **Mac Ailey**[13] 7405 3-9-2 54 .... DavidAllan 5 50
(Tim Easterby) *hld up: hdwy and swtchd lft over 1f out: nt clr run ins fnl f: nt trble ldrs (jockey said gelding was denied a clear run inside the final furlong)* 4/1[2]
5006 10 ½ **Sooqaan**[14] 7385 8-9-6 54 .... (p) CamHardie 4 47
(Antony Brittain) *prom: racd keenly: rdn over 1f out: wknd ins fnl f* 50/1
3053 11 2 **With Approval (IRE)**[34] 6666 7-9-1 52 .... (b) GemmaTutty(3) 12 41
(Karen Tutty) *chsd ldrs on outer: led over 6f out: hdd 2f out: wknd ins fnl f* 12/1
663 12 2 ½ **Zero To Hero (IRE)**[19] 7177 4-9-7 55 .... AdamMcNamara 2 39
(Archie Watson) *hld up: sme hdwy u.p over 1f out: wknd fnl f* 50/1
00/0 13 2 ¼ **True Colors**[17] 7282 5-9-2 50 .... CharlieBennett 13 29
(Mark Pattinson) *hld up: drvn along over 3f out: wknd 2f out* 100/1

1m 48.58s (-1.52) **Going Correction** -0.175s/f (Stan) 13 Ran SP% 125.4
WFA 3 from 4yo+ 4lb
Speed ratings (Par 101): **99,98,97,97,97 96,95,95,93,92 91,88,86**
CSF £27.77 CT £171.99 TOTE £11.40: £3.90, £1.10, £2.60; EX 39.60 Trifecta £184.80.
Owner Nigel Morris **Bred** Alvediston Stud & Partners **Trained** Kingsclere, Hants

FOCUS
A moderate end to proceedings but it was a close finish and favourite backers were denied by a determined winner.
T/Plt: £47.10 to a £1 stake. Pool: £59,574.74 - 923.18 winning units T/Qpdt: £8.50 to a £1 stake. Pool: £8,542.62 - 740.47 winning units **Colin Roberts**

7505 COMPIEGNE (L-H)
Thursday, October 3

OFFICIAL GOING: Turf: very soft

7860a PRIX DE JONQUIERES (CLAIMER) (4YO+) (TURF) — 1m 6f
1:07 4-Y-O+
£8,558 (£3,423; £2,567; £1,711; £855)

RPR
1 **Attentionadventure**[542] 8-8-11 0 .... CristianDemuro 8 78
(Frau S Steinberg, Germany) 7/1
2 1 **Nabunga (FR)**[33] 6790 7-9-4 0 .... StephanePasquier 6 84
(J Phelippon, France) 10/1
3 4 **Dhangadhi (FR)**[13] 7-8-3 0 .... (b) DamienBoche(5) 3 68
(L Gadbin, France) 11/2
4 shd **Cutty Pie (IRE)**[6] 7676 5-9-1 0 .... (p) AlexisBadel 2 75
(J Phelippon, France) 9/1
5 6 **Carnageo (FR)**[10] 7536 6-9-2 0 .... (b) Pierre-CharlesBoudot 1 67
(P Monfort, France) 49/10[2]
6 nse **Wisperwind (GER)**[24] 7-9-1 0 .... (p) ChristopheSoumillon 7 66
(Henk Grewe, Germany) 9/5[1]
7 18 **Panatos (FR)**[35] 6642 4-8-11 0 .... (p) MickaelBarzalona 4 37
(Alexandra Dunn) *led: shkn up over 2f out: rdn and hdd 2f out: wknd and eased over 1f out* 27/1
P **Classic Joy (FR)**[77] 5115 4-9-4 0 .... (p) MaximeGuyon 5
(L Viel, France) 51/10[3]

3m 7.51s 8 Ran SP% 119.6
PARI-MUTUEL (all including 1 euro stake): WIN 8.00; PLACE 2.30, 3.10, 2.00; DF 30.40.
Owner Stall Salzburg **Bred** Hofgut Heymann Kg **Trained** Germany

7861a PRIX DE JAUX (CLAIMER) (4YO+) (TURF) — 1m
2:17 4-Y-O+
£8,558 (£3,423; £2,567; £1,711; £855)

RPR
1 **Rogue**[29] 6863 4-9-1 0 .... (p) MickaelBarzalona 1 83
(Alexandra Dunn) *wl into stride: led: mde all: rowed along 2f out: rdn over 1f out: drvn to hold chalr ins fnl f: kpt on gamely* 61/10[3]
2 nk **Domagnano (IRE)**[7] 4-8-11 0 .... AlexisBadel 2 78
(D Smaga, France) 18/1
3 2 **Admire Fuji (IRE)**[12] 9-9-2 0 .... VincentCheminaud 5 79
(D De Waele, France) 15/1
4 nk **Shamdor**[135] 2956 4-9-1 0 .... ChristopheSoumillon 13 77
(A De Royer-Dupre, France) 9/1
5 2 **Inseo (FR)**[21] 7136 8-9-1 0 .... (p) HugoJourniac 4 72
(M Boutin, France) 29/1
6 nse **Hautot (FR)**[104] 4090 4-9-2 0 .... AlexandreChesneau(3) 11 76
(Gerald Geisler, Germany) 10/1
7 2 **Sa Mola (GER)**[41] 4-8-9 0 .... ThomasTrullier(6) 12 68
(N Clement, France) 9/1
8 1 ¼ **Hanabaal Tun (FR)**[37] 5-8-9 0 .... (b) QuentinPerrette(6) 6 65
(R Le Dren Doleuze, France) 12/1
9 snk **Cloud Dancer (FR)**[21] 7136 4-8-11 0 .... IoritzMendizabal 9 60
(Mario Hofer, Germany) 5/1[2]
10 ¾ **Gran Pierino (ITY)**[90] 5-8-7 0 .... MlleLeaBails(9) 10 64
(Andrea Marcialis, France) 12/1
11 snk **Undiscovered Angel (FR)**[153] 5-8-5 0 .... DelphineSantiago(3) 8 55
(Mlle K Hoste, Belgium) 78/1
12 1 **Lucky Lips (GER)**[70] 5-9-5 0 .... MaximeGuyon 7 64
(Mario Hofer, Germany) 29/10[1]
13 3 **Copper Baked (FR)**[21] 7136 5-8-6 0 .... MlleSophieTison(9) 3 53
(L Rovisse, France) 43/1

1m 39.91s 13 Ran SP% 119.3
PARI-MUTUEL (all including 1 euro stake): WIN 7.10; PLACE 3.00, 5.40, 4.10; DF 48.60.
Owner Helium Racing Ltd **Bred** Maywood Stud **Trained** West Buckland, Somerset

6006 HOPPEGARTEN (R-H)

Thursday, October 3

OFFICIAL GOING: Turf: good to soft

7862a PFERDEWETTEN.DE - 29TH PREIS DER DEUTSCHEN EINHEIT (GROUP 3) (3YO+) (TURF) 1m 2f

3:45 3-Y-O+ **£28,828** (£10,810; £5,405; £2,702; £1,801)

RPR

1 **Itobo (GER)**[40] 6487 7-9-4 0 .... MarcoCasamento 2 114
(H-J Groschel, Germany) *trckd ldr: urged along over 2f out: rdn to chal over 1f out: drvn ins fnl f: led on post* **43/5[3]**

2 *nse* **Laccario (GER)**[32] 6771 3-9-0 0 .... EduardoPedroza 3 115
(A Wohler, Germany) *settled in 2nd: pushed along 2f out: rdn to chal over 1f out: led 1f out: drvn and sustained battle w wnr ins fnl f: hdd on post* **3/5[1]**

3 *½* **Be My Sheriff (GER)**[40] 6487 5-9-4 0 .... AdriedeVries 6 113
(Henk Grewe, Germany) *led: rowed along 2f out: rdn and strly chal over 1f out: hdd 1f out: drvn and ev ch ins fnl f: no ex fnl 75yds* **21/10[2]**

4 *11* **Ismene (GER)**[40] 6487 3-8-10 0 .... FilipMinarik 1 88
(Jean-Pierre Carvalho, Germany) *hld up in rr: urged along over 2f out: rdn and outpcd over 1f out: no ex ins fnl f* **148/10**

5 *3½* **Preciosa (GER)**[68] 5470 3-8-10 0 .... BauyrzhanMurzabayev 4 81
(R Dzubasz, Germany) *settled bhd ldrs in 4th: pushed along over 2f out: rdn w limited rspnse over 1f out: wknd fnl f* **10/1**

2m 10.93s (4.23)
WFA 3 from 5yo+ 4lb **5 Ran SP% 120.6**
PARI-MUTUEL (all including 1 euro stake): WIN 9.60 PLACE: 2.20, 1.30; SF: 14.00.
Owner Stall Totti **Bred** Gestut Gorlsdorf **Trained** Germany

6948 ASCOT (R-H)

Friday, October 4

OFFICIAL GOING: Soft (heavy in places on round course; str, 5.9, rnd 5.5)
Wind: Almost nil Weather: Overcast with rain before racing

7863 MAR-KEY GROUP CLASSIFIED STKS 1m (S)

2:00 (2:03) (Class 3) 3-Y-O+ **£9,703** (£2,887; £1,443; £721) **Stalls** High

Form RPR

-300 1 **Sawwaah**[28] 6923 4-9-3 90 .... (b[1]) JimCrowley 9 97
(Owen Burrows) *racd towards nr side and on his own for 1st 3f: mde virtually all: rdn 2f out: jnd over 1f out: kpt on wl u.p fnl f* **9/1**

0002 2 *hd* **Tulfarris**[28] 6914 3-9-0 90 .... StevieDonohoe 7 96
(Charlie Fellowes) *prom: moved across to trck wnr towards nr side after 3f: rdn to chal and upsides over 1f out: stl ev ch ins fnl f: nt qckn nr fin* **4/1[2]**

530 3 *3* **Model Guest**[6] 7697 3-9-0 90 .... TomQueally 5 89
(George Margarson) *hld up in main gp in centre: gng bttr than most whn prog 2f out: rdn to take 3rd over 1f out: no threat to ldng pair* **50/1**

6303 4 *½* **Trolius (IRE)**[28] 6914 3-9-0 90 .... (p) JamesDoyle 1 88
(Simon Crisford) *trckd ldrs in main gp in centre: rdn over 2f out: kpt on over 1f out to press for 3rd fnl f* **10/1**

3465 5 *nk* **Mr Top Hat**[29] 6895 4-8-12 87 .... RayDawson[(5)] 6 87
(David Evans) *trckd ldrs in main gp in centre: rdn over 2f out and sn lost pl: kpt on again fnl f* **12/1**

544 6 *½* **Target Zone**[76] 5194 3-9-0 89 .... GeraldMosse 8 86
(David Elsworth) *hld up in last pair: swtchd across towards nr side after 3f: rdn 3f out and struggling: no ch fnl 2f but kpt on fnl f* **10/1**

1-45 7 *nk* **Mostawaa**[20] 7191 3-9-0 84 .... DavidEgan 2 85
(Heather Main) *prom in centre: led gp 1/2-way but nt on terms w wnr: fdd over 1f out* **25/1**

-525 8 *4* **Herculean**[49] 6151 4-9-3 90 .... JasonWatson 3 76
(Roger Charlton) *led main gp in centre to 1/2-way: steadily lost pl: rdn and wknd 2f out (trainer's rep could offer no explanation for the gelding's performance)* **15/8[1]**

035 9 *4* **Lush Life (IRE)**[27] 6951 4-9-3 90 .... (p) JamieSpencer 10 67
(Jamie Osborne) *stdd s: hld up in detached last: pushed along and briefest of effrts jst over 2f out: eased whn no ch fnl f (trainer could offer no explanation for the filly's performance)* **8/1[3]**

3160 10 *7* **Fox Leicester (IRE)**[56] 5666 3-9-0 87 .... SilvestreDeSousa 4 51
(Andrew Balding) *chsd ldrs in main gp in centre: rdn and wknd over 2f out: t.o* **14/1**

1m 47.52s (6.12) **Going Correction** +0.975s/f (Soft)
WFA 3 from 4yo 3lb **10 Ran SP% 114.2**
Speed ratings (Par 107): **108,107,104,104,104 103,103,99,95,88**
CSF £43.99 TOTE £8.40: £2.90, £1.50, £9.90; EX 55.80 Trifecta £1130.20.
Owner Hamdan Al Maktoum **Bred** Shadwell Estate Company Limited **Trained** Lambourn, Berks

FOCUS
There was 2mm of rain overnight and the going was given as soft, heavy in places on the Round course (GoingStick 5.5) and soft on the Straight course (GoingStick 5.9). The rail on the round course was 3yds out from its innermost position from the 1m4f start, increasing to 14yds out at the home straight where the rail finished in a cutaway. The straight course was divided in two with a rail in the middle of the course from the 1m start to approx 2.5f from the winning line, with the stands' side in use for this meeting. A competitive heat but the first two pulled nicely clear and the winner rates back to his best.

7864 LONDONMETRIC NOEL MURLESS STKS (LISTED RACE) 1m 6f 34y

2:35 (2:35) (Class 1) 3-Y-O

£45,368 (£17,200; £8,608; £4,288; £2,152; £1,080) **Stalls** Centre

Form RPR

3111 1 **Hereby (IRE)**[21] 7144 3-8-10 88 .... HarryBentley 2 102+
(Ralph Beckett) *led 2f: trckd ldng pair tl shkn up to ld wl over 1f out: hrd pressed after: kpt on really wl fnl f* **9/2[2]**

3214 2 *1½* **Sapa Inca (IRE)**[35] 6657 3-8-10 90 .... HayleyTurner 1 99
(Mark Johnston) *hld up in 5th: stdy prog over 2f out: rdn to take 2nd over 1f out and sn chalng: kpt on but hld ins fnl f* **9/1**

5456 3 *1½* **Almania (IRE)**[41] 6471 3-9-1 95 .... RyanMoore 3 102
(Sir Michael Stoute) *trckd ldr after 3f: rdn to ld over 2f out: hdd wl over 1f out and sn in 3rd: kpt on same pce after* **5/2[1]**

3152 4 *3¼* **I'll Have Another (IRE)**[9] 7566 3-8-10 98 .... FrannyNorton 5 92
(Mark Johnston) *trckd ldng trio: rdn and nt qckn over 2f out: one pce and wl hld after* **8/1**

1151 5 *5* **Just Hubert (IRE)**[20] 7209 3-9-1 91 .... TomMarquand 4 90
(William Muir) *in tch but nvr gng that wl: drvn over 2f out and stl in tch: wknd over 1f out* **5/1[3]**

3232 6 *6* **Funny Man**[12] 7493 3-9-1 80 .... (b) JimCrowley 6 82
(David O'Meara) *hld up in last: effrt 5f out: urged along over 3f out: wknd over 2f out* **25/1**

1026 7 *2* **Tribal Craft**[34] 6712 3-8-10 91 .... DavidProbert 7 74
(Andrew Balding) *led after 2f: hdd & wknd qckly over 2f out (jockey said filly ran too free)* **8/1**

4000 8 *75* **Cap Francais**[27] 6952 3-9-1 97 .... JamieSpencer 8
(Ed Walker) *hld up in last pair: rdn 5f out: sn btn: virtually p.u over 1f out (trainer's rep said gelding was unsuited by the going and would prefer a quicker surface)* **13/2**

3m 14.77s (10.47) **Going Correction** +0.975s/f (Soft) **8 Ran SP% 112.8**
Speed ratings (Par 109): **109,108,107,105,102 99,98,55**
CSF £42.69 TOTE £4.80: £1.50, £2.30, £1.40; EX 38.90 Trifecta £183.70.
Owner J H Richmond-Watson **Bred** Lawn Stud **Trained** Kimpton, Hants

FOCUS
Add 33yds. An ordinary Listed race, rated around the third to his Melrose run, but the winner is progressive.

7865 AMATEUR JOCKEYS ASSOCIATION H'CAP (FOR GENTLEMAN AMATEUR RIDERS) 7f

3:10 (3:10) (Class 3) (0-95,94) 3-Y-O+ **£8,110** (£2,515; £1,257; £629) **Stalls** High

Form RPR

5105 1 **King's Pavilion (IRE)**[20] 7184 6-10-9 **87** .... MrEireannCagney[(5)] 8 94
(Jason Ward) *w ldr at decent pce: led 1/2-way: jnd and urged along over 1f out: hld on wl fnl f* **7/1[3]**

025 2 *nk* **Hawridge Storm (IRE)**[21] 7159 3-10-2 **77** .... MrPatrickMillman 2 82
(Rod Millman) *s.i.s: in tch: trckd ldrs 3f out: drvn over 1f out: kpt on steadily fnl f and tk 2nd nr fin but a jst hld* **16/1**

3440 3 *nk* **Cliffs Of Capri**[34] 6706 5-11-6 **93** .... (p) MrAlexFerguson 3 98
(Jamie Osborne) *trckd ldrs: wnt 2nd over 1f out and sn chalng: stl upsides u.str.p ins fnl f: no ex and lost 2nd nr fin* **7/2[2]**

0143 4 *2¾* **Marshal Dan (IRE)**[41] 6468 4-10-6 **79** .... MrJamesHarding 6 77
(Heather Main) *led at decent pce to 1/2-way: pressed wnr to over 1f out: steadily fdd* **7/2[2]**

4353 5 *12* **Raydiance**[13] 7435 4-11-5 **92** .... MrSimonWalker 1 59
(K R Burke) *trckd ldrs: rdn 3f out: wknd over 2f out* **7/4[1]**

2010 6 *6* **Parys Mountain (IRE)**[15] 7362 5-10-8 **81** .... (t) MrWilliamEasterby 5 32
(Tim Easterby) *in tch to 1/2-way: sn wknd and bhd* **9/1**

U **Rafiot (USA)**[165] 3-10-4 **82** .... MrGeorgeGorman[(3)] 4
(Gary Moore) *trcking ldrs whn stmbld and uns rdr over 5f out* **20/1**

1m 35.12s (7.62) **Going Correction** +0.975s/f (Soft)
WFA 3 from 4yo+ 2lb **7 Ran SP% 114.0**
Speed ratings (Par 107): **95,94,94,91,77 70,**
CSF £102.03 CT £456.21 TOTE £7.10: £3.60, £6.20; EX 117.10 Trifecta £379.80.
Owner Peter Ward **Bred** Darley **Trained** Sessay, N Yorks

FOCUS
There wasn't much between the first three at the line but the winner was always holding on and is rated to this year's form.

7866 CANACCORD GENUITY GORDON CARTER H'CAP 1m 7f 209y

3:45 (3:45) (Class 3) (0-95,96) 3-Y-O+ **£8,409** (£2,502; £1,250; £625) **Stalls** Centre

Form RPR

6522 1 **Landa Beach (IRE)**[28] 6924 3-8-10 **81** .... (p) DavidProbert 11 90
(Andrew Balding) *dwlt: hld up in last trio: rdn wl over 2f out: racd awkwardly and no immediate prog: sed to run on wl over 1f out: styd on strly fnl f to ld last strides* **6/1[3]**

-051 2 *hd* **Darksideoftarnside (IRE)**[52] 6044 5-9-6 **82** .... (v[1]) JimCrowley 5 90
(Ian Williams) *trckd ldrs: hrd rdn wl over 2f out: racd awkwardly but drvn ahd 1f out: hung lft after: hdd last strides* **7/1**

02R3 3 *3¼* **Platitude**[8] 7615 6-9-13 **96** .... MarcoGhiani[(7)] 10 100
(Amanda Perrett) *taken down early: trckd ldrs: rdn over 2f out: clsd to ld briefly jst over 1f out: pressing ldr but hld whn impeded 150yds out: fdd* **12/1**

-543 4 *1* **Quloob**[31] 6848 5-10-0 **90** .... HectorCrouch 6 93
(Gary Moore) *wl in tch in midfield: rdn wl over 2f out: kpt on one pce fnl 2f and n.d* **16/1**

5-06 5 *1* **Altra Vita**[70] 5404 4-9-12 **88** .... (p w) RyanTate 3 90
(Sir Mark Prescott Bt) *trckd ldr: led 5f out to over 3f out: fdd u.p over 1f out* **25/1**

4216 6 *½* **Laafy (USA)**[27] 6955 3-9-4 **89** .... (v) RyanMoore 1 90+
(Sir Michael Stoute) *sn trckd ldng pair: led over 3f out gng strly: rdn over 2f out: hdd & wknd jst over 1f out* **2/1[1]**

1111 7 *8* **Platform Nineteen (IRE)**[26] 7001 3-9-0 **85** .... (p) CliffordLee 2 77
(Michael Bell) *taken down early: wl in tch: rdn over 2f out and no prog: wknd over 1f out (trainer was unsuited by the going and would prefer a firmer surface)* **3/1[2]**

6122 8 *6* **Horatio Star**[31] 6848 4-9-0 **76** .... (p) TomMarquand 8 60
(Brian Meehan) *led at gd clip: taken wd fr 7f out: hdd 5f out: styd pressing ldrs tl drvn and wknd over 2f out* **20/1**

4013 9 *2* **Battle Of Marathon (USA)**[13] 7436 7-8-10 **79** .... LauraPearson[(7)] 9 61
(John Ryan) *hld up in last: sme prog 6f out: rdn and no hdwy over 2f out: wknd* **14/1**

0006 10 *21* **Nakeeta**[31] 6834 8-9-11 **87** .... (h) RobertHavlin 7 44
(Linda Jewell) *dwlt: a in rr: rdn 3f out: wknd 2f out: t.o* **40/1**

-404 11 *42* **Alfredo (IRE)**[28] 6929 7-9-12 **88** .... (tp) TomQueally 4
(Seamus Durack) *a in rr: dropped to last and struggling over 5f out: t.o* **50/1**

3m 43.55s (10.25) **Going Correction** +0.975s/f (Soft)
WFA 3 from 4yo+ 9lb **11 Ran SP% 118.4**
Speed ratings (Par 107): **113,112,111,110,110 110,106,103,102,91 70**
CSF £46.01 CT £494.25 TOTE £7.00: £2.00, £2.40, £3.40; EX 47.40 Trifecta £772.80.
Owner Philip Fox & Partner **Bred** Powerstown Stud Ltd **Trained** Kingsclere, Hants

FOCUS
Add 33yds. A proper test of stamina in the conditions.

7867 VEOLIA NOVICE STKS — 1m 3f 211y
4:20 (4:20) (Class 3) 3-Y-O+ — £9,703 (£2,887; £1,443; £721) Stalls Low

Form — RPR

4232 **1** **Caravan Of Hope (IRE)**[36] 6641 3-9-5 80........................ RyanMoore 1 — 85
(Hugo Palmer) *hld up in last pair: shkn up 3f out: rdn 2f out and mde limited imp over 1f out: styd on ins fnl f to ld last 75yds* — 5/6[1]

-232 **2** ¾ **Pianissimo**[15] 7382 3-9-5 78.......................(b) RobertHavlin 4 — 83
(John Gosden) *trckd ldng pair: wnt 2nd over 3f out: stl gng strly over 2f out: clsd on ldr v grad whn shkn up: eventually led ins fnl f but immediately hdd and outpcd* — 11/2[3]

3234 **3** 1 **Two Bids**[21] 7143 3-9-5 80.......................(p[1]) TomMarquand 5 — 81
(William Haggas) *t.k.h: led after 1f and sn clr: rdn and stl 3 l ahd 2f out: hdd and fdd ins fnl f* — 7/1

2303 **4** shd **King Power**[36] 6633 3-9-0 80........................ SilvestreDeSousa 3 — 76
(Andrew Balding) *t.k.h early: hld up in last pair: rdn over 2f out: kpt on over 1f out and grad clsng at fin but nvr looked keen enough to chal* — 3/1[2]

44 **5** 64 **Its Nice Tobe Nice**[21] 7159 3-9-0 0........................ JasonWatson 2
(William Muir) *led 1f: chsd ldr to over 3f out: sn wknd: t.o* — 50/1

2m 44.41s (11.81) **Going Correction** +0.975s/f (Soft) — 5 Ran SP% **109.4**
Speed ratings (Par 107): **99,98,97,97,55**
CSF £5.86 TOTE £1.90: £1.30, £1.80; EX 5.10 Trifecta £14.40.
Owner Dr Ali Ridha **Bred** Oak Hill Stud **Trained** Newmarket, Suffolk

FOCUS
Add 25yds. They finished in a heap in this novice but the winner has been rated to form.

7868 ORIGINAL HARROGATE WATER H'CAP — 6f
4:55 (4:56) (Class 2) (0-105,104) 3-Y-O — £18,675 (£5,592; £2,796; £1,398; £699; £351) Stalls High

Form — RPR

6321 **1** **Tinto**[15] 7397 3-8-6 **96**........................ MarcoGhiani(7) 2 — 106
(Amanda Perrett) *hld up in last: stdy prog on outer 2f out: rdn to ld 1f out: hrd pressed after: hld on wl* — 16/1

1614 **2** nk **Aplomb (IRE)**[48] 6222 3-8-10 **93**........................ TomMarquand 9 — 102
(William Haggas) *trckd ldrs: clsd to ld over 1f out: rdn and hdd 1f out: pressed wnr after: kpt on wl but a hld* — 4/1[2]

4103 **3** 2½ **Revich (IRE)**[21] 7142 3-8-6 **89**........................ HarryBentley 4 — 90
(Richard Spencer) *hld up in last trio: prog 2f out: rdn and hanging rt over 1f out: styd on fnl f to take 3rd nr fin* — 20/1

6310 **4** ½ **Dazzling Dan (IRE)**[20] 7193 3-9-7 **104**........................ DavidProbert 3 — 103
(Pam Sly) *trckd ldrs: moved up gng strly to ld 2f out: sn shkn up and hdd over 1f out: fdd fnl f* — 8/1[3]

015 **5** 1½ **Lihou**[48] 6222 3-8-2 **85** oh2........................ HollieDoyle 5 — 80
(David Evans) *trckd ldrs: rdn 2f out: no imp over 1f out: wknd fnl f* — 16/1

1045 **6** ¾ **Dominus (IRE)**[42] 6413 3-8-4 **87**.......................(t) DavidEgan 7 — 79
(Brian Meehan) *w ldrs: upsides 2f out: rdn and wknd over 1f out* — 16/1

41-1 **7** 1¼ **Mubakker (USA)**[31] 6838 3-8-13 **96**........................ JimCrowley 8 — 84
(Sir Michael Stoute) *dwlt: a in rr: rdn and no prog 2f out* — 3/1[1]

5560 **8** 1¾ **Barbill (IRE)**[13] 7433 3-8-12 **95**.......................(p[1]) JFEgan 6 — 78
(Mick Channon) *trckd ldrs: pushed along 1/2-way: nt clr run and swtchd rt 2f out: sn rdn and wknd* — 10/1

2500 **9** 4½ **Lincoln Park**[13] 7431 3-8-4 **87**.......................(t[1]) GeorgeWood 11 — 55
(Michael Appleby) *led to 2f out: wknd qckly over 1f out* — 25/1

3131 **10** 9 **Roulston Scar (IRE)**[26] 7002 3-8-12 **98**........................ MeganNicholls(3) 10 — 37+
(Kevin Ryan) *stmbld bdly s: t.k.h and sn rcvrd to join ldr: wknd rapidly 2f out: t.o* — 3/1[1]

1m 17.03s (3.33) **Going Correction** +0.975s/f (Soft) — 10 Ran SP% **122.3**
Speed ratings (Par 107): **116,115,112,111,109 108,106,104,98,86**
CSF £79.02 CT £1338.11 TOTE £16.80: £3.90, £1.60, £4.60; EX 101.40 Trifecta £1419.70.
Owner D James, S Jenkins & M Quigley **Bred** Llety Farms **Trained** Pulborough, W Sussex

FOCUS
A good sprint handicap won by a progressive sort.
T/Jkpt: Not Won. T/Plt: £1,117.40 to a £1 stake. Pool: £126,991.23 - 82.96 winning units T/Qpdt: £193.50 to a £1 stake. Pool: £11,591.20 - 44.32 winning units **Jonathan Neesom**

7626 SOUTHWELL (L-H)
Friday, October 4

OFFICIAL GOING: Fibresand: standard
Wind: Virtually nil Weather: Cloudy with showers

7869 SOUTHWELL GOLF CLUB H'CAP — 6f 16y(F)
5:25 (5:31) (Class 6) (0-65,67) 3-Y-O+ — £2,781 (£827; £413; £400; £400; £400) Stalls Low

Form — RPR

3102 **1** **Requited (IRE)**[8] 7632 3-9-11 **67**........................ CharlieBennett 2 — 75
(Hughie Morrison) *trckd ldr: cl up 1/2-way: led wl over 1f out: rdn and kpt on fnl f* — 2/1[1]

1000 **2** 1½ **Bee Machine (IRE)**[15] 7384 4-8-5 **53**.......................(bt) ZakWheatley(7) 6 — 57
(Declan Carroll) *in tch: pushed along over 2f out: rdn over 1f out: str run ins fnl f: nrst fin (jockey said gelding anticipated the start and missed the break as a result)* — 16/1

3040 **3** 1 **Champagne Mondays**[46] 6277 3-8-4 **46** oh1.......................(b) KieranO'Neill 1 — 47
(Scott Dixon) *led: jnd and rdn over 2f out: hdd wl over 1f out: drvn and kpt on same pce fnl f* — 20/1

6055 **4** 1¼ **Essenza (IRE)**[15] 7384 3-8-13 **58**........................ SeanDavis(3) 10 — 55
(Richard Fahey) *chsd ldrs: rdn along 2f out: drvn and edgd lft fnl f: no imp* — 13/2[3]

4004 **5** 1¼ **Always Amazing**[15] 7371 5-8-7 **48**.......................(b) LukeMorris 5 — 41
(Robyn Brisland) *chsd ldng pair: rdn along on outer and wd st: drvn wl over 1f out: grad wknd (vet said gelding bled from the nose)* — 16/1

6000 **6** ½ **Newstead Abbey**[11] 7507 9-9-5 **60**.......................(p) TomEaves 3 — 52
(Rebecca Bastiman) *chsd ldrs on inner: rdn along over 2f out: drvn wl over 1f out: sn no imp* — 20/1

5000 **7** 1¼ **The Gingerbreadman**[65] 5558 4-8-0 **46** oh1........................ PaulaMuir(5) 7 — 34
(Chris Fairhurst) *a towards rr (jockey said gelding anticipated the start and missed the break as a result)* — 28/1

0212 **8** shd **Senorita Grande (IRE)**[13] 7446 3-9-2 **61**.......................(v) CierenFallon(3) 11 — 48
(John Quinn) *wnt rt s: towards rr: bhd and wd st: n.d* — 3/1[2]

0000 **9** 2 **Murqaab**[13] 7472 3-9-3 **59**.......................(b) LewisEdmunds 9 — 40
(John Balding) *chsd ldrs: rdn along 2f out: sn drvn and wknd over 1f out* — 33/1

5262 **10** 3 **Fairy Fast (IRE)**[18] 7286 3-9-9 **65**.......................(p) JackMitchell 8 — 37+
(George Boughey) *dwlt: a bhd (jockey said filly was slowly away)* — 7/1

000 **11** 2 **Thespinningwheel (IRE)**[99] 4305 4-8-5 **46** oh1.......................(b[1]) RyanPowell 4 — 12
(Adam West) *s.i.s: a bhd* — 66/1

1m 14.24s (-2.26) **Going Correction** -0.35s/f (Stan)
WFA 3 from 4yo+ 1lb — 11 Ran SP% **113.3**
Speed ratings (Par 101): **101,99,97,96,94 93,92,91,89,85 82**
CSF £32.07 CT £500.66 TOTE £2.60: £1.10, £4.30, £5.80; EX 27.50 Trifecta £260.70.
Owner H Morrison **Bred** Barry Noonan And Denis Noonan **Trained** East Ilsley, Berks

FOCUS
There was 5mm of overnight rain but the going as ever was standard. A competitive Class 6 to start things off.

7870 SKY SPORTS RACING ON SKY 415 NOVICE STKS — 7f 14y(F)
6:00 (6:02) (Class 5) 2-Y-O — £3,428 (£1,020; £509; £254) Stalls Low

Form — RPR

50 **1** **Tafish (IRE)**[28] 6926 2-9-2 0........................ ShaneKelly 11 — 81
(Richard Hughes) *chsd ldrs: rdn along on outer 3f out: hdwy wl over 1f out: sn chal: drvn to ld ent fnl f: kpt on strly (jockey said colt jumped left out of the stalls)* — 4/1[3]

3 **2** 2½ **Animal Instinct**[13] 7445 2-9-2 0........................ LukeMorris 3 — 74
(Sir Mark Prescott Bt) *chsd ldng trio: pushed along over 3f out: rdn wl over 2f out: drvn over 1f out: edgd lft ins fnl f: kpt on wl towards fin* — 9/2

3231 **3** nse **Jump The Gun (IRE)**[15] 7386 2-9-3 78........................ CierenFallon(3) 1 — 78
(Jamie Osborne) *clsd up on inner: led 3f out: rdn along 2f out: drvn and hdd ent fnl f: kpt on same pce* — 7/2[2]

32 **4** 4 **Challet (IRE)**[18] 7285 2-9-2 0........................ CallumRodriguez 12 — 63
(Michael Dods) *slt ld: hdd 3f out: cl up: rdn over 2f out: drvn and ev ch over 1f out: wknd ent fnl f* — 5/2[1]

04 **5** 7 **Seven Emirates (IRE)**[20] 7179 2-9-2 0........................ BenCurtis 2 — 45
(K R Burke) *t.k.h: cl up: disp ld 1/2-way: rdn along over 2f out: grad wknd* — 5/1

00 **6** 1½ **El Jefe (IRE)**[15] 7388 2-9-2 0........................ BenRobinson 8 — 41
(Brian Ellison) *dwlt and swtchd lft s: towards rr: sme hdwy fnl 2f: n.d* — 100/1

7 6 **Walls Have Ears (IRE)** 2-8-8 0........................ GabrieleMalune(3) 10 — 21
(Ivan Furtado) *a towards rr* — 50/1

8 2½ **Warne's Army** 2-8-11 0........................ RichardKingscote 9 — 14
(Mark Johnston) *green a in rr* — 25/1

55 **9** 1¾ **Ami Li Bert (IRE)**[15] 7388 2-8-11 0........................ TheodoreLadd(5) 6 — 15
(Michael Appleby) *dwlt: a in rr* — 66/1

0 **10** 7 **Ochre Riu (IRE)**[28] 6943 2-9-2 0........................ DavidAllan 4
(Ivan Furtado) *in tch: rdn along 3f out: sn wknd* — 100/1

00 **11** 5 **Handsome Yank (USA)**[15] 7361 2-9-2 0........................ DougieCostello 5
(Ivan Furtado) *a towards rr* — 50/1

1m 27.3s (-3.00) **Going Correction** -0.35s/f (Stan) — 11 Ran SP% **116.9**
Speed ratings (Par 95): **103,100,100,95,87 85,78,76,74,66 60**
CSF £21.56 TOTE £5.70: £1.90, £1.60, £1.90; EX 31.00 Trifecta £112.60.
Owner Jaber Abdullah **Bred** Kildaragh Stud **Trained** Upper Lambourn, Berks

FOCUS
An interesting novice for the course with the five at the head of the market clear from halfway.

7871 FOLLOW AT THE RACES ON TWITTER NURSERY H'CAP — 7f 14y(F)
6:30 (6:30) (Class 5) (0-75,77) 2-Y-O — £3,428 (£1,020; £509; £400; £400; £400) Stalls Low

Form — RPR

451 **1** **Borsdane Wood**[15] 7388 2-9-10 **77**........................ BenCurtis 7 — 83
(K R Burke) *trckd ldrs on outer: hdwy over 2f out: rdn to ld ent fnl f: kpt on strly* — 1/1[1]

443 **2** 1¼ **Creativity**[15] 7388 2-9-0 **67**........................ TonyHamilton 3 — 70
(Richard Fahey) *in tch: hdwy 2f out: rdn over 1f out: styd on fnl f* — 12/1

4301 **3** 1½ **Najm**[14] 7419 2-9-9 **76**.......................(b) LukeMorris 6 — 75
(Sir Mark Prescott Bt) *led: rdn along 2f out: drvn over 1f out: edgd lft and hdd ent fnl f: sn drvn and kpt on same pce* — 7/1[3]

0050 **4** 1¼ **Iva Reflection (IRE)**[21] 7140 2-9-9 **76**.......................(p) RichardKingscote 4 — 72
(Tom Dascombe) *trckd ldrs on inner: pushed along over 2f out: rdn wl over 1f out: drvn ent fnl f: kpt on same pce* — 8/1

5430 **5** 1¼ **Swinley Forest (IRE)**[22] 7119 2-9-9 **76**.......................(p) LiamKeniry 8 — 68
(Brian Meehan) *prom: pushed along over 2f out: rdn wl over 1f out: grad wknd appr fnl f* — 11/2[2]

0624 **6** 1 **Kilig**[9] 7582 2-8-9 **62**.......................(t[1]) DavidAllan 5 — 52
(Tim Easterby) *cl up: rdn along 2f out: sn drvn and wknd over 1f out* — 14/1

2403 **7** 8 **Pentewan**[14] 7419 2-9-4 **74**.......................(b) RowanScott(3) 2 — 43
(Phillip Makin) *dwlt: a in rr* — 16/1

0150 **8** 10 **Big City**[14] 7399 2-9-2 **74**........................ PaulaMuir(5) 1 — 17
(Roger Fell) *dwlt: a in rr (jockey said gelding fly leapt leaving the stalls)* — 40/1

1m 28.12s (-2.18) **Going Correction** -0.35s/f (Stan) — 8 Ran SP% **111.7**
Speed ratings (Par 95): **98,96,94,93,92 90,81,70**
CSF £13.82 CT £55.56 TOTE £1.50: £1.10, £2.30, £2.40; EX 14.10 Trifecta £78.10.
Owner David W Armstrong **Bred** Highfield Farm Llp **Trained** Middleham Moor, N Yorks

FOCUS
A decent nursery with course form again coming to the fore.

7872 ALL WEATHER CHAMPIONSHIP SEASON 7 H'CAP — 1m 4f 14y(F)
7:00 (7:01) (Class 4) (0-85,86) 3-Y-O+ — £5,207 (£1,549; £774; £400; £400; £400) Stalls Low

Form — RPR

6432 **1** **Asian Angel (IRE)**[9] 7577 3-9-6 **83**........................ FrannyNorton 3 — 94
(Mark Johnston) *trckd ldrs: hdwy 3f out: led 2f out: jnd and rdn over 1f out: drvn ins fnl f: kpt on wl towards fin* — 4/1[3]

260- **2** 1¼ **Jus Pires (USA)**[400] 6714 5-9-10 **81**.......................(t) DavidNolan 8 — 89
(Declan Carroll) *hld up in rr: smooth hdwy on inner over 2f out: chal over 1f out: sn rdn and ev ch: drvn ins fnl f: kpt on same pce towards fin* — 20/1

4101 **3** 3¼ **Blowing Dixie**[8] 7629 3-8-4 **67** 6ex........................ JosephineGordon 6 — 71
(Jane Chapple-Hyam) *trckd ldrs: dropped to rr after 4f: hdwy on outer and v wd st: rdn to chse ldrs 2f out: ev ch and drvn over 1f out: kpt on same pce* — 6/5[1]

4101 **4** 1½ **Regal Mirage (IRE)**[16] 7332 5-9-5 **76**........................ DavidAllan 7 — 76
(Tim Easterby) *hld up in tch: hdwy over 2f out: rdn to chse ldrs over 1f out: sn drvn and no imp* — 9/1

0405 **5** ½ **Royal Cosmic**[9] 7577 5-8-12 **72**........................ SeanDavis(3) 2 — 72
(Richard Fahey) *cl up: slt ld 3f out: sn rdn: hdd 2f out: sn drvn and grad wknd* — 20/1

The Form Book Flat 2019, Raceform Ltd, Newbury, RG14 5SJ

2042 **6** *5* **Sputnik Planum (USA)**[48] 6211 5-9-8 **86**....................(t) MarkCrehan(7) 4 78
(Michael Appleby) *trckd ldng pair: pushed along 3f out: rdn over 2f out: drvn wl over 1f out: sn btn* **7/2**[2]
0500 **7** *3 ¾* **Dragon Mountain**[11] 7513 4-8-10 **67**..............................(h[1]) GrahamLee 9 53
(Keith Dalgleish) *hld up towards rr: hdwy to trck ldrs 1/2-way: pushed along 4f out: rdn over 3f out and wd st: sn drvn and wknd* **28/1**
04-0 **8** *17* **Into The Zone**[74] 5254 3-8-7 **70**..............................(t) LukeMorris 1 29
(Simon Crisford) *led: rdn along and hdd 3f out: sn wknd* **20/1**
2m 35.45s (-5.55) **Going Correction** -0.35s/f (Stan)
WFA 3 from 4yo+ 6lb **8** Ran SP% **115.4**
Speed ratings (Par 105): **104,103,101,100,99 96,93,82**
CSF £78.02 CT £149.94 TOTE £4.90: £1.70, £5.30, £1.10; EX 118.40 Trifecta £397.80.
Owner Dr J Walker **Bred** Skymarc Farm **Trained** Middleham Moor, N Yorks
■ Wanaasah was withdrawn. Price at time of withdrawal 12-1. Rule 4 applies to bets places prior to withdrawal but not to SP bets - deduction 5p in the pound.. New market formed
■ Stewards' Enquiry : David Nolan two-day ban: misuse of whip (Oct 18, 21)
FOCUS
A competitive middle-distance handicap which looked to be slowly run. A pb from the winner.

7873 SKY SPORTS RACING ON VIRGIN 535 H'CAP 1m 4f 14y(F)
7:30 (7:31) (Class 6) (0-60,61) 3-Y-O+

£2,781 (£827; £413; £400; £400; £400) **Stalls** Low

Form RPR
1200 **1** **Cold Harbour**[8] 7629 4-10-2 **61**..............................(t) KieranO'Neill 8 68
(Robyn Brisland) *trckd ldrs: smooth hdwy over 4f out: led 3f out: clr 2f out: rdn and jnd jst over 1f out: sn drvn and kpt on wl towards fin (trainer said regarding apparent improvement in from that the gelding benefitted from a drop in grade and a less competitive race)* **8/1**
3021 **2** *¾* **Loose Chippings (IRE)**[23] 7087 5-9-7 **55**.............. GabrieleMalune(3) 2 61
(Ivan Furtado) *trckd ldrs on inner: n.m.r bnd 4f out: hdwy 3f out: chsd wnr wl over 1f out: sn rdn to chal: drvn and ev ch ins fnl f tl no ex last 75yds* **9/2**[2]
3066 **3** *3 ½* **Mongolia**[18] 7270 3-9-1 **52**.............................. LukeMorris 14 53
(Michael Appleby) *hld up in midfield: pushed along and hdwy over 3f out: sn rdn: styd on to chse ldng pair wl over 1f out: sn drvn and kpt on same pce* **22/1**
0054 **4** *½* **Tyrsal (IRE)**[39] 6550 8-9-0 **45**..............................(p) JosephineGordon 6 44
(Shaun Keightley) *in rr: hdwy over 3f out: carried wd st: sn swtchd lft and rdn: kpt on u.p to fnl 2f: nrst fin* **33/1**
3320 **5** *2* **Dolly Dupree**[18] 7280 3-8-12 **54**.............................. TheodoreLadd(5) 9 51
(Paul D'Arcy) *hld up towards rr: hdwy 4f out: rdn along and wd st: chsd ldrs 2f out: drvn and edgd lft wl over 1f out: sn no imp (jockey said filly fly leapt leaving the stalls)* **11/2**[3]
-061 **6** *2* **Para Queen (IRE)**[54] 5987 3-8-11 **51**.............................. JaneElliott(3) 10 45
(Heather Main) *dwlt and reminders s: in rr: hdwy 4f out: rdn along and wd st: drvn 2f out: plugged on one pce (jockey said filly was never travelling; trainer said that the filly was unsuited by the fibresand surface)* **15/2**
-030 **7** *1 ¼* **Amber Rock (USA)**[81] 4998 3-8-5 **45**..............................(t[1]) SeanDavis(3) 3 37
(Les Eyre) *t.k.h: prom: cl up 1/2-way: led over 4f out: rdn along and hdd over 3f out: sn drvn and wknd over 2f out (jockey said gelding ran too free)* **25/1**
0600 **8** *3 ½* **Foxrush Take Time (FR)**[5] 7732 4-9-0 **45**..............................(e) FrannyNorton 11 30
(Richard Guest) *prom: pushed along whn n.m.r bnd 4f out: sn rdn and wknd over 2f out* **16/1**
3430 **9** *10* **Going Native**[142] 2737 4-9-7 **52**.............................. JackMitchell 13 21
(Olly Williams) *midfield: hdwy and in tch 1/2-way: chsd ldrs 4f out: rdn along over 3f out: wd st and sn btn* **20/1**
/460 **10** *½* **Another Lincolnday**[70] 4510 8-9-6 **51**.............................. GrahamLee 12 20
(Rebecca Menzies) *a towards rr* **25/1**
3000 **11** *2* **Zahraani**[31] 6843 4-9-1 **46**..............................(p[1]) ShaneKelly 4 11
(J R Jenkins) *a towards rr* **50/1**
4242 **12** *6* **Duke Of Alba (IRE)**[7] 7643 4-10-2 **61**.............................. BenCurtis 1 17
(John Mackie) *trckd ldrs on inner: reminders 1/2-way: sn rdn along: outpcd and bhd fr 4f out (trainer's rep said that the gelding ran flat having raced 7 days earlier)* **9/4**[1]
0000 **13** *22* **Dream Model (IRE)**[15] 7385 3-8-8 **45**..............................(p) AndrewMullen 7
(Mark Loughnane) *chsd ldrs: rdn along over 4f out: sn wknd* **66/1**
2200 **14** *52* **Thecornishbarron (IRE)**[135] 2963 7-9-2 **47**.............................. EoinWalsh 5
(Aytach Sadik) *led: hdd over 4f out: sn wknd and bhd fnl 3f (vet said gelding was struck into on its left hind)* **66/1**
2m 38.67s (-2.33) **Going Correction** -0.35s/f (Stan)
WFA 3 from 4yo+ 6lb **14** Ran SP% **117.8**
Speed ratings (Par 101): **93,92,90,89,88 87,86,84,77,77 75,71,57,22**
CSF £39.03 CT £767.89 TOTE £7.10: £2.30, £1.90, £4.80; EX 39.90 Trifecta £960.30.
Owner Mrs Jo Brisland **Bred** Exors Of The Late Mrs Liz Nelson **Trained** Danethorpe, Notts
FOCUS
An ordinary contest with another multiple course winner.

7874 SKY SPORTS RACING ON SKY 415 NURSERY H'CAP 1m 13y(F)
8:00 (8:00) (Class 5) (0-75,75) 2-Y-O

£3,428 (£1,020; £509; £400; £400; £400) **Stalls** Low

Form RPR
0265 **1** **Bermuda Schwartz**[34] 6718 2-9-6 **74**.............................. ShaneKelly 3 78
(Richard Hughes) *trckd ldrs: smooth hdwy over 2f out: rdn to chal over 1f out: slt ld and drvn ins fnl f: hld on wl* **13/2**[3]
6651 **2** *hd* **Kuwait Shield**[13] 7438 2-9-5 **73**.............................. TonyHamilton 5 77
(Richard Fahey) *cl up: led over 2f out: jnd and rdn over 1f out: drvn and hdd narrowly ins fnl f: kpt on gamely u.p: jst hld* **13/2**[3]
5066 **3** *4* **Hooroo (IRE)**[36] 6625 2-8-12 **66**.............................. BenCurtis 6 60
(K R Burke) *cl up on outer: pushed along and sltly outpcd 3f out: hdwy over 2f out: sn rdn and ev ch tl drvn over 1f out and kpt on same pce* **7/2**[2]
3322 **4** *6* **Expensive Dirham**[8] 7620 2-9-7 **75**.............................. FrannyNorton 4 56
(Mark Johnston) *trckd ldrs: pushed along and lost pl after 2f: sn in rr and swtchd rt: sme hdwy 3f out: drvn over 2f out and plugged on one pce* **5/4**[1]
042 **5** *9* **Alibaba**[40] 6497 2-9-3 **71**.............................. ShelleyBirkett 1 31
(Julia Feilden) *cl up on inner: led over 4f out: rdn along 3f out: hdd over 2f out: sn drvn and wknd* **16/1**
040 **6** *3 ½* **Forus**[62] 5676 2-9-1 **69**.............................. NicolaCurrie 2 21
(Jamie Osborne) *slt ld: hdd over 4f out: rdn along over 3f out: sn wknd* **14/1**
330 **7** *7* **Handlebars (IRE)**[15] 7361 2-8-10 **64**.............................. GrahamLee 7
(Keith Dalgleish) *dwlt: a towards rr* **14/1**
1m 41.26s (-2.44) **Going Correction** -0.35s/f (Stan) **7** Ran SP% **112.5**
Speed ratings (Par 95): **98,97,93,87,78 75,68**
CSF £45.68 TOTE £5.60: £3.60, £2.50; EX 74.40 Trifecta £170.90.
Owner Alex Smith **Bred** P J Gleeson **Trained** Upper Lambourn, Berks
FOCUS
Bit of a turn-up in this mile nursery and the winner has been rated to his best.

7875 VISIT ATTHERACES.COM H'CAP 1m 13y(F)
8:30 (8:31) (Class 5) (0-70,71) 3-Y-O+

£3,428 (£1,020; £509; £400; £400; £400) **Stalls** Low

Form RPR
6431 **1** **Makambe (IRE)**[31] 6839 4-9-5 **66**..............................(p) JoeyHaynes 3 75
(Chelsea Banham) *in tch: n.m.r and hmpd over 4f out: hdwy to trck ldrs over 3f out: effrt on inner and cl up over 2f out: rdn to ld wl over 1f out: kpt on strly* **5/1**[2]
6000 **2** *1 ¼* **Love Your Work (IRE)**[23] 7083 3-9-4 **68**.............................. CharlieBennett 6 73
(Adam West) *cl up: led 3f out: rdn and hdd wl over 1f out: sn drvn: kpt on* **10/1**
4061 **3** *¾* **French Twist**[34] 6731 3-8-7 **62**..............................(p) ThomasGreatrex(5) 14 65
(David Loughnane) *prom: cl up over 3f out: rdn along over 2f out: drvn over 1f out: edgd lft ent fnl f: kpt on same pce* **20/1**
0002 **4** *1* **My Amigo**[8] 7609 6-9-0 **64**..............................(p) JaneElliott(3) 10 65
(Marjorie Fife) *in rr: pushed along over 3f out: rdn over 2f out: styd on wl fr over 1f out: nrst fin* **12/1**
0051 **5** *½* **Muqarred (USA)**[15] 7385 7-9-1 **65**..............................(b) GemmaTutty(3) 13 65
(Karen Tutty) *midfield: wd st: rdn along over 2f out: styd on wl fnl f* **15/2**[3]
0011 **6** *shd* **Break The Silence**[15] 7384 5-8-8 **55**..............................(b) KieranO'Neill 8 55
(Scott Dixon) *cl up: rdn and ev ch 2f out: drvn over 1f out: kpt on same pce* **10/1**
2 **7** *1* **Snow Ocean (IRE)**[22] 7114 3-9-6 **70**..............................(h) EoinWalsh 2 67
(David Evans) *bhd and green early: hdwy over 2f out: sn rdn: kpt on fnl f: n.d (jockey said gelding hung left)* **20/1**
3332 **8** *½* **Elhafei (USA)**[21] 7166 4-9-10 **71**..............................(p) AlistairRawlinson 9 67
(Michael Appleby) *in tch: effrt and wd st: sn rdn and no imp* **7/2**[1]
5000 **9** *½* **Bond Angel**[23] 7084 4-8-11 **63**.............................. RayDawson(5) 11 58
(David Evans) *towards rr: v wd st: rdn along nr stands' rail 2f: nvr nr ldrs* **10/1**
0114 **10** *¾* **Dawn Breaking**[36] 6628 4-8-11 **58**..............................(b) PhilDennis 7 51
(Richard Whitaker) *cl up: rdn over 3f out: wknd over 2f out* **12/1**
0213 **11** *5* **Dreamseller (IRE)**[14] 7404 3-8-10 **60**..............................(p) DavidAllan 5 42
(Tim Easterby) *led: rdn and hdd 3f out: sn wknd* **8/1**
0000 **12** *7* **Watheer**[59] 5770 4-9-1 **62**..............................(b) BenCurtis 4 28
(Roger Fell) *chsd ldrs: rdn along 3f out: sn wknd (jockey said gelding hung left)* **16/1**
2020 **13** *1 ½* **Thornaby Nash**[9] 7587 8-9-7 **68**..............................(b) TomEaves 12 30
(Jason Ward) *a towards rr* **50/1**
-205 **14** *8* **Ambersand (IRE)**[22] 7129 3-9-2 **66**.............................. TonyHamilton 1 10
(Richard Fahey) *chsd ldrs: n.m.r over 4f out: sn rdn along and lost pl: bhd and eased over 2f out* **33/1**
1m 41.47s (-2.23) **Going Correction** -0.35s/f (Stan)
WFA 3 from 4yo+ 3lb **14** Ran SP% **124.7**
Speed ratings (Par 103): **97,95,95,94,93 93,92,91,91,90 85,78,77,69**
CSF £54.13 CT £974.63 TOTE £5.80: £2.30, £3.60, £6.90; EX 74.40 Trifecta £1168.00.
Owner Turrloo F Parrett **Bred** Mrs F Hay **Trained** Cowlinge, Suffolk
■ Stewards' Enquiry : Kieran O'Neill one-day ban; failing to ride out (Oct 18)
FOCUS
They appeared to go some gallop in this Class 5 handicap.
T/Plt: £49.00 to a £1 stake. Pool: £79,092.36 - 1178.14 winning units T/Qpdt: £14.70 to a £1 stake. Pool: £10,040.10 - 504.62 winning units **Joe Rowntree**

7664 DUNDALK (A.W) (L-H)
Friday, October 4

OFFICIAL GOING: Polytrack: standard

7876a IRISH STALLION FARMS EBF RACE (PLUS 10 RACE) 5f (P)
5:10 (5:11) 2-Y-O

£10,648 (£3,441; £1,639; £738; £378; £198)

RPR
1 **Brunelle (IRE)**[35] 6690 2-9-2 0.............................. ColinKeane 3 84+
(G M Lyons, Ire) *racd in mid-div: clsr to chse ldrs over 1f out: rdn to ld ins fnl 150yds: kpt on wl clsng stages* **2/1**[1]
2 *1 ¼* **Phase After Phase (IRE)**[37] 6617 2-9-7 **94**..............(tp) DonnachaO'Brien 6 84+
(Joseph Patrick O'Brien, Ire) *racd in mid-div tl clsr on outer appr fnl f: wnt 4th fnl 150yds: styd on wl into 2nd clsng stages: nt rch wnr* **5/1**
3 *hd* **Cool Sphere (USA)**[29] 6899 2-9-7 0.............................. WJLee 8 83
(Robert Cowell) *settled off ldrs in 4th: clsr under 2f out into 2nd: rdn and no imp on wnr fnl 100yds: kpt on wl: dropped to 3rd clsng stages* **9/2**[3]
4 *1 ½* **George Cornelius (IRE)**[173] 1786 2-9-7 0.............................. MarkGallagher 1 78
(Kieran P Cotter, Ire) *sn led: t.k.h: edgd rt appr fnl f: hdd fnl 150yds: sn no ex in 4th* **9/4**[2]
5 *1* **Lady Maura (IRE)**[16] 7358 2-8-11 0.............................. NGMcCullagh 4 64
(J P Murtagh, Ire) *bit slowly away and racd towards rr: prog over 1f out: kpt on same pce fnl f into 5th clsng stages: nvr on terms* **16/1**
6 *½* **True Motion (IRE)**[37] 6617 2-9-2 **82**.............................. OisinMurphy 7 67
(Aidan F Fogarty, Ire) *broke wl and led briefly: sn hdd and chsd ldr in 3rd: nt qckn over 1f out: wknd ins fnl f* **12/1**
7 *nk* **On Tick (IRE)**[16] 7358 2-8-6 0.............................. SiobhanRutledge(10) 2 66
(Miss Katy Brown, Ire) *bit slowly away and racd in rr for most: kpt on one pce fnl f: nvr a factor* **25/1**
8 *6 ½* **Sampers Seven (IRE)** 2-8-11 0.............................. RonanWhelan 9 38
(M Halford, Ire) *sn trckd ldr in 2nd: pushed along and nt qckn over 1f out: sn wknd: nt hrd rdn clsng stages* **25/1**
59.0s (-0.40) **Going Correction** +0.15s/f (Slow) **8** Ran SP% **120.2**
Speed ratings: **109,107,106,104,102 101,101,91**
CSF £13.45 TOTE £2.70: £1.02, £2.00, £1.60; DF 9.50 Trifecta £34.70.
Owner Anamoine Limited **Bred** Windflower Overseas **Trained** Dunsany, Co Meath

FOCUS
A decent juvenile sprint for this time of year. The third and seventh limit the level.

7877a - 7878a (Foreign Racing) - See Raceform Interactive

7879a BOYLESPORTS IRISH EBF STAR APPEAL STKS (LISTED RACE) 7f (P)
6:45 (6:45) 2-Y-O £39,864 (£12,837; £6,081; £2,702; £1,351; £675)

RPR
1 **Fort Myers (USA)**[20] 7195 2-9-3 106 DonnachaO'Brien 4 105+
(A P O'Brien, Ire) *led for 1f: trckd ldrs in 3rd: swtchd rt 2f out and rdn: on terms ent fnl f and led fnl 150yds: kpt on wl clsng stages* 1/1[1]
2 1 **Justifier (IRE)**[42] 6430 2-9-6 103 (t) ColinKeane 7 105
(G M Lyons, Ire) *towards rr early: sn gd prog on outer to ld after 1f: strly pressed under 2f out: hdd fnl 150yds: kpt on same pce in 2nd wout matching wnr* 9/2[3]
3 hd **Punita Arora (IRE)**[20] 7215 2-8-12 98 ShaneFoley 5 97
(Mrs John Harrington, Ire) *hld up in 4th: pushed along 2f out: prog towards outer ent fnl f: kpt on wl into 3rd cl home: nvr nrr* 10/1
4 nk **Unforgetable (IRE)**[22] 7119 2-8-12 97 ShaneCrosse 3 96
(Joseph Patrick O'Brien, Ire) *racd in 5th: prog towards inner appr fnl f: briefly short of room fnl 150yds: styd on wl clsng stages in 4th* 10/1
5 2 **Chrysalism (IRE)**[11] 7528 2-8-12 85 DeclanMcDonogh 2 91
(Joseph Patrick O'Brien, Ire) *in rr for most: styd on wl on outer ins fnl f into 5th cl home: nvr on terms* 25/1
6 ½ **Above (FR)**[34] 6746 2-9-3 100 OisinMurphy 6 95
(Archie Watson) *trckd ldr in 2nd: rdn and almost on terms under 2f out: hdd ins fnl f: sn no ex* 10/3[2]

1m 25.28s (0.18) **Going Correction** +0.15s/f (Slow) 6 Ran SP% 113.3
Speed ratings: **105,103,103,103,101 100**
CSF £6.05 TOTE £1.80: £1.02, £2.60; DF 5.80 Trifecta £21.30.
Owner Michael Tabor & Derrick Smith & Mrs John Magnier **Bred** Orpendale, Chelston & Wynatt **Trained** Cashel, Co Tipperary

FOCUS
A disappointing turnout for the prize-money on offer. It did not deviate much from the anticipated script as the favourite ran to his mark and always looked like doing enough.

7880 - 7884a (Foreign Racing) - See Raceform Interactive

7674 SAINT-CLOUD (L-H)
Friday, October 4

OFFICIAL GOING: Turf: very soft

7885a PRIX DAHLIA - FONDS EUROPEEN DE L'ELEVAGE (LISTED RACE) (4YO+ FILLIES & MARES) (TURF) 1m 2f
12:50 4-Y-O+ £21,621 (£8,648; £6,486; £4,324; £2,162)

RPR
1 **Lanana (FR)**[27] 6992 4-8-11 0 EddyHardouin 4 101
(Robert Collet, France) 63/10
2 ¾ **Magic Lily**[721] 8004 4-8-11 0 WilliamBuick 6 100
(Charlie Appleby) *plld hrd: hld up in 3rd: chsd ldr 3 1/2f out: pushed along w 2 1/2f to run: styd on u.p fr 1 1/2f out: nt pce of wnr ins fnl f* 6/4[1]
3 1¼ **Tosen Gift (IRE)**[27] 6992 4-9-2 0 YutakaTake 7 102
(S Kobayashi, France) 49/10[3]
4 snk **Palmyre (FR)**[27] 6992 4-8-11 0 AlexisBadel 2 97
(H-F Devin, France) 16/1
5 snk **Shahnaza (FR)**[82] 4962 4-9-2 0 ChristopheSoumillon 5 102
(A De Royer-Dupre, France) 7/2[2]
6 3 **Golden Rajsa (FR)**[17] 5-8-11 0 (b) MickaelBarzalona 1 91
(Pauline Menges, France) 58/10
7 nk **Skill Set (IRE)**[51] 6082 4-8-11 0 Pierre-CharlesBoudot 3 90
(Henry Candy) *led: hdd after 1f: trckd new ldr: drvn and nt qckn wl over 2f out: wknd u.p appr fnl f* 18/1

2m 16.54s (0.54) 7 Ran SP% 118.7
PARI-MUTUEL (all including 1 euro stake): WIN 7.30; PLACE 2.70, 1.90; SF 29.20.
Owner Ballantines Racing Stud Ltd **Bred** Aleyrion Bloodstock **Trained** Chantilly, France

7886a PRIX MATCHEM (LISTED RACE) (3YO) (TURF) 7f
2:32 3-Y-O £24,774 (£9,909; £7,432; £4,954; £2,477)

RPR
1 **Matematica (GER)**[29] 6910 3-8-10 0 OlivierPeslier 7 102+
(C Laffon-Parias, France) 76/10
2 1¼ **Milord's Song (FR)**[48] 6252 3-9-0 0 TheoBachelot 8 103
(S Wattel, France) 41/5
3 nse **Firebird Song (IRE)**[19] 7250 3-9-0 0 MickaelBarzalona 2 102+
(H-A Pantall, France) *racd in fnl trio on inner: clsd ins fnl 2 1/2f: 5th whn stdd and angled out wl over 1f out: drvn and r.o fnl f: jst missed 2nd* 12/1
4 nse **Pretty Boy (IRE)**[22] 3-9-0 0 CristianDemuro 9 102
(Mme Pia Brandt, France) 73/10
5 1½ **Feliciana De Vega**[55] 5949 3-8-10 0 AlexisBadel 1 95+
(Ralph Beckett) *cl 3rd on inner and ev ch 2f out: nt clr run fr there tl ins fnl f: nt rcvr: eased late on* 27/10[1]
6 1¼ **Moni (FR)**[14] 3-9-0 0 (b) CyrilleStefan 6 95
(S Culin, France) 33/1
7 1¾ **Shendam (FR)**[48] 6249 3-9-0 0 (b[1]) ChristopheSoumillon 5 90
(M Delzangles, France) 87/10
8 2 **Urwald**[48] 6249 3-9-3 0 Pierre-CharlesBoudot 4 88
(A Fabre, France) 7/1[3]
9 7½ **Zazen**[27] 3-8-10 0 MaximeGuyon 3 61
(A Fabre, France) 31/10[2]

1m 29.76s (-2.44) 9 Ran SP% 119.4
PARI-MUTUEL (all including 1 euro stake): WIN 8.60; PLACE 2.50, 2.80, 4.00; DF 26.80.
Owner Wertheimer & Frere **Bred** Wertheimer & Frere **Trained** Chantilly, France

7887a PRIX THOMAS BRYON JOCKEY CLUB DE TURQUIE (GROUP 3) (2YO) (TURF) 7f
3:06 2-Y-O £36,036 (£14,414; £10,810; £7,207; £3,603)

RPR
1 **King's Command**[54] 6002 2-8-13 0 MickaelBarzalona 3 116
(Charlie Appleby) *mde all: kicked for home wl over 2f out: styd on strly fnl f: unchal* 93/10
2 3½ **Royal Crusade**[20] 7195 2-8-13 0 WilliamBuick 5 107
(Charlie Appleby) *settled in 4th: chsd ldr appr 2f out: styd on u.p: nvr trbld wnr* 1/1[1]
3 nk **Wooded (IRE)**[33] 6777 2-8-13 0 Pierre-CharlesBoudot 6 106
(F-H Graffard, France) *hld up in fnl pair on outer: hdwy 1 1/2f fr home: styd on fnl f but a hld for 2nd* 3/1[2]
4 3 **Happy Bere (FR)**[26] 7005 2-8-13 0 OlivierPeslier 2 98
(A De Watrigant, France) *racd keenly: trckd ldr on inner: rdn but nt qckn 2f out: dropped away appr fnl f* 63/10
5 ¾ **Chill Chainnigh (FR)**[36] 2-8-13 0 JeromeCabre 1 96
(Y Barberot, France) *settled in fnl pair on inner: rdn and effrt 1 1/2f out: sn no further imp: wl hld fnl f* 23/1
6 15 **Oxalis (IRE)**[21] 2-8-13 0 MaximeGuyon 4 57
(F Head, France) *racd keenly: restrained bhd ldr on outer: outpcd and pushed along over 2f out: adrift in last fr 1 1/2f out: hld whn eased ins fnl f* 23/5[3]

1m 31.49s (-0.71) 6 Ran SP% 120.4
PARI-MUTUEL (all including 1 euro stake): WIN 10.30; PLACE 3.30, 1.40; SF 18.50.
Owner Godolphin **Bred** Godolphin **Trained** Newmarket, Suffolk

7888 - (Foreign Racing) - See Raceform Interactive

7863 ASCOT (R-H)
Saturday, October 5

OFFICIAL GOING: Soft (heavy in places on round course; str 6.2, rnd 5.4)
Wind: Almost nil Weather: Overcast

7889 UK HI-FI SHOW LIVE ROUS STKS (LISTED RACE) 5f
2:00 (2:01) (Class 1) 3-Y-O+
£25,519 (£9,675; £4,842; £2,412; £1,210; £607) Stalls High

Form RPR
1112 1 **Dakota Gold**[14] 7454 5-9-3 110 ConnorBeasley 6 115
(Michael Dods) *racd freely: mde all: rdn and pressed over 1f out: styd on stoutly fnl f* 15/8[1]
3240 2 1½ **Arecibo (FR)**[14] 7433 4-9-0 100 (v) DanielTudhope 1 107
(David O'Meara) *hld up towards rr: prog 2f out: rdn over 1f out: styd on to take 2nd last 75yds: unable to chal* 12/1
1342 3 nk **Danzeno**[27] 6999 8-9-0 105 AlistairRawlinson 7 106
(Michael Appleby) *trckd ldng pair: rdn to chse wnr wl over 1f out and sn trying to chal: hld fnl f and lost 2nd last 75yds* 6/1[3]
2154 4 1 **Tis Marvellous**[24] 7073 5-9-0 109 (t) AdamKirby 9 102
(Clive Cox) *chsd ldrs: outpcd 2f out: kpt on same pce fnl f* 7/1
4320 5 ¾ **Stake Acclaim (IRE)**[20] 7254 7-9-0 105 FrannyNorton 4 99
(Dean Ivory) *chsd wnr to wl over 1f out: fdd fnl f* 10/1
1351 6 ¾ **Maygold**[28] 6960 4-8-9 97 LiamKeniry 2 92
(Ed Walker) *t.k.h: hld up in rr: swtchd rt and effrt wl over 1f out: kpt on fnl f but nvr enough pce to be involved (vet said filly lost its right fore shoe)* 11/2[2]
4340 7 nk **Poetry**[20] 7254 3-8-9 98 AndreaAtzeni 5 91
(Michael Bell) *chsd ldrs: outpcd 2f out: no imp after* 25/1
4040 8 1½ **True Mason**[20] 7243 3-9-0 95 (v) BenCurtis 3 91
(K R Burke) *s.i.s: pushed along in rr: effrt on outer 2f out: no hdwy fnl f* 16/1
2500 9 4 **The Cruising Lord**[56] 5932 3-9-0 97 LukeMorris 10 77
(Michael Attwater) *rdn in midfield bef 1/2-way: sn struggling: bhd fnl f (vet said gelding lost its right fore shoe)* 50/1
3300 10 ¾ **Reticent Angel (IRE)**[15] 7401 3-8-9 90 (p) HectorCrouch 11 69
(Clive Cox) *a in rr: rdn and no prog 1/2-way: bhd fnl f* 66/1
606 11 1 **Intense Romance (IRE)**[28] 6960 5-8-9 97 SilvestreDeSousa 8 64
(Michael Dods) *dwlt: a wl in rr: rdn and no prog 1/2-way: bhd fnl f* 12/1

1m 1.12s (0.42) **Going Correction** +0.50s/f (Yiel) 11 Ran SP% 114.6
Speed ratings (Par 111): **116,113,113,111,110 109,108,106,99,98 97**
CSF £25.45 TOTE £2.40: £1.10, £3.50, £2.30; EX 25.00 Trifecta £132.60.
Owner Doug Graham & Ian Davison **Bred** Redgate Bstock & Peter Bottowley Bstock **Trained** Denton, Co Durham

FOCUS
Straight course divided into two from 1m to 2.5f and stands' side of track used. After 6mm of rain on Friday, the ground was officially described as soft on the straight course and soft, heavy in places on the round course. A strong-looking edition of this Listed sprint. The winner and second rate to form.

7890 PROPERTY RACEDAY TARGETS £3M CUMBERLAND LODGE STKS (GROUP 3) 1m 3f 211y
2:35 (2:35) (Class 1) 3-Y-O+
£34,026 (£12,900; £6,456; £3,216; £1,614; £810) Stalls Low

Form RPR
0402 1 **Morando (FR)**[49] 6213 6-9-5 112 SilvestreDeSousa 3 119
(Andrew Balding) *hld up in 4th tl trckd ldng pair 1/2-way: shkn up to ld over 1f out: qckly drew clr: styd on strly* 2/1[1]
1141 2 6 **Sextant**[21] 7180 4-9-2 108 LouisSteward 1 106
(Sir Michael Stoute) *dwlt: hld up in 6th: rdn and prog jst over 2f out: kpt on to take 2nd jst ins fnl f but wnr wl clr* 7/1[3]
2013 3 1½ **Vivid Diamond (IRE)**[23] 7118 3-8-7 106 FrannyNorton 5 102
(Mark Johnston) *trckd ldr: rdn to ld over 2f out: hdd and qckly outpcd over 1f out: lost 2nd jst ins fnl f* 9/1
1121 4 1¼ **Faylaq**[10] 7574 3-8-10 107 DaneO'Neill 4 103
(William Haggas) *hld up in 5th: gng wl enough 3f out: shkn up 2f out: limited prog over 1f out and no hdwy after* 4/1[2]
-051 5 ½ **Raakib Alhawa (IRE)**[42] 6466 3-8-10 107 AndreaAtzeni 2 102
(David Simcock) *dwlt: hld up in last: rdn wl over 2f out: plugged on but nvr a factor* 8/1
3551 6 1¾ **Surrey Thunder (FR)**[44] 6385 3-8-10 104 CharlesBishop 7 99
(Joseph Tuite) *t.k.h: trckd ldng pair to 1/2-way: rdn wl over 2f out: steadily wknd* 20/1
-100 7 30 **Wells Farhh Go (IRE)**[42] 6473 4-9-2 110 DavidAllan 6 50
(Tim Easterby) *racd v freely: led and clr to 1/2-way: hdd & wknd qckly over 2f out: virtually p.u nr fin (jockey said colt ran too free; vet said colt had struck into its right fore)* 4/1[2]

2m 40.07s (7.47) **Going Correction** +0.50s/f (Yiel)
WFA 3 from 4yo+ 6lb 7 Ran SP% 111.7
Speed ratings (Par 113): **95,91,90,89,88 87,67**
CSF £15.82 TOTE £2.70: £1.50, £2.60; EX 14.90 Trifecta £98.90.
Owner King Power Racing Co Ltd **Bred** Guy Pariente Holding Sprl **Trained** Kingsclere, Hants

FOCUS
Add 25 yards. This Group 3 was taken apart by the well-fancied Morando, who relished the underfoot conditions and there's a case for rating this as a clear pb, but there are enough doubts to just have him matching his best.

7891 BET365 CHALLENGE CUP (HERITAGE H'CAP) 7f
3:10 (3:10) (Class 2) 3-Y-0+

£112,050 (£33,552; £16,776; £8,388; £4,194; £2,106) **Stalls** High

Form — RPR

2532 **1** **Kynren (IRE)**[14] 7430 5-9-2 **101** .... BenCurtis 17 — 112
(David Barron) *trckd ldng pair: shkn up to ld over 1f out: pressed after but rdn out and styd on wl* **11/4**[1]

345 **2** ½ **Greenside**[91] 4666 8-8-2 **94** .... MarcoGhiani(7) 9 — 104
(Henry Candy) *trckd ldng pair: clsd to chal over 1f out: pressed wnr after and clr of rest but nt qckn last 100yds* **14/1**

1354 **3** 3¼ **Escobar (IRE)**[28] 6950 5-9-6 **105** .... (t) AdamKirby 6 — 107
(David O'Meara) *hld up wl in rr: prog on outer of gp 2f out: drvn and styd on to take 3rd ins fnl f: no threat to ldng pair* **14/1**

424 **4** nk **Summerghand (IRE)**[14] 7433 5-9-3 **102** .... DanielTudhope 5 — 103
(David O'Meara) *hld up wl in rr: prog on outer of gp 2f out: drvn and styd on fnl f: no threat to ldng pair* **16/1**

2511 **5** nse **Casanova**[22] 7163 3-8-10 **97** .... AndreaAtzeni 13 — 97+
(John Gosden) *racd freely: mde most to over 1f out: sn lft bhd: kpt on fnl f* **6/1**[2]

2512 **6** hd **Bedouin's Story**[23] 7106 4-9-4 **103** .... (p) HectorCrouch 3 — 103
(Saeed bin Suroor) *stdd s: towards rr: prog on outer of gp into midfield 1/2-way: hdd 2f out to chse ldng pair jst over 1f out: one pce and lost pls ins fnl f* **9/1**

0104 **7** ½ **Cold Stare (IRE)**[7] 7701 4-8-13 **98** ow1 .... (t) RobbieDowney 15 — 97
(David O'Meara) *hld up towards rr: drvn and prog 2f out: styd on same pce fnl f: nvr nrr* **33/1**

1611 **8** 2 **Qaysar (FR)**[21] 7198 4-9-6 **105** .... PatDobbs 16 — 99
(Richard Hannon) *trckd ldrs: rdn and no prog 2f out: steadily fdd* **20/1**

3535 **9** 1 **Raydiance**[1] 7865 4-8-7 **92** .... JoeyHaynes 14 — 83
(K R Burke) *chsd ldrs: rdn over 2f out: lost pl wl over 1f out: n.d after* **40/1**

5600 **10** 1¼ **Keyser Soze (IRE)**[35] 6706 5-8-13 **98** .... LukeMorris 10 — 86
(Richard Spencer) *blindfold off sltly late and slowly away: mostly in last pair: rdn wl over 2f out: sme prog over 1f out but nvr a danger* **33/1**

0000 **11** ¾ **Lake Volta (IRE)**[21] 7188 4-8-9 **94** .... FrannyNorton 12 — 80
(Mark Johnston) *w ldr to 2f out: wknd* **20/1**

-153 **12** 1½ **Silver Line (IRE)**[17] 7340 5-9-7 **106** .... CallumShepherd 2 — 88
(Saeed bin Suroor) *trckd ldrs: rdn 2f out: wknd over 1f out* **25/1**

6422 **13** hd **Ripp Orf (IRE)**[28] 6950 5-8-11 **96** .... (t) GeraldMosse 8 — 77
(David Elsworth) *hld up towards rr: rdn and no prog over 2f out: n.d after (trainer's rep said gelding was unsuited by the going and would prefer a quicker surface)* **7/1**[3]

0003 **14** ¾ **So Beloved**[22] 7164 9-8-6 **98** .... AngusVilliers(7) 18 — 77
(David O'Meara) *trckd ldrs: rdn and no prog over 2f out: wknd over 1f out* **14/1**

P440 **15** 1 **Remarkable**[49] 6207 6-8-11 **96** .... (b) RossaRyan 1 — 73
(David O'Meara) *racd on outer of gp: in tch in midfield but racd awkwardly: no prog 2f out: wknd over 1f out* **33/1**

4313 **16** nk **Raising Sand**[28] 6956 7-9-10 **109** .... NicolaCurrie 11 — 85
(Jamie Osborne) *a in last quartet: urged along and nt gng wl 3f out: nvr a factor (trainer's rep could offer no explanation for the gelding's performance)* **7/1**[3]

4554 **17** 2 **Battered**[7] 7697 5-8-11 **96** .... SilvestreDeSousa 7 — 67
(Ralph Beckett) *a wl in rr: shkn up and no prog over 2f out* **12/1**

1m 28.54s (1.04) **Going Correction** +0.50s/f (Yiel)
WFA 3 from 4yo+ 2lb — **17 Ran SP% 134.2**
Speed ratings (Par 109): **114,113,109,109,109 109,108,106,105,103 102,101,100,100,98 98,96**
CSF £45.12 CT £522.32 TOTE £3.50: £1.40, £3.90, £2.70, £4.60; EX 45.40 Trifecta £1036.50.
Owner Elliott Brothers & Peacock & Partner **Bred** Rathasker Stud **Trained** Maunby, N Yorks

FOCUS
A typically competitive heritage handicap, though a lot of these struggled in the conditions and two came clear in the final furlong. This rates a pb from the winner.

7892 JOHN GUEST RACING BENGOUGH STKS (GROUP 3) 6f
3:40 (3:44) (Class 1) 3-Y-0+

£39,697 (£15,050; £7,532; £3,752; £1,883; £945) **Stalls** High

Form — RPR

1103 **1** **Cape Byron**[42] 6472 5-9-2 113 .... AndreaAtzeni 6 — 117
(Roger Varian) *awkward s: trckd ldrs: shkn up to ld over 1f out: wl in command fnl f: drvn out* **13/8**[1]

2406 **2** 2 **Donjuan Triumphant (IRE)**[49] 6215 6-9-2 107 .... SilvestreDeSousa 7 — 110
(Andrew Balding) *hld up in rr: prog over 2f out: rdn and styd on to take 2nd ins fnl f: no ch w wnr* **9/2**[3]

0364 **3** nk **Keystroke**[14] 7454 7-9-5 108 .... (t) AdamKirby 10 — 112+
(Stuart Williams) *stdd s: hld up in last: swtchd rt and effrt wl over 1f out: urged along and styd on to press for 2nd ins fnl f: no ch w wnr* **12/1**

4131 **4** 1¼ **Raucous**[42] 6453 6-9-2 106 .... (tp) AlistairRawlinson 5 — 105
(Robert Cowell) *in tch: rdn 2f out: pressed for a pl fnl f: one pce last 100yds* **16/1**

0100 **5** 2½ **Good Effort (IRE)**[14] 7433 4-9-2 97 .... (p[1]) BenCurtis 2 — 97
(Ismail Mohammed) *led at gd pce: hdd over 1f out: wknd ins fnl f* **25/1**

01-1 **6** ½ **Tabdeed**[63] 5658 4-9-2 103 .... DaneO'Neill 9 — 95
(Owen Burrows) *s.i.s: hld up in rr: rdn and no rspnse 2f out: no great prog after (trainer's rep said colt was unsuited by the soft going on this occasion, which in their opinion was riding tacky)* **2/1**[2]

0130 **7** ¾ **Richenza (FR)**[49] 6229 4-8-13 94 .... RobHornby 8 — 90
(Ralph Beckett) *chsd ldrs: rdn 2f out: sn lft bhd* **40/1**

2235 **8** 1½ **Rock On Baileys**[27] 6999 4-8-13 99 .... (b) NicolaCurrie 3 — 85
(Amy Murphy) *t.k.h: hld up in rr: effrt on outer 2f out: no prog over 1f out* **66/1**

5110 **9** 7 **Green Power**[21] 7193 4-9-2 98 .... HectorCrouch 4 — 66
(John Gallagher) *w ldr to 1/2-way: wknd qckly 2f out* **33/1**

1- **10** 10 **Thrilla In Manila**[344] 8606 3-9-1 0 .... LukeMorris 1 — 34
(Richard Spencer) *plld hrd: chsd ldrs to 1/2-way: sn wknd: t.o (jockey said colt ran too free)* **33/1**

1m 15.63s (1.93) **Going Correction** +0.50s/f (Yiel)
WFA 3 from 4yo+ 1lb — **10 Ran SP% 116.8**
Speed ratings (Par 113): **107,104,103,102,98 98,97,95,85,72**
CSF £8.99 TOTE £2.20: £1.10, £1.40, £3.10; EX 9.30 Trifecta £63.60.
Owner Sheikh Mohammed Obaid Al Maktoum **Bred** Darley **Trained** Newmarket, Suffolk

FOCUS
This Group 3 prize was won with plenty of authority by course specialist Cape Byron, who rates back to his Wokingham form.

7893 CHILD BEREAVEMENT UK BRITISH EBF STKS (LISTED RACE) (F&M) 7f
4:15 (4:18) (Class 1) 3-Y-0+

£22,684 (£8,600; £4,304; £2,144; £1,076; £540) **Stalls** High

Form — RPR

3240 **1** **Di Fede (IRE)**[22] 7146 4-9-0 101 .... SilvestreDeSousa 3 — 106
(Ralph Beckett) *hld up in last of quartet towards far side: stdy prog jst over 2f out: clsd over 1f out: rdn to ld ins fnl f: styd on wl* **7/4**[1]

1332 **2** ¾ **Miss Celestial (IRE)**[34] 6769 3-8-12 97 .... (p) LukeMorris 9 — 103
(Sir Mark Prescott Bt) *taken down early: t.k.h: trckd ldrs towards nr side: angled across to middle over 2f out: chal and on terms over 1f out: styd on but jst outpcd last 100yds* **16/1**

1435 **3** ½ **Muchly**[56] 5949 3-8-12 98 .... AndreaAtzeni 8 — 102+
(John Gosden) *led gp towards nr side: overall ldr over 2f out to ins fnl f: styd on* **11/1**

4400 **4** 1¾ **Shepherd Market (IRE)**[8] 7657 4-9-0 94 .... (b[1]) HectorCrouch 1 — 98
(Clive Cox) *trckd ldr in quartet towards far side: led gp jst over 2f out to over 1f out: fdd ins fnl f* **33/1**

0110 **5** hd **Beauty Filly**[35] 6706 4-9-3 102 .... DanielTudhope 2 — 101
(William Haggas) *trckd ldng pair in quartet towards far side: chal and on terms over 1f out: fdd ins fnl f (vet said filly lost its right hind shoe)* **13/2**[2]

-000 **6** 2¼ **Blizzard**[37] 6646 4-9-0 98 .... RossaRyan 10 — 92
(Ralph Beckett) *trckd ldr towards nr side: cl up 2f out: rdn and wknd over 1f out* **16/1**

5200 **7** 4½ **Red Starlight**[15] 7411 4-9-0 97 .... PatDobbs 5 — 80
(Richard Hannon) *hld up in tch gp towards nr side: rdn 2f out: sn wknd* **14/1**

3011 **8** nk **Excellent Times**[28] 6974 4-9-0 92 .... DavidAllan 6 — 79
(Tim Easterby) *towards rr of nr side gp: rdn and no prog over 2f out: sn btn* **14/1**

2110 **9** ¾ **Tapisserie**[48] 6257 3-9-1 100 .... BenCurtis 12 — 79
(William Haggas) *taken down early: sltly awkward s: hld up in rr in gp towards nr side: stl gng wl enough over 2f out: shkn up and no prog wl over 1f out* **10/1**

2-10 **10** 2½ **Dandhu**[153] 2443 3-9-3 107 .... GeraldMosse 7 — 75
(David Elsworth) *a towards rr of gp towards nr side: struggling over 2f out* **8/1**[3]

-100 **11** 1¼ **Lyzbeth (FR)**[44] 6379 3-8-12 96 .... RobHornby 11 — 67
(Martyn Meade) *nvr beyond midfield of gp towards nr side: rdn and struggling wl over 2f out* **12/1**

4164 **12** 8 **Jadeerah**[56] 5944 3-8-12 90 .... (h) DaneO'Neill 4 — 46
(John Gosden) *overall ldr in quartet towards far side to over 2f out: wknd rapidly sn after* **18/1**

1m 29.53s (2.03) **Going Correction** +0.50s/f (Yiel)
WFA 3 from 4yo 2lb — **12 Ran SP% 119.2**
Speed ratings (Par 111): **108,107,106,104,104 101,96,96,95,92 91,82**
CSF £33.62 TOTE £2.30: £1.30, £5.00, £3.60; EX 31.40 Trifecta £241.70.
Owner Robert Ng **Bred** Robert Ng **Trained** Kimpton, Hants

FOCUS
With only four of these rated in excess of 100, it wasn't the deepest of Listed races. The market was dominated by Di Fede and she made it back-to-back wins in the race, rated to the same level as in 2018.

7894 MCGEE GROUP H'CAP 5f
4:50 (4:51) (Class 3) (0-95,97) 3-Y-0+ **£12,938** (£3,850; £1,924; £962) **Stalls** High

Form — RPR

2325 **1** **Pendleton**[15] 7402 3-8-12 **85** .... (p) CallumRodriguez 3 — 96+
(Michael Dods) *w ldrs: rdn to take narrow ld over 1f out: hrd pressed fnl f: hld on wl* **6/1**[2]

6001 **2** nk **Came From The Dark (IRE)**[29] 6921 3-9-3 **90** .... GeraldMosse 12 — 100+
(Ed Walker) *hld up towards rr: rdn and prog wl over 1f out: styd on wl fnl f: tk 2nd last 50yds and clsd on wnr: too late* **9/2**[1]

0000 **3** ½ **Teruntum Star (FR)**[21] 7193 7-9-2 **89** .... (p) DavidAllan 1 — 96
(David C Griffiths) *prom on outer: rdn to chal and w wnr over 1f out tl nt qckn ins fnl f: lost 2nd last 50yds* **40/1**

1604 **4** nk **Camacho Chief (IRE)**[28] 6960 4-9-10 **97** .... ConnorBeasley 16 — 103
(Michael Dods) *hld up wl in rr: rdn and prog over 1f out: n.m.r briefly ins fnl f: styd on wl nr fin* **8/1**

0244 **5** ½ **Saaheq**[17] 7348 5-8-7 **87** .... AngusVilliers(7) 2 — 91
(Michael Appleby) *hld up in midfield: prog over 1f out: styd on fnl f but nvr quite pce to chal (jockey said gelding hung left-handed under pressure)* **8/1**

521 **6** hd **Call Me Ginger**[18] 7313 3-9-0 **87** .... DanielTudhope 4 — 91
(Jim Goldie) *hld up in rr: prog on outer of gp over 1f out: styd on fnl f but nt pce to chal* **10/1**

1525 **7** ½ **Blue De Vega (GER)**[17] 7348 6-9-2 **89** .... (tp) HectorCrouch 7 — 91
(Robert Cowell) *chsd ldrs: rdn over 1f out: one pce and no imp fnl f* **20/1**

3003 **8** ½ **Spoof**[12] 7524 4-9-0 **87** .... (h) AndreaAtzeni 10 — 87
(Charles Hills) *stdd s: hld up in rr: nudged along to make prog over 1f out: nt clr run briefly jst ins fnl f: kpt on but nvr a threat* **20/1**

000 **9** shd **Erissimus Maximus (FR)**[14] 7467 5-8-4 **84** .... (b) SeanKirrane(7) 9 — 83
(Amy Murphy) *w ldrs: led 1/2-way to over 1f out: wknd ins fnl f* **14/1**

5413 **10** ¾ **Pettochside**[5] 7757 10-8-0 **80** oh12 .... GeorgeRooke(7) 18 — 77
(John Bridger) *sn wl in rr: prog nr side over 1f out: no hdwy fnl f* **33/1**

1600 **11** ¾ **Tawny Port**[29] 6920 5-8-4 **84** .... MarcoGhiani(7) 5 — 78
(Stuart Williams) *led to 1/2-way: wknd over 1f out* **14/1**

2111 **12** 2¾ **Celsius (IRE)**[65] 5589 3-8-13 **86** .... (t) LukeMorris 6 — 71
(Tom Clover) *stdd s and awkwardly away: t.k.h and hld up in rr: effrt over 1f out: no great hdwy* **16/1**

-201 **13** 1¼ **Alaadel**[29] 6920 6-9-7 **94** .... (t) AdamKirby 11 — 74
(Stuart Williams) *dwlt: mostly struggling in rr: nvr a factor (trainer said gelding was unsuited by being slowly away over 5f)* **10/1**

324 **14** 2½ **Mercenary Rose (IRE)**[50] 6148 3-8-7 **80** oh1 .... (t) FrannyNorton 8 — 52
(Paul Cole) *chsd ldrs: rdn 2f out: losing pl qckly whn impeded 1f out (jockey said filly suffered interference in running)* **33/1**

121 **15** 1½ **Texting**[28] 6954 3-8-5 **83** .... SeamusCronin(5) 13 — 49
(Mohamed Moubarak) *w ldrs to 2f out: wkng qckly whn impeded 1f out* **7/1**[3]

0101 **16** 2¼ **Han Solo Berger (IRE)**[18] 7321 4-8-7 **80** oh3 .... (p) GeorgeWood 14 — 37
(Chris Wall) *nvr gng the pce and a struggling in rr (trainer's rep said gelding was unsuited by the going and would prefer a quicker surface)* **33/1**

0304 **17** 1 1/4 **Quench Dolly**[10] 7564 5-8-7 **80** oh4.................. LiamJones 15 33
(John Gallagher) *dwlt: sn w ldrs: wknd rapidly 2f out* **40/1**

1m 2.0s (1.30) **Going Correction** +0.50s/f (Yiel) **17 Ran SP% 127.8**
Speed ratings (Par 107): **109,108,107,107,106 106,105,104,104,103 101,97,95,91,89 85,83**
CSF £31.82 CT £1062.03 TOTE £6.80: £1.90, £1.80, £20.20, £2.00; EX 45.80 Trifecta £1665.90.

Owner David W Armstrong **Bred** Highfield Farm Llp **Trained** Denton, Co Durham

FOCUS
This looked competitive beforehand and they finished in a bit of a heap behind the consistent winner. The first two rate on the upgrade.
T/Jkpt: £2,387.90 to a £1 stake. Pool: £26,906.97 - 8.00 winning units T/Plt: £35.50 to a £1 stake. Pool: £182,246.05 - 3,737.64 winning units T/Qpdt: £13.60 to a £1 stake. Pool: £15,731.96 - 854.41 winning units **Jonathan Neesom**

7691 **NEWMARKET** (R-H)
Saturday, October 5

OFFICIAL GOING: Good to soft (6.6)
Wind: Light against Weather: Cloudy with sunny spells

7895 BRITISH EBF PREMIER FILLIES' H'CAP 1m 2f
1:40 (1:42) (Class 2) 3-Y-O+

£31,125 (£9,320; £4,660; £2,330; £1,165; £585) **Stalls** Low

Form RPR
3121 **1** **Eva Maria**[16] 7366 3-9-0 **88**.................. PaulHanagan 1 98+
(Richard Fahey) *trckd ldrs: wnt 2nd over 2f out: shkn up to ld over 1f out: rdn and hung lft ins fnl f: r.o* **4/1**[1]

-114 **2** 1 **Ghaziyah**[43] 6406 3-9-0 **88**.................. PJMcDonald 12 96+
(William Haggas) *hld up: hdwy over 1f out: sn rdn: r.o to go 2nd post: nt rch wnr* **8/1**

224 **3** *shd* **Nkosikazi**[35] 6721 4-9-2 **89**.................. CierenFallon(3) 2 96
(William Haggas) *led: rdn: edgd lft and hdd over 1f out: styd on same pce towards fin* **11/1**

3616 **4** *nk* **Hyanna**[14] 7457 4-9-5 **94**.................. GeorgiaDobie(5) 3 100
(Eve Johnson Houghton) *s.i.s: hdwy 1/2-way: rdn over 1f out: styd on* **8/1**

0460 **5** 1 1/2 **Bubble And Squeak**[13] 7499 4-9-1 **90**.................. WilliamCarver(5) 4 93
(Sylvester Kirk) *chsd ldrs: rdn over 2f out: styd on same pce wl ins fnl f* **25/1**

2210 **6** 2 3/4 **Gallic**[17] 7347 3-8-13 **87**.................. RyanMoore 8 86
(Ed Walker) *sn chsng ldr: ev ch over 2f out: sn rdn and lost 2nd: edgd rt and no ex ins fnl f* **12/1**

4310 **7** 2 3/4 **Alemagna**[28] 6955 3-8-8 **82**.................. HarryBentley 6 75
(David Simcock) *hld up in tch: racd keenly: rdn and edgd rt over 1f out: styd on same pce* **13/2**[3]

2201 **8** *nk* **Nearooz**[30] 6902 3-9-3 **91**.................. DavidEgan 11 84+
(Roger Varian) *hld up: hdwy over 4f out: rdn over 1f out: wknd ins fnl f (trainer's rep said filly was unsuited by the ground and would prefer a faster surface)* **12/1**

3213 **9** 1 1/4 **Shrewdness**[35] 6709 3-8-7 **81**.................. TomMarquand 13 71
(William Haggas) *hld up: rdn over 2f out: nvr on terms* **20/1**

3216 **10** 1 **Alnaseem**[43] 6408 3-8-7 **81**..................(h) KieranO'Neill 5 69
(Luke McJannet) *hld up: rdn over 3f out: n.d* **50/1**

2312 **11** 1 1/4 **Escape The City**[8] 7663 4-8-4 **74**.................. HollieDoyle 7 59
(Hughie Morrison) *prom: nt clr run 8f out: rdn over 3f out: wknd wl over 1f out* **12/1**

0312 **12** 1 1/4 **Torochica**[22] 7141 3-8-9 **83** ow2.................. KierenFox 14 66
(John Best) *hld up: hdwy over 6f out: rdn over 4f out: wknd over 2f out* **16/1**

2151 **13** 3 1/4 **Scentasia**[17] 7349 3-9-9 **97**.................. RobertHavlin 9 74
(John Gosden) *s.i.s: hld up: plld hrd: hmpd 8f out: hdwy over 2f out: rdn and wknd over 1f out (jockey said filly hung left-handed and ran too freely)* **5/1**[2]

3112 **14** 10 **Geetanjali (IRE)**[31] 6854 4-9-1 **85**..................(v) OisinMurphy 10 41
(Michael Bell) *prom: rdn over 2f out: hung lft and wknd over 1f out* **20/1**

2m 9.24s (3.84) **Going Correction** +0.35s/f (Good)
WFA 3 from 4yo 4lb **14 Ran SP% 124.8**
Speed ratings (Par 96): **98,97,97,96,95 93,91,91,90,89 88,87,84,76**
CSF £35.37 CT £339.99 TOTE £3.30: £1.30, £3.90, £4.00; EX 55.70 Trifecta £644.10.
Owner W J and T C O Gredley **Bred** Stetchworth & Middle Park Studs Ltd **Trained** Musley Bank, N Yorks

FOCUS
Far side course used. Stalls: far side, except 1m4f: centre. The ground had dried out a little from the overnight good to soft, soft in places. A valuable and competitive fillies' handicap. Most of the principals raced prominently in a race which wasn't run at a strong initial gallop. A position near the rail proved advantageous, with the four lowest drawn all finishing in the first five. The winner progressed again.

7896 £150,000 TATTERSALLS OCTOBER AUCTION STKS 6f
2:15 (2:17) (Class 2) 2-Y-O

£81,165 (£33,210; £14,775; £7,365; £3,690; £1,470) **Stalls** Low

Form RPR
1454 **1** **Under The Stars (IRE)**[8] 7659 2-8-10 105.................. OisinMurphy 11 94+
(James Tate) *racd far side: chsd ldrs: carried lft and rdn to ld wl ins fnl f: r.o: 1st of 15 in gp* **5/4**[1]

1310 **2** *shd* **Mild Illusion (IRE)**[7] 7696 2-8-6 81.................. JosephineGordon 9 90
(Jonathan Portman) *led far side: led overall over 1f out: sn rdn and hung lft: hdd ins fnl f: styd on: 2nd of 15 in gp (jockey said filly hung left-handed in the closing stages)* **20/1**

1 **3** 2 1/2 **Bond's Boy**[42] 6457 2-8-7 0.................. PaulHanagan 8 84
(Richard Fahey) *racd far side: hld up: hdwy 1/2-way: rdn over 1f out: styd on: 3rd of 15 in gp* **13/2**[2]

4102 **4** 1 **Indian Creak (IRE)**[15] 7409 2-8-13 89.................. TomMarquand 12 87
(Mick Channon) *hld up: hdwy over 2f out: rdn and hung lft over 1f out: styd on same pce ins fnl f: 4th of 15 in gp* **22/1**

6042 **5** 1/2 **Keep Busy (IRE)**[7] 7679 2-8-8 80.................. JFEgan 5 80
(John Quinn) *racd far side: chsd ldrs: rdn over 1f out: no ex ins fnl f: 5th of 15 in gp* **16/1**

104 **6** 4 **Commanche Falls**[56] 5934 2-8-7 73..................(p[1]) AndrewMullen 18 74+
(Michael Dods) *racd stands' side: hld up: hdwy over 1f out: rdn to ld his gp ins fnl f: no ch w far side: 1st of 13 in gp* **66/1**

0426 **7** 1/2 **Lambeth Walk**[14] 7432 2-8-6 96.................. HollieDoyle 6 65
(Archie Watson) *racd far side: chsd ldrs: rdn over 2f out: wknd fnl f: 6th of 15 in gp* **8/1**[3]

00 **8** 1/2 **Acquire**[30] 6906 2-8-3 ow1.................. ThoreHammerHansen 10 60
(Richard Hannon) *racd far side: mid-div: pushed along 1/2-way: hdwy over 2f out: wknd over 1f out: 7th of 15 in gp* **100/1**

1115 **9** *shd* **Bettys Hope**[40] 6542 2-8-8 89.................. CharlieBennett 23 72+
(Rod Millman) *racd stands' side: hld up: nt clr run over 2f out: hdwy and swtchd rt over 1f out: nt trble ldrs: 2nd of 13 in gp* **22/1**

42 **10** *hd* **One Night Stand**[18] 7316 2-8-9 0.................. KieranShoemark 22 72+
(William Jarvis) *racd stands' side: hld up: hdwy over 2f out: led that gp over 1f out tl hdd and no ex ins fnl f: 3rd of 13 in gp (jockey said gelding ran too freely)* **25/1**

3254 **11** 1 1/4 **No Mercy**[27] 6997 2-8-13 77..................(t[1]) PJMcDonald 7 65
(K R Burke) *racd far side: hld up in tch: rdn over 2f out: wknd fnl f: 8th of 15 in gp* **50/1**

5035 **12** 1 1/4 **Emten (IRE)**[22] 7149 2-8-9 89 ow1.................. ShaneKelly 15 58
(Jamie Osborne) *racd far side: hld up: stmbld over 4f out: hdwy over 2f out: wknd fnl f: 9th of 15 in gp* **22/1**

0300 **13** 1 1/2 **Trevie Fountain**[15] 7419 2-8-12 68 ow3.................. MeganNicholls 1 56
(Richard Fahey) *racd far side: in rr: hdwy over 1f out: wknd ins fnl f: 10th of 15 in gp (jockey said colt hung left-handed throughout)* **100/1**

01 **14** 1 3/4 **Intimate Moment**[87] 4802 2-8-2 0.................. RayDawson 25 48+
(Philip McBride) *s.i.s: racd stands' side: hld up: effrt and nt clr run over 2f out: nvr on terms: 4th of 13 in gp* **40/1**

2623 **15** 1 1/4 **Seraphinite (IRE)**[36] 6667 2-8-6 77.................. EdwardGreatrex 29 48+
(Jamie Osborne) *racd stands' side: hld up: hdwy over 2f out: hmpd over 1f out: sn wknd: 5th of 13 in gp* **80/1**

1646 **16** 3/4 **Ebony Adams**[12] 7522 2-8-3 65 ow1..................(b[1]) MartinDwyer 28 43+
(Brian Meehan) *racd stands' side: chsd ldrs: led all over 3f out tl over 2f out: wknd fnl f: 6th of 13 in gp* **100/1**

1024 **17** *hd* **Don't Stop Dancing (IRE)**[32] 6845 2-8-9 84 ow2.................. RobertHavlin 24 48+
(Ronald Harris) *racd stands' side: hld up in tch: rdn over 2f out: wknd over 1f out: 7th of 13 in gp* **33/1**

6413 **18** 3 1/2 **Angel Grey (IRE)**[32] 6833 2-8-6 82.................. DavidProbert 3 28
(Andrew Balding) *racd far side: hld up in tch: racd keenly: rdn over 2f out: wknd over 1f out: 11th of 15 in gp* **11/1**

0341 **19** 1 1/4 **Craigburn**[19] 7284 2-8-7 63..................(p) CierenFallon 26 32+
(Tom Clover) *racd stands' side: hdwy over 3f out: nt clr run over 2f out: wknd over 1f out: 8th of 13 in gp (jockey said gelding was denied a clear run approximately 2 1/2f out; vet said gelding lost its right fore shoe)* **100/1**

3031 **20** 2 **Solemn Pledge**[10] 7584 2-8-8 68.................. HarrisonShaw 30 27+
(K R Burke) *racd stands' side: chsd ldrs: rdn over 2f out: wknd over 1f out: 9th of 13 in gp* **66/1**

004 **21** 1 3/4 **Flashy Flyer**[126] 3350 2-8-2 49.................. SophieRalston 14 9
(Dean Ivory) *racd far side: chsd ldrs: rdn and wknd over 1f out: 12th of 15 in gp* **150/1**

5011 **22** 1/2 **Bushtucker Trial (IRE)**[41] 6498 2-8-11 80.................. HayleyTurner 13 16
(Michael Bell) *racd far side: sn pushed along in rr: wknd over 2f out: 13th of 15 in gp* **33/1**

0 **23** *nk* **Uncle Sid**[18] 7316 2-8-7 0.................. RyanTate 2 11
(William Jarvis) *racd far side: hld up: wknd 2f out: 14th of 15 in gp* **100/1**

0060 **24** 3/4 **Hot Date**[46] 6313 2-8-2 42.................. RyanPowell 21 +
(George Margarson) *racd stands' side: led overall: hdd over 3f out: wknd over 1f out: 10th of 13 in gp* **150/1**

103 **25** *nk* **Silver Start**[119] 3573 2-8-2 76.................. DavidEgan 20 +
(Charles Hills) *racd stands' side: chsd ldrs: led overall over 2f out tl over 1f out: wknd fnl f: 11th of 13 in gp* **33/1**

5 **26** 1 **Bavardages (IRE)**[9] 7627 2-8-7 0.................. HarryBentley 4
(Mark Johnston) *racd far side: prom over 3f: last of 15 in gp* **66/1**

0 **27** 5 **Love Not Money**[9] 7605 2-8-2 0.................. RaulDaSilva 27 +
(Robert Cowell) *racd stands' side: chsd ldrs: rdn 1/2-way: wknd over 1f out: 12th of 13 in gp* **150/1**

0150 **28** 2 3/4 **D Day (IRE)**[23] 7119 2-8-7 83.................. KieranO'Neill 19 +
(Richard Hannon) *racd stands' side: pushed along and prom: lost pl 1/2-way: sn bhd: last of 13 in gp* **66/1**

1m 14.06s (2.16) **Going Correction** +0.35s/f (Good) **28 Ran SP% 132.1**
Speed ratings (Par 101): **99,98,95,94,93 88,87,86,86,86 84,83,81,78,77 76,75,71,69,66 64,63,63,62,62 60,54,50**
CSF £33.32 TOTE £2.20: £1.50, £5.20, £2.50; EX 27.40 Trifecta £242.40.
Owner Saeed Manana **Bred** Rabbah Bloodstock Limited **Trained** Newmarket, Suffolk

FOCUS
A huge field and the usual wide disparity in ability in this richly endowed sales race. They split into two groups and the first five home came from the larger group who raced centre-to-far side, with the principals drifting over to the stands' side in the latter stages.

7897 LETTERGOLD BRITISH EBF NOVICE STKS (PLUS 10 RACE) 1m
2:50 (2:52) (Class 4) 2-Y-O

£6,469 (£1,925; £962; £481) **Stalls** Low

Form RPR
1 **1** **White Moonlight (USA)**[29] 6928 2-9-3 0.................. OisinMurphy 5 93
(Saeed bin Suroor) *mde all: pushed clr over 1f out: comf* **5/1**

0 **2** 3 3/4 **Arthurian Fable (IRE)**[17] 7338 2-9-2 0.................. MartinDwyer 1 84+
(Brian Meehan) *hld up in tch: outpcd over 3f out: hdwy over 2f out: wnt 2nd fnl f: no ch w wnr* **100/1**

3 1 3/4 **Grain Of Sense (IRE)** 2-9-2 0.................. HarryBentley 10 80+
(Ralph Beckett) *s.s: rn green in rr: r.o ins fnl f: nrst fin* **33/1**

4 1 3/4 **Aquileo (IRE)** 2-9-2 0.................. DavidEgan 9 76+
(Roger Varian) *s.s: rn green in rr: hdwy over 1f out: nt trble ldrs (jockey said colt was slowly away)* **25/1**

5 1/2 **Shoshone Warrior (IRE)**[36] 6688 2-9-2 0.................. RyanMoore 4 75
(A P O'Brien, Ire) *hld up in tch: swtchd lft over 3f out: rdn over 1f out: styd on same pce* **7/2**[2]

6 1 **Duck And Vanish** 2-9-2 0.................. TomMarquand 6 73
(William Haggas) *hld up: pushed along over 2f out: nt trble ldrs* **20/1**

7 1/2 **Sly Minx** 2-8-11 0.................. HollieDoyle 13 67
(Mick Channon) *sn pushed along in rr: nt trble ldrs* **100/1**

8 *hd* **Fly Falcon (IRE)** 2-9-2 0.................. KieranO'Neill 8 71
(Richard Hannon) *hld up: hdwy over 3f out: wknd over 1f out* **50/1**

32 **9** 3/4 **Never Alone**[17] 7338 2-9-2 0.................. PJMcDonald 3 70
(Charlie Appleby) *chsd ldrs: chsd wnr 2f out tl rdn over 1f out: wknd fnl f* **15/8**[1]

10 4 **Al Khabeer** 2-9-2 0.................. JackMitchell 2 61
(Simon Crisford) *hld up in tch: pushed along and lost pl 1/2-way: n.d after* **20/1**

015 **11** 1 1/4 **Eshaasy**[35] 6727 2-9-8 90.................. RobertHavlin 14 64
(John Gosden) *chsd ldrs: rdn over 2f out: wknd over 1f out* **10/1**

142 **12** *nk* **Man Of The Night (FR)**[15] 7410 2-9-8 94........................ SeanLevey 11 63
(Richard Hannon) *chsd ldr tl rdn 2f out: wknd over 1f out* **9/2**[3]

1m 40.01s (1.61) **Going Correction** +0.35s/f (Good) 12 Ran SP% **121.2**
Speed ratings (Par 97): **105,101,99,97,97 96,95,95,94,90 89,89**
CSF £445.23 TOTE £5.10: £2.10, £25.40, £15.60; EX 491.10.
Owner Godolphin **Bred** Godolphin **Trained** Newmarket, Suffolk

FOCUS
An impressive winner of this novice event, although some of her market rivals were below par.

7898 KINGDOM OF BAHRAIN SUN CHARIOT STKS (GROUP 1) (BRITISH CHAMPIONS SERIES) (F&M) 1m

3:25 (3:25) (Class 1) 3-Y-0+

£151,344 (£57,378; £28,715; £14,304; £7,178; £3,602) **Stalls** Low

Form RPR

0121 **1** **Billesdon Brook**[64] 5608 4-9-3 106........................ SeanLevey 1 116
(Richard Hannon) *prom: hmpd and lost pl 7f out: hdwy and nt clr run over 2f out: rdn to ld wl ins fnl f: r.o* **16/1**

4341 **2** *1 ½* **Veracious**[85] 4885 4-9-3 113........................(t) OisinMurphy 4 113
(Sir Michael Stoute) *s.i.s: sn prom: led over 1f out: rdn and hdd wl ins fnl f: styd on same pce* **10/1**

4101 **3** *½* **Iridessa (IRE)**[21] 7221 3-9-0 116........................ DonnachaO'Brien 3 112
(Joseph Patrick O'Brien, Ire) *chsd ldrs: rdn over 1f out: styd on* **4/1**[2]

1201 **4** *1 ¼* **Lavender's Blue (IRE)**[35] 6726 3-9-0 107........................ RobertHavlin 6 109
(Amanda Perrett) *hld up: nt clr run over 1f out: r.o ins fnl f: nt rch ldrs* **8/1**[3]

3345 **5** *2* **I Can Fly**[21] 7221 4-9-3 112........................ SeamieHeffernan 9 104
(A P O'Brien, Ire) *s.i.s: hld up: hdwy on outer over 2f out: rdn over 1f out: no ex ins fnl f* **12/1**

261 **6** *½* **Madeleine Must (FR)**[30] 6910 3-9-0 105........................ HarryBentley 8 103
(H-A Pantall, France) *s.i.s: hld up: rdn over 1f out: nt rch ldrs* **25/1**

6124 **7** *1 ¼* **Laurens (FR)**[21] 7221 4-9-3 116........................ PJMcDonald 2 100
(K R Burke) *led: hdd over 1f out: wknd ins fnl f* **5/2**[1]

1202 **8** *nk* **Hermosa (IRE)**[21] 7221 3-9-0 116........................ RyanMoore 7 100
(A P O'Brien, Ire) *chsd ldr tl rdn 2f out: wknd ins fnl f (trainer could offer no explanation for the filly's performance)* **5/2**[1]

24-5 **9** *11* **Crown Walk**[41] 4-9-3 103........................ VincentCheminaud 5 74
(H-A Pantall, France) *trckd ldrs: plld hrd: shkn up over 2f out: wknd over 1f out* **33/1**

1m 38.01s (-0.39) **Going Correction** +0.35s/f (Good)
WFA 3 from 4yo 3lb 9 Ran SP% **117.7**
Speed ratings (Par 117): **115,113,113,111,109 109,108,107,96**
CSF £167.35 CT £772.80 TOTE £25.20: £4.80, £2.50, £1.70; EX 149.10 Trifecta £2453.00.
Owner Pall Mall Partners & Mrs R J McCreery **Bred** Stowell Hill Partners **Trained** East Everleigh, Wilts

FOCUS
The rates a below-average renewal but the winner came back to her best, with the second and third close to form.

7899 WEATHERBYS DESIGN AND PRINT NOVICE STKS (PLUS 10 RACE) 7f

4:00 (4:00) (Class 4) 2-Y-0 **£5,175** (£1,540; £769; £384) **Stalls** Low

Form RPR

1 **Kinross** 2-9-2 0........................ HarryBentley 10 101+
(Ralph Beckett) *s.i.s: hld up: racd keenly: hdwy over 3f out: edgd rt over 2f out: led over 1f out: shkn up and qcknd clr ins fnl f: impressive* **3/1**[2]

1 **2** *8* **Raaeb (IRE)**[22] 7151 2-9-8 0........................ OisinMurphy 3 87
(Saeed bin Suroor) *led: racd keenly: shkn up and hdd over 1f out: wknd wl ins fnl f* **5/2**[1]

33 **3** *3 ¼* **Finest Sound (IRE)**[17] 7338 2-9-2 0........................ DavidEgan 8 73
(Simon Crisford) *prom: chsd ldr over 4f out: rdn and ev ch wl over 1f out: wknd ins fnl f (jockey said colt hung left-handed throughout)* **10/3**[3]

4 *nk* **Al Qaqaa (USA)** 2-9-2 0........................ TomMarquand 13 72+
(William Haggas) *hld up: hdwy over 2f out: nt trble ldrs* **20/1**

5 *hd* **Vatican City (IRE)** 2-9-2 0........................ RyanMoore 14 72+
(A P O'Brien, Ire) *hld up: shkn up 1/2-way: nt clr run and swtchd lft over 1f out: edgd rt and r.o ins fnl f: nt rch ldrs* **4/1**

6 **6** *4* **Albert Edward (IRE)**[15] 7406 2-9-2 0........................ MartinDwyer 5 62
(Brian Meehan) *chsd ldrs: rdn over 2f out: wknd over 1f out* **25/1**

0 **7** *9* **Gigi's Beach**[17] 7346 2-9-2 0........................ PaulHanagan 6 39
(Hugo Palmer) *chsd ldrs: rdn and edgd rt over 2f out: sn wknd* **66/1**

0 **8** *nse* **Jadeer (IRE)**[14] 7458 2-9-2 0........................ DavidProbert 11 39
(Mick Channon) *s.i.s: hld up: plld hrd: hung rt and wknd over 1f out (jockey said colt hung right-handed throughout)* **66/1**

65 **9** *1 ¼* **Maximilius (GER)**[23] 7113 2-9-2 0........................ SeanLevey 7 36
(Ralph Beckett) *mid-div: drvn along over 4f out: wknd over 2f out* **66/1**

10 *2 ¾* **Big Jimbo** 2-9-2 0........................ ShaneKelly 1 29
(Gary Moore) *sn outpcd* **50/1**

0 **11** *hd* **Jungle Capers (IRE)**[15] 7406 2-9-2 0........................ HollieDoyle 9 29
(Mick Channon) *prom: rdn over 2f out: wknd over 1f out* **66/1**

12 *hd* **Captivated** 2-9-2 0........................ RobertHavlin 15 28
(John Gosden) *s.i.s: hdwy over 5f out: edgd rt and wknd over 1f out* **16/1**

0 **13** *12* **Theydon Bagel**[14] 7461 2-8-6 0........................ WilliamCarver(5) 2
(Peter Charalambous) *s.i.s: outpcd* **100/1**

0 **14** *4 ½* **Theydon Louboutin**[14] 7461 2-8-6 0........................ ThoreHammerHansen(5) 12
(Peter Charalambous) *s.i.s: sn prom: rdn over 2f out: sn wknd* **100/1**

0 **15** *6* **The Simple Truth (FR)**[41] 6504 2-8-13 0........................ MeganNicholls(3) 4
(John Berry) *sn pushed along in rr: wknd over 2f out* **100/1**

1m 26.02s (0.62) **Going Correction** +0.35s/f (Good) 15 Ran SP% **122.0**
Speed ratings (Par 97): **110,100,97,96,96 92,81,81,80,77 76,76,62,57,50**
CSF £10.46 TOTE £3.60: £1.50, £2.20, £1.30; EX 11.80 Trifecta £38.90.
Owner J H Richmond-Watson **Bred** Lawn Stud **Trained** Kimpton, Hants

FOCUS
An impressive, wide-margin winner of this novice stakes, in which they finished well strung out. The time was good, 1.42sec quicker than the concluding Class 3 handicap.

7900 BRITISH EBF PREMIER FILLIES' H'CAP 1m 4f

4:35 (4:38) (Class 2) 3-Y-0+

£31,125 (£9,320; £4,660; £2,330; £1,165; £585) **Stalls** Centre

Form RPR

4122 **1** **Specialise**[30] 6893 3-8-13 87........................ DavidEgan 10 95
(Roger Varian) *hld up in tch: nt clr run over 2f out: rdn over 1f out: styd on to ld wl ins fnl f* **9/2**[3]

5/ **2** *¾* **Melburnian (FR)**[22] 7170 4-8-7 75 ow1........................ TomMarquand 4 81
(A J Martin, Ire) *hld up: hdwy over 2f out: led over 1f out: rdn and hdd wl ins fnl f* **6/1**

1341 **3** *½* **Maybe Today**[24] 7075 4-9-10 92........................(p) RyanMoore 12 97
(Simon Crisford) *hld up: hdwy over 2f out: rdn over 1f out: hung rt ins fnl f: styd on* **7/1**

125- **4** *½* **Giving Glances**[224] 7696 4-9-3 85........................ DavidProbert 11 89+
(Alan King) *hld up: nt clr run over 2f out: r.o ins fnl f: nt rch ldrs (jockey said filly was denied a clear run)* **25/1**

3211 **5** *¾* **Oh It's Saucepot**[16] 7395 5-9-5 87........................ HollieDoyle 5 90
(Chris Wall) *chsd ldrs: rdn and ev ch over 2f out: styd on same pce ins fnl f* **4/1**[2]

1421 **6** *4* **Colony Queen**[17] 7343 3-7-9 74 oh5........................ AndrewBreslin(5) 13 72
(Steve Gollings) *hld up: hdwy over 4f out: rdn and ev ch over 2f out: wknd ins fnl f* **40/1**

3124 **7** *4* **Lightening Dance**[16] 7395 5-8-9 77........................(b) RobertHavlin 8 67
(Amanda Perrett) *s.i.s: hld up: effrt and nt clr run over 2f out: wknd over 1f out* **16/1**

54 **8** *nk* **Amourice (IRE)**[135] 3016 4-8-9 82........................ RayDawson(5) 1 72
(Jane Chapple-Hyam) *chsd ldr: rdn over 3f out: ev ch over 2f out: wknd over 1f out* **16/1**

221 **9** *1 ¼* **Strelka**[24] 7081 3-8-7 81........................ HarryBentley 7 70
(Ralph Beckett) *trckd ldrs: rdn and ev ch over 2f out: wknd over 1f out (trainer's rep could offer no explanation for the filly's performance)* **9/4**[1]

14-0 **10** *¾* **Koduro (IRE)**[16] 7366 3-8-6 80........................ AndrewMullen 3 68
(K R Burke) *hld up in tch: rdn and lost pl 3f out: wknd over 1f out* **66/1**

0503 **11** *nse* **Garrel Glen**[14] 7466 3-9-0 88........................ TomQueally 2 75
(James Eustace) *hld up: plld hrd: rdn over 3f out: n.d* **33/1**

5P-4 **12** *1 ¾* **Belisa (IRE)**[36] 6661 5-8-13 81........................ PaulHanagan 9 65
(Ivan Furtado) *led: rdn and hdd over 1f out: wknd fnl f* **50/1**

2m 36.14s (3.64) **Going Correction** +0.35s/f (Good)
WFA 3 from 4yo+ 6lb 12 Ran SP% **120.2**
Speed ratings (Par 96): **101,100,100,99,99 96,94,93,92,92 92,91**
CSF £30.92 CT £190.65 TOTE £6.40: £2.00, £1.90, £2.00; EX 38.40 Trifecta £337.20.
Owner Saif Ali **Bred** Newsells Park Stud **Trained** Newmarket, Suffolk

FOCUS
A good prize, and solid fillies' form.

7901 SAMANTHA COOPER FILLIES' H'CAP 7f

5:10 (5:11) (Class 3) (0-90,91) 3-Y-0+ **£9,056** (£2,695; £1,346; £673) **Stalls** Low

Form RPR

-004 **1** **Dutch Treat**[23] 7123 3-9-5 85........................ DavidProbert 5 93
(Andrew Balding) *hld up: hdwy over 2f out: rdn and r.o to ld nr fin (trainer said, regarding the improved form shown, the filly had benefited from running on the easier surface)* **16/1**

6533 **2** *nk* **Clara Peeters**[17] 7341 3-9-6 86........................ TomMarquand 6 93
(Gary Moore) *chsd ldrs: rdn to ld wl ins fnl f: hdd nr fin* **8/1**

340 **3** *1 ¾* **Material Girl**[28] 6974 3-8-5 71........................(v) HollieDoyle 12 73
(Richard Spencer) *pushed along early in rr: hdwy over 2f out: rdn over 1f out: styd on* **8/1**

6425 **4** *½* **Hunni**[22] 7165 4-8-8 72........................ JosephineGordon 4 74
(Tom Clover) *led: hdd over 5f out: chsd ldr tl led again over 2f out: rdn over 1f out: hdd and unable qck wl ins fnl f* **11/2**[2]

-632 **5** *nse* **Canton Queen (IRE)**[28] 6951 3-9-11 91........................ TomQueally 3 92+
(Richard Hannon) *hld up: pushed along 1/2-way: hdwy and nt clr run over 1f out: nt rch ldrs* **7/1**

0330 **6** *shd* **Amber Spark (IRE)**[16] 7366 3-8-11 77........................ PaulHanagan 1 77
(Richard Fahey) *s.s: pushed along in rr: r.o ins fnl f: nvr nrr (jockey said filly hung left-handed)* **20/1**

6336 **7** *shd* **Jungle Juice (IRE)**[12] 7514 3-8-6 72........................ DavidEgan 9 72
(Mick Channon) *hld up: rdn over 2f out: nt clr run over 1f out: r.o ins fnl f: nt trble ldrs* **28/1**

2233 **8** *3 ¼* **Rhossili Down**[91] 4655 3-8-8 74........................(w) HarryBentley 2 65
(Charles Hills) *hld up: hdwy 1/2-way: rdn over 1f out: wknd wl ins fnl f* **11/1**

306 **9** *½* **Praxidice**[14] 7471 3-8-5 71 oh1........................(t[1]) AndrewMullen 11 61
(K R Burke) *s.i.s: sn prom: rdn over 1f out: wknd ins fnl f* **16/1**

3-10 **10** *2 ½* **Clerisy**[141] 2806 3-9-5 85........................ RyanMoore 7 68
(Sir Michael Stoute) *hld up: nt clr run over 2f out: hmpd over 1f out: n.d after* **6/1**[3]

0513 **11** *1 ¾* **Warning Fire**[6] 7735 3-9-10 90........................ OisinMurphy 8 68
(Mark Johnston) *prom: nt clr run over 1f out: wknd fnl f (jockey said filly had no more to give)* **5/1**[1]

5266 **12** *2 ½* **Fabulist**[28] 6968 3-9-2 82........................(b[1]) RobertHavlin 10 54
(John Gosden) *racd freely: led over 5f out: hdd over 2f out: wknd over 1f out* **8/1**

1m 27.44s (2.04) **Going Correction** +0.35s/f (Good)
WFA 3 from 4yo 2lb 12 Ran SP% **120.5**
Speed ratings (Par 104): **102,101,99,99,99 98,98,95,94,91 89,86**
CSF £140.79 CT £1135.64 TOTE £20.90: £6.50, £3.00, £3.60; EX 209.10 Trifecta £1889.90.
Owner Mildmay Racing & D H Caslon **Bred** Exors Of The Late Sir Eric Parker **Trained** Kingsclere, Hants

FOCUS
Decent fillies' form.
T/Plt: £81.60 to a £1 stake. Pool: £98,358.65 - 879.12 winning units T/Qpdt: £32.40 to a £1 stake. Pool: £7,757.49 - 176.84 winning units **Colin Roberts**

7584 REDCAR (L-H)

Saturday, October 5

OFFICIAL GOING: Heavy (soft in places; 6.4)
Wind: light largely behind Weather: overcast

7902 ANDY CURTIS TRIPLE PARALYMPIAN 50TH BIRTHDAY EBF STALLIONS NOVICE STKS (PLUS 10 RACE) 7f

1:45 (1:48) (Class 4) 2-Y-0 **£4,851** (£1,443; £721; £360) **Stalls** Centre

Form RPR

3320 **1** **Embolden (IRE)**[22] 7140 2-9-2 79........................(v) TonyHamilton 6 79
(Richard Fahey) *mde all: racd keenly: rdn 2f out: strly pressed ins fnl f: drvn and kpt on wl* **7/1**

21 **2** *1* **Gravity Force**[15] 7398 2-9-8 0........................ CliffordLee 12 83
(K R Burke) *trckd ldrs: rdn over 2f out: drvn over 1f out: chal strly ins fnl f: one pce fnl 75yds* **11/1**

15 **3** *nk* **Duesenberg (IRE)**[15] 7398 2-9-5 0........................ SeanDavis(3) 3 82
(Richard Fahey) *hld up: pushed along and hdwy over 2f out: rdn to chse ldng pair appr fnl f: kpt on ins fnl f* **6/1**[3]

0 **4** *5* **Got The T Shirt**[15] 7398 2-9-2 0........................ ShaneGray 8 63
(Keith Dalgleish) *in tch: rdn 2f out: outpcd over 1f out: plugged on* **33/1**

6 **5** *1 ½* **Dilithium (FR)**[45] 6337 2-9-2 0 SamJames 4 60
(Kevin Ryan) *trckd ldrs: rdn 2f out: edgd lft over 1f out: wknd ins fnl f* **16/1**

020 **6** *¾* **Abbey Wharf (IRE)**[42] 6457 2-8-8 68 RowanScott(3) 1 53
(Nigel Tinkler) *midfield: rdn over 2f out: plugged on ins fnl f* **16/1**

7 *1 ¼* **Sports Reporter** 2-9-2 0 BarryMcHugh 2 55+
(Richard Fahey) *midfield: pushed along and sme hdwy 2f out: rdn and wknd fnl f* **4/1**[2]

2 **8** *1 ¼* **Vega Magic (IRE)**[27] 7000 2-9-2 0 TomEaves 9 51
(Kevin Ryan) *prom: rdn and edgd lft 2f out: sn wknd (vet said colt to be lame on its right hind)* **2/1**[1]

9 *shd* **Camouflaged (IRE)** 2-9-2 0 JoeFanning 5 51
(Mark Johnston) *wnt rt s: green in rr: sme late hdwy: nvr involved* **11/1**

10 *3 ¼* **I'm Easy** 2-8-11 0 GerO'Neill(5) 7 43
(Michael Easterby) *s.i.s: hld up: nvr threatened* **80/1**

00 **11** *½* **Twin Paradox**[16] 7361 2-9-2 0 BenRobinson 13 42
(John Quinn) *midfield: pushed along over 2f out: wknd over 1f out* **100/1**

0 **12** *1* **Starbo (IRE)**[19] 7285 2-9-2 0 RichardKingscote 14 39
(John Quinn) *hld up: nvr threatened* **66/1**

13 *4 ½* **Binyon** 2-9-2 0 GrahamLee 10 28
(David Barron) *midfield: pushed along 3f out: rdn and wknd 2f out* **66/1**

14 *9* **Itojeh** 2-9-2 0 NathanEvans 11 6
(Michael Easterby) *dwlt: a in rr* **100/1**

1m 27.2s (1.80) **Going Correction** +0.425s/f (Yiel) **14** Ran SP% **117.7**
Speed ratings (Par 97): **106,104,104,98,97 96,94,93,93,89 88,87,82,72**
CSF £78.32 TOTE £8.20: £2.20, £2.70, £2.10; EX 83.20 Trifecta £471.30.
Owner Peter O'Callaghan **Bred** Ringfort Stud Ltd **Trained** Musley Bank, N Yorks

FOCUS
Following a wet week the going was heavy, soft in places. This is usually a competitive novice event which has thrown up some very useful winners over the years, but this was probably just an ordinary edition. The first three finished clear.

7903 EVERY RACE LIVE ON RACING TV (S) STKS 1m 2f 1y
2:20 (2:20) (Class 5) 3-5-Y-O

£3,737 (£1,112; £555; £300; £300; £300) **Stalls** Low

Form RPR

5400 **1** **Lightning Attack**[16] 7363 3-8-13 72 TonyHamilton 7 72
(Richard Fahey) *in tch: trckd ldr gng wl over 2f out: rdn to chal strly over 1f out: led 75yds out: drvn out* **5/2**[2]

6305 **2** *1 ¼* **Indomeneo**[13] 7489 4-9-5 73 SeanDavis(3) 1 74
(Richard Fahey) *led: drvn and strly pressed over 1f out: hdd 75yds out: one pce* **4/1**[3]

0620 **3** *6* **Knightly Spirit**[12] 7513 4-9-8 57 JoeFanning 5 63
(Iain Jardine) *midfield: rdn along 3f out: wnt 3rd over 1f out: plugged on* **9/1**

1000 **4** *12* **Finniston Farm**[29] 6923 4-9-8 93 (p) RichardKingscote 6 41
(Tom Dascombe) *trckd ldr: rdn over 2f out: sn outpcd: wknd over 1f out* **5/4**[1]

0600 **5** *3* **Irish Minister (USA)**[36] 6663 4-9-3 56 (b) CamHardie 4 31
(David Thompson) *hld up: rdn 4f out: wknd 2f out* **20/1**

0-00 **6** *15* **Littlebitofmagic**[56] 5969 3-8-13 53 TomEaves 2 5
(Michael Dods) *trckd ldr: rdn along and lost pl over 5f out: wknd and bhd fnl 3f* **25/1**

000- **7** *1 ¾* **Newgate Duchess**[312] 9272 5-8-12 28 DougieCostello 8
(Tony Coyle) *a in rr* **100/1**

460/ **8** *2 ½* **Red Star Dancer (IRE)**[711] 8314 5-9-3 45 JamesSullivan 3
(David Thompson) *hld up in midfield: pushed along over 6f out: wknd and bhd fnl 3f* **66/1**

2m 11.99s (5.09) **Going Correction** +0.425s/f (Yiel)
WFA 3 from 4yo+ 4lb **8** Ran SP% **114.1**
Speed ratings (Par 103): **96,95,90,80,78 66,64,62**
CSF £12.44 TOTE £3.60: £1.10, £1.30, £2.10; EX 11.20 Trifecta £60.50.The winner was sold to Tony Newcombe for £12,000. Finniston Farm was claimed by Mrs S. V. O. Leech for £10,000.
Owner Peter Timmins **Bred** Mrs F M Gordon **Trained** Musley Bank, N Yorks

FOCUS
There was a wide range of abilities in this non-handicap seller and not surprisingly they finished well strung out. The favourite was clear top on ratings but ran well below his best.

7904 RACING TV REDCAR TWO YEAR OLD TROPHY (LISTED RACE) 5f 217y
2:55 (2:56) (Class 1) 2-Y-O

£99,242 (£37,625; £18,830; £9,380; £4,707; £2,362) **Stalls** Centre

Form RPR

1653 **1** **Summer Sands**[7] 7693 2-8-3 109 BarryMcHugh 8 92+
(Richard Fahey) *pressed ldr towards far side: pushed along to ld 2f out: pressed appr fnl f: drvn and kpt on wl to draw clr ins fnl f* **11/8**[1]

1112 **2** *2 ¾* **Troubador (IRE)**[45] 6356 2-8-12 101 PaulMulrennan 9 93+
(Michael Dods) *prom on outer of far side gp: rdn to chal strly appr fnl f: kpt on same pce ins fnl f and sn hld in 2nd* **13/2**

11 **3** *¾* **Desert Safari (IRE)**[10] 7569 2-9-0 95 RichardKingscote 4 93
(Mark Johnston) *racd far side: led narrowly: rdn and hdd 2f out: one pce ins fnl f* **6/1**[3]

1441 **4** *nk* **Aberama Gold**[15] 7399 2-8-6 81 ShaneGray 18 84+
(Keith Dalgleish) *hld up towards stands' side: swtchd lft over 2f out: sn hdwy: rdn and edgd lft towards far side gp 1f out: kpt on wl* **66/1**

42 **5** *2 ¼* **Amarillo Star (IRE)**[29] 6911 2-9-2 0 StevieDonohoe 11 87
(Charlie Fellowes) *swtchd lft after s to r against far rail: chsd ldrs: rdn over 2f out: outpcd ins fnl f* **40/1**

521 **6** *shd* **Hartswood**[19] 7285 2-8-9 78 SeanDavis 12 80
(Richard Fahey) *hld up far side: rdn over 2f out: kpt on ins fnl f: nrst fin* **33/1**

2104 **7** *shd* **Vintage Times**[21] 7182 2-8-1 76 DuranFentiman 13 72
(Tim Easterby) *midfield far side: hdwy and chsd ldrs over 2f out: sn rdn: wknd ins fnl f* **66/1**

1022 **8** *1 ¾* **Know No Limits (IRE)**[22] 7140 2-8-4 88 JamesSullivan 10 69
(Tom Dascombe) *midfield towards outer of far side gp: rdn over 2f out: no imp* **20/1**

0202 **9** *¾* **Clay Regazzoni**[4] 7778 2-8-9 76 (b[1]) SamJames 15 72
(Keith Dalgleish) *hld up towards far side: rdn over 2f out: kpt on ins fnl f: nvr a threat* **66/1**

1330 **10** *¾* **Dubai Station**[43] 6422 2-9-2 101 CliffordLee 6 77
(K R Burke) *trckd ldrs far side: rdn over 2f out: wknd fnl f* **10/1**

1301 **11** *nk* **Glasvegas (IRE)**[12] 7506 2-8-9 97 (p[1]) GrahamLee 1 69
(Keith Dalgleish) *chsd ldrs far side: sn pushed along: wknd fnl f* **5/1**[2]

2206 **12** *1 ¼* **Dylan De Vega**[15] 7400 2-8-12 92 TonyHamilton 2 68
(Richard Fahey) *midfield far side: rdn over 2f out: wknd fnl f* **16/1**

3220 **13** *3* **Leapers Wood**[27] 6997 2-8-9 79 TomEaves 14 56
(Michael Dods) *dwlt: a towards rr far side* **80/1**

4260 **14** *shd* **Kilham**[36] 6653 2-9-2 68 CamHardie 7 63
(Declan Carroll) *midfield far side rdn over 3f out: wknd 2f out (jockey said gelding was unable to get a desired prominent position having been slightly slowly away)* **150/1**

0030 **15** *1 ¾* **River Of Kings (IRE)**[10] 7582 2-9-2 59 (h) RowanScott 5 58
(Keith Dalgleish) *v.s.a: a in rr far side (jockey said gelding was slowly away)* **200/1**

2221 **16** *7* **Laikaparty (IRE)**[31] 6852 2-8-12 84 (b) AdamMcNamara 17 33
(Archie Watson) *racd stands' side: midfield overall: rdn over 2f out: sn wknd (trainer said gelding was unsuited by the ground and would prefer a quicker surface)* **66/1**

1401 **17** *2* **Praxeology (IRE)**[21] 7182 2-9-2 91 JoeFanning 16 31
(Mark Johnston) *racd stands' side: chsd ldrs overall: rdn 3f out: sn wknd (trainer's rep said colt was unsuited by the high draw which was away from the pace)* **40/1**

1m 12.6s (0.80) **Going Correction** +0.425s/f (Yiel) **17** Ran SP% **122.3**
Speed ratings (Par 103): **111,107,106,105,102 102,102,100,99,98 97,96,92,92,89 80,77**
CSF £9.69 TOTE £1.90: £1.10, £2.10, £2.80; EX 10.60 Trifecta £54.80.
Owner The Cool Silk Partnership **Bred** Koharu Partnership **Trained** Musley Bank, N Yorks

FOCUS
This wouldn't have been the most competitive runnings of this valuable event, but the winner is a classy performer and with the right horses coming to the fore, the form should work out. The main action took place on the far side with the first three all being drawn in single figures.

7905 RACING TV EBF STALLIONS GUISBOROUGH STKS (LISTED RACE) 7f
3:35 (3:38) (Class 1) 3-Y-O+

£28,355 (£10,750; £5,380; £2,680; £1,345; £675) **Stalls** Centre

Form RPR

0100 **1** **Main Edition (IRE)**[71] 5369 3-9-0 105 JoeFanning 1 111
(Mark Johnston) *prom: led 5f out: pushed along 2f out: in command appr fnl f: rdn out fnl 110yds: comf* **8/1**

3366 **2** *2* **First Contact (IRE)**[157] 2271 4-9-0 106 BrettDoyle 2 104
(Charlie Appleby) *trckd ldrs: pushed along to chse ldr over 2f out: drvn over 1f out: kpt on same pce and sn hld in 2nd* **3/1**[2]

5450 **3** *1* **Mitchum Swagger**[108] 3987 7-9-0 105 RichardKingscote 3 101
(Ralph Beckett) *in tch: rdn over 2f out: kpt on same pce in 3rd fnl f* **15/8**[1]

010 **4** *4 ½* **Makzeem**[70] 5413 6-9-0 104 (t) JasonWatson 5 90
(Roger Charlton) *dwlt: hld up: pushed along over 2f out: drvn and sme hdwy over 1f out: wknd ins fnl f* **7/2**[3]

5053 **5** *1 ¼* **Breton Rock (IRE)**[21] 7194 9-9-0 104 StevieDonohoe 4 86
(David Simcock) *hld up: rdn over 2f out: sn btn* **8/1**

2-20 **6** *¾* **Muntadab (IRE)**[7] 7701 7-9-0 105 PaulMulrennan 7 84
(Roger Fell) *led for 2f: remained cl up: rdn over 2f out: wknd over 1f out* **25/1**

1m 25.7s (0.30) **Going Correction** +0.425s/f (Yiel)
WFA 3 from 4yo+ 2lb **6** Ran SP% **108.1**
Speed ratings (Par 111): **115,112,111,106,105 104**
CSF £29.60 TOTE £8.30: £3.70, £1.60; EX 37.80 Trifecta £73.00.
Owner Saif Ali **Bred** Minch Bloodstock **Trained** Middleham Moor, N Yorks

FOCUS
A tightly knit Listed event with little between the six on official ratings. The pace was fair and the winner scored in good style.

7906 RACING TV STRAIGHT-MILE SERIES FINAL H'CAP 7f 219y
4:10 (4:11) (Class 2) 3-Y-O+

£28,012 (£8,388; £4,194; £2,097; £1,048; £526) **Stalls** Centre

Form RPR

2341 **1** **Give It Some Teddy**[18] 7312 5-9-0 81 DuranFentiman 4 90
(Tim Easterby) *trckd ldrs: pushed into ld over 1f out: kpt on wl: rdn out towards fin* **7/2**[2]

5000 **2** *1 ¾* **Kripke (IRE)**[27] 6998 4-8-13 80 TomEaves 11 85
(David Barron) *led: rdn over 2f out: hdd over 1f out: one pce ins fnl f* **7/1**

1522 **3** *hd* **Star Shield**[18] 7312 4-9-4 85 DavidNolan 1 90
(David O'Meara) *midfield on inner: pushed along 2f out: angled rt and chsd ldng pair jst ins fnl f: rdn and kpt on* **10/3**[1]

1203 **4** *¾* **One To Go**[12] 7512 3-8-0 70 oh3 (v[1]) CamHardie 2 73
(Tim Easterby) *trckd ldrs: n.m.r and angled rt appr fnl f: drvn and kpt on same pce* **14/1**

6530 **5** *½* **Zip**[28] 6961 3-8-0 73 SeanDavis(3) 8 75
(Richard Fahey) *dwlt: hld up in midfield: pushed along over 2f out: drvn over 1f out: kpt on ins fnl f: nvr trbld ldrs* **9/1**

6104 **6** *1 ¼* **Breanski**[18] 7312 5-9-2 86 FinleyMarsh(3) 3 85
(Jedd O'Keeffe) *hld up in midfield: pushed along over 2f out: rdn over 1f out: nvr a threat* **4/1**[3]

5344 **7** *4* **Creek Island (IRE)**[12] 7512 3-8-0 70 oh1 JoeFanning 7 60
(Mark Johnston) *prom: rdn 2f out: wknd ins fnl f* **20/1**

0066 **8** *2* **Hayadh**[18] 7312 6-9-4 85 PhilDennis 6 70
(Rebecca Bastiman) *trckd ldrs: rdn over 2f out: wknd over 1f out* **16/1**

0156 **9** *¾* **Universal Gleam**[14] 7434 4-9-10 91 GrahamLee 5 74
(Keith Dalgleish) *dwlt: hld up: rdn over 2f out: nvr threatened* **11/1**

2010 **10** *1 ¼* **Calvados Spirit**[21] 7212 6-8-11 78 TonyHamilton 12 58
(Richard Fahey) *dwlt and swtchd lft after s: a towards rr* **50/1**

1m 38.97s (2.37) **Going Correction** +0.425s/f (Yiel)
WFA 3 from 4yo+ 3lb **10** Ran SP% **115.4**
Speed ratings (Par 109): **105,103,103,102,101 100,96,94,93,92**
CSF £28.03 CT £89.84 TOTE £4.40: £2.10, £3.70, £1.30; EX 33.20 Trifecta £139.10.
Owner Lee Bond **Bred** Usk Valley Stud **Trained** Great Habton, N Yorks

FOCUS
Just a fair gallop to this series final in which they all raced over towards the far side and the winner was repeating his success of 2018.

7907 MARKET CROSS JEWELLERS H'CAP 1m 2f 1y
4:45 (4:45) (Class 4) (0-80,82) 3-Y-O+

£5,692 (£1,694; £846; £423; £300; £300) **Stalls** Low

Form RPR

4223 **1** **Olympic Conqueror (IRE)**[14] 7452 3-8-11 70 BarryMcHugh 1 80
(James Fanshawe) *trckd ldr: drvn to chal over 1f out: styd on to ld fnl 75yds* **11/4**[1]

330 **2** *1* **Railport Dolly**[16] 7379 4-9-4 73 (h) JoeFanning 2 80
(David Barron) *sn led: rdn over 2f out: drvn and strly pressed over 1f out: hdd 75yds out: one pce* **9/2**[2]

1043 **3** *1 ½* **Delph Crescent (IRE)**[10] 7589 4-9-2 **74**........................(p) SeanDavis(3) 3 78
(Richard Fahey) *in tch on inner: pushed and hdwy 3f out: drvn to chse ldng pair 2f out: kpt on fnl f* **7/1**[3]
6003 **4** *½* **Dance King**[9] 7625 9-8-13 **68**........................(t) PhilDennis 10 71
(Tim Easterby) *slowly away: hld up in midfield: pushed along and hdwy over 3f out: swtchd rt 2f out: sn drvn: kpt on fnl f* **12/1**
3340 **5** *3 ¾* **Detachment**[4] 7782 6-9-4 **73**........................ PaulMulrennan 14 69
(Roger Fell) *hld up: rdn along and sme hdwy over 2f out: kpt on: nvr a threat* **16/1**
5545 **6** *4 ½* **Stonific (IRE)**[12] 7510 6-9-13 **82**........................ DavidNolan 7 69
(David O'Meara) *midfield inner: rdn along and sme hdwy over 2f out: sn drvn: wknd over 1f out* **14/1**
1400 **7** *3* **Bit Of A Quirke**[21] 7185 6-9-2 **71**........................ GrahamLee 4 52
(Mark Walford) *chsd ldrs: rdn along over 4f out: wknd 2f out* **33/1**
5226 **8** *½* **Al Erayg (IRE)**[37] 6626 6-9-7 **76**........................(p) RachelRichardson 12 56
(Tim Easterby) *hld up: nvr threatened* **16/1**
1034 **9** *9* **Assembled**[51] 6129 3-9-2 **75**........................(p[1]) JasonWatson 13 38
(Hugo Palmer) *hld up in midfield: rdn over 3f out: sn wknd* **9/1**
0366 **10** *13* **Guildhall**[23] 7126 3-9-0 **73**........................(t[1]) RichardKingscote 9 10
(Ralph Beckett) *hld up: drvn 3f out: wknd* **14/1**
-000 **11** *16* **Jamih**[10] 7589 4-9-3 **72**........................ JamesSullivan 8
(Tina Jackson) *prom: rdn over 3f out: wknd over 2f out* **66/1**
1643 **12** *½* **Trinity Lake**[22] 7141 3-9-7 **80**........................ TomEaves 5
(Declan Carroll) *midfield: drvn over 3f out: sn wknd (trainer could offer no explanation for the gelding's performance)* **9/1**
0000 **13** *3 ¼* **New Look (FR)**[16] 7378 4-8-10 **65** oh1........................(b) DuranFentiman 6
(Tim Easterby) *in tch on outer: rdn along and lost pl over 4f out: sn wknd (vet said gelding had bled from the nose)* **40/1**

2m 11.77s (4.87) **Going Correction** +0.425s/f (Yiel)
WFA 3 from 4yo+ 4lb **13** Ran SP% **117.0**
Speed ratings (Par 105): **97,96,95,94,91 88,85,85,78,67 54,54,51**
CSF £13.52 CT £78.55 TOTE £3.00: £1.50, £1.90, £1.30; EX 14.60 Trifecta £34.80.
Owner The Cool Silk Partnership **Bred** M K & A Doyle **Trained** Newmarket, Suffolk

FOCUS
Mainly exposed sorts in this 66-80 handicap which was run at a fair gallop. Few got into it and they finished strung out.

7908 WATCH RACE REPLAYS AT RACINGTV.COM H'CAP 5f
5:20 (5:22) (Class 4) (0-85,83) 3-Y-O+

£5,692 (£1,694; £846; £423; £300; £300) **Stalls** Centre

Form RPR
4311 **1** **Fairy Stories**[12] 7511 3-8-12 **77**........................ SeanDavis(3) 3 87
(Richard Fahey) *trckd ldr: pushed into narrow ld over 1f out: drvn fnl f: kpt on wl* **9/4**[1]
-00 **2** *nk* **Jewel Maker (IRE)**[18] 7310 4-8-8 **70**........................ DuranFentiman 7 78
(Tim Easterby) *trckd ldr: pushed along to chal strly over 1f out: drvn fnl f: kpt on wl but a jst hld* **16/1**
2333 **3** *1* **Sheepscar Lad (IRE)**[9] 7624 5-8-2 **69**........................ FayeMcManoman(5) 8 73
(Nigel Tinkler) *in tch: pushed along over 1f out: kpt on in 3rd ins fnl f* **6/1**
0162 **4** *1* **Hawaam (IRE)**[9] 7624 4-9-5 **81**........................(p) CamHardie 2 82
(Roger Fell) *led: rdn and hdd over 1f out: no ex ins fnl f* **5/1**[3]
0030 **5** *2 ¼* **Lathom**[7] 7700 6-9-5 **81**........................ TomEaves 1 74
(Paul Midgley) *hld up: pushed along over 2f out: nvr a threat* **9/2**[2]
0663 **6** *hd* **Manshood (IRE)**[24] 7077 6-9-4 **80**........................(b) PaulMulrennan 5 72
(Paul Midgley) *hld up in tch: pushed along and n.m.r over 1f out: rdn and sn btn* **15/2**
0206 **7** *nse* **Tomily (IRE)**[7] 7700 5-9-7 **83**........................(p) DavidNolan 4 75
(David O'Meara) *chsd ldrs: rdn 2f out: wknd fnl f* **5/1**[3]

1m 0.11s (1.61) **Going Correction** +0.425s/f (Yiel) **7** Ran SP% **128.5**
Speed ratings (Par 105): **104,103,101,100,96 96,96**
CSF £39.75 CT £191.77 TOTE £2.60: £1.50, £6.20; EX 39.50 Trifecta £162.50.
Owner Richard Fahey Ebor Racing Club Ltd **Bred** Mrs Sheila Oakes **Trained** Musley Bank, N Yorks

FOCUS
Quite a competitive 5f handicap in which two dominated the closing stages and the progressive winner completed a hat-trick.
T/Plt: £78.80 to a £1 stake. Pool: £54,578.23 - 505.39 winning units T/Qpdt: £8.40 to a £1 stake. Pool: £6,005.20 - 525.22 winning units **Andrew Sheret**

[7853] WOLVERHAMPTON (A.W) (L-H)
Saturday, October 5

OFFICIAL GOING: Tapeta: standard
Wind: Light, half behind in nearly 2f of home straight

7909 CASH OUT AT BET365 H'CAP 1m 1f 104y (Tp)
5:30 (5:30) (Class 6) (0-55,55) 3-Y-O

£2,781 (£827; £413; £400; £400; £400) **Stalls** Low

Form RPR
600 **1** **Chamomile**[21] 7190 3-9-6 **54**........................ PatCosgrave 5 60
(Daniel Kubler) *t.k.h early: in tch: hdwy over 2f out: rdn to ld over 1f out: kpt on wl fnl f* **7/1**
0044 **2** *1 ¼* **Impressionable**[19] 7281 3-9-2 **53**........................(t) JaneElliott(3) 6 57
(William Muir) *slowly away and fly-jmpd s: hld up in last pl: hdwy on wd outside over 2f out: gd hdwy to chse wnr ins fnl f: r.o (jockey said filly missed the break and also hung right-handed off the final bend)* **14/1**
5020 **3** *hd* **Tails I Win (CAN)**[10] 7578 3-8-13 **52**........................ PaulaMuir(5) 8 55
(Roger Fell) *t.k.h: midfield on outside: hdwy and pushed along over 2f out: rdn and chsd wnr briefly ins fnl f: kpt on: hld nr fin* **9/2**[1]
1504 **4** *4* **Lippy Lady (IRE)**[18] 7295 3-8-13 **52**........................(h) RhiainIngram(5) 9 48
(Paul George) *hld up towards rr: stdy hdwy 1/2-way: rdn and outpcd over 2f out: rallied to chse clr ldng trio ins fnl f: kpt on: no imp* **12/1**
2054 **5** *nk* **Picture Poet (IRE)**[16] 7376 3-9-4 **55**........................ CierenFallon(3) 1 50
(Henry Spiller) *midfield: drvn along over 2f out: kpt on ins fnl f: no imp* **9/2**[1]
012 **6** *1* **Olaf**[20] 7228 3-9-6 **54**........................ KieranShoemark 4 47
(George Boughey) *led: rdn over 2f out: hdd over 1f out: wknd ins fnl f* **5/1**[2]
6606 **7** *1 ¾* **Transpennine Gold**[28] 6983 3-9-1 **52**........................(p) HarrisonShaw(3) 7 42
(Michael Dods) *t.k.h early: pressed ldr to over 2f out: rdn and wknd over 1f out* **9/1**
0006 **8** *hd* **Mr Spirit (IRE)**[35] 6731 3-9-0 **55**........................(p[1]) StefanoCherchi(7) 11 44
(Marco Botti) *dwlt and swtchd lft s: hld up: rdn over 2f out: no imp fr over 1f out* **16/1**
200 **9** *1 ¼* **Bumblekite**[87] 4794 3-8-11 **50**........................ TobyEley(5) 2 37
(Steph Hollinshead) *cl up: drvn along over 2f out: edgd lft and wknd over 1f out (jockey said filly hung left-handed under pressure)* **40/1**
3400 **10** *hd* **Bader**[20] 7232 3-9-3 **51**........................(b) JohnFahy 3 38
(Richard Hannon) *s.i.s: hld up on ins: rdn and shortlived effrt over 2f out: wknd over 1f out* **11/2**[3]

1m 59.57s (-1.23) **Going Correction** -0.15s/f (Stan) **10** Ran SP% **113.6**
Speed ratings (Par 99): **99,97,97,94,93 93,91,91,90,89**
CSF £97.13 CT £487.36 TOTE £7.10: £2.90, £2.60, £1.70; EX 90.30 Trifecta £511.90.
Owner Mr & Mrs G Middlebrook **Bred** Rabbah Bloodstock Limited **Trained** Lambourn, Berks

FOCUS
A moderate affair that went to a handicap debutante.

7910 BET365 NURSERY H'CAP 1m 142y (Tp)
6:00 (6:02) (Class 6) (0-60,63) 2-Y-O

£2,781 (£827; £413; £400; £400; £400) **Stalls** Low

Form RPR
0251 **1** **Inflamed**[19] 7277 2-9-8 **61**........................ PatCosgrave 11 68
(Ed Walker) *hld up on outside: hdwy 3f out: chsd ldr and rdn over 1f out: led ins fnl f: sn clr* **5/2**[1]
4032 **2** *4* **Grace Plunkett**[12] 7516 2-9-0 **53**........................(b) KieranShoemark 3 52
(Richard Spencer) *led: rdn 3f clr 2f out: rdn and hung lft over 1f out: hdd ins fnl f: no ch w wnr* **6/1**[3]
6565 **3** *shd* **Treaty Of Dingle**[19] 7275 2-9-3 **56**........................ CharlieBennett 5 54
(Hughie Morrison) *dwlt: hld up: rdn over 2f out: edgd lft and hdwy to take 3rd wl ins fnl f: r.o* **8/1**
4245 **4** *1 ¼* **Lexington Quest (IRE)**[19] 7277 2-9-9 **62**........................(b[1]) JohnFahy 6 58
(Richard Hannon) *s.i.s: hld up: hdwy and prom after 3f: effrt and chsd ldr over 2f out to over 1f out: no ex and lost 3rd wl ins fnl f* **11/1**
540 **5** *1 ½* **Wallaby (IRE)**[55] 5992 2-9-3 **61**........................ TylerSaunders(5) 10 54
(Jonathan Portman) *prom: drvn along and outpcd over 2f out: no imp fr over 1f out* **12/1**
0640 **6** *½* **Boy George**[52] 6071 2-9-5 **58**........................ CallumShepherd 7 51
(Dominic Ffrench Davis) *t.k.h: hld up: hmpd bnd after 1f: effrt and rdn over 2f out: no imp over 1f out: lost hind shoe* **18/1**
P000 **7** *hd* **Austin Taetious**[12] 7516 2-8-6 **45**........................(p[1]) RyanPowell 8 36
(Adam West) *hld up towards rr: drvn along over 2f out: effrt wl over 1f out: hung lft and no imp fnl f: lost front shoe* **80/1**
005 **8** *6* **Gifted Dreamer (IRE)**[57] 5907 2-7-13 **45**........................(w) IsobelFrancis(7) 4 24
(Mark Usher) *trckd ldrs tl rdn and wknd wl over 1f out (jockey said gelding hung right-handed in the straight)* **40/1**
0601 **9** *1* **Hermano Bello (FR)**[12] 7516 2-9-3 **63**........................(b) MarkCrehan(7) 1 39
(Richard Hannon) *in tch on ins: rdn and struggling over 2f out: btn over 1f out* **3/1**[2]
0000 **10** *6* **Lightning Bug (IRE)**[23] 7111 2-8-3 **45**........................ JaneElliott(3) 12 9
(Suzy Smith) *racd wd early: pressed ldr to over 2f out: sn drvn and wknd* **100/1**
0606 **11** *16* **Dark Side Division**[18] 7315 2-8-10 **52**........................(b[1]) CierenFallon(3) 9
(John Ryan) *t.k.h: prom: lost pl after 3f: struggling over 2f out: sn lost tch: t.o (vet said gelding was struck into on his left hind)* **16/1**
0005 **U** **Lafontaine (FR)**[12] 7516 2-8-1 **47**........................ ElinorJones(7) 2
(Sylvester Kirk) *s.i.s: t.k.h towards rr: sddle slipped and uns rdr after 2f* **16/1**

1m 49.88s (-0.22) **Going Correction** -0.15s/f (Stan) **12** Ran SP% **116.7**
Speed ratings (Par 93): **94,90,90,89,87 87,87,81,81,75 61,**
CSF £17.37 CT £106.54 TOTE £2.80: £1.50, £2.10, £2.70; EX 14.40 Trifecta £79.90.
Owner P K Siu **Bred** Theakston Stud **Trained** Upper Lambourn, Berks
■ Stewards' Enquiry : Ryan Powell four-day ban: interference & careless riding (Oct 21-24)

FOCUS
An ordinary nursery, but it was won in good style by a progressive sort.

7911 BET365 NOVICE STKS 7f 36y (Tp)
6:30 (6:32) (Class 5) 2-Y-O **£3,428** (£1,020; £509; £254) **Stalls** High

Form RPR
1 **San Rafael (IRE)** 2-9-5 0........................ JFEgan 1 72
(Mark Johnston) *mde virtually all: rdn 2f out: hld on wl fnl f* **9/1**
4 **2** *½* **Sunset Breeze**[9] 7627 2-9-5 0........................ RyanTate 12 71
(Sir Mark Prescott Bt) *t.k.h: early ldr: pressed wnr: rdn along 2f out: kpt on fnl f: hld towards fin (jockey said colt hung left-handed throughout)* **17/2**[3]
3 *hd* **Abwaaq (USA)** 2-9-5 0........................ JackMitchell 8 70+
(Simon Crisford) *t.k.h: sn chsng ldrs: drvn over 1f out: edgd lft: kpt on fnl f: no ex towards fin* **5/2**[1]
4 *nk* **Daysaq (IRE)** 2-9-5 0........................ KieranShoemark 7 70+
(Owen Burrows) *hld up: hdwy and angled rt over 1f out: kpt on ins fnl f: nrst fin* **7/2**[2]
5 *1 ½* **Emirates Currency** 2-9-2 0........................ WilliamCox(3) 10 66+
(Clive Cox) *dwlt: hld up: pushed along and green over 2f out: edgd lft and kpt on fnl f: bttr for r (jockey said colt was slowly away and ran green)* **16/1**
04 **6** *nk* **Fansurper (IRE)**[7] 7698 2-9-0 0........................ PaulaMuir(5) 3 65
(Roger Fell) *trckd ldrs: drvn along over 2f out: no ex fnl f* **50/1**
7 *1* **Bold Suitor** 2-9-5 0........................ PatCosgrave 6 63
(Ed Walker) *dwlt: hld up: rdn along over 2f out: kpt on fnl f: nvr able to chal* **10/1**
5 **8** *1 ¼* **Abnaa**[15] 7407 2-9-5 0........................ CallumShepherd 11 60
(Brian Meehan) *hld up: drvn along over 3f out: no imp fr 2f out* **7/2**[2]
60 **9** *nse* **Blairlogie**[14] 7453 2-8-12 0........................ GeorgeBass(7) 5 60
(Mick Channon) *hld up on ins: drvn and outpcd over 2f out: btn over 1f out* **50/1**
10 *½* **Bee Magic (IRE)** 2-9-5 0........................ LewisEdmunds 4 58
(William Muir) *dwlt: sn pushed along and in tch: drvn along over 2f out: wknd appr fnl f* **22/1**

1m 29.64s (0.84) **Going Correction** -0.15s/f (Stan) **10** Ran SP% **116.8**
Speed ratings (Par 95): **89,88,88,87,86 85,84,83,83,82**
CSF £81.64 TOTE £10.90: £2.80, £2.10, £1.50; EX 66.80 Trifecta £238.10.
Owner Middleham Park Racing XCIX **Bred** L O'Toole **Trained** Middleham Moor, N Yorks

FOCUS
A tactical affair in which it was an advantage to be handy.

7912 BET365 MAIDEN FILLIES' STKS 7f 36y (Tp)
7:00 (7:04) (Class 5) 3-Y-O+ **£3,428** (£1,020; £509; £254) **Stalls** High

Form RPR
1 **Kahala Queen (IRE)** 3-9-0 0........................ JackMitchell 3 63+
(Roger Varian) *dwlt: hld up in tch: pushed along and green over 2f out: hdwy over 1f out: kpt on wl last 100yds to ld cl home* **4/5**[1]

6234 **2** *nse* **Society Guest (IRE)**^{7} 7681 3-9-0 65 (v^{1}) CallumShepherd 7 62
(Mick Channon) *disp ldr: rdn to ld over 1f out: hung (lft) to far rail ins fnl f: kpt on: hdd cl home* **11/4^{2}**

0-32 **3** *1 ½* **City Of Love**^{9} 7608 3-9-0 74 DanielMuscutt 8 58
(David Lanigan) *trckd ldrs: effrt and wnt 2nd over 1f out: hdd and one pce last 100yds (jockey said filly hung left-handed under pressure)* **4/1^{3}**

4050 **4** *4 ½* **Caledonian Gold**^{14} 7470 6-8-9 43 (h) GavinAshton$^{(7)}$ 1 47
(Lisa Williamson) *led: rdn over 2f out: hdd over 1f out: wknd fnl f* **150/1**

6 **5** *2 ¾* **Petit Bay**^{52} 6074 3-9-0 0 RyanTate 2 39
(Sir Mark Todd) *hld up: drvn and outpcd over 2f out: n.d after* **20/1**

60- **6** *¾* **Santana Slew**^{298} 9490 3-8-9 0 (w) ThomasGreatrex$^{(5)}$ 4 37
(James Given) *t.k.h prom: rdn over 2f out: wknd over 1f out* **25/1**

7 *1 ¾* **Highland Sun (IRE)** 3-8-11 0 JaneElliott$^{(3)}$ 6 32
(Richard Phillips) *dwlt: bhd: outpcd after 3f: nvr on terms (jockey said filly ran green)* **66/1**

1m 27.85s (-0.95) **Going Correction** -0.15s/f (Stan) 7 Ran SP% **113.0**
WFA 3 from 6yo 2lb
Speed ratings (Par 100): **99,98,97,92,88 88,86**
CSF £3.11 TOTE £1.60: £1.30, £1.60; EX 3.20 Trifecta £5.70.
Owner Sheikh Mohammed Obaid Al Maktoum **Bred** New England Stud & Mount Coote Stud **Trained** Newmarket, Suffolk

FOCUS
A modest fillies' maiden, with the fourth limiting the level.

7913 BET365 H'CAP — 6f 20y (Tp)

7:30 (7:33) (Class 3) (0-95,97) 3-Y-O- £7,246 (£2,168; £1,084; £542; £270) **Stalls Low**

Form RPR

4341 **1** **Motagally**^{19} 7268 3-8-8 82 (b) KieranShoemark 3 96
(Charles Hills) *in tch: smooth hdwy to trck ldrs 1/2-way: rdn to ld ins fnl f: sn clr: readily* **13/2**

-501 **2** *2 ½* **Power Link (USA)**^{46} 6319 3-9-1 89 (p) CallumShepherd 11 95
(James Tate) *hld up towards rr: hdwy over 2f out: chsd (clr) wnr ins fnl f: r.o: nt pce to chal* **9/2^{1}**

0030 **3** *¾* **Intisaab**^{14} 7433 8-9-7 97 (vt) CierenFallon$^{(3)}$ 9 101
(David O'Meara) *dwlt: hld up: hdwy on wd outside over 1f out: edgd lft and wnt 3rd wl ins fnl f: nrst fin* **5/1^{2}**

5501 **4** *¾* **Walk On Walter (IRE)**^{21} 7175 4-9-7 94 (h) NicolaCurrie 10 95
(Jonathan Portman) *midfield on outside: drvn and outpcd over 2f out: rallied over 1f out: kpt on ins fnl f* **7/1**

3005 **5** *1* **Dream Today (IRE)**^{16} 7372 4-9-6 93 DougieCostello 6 91
(Jamie Osborne) *hld up on ins: drvn along whn nt clr run briefly over 2f out: hdwy and edgd lft ins fnl f: nvr able to chal* **8/1**

350 **6** *¾* **Watchable**^{21} 7193 9-9-6 96 (p) HarrisonShaw$^{(3)}$ 5 92
(David O'Meara) *sn led and hrd pressed: rdn along over 2f out: hdd ins fnl f: sn btn* **9/1**

2000 **7** *nk* **Junius Brutus (FR)**^{21} 7187 3-9-5 93 SilvestreDeSousa 2 88
(Ralph Beckett) *sn disputing ld: drvn along 2f out: wknd ins fnl f* **11/2^{3}**

0030 **8** *¾* **Reflektor (IRE)**^{62} 5705 6-8-9 87 ThomasGreatrex$^{(5)}$ 8 79
(Tom Dascombe) *early ldr: trckd ldrs tl rdn and wknd over 1f out* **11/1**

5100 **9** *¾* **Amplify (IRE)**^{28} 6954 3-9-1 89 LiamKeniry 7 79
(Brian Meehan) *hld up on ins: rdn over 2f out: wknd over 1f out* **33/1**

4006 **10** *1 ¼* **Moonraker**^{18} 7321 7-8-12 92 (p^{1}) MarkCrehan$^{(7)}$ 4 78
(Michael Appleby) *slowly away: bhd: struggling over 2f out: btn whn hung rt ins fnl f* **33/1**

46-0 **11** *16* **Restive Spirit**^{16} 7372 4-9-2 89 (p) JackMitchell 1 24
(Charlie Wallis) *prom: drvn and outpcd over 2f out: lost tch over 1f out: eased whn no ch fnl f* **80/1**

1m 11.59s (-2.91) **Going Correction** -0.15s/f (Stan) 11 Ran SP% **112.6**
WFA 3 from 4yo+ 1lb
Speed ratings (Par 107): **113,109,108,107,106 105,104,103,102,101 79**
CSF £33.82 CT £159.67 TOTE £5.90: £2.40, £2.00, £1.80; EX 38.30 Trifecta £181.90.
Owner Hamdan Al Maktoum **Bred** Whitsbury Manor Stud **Trained** Lambourn, Berks

FOCUS
A good sprint run at a strong pace and the winner impressed, posting a clear pb.

7914 BET365 FILLIES' H'CAP — 6f 20y (Tp)

8:00 (8:00) (Class 4) (0-85,86) 3-Y-O+
£5,207 (£1,549; £774; £400; £400; £400) **Stalls Low**

Form RPR

1243 **1** **Betsey Trotter (IRE)**^{16} 7380 4-9-12 86 (p) HarrisonShaw$^{(3)}$ 3 93
(David O'Meara) *trckd ldrs: effrt and rdn over 1f out: led ins fnl f: kpt on strly* **7/2^{2}**

1256 **2** *1* **Sundiata**^{84} 4926 3-8-12 70 KieranShoemark 2 74
(Charles Hills) *s.i.s: hld up: stdy hdwy over 2f out: rdn: flashed tail and chsd wnr ins fnl f: r.o* **8/1^{3}**

5023 **3** *½* **Chitra**^{21} 7206 3-9-4 79 CierenFallon$^{(3)}$ 6 81
(Daniel Kubler) *t.k.h: led: rdn along 2f out: edgd rt and hdd ins fnl f: kpt on same pce* **7/2^{2}**

0022 **4** *nk* **Turanga Leela**^{14} 7471 5-8-11 73 (b) TobyEley$^{(5)}$ 5 74
(John Mackie) *prom: effrt on outside over 2f out: drvn and outpcd wl over 1f out: kpt on ins fnl f* **3/1^{1}**

3114 **5** *1* **Lapidary**^{45} 6346 3-9-6 78 LukeMorris 4 76
(Heather Main) *t.k.h: pressed ldr: drvn over 2f out: outpcd appr fnl f* **7/2^{2}**

4550 **6** *5* **Alicia Darcy (IRE)**^{5} 7760 3-9-1 73 (b) AdamMcNamara 1 55
(Archie Watson) *s.i.s: hld up: drvn and outpcd over 2f out: edgd lft and wknd wl over 1f out (jockey said filly was never travelling)* **9/1**

1m 13.57s (-0.93) **Going Correction** -0.15s/f (Stan) 6 Ran SP% **112.8**
WFA 3 from 4yo+ 1lb
Speed ratings (Par 102): **100,98,98,97,96 89**
CSF £30.13 TOTE £4.10: £1.90, £4.00; EX 31.60 Trifecta £133.50.
Owner F Gillespie **Bred** James Hughes **Trained** Upper Helmsley, N Yorks

FOCUS
This looks ordinary fillies' form but a small pb from the winner.

7915 BET365.COM H'CAP — 1m 4f 51y (Tp)

8:30 (8:31) (Class 5) (0-75,75) 3-Y-O+
£3,428 (£1,020; £509; £400; £400; £400) **Stalls Low**

Form RPR

3431 **1** **Monsieur Lambrays**^{36} 6687 3-9-4 75 (b) JackMitchell 11 83
(Tom Clover) *trckd ldrs: wnt 2nd after 2f: led 3f out: rdn 2f out: kpt on wl fnl f: jst hld on* **4/1^{3}**

00-2 **2** *nse* **All Points West**^{9} 7625 3-8-11 68 LukeMorris 3 76+
(Sir Mark Prescott Bt) *in tch: pushed along briefly after 6f: hdwy to chse wnr over 2f out: rdn and kpt on wl u.p fnl f: jst failed* **3/1^{1}**

4105 **3** *3* **Beguiling Charm (IRE)**^{36} 6672 3-9-1 72 LiamKeniry 4 75
(Ed Walker) *in tch: effrt over 2f out: chsd clr ldng pair over 1f out: edgd lft ins fnl f: kpt on: no imp* **14/1**

0140 **4** *½* **Trailboss (IRE)**^{26} 7026 4-9-5 70 (v^{1}) StevieDonohoe 1 71+
(Ed Vaughan) *dwlt: hld up: rdn and hdwy over 2f out: kpt on fnl f: nrst fin (jockey said gelding was slowly away)* **14/1**

0342 **5** *½* **Dobrianka**^{29} 6931 3-9-3 74 (p^{1}) RobHornby 12 75
(Ralph Beckett) *racd wd early: led 2f: chsd ldrs: drvn over 2f out: no ex appr fnl f* **7/2^{2}**

4010 **6** *4 ½* **Valence**^{113} 3808 3-9-2 73 (p) EdwardGreatrex 10 67
(Ed Dunlop) *hld up in midfield: rdn along over 2f out: edgd lft over 1f out: wknd ins fnl f* **20/1**

1013 **7** *½* **Bug Boy (IRE)**^{23} 7116 3-8-12 70 (p) RhiainIngram$^{(5)}$ 8 63
(Paul George) *blkd early: t.k.h: hld up on outside: shortlived effrt over 2f out: wknd over 1f out* **16/1**

4200 **8** *nse* **Cherries At Dawn (IRE)**^{85} 4869 4-9-3 68 CallumShepherd 9 60
(Dominic Ffrench Davis) *dwlt: hld up: rdn along over 2f out: nvr rchd ldrs* **33/1**

1000 **9** *2 ½* **Tralee Hills**^{70} 5417 5-9-5 75 (p) TobyEley$^{(5)}$ 6 63
(Peter Hedger) *slowly away: in rr: drvn along over 2f out: nvr on terms (trainer said gelding missed the kick; jockey said gelding was never travelling thereafter)* **25/1**

0030 **10** *6* **Fume (IRE)**^{76} 5215 3-8-8 68 (h^{1}) JaneElliott$^{(3)}$ 2 48
(James Bethell) *plld hrd early: midfield on ins: rdn over 4f out: wknd over 2f out* **14/1**

0245 **11** *4* **Smiley Bagel (IRE)**^{131} 3155 6-8-12 68 KevinLundie$^{(5)}$ 5 40
(Mark Loughnane) *hld up on ins: rdn over 3f out: wknd over 2f out* **50/1**

0035 **12** *3* **Robert L'Echelle (IRE)**^{19} 7279 3-9-0 71 (b^{1}) CharlieBennett 7 40
(Hughie Morrison) *dwlt: hdwy to ld after 2f: rdn and hdd 3f out: wknd qckly wl over 1f out* **13/2**

2m 37.78s (-3.02) **Going Correction** -0.15s/f (Stan) 12 Ran SP% **119.9**
WFA 3 from 4yo+ 6lb
Speed ratings (Par 103): **104,103,101,101,101 98,97,97,96,92 89,87**
CSF £15.91 CT £156.11 TOTE £5.80: £2.00, £1.30, £6.30; EX 21.50 Trifecta £185.30.
Owner Exors The Late J T Habershon-Butcher **Bred** Glebe Stud **Trained** Newmarket, Suffolk

FOCUS
They went an ordinary gallop and few got involved, the first two having it between them from the turn in.
T/Plt: £79.50 to a £1 stake. Pool: £77,299.54 - 709.40 winning units T/Qpdt: £15.60 to a £1 stake. Pool: £10,946.42 - 518.0 winning units **Richard Young**

7916a - 7919a (Foreign Racing) - See Raceform Interactive

7884 KEENELAND (L-H)

Saturday, October 5

OFFICIAL GOING: Dirt: fast; turf: firm

7920a FIRST LADY STKS (GRADE 1) (3YO+ FILLIES & MARES) (TURF) — 1m (T)

10:04 3-Y-O+

£188,976 (£62,992; £31,496; £15,748; £9,448; £787)

RPR

1 **Uni**^{56} 5977 5-8-12 0 JoelRosario 4 113
(Chad C Brown, U.S.A) *hld up in rr on ins: plenty to do whn angled to outside and gd hdwy fr 2f out: sustained run to ld ins fnl f: sn clr* **3/1^{2}**

2 *2 ½* **Juliet Foxtrot**^{34} 4-8-12 0 FlorentGeroux 3 107
(Brad H Cox, U.S.A) *hld up in tch: smooth hdwy to chse ldr over 2f out: shkn up to ld over 1f out: drvn and hdd ins fnl f: nt pce of wnr* **83/10**

3 *1 ¼* **Vasilika (USA)**^{34} 5-8-12 0 (b) FlavienPrat 6 104
(Jerry Hollendorfer, U.S.A) *hld up in rr: last and plenty to do bnd over 2f out: gd hdwy over 1f out: chsd clr ldng pair ins fnl f: clsng at fin* **23/5^{3}**

4 *1 ½* **Rushing Fall (USA)**^{84} 4950 4-8-12 0 JavierCastellano 10 101
(Chad C Brown, U.S.A) *hld up midfield: hdwy over 2f out: effrt and chsd clr ldng pair briefly ins fnl f: sn no ex* **13/10^{1}**

5 *hd* **Hanalei Moon (USA)**^{35} 4-8-12 0 (b) TylerGaffalione 13 100
(Mark Casse, Canada) *stdd fr wdst draw and swtchd lft s: bhd and detached early: plenty to do over 2f out: gd hdwy and weaved through over 1f out: kpt on: nrst fin* **77/1**

6 *3 ¾* **Awesometank**^{21} 7225 4-8-12 0 JamesDoyle 2 91
(William Haggas) *hld up on ins: effrt and shkn up whn n.m.r over 2f out: no imp whn nt clr run briefly ent fnl f: n.d* **36/1**

7 *hd* **Just Wonderful (USA)**^{21} 7221 3-8-9 0 (h) WayneLordan 12 91
(A P O'Brien, Ire) *hld up on outside: drvn and outpcd wl over 2f out: sme late hdwy: nvr rchd ldrs* **18/1**

8 *¾* **Mitchell Road (USA)**^{28} 4-8-12 0 JulienRLeparoux 8 89
(William Mott, U.S.A) *chsd clr ldng pair: effrt and rdn over 2f out: edgd lft and wknd appr fnl f* **33/1**

9 *1 ¾* **Storm The Hill (USA)**^{28} 5-8-12 0 AdamBeschizza 9 85
(Philip D'Amato, U.S.A) *hld up midfield: drvn along 3f out: wknd over 1f out* **105/1**

10 *1 ½* **Ms Bad Behavior (CAN)**^{28} 4-8-12 0 JoseLOrtiz 11 82
(Richard Baltas, U.S.A) *led: drvn along and hdd over 1f out: wknd fnl f* **37/1**

11 *1 ¾* **Indian Blessing**^{42} 6491 5-8-12 0 JamieSpencer 7 78
(Ed Walker) *hld up on ins: shkn up whn nt clr run over 1f out: sn n.d: eased whn no ch ins fnl f* **212/10**

12 *1 ¾* **Marina's Legacy (USA)**^{32} 5-8-12 0 JesusLopezCastanon 5 74
(Aaron M West, U.S.A) *prom: drvn along over 3f out: wknd wl over 1f out* **108/1**

13 *11 ¾* **Conquest Hardcandy (USA)**^{42} 6491 5-8-12 0 JamesGraham 1 47
(Michelle Nihei, U.S.A) *pressed wnr and 3 l clr of rest: drvn along over 3f out: sn wknd: lost tch fnl f* **100/1**

1m 32.87s 13 Ran SP% **119.3**
WFA 3 from 4yo+ 3lb
PARI-MUTUEL (all including 2 unit stake): WIN 8.00; PLACE (1-2) 4.40, 8.20; SHOW (1-2-3) 3.00, 5.00, 3.60; SF 57.60.
Owner Michael Dubb, Head Of Plains Partners LLC Et Al **Bred** Haras D'Etreham **Trained** USA

7921a (Foreign Racing) - See Raceform Interactive

The Form Book Flat 2019, Raceform Ltd, Newbury, RG14 5SJ

7922a SHADWELL TURF MILE STKS (GRADE 1) (3YO+) (TURF) 1m (T)

11:15 3-Y-0+

£472,440 (£157,480; £78,740; £39,370; £23,622; £1,750)

RPR

1 **Bowies Hero (USA)**[47] 5-9-0 0 ....(b) FlavienPrat 5 109+
(Philip D'Amato, U.S.A) *midfield: hdwy on outside fr 2 1/2f out: rdn 2f out: drvn 1 1/2f out: styd on wl to ld 75yds out: drvn out* **41/5[3]**

2 ¾ **Diamond Oops (USA)**[70] 4-9-0 0 ....(b) JulienRLeparoux 7 107
(Patrick L Biancone, U.S.A) *led: hdd after 2f: led over 2f out: rdn 2f out: sn pressed: kpt on gamely: hdd 75yds out* **122/10**

3 *nse* **Suedois (FR)**[21] 7220 8-9-0 0 ....(p) JamieSpencer 12 107
(David O'Meara) *hld up towards rr of midfield: wd into st: rdn 2f out: drvn and styd on wl fr over 1f out: nt rch wnr* **20/1**

4 *nse* **First Premio (USA)**[35] 5-9-0 0 ....(b) MiguelMena 9 107+
(Mark Casse, Canada) *towards rr of midfield: dropped towards rr over 2f out: rdn 2f out: styd on strly fnl 150yds: nrst fin* **28/1**

5 *nse* **March To The Arch (USA)**[33] 4-9-0 0 ....(b) TylerGaffalione 11 107
(Mark Casse, Canada) *hld up towards rr: rdn 2f out: drvn and styd on wl fr over 1f out: nrst fin* **214/10**

6 *nse* **Next Shares (USA)**[35] 6-9-0 0 ....(b) CoreyJLanerie 1 107
(Richard Baltas, U.S.A) *towards rr: rdn and gd hdwy on inner fr 2f out: chsd ldrs ent fnl f: kpt on* **185/10**

7 ½ **Divisidero (USA)**[34] 7-9-0 0 .... JulianPimentel 13 106
(Kelly Rubley, U.S.A) *in tch in midfield on outside: hdwy to trck ldrs 2 1/2f out: rdn 2f out: ev ch appr fnl f: drvn ins fnl f: no ex fnl 75yds* **247/10**

8 ½ **Bandua (USA)**[55] 6001 4-9-0 0 .... AdamBeschizza 3 102
(Jack Sisterson, U.S.A) *trckd ldrs: rdn and pressed ldr 2f out: ev ch 1f out: no ex fnl 100yds* **32/5[2]**

8 *dht* **Van Beethoven (CAN)**[56] 5979 3-8-11 0 .... WayneLordan 2 105
(A P O'Brien, Ire) *midfield: rdn 2f out: kpt on fnl f: nt clr run fnl 100yds: nrst fin* **18/1**

10 1 **Valid Point (USA)**[56] 5979 3-8-11 0 .... JavierCastellano 4 100
(Chad C Brown, U.S.A) *in tch: rdn over 2f out: kpt on fr 1f out: nt clr run fnl 150yds* **11/5[1]**

11 *nk* **Admission Office (USA)**[111] 4-9-0 0 ....(b) JoseLOrtiz 6 99
(Brian A Lynch, Canada) *in rr rdn 2f out: styd on fr over 1f out: nt clr run fnl 150yds* **32/5[2]**

12 2¼ **Vintager**[34] 6770 4-9-0 0 .... JamesDoyle 8 94
(Charlie Appleby) *in tch in midfield: rdn over 2f out: wknd fnl 100yds* **108/10**

13 6¼ **Robin Of Navan (FR)**[27] 7007 6-9-0 0 .... FlorentGeroux 10 80
(Harry Dunlop) *towards rr of midfield: dropped towards rr over 2f out: rdn and outpcd fr over 1f out* **51/1**

14 8¼ **Real Story (USA)**[35] 4-9-0 0 .... JoeBravo 14 61
(Ignacio Correas IV, U.S.A) *led after 2f: rdn and hdd over 2f out: wknd 1 1/2f out: sn eased* **168/10**

1m 34.2s
WFA 3 from 4yo+ 3lb **14** Ran SP% **119.7**
PARI-MUTUEL (all including 2 unit stake): WIN 18.40; PLACE (1-2) 8.80, 13.00; SHOW (1-2-3) 6.60, 8.80, 11.80; SF 214.80.
Owner Agave Racing Stable, ERJ Racing LLC & Madaket Stab **Bred** Pope McLean, Pope McLean Jr & Marc McLean **Trained** North America

7477 LONGCHAMP (R-H)

Saturday, October 5

OFFICIAL GOING: Turf: very soft

7923a QATAR PRIX DOLLAR (GROUP 2) (3YO+) (GRANDE COURSE: 2ND POST) (TURF) 1m 1f 165y

12:30 3-Y-0+ £102,702 (£39,639; £18,918; £12,612; £6,306)

RPR

1 **Skalleti (FR)**[41] 4-9-2 0 .... Pierre-CharlesBoudot 6 113+
(J Reynier, France) *stdd s: confidently rdn in last pl: rdn and hdwy against far rail over 1f out: angled lft and led wl ins fnl f: kpt on* **31/10[2]**

2 ¾ **Mountain Angel (IRE)**[51] 6144 5-9-2 0 .... OlivierPeslier 3 111
(Roger Varian) *dwlt: t.k.h: led after 1f and dictated ordinary gallop: rdn and qcknd over 1f out: hdd and no ex wl ins fnl f* **77/10[3]**

3 1¼ **Line of Duty (IRE)**[27] 7007 3-8-11 0 ....(p) WilliamBuick 5 108
(Charlie Appleby) *prom: drvn and sltly outpcd 2f out: rallied appr fnl f: one pce fnl 100yds* **7/10[1]**

4 1½ **Leo De Fury (IRE)**[21] 7218 3-8-11 0 .... ShaneFoley 4 105
(Mrs John Harrington, Ire) *led at stdy gallop for 1f: chsd ldr: drvn along 2f out: kpt on same pce ins fnl f* **13/1**

5 ½ **Villa Rosa (FR)**[19] 7293 4-8-13 0 .... AlexisBadel 1 101
(H-F Devin, France) *trckd ldrs: drvn along and outpcd over 1f out: no imp fnl f* **87/10**

6 5 **Flambeur (USA)**[26] 7045 3-8-11 0 .... MaximeGuyon 2 94
(C Laffon-Parias, France) *hld up in tch: drvn and outpcd wl over 1f out: wknd fnl f: eased whn no ch last 50yds* **9/1**

2m 6.56s (3.66) **Going Correction** +1.125s/f (Soft)
WFA 3 from 4yo+ 4lb **6** Ran SP% **122.2**
Speed ratings: **117,116,115,114,113 109**
PARI-MUTUEL (all including 1 euro stake): WIN 4.10; PLACE 2.50, 2.80; SF 20.00.
Owner Jean-Claude Seroul **Bred** Guy Pariente Holding **Trained** France

FOCUS
The first of the Group races over Arc weekend hadn't been the best for British raiders in recent times, with John Gosden's Pipedreamer in 2009 that last non-French or German-trained runner to collect the prize. The official going was given as very soft and plenty of turf was being cut up during the race.

7924a QATAR PRIX DANIEL WILDENSTEIN (GROUP 2) (3YO+) (GRANDE COURSE) (TURF) 1m

1:35 3-Y-0+ £102,702 (£39,639; £18,918; £12,612; £6,306)

RPR

1 **The Revenant**[128] 3287 4-9-4 0 ....(h) Pierre-CharlesBoudot 2 118
(F-H Graffard, France) *in tch: stdy hdwy after 3f: angled lft and effrt 2f out: led 1f out: pushed along and sn qcknd clr: readily* **16/5**

2 4½ **Olmedo (FR)**[27] 7007 4-9-2 0 .... CristianDemuro 1 106
(J-C Rouget, France) *t.k.h: trckd ldrs: smooth hdwy to chal 2f out: sn rdn: chsd (clr) wnr ins fnl f: no imp* **9/5[1]**

3 ¾ **Shaman (IRE)**[27] 7007 3-8-13 0 .... MaximeGuyon 5 104
(C Laffon-Parias, France) *pressed ldr: led and rdn 2f out: hdd 1f out: sn one pce* **31/10[3]**

4 1¼ **Impulsif**[76] 4-9-2 0 .... MickaelBarzalona 4 101
(A Fabre, France) *t.k.h: led at ordinary gallop: rdn and hdd 2f out: outpcd fnl f* **13/5[2]**

5 3½ **Tauran Shaman (IRE)**[66] 5568 3-8-13 0 .... ShaneFoley 3 93
(Mrs John Harrington, Ire) *t.k.h: stdd in last pl: rdn and outpcd over 2f out: btn over 1f out* **12/1**

1m 43.9s (5.50) **Going Correction** +1.125s/f (Soft)
WFA 3 from 4yo 3lb **5** Ran SP% **119.4**
Speed ratings: **117,112,111,110,107**
PARI-MUTUEL (all including 1 euro stake): WIN 4.20; PLACE 1.70, 1.60; SF 15.30.
Owner Al Asayl France **Bred** Al Asayl Bloodstock Ltd **Trained** France

FOCUS
A small but classy field for this Group 2 contest, although the form can be picked apart due to some not handling the ground and the race becoming a sprint in the home straight.

7925a HARAS DE BOUQUETOT - CRITERIUM DE LA VENTE D'OCTOBRE ARQANA (CONDITIONS) (2YO) (GRANDE COURSE)(TURF) 1m

2:50 2-Y-0

£123,873 (£64,414; £34,684; £14,864; £2,477; £2,477)

RPR

1 **Into Faith (FR)**[36] 6669 2-9-0 0 .... Pierre-CharlesBoudot 9 81
(David Menuisier) *racd towards rr of midfield: pushed along rnd fnl bnd on inner: rdn to chal 1 1/2f out: sn qcknd: led ent fnl f: kpt on wl u.p* **228/10**

2 1¼ **Ceinture Noire (FR)**[30] 2-8-10 0 .... StephanePasquier 2 75
(R Le Dren Doleuze, France) **16/1**

3 *nk* **Luigi Vampa (FR)**[22] 7154 2-9-2 0 .... ChristopheSoumillon 7 80
(David Menuisier) *mostly racd in 3rd: pushed along 2f out: rdn to chse ldrs over 1f out: drvn fnl f: styd on wl u.p* **36/5[3]**

4 *hd* **Ladysane (FR)**[22] 2-8-10 0 .... AlexisBadel 14 74
(J Boisnard, France) **13/1**

5 ¾ **C'Moi Cesar (FR)**[45] 2-9-0 0 .... AntoineHamelin 6 76
(Laurent Loisel, France) **128/1**

6 ¾ **Gold Moonlight (FR)**[17] 2-9-0 0 .... AurelienLemaitre 13 74+
(F Head, France) **57/1**

7 *nk* **La Venus Espagnola (IRE)**[22] 2-8-10 0 .... OlivierPeslier 8 70
(C Laffon-Parias, France) **27/10[2]**

8 ½ **Shut Down (FR)**[34] 6776 2-9-0 0 .... IoritzMendizabal 3 73
(Mario Hofer, Germany) **26/1**

9 2½ **Torpen (FR)**[37] 2-9-0 0 ....(p) CristianDemuro 12 67
(P Monfort, France) **11/1**

10 *snk* **Secret Time (GER)**[27] 7006 2-8-10 0 .... MickaelBarzalona 11 63
(F Chappet, France) **13/5[1]**

11 2 **Tag (FR)** 2-9-0 0 .... MaximeGuyon 4 62
(F Rossi, France) **15/2**

12 *nk* **Bassmatchi (FR)** 2-9-0 0 .... SebastienMaillot 1 62
(C Boutin, France) **123/1**

13 2½ **Angela (FR)**[21] 2-8-10 0 .... TonyPiccone 5 52
(Miss V Haigh, France) **87/1**

14 1½ **Troilus (FR)**[27] 7005 2-9-0 0 .... TheoBachelot 10 53
(S Wattel, France) **12/1**

1m 46.08s (7.68) **Going Correction** +1.125s/f (Soft) **14** Ran SP% **120.2**
Speed ratings: **106,104,104,104,103 102,102,101,99,99 97,97,94,93**
PARI-MUTUEL (all including 1 euro stake): WIN 23.80; PLACE 6.40, 4.90, 3.20; DF 118.40.
Owner All For One Racing **Bred** The Kathryn Stud **Trained** Pulborough, W Sussex

7926a QATAR PRIX DE ROYALLIEU (GROUP 1) (3YO+ FILLIES & MARES) (GRANDE COURSE) (TURF) 1m 6f

3:25 3-Y-0+ £154,432 (£61,783; £30,891; £15,432; £7,729)

RPR

1 **Anapurna**[20] 7252 3-8-10 0 .... FrankieDettori 4 113+
(John Gosden) *mde all at ordinary pce: taken wd fr over 4f out: rdn over 2f out: edgd lft u.p wl ins fnl f: kpt on wl* **17/5[2]**

2 1¼ **Delphinia (IRE)**[23] 7118 3-8-10 0 .... ChristopheSoumillon 9 111
(A P O'Brien, Ire) *chsd wnr to 6f out: cl up: effrt and drvn over 2f out: blkd over 1f out: n.m.r and bmpd three times wl ins fnl f: kpt on to take 2nd last stride* **89/10**

3 *shd* **Enbihaar (IRE)**[23] 7118 4-9-3 0 .... JimCrowley 5 109
(John Gosden) *hld up towards rr: hdwy and prom over 3f out: rdn: edgd rt and pressed wnr 2f out: keeping on whn bmpd three times wl ins fnl f: lost 2nd last stride* **21/10[1]**

4 1¼ **Lah Ti Dar**[44] 6377 4-9-3 0 .... WilliamBuick 1 107
(John Gosden) *t.k.h early: cl up: chal over 4f out to over 2f out: drvn and one pce fr over 1f out* **7/1**

5 1½ **Pilaster**[63] 5663 4-9-3 0 .... MaximeGuyon 6 105
(Roger Varian) *hld up on outside: rdn and outpcd over 3f out: rallied over 1f out: kpt on fnl f: nvr able to chal* **37/1**

6 ¾ **Satomi (GER)**[35] 6747 3-8-10 0 .... IoritzMendizabal 3 106
(Markus Klug, Germany) *prom: rdn along over 3f out: outpcd fr over 1f out* **56/1**

7 1 **South Sea Pearl (IRE)**[23] 7118 3-8-10 0 .... Pierre-CharlesBoudot 8 105
(A P O'Brien, Ire) *hld up in rr: drvn along over 3f out: no imp fr over 1f out* **20/1**

8 ¾ **Musis Amica (IRE)**[20] 7252 4-9-3 0 .... MickaelBarzalona 7 102
(A Fabre, France) *hld up: drvn along bnd over 2f out: no imp fr over 1f out* **39/10[3]**

9 2½ **Mutamakina**[20] 7253 3-8-10 0 .... OlivierPeslier 2 100
(C Laffon-Parias, France) *hld up in tch: drvn along over 3f out: wknd wl over 1f out* **36/5**

3m 10.98s
WFA 3 from 4yo 7lb **9** Ran SP% **119.3**
PARI-MUTUEL (all including 1 euro stake): WIN 4.40; PLACE 1.70, 2.30, 1.50; DF 22.40.
Owner Helena Springfield Ltd **Bred** Meon Valley Stud **Trained** Newmarket, Suffolk

FOCUS
A race promoted to Group 1 status this season, plus with another furlong and a half added to the previous distance, this was mostly dominated by those who raced close up. Things got tight close to the line but the placings remained unchanged.

7927a QATAR PRIX CHAUDENAY (GROUP 2) (3YO) (MOYENNE COURSE) (TURF) 1m 7f
4:00 3-Y-O **£102,702** (£39,639; £18,918; £12,612; £6,306)

RPR

1 **Technician (IRE)**[21] 7196 3-9-2 0........................ Pierre-CharlesBoudot 2 108+
(Martyn Meade) *hld up: stdy hdwy over 3f out: effrt and chsd clr ldr over 1f out: sustained run to ld last 100yds: rdn out* **69/10**[3]

2 ¾ **Moonlight Spirit (IRE)**[34] 6773 3-9-2 0........................ WilliamBuick 5 107+
(Charlie Appleby) *led: qcknd clr over 3f out: rdn 2f out: edgd rt appr fnl f: hdd last 100yds: kpt on same pce* **8/5**[1]

3 2 **Iskanderhon (USA)**[23] 3-9-2 0........................ FrankPanicucci 1 104
(I Endaltsev, Czech Republic) *s.i.s: hld up: rdn and hdwy to chse clr ldng pair over 1f out: kpt on ins fnl f* **98/1**

4 2 **Muette**[23] 7137 3-8-13 0........................ MaximeGuyon 6 99
(A Fabre, France) *prom: drvn and outpcd over 3f out: rallied over 1f out: kpt on same pce fnl f* **76/10**

5 1 **Ashrun (FR)**[34] 6771 3-9-2 0........................ BauyrzhanMurzabayev 10 101
(A Wohler, Germany) *hld up in midfield: drvn along over 3f out: effrt over 2f out: no imp fr over 1f out* **23/1**

6 1½ **Golden Box (USA)**[23] 7137 3-8-13 0........................ ChristopheSoumillon 3 96
(A De Royer-Dupre, France) *hld up: effrt and drvn along over 2f out: no imp fr over 1f out* **14/1**

7 4½ **Nayef Road (IRE)**[21] 7196 3-9-2 0........................ FrankieDettori 8 94
(Mark Johnston) *prom: taken wd briefly 1/2-way: sn chsng ldr: drvn along 3f out: edgd rt and lost 2nd over 1f out: wknd fnl f* **31/10**[2]

8 2 **San Huberto (IRE)**[28] 6994 3-9-2 0........................ TonyPiccone 4 91
(F Chappet, France) *hld up: rdn along 3f out: no imp 2f out: btn and eased ins fnl f* **14/1**

9 3 **Dashing Willoughby**[21] 7196 3-9-2 0........................ JimCrowley 9 88
(Andrew Balding) *in tch: rdn along over 3f out: wknd wl over 1f out* **9/1**

10 5½ **Lucky Lycra (IRE)**[31] 6875 3-8-13 0........................ Francois-XavierBertras 7 78
(F Rohaut, France) *chsd ldr to 1/2-way: cl up tl rdn and wknd over 2f out* **23/1**

3m 19.86s (3.86) **Going Correction** +1.125s/f (Soft) **10 Ran SP% 119.8**
Speed ratings: **115,114,113,112,111 111,108,107,106,103**
PARI-MUTUEL (all including 1 euro stake): WIN 7.90; PLACE 2.40, 1.50, 11.10; DF 6.90.
Owner Team Valor 1 **Bred** Barronstown Stud **Trained** Manton, Wilts

FOCUS
Prior to the off the majority of this field could be handed good reasons for landing the prize, so this should be decent form.

7928a QATAR PRIX DU CADRAN (GROUP 1) (4YO+) (NEW & GRANDE COURSE) (TURF) 2m 4f
4:35 4-Y-O+ **£154,432** (£61,783; £30,891; £15,432; £7,729)

RPR

1 **Holdthasigreen (FR)**[83] 4962 7-9-2 0........................ TonyPiccone 8 115
(B Audouin, France) *mde all: rdn and qcknd over 2f out: hld on wl fnl f* **138/10**

2 ¾ **Call The Wind**[48] 6266 5-9-2 0........................ AurelienLemaitre 9 114
(F Head, France) *hld up: effrt and hdwy on outside over 2f out: chsd wnr over 1f out: edgd rt and kpt on fnl f: hld nr fin* **4/1**[2]

3 ¾ **Dee Ex Bee**[43] 6421 4-9-2 0........................ MickaelBarzalona 7 114
(Mark Johnston) *chsd wnr: drvn along over 3f out: outpcd and lost 2nd over 1f out: rallied ent fnl f: one pce fnl 100yds* **11/10**[1]

4 5½ **Who Dares Wins (IRE)**[77] 5183 7-9-2 0........(p) Pierre-CharlesBoudot 5 108
(Alan King) *hld up: rdn over 2f out: hdwy and edgd rt over 1f out: kpt on steadily fnl f: no imp* **15/1**

5 1¼ **Falcon Eight (IRE)**[43] 6421 4-9-2 0........................(p) FrankieDettori 3 107
(D K Weld, Ire) *t.k.h: hld up in tch on ins: effrt whn nt clr run briefly over 3f out: rdn over 2f out: sn no imp: btn over 1f out* **11/1**

6 snk **Way To Paris**[20] 7251 6-9-2 0........................ CristianDemuro 1 107
(Andrea Marcialis, France) *t.k.h: trckd ldrs: rdn over 2f out: wknd over 1f out* **11/2**[3]

7 10 **Cleonte (IRE)**[22] 7148 6-9-2 0........................ JimCrowley 4 97
(Andrew Balding) *midfield: effrt and drvn along 3f out: wknd over 1f out* **15/1**

8 4 **Mille Et Mille**[48] 6266 9-9-2 0........................ ChristopheSoumillon 10 93
(C Lerner, France) *t.k.h early: trckd ldrs tl rdn and wknd fr 2f out* **23/1**

9 20 **Line Des Ongrais (FR)**[27] 7008 8-8-13 0........................(p) MorganDelalande 6 70
(P Chemin & C Herpin, France) *hld up: drvn and outpcd over 2f out: sn btn: t.o* **68/1**

10 dist **Funny Kid (USA)**[71] 5409 6-9-2 0........................ MaximeGuyon 2
(C Ferland, France) *hld up on ins: rdn and lost pl qckly over 2f out: eased whn btn fnl 2f* **32/1**

4m 41.83s (23.83) **Going Correction** +1.125s/f (Soft) **10 Ran SP% 119.2**
Speed ratings: **97,96,96,94,93 93,89,88,80,**
PARI-MUTUEL (all including 1 euro stake): WIN 14.80; PLACE 2.10, 1.40, 1.20; DF 14.80.
Owner Jean Gilbert & Claude Le Lay **Bred** J Gilbert & C Le Lay **Trained** France

FOCUS
Despite there being a few in the line up who either usually lead or at least push the pace, the early gallop was moderate, which meant the winner had it all his own way and those held up had little chance.

7929a - 7933a (Foreign Racing) - See Raceform Interactive

6644 TIPPERARY (L-H)
Sunday, October 6

OFFICIAL GOING: Flat - soft to heavy; jumps - good to yielding

7934a COOLMORE STUD HOME OF CHAMPIONS CONCORDE STKS (GROUP 3) 7f 100y
2:30 (2:32) 3-Y-O+
£34,549 (£11,126; £5,270; £2,342; £1,171; £585)

RPR

1 **Yulong Gold Fairy**[122] 3521 4-9-2 100........................ KevinManning 9 102
(J S Bolger, Ire) *chsd ldrs in 6th early tl dropped to 8th after 1f: disp 6th at 1/2-way: pushed along and hdwy over 2f out: disp 2nd whn struck by rivals whip 1 1/2f out: sn rdn and kpt on wl to ld ins fnl f* **5/1**[2]

2 ¾ **Imaging**[129] 3287 4-9-8 107........................ OisinOrr 2 106
(D K Weld, Ire) *chsd ldrs: 4th 1/2-way: impr into 2nd gng wl under 3f out: rdn 1 1/2f out and kpt on wl to dispute ld briefly ins fnl f tl sn hdd: kpt on wl wout matching wnr nr fin* **7/4**[1]

3 ¾ **Crafty Madam (IRE)**[45] 6379 5-9-2 88........................(t) WJLee 6 98
(K J Condon, Ire) *hld up towards rr: 11th 1/2-way: rdn nr side under 2f out and hdwy: r.o wl nr side into nvr threatening 3rd cl home: nrst fin* **16/1**

4 1¼ **Psychedelic Funk**[5] 7794 5-9-5 99........................(b) ColinKeane 3 98
(G M Lyons, Ire) *cl up tl sn led: 1 l clr at 1/2-way: stl gng wl into st: rdn under 2f out: jnd and hdd u.p ins fnl f: no ex in 3rd wl ins fnl f: wknd into 4th cl home* **10/1**

5 2½ **Wisdom Mind (IRE)**[5] 7794 4-9-2 93........................(t) ShaneCrosse 8 89
(Joseph Patrick O'Brien, Ire) *in rr of mid-div: 8th 1/2-way: pushed along over 2f out and sme hdwy u.p 1 1/2f out: no imp on ldrs in 6th ins fnl f: kpt on in 5th nr fin* **16/1**

6 1¾ **Black Magic Woman (IRE)**[22] 7222 3-9-0 97........................ GaryHalpin 1 83
(Jack W Davison, Ire) *broke wl and prom early tl sn settled bhd ldrs: pushed along and disp 6th fr 1/2-way: sme hdwy to dispute 4th 2f out: no imp on ldrs u.p 1 1/2f out: one pce fnl f: jst hld 6th (jockey said that his mount did not handle todays ground)* **10/1**

7 shd **Quizical (IRE)**[8] 7716 4-9-5 90........................ RobbieColgan 5 87
(Ms Sheila Lavery, Ire) *mid-div early: 9th 1/2-way: rdn over 2f out: sme hdwy u.p far side under 2f out: no ex disputing 6th ins fnl f: kpt on again in 7th nr fin: jst failed for 6th* **22/1**

8 4¾ **Saltonstall**[21] 7248 5-9-5 97........................(tp) ChrisHayes 10 75
(Adrian McGuinness, Ire) *mid-div: impr to chse ldrs after 1f: clsr in 3rd bef 1/2-way: pushed along bhd ldrs under 3f out and no ex 2f out where rdn: wknd* **8/1**[3]

9 hd **Bowerman**[10] 7637 5-9-5 98........................ DeclanMcDonogh 12 75
(Adrian McGuinness, Ire) *s.i.s and pushed along in rr early: tk clsr order after 1f: pushed along in 10th fr bef 1/2-way: no imp u.p in rr over 2f out: kpt on one pce fnl 2f* **12/1**

10 6 **Chocolate Music (IRE)**[50] 6235 3-9-0 93........................ NGMcCullagh 11 56
(Mrs John Harrington, Ire) *hld up towards rr: last at 1/2-way: pushed along and no imp over 2f out: nvr a factor* **50/1**

11 12 **On A Session (USA)**[37] 6693 3-9-3 95........................ LeighRoche 4 29
(Aidan F Fogarty, Ire) *chsd ldrs: 5th 1/2-way: pushed along over 2f out and sn wknd: eased ins fnl f* **16/1**

12 22 **Dubai Dominion**[31] 6894 3-9-3 99........................(b) SeamieHeffernan 7
(Ed Vaughan) *sn led briefly tl hdd and settled bhd ldr: pushed along in 2nd fr 1/2-way and wknd into st: eased over 1f out* **12/1**

1m 43.45s
WFA 3 from 4yo+ 2lb **12 Ran SP% 121.7**
CSF £14.43 TOTE £6.00: £1.50, £1.30, £4.60; DF 15.10 Trifecta £254.60.
Owner Zhang Yuesheng **Bred** Lady Fairhaven **Trained** Coolcullen, Co Carlow

FOCUS
Back-to-back wins in this race for Yulong Gold Fairy, who was making an immediate impact for this stable. The second, third and fourth set the standard.

7935 - 7936a (Foreign Racing) - See Raceform Interactive

7499 COLOGNE (R-H)
Sunday, October 6

OFFICIAL GOING: Turf: soft

7937a PREIS DES WINTERFAVORITEN (GROUP 3) (2YO) (TURF) 1m
4:00 2-Y-O **£76,576** (£27,927; £18,468; £9,279; £4,954)

RPR

1 **Rubaiyat (FR)**[28] 7004 2-9-2 0........................ ClementLecoeuvre 7 111
(Henk Grewe, Germany) *racd a little keenly early: hld up in fnl trio: pushed along to chal 2f out: rdn over 1f out: responded for press to ld jst ins fnl f: kpt on strly clsng stages* **6/5**[1]

2 ¾ **Wonderful Moon (GER)**[70] 2-9-2 0........................ BauyrzhanMurzabayev 6 109+
(Henk Grewe, Germany) *stmbld bdly leaving stalls: rcvrd to trck ldr after 2f: led jst under 3f out: sn asked to qckn: pressed over 1f out: hdd jst ins fnl f: kpt on but a hld* **17/10**[2]

3 11¼ **Palao (GER)** 2-9-2 0........................ MartinSeidl 5 85
(Markus Klug, Germany) *in tch: pushed along over 3f out: limited rspnse and sn rdn: kpt on into v modest 3rd ins fnl f: nvr threatened* **17/2**

4 1½ **Palimero (GER)** 2-9-2 0........................ LukasDelozier 3 81
(Mario Hofer, Germany) *hld up in rr: effrt over 3f out: stmbld whn making sme hdwy 2f out: sn one pce: lost 3rd ins fnl f* **68/10**

5 6 **More No Never (GER)** 2-9-2 0........................ MichaelCadeddu 4 68
(Jean-Pierre Carvalho, Germany) *led: hdd jst under 3f out: sn drvn: dropped to rr over 1f out: eased ins fnl f* **63/10**[3]

1m 41.52s (3.13) **5 Ran SP% 119.5**
PARI-MUTUEL (all including 1 euro stake): WIN 2.20 PLACE: 1.30, 1.40; SF: 3.20.
Owner Darius Racing **Bred** Gestut Karlshof **Trained** Germany

7938 - (Foreign Racing) - See Raceform Interactive

7923 LONGCHAMP (R-H)
Sunday, October 6

OFFICIAL GOING: Turf: very soft

7939a QATAR PRIX MARCEL BOUSSAC - CRITERIUM DES POULICHES (GROUP 1) (2YO FILLIES) (GRANDE COURSE) (TURF) 1m
1:15 2-Y-O **£205,909** (£82,378; £41,189; £20,576; £10,306)

RPR

1 **Albigna (IRE)**[21] 7244 2-8-11 0........................ ShaneFoley 7 112+
(Mrs John Harrington, Ire) *in tch: hdwy on outer 2 1/2f out: rdn sn after: r.o to go 2nd ent fnl f: led 1/2f out: drew clr clsng stages* **42/10**[3]

2 2½ **Marieta (FR)**[50] 6248 2-8-11 0........................ TonyPiccone 3 107
(M Delcher Sanchez, France) *led: rdn to assert 2f out and briefly extended advantage: no ex whn hdd 1/2f out: hld on for 2nd* **58/10**

3 ½ **Flighty Lady (IRE)**[28] 7006 2-8-11 0........................ MaximeGuyon 5 105
(Gavin Hernon, France) *chsd ldrs: asked for effrt 2 1/2f out: moved to ins rail 1 1/2f out: r.o for 3rd ins fnl f: nt quite make 2nd* **9/1**

4 1½ **Bionic Woman (IRE)**[23] 2-8-11 0........................ MickaelBarzalona 2 102
(A Fabre, France) *trckd ldr in 2nd: briefly lost position nring 1/2-way: reclaimed 2nd and shkn up 2f out: no imp on ldr: one pce ins fnl f* **42/10**[3]

5 1 **Plegastell (FR)**[36] 6750 2-8-11 0........................ Pierre-CharlesBoudot 1 100
(Edouard Monfort, France) *chsd ldr on inner: rdn to chal 2f out: no imp: wknd ins fnl f* **41/10**[2]

6 6 ½ **Fee Historique (FR)**[31] 2-8-11 0........................ GregoryBenoist 6 86
(Hiroo Shimizu, France) *towards rr on inner: effrt over 2f out: kpt on for mild prog ins fnl f: nvr trbld ldrs* **83/1**

7 ¾ **Savarin (JPN)**[28] 7006 2-8-11 0........................ YutakaTake 4 84
(A Fabre, France) *mid-div on inner: rdn 2f out: no imp* **14/5**[1]

8 3 ½ **Kenlova (FR)**[28] 7006 2-8-11 0........................ TheoBachelot 8 76
(P Bary, France) *a in rr: nvr involved* **17/1**

9 dist **Nunzia (FR)**[28] 7006 2-8-11 0........................ ChristopheSoumillon 9
(F Vermeulen, France) *plld hrd in rr: sn moved up on outer to go 2nd appr 1/2-way: qckly lost grnd 3f out: eased and t.o* **26/1**

1m 41.26s (2.86) **Going Correction** +0.775s/f (Yiel) 9 Ran SP% **119.5**
Speed ratings: **116,113,113,111,110 104,103,99,**
PARI-MUTUEL (all including 1 euro stake): WIN 5.20; PLACE 2.00, 2.10, 2.50; DF 17.60.
Owner Niarchos Family **Bred** Niarchos Family **Trained** Moone, Co Kildare

FOCUS
This has been won by some good horses, most notably Found in the past decade. This latest winner rates to the ten-year par. The early leader made this a decent enough gallop, so the form should be reliable in similar ground. Jockeys who rode in the first race described the going as a mixture of soft and heavy.

7940a QATAR PRIX JEAN-LUC LAGARDERE SPONSORISE PAR MANATEQ (GROUP 1) (2YO COLTS & FILLIES) (GRANDE COURSE) 1m

1:50 2-Y-0 **£205,909** (£82,378; £41,189; £20,576; £10,306)

RPR

1 **Victor Ludorum**[22] 2-9-0 0........................ MickaelBarzalona 4 113+
(A Fabre, France) *in tch in midfield: rdn and hdwy fr under 2f out: led 100yds out: kpt on strly: readily* **9/5**[1]

2 ¾ **Alson (GER)**[36] 6746 2-9-0 0........................ FrankieDettori 1 111
(Jean-Pierre Carvalho, Germany) *racd keenly: led: rdn 2f out: hdd 100yds out: kpt on* **87/10**

3 snk **Armory (IRE)**[21] 7245 2-9-0 0........................ RyanMoore 5 111
(A P O'Brien, Ire) *chsd ldr: rdn 2f out: ev ch over 1f out: kpt on fnl f* **11/5**[2]

4 snk **Ecrivain (FR)**[28] 7005 2-9-0 0........................ MaximeGuyon 3 111
(C Laffon-Parias, France) *trckd ldrs: rdn and effrt 2f out: kpt on tl no ex fnl 50yds* **19/5**[3]

5 nk **Helter Skelter (FR)**[50] 6251 2-9-0 0........................ YutakaTake 7 110+
(J-C Rouget, France) *hld up in rr: pushed along and kpt on wl fr 1 1/2f out: nrst fin* **13/1**

6 4 ½ **Chachnak (FR)**[31] 2-9-0 0........................ CristianDemuro 6 100
(F Vermeulen, France) *hld up: rdn and no imp fr 2f out* **32/1**

7 1 ¼ **Kenway (FR)**[35] 6777 2-9-0 0........................ Pierre-CharlesBoudot 2 97
(F Rossi, France) *towards rr of midfield: rdn under 2f out: wknd fnl f* **8/1**

1m 44.15s (5.75) **Going Correction** +0.775s/f (Yiel) 7 Ran SP% **119.4**
Speed ratings: **102,101,101,100,100 96,94**
PARI-MUTUEL (all including 1 euro stake): WIN 2.80; PLACE 1.90, 3.70; SF 18.90.
Owner Godolphin SNC **Bred** Godolphin **Trained** Chantilly, France

FOCUS
The runner-up set a modest pace and the time was almost three seconds slower than the Prix Marcel Boussac. It's hard to be overly positive about this result considering five finished on top of each other, so it remains to be seen quite how good the unexposed winner turns out to be. His RPR is among the lower end of what has been achieved in the past decade as a result, in line with a similar horse Ultra, who was owned, trained and ridden by the same connections.

7941a QATAR PRIX DE L'ARC DE TRIOMPHE (GROUP 1) (3YO+) (GRANDE COURSE) (TURF) 1m 4f

3:05 3-Y-0+ **£2,573,873** (£1,029,729; £514,864; £257,207; £128,828)

RPR

1 **Waldgeist**[21] 7251 5-9-5 0........................ Pierre-CharlesBoudot 3 128
(A Fabre, France) *hld up towards rr of midfield: rdn and hdwy fr over 2f out: swtchd to outside 1 1/2f out: styd on wl to ld 50yds out: rdn out* **131/10**

2 1 ¾ **Enable**[45] 6377 5-9-2 0........................ FrankieDettori 9 123
(John Gosden) *in tch: trckd ldrs 3f out: rdn to ld 2f out: drvn 1 1/2f out: hdd 50yds out: sn no ex* **1/2**[1]

3 1 ¾ **Sottsass (FR)**[21] 7253 3-8-13 0........................ CristianDemuro 1 123
(J-C Rouget, France) *in tch in midfield: hdwy to chse ldrs appr 2f out: sn rdn: drvn and kpt on same pce fr 1 1/2f out* **66/10**[2]

4 ½ **Japan**[46] 6354 3-8-13 0........................ RyanMoore 10 123
(A P O'Brien, Ire) *hld up towards rr of midfield: rdn and hdwy on outside fr under 3f out: chsd ldrs 1 1/2f out: sn drvn: kpt on same pce* **9/1**[3]

5 6 **Magical (IRE)**[22] 7219 4-9-2 0........................ DonnachaO'Brien 8 109+
(A P O'Brien, Ire) *chsd ldr: led gng wl 2 1/2f out: rdn and hdd 2f out: wknd 1 1/2f out* **19/1**

6 3 ½ **Soft Light (FR)**[42] 6522 3-8-13 0........................ YutakaTake 6 107
(J-C Rouget, France) *dwlt: towards rr: pushed along and kpt on steadily fr 2 1/2f out: n.d* **85/1**

7 8 **Kiseki (JPN)**[21] 7251 5-9-5 0........................ ChristopheSoumillon 7 94
(Katsuhiko Sumii, Japan) *towards rr of midfield: rdn under 3f out: wknd 2f out* **44/1**

8 4 ½ **Nagano Gold**[42] 6522 5-9-5 0........................ MickaelBarzalona 11 86
(Vaclav Luka Jr, Czech Republic) *in rr: rdn and plugged on fr 2 1/2f out: nvr in contention* **85/1**

9 4 ½ **French King**[56] 6007 4-9-5 0........................ OlivierPeslier 5 79
(H-A Pantall, France) *towards rr: eased whn btn 2f out* **41/1**

10 2 ½ **Ghaiyyath (IRE)**[35] 6771 4-9-5 0........................ WilliamBuick 12 75
(Charlie Appleby) *led: rdn under 3f out: hdd 2 1/2f out: wknd qckly 2f out: eased fr 1 1/2f out* **13/1**

11 nse **Blast Onepiece (JPN)**[49] 4-9-5 0........................ YugaKawada 4 75
(Masahiro Otake, Japan) *midfield: rdn 3f out: lost pl 2 1/2f out: sn struggling* **58/1**

12 15 **Fierement (JPN)**[49] 4-9-5 0........................ Christophe-PatriceLemaire 2 51
(Takahisa Tezuka, Japan) *trckd ldrs: lost pl under 3f out: sn struggling: eased fr 2f out* **36/1**

2m 31.97s (1.57) **Going Correction** +0.775s/f (Yiel)
WFA 3 from 4yo+ 6lb 12 Ran SP% **120.4**
Speed ratings: **125,123,122,122,118 116,110,107,104,103 102,92**
PARI-MUTUEL (all including 1 euro stake): WIN 14.10; PLACE 1.60, 1.10, 1.70; DF 7.40.
Owner Gestut Ammerland & Newsells Park **Bred** The Waldlerche Partnership **Trained** Chantilly, France

FOCUS
While all eyes were on the market leader, this was a pretty strong Arc with all bar a top 3yo filly lining up. The gallop was strong and several were beaten off early in the home straight. Conditions were testing but the right horses were involved in the finish, with none of the rank outsiders making an impression. This rates a career best from the winner, with the runner-up 6lb off her 2017 best.

7942a PRIX DE L'OPERA LONGINES (GROUP 1) (3YO+ FILLIES & MARES) (GRANDE COURSE) (TURF) 1m 2f

3:55 3-Y-0+ **£257,387** (£102,972; £51,486; £25,720; £12,882)

RPR

1 **Villa Marina**[21] 7252 3-8-11 0........................ OlivierPeslier 7 115
(C Laffon-Parias, France) *midfield on outside: stdy hdwy fr 3f out: chsd ldrs whn rdn 2f out: hung rt fnl f: led 150yds out: drvn and hld on wl whn pressed clsng stages* **199/10**

2 snk **Fleeting (IRE)**[21] 7252 3-8-11 0........................ WayneLordan 12 115+
(A P O'Brien, Ire) *hld up in rr pair: rdn over 2f out: briefly nt clr run 1 1/2f out: styd on strly fr over 1f out: pressed wnr clsng stages* **19/1**

3 ¾ **Watch Me (FR)**[56] 6004 3-8-11 0........................ Pierre-CharlesBoudot 11 114+
(F-H Graffard, France) *hld up in rr pair: rdn over 2f out: keeping on whn nt clr run and forced to switch 1f out: styd on wl fnl f: nt clr run clsng stages* **9/1**

4 nk **Commes (FR)**[52] 6142 3-8-11 0........................ YutakaTake 4 113
(J-C Rouget, France) *in tch: trckd ldrs on outside 3f out: rdn to ld over 2f out: hdd 1 1/2f out: pushed along and kpt on same pce* **12/1**

5 snk **Terebellum (IRE)**[50] 6250 3-8-11 0........................ MickaelBarzalona 9 113
(John Gosden) *trckd ldrs: chsd ldr 1/2-way: rdn 2f out: led 1 1/2f out: drvn over 1f out: hdd 150yds out: wknd clsng stages* **59/10**[2]

6 1 ¼ **With You**[49] 6265 4-9-2 0........................(b) AurelienLemaitre 1 110
(F Head, France) *chsd ldr: dropped to 3rd 1/2-way: rdn 2 1/2f out: fdd fnl f* **13/2**[3]

7 ½ **Ligne D'Or**[21] 7252 4-9-2 0........................ VincentCheminaud 2 109
(A Fabre, France) *midfield: in tch whn rdn 2 1/2f out: kpt on same pce tl no ex fnl 50yds* **24/1**

8 5 **Pink Dogwood (IRE)**[21] 7252 3-8-11 0........................ RyanMoore 8 99
(A P O'Brien, Ire) *hld up towards rr: rdn over 2f out: kpt on steadily fnl f: n.d* **12/1**

9 1 ¼ **Etoile (FR)**[50] 6250 3-8-11 0........................ CristianDemuro 5 97
(J-C Rouget, France) *in tch in midfield: rdn over 2f out: wknd over 1f out* **34/1**

10 2 ½ **Mehdaayih**[66] 5586 3-8-11 0........................ FrankieDettori 3 92
(John Gosden) *led: rdn and hdd over 2f out: wknd 1 1/2f out* **6/5**[1]

11 6 **Cartiem (FR)**[50] 6250 3-8-11 0........................ MaximeGuyon 10 80
(J-C Rouget, France) *a towards rr: rdn 2 1/2f out: wknd over 1f out* **79/1**

P **Goddess (USA)**[21] 7242 3-8-11 0........................ ChristopheSoumillon 6
(A P O'Brien, Ire) *towards rr of midfield: rdn 2f out: keeping on at same pce whn wnt wrong over 1f out: sn p.u* **25/1**

2m 9.09s (5.09) **Going Correction** +0.775s/f (Yiel)
WFA 3 from 4yo 4lb 12 Ran SP% **120.4**
Speed ratings: **110,109,109,109,108 107,107,103,102,100 95,**
PARI-MUTUEL (all including 1 euro stake): WIN 20.90; PLACE 4.90, 6.70, 3.60; DF 116.70.
Owner Sarl Darpat France **Bred** Sarl Darpat France **Trained** Chantilly, France

FOCUS
There was a steady early pace, they were well bunched entering the straight and finished in a bit of a heap.

7943a PRIX DE L'ABBAYE DE LONGCHAMP LONGINES (GROUP 1) (2YO+) (SPRINT COURSE) (TURF) 5f (S)

4:30 2-Y-0+ **£180,171** (£72,081; £36,040; £18,004; £9,018)

RPR

1 **Glass Slippers**[21] 7254 3-9-7 0........................ TomEaves 3 117
(Kevin Ryan) *led after 1 1/2f: mde rest: rdn 2 1/2f out: drvn and grad drew clr fr under 2f out: kpt on strly* **128/10**

2 3 **So Perfect (USA)**[21] 7243 3-9-7 0........................ DonnachaO'Brien 1 106+
(A P O'Brien, Ire) *in tch in midfield: rdn and swtchd off rail 2f out: styd on fnl f: snatched 2nd cl home: no imp on wnr* **27/1**

3 nk **El Astronaute (IRE)**[25] 7073 6-9-11 0........................ JasonHart 4 108
(John Quinn) *led: hdd after 1 1/2f: chsd ldr: rdn 2 1/2f out: kpt on wl tl no ex and lost 2nd cl home* **84/1**

4 shd **Invincible Army (IRE)**[21] 7243 4-9-11 0........................(p) OisinMurphy 5 108
(James Tate) *trckd ldrs: rdn 2 1/2f out: kpt on wl: nt able to chal* **21/1**

5 1 **Mabs Cross**[21] 7243 5-9-7 0........................ GeraldMosse 8 100+
(Michael Dods) *towards rr of midfield: rdn along fr 3f out: kpt on fr over 1f out: nrst fin* **10/1**[3]

6 2 **Gold Vibe (IRE)**[21] 7254 6-9-11 0........................(b) CristianDemuro 2 97
(P Bary, France) *in tch: rdn 2 1/2f out: no ex ins fnl f* **30/1**

7 ¾ **Finsbury Square (IRE)**[9] 7-9-11 0........................ TonyPiccone 7 94
(M Delcher Sanchez, France) *towards rr of midfield: rdn over 2f out: kpt on fnl f: n.d* **86/1**

8 shd **Sestilio Jet (FR)**[21] 7254 4-9-11 0........................ FrankieDettori 14 94
(Andrea Marcialis, France) *in rr: rdn 2f out: kpt on fr 1 1/2f out: n.d* **17/1**

9 nk **Spinning Memories (IRE)**[42] 6520 4-9-7 0........ ChristopheSoumillon 6 89
(P Bary, France) *midfield: rdn and unable qck under 2f out: wknd steadily fnl f* **67/10**[2]

10 4 **Fairyland (IRE)**[21] 7243 3-9-7 0........................ RyanMoore 9 75
(A P O'Brien, Ire) *towards rr of midfield: rdn and no imp fr 2 1/2f out* **18/1**

11 1 **Shades Of Blue (IRE)**[21] 7254 3-9-7 0........................(p) AdamKirby 10 72
(Clive Cox) *towards rr: rdn 3f out: kpt on steadily fr 1 1/2f out: nvr in contention* **23/1**

12 1 ¼ **Jolie (FR)**[20] 7292 2-8-4 0........................(b[1]) YutakaTake 16 62
(Andrea Marcialis, France) *a towards rr* **74/1**

13 2 ½ **Recon Mission (IRE)**[43] 6476 3-9-11 0........................ TomMarquand 12 62
(Tony Carroll) *towards rr of midfield: rdn over 3f out: dropped towards 1/2-way: sn no imp* **119/1**

14 1 ½ **Battaash (IRE)**[44] 6423 5-9-11 0........................ JimCrowley 11 56
(Charles Hills) *in tch: rdn over 2f out: wknd qckly 1 1/2f out: eased fnl f* **9/10**[1]

15 1 ¼ **Soldier's Call**[21] 7243 3-9-11 0........................ DanielTudhope 15 52
(Archie Watson) *towards rr of midfield: rdn under 3f out: wknd under 2f out* **21/1**

16 20 **Ken Colt (IRE)**[71] 5471 4-9-11 0........................ StephanePasquier 13
(F Chappet, France) *midfield: lost pl 1/2-way: sn struggling: eased fnl 1 1/2f* **34/1**

58.04s (1.74) **Going Correction** +0.775s/f (Yiel) 16 Ran SP% **120.2**
Speed ratings: **117,112,111,111,109 106,105,105,104,98 96,94,90,88,86 54**
PARI-MUTUEL (all including 1 euro stake): WIN 13.80; PLACE 4.30, 8.80, 19.50; DF 84.70.
Owner Bearstone Stud Limited **Bred** Bearstone Stud Ltd **Trained** Hambleton, N Yorks

FOCUS
There was always the possibility of trouble in running with a field of this size but it looked a really clean race, with the winner landing the prize with loads to spare, and two 3yo fillies filling the first two positions. That said, those drawn high might as well have stayed in their stables.

7944a QATAR PRIX DE LA FORET (GROUP 1) (3YO+) (NEW COURSE: 2ND POST) (TURF) 7f

5:05 3-Y-O+ £180,171 (£72,081; £36,040; £18,004; £9,018)

RPR

1 **One Master**[63] 5716 5-8-13 0........................ Pierre-CharlesBoudot 6 117
(William Haggas) *racd towards rr of midfield: swtchd lft and pushed along jst under 2f out: hdwy to chal ent fnl f: sn led: kpt on wl clsng stages: a doing enough* **17/5**[2]

2 ½ **City Light (FR)**[21] 7255 5-9-2 0........................ ChristopheSoumillon 1 118
(S Wattel, France) *prom on inner: pushed along between rivals over 1 1/2f out: ev ch ent fnl f: kpt on wl clsng stages but a hld* **13/5**[1]

3 3 ½ **Speak In Colours**[8] 7713 4-9-2 0........................ DonnachaO'Brien 11 109
(Joseph Patrick O'Brien, Ire) *midfield on outer: asked for effrt over 2f out: prog to press ldrs over 1f out: led narrowly ent fnl f: sn hdd: kpt on same pce clsng stages* **23/1**

4 ¾ **Safe Voyage (IRE)**[50] 6215 6-9-2 0........................ FrankieDettori 2 107
(John Quinn) *midfield: pushed along between horses over 2f out: no immediate rspnse: kpt on u.p into modest 4th ins fnl f* **87/10**

5 snk **Graignes (FR)**[21] 7255 3-9-0 0........................ CristianDemuro 12 106
(Y Barberot, France) *hld up in rr: angled out and pushed along jst under 2f out: r.o wl fr over 1f out: nrst fin* **12/1**

6 1 ¼ **Hey Gaman**[50] 6215 4-9-2 0........................ OisinMurphy 3 103
(James Tate) *led: tried to qckn over 2f out: sn rdn: hdd over 1f out: grad wknd ins fnl f: no ex* **16/1**

7 nk **Forever In Dreams (IRE)**[29] 6959 3-8-10 0........................ RonanWhelan 5 97
(Aidan F Fogarty, Ire) *cl up: pushed along to press ldr over 2f out: rdn 1 1/2f out: unable qck w ldrs ent fnl f: kpt on same pce* **42/1**

8 1 **Wasmya (FR)**[35] 6769 3-8-10 0........................ MaximeGuyon 7 95
(F-H Graffard, France) *hld up in fnl trio: outpcd and pushed along jst under 3f out: no imp and wl hld ent fnl f* **12/1**

9 snk **Glorious Journey**[50] 6215 4-9-2 0........................ WilliamBuick 8 99
(Charlie Appleby) *racd a little keenly: prom on outer: pushed along to chse ldr 2 1/2f out: unable qck: wknd fr over 1f out* **69/10**[3]

10 snk **Sir Dancealot (IRE)**[22] 7194 5-9-2 0........................ GeraldMosse 4 99
(David Elsworth) *midfield on inner: struggling to go pce and pushed along 3f out: no rspnse: btn ent fnl f* **16/1**

11 shd **Marianafoot (FR)**[21] 7255 4-9-2 0........................ MickaelBarzalona 9 99
(J Reynier, France) *towards rr of midfield: asked for effrt over 2f out: no imp and sn struggling: wknd ins fnl f* **26/1**

12 2 ½ **Waldpfad (GER)**[29] 6959 5-9-2 0........................ AndreaAtzeni 10 92
(D Moser, Germany) *hld up in fnl pair: pushed along over 2f out: dropped to rr over 1f out and wl btn: nvr a factor* **11/1**

1m 23.66s (2.96) **Going Correction** +0.775s/f (Yiel)
WFA 3 from 4yo+ 2lb **12** Ran SP% **119.2**
Speed ratings: **114,113,109,108,108 106,106,105,105,105 105,102**
PARI-MUTUEL (all including 1 euro stake): WIN 4.40; PLACE 1.60, 1.60, 4.60; DF 8.30.
Owner Lael Stable **Bred** Lael Stables **Trained** Newmarket, Suffolk

FOCUS
This looked quite a competitive Group 1, but the first two in the betting finished clear of the rest.

7945a - 7955a (Foreign Racing) - See Raceform Interactive

7819 NEWCASTLE (A.W) (L-H)

Monday, October 7

OFFICIAL GOING: Tapeta: standard
Wind: Breezy, across

7956 C H SERVICES H'CAP 1m 2f 42y (Tp)

5:30 (5:30) (Class 6) (0-60,60) 3-Y-O+
£2,846 (£847; £423; £400; £400; £400) **Stalls High**

Form RPR

2300 **1** **Menin Gate (IRE)**[27] 7048 3-9-3 **57**........................ TonyHamilton 13 65
(Richard Fahey) *hld up towards rr: stdy hdwy over 2f out: effrt and rdn over 1f out: nt clr run and swtchd rt ins fnl f: kpt on wl to ld cl home* **9/1**

-033 **2** nk **Troop**[12] 7581 4-9-1 **51**........................ FrannyNorton 8 57
(Ann Duffield) *t.k.h: hld up in midfield: hdwy over 2f out: rdn to ld ins fnl f: kpt on: hdd cl home (jockey said gelding hung right under pressure)* **4/1**[2]

0331 **3** nk **Corked (IRE)**[12] 7578 6-9-7 **57**........................ PJMcDonald 14 63
(Alistair Whillans) *hld up on outside: hdwy over 2f out: effrt and led over 1f out: edgd lft and hdd ins fnl f: rallied: hld nr fin* **7/2**[1]

0640 **4** 1 ¼ **Thawry**[17] 7415 4-9-4 **59**........................ KieranSchofield(5) 3 63
(Antony Brittain) *hld up: hdwy over 2f out: effrt and ev ch over 1f out to ins fnl f: rdn and one pce fnl 75yds* **11/1**

0625 **5** 1 **Jazz Hands (IRE)**[12] 7581 3-8-10 **53**........................ SeanDavis(3) 12 56
(Richard Fahey) *hld up: hdwy over 2f out: effrt and prom over 1f out: rdn and one pce fnl f* **16/1**

0000 **6** 1 ¼ **False Id**[17] 7418 6-9-10 **60**........................(v[1]) ShaneGray 6 60
(Fred Watson) *dwlt: hld up: effrt whn nt clr run over 2f out: rdn and hdwy over 1f out: r.o ins fnl f: nt pce to chal* **80/1**

4504 **7** 2 ½ **Sir Gnet (IRE)**[25] 7109 5-9-10 **60**........................(h) DanielMuscutt 2 55
(Ed Dunlop) *hld up in midfield: stdy hdwy over 2f out: rdn wl over 1f out: sn no ex* **18/1**

0300 **8** nk **Charlie's Boy (IRE)**[17] 7404 3-9-0 **54**........................ PaulMulrennan 10 50
(Michael Dods) *t.k.h: chsd clr ldng pair: clsd 1/2-way: effrt and ev ch over 2f out: wknd over 1f out* **11/1**

0240 **9** 4 ½ **Poyle George Two**[14] 7508 4-8-7 **48**........................ AndrewBreslin(5) 4 34
(John Hodge) *prom: drvn along 3f out: wknd fr 2f out* **33/1**

0365 **10** 1 ¾ **Ningaloo (GER)**[14] 7513 5-9-7 **57**........................ DanielTudhope 1 40
(Rebecca Bastiman) *s.i.s: hld up: drvn along 3f out: nvr rchd ldrs (vet said gelding was lame left hind post-race)* **5/1**[3]

2506 **11** ½ **Bahkit (IRE)**[81] 5096 5-9-2 **59**........................ NickBarratt-Atkin(7) 7 41
(Philip Kirby) *t.k.h: w ldr and clr of rest: led 1/2-way: rdn and hdd over 1f out: sn wknd* **28/1**

5102 **12** 2 ½ **Graceful Act**[42] 6545 11-8-8 **49**........................ PaulaMuir(5) 9 27
(Ron Barr) *hld up in tch: effrt and rdn over 2f out: wknd over 1f out* **50/1**

0000 **13** 1 ¼ **Anchises**[39] 6628 4-9-4 **57**........................(t[1] w) HarrisonShaw(3) 11 33
(Rebecca Menzies) *s.i.s: bhd: struggling 3f out: sn btn* **33/1**

6560 **14** 20 **Airplane (IRE)**[15] 7492 4-9-7 **57**........................(p[1]) JamesSullivan 5
(Paul Collins) *t.k.h: led at decent gallop to 1/2-way: lost pl qckly over 2f out: lost tch and eased fr over 1f out* **66/1**

2m 10.28s (-0.12) **Going Correction** +0.10s/f (Slow)
WFA 3 from 4yo+ 4lb **14** Ran SP% **110.7**
Speed ratings (Par 101): **104,103,103,102,101 100,98,98,94,93 93,91,90,74**
CSF £39.17 CT £144.10 TOTE £8.20: £2.70, £1.70, £1.30; EX 50.30 Trifecta £263.00.
Owner A Long Long Way To Run **Bred** Ringfort Stud **Trained** Musley Bank, N Yorks
■ Stewards' Enquiry : Franny Norton two-day ban; misuse of whip (Oct 21-22)

FOCUS
A modest handicap. Straightforward form, the fifth among those to set the level.

7957 DFE ELECTRICAL MAIDEN STKS 1m 2f 42y (Tp)

6:00 (6:06) (Class 5) 2-Y-O £3,493 (£1,039; £519; £259) **Stalls High**

Form RPR

23 **1** **Live Your Dream (IRE)**[18] 7392 2-9-5 0........................ HectorCrouch 3 77+
(Saeed bin Suroor) *dwlt: sn led: mde rest: rdn clr fr over 1f out: eased nr fin* **1/6**[1]

2 6 **Warranty (FR)** 2-9-5 0........................ FrannyNorton 1 67
(Mark Johnston) *chsd wnr: rdn over 2f out: outpcd fr over 1f out: bttr for r* **6/1**[2]

6 **3** 3 ½ **Three Dragons**[26] 7067 2-9-5 0........................ AndrewMullen 4 60
(Ben Haslam) *walked to s: stdd in last pl: stdy hdwy to chse ldng pair 4f out: rdn over 2f out: sn no imp* **25/1**[3]

0400 **4** 30 **Thomas Hawk**[11] 7626 2-9-5 **35**........................ DavidNolan 6 6
(Alan Brown) *early ldr: chsd clr ldng pair to 4f out: rdn and lost tch over 2f out* **250/1**

2m 11.37s (0.97) **Going Correction** +0.10s/f (Slow) **4** Ran SP% **104.2**
Speed ratings (Par 95): **100,95,92,68**
CSF £1.32 TOTE £1.10; EX 1.50 Trifecta £1.80.
Owner Godolphin **Bred** Godolphin **Trained** Newmarket, Suffolk

FOCUS
A fair little staying juvenile maiden. The winning time was over a second slower than the opening C&D handicap and the third may prove the anchor to the form in time.

7958 FORD MEDIAN AUCTION MAIDEN STKS 7f 14y (Tp)

6:30 (6:35) (Class 5) 2-Y-O £3,493 (£1,039; £519; £259) **Stalls Centre**

Form RPR

1 **High Accolade (IRE)** 2-9-5 0........................ PJMcDonald 11 78+
(James Tate) *prom: hdwy over 2f out: shkn up to ld over 1f out: hrd pressed ins fnl f: rdn and r.o wl towards fin* **11/10**[1]

2223 **2** ½ **Saint Of Katowice (IRE)**[44] 6450 2-9-5 **77**........................ TonyHamilton 9 77
(Richard Fahey) *hld up: hdwy over 2f out: rdn and ev ch ins fnl f: kpt on same pce towards fin* **10/3**[2]

0 **3** 5 **Secret Diary**[13] 7538 2-9-0 0........................ DanielTudhope 10 60
(Declan Carroll) *led: rdn and hdd over 1f out: sn outpcd by first two* **28/1**

0 **4** 1 ¾ **Itwouldberudenotto**[156] 2415 2-9-5 0........................ DavidNolan 4 60
(Richard Fahey) *prom: rdn along over 2f out: kpt on same pce fnl f* **20/1**

33 **5** 1 **Dandy's Angel (IRE)**[26] 7063 2-8-11 0........................ SeanDavis(3) 1 53
(John Wainwright) *hld up on outside: rdn and outpcd over 2f out: rallied over 1f out: no imp fnl f* **20/1**

05 **6** ½ **La Trinidad**[13] 7539 2-9-0 0........................ PaulaMuir(5) 7 60+
(Roger Fell) *t.k.h: hld up: shkn up and stdy hdwy over 1f out: nvr nr ldrs (enq held into the running and riding of the gelding which was slowly away before staying on strongly to finish sixth of eleven beaten 8¾ lengths. Jockey said her instructions were that as the gelding had dwelt in its last two races, to get him settled a* **50/1**

7 ¾ **Villa Paloma (IRE)** 2-9-0 0........................ JoeFanning 8 50
(Mark Johnston) *prom: rdn over 2f out: wknd over 1f out* **14/1**

45 **8** 2 **Reggino (FR)**[17] 7416 2-9-5 0........................ CliffordLee 6 50
(Jedd O'Keeffe) *t.k.h: cl up: rdn along over 2f out: wknd over 1f out* **20/1**

9 2 **Hajey** 2-9-5 0........................ FrannyNorton 3 45
(Mark Johnston) *cl up: rdn and outpcd over 2f out: btn over 1f out* **13/2**[3]

0 **10** 3 ¼ **Bouncing Bobby (IRE)**[18] 7361 2-9-5 0........................ CallumRodriguez 5 36
(Michael Dods) *hld up: pushed along and outpcd over 2f out: sn struggling* **25/1**

11 23 **Charmore** 2-9-0 0........................ ShaneGray 2
(Ann Duffield) *t.k.h: hld up: hung bdly lft after 3f: sn lost tch: t.o (jockey said filly hung left)* **100/1**

1m 27.72s (1.52) **Going Correction** +0.10s/f (Slow) **11** Ran SP% **115.2**
Speed ratings (Par 95): **95,94,88,86,85 85,84,81,79,75 49**
CSF £3.86 TOTE £2.10: £1.20, £1.20, £1.60; EX 6.00 Trifecta £83.30.
Owner Saeed Manana **Bred** James F Hanly **Trained** Newmarket, Suffolk

FOCUS
A fair juvenile maiden. The form could be rated higher but a cautious view has been taken.

7959 SCE ELECTRICAL LTD H'CAP 5f (Tp)

7:00 (7:05) (Class 6) (0-65,65) 3-Y-O+
£2,846 (£847; £423; £400; £400; £400) **Stalls Centre**

Form RPR

0442 **1** **Swiss Connection**[20] 7307 3-9-4 **62**........................(h) GrahamLee 8 68
(Bryan Smart) *prom in centre of gp: effrt and pressed ldr over 1f out: kpt on wl fnl f to ld cl home* **11/4**[1]

1330 **2** shd **The Grey Zebedee**[20] 7307 3-9-0 **58**........................(b) DuranFentiman 6 64
(Tim Easterby) *led in centre of gp: rdn along over 1f out: kpt on fnl f: hdd cl home* **20/1**

0065 **3** ¾ **Shepherd's Purse**[12] 7576 7-9-0 **58**........................(p) JamesSullivan 10 60
(Ruth Carr) *t.k.h: cl up towards nr side of gp: drvn along 2f out: kpt on ins fnl f: hld towards fin* **10/1**

-001 **4** ½ **Gleaming Arch**[20] 7307 5-8-11 **58**........................ SeanDavis(3) 7 58
(Fred Watson) *hld up in centre of gp: rdn and hdwy over 1f out: kpt on fnl f: nt pce to chal* **6/1**[2]

4110 **5** ½ **Fard**[10] 7654 4-8-13 **62**........................ PaulaMuir(5) 4 60
(Roger Fell) *towards rr on far side of gp: rdn along 1/2-way: hdwy over 1f out: kpt on fnl f: no imp* **6/1**[2]

0660 **6** nk **Lord Of The Glen**[8] 7737 4-8-3 **47**........................(v) JamieGormley 12 44
(Jim Goldie) *hld up in centre of gp: rdn and hdwy over 1f out: kpt on fnl f: no imp (jockey said gelding was denied a clear run in the final furlong)* **17/2**[3]

2044 **7** hd **Longroom**[34] 6829 7-9-6 **64**........................(t) PhilDennis 3 61
(Noel Wilson) *t.k.h early: prom in centre of gp: rdn and effrt over 1f out: no ex ins fnl f* **22/1**

6000 **8** 1 ½ **Inner Charm**[15] 7486 3-8-11 **55**........................(t[1]) SamJames 2 47
(Kevin Ryan) *in tch on far side of gp: stdy hdwy 1/2-way: effrt over 1f out: rdn and wknd ins fnl f* **25/1**

5145 **9** *nk* **Northern Society (IRE)**[12] 7588 3-9-3 **61** ShaneGray 14 52
(Keith Dalgleish) *unruly on way to post: hld up on nr side of gp: effrt over 2f out: outpcd over 1f out: n.d after* **22/1**

0010 **10** *1* **Spirit Power**[58] 5952 4-9-4 **65** HarrisonShaw(3) 11 51
(Eric Alston) *cl up on nr side of gp tl rdn and wknd over 1f out* **10/1**

346 **11** *nse* **Gupta**[196] 1336 3-9-6 **64** DavidNolan 13 51
(David Brown) *reluctant to enter stalls: hld up on nr side of gp: hdwy and prom 2f out: rdn and wknd fnl f* **28/1**

6200 **12** *1 1/4* **Willow Brook**[60] 5854 3-8-8 **52** (h) CliffordLee 1 35
(Julie Camacho) *bhd on far side of gp: drvn along 1/2-way: sn struggling* **80/1**

240- **13** *1 3/4* **Excellently Poised**[59] 5924 4-9-5 **63** BarryMcHugh 5 38
(Mark Loughnane) *towards rr on far side of gp: drvn and struggling 1/2-way: nvr on terms* **14/1**

6600 **14** *7* **Kyroc (IRE)**[8] 7737 3-7-12 **47** ow1 AndrewBreslin(5) 9
(Susan Corbett) *taken early to post: bhd and sn outpcd in centre: no ch fr 1/2-way (jockey said filly moved poorly throughout)* **200/1**

59.99s (0.49) **Going Correction** +0.10s/f (Slow) 14 Ran SP% **113.1**
Speed ratings (Par 101): **100,99,98,97,97 96,96,93,93,91 91,89,86,75**
CSF £63.84 CT £477.21 TOTE £3.30: £1.50, £4.70, £2.90; EX 30.70 Trifecta £670.20.
Owner Woodcock Electrical Ltd **Bred** Natton House Thoroughbreds **Trained** Hambleton, N Yorks

FOCUS
A modest sprint handicap but pretty deep/competitive for the time of year.

7960 MOUNSEY H'CAP 1m 5y (Tp)
7:30 (7:33) (Class 6) (0-55,55) 3-Y-O+
£2,846 (£847; £423; £400; £400; £400) **Stalls** Centre

Form RPR
2204 **1** **Perfect Swiss**[23] 7207 3-9-3 **54** RachelRichardson 13 68+
(Tim Easterby) *hld up in last pl on nr side of gp: gd hdwy to ld over 1f out: sn clr: eased fnl 50yds: readily* **8/1**

0560 **2** *5* **Rebel State (IRE)**[10] 7654 6-8-8 **49** OwenPayton(7) 7 52
(Jedd O'Keeffe) *hld up in centre: effrt and edgd lft over 2f out: chsd (clr) wnr fnl f: kpt on: no imp* **10/1**

660 **3** *1 1/2* **High Fort (IRE)**[71] 5477 4-9-4 **52** CliffordLee 2 52
(Karen McLintock) *led in centre of gp: drvn over 2f out: hdd over 1f out: kpt on same pce ins fnl f* **20/1**

0134 **4** *hd* **Gunnison**[18] 7385 3-9-3 **54** (p) TonyHamilton 9 53
(Richard Fahey) *hld up towards centre of gp: hdwy over 2f out: drvn over 1f out: kpt on same pce ins fnl f* **13/2**[3]

3626 **5** *1 3/4* **Mr Cool Cash**[14] 7508 7-8-10 **47** (t) SeanDavis(3) 11 42
(John Davies) *hld up: effrt in centre of gp whn hmpd and rdn over 1f out: kpt on fnl f: no imp* **28/1**

-040 **6** *nse* **Calevade (IRE)**[59] 5915 3-9-1 **52** (p[1]) PaulMulrennan 10 47
(Ben Haslam) *dwlt: hld up in centre of gp: rdn over 2f out: no imp fr over 1f out* **15/2**

2360 **7** *3/4* **Molten Lava (IRE)**[138] 2972 7-9-4 **52** (p) PJMcDonald 8 46
(Steve Gollings) *t.k.h: trckd ldrs in centre of gp: rdn along over 2f out: no ex fr over 1f out* **14/1**

4200 **8** *1 1/2* **Don't Be Surprised**[55] 6036 4-9-5 **53** (v[1]) BenRobinson 12 43
(Seb Spencer) *in tch on nr side of gp: rdn and ev ch over 1f out: wknd ins fnl f* **5/1**[1]

5003 **9** *3/4* **Shamaheart (IRE)**[12] 7587 9-9-7 **55** (tp) SamJames 1 44
(Geoffrey Harker) *in tch on far side of gp: drvn over 2f out: fdd over 1f out* **33/1**

0-65 **10** *3* **Shouranour (IRE)**[18] 7385 9-9-7 **55** (b) DavidNolan 14 37
(Peter Niven) *hld up on nr side of gp: rdn over 2f out: wknd over 1f out* **12/1**

345/ **11** *nk* **Poetic Choice**[157] 2386 8-9-4 **52** (b) RobbieDowney 5 33
(Keith Henry Clarke, Ire) *slowly away: hld up on far side of gp: drvn over 2f out: no imp fr over 1f out (trainers rep could offer no explanation for the poor performance)* **8/1**

0025 **12** *1 1/4* **Key Choice**[30] 6983 3-9-3 **54** PhilDennis 6 33
(Eric Alston) *cl up on nr side of gp tl rdn and wknd over 1f out* **11/2**[2]

0050 **13** *5* **Pumaflor (IRE)**[31] 6937 7-8-7 **48** (p) NickBarratt-Atkin(7) 3 16
(Philip Kirby) *cl up on far side of gp: drvn and ev ch over 2f out: wknd over 1f out* **80/1**

1m 39.77s (1.17) **Going Correction** +0.10s/f (Slow)
WFA 3 from 4yo+ 3lb 13 Ran SP% **115.2**
Speed ratings (Par 101): **98,93,91,91,89 89,88,87,86,83 83,81,76**
CSF £79.29 CT £1589.82 TOTE £9.10: £3.50, £3.00, £6.40; EX 81.20 Trifecta £2497.10.
Owner Craig Wilson & Partner **Bred** Mildmay Bloodstock Ltd **Trained** Great Habton, N Yorks

FOCUS
A modest handicap.

7961 GREENSLEEVES LAWN CARE TREATMENT SERVICES H'CAP 7f 14y (Tp)
8:00 (8:03) (Class 6) (0-55,54) 3-Y-O+
£2,846 (£847; £423; £400; £400; £400) **Stalls** Centre

Form RPR
0002 **1** **Billy Wedge**[10] 7654 4-9-6 **52** BarryMcHugh 13 60
(Tracy Waggott) *hld up on nr side of gp: hdwy to ld wl over 1f out: drvn out ins fnl f* **11/8**[1]

5006 **2** *1 1/4* **Joyful Star**[23] 7207 9-8-12 **47** SeanDavis(3) 1 52
(Fred Watson) *hld up on far side of gp: effrt and angled lft over 2f out: ev ch over 1f out to ins fnl f: one pce fnl 50yds* **10/1**[3]

0000 **3** *nk* **The Retriever (IRE)**[23] 7207 4-9-0 **46** GrahamLee 11 50
(Micky Hammond) *prom on nr side of gp: effrt and ev ch briefly wl over 1f out: kpt on fnl f: no ex fnl 50yds* **14/1**

000 **4** *3/4* **Dixieland (IRE)**[27] 7051 3-9-6 **54** DanielTudhope 6 55
(Marjorie Fife) *hld up in tch centre: drvn along over 2f out: kpt on fnl f: nt pce to chal* **22/1**

0005 **5** *3/4* **Lord Rob**[12] 7587 8-8-11 **46** HarrisonShaw(3) 9 46
(David Thompson) *bhd on far side of gp: rdn over 2f out: hdwy over 1f out: no imp ins fnl f* **50/1**

0020 **6** *3/4* **Breathoffreshair**[11] 7606 5-8-7 **46** (bt) HarryRussell(7) 8 45
(Richard Guest) *hld up: effrt and rdn on nr side of gp over 1f out: kpt on fnl f: nt pce to chal* **22/1**

-P04 **7** *hd* **Roca Magica**[21] 7282 3-9-3 **51** TomEaves 7 48
(Ed Dunlop) *hld up towards far side of gp: effrt and rdn 2f out: no imp fnl f* **20/1**

5343 **8** *2* **Puchita (IRE)**[14] 7527 4-9-5 **51** (p) CamHardie 3 44
(Antony Brittain) *prom towards centre of gp: effrt and ev ch over 2f out to over 1f out: edgd rt and wknd ins fnl f* **7/1**[2]

0400 **9** *hd* **Gun Case**[10] 7654 7-9-0 **51** (p) AndrewBreslin(5) 10 44
(Alistair Whillans) *s.i.s: sn pushed along in rr on nr side of gp: edgd lft and kpt on steadily fnl f: n.d* **10/1**[3]

4040 **10** *1 1/2* **Black Hambleton**[147] 2681 6-9-0 **46** PaulMulrennan 2 35
(Bryan Smart) *prom on far side of gp: rdn over 2f out: wknd over 1f out* **16/1**

0003 **11** *2* **Extrasolar**[17] 7420 9-9-7 **53** (t) SamJames 5 37
(Geoffrey Harker) *cl up in centre of gp: effrt and ev ch over 2f out to over 1f out: sn wknd* **16/1**

1250 **12** *2* **Kodimoor (IRE)**[16] 7444 6-9-1 **47** (p) DougieCostello 4 26
(Mark Walford) *w ldr in centre of gp: led 1/2-way to wl over 1f out: sn wknd* **16/1**

0250 **13** *2* **Tavener**[7] 7770 7-9-5 **51** PhilDennis 14 25
(David C Griffiths) *led on nr side of gp to 1/2-way: rdn and wknd over 2f out* **22/1**

1m 27.72s (1.52) **Going Correction** +0.10s/f (Slow)
WFA 3 from 4yo+ 2lb 13 Ran SP% **116.9**
Speed ratings (Par 101): **95,93,93,92,91 90,90,88,87,86 83,81,79**
CSF £13.28 CT £144.81 TOTE £2.20: £1.20, £2.90, £4.90; EX 18.10 Trifecta £235.60.
Owner David Tate **Bred** David Tate **Trained** Spennymoor, Co Durham

FOCUS
Another modest handicap. The form could be rated a bit better through the runner-up.

7962 GREENSLEEVES LAWNCARE TREATMENT SERVICES CLASSIFIED STKS 6f (Tp)
8:30 (8:34) (Class 6) 3-Y-O+
£2,846 (£847; £423; £400; £400; £400) **Stalls** Centre

Form RPR
6052 **1** **Jeffrey Harris**[8] 7737 4-9-1 50 DanielTudhope 3 59
(Jim Goldie) *hld up in centre of gp: effrt and angled rt over 2f out: led appr fnl f: rdn clr: comf* **12/1**

0334 **2** *3* **Red Allure**[12] 7591 4-9-1 47 NathanEvans 5 50
(Michael Mullineaux) *cl up in centre of gp: led over 2f out: edgd lft and hdd over 1f out: sn chsng wnr: kpt on same pce fnl f* **18/1**

0025 **3** *1/2* **Eldelbar (SPA)**[16] 7443 5-9-1 50 (h) SamJames 4 49
(Geoffrey Harker) *hld up on far side of gp: hdwy and prom over 2f out: sn rdn: kpt on ins fnl f* **4/1**[2]

5043 **4** *3/4* **Rockley Point**[5] 7824 6-9-1 50 (b) PhilDennis 11 46
(Katie Scott) *cl up on nr side of gp: ev ch fr 1/2-way to over 1f out: rdn and one pce ins fnl f* **10/3**[1]

4030 **5** *1 1/4* **Loulin**[138] 2958 4-9-1 50 (t[1] w) JamesSullivan 10 43
(Ruth Carr) *led to over 2f out: rallied and ev ch over 1f out: drvn and no ex ins fnl f* **20/1**

3006 **6** *1* **Josiebond**[15] 7486 3-9-0 49 LewisEdmunds 14 40
(Rebecca Bastiman) *hld up on nr side of gp: rdn over 2f out: hdwy and edgd lft over 1f out: kpt on fnl f: no imp* **22/1**

006 **7** *1 3/4* **Hasili Filly**[10] 7655 3-9-0 35 PaulMulrennan 13 34
(Lawrence Mullaney) *midfield towards centre of gp: drvn along over 2f out: no imp over 1f out* **25/1**

3150 **8** *1* **Someone Exciting**[12] 7591 6-8-12 50 HarrisonShaw(3) 12 31
(David Thompson) *in tch on nr side of gp: rdn over 2f out: wknd over 1f out* **11/2**[3]

0000 **9** *3 3/4* **Deeds Not Words (IRE)**[12] 7591 8-9-1 50 (p) BarryMcHugh 7 20
(Tracy Waggott) *s.i.s: bhd on nr side of gp: drvn 1/2-way: sme late hdwy: nvr on terms* **20/1**

2460 **10** *nse* **Picks Pinta**[68] 5559 8-9-1 47 (p) JamieGormley 6 20
(John David Riches) *in tch in centre of gp: drvn and outpcd over 2f out: btn fnl f* **22/1**

0043 **11** *nk* **Raffle King (IRE)**[11] 7628 5-8-12 46 ConnorMurtagh(3) 8 19
(Julia Brooke) *t.k.h: in tch in centre of gp: drvn and outpcd over 2f out: wknd over 1f out (trainers rep said, regards the poor performance, gelding may have been unsuited by the removal of a visor on this occasion)* **22/1**

0420 **12** *2 3/4* **Lyons Lane**[11] 7628 3-9-0 47 CallumRodriguez 2 11
(Michael Dods) *in tch on far side of gp: rdn over 2f out: wknd wl over 1f out* **11/1**

0006 **13** *1* **Temple Of Wonder (IRE)**[10] 7654 3-9-0 49 (p) JackGarritty 1 8
(Liam Bailey) *midfield on far side of gp: struggling over 2f out: sn btn* **25/1**

0-00 **14** *3/4* **Mixed Up Miss (IRE)**[10] 7651 3-9-0 45 (b) GrahamLee 9 5
(Bryan Smart) *walked to post: bhd in centre of gp: struggling over 3f out: nvr on terms* **66/1**

1m 12.46s (-0.04) **Going Correction** +0.10s/f (Slow)
WFA 3 from 4yo+ 1lb 14 Ran SP% **111.5**
Speed ratings (Par 101): **104,100,99,98,96 95,93,91,86,86 86,82,81,80**
CSF £164.85 TOTE £8.70: £2.30, £4.60, £1.90; EX 139.20 Trifecta £710.20.
Owner Mrs & Exors The Late Philip C Smith **Bred** Philip C Smith & Mrs Joyce W Smith **Trained** Uplawmoor, E Renfrews

FOCUS
A moderate classified stakes.
T/Plt: £20.00 to a £1 stake. Pool: £80,531.20 - 2,937.00 winning units T/Qpdt: £15.60 to a £1 stake. Pool: £11,106.54 - 526.48 winning units **Richard Young**

7619 PONTEFRACT (L-H)
Monday, October 7
7963 Meeting Abandoned - Waterlogged

6806 WINDSOR (R-H)
Monday, October 7

OFFICIAL GOING: Soft
Wind: Light, behind Weather: Overcast, drizzly

7971 KINGSTONE PRESS NURSERY H'CAP 1m 31y
2:10 (2:15) (Class 4) (0-80,79) 2-Y-O
£4,463 (£1,328; £663; £331; £300; £300) **Stalls** Centre

Form RPR
4053 **1** **Sir Arthur Dayne (IRE)**[16] 7429 2-9-5 **77** (v) TomMarquand 3 83
(Mick Channon) *trckd ldr: rdn to chal over 2f out and grabbed far rail: upsides whn new ldr wnt by over 1f out: rallied u.p to ld fnl 75yds* **9/2**[3]

The Form Book Flat 2019, Raceform Ltd, Newbury, RG14 5SJ

553 **2** *hd* **Talap**[12] 7586 2-9-0 **72**.................................(p) DavidEgan 4 78
(Roger Varian) *trckd ldng pair: shkn up to ld over 1f out and looked sure to win: drvn fnl f: hdd fnl 75yds: kpt on (vet said colt lost both it's front shoes)* **7/2**[2]

322 **3** *4* **Arabian Moon**[24] 7151 2-9-7 **79**................................. RobHornby 2 76
(Ralph Beckett) *led: hanging lft bnd 6f out to over 4f out: tk field to far side 3f out: rdn and hdd over 1f out: one pce* **9/2**[3]

054 **4** *4 ½* **Wild Hero (IRE)**[24] 7139 2-9-1 **73**................................. OisinMurphy 5 60+
(Andrew Balding) *propped bdly s: hld up in last: lft bhd 3f out: no ch after but kpt on to take modest 4th ins fnl f (jockey said colt stumbled leaving the stalls)* **11/4**[1]

434 **5** *2 ½* **Three Fans (FR)**[49] 6287 2-9-1 **73**................................. RichardKingscote 6 54
(Tom Dascombe) *in tch: effrt over 3f out but sn outpcd: no prog after* **15/2**

0060 **6** *shd* **Party Potential (USA)**[26] 7079 2-8-0 **58** oh1.................(v[1]) RyanPowell 8 39
(Alan King) *slowly away: in rr: urged along 1/2-way: lft bhd 3f out: hanging lft and no ch fnl 2f* **50/1**

526 **7** *shd* **Rocket Dancer**[33] 6858 2-8-13 **74**................................. CierenFallon(3) 7 55
(Sylvester Kirk) *chsd ldng trio: outpcd 3f out: wknd over 1f out* **11/1**

0260 **8** *12* **Jim 'N' Tomic (IRE)**[31] 6911 2-9-3 **75**................................. CallumShepherd 1 30
(Dominic Ffrench Davis) *in tch: lft bhd 3f out: wknd 2f out: t.o* **25/1**

1m 50.8s (6.30) **Going Correction** +0.70s/f (Yiel) **8 Ran SP% 111.2**
Speed ratings (Par 97): **96,95,91,87,84 84,84,72**
CSF £19.42 CT £70.84 TOTE £4.90: £1.40, £1.30, £1.50; EX 18.40 Trifecta £52.80.
Owner M Channon **Bred** Tally-Ho Stud **Trained** West Ilsley, Berks

FOCUS
The rail on the bend and from the 6f marker to the intersection was 6yds out. The far side of the straight from the intersection to the winning line was dolled out by 6yds to save ground. Due to remedial work on the track the grass coverage was described as variable but fit to race. Add 23yds. They finished strung out behind the first two in this nursery. Late season and soft ground, but even so a pb from the runner-up.

7972 KALTENBURG EBF NOVICE STKS 1m 31y
2:40 (2:50) (Class 5) 2-Y-O £3,428 (£1,020; £509; £127) **Stalls** Centre

Form RPR

1 **Vintage Rascal (FR)** 2-9-5 0................................. TomMarquand 1 80+
(Tom Ward) *trckd ldrs: clsd over 2f out: rdn to ld over 1f out: styd on wl and drew clr fnl f* **8/1**

52 **2** *4 ½* **Tinnahalla (IRE)**[18] 7388 2-9-5 0................................. NicolaCurrie 12 70
(Jamie Osborne) *racd freely: led: rdn and hdd over 1f out: kpt on but no ch w wnr after* **15/2**[3]

4 **3** *1 ½* **Bottom Bay**[27] 7055 2-9-5 0................................. JamesDoyle 2 67
(Michael Bell) *trckd ldr to over 3f out: wnt 2nd again briefly over 2f out: rdn and kpt on same pce after* **7/4**[1]

04 **4** *hd* **Alargedram (IRE)**[16] 7473 2-9-2 0................................. MeganNicholls(3) 10 66
(Alan King) *wl in tch: shkn up and no prog over 2f out: styd on steadily ins fnl f* **7/1**[2]

4 *dht* **Bannister (FR)** 2-9-5 0................................. KieranShoemark 3 66+
(Tom George) *dwlt: t.k.h: wl in rr and wd bnd over 5f out: rapid prog to chse ldr over 3f out to over 2f out: kpt on one pce after (jockey said gelding ran too free)* **8/1**

6 *nse* **Arij (IRE)** 2-9-5 0................................. JackMitchell 5 66+
(Simon Crisford) *s.i.s: wl in rr: pushed along 3f out: styd on fr over 1f out: nrst fin* **8/1**

0 **7** *¾* **Isayalittleprayer**[67] 5588 2-9-0 0................................. JasonWatson 9 60
(Gary Moore) *chsd ldrs: shkn up over 2f out: kpt on one pce and no imp after* **20/1**

8 *1* **Mr Rusty (IRE)** 2-9-5 0................................. RossaRyan 13 62
(Richard Hannon) *chsd ldrs: rdn over 2f out: one pce no imp after* **25/1**

9 *1* **Elham Valley (FR)** 2-9-5 0................................. OisinMurphy 8 60+
(Andrew Balding) *wl in rr: last 1/2-way: no ch 3f out: kpt on steadily over 1f out (jockey said colt ran green)* **14/1**

0 **10** *6* **Arthalot (IRE)**[22] 7235 2-9-5 0................................. LukeMorris 4 47
(Karen George) *chsd ldrs but pushed along: lost pl 1/2-way: struggling in rr 3f out* **50/1**

11 *3* **Spring To Mind** 2-9-0 0................................. RobHornby 6 35
(Ralph Beckett) *chsd ldrs: lost pl 1/2-way: struggling in rr over 2f out* **16/1**

12 *3 ¼* **Ginger Box** 2-9-0 0.................................(p[1]) JFEgan 14 28
(Karen George) *dwlt: a in rr: lft bhd 3f out* **66/1**

0 **13** *10* **Majestyk Fire (IRE)**[37] 6718 2-9-5 0.................................(t) TomQueally 7 11
(David Flood) *s.i.s: a in rr: lft bhd fr 3f out* **100/1**

1m 50.62s (6.12) **Going Correction** +0.70s/f (Yiel) **13 Ran SP% 119.6**
Speed ratings (Par 95): **97,92,91,90,90 90,90,89,88,82 79,75,65**
CSF £64.23 TOTE £11.50: £3.40, £1.90, £1.10; EX 99.10 Trifecta £496.50.
Owner Charlie Rosier & Mrs Julia Rosier **Bred** Berend Van Dalfsen **Trained** Upper Lambourn, Berks

■ Back From Dubai was withdrawn, price at time of withdrawal 11/2. Rule 4 applies to board prices prior to withdrawal, but not to SP bets. Deduction of 15p in the pound. New market formed.

FOCUS
Add 23yds. Few got into this, the pace holding up pretty well. The winner did it well but the form's rated conservatively around the next three home.

7973 61 DEEP CLAIMING STKS 1m 2f
3:10 (3:17) (Class 6) 3-4-Y-O £2,781 (£827; £413; £300; £300; £300) **Stalls** Centre

Form RPR

6623 **1** **Dawn Treader (IRE)**[21] 7270 3-8-3 **63**........ ThoreHammerHansen(5) 12 69
(Richard Hannon) *hld up towards rr: prog over 3f out: chsd clr ldr over 2f out: rdn to cl over 1f out: styd on to ld nr fin: eased last strides* **5/1**

4241 **2** *shd* **Elegant Love**[20] 7295 3-8-7 **65**................................. DavidEgan 7 68
(David Evans) *mde most: dashed for home over 3f out and sn clr: racd against far side rail over 2f out: kpt on but hdd and hld nr fin* **7/2**[3]

06 **3** *7* **Tops No**[26] 7081 4-8-6 0................................. GeorgeWood 6 49
(William Muir) *hld up in rr: prog over 3f out: chsd ldrs over 2f out: outpcd by ldng pair after but kpt on* **100/1**

5552 **4** *shd* **Plait**[12] 7567 4-9-5 **82**................................. CallumShepherd 13 62
(Michael Bell) *cl up: rdn to chse clr ldrs 3f out to over 2f out: sn outpcd and btn* **15/8**[1]

2360 **5** *4 ½* **Steeve**[16] 7465 3-9-2 **67**.................................(p) OisinMurphy 3 56
(Rod Millman) *in tch: dropped to rr and struggling over 3f out: n.d after* **3/1**[2]

-510 **6** *¾* **Sea Battle (FR)**[16] 7450 3-8-7 **65**................................. RayDawson(5) 11 51
(Jane Chapple-Hyam) *awkward s and dwlt: wl in tch: rdn over 3f out: sn outpcd and btn* **10/1**

2650 **7** *8* **Overtrumped**[10] 7643 4-8-6 **57**.................................(v) JosephineGordon 4 25
(Mike Murphy) *a in rr: struggling u.p fr 1/2-way* **16/1**

00 **8** *¾* **Counterfeit**[53] 6107 4-8-6 **47** ow1.................................(p) JFEgan 9 24
(Paul George) *dwlt: sn prom: wknd over 3f out* **100/1**

0000 **9** *2 ½* **Face Like Thunder**[7] 7758 4-8-8 **57**................................. DarraghKeenan(3) 10 24
(John Butler) *t.k.h: pressed ldr to over 3f out: sn wknd qckly (jockey said gelding ran too free)* **50/1**

0000 **10** *19* **Poet Pete (IRE)**[33] 6860 3-8-3 **32**.................................(p) WilliamCox(3) 8
(Mark Usher) *chsd ldrs: rdn 4f out: sn wknd: t.o (jockey said gelding stopped quickly)* **150/1**

6-00 **P** **Time Trialist**[53] 6117 3-8-8 **51**................................. CharlieBennett 1
(Pat Phelan) *dwlt: sn bhd: t.o whn p.u over 4f out: dismntd (trainer said gelding had a breathing problem)* **100/1**

2m 15.16s (6.16) **Going Correction** +0.70s/f (Yiel)
WFA 3 from 4yo 4lb **11 Ran SP% 119.2**
Speed ratings (Par 101): **103,102,97,97,93 93,86,86,84,68**
CSF £23.37 TOTE £5.30: £1.60, £1.80, £27.90; EX 23.20 Trifecta £812.20.Dawn Treader was claimed by Mrs S. V. O. Leech for £6000.
Owner C M Graham **Bred** Zalim Bikov **Trained** East Everleigh, Wilts

FOCUS
Add 23yds. The first two finished clear in this modest affair, both running to their respective marks.

7974 IVOR LAWS MEMORIAL H'CAP 1m 3f 99y
3:40 (3:47) (Class 3) (0-95,93) 3-Y-O+ £7,246 (£2,168; £1,084; £542; £270) **Stalls** Centre

Form RPR

011 **1** **Torcello (IRE)**[8] 7727 5-8-13 **83** 5ex................................. MeganNicholls(3) 2 92
(Shaun Lycett) *trckd ldr: led over 2f out: drvn and hrd pressed fnl f: jst clung on* **2/1**[1]

-433 **2** *shd* **Escapability (IRE)**[161] 2207 4-8-10 **77**................................. OisinMurphy 9 85
(Alan King) *sn trckd ldng pair: rdn to chse wnr wl over 1f out: chal fnl f: kpt on wl nr fin: jst failed* **9/1**

2404 **3** *1 ¾* **Top Power (FR)**[24] 7141 3-8-7 **79**................................. SilvestreDeSousa 3 84
(Andrew Balding) *led at gd pce: drvn and hdd over 2f out: lost 2nd wl over 1f out but kpt on* **11/2**[2]

/0-1 **4** *½* **Lightly Squeeze**[32] 6896 5-8-10 **77**.................................(h) TomMarquand 10 81
(Harry Fry) *slowly away: hld up in last pair: shkn up over 3f out: prog over 2f out: kpt on u.p but nvr able to chal (jockey said gelding was slowly away)* **6/1**[3]

044/ **5** *¾* **Chesterfield (IRE)**[315] 7223 9-9-2 **83**................................. RobHornby 5 86
(Seamus Mullins) *hld up in last trio: pushed along and prog 3f out: rdn to chse ldrs over 1f out: one pce fnl f* **66/1**

426 **6** *½* **Autumn War (IRE)**[32] 6895 4-9-4 **85**................................. KieranShoemark 8 87
(Charles Hills) *hld up in last pair: stl there jst over 2f out: swtchd to outer and rdn wl over 1f out: kpt on but too late to threaten* **28/1**

4314 **7** *3 ¼* **Fannie By Gaslight**[6] 7782 4-8-9 **76**................................. DavidEgan 7 73
(Mick Channon) *chsd ldrs: rdn 3f out: no imp 2f out: wknd over 1f out (jockey said filly ran flat)* **7/1**

244 **8** *nse* **Dragons Voice**[32] 6895 5-9-4 **85**................................. JasonWatson 6 81
(David Menuisier) *hld up towards rr: rdn over 3f out: no prog 2f out: fdd over 1f out* **16/1**

-515 **9** *2 ½* **Sandyman**[30] 6967 3-8-6 **78**................................. LukeMorris 4 70
(Paul Cole) *chsd ldrs: rdn over 3f out: wknd 2f out* **22/1**

0300 **10** *5* **Crystal King**[30] 6958 4-9-12 **93**................................. RyanMoore 1 77
(Sir Michael Stoute) *wl in tch: shkn up over 3f out: wknd 2f out: eased fnl f (trainers rep could offer no explanation for the poor performance)* **13/2**

2m 35.02s (5.32) **Going Correction** +0.70s/f (Yiel)
WFA 3 from 4yo+ 5lb **10 Ran SP% 114.0**
Speed ratings (Par 107): **108,107,106,106,105 105,103,102,101,97**
CSF £20.11 CT £85.52 TOTE £2.50: £1.10, £2.80, £2.10; EX 22.50 Trifecta £130.10.
Owner Dan Gilbert **Bred** Rathasker Stud **Trained** Leafield, Oxon

FOCUS
Add 23yds. It didn't pay to be too far off the pace. The winner was a bit below his Epsom form.

7975 BARRY GOULD MEMORIAL H'CAP 1m 31y
4:10 (4:18) (Class 4) (0-80,80) 3-Y-O+ £5,207 (£1,549; £774; £387; £300; £300) **Stalls** Centre

Form RPR

0046 **1** **Leader Writer (FR)**[11] 7618 7-9-0 **73**.................................(p) HayleyTurner 2 83
(David Elsworth) *dwlt: hld up in last pair: stdy prog fr 3f out: rdn to ld 1f out: pushed out fnl 100yds: readily* **11/1**

1035 **2** *1 ¼* **I'lletyougonow**[19] 7341 3-8-10 **72**.................................(p) SilvestreDeSousa 6 79
(Mick Channon) *chsd ldr 2f: styd prom: rdn on outer 3f out: led 2f out to 1f out: styd on* **10/1**

0005 **3** *3 ½* **George Of Hearts (FR)**[17] 7413 4-9-3 **79**.................(t) CierenFallon(3) 13 78
(George Baker) *dwlt: sn in midfield: prog to chse ldrs 3f out: sn rdn: no hdwy 2f out: styd on u.p to take 3rd nr fin* **15/2**

1102 **4** *¾* **Fortune And Glory (USA)**[31] 6925 6-9-0 **73**................................. DavidEgan 8 70
(Joseph Tuite) *dwlt: hld up wl in rr: prog 3f out: rdn to chal wl over 1f out: one pce after* **10/1**

0425 **5** *1 ¼* **Scofflaw**[9] 7680 5-9-7 **80**.................................(b) StevieDonohoe 10 74
(David Evans) *sn prom: chsd ldr 5f out: led over 3f out to 2f out: fdd (jockey said gelding ran too free)* **25/1**

0-40 **6** *½* **Tanqeeb**[23] 7204 3-8-0 **69**................................. RPWalsh(7) 12 62
(Ian Williams) *dwlt: towards rr and wd bnd over 5f out: prog against far rail over 2f out: drvn and ch wl over 1f out: fdd* **66/1**

1203 **7** *6* **Los Camachos (IRE)**[12] 7567 4-9-4 **77**................................. TomMarquand 14 56
(John Gallagher) *won battle for ld and set str pce early: hdd over 3f out: wknd over 2f out* **18/1**

4201 **8** *nk* **Secret Return (IRE)**[51] 6201 6-9-6 **79**................................. JFEgan 5 58
(Paul George) *dwlt: towards rr: prog over 2f out: rdn and ch wl over 1f out: sn wknd qckly (jockey said mare lost it's action)* **7/1**[3]

4620 **9** *½* **Sir Roderic (IRE)**[24] 7164 6-8-13 **72**.................................(v) CharlieBennett 11 50
(Rod Millman) *prom: chsd ldr 6f out to 5f out: rt on terms 2f out: sn wknd qckly* **20/1**

4250 **10** *2 ¼* **Oloroso (IRE)**[16] 7460 3-8-9 **71**................................. OisinMurphy 7 43
(Andrew Balding) *hld up in rr: shkn up and no prog over 2f out: nvr in it* **3/1**[1]

6234 **11** *16* **Medieval (IRE)**[44] 6468 5-9-3 **76**.................................(p) RossaRyan 1 12
(Paul Cole) *prom: n.m.r after 2f: sn lost pl: wknd over 2f out: t.o* **5/1**[2]

1230 **12** *5* **Conspiritor**[25] 7129 3-8-9 **71**................................. KieranShoemark 4
(Charles Hills) *a in rr: wknd 3f out: t.o (trainers rep said, regards the poor performance, gelding was unsuited by the ground and would prefer a quicker surface; vet said gelding lost it's left fore shoe)* **40/1**

0066 **13** *10* **Nightingale Valley**[46] 6362 6-8-13 **72**.................................(v) RobHornby 3
(Stuart Kittow) *chsd ldrs: lost pl 1/2-way: wknd over 2f out: t.o* **12/1**

1m 48.62s (4.12) **Going Correction** +0.70s/f (Yiel)
WFA 3 from 4yo+ 3lb **13 Ran SP% 117.9**
Speed ratings (Par 105): **107,105,102,101,100 99,93,93,92,90 74,69,59**
CSF £110.84 CT £917.76 TOTE £12.40: £4.20, £3.50, £2.90; EX 137.20 Trifecta £1465.90.

Owner G B Partnership **Bred** Guy Heald **Trained** Newmarket, Suffolk

FOCUS

Add 23yds. A fair handicap in which they finished well stretched out. The winner's best form since his reappearance.

7976 ESTRELLA DAMM MAIDEN STKS — 6f 12y

4:40 (4:46) (Class 5) 3-Y-0+ — £3,428 (£1,020; £509; £254) Stalls Centre

Form — RPR

0020 1 **True Belief (IRE)**[55] 6052 3-9-5 59 ....(h) RossaRyan 4 — 70
(Brett Johnson) *taken down early: stdd s: t.k.h: hld up in last pair: prog 1/2-way: drvn and tending to hang lft 2f out: clsd to ld jst ins fnl f: styd on (trainer said, regards the apparent improvement in form, gelding was badly hampered at Lingfield)* **20/1**

5340 2 1 1/4 **Mrs Worthington (IRE)**[5] 7812 3-9-0 61 .... RobHornby 6 — 61
(Jonathan Portman) *trckd ldrs: prog to chal 2f out: upsides tl wnr wnt past fnl f: nt qckn* **11/4**[2]

2232 3 1 **Lofty**[102] 4286 3-9-5 73 .... TomMarquand 8 — 63
(David Barron) *prom: trckd ldr over 3f out: led jst over 2f out: sn jnd: hdd and one pce jst ins fnl f* **1/1**[1]

0 4 1 **Maqboola (USA)**[65] 5650 3-8-11 0 .... FinleyMarsh(3) 9 — 55
(Richard Hughes) *led to jst over 2f out: nt qckn u.p wl over 1f out: one pce after* **40/1**

40 5 4 1/2 **Hellovasinger**[20] 7319 3-9-5 0 .... StevieDonohoe 7 — 45
(Richard Hughes) *mostly in last pair: outpcd 1/2-way: sme prog past toiling rivals 2f out: no ch w ldrs* **33/1**

00 6 3 3/4 **Jane Camille**[21] 7278 3-9-0 0 .... NicolaCurrie 10 — 28
(Peter Hedger) *sn in rr: nvr a factor: no ch over 1f out* **100/1**

44 7 hd **Festina**[20] 7303 3-9-0 0 .... LukeMorris 5 — 28
(Sir Mark Prescott Bt) *chsd ldrs to 1/2-way: sn wknd* **16/1**

0-00 8 1 1/2 **Shaffire**[125] 3442 3-9-0 55 .... CharlesBishop 1 — 23
(Joseph Tuite) *taken down early: a in rr: struggling over 2f out* **20/1**

35 9 1 1/4 **Moudallal**[17] 7417 3-9-0 0 .... HayleyTurner 2 — 19
(Robert Cowell) *a wl in rr and sn pushed along: no prog* **50/1**

6-6 10 3 1/4 **Doubly Beautiful (IRE)**[40] 6594 3-9-5 0 .... KieranShoemark 3 — 13
(Ed de Giles) *chsd ldr over 2f: wknd qckly over 2f out (trainers rep said gelding was unsuited by the ground on this occasion and would prefer a quicker surface)* **5/1**[3]

1m 16.31s (4.21) **Going Correction** +0.70s/f (Yiel) — **10 Ran SP% 117.1**

Speed ratings (Par 103): **99,97,96,94,88 83,83,81,79,75**

CSF £71.94 TOTE £18.20: £3.90, £1.30, £1.10; EX 97.00 Trifecta £278.30.

Owner Colin Westley **Bred** River Downs Stud **Trained** Epsom, Surrey

FOCUS

Modest maiden form, and a hard race to rate accurately.

7977 AMATEUR JOCKEYS ASSOCIATION NOVICE AMATEUR RIDERS' H'CAP (FOR AMATEURS WITH NO MORE THAN 3 WINS) — 6f 12y

5:10 (5:17) (Class 6) (0-65,67) 3-Y-0+ — £2,682 (£832; £415; £300; £300; £300) Stalls Centre

Form — RPR

3230 1 **Smokey Lane (IRE)**[20] 7299 5-11-7 67 .... MrPhilipThomas(3) 3 — 75
(David Evans) *chsd ldrs: pushed along to cl 2f out: rdn to ld over 1f out: kpt on u.p* **7/2**[1]

2260 2 1 1/4 **Bahuta Acha**[57] 5986 4-11-4 64 .... MrBradleyRoberts(3) 7 — 68
(David Loughnane) *chsd ldrs: rdn 2f out: tk 2nd 1f out: kpt on but nvr able to chal* **12/1**

0005 3 1 1/2 **Just An Idea (IRE)**[11] 7603 5-10-4 50 oh3 ....(b) MissCamillaSwift(3) 10 — 50
(Roger Ingram) *trckd ldr: upsides 2f out to over 1f out: one pce* **33/1**

3300 4 nk **Arctic Flower (IRE)**[8] 7731 6-10-7 50 oh1 .... MissAntoniaPeck 12 — 49
(John Bridger) *trckd ldrs: pushed along 2f out and cl enough: one pce over 1f out* **11/2**[3]

0060 5 1 1/2 **Ocean Temptress**[55] 6058 5-10-7 50 oh5 ....(v) MrGeorgeEddery 9 — 44
(Louise Allan) *chsd ldrs: rdn 2f out: no imp over 1f out: fdd fnl f* **20/1**

1060 6 1 1/2 **Mama Africa (IRE)**[68] 5560 5-11-3 60 ....(p) MissImogenMathias 5 — 50
(John Flint) *chsd ldrs but nvr on terms w them: one pce and no imp over 1f out* **25/1**

3246 7 1 **Lalania**[19] 7345 4-11-4 64 .... MissJuliaEngstrom(3) 1 — 51
(Stuart Williams) *racd alone against nr side: wl in rr: kpt on over 1f out but nvr on terms* **10/1**

100 8 3 1/2 **Sovereign State**[62] 5768 4-10-11 54 .... MrEireannCagney 8 — 30
(Tony Newcombe) *dwlt: a wl off the pce in rr* **12/1**

0004 9 3/4 **Mercers**[49] 6284 5-10-9 52 ....(b) MissMeganTrainor 4 — 26
(Paddy Butler) *racd freely: led to 2f out: wknd qckly* **16/1**

6144 10 1 1/2 **Secondo (FR)**[46] 6363 9-11-6 63 ....(v) MrCraigDowson 11 — 33
(Robert Stephens) *dwlt: a wl off the pce in rr* **16/1**

0060 11 2 1/2 **Who Told Jo Jo (IRE)**[7] 7757 5-10-9 55 .... MrsCharlottePownall(3) 2 — 17
(Joseph Tuite) *a wl in rr and nvr a factor* **25/1**

6214 12 6 **Stay Forever (FR)**[54] 6084 3-11-5 66 .... MissMeganFox(3) 6 — 10
(Andrew Balding) *dwlt: outpcd and a bhd* **5/1**[2]

1m 16.53s (4.43) **Going Correction** +0.70s/f (Yiel)

WFA 3 from 4yo+ 1lb — **12 Ran SP% 105.9**

Speed ratings (Par 101): **98,96,94,93,91 89,88,83,82,80 77,69**

CSF £34.91 CT £865.91 TOTE £3.90: £1.40, £3.00, £9.30; EX 36.20 Trifecta £606.40.

Owner Mrs E Evans **Bred** Miss Philippa Proctor Quinn **Trained** Pandy, Monmouths

■ Aegean Mist was withdrawn, price at time of withdrawal 8/1. Rule 4 applies to all bets. Deduction of 10p in the pound.

FOCUS

An ordinary sprint handicap for inexperienced amateur riders. The second and third help set a straightforward level. This was Philip Thomas's first winner under rules.

T/Jkpt: Not Won. T/Plt: £65.80 to a £1 stake. Pool: £84,382.03 - 934.88 winning units T/Qpdt: £28.40 to a £1 stake. Pool: £8,151.19 - 212.33 winning units **Jonathan Neesom**

7860

COMPIEGNE (L-H)

Monday, October 7

OFFICIAL GOING: Turf: very soft

7978a PRIX CHARLES LAFFITTE (LISTED RACE) (3YO FILLIES) (TURF) — 1m 2f

1:42 3-Y-O — £24,774 (£9,909; £7,432; £4,954; £2,477)

RPR

1 **Mashael (FR)**[59] 3-9-0 0 .... VincentCheminaud 1 — 105
(A Fabre, France) **37/10**[2]

2 4 **Bighearted**[19] 7347 3-9-0 0 .... CameronNoble 6 — 97
(Michael Bell) *wl into stride: led: urged along 2f out: rdn to hold advantage over 1f out: hdd 1f out: drvn and kpt on ins fnl f* **63/10**[3]

3 2 **Samothrace (FR)**[44] 3-9-0 0 .... ChristopheSoumillon 2 — 93
(F-H Graffard, France) **15/1**

4 2 1/2 **Ebony (FR)**[31] 6946 3-9-0 0 ....(b[1]) CristianDemuro 13 — 88
(J-C Rouget, France) **16/5**[1]

5 2 **Tilda (IRE)**[20] 3-9-0 0 .... Pierre-CharlesBoudot 10 — 84
(A Fabre, France) **81/10**

6 1 **Wanderwell**[19] 3-9-0 0 .... MickaelBarzalona 3 — 82
(A Fabre, France) *settled midfield: rowed along 2f out: rdn over 1f out: kpt on same pce ins fnl f* **18/1**

7 1/2 **Terra Dina (FR)**[31] 6946 3-9-0 0 .... AlexisBadel 11 — 81
(H-F Devin, France) **25/1**

8 snk **Mythic (FR)**[16] 7477 3-9-0 0 .... StephanePasquier 4 — 81
(A De Royer-Dupre, France) **74/10**

9 1/2 **Sand Share**[36] 6775 3-9-0 0 .... HarryBentley 14 — 80
(Ralph Beckett) *dwlt: hld up in rr: shkn up over 2f out: rdn over 1f out: nvr on terms and one pce fnl f* **16/1**

10 3 1/2 **Sakura Zensen (FR)**[24] 7171 3-9-0 0 ....(b) GregoryBenoist 8 — 73
(Hiroo Shimizu, France) **15/1**

11 1/2 **Freedom Rising (GER)**[15] 7499 3-9-0 0 .... AntoineHamelin 5 — 72
(Yasmin Almenrader, Germany) **37/1**

12 1 **Houesville (FR)**[33] 3-9-0 0 .... MlleAlisonMassin 7 — 70
(C Lerner, France) **33/1**

13 15 **Mythica (IRE)**[15] 7499 3-9-0 0 .... TheoBachelot 9 — 40
(Jean-Pierre Carvalho, Germany) **20/1**

2m 10.04s — **13 Ran SP% 119.5**

PARI-MUTUEL (all including 1 euro stake): WIN 4.70; PLACE 2.10, 2.50, 3.70; DF 13.10.

Owner HE Sh Joaan Bin Hamad Al Thani **Bred** Al Shaqab Racing **Trained** Chantilly, France

7979 - (Foreign Racing) - See Raceform Interactive

7268

BRIGHTON (L-H)

Tuesday, October 8

OFFICIAL GOING: Good to soft (6.3)

Weather: overcast with sunny periods

7980 BONUSCODEBETS.CO.UK NURSERY H'CAP — 6f 210y

2:00 (2:02) (Class 5) (0-75,75) 2-Y-O — £3,428 (£1,020; £509; £300; £300; £300) Stalls Centre

Form — RPR

4505 1 **More Than A Prince**[14] 7548 2-9-5 73 .... RossaRyan 9 — 79
(Richard Hannon) *midfield in tch: effrt to chse ldr 2f out: rdn to ld over 1f out: rdn out and styd on wl* **11/2**[2]

002 2 2 1/4 **Awesome Gary**[29] 7023 2-8-13 67 .... BrettDoyle 4 — 67
(Tony Carroll) *prom: pushed along and no immediate imp 2f out: rdn and wnt 2nd 1f out: kpt on but nt match wnr* **11/1**

034 3 3/4 **Anglo Saxson (IRE)**[20] 7346 2-9-7 75 .... StevieDonohoe 6 — 73
(Charlie Fellowes) *in tch in midfield: hdwy u.p in centre of trck 2f out: rdn and wnt 3rd 1f out: kpt on* **3/1**[1]

0000 4 3/4 **Comvida (IRE)**[22] 7275 2-8-0 54 oh9 ....(b[1]) JimmyQuinn 8 — 50
(Hugo Palmer) *led: shifted rt 6f out: led field towards stands' side off home bnd: rdn along and hdd by wnr over 1f out: wknd fnl f* **20/1**

3504 5 2 **Global Agreement**[8] 7754 2-8-12 66 .... KieranO'Neill 7 — 57
(Milton Harris) *walked to post: in rr of midfield: rdn and no imp 2f out: drvn and mde sme late hdwy fnl f* **7/1**[3]

020 6 3/4 **Moondance**[13] 7570 2-8-12 66 .... HectorCrouch 1 — 55
(Gary Moore) *in rr of midfield: pushed along and struggling over 2f out: rdn and minor hdwy over 1f out: kpt on one pce fnl f* **25/1**

3405 7 nk **Brazen Safa**[47] 6369 2-9-5 73 .... HayleyTurner 5 — 61
(Michael Bell) *hld up in last pair: rdn and c wdst of all off home bnd: drvn along over 1f out: plugged on past btn horses fnl f: nrst fin* **10/1**

053 8 2 3/4 **Pure Purfection (IRE)**[26] 7124 2-8-5 59 .... DavidEgan 2 — 40
(Jim Boyle) *midfield on inner: rdn along and outpcd 2f out: drvn and no hdwy 1f out: plugged on* **33/1**

0001 9 1 1/4 **Kyllwind**[13] 7582 2-9-5 73 .... RobHornby 11 — 51
(Martyn Meade) *trckd ldr to 2f out: rdn and lost pl over 1f out: wknd fnl f* **8/1**

6430 10 2 1/2 **Positive Light (IRE)**[39] 6683 2-8-4 58 ....(p[1]) LukeMorris 12 — 29
(Sir Mark Prescott Bt) *racd freely on outer in 3rd: rdn along and outpcd 2f out: plugged on one pce fnl f* **25/1**

665 11 15 **Wilfy**[18] 7406 2-9-4 72 .... LiamKeniry 13 — 4
(Sylvester Kirk) *restless in stalls: s.i.s: midfield on outer: wknd u.p 2f out: no ex* **8/1**

654 12 4 **Ocho Grande (IRE)**[26] 7113 2-8-13 67 .... CharlesBishop 10
(Eve Johnson Houghton) *dwlt and racd in rr: nvr on terms* **9/1**

060 13 3 3/4 **Hootenanny (IRE)**[13] 7569 2-8-3 57 ....(b[1]) MartinDwyer 3
(Adam West) *restrained s and racd in rr: a bhd* **50/1**

1m 26.66s (2.86) **Going Correction** +0.475s/f (Yiel) — **13 Ran SP% 119.9**

Speed ratings (Par 95): **102,99,98,97,95 94,94,91,89,86 69,65,60**

CSF £60.47 CT £217.99 TOTE £5.90: £2.50, £2.90, £1.30; EX 58.50 Trifecta £294.30.

Owner Lady Bamford **Bred** Lady Bamford **Trained** East Everleigh, Wilts

FOCUS

Following 6mm of overnight rain, the ground was given as good to soft, good in places (GoingStick 6.3). All distances as advertised. A nursery run at a sound pace with a result that gives the form a solid look, the well-bred winner improving on the back of market confidence to get the better of a pair that arrived in form. They ended up spread across the track and while the winner was more towards the stands' rail than the placed pair, it's hard to know if he was at any great advantage. The runner-up built on his figure behind a decent horse here last time.

7981 EBF NOVICE MEDIAN AUCTION STKS — 6f 210y

2:30 (2:34) (Class 5) 2-Y-O — £3,428 (£1,020; £509; £254) Stalls Centre

Form — RPR

02 1 **Overwrite (IRE)**[10] 7677 2-9-5 0 .... FrannyNorton 11 — 83+
(Mark Johnston) *mde all: led field stands' side off home bnd: rdn and qckly asserted over 1f out: hung lft ins fnl f but wl in command* **11/10**[1]

2 6 **Dashing Roger** 2-9-5 0 .... EdwardGreatrex 16 — 67+
(William Stone) *in tch on outer: effrt in midfield 2f out: sn rdn and mde gd hdwy over 1f out: rdn and kpt on wl to go remote 2nd wl ins fnl f: no ch w wnr (jockey said gelding hung right-handed throughout)* **40/1**

3 3/4 **Capla Cubiste** 2-9-0 0 .... LukeMorris 2 — 60
(Sir Mark Prescott Bt) *prom on inner: a little green at times: rdn to chse ldr over 2f out: readily outpcd by wnr and hung lft over 1f out: kpt on but lost 2nd wl ins fnl f* **14/1**

	4	5	**Casa Loupi** 2-9-5 0 ... HectorCrouch 4 (Gary Moore) *midfield: pushed along and green over 3f out: rdn and hdwy over 1f out: kpt on one pce fnl f*	**25/1**	52+
0	5	1 ¼	**Burning (IRE)**[63] 5774 2-9-5 0 ... StevieDonohoe 9 (Charlie Fellowes) *in rr of midfield: hdwy u.p in centre of trck 2f out: sn rdn and one pce: lost 4th cl home*	**5/1**[2]	49+
	6	hd	**Voice Of Dubawi** 2-9-0 0 ... MartinDwyer 7 (Paul Webber) *dwlt and racd in rr: prog into midfield 2f out: rdn and sme late hdwy ins fnl f*	**66/1**	44
0	7	1 ¾	**Edebez (IRE)**[35] 6845 2-9-5 0 ... JimmyQuinn 6 (Seamus Mullins) *hld up: hdwy into midfield over 2f out: pushed along and no real imp over 1f: kpt on one pce fnl f under mostly hands and heels*	**20/1**	44
06	8	1 ¼	**Scallywagtail (IRE)**[26] 7124 2-9-5 0 ... DavidProbert 8 (Gary Moore) *midfield: minor hdwy to chse ldrs over 2f out: sn rdn and wknd 1f out*	**33/1**	41
	9	nse	**Rains Of Castamere** 2-9-5 0 ... CharlesBishop 12 (Mick Channon) *prom early: rdn along and outpcd over 1f out: wknd fnl f*	**10/1**	41
0	10	1	**Vintage Port (IRE)**[18] 7406 2-9-5 0 ... RossaRyan 1 (Tony Carroll) *settled in tch on inner: rdn along and outpcd 2f out: wknd over 1f out*	**40/1**	38
00	11	2 ¾	**By Jove**[20] 7346 2-9-5 0 ... HayleyTurner 15 (Michael Bell) *hld up: rdn in rr over 2f out: nvr on terms*	**28/1**	31
45	12	¾	**Kuwaity**[22] 7285 2-9-5 0 ... DavidEgan 10 (Mohamed Moubarak) *chsd ldr tl 2f out: sn rdn and lost pl over 1f out: no ex*	**9/1**[3]	29
0	13	2 ¾	**Lady Sarah**[18] 7406 2-9-0 0 ... BrettDoyle 14 (Tony Carroll) *hld up: a bhd*	**100/1**	17
	14	1 ¾	**Eight Bells** 2-9-5 0 ... CallumShepherd 3 (Michael Bell) *racd in midfield: pushed along and no hdwy over 2f out: rdn and wknd fr over 1f out*	**14/1**	17
00	15	14	**Viking Honour (IRE)**[18] 7407 2-9-5 0 ... (p[1]) RobHornby 5 (Joseph Tuite) *in tch: rdn along and outpcd over 2f out: sn wknd*	**100/1**	
00	16	1 ¼	**Mr Jack Daniels**[40] 6640 2-9-5 0 ... (h[1]) KieranO'Neill 13 (Peter Hiatt) *awkward on way to s: hld up: a bhd*	**100/1**	

1m 26.67s (2.87) **Going Correction** +0.475s/f (Yiel) **16** Ran SP% **121.0**
Speed ratings (Par 95): **102,95,94,88,87 86,84,83,83,82 79,78,75,73,57 55**
CSF £71.13 TOTE £1.80: £1.10, £9.30, £3.10; EX 40.60 Trifecta £475.80.
Owner Sheikh Hamdan bin Mohammed Al Maktoum **Bred** Mrs H M Smith & James Murtagh **Trained** Middleham Moor, N Yorks

FOCUS
Plenty were green and/or floundered in the conditions, leaving Overwrite with a simple task, but the way he cleared away was still most impressive, and there was some mild promise from some of the newcomers. Once again the field made their way to the near side in the straight and the first pair were closer to the rail than most. The winner routed them, and it's rated as very ordinary form behind him.

7982 42 BEDFORD ROW CHAMBERS H'CAP 7f 211y

3:05 (3:05) (Class 6) (0-65,65) 3-Y-O+
£2,781 (£827; £413; £300; £300; £300) **Stalls** Centre

Form					RPR
0065	1		**Hedging (IRE)**[46] 6414 5-9-4 **59** ... (v) CharlesBishop 14 (Eve Johnson Houghton) *prom early: decisive move to get to nr rail 3f out and ld: rdn along over 1f out: kpt on strly fnl f*	**14/1**	70
1051	2	2 ¾	**Kyllachys Tale (IRE)**[23] 7237 5-9-7 **65** ... CierenFallon[(3)] 4 (Roger Teal) *hld up: hdwy u.p over 2f out: rdn and hdwy to go 2nd ins fnl f: kpt on*	**6/1**[2]	70
23	3	2 ½	**Silverturnstogold**[29] 7024 4-8-12 **60** ... AngusVilliers[(7)] 9 (Tony Carroll) *hld up: hdwy u.p to chse ldrs in centre of trck 2f out: rdn along to go 2nd briefly 1f out: no ex fnl f*	**9/2**[1]	59
0130	4	½	**Good Luck Charm**[37] 6758 10-8-13 **61** ... (v) RhysClutterbuck[(7)] 10 (Gary Moore) *hld up: pushed along to chse ldrs over 2f out: rdn and hung lft 1f out: one pce fnl f*	**33/1**	59
5522	5	1	**Duke Of North (IRE)**[29] 7028 7-8-11 **52** ... (p) CharlieBennett 13 (Jim Boyle) *chsd ldrs: rdn along and unable qck over 1f out: one pce fnl f*	**14/1**	48
1312	6	1 ¾	**Joyful Dream (IRE)**[22] 7273 5-9-0 **58** ... (b) DarraghKeenan[(3)] 8 (John Butler) *hld up: gd hdwy on to heels of ldrs 2f out: sn rdn and sltly hmpd over 1f out: no ex fnl f (jockey said mare anticipated the start and hit her head on the gates)*	**10/1**	51
3202	7	1 ¾	**Duchess Of Avon**[35] 6844 4-9-6 **61** ... ShaneKelly 6 (Gary Moore) *racd in midfield: rdn along and no imp over 1f out: wknd fnl f*	**8/1**[3]	49
6206	8	1 ¼	**My Lady Claire**[54] 6123 3-8-9 **53** ... (p[1]) DavidProbert 16 (Patrick Chamings) *prom: rdn along to chse wnr over 2f out: hung lft u.p over 1f out and sn lost 2nd: wknd fnl f*	**20/1**	39
1023	9	1 ½	**Toro Dorado**[21] 7305 3-9-4 **62** ... EdwardGreatrex 12 (Ed Dunlop) *in rr of midfield: effrt to cl 3f out: sn rdn and no imp over 1f out: wknd fnl f*	**10/1**	44
3100	10	¾	**Wilson (IRE)**[22] 7272 4-9-9 **64** ... (p) ShelleyBirkett 2 (Julia Feilden) *hld up: rdn and no hdwy 2f out: nvr a factor*	**33/1**	45
200	11	¾	**Master Poet**[22] 7282 4-8-11 **52** ... (p) LukeMorris 1 (Gary Moore) *prom on inner: rdn along in centre of trck over 2f out: hung lft over 1f out: one pce after*	**16/1**	31
6443	12	½	**Penarth Pier (IRE)**[14] 7549 3-8-10 **54** ... FrannyNorton 5 (Christine Dunnett) *racd in midfield: rdn and no imp 2f out: sn bhd*	**16/1**	32
2300	13	7	**Confrerie (IRE)**[8] 7758 4-9-6 **61** ... KieranO'Neill 7 (George Baker) *hld up and racd keenly: a in rr*	**10/1**	24
0614	14	10	**Kennocha (IRE)**[17] 7472 3-9-1 **59** ... (tp) DavidEgan 15 (Amy Murphy) *led: rdn along and hdd in centre of trck 3f out: sn wknd and lost pl 2f out (trainers rep said filly was unsuited by the ground and would prefer a sounder surface)*	**10/1**	
6414	15	17	**Imbucato**[37] 6758 5-8-12 **53** ... (p) BrettDoyle 11 (Tony Carroll) *chsd ldrs: rdn along and hmpd over 2f out: sn wknd and bhd (jockey said gelding hung left-handed)*	**11/1**	
0000	16	4 ½	**Margie's Choice (GER)**[104] 4249 4-9-2 **57** ... LiamKeniry 3 (Michael Madgwick) *prom: rdn and short of room over 2f out: sn wknd and t.o*	**50/1**	

1m 40.22s (3.32) **Going Correction** +0.475s/f (Yiel) **16** Ran SP% **126.0**
WFA 3 from 4yo+ 3lb
Speed ratings (Par 101): **102,99,96,96,95 93,91,90,89,88 87,87,80,70,53 48**
CSF £95.66 CT £473.32 TOTE £14.70: £3.20, £2.30, £1.70, £5.70; EX 147.80 Trifecta £1083.60.
Owner Eden Racing Club **Bred** Old Carhue & Graeng Bloodstock **Trained** Blewbury, Oxon

FOCUS
No doubt the track bias had an impact on this low-grade handicap, the winner the only one to stay glued to the stands' rail in the straight. He was entitled to win off this mark. The pace was strong from the outset.

7983 BRITISH EBF NOVICE STKS 7f 211y

3:35 (3:37) (Class 5) 2-Y-O
£3,428 (£1,020; £509; £254) **Stalls** Centre

Form					RPR
1	1		**Oleksander**[25] 7154 2-9-6 0 ... DavidEgan 1 (Archie Watson) *trckd ldr: pushed along to ld over 2f out: rdn and hdd by rival over 1f out: rallied wl u.p to ld again 1f out: styd on wl*	**9/4**[2]	82
5204	2	1	**Light Angel**[12] 7612 2-9-6 90 ... CierenFallon[(3)] 6 (John Gosden) *chsd ldrs: pushed along and wnt 2nd over 2f out: rdn to ld over 1f out: sn drvn and hdd by wnr 1f out: kpt on*	**10/11**[1]	83
352	3	nk	**Inca Man (FR)**[14] 7555 2-9-2 0 ... RossaRyan 2 (Paul Cole) *midfield and green at times: effrt to cl over 2f out: sn rdn and outpcd by ldng pair over 1f out: r.o wl again fnl f*	**11/2**[3]	75
0	4	12	**Rally Driver**[12] 7623 2-9-2 0 ... CallumShepherd 4 (Mick Channon) *hld up: pushed along and outpcd 2f out: sn bhd*	**50/1**	47
2	5	3 ½	**Herodotus (IRE)**[37] 6757 2-9-2 0 ... DavidProbert 5 (Andrew Balding) *led and racd freely: led field stands' side 3f out: sn rdn and hdd by wnr over 2f out: sn wknd*	**12/1**	39
0	6	8	**Fear Naught**[20] 7338 2-9-2 0 ... LiamKeniry 3 (George Baker) *hld up: hdwy on outer over 2f out: rdn and wknd over 1f out*	**33/1**	21

1m 41.39s (4.49) **Going Correction** +0.475s/f (Yiel) **6** Ran SP% **111.1**
Speed ratings (Par 95): **96,95,94,82,79 71**
CSF £4.53 TOTE £3.60: £2.00, £1.10; EX 5.20 Trifecta £12.00.
Owner Nurlan Bizakov **Bred** Hesmonds Stud Ltd **Trained** Upper Lambourn, W Berks

FOCUS
The crucial point in this very useful novice was when Oleksander managed to secure the rail before his main rival, that arguably the difference between them. The pace was steady until it lifted after halfway. The runner-up has been rated as slightly below his best.

7984 CYRIL'S BIRTHDAY CELEBRATION H'CAP 1m 1f 207y

4:10 (4:11) (Class 6) (0-65,65) 3-Y-O+
£2,781 (£827; £413; £300; £300; £300) **Stalls** Centre

Form					RPR
3364	1		**Hermocrates (FR)**[12] 7625 3-9-8 **65** ... (b) RossaRyan 3 (Richard Hannon) *prom on inner: pushed along to chse ldr 3f out: rdn to ld over 1f out: hung lft u.str.p fnl f but kpt on wl*	**10/1**	74
3322	2	2 ¾	**Hammy End (IRE)**[22] 7290 3-9-1 **61** ... (h) CierenFallon[(3)] 15 (William Muir) *hld up: smooth hdwy to go 2nd over 3f out: c over to stands' side to ld 3f out: rdn along and hdd by wnr over 1f out: kpt on one pce fnl f (jockey said gelding hung left-handed)*	**11/2**[2]	65
	3	½	**Zamani (GER)**[86] 3-9-0 **62** ... PoppyBridgwater[(5)] 13 (David Bridgwater) *midfield on outer: effrt to chse ldr over 2f out: rdn and kpt on wl to go 3rd ins fnl f*	**20/1**	65
1234	4	½	**Shifting Gold (IRE)**[20] 7343 3-9-4 **61** ... CallumShepherd 4 (William Knight) *dwlt and racd in rr: hdwy rt against stands' rail 3f out: rdn and sme hdwy over 1f out: nrst fin*	**9/1**	63
2461	5	shd	**Light Of Air (FR)**[16] 6760 6-9-1 **61** ... (b) LouisGaroghan[(7)] 11 (Gary Moore) *hld up: pushed along and hung lft to far side over 2f out: sn rdn and kpt on one pce fnl f*	**14/1**	62
1054	6	2 ¾	**Spirit Of Angel (IRE)**[32] 6931 3-9-6 **63** ... (v[1]) MartinDwyer 6 (Marcus Tregoning) *hld up: pushed along and outpcd 3f out: rdn and minor hdwy 2f out: kpt on steadily*	**9/1**	59
4043	7	½	**Jumping Jack (IRE)**[16] 6507 5-9-10 **63** ... (p) CharlesBishop 7 (Chris Gordon) *racd in midfield: racd along on fair rail 3f out: rdn and no imp 2f out: one pce fnl f*	**16/1**	58
2635	8	3	**Banksy's Art**[58] 5993 4-9-1 **61** ... AngusVilliers[(7)] 12 (Amanda Perrett) *chsd ldrs early: rdn along and outpcd 2f out: no imp u.p over 1f out: no ex*	**9/2**[1]	50
6400	9	2 ¼	**Buzz Lightyere**[19] 7376 6-8-11 **50** ... (v) DavidProbert 2 (Patrick Chamings) *racd in midfield: rdn and no imp 2f out: one pce fnl f*	**20/1**	35
	10	3 ¾	**Tremwedge**[162] 2225 3-8-13 **56** ... LiamKeniry 10 (Miss Ellmarie Holden, Ire) *in tch in midfield: rdn along over 3f out: sn drvn and lost pl 2f out*	**6/1**[3]	34
6450	11	1 ¾	**Allocated (IRE)**[24] 7192 3-9-4 **64** ... (p[1]) DarraghKeenan[(3)] 5 (John Butler) *chsd ldrs: rdn along and outpcd 2f out: lost pl and wknd over 1f out*	**33/1**	39
1135	12	4 ½	**Cafe Sydney (IRE)**[20] 7343 3-9-1 **58** ... BrettDoyle 14 (Tony Carroll) *hld up: hdwy into midfield: 3f out: rdn and briefly short of room 2f out: sn drvn and wknd over 1f out*	**12/1**	25
5633	13	2 ½	**Beer With The Boys**[7] 7790 4-9-6 **59** ... (v) ShaneKelly 1 (Mick Channon) *midfield: rdn along and struggling 3f out: bmpd by rival over 2f out and sn struggling*	**8/1**	20
0435	14	5	**Couldn't Could She**[23] 7229 4-9-9 **62** ... CharlieBennett 16 (Adam West) *hld up: outpcd 3f out: a bhd (jockey said filly stopped quickly)*	**14/1**	13
6366	15	13	**Cedar**[75] 5354 3-8-3 **46** ... KieranO'Neill 8 (Mohamed Moubarak) *led: rdn along and hdd 3f out: wknd qckly 2f out*	**66/1**	

2m 11.0s (6.00) **Going Correction** +0.675s/f (Yiel) **15** Ran SP% **128.9**
WFA 3 from 4yo+ 4lb
Speed ratings (Par 101): **103,100,100,100,99 97,97,94,93,90 88,85,83,79,68**
CSF £65.77 CT £1124.32 TOTE £11.90: £3.50, £2.00, £4.90; EX 51.60 Trifecta £932.30.
Owner Michael Pescod **Bred** D R Tucker & Silfield Bloodstock **Trained** East Everleigh, Wilts
■ Stewards' Enquiry : Martin Dwyer caution; careless riding

FOCUS
Surprisingly, they shunned the stands' rail this time and there was no obvious bias in this well-run, modest handicap. A competitive race for the grade.

7985 BLIND VETERANS UK APPRENTICE H'CAP (HANDS AND HEELS RACE) (RACING EXCELLENCE INITIATIVE) 1m 3f 198y

4:45 (4:47) (Class 6) (0-55,55) 3-Y-O+
£2,781 (£827; £413; £300; £300; £300) **Stalls** High

Form					RPR
0322	1		**Royal Dancer**[14] 7553 3-8-10 **53** ... ElinorJones[(8)] 3 (Sylvester Kirk) *prom: smooth hdwy to chse ldrs 2f out: pushed along to ld over 1f out: rdn and hung lft ins fnl f: all out*	**9/2**[3]	60

The Form Book Flat 2019, Raceform Ltd, Newbury, RG14 5SJ

3200 **2** *shd* **Mistress Nellie**[21] 7318 4-9-4 47 GeorgiaDobie 7 53
(William Stone) *hld up: smooth hdwy wdst of all against stands' rail 2f out: sn rdn and wnt 2nd 1f out: hung lft and clsd all the way to the line: jst failed (jockey said filly hung left-handed)* **4/1**[2]

0050 **3** *2 1/4* **Pecorino**[23] 7240 3-9-3 55 AngusVilliers(3) 11 58
(Richard Hughes) *dwlt and racd in rr: hdwy u.p into midfield 3f out: sn rdn and clsd to go 3rd ins fnl f: kpt on* **8/1**

4523 **4** *2 3/4* **General Brook (IRE)**[16] 7492 9-9-9 55 (p) KateLeahy(3) 2 53
(John O'Shea) *prom: wnt 2nd to chse ldr 5f out: sn rdn and lost pl over 2f out: wknd fnl f* **10/1**

0003 **5** *8* **Millie May**[22] 7271 5-9-3 46 oh1 GavinAshton 4 32
(Jimmy Fox) *hld up way off pce: hdwy on outer over 3f out: sn rdn and no imp 2f out: wknd fnl f* **16/1**

6000 **6** *1/2* **Affair**[24] 7202 5-9-1 47 (v1) IsobelFrancis(3) 9 33+
(Hughie Morrison) *led and sn clr 1/2-way: much reduced advantage over 2f out: rdn and hdd over 1f out: no ex (jockey said mare ran too free)* **10/1**

0240 **7** *4 1/2* **Iballisticvin**[35] 6843 6-9-4 53 (v) RhysClutterbuck(6) 10 32
(Gary Moore) *hld up: hdwy to chse ldrs over 2f out: sn rdn and no imp over 1f out: wknd fnl f* **17/2**

00-6 **8** *1/2* **Poucor**[23] 7240 4-9-4 47 AmeliaGlass 6 25
(Mick Channon) *prom: rdn along to chse ldrs 3f out: wknd 2f out: sn bhd* **10/3**[1]

4000 **9** *8* **Perique**[90] 4803 3-9-2 54 GeorgeRooke(3) 8 21
(Peter Hiatt) *hld up: clsd on ldrs gng wl 3f out: rdn and fnd little 2f out: sn wknd* **25/1**

/50- **10** *3/4* **Hermosa Vaquera (IRE)**[16] 8737 9-9-6 55 (p) LouisGaroghan(6) 1 20
(Gary Moore) *prom in chsng pack: rdn and wknd 4f out: t.o* **33/1**

400 **11** *3/4* **Lady Of Mercia**[56] 6043 3-8-13 48 GraceMcEntee 5 13
(John Flint) *midfield: rdn and wknd 4f out: t.o* **50/1**

2m 44.32s (8.32) **Going Correction** +0.675s/f (Yiel)
WFA 3 from 4yo+ 6lb **11** Ran SP% **115.7**
Speed ratings (Par 101): **99,98,97,95,90 89,86,86,81,80 80**
CSF £22.06 CT £139.71 TOTE £3.30: £1.90, £1.90, £2.60; EX 21.60 Trifecta £238.90.
Owner Gerry Dolan **Bred** Littleton Stud **Trained** Upper Lambourn, Berks

FOCUS
A basement handicap in which \bAffair\p set a furious gallop but was largely ignored by the others. There were no hard-luck stories. The winner is rated in line with his previous best.

7986 SUSSEX ART FAIR (EAST) 12 OCTOBER H'CAP 5f 60y
5:15 (5:15) (Class 6) (0-65,66) 3-Y-0+
£2,781 (£827; £413; £300; £300; £300) **Stalls** Low

Form RPR

5332 **1** **Firenze Rosa (IRE)**[8] 7757 4-8-1 50 AledBeech(7) 7 58
(John Bridger) *in tch in midfield: gd hdwy u.p to cl 2f out: rdn to ld over 1f out: rdn out fnl f* **11/2**[3]

0600 **2** *1 1/4* **Major Pusey**[13] 7568 7-9-7 66 CierenFallon(3) 11 70
(John Gallagher) *hld up: hdwy into midfield 1/2-way: sn rdn and styd on strly on outer fnl f: nt rch wnr* **4/1**[1]

6645 **3** *1/2* **Kraka (IRE)**[14] 7552 4-9-4 60 KieranO'Neill 3 62
(Christine Dunnett) *chsd ldrs: rdn along and ev ch appr fnl f: unable to match front pair fnl 100yds* **4/1**[1]

2254 **4** *shd* **Valentino Sunrise**[13] 7568 3-9-2 58 CallumShepherd 9 61
(Mick Channon) *chsd ldrs: rdn along to hold position 2f out: drvn and one pce ins fnl f* **13/2**

3466 **5** *2 1/2* **Pharoh Jake**[56] 6048 11-7-10 45 IsobelFrancis(7) 1 38
(John Bridger) *racd in midfield: hdwy u.p 2f out: sn rdn and no imp 1f out: wknd fnl f* **40/1**

3463 **6** *nk* **Cool Strutter (IRE)**[54] 6107 7-8-5 47 (p) HayleyTurner 13 39
(John Spearing) *prom on outer: rdn along to cl over 1f out: wknd fnl f* **12/1**

3450 **7** *1/2* **Flowing Clarets**[7] 7784 6-8-4 46 LiamJones 5 37
(John Bridger) *midfield and racd freely: effrt to cl 2f out: sn rdn and hung lft over 1f out: wknd fnl f* **16/1**

312 **8** *1 1/2* **Toni's A Star**[11] 7651 7-9-0 63 AngusVilliers(7) 10 48
(Tony Carroll) *trckd ldr: rdn along and lost pl over 1f out: wknd fnl f* **5/1**[2]

4350 **9** *5* **Roundabout Magic (IRE)**[10] 7690 5-9-3 59 NickyMackay 2 27
(Simon Dow) *led: c stands' side in st: rdn along and hung sltly lft 2f out: hdd by wnr over 1f out: wknd fnl f* **14/1**

0604 **10** *1* **Autumn Splendour (IRE)**[8] 7757 3-9-3 59 (p) PhilipPrince 12 25+
(Milton Bradley) *dwlt and sn bhd: drifted to far rail over 1f out: nvr on terms (jockey said gelding was slowly away)* **25/1**

1160 **11** *2 1/4* **Pocket Warrior**[123] 3527 8-8-11 53 (t) ShaneKelly 6 10
(Paul D'Arcy) *dwlt and bmpd leaving stalls: sn rdn and bhd* **22/1**

0550 **12** *1 1/4* **Alfie's Angel (IRE)**[38] 6703 5-8-3 45 JimmyQuinn 8
(Milton Bradley) *dwlt and racd in rr: outpcd and detached 2f out* **40/1**

1m 5.63s (2.63) **Going Correction** +0.475s/f (Yiel) **12** Ran SP% **118.7**
Speed ratings (Par 101): **98,96,95,95,91 90,89,87,79,77 74,72**
CSF £26.72 CT £99.32 TOTE £6.70: £2.20, £2.10, £1.90; EX 29.70 Trifecta £171.90.
Owner Mr & Mrs K Finch **Bred** Gervin Creaner **Trained** Liphook, Hants
■ Stewards' Enquiry : Angus Villiers two-day ban; misuse of whip (Oct 22-23)

FOCUS
A modest sprint handicap in which plenty were a long way back at halfway, including the runner-up who caught the eye. The form looks solid otherwise, with the winner close to her recent form.
T/Jkpt: Not Won. T/Plt: £32.00 to a £1 stake. Pool: £82,700.65 - 1,881.50 winning units T/Qpdt: £12.10 to a £1 stake. Pool: £9,393.38 - 571.09 winning units **Mark Grantham**

7437 CATTERICK (L-H)
Tuesday, October 8
7987 Meeting Abandoned - Waterlogged

7832 CHELMSFORD (A.W) (L-H)
Tuesday, October 8
OFFICIAL GOING: Polytrack: standard
Wind: medium, half behind Weather: showers and bright spells

7994 BET TOTEPLACEPOT AT TOTESPORT.COM CLAIMING STKS 7f (P)
4:40 (4:42) (Class 5) 2-Y-O
£4,204 (£1,251; £625; £400; £400; £400) **Stalls** Low

Form RPR

5140 **1** **Dragon Command**[68] 5587 2-9-7 77 (p) HarryBentley 6 74
(George Scott) *wnt rt s and dwlt: rcvrd to press ldr after 1f: led 5f out: rdn ent fnl 2f: kpt on ins fnl f* **13/8**[1]

1164 **2** *1* **Mac McCarthy (IRE)**[24] 7173 2-9-4 72 (p1) FinleyMarsh(3) 4 71
(Richard Hughes) *led early: sn hdd and hld up wl in tch: swtchd rt and nt clr run over 1f out: hung lft and racd awkwardly over 1f out: kpt on ins fnl f to snatch 2nd last strides* **3/1**[2]

4061 **3** *nk* **Chromium**[17] 7469 2-8-4 62 (v) JosephineGordon 3 54
(Mark Usher) *chsd ldrs tl chsd wnr 4f out: rdn over 2f out: kpt on same pce u.p fnl 100yds: lost 2nd last strides* **10/1**

03 **4** *3/4* **Cadeo**[12] 7605 2-9-0 0 (h) StefanoCherchi(7) 1 69
(Marco Botti) *taken down early and led to post: hld up wl in tch: effrt on inner over 1f out: no imp fnl 100yds* **6/1**

3066 **5** *nk* **Constanzia**[15] 7515 2-8-6 65 NicolaCurrie 5 53
(Jamie Osborne) *sn led: hdd 5f out: styd chsng ldrs: effrt 2f out: keeping on same pce whn short of room 100yds out: swtchd lft and no imp after* **9/2**[3]

0502 **6** *9* **Serious Jockin**[8] 7768 2-8-4 44 GeorgeBass(7) 2 34
(Mick Channon) *taken down early: t.k.h: hld up in tch: effrt in centre over 1f out: hung lft and wknd fnl f* **16/1**

1m 26.52s (-0.68) **Going Correction** -0.175s/f (Stan) **6** Ran SP% **110.5**
Speed ratings (Par 95): **96,94,94,93,93 83**
CSF £6.43 TOTE £2.20: £1.40, £1.70; EX 6.20 Trifecta £32.40.Dragon Command was claimed by Mr G. O. Scott for £20000, Chromium was claimed by Mr M. J. Attwater for £8000
Owner The Black Dragon **Bred** Saleh Al Homaizi & Imad Al Sagar **Trained** Newmarket, Suffolk

FOCUS
This claimer was dominated from the front by the winner, who was the highest rated runner in the line-up. The fourth was the only improver of note.

7995 BET TOTEEXACTA AT TOTESPORT.COM FILLIES' NOVICE STKS (PLUS 10 RACE) 6f (P)
5:10 (5:14) (Class 4) 2-Y-O **£6,080** (£1,809; £904; £452) **Stalls** Centre

Form RPR

0250 **1** **Taste The Nectar (USA)**[26] 7117 2-9-0 69 (p) SilvestreDeSousa 7 70
(Robert Cowell) *pushed along in midfield early: clsd to trck ldrs on inner over 3f out: effrt to chal between rivals over 1f out: led 1f out: drvn and asserted ins fnl f: eased cl home* **6/1**

2463 **2** *1 1/4* **Hidden Spell (IRE)**[19] 7377 2-9-0 71 DanielTudhope 1 66
(K R Burke) *chsd ldr: effrt and ev ch over 1f out: drvn and unable to match pce of wnr ins fnl f: kpt on same pce fnl 100yds* **7/4**[1]

06 **3** *3 1/4* **Falacho (IRE)**[14] 7546 2-8-9 0 ThomasGreatrex(5) 5 56
(David Loughnane) *sn led: rdn and hrd pressed over 1f out: hdd 1f out: no ex and wknd ins fnl f* **25/1**

54 **4** *2* **Vintage Polly (IRE)**[19] 7393 2-9-0 0 JamesDoyle 2 50
(Hugo Palmer) *t.k.h: chsd ldrs: effrt in 4th but struggling to qckn over 2f out: wl hld and swtchd rt 1f out* **5/2**[2]

0 **5** *3/4* **Gently Spoken (IRE)**[81] 5132 2-9-0 0 RobHornby 3 48+
(Martyn Meade) *wl in tch in midfield: pushed along and outpcd in 5th over 2f out: wl hld and plugged on same pce fr over 1f out* **3/1**[3]

0 **6** *4 1/2* **Tiger Balm**[14] 7546 2-9-0 0 StevieDonohoe 6 35
(George Boughey) *stdd s: t.k.h: hld up in rr of main gp: modest prog into midfield over 2f out: no prog after and wl btn over 1f out* **40/1**

00 **7** *2 1/4* **Alcance (FR)**[49] 6300 2-9-0 0 HectorCrouch 9 28
(Clive Cox) *in tch in midfield: rn green and wnt rt 4f out: rdn and outpcd over 2f out: wl btn over 1f out* **20/1**

6 **8** *5* **Red's Rocket**[26] 7103 2-9-0 0 NicolaCurrie 10 13
(Laura Mongan) *a off the pce in rr of main gp: nvr involved* **50/1**

9 *5* **Littlemissattitude** 2-9-0 0 LewisEdmunds 4
(Derek Shaw) *s.i.s and wnt lft leaving stalls: rn green and a off the pce in rr of main gp: wl bhd fnl 2f* **50/1**

10 *53* **Neroli** 2-9-0 0 KierenFox 8
(Derek Shaw) *s.i.s: rn green and flashing tail leaving stalls: sn lost tch: t.o* **50/1**

1m 12.46s (-1.24) **Going Correction** -0.175s/f (Stan) **10** Ran SP% **149.7**
Speed ratings (Par 94): **101,99,95,92,91 85,82,75,69,**
CSF £16.86 TOTE £7.00: £1.60, £1.10, £8.00; EX 24.80 Trifecta £235.10.
Owner T W Morley **Bred** Winstar Farm Llc, B P Walden Jr Et Al **Trained** Six Mile Bottom, Cambs

FOCUS
It didn't pay to be too far off the pace here. Modest form, rated around the front pair.

7996 BET TOTEQUADPOT AT TOTESPORT.COM NOVICE STKS 1m (P)
5:40 (5:42) (Class 5) 2-Y-O **£4,204** (£1,251; £625; £312) **Stalls** Low

Form RPR

0 **1** **Prince Imperial (USA)**[46] 6409 2-9-5 0 (v1) JimCrowley 5 80
(Sir Michael Stoute) *pressed ldr: effrt ent fnl 2f: maintained chal and drvn 1f out: led wl ins fnl f: styd on* **5/1**[3]

6 **2** *1 1/4* **Buwardy**[11] 7661 2-9-5 0 RobertHavlin 6 77
(John Gosden) *swtchd lft sn after s: wl in tch in midfield: effrt to chse ldrs over 2f out: kpt on same pce ins fnl f: snatched 2nd last strides* **11/1**

5 **3** *hd* **Imperial Square (IRE)**[13] 7579 2-9-5 0 DanielTudhope 3 77
(Mark Johnston) *led: rdn ent fnl 2f: kpt on and drvn 1f out: hdd wl ins fnl f: no ex and outpcd cl home: lost 2nd last strides* **16/1**

4 *2 3/4* **Secret Victory** 2-9-5 0 WilliamBuick 2 70
(Charlie Appleby) *awkward leaving stalls: trckd ldrs: rdn over 2f out: unable qck and outpcd over 1f out: wl hld 4th and kpt on same pce ins fnl f* **1/1**[1]

5 **5** *4 1/2* **Turn On The Charm (FR)**[32] 6927 2-9-5 0 GeorgeWood 4 60
(James Fanshawe) *stdd after s: t.k.h: hld up in tch in last pair: effrt and hung lft over 1f out: sn outpcd and wknd ins fnl f* **7/2**[2]

6 5 **Chairman Power** 2-9-5 0 SilvestreDeSousa 1 48
(Sir Michael Stoute) *hld up in tch in rr: effrt over 2f out: sn struggling and outpcd: bhd ins fnl f* **10/1**

1m 39.5s (-0.40) **Going Correction** -0.175s/f (Stan) **6 Ran SP% 112.2**
Speed ratings (Par 95): **95,93,93,90,86 81**
CSF £53.00 TOTE £5.20: £2.50, £3.40; EX 51.80 Trifecta £271.90.
Owner K Abdullah **Bred** Juddmonte Farms Inc **Trained** Newmarket, Suffolk

FOCUS
One or two didn't run up to expectations in this novice, but the winner was well supported. Fluid ratings with not too much to go on.

7997 BET TOTETRIFECTA AT TOTESPORT.COM CONDITIONS STKS 1m (P)
6:10 (6:12) (Class 3) 3-Y-O+ **£9,703** (£2,887; £1,443) **Stalls** Low

Form RPR

0102 1 **Habub (USA)**[24] 7188 4-9-3 99 JimCrowley 2 109
(Owen Burrows) *racd keenly: mde all: rdn and edgd lft over 1f out: in command and styd on wl ins fnl f: comf* **5/4**[1]

1-52 2 3 ¼ **Arctic Sound**[142] 2889 3-9-0 108 JoeFanning 1 102
(Mark Johnston) *trckd rivals: rdn 3f out: unable qck over 1f out: chsd wnr and no imp fnl 100yds* **3/1**[3]

0033 3 nk **Ambassadorial (USA)**[30] 7011 5-9-3 104 (e) DavidEgan 3 101
(Jane Chapple-Hyam) *chsd wnr: c towards centre and unable qck over 1f out: kpt on same pce and lost 2nd 100yds out* **13/8**[2]

1m 37.54s (-2.36) **Going Correction** -0.175s/f (Stan)
WFA 3 from 4yo+ 3lb **3 Ran SP% 107.5**
Speed ratings (Par 107): **104,100,100**
CSF £4.81 TOTE £2.10; EX 4.60.
Owner Hamdan Al Maktoum **Bred** Summer Wind Farm **Trained** Lambourn, Berks

FOCUS
A good little race, but inevitably it was tactical, and the favourite was always in pole position to quicken first entering the straight. Only the winner ran his race.

7998 BET TOTESWINGER AT TOTESPORT.COM H'CAP 2m (P)
6:40 (6:42) (Class 6) (0-65,65) 3-Y-O+
£3,105 (£924; £461; £400; £400; £400) **Stalls** Low

Form RPR

-503 1 **Jeweller**[24] 7192 3-9-2 62 (b[1]) JimCrowley 4 81
(Sir Michael Stoute) *short of room sn after s: sn rcvrd and trckd ldrs after 2f: swtchd rt and clsd to join ldr over 3f out: led over 2f out: sn pushed clr: eased wl ins fnl f: v easily* **11/8**[1]

4424 2 13 **Volcanique (IRE)**[19] 7390 3-8-0 46 (v[1]) LukeMorris 1 48
(Sir Mark Prescott Bt) *led: rdn and hdd over 2f out: sn outpcd and wl btn 2f out: plugged on to hold modest 2nd fnl f* **9/2**[3]

6/00 3 2 ¼ **Zamoyski**[39] 6674 9-9-11 62 (p) TomMarquand 5 59
(Steve Gollings) *in tch in last trio: rdn 5f out: 7th and outpcd over 2f out: no ch w wnr after but plugged on and swtchd rt 1f out: wnt modest 3rd towards fin* **50/1**

0-11 4 1 ¾ **Spice War**[14] 7553 4-9-9 65 ThomasGreatrex(5) 6 60+
(Oliver Sherwood) *chsd ldrs on outer: shuffled bk into midfield 1/2-way: rdn wl over 3f out: outpcd by wnr and wl hld 2f out: modest 3rd over 1f out: no imp* **7/4**[2]

0420 5 1 ¾ **Mr Nice Guy (IRE)**[24] 7202 3-8-10 56 DavidEgan 3 51
(Clare Hobson) *midfield: reminders over 6f out: rdn over 4f out: outpcd and no ch w wnr over 2f out: plugged on* **14/1**

3000 6 2 ¾ **Garrison Law**[10] 7685 3-8-7 53 (p[1]) HarryBentley 2 45
(David Simcock) *chsd ldr tl 9f out: chsd ldrs after: 4th and outpcd over 2f out: wl btn over 1f out* **12/1**

4200 7 11 **Princess Harley (IRE)**[47] 6371 4-9-11 62 FrannyNorton 7 39
(Mick Quinn) *t.k.h: hld up in tch in midfield: swtchd rt and hdwy to press wnr 9f out tl over 3f out: sn u.p and struggling: wl bhd and eased ins fnl f* **25/1**

-000 8 30 **Zarrar (IRE)**[7] 7790 4-9-11 62 (b) RyanTate 8 3
(Camilla Poulton) *a in rr: lost tch and eased wl over 1f out: t.o* **50/1**

3m 27.53s (-2.47) **Going Correction** -0.175s/f (Stan)
WFA 3 from 4yo+ 9lb **8 Ran SP% 118.8**
Speed ratings (Par 101): **99,92,91,90,89 88,82,67**
CSF £8.53 CT £206.07 TOTE £2.00: £1.10, £1.30, £10.50; EX 7.90 Trifecta £91.70.
Owner Cheveley Park Stud **Bred** Cheveley Park Stud Ltd **Trained** Newmarket, Suffolk

FOCUS
This proved pretty uncompetitive, the favourite bolting up on his first try over 2m.

7999 BET TOTESCOOP6 AT TOTESPORT.COM MAIDEN STKS 1m 2f (P)
7:10 (7:16) (Class 5) 3-4-Y-O **£4,948** (£1,472; £735; £367) **Stalls** Low

Form RPR

-643 1 **To The Moon**[48] 6346 3-9-0 77 RobertHavlin 6 74+
(John Gosden) *wnt rt leaving stalls: led after over 1f: mde rest: rdn: rn green and hung rt bnd 2f out: rdn clr over 1f out: styd on wl* **6/5**[1]

44 2 4 ½ **Exmoor Beast**[14] 7559 3-9-5 0 DavidEgan 5 70
(Peter Charalambous) *in tch in midfield: rdn over 3f out: drvn over 2f out: chsd wnr over 1f out: no imp and plugged on same pce ins fnl f* **14/1**

6064 3 3 ½ **Aubretia (IRE)**[22] 7272 3-9-0 62 (b[1]) TomMarquand 9 59
(Richard Hannon) *led for over 1f: chsd wnr tl over 6f out: styd chsng ldrs: rdn over 2f out: hung lft and btn 3rd 1f out: wknd ins fnl f* **14/1**

3 4 2 **End Over End**[12] 7630 3-9-0 0 AdamMcNamara 7 55
(Archie Watson) *in rr of main gp: rdn 7f out: drvn 3f out: plugged on to pass btn ins fnl f: no ch w wnr* **33/1**

6-2 5 2 **Malika I Jahan (FR)**[17] 7451 3-9-0 0 DanielMuscutt 1 51
(David Lanigan) *t.k.h: hld up in tch in rr of main gp: hdwy and rdn over 2f out: chsd wnr briefly 2f out: 4th and btn over 1f out: wknd ins fnl f* **4/1**[3]

66 6 4 ½ **Dr Jekyll (IRE)**[19] 7373 3-9-5 0 JamieSpencer 8 55
(David Simcock) *s.i.s: hdwy to chse ldrs 8f out: chsd wnr over 6f out: drvn over 2f out: lost 2nd 2f out: sn btn and wknd fnl f* **5/2**[2]

05 7 17 **Gustave Aitch (FR)**[29] 7035 3-9-5 0 LiamKeniry 3 15
(Sophie Leech) *chsd ldrs: lost pl over 2f out: wl bhd and eased ins fnl f* **50/1**

6 8 29 **Smart Samba (IRE)**[15] 7525 3-9-5 0 GeorgeWood 2
(Chris Wall) *s.i.s: nvr gng and sn wl detached: t.o* **50/1**

2m 6.46s (-2.14) **Going Correction** -0.175s/f (Stan)
WFA 3 from 4yo 4lb **8 Ran SP% 114.2**
Speed ratings (Par 103): **101,97,94,93,91 87,74,51**
CSF £20.32 TOTE £1.80: £1.10, £2.50, £2.40; EX 17.80 Trifecta £101.10.
Owner Lady Bamford **Bred** Lady Bamford **Trained** Newmarket, Suffolk
■ Overbeck was withdrawn. Price at time of withdrawal 33/1. Rule 4 does not apply

FOCUS
This proved easy enough for the favourite, who was always in control up front. She didn't need to improve with her form rivals not at their bests.

8000 BOOK YOUR CHRISTMAS PARTY HERE H'CAP (DIV I) 1m 2f (P)
7:40 (7:47) (Class 6) (0-55,57) 3-Y-O+
£3,105 (£924; £461; £400; £400; £400) **Stalls** Low

Form RPR

0225 1 **Hidden Dream (IRE)**[66] 5653 4-8-13 46 (p) KieranO'Neill 5 51
(Christine Dunnett) *led for 2f: chsd ldr tl led again over 2f out: sn rdn and clr over 1f out: all out but a jst doing enough towards fin* **10/1**

020 2 ½ **Seaquinn**[12] 7609 4-8-12 45 KierenFox 1 49
(John Best) *chsd ldrs: effrt ent fnl 2f: chsd wnr ent fnl f: grad clsd u.p: nt quite rch wnr* **5/1**[2]

0020 3 nk **Red Gunner**[23] 7232 5-9-5 52 EdwardGreatrex 6 57+
(Mark Loughnane) *hld up in midfield: effrt: swtchd rt and nt clr run over 1f out: shifting lft and hdwy 1f out: kpt on wl u.p ins fnl f: nt rch wnr (jockey said gelding was denied a clear run)* **14/1**

6002 4 ¾ **Golden Deal (IRE)**[38] 6723 4-9-1 48 LukeMorris 2 50
(Richard Phillips) *t.k.h: hld up in tch in midfield: effrt and edgd lft over 1f out: kpt on ins fnl f: nt rch ldrs* **7/1**[3]

5204 5 2 **Falls Creek (USA)**[55] 6077 4-8-13 46 (b) DavidProbert 9 44
(Andrew Balding) *hld up towards rr: swtchd rt and effrt over 1f out: styd on ins fnl f: nt rch ldrs* **9/2**[1]

5431 6 ¾ **Sharp Operator**[14] 7550 6-9-7 54 (h) DavidEgan 7 51
(Charlie Wallis) *hld up in tch in midfield: effrt and hdwy over 1f out: chsd ldrs 1f out: no imp ins fnl f: wknd towards fin* **7/1**[3]

0056 7 shd **Dutch Artist (IRE)**[14] 7545 7-8-9 47 (p) FayeMcManoman(5) 3 44
(Nigel Tinkler) *s.i.s: hld up towards rr: effrt on inner over 1f out: keeping on whn nt clr run and swtchd rt ins fnl f: nvr trbld ldrs* **12/1**

1600 8 nk **Arlecchino's Arc (IRE)**[104] 4232 4-9-5 57 (v) ThomasGreatrex(5) 4 53
(Mark Usher) *in tch in midfield: effrt u.p over 2f out: unable qck over 1f out: one pce ins fnl f* **10/1**

0052 9 nk **Waterproof**[22] 7280 3-8-12 49 (p) JosephineGordon 8 46
(Shaun Keightley) *chsd wnr for over 1f: styd chsng ldrs: rdn over 2f out: unable qck u.p and btn over 1f out: wknd ins fnl f* **9/2**[1]

0-50 10 ½ **Mrs Ivy**[29] 7035 3-9-4 55 (b[1]) HarryBentley 11 52
(Ralph Beckett) *hld up in rr: effrt over 1f out: sme hdwy ins fnl f but no threat to ldrs: nt clr run and no imp towards fin* **16/1**

0050 11 1 ¼ **Salmon Fishing (IRE)**[11] 7654 3-8-10 52 (p) SeamusCronin(5) 12 45
(Mohamed Moubarak) *stdd and swtchd lft after s: hld up in rr: swtchd rt and effrt over 1f out: kpt on ins fnl f: nvr involved* **20/1**

05-0 12 2 **Indian Sea**[24] 7190 3-8-5 45 DarraghKeenan(3) 13 34
(Dr Jon Scargill) *mounted in chute: hdwy to ld after 2f: rdn and hdd over 2f out: no ex u.p and lost 2nd ent fnl f: wknd ins fnl f* **50/1**

0000 13 4 ½ **Rocksette**[19] 7375 5-9-5 52 (p) RobertHavlin 10 32
(Adam West) *n.m.r sn after s: hld up in last pair: effrt over 1f out: no prog and wl btn fnl f (jockey said mare suffered interference when leaving the stalls)* **33/1**

2m 6.56s (-2.04) **Going Correction** -0.175s/f (Stan)
WFA 3 from 4yo+ 4lb **13 Ran SP% 128.1**
Speed ratings (Par 101): **101,100,100,99,98 97,97,97,97,96 95,94,90**
CSF £61.78 CT £728.52 TOTE £13.00: £3.20, £2.40, £3.80; EX 74.00 Trifecta £1385.10.
Owner Machin, Milner, Sparkes & Dunnett **Bred** Anything & Everything Asociates **Trained** Hingham, Norfolk

FOCUS
The first division of a low-grade handicap. It was marginally the slower of the two legs and the winner was close to last year's form here.

8001 BOOK YOUR CHRISTMAS PARTY HERE H'CAP (DIV II) 1m 2f (P)
8:10 (8:16) (Class 6) (0-55,56) 3-Y-O+
£3,105 (£924; £461; £400; £400; £400) **Stalls** Low

Form RPR

03 1 **Dreamboat Dave (IRE)**[10] 7685 3-9-3 55 EoinWalsh 1 64
(Sarah Humphrey) *w ldrs early: settled bk and in tch in midfield: effrt on inner and hdwy u.p to ld over 1f out: r.o strly ins fnl f* **7/1**[3]

0031 2 2 ½ **Masai Spirit**[14] 7549 3-9-4 56 KieranShoemark 5 60
(Philip McBride) *led for 2f: chsd ldr tl 6f out: styd chsng ldrs: drvn and ev ch over 1f out: nt match pce of wnr and one pce fnl f* **5/1**[2]

0000 3 2 ¼ **Dyagilev**[10] 7685 4-9-0 48 (b) DanielMuscutt 10 50+
(Lydia Pearce) *std and short of room sn after s: hld up towards rr: effrt and nt clr run wl over 1f out: hdwy 1f out: r.o wl ins fnl f: no threat to wnr* **20/1**

1042 4 ½ **Billie Beane**[19] 7376 4-9-3 54 DarraghKeenan(3) 3 52
(Dr Jon Scargill) *chsd ldrs: effrt and ev ch over 1f out: sn rdn and unable to match pce of wnr: wl hld and one pce ins fnl f: lost 3rd towards fin* **7/1**[3]

4043 5 1 ¾ **Cash N Carrie (IRE)**[19] 7375 5-8-12 46 oh1 LukeMorris 11 41
(Michael Appleby) *chsd ldr for 2f: chsd ldr again 6f out tl over 1f out: wknd ins fnl f* **25/1**

205 6 3 ¾ **Heatherdown (IRE)**[19] 7376 3-8-9 52 (p) ThomasGreatrex(5) 4 41
(Ian Williams) *bustled along early: in tch in midfield: keen 5f out: effrt u.p over 1f out: no imp and wknd ins fnl f* **9/1**

2246 7 4 **Chakrii (IRE)**[19] 7375 3-8-13 51 HayleyTurner 12 32
(Henry Spiller) *stdd s: hld up in rr: nt clrest of runs wl over 1f out: swtchd rt ins fnl f: kpt on: nvr trbld ldrs* **14/1**

2500 8 nk **Nabvutika (IRE)**[19] 7375 3-8-11 49 LiamKeniry 2 29
(John Butler) *midfield: no hdwy u.p and btn over 1f out: wknd ins fnl f* **33/1**

3234 9 2 **Percy Toplis**[21] 7318 5-8-13 47 (p) KieranO'Neill 9 23
(Christine Dunnett) *midfield and rousted along on outer early: hdwy to ld after 2f: drvn over 2f out: hdd over 1f out: sn btn and wknd ins fnl f* **14/1**

00-0 10 nse **Sunshine Coast**[19] 7375 4-9-7 55 NicolaCurrie 8 31
(Jamie Osborne) *midfield: no hdwy u.p and btn over 1f out: wknd ins fnl f* **40/1**

3122 11 6 **Poetic Legacy (IRE)**[5] 7859 3-9-4 56 DanielTudhope 6 21
(Mark Johnston) *towards rr: sme hdwy on outer 4f out: rdn over 2f out: sn struggling and btn over 1f out: wknd fnl f (jockey said filly ran flat)* **11/8**[1]

6004 12 3 ¾ **Sittin Handy (IRE)**[14] 7550 3-8-8 46 oh1 (p) JoeyHaynes 7 4
(Dean Ivory) *stdd after s: hld up towards rr: nvr involved* **33/1**

2m 6.28s (-2.32) **Going Correction** -0.175s/f (Stan)
WFA 3 from 4yo+ 4lb **12 Ran SP% 127.0**
Speed ratings (Par 101): **102,100,98,97,96 93,90,89,88,88 83,80**
CSF £41.50 CT £691.11 TOTE £8.50: £2.30, £1.40, £5.40; EX 46.70 Trifecta £406.40.
Owner The Old Etonians **Bred** Tally-Ho Stud **Trained** West Wratting, Cambs

FOCUS
The quicker of the two divisions by 0.28sec. The winner was well weighted on this year's Irish form.
T/Plt: £170.20 to a £1 stake. Pool: £39,693.04 - 233.10 winning units T/Qpdt: £56.60 to a £1 stake. Pool: £5,900.16 - 104.19 winning units **Steve Payne**

7521 **LEICESTER (R-H)**
Tuesday, October 8

OFFICIAL GOING: Heavy (4.2)
Wind: Light half behind Weather: Cloudy with sunny spells

8002 BROCK HILL BADGER H'CAP — 1m 3f 179y
1:50 (1:50) (Class 4) (0-85,83) 3-Y-O
£5,789 (£1,722; £860; £430; £300; £300) Stalls Low

Form RPR
3112 1 **Tavus (IRE)**[19] 7370 3-8-5 72 ow1 ThomasGreatrex(5) 4 83
(Roger Charlton) *chsd ldrs: rdn to ld over 2f out: hdd over 1f out: rallied to ld post* 4/1[2]
-134 2 shd **Baltic Song (IRE)**[41] 6597 3-9-5 81 RobertHavlin 9 91
(John Gosden) *a.p on outer: rdn over 2f out: led over 1f out: edgd rt: hdd post* 11/1
1324 3 5 **Proton (IRE)**[21] 7302 3-9-3 79 PaulMulrennan 2 81
(Jedd O'Keeffe) *led after 1f: hdd over 9f out: chsd ldr: rdn and ev ch 2f out: no ex ins fnl f* 15/2
2562 4 1 ½ **Pour Me A Drink**[18] 7413 3-9-7 83 AdamKirby 5 82
(Clive Cox) *led 1f: led again over 9f out: rdn and hdd over 2f out: styd on same pce fr over 1f out* 9/4[1]
-226 5 7 **Group Stage (GER)**[92] 4739 3-8-6 71 MeganNicholls(3) 7 59
(Alan King) *hld up: outpcd over 3f out: n.d after* 5/1[3]
1151 6 2 **Earl Of Harrow**[59] 5954 3-9-0 76 AndreaAtzeni 6 61
(Mick Channon) *broke wl: stdd sn after s: hld up: sme hdwy over 3f out: rdn and wknd over 2f out* 12/1
2115 7 42 **Fantastic Blue**[17] 7459 3-9-6 82 JackMitchell 8
(Ismail Mohammed) *hld up: rdn: hung rt and wknd over 3f out: eased over 1f out (trainers rep said colt was unsuited by the ground and would prefer a faster surface)* 12/1
011P 8 99 **Tigerskin**[23] 7239 3-8-12 74 (bt) HarryBentley 1
(Ralph Beckett) *prom: pushed along at times: lost pl 5f out: sn bhd: eased (trainers rep said gelding had a breathing problem)* 8/1
2m 45.18s (10.18) **Going Correction** +1.225s/f (Soft) 8 Ran SP% **114.0**
Speed ratings (Par 103): **109,108,105,104,99 98,70,4**
CSF £46.14 CT £315.69 TOTE £3.60: £1.10, £3.20, £2.20; EX 53.20 Trifecta £283.70.
Owner Tony Bloom **Bred** Gillian, Lady Howard De Walden **Trained** Beckhampton, Wilts
FOCUS
Add 15yds to races 1, 2 and 4. The front pair drew clear late in what was a fair 3yo handicap. Both have been rated as running pbs.

8003 STOAT (S) STKS — 1m 2f
2:20 (2:20) (Class 5) 3-Y-O £2,911 (£866; £432; £216) Stalls Low

Form RPR
-666 1 **Lord Howard (IRE)**[21] 7295 3-8-12 46 (v1) AndreaAtzeni 2 54
(Mick Channon) *prom: racd keenly: rdn over 3f out: sn outpcd: swtchd lft wl over 1f out: hdwy sn after: styd on u.p to ld wl ins fnl f* 13/2
6650 2 1 ¼ **Max Guevara (IRE)**[19] 7375 3-8-6 54 ow1 (b1) Pierre-LouisJamin(7) 10 53
(William Muir) *s.i.s: hld up: swtchd lft over 3f out: hdwy on outer to ld over 2f out: rdn over 1f out: hdd and unable qck wl ins fnl f* 6/1[3]
6050 3 ¾ **Keith**[36] 6805 3-8-9 45 MeganNicholls(3) 7 51
(Rod Millman) *chsd ldrs: rdn over 2f out: styd on* 11/1
2430 4 hd **Risk Mitigation (USA)**[29] 7025 3-8-12 50 CliffordLee 3 50
(David Evans) *hld up: drvn along over 4f out: r.o u.p ins fnl f: nt rch ldrs* 3/1[1]
6003 5 ¾ **Bonneville (IRE)**[21] 7295 3-8-12 50 (b) PaulMulrennan 1 49
(Rod Millman) *w ldr tl led over 6f out: rdn and hdd over 2f out: styd on same pce wl ins fnl f* 9/1
1500 6 5 **Lieutenant Conde**[36] 6810 3-9-3 62 (vt1) RobertHavlin 11 45
(Hughie Morrison) *hld up: rdn whn hmpd wl over 1f out: hung rt and styd on ins fnl f: nvr nrr* 8/1
4250 7 2 ½ **Goodwood Sonnet (IRE)**[31] 6982 3-8-12 49 (v) KieranShoemark 4 35
(William Knight) *s.i.s: hld up: hdwy over 3f out: sn rdn: wknd over 1f out* 5/1[2]
304 8 8 **Little Tipple**[60] 5880 3-8-1 46 ow1 (t1) LauraPearson(7) 9 17
(John Ryan) *prom on outer: rdn over 3f out: wknd over 1f out* 22/1
0400 9 7 **Lady Muk**[40] 6624 3-8-7 53 (p) GeorgeWood 8 3
(Steph Hollinshead) *led: hdd over 6f out: chsd ldr: rdn over 3f out: lost 2nd over 2f out: wknd over 1f out* 33/1
0606 10 13 **Cinzento (IRE)**[24] 7192 3-8-12 44 (t1) KevinStott 5
(Stuart Williams) *s.i.s: hdwy over 8f out: rdn and wknd over 2f out* 13/2
U **Inceyquincyspider (IRE)**[65] 3-8-5 0 SeanKirrane(7) 6
(Julia Feilden) *s.i.s: in rr whn hung lft and uns rdr wl over 5f out* 33/1
2m 22.31s (13.11) **Going Correction** +0.95s/f (Soft) 11 Ran SP% **122.3**
Speed ratings (Par 101): **85,84,83,83,82 78,76,70,64,54**
CSF £46.32 TOTE £7.90: £2.40, £1.80, £2.20; EX 60.30 Trifecta £1325.80.There was no bid for the winner.
Owner M Channon **Bred** Mount Coote Stud **Trained** West Ilsley, Berks
FOCUS
Add 15yds. Lowly selling form.

8004 RACINGTV AUTUMN SPRINT H'CAP (96PLUS RACE) — 5f
2:55 (2:55) (Class 2) (0-110,105) 3-Y-O+ £12,602 (£3,772; £1,886) Stalls High

Form RPR
1100 1 **Archer's Dream (IRE)**[27] 7073 3-9-0 98 GeorgeWood 1 103
(James Fanshawe) *trckd ldr: chal over 1f out: rdn ins fnl f: r.o to ld post* 5/2[2]
5001 2 nse **Tarboosh**[14] 7541 6-9-3 101 KevinStott 3 105
(Paul Midgley) *stdd s: hld up: racd keenly: swtchd rt 1/2-way: hdwy to ld over 1f out: rdn ins fnl f: hdd post* 4/6[1]
0500 3 2 **Copper Knight (IRE)**[24] 7193 5-9-7 105 (t) RachelRichardson 2 102
(Tim Easterby) *led: shkn up and hdd over 1f out: styd on same pce ins fnl f* 4/1[3]
1m 5.47s (3.67) **Going Correction** +0.95s/f (Soft) 3 Ran SP% **108.6**
Speed ratings (Par 109): **108,107,104**
CSF £4.72 TOTE £2.50; EX 4.40 Trifecta £6.30.
Owner Fred Archer Racing - Wheel Of Fortune **Bred** Ms Anne Coughlan **Trained** Newmarket, Suffolk
FOCUS
Just the three runners, but useful sprinting form. A small pb from the winner.

8005 SQUIRREL H'CAP (96PLUS RACE) — 1m 3f 179y
3:25 (3:25) (Class 2) (0-110,100) 3-Y-O+ £12,602 (£3,772; £1,886; £944) Stalls Low

Form RPR
0410 1 **Indianapolis (IRE)**[46] 6420 4-9-5 97 (p) PaulMulrennan 1 105
(James Given) *chsd ldr tl led over 6f out: rdn over 2f out: edgd lft ins fnl f: styd on wl* 9/2
-013 2 1 ¾ **Spanish Archer (FR)**[33] 6895 4-9-6 98 (h) DanielMuscutt 3 103
(James Fanshawe) *s.s: hdwy over 10f out: ev ch fr over 2f out tl rdn and no ex ins fnl f* 5/2[2]
6104 3 8 **Getchagetchagetcha**[13] 7565 3-9-2 100 (p1) AdamKirby 2 93
(Clive Cox) *trckd ldrs: racd keenly: rdn over 2f out: wknd fnl f* 11/4[3]
-502 4 30 **Spirit Ridge**[12] 7616 4-9-4 96 KieranShoemark 4 40
(Amanda Perrett) *led: hdd over 6f out: chsd ldr tl rdn over 3f out: wknd over 2f out (trainer said gelding was unsuited by the ground and would prefer a quicker surface)* 7/4[1]
2m 50.24s (15.24) **Going Correction** +1.225s/f (Soft)
WFA 3 from 4yo 6lb 4 Ran SP% **109.8**
Speed ratings (Par 109): **98,96,91,71**
CSF £15.53 TOTE £6.30; EX 16.00 Trifecta £50.40.
Owner Alex Owen **Bred** Smithfield Inc **Trained** Willoughton, Lincs
FOCUS
Add 15yds. Questionable form with a couple of these, including the favourite, failing to give their running. The form could be worth a bit better at face value.

8006 BRITISH EBF DORMOUSE NOVICE STKS — 7f
4:00 (4:00) (Class 5) 3-Y-O+ £4,463 (£1,328; £663; £331) Stalls High

Form RPR
00 1 **Dansepo**[13] 7572 3-9-3 0 KieranShoemark 6 61
(Adam West) *chsd ldrs: lost pl 1/2-way: hdwy over 1f out: rdn: edgd lft and styd on to ld wl ins fnl f (trainers rep said, regards apparent improvement in form, gelding appears to be improving with every run and has been working well at home)* 66/1
2 1 ½ **Sommer Katze (FR)** 3-9-3 0 DavidNolan 1 57
(Declan Carroll) *s.i.s: sn prom: led over 1f out: sn edgd lft and rdn: hdd wl ins fnl f* 6/1[3]
0600 3 1 ½ **Tilsworth Diamond**[33] 6897 4-8-7 44 SeanKirrane(7) 5 49
(Mike Murphy) *s.i.s: hld up: hdwy over 2f out: swtchd rt and rdn over 1f out: styd on* 28/1
34 4 3 ¾ **Karisoke**[19] 7373 3-9-3 0 JackMitchell 3 43
(Simon Crisford) *led 1f: chsd ldr: led again over 2f out: rdn and hdd over 1f out: wknd ins fnl f* 2/5[1]
00- 5 2 ½ **Blue Battalion**[379] 7612 3-9-3 0 TomQueally 2 37
(John Gallagher) *sn pushed along in rr: hdwy 1/2-way: wknd over 1f out* 50/1
20-5 6 57 **Revolutionary Man (IRE)**[33] 6898 4-9-5 73 (tp) AdamKirby 4
(Mark Loughnane) *led 6f out: rdn: hdd & wknd over 2f out (trainer said gelding was unsuited by the ground and would prefer a quicker surface)* 4/1[2]
1m 33.16s (7.46) **Going Correction** +0.95s/f (Soft)
WFA 3 from 4yo 2lb 6 Ran SP% **112.6**
Speed ratings (Par 103): **95,93,91,87,84 19**
CSF £402.01 TOTE £34.10: £9.20, £2.30; EX 252.50 Trifecta £2052.20.
Owner Frank Hutchinson **Bred** A M Wragg **Trained** Epsom, Surrey
FOCUS
A right old turn up in this novice, the complete outsider triumphing. Moderate form, the form pair both disappointing.

8007 RED DEER H'CAP — 6f
4:35 (4:35) (Class 5) (0-70,72) 3-Y-O+
£4,140 (£1,232; £615; £307; £300; £300) Stalls High

Form RPR
2301 1 **Smokey Lane (IRE)**[1] 7977 5-9-11 72 5ex CliffordLee 1 81
(David Evans) *hld up in tch: chsd ldr over 2f out: rdn over 1f out: styd on to ld wl ins fnl f* 11/4[2]
006 2 nk **Zapper Cass (FR)**[6] 7828 6-9-2 68 TheodoreLadd(5) 4 76
(Michael Appleby) *led: rdn over 1f out: sn hung rt: hdd wl ins fnl f* 5/1[3]
0000 3 8 **Dodgy Bob**[17] 7468 6-8-7 54 oh6 (v) NathanEvans 6 36
(Michael Mullineaux) *prom: pushed along over 4f out: styd on same pce fr over 1f out (jockey said colt hung right)* 50/1
5602 4 hd **Elzaam's Dream (IRE)**[40] 6638 3-8-9 57 (h) RaulDaSilva 7 39
(Ronald Harris) *sn pushed along in rr: rdn over 2f out: hung rt and styd on ins fnl f: nvr nrr* 10/1
-200 5 1 ¾ **Your Choice**[54] 6120 4-8-12 62 (p) MeganNicholls(3) 3 38
(Laura Mongan) *chsd ldrs: rdn over 2f out: wknd over 1f out* 20/1
3025 6 1 ½ **Hey Ho Let's Go**[46] 6418 3-8-11 62 (h) WilliamCox(3) 8 33
(Clive Cox) *w ldr: rdn over 2f out: hung rt and wknd over 1f out (jockey said colt hung right)* 10/1
1252 7 11 **Quirky Gertie (IRE)**[8] 7762 3-9-10 72 AndreaAtzeni 2 8
(Mick Channon) *hld up: pushed along 1/2-way: rdn and wknd over 1f out (jockey said filly stopped quickly; trainers rep said filly may have been feeling the affects of a hard race on similar ground eight days ago)* 13/8[1]
2451 R **Miss Liberty Belle (AUS)**[17] 7446 3-8-10 58 KieranShoemark 5
(William Jarvis) *ref to r* 11/1
1m 16.07s (3.97) **Going Correction** +0.95s/f (Soft)
WFA 3 from 4yo+ 1lb 8 Ran SP% **114.7**
Speed ratings (Par 103): **107,106,95,95,93 91,76,**
CSF £17.04 CT £551.49 TOTE £3.50: £1.30, £2.80, £10.90; EX 15.80 Trifecta £778.90.
Owner Mrs E Evans **Bred** Miss Philippa Proctor Quinn **Trained** Pandy, Monmouths
FOCUS
The front pair pulled clear in this sprint handicap. The winner backed up his win the previous day, with the second rated in line with his turf form from the past year.

8008 LEVERET APPRENTICE H'CAP (DIV I) — 7f
5:05 (5:05) (Class 6) (0-65,66) 3-Y-O+
£3,687 (£1,097; £548; £300; £300; £300) Stalls High

Form RPR
0253 1 **Stallone (IRE)**[6] 7828 3-9-10 66 (v) SeanKirrane(3) 7 75
(Richard Spencer) *prom: racd keenly: chsd ldr 1/2-way: led over 2f out: rdn out* 5/2[1]
3640 2 5 **Cottingham**[13] 7578 4-8-9 46 oh1 ThoreHammerHansen 4 44
(Kevin Frost) *hld up in tch: chsd wnr over 1f out: sn rdn: styd on same pce fnl f* 13/2[3]

The Form Book Flat 2019, Raceform Ltd, Newbury, RG14 5SJ

0435 **3** 1 1/4 **Snooker Jim**[7] 7776 4-8-8 **48**....................(t) TobyEley(3) 2 42
(Steph Hollinshead) *s.i.s: hld up: hdwy 1/2-way: rdn over 2f out: no ex ins fnl f* **7/2**[2]

5226 **4** *nk* **Classic Star**[46] 6389 3-9-3 **61**.................... LukeBacon(5) 8 54
(Dean Ivory) *s.i.s: hdwy over 5f out: nt clr run and lost pl 1/2-way: swtchd rt over 2f out: styd on fr over 1f out* **7/2**[2]

6000 **5** 3/4 **Lily Of Year (FR)**[54] 6107 4-8-3 **47**.................... MichaelPitt(7) 6 39
(Denis Coakley) *dwlt: hld up: swtchd rt 1/2-way: styd on fr over 1f out: nt trble ldrs* **20/1**

0426 **6** 3 **Tobeornottobee**[13] 7591 3-8-13 **59**.................... JessicaAnderson(7) 10 42
(Declan Carroll) *plld hrd and prom: led 4f out: hdd over 2f out: wknd fnl f* **7/1**

454 **7** 8 **Sally Hope**[26] 7114 3-9-1 **54**.................... ScottMcCullagh 9 17
(John Gallagher) *led 3f: wknd 2f out (jockey said filly ran too free)* **20/1**

3006 **8** 6 **Lonicera**[23] 7236 3-8-9 **55**.................... EmmaTaff(7) 3 3
(Henry Candy) *racd keenly on outer: prom: rdn over 2f out: wknd over 1f out* **12/1**

0500 **9** 1 3/4 **Magic Ship (IRE)**[63] 5787 4-8-4 **46** oh1.................... ZakWheatley(5) 11
(John Norton) *chsd ldrs: pushed along and lost pl 1/2-way: wknd over 2f out* **66/1**

1m 31.81s (6.11) **Going Correction** +0.95s/f (Soft)
WFA 3 from 4yo+ 2lb **9 Ran SP% 117.6**
Speed ratings (Par 101): **103,97,95,95,94 91,82,75,73**
CSF £19.36 CT £57.99 TOTE £2.90: £1.10, £2.30, £1.40; EX 19.70 Trifecta £80.20.
Owner Rebel Racing Premier **Bred** Ms Marie Higgins **Trained** Newmarket, Suffolk

FOCUS
The first leg of a moderate handicap, it was turned into a bit of a rout. The form's taken with a pinch of salt given the conditions.

8009 LEVERET APPRENTICE H'CAP (DIV II) 7f
5:35 (5:36) (Class 6) (0-65,65) 3-Y-O+
£3,687 (£1,097; £548; £300; £300; £300) **Stalls High**

Form RPR

3236 **1** **Milan Reef (IRE)**[118] 3720 4-9-0 **54**.................... MarkCrehan(3) 7 64
(David Loughnane) *mde all: rdn over 1f out: styd on* **7/2**[2]

0505 **2** 2 **Field Of Vision (IRE)**[22] 7273 6-8-13 **50**....................(b) WilliamCarver 2 55
(John Flint) *a.p: chsd wnr and hung rt fnl 3f: rdn over 1f out: nt run on (jockey said gelding hung right)* **7/2**[2]

2405 **3** 7 **Cotubanama**[15] 7527 3-9-11 **64**....................(v[1]) ScottMcCullagh 5 51
(Mick Channon) *s.i.s: hdwy over 2f out: rdn over 1f out: styd on same pce* **11/1**

0550 **4** *shd* **Cheerful**[19] 7374 3-8-9 **55**.................... AliceBond(7) 3 41
(Philip McBride) *s.i.s: sn pushed along in rr: hdwy over 2f out: rdn over 1f out: styd on same pce* **20/1**

0060 **5** 8 **Vicky Cristina (IRE)**[50] 6275 4-8-6 **46** oh1....................(v) TobyEley(3) 8 13
(John Holt) *s.i.s: hdwy 1/2-way: rdn and wknd over 1f out* **40/1**

364 **6** 1 **My Law**[114] 3887 3-8-13 **57**.................... LukeCatton(5) 4 21
(Jim Boyle) *chsd ldrs: rdn over 2f out: wknd over 1f out* **8/1**

3360 **7** 2 1/2 **Cooperess**[22] 7286 6-8-6 **46** oh1.................... Pierre-LouisJamin(3) 11 5
(Adrian Wintle) *prom: racd keenly: rdn over 2f out: wknd over 1f out* **14/1**

0032 **8** 1/2 **Jean Valjean**[15] 7523 3-9-9 **65**....................(h) SeanKirrane(3) 6 21
(Richard Spencer) *prom: rdn over 2f out: sn wknd (jockey said gelding jumped right leaving the stalls)* **5/2**[1]

0000 **9** 18 **Plissken**[15] 7526 3-8-11 **50**.................... TheodoreLadd 9
(Richard Price) *hld up in tch: lost pl over 4f out: sn bhd (jockey said filly hung badly right)* **50/1**

001 **10** 71 **Another Boy**[55] 6084 6-9-1 **57**....................(p) CharlotteBennett(5) 1
(Ralph Beckett) *s.i.s: sn prom: jnd wnr over 4f out tl pushed along 1/2-way: sn wknd (vet said gelding bled from the nose)* **7/1**[3]

1m 30.86s (5.16) **Going Correction** +0.95s/f (Soft)
WFA 3 from 4yo+ 2lb **10 Ran SP% 120.8**
Speed ratings (Par 101): **106,103,95,95,86 85,82,81,61,**
CSF £16.62 CT £128.50 TOTE £4.70: £1.60, £1.10, £3.30; EX 16.20 Trifecta £132.30.
Owner Martin Godfrey **Bred** Pat Beirne **Trained** Tern Hill, Shropshire

FOCUS
Similar to the first leg it proved quite uncompetitive, with two of the runners dominating. Probably not form to take too literally.
T/Plt: £4,705.80 to a £1 stake. Pool: £52,537.84 - 8.15 winning units T/Qpdt: £390.60 to a £1 stake. Pool: £5,532.95 - 10.48 winning units **Colin Roberts**

8010a (Foreign Racing) - See Raceform Interactive

7811 KEMPTON (A.W) (R-H)
Wednesday, October 9

OFFICIAL GOING: Polytrack: standard to slow
Wind: light, across Weather: fine

8011 CLOSE BROTHERS/BRITISH STALLION STUDS EBF NOVICE STKS (DIV I) 7f (P)
4:35 (4:36) (Class 5) 2-Y-O
£3,881 (£1,155; £577; £288) **Stalls Low**

Form RPR

1 **Desert Peace (USA)** 2-9-5 0.................... WilliamBuick 2 84+
(Charlie Appleby) *chsd ldrs: effrt ent fnl 2f: clsd 1f out: led ins fnl f: styd on strly and wl in command at fin* **7/4**[1]

4 **2** 1 3/4 **Nugget**[19] 7406 2-9-5 0.................... SeanLevey 5 80
(Richard Hannon) *pressed ldr: rdn and ev ch ent fnl 2f: led over 1f out: sn drvn: hdd ins fnl f: kpt on wl but a hld* **7/2**[3]

3140 **3** 3 3/4 **Banmi (IRE)**[15] 7548 2-9-4 **70**.................... TomMarquand 12 69
(Mohamed Moubarak) *chsd ldrs: effrt over 2f out: 4th and no imp over 1f out: kpt on ins fnl f: wnt 3rd cl home: no threat to ldrs* **50/1**

4 1/2 **Raajin** 2-9-5 0.................... JimCrowley 1 69
(Charles Hills) *led and rn green: pressed and rdn 2f out: hdd over 1f out: no ex jst ins fnl f: wknd towards fin and lost 3rd cl home* **5/1**

5 1/2 **Beauty Choice** 2-9-5 0.................... StevieDonohoe 8 67+
(Charlie Fellowes) *hld up in tch in midfield: effrt over 2f out: sn outpcd and wl hld in 5th over 1f out: kpt on steadily ins fnl f* **50/1**

6 1 1/2 **The Turpinator (IRE)** 2-9-5 0.................... DaneO'Neill 9 64+
(David Elsworth) *swtchd rt sn after s: racd in last trio: effrt: rn green and outpcd over 2f out: rallied and swtchd lft ent fnl f: styd on wl ins fnl f: eased fnl 50yds: promising* **50/1**

0 **7** 1 **Siberian Night (IRE)**[62] 6891 2-9-5 0.................... LiamKeniry 6 61
(Ed Walker) *hld up in midfield: effrt over 2f out: sn outpcd: wl hld and kpt on same pce fr over 1f out* **28/1**

50 **8** 1 3/4 **Tiger Zone (IRE)**[16] 7521 2-9-5 0.................... AdamKirby 10 56
(Clive Cox) *stdd and dropped in bhd after s: hld up in rr: effrt over 2f out: sn outpcd and wl btn fnl 2f* **66/1**

02 **9** 1 1/4 **Mars Landing (IRE)**[21] 7339 2-9-5 0.................... RyanMoore 13 53
(Sir Michael Stoute) *restless in stalls: awkward leaving stalls and dwlt: rcvrd and hdwy into midfield after 2f: rdn over 2f out: sn outpcd and wl hld over 1f out: wknd fnl f* **9/4**[2]

10 13 **Punctuate (FR)** 2-9-5 0.................... RossaRyan 7 19
(Richard Hannon) *swtchd rt after s: hld up in tch in midfield: effrt over 2f out: awkward hd carriage and sn outpcd: hung rt and wknd over 1f out (jockey said colt hung right-handed)* **50/1**

11 16 **Heer I Am** 2-9-5 0....................(t[1]) JFEgan 11
(Paul George) *a towards rr: last ent fnl 3f: sn lost tch: t.o* **100/1**

1m 26.42s (0.42) **Going Correction** -0.025s/f (Stan) **11 Ran SP% 119.8**
Speed ratings (Par 95): **96,94,89,89,88 86,85,83,82,67 49**
CSF £8.25 TOTE £2.30: £1.10, £1.40, £5.80; EX 7.30 Trifecta £140.10.
Owner Godolphin **Bred** Doug Branham & Felicia Branham **Trained** Newmarket, Suffolk

FOCUS
Plenty of this field started at longish odds, and made no impression. The first two home were second and third early on.

8012 CLOSE BROTHERS/BRITISH STALLION STUDS EBF NOVICE STKS (DIV II) 7f (P)
5:10 (5:14) (Class 5) 2-Y-O
£3,881 (£1,155; £577; £288) **Stalls Low**

Form RPR

1 **Higher Kingdom** 2-9-5 0.................... DanielTudhope 4 83+
(Archie Watson) *led for over 1f: styd pressing ldr tl shkn up to ld again 2f out: sn qcknd clr and r.o strly ins fnl f: v readily* **8/11**[1]

54 **2** 4 **Star Of Wells (IRE)**[54] 6185 2-9-5 0.................... TomMarquand 9 69
(William Haggas) *midfield: rdn over 4f out: hdwy on inner to chse ldrs and flashed tail over 1f out: chsd clr wnr 1f out: no imp: kpt on and hung on to 2nd towards fin* **7/2**[2]

0 **3** *hd* **Zambezi Magic**[16] 7521 2-9-5 0....................(h) AdamKirby 12 68
(Clive Cox) *wnt lft leaving stalls: in rr of main gp: hdwy between rivals over 1f out: battling for 2nd and kpt on wl fnl 100yds: no threat to wnr* **16/1**

6 **4** 3/4 **HMS President (IRE)**[44] 6528 2-9-5 0.................... TomQueally 6 66
(Eve Johnson Houghton) *edgd lft leaving stalls: towards rr of main gp: effrt over 2f out: hdwy 1f out: kpt on ins fnl f: no ch w wnr* **20/1**

5 3/4 **Blue Skyline (IRE)** 2-9-5 0.................... GeraldMosse 11 64
(David Elsworth) *midfield: effrt over 2f out: rn green and hung rt 2f out: no threat to wnr but kpt steadily ins fnl f* **16/1**

0 **6** 3 1/4 **Old Friend (FR)**[33] 6912 2-9-5 0.................... LiamKeniry 2 56
(Ed Walker) *chsd ldrs: effrt over 2f out: chsd clr wnr over 1f out tl 1f out: wknd ins fnl f* **12/1**

7 3 3/4 **Cobnut (IRE)** 2-9-5 0.................... GeorgeWood 8 46
(James Fanshawe) *a in rr of main gp: rdn and no hdwy over 2f out: sn wl btn (jockey said colt ran green)* **10/1**[3]

8 3/4 **Saffron Lane** 2-9-0 0.................... SeanLevey 7 38
(Harry Dunlop) *chsd ldrs: rdn over 2f out: unable qck and lost pl over 1f out: wknd ins fnl f* **66/1**

0 **9** 1 1/2 **Quimerico**[91] 4798 2-9-5 0.................... KierenFox 10 39
(John Best) *pushed along early to go prom: led after over 1f: rdn and hdd 2f out: lost pl over 1f out: wknd fnl f* **50/1**

10 29 **Purple Sandpiper** 2-9-5 0.................... LukeMorris 1
(Robyn Brisland) *rn green and sn detached in last: lost tch over 2f out: t.o (jockey said colt was slowly away and ran green)* **33/1**

1m 25.76s (-0.24) **Going Correction** -0.025s/f (Stan) **10 Ran SP% 119.8**
Speed ratings (Par 95): **100,95,95,94,93 89,85,84,82,49**
CSF £3.33 TOTE £1.60: £1.10, £1.10, £2.90; EX 3.80 Trifecta £23.90.
Owner Clipper Logistics **Bred** South Acre Bloodstock **Trained** Upper Lambourn, W Berks
■ On The Right Track was withdrawn. Price at time of withdrawal 18-1.\n\x\x Rule 4 does not appl

FOCUS
Much like the first division of this novice event, which had been run in a slightly slower time, only a few were fancied in the betting but the winner, and market leader, proved to be much the best. The level is a bit fluid in behind the winner.

8013 CLOSE BROTHERS BUSINESS FINANCE MAIDEN FILLIES' STKS 1m 2f 219y(P)
5:40 (5:43) (Class 5) 3-Y-O+
£3,881 (£1,155; £577; £288) **Stalls Low**

Form RPR

-223 **1** **Maximum Effect**[34] 6886 3-9-0 **77**.................... NickyMackay 3 82
(John Gosden) *chsd ldrs: effrt to chal and hung rt jst over 2f out: led 2f out: in command and styd on wl ins fnl f* **5/2**[2]

2 2 **Casual Reply** 3-9-0 0.................... AdamMcNamara 6 78+
(Roger Charlton) *hld up in midfield: hdwy over 2f out: rdn and clsd over 1f out: chsd wnr 1f out: kpt on wl but nvr getting on terms w wnr* **16/1**

20 **3** 2 3/4 **Brown Honey**[21] 7347 3-9-0 0.................... SeanLevey 2 72
(Ismail Mohammed) *chsd ldrs: effrt over 2f out: unable qck over 1f out: chsd ldng pair and no imp fnl 100yds* **7/1**

0322 **4** 1 **Dubious Affair (IRE)**[37] 6812 3-9-0 **76**....................(v[1]) RyanMoore 9 70
(Sir Michael Stoute) *led: rdn and hdd 2f out: outpcd and btn whn lost 2nd 1f out: wknd ins fnl f* **11/4**[3]

5 1 1/4 **Bye Bye Lady (FR)** 3-9-0 0.................... SilvestreDeSousa 4 68+
(Andrew Balding) *midfield: effrt on inner ent fnl 2f: swtchd lft over 1f out: no threat to ldrs but kpt on ins fnl f* **9/4**[1]

5 **6** 3 1/2 **Mystic Dragon**[11] 7704 3-9-0 0.................... GeraldMosse 1 61?
(Mrs Ilka Gansera-Leveque) *t.k.h early: chsd ldrs: rdn over 2f out: unable qck and btn over 1f out: wknd ins fnl f* **66/1**

00 **7** 1 1/4 **High Gloss**[50] 6316 3-9-0 0.................... DanielMuscutt 8 58+
(James Fanshawe) *hld up in last trio: effrt over 2f out: no imp and wl hld over 1f out* **50/1**

00-3 **8** 3/4 **Summer Skies**[24] 7228 3-9-0 **67**....................(v[1]) HayleyTurner 7 57
(Marcus Tregoning) *midfield: rdn and racd awkwardly over 3f out: outpcd over 2f out: wl btn over 1f out* **33/1**

05 **9** 2 1/4 **War Empress (IRE)**[164] 2148 3-9-0 0.................... ShelleyBirkett 11 52
(Julia Feilden) *a in rr: nvr involved* **100/1**

0 **10** 1 **Anything For You**[20] 7373 3-9-0 0.................... RobHornby 10 50
(Jonathan Portman) *sn chsd ldr: rdn and lost 2nd jst over 2f out: lost pl and wknd over 1f out* **66/1**

11 26 **Justlookatmenow** 3-9-0 0.................... LukeMorris 5
(Karen George) *sn dropped towards rr: rdn over 2f out: sn bhd: t.o* **100/1**

2m 22.6s (1.60) **Going Correction** -0.025s/f (Stan) **11 Ran SP% 114.3**
Speed ratings (Par 100): **96,94,92,91,90 88,87,86,85,84 65**
CSF £37.73 TOTE £3.20: £1.10, £3.60, £1.50; EX 41.40 Trifecta £263.70.
Owner Lady Bamford **Bred** Denniff Farms Ltd **Trained** Newmarket, Suffolk

The Form Book Flat 2019, Raceform Ltd, Newbury, RG14 5SJ

FOCUS
With a valuable win in the offing for one of these fillies to eventually head to stud with, this was a competitive event. The third has been rated close to her debut form.

8014 32RED.COM H'CAP (LONDON MIDDLE DISTANCE SERIES QUALIFIER) 1m 2f 219y(P)
6:10 (6:14) (Class 4) (0-80,80) 3-Y-O+

£6,469 (£1,925; £962; £481; £400; £400) **Stalls** Low

Form RPR

6140 **1** **Regal Director (IRE)**[18] 7465 4-9-9 **79**........................ DanielTudhope 6 91
(Archie Watson) *sn led and mde rest: rdn and qcknd clr 2f out: drvn and reduced ld ins fnl f: all out towards fin: jst hld on* **3/1**[1]

1040 **2** *hd* **Singing Sheriff**[123] 3567 4-9-2 **72**........................ LiamKeniry 10 83+
(Ed Walker) *hld up in midfield: swtchd lft and effrt 2f out: chsd clr wnr over 1f out: styd on wl and clsd ins fnl f: jst failed* **16/1**

0000 **3** *3 ¾* **Kyllachy Gala**[121] 3663 6-9-7 **80**........................ GabrieleMalune(3) 7 84
(Marco Botti) *hld up in tch in midfield: effrt over 2f out: hdwy over 1f out: styd on wl ins fnl f: wnt 3rd nr fin: nvr getting to ldrs* **8/1**[3]

3613 **4** *hd* **C'Est No Mour (GER)**[27] 7127 6-9-8 **78**........................(b[1]) TomMarquand 2 82+
(Peter Hedger) *dwlt: hld up in rr: effrt and plenty to do over 2f out: swtchd lft and hdwy over 1f out: styd on strly ins fnl f: wnt 4th last strides: no threat to ldrs* **9/1**

1122 **5** *nk* **Geranium**[18] 7465 4-9-4 **74**........................ DavidProbert 1 77
(Hughie Morrison) *in tch in midfield: effrt to chse clr wnr 2f out: sn drvn: lost 2nd over 1f out: kpt on but no real imp ins fnl f: lost 2 pls nr fin* **6/1**[2]

1210 **6** *2 ¼* **Blue Medici**[31] 7003 5-9-5 **75**........................ OisinMurphy 14 74
(Mark Loughnane) *hld up in midfield: effrt over 2f out: nt clr run 2f out: kpt on ins fnl f: nvr trbld ldrs* **16/1**

5014 **7** *2 ¾* **El Borracho (IRE)**[20] 7370 4-9-7 **77**........................(h) PJMcDonald 13 71
(Simon Dow) *swtchd rt after s: hld up in rr: effrt and stl plenty to do over 2f out: kpt on ins fnl f: nvr trbld ldrs* **16/1**

1056 **8** *½* **Ashazuri**[30] 7026 5-9-3 **73**........................(h) NicolaCurrie 3 66
(Jonathan Portman) *t.k.h: hld up towards rr: effrt and plenty to do over 2f out: edgd rt 2f out: kpt on ins fnl f: nvr trbld ldrs (jockey said mare was short of room entering the first bend)* **33/1**

0243 **9** *¾* **Grey D'Ars (FR)**[23] 7279 3-9-5 **80**........................ CallumShepherd 8 73
(Nick Littmoden) *chsd ldrs tl chsd wnr 6f out tl 2f out: sn lost pl u.p: wknd ins fnl f (jockey said colt ran flat)* **6/1**[2]

3440 **10** *¾* **Final Rock**[62] 5840 4-9-6 **76**........................(p) LukeMorris 4 67
(Sir Mark Prescott Bt) *t.k.h: mostly chsd wnr tl 6f out: unable qck ent fnl 2f: sn lost pl and wknd fnl f* **14/1**

3406 **11** *¾* **Sheberghan (IRE)**[20] 7379 4-9-7 **77**........................ JimCrowley 11 66
(Ed Dunlop) *hld up towards rr: effrt and plenty to do over 2f out: n.d* **8/1**[3]

-040 **12** *1* **Seven Clans (IRE)**[25] 7185 7-9-8 **78**........................(b) AdamKirby 9 65
(Neil Mulholland) *in tch in midfield: effrt over 2f out: sn struggling and outpcd: wknd over 1f out* **66/1**

4066 **13** *10* **Grand Inquisitor**[13] 7610 7-9-7 **77**........................(b) HayleyTurner 5 46
(Conor Dore) *t.k.h: chsd ldrs tl hung lft and struggling over 2f out: sn wknd* **50/1**

0/45 **14** *55* **Banish (USA)**[37] 6804 6-9-7 **77**........................(bt) CharlesBishop 12
(Tom George) *chsd ldrs: wd and losty pl over 3f out: t.o ins fnl f (jockey said gelding stopped quickly)* **66/1**

2m 18.54s (-2.46) **Going Correction** -0.025s/f (Stan)
WFA 3 from 4yo+ 5lb **14 Ran SP% 118.0**
Speed ratings (Par 105): **111,110,108,107,107 106,104,103,103,102 102,101,94,54**
CSF £54.03 CT £352.79 TOTE £3.50: £1.50, £5.10, £4.30; EX 56.90 Trifecta £764.30.
Owner The Real Quiz **Bred** Sheikh Mohammed Obaid Al Maktoum **Trained** Upper Lambourn, W Berks

FOCUS
A competitive event was taken by a well-judged ride by Danny Tudhope. Therefore, the form may not be reliable in the coming weeks. The winner has been rated in line with his Redcar win on his stable debut.

8015 EBFSTALLIONS.COM CONDITIONS STKS 6f (P)
6:40 (6:40) (Class 2) 3-Y-O+

£12,450 (£3,728; £1,864; £932; £466; £234) **Stalls** Low

Form RPR

5201 **1** **Enjazaat**[26] 7152 4-9-6 103........................ JimCrowley 4 111
(Owen Burrows) *hld up in tch: effrt and hdwy over 1f out: drvn to ld 1f out: styd on strly and asserted 100yds out: gng away at fin* **7/4**[2]

0011 **2** *1 ¾* **Royal Birth**[11] 7687 8-9-6 102........................(t) OisinMurphy 5 105
(Stuart Williams) *cl up: pressed ldr after over 1f: effrt and ev ch over 1f out: chsd wnr but no ex 100yds out: one pce* **11/2**[3]

0230 **3** *½* **Marnie James**[25] 7193 4-9-2 101........................ DanielTudhope 1 99
(Jedd O'Keeffe) *t.k.h: hld up in tch: effrt on inner 2f out: chsd ldrs and drvn 1f out: no ex and outpcd fnl 100yds* **13/8**[1]

0236 **4** *1* **Danzan (IRE)**[33] 6920 4-9-2 92........................ DavidProbert 3 96
(Andrew Balding) *led: rdn 2f out: hdd 1f out: no ex and wknd fnl 100yds* **10/1**

135 **5** *5* **Tropics (USA)**[11] 7687 11-9-6 107........................(h) SophieRalston 2 84
(Dean Ivory) *awkward and wnt lft leaving stalls: t.k.h: chsd ldr for over 1f out: styd cl up: effrt over 1f out: no ex 1f out: sn wknd* **16/1**

6104 **6** *2 ¾* **Unabated (IRE)**[20] 7372 5-9-6 88........................(t) RayDawson 6 75
(Jane Chapple-Hyam) *t.k.h: hld up in tch: effrt ent fnl 2f: unable qck and outpcd over 1f out: bhd fnl f* **20/1**

1m 12.12s (-0.98) **Going Correction** -0.025s/f (Stan) **6 Ran SP% 109.6**
Speed ratings (Par 109): **105,102,102,100,94 90**
CSF £11.09 TOTE £2.50: £1.30, £2.80; EX 6.90 Trifecta £18.70.
Owner Hamdan Al Maktoum **Bred** C J Mills **Trained** Lambourn, Berks

FOCUS
A mainly smart field lined up for this sprint, but the early pace looked slow and the dash started at around the 2f post. The second helps set the standard.

8016 32RED H'CAP 7f (P)
7:10 (7:11) (Class 3) (0-95,95) 3-Y-O+

£9,337 (£2,796; £1,398; £699; £349; £175) **Stalls** Low

Form RPR

3321 **1** **Intuitive (IRE)**[25] 7187 3-9-7 **95**........................ PJMcDonald 3 106+
(James Tate) *trckd ldrs: clsd and upsides ldrs travelling strly wl over 1f out: sn led: rdn: edgd rt and asserted ins fnl f: r.o wl* **13/8**[1]

0060 **2** *1* **Kimifive (IRE)**[32] 6950 4-9-4 **90**........................ JimmyQuinn 6 100
(Joseph Tuite) *hld up in tch in midfield: clsd to chal and rdn over 1f out: short of room ins fnl f: kpt on same pce and hld whn short of room and swtchd lft towards fin* **16/1**

6610 **3** *3 ¼* **Turn 'n Twirl (USA)**[25] 7188 3-9-0 **88**........................ JimCrowley 12 87
(Simon Crisford) *in tch in midfield: effrt ent fnl 2f: drvn over 1f out: kpt on to snatch 3rd on post: no threat to ldng pair* **12/1**

0000 **4** *nse* **Gossiping**[11] 7697 7-8-13 **85**........................ ShaneKelly 2 85
(Gary Moore) *hld up in tch in midfield: clsd and swtchd rt 2f out: chsd ldrs but outpcd u.p jst over 1f out: wl hld and one pce ins fnl f: lost 3rd on post* **16/1**

3503 **5** *¾* **Nick Vedder**[13] 7607 5-8-10 **82**........................ DavidProbert 13 80
(Robyn Brisland) *dropped on after s: hld up in rr: clsd and nt clr run over 1f out: wnt between rivals jst over 1f out: styd on ins fnl f: nvr trbld ldrs (jockey said gelding hung left-handed)* **40/1**

0601 **6** *¾* **Markazi (FR)**[20] 7362 5-9-4 **90**........................(v) DanielTudhope 4 86
(David O'Meara) *w ldr tl rdn to ld 2f out: hdd over 1f out: sn outpcd and wknd ins fnl f* **13/2**[3]

6020 **7** *½* **Diocles Of Rome (IRE)**[25] 7188 4-9-2 **88**........................ HarryBentley 7 82
(Ralph Beckett) *dwlt: hld up towards rr of main gp: effrt over 2f out: kpt on ins fnl f: nvr trbld ldrs* **7/1**

0303 **8** *¾* **Exchequer (IRE)**[14] 7591 8-8-8 **87**........................(tp) HarryRussell(7) 5 79
(Richard Guest) *mounted in chute: dwlt and swtchd rt leaving stalls: hld up in tch: effrt and swtchd rt 2f out: kpt on but nvr threatened ldrs* **50/1**

3104 **9** *1* **Jaleel**[15] 7551 3-8-11 **85**........................(b) JackMitchell 9 74
(Roger Varian) *dwlt: hld up towards rr of main gp: effrt over 2f out: no real imp u.p over 1f out: nvr involved* **8/1**

6060 **10** *1* **Eljaddaaf (IRE)**[20] 7372 8-8-12 **89**........................(h) SophieRalston(5) 10 76
(Dean Ivory) *dropped in bhd after s: hld up in rr: nvr involved* **66/1**

1150 **11** *½* **Gentle Look**[74] 5434 3-9-0 **88**........................(p[1]) OisinMurphy 8 73
(Saeed bin Suroor) *t.k.h: chsd ldrs: rdn ent fnl 2f: unable qck and outpcd over 1f out: wknd ins fnl f* **11/2**[2]

264- **12** *1 ¼* **Easy Tiger**[389] 7272 7-9-1 **87**........................ LiamKeniry 1 69
(David Weston) *led: rdn and hdd 2f out: lost pl over 1f out: wknd fnl f* **66/1**

2553 **13** *2 ¼* **Jack's Point**[18] 7448 3-9-5 **93**........................(p) CharlesBishop 11 68
(William Muir) *chsd ldrs on outer: rdn and struggling over 2f out: lost pl and wknd over 1f out* **33/1**

1m 24.47s (-1.53) **Going Correction** -0.025s/f (Stan)
WFA 3 from 4yo+ 2lb **13 Ran SP% 120.2**
Speed ratings (Par 107): **107,105,102,102,101 100,99,98,97,96 96,94,92**
CSF £31.77 CT £256.09 TOTE £2.10: £1.10, £4.80, £4.20; EX 30.70 Trifecta £306.60.
Owner Sheikh Hamed Dalmook Al Maktoum **Bred** Domenico Fonzo & Maria Teresa Matouani **Trained** Newmarket, Suffolk

FOCUS
A strong looking race became a two-horse affair in the latter stages. The second has been rated close to his best.

8017 32RED CASINO H'CAP 7f (P)
7:40 (7:41) (Class 4) (0-80,80) 3-Y-O+

£6,469 (£1,925; £962; £481; £400; £400) **Stalls** Low

Form RPR

0304 **1** **Invasion Day (IRE)**[12] 7653 3-9-5 **80**........................(p) DanielTudhope 5 91+
(David O'Meara) *hld up towards rr: gd hdwy over 1f out: rdn and str run to ld ins fnl f: in command and pushed out towards fin* **9/1**

1021 **2** *1* **Delilah Park**[32] 6968 5-9-7 **80**........................ JackMitchell 13 86
(Chris Wall) *taken down early: t.k.h: prom: chsd ldr after 2f: drvn and ev ch over 1f out: led ins fnl f: sn hdd and one pce towards fin* **13/2**[3]

2100 **3** *¾* **Alhakmah (IRE)**[111] 4023 3-9-5 **80**........................ SeanLevey 11 83
(Richard Hannon) *t.k.h: chsd ldrs: effrt ent fnl 2f: drvn and pressing ldrs: kpt on ins fnl f* **33/1**

0630 **4** *nk* **Azzeccagarbugli (IRE)**[26] 7164 6-9-6 **79**........................(p) RossaRyan 12 82
(Mike Murphy) *pushed along leaving stalls: led after 1f: rdn ent fnl 2f: drvn and battled on wl tl hdd ins fnl f: no ex and outpcd fnl 100yds* **33/1**

4454 **5** *nk* **Maksab (IRE)**[25] 7205 4-9-6 **79**........................(p[1]) SilvestreDeSousa 7 81
(Mick Channon) *led for 1f: pressed ldr after: drvn and ev ch over 1f out tl no ex and outpcd fnl 100yds* **15/2**

0215 **6** *½* **Indian Viceroy**[27] 7128 3-9-3 **78**........................(p) OisinMurphy 6 78
(Hughie Morrison) *wnt lft leaving stalls: hld up in tch in midfield: effrt ent fnl 2f: clsd and chsd ldrs u.p 1f out: sn no ex and outpcd ins fnl f* **9/1**

6605 **7** *hd* **Indomitable (IRE)**[37] 6801 3-8-11 **72**........................(p[1]) DavidProbert 3 71
(Andrew Balding) *midfield: effrt jst over 2f out: kpt on u.p ins fnl f: nvr enough pce to chal* **16/1**

4204 **8** *1 ¾* **Majestic Mac**[18] 7460 3-9-1 **76**........................ PJMcDonald 1 71
(Hughie Morrison) *in tch in midfield: effrt and hdwy 2f out: no ex and no hdwy 1f out: wknd ins fnl f* **6/1**[2]

4424 **9** *1 ¾* **Ginger Fox**[18] 7465 3-9-1 **76**........................(v) JimCrowley 9 66
(Ian Williams) *s.i.s: t.k.h: hld up in tch towards rr: effrt over 2f out: nvr trbld ldrs (jockey said gelding was slowly away)* **7/1**

3-21 **10** *1* **Molivaliente (USA)**[91] 4793 3-9-2 **77**........................ KierenFox 10 64
(John Best) *s.i.s: t.k.h: hld up in rr: n.d (jockey said colt was slowly away and ran too free)* **9/2**[1]

1235 **11** *nse* **Leo Davinci (USA)**[79] 5255 3-9-1 **76**........................(tp) HarryBentley 2 63
(George Scott) *hld up in tch in last quintet: effrt on inner over 1f out: no imp and wl hld fnl f* **16/1**

0440 **12** *6* **Baltic Prince (IRE)**[26] 7145 9-9-1 **74**........................ TomMarquand 4 46
(Tony Carroll) *chsd ldrs: lost pl u.p over 1f out: wknd fnl f* **16/1**

5606 **13** *4 ½* **Jellmood**[76] 5343 4-8-11 **70**........................(t) CharlesBishop 8 30
(Chris Gordon) *v.s.a: a in rr (jockey said gelding was slowly away)* **80/1**

1m 25.61s (-0.39) **Going Correction** -0.025s/f (Stan)
WFA 3 from 4yo+ 2lb **13 Ran SP% 114.8**
Speed ratings (Par 105): **101,99,99,98,98 97,97,95,93,92 92,85,80**
CSF £63.07 CT £1898.27 TOTE £10.40: £3.20, £2.60, £6.60; EX 72.70 Trifecta £1689.60.
Owner Clipper Logistics **Bred** Cloughmealy Stud **Trained** Upper Helmsley, N Yorks

FOCUS
As the betting suggested, this was an open event, but the winner claimed the prize in taking style.

8018 32RED ON THE APP STORE H'CAP 6f (P)
8:10 (8:11) (Class 6) (0-55,55) 3-Y-O+ **£3,105** (£924; £461; £400; £400) **Stalls** Low

Form RPR

2525 **1** **Terri Rules (IRE)**[34] 6889 4-9-5 **54**........................ DanielMuscutt 9 61
(Lee Carter) *chsd ldrs tl clsd to ld wl over 1f out: sn hrd pressed and rdn: hdd ins fnl f: battled bk to ld again last stride* **16/1**

5300 **2** *shd* **Halle's Harbour**[9] 7770 3-9-5 **55**........................(v) OisinMurphy 6 62
(Paul George) *hld up in midfield: clsd to chse ldrs 2f out: effrt and chal over 1f out: led ins fnl f: hdd last stride* **7/1**[2]

0202 **3** *2* **Garth Rockett**[7] 7811 5-9-6 **55**........................(tp) LukeMorris 3 56
(Mike Murphy) *in tch in midfield: clsd and effrt 2f out: chsd ldrs and kpt on same pce ins fnl f* **13/8**[1]

4514 **4** 3/4 **Dandilion (IRE)**[9] 7770 6-8-12 52 ThoreHammerHansen(5) 12 50
(Alex Hales) *swtchd sharply rt after s: hld up in rr: swtchd lft and effrt 2f out: hdwy 1f out: r.o wl ins fnl f: nvr trbld ldrs (jockey said mare ducked violently right-handed leaving the stalls)* **17/2**[3]

342 **5** 2 **Mad Endeavour**[55] 6107 8-9-3 52 (b) FergusSweeney 2 44
(Stuart Kittow) *in tch in midfield: effrt on inner to chse ldrs over 1f out: no ex 1f out: wknd ins fnl f* **14/1**

00-0 **5** dht **Simply Sin (IRE)**[114] 3946 4-9-2 51 (h[1]) LiamKeniry 1 43
(Neil Mulholland) *s.i.s and pushed along early: towards rr: hdwy on inner 2f out: kpt on same pce ins fnl f* **20/1**

0103 **7** 2 **Classy Cailin (IRE)**[40] 6682 4-9-3 52 ShaneKelly 5 39
(Pam Sly) *hld up in last trio: hmpd bnd over 4f out: swtchd lft over 1f out: kpt on ins fnl f: nvr trbld ldrs* **10/1**

0060 **8** 3/4 **Wiff Waff**[25] 7172 4-9-6 55 (v[1]) CharlesBishop 11 39
(Chris Gordon) *chsd ldrs: rdn over 2f out: unable qck and outpcd over 1f out: wknd ins fnl f* **40/1**

4035 **9** 3/4 **Mayfair Madame**[9] 7757 3-9-4 54 RobHornby 4 36
(Stuart Kittow) *in tch in midfield: effrt over 2f out: no imp over 1f out: wl hld ins fnl f* **11/1**

6-30 **10** shd **Catheadans Fiyah**[42] 6598 3-9-2 52 (h[1]) GeorgeWood 7 34
(Martin Bosley) *short of room leaving stalls: hld up towards rr: rdn and hdwy over 1f out: no imp ins fnl f* **33/1**

0263 **11** 2 1/2 **Rock In Society (IRE)**[23] 7281 4-9-1 53 (b) DarraghKeenan(3) 8 27
(John Butler) *led: rdn and hdd wl over 1f out: wknd ins fnl f* **7/1**[2]

4040 **12** 4 **Alba Del Sole (IRE)**[9] 7770 4-8-12 54 SeanKirrane(7) 10 16
(Charlie Wallis) *chsd ldr tl 2f out: lost pl u.p over 1f out: wknd fnl f* **25/1**

1m 12.88s (-0.22) **Going Correction** -0.025s/f (Stan)
WFA 3 from 4yo+ 1lb 12 Ran SP% **117.6**
Speed ratings (Par 101): **100,99,97,96,93 93,90,89,88,88 85,80**
CSF £117.94 CT £289.68 TOTE £18.20: £3.10, £2.30, £1.20; EX 144.20 Trifecta £809.20.
Owner Kestonracingclub **Bred** John Joe Ronayne **Trained** Epsom, Surrey

FOCUS
This mainly moderate handicap saw quite a short-priced favourite considering he hadn't won for a while. The winner has been rated near her recent selling form.
T/Plt: £41.70. to a £1 stake. Pool: £51,675.45 - 902.92 winning units T/Qpdt: £30.60 to a £1 stake. Pool: £7,780.34 - 188.10 winning units **Steve Payne**

7956 NEWCASTLE (A.W) (L-H)
Wednesday, October 9

OFFICIAL GOING: Tapeta: standard
Wind: Fairly strong, half against on the straight course and in over 3f of home straight in races on the r Weather: Dry

8019 RAMSIDE HALL HOTEL, GOLF & SPA H'CAP 1m 4f 98y (Tp)
5:25 (5:26) (Class 6) (0-65,65) 3-Y-O+
£2,781 (£827; £413; £400; £400; £400) **Stalls** High

Form RPR

2111 **1** **Trouble Shooter (IRE)**[28] 7082 3-9-3 64 (v) JosephineGordon 4 74+
(Shaun Keightley) *t.k.h: hld up in tch: smooth hdwy on outside to ld over 2f out: hrd pressed and rdn over 1f out: pushed clr ins fnl f: comf* **9/2**[3]

6424 **2** 2 1/4 **Vibrance**[23] 7287 3-9-4 65 PaulMulrennan 10 72+
(James Fanshawe) *dwlt: hld up towards rr: hdwy 3f out: effrt and ev ch briefly over 1f out: kpt on ins fnl f: nt pce of wnr* **7/2**[2]

1306 **3** 2 3/4 **Glorious Dane**[60] 5975 3-9-3 64 ShaneGray 5 67
(Stef Keniry) *hld up: hdwy on outside over 2f out: effrt over 1f out: no ex ins fnl f* **33/1**

0046 **4** 1/2 **Straitouttacompton**[18] 7441 3-9-3 64 (t) DougieCostello 3 66
(Ivan Furtado) *hld up in midfield: effrt whn nt clr run over 2f out to wl over 1f out: rdn and kpt on ins fnl f: nt pce to chal* **33/1**

4325 **5** 3/4 **Remember Rocky**[20] 7368 10-9-2 62 (b) PaulaMuir(5) 11 62
(Lucy Normile) *t.k.h early: prom: rdn over 2f out: edgd lft and outpcd fr over 1f out* **33/1**

0310 **6** 2 3/4 **Kirtling**[22] 7318 8-9-6 61 (t) BenCurtis 9 57
(Andi Brown) *missed break: hld up: smooth hdwy and prom 2f out: sn rdn: wknd ins fnl f (jockey said gelding was slowly away)* **9/1**

5044 **7** 3/4 **Zihaam**[21] 7332 5-9-10 65 (p) DavidEgan 12 59
(Roger Fell) *pressed ldr: ev ch and rdn over 2f out: wknd over 1f out* **40/1**

2010 **8** hd **Myklachi (FR)**[20] 7368 3-9-4 65 DavidNolan 14 60
(David O'Meara) *hld up: rdn along 3f out: hdwy over 1f out: no imp fnl f* **10/1**

5630 **9** 2 **Royal Flag**[7] 7830 9-9-7 62 BenRobinson 1 53
(Brian Ellison) *chsd ldrs: drvn along over 3f out: rallied: wknd over 1f out* **18/1**

3414 **10** 1/2 **Esspeegee**[37] 6796 6-9-7 65 (v) CierenFallon(3) 7 55
(Alan Bailey) *hld up: rdn along over 2f out: nvr able to chal (jockey said gelding was slowly away)* **16/1**

5424 **11** 17 **Wadacre Galoubet**[18] 7450 3-9-4 65 JoeFanning 13 31
(Mark Johnston) *chsd ldrs: rdn over 2f out: wkng whn hmpd over 1f out* **14/1**

1400 **12** 1 3/4 **Ezanak (IRE)**[17] 7492 6-9-10 65 (p) TomEaves 6 27
(John Wainwright) *midfield: rdn over 4f out: wknd fnl 3f* **150/1**

13 **13** 1 **Chica Buena (IRE)**[10] 7732 4-9-2 57 GrahamLee 2 18
(Keith Dalgleish) *led to over 2f out: rdn and wknd wl over 1f out (trainers rep could offer no explanation for the poor performance)* **10/3**[1]

2m 41.0s (-0.10) **Going Correction** +0.075s/f (Slow)
WFA 3 from 4yo+ 6lb 13 Ran SP% **112.3**
Speed ratings (Par 101): **103,101,99,99,98 97,96,96,95,94 83,82,81**
CSF £18.42 CT £450.84 TOTE £4.60: £2.30, £1.90, £12.80; EX 22.10 Trifecta £775.60.
Owner Simon Lockyer **Bred** Kildaragh Stud & M Downey **Trained** Newmarket, Suffolk

FOCUS
Just an average class 6 handicap with the exception of the front pair who are going the right way and pulled comfortably clear. The gallop steadied briefly around halfway but it was a fair test. It looks sound form as rated.

8020 COLONEL PORTERS BAR DEAN ST NEWCASTLE NOVICE STKS 1m 4f 98y (Tp)
5:55 (5:56) (Class 5) 3-Y-O+
£3,428 (£1,020; £509; £254) **Stalls** High

Form RPR

31 **1** **Good Tidings (FR)**[15] 7559 3-9-9 0 RobertHavlin 2 84+
(John Gosden) *plld hrd early: trckd ldrs: rdn to ld over 1f out: edgd rt: drew clr ins fnl f: comf* **30/100**[1]

3 **2** 3 **Goobinator (USA)**[57] 6034 3-9-2 0 PaulMulrennan 3 72
(Donald McCain) *t.k.h: pressed ldr: led over 2f out to over 1f out: kpt on ins fnl f: nt pce of wnr* **16/1**

3 1/2 **Mother's Approach (IRE)**[51] 6296 3-8-11 0 JoeFanning 5 66
(Gavin Cromwell, Ire) *hld up: hdwy and prom over 1f out: rdn and kpt on ins fnl f* **22/1**

2553 **4** 1 1/4 **Lady Scatterley (FR)**[11] 7704 3-8-11 68 DavidAllan 6 64
(Tim Easterby) *led to over 2f out: rallied: rdn and outpcd fnl f* **11/1**[3]

243 **5** nk **Final Orders**[15] 7559 3-9-2 78 (p) GrahamLee 7 69
(Simon Crisford) *prom: hdwy whn n.m.r briefly over 2f out: rdn and edgd lft over 1f out: sn no imp (jockey said gelding hung left-handed under pressure)* **9/2**[2]

-6 **6** 1 1/4 **Abwab (IRE)**[93] 4732 3-8-11 0 GerO'Neill(5) 1 67?
(Michael Easterby) *hld up: pushed along and outpcd 3f out: rallied over 1f out: sn no imp (jockey said gelding hung right-handed)* **125/1**

5 **7** 45 **Spy Fi**[40] 6662 5-9-3 0 JackGarritty 8
(John Norton) *hld up: rdn along over 4f out: lost tch over 2f out: t.o* **250/1**

2m 41.09s (-0.01) **Going Correction** +0.075s/f (Slow)
WFA 3 from 5yo 6lb 7 Ran SP% **114.9**
Speed ratings (Par 103): **103,101,100,99,99 98,68**
CSF £7.48 TOTE £1.20: £1.10, £3.10; EX 6.10 Trifecta £28.30.
Owner HH Sheikh Zayed bin Mohammed Racing **Bred** David Powell **Trained** Newmarket, Suffolk

FOCUS
No surprises in this, the market leader confirming that he was a cut above the remainder, with a steady pace meaning those behind him finished in a bunch. Muddling form, but the second has been rated close to his debut form.

8021 LANCASTRIAN SUITE FILLIES' NOVICE STKS (PLUS 10 RACE) 1m 5y (Tp)
6:25 (6:29) (Class 5) 2-Y-O
£3,428 (£1,020; £509; £254) **Stalls** Centre

Form RPR

1 **Tiempo Vuela** 2-9-0 0 RobertHavlin 8 83+
(John Gosden) *hld up in midfield: rdn and hdwy 2f out: qcknd to ld ins fnl f: drifted lft and sn clr: promising* **5/1**[3]

233 **2** 3 **Tulip Fields**[33] 6918 2-9-0 81 JoeFanning 4 76
(Mark Johnston) *t.k.h: led: rdn along over 1f out: hdd ins fnl f: nt pce of wnr* **9/4**[2]

02 **3** 2 3/4 **Eventful**[21] 7330 2-9-0 0 BenCurtis 3 70
(Hugo Palmer) *dwlt: sn cl up: effrt and edgd lft over 1f out: drvn and no ex ins fnl f* **11/1**

3 **4** 3 **Red Line Alexander (IRE)**[32] 6949 2-9-0 0 GrahamLee 7 63
(Simon Crisford) *chsd ldr: rdn and effrt 2f out: wknd ins fnl f* **6/4**[1]

5 1 1/2 **Easy Desire** 2-9-0 0 TonyHamilton 1 60
(Richard Fahey) *slowly away: hld up: effrt and rn green over 2f out: sn outpcd: no imp after* **28/1**

6 1 1/2 **Zere** 2-9-0 0 DavidEgan 2 57
(Archie Watson) *chsd ldrs: drvn and outpcd over 2f out: n.d after* **14/1**

7 1 1/4 **Presidential Sweet (ITY)** 2-8-11 0 CierenFallon(3) 9 54
(Marco Botti) *slowly away: bhd: hdwy to tag onto bk of gp bef 1/2-way: drvn and green over 2f out: n.d after (jockey said filly ran green)* **16/1**

06 **8** 8 **Ventura Destiny (FR)**[10] 7733 2-9-0 0 ShaneGray 10 36
(Keith Dalgleish) *hld up in midfield: rdn and struggling over 2f out: sn wknd* **125/1**

00 **9** 2 1/4 **Just Call Me Ella**[22] 7304 2-9-0 0 CamHardie 6 31
(Rebecca Menzies) *hld up: rdn and outpcd over 2f out: sn btn* **250/1**

10 6 **High Moor Flyer** 2-9-0 0 JackGarritty 5 18
(Jedd O'Keeffe) *hld up: drvn over 3f out: wknd over 2f out* **80/1**

0 **11** 4 1/2 **Poco Contante**[32] 6970 2-9-0 0 BenRobinson 11 8
(David Thompson) *hld up: rdn over 3f out: wknd over 2f out* **250/1**

1m 40.58s (1.98) **Going Correction** +0.075s/f (Slow) 11 Ran SP% **114.6**
Speed ratings (Par 92): **93,90,87,84,82 81,80,72,69,63 59**
CSF £16.22 TOTE £5.00: £1.90, £1.10, £2.20; EX 16.70 Trifecta £100.10.
Owner A E Oppenheimer And Sophie **Bred** Hascombe & Valiant Stud Ltd **Trained** Newmarket, Suffolk

FOCUS
An interesting novice in which an above-average filly overcame one with solid previous form. The pace was even and there was no obvious bias. The second has been rated close to form.

8022 BOWBURN HALL HOTEL NURSERY H'CAP 7f 14y (Tp)
6:55 (6:57) (Class 6) (0-65,67) 2-Y-O
£2,781 (£827; £413; £400; £400; £400) **Stalls** Centre

Form RPR

0501 **1** **Idoapologise**[23] 7283 2-9-9 67 (h) KevinStott 10 72+
(James Bethell) *hld up stands' side gp: smooth hdwy over 2f out: rdn to ld ins fnl f: r.o wl* **2/1**[1]

660 **2** nk **Guipure**[96] 4605 2-9-6 64 BenCurtis 11 68
(K R Burke) *in tch stands' side gp: hdwy over 2f out: sn drvn: chsd wnr ins fnl f: kpt on: hld nr fin* **14/1**

5500 **3** 1 1/2 **Bryn Du**[14] 7585 2-8-12 59 (t[1]) CierenFallon(3) 12 60
(William Haggas) *led stands' side gp: rdn and overall ldr briefly over 1f out: hdd ins fnl f: kpt on same pce last 50yds* **7/1**[3]

4500 **4** nk **Don Ramiro (IRE)**[14] 7582 2-9-4 62 TomEaves 9 62
(Kevin Ryan) *hld up stands' side gp: drvn along over 2f out: hdwy over 1f out: kpt on ins fnl f: nt pce to chal* **13/2**[2]

0240 **5** 1 **Bendy Spirit (IRE)**[24] 7247 2-9-9 67 TonyHamilton 4 64
(Richard Fahey) *hld up in centre gp: hdwy over 2f out: drvn and prom over 1f out: no ex ins fnl f* **10/1**

406 **6** 1 1/2 **Pearl Stream**[14] 7584 2-8-13 57 ConnorBeasley 3 51
(Michael Dods) *hld up in centre gp: drvn and outpcd over 2f out: rallied on far side of gp over 1f out: kpt on fnl f: no imp* **28/1**

0140 **7** 1 1/2 **Our Dave**[22] 7306 2-9-2 60 (v) DavidAllan 8 50
(John Quinn) *prom in centre gp: drvn along over 2f out: wknd over 1f out* **28/1**

052 **8** 4 **Grace Note**[23] 7269 2-9-4 62 (b) PaulMulrennan 7 42
(Archie Watson) *led and overall ldr in centre gp: rdn and hdd over 1f out: sn wknd* **33/1**

0005 **9** 1/2 **Inductive**[14] 7582 2-8-11 55 (p[1]) CallumRodriguez 6 34
(Michael Dods) *chsd ldr in centre gp: rdn over 2f out: wknd over 1f out* **8/1**

0000 **10** 3 1/2 **Hands Down (IRE)**[33] 6919 2-8-5 54 FayeMcManoman(5) 1 24
(Nigel Tinkler) *hld up in centre gp: rdn and struggling over 2f out: sn btn (trainers rep said filly had a breathing problem)* **50/1**

5303 **11** 4 **Puerto Sol (IRE)**[14] 7584 2-8-13 57 BenRobinson 2 17
(Brian Ellison) *missed break: bhd in centre gp: rdn over 2f out: edgd rt and wknd wl over 1f out* **33/1**

0444 **12** 2 3/4 **Red Maharani**[22] 7306 2-9-0 58 BarryMcHugh 5 11
(James Given) *hld up in centre gp: drvn along over 2f out: sn wknd* **16/1**

6002 **13** *17* **Breck's Selection (FR)**[25] 7173 2-9-7 **65**.......................... DavidEgan 13
(Mark Johnston) *hld up in stands' side gp: drvn and struggling 3f out: lost tch fnl 2f: t.o (trainers rep could offer no explanation for the poor performance)* **12/1**

1m 27.15s (0.95) **Going Correction** +0.075s/f (Slow) **13 Ran SP% 114.3**
Speed ratings (Par 93): **97,96,94,94,93 91,90,85,84,80 76,73,53**
CSF £29.03 CT £153.82 TOTE £2.50: £1.10, £3.50, £2.80; EX 35.80 Trifecta £222.60.
Owner Clarendon Thoroughbred Racing **Bred** The Shiba Partnership **Trained** Middleham Moor, N Yorks

FOCUS
The draw certainly played a part in this modest nursery, with the group that came stands' side dominating the finish. That said, the front pair should still be viewed positively. The second and third have been rated as stepping forward.

8023 HARDWICK HALL HOTEL SEDGEFIELD H'CAP — 5f (Tp)
7:25 (7:28) (Class 4) (0-80,80) 3-Y-O+

£5,207 (£1,549; £774; £400; £400; £400) **Stalls** Centre

Form RPR

0300 **1** **Secretinthepark**[28] 7077 9-9-3 **76**....................................(b) JackGarritty 11 84
(Michael Mullineaux) *mde all on nr side of gp: drvn along 2f out: hld on wl fnl f* **25/1**

5032 **2** *nk* **Foxy Forever (IRE)**[9] 7771 9-9-5 **78**.........................(bt) RobbieDowney 14 85
(Michael Wigham) *hld up on nr side of gp: effrt and rdn over 1f out: chsd wnr last 100yds: kpt on fin* **5/1**[1]

0044 **3** *1 ¼* **Excessable**[21] 7334 6-8-9 **68**...............................(tp) RachelRichardson 12 71
(Tim Easterby) *cl up on nr side of gp: rdn along over 2f out: kpt on same pce ins fnl f* **12/1**

4603 **4** *½* **Royal Brave (IRE)**[10] 7736 8-9-7 **80**.............................. DavidAllan 9 81
(Rebecca Bastiman) *hld up in centre of gp: rdn and hdwy over 1f out: kpt on ins fnl f: nrst fin* **22/1**

5503 **5** *hd* **Canford Bay (IRE)**[11] 7700 5-9-7 **80**.............................. CamHardie 1 80+
(Antony Brittain) *hld up in midfield on far side of gp: rdn over 2f out: kpt on fnl f: nvr able to chal* **16/1**

2100 **6** *hd* **Sonja Henie (IRE)**[20] 7380 3-9-2 **80**.............. ThomasGreatrex(5) 5 80+
(David Loughnane) *prom on far side of gp: drvn along 1/2-way: one pce appr fnl f* **8/1**

4406 **7** *¾* **Bowson Fred**[14] 7588 7-8-9 **68**.................................. GrahamLee 10 65
(Michael Easterby) *dwlt: midfield on nr side of gp: rdn and effrt 2f out: outpcd ins fnl f* **11/2**[2]

6454 **8** *1 ¼* **Tathmeen (IRE)**[18] 7470 4-8-12 **71**........................ CallumRodriguez 4 63
(Antony Brittain) *dwlt: hld up towards far side of gp: rdn along over 1f out: checked ins fnl f: no imp* **6/1**[3]

6500 **9** *shd* **Little Legs**[20] 7387 3-9-7 **80**.. BenRobinson 13 73
(Brian Ellison) *bhd on nr side of gp: drvn along over 2f out: no imp fnl f* **16/1**

4205 **10** *¾* **Chookie Dunedin**[41] 6631 4-8-9 **68**.............................. TomEaves 7 57
(Keith Dalgleish) *cl up in centre of gp: drvn along over 2f out: fdd over 1f out* **12/1**

5040 **11** *1* **Spirit Of Wedza (IRE)**[42] 6591 7-8-11 **70**...................... KevinStott 2 55
(Julie Camacho) *hld up on far side of gp: rdn 2f out: sn n.d: btn fnl f* **28/1**

1020 **12** *3 ¼* **Archimedes (IRE)**[6] 7855 6-8-10 **69**...............................(vt) PhilDennis 6 43
(David C Griffiths) *cl up in centre of gp: drvn along 1/2-way: wknd over 1f out* **28/1**

0664 **13** *shd* **Henley**[11] 7700 7-8-10 **69**... BarryMcHugh 3 42
(Tracy Waggott) *cl up on far side of gp: lost pl 1/2-way: sn struggling* **16/1**

0604 **14** *4 ½* **Mutawaffer (IRE)**[98] 4495 3-9-6 **79**............................ BenCurtis 8 37
(Phillip Makin) *t.k.h: hld up in centre of gp: drvn along over 2f out: wknd over 1f out* **9/1**

59.27s (-0.23) **Going Correction** +0.075s/f (Slow) **14 Ran SP% 115.6**
Speed ratings (Par 105): **104,103,101,100,100 100,98,96,96,95 93,88,88,81**
CSF £135.55 CT £1094.20 TOTE £32.10: £6.70, £1.80, £4.30; EX 200.10 Trifecta £1786.50.
Owner Mia Racing **Bred** Mia Racing **Trained** Alpraham, Cheshire

FOCUS
A well-contested sprint handicap in which high draws were seen to advantage once more and, despite a sound gallop, few got involved from the rear. The winner has been rated to his best since 2015, with the second in line with his recent form and the third to his recent efforts.

8024 IMPECCABLE PIG SEDGEFIELD H'CAP — 1m 5y (Tp)
7:55 (7:56) (Class 4) (0-85,85) 3-Y-O+

£5,207 (£1,549; £774; £400; £400; £400) **Stalls** Centre

Form RPR

520 **1** **Fennaan (IRE)**[31] 6998 4-9-6 **83**...................................... BenCurtis 7 92+
(Phillip Makin) *slowly away: hld up in centre of gp: swtchd to stands' rail and gd hdwy over 1f out: led ins fnl f: ears pricked nr fin: comf* **11/2**[2]

-600 **2** *¾* **Tangled (IRE)**[11] 7678 4-9-3 **80**................................(h[1]) ShaneGray 4 86
(Karen Tutty) *hld up in centre of gp: pushed along over 2f out: hdwy and edgd lft over 2f out: ev ch briefly ins fnl f: kpt on* **14/1**

2060 **3** *½* **Saisons D'Or (IRE)**[22] 7310 4-8-8 **78**.................. OwenPayton(7) 13 83
(Jedd O'Keeffe) *led on nr side of gp: rdn and hdd over 1f out: rallied: kpt on ins fnl f* **40/1**

2133 **4** *1 ¼* **Eligible (IRE)**[39] 6729 3-9-2 **82**................................. HectorCrouch 12 84+
(Clive Cox) *in tch on nr side of gp: effrt over 2f out: rdn to ld over 1f out: hung lft and hdd ins fnl f: sn no ex* **13/2**[3]

422F **5** *3* **Alnadir (USA)**[47] 6390 3-9-5 **85**...............................(p) RobertHavlin 9 80
(Simon Crisford) *hld up in centre of gp: rdn over 2f out: hdwy fnl f: kpt on: nvr able to chal* **13/2**[3]

6026 **6** *7* **Banksea**[26] 7153 6-9-7 **84**..(h) SamJames 6 63
(Marjorie Fife) *t.k.h: in tch in centre of gp: outpcd and hung lft over 2f out: no imp over 1f out* **28/1**

2050 **7** *2 ½* **Mardle**[19] 7404 3-9-0 **80**.. CliffordLee 3 53
(K R Burke) *hld up on far side of gp: hdwy and prom over 2f out: wknd over 1f out* **16/1**

6114 **8** *¾* **Image Of The Moon**[18] 7471 3-8-13 **79**..............(p) JosephineGordon 1 51
(Shaun Keightley) *t.k.h: prom on far side of gp: rdn over 2f out: wknd over 1f out* **12/1**

6031 **9** *2 ¾* **Brother McGonagall**[25] 7212 5-9-5 **82**.......................... DavidAllan 2 47
(Tim Easterby) *hld up towards far side of gp: rdn and outpcd over 2f out: n.d after* **16/1**

4054 **10** *8* **Florenza**[23] 7288 6-8-11 **74**.. TomEaves 8 21
(Chris Fairhurst) *racd in centre of gp: w ldrs to over 3f out: drvn and wknd fr 2f out* **33/1**

20P0 **11** *¾* **Rey Loopy (IRE)**[22] 7312 5-9-7 **84**........................... PaulMulrennan 11 29
(Ben Haslam) *hld up on nr side of gp: rdn and hdwy wl over 1f out: wknd ins fnl f* **12/1**

6140 **12** *½* **Glengarry**[20] 7362 6-9-5 **82**.................................. CallumRodriguez 10 26
(Keith Dalgleish) *in tch in centre of gp: drvn along over 2f out: wknd over 1f out (trainers rep could offer no explanation for the poor performance)* **5/1**[1]

025 **13** *27* **Helovaplan (IRE)**[44] 6543 5-9-8 **85**............................. GrahamLee 14
(Bryan Smart) *midfield on nr side of gp: drvn and struggling over 2f out: sn lost tch: t.o (trainer could offer no explanation for the poor performance other than the jockey said gelding became upset in the stalls)* **9/1**

00-5 **14** *hd* **Keswick**[14] 7567 5-9-3 **80**.......................................(t) DavidEgan 5
(Heather Main) *w ldrs to over 3f out: rdn and wknd over 2f out: t.o (trainers rep said it could offer no explanation for the poor performance)* **22/1**

1m 38.87s (0.27) **Going Correction** +0.075s/f (Slow) **14 Ran SP% 115.7**
WFA 3 from 4yo+ 3lb
Speed ratings (Par 105): **101,100,99,98,95 88,86,85,82,74 73,73,46,46**
CSF £73.61 CT £2843.69 TOTE £6.70: £2.60, £3.80, £12.10; EX 87.80 Trifecta £1951.70.
Owner Mrs Wendy Burdett **Bred** Minch Bloodstock And Castletown Stud **Trained** Easingwold, N Yorks

■ Stewards' Enquiry : Hector Crouch caution; careless riding

FOCUS
The pace was sound in this useful handicap and the field finished well strung out, so there's little reason to doubt the result acknowledging three of the first four home made their challenge towards the near side. The third looks the key to the form. The winner has been rated in line with his early 2019 form.

8025 WONDERBAR THE GATE NEWCASTLE H'CAP — 7f 14y (Tp)
8:25 (8:28) (Class 5) (0-75,75) 3-Y-O

£3,428 (£1,020; £509; £400; £400; £400) **Stalls** Centre

Form RPR

0103 **1** **Castle Quarter (IRE)**[19] 7418 3-8-11 **65**....................(b[1]) BenRobinson 8 74
(Seb Spencer) *prom on far side of gp: effrt and rdn over 1f out: led ins fnl f: hld on wl cl home* **5/1**[2]

2155 **2** *shd* **Northernpowerhouse**[39] 6700 3-9-7 **75**........................(p) GrahamLee 11 83
(Bryan Smart) *in tch in centre of gp: stdy hdwy whn checked over 1f out: drvn and ev ch ins fnl f: kpt on: jst hld* **11/2**[3]

0031 **3** *2* **Ghathanfar (IRE)**[33] 6945 3-8-9 **63**.................................. CamHardie 3 66+
(Tracy Waggott) *t.k.h: cl up on far side of gp: led over 1f out to ins fnl f: hung lft and sn one pce* **9/2**[1]

645 **4** *nk* **Double Martini (IRE)**[17] 7486 3-8-13 **67**............................... BenCurtis 1 69
(Roger Fell) *hld up on far side of gp: pushed along over 2f out: hdwy over 1f out: kpt on fnl f: no imp* **40/1**

1404 **5** *¾* **Ascended (IRE)**[25] 7206 3-9-4 **75**........................ CierenFallon(3) 12 75+
(William Haggas) *midfield on far side of gp: pushed along over 2f out: hdwy over 1f out: one pce whn checked ins fnl f* **11/2**[3]

0420 **6** *1 ¾* **Barbarosa (IRE)**[33] 6945 3-8-7 **61** oh1.................................. PhilDennis 6 57
(Michael Herrington) *dwlt: hld up: rdn over 2f out: hdwy over 1f out: no imp ins fnl f* **25/1**

0123 **7** *1 ½* **Termonator**[134] 3204 3-8-10 **64**... SamJames 13 56
(Grant Tuer) *hld up on nr side of gp: rdn and effrt whn nt clr run appr fnl f: sn no imp* **12/1**

4320 **8** *½* **Coolagh Magic**[15] 7540 3-9-7 **75**.. NathanEvans 2 66
(Seb Spencer) *hld up in centre of gp: drvn along over 2f out: no imp fr over 1f out (jockey said gelding was denied a clear run on more than one occasion approaching two furlongs out)* **25/1**

3520 **9** *½* **Lady Calcaria**[13] 7613 3-9-4 **72**.. DavidAllan 7 62
(Tim Easterby) *hld up towards rr in centre of gp: drvn along and outpcd over 2f out: n.d after* **16/1**

4040 **10** *2 ¾* **Jem Scuttle (USA)**[19] 7404 3-9-0 **68**............................(t) TomEaves 4 51
(Declan Carroll) *t.k.h: led in centre of gp: drvn and hdd over 1f out: sn wknd* **20/1**

1-50 **11** *¾* **Island Glen (USA)**[122] 3638 3-9-3 **71**................................ DavidEgan 5 52
(Heather Main) *hld up on nr side of gp: effrt and rdn over 2f out: wknd wl over 1f out* **14/1**

0102 **12** *nk* **Sharp Talk (IRE)**[18] 7472 3-8-11 **65**........................ JosephineGordon 10 45
(Shaun Keightley) *prom on nr side of gp: rdn over 2f out: wknd over 1f out (trainer could offer no explanation for the poor performance)* **9/1**

5453 **13** *1 ¾* **Balata Bay**[16] 7523 3-8-10 **71**......................................(b) EllaMcCain(7) 14 47
(Donald McCain) *chsd ldrs tl rdn and wknd wl over 1f out* **33/1**

0460 **14** *4 ½* **Spotton (IRE)**[17] 7486 3-8-7 **61** oh16.............................. JamieGormley 9 25
(Rebecca Bastiman) *hld up in centre of gp: drvn and outpcd 3f out: sn struggling* **150/1**

1m 26.68s (0.48) **Going Correction** +0.075s/f (Slow) **14 Ran SP% 114.4**
Speed ratings (Par 101): **100,99,97,97,96 94,92,92,91,88 87,87,85,80**
CSF £28.32 CT £135.13 TOTE £5.50: £1.90, £2.50, £1.70; EX 32.60 Trifecta £97.20.
Owner R Postlethwaite **Bred** Mrs T Brudenell **Trained** Malton, N Yorks

FOCUS
Some improving sorts dominated the finish after they'd gone a solid pace, so this is better form than the average 0-75 at this track. The winner has been rated as finding a bit on his recent course form.
T/Jkpt: Not Won. T/Plt: £230.30 to a £1 stake. Pool: £77,467.85 - 245.50 winning units T/Qpdt: £147.10 to a £1 stake. Pool: £10,488.48 - 52.74 winning units **Richard Young**

7825 NOTTINGHAM (L-H)
Wednesday, October 9

OFFICIAL GOING: Soft (5.6)
Wind: Light against Weather: Sunny periods

8026 BRITISH STALLION STUDS EBF NOVICE STKS — 6f 18y
1:25 (1:29) (Class 5) 2-Y-O **£3,881** (£1,155; £577; £288) **Stalls** Centre

Form RPR

5 **1** **Moosmee (IRE)**[34] 6891 2-9-2 0.. JamesDoyle 10 82
(William Haggas) *mde all: rdn along wl over 1f out: drvn ins fnl f: kpt on wl* **9/4**[1]

2203 **2** *½* **Asmund (IRE)**[19] 7399 2-9-2 **80**... BenCurtis 11 80
(K R Burke) *trckd ldrs: hdwy over 2f out: chsd wnr wl over 1f out: sn rdn: ev ch whn drvn and edgd lft ins fnl f: kpt on towards fin* **5/2**[2]

665 **3** *5* **Clegane**[22] 7304 2-8-11 72................................... RichardKingscote 9 60
(Ed Walker) *hld up in tch: hdwy to trck ldrs wl over 2f out: effrt to chse ldng pair wl over 1f out: sn rdn: edgd lft and one pce* **11/2**[3]

05 **4** *¾* **Triple Spear**[21] 7333 2-8-11 0.................................. TheodoreLadd(5) 3 63
(Michael Appleby) *prom on outer: cl up 1/2-way: sn pushed along: rdn 2f out and kpt on one pce (jockey said gelding hung right)* **16/1**

5 2 **Park Lane Dancer (IRE)** 2-9-2 0 ... PaulHanagan 1 57
(John Quinn) *s.i.s: green and wl bhd: pushed along bef 1/2-way: rdn and hdwy over 2f out: kpt on wl fnl f: nrst fin* **33/1**

0 **6** 3/4 **Cesifire (IRE)**[36] 6846 2-8-11 0 ... DavidProbert 6 50
(Adam West) *towards rr: hdwy over 2f out: sn rdn along: kpt on fnl f* **28/1**

6 **7** 2 **Passing Nod**[114] 3942 2-8-13 0 ...(h[1]) GeorgiaCox(3) 12 49
(William Haggas) *chsd ldrs: pushed along 1/2-way: sn rdn and wknd* **25/1**

04 **8** 3/4 **Brazen Point**[13] 7619 2-9-2 0 ...(t) DuranFentiman 2 46
(Tim Easterby) *a towards rr* **14/1**

10 **9** 1 1/2 **Deb's Delight**[25] 7179 2-9-9 0 ... DavidNolan 5 49
(Richard Fahey) *hld up: hdwy and in tch 1/2-way: chsd ldrs and rdn along 2f out: sn wknd* **8/1**

00 **10** 24 **Saracen Spirit**[13] 7619 2-9-2 0 ... FrannyNorton 8
(Mick Channon) *cl up: rdn along 1/2-way: sn wknd* **100/1**

1m 17.76s (3.96) **Going Correction** +0.475s/f (Yiel) **10 Ran SP% 109.6**
Speed ratings (Par 95): **92,91,84,83,81 80,77,76,74,42**
CSF £6.87 TOTE £3.10: £1.40, £1.20, £1.50; EX 6.30 Trifecta £28.60.
Owner Sheikh Ahmed Al Maktoum **Bred** Ms Ellen Fox **Trained** Newmarket, Suffolk
■ Hong Kong Harry was withdrawn. Price at time of withdrawal 14-1. Rule applies to all bets - deduction 5p in the pound.

FOCUS
Outer track used. The front two pulled clear in this novice event run in testing conditions. They raced towards the stands' rail and there was a headwind in the straight. The winner has been rated as improving from Haydock.

8027 TBA SUPPORTING BRITISH BREEDERS FILLIES' H'CAP 1m 6f
1:55 (1:55) (Class 3) (0-95,79) 3-Y-O+
£12,450 (£3,728; £1,864; £932; £466; £234) **Stalls Low**

Form RPR

1151 **1** **Maid In Manhattan (IRE)**[7] 7830 5-9-13 79 5ex...(h) HarrisonShaw(3) 5 87
(Rebecca Menzies) *trckd ldng pair: hdwy over 3f out: cl up over 2f out: led 1 1/2f out and sn rdn: drvn ins fnl f: hld on wl towards fin* **11/8[1]**

45-0 **2** shd **Methag (FR)**[198] 1330 6-8-11 65 ... ThoreHammerHansen(5) 1 72
(Alex Hales) *hld up in rr: hdwy on inner 3f out: cl up wl over 1f out: rdn to chal ent fnl f: sn drvn and ev ch: kpt on wl: jst hld* **14/1[3]**

0400 **3** 2 **Double Reflection**[20] 7366 4-9-0 70 ... RhonaPindar(7) 6 74
(K R Burke) *stdd s and hld up in rr: hdwy on outer to trck ldrs wl over 2f out: effrt to chse ldng pair over 1f out: rdn and kpt on same pce fnl f* **25/1**

55-5 **4** 2 3/4 **All My Love (IRE)**[189] 469 7-9-3 69 ... WilliamCox(3) 7 70
(Pam Sly) *led 1f: trckd ldr: cl up over 4f out: led wl over 3f out: rdn along and hdd over 2f out: sn drvn and grad wknd* **16/1**

2511 **5** hd **Well Funded (IRE)**[11] 7683 3-9-5 75 ... PaulHanagan 2 78
(James Bethell) *trckd ldng pair: hdwy over 4f out: cl up over 3f out: led wl over 2f out: sn rdn: hdd 1 1/2f out: sn drvn and wknd (trainer could offer no explanation for the poor performance other than the filly may have been unsuited by the uneven pace of the race on this occasion)* **11/8[1]**

1510 **6** 1/2 **Donnachies Girl (IRE)**[16] 7510 6-8-8 62 ... KieranSchofield(5) 3 62
(Alistair Whillans) *pushed along s and cl up: led after 1f: pushed along 5f out: rdn over 4f out: sn hdd: wknd over 2f out* **11/1[2]**

3m 19.24s (12.84) **Going Correction** +0.475s/f (Yiel) **6 Ran SP% 108.9**
WFA 3 from 4yo+ 7lb
Speed ratings (Par 104): **82,81,80,79,79 78**
CSF £21.39 TOTE £2.60: £1.60, £3.60; EX 23.50 Trifecta £167.20.
Owner Stoneleigh Racing **Bred** John Breslin **Trained** Mordon, Durham

FOCUS
Add 6yds. A tight finish for this staying handicap, with the winner recording her sixth success of the campaign. They raced towards the far rail this time. The form could be rated a bit higher if the third confirms this effort.

8028 BRITISH EBF MATCHBOOK FUTURE STAYERS OATH RESTRICTED MAIDEN STKS (PLUS 10) (SIRE/DAM RESTRICTED) 1m 75y
2:25 (2:27) (Class 2) 2-Y-O
£10,350 (£3,080; £1,539; £769) **Stalls Centre**

Form RPR

52 **1** **King Carney**[40] 6664 2-9-5 0 ... RichardKingscote 2 80
(Charlie Fellowes) *sn led: pushed along 3f out: rdn wl over 1f out: drvn and kpt on wl fnl f* **5/1[3]**

04 **2** 2 **Damage Control**[9] 7755 2-9-5 0 ... OisinMurphy 8 76
(Andrew Balding) *cl up: pushed along wl over 2f out: rdn over 1f out: drvn and edgd lft ent fnl f: kpt on: no imp* **4/1[2]**

3 nk **Annie De Vega** 2-9-0 0 ... HarryBentley 9 70+
(Ralph Beckett) *midfield: hdwy over 3f out: trckd ldrs over 2f out: rdn to chse ldng pair over 1f out: kpt on u.p fnl f* **11/4[1]**

4 1/2 **Too Big To Fail (IRE)** 2-9-0 0 ... FrannyNorton 1 69+
(Mark Johnston) *green and towards rr: hdwy on inner over 4f out: n.m.r and swtchd rt to outer over 2f out: sn rdn to chse ldrs: kpt on fnl f* **12/1**

60 **5** 7 **Molinari (IRE)**[9] 7755 2-9-5 0 ... KieranShoemark 4 58
(William Muir) *chsd ldng pair: rdn along over 3f out: drvn 2f out: grad wknd* **66/1**

6 3 1/4 **Favorite Moon (GER)** 2-9-5 0 ... JamesDoyle 5 51+
(William Haggas) *awkward and dwlt s: bhd: hdwy 1/2-way: rdn along and in tch 2 1/2f out: sn wknd* **5/1[3]**

7 2 3/4 **Crossing The Bar (IRE)** 2-9-5 0 ... DavidProbert 6 45
(Sir Michael Stoute) *dwlt: green and a in rr* **16/1**

8 3 **Chankaya** 2-9-5 0 ... JackMitchell 7 39+
(Hugo Palmer) *awkward and dwlt s: sme hdwy over 4f out: rdn along over 3f out: sn wknd (jockey said colt was slowly away)* **8/1**

9 nk **Quickthorn** 2-9-5 0 ... CharlieBennett 3 38
(Hughie Morrison) *green: sn pushed along and a in rr* **50/1**

5 **10** 5 **Master Spy (IRE)**[90] 4839 2-9-5 0 ... PaulHanagan 10 27
(Paul Cole) *chsd ldrs: rdn along over 3f out: sn wknd* **25/1**

1m 49.64s (2.94) **Going Correction** +0.475s/f (Yiel) **10 Ran SP% 112.0**
Speed ratings (Par 101): **104,102,101,101,94 90,88,85,84,79**
CSF £23.91 TOTE £5.90: £2.10, £1.90, £1.40; EX 22.90 Trifecta £93.90.
Owner Mrs Susan Roy **Bred** Select Bloodstock **Trained** Newmarket, Suffolk

FOCUS
Add 6yds. An informative maiden on paper and the winner put them to the sword. The level is fluid.

8029 BRITISH EBF NURSERY H'CAP 1m 2f 50y
2:55 (2:55) (Class 2) 2-Y-O
£16,172 (£4,812; £2,405; £1,202) **Stalls Low**

Form RPR

4315 **1** **Dubai Souq (IRE)**[32] 6965 2-9-3 85 ...(p[1]) OisinMurphy 5 97
(Saeed bin Suroor) *t.k.h: mde all: rdn clr wl over 2f out: styd on strly* **7/2[2]**

4010 **2** 6 **Magna Moralia (IRE)**[32] 6969 2-8-1 72 ow1 ... SeanDavis(3) 2 73
(John Quinn) *towards rr: hdwy on inner 1/2-way: trckd ldrs over 3f out: rdn to chse wnr 2f out: sn drvn and no imp* **20/1**

023 **3** 3 1/2 **Green Book (FR)**[13] 7623 2-8-8 76 ... PaulHanagan 8 71
(Brian Ellison) *hld up towards rr: hdwy 3f out: rdn over 2f out: kpt on fnl f: n.d* **11/2[3]**

065 **4** 1/2 **Duke Of Condicote**[14] 7562 2-8-1 74 ow1 ... ThoreHammerHansen(5) 6 68+
(Alan King) *midfield: dropped to rr after 3f: hdwy on inner 4f out: swtchd rt towards outer 3f out and sn rdn along: drvn fnl 2f: one pce* **11/4[1]**

054 **5** 7 **Sky Flyer**[43] 6564 2-8-3 71 ... JimmyQuinn 9 52
(Ralph Beckett) *hld up towards rr: hdwy over 3f out: sn swtchd rt to outer and rdn along over 2f out: sn drvn and wknd* **14/1**

1131 **6** 2 3/4 **Walkonby**[13] 7620 2-8-5 73 ... NathanEvans 3 49
(Mick Channon) *chsd ldrs: rdn along 3f out: sn drvn and wknd fnl 2f* **7/1**

3111 **7** 1 1/4 **Gallaside (FR)**[33] 6942 2-9-7 89 ... HollieDoyle 1 63
(Archie Watson) *trckd wnr: rdn along 3f out: drvn over 2f out: sn wknd (jockey said colt hung left in the home straight)* **7/1**

031 **8** 21 **Island Storm (IRE)**[19] 7416 2-8-3 76 ... TheodoreLadd(5) 7 12
(Heather Main) *in rr whn rn wd bnd over 6f out: nvr a factor (jockey said colt had blood in it's mouth post-race; vet said colt had a loose tooth)* **25/1**

2121 **9** 24 **Flylikeaneagle (IRE)**[21] 7331 2-9-3 85 ... FrannyNorton 4
(Mark Johnston) *chsd ldrs: rdn along wl over 3f out: hmpd 3f out and sn wknd (trainers rep could offer no explanation for the poor performance other than the colt suffered interference four furlongs out)* **10/1**

2m 14.49s (1.09) **Going Correction** +0.475s/f (Yiel) **9 Ran SP% 113.6**
Speed ratings (Par 101): **114,109,106,106,100 98,97,80,61**
CSF £68.09 CT £376.29 TOTE £3.00: £1.30, £6.10, £2.40; EX 55.80 Trifecta £467.80.
Owner Godolphin **Bred** Godolphin **Trained** Newmarket, Suffolk
■ Stewards' Enquiry : Jimmy Quinn two-day ban; careless riding (Oct 23-24)

FOCUS
Add 6yds. A competitive nursery turned into a rout by a horse winning his first race on turf, and it was another front-running winner.

8030 LIKE RACING TV ON FACEBOOK H'CAP (DIV I) 1m 75y
3:30 (3:31) (Class 5) (0-73,75) 3-Y-O+
£3,881 (£1,155; £577; £300; £300; £300) **Stalls Centre**

Form RPR

2426 **1** **Al Moataz (IRE)**[16] 7519 3-8-11 73 ... StefanoCherchi(7) 9 82
(Marco Botti) *hld up towards rr: smooth hdwy on inner 3f out: trckd ldrs over 2f out: swtchd rt and rdn to ld over 1f out: kpt on wl* **7/1**

3401 **2** 1 1/4 **Espresso Freddo (IRE)**[9] 7758 5-8-10 62 5ex...(v) KieranShoemark 7 68
(Robert Stephens) *hld up towards rr: hdwy on outer 3f out: chsd ldrs 2f out: sn rdn: styd on to chse wnr ins fnl f: no imp towards fin* **11/2[3]**

0642 **3** 1 **Thorn**[27] 7129 3-8-13 68 ...(h) PaulHanagan 4 72
(Peter Hiatt) *trckd ldr: hdwy and cl up 3f out: rdn along 2f out: sn ev ch: drvn ent fnl f and kpt on same pce* **16/1**

0004 **4** 3/4 **Vive La Difference (IRE)**[10] 7738 5-9-2 68 ...(p[1]) DuranFentiman 11 70
(Tim Easterby) *trckd ldrs: hdwy over 3f out: pushed along and ch over 2f out: sn rdn and kpt on same pce* **10/1**

2240 **5** hd **Salt Whistle Bay (IRE)**[64] 5776 5-9-9 75 ... RichardKingscote 1 77
(Rae Guest) *led: pushed along over 3f out: rdn over 2f out: drvn and hdd over 1f out: grad wknd* **5/1[2]**

4410 **6** 3 1/4 **Inner Circle (IRE)**[39] 6734 5-9-6 72 ...(p) EdwardGreatrex 5 66
(Mark Loughnane) *chsd ldrs: rdn along wl over 2f out: sn drvn and btn (jockey said gelding ran too free)* **25/1**

5232 **7** nk **Quarry Beach**[18] 7460 3-9-3 72 ... HollieDoyle 3 66
(Henry Candy) *trckd ldng pair: pushed along 3f out: rdn 2f out: hld whn n.m.r and wknd over 1f out* **5/1[2]**

6320 **8** 2 3/4 **Rudy Lewis (IRE)**[18] 7452 3-9-5 74 ... JamesDoyle 10 61
(Charlie Fellowes) *trckd ldrs: hdwy 4f out: rdn along 3f out: sn wknd (jockey said gelding stopped quickly; trainers rep could offer no explanation for the poor performance)* **7/2[1]**

1000 **9** 1/2 **Pushmi Pullyu (IRE)**[47] 6412 3-8-6 64 ... DarraghKeenan(3) 2 50
(Jane Chapple-Hyam) *trckd ldrs on inner: n.m.r after 2f: rdn along wl over 3f out: sn wknd* **10/1**

60-0 **10** 16 **Dark Mystique**[54] 6169 3-8-7 62 ... JoeyHaynes 6 11
(Dean Ivory) *a towards rr* **50/1**

1m 50.37s (3.67) **Going Correction** +0.475s/f (Yiel) **10 Ran SP% 113.3**
WFA 3 from 5yo+ 3lb
Speed ratings (Par 103): **100,98,97,97,96 93,93,90,90,74**
CSF £43.93 CT £591.54 TOTE £7.50: £2.70, £2.20, £3.70; EX 47.70 Trifecta £572.00.
Owner Mubarak Al Naemi **Bred** Mubarak Al Naemi **Trained** Newmarket, Suffolk

FOCUS
Add 6yds. A strong gallop for this mile handicap, with two hold-up performers coming to the fore. The second has been rated close to his Bath figure, and the third in line with his Epsom latest.

8031 LIKE RACING TV ON FACEBOOK H'CAP (DIV II) 1m 75y
4:00 (4:01) (Class 5) (0-73,74) 3-Y-O+
£3,881 (£1,155; £577; £300; £300; £300) **Stalls Centre**

Form RPR

652 **1** **Eponina (IRE)**[23] 7288 5-8-5 62 ... TheodoreLadd(5) 8 71
(Michael Appleby) *sn led: pushed along 3f out: rdn clr 2f out: kpt on strly* **11/2[2]**

0365 **2** 2 1/4 **Make Me**[20] 7363 4-8-9 61 ... JamesSullivan 10 65
(Tim Easterby) *trckd ldrs: effrt and n.m.r over 2f out and again wl over 1f out: sn rdn: styd on fnl f: nrst fin* **7/1[3]**

2300 **3** nk **Moxy Mares**[28] 7069 4-9-3 74 ...(p) KevinLundie(5) 4 77
(Mark Loughnane) *trckd ldrs on inner: hdwy 3f out: rdn along 2f out: chsd wnr and drvn over 1f out: kpt on same pce fnl f* **16/1**

612 **4** 2 1/2 **My Ukulele (IRE)**[10] 7735 3-9-0 72 ... SeanDavis(3) 3 70
(John Quinn) *hld up towards rr: hdwy over 2f out: sn rdn and kpt on fnl f* **7/1[3]**

0656 **5** 2 1/4 **Hitman**[14] 7581 6-8-7 59 oh3 ... DuranFentiman 2 52
(Rebecca Bastiman) *hld up towards rr: hdwy on inner 3f out: rdn along over 2f out: drvn over 1f out: kpt on: n.d* **33/1**

0213 **6** nk **Classic Charm**[54] 6170 4-9-6 72 ... JoeyHaynes 6 64
(Dean Ivory) *chsd ldng pair: rdn ovr 1f out: wknd fnl f* **7/2[1]**

0600 **7** 1/2 **Fitzrovia**[12] 7652 4-8-12 64 ... KieranShoemark 5 55
(Ed de Giles) *hld up in rr: hdwy on wd outside wl over 2f out: rdn wl over 1f out: sn no imp* **12/1**

1002 **8** 1/2 **Mujassam**[14] 7601 7-9-4 73 ...(v) WilliamCox(3) 11 63
(Sophie Leech) *hld up: hdwy on outer and in tch over 3f out: rdn along wl over 2f out: sn btn* **33/1**

0620 **9** 1/2 **Sir Plato (IRE)**[34] 6904 5-9-1 67 ... HollieDoyle 7 56
(Rod Millman) *sn chsng wnr: rdn along over 3f out: wknd over 2f out* **7/1[3]**

2655 **10** *1* **Imperial State**[26] 7145 6-9-5 **71**......(t) NathanEvans 9 58
(Michael Easterby) *hld up towards rr: hdwy 3f out: rdn to chse ldrs 2f out: drvn and wknd over 1f out* **14/1**

1m 49.77s (3.07) **Going Correction** +0.475s/f (Yiel)
WFA 3 from 4yo+ 3lb **10** Ran SP% **101.2**
Speed ratings (Par 103): **103,100,100,97,95 95,94,94,93,92**
CSF £33.98 CT £409.67 TOTE £4.70: £1.60, £2.20, £4.20; EX 37.50 Trifecta £360.80.
Owner Mrs Elisabeth Cash **Bred** Rev John Naughton **Trained** Oakham, Rutland

■ Knowing glance was withdrawn. Price at time of withdrawal 6-1. Rule 4 applies to all bets - deduction 10p in the pound.

FOCUS
Add 6yds. Once more if paid to be handy in the second division of the mile handicap. The second has been rated close to his most recent figures, with the third in line with this year's form in Britain.

8032 JOIN RACING TV NOW H'CAP 1m 2f 50y
4:30 (4:31) (Class 4) (0-85,83) 3-Y-0+ **£5,822** (£1,732; £865; £432; £300) **Stalls** Low

Form RPR
105 **1** **Rake's Progress**[53] 6218 5-8-9 **75**...... AngusVilliers[(7)] 1 84
(Heather Main) *trckd ldrs: pushed along 3f out: rdn over 1f out: chal ent fnl f: kpt on wl to ld last 110yds* **5/2**[2]

436 **2** *3 ¾* **Sod's Law**[73] 5474 4-9-6 **79**...... JamesDoyle 3 81
(Hughie Morrison) *hld up: hdwy on outer 3f out: rdn to chal 2f out: sn led and edgd lft: jnd and drvn jst ins fnl f: sn wandered: hdd and no ex last 110yds* **6/4**[1]

203- **3** *5* **Royal Big Night (USA)**[374] 7798 3-9-3 **80**...... FrannyNorton 2 72
(Mark Johnston) *cl up: led after 2f: hdd over 5f out: cl up and pushed along 4f out: rdn over 3f: sn drvn and outpcd over 2f out: kpt on appr fnl f* **12/1**

0064 **4** *nk* **Villette (IRE)**[131] 3300 5-9-5 **78**...... JoeyHaynes 6 68
(Dean Ivory) *trckd ldng pair: smooth hdwy to ld wl over 3f out: rdn along 2f out: sn hdd: drvn and wknd* **5/1**[3]

U4/6 **5** *67* **First Voyage (IRE)**[131] 3300 6-9-1 **74**...... AlistairRawlinson 7
(Michael Appleby) *led 2f: cl up: led again over 5f out: pushed along over 4f out: hdd wl over 3f out: sn wknd (vet said gelding bled from the nose)* **13/2**

2m 16.61s (3.21) **Going Correction** +0.475s/f (Yiel)
WFA 3 from 4yo+ 4lb **5** Ran SP% **106.3**
Speed ratings (Par 105): **106,103,99,98,45**
CSF £6.16 TOTE £2.80: £1.60, £1.50; EX 7.80 Trifecta £27.70.
Owner Coxwell Partnership **Bred** Mr & Mrs A E Pakenham **Trained** Kingston Lisle, Oxon

FOCUS
Add 6yds. They went quickly in this attritional contest. The front two came well clear. There's a case for rating the winner as having run a pb.

8033 FOLLOW @RACINGTV ON TWITTER APPRENTICE H'CAP 1m 2f 50y
5:00 (5:02) (Class 5) (0-70,72) 3-Y-0+
£3,881 (£1,155; £577; £300; £300; £300) **Stalls** Low

Form RPR
1631 **1** **Deinonychus**[7] 7829 8-9-11 **67** 4ex......(h) TheodoreLadd 7 75
(Michael Appleby) *hld up in rr: hdwy over 2f out: rdn to chse ldrs over 1f out: str run ent fnl f: led towards fin* **11/8**[1]

422 **2** *1* **Bruyere (FR)**[55] 6123 3-9-4 **64**......(h) SebastianWoods 12 70
(Dean Ivory) *hld up in midfield: gd hdwy on inner 3f out: chsd ldrs 2f out: rdn over 1f out: slt ld ins fnl f: hdd and no ex towards fin* **12/1**

006- **3** *nk* **Westbrook Bertie**[237] 8901 4-10-2 **72**...... ScottMcCullagh 10 77
(Mick Channon) *in tch: hdwy to chse ldrs 4f out: rdn over 2f out: drvn and ev ch ins fnl f: n.m.r and swtchd rt last 100yds: kpt on* **14/1**

2040 **4** *1 ½* **Cosmic Ray**[15] 7545 7-8-13 **55**......(h) WilliamCarver 9 57
(Les Eyre) *chsd ldr: led wl over 5f out: rdn along 3f out: drvn over 1f out: hdd ins fnl f: kpt on same pce* **16/1**

-005 **5** *1 ½* **Sociologist (FR)**[13] 7629 4-9-1 **60**......(p) KieranSchofield[(3)] 1 59
(Scott Dixon) *trckd ldng pair: hdwy to chse ldr over 4f out: rdn along 3f out: drvn wl over 1f out: kpt on same pce fnl f* **25/1**

4400 **6** *1* **Country'N'Western (FR)**[29] 7053 7-9-4 **63**...... AledBeech[(3)] 6 60
(Robert Eddery) *hld up and bhd: hdwy on inner over 3f out: rdn along 2f out: sn drvn: kpt on fnl f* **33/1**

3540 **7** *nk* **Dutch Uncle**[39] 6736 7-9-13 **72**......(p) AngusVilliers[(3)] 13 68
(Tom Clover) *hld up in rr: stdy hdwy on outer over 4f out: chsd ldrs on outer 3f out: rdn over 2f out: sn no imp* **16/1**

5520 **8** *3 ¾* **Militry Decoration (IRE)**[28] 7083 4-8-13 **60**...... ZakWheatley[(5)] 8 49
(Dr Jon Scargill) *chsd ldrs: rdn along over 3f out: drvn 2f out: grad wknd* **13/2**[2]

6240 **9** *3 ¾* **Beatbybeatbybeat**[16] 7526 6-9-9 **65**......(v) WilliamCox 14 46
(Antony Brittain) *hld up in rr: hdwy on outer over 3f out: rdn along wl over 2f out: n.d* **50/1**

5053 **10** *nk* **Cheeky Rascal (IRE)**[9] 7756 4-9-6 **67**......(v) LukeCatton[(5)] 15 48
(Tom Ward) *a in rr* **20/1**

5304 **11** *3 ½* **Tangramm**[15] 7560 7-9-6 **67**......(p) LukeBacon[(5)] 11 41
(Dean Ivory) *chsd ldrs: rn wd bnd 7f out: rdn along over 3f out: sn drvn and wknd* **10/1**

6406 **12** *3 ½* **Spencers Son (IRE)**[33] 6925 3-9-4 **67**......(p) SeanKirrane[(3)] 16 35
(Richard Spencer) *hld up: a in rr* **40/1**

0000 **13** *9* **Bated Beauty (IRE)**[47] 6412 4-9-5 **61**...... DarraghKeenan 3 10
(John Butler) *dwlt: sn in midfield: rdn along over 4f out: sn wknd* **50/1**

3514 **14** *1 ½* **Dame Freya Stark**[13] 7629 3-9-11 **71**...... AndrewBreslin 4 18
(Mark Johnston) *chsd ldrs: rdn along over 4f out: wknd over 3f out* **16/1**

2006 **15** *13* **Cormier (IRE)**[12] 7643 3-9-4 **64**......(v[1]) HarrisonShaw 5
(Stef Keniry) *led: hdd 7f out: prom tl rdn along and wknd over 3f out (trainer said gelding did not face the first-time visor)* **9/1**[3]

2m 16.41s (3.01) **Going Correction** +0.475s/f (Yiel)
WFA 3 from 4yo+ 4lb **15** Ran SP% **124.4**
Speed ratings (Par 103): **107,106,105,104,103 102,102,99,96,96 93,90,83,82,71**
CSF £18.17 CT £180.25 TOTE £1.90: £1.70, £2.50, £3.80; EX 9.70 Trifecta £232.30.
Owner I R Hatton **Bred** Howdale Bloodstock Ltd **Trained** Oakham, Rutland

FOCUS
Add 6yds. A weak apprentice handicap which produced a good finish. The winner has been rated similar to his C&D latest, with the third close to the balance of his form and the fourth close to his recent level.

T/Plt: £161.10 to a £1 stake. Pool: £55,619.92 - 251.89 winning units T/Qpdt: £58.50 to a £1 stake. Pool: £5,342.13 - 67.56 winning units **Joe Rowntree**

8034 - 8050a (Foreign Racing) - See Raceform Interactive

7776 AYR (L-H)
Thursday, October 10
8051 Meeting Abandoned - Waterlogged track

8011 KEMPTON (A.W) (R-H)
Thursday, October 10

OFFICIAL GOING: Polytrack: standard to slow
Wind: light, across Weather: light cloud

8058 BET AT RACINGTV.COM NOVICE AUCTION STKS 7f (P)
5:00 (5:02) (Class 5) 2-Y-0 **£3,881** (£1,155; £577; £288) **Stalls** Low

Form RPR
4 **1** *nse* **Broughtons Gold**[147] 2761 2-8-13 0...... HayleyTurner 9 72
(Tom Clover) *wnt rt leaving stalls: t.k.h: chsd ldrs: effrt to press ldrs over 1f out: drvn and str chal ins fnl f: carried lft but kpt on wl: jst hld: fin 2nd: awrdd r* **9/4**[2]

03 **2** **Sterling Stamp (IRE)**[15] 7569 2-8-13 0...... RossaRyan 2 72
(Paul Cole) *t.k.h: chsd ldr tl over 4f out: effrt to chal between rivals over 1f out: rdn to ld 1f out: hrd pressed and edgd lft ins fnl f: jst hld on: fin 1st: disqualified and plcd 2nd* **11/10**[1]

6606 **3** *2 ¾* **Mungo's Quest (IRE)**[14] 7605 2-8-13 48...... HectorCrouch 3 65?
(Simon Dow) *in tch in midfield: effrt ent fnl 2f: sltly outpcd and swtchd lft jst over 1f out: kpt on ins fnl f: wnt 3rd towards fin* **40/1**

4 **4** *¾* **Stony Look (IRE)**[17] 7515 2-8-7 0...... DavidProbert 12 57
(Andrew Balding) *chsd ldrs: wnt 2nd over 4f out: effrt and ev ch 2f out: no ex 1f out: wknd and lost 3rd towards fin* **15/2**[3]

0 **5** *½* **Island Nation (IRE)**[19] 7453 2-9-2 0...... RichardKingscote 10 64
(Heather Main) *edgd rt leaving stalls: midfield: effrt over 2f out: styd on ins fnl f: no threat to ldrs* **20/1**

6 *¾* **Rock Of Redmond (IRE)** 2-8-2 0...... SophieRalston[(5)] 11 54
(Dean Ivory) *sn led: rdn and hrd pressed wl over 1f out: hdd 1f out: wknd ins fnl f* **50/1**

7 *nk* **Licit (IRE)** 2-8-4 0...... MarcoGhiani[(5)] 8 55
(Mohamed Moubarak) *stdd s: t.k.h: hld up in midfield on outer: effrt and outpcd ent fnl 2f: rallied and kpt on ins fnl f: no threat to ldrs* **33/1**

8 *1 ½* **Morlaix** 2-8-11 0...... PoppyBridgwater[(5)] 7 58
(David Simcock) *hld up in rr: effrt over 2f out: nvr involved* **14/1**

0 **9** *5* **The Fitzpiers Lion (IRE)**[28] 7113 2-9-0 0...... RaulDaSilva 5 43
(Ronald Harris) *hld up towards rr: rdn over 2f out: sn outpcd and wl btn over 1f out* **40/1**

10 *4 ½* **Tazaman** 2-8-13 0...... KieranShoemark 4 30
(Kevin Frost) *s.i.s: a bhd (jockey said gelding was slowly away)* **25/1**

0 **11** *5* **Scorpio's Dream**[15] 7570 2-9-0 0...... CallumShepherd 1 18
(Charlie Wallis) *in tch in midfield: rdn over 2f out: sn outpcd and btn: wknd over 1f out* **100/1**

1m 27.66s (1.66) **Going Correction** 0.0s/f (Stan) **11** Ran SP% **116.2**
Speed ratings (Par 95): **89,90,86,85,85 84,84,82,76,71 65**
CSF £4.62 TOTE £3.10: £1.10, £1.40, £8.20; EX 6.20 Trifecta £83.90.
Owner Broughton Thermal Insulation **Bred** Broughton Bloodstock **Trained** Newmarket, Suffolk
■ Dancing Girl was withdrawn. Price at time of withdrawal 50-1. Rule 4 does not apply.

FOCUS
A run-of-the-mill 2yo novice event in which the two market leaders came clear in a tight finish. The first past the post has been rated to his pre-race figure.

8059 32RED CASINO NOVICE STKS (DIV I) 6f (P)
5:30 (5:31) (Class 5) 2-Y-0 **£3,881** (£1,155; £577; £288) **Stalls** Low

Form RPR
321 **1** **Smokey Bear (IRE)**[20] 7407 2-9-4 86...... ThomasGreatrex[(5)] 5 85
(Roger Charlton) *t.k.h: trckd ldrs: swtchd rt and effrt to chal over 1f out: rdn to ld 1f out: styd on wl ins fnl f* **1/1**[1]

02 **2** *¾* **Great Image (IRE)**[19] 7437 2-9-2 0...... OisinMurphy 9 76
(Saeed bin Suroor) *pressed ldr tl led over 2f out: hrd pressed and rdn over 1f out: hdd 1f out: kpt on but a hld ins fnl f* **4/1**[3]

0 **3** *3 ¼* **Juan Les Pins**[19] 7458 2-9-2 0...... TomMarquand 8 66
(Ed Walker) *stdd s: hld up in tch in midfield: effrt ent fnl 2f: 5th and no imp over 1f out: kpt on to go 3rd ins fnl f: no threat to ldrs* **40/1**

653 **4** *½* **Roman Melody**[20] 7406 2-9-2 76...... GeraldMosse 3 65
(David Elsworth) *pushed along leaving stalls: sn chsng ldrs: rdn ent fnl 2f: chsd clr ldng pair and no imp over 1f out: kpt on same pce and lost 3rd ins fnl f* **7/2**[2]

6 **5** *nk* **Badri**[47] 6449 2-9-2 0...... JimCrowley 4 64+
(Charles Hills) *hld up in last pair: effrt over 2f out: no imp and stl plenty to do 2f out: hdwy and reminder 1f out: styd on wl ins fnl f: no threat to ldrs* **10/1**

55 **6** *3* **Barking Mad**[35] 6899 2-9-2 0...... PJMcDonald 2 55
(David Evans) *wl in tch in midfield: rdn and outpcd jst over 2f out: wl hld over 1f out* **20/1**

7 *hd* **Tidal Racer** 2-9-2 0...... AdamKirby 1 54
(Clive Cox) *pushed along leaving stalls: in tch in midfield: effrt over 2f out: sn outpcd and wl hld over 1f out* **20/1**

0 **8** *¾* **Sacred Legacy (IRE)**[34] 6911 2-9-2 0...... DavidProbert 6 52
(Ronald Harris) *led: rdn and hdd over 1f out: hung rt and wknd over 1f out (jockey said colt hung right-handed)* **50/1**

60 **9** *15* **Theheartneverlies**[10] 7769 2-8-9 0...... GavinAshton[(7)] 11 7
(Sir Mark Prescott Bt) *stdd s: a towards rr: lost tch over 2f out* **100/1**

0 **10** *6* **Total Perfection (IRE)**[16] 7555 2-9-2 0...... SeanLevey 10
(Richard Hannon) *hld up in last trio: effrt over 2f out: sn outpcd and wl btn: tch 2f out* **66/1**

1m 13.58s (0.48) **Going Correction** 0.0s/f (Stan) **10** Ran SP% **117.7**
Speed ratings (Par 95): **96,95,90,90,89 85,85,84,64,56**
CSF £4.92 TOTE £2.40: £1.50, £1.30, £10.30; EX 6.10 Trifecta £68.70.
Owner De Zoete, Inglett & Jones **Bred** Cordulf Stud **Trained** Beckhampton, Wilts

FOCUS
The first pair had to this to themselves a fair way out and it's juvenile useful form. It's been rated at face value.

8060 32RED CASINO NOVICE STKS (DIV II) 6f (P)
6:00 (6:00) (Class 5) 2-Y-O
£3,881 (£1,155; £577; £288) **Stalls** Low

Form RPR
2 **1** **Premier Power**[54] 6219 2-9-2 0 SilvestreDeSousa 7 100+
(Roger Varian) *t.k.h: trckd ldrs: swtchd lft and cruised into ld over 1f out: drew wl clr fnl f: v easily* **1/3**[1]

0 **2** 5 **Tom Collins**[53] 6891 2-9-2 0 GeraldMosse 6 82
(David Elsworth) *edgd lft leaving stalls: sn pressing ldr: rdn to chal 2f out: led over 1f out: sn hdd: kpt on but no ch w wnr fnl f* **14/1**

3 **3** 4 ½ **Well Prepared**[17] 7521 2-9-2 0 OisinMurphy 3 68
(Richard Hannon) *led: rdn and hrd pressed 2f out: hdd over 1f out: sn outpcd and wl btn 3rd ins fnl f* **3/1**[2]

30 **4** 1 **Tommy Rock (IRE)**[20] 7406 2-9-2 0 AdamKirby 1 65
(Clive Cox) *hld up in last trio: effrt over 2f out: kpt on ins fnl f: no ch w wnr* **9/1**[3]

0 **5** 2 ½ **Alezan**[20] 7412 2-8-11 0 (h[1]) CharlesBishop 5 53
(Eve Johnson Houghton) *taken down early: stdd s: t.k.h: hld up in rr: effrt over 2f out: n.d* **25/1**

6 ½ **Step To The Beat** 2-9-2 0 HectorCrouch 9 56
(Clive Cox) *restless in stalls: off the pce in midfield: rdn over 2f out: no imp and wl btn over 1f out* **25/1**

00 **7** 1 ¼ **Bonus**[28] 7124 2-9-2 0 CharlieBennett 2 52
(Jim Boyle) *chsd ldrs and clr in ldng quintet: rdn ent fnl 2f: 4th and outpcd over 1f out: sn wknd* **50/1**

8 10 **Callherwhatyoulike** 2-8-11 0 MartinDwyer 10 17
(Tim Pinfield) *wnt lft leaving stalls: rn green and a towards rr* **66/1**

1m 12.89s (-0.21) **Going Correction** 0.0s/f (Stan) 8 Ran SP% **127.8**
Speed ratings (Par 95): **101,94,88,87,83 83,81,68**
CSF £9.07 TOTE £1.10: £1.02, £3.20, £1.10; EX 8.00 Trifecta £13.70.
Owner King Power Racing Co Ltd **Bred** Newsells Park Stud **Trained** Newmarket, Suffolk

FOCUS
This second division of the 6f novice proved one-way traffic and it was 0.69sec quicker than the first. It's been rated at something like face value.

8061 WISE BETTING AT RACINGTV.COM NURSERY H'CAP 1m (P)
6:30 (6:32) (Class 6) (0-65,65) 2-Y-O
£3,105 (£924; £461; £400; £400; £400) **Stalls** Low

Form RPR
0033 **1** **Souter Johnnie (IRE)**[29] 7079 2-9-5 63 AdamKirby 10 67+
(Richard Hughes) *dwlt and rousted along early: hld up towards rr: hdwy on outer 1/2-way: swtchd lft over 2f out: hdwy u.p over 1f out: led ins fnl f: styd on strly* **3/1**[1]

556 **2** 1 ¼ **Utopian Lad (IRE)**[60] 5980 2-9-5 63 (p[1]) RichardKingscote 5 64+
(Tom Dascombe) *hld up in last quartet: nt clr run and swtchd lft over 2f out: rdn and hdwy over 1f out: styd on wl ins fnl f: wnt 2nd last strides: nt rch wnr* **7/2**[2]

3532 **3** nk **Rochford (IRE)**[23] 7306 2-9-0 61 CierenFallon(3) 1 61
(Henry Spiller) *wl in tch in midfield: effrt and hdwy on inner ent fnl 2f: rdn to ld over 1f out: hdd and one pce ins fnl f: lost 2nd last strides* **6/1**[3]

005U **4** 1 **Lafontaine (FR)**[5] 7910 2-8-3 47 DavidEgan 6 45
(Sylvester Kirk) *led: rdn and hdd over 1f out: kpt on same pce ins fnl f* **16/1**

6606 **5** nk **Divine Connection**[24] 7277 2-9-4 62 RobHornby 8 59
(Jonathan Portman) *in tch in midfield: nt clrest of runs ent fnl 2f: hdwy u.p 1f out: kpt on ins fnl f* **20/1**

640 **6** 2 **Jack Ruby (IRE)**[34] 6926 2-9-0 63 ThoreHammerHansen(5) 3 56
(Richard Hannon) *dwlt and pushed along leaving stalls: rcvrd and hdwy to chse ldrs after 2f: unable qck u.p over 1f out: wknd ins fnl f* **16/1**

6332 **7** nk **Bacchalot (IRE)**[10] 7767 2-9-6 64 OisinMurphy 9 56
(Richard Hannon) *chsd ldr: unable qck u.p over 1f out: wknd ins fnl f* **8/1**

0230 **8** hd **Hiconic**[29] 7079 2-9-3 61 DavidProbert 14 53
(Alex Hales) *hld up in last pair: swtchd lft and effrt over 2f out: kpt on but nvr threatened ldrs* **66/1**

0004 **9** ½ **Camacho Man (IRE)**[10] 7767 2-8-11 55 RossaRyan 12 46
(Jennie Candlish) *hmpd sn after s: hld up in rr: nt clr run and swtchd lft 2f out: hdwy 1f out: kpt on ins fnl f: nvr trbld ldrs (jockey said colt was hampered leaving the stalls)* **14/1**

0000 **10** nk **Grimsthorpe Castle**[17] 7516 2-8-9 53 HarryBentley 4 45
(Ed Walker) *chsd ldrs tl short of room and shuffled bk to midfield after 1f: effrt ent fnl 2f: no imp over 1f out: wknd ins fnl f* **25/1**

6063 **11** 1 **Disarming (IRE)**[17] 7516 2-9-0 58 HollieDoyle 2 46
(Dr Jon Scargill) *in tch in midfield: effrt on inner 2f out: no imp over 1f out: wknd ins fnl f (jockey said filly ran in snatches)* **9/1**

055 **12** 2 ½ **Mr Kodi (IRE)**[43] 6604 2-8-12 56 (v) PJMcDonald 7 38
(David Evans) *chsd ldrs: rdn 3f out: hung rt and no imp over 2f out: wknd over 1f out (jockey said gelding hung right-handed)* **33/1**

0000 **13** 11 **Thank The Irish (IRE)**[16] 7548 2-9-7 65 NicolaCurrie 11 22
(Jamie Osborne) *chsd ldrs on outer: rdn over 2f out: lost pl and wknd over 1f out: wl bhd ins fnl f (jockey said colt stopped quickly)* **25/1**

1m 41.58s (1.78) **Going Correction** 0.0s/f (Stan) 13 Ran SP% **117.9**
Speed ratings (Par 93): **91,89,89,88,88 86,85,85,85,84 83,81,70**
CSF £12.02 CT £61.20 TOTE £4.60: £2.00, £2.00, £1.50; EX 17.70 Trifecta £57.70.
Owner The Caledonian Racing Society **Bred** Kevin Murphy **Trained** Upper Lambourn, Berks

FOCUS
An ordinary nursery. Small improvement from the first two.

8062 32RED OPTIONAL CLAIMING H'CAP 1m (P)
7:00 (7:02) (Class 2) 4-Y-O+
£18,675 (£5,592; £2,796; £1,398; £699; £351) **Stalls** Low

Form RPR
6660 **1** **Via Serendipity**[49] 6376 5-10-0 104 (t) AdamKirby 7 112
(Stuart Williams) *wl in tch in midfield: effrt 2f out: clsd to chse ldr and drvn jst over 1f out: styd on to ld ins fnl f: rdn out (trainer said, regarding the improved form shown, the gelding had appreciated a return to the all-weather where he has won previously)* **16/1**

2120 **2** 1 ½ **Pinnata (IRE)**[22] 7350 5-9-4 94 (t) SeanLevey 6 99
(Stuart Williams) *sn led: rdn and kicked on 2f out: hdd and one pce ins fnl f* **7/1**

0642 **3** ½ **Pactolus (IRE)**[21] 7396 8-9-12 102 (t) OisinMurphy 10 106
(Stuart Williams) *hld up wl in tch in midfield: nt clrest of runs 2f out: hdwy u.p ins fnl f: kpt on* **33/1**

-011 **4** hd **Kasbaan**[33] 6964 4-9-7 97 AlistairRawlinson 8 100+
(Michael Appleby) *chsd ldr early: settled bk and wl in tch in midfield: effrt ent fnl 2f: unable qck and no imp over 1f out: kpt on ins fnl f: nt enough pce to threaten ldrs* **6/4**[1]

0310 **5** hd **Love Dreams (IRE)**[15] 7563 5-8-7 83 (p) NicolaCurrie 14 86
(Jamie Osborne) *in tch in midfield: effrt ent fnl 2f: hdwy 1f out: kpt on ins fnl f: nvr trbld ldrs* **33/1**

3000 **6** nk **Silent Attack**[224] 961 6-9-10 100 GeorgeDowning 3 102+
(Tony Carroll) *hld up in last trio: hdwy over 1f out: kpt on ins fnl f: nvr trbld ldrs* **66/1**

4504 **7** ½ **Chiefofchiefs**[34] 6915 6-9-8 98 (p) RichardKingscote 1 99
(Charlie Fellowes) *chsd ldrs: effrt ent fnl 2f: drvn over 1f out: no ex ins fnl f: wknd towards fin* **11/2**[3]

2000 **8** ½ **Florencio**[16] 7551 6-8-0 76 oh1 (p) HollieDoyle 9 76
(Jamie Osborne) *sn chsd ldr: rdn ent fnl 2f: unable qck and lost 2nd jst over 1f out: wknd towards fin* **100/1**

-526 **9** shd **George William**[54] 6214 6-9-2 92 TomMarquand 5 92
(Ed Walker) *hld up in tch in midfield: swtchd lft and effrt jst over 2f out: nvr trbld ldrs* **12/1**

4204 **10** 1 ¼ **Shady McCoy (USA)**[15] 7563 9-8-12 88 ow1 JimCrowley 2 85
(Ian Williams) *hld up in last quartet: effrt and swtchd rt ent fnl 2f: sme hdwy over 1f out but nvr getting to ldrs: wknd ins fnl f* **33/1**

4435 **11** hd **Seniority**[34] 6915 5-9-10 100 JamesDoyle 13 96
(William Haggas) *stdd after s: hld up in rr: effrt and swtchd rt ent fnl 2f: sme hdwy over 1f out: nvr getting on terms and wknd ins fnl f* **5/1**[2]

336 **12** 3 **Enigmatic (IRE)**[34] 6914 5-8-8 87 CierenFallon(3) 4 76
(Alan Bailey) *midfield: rdn over 2f out: sn struggling and outpcd over 1f out: wknd ins fnl f* **33/1**

0510 **13** 1 **Bacacarat (IRE)**[124] 3581 4-8-8 84 SilvestreDeSousa 11 71
(Andrew Balding) *stdd after s: t.k.h: hld up in last pair: nvr involved* **16/1**

0240 **14** 2 ½ **Masham Star (IRE)**[83] 5155 5-9-0 90 (w) PJMcDonald 12 71
(Mark Johnston) *chsd ldrs tl rdn and lost pl over 2f out: wknd over 1f out* **14/1**

1m 37.65s (-2.15) **Going Correction** 0.0s/f (Stan) 14 Ran SP% **124.9**
Speed ratings (Par 109): **110,108,108,107,107 107,106,106,106,104 104,101,100,98**
CSF £123.82 CT £3686.13 TOTE £19.00: £4.40, £2.50, £6.70; EX 109.30 Trifecta £1808.90.
Owner Happy Valley Racing & Breeding Limited **Bred** R Shaykhutdinov **Trained** Newmarket, Suffolk

FOCUS
This feature handicap was run at a fair pace and it saw a 1-2-3 for trainer Stuart Williams. A clear pb from the winner, with the second and third setting the level.

8063 32RED ON THE APP STORE H'CAP 6f (P)
7:30 (7:30) (Class 5) (0-75,75) 3-Y-O+
£3,752 (£1,116; £557; £400; £400; £400) **Stalls** Low

Form RPR
0252 **1** **Busby (IRE)**[9] 7789 4-9-4 75 (p) CierenFallon(3) 3 81
(Conrad Allen) *chsd ldrs: rdn over 2f out: drvn and kpt on ins fnl f to ld 50yds out: all out* **5/4**[1]

6153 **2** nk **Secret Potion**[8] 7831 5-9-1 69 DavidProbert 1 74
(Ronald Harris) *hld up in tch in midfield: effrt ent fnl 2f: clsd u.p to chse ldrs 1f out: kpt on and ev ch wl ins fnl f: jst hld cl home* **20/1**

0114 **3** hd **Top Boy**[25] 7230 9-9-1 69 TomMarquand 11 73+
(Tony Carroll) *hld up in last trio: effrt ent fnl 2f: hdwy u.p 1f out: styd on strly u.p ins fnl f: nt quite rch ldrs* **14/1**

0550 **4** ¾ **Human Nature (IRE)**[85] 5050 6-9-4 72 (t) OisinMurphy 10 74
(Stuart Williams) *led: rdn and hdd over 1f out: kpt on and stl ev ch tl no ex and jst outpcd wl ins fnl f* **12/1**

1101 **5** shd **Fantastic Flyer**[16] 7552 4-9-7 75 (p) JoeyHaynes 8 77
(Dean Ivory) *press ldr: rdn to ld narrowly over 1f out: drvn and hdd 50yds: no ex and outpcd towards fin* **12/1**

4130 **6** 1 **Cent Flying**[15] 7564 4-9-5 73 (t) MartinDwyer 5 71
(William Muir) *in tch in midfield: effrt 2f out: unable qck u.p 1f out: kpt on same pce ins fnl f* **16/1**

0106 **7** hd **Broughtons Flare (IRE)**[42] 6631 3-8-13 68 HayleyTurner 12 66
(Philip McBride) *in tch in midfield: effrt over 2f out: kpt on ins fnl f: nt enough pce to chal* **16/1**

0016 **8** nk **Dream Catching (IRE)**[15] 7568 4-8-13 72 WilliamCarver(5) 2 77+
(Andrew Balding) *half-rrd as stalls opened and slowly away: hld up in rr: effrt on inner 2f out: clsd u.p over 1f out: chsd ldrs whn nt clr run ins fnl f: nowhere to go and no imp fnl 100yds (jockey said gelding was slowly away losing many lengths and was denied a clear run in the closing stages)* **11/2**[2]

6203 **9** 1 **Leo Minor (USA)**[12] 7690 5-8-13 67 (t) RichardKingscote 7 61
(Robert Cowell) *hld up in tch in last trio: effrt 2f out: nt clr run 1f out: nvr trbld ldrs* **25/1**

5040 **10** 2 ½ **Lightning Charlie**[34] 6916 7-9-2 70 JimCrowley 6 56
(Amanda Perrett) *chsd ldrs: effrt 2f out: unable qck over 1f out: wknd ins fnl f* **6/1**[3]

1m 12.48s (-0.62) **Going Correction** 0.0s/f (Stan)
WFA 3 from 4yo+ 1lb 10 Ran SP% **116.5**
Speed ratings (Par 103): **104,103,103,102,102 100,100,100,98,95**
CSF £31.32 CT £258.69 TOTE £2.10: £1.20, £5.90, £2.50; EX 30.80 Trifecta £367.80.
Owner John C Davies **Bred** J C Davies **Trained** Newmarket, Suffolk

FOCUS
The strong early pace collapsed late on in this modest sprint handicap. The second has been rated back to his old best for now.

8064 32RED CASINO FILLIES' H'CAP 1m 3f 219y(P)
8:00 (8:01) (Class 4) (0-85,85) 3-Y-O+
£6,469 (£1,925; £962; £481; £400; £400) **Stalls** Low

Form RPR
0416 **1** **Hermosura**[24] 7279 3-8-9 72 (v[1]) HarryBentley 4 81
(Ralph Beckett) *mde all: rdn over 2f out: styd on wl u.p and clr ins fnl f: eased towards fin* **12/1**

5121 **2** 2 ¾ **Chicago Doll**[40] 6736 3-9-5 82 TomMarquand 2 87
(Alan King) *chsd ldrs: effrt on inner ent fnl 2f: chsd wnr 1f out: no imp and one pce after* **3/1**[1]

21 **3** ½ **Mina Vagante**[22] 7344 3-8-10 76 CierenFallon(3) 6 80
(Hugo Palmer) *chsd wnr: rdn ent fnl 2f: unable to match pce of wnr and lost 2nd 1f out: kpt on same pce after* **7/1**

2340 **4** 2 ¼ **Manorah (IRE)**[28] 7137 3-9-2 79 (p[1]) JackMitchell 5 79
(Roger Varian) *chsd ldrs: effrt over 2f out: drvn and unable qck over 1f out: wknd ins fnl f* **8/1**

The Form Book Flat 2019, Raceform Ltd, Newbury, RG14 5SJ

5262 **5** *hd* **Point In Time (IRE)**[19] 7466 4-9-5 **76**.................................... DavidProbert 9 75
(Mark Usher) *hld up in rr: effrt over 2f out: kpt on ins fnl f: nvr trbld ldrs* **25/1**

2044 **6** *hd* **Dono Di Dio**[15] 7566 4-9-4 **80**.................................(b) ScottMcCullagh(5) 8 79
(Michael Madgwick) *stdd s: hld up in rr: hdwy on outer 1/2-way: chsd ldrs 5f out: rdn and outpcd over 2f out: no ch but kpt on again ins fnl f* **16/1**

4-01 **7** *½* **Lucky Turn (IRE)**[7] 7835 3-8-10 **73** 6ex.......................... HayleyTurner 1 72
(Michael Bell) *hld up in tch towards rr: effrt and swtchd lft over 2f out: 6th and no imp u.p over 1f out: wl hld fnl f* **9/2[2]**

5120 **8** *½* **Norma**[22] 7347 3-9-8 **85**.. GeorgeWood 3 83+
(James Fanshawe) *t.k.h early: in tch in midfield: clsd to chse ldrs and nt clrest of runs 2f: gap sn opened and rdn: no ex 1f out: wknd ins fnl f* **13/2[3]**

0513 **9** *nse* **Maroon Bells (IRE)**[26] 7200 4-8-10 **67**............................ DavidEgan 10 64
(David Menuisier) *in tch in midfield: effrt 3f out: no imp and wl hld over 1f out* **40/1**

-633 **10** *½* **Honfleur (IRE)**[21] 7395 3-8-2 **70**...............................(b[1]) MarcoGhiani(5) 7 67
(Sir Michael Stoute) *dwlt: hld up in tch towards rr: effrt over 2f out: no real imp: nvr a threat* **13/2[3]**

2m 34.55s (0.05) **Going Correction** 0.0s/f (Stan)
WFA 3 from 4yo 6lb **10** Ran SP% **113.3**
Speed ratings (Par 102): **99,97,96,95,95 95,94,94,94,94**
CSF £46.64 CT £275.63 TOTE £13.60: £3.70, £1.30, £3.00; EX 51.70 Trifecta £343.40.
Owner Newsells Park Stud **Bred** Newsells Park Stud **Trained** Kimpton, Hants

FOCUS
Racing handily was a must in this fair 3yo fillies' handicap. The second and third have been rated close to form.

8065 100% PROFIT BOOST AT 32REDSPORT.COM H'CAP 1m 3f 219y(P)
8:30 (8:31) (Class 6) (0-65,67) 3-Y-0+
£3,105 (£924; £461; £400; £400; £400) **Stalls** Low

Form RPR

0640 **1** **Philonikia**[54] 6232 3-9-5 **65**.. HarryBentley 5 74+
(Ralph Beckett) *hld up in tch in midfield: clsd and swtchd rt jst over 2f out: rdn to ld over 1f out: styd on strly ins fnl f* **7/1[3]**

6042 **2** *2 ¼* **Miss M (IRE)**[9] 7790 5-9-7 **61**.. MartinDwyer 11 65
(William Muir) *rousted along leaving stalls: sn clsd to chse ldrs: effrt ent fnl 2f: chal over 1f out: no ex and outpcd ins fnl f* **15/2**

0532 **3** *1 ½* **Avenue Foch**[26] 7192 3-9-5 **65**.. TomMarquand 4 68
(James Fanshawe) *in tch in midfield: clsd and nt clrest of runs ent fnl 2f: sn in the clr and hdwy u.p: 3rd and one pce ins fnl f* **9/4[1]**

3353 **4** *1 ¼* **Murhib (IRE)**[51] 6320 7-9-3 **57**...............................(h) RichardKingscote 12 57
(Lydia Richards) *led: rdn ent fnl 2f: hdd over 1f out: no ex and outpcd ins fnl f* **10/1**

3424 **5** *½* **Brittanic (IRE)**[16] 7553 5-9-5 **64**................................(p) DylanHogan(5) 6 63
(David Simcock) *hld up towards rr: effrt over 2f out: kpt on ins fnl f: nvr trbld ldrs* **25/1**

2153 **6** *1 ½* **No Thanks**[23] 7318 3-9-2 **62**... CallumShepherd 2 60
(William Jarvis) *led: sn hdd and chsd ldrs: effrt to chal over 1f out: no ex 1f out and wknd ins fnl f* **8/1**

2123 **7** *1 ¼* **Sea Of Mystery (IRE)**[14] 7629 6-9-3 **64**.......................... MarkCrehan(7) 10 59+
(Michael Appleby) *midfield: hdwy 1/2-way: outpcd u.p over 2f out: rallied and kpt on ins fnl f: no threat to ldrs* **25/1**

4460 **8** *nk* **Geomatrician (FR)**[41] 6681 3-9-2 **62**..............................(v) OisinMurphy 3 57
(Andrew Balding) *chsd ldr after 2f tl unable qck and lost pl over 1f out: wknd ins fnl f* **4/1[2]**

0-00 **9** *2 ¼* **Sea Sovereign (IRE)**[54] 6218 6-9-10 **64**........................... CharlesBishop 1 55
(Ian Williams) *hld up towards rr: effrt over 2f out: nvr trbld ldrs* **14/1**

3206 **10** *3* **War Of Succession**[44] 6560 5-9-0 **54**................................ HayleyTurner 8 40
(Tony Newcombe) *stdd s: hld up in rr: rdn over 4f out: nvr involved* **40/1**

2163 **11** *¾* **Heron (USA)**[62] 5891 5-9-12 **66**.. DanielMuscutt 13 51
(Brett Johnson) *stdd after s: hld up in rr: effrt over 2f out: no prog: nvr involved* **20/1**

4544 **12** *8* **Bartholomew J (IRE)**[38] 6812 5-9-13 **67**.........................(p) GeorgeWood 14 39
(Lydia Pearce) *wl in tch in midfield: rdn over 3f out: sn struggling and lost pl over 2f out: bhd ins fnl f* **40/1**

4140 **13** *12* **Music Major**[191] 1498 6-9-4 **58**.. DavidProbert 9 11
(Michael Attwater) *t.k.h: prom early: sn settled bk into midfield: effrt ent fnl 2f: sn btn and wknd over 1f out (jockey said gelding stopped quickly)* **50/1**

2m 33.75s (-0.75) **Going Correction** 0.0s/f (Stan)
WFA 3 from 4yo+ 6lb **13** Ran SP% **121.2**
Speed ratings (Par 101): **102,100,99,98,98 97,96,96,94,92 92,86,78**
CSF £54.95 CT £158.44 TOTE £7.00: £2.00, £2.10, £1.60; EX 66.60 Trifecta £282.70.
Owner Mr and Mrs David Aykroyd **Bred** Mr & Mrs David Aykroyd **Trained** Kimpton, Hants

FOCUS
They were soon strung out in this ordinary handicap. The second, third and fourth set a straightforward level.
T/Plt: £37.50 to a £1 stake. Pool: £53,504.55. 1,040.51 winning units. T/Qpdt: £22.80 to a £1 stake. Pool: £7,323.31. 237.55 winning units. **Steve Payne**

7869 SOUTHWELL (L-H)
Thursday, October 10

OFFICIAL GOING: Fibresand: standard
Wind: Moderate, across Weather: Cloudy

8066 VISIT ATTHERACES.COM H'CAP 4f 214y(F)
5:10 (5:11) (Class 5) (0-75,74) 3-Y-0+
£3,428 (£1,020; £509; £400; £400; £400) **Stalls** Centre

Form RPR

2000 **1** **Samovar**[21] 7387 4-9-3 **70**..(b) KieranO'Neill 10 78
(Scott Dixon) *dwlt and towards stands' side: sn chsng ldrs: hdwy and cl up 2f out: rdn to ld over 1f out: drvn and edgd lft ins fnl f: kpt on wl towards fin* **14/1**

5642 **2** *nk* **Miningggold**[21] 7387 6-9-4 **71**....................................(p) AndrewMullen 11 78
(Michael Dods) *racd towards stands' side: trckd ldrs whn n.m.r and checked 3f out: swtchd lft and hdwy 2f out: rdn over 1f out: chsd wnr ins fnl f: drvn and kpt on wl towards fin* **5/1[2]**

2003 **3** *1 ¼* **Kyllachy Warrior (IRE)**[34] 6944 3-9-0 **67**........................ PhilDennis 9 71
(Lawrence Mullaney) *swtchd lft s: sn cl up centre: led 1/2-way: jnd 2f out and sn rdn: drvn and hdd over 1f out: kpt on same pce fnl f* **12/1**

5606 **4** *1* **Sandridge Lad (IRE)**[21] 7387 3-9-4 **71**.............................. StevieDonohoe 4 71+
(John Ryan) *racd towards far side: chsd ldrs: rdn along and outpcd 1/2-way: hdwy over 1f out: kpt on u.p fnl f* **9/1**

4106 **5** *1 ½* **Red Pike (IRE)**[40] 6699 8-9-7 **74**.. GrahamLee 3 68+
(Bryan Smart) *dwlt and rr far side: swtchd lft to far rail after 1f: rdn along 2f out: styd on wl fnl f* **8/1[3]**

0226 **6** *nse* **Tan**[22] 7334 5-8-5 **63**.. TheodoreLadd(5) 12 56
(Michael Appleby) *racd nr stands' rail: trckd ldrs: effrt 2f out: sn rdn and hung lft over 1f out: sn no imp (jockey said gelding hung left-handed throughout)* **7/2[1]**

1331 **7** *shd* **Red Stripes (USA)**[12] 7690 7-8-6 **64**...........................(b) SeamusCronin(5) 5 57
(Lisa Williamson) *led centre: hdd 1/2-way: cl up and rdn 2f out: drvn over 1f out: grad wknd fnl f* **5/1[2]**

3500 **8** *hd* **First Excel**[84] 5107 7-8-12 **65**....................................(b[1]) LewisEdmunds 2 57
(Roy Bowring) *racd towards far side: prom: cl up 1/2-way: rdn along wl over 1f out: grad wknd appr fnl f* **10/1**

10R0 **9** *1 ¾* **Red Invader (IRE)**[14] 7632 9-8-7 **63**........................... DarraghKeenan(3) 1 49
(John Butler) *dwlt: sn outpcd and bhd tl styd on fr over 1f out: n.d* **50/1**

4022 **10** *2 ¾* **Lydiate Lady**[15] 7588 7-8-8 **61**.. JasonHart 7 37
(Eric Alston) *cl up centre: rdn along over 2f out: sn wknd* **12/1**

3006 **11** *1* **Billy Dylan (IRE)**[21] 7383 4-9-3 **70**..................................(p) DavidNolan 8 42
(David O'Meara) *prom towards stands' side: rdn along bef 1/2-way: sn wknd* **18/1**

2000 **12** *8* **Granny Roz**[135] 3207 5-9-1 **68**.. JimmyQuinn 6 12
(Ray Craggs) *in tch centre: rdn along 1/2-way: sn outpcd and bhd* **66/1**

58.86s (-0.84) **Going Correction** -0.125s/f (Stan) **12** Ran SP% **116.5**
Speed ratings (Par 103): **101,100,98,96,94 94,94,93,91,86 85,72**
CSF £81.18 CT £639.50 TOTE £15.00: £3.80, £2.20, £4.50; EX 96.50 Trifecta £870.00.
Owner P J Dixon, Chrystal Maze & Ashley Severn **Bred** Paul Dixon & Crystal Maze Partnership **Trained** Babworth, Notts

FOCUS
This fair sprint handicap was well run. Being drawn high was a positive.

8067 SKY SPORTS RACING ON VIRGIN 535 MAIDEN STKS 4f 214y(F)
5:45 (5:46) (Class 5) 2-Y-O £3,428 (£1,020; £509; £254) **Stalls** Centre

Form RPR

4222 **1** **Daily Times**[38] 6793 2-9-0 78...................................(t[1]) RobertHavlin 7 75+
(John Gosden) *led 1f: cl up centre: led over 2f out: rdn clr wl over 1f out: readily* **5/6[1]**

4560 **2** *5* **Hollaback Girl**[7] 7853 2-9-0 57.................................(v[1]) StevieDonohoe 5 57
(Richard Spencer) *racd centre: in rr and rdn along bef 1/2-way: hdwy u.p wl over 1f out: drvn and kpt on wl fnl f: tk 2nd nr line: no ch w wnr* **12/1**

5 **3** *hd* **Quaint (IRE)**[101] 4448 2-9-0 0... GrahamLee 1 56
(Hughie Morrison) *dwlt: racd far side: sn cl up: rdn along 2f out: drvn over 1f out: kpt on same pce fnl f: lost 2nd nr line* **11/2[3]**

00 **4** *2* **Heartstar**[10] 7769 2-8-9 0.. TobyEley(5) 2 49
(John Mackie) *cl up centre: rdn along 2f out: sn drvn and wknd over 1f out* **50/1**

60 **5** *1* **Orange Justice**[21] 7377 2-9-0 0.. LukeMorris 6 45
(David Loughnane) *cl up centre: rdn along bef 1/2-way: sn lost pl and bhd* **40/1**

00 **6** *1 ½* **The Grey Bay (IRE)**[10] 7769 2-9-5 0................................... JasonHart 10 45
(Julie Camacho) *dwlt and sltly hmpd s: racd towards stands' side: in tch: chsd ldrs 3f out: sn rdn and edgd lft: wknd fnl 2f* **16/1**

2643 **7** *1 ¼* **Point Of Order**[19] 7440 2-9-5 75..................................(b[1]) AndrewMullen 4 41
(Archie Watson) *cl up centre: slt ld after 1f: rdn along and hdd jst over 2f out: sn drvn and wknd over 1f out* **2/1[2]**

50 **8** *4 ½* **Dark Moonlight (IRE)**[105] 4282 2-8-12 0....................... GraceMcEntee(7) 9 24
(Phil McEntee) *in rr: outpcd and bhd fr 1/2-way* **50/1**

00 **9** *4* **Worthamonkey**[10] 7768 2-9-5 0... DannyBrock 8 10
(Denis Quinn) *in rr: outpcd and bhd fr 1/2-way* **100/1**

59.29s (-0.41) **Going Correction** -0.125s/f (Stan) **9** Ran SP% **124.2**
Speed ratings (Par 95): **98,90,89,86,84 82,80,73,66**
CSF £14.90 TOTE £1.60: £1.10, £3.10, £1.60; EX 20.50 Trifecta £88.10.
Owner Allan Belshaw **Bred** Times Of Wigan Ltd **Trained** Newmarket, Suffolk

FOCUS
An ordinary maiden won easily by the odds-on favourite. It's been rated conservatively.

8068 FOLLOW AT THE RACES ON TWITTER H'CAP 1m 13y(F)
6:15 (6:20) (Class 6) (0-60,60) 3-Y-O+
£2,781 (£827; £413; £400; £400; £400) **Stalls** Low

Form RPR

6003 **1** **Atalanta Queen**[21] 7385 4-8-9 **48**...............................(b) KieranO'Neill 14 55
(Robyn Brisland) *cl up: disp ld 3f out: rdn along 2f out: drvn ent fnl f: kpt on to ld nr fin* **6/1[2]**

0116 **2** *nk* **Break The Silence**[6] 7875 5-8-9 **55**........................(b) JonathanFisher(7) 12 61
(Scott Dixon) *cl up: led after 2f: rdn along over 2f out: drvn ent fnl f: hdd and no ex nr fin* **2/1[1]**

5006 **3** *1 ½* **Mr Strutter (IRE)**[14] 7632 5-9-7 **60**.................................. AndrewElliott 3 63
(Ronald Thompson) *towards rr: rdn along on inner 1/2-way: swtchd rt and wd st: hdwy 2f out: styd on to chse ldrs over 1f out: drvn and edgd lft ins fnl f: kpt on* **6/1[2]**

0240 **4** *1 ¾* **Fly True**[21] 7384 6-9-6 **59**.. NickyMackay 5 58
(Ivan Furtado) *towards rr: smooth hdwy 3f out: chsd ldrs wl over 1f out: sn rdn and no imp fnl f* **20/1**

4004 **5** *2* **Searanger (USA)**[21] 7384 6-8-8 **47**..............................(vt) AndrewMullen 11 41
(Rebecca Menzies) *dwlt: sn swtchd rt and hdwy on outer to go cl up after 1f: disp ld 1/2-way: wd st: rdn along over 2f out: drvn and drifted rt to stands' rail over 1f out: grad wknd* **16/1**

4000 **6** *hd* **Olivia R (IRE)**[31] 7032 3-9-1 **57**.. ShaneKelly 9 51
(David Barron) *chsd ldrs: rdn along wl over 2f out: drvn over 1f out: kpt on same pce* **50/1**

-200 **7** *1 ½* **Lily Ash (IRE)**[23] 7318 6-9-1 **54**.................................... JosephineGordon 8 47+
(Mike Murphy) *dwlt: hmpd and stmbld bdly after 150yds: bhd: hdwy and wd st: rdn over 2f out: kpt on (jockey said mare suffered interference leaving the stalls)* **33/1**

-040 **8** *½* **Is It Off (IRE)**[29] 7084 4-9-6 **59**.. LiamKeniry 6 48
(Sean Curran) *chsd ldrs: rdn along over 2f out: sn drvn and wknd* **25/1**

0005 **9** *3 ¼* **Seven For A Pound (USA)**[62] 5905 3-8-8 **50**....................... BarryMcHugh 4 32
(Richard Fahey) *a towards rr* **7/1[3]**

5036 **10** *1 ¾* **Tellovoi (IRE)**[14] 7603 11-8-10 **49** oh1 ow3..................(p) PhilipPrince 1 27
(Richard Guest) *a in rr* **66/1**

0630 **11** *7* **Squire**[16] 7550 8-8-12 **51**...(bt[1]) LukeMorris 2 13
(Marjorie Fife) *in tch: hdwy to chse ldrs over 3f out: rdn along wl over 2f out: sn wknd* **33/1**

5040 **12** *11* **Little Choosey**[84] 5106 9-8-7 **46** oh1....................(bt) JimmyQuinn 10
(Roy Bowring) *t.k.h: trckd ldrs whn n.m.r and swtchd rt after 2f: chsd ldrs: rdn along 3f out: wknd over 2f out* **100/1**

0200 **13** *1 1/4* **Bold Show**[15] 7581 3-8-9 **54**....................(v) MeganNicholls(3) 7
(Richard Fahey) *sn rdn along towards rr: outpcd and bhd fnl 3f (jockey said gelding suffered interference leaving the stalls)* **17/2**

5005 **14** *6* **Just Later**[12] 7685 3-9-3 **59**....................(t) JasonHart 13
(Amy Murphy) *slt ld 2f: prom: rdn along wl over 3f out: sn wknd* **8/1**

1m 43.63s (-0.07) **Going Correction** -0.125s/f (Stan) **14** Ran SP% **120.9**
WFA 3 from 4yo+ 3lb
Speed ratings (Par 101): **95,94,93,91,89 89,87,87,84,82 75,64,63,57**
CSF £17.34 CT £80.25 TOTE £7.70: £2.40, £2.50, £2.90; EX 18.30 Trifecta £122.60.
Owner Ferrybank Properties Limited **Bred** R T Dunne **Trained** Danethorpe, Notts

FOCUS
There was a wide range of ability on show in what was basically a moderate event. The pace was strong early but not many got into this. The winner has been rated in line with this year's best form.

8069 BRAMLEY APPLE MAIDEN STKS 7f 14y(F)
6:45 (6:48) (Class 5) 2-Y-O
£3,428 (£1,020; £509; £254) **Stalls** Low

Form RPR

53 **1** **Bill The Butcher (IRE)**[28] 7103 2-9-5 0.................... StevieDonohoe 2 82+
(Richard Spencer) *trckd ldrs: hdwy over 2f out: chal over 1f out: rdn to ld and edgd lft ins fnl f: sn clr* **11/4**[2]

6042 **2** *4* **Live In The Moment (IRE)**[10] 7754 2-9-5 73.................... RobertHavlin 1 72
(Adam West) *cl up on inner: led jst over 3f out: rdn along 2f out: drvn ent fnl f: sn hdd and kpt on same pce* **11/2**

06 **3** *1 1/4* **Summeronsevenhills (USA)**[22] 7339 2-9-5 0.................... ShaneKelly 9 68
(Richard Hughes) *trckd ldrs on outer: reminders and hdwy 3f out: sn cl up: rdn and ev ch over 1f out: sn drvn and kpt on same pce* **9/4**[1]

4 **4** *6* **Perfect Empire**[9] 7778 2-9-5 0.................... FrannyNorton 3 53
(Mark Johnston) *in tch: hdwy on inner 3f out: sn rdn along: plugged on same pce fnl 2f* **9/2**[3]

0 **5** *1* **Class Clown (IRE)**[24] 7285 2-9-5 0.................... RobbieDowney 8 50
(David Barron) *cl up: rdn along 3f out: drvn and hld whn n.m.r and edgd lft wl over 1f out: sn wknd* **66/1**

0 **6** *8* **Rulers Kingdom (IRE)**[15] 7586 2-9-5 0.................... JasonHart 5 29
(Mark Johnston) *towards rr and swtchd markedly rt to outer after 1 1/2f: outpcd and bhd after* **7/1**

00 **7** *2* **Goddess Of Rome (IRE)**[17] 7515 2-9-0 0.................... RyanPowell 4 19
(Simon Crisford) *dwlt: a in rr (jockey said filly hung right-handed throughout)* **50/1**

60 **8** *2 3/4* **Sheung Wan**[14] 7627 2-9-5 0.................... DavidNolan 7 17
(Richard Fahey) *slt ld: hdd over 3f out: sn rdn and wknd 2f out* **25/1**

6 **9** *24* **Toolmaker**[24] 7269 2-8-12 0.................... EllieMacKenzie(7) 6
(David Flood) *chsd ldrs: rdn along wl over 2f out: sn wknd (jockey said colt did not face the kick back)* **100/1**

1m 27.84s (-2.46) **Going Correction** -0.125s/f (Stan) **9** Ran SP% **111.8**
Speed ratings (Par 95): **109,104,103,96,95 85,83,80,53**
CSF £17.16 TOTE £3.90: £1.10, £1.60, £1.60; EX 13.10 Trifecta £33.90.
Owner Rebel Racing Premier II **Bred** Manister House Stud **Trained** Newmarket, Suffolk

FOCUS
A fair maiden and a nice performance from the winner, who finished well on top.

8070 WATCH SKY SPORTS RACING IN HD H'CAP 7f 14y(F)
7:15 (7:16) (Class 5) (0-70,70) 3-Y-O+
£3,428 (£1,020; £509; £400; £400; £400) **Stalls** Low

Form RPR

5535 **1** **Awa Bomba**[14] 7632 3-8-9 **63**....................(h[1]) DarraghKeenan(3) 6 73
(Tony Carroll) *hld up in tch: hdwy 3f out: cl up over 2f out: rdn to take slt ld 1 1/2f out: drvn and edgd lft ins fnl f: kpt on wl towards fin* **9/2**[2]

5554 **2** *3/4* **Esprit De Corps**[24] 7289 5-9-7 **70**.................... ShaneKelly 5 79
(David Barron) *hld up in tch: hdwy over 2f out: rdn over 1f out: drvn to chse wnr and ev ch ins fnl f: no ex last 75yds* **5/1**[3]

6430 **3** *2* **Primeiro Boy (IRE)**[13] 7652 3-8-12 **63**.................... BarryMcHugh 7 66
(Richard Fahey) *chsd ldrs on outer: hdwy 3f out: cl up 2f out: sn rdn: ev ch and drvn whn edgd lft ent fnl f: kpt on same pce after* **14/1**

0500 **4** *4* **Gremoboy**[11] 7732 3-9-3 **68**....................(p) DuranFentiman 2 60
(Tim Easterby) *in tch: hdwy 3f out: sn chsng ldrs: rdn wl over 1f out: no imp fnl f* **25/1**

0613 **5** *3/4* **French Twist**[6] 7875 3-8-11 **62**....................(p) JasonHart 3 52
(David Loughnane) *trckd ldrs on inner: hdwy and cl up 3f out: rdn and ev ch 2f out: sn drvn and btn* **4/1**[1]

0000 **6** *1* **Watheer**[6] 7875 4-8-8 **62**.................... PaulaMuir(5) 1 50
(Roger Fell) *chsd ldrs on inner: rdn along over 3f out: hdwy over 2f out: drvn wl over 1f out and sn wknd* **33/1**

210 **7** *1 1/4* **Liamba**[127] 3470 4-9-7 **70**....................(v) DavidNolan 4 55
(David O'Meara) *slt ld: pushed along 3f out: rdn over 2f out: sn drvn: hdd & wknd wl over 1f out* **11/2**

0060 **8** *2 1/2* **London Protocol (FR)**[33] 6961 6-9-2 **70**....................(b) TobyEley(5) 12 48
(John Mackie) *dwlt and wnt rt s: a in rr (jockey said gelding was slowly away)* **12/1**

0002 **9** *nse* **Intense Style (IRE)**[15] 7587 7-8-12 **61**.................... DannyBrock 11 39
(Denis Quinn) *s.i.s: a in rr (jockey said gelding was slowly away and hung left-handed)* **50/1**

1420 **10** *11* **Kendergarten Kop (IRE)**[7] 7839 4-9-6 **69**....................(p) LukeMorris 8 17
(David Flood) *cl up: rdn along 3f out: sn drvn and wknd* **7/1**

3440 **11** *14* **Stronsay (IRE)**[55] 6176 3-9-4 **69**....................(p) GrahamLee 10
(Bryan Smart) *cl up on outer: rdn along over 3f out: drvn and wknd wl over 2f out* **12/1**

1m 28.27s (-2.03) **Going Correction** -0.125s/f (Stan) **11** Ran SP% **113.5**
WFA 3 from 4yo+ 2lb
Speed ratings (Par 103): **106,105,102,98,97 96,94,92,91,79 63**
CSF £25.77 CT £287.82 TOTE £5.70: £1.70, £1.80, £4.40; EX 25.20 Trifecta £248.10.
Owner Mrs Katie Morgan **Bred** Mr And Mrs L Norris **Trained** Cropthorne, Worcs

FOCUS
This didn't look an overly strong race for the level but the winner did it nicely.

8071 SKY SPORTS RACING ON VIRGIN 535 H'CAP 6f 16y(F)
7:45 (7:46) (Class 6) (0-60,61) 3-Y-O+
£2,781 (£827; £413; £400; £400; £400) **Stalls** Low

Form RPR

0511 **1** **Queen Of Kalahari**[14] 7632 4-9-7 **58**....................(p) LewisEdmunds 11 67
(Les Eyre) *mde most: rdn clr wl over 1f out: drvn ins fnl f: kpt on wl towards fin* **11/8**[1]

4030 **2** *3/4* **Tease Maid**[8] 7823 3-9-5 **57**....................(p[1]) JasonHart 4 64
(John Quinn) *midfield: hdwy and wd st: rdn to chse wnr wl over 1f out: drvn and kpt on wl fnl f* **11/1**

3532 **3** *3 3/4* **Poeta Brasileiro (IRE)**[12] 7690 4-9-7 **61**....................(t) GabrieleMalune(3) 2 57
(David Brown) *hld up: hdwy 3f out: chsd ldrs 2f out: sn rdn: styd on u.p fnl f* **4/1**[2]

6006 **4** *3/4* **Painted Dream**[28] 7105 3-9-7 **59**....................(b[1]) TomQueally 7 52
(George Margarson) *dwlt and towards rr: hdwy and wd st: rdn over 2f out: kpt on wl fnl f* **14/1**

0164 **5** *3 1/2* **Jill Rose**[14] 7632 3-9-9 **61**....................(b) PhilDennis 10 44
(Richard Whitaker) *chsd ldrs: wd st: rdn over 2f out: sn one pce* **9/1**[3]

0324 **6** *nk* **Guardia Svizzera (IRE)**[17] 7507 5-9-0 **56**....................(h) PaulaMuir(5) 3 38
(Roger Fell) *in rr: hdwy over 2f out: sn rdn and kpt on: n.d* **14/1**

6316 **7** *shd* **Aquarius (IRE)**[19] 7446 3-9-6 **58**.................... LiamJones 5 40
(Michael Appleby) *nvr bttr than midfield* **20/1**

1055 **8** *1* **Amelia R (IRE)**[45] 6547 3-9-6 **58**.................... JimmyQuinn 1 37
(Ray Craggs) *a towards rr* **20/1**

0-50 **9** *1/2* **Robbian**[107] 4212 8-8-1 **45**.................... AledBeech(7) 6 22
(Charles Smith) *chsd ldrs: rdn along 1/2-way: sn outpcd* **100/1**

00-2 **10** *nk* **Blackcurrent**[14] 7628 3-9-0 **52**.................... GrahamLee 12 28
(Alan Brown) *cl up: rdn along 3f out: drvn over 2f out: sn wknd* **33/1**

2110 **11** *3 1/2* **Jazz Legend (USA)**[155] 2532 6-9-1 **55**.................... WilliamCox(3) 9 21
(Mandy Rowland) *chsd ldrs: rdn along wl over 2f out: sn wknd* **20/1**

050 **12** *1 1/2* **Vikivaki (USA)**[19] 7472 3-9-6 **58**....................(p[1]) LukeMorris 8 19
(David Loughnane) *chsd ldrs on inner: rdn along 3f out: sn drvn and btn* **20/1**

3000 **13** *14* **Alban's Dream**[41] 6685 3-9-3 **58**....................(b) DarraghKeenan(3) 13
(Robert Eddery) *cl up on outer: rdn along 3f out: sn wknd (jockey said his saddle slipped)* **66/1**

1m 16.05s (-0.45) **Going Correction** -0.125s/f (Stan) **13** Ran SP% **118.2**
WFA 3 from 4yo+ 1lb
Speed ratings (Par 101): **98,97,92,91,86 85,85,84,83,83 78,76,58**
CSF £15.69 CT £54.07 TOTE £2.30: £1.10, £3.50, £1.50; EX 22.40 Trifecta £102.80.
Owner Les Eyre Racing Partnership I **Bred** Minster Stud **Trained** Catwick, N Yorks

FOCUS
The in-form and well-treated winner notched up another C&D success. The second has been rated to her previous best here.

8072 VISIT SOUTHWELL H'CAP 1m 4f 14y(F)
8:15 (8:17) (Class 6) (0-55,55) 3-Y-O+
£2,781 (£827; £413; £400; £400; £400) **Stalls** Low

Form RPR

1421 **1** **Blyton Lass**[33] 6982 4-9-3 **51**.................... BarryMcHugh 9 57
(James Given) *hld up towards rr: stdy hdwy over 4f out: chsd ldrs 2f out: rdn to chal wl over 1f out: led appr fnl f: drvn and kpt on strly* **7/1**

0550 **2** *3/4* **Seventii**[26] 7202 5-8-9 **46** oh1.................... DarraghKeenan(3) 10 51
(Robert Eddery) *trckd ldr: effrt 2f out: rdn and ev ch whn n.m.r and sltly hmpd over 1f out: drvn to chse wnr ins fnl f: kpt on* **28/1**

0212 **3** *3/4* **Loose Chippings (IRE)**[6] 7873 5-9-4 **55**....................(p[1]) GabrieleMalune(3) 4 59
(Ivan Furtado) *sn led: pushed along 3f out: rdn 2f out: drvn and edgd rt over 1f out: sn hdd and drvn: kpt on same pce fnl f* **2/1**[1]

-050 **4** *1* **Archie's Sister**[23] 7314 3-8-6 **46** oh1....................(t) RyanPowell 3 51+
(Philip Kirby) *awkward and fly jumping s: slowly away and bhd: hdwy 4f out: rdn along and in tch over 2f out: chsd ldrs and styng on whn n.m.r and swtchd rt ins fnl f: kpt on wl towards fin (jockey said filly fly leapt leaving the stalls)* **66/1**

0052 **5** *nk* **Postie**[21] 7390 3-8-9 **49**.................... RyanTate 12 52
(James Eustace) *trckd ldrs: hdwy 3f out: rdn along over 2f out: drvn over 1f out: kpt on same pce fnl f (jockey said that approaching the line, the filly was caught on the heels of Loose Chippings, causing him to sit up briefly and possibly lose fourth place)* **3/1**[2]

0-50 **6** *hd* **Call Me Madam**[30] 7048 4-8-13 **47**.................... JosephineGordon 14 48
(James Bethell) *trckd ldng trio: effrt and hdwy on outer over 3f out: rdn along over 2f out: sn drvn and kpt on same pce* **25/1**

0323 **7** *3/4* **Point Of Honour (IRE)**[15] 7578 4-8-12 **46**....................(p) GrahamLee 13 46
(Phillip Makin) *s.i.s and towards rr: hdwy on outer and in tch 1/2-way: rdn along and wd st: chsd ldrs over 2f out: sn drvn and no imp fr over 1f out (jockey said gelding was restless in the stalls)* **13/2**[3]

3205 **8** *3 3/4* **Dolly Dupree**[6] 7873 3-8-9 **54**.................... TheodoreLadd(5) 6 49
(Paul D'Arcy) *trckd ldrs on inner: effrt 3f out: rdn along 2f out: sn drvn and grad wknd* **7/1**

6000 **9** *4* **Foxrush Take Time (FR)**[6] 7873 4-8-12 **46** oh1..........(e) PhilipPrince 11 34
(Richard Guest) *a towards rr* **33/1**

0000 **10** *11* **Daniel Dravot**[8] 7818 3-8-6 **46** oh1.................... AndrewMullen 7 17
(Michael Attwater) *trckd ldrs: pushed along 5f out: rdn 4f out: sn wknd* **50/1**

2-00 **11** *15* **Ruler Of The Nile**[249] 589 7-9-2 **53**....................(b) MeganNicholls(3) 5
(Marjorie Fife) *a in rr* **40/1**

000- **12** *13* **Crakehall Lad (IRE)**[36] 6036 8-8-12 **46** oh1....................(b[1]) KieranO'Neill 2
(Andrew Crook) *s.i.s: sn rdn along and a bhd: t.o fnl 4f* **80/1**

5004 **13** *19* **Inflexiball**[58] 6059 7-8-12 **46** oh1.................... FrannyNorton 8
(John Mackie) *chsd ldrs: reminders 1/2-way: rdn along 5f out: sn lost pl: bhd and eased fnl 3f* **33/1**

2m 39.69s (-1.31) **Going Correction** -0.125s/f (Stan) **13** Ran SP% **117.0**
WFA 3 from 4yo+ 6lb
Speed ratings (Par 101): **99,98,98,97,97 97,96,94,91,84 74,65,52**
CSF £186.82 CT £535.89 TOTE £7.30: £2.30, £7.10, £1.20; EX 244.20 Trifecta £1072.50.
Owner Andy Clarke **Bred** Mrs V J Lovelace **Trained** Willoughton, Lincs

FOCUS
A moderate middle-distance contest which produced a comfortable winner. Straightforward form.
T/Plt: £17.30 to a £1 stake. Pool: £64,979.93. 2,727.22 winning units. T/Qpdt: £3.80 to a £1 stake. Pool: £10,383.31. 1,982.71 winning units. **Joe Rowntree**

8073 - 8080a (Foreign Racing) - See Raceform Interactive

[8019]NEWCASTLE (A.W) (L-H)

Friday, October 11

OFFICIAL GOING: Tapeta: standard

Wind: Fairly strong, half against in races on the straight course and in over 3f of home straight in races Weather: Dry

8081 CRONNIE CREATIVE LIGHTS CAMERA ACTION H'CAP 2m 56y (Tp)

5:25 (5:26) (Class 6) (0-55,57) 3-Y-0+

£2,781 (£827; £413; £400; £400; £400) **Stalls** Low

Form RPR

4620 **1** **Nataleena (IRE)**[21] 7415 3-8-12 **55** AndrewMullen 8 65+
(Ben Haslam) *hld up: hdwy and angled rt over 2f out: rdn to ld over 1f out: edgd lft and drew clr last 150yds* **5/1**[3]

-426 **2** *6* **Aussie Breeze**[34] 6982 3-8-7 **50** ShaneGray 7 53
(Tom George) *chsd ldr: led over 3f out: rdn and hdd over 1f out: no ch w wnr* **6/1**

6-02 **3** *1* **Oromo (IRE)**[14] 7670 6-8-12 **46** oh1 (t) DougieCostello 12 46+
(Karl Thornton, Ire) *hld up in rr: rdn over 2f out: edgd lft and hdwy over 1f out: tk 3rd wl ins fnl f: no imp (jockey said gelding hung left under pressure)* **14/1**

050- **4** *1 ¼* **Our Cilla**[153] 8613 5-9-2 **50** (b) BenRobinson 6 48
(Andrew Crook) *prom: hdwy to press ldr over 2f out to over 1f out: drvn and outpcd fnl f* **100/1**

0022 **5** *1 ½* **Put The Law On You (IRE)**[30] 7070 4-9-0 **48** (p) JamieGormley 3 45
(Alistair Whillans) *trckd ldrs: effrt and rdn over 2f out: outpcd appr fnl f (jockey said gelding hung left throughout)* **9/4**[1]

-000 **6** *¾* **Duration (IRE)**[30] 6601 4-9-7 **55** (b[1]) DavidNolan 10 51
(J R Jenkins) *t.k.h: hld up in midfield: effrt and rdn over 2f out: wknd ins fnl f* **50/1**

0262 **7** *11* **Urban Spirit (IRE)**[100] 4510 5-9-7 **55** CliffordLee 2 37
(Karen McLintock) *t.k.h: prom: rdn along over 2f out: wknd over 1f out* **7/2**[2]

0000 **8** *18* **Angel Black (IRE)**[18] 7520 3-8-4 **47** oh1 ow1 (p[1]) JosephineGordon 11 10
(Shaun Keightley) *dwlt: t.k.h and sn midfield: outpcd whn hung lft 3f out: sn btn: t.o* **50/1**

4600 **9** *¾* **Another Lincolnday**[7] 7873 8-9-0 **51** (p) HarrisonShaw(3) 9 11
(Rebecca Menzies) *in tch: drvn along and effrt over 3f out: wknd over 2f out: t.o* **12/1**

0640 **10** *10* **Ozark**[32] 7035 3-8-3 **46** oh1 DuranFentiman 4
(Jennie Candlish) *hld up: drvn and outpcd over 3f out: sn btn: t.o* **80/1**

-000 **11** *9* **Bigdabog**[42] 6663 4-8-9 **46** oh1 (p[1]) ConnorMurtagh(3) 5
(Stella Barclay) *hld up on ins: drvn along 4f out: sn struggling: t.o* **150/1**

360 **12** *13* **Sweetest Smile (IRE)**[24] 7300 4-8-12 **46** oh1 (b) JackMitchell 13
(Ed de Giles) *t.k.h: led to over 2f out: sn btn: eased whn no ch fr over 1f out* **8/1**

3m 36.26s (1.26) **Going Correction** +0.225s/f (Slow)
WFA 3 from 4yo+ 9lb **12 Ran SP% 116.2**
Speed ratings (Par 101): **105,102,101,100,100 99,94,85,84,79 75,68**
CSF £34.13 CT £395.32 TOTE £5.90: £2.30, £1.90, £3.50; EX 38.30 Trifecta £320.60.
Owner Shapiro,Milner,Rees,Nicol,Feeney,Haslam **Bred** London Thoroughbred Services Ltd **Trained** Middleham Moor, N Yorks

FOCUS
A moderate staying handicap, rated around the runner-up to her mark.

8082 CRONNIE CREATIVE MAKE IT AWESOME H'CAP 1m 4f 98y (Tp)

6:00 (6:00) (Class 4) (0-85,86) 3-Y-0+

£5,207 (£1,549; £774; £400; £400; £400) **Stalls** High

Form RPR

2101 **1** **Paths Of Glory**[24] 7294 4-9-10 **84** (t) JackMitchell 5 93+
(Hugo Palmer) *dwlt: hld up: shkn up: swtchd to far rail and gd hdwy to ld over 1f out: rdn and r.o strly fnl f: eased cl home* **11/8**[1]

1220 **2** *2* **Arabic Culture (USA)**[33] 7003 5-9-3 **77** SamJames 3 82
(Grant Tuer) *t.k.h early: hld up on ins: hdwy over 2f out: effrt and rdn over 1f out: wnt 2nd wl ins fnl f: nt rch wnr* **8/1**

5261 **3** *hd* **Lopes Dancer (IRE)**[16] 7577 7-9-3 **77** BenRobinson 4 82
(Brian Ellison) *prom: effrt and ev ch over 1f out: chsd wnr to wl ins fnl f: r.o* **11/1**

5100 **4** *2 ¾* **Beyond The Clouds**[20] 7436 6-9-9 **83** TomEaves 9 83
(Kevin Ryan) *trckd ldr: led gng wl 3f out: rdn and hdd over 1f out: outpcd ins fnl f* **5/1**[2]

5530 **5** *¾* **Mistiroc**[20] 7436 8-9-9 **86** (v) CierenFallon(3) 7 85
(John Quinn) *hld up in tch: pushed along over 1f out: effrt over 1f out: fdd ins fnl f* **7/1**[3]

1043 **6** *¾* **Autretot (FR)**[16] 7577 4-9-9 **83** DavidNolan 6 81
(David O'Meara) *hld up: hdwy on outside over 2f out: rdn over 1f out: fdd ins fnl f* **8/1**

00-5 **7** *13* **Paddyplex**[210] 1220 6-9-8 **82** CliffordLee 1 59
(Karen McLintock) *led tl hdd 3f out: rallied: rdn and wknd wl over 1f out* **40/1**

6116 **8** *7* **Global Falcon**[62] 5943 3-8-13 **79** AndrewMullen 8 46
(Charles Hills) *prom: drvn and outpcd over 2f out: sn btn: fin lame (vet said colt finished lame left fore)* **14/1**

212 **9** *¾* **Roman Stone (USA)**[19] 7490 3-9-2 **82** ShaneGray 2 48
(Keith Dalgleish) *trckd ldrs: drvn along over 3f out: wknd over 2f out* **28/1**

2m 40.14s (-0.96) **Going Correction** +0.225s/f (Slow)
WFA 3 from 4yo+ 6lb **9 Ran SP% 114.4**
Speed ratings (Par 105): **112,110,110,108,108 107,99,94,93**
CSF £12.96 CT £86.65 TOTE £2.00: £1.10, £2.00, £3.00; EX 11.20 Trifecta £39.50.
Owner China Horse Club International Limited **Bred** Dayton Investments Ltd **Trained** Newmarket, Suffolk

FOCUS
The feature contest was a decent middle-distance handicap. The winner built on his Chepstow win.

8083 CRONNIE CREATIVE CAPTURE THE GOOD TIMES APPRENTICE H'CAP 6f (Tp)

6:30 (6:34) (Class 6) (0-65,65) 3-Y-0+

£2,781 (£827; £413; £400; £400; £400) **Stalls** Centre

Form RPR

0054 **1** **Axe Axelrod (USA)**[14] 7652 3-9-7 **62** (b) BenRobinson 12 70
(Michael Dods) *hld up: hdwy on nr side of gp over 2f out: led over 1f out: rdn and r.o strly fnl f* **5/1**[2]

0016 **2** *¾* **Peachey Carnehan**[11] 7770 5-8-12 **57** (v) AmeliaGlass(5) 8 63
(Michael Mullineaux) *dwlt: hld up in centre of gp: effrt and swtchd rt 2f out: hdwy to chse wnr wl ins fnl f: r.o* **10/1**

6240 **3** *½* **Kaafy (IRE)**[13] 7703 3-9-7 **62** SeanDavis 6 66
(Grant Tuer) *hld up on far side of gp: hdwy and rdn 2f out: hung rt and chsd wnr 1f out: no ex and lost 2nd wl ins fnl f* **33/1**

3043 **4** *2 ¼* **Mr Wagyu (IRE)**[24] 7311 4-9-11 **65** (v) CierenFallon 3 63
(John Quinn) *cl up on far side of gp: effrt and ev ch over 1f out: chsd wnr to ins fnl f: sn no ex* **12/1**

54 **5** *¾* **Scandinavian Lady (IRE)**[20] 7443 3-9-2 **57** GabrieleMalune 5 52
(Ivan Furtado) *in tch in centre of gp: effrt and angled lft over 2f out: drvn and one pce fr over 1f out* **9/1**

65 **6** *1 ¼* **Pinarella (FR)**[31] 7050 3-9-4 **64** (p) HarryRussell(5) 10 56
(Ben Haslam) *t.k.h: hld up on nr side of gp: drvn and outpcd over 2f out: rallied ins fnl f: kpt on: nvr able to chal* **33/1**

6302 **7** *hd* **My Town Chicago (USA)**[16] 7576 4-9-4 **61** ThoreHammerHansen(3) 7 52
(Kevin Frost) *led in centre of gp: rdn over 2f out: hdd over 1f out: wknd ins fnl f* **10/1**

3001 **8** *1 ¼* **I Know How (IRE)**[30] 7066 4-9-9 **63** (b) HarrisonShaw 11 50
(Julie Camacho) *hld up on nr side of gp: drvn and outpcd over 2f out: n.d after* **6/1**[3]

4655 **9** *2* **Mutabaahy (IRE)**[13] 7703 4-9-3 **62** KieranSchofield(5) 4 43
(Antony Brittain) *cl up in centre of gp: effrt and rdn over 2f out: wknd ent fnl f* **9/2**[1]

0025 **10** *4* **Sepahi**[29] 7105 3-9-3 **61** (p) DylanHogan(3) 2 30
(Henry Spiller) *taken early to post: dwlt: hld up on far side of gp: drvn over 2f out: sn btn* **50/1**

1004 **11** *2 ¼* **Hawk In The Sky**[15] 7624 3-9-2 **62** GavinAshton(5) 9 24
(Richard Whitaker) *t.k.h: prom towards nr side of gp: rdn and hung lft over 2f out: wknd wl over 1f out* **16/1**

2130 **12** *½* **Mochalov**[8] 7839 4-9-8 **62** DarraghKeenan 1 23
(Jane Chapple-Hyam) *hld up on far side of gp: drvn and outpcd over 2f out: sn btn* **8/1**

3020 **13** *19* **Avenue Of Stars**[18] 7507 6-9-8 **62** (v) ConnorMurtagh 13
(Karen McLintock) *s.v.s: t.o thrght (jockey said gelding panicked in the stalls and as a result missed the break and lost many lengths)* **12/1**

1m 13.51s (1.01) **Going Correction** +0.225s/f (Slow)
WFA 3 from 4yo+ 1lb **13 Ran SP% 117.5**
Speed ratings (Par 101): **102,101,100,97,96 94,94,92,90,84 81,81,55**
CSF £52.72 CT £1539.27 TOTE £7.60: £2.60, £2.90, £8.40; EX 60.90 Trifecta £2776.80.
Owner Merchants and Missionaries **Bred** Hurstland Farm Inc & William Kartozian **Trained** Denton, Co Durham

FOCUS
A modest apprentice riders' handicap. The winner cashed in on a very fair mark.

8084 CRONNIE CREATIVE/EBF NOVICE STKS 6f (Tp)

7:00 (7:03) (Class 5) 2-Y-0

£3,816 (£1,135; £567; £283) **Stalls** Centre

Form RPR

1 **Yes Always (IRE)** 2-9-0 0 BenCurtis 9 76+
(K R Burke) *in tch towards centre of gp: smooth hdwy to ld over 1f out: rdn: edgd lft and qcknd clr ins fnl f: pricked ears and eased cl home* **5/2**[2]

2 *2* **Perfect Focus (IRE)** 2-9-5 0 JackMitchell 1 75+
(Simon Crisford) *hld up in tch on far side of gp: shkn up: hdwy and pressed wnr over 1f out: kpt on same pce last 100yds* **6/4**[1]

3 **3** *1 ¾* **Lairig Ghru**[15] 7619 2-9-5 0 AndrewMullen 7 70
(Micky Hammond) *t.k.h: cl up in centre of gp: effrt and rdn over 1f out: kpt on same pce ins fnl f* **20/1**

0 **4** *½* **Slingshot**[43] 6622 2-9-0 0 GrahamLee 10 64+
(Bryan Smart) *hld up in centre of gp: pushed along and plenty to do over 1f out: kpt on fnl f: nrst fin* **16/1**

55 **5** *1* **Pretty Lady (IRE)**[11] 7769 2-9-0 0 FrannyNorton 3 61
(Mark Johnston) *led at decent gallop in centre of gp: drvn and hdd over 1f out: wknd ins fnl f* **33/1**

05 **6** *½* **Penmellyn (IRE)**[147] 2783 2-9-0 0 (h) ShaneGray 5 59
(Phillip Makin) *t.k.h in midfield in centre of gp: shkn up and outpcd over 1f out: n.d after* **50/1**

5 **7** *nk* **Momentum**[16] 7580 2-9-0 0 CamHardie 14 58
(Antony Brittain) *bhd in centre of gp: rdn over 2f out: hdwy and edgd lft over 1f out: kpt on fnl f: no imp* **80/1**

8 *nse* **Dream Academy (IRE)** 2-9-5 0 TomEaves 12 63+
(Kevin Ryan) *hld up on nr side of gp: rdn and effrt over 2f out: no imp over 1f out* **11/2**[3]

8 *dht* **Cindy Looper** 2-9-0 0 PhilDennis 8 58
(Richard Whitaker) *dwlt: bhd in centre of gp: rdn over 2f out: no imp fr over 1f out* **100/1**

10 *¾* **Innings** 2-9-5 0 TonyHamilton 13 61
(Richard Fahey) *hld up on nr side of gp: hdwy over 2f out: wknd fnl f* **9/1**

60 **11** *¾* **Full House**[18] 7506 2-9-5 0 SamJames 4 58
(John Davies) *cl up on far side of gp: rdn over 2f out: wknd over 1f out* **100/1**

12 *2 ¼* **Dutch Monument** 2-8-11 0 SeanDavis(3) 11 47
(Richard Fahey) *hld up towards centre of gp: rn green and outpcd over 2f out: sn btn* **25/1**

0 **13** *2 ½* **Niamh's Starlight (IRE)**[30] 7063 2-8-11 0 HarrisonShaw(3) 6 39
(Bryan Smart) *dwlt: bhd far side: struggling over 2f out: sn btn* **100/1**

1m 13.62s (1.12) **Going Correction** +0.225s/f (Slow) **13 Ran SP% 117.6**
Speed ratings (Par 95): **101,98,96,95,94 93,92,92,92,91 90,87,84**
CSF £6.08 TOTE £3.70: £1.40, £1.10, £4.70; EX 8.30 Trifecta £69.60.
Owner The Cool Silk Partnership **Bred** Whisperview Trading Ltd **Trained** Middleham Moor, N Yorks
■ Carla Erangey was withdrawn. Price at time of withdrawal 50-1. Rule 4 does not apply

FOCUS
A fair juvenile novice contest. The second-favourite won well and her winning time was marginally slower than the previous C&D handicap. Probably ordinary form down the field.

8085 CRONNIE CREATIVE LIGHTS CAMERA ACTION NURSERY H'CAP 6f (Tp)

7:30 (7:33) (Class 6) (0-65,65) 2-Y-0

£2,781 (£827; £413; £400; £400; £400) **Stalls** Centre

Form RPR

0020 **1** **Holloa**[16] 7584 2-9-4 **62** DuranFentiman 8 66
(Tim Easterby) *hld up in centre of gp: nt clr run over 2f out and over 1f out: rdn and gd hdwy to ld ins fnl f: kpt on strly* **16/1**

004 **2** *¾* **Jems Bond**[14] 7645 2-9-0 **58** GrahamLee 10 60
(Alan Brown) *hld up in centre of gp: effrt whn nt clr run over 2f out to over 1f out: sn hmpd: rdn: edgd lft and gd hdwy to chse wnr last 25yds: r.o (jockey said gelding was denied a clear run continuously from 2f out to the final furlong)* **20/1**

4543 **3** ½ **Dancing Leopard (IRE)**[22] 7386 2-9-2 **63**..............(v) HarrisonShaw(3) 2 63
(K R Burke) hld up on far side of gp: rdn and hdwy over 1f out: kpt on ins fnl f to take 3rd cl home: nrst fin (jockey said filly was slowly away) **11/1**

004 **4** hd **Panist (IRE)**[20] 7437 2-9-6 **64**.............................. FrannyNorton 1 64
(Mark Johnston) cl up on far side of gp: rdn: edgd rt and led over 1f out: hdd ins fnl f: one pce and lost two pls last 25yds **15/2**[3]

0340 **5** ¾ **Street Life**[24] 7309 2-8-10 **57**..............................(v1) SeanDavis(3) 13 54
(Richard Fahey) chsd ldrs on nr side of gp: effrt and ev ch over 1f out to ins fnl f: sn no ex **9/1**

005 **6** ¾ **Captain Corelli (IRE)**[15] 7619 2-9-2 **60**..................... CallumRodriguez 9 55
(Julie Camacho) hld up in centre of gp: effrt whn nt clr run and angled (rt) to stands' rail over 1f out: kpt on fnl f: no imp **4/1**[1]

003 **7** nk **Somekindasuperstar**[16] 7580 2-9-7 **65**................. JosephineGordon 12 59
(Paul Collins) dwlt: hld up on nr side of gp: effrt over 2f out: rdn and no imp over 1f out **28/1**

540 **8** 1 **My Dandy Doc (IRE)**[41] 6697 2-9-5 **63**............................ BenCurtis 14 54
(John Quinn) hld up on nr side of gp: hdwy over 2f out: rdn and no ex fr over 1f out **7/1**[2]

0565 **9** shd **Maurice Dancer**[25] 7284 2-9-4 **62**............................(p1) PaulMulrennan 5 53
(Julie Camacho) hld up on far side of gp: effrt and rdn over 1f out: sn no imp: btn fnl f **8/1**

4000 **10** 2¾ **Newsical**[16] 7584 2-9-0 **58**.............................. DougieCostello 4 41
(Mark Walford) hld up on far side of gp: rdn wl over 1f out: wknd fnl f **16/1**

3460 **11** 1½ **Zain Storm (FR)**[36] 6883 2-9-7 **65**............................ PaddyMathers 7 43
(John Butler) hld up in centre of gp: rdn and angled rt 2f out: sn n.d **16/1**

5500 **12** 3¼ **Callipygian**[24] 7306 2-8-12 **56**..............................(t) TomEaves 11 24
(James Given) led in centre of gp: rdn over 2f out: hdd & wknd over 1f out **25/1**

2326 **13** 1¼ **Bertie's Princess (IRE)**[17] 7539 2-9-4 **65**.................. CierenFallon(3) 6 30
(Nigel Tinkler) t.k.h: cl up in centre of gp: rdn wl over 1f out: sn wknd **15/2**[3]

1m 15.81s (3.31) **Going Correction** +0.225s/f (Slow) 13 Ran SP% **115.2**
Speed ratings (Par 93): **86,85,84,84,83 82,81,80,80,76 74,70,68**
CSF £297.95 CT £3749.39 TOTE £16.20: £5.10, £5.20, £4.10; EX 244.50 Trifecta £2748.40.
Owner The Hecklers **Bred** Mrs Mary Taylor And James F Taylor **Trained** Great Habton, N Yorks

FOCUS
A modest nursery run at a steady tempo. The winning time was significantly slower than the previous C&D juvenile novice contest. The winner's Thirsk run could be rated this high.

8086 CRONNIE CREATIVE UP YOUR EXPOSURE MEDIAN AUCTION MAIDEN STKS 1m 5y (Tp)

8:00 (8:01) (Class 5) 3-5-Y-O

£3,428 (£1,020; £509; £254) **Stalls Centre**

Form RPR

232 **1** **Aegeus (USA)**[62] 5955 3-9-5 **74**.............................. GrahamLee 1 73
(Amanda Perrett) t.k.h: cl up: shkn up to ld over 1f out: hrd pressed ins fnl f: kpt on wl towards fin **2/1**[1]

25 **2** hd **Ravenscar (IRE)**[24] 7303 3-9-0 **0**............................ SamJames 7 68
(Grant Tuer) hld up: hdwy on outside to press wnr over 1f out: rdn and ev ch ins fnl f: kpt on: hld cl home **9/1**

3 ¾ **Hill Hollow (IRE)** 3-9-0 **0**.............................. DylanHogan(5) 4 71
(David Simcock) dwlt: hld up in tch: rdn and hdwy to chse ldrs over 2f out: hung rt ins fnl f: kpt on **8/1**

320 **4** nk **Don't Jump George (IRE)**[25] 7278 4-9-8 **0**..................(t) RossaRyan 9 70
(Shaun Lycett) stdd in tch: effrt whn n.m.r and angled lft wl over 1f out: sn hung lft: rdn and kpt on fnl f **5/1**[3]

353 **5** 3¼ **Blistering Barney (IRE)**[24] 7303 3-9-5 **66**..................... AndrewElliott 8 63
(Christopher Kellett) led to over 3f out: rallied: effrt whn nt clr run briefly over 1f out: sn wknd **8/1**

0000 **6** 2¼ **Uponastar (IRE)**[63] 5890 3-9-0 **44**.............................. AndrewMullen 2 52?
(Ben Haslam) hld up: pushed along wl over 1f out: sn outpcd **150/1**

02 **7** 7 **Extrodinair**[22] 7373 4-9-3 **0**.............................. RayDawson(5) 5 41
(Jane Chapple-Hyam) t.k.h: cl up: led over 3f out to over 1f out: rdn and wknd fnl f (jockey said gelding stopped quickly) **5/2**[2]

-000 **8** nse **Jazz Magic (IRE)**[43] 6627 4-9-8 **43**..............................(p) CamHardie 3 41
(Lynn Siddall) hld up: drvn and struggling 3f out: sn wknd **66/1**

9 nse **What A Turnup (IRE)** 4-9-3 **0**.............................. DougieCostello 6 36
(Mark Walford) prom: rdn and lost pl wl over 2f out: sn wknd **50/1**

1m 42.14s (3.54) **Going Correction** +0.225s/f (Slow)
WFA 3 from 4yo 3lb 9 Ran SP% **114.9**
Speed ratings (Par 103): **91,90,90,89,86 84,77,77,77**
CSF £21.02 TOTE £2.50: £1.10, £2.60, £3.10; EX 13.30 Trifecta £100.30.
Owner K Abdullah **Bred** Juddmonte Farms Inc **Trained** Pulborough, W Sussex

FOCUS
An ordinary median auction maiden in which the winner is rated to form.

8087 CRONNIE CREATIVE ADJUST YOUR FOCUS H'CAP 1m 5y (Tp)

8:30 (8:32) (Class 5) (0-70,72) 3-Y-O+

£3,428 (£1,020; £509; £400; £400; £400) **Stalls Centre**

Form RPR

1622 **1** **Home Before Dusk**[14] 7653 4-9-12 **72**..............(p) CallumRodriguez 13 84+
(Keith Dalgleish) hld up on nr side of chsng gp: hdwy to chse clr ldng pair over 2f out: led over 1f out: sn clr: drifted lft ins fnl f: kpt on strly **3/1**[1]

2323 **2** 1¾ **Stormbomber (CAN)**[17] 7560 3-9-6 **69**.............................. CliffordLee 3 76
(Ed Walker) dwlt: hld up on far side of chsng gp: effrt over 2f out: hdwy to chse (clr) wnr ins fnl f: clsng at fin **3/1**[1]

0200 **3** ¾ **Stoney Lane**[15] 7621 4-9-11 **71**.............................. PhilDennis 12 76
(Richard Whitaker) hld up on nr side of chsng gp: hdwy to chse (clr) wnr 1f out to ins fnl f: kpt on same pce **14/1**

0032 **4** 2¾ **Traveller (FR)**[16] 7581 5-8-11 **57**..............................(tp) CamHardie 8 56
(Antony Brittain) blkd s: sn prom in centre of chsng gp: rdn and outpcd over 2f out: rallied fnl f: no imp **16/1**

6105 **5** shd **Placebo Effect (IRE)**[17] 7542 4-9-6 **66**....................(p) BenRobinson 14 65
(Ollie Pears) hld up on nr side of chsng gp: hdwy to chse (clr) wnr briefly over 1f out: rdn and no ex ins fnl f (jockey said gelding ran too free) **16/1**

4335 **6** 3¾ **Bollihope**[15] 7610 7-9-6 **66**.............................. JosephineGordon 7 56
(Shaun Keightley) racd in centre of chsng gp: chsd clr ldng pair to over 2f out: drvn and outpcd wl over 1f out: n.d after **8/1**[3]

6206 **7** 1 **Newmarket Warrior (IRE)**[24] 7305 8-9-3 **66**............(p) CierenFallon(3) 6 54
(Iain Jardine) dwlt: hld up in centre of chsng gp: rdn over 2f out: no imp over 1f out **22/1**

0004 **8** ½ **Armed (IRE)**[24] 7305 4-9-6 **66**.............................. PaulMulrennan 9 53
(Phillip Makin) hld up on nr side of chsng gp: drvn along over 2f out: wknd over 1f out **15/2**[2]

0263 **9** ¾ **Straight Ash (IRE)**[17] 7542 4-8-11 **60**.............................. HarrisonShaw(3) 5 45
(Ollie Pears) cl up towards far side of chsng gp: drvn over 2f out: sn outpcd: btn over 1f out **33/1**

0616 **10** 4 **So Macho (IRE)**[24] 7310 4-9-4 **64**.............................. SamJames 1 40
(Grant Tuer) hld up on far side of chsng gp: rdn and hung lft wl over 1f out: sn wknd (jockey said gelding hung left throughout) **33/1**

0151 **11** 1 **Insurplus (IRE)**[14] 7652 6-9-11 **71**.............................. PaddyMathers 2 44
(Jim Goldie) hld up in centre of chsng gp: struggling 2f out: sn btn (trainer could offer no explanation for the gelding's performance; vet found the gelding to be lame left fore) **20/1**

0003 **12** 7 **Destroyer**[22] 7378 6-9-7 **67**.............................. JamesSullivan 10 24
(Tom Tate) led at str gallop and sn clr w one other: rdn and hdd over 1f out: wknd qckly **9/1**

3343 **13** 11 **Eesha's Smile (IRE)**[50] 6370 3-8-13 **65**..............(p) GabrieleMalune(3) 4
(Ivan Furtado) disp ld at str gallop and sn clr of rest: drvn over 2f out: wknd qckly over 1f out **25/1**

1m 40.04s (1.44) **Going Correction** +0.225s/f (Slow)
WFA 3 from 4yo+ 3lb 13 Ran SP% **120.1**
Speed ratings (Par 103): **101,99,98,95,95 91,90,90,89,85 84,77,66**
CSF £9.57 CT £111.44 TOTE £3.90: £1.40, £1.50, £4.80; EX 16.70 Trifecta £142.50.
Owner G R Leckie **Bred** G L S Partnership **Trained** Carluke, S Lanarks

FOCUS
An ordinary handicap. One of the joint-favourites won well in a notably quicker time than the previous C&D maiden. The winner is rated better than ever.
T/Plt: £149.20 to a £1 stake. Pool: £68,286.14 - 333.93 winning units. T/Qpdt: £41.80 to a £1 stake. Pool: £8,418.06 - 148.80 winning units. **Richard Young**

7895 NEWMARKET (R-H)

Friday, October 11

OFFICIAL GOING: Good to soft (6.4)
Wind: strong, half behind Weather: overcast, windy

8088 NEWMARKET ACADEMY GODOLPHIN BEACON PROJECT CORNWALLIS STKS (GROUP 3) 5f

1:50 (1:51) (Class 1) 2-Y-O

£34,026 (£12,900; £6,456; £3,216; £1,614; £810) **Stalls Low**

Form RPR

5036 **1** **Good Vibes**[36] 6907 2-8-12 **101**.............................. RichardKingscote 3 104
(David Evans) taken down early and led to s: stdd s: t.k.h: hdwy to chse ldr over 3f out: effrt and ev ch ent fnl 2f: led jst ins fnl f: hld on wl (trainer said, regarding the improved form shown, the filly benefited from the drop in trip to 5f from 6f and the Good to Soft going) **12/1**

6664 **2** nk **Pistoletto (USA)**[18] 7532 2-9-1 **95**.............................. RyanMoore 8 106
(A P O'Brien, Ire) looked wl; chsd ldrs: effrt to press ldrs 2f out: ev ch over 1f out: kpt on u.p but hld wl ins fnl f **12/1**

6145 **3** ½ **Jouska**[36] 6907 2-8-12 **89**.............................. ShaneFoley 12 101
(Henry Candy) sltly on toes; hld up in rr: rdn over 2f out: stl last 1f out: hdwy ins fnl f: styd on strly fnl 100yds: nt rch ldrs **20/1**

5260 **4** ¾ **Kemble (IRE)**[36] 6907 2-8-12 **91**.............................. SeanLevey 4 98
(Richard Hannon) led: rdn ent fnl 2f: drvn and hdd jst ins fnl f: no ex and one pce fnl 100yds **50/1**

611 **5** nse **Golden Dragon (IRE)**[48] 6464 2-9-1 **89**.............................. JamesDoyle 6 101
(Stuart Williams) str; chsd ldr for over 1f out: effrt and ev ch 2f out: jst getting outpcd whn sltly impeded ins fnl f: kpt on same pce towards fin **16/1**

0134 **6** nk **Flaming Princess (IRE)**[28] 7149 2-8-12 **98**................. BarryMcHugh 11 97
(Richard Fahey) hld up in tch in last trio: effrt and hung lft over 1f out: kpt on ins fnl f: nt rch ldrs **12/1**

2251 **7** ¾ **Platinum Star (IRE)**[46] 6542 2-9-1 **106**.............................. OisinMurphy 7 97
(Saeed bin Suroor) hld up in tch in midfield: effrt 2f out: sme hdwy u.p 1f out: no imp ins fnl f: wknd towards fin **5/4**[1]

11 **8** hd **Lazuli (IRE)**[30] 7071 2-9-1 **100**.............................. WilliamBuick 10 97
(Charlie Appleby) str; hld up in tch in last trio: effrt over 1f out: sme hdwy u.p 1f out: sn no imp: wknd wl ins fnl f **5/1**[2]

1030 **9** 1¼ **Flippa The Strippa (IRE)**[50] 6374 2-8-12 **94**.......... KieranShoemark 1 89
(Charles Hills) in tch in midfield: effrt on far side over 1f out: no imp 1f out: wknd ins fnl f **33/1**

1 **10** ¾ **Jamaheery (IRE)**[22] 7393 2-8-12 **0**.............................. JimCrowley 13 87
(Richard Hannon) hld up in tch in midfield: effrt ent fnl 2f: no ex u.p 1f out: wknd ins fnl f **8/1**[3]

1R03 **11** 1 **Ickworth (IRE)**[21] 7400 2-8-12 **97**.............................. WJLee 9 83
(W McCreery, Ire) in tch in midfield: effrt u.p jst over 1f out: sn no imp and losing pl whn short of room ins fnl f: wknd fnl 100yds **16/1**

2221 **12** ½ **Poets Dance**[36] 6899 2-8-12 **78**.............................. SilvestreDeSousa 2 81
(Rae Guest) t.k.h: chsd ldrs: effrt 2f out: unable qck and lost pl over 1f out: wknd ins fnl f **33/1**

59.27s (0.17) **Going Correction** +0.075s/f (Good) 12 Ran SP% **119.7**
Speed ratings (Par 105): **101,100,99,98,98 97,96,96,94,93 91,90**
CSF £143.36 TOTE £16.90: £3.90, £3.40, £5.90; EX 179.10 Trifecta £3620.00.
Owner Paul & Clare Rooney **Bred** Whitsbury Manor Stud **Trained** Pandy, Monmouths

FOCUS
Stands'-side course used. Stalls Far-side except 1m2f: centre. Good to soft going (GoingStick 6.4) for this high-class card. Richard Kingscote described the ground as "dead" after winning the opener, and Joe Fanning felt it was "loose" in the second. There was quite a stiff crosswind too. Something of a compressed finish to this sprinting Group 3, in which most of the principals raced prominently, and it rates a fairly ordinary renewal. The time was only 1.77sec outside the standard.

8089 GODOLPHIN LIFETIME CARE OH SO SHARP STKS (GROUP 3) (FILLIES) 7f

2:25 (2:25) (Class 1) 2-Y-O

£34,026 (£12,900; £6,456; £3,216; £1,614; £810) **Stalls Low**

Form RPR

1341 **1** **Rose Of Kildare (IRE)**[20] 7432 2-9-3 **99**.............................. JoeFanning 1 104
(Mark Johnston) chsd ldrs: effrt and shkn up to chal 2f out: drvn to ld ent fnl f: edgd lft and hld on gamely ins fnl f: all out **12/1**

2 nk **Valeria Messalina (IRE)**[23] 7357 2-9-0 **0**.............................. ShaneFoley 9 100+
(Mrs John Harrington, Ire) unfurnished; in tch in midfield: effrt and clsd to chse ldrs over 1f out: hung rt and wnt 2nd ins fnl f: ev ch fnl 100yds: kpt on but hld towards fin **9/1**

0012 **3** nk **Separate**[13] 7696 2-9-0 **95**..............................(b) SeanLevey 7 100
(Richard Hannon) hld up in tch in last trio: effrt 2f out: clsd to chse ldrs and swtchd rt ent fnl f: hdwy u.p and ev ch wl ins fnl f: kpt on **8/1**

5 **4** hd **Nope (IRE)**[12] 7742 2-9-0 **92**.............................. WJLee 8 99+
(Mrs John Harrington, Ire) compact; hld up in tch in rr: effrt over 1f out: clsd u.p and pressed ldrs 100yds out: kpt on but nvr quite getting to ldrs **16/1**

611 **5** *1 3/4* **Belle Anglaise**[17] 7547 2-9-0 80 .... RichardKingscote 4 95
(Stuart Williams) *athletic; in tch in midfield: clsd to press ldrs 2f out: sn rdn: jst getting outpcd whn carried rt ins fnl f: wknd towards fin* **50/1**

133 **6** *2 1/2* **Final Song (IRE)**[91] 4883 2-9-0 103 .... OisinMurphy 3 88
(Saeed bin Suroor) *looked wl; trckd ldrs and travelled strly: clsd to ld jst over 2f out: rdn and hdd ent fnl f: edgd rt and wknd ins fnl f* **2/1**[1]

2422 **7** *3 1/2* **Stylistique**[14] 7659 2-9-0 105 .... AndreaAtzeni 6 80
(Roger Varian) *dwlt: hld up in tch in rr: no hdwy u.p over 1f out: wknd ins fnl f (trainer said filly ran flat having had a busy season)* **7/2**[2]

15 **8** *8* **Wejdan (FR)**[50] 6374 2-9-0 0 .... JamesDoyle 2 60
(William Haggas) *led tl jst over 2f out: sn rdn and lost pl over 1f out: wknd fnl f (trainer could offer no explanation for the filly's performance)* **4/1**[3]

31 **9** *6* **Vividly**[71] 5588 2-9-0 0 .... KieranShoemark 5 45
(Charles Hills) *sltly on toes; pressed ldr tl over 2f out: sn rdn and lost pl: bhd and eased wl ins fnl f (vet said filly lost its right hind shoe)* **20/1**

1m 25.01s (-0.39) **Going Correction** +0.075s/f (Good) 9 Ran SP% **117.0**
Speed ratings (Par 102): **105,104,104,104,102 99,95,86,79**
CSF £115.67 TOTE £12.30: £3.10, £3.00, £2.40; EX 122.10 Trifecta £680.50.
Owner Kingsley Park 14 **Bred** Wansdyke Farms Ltd **Trained** Middleham Moor, N Yorks

FOCUS
Probably a modest edition of this Group 3, with necks and heads separating the first four. The leaders dropped away, suggesting that the early pace was quite strong. The form has been rated cautiously.

8090 GODOLPHIN STUD & STABLE STAFF AWARDS CHALLENGE STKS (GROUP 2) 7f
3:00 (3:01) (Class 1) 3-Y-O+ **£68,052** (£25,800; £12,912; £6,432; £3,228) **Stalls** Low

Form RPR

3105 **1** **Mustashry**[97] 4668 6-9-8 121 .... JimCrowley 5 122
(Sir Michael Stoute) *looked wl; mde virtually all: rdn and qcknd ent fnl 2f: styd on strly and a doing enough ins fnl f* **2/1**[2]

4106 **2** *1 1/4* **Limato (IRE)**[47] 6508 7-9-3 114 .... RyanMoore 1 114
(Henry Candy) *hld up in tch in last pair: effrt 2f out: chsd wnr over 1f out: kpt on but a hld ins fnl f* **4/1**[3]

2501 **3** *2 3/4* **Oh This Is Us (IRE)**[41] 6711 6-9-3 108 .... AndreaAtzeni 2 107
(Richard Hannon) *hld up in tch in last pair: effrt 2f out: chsd ldng pair 1f out: no imp and kpt on same pce ins fnl f* **12/1**

2040 **4** *4* **Solar Gold (IRE)**[28] 7146 4-9-0 98 .... JamesDoyle 4 93
(William Haggas) *chsd ldr: rdn ent fnl 2f: lost pl over 1f out: wknd ins fnl f* **11/1**

1614 **5** *2 3/4* **Shine So Bright**[27] 7194 3-9-4 115 .... SilvestreDeSousa 3 91
(Andrew Balding) *stdd s: t.k.h: sn chsng ldng pair: rdn ent fnl 2f: lost pl over 1f out: wknd ins fnl f (trainer's rep said colt was unsuited by the going and would prefer a quicker surface)* **6/4**[1]

1m 24.91s (-0.49) **Going Correction** +0.075s/f (Good)
WFA 3 from 4yo+ 2lb 5 Ran SP% **109.4**
Speed ratings (Par 115): **105,103,100,95,92**
CSF £10.04 TOTE £3.20: £1.80, £1.30; EX 10.40 Trifecta £48.60.
Owner Hamdan Al Maktoum **Bred** Shadwell Estate Company Limited **Trained** Newmarket, Suffolk

FOCUS
A smaller field than usual for this event, perhaps not helped by its proximity in the calendar to the Prix de la Foret. This could rate a pb from Mustashry, but he had the run of the race.

8091 BET365 FILLIES' MILE (GROUP 1) 1m
3:35 (3:40) (Class 1) 2-Y-O
£321,829 (£122,012; £61,063; £30,418; £15,265; £7,661) **Stalls** Low

Form RPR

11 **1** **Quadrilateral**[21] 7412 2-9-0 103 .... JasonWatson 5 115+
(Roger Charlton) *looked wl; in tch in midfield: effrt over 2f out: clsd u.p to chse ldrs and shifted rt jst over 1f out: chsd ldr ins fnl f: styd on wl u.p to ld towards fin* **9/4**[1]

11 **2** *hd* **Powerful Breeze**[29] 7120 2-9-0 105 .... JamesDoyle 9 114+
(Hugo Palmer) *unfurnished; scope; on toes; stdd s: t.k.h: hld up in tch in rr: hdwy to chse ldrs 3f out: rdn to ld and edgd rt over 1f out: hdd and no ex towards fin* **7/1**

151 **3** *1 1/2* **Love (IRE)**[26] 7244 2-9-0 110 .... RyanMoore 8 111
(A P O'Brien, Ire) *compact; wl in tch in midfield: clsd to ld narrowly 1/2-way: hdd 3f out but styd upsides ldr: unable qck and carried rt ent fnl f: 3rd and kpt on same pce fnl 100yds* **4/1**[3]

1 **4** *1 1/4* **Cayenne Pepper (IRE)**[42] 6689 2-9-0 109 .... ShaneFoley 3 108+
(Mrs John Harrington, Ire) *str; looked wl; chsd ldr: ev ch 1/2-way: rdn over 2f out: outpcd on downhill run over 1f out: sltly impeded ent fnl f: swtchd lft: rallied and kpt on ins fnl f: no threat to ldrs* **11/4**[2]

4112 **5** *nk* **Boomer**[29] 7120 2-9-0 102 .... RichardKingscote 6 108
(Tom Dascombe) *chsd ldrs tl upsides ldrs 1/2-way: led 3f out: rdn over 2f out: hdd over 1f out: hung rt: lost 2nd and btn ins fnl f: wknd towards fin* **10/1**

21 **6** *2 1/4* **Queen Daenerys (IRE)**[20] 7461 2-9-0 0 .... WilliamBuick 4 103+
(Roger Varian) *stdd s: hld up in tch in last trio: effrt over 2f out: sme hdwy over 1f out but nvr getting on terms: plugged on same pce ins fnl f* **16/1**

3155 **7** *7* **Ananya**[29] 7120 2-9-0 97 .... BrettDoyle 1 87
(Peter Chapple-Hyam) *tall; chsd ldrs tl lost pl 1/2-way: wknd over 1f out* **50/1**

41 **8** *7* **Anastarsia (IRE)**[16] 7579 2-9-0 0 .... FrankieDettori 7 72
(John Gosden) *t.k.h: hld up in tch in last trio: effrt over 2f out: sn btn and wknd over 1f out* **20/1**

1510 **9** *8* **West End Girl**[29] 7120 2-9-0 101 .... AdamKirby 2 54
(Mark Johnston) *led tl 1/2-way: sn lost pl: bhd fnl 2f* **33/1**

1m 37.75s (-0.65) **Going Correction** +0.075s/f (Good) 9 Ran SP% **114.6**
Speed ratings (Par 106): **106,105,104,103,102 100,93,86,78**
CSF £18.15 CT £59.58 TOTE £2.50: £1.30, £2.20, £1.40; EX 18.00 Trifecta £68.20.
Owner K Abdullah **Bred** Juddmonte Farms Ltd **Trained** Beckhampton, Wilts

FOCUS
This looked an up-to-scratch edition of this prestigious event, with the third and fourth decent guides. The previous four winners all went on to earn Group 1 honours at three.

8092 BET365 OLD ROWLEY CUP H'CAP (HERITAGE HANDICAP) 1m 4f
4:10 (4:16) (Class 2) 3-Y-O
£74,700 (£22,368; £11,184; £5,592; £2,796; £1,404) **Stalls** Centre

Form RPR

-112 **1** **Trueshan (FR)**[34] 6955 3-9-0 93 .... WilliamBuick 17 109
(Alan King) *wl in tch in midfield: clsd to press ldrs 3f out: upsides ldr over 2f out: rdn to ld wl over 1f out: styd on strly and drew clr ins fnl f: readily* **13/2**[1]

1120 **2** *3 3/4* **First In Line**[34] 6955 3-9-7 100 .... FrankieDettori 7 110
(John Gosden) *looked wl; hld up in midfield: swtchd lft and clsd 4f out: hdwy to chse ldrs 3f out: rdn to chse wnr over 1f out: no imp and btn 1f out: kpt on same pce* **7/1**[2]

0316 **3** *4* **Rhythmic Intent (IRE)**[34] 6952 3-8-5 84 .... HayleyTurner 19 88
(Stuart Williams) *looked wl; hld up in midfield: effrt over 3f out: edgd rt: sltly impeded and kpt on u.p over 1f out: wnt 3rd ins fnl f: no threat to ldng pair* **10/1**

2320 **4** *1 3/4* **The Trader (IRE)**[20] 7434 3-8-12 91 .... JoeFanning 8 92
(Mark Johnston) *chsd ldr early: chsd ldrs tl clsd to ld 3f out: rdn and hrd pressed over 2f out: hdd wl over 1f out: sn outpcd: wknd ins fnl f* **33/1**

3214 **5** *1* **Cardano (USA)**[22] 7396 3-8-5 89 ow1 .... ThomasGreatrex(5) 12 88
(Ian Williams) *hld up in midfield: effrt and hdwy to chse ldrs 3f out: unable qck and no imp whn edgd lft over 1f out: wknd ins fnl f* **50/1**

1411 **6** *1 3/4* **Derevo**[76] 5437 3-9-3 96 .... RyanMoore 9 92
(Sir Michael Stoute) *looked wl; hld up in midfield: effrt 3f out: no imp u.p and btn over 1f out: wknd ins fnl f* **8/1**[3]

1421 **7** *1/2* **Dreamweaver (IRE)**[24] 7301 3-8-3 82 .... NicolaCurrie 15 78
(Ed Walker) *hld up towards rr: effrt end fnl 3f: sme hdwy u.p over 2f out: no imp and btn whn edgd rt 1f out: wknd ins fnl f (jockey said gelding lugged left throughout)* **33/1**

114 **8** *nk* **Country**[41] 6725 3-9-0 93 .... JamesDoyle 10 88
(William Haggas) *compact; t.k.h: hld up in midfield: effrt over 2f out: no imp u.p over 1f out: wknd ins fnl f* **10/1**

3212 **9** *3/4* **Cape Cavalli (IRE)**[23] 7342 3-8-4 83 .... (b[1]) SilvestreDeSousa 13 77
(Simon Crisford) *stdd s: hld up in rr: swtchd lft and clsd over 2f out: no imp u.p and btn over 1f out: wknd fnl f* **12/1**

1321 **10** *shd* **Apparate**[34] 6952 3-9-0 93 .... AndreaAtzeni 18 87
(Roger Varian) *looked wl; wl in tch in midfield: clsd to chse ldrs 3f out: sn u.p: unable qck over 1f out: wknd fnl f* **12/1**

5414 **11** *4* **Skymax (GER)**[48] 6471 3-8-11 90 .... (b) RichardKingscote 14 77
(Ralph Beckett) *chsd ldrs tl led after over 1f: sn hdd and chsd ldr: rdn and ev ch 3f out: sn outpcd: wknd over 1f out* **11/1**

6122 **12** *1 1/4* **Natty Night**[24] 7302 3-7-9 79 oh2 .... RhiainIngram(5) 16 64
(William Muir) *chsd ldrs tl led after 2f: rdn and hdd jst over 3f out: outpcd over 2f out: wknd over 1f out* **25/1**

2032 **13** *8* **Sinjaari (IRE)**[36] 6895 3-9-3 96 .... OisinMurphy 11 69
(William Haggas) *hld up in last trio: effrt over 2f out: nvr threatened to get on terms: wl btn over 1f out: wknd (trainer said colt was never travelling)* **8/1**[3]

1230 **14** *13* **Kiefer**[48] 6471 3-8-9 88 ow1 .... CharlesBishop 5 40
(Eve Johnson Houghton) *hld up in midfield: rdn 4f out: sn lost pl and bhd: t.o* **9/1**

15 *hd* **Le Baol (FR)**[119] 3833 3-9-3 96 .... GeraldMosse 2 47
(Hughie Morrison) *t.k.h: led early: chsd ldrs: swtchd lft and clsd 4f out: rdn to ld jst over 3f out: sn hdd and lost pl qckly ent fnl 2f: eased over 1f out: t.o (jockey said colt ran too free)* **14/1**

2216 **16** *3* **Starfighter**[21] 7413 3-8-1 80 .... NickyMackay 1 27
(Ed Walker) *hld up in midfield: effrt 4f out: no imp and wl hld over 2f out: eased over 1f out: t.o* **33/1**

3302 **17** *13* **Power Of States (IRE)**[20] 7452 3-8-0 79 oh1 .... (bt) JimmyQuinn 3 5
(Hugo Palmer) *wl in tch in midfield: rdn over 3f out: sn struggling and wl bhd fnl 2f: eased: t.o* **50/1**

1062 **18** *5* **Babbo's Boy (IRE)**[16] 7574 3-8-10 89 .... JasonWatson 4 7
(Michael Bell) *hld up in midfield: swtchd lft and effrt over 3f out: no imp and wl btn 2f out: eased: t.o* **25/1**

221 **19** *9* **Battle of Paradise (USA)**[36] 6887 3-8-0 79 oh1 .... LukeMorris 6
(Sir Mark Prescott Bt) *str; stdd s: a towards rr: rdn over 4f out: sn btn: bhd and eased fnl 2f: t.o (trainer said gelding was never travelling)* **9/1**

2m 29.85s (-2.65) **Going Correction** +0.075s/f (Good) **19** Ran SP% **137.1**
Speed ratings (Par 107): **111,108,105,104,104 102,102,102,101,101 99,98,92,84,84 82,73,70,64**
CSF £52.63 CT £479.96 TOTE £7.40: £2.00, £1.80, £2.70, £7.40; EX 37.80 Trifecta £996.10.
Owner Barbury Lions 5 **Bred** Didier Blot **Trained** Barbury Castle, Wilts

FOCUS
Add 13yds to race distance. A classy and highly competitive handicap, which appeared to be soundly run. They finished nicely strung out and the form appears solid. Another clear pb from the winner and the form could rate higher.

8093 GODOLPHIN UNDER STARTERS ORDERS MAIDEN FILLIES' STKS (PLUS 10 RACE) 7f
4:45 (4:51) (Class 3) 2-Y-O **£6,469** (£1,925; £962; £481) **Stalls** Low

Form RPR

1 **Spring Of Love** 2-9-0 0 .... WilliamBuick 12 82+
(Charlie Appleby) *str; chsd ldrs and travelled strly: clsd to ld 2f out: rdn over 1f out: asserted but rn green and edgd rt 1f out: styd on wl* **5/1**[2]

2 *1 1/4* **Waliyak (FR)** 2-9-0 0 .... AndreaAtzeni 4 77+
(Roger Varian) *str; t.k.h: chsd ldrs: stuck bhd and wall of horses and swtchd lft 2f out: rdn and kpt on wl ins fnl f: chsd wnr 50yds out: no imp* **5/2**[1]

03 **3** *3/4* **Rhyme Scheme (IRE)**[27] 7203 2-9-0 0 .... GeraldMosse 8 75
(Mick Channon) *unfurnished; chsd ldrs: clsd and upsides ldrs over 2f out: rdn over 1f out: unable to match pce of wnr 1f out: kpt on same pce ins fnl f* **25/1**

4 *1/2* **Elfin Queen (USA)**[23] 7353 2-9-0 0 .... RyanMoore 3 74
(A P O'Brien, Ire) *athletic; chsd ldr: rdn and ev ch over 2f out: unable to match pce of wnr 1f out: chsd wnr but no imp ins fnl f: one pce and lost 2 pls fnl 50yds* **7/1**

5 *2* **Sparkling Olly (IRE)** 2-9-0 0 .... HayleyTurner 10 69+
(Michael Bell) *unfurnished; in tch in midfield: clsd and effrt 2f out: unable qck: rn green and hung rt over 1f out: kpt on same pce ins fnl f* **33/1**

6 *1/2* **Beauty Stone (IRE)** 2-9-0 0 .... JamesDoyle 7 68+
(Charlie Appleby) *ly; looked wl; chsd ldrs: effrt ent fnl 2f: rn green and outpcd in dip over 1f out: kpt on same pce fnl f* **13/2**[3]

7 *2* **Ragtime Sally** 2-9-0 0 .... JasonWatson 6 63
(Harry Dunlop) *workmanlike; sltly unfurnished; led: hdd 2f: rdn and struggling to qckn whn squeezed for room jst over 1f out: wknd ins fnl f* **66/1**

0 **8** *1* **Greek Oasis**[22] 7393 2-9-0 0 .... GeorgeWood 17 60+
(Chris Wall) *str; hld up in tch in midfield: effrt jst over 2f out: unable qck and outpcd over 1f out: wknd ins fnl f* **66/1**

9 *nk* **Make It Rain (IRE)** 2-9-0 0 .... SilvestreDeSousa 14 59+
(Simon Crisford) *compact; stdd s: hld up in tch: effrt 2f out: no imp and edgd rt over 1f out: nvr threatened ldrs* **8/1**

10 2 **Katara (FR)** 2-9-0 0........................ RichardKingscote 5 54+
(Sir Michael Stoute) *athletic; s.i.s and stmbld bdly leaving stalls: a towards rr: outpcd over 2f out: no ch after (jockey said filly stumbled leaving the stalls)* **17/2**

5 11 3/4 **Summer Valley**[44] 6603 2-9-0 0........................ ShaneKelly 13 52
(Gary Moore) *str; hld up in tch: effrt over 2f out: sn outpcd and wknd over 1f out* **66/1**

12 3 1/4 **Echo's Love (IRE)** 2-9-0 0........................ NickyMackay 2 44
(John Gosden) *compact; in tch in midfield: effrt over 2f out: sn struggling and btn over 1f out: wknd fnl f* **12/1**

13 1 **Dramatica (IRE)** 2-9-0 0........................ OisinMurphy 9 42+
(Stuart Williams) *str; hld up in tch: pushed along and outpcd over 2f out: wl btn over 1f out* **13/2[3]**

06 14 10 **Lovers' Gait (IRE)**[27] 7203 2-9-0 0........................(h[1]) EdwardGreatrex 11 17
(Ed Dunlop) *compact; hld up towards rr: struggling whn impeded over 2f out: sn wl bhd (vet said filly lost its left hind shoe)* **66/1**

15 1/2 **Some Picture (IRE)** 2-9-0 0........................ StevieDonohoe 16 16
(Mick Channon) *compact; t.k.h: hld up in rr: hung lft and lost tch 3f out* **66/1**

16 1 1/4 **Fryerns** 2-9-0 0........................(h[1]) DanielMuscutt 1
(George Scott) *str; awkward and veered rt leaving stalls: a in rr: lost tch wl over 2f out (jockey said filly was slowly away)* **50/1**

1m 26.52s (1.12) **Going Correction** +0.075s/f (Good) **16 Ran SP% 129.9**
Speed ratings (Par 96): **96,94,93,93,90 90,88,86,86,84 83,79,78,67,66 65**
CSF £18.42 TOTE £5.20: £2.10, £1.40, £6.50; EX 26.30 Trifecta £432.10.
Owner Godolphin **Bred** Godolphin **Trained** Newmarket, Suffolk

FOCUS
Probably fairly useful maiden form. The time was a second and a half slower than that of the Oh So Sharp Stakes.

8094 DARLEY PRIDE STKS (GROUP 3) (F&M) 1m 2f
5:20 (5:24) (Class 1) 3-Y-O+
£34,026 (£12,900; £6,456; £3,216; £1,614; £810) **Stalls Low**

Form RPR

0111 1 **Fanny Logan (IRE)**[23] 7347 3-8-13 106........................(h) FrankieDettori 3 108+
(John Gosden) *hld up in midfield: clsd 1/2-way: effrt to chse ldng trio over 2f out: rdn and pressing ldrs 1f out: led wl ins fnl f: sn in command and eased cl home* **4/5[1]**

22 2 1 **Queen (FR)**[20] 7478 3-8-13 101........................ TheoBachelot 8 106
(Mme Pia Brandt, France) *str; looked wl; t.k.h: chsd ldrs: effrt over 2f out: ev ch u.p over 1f out: led ins fnl f: hdd and one pce wl ins fnl f* **7/1[3]**

2252 3 1/2 **Simply Beautiful (IRE)**[14] 7658 3-8-13 103........................ RyanMoore 7 105
(A P O'Brien, Ire) *pressed ldr: rdn and ev ch over 2f out tl no ex and one pce fnl 100yds* **5/1[2]**

3035 4 nk **Trethias**[26] 7242 3-8-13 103........................(p[1]) ShaneFoley 6 104
(Mrs John Harrington, Ire) *led: rdn ent fnl 2f: hdd ins fnl f: no ex and one pce fnl 100yds* **14/1**

6203 5 10 **Tipitena**[15] 7635 4-9-3 100........................ WJLee 4 83
(W McCreery, Ire) *stdd s: hld up in last trio: effrt over 2f out: sn outpcd: modest 5th over 1f out: wknd ins fnl f* **25/1**

4645 6 8 **Exhort**[14] 7657 4-9-3 100........................ JamesDoyle 2 67
(Richard Fahey) *s.i.s: hld up in rr: effrt over 2f out: sn struggling and wl btn over 1f out: wknd fnl f* **18/1**

1-10 7 1 1/4 **Tamniah (FR)**[26] 7252 3-9-2 100........................ OisinMurphy 5 69
(A Fabre, France) *compact; t.k.h: chsd ldrs tl over 2f out: sn btn and wknd over 1f out* **11/1**

1213 8 10 **Sweet Promise**[40] 6775 3-8-13 101........................ GeorgeWood 1 46
(James Fanshawe) *t.k.h: hld up in midfield: effrt over 2f out: sn struggling: wl btn over 1f out: wknd* **11/1**

2m 3.68s (-1.72) **Going Correction** +0.075s/f (Good) **8 Ran SP% 117.2**
WFA 3 from 4yo 4lb
Speed ratings (Par 113): **109,108,107,107,99 93,92,84**
CSF £7.35 TOTE £1.60: £1.10, £2.10, £1.40; EX 6.60 Trifecta £29.80.
Owner HH Sheikha Al Jalila Racing **Bred** Godolphin **Trained** Newmarket, Suffolk

FOCUS
Not many really figured in what looked to be quite a weak Group 3. It's rated around the second, third and fourth. Only three of the field were British-trained.
T/Jkpt: Not won. T/Plt: £2494.10 to a £1 stake. Pool: £121052.26 - 35.43 winning units. T/Qpdt: £13.20 to a £1 stake. Pool: £16628.78 - 928.68 winning units. **Steve Payne**

6997 YORK (L-H)
Friday, October 11

OFFICIAL GOING: Soft (6.1)
Wind: Fresh across Weather: Cloudy

8095 TSG AND BREWIN DOLPHIN NURSERY H'CAP 5f 89y
2:00 (2:01) (Class 3) (0-95,88) 2-Y-O **£9,703** (£2,887; £1,443; £721) **Stalls High**

Form RPR

4232 1 **Ainsdale**[27] 7182 2-8-8 75........................ BenCurtis 3 90+
(K R Burke) *wnt lft s: sn in tch: hdwy on outer over 2f out: chal wl over 1f out: rdn to ld jst ins fnl f: sn clr: kpt on strly* **6/1[1]**

2200 2 4 **Vardon Flyer**[51] 6356 2-8-10 77........................ NathanEvans 1 79
(Michael Easterby) *cl up: led over 2f out: jnd and rdn wl over 1f out: drvn and hdd jst ins fnl f: kpt on* **6/1[1]**

2234 3 1 1/2 **Cruising**[51] 6337 2-8-5 72........................(h[1]) CamHardie 7 69
(David Brown) *in tch: pushed along 1/2-way: n.m.r and checked sltly over 2f out: sn rdn: styd on wl fnl f* **25/1**

011 4 nk **Romantic Vision (IRE)**[20] 7437 2-9-2 83........................ DanielTudhope 4 79
(Kevin Ryan) *cl up: rdn along 2f out: drvn over 1f out: kpt on same pce* **15/2[3]**

1201 5 3/4 **Singe Anglais (IRE)**[30] 7064 2-8-0 72........................ FayeMcManoman(5) 6 66+
(Nigel Tinkler) *sn outpcd and bhd: rdn along and detached bef 1/2-way: swtchd rt to stands' rail and hdwy 2f out: styd on u.p fnl f: nrst fin* **14/1**

2341 6 1 **Clan Royale**[33] 6997 2-9-6 87........................(b) DavidEgan 5 78
(Roger Varian) *cl up: led over 4f out: pushed along and hdd over 2f out: sn rdn and kpt on same pce* **7/1[2]**

4212 7 2 1/4 **Music Therapist (IRE)**[10] 7785 2-8-10 77........................ HarryBentley 8 60
(George Scott) *dwlt and towards rr: hdwy into midfield over 3f out: swtchd lft to outer and hdwy to chse ldrs wl over 1f out: sn rdn and no imp* **12/1**

1323 8 1/2 **What A Business (IRE)**[9] 7827 2-8-3 75........................ PaulaMuir(5) 15 57+
(Roger Fell) *chsd ldrs: rdn along over 2f out: sn drvn and grad wknd* **8/1**

012 9 2 **Reassure**[23] 7333 2-8-10 77........................ TomMarquand 11 52+
(William Haggas) *slt ld early: hdd over 4f out: cl up: rdn along wl over 2f out: sn wknd* **16/1**

1040 10 1 1/2 **Vintage Times**[6] 7904 2-8-9 76........................ DavidAllan 14 47
(Tim Easterby) *hld up: hdwy over 2f out: rdn along wl over 1f out: n.d* **8/1**

3000 11 1 1/2 **Coastal Mist (IRE)**[26] 7247 2-8-7 74........................ AndrewMullen 12 40
(John Quinn) *a towards rr* **25/1**

1105 12 6 **Pop Dancer (IRE)**[13] 7679 2-9-7 88........................ TonyHamilton 10 35
(Richard Fahey) *dwlt: a in rr (jockey said colt reared as the stalls opened and was slowly away)* **20/1**

4311 13 6 **Stone Soldier**[13] 7679 2-9-4 85........................ TomEaves 13 12+
(James Given) *chsd ldrs: rdn along and lost pl 1/2-way: sn bhd (trainer could offer no explanation for the colt's performance)* **10/1**

023 14 3 1/2 **Dazzling Des (IRE)**[22] 7369 2-9-0 81........................(p[1]) DavidProbert 9
(David O'Meara) *chsd ldrs: rdn along wl over 2f out: sn wknd* **40/1**

1m 7.52s (3.92) **Going Correction** +0.775s/f (Yiel) **14 Ran SP% 119.3**
Speed ratings (Par 99): **99,92,90,89,88 86,83,82,79,76 74,64,55,49**
CSF £38.07 CT £849.67 TOTE £6.30: £2.30, £2.50, £7.20; EX 40.60 Trifecta £1481.80.
Owner David W Armstrong **Bred** Highfield Farm Llp **Trained** Middleham Moor, N Yorks

FOCUS
The rail around home bend from 9f to entrance to the home straight was moved out 6m. After riding in the opener Cam Hardie and Nathan Evans called the ground soft, while Ben Curtis said: "It's soft to heavy".\n\x\x This fair nursery proved hard work with runners kicking up the turf and the first pair dominated the finish. Low numbers did notably best.

8096 RACEBETS MONEY BACK 2ND 3RD 4TH H'CAP 7f 192y
2:40 (2:40) (Class 2) (0-100,100) 4-Y-O+
£15,562 (£4,660; £2,330; £1,165; £582; £292) **Stalls Low**

Form RPR

U36F 1 **Crownthorpe**[50] 6376 4-8-9 91........................ SeanDavis(3) 4 101
(Richard Fahey) *hld up in tch: effrt over 2f out: rdn to ld over 1f out: clr ins fnl f: kpt on strly* **12/1**

4546 2 2 1/4 **Firmament**[13] 7697 7-9-4 97........................(p) DanielTudhope 12 102
(David O'Meara) *hld up in midfield: stdy hdwy whn checked over 2f out: sn rdn: effrt over 1f out: chsd (clr) wnr ins fnl f: r.o* **6/1[2]**

4331 3 nk **Alemaratalyoum (IRE)**[16] 7563 5-8-13 97........................(t) MarcoGhiani(5) 3 101
(Stuart Williams) *t.k.h: chsd ldr: gng easily over 2f out: effrt and rdn over 1f out: disp 2nd ins fnl f: no ex towards fin* **4/1[1]**

1051 4 1 1/2 **King's Pavilion (IRE)**[7] 7865 6-8-13 92 5ex........................ TomEaves 2 93
(Jason Ward) *led: rdn over 2f out: hdd over 1f out: no ex and lost two pls ins fnl f* **14/1**

0041 5 1/2 **Waarif (IRE)**[20] 7430 6-9-4 97........................ RobbieDowney 15 97
(David O'Meara) *dwlt: hld up: stdy hdwy 3f out: rdn 2f out: kpt on ins fnl f: nt pce to chal* **9/1**

0016 6 nk **Young Fire (FR)**[10] 7781 4-8-10 89........................ HarryBentley 13 88
(David O'Meara) *hld up: stdy hdwy over 2f out: rdn wl over 1f out: kpt on same pce ins fnl f* **14/1**

310 7 1/2 **Hortzadar**[42] 6693 4-9-1 94........................ DavidNolan 16 92
(David O'Meara) *hld up in tch: effrt and drvn along over 2f out: no ex fr over 1f out* **9/1**

0-0P 8 nk **Humbert (IRE)**[181] 1753 5-9-3 96........................(p) DavidProbert 9 93
(David O'Meara) *trckd ldrs: drvn along over 2f out: fdd over 1f out* **40/1**

0226 9 2 3/4 **Donncha (IRE)**[18] 7517 8-8-3 87........................ RayDawson(5) 1 78
(Seb Spencer) *hld up on ins: drvn along 3f out: no imp fr 2f out* **8/1[3]**

5510 10 6 **Wahoo**[20] 7435 4-8-9 88........................ AndrewMullen 8 65
(Michael Dods) *t.k.h: prom: rdn and edgd rt over 2f out: wknd wl over 1f out* **25/1**

5020 11 1 1/4 **Gulf Of Poets**[20] 7430 7-8-11 90........................ NathanEvans 6 64
(Michael Easterby) *hld up: drvn and struggling 3f out: sn btn* **20/1**

500 12 1 **Zap**[27] 7188 4-8-7 86........................ PaulHanagan 14 58
(Richard Fahey) *hld up: rdn over 3f out: nvr on terms* **14/1**

4205 13 2 1/4 **Alfred Richardson**[20] 7430 5-8-8 87........................ HollieDoyle 11 54
(John Davies) *towards rr: drvn along 4f out: sn struggling* **14/1**

3146 14 3 1/2 **Mikmak**[30] 7068 6-8-7 86 oh1........................(p) DuranFentiman 5 44
(Tim Easterby) *hld up: rdn along 3f out: sn btn* **14/1**

50 15 7 **Sanaadh**[34] 6950 6-8-12 91........................(t) FrannyNorton 7 33
(Michael Wigham) *hld up: rdn over 3f out: sn wknd* **22/1**

1m 42.53s (5.03) **Going Correction** +0.775s/f (Yiel) **15 Ran SP% 121.8**
Speed ratings (Par 109): **105,102,102,100,100 100,99,99,96,90 89,88,86,82,75**
CSF £78.94 CT £354.96 TOTE £13.80: £4.30, £1.80, £2.70; EX 100.70 Trifecta £1225.00.
Owner Richard Fahey Ebor Racing Club Ltd **Bred** Mrs Sheila Oakes **Trained** Musley Bank, N Yorks

FOCUS
It proved hard to make up significant ground in this decent handicap, but it's solid form nevertheless. The winner is rated better than ever. Add 17yds.

8097 MORAG'S 10 YEARS AT RACING TO SCHOOL EBF NOVICE STKS (PLUS 10 RACE) 5f
3:15 (3:17) (Class 3) 2-Y-O **£9,703** (£2,887; £1,443; £721) **Stalls High**

Form RPR

3 1 **Art Power (IRE)**[35] 6943 2-9-2 0........................ DavidAllan 5 93+
(Tim Easterby) *trckd ldng pair: smooth hdwy and cl up 2f out: led over 1f out: sn rdn and qcknd clr: readily* **9/1**

2 5 **Minhaaj (IRE)** 2-8-11 0........................ DaneO'Neill 4 71+
(William Haggas) *rn green: outpcd and bhd: hdwy over 2f out: swtchd rt towards stands' rail and rdn wl over 1f out: styd on strly fnl f* **14/1**

2 3 nk **The Bell Conductor (IRE)**[130] 3411 2-9-2 0........................ BenCurtis 1 71+
(Phillip Makin) *racd wd: led: pushed along and jnd 2f out: sn rdn: hdd over 1f out: kpt on same pce* **9/4[1]**

2413 4 4 **Strong Power (IRE)**[46] 6548 2-9-8 84........................ HarryBentley 3 63
(George Scott) *chsd ldrs: rdn along 2f out: kpt on same pce* **7/2[2]**

21 5 3 1/4 **Spirit Of The Sky**[9] 7825 2-9-3 0........................ TonyHamilton 7 47
(Richard Fahey) *in tch: rdn along over 2f out: sn no imp* **10/1**

210 6 3/4 **Abstemious**[49] 6422 2-9-8 90........................ TomEaves 2 49
(Kevin Ryan) *prom: rdn along over 2f out: sn wknd* **4/1[3]**

1 7 nk **Rosa (IRE)**[10] 7786 2-9-3 0........................ HollieDoyle 9 43+
(Archie Watson) *chsd ldrs: rdn along wl over 2f out: sn wknd* **8/1**

4 8 3 1/4 **Evora Knights**[22] 7386 2-9-2 0........................ NathanEvans 8 31+
(Michael Easterby) *a in rr* **66/1**

450 9 4 1/2 **Sam's Call**[15] 7619 2-8-11 69........................ GerO'Neill(5) 6 15+
(Michael Easterby) *a in rr (trainer's rep said colt was unsuited by the going and would prefer a quicker surface)* **25/1**

1m 1.52s (3.32) **Going Correction** +0.775s/f (Yiel) **9 Ran SP% 115.2**
Speed ratings (Par 99): **104,96,95,89,83 82,82,77,69**
CSF £124.83 TOTE £9.70: £2.30, £3.90, £1.30; EX 128.60 Trifecta £324.30.
Owner King Power Racing Co Ltd **Bred** Owenstown Bloodstock Ltd **Trained** Great Habton, N Yorks

The Form Book Flat 2019, Raceform Ltd, Newbury, RG14 5SJ

FOCUS
This was a good-quality novice event for 2yos, but the ground played a big part in stringing out the field. The winner looks useful.

8098 RACEBETS H'CAP — 1m 5f 188y
3:50 (3:52) (Class 2) 3-Y-O

£62,250 (£18,640; £9,320; £4,660; £2,330; £1,170) Stalls Low

Form RPR

2131 1 **Hamish**[48] 6471 3-9-7 98 .... DanielTudhope 9 114+
(William Haggas) *hld up in midfield: smooth hdwy to ld over 2f out: shkn up and qcknd clr over 1f out: eased last 150yds: impressive* **13/8**[1]

-613 2 2 ¾ **Elysian Flame**[34] 6955 3-8-12 89 ....(b[1]) NathanEvans 8 95
(Michael Easterby) *hld up: rdn over 3f out: hdwy over 2f out: chsd (clr) wnr ins fnl f: no imp* **9/1**[3]

2501 3 2 ¼ **Holy Kingdom (IRE)**[13] 7689 3-8-2 82 .... SeanDavis(3) 5 84
(Tom Clover) *trckd ldrs: smooth hdwy to ld briefly over 2f out: chsd wnr tl ins fnl f: no ex* **33/1**

1130 4 1 ¼ **Future Investment**[72] 5541 3-8-12 89 .... BenCurtis 2 89
(Ralph Beckett) *prom: hdwy and ev ch briefly over 2f out: disp 2nd tl ins fnl f: no ex* **7/1**[2]

1150 5 hd **Jackamundo (FR)**[34] 6955 3-8-2 79 .... CamHardie 3 79
(Declan Carroll) *hld up: hdwy and in tch over 2f out: sn rdn: no imp fr over 1f out* **25/1**

1114 6 2 ¼ **Moon King (FR)**[34] 6955 3-9-0 91 .... HarryBentley 12 87
(Ralph Beckett) *hld up on outside: rdn over 3f out: hdwy and in tch over 2f out: wknd over 1f out* **7/1**[2]

4132 7 3 ¾ **Space Walk**[62] 5943 3-8-5 82 ....(t) MartinDwyer 6 72
(William Haggas) *s.i.s: t.k.h in rr: effrt and drvn over 2f out: no further imp over 1f out: wknd fnl f* **16/1**

1555 8 2 **Mondain**[34] 6955 3-8-10 87 .... JasonHart 10 74
(Mark Johnston) *led: rdn and hdd over 2f out: wknd over 1f out* **33/1**

3162 9 3 **Fox Vardy (USA)**[49] 6411 3-8-6 83 .... DavidProbert 18 65
(Martyn Meade) *hld up in tch on outside: drvn and outpcd over 2f out: n.d after (jockey said colt hung left-handed throughout)* **10/1**

5042 10 ½ **Kosciuszko (IRE)**[20] 7459 3-8-11 88 .... RobertHavlin 11 70
(John Gosden) *s.i.s: hld up: rdn and hdwy over 3f out: wknd wl over 1f out* **20/1**

3413 11 2 ¼ **Emirates Knight (IRE)**[16] 7574 3-8-11 88 .... DavidEgan 13 66
(Roger Varian) *hld up in tch: rdn over 3f out: wknd over 2f out* **40/1**

-221 12 2 ¾ **Navajo Pass**[51] 6340 3-8-8 85 .... GrahamLee 1 59
(Donald McCain) *t.k.h early: trckd ldrs: drvn along over 3f out: wknd fr 2f out* **10/1**

-541 13 5 **Art Of Diplomacy**[19] 7493 3-7-9 77 oh7 .... KieranSchofield(5) 15 43
(Michael Easterby) *s.i.s: hld up: drvn and struggling over 3f out: nvr on terms* **33/1**

5233 14 11 **Agravain**[27] 7209 3-8-0 77 oh8 .... JamesSullivan 14 25
(Tim Easterby) *t.k.h: hld up towards rr: struggling over 3f out: sn btn: t.o* **66/1**

0121 15 16 **Deal A Dollar**[24] 7302 3-9-6 97 ....(bt) LouisSteward 4 19
(Sir Michael Stoute) *midfield on ins: drvn and struggling over 3f out: sn wknd: t.o* **16/1**

1100 16 2 ¾ **Euro Implosion (IRE)**[20] 7441 3-8-0 80 oh2 ow3.. GabrieleMalune(3) 17
(Keith Dalgleish) *chsd ldr to over 3f out: sn lost pl and struggling: t.o* **50/1**

6321 17 1 ¾ **Mister Chiang**[15] 7631 3-8-7 84 ....(v) FrannyNorton 7
(Mark Johnston) *midfield on outside: hdwy to chse ldrs after 3f: drvn and lost pl over 3f out: sn struggling: t.o* **33/1**

3m 8.31s (8.11) **Going Correction** +0.775s/f (Yiel) **17 Ran SP% 129.3**
Speed ratings (Par 107): **107,105,104,103,103 102,99,98,97,96 95,93,91,84,75 74,73**
CSF £15.64 CT £394.79 TOTE £2.60: £1.30, £2.00, £5.70, £2.10; EX 20.30 Trifecta £372.00.
Owner B Haggas **Bred** J B Haggas **Trained** Newmarket, Suffolk

FOCUS
A classy 3yo staying handicap. It was run at a routine pace and proved one-way traffic from 2f out. The winner looks a Group horse, with the runner-up rated to form. Add 22yds.

8099 PARSONAGE HOTEL AND CLOISTERS SPA H'CAP — 5f
4:20 (4:24) (Class 3) (0-95,91) 3-Y-O+

£12,450 (£3,728; £1,864; £932; £466; £234) Stalls Centre

Form RPR

1122 1 **Moss Gill (IRE)**[48] 6476 3-9-6 90 .... PJMcDonald 5 105+
(James Bethell) *racd towards far side: trckd ldrs: swtchd rt and hdwy 2f out: rdn to ld ent fnl f: sn clr: readily* **7/2**[1]

1021 2 2 **Count D'orsay (IRE)**[13] 7700 3-9-5 89 .... DavidAllan 14 97+
(Tim Easterby) *hld up towards rr centre: hdwy wl over 1f out: rdn ent fnl f: kpt on wl: nt rch wnr* **20/1**

6100 3 2 ¼ **Orvar (IRE)**[27] 7193 6-9-7 91 .... DanielTudhope 17 90
(Paul Midgley) *racd towards centre: trckd ldrs and hdwy 2f out: rdn over 1f out: drvn and kpt on same pce fnl f* **16/1**

2441 4 hd **The Daley Express (IRE)**[11] 7771 5-9-6 90 5ex........ DavidProbert 12 88
(Ronald Harris) *racd centre: hld up: hdwy and n.m.r 1f out: nt clr run and hmpd over 1f out: rdn and styd on wl fnl f* **40/1**

2050 5 ½ **Savalas (IRE)**[20] 7431 4-9-3 87 ....(v) KevinStott 8 83
(Kevin Ryan) *slt ld centre: rdn along 2f out: sn hdd: cl up tl drvn and kpt on same pce fnl f* **25/1**

1302 6 1 ¼ **Only Spoofing (IRE)**[13] 7714 5-9-0 89 .... MarcoGhiani(5) 2 81
(Jedd O'Keeffe) *chsd ldrs towards far side: rdn along wl over 1f out: drvn and kpt on same pce fnl f* **8/1**[3]

602 7 ½ **Broken Spear**[13] 7700 3-8-12 87 ....(v) GeorgiaDobie(5) 20 78
(Tony Coyle) *towards rr: hdwy towards stands' side wl over 1f out: sn rdn: kpt on fnl f* **25/1**

1221 8 hd **Fantasy Keeper**[9] 7828 5-8-8 85 5ex .... AngusVilliers(7) 10 74+
(Michael Appleby) *racd centre: trckd ldrs early: sn pushed along: lost pl and towards rr 1/2-way: rdn 2f out and sn n.m.r: kpt on u.p fnl f* **8/1**[3]

0300 9 nk **Jawwaal**[20] 7431 4-9-3 87 ....(p) CallumRodriguez 4 75
(Michael Dods) *cl up towards far side: led 2f out: sn rdn: hdd and drvn ent fnl f: sn wknd* **5/1**[2]

0260 10 shd **Bossipop**[13] 7701 6-8-12 82 ....(b) CamHardie 11 70
(Tim Easterby) *chsd ldrs centre: rdn along 2f out: wkng whn hmpd wl over 1f out* **40/1**

0034 11 ¾ **Free Love**[18] 7524 3-8-12 87 .... TheodoreLadd(5) 21 73
(Michael Appleby) *nvr bttr than midfield* **66/1**

0211 12 1 **Music Society (IRE)**[21] 7402 4-9-2 86 .... PaulMulrennan 1 68
(Tim Easterby) *racd towards far side: chsd ldrs: rdn along 2f out: sn drvn and grad wknd* **5/1**[2]

0336 13 hd **Storm Over (IRE)**[117] 3883 5-9-4 88 .... TonyHamilton 22 69
(Phillip Makin) *a towards rr* **66/1**

220 14 shd **War Whisper (IRE)**[30] 7077 6-8-12 82 .... HarryBentley 9 63
(Paul Midgley) *in tch centre: rdn along and n.m.r 2f out: sn wknd* **25/1**

0060 15 1 **Dark Defender**[21] 7402 6-8-12 82 ....(b) PhilDennis 7 59
(Rebecca Bastiman) *a towards rr* **22/1**

0234 16 2 **Duke Of Firenze**[17] 7541 10-9-7 91 .... NathanEvans 16 61
(David C Griffiths) *a in rr* **25/1**

4412 17 shd **Holmeswood**[23] 7348 5-9-6 90 ....(p) KieranO'Neill 3 59
(Julie Camacho) *racd towards far side: in tch: rdn along over 2f out: sn wknd* **11/1**

020 18 nk **Lord Riddiford (IRE)**[18] 7524 4-9-6 90 .... JasonHart 18 58
(John Quinn) *racd towards stands' side: chsd ldrs: rdn along over 2f out: sn wknd* **40/1**

0140 19 1 ¾ **Merry Banter**[11] 7771 5-8-11 84 .... JaneElliott(3) 15 46
(Paul Midgley) *prom centre: rdn along 2f out: sn drvn: edgd lft and wknd* **66/1**

0362 20 2 ¼ **Dark Shot**[17] 7541 6-9-1 85 ....(p) PaddyMathers 19 39
(Scott Dixon) *racd towards stands' side: chsd ldrs: rdn along over 2f out: sn wknd* **25/1**

0005 21 nk **Foolaad**[34] 6960 8-9-7 91 ....(t) LewisEdmunds 13 44
(Roy Bowring) *a in rr* **25/1**

0060 22 1 ¾ **Harome (IRE)**[35] 6920 5-8-12 87 .... PaulaMuir(5) 6 34
(Roger Fell) *chsd ldrs towards far side: rdn along over 2f out: sn wknd (jockey said gelding hung right-handed throughout)* **40/1**

1m 1.25s (3.05) **Going Correction** +0.775s/f (Yiel) **22 Ran SP% 138.4**
Speed ratings (Par 107): **106,102,99,98,98 96,95,94,94,94 93,91,91,91,89 86,86,85,82,79 78,75**
CSF £82.89 CT £1082.14 TOTE £4.60: £1.50, £4.50, £4.60, £8.60; EX 63.80 Trifecta £1829.30.
Owner G Van Cutsem & Partner **Bred** Camas Park & Lynch Bages **Trained** Middleham Moor, N Yorks

FOCUS
Being drawn low was a big help in this decent sprint handicap, although it's hard to crab the form. The winner progressed again.

8100 ELEVATOR COMPANY EBF NOVICE AUCTION STKS (PLUS 10 RACE) — 7f 192y
4:55 (4:56) (Class 3) 2-Y-O

£9,703 (£2,887; £1,443; £721) Stalls Low

Form RPR

4203 1 **Sword Beach (IRE)**[20] 7473 2-9-3 84 .... TomMarquand 7 85
(Eve Johnson Houghton) *t.k.h: led 1f: trckd ldrs: effrt and disputing ld whn carried lft over 1f out: led ins fnl f: hld on wl u.p cl home* **4/1**[3]

42 2 hd **Arch Moon**[22] 7361 2-9-3 0 .... CallumRodriguez 10 85
(Michael Dods) *t.k.h: prom: rdn and outpcd over 1f out: edgd lft and rallied to press wnr wl ins fnl f: kpt on: jst hld* **10/3**[2]

2212 3 1 **Yoshimi (IRE)**[20] 7429 2-9-5 85 .... PaulHanagan 11 84
(Richard Fahey) *pressed ldr: rdn and led over 1f out: drifted lft and hdd ins fnl f: kpt on same pce towards fin (jockey said colt hung left-handed)* **7/4**[1]

4 1 **Bucephalus (GER)** 2-9-3 0 .... HectorCrouch 9 80+
(Ed Walker) *hld up on outside: effrt over 2f out: rdn and sltly outpcd over 1f out: edgd lft and rallied ins fnl f: kpt on fin* **25/1**

5 2 ¼ **Tenfold (IRE)** 2-8-13 0 .... DavidProbert 4 71
(Martyn Meade) *dwlt: t.k.h and led after 1f: rdn and hdd over 1f out: sn no ex* **8/1**

003 6 ½ **Violette Szabo (IRE)**[41] 6697 2-8-3 67 .... FayeMcManoman(5) 5 65
(Nigel Tinkler) *hld up in midfield: rdn over 2f out: outpcd fr over 1f out* **40/1**

7 ½ **La Foglietta** 2-8-12 0 .... HarryBentley 3 68
(Ralph Beckett) *missed break: hld up: rdn and hdwy over 2f out: no further imp over 1f out: btn fnl f* **10/1**

5 8 4 ½ **Sweet Reward (IRE)**[47] 6504 2-9-3 0 .... DanielTudhope 2 66+
(Jonathan Portman) *in tch: hdwy and ev ch over 2f out: rdn and wknd over 1f out: eased whn btn ins fnl f (jockey said colt stopped quickly; trainer's rep said colt is an immature type that got tired in the soft going)* **16/1**

6 9 20 **Puckle**[16] 7586 2-8-8 0 .... JamesSullivan 1 10
(Tim Easterby) *bhd: drvn along and outpcd 3f out: sn btn: t.o* **40/1**

0 10 1 ¼ **Fiannoglaigh (IRE)**[25] 7285 2-8-12 0 .... DavidAllan 8 11
(Rebecca Menzies) *hld up: rdn over 4f out: struggling fnl 3f: t.o* **66/1**

11 4 **Anno Maximo (GER)** 2-9-1 0 .... CallumShepherd 6 6
(Michael Bell) *rn green in rr: struggling 3f out: sn btn: t.o (jockey said colt ran green)* **40/1**

1m 45.75s (8.25) **Going Correction** +0.775s/f (Yiel) **11 Ran SP% 118.2**
Speed ratings (Par 99): **89,88,87,86,84 84,83,79,59,57 53**
CSF £17.18 TOTE £4.20: £1.50, £1.40, £1.20; EX 16.90 Trifecta £36.90.
Owner HP Racing Sword Beach **Bred** Colin Kennedy **Trained** Blewbury, Oxon

FOCUS
This was a fair novice event. Again the far side was the place to be in the home straight. The winner and third are rated back to their best. Add 17yds.

8101 IRISH THOROUGHBRED MARKETING H'CAP — 7f
5:30 (5:33) (Class 4) (0-85,85) 3-Y-O+

£9,962 (£2,964; £1,481; £740; £300; £300) Stalls Low

Form RPR

3225 1 **Hafeet Alain (IRE)**[123] 3654 3-9-0 80 .... ConnorBeasley 13 94
(Adrian Nicholls) *trckd ldrs: swtchd rt and hdwy to ld 2f out: rdn clr over 1f out: kpt on strly* **16/1**

0053 2 3 ¾ **Flying Pursuit**[13] 7701 6-9-7 85 ....(tp) RachelRichardson 15 90
(Tim Easterby) *chsd ldr: pushed along over 2f out: rdn wl over 1f out: kpt on same pce fnl f* **12/1**

030 3 1 **Captain Jameson (IRE)**[21] 7402 4-9-3 81 .... JasonHart 3 83
(John Quinn) *trckd ldrs: hdwy over 2f out: rdn over 1f out: styd on fnl f* **17/2**[3]

0044 4 ¾ **Dance Diva**[12] 7735 4-9-7 85 ....(v) PaulHanagan 1 85
(Richard Fahey) *trckd ldrs: hdwy over 2f out: rdn wl over 1f out: drvn and edgd lft ins fnl f: one pce after* **12/1**

0031 5 ½ **Jabalaly (IRE)**[18] 7519 3-9-1 81 ....(b) DaneO'Neill 6 79+
(Ed Dunlop) *towards rr: hdwy 2f out: sn rdn: kpt on fnl f* **9/1**

1106 6 1 ¼ **Mr Orange (IRE)**[15] 7621 6-9-0 78 ....(p) KieranO'Neill 5 74
(Paul Midgley) *midfield: rdn along and sltly outpcd over 3f out: kpt on fr over 1f out* **40/1**

0005 7 ½ **King Of Tonga (IRE)**[22] 7362 3-9-4 84 .... DanielTudhope 4 78
(David O'Meara) *in tch: hdwy to chse ldrs 2f out: rdn over 1f out: hld whn n.m.r and hmpd ins fnl f* **7/1**[1]

5453 8 hd **Tommy Taylor (USA)**[22] 7362 5-9-2 83 .... MeganNicholls(3) 20 77
(Kevin Ryan) *hld up: hdwy on wd outside over 2f out: rdn to chse ldrs wl over 1f out: sn drvn and btn* **15/2**[2]

6621 **9** 1 3/4 **Highly Sprung (IRE)**[15] 7621 6-9-3 **81**........................ LewisEdmunds 2 71
(Les Eyre) *chsd ldrs: rdn along over 2f out: sn drvn and grad wknd* **20/1**

6221 **10** 3/4 **Mogsy (IRE)**[20] 7442 3-9-0 **83**........................ JaneElliott(3) 10 70
(Tom Dascombe) *led: rdn along over 2f out: sn hdd & wknd (jockey said gelding ran too free)* **20/1**

3412 **11** nse **Sparklealot (IRE)**[22] 7362 3-9-5 **85**........................(p) DavidProbert 14 71
(Ivan Furtado) *chsd ldng pair: rdn along over 2f out: sn drvn and wknd* **7/1**[1]

2316 **12** shd **Lucky Louie**[29] 7121 6-9-0 **78**........................(p) RossaRyan 11 65
(Roger Teal) *wnt rt s: a towards rr* **12/1**

1352 **13** 2 **Hesslewood (IRE)**[111] 4107 3-9-4 **84**........................ PJMcDonald 8 65
(James Bethell) *a towards rr* **16/1**

1100 **14** 3/4 **Irv (IRE)**[24] 7312 3-9-4 **84**........................ JamesSullivan 17 63
(Micky Hammond) *a in rr* **40/1**

2150 **15** 3 1/4 **Twin Appeal (IRE)**[8] 7856 8-8-12 **79**........................ GemmaTutty(3) 7 51
(Karen Tutty) *in tch: rdn along over 2f out: sn wknd* **25/1**

544 **16** 1 **Balgair**[23] 7350 5-9-5 **83**........................ DavidEgan 19 52
(Tom Clover) *a in rr* **20/1**

0210 **17** nk **Queen's Sargent (FR)**[22] 7362 4-9-4 **82**........................ KevinStott 18 50
(Kevin Ryan) *in tch: hdwy on outer to chse ldrs 3f out: rdn along whn n.m.r over 2f out: sn wknd* **9/1**

0200 **18** 5 **James Watt (IRE)**[20] 7431 3-9-0 **83**........................ CameronNoble(3) 9 37
(Michael Bell) *a in rr* **40/1**

2-00 **19** 3/4 **Nordic Fire**[20] 7435 3-9-2 **82**........................ HarryBentley 12 34
(David O'Meara) *sltly hmpd and dwlt s: a in rr* **50/1**

1m 28.21s (3.61) **Going Correction** +0.775s/f (Yiel) **19** Ran SP% **129.5**
WFA 3 from 4yo+ 2lb
Speed ratings (Par 105): **110,105,104,103,103 101,101,100,98,98 98,97,95,94,91 89,89,83,82**
CSF £185.81 CT £1813.05 TOTE £21.60: £4.60, £3.00, £2.60, £3.20; EX 310.50 Trifecta £1691.40.
Owner Mohd Al Aassar **Bred** Miss Samantha Jarrom **Trained** Sessay, N Yorks

FOCUS
This looked ultra-competitive, but it paid to be handy and the going again caught out most. A clear pb from the winner.
T/Plt: £36.10 to a £1 stake. Pool: £112492.16 - 2274.20 winning units. T/Qpdt: £10.40 to a £1 stake. Pool: £10815.56 - 763.33 winning units. **Joe Rowntree & Richard Young**

8102 - 8109a (Foreign Racing) - See Raceform Interactive

8088
NEWMARKET (R-H)
Saturday, October 12

OFFICIAL GOING: Soft (ovr 5.6; stands' 5.4, ctr 5.6, far 5.7)
Wind: half behind Weather: OVERCAST

8110 DUBAI NURSERY H'CAP 7f
1:45 (1:46) (Class 2) 2-Y-O

£12,450 (£3,728; £1,864; £932; £466; £234) **Stalls** High

Form RPR

1115 **1** **Tomfre**[29] 7150 2-9-7 **90**........................ HarryBentley 6 96
(Ralph Beckett) *ly; looked wl; racd towards centre: stdd s: t.k.h: hld up in tch: effrt and hdwy over 2f out: rdn and chal over 1f out: led and edgd lft jst ins fnl f: hld on wl* **7/1**[3]

0U53 **2** 1/2 **Milltown Star**[16] 7612 2-9-4 **87**........................ RonanWhelan 12 92
(Mick Channon) *racd nr stands' rail: hld up in tch in last trio: clsd 3f out: rdn to ld and edgd rt over 1f out: hdd jst ins fnl f: kpt on wl but hld towards fin* **8/1**

3122 **3** 1/2 **Visible Charm (IRE)**[49] 6450 2-9-0 **83**........................ WilliamBuick 2 87
(Charlie Appleby) *looked wl; racd towards centre: wnt rt leaving stalls: hld up in tch in midfield: clsd and chal 2f out: maintained effrt and ev ch after: one pce and hld towards fin* **7/1**[3]

011 **4** 1 3/4 **Ascension**[36] 6943 2-9-4 **87**........................ RyanMoore 11 86
(Roger Varian) *str; racd towards centre: dwlt and short of room leaving stalls: hld up in tch in last trio: effrt over 2f out: n.m.r over 1f out: hdwy 1f out: styd on ins fnl f: no threat to ldrs* **3/1**[1]

6311 **5** 1/2 **Powertrain (IRE)**[29] 7140 2-9-4 **87**........................ OisinMurphy 10 85
(Hugo Palmer) *str; racd nr stands' rail: wnt lft leaving stalls: led gp and chsd ldrs overall: clsd to press ldrs 3f out: rdn and ev ch 2f out: no ex 1f out: wknd ins fnl f* **5/1**[2]

5351 **6** 1 3/4 **Old News**[20] 7495 2-9-3 **86**........................(p) ShaneKelly 9 80
(Richard Hughes) *racd nr stands' rail: wnt lft leaving stalls: in tch in midfield overall: effrt jst over 2f out: no imp and drifting rt over 1f out: wknd ins fnl f* **25/1**

3123 **7** nk **Be Prepared**[14] 7698 2-9-4 **87**........................ JackMitchell 8 80
(Simon Crisford) *compact; looked wl; racd towards centre: t.k.h: clsd to chse ldrs 2f out: sn rdn and unable qck over 1f out: wknd ins fnl f* **16/1**

0616 **8** 1 3/4 **Winning Streak**[14] 7679 2-8-10 **84**........................(t) MarcoGhiani(5) 7 72
(Stuart Williams) *racd towards centre: t.k.h: chsd overall ldr tl over 2f out: wnt lft and outpcd over 1f out: wknd ins fnl f* **20/1**

2106 **9** 1 3/4 **Ethic**[31] 7072 2-9-1 **84**........................ JamesDoyle 3 68
(William Haggas) *racd towards centre: chsd ldrs: clsd and rdn ent fnl 2f: unable qck and outpcd over 1f out: wknd ins fnl f* **16/1**

462 **10** 1 **Shoot To Kill (IRE)**[30] 7103 2-8-8 **77**........................ HayleyTurner 5 59
(George Scott) *racd towards centre: overall ldr: rdn wl over 1f out: hdd and edgd lft over 1f out: wknd ins fnl f* **20/1**

5121 **11** 1 1/4 **Bravo Faisal (IRE)**[31] 7072 2-9-1 **84**........................ FrankieDettori 13 62
(Richard Fahey) *compact; racd nr stands' rail: midfield: struggling over 2f out: wl hld over 1f out: wknd ins fnl f* **14/1**

0260 **12** 2 1/2 **What An Angel**[16] 7612 2-8-10 **79**........................ SeanLevey 1 51
(Richard Hannon) *racd towards centre: t.k.h: hld up in rr: effrt ent fnl 2f: no hdwy and wknd fnl f* **9/1**

1m 29.01s (3.61) **Going Correction** +0.50s/f (Yiel) **12** Ran SP% **119.6**
Speed ratings (Par 101): **99,98,97,95,95 93,92,90,88,87 86,83**
CSF £60.73 CT £417.91 TOTE £8.40: £2.40, £2.80, £2.70; EX 55.60 Trifecta £405.10.
Owner Mrs Philip Snow & Partners **Bred** Mrs P Snow & Partners **Trained** Kimpton, Hants

FOCUS
Stands' side course used. Stalls stands' side except 1m6f: far side. Race 5 increased by 13yds. A total 8mm of overnight rain ensured the going was downgraded to soft all over prior to the opener, the time of which suggested it was definitely the case. Unlike the previous day, there was minimal wind across the track. This was a good nursery in which the main action developed towards the centre of the course. Another step forward from the second.

8111 GODOLPHIN FLYING START ZETLAND STKS (GROUP 3) 1m 2f
2:20 (2:21) (Class 1) 2-Y-O

£34,026 (£12,900; £6,456; £3,216; £1,614; £810) **Stalls** High

Form RPR

21 **1** **Max Vega (IRE)**[16] 7623 2-9-2 0........................ HarryBentley 1 105+
(Ralph Beckett) *neat; hld up in tch in midfield: effrt and hdwy to chal 2f out: led and edgd lft u.p over 1f out: styd on strly and drew clr ins fnl f: readily* **7/1**

11 **2** 3 **Miss Yoda (GER)**[29] 7162 2-8-13 86........................ FrankieDettori 9 97
(John Gosden) *compact; taken down early: stdd s: t.k.h: hld up in tch: hdwy to chse ldr 8f tl 5f out: styd handy tl clsd to ld 2f out: rdn and hdd over 1f out: nt match pce of wnr and btn ins fnl f* **9/2**[2]

441 **3** 3/4 **Berkshire Rocco (FR)**[42] 6710 2-9-2 84........................ OisinMurphy 7 98
(Andrew Balding) *str; chsd ldr for 2f: in tch in midfield: effrt over 2f out: shkn up and effrt 2f out: chsd ldng pair and plugged on same pce ins fnl f* **16/1**

4 2 3/4 **Mythical (FR)**[16] 7634 2-9-2 0........................ RyanMoore 2 93
(A P O'Brien, Ire) *str; looked wl; hld up in tch: effrt and stuck bhd a wall of horses ent fnl 2f: hdwy and shifted rt 1f out: wl hld 4th and no imp ins fnl f* **2/1**[1]

411 **5** 2 3/4 **Tritonic**[22] 7410 2-9-2 94........................ JamesDoyle 8 88
(Alan King) *stdd s: t.k.h: hld up in tch in rr: hdwy 4f out: chsd ldrs and rdn ent fnl 2f: no ex over 1f out: wknd ins fnl f* **6/1**[3]

21 **6** 1 **Volkan Star (IRE)**[50] 6402 2-9-2 0........................ WilliamBuick 4 87
(Charlie Appleby) *str; t.k.h: chsd ldrs tl wnt 2nd 5f out tl over 2f out: no ex u.p and bumping w rival over 1f out: wknd ins fnl f* **9/2**[2]

1624 **7** 1/2 **Subjectivist**[35] 6957 2-9-2 97........................ FrannyNorton 3 86
(Mark Johnston) *tall; t.k.h: led: hdd 2f out: sn struggling and bumping w rival over 1f out: wknd ins fnl f* **14/1**

5121 **8** 22 **Tell Me All**[21] 7429 2-9-2 90........................ LukeMorris 5 46
(Sir Mark Prescott Bt) *athletic; stdd after s: t.k.h: hld up in last pair: effrt over 2f out: sn btn: bhd and heavily eased ins fnl f* **16/1**

2m 9.5s (4.10) **Going Correction** +0.50s/f (Yiel) **8** Ran SP% **114.9**
Speed ratings (Par 105): **103,100,100,97,95 94,94,76**
CSF £38.63 TOTE £8.50: £2.10, £1.40, £3.90; EX 40.00 Trifecta £789.10.
Owner The Pickford Hill Partnership **Bred** Tullpark Ltd **Trained** Kimpton, Hants

FOCUS
This year's Zetland Stakes was run at a muddling pace and the ground seemed to find out most. The second and third have been rated as taking a step forward.

8112 DUBAI AUTUMN STKS (GROUP 3) 1m
2:55 (2:56) (Class 1) 2-Y-O

£34,026 (£12,900; £6,456; £3,216; £1,614; £810) **Stalls** High

Form RPR

1 **1** **Military March**[77] 5439 2-9-1 0........................ OisinMurphy 8 113+
(Saeed bin Suroor) *ly; str; looked wl; led: rdn and clr w runner-up over 1f out: hdd 1f out: battled bk gamely u.p to ld again wl ins fnl f: styd on* **4/1**[2]

213 **2** 1/2 **Al Suhail**[42] 6727 2-9-1 105........................(h) WilliamBuick 9 112
(Charlie Appleby) *str; sltly on toes; t.k.h: hld up in tch: clsd to trck ldrs 6f out: jnd wnr ent fnl 2f: drvn to ld 1f out: hdd wl ins fnl f: no ex* **4/1**[2]

3353 **3** 7 **Ropey Guest**[16] 7614 2-9-1 97........................ ShaneKelly 6 97
(George Margarson) *hld up in tch in last trio: effrt and hdwy over 1f out: chsd clr ldng pair and edgd rt jst ins fnl f: kpt on but no imp* **33/1**

211 **4** nk **Molatham**[29] 7150 2-9-1 102........................ JimCrowley 2 96
(Roger Varian) *str; stdd s: hld up in tch in last trio: clsd over 3f out: effrt to chse ldrs 2f out: outpcd and edgd lft ent fnl f: battling for wl hld 3rd ins fnl f* **5/2**[1]

5 4 1/2 **Persia (IRE)**[25] 7322 2-9-1 0........................ RyanMoore 7 86
(A P O'Brien, Ire) *compact; looked wl; chsd ldrs: rdn over 3f out: outpcd u.p and btn over 1f out: wknd and edgd rt ins fnl f* **9/2**[3]

411 **6** 5 **Johan**[13] 7733 2-9-1 88........................ JamesDoyle 5 75
(William Haggas) *athletic; w wnr tl over 2f out: outpcd u.p and btn over 1f out: wknd fnl f* **11/1**

11 **7** 3/4 **Cherokee Trail (USA)**[21] 7453 2-9-1 94........................ FrankieDettori 1 73
(John Gosden) *stdd and dropped in bhd after s: hld up in rr: hdwy 4f out: rdn over 2f out: unable qck and btn over 1f out: wknd fnl f (jockey said colt lost action in the dip)* **7/1**

11 **8** 2 **Dontaskmeagain (USA)**[18] 7539 2-9-1 92........................ FrannyNorton 3 69
(Mark Johnston) *athletic; chsd ldrs: rdn over 2f out: unable qck and lost pl qckly over 1f out: bhd fnl f* **16/1**

1m 40.47s (2.07) **Going Correction** +0.50s/f (Yiel) **8** Ran SP% **116.4**
Speed ratings (Par 105): **109,108,101,101,96 91,90,88**
CSF £20.82 TOTE £5.00: £1.60, £1.60, £5.50; EX 19.30 Trifecta £257.40.
Owner Godolphin **Bred** Godolphin **Trained** Newmarket, Suffolk

FOCUS
A juvenile Group 3 that's been significantly boosted in recent seasons, mainly thanks to two subsequent Guineas winners fighting it out in 2018. This year's edition was fascinating and, on deep going, it proved more of a stamina test, with two classy Godolphin colts coming well clear on the stands' side. It's been rated as one of the better renewals, the third offering some perspective as to the level.

8113 DARLEY DEWHURST STKS (GROUP 1) (C&F) 7f
3:30 (3:36) (Class 1) 2-Y-O

£302,689 (£114,756; £57,431; £28,609; £14,357; £7,205) **Stalls** High

Form RPR

1111 **1** **Pinatubo (IRE)**[27] 7245 2-9-1 128........................ WilliamBuick 2 122
(Charlie Appleby) *hld up in tch in midfield: clsd to chse ldrs 2f out: rdn to chal over 1f out: led and edgd sltly lft ins fnl f: styd on* **1/3**[1]

143 **2** 2 **Arizona (IRE)**[27] 7245 2-9-1 108........................ SeamieHeffernan 5 117
(A P O'Brien, Ire) *looked wl; led: rdn over 1f out: hdd ins fnl f: no ex and one pce towards fin* **14/1**

21 **3** 2 3/4 **Wichita (IRE)**[16] 7614 2-9-1 114........................ RyanMoore 7 110
(A P O'Brien, Ire) *chsd ldrs: clsd 3f out: pressing ldrs 2f out: sn rdn and unable qck over 1f out: wl hld and plugged on same pce ins fnl f* **7/2**[2]

004 **4** 2 **Year Of The Tiger (IRE)**[14] 7691 2-9-1 100........................ PBBeggy 8 105
(A P O'Brien, Ire) *athletic; sweating; hld up in tch: clsd over 2f out: rdn and no imp whn hung rt over 1f out: wl hld: plugged on and stl hanging ins fnl f* **50/1**

220 **5** *2 ¾* **Monarch Of Egypt (USA)**[14] 7693 2-9-1 111................ WayneLordan 3 98
(A P O'Brien, Ire) *athletic; chsd ldrs tl wnt 2nd over 3f out: rdn to press ldr 2f out: outpcd and btn over 1f out: wknd ins fnl f* **16/1**

121 **6** *2 ¼* **Positive**[42] 6727 2-9-1 109.. AdamKirby 6 93
(Clive Cox) *hld up in tch: effrt and shifted rt over 2f out: sn u.p and no hdwy: wl btn over 1f out (trainer could offer no explanation for the colt's performance)* **8/1**[3]

1162 **7** *3 ¼* **Mystery Power (IRE)**[21] 7456 2-9-1 110......................... OisinMurphy 1 84
(Richard Hannon) *hld up in tch in midfield: effrt jst over 2f out: sn struggling and wknd over 1f out* **20/1**

4104 **8** *7* **Royal Commando (IRE)**[21] 7456 2-9-1 101............. KieranShoemark 4 67
(Charles Hills) *hld up in rr: clsd over 2f: effrt ent fnl 2f: sn btn* **50/1**

0103 **9** *9* **Iffraaz (IRE)**[31] 7072 2-9-1 92...................................... JamesDoyle 9 44
(Mark Johnston) *on toes; chsd ldr tl over 3f out: lost pl and wl bhd over 1f out* **66/1**

1m 26.55s (1.15) **Going Correction** +0.50s/f (Yiel) **9** Ran SP% **131.1**
Speed ratings (Par 109): **113,110,107,105,102 99,95,87,77**
CSF £9.64 CT £14.58 TOTE £1.20: £1.02, £3.70, £1.40; EX 7.90 Trifecta £23.30.
Owner Godolphin **Bred** Godolphin **Trained** Newmarket, Suffolk

FOCUS
This season's Dewhurst was all about the brilliant winner and he didn't disappoint, for all that the race rather fell apart on the testing surface. The placed horses at least give it a solid look. It's been rated as a decent renewal, with the second posting his best effort yet, but the third below his Tattersalls Stakes form.

8114 EMIRATES CESAREWITCH STKS (HERITAGE H'CAP) 2m 2f
4:10 (4:18) (Class 2) 3-Y-O+

£217,875 (£65,240; £32,620; £16,310; £8,155; £4,095) **Stalls** Low

Form RPR

00-0 **1** **Stratum**[34] 6484 6-9-7 **101**.. JasonWatson 20 110
(W P Mullins, Ire) *hld up in tch in midfield: effrt ent fnl 3f: swtchd lft and clsd over 2f out: drvn to chal over 1f out: sn led: styd on wl and a jst holding rivals* **25/1**

5 **2** *½* **Party Playboy (GER)**[38] 6872 5-8-2 **82**...................... NGMcCullagh 23 90
(Anthony Mullins, Ire) *looked wl; hld up in midfield: clsd to chse ldrs and travelling strly over 3f out: shkn up 2f out: rdn and edgd rt over 1f out: kpt on wl but a jst hld ins fnl f: snatched 2nd last stride* **50/1**

0461 **3** *shd* **Summer Moon**[23] 7394 3-8-5 **95** 4ex.......................... FrannyNorton 28 103
(Mark Johnston) *chsd ldr after 3f tl 8f out: styd chsng ldrs: swtchd rt and chsd ldr again over 3f out: rdn to ld wl over 1f out: hdd ent fnl f: kpt on wl but a jst hld ins fnl f: lost 2nd last stride* **50/1**

4420 **4** *6* **Not So Sleepy**[35] 6958 7-9-0 **94**..................................(t) ConnorBeasley 6 96
(Hughie Morrison) *t.k.h: chsd ldrs tl clsd to ld 5f out: rdn over 2f out: hdd wl over 1f out: sn outpcd: 4th and plugged on same pce fnl f (jockey said gelding ran too free)* **33/1**

/1-0 **5** *5* **Mr Everest (IRE)**[30] 5508 6-8-6 **86**...(t) JFEgan 8 83
(A J Martin, Ire) *hld up in midfield: stdy prog 5f out: rdn wl over 2f out: hung rt and no prog 2f out: wl hld over 1f out* **13/2**[3]

0 **6** *nk* **Great Trango (IRE)**[70] 5508 6-8-3 **83**.........................(b) WayneLordan 19 80
(David Harry Kelly, Ire) *hld up towards rr: effrt 3f out: kpt on over 1f out: plugged on to pass btn horses ins fnl f: no ch w ldrs* **25/1**

2144 **7** *nk* **Who Dares Wins (IRE)**[7] 7928 7-9-3 **104**.................(p) AngusVilliers[(7)] 7 100
(Alan King) *hld up in midfield: nt clr run 4f out: effrt over 3f out: swtchd lft over 2f out: kpt on u.p over 1f out: plugged on to pass btn horses ins fnl f: no threat to ldrs* **16/1**

5 **8** *1 ¾* **Sneaky Getaway (IRE)**[29] 7148 6-9-7 **101**...................... RonanWhelan 9 96
(Emmet Mullins, Ire) *hld up in tch in midfield: nt clr run 4f out: sn swtchd lft and rdn: no imp u.p and btn 2f out: wknd ins fnl f* **33/1**

-200 **9** *nk* **Dubawi Fifty**[52] 6355 6-9-5 **99**.......................................(v[1]) AdamKirby 13 93
(Karen McLintock) *looked wl; midfield: effrt u.p 4f out: no imp u.p over 2f out: wl hld after* **33/1**

64-1 **10** *2 ¼* **Great White Shark (FR)**[26] 5508 5-8-9 **89**.................... WilliamBuick 10 81
(W P Mullins, Ire) *uns rdr 2f bef arriving at s: hld up in midfield: nt clr run and shuffled bk 5f out: swtchd lft: rt and tried to rally 4f out: no ch but plugged on to pass btn horses fr over 1f out* **7/1**

0-22 **11** *3 ½* **Buildmeupbuttercup**[28] 7216 5-9-0 **94**........................(t) FrankieDettori 21 83
(W P Mullins, Ire) *hld up towards rr: clsd 5f out: swtchd rt and hdwy 4f out: chsd ldrs 3f out: no ex u.p and btn over 1f out: wknd fnl f* **6/1**[2]

1122 **12** *¾* **Nuits St Georges (IRE)**[27] 7239 4-8-3 **83** ow1............. GeorgeWood 22 71
(David Menuisier) *t.k.h: led: sn hdd and styd chsng ldrs: u.p and struggling over 3f out: btn whn hmpd 2f out: sn wknd* **66/1**

0512 **13** *6* **Darksideoftarnside (IRE)**[8] 7866 5-7-13 **82**.......(v) GabrieleMalune[(3)] 25 64
(Ian Williams) *hld up in tch in midfield: clsd to join ldrs 5f out: rdn 4f out: sn struggling to qckn: losing pl and btn whn edgd lft 2f out: sn wknd* **33/1**

0002 **14** *3 ¼* **Cypress Creek (IRE)**[14] 7717 4-9-9 **103**......................(b) RyanMoore 17 82
(A P O'Brien, Ire) *hld up towards rr: effrt u.p 4f out: nvr threatened to get on terms: wl btn whn edgd rt over 2f out: eased ins fnl f* **33/1**

1551 **15** *4* **Ranch Hand**[35] 6955 3-8-8 **98** 4ex................................... OisinMurphy 4 76
(Andrew Balding) *looked wl; t.k.h: chsd ldrs: rdn over 3f out: sn struggling and wl btn 2f out: eased fnl f (trainer's rep could offer no explanation for the gelding's performance)* **11/2**[1]

3120 **16** *5* **Graceful Lady**[21] 7464 6-7-10 **81**............................ AndrewBreslin[(5)] 29 51
(Robert Eddery) *hld up towards rr: hdwy 5f out: no hdwy u.p 3f out: wknd 2f out: eased ins fnl f: t.o* **66/1**

5011 **17** *2 ¾* **Eddystone Rock (IRE)**[52] 6355 7-9-5 **99**........................ KierenFox 26 66
(John Best) *hld up in midfield: drvn over 4f out: sn struggling and outpcd over 3f out: wknd over 2f out: eased fnl f: t.o* **33/1**

0605 **18** *4* **Hermoso Mundo (SAF)**[23] 7394 7-8-12 **92**.................... SeanLevey 14 55
(Hughie Morrison) *hld up in midfield: effrt u.p 4f out: no imp and wl btn 2f out: eased ins fnl f: t.o* **100/1**

1130 **19** *12* **Rochester House (IRE)**[49] 6471 3-8-4 **94**...................... JoeFanning 24 48
(Mark Johnston) *t.k.h: chsd ldrs tl lost pl qckly and short of room 4f out: sn swtchd lft and eased: t.o* **50/1**

5121 **20** *1 ¼* **Themaxwecan (IRE)**[39] 6834 3-8-12 **102** 4ex................. JamesDoyle 2 55
(Mark Johnston) *looked wl; hld up in tch in midfield: shuffled bk and n.m.r over 4f out: swtchd lft and no rspnse to press over 3f out: eased over 2f out: t.o* **20/1**

4/10 **21** *shd* **Rainbow Dreamer**[35] 6958 6-8-13 **93**........................(v) JimCrowley 16 42
(Alan King) *hld up in tch in midfield clsd to chse ldrs 5f out: rdn 4f out: sn struggling and btn: eased fnl f: t.o* **50/1**

6234 **22** *¾* **Seinesational**[22] 7403 4-8-5 **85**.....................................(v) KieranO'Neill 31 34
(William Knight) *t.k.h: chsd ldrs: u.p 4f out: sn drvn and btn: eased over 1f out: t.o* **66/1**

0-10 **23** *1* **Coeur Blimey (IRE)**[112] 4096 8-8-9 **89**........................ ShaneKelly 27 37
(Sue Gardner) *sn led: rdn and hdd 5f out: lost pl u.p and btn 3f out: eased wl over 1f out: t.o* **25/1**

1533 **24** *1* **Coeur De Lion**[84] 5183 6-8-13 **93**.....................................(p) ShaneFoley 1 40
(Alan King) *in tch in midfield: u.p and btn over 3f out: eased over 2f out: t.o (jockey said gelding stopped quickly)* **20/1**

0011 **25** *½* **Time To Study (FR)**[35] 6958 5-9-0 **97** 4ex..............(p) CierenFallon[(3)] 15 43
(Ian Williams) *looked wl; hld up in midfield: effrt 4f out: sn drvn and no prog: wl btn over 2f out: eased over 1f out: t.o* **20/1**

0-42 **26** *4* **Sovereign Duke (GER)**[77] 5443 4-8-10 **90**..................... HarryBentley 5 32
(Henry Candy) *in tch in midfield: u.p and struggling 4f out: sn btn: eased over 2f out: t.o* **50/1**

1311 **27** *28* **Land Of Oz**[21] 7464 3-8-1 **91** 7ex.................................... DavidEgan 30 8
(Sir Mark Prescott Bt) *looked wl; t.k.h: hld up towards rr: rapid move to join ldr 8f out: lost pl qckly 4f out: sn wl bhd: eased over 2f out: t.o (jockey said colt ran too free)* **15/2**

11-1 **28** *3 ½* **Timoshenko**[73] 5540 4-8-6 **86**...(p) LukeMorris 12
(Sir Mark Prescott Bt) *hld up in midfield: u.p over 5f out: sn lost pl: wl btn and eased over 3f out: t.o (trainer said the gelding was unsuited by the soft ground and would prefer a quicker surface)* **12/1**

4-15 **29** *18* **Garbanzo (IRE)**[35] 6958 5-8-10 **90**..................................... LiamKeniry 3
(Ed Walker) *in tch in midfield: rdn and lost pl qckly over 5f out: lost tch 4f out: eased: t.o* **50/1**

520 **30** *30* **Billy Ray**[63] 5928 4-8-7 **92**...............................(v[1] w) ScottMcCullagh[(5)] 18
(Mick Channon) *a in rr: rdn over 5f out: sn lost tch: eased: t.o (jockey said colt was never travelling)* **33/1**

3m 58.64s (3.14) **Going Correction** +0.50s/f (Yiel)
WFA 3 from 4yo+ 10lb **30** Ran SP% **144.5**
Speed ratings (Par 109): **113,112,112,110,107 107,107,106,106,105 104,103,101,99,97 95,94,92,87,86 86,86,85,85,85 83,71**
CSF £979.03 CT £44123.38 TOTE £39.80: £7.40, £16.90, £14.90, £10.50; EX 2940.10 Trifecta £29602.30.
Owner Tony Bloom **Bred** Al Asayl Bloodstock Ltd **Trained** Muine Bheag, Co Carlow

FOCUS
Another fascinating Cesarewitch. Predictably there was a solid pace on and the ground played its part, with the principals coming clear inside the final furlong. Add 13yds due to re-positioning of bend into the home straight. A clear pb from the second and a lesser pb from the third.

8115 DUBAI BRITISH EBF BOADICEA STKS (LISTED RACE) (F&M) 6f
4:45 (4:54) (Class 1) 3-Y-O+

£22,684 (£8,600; £4,304; £2,144; £1,076; £540) **Stalls** High

Form RPR

1300 **1** **Richenza (FR)**[7] 7892 4-9-1 93.. HarryBentley 16 104
(Ralph Beckett) *mid-div: hdwy over 2f out: rdn to ld wl over 1f out: kpt on strly fnl f* **11/1**[3]

1006 **2** *1 ¾* **Invitational**[42] 6721 3-9-0 88.. DavidEgan 14 98
(Roger Varian) *slowly away: sn trcking ldrs: rdn to ld over 2f out: hdd wl over 1f out: kpt on but a being hld fnl f* **33/1**

-020 **3** *1 ¾* **Bravo Sierra**[27] 7255 3-9-0 100.. FrankieDettori 5 92+
(A Fabre, France) *athletic; mid-div: hdwy but nt clrest of runs over 2f out: kpt on whn clr over 1f out: wnt 3rd ins fnl f but nvr gng pce to get on terms* **9/4**[1]

2024 **4** *1 ½* **Gypsy Spirit**[20] 7496 3-9-0 95.. SeanLevey 4 88
(Tom Clover) *on toes; mid-div: hdwy over 2f out: sn rdn: disp cl 3rd over 1f out: kpt on same pce fnl f* **14/1**

6660 **5** *¾* **Yolo Again (IRE)**[34] 6999 3-9-0 89............................... JimmyQuinn 17 85
(Roger Fell) *hld up towards rr: rdn and stdy prog fr 2f out: styd on into 5th ins fnl f but nvr gng pce to rch ldrs* **50/1**

1410 **6** *¾* **Raincall**[22] 7401 4-9-1 80.. ShaneFoley 3 83
(Henry Candy) *looked wl; prom: rdn and ev ch over 2f out tl ent fnl f: no ex* **33/1**

1105 **7** *¾* **Beauty Filly**[7] 7893 4-9-4 101.. JamesDoyle 1 83
(William Haggas) *hld up towards rr: hdwy 3f out: rdn to dispute 4th over 1f out: fdd ins fnl f* **5/1**[2]

21-5 **8** *½* **Lady Aria**[163] 2319 3-9-0 95.. JasonWatson 2 79
(Michael Bell) *outpcd in last over 3f out: hdwy 2f out: styd on fnl f but nvr any threat* **20/1**

3453 **9** *1 ¼* **Gold Filigree (IRE)**[22] 7401 4-9-1 97............................(b[1]) ShaneKelly 11 75
(Richard Hughes) *prom: rdn and ev ch over 2f out tl jst over 1f out: wknd fnl f (jockey said filly became unbalanced in the dip)* **16/1**

0116 **10** *1 ¾* **Farzeen**[29] 7146 3-9-0 93.. JackMitchell 7 69
(Roger Varian) *athletic; chsd ldrs: rdn over 2f out: wknd jst over 1f out* **5/1**[2]

5316 **11** *hd* **Maid Of Spirit (IRE)**[40] 6809 4-9-1 77.............................. AdamKirby 15 69
(Clive Cox) *trckd ldrs: rdn over 2f out: wknd jst over 1f out* **33/1**

1114 **12** *shd* **Last Empire**[22] 7401 3-9-0 95.................................... KieranShoemark 12 68
(Kevin Ryan) *little slowly away: towards rr: rdn over 2f out: nvr any imp* **5/1**[2]

0206 **13** *4* **Treasure Me**[106] 4340 4-9-1 87.......................................(v) StevieDonohoe 13 55
(Charlie Fellowes) *on toes; led: rdn and hdd over 2f out: wknd jst over 1f out* **33/1**

2213 **14** *2 ½* **Restless Rose**[16] 7613 4-9-1 82.. JimCrowley 9 47
(Stuart Williams) *prom: rdn over 2f out: wknd over 1f out* **25/1**

2124 **15** *6* **Whisper Aloud**[16] 7613 3-9-0 80.. OisinMurphy 10 28
(Archie Watson) *looked wl; mid-div: rdn over 2f out: sn wknd (trainer's rep said the filly was unsuited by the soft ground and would prefer a quicker surface)* **33/1**

1m 14.25s (2.35) **Going Correction** +0.50s/f (Yiel)
WFA 3 from 4yo+ 1lb **15** Ran SP% **126.9**
Speed ratings (Par 111): **104,101,99,97,96 95,94,93,92,89 89,89,83,80,72**
CSF £346.15 TOTE £12.90: £3.60, £11.40, £1.30; EX 472.70 Trifecta £2902.80.
Owner Mrs Lynn Turner & Guy Brook **Bred** S A Le Thenney **Trained** Kimpton, Hants

FOCUS
Plenty of runners but not much strength in depth to this Listed event for fillies and mares. This was the first winner to be over the age of three for six years and she benefited from a run along the near real, although she won convincingly. It's been rated around the better view of the winner's form.

8116 DARLEY STKS (GROUP 3) 1m 1f
5:20 (5:26) (Class 1) 3-Y-O+

£34,026 (£12,900; £6,456; £3,216; £1,614; £810) **Stalls** High

Form RPR

1-35 **1** **Feliciana De Vega**[8] 7886 3-8-10 98.............................. HarryBentley 4 111
(Ralph Beckett) *travelled wl bhd ldrs: hdwy to ld over 2f out: kpt on strly fnl f: rdn out* **4/1**[2]

2110 **2** *3* **Indeed**[71] 5610 4-9-3 107.. LiamKeniry 9 107
(Dominic Ffrench Davis) *hld up in tch: rdn and hdwy fr 2f out: wnt 3rd ins fnl f: kpt on to snatch 2nd fnl stride: no threat to wnr* **5/1**[3]

35-4 **3** *shd* **Prince Eiji**[24] 7340 3-8-13 104 .... WilliamBuick 5 108
(Roger Varian) *looked wl: hld up in last trio: swtchd rt and hdwy over 2f out: rdn to chse wnr over 1f out: kpt on but nt pce to chal: lost 2nd fnl stride* **9/1**

0222 **4** *1 3/4* **Matterhorn (IRE)**[28] 7220 4-9-3 112 .... FrannyNorton 7 103
(Mark Johnston) *disp ld tl rdn over 2f out: kpt on tl no ex fnl 100yds* **7/2**[1]

5532 **5** *hd* **Pincheck (IRE)**[11] 7794 5-9-3 109 .... ShaneFoley 11 103
(Mrs John Harrington, Ire) *hld up in last pair: swtchd rt 2f out: sn drvn and hdwy: styd on to press for 4th fnl 100yds: nt pce to threaten ldrs* **7/1**

0045 **6** *shd* **Aquarium**[64] 5909 4-9-3 100 .... JFEgan 6 102
(Jane Chapple-Hyam) *s.i.s: in last pair: rdn 2f out: hdwy ent fnl f: kpt on but nt pce to get on terms* **20/1**

1122 **7** *5* **Duneflower (IRE)**[21] 7477 3-8-10 105 .... KieranO'Neill 2 90
(John Gosden) *trckd ldrs: rdn whn short of room over 2f out: sn hld: wknd ins fnl f* **7/1**

0041 **8** *nk* **Dolphin Vista (IRE)**[64] 5926 6-9-3 105 .... JamesDoyle 1 91
(Ralph Beckett) *disp ld tl rdn over 2f out: hld disputing cl 3rd over 1f out: wknd ins fnl f* **7/1**

04-0 **9** *5* **Chilean**[115] 3987 4-9-3 98 ....(b[1]) SeanLevey 8 81
(Martyn Meade) *trckd ldrs: rdn over 2f out: wknd over 1f out* **16/1**

1m 54.38s (3.28) **Going Correction** +0.50s/f (Yiel)
WFA 3 from 4yo+ 4lb **9** Ran SP% **117.0**
Speed ratings (Par 113): **105,102,102,100,100 100,95,95,91**
CSF £24.74 TOTE £4.50: £1.60, £2.00, £2.50; EX 27.50 Trifecta £242.60.
Owner Waverley Racing **Bred** Ed's Stud Ltd **Trained** Kimpton, Hants

FOCUS
This fair Group 3 was run at a routine sort of pace. The level is a bit fluid. The race could be rated a bit higher based around the second's July course handicap win.
T/Jkpt: Not Won. T/Plt: £3,607.10 to a £1 stake. Pool: £163,312.14 - 33.05 winning units T/Qpdt: £323.90 to a £1 stake. Pool: £19,885.33 - 45.43 winning units **Steve Payne & Tim Mitchell**

7909 WOLVERHAMPTON (A.W) (L-H)
Saturday, October 12

OFFICIAL GOING: Tapeta: standard
Wind: Light behind Weather: Overcast

8117 COMPARE BOOKMAKER SITES AT BONUSCODEBETS.CO.UK H'CAP — 5f 21y (Tp)
5:25 (5:26) (Class 5) (0-70,74) 3-Y-O+
£3,428 (£1,020; £509; £400; £400; £400) **Stalls** Low

Form RPR

51-0 **1** **Ty Rock Brandy (IRE)**[45] 6618 4-8-10 **59** .... CallumShepherd 2 66
(Miss Natalia Lupini, Ire) *hld up: hdwy over 1f out: r.o u.p to ld nr fin* **8/1**

6233 **2** *1/2* **Show Me The Bubbly**[9] 7855 3-9-3 **73** .... KateLeahy[(7)] 4 79
(John O'Shea) *chsd ldr after 1f: hung rt fr over 3f out tl led 1/2-way: rdn over 1f out: edgd lft ins fnl f: hdd nr fin (jockey said filly hung right-handed)* **9/2**[2]

-321 **3** *nk* **Spirited Guest**[9] 7854 3-9-8 **74** .... JaneElliott[(3)] 8 79
(George Margarson) *prom: racd keenly: hung rt 1/2-way: chsd ldr over 1f out: rdn and edgd lft ins fnl f: styd on* **6/5**[1]

1500 **4** *2* **Major Blue**[9] 7837 3-9-7 **70** ....(b) NicolaCurrie 11 68
(James Eustace) *s.i.s: hld up: hdwy over 1f out: rdn and edgd lft ins fnl f: r.o: nt rch ldrs* **18/1**

2622 **5** *hd* **Thegreyvtrain**[41] 6754 3-9-1 **64** .... DavidProbert 5 61
(Ronald Harris) *hld up: nt clr run 3f out: hdwy 1/2-way: rdn over 1f out: styd on same pce wl ins fnl f* **20/1**

0003 **6** *2 1/4* **Dodgy Bob**[4] 8007 6-8-7 **56** oh8 ....(v) CharlieBennett 1 44
(Michael Mullineaux) *pushed along to chse ldrs: rdn over 1f out: nt clr run and swtchd rt ins fnl f: no ex* **40/1**

0022 **7** *1* **Teepee Time**[54] 6277 6-8-7 **56** oh11 ....(b) PhilDennis 6 41
(Michael Mullineaux) *led to 1/2-way: rdn over 1f out: wknd ins fnl f* **50/1**

110 **8** *3 1/4* **Awsaaf**[27] 7230 4-9-8 **71** ....(t) NickyMackay 3 44
(Michael Wigham) *n.m.r after s: sn pushed along in rr: rdn over 1f out: nt trble ldrs* **13/2**[3]

0064 **9** *1 1/4* **The Defiant**[23] 7367 3-9-4 **67** .... BenRobinson 10 36
(Paul Midgley) *hld up: racd keenly: hung rt over 3f out tl rdn and edgd lft over 1f out: n.d (jockey said gelding hung right-handed throughout)* **16/1**

0030 **10** *2 1/2* **David's Beauty (IRE)**[12] 7757 6-8-2 **56** oh4 ....(b) KieranSchofield[(5)] 7 15
(Brian Baugh) *chsd ldrs over 3f* **33/1**

1000 **11** *9* **Superseded (IRE)**[17] 7588 3-9-0 **66** .... DarraghKeenan[(3)] 9
(John Butler) *chsd ldrs on outer: hung rt and wknd 1/2-way* **10/1**

1m 0.82s (-1.08) **Going Correction** -0.125s/f (Stan) **11** Ran SP% **120.4**
Speed ratings (Par 103): **103,102,101,98,98 94,93,87,85,81 67**
CSF £43.62 CT £75.65 TOTE £9.10: £2.20, £1.10, £1.30; EX 54.10 Trifecta £190.60.
Owner T Heatrick **Bred** D Laverty **Trained** Gilford, Co Down
■ Stewards' Enquiry : Phil Dennis one-day ban: failure to ride to their draw (Oct 28)

FOCUS
The going was standard. Stalls - 7f: outside; Remainder: inside. A competitive sprint handicap. Three of the fancied horses fought out the finish and the form should work out. The second has been rated in line with her best, with the third confirming his latest improved novice win.

8118 BLACK COUNTRY CHAMBER OF COMMERCE (S) STKS — 6f 20y (Tp)
6:00 (6:00) (Class 5) 2-Y-O
£3,428 (£1,020; £509; £400; £400; £400) **Stalls** Low

Form RPR

5304 **1** **Speed Merchant (IRE)**[16] 7626 2-8-7 60 ....(p[1]) ThomasGreatrex[(5)] 6 62+
(Brian Meehan) *pushed along in rr: hdwy over 2f out: rdn to ld and edgd lft ins fnl f: r.o* **11/2**[2]

6660 **2** *2 3/4* **Kocasandra (IRE)**[12] 7754 2-8-7 70 ....(b) DavidProbert 3 49
(Archie Watson) *chsd ldrs: pushed along over 2f out: styd on same pce u.p ins fnl f: wnt 2nd nr fin* **4/5**[1]

0453 **3** *nk* **Village Rock (IRE)**[12] 7768 2-8-9 52 ....(b) FinleyMarsh[(3)] 5 53
(Richard Hughes) *prom: chsd ldr over 2f out: rdn to ld and hung lft fr over 1f out: hdd and no ex ins fnl f* **7/1**

0600 **4** *1* **Candid (IRE)**[27] 7234 2-8-7 48 ....(p[1]) CharlieBennett 8 45
(Jonathan Portman) *prom: rdn over 2f out: kpt on (jockey said filly hung right-handed on the bend)* **40/1**

0246 **5** *1 3/4* **Call Me Cheers**[9] 7853 2-8-12 58 .... CliffordLee 7 45
(David Evans) *hld up: rdn and hung rt over 2f out: styd on ins fnl f: nvr on terms (jockey said gelding hung right-handed)* **6/1**[3]

6610 **6** *1/2* **Twittering (IRE)**[12] 7767 2-9-3 63 ....(b) NicolaCurrie 11 48
(Jamie Osborne) *led: shkn up and hdd over 1f out: nt clr run and no ex ins fnl f* **9/1**

3405 **7** *1 3/4* **Baracca Rocks**[21] 7469 2-8-4 53 ....(v) HarrisonShaw[(3)] 9 33
(K R Burke) *disp ld 1f: chsd ldr tl rdn over 2f out: wknd ins fnl f* **16/1**

060 **8** *2 1/2* **Goodman Square**[9] 7833 2-8-0 34 .... IsobelFrancis[(7)] 10 25
(Mark Usher) *hung lft thrght: n.d* **100/1**

500 **9** *2* **Dark Moonlight (IRE)**[2] 8067 2-8-5 0 .... GraceMcEntee[(7)] 4 24
(Phil McEntee) *s.i.s: nt clr run wl over 3f out and again 2f out: sme hdwy u.p over 1f out: wknd ins fnl f* **50/1**

00 **10** *10* **Rosa P**[31] 7063 2-8-4 0 .... WilliamCox[(3)] 2
(Steph Hollinshead) *s.i.s: a in rr (jockey said filly was never travelling)* **100/1**

6600 **11** *3/4* **Koovers (IRE)**[9] 7853 2-8-5 52 ....(v[1]) AidenSmithies[(7)] 1
(Gay Kelleway) *hit rails over 4f out: sn outpcd (jockey said gelding jinked left-handed and hit the rail approximately 5f out)* **40/1**

1m 13.91s (-0.59) **Going Correction** -0.125s/f (Stan) **11** Ran SP% **122.4**
Speed ratings (Par 95): **98,94,93,92,90 89,87,83,81,67 66**
CSF £10.62 TOTE £5.70: £1.20, £1.20, £2.10; EX 15.00 Trifecta £46.50.The winner was sold to Mick Appleby for £11,000. Twittering was claimed by Mr O. Signy for £6,000
Owner Manton Thoroughbreds Iv **Bred** J McAteer & L McAteer **Trained** Manton, Wilts

FOCUS
A weak seller. The winner did it nicely, though, and should make his mark back in handicap company. The winner has been rated back to his best.

8119 WOLVERHAMPTON HOLIDAY INN CLASSIFIED STKS — 6f 20y (Tp)
6:30 (6:31) (Class 6) 3-Y-O+
£2,781 (£827; £413; £400; £400; £400) **Stalls** Low

Form RPR

1544 **1** **Sharrabang**[21] 7444 3-8-11 53 .... MeganNicholls[(3)] 2 54+
(Stella Barclay) *prom: pushed along over 2f out: hung lft and nt clr run over 1f out: swtchd rt: rdn and r.o to ld nr fin* **2/1**[1]

6043 **2** *nk* **Obsession For Gold (IRE)**[9] 7838 3-9-0 49 ....(t) DanielMuscutt 7 53
(Mrs Ilka Gansera-Leveque) *a.p: racd keenly: rdn to ld and hung lft over 1f out: hdd nr fin* **3/1**[2]

2406 **3** *1/2* **Isabella Ruby**[14] 7681 4-8-8 44 ....(h) GavinAshton[(7)] 8 52
(Lisa Williamson) *s.i.s: hdwy on outer over 1f out: rdn and edgd lft ins fnl f: styd on* **20/1**

3050 **4** *1 3/4* **North Korea (IRE)**[28] 7172 3-8-9 43 .... GeorgiaDobie[(5)] 12 46
(Brian Baugh) *broke wl enough: sn lost pl: rdn and r.o ins fnl f: nt rch ldrs* **50/1**

0430 **5** *hd* **Molly Blake**[12] 7757 3-8-11 53 .... WilliamCox[(3)] 3 46
(Clive Cox) *chsd ldrs: rdn and swtchd rt over 1f out: styd on* **8/1**[3]

064 **6** *nk* **Penwood (FR)**[11] 7784 4-9-1 47 ....(b[1]) GeorgeDowning 4 45
(Joseph Tuite) *s.i.s: sn pushed along in rr: rdn and r.o ins fnl f: nvr nrr (jockey said filly was slowly away)* **20/1**

0006 **7** *3/4* **Griggy (IRE)**[110] 4192 3-8-11 55 .... DarraghKeenan[(3)] 5 43
(John Butler) *hld up: rdn 1f out: styd on ins fnl f: nt trble ldrs* **3/1**[2]

0400 **8** *1 1/2* **Alba Del Sole (IRE)**[3] 8018 4-9-1 52 ....(p) CallumShepherd 1 38
(Charlie Wallis) *s.i.s: hld up: hdwy u.p over 1f out: no ex ins fnl f* **14/1**

0300 **9** *2 1/2* **Moneta**[17] 7573 3-9-0 52 .... DavidProbert 6 31
(Ronald Harris) *prom: stdd and lost pl after 1f: hdwy over 2f out: rdn and nt clr run wl over 1f out: wknd ins fnl f* **18/1**

5050 **10** *nk* **Hanati (IRE)**[25] 7307 3-9-0 52 .... BenRobinson 13 30
(Brian Ellison) *pushed along and prom: jnd ldr over 4f out tl led over 2f out: rdn and hdd over 1f out: wknd ins fnl f* **28/1**

0006 **11** *3/4* **Wye Bother (IRE)**[16] 7606 3-8-9 43 ....(t) SeanKirrane[(5)] 9 27
(Milton Bradley) *led: hdd over 4f out: rdn over 2f out: wknd fnl f* **50/1**

255 **12** *3/4* **Celerity (IRE)**[44] 6639 5-8-10 45 ....(p) SeamusCronin[(5)] 11 25
(Lisa Williamson) *chsd ldrs: led over 4f out: hdd over 2f out: wknd fnl f* **66/1**

1m 14.33s (-0.17) **Going Correction** -0.125s/f (Stan)
WFA 3 from 4yo+ 1lb **12** Ran SP% **124.8**
Speed ratings (Par 101): **96,95,94,92,92 91,90,88,85,85 84,83**
CSF £7.88 TOTE £3.10: £1.30, £1.50, £4.90; EX 9.70 Trifecta £112.30.
Owner Matt Watkinson Racing Club **Bred** The Bounty Hunters **Trained** Garstang, Lancs
■ Stewards' Enquiry : Sean Kirrane one-day ban: failure to ride to their draw (Oct 28)

FOCUS
Ordinary fare. The winner did it quite well despite having an interrupted passage. The third limits the level.

8120 FOLLOW US ON TWITTER @WOLVESRACES H'CAP — 1m 5f 219y (Tp)
7:00 (7:02) (Class 4) (0-85,84) 3-Y-O+
£5,207 (£1,549; £774; £400; £400; £400) **Stalls** Low

Form RPR

2114 **1** **Seaborn (IRE)**[17] 7575 5-9-6 **76** .... DavidProbert 6 85
(Patrick Chamings) *chsd ldrs: stdd and lost pl after 1f: hdwy over 3f out: chsd ldr over 2f out: led over 1f out: rdn out* **11/1**

2421 **2** *1 1/4* **Australis (IRE)**[30] 7108 3-9-2 **79** ....(b) RossaRyan 3 86
(Roger Varian) *s.s: rcvrd to chse ldr after 1f: led over 3f out: rdn and hdd over 1f out: styd on same pce ins fnl f* **5/2**[2]

131 **3** *2 1/2* **Charlie D (USA)**[27] 7231 4-9-11 **84** ....(tp) JaneElliott[(3)] 5 88+
(Tom Dascombe) *hld up: nt clr run over 2f out: hdwy over 1f out: rdn: edgd rt and rdr dropped rein ins fnl f: r.o: nt rch ldrs* **6/1**

3222 **4** *5* **Houlton**[33] 7033 4-9-4 **81** ....(tp) StefanoCherchi[(7)] 4 78
(Marco Botti) *prom: rdn over 2f out: wknd fnl f* **5/1**[3]

0323 **5** *2 1/4* **Sufi**[17] 7575 5-9-0 **73** ....(t) MeganNicholls[(3)] 2 66
(Milton Harris) *s.i.s: hld up: hdwy on outer over 2f out: rdn and wknd over 1f out (trainer said gelding had a breathing problem)* **16/1**

3333 **6** *8* **Albanita**[27] 7229 3-8-11 **74** ....(p) LukeMorris 1 58
(Sir Mark Prescott Bt) *chsd ldrs: rdn over 2f out: wknd over 1f out (trainer's rep said the filly did not stay the 1 mile and 6 furlong trip on the occasion)* **8/1**

3642 **7** *32* **Great Bear**[31] 7082 3-8-13 **81** ....(p) ThomasGreatrex[(5)] 7 20
(Roger Charlton) *led: rdn and hdd over 3f out: wknd over 2f out (trainer's rep could offer no explanation for the colt's performance other than that the jockey said the colt stopped very quickly)* **9/4**[1]

2m 58.85s (-2.15) **Going Correction** -0.125s/f (Stan)
WFA 3 from 4yo+ 7lb **7** Ran SP% **115.6**
Speed ratings (Par 105): **101,100,98,96,94 90,71**
CSF £39.63 TOTE £11.80: £3.90, £2.50; EX 58.20 Trifecta £524.00.
Owner Ian Beach **Bred** Michael Fennessy **Trained** Baughurst, Hants

FOCUS
A decent staying handicap. The winner travelled well and did it nicely. The third has been rated close to his best.

8121 BRITISH STALLION STUDS EBF NOVICE STKS 1m 1f 104y (Tp)
7:30 (7:36) (Class 5) 2-Y-O £3,428 (£1,020; £509; £254) Stalls Low

Form RPR
1 **Emissary** 2-9-2 0 JackMitchell 4 86+
(Hugo Palmer) *hld up: hdwy on outer over 2f out: chsd ldr over 1f out: shkn up to ld ins fnl f: edgd lft and r.o wl: comf* 4/1[2]
2 2 2 ¼ **Glenties (USA)**[10] 7821 2-9-2 0 JoeFanning 11 82+
(Mark Johnston) *chsd ldr after 1f: led over 2f out: rdn over 1f out: hdd ins fnl f: sn outpcd* 7/2[1]
3 9 **Miraz (IRE)** 2-9-2 0 RossaRyan 7 65
(Richard Hannon) *led 1f: chsd ldrs: rdn and hung lft over 1f out: wknd ins fnl f* 22/1
4 4 nse **Pot Of Paint**[50] 6424 2-8-13 0 JaneElliott(3) 9 65
(Tom Dascombe) *led over 8f out: hung rt: hdd over 2f out: wknd fnl f* 7/2[1]
05 5 5 **Looktothelight (USA)**[36] 6926 2-9-2 0 NicolaCurrie 2 55
(Jamie Osborne) *s.i.s: sn rcvrd into mid-div: shkn up over 2f out: wknd over 1f out* 9/1
6522 6 nk **Wild Thunder (IRE)**[28] 7197 2-9-9 90 TomMarquand 1 62
(Richard Hannon) *chsd ldrs: rdn over 2f out: hung lft and wknd over 1f out* 4/1[2]
0 7 1 ¼ **Walls Have Ears (IRE)**[8] 7870 2-8-8 0 GabrieleMalune(3) 3 47
(Ivan Furtado) *mid-div: effrt over 3f out: wknd wl over 1f out* 100/1
8 nse **Perfect Arch (IRE)** 2-9-2 0 CallumShepherd 5 52
(Saeed bin Suroor) *s.i.s: hld up: drvn along 1/2-way: n.d* 9/2[3]
9 3 ½ **Recall It All** 2-9-2 0 DougieCostello 6 46
(Ivan Furtado) *s.i.s: a in rr (jockey said gelding was slowly away)* 80/1
50 10 28 **Belle Rousse**[16] 7605 2-8-11 0 LukeMorris 8
(Sir Mark Prescott Bt) *sn drvn along in rr and outpcd* 100/1

1m 57.99s (-2.81) **Going Correction** -0.125s/f (Stan) 10 Ran SP% 120.2
Speed ratings (Par 95): **107,105,97,96,92 92,91,91,87,63**
CSF £18.89 TOTE £4.20: £1.50, £1.20, £7.50; EX 17.30 Trifecta £182.50.
Owner K Abdullah **Bred** Juddmonte Farms (east) Ltd **Trained** Newmarket, Suffolk

FOCUS
Potentially an above-average AW novice. The first two finished clear and the well-bred winner looks very promising.

8122 GRAND THEATRE WOLVERHAMPTON H'CAP 1m 142y (Tp)
8:00 (8:04) (Class 5) (0-75,75) 3-Y-O+ £3,428 (£1,020; £509; £400; £400; £400) Stalls Low

Form RPR
6006 1 **Sea Fox (IRE)**[148] 2799 5-9-9 75 (w) CliffordLee 8 80
(David Evans) *chsd ldrs: shkn up over 1f out: hung lft and r.o u.p to ld post* 11/1
4520 2 shd **Robero**[15] 7653 7-9-2 73 (e) TobyEley(5) 2 77
(Gay Kelleway) *trckd ldrs: rdn to ld wl ins fnl f: hdd post (vet reported gelding lost its left-fore shoe; jockey said gelding hung left-handed)* 5/1[2]
5446 3 hd **Sheila's Showcase**[15] 7663 3-9-2 72 CharlesBishop 9 77
(Denis Coakley) *a.p: chsd ldr over 6f out: rdn and ev ch whn hung lft and rt over 1f out: led ins fnl f: sn hdd: styd on (vet reported gelding lost its left fore shoe)* 20/1
53-5 4 shd **Rangali Island (IRE)**[161] 2395 3-9-3 73 CallumShepherd 12 78+
(David Simcock) *hld up: rdn and r.o wl ins fnl f: hmpd nr fin* 9/1
3531 5 ¾ **Jack D'Or**[26] 7278 3-9-5 75 LukeMorris 7 79+
(Ed Walker) *hld up: hdwy and nt clr run over 1f out: r.o* 3/1[1]
4613 6 nk **Universal Effect**[59] 6075 3-9-3 73 (h) LiamJones 5 75
(Mark Loughnane) *hld up in tch: shkn up over 1f out: rdn and edgd rt ins fnl f: r.o* 18/1
1404 7 2 **Street Poet (IRE)**[9] 7856 6-9-7 73 PhilDennis 4 70
(Michael Herrington) *chsd ldrs: rdn over 1f out: no ex ins fnl f* 9/1
4404 8 1 ¾ **Oneovdem**[18] 7554 5-9-3 74 (v[1]) TheodoreLadd(5) 6 67
(Tim Pinfield) *led: rdn over 1f out: hdd and no ex ins fnl f* 17/2[3]
0-21 9 ¾ **Mac Jetes**[12] 7772 3-8-11 72 ThomasGreatrex(5) 10 64
(David Loughnane) *hld up: hdwy on outer over 2f out: rdn over 1f out: styd on same pce fnl f* 11/1
5205 10 ½ **Entertaining (IRE)**[110] 4188 3-9-4 74 TomMarquand 13 65
(Richard Hannon) *s.i.s: nvr on terms* 20/1
1050 11 1 ½ **Alfa McGuire (IRE)**[26] 7289 4-9-5 74 MeganNicholls(3) 11 60
(Phillip Makin) *hld up in tch: shkn up over 2f out: wknd over 1f out* 10/1
30 12 ¾ **Whatwouldyouknow (IRE)**[31] 7074 4-9-3 69 (h[1]) PhilipPrince 3 54
(Richard Guest) *hld up: rdn over 1f out: n.d (trainer's rep said gelding had a breathing problem)* 14/1
356 13 2 ¼ **Amor Fati (IRE)**[23] 7378 4-9-2 68 EoinWalsh 1 48
(David Evans) *s.s: a in rr (jockey said gelding was slowly away)* 20/1

1m 47.88s (-2.22) **Going Correction** -0.125s/f (Stan)
WFA 3 from 4yo+ 4lb 13 Ran SP% 124.2
Speed ratings (Par 103): **104,103,103,103,102 102,100,99,98,98 96,96,94**
CSF £65.80 CT £1129.65 TOTE £12.50: £4.40, £2.20, £7.60; EX 80.70 Trifecta £1280.80.
Owner Eric Griffiths & P D Evans **Bred** Tally-Ho Stud **Trained** Pandy, Monmouths
■ Stewards' Enquiry : Phil Dennis caution: careless riding

FOCUS
A run of the mill handicap, but it produced a thrilling finish. Ordinary form rated around the third to this year's form.

8123 SKY SPORTS RACING VIRGIN 535 H'CAP 7f 36y (Tp)
8:30 (8:32) (Class 6) (0-55,57) 3-Y-O+ £2,781 (£827; £413; £400; £400; £400) Stalls High

Form RPR
0301 1 **Viola Park**[12] 7770 5-9-9 57 (p) DavidProbert 7 63
(Ronald Harris) *hld up in tch: shkn up over 1f out: rdn to ld and hung lft ins fnl f: r.o* 4/1[2]
6316 2 ½ **Brigand**[26] 7282 4-9-3 54 DarraghKeenan(3) 3 59
(John Butler) *a.p: chsd ldr 2f out: rdn to ld ins fnl f: sn hdd: kpt on* 9/1
4 3 2 ¼ **Sagittarian Wind**[25] 7298 3-9-2 52 AdamMcNamara 1 50
(Archie Watson) *chsd ldr tl led over 2f out: rdn: hdd and no ex ins fnl f* 9/5[1]
6030 4 1 **Mooroverthebridge**[27] 7236 5-9-3 51 (b[1]) RossaRyan 5 48
(Grace Harris) *s.s: hld up: hdwy u.p over 1f out: hung lft ins fnl f: nt rch ldrs* 15/2
0000 5 hd **Capla Demon**[54] 6273 4-9-2 55 KieranSchofield(5) 9 51
(Antony Brittain) *s.i.s: hld up: plld hrd: r.o ins fnl f (jockey said gelding stumbled leaving the stalls)* 33/1
210 6 1 ¼ **Captain Sedgwick (IRE)**[27] 7236 5-8-12 49 JaneElliott(3) 10 42
(John Spearing) *s.i.s: hld up: hung lft and styng on whn nt clr run wl ins fnl f (jockey said mare suffered interference when leaving the stalls)* 16/1
2000 7 ½ **Robben Rainbow**[13] 7738 5-9-1 49 PhilDennis 4 41
(Katie Scott) *s.i.s: hld up: rdn over 1f out: nvr on terms* 12/1
00 8 1 **Dreamboat Annie**[9] 7837 4-8-11 52 EllieMacKenzie(7) 6 42
(Mark Usher) *led: hdd over 2f out: wknd ins fnl f* 28/1
0350 9 2 ¼ **Itmakesyouthink**[25] 7299 5-9-7 55 (h) EdwardGreatrex 8 39
(Mark Loughnane) *s.i.s: hld up: rdn over 1f out: n.d (jockey said gelding was slowly away and hung right-handed in the straight)* 11/2[3]
3160 10 2 ¾ **Kellington Kitty (USA)**[22] 7420 4-9-4 52 (p) DanielMuscutt 2 29
(Mike Murphy) *prom: rdn over 2f out: wknd and eased fnl f* 20/1
0550 11 2 ¾ **Elusif (IRE)**[87] 5051 4-8-13 54 GavinAshton(7) 12 25
(Shaun Keightley) *hld up: racd wd: hdwy 1/2-way: wknd over 2f out (jockey said gelding jumped left handed when leaving the stalls)* 20/1

1m 28.03s (-0.77) **Going Correction** -0.125s/f (Stan)
WFA 3 from 4yo+ 2lb 11 Ran SP% 122.4
Speed ratings (Par 101): **99,98,95,94,94 93,92,91,88,85 82**
CSF £39.39 CT £89.87 TOTE £5.40: £1.90, £2.30, £1.20; EX 41.30 Trifecta £127.40.
Owner John & Margaret Hatherell & RHS Ltd **Bred** Limestone Stud **Trained** Earlswood, Monmouths

FOCUS
Only a moderate contest. The winner underlined his liking for Tapeta. Straightforward form rated around the first three.
T/Plt: £58.80 to a £1 stake. Pool: £70,493.78 - 874.49 winning units T/Qpdt: £44.00 to a £1 stake. Pool: £9,635.51 - 161.72 winning units **Colin Roberts**

8095 YORK (L-H)
Saturday, October 12

OFFICIAL GOING: Soft (ovr 6.1; far 6.0, ctr 6.1, stands' 5.9)
Wind: moderate half behind Weather: Cloudy

8124 PLAY CORRECT4 FOR FREE WITH CORAL NURSERY H'CAP 7f 192y
2:05 (2:05) (Class 2) 2-Y-O £18,675 (£5,592; £2,796; £1,398; £699; £351) Stalls Low

Form RPR
5131 1 **Lucander (IRE)**[28] 7197 2-9-4 84 BenCurtis 1 88+
(Ralph Beckett) *hld up towards rr: hdwy over 2f out: rdn to chse ldrs whn bmpd over 1f out: styd on wl u.p fnl f to ld nr line* 9/2[2]
661 2 shd **Convict**[17] 7586 2-9-3 83 TomMarquand 7 87+
(William Haggas) *hld up towards rr: pushed along and sltly outpcd over 3f out: swtchd lft and hdwy over 2f out: led 1 1/2f out and sn rdn: drvn ins fnl f: hdd and no ex nr line* 13/8[1]
5315 3 1 **International Lion**[21] 7429 2-8-0 66 oh2 PaddyMathers 5 68
(Richard Fahey) *hld up towards rr: stdy hdwy on inner over 3f out: led over 2f out: sn jnd and rdn: hdd 1 1/2f out: sn drvn and ev ch tl n.m.r and no ex last 50yds* 9/1
1132 4 1 **Rich Belief**[36] 6942 2-9-7 87 (b[1]) PJMcDonald 8 86
(James Bethell) *hld up in rr: hdwy on inner over 3f out: rdn to chal 2f out: ev ch whn edgd lft ent fnl f: kpt on same pce* 12/1
1323 5 1 **The New Marwan**[29] 7139 2-9-0 80 PaulHanagan 9 77
(Richard Fahey) *trckd ldr: hdwy 3f out: rdn along on outer whn hung lft jst over 1f out: sn drvn and kpt on same pce* 12/1
3250 6 2 ½ **Viceregent**[21] 7429 2-8-2 71 SeanDavis(3) 2 63
(Richard Fahey) *trckd ldr: hdwy 3f out: cl up over 2f out: sn rdn: drvn and wknd wl over 1f out* 16/1
4541 7 shd **Breguet Boy (IRE)**[17] 7585 2-8-6 72 ShaneGray 6 63
(Keith Dalgleish) *chsd ldrs: rdn along 3f out: wknd 2f out* 9/1
1016 8 10 **Love Destiny**[16] 7612 2-9-0 80 SilvestreDeSousa 3 49
(Mark Johnston) *led: pushed along over 3f out: rdn and hdd wl over 2f out: sn wknd* 6/1[3]
5260 9 13 **Rocket Dancer**[5] 7971 2-8-8 74 RobertHavlin 10 15+
(Sylvester Kirk) *trckd ldrs: pushed along 1/2-way: rdn over 3f out: sn wknd* 33/1

1m 41.13s (3.63) **Going Correction** +0.675s/f (Yiel) 9 Ran SP% 114.8
Speed ratings (Par 101): **108,107,106,105,104 102,102,92,79**
CSF £12.10 CT £62.45 TOTE £5.00: £1.70, £1.30, £2.40; EX 13.70 Trifecta £119.00.
Owner Mrs M E Slade & B Ohlsson **Bred** John Connolly **Trained** Kimpton, Hants
■ Stewards' Enquiry : Paddy Mathers four-day ban: misuse of the whip (Oct 28-31)

FOCUS
The official going was soft (GoingStick: far side in home straight 6.0, centre 6.1, stands side 5.9; general 6.1). Racing on inner racing line, so race distances as advertised. A valuable nursery to start the card and the leaders may have gone off too quick, with the principals coming from off the pace. Ben Curtis said: "The ground is tacky and gluey" and Tom Marquand said: "It's harder work than yesterday as it's not wet any more." The time was 5.53sec outside standard. Solid form.

8125 CORAL.CO.UK ROCKINGHAM STKS (LISTED RACE) 6f
2:40 (2:45) (Class 1) 2-Y-O £28,355 (£10,750; £5,380; £2,680; £1,345; £675) Stalls High

Form RPR
4414 1 **Aberama Gold**[7] 7904 2-9-1 85 ShaneGray 6 102
(Keith Dalgleish) *mde most: rdn wl over 1f out: edgd rt to stands' rail ent fnl f: kpt on wl* 10/1[2]
1150 2 ¾ **Ventura Lightning (FR)**[17] 7602 2-9-1 100 TonyHamilton 3 100
(Richard Fahey) *hld up: hdwy on wd outside over 2f out: rdn over 1f out: chsd wnr and drvn ins fnl f: kpt on wl towards fin* 12/1[3]
1414 3 2 **Orlaith (IRE)**[21] 7432 2-8-13 99 PaulMulrennan 5 92
(Iain Jardine) *trckd ldrs: pushed along and sltly outpcd 2f out: sn rdn: styd on wl u.p fnl f* 12/1[3]
113 4 nk **Huraiz (IRE)**[35] 6966 2-9-1 101 DaneO'Neill 2 93
(Mark Johnston) *hld up in tch: hdwy and prom 1/2-way: rdn to chal 2f out: ev ch over 1f out: sn drvn and wknd fnl f* 12/1[3]
61 5 ¾ **Stormy Girl (IRE)**[31] 7063 2-8-10 0 ThomasGreatrex 7 86
(David Loughnane) *cl up: rdn along 2f out: sn drvn and grad wknd* 16/1
21 6 1 ¼ **Cobra Eye**[74] 5523 2-9-1 0 TomMarquand 11 87+
(John Quinn) *towards rr: hdwy 1/2-way: rdn along and edgd lft 2 1/2f out: drvn wl over 1f out: kpt on: nvr nr ldrs* 18/1
532 7 7 **Jamais Assez (USA)**[15] 7645 2-9-1 78 BenCurtis 9 66
(K R Burke) *hld up: a towards rr* 33/1
11 8 1 **Lampang (IRE)**[14] 7698 2-9-1 97 SilvestreDeSousa 12 63+
(Tim Easterby) *dwlt and swtchd lft s: hld up in rr: pushed along 1/2-way: swtchd rt 2 1/2f out: sn rdn and btn (trainer said the colt was unsuited by the soft going and would prefer a quicker surface)* 1/1[1]

4141 **9** *1* **Stone Circle (IRE)**[27] 7247 2-9-1 94........................ CallumShepherd 8 60+
(Michael Bell) *prom: rdn along wl over 2f out: sn wknd* **16/1**

2602 **10** *nse* **Misty Grey (IRE)**[31] 7071 2-9-1 98........................ PJMcDonald 1 60
(Mark Johnston) *chsd ldrs: rdn along over 2f out: sn wknd* **10/1**[2]

310 **11** *21* **Treble Treble (IRE)**[49] 6474 2-9-1 87........................ KevinStott 4
(Kevin Ryan) *a in rr* **22/1**

10 **12** *2 1/4* **Yorkshire Gold**[52] 6352 2-9-1 0........................ TomEaves 10 +
(Kevin Ryan) *towards rr: pushed along whn n.m.r and hmpd wl over 2f out: bhd after* **25/1**

1m 16.3s (4.70) **Going Correction** +0.675s/f (Yiel) **12** Ran SP% **119.4**
Speed ratings (Par 103): **95,94,91,90,89 88,78,77,76,76 48,45**
CSF £122.13 TOTE £11.40: £2.50, £3.20, £3.40; EX 149.30 Trifecta £2597.50.
Owner Weldspec Glasgow Limited **Bred** Mrs J McMahon **Trained** Carluke, S Lanarks

FOCUS
A race that has been won by Group-class performers such as Mattmu, Donjuan Triumphant and Sir Dancealot in recent years. This was a one-horse race according to the market, but it didn't turn out that way. It's been rated around the second for now.

8126 SMART MONEY'S ON CORAL H'CAP (96PLUS RACE) 1m 2f 56y
3:15 (3:15) (Class 2) (0-110,110) 3-Y-0+
£18,675 (£5,592; £2,796; £1,398; £699; £351) **Stalls** Low

Form RPR

6001 **1** **Coolagh Forest (IRE)**[34] 6998 3-8-6 **96**........................ PaulHanagan 1 107
(Richard Fahey) *trckd ldr: hdwy over 2f out: led wl over 1f out: rdn ent fnl f: kpt on strly* **7/2**[2]

0620 **2** *3* **Johnny Drama (IRE)**[21] 7457 4-8-13 **99**........................ SilvestreDeSousa 6 104
(Andrew Balding) *hld up in rr: hdwy wl over 2f out: rdn over 1f out: chsd wnr ent fnl f: sn rdn and edgd lft: kpt on same pce* **2/1**[1]

0656 **3** *4* **Dark Vision (IRE)**[14] 7694 3-8-10 **100**........................(v) PJMcDonald 3 97
(Mark Johnston) *trckd ldrs: hdwy over 3f out: rdn along and cl up 2f out: sn ev ch: drvn and wknd over 1f out* **11/2**

1666 **4** *4* **Forest Ranger (IRE)**[23] 7365 5-9-10 **110**........................ TonyHamilton 2 99
(Richard Fahey) *trckd ldng pair: hdwy 3f out: rdn along over 2f out: drvn wl over 1f out: sn btn* **15/2**

0543 **5** *1/2* **Big Country (IRE)**[23] 7365 6-8-11 **104**........................(p) MarkCrehan(7) 5 92
(Michael Appleby) *trckd ldrs: pushed along over 3f out: rdn over 2f out: sn wknd* **14/1**

1540 **6** *1 1/2* **Victory Command (IRE)**[21] 7457 3-8-9 **99**........................ JasonHart 7 84
(Mark Johnston) *led: pushed along over 3f out: rdn over 2f out: hdd wl over 1f out: sn wknd* **20/1**

1331 **7** *27* **Harrovian**[23] 7396 3-8-8 **98** ow2........................(b) RobertHavlin 4 29
(John Gosden) *hld up towards rr: pushed along over 3f out: sn rdn and btn: eased fnl 2f (trainer's rep said the colt was unsuited by the soft going and would prefer a quicker surface)* **4/1**[3]

2m 13.06s (2.76) **Going Correction** +0.675s/f (Yiel)
WFA 3 from 4yo+ 4lb **7** Ran SP% **114.1**
Speed ratings (Par 109): **114,111,108,105,104 103,82**
CSF £10.90 TOTE £4.30: £2.20, £1.70; EX 14.20 Trifecta £65.50.
Owner Alan Harte **Bred** Leaf Stud **Trained** Musley Bank, N Yorks
■ Stewards' Enquiry : Mark Crehan two-day ban: misuse of the whip (Oct 28-29)

FOCUS
A good handicap, but not many got into it. A 3yo was winning it for the fifth time in seven years. The second has been rated close to form.

8127 CORAL SPRINT TROPHY H'CAP 6f
3:50 (3:53) (Class 2) (0-105,105) 3-Y-0+
£62,250 (£18,640; £9,320; £4,660; £2,330; £1,170) **Stalls** Centre

Form RPR

0033 **1** **Gulliver**[21] 7433 5-9-5 **100**........................(tp) JasonHart 5 108
(David O'Meara) *in tch centre: hdwy 2f out: swtchd rt and rdn to chse ldrs over 1f out: styd on wl fnl f to ld nr fin* **16/1**

0230 **2** *nk* **Hyperfocus (IRE)**[21] 7431 5-8-13 **94**........................(p) DavidAllan 4 101
(Tim Easterby) *racd centre: led: rdn along wl over 1f out: drvn and hdd briefly ins fnl f: sn led again tl hdd and no ex nr fin* **16/1**

3423 **3** *3/4* **Danzeno**[7] 7889 8-9-5 **105**........................ TheodoreLadd(5) 10 110
(Michael Appleby) *trckd ldrs centre: hdwy 2f out: rdn and edgd lft over 1f out: led narrowly and briefly ins fnl f: hanging lft and drvn sn hdd and no ex towards fin (jockey said gelding hung right-handed throughout)* **12/1**

2346 **4** *3/4* **Louie De Palma**[21] 7433 7-9-0 **95**........................ HectorCrouch 3 97
(Clive Cox) *chsd ldrs towards centre: hdwy 2f out: rdn over 1f out: drvn and kpt on fnl f* **10/1**

1620 **5** *nk* **Lahore (USA)**[21] 7431 5-9-2 **97**........................ PaulMulrennan 2 98
(Phillip Makin) *hld up towards rr centre: hdwy whn n.m.r wl over 1f out: sn rdn: styd on strly fnl f* **12/1**

2010 **6** *1 3/4* **Alaadel**[7] 7894 6-8-13 **94**........................(t) GeraldMosse 1 90
(Stuart Williams) *in tch on inner: hdwy 2f out: rdn over 1f out: kpt on fnl f: nrst fin* **12/1**

0000 **7** *nk* **Soldier's Minute**[21] 7433 4-9-1 **96**........................(h) ShaneGray 8 91
(Keith Dalgleish) *chsd ldrs centre: rdn along 2f out: swtchd rt: drvn and wknd over 1f out* **33/1**

0025 **8** *4* **Ice Age (IRE)**[23] 7397 6-8-12 **93**........................ CharlesBishop 7 75
(Eve Johnson Houghton) *chsd ldrs centre: rdn along 2f out: swtchd rt: drvn and wknd over 1f out* **25/1**

0303 **9** *1/2* **Intisaab**[7] 7913 8-9-2 **97**........................(vt) SilvestreDeSousa 12 77
(David O'Meara) *towards rr centre tl styd on fnl 2f: n.d* **16/1**

4244 **10** *3/4* **Summerghand (IRE)**[7] 7891 5-9-7 **102**........................ DavidNolan 13 80
(David O'Meara) *in tch centre: rdn along 2f out: sn no imp* **12/1**

621 **11** *3 1/4* **Bernardo O'Reilly**[50] 6396 5-8-13 **94**........................ MartinDwyer 11 61
(Richard Spencer) *bhd centre tl styd on u.p fnl 2f: n.d* **20/1**

0162 **12** *1 1/2* **Growl**[21] 7433 7-9-3 **98**........................ TonyHamilton 16 61
(Richard Fahey) *in tch and swtchd towards centre after 1f: chsd ldrs 1/2-way: rdn along 2f out: grad wknd* **20/1**

4603 **13** *shd* **Lancelot Du Lac (ITY)**[14] 7687 9-9-0 **95**........................(h) JoeyHaynes 9 57
(Dean Ivory) *racd centre: midfield: rdn along over 2f out: n.d* **50/1**

0002 **14** *3/4* **Gunmetal (IRE)**[14] 7701 6-9-3 **98**........................ PJMcDonald 15 58
(David Barron) *in tch centre: chsd ldrs 1/2-way: rdn along over 2f out: sn wknd* **25/1**

0200 **15** *1* **Hey Jonesy (IRE)**[21] 7433 4-9-6 **101**........................ KevinStott 20 58
(Kevin Ryan) *racd stands' side: sn outpcd and rdn along in rr: bhd and detached 1/2-way* **8/1**[2]

1040 **16** *1/2* **Cold Stare (IRE)**[7] 7891 4-9-0 **95**........................(t) RobbieDowney 21 50
(David O'Meara) *racd towards stands' side: a towards rr* **25/1**

1010 **17** *3/4* **Air Raid**[70] 5664 4-9-5 **100**........................ JackGarritty 6 53
(Jedd O'Keeffe) *cl up centre: disp ld 1/2-way: rdn along 2f out: drvn and hld whn n.m.r and hmpd jst over 1f out: sn wknd* **9/1**[3]

3050 **18** *1 1/4* **Staxton**[21] 7433 4-9-2 **97**........................(p) DuranFentiman 22 46
(Tim Easterby) *racd towards stands' side: a towards rr* **33/1**

3631 **19** *1/2* **Get Knotted (IRE)**[11] 7781 7-9-0 **95**........................(p) CallumRodriguez 19 42
(Michael Dods) *a in rr towards stands' side* **10/1**

2250 **20** *1/2* **Pass The Vino (IRE)**[34] 7010 3-9-2 **98**........................ TomQueally 14 44
(Paul D'Arcy) *dwlt: a bhd* **33/1**

6142 **21** *1 3/4* **Aplomb (IRE)**[8] 7868 3-9-1 **97**........................ TomMarquand 17 37
(William Haggas) *racd towards stands' side: towards rr: rdn along 1/2-way: sn bhd (trainer's rep could offer no explanation for the gelding's performance)* **7/1**[1]

0000 **22** *2* **George Bowen (IRE)**[21] 7433 7-8-12 **93**........................(v) PaulHanagan 18 27
(Richard Fahey) *racd towards stands' side: a towards rr* **50/1**

1m 14.54s (2.94) **Going Correction** +0.675s/f (Yiel)
WFA 3 from 4yo+ 1lb **22** Ran SP% **134.0**
Speed ratings (Par 109): **107,106,105,104,104 101,101,96,95,94 90,88,88,87,85 85,84,82,81,81 78,76**
CSF £238.72 CT £3210.74 TOTE £23.00: £5.10, £3.80, £2.80, £3.40; EX 366.10 Trifecta £7789.20.
Owner Withernsea Thoroughbred Limited **Bred** S A Douch **Trained** Upper Helmsley, N Yorks

FOCUS
A wide-open sprint handicap in which more than half the field had run in the Ayr Gold Cup. Six of the last eight winners of the race had defied a three-figure official rating and today's winner continued that trend, but the most notable aspect of the race was the draw as those drawn in the top half may as well have stayed at home. The winner has been rated close to his best.

8128 JOIN THE CORAL BET & GET CLUB EBFSTALLIONS.COM NOVICE STKS (PLUS 10 RACE) 7f
4:25 (4:27) (Class 3) 2-Y-O **£9,703** (£2,887; £1,443; £721) **Stalls** Low

Form RPR

5 **1** **Al Rufaa (FR)**[9] 7842 2-9-5 0........................ RobertHavlin 1 82
(John Gosden) *t.k.h: led: rdn along 2f out: hdd narrowly and drvn over 1f out: led again jst ins fnl f: drvn and edgd lft last 100yds: kpt on* **11/2**[3]

30 **2** *nk* **Fox Duty Free (IRE)**[50] 6424 2-9-5 0........................ SilvestreDeSousa 5 81
(Andrew Balding) *trckd ldng pair: hdwy and cl up on inner over 1f out: sn rdn and ev ch: drvn and kpt on fnl f* **9/4**[2]

22 **3** *1/2* **El Naseri (IRE)**[22] 7398 2-9-5 0........................ PaulMulrennan 7 80
(Michael Dods) *chsd ldrs: rdn along over 2f out: drvn over 1f out: edgd lft ins fnl f: kpt on same pce* **11/2**[3]

4 *hd* **Splinter** 2-9-5 0........................ TonyHamilton 6 79
(Richard Fahey) *dwlt and in rr: hdwy 3f out: rdn along to chse ldrs wl over 1f out: drvn and keeping on whn carried lft and sltly hmpd last 100yds: no ex* **16/1**

5 **5** *2* **Gold Desert**[24] 7338 2-9-5 0........................ TomMarquand 9 74+
(Richard Hannon) *towards rr: hdwy 3f out: rdn along to chse ldrs wl over 1f out: kpt on same pce* **12/1**

2 **6** *1 1/2* **Colour Image (IRE)**[15] 7661 2-9-5 0........................ TomQueally 2 74+
(Saeed bin Suroor) *t.k.h: trckd ldr: hdwy and cl up 2f out: led narrowly jst over 1f out: sn rdn: hdd jst ins fnl f: wknd* **13/8**[1]

00 **7** *13* **Gigi's Beach**[7] 7899 2-9-5 0........................ BenCurtis 10 38
(Hugo Palmer) *in tch: rdn along wl over 2f out: sn outpcd and bhd* **33/1**

8 *1/2* **Power Point** 2-9-5 0........................ TomEaves 8 37
(John Wainwright) *a in rr: bhd fr 1/2-way* **66/1**

000 **9** *3 3/4* **Hovingham (IRE)**[18] 7539 2-9-0 41........................ FayeMcManoman(5) 3 27
(Nigel Tinkler) *a in rr: bhd fr 1/2-way* **100/1**

1m 29.81s (5.21) **Going Correction** +0.675s/f (Yiel) **9** Ran SP% **118.6**
Speed ratings (Par 99): **97,96,96,95,93 91,77,76,72**
CSF £18.79 TOTE £6.40: £1.70, £1.20, £1.60; EX 20.40 Trifecta £95.60.
Owner Al Shaqab Racing **Bred** J P J Dubois **Trained** Newmarket, Suffolk

FOCUS
Not a great deal of depth to this novice and the first four finished in a heap. It's been rated tentatively around the second's debut.

8129 FREE BETS FOR LENGTHS WITH CORAL H'CAP 2m 56y
5:00 (5:00) (Class 3) (0-90,90) 4-Y-O+ **£9,703** (£2,887; £1,443; £721) **Stalls** Low

Form RPR

4535 **1** **Sassie (IRE)**[10] 7830 4-8-10 **79**........................ PaulHanagan 8 88
(Michael Easterby) *hld up towards rr: hdwy 4f out: chsd ldrs wl over 1f out: rdn to ld jst ins fnl f: kpt on strly* **5/1**[2]

2540 **2** *3* **Orin Swift (IRE)**[49] 6448 5-8-12 **81**........................ AlistairRawlinson 7 86
(Jonathan Portman) *hld up towards rr: hdwy 4f out: chal 2f out: sn rdn and led narrowly jst over 1f out: hdd and drvn jst ins fnl f: kpt on same pce* **20/1**

36-2 **3** *nse* **River Icon**[19] 7510 7-8-11 **80**........................(p) PaulMulrennan 9 85
(Iain Jardine) *trckd ldng trio: hdwy 4f out: led 2f out: sn rdn and hdd jst over 1f out: drvn and kpt on same pce fnl f* **12/1**

1-00 **4** *1* **Arrowtown**[22] 7403 7-9-2 **90**........................(h) GerO'Neill(5) 2 94
(Michael Easterby) *hld up in rr: hdwy over 3f out: rdn along 2f out: styd on u.p fnl f* **3/1**[1]

4245 **5** *nk* **Doctor Cross (IRE)**[21] 7436 5-8-6 **75**........................ BarryMcHugh 10 78
(Richard Fahey) *in tch: hdwy 4f out: chsd ldrs and n.m.r wl over 1f out: sn rdn and kpt on same pce fnl f (jockey said gelding was denied a clear run in the closing stages)* **11/1**

1344 **6** *1* **Contrebasse**[10] 7830 4-8-2 **71** oh2........................(p) JamesSullivan 3 73
(Tim Easterby) *trckd ldrs on inner: n.m.r and swtchd rt 3f out: effrt and n.m.r on inner over 1f out: sn rdn and kpt on same pce* **13/2**

2016 **7** *5* **Knight Crusader**[78] 5368 7-9-1 **84**........................ BenCurtis 11 80
(John O'Shea) *hld up and bhd: hdwy 3f out: swtchd markedly rt to outer and rdn over 2f out: n.d* **20/1**

111 **8** *6* **Rubenesque (IRE)**[10] 7819 7-8-8 **77**........................(t) JasonHart 6 66
(Tristan Davidson) *trckd ldr: hdwy to ld 4f out: rdn along 3f out: hdd 2f out and sn wknd* **11/2**[3]

6122 **9** *1 3/4* **Forewarning**[23] 7381 5-8-2 **71** oh1........................(p[1]) CamHardie 4 58
(Julia Brooke) *hld up: a towards rr* **8/1**

4055 **10** *1/2* **Royal Cosmic**[8] 7872 5-7-13 **71** oh1........................ SeanDavis(3) 12 57
(Richard Fahey) *hld up: a towards rr (jockey said mare hung left-handed)* **25/1**

0 **11** *13* **Manzil (IRE)**[21] 7436 4-8-11 **80**........................(b[1]) NathanEvans 5 51
(Michael Easterby) *led: rdn along and hdd 4f out sn wknd* **33/1**

5060 **12** *8* **Aircraft Carrier (IRE)**[21] 7464 4-9-7 **90**........................(b) SilvestreDeSousa 1 51
(John Ryan) *trckd ldng pair: rdn along 4f out: sn wknd (jockey said gelding had no more to give on testing ground)* **10/1**

3m 43.34s (9.44) **Going Correction** +0.675s/f (Yiel) **12** Ran SP% **122.9**
Speed ratings (Par 107): **103,101,101,100,100 100,97,94,93,93 87,83**
CSF £108.28 CT £1162.71 TOTE £5.20: £1.70, £6.20, £3.90; EX 136.00 Trifecta £1040.00.
Owner L Vincent, S Hull & S Hollings **Bred** Worksop Manor Stud **Trained** Sheriff Hutton, N Yorks

FOCUS
A good staying handicap, but they didn't go very quick. Unlike in the earlier races, the runners stuck to the inside rail on reaching the straight. It's been rated around the well placed third.

8130 COLDSTREAM GUARDS ASSOCIATION CUP H'CAP — 1m 2f 56y
5:35 (5:36) (Class 3) (0-95,95) 3-Y-O+ £9,703 (£2,887; £1,443; £721) Stalls Low

Form | | | | RPR
61-1 **1** **Dubai Icon**23 7373 3-9-2 **89** JosephineGordon 10 99+
(Saeed bin Suroor) *hld up in midfield: hdwy over 2f out: chsd ldrs over 1f out: rdn to ld jst ins fnl f: kpt on wl (vet reported colt had blood in its left nostril which was due to the colt rearing and hitting its head in the stalls)* **3/1**1

2300 **2** 3/4 **Cockalorum (IRE)**14 7694 4-9-4 **87** (b) BenCurtis 4 93
(Roger Fell) *in tch: hdwy over 2f out: rdn along wl over 1f out: drvn and n.m.r ent fnl f: kpt on wl u.p towards fin* **12/1**

4102 **3** nk **Ladies First**23 7366 5-9-1 **84** NathanEvans 12 89
(Michael Easterby) *hld up in midfield: hdwy on outer over 3f out: led over 2f out: sn rdn and hdd 1 1/2f out: cl up and drvn ins fnl f: kpt on same pce towards fin* **14/1**

1000 **4** 1/2 **Badenscoth**14 7694 5-9-7 **90** JoeyHaynes 18 94
(Dean Ivory) *stdd and swtchd lft s: hld up in rr: hdwy on inner 3f out: chsd ldrs over 1f out: rdn to ld 1 1/2f out: drvn and edgd rt ent fnl f: sn hdd: kpt on same pce towards fin (jockey said gelding stumbled shortly after the start)* **25/1**

0003 **5** 3 **Awake My Soul (IRE)**16 7622 10-9-0 **83** JamesSullivan 14 81
(Tom Tate) *hld up towards rr: hdwy 3f out: rdn along to chse ldrs 2f out: sn drvn and no imp* **16/1**

0504 **6** 1 1/4 **Society Red**21 7434 5-9-2 **85** PaulHanagan 8 81
(Richard Fahey) *trckd ldrs: hdwy and cl up over 2f out: rdn wl over 1f out: drvn and wknd appr fnl f* **14/1**

5321 **7** 1 1/2 **Addis Ababa (IRE)**11 7782 4-9-7 **90** (p) DavidNolan 9 83
(David O'Meara) *cl up: led over 3f out: rdn along and hdd over 2f out: sn drvn: wknd over 1f out* **10/1**3

6053 **8** 1 **Anythingtoday (IRE)**21 7434 5-9-12 **95** (v) SilvestreDeSousa 17 86
(David O'Meara) *hld up in rr: hdwy 3f out: rdn along 2f out: kpt on same pce* **20/1**

0401 **9** shd **Scottish Summit (IRE)**17 7589 6-9-0 **83** SamJames 1 73
(Geoffrey Harker) *hld up: hdwy on inner 4f out: cl up over 2f out: rdn wl over 1f out: ev ch: wknd appr fnl f* **22/1**

0411 **10** 4 **Ayutthaya (IRE)**16 7622 4-9-9 **92** TomEaves 13 74
(Kevin Ryan) *a towards rr* **11/1**

6314 **11** hd **Benadalid**29 7153 4-8-13 **82** JasonHart 3 64
(Chris Fairhurst) *a towards rr* **25/1**

405 **12** 2 1/2 **First Sitting**30 7122 8-9-9 **92** GeraldMosse 16 69
(Chris Wall) *a towards rr* **25/1**

0216 **13** 3/4 **Furzig**49 6475 4-9-2 **88** SeanDavis(3) 19 63
(Richard Fahey) *hld up towards rr: hdwy and in tch 3f out: sn rdn and wknd* **16/1**

6020 **14** nse **Poet's Dawn**21 7434 4-9-1 **84** DavidAllan 11 59
(Tim Easterby) *t.k.h: prom: cl up 4f out: rdn along wl over 2f out: sn wknd* **14/1**

3540 **15** 1 **Freerolling**21 7457 4-9-0 **83** (h1) PaulMulrennan 2 56
(Charlie Fellowes) *t.k.h: trckd ldng trio: pushed along over 3f out: rdn and wknd over 2f out* **11/1**

5106 **16** shd **Mutamaded (IRE)**14 7702 6-9-2 **85** AndrewMullen 20 58
(Ruth Carr) *in tch on outer: rdn along over 3f out: sn wknd* **50/1**

-050 **17** 3 3/4 **Star Archer**21 7434 5-9-3 **86** CamHardie 15 52
(Michael Easterby) *a in rr* **50/1**

2 **18** 3 1/4 **Lord Of The Rock (IRE)**70 5693 7-9-1 **84** GrahamLee 7 43
(Lawrence Mullaney) *led: pushed along 4f out: sn hdd & wknd* **12/1**

4221 **19** 2 1/4 **Cape Victory (IRE)**28 7213 3-9-6 **93** PJMcDonald 6 49
(James Tate) *chsd ldrs: rdn along over 3f out: sn wknd (trainer's rep said the colt was unsuited by the soft going and would prefer a quicker surface)* **8/1**2

2m 14.61s (4.31) **Going Correction** +0.675s/f (Yiel)
WFA 3 from 4yo+ 4lb **19 Ran SP% 133.6**
Speed ratings (Par 107): **109,108,108,107,105 104,103,102,102,99 98,96,96,96,95 95,92,89,88**
CSF £38.55 CT £473.88 TOTE £3.60: £1.70, £3.60, £2.70, £7.70; EX 57.40 Trifecta £1037.50.
Owner Godolphin **Bred** Godolphin **Trained** Newmarket, Suffolk

FOCUS
Another big-field handicap to end, but there was an unexposed 3yo lurking in the field and he made no mistake. The second and third have been rated in line with the better view of their form.
T/Plt: £1,256.40 to a £1 stake. Pool: £143,199.97 - 83.20 winning units T/Qpdt: £72.20 to a £1 stake. Pool: £12,767.17 - 130.80 winning units **Joe Rowntree**

8131 - 8133a (Foreign Racing) - See Raceform Interactive

7748 CAULFIELD (R-H)
Saturday, October 12

OFFICIAL GOING: Turf: good

8134a LADBROKES HERBERT POWER STKS (GROUP 2 H'CAP) (3YO+) (TURF) — 1m 4f
4:35 3-Y-O+
£133,149 (£39,779; £19,889; £9,944; £5,524; £4,419)

| | | | RPR
1 **The Chosen One (NZ)**13 7748 4-8-8 (b) DamianLane 7 108+
(Murray Baker & Andrew Forsman, New Zealand) **11/2**1

2 1/2 **Prince Of Arran**35 6962 6-9-2 **0** MichaelWalker 10 113
(Charlie Fellowes) *sn settled in midfield: tk clsr order under 4f out: pressed ldrs turning in: rdn along to ld 1 1/2f out: hrd pressed 100yds out: hdd 50yds out: no ex* **15/2**3

3 3 **Sully (NZ)**15 5-8-8 **0** (bt) BrettPrebble 4 100
(Trent Busuttin & Natalie Young, Australia) **17/2**

4 3/4 **Wall Of Fire (IRE)**15 6-8-5 **0** (b) MichaelDee 6 96
(Ciaron Maher & David Eustace, Australia) **100/1**

5 1 1/4 **Hang Man (IRE)**15 5-8-5 **0** KerrinMcEvoy 9 94
(Michael Moroney, Australia) **13/2**2

6 1 1/4 **Raheen House (IRE)**49 6473 5-9-2 **0** JamieSpencer 8 103
(William Haggas) *dwlt s: settled towards rr: pushed along 3f out: stl towards rr and rdn 1 1/2f out: styd on fnl f: nvr trbld ldrs* **17/2**

7 shd **Ventura Storm (IRE)**7 6-8-13 **0** (b) MarkZahra 1 100
(David A & B Hayes & Tom Dabernig, Australia) **14/1**

8 shd **Qafila (AUS)**13 4-8-8 **0** CoryParish 3 97
(David A & B Hayes & Tom Dabernig, Australia) *led 1f: trckd ldr: pushed along to ld narrowly 3f out: rdn and hdd 1 1/2f out: wknd fnl f* **16/1**

9 1 1/4 **Glory Days (NZ)**15 7-9-0 **0** CraigAWilliams 2 99
(Bill Thurlow, New Zealand) **10/1**

10 3 1/4 **Super Titus**13 7748 5-8-8 **0** JamieKah 12 87
(David A & B Hayes & Tom Dabernig, Australia) **17/1**

11 shd **Haky (IRE)**34 7008 5-9-0 **0** LindaMeech 11 93
(J E Hammond, France) **11/2**1

12 1/2 **Sweet Thomas (GER)**22 7-8-10 **0** DwayneDunn 5 89
(Matthew A Smith, Australia) **100/1**

13 10 **Self Sense (AUS)**14 9-8-8 **0** (bt) LukeNolen 13 71
(David Brideoake, Australia) **100/1**

2m 27.52s **13 Ran SP% 107.1**

Owner R L Bonnington, A G, C P, G, K J, Mrs P A & P R De **Bred** A G, K J, M C & P R Dennis **Trained** New Zealand

8135a SCHWEPPES THOUSAND GUINEAS (GROUP 1) (3YO FILLIES) (TURF) — 1m
5:10 3-Y-O
£333,149 (£99,447; £49,723; £24,861; £13,812; £11,049)

| | | | RPR
1 **Flit (AUS)**13 3-8-10 0 HughBowman 2 101
(James Cummings, Australia) *qckly into stride: sn settled in midfield: shkn up and styd on fr over 1 1/2f out: wnt 2nd 110yds out: clsd on ldr and jst led on line* **27/20**1

2 nse **Missile Mantra (AUS)**13 3-8-10 0 (b1) DamianLane 10 101
(Peter & Paul Snowden, Australia) **15/2**

3 shd **Southbank (AUS)**13 3-8-10 0 JamesMcDonald 4 101
(Anthony Freedman, Australia) **16/1**

4 1 3/4 **Lyre (AUS)**13 3-8-10 0 (t) MarkZahra 3 97
(Anthony Freedman, Australia) *prom 1f: trckd ldr: drvn along 2f out: rdn in 2nd over 1f out: sn outpcd by ldr and wknd fnl 150yds: rdn out* **19/5**2

5 1 **Acting (NZ)**13 3-8-10 0 (t) CraigAWilliams 6 95
(Trent Busuttin & Natalie Young, Australia) **6/1**3

6 1 **Emeralds (AUS)**21 3-8-10 0 BenMelham 8 92
(John Sargent, Australia) **10/1**

7 1 3/4 **Tenley (AUS)**13 3-8-10 0 (b) KerrinMcEvoy 7 88
(James Cummings, Australia) *in rr of midfield: pushed along 3f out: ct wd turning in: stl towards rr and rdn along over 1f out: kpt on same pce: nvr a factor* **25/1**

8 shd **I Am Eloquent (AUS)**21 3-8-10 0 (t) StephenBaster 5 88
(Trent Busuttin & Natalie Young, Australia) **50/1**

9 hd **Barbie's Fox (AUS)**13 3-8-10 0 (p) DamienOliver 1 88
(Louise Bonella, Australia) **50/1**

10 5 **St Edward's Crown (AUS)**13 3-8-10 0 (b1) DamienThornton 9 76
(Shane Fliedner, Australia) **70/1**

1m 37.19s **10 Ran SP% 113.6**

Owner Godolphin **Bred** Godolphin Australia **Trained** Australia

8136a LADBROKES STKS (GROUP 1) (3YO+) (TURF) — 1m 2f
5:50 3-Y-O+
£333,011 (£99,447; £49,723; £24,861; £13,812; £11,049)

| | | | RPR
1 **Cape Of Good Hope (IRE)**69 5721 3-8-13 0 MarkZahra 6 112+
(David A & B Hayes & Tom Dabernig, Australia) *settled in rr of midfield: angled out and asked for effrt under 1 1/2f out: styd on to chal fnl 50yds: led fnl stride* **20/1**

2 shd **Black Heart Bart (AUS)**13 7748 9-9-4 0 (t) BradRawiller 8 112
(Lindsey Smith, Australia) **20/1**

3 1 1/2 **Harlem**13 7748 7-9-4 0 (b) DwayneDunn 5 109
(David A & B Hayes & Tom Dabernig, Australia) **25/1**

4 shd **Avilius**21 7482 5-9-4 0 KerrinMcEvoy 7 109+
(James Cummings, Australia) *settled towards rr: drvn along on outer 2f out: hdwy and rdn under 1f out: continued prog: nt pce to get on terms w ldrs: rdn out* **21/20**1

5 shd **Humidor (NZ)**13 7748 7-9-4 0 JohnAllen 4 109
(Ciaron Maher & David Eustace, Australia) **18/1**

6 shd **Homesman (USA)**13 7748 5-9-4 0 (b) BenMelham 2 108
(Liam Howley, Australia) **17/5**2

7 hd **Gailo Chop (FR)**13 7748 8-9-4 0 DamienOliver 1 108
(Matthew Williams, Australia) **8/1**3

8 1 3/4 **Suzuka Devious (JPN)**90 8-9-4 0 MichaelDee 3 105
(Mitsuru Hashida, Japan) **50/1**

9 1 1/2 **Dream Castle**116 3948 5-9-4 0 PatCosgrave 9 102
(Saeed bin Suroor) *in 3rd on outer: drvn along over 2f out: sn lost position and rdn along: wl hld fnl 100yds* **15/1**

10 3/4 **Gatting (AUS)**13 7748 6-9-4 0 (b) JamieKah 10 100
(Darren McAuliffe, Australia) **19/1**

2m 2.51s
WFA 3 from 4yo+ 4lb **10 Ran SP% 114.5**

Owner Coolmore, D Hayes Et Al **Bred** Hveger Syndicate **Trained** Australia

8137a LADBROKES CAULFIELD GUINEAS (GROUP 1) (3YO) (TURF) — 1m
6:30 3-Y-O
£667,679 (£198,895; £99,447; £49,723; £27,624; £22,099)

| | | | RPR
1 **Super Seth (AUS)**13 3-8-13 0 (p) MarkZahra 4 111
(Anthony Freedman, Australia) **13/2**3

2 nse **Alligator Blood (AUS)**13 3-8-13 0 RyanMaloney 11 111
(David Vandyke, Australia) **4/1**2

3 2 1/4 **Groundswell (AUS)**13 3-8-13 0 (b) KerrinMcEvoy 10 106
(Anthony Freedman, Australia) **12/1**

4 3/4 **Subedar (AUS)**14 3-8-13 0 (b) BradRawiller 6 104
(James Cummings, Australia) *settled in rr of midfield: rdn along w plenty to do under 1 1/2f out: styd on wl to go 4th cl home: nt rching ldrs: rdn out* **15/1**

5 1/2 **Dalasan (AUS)**13 3-8-13 0 (b1) HughBowman 16 103
(Leon Macdonald & Andrew Gluyas, Australia) **13/5**1

6 *hd* **Conqueror (AUS)**[15] 3-8-13 0..........(b) DamianLane 2 102
(David A & B Hayes & Tom Dabernig, Australia) *midfield: pushed along turning in: rdn 1 1/2f out: kpt on: no imp on ldrs: rdn on out* **50/1**
7 *1* **Vegas Knight (AUS)**[15] 3-8-13 0.......... CraigAWilliams 9 100
(Colin Little, Australia) **40/1**
8 *hd* **Soul Patch (AUS)**[17] 3-8-13 0.......... DwayneDunn 12 100
(Ken Keys, Australia) **16/1**
9 *3/4* **Skiddaw (AUS)**[21] 3-8-13 0..........(t) DamienOliver 5 98
(Danny O'Brien, Australia) **40/1**
10 *shd* **Stand To Attention (AUS)**[17] 3-8-13 0..........(b) JamesWinks 3 98
(Leon & Troy Corstens, Australia) **150/1**
11 *shd* **Roccabascerana (AUS)**[13] 3-8-13 0.......... LindaMeech 1 97
(David Jolly, Australia) **25/1**
12 *shd* **Express Pass (AUS)**[13] 3-8-13 0..........(tp) BenMelham 7 97
(Nick Ryan, Australia) **20/1**
13 *3/4* **Yourdeel (NZ)**[13] 3-8-13 0..........(bt) MichaelWalker 8 95
(David A & B Hayes & Tom Dabernig, Australia) **30/1**
14 *shd* **Kubrick (AUS)**[14] 7722 3-8-13 0.......... JamesMcDonald 15 95
(Chris Waller, Australia) **13/2**[3]
15 *3* **Eric The Eel (AUS)**[14] 3-8-13 0.......... BrettPrebble 14 88
(Stuart Kendrick, Australia) **30/1**
16 *3 1/4* **Exeter (AUS)**[13] 3-8-13 0..........(p) LukeNolen 13 81
(David A & B Hayes & Tom Dabernig, Australia) **200/1**

1m 36.44s **16** Ran SP% **117.3**

Owner Pinecliff Racing, Railway Regulars Et Al **Bred** Arrowfield Pastoral Pty Ltd & Planette Thoroughbre **Trained** Australia

8138a LAMARO'S HOTEL STH MELBOURNE TOORAK H'CAP (GROUP 1) (2YO+) (TURF) 1m

7:10 2-Y-O+
£167,265 (£49,723; £24,861; £12,430; £6,906; £5,524)

RPR
1 **Fierce Impact (JPN)**[21] 5-8-8 **0**..........(b) CraigAWilliams 15 108
(Matthew A Smith, Australia) **17/1**
2 *1 3/4* **Night's Watch (NZ)**[28] 6-8-11 **0**..........(t) JamesMcDonald 9 107
(Chris Waller, Australia) **6/1**[1]
3 *3/4* **Age Of Chivalry (NZ)**[21] 7475 4-8-8 **0**.......... KerrinMcEvoy 10 102
(Mathew Ellerton & Simon Zahra, Australia) **8/1**[3]
4 *shd* **Sikandarabad (IRE)**[21] 6-8-11 **0**..........(b) MarkZahra 5 105
(David A & B Hayes & Tom Dabernig, Australia) **12/1**
5 *1* **Waging War (AUS)**[13] 6-8-3 **0**..........(b) RaquelClark 4 95
(Leon Macdonald & Andrew Gluyas, Australia) **6/1**[1]
6 *1/2* **Cliff's Edge (AUS)**[21] 7475 5-9-1 **0**..........(b) JohnAllen 6 106
(Ciaron Maher & David Eustace, Australia) **25/1**
7 *shd* **Madison County (NZ)**[21] 7475 4-9-2 **0**.......... DamianLane 17 106
(Murray Baker & Andrew Forsman, New Zealand) **15/1**
8 *shd* **Miss Siska (AUS)**[15] 6-8-3 **0**.......... DeanYendall 11 93
(Grahame Begg, Australia) **25/1**
9 *hd* **Widgee Turf (AUS)**[21] 7475 6-9-1 **0**.......... BillyEgan 8 105
(Patrick Payne, Australia) **11/1**
10 *hd* **Mahamedeis (AUS)**[13] 5-8-8 **0**..........(bt) BenMelham 1 97
(Nick Ryan, Australia) **14/1**
11 *shd* **Streets Of Avalon (AUS)**[21] 7475 5-8-11 **0**..........(bt) ZacSpain 14 100
(Shane Nichols, Australia) **50/1**
12 *shd* **Princess Jenni (NZ)**[15] 4-8-8 **0**.......... DamienOliver 13 97
(David Brideoake, Australia) **13/2**[2]
13 *3/4* **Chief Ironside**[99] 4612 4-8-3 **0**.......... AnthonyDarmanin 2 90
(David Menuisier) *dwlt: settled in midfield on inner: drvn along 1 1/2f out: sn nt clr run: no ch after* **25/1**
14 *3/4* **So Si Bon (AUS)**[21] 7475 6-9-2 **0**.......... LukeNolen 18 101
(David A & B Hayes & Tom Dabernig, Australia) **20/1**
15 *hd* **Amphitrite (AUS)**[21] 7475 4-8-9 **0**..........(b[1]) JamieKah 3 94
(David A & B Hayes & Tom Dabernig, Australia) **16/1**
16 *3 3/4* **Order Again (NZ)**[13] 6-8-7 **0**..........(t) LarryCassidy 12 83
(Brian Smith, Australia) **100/1**
17 *1/2* **Wyndspelle (NZ)**[21] 6-8-11 **0**..........(bt) MichaelDee 7 86
(Johno Benner, New Zealand) **60/1**
18 *hd* **Dyslexic (AUS)**[13] 5-8-3 **0**.......... DamienThornton 16 78
(Michael, Wayne & John Hawkes, Australia) **30/1**

1m 35.19s **18** Ran SP% **117.5**

Owner Seymour Bloodstock, Denns Racing Et Al **Bred** Keiai Orthopedic Appliance Co Ltd **Trained** Australia

7938 KEENELAND (L-H)
Saturday, October 12

OFFICIAL GOING: Turf: firm

8139a QUEEN ELIZABETH II CHALLENGE CUP STKS PRESENTED BY LANE'S END (GRADE 1) (3YO FILLIES) (TURF) 1m 1f (T)

10:30 3-Y-O
£236,220 (£78,740; £39,370; £19,685; £11,811; £2,625)

RPR
1 **Cambier Parc (USA)**[55] 6268 3-8-9 0.......... JohnRVelazquez 2 107
(Chad C Brown, U.S.A) *mde all: rdn and kicked for home under 2f out: kpt on strly fnl f: drvn out* **9/5**[1]
2 *1* **Castle Lady (IRE)**[113] 4051 3-8-9 0.......... MickaelBarzalona 4 104
(H-A Pantall, France) *in tch: trckd ldrs 2f out: rdn under 2f out: jostled w rival 1 1/2f out: drvn and kpt on wl fnl f: no imp on wnr* **33/10**[2]
3 *1 3/4* **Princesa Carolina (USA)**[34] 3-8-9 0.......... JoseLOrtiz 3 101
(Kenneth McPeek, U.S.A) *in tch in midfield: rdn over 1f out: styd on fnl f* **128/10**
4 *nk* **Cafe Americano (USA)**[62] 3-8-9 0.......... IradOrtizJr 5 100
(Chad C Brown, U.S.A) *towards rr: rdn 2f out: drvn and styd on fnl f: nrst fin* **49/10**[3]
5 *nse* **Varenka (USA)**[56] 3-8-9 0.......... JavierCastellano 7 100
(H Graham Motion, U.S.A) *towards rr of midfield: shkn up and hdwy on outside fr 2 1/2f out: rdn and kpt on fr under 2f out* **7/1**
6 *1* **Regal Glory (USA)**[56] 3-8-9 0.......... LuisSaez 8 98
(Chad C Brown, U.S.A) *veered rt leaving stalls: sn rcvrd and trckd ldrs: rdn under 2f out: jostled w rival 1 1/2f out: fdd fnl f* **84/10**
7 *3/4* **Kelsey's Cross (USA)**[28] 3-8-9 0..........(b) JulienRLeparoux 1 96
(Patrick L Biancone, U.S.A) *a towards rr* **39/1**
8 *1/2* **Magnetic Charm**[28] 7224 3-8-9 0.......... FlorentGeroux 6 95
(William Haggas) *w ldr: outpcd 2f out: nt clr run and lost pl under 2f out: sn rdn: wknd over 1f out* **15/2**

1m 49.54s (-0.26) **8** Ran SP% **120.6**
PARI-MUTUEL (all including 2 unit stake): WIN 5.60; PLACE (1-2) 3.20, 4.60; SHOW (1-2-3) 2.80, 3.60, 5.00; SF 25.00.
Owner OXO Equine LLC **Bred** Bonne Chance Farm Llc **Trained** USA

7799 MAISONS-LAFFITTE (R-H)
Saturday, October 12

OFFICIAL GOING: Turf: very soft

8140a CRITERIUM DE MAISONS-LAFFITTE (GROUP 2) (2YO) (TURF) 6f

1:35 2-Y-O
£97,567 (£37,657; £17,972; £11,981; £5,990)

RPR
1 **Shadn (IRE)**[21] 7456 2-8-13 0.......... Pierre-CharlesBoudot 6 107
(Andrew Balding) *bmpd w rival leaving stalls: settled in fnl trio: niggled along 1/2-way: hdwy u.p to chse ldr over 1f out: sustained chal ins fnl f: led cl home* **23/5**
2 *hd* **Devil (IRE)**[26] 7292 2-9-2 0.......... AurelienLemaitre 4 109
(F Head, France) *w.w in rr: hdwy u.p to ld on outer over 1 1/2f out: styd on whn chal ins fnl f: hdd cl home* **23/10**[1]
3 *1 3/4* **Sir Boris (IRE)**[19] 7532 2-9-2 0.......... RichardKingscote 5 104
(Tom Dascombe) *led: drvn whn pressed ins fnl 2 1/2f: sn rdn and hdd over 1 1/2f out: kpt on u.p but nt pce of front two fnl f* **43/10**[3]
4 *nse* **Lady Penelope (IRE)**[22] 7400 2-8-13 0.......... ChristopheSoumillon 1 101
(Joseph Patrick O'Brien, Ire) *awkward leaving stalls: racd in fnl trio: hdwy 1 1/2f fr home: styd on u.p: jst missed 3rd but nvr trbld ldrs* **66/10**
5 *1/2* **Alocasia**[17] 7602 2-8-13 0.......... AlexisBadel 7 100
(H-F Devin, France) *bmpd w rival leaving stalls: sn chsng ldr: pushed along fr 2 1/2f out: rdn and ev ch over 1 1/2f out: dropped away u.p fnl f* **42/10**[2]
6 *1 1/4* **Spartan Fighter**[50] 6422 2-9-2 0.......... DanielTudhope 8 99
(Declan Carroll) *chsd ldrs on outer: rdn to chse front two 1 1/2f out: wknd fnl f* **14/1**
7 *snk* **Lady Galore (IRE)**[42] 6791 2-8-13 0.......... JulienAuge 2 96
(C Ferland, France) *racd keenly: chsd ldrs on inner: outpcd and scrubbed along 2 1/2f out: wl hld fnl f* **26/1**
8 *snk* **Jessely (FR)**[17] 7602 2-8-13 0.......... CristianDemuro 3 95
(Andrea Marcialis, France) *midfield between horses: outpcd and rdn ins fnl 2f: sn btn* **9/1**

1m 12.23s (-1.17) **8** Ran SP% **119.8**
PARI-MUTUEL (all including 1 euro stake): WIN 5.60; PLACE 1.60, 1.40, 1.70; DF 7.30.
Owner Alrabban Racing **Bred** Barronstown Stud **Trained** Kingsclere, Hants

FOCUS
The field was fairly compressed at the finish and it's been rated as a slightly lesser renewal.

8141a PRIX DE BONNEVAL (LISTED RACE) (3YO+) (TURF) 5f 110y

2:50 3-Y-O+
£23,423 (£9,369; £7,027; £4,684; £2,342)

RPR
1 **Tour To Paris (FR)**[27] 7255 4-8-13 0.......... CristianDemuro 11 108
(Mme Pia Brandt, France) **17/5**[2]
2 *nse* **The Right Man**[133] 3369 7-8-13 0.......... Francois-XavierBertras 1 108
(D Guillemin, France) **14/5**[1]
3 *2* **Trois Mille (FR)**[56] 6252 3-8-13 0.......... AlexisBadel 2 102
(S Cerulis, France) **15/2**
4 *snk* **Flaming Star (FR)**[99] 4621 3-8-9 0.......... VincentCheminaud 7 98
(H-A Pantall, France) **25/1**
5 *snk* **Maygold**[7] 7889 4-8-9 0.......... AntoineHamelin 5 96
(Ed Walker) *racd keenly in midfield: pushed along 2f out: sn rdn and hdwy ent fnl f: kpt on wl u.p* **15/1**
6 *shd* **Tertius (FR)**[48] 6520 3-9-3 0.......... TheoBachelot 3 105
(M Nigge, France) **61/10**[3]
7 *1/2* **Mubaalegh**[15] 5-8-13 0.......... RonanThomas 9 98
(J E Hammond, France) *plld hrd first 2f: led: hdd 2f out: rdn to chal: grad lft bhd* **16/1**
8 *hd* **Bakoel Koffie (IRE)**[34] 7010 5-9-3 0.......... TonyPiccone 6 102
(M Delcher Sanchez, France) **16/1**
9 *6* **Kenbaio (FR)**[69] 5714 3-8-13 0.......... Pierre-CharlesBoudot 10 79
(P Bary, France) **15/2**
10 *2 1/2* **Inspired Thought (IRE)**[22] 7401 3-8-9 0..........(p) HollieDoyle 8 67
(Archie Watson) *dwlt: racd in midfield: shkn up over half way: hrd rdn ent fnl 2f: sn drvn and no imp: outpcd by ldrs* **35/1**
11 *2* **Comedia Eria (FR)**[27] 7254 7-8-9 0.......... StephanePasquier 4 59
(P Monfort, France) **12/1**

1m 4.45s (-2.85) **11** Ran SP% **119.0**
PARI-MUTUEL (all including 1 euro stake): WIN 4.40; PLACE 1.80, 1.60, 2.30; DF 7.90.
Owner A Jathiere & G Augustin-Normand **Bred** Earl Haras Du Quesnay **Trained** France

8142 - 8152a (Foreign Racing) - See Raceform Interactive

7724 SAN SIRO (R-H)
Saturday, October 12

OFFICIAL GOING: Turf: good

8153a PREMIO VERZIERE MEMORIAL ALDO CIRLA (GROUP 3) (3YO+) (GRANDE COURSE) (TURF) 1m 2f

3:45 3-Y-O+
£31,528 (£13,873; £7,568; £3,781)

RPR
1 **Call Me Love**[41] 3-8-9 0.......... FabioBranca 6 104
(A Botti, Italy) *hld up in fnl trio: hdwy 2f out: led appr fnl f: sn clr: comf* **25/12**[2]
2 *3 1/2* **Elisa Again**[13] 3-8-9 0..........(tp) AndreaMezzatesta 5 97
(R Biondi, Italy) *chsd ldr between horses: 2nd and ev ch ins fnl 2f: styd on but nt match pce of wnr fnl f* **83/100**[1]

3 1 1/4 **Binti Al Nar (GER)**[20] 7503 4-9-0 0....................(b) CarloFiocchi 4 95
(P Schiergen, Germany) *racd keenly: led under restraint: hdd after 1 1/2f and chsd ldr: qcknd to ld more than 2f out: drvn but hdd appr fnl f: kpt on at one pce* **74/10**

4 1 1/4 **Queen Josephine (GER)** 3-8-9 0.................... SibylleVogt 3 92
(M Figge, Germany) *hld up in fnl trio: styd on ins fnl f: nvr nrr* **111/10**

5 3 **Light My Fire (FR)**[58] 4-9-0 0....................(t) AntonioFresu 1 86
(Karoly Kerekes, Germany) *chsd ldr on inner: rdn and nt qckn 2f out: dropped away fnl f* **34/1**

6 3/4 **Great Aventura (IRE)**[13] 5-9-0 0.................... SilvanoMulas 7 85
(Cristiano Davide Fais, Italy) *chsd ldr on outer: led after 1 1/2f: hdd on run to 2f out: rdn and wknd ins fnl f* **188/10**

7 6 **Must Be Late (IRE)**[111] 4171 3-8-9 0....................(b) DarioVargiu 2 73
(A Botti, Italy) *w.w in rr: shkn up but no imp fr 2f out: wl hld whn eased ins fnl f* **57/10**[3]

2m 3.4s (-3.30)
WFA 3 from 4yo+ 4lb **7 Ran SP% 130.1**
PARI-MUTUEL (all including 1 euro stake): WIN 3.08; PLACE 1.30, 1.15; DF 2.34.
Owner Scuderia Effevi SRL **Bred** Grundy Bloodstock Ltd **Trained** Italy

7266 WOODBINE (L-H)
Saturday, October 12
OFFICIAL GOING: Turf: yielding changing to good after race 7 (9.30)

8154a E.P. TAYLOR STKS (GRADE 1) (3YO+ FILLIES & MARES) (TURF) 1m 2f (T)
10:05 3-Y-O+
£206,896 (£68,965; £34,482; £17,241; £8,275; £3,448)

RPR

1 **Starship Jubilee (USA)**[28] 7224 6-8-12 0.................... LuisContreras 8 106+
(Kevin Attard, Canada) *w ldr: led gng wl 2 1/2f out: rdn and kpt on wl fr 2f out: readily* **7/2**[2]

2 1 **Durance (GER)**[42] 6747 3-8-8 0....................(p) LukasDelozier 6 104
(P Schiergen, Germany) *in tch in midfield: sltly hmpd and forced to switch 2f out: sn rdn: styd on fr over 1f out: nt rch wnr* **166/10**

3 hd **Platane**[56] 6250 3-8-8 0.................... MaximeGuyon 9 104
(C Laffon-Parias, France) *towards rr of midfield: rdn 2 1/2f out: styd on fr 1 1/2f out: drvn ins fnl f: nt rch wnr* **173/10**

4 1 **Imperial Charm**[37] 6910 3-8-8 0.................... AndreaAtzeni 7 102
(Simon Crisford) *trckd ldrs: rdn over 2f out: drvn 1 1/2f out: no ex fnl 75yds* **67/10**

5 2 1/4 **Holy Helena (CAN)**[28] 7224 5-8-12 0............ RafaelManuelHernandez 5 97
(James Jerkens, U.S.A) *in tch: trckd ldrs 1/2-way: rdn 2 1/2f out: wknd steadily fr over 1f out* **76/10**

6 nk **Si Que Es Buena (ARG)**[259] 6-8-12 0.................... ChrisLanderos 4 96
(H Graham Motion, U.S.A) *t.k.h: towards rr: rdn 2f out: kpt on fnl f: n.d* **5/1**[3]

7 nse **Gaining**[30] 5-8-12 0.................... JoseValdiviaJr 1 96
(Brad H Cox, U.S.A) *midfield: rdn under 2f out: nt clr run 1f out: no imp fnl f* **109/10**

8 3/4 **Red Tea**[55] 6265 6-8-12 0.................... EuricoRosaDaSilva 2 94
(Joseph Patrick O'Brien, Ire) *led: hdd 2 1/2f out: rdn 2f out: wknd wl over 1f out* **67/20**[1]

9 1/2 **A. A. Azula's Arch (USA)**[34] 4-8-12 0.................... KazushiKimura 3 93
(Kevin Attard, Canada) *a towards rr* **37/1**

10 1/2 **Secret Message (USA)**[49] 6491 4-8-12 0....................(b) TrevorMcCarthy 10 92
(H Graham Motion, U.S.A) *a in rr* **97/10**

2m 3.29s (-0.73)
WFA 3 from 4yo+ 4lb **10 Ran SP% 118.0**
PARI-MUTUEL (all including 2 unit stake): WIN 9.00; PLACE (1-2) 5.30, 8.80; SHOW (1-2-3) 3.60, 5.30, 8.50; SF 115.90.
Owner Blue Heaven Farm LLC **Bred** William P Sorren **Trained** Canada

FOCUS
The second and third have been rated to their marks.

8155a PATTISON CANADIAN INTERNATIONAL STKS (GRADE 1) (3YO+) (TURF) 1m 4f (T)
10:42 3-Y-O+
£275,862 (£91,954; £50,574; £27,586; £9,195; £4,597)

RPR

1 **Desert Encounter (IRE)**[21] 7455 7-9-0 0.................... AndreaAtzeni 4 111+
(David Simcock) *missed break: in rr: rdn under 2f out: styd on wl and weaved through field fr 1 1/2f out: led 125yds out: kpt on strly* **6/4**[2]

2 1/2 **Alounak (FR)**[49] 6487 4-9-0 0.................... ClementLecoeuvre 5 110
(Waldemar Hickst, Germany) *hld up in tch: rdn and styd on wl fr 2f out: nt able to chal* **136/10**

3 nk **Ziyad**[48] 6522 4-9-0 0.................... MaximeGuyon 1 110
(C Laffon-Parias, France) *led: rdn under 2f out: hdd 125yds out: kpt on* **23/20**[1]

4 nk **Pivoine (IRE)**[21] 7455 5-9-0 0....................(b) RobHornby 2 109
(Andrew Balding) *trckd ldrs: rdn and kpt on same pce fr under 2f out* **122/10**

5 2 3/4 **Pumpkin Rumble (USA)**[21] 8-9-0 0.................... EuricoRosaDaSilva 6 105
(Kevin Attard, Canada) *chsd ldr: rdn 2f out: wknd fr wl over 1f out* **119/10**

6 1/2 **Nessy (USA)**[28] 7226 6-9-0 0....................(b) ChrisLanderos 3 104
(Ian R Wilkes, U.S.A) *hld up in tch: rdn over 2f out: outpcd fr 1 1/2f out* **91/10**[3]

2m 28.62s (-0.98) **6 Ran SP% 118.6**
PARI-MUTUEL (all including 2 unit stake): WIN 5.00; PLACE (1-2) 3.60, 10.90; SHOW (1-2-3) 2.20, 4.60, 2.10; SF 41.70.
Owner Abdulla Al Mansoori **Bred** Tally-Ho Stud **Trained** Newmarket, Suffolk

FOCUS
The level is set by the second, fifth and sixth.

7562 GOODWOOD (R-H)
Sunday, October 13
8156 Meeting Abandoned - Waterlogged

8163 - (Foreign Racing) - See Raceform Interactive

7740 CURRAGH (R-H)
Sunday, October 13
OFFICIAL GOING: Straight course - soft to heavy; round course - soft

8164a IRISH STALLION FARMS EBF LEGACY STKS (LISTED RACE) 6f
2:05 (2:05) 2-Y-O
£29,234 (£9,414; £4,459; £1,981; £990; £495) **Stalls** Centre

RPR

1 **Tango (IRE)**[15] 7692 2-9-0 103 ow2.................... DonnachaO'Brien 8 105
(A P O'Brien, Ire) *chsd ldrs nr side: hdwy travelling wl to ld over 1f out: rdn and qcknd clr ins fnl f: easily* **11/8**[1]

2 6 **Schroders Mistake (IRE)**[20] 7530 2-8-12 85.................... WJLee 4 85
(K J Condon, Ire) *cl up far side: disp ld fr 1/2-way and led narrowly over 2f out: rdn and strly pressed 1 1/2f out: sn hdd and no imp on easy wnr ins fnl f: kpt on same pce* **8/1**

3 1 1/2 **Silver Spear (IRE)**[20] 7531 2-8-12 84.................... AndrewSlattery 7 81
(Andrew Slattery, Ire) *chsd ldrs nr side: almost on terms at 1/2-way: effrt 1 1/2f out: no imp on easy wnr ins fnl f: kpt on same pce* **16/1**

4 1 3/4 **Kondratiev Wave (IRE)**[14] 7740 2-9-3 0.................... ShaneFoley 3 80
(Kieran P Cotter, Ire) *led narrowly far side: jnd fr 1/2-way: drvn and hdd over 2f out: u.p in 4th over 1f out: kpt on same pce* **14/1**

5 3/4 **French Rain (IRE)**[51] 6429 2-8-12 0.................... ColinKeane 5 73
(G M Lyons, Ire) *w.w towards rr nr side: tk clsr order fr 1/2-way: rdn and no imp on ldrs 2f out: kpt on one pce in 5th ins fnl f* **15/2**[3]

6 2 1/2 **Lady Jane Wilde (IRE)**[29] 7215 2-8-12 0.................... NGMcCullagh 6 66
(John M Oxx, Ire) *hld up in rr nr side: rdn 2f out and kpt on one pce: nvr trbld ldrs* **8/1**

7 1 1/4 **Lil Grey (IRE)**[15] 7692 2-8-12 95.................... RobbieColgan 2 62
(Ms Sheila Lavery, Ire) *trckd ldrs far side: almost on terms at 1/2-way: rdn and no ex 2f out: sn wknd* **4/1**[2]

8 4 1/2 **Arranmore**[44] 6690 2-9-3 91.................... KevinManning 1 53
(J S Bolger, Ire) *hooded to load: settled bhd ldrs far side: drvn after 1/2-way and sn no ex u.p: wknd over 1f out* **12/1**

1m 17.4s (3.20) **Going Correction** +0.925s/f (Soft) **8 Ran SP% 116.3**
Speed ratings: **115,107,105,102,101 98,96,90**
CSF £13.63 TOTE £1.90: £1.02, £2.50, £4.50; DF 10.90 Trifecta £147.30.
Owner Michael Tabor & Derrick Smith & Mrs John Magnier **Bred** Fastnet Stud Ltd **Trained** Cashel, Co Tipperary

FOCUS
What looked quite an intriguing affair beforehand developed into a rout. The winner proved in a different league and was impressive. She's been rated in line with her recent improved form in better races.

8165a STAFFORDSTOWN STUD STKS (LISTED RACE) (FILLIES) 1m
2:40 (2:41) 2-Y-O
£26,576 (£8,558; £4,054; £1,801; £900; £450)

RPR

1 **Fancy Blue (IRE)**[25] 7356 2-9-0 0.................... SeamieHeffernan 5 100
(A P O'Brien, Ire) *dwlt sltly: w.w in rr: last at 1/2-way: swtchd lft over 2f out and hdwy nr side: rdn in 4th and r.o wl ins fnl f to ld fnl strides* **4/1**[3]

2 hd **A New Dawn (IRE)**[14] 7742 2-9-0 102.................... DonnachaO'Brien 8 100
(Joseph Patrick O'Brien, Ire) *sn settled towards rr: 5th 1/2-way: prog to chal 2f out: rdn to ld narrowly ent fnl f: kpt on wl ins fnl f: hdd fnl strides* **15/8**[1]

3 1/2 **Auxilia (IRE)**[69] 5755 2-9-0 0.................... ColinKeane 7 99
(G M Lyons, Ire) *led narrowly briefly tl sn settled bhd ldrs: 4th at 1/2-way: rdn to chal under 2f out and sn disp ld briefly tl hdd: kpt on u.p ins fnl f: hld cl home* **5/2**[2]

4 hd **Shehreen (IRE)**[14] 7742 2-9-0 93.................... ChrisHayes 1 98
(D K Weld, Ire) *sn led: narrow advantage 3f out: drvn over 2f out and sn jnd: hdd over 1f out: kpt on u.p ins fnl f: hld cl home* **13/2**

5 1 1/4 **Celestial Object (IRE)**[17] 7633 2-9-0 0.................... ShaneFoley 3 96
(Mrs John Harrington, Ire) *disp briefly early tl sn settled bhd ldr: cl 2nd at 1/2-way: pushed along 3f out: effrt on terms 2f out: sn hdd and dropped to 5th: kpt on ins fnl f* **7/1**

6 4 1/2 **Lady Georgie (IRE)**[30] 7167 2-9-0 0.................... RossCoakley 2 86
(John C McConnell, Ire) *chsd ldrs: 3rd 3f out: rdn bhd ldrs 2f out and no imp over 1f out* **50/1**

7 3/4 **Zofar Zogood (IRE)**[17] 7633 2-9-0 0....................(t[1]) DeclanMcDonogh 6 84
(Joseph Patrick O'Brien, Ire) *w.w towards rr: rn freely early: rdn and no ex over 2f out* **33/1**

1m 53.09s (12.49) **Going Correction** +0.925s/f (Soft) **7 Ran SP% 114.1**
Speed ratings: **74,73,73,73,71 67,66**
CSF £11.89 TOTE £4.40: £2.00, £1.40; DF 10.00 Trifecta £28.60.
Owner Michael Tabor & Derrick Smith & Mrs John Magnier **Bred** Coolmore **Trained** Cashel, Co Tipperary

FOCUS
A thrilling finish to this Listed prize for fillies, which was run at a sensible clip in the conditions. The first four home were separated by less than a length. The second has been rated just off her latest effort.

8166a WATERFORD TESTIMONIAL STKS (LISTED RACE) 6f
3:15 (3:16) 3-Y-O+
£23,918 (£7,702; £3,648; £1,621; £810; £405) **Stalls** Centre

RPR

1 **Make A Challenge (IRE)**[15] 7714 4-9-6 109.................... JoeDoyle 1 115+
(Denis Gerard Hogan, Ire) *trckd ldrs: 3rd 1/2-way: gng wl in 2nd after 1/2-way: impr to ld ent fnl f and rdn clr: kpt on wl clsng stages where wnt rt: easily* **9/4**[1]

2 4 1/2 **Downforce (IRE)**[15] 7713 7-9-6 106....................(v) WJLee 3 101
(W McCreery, Ire) *led: drvn and strly pressed over 1f out: sn hdd and no imp on easy wnr ins fnl f: kpt on same pce* **9/4**[1]

3 1 1/2 **Urban Beat (IRE)**[15] 7714 4-9-9 101.................... ShaneFoley 4 99
(J P Murtagh, Ire) *hld up towards rr: disp 6th at 1/2-way: prog 2f out: no imp on easy wnr u.p in 3rd ins fnl f: kpt on same pce* **4/1**[2]

4 2 3/4 **Fairy Falcon**[23] 7401 4-9-1 99....................(p[1]) DeclanMcDonogh 8 82
(Bryan Smart) *chsd ldrs: 4th 1/2-way: rdn bhd ldrs 2f out and no ex over 1f out: one pce after* **14/1**

5 1 1/2 **Flight Risk (IRE)**[57] 6235 8-9-11 110 KevinManning 2 87
(J S Bolger, Ire) *hld up bhd ldrs: 5th 1/2-way: rdn 2f out and no imp in 5th ent fnl f: kpt on one pce* **5/1**[3]
6 shd **Independent Missy (IRE)**[121] 3826 3-9-0 86 RonanWhelan 10 77
(Tracey Collins, Ire) *s.i.s and in rr early: rdn 2f out and no imp disputing 6th ent fnl f: kpt on one pce* **14/1**
7 5 **Rhydwyn (IRE)**[28] 7241 3-9-5 92 (t) ColinKeane 9 66
(T Hogan, Ire) *hld up towards rr: disp 6th at 1/2-way: rdn 2f out and no imp disputing 6th ent fnl f: wknd* **25/1**
8 3 1/2 **Zodiacus (IRE)**[4] 8038 3-9-0 75 (t) RobbieColgan 7 50
(T G McCourt, Ire) *cl up bhd ldr: 2nd 1/2-way: wknd fr over 2f out* **66/1**
1m 16.7s (2.50) **Going Correction** +0.925s/f (Soft)
WFA 3 from 4yo+ 1lb **8** Ran SP% **116.9**
Speed ratings: **120,114,112,108,106 106,99,94**
CSF £7.44 TOTE £2.70: £1.02, £1.20, £1.60; DF 5.70 Trifecta £16.70.
Owner M G Hogan & Walter O'Connor & James Joseph Reilly **Bred** Godolphin **Trained** Cloughjordan, Co Tipperary
FOCUS
A lot of these arrived here out of sorts, so it could be worth taking the winner's performance with a pinch of salt, but the way in which he sprinted clear in the closing stages was very easy on the eye. This was seriously impressive visually. The second, third and fourth have been rated in line with their recent efforts.

8167 - 8170a (Foreign Racing) - See Raceform Interactive

7862 HOPPEGARTEN (R-H)
Sunday, October 13

OFFICIAL GOING: Turf: good

8171a SILBERNES PFERD (GROUP 3) (3YO+) (TURF) 1m 7f
1:05 3-Y-O+ £28,828 (£10,810; £5,405; £2,702; £1,801)

RPR
1 **Ladykiller (GER)**[56] 3-8-10 0 BauyrzhanMurzabayev 6 106
(A Wohler, Germany) *mde all: shkn up to assert 2 1/2f out: kpt on wl whn chal ins fnl f: a doing enough* **27/10**[2]
2 1 1/2 **Nacida (GER)**[28] 7249 5-9-1 0 AdriedeVries 1 99
(Yasmin Almenrader, Germany) *settled in 3rd: hdwy to go 2nd over 3f out: sn rdn: r.o: nt match wnr ins fnl f* **114/10**
3 1 1/4 **Lillian Russell (IRE)**[56] 6266 4-8-13 0 VincentCheminaud 5 96
(H-A Pantall, France) *chsd ldng trio: rdn 3f out where proged to 3rd: r.o: no imp on ldng pair* **17/10**[1]
4 hd **Enjoy The Moon (IRE)**[74] 3-8-8 0 LukasDelozier 4 100
(P Schiergen, Germany) *cl up: pushed along 3 1/2f out: rdn 2 1/2f out: kpt on one pce* **9/2**
5 5 **Moonshiner (GER)**[28] 7249 6-9-2 0 (p) FilipMinarik 2 92
(Jean-Pierre Carvalho, Germany) *in rr: hdwy on outer over 3f out: sn rdn: no imp on ldrs* **7/2**[3]
6 31 **Amarone (GER)**[14] 4-8-13 0 JozefBojko 3 52
(Eva Fabianova, Germany) *trckd ldr on outer: lost position 3f out: sn wknd rapidly* **15/1**
3m 19.37s
WFA 3 from 4yo+ 8lb **6** Ran SP% **118.8**
PARI-MUTUEL (all including 1 euro stake): WIN 3.7 PLACE: 1.9, 4.8; SF: 40.0.
Owner Rennstall Gestut Hachtsee **Bred** Gestut Karlshof **Trained** Germany

8172 - 8179a (Foreign Racing) - See Raceform Interactive

7732 MUSSELBURGH (R-H)
Monday, October 14

OFFICIAL GOING: Soft (7.2)
Wind: Breezy, half behind in sprints and in approximately 4f of home straight in races on the round course Weather: Fine, dry

8180 RACINGTV.COM NURSERY H'CAP 5f 1y
1:20 (1:20) (Class 6) (0-65,64) 2-Y-O
£3,105 (£924; £461; £300; £300; £300) Stalls High

Form RPR
4300 1 **Carmel**[14] 7767 2-9-0 57 (b[1]) DanielTudhope 4 60
(Archie Watson) *w ldr: drvn along over 2f out: led fnl 150yds: drew clr towards fin* **3/1**[2]
6054 2 2 1/2 **Garnock Valley**[21] 7506 2-8-13 56 PJMcDonald 5 50
(R Mike Smith) *in tch: drvn and outpcd over 1f out: rallied ins fnl f: kpt on to take 2nd last stride* **8/1**
0400 3 nse **Wade's Magic**[12] 7827 2-9-5 62 (b) DavidAllan 1 56
(Tim Easterby) *t.k.h early: led: rdn over 1f out: hdd fnl 150yds: no ex and lost 2nd last stride* **2/1**[1]
4324 4 3/4 **Maybellene (IRE)**[15] 7734 2-9-6 63 CamHardie 8 54
(Alan Berry) *trckd ldrs: effrt and drvn along 2f out: kpt on same pce ins fnl f* **11/2**
4020 5 1 **Summer Heights**[15] 7734 2-8-13 56 PaddyMathers 7 44
(Jim Goldie) *s.i.s: bhd and sn outpcd: sme late hdwy: nvr rchd ldrs* **12/1**
0633 6 nk **Not On Your Nellie (IRE)**[15] 7734 2-9-7 64 (t[1]) TomEaves 2 50
(Nigel Tinkler) *t.k.h early: chsd ldrs: shkn up and ev ch over 1f out: drvn and wknd fnl 100yds* **9/2**[3]
1m 3.2s (3.50) **Going Correction** +0.45s/f (Yiel) **6** Ran SP% **110.7**
Speed ratings (Par 93): **90,86,85,84,83 82**
CSF £25.10 CT £54.40 TOTE £6.40: £2.90, £4.30; EX 35.40 Trifecta £102.70.
Owner Mrs Julie Martin And David R Martin **Bred** Julie Routledge-Martin **Trained** Upper Lambourn, W Berks
FOCUS
The stands' bend was out 2yds. \n\x\x Those racing nearer the stands' rail were at an advantage in this moderate nursery. The time backed up an official description of soft going. Late-season form, the winner rated back to her best.

8181 LIKE RACING TV ON FACEBOOK H'CAP 7f 33y
1:50 (1:51) (Class 5) (0-75,75) 3-Y-O+
£3,428 (£1,020; £509; £300; £300; £300) Stalls Low

Form RPR
3256 1 **Black Friday**[24] 7418 4-9-3 69 (p) JasonHart 4 82+
(Karen McLintock) *in tch in chsng gp: shkn up and hdwy to ld over 2f out: rdn clr fnl f: eased cl home* **3/1**[1]
2001 2 3 1/4 **How Bizarre**[15] 7738 4-9-6 72 DavidNolan 1 76
(Liam Bailey) *chsd clr ldr: rdn over 2f out: chsd wnr over 1f out: kpt on same pce fnl f* **7/1**[3]
6550 3 1 1/2 **Imperial State**[5] 8031 6-9-5 71 (t) TomEaves 5 74+
(Michael Easterby) *slowly away: hld up: effrt whn nt clr run over 2f out to over 1f out: hdwy to chse clr ldng pair ins fnl f: r.o fin* **9/1**
4000 4 nk **Highlight Reel (IRE)**[28] 7289 4-9-2 68 PhilDennis 6 68
(Rebecca Bastiman) *hld up in midfield: effrt over 2f out: chsd clr ldng pair over 1f out to ins fnl f: no ex* **17/2**
0-60 5 3 3/4 **Najib (IRE)**[150] 2795 3-9-4 72 BenCurtis 10 61
(Roger Fell) *hld up towards rr: drvn along 3f out: hdwy over 1f out: no imp fnl f* **16/1**
1164 6 nse **Ugo Gregory**[12] 7828 3-9-0 68 DavidAllan 2 57
(Tim Easterby) *s.i.s: hld up in midfield: effrt and rdn over 2f out: no imp over 1f out* **9/2**[2]
1550 7 2 1/4 **Ramesses**[44] 6700 3-9-5 73 PaddyMathers 12 56
(Richard Fahey) *in tch in chsng gp on outside: drvn along over 2f out: wknd over 1f out* **20/1**
305 8 3/4 **Mostahel**[24] 7418 5-9-1 67 PaulMulrennan 9 49
(Paul Midgley) *s.i.s: hld up: pushed along over 2f out: no imp fr over 1f out* **12/1**
6000 9 1/2 **Arcavallo (IRE)**[28] 7289 4-9-2 68 (b) CallumRodriguez 3 49
(Michael Dods) *t.k.h: led and sn clr: hdd over 2f out: wknd over 1f out* **16/1**
4000 10 2 1/2 **Shining Armor**[34] 7049 3-9-7 75 CamHardie 7 48
(John Ryan) *prom in chsng gp: drvn along 4f out: wknd wl over 1f out* **40/1**
0 11 1 **Western Dawn (IRE)**[17] 7653 3-9-6 74 ShaneGray 11 45
(Phillip Makin) *s.i.s: bhd: drvn along over 3f out: nvr on terms* **40/1**
1442 12 1/2 **Ollivander (IRE)**[20] 7540 3-9-7 75 (v) DanielTudhope 8 44
(David O'Meara) *prom in chsng gp: rdn along over 3f out: wknd over 2f out (trainer's rep could offer no explanation for the gelding's performance)* **7/1**[3]
1m 31.55s (2.55) **Going Correction** +0.45s/f (Yiel)
WFA 3 from 4yo+ 2lb **12** Ran SP% **117.8**
Speed ratings (Par 103): **103,99,97,97,92 92,90,89,88,86 84,84**
CSF £23.21 CT £169.08 TOTE £4.50: £2.10, £2.60, £3.00; EX 20.10 Trifecta £150.70.
Owner Miss S A Booth & Don Eddy **Bred** Catridge Farm Stud & Partners **Trained** Ingoe, Northumberland
FOCUS
There was no hiding place in this modest handicap. The winner built on his Carlisle form.

8182 BREEDERS BACKING RACING EBF FLYING SCOTSMAN CONDITIONS STKS 5f 1y
2:20 (2:27) (Class 3) 3-Y-O+ £9,337 (£2,796; £1,398; £699; £349) Stalls High

Form RPR
0012 1 **Tarboosh**[6] 8004 6-9-5 101 KevinStott 3 109+
(Paul Midgley) *sn trcking ldrs: smooth hdwy to ld ins fnl f: shkn up and qcknd clr fnl 100yds: eased cl home: readily* **10/11**[1]
5003 2 2 1/2 **Copper Knight (IRE)**[6] 8004 5-9-7 105 (t) DavidAllan 5 102
(Tim Easterby) *pressed ldr: led and rdn over 1f out: edgd lft and hdd ins fnl f: sn no ch w ready wnr* **4/1**[2]
0600 3 3/4 **Merhoob (IRE)**[23] 7433 7-9-5 97 BenCurtis 2 97
(John Ryan) *prom: effrt on outside and rdn over 1f out: kpt on same pce ins fnl f* **9/1**
-613 4 3 1/4 **Kyllang Rock (IRE)**[20] 7541 5-9-2 102 PJMcDonald 1 83
(James Tate) *stdd and swtchd lft s: hld up in last pl: angled rt and effrt over 1f out: sn no imp: btn ins fnl f* **9/2**[3]
6020 5 1 1/2 **Broken Spear**[3] 8099 3-9-2 87 (p) DougieCostello 6 78
(Tony Coyle) *led: drvn along over 2f out: hdd over 1f out: wknd fnl f* **14/1**
1m 0.7s (1.00) **Going Correction** +0.45s/f (Yiel) **5** Ran SP% **107.2**
Speed ratings (Par 107): **110,106,104,99,97**
CSF £4.49 TOTE £1.80: £1.10, £1.70; EX 4.60 Trifecta £11.70.
Owner The Guys & Dolls & Sandfield Racing **Bred** Landmark Racing Limited **Trained** Westow, N Yorks
FOCUS
The high numbers were again favoured despite the small field in this decent conditions sprint. Straightforward form, rated around the runner-up.

8183 FOLLOW RACINGTV @RACINGTV ON TWITTER H'CAP 5f 1y
2:55 (2:57) (Class 5) (0-75,75) 3-Y-O+
£3,428 (£1,020; £509; £300; £300; £300) Stalls High

Form RPR
5401 1 **Militia**[25] 7367 4-9-2 70 PaulHanagan 10 79
(Richard Fahey) *mde all against stands' rail: rdn along wl over 1f out: edgd rt ins fnl f: kpt on strly* **7/2**[2]
0130 2 1 **Show Palace**[38] 6921 6-9-7 75 JoeFanning 3 80
(Jennie Candlish) *pressed wnr thrght: rdn over 1f out: kpt on same pce ins fnl f* **4/1**[3]
-002 3 1 1/4 **Jewel Maker (IRE)**[9] 7908 4-9-5 73 DavidAllan 8 74
(Tim Easterby) *prom: effrt and rdn over 1f out: kpt on ins fnl f: nt rch first two* **15/8**[1]
1562 4 1 1/2 **Boudica Bay (IRE)**[15] 7736 4-8-8 62 JasonHart 2 58
(Eric Alston) *trckd ldrs: effrt and rdn over 1f out: no ex ins fnl f* **9/2**
4000 5 1 **Our Place In Loule**[21] 7511 6-8-8 62 PhilDennis 11 54
(Noel Wilson) *s.i.s: chsd ldng gp: rdn and outpcd 1/2-way: edgd rt over 1f out: kpt on ins fnl f: no imp* **33/1**
3002 6 1/2 **B Fifty Two (IRE)**[16] 7703 10-8-4 65 (tp) NickBarratt-Atkin(7) 4 55
(Marjorie Fife) *dwlt and n.m.r s: bhd: short-lived effrt on outside over 1f out: no imp fnl f* **20/1**
3205 7 1/2 **Economic Crisis (IRE)**[15] 7736 10-8-10 64 TomEaves 9 52
(Alan Berry) *dwlt: bhd and sn outpcd: drvn along after 2f: nvr rchd ldrs* **20/1**
3041 8 1/2 **Astrophysics**[15] 7737 7-8-5 59 (p) CamHardie 1 46
(Lynn Siddall) *chsd ldng gp: rdn over 2f out: edgd rt and wknd fnl f* **10/1**
1m 1.8s (2.10) **Going Correction** +0.45s/f (Yiel) **8** Ran SP% **116.7**
Speed ratings (Par 103): **101,99,97,95,93 92,91,91**
CSF £17.80 CT £33.74 TOTE £4.10: £1.10, £1.40, £1.70; EX 23.40 Trifecta £74.80.
Owner Middleham Park Racing Cxvi & Partner **Bred** Jnp Bloodstock Ltd **Trained** Musley Bank, N Yorks

FOCUS
Yet again the stands' rail was the place to be in this competitive-looking sprint. Pace held up.

8184 JOIN RACINGTV NOW H'CAP 7f 33y
3:25 (3:31) (Class 2) (0-100,102) 3-Y-O+
£12,450 (£3,728; £1,864; £932; £466; £234) **Stalls** Low

Form RPR
0005 1 **Blown By Wind**[41] 6841 3-9-0 **93** JoeFanning 2 106
(Mark Johnston) *s.i.s: hld up in last pl: shkn up and angled to outside over 2f out: hdwy over 1f out: edgd rt and sustained run to ld ins fnl f: sn clr* **12/1**
-113 2 3 **Montatham**[26] 7349 3-8-9 **88** PaulHanagan 1 93
(William Haggas) *hld up in tch on ins: angled rt and drvn along over 2f out: hdwy to chse (clr) wnr wl ins fnl f: kpt on* **7/2**[2]
6016 3 ¾ **Three Saints Bay (IRE)**[39] 6894 4-9-8 **99** DanielTudhope 6 103
(David O'Meara) *t.k.h: led: clr 4f out to over 1f out: drvn and hdd ins fnl f: no ex and lost 2nd nr fin* **12/1**
14-1 4 2¼ **Tribal Warrior**[103] 4511 4-8-11 **88** DavidAllan 10 86+
(James Tate) *t.k.h: hld up: stdy hdwy on outside over 2f out: rdn and edgd rt over 1f out: no imp ins fnl f* **9/2**
2143 5 ½ **Barristan The Bold**[44] 6711 3-9-2 **95** RichardKingscote 4 91
(Tom Dascombe) *prom: effrt and chsd (clr) ldr over 2f out to over 1f out: rdn and no ex ins fnl f* **4/1**[3]
110 6 2½ **Shawaamekh**[30] 7222 5-8-13 **90** (t) KevinStott 8 81+
(Declan Carroll) *t.k.h: prom: rdn and outpcd over 2f out: btn over 1f out (trainer's rep could offer no explanation for the gelding's performance)* **3/1**[1]
2043 7 2¼ **Arcanada (IRE)**[16] 7678 6-8-8 **85** (p) CamHardie 9 70
(Tom Dascombe) *s.i.s: hld up: rdn and outpcd 3f out: nvr on terms* **20/1**
-206 8 2½ **Muntadab (IRE)**[9] 7905 7-9-11 **102** BenCurtis 3 80
(Roger Fell) *chsd ldr to over 2f out: sn rdn and wknd* **16/1**
0110 9 1¼ **Excellent Times**[9] 7893 4-9-1 **92** PhilDennis 7 67
(Tim Easterby) *hld up on ins: drvn and outpcd over 2f out: sn btn* **20/1**

1m 30.4s (1.40) **Going Correction** +0.45s/f (Yiel)
WFA 3 from 4yo+ 2lb **9 Ran SP% 116.2**
Speed ratings (Par 109): **110,106,105,103,102 99,97,94,92**
CSF £54.19 CT £520.64 TOTE £14.70: £3.90, £2.10, £4.10; EX 71.40 Trifecta £828.60.
Owner Sheikh Hamdan bin Mohammed Al Maktoum **Bred** Godolphin **Trained** Middleham Moor, N Yorks

FOCUS
Add 7yds. They went a fair pace in this decent handicap and it's solid form. Improvement from the winner.

8185 EVERY RACE LIVE ON RACINGTV (S) STKS 1m 4f 104y
4:00 (4:00) (Class 4) 3-Y-O+
£5,207 (£1,549; £774; £387; £300; £300) **Stalls** Low

Form RPR
0130 1 **Battle Of Marathon (USA)**[10] 7866 7-9-8 79 BenCurtis 5 81
(John Ryan) *chsd ldrs: hdwy to ld over 5f out: clr over 3f out: rdn 2f out: kpt on strly fnl f: unchal* **3/1**[2]
0/50 2 5 **Tamleek (USA)**[72] 5657 5-9-4 90 DanielTudhope 7 72
(David O'Meara) *pressed ldr to 1/2-way: cl up: chsd (clr) wnr over 3f out: effrt and rdn over 2f out: edgd rt and no imp fnl f* **5/4**[1]
6203 3 7 **Knightly Spirit**[9] 7903 4-9-8 57 DavidAllan 4 63
(Iain Jardine) *t.k.h: prom: drvn and outpcd over 2f out: rallied to chse clr ldng pair ins fnl f: no imp* **22/1**
5456 4 nk **Stonific (IRE)**[9] 7907 6-10-0 80 (v[1]) DavidNolan 1 69
(David O'Meara) *hld up: rdn along 3f out: sme hdwy over 1f out: no imp ins fnl f* **8/1**[3]
3423 5 1 **Employer (IRE)**[13] 7782 4-9-8 75 PaulMulrennan 6 61
(Jim Goldie) *plld hrd early: hld up: stdy hdwy 1/2-way: effrt and chsd ldng pair over 2f out: rdn and wknd appr fnl f* **3/1**[2]
0-0 6 40 **Exchequer (FR)**[18] 7213 3-8-5 66 RhonaPindar[(7)] 3
(Lucinda Russell) *t.k.h: led to 1/2-way: chsd wnr to over 3f out: sn struggling: lost tch fr over 2f out: t.o* **66/1**

2m 53.01s (8.51) **Going Correction** +0.875s/f (Soft)
WFA 3 from 4yo+ 6lb **6 Ran SP% 111.4**
Speed ratings (Par 105): **106,102,98,97,97 70**
CSF £7.05 TOTE £3.70: £1.60, £1.40; EX 8.30 Trifecta £55.50.There was no bid for the winner.
Owner Gerry McGladery **Bred** Galleria Bloodstock & Rhinestone B/Stock **Trained** Newmarket, Suffolk

FOCUS
By selling standards this was an interesting affair. It's rated around the winner and third. Add 7yds.

8186 WATCH RACINGTV NOW AMATEUR RIDERS' H'CAP 1m 208y
4:30 (4:38) (Class 5) (0-70,70) 3-Y-O+
£3,306 (£1,025; £512; £300; £300; £300) **Stalls** Low

Form RPR
2122 1 **Luna Magic**[43] 6760 5-10-12 **68** MissBrodieHampson 3 78
(Archie Watson) *cl up: led over 3f out: rdn clr fr over 2f out: kpt on wl fnl f: unchal* **9/2**[2]
5156 2 1¾ **Zealous (IRE)**[21] 7513 6-9-12 **61** (p) MrConnorWood[(7)] 8 66
(Alistair Whillans) *hld up: shkn up and hdwy over 2f out: chsd (clr) wnr ins fnl f: kpt on: nt pce to chal* **16/1**
0635 3 ¾ **Star Ascending (IRE)**[20] 7544 7-9-9 **56** (p) MrRyanHolmes[(5)] 12 60
(Jennie Candlish) *hld up: stdy hdwy on outside over 2f out: pushed along and hung rt over 1f out: disp 2nd pl briefly ins fnl f: one pce towards fin* **25/1**
3231 4 2¼ **Catch My Breath**[47] 6610 3-10-5 **65** MrSimonWalker 2 65
(John Ryan) *in tch: hdwy to chse wnr over 3f out: rdn 2f out: no ex and lost two pls ins fnl f* **10/3**[1]
4001 5 hd **Spirit Of Sarwan (IRE)**[21] 7513 5-10-8 **67** (v) MissSarahBowen[(3)] 10 66
(Stef Keniry) *s.i.s: hld up: hdwy on wd outside over 2f out: shkn up and no further imp ins fnl f* **22/1**
0324 6 ¾ **Star Of Valour (IRE)**[21] 7513 4-10-0 **56** MissEmmaTodd 13 53
(Lynn Siddall) *t.k.h: hld up: stdy hdwy 3f out: shkn up 2f out: wknd ins fnl f* **7/1**
4526 7 ¾ **Zeshov (IRE)**[30] 7212 8-10-10 **66** (p) MissSerenaBrotherton 14 61
(Rebecca Bastiman) *hld up in tch: shkn up over 2f out: effrt and edgd lft over 1f out: wknd ins fnl f* **20/1**
2034 8 2½ **One To Go**[9] 7906 3-10-9 **69** (v) MissEmilyEasterby 7 60
(Tim Easterby) *t.k.h: hld up towards rr: shkn up 2f out: sn no imp: btn fnl f* **6/1**
01-2 9 2½ **Firlinfeu**[22] 7489 4-11-0 **70** MrJamesHarding 4 55
(Jim Goldie) *bhd: struggling over 3f out: sme late hdwy: nvr on terms (vet reported gelding was mildly lame right fore)* **11/2**[3]
5206 10 3½ **Agar's Plough**[25] 7363 4-10-11 **67** (b) MissJoannaMason 9 45
(Michael Easterby) *t.k.h: hld up in tch: rdn and outpcd over 2f out: sn btn* **12/1**
0116 11 ¾ **Lagenda**[15] 7738 6-10-1 **64** MrAndrewMcBride[(7)] 6 40
(Liam Bailey) *trckd ldrs: rdn over 3f out: wknd fr 2f out* **40/1**
460- 12 5 **Imperial Focus (IRE)**[153] 9551 6-10-3 **59** MissAmieWaugh 5 25
(Simon Waugh) *led to over 3f out: rdn and wknd over 2f out* **50/1**
20/0 13 ¾ **Dance Of Fire**[33] 7069 7-10-9 **65** MrKitAlexander 1 29
(N W Alexander) *slowly away: bhd: struggling 4f out: nvr on terms (jockey said gelding was slowly away)* **50/1**
0400 14 1¾ **Guvenor's Choice (IRE)**[34] 7060 4-9-12 **59** (t) MissAmyCollier[(5)] 11 19
(Marjorie Fife) *t.k.h early: trckd ldrs: lost pl 3f out: sn struggling* **28/1**

2m 0.09s (6.99) **Going Correction** +0.875s/f (Soft)
WFA 3 from 4yo+ 4lb **14 Ran SP% 119.8**
Speed ratings (Par 103): **103,101,100,98,98 97,97,95,92,89 89,84,83,82**
CSF £67.30 CT £1663.92 TOTE £5.40: £1.70, £4.30, £7.40; EX 69.50 Trifecta £1325.10.
Owner Marco Polo **Bred** Lady Jennifer Green **Trained** Upper Lambourn, W Berks

FOCUS
An ordinary handicap, confined to amateur riders. A pb from the winner.
T/Plt: £96.00 to a £1 stake. Pool: £36,967.45 - 280.93 winning units T/Qpdt: £8.80 to a £1 stake. Pool: £7,736.97 - 650.5 winning units **Richard Young**

7971 WINDSOR (R-H)
Monday, October 14
8187 Meeting Abandoned - Waterlogged

8117 WOLVERHAMPTON (A.W) (L-H)
Monday, October 14

OFFICIAL GOING: Tapeta: standard
Wind: Light against Weather: Overcast

8194 COMPARE BOOKMAKER SITES AT BONUSCODEBETS.CO.UK FILLIES' H'CAP 5f 21y (Tp)
5:25 (5:30) (Class 5) (0-70,68) 3-Y-O+
£3,428 (£1,020; £509; £400; £400; £400) **Stalls** Low

Form RPR
4601 1 **Powerful Dream (IRE)**[14] 7757 6-9-7 **68** (p) DavidProbert 1 76
(Ronald Harris) *s.i.s: hld up: hdwy over 1f out: rdn to ld ins fnl f: r.o* **5/2**[1]
0100 2 ½ **Compton Poppy**[32] 7112 5-8-12 **59** GeorgeDowning 6 65
(Tony Carroll) *hld up: hdwy on outer over 1f out: rdn and edgd lft ins fnl f: r.o* **18/1**
5310 3 2¼ **Miss Gargar**[20] 7557 3-8-7 **59** (v) ThomasGreatrex[(5)] 9 58
(Harry Dunlop) *s.i.s: in rr and pushed along whn hung rt 1/2-way: r.o ins fnl f: wnt 3rd post: nt rch ldrs (jockey said filly was slowly away and unable to get a prominent position from stall nine)* **8/1**
600 4 hd **Angel Force (IRE)**[19] 7588 4-9-4 **65** (b) SilvestreDeSousa 4 62
(David C Griffiths) *chsd ldr: rdn to ld over 1f out: hdd ins fnl f: styd on same pce* **7/2**[2]
1602 5 nk **Aquadabra (IRE)**[11] 7844 4-8-12 **59** CallumShepherd 2 55
(Christopher Mason) *chsd ldrs: n.m.r over 1f out: sn rdn and ev ch: no ex wl ins fnl f* **7/1**
4415 6 nk **Precious Plum**[16] 7690 5-9-4 **65** (p) JamesSullivan 5 60
(Charlie Wallis) *chsd ldrs: rdn over 1f out: styd on same pce fnl f* **11/2**[3]
5020 7 1 **Raspberry**[17] 7656 3-9-3 **67** DarraghKeenan[(3)] 3 60
(Olly Williams) *prom: lost pl 4f out: r.o ins fnl f* **25/1**
3125 8 ½ **Society Star**[34] 7047 3-8-10 **64** (p) AngusVilliers[(7)] 10 55
(Robert Cowell) *s.i.s: r.o ins fnl f: nvr on terms* **16/1**
0054 9 2¾ **Country Rose (IRE)**[40] 6851 3-9-4 **65** (bt[1]) RaulDaSilva 8 46
(Ronald Harris) *led: racd freely: clr over 3f out tl 2f out: rdn: edgd rt and hdd over 1f out: wknd ins fnl f* **25/1**

1m 0.99s (-0.91) **Going Correction** -0.15s/f (Stan) **9 Ran SP% 108.6**
Speed ratings (Par 100): **101,100,96,96,95 95,93,92,88**
CSF £44.68 CT £278.87 TOTE £2.60: £1.20, £3.30, £1.90; EX 41.90 Trifecta £233.30.
Owner Ridge House Stables Ltd **Bred** Ballyhane Stud **Trained** Earlswood, Monmouths
■ Fairy Fast was withdrawn, price at time of withdrawal 11/1. Rule 4 applies to board prices prior to withdrawal, but not to SP bets. Deduction of 5p in the pound. New market formed.

FOCUS
The track was harrowed to a depth of 3.5 to 4 inches and reinstated with a gallop master finish. The podium was locked out by closers in this modest fillies' sprint handicap. Ordinary form, rated around the runner-up.

8195 WOLVERHAMPTON-RACECOURSE.CO.UK MAIDEN AUCTION STKS 5f 21y (Tp)
5:55 (5:56) (Class 5) 2-Y-O
£3,428 (£1,020; £509; £254) **Stalls** Low

Form RPR
3 1 **Be Ahead**[35] 7044 2-8-13 0 DaneO'Neill 9 74+
(E J O'Neill, France) *sn w ldr: led 1/2-way: hung lft over 1f out: r.o wl: comf* **11/10**[1]
4055 2 2¾ **Lilkian**[20] 7556 2-9-2 64 JosephineGordon 7 63+
(Shaun Keightley) *edgd rt s: pushed along early in rr: racd wd: rdn: edgd lft and r.o to go 2nd wl ins fnl f: no ch w wnr* **4/1**[2]
3 1¼ **Dark Phoenix (IRE)** 2-9-3 0 KieranO'Neill 1 60
(Paul Cole) *prom: outpcd over 3f out: rdn and hung lft over 1f out: r.o ins fnl f: wnt 3rd nr fin (jockey said colt ran green; vet said colt lost it's left hind shoe)* **25/1**
230 4 hd **On Tick (IRE)**[10] 7876 2-8-8 0 (t[1]) SiobhanRutledge[(7)] 6 59+
(Miss Katy Brown, Ire) *s.i.s and hmpd s: sn pushed along in rr: rdn and swtchd lft over 1f out: r.o ins fnl f: nt trble ldrs* **6/1**[3]
00 5 hd **Love Not Money**[9] 7896 2-8-3 0 AngusVilliers[(7)] 3 51
(Robert Cowell) *chsd ldrs: rdn over 1f out: styd on same pce fnl f* **50/1**
30 6 ½ **Castlehill Retreat**[125] 3702 2-9-4 0 JamesSullivan 4 57
(Ben Haslam) *edgd rt s: pushed along early in rr: rdn over 1f out: styd on ins fnl f: nvr nrr* **16/1**
0040 7 ½ **Rushcutters Bay**[14] 7754 2-9-0 58 (b[1]) CierenFallon[(3)] 2 54
(Hugo Palmer) *led to 1/2-way: rdn over 1f out: wknd ins fnl f* **9/1**

5034 **8** 1 1/4 **Dynamighty**[20] 7556 2-9-0 65.................(p[1]) KieranShoemark 5 47
(Richard Spencer) *hmpd s: sn pushed along and prom: rdn over 1f out: wknd ins fnl f* **11/1**

40 **9** 1/2 **Knock Knock (IRE)**[20] 7538 2-9-4 0.............................(t[1]) RobHornby 8 49
(Sylvester Kirk) *chsd ldrs: rdn over 1f out: wknd ins fnl f* **100/1**

1m 1.66s (-0.24) **Going Correction** -0.15s/f (Stan) **9** Ran SP% **112.9**
Speed ratings (Par 95): **95,90,88,88,87 87,86,84,83**
CSF £5.25 TOTE £1.80: £1.10, £1.10, £6.90; EX 6.20 Trifecta £44.90.
Owner Khalifa Dasmal **Bred** K A Dasmal **Trained** France
■ Tattletime was withdrawn, price at time of withdrawal 100/1. Rule 4 does not apply.

FOCUS
One-way traffic for the favourite in this moderate sprint juvenile maiden, a first runner in Britain this year for Eoghan O'Neill. Modest form in behind the winner.

8196 WOLVERHAMPTON RUM FESTIVAL 23RD NOVEMBER H'CAP 1m 5f 219y (Tp)
6:25 (6:26) (Class 6) (0-65,67) 3-Y-O+
£2,781 (£827; £413; £400; £400; £400) **Stalls Low**

Form RPR

0406 **1** **Red Secret (CAN)**[12] 7817 3-8-13 **57**.................(b[1]) SilvestreDeSousa 10 64+
(Ed Dunlop) *s.i.s: hdwy on outer 9f out: led 8f out: rdn clr over 2f out: edgd rt over 1f out: styd on* **3/1**[1]

4600 **2** 2 1/4 **Noble Behest**[37] 6967 5-9-7 **65**.........................(p) RPWalsh[(7)] 1 67
(Ian Williams) *w ldr 2f: remained handy: chsd wnr over 2f out: rdn over 1f out: styd on same pce towards fin* **15/2**[3]

6000 **3** 1 1/4 **Blue Beirut (IRE)**[23] 7450 3-8-2 **46** oh1..................... HollieDoyle 8 48
(William Muir) *hld up in tch: outpcd over 3f out: hdwy over 1f out: r.o* **14/1**

1124 **4** 1 **Affluence (IRE)**[28] 6830 4-9-9 **67**.............................(p) JacobClark[(7)] 11 66
(Martin Smith) *mid-div: hdwy on outer over 4f out: rdn over 1f out: styd on same pce ins fnl f* **14/1**

0042 **5** 2 1/2 **Reassurance**[27] 7314 4-9-10 **61**.............................(b) JamesSullivan 13 56
(Tim Easterby) *chsd ldrs: led over 11f out: hdd 8f out: chsd wnr tl rdn over 2f out: wknd fnl f* **11/1**

2034 **6** 3/4 **Bolt N Brown**[17] 7650 3-9-1 **62**...............................(t) CierenFallon[(3)] 6 58
(Gay Kelleway) *led: hdd over 11f out: chsd ldrs: rdn over 2f out: wknd over 1f out* **8/1**

2-00 **7** 1 1/4 **Doctor Jazz (IRE)**[14] 7756 4-9-5 **63**........................ MarkCrehan[(7)] 12 55
(Michael Appleby) *chsd ldrs tl rdn and wknd over 1f out* **66/1**

P022 **8** 1 3/4 **Continuum**[20] 7558 10-10-1 **66**...............................(v) NicolaCurrie 5 55
(Peter Hedger) *s.s: nvr on terms (jockey said gelding was denied a clear run two furlongs out)* **8/1**

0634 **9** 2 1/2 **Alpasu (IRE)**[28] 7290 3-9-3 **61**.............................. BarryMcHugh 4 49
(Adrian Nicholls) *hld up: nt clr run over 2f out: n.d* **8/1**

2300 **10** hd **Guaracha**[12] 7818 8-8-2 **46** oh1.............................(v) AngusVilliers[(7)] 9 32
(Alexandra Dunn) *broke wl: sn pushed along and lost pl: n.d after* **80/1**

2510 **11** shd **Filament Of Gold (USA)**[29] 7231 8-9-3 **54**...............(b) KieranO'Neill 3 39
(Roy Brotherton) *s.i.s: hld up: hdwy on outer over 2f out: rdn and wknd over 1f out* **50/1**

3655 **12** 4 **Tucson**[84] 5242 3-9-7 **65**.............................. JosephineGordon 7 47
(James Bethell) *s.i.s: sn pushed along and a in rr (jockey said gelding was never travelling)* **11/2**[2]

0534 **13** 3 **Shovel It On (IRE)**[11] 7857 4-8-11 **48**.....................(bt) RaulDaSilva 2 23
(Steve Flook) *prom: rdn over 3f out: wknd over 2f out* **28/1**

3m 2.5s (1.50) **Going Correction** -0.15s/f (Stan)
WFA 3 from 4yo+ 7lb **13** Ran SP% **115.3**
Speed ratings (Par 101): **89,87,87,86,85 84,83,82,81,81 81,78,77**
CSF £23.70 CT £271.77 TOTE £2.90: £1.50, £2.80, £4.40; EX 26.80 Trifecta £309.30.
Owner The Hon R J Arculli **Bred** William D Graham **Trained** Newmarket, Suffolk

FOCUS
A deft move by De Sousa as the pace sagged nearing halfway, allied to the transformative effect of the first-time blinkers, won the day in this moderate stayers' handicap. The third helps with the level.

8197 VISIT ATTHERACES.COM H'CAP 1m 142y (Tp)
6:55 (6:57) (Class 4) (0-80,80) 3-Y-O+
£5,207 (£1,549; £774; £400; £400; £400) **Stalls Low**

Form RPR

5160 **1** **Kaser (IRE)**[18] 7610 4-9-3 **78**...................... ThomasGreatrex[(5)] 4 87
(David Loughnane) *prom: lost pl after 1f: hdwy on outer over 1f out: rdn to ld and hung lft wl ins fnl f: r.o* **11/2**[2]

4351 **2** 1 1/2 **Zafaranah (USA)**[18] 7608 5-9-6 **76**........................ RobHornby 1 82
(Pam Sly) *chsd ldrs: rdn to ld 1f out: hdd and unable qck wl ins fnl f* **16/1**

0403 **3** 1 1/4 **Storm Ahead (IRE)**[25] 7363 6-9-5 **75**.....................(b) NathanEvans 11 78
(Tim Easterby) *hld up: rdn over 1f out: r.o wl ins fnl f: nt rch ldrs* **18/1**

3325 **4** 1/2 **Alhaazm**[39] 6909 3-9-5 **79**..................................(t) DaneO'Neill 2 82
(Sir Michael Stoute) *sn led: rdn and hdd 1f out: styd on same pce wl ins fnl f* **4/1**[1]

2042 **5** nk **Fares Poet (IRE)**[20] 7554 3-8-13 **76**......................(h) CierenFallon[(3)] 13 78
(Marco Botti) *chsd ldrs: wnt 2nd over 2f out tl rdn over 1f out: styd on same pce ins fnl f* **17/2**

0-00 **6** 1 **Chai Chai (IRE)**[110] 4249 4-9-2 **72**.....................(t) SilvestreDeSousa 12 71
(Tom Dascombe) *hld up: plld hrd: swtchd rt and hdwy over 1f out: sn rdn: styd on same pce ins fnl f* **33/1**

1226 **7** 3/4 **Chosen World**[167] 2242 5-9-3 **73**.............................. BarryMcHugh 3 70
(Julie Camacho) *hld up in tch: rdn over 1f out: wknd ins fnl f* **40/1**

5543 **8** 3/4 **Global Art**[23] 7465 4-9-10 **80**.............................(v[1]) HollieDoyle 7 75
(Ed Dunlop) *s.i.s: in rr: rdn and edgd lft ins fnl f: nvr on terms (jockey said gelding was denied a clear run in the final furlong)* **13/2**[3]

3204 **9** nk **Dourado (IRE)**[15] 7731 5-9-9 **79**........................ DavidProbert 6 73
(Patrick Chamings) *hld up: hdwy over 5f out: rdn over 1f out: wknd ins fnl f* **7/1**

5005 **10** 1/2 **My Target (IRE)**[224] 1018 8-9-9 **79**........................ NickyMackay 9 72
(Michael Wigham) *hld up: nt clr run fr over 1f out tl swtchd lft ins fnl f: nvr on terms (jockey said gelding was denied a clear run in the final furlong)* **66/1**

6261 **11** 1/2 **Pytilia (USA)**[20] 7554 3-8-12 **79**........................ AngusVilliers[(7)] 8 72
(Richard Hughes) *prom: nt clr run and lost pl over 7f out: racd keenly on outer over 5f out: rdn over 2f out: n.d after (trainers rep could offer no explanation for the poor performance; filly was routine tested)* **11/2**[2]

1550 **12** nk **Made Of Honour (IRE)**[11] 7856 5-9-10 **80**...............(b) RossaRyan 10 71
(David Loughnane) *pushed along to chse ldr over 7f out tl rdn over 2f out: wknd fnl f* **66/1**

3611 **13** 2 1/4 **Kingston Kurrajong**[32] 7125 6-9-10 **80**.................... CallumShepherd 5 66
(William Knight) *s.i.s: hld up: hdwy over 2f out: wknd fnl f* **12/1**

1m 47.39s (-2.71) **Going Correction** -0.15s/f (Stan)
WFA 3 from 4yo+ 4lb **13** Ran SP% **114.3**
Speed ratings (Par 105): **106,104,103,103,102 101,101,100,100,99 99,99,97**
CSF £84.10 CT £1516.75 TOTE £7.30: £2.30, £4.10, £5.10; EX 89.30 Trifecta £1933.40.
Owner Lowe, Lewis And Hoyland **Bred** Irish National Stud **Trained** Tern Hill, Shropshire

FOCUS
Not many got involved in this extended mile handicap, but the winner still came from quite some way back. The form has a sound look to it.

8198 VISIT THE BLACK COUNTRY FILLIES' NOVICE AUCTION STKS 7f 36y (Tp)
7:25 (7:27) (Class 6) 2-Y-O
£2,781 (£827; £413; £206) **Stalls High**

Form RPR

4140 **1** **Lethal Talent**[31] 7155 2-9-2 69........................ TylerSaunders[(5)] 9 78
(Jonathan Portman) *chsd ldr tl led over 1f out: sn rdn clr: easily* **9/2**

2 1 3/4 **Trinity Girl** 2-9-0 0........................ SilvestreDeSousa 8 65+
(Mark Johnston) *s.i.s: pushed along early in rr: hdwy on outer over 1f out: rdn: hung lft and r.o to go 2nd wl ins fnl f: no ch w wnr (jockey said filly hung left and ran green)* **5/2**[1]

5 **3** 3 3/4 **Untouchable Beauty**[21] 7515 2-8-11 0........................ CierenFallon[(3)] 4 56
(Hugo Palmer) *hld up in tch: hmpd 6f out: swtchd rt and shkn up over 1f out: styd on same pce fnl f* **7/2**[2]

0 **4** nse **Berkshire Philly**[13] 7787 2-9-0 0........................ RobHornby 10 55
(Andrew Balding) *sn prom: shkn up over 1f out: styd on same pce fnl f* **40/1**

2 **5** 4 1/2 **River Sprite**[28] 7276 2-9-0 0........................ KieranShoemark 2 44
(Daniel Kubler) *led: rdn and hdd over 1f out: wknd ins fnl f* **4/1**[3]

0500 **6** nk **Mayflower Lady (IRE)**[32] 7110 2-9-0 32.....................(b) RaulDaSilva 6 44
(Ronald Harris) *chsd ldrs: rdn over 2f out: edgd lft over 1f out: wknd fnl f* **200/1**

106 **7** 1 1/2 **Anna Of Sussex (IRE)**[24] 7412 2-9-0 73........................ ShariqMohd[(7)] 5 47
(Sylvester Kirk) *prom: rdn over 2f out: wknd over 1f out* **9/1**

8 3/4 **Alpine Mistral (IRE)** 2-9-0 0........................ JosephineGordon 7 38
(Shaun Keightley) *s.s: hung lft fr over 2f out: nvr on terms (jockey said filly was slowly away and hung left in the home straight)* **16/1**

0 **9** nk **Prairie Moppins (USA)**[60] 6118 2-9-0 0........................ NicolaCurrie 1 37
(Sylvester Kirk) *s.i.s: hld up: nvr on terms (jockey said filly ran green)* **33/1**

10 6 **Lady Dandy (IRE)** 2-9-0 0........................ LewisEdmunds 3 23
(Ivan Furtado) *s.i.s: a in rr* **50/1**

11 18 **Dark Discretion** 2-9-0 0........................ RossaRyan 11
(Kevin Frost) *s.s: outpcd (jockey said filly ran green)* **100/1**

1m 28.26s (-0.54) **Going Correction** -0.15s/f (Stan) **11** Ran SP% **113.7**
Speed ratings (Par 90): **97,95,90,90,85 85,83,82,82,75 54**
CSF £15.32 TOTE £5.30: £2.00, £1.10, £1.70; EX 19.70 Trifecta £97.40.
Owner Whitcoombe Park Racing **Bred** Bickmarsh Stud **Trained** Upper Lambourn, Berks

FOCUS
Very few got meaningfully involved in this moderate fillies' novice, and the penalised winner could easily have won by further.

8199 GRAND THEATRE WOLVERHAMPTON H'CAP 7f 36y (Tp)
7:55 (7:56) (Class 6) (0-65,65) 4-Y-O+
£2,781 (£827; £413; £400; £400; £400) **Stalls High**

Form RPR

1440 **1** **Secondo (FR)**[7] 7977 9-9-4 **63**.............................(v) DaneO'Neill 2 70
(Robert Stephens) *s.i.s: hld up: hdwy over 1f out: rdn to ld wl ins fnl f: r.o (trainer said, regards apparent improvement in form, gelding appreciated the return to the Tapeta surface at Wolvehampton where the gelding has run well previously; gelding was routine tested)* **16/1**

5033 **2** 1 1/4 **Gottardo (IRE)**[11] 7837 4-9-5 **64**........................ HollieDoyle 10 68
(Ed Dunlop) *hld up: swtchd rt over 1f out: rdn and r.o wl ins fnl f: wnt 2nd nr fin* **8/1**[3]

0414 **3** 1/2 **Our Charlie Brown**[48] 6572 5-9-6 **65**.....................(p) JamesSullivan 7 68
(Tim Easterby) *chsd ldrs: rdn to ld ins fnl f: sn edgd lft and hdd: styd on same pce* **17/2**

331 **4** nk **Fiery Breath**[34] 7052 4-9-3 **65**.........................(h) DarraghKeenan[(3)] 1 67
(Robert Eddery) *hld up: plld hrd: hdwy over 1f out: nt clr run and swtchd rt ins fnl f: r.o (jockey said gelding hung right)* **11/1**

5014 **5** nk **Ubla (IRE)**[17] 7654 6-8-13 **61**.............................(e) CierenFallon[(3)] 6 62
(Gay Kelleway) *hld up in tch: racd keenly: nt clr run ins fnl f: r.o* **12/1**

0314 **6** 1/2 **Napping**[23] 7446 6-9-5 **64**........................ SilvestreDeSousa 5 64
(Amy Murphy) *sn prom: racd keenly: rdn and ev ch ins fnl f: styd on same pce* **17/2**

4524 **7** 1 1/4 **Rock Boy Grey (IRE)**[24] 7418 4-9-6 **65**.....................(t[1]) LiamJones 8 65
(Mark Loughnane) *s.i.s: hld up: hdwy over 1f out: nt clr run sn after: hmpd ins fnl f: nt rcvr* **7/2**[1]

4040 **8** hd **Gold Hunter (IRE)**[27] 7299 9-9-6 **65**.....................(tp) RaulDaSilva 4 61
(Steve Flook) *sn prom: rdn over 1f out: no ex ins fnl f* **33/1**

1045 **9** shd **Hic Bibi**[25] 7383 4-9-0 **64**........................ ThomasGreatrex[(5)] 3 60
(David Loughnane) *chsd ldr tl over 4f out: wnt 2nd again over 2f out: rdn to ld over 1f out: hdd ins fnl f: wknd towards fin* **14/1**

1026 **10** 1 1/2 **Al Ozzdi**[17] 7652 4-9-0 **64**........................ PaulaMuir[(5)] 9 57
(Roger Fell) *stdd s: hld up: nvr on terms (jockey said gelding hung right)* **9/1**

-120 **11** nk **Scoffsman**[14] 7758 4-9-3 **62**........................ RossaRyan 11 54
(Kevin Frost) *s.i.s: plld hrd and hung rt: hdwy on outer over 5f out: led 1/2-way: rdn and hdd over 1f out: wknd wl ins fnl f* **5/1**[2]

0140 **12** 2 3/4 **Echo Of Lightning**[25] 7383 9-8-12 **64**.....................(p) AngusVilliers[(7)] 12 49
(Roger Fell) *led to 1/2-way: wknd fnl f* **66/1**

1m 27.78s (-1.02) **Going Correction** -0.15s/f (Stan) **12** Ran SP% **114.1**
Speed ratings (Par 101): **99,97,97,96,96 95,94,94,93,92 91,88**
CSF £133.43 CT £1186.22 TOTE £17.50: £4.50, £1.90, £2.20; EX 205.90 Trifecta £1516.20.
Owner Robert Stephens Racing Club **Bred** John Deer **Trained** Penhow, Newport

FOCUS
The faster of the two 7f contests on the card by just under half a second, and the complexion of the race changed completely in the final furlong as the leaders were swamped.

8200 WATCH SKY SPORTS RACING IN HD "CONFINED" H'CAP (NOT WON A FLAT RACE IN 2019) 1m 4f 51y (Tp)
8:25 (8:27) (Class 6) (0-65,65) 3-Y-O+
£2,781 (£827; £413; £400; £400; £400) **Stalls Low**

Form RPR

6332 **1** **Forbidden Dance**[23] 7474 3-9-4 **65**.....................(b) SilvestreDeSousa 7 73+
(Hughie Morrison) *chsd ldrs: edgd rt 1f out: rdn to ld ins fnl f: styd on* **9/4**[1]

The Form Book Flat 2019, Raceform Ltd, Newbury, RG14 5SJ

5553 **2** 1¼ **Guroor**[12] 7817 3-8-8 **62**.................... StefanoCherchi(7) 4 68
(Marco Botti) *chsd ldr tl led over 2f out: rdn and edgd rt fr over 1f out: hdd ins fnl f: styd on same pce* **3/1**[2]

0203 **3** 1¼ **Circle Of Stars (IRE)**[23] 7474 3-8-10 **64**.................... AledBeech(7) 5 68
(Charlie Fellowes) *hld up in tch: rdn and nt clr run 1f out: styd on same pce ins fnl f* **7/1**

3603 **4** 3¼ **Star Talent (IRE)**[35] 7035 3-8-12 **62**....................(e) CierenFallon(3) 2 61
(Gay Kelleway) *trckd ldrs: rdn and hung lft over 1f out: no ex ins fnl f* **9/1**

4336 **5** shd **What Will Be (IRE)**[22] 3311 3-9-0 **61**.................... KieranShoemark 8 60
(Olly Murphy) *hld up: hdwy over 1f out: nt rch ldrs* **4/1**[3]

2000 **6** 1¾ **Cherries At Dawn (IRE)**[9] 7915 4-9-10 **65**..........(t[1]) CallumShepherd 11 60
(Dominic Ffrench Davis) *s.i.s: hld up: rdn over 1f out: nt trble ldrs* **25/1**

-004 **7** ¾ **Major Snugfit**[20] 7545 3-9-2 **63**....................(b[1]) NathanEvans 1 58
(Michael Easterby) *chsd ldrs: rdn over 2f out: wknd ins fnl f* **12/1**

0604 **8** ¾ **So Hi Cardi (FR)**[15] 7739 3-7-13 **51** oh2....................(h) PaulaMuir(5) 10 44
(Roger Fell) *s.i.s: hld up: rdn over 3f out: nvr on terms* **80/1**

6402 **9** 3¾ **Teemlucky**[30] 7200 3-8-6 **53**.................... JosephineGordon 3 40
(Ian Williams) *led: hdd over 2f out: wknd fnl f* **25/1**

00 **10** 13 **Dr Richard Kimble (IRE)**[59] 6180 4-9-0 **60**......(p) FayeMcManoman(5) 9 26
(Marjorie Fife) *hld up: rdn over 2f out: sn wknd (jockey said gelding stopped quickly)* **125/1**

114/ **11** 8 **Babouska**[990] 434 5-8-13 **57**....................(p[1]) WilliamCox(3) 12 10
(John Flint) *hld up: rdn over 4f out: lost tch fnl 3f* **100/1**

2m 39.0s (-1.80) **Going Correction** -0.15s/f (Stan)
WFA 3 from 4yo+ 6lb **11** Ran SP% **116.7**
Speed ratings (Par 101): **100,99,98,96,96 94,94,93,91,82 77**
CSF £8.64 CT £39.97 TOTE £3.00: £1.20, £1.40, £2.50; EX 10.00 Trifecta £42.60.
Owner Brooke Pilkington Rogers **Bred** Meon Valley Stud **Trained** East Ilsley, Berks

FOCUS
A very steady pace only finally ratcheted up a few notches leaving the final back straight, but the right horses still came to the fore.
T/Plt: £179.60 to a £1 stake. Pool: £90,054.35 - 365.87 winning units T/Qpdt: £63.20 to a £1 stake. Pool: £12,797.52 - 149.63 winning units **Colin Roberts**

7391 YARMOUTH (L-H)

Monday, October 14

OFFICIAL GOING: Heavy (soft in places; 5.1)
Wind: Medium becoming strong, half against Weather: Overcast, light rain at times

8201 PALM COURT HOTEL OF GREAT YARMOUTH NURSERY H'CAP 7f 3y

2:10 (2:18) (Class 5) (0-70,70) 2-Y-O

£3,428 (£1,020; £509; £300; £300; £300) **Stalls** Centre

Form RPR

054 **1** **Parikarma (IRE)**[27] 7304 2-9-7 **70**.................... RobertHavlin 3 72
(Ed Dunlop) *hld up in tch in midfield: effrt and swtchd rt over 1f out: rdn to chse ldr fnl 100yds: styd on wl to ld cl home* **11/2**[3]

2440 **2** shd **Light The Fuse (IRE)**[12] 7827 2-9-4 **70**.................... HarrisonShaw(3) 2 72
(K R Burke) *chsd ldrs: effrt to chse ldr wl over 1f out: clsd and drvn to ld ins fnl f: sn hung rt and hdd cl home* **5/1**[2]

4635 **3** 1½ **Robert Guiscard (IRE)**[24] 7419 2-9-7 **70**.................... FrannyNorton 5 68
(Mark Johnston) *wnt lft leaving stalls: in tch in midfield: stmbld path over 5f out: effrt 3f out: rdn over 2f out: kpt on ins fnl f* **5/1**[2]

506 **4** nk **Burniston Rocks**[42] 6807 2-9-3 **66**.................... StevieDonohoe 6 63
(Ed Vaughan) *sn in rr: pushed along 1/2-way: rdn over 2f out: swtchd lft and clsd 1f out: kpt on wl ins fnl f: nt rch ldrs* **6/1**

2346 **5** ¾ **Red Jasper**[12] 7827 2-8-12 **61**.................... LiamJones 4 56
(Michael Appleby) *dwlt and short of room leaving stalls: in tch: clsd and swtchd rt 2f out: drvn to chse ldrs 1f out: no ex and one pce fnl 100yds* **9/1**

0344 **6** ¾ **Little Ted**[23] 7438 2-8-11 **60**....................(b) DuranFentiman 8 54
(Tim Easterby) *led: j. path over 5f out: rdn over 1f out: drvn and hrd pressed 1f out: hdd ins fnl f: wknd fnl 50yds* **9/2**[1]

0425 **7** 4½ **Alibaba**[10] 7874 2-9-6 **69**.................... ShelleyBirkett 1 51
(Julia Feilden) *chsd ldrs tl 2f out: sn lost pl: wknd fnl f (jockey said gelding ran flat after a long season)* **12/1**

002R **8** 3¼ **Kitos**[19] 7582 2-8-0 **49** oh1....................(b) LukeMorris 9 23
(Sir Mark Prescott Bt) *chsd ldr tl wl over 1f out: sn outpcd: wknd fnl f* **12/1**

352 **9** 19 **Freshwater Cliffs**[18] 7605 2-9-7 **70**.................... RyanMoore 7
(Richard Hughes) *stdd s: t.k.h: hld up in tch: rdn and struggling whn impeded 2f out: sn bhd* **9/1**

1m 30.65s (5.55) **Going Correction** +0.775s/f (Yiel) **9** Ran SP% **116.6**
Speed ratings (Par 95): **99,98,97,96,95 95,89,86,64**
CSF £33.47 CT £147.20 TOTE £6.50: £2.50, £2.30, £1.60; EX 44.50 Trifecta £251.30.
Owner Mrs Susan Roy **Bred** Minch Bloodstock **Trained** Newmarket, Suffolk

FOCUS
Testing ground, with the description of heavy an accurate one. They raced centre-field in this nursery, although the main action unfolded late more centre-to-stands' side.

8202 BRITISH EBF NOVICE STKS (PLUS 10 RACE) 6f 3y

2:45 (2:48) (Class 4) 2-Y-O **£4,463** (£1,328; £663; £331) **Stalls** Centre

Form RPR

3 **1** **Donnybrook (IRE)**[38] 6928 2-9-0 0....................(h) RobertHavlin 6 75+
(John Gosden) *taken down early: dwlt: rcvrd to chse ldr over 4f out: led over 2f out: rdn over 1f out: edgd rt 1f out: forged ahd and edgd lft wl ins fnl f: kpt on* **4/11**[1]

4 **2** ½ **Baileys Blues (FR)**[12] 7825 2-9-5 0.................... FrannyNorton 11 79
(Mark Johnston) *led: hdd but styd pressing wnr over 2f out: rdn over 1f out: drvn ins fnl f: edgd rt and no ex wl ins fnl f* **12/1**

3 ½ **Lady Isabel (IRE)** 2-9-0 0.................... DavidEgan 12 72+
(Alan Bailey) *rn green in last pair: rdn: hung lft and struggling 3f out: swtchd rt and hdwy over 1f out: chsd clr ldng pair: clsng to press ldrs whn short of room and hmpd towards fin* **50/1**

4 7 **Gmasha** 2-9-0 0.................... LukeMorris 4 51
(Robert Cowell) *in tch in midfield: effrt ent fnl 2f: outpcd and btn over 1f out: wl hld but plugged on ins fnl f* **33/1**

5 nk **Harbour Point** 2-8-9 0.................... TheodoreLadd(5) 5 50
(Michael Appleby) *hld up in tch in midfield: effrt to chse ldng pair over 1f out: hung lft and no imp 1f out: wknd ins fnl f* **50/1**

6 1¼ **Boom Boom Boom** 2-9-5 0....................(t[1]) DanielMuscutt 1 51
(Stuart Williams) *dwlt: rn green in last pair: effrt 2f out: swtchd rt and no hdwy over 1f out: nvr involved* **9/1**

60 **7** shd **Passing Nod**[5] 8026 2-8-12 0....................(h) GianlucaSanna(7) 2 51
(William Haggas) *chsd ldrs: rdn over 2f out: outpcd u.p over 1f out: wknd ins fnl f* **7/1**[3]

4 **8** nk **Main Reef**[164] 2367 2-9-5 0.................... AndreaAtzeni 3 50
(David Simcock) *chsd ldr for over 1f: in tch in midfield after: rdn over 2f out: outpcd and btn over 1f out: wknd ins fnl f* **9/2**[2]

1m 17.03s (4.43) **Going Correction** +0.775s/f (Yiel) **8** Ran SP% **128.6**
Speed ratings (Par 97): **101,100,99,90,89 88,88,87**
CSF £8.56 TOTE £1.30: £1.10, £2.20, £8.00; EX 7.80 Trifecta £84.20.
Owner Godolphin **Bred** Mayhem Syndicate **Trained** Newmarket, Suffolk

■ Stewards' Enquiry : Franny Norton caution: careless riding

FOCUS
Little got into this uncompetitive novice and the red-hot favourite was all out to score. The action unfolded near to the stands' rail late on.

8203 BRITISH STALLION STUDS EBF NOVICE STKS (PLUS 10 RACE) 7f 3y

3:15 (3:22) (Class 4) 2-Y-O **£4,916** (£1,463; £731; £365) **Stalls** Centre

Form RPR

4 **1** **Society Lion**[17] 7661 2-9-5 0.................... RyanMoore 4 80
(Sir Michael Stoute) *t.k.h: chsd ldr: rdn to ld over 1f out: edgd rt and styd on wl ins fnl f: rdn out* **6/4**[1]

5 **2** 2½ **Jumaira Bay (FR)**[19] 7571 2-9-5 0.................... AndreaAtzeni 7 74
(Roger Varian) *led: rdn and hdd over 1f out: hung lft and one pce ins fnl f* **7/1**[3]

3 nk **Naizagai** 2-9-5 0.................... DavidEgan 12 73
(Roger Varian) *chsd ldrs: kpt on same pce u.p ins fnl f* **8/1**

4 1¼ **Mishriff (IRE)** 2-9-5 0.................... RobertHavlin 8 70+
(John Gosden) *s.i.s: hld up towards rr: wnt lft 4f out: shkn and stl plenty to do in 5th over 1f out: sn swtchd rt: kpt on ins fnl f: no threat to ldrs* **5/2**[2]

5 2¾ **Master The Stars (GER)** 2-9-5 0.................... EdwardGreatrex 3 63
(Ed Dunlop) *t.k.h: hld up in tch in midfield: effrt to chse ldrs over 1f out: no ex and btn 1f out: wknd ins fnl f* **14/1**

60 **6** 6 **Revolver (IRE)**[11] 7842 2-9-5 0.................... LukeMorris 1 48
(Sir Mark Prescott Bt) *t.k.h: chsd ldrs: effrt ent fnl 2f: outpcd and btn over 1f out: wknd fnl f* **100/1**

5 **7** ½ **Frankly Mr Shankly (GER)**[26] 7346 2-9-5 0..........(h) StevieDonohoe 11 47
(Michael Bell) *taken down early: awkward leaving stalls: hld up in tch: effrt over 2f out: no imp and outpcd over 1f out: wknd fnl f* **7/1**[3]

8 ¾ **London (GER)** 2-9-0 0.................... BrettDoyle 2 40
(Mrs Ilka Gansera-Leveque) *s.i.s: t.k.h: sn rcvrd and in tch in midfield: effrt 2f out: sn outpcd: wknd fnl f* **18/1**

0 **9** 8 **Flying Standard (IRE)**[26] 7346 2-9-5 0.................... GeorgeWood 9 25
(Chris Wall) *t.k.h: in tch in midfield tl dropped to rr over 2f out: sn rdn and wknd over 1f out* **66/1**

10 3½ **Moment Of Peace** 2-9-5 0.................... EoinWalsh 6 16
(Christine Dunnett) *s.i.s: a towards rr: rdn over 2f out: bhd over 1f out* **200/1**

1m 32.27s (7.17) **Going Correction** +0.775s/f (Yiel) **10** Ran SP% **119.6**
Speed ratings (Par 97): **90,87,86,85,82 75,74,73,64,60**
CSF £13.58 TOTE £2.40: £1.40, £1.90, £2.30; EX 14.30 Trifecta £60.80.
Owner K Abdullah **Bred** Juddmonte Farms Ltd **Trained** Newmarket, Suffolk

FOCUS
Little pace on here with several racing keenly. They raced stands' side.

8204 MOMENTS RESTAURANT OF SCRATBY H'CAP 1m 3f 104y

3:50 (3:51) (Class 6) (0-55,61) 3-Y-O+

£2,781 (£827; £413; £300; £300; £300) **Stalls** Low

Form RPR

5302 **1** **Cheng Gong**[37] 6982 3-8-9 **48**.................... DavidEgan 10 56
(Tom Clover) *chsd ldrs: effrt to chse ldr 2f out: drvn to ld over 1f out: kpt on ins fnl f: rdn out* **5/1**[3]

0-60 **2** 1¼ **Poucor**[6] 7985 4-8-13 **47**.................... AndreaAtzeni 7 52
(Mick Channon) *chsd ldrs: rdn over 3f out: kpt on and pressing ldrs over 1f out: chsd wnr wl ins fnl f: no imp* **4/1**[2]

0205 **3** shd **Das Kapital**[20] 7553 4-8-12 **46**....................(p) FrannyNorton 8 51
(John Berry) *hld up in tch in midfield: clsd over 3f out: rdn and ev ch over 1f out: chsd wnr and kpt on same pce after: lost 2nd wl ins fnl f* **11/1**

0003 **4** 2¾ **Dyagilev**[6] 8001 4-8-9 **48**....................(b) RayDawson(5) 9 49
(Lydia Pearce) *dwlt: towards rr: effrt and sme hdwy over 2f out: kpt on ins fnl f: wnt 4th towards fin: nvr trbld ldrs* **10/1**

2002 **5** 1 **Mistress Nellie**[6] 7985 4-8-8 **47**....................(p) GeorgiaDobie(5) 15 46
(William Stone) *t.k.h: in tch in midfield: clsd to chse ldr over 3f out: led wl over 2f out: rdn and hdd over 1f out: sn outpcd and wknd ins fnl f* **7/2**[1]

5003 **6** ½ **Famous Dynasty (IRE)**[14] 7759 5-9-0 **48**.................... DanielMuscutt 11 46
(Michael Blanshard) *hld up towards rr: clsd over 2f out: no imp u.p over 1f out: wl hld and plugged on same pce ins fnl f* **10/1**

0334 **7** 11 **Tamok (IRE)**[37] 6982 3-8-8 **47**....................(v) HayleyTurner 12 29
(Michael Bell) *hld up in midfield: rdn 6f out: nvr threatened to get on terms: 7th and wknd over 1f out* **7/1**

6030 **8** 1 **Grasmere (IRE)**[25] 7376 4-8-12 **46** oh1....................(t) BrettDoyle 3 26
(Alan Bailey) *led tl 4f out: rdn and lost pl over 2f out: wknd over 1f out* **50/1**

5635 **9** 3¼ **Homesick Boy (IRE)**[11] 7857 3-8-13 **52**....................(b[1]) RobertHavlin 13 28
(Ed Dunlop) *s.i.s: a towards rr: nvr involved* **10/1**

2340 **10** 4½ **Percy Toplis**[6] 8001 5-8-13 **47**.................... EoinWalsh 14 15
(Christine Dunnett) *in rr of main gp: effrt over 3f out: no prog and wl btn fnl 2f* **14/1**

6-00 **11** 4 **Bostonian**[32] 7116 9-9-7 **55**....................(p[1]) LukeMorris 5 17
(Shaun Lycett) *t.k.h: w ldr tl led 4f out: hdd wl over 2f out: sn lost pl u.p: wl bhd ins fnl f* **33/1**

0400 **12** 4½ **Bricklebrit**[46] 6636 3-8-13 **52**.................... JFEgan 2 8
(Rae Guest) *wl in tch in midfield: lost pl u.p 4f out: wl bhd fnl f* **33/1**

0600 **13** 1 **Rent's Dew (IRE)**[34] 7048 3-8-10 **49**.................... DuranFentiman 1
(Tim Easterby) *s.i.s: in tch in midfield: rdn 3f out: sn struggling and btn: wl bhd fnl f* **18/1**

2m 35.17s (7.37) **Going Correction** +0.775s/f (Yiel)
WFA 3 from 4yo+ 5lb **13** Ran SP% **126.8**
Speed ratings (Par 101): **104,103,103,101,100 99,91,91,88,85 82,79,78**
CSF £26.68 CT £222.03 TOTE £5.20: £1.70, £2.00, £4.60; EX 31.90 Trifecta £460.20.
Owner R & S Marchant, D Fawdon & G Jarvis **Bred** Miss K Rausing **Trained** Newmarket, Suffolk

FOCUS
Moderate handicap form, they headed centre-field in the straight and it was no surprise to see one of the 3yos come out on top.

8205 BEST ODDS GUARANTEED AT MANSIONBET H'CAP — 1m 2f 23y
4:20 (4:26) (Class 6) (0-60,61) 3-Y-O

£2,781 (£827; £413; £300; £300; £300) Stalls Low

Form — RPR

5050 **1** **Mac Ailey**[11] 7859 3-9-0 **52** RachelRichardson 2 — 61
(Tim Easterby) *chsd ldrs tl led travelling strly jst over 2f out: rdn clr over 1f out: styd on wl ins fnl f* — 13/2

4310 **2** 2 1/2 **Ragstone Cowboy (IRE)**[12] 7817 3-9-7 **59** (v) ShaneKelly 10 — 64
(Gary Moore) *wl in tch in midfield: clsd and upsides ldrs 3f out: rdn ent fnl 2f: clr 2nd but no imp on wnr ins fnl f* — 8/1

2050 **3** 3 1/2 **Dolly Dupree**[4] 8072 3-8-9 **47** JFEgan 6 — 45
(Paul D'Arcy) *hld up in tch in midfield: effrt over 2f out: unable qck and wl hld by ldng pair over 1f out: plugged on to go 3rd wl ins fnl f* — 11/2[3]

0000 **4** 3/4 **Lynchpin (IRE)**[12] 7817 3-8-9 **47** ow1 (b) BrettDoyle 4 — 44
(Lydia Pearce) *dwlt: hld up towards rr: gd hdwy and c towards stands' side over 4f out: rdn and ev ch 3f out: outpcd and btn over 1f out: wknd ins fnl f* — 33/1

4230 **5** nk **Reddiac (IRE)**[16] 7685 3-9-5 **57** (p) RobertHavlin 1 — 53
(Ed Dunlop) *t.k.h: hld up towards rr: hdwy over 3f out: unable qck and no imp over 1f out: wknd ins fnl f* — 16/1

6661 **6** 1 1/4 **Lord Howard (IRE)**[6] 8003 3-9-0 **52** 6ex (v) AndreaAtzeni 11 — 46
(Mick Channon) *dwlt and rousted along early: in tch in midfield: rdn ent fnl 3f: unable qck and outpcd 2f out: no ch but plugged on again ins fnl f* — 4/1[1]

0300 **7** 1/2 **Amber Rock (USA)**[10] 7873 3-8-5 **46** ow1 (tp) GabrieleMalune(3) 16 — 39
(Les Eyre) *prom tl led after 2f: rdn and hdd jst over 2f out: outpcd and btn over 1f out: wknd ins fnl f* — 9/1

0052 **8** 1 1/2 **Princess Florence (IRE)**[15] 7738 3-9-0 **52** StevieDonohoe 5 — 42
(John Ryan) *hld up in rr: hdwy and effrt 2f out: no imp over 1f out: wknd ins fnl f* — 22/1

0342 **9** 3/4 **Osmosis**[20] 7542 3-9-9 **61** FrannyNorton 9 — 50
(Jason Ward) *hld up in tch in midfield: effrt over 2f out: unable qck and btn over 1f out: wknd ins fnl f* — 5/1[2]

5440 **10** 1 1/2 **Loveheart**[18] 7609 3-9-5 **57** RyanMoore 15 — 43
(Michael Bell) *hld up in tch towards rr: clsd over 2f out: rdn and no prog wl over 1f out: sn wknd* — 12/1

4300 **11** 1 1/4 **Closer Than Close**[53] 6367 3-9-9 **61** (h) DanielMuscutt 14 — 45
(Jonathan Portman) *chsd ldrs: wnt 2nd 4f out tl ent fnl 2f: sn lost pl: wknd over 1f out* — 12/1

000 **12** 23 **Best Haaf**[151] 2764 3-8-13 **56** TheodoreLadd(5) 12
(Michael Appleby) *t.k.h: led for 2f: chsd ldr tl 4f out: dropped out and t.o whn heavily eased ins fnl f (jockey said gelding ran too freely)* — 16/1

0540 **13** 20 **Mousquetaire (FR)**[44] 6723 3-8-11 **49** (h) DavidEgan 8
(David Menuisier) *chsd ldrs early: stdd bk to rr after 2f: sme hdwy 4f out: rdn and btn over 2f out: t.o and eased ins fnl f* — 20/1

2m 17.16s (8.36) **Going Correction** +0.775s/f (Yiel) — **13 Ran SP% 125.7**
Speed ratings (Par 99): **97,95,92,91,91 90,89,88,88,86 85,67,51**
CSF £59.53 CT £315.51 TOTE £6.60: £2.50, £2.70, £2.30; EX 71.90 Trifecta £389.40.
Owner Dubelem (racing) Limited & Partner **Bred** Bearstone Stud Ltd **Trained** Great Habton, N Yorks

FOCUS
A moderate handicap run at a steady pace, they came centre-to-stands' side in the straight.

8206 OPTIMIST DESIGN LTD H'CAP — 1m 3y
4:55 (5:01) (Class 5) (0-70,72) 3-Y-O+

£3,428 (£1,020; £509; £300; £300; £300) Stalls Centre

Form — RPR

5131 **1** **Purgatory**[33] 7084 3-9-4 **69** (b) AndreaAtzeni 8 — 82+
(Chris Wall) *hld up in midfield: clsd nt clr run and nudged way through ent fnl 2f: trckd ldr and travelling strly over 1f out: rdn to ld 100yds out: sn readily wnt clr: comf* — 3/1[1]

0-00 **2** 2 3/4 **Sir Hamilton (IRE)**[160] 2516 4-9-1 **68** (p) MarcoGhiani(5) 4 — 71
(Luke McJannet) *t.k.h: hld up in midfield: hdwy to chse ldr over 4f out: led wl over 1f out: rdn and edgd rt 1f out: hdd and outpcd fnl 100yds* — 20/1

563 **3** 2 3/4 **Uzincso**[28] 7278 3-9-3 **68** DanielMuscutt 12 — 65
(John Butler) *bmpd leaving stalls: hld up in tch: effrt ent fnl 2f: kpt on u.p ins fnl f to snatch 3rd cl home: no threat to ldrs* — 12/1

4060 **4** 1/2 **Spencers Son (IRE)**[5] 8033 3-9-2 **67** (b[1]) StevieDonohoe 9 — 63
(Richard Spencer) *racd keenly: led: rdn and hdd wl over 1f out: 3rd and btn whn edgd lft 1f out: plugged on same pce after: lost 3rd cl home* — 25/1

063 **5** shd **Squelch**[19] 7572 3-9-7 **72** LukeMorris 3 — 68
(Rae Guest) *in tch in midfield: effrt over 2f out: drvn and chsng ldrs but no imp over 1f out: wl hld and plugged on same pce fnl f* — 14/1

4530 **6** 1 3/4 **Noble Peace**[20] 7560 6-8-11 **64** (b) RayDawson(5) 13 — 56
(Lydia Pearce) *in tch in midfield: effrt and chsd ldrs u.p 2f out: no ex over 1f out: wknd ins fnl f* — 7/1[3]

3454 **7** hd **Coverham (IRE)**[16] 7684 5-9-7 **69** RyanTate 14 — 60
(James Eustace) *in tch in midfield: effrt ent fnl 2f: chsd ldrs but unable qck u.p fnl f: wknd ins fnl f* — 8/1

0044 **8** 3 **Vive La Difference (IRE)**[5] 8030 5-9-6 **68** (p) DuranFentiman 2 — 52
(Tim Easterby) *hld up in rr: clsd over 3f out: effrt ent fnl 2f: nvr threatened to get on terms and btn over 1f out: wknd ins fnl f* — 7/2[2]

-045 **9** 3 **Robsdelight (IRE)**[115] 4061 4-9-2 **71** (p) AidenSmithies(7) 10 — 48
(Gay Kelleway) *wnt lft leaving stalls: chsd ldr tl over 5f out: rdn and losing pl and nudged lft over 1f out: wknd over 1f out* — 8/1

6306 **10** hd **Pamper**[28] 7278 3-9-2 **67** (v) RyanMoore 11 — 44
(James Fanshawe) *squeezed for room and leaving stalls: a towards rr: rdn 3f out: nvr a threat* — 10/1

235- **11** 25 **Flaunt It (IRE)**[292] 9708 3-9-1 **66** JFEgan 1
(Jane Chapple-Hyam) *chsd ldrs: wnt 2nd over 5f out tl over 4f out: lost pl and bhd 2f out: wknd: t.o* — 33/1

0-43 **12** 19 **Swiss Cheer (FR)**[201] 1352 3-9-7 **72** RobertHavlin 5
(Jonathan Portman) *keen to post: t.k.h: hld up in rr: lost tch 3f out: sn eased: t.o* — 16/1

1m 44.72s (6.52) **Going Correction** +0.775s/f (Yiel)
WFA 3 from 4yo+ 3lb — **12 Ran SP% 122.8**
Speed ratings (Par 103): **98,95,92,92,91 90,89,86,83,83 58,39**
CSF £70.60 CT £666.30 TOTE £4.00: £1.80, £7.60, £3.90; EX 97.50 Trifecta £1044.80.
Owner Des Thurlby **Bred** Des Thurlby **Trained** Newmarket, Suffolk
■ Stewards' Enquiry : Aiden Smithies caution: careless riding

FOCUS
Modest enough handicap form, they raced centre-field and appeared to go an okay gallop. Another pb from the winner but the form is potentially a bit shaky.

8207 MANSIONBET'S BEATEN BY A HEAD H'CAP — 7f 3y
5:30 (5:31) (Class 6) (0-65,66) 3-Y-O+

£2,781 (£827; £413; £300; £300; £300) Stalls Centre

Form — RPR

2531 **1** **Stallone (IRE)**[6] 8008 3-9-3 **66** (v) SeanKirrane(5) 12 — 75
(Richard Spencer) *chsd ldrs tl wnt 2nd ent fnl 2f: rdn to chal over 1f out: drvn and led narrowly ins fnl f: kpt on* — 10/11[1]

0120 **2** hd **Dutch Story**[41] 6840 3-8-12 **56** (p) MartinDwyer 3 — 65
(Amanda Perrett) *racd centre to far side: pressed ldr tl led 4f out: rdn and hrd press over 1f out: hdd ins fnl f: kpt on but jst hld cl home* — 7/1[2]

0200 **3** 5 **Secret Treaties**[28] 7281 3-8-7 **51** HayleyTurner 1 — 47
(Christine Dunnett) *trckd rival centre to far side: clsd 3rd and effrt wl over 1f out: no ex 1f out: outpcd ins fnl f* — 33/1

3440 **4** 2 1/2 **Reasoned (IRE)**[11] 7835 3-9-0 **58** RyanTate 10 — 48
(James Eustace) *in tch in midfield: effrt ent fnl 2f: 4th and no imp u.p over 1f out: wl hld ins fnl f* — 11/1

5043 **5** 2 3/4 **Bullington Boy (FR)**[16] 7681 3-9-7 **65** JFEgan 8 — 48
(Jane Chapple-Hyam) *t.k.h: hld up in tch: effrt over 2f out: edgd lft u.p and no imp: wknd ins fnl f* — 8/1[3]

0000 **6** 3/4 **Lacan (IRE)**[47] 6605 8-8-8 **57** JoeBradnam(7) 7 — 39
(Michael Bell) *hld up in rr: effrt 2f out: no imp and wl hld 6th 1f out* — 50/1

0000 **7** 2 1/4 **Face Like Thunder**[7] 7973 4-8-13 **55** DannyBrock 13 — 31
(John Butler) *in tch in midfield: effrt over 2f out: sn btn: wknd over 1f out* — 33/1

6256 **8** 1 1/2 **Reconnaissance**[35] 7027 3-9-0 **58** (t) DavidEgan 2 — 30
(Tom Clover) *in tch in midfield: effrt over 2f out: no imp and btn over 1f out: wknd ins fnl f* — 7/1[2]

0005 **9** nk **Any Smile (IRE)**[18] 7608 3-8-9 **53** (p) ShelleyBirkett 11 — 24
(Julia Feilden) *led tl 4f out: chsd ldr tl ent fnl 2f: sn lost pl: wknd fnl f* — 50/1

5023 **10** 19 **Mitigator**[24] 7405 3-9-8 **66** (b) BrettDoyle 15 — s
(Lydia Pearce) *racd nr stands' side: midfield: rdn over 2f out: sn btn: wl bhd and eased ins fnl f* — 10/1

0-04 **11** 27 **Pecheurs De Perles (IRE)**[253] 590 5-8-2 **49** oh4 AndrewBreslin(5) 14
(John Butler) *t.k.h: hld up in tch: rdn over 3f out: sn btn: wl bhd and eased fnl f: t.o* — 18/1

1m 30.51s (5.41) **Going Correction** +0.775s/f (Yiel)
WFA 3 from 4yo+ 2lb — **11 Ran SP% 121.0**
Speed ratings (Par 101): **100,99,94,91,88 87,84,82,82,60 30**
CSF £7.82 CT £134.18 TOTE £1.50: £1.10, £2.20, £8.60; EX 9.20 Trifecta £201.40.
Owner Rebel Racing Premier **Bred** Ms Marie Higgins **Trained** Newmarket, Suffolk

FOCUS
The front pair came clear in this moderate handicap, with the action unfolding centre-field. Straightforward form.

T/Jkpt: £11,851.60 to a £1 stake. Pool: £100,154.95 - 6.0 winning units T/Plt: £129.80 to a £1 stake. Pool: £70,583.38 - 396.92 winning units T/Qpdt: £51.80 to a £1 stake. Pool: £7,294.07 - 104.08 winning units **Steve Payne**

8208 - 8216a (Foreign Racing) - See Raceform Interactive

8058
KEMPTON (A.W) (R-H)
Tuesday, October 15

OFFICIAL GOING: Polytrack: standard to slow

8217 100% PROFIT BOOST AT 32REDSPORT.COM H'CAP — 6f (P)
5:00 (5:04) (Class 6) (0-65,65) 3-Y-O+

£3,105 (£924; £461; £400; £400; £400) Stalls Low

Form — RPR

0125 **1** **Lordsbridge Boy**[39] 6930 3-8-12 **62** SophieRalston(5) 7 — 69
(Dean Ivory) *mde all: racd keenly: swtchd rt sn after s: shkn up over 1f out: pushed out* — 5/2[1]

0201 **2** nk **True Belief (IRE)**[8] 7976 3-9-6 **65** 6ex (h) RossaRyan 5 — 71
(Brett Johnson) *s.s: hld up: hdwy over 1f out: sn rdn: r.o* — 9/1

0050 **3** 1/2 **The Lacemaker**[20] 7576 5-9-1 **59** (p) HollieDoyle 3 — 64
(Milton Harris) *prom: hmpd sn after s: rdn over 1f out: r.o* — 33/1

0141 **4** 1/2 **Holdenhurst**[24] 7470 4-9-7 **65** EoinWalsh 8 — 68
(Bill Turner) *w wnr 1f: remained handy: rdn over 1f out: styd on* — 8/1

440 **5** 1 **Papa Delta**[54] 6363 5-9-2 **60** GeorgeDowning 4 — 60
(Tony Carroll) *hld up: hdwy and n.m.r fnl f: r.o (vet said gelding was struck into on it's right hind)* — 10/3[2]

P20 **6** 3/4 **Catheadans Fury**[30] 7230 5-9-1 **59** (t) GeorgeWood 9 — 57
(Martin Bosley) *s.i.s: hld up: racd keenly: rdn over 1f out: r.o ins fnl f: nrst fin* — 25/1

-500 **7** 1 1/2 **Shellebeau (IRE)**[95] 4870 3-9-6 **65** RobertHavlin 12 — 58
(Alexandra Dunn) *sn prom: rdn over 1f out: no ex ins fnl f* — 66/1

6655 **8** 1/2 **Alabama Dreaming**[13] 7811 3-9-2 **64** (b[1]) MeganNicholls(3) 2 — 56
(George Scott) *s.i.s: hld up: hdwy over 2f out: rdn over 1f out: no ex ins fnl f* — 6/1[3]

0240 **9** 1/2 **Ghepardo**[29] 7274 4-9-2 **60** (p[1]) TomMarquand 11 — 50
(Patrick Chamings) *hld up: rdn over 2f out: n.d* — 33/1

1044 **10** nk **Olaudah**[24] 7447 5-9-2 **60** DavidProbert 1 — 49
(Henry Candy) *prom: hmpd sn after s: chsd wnr wl over 1f out: sn rdn: wknd ins fnl f* — 6/1[3]

0406 **11** 7 **Alliseeisnibras (IRE)**[28] 7320 3-9-6 **65** (p[1]) SeanLevey 10 — 33
(Ismail Mohammed) *chsd wnr after 1f tl rdn over 2f out: wknd fnl f* — 33/1

1m 12.32s (-0.78) **Going Correction** -0.025s/f (Stan)
WFA 3 from 4yo+ 1lb — **11 Ran SP% 115.5**
Speed ratings (Par 101): **104,103,102,102,100 99,97,97,96,96 86**
CSF £24.05 CT £595.19 TOTE £3.10: £1.40, £2.60, £8.60; EX 30.50 Trifecta £853.10.
Owner Roger S Beadle **Bred** Mrs I L Sneath **Trained** Radlett, Herts
■ Stewards' Enquiry : Sophie Ralston three-day ban; careless riding (Oct 29-31)

FOCUS
A modest sprint.

8218 32RED CASINO/BRITISH STALLION STUDS EBF MAIDEN FILLIES' STKS (PLUS 10 RACE) — 6f (P)
5:30 (5:31) (Class 5) 2-Y-O

£3,881 (£1,155; £577; £288) Stalls Low

Form — RPR

23 **1** **Tambourine Girl**[97] 4790 2-9-0 **0** AdamMcNamara 12 — 75
(Roger Charlton) *chsd ldr tl rdn over 1f out: styd on u.p to ld wl ins fnl f: jst hld on* — 5/1[3]

0 **2** *shd* **Depose**[90] 5045 2-9-0 0........(h) JackMitchell 6 75
(Hugo Palmer) *hld up: hdwy over 1f out: sn rdn: swtchd rt ins fnl f: r.o wl* **6/1**

54 **3** *shd* **Rakassah (IRE)**[21] 7539 2-9-0 0........ ShaneKelly 2 74
(Richard Hughes) *chsd ldrs: led over 1f out: rdn and hdd wl ins fnl f: r.o* **9/2**[2]

03 **4** *3 1/4* **Catechism**[21] 7546 2-9-0 0........ KieranShoemark 8 65
(Richard Spencer) *sn led: rdn and hdd over 1f out: no ex wl ins fnl f* **9/1**

6 **5** *shd* **Rock Of Fame**[20] 7580 2-9-0 0........ AndreaAtzeni 4 64+
(Roger Varian) *hld up: pushed along over 3f out: r.o ins fnl f: nt rch ldrs* **4/1**[1]

6 **6** *1 1/4* **Twelve Diamonds (IRE)**[20] 7569 2-9-0 0........ JimCrowley 1 61
(Charles Hills) *prom: rdn over 1f out: no ex ins fnl f* **16/1**

7 *1/2* **Able Grace (IRE)** 2-9-0 0........ HectorCrouch 10 59
(Clive Cox) *prom: racd keenly: nt clr run and lost pl after 1f: n.d after* **50/1**

4 **8** *hd* **Urtzi (IRE)**[14] 7786 2-9-0 0........ RobertHavlin 5 59
(Michael Attwater) *s.i.s and stmbld s: styd on ins fnl f: nvr nrr* **66/1**

9 *hd* **Aljalela (FR)** 2-9-0 0........ RossaRyan 9 58
(Richard Hannon) *s.i.s: pushed along over 3f out: n.d* **25/1**

4 **10** *1/2* **Spinacia (IRE)**[13] 7813 2-8-9 0........ GeorgiaDobie(5) 7 56
(Eve Johnson Houghton) *s.i.s and stmbld s: nvr on terms* **11/1**

5 **11** *3/4* **Trecco Bay**[14] 7786 2-9-0 0........ GeraldMosse 3 54
(David Elsworth) *chsd ldrs: rdn over 2f out: wknd fnl f* **5/1**[3]

1m 12.61s (-0.49) **Going Correction** -0.025s/f (Stan) **11** Ran SP% **117.3**
Speed ratings (Par 92): **102,101,101,97,97 95,94,94,94,93 92**
CSF £34.61 TOTE £3.00: £1.30, £2.80, £1.40; EX 42.60 Trifecta £214.10.
Owner Owners Group 041 **Bred** Highclere Stud **Trained** Beckhampton, Wilts

FOCUS
Just a fair maiden.

8219 32RED.COM NURSERY H'CAP — 6f (P)

6:00 (6:01) (Class 4) (0-85,84) 2-Y-O

£6,469 (£1,925; £962; £481; £400; £400) **Stalls** Low

Form / RPR

521 **1** **Epsom Faithfull**[52] 6442 2-8-8 **71**........ CharlieBennett 6 75
(Pat Phelan) *edgd lft s: sn chsng ldr: rdn over 1f out: r.o to ld nr fin* **16/1**

1221 **2** *hd* **Audio**[26] 7369 2-9-3 **80**........(t) SeanLevey 1 83
(Richard Hannon) *trckd ldrs: plld hrd: rdn over 1f out: led wl ins fnl f: hdd nr fin (jockey said gelding hung left-handed)* **8/1**[3]

5333 **3** *1 1/2* **Glamorous Anna**[13] 7813 2-9-3 **83**........ MitchGodwin(3) 5 82
(Christopher Mason) *sn led: pushed along and qcknd over 2f out: rdn clr and edgd rt over 1f out: hdd wl ins fnl f* **9/1**

2211 **4** *shd* **X Force (IRE)**[45] 6705 2-9-7 **84**........ HollieDoyle 8 83
(Archie Watson) *hld up in tch: plld hrd: lost pl over 3f out: hdwy over 1f out: sn rdn: r.o (jockey said gelding hung left-handed)* **11/4**[1]

4144 **5** *1 1/2* **Champagne Supanova (IRE)**[26] 7369 2-8-9 **72**...(v) KieranShoemark 3 66
(Richard Spencer) *s.i.s: hdwy over 3f out: rdn over 1f out: styd on* **20/1**

0510 **6** *1* **Port Winston (IRE)**[26] 7391 2-8-11 **74**........(h) DavidProbert 7 65
(Alan King) *s.i.s and hmpd s: hld up: styd on ins fnl f: nvr on terms (jockey said gelding was slowly away)* **50/1**

1500 **7** *hd* **Fantom Force (IRE)**[26] 7391 2-8-11 **74**........ RossaRyan 4 65
(Richard Hannon) *chsd ldrs: rdn over 2f out: styd on same pce fr over 1f out* **25/1**

2054 **8** *4* **St Ives**[17] 7679 2-8-9 **75**........(p) CierenFallon(3) 9 54
(William Haggas) *hld up in tch on outer: lost pl over 4f out: shkn up and hung rt over 2f out: n.d after* **4/1**[2]

1m 12.79s (-0.31) **Going Correction** -0.025s/f (Stan) **8** Ran SP% **84.2**
Speed ratings (Par 97): **101,100,98,98,96 95,95,89**
CSF £69.54 CT £448.29 TOTE £10.60: £2.20, £2.10, £2.10; EX 71.00 Trifecta £264.80.
Owner Epsom Racegoers No. 2 **Bred** James Patton **Trained** Epsom, Surrey
■ Predictable Tully was withdrawn. Price at time of withdrawal 11/4J. Rule 4 applies to all bets. Deduction - 25p in the pound.

FOCUS
There was a tight finish to this nursery.

8220 32RED ON THE APP STORE H'CAP (DIV I) — 7f (P)

6:30 (6:31) (Class 5) (0-75,77) 3-Y-O+

£3,752 (£1,116; £557; £400; £400; £400) **Stalls** Low

Form / RPR

0122 **1** **Highfaluting (IRE)**[22] 7519 5-9-6 **74**........ GeraldMosse 2 84+
(James Eustace) *chsd ldrs: shkn up to ld over 1f out: rdn and edgd lft ins fnl f: styd on* **10/11**[1]

0616 **2** *1* **In The Cove (IRE)**[31] 7189 3-9-3 **73**........(b) RossaRyan 8 77
(Richard Hannon) *disp ld early: plld hrd in 2nd: rdn and ev ch over 1f out: styd on* **8/1**[3]

415 **3** *2 1/2* **The Groove**[28] 7299 6-9-0 **68**........ EoinWalsh 12 66
(David Evans) *hld up: hdwy over 1f out: r.o: nt rch ldrs* **40/1**

3 **4** *1 1/4* **Mid Atlantic Storm (IRE)**[90] 5041 3-8-10 **66**........ TomMarquand 3 60
(Tom Ward) *s.i.s: sn prom: rdn and ev ch over 1f out: no ex ins fnl f (jockey said gelding hung left-handed under pressure)* **20/1**

4336 **5** *hd* **Consequences (IRE)**[19] 7607 4-9-3 **74**........ CierenFallon(3) 5 68
(Ian Williams) *hld up: rdn over 2f out: hdwy over 1f out: r.o* **16/1**

0033 **6** *nk* **Danecase**[28] 7299 6-9-1 **69**........(tp) JosephineGordon 10 63
(David Dennis) *sn led: rdn and hdd over 1f out: no ex ins fnl f* **20/1**

5646 **7** *1 1/2* **Red Bravo (IRE)**[16] 7731 3-8-12 **68**........(b[1]) KieranShoemark 1 56
(Charles Hills) *s.i.s: hmpd over 6f out: hdwy over 2f out: rdn over 1f out: wknd ins fnl f* **10/1**

-666 **8** *1 1/4* **Kyllachy Dragon (IRE)**[225] 1018 4-9-7 **75**........ RobHornby 7 61
(Mark Rimell) *disp ld early: chsd ldrs: rdn over 1f out: wknd fnl f* **33/1**

-325 **9** *3/4* **Scorched Breath**[195] 1516 3-9-1 **71**........(h[1]) JimCrowley 11 54
(Charlie Fellowes) *hld up: racd keenly: nvr on terms* **9/2**[2]

2000 **10** *1/2* **Rock Of Estonia (IRE)**[14] 7789 4-9-5 **73**........ DanielMuscutt 6 56
(Michael Squance) *hld up: plld hrd: n.d (vet said gelding was lame)* **66/1**

1200 **11** *7* **Lestrade**[12] 7856 3-9-7 **77**........(h) DavidProbert 9 40
(David O'Meara) *plld hrd and sn prom: rdn and wknd over 1f out* **20/1**

1m 26.12s (0.12) **Going Correction** -0.025s/f (Stan)
WFA 3 from 4yo+ 2lb **11** Ran SP% **117.8**
Speed ratings (Par 103): **98,96,94,92,92 92,90,88,88,87 79**
CSF £7.65 CT £182.93 TOTE £1.70: £1.10, £2.70, £10.40; EX 8.10 Trifecta £175.70.
Owner David Batten **Bred** Bloomsbury Stud **Trained** Newmarket, Suffolk

FOCUS
A comfortable success for the odds-on favourite. It was the slower division by 1.11sec and the second helps with the standard.

8221 32RED ON THE APP STORE H'CAP (DIV II) — 7f (P)

7:00 (7:01) (Class 5) (0-75,76) 3-Y-O+

£3,752 (£1,116; £557; £400; £400; £400) **Stalls** Low

Form / RPR

2042 **1** **Little Palaver**[34] 7080 7-8-10 **71**........(p) AmeliaGlass(7) 12 79
(Clive Cox) *plld hrd: led 6f out: rdn over 1f out: styd on* **14/1**

1060 **2** *nk* **Mendoza (IRE)**[39] 6930 3-9-2 **72**........ RyanTate 5 78
(James Eustace) *led 1f: chsd ldrs: rdn over 1f out: styd on u.p to go 2nd nr fin* **25/1**

5615 **3** *hd* **Final Frontier (IRE)**[42] 6826 6-9-0 **68**........ JackGarritty 8 74
(Ruth Carr) *prom: chsd wnr over 5f out: rdn over 1f out: styd on* **33/1**

2642 **4** *1 1/4* **Turn To Rock (IRE)**[13] 7812 3-8-11 **67**........ HectorCrouch 2 69
(Ed Walker) *hld up: hdwy over 2f out: rdn over 1f out: r.o* **6/1**[2]

/305 **5** *3/4* **I Can (IRE)**[17] 7684 4-9-1 **69**........ NicolaCurrie 1 70
(Sir Mark Todd) *hld up: hdwy over 1f out: sn rdn: styd on* **7/1**[3]

5644 **6** *1* **Kamikaze Lord (USA)**[22] 7519 3-9-1 **71**........(t) RobertHavlin 11 68
(John Butler) *hld up: rdn over 1f out: styd on ins fnl f: nt trble ldrs* **8/1**

1362 **7** *nk* **Fighting Temeraire (IRE)**[31] 7205 6-9-7 **75**........ JoeyHaynes 6 73
(Dean Ivory) *hld up in tch: plld hrd: outpcd over 2f out: styd on u.p fnl f* **12/1**

2333 **8** *1/2* **Mums Hope**[14] 7788 3-9-3 **76**........(b) CierenFallon(3) 3 71
(Hughie Morrison) *s.i.s: hld up: rdn over 1f out: nvr nrr (jockey said filly was slowly away)* **4/1**[1]

1200 **9** *1 1/4* **Pentland Lad (IRE)**[133] 3440 3-8-10 **66**........(t) DavidProbert 4 58
(Charlie Fellowes) *hld up in tch: rdn over 2f out: no ex fnl f* **9/1**

0000 **10** *2* **Ghayadh**[28] 7305 4-9-4 **72**........(h) JamieSpencer 7 59
(George Boughey) *s.i.s: hld up: nvr on terms* **20/1**

1141 **11** *1 1/4* **Bounty Pursuit**[28] 7299 7-9-4 **75**........ MeganNicholls(3) 10 59
(Michael Blake) *s.i.s: hld up: pushed along on outer over 3f out: n.d (jockey said gelding hung left-handed throughout)* **11/1**

5304 **12** *4 1/2* **Water Diviner (IRE)**[52] 6469 3-9-6 **76**........ SeanLevey 9 47
(Richard Hannon) *chsd ldrs tl wknd over 1f out* **8/1**

1m 25.01s (-0.99) **Going Correction** -0.025s/f (Stan)
WFA 3 from 4yo+ 2lb **12** Ran SP% **113.2**
Speed ratings (Par 103): **104,103,103,102,101 100,99,99,97,95 93,88**
CSF £315.94 CT £10834.35 TOTE £17.70: £5.10, £7.70, £8.00; EX 263.50 Trifecta £2810.30.
Owner Trevor Fox **Bred** Mrs Sandra Fox **Trained** Lambourn, Berks

FOCUS
This was run in a time 1.11sec faster than the first division and the winner made most, while the placed horses raced close up. Ordinary form, with the first three to their marks.

8222 32RED H'CAP — 1m (P)

7:30 (7:30) (Class 2) (0-100,100) 3-Y-O

£15,562 (£4,660; £2,330; £1,165; £582; £292) **Stalls** Low

Form / RPR

-211 **1** **Alrajaa**[12] 7836 3-9-0 **93**........ JimCrowley 8 105+
(John Gosden) *chsd ldr: rdn to ld over 1f out: r.o wl* **6/4**[1]

5121 **2** *2 1/4* **Kuwait Currency (USA)**[13] 7815 3-9-7 **100**........(t) SeanLevey 5 105
(Richard Hannon) *led: rdn and hdd over 1f out: styd on same pce ins fnl f* **3/1**[2]

3046 **3** *nk* **Rectory Road**[13] 7815 3-8-1 **83**........(h[1]) WilliamCox(3) 7 87
(Andrew Balding) *s.i.s: hld up: racd keenly: swtchd lft over 2f out: rdn and r.o ins fnl f: nt rch ldrs* **14/1**

303 **4** *1/2* **Model Guest**[11] 7863 3-8-9 **88**........(b[1]) DavidProbert 2 91
(George Margarson) *chsd ldrs: rdn over 1f out: styd on same pce ins fnl f* **16/1**

500 **5** *hd* **Creationist (USA)**[109] 4342 3-8-13 **92**........(w) AdamMcNamara 6 95
(Roger Charlton) *prom on outer: racd keenly: rdn over 1f out: styd on (jockey said gelding ran too free)* **16/1**

5241 **6** *hd* **Sir Busker (IRE)**[22] 7517 3-8-13 **92**........ JamieSpencer 4 94
(William Knight) *stdd s: hld up: swtchd lft over 1f out: r.o ins fnl f: nvr nrr* **11/2**[3]

1513 **7** *1 3/4* **Siglo Six**[32] 7163 3-8-9 **88**........(h) KieranShoemark 1 86
(Hugo Palmer) *hld up: plld hrd: hdwy over 1f out: styd on same pce fnl f* **10/1**

-612 **8** *1/2* **Listen To The Wind (IRE)**[104] 4497 3-8-5 **87**........ CierenFallon(3) 3 84
(William Haggas) *prom: rdn over 2f out: no ex fnl f* **12/1**

1m 39.33s (-0.47) **Going Correction** -0.025s/f (Stan) **8** Ran SP% **115.6**
Speed ratings (Par 107): **101,98,98,97,97 97,95,95**
CSF £6.07 CT £42.93 TOTE £1.90: £1.10, £1.50, £3.40; EX 6.30 Trifecta £55.70.
Owner Hamdan Al Maktoum **Bred** Shadwell Estate Company Limited **Trained** Newmarket, Suffolk

FOCUS
This was steadily run and favoured those up front, but the progressive winner still impressed. Another clear pb from him.

8223 WISE BETTING AT RACINGTV.COM H'CAP — 1m (P)

8:00 (8:00) (Class 6) (0-60,60) 3-Y-O+

£3,105 (£924; £461; £400; £400; £400) **Stalls** Low

Form / RPR

454 **1** **Takeonefortheteam**[42] 6839 4-9-6 **59**........ LiamJones 8 67+
(Mark Loughnane) *hld up: nt clr run fr over 2f out tl swtchd lft over 1f out: shkn up and qcknd to ld wl ins fnl f: comf* **5/1**

5201 **2** *1 1/4* **Cauthen (IRE)**[29] 7282 3-8-13 **58**........(h[1]) FinleyMarsh(3) 12 63
(Milton Harris) *hld up: hdwy over 1f out: rdn and ev ch ins fnl f: styd on same pce towards fin* **7/1**

000 **3** *shd* **Medici Moon**[47] 6643 5-9-3 **56**........(p) RobHornby 7 61
(Richard Price) *sn led: rdn and hung lft over 1f out: hdd wl ins fnl f* **33/1**

4554 **4** *3/4* **Cashel (IRE)**[19] 7609 4-9-6 **59**........ AlistairRawlinson 9 62
(Michael Appleby) *awkward s: pushed along early in rr: hdwy u.p fnl f: kpt on* **3/1**[1]

5060 **5** *1 1/2* **God Has Given**[56] 6304 3-9-1 **60**........(t[1]) GabrieleMalune(3) 3 60
(Ivan Furtado) *chsd ldr 1f: remained handy: rdn over 1f out: styd on same pce ins fnl f* **11/1**

26-0 **6** *1/2* **Havana Sunset**[20] 7573 3-9-3 **59**........ RossaRyan 6 58
(Mike Murphy) *plld hrd and prom: rdn over 1f out: no ex wl ins fnl f* **20/1**

0050 **7** *nk* **The Warrior (IRE)**[83] 5309 7-9-7 **60**........(v) DanielMuscutt 4 58
(Lee Carter) *hld up in tch: rdn over 1f out: no ex ins fnl f* **9/2**[3]

1346 **8** *1/2* **Jupiter**[13] 7812 4-8-10 **56**........(v) LukeCatton(7) 13 53
(Alexandra Dunn) *chsd ldr after 1f tl rdn over 1f out: no ex ins fnl f* **25/1**

0030 **9** *2 ¼* **Rifft (IRE)**[42] 7558 6839 4-9-6 **59**..............................(t[1]) CallumShepherd 11 51
(Lydia Richards) *hld up in tch: rdn over 2f out: n.m.r over 1f out: wknd ins fnl f* **25/1**

3365 **10** *nk* **Annexation (FR)**[19] 7609 3-9-3 **59**..............................(p[1]) RobertHavlin 10 50
(Ed Dunlop) *hld up: plld hrd: hdwy on outer over 3f out: n.m.r over 1f out: wknd fnl f (jockey said colt ran too free)* **4/1**[2]

1m 40.29s (0.49) **Going Correction** -0.025s/f (Stan)
WFA 3 from 4yo+ 3lb **10** Ran SP% **116.1**
Speed ratings (Par 101): **96,94,94,93,92 91,91,91,88,88**
CSF £37.37 CT £1072.00 TOTE £6.10: £1.60, £1.90, £8.90; EX 38.40 Trifecta £883.80.
Owner S & A Mares **Bred** G S Shropshire **Trained** Rock, Worcs

FOCUS
They finished pretty bunched up here, the closers having their day but the long-time leader not beaten far in third.

8224 BET AT RACINGTV.COM H'CAP 1m 3f 219y(P)
8:30 (8:32) (Class 6) (0-60,60) 3-Y-O+
£3,105 (£924; £461; £400; £400; £400) **Stalls** Low

Form RPR

4343 **1** **Banta Bay**[21] 7558 5-8-13 **49**.............................. JosephineGordon 13 57
(John Best) *chsd ldrs: rdn and edgd rt fr over 1f out: led ins fnl f: styd on wl* **7/1**[2]

060 **2** *1 ½* **Master Milliner (IRE)**[29] 7278 3-9-1 **57**.............................. RobertHavlin 8 63
(Emma Lavelle) *sn prom: nt clr run and lost pl over 2f out: rallied over 1f out: r.o to go 2nd wl ins fnl f* **14/1**

0544 **3** *¾* **Passing Clouds**[22] 7518 4-9-1 **51**.............................. KierenFox 12 55
(Michael Attwater) *s.i.s: rcvrd to ld after 1f: rdn over 1f out: hdd ins fnl f: styd on same pce (jockey said gelding hung left-handed in the closing stages)* **12/1**

0203 **4** *nk* **Red Gunner**[7] 8000 5-9-2 **52**.............................. EdwardGreatrex 2 56
(Mark Loughnane) *hld up: hdwy over 2f out: rdn over 1f out: styd on same pce ins fnl f* **7/1**[2]

3221 **5** *nk* **Royal Dancer**[7] 7985 3-8-11 **53**.............................. LukeMorris 4 57
(Sylvester Kirk) *chsd ldrs: wnt 2nd over 3f out: rdn and ev ch over 1f out: styd on same pce ins fnl f* **5/1**[1]

0/60 **6** *shd* **Tulane (IRE)**[120] 3941 4-9-4 **57**.............................. JaneElliott[(3)] 1 60
(Richard Phillips) *hld up: gd hdwy over 1f out: sn rdn: no ex wl ins fnl f* **10/1**[3]

5605 **7** *½* **Movie Star (GER)**[28] 7318 4-9-10 **60**..............................(t) JamieSpencer 6 62
(Amy Murphy) *hld up: hdwy over 2f out: sn rdn: styd on* **5/1**[1]

40-2 **8** *4 ½* **Vlannon**[166] 2344 4-9-1 **51**.............................. LiamKeniry 7 46
(Michael Madgwick) *s.i.s: rdn over 3f out: nt trble ldrs* **16/1**

2654 **9** *8* **Hummdinger (FR)**[23] 5954 3-9-4 **60**..............................(v) DavidProbert 5 43
(Alan King) *hld up in tch: rdn over 2f out: wknd over 1f out* **5/1**[1]

06-0 **10** *3 ½* **Finisher (USA)**[21] 7560 4-9-7 **60**.............................. TimClark[(3)] 3 36
(Mark Gillard) *s.i.s: in rr and pushed along 10f out: nvr on terms (jockey said gelding was slowly away)* **100/1**

000 **11** *nk* **Binmar's Sexy Lexy (CAN)**[47] 6641 3-8-2 **47**.............................. WilliamCox[(3)] 9 24
(Stuart Kittow) *mid-div: rdn over 5f out: wknd over 2f out* **66/1**

0000 **12** *7* **River Dart (IRE)**[56] 6303 7-9-9 **59**.............................. TomMarquand 10 24
(Tony Carroll) *s.i.s: pushed along and hdwy to chse ldr 10f out tl rdn over 3f out: wknd over 2f out* **25/1**

2000 **13** *14* **Monsieur Fox**[60] 6152 4-9-4 **54**.............................. CallumShepherd 11
(Lydia Richards) *in rr and pushed along 10f out: rdn and hung lft over 3f out: sn wknd* **40/1**

0540 **14** *43* **Sweet Nature (IRE)**[14] 7790 4-9-4 **54**..............................(p) NicolaCurrie 14
(Laura Mongan) *s.i.s: hdwy on outer to go prom over 10f out: rdn and wknd over 3f out* **25/1**

2m 33.93s (-0.57) **Going Correction** -0.025s/f (Stan)
WFA 3 from 4yo+ 6lb **14** Ran SP% **116.9**
Speed ratings (Par 101): **100,99,98,98,98 98,97,94,89,87 86,82,72,44**
CSF £93.90 CT £1158.83 TOTE £7.20: £2.00, £5.20, £4.10; EX 100.90 Trifecta £678.30.
Owner Jones, Fuller & Paine **Bred** R, J D & M R Bromley Gardner **Trained** Oad Street, Kent

FOCUS
A moderate affair, but a competitive one.
T/Plt: £462.20 to a £1 stake. Pool: £62,856.22 - 99.26 winning units T/Qpdt: £140.80 to a £1 stake. Pool: £14,664.96 - 77.02 winning units **Colin Roberts**

8002 LEICESTER (R-H)
Tuesday, October 15
8225 Meeting Abandoned - Waterlogged

8180 MUSSELBURGH (R-H)
Tuesday, October 15

OFFICIAL GOING: Soft (7.1)
Wind: Almost nil Weather: Overcast, dry

8232 JOIN RACINGTV NOW NOVICE STKS 7f 33y
2:05 (2:10) (Class 5) 2-Y-O
£4,140 (£1,232; £615; £307) **Stalls** Low

Form RPR

603 **1** **Alix James**[17] 7679 2-9-2 **73**.............................. PaulMulrennan 1 73
(Iain Jardine) *t.k.h: mde all: rdn over 1f out: kpt on wl fnl f: unchal* **11/10**[1]

3 **2** *1 ¼* **Hua Mulan (IRE)**[16] 7733 2-8-11 **0**.............................. GrahamLee 5 65
(Keith Dalgleish) *prom: effrt and pushed along over 2f out: chsd wnr over 1f out: kpt on ins fnl f: nt pce to chal* **12/1**[3]

0 **3** *1 ¾* **Warne's Army**[11] 7870 2-8-11 **0**.............................. JoeFanning 3 61+
(Mark Johnston) *bhd: rdn over 3f out: drifted lft 2f out: hdwy to chse clr ldng pair ins fnl f: kpt on: nrst fin* **25/1**

42 **4** *2 ¾* **Le Chiffre**[38] 6970 2-9-2 **0**.............................. DanielTudhope 8 59
(David O'Meara) *reluctant to enter stalls: trckd ldrs: rdn over 2f out: edgd rt and outpcd over 1f out: btn ins fnl f* **5/4**[2]

0 **5** *1 ½* **Sea Ewe**[20] 7580 2-8-11 **0**.............................. JamesSullivan 6 50
(Alistair Whillans) *hld up: rdn along 3f out: no imp fr over 1f out* **80/1**

64 **6** *5* **Funky Dunky (IRE)**[15] 7765 2-8-13 **0**.............................. SeanDavis[(3)] 2 42
(Keith Dalgleish) *chsd wnr: rdn over 2f out: hung rt and wknd over 1f out* **50/1**

5 **7** *1 ½* **Grandads Best Girl**[16] 7733 2-8-11 **0**.............................. BenRobinson 7 34
(Linda Perratt) *s.i.s and swtchd rt s: hld up: rdn and effrt over 2f out: wknd over 1f out: eased whn btn ins fnl f* **33/1**

1m 33.49s (4.49) **Going Correction** +0.725s/f (Yiel) **7** Ran SP% **109.7**
Speed ratings (Par 95): **103,101,99,96,94 89,87**
CSF £12.74 TOTE £2.10: £1.10, £3.40; EX 10.00 Trifecta £63.60.
Owner James Property Ltd **Bred** Plantation Stud **Trained** Carrutherstown, D'fries & G'way

FOCUS
The going was soft for the second day of this meeting. This was an uncompetitive and ordinary-looking juvenile novice and, with the second favourite running below expectations, it took little winning. The field tacked across towards the stands' side in the straight.

8233 LIKE RACINGTV ON FACEBOOK H'CAP (DIV I) 7f 33y
2:40 (2:44) (Class 6) (0-60,60) 3-Y-O+
£3,493 (£1,039; £519; £300; £300; £300) **Stalls** Low

Form RPR

0032 **1** **Forever A Lady (IRE)**[14] 7780 6-9-6 **59**.............................. JoeFanning 1 66
(Keith Dalgleish) *hld up in midfield: shkn up and hdwy over 2f out: bk on bridle and led over 1f out: rdn and edgd lft ins fnl f: r.o wl* **7/2**[1]

4600 **2** *1 ¾* **Tarnhelm**[24] 7443 4-8-4 **50**.............................. RhonaPindar[(7)] 6 53
(Wilf Storey) *missed break: hld up: pushed along and hdwy 2f out: chsd wnr ent fnl f: edgd rt: kpt on: nt pce to chal* **9/1**

5004 **3** *1 ¼* **Gremoboy**[5] 8070 3-8-6 **47**..............................(p) DuranFentiman 3 46
(Tim Easterby) *led: rdn and hrd pressed fr over 2f out: hdd over 1f out: rallied: kpt on same pce wl ins fnl f* **7/2**[1]

5450 **4** *1* **Colour Contrast (IRE)**[35] 6572 6-9-5 **58**..............................(b) JamieGormley 11 55
(Iain Jardine) *t.k.h: hld up in tch: effrt over 2f out: ev ch briefly over 1f out: no ex ins fnl f* **16/1**

1400 **5** *hd* **Roaring Forties (IRE)**[21] 7540 6-9-7 **60**..............................(b) DanielTudhope 2 57
(Rebecca Bastiman) *prom: rdn over 2f out: hdwy and ev ch briefly over 1f out: fdd ins fnl f* **4/1**[2]

0006 **6** *1* **Archies Lad**[23] 7489 3-8-12 **53**.............................. LewisEdmunds 9 46
(R Mike Smith) *towards rr: pushed along and hdwy over 2f out: rdn and no imp fnl f* **28/1**

0005 **7** *2 ¾* **Star Cracker (IRE)**[18] 7651 7-8-7 **46** oh1.............................. PhilDennis 8 33
(Jim Goldie) *pressed ldr: ev ch over 2f out to over 1f out: rdn and wknd fnl f (trainer said gelding was unsuited by the soft ground and would prefer a faster surface)* **40/1**

5503 **8** *1 ½* **Prince Of Time**[15] 7761 7-8-2 **46** oh1..............................(p) PaulaMuir[(5)] 12 29
(Stella Barclay) *in tch: drvn along over 2f out: wknd over 1f out* **25/1**

0006 **9** *½* **Newstead Abbey**[11] 7869 9-8-11 **50**.............................. TomEaves 7 32
(Rebecca Bastiman) *hld up in tch: drvn along over 2f out: wknd wl over 1f out* **14/1**

3435 **10** *hd* **Midnight In Havana**[24] 7444 3-9-2 **57**.............................. GrahamLee 10 38
(Bryan Smart) *cl up: rdn over 2f out: wknd over 1f out* **6/1**[3]

0605 **11** *4* **Gilmer (IRE)**[15] 7761 8-8-4 **46**..............................(v) HarrisonShaw[(3)] 4 18
(Stef Keniry) *s.i.s: bhd: drvn along and outpcd 3f out: sn btn* **20/1**

0000 **12** *11* **Griffin Street**[16] 7737 6-8-2 **46** oh1..............................(b) AndrewBreslin[(5)] 5
(Alistair Whillans) *missed break: bhd: struggling 3f out: lost tch fnl 2f* **80/1**

1m 33.63s (4.63) **Going Correction** +0.725s/f (Yiel)
WFA 3 from 4yo+ 2lb **12** Ran SP% **117.0**
Speed ratings (Par 101): **102,100,98,97,97 96,92,91,90,90 85,73**
CSF £33.03 CT £120.12 TOTE £3.60: £1.50, £2.40, £2.10; EX 36.40 Trifecta £235.10.
Owner Ken McGarrity **Bred** Mick McGinn **Trained** Carluke, S Lanarks

FOCUS
The first division of a 46-60 handicap but it is unlikely to be a race that throws up many future winners. Once again the field came centre to stand side in the straight. The pace was no more than fair.

8234 LIKE RACINGTV ON FACEBOOK H'CAP (DIV II) 7f 33y
3:10 (3:17) (Class 6) (0-60,60) 3-Y-O+
£3,493 (£1,039; £519; £300; £300; £300) **Stalls** Low

Form RPR

65-F **1** **Cawthorne Lad**[132] 3478 3-8-12 **53**.............................. DuranFentiman 2 60+
(Tim Easterby) *hld up on ins: stdy hdwy over 2f out: rdn and chsd ldr over 1f out: led ins fnl f: kpt on wl* **18/1**

2130 **2** *1 ¼* **Dreamseller (IRE)**[11] 7875 3-9-5 **60**..............................(p) DavidAllan 5 64
(Tim Easterby) *t.k.h early: trckd ldrs: led gng wl over 1f out: sn rdn: hdd ins fnl f: one pce towards fin* **9/4**[1]

3433 **3** *3 ¾* **Be Bold**[14] 7780 7-8-12 **51**..............................(b) LewisEdmunds 11 47
(Rebecca Bastiman) *led: rdn: edgd lft and hdd over 1f out: outpcd by first two fnl f* **6/1**

1400 **4** *1* **Naples Bay**[15] 7766 5-8-11 **53**.............................. HarrisonShaw[(3)] 1 46
(Katie Scott) *plld hrd early: prom: rdn over 2f out: kpt on same pce fnl f (jockey said gelding ran too free)* **10/1**

0040 **5** *½* **Cliff Bay (IRE)**[14] 7776 5-8-9 **48**..............................(v[1]) GrahamLee 12 40
(Keith Dalgleish) *sn w ldr: rdn over 2f out: outpcd over 1f out: no further imp fnl f* **7/1**

5060 **6** *hd* **Darwina**[14] 7776 3-8-0 **46**..............................(h) AndrewBreslin[(5)] 10 36
(Alistair Whillans) *dwlt: bhd and sn detached: rdn and hdwy over 2f out: no imp fr over 1f out* **20/1**

4P03 **7** *1* **Leeshaan (IRE)**[14] 7779 4-8-7 **46** oh1.............................. PhilDennis 7 35
(Rebecca Bastiman) *dwlt: hld up: drvn along over 2f out: no imp fr over 1f out: btn fnl f* **5/1**[2]

3306 **8** *½* **Cameo Star (IRE)**[14] 7779 4-9-4 **60**..............................(p) SeanDavis[(3)] 8 48
(Richard Fahey) *hld up: drvn along over 3f out: rallied over 2f out: edgd rt and no imp over 1f out: btn fnl f* **11/2**[3]

0005 **9** *4* **Haymarket**[16] 7738 10-8-7 **46** oh1.............................. JamesSullivan 9 24
(R Mike Smith) *prom: rdn and struggling over 2f out: hung rt and sn btn* **50/1**

1m 33.68s (4.68) **Going Correction** +0.725s/f (Yiel)
WFA 3 from 4yo+ 2lb **9** Ran SP% **110.7**
Speed ratings (Par 101): **102,100,96,95,94 94,93,92,88**
CSF £55.12 CT £269.34 TOTE £15.60: £4.10, £1.40, £1.90; EX 70.60 Trifecta £534.60.
Owner E A Brook **Bred** E A Brook **Trained** Great Habton, N Yorks

The Form Book Flat 2019, Raceform Ltd, Newbury, RG14 5SJ

FOCUS
This was the second and stronger division of the 46-60 handicap. The pace was fair, they all came towards the stand side and the first two, who are stable companions, finished clear.

8235 RACINGTV.COM H'CAP 5f 1y
3:45 (3:48) (Class 6) (0-60,61) 3-Y-O+
£3,493 (£1,039; £519; £300; £300; £300) **Stalls** High

Form RPR
0441 **1** **Quanah (IRE)**[15] 7764 3-9-7 **60**.................................... DanielTudhope 9 66
(Liam Bailey) *midfield: rdn along 1/2-way: hdwy on outside wl over 1f out: led ins fnl f: kpt on wl cl home* **5/2**[1]
4024 **2** *nk* **Mr Greenlight**[13] 7831 4-9-7 **60**..(p) DavidAllan 1 64
(Tim Easterby) *sn led: rdn and edgd lft over 1f out: hdd ins fnl f: rallied: hld cl home* **15/2**[3]
6036 **3** *shd* **Burmese Blazer (IRE)**[15] 7761 4-9-2 **55**....................(p) PaddyMathers 3 59
(Jim Goldie) *prom: effrt and rdn over 1f out: ev ch ins fnl f: kpt on: hld nr fin* **5/1**[2]
2014 **4** *1 3/4* **Popping Corks (IRE)**[15] 7766 3-8-13 **52**...................... BenRobinson 4 50
(Linda Perratt) *early ldr: w ldr to 2f out: sn drvn along: one pce ins fnl f (jockey said filly hung right throughout)* **9/1**
0003 **5** *1* **Corton Lass**[16] 7737 4-8-7 **46** oh1.............................. JoeFanning 10 40
(Keith Dalgleish) *prom: effrt whn nt clr run briefly over 1f out: edgd rt and one pce fnl f* **16/1**
0400 **6** *nk* **Spenny's Lass**[31] 7214 4-8-7 **46** oh1..........................(v[1]) AndrewMullen 12 39
(John Ryan) *towards rr: drvn along over 3f out: kpt on ins fnl f: nrst fin* **16/1**
0506 **7** *nk* **Pavers Pride**[16] 7736 5-9-5 **58**.. GrahamLee 6 50
(Noel Wilson) *towards rr and sn pushed along: hdwy over 1f out: no imp ins fnl f* **15/2**[3]
0110 **8** *1 1/4* **Night Law**[34] 7066 5-9-3 **56**..(b) PhilDennis 2 43
(Katie Scott) *w ldrs to over 2f out: rdn and wknd over 1f out* **14/1**
3000 **9** *1 1/4* **Classic Pursuit**[23] 7488 8-9-4 **57**..............................(v) JamesSullivan 5 40
(Marjorie Fife) *prom: outpcd and edgd rt 1/2-way: wknd over 1f out* **25/1**
1450 **10** *1/2* **Northern Society (IRE)**[8] 7959 3-9-5 **61**........................ SeanDavis(3) 8 43
(Keith Dalgleish) *reluctant to enter stalls: bhd and sn rdn along: hdwy whn nt clr run over 1f out to ins fnl f: no imp whn hmpd and snatched up wl ins fnl f* **12/1**
0400 **11** *3 3/4* **Beechwood Izzy (IRE)**[25] 7405 3-8-12 **56**...........(b[1]) AndrewBreslin(5) 7 24
(Keith Dalgleish) *dwlt and blkd s: bhd and sn detached: nvr on terms* **25/1**
1m 2.77s (3.07) **Going Correction** +0.725s/f (Yiel) **11** Ran SP% **112.6**
Speed ratings (Par 101): **104,103,103,100,98 98,98,96,94,93 87**
CSF £19.96 CT £86.38 TOTE £2.70: £1.10, £2.10, £2.70; EX 16.50 Trifecta £63.40.
Owner Mrs Ailsa Stirling **Bred** Stonecross Stud **Trained** Middleham, N Yorks
FOCUS
A run-of-the-mill 5f handicap with most of the runners exposed sorts.

8236 EVERY RACE LIVE ON RACINGTV H'CAP 1m 7f 217y
4:15 (4:21) (Class 5) (0-75,76) 3-Y-O+
£3,428 (£1,020; £509; £300; £300; £300) **Stalls** High

Form RPR
1254 **1** **Beechwood Jude (FR)**[24] 7436 3-9-3 **73**..........................(p) JoeFanning 1 79
(Keith Dalgleish) *trckd ldr: effrt and rdn over 2f out: led appr fnl f: edgd lft last 50yds: kpt on wl* **3/1**[2]
6-25 **2** *3/4* **Normal Norman**[31] 7212 5-10-1 **76**.................................... DavidAllan 2 81
(John Ryan) *t.k.h early: hld up in midfield: hdwy 3f out: effrt and cl up over 1f out: chsd wnr ins fnl f: r.o* **2/1**[1]
5446 **3** *1* **Bodacious Name (IRE)**[127] 3653 5-9-6 **67**...................... JasonHart 11 71+
(John Quinn) *slowly away: t.k.h in rr: rdn over 2f out: kpt on wl fnl f to take 3rd last stride* **11/2**
5464 **4** *hd* **Tor**[39] 6933 5-9-8 **69**.. DanielTudhope 4 73
(Marjorie Fife) *led at modest gallop: qckd 4f out: drvn and hdd appr fnl f: one pce whn checked last 50yds: lost 3rd last stride* **9/2**[3]
312/ **5** *nk* **Arthurs Secret**[161] 5758 9-9-7 **68**............................ PaulMulrennan 6 71
(Sandy Thomson) *t.k.h: prom: rdn and outpcd over 2f out: rallied fnl f: nt pce to chal* **20/1**
310- **6** *6* **Gripper**[43] 7455 4-8-13 **67**...(p) RhonaPindar(7) 7 63
(Lucinda Russell) *chsd ldrs: drvn along over 2f out: wknd wl over 1f out* **66/1**
6560 **7** *nk* **Maulesden May (IRE)**[22] 7510 6-9-8 **69**........................ GrahamLee 9 65
(Keith Dalgleish) *dwlt: hld up: rdn along 3f out: hung lft and no imp over 1f out* **40/1**
0000 **8** *1/2* **Shrewd**[26] 7368 9-9-3 **67**..(v[1]) HarrisonShaw(3) 3 62
(Iain Jardine) *hld up bhd ldng gp: drvn and outpcd over 2f out: n.d after* **9/1**
20-0 **9** *3 3/4* **Astute Boy (IRE)**[24] 7436 5-9-9 **70**..........................(tp) JamesSullivan 10 61
(R Mike Smith) *hld up: rdn and struggling over 2f out: sn btn* **50/1**
50/6 **10** *6* **Ballynanty (IRE)**[136] 3361 7-10-0 **75**.......................(t) LucyAlexander 8 59
(N W Alexander) *hld up bhd ldng gp on outside: rdn and outpcd 3f out: wknd fnl 2f* **50/1**
3m 53.46s (21.96) **Going Correction** +0.725s/f (Yiel)
WFA 3 from 4yo+ 9lb **10** Ran SP% **114.5**
Speed ratings (Par 103): **74,73,73,73,72 69,69,69,67,64**
CSF £8.85 CT £29.91 TOTE £3.30: £1.10, £1.10, £2.90; EX 9.30 Trifecta £36.10.
Owner Middleham Park Racing LXXXIV **Bred** T De La Heronniere & J Hebert **Trained** Carluke, S Lanarks
■ Stewards' Enquiry : Joe Fanning caution; careless riding
FOCUS
Add 7 yards. This wasn't the most competitive of staying handicaps. It was run at a modest gallop and the form is unlikely to prove reliable as the prominent racers were favoured. Once again the field came across towards the stands' side in the straight. The winner's rated in line with a better view of his form.

8237 WATCH RACINGTV NOW H'CAP 1m 2y
4:50 (4:54) (Class 4) (0-80,78) 3-Y-O+
£5,822 (£1,732; £865; £432; £300; £300) **Stalls** Low

Form RPR
0625 **1** **Greek Hero**[38] 6961 3-9-7 **78**.. DanielTudhope 10 87
(Declan Carroll) *s.i.s: hld up: rdn over 2f out: hdwy over 1f out: led ins fnl f: kpt on strly towards fin* **9/2**[1]
2260 **2** *3/4* **Al Erayg (IRE)**[10] 7907 6-9-6 **74**.......................................(p) DavidAllan 2 81
(Tim Easterby) *prom: effrt and rdn wl over 1f out: ev ch ins fnl f: kpt on: hld nr fin* **11/2**[3]
0032 **3** *1 1/2* **Glasses Up (USA)**[14] 7782 4-9-9 **77**.............................. JamesSullivan 9 81
(R Mike Smith) *t.k.h: hld up in midfield on outside: rdn and outpcd over 2f out: rallied fnl f: kpt on: nt pce to chal* **9/1**
3661 **4** *1/2* **Gometra Ginty (IRE)**[16] 7735 3-9-7 **78**.........................(p) JoeFanning 11 81
(Keith Dalgleish) *cl up: rdn over 2f out: led over 1f out to ins fnl f: sn one pce* **12/1**
0613 **5** *2* **Donnelly's Rainbow (IRE)**[16] 7738 6-8-13 **67**............. JamieGormley 4 65
(Rebecca Bastiman) *in tch: drvn along over 2f out: kpt on same pce fnl f* **9/1**
0012 **6** *1 1/4* **How Bizarre**[1] 8181 4-8-11 **72**................................ JonathanFisher(7) 13 67
(Liam Bailey) *t.k.h: led on outside: rdn and hdd over 1f out: wknd ins fnl f* **5/1**[2]
5300 **7** *shd* **Ghalib (IRE)**[13] 7829 7-9-8 **76**.................................... LewisEdmunds 5 71
(Rebecca Bastiman) *trckd ldrs: rdn and effrt over 2f out: wknd fnl f* **13/2**
6510 **8** *1 3/4* **Pioneering (IRE)**[22] 7513 5-8-10 **69**................................(p) PaulaMuir(5) 8 60
(Roger Fell) *prom: rdn over 2f out: wknd over 1f out* **22/1**
-044 **9** *8* **Falmouth Light (FR)**[125] 3726 4-9-9 **77**......................... PaulMulrennan 1 50
(Iain Jardine) *dwlt: hld up: rdn along over 2f out: wknd wl over 1f out* **16/1**
0300 **10** *1/2* **Dancin Boy**[14] 7782 3-9-7 **78**.. TomEaves 7 49
(Michael Dods) *t.k.h: hld up: drvn and outpcd over 2f out: sn btn* **22/1**
331 **11** *16* **Be Kool (IRE)**[20] 7587 6-9-9 **77**......................................(v) BenRobinson 6 12
(Brian Ellison) *plld hrd: prom: lost pl over 2f out: sn struggling: lost tch fnl f (jockey said gelding hung right in the closing stages)* **12/1**
4505 **12** *2 1/4* **Battle Of Waterloo (IRE)**[18] 7663 3-9-3 **77**................... SeanDavis(3) 3 6
(John Ryan) *slowly away: hld up: drvn along 3f out: wknd 2f out: eased whn no ch fnl f* **25/1**
1m 45.73s (5.73) **Going Correction** +0.725s/f (Yiel)
WFA 3 from 4yo+ 3lb **12** Ran SP% **117.4**
Speed ratings (Par 105): **100,99,97,97,95 94,93,92,84,83 67,65**
CSF £27.61 CT £218.17 TOTE £7.00: £3.00, £2.60, £2.40; EX 30.50 Trifecta £158.90.
Owner Clipper Logistics **Bred** Scuderia Archi Romani **Trained** Malton, N Yorks
FOCUS
A competitive mile handicap and although it was run at a fairly modest gallop there seemed no pace bias for the winner, who came from last to first. The form looks sound.

8238 FOLLOW RACINGTV ON RACINGTV.COM H'CAP 1m 5f
5:25 (5:25) (Class 6) (0-60,61) 3-Y-O+
£3,493 (£1,039; £519; £300; £300; £300) **Stalls** Low

Form RPR
0521 **1** **Smart Lass (IRE)**[16] 7732 4-9-2 **52**................................ JamieGormley 4 61
(Iain Jardine) *t.k.h early: cl up: jnd ldr 1/2-way: led over 4f out: drew clr 3f out: rdn and drifted lft over 1f out: kpt on wl: unchal* **2/1**[1]
0000 **2** *7* **Starplex**[122] 2842 9-9-10 **60**.. JoeFanning 6 60
(Keith Dalgleish) *t.k.h early: prom: hdwy to chse (clr) wnr over 2f out: sn rdn: kpt on fnl f: nt pce to chal* **3/1**[2]
00-0 **3** *nk* **Mamdood (IRE)**[20] 7581 5-8-10 **49**....................(vt[1]) HarrisonShaw(3) 11 48
(Stef Keniry) *dwlt: hld up: rdn 3f out: kpt on fnl f to take 3rd cl home: nrst fin* **40/1**
0002 **4** *2 1/2* **Gworn**[16] 7739 9-8-11 **50**.. ConnorMurtagh(3) 1 46
(R Mike Smith) *in tch: hdwy and disp 2nd pl over 2f out to ins fnl f: wknd and lost 3rd cl home* **28/1**
4564 **5** *1* **Elite Icon**[34] 7070 5-8-10 **46** oh1..................................(v) PaddyMathers 7 40
(Jim Goldie) *t.k.h: hld up in midfield: rdn and outpcd over 2f out: rallied ins fnl f: nvr rchd ldrs* **20/1**
2000 **6** *3* **Majeste**[14] 7783 5-9-11 **61**... TomEaves 12 51
(Rebecca Bastiman) *t.k.h: hld up in midfield: rdn over 2f out: no further imp fr over 1f out* **25/1**
0106 **7** *2 3/4* **Lizzie Loch**[23] 7493 3-9-1 **57**.. AndrewMullen 8 46
(Alistair Whillans) *cl up: rdn over 3f out: wknd wl over 1f out* **50/1**
5534 **8** *nk* **Gemologist (IRE)**[16] 7732 4-8-10 **51**.......................(t) FayeMcManoman(5) 3 37
(Lucinda Russell) *hld up: rdn along 3f out: no imp fr 2f out* **28/1**
5-60 **9** *1* **Something Brewing (FR)**[34] 7070 5-9-5 **55**...........(v[1]) PaulMulrennan 9 40
(Iain Jardine) *t.k.h: hld up towards rr: rdn over 3f out: nvr able to chal* **50/1**
4302 **10** *1 1/2* **Lincoln Tale (IRE)**[16] 7732 3-9-4 **60**............................ DanielTudhope 2 45
(David O'Meara) *hld up in tch: effrt and drvn along 3f out: wknd over 1f out* **7/2**[3]
6066 **11** *6* **Pammi**[14] 7783 4-8-10 **46** oh1..(p) BenRobinson 5 21
(Jim Goldie) *led to 1/2-way: chsd wnr to over 2f out: wknd wl over 1f out* **25/1**
4003 **12** *1 1/2* **Doon Star**[16] 7739 4-8-10 **46** oh1.................................... PhilDennis 14 19
(Jim Goldie) *hld up on outside: drvn along 3f out: sn no imp: btn fnl 2f* **16/1**
3555 **13** *nk* **Nearly There**[35] 7048 6-9-3 **53**.................................(t) DuranFentiman 13 25
(Wilf Storey) *hld up: drvn and struggling over 3f out: sn btn (trainer said gelding was unsuited by the ground and would prefer a sounder surface)* **25/1**
4145 **14** *hd* **Cuba Ruba**[23] 7493 3-9-2 **58**...(p) DavidAllan 10 32
(Tim Easterby) *plld hrd in rr: drvn along 3f out: wknd 2f out (jockey said gelding ran too free)* **10/1**
3m 1.35s (9.65) **Going Correction** +0.725s/f (Yiel)
WFA 3 from 4yo+ 6lb **14** Ran SP% **125.1**
Speed ratings (Par 101): **99,94,94,92,92 90,88,88,88,87 83,82,82,82**
CSF £7.11 CT £188.70 TOTE £2.90: £1.40, £1.20, £14.00; EX 9.80 Trifecta £249.60.
Owner Gerry McGladery **Bred** Ben Browne **Trained** Carrutherstown, D'fries & G'way
FOCUS
Add 7yds to the official distance. Although this was a 14-runner handicap they bet double figures bar three. The early gallop was ordinary and under a good ride the easy winner got first run on her rivals.
T/Jkpt: Partly won. £10,000.00 to a £1 stake. Pool: £10,000.00 - 0.5 winning units. T/Plt: £14.10 to a £1 stake. Pool: £54,888.48 - 2,824.80 winning units T/Qpdt: £5.40 to a £1 stake. Pool: £5,332.06 - 723.28 winning units **Richard Young**

The Form Book Flat 2019, Raceform Ltd, Newbury, RG14 5SJ

7774 CHANTILLY (R-H)

Tuesday, October 15

OFFICIAL GOING: Polytrack: standard; turf: soft

8239a PRIX DE L'ALLEE MASSINE (CLAIMER) (2YO) (ALL-WEATHER TRACK) (POLYTRACK) 7f (P)

2:00 2-Y-O **£10,360** (£4,144; £3,108; £2,072; £1,036)

RPR

1 **Najm**[11] 7871 2-8-11 0..(b) CristianDemuro 7 72
(P Monfort, France) **43/10**[3]

2 3/4 **Hernan**[36] 7043 2-9-4 0.. Pierre-CharlesBoudot 2 77+
(Andrea Marcialis, France) **3/1**[1]

3 hd **Magic Timing**[34] 7064 2-9-4 0...............................(b) MickaelBarzalona 4 77+
(Tim Fitzgerald) *squeezed s: sn settled in fnl pair but cl up: rdn whn gap appeared over 1 1/2f out: r.o strly fnl f: nvr nrr* **31/10**[2]

4 2 **Thaniella (FR)**[18] 2-8-8 0.. MaximeGuyon 3 61
(P Bary, France) **3/1**[1]

5 2 1/2 **Goldmembers (FR)**[18] 7674 2-8-5 0.............................(b[1]) MlleLeaBails[(6)] 6 58
(M Boutin, France) **26/1**

6 1 1/2 **Calle Nevada (FR)**[15] 2-8-11 0.................................... VincentCheminaud 1 54
(D Windrif, France) **9/1**

7 1 1/2 **Mequinenza (IRE)**[59] 2-8-8 0.. EddyHardouin 10 47
(Vaclav Luka Jr, Czech Republic) **39/1**

8 1 3/4 **Mehanydream (FR)**[49] 6584 2-8-4 0.............................. HugoMouesan[(7)] 8 45
(C Boutin, France) **23/1**

9 1 3/4 **Roselane (FR)**[79] 2-8-0 0.................................. Joseph-MathieuMighty[(8)] 5 38
(M Delcher Sanchez, France) **28/1**

10 9 **Can't Beat It**[12] 2-8-11 0..(b[1]) AntoineHamelin 9 18
(Gavin Hernon, France) **31/1**

1m 26.19s **10 Ran SP% 120.2**
PARI-MUTUEL (all including 1 euro stake): WIN 5.30; PLACE 1.60, 1.60, 1.60; DF 6.30.
Owner Gerard L Ferron **Bred** Malih L Al Basti **Trained** France

8240a PRIX DE LA COURTILLE (CONDITIONS) (4YO+) (ALL-WEATHER TRACK) (POLYTRACK) 1m 1f 110y(P)

2:35 4-Y-0+

£12,612 (£4,792; £3,531; £2,018; £1,009; £756)

RPR

1 **Magical Forest (IRE)**[22] 7536 5-8-13 0.............................. CristianDemuro 8 83
(H Blume, Germany) **13/2**

2 1/2 **Miracle Des Aigles (FR)**[164] 2429 6-8-3 0..... MlleFriedaValleSkar[(8)] 10 80
(Mme C Barande-Barbe, France) **73/10**

3 3/4 **Mainsail Atlantic (USA)**[27] 7350 4-8-11 0...........(p) MickaelBarzalona 9 78
(James Fanshawe) *broke wl: w ldrs early: sn settled in 5th on outer: pushed along w 1 1/2f to run: styd on u.p fnl f: nt pce to chal* **22/5**[2]

4 1/2 **Szoff (GER)**[201] 9-9-0 0.. StephanePasquier 2 80
(Yasmin Almenrader, Germany) **12/1**

5 3/4 **Garlizain (FR)** 4-9-0 0................................ Roberto-CarlosMontenegro 3 79
(Alexandros Giatras, Greece) **13/1**

6 1 **I Am Charlie (FR)**[105] 6-8-8 0.............................. MlleMarieVelon[(8)] 11 80
(J-P Gauvin, France) **56/10**[3]

7 nk **Lucknow**[873] 3017 5-8-11 0...................................... ValentinSeguy 12 73
(Alexandros Giatras, Greece) **45/1**

8 1 **Galope Americano (BRZ)**[29] 5-9-0 0.............................. MaximeGuyon 7 74
(Mme Pia Brandt, France) **5/2**[1]

9 3/4 **Historic Event (IRE)**[885] 2630 5-8-8 0............................ AntoineHamelin 5 67
(Alexandros Giatras, Greece) **10/1**

10 3/4 **Damavand (GER)**[15] 4-9-4 0...................................... MichaelCadeddu 6 75
(Mario Hofer, Germany) **32/1**

11 1 1/2 **Dark Dream (FR)**[36] 8-8-11 0...................................... EddyHardouin 1 65
(Mlle M Henry, France) **41/1**

12 dist **The One Maybe (FR)** 4-8-8 0...................................... StephaneBreux 4
(Stephanie Gachelin, France) **119/1**

1m 54.11s **12 Ran SP% 120.0**
PARI-MUTUEL (all including 1 euro stake): WIN 7.50; PLACE 2.30, 2.70, 2.20; DF 28.40.
Owner Christoph Holschbach & Oliver Post **Bred** Adrian McMullan & Mairead O'Grady **Trained** Germany

8241 (Void numbering)

7754 BATH (L-H)

Wednesday, October 16

OFFICIAL GOING: Soft (6.1)
Wind: light across Weather: sunny periods

8242 DOWNLOAD THE STAR SPORTS APP NOW H'CAP 5f 160y

1:40 (1:40) (Class 5) (0-70,72) 3-Y-0+

£3,428 (£1,020; £509; £300; £300; £300) **Stalls** Centre

Form RPR

302 1 **Doc Sportello (IRE)**[28] 7337 7-9-10 **72**.............................. TomMarquand 3 81
(Tony Carroll) *slowly away: sn pushed along in last: swtchd rt and hdwy over 2f out: edgd sltly lft: led fnl 130yds: kpt on strly (jockey said gelding hung left-handed under pressure)* **11/2**[3]

3321 2 1/2 **Firenze Rosa (IRE)**[8] 7986 4-8-0 **55** 5ex.............................. AledBeech[(7)] 10 62
(John Bridger) *mid-div: hdwy over 2f out: led ent fnl f: hdd fnl 130yds: kpt on but no ex towards fin* **8/1**

1532 3 3 **Secret Potion**[6] 8063 5-9-6 **68**.. DavidProbert 7 65
(Ronald Harris) *in last trio: swtchd to centre and hdwy 2f out: wnt 3rd ent fnl f: kpt on but nt pce to get on terms* **5/1**[2]

0-06 4 shd **Hieronymus**[71] 5773 3-9-9 **72**.......................................(t[1]) OisinMurphy 2 69
(Seamus Durack) *hld up towards rr: prog 2f out: sn rdn: chal for hld 3rd ent fnl f: kpt on same pce* **20/1**

5 3 3/4 **Dormio**[101] 3-9-4 **70**.. MeganNicholls[(3)] 11 54
(Stuart Kittow) *trckd ldrs: rdn over 2f out: sn one pce* **11/1**

6512 6 1 1/4 **Our Oystercatcher**[33] 7161 5-9-10 **72**.............................. HectorCrouch 9 52
(Mark Pattinson) *led: rdn and hdd ent fnl f: sn wknd* **11/4**[1]

3402 7 2 1/4 **Mrs Worthington (IRE)**[9] 7976 3-8-10 **59**.............................. HollieDoyle 1 32
(Jonathan Portman) *s.i.s: sn mid-div: hdwy over 2f out: nt pce to chal: fdd fnl f* **7/1**

1021 8 2 1/2 **Requited (IRE)**[12] 7869 3-9-4 **67**.............................. CharlieBennett 5 32
(Hughie Morrison) *trckd ldr: rdn 2f out: sn edgd lft and wknd* **16/1**

3320 9 2 3/4 **Princely**[16] 7757 4-9-2 **64**.. EoinWalsh 6 20
(Tony Newcombe) *trckd ldr: rdn 2f out: wknd jst over 1f out* **12/1**

0520 10 3 **Porto Ferro (IRE)**[28] 7337 5-8-8 **56**..............................(t) KieranO'Neill 4
(John Bridger) *trckd ldr: rdn over 2f out: sn wknd (vet said mare lost her right fore shoe)* **14/1**

240- 11 2 3/4 **Grandma Tilly**[532] 2282 4-8-12 **60**.................................. FrannyNorton 8
(Steph Hollinshead) *mid-div: effrt over 2f out: wknd over 1f out* **50/1**

1m 13.45s (2.35) **Going Correction** +0.35s/f (Good)
WFA 3 from 4yo+ 1lb **11 Ran SP% 117.6**
Speed ratings (Par 103): **98,97,93,93,88 86,83,80,76,72 68**
CSF £49.14 CT £240.14 TOTE £6.60: £2.30, £2.60, £2.10; EX 60.70 Trifecta £286.60.
Owner George Nixon **Bred** J Hutchinson **Trained** Cropthorne, Worcs

FOCUS
An ordinary sprint handicap in which the first four home were played later on the soft ground. The runner-up is the best guide.

8243 STARSPORTS.BET NOVICE STKS 5f 10y

2:10 (2:10) (Class 5) 2-Y-O **£4,140** (£1,232; £615; £307) **Stalls** Centre

Form RPR

1 **Raasel** 2-9-5 0.. JimCrowley 2 82+
(Marcus Tregoning) *trckd ldr: led 2f out: edgd sltly rt jst over 1f out: kpt on finding for press fnl f: readily* **7/2**[2]

425 2 1/2 **Amarillo Star (IRE)**[11] 7904 2-8-12 89.............................. AledBeech[(7)] 7 80+
(Charlie Fellowes) *s.i.s: in last pair: hdwy over 2f out: drifted lft over 1f out: sn rdn to chal: kpt on but a being hld ins fnl f* **4/7**[1]

412 3 4 **Jeanie B**[16] 7765 2-9-4 77.. FrannyNorton 5 65
(Mick Channon) *cl up: rdn 2f out: sn hung rt: kpt on but nt pce of front pair fnl f (jockey said filly hung right-handed)* **7/2**[2]

00 4 1 3/4 **The Red Witch**[104] 4557 2-9-0 0.. RobertHavlin 1 55
(Steph Hollinshead) *trckd ldr: rdn 2f out: sn one pce* **100/1**

0603 5 1 3/4 **Shani**[16] 7754 2-9-0 59..(p) KieranO'Neill 6 48
(John Bridger) *led: rdn and hdd 2f out: sn edgd rt: wknd fnl f* **28/1**[3]

60 6 4 **Wrath Of Hector**[63] 6078 2-9-5 0.. EoinWalsh 4 39
(Tony Newcombe) *s.i.s: in last pair and sn rousted along: drvn over 2f out: nvr any imp* **100/1**

060 7 7 **Erika**[16] 7755 2-9-0 0..(b[1]) RossaRyan 3 9
(Neil Mulholland) *in tch: rdn over 2f out: wknd over 1f out* **125/1**

1m 3.27s (1.27) **Going Correction** +0.35s/f (Good) **7 Ran SP% 114.3**
Speed ratings (Par 95): **103,102,95,93,90 83,72**
CSF £5.98 TOTE £3.40: £1.20, £1.30; EX 6.30 Trifecta £12.90.
Owner Hamdan Al Maktoum **Bred** Bearstone Stud **Trained** Whitsbury, Hants

FOCUS
A fairly decent juvenile novice sprint. The odds-on favourite couldn't quite get to grips with a talented newcomer in the closing stages.

8244 DOWNLOAD THE STAR SPORTS APP NOW/EBF NOVICE STKS 1m 2f 37y

2:45 (2:46) (Class 5) 2-Y-O **£4,140** (£1,232; £615; £307) **Stalls** Low

Form RPR

5 1 **Midnights Legacy**[16] 7755 2-9-5 0.. TomMarquand 3 79+
(Alan King) *mid-div: rdn and hdwy over 2f out: led jst ins fnl f: styd on strly* **11/2**

3 2 2 1/4 **Salamanca School (FR)**[27] 7361 2-9-5 0.............................. FrannyNorton 1 75
(Mark Johnston) *pressed ldr: led over 6f out: rdn and strly chal fr over 2f out: hdd jst ins fnl f: styd on same pce (jockey said colt hung right-handed)* **6/1**

634 3 shd **Herman Hesse**[21] 7562 2-9-5 76.............................. RobertHavlin 8 75
(John Gosden) *trckd ldrs: rdn over 2f out: ev ch over 1f out: styd on same pce ins fnl f* **3/1**[2]

33 4 nk **Stag Horn**[21] 7562 2-9-5 0.. OisinMurphy 12 74
(Archie Watson) *trckd ldrs: rdn to chal 2f out: ev ch ent fnl f: styd on same pce* **5/2**[1]

552 5 1 3/4 **Tantivy**[21] 7562 2-9-5 77.. SeanLevey 5 71
(Richard Hannon) *led tl over 6f out: remained upsides: rdn for str chal over 2f out: ev ch ent fnl f: styd on tl no ex fnl 120yds* **9/2**[3]

00 6 4 1/2 **Arthalot (IRE)**[9] 7972 2-9-2 0.............................. MeganNicholls[(3)] 4 63
(Karen George) *sn pushed along in last pair: styd on fr over 2f out but nvr threatened to get on terms w ldrs (jockey said gelding hung left-handed)* **80/1**

7 2 **Justified** 2-9-5 0.. HarryBentley 2 59+
(Mark Johnston) *trckd ldrs: rdn over 2f out: wknd over 1f out* **16/1**

550 8 4 **Buto**[21] 7562 2-9-5 63.. EdwardGreatrex 7 52
(Eve Johnson Houghton) *last pair: struggling 4f out: nvr on terms (jockey said gelding was never travelling)* **40/1**

00 9 12 **Derek Le Grand**[16] 7755 2-9-5 0.. RossaRyan 6 31
(Grace Harris) *mid-div: rdn wl over 2f out: sn wknd* **66/1**

04 10 9 **Rally Driver**[8] 7983 2-9-5 0.. DavidProbert 9 14
(Mick Channon) *mid-div: rdn over 4f out: wknd over 2f out* **100/1**

03 11 32 **Margaretha (IRE)**[43] 6832 2-9-0 0.. GeorgeWood 10
(Amy Murphy) *mid-div tl wknd over 3f out (jockey said filly ran green; trainer's rep said filly was not suited by the soft going and would appreciate a return to a quicker surface)* **125/1**

2m 13.75s (2.65) **Going Correction** +0.35s/f (Good) **11 Ran SP% 114.3**
Speed ratings (Par 95): **103,101,101,100,99 95,94,91,81,74 48**
CSF £36.91 TOTE £6.50: £2.00, £2.60, £1.50; EX 48.20 Trifecta £224.50.
Owner Pitchall Stud Partnership **Bred** Pitchall Stud **Trained** Barbury Castle, Wilts

FOCUS
A fair juvenile staying novice contest in which the right five horses came to the fore. Improvement from the winner, with the third, fourth and fifth all coming from the same Goodwood race.

8245 BRITISH STALLION STUDS EBF BECKFORD STKS (LISTED RACE) (F&M) 1m 6f

3:20 (3:20) (Class 1) 3-Y-O+

£22,684 (£8,600; £4,304; £2,144; £1,076; £540) **Stalls** High

Form RPR

2142 1 **Sapa Inca (IRE)**[12] 7864 3-8-11 94.............................. HayleyTurner 7 99+
(Mark Johnston) *hld up in last pair: gd hdwy under hands and heels over 2f out: led over 1f out but drifting to stands' side rails: in command fnl f: comf* **7/2**[2]

3015 2 1 3/4 **Hulcote**[115] 4145 4-9-4 87.. HectorCrouch 9 95
(Clive Cox) *hld up towards rr: c wd and hdwy 3f out: led 2f: rdn and hdd over 1f out: styd on same pce fnl f* **16/1**

The Form Book Flat 2019, Raceform Ltd, Newbury, RG14 5SJ

2056 **3** *hd* **Dance Legend**[44] 6820 4-9-4 92 DaneO'Neill 3 95
(Rae Guest) *mid-div: swtchd to stands' side and hdwy early in the st: rdn and ev ch 2f out tl jst over 1f out: styd on same pce* **10/1**

4023 **4** *2 1/4* **Grace And Danger (IRE)**[32] 7180 3-8-11 102 DavidProbert 5 92+
(Andrew Balding) *hld up towards rr: rdn and hdwy 2f out: styd on into 4th jst ins fnl f: nt pce to threaten ldrs* **9/2[3]**

03-0 **5** *3/4* **Bongiorno (IRE)**[29] 7326 4-9-4 93 (p) WJLee 10 91
(W McCreery, Ire) *kpt wd early: mid-div: hdwy to sit promly 6f out: led 3f out: rdn and hdd 2f out: styd on same pce* **16/1**

0403 **6** *1* **Lorelina**[21] 7566 6-9-4 91 OisinMurphy 1 89
(Andrew Balding) *led tl 3f out: sn rdn: one pce fnl 2f* **14/1**

7 *1* **Diamond Hill (IRE)**[29] 7326 6-9-7 99 ShaneFoley 8 91
(W P Mullins, Ire) *little slowly away: last: rdn over 2f out: styd on steadily but little imp on ldrs (jockey said mare was never travelling)* **6/4[1]**

5411 **8** *1/2* **Vindolanda**[19] 7643 3-8-11 75 KieranShoemark 4 87
(Charles Hills) *prom: rdn and ev ch over 2f out tl over 1f out: wknd ent fnl f* **33/1**

3620 **9** *2 1/4* **Claire Underwood (IRE)**[26] 7403 4-9-4 87 SeanDavis 2 84
(Richard Fahey) *trckd ldrs: rdn over 2f out: sn wknd* **50/1**

3232 **10** *11* **Noble Music (GER)**[23] 7518 3-8-11 77 HarryBentley 6 68
(Ralph Beckett) *trckd ldrs: switch to stands' side ent st: sn wknd* **25/1**

3m 9.59s (3.49) **Going Correction** +0.35s/f (Good)
WFA 3 from 4yo+ 7lb **10** Ran SP% **116.7**
Speed ratings (Par 111): **104,103,102,101,101 100,100,99,98,92**
CSF £56.41 TOTE £3.60: £1.60, £4.00, £2.80; EX 51.60 Trifecta £324.80.
Owner China Horse Club International Limited **Bred** Desert Star Phoenix Jvc **Trained** Middleham Moor, N Yorks

FOCUS
The feature race was a good-quality Listed staying contest for fillies and mares. The first three races towards the stands' side. The winner is rated similar to her latest form.

8246 BATH LUXURY TOILET HIRE H'CAP 2m 1f 24y
3:50 (3:51) (Class 5) (0-70,72) 3-Y-0+
£3,428 (£1,020; £509; £300; £300; £300) **Stalls** Low

Form RPR

3654 **1** **Cochise**[23] 7520 3-8-10 62 ThomasGreatrex(5) 10 75+
(Roger Charlton) *racd keenly: trckd ldrs: in tch 6f out: smooth hdwy over 2f out: led wl over 1f out: styd on wl: comf* **6/1[3]**

3512 **2** *2 1/2* **Land Of Winter (FR)**[20] 7629 3-9-1 62 DavidProbert 8 70
(Rae Guest) *hld up towards rr: tk clsr order 6f out: rdn in cl 3rd 2f out: styd on to go 2nd ins fnl f but no threat to wnr* **3/1[2]**

3 *nk* **Quel Destin (FR)**[215] 4-9-10 66 (t[1]) MeganNicholls(3) 1 73
(Paul Nicholls) *led for over 4f: trckd ldrs: led gng strly over 2f out: shkn up and hdd over 1f out: sn outpcd by wnr: no ex whn losing 2nd towards fin* **4/5[1]**

0/00 **4** *16* **Montys Angel (IRE)**[22] 7558 9-8-2 48 oh3 (p) AledBeech(7) 9 39
(John Bridger) *mid-div: outpcd by ldrs over 2f out: wnt modest 4th over 1f out: nvr any threat to front three* **150/1**

0503 **5** *6* **Bambys Boy**[54] 6400 8-9-4 57 (t[1]) FrannyNorton 2 42
(Neil Mulholland) *stdd s: racd keenly: sn midfield: hdwy to ld after 4f: rdn and hdd over 2f out: wknd over 1f out (jockey said gelding ran too freely.)* **9/1**

1260 **6** *10* **Master Grey (IRE)**[62] 6105 4-10-5 72 OisinMurphy 12 47
(Rod Millman) *hld up towards rr: rdn over 3f out: little imp: wknd 2f out* **20/1**

5 **7** *10* **True Thoughts (IRE)**[13] 3000 4-8-8 52 (b) PoppyBridgwater(5) 4 17
(Laura Young) *a towards rr* **200/1**

5-0 **8** *2 1/4* **Samson's Reach**[158] 1989 6-8-6 48 oh3 WilliamCox(3) 5 10
(Richard Price) *struggling over 3f out: a towards rr* **100/1**

0360 **9** *1 3/4* **The Way You Dance (IRE)**[13] 7845 7-9-4 62 SeamusCronin(5) 7 23
(Michael Attwater) *w ldr for 4f: trckd ldrs: rdn over 3f out: wknd over 2f out* **66/1**

0-00 **10** *18* **War Drums**[49] 6601 5-9-9 62 (h) RossaRyan 3 5
(Alexandra Dunn) *trckd ldrs: in tch whn reminders over 6f out: wknd over 2f out (vet said gelding lost his right hind-shoe)* **33/1**

5203 **11** *99* **Arthur Pendragon (IRE)**[48] 6642 3-9-10 71 (bt w) MartinDwyer 11
(Brian Meehan) *trckd ldrs: rdn over 4f out: sn bhd: eased fr over 2f out (jockey said colt stopped quickly)* **14/1**

3m 58.64s (7.24) **Going Correction** +0.35s/f (Good)
WFA 3 from 4yo+ 8lb **11** Ran SP% **122.9**
Speed ratings (Par 103): **97,95,95,88,85 80,75,74,74,65 18**
CSF £25.07 CT £30.30 TOTE £8.80: £2.00, £1.20, £1.10; EX 25.90 Trifecta £66.40.
Owner Philip Newton **Bred** Philip Newton **Trained** Beckhampton, Wilts

FOCUS
An ordinary staying handicap. The third-favourite won readily on soft ground he relished, but in a modest comparative time. The first three came clear with a pb from the winner.

8247 NAILSEA ELECTRICAL KITCHEN AND APPLIANCE FILLIES' H'CAP 1m
4:25 (4:28) (Class 5) (0-70,71) 3-Y-0+
£3,428 (£1,020; £509; £300; £300; £300) **Stalls** Low

Form RPR

0021 **1** **Gamesters Icon**[15] 7776 4-8-11 60 (tp) MeganNicholls(3) 11 79
(Oliver Greenall) *trckd ldrs: led jst over 2f out: sn pushed clr: easily* **2/1[1]**

1426 **2** *7* **Capriolette (IRE)**[16] 7756 4-9-10 70 DavidProbert 10 73
(Ed Walker) *trckd ldr: led briefly over 2f out: styd on but sn outpcd by wnr* **8/1**

0000 **3** *1 1/2* **Vixen (IRE)**[35] 7084 5-9-2 62 (h) EdwardGreatrex 8 61
(Emma Lavelle) *hld up towards rr: hdwy over 2f out: sn rdn: chsd ldng pair over 1f out: styd on same pce fnl f* **25/1**

30 **4** *2* **Triple Nickle (IRE)**[18] 7682 3-8-8 62 (p) ThomasGreatrex(5) 14 56
(Bernard Llewellyn) *hld up towards rr: hdwy 2f out: wnt 4th over 1f out: styd on same pce fnl f* **20/1**

-005 **5** *1/2* **Born To Please**[41] 6896 5-7-12 51 oh2 (b[1]) IsobelFrancis(7) 6 45
(Mark Usher) *mid-div: rdn over 3f out: styd on same pce fnl 2f* **33/1**

0105 **6** *1 3/4* **Incentive**[16] 7758 5-8-11 64 (p) AngusVilliers(7) 12 54
(Stuart Kittow) *hld up towards rr: rdn over 2f out: nt best of runs over 1f out: styd on but nvr any threat* **50/1**

2361 **7** *shd* **Milan Reef (IRE)**[8] 8009 4-8-5 54 SeanDavis(3) 9 43
(David Loughnane) *led: rdn and hdd over 2f out: sn hld: wknd fnl f* **9/2[3]**

252 **8** *3/4* **Lady Alavesa**[18] 7682 4-9-4 64 OisinMurphy 3 52
(Michael Herrington) *in tch: rdn 2f out: nt pce to chal: fdd ins fnl f* **9/4[2]**

0414 **9** *nk* **Diamond Shower (IRE)**[42] 6856 3-8-11 63 WilliamCox(3) 5 49
(John Flint) *in tch: struggling 5f out: wknd fnl f* **50/1**

3360 **10** *nse* **Jungle Juice (IRE)**[11] 7901 3-9-2 70 ScottMcCullagh(5) 1 56
(Mick Channon) *trckd ldrs: rdn over 2f out: wknd ent fnl f* **20/1**

002/ **11** *1/2* **Hijran (IRE)**[179] 5760 6-8-11 62 (w) PoppyBridgwater(5) 4 48
(Henry Oliver) *mid-div: rdn over 2f out: wknd ent fnl f* **33/1**

5-50 **12** *4 1/2* **Rollicking (IRE)**[13] 7839 3-9-8 71 RossaRyan 7 45
(Richard Hannon) *a towards rr* **33/1**

0000 **13** *51* **Plissken**[8] 8009 3-7-11 51 oh1 (h) RhiainIngram(5) 2
(Richard Price) *dwlt bdly: a wl bhd (jockey said filly was slowly away)* **100/1**

1m 42.78s (1.08) **Going Correction** +0.35s/f (Good)
WFA 3 from 4yo+ 3lb **13** Ran SP% **120.5**
Speed ratings (Par 100): **108,101,99,97,97 95,95,94,94,94 93,89,38**
CSF £16.66 CT £320.14 TOTE £2.80: £1.40, £2.40, £6.20; EX 21.00 Trifecta £265.20.
Owner Gamesters Partnership **Bred** D V Williams **Trained** Oldcastle Heath, Cheshire

FOCUS
An ordinary fillies' handicap with no depth. The favourite fairly routed this opposition and is rated back to her best.

8248 SILVESTRE DE SOUSA'S EXCLUSIVE BLOG STARSPORTSBET.CO.UK H'CAP 1m 3f 137y
4:55 (5:01) (Class 5) (0-70,71) 3-Y-0+
£3,428 (£1,020; £509; £300; £300; £300) **Stalls** Low

Form RPR

602 **1** **Manucci (IRE)**[17] 7730 3-9-4 70 MartinDwyer 8 79+
(Amanda Perrett) *trckd ldrs: led over 2f out: in command and styd on wl fnl f* **6/1[3]**

6330 **2** *1 1/2* **Beer With The Boys**[8] 7984 4-8-9 60 ow1 (v) ScottMcCullagh(5) 3 66
(Mick Channon) *hld up towards rr: reminder over 4f out: hdwy on inner 3f out: sn rdn: styd on into 2nd ins fnl f: a being hld* **12/1**

2325 **3** *3/4* **Luck Of Clover**[62] 6125 3-8-12 64 DavidProbert 1 69
(Andrew Balding) *mid-div: hdwy on outer over 3f out: rdn to chse wnr over 2f out: nt pce to chal: styd on but no ex whn losing 2nd ins fnl f* **9/2[2]**

3025 **4** *1 1/4* **Galactic Spirit**[14] 7816 4-9-10 70 FergusSweeney 6 73
(James Evans) *s.i.s: nt travelling in rr: hdwy swtchd to stands' side over 2f out: wnt 6th over 1f out: styd on into 4th ins fnl f* **16/1**

3222 **5** *3/4* **Hammy End (IRE)**[8] 7984 3-8-6 61 (h) GeorgiaCox(3) 11 62
(William Muir) *hld up towards rr: gd hdwy swtchd to stands' side wl over 2f out: chal for 2nd over 1f out: no ex ins fnl f* **3/1[1]**

1450 **6** *hd* **Ascot Day (FR)**[18] 7683 5-9-5 70 (p) ThomasGreatrex(5) 4 71
(Bernard Llewellyn) *hld up towards rr: rdn and hdwy over 2f out: chsd ldrs over 1f out: nt pce to chal: no ex ex fnl 100yds* **7/1**

0155 **7** *3 1/4* **Tiar Na Nog (IRE)**[44] 6812 7-9-11 71 OisinMurphy 9 67
(Denis Coakley) *mid-div: hdwy over 3f out: rdn over 2f out: nvr quite on terms: wknd fnl f* **8/1**

-420 **8** *4 1/2* **Love And Be Loved**[113] 4220 5-9-2 65 (h) WilliamCox(3) 5 53
(John Flint) *led: rdn and hdd over 2f out: wknd fnl f (jockey said mare stopped quickly)* **16/1**

-100 **9** *3 3/4* **Bombero (IRE)**[19] 7643 5-9-10 70 (b[1]) RossaRyan 12 52
(Ed de Giles) *mid-div: hdwy over 3f out: effrt in 4th over 2f out: wknd over 1f out* **12/1**

040 **10** *2* **Sherwood Forrester**[76] 5578 3-8-5 60 MeganNicholls(3) 13 40
(Paul George) *racd keenly: trckd ldrs: rdn over 2f out: sn wknd (jockey said gelding ran too freely)* **16/1**

636 **11** *1/2* **Maroc**[50] 6568 6-9-6 69 (p) SeanDavis(3) 2 47
(Nikki Evans) *prom: rdn 3f out: sn wknd* **50/1**

0500 **12** *68* **Enmeshing**[39] 6977 6-8-10 56 EdwardGreatrex 7
(Alexandra Dunn) *trckd ldrs tl lost pl 6f out: wknd 3f out: sn eased (jockey said gelding was never travelling and also stopped quickly)* **28/1**

2m 35.6s (4.80) **Going Correction** +0.35s/f (Good)
WFA 3 from 4yo+ 6lb **12** Ran SP% **119.5**
Speed ratings (Par 103): **98,97,96,95,95 95,92,89,87,86 85,40**
CSF £76.76 CT £359.13 TOTE £5.60: £2.10, £3.40, £1.90; EX 76.90 Trifecta £332.90.
Owner John Connolly & Odile Griffith **Bred** B Flay Thoroughbreds Inc **Trained** Pulborough, W Sussex

FOCUS
An ordinary middle-distance handicap in which the winner progressed again.
T/Jkpt: Not won. T/Plt: £73.60 to a £1 stake. Pool: £65,803.04 - 652.34 winning units T/Qpdt: £27.00 to a £1 stake. Pool: £6,823.10 - 186.32 winning units **Tim Mitchell**

8217 KEMPTON (A.W) (R-H)
Wednesday, October 16

OFFICIAL GOING: Polytrack: standard to slow
Wind: Light, across Weather: Fine

8249 100% PROFIT BOOST AT 32REDSPORT.COM CLASSIFIED STKS 6f (P)
4:40 (4:43) (Class 6) 3-Y-0+
£3,105 (£924; £461; £400; £400; £400) **Stalls** Low

Form RPR

4602 **1** **Twilighting**[15] 7784 3-9-0 49 NicolaCurrie 10 55+
(Henry Candy) *in tch in midfield: shkn up and prog over 2f out: swtchd to inner and clsd to ld jst over 1f out: edgd lft fnl f but styd on wl* **10/3[3]**

0062 **2** *1 3/4* **Aiguillette**[20] 7606 3-9-0 45 ShaneKelly 2 49
(Gary Moore) *prom: lost pl after 2f: rdn and prog 2f out: styd on to take 2nd last 100yds: no imp on wnr* **11/4[1]**

0553 **3** *hd* **Jaganory (IRE)**[15] 7784 7-9-1 48 (v) CallumShepherd 3 44
(Christopher Mason) *chsd ldrs: rdn 2f out: nt qckn over 1f out: kpt on to press for 3rd and impeded nr fin: fin 4th: promoted to 3rd* **11/2**

-000 **4** *1 1/2* **Carla Koala**[168] 2300 3-8-7 48 (p[1]) EllieMacKenzie(7) 7 44
(Natalie Lloyd-Beavis) *led: rdn 2f out: hdd jst over 1f out: one pce and edgd lft ins fnl f: fin 3rd: disqualified and plcd 4th* **66/1**

4231 **5** *1* **Catapult**[13] 7838 4-9-1 48 (p) JosephineGordon 9 41
(Shaun Keightley) *prog out wd to go prom over 4f out: rdn and nt qckn 2f out: one pce after (jockey said gelding hung left-handed round the bend)* **3/1[2]**

4505 **6** *hd* **Disey's Edge**[29] 7298 3-8-11 48 (p) MitchGodwin(3) 4 40
(Christopher Mason) *sn urged along in last pair: nvr on terms but styd on fr over 1f out* **20/1**

00-4 **7** *1/2* **Miss Gradenko**[13] 7854 3-9-0 50 RaulDaSilva 5 39
(Robert Cowell) *pressed ldr: rdn and nt qckn 2f out: fdd fnl f* **16/1**

030 **8** *1 1/4* **Plum Duff**[29] 7298 3-9-0 43 CharlesBishop 6 35
(Michael Blanshard) *stdd s: hld up in last: prog into midfield over 1f out: pushed along and no hdwy fnl f: nt disgracd (jockey said filly suffered interference shortly after leaving the stalls)* **40/1**

0-55 **9** *5* **Maerchengarten**[13] 7854 3-8-11 50........................ JaneElliott(3) 11 20
(Ed de Giles) *slowly away: a in rr: shkn up and no prog over 2f out (jockey said filly hung left-handed round the bend)* **25/1**

0000 **10** *2* **Just For The Craic (IRE)**[58] 6273 4-9-1 48..................(t[1]) LiamKeniry 8 14
(Neil Mulholland) *awkward s: rushed up to press ldr over 4f out: wknd qckly 2f out* **25/1**

0-04 **11** *2 1/4* **On The Bob**[139] 3253 3-9-0 47..............................(p[1]) JoeyHaynes 1 7
(Paddy Butler) *a towards rr: wknd 2f out* **100/1**

1m 13.16s (0.06) **Going Correction** -0.05s/f (Stan)
WFA 3 from 4yo+ 1lb **11** Ran SP% **113.4**
Speed ratings (Par 101): **97,94,92,92,91 90,90,88,81,79 76**
CSF £11.48 TOTE £2.90: £1.10, £1.60, £13.60, £1.90; EX 15.50.
Owner Six Too Many **Bred** Peter Balding & Lady Whent **Trained** Kingston Warren, Oxon

FOCUS
A weak classified race, but the winner appears to be getting her act together now. Very modest form.

8250 32RED CASINO NOVICE MEDIAN AUCTION STKS 6f (P)
5:10 (5:15) (Class 5) 2-Y-O £3,881 (£1,155; £577; £288) **Stalls** Low

Form RPR

2 **1** **Pepper Bay**[21] 7570 2-9-0 0.................................. HollieDoyle 1 76+
(Archie Watson) *trckd ldr: pushed into ld wl over 1f out: nrly 3 l clr fnl f: ld dwindled and rdn out but nvr in any danger* **1/1**[1]

2 *1* **Cry Havoc (IRE)** 2-9-0 0.................................. RobHornby 4 73
(Rae Guest) *chsd ldrs: pushed along over 2f out: rdn to cl on inner over 1f out: tk 2nd last 100yds: styd on wl but nvr able to chal* **20/1**

0 **3** *3/4* **Captivated**[11] 7899 2-9-5 0.................................. RobertHavlin 6 76
(John Gosden) *trckd ldng pair: rdn to chse wnr over 1f out: no imp and lost 2nd last 100yds: styd on* **3/1**[2]

42 **4** *2 3/4* **Qasbaz (IRE)**[21] 7569 2-9-5 0.................................. NicolaCurrie 8 68
(Jamie Osborne) *chsd ldrs: outpcd fr 2f out: kpt on same pce after and clr of rest* **4/1**[3]

0 **5** *5* **Quiet Word (FR)**[159] 2579 2-9-0 0.................................. AdamMcNamara 7 48+
(Archie Watson) *t.k.h: led and sn 3 l clr: hdd & wknd wl over 1f out* **25/1**

40 **6** *2 1/2* **Populaire (FR)**[26] 7406 2-9-0 0..............................(h[1]) JimCrowley 11 40
(Amanda Perrett) *dwlt: rchd midfield by 1/2-way but nt on terms w ldrs: no hdwy after* **14/1**

7 *1* **Various (IRE)** 2-9-5 0.................................. CharlesBishop 12 42
(Eve Johnson Houghton) *chsd ldrs but nt on terms: rdn over 2f out: sn btn* **50/1**

8 *1/2* **Etheric** 2-9-0 0.................................. TomMarquand 3 36
(Marco Botti) *a wl in rr: no ch over 2f out (jockey said filly was never travelling)* **25/1**

9 *2* **May Happen** 2-8-7 0.................................. ElinorJones(7) 2 30
(Jamie Osborne) *slowly away: a towards rr: bhd over 1f out* **66/1**

10 *1 1/2* **Tyger Bay** 2-9-5 0..............................(t[1]) JosephineGordon 5 30
(Shaun Keightley) *s.s: a wl in rr: bhd over 1f out* **66/1**

11 *4 1/2* **Bo Taifan (IRE)** 2-9-5 0.................................. ShaneKelly 9 17
(Richard Hughes) *s.v.s: a wl bhd* **66/1**

1m 12.84s (-0.26) **Going Correction** -0.05s/f (Stan) **11** Ran SP% **120.6**
Speed ratings (Par 95): **99,97,96,93,86 83,81,81,78,76 70**
CSF £29.81 TOTE £1.70: £1.10, £4.40, £1.20; EX 21.30 Trifecta £71.60.
Owner Pepper Bay Syndicate **Bred** Highclere Stud & Jake Warren Ltd **Trained** Upper Lambourn, W Berks

FOCUS
Just a fair novice. Pace held up.

8251 WISE BETTING AT RACINGTV.COM CLASSIFIED STKS 1m (P)
5:40 (5:42) (Class 6) 3-Y-O+ £3,105 (£924; £461; £400; £400; £400) **Stalls** Low

Form RPR

032 **1** **Necoleta**[18] 7685 3-9-0 48.................................. LiamKeniry 3 59
(Sylvester Kirk) *wl in tch in midfield: rdn and prog over 2f out: chal over 1f out: narrow ld last 100yds: styd on wl* **7/1**

0003 **2** *nk* **Pearl Jam**[41] 6885 3-9-0 47.................................. TomMarquand 7 58
(James Fanshawe) *trckd ldrs: prog to ld over 1f out but sn pressed: narrowly hdd last 100yds: styd on and clr of rest but hld after* **5/2**[1]

6004 **3** *5* **Rosarno (IRE)**[23] 7508 5-9-3 49..............................(b) JoeyHaynes 13 48
(Chelsea Banham) *hld up towards rr gng strly: shkn up over 2f out and hanging rt: prog over 1f out: kpt on to take 3rd last 75yds* **4/1**[2]

0200 **4** *1* **Sir Magnum**[57] 6327 4-9-3 49.................................. BrettDoyle 12 46
(Tony Carroll) *trckd ldr after 1f to wl over 1f out: fdd* **20/1**

0025 **5** *1 1/4* **Cat Royale (IRE)**[46] 6723 6-9-3 49..............................(b) DannyBrock 8 44
(John Butler) *w ldrs early and trckd them after 1f: drvn 2f out and briefly nt clr run: outpcd over 1f out: one pce after* **14/1**

400 **6** *1/2* **Kafeel (USA)**[57] 6317 8-9-3 50..............................(b) RobertHavlin 11 41
(Alexandra Dunn) *sn led: hdd & wknd over 1f out* **20/1**

1000 **7** *2 1/4* **Miss Recycled**[28] 7343 4-9-3 48.................................. GeorgeWood 1 36
(Michael Madgwick) *wl in rr: rdn 3f out: sme prog into midfield over 1f out but no ch: no hdwy after (vet said filly had lost her right-fore shoe)* **25/1**

000 **8** *nk* **Dee Dee Dottie**[72] 5748 3-8-9 39.................................. KevinLundie(5) 4 35
(Mark Loughnane) *towards rr whn impeded and snatched up after 2f: rdn and no real prog over 2f out* **50/1**

4000 **9** *1 1/4* **Bader**[11] 7909 3-9-0 50..............................(b) SeanLevey 9 32
(Richard Hannon) *w ldrs early: clsd up: rdn over 2f out: wknd qckly on inner over 1f out* **12/1**

0302 **10** *3/4* **Clipsham Tiger (IRE)**[28] 7335 3-8-7 49..................(h) GeorgeRooke(7) 10 30
(Michael Appleby) *t.k.h: trckd ldrs on outer tl wknd rapidly wl over 1f out* **14/1**

0456 **11** *1/2* **Incredible Dream (IRE)**[29] 7318 6-8-12 50..........(tp) WilliamCarver(5) 2 30
(Conrad Allen) *t.k.h: hld up in last pair: rdn and no prog over 2f out: no ch* **9/2**[3]

6003 **12** *10* **Tilsworth Diamond**[8] 8006 4-8-12 44.................................. SeanKirrane(5) 6 7
(Mike Murphy) *in tch in midfield to over 3f out: wknd: t.o* **66/1**

0000 **13** *hd* **Mazmerize**[62] 6128 3-9-0 28..............................(vt[1]) EoinWalsh 5 5
(Christine Dunnett) *prog on outer into midfield bnd over 3f out: wknd rapidly over 2f out: t.o* **100/1**

-000 **14** *6* **Redemptress (IRE)**[51] 6531 3-8-7 33..............................(p[1]) KateLeahy(7) 14
(John O'Shea) *a bhd: t.o* **100/1**

1m 38.86s (-0.94) **Going Correction** -0.05s/f (Stan)
WFA 3 from 4yo+ 3lb **14** Ran SP% **119.1**
Speed ratings (Par 101): **102,101,96,95,94 93,91,91,90,89 88,78,78,72**
CSF £23.11 TOTE £8.20: £2.20, £1.50, £1.70; EX 23.50 Trifecta £87.80.
Owner Miss A Jones **Bred** Saleh Al Homaizi & Imad Al Sagar **Trained** Upper Lambourn, Berks

FOCUS
A pretty weak race, but the first two finished clear and are in-form 3yos capable of improving.

8252 32RED.COM NURSERY H'CAP 1m (P)
6:10 (6:11) (Class 4) (0-85,84) 2-Y-O £6,469 (£1,925; £962; £481; £400; £400) **Stalls** Low

Form RPR

5300 **1** **Impatient**[13] 7840 2-8-12 75..............................(v[1]) HarryBentley 7 81+
(Ralph Beckett) *trckd ldr: shkn up to ld wl over 1f out: drvn and wl in command fnl f: decisively* **7/1**

4154 **2** *1 1/4* **Incinerator**[13] 7840 2-9-5 82..............................(t) JamesDoyle 6 85
(Hugo Palmer) *trckd ldng pair: rdn 2f out: chsd wnr jst over 1f out: styd on but no imp and wl hld* **4/1**[3]

6216 **3** *1 1/2* **Atheeb**[25] 7429 2-9-3 80.................................. JimCrowley 3 80
(Sir Michael Stoute) *hld up disputing 5th: pushed along 2f out: outpcd over 1f out: shkn up and styd on to take 3rd ins fnl f: no threat to ldng pair* **5/2**[1]

2010 **4** *1 1/4* **Cheat (IRE)**[26] 7409 2-9-3 80.................................. HollieDoyle 5 77
(Richard Hannon) *t.k.h: hld up in last pair: prog over 1f out: kpt on to take 4th nr fin: n.d* **13/2**

11 **5** *hd* **Cobber Kain**[20] 7605 2-9-7 84.................................. RobertHavlin 8 80
(John Gosden) *led: shkn up and hdd wl over 1f out: steadily wknd* **10/3**[2]

2601 **6** *3/4* **Blausee (IRE)**[29] 7315 2-8-11 74 ow1.................................. TomMarquand 4 69
(Philip McBride) *hld up in last pair: prog on inner 2f out: no imp on ldrs fnl f* **16/1**

0410 **7** *1 1/2* **Top Buck (IRE)**[25] 7429 2-9-0 77..............................(p) LiamKeniry 2 68
(Brian Meehan) *trckd ldng pair: rdn and nt qckn 2f out: fdd fnl f* **20/1**

240 **8** *2 1/2* **Forbidden Land (IRE)**[13] 7840 2-9-2 79.................................. SeanLevey 1 64
(Richard Hannon) *t.k.h: hld up disputing 5th: rdn and no prog 2f out: wknd over 1f out* **14/1**

1m 40.44s (0.64) **Going Correction** -0.05s/f (Stan) **8** Ran SP% **114.8**
Speed ratings (Par 97): **94,92,91,90,89 89,87,85**
CSF £35.24 CT £89.88 TOTE £8.20: £2.80, £1.10, £1.30; EX 38.50 Trifecta £136.70.
Owner J H Richmond-Watson **Bred** Lawn Stud **Trained** Kimpton, Hants

FOCUS
A competitive nursery but it was a tactical affair that was run at a fairly steady early gallop and turned into a dash up the straight. Improved form from the winner.

8253 32RED H'CAP 1m (P)
6:40 (6:42) (Class 3) (0-90,90) 3-Y-O+ £9,337 (£2,796; £1,398; £699; £349; £175) **Stalls** Low

Form RPR

1-52 **1** **Khuzaam (USA)**[28] 7349 3-9-3 89.................................. JimCrowley 8 105
(Roger Varian) *led 2f: styd v cl up: led again 2f out and immediately bounded clr: impressive* **10/11**[1]

3315 **2** *7* **Lawmaking**[23] 7517 6-9-3 86..............................(b) LiamKeniry 2 87
(Michael Scudamore) *hld up in midfield: prog 2f out: rdn to take 2nd fnl f but absolutely no ch w wnr* **8/1**[3]

1435 **3** *nse* **Graphite Storm**[25] 7462 5-9-1 84.................................. HectorCrouch 14 85
(Clive Cox) *hld up wl in rr fr wdst draw: gd prog 2f out: drvn to chal for 2nd fnl f: no ch w wnr* **25/1**

0605 **4** *1/2* **Chairmanoftheboard (IRE)**[28] 7349 3-8-13 85........ CallumShepherd 3 84
(Mick Channon) *hld up in midfield: shkn up and no prog jst over 2f out: hdwy over 1f out: styd on fnl f to press for a pl nr fin* **33/1**

6110 **5** *1 1/4* **Kingston Kurrajong**[2] 8197 6-8-4 80.................................. Pierre-LouisJamin(7) 1 77
(William Knight) *hld up towards rr: prog on inner over 2f out: chsd ldrs 1f out: kpt on same pce after* **16/1**

0004 **6** *1* **Exec Chef (IRE)**[17] 7727 4-9-7 90.................................. CharlieBennett 6 85
(Jim Boyle) *chsd ldrs: rdn and nt qckn on outer 2f out: lost pl over 1f out: kpt on* **10/1**

141 **7** *1/2* **De Vegas Kid (IRE)**[70] 5804 5-9-2 85.................................. GeorgeDowning 4 78
(Tony Carroll) *hld up wl in rr: pushed along fr over 2f out: kpt on steadily over 1f out: reminders nr fin: nvr remotely involved* **33/1**

5065 **8** *3/4* **Dark Jedi (IRE)**[20] 7617 3-8-12 84..............................(b[1]) KieranShoemark 11 75
(Charles Hills) *prog to ld after 2f: hdd 2f out: lost 2nd and wknd fnl f* **50/1**

3000 **9** *1/2* **Apex King (IRE)**[73] 5711 5-9-5 88.................................. HollieDoyle 9 79
(Mark Usher) *prom: rdn over 2f out: wknd over 1f out* **50/1**

3034 **10** *nse* **Trolius (IRE)**[12] 7863 3-9-1 87..............................(p) JamesDoyle 10 76
(Simon Crisford) *snatched up after 100yds and in rr after: rdn on outer over 2f out: no great prog* **8/1**[3]

5430 **11** *1/2* **Name The Wind**[25] 7448 3-9-4 90.................................. TomMarquand 5 78
(James Tate) *prom: rdn over 2f out: sing to weaken whn n.m.r on inner jst over 1f out* **5/1**[2]

0605 **12** *1 1/2* **The Emperor Within (FR)**[33] 7163 4-9-4 87..........(p[1]) GeorgeWood 13 73
(Martin Smith) *prom: chsd ldr over 5f out to over 2f out: wknd qckly over 1f out* **25/1**

-600 **13** *4 1/2* **Golden Wolf (IRE)**[14] 7815 5-9-0 83.................................. ShaneKelly 12 58
(Tony Carroll) *dropped in fr wd draw and hld up in last pair: rdn and no prog over 2f out* **100/1**

0014 **14** *7* **Secret Art (IRE)**[33] 7166 9-9-0 83.................................. HarryBentley 7 42
(Gary Moore) *a towards rr: rdn and wknd over 2f out* **33/1**

1m 36.69s (-3.11) **Going Correction** -0.05s/f (Stan)
WFA 3 from 4yo+ 3lb **14** Ran SP% **127.7**
Speed ratings (Par 107): **113,106,105,105,104 103,102,101,101,101 100,99,94,87**
CSF £8.85 CT £136.47 TOTE £1.70: £1.10, £2.50, £5.80; EX 13.10 Trifecta £233.00.
Owner Hamdan Al Maktoum **Bred** Shadwell Farm LLC **Trained** Newmarket, Suffolk

FOCUS
The favourite proved a blot on the handicap here and won as he liked.

8254 32RED ON THE APP STORE FILLIES' H'CAP 7f (P)
7:10 (7:16) (Class 5) (0-70,71) 3-Y-O+ £3,752 (£1,116; £557; £400; £400; £400) **Stalls** Low

Form RPR

654 **1** **Dawaaween (IRE)**[120] 3972 3-9-8 68.................................. JimCrowley 3 78
(Owen Burrows) *trckd ldng quartet: clsd 2f out: rdn to ld over 1f out: styd on and in command last 100yds* **2/1**[1]

2421 **2** *1 1/2* **Sonnet Rose (IRE)**[18] 7684 5-9-1 64..............................(bt) WilliamCarver(5) 2 71
(Conrad Allen) *led 1f: styd v cl up: rdn to chal over 1f out: kpt on to chse wnr ins fnl f: a hld* **9/2**[2]

3340 **3** *1* **Chloellie**[43] 6839 4-9-10 68.................................. HarryBentley 10 72
(J R Jenkins) *trckd ldr over 5f out: rdn to chal 2f out: nt qckn over 1f out: lost 2nd and one pce ins fnl f* **9/1**[3]

1503 **4** *3/4* **Devils Roc**[13] 7843 3-9-10 70.................................. RobHornby 6 71
(Jonathan Portman) *wl in tch: rdn 2f out: kpt on same pce and nvr able to chal* **16/1**

The Form Book Flat 2019, Raceform Ltd, Newbury, RG14 5SJ

6041 **5** *nk* **Redemptive**[25] 7472 3-9-6 **66** .... HollieDoyle 8 66
(John Butler) *trckd ldng trio: rdn and nt qckn jst over 2f out: one pce after* **10/1**

2456 **6** *1/2* **Di Matteo**[65] 6027 3-9-0 **67** .... StefanoCherchi(7) 12 66
(Marco Botti) *hld up in rr: prog on inner 2f out: urged along and one pce fnl f* **33/1**

2260 **7** *1/2* **Roman Spinner**[35] 7080 4-9-11 **69** ....(t) ShaneKelly 14 68
(Rae Guest) *dropped in fr wdst draw and hld up in last: prog between rivals fr 2f out: keeping on but no ch whn hmpd ins fnl f (jockey said filly was denied a clear run in the final furlong)* **12/1**

44-0 **8** *hd* **Dove Divine (FR)**[134] 3440 3-9-9 **69** .... RobertHavlin 7 66
(Hughie Morrison) *hld up wl in rr: stl there and pushed along 2f out: swtchd lft over 1f out: styd on ins fnl f: nvr in it* **16/1**

6230 **9** *nk* **Midas Girl (FR)**[23] 7519 3-9-5 **65** .... LiamKeniry 4 61
(Ed Walker) *sn in midfield: rdn wl over 2f out and struggling: kpt on same pce over 1f out* **20/1**

2444 **10** *hd* **Bint Dandy (IRE)**[13] 7843 8-9-10 **68** ....(b) FrannyNorton 5 65
(Charlie Wallis) *hld up towards rr: rdn and nt qckn jst over 2f out: kpt on fnl f but too late to threaten* **12/1**

2005 **11** *1 3/4* **Your Choice**[8] 8007 4-9-4 **62** ....(v[1]) NicolaCurrie 9 54
(Laura Mongan) *led after 1f to over 1f out: wknd fnl f* **66/1**

4405 **12** *9* **Padura Brave**[21] 7573 3-8-11 **57** ....(p) JosephineGordon 11 24
(Mark Usher) *racd wd: in tch: wknd wl over 2f out* **20/1**

025 **13** *8* **Serenading**[32] 7190 3-9-10 **70** .... JamesDoyle 13 15
(James Fanshawe) *t.k.h: racd v wd: dropped to rr bnd 3f out: sn bhd: t.o (jockey said filly was carried wide on the bend and never picked up in the straight)* **12/1**

1m 25.04s (-0.96) **Going Correction** -0.05s/f (Stan)
WFA 3 from 4yo+ 2lb **13** Ran SP% **119.4**
Speed ratings (Par 100): **103,101,100,99,98 98,97,97,97,97 95,84,75**
CSF £9.42 CT £69.54 TOTE £2.60: £1.50, £1.30, £3.40; EX 11.00 Trifecta £78.90.
Owner Hamdan Al Maktoum **Bred** Shadwell Estate Company Limited **Trained** Lambourn, Berks

FOCUS
It didn't pay to be too far off the pace here.

8255 BET AT RACINGTV.COM H'CAP (DIV I) 7f (P)
7:40 (7:44) (Class 6) (0-55,57) 3-Y-0+

£3,105 (£692; £692; £400; £400; £400) **Stalls** Low

Form RPR

4430 **1** **Penarth Pier (IRE)**[8] 7982 3-9-6 **54** .... RobertHavlin 9 64
(Christine Dunnett) *trckd ldrs: prog on inner over 2f out: led over 1f out: styd on wl and clr fnl f* **12/1**

420 **2** *3 1/4* **Glamorous Crescent**[31] 7236 3-9-9 **57** .... RossaRyan 1 59
(Grace Harris) *taken down early: prom: rdn to chal 2f out: nt qckn over 1f out and sn outpcd by wnr: kpt on* **10/1**

1006 **2** *dht* **Three C's (IRE)**[22] 7549 5-9-2 **48** ....(p) HarryBentley 5 51
(George Boughey) *chsd ldrs: rdn over 2f out: kpt on over 1f out: no threat to wnr (starter reported that the gelding was the subject of a third criteria failure; trainer was informed that the gelding could not run until the day after passing a stalls test)* **7/1[3]**

0000 **4** *3/4* **Sherella**[77] 5552 3-8-11 **45** .... DavidProbert 13 45
(J R Jenkins) *hld up in rr: prog over 2f out: rdn and styd on to press for a pl fnl f* **50/1**

4360 **5** *1 3/4* **Agent Of Fortune**[27] 7374 4-9-7 **53** ....(p) LiamKeniry 4 51+
(Christine Dunnett) *hld up wl in rr: pushed along whn stuck bhd rivals over 1f out tl ins fnl f and eased: rdn and r.o wl last 150yds but ch had gone* **10/1**

2023 **6** *nk* **Garth Rockett**[7] 8018 5-9-5 **56** ....(tp) SeanKirrane(5) 3 51
(Mike Murphy) *taken down early: hld up towards rr: rdn over 2f out: sme prog on outer over 1f out: no hdwy after* **2/1[1]**

6036 **7** *1 1/2* **Powerage (IRE)**[55] 6361 3-8-13 **47** .... FrannyNorton 10 37
(Malcolm Saunders) *mostly in midfield: pushed along and no prog 2f out: nvr involved* **25/1**

64P/ **8** *3/4* **Ultimat Power (IRE)**[1059] 8046 5-8-8 **45** .... SeamusCronin(5) 6 34
(Frank Bishop) *awkward s: t.k.h and hld up in last pair: looked like dropping away over 2f out: kpt on again on wd outside over 1f out* **50/1**

43 **9** *shd* **Sagittarian Wind**[4] 8123 3-9-4 **52** .... HollieDoyle 12 40
(Archie Watson) *blasted off in clr ld: hdd & wknd over 1f out* **11/4[2]**

6156 **10** *1/2* **Cristal Pallas Cat (IRE)**[37] 7028 4-8-10 **47** .... RhiainIngram(5) 7 35
(Roger Ingram) *pressed ldrs to over 2f out: sn wknd* **12/1**

0046 **11** *1 1/4* **Yet Another (IRE)**[42] 6857 4-8-10 **45** ....(p[1]) WilliamCox(3) 8 30
(Grace Harris) *chsd ldrs: rdn and wknd 2f out* **100/1**

-000 **12** *hd* **Shoyd**[13] 7843 4-8-10 **49** .... MarkCrehan(7) 11 33
(Richard Hannon) *slow to get gng and rousted: drvn in rr over 2f out and no prog* **50/1**

000 **13** *1/2* **Paco Dawn**[31] 7237 5-8-13 **45** ....(h[1]) TomMarquand 2 28
(Tony Carroll) *nvr bttr than midfield: rdn and no prog 2f out* **50/1**

000 **14** *10* **Be Together**[63] 6074 3-8-11 **45** .... KieranShoemark 14 1
(Charles Hills) *a in rr: wknd over 2f out: t.o (vet said filly had bled from the nose)* **50/1**

1m 25.64s (-0.36) **Going Correction** -0.05s/f (Stan)
WFA 3 from 4yo+ 2lb **14** Ran SP% **120.7**
Speed ratings (Par 101): **100,96,96,95,93 93,91,90,90,89 88,88,87,76**
WIN: 14.60 Penarth Pier; PL: 3.20 Glamorous Crescent 2.90 Penarth Pier 2.30 Three C's; EX: 42.20 82.30; CSF: 61.31 45.49; TC: 469.13 453.81; TF: 289.20 538.70 CSF £61.31 CT £469.13 TOTE £14.60: £2.90, £3.20; EX 82.30 Trifecta £538.70.
Owner Ron Spore & P D West **Bred** Athassel House Stud Ltd **Trained** Hingham, Norfolk

FOCUS
A moderate handicap but the quicker of the two divisions by 0.36sec. The second, third and fourth offer perspective.

8256 BET AT RACINGTV.COM H'CAP (DIV II) 7f (P)
8:10 (8:13) (Class 6) (0-55,56) 3-Y-0+

£3,105 (£924; £461; £400; £400; £400) **Stalls** Low

Form RPR

6054 **1** **Maisie Moo**[72] 5730 3-9-0 **50** .... JosephineGordon 4 57
(Shaun Keightley) *trckd ldrs: prog to take 2nd wl over 1f out: rdn and grad clsd on ldr fnl f: led last 50yds* **10/3[1]**

2630 **2** *nk* **Rock In Society (IRE)**[7] 8018 4-9-0 **53** ....(b) DylanHogan(5) 13 60
(John Butler) *led fr wdst draw: rdn 2f out: stl 2 l up 1f out: kpt on but collared last 50yds* **16/1**

4300 **3** *2 1/2* **Global Acclamation**[39] 6983 3-9-3 **53** ....(b) RobertHavlin 3 53
(Ed Dunlop) *chsd ldrs: shkn up and prog over 2f out to chse ldng pair jst over 1f out: kpt on but no imp* **13/2**

4612 **4** *1 3/4* **Mabo**[16] 7758 4-9-7 **55** ....(b) RossaRyan 10 51
(Grace Harris) *sn in rr: swtchd lft and rdn over 2f out: styd on over 1f out to take 4th nr fin: too late to threaten* **5/1[3]**

6402 **5** *nk* **Cottingham**[8] 8008 4-8-12 **46** oh1 ....(p[1]) KieranShoemark 8 41
(Kevin Frost) *dwlt: mostly in last: shkn up and swtchd to wd outside over 2f out: styd on wl fr over 1f out to take 5th nr fin (jockey said gelding was slowly away)* **8/1**

0600 **6** *3/4* **Dalness Express**[27] 7384 6-8-12 **46** oh1 ....(bt) HollieDoyle 1 39
(Archie Watson) *wl in rr: rdn and prog 2f out: no hdwy fnl f* **4/1[2]**

562 **7** *hd* **Ecstasea (IRE)**[57] 6302 3-9-6 **56** .... DavidProbert 9 48
(Rae Guest) *chsd ldrs: rdn and nt pce to cl fr 2f out: n.d fnl f* **9/1**

6050 **8** *3* **Reshaan (IRE)**[20] 7632 4-8-12 **46** oh1 ....(p) CallumShepherd 11 31
(Alexandra Dunn) *pressed ldrs: rdn over 2f out: wknd over 1f out* **20/1**

60/3 **9** *1 1/2* **Sixth Of June**[20] 7603 5-8-9 **46** oh1 .... WilliamCox(3) 5 27
(Simon Earle) *a towards rr: rdn and struggling over 2f out* **33/1**

1020 **10** *1* **Seafaring Girl (IRE)**[25] 7443 3-9-1 **51** ....(p) TomMarquand 6 29
(Mark Loughnane) *chsd ldr to wl over 1f out: wknd* **20/1**

3400 **11** *hd* **Amberine**[32] 7172 5-8-12 **46** oh1 .... FrannyNorton 7 24
(Malcolm Saunders) *nvr beyond midfield: rdn 2f out: wknd over 1f out* **25/1**

0660 **12** *1/2* **Iris's Spirit**[69] 5842 3-8-10 **46** oh1 .... BrettDoyle 12 22
(Tony Carroll) *a towards rr on outer: struggling over 2f out: no prog after* **66/1**

1m 26.0s **Going Correction** -0.05s/f (Stan)
WFA 3 from 4yo+ 2lb **12** Ran SP% **117.9**
Speed ratings (Par 101): **98,97,94,92,92 91,91,87,86,85 84,84**
CSF £53.71 CT £338.78 TOTE £3.80: £1.60, £5.10, £1.90; EX 61.10 Trifecta £237.30.
Owner Simon Lockyer & Tim Clarke **Bred** Natton House Thoroughbreds **Trained** Newmarket, Suffolk

FOCUS
The second leg of this low-grade handicap was run in a time 0.36sec slower than the first division. The first pair came clear.
T/Plt: £8.00 to a £1 stake. Pool: £50,762.85 - 4,629.15 winning units T/Qpdt: £5.50 to a £1 stake. Pool: £7,729.26 - 1,036.01 winning units **Jonathan Neesom**

8026 NOTTINGHAM (L-H)
Wednesday, October 16

OFFICIAL GOING: Heavy (5.3)
Wind: Light across Weather: Overcast

8257 KIER CONSTRUCTION NOTTINGHAM EBF MAIDEN STKS 1m 75y
1:55 (1:56) (Class 5) 2-Y-O **£3,881** (£1,155; £577; £288) **Stalls** Centre

Form RPR

32 **1** **Zegalo (IRE)**[22] 7539 2-9-5 0 .... AndreaAtzeni 6 76+
(Roger Varian) *led early: chsd ldr tl led again over 5f out: rdn over 1f out: edgd lft ins fnl f: styd on (vet said colt lost its left-fore shoe)* **8/13[1]**

2 *1 3/4* **Phoenix Aquilus (IRE)** 2-9-5 0 .... TomQueally 3 71
(Seamus Durack) *s.i.s: hdwy to chse ldrs after 1f: shkn up over 1f out: styd on same pce ins fnl f* **66/1**

06 **3** *hd* **Nibras Wish (IRE)**[28] 7346 2-9-5 0 .... BenCurtis 2 71
(Ismail Mohammed) *sn led: hdd over 5f out: chsd wnr: ev ch over 2f out: rdn over 1f out: styd on same pce ins fnl f (vet said colt lost its left-fore shoe)* **18/1**

4 *4 1/2* **Chichester** 2-9-5 0 .... RyanMoore 11 61
(Sir Michael Stoute) *broke wl: sn lost pl: hdwy over 2f out: rdn over 1f out: styd on same pce* **11/1**

4 **5** *1 1/2* **Thai Power (IRE)**[20] 7611 2-9-5 0 .... SilvestreDeSousa 8 58
(Andrew Balding) *chsd ldrs: shkn up over 2f out: sn lost pl* **7/2[2]**

6 *nk* **Gibraltar (IRE)** 2-9-5 0 .... RichardKingscote 1 58
(Michael Bell) *s.i.s: hld up: rdn over 2f out: nvr on terms* **9/1[3]**

0 **7** *nse* **Purple Sandpiper**[7] 8012 2-9-5 0 .... PaulMulrennan 5 58
(Robyn Brisland) *chsd ldrs: lost pl after 1f: hdwy over 3f out: rdn over 1f out: wknd fnl f* **150/1**

1m 57.16s (10.46) **Going Correction** +1.025s/f (Soft) **7** Ran SP% **109.9**
Speed ratings (Par 95): **88,86,86,81,80 79,79**
CSF £45.53 TOTE £1.60: £1.40, £26.40; EX 36.80 Trifecta £482.90.
Owner Hussain Alabbas Lootah **Bred** H A Lootah **Trained** Newmarket, Suffolk

FOCUS
Outer Track. Rail was out 4yds on the home bend. \n\x\x This was a proper test for these 2yos and the race should throw up future middle-distance winners, but the field finished quite compressed. Add 12yds.

8258 WEIR SKIPS (CONSTRUCTION & DEMOLITION) EBF MAIDEN FILLIES' STKS (PLUS 10 RACE) 1m 75y
2:30 (2:34) (Class 5) 2-Y-O **£3,881** (£1,155; £577; £288) **Stalls** Centre

Form RPR

2 **1** **So I Told You (IRE)**[16] 7755 2-9-0 0 .... RyanMoore 2 78+
(Richard Hughes) *led: hdd 5f out: led again over 3f out: rdn over 1f out: styd on wl* **1/2[1]**

2 *2 1/4* **Magic Dust** 2-8-7 0 .... StefanoCherchi(7) 1 73
(Marco Botti) *chsd ldrs: rdn to chse wnr fnl f: styd on same pce* **8/1**

3 *3 1/4* **Isola Bella May (IRE)** 2-9-0 0 .... JackGarritty 9 66
(Jedd O'Keeffe) *s.i.s: hld up: hdwy over 3f out: chsd wnr over 3f out tl rdn and lost 2nd 1f out: no ex* **20/1**

0 **4** *5* **Girl From Mars (IRE)**[18] 7677 2-9-0 0 .... RichardKingscote 8 56
(Tom Dascombe) *chsd wnr tl over 6f out: remained handy: rdn over 3f out: wknd over 2f out* **7/1[3]**

5 *1/2* **Ampney Red** 2-9-0 0 .... GeraldMosse 6 55
(Hughie Morrison) *s.i.s: in rr: wnt centre over 4f out: hdwy over 3f out: led that pair over 2f out and up w the pce far side: rdn: hung lft and wknd over 1f out* **11/2[2]**

00 **6** *8* **Lismore (IRE)**[14] 7814 2-9-0 0 .... LukeMorris 10 38
(Sir Mark Prescott Bt) *prom: rdn over 3f out: wknd over 2f out* **40/1**

0 **7** *16* **Lightning Blue**[14] 7826 2-9-0 0 .... SilvestreDeSousa 3
(Mick Channon) *chsd wnr over 6f out: led 5f out: wnt centre over 4f out: hdd over 3f out: sn rdn and hung lft: wknd and eased wl over 1f out (jockey said filly had no more to give)* **25/1**

1m 55.82s (9.12) **Going Correction** +1.025s/f (Soft) **7** Ran SP% **116.7**
Speed ratings (Par 92): **95,92,89,84,84 76,60**
CSF £5.41 TOTE £1.20: £1.10, £2.10; EX 5.50 Trifecta £41.80.
Owner Flaxman Stables Ireland Ltd **Bred** Flaxman Stables Ireland Ltd **Trained** Upper Lambourn, Berks

■ Mums The Law was withdrawn. Price at time of withdrawal 10/1. Rule 4 applies to all bets - deduction 5p in the £.

The Form Book Flat 2019, Raceform Ltd, Newbury, RG14 5SJ

FOCUS
The far rail was the place to be in this modest fillies' maiden and it was hard work. The winner built on her debut promise. Add 12yds.

8259 WHO IS GETTING THE BEERS IN HOPHOUSE13 NURSERY H'CAP 1m 75y
3:05 (3:05) (Class 5) (0-70,72) 2-Y-O
£3,881 (£1,155; £577; £300; £300; £300) Stalls Centre

Form RPR

062 1 **She's A Unicorn**[20] 7623 2-8-13 67..........................(v1) PoppyFielding(7) 1 72
(Tom Dascombe) *s.i.s: in rr: hdwy over 1f out: styd on to ld wl ins fnl f: comf* **20/1**

4060 2 2 1/2 **Ambyfaeirvine (IRE)**[14] 7827 2-9-4 65..........................(v1) JasonHart 7 65
(Ivan Furtado) *led 1f: chsd ldr tl led again over 3f out: rdn over 1f out: hdd wl ins fnl f* **16/1**

5230 3 nk **Jungle Book (GER)**[16] 7767 2-9-3 64.................. RichardKingscote 4 63
(Jonathan Portman) *hld up: hdwy over 2f out: rdn and swtchd rt 1f out: kpt on* **3/1**[1]

3046 4 1 1/4 **Richard R H B (IRE)**[55] 6372 2-9-6 67........................ DavidEgan 9 63
(David Loughnane) *prom: rdn to chse ldr over 1f out tl no ex ins fnl f* **10/1**

543 5 8 **King's Charisma (IRE)**[30] 7285 2-9-7 68...................... DavidNolan 3 48
(David O'Meara) *hld up: hdwy over 2f out: wknd over 1f out* **8/1**

6010 6 1 3/4 **Bankawi**[39] 6969 2-8-7 54.. NathanEvans 11 30
(Michael Easterby) *chsd ldrs: wnt 2nd 3f out tl rdn over 1f out: wknd fnl f* **5/1**[2]

1642 7 6 **Mac McCarthy (IRE)**[8] 7994 2-9-11 72..........................(p) RyanMoore 6 35
(Richard Hughes) *broke wl: sn lost pl: n.d after (trainer's rep said gelding was unsuited by the going and would prefer a faster surface)* **8/1**

346 8 6 **Sweet Sixteen (GER)**[48] 6629 2-9-1 62............(b1) SilvestreDeSousa 10 13
(Amy Murphy) *led and flashed tail 7f out: racd freey: hdd & wknd over 3f out (jockey said filly ran too free)* **16/1**

0352 9 hd **Sir Havelock (IRE)**[21] 7582 2-8-11 58..........................(p) TonyHamilton 8 8
(Richard Fahey) *s.i.s: hld up: a in rr: bhd fnl 3f* **6/1**[3]

4512 10 24 **Interrupted Dream**[20] 7626 2-9-4 65.......................... LukeMorris 2
(Gay Kelleway) *hld up in tch: rdn over 3f out: hmpd and wknd wl over 2f out (trainer said colt was unsuited by the going and would prefer an all-weather surface)* **12/1**

064 11 15 **Clifftop Heaven**[30] 7285 2-9-6 67........................ DougieCostello 5
(Mark Walford) *hld up: wknd over 3f out (jockey said gelding was never travelling; trainer said gelding was unsuited by the going and would prefer a faster surface)* **20/1**

1m 56.14s (9.44) **Going Correction** +1.025s/f (Soft) 11 Ran SP% **116.2**
Speed ratings (Par 95): **93,90,90,88,80 79,73,67,67,43 28**
CSF £301.86 CT £1250.24 TOTE £15.50: £4.20, £6.70, £1.50; EX 394.10 Trifecta £2656.20.
Owner T Dascombe **Bred** Hall Of Fame Stud **Trained** Malpas, Cheshire

FOCUS
There was a slow-motion finish in this ordinary nursery and the stands' side was again favoured. The form is rated a shade cautiously. Add 12yds.

8260 KIER PARTNERING WITH PASIC H'CAP 1m 2f 50y
3:40 (3:42) (Class 3) (0-90,89) 3-Y-O+
£9,337 (£2,796; £1,398; £699; £349; £175) Stalls Low

Form RPR

0035 1 **Majestic Dawn (IRE)**[18] 7694 3-9-7 89........................ DavidEgan 5 101
(Paul Cole) *mde all: rdn over 1f out: sn hung rt: styd on* **9/4**[1]

521 2 1/2 **Junooh (IRE)**[22] 7543 3-8-10 78.......................... AndreaAtzeni 2 89
(Sir Michael Stoute) *prom: chsd wnr over 7f out: rdn over 1f out: edgd rt ins fnl f: styd on* **4/1**[3]

2631 3 3 1/4 **Skyman**[47] 6671 3-8-11 79.............................. SilvestreDeSousa 8 83
(Roger Charlton) *hld up: swtchd rt over 2f out: sn rdn: hdwy over 1f out: styd on same pce wl ins fnl f* **3/1**[2]

6603 4 1 1/2 **Music Seeker (IRE)**[14] 7829 5-8-10 81.......................(t) ZakWheatley(7) 10 81
(Declan Carroll) *chsd ldrs: rdn over 1f out: no ex ins fnl f* **10/1**

4655 5 3 **Mr Top Hat**[12] 7863 4-9-9 87.. BenCurtis 3 81
(David Evans) *prom: rdn over 2f out: wknd fnl f* **9/1**

0333 6 5 **Global Gift (FR)**[18] 7680 3-9-7 89........................ GeraldMosse 7 74
(Ed Dunlop) *hld up: hdwy 2f out: wknd over 1f out* **7/1**

/05- 7 7 **Novelty Seeker (USA)**[497] 3453 10-8-13 77................ NathanEvans 4 47
(Michael Easterby) *s.i.s: hld up: hdwy over 3f out: wknd 2f out* **66/1**

0426 8 5 **Sputnik Planum (USA)**[12] 7872 5-9-8 86.......................(t) LukeMorris 9 46
(Michael Appleby) *hld up: rdn over 3f out: hung lft and wknd over 2f out* **16/1**

000/ 9 1 **Flight Officer**[837] 4355 8-9-1 79.............................. CamHardie 6 37
(Michael Easterby) *hld up in tch: wknd 3f out* **66/1**

00-5 10 13 **Jamil (IRE)**[20] 7622 4-9-2 80.............................. JamesSullivan 1 12
(Tina Jackson) *chsd ldr over 2f: remained handy tl rdn over 2f out: sn wknd and eased* **50/1**

2m 20.46s (7.06) **Going Correction** +1.025s/f (Soft)
WFA 3 from 4yo+ 4lb 10 Ran SP% **118.2**
Speed ratings (Par 107): **112,111,109,107,105 101,95,91,91,80**
CSF £11.60 CT £27.04 TOTE £3.00: £1.10, £1.80, £1.50; EX 12.90 Trifecta £39.40.
Owner Green & Norman **Bred** Hall Of Fame Stud Ltd **Trained** Whatcombe, Oxon
■ Stewards' Enquiry : Andrea Atzeni four-day ban: used whip in the incorrect place on the run to the line (Oct 30-31, Nov 1-2)

FOCUS
The first two were clear at the finish in this feature handicap, which was dominated by 3yos. Add 12yds.

8261 MODULYSS CARPET TILES NURSERY H'CAP 5f 8y
4:10 (4:10) (Class 4) (0-85,83) 2-Y-O £6,469 (£1,925; £962; £481; £300) Stalls High

Form RPR

2321 1 **Ainsdale**[5] 8095 2-9-5 81 6ex.................................... BenCurtis 4 90+
(K R Burke) *w ldr: led and edgd rt over 1f out: styd on wl* **4/7**[1]

2203 2 2 1/2 **Sermon (IRE)**[25] 7437 2-9-3 79..........................(p) RichardKingscote 5 77
(Tom Dascombe) *led: rdn and hdd over 1f out: styd on same pce ins fnl f* **12/1**

0401 3 1 1/2 **Ventura Flame (IRE)**[16] 7765 2-9-7 83.................. JoeFanning 2 76
(Keith Dalgleish) *chsd ldrs: rdn over 1f out: no ex wl ins fnl f* **6/1**[3]

3520 4 1 1/4 **Tom Tulliver**[26] 7399 2-9-5 81................................ DavidNolan 1 69
(Declan Carroll) *s.i.s and edgd lft s: hdwy 3f out: rdn 1/2-way: no ex ins fnl f* **10/1**

5555 5 1 1/4 **Go Well Spicy (IRE)**[23] 7522 2-8-11 73.................. SilvestreDeSousa 3 60
(Mick Channon) *chsd ldrs: rdn over 1f out: eased whn btn ins fnl f (jockey said filly had no more to give; trainer's rep said filly was unsuited by the going and would prefer a faster surface)* **11/2**[2]

1m 4.42s (4.22) **Going Correction** +0.775s/f (Yiel) 5 Ran SP% **110.1**
Speed ratings (Par 97): **97,93,90,88,86**
CSF £8.43 TOTE £1.40: £1.40, £2.80; EX 7.10 Trifecta £18.20.
Owner David W Armstrong **Bred** Highfield Farm Llp **Trained** Middleham Moor, N Yorks

FOCUS
They kept stands' side in this fair little nursery and it's straightforward form.

8262 HARLOW TIMBER H'CAP 5f 8y
4:45 (4:46) (Class 4) (0-85,84) 3-Y-O+
£6,469 (£1,925; £962; £481; £300; £300) Stalls High

Form RPR

0251 1 **Wrenthorpe**[14] 7831 4-9-1 78.................................... GrahamLee 5 87
(Bryan Smart) *chsd ldr tl led over 1f out: edgd lft ins fnl f: styd on* **9/2**[2]

400 2 nk **Bellevarde (IRE)**[14] 7828 5-8-7 70 oh3........................ DavidEgan 12 78
(Richard Price) *chsd ldrs: rdn and hung lft fr over 1f out: r.o wl (jockey said mare hung left-handed in the final furlong)* **25/1**

1610 3 1 1/2 **Afandem (IRE)**[14] 7828 5-9-3 80..........................(p) DavidAllan 13 83
(Tim Easterby) *hld up: rdn 1/2-way: hdwy over 1f out: carried lft ins fnl f: styd on* **14/1**

2060 4 nk **Peggie Sue**[14] 7828 4-9-0 82.................................... TobyEley(5) 6 84
(Adam West) *hld up: racd keenly: hdwy over 1f out: styd on* **9/1**

1624 5 3/4 **Hawaam (IRE)**[11] 7908 4-8-12 80..........................(p) PaulaMuir(5) 11 79
(Roger Fell) *led over 3f: no ex ins fnl f* **20/1**

1046 6 hd **Abate**[71] 5791 3-8-8 71.. AndrewMullen 14 70
(Adrian Nicholls) *s.i.s: hld up: rdn over 1f out: stmbld and r.o wl ins fnl f: nt rch ldrs* **14/1**

5250 7 nse **Youkan (IRE)**[21] 7564 4-9-2 79..........................(p1) RichardKingscote 1 77
(Stuart Kittow) *s.i.s: hdwy u.p on outer over 1f out: nt rch ldrs* **12/1**

0000 8 2 1/2 **Erissimus Maximus (FR)**[11] 7894 5-9-5 82........(v1) SilvestreDeSousa 2 71
(Amy Murphy) *chsd ldrs: rdn and lost pl 1/2-way: sn hung lft: n.d after* **15/2**[3]

2130 9 nse **Green Door (IRE)**[68] 5888 8-8-11 79..........................(v) MarcoGhiani(5) 3 68
(Robert Cowell) *s.i.s: n.d* **20/1**

3040 10 1 **Quench Dolly**[11] 7894 5-8-12 75.................................. TomQueally 10 60
(John Gallagher) *hld up: pushed along 1/2-way: n.d* **33/1**

4612 11 2 1/4 **Prestbury Park (USA)**[13] 7855 4-8-11 74.................. PaulMulrennan 8 51
(Paul Midgley) *prom: rdn 1/2-way: wknd over 1f out* **10/1**

2210 12 10 **Fantasy Keeper**[5] 8099 5-9-7 84.............................. GeraldMosse 7 25
(Michael Appleby) *s.i.s: sn pushed along in rr: wknd and eased wl over 1f out (trainer said gelding was never travelling)* **15/8**[1]

1m 2.89s (2.69) **Going Correction** +0.775s/f (Yiel) 12 Ran SP% **121.2**
Speed ratings (Par 105): **109,108,106,105,104 104,104,100,99,98 94,78**
CSF £120.24 CT £1505.21 TOTE £6.50: £2.20, £8.00, £4.20; EX 142.80 Trifecta £976.00.
Owner Dan Maltby Bloodstock Ltd & B Smart **Bred** C J Mills **Trained** Hambleton, N Yorks

FOCUS
Competitive stuff, rated around the second and third.

8263 COUNTRYSIDE PROPERTIES H'CAP 5f 8y
5:15 (5:19) (Class 6) (0-65,67) 3-Y-O+
£3,234 (£962; £481; £300; £300; £300) Stalls High

Form RPR

0534 1 **Skeetah**[54] 6397 3-8-13 57.. JasonHart 5 64
(John Quinn) *chsd ldrs: rdn over 1f out: led ins fnl f: r.o* **16/1**

0600 2 1 1/4 **Van Gerwen**[30] 7286 6-9-5 63.................................. KevinStott 6 65
(Paul Midgley) *hld up: pushed along and hdwy 1/2-way: rdn over 1f out: r.o* **15/2**[3]

0-00 3 1 **Ebitda**[51] 6549 5-9-0 65.................................. JonathanFisher(7) 7 63
(Scott Dixon) *chsd ldrs: led 1/2-way: rdn over 1f out: hdd ins fnl f: styd on same pce* **14/1**

3165 4 1/2 **Carlovian**[14] 7824 6-8-9 53..........................(p) DuranFentiman 3 49
(Mark Walford) *chsd ldrs: rdn over 1f out: styd on* **14/1**

0062 5 nse **Zapper Cass (FR)**[8] 8007 6-9-4 67........................ TheodoreLadd(5) 8 63
(Michael Appleby) *pushed along towards rr: hdwy 3f out: rdn over 1f out: styd on (jockey said gelding ran flat; trainer said the race may have came too soon for the gelding having only ran 8 days previously)* **11/8**[1]

-500 6 3/4 **Robbian**[6] 8071 8-8-7 51 oh6.. JohnFahy 2 44
(Charles Smith) *chsd ldrs: lost pl over 3f out: rallied over 1f out: no ex wl ins fnl f* **50/1**

040 7 1/2 **The Golden Cue**[16] 7757 4-8-4 53.............................. TobyEley(5) 11 44
(Steph Hollinshead) *sn pushed along in rr: r.o ins fnl f: nvr nrr* **16/1**

3246 8 1/2 **Guardia Svizzera (IRE)**[6] 8071 5-8-12 61..........(h) PaulaMuir(5) 16 51
(Roger Fell) *prom: rdn and hung lft fr 2f out: no ex fnl f (jockey said gelding hung left-handed)* **14/1**

2544 9 3 3/4 **Valentino Sunrise**[8] 7986 3-9-0 58.................. SilvestreDeSousa 12 35
(Mick Channon) *prom: rdn 1/2-way: wknd fnl f* **4/1**[2]

3000 10 5 **Glyder**[20] 7628 5-8-7 51 oh6..........................(p) LiamJones 4 9
(John Holt) *s.i.s: hdwy over 3f out: rdn and wknd over 1f out (starter reported that the mare was the subject of a third criteria failure; trainer was informed that the mare could not run until the day after passing a stalls test)* **66/1**

004 11 1 3/4 **Angel Force (IRE)**[2] 8194 4-9-7 65..........................(b) DavidAllan 1 17
(David C Griffiths) *led to 1/2-way: wknd over 1f out* **25/1**

4620 12 hd **Maid From The Mist**[14] 7824 3-8-7 51 oh1.................. DavidEgan 13 3
(John Gallagher) *mid-div: sn pushed along: n.d* **20/1**

0000 13 7 **Point Of Woods**[36] 7051 6-8-6 57.............................. EllaMcCain(7) 14
(Tina Jackson) *s.i.s: outpcd* **50/1**

5035 14 1 3/4 **Honey Gg**[14] 7831 4-9-6 64.................................. DavidNolan 17
(Declan Carroll) *hld up in tch: nt clr run over 3f out: rdn and wknd over 1f out* **16/1**

0000 15 3/4 **Hellofagame**[23] 7527 4-8-2 51 oh6..........................(v1) SophieRalston(5) 10
(Richard Price) *sn outpcd* **80/1**

0466 16 8 **George Thomas**[29] 7319 3-9-2 60..............................(v1) TomQueally 15
(Mick Quinn) *prom: chsd ldrs to 1/2-way* **50/1**

1534 17 hd **Ginvincible**[46] 6715 3-9-6 64.................................. BarryMcHugh 9
(James Given) *restless in stalls: hld up: wknd over 1f out* **16/1**

1m 4.03s (3.83) **Going Correction** +0.775s/f (Yiel) 17 Ran SP% **134.6**
Speed ratings (Par 101): **100,98,96,95,95 94,93,92,86,78 75,75,64,61,60 47,47**
CSF £138.73 CT £1783.35 TOTE £18.70: £4.10, £1.10, £4.70, £3.20; EX 161.70 Trifecta £1406.90.
Owner The Jam Partnership **Bred** Facts & Figures **Trained** Settrington, N Yorks

FOCUS
The main action unfolded down the middle in this moderate sprint handicap. The winner ran her previous best figure on soft.
T/Plt: £20.50 to a £1 stake. Pool: £ - 1,654.14 winning units T/Qpdt: £16.10 to a £1 stake. Pool: £ - 217.24 winning units **Colin Roberts**

[8066]SOUTHWELL (L-H)
Wednesday, October 16

OFFICIAL GOING: Fibresand: standard
Wind: Light across Weather: Clear skies

8264 SKY SPORTS RACING ON SKY 415 H'CAP 6f 16y(F)
5:25 (5:28) (Class 6) (0-60,61) 3-Y-O+
£2,781 (£827; £413; £400; £400; £400) **Stalls Low**

Form RPR
5323 1 **Poeta Brasileiro (IRE)**[6] 8071 4-9-6 **61**......................(t) CierenFallon(3) 5 71+
(David Brown) *trckd ldrs: pushed along wl over 2f out: swtchd lft and hdwy wl over 1f out: rdn to ld over 1f out: clr fnl f* **15/8**[1]
0361 2 2 ½ **Vallarta (IRE)**[16] 7761 9-8-13 **51**.............................. JamesSullivan 6 54
(Ruth Carr) *trckd ldrs: pushed along and wd st: rdn wl over 1f out: chsd wnr ent fnl f: no imp* **11/1**
545 3 1 ¾ **Scandinavian Lady (IRE)**[5] 8083 3-9-4 **57**.................. TonyHamilton 7 54
(Ivan Furtado) *towards rr: hdwy towards inner over 2f out: rdn wl over 1f out: kpt on fnl f* **9/2**[3]
5313 4 ¾ **Round The Island**[21] 7590 6-9-7 **59**........................... PhilDennis 4 54
(Richard Whitaker) *towards rr: pushed along and hdwy on inner 2f out: rdn wl over 1f out: kpt on fnl f* **7/1**
0000 5 ½ **Murqaab**[12] 7869 3-9-3 **56**.............................. LewisEdmunds 1 50
(John Balding) *cl up on inner: rdn along over 2f out: sn drvn and wknd over 1f out* **33/1**
0046 6 6 **Montalvan (IRE)**[18] 7703 3-9-8 **61**..............................(p) BenCurtis 3 37
(Roger Fell) *chsd ldng pair: rdn along over 2f out: sn wknd* **7/2**[2]
5553 7 nk **Ghost Buy (FR)**[110] 4328 3-9-4 **57**..........................(t w) DougieCostello 8 32
(Ivan Furtado) *trckd ldrs and wd st: sn rdn: n.d* **12/1**
4040 8 1 **Normal Equilibrium**[35] 7077 9-9-2 **57**.................. GabrieleMalune(3) 2 29
(Ivan Furtado) *slt ld: rdn along over 2f out: drvn wl over 1f out: sn hdd & wknd* **25/1**

1m 14.54s (-1.96) **Going Correction** -0.275s/f (Stan)
WFA 3 from 4yo+ 1lb 8 Ran SP% **110.5**
Speed ratings (Par 101): **102,98,96,95,94 86,86,84**
CSF £22.38 CT £76.13 TOTE £2.80: £1.20, £1.90, £1.40; EX 15.20 Trifecta £73.60.
Owner Patrick Moyles **Bred** Kildaragh Stud **Trained** Averham Park, Notts

FOCUS
The market leader went off a short price but plenty of those just behind him in the betting were fairly close together, suggesting this was a competitive event. The winner's rated within 4lb of his best.

8265 SKY SPORTS RACING ON SKY 415 MAIDEN STKS 7f 14y(F)
5:55 (5:56) (Class 5) 2-Y-O £3,428 (£1,020; £509; £254) **Stalls Low**

Form RPR
00 1 **Escalade (IRE)**[13] 7832 2-9-0 0.............................. RyanTate 5 75+
(Sir Mark Prescott Bt) *cl up: led 1/2-way: pushed along over 2f out: rdn along over 1f out: kpt on wl* **33/1**
024 2 1 ¾ **Baadirr**[103] 4596 2-9-2 82.............................. CierenFallon(3) 1 74
(William Haggas) *trckd ldng pair on inner: effrt over 2f out and sn pushed along: rdn to chse wnr ent fnl f: sn ev ch: kpt on same pce last 100yds* **11/10**[1]
2302 3 1 ¼ **Born To Destroy**[39] 6963 2-9-5 81.............................. LukeMorris 3 71
(Richard Spencer) *trckd ldng pair: pushed along 1/2-way: rdn along on outer over 2f out: drvn over 1f out: sn one pce* **11/10**[1]
06 4 ½ **Fear Naught**[8] 7983 2-9-5 0.............................. PJMcDonald 4 70+
(George Baker) *slt ld: hdd 1/2-way: cl up: rdn along 2f out: kpt on one pce* **25/1**[3]
5 16 **Bulldozer (IRE)** 2-9-5 0.............................. AlistairRawlinson 2 28
(Michael Appleby) *dwlt: green and swtchd rt to outer sn after s: a outpcd in rr* **11/1**[2]

1m 28.22s (-2.08) **Going Correction** -0.275s/f (Stan) 5 Ran SP% **110.4**
Speed ratings (Par 95): **100,98,96,96,77**
CSF £71.38 TOTE £39.70: £9.50, £1.20; EX 86.90 Trifecta £190.60.
Owner Mr & Mrs John Kelsey-Fry **Bred** John Kelsey-Fry **Trained** Newmarket, Suffolk

FOCUS
Punters had this between two but it was an outsider who landed this in good style. If anything she was value for extra, but the form is rated cautiously.

8266 SKY SPORTS RACING ON VIRGIN 535 H'CAP 7f 14y(F)
6:25 (6:26) (Class 6) (0-65,69) 3-Y-O+
£2,781 (£827; £413; £400; £400; £400) **Stalls Low**

Form RPR
5351 1 **Awa Bomba**[6] 8070 3-9-8 **69** 6ex..............................(h) DarraghKeenan(3) 2 79+
(Tony Carroll) *hld up: gd hdwy on outer wl over 2f out: chsd ldr and edgd lft wl over 1f out: rdn to ld appr fnl f: kpt on wl* **11/10**[1]
0515 2 1 ¾ **Muqarred (USA)**[12] 7875 7-9-6 **65**..............................(b) GemmaTutty(3) 5 71
(Karen Tutty) *chsd ldrs: hdwy 3f out: rdn to chse ldr 2f out: drvn over 1f out: kpt on same pce* **4/1**[2]
3030 3 5 **Freedom And Wheat (IRE)**[107] 4454 3-9-3 **61**...........(v) KieranO'Neill 6 53
(Mark Usher) *slt ld on inner: pushed along 3f out: rdn over 2f out: drvn wl over 1f out: hdd appr fnl f: kpt on same pce (jockey said gelding hung left in the home straight)* **16/1**
0000 4 ½ **The Gingerbreadman**[12] 7869 4-7-13 **46** oh1................. PaulaMuir(5) 4 38
(Chris Fairhurst) *in rr: hdwy over 2f out: sn rdn along: kpt on u.p fnl f* **33/1**
0002 5 nk **Bee Machine (IRE)**[12] 7869 4-8-4 **53**..............................(bt) ZakWheatley(7) 7 44
(Declan Carroll) *t.k.h: cl up: disp ld over 4f out: rdn along over 2f out: sn drvn and wknd* **9/2**[3]
6400 6 1 ¼ **Epona**[86] 5237 3-9-5 **63**..............................(w) JoeFanning 1 50+
(Keith Dalgleish) *rrd and lost five l s: a towards rr (jockey said filly reared as the stalls opened and was slowly away as a result)* **16/1**
5353 7 ½ **Amazing Grazing (IRE)**[15] 7777 5-9-7 **63**.............................. PhilDennis 3 50
(Rebecca Bastiman) *chsd ldng pair: rdn along 3f out: wknd over 2f out* **9/1**
0000 8 4 ½ **Bevsboy (IRE)**[27] 7389 5-8-4 **46** oh1..............................(p) CamHardie 9 21
(Lynn Siddall) *a towards rr* **100/1**
042 9 3 ¼ **Cosmic Chatter**[16] 7761 9-8-5 **47**..............................(p) JamesSullivan 8 14
(Ruth Carr) *in rr and wd st: sn bhd* **25/1**

1m 28.03s (-2.27) **Going Correction** -0.275s/f (Stan)
WFA 3 from 4yo+ 2lb 9 Ran SP% **115.3**
Speed ratings (Par 101): **101,99,93,92,92 90,90,85,81**
CSF £5.48 CT £43.58 TOTE £1.70: £1.10, £1.70, £4.20; EX 6.30 Trifecta £67.90.
Owner Mrs Katie Morgan **Bred** Mr And Mrs L Norris **Trained** Cropthorne, Worcs

FOCUS
They appeared to go off quickly in this modest handicap, so it wasn't a surprise when a couple from behind proved best in the final stages. The first pair finished clear.

8267 STOBART RAIL & CIVILS H'CAP 4f 214y(F)
6:55 (6:57) (Class 4) (0-85,87) 3-Y-O+
£5,207 (£1,549; £774; £400; £400; £400) **Stalls Centre**

Form RPR
2445 1 **Saaheq**[11] 7894 5-9-4 **87**..............................(be[1]) TheodoreLadd(5) 9 96+
(Michael Appleby) *hld up towards stands' side: effrt and n.m.r over 2f out: hdwy wl over 1f out: sn rdn to chal: qcknd to ld ins fnl f: readily* **10/3**[1]
0001 2 1 ¼ **Samovar**[6] 8066 4-8-11 **75** 5ex..............................(b) KieranO'Neill 5 79
(Scott Dixon) *cl up centre: rdn wl over 1f out: ev ch and drvn ent fnl f: no ex last 75yds* **12/1**
1-03 3 hd **Magic J (USA)**[19] 7655 3-9-4 **85**.............................. CierenFallon(3) 4 89
(Ed Vaughan) *n.m.r and sltly hmpd s: swtchd rt after 1f and sn trcking ldrs: hdwy 2f out: rdn and ev ch whn edgd lft ent fnl f: sn drvn and kpt on same pce* **4/1**[2]
011 4 ½ **Harry Hurricane**[44] 6809 7-9-6 **84**..............................(p) PJMcDonald 1 85
(George Baker) *racd towards far side: trckd ldrs: hdwy and cl up wl over 1f out: sn rdn and ev ch: drvn and kpt on same pce fnl f* **10/1**
3620 5 ½ **Dark Shot**[5] 8099 6-9-7 **85**..............................(v[1]) BenCurtis 3 85
(Scott Dixon) *racd centre: slt ld: rdn along 2f out: drvn over 1f out: hdd jst ins fnl f: kpt on same pce* **11/2**[3]
6064 6 ¾ **Sandridge Lad (IRE)**[6] 8066 3-8-7 **71**..............................(p[1]) JoeFanning 11 69
(John Ryan) *racd nr stands' rail: prom: rdn along 2f out: drvn over 1f out: wknd fnl f* **12/1**
6141 7 1 ½ **Crosse Fire**[27] 7387 7-9-5 **83**..............................(b) LukeMorris 8 75
(Scott Dixon) *cl up centre: rdn along over 2f out: drvn and hld whn n.m.r wl over 1f out: sn wknd* **16/1**
5035 8 1 ¾ **Nick Vedder**[7] 8016 5-9-4 **82**.............................. PaulMulrennan 7 67
(Robyn Brisland) *in rr and swtchd markedly lft towards far side wl over 3f out: bhd tl styd on fr over 1f out* **7/1**
6422 9 ¾ **Miningggold**[6] 8066 6-8-7 **71**..............................(p) AndrewMullen 10 54
(Michael Dods) *trckd ldrs towards stands' side: swtchd rt and rdn wl over 1f out: sn no imp* **15/2**
1-50 10 3 ½ **Laith Alareen**[56] 6332 4-9-5 **83**..............................(t) DougieCostello 2 53
(Ivan Furtado) *cl up centre: rdn along over 2f out: sn wknd* **50/1**
1050 11 ¾ **Cool Spirit**[40] 6921 4-8-11 **78**.............................. ConnorMurtagh(3) 6 45
(Olly Williams) *racd centre: outpcd and bhd fr 1/2-way* **50/1**

57.9s (-1.80) **Going Correction** -0.275s/f (Stan) 11 Ran SP% **117.0**
Speed ratings (Par 105): **103,101,100,99,99 97,95,92,91,85 84**
CSF £44.46 CT £167.35 TOTE £4.20: £1.90, £3.70, £1.60; EX 42.30 Trifecta £225.30.
Owner The Horse Watchers **Bred** Cliveden Stud Ltd **Trained** Oakham, Rutland

FOCUS
There was plenty of pace on early and the winner, who sat off the gallop, was nicely on top passing the line. He can better this on the AW.

8268 8TH NOVEMBER 30TH ANNIVERSARY DINNER MAIDEN STKS 4f 214y(F)
7:25 (7:26) (Class 5) 3-Y-O+ £3,428 (£1,020; £509; £254) **Stalls Centre**

Form RPR
44 1 **Hareem Queen (IRE)**[173] 2077 3-9-0 0.............................. PJMcDonald 1 63+
(K R Burke) *cl up centre: led 1/2-way: pushed clr wl over 1f out: easily* **9/4**[2]
036 2 4 ½ **Sambucca Spirit**[19] 7651 3-9-5 45.............................. PaulMulrennan 2 52
(Paul Midgley) *in tch towards far side: rdn along and hdwy wl over 1f out: kpt on u.p fnl f: no ch w wnr* **16/1**
6204 3 ¾ **Great Suspense**[19] 7651 3-9-5 61.............................. CamHardie 3 49
(David O'Meara) *trckd ldng pair centre: rdn along over 2f out: drvn and wknd over 1f out* **5/1**[3]
0005 4 3 **Filbert Street**[20] 7606 4-9-5 48..............................(b) LukeMorris 4 38
(Michael Appleby) *led centre: hdd 1/2-way: sn pushed along: rdn wl over 1f out: sn wknd* **12/1**
50 5 nk **Ginger Max**[165] 2397 3-9-5 0.............................. TonyHamilton 7 37
(Richard Fahey) *in rr and outpcd tl kpt on fnl 2f* **8/1**
2323 6 2 ¾ **Lofty**[9] 7976 3-9-5 73.............................. BenCurtis 6 28
(David Barron) *trckd ldrs centre: effrt 2f out: sn rdn: drvn over 1f out: sn btn (trainer said gelding was unsuited by the drop in trip to 5f on this occasion)* **6/4**[1]

57.84s (-1.86) **Going Correction** -0.275s/f (Stan) 6 Ran SP% **112.1**
Speed ratings (Par 103): **103,95,94,89,89 84**
CSF £33.77 TOTE £2.50: £1.50, £5.10; EX 35.00 Trifecta £171.50.
Owner John Dance **Bred** Corduff Stud **Trained** Middleham Moor, N Yorks

FOCUS
Not much got into this ordinary contest, but the winner might be able to progress into a fair handicapper. The time was marginally quicker than the 0-85 handicap that preceded it. The runner-up is key to the form.

8269 FOLLOW AT THE RACES ON TWITTER H'CAP 1m 4f 14y(F)
7:55 (7:55) (Class 6) (0-60,60) 3-Y-O+
£2,781 (£827; £413; £400; £400; £400) **Stalls Low**

Form RPR
0663 1 **Mongolia**[12] 7873 3-8-10 **52**.............................. LukeMorris 1 62
(Michael Appleby) *trckd ldrs: hdwy 3f out: led 2f out: rdn clr over 1f out: kpt on wl* **4/1**[2]
4304 2 3 ¾ **Risk Mitigation (USA)**[8] 8003 3-8-8 **50**..............................(v) BenCurtis 2 54
(David Evans) *led 2f: prom: pushed along 3f out: ev ch 2f out: sn rdn: kpt on same pce* **6/1**
2123 3 3 **Loose Chippings (IRE)**[6] 8072 5-9-7 **57**.............................. DougieCostello 6 55
(Ivan Furtado) *t.k.h and stdd s: hld up in rr: trckd ldrs over 3f: effrt on outer wl over 1f out: sn rdn and n.d* **13/8**[1]
0061 4 nk **Feebi**[30] 7290 3-8-3 **50**.............................. PaulaMuir(5) 5 49
(Chris Fairhurst) *hld up in rr: hdwy over 3f out: rdn along on inner over 2f out: kpt on fnl f* **5/1**[3]
5 4 **Angel Of My Heart (IRE)**[108] 4-9-7 **57**.............................. PaulMulrennan 7 48
(Michael Easterby) *trckd ldrs: cl up 1/2-way: rdn along to take slt ld wl over 2f out: hdd and drvn 2f out: sn wknd* **7/1**

36-0 **6** *3* **It's Never Enough**[79] 5486 5-9-8 **58**.....................(h[1] w) LucyAlexander 3 45
(James Ewart) *t.k.h: cl up: led after 3f: rdn along over 3f out: hdd wl over 2f out: sn wknd (jockey said gelding hung right throughout)* **16/1**

0000 **7** *23* **Mountain Of Stars**[120] 3970 4-8-5 **46** oh1........... FayeMcManoman(5) 8
(Suzzanne France) *trckd ldrs: cl up 1/2-way: rdn along over 3f out: sn wknd* **80/1**

2m 36.5s (-4.50) **Going Correction** -0.275s/f (Stan)
WFA 3 from 4yo+ 6lb 7 Ran SP% **108.7**
Speed ratings (Par 101): **104,101,99,99,96 94,79**
CSF £24.94 CT £46.86 TOTE £3.30: £1.90, £2.20; EX 9.10 Trifecta £93.80.
Owner Robin Oliver **Bred** Stowell Hill Partners **Trained** Oakham, Rutland

FOCUS
A modest middle-distance event.

8270 VISIT ATTHERACES.COM H'CAP 1m 13y(F)
8:25 (8:28) (Class 6) (0-60,62) 3-Y-O+
£2,781 (£827; £413; £400; £400; £400) **Stalls** Low

Form RPR

0000 **1** **Bond Angel**[12] 7875 4-9-10 **62**................................ BenCurtis 12 68
(David Evans) *hld up towards rr: hdwy 3f out: effrt on outer to chse ldrs wl over 1f out and sn rdn: chal ins fnl f: styd on wl to ld nr line* **4/1**[2]

6440 **2** *nk* **Oblate**[62] 6101 3-9-3 **58**................................(p[1]) KieranO'Neill 8 62+
(Robyn Brisland) *s.i.s and bhd: hdwy into midfield 1/2-way: chsd ldrs wl over 2f out: rdn to chse ldr over 1f out: drvn to chal ent fnl f: ev ch tl no ex nr fin (jockey said filly missed the break)* **33/1**

1162 **3** *shd* **Break The Silence**[6] 8068 5-8-10 **55**....................(b) JonathanFisher(7) 10 60
(Scott Dixon) *sn cl up: led over 3f out: rdn along wl over 1f out: jnd and drvn ent fnl f: kpt on gamely: hdd and no ex nr line* **11/4**[1]

3163 **4** *1 1/4* **Savitar (IRE)**[14] 7811 4-9-3 **62**..............................(p[1]) LukeCatton(7) 9 64
(Jim Boyle) *towards rr: hdwy whn n.m.r and sltly hmpd bnd 3f out: sn swtchd rt and hdwy 2f out: rdn wl over 1f out: styd on wl fnl f: nrst fin* **7/1**

0063 **5** *1 1/2* **Mr Strutter (IRE)**[6] 8068 5-9-8 **60**................................ AndrewElliott 5 59
(Ronald Thompson) *slt ld: hdd over 3f out: cl up and rdn along over 2f out: drvn wl over 1f out: kpt on same pce* **5/1**[3]

0046 **6** *2* **Fiction Writer (USA)**[20] 7609 3-9-6 **61**......................(b[1]) PJMcDonald 3 55
(Mark Johnston) *in tch: hdwy 3f out: rdn to chse ldrs over 2f out: drvn wl over 1f out: no imp* **15/2**

5033 **7** *1* **Abie's Hollow**[16] 7764 3-9-5 **60**................................ BenRobinson 2 51
(Tony Coyle) *in tch: hdwy on inner 3f out: rdn along 2f out: sn drvn and n.d (jockey said gelding hung left)* **10/1**

0000 **8** *7* **Roser Moter (IRE)**[22] 7549 4-8-8 **46** oh1......................(tp) LukeMorris 13 23
(Michael Appleby) *a towards rr* **100/1**

4120 **9** *2 3/4* **Crazy Spin**[118] 4029 3-8-8 **52**..............................(p) GabrieleMalune(3) 11 22
(Ivan Furtado) *towards rr and swtchd rt towards outer after 1f: nvr a factor* **22/1**

0006 **10** *1 1/4* **Watheer**[6] 8070 4-9-2 **59**................................ PaulaMuir(5) 1 27
(Roger Fell) *trckd ldrs on inner: hdwy to chse ldng pair 1/2-way: rdn along 3f out: drvn over 2f out and sn wknd* **20/1**

45-0 **11** *3/4* **Wicklow Warrior**[275] 241 4-8-8 **46** oh1......................(p) NathanEvans 7 13
(Peter Niven) *chsd ldrs: hdwy over 3f out: rdn along wl over 2f out: grad wknd* **66/1**

0000 **12** *10* **Pinkie Pie (IRE)**[15] 7780 3-8-5 **46** oh1......................(b[1]) CamHardie 14
(Andrew Crook) *a towards rr* **100/1**

400- **13** *3* **Bunker Hill Lad**[421] 6397 4-9-3 **55**................................ AlistairRawlinson 6
(Michael Appleby) *a bhd* **50/1**

0056 **14** *6* **The Thorny Rose**[27] 7384 3-8-8 **49**................................ AndrewMullen 4
(Michael Dods) *chsd ldrs: rdn along* **25/1**

1m 42.02s (-1.68) **Going Correction** -0.275s/f (Stan)
WFA 3 from 4yo+ 3lb 14 Ran SP% **118.0**
Speed ratings (Par 101): **97,96,96,95,93 91,90,83,81,79 79,69,66,60**
CSF £137.62 CT £424.33 TOTE £5.20: £2.00, £9.80, £1.60; EX 182.90 Trifecta £918.10.
Owner M W Lawrence **Bred** R C Bond **Trained** Pandy, Monmouths

FOCUS
A few held some sort of chance inside the final 2f, so this may well be reliable form for the level at this track.
T/Plt: £41.20 to a £1 stake. Pool: £62,586.25 - 1,107.83 winning units T/Qpdt: £14.80 to a £1 stake. Pool: £8,124.45 - 405.60 winning units **Joe Rowntree**

8271 - 8278a (Foreign Racing) - See Raceform Interactive

7980
BRIGHTON (L-H)
Thursday, October 17

OFFICIAL GOING: Soft (heavy in places; 5.7) (races 3 to 6 abandoned - false ground)

8279 BONUSCODEBETS.CO.UK H'CAP 5f 215y
1:25 (1:26) (Class 6) (0-55,55) 3-Y-O+
£2,781 (£827; £413; £300; £300; £300) **Stalls** Low

Form RPR

0501 **1** **Wild Flower (IRE)**[21] 7604 7-9-0 **48**..............................(p) KieranO'Neill 10 58
(Luke McJannet) *chsd ldr tl led over 2f out: rdn and extended advantage ent fnl f: drvn and kpt on: all out* **14/1**

0022 **2** *hd* **Mister Freeze (IRE)**[28] 7384 5-8-12 **46** oh1..............(vt) DavidProbert 1 55
(Patrick Chamings) *hld up in rr: hdwy on nr side u.p into 4th over 1f out: styd on strly ins fnl f clsng all the way to the line: jst failed* **7/1**[3]

3212 **3** *4* **Firenze Rosa (IRE)**[1] 8242 4-9-0 **55** 5ex................................ AledBeech(7) 7 52
(John Bridger) *racd in midfield in tch: clsd on ldrs gng wl over 1f out: rdn and ev ch 1f out: unable to sustain effrt fnl f* **11/8**[1]

0040 **4** *1/2* **Bahamian Sunrise**[17] 7757 7-9-7 **55**..............................(b) HectorCrouch 6 51
(John Gallagher) *racd in midfield: effrt on far side 2f out: rdn and no imp over 1f out: one pce fnl f* **6/1**[2]

4665 **5** *1 1/2* **Pharoh Jake**[9] 7986 11-8-12 **46** oh1................................ LukeMorris 5 37
(John Bridger) *prom: rdn along and outpcd 2f out: hdwy u.p into 5th over 1f out: one pce after* **33/1**

0605 **6** *1/2* **Ocean Temptress**[10] 7977 5-8-7 **46** oh1..............(b) RayDawson(5) 14 36
(Louise Allan) *prom on outer: rdn and qckly outpcd over 2f out: picked up again for press wl ins fnl f and passed btn horses* **9/1**

4500 **7** *1* **Flowing Clarets**[9] 7986 6-8-9 **46** oh1................................ MitchGodwin(3) 13 33
(John Bridger) *walked to post: led: rdn along and hdd by wnr over 2f out: wknd fr 1f out* **16/1**

-000 **8** *1* **Shaffire**[10] 7976 3-9-6 **55**................................ CharlesBishop 3 39
(Joseph Tuite) *hld up: a in rr* **50/1**

4636 **9** *1* **Cool Strutter (IRE)**[9] 7986 7-8-13 **47**..............................(p) RyanTate 12 28
(John Spearing) *racd in midfield: rdn and unable qck over 1f out: plugged on one pce fnl f* **10/1**

0040 **10** *5* **Mercers**[10] 7977 5-9-4 **52**..............................(b) CallumShepherd 11 18
(Paddy Butler) *racd in rr: rdn wl off pce 2f out: nvr on terms* **33/1**

R00 **11** *11* **Free Talkin**[82] 5430 4-8-12 **46** oh1..............................(p) KierenFox 8
(Michael Attwater) *wnt to post early: v.s.a: rcvrd into midfield: rdn and lost pl over 2 out: sn bhd (jockey said filly jumped awkwardly from the stalls)* **100/1**

1m 15.36s (4.26) **Going Correction** +0.60s/f (Yiel)
WFA 3 from 4yo+ 1lb 11 Ran SP% **109.4**
Speed ratings (Par 101): **95,94,89,88,86 86,84,83,82,75 60**
CSF £93.71 CT £199.36 TOTE £11.90: £2.30, £1.90, £1.20; EX 69.90 Trifecta £130.80.
Owner Miss Rebecca Dennis **Bred** Peter Harms **Trained** Newmarket, Suffolk

FOCUS
A largish field for this low-grade sprint handicap. They finished pretty tired in the ground with the first two coming clear, and very few getting involved from off the pace.

8280 EBF NOVICE STKS 5f 215y
1:55 (1:55) (Class 5) 2-Y-O
£3,428 (£1,020; £509; £254) **Stalls** Low

Form RPR

32 **1** **Silver Samurai**[35] 7104 2-9-2 0................................ DanielMuscutt 4 77
(Marco Botti) *trckd ldng pair: smooth hdwy to chal 2f out: effrt to ld over 1f out: asserted ins fnl f: comf* **1/1**[1]

42 **2** *4 1/2* **Sunset Breeze**[12] 7911 2-9-2 0................................ LukeMorris 5 64
(Sir Mark Prescott Bt) *led for 2f then led again 2f out: rdn along: hdd and readily outpcd by wnr over 1f out: kpt on u.p for remote 2nd* **2/1**[2]

3 *nk* **Rain Prancer (IRE)** 2-8-13 0................................ MeganNicholls(3) 3 63
(Richard Spencer) *hld up in last: hdwy on stands' rail 2f out: sn rdn kpt on ins fnl f in battle for 2nd* **12/1**

5302 **4** *5* **Santorini Sal**[35] 7110 2-8-8 57................................ MitchGodwin(3) 1 43
(John Bridger) *racd in 4th: hdwy whn briefly short of room 2f out: sn rdn and fnd little: wknd fnl f* **9/1**[3]

50 **5** *nk* **Bavardages (IRE)**[12] 7896 2-9-2 0................................ FrannyNorton 6 47
(Mark Johnston) *led after 2f: led field to nr side 3f out: rdn and hdd 2f out: sn wknd over 1f out* **12/1**

1m 15.37s (4.27) **Going Correction** +0.60s/f (Yiel) 5 Ran SP% **108.7**
Speed ratings (Par 95): **95,89,88,81,81**
CSF £3.10 TOTE £1.90: £1.30, £1.50; EX 3.30 Trifecta £17.70.
Owner What A Time To Be Alive 1 **Bred** Seaton Partnership **Trained** Newmarket, Suffolk

FOCUS
Distance reduced by 20yds. An ordinary juvenile novice and the time was almost the same as the opening handicap. The next four races were abandoned due to a patch of false ground at the 6f marker. It's hard to be sure of the exact merit but this was surely a step up from the winner.

8281 WILLIAM HENRY ALBERT HEDINGTON MEMORIAL H'CAP 7f 211y
(2:30) (Class 5) (0-75,) 3-Y-O+
£

8282 IRISH STALLION FARMS EBF NOVICE MEDIAN AUCTION STKS (PLUS 10 RACE) 7f 211y
(3:05) (Class 4) 2-Y-O
£

8283 NORTH ROAD TIMBER H'CAP 1m 1f 207y
(3:35) (Class 6) (0-60,) 3-Y-O+
£

8284 BARRY BONES 60TH BIRTHDAY H'CAP 6f 210y
(4:10) (Class 6) (0-60,) 3-Y-O+
£

8285 JINGLE & MINGLE CHRISTMAS PARTY NIGHTS H'CAP 5f 60y
4:40 (4:40) (Class 5) (0-75,77) 3-Y-O+
£3,428 (£1,020; £509; £300; £300; £300) **Stalls** Centre

Form RPR

6454 **1** **Michaels Choice**[29] 7337 3-8-12 **66**..............................(b) DavidProbert 9 74
(William Jarvis) *midfield in tch: hdwy on to heels of ldrs 2f out: rdn and wnt 2nd appr fnl f: styd on wl to ld ins fnl 50yds* **10/1**

5102 **2** *1/2* **The Lamplighter (FR)**[17] 7760 4-9-2 **73**..............(tp) MeganNicholls(3) 5 78
(George Baker) *midfield: gd hdwy to cl on ldrs 2f out: rdn and led over 1f out: immediately hung lft towards far rail: drvn and kpt on fnl f: hdd by wnr fnl 50yds (jockey said gelding hung left-handed)* **5/1**

5001 **3** *2 1/4* **Spanish Star (IRE)**[17] 7760 4-8-12 **73**................................ GeorgeRooke(7) 10 70
(Patrick Chamings) *hld up: hdwy u.p on outer 2f out: sn rdn and styd on wl fnl f: nt rch ldng pair* **6/1**

4130 **4** *3 1/4* **Pettochside**[12] 7894 10-9-4 **72**................................ KieranO'Neill 2 58
(John Bridger) *midfield: hdwy to ld v briefly 2f out: sn hdd over 1f out: one pce fnl f* **9/2**[3]

312 **5** *3 1/4* **Hassaad**[14] 7854 3-9-4 **72**................................ HollieDoyle 8 48
(Archie Watson) *prom in 3rd and keen early: rdn and outpcd over 1f out: one pce fnl f* **4/1**[2]

1635 **6** *4* **Harrogate (IRE)**[31] 7268 4-9-9 **77**..............................(b) CharlieBennett 1 38
(Jim Boyle) *chsd ldr tl 2f out: sn rdn and lost pl over 1f out: wknd fnl f* **12/1**

6002 **7** *nk* **Major Pusey**[9] 7986 7-8-12 **66**................................ HectorCrouch 3 26
(John Gallagher) *hld up in last: styd on far side 3f out: rdn and only minor hdwy 2f out: nvr on terms (jockey said gelding resented the kickback)* **5/2**[1]

4206 **8** *5* **King Crimson**[15] 7831 7-8-13 **70**................................ DarraghKeenan(3) 4 12
(John Butler) *led: rdn along and hdd 2f out: sn wknd* **28/1**

1m 5.47s (2.47) **Going Correction** +0.60s/f (Yiel) 8 Ran SP% **117.9**
Speed ratings (Par 103): **104,103,99,94,89 82,82,74**
CSF £60.95 CT £332.83 TOTE £11.20: £3.20, £1.80, £2.20; EX 80.20 Trifecta £655.20.
Owner The Music Makers **Bred** Fernham Farm Ltd **Trained** Newmarket, Suffolk

FOCUS
This fair sprint looked quite competitive beforehand but they finished quite spread out.
T/Plt: £1.10 to a £1 stake. Pool £43,651.77 - 43,906.96 winning units T/Qpdt: Void
Mark Grantham

[7994] CHELMSFORD (A.W) (L-H)

Thursday, October 17

OFFICIAL GOING: Polytrack: standard

Wind: light, behind Weather: light cloud

8286 BET AT TOTESPORT.COM NURSERY H'CAP — 1m 2f (P)

5:30 (5:34) (Class 5) (0-70,71) 2-Y-O

£5,175 (£1,540; £769; £400; £400; £400) **Stalls** Low

Form — RPR

036 **1** — **Good Reason**[48] 6675 2-9-7 **68** .... OisinMurphy 5 — 79+
(Saeed bin Suroor) *trckd ldrs and travelled strly: swtchd rt and clsd wl over 1f out: rdn and qckd to ld ent fnl f: in command fnl f: comf* **9/2**[2]

0501 **2** 3 ¾ **Sophar Sogood (IRE)**[21] 7626 2-8-9 **56** .... JFEgan 12 — 58
(Paul D'Arcy) *bmpd leaving stalls: in tch: effrt on outer over 3f out: flashing tail but styd on u.p ins fnl f: snatched 2nd last strides: no threat to wnr* **10/1**

3034 **3** hd **Moorland Spirit (IRE)**[31] 7277 2-9-2 **63** ....(b) AdamMcNamara 11 — 66
(Archie Watson) *wnt rt leaving stalls: chsd ldrs: effrt over 2f out: edgd lft u.p ins fnl f: chsd clr wnr 100yds out: no imp: lost 2nd last strides* **14/1**

000 **4** 2 ¼ **Prestigious (IRE)**[50] 6592 2-8-10 **57** ....(p[1]) TomMarquand 4 — 55
(Archie Watson) *chsd ldrs for 2f: settled bk into midfield: n.m.r over 1f out: keeping on whn carried lft ins fnl f: plugged on but no ch w wnr* **20/1**

0540 **5** nse **Selsey Sizzler**[22] 7562 2-9-1 **62** .... JimCrowley 7 — 60
(William Knight) *midfield early: sn lost pl and niggled along towards rr: wd and hdwy u.p 1f out: kpt on ins fnl f: no ch w wnr* **6/1**[3]

0066 **6** nk **My Havana**[22] 7582 2-8-7 **54** ....(p) SilvestreDeSousa 1 — 51
(Nigel Tinkler) *led: drvn ent fnl f: hdd ent fnl f: sn outpcd: lost 2nd and wknd fnl 100yds (jockey said gelding lugged right-handed inside the final furlong)* **8/1**

5546 **7** ½ **Webuyanyhorse**[23] 7548 2-9-10 **71** .... NicolaCurrie 6 — 67
(Jamie Osborne) *t.k.h: pressed ldr: rdn over 2f out: unable qck and edgd rt over 1f out: wknd ins fnl f (vet said gelding had lame left fore)* **11/1**

6000 **8** 1 **Speed Dating (FR)**[17] 7767 2-8-8 **55** ....(v) LewisEdmunds 9 — 49
(Derek Shaw) *t.k.h: hld up towards rr: effrt and hdwy on inner over 1f out: no imp and wl hld whn nt clrest of runs ins fnl f* **66/1**

5405 **9** hd **Wallaby (IRE)**[12] 7910 2-8-12 **59** .... RobHornby 10 — 53
(Jonathan Portman) *midfield early: dropped towards rr 6f out: drvn over 1f out: no imp and wl hld ins fnl f* **25/1**

406 **10** hd **Forus**[13] 7874 2-9-6 **67** .... DougieCostello 2 — 61
(Jamie Osborne) *v.s.a: hld up in rr: effrt and wnt lft over 1f out: nvr involved (jockey said colt was slowly away and ran green down the back straight)* **50/1**

050 **11** ½ **Debt Of Honour**[20] 7661 2-8-8 **58** ....(v[1]) CameronNoble[(3)] 8 — 51
(Michael Bell) *midfield: hdwy to chse ldrs on outer over 7f out: rdn over 3f out: lost pl over 1f out: wknd fnl f* **25/1**

0331 **12** ¾ **Souter Johnnie (IRE)**[7] 8061 2-9-8 **69** 6ex ....(b[1]) JamesDoyle 3 — 60
(Richard Hughes) *awkward leaving stalls: hld up in tch: effrt over 1f out: no imp whn carried lft ins fnl f: wknd fnl 100yds (trainer's rep said gelding ran too free and did not stay the trip)* **7/4**[1]

2m 10.07s (1.47) **Going Correction** -0.05s/f (Stan) — **12 Ran SP% 119.9**
Speed ratings (Par 95): **92,89,88,87,87 86,86,85,85,85 84,84**
CSF £46.45 CT £593.34 TOTE £4.60: £1.70, £4.00; EX 48.40 Trifecta £214.70.

Owner Godolphin **Bred** Godolphin **Trained** Newmarket, Suffolk

FOCUS
This was a long way for 2yos, so expect those who finished close up to contest middle-distance events at the very least next year. The runner-up is rated in line with his Southwell form.

8287 TOTEPOOL CASHBACK CLUB AT TOTESPORT.COM EBF NOVICE AUCTION STKS — 1m (P)

6:00 (6:07) (Class 5) 2-Y-O

£4,204 (£1,251; £625; £312) **Stalls** Low

Form — RPR

12 **1** — **Bronze River**[33] 7174 2-9-2 **0** .... WilliamCarver[(5)] 14 — 84+
(Andrew Balding) *midfield and pushed along leaving stalls: hdwy to ld after 2f: mde rest: pushed along and readily asserted over 1f out: r.o strly: readily* **7/2**[2]

2 2 **Rhubarb Bikini (IRE)** 2-9-2 **0** .... AdamMcNamara 13 — 74
(Archie Watson) *midfield: hdwy to chse wnr after 2f: effrt and unable to match pce of wnr over 1f out: rn green and hung lft ins fnl f: kpt on same pce* **22/1**

4 **3** 2 **Aquascape (IRE)**[23] 7555 2-9-2 **0** .... AndreaAtzeni 1 — 70
(Harry Dunlop) *led for 2f: chsd ldrs after: effrt in cl 3rd over 2f out: unable qck and edgd rt over 1f out: kpt on same pce ins fnl f* **8/1**

5 **4** ½ **Gonna Dancealot (IRE)**[89] 5189 2-8-10 **0** .... JFEgan 3 — 63
(Jane Chapple-Hyam) *t.k.h: in tch in midfield: effrt and outpcd over 1f out: kpt on but no threat to wnr ins fnl f* **6/1**

5 ¾ **Whisper Not** 2-9-1 **0** .... SeanLevey 12 — 66+
(Richard Hannon) *dwlt and short of room leaving stalls: hdwy into midfield and t.k.h after 2f: effrt and c wd 2f out: rn green: hung lft but kpt on ins fnl f: no threat to wnr* **7/1**

6 2 **School Of Thought** 2-9-0 **0** .... OisinMurphy 5 — 60
(James Tate) *dwlt: in tch: nt clrest of run ent fnl f: swtchd lft and effrt on inner over 1f out: nvr threatened ldrs and kpt on same pce ins fnl f* **5/2**[1]

6440 **7** 5 **Pettinger**[27] 7419 2-8-10 **64** .... KieranShoemark 2 — 45
(Charles Hills) *wl in tch in midfield on inner: effrt and swtchd rt over 1f out: wknd ins fnl f* **20/1**

0 **8** 4 ½ **Enchantee (IRE)**[16] 7787 2-8-10 **0** .... TomMarquand 6 — 34
(Sir Mark Todd) *chsd ldr for over 1f: chsd ldrs tl outpcd over 1f out: btn whn sltly squeezed for room 1f out: sn wknd* **66/1**

30 **9** 1 ¼ **Looks Good (IRE)**[38] 7031 2-8-11 **0** .... ShaneKelly 9 — 33
(Richard Hughes) *hld up in tch towards rr: effrt 2f out: sn outpcd and btn* **33/1**

00 **10** 2 ¼ **Lenny The Lion**[16] 7787 2-8-7 **0** .... RayDawson[(5)] 8 — 28
(Lydia Pearce) *a towards rr: rdn over 2f out: sn struggling and wknd over 1f out* **100/1**

600 **11** shd **Opine (IRE)**[16] 7787 2-9-1 **0** .... HayleyTurner 4 — 31
(Michael Bell) *sn in rr: effrt over 2f out: sn btn and wknd over 1f out* **25/1**

3 **12** 10 **Diamond Falls (IRE)**[16] 7787 2-8-13 **0** .... JimCrowley 7 — 6
(Amanda Perrett) *restless in stalls: t.k.h: chsd ldrs: effrt over 2f out: sn btn and lost pl over 1f out: wknd fnl f (jockey said gelding upset in the stalls)* **4/1**[3]

13 15 **Last Days Of May** 2-8-4 **0** .... GabrieleMalune[(3)] 10
(Christine Dunnett) *in tch on outer: rdn over 2f out: sn dropped to rr and bhd over 1f out* **66/1**

1m 40.15s (0.25) **Going Correction** -0.05s/f (Stan) — **13 Ran SP% 128.6**
Speed ratings (Par 95): **96,94,92,91,90 88,83,79,78,75 75,65,50**
CSF £87.42 TOTE £4.30: £1.30, £7.40, £2.50; EX 81.70 Trifecta £565.10.

Owner Mick and Janice Mariscotti **Bred** Meon Valley Stud **Trained** Kingsclere, Hants

FOCUS
The first two home were in the same positions from some way out, so those held up struggled to make any impact. The winner is the type to progress further.

8288 EXTRA PLACES AT TOTESPORT.COM NOVICE STKS — 7f (P)

6:30 (6:35) (Class 5) 2-Y-O

£4,204 (£1,251; £625; £312) **Stalls** Low

Form — RPR

4323 **1** — **Always Fearless (IRE)**[40] 6965 2-9-5 **77** .... SilvestreDeSousa 4 — 77
(Richard Hannon) *restless in stalls: led for 1f: styd chsng ldrs: swtchd ins and effrt to chal over 1f out: sn drvn: led ins fnl f: kpt on u.p* **5/2**[1]

2 nk **Law Of One (IRE)** 2-9-5 **0** .... JimCrowley 1 — 78+
(Sir Michael Stoute) *restless in stalls: dwlt: in tch towards rr: effrt on inner and briefly squeezed for room over 1f out: rdn and hdwy 1f out: styd on wl to chse wnr towards fin: nvr quite getting to wnr* **5/2**[1]

3 ¾ **Canagat** 2-9-5 **0** .... DavidEgan 10 — 74
(Archie Watson) *dwlt: hdwy to ld after 1f: rdn over 1f out: drvn 1f out: hdd ins fnl f: kpt on same pce and lost 2nd towards fin* **4/1**[3]

4 1 ½ **Zeimaam (IRE)** 2-9-5 **0** .... KieranShoemark 7 — 70
(Owen Burrows) *in tch in midfield: hdwy to chse ldr over 4f out tl unable qck over 1f out: kpt on same pce ins fnl f* **16/1**

5 nk **Soyounique (IRE)** 2-9-5 **0** .... NicolaCurrie 3 — 70
(Sir Mark Todd) *in tch in midfield: effrt: rn green and edgd lft over 1f out: kpt on same pce ins fnl f* **25/1**

0 **6** 2 **Vandad (IRE)**[27] 7406 2-9-5 **0** .... OisinMurphy 6 — 64
(Richard Hughes) *pressed ldr early: sn settled bk and wl in tch in midfield: effrt over 1f out: unable qck and btn over 1f out: wknd ins fnl f* **7/2**[2]

00 **7** 6 **Break Cover**[112] 4282 2-9-5 **0** .... RyanTate 5 — 49
(James Eustace) *in tch towards rr: effrt and c wd 2f out: sn outpcd and btn: wknd fnl f* **50/1**

44 **8** 1 **Costello**[21] 7605 2-9-5 **0** .... HayleyTurner 9 — 46
(Mike Murphy) *stdd s: hld up in tch in rr: pushed along over 3f out: wknd over 1f out* **25/1**

1m 26.84s (-0.36) **Going Correction** -0.05s/f (Stan) — **8 Ran SP% 114.9**
Speed ratings (Par 95): **100,99,98,97,96 94,87,86**
CSF £8.75 TOTE £3.10: £1.20, £1.20, £1.40; EX 10.10 Trifecta £39.50.

Owner King Power Racing Co Ltd **Bred** Diomed Bloodstock Ltd **Trained** East Everleigh, Wilts

FOCUS
While this form isn't going to be reliable with so many finishing close up, winners should emerge from it.

8289 IRISH LOTTO AT TOTESPORT.COM H'CAP — 7f (P)

7:00 (7:04) (Class 4) (0-85,87) 3-Y-O+

£5,530 (£1,645; £822; £411; £400; £400) **Stalls** Low

Form — RPR

0456 **1** — **Dominus (IRE)**[13] 7868 3-9-6 **85** .... OisinMurphy 5 — 94
(Brian Meehan) *t.k.h: chsd ldrs tl wnt 2nd over 5f out: effrt to chal over 1f out: rdn to ld jst ins fnl f: styd on* **3/1**[1]

14-0 **2** 1 ¼ **Madkhal (USA)**[23] 7551 3-9-8 **87** .... JimCrowley 1 — 93
(Saeed bin Suroor) *trckd ldrs on inner: nt clr run ent fnl 2f: swtchd out rt over 1f out: effrt ent fnl f: styd on to chse wnr wl ins fnl f: nvr getting to wnr* **5/1**[3]

6410 **3** 1 **Corazon Espinado (IRE)**[112] 4299 4-9-7 **84** .... SilvestreDeSousa 3 — 88
(Simon Dow) *led: rdn and hrd pressed over 1f out: hdd jst ins fnl f: no ex and lost 2nd wl ins fnl f* **8/1**

0030 **4** ½ **Commander Han (FR)**[14] 7836 4-9-1 **78** ....(p) DougieCostello 9 — 81
(Jamie Osborne) *stdd after s: hld up towards rr: effrt over 1f out: hdwy 1f out: swtchd rt and styd on ins fnl f: nvr trbld ldrs* **25/1**

2542 **5** ½ **Philamundo (IRE)**[33] 7191 4-9-0 **77** ....(b) KieranShoemark 2 — 78
(Richard Spencer) *sn in rr: effrt on inner over 1f out: hung lft and styd on ins fnl f: nvr trbld ldrs* **6/1**

2430 **6** 1 ¼ **Quick Breath**[24] 7517 4-9-0 **82** .... TylerSaunders[(5)] 13 — 83+
(Jonathan Portman) *swtchd lft sn after s: hld up in tch: effrt whn squeezed for room and hmpd over 1f out: swtchd rt and rallied 1f out: styd on ins fnl f: no threat to ldrs* **9/1**

2220 **7** ½ **Atletico (IRE)**[19] 7678 7-9-1 **78** .... HarryBentley 7 — 75
(David Evans) *hld up in tch: effrt and nt clrest of runs over 1f out: swtchd lft and kpt on ins fnl f: no threat to ldrs* **10/1**

1624 **8** ¾ **Aluqair (IRE)**[14] 7836 3-9-3 **82** .... JamesDoyle 10 — 76
(Simon Crisford) *t.k.h: sn prom fr wd draw: unable to u.p and edgd rt over 1f out: wknd ins fnl f* **4/1**[2]

0060 **9** ½ **Quiet Endeavour (IRE)**[22] 7564 3-9-4 **83** .... ShaneKelly 8 — 75
(George Baker) *chsd ldr tl over 5f out: nt clr run and wnt rt over 1f out: unable qck and btn whn sltly impeded ins fnl f: wknd* **25/1**

0600 **10** ½ **Normandy Barriere (IRE)**[21] 7621 7-8-12 **78** .... RowanScott[(3)] 12 — 70
(Nigel Tinkler) *in tch in midfield: effrt whn pushed rt and short of room over 1f out: no imp and wl hld ins fnl f* **20/1**

3114 **11** 9 **Amorously (IRE)**[33] 7176 3-8-13 **78** .... SeanLevey 6 — 45
(Richard Hannon) *in tch in midfield: effrt over 2f out: unable qck and btn over 1f out: wknd ins fnl f* **25/1**

0000 **12** 3 ½ **In The Red (IRE)**[31] 7268 6-8-12 **75** ....(p) EoinWalsh 4 — 33
(Martin Smith) *hld up in tch towards rr: nt clr run and shuffled bk to last over 2f out: swtchd rt and no hdwy over 1f out: sn bhd* **50/1**

1m 25.82s (-1.38) **Going Correction** -0.05s/f (Stan)
WFA 3 from 4yo+ 2lb — **12 Ran SP% 124.4**
Speed ratings (Par 105): **105,103,102,101,101 99,99,98,97,97 87,83**
CSF £17.66 CT £114.75 TOTE £3.60: £1.60, £1.60, £2.70; EX 21.80 Trifecta £120.30.

Owner G P M Morland & J W Edgedale **Bred** Morgan Cahalan **Trained** Manton, Wilts

■ Stewards' Enquiry : Rowan Scott three-day ban: interference & careless riding (Oct 31, Nov 1-2)
Dougie Costello caution: careless riding
Shane Kelly three-day ban: interference & careless riding (Oct 31, Nov 1-2)

FOCUS
This didn't look a particularly strong race for a 0-85, and it was a positive to be positioned close to the lead.

8290 BET IN PLAY AT TOTESPORT.COM NOVICE STKS 7f (P)
7:30 (7:33) (Class 5) 3-Y-O+ £4,948 (£1,472; £735; £367) Stalls Low

Form RPR
1 **Healing Power** 3-9-0 0 GabrieleMalune(3) 3 76
(Ivan Furtado) *sn led and mde rest: 3 l clr and stl travelling strly 2f out: rdn over 1f out: kpt on and a gng to hold on towards fin* **25/1**

6 2 1 **Pentimento**[71] 5808 3-9-3 0 KierenFox 12 73+
(John Best) *hld up towards rr: plenty to do whn swtchd rt and effrt over 1f out: swtchd rt again 1f out: str run u.p ins fnl f: wnt 2nd 50yds out: clsng but nt getting to wnr whn r.o to heels of wnr cl home (jockey said gelding ran green)* **33/1**

3432 3 ¾ **Ghaith**[77] 5579 4-9-5 74 (p[1]) JamesDoyle 10 72
(Hugo Palmer) *chsd ldrs: effrt and forced wd wl over 1f out: chse clr wnr over 1f out: hung lft ins fnl f: kpt on but nvr getting to wnr: lost 2nd towards fin* **11/4[2]**

3- 4 1 **Furqaan (IRE)**[320] 9354 3-8-12 0 JimCrowley 7 63
(Owen Burrows) *hld up in tch in midfield: effrt and swtchd rt 2f out: hdwy to chse ldng pair and hung lft ins fnl f: kpt on but nvr getting to wnr* **6/5[1]**

5 1 ¼ **Alvaro** 3-9-3 0 JimmyQuinn 11 65
(Michael Wigham) *hld up in rr and rn green early: hdwy and switching rt over 1f out: clsd: rn green and hung lft ins fnl f: no threat to ldrs but gng on wl at fin (jockey said gelding hung left-handed)* **66/1**

2342 6 2 ½ **Society Guest (IRE)**[12] 7912 3-8-12 65 (v) CallumShepherd 6 53
(Mick Channon) *hld up in tch in midfield: effrt over 1f out: fnd little: wl hld and kpt on same pce ins fnl f* **9/1**

55 7 1 ¾ **The Grey Goat (IRE)**[14] 7841 3-9-3 0 DavidEgan 5 53
(Peter Charalambous) *in tch in midfield: nt clr run ent fnl 2f: swtchd rt and effrt over 1f out: no imp and wl hld fnl f* **16/1**

06 8 ¾ **Urban Scene**[59] 6283 3-8-12 0 HayleyTurner 2 46
(Linda Jewell) *hld up in tch towards rr: effrt on inner over 1f out: nt clrest of runs 1f out: swtchd rt and kpt on ins fnl f: nvr involved* **66/1**

4 9 nk **Six Til Twelve (IRE)**[21] 7630 3-9-3 0 TomMarquand 4 51
(Robyn Brisland) *t.k.h: led briefly: chsd ldrs after over 1f: drvn over 2f out: chsd wnr briefly again wl over 1f out: wknd ins fnl f* **50/1**

-053 10 ½ **Mary Somerville**[21] 7608 3-8-12 74 NickyMackay 13 44
(John Gosden) *s.i.s: nvr travelling enough: in tch on outer: effrt over 1f out: sn impeded: no real imp and wl hld fnl f* **7/1[3]**

60 11 5 **Forgotten Girl**[31] 7278 3-8-12 0 EoinWalsh 1 31
(Christine Dunnett) *in tch in midfield: effrt on inner over 1f out: no imp and wknd ins fnl f* **66/1**

12 shd **Berties Mission (USA)**[15] 3-9-3 0 LewisEdmunds 9 35
(Derek Shaw) *taken down early: t.k.h: hld up in rr: effrt over 1f out: no imp: wknd ins fnl f* **66/1**

032 13 3 **Mr Carpenter (IRE)**[41] 6941 3-9-3 80 (t[1]) DanielMuscutt 8 27
(David Lanigan) *pushed along leaving stalls: sn chsng ldrs: wnt 2nd over 5f out: drifted rt off bnd wl over 1f out: sn lost pl: wknd fnl f (jockey said gelding stopped quickly)* **8/1**

1m 25.97s (-1.23) **Going Correction** -0.05s/f (Stan) 13 Ran SP% 126.3
WFA 3 from 4yo 2lb
Speed ratings (Par 103): **105,103,103,101,100 97,95,94,94,93 88,87,84**
CSF £666.44 TOTE £36.20: £7.20, £9.00; EX 2038.20 Trifecta £2693.20.
Owner Carl Hodgson **Bred** St Albans Bloodstock Ltd **Trained** Wiseton, Nottinghamshire

FOCUS
Older-horse novice events at this stage of the season don't take a lot of winning so it wasn't any great shock that the market principals were overturned. The time was good when compared to the 0-85 handicap that preceded it.

8291 DOUBLE DELIGHT HAT-TRICK HEAVEN AT TOTESPORT.COM H'CAP 1m (P)
8:00 (8:04) (Class 6) (0-65,66) 3-Y-O+ £3,105 (£924; £461; £400; £400; £400) Stalls Low

Form RPR
6313 1 **Zefferino**[21] 7609 5-9-3 61 (t) GeorgeWood 5 70
(Martin Bosley) *hld up in rr: effrt ent fnl 2f: edgd out rt and gd hdwy over 1f out: chsd ldr 1f out: r.o to ld wl ins fnl f: sn clr* **6/1**

2311 2 2 ¼ **Parknacilla (IRE)**[28] 7374 3-8-3 57 (p) AngusVilliers(7) 7 60
(Henry Spiller) *dwlt and rousted along leaving stalls: hld up towards rr: effrt and hdwy over 1f out: nt clr run and swtchd rt 1f out: str run ins fnl f to snatch 2nd last strides: no threat to wnr (jockey said filly was denied a clear run)* **4/1[2]**

0024 3 nk **My Amigo**[13] 7875 6-9-7 65 (p) HollieDoyle 3 68+
(Marjorie Fife) *wnt rt leaving stalls: chsd ldr: rdn and ev ch over 2f out: led over 1f out: sn drvn: hdd wl ins fnl f: no ex and lost 2nd last strides (jockey said gelding had jumped right-handed)* **3/1[1]**

4460 4 ¾ **Beepeecee**[190] 1675 5-9-5 63 ShaneKelly 6 65
(Thomas Gallagher) *in tch in midfield: swtchd rt and effrt to chse ldrs over 1f out: kpt on same pce ins fnl f* **33/1**

5106 5 nk **Sea Battle (FR)**[10] 7973 3-8-13 65 RayDawson(5) 2 65
(Jane Chapple-Hyam) *uns rdr on way to post who then led him to post: in tch in midfield: effrt over 2f out: kpt on same pce u.p ins fnl f* **8/1**

4530 6 1 ½ **Toybox**[29] 7343 3-9-1 62 (p) RobHornby 10 58
(Jonathan Portman) *hld up in tch towards rr: nt clr run over 1f out: gap opened and effrt jst ins fnl f: no imp 100yds out: wknd towards fin* **12/1**

233 7 3 ½ **Harry Beau**[50] 6602 5-9-3 61 (vt) HarryBentley 12 50
(David Evans) *chsd ldrs: 4th and drvn over 2f out: unable qck over 1f out: wknd ins fnl f* **16/1**

0043 8 ¾ **Letsbe Avenue (IRE)**[36] 7084 4-9-7 65 (b) SeanLevey 4 53
(Richard Hannon) *dwlt: sn swtchd lft and hdwy to chse ldrs after 1f out: 3rd and drvn over 2f out: unable qck over 1f out: wknd ins fnl f* **9/2[3]**

3246 9 1 **Ifton**[26] 7460 3-9-0 61 RossaRyan 8 45
(Ruth Carr) *hld up in tch in midfield: c wd and effrt over 1f out: sn hung lft and no hdwy: wknd ins fnl f* **7/1**

000 10 shd **Gennaro (IRE)**[35] 7129 3-8-8 58 (tp[1]) GabrieleMalune(3) 1 42
(Ivan Furtado) *taken down early: led: rdn and hdd over 1f out: no ex and lost 2nd 1f out: sn wknd* **22/1**

-000 11 5 **Sunvisor (IRE)**[26] 7460 3-9-1 62 TomMarquand 13 35
(William Muir) *a in rr: rdn over 2f out: no prog and sn outpcd: wl bhd fnl f* **25/1**

2015 12 hd **Blessed To Empress (IRE)**[45] 6795 4-9-3 66 (v) SeanKirrane(5) 9 39
(Amy Murphy) *in tch in midfield: no hdwy u.p and leaned on over 1f out: wknd ins fnl f* **22/1**

1m 38.94s (-0.96) **Going Correction** -0.05s/f (Stan)
WFA 3 from 4yo+ 3lb 12 Ran SP% 130.1
Speed ratings (Par 101): **102,99,99,98,98 96,93,92,91,91 86,86**
CSF £32.01 CT £91.77 TOTE £7.90: £2.30, £1.50, £1.70; EX 50.70 Trifecta £138.90.
Owner John Carey **Bred** Saleh Al Homaizi & Imad Al Sagar **Trained** Chalfont St Giles, Bucks
■ Stewards' Enquiry : Ray Dawson seven-day ban: used whip above permitted level (Oct 31, Nov 1-2, 4-7)

FOCUS
A modest event, in which being held up proved to be beneficial. The winner is edging back towards last year's best.

8292 CHRISTMAS PARTIES HERE H'CAP 2m (P)
8:30 (8:32) (Class 6) (0-60,68) 3-Y-O £3,105 (£924; £461; £400; £400) Stalls Low

Form RPR
5031 1 **Jeweller**[9] 7998 3-10-7 68 6ex (b) JimCrowley 5 78+
(Sir Michael Stoute) *mde all: pushed along ent fnl 2f: rdn over 1f out: asserted u.p 1f out: styd on wl* **1/6[1]**

00-0 2 3 ¾ **Que Quieres (USA)**[24] 7518 3-9-1 48 TomMarquand 2 51
(Simon Dow) *stdd s: t.k.h: hld up in rr: effrt 3f out: c wd wl over 1f out: kpt on ins fnl f: wnt 2nd towards fin: no threat to wnr* **25/1**

-005 3 1 **Miss Swift**[26] 7450 3-8-12 45 RaulDaSilva 3 47
(Marcus Tregoning) *chsd wnr for 4f: chsd ldrs tl wnt 2nd again 3f out: sn rdn: swtchd rt over 1f out: sn hung rt and no imp: lost 2nd towards fin* **20/1**

0433 4 1 ¼ **Sibylline**[26] 7450 3-9-3 50 StevieDonohoe 4 50
(David Simcock) *hld up in tch 4th: effrt u.p over 2f out: no threat to wnr and kpt on same pce fnl f* **10/1[3]**

0562 5 46 **Fountain Of Life**[26] 7450 3-9-2 54 RayDawson(5) 1
(Philip McBride) *chsd ldrs: wnt 2nd 12f out tl 3f out: lost pl and bhd over 1f out: virtually p.u ins fnl f: t.o (trainer said gelding would be better suited by a re-application of blinkers and a stronger pace)* **6/1[2]**

3m 35.19s (5.19) **Going Correction** -0.05s/f (Stan) 5 Ran SP% 117.7
Speed ratings (Par 99): **85,83,82,82,59**
CSF £8.94 TOTE £1.10: £1.10, £8.00; EX 10.50 Trifecta £47.60.
Owner Cheveley Park Stud **Bred** Cheveley Park Stud Ltd **Trained** Newmarket, Suffolk

FOCUS
The market leader went to the front soon after the start and predictably remained there. The form's rated cautiously.
T/Plt: £76.90 to a £1 stake. Pool: £44,586.64 - 579.61 winning units T/Qpdt: £10.40 to a £1 stake. Pool: £6,464.73 - 619.11 winning units **Steve Payne**

8194 WOLVERHAMPTON (A.W) (L-H)
Thursday, October 17

OFFICIAL GOING: Tapeta: standard
Wind: Light behind Weather: Overcast

8293 HOTEL & CONFERENCING AT WOLVERHAMPTON APPRENTICE H'CAP 1m 4f 51y (Tp)
5:10 (5:10) (Class 6) (0-60,62) 3-Y-O £2,781 (£827; £413; £400; £400; £400) Stalls Low

Form RPR
5532 1 **Guroor**[3] 8200 3-9-2 62 StefanoCherchi(7) 6 74
(Marco Botti) *hld up in tch: shkn up to ld over 1f out: rdn clr ins fnl f: comf* **13/8[1]**

01 2 5 **Charlie Arthur (IRE)**[19] 7685 3-9-9 62 FinleyMarsh 1 66
(Richard Hughes) *chsd ldr over 6f: remained handy: rdn over 1f out: wnt 2nd again ins fnl f: styd on same pce* **9/2[2]**

245 3 ¾ **Sinndarella (IRE)**[15] 7818 3-8-3 47 (p) TobyEley(5) 9 50
(Sarah Hollinshead) *hld up: racd keenly: hdwy over 2f out: rdn and hung lft over 1f out: styd on to go 3rd wl ins fnl f (jockey said filly ran too free)* **16/1**

3314 4 1 ¾ **Hooflepuff (IRE)**[27] 7415 3-9-2 60 (p w) HarryRussell(5) 2 60
(Brian Ellison) *chsd ldrs: lost pl over 5f out: hdwy over 2f out: rdn over 1f out: hung lft and styd on same pce fnl f* **9/2[2]**

0520 5 ¾ **Waterproof**[9] 8000 3-8-3 49 (p) GavinAshton(7) 8 48
(Shaun Keightley) *s.i.s: hld up: hdwy on outer over 5f out: chsd ldr over 2f out: rdn and ev ch over 1f out: sn hung lft: wknd ins fnl f* **9/1[3]**

3 6 ½ **Zamani (GER)**[9] 7984 3-9-6 62 PoppyBridgwater(3) 5 60
(David Bridgwater) *chsd ldrs: wnt 2bd over 5f out: led over 3f out: rdn and hdd over 1f out: wknd ins fnl f* **9/2[2]**

-400 7 11 **Swerved (IRE)**[128] 3708 3-9-1 54 BenRobinson 4 34
(Ollie Pears) *hld up: rdn over 3f out: wknd over 2f out* **25/1**

4060 8 19 **Riverina**[24] 7520 3-8-4 46 (b) TheodoreLadd(3) 10
(Harry Dunlop) *s.i.s: hld up: wknd 4f out* **33/1**

5 9 4 **Quare Lucky (IRE)**[30] 7295 3-8-13 52 (p[1]) WilliamCox 3
(Mark Loughnane) *led over 8f: rdn and wknd over 2f out (jockey said filly hung right throughout)* **50/1**

2m 40.4s (-0.40) **Going Correction** -0.15s/f (Stan) 9 Ran SP% 117.3
Speed ratings (Par 99): **95,91,91,90,89 89,81,69,66**
CSF £9.10 CT £86.17 TOTE £2.20: £1.10, £1.40, £2.60; EX 9.60 Trifecta £84.60.
Owner Fabfive **Bred** Essafinaat Ltd **Trained** Newmarket, Suffolk

FOCUS
A comfortable winner of this moderate event, which took 5.40sec longer than standard. This was a step up on her win here last week.

8294 GRAND THEATRE NOVICE STKS 1m 142y (Tp)
5:45 (5:46) (Class 5) 3-Y-O+ £3,428 (£1,020; £509; £254) Stalls Low

Form RPR
1- 1 **Dawaam (USA)**[331] 9165 3-9-9 0 DaneO'Neill 2 100+
(Owen Burrows) *s.i.s: hdwy over 5f out: nt clr run and swtchd lft over 1f out: swtchd rt 1f out: shkn up and qcknd to ld ins fnl f: r.o wl: impressive* **1/1[1]**

1 2 2 ¾ **Nabeyla**[240] 795 3-9-4 0 JackMitchell 11 82
(Roger Varian) *sn led: rdn over 1f out: hdd ins fnl f: sn outpcd* **7/2[3]**

32 3 shd **Informed Front (USA)**[22] 7572 3-9-2 0 (t) RobertHavlin 3 80
(John Gosden) *chsd ldrs: rdn over 1f out: styd on same pce ins fnl f* **5/2[2]**

03 4 2 ¼ **Fields Of Dreams**[178] 1984 3-9-2 0 JasonWatson 10 75
(Roger Charlton) *hld up: shkn up and swtchd rt over 2f out: hdwy and edgd lft over 1f out: nt rch ldrs* **50/1**

13 **5** 1 **Perfect Number**[15] 7822 3-9-4 0 .... JosephineGordon 9 74
(Saeed bin Suroor) *s.i.s: hdwy on outer over 6f out: rdn over 1f out: no ex ins fnl f (jockey said filly suffered interference shortly after leaving stalls)* **8/1**

6 3 1/4 **Wemyss Ware (IRE)** 3-9-2 0 .... PJMcDonald 1 65
(Sir Michael Stoute) *s.i.s: pushed along in rr: styd on ins fnl f: nvr nrr* **20/1**

7 nk **Archon** 3-9-2 0 .... NathanEvans 8 64
(Michael Easterby) *racd keenly: wnt 2nd over 7f out tl rdn over 1f out: wknd ins fnl f* **80/1**

2/3- **8** 1 1/2 **Profound (IRE)**[371] 8141 4-9-6 80 .... TomQueally 6 61
(Mark Usher) *hld up: nvr on terms* **66/1**

03- **9** 1/2 **Clooney**[468] 4617 4-8-13 0 .... MorganCole(7) 5 60
(Lydia Pearce) *hld up: shkn up over 1f out: n.d* **150/1**

50 **10** 4 1/2 **Calima Calling (IRE)**[33] 7190 3-8-11 0 .... AlistairRawlinson 4 44
(Michael Appleby) *led early: plld hrd: lost pl 7f out: n.d after* **100/1**

0 **11** 3 3/4 **Gms Princess**[47] 6732 3-8-11 0 .... JoeyHaynes 7 36
(Sarah Hollinshead) *chsd ldrs: rdn over 3f out: wknd over 1f out* **100/1**

1m 48.72s (-1.38) **Going Correction** -0.15s/f (Stan)
WFA 3 from 4yo 4lb **11** Ran SP% **124.0**
Speed ratings (Par 103): **100,97,97,95,94 91,91,90,89,85 82**
CSF £5.24 TOTE £2.00: £1.10, £1.10, £1.20; EX 6.80 Trifecta £13.90.
Owner Hamdan Al Maktoum **Bred** Baumann Stables, E Bradley & A Sones **Trained** Lambourn, Berks

FOCUS
A smart performance from the favourite, and a race that could produce a few winners.

8295 RENAULT TRUCKS MIDLANDS CLASSIFIED STKS 7f 36y (Tp)
6:15 (6:17) (Class 6) 3-Y-O+
£2,781 (£827; £413; £400; £400; £400) **Stalls** High

Form RPR

4400 **1** **So Claire**[56] 6361 3-8-11 45 .... JaneElliott(3) 12 50
(William Muir) *hld up in tch on outer: rdn over 1f out: r.o to ld nr fin* **16/1**

0045 **2** nk **Searanger (USA)**[7] 8068 6-9-2 47 ....(vt) PJMcDonald 11 50
(Rebecca Menzies) *s.s: hld up: gd hdwy fnl f: sn rdn: r.o wl to go 2nd post: nt quite rch wnr (jockey said gelding was slowly away)* **9/2**[2]

4000 **3** nk **The King's Steed**[101] 4733 6-9-2 50 ....(bt) JasonWatson 9 49
(Shaun Lycett) *chsd ldrs: pushed along 1/2-way: rdn to ld ins fnl f: hdd nr fin* **11/4**[1]

66P0 **4** 1 1/4 **Caesonia**[31] 7282 3-9-0 50 ....(p[1]) BenCurtis 10 45
(Charles Hills) *chsd ldr tl led over 2f out: rdn and hdd ins fnl f: no ex towards fin* **16/1**

0036 **5** shd **Dodgy Bob**[5] 8117 6-9-2 48 ....(v) NathanEvans 3 46
(Michael Mullineaux) *pushed along to chse ldrs: lost pl 1/2-way: swtchd rt and hdwy on outer over 2f out: rdn over 1f out: styd on* **6/1**

0005 **6** 1 1/2 **Kyllachy Castle**[57] 6338 3-9-0 45 .... CamHardie 5 41
(Lynn Siddall) *hld up: hdwy over 1f out: nt rch ldrs* **12/1**

0006 **7** 2 1/4 **Manzoni**[14] 7838 3-9-0 47 ....(p[1]) RobbieDowney 1 36
(Mohamed Moubarak) *chsd ldrs: rdn 1/2-way: wknd wl ins fnl f* **8/1**

6502 **8** 1 1/2 **Prince Consort (IRE)**[19] 7681 4-9-2 48 ....(b) TomEaves 6 33
(John Wainwright) *chsd ldrs: rdn over 2f out: wknd ins fnl f* **16/1**

05-0 **9** 1 1/2 **Badger Berry**[28] 7371 3-8-9 45 ....(e) PoppyBridgwater(5) 2 29
(Nick Littmoden) *hld up: racd keenly: hdwy whn nt clr run over 1f out: nt trble ldrs* **25/1**

4600 **10** 1 3/4 **Picks Pinta**[10] 7962 8-9-2 47 ....(p) JamieGormley 7 25
(John David Riches) *s.s: outpcd (jockey said gelding ran flat)* **18/1**

000 **11** 1 1/2 **Jazzameer**[80] 5494 4-9-2 31 .... JoeyHaynes 8 21
(Debbie Hughes) *hld up: rdn 1/2-way: a in rr* **66/1**

0040 **12** 3 1/2 **Cuban Spirit**[42] 6885 4-8-11 49 .... SeamusCronin(5) 4 12
(Lee Carter) *led over 4f: edgd lft over 1f out: wknd fnl f* **11/2**[3]

1m 28.59s (-0.21) **Going Correction** -0.15s/f (Stan)
WFA 3 from 4yo+ 2lb **12** Ran SP% **121.6**
Speed ratings (Par 101): **95,94,94,92,92 91,88,86,85,83 81,77**
CSF £88.84 TOTE £28.90: £5.90, £1.70, £1.10; EX 120.80 Trifecta £1528.80.
Owner Foursome Thoroughbreds **Bred** Foursome Thoroughbreds **Trained** Lambourn, Berks

FOCUS
They went a decent gallop in this very moderate event, which was dominated by those drawn high.

8296 WOLVERHAMPTON-RACECOURSE.CO.UK H'CAP 5f 21y (Tp)
6:45 (6:45) (Class 5) (0-70,70) 3-Y-O+
£3,428 (£1,020; £509; £400; £400; £400) **Stalls** Low

Form RPR

0653 **1** **Shepherd's Purse**[10] 7959 7-8-9 **58** ....(b[1]) JamesSullivan 3 67
(Ruth Carr) *trckd ldrs: nt clr run over 1f out: shkn up to ld ins fnl f: r.o: comf* **6/1**[3]

1360 **2** 1 1/4 **It Must Be Faith**[14] 7855 9-8-7 **59** ....(p) JaneElliott(3) 9 64
(Michael Appleby) *stdd s: hld up: hdwy and hung lft ins fnl f: r.o: nt rch wnr* **33/1**

0440 **3** 1 1/2 **Longroom**[10] 7959 7-9-1 **64** .... PhilDennis 8 63
(Noel Wilson) *w wnr tl led 2f out: rdn and hdd ins fnl f: styd on same pce* **12/1**

1214 **4** 3/4 **Knockabout Queen**[24] 7523 3-9-5 **68** .... JackMitchell 5 65
(Tony Carroll) *s.i.s: hld up: r.o ins fnl f: nt trble ldrs* **7/1**

4104 **5** 1/2 **Landing Night (IRE)**[14] 7855 7-9-3 **66** ....(bt) PJMcDonald 10 61
(Rebecca Menzies) *hld up: shkn up and swtchd rt over 1f out: r.o ins fnl f: nrst fin* **11/1**

3310 **6** 3/4 **Red Stripes (USA)**[7] 8066 7-8-10 **64** ....(b) SeamusCronin(5) 1 56
(Lisa Williamson) *led 3f: sn rdn: wknd ins fnl f* **10/1**

301 **7** hd **Hard Solution**[22] 7588 3-9-1 **67** .... HarrisonShaw(3) 4 67+
(David O'Meara) *hld up: hdwy over 1f out: nt clr run ins fnl f: n.d (jockey said gelding was denied a clear run approaching the final furlong)* **9/2**[2]

0040 **8** nk **Angel Force (IRE)**[1] 8263 4-9-2 **65** ....(b) DavidAllan 6 55
(David C Griffiths) *chsd ldrs: rdn over 1f out: wknd ins fnl f* **9/1**

5004 **9** 1/2 **Major Blue**[5] 8117 3-9-7 **70** ....(b) JasonWatson 2 59
(James Eustace) *s.i.s: hld up: hdwy over 1f out: sn rdn: wknd ins fnl f (jockey said gelding was was slowly into stride; vet said gelding had lost its right fore shoe)* **2/1**[1]

1m 0.06s (-1.84) **Going Correction** -0.15s/f (Stan) **9** Ran SP% **116.4**
Speed ratings (Par 103): **108,106,103,102,101 100,100,99,98**
CSF £173.42 CT £2301.85 TOTE £8.40: £2.20, £5.60, £5.10; EX 63.20 Trifecta £1149.00.
Owner The Chancers And Mrs R Carr **Bred** F Stribbling **Trained** Huby, N Yorks

FOCUS
A fairly modest sprint in which they went hard up front.

8297 BRITISH STALLION STUDS EBF NOVICE AUCTION STKS (PLUS 10 RACE) 6f 20y (Tp)
7:15 (7:16) (Class 4) 2-Y-O
£4,463 (£1,328; £663; £331) **Stalls** Low

Form RPR

031 **1** **Progressive Rating**[31] 7276 2-9-9 87 .... JasonWatson 6 83
(William Knight) *mde virtually all: rdn over 1f out: styd on* **11/8**[1]

1030 **2** nk **Odyssey Girl (IRE)**[32] 7247 2-9-4 75 .... LukeMorris 8 77
(Richard Spencer) *a.p: chsd wnr over 3f out: rdn and hung lft fr over 1f out: styd on u.p* **14/1**

0 **3** 3 1/4 **I'm Watching You**[35] 7113 2-9-2 0 .... TomQueally 7 65
(Ronald Harris) *hld up: hdwy over 2f out: rdn: edgd lft and no ex ins fnl f* **80/1**

432 **4** nse **Stroxx (IRE)**[33] 7179 2-9-2 75 .... DavidAllan 4 65
(Tim Easterby) *s.i.s: plld hrd and hdwy over 3f out: rdn and edgd lft over 1f out: styd on same pce fnl f (jockey said colt ran too free)* **3/1**[3]

3251 **5** 6 **Second Love (IRE)**[42] 6883 2-9-9 81 .... CliffordLee 1 60+
(K R Burke) *pushed along and prom: hmpd over 5f out: rdn and swtchd rt 2f out: wknd fnl f* **11/4**[2]

6 3 1/4 **Star Prize (IRE)** 2-8-6 0 .... FayeMcManoman(5) 9 32
(Noel Wilson) *s.i.s: nvr on terms* **100/1**

0 **7** 2 1/2 **Knockacurra (IRE)**[131] 3595 2-9-2 0 .... EdwardGreatrex 5 30
(Mark Loughnane) *chsd ldrs: lost pl over 3f out: wknd over 2f out* **100/1**

0 **8** nk **Evaporust (IRE)**[41] 6911 2-8-9 0 .... EllieMacKenzie(7) 10 29
(Mark Usher) *bhd and swtchd lft over 5f out: a in rr* **150/1**

031 **9** 1 3/4 **Sterling Stamp (IRE)**[7] 8058 2-9-2 0 .... BenCurtis 3 24+
(Paul Cole) *plld hrd: hung lft thrght: wnt 2nd over 5f out tl over 3f out: almost p.u fr over 1f out (jockey said colt hung badly left and was unrideable)* **9/2**

1m 13.46s (-1.04) **Going Correction** -0.15s/f (Stan) **9** Ran SP% **122.5**
Speed ratings (Par 97): **100,99,95,95,87 82,79,79,76**
CSF £26.16 TOTE £2.30: £1.10, £3.20, £9.80; EX 23.50 Trifecta £246.40.
Owner P Chan & A Hetherton **Bred** Peter Winkworth **Trained** Angmering, W Sussex

FOCUS
A bit of a rough race but a promising winner. The form's rated around the runner-up.

8298 SKY SPORTS RACING ON SKY 415 H'CAP 1m 4f 51y (Tp)
7:45 (7:45) (Class 5) (0-75,75) 3-Y-O+
£3,428 (£1,020; £509; £400; £400; £400) **Stalls** Low

Form RPR

6-30 **1** **Purdey's Gift**[15] 7816 3-9-3 **74** .... RobertHavlin 12 86+
(Andrew Balding) *s.i.s: hld up: hdwy on outer over 2f out: rdn: r.o to ld and hung lft wl ins fnl f* **7/1**

2235 **2** 1 1/4 **Sweet Celebration (IRE)**[20] 7650 3-8-4 **68** .... StefanoCherchi(7) 7 76
(Marco Botti) *hld up: pushed and hdwy over 3f out: rdn and ev ch wl ins fnl f: styd on same pce* **22/1**

4126 **3** nk **Iron Mike**[16] 7782 3-8-12 **69** ....(b) JoeFanning 4 76
(Keith Dalgleish) *trckd ldrs: swtchd rt 4f out: led over 3f out: rdn: edgd lft and hdd wl ins fnl f* **8/1**

0221 **4** 3/4 **Verify**[45] 6810 3-9-0 **71** .... PJMcDonald 3 77
(Ed Walker) *hld up: hdwy 1/2-way: chsd ldr over 2f out: rdn and ev ch ins fnl f: styd on same pce* **3/1**[2]

0302 **5** nk **Ned Pepper (IRE)**[72] 5778 3-9-1 **72** .... TomQueally 1 77+
(Alan King) *hld up: pushed along over 3f out: hdwy u.p over 1f out: r.o: nt rch ldrs* **9/1**

400 **6** 13 **Cafe Espresso**[22] 7575 3-9-4 **75** .... JoeyHaynes 2 60
(Chelsea Banham) *hld up: nvr on terms* **66/1**

/45- **7** hd **Adams Park**[445] 2140 4-9-5 **75** .... TheodoreLadd(5) 5 58
(Michael Appleby) *w ldr 1f: remained handy: rdn over 3f out: wknd 2f out (jockey said gelding was denied clear run approaching home turn)* **50/1**

0-22 **8** 1 3/4 **All Points West**[12] 7915 3-9-2 **73** .... LukeMorris 6 55
(Sir Mark Prescott Bt) *s.i.s: hld up: hdwy u.p over 1f out: sn edgd lft and wknd* **7/2**[3]

3120 **9** 3 3/4 **Ad Libitum**[15] 7816 4-9-2 **67** ....(p) BenCurtis 9 42
(Roger Fell) *chsd ldr over 10f out tl rdn over 3f out: wknd 2f out* **50/1**

2221 **10** 7 **Mojave**[33] 7177 3-9-4 **75** .... JasonWatson 8 39
(Roger Charlton) *led over 8f: sn rdn: wknd 2f out (jockey said gelding stopped quickly)* **5/2**[1]

150- **11** 21 **Arabian Oasis**[512] 2990 7-8-3 **61** oh4................(p) MorganCole(7) 11
(Lydia Pearce) *hld up: rdn over 4f out: wknd over 3f out* **100/1**

55-0 **12** 13 **Numero Uno**[281] 134 3-8-10 **67** .... EdwardGreatrex 10
(Tim Vaughan) *hld up: rdn over 5f out: sn wknd (jockey said gelding was never travelling)* **66/1**

2m 36.32s (-4.48) **Going Correction** -0.15s/f (Stan)
WFA 3 from 4yo+ 6lb **12** Ran SP% **121.6**
Speed ratings (Par 103): **108,107,106,106,106 97,97,96,93,89 75,66**
CSF £153.47 CT £1272.43 TOTE £6.30: £3.40, £5.10, £2.80; EX 140.30 Trifecta £1838.00.
Owner Sheikh Juma Dalmook Al Maktoum **Bred** Horizon Bloodstock Limited **Trained** Kingsclere, Hants

FOCUS
A competitive race for the grade, run no less than 4.08sec quicker than the opening Class 6 handicap. The first five finished well clear.

8299 YOUR ULTIMATE JUMPS GUIDE ON ATTHERACES.COM/JUMPS H'CAP 1m 1f 104y (Tp)
8:15 (8:16) (Class 6) (0-55,55) 3-Y-O+
£2,781 (£827; £413; £400; £400; £400) **Stalls** Low

Form RPR

3303 **1** **Pike Corner Cross (IRE)**[14] 7859 7-9-3 **50** ....(vt) CliffordLee 8 56
(David Evans) *chsd ldrs: led 2f out: rdn over 1f out: jst hld on* **4/1**[1]

0442 **2** hd **Impressionable**[12] 7909 3-9-1 **55** .... JaneElliott(3) 12 61
(William Muir) *uns rdr to post: hld up: plld hrd: hdwy on outer over 1f out: edgd lft and r.o ins fnl f: nt quite rch wnr (jockey said filly hung right)* **11/2**[2]

0445 **3** nk **Four Mile Bridge (IRE)**[15] 7817 3-9-1 **52** ....(p[1]) JosephineGordon 11 57
(Mark Usher) *wnt prom on outer after 1f: pushed along and lost pl over 6f out: hdwy on outer and edgd rt over 2f out: rdn to chse wnr over 1f out: r.o (jockey said gelding hung right)* **13/2**[3]

0203 **4** 2 1/2 **Tails I Win (CAN)**[12] 7909 3-9-2 **53** ....(h) BenCurtis 10 53
(Roger Fell) *hld up: hdwy over 1f out: sn rdn: styd on* **4/1**[1]

0405 **5** shd **Steal The Scene (IRE)**[14] 7859 7-9-7 **54** ....(tp) PJMcDonald 3 54
(Kevin Frost) *hld up in tch: rdn over 1f out: edgd lft and no ex wl ins fnl f* **10/1**

0360 **6** 2 **Duke Of Dunabar**[15] 7817 3-8-13 **50** ... JasonWatson 6 46
(Roger Teal) *chsd ldrs: rdn over 1f out: no ex ins fnl f* **17/2**
4200 **7** 3/4 **Zappiness (USA)**[30] 7318 3-9-4 **55** ... (b[1]) JackMitchell 5 50
(Peter Chapple-Hyam) *hld up in tch: rdn over 1f out: no ex* **20/1**
0560 **8** nk **Dutch Artist (IRE)**[9] 8000 7-8-9 **47** ... (p) FayeMcManoman(5) 13 41
(Nigel Tinkler) *s.i.s: hld up: styd on ins fnl f: nvr nrr* **16/1**
0010 **9** 1 1/2 **Silvington**[24] 7527 4-9-2 **49** ... (p) EdwardGreatrex 7 40
(Mark Loughnane) *hld up: rdn over 1f out: nvr on terms* **40/1**
000 **10** 5 **Bob's Girl**[29] 7335 4-8-6 **46** ... (b) AmeliaGlass(7) 4 28
(Michael Mullineaux) *led: hung rt over 6f out: hdd 2f out: wknd fnl f* **50/1**
1500 **11** hd **Sumner Beach**[28] 7385 5-9-6 **53** ... BenRobinson 9 35
(Brian Ellison) *s.i.s: hld up: a in rr (jockey said gelding was denied a clear run between 2f and 1f out)* **16/1**
0003 **12** 1 1/4 **Final Attack (IRE)**[14] 7857 8-8-12 **48** ... (p) WilliamCox(3) 1 27
(Sarah Hollinshead) *s.i.s: hdwy 7f out: rdn and nt clr run over 1f out: sn wknd* **20/1**
6530 **13** 4 **Midnight Mood**[14] 7857 6-9-3 **50** ... (b[1]) LukeMorris 2 22
(Dominic Ffrench Davis) *prom: chsd ldr over 5f out tl rdn 2f out: wknd over 1f out: eased (jockey said mare stopped quickly)* **11/1**

1m 59.69s (-1.11) **Going Correction** -0.15s/f (Stan)
WFA 3 from 4yo+ 4lb **13** Ran SP% **122.4**
Speed ratings (Par 101): **98,97,97,95,95 93,92,92,91,86 86,85,81**
CSF £24.84 CT £144.86 TOTE £5.10: £1.70, £2.10, £2.80; EX 33.20 Trifecta £236.80.
Owner John Abbey & Emma Evans **Bred** Rockfield Farm **Trained** Pandy, Monmouths

FOCUS
Very modest form. The winner was on a fair mark on the best of this year's form.
T/Plt: £235.20 to a £1 stake. Pool: £55,125.23 - 234.33 winning units T/Qpdt: £109.40 to a £1 stake. Pool: £7,207.95 - 65.87 winning units **Colin Roberts**

8081
NEWCASTLE (A.W) (L-H)
Friday, October 18

OFFICIAL GOING: Tapeta: standard
Wind: Almost nil Weather: Dry

8300 JPS LTD H'CAP 1m 2f 42y (Tp)
5:00 (5:05) (Class 5) (0-70,70) 3-Y-O+
£3,428 (£1,020; £509; £400; £400; £400) **Stalls** High

Form RPR
2356 **1** **Kannapolis (IRE)**[37] 7074 4-9-8 **69** ... GrahamLee 2 76
(Michael Easterby) *in tch: hdwy to chse clr ldr over 2f out: hdwy to ld 1f out: sn pressed: kpt on wl towards fin* **5/1**[2]
6243 **2** 1/2 **Kilbaha Lady (IRE)**[15] 7835 5-8-13 **65** ... FayeMcManoman(5) 14 71
(Nigel Tinkler) *t.k.h early: hld up in midfield: hdwy whn nt clr run and swtchd lft over 1f out: rdn and pressed wnr ins fnl f: no ex towards fin* **4/1**[1]
1632 **3** 1/2 **Debbonair (IRE)**[18] 7756 3-9-2 **67** ... (b) KieranShoemark 6 72
(Hugo Palmer) *hld up: rdn and gd hdwy to chse ldrs over 1f out: r.o ins fnl f* **17/2**
4242 **4** 3 **Granite City Doc**[25] 7513 6-9-1 **67** ... PaulaMuir(5) 9 66
(Lucy Normile) *hld up: rdn over 2f out: hdwy over 1f out: kpt on fnl f: no imp* **13/2**
255- **5** 3/4 **Gift Of Raaj (IRE)**[423] 6394 4-9-9 **70** ... (p[1]) AndreaAtzeni 11 68
(Ivan Furtado) *pressed ldr to over 2f out: sn drvn along: outpcd fnl f* **12/1**
000 **6** 2 1/4 **Briardale (IRE)**[29] 7379 7-9-8 **69** ... (p) PJMcDonald 1 62
(James Bethell) *led: qckn clr 3f out: rdn and hdd 1f out: sn wknd* **18/1**
1400 **7** 3/4 **Trinity Star (IRE)**[21] 7643 8-9-5 **69** ... (v) SeanDavis(3) 13 61
(Karen McLintock) *s.i.s: hld up: rdn and hung lft over 2f out: kpt on fnl f: nvr able to chal* **33/1**
5020 **8** 1 **Cuban Sun**[20] 7682 3-9-3 **68** ... BarryMcHugh 7 58
(James Given) *prom: drvn along over 2f out: wknd over 1f out* **25/1**
5100 **9** 3 **Pioneering (IRE)**[3] 8237 5-9-8 **69** ... BenCurtis 4 53
(Roger Fell) *t.k.h: prom: rdn along on outside over 2f out: wknd over 1f out* **6/1**[3]
3 **10** nk **Zane Daddy (USA)**[24] 7543 3-9-4 **69** ... FrannyNorton 5 55+
(Mark Johnston) *t.k.h: hld up on ins: drvn and outpcd over 2f out: sn btn* **11/1**
2001 **11** 4 1/2 **Cold Harbour**[14] 7873 4-9-4 **65** ... (t) KieranO'Neill 10 39
(Robyn Brisland) *t.k.h: chsd ldrs tl rdn and wknd fr 2f out* **10/1**
0000 **12** 2 1/4 **Jamih**[13] 7907 4-9-7 **68** ... JamesSullivan 12 37
(Tina Jackson) *t.k.h: hld up in midfield on outside: drvn along over 2f out: sn wknd* **80/1**
4140 **13** 89 **Dutch Coed**[25] 7513 7-9-0 **64** ... RowanScott(3) 3
(Nigel Tinkler) *s.i.s: hld up: rdn over 4f out: lost tch over 3f out: t.o* **33/1**

2m 10.91s (0.51) **Going Correction** +0.125s/f (Slow)
WFA 3 from 4yo+ 4lb **13** Ran SP% **116.2**
Speed ratings (Par 103): **103,102,102,99,99 97,96,96,93,93 87,87,16**
CSF £23.72 CT £166.95 TOTE £6.50: £2.30, £1.50, £3.40; EX 30.00 Trifecta £295.30.
Owner A Stott & E Brook **Bred** Old Carhue Stud **Trained** Sheriff Hutton, N Yorks

FOCUS
A modest handicap. The winner has been rated in line with this year's form.

8301 CCF LTD H'CAP 1m 5y (Tp)
5:35 (5:38) (Class 6) (0-55,60) 3-Y-O+
£2,781 (£827; £413; £400; £400; £400) **Stalls** Centre

Form RPR
2041 **1** **Perfect Swiss**[11] 7960 3-9-9 **60** 6ex ... RachelRichardson 6 69+
(Tim Easterby) *dwlt: hld up on far side of gp: smooth hdwy over 2f out: effrt and edgd rt over 1f out: led ins fnl f: drvn out* **11/8**[1]
0332 **2** 3/4 **Troop**[11] 7956 4-9-3 **51** ... (p) FrannyNorton 5 59
(Ann Duffield) *cl up towards far side of gp: led over 2f out: rdn and edgd rt over 1f out: hdd ins fnl f: rallied: hld nr fin (jockey said gelding hung right-handed)* **3/1**[2]
5602 **3** 3 3/4 **Rebel State (IRE)**[11] 7960 6-8-8 **49** ... OwenPayton(7) 12 49
(Jedd O'Keeffe) *in tch on nr side of gp: hdwy and ev ch briefly 2f out: rdn and kpt on fnl f: nt pce of first two* **11/1**
3000 **4** 2 1/2 **Charlie's Boy (IRE)**[11] 7956 3-9-3 **54** ... PaulMulrennan 13 47
(Michael Dods) *in tch on nr side of gp: rdn and outpcd over 1f out: rallied ins fnl f: no imp* **8/1**[3]
5020 **5** 1 **Silk Mill Blue**[23] 7578 5-9-1 **49** ... PhilDennis 8 41
(Richard Whitaker) *hld up in midfield in centre of gp: effrt and rdn over 1f out: no imp fnl f* **33/1**
004 **6** hd **Dixieland (IRE)**[11] 7961 3-9-3 **54** ... SamJames 4 45
(Marjorie Fife) *hld up on far side of gp: rdn over 2f out: hdwy over 1f out: no imp fnl f* **33/1**
0000 **7** 1/2 **Deeds Not Words (IRE)**[11] 7962 8-9-2 **50** ... (p) BarryMcHugh 2 41
(Tracy Waggott) *dwlt: sn swtchd to nr side of gp: hld up: effrt and drvn along over 2f out: no further imp over 1f out* **125/1**
1344 **8** 1/2 **Gunnison**[11] 7960 3-9-0 **54** ... (p) SeanDavis(3) 14 42
(Richard Fahey) *t.k.h: midfield on nr side of gp: rdn over 2f out: outpcd over 1f out* **16/1**
0-00 **9** shd **Amood (IRE)**[23] 7581 8-9-4 **55** ... RowanScott(3) 3 44
(Simon West) *hld up in centre of gp: effrt and rdn 2f out: nvr able to chal* **66/1**
6005 **10** 1 1/4 **Irish Minister (USA)**[13] 7903 4-9-6 **54** ... (bt) PJMcDonald 11 40
(David Thompson) *dwlt: bhd on nr side of gp: drvn along 3f out: sn no imp: btn over 1f out* **33/1**
5034 **11** shd **Klipperty Klopp**[30] 7335 3-9-2 **53** ... CamHardie 10 38
(Antony Brittain) *midfield in centre of gp: drvn along 2f out: sn n.d: btn fnl f* **25/1**
0005 **12** nk **Rosin Box (IRE)**[17] 7783 6-9-1 **49** ... DuranFentiman 9 35
(Tristan Davidson) *in tch in centre of gp: rdn over 2f out: wknd over 1f out (jockey said mare ran too free)* **25/1**
0530 **13** 1 **With Approval (IRE)**[15] 7859 7-9-0 **51** ... GemmaTutty(3) 7 34
(Karen Tutty) *led in centre of gp to over 2f out: rdn and wknd over 1f out* **14/1**
3026 **14** 3 3/4 **Clement (IRE)**[164] 2513 9-9-2 **53** ... (p) JaneElliott(3) 1 28
(Marjorie Fife) *t.k.h: hld up on far side of gp: rdn and struggling over 2f out: sn btn (jockey said gelding ran too free)* **80/1**

1m 41.5s (2.90) **Going Correction** +0.125s/f (Slow)
WFA 3 from 4yo+ 3lb **14** Ran SP% **119.1**
Speed ratings (Par 101): **90,89,85,83,82 81,81,80,80,79 79,79,78,74**
CSF £4.58 CT £33.17 TOTE £1.80: £1.30, £1.30, £3.00; EX 5.80 Trifecta £46.10.
Owner Craig Wilson & Partner **Bred** Mildmay Bloodstock Ltd **Trained** Great Habton, N Yorks

FOCUS
They went fairly steady early on, but the big two in the market still came clear.

8302 JPS STEEL FRAMES NOVICE AUCTION STKS 7f 14y (Tp)
6:05 (6:08) (Class 6) 2-Y-O
£2,781 (£827; £413; £206) **Stalls** Centre

Form RPR
66 **1** **Wadi Al Salaam (IRE)**[27] 7437 2-9-2 0 ... DuranFentiman 5 74
(Tim Easterby) *in tch in centre of gp: hdwy to press ldr over 1f out: slt ld ins fnl f: hld on wl cl home* **40/1**
1 **2** shd **Zabeel Champion**[34] 7174 2-9-9 0 ... FrannyNorton 6 81
(Mark Johnston) *led in centre of gp: rdn 2f out: edgd lft and hdd ins fnl f: styd upsides wnr: kpt on: jst hld* **8/11**[1]
50 **3** 2 3/4 **Master Spy (IRE)**[9] 8028 2-9-2 0 ... BenCurtis 3 67
(Paul Cole) *hld up in midfield on far side of gp: rdn and hdwy 2f out: kpt on ins fnl f: nt rch first two* **18/1**
2223 **4** 1/2 **River Cam**[31] 7308 2-8-11 71 ... PJMcDonald 2 61
(James Tate) *cl up towards far side of gp: effrt and rdn over 1f out: ev ch briefly ent fnl f: outpcd last 100yds* **10/3**[2]
04 **5** 1 1/4 **Got The T Shirt**[13] 7902 2-8-11 0 ... BenSanderson(5) 1 63
(Keith Dalgleish) *in tch on far side of gp: effrt and rdn over 1f out: outpcd ins fnl f* **11/1**
04 **6** nk **Itwouldberudenotto**[11] 7958 2-9-2 0 ... PaulHanagan 11 62
(Richard Fahey) *hld up on nr side of gp: rdn and hdwy 2f out: no imp ins fnl f* **28/1**
0 **7** hd **Binyon**[13] 7902 2-9-2 0 ... BenRobinson 4 62
(David Barron) *hld up in centre of gp: hdwy and prom wl over 1f out: wknd ins fnl f* **80/1**
3031 **8** 1 1/4 **Never In Red (IRE)**[32] 7269 2-9-9 72 ... KieranO'Neill 7 65
(Robyn Brisland) *plld hrd: cl up in centre of gp: ev ch over 2f out to over 1f out: wknd fnl f* **8/1**[3]
60 **9** hd **Top Flight Cool**[32] 7285 2-9-2 0 ... PhilDennis 8 58
(Tim Easterby) *dwlt: plld hrd: hld up in centre of gp: rdn 2f out: sn n.d: btn fnl f* **50/1**
00 **10** 5 **Peerless Percy (IRE)**[23] 7586 2-9-2 0 ... PaulMulrennan 9 45
(Michael Dods) *hld up in centre of gp: drvn along and outpcd over 2f out: btn over 1f out* **50/1**
0 **11** 9 **Villa Paloma (IRE)**[11] 7958 2-8-11 0 ... AndreaAtzeni 10 18
(Mark Johnston) *prom on nr side of gp: rdn and outpcd over 2f out: btn over 1f out* **33/1**
06 **12** 1/2 **Copperlight (IRE)**[28] 7416 2-9-2 0 ... AndrewMullen 13 22
(Ben Haslam) *dwlt: bhd on nr side of gp: struggling 3f out: sn wknd* **125/1**
0 **13** 3 1/2 **Charmore**[11] 7958 2-8-11 0 ... ShaneGray 12 8
(Ann Duffield) *bhd on nr side of gp: struggling over 2f out: sn wknd* **250/1**

1m 28.65s (2.45) **Going Correction** +0.125s/f (Slow) **13** Ran SP% **120.9**
Speed ratings (Par 93): **91,90,87,87,85 85,85,83,83,77 67,66,62**
CSF £70.64 TOTE £60.80: £8.50, £1.10, £3.90; EX 177.50 Trifecta £1479.20.
Owner E A Al Afoo **Bred** John Cullinan **Trained** Great Habton, N Yorks

FOCUS
A bit of a surprise here, but there looked no fluke about it.

8303 ROCKFON FILLIES' NURSERY H'CAP 7f 14y (Tp)
6:35 (6:37) (Class 4) (0-80,82) 2-Y-O
£4,463 (£1,328; £663; £400; £400; £400) **Stalls** Centre

Form RPR
2035 **1** **Onassis (IRE)**[20] 7696 2-9-4 **75** ... HayleyTurner 1 81+
(Charlie Fellowes) *hld up: shkn up and hdwy over 1f out: rdn to ld ins fnl f: pushed out: comf* **15/8**[1]
2544 **2** 2 **African Swift (USA)**[24] 7548 2-9-3 **74** ... FrannyNorton 3 75
(Mark Johnston) *t.k.h early: led: rdn 2f out: hdd ins fnl f: kpt on: nt pce of wnr* **11/2**
410 **3** 1 1/2 **Angel Of Delight (IRE)**[55] 6444 2-9-11 **82** ... BenCurtis 4 79
(Hugo Palmer) *dwlt: sn trcking ldrs: edgd rt and wnt 2nd briefly wl over 1f out: rdn and one pce ins fnl f* **9/2**[3]
5364 **4** 1 3/4 **Charming Spirit (IRE)**[25] 7522 2-9-3 **74** ... AndreaAtzeni 7 67
(Roger Varian) *hld up in tch: effrt and drvn along 2f out: no imp appr fnl f* **7/2**[2]
5103 **5** 6 **Red Treble**[27] 7438 2-9-5 **76** ... (h) CamHardie 8 54
(Rebecca Menzies) *stdd s: t.k.h: hld up: hdwy over 2f out: rdn and hung rt over 1f out: sn wknd (jockey said filly hung right-handed under pressure)* **12/1**
6140 **6** 3 3/4 **Miss Villanelle**[45] 6833 2-9-6 **77** ... KieranShoemark 2 46
(Charles Hills) *t.k.h: pressed ldr: drvn over 2f out: wknd wl over 1f out* **16/1**

5564 **7** *nk* **Bye Bye Euro (IRE)**[27] 7429 2-8-6 **63**.............................. ShaneGray 5 31
(Keith Dalgleish) *prom tl rdn and wknd fr 2f out* **12/1**

1m 27.41s (1.21) **Going Correction** +0.125s/f (Slow) **7** Ran SP% **111.8**
Speed ratings (Par 94): **98,95,94,92,85 80,80**
CSF £12.01 CT £38.88 TOTE £2.50: £2.20, £2.10; EX 13.20 Trifecta £73.30.
Owner Triermore Stud & The Hon P Stanley **Bred** C O P Hanbury **Trained** Newmarket, Suffolk

FOCUS
A fair fillies' nursery.

8304 JPS CEILINGS & PARTITIONS H'CAP 6f (Tp)

7:05 (7:05) (Class 5) (0-75,75) 3-Y-O+
£3,428 (£1,020; £509; £400; £400; £400) **Stalls** Centre

Form RPR

512 **1** **Futuristic (IRE)**[21] 7655 3-9-6 **75**.............................. PJMcDonald 1 90+
(James Tate) *cl up: rdn to ld over 1f out: clr ins fnl f: kpt on strly* **2/1**[1]

0224 **2** *2 ¼* **Epeius (IRE)**[21] 7656 6-9-5 **73**..............................(v) AndrewMullen 9 79
(Ben Haslam) *wnt lft s: in tch: effrt and rdn 2f out: chsd (clr) wnr ins fnl f: r.o* **8/1**[3]

6000 **3** *½* **Bugler Bob (IRE)**[29] 7383 3-9-1 **70**.............................. BenCurtis 10 74
(John Quinn) *in tch: rdn over 2f out: kpt on fnl f: nrst fin* **14/1**

6203 **4** *hd* **Three Card Trick**[24] 7552 3-9-3 **72**.............................. TomEaves 8 75
(Kevin Ryan) *carried lft and bmpd s: led: rdn and hdd over 1f out: no ex and lost two pls ins fnl f* **16/1**

4045 **5** *½* **Ascended (IRE)**[9] 8025 3-9-6 **75**.............................. AndreaAtzeni 5 77+
(William Haggas) *bdly hmpd s: bhd: rdn and hdwy over 2f out: no further imp ins fnl f* **15/2**[2]

4604 **6** *2* **Upstaging**[28] 7402 7-9-7 **75**..............................(p) RossaRyan 12 70
(Noel Wilson) *t.k.h: hld up: rdn and hdwy over 1f out: kpt on fnl f* **20/1**

0006 **7** *1 ¼* **Nibras Again**[18] 7771 5-9-7 **75**.............................. PaulMulrennan 13 66
(Paul Midgley) *plld hrd: cl up: rdn along 2f out: wknd ins fnl f* **14/1**

0142 **8** *1 ¼* **Great Shout (IRE)**[30] 7345 3-9-2 **71**..............................(t) GeorgeWood 11 58+
(Amy Murphy) *rrd s: sn stmbld: hld up: rdn over 2f out: no imp over 1f out (jockey said filly reared as the stalls opened and was slowly away)* **8/1**[3]

5106 **9** *hd* **Oriental Lilly**[23] 7583 5-8-9 **70**..............................(p) CoreyMadden(7) 2 57
(Jim Goldie) *dwlt: bhd: rdn and outpcd over 2f out: n.d after* **25/1**

5000 **10** *3 ¾* **Ower Fly**[16] 7820 6-9-0 **71**.............................. JaneElliott(3) 7 46
(Ruth Carr) *carried lft and bmpd s: bhd: struggling over 2f out: nvr on terms (jockey said gelding suffered interference at the start)* **66/1**

0000 **11** *3 ½* **Drogon (IRE)**[27] 7435 3-9-6 **75**.............................. PaulHanagan 4 39
(Jackie Stephen) *midfield: drvn along over 2f out: wknd wl over 1f out* **40/1**

205 **12** *3 ½* **Somewhere Secret**[18] 7766 5-9-1 **69**..............................(p) JackGarritty 6 21+
(Michael Mullineaux) *bdly hmpd s: bhd: struggling over 2f out: sn btn (jockey said gelding suffered interference at the start)* **18/1**

0502 **13** *17* **Final Go**[21] 7656 4-9-4 **72**.............................. SamJames 3
(Grant Tuer) *in tch: rdn over 2f out: sn wknd: t.o (jockey said gelding moved poorly in the final 2f)* **15/2**[2]

1m 12.0s (-0.50) **Going Correction** +0.125s/f (Slow)
WFA 3 from 4yo+ 1lb **13** Ran SP% **116.1**
Speed ratings (Par 103): **108,105,104,104,103 100,99,97,97,92 87,82,60**
CSF £16.22 CT £183.15 TOTE £2.90: £1.20, £2.60, £3.60; EX 24.90 Trifecta £250.40.
Owner Saeed Manana **Bred** Rabbah Bloodstock Limited **Trained** Newmarket, Suffolk

FOCUS
This went the way of the least exposed runner in the line-up. The runner-up helps set the standard.

8305 HADLEY STEEL FRAMING H'CAP 1m 5y (Tp)

7:35 (7:37) (Class 5) (0-75,77) 3-Y-O+
£3,428 (£1,020; £509; £400; £400; £400) **Stalls** Centre

Form RPR

6221 **1** **Home Before Dusk**[7] 8087 4-9-5 **77** 5ex..............................(p) BenSanderson(5) 3 91+
(Keith Dalgleish) *dwlt: hld up on far side of gp: hdwy over 2f out: rdn and led ins fnl f: sn clr* **5/2**[1]

0-00 **2** *3 ¼* **La Rav (IRE)**[29] 7362 5-9-8 **75**.............................. NathanEvans 13 81
(Michael Easterby) *hld up on nr side of gp: smooth hdwy to ld 2f out: rdn and hdd ins fnl f: kpt on same pce* **7/1**[3]

5-00 **3** *nk* **Elusive Heights (IRE)**[29] 7363 6-9-1 **68**.............................. PaulMulrennan 14 73
(Roger Fell) *t.k.h: hld up in centre of gp: rdn and hdwy over 1f out: kpt on fnl f: nt pce to chal* **14/1**

664 **4** *nk* **Plunger**[15] 7839 4-9-8 **75**..............................(p) PJMcDonald 10 79
(Paul Cole) *led in centre of gp: rdn and hdd over 1f out: kpt on same pce ins fnl f* **11/2**[2]

2103 **4** *dht* **Valley Of Fire**[24] 7540 7-9-1 **68**..............................(p) LewisEdmunds 7 72
(Les Eyre) *midfield in centre of gp: hdwy and prom over 1f out: rdn and one pce ins fnl f* **33/1**

0030 **6** *11* **Destroyer**[7] 8087 6-9-0 **67**.............................. AndrewMullen 4 46
(Tom Tate) *cl up in centre of gp: rdn over 2f out: wknd over 1f out* **20/1**

2030 **7** *nk* **Ideal Candy (IRE)**[32] 7288 4-9-0 **70**..............................(h) GemmaTutty(3) 11 48
(Karen Tutty) *t.k.h: hld up on nr side of gp: rdn over 2f out: hung lft and sn struggling* **100/1**

5312 **8** *nse* **Lucky Number**[52] 6558 3-9-2 **75**.............................. GeorgiaCox(3) 6 52
(William Haggas) *t.k.h: cl up in centre of gp: drvn along over 2f out: wknd over 1f out* **7/1**[3]

2422 **9** *¾* **Zoravan (USA)**[21] 7652 6-8-9 **67**..............................(b) AndrewBreslin(5) 12 43
(Keith Dalgleish) *missed break and sn swtchd lft: hld up on far side of gp: rdn and outpcd over 2f out: sn btn* **28/1**

0052 **10** *shd* **Elixsoft (IRE)**[23] 7583 4-9-7 **74**..............................(p) BenCurtis 1 50
(Roger Fell) *midfield on far side of gp: drvn along over 2f out: sn wknd* **28/1**

3306 **11** *4 ½* **Amber Spark (IRE)**[13] 7901 3-9-5 **75**.............................. PaulHanagan 9 40
(Richard Fahey) *hld up on far side of gp: drvn and outpcd 3f out: sn btn* **10/1**

2454 **12** *2 ½* **Nooshin**[23] 7583 3-9-3 **73**..............................(t) AndreaAtzeni 5 32
(Amy Murphy) *dwlt: sn prom on far side of gp: drvn and outpcd over 2f out: wknd wl over 1f out* **12/1**

2211 **13** *10* **Dubai Acclaim (IRE)**[24] 7540 4-9-5 **75**..............................(p) SeanDavis(3) 8 12
(Richard Fahey) *hld up on nr side of gp: drvn and struggling wl over 2f out: sn wknd (jockey could offer no explanation for the gelding's performance)* **12/1**

1230 **14** *hd* **Moongazer**[94] 5030 3-9-4 **74**.............................. KieranShoemark 2 10
(Charles Hills) *hld up in midfield towards centre of gp: rdn and struggling wl over 2f out: sn btn* **33/1**

1m 38.53s (-0.07) **Going Correction** +0.125s/f (Slow)
WFA 3 from 4yo+ 3lb **14** Ran SP% **118.6**
Speed ratings (Par 103): **105,101,101,101,101 90,89,89,89,88 84,81,71,71**
CSF £17.50 CT £213.57 TOTE £3.10: £1.20, £3.50, £5.60; EX 34.50 Trifecta £355.70.
Owner G R Leckie **Bred** G L S Partnership **Trained** Carluke, S Lanarks

FOCUS
This was run to suit those held up off the pace and the winner posted another pb.

8306 JPS FLOORING H'CAP 7f 14y (Tp)

8:05 (8:07) (Class 6) (0-60,60) 3-Y-O+
£2,781 (£827; £413; £400; £400; £400) **Stalls** Centre

Form RPR

3060 **1** **Cameo Star (IRE)**[3] 8234 4-9-4 **60**..............................(p) SeanDavis(3) 13 68
(Richard Fahey) *dwlt: hld up on nr side of gp: led over 1f out: edgd lft ins fnl f: drvn out* **16/1**

4003 **2** *1 ¾* **Uncle Charlie (IRE)**[27] 7444 5-9-6 **59**.............................. FrannyNorton 4 63
(Ann Duffield) *t.k.h: hld up in centre of gp: hdwy gng wl whn nt clr run over 2f out to over 1f out: effrt and chsd wnr ins fnl f: r.o* **11/2**[2]

0012 **3** *1* **Jack Randall**[52] 6575 3-9-3 **58**.............................. DuranFentiman 14 59
(Tim Easterby) *t.k.h: in tch on nr side of gp: effrt and rdn wl over 1f out: kpt on ins fnl f* **10/1**

000 **4** *½* **Ishebayorgrey (IRE)**[16] 7823 7-9-4 **57**.............................. JamieGormley 2 57
(Iain Jardine) *t.k.h: prom on far side of gp: hdwy and chsd wnr over 1f out to ins fnl f: edgd rt and sn no ex* **25/1**

0021 **5** *hd* **Billy Wedge**[11] 7961 4-9-4 **57** 5ex.............................. BarryMcHugh 5 57
(Tracy Waggott) *dwlt: t.k.h and swtchd rt s: hld up in centre of gp: swtchd lft wl over 2f out: effrt and rdn over 1f out: one pce ins fnl f* **9/2**[1]

1140 **6** *shd* **Dawn Breaking**[14] 7875 4-9-4 **57**.............................. PhilDennis 12 57
(Richard Whitaker) *hld up towards nr side of gp: rdn and angled rt over 1f out: kpt on fnl f: nvr able to chal* **12/1**

0162 **7** *1 ¼* **Peachey Carnehan**[7] 8083 5-9-4 **57**..............................(v) JamesSullivan 7 55
(Michael Mullineaux) *midfield in centre of gp: rdn whn n.m.r briefly over 1f out: sn outpcd: n.d after* **6/1**[3]

0605 **8** *1* **Majdool (IRE)**[55] 6441 6-9-4 **57**..............................(e) DavidNolan 3 51
(Noel Wilson) *hld up on far side of gp: rdn over 2f out: hdwy and in tch over 1f out: wknd ins fnl f* **14/1**

0333 **9** *½* **Gorgeous General**[21] 7651 4-9-5 **58**.............................. PaulMulrennan 1 51
(Lawrence Mullaney) *prom on far side of gp: rdn over 2f out: wknd over 1f out* **20/1**

4266 **10** *1 ½* **Tobeeornottobee**[10] 8008 3-8-11 **59**.............................. JessicaAnderson(7) 10 47
(Declan Carroll) *t.k.h: cl up on nr side of gp: drvn and ev ch briefly wl over 1f out: wknd fnl f* **10/1**

2120 **11** *2 ½* **Sophia Maria**[16] 7823 3-9-5 **60**..............................(p) PJMcDonald 8 42
(James Bethell) *cl up in centre of gp: hdwy and overall ldr over 2f out: rdn and hdd over 1f out: wknd fnl f* **8/1**

6601 **12** *½* **Christmas Night**[27] 7443 4-9-1 **57**.............................. HarrisonShaw(3) 6 38
(Ollie Pears) *cl up towards centre of gp: drvn and outpcd over 2f out: sn wknd* **16/1**

13 *2 ½* **Hummingbird (IRE)**[60] 6295 3-8-11 **57**.............................. ThomasGreatrex(5) 9 31
(David Loughnane) *led in centre of gp to over 2f out: rdn and wknd over 1f out* **50/1**

0400 **14** *2 ¾* **Dirchill (IRE)**[42] 6945 5-9-5 **58**..............................(b) AndrewMullen 11 26
(David Thompson) *t.k.h: sn swtchd to r alone next to stands' rail: overall ldr to over 2f out: sn rdn and wknd (jockey said gelding ran too free)* **66/1**

1m 27.67s (1.47) **Going Correction** +0.125s/f (Slow)
WFA 3 from 4yo+ 2lb **14** Ran SP% **115.3**
Speed ratings (Par 101): **96,94,92,92,92 91,90,89,88,87 84,83,80,77**
CSF £94.32 CT £961.66 TOTE £17.80: £6.80, £2.40, £3.50; EX 117.40 Trifecta £2401.80.
Owner Let's Go Racing 2 **Bred** Mrs P O'Rourke **Trained** Musley Bank, N Yorks

FOCUS
An ordinary handicap.
T/Plt: £13.10 to a £1 stake. Pool £64,525.76 - winning units T/Qpdt: £8.10 to a £1 stake. Pool £7,724.39 - 699.25 winning units **Richard Young**

7902 REDCAR (L-H)

Friday, October 18

8307 Meeting Abandoned - Waterlogged Course

8293 WOLVERHAMPTON (A.W) (L-H)

Friday, October 18

OFFICIAL GOING: Tapeta: standard
Wind: breezy Weather: showers, cool

8315 HOTEL & CONFERENCING AT WOLVERHAMPTON NURSERY H'CAP 5f 21y (Tp)

5:25 (5:25) (Class 5) (0-75,76) 2-Y-O
£3,557 (£1,058; £529; £400; £400; £400) **Stalls** Low

Form RPR

5200 **1** **Get Boosting**[18] 7765 2-9-5 **71**.............................. TomMarquand 6 77
(Keith Dalgleish) *hld up: pushed along 2f out: hdwy on outer over 1f out: rdn ent fnl f: r.o wl to ld last 25yds: pushed out nr fin* **16/1**

4553 **2** *½* **Swinley (IRE)**[17] 7785 2-9-5 **71**.............................. JamesDoyle 8 75
(Richard Hughes) *chsd ldrs on outer: rdn to ld 1f out: r.o fnl f: hdd last 25yds* **10/3**[2]

4243 **3** *2 ¾* **Hot Heels**[34] 7182 2-9-10 **76**.............................. RichardKingscote 4 70
(Tom Dascombe) *racd in cl 2nd: shkn up to ld 1 1/2f out: hdd 1f out: rdn and no ex fnl f* **15/8**[1]

3405 **4** *nk* **Street Life**[7] 8085 2-8-5 **57**..............................(v) PaddyMathers 9 50
(Richard Fahey) *slowly away: bhd: pushed along 1 1/2f out: drvn and hdwy ent fnl f: kpt on* **25/1**

4210 **5** *1 ¼* **Aryaaf (IRE)**[41] 6980 2-9-7 **73**.............................. JimCrowley 2 62
(Simon Crisford) *trckd ldrs on inner: drvn 2f out: rdn fnl f: no ex* **5/1**[3]

6230 **6** *nse* **Seraphinite (IRE)**[13] 7896 2-9-10 **76**..............................(b[1]) NicolaCurrie 5 65
(Jamie Osborne) *dwlt: bhd: drvn in rr 2f out: rdn fnl f: mod late hdwy* **9/1**

51 **7** *shd* **A Go Go**[15] 7853 2-8-3 **55**.............................. DavidEgan 1 43
(David Evans) *led: drvn 2f out: rdn and hdd 1 1/2f out: wknd fnl f: lost shoe* **11/1**

3534 **8** *1* **Too Hard To Hold (IRE)**[17] 7785 2-9-6 **72**.............................. JoeFanning 7 57+
(Mark Johnston) *chsd ldrs: stmbld and dropped to midfield after 1f: drvn 1 1/2f out: wknd fnl f* **7/1**

000 **9** *nk* **Hot Hot Hot**[28] 7407 2-8-2 **54** oh7 ow2.............................. RaulDaSilva 3 38
(Tony Carroll) *hld up: drvn 1 1/2f out: reminder 1f out: wknd fnl f* **66/1**

1m 0.63s (-1.27) **Going Correction** -0.225s/f (Stan) **9** Ran SP% **116.6**
Speed ratings (Par 95): **101,100,95,95,93 93,93,91,91**
CSF £69.61 CT £152.20 TOTE £19.60: £4.40, £2.30, £1.30; EX 102.70 Trifecta £277.20.

The Form Book Flat 2019, Raceform Ltd, Newbury, RG14 5SJ

Owner Provan,Mclaughlin,Mcfarlane,Vanderhoeven **Bred** Glebe Farm Stud **Trained** Carluke, S Lanarks

FOCUS
This fixture replaced an abandoned card at Haydock. A surprise winner of this modest nursery.

8316 GRAND THEATRE FILLIES' NOVICE STKS (PLUS 10 RACE) 6f 20y (Tp)
5:55 (5:57) (Class 4) 2-Y-O £4,528 (£1,347; £673; £336) **Stalls** Low

Form RPR

1 **1** **Chasing Dreams**[185] 1833 2-9-6 0 ....(h) WilliamBuick 1 88+
(Charlie Appleby) *mde all: t.k.h: pushed along 2f out: reminder in narrow ld 1 1/2f out: 1 l ld 1f out: reminder fnl f: sn plld clr* **2/9**[1]

42 **2** *3* **Quick Recap (IRE)**[21] 7644 2-9-0 0 .... RichardKingscote 4 73+
(Tom Dascombe) *chsd ldr: cl 2nd 2f out: drvn 1 1/2f out: no ex as wnr asserted ins fnl f* **7/2**[2]

4 **3** *3* **Grace And Virtue (IRE)**[23] 7580 2-9-0 0 .... TonyHamilton 9 62
(Richard Fahey) *trckd ldrs: pushed along in 3rd 2f out: rdn fnl f: one pce* **25/1**[3]

6 **4** *shd* **Superiority (IRE)**[22] 7619 2-8-7 0 .... RhonaPindar(7) 7 62
(K R Burke) *chsd ldrs on outer: drvn 1 1/2f out: one pce fnl f* **80/1**

04 **5** *hd* **Brainchild**[52] 6577 2-9-0 0 .... JoeFanning 10 61
(Keith Dalgleish) *hld up: pushed along 2f out: drvn and hdwy over 1f out: reminders fnl f: one pce* **33/1**

00 **6** *6* **Oasis Song**[36] 7104 2-9-0 0 .... TomMarquand 11 43
(Hughie Morrison) *hld up: drvn 2f out: sn wknd* **40/1**

7 *hd* **Barbelo (IRE)** 2-9-0 0 .... LukeMorris 3 43
(Richard Spencer) *dwlt: t.k.h in rr: drvn 2f out: no imp* **80/1**

1m 13.51s (-0.99) **Going Correction** -0.225s/f (Stan) 7 Ran SP% **115.8**
Speed ratings (Par 94): **97,93,89,88,88 80,80**
CSF £1.34 TOTE £1.10: £1.10, £1.30; EX 1.50 Trifecta £4.00.
Owner Godolphin **Bred** Ors Bloodstock & Stanley House Stud **Trained** Newmarket, Suffolk

FOCUS
Only two mattered in this.

8317 COME TO GENTLEMAN'S EVENING - 23RD NOVEMBER H'CAP 6f 20y (Tp)
6:25 (6:27) (Class 3) (0-95,94) 3-Y-O+ £7,762 (£2,310; £1,154; £577) **Stalls** Low

Form RPR

5012 **1** **Power Link (USA)**[13] 7913 3-9-2 **90** ....(p) JamesDoyle 3 100+
(James Tate) *hld up: drvn 1 1/2f out: rdn and hdwy on outer fnl f: r.o wl to ld last 50yds* **6/4**[1]

233 **2** *hd* **Baby Steps**[34] 7183 3-8-6 **80** oh1 .... DavidEgan 2 87
(David Loughnane) *t.k.h: mid-div: 4th 2f out: drvn 1 1/2f out: rdn and hdwy fnl f: sn ev ch: r.o wl* **6/1**[3]

0022 **3** *½* **Gabrial The Saint (IRE)**[27] 7431 4-9-5 **92** .... TonyHamilton 9 97
(Richard Fahey) *unruly at s: prom: cl 2nd 2f out: rdn to ld over 1f out: kpt on fnl f: hdd last 50yds* **9/1**

4330 **4** *½* **El Hombre**[76] 5664 5-9-4 **91** .... JoeFanning 1 94
(Keith Dalgleish) *hld up: drvn 1 1/2f out: hdwy ent fnl f: rdn and no ex nr fin* **7/2**[2]

3506 **5** *1 ¼* **Watchable**[13] 7913 9-9-0 **94** ....(p) AngusVilliers(7) 5 93
(David O'Meara) *trckd ldrs: pushed along in 3rd 2f out: drvn and wknd fnl f* **9/1**

0060 **6** *3* **Moonraker**[13] 7913 7-9-3 **90** .... AlistairRawlinson 8 80
(Michael Appleby) *t.k.h: hld up: pushed along over 2f out: rdn over 1f out: no imp* **50/1**

0300 **7** *½* **Reflektor (IRE)**[13] 7913 6-8-12 **85** .... RichardKingscote 7 73
(Tom Dascombe) *led: pushed along in narrow ld 2f out: rdn and hdd over 1f out: wknd fnl f* **8/1**

10 **8** *hd* **Last Page**[104] 4649 4-8-10 **83** .... TomMarquand 4 71
(Tony Carroll) *slowly away: bhd: drvn on outer 1 1/2f out: sn rdn: no imp* **20/1**

1m 12.62s (-1.88) **Going Correction** -0.225s/f (Stan)
WFA 3 from 4yo+ 1lb 8 Ran SP% **114.3**
Speed ratings (Par 107): **103,102,102,101,99 95,95,94**
CSF £11.02 CT £60.23 TOTE £1.70: £1.10, £1.40, £3.20; EX 9.30 Trifecta £51.70.
Owner Sheikh Rashid Dalmook Al Maktoum **Bred** SF Bloodstock LLC **Trained** Newmarket, Suffolk

FOCUS
A decent sprint handicap run at a solid gallop. The two 3yos in the field finished 1-2, both posting pbs, rated around the third.

8318 VISIT ATTHERACES.COM NURSERY H'CAP 7f 36y (Tp)
6:55 (6:55) (Class 4) (0-85,87) 2-Y-O £4,463 (£1,328; £663; £400; £400; £400) **Stalls** High

Form RPR

0103 **1** **Mischief Star**[35] 7140 2-9-2 **75** .... JimCrowley 7 79
(David O'Meara) *hld up: pushed along and hdwy on outer over 1f out: rdn and str run fnl f: led 50yds out: sn clr* **11/1**

0513 **2** *1 ¼* **Last Surprise (IRE)**[20] 7696 2-9-11 **87** .... MeganNicholls(3) 4 88+
(Simon Crisford) *chsd ldrs: wnt 2nd 1/2-way: led 2f out: drvn in 2 l ld 1f out: rdn fnl f: hdd last 50yds* **13/8**[1]

2032 **3** *hd* **Asmund (IRE)**[9] 8026 2-9-7 **80** .... CliffordLee 9 81
(K R Burke) *hld up on outer: drvn and hdwy 1 1/2f out: rdn into 2nd 1f out: kpt on but dropped to 3rd fnl f* **6/1**[2]

3133 **4** *3 ¼* **Hubert (IRE)**[19] 7725 2-9-4 **77** .... LukeMorris 1 69
(Sylvester Kirk) *chsd ldr: dropped to 3rd 1/2-way: drvn 2f out: rdn 1 1/2f out: no ex u.p fnl f* **11/1**

1556 **5** *shd* **One Bite (IRE)**[28] 7399 2-9-0 **73** .... JoeFanning 3 65
(Keith Dalgleish) *mid-div: pushed along 1 1/2f out: reminder and no ex fnl f* **16/1**

2544 **6** *nk* **Fair Pass (IRE)**[39] 7029 2-8-11 **70** .... TomMarquand 5 61
(Marco Botti) *hld up: drvn 2f out: rdn fnl f: no imp* **8/1**[3]

5134 **7** *½* **Silver Mission (IRE)**[48] 6728 2-9-2 **75** .... TonyHamilton 6 65
(Richard Fahey) *bhd: pushed along on inner 1 1/2f out: sn nt clr run: swtchd over 1f out: rdn and one pce fnl f* **12/1**

4305 **8** *2 ¼* **Swinley Forest (IRE)**[14] 7871 2-9-1 **74** ....(p) RobertHavlin 8 59
(Brian Meehan) *hld up: hdwy 3f out: drvn 2f out: rdn and wknd fnl f* **8/1**[3]

5511 **9** *6* **Lets Go Lucky**[18] 7767 2-9-1 **74** ....(h) JamesDoyle 2 44
(David Evans) *led: drvn and hdd 2f out: sn rdn and wknd* **8/1**[3]

1m 27.96s (-0.84) **Going Correction** -0.225s/f (Stan) 9 Ran SP% **116.0**
Speed ratings (Par 97): **95,93,93,89,89 89,88,86,79**
CSF £29.42 CT £123.68 TOTE £11.40: £2.70, £1.10, £3.00; EX 35.90 Trifecta £148.40.
Owner Three Men And A Trainer **Bred** The Red Mischief Partnership **Trained** Upper Helmsley, N Yorks

FOCUS
A fair nursery in which they went a reasonable gallop.

8319 BRITISH STALLION STUDS EBF NOVICE STKS (PLUS 10 RACE) 1m 142y (Tp)
7:25 (7:26) (Class 4) 2-Y-O £4,528 (£1,347; £673; £336) **Stalls** Low

Form RPR

03 **1** **Fashion Royalty**[33] 7235 2-8-11 0 .... JasonWatson 7 76
(Roger Charlton) *mde all: pushed along in 2 l ld 2f out: rdn over 1f out: r.o in diminishing ld fnl f: jst hld on* **12/1**

2 *nse* **Poet's Mind (USA)** 2-9-2 0 .... JamesDoyle 6 81
(Charlie Appleby) *mid-div: pushed along and hdwy into 2nd 2f out: reminder over 1f out: rdn and r.o wl to cl on wnr fnl f: jst failed* **9/2**[3]

3 *½* **Spirit Dancer** 2-9-2 0 .... TonyHamilton 1 80+
(Richard Fahey) *hld up: pushed along and hdwy 2f out: drvn into 3rd over 1f out: rdn fnl f: r.o wl: clsng on front two nr fin* **28/1**

4 *1 ¾* **In The Night (IRE)** 2-9-2 0 .... WilliamBuick 2 76+
(Charlie Appleby) *slowly away: bhd: drvn 2f out: reminders 1f out: kpt on steadily under hand riding ins fnl f* **5/6**[1]

31 **5** *3 ¾* **Maqtal (USA)**[30] 7346 2-9-8 0 .... JimCrowley 4 74
(Roger Varian) *prom: drvn 3f out: lost pl 2f out: dropped away over 1f out* **11/4**[2]

60 **6** *9* **Deverell**[48] 6708 2-9-2 0 .... RobertHavlin 3 49
(John Gosden) *t.k.h: mid-div: 3rd 3f out: pushed along and lost pl 2f out: sn wknd* **16/1**

1m 48.68s (-1.42) **Going Correction** -0.225s/f (Stan) 6 Ran SP% **116.4**
Speed ratings (Par 97): **97,96,96,94,91 83**
CSF £65.98 TOTE £12.60: £5.70, £2.10; EX 66.90 Trifecta £648.10.
Owner Andrew Rosen **Bred** Andrew Rosen **Trained** Beckhampton, Wilts

FOCUS
An interesting novice event despite the absence of the paper favourite.

8320 WOLVERHAMPTON-RACECOURSE.CO.UK H'CAP 1m 142y (Tp)
7:55 (7:56) (Class 3) (0-95,97) 3-Y-O+ £7,762 (£2,310; £1,154; £577) **Stalls** Low

Form RPR

2405 **1** **Rampant Lion (IRE)**[29] 7364 4-8-10 **82** ....(p) DavidProbert 5 89
(William Jarvis) *hld up: pushed along and hdwy over 1f out: chal ins fnl f: rdn to ld 50yds out: gng away at fin* **40/1**

6124 **2** *¾* **Calder Prince (IRE)**[20] 7678 6-9-5 **91** ....(p) RichardKingscote 6 96
(Tom Dascombe) *chsd ldrs: pushed along in 3rd 2f out: drvn to chse ldr 1 1/2f out: rdn to ld 1f out: r.o in narrow ld ins fnl f: hdd 50yds out: no ex* **20/1**

211 **3** *½* **New Arrangement**[33] 7228 3-9-2 **92** .... TomMarquand 9 96
(James Tate) *mid-div: drvn 1 1/2f out: rdn and hdwy 1f out: r.o fnl f* **9/1**

2-11 **4** *hd* **Tempus**[128] 3727 3-9-1 **91** .... JasonWatson 2 95
(Roger Charlton) *chsd ldrs: pushed along in 4th 2f out: sn drvn: cl up and rdn 1f out: one pce fnl f* **5/2**[1]

1240 **5** *shd* **Fields Of Athenry (USA)**[63] 6150 3-9-1 **91** .... WilliamBuick 8 94
(James Tate) *hld up: drvn 2f out: rdn on outer over 1f out: kpt on fnl f* **15/2**[2]

1063 **6** *hd* **Harbour Spirit (FR)**[34] 7191 3-8-8 **84** ....(p) DavidEgan 7 87
(Richard Hughes) *fly j. leaving stalls losing several l: bhd: drvn and hdwy on outer 1 1/2f out: sn rdn: kpt on fnl f* **14/1**

4403 **7** *5* **Cliffs Of Capri**[14] 7865 5-9-7 **93** ....(p) DougieCostello 4 85
(Jamie Osborne) *hld up: drvn on inner 1 1/2f out: wknd fnl f* **22/1**

5115 **8** *½* **Casanova**[13] 7891 3-9-7 **97** ....(h[1]) RobertHavlin 10 87
(John Gosden) *trckd across fr wd draw to go prom: pushed into ld over 2f out: rdn over 1f out: sn hdd: wknd fnl f: lost shoe* **5/2**[1]

0043 **9** *8* **Hot Team (IRE)**[19] 7728 3-9-0 **90** ....(v) JamesDoyle 3 62
(Hugo Palmer) *hld up: pushed along in rr over 2f out: rdn 1 1/2f out: no imp* **8/1**[3]

4110 **10** *6* **Attainment**[16] 7815 3-9-4 **94** .... JoeFanning 1 52
(James Tate) *led: pushed along and hdd over 2f out: sn dropped away: eased fnl f* **16/1**

1m 46.24s (-3.86) **Going Correction** -0.225s/f (Stan)
WFA 3 from 4yo+ 4lb 10 Ran SP% **114.1**
Speed ratings (Par 107): **108,107,106,106,106 106,102,101,94,89**
CSF £648.38 CT £7603.42 TOTE £29.60: £6.30, £6.10, £4.20; EX 328.90.
Owner Dr J Walker **Bred** R J Cornelius **Trained** Newmarket, Suffolk

FOCUS
The leaders went off quickly in this competitive handicap and the field was soon stretched out, but there was still a compressed finish. The winner has been rated close to his best.

8321 VISIT THE BLACK COUNTRY H'CAP 2m 120y (Tp)
8:25 (8:25) (Class 4) (0-85,85) 3-Y-O+ £5,433 (£1,617; £808; £404; £400; £400) **Stalls** Low

Form RPR

2331 **1** **Selino**[55] 6459 3-9-7 **85** ....(v) DanielMuscutt 4 103+
(James Fanshawe) *t.k.h: mid-div: smooth hdwy to ld over 2f out: sn opened up 6 l ld: rdn in 10 l ld 1f out: in total command fnl f: eased last 100yds: v easily* **15/8**[2]

1313 **2** *10* **Charlie D (USA)**[6] 8120 4-10-0 **84** ....(tp) RichardKingscote 5 87
(Tom Dascombe) *led: hdd 1/2-way: trckd ldrs: drvn 2f out: wnt into 6 l 2nd 1 1/2f out: sn rdn: kpt on fnl f: no ch w v easy wnr* **7/4**[1]

4132 **3** *6* **Sir Prize**[23] 7575 4-9-2 **77** .... SophieRalston(5) 2 73
(Dean Ivory) *t.k.h: hld up: drvn and hdwy on outer 3f out: sn rdn: wnt 3rd 1 1/2f out: one pce fnl f* **9/2**[3]

4452 **4** *4 ½* **Tigray (USA)**[22] 7631 3-8-5 **74** .... TheodoreLadd(5) 7 65
(Michael Appleby) *hld up in rr: pushed along over 2f out: kpt on into 4th fr over 1f out* **25/1**

1140 **5** *shd* **Champagne Marengo (IRE)**[34] 7209 3-8-7 **71** ....(v) DavidEgan 3 62
(Ian Williams) *hld up: hdwy on outer to ld 1/2-way: rdn and hdd over 2f out: wknd* **8/1**

3652 **6** *8* **Vampish**[39] 7034 4-9-0 **70** ....(b[1]) TomMarquand 1 51
(Philip McBride) *trckd ldrs: lost pl 1/2-way: drvn 3f out: sn rdn and wknd* **16/1**

0163 **7** *16* **Toshima (IRE)**[43] 6348 4-9-12 **82** ....(vt[1]) JimCrowley 6 43
(Robert Stephens) *prom: drvn and lost pl over 2f out: sn dropped away: lame* **14/1**

3m 36.64s (-2.66) **Going Correction** -0.225s/f (Stan)
WFA 3 from 4yo 8lb 7 Ran SP% **116.8**
Speed ratings (Par 105): **97,92,89,87,87 83,76**
CSF £5.81 TOTE £2.30: £1.10, £1.90; EX 6.00 Trifecta £15.70.
Owner Dr Catherine Wills **Bred** St Clare Hall Stud **Trained** Newmarket, Suffolk

FOCUS
A dominant winner of what had looked an open staying handicap and this rates a big step forward.

T/Plt: £139.90 to a £1 stake. Pool £72,049.08 - 375.81 winning units T/Qpdt: £49.10 to a £1 stake. Pool £8,043.74 - 121.15 winning units **Keith McHugh**

8322 - 8327a (Foreign Racing) - See Raceform Interactive

8102

DUNDALK (A.W) (L-H)

Friday, October 18

OFFICIAL GOING: Polytrack: standard

8328a AL BASTI EQUIWORLD MERCURY STKS (GROUP 3) 5f (P)

8:15 (8:26) 2-Y-O+

£39,864 (£12,837; £6,081; £2,702; £1,351; £675)

RPR

1 **Dr Simpson (FR)**[28] 7400 2-8-4 93 .... RoryCleary 6 102
(Tom Dascombe) *led narrowly early tl sn jnd and disp ld: pushed along in cl 2nd at 1/2-way: rdn under 2f out and regained ld 1f out: extended advantage ins fnl f and kpt on wl: reduced ld cl home* **16/1**

2 ¾ **Dream Shot (IRE)**[35] 7149 2-8-7 105 .... ChrisHayes 8 104+
(James Tate) *mid-div: pushed along briefly in 8th over 3f out: tk clsr order fr 1/2-way and pushed along again: rdn over 2f out and n.m.r over 1f out: sn swtchd rt in 7th and r.o wl into nvr nrr 2nd fnl strides* **6/1[3]**

3 *hd* **Corinthia Knight (IRE)**[26] 7497 4-9-11 99 .... HollieDoyle 12 108
(Archie Watson) *chsd ldrs: drvn in 6th over 3f out and clsd u.p into 2nd wl ins fnl f where no imp on wnr: denied 2nd fnl strides* **20/1**

4 1 ¾ **Hit The Bid**[27] 7454 5-9-11 105 .... (t) RonanWhelan 1 102
(D J Bunyan, Ire) *on toes behand: mounted on trck: pushed along briefly fr s and sn disp ld: narrow advantage at 1/2-way: rdn far side 2f out and hdd u.p 1f out: no ex wl ins fnl f and dropped to 4th* **9/10[1]**

5 ½ **Alfredo Arcano (IRE)**[21] 7664 5-9-11 101 .... (t) OisinOrr 2 100
(David Marnane, Ire) *sn chsd ldrs: disp 4th at 1/2-way: rdn bhd ldrs 2f out and no imp on wnr u.p in 5th wl ins fnl f: kpt on same pce* **10/1**

6 *nk* **Blue Uluru (IRE)**[21] 7664 4-9-8 101 .... ColinKeane 5 96
(G M Lyons, Ire) *chsd ldrs: disp 4th at 1/2-way: rdn under 2f out and no imp on ldrs ent fnl f* **5/1[2]**

7 *hd* **Leodis Dream (IRE)**[27] 7449 3-9-11 104 .... DanielTudhope 11 99
(David O'Meara) *chsd ldrs: 3rd at 1/2-way: rdn under 2f out and no ex ent fnl f: sn wknd* **7/1**

8 *hd* **Ickworth (IRE)**[7] 8088 2-8-4 95 .... LeighRoche 10 88
(W McCreery, Ire) *in rr of mid-div: pushed along in 11th over 3f out: sme hdwy u.p nr side 1f out: kpt on one pce* **25/1**

9 1 ¼ **Primo Uomo (IRE)**[21] 7664 7-9-11 99 .... (t) NGMcCullagh 3 93
(Gerard O'Leary, Ire) *in rr of mid-div: pushed along in 9th over 3f out: no imp far side over 1f out: one pce fnl f* **14/1**

10 *nk* **Deia Glory**[28] 7401 3-9-8 92 .... DonnachaO'Brien 13 90
(Michael Dods) *sn settled in rr: last at 1/2-way: swtchd lft stl in rr over 1f out and sme modest hdwy u.p clsng stages* **33/1**

11 *hd* **Rapid Reaction (IRE)**[20] 7714 4-9-8 97 .... (p[1]) AndrewSlattery 9 88
(J F Grogan, Ire) *mid-div: 7th 3f out: rdn and imp under 2f out: wknd and eased ins fnl f* **33/1**

12 ½ **Lethal Promise (IRE)**[86] 5325 3-9-8 98 .... (h) WJLee 7 87
(W McCreery, Ire) *dwlt: in rr early tl sn tk clsr order: 12th 3f out: rdn and no imp 2f out: eased nr fin* **20/1**

13 1 **Julia's Magic (IRE)**[50] 6648 4-9-8 86 .... GaryCarroll 15 83
(Mrs Denise Foster, Ire) *in rr of mid-div: 10th 3f out: drvn fr 1/2-way and no ex u.p under 2f out: sn wknd: eased cl home* **50/1**

58.36s (-1.04) **Going Correction** +0.225s/f (Slow) **13 Ran SP% 138.9**
Speed ratings: **117,115,115,112,111 111,111,110,108,108 107,107,105**
CSF £118.25 TOTE £38.90: £8.80, £2.30, £5.10; DF 289.60 Trifecta £1073.10.
Owner Russell Jones **Bred** Mme Debbiella Camacho **Trained** Malpas, Cheshire
■ El Astronaute was withdraw. Price at time of withdrawal 2-1. Rule 4\n\x\x applies to board prices, but not to SP bets - deduction 30p in the pound. New market formed

FOCUS
A race that changed complexion when El Astronaute broke out from the front of the stalls and was withdrawn. The winner rates an improver, with the next four finishers and the tenth helping the standard.

8329 - (Foreign Racing) - See Raceform Interactive

8140

MAISONS-LAFFITTE (R-H)

Friday, October 18

OFFICIAL GOING: Turf: heavy

8330a PRIX DES PETRONS (CLAIMER) (2YO) (TURF) 5f 110y

1:58 2-Y-O **£8,558** (£3,423; £2,567; £1,711; £855)

RPR

1 **Autumnal (FR)**[102] 2-8-3 0 .... DamienBoche(5) 9 70
(L Gadbin, France) **186/10**

2 *shd* **Thunderdome (FR)**[32] 7276 2-8-9 0 .... QuentinPerrette(6) 10 77
(Gay Kelleway) *racd in rr: niggled along early: began to make hdwy at 1/2-way: styd on strly to chal ins fnl f: jst denied* **10/1**

3 3 **Trentatre (FR)**[170] 2315 2-8-0 0 ow1 .... MlleLeaBails(9) 1 61
(Andrea Marcialis, France) **33/1**

4 *shd* **Mehanydream (FR)**[3] 8239 2-9-2 0 .... SebastienMaillot 2 68
(C Boutin, France) **9/1**

5 *snk* **Atocha (FR)** 2-9-4 0 .... (b[1]) TonyPiccone 5 69
(M Delcher Sanchez, France) **13/1**

6 2 **Cristal Marvelous (FR)**[18] 2-8-11 0 .... MlleCoraliePacaut(4) 4 60
(M Boutin, France) **74/10**

7 2 ½ **Melrose (IRE)**[22] 7641 2-8-11 0 .... (p) StephanePasquier 12 47
(E Lyon, France) **9/1**

8 *hd* **Ma Boy Harris (IRE)**[32] 7283 2-9-1 0 .... (p) ThomasTrullier(3) 11 54
(P Monfort, France) **48/10[2]**

9 *shd* **Spinning Mist**[18] 2-9-3 0 .... (b) MickaelBarzalona 8 52
(J Phelippon, France) **5/2[1]**

10 1 ¼ **Spencer**[28] 2-8-3 0 .... (p) MlleAmbreMolins(8) 13 42
(J Phelippon, France) **33/1**

11 10 **Hong Kong Star (FR)**[48] 2-8-8 0 .... TheoBachelot 7 6
(O Trigodet, France) **68/10[3]**

12 3 **Hudson Hornet (FR)**[74] 5763 2-9-1 0 .... (b[1]) AlexandreChesneau(3) 3 6
(Jiri Chaloupka, Czech Republic) **58/1**

1m 6.21s (-1.09) **12 Ran SP% 119.5**
PARI-MUTUEL (all including 1 euro stake): WIN 19.60; PLACE 6.20, 4.70, 9.40; DF 71.40.
Owner Gerard Dufit **Bred** Mlle K Aalen **Trained** France

7889

ASCOT (R-H)

Saturday, October 19

OFFICIAL GOING: Straight course - heavy (5.3); inner flat course - good to soft (soft in places; 6.6) changing to soft after race 2 (2:10)
Wind: Moderate, half against Weather: Fine but cloudy, shower race 2

8331 QIPCO BRITISH CHAMPIONS SPRINT STKS (GROUP 1) 6f

1:35 (1:37) (Class 1) 3-Y-O+

£330,693 (£125,372; £62,744; £31,255; £15,686; £7,872) **Stalls** Low

Form RPR

4062 1 **Donjuan Triumphant (IRE)**[14] 7892 6-9-2 107 .... SilvestreDeSousa 4 120+
(Andrew Balding) *hld up in midfield: nt clr run 2f out: swtchd lft and hmpd over 1f out: str run fnl f whn in the clr to ld 75yds: won gng away* **33/1**

3251 2 1 **One Master**[13] 7944 5-8-13 115 .... Pierre-CharlesBoudot 10 114+
(William Haggas) *hld up towards rr: pushed along whn nt clr run 2f out: prog whn nt clr run over 1f out and swtchd lft: gd prog fnl f: r.o but jst outpcd by wnr* **4/1[1]**

1200 3 *nk* **Forever In Dreams (IRE)**[13] 7944 3-8-12 112 .... JamieSpencer 7 113
(Aidan F Fogarty, Ire) *trckd ldrs: rdn to cl over 1f out: disp ld briefly 100yds out: outpcd nr fin* **66/1**

1024 4 *nse* **Brando**[42] 6959 7-9-2 116 .... TomEaves 12 116
(Kevin Ryan) *hld up wl in rr: rdn and gd prog wl over 1f out: clsd on outer to chal ins fnl f and upsides 75yds out: no ex nr fin* **25/1**

121 5 1 ½ **Make A Challenge (IRE)**[6] 8166 4-9-2 111 .... (p) JoeDoyle 16 111
(Denis Gerard Hogan, Ire) *taken down early: pressed ldrs: gng strly 2f out: shkn up to ld jst over 1f out: hdd & wknd last 75yds* **9/1[3]**

4413 6 1 **Speak In Colours**[13] 7944 4-9-2 111 .... (t) DonnachaO'Brien 9 108
(Joseph Patrick O'Brien, Ire) *hld up in rr: rdn 2f out: prog jst over 1f out: styd on and nvr nrr but no threat to ldrs* **22/1**

0121 7 *hd* **Advertise**[76] 5716 3-9-1 119 .... (b) FrankieDettori 2 108
(Martyn Meade) *chsd ldrs: rdn wl over 1f out: one pce and no imp* **4/1[1]**

4131 8 ½ **Hello Youmzain (FR)**[42] 6959 3-9-1 118 .... JamesDoyle 5 106
(Kevin Ryan) *led and tk field to far side: hdd jst over 1f out: wknd ins fnl f: eased nr fin (jockey said colt suffered interference on the run to the line)* **6/1[2]**

4465 9 ½ **Mabs Cross**[13] 7943 5-8-13 112 .... GeraldMosse 15 102
(Michael Dods) *hld up wl in rr: rdn and no prog 2f out: styd on fnl f: nvr nrr* **28/1**

3643 10 *shd* **Keystroke**[14] 7892 7-9-2 109 .... (t) AdamKirby 14 105
(Stuart Williams) *hld up in last: modest prog and no ch whn nt clr run 1f out: drvn and styd on wl last 150yds: nvr nrr* **66/1**

0210 11 ¾ **Khaadem (IRE)**[42] 6959 3-9-1 116 .... JimCrowley 6 102
(Charles Hills) *chsd ldrs: rdn whn n.m.r briefly over 1f out: wknd* **50/1**

1031 12 2 **Cape Byron**[14] 7892 5-9-2 113 .... AndreaAtzeni 8 96
(Roger Varian) *pressed ldrs tl wknd over 1f out* **9/1[3]**

3602 13 ¾ **The Tin Man**[42] 6959 7-9-2 117 .... OisinMurphy 11 94
(James Fanshawe) *dwlt: sn trckd ldrs: rdn and no prog 2f out: wknd over 1f out* **10/1**

-630 14 1 ½ **Sands Of Mali (FR)**[119] 4094 4-9-2 116 .... DanielTudhope 3 90
(Richard Fahey) *pressed ldr: stl upsides 2f out: wknd over 1f out (vet said colt lost its right fore shoe)* **12/1**

00-2 15 4 ½ **Librisa Breeze**[63] 6215 7-9-2 113 .... JoeyHaynes 17 76
(Dean Ivory) *a in rr: wknd 2f out* **16/1**

1200 16 1 **Dream Of Dreams (IRE)**[42] 6959 5-9-2 118 .... WilliamBuick 13 73
(Sir Michael Stoute) *racd on outer: nvr beyond midfield: wknd over 2f out* **20/1**

3022 17 2 ¼ **So Perfect (USA)**[13] 7943 3-8-12 111 .... SeamieHeffernan 1 63
(A P O'Brien, Ire) *chsd ldng pair to over 2f out: sn wknd* **33/1**

1m 16.43s (2.73) **Going Correction** +0.875s/f (Soft)
WFA 3 from 4yo+ 1lb **17 Ran SP% 124.2**
Speed ratings (Par 117): **116,114,114,114,112 110,110,109,109,109 108,105,104,102,96 95,92**
CSF £151.53 CT £8654.00 TOTE £48.90: £8.40, £2.10, £15.40; EX 285.60 Trifecta £12381.20.
Owner King Power Racing Co Ltd **Bred** Patrick Cosgrove & Dream Ahead Syndicate **Trained** Kingsclere, Hants

FOCUS
An abnormal amount of rain resulted in patches of waterlogged ground so the three races scheduled for the round course were switched to the inner Flat (hurdles) track. The ground was much more testing on the straight course but there was no further rain after Friday evening. After race two the going was changed on the inner Flat course to soft from good to soft, soft in places. No King's Stand/Diamond Jubilee winner Blue Point (retired) or July Cup victor Ten Sovereigns (ran in the Everest at Randwick earlier in the day) but still a strong field in which the last three winners of the race were in the line-up, plus all this season's domestic (and French) Group 1 events over sprint distances for 3yos and older were represented in some form. However, a couple of the leading players weren't at their best and this threw up a bit of a shock The pace was a decent one in the conditions and those held up came to the fore in the closing stages. The field raced far side.

8332 QIPCO BRITISH CHAMPIONS LONG DISTANCE CUP (GROUP 2) 1m 7f 127y

2:10 (2:11) (Class 1) 3-Y-O+

£255,195 (£96,750; £48,420; £24,120; £12,105; £6,075) **Stalls** Low

Form RPR

-222 1 **Kew Gardens (IRE)**[34] 7246 4-9-7 118 .... DonnachaO'Brien 3 122
(A P O'Brien, Ire) *trckd ldng pair: gng easily 3f out: led jst over 2f out: drvn and hdd jst over 1f out: styd on wl to ld again last strides* **7/2[2]**

1111 2 *nse* **Stradivarius (IRE)**[36] 7148 5-9-7 121 .... FrankieDettori 6 121
(John Gosden) *trckd ldrs: nudged along over 4f out: drvn and gd prog 2f out to ld narrowly jst over 1f out: styd on after but hdd last strides and jst pipped (jockey said horse hung right-handed under pressure)* **8/13[1]**

1-41 3 5 **Royal Line**[42] 6962 5-9-7 111 .... RobertHavlin 5 115
(John Gosden) *hld up in rr: stl gng strly 3f out: shkn up and prog to chse ldng pair over 1f out: no imp and lft further bhd fnl f* **12/1**

2020 4 1 ¼ **Mekong**[56] 6473 4-9-7 108 .... JimCrowley 10 113
(Sir Michael Stoute) *reluctant to leave stall and lft 8 l: sn in tch in last: rdn and prog over 2f out: tk 4th over 1f out: no further hdwy (jockey said gelding was slowly away)* **20/1**

-101 5 3 ½ **Withhold**[23] 7615 6-9-7 113 .... (p) JasonWatson 4 109
(Roger Charlton) *mde most: rdn and hdd jst over 2f out: wknd over 1f out (jockey said gelding hung badly left-handed throughout)* **15/2[3]**

6403 6 ½ **Capri (IRE)**[21] 7717 5-9-7 111 .... SeamieHeffernan 7 108
(A P O'Brien, Ire) *pushed up to join ldr: drvn and stl upsides 3f out: lost pl and squeezed out jst over 2f out: dropped away qckly* **25/1**

3020 **7** *6* **Cleonte (IRE)**[14] 7928 6-9-7 108.......................... SilvestreDeSousa 2 101
(Andrew Balding) *wl in tch: drvn on inner over 2f out: wknd qckly over 1f out* **40/1**

-303 **8** *nk* **Max Dynamite (FR)**[36] 7148 9-9-7 107.......................... OisinMurphy 8 101
(W P Mullins, Ire) *hld up in rr: rdn and no prog over 2f out: sn wknd* **33/1**

1331 **9** *1 3/4* **Bin Battuta**[21] 7686 5-9-7 110.......................... (p) HectorCrouch 9 99
(Saeed bin Suroor) *hld up towards rr: no prog u.p over 2f out: sn wknd* **25/1**

3m 29.49s
WFA 3 from 4yo+ 8lb **9** Ran SP% **121.4**
CSF £6.01 CT £23.71 TOTE £4.50: £1.40, £1.10, £3.10; EX 7.20 Trifecta £35.50.
Owner Derrick Smith & Mrs John Magnier & Michael Tabor **Bred** Barronstown Stud **Trained** Cashel, Co Tipperary

FOCUS
The switch to the inner Flat course meant the distance was reduced by 82yds from the original 1m 7f 209yds. A race in which the majority of the pre-race focus naturally centred on Stradivarius but his winning streak came to an end. The gallop was a sensible one in driving rain and the first two deserve credit for pulling clear in the last furlong. This rates a small pb from the winner, with the runner-up a bit below form.

8333 QIPCO BRITISH CHAMPIONS FILLIES & MARES STKS (GROUP 1) 1m 3f 133y
2:45 (2:48) (Class 1) 3-Y-O+

£311,905 (£118,250; £59,180; £29,480; £14,795; £7,425) **Stalls** High

Form RPR

3111 **1** **Star Catcher**[34] 7252 3-8-13 114.......................... FrankieDettori 11 115
(John Gosden) *t.k.h early: trckd ldng trio: rdn 2f out: clsd between rivals to chal fnl f: narrow ld last 100yds: pushed out nr fin and a jst holding on* **7/4**[1]

5322 **2** *shd* **Delphinia (IRE)**[14] 7926 3-8-13 113.......................... SeamieHeffernan 2 114
(A P O'Brien, Ire) *led at gd pce: rdn 2f out: jnd jst over 1f out: hdd last 100yds: kpt on wl but jst hld* **20/1**

1144 **3** *1* **Sun Maiden**[42] 6962 4-9-5 106.......................... JimCrowley 12 112
(Sir Michael Stoute) *t.k.h early: trckd ldrs in 6th: prog 2f out: rdn to join ld jst over 1f out tl no ex last 150yds* **25/1**

2452 **4** *nk* **Fleeting (IRE)**[13] 7942 3-8-13 113.......................... DonnachaO'Brien 5 113+
(A P O'Brien, Ire) *hld up in 7th: clsd 2f out: swtchd towards inner and prog to trck ldng trio over 1f out: gap clsd sn after: swtchd arnd and r.o last 100yds but nt rcvr* **9/2**[2]

2133 **5** *2 1/2* **Klassique**[62] 6263 4-9-5 106.......................... JamesDoyle 7 108
(William Haggas) *hld up in 8th: rdn and prog on outer 2f out: chsd ldrs 1f out: fdd last 150yds* **28/1**

10-1 **6** *shd* **Antonia De Vega (IRE)**[128] 3762 3-8-13 104.......................... HarryBentley 10 108
(Ralph Beckett) *hld up in 9th: drvn over 2f out: nvr a threat but kpt on u.p over 1f out* **8/1**

0440 **7** *2 1/4* **South Sea Pearl (IRE)**[14] 7926 3-8-13 104.......................... SeanLevey 3 104
(A P O'Brien, Ire) *trckd ldr: drvn 3f out: wknd wl over 1f out* **66/1**

3300 **8** *3/4* **Pink Dogwood (IRE)**[13] 7942 3-8-13 110.......... Pierre-CharlesBoudot 9 103
(A P O'Brien, Ire) *hld up in last: pushed along 5f out: drvn and no hdwy 3f out: modest late prog (jockey said filly lost its action down the back straight)* **16/1**

1011 **9** *1 1/4* **Tarnawa (IRE)**[34] 7242 3-8-13 108.......................... ChrisHayes 8 101
(D K Weld, Ire) *trckd ldrs in 5th: rdn over 2f out: sn lost pl: wkng whn short of room over 1f out* **10/1**

4106 **10** *shd* **Nausha**[34] 7242 3-8-13 102.......................... AndreaAtzeni 4 101
(Roger Varian) *stdd s: hld up in last pair: rdn and no prog over 2f out* **80/1**

1101 **11** *2 1/4* **Anapurna**[14] 7926 3-8-13 115.......................... WilliamBuick 1 97
(John Gosden) *slipped up on way to s: t.k.h: trckd ldr: rdn 3f out: wknd qckly wl over 1f out (vet said filly lost its right fore shoe)* **6/1**[3]

1033 **12** *9* **Sparkle Roll (FR)**[91] 5190 3-8-13 106.......................... OisinMurphy 6 83
(John Gosden) *stdd s: hld up in last trio: rdn and wknd wl over 2f out* **14/1**

2m 28.48s
WFA 3 from 4yo 6lb **12** Ran SP% **116.4**
CSF £45.86 CT £665.87 TOTE £2.20: £1.20, £3.60, £7.00; EX 39.90 Trifecta £386.50.
Owner A E Oppenheimer **Bred** Hascombe And Valiant Studs **Trained** Newmarket, Suffolk
■ Stewards' Enquiry : Seamie Heffernan two-day ban: used whip above the permitted level (Nov 2, 4)

FOCUS
The switch to the inner course saw the official distance reduced by 78yds from the original 1m 3f 211yds, and the ground changed to soft before this race. Magical, Coronet and Deirdre - three of the world's leading older fillies and mares on turf - contested the Champion Stakes later on the card thus leaving the way open for the year's top 3yos to continue their recent domination of this event. The gallop seemed reasonable and the fourth was unlucky not to have finished closer. It rates ordinary form for the grade but with the winner to her best.

8334 QUEEN ELIZABETH II STKS (GROUP 1) (SPONSORED BY QIPCO) (BRITISH CHAMPIONS MILE) 1m (S)
3:20 (3:25) (Class 1) 3-Y-O+

£623,810 (£236,500; £118,360; £58,960; £29,590; £14,850) **Stalls** Low

Form RPR

-121 **1** **King Of Change**[31] 7340 3-9-1 115.......................... SeanLevey 12 122+
(Richard Hannon) *wl plcd: swift prog 2f out to ld over 1f out and sn 2 l clr: hung lft fnl f and bdly so nr fin: a in command* **12/1**

1111 **2** *1 1/4* **The Revenant**[14] 7924 4-9-4 120.......................... (h) Pierre-CharlesBoudot 10 120
(F-H Graffard, France) *wl in tch: rdn and prog 2f out: chsd wnr ins fnl f: keeping on but wl hld whn impeded 100yds out* **4/1**[2]

1334 **3** *1 1/2* **Safe Voyage (IRE)**[13] 7944 6-9-4 113.......................... JamieSpencer 8 117
(John Quinn) *stdd s: hld up in last pair: prog jst over 2f out: drvn over 1f out: styd on to take 3rd last 100yds* **40/1**

3412 **4** *1 1/2* **Veracious**[14] 7898 4-9-1 113.......................... (t) JasonWatson 6 111
(Sir Michael Stoute) *led at gd clip and sn 3 l clr: hdd over 1f out: grad fdd* **20/1**

11-1 **5** *3/4* **Mohaather**[189] 1752 3-9-1 114.......................... JimCrowley 2 111+
(Marcus Tregoning) *hld up in rr: prog 2f out: rdn over 1f out: kpt on same pce fnl f* **16/1**

0435 **6** *1 1/2* **Happy Power (IRE)**[22] 7660 3-9-1 114.......................... SilvestreDeSousa 5 107
(Andrew Balding) *trckd ldr: rdn 2f out: hanging rt over 1f out and fdd fnl f* **25/1**

-240 **7** *nk* **Century Dream (IRE)**[203] 1445 5-9-4 114.......................... (t) WilliamBuick 11 108
(Simon Crisford) *hld up wl in rr: prog on outer 2f out: rdn and kpt on same pce fnl f* **22/1**

0156 **8** *2* **Lord Glitters (FR)**[59] 6354 6-9-4 117.......................... DanielTudhope 15 103
(David O'Meara) *sn in last pair: cajoled along 3f out and no rspnse: consented to run on over 1f out: nvr nrr* **11/2**[3]

3130 **9** *2 1/4* **Raising Sand**[14] 7891 7-9-4 109.......................... NicolaCurrie 3 98
(Jamie Osborne) *hld up towards rr: rdn wl over 2f out: kpt on but nvr enough pce enough to figure* **80/1**

1665 **10** *3/4* **Phoenix Of Spain (IRE)**[41] 7007 3-9-1 118.......................... JamesDoyle 7 95
(Charles Hills) *t.k.h: trckd ldr to 2f out: wknd* **20/1**

4023 **11** *3/4* **Accidental Agent**[56] 6467 5-9-4 110.......................... (p w) CharlesBishop 9 94
(Eve Johnson Houghton) *wl in tch tl wknd wl over 1f out (starter reported that the horse was the subject of a third criteria failure; trainer was informed that the colt could not run until the day after passing a stalls test)* **50/1**

2-16 **12** *5* **Move Swiftly**[83] 5479 4-9-1 112.......................... (p[1]) TomMarquand 4 80
(William Haggas) *dwlt: wl in rr: rdn over 2f out: no significant prog* **33/1**

1242 **13** *1 1/2* **King Of Comedy (IRE)**[22] 7660 3-9-1 118.......................... (p[1]) FrankieDettori 14 79
(John Gosden) *reluctant to go to post and had to be dismntd and led: dwlt: hld up in rr: shkn up over 2f out: no real hdwy* **9/1**

1-15 **14** *12* **Magna Grecia (IRE)**[147] 3104 3-9-1 120.......................... DonnachaO'Brien 1 51
(A P O'Brien, Ire) *prom on inner tl wknd rapidly over 2f out: t.o (trainer said colt may have become tired on the heavy going)* **13/2**

1122 **15** *1 1/2* **Imaging**[13] 7934 4-9-4 107.......................... ChrisHayes 16 48
(D K Weld, Ire) *nvr beyond midfield: wknd rapidly over 2f out: t.o* **28/1**

12-1 **16** *11* **Benbatl**[22] 7660 5-9-4 126.......................... (t) OisinMurphy 13 23
(Saeed bin Suroor) *trckd ldrs: wknd v rapidly over 2f out: t.o (trainer's rep said horse was unsuited by the heavy going and would prefer a quicker surface)* **7/2**[1]

1m 44.88s (3.48) **Going Correction** +0.875s/f (Soft)
WFA 3 from 4yo+ 3lb **16** Ran SP% **124.3**
Speed ratings (Par 117): **117,115,114,112,112 110,110,108,105,105 104,99,97,85,84 73**
CSF £54.00 CT £1925.25 TOTE £12.90: £3.60, £1.90, £11.00; EX 73.60 Trifecta £1969.80.
Owner Ali Abdulla Saeed **Bred** Rabbah Bloodstock Limited **Trained** East Everleigh, Wilts

FOCUS
No Too Darn Hot (retired) or Moulin/Jacques Le Marois winners Circus Maximus and Romanised so just ordinary form of its type. But still, this rates a clear pb from the winner to back up his Guineas run. The gallop was sound. The field again raced on the far side of the course.

8335 QIPCO CHAMPION STKS (BRITISH CHAMPIONS MIDDLE DISTANCE) (GROUP 1) 1m 2f
4:00 (4:05) (Class 1) 3-Y-O+

£770,547 (£292,131; £146,201; £72,829; £36,550; £18,343) **Stalls** Low

Form RPR

2215 **1** **Magical (IRE)**[13] 7941 4-9-2 122.......................... DonnachaO'Brien 8 121
(A P O'Brien, Ire) *trckd ldr: shkn up to ld wl over 1f out: drvn and pressed fnl f: styd on wl* **1/1**[1]

4121 **2** *3/4* **Addeybb (IRE)**[70] 5950 5-9-5 114.......................... (p) JamesDoyle 3 122
(William Haggas) *trckd ldrs: prog to chse wnr over 1f out: hrd rdn and tried to chal fnl f: styd on but no imp last 100yds* **5/1**[3]

4614 **3** *2 1/4* **Deirdre (JPN)**[35] 7219 5-9-2 116.......................... OisinMurphy 1 115
(Mitsuru Hashida, Japan) *hld up towards rr: shkn up and prog 2f out: rdn and kpt on fnl f to take 3rd last stride* **10/1**

43-1 **4** *hd* **Fox Tal**[38] 7076 3-9-1 110.......................... SilvestreDeSousa 2 117
(Andrew Balding) *t.k.h early: trckd ldng pair: rdn 2f out: outpcd over 1f out: one pce after: lost 3rd last stride* **20/1**

0120 **5** *1* **Mehdaayih**[13] 7942 3-8-12 113.......................... RobertHavlin 6 112
(John Gosden) *hld up in last pair: gng wl 3f out: shkn up and prog 2f out: rdn and kpt on same pce fnl f: n.d* **16/1**

-411 **6** *5* **Coronet**[62] 6265 5-9-2 115.......................... FrankieDettori 5 102
(John Gosden) *hld up in tch: rdn and floundering over 2f out: sn btn* **4/1**[2]

3455 **7** *3/4* **I Can Fly**[14] 7898 4-9-2 112.......................... SeamieHeffernan 4 101
(A P O'Brien, Ire) *slowly away: a in rr: rdn and no prog 2f out: wknd over 1f out* **22/1**

1345 **8** *1/2* **Regal Reality**[59] 6354 4-9-5 120.......................... JimCrowley 9 103
(Sir Michael Stoute) *led: rdn and hdd wl over 1f out: wknd qckly* **16/1**

6223 **9** *8* **Pondus**[28] 7455 3-9-1 107.......................... DanielMuscutt 7 87
(James Fanshawe) *t.k.h early: hld up in rr: last and struggling over 2f out: sn wl btn* **33/1**

2m 8.42s
WFA 3 from 4yo+ 4lb **9** Ran SP% **119.6**
CSF £6.41 CT £33.98 TOTE £1.80: £1.10, £1.60, £2.10; EX 7.50 Trifecta £63.30.
Owner Derrick Smith & Mrs John Magnier & Michael Tabor **Bred** Orpendale, Chelston & Wynatt **Trained** Cashel, Co Tipperary

FOCUS
Despite no recent success in this contest, fillies and mares dominated the market. Indeed, nothing of that sex until this running had been successful since the race was moved to this track, and Pride was the last in 2006 when it took place at Newmarket. Aidan O'Brien, whose Found finished second twice in 2015 and 2016, gained his first win in this event with a really tough and talented filly.

8336 BALMORAL H'CAP (SPONSORED BY QIPCO) 1m (S)
4:40 (4:43) (Class 2) 3-Y-O+

£155,625 (£46,600; £23,300; £11,650; £5,825; £2,925) **Stalls** Low

Form RPR

3543 **1** **Escobar (IRE)**[14] 7891 5-9-6 **105**.......................... (t) AdamKirby 21 115
(David O'Meara) *hld up in last pair: prog over 2f out and stl swinging along: swtchd to outer and rdn over 1f out: swept into the ld jst ins fnl f: hung rt but styd on and drew clr* **16/1**

1021 **2** *2 1/4* **Lord North (IRE)**[21] 7694 3-9-8 **110**.......................... FrankieDettori 20 114
(John Gosden) *hld up towards rr: prog 1/2-way to join ldrs 3f out: rdn to chal 2f out: kpt on but outpcd fnl f (starter reported that the gelding was the subject of a third criteria failure; trainer was informed that the gelding could not run until the day after passing a stalls test)* **3/1**[1]

4503 **3** *1* **Mitchum Swagger**[14] 7905 7-9-6 **105**.......................... RobHornby 4 108
(Ralph Beckett) *trckd ldrs: shkn up 2f out: nt qckn over 1f out: kpt on same pce to take 3rd nr fin (jockey said gelding was denied a clear run)* **28/1**

2-52 **4** *3/4* **Glen Shiel**[24] 7563 5-9-1 **100**.......................... HollieDoyle 7 101
(Archie Watson) *prom: led 3f out: drvn 2f out: hdd and one pce jst ins fnl f* **18/1**

0415 **5** *1 3/4* **Waarif (IRE)**[8] 8096 6-8-12 **97**.......................... DanielTudhope 15 94
(David O'Meara) *prom: trckd ldr 3f out gng strly: rdn 2f out: carried hd awkwardly and fnd little u.p over 1f out: wknd fnl f* **18/1**

5321 **6** *nse* **Kynren (IRE)**[14] 7891 5-9-8 **107** 6ex.......................... BenCurtis 19 104
(David Barron) *prom on outer: hrd rdn 2f out: one pce over 1f out* **6/1**[2]

0030 **7** *3/4* **So Beloved**[14] 7891 9-8-13 **98**.......................... GeraldMosse 10 93
(David O'Meara) *towards rr: pushed along over 2f out: kpt on over 1f out but nvr enough pce to threaten* **66/1**

0010 **8** 3/4 **Pogo (IRE)**[42] 6950 3-9-2 **104**.................................... KieranShoemark 22 96
(Charles Hills) *hld up in midfield: prog on outer to trck ldrs 2f out: sn rdn: fdd fnl f* **66/1**

5040 **9** nk **Chiefofchiefs**[9] 8062 6-8-13 **98**...........................(vt[1]) RichardKingscote 6 91
(Charlie Fellowes) *trckd ldrs: rdn and cl up 2f out to over 1f out: fdd fnl f* **50/1**

2105 **10** 1 3/4 **Biometric**[57] 6425 3-8-13 **101**.. HarryBentley 11 89
(Ralph Beckett) *hld up in midfield: rdn to chse ldrs over 1f out but hanging rt: wknd fnl f* **8/1**

6563 **11** nk **Dark Vision (IRE)**[7] 8126 3-8-12 **100**..........................(v) WilliamBuick 13 87
(Mark Johnston) *hld up wl in rr: rdn and no great prog on outer 2f out* **16/1**

5000 **12** nk **Clon Coulis (IRE)**[22] 7657 5-9-0 **99**...........................(h) JamieSpencer 1 86
(David Barron) *stdd s: hld up in last pair: shkn up and modest prog over 2f out: no hdwy over 1f out* **13/2**[3]

1060 **13** 1/2 **Saltonstall**[13] 7934 5-8-12 **97**....................................(tp) JasonWatson 17 83
(Adrian McGuinness, Ire) *hld up towards rr: prog over 2f out: rdn and wknd over 1f out* **50/1**

344 **14** 4 1/2 **Amedeo Modigliani (IRE)**[18] 7794 4-8-13 **98**.....(t) DonnachaO'Brien 12 74
(A P O'Brien, Ire) *hld up in midfield: gng bttr than most over 2f out: shkn up wl over 1f out: hanging and fnd nil: sn lost pl and sltly impeded: wknd* **7/1**

-522 **15** 7 **Arctic Sound**[11] 7997 3-9-6 **108**.............................. SilvestreDeSousa 23 67
(Mark Johnston) *in tch on outer: rdn and no prog over 2f out: wknd over 1f out* **40/1**

0100 **16** 2 1/4 **Circus Couture (IRE)**[91] 5192 7-8-11 **96**............................ JFEgan 5 51
(Jane Chapple-Hyam) *chsd ldrs to 3f out: wknd qckly 2f out* **66/1**

1-50 **17** 3/4 **Flaming Spear (IRE)**[63] 6215 7-9-8 **107**.......................... JoeyHaynes 16 60
(Dean Ivory) *s.s: hld up wl in rr: sme prog 3f out: wknd qckly 2f out* **28/1**

0011 **18** 6 **Coolagh Forest (IRE)**[7] 8126 3-9-0 **102** 6ex................ PaulHanagan 14 40
(Richard Fahey) *led to 3f out: lost pl rapidly and sn bhd* **11/1**

0001 **19** 37 **Kick On**[65] 6122 3-9-6 **108**.. OisinMurphy 2
(John Gosden) *prom: shkn up and wknd qckly over 2f out: heavily eased fnl f: t.o (jockey said colt boiled over in the preliminaries)* **11/1**

0-32 **20** 4 1/2 **Commander Cole**[21] 7686 5-9-0 **102**.......................... CierenFallon(3) 3
(Saeed bin Suroor) *w ldrs to over 3f out: wknd rapidly and t.o 2f out: eased (trainer's rep said gelding was unsuited by the heavy going and would prefer a quicker surface)* **28/1**

1m 45.8s (4.40) **Going Correction** +0.875s/f (Soft)
WFA 3 from 4yo+ 3lb **20** Ran SP% **136.4**
Speed ratings (Par 109): **113,110,109,109,107 107,106,105,105,103 103,103,102,98,91 88,88,82,45,40**
CSF £65.60 CT £1464.57 TOTE £14.20: £2.60, £1.70, £5.90, £4.30; EX 88.40 Trifecta £4781.50.

Owner Withernsea Thoroughbred Limited **Bred** Peter Evans **Trained** Upper Helmsley, N Yorks

FOCUS
There was always the chance that a track bias would show itself with the field spread across the width of the track, but everything headed towards the middle to far side. That looked like it would rule out those drawn really high (stands' side), but they still provided the first two home.
T/Jkpt: Not Won. T/Plt: £76.70 to a £1 stake. Pool: £319,493.77 - 3,040.44 winning units T/Qpdt: £16.80 to a £1 stake. Pool: £27,930.00 - 1,230.0 winning units **Jonathan Neesom**

7437

CATTERICK (L-H)

Saturday, October 19

OFFICIAL GOING: Soft (heavy in places; 6.9)
Wind: virtually nil Weather: overcast, drizzle after race 4

8337 BEST FLAT RACES LIVE ON RACING TV NOVICE MEDIAN AUCTION STKS 5f 212y

1:40 (1:42) (Class 5) 2-Y-O **£4,140** (£1,232; £615; £307) **Stalls** Low

Form RPR

2 **1** **Felicia Blue**[122] 4006 2-8-11 0.. PaddyMathers 2 72
(Richard Fahey) *prom: styd centre st initially: rdn into narrow ld over 1f out: edgd lft towards far side ent fnl f: kpt on wl* **7/1**

36 **2** 1 1/4 **Seas Of Elzaam (IRE)**[30] 7377 2-9-2 0.......................... ShaneGray 6 73
(David O'Meara) *trckd ldrs: c stands' side st: rdn over 1f out: kpt on fnl f* **18/1**

2313 **3** 3/4 **Jump The Gun (IRE)**[15] 7870 2-9-9 78.......................... PJMcDonald 1 78
(Jamie Osborne) *trckd ldrs: styd far side st: rdn to chal strly over 1f out: drvn ins fnl f no ex towards fin (starter reported that the colt was the subject of a third criteria failure; trainer was informed that the colt could not run until the day after passing a stalls test)* **2/1**[1]

22 **4** 1 1/4 **Rebel Soldier Boy**[25] 7538 2-9-2 0.............................. DavidNolan 4 67
(David O'Meara) *midfield: c stands' side st: rdn and hdwy to chse ldrs over 1f out: kpt on same pce ins fnl f* **9/2**[3]

2 **5** 2 3/4 **Leoch**[26] 7506 2-9-2 0.. KevinStott 10 62
(Kevin Ryan) *trckd ldrs: racd quite keenly: c stands' side st: rdn over 1f out: wknd and eased fnl 75yds* **9/4**[2]

6 4 1/2 **Where's Mick (IRE)** 2-9-2 0.. JackGarritty 5 45
(Jedd O'Keeffe) *s.i.s: hld up: styd far side st: hdwy and briefly chsd ldrs 2f out: wknd appr fnl f* **40/1**

00 **7** nk **Apache Bay**[30] 7377 2-8-11 0.. BenRobinson 12 39
(John Quinn) *across fr wd stall and sn led: c towards stands' side st: rdn and hdd over 1f out: sn wknd* **66/1**

8 7 **Cuban Affair** 2-8-11 0.. TonyHamilton 9 18
(Richard Fahey) *midfield on outer: c stands' side st: sn pushed along: wknd over 1f out* **20/1**

9 11 **Gowanlad** 2-9-2 0.. PhilDennis 8
(Philip Kirby) *hld up: racd keenly: racd centre st: wknd over 2f out* **50/1**

0 **10** 3 1/4 **Brass Clankers**[23] 7627 2-9-2 0.................................. PaulMulrennan 11
(Robyn Brisland) *hld up: rdn 3f out: sn wknd and bhd* **40/1**

0 **11** 19 **Belle Voci**[30] 7377 2-8-11 0.. CamHardie 3
(Stella Barclay) *sn pushed along towards rr: t.o fnl 3f* **100/1**

1m 19.33s (5.73) **Going Correction** +1.025s/f (Soft) **11** Ran SP% **114.1**
Speed ratings (Par 95): **95,93,92,90,87 81,80,71,56,52 26**
CSF £106.06 TOTE £6.40: £1.80, £4.30, £2.00; EX 167.00 Trifecta £404.70.
Owner Mrs Jane Newett & Partner **Bred** Mrs J Newett & R A Fahey **Trained** Musley Bank, N Yorks

FOCUS
After another 5mm of rain overnight the going was soft, heavy in places with a stick reading of 5.9 (the lowest reading since April 2016). All race distances were as advertised. A competitive novice auction to start things off and they spread right across the track up the straight but it appeared to make little difference.

8338 BRITISH EBF FILLIES' NOVICE STKS (PLUS 10 RACE) 7f 6y

2:15 (2:18) (Class 4) 2-Y-O **£6,663** (£1,982; £990; £495) **Stalls** Centre

Form RPR

0 **1** **Bound For Heaven**[24] 7580 2-9-0 0.............................. PJMcDonald 1 72
(K R Burke) *led: hdd over 4f out: remained cl up: rdn to ld again jst ins fnl f: drvn out* **9/2**[2]

2 3/4 **Golden Hind** 2-9-0 0.. ShaneGray 9 70+
(David O'Meara) *dwlt: hld up: pushed along over 3f out: rdn and hdwy on wd outside over 1f out: kpt on wl: wnt 2nd towards fin* **5/1**[3]

3 3/4 **Savage Beauty (IRE)** 2-9-0 0.. TonyHamilton 5 68
(Richard Fahey) *in tch: sltly hmpd and shuffled bk sltly over 2f out: pushed along and hdwy to chse ldrs appr fnl f: rdn and hung lft ins fnl f: kpt on same pce (vet said filly lost its left fore shoe)* **8/1**

3 **4** nk **Samille (IRE)**[31] 7330 2-9-0 0.. KevinStott 8 68
(Amy Murphy) *midfield: rdn and hdwy over 2f out: drvn to chse ldrs appr fnl f: kpt on same pce* **14/1**

33 **5** 1 3/4 **Let Her Loose (IRE)**[18] 7778 2-8-11 0.......................... SeanDavis(3) 7 63
(Richard Fahey) *hld up: pushed along over 3f out: rdn and hdwy on outer over 1f out: hung lft and one pce ins fnl f* **9/4**[1]

06 **6** 1 1/4 **Gina D'Cleaner**[35] 7211 2-9-0 0.. JoeFanning 11 60
(Keith Dalgleish) *trckd ldrs on outer: racd quite keenly: led over 4f out: rdn 2 l clr 2f out: hdd jst ins fnl f: sn wknd* **22/1**

0 **7** 1 1/4 **Ramsha (IRE)**[16] 7832 2-9-0 0.. DaneO'Neill 2 60
(Mark Johnston) *trckd ldrs: rdn over 2f out: keeping on at same pce whn hmpd ins fnl f: eased fnl 50yds (jockey said filly was denied a clear run in the final furlong)* **20/1**

64 **8** 3/4 **Al Jawhra (IRE)**[31] 7330 2-9-0 0.. DavidAllan 13 55
(Tim Easterby) *midfield: rdn over 2f out: one pce and nvr threatened* **16/1**

9 1 **Athabasca (IRE)** 2-9-0 0.. SamJames 3 53
(Grant Tuer) *trckd ldrs: lost pl 5f out: sn shuffled bk towards rr: rdn and sme hdwy over 1f out: wknd ins fnl f* **20/1**

10 21 **Secret Smile (IRE)** 2-9-0 0.. FrannyNorton 12
(Mark Johnston) *s.i.s: hld up: hdwy on outside and trckd ldrs over 4f out: rdn over 2f out: wknd over 1f out and eased* **10/1**

00 **11** 4 1/2 **Mist In The Valley**[144] 3196 2-9-0 0.............................. GrahamLee 4
(David Brown) *hld up in rr: wknd and bhd over 2f out* **66/1**

1m 35.76s (8.36) **Going Correction** +1.025s/f (Soft) **11** Ran SP% **113.7**
Speed ratings (Par 94): **93,92,91,90,88 87,86,85,84,60 54**
CSF £24.83 TOTE £4.10: £1.40, £1.60, £2.50; EX 30.70 Trifecta £120.60.
Owner John Dance **Bred** C J Murfitt **Trained** Middleham Moor, N Yorks

FOCUS
A handful of interesting fillies in this novice and the field closed right up near the line. The winner stepped forward from her debut.

8339 WILLIAM HILL LEADING RACECOURSE BOOKMAKER VETERANS' H'CAP 5f 212y

2:50 (2:52) (Class 5) (0-75,76) 6-Y-O+
£6,080 (£1,809; £904; £452; £300; £300) **Stalls** Low

Form RPR

1135 **1** **Captain Dion**[23] 7621 6-8-12 **69**..........................(b) GabrieleMalune(3) 2 79
(Ivan Furtado) *mde all: pushed along and in command over 1f out: rdn out ins fnl f: unchal* **7/2**[2]

3040 **2** 2 1/4 **Magical Effect (IRE)**[23] 7621 7-9-7 **75**.......................(p) JamieGormley 5 78
(Ruth Carr) *hld up: rdn and hdwy 2f out: wnt 2nd ins fnl f: kpt on but no threat wnr* **8/1**[3]

0026 **3** 1 3/4 **B Fifty Two (IRE)**[5] 8183 10-8-8 **65**........................(tp) JaneElliott(3) 9 62
(Marjorie Fife) *midfield: rdn over 2f out: kpt on fnl f* **9/1**

3410 **4** nk **Kenny The Captain (IRE)**[17] 7828 8-8-13 **67**.............. DavidAllan 4 63
(Tim Easterby) *chsd ldr: rdn over 2f out: one pce* **7/2**[2]

063/ **5** 5 **Star Citizen**[842] 4249 7-8-11 **65**.. KevinStott 1 45
(Fred Watson) *midfield: rdn over 2f out: wknd ins fnl f* **40/1**

2050 **6** nk **Economic Crisis (IRE)**[5] 8183 10-8-7 **64**.................. HarrisonShaw(3) 10 43
(Alan Berry) *hld up: rdn over 2f out: nvr threatened* **16/1**

3165 **7** 1 **Case Key**[32] 7321 6-8-11 **70**.................................(b) TheodoreLadd(5) 3 46
(Michael Appleby) *dwlt: a towards rr* **12/1**

6630 **8** 2 3/4 **Gin In The Inn (IRE)**[23] 7621 6-9-2 **73**.......................... SeanDavis(3) 7 40
(Richard Fahey) *chsd ldr: rdn over 2f out: wknd fnl f* **10/1**

6002 **9** 1 1/4 **Van Gerwen**[3] 8263 6-8-9 **63**.. GrahamLee 6 26
(Paul Midgley) *hld up in midfield: rdn over 2f out: sn wknd (trainer's rep said gelding ran flat having ran only 3 days previously)* **3/1**[1]

1m 18.77s (5.17) **Going Correction** +1.025s/f (Soft) **9** Ran SP% **115.7**
Speed ratings: **99,96,93,93,86 86,84,81,79**
CSF £31.68 CT £234.67 TOTE £4.40: £1.70, £2.10, £2.30; EX 27.10 Trifecta £147.60.
Owner Daniel Macauliffe & Anoj Don **Bred** Miss R J Dobson **Trained** Wiseton, Nottinghamshire

FOCUS
An open-looking veterans' sprint but it was turned into a procession.

8340 WILLIAM HILL CATTERICK DASH H'CAP 5f

3:25 (3:28) (Class 2) (0-100,102) 3-Y-O+
£21,787 (£6,524; £3,262; £1,631; £815; £409) **Stalls** Low

Form RPR

0212 **1** **Count D'orsay (IRE)**[8] 8099 3-9-0 **91**.............................. DavidAllan 3 100
(Tim Easterby) *chsd ldrs towards far side: rdn to ld over 1f out: drvn and kpt on wl* **5/1**[2]

3116 **2** 1/2 **Four Wheel Drive**[26] 7524 3-8-10 **87**..........................(p) JoeFanning 4 94
(David Brown) *chsd ldrs far side: rdn 2f out: kpt on fnl f* **20/1**

0205 **3** 1 1/4 **Broken Spear**[5] 8182 3-8-9 **86**..................................(p) BarryMcHugh 2 89
(Tony Coyle) *chsd ldrs far side: rdn over 2f out: one pce ins fnl f* **18/1**

6205 **4** 1 **Dark Shot**[3] 8267 6-8-7 **84** oh2..................................(v) PaddyMathers 1 82
(Scott Dixon) *hld up towards far side: rdn over 2f out: kpt on fnl f* **22/1**

0003 **5** 1 3/4 **Teruntum Star (FR)**[14] 7894 7-8-13 **90**................(p) AlistairRawlinson 12 82+
(David C Griffiths) *hld up centre: rdn along 3f out: kpt on ins fnl f: nvr trbld ldrs* **20/1**

2302 **6** 3/4 **Hyperfocus (IRE)**[7] 8127 5-9-6 **97**..............................(p) DuranFentiman 5 86
(Tim Easterby) *in tch centre: rdn 2f out: edgd lft and one pce ins fnl f* **10/1**

1040 **7** 1 1/4 **Makanah**[35] 7193 4-9-6 **97**.. PaulMulrennan 13 81
(Julie Camacho) *chsd ldr centre: rdn 2f out: no ex ins fnl f* **8/1**

2511 **8** 1 ¾ **Wrenthorpe**[3] 8262 4-8-8 **85** 5ex ow1 .... GrahamLee 6 63
(Bryan Smart) *racd centre: led narrowly: rdn and hdd over 1f out: wknd ins fnl f* **7/1**[3]

1221 **9** shd **Moss Gill (IRE)**[8] 8099 3-9-7 **98** .... PJMcDonald 11 77
(James Bethell) *midfield in centre: rdn and outpcd over 2f out: nvr involved (trainer's rep said gelding was unsuited by the ground on this occasion which in her opinion was riding very testing)* **5/2**[1]

2402 **10** 3 **Arecibo (FR)**[14] 7889 4-9-11 **102** ....(v) DavidNolan 14 69
(David O'Meara) *hld up in centre: nvr threatened (jockey said gelding stumbled 2 furlongs out)* **14/1**

0340 **11** 2 **Free Love**[8] 8099 3-8-4 **86** .... TheodoreLadd(5) 7 47
(Michael Appleby) *chsd ldrs centre: rdn over 2f out: wknd over 1f out* **20/1**

2340 **12** 1 ½ **Duke Of Firenze**[8] 8099 10-8-12 **89** .... PhilDennis 10 43
(David C Griffiths) *hld up in rr centre: nvr threatened* **50/1**

0403 **13** 6 **She Can Boogie (IRE)**[42] 6960 3-8-9 **89** .... JaneElliott(3) 9 23
(Tom Dascombe) *chsd ldrs centre: rdn and lost pl over 2f out: wknd over 1f out* **14/1**

6245 **14** 1 ¼ **Hawaam (IRE)**[3] 8262 4-8-7 **84** oh4 ....(p) JamieGormley 8 12
(Roger Fell) *dwlt: sn chsd ldrs in centre: rdn and lost pl over 2f out: sn wknd* **50/1**

1m 2.91s (2.41) **Going Correction** +1.025s/f (Soft) **14 Ran SP% 119.1**
Speed ratings (Par 109): **114,113,111,109,106 105,103,100,100,95 92,90,80,78**
CSF £108.62 CT £1121.56 TOTE £5.40: £2.30, £6.10, £6.00; EX 131.90 Trifecta £1074.30.
Owner Ambrose Turnbull & John Cruces **Bred** Corrin Stud **Trained** Great Habton, N Yorks

FOCUS
A competitive and valuable feature sprint handicap with a red-hot 3yo favourite. The draw looked to do for him and others.

8341 FOLLOW @WILLHILLRACING ON TWITTER H'CAP 1m 4f 13y
3:55 (3:57) (Class 4) (0-80,81) 3-Y-O+

£8,964 (£2,684; £1,342; £671; £335; £300) **Stalls Low**

Form RPR

2112 **1** **Anna Bunina (FR)**[30] 7379 3-9-4 **80** .... JackGarritty 5 93
(Jedd O'Keeffe) *prom: led 3f out: sn pushed along: drvn over 1f out: styd on wl* **11/4**[1]

2-26 **2** 3 ¾ **Wolf Prince (IRE)**[21] 7683 3-9-0 **76** .... PJMcDonald 3 82
(Amy Murphy) *led: rdn along and hdd 3f out: drvn over 1f out: styd on ins fnl f* **11/2**[3]

55 **3** 2 ¼ **Unit Of Assessment (IRE)**[24] 7575 5-9-10 **80** ....(vt) DaneO'Neill 2 82
(William Knight) *trckd ldrs: rdn over 3f out: drvn to dispute 2nd over 1f out: no ex fnl 110yds* **10/1**

1110 **4** 3 ½ **Gylo (IRE)**[28] 7441 3-8-10 **75** .... HarrisonShaw(3) 10 71
(David O'Meara) *in tch: rdn over 3f out: swtchd rt to stands' side over 2f out: plugged on* **12/1**

2105 **5** 8 **Qawamees (IRE)**[29] 7403 4-9-7 **77** ....(bt) GrahamLee 1 61
(Michael Easterby) *hld up: sme hdwy 4f out: rdn 3f out: wknd over 1f out* **14/1**

3405 **6** 8 **Detachment**[14] 7907 6-8-12 **71** .... CameronNoble(3) 12 42
(Roger Fell) *hld up in midfield: rdn over 3f out: nvr involved* **20/1**

1230 **7** 3 **Sea Of Mystery (IRE)**[9] 8065 6-8-5 **66** oh3 ....(tp) TheodoreLadd(5) 9 32
(Michael Appleby) *hld up in midfield: rdn over 3f out: nvr involved* **14/1**

5664 **8** 1 ¾ **Billy No Mates (IRE)**[21] 7702 3-9-3 **79** .... PaulMulrennan 8 42
(Michael Dods) *trckd ldrs: rdn over 3f out: wknd 2f out (trainer's rep could offer no explanation for the gelding's performance)* **10/3**[2]

0540 **9** 4 **Super Kid**[21] 7702 7-9-2 **72** ....(tp) RachelRichardson 4 29
(Tim Easterby) *a towards rr* **33/1**

0663 **10** 4 ½ **Cape Islay (FR)**[31] 7332 3-9-5 **81** .... FrannyNorton 6 31
(Mark Johnston) *midfield: rdn over 3f out: wknd over 2f out* **33/1**

0560 **11** 6 **Winged Spur (IRE)**[32] 7294 4-9-7 **77** .... JoeFanning 7 17
(Mark Johnston) *dwlt: a in rr* **33/1**

040 **12** 47 **Appointed**[21] 7702 5-9-4 **74** ....(t) DavidAllan 11
(Tim Easterby) *trckd ldrs: rdn over 4f out: sn wknd: eased and t.o fnl 2f* **12/1**

2m 50.69s (10.09) **Going Correction** +1.025s/f (Soft) **12 Ran SP% 116.5**
WFA 3 from 4yo+ 6lb
Speed ratings (Par 105): **107,104,103,100,95 90,88,86,84,81 77,45**
CSF £16.67 CT £127.54 TOTE £4.00: £1.50, £2.90, £2.20; EX 19.80 Trifecta £141.30.
Owner Highbeck Racing 3 **Bred** Dermot Cantillon **Trained** Middleham Moor, N Yorks

FOCUS
Lots of chances in this middle-distance handicap but it was attritional stuff and the strongest stayer won it.

8342 GET SO MUCH MORE WITH RACING TV H'CAP 7f 6y
4:30 (4:33) (Class 4) (0-80,81) 3-Y-O+

£8,964 (£2,684; £1,342; £671; £335; £300) **Stalls Centre**

Form RPR

000 **1** **Rolladice**[42] 6972 4-8-9 **67** .... NathanEvans 8 76
(Michael Easterby) *prom: pushed along over 3f out: rdn into narrow ld over 2f out: drvn and hdd 1f out: rallied to ld again towards fin* **40/1**

303 **2** nk **Captain Jameson (IRE)**[8] 8101 4-9-9 **81** ....(p) PJMcDonald 4 89
(John Quinn) *in tch: pushed along and hdwy to chse ldrs over 2f out: rdn to ld 1f out: sn drvn: no ex and hdd towards fin* **3/1**[1]

5305 **3** 2 ½ **Zip**[14] 7906 3-8-12 **72** .... TonyHamilton 7 73
(Richard Fahey) *hld up in midfield: rdn and hdwy 2f out: kpt on to go 3rd fnl 75yds* **11/2**[2]

4631 **4** ½ **Confrontational (IRE)**[21] 7678 5-9-7 **79** ....(p) ShaneGray 3 79
(Jennie Candlish) *chsd ldrs: rdn over 2f out: kpt on same pce* **11/2**[2]

4660 **5** 1 ¼ **Airglow (IRE)**[29] 7402 4-8-12 **75** ....(h) GerO'Neill(5) 9 72
(Michael Easterby) *trckd ldrs: drvn to chal over 1f out: wknd fnl 110yds* **10/1**

2142 **6** ¾ **Global Spirit**[50] 6677 4-9-6 **78** ....(p) PaulMulrennan 2 73
(Roger Fell) *hld up: rdn over 2f out: plugged on fr over 1f out: nvr threatened* **16/1**

3006 **7** 1 ¼ **Jackpot Royale**[31] 7350 4-9-1 **78** .... TheodoreLadd(5) 14 70
(Michael Appleby) *hld up: swtchd rt to stands' side over 2f out: plugged on nvr threatened* **20/1**

0400 **8** 3 **Start Time (IRE)**[23] 7621 6-9-0 **72** .... KevinStott 11 56
(Paul Midgley) *midfield on outer: rdn over 2f out: wknd fnl f* **16/1**

0106 **9** 3 **Parys Mountain (IRE)**[15] 7865 5-9-8 **80** ....(t) DavidAllan 5 56
(Tim Easterby) *led: rdn and hdd over 2f out: wknd fnl f* **14/1**

1066 **10** ½ **Mr Orange (IRE)**[8] 8101 6-9-5 **77** ....(p) GrahamLee 13 52
(Paul Midgley) *hld up: nvr threatened* **20/1**

4606 **11** ½ **Beryl The Petal (IRE)**[39] 7049 3-9-1 **78** ....(v) HarrisonShaw(3) 6 51
(David O'Meara) *midfield: rdn over 2f out: wknd fnl f* **40/1**

3462 **12** ¾ **Self Assessment (IRE)**[39] 7049 3-8-13 **73** .... CliffordLee 10 44
(K R Burke) *hld up: nvr threatened* **14/1**

5000 **13** 2 ¼ **Right Action**[30] 7362 5-9-2 **77** .... ConnorMurtagh(3) 1 43
(Richard Fahey) *midfield on inner: rdn over 2f out: wknd over 1f out* **9/1**[3]

0400 **14** 12 **Wasntexpectingthat**[18] 7781 3-8-8 **68** .... PaddyMathers 12 2
(Richard Fahey) *hld up: rdn over 2f out: wknd over 1f out: eased ins fnl f* **40/1**

5300 **15** 9 **Summer Daydream (IRE)**[20] 7735 3-9-3 **77** ....(v[1]) JoeFanning 15
(Keith Dalgleish) *a in rr: eased over 1f out* **25/1**

1m 33.9s (6.50) **Going Correction** +1.025s/f (Soft) **15 Ran SP% 120.6**
WFA 3 from 4yo+ 2lb
Speed ratings (Par 105): **103,102,99,99,97 96,95,92,88,88 87,86,84,70,60**
CSF £148.08 CT £793.90 TOTE £49.40: £11.50, £1.60, £1.60; EX 236.20 Trifecta £1796.30.
Owner A Pollock And J Blackburn **Bred** Mrs R D Peacock **Trained** Sheriff Hutton, N Yorks
■ Stewards' Enquiry : Nathan Evans four-day ban: used whip above the permitted level (Nov 2, 4-6)

FOCUS
An open contest but once again a prominent position was key.

8343 GO RACING IN YORKSHIRE APPRENTICE H'CAP (GO RACING IN YORKSHIRE FUTURE STARS SERIES) (DIV I) 1m 5f 192y
5:00 (5:04) (Class 6) (0-60,61) 3-Y-O+

£3,946 (£1,174; £586; £300; £300; £300) **Stalls Low**

Form RPR

0564 **1** **Miss Ranger (IRE)**[32] 7314 7-9-2 **48** .... PaulaMuir 1 55
(Roger Fell) *trckd ldrs: rdn to ld appr fnl f: styd on wl* **8/1**[3]

-500 **2** 2 ¼ **Lady Kyria (FR)**[28] 7441 5-9-4 **57** ....(h) NickBarratt-Atkin(7) 8 61
(Philip Kirby) *midfield: rdn over 2f out: hdwy over 1f out: styd on to go 2nd ins fnl f* **9/1**

000 **3** 1 ¾ **Fasterkhani**[130] 3680 3-8-7 **46** .... TheodoreLadd 6 49
(Philip Kirby) *led: jnd 4f out: rdn over 2f out: hdd appr fnl f: no ex ins fnl f* **20/1**

-000 **4** 6 **Ruler Of The Nile**[9] 8072 7-8-10 **45** .... RhonaPindar(3) 3 38
(Marjorie Fife) *trckd ldr: jnd ldr 4f out: rdn over 2f out: wknd appr fnl f* **40/1**

2135 **5** 3 ¼ **Jan De Heem**[28] 7441 9-9-9 **58** ....(v) EllaMcCain(3) 10 46
(Tina Jackson) *hld up: lot to do whn rdn along over 2f out: nvr a threat* **5/1**[2]

0631 **6** 1 **Beaufort (IRE)**[29] 7415 3-9-8 **61** .... SeamusCronin 5 49
(Michael Dods) *v.s.a and lost 20 l s: in tch w main field 9f out: rdn over 2f out: sn btn (jockey said gelding became upset in the stalls and as a result missed the break, losing many lengths)* **2/1**[1]

000 **7** 6 **Excalibur (POL)**[13] 6343 6-8-13 **45** ....(p) AndrewBreslin 4 23
(Micky Hammond) *midfield: rdn over 3f out: wknd over 2f out* **14/1**

3m 31.97s (24.37) **Going Correction** +1.025s/f (Soft) **7 Ran SP% 85.0**
WFA 3 from 5yo+ 7lb
Speed ratings (Par 101): **71,69,68,65,63 62,59**
CSF £38.85 CT £479.01 TOTE £6.60: £2.00, £3.20; EX 35.40 Trifecta £450.60.
Owner Jane Greetham & Victoria Greetham **Bred** J F Tuthill **Trained** Nawton, N Yorks
■ Soft Summer Rain was withdrawn. Price at time of withdrawal 5/2. Rule 4 applies to all bets - deduction 25p in the pound

FOCUS
An uncompetitive apprentice handicap over a staying trip.

8344 GO RACING IN YORKSHIRE APPRENTICE H'CAP (GO RACING IN YORKSHIRE FUTURE STARS SERIES) (DIV II) 1m 5f 192y
5:35 (5:35) (Class 6) (0-60,62) 3-Y-O+

£3,946 (£1,174; £586; £300; £300; £300) **Stalls Low**

Form RPR

0056 **1** **Gordalan**[50] 6660 3-8-6 **52** ....(v[1]) ZakWheatley(5) 3 63
(Philip Kirby) *mde all: racd keenly: slipped clr 9f out: sn 15 l up: rdn out fr over 1f out: unchal (trainer said, regarding the improved form shown, the gelding may have appreciated the first-time application of a visor)* **18/1**

3006 **2** 8 **Masters Apprentice (IRE)**[13] 7314 4-9-6 **54** ....(p) PaulaMuir 8 51+
(Mark Walford) *midfield: rdn along 3f out: plugged on to go poor 2nd ins fnl f (jockey said gelding hung left)* **4/1**[2]

0643 **3** hd **St Andrews (IRE)**[39] 7053 6-9-0 **53** ....(v) OliverStammers(5) 9 50+
(Gillian Boanas) *midfield: rdn and outpcd over 3f out: plugged on fr over 1f out to dispute poor 2nd ins fnl f* **3/1**[1]

0000 **4** 6 **Richard Strauss (IRE)**[9] 5766 5-8-8 **49** ....(p) NickBarratt-Atkin(7) 4 37
(Philip Kirby) *prom: chsd clr ldr 9f out: rdn 3f out: wknd ins fnl f* **25/1**

0-01 **5** 10 **Only Orsenfoolsies**[15] 3294 10-9-7 **60** ....(p) AidenBlakemore(5) 2 34
(Micky Hammond) *midfield: rdn over 3f out: sn wknd* **9/2**[3]

506- **6** nk **Legalized**[189] 8416 5-8-12 **46** oh1 .... DannyRedmond 5 19
(Dianne Sayer) *in tch: rdn over 3f out: wknd fnl f and eased* **4/1**[2]

0504 **7** 17 **Archie's Sister**[9] 8072 3-8-5 **46** oh1 ....(t) TheodoreLadd 10
(Philip Kirby) *v.s.a: a in rr (jockey said filly fly lept leaving the stalls)* **9/2**[3]

05 **8** 22 **Late For The Sky**[94] 5043 5-8-7 **46** oh1 .... GavinAshton(5) 6
(Stella Barclay) *hld up: rdn 4f out: wknd and t.o* **50/1**

3m 25.31s (17.71) **Going Correction** +1.025s/f (Soft) **8 Ran SP% 112.4**
WFA 3 from 4yo+ 7lb
Speed ratings (Par 101): **90,85,85,81,76 76,66,53**
CSF £85.58 CT £280.58 TOTE £23.40: £3.80, £1.20, £1.40; EX 104.80 Trifecta £215.70.
Owner Buckingham Flooring **Bred** Jarvis Associates **Trained** East Appleton, N Yorks

FOCUS
The second division of the staying handicap for apprentices and it was stolen by Zak Wheatley.
T/Plt: £337.00 to a £1 stake. Pool: £50,602.22 - 109.60 winning units T/Qpdt: £100.80 to a £1 stake. Pool: £4,730.00 - 34.72 winning units **Andrew Sheret**

8315 WOLVERHAMPTON (A.W) (L-H)
Saturday, October 19

OFFICIAL GOING: Tapeta: standard
Wind: partly cloudy, quite cool Weather: light breeze

8345 INVADES STUDENT RACING EXTRAVAGANZA H'CAP 1m 142y (Tp)
5:05 (5:10) (Class 6) (0-60,60) 3-Y-O+

£2,781 (£827; £413; £400; £400; £400) **Stalls Low**

Form RPR

2021 **1** **Colonel Slade (IRE)**[24] 7581 3-9-2 **60** ....(t[1]) JackMitchell 7 70
(Phillip Makin) *mde all: pushed along in 1 1/2 l ld 2f out: rdn over 1f out: drifted rt ent fnl f where 2 l clr: r.o wl: comf* **6/4**[1]

0324 **2** 2 1/2 **Traveller (FR)**[8] 8087 5-9-3 **57**...(tp) CamHardie 13 62
(Antony Brittain) *chsd ldrs on outer: pushed along in 4th 2f out: rdn and hdwy to chse ldr 1f out: kpt on but no imp ins fnl f* 7/2[2]

5456 **3** 2 1/4 **Storm Eleanor**[23] 7629 3-9-2 **60**... CharlieBennett 9 60
(Hughie Morrison) *hld up: pushed along over 2f out: reminder 1 1/2f out: rdn and r.o fnl f: tk 3rd last two strides* 12/1

- **4** nk **Kudbegood (IRE)**[21] 7715 4-9-1 **60**...(t) DylanHogan(5) 6 60
(John C McConnell, Ire) *trckd ldrs: pushed along in 3rd 2f out: rdn into 2nd 1 1/2f out: wknd fnl f: lost 3rd last two strides* 11/2[3]

5305 **5** 3 1/2 **Air Of York (IRE)**[46] 6844 7-9-6 **60**...(p) LukeMorris 4 52
(Grace Harris) *hld up: drvn over 2f out: rdn in mid-div 1 1/2f out: sn wknd* 20/1

0/23 **6** 2 1/4 **Pushaq (IRE)**[87] 5326 6-9-2 **56**...(t) ShaneKelly 11 44
(Anthony McCann, Ire) *prom: rdn in 2nd 2f out: lost pl 1 1/2f out: sn wknd* 9/1

5600 **7** 6 **Bobby Joe Leg**[29] 7418 5-9-4 **58**... JamesSullivan 10 33
(Ruth Carr) *in rr: reminders bef 1/2-way: hdwy on outer over 2f out: sn drvn: rdn and wknd over 1f out* 20/1

5000 **8** 6 **Arlecchino's Leap**[38] 7084 7-9-4 **58**...(p) DavidProbert 1 20
(Mark Usher) *hld up: rdn over 2f out: wl bhd fr 1 1/2f out* 12/1

0000 **9** 1/2 **Staplegrove (IRE)**[17] 7820 4-9-2 **56**... DougieCostello 5 17
(Stella Barclay) *mid-div: drvn and lost pl over 2f out: no ch fr 1 1/2f out* 50/1

3006 **10** 1/2 **William McKinley**[67] 6052 3-9-2 **60**...(b) RossaRyan 2 20
(Ali Stronge) *bhd: reminders after 2f: drvn and dropped to last 3f out: sn wl bhd* 16/1

1m 47.15s (-2.95) **Going Correction** -0.15s/f (Stan)
WFA 3 from 4yo+ 4lb **10** Ran SP% **120.4**
Speed ratings (Par 101): **107,104,102,102,99 97,92,86,86,85**
CSF £6.63 CT £47.16 TOTE £2.00: £1.10, £1.30, £3.70; EX 7.50 Trifecta £50.00.
Owner P J Makin **Bred** Kellsgrange Stud & T & J Hurley **Trained** Easingwold, N Yorks

FOCUS
An ordinary handicap run at a fair pace. The progressive winner edged into the centre of the course in the straight.

8346 UNIVERSITY OF BIRMINGHAM INVADES NOVICE STKS 1m 142y (Tp)
5:40 (5:44) (Class 5) 2-Y-O £3,428 (£1,020; £509; £254) **Stalls** Low

Form RPR

00 **1** **Chinese Whisperer (FR)**[17] 7814 2-9-5 0... TomQueally 5 73
(Alan King) *prom: cl 2nd 2f out: pushed into ld 1 1/2f out: rdn into 2 l ld ins fnl f: r.o wl: ld diminishing nr fin* 20/1

2 nk **King Of Arms** 2-9-5 0... KieranO'Neill 2 72+
(John Gosden) *trckd ldrs: 3rd 2f out: drvn 1 1/2f out: drifted rt and reminder ins fnl f: r.o wl: gaining on wnr nr fin* 7/4[2]

3 1 1/4 **My Vision** 2-9-5 0... CallumShepherd 6 70+
(Saeed bin Suroor) *bked out of stalls sharply during loading but consented 2nd time: slowly away: sn rcvrd to r in midfield: pushed along in 5th 2f out: drvn on inner over 1f out: reminder and wnt 3rd ins fnl f: kpt on* 4/1[3]

0 **4** hd **Sefton Warrior**[31] 7346 2-9-5 0... StevieDonohoe 9 69
(Richard Spencer) *mid-div: drvn on outer 1 1/2f out: reminder fnl f: r.o* 25/1

00 **5** 1 **Kings Creek (IRE)**[24] 7571 2-9-5 0... GeorgeWood 3 67
(Alan King) *t.k.h: chsd ldrs: drvn in 4th 2f out: lost pl over 1f out: rdn fnl f: no ex* 50/1

32 **6** hd **Crystal Pegasus**[24] 7579 2-9-5 0... LouisSteward 1 67
(Sir Michael Stoute) *led: pushed along in narrow ld 2f out: hdd 1 1/2f out: sn rdn: wknd fnl f* 11/8[1]

7 1/2 **Kitten's Dream** 2-9-2 0... SeanDavis(3) 8 65+
(Richard Fahey) *hld up: pushed along over 2f out: drvn 1 1/2f out: r.o steadily under hand riding fnl f* 20/1

0 **8** shd **Savanna Gold (IRE)**[17] 7814 2-9-5 0... JackMitchell 4 65+
(Hugo Palmer) *hld up: drvn over 2f out: reminders ent fnl f: kpt on* 20/1

9 23 **Colada Cove (IRE)** 2-9-5 0... DavidProbert 7 15
(Tom Ward) *in rr: drvn over 2f out: sn lost tch* 28/1

1m 50.57s (0.47) **Going Correction** -0.15s/f (Stan) **9** Ran SP% **122.0**
Speed ratings (Par 95): **91,90,89,89,88 88,87,87,67**
CSF £54.89 TOTE £44.50: £6.80, £1.10, £1.80; EX 138.40 Trifecta £1367.60.
Owner Barbury Lions 5 **Bred** Berend Van Dalfsen **Trained** Barbury Castle, Wilts

FOCUS
A falsely run race in which several finished in a bit of a heap and this bare form doesn't look reliable. The market leader disappointed and the runner-up and third are the ones to take from the race.

8347 ASTON UNIVERSITY INVADES H'CAP 2m 120y (Tp)
6:15 (6:17) (Class 6) (0-60,60) 4-Y-O+ £2,781 (£827; £413; £400; £400; £400) **Stalls** Low

Form RPR

0/0- **1** **Yamato (IRE)**[22] 7670 6-8-6 **48**...(t) SeanDavis(3) 8 58+
(John C McConnell, Ire) *mid-div: hdwy over 3f out: led 2f out: drvn into 3 l ld 1f out: 6 l clr wl ins fnl f: heavily eased and ld much reduced last 100yds: jst hld on* 6/1

3506 **2** shd **Falcon Cliffs (IRE)**[16] 7845 5-9-2 **55**... TomMarquand 9 60
(Tony Carroll) *hld up: drvn and hdwy on outer 1 1/2f out: rdn fnl f: r.o wl: clsd rapidly on eased down wnr last 100yds: jst failed* 11/4[1]

4620 **3** 3/4 **Butterfield (IRE)**[19] 7759 6-8-11 **50**... EoinWalsh 4 54
(Brian Forsey) *hld up: drvn and hdwy on outer over 2f out: wnt 3rd 1 1/2f out: rdn to chse wnr ent fnl f: kpt on: flattered by proximity to eased down wnr* 33/1

4203 **4** 3 1/4 **Yasir (USA)**[17] 7818 11-9-0 **53**... DavidProbert 6 53
(Sophie Leech) *slowly away: in rr: hdwy on outer over 2f out: drvn 1 1/2f out: sn rdn: kpt on into 4th fnl f* 5/1[3]

2352 **5** 3/4 **Givepeaceachance**[19] 7759 4-9-2 **55**... ShaneKelly 10 54
(Denis Coakley) *prom: led after 5f: rdn and hdd 2f out: wknd fnl f* 7/2[2]

006/ **6** 3 **Never A Word (USA)**[9] 9270 5-9-4 **60**...(bt) MeganNicholls(3) 7 56
(Oliver Greenall) *hld up: drvn 1 1/2f out: rdn over 1f out: one pce fnl f (jockey said gelding was slowly away)* 20/1

6220 **7** shd **Sacred Sprite**[45] 6853 4-9-2 **60**... DylanHogan(5) 11 56
(John Berry) *hld up: drvn on outer 3f out: rdn 1 1/2f out: no imp* 15/2

3600 **8** 1 **Sweetest Smile (IRE)**[8] 8081 4-8-4 **46** oh1... WilliamCox(3) 13 40
(Ed de Giles) *chsd ldrs: drvn and lost pl over 2f out: sn rdn and wknd* 33/1

2340 **9** 2 **Danglydontask**[25] 7558 8-8-8 **47**...(b) LukeMorris 3 39
(Mike Murphy) *chsd ldrs: wnt 2nd 1/2-way: rdn 3f out: dropped away fr 1 1/2f out* 25/1

3350 **10** 1 1/2 **Konigin**[32] 7318 4-9-6 **59**...(tp) HectorCrouch 1 49
(John Berry) *hld up: pushed along 2f out: rdn over 1f out: no imp (jockey said filly was denied a clear run approaching the home turn)* 9/1

4306 **11** 1 1/4 **Normandy Blue**[19] 7759 4-8-7 **46** oh1...(p) KieranO'Neill 12 35
(Luke McJannet) *hld up: drvn in mid-div and nt clr run over 2f out: sn rdn and wknd* 14/1

05-3 **12** 11 **Helf (IRE)**[21] 185 5-9-1 **54**...(tp) JamesSullivan 2 29
(Oliver Greenall) *mid-div: drvn and lost pl over 3f out: rdn and wknd over 2f out* 28/1

6/ **13** 8 **Authorative (IRE)**[22] 1717 9-8-7 **46** oh1...(tp) CamHardie 5 12
(Anthony McCann, Ire) *led: hdd after 5f: dropped to 3rd 1/2-way: rdn and wknd 3f out* 40/1

3m 39.08s (-0.22) **Going Correction** -0.15s/f (Stan) **13** Ran SP% **128.7**
Speed ratings (Par 101): **94,93,93,92,91 90,90,89,88,88 87,82,78**
CSF £22.95 CT £539.60 TOTE £7.70: £2.30, £1.20, £10.40; EX 31.50 Trifecta £1669.90.
Owner Singing The Blues Syndicate **Bred** T Kimura **Trained** Stamullen, Co Meath

FOCUS
A moderate handicap run at a reasonable gallop and one that would have seen Yamato run out a comfortable winner had his rider not dropped his hands in the last 100yds.

8348 UNIVERSITY COLLEGE BIRMINGHAM INVADES H'CAP 1m 1f 104y (Tp)
6:45 (6:45) (Class 6) (0-60,60) 3-Y-O+ £2,781 (£827; £413; £400; £400; £400) **Stalls** Low

Form RPR

024 **1** **Miss Elsa**[17] 7817 3-8-13 **57**... GeorgiaDobie(5) 5 64
(Eve Johnson Houghton) *mid-div: pushed along and hdwy 1 1/2f out: drvn to ld 1f out: rdn clr fnl f* 5/1[3]

4334 **2** 2 **Vipin (FR)**[19] 7758 4-9-7 **59**... GeorgiaCox(3) 3 62
(William Muir) *chsd ldrs: pushed along in 3rd 2f out: drvn to ld on inner over 1f out: sn hdd: rdn and kpt on fnl f: nt pce of wnr* 9/2[2]

4-06 **3** nk **Rusper's Gift (IRE)**[40] 7034 3-9-7 **60**... DougieCostello 8 63
(Jamie Osborne) *chsd ldrs: drvn over 2f out: cl up and rdn over 1f out: kpt on into 3rd fnl f* 50/1

6404 **4** 1/2 **Thawry**[12] 7956 4-9-10 **59**... CamHardie 2 61
(Antony Brittain) *hld up: pushed along and hdwy 1 1/2f out: nt clr run over 1f out: rdden and kpt on into 4th fnl f* 8/1

004 **5** nse **Pilot Wings (IRE)**[16] 7858 4-9-10 **59**...(tp) DavidProbert 6 61
(David Dennis) *hld up: pushed along on outer 1 1/2f out: drvn and hdwy 1f out: rdn fnl f: kpt on* 11/1

02-0 **6** hd **Earl Of Bunnacurry (IRE)**[72] 5876 5-9-9 **58**... KieranO'Neill 1 59
(Gavin Cromwell, Ire) *disp ld tl led on own over 3f out: rdn in 1 l ld 2f out: hdd over 1f out: wknd fnl f* 13/8[1]

0206 **7** 1 **Thunderoad**[21] 7685 3-9-7 **60**...(p) ShaneKelly 7 59
(Tony Carroll) *hld up: smooth hdwy on outer 2f out: cl up over 1f out: rdn and wknd fnl f* 7/1

0655 **8** 4 **Zest Of Zambia (USA)**[34] 7238 3-9-4 **57**... CharlieBennett 9 49
(Dai Burchell) *disp ld tl hdd over 3f out: drvn and lost pl 1 1/2f out: sn rdn and wknd* 50/1

0600 **9** 1 **Raven's Raft (IRE)**[32] 7300 4-9-7 **56**... StevieDonohoe 11 46
(David Loughnane) *mid-div: drvn and lost pl 2f out: sn wknd* 20/1

4-00 **10** 2 1/4 **Island Reel (IRE)**[158] 2719 3-9-4 **60**... JaneElliott(3) 4 46
(Heather Main) *hld up: rdn 1 1/2f out: lost tch 1f out (jockey said filly was slowly away)* 22/1

3600 **11** 3 1/2 **Uh Oh Chongo**[18] 7776 3-9-3 **56**... JamesSullivan 13 35
(Michael Easterby) *hld up: rdn and lost tch 1 1/2f out* 25/1

2m 0.12s (-0.68) **Going Correction** -0.15s/f (Stan)
WFA 3 from 4yo+ 4lb **11** Ran SP% **121.8**
Speed ratings (Par 101): **97,95,94,94,94 94,93,89,88,86 83**
CSF £27.13 CT £1023.06 TOTE £5.40: £1.80, £1.80, £15.60; EX 31.00 Trifecta £1249.20.
Owner Eden Racing Club **Bred** Eve Johnson Houghton **Trained** Blewbury, Oxon

FOCUS
A low-grade handicap in which the gallop soon steadied before picking up again on the approach to the home straight.

8349 BIRMINGHAM CITY UNIVERSITY INVADES FILLIES' H'CAP 6f 20y (Tp)
7:15 (7:16) (Class 4) (0-85,83) 3-Y-O+ £5,207 (£1,549; £774; £400; £400; £400) **Stalls** Low

Form RPR

513 **1** **Dizzy G (IRE)**[29] 7402 4-9-7 **80**... AndrewMullen 2 88
(K R Burke) *trckd ldrs: drvn in 5th 2f out: rdn over 1f out: hdwy ins fnl f: str run nr fin: led last stride* 15/2

4201 **2** nse **With Caution (IRE)**[23] 7607 3-9-9 **83**... TomMarquand 5 91
(James Tate) *prom: pushed along in cl 2nd 2f out: rdn 1f out: led 1/2f out: strly pressed nr fin: hdd last stride* 11/4[1]

1240 **3** 1/2 **Whisper Aloud**[7] 8115 3-8-13 **80**... Pierre-LouisJamin(7) 6 86
(Archie Watson) *led: drvn in narrow ld 2f out: rdn 1f out: hdd 1/2f out: kpt on* 9/2[2]

0516 **4** 1 **Irene May (IRE)**[23] 7613 3-9-7 **81**... LukeMorris 4 84
(Sylvester Kirk) *hld up: drvn over 2f out: rdn 1 1/2f out: r.o into 4th fnl f: nvr nrr* 12/1

3154 **5** 1 1/4 **Lethal Angel**[16] 7837 4-8-13 **72**...(p) KieranO'Neill 1 71
(Stuart Williams) *hld up: drvn and effrt 1 1/2f out: rdn over 1f out: one pce fnl f* 6/1[3]

1003 **6** hd **Alhakmah (IRE)**[10] 8017 3-9-6 **80**... RossaRyan 8 78
(Richard Hannon) *t.k.h: chsd ldrs: drvn in 3rd 2f out: rdn and wknd over 1f out* 9/2[2]

5300 **7** 1 **Fizzy Feet (IRE)**[73] 5819 3-8-12 **77**... ThomasGreatrex(5) 3 72
(David Loughnane) *chsd ldrs: drvn 2f out: rdn over 1f out: wknd fnl f* 20/1

0433 **8** 1/2 **Rose Berry**[75] 5736 5-9-7 **80**...(h) HectorCrouch 7 74
(Charlie Wallis) *hld up: drvn on outer over 2f out: rdn over 1f out: no imp* 12/1

1155 **9** 1 3/4 **Gilt Edge**[19] 7760 3-8-7 **72**... RhiainIngram(5) 10 60
(Christopher Mason) *bhd: drvn in last 2f out: nvr involved* 25/1

0500 **10** nk **Machree (IRE)**[35] 7183 4-9-9 **82**... CallumShepherd 9 69
(Declan Carroll) *bhd: drvn 2f out: brief hdwy over 1f out: no ex and eased fnl f* 20/1

1m 12.45s (-2.05) **Going Correction** -0.15s/f (Stan)
WFA 3 from 4yo+ 1lb **10** Ran SP% **117.8**
Speed ratings (Par 102): **107,106,106,104,103 103,101,101,98,98**
CSF £27.94 CT £106.31 TOTE £5.00: £1.10, £1.50, £2.30; EX 22.20 Trifecta £78.60.
Owner Mrs Melba Bryce **Bred** Laurence & David Gleeson **Trained** Middleham Moor, N Yorks

FOCUS
A reasonable handicap but, although the pace seemed sound, those held up were at a disadvantage.

8350 HARDWICK BADGER INVADES H'CAP — 1m 4f 51y (Tp)
7:45 (7:45) (Class 3) (0-95,94) 3-Y-O- **£7,246** (£2,168; £1,084; £542; £270) **Stalls** Low

Form RPR

1011 **1** **Paths Of Glory**[8] 8082 4-9-5 **89**........(t) JackMitchell 11 103+
(Hugo Palmer) *mid-div: pushed along and hdwy into 3rd 2f out: drvn to chse ldr 1 1/2f out: rdn fnl f: r.o wl to cl down ldr last 100yds: won on nod* **15/8**[1]

0212 **2** *shd* **El Misk**[32] 7317 3-9-3 **93**........KieranO'Neill 8 105+
(John Gosden) *trckd ldr: dropped to 3rd bef 1/2-way: hdwy to ld 2f out: rdn in 1 l ld 1f out: r.o wl: clsd down by wnr last 100yds: lost on nod* **7/2**[2]

2110 **3** *2 1/4* **Dubai Tradition (USA)**[80] 5541 3-8-12 **88**........HectorCrouch 1 97+
(Saeed bin Suroor) *trckd ldrs: pushed along in 4th 2f out: drvn into 3rd 1f out: rdn fnl f: one pce* **7/2**[2]

1536 **4** *3* **Flaming Marvel (IRE)**[30] 7394 5-9-5 **89**........DavidProbert 3 93
(James Fanshawe) *hld up: hdwy 2f out: drvn on outer 1 1/2f out: rdn 1f out: no ex fnl f* **10/1**

104 **5** *1 1/2* **Yellow Tiger (FR)**[70] 5931 3-8-3 **82**........(p) GabrieleMalune(3) 10 84
(Ian Williams) *hld up in rr: pushed along and hdwy over 2f out: sn rdn: no ex fr over 1f out* **20/1**

5035 **6** *3* **Al Hamdany (IRE)**[84] 5437 5-9-6 **90**........LukeMorris 9 87
(Marco Botti) *hld up: bmpd along over 2f out: rdn fnl f: no imp* **25/1**

4321 **7** *2 3/4* **Asian Angel (IRE)**[15] 7872 3-8-11 **87**........FrannyNorton 6 79
(Mark Johnston) *mid-div on outer: lost pl 2f out: sn drvn and wknd* **9/1**[3]

4010 **8** *1/2* **Jersey Wonder (IRE)**[78] 5614 3-8-12 **88**........NicolaCurrie 5 80
(Jamie Osborne) *led: drvn and hdd 2f out: sn wknd* **33/1**

0645 **9** *7* **Manjaam (IRE)**[21] 7688 6-8-5 **80**........(b) ThomasGreatrex(5) 7 60
(Ian Williams) *hld up on outer: hdwy to go prom bef 1/2-way: sn racing in 2nd: drvn and lost pl over 2f out: wknd* **20/1**

3056 **10** *1 1/2* **Cosmelli (ITY)**[84] 5437 6-9-7 **94**........(b) MeganNicholls(3) 2 72
(Gay Kelleway) *mid-div: drvn and lost pl over 2f out: reminders over 1f out: wknd* **40/1**

0004 **11** *9* **Dunkerron**[105] 4648 3-9-2 **92**........TomQueally 4 56
(Alan King) *t.k.h: hld up: dropped to last over 2f out: sn rdn and lost tch* **25/1**

2m 33.44s (-7.36) **Going Correction** -0.15s/f (Stan) course record
WFA 3 from 4yo+ 6lb **11** Ran SP% **120.9**
Speed ratings (Par 107): **112,111,110,108,107 105,103,103,98,97 91**
CSF £7.72 CT £21.92 TOTE £2.60: £1.50, £1.60, £1.50; EX 10.10 Trifecta £39.50.
Owner China Horse Club International Limited **Bred** Dayton Investments Ltd **Trained** Newmarket, Suffolk

FOCUS
A good-quality event and one run at a respectable gallop. The three market leaders - all progressive types - filled the first three placings and it's worth viewing the form in a positive light.

8351 INVADES ROUND TWO COMING SOON NOVICE STKS — 1m 1f 104y (Tp)
8:15 (8:16) (Class 5) 3-Y-O+ **£3,428** (£1,020; £509; £254) **Stalls** Low

Form RPR

2 **1** **Nsnas (IRE)**[25] 7559 3-9-2 0........CallumShepherd 2 85+
(Saeed bin Suroor) *trckd ldrs: drvn in 3rd 2f out: rdn to chal on inner 1f out: led 1/2f out: sn clr: comf* **5/4**[1]

34 **2** *2 1/4* **Big Daddy Kane**[24] 7572 3-9-2 0........DanielMuscutt 10 78
(Marco Botti) *t.k.h: prom: pushed along in 1/2 l 2nd 2f out: drvn to chal over 1f out: rdn and dropped to 3rd fnl f: r.o to take 2nd nr fin* **9/1**

0 **3** *nk* **Classic Design (IRE)**[23] 7630 3-9-2 0........JackMitchell 6 77
(Simon Crisford) *led: drvn in 1/2 l ld 2f out: rdn 1f out: hdd 1/2f out: no ex: lost 2nd nr fin* **28/1**

31 **4** *1/2* **Shauyra (IRE)**[43] 6941 3-9-1 0........GeorgiaCox(3) 1 78
(William Haggas) *t.k.h: mid-div: drvn in 4th 2f out: rdn over 1f out: kpt on fnl f* **5/2**[2]

3-5 **5** *2 1/4* **Tofan**[278] 239 4-9-6 0........(t w) LukeMorris 9 72
(Marco Botti) *hld up: drvn 1 1/2f out: one pce fr over 1f out* **25/1**

0 **6** *1* **Raining Fire (IRE)**[155] 2795 3-9-2 0........DavidProbert 4 69+
(James Fanshawe) *hld up: drvn 2f out: reminder 1 1/2f out: no imp* **4/1**[3]

7 *3 3/4* **Tactical Approach (IRE)**[23] 7636 3-9-2 0........(t) KieranO'Neill 7 62
(Gavin Cromwell, Ire) *hld up: drvn on outer over 2f out: rdn and wknd over 1f out* **20/1**

00- **8** *8* **Pukka Tique**[364] 8420 3-9-2 0........(t[1]) DougieCostello 3 45
(Ivan Furtado) *trckd ldrs: drvn 3f out: wknd over 2f out (jockey said gelding ran green and hung right-handed on the bend)* **66/1**

9 *3* **Orion's Shore (IRE)** 3-9-2 0........NicolaCurrie 5 39
(Jamie Osborne) *a in rr: lost tch 2f out (jockey said colt ran green)* **50/1**

1m 59.29s (-1.51) **Going Correction** -0.15s/f (Stan)
WFA 3 from 4yo 4lb **9** Ran SP% **118.5**
Speed ratings (Par 103): **100,98,97,97,95 94,91,83,81**
CSF £13.43 TOTE £2.00: £1.10, £2.80, £5.40; EX 11.90 Trifecta £113.60.
Owner Godolphin **Bred** Progeny Stallions Ltd **Trained** Newmarket, Suffolk

FOCUS
A fair novice event in which the gallop was on the steady side and those held up were at a disadvantage.
T/Plt: £40.00 to a £1 stake. Pool: £63,509.85 - 1,157.10 winning units T/Qpdt: £14.80 to a £1 stake. Pool: £13,192.58 - 658.31 winning units **Keith McHugh**

8352-8355a (Foreign Racing) - See Raceform Interactive

7215 LEOPARDSTOWN (L-H)
Saturday, October 19

OFFICIAL GOING: Soft changing to soft to heavy after race 2 (1.55)

8356a KILLAVULLAN STKS (GROUP 3) — 7f
3:40 (3:40) 2-Y-O **£31,891** (£10,270; £4,864; £2,162; £1,081)

RPR

1 **Stela Star (IRE)**[22] 7666 2-9-0 78........ColinKeane 2 102
(Thomas Mullins, Ire) *mde all: pressed ent fnl f: styd on wl for press to extend advantage clsng stages* **33/1**

2 *1 1/2* **Iberia (IRE)**[21] 7691 2-9-3 104........WayneLordan 3 101
(A P O'Brien, Ire) *chsd ldrs in 3rd: pushed along under 2f out: kpt on same pce into 2nd clsng stages: nt rch wnr* **6/4**[1]

3 *hd* **Katiba (IRE)**[20] 7745 2-9-0 0........OisinOrr 1 98
(D K Weld, Ire) *trckd ldr in 2nd: pushed along under 2f out on inner in 4th: kpt on same pce into 3rd fnl 100yds* **3/1**[3]

4 *1 3/4* **Camachita (IRE)**[8] 8103 2-9-0 89........AndrewSlattery 5 93
(J P Murtagh, Ire) *chsd ldrs in 4th: clsr in 2nd under 2f out: no imp ins fnl 100yds in 4th: kpt on same pce* **8/1**

5 *7 1/2* **Geometrical (IRE)**[34] 7245 2-9-3 103........KevinManning 4 77
(J S Bolger, Ire) *a in rr: pushed along 2f out and sn no imp: detached ent fnl f* **2/1**[2]

1m 37.16s (6.76) **Going Correction** +1.15s/f (Soft) **5** Ran SP% **112.4**
Speed ratings: **107,105,105,103,94**
CSF £84.92 TOTE £16.10: £2.60, £1.02; DF 46.60 Trifecta £94.10.
Owner Mrs Helen Mullins **Bred** Vimal & Gillian Khosla **Trained** Goresbridge, Co Kilkenny

FOCUS
As the old saying goes, you need to speculate to accumulate and Tom Mullins was rewarded big time for what looked a fanciful entry with Stela Star. This race has been rated at the bottom end of recent averages but it rates a massive step forward from the winner however viewed.

8357 - 8359a (Foreign Racing) - See Raceform Interactive

8134 CAULFIELD (R-H)
Saturday, October 19

OFFICIAL GOING: Turf: good

8360a LADBROKES MOONGA STKS (GROUP 3) (3YO+) (TURF) — 7f
6:30 3-Y-O+
£66,712 (£19,889; £9,944; £4,972; £2,762; £2,209)

RPR

1 **Streets Of Avalon (AUS)**[7] 8138 5-9-3 0........(bt) BenMelham 9 112
(Shane Nichols, Australia) **4/1**[3]

2 *1* **Variation (AUS)**[49] 6-9-0 0........DamienOliver 6 106
(Stephen Miller, Australia) **13/1**

3 *hd* **Royal Meeting (IRE)**[356] 8668 3-9-6 0........PatCosgrave 8 112
(Saeed bin Suroor) *dwlt: slow to stride: sn rcvrd to be prom on outer: drvn wl over 1 1/2f out: styd on ins fnl f: nvr able to chal* **13/5**[1]

4 *1 1/4* **Manolo Blahniq (NZ)**[7] 6-9-2 0........(b) JakeNoonan 1 104
(Tony Noonan, Australia) **11/1**

5 *hd* **Land Of Plenty (AUS)**[196] 1610 6-9-6 ....(vt[1]) DamianLane 2 108
(Peter & Paul Snowden, Australia) **4/1**[3]

6 *shd* **Moss 'N' Dale (NZ)**[147] 7-9-3 0........(t) JackMartin 7 104
(Peter Gelagotis, Australia) **50/1**

7 *1* **Tom Melbourne (IRE)**[21] 8-9-2 0........MichaelWalker 3 101
(Chris Waller, Australia) **14/1**

8 *3 1/2* **Terbium (AUS)**[28] 4-9-3 0........LukeNolen 4 92
(Phillip Stokes, Australia) **30/1**

9 *1* **Desert Lord (AUS)**[14] 7930 5-9-0 0........(p) DwayneDunn 5 86
(Michael, Wayne & John Hawkes, Australia) **18/5**[2]

1m 23.94s
WFA 3 from 4yo+ 2lb **9** Ran SP% **116.8**

Owner Warren Racing, D Healy Et Al **Bred** Warren Racing Pty Ltd **Trained** Australia

8361a STELLA ARTOIS CAULFIELD CUP (GROUP 1 H'CAP) (3YO+) (TURF) — 1m 4f
7:15 3-Y-O+
£1,740,331 (£386,740; £193,370; £110,497; £82,872; £66,298)

RPR

1 **Mer De Glace (JPN)**[76] 4-8-10 0........(b) DamianLane 17 115
(Hisashi Shimizu, Japan) *w.w towards rr: 2nd last and plenty to do 1/2-way: tk clsr order towards outer more than 2f fr home: str run to ld ins fnl f: sn asserted: readily* **7/1**[3]

2 *1* **Vow And Declare (AUS)**[14] 7918 4-8-4 0........CraigAWilliams 7 107
(Danny O'Brien, Australia) *hld up towards rr: hdwy wl over 2f out: styd on u.p to go 2nd last 50yds: nt trble wnr* **7/1**[3]

3 *hd* **Mirage Dancer**[78] 5613 5-8-11 0........BenMelham 9 114
(Trent Busuttin & Natalie Young, Australia) *prom between horses: rdn and battled for pls fr 1 1/2f out: styd on u.p* **15/1**

4 *hd* **Constantinople (IRE)**[59] 6353 3-8-5 0........(p) LukeNolen 5 115+
(David A & B Hayes & Tom Dabernig, Australia) *midfield: n.m.r and shuffled bk over 3f out: towards rr 2f out: nt clr run w 1 1/2f to run and snatched up: styd on ins fnl f* **11/2**[1]

5 *hd* **Finche**[14] 7918 5-8-8 0........MichaelWalker 15 110
(Chris Waller, Australia) *prom on outer: dropped into midfield 1/2-way: drvn to chse ldrs 2f out: 2nd and rdn w 1 1/2f to run: led appr fnl f: hdd ins fnl f: no ex* **13/2**[2]

6 *hd* **Mustajeer**[56] 6473 6-8-10 0........DamienOliver 12 112
(Kris Lees, Australia) *fnl pair: hdwy 2 1/2f out: shuffled wd and bk w 2f to travel: last and n.m.r 1 1/2f out: in clr and r.o u.p fnl f: nvr nrr* **11/1**

7 *1 1/4* **Hartnell**[14] 7918 8-9-2 0........BradRawiller 13 116
(James Cummings, Australia) *chsd ldrs: rdn and nt qckn fr 2f out: one pce fnl f* **25/1**

8 *3/4* **Red Verdon (USA)**[56] 6473 6-8-8 0........(b) PatCosgrave 11 107
(Ed Dunlop) *hld up in midfield: chsd front rnk w more than 1 1/2f to run: n.m.r and sltly impeded over 1f out: no further imp* **70/1**

9 *shd* **The Chosen One (NZ)**[7] 8134 4-8-3 0........(b) StephenBaster 18 102+
(Murray Baker & Andrew Forsman, New Zealand) *adrift in rr: clsd on outer 2 1/2f fr home: kpt on same pce last 1 1/2f: nvr in contention* **12/1**

10 *shd* **Sound (GER)**[14] 7918 6-8-7 0........JamesWinks 6 106
(Michael Moroney, Australia) *hld up in midfield: clsd to be win striking dist of ldrs 2f out: kpt on one pce u.p* **100/1**

11 *hd* **Mr Quickie (AUS)**[14] 7918 4-8-5 0........(b) JohnAllen 8 103+
(Phillip Stokes, Australia) *dwlt: towards rr: styd on fnl f: nvr nrr* **7/1**[3]

12 *hd* **Gold Mount**[98] 4933 6-8-8 0........MarkDuPlessis 2 106
(Ian Williams) *towards rr on inner: clsd into midfield 1/2-way: dropped towards rr 2 1/2f out: effrt but nt clr run on inner 1 1/2f fr home: styd on late: nvr trbld ldrs* **25/1**

13 *1* **Wolfe (JPN)**[3] 4-7-12 0........BeauMertens 3 94
(Gai Waterhouse & Adrian Bott, Australia) *led: hrd pressed and drvn fr over 2f out: hdd appr fnl f: sn btn* **20/1**

14 *shd* **Brimham Rocks**[14] 7931 5-8-3 0........(t) MichaelDee 16 99
(Chris Waller, Australia) *prom on outer: chsd ldrs 2f fr home: sn rdn and no imp: one pce fnl 1 1/2f* **30/1**

15 *shd* **Angel Of Truth (AUS)**[14] 4-8-7 0........DeanYendall 10 103
(Gwenda Markwell, Australia) *chsd ldrs: lost pl 2 1/2f out: wl hld fnl f* **40/1**

16 1 1/2 **Rostropovich (IRE)**[14] 7918 4-8-10 0........................ DwayneDunn 14 104
(David A & B Hayes & Tom Dabernig, Australia) *dwlt: towards rr: rushed up on outer to press ldr 1/2-way: outpcd and rdn 1 1/2f out: dropped away fnl f* **30/1**

17 1/2 **Qafila (AUS)**[7] 8134 4-8-2 0........................(p) CoryParish 4 95
(David A & B Hayes & Tom Dabernig, Australia) *prom on inner: rdn and no imp 2f out: sn btn* **40/1**

18 91 **Big Duke (IRE)**[14] 7931 7-8-7 0........................ BrettPrebble 1
(Kris Lees, Australia) *midfield on inner: lost pl qckly 3 1/2f out: t.o* **40/1**

2m 30.16s
WFA 3 from 4yo+ 6lb **18 Ran SP% 117.1**

Owner U Carrot Farm **Bred** Northern Farm **Trained** Japan

FOCUS

This was an interesting mix of horses for one of Australia's most prestigious races, but the whole field finished close up, suggesting the early pace wasn't frenetic. That said, it was some effort by the winner, who emerged from a wide stall. With regards to doing the double, landing this and going on to glory in the Melbourne Cup, you have to go back to 2001 for the last time that happened.

8142 RANDWICK (L-H)

Saturday, October 19

OFFICIAL GOING: Turf: good

8362a THE TAB EVEREST (CONDITIONS) (2YO+) (TURF) 6f
6:15 2-Y-O+

£3,645,856 (£1,182,320; £685,082; £497,237; £375,690; £248,618)

RPR

1 **Yes Yes Yes (AUS)**[21] 7722 3-8-5 0........................(b[1]) GlenBoss 9 118+
(Chris Waller, Australia) **8/1**

2 1/2 **Santa Ana Lane (AUS)**[14] 7-9-3 0........................ MarkZahra 2 120+
(Anthony Freedman, Australia) **9/2[2]**

3 1/2 **Trekking (AUS)**[7] 5-9-3 0........................ JoshuaParr 5 118
(James Cummings, Australia) *in rr: effrt 2f out: gd hdwy on outer fnl f: clst fin: rdn out* **30/1**

4 1/2 **Nature Strip (AUS)**[22] 7672 5-9-3 0........................(t) TimothyClark 12 116
(Chris Waller, Australia) **20/1**

5 nk **Pierata (AUS)**[28] 7481 5-9-3 0........................(b) TommyBerry 1 115
(Gregory Hickman, Australia) **6/1[3]**

6 1 **Classique Legend (AUS)**[14] 4-9-3 0........................ NashRawiller 8 112
(Les Bridge, Australia) **17/1**

7 1/2 **Alizee (AUS)**[49] 6748 5-8-13 0........................ HughBowman 10 107
(James Cummings, Australia) *settled in midfield: shkn up 1 1/2f out: kpt on: outpcd fnl f* **8/1**

8 1 **Redzel (AUS)**[28] 7481 7-9-3 0........................(b) KerrinMcEvoy 7 107
(Peter & Paul Snowden, Australia) **12/1**

9 hd **In Her Time (AUS)**[224] 1107 7-8-13 0........................ BrentonAvdulla 4 103
(Kris Lees, Australia) *midfield: angled out over 2f out: drvn along 1 1/2f out: one pce and lost position ins fnl f* **20/1**

10 nk **Sunlight (AUS)**[14] 4-8-13 0........................(t) LukeCurrie 6 102
(Tony McEvoy & Calvin McEvoy, Australia) **12/1**

11 hd **Arcadia Queen (AUS)**[35] 4-8-13 0........................(t) JamesMcDonald 3 101
(Chris Waller, Australia) **4/1[1]**

12 1/2 **Ten Sovereigns (IRE)**[57] 6423 3-9-2 0........................ RyanMoore 11 104
(A P O'Brien, Ire) *settled towards rr: drvn along in last 2f out: outpcd and rdn along over 1f out: wl hld fnl f* **19/1**

1m 7.32s
WFA 3 from 4yo+ 1lb **12 Ran SP% 113.4**

Owner Yes Yes Yes, B Sokolski Et Al **Bred** Arlington Park Racing **Trained** Australia

8363 - 8366a (Foreign Racing) - See Raceform Interactive

7352 NAAS (L-H)

Sunday, October 20

OFFICIAL GOING: Soft to heavy (heavy in places on round course)

8367a NAAS RACECOURSE BUSINESS CLUB IRISH EBF GARNET STKS (LISTED RACE) (F&M) 1m
3:30 (3:31) 3-Y-O+

£29,234 (£9,414; £4,459; £1,981; £990; £495)

RPR

1 **Silk Forest (IRE)**[66] 6136 3-9-0 91........................ WJLee 3 104+
(P Twomey, Ire) *mde all: narrow advantage at 1/2-way: stl gng wl nr side over 2f out: rdn under 2f out and styd on strly to assert ins fnl f: easily* **7/1[3]**

2 5 **Trethias**[9] 8094 3-9-3 103........................(p) ShaneFoley 13 95
(Mrs John Harrington, Ire) *prom tl sn settled bhd ldrs: cl 3rd after 1/2-way: rdn nr side over 2f out and no imp on wnr u.p in 2nd ins fnl f: kpt on same pce* **4/1[2]**

3 1/2 **Jumellea (IRE)**[9] 8106 3-9-0 87........................(bt) DeclanMcDonogh 4 91
(Joseph Patrick O'Brien, Ire) *dwlt and pushed along briefly early where reminder: sn rr: 13th after 1/2-way: nt clr run 2f out: sn swtchd rt and rdn: r.o wl u.p nr side ins fnl f into nvr threatening 3rd cl home* **11/1**

4 1 1/4 **Shepherd Market (IRE)**[15] 7893 4-9-3 95........................(v[1]) ColinKeane 14 89
(Clive Cox) *hld up in tch: disp 6th after 1/2-way: rdn bhd ldrs over 2f out and no imp on wnr u.p in 3rd ins fnl f: dropped to 4th cl home* **8/1**

5 1/2 **Come September (IRE)**[24] 7635 3-9-0 94........................ GaryCarroll 5 87
(Gavin Cromwell, Ire) *mid-div: disp 6th after 1/2-way: rdn over 2f out and no imp in 5th 1f out: kpt on same pce* **20/1**

6 nk **Frosty (IRE)**[24] 7635 3-9-0 99........................ DonnachaO'Brien 9 86
(A P O'Brien, Ire) *settled bhd ldr: cl 2nd at 1/2-way: swtchd lft 2f out and rdn: sn no imp on wnr u.p in 3rd: wknd far side ins fnl f* **8/1**

7 2 1/4 **Wisdom Mind (IRE)**[14] 7934 4-9-3 93........................(t) SeamieHeffernan 8 82
(Joseph Patrick O'Brien, Ire) *hld up towards rr: 12th after 1/2-way: rdn and sme hdwy far side 2f out: no imp on wnr u.p in 6th ent fnl f: kpt on one pce* **16/1**

8 1 **Stormy Belle (IRE)**[11] 8040 5-9-3 82........................(t) KevinManning 12 80
(P A Fahy, Ire) *in rr of mid-div: 11th after 1/2-way: bmpd sltly into st: rdn nr side 2f out and sme hdwy u.p 1f out: kpt on one pce* **50/1**

9 1/2 **Chocolate Music (IRE)**[14] 7934 3-9-0 93........................ TomMadden 10 78
(Mrs John Harrington, Ire) *dwlt and pushed along in rr early: pushed along again in rr into st and no imp over 2f out: kpt on nr side ins fnl f: nvr nrr* **33/1**

10 3/4 **Mia Maria (IRE)**[24] 7637 3-9-0 92........................(v[1]) OisinOrr 2 76
(D K Weld, Ire) *chsd ldrs: 5th 1/2-way: rdn over 2f out and sn no ex u.p down centre: wknd fr over 1f out* **16/1**

11 nk **Titanium Sky (IRE)**[8] 8177 3-9-0 95........................(p[1]) ChrisHayes 7 75
(D K Weld, Ire) *hld up towards rr early: disp 9th after 1/2-way: rdn briefly under 2f out and no imp* **14/1**

12 nk **Angels**[41] 7041 4-9-3 71........................ NGMcCullagh 6 75
(J P Murtagh, Ire) *in rr of mid-div: disp 9th after 1/2-way: drvn over 2f out sn no ex* **50/1**

13 3/4 **Iconic Choice**[31] 7365 3-9-0 102........................ RichardKingscote 11 73
(Tom Dascombe) *hld up in tch: drvn in 8th after 1/2-way and sltly bmpd rival into st: no imp u.p under 3f out: wkng whn n.m.r and hmpd 2f out* **7/2[1]**

14 3/4 **Lovee Dovee**[22] 7718 3-9-0 89........................ ShaneCrosse 1 71
(Joseph Patrick O'Brien, Ire) *chsd ldrs: 4th after 1/2-way: drvn bhd ldrs far side and no ex fr over 2f out: sn wknd: eased ins fnl f* **7/1[3]**

1m 46.16s (6.16)
WFA 3 from 4yo+ 3lb **14 Ran SP% 127.8**
CSF £36.33 TOTE £8.40: £2.50, £1.70, £3.50; DF 34.60 Trifecta £392.00.
Owner Tan Kai Chah **Bred** J Ryan **Trained** Cashel, Co Tipperary

FOCUS

An impressive display from Silk Forest, especially given this was just her fourth career start. She looks a future Group-race contender.

8368a IRISH STALLION FARMS EBF BLUEBELL STKS (LISTED RACE) (F&M) 1m 3f 190y
4:00 (4:01) 3-Y-O+

£29,234 (£9,414; £4,459; £1,981; £990; £495)

RPR

1 **Solage**[24] 7635 3-9-0 94........................ KevinManning 4 98
(J S Bolger, Ire) *mid-div: disp 6th bef st: hdwy far side 2f out: disp ld u.p ent fnl f: led narrowly ins fnl f and kpt on wl clsng stages: all out* **14/1**

2 3/4 **Warnaq (IRE)**[33] 7326 5-9-6 94........................ ColinKeane 7 96
(Matthew J Smith, Ire) *broke wl to ld: rdn 2f out and pressed clly: jnd u.p ent fnl f: hdd narrowly ins fnl f: kpt on wl clsng stages wout matching wnr* **7/1**

3 hd **Camphor (IRE)**[33] 7326 3-9-0 97........................ ShaneFoley 10 97
(Mrs John Harrington, Ire) *hld up towards rr: gng wl in 11th bef st: hdwy nr side over 2f out to chse ldrs: rdn over 1f out and clsd u.p nr side ins fnl f: hld in 3rd cl home* **5/1[3]**

4 3/4 **Loveisthehigherlaw**[59] 6381 3-9-0 99........................ WJLee 8 95
(P Twomey, Ire) *chsd ldrs: rn freely early: 3rd 1/2-way: rdn bhd ldrs nr side 2f out and u.p in 6th over 1f out: kpt on into 4th wl ins fnl f: nt trble wnr* **9/2[2]**

5 1 **Quote**[16] 7883 3-9-0 80........................(t) MichaelHussey 1 94
(A P O'Brien, Ire) *hld up towards rr: hdwy far side over 2f out to chal 1 1/2f out: got on terms briefly u.p over 1f out: no ex bhd ldrs and one pce ins fnl f* **33/1**

6 3/4 **Snapraeceps (IRE)**[24] 7635 3-9-0 100........................ ShaneCrosse 11 93
(Joseph Patrick O'Brien, Ire) *chsd ldrs: 5th 1/2-way: rdn 2f out and no ex u.p nr side ent fnl f: one pce after* **25/1**

7 nk **Winiata (IRE)**[41] 7038 3-9-0 94........................ NGMcCullagh 3 92
(J P Murtagh, Ire) *hld up in rr of mid-div early: disp 6th bef st: rdn nr side 2f out and sn no ex* **14/1**

8 4 1/2 **Simply Beautiful (IRE)**[9] 8094 3-9-0 103........................ DonnachaO'Brien 9 85
(A P O'Brien, Ire) *cl up bhd ldr in 2nd: rdn over 2f out and sn u.p in 3rd: wknd over 1f out: eased ins fnl f* **11/4[1]**

9 1 3/4 **Chablis (IRE)**[35] 7242 3-9-0 97........................ SeamieHeffernan 5 82
(A P O'Brien, Ire) *hld up in rr: gd hdwy on inner 3f out to chse ldrs far side: rdn disputing cl 2nd 2f out and no ex over 1f out: wknd and eased ins fnl f* **14/1**

10 4 1/2 **Kiss For A Jewel (IRE)**[27] 7535 3-9-0 93........................(p) ChrisHayes 6 75
(D K Weld, Ire) *chsd ldrs: 4th 1/2-way: rdn bhd ldrs 2f out and no ex u.p 1 1/2f out: sn wknd: eased ins fnl f* **9/2[2]**

11 9 1/2 **Terzetto (IRE)**[24] 7635 4-9-6 97........................ RossCoakley 12 59
(M Halford, Ire) *hld up: drvn in rr of mid-div under 4f out and sn no ex u.p in rr: wknd: eased ins fnl f* **50/1**

12 3 3/4 **Invitation (IRE)**[33] 7326 3-9-0 84........................ PBBeggy 2 54
(A P O'Brien, Ire) *mid-div: pushed along under 4f out and sn no imp towards rr under 3f out: wknd and eased* **50/1**

2m 43.82s
WFA 3 from 4yo+ 6lb **12 Ran SP% 122.9**
CSF £109.97 TOTE £19.20: £3.90, £2.70, £1.80; DF 154.60 Trifecta £1081.30.
Owner Ballylinch Stud & Ecurie Des Charmes **Bred** Ecurie Des Monceaux **Trained** Coolcullen, Co Carlow

FOCUS

Any amount of these held a chance a furlong out with the lightly raced Solage battling best. The first two rate as improvers.

8369 - 8370a (Foreign Racing) - See Raceform Interactive

6769 BADEN-BADEN (L-H)

Sunday, October 20

OFFICIAL GOING: Turf: heavy

8371a PREIS DER WINTERKONIGIN (GROUP 3) (2YO FILLIES) (TURF) 1m
2:20 2-Y-O

£54,054 (£20,720; £9,909; £5,405; £2,702; £1,801)

RPR

1 **Ocean Fantasy (FR)** 2-9-2 0........................ MichaelCadeddu 9 100
(Jean-Pierre Carvalho, Germany) *towards rr: pushed along 2 1/2f out: hdwy and rdn ins fnl 2f: continued to stay on to ld 150yds out: hrd pressed and battled on wl to hold on* **107/10**

2 shd **Tickle Me Green (GER)** 2-9-2 0........................ MaximPecheur 1 100
(Markus Klug, Germany) *trckd ldrs: led 2f out: sn shkn up: hdd 150yds out: rallied: jst hld* **22/5[2]**

3 5 1/2 **Tabera**[21] 2-9-2 0 EduardoPedroza 3 88
(M G Mintchev, Germany) *led: hdd 2f out: sn shkn up: kpt on wl bef outpcd by front pair fnl 150yds: drvn out* **51/10**[3]

4 1 1/2 **Shenouni (GER)** 2-9-2 0 FilipMinarik 2 84
(Jean-Pierre Carvalho, Germany) *midfield: effrt and tk clsr order 2f out: rdn along and outpcd fnl f: rdn out* **164/10**

5 1 1/4 **Nona (GER)**[50] 6746 2-9-2 0 AndreBest 5 82
(Mario Hofer, Germany) *in rr of midfield: tk clsr order and rdn along ins fnl 2f: kpt on same pce: rdn out* **226/10**

6 1 **Schwesterherz (FR)**[64] 6248 2-9-2 0 BauyrzhanMurzabayev 6 81
(Henk Grewe, Germany) *settled bhd ldng pair: effrt 2f out: one pce: kpt on wout troubling ldrs* **33/10**[1]

7 shd **Flamingo Girl (GER)**[21] 7749 2-9-2 0 BayarsaikhanGanbat 7 79
(Henk Grewe, Germany) *cl up: pushed along to hold position 3f out: stl in tch and rdn along 2f out: sn lost position: plugged on* **161/10**

8 7 1/2 **A Racing Beauty (GER)** 2-9-2 0 MickaelBerto 10 63
(Henk Grewe, Germany) *towards rr: effrt over 2f out: no imp and wl hld fnl f* **59/10**

9 2 1/4 **Stellina (GER)** 2-9-2 0 LukasDelozier 4 58
(P Schiergen, Germany) *in rr of midfield: effrt over 2f out: plugged on same pce: eased fnl f* **118/10**

10 8 1/2 **Alison (SWE)** 2-9-2 0 JozefBojko 12 39
(H-J Groschel, Germany) *towards rr: tk clsr order 1/2-way: outpcd ins fnl 2f: sn wl bhd* **93/10**

11 19 **Vive En Liberte (GER)**[112] 2-9-2 0 AdriedeVries 8
(Yasmin Almenrader, Germany) *midfield: rdn and dropped to rr over 2f out: sn eased* **26/1**

1m 48.01s (8.90) **11 Ran SP% 118.3**
PARI-MUTUEL (all including 1 euro stake): WIN 11.70 PLACE: 2.80, 2.00, 2.10; SF: 56.10.
Owner Gestut Hony-Hof **Bred** Haras Du Mezeray **Trained** Germany

8372a BADEN-WURTTEMBERG-TROPHY - LE DEFI DU GALOP (GROUP 3) (3YO+) (TURF) 1m 2f
4:05 3-Y-0+ **£28,828** (£10,810; £5,405; £2,702; £1,801)

RPR

1 **Nancho (GER)** 4-9-0 0 BayarsaikhanGanbat 2 109
(Gabor Maronka, Hungary) *chsd ldr on inner: led ins fnl 3f: drvn along 1 1/2f out: forged clr fnl f: readily* **42/10**[3]

2 7 1/2 **Say Good Buy (GER)**[105] 3-8-9 0 AlexanderPietsch 6 94
(P Schiergen, Germany) *led: hdd ins fnl 3f and outpcd by new ldrs sn after: rallied u.p 1 1/2f out: styd on to regain 2nd wl ins fnl f: nt trble wnr* **101/10**

3 1/2 **Be My Sheriff (GER)**[17] 7862 5-9-0 0 AdriedeVries 5 93
(Henk Grewe, Germany) *chsd ldr outside rival: drvn to chse new ldr over 2 1/2f out: kpt on u.p tl laboured ins fnl f: lost 2nd fnl 75yds* **1/1**[1]

4 6 **Itobo (GER)**[17] 7862 7-9-4 0 MichaelCadeddu 4 85
(H-J Groschel, Germany) *racd in fnl pair: drvn and effrt 2 1/2f out: sn rdn and btn* **7/2**[2]

5 10 **Rolando (IRE)**[21] 7753 5-9-0 0 BauyrzhanMurzabayev 1 61
(A Wohler, Germany) *prom: outpcd and rdn 2 1/2f out: sn wknd: t.o* **69/10**

6 9 1/2 **Ronaldo (GER)**[246] 766 5-9-0 0 (b) FilipMinarik 7 42
(Andreas Suborics, Germany) *settled in rr: drvn 2 1/2f out but no imp: sn wknd: t.o* **173/10**

2m 14.21s (9.22) **6 Ran SP% 118.6**
WFA 3 from 4yo+ 4lb
PARI-MUTUEL (all including 1 euro stake): WIN 5.20 PLACE: 3.00, 6.10; SF: 55.90.
Owner Intergaj **Bred** H Johanpeter **Trained** Hungary

7223 CHOLET (R-H)
Sunday, October 20

OFFICIAL GOING: Turf: heavy

8373a GRAND PRIX DE CHOLET (CONDITIONS) (3YO+) (TURF) 6f 165y
3:42 3-Y-0+ **£14,414** (£5,477; £4,036; £2,306; £1,153; £864)

RPR

1 **Elegant Light**[21] 3-8-10 0 SoufianeSaadi 6 93
(H-A Pantall, France) *sn chsng front rnk: drvn and nt clr run whn coming towards stands' side 2f out: angled ins and clsd 1 1/2f out: led ent fnl f: sn clr: comf* **13/5**[2]

2 4 **Roncey (FR)**[36] 5-9-10 0 (b) AlexandreRoussel 1 94
(Edouard Monfort, France) **2/1**[1]

3 nk **Soho Starlight**[63] 6-9-5 0 (p) JulienGuillochon 5 89
(H-A Pantall, France) **73/10**

4 4 **No Faith (FR)**[323] 9364 4-8-11 0 AugustinMadamet 3 69
(C Ferland, France) **43/10**

5 5 1/2 **Euryale (IRE)**[34] 5-9-5 0 PierreBazire 4 61
(J-V Toux, France) **33/10**[3]

6 19 **Cold Fusion (IRE)**[137] 9383 6-8-9 0 JeromeMoutard 2
(Dai Williams) *w ldrs between horses: lost pl 1 1/2f out: wl detached in last bef 1/2-way: t.o* **20/1**

1m 26.21s **6 Ran SP% 120.0**
WFA 3 from 4yo+ 2lb
PARI-MUTUEL (all including 1 euro stake): WIN 3.60; PLACE 1.90, 1.70; SF 10.70.
Owner Godolphin SNC **Bred** Godolphin **Trained** France

8374 - (Foreign Racing) - See Raceform Interactive

4418 LA ZARZUELA (R-H)
Sunday, October 20

OFFICIAL GOING: Turf: soft

8375a GRAN PREMIO MEMORIAL DUQUE DE TOLEDO (LISTED RACE) (3YO+) (TURF) 1m 4f
12:35 3-Y-0+ **£40,540** (£16,216; £8,108; £4,054)

RPR

1 **Cnicht (FR)**[66] 6145 5-9-3 0 ThomasHenderson 6 95
(D Henderson, France) **244/10**

2 1 1/4 **Solmina (FR)**[48] 6820 7-9-0 0 AnthonyCrastus 2 90
(J-L Dubord, France) **107/10**

3 1 **Hipodamo De Mileto (FR)**[113] 4418 5-9-3 0 ClementCadel 12 91
(J Calderon, Spain) **12/5**[2]

4 1 3/4 **Federico**[66] 6145 6-9-3 0 HayleyTurner 1 89
(Enrique Leon Penate, Spain) **191/10**

5 nk **Most Empowered (IRE)**[130] 5-9-0 0 BorjaFayosMartin 11 85
(Enrique Leon Penate, Spain) **5/1**[3]

6 5 1/2 **Amazing Red (IRE)**[28] 7498 6-9-3 0 JoseLuisMartinez 5 79
(Ed Dunlop) *racd keenly: hld up towards rr on outer: drvn 2 1/2f out but no immediate imp: sme prog appr fnl f: nt persevered w whn clr nt gng to trble ldrs fnl 75yds* **11/5**[1]

7 1 **Tuvalu**[66] 6145 7-9-3 0 JaimeGelabertBautista 8 78
(J-M Osorio, Spain) **231/10**

8 1/2 **Putumayo (FR)**[113] 4418 4-9-3 0 NicolasDeJulian 7 77
(J-M Osorio, Spain) **30/1**

9 11 1/2 **Atty Persse (IRE)**[66] 6145 5-9-3 0 RicardoSousa 3 59
(Enrique Leon Penate, Spain) **66/10**

10 3/4 **Emin (IRE)**[549] 4-9-3 0 TomMarquand 10 57
(Enrique Leon Penate, Spain) **168/10**

11 2 1/2 **Molly King (GER)**[1158] 6-9-3 0 JoseLuisBorrego 9 53
(V B Buda, Spain) **30/1**

2m 35.08s **11 Ran SP% 124.2**
WFA 3 from 4yo+ 6lb
Owner Nicholas J Hughes **Bred** N Hughes **Trained** France

7939 LONGCHAMP (R-H)
Sunday, October 20

OFFICIAL GOING: Turf: heavy

8376a PRIX DE SAINT-CYR (LISTED RACE) (3YO FILLIES) (NEW COURSE: 2ND POST) (TURF) 7f
2:15 3-Y-0 **£24,774** (£9,909; £7,432; £4,954; £2,477)

RPR

1 **Aviatress (IRE)**[45] 6910 3-8-10 0 StephanePasquier 2 101+
(A De Royer-Dupre, France) **114/10**

2 1/2 **Orchid Star**[187] 1832 3-8-10 0 WilliamBuick 8 100
(Charlie Appleby) *led: gng wl and pushed along 2f out: rdn along under 1f out: hdd cl home* **11/1**

3 2 1/2 **Jet Setteuse (FR)**[20] 3-8-10 0 AlexisBadel 1 93
(F Rohaut, France) **36/5**[3]

4 snk **K Club (IRE)**[21] 3-8-10 0 EddyHardouin 7 92
(J Hirschberger, Germany) **21/1**

5 1 3/4 **Nuala (FR)**[32] 7360 3-8-10 0 Pierre-CharlesBoudot 11 88
(A Fabre, France) **54/10**[2]

6 snk **Matematica (GER)**[16] 7886 3-9-0 0 MaximeGuyon 6 91+
(C Laffon-Parias, France) **13/5**[1]

7 1/2 **Ghislaine**[21] 3-9-0 0 VincentCheminaud 5 90
(A Wohler, Germany) **9/1**

8 snk **Grace Spirit**[32] 7360 3-8-10 0 AntoineHamelin 10 86
(A De Royer-Dupre, France) **12/1**

9 1 **Waldblumchen (GER)**[30] 3-8-10 0 CristianDemuro 12 83
(G Botti, France) **15/1**

10 2 **Firebird Song (IRE)**[16] 7886 3-9-0 0 MickaelBarzalona 13 82
(H-A Pantall, France) *settled in midfield on outer: drvn along and outpcd under 2f out: wl hld fnl f* **87/10**

11 1/2 **Castle Of May (IRE)**[21] 3-8-10 0 RonanThomas 4 76
(F-H Graffard, France) **12/1**

12 1 1/4 **Amatriciana (FR)**[28] 7499 3-8-10 0 AntoineCoutier 9 73
(Carina Fey, France) **46/1**

1m 30.26s (9.56) **12 Ran SP% 120.6**
PARI-MUTUEL (all including 1 euro stake): WIN 12.40; PLACE 3.90, 4.60, 3.00; DF 87.50.
Owner LNJ Foxwoods **Bred** Ecurie Des Monceaux **Trained** Chantilly, France

FOCUS
The first two have been rated as on the upgrade.

8377a PRIX CASIMIR DELAMARRE - FONDS EUROPEEN DE L'ELEVAGE (LISTED RACE) (3YO+ F & M) (MOYENNE COURSE) 1m 1f
2:50 3-Y-0+ **£23,423** (£9,369; £7,027; £4,684; £2,342)

RPR

1 **Dariyza (FR)**[29] 7477 3-8-11 0 StephanePasquier 7 101+
(A De Royer-Dupre, France) **9/2**[2]

2 1 **Wishfully (IRE)**[28] 7499 3-8-11 0 MickaelBarzalona 3 98
(H-A Pantall, France) *midfield on inner: drvn along and hdwy 2f out: led and rdn along over 1f out: pressed wl ins fnl f: hdd 50yds out: no ex* **53/10**[3]

3 1 1/4 **Made To Lead (FR)**[15] 4-9-1 0 (p) JeromeClaudic 2 95
(E Lyon, France) **66/10**

4 3 **Bubble And Squeak**[15] 7895 4-9-1 0 TheoBachelot 6 89
(Sylvester Kirk) *midfield: drvn along 2f out: tk clsr order and rdn along over 1f out: outpcd by ldrs ins fnl f: kpt on wl: drvn out* **12/1**

5 hd **Excellency (FR)**[25] 3-8-11 0 AlexisBadel 8 89
(H-F Devin, France) **54/10**

6 3 **Bowled Over (IRE)**[32] 7360 3-8-11 0 Pierre-CharlesBoudot 4 82
(F-H Graffard, France) **17/5**[1]

7 2 1/2 **Over The Moon (IRE)**[76] 3-8-11 0 AurelienLemaitre 1 77
(P Sogorb, France) **30/1**

8 3/4 **Kanuka (FR)**[44] 6946 3-8-11 0 CristianDemuro 9 75
(J Reynier, France) **6/1**

9 4 1/2 **Valrose (FR)**[28] 3-8-11 0 EddyHardouin 5 66
(Claudia Erni, Switzerland) **11/1**

2m 5.5s (13.90) **9 Ran SP% 119.1**
WFA 3 from 4yo 4lb
PARI-MUTUEL (all including 1 euro stake): WIN 5.50; PLACE 2.10, 2.10, 2.20; DF 11.00.
Owner H H Aga Khan **Bred** S.A. Aga Khan **Trained** Chantilly, France

8378a PRIX DU CONSEIL DE PARIS (GROUP 2) (3YO+) (GRANDE COURSE) (TURF) 1m 3f
3:25 3-Y-0+ £66,756 (£25,765; £12,297; £8,198; £4,099)

RPR
1 **Subway Dancer (IRE)**[12] 8010 7-9-2 0........................(p) RadekKoplik 3 115
(Z Koplik, Czech Republic) *led 2f: trckd ldr: shkn up to ld 1 1/2f out: r.o wl fnl f* **38/1**
2 1 3/4 **Edisa (USA)**[43] 6993 3-8-7 0........................ StephanePasquier 5 109+
(A De Royer-Dupre, France) *in rr of midfield: effrt 2f out: hdwy and rdn along 1f out: wnt 2nd 100yds out: nt pce to chal* **43/10**[3]
3 2 1/2 **Silverwave (FR)**[35] 7251 7-9-2 0........................ MickaelBarzalona 8 107
(F Vermeulen, France) *led after 2f: pressed and drvn along 2f out: hdd 1 1/2f out: sn rdn: kpt on* **9/1**
4 nk **Soudania**[29] 7478 3-8-9 0........................ MaximeGuyon 2 105
(F Head, France) *midfield: shkn up and briefly threatened 1 1/2f out: outpcd fnl 150yds: drvn out* **21/10**[1]
5 1 1/2 **Monsieur Croco (FR)**[21] 7753 4-9-2 0........................ GregoryBenoist 6 104
(Mlle Y Vollmer, France) *in rr: angled out and effrt under 2f out: hdwy into midfield: edgd rt u.p 1f out: one pce fnl f: nvr on terms w ldrs* **23/5**
6 9 **Winterfuchs (GER)**[29] 7478 3-8-13 0........................ SibylleVogt 1 91
(Carmen Bocskai, Germany) *midfield: drvn along over 2f out: lost position and sn rdn: plugged on same pce* **20/1**
7 18 **Intellogent (IRE)**[34] 7293 4-9-2 0........................(p) CristianDemuro 4 55
(F Chappet, France) *prom: shkn up 2f out: sn outpcd and lost position: eased fnl f* **9/1**
8 7 **Pelligrina (IRE)**[140] 3391 3-8-10 0 ow1........................ Pierre-CharlesBoudot 7 43
(A Fabre, France) *towards rr: pushed along and dropped to last over 2f out: eased fnl 2f* **16/5**[2]

2m 29.57s (9.67)
WFA 3 from 4yo+ 5lb 8 Ran SP% **120.1**
PARI-MUTUEL (all including 1 euro stake): WIN 39.10; PLACE 8.20, 2.50, 2.50; DF 84.90.
Owner Bonanza **Bred** Scea Haras De Saint Pair **Trained** Czech Republic

FOCUS
The surprise winner has been rated to his best.

8379a PRIX DU RANELAGH (LISTED RACE) (3YO+) (GRANDE COURSE) (TURF) 1m
4:35 3-Y-0+ £23,423 (£9,369; £7,027; £4,684; £2,342)

RPR
1 **Qualisaga (FR)**[161] 2670 5-8-13 0........................ EddyHardouin 3 107
(Carina Fey, France) **68/10**
2 3/4 **Magny Cours (USA)**[217] 1244 4-9-2 0........................ Pierre-CharlesBoudot 5 108
(A Fabre, France) *last: drvn along and hdwy over 1 1/2f out: chal 150yds out: nt pce of wnr cl home* **39/10**[3]
3 2 **History Writer (IRE)**[22] 7694 4-9-2 0........................ MaximeGuyon 1 103
(David Menuisier) *hld up in fnl trio on inner: clsd to chse ldrs 1/2-way: led narrowly wl over 3f out: drvn 2f out: hdd 1f out: no ex* **59/10**
4 snk **Mount Pelion (IRE)**[38] 4-9-2 0........................ MickaelBarzalona 7 103
(A Fabre, France) *settled in rr of midfield: tk clsr order and drvn along 2f out: hdwy to chal 1f out: outpcd by ldrs fnl f: drvn out* **29/10**[1]
5 5 **Larno (FR)**[10] 5-9-2 0........................ TonyPiccone 4 92
(M Boutin, France) **41/5**
6 7 **Wootton (FR)**[32] 7340 4-9-7 0........................ WilliamBuick 2 80
(Charlie Appleby) *towards rr: drvn along over 2f out: no imp: eased fnl f* **31/10**[2]
7 3 **Broderie**[21] 7750 4-9-2 0........................ VincentCheminaud 8 69
(H-A Pantall, France) *trckd ldr: shkn up 2f out: briefly threatened: outpcd 1f out: sn btn* **17/2**

1m 48.26s (9.86) 7 Ran SP% **119.1**
PARI-MUTUEL (all including 1 euro stake): WIN 7.80; PLACE 2.80, 1.70, 2.90; DF 20.40.
Owner Torsten Raber **Bred** Mme N Malatier & J-P-J Dubois **Trained** France

8340- 8389a (Foreign Racing) - See Raceform Interactive

8153 SAN SIRO (R-H)
Sunday, October 20

OFFICIAL GOING: Turf: heavy

8390a GRAN CRITERIUM (GROUP 2) (2YO COLTS & FILLIES) (MEDIA COURSE) (TURF) 7f 110y
2:30 2-Y-0 £117,117 (£51,531; £28,108; £14,054)

RPR
1 **Rubaiyat (FR)**[14] 7937 2-8-11 0........................ ClementLecoeuvre 2 114+
(Henk Grewe, Germany) *racd keenly: chsd front pair: drvn to chal ent fnl 2f: sn rdn and led over 1f out: forged clr ins fnl f* **8/11**[1]
2 5 **Cima Emergency (IRE)** 2-8-11 0........................(t) FabioBranca 1 102
(Grizzetti Galoppo SRL, Italy) *racd keenly: pressed ldr on inner tl wnt on after 1 1/2f: stl travelling strly whn eventual wnr chal ent fnl 2f: rdn but no match for wnr whn hdd over 1f out: kpt on for 2nd* **98/10**
3 1 3/4 **Elaire Noire (IRE)**[22] 2-8-11 0........................(t) AndreaMezzatesta 3 98
(R Biondi, Italy) *led on outer: hdd after 1 1/2f and chsd new ldr: sltly outpcd and rdn 2f out: kpt on at one pce for 3rd* **63/20**[2]
4 1 3/4 **Sicomoro (ITY)**[119] 4172 2-8-11 0........................ SergioUrru 4 94
(Nicolo Simondi, Italy) *racd keenly: hld up in midfield on inner: rdn and nt qckn 2f out: plugged on at one pce* **232/10**
5 snk **Gerardino Jet (IRE)**[22] 2-8-11 0........................ AntonioFresu 5 94
(Mario Marcialis, Italy) *racd in fnl pair on inner: drvn and no real imp over 2f out: one pce fr there* **11/1**
6 2 1/2 **Smart Rag (IRE)**[14] 2-8-11 0........................ DarioVargiu 6 88
(A Botti, Italy) *racd in fnl pair on outer: rdn and shortlived effrt 2f out: sn btn* **10/3**[3]
7 5 **Urus** 2-8-11 0........................(t) SilvanoMulas 7 76
(Grizzetti Galoppo SRL, Italy) *plld hrd: hld up in midfield on outer: rdn and wknd over 1 1/2f out* **26/1**

1m 36.4s (0.90) 7 Ran SP% **130.5**
PARI-MUTUEL (all including 1 euro stake): WIN 1.74; PLACE 1.26, 2.57; DF 8.23.
Owner Darius Racing **Bred** Gestut Karlshof **Trained** Germany

8391a GRAN PREMIO DEL JOCKEY CLUB (GROUP 2) (3YO+) (GRANDE COURSE) (TURF) 1m 4f
3:10 3-Y-0+ £105,405 (£46,378; £25,297; £12,648)

RPR
1 **Donjah (GER)**[28] 7500 3-8-9 0........................ ClementLecoeuvre 4 110
(Henk Grewe, Germany) *w.w one fr last in single-file field: prog over 2f out: drvn to ld appr fnl f: sn clr: v comf* **8/11**[1]
2 4 1/2 **Chasedown (IRE)**[497] 5-9-4 0........................ DarioVargiu 2 105
(A Botti, Italy) *led: hdd over 2f out: rallied u.p over 1f out: regained 2nd ins fnl f: kpt on but no match for wnr* **13/8**[2]
3 3 3/4 **Colomano**[28] 7500 5-9-4 0........................ MartinSeidl 3 99
(Markus Klug, Germany) *racd keenly: chsd clr ldr: led over 2f out: hdd appr fnl f: sn labouring and lost 2nd: plugged on at one pce* **10/3**[3]
4 5 **Khan (GER)**[63] 6266 5-9-4 0........................(p) JackMitchell 5 91
(Henk Grewe, Germany) *detached in rr: rdn along 3f out: sme late prog but needed plenty of urging: nvr in contention* **8/11**[1]
5 18 **Chestnut Honey (IRE)**[28] 7504 3-8-13 0........................ FabioBranca 1 64
(A Botti, Italy) *settled in 3rd: drvn to cl over 2f out: sn no further imp and wknd: wl hld fnl f and eased* **13/8**[2]

2m 35.8s (4.30)
WFA 3 from 5yo 6lb 5 Ran SP% **215.1**
PARI-MUTUEL (all including 1 euro stake): WIN 1.72; PLACE 1.34, 2.05; DF 7.51.
Owner Darius Racing **Bred** Gestut Karlshof **Trained** Germany

8392a PREMIO VITTORIO DI CAPUA (GROUP 2) (3YO+) (GRANDE COURSE) (TURF) 1m
3:50 3-Y-0+ £105,405 (£46,378; £25,297; £12,648)

RPR
1 **Out Of Time (ITY)**[112] 4432 3-8-11 0........................ DarioVargiu 4 112
(A Botti, Italy) *in rr: began to cl fr 3f out: sn drvn and sustained run to ld ent fnl f: grad asserted* **13/2**
2 1 3/4 **Anda Muchacho (IRE)**[28] 7502 5-9-1 0........................ AntonioFresu 8 110
(Nicolo Simondi, Italy) *chsd ldr on outer: drvn to ld 1 1/2f out: sn chal and hdd ent fnl f: kpt on at same pce: pair clr* **154/100**[1]
3 5 **Robin Of Navan (FR)**[15] 7922 6-9-1 0........................(p) GeraldMosse 6 98
(Harry Dunlop) *racd keenly: restrained in 4th: drvn to ld ent fnl 2f: hdd 1 1/2f out: no ex* **69/20**[2]
4 3 **Nica (GER)**[21] 7750 4-8-11 0........................ RenePiechulek 3 88
(Dr A Bolte, Germany) *hld up in 5th: lost pl and adrift over 2 1/2f out: styd on u.p ins fnl f: wnt 4th fnl 50yds* **59/10**
5 2 1/4 **Ninario (GER)**[21] 7750 4-9-1 0........................ FabioBranca 2 86
(Waldemar Hickst, Germany) *towards rr on inner: rdn and prog over 2f out: run petered out appr fnl f: plugged on at one pce* **51/10**
6 2 1/2 **Zargun (GER)**[49] 6770 4-9-1 0........................(p) ClementLecoeuvre 1 81
(Henk Grewe, Germany) *chsd ldr on inner: drvn to ld ins fnl 2 1/2f: hdd 2f out: sn wknd* **227/10**
7 11 **Greg Pass (IRE)**[28] 7502 7-9-1 0........................ WalterGambarota 7 55
(Nicolo Simondi, Italy) *led: drvn and hdd 2 1/2f out: wknd fnl 1 1/2f* **154/100**[1]
8 dist **Mission Boy**[28] 7502 3-8-11 0........................ CarloFiocchi 5
(A Botti, Italy) *towards rr on outer: lost tch wl over 2f out: t.o* **41/10**[3]

1m 39.9s (-2.20)
WFA 3 from 4yo+ 3lb 8 Ran SP% **169.3**
PARI-MUTUEL (all including 1 euro stake): WIN 7.51; PLACE 1.92, 1.33, 1.68; DF 10.85.
Owner Scuderia Del Giglio Sardo Srl **Bred** Rz Del Velino Srl **Trained** Italy

8393a PREMIO DORMELLO (GROUP 2) (2YO FILLIES) (MEDIA COURSE) (TURF) 1m
4:30 2-Y-0 £105,405 (£46,378; £25,297; £12,648)

RPR
1 **Night Colours (IRE)**[21] 7726 2-8-11 0........................ FabioBranca 6 103
(Simon Crisford) *sltly s.i.s: sn settled in fnl pair: hdwy 2 1/2f out: drvn to chal 1 1/2f out: sustained run u.p fnl f: led fnl 75yds and hld on* **5/4**[1]
2 shd **Rose Secret (ITY)**[35] 2-8-11 0........................ DarioVargiu 7 103
(A Botti, Italy) *towards rr: clsd after 1/2-way: chsd ldrs 1 1/2f out: led appr fnl f: hrd pressed fr there: hdd fnl 75yds: rallied gamely* **5/1**[3]
3 1 3/4 **Romsey**[21] 7749 2-8-11 0........................ GeraldMosse 2 99
(Hughie Morrison) *sn prom: chsd ldr 3f out: sn rdn and led 2f out: hdd appr fnl f: no ex fnl 100yds* **51/20**[2]
4 2 1/2 **Ancona (IRE)**[22] 7724 2-8-11 0........................(h) RenePiechulek 9 93
(Andreas Suborics, Germany) *towards rr on outer: rushed up to chse ldrs after 2f: rdn and nt qckn over 2f out: grad dropped away* **93/10**
5 4 **Faccio Io**[49] 2-8-11 0........................(t) CarloFiocchi 4 84
(Grizzetti Galoppo SRL, Italy) *plld hrd: sn restrained in midfield: one pce u.p fnl 2f* **43/5**
6 3 1/2 **Golden Lips (IRE)**[36] 7203 2-8-11 0........................ OlivierPeslier 5 76
(Harry Dunlop) *midfield: dropped into fnl trio after 2 1/2f: sme mod last prog: nvr trbld ldrs* **705/100**
7 2 1/2 **Always Dreaming (GER)**[21] 2-8-11 0........................ ClementLecoeuvre 3 70
(Waldemar Hickst, Germany) *prom on inner: dropped into midfield bef 1/2-way: rdn and btn fnl 2f* **12/1**
8 2 3/4 **Sa Paradura**[92] 2-8-11 0........................(t) SilvanoMulas 8 64
(Grizzetti Galoppo SRL, Italy) *prom on outer: drvn and no imp 2 1/2f out: sn wknd* **35/1**
9 nse **Diavolaccia (ITY)** 2-8-11 0........................(t) ClaudioColombi 1 64
(Nicolo Simondi, Italy) *led: hdd 2f out: sn wknd u.p* **173/10**
10 11 **Visions (IRE)** 2-8-11 0........................(t) NicolaPinna 10 38+
(Grizzetti Galoppo SRL, Italy) *a among bkmarkers: lost tch fnl 2f* **34/1**

1m 37.8s (-4.30) 10 Ran SP% **140.6**
PARI-MUTUEL (all including 1 euro stake): WIN 2.24; PLACE 1.16, 1.42, 1.21; DF 19.32.
Owner Hussain Alabbas Lootah **Bred** Grenane House Stud **Trained** Newmarket, Suffolk

[7619] PONTEFRACT (L-H)

Monday, October 21

OFFICIAL GOING: Soft (heavy in places; 5.9)

Wind: Light behind Weather: Heavy Cloud and showers

8394 FARMER COPLEYS PUMPKIN FESTIVAL 2019 NURSERY H'CAP — 1m 6y

2:20 (2:21) (Class 5) (0-75,74) 2-Y-O

£3,881 (£1,155; £577; £300; £300; £300) **Stalls Low**

Form — RPR

6602 **1** **Guipure**[12] 8022 2-9-1 **68** ... BenCurtis 2 — 74+
(K R Burke) *trckd ldrs: pushed along and hdwy on inner over 2f out: swtchd rt and wd st: sn chsng ldr and rdn: led jst ins fnl f: drvn out* **10/1**

0102 **2** *3 ¼* **Magna Moralia (IRE)**[12] 8029 2-9-5 **72** ... DanielTudhope 1 — 71
(John Quinn) *dwlt and in rr: hdwy over 2f out: rdn wl over 1f out: styd on fnl f* **5/4**[1]

006 **3** *½* **El Jefe (IRE)**[17] 7870 2-8-2 **55** ... CamHardie 7 — 53+
(Brian Ellison) *dwlt and towards rr: hdwy 1/2-way: chsd ldrs and rdn along 2f out: styd on fnl f* **20/1**

5410 **4** *1* **Breguet Boy (IRE)**[9] 8124 2-8-13 **71** ... BenSanderson(5) 3 — 69
(Keith Dalgleish) *trckd ldrs: hdwy and pushed along whn clipped heels and stmbld bdly home turn 2f out: sn rdn: kpt on same pce* **7/1**[3]

663 **5** *1* **Hooroo (IRE)**[17] 7874 2-8-11 **64** ... CliffordLee 10 — 57
(K R Burke) *hld up in rr: hdwy and wd st: rdn wl over 1f out: kpt on fnl f (vet said gelding sustained a wound to its left-fore)* **28/1**

650 **6** *nk* **Maximilius (GER)**[16] 7899 2-8-8 **61** ... HarryBentley 9 — 54
(Ralph Beckett) *hld up towards rr: hdwy over 2f out: rdn along wl over 1f out: plugged on one pce* **9/1**

0602 **7** *nk* **Ambyfaeirvine (IRE)**[5] 8259 2-8-13 **66** ow1 ... (v) DavidAllan 5 — 58+
(Ivan Furtado) *led: rdn along and clr wl over 1f out: hdd and drvn jst ins fnl f: grad wknd (jockey said colt ran too free)* **5/1**[2]

3054 **8** *7* **Lawaa (FR)**[23] 7699 2-9-1 **68** ... (p[1]) PaulHanagan 4 — 45
(Richard Fahey) *chsd ldrs: rdn along over 2f out: sn drvn and wknd* **28/1**

003 **9** *3 ¾* **Genever Dragon (IRE)**[79] 5655 2-9-7 **74** ... (p[1]) RichardKingscote 8 — 42
(Tom Dascombe) *trckd ldrs: pushed along over 2f out: sn rdn and wknd* **14/1**

0004 **10** *17* **Comvida (IRE)**[13] 7980 2-8-0 **53** oh1 ... (b) JimmyQuinn 6
(Hugo Palmer) *chsd ldr: rdn along 3f out: drvn over 2f out: sn wknd* **25/1**

3152 **11** *2 ½* **Out Of Breath**[26] 7585 2-9-7 **74** ... SamJames 11
(Grant Tuer) *a towards rr* **20/1**

1m 50.36s (4.46) **Going Correction** +0.625s/f (Yiel) — 11 Ran SP% **119.6**

Speed ratings (Par 95): **102,98,98,97,96 95,95,88,84,67 65**

CSF £21.70 CT £262.20 TOTE £10.70: £2.10, £1.30, £6.60; EX 32.40 Trifecta £1164.00.

Owner Cheveley Park Stud **Bred** Cheveley Park Stud Ltd **Trained** Middleham Moor, N Yorks

FOCUS

As in previous seasons for this meeting, the rail was dolled out by up to 3yds between the 3f and 2f markers, adding approximately 5yds to all races. They didn't hang around in this modest nursery and the centre of the home straight proved the place to be. A winning time 8.56sec slower than RP standard advertised going more like heavy all over.

8395 NAPOLEONS CASINO BRADFORD NOVICE AUCTION STKS — 6f

2:50 (2:56) (Class 5) 2-Y-O — **£3,881** (£1,155; £577; £288) **Stalls Low**

Form — RPR

4632 **1** **Hidden Spell (IRE)**[13] 7995 2-8-12 **70** ... BenCurtis 7 — 72
(K R Burke) *cl up: led after 1f: rdn along and wd st: drvn and kpt on wl fnl f* **10/3**[2]

4042 **2** *1 ¾* **Spygate**[21] 7763 2-9-4 **76** ... DanielTudhope 2 — 73
(Richard Fahey) *trckd ldng pair on inner: hdwy over 2f out: rdn to chse wnr over 1f out: drvn and ch ent fnl f: kpt on same pce* **11/10**[1]

0 **3** *2 ¾* **Twist Of Hay**[66] 6175 2-8-11 **0** ... TomEaves 11 — 59+
(Michael Dods) *dwlt and in rr: hdwy over 2f out: rdn along wl over 1f out: kpt on fnl f: nrst fin* **20/1**

0 **4** *nk* **Clotherholme (IRE)**[23] 7698 2-9-4 **0** ... PaulMulrennan 8 — 64
(Ann Duffield) *trckd ldrs: pushed along over 2f out: rdn wl over 1f out: drvn and kpt on same pce fr over 1f out* **66/1**

4 **5** *1* **Lincoln Gamble**[34] 7308 2-9-0 **0** ... PaulHanagan 1 — 57
(Richard Fahey) *trckd ldrs: hdwy on inner over 2f out: rdn along wl over 1f out: grad wknd* **9/2**[3]

32 **6** *½* **Simply Silca (IRE)**[51] 6719 2-8-13 **0** ... ShaneKelly 6 — 54
(Richard Hughes) *cl up: rdn along over 2f out: drvn wl over 1f out: grad wknd fr over 1f out* **16/1**

5 **7** *12* **Bulldozer (IRE)**[5] 8265 2-9-5 **0** ... AlistairRawlinson 4 — 24
(Michael Appleby) *in tch: pushed along 3f out: rdn over 2f out: sn wknd* **66/1**

00 **8** *7* **Starbo (IRE)**[16] 7902 2-9-0 **0** ... BenRobinson 3
(John Quinn) *green and sn outpcd in rr: hdwy 2f out: sn rdn and n.d* **16/1**

0 **9** *2 ½* **Cindy Looper**[10] 8084 2-8-10 **0** ... PhilDennis 10
(Richard Whitaker) *in tch: rdn along 2 1/2f out: sn wknd* **25/1**

10 *4 ½* **Jack Is Back** 2-9-0 **0** ... GrahamLee 9
(Lawrence Mullaney) *dwlt: a in rr* **33/1**

11 *13* **Lakeland Magic (IRE)** 2-9-3 **0** ... SamJames 5
(Grant Tuer) *dwlt: green: sn outpcd and bhd (starter said gelding was reluctant to enter stalls; trainer told gelding couldn't run again until passing a stalls test)* **33/1**

1m 20.89s (3.79) **Going Correction** +0.625s/f (Yiel) — 11 Ran SP% **118.1**

Speed ratings (Par 95): **99,96,93,92,91 90,74,65,61,55 38**

CSF £6.90 TOTE £4.00: £1.50, £1.10, £4.60; EX 7.60 Trifecta £65.90.

Owner Clipper Logistics **Bred** Nanallac Stud **Trained** Middleham Moor, N Yorks

FOCUS

Add 5yds. The middle of the home straight was again favoured in this ordinary novice event. It's been rated at face value.

8396 KC ETHICAL AND SUSTAINABLE BRITISH CAVIAR H'CAP — 1m 2f 5y

3:20 (3:24) (Class 4) (0-85,82) 3-Y-O+

£5,336 (£1,588; £793; £396; £300; £300) **Stalls Low**

Form — RPR

3323 **1** **Bo Samraan (IRE)**[156] 2845 3-9-0 **79** ... JoeFanning 4 — 90
(Mark Johnston) *trckd ldr: led over 7f out: pushed along over 2f out and wd st: rdn over 1f out: drvn and hdd narrowly ins fnl 100yds: rallied gamely to ld again towards fin* **6/1**[2]

362 **2** *hd* **Sod's Law**[12] 8032 4-9-3 **78** ... DanielTudhope 2 — 88
(Hughie Morrison) *trckd ldrs: hdwy over 2f out: wd st and rdn to chal over 1f out: drvn along nr stands' rail to take slt ld last 100yds: hdd and no ex towards fin* **9/2**[1]

0035 **3** *10* **Awake My Soul (IRE)**[9] 8130 10-9-6 **81** ... JamesSullivan 5 — 71
(Tom Tate) *dwlt and in rr: hdwy over 2f out: rdn along to chse ldrs over 1f out: no imp fnl f* **7/1**[3]

0230 **4** *3 ¼* **Archaeology**[24] 7653 3-9-2 **81** ... JackGarritty 11 — 65
(Jedd O'Keeffe) *trckd ldng pair: effrt on inner 3f out: rdn along over 2f out: sn drvn and kpt on same pce* **25/1**

051 **5** *5* **Rake's Progress**[12] 8032 5-8-11 **79** ... StefanoCherchi(7) 3 — 52
(Heather Main) *dwlt and in rr: hdwy over 2f out: sn rdn along: plugged on: n.d* **7/1**[3]

2613 **6** *1 ¼* **Lopes Dancer (IRE)**[10] 8082 7-9-2 **77** ... BenRobinson 9 — 48
(Brian Ellison) *a towards rr* **8/1**

1014 **7** *4* **Regal Mirage (IRE)**[17] 7872 5-9-1 **76** ... DavidAllan 8 — 39
(Tim Easterby) *t.k.h: hld up in midfield: hdwy over 3f out: pushed along to chse ldrs 2f out: sn rdn and wknd over 1f out (vet said gelding had lost its left hind shoe)* **14/1**

1620 **8** *4 ½* **Illustrissime (USA)**[51] 3502 6-9-7 **82** ... DougieCostello 1 — 36
(Mark Walford) *hld up: hdwy on inner over 2f out: rdn along wl over 1f out: sn drvn and n.d* **50/1**

3021 **9** *3 ½* **Power Player**[31] 7405 3-8-6 **71** ... BenCurtis 12 — 19
(K R Burke) *trckd ldrs: pushed along 3f out: rdn 2f out: sn wknd* **12/1**

0323 **10** *11* **Glasses Up (USA)**[6] 8237 4-9-2 **77** ... PaulMulrennan 13 — 2
(R Mike Smith) *chsd ldrs on outer: rdn along wl over 2f out: sn wknd* **8/1**

0045 **11** *2* **Frankelio (FR)**[23] 7678 4-8-11 **72** ... GrahamLee 14
(Micky Hammond) *in tch: hdwy to chse ldrs on outer over 3f out: rdn along over 2f out: sn wknd* **16/1**

1654 **12** *2 ½* **Medalla De Oro**[37] 7185 5-9-4 **79** ... (h) HarryBentley 6
(Tom Clover) *sn led: hdd over 7f out: cl up: rdn along over 2f out: sn wknd* **14/1**

0433 **13** *6* **Delph Crescent (IRE)**[16] 7907 4-8-12 **73** ... (p) PaulHanagan 15
(Richard Fahey) *a towards rr* **16/1**

00/0 **14** *1 ¼* **Flight Officer**[5] 8260 8-8-13 **79** ... GerO'Neill(5) 10
(Michael Easterby) *a towards rr* **66/1**

2m 19.5s (4.50) **Going Correction** +0.625s/f (Yiel)

WFA 3 from 4yo+ 4lb — 14 Ran SP% **119.8**

Speed ratings (Par 105): **107,106,98,96,92 91,88,84,81,72 71,69,64,63**

CSF £32.50 CT £197.59 TOTE £7.00: £2.70, £2.00, £2.70; EX 38.10 Trifecta £244.10.

Owner Jaber Abdullah **Bred** Sunderland Holdings Inc **Trained** Middleham Moor, N Yorks

FOCUS

Add 5yds. Racing handily was a must in this fair handicap and two came right away on the stands' side. The winner has been rated in line with his Chester form two starts back.

8397 EBFSTALLIONS.COM SILVER TANKARD STKS (LISTED RACE) — 1m 6y

3:50 (3:51) (Class 1) 2-Y-O

£19,848 (£7,525; £3,766; £1,876; £941; £472) **Stalls Low**

Form — RPR

521 **1** **King Carney**[12] 8028 2-9-3 **82** ... DanielTudhope 5 — 96+
(Charlie Fellowes) *mde all: rdn along and wd st to stands' side: jnd wl over 1f out: drvn ins fnl f: kpt on wl towards fin* **7/2**[2]

131 **2** *¾* **Wyclif**[43] 7000 2-9-3 **90** ... HarryBentley 1 — 94
(Ralph Beckett) *hld up in rr: hdwy on inner to trck ldrs and wd st: rdn along to chse wnr over 1f out: drvn to chal ins fnl f: ev ch tl no ex towards fin* **15/8**[1]

411 **3** *½* **Grand Rock (IRE)**[22] 7726 2-9-3 **93** ... JamesDoyle 4 — 93
(William Haggas) *hld up in rr: hdwy and wd st: sn rdn and chsng wnr: ch and drvn ins fnl f: kpt on same pce last 100yds* **7/2**[2]

216 **4** *15* **He's A Keeper (IRE)**[44] 6957 2-9-3 **93** ... RichardKingscote 3 — 60
(Tom Dascombe) *trckd ldrs: hdwy 1/2-way: chsd wnr over 2f out: sn rdn along and wd st: sn drvn and outpcd appr fnl f (vet said colt had lost its left-fore shoe)* **7/1**[3]

0531 **5** *6* **Sir Arthur Dayne (IRE)**[14] 7971 2-9-3 **83** ... (v) SilvestreDeSousa 2 — 47
(Mick Channon) *trckd ldng pair: hdwy on inner 3f out: rdn along 2f out: sn drvn and wknd wl over 1f out* **11/1**

211 **6** *18* **Freyja (IRE)**[33] 7330 2-8-12 **87** ... JoeFanning 6
(Mark Johnston) *trckd wnr: pushed along over 3f out: rdn wl over 2f out: sn outpcd and bhd* **8/1**

1m 50.76s (4.86) **Going Correction** +0.625s/f (Yiel) — 6 Ran SP% **111.2**

Speed ratings (Par 103): **100,99,98,83,77 59**

CSF £10.29 TOTE £4.40: £1.70, £1.90; EX 11.30 Trifecta £39.00.

Owner Mrs Susan Roy **Bred** Select Bloodstock **Trained** Newmarket, Suffolk

FOCUS

Add 5yds. An average edition of this 2yo Listed prize. Again they came stands' side off the home turn and the principals dominated.

8398 LESLIE BURTON (FISHER) MAIDEN STKS — 1m 4f 5y

4:20 (4:21) (Class 5) 3-Y-O+ — **£3,881** (£1,155; £577; £288) **Stalls Low**

Form — RPR

5534 **1** **Lady Scatterley (FR)**[12] 8020 3-9-0 **67** ... DavidAllan 5 — 74
(Tim Easterby) *mde all: rdn clr and wd st 2f out: drvn and kpt on wl fnl f* **12/1**

506 **2** *2 ½* **Fox Fearless**[94] 5127 3-9-5 **68** ... CliffordLee 2 — 75
(K R Burke) *hld up: hdwy and in tch 5f out: pushed along to chse ldrs 3f out: rdn to chse wnr wl over 1f out: sn drvn and kpt on same pce fnl f* **20/1**

3224 **3** *6* **Dante's View (IRE)**[26] 7577 3-9-5 **79** ... DanielTudhope 3 — 65
(Sir Michael Stoute) *hld up towards rr: hdwy 4f out: pushed along 3f out: kpt on to chse ldng pair fr wl over 1f out: no imp* **7/2**[2]

3034 **4** *28* **King Power**[17] 7867 3-9-0 **77** ... SilvestreDeSousa 1 — 16
(Andrew Balding) *prom: trckd wnr after 4f: effrt over 3f out: sn rdn along: drvn and wknd 2f out: sn wknd* **11/8**[1]

3322 **5** *9* **Swift Wing**[23] 7689 3-9-5 **79** ... (v[1]) RobertHavlin 4 — 6
(John Gosden) *trckd ldrs: hdwy 5f out: rdn along 3f out: sn drvn and wknd (trainer's rep said gelding was unsuited by the uphill finish on testing conditions)* **4/1**[3]

4242 **6** *1* **Vibrance**[12] 8019 3-9-0 **67** ... JoeFanning 10
(James Fanshawe) *hld up: pushed along over 4f out: sn rdn and n.d* **9/1**

4 **7** *28* **Montelimar**[27] 7543 4-9-1 **0** ... AndrewBreslin(5) 7
(Andrew Crook) *a bhd* **200/1**

32 **8** *6* **Rory And Me (FR)**[23] 7704 4-9-11 **0** ... (t) GrahamLee 8
(Micky Hammond) *prom: rdn along on outer 4f out: sn wknd* **14/1**

2 **9** *53* **Education**[37] 7177 3-9-5 **0** ... HarryBentley 9
(Ismail Mohammed) *a bhd* **66/1**

10 9 **Hart Fell** 3-9-5 0 PaulMulrennan 6
(Kevin Frost) *a bhd* **100/1**
2m 49.82s (8.72) **Going Correction** +0.625s/f (Yiel)
WFA 3 from 4yo 6lb **10** Ran SP% **116.4**
Speed ratings (Par 103): **95,93,89,70,64 64,45,41,6,**
CSF £210.27 TOTE £16.80: £3.40, £4.90, £1.60; EX 259.80 Trifecta £1650.00.

Owner Mrs T Whatley **Bred** Mlle Moa Sundstrom **Trained** Great Habton, N Yorks

FOCUS
Add 5yds. The majority of these were struggling on the ground 3f out and there was another winner from the front. The second has been rated close to last year's turf form.

8399 PHIL BULL TROPHY CONDITIONS STKS (ROUND 8 OF THE PONTEFRACT STAYERS CHAMPIONSHIP) 2m 2f 2y
4:50 (4:51) (Class 2) 3-Y-O+

£12,318 (£3,708; £1,854; £924; £464; £234) **Stalls** Low

Form RPR
5400 1 **Fun Mac (GER)**[37] 7181 8-9-4 84 (t) RobertHavlin 5 90
(Hughie Morrison) *hld up in rr: hdwy 4f out: chsd ldrs and rdn over 1f out: chal and n.m.r ins fnl f: sn rdn: styd on wl to ld towards fin (trainer's rep could offer no explanation for the gelding's improved form)* **11/4**[2]

-004 2 ½ **Arrowtown**[9] 8129 7-8-13 89 (h) GrahamLee 1 84
(Michael Easterby) *trckd ldrs on inner: hdwy 4f out: chsd ldr and wd st: rdn to chal over 1f out: drvn to take narrow ld ins fnl f: sn edgd lft: hdd and no ex towards fin* **5/6**[1]

1110 3 2¼ **Rubenesque (IRE)**[9] 8129 7-8-13 77 (t) PhilDennis 4 82
(Tristan Davidson) *led: pushed along over 2f out: rdn and wd st: sn jnd and drvn: hdd ins fnl f: kpt on same pce* **6/1**

/36- 4 10 **Taxmeifyoucan (IRE)**[17] 9775 5-9-4 86 (p) JoeFanning 3 79
(Keith Dalgleish) *trckd ldng pair: hdwy over 3f out: cl up and wd st: rdn along wl over 1f out: sn one pce* **5/1**[3]

0 5 47 **Notwhatiam (IRE)**[23] 7681 9-9-4 0 ConnorMurtagh 6 30
(Alan Berry) *cl up: rdn along 4f out: sn wknd (jockey said gelding hung left-handed throughout)* **100/1**

660/ 6 8 **Hartside (GER)**[141] 1703 10-9-4 57 PaulMulrennan 2 22
(Peter Winks) *hld up: a in rr: outpcd and bhd fnl 4f* **100/1**
4m 30.0s (22.30) **Going Correction** +0.625s/f (Yiel) **6** Ran SP% **114.2**
Speed ratings (Par 109): **75,74,73,69,48 44**
CSF £5.56 TOTE £3.40: £1.40, £1.30; EX 7.20 Trifecta £15.10.

Owner Mrs Angela McAlpine & Partners **Bred** Gestut Gorlsdorf **Trained** East Ilsley, Berks

FOCUS
Add 5yds. This fair marathon event proved tactical. The second has been rated to form.

8400 THANK YOU FOR EVERYTHING COLIN MAKEPEACE H'CAP 5f 3y
5:20 (5:22) (Class 4) (0-85,85) 3-Y-O+

£5,336 (£1,588; £793; £396; £300; £300) **Stalls** Low

Form RPR
100 1 **Our Little Pony**[44] 6972 4-8-9 78 FayeMcManoman(5) 6 86
(Lawrence Mullaney) *hld up towards rr: hdwy wl over 1f out: chsd ldrs and rdn ent fnl f: sn chal: kpt on wl to ld last 50yds* **9/1**[3]

2450 2 ½ **Hawaam (IRE)**[2] 8340 4-9-2 80 (p) RobertHavlin 1 86
(Roger Fell) *prom on inner: led over 3f out: rdn wl over 1f out: drvn ins fnl f: hdd and no ex last 50yds* **11/1**

4011 3 2¾ **Militia**[7] 8183 4-8-11 75 5ex PaulHanagan 2 71
(Richard Fahey) *cl up: wd st: rdn along wl over 1f out: ev ch tl drvn ins fnl f and kpt on same pce* **3/1**[1]

3333 4 1¼ **Sheepscar Lad (IRE)**[16] 7908 5-8-7 71 oh2 JoeFanning 5 63
(Nigel Tinkler) *t.k.h: hld up towards rr: hdwy 2f out: rdn to chse ldrs over 1f out: drvn and no imp fnl f* **9/1**[3]

043 5 ¾ **Gamesome (FR)**[32] 7367 8-8-4 71 oh1 HarrisonShaw(3) 4 60
(Paul Midgley) *hld up in rr: effrt on inner and nt clr run home turn 2f out: sn rdn: styd on fnl f* **16/1**

4004 6 ½ **Roundhay Park**[40] 7077 4-9-0 81 RowanScott(3) 7 68
(Nigel Tinkler) *towards rr: hdwy wl over 1f out: sn rdn: kpt on fnl f* **8/1**[2]

2200 7 1¼ **War Whisper (IRE)**[10] 8099 6-9-2 80 KevinStott 3 63
(Paul Midgley) *chsd ldrs: swtchd rt and rdn wl over 1f out: drvn and kpt on same pce fnl f* **12/1**

3360 8 1¼ **Storm Over (IRE)**[10] 8099 5-9-7 85 PaulMulrennan 8 63
(Phillip Makin) *chsd ldrs: rdn along wl over 1f out: sn drvn and wknd* **14/1**

6120 9 2 **Prestbury Park (USA)**[5] 8262 4-8-10 74 GrahamLee 10 45
(Paul Midgley) *chsd ldrs: rdn along 2f out: wd st: sn drvn and one pce* **12/1**

0001 10 1¼ **Rolladice**[2] 8342 4-8-3 72 5ex AndrewBreslin(5) 11 38
(Michael Easterby) *a outpcd in rr* **8/1**[2]

2214 11 1½ **Desert Ace (IRE)**[22] 7736 8-8-5 72 ConnorMurtagh(3) 9 33
(Paul Midgley) *slt ld 1 1/2f: cl up: rdn along 2f out: sn drvn and wknd over 1f out* **33/1**

2041 12 6 **Penny Pot Lane**[23] 7703 6-8-7 71 oh1 (p) PhilDennis 12 10
(Richard Whitaker) *racd wd: a in rr* **22/1**

2121 13 17 **Autumn Flight (IRE)**[21] 7766 3-8-12 76 (b) DavidAllan 13
(Tim Easterby) *prom on wd outside: rdn along over 2f out: sn wknd (trainer's rep could offer no explanation for the gelding's performance)* **8/1**[2]
1m 5.89s (1.99) **Going Correction** +0.625s/f (Yiel) **13** Ran SP% **121.9**
Speed ratings (Par 105): **109,108,103,101,100 99,97,95,92,90 88,78,51**
CSF £106.50 CT £373.80 TOTE £11.60: £2.70, £4.20, £1.90; EX 99.70 Trifecta £512.70.

Owner Richard Swift **Bred** Mel Roberts & Ms Nicola Meese **Trained** Great Habton, N Yorks

■ Stewards' Enquiry : Joe Fanning jockey cautioned: careless riding

FOCUS
Add 5yds. This closing sprint handicap looked wide-open. The first two have been rated to their best.
T/Jkpt: Not won. T/Plt: £40.80 to a £1 stake. Pool: £61,568.84 - 1,101.30 winning units T/Qpdt: £23.00 to a £1 stake. Pool: £5,783.50 - 185.99 winning units **Joe Rowntree**

8264 SOUTHWELL (L-H)
Monday, October 21

OFFICIAL GOING: Fibresand: standard
Wind: Light across Weather: Overcast

8401 SKY SPORTS RACING ON SKY 415 H'CAP 4f 214y(F)
5:30 (5:31) (Class 6) (0-60,62) 3-Y-O+

£2,781 (£827; £413; £400; £400; £400) **Stalls** Centre

Form RPR
5031 1 **Young Tiger**[19] 7824 6-9-1 54 (h) AndrewMullen 8 64
(Tom Tate) *s.i.s: hdwy 1/2-way: rdn to ld over 1f out: r.o* **13/2**

U636 2 1¾ **Arzaak (IRE)**[23] 7690 5-9-8 61 (b) JosephineGordon 5 65
(Charlie Wallis) *led 1f: chsd ldrs: shkn up over 1f out: r.o to go 2nd post* **5/1**[2]

1603 3 nse **Piazon**[26] 7588 8-9-7 60 (be) NathanEvans 3 64
(Julia Brooke) *prom: outpcd over 3f out: hdwy u.p and edgd rt over 1f out: styd on* **4/1**[1]

3065 4 1¼ **Tadaany (IRE)**[25] 7628 7-8-9 48 (v) TomEaves 6 47
(Ruth Carr) *led 4f out: hdd 1/2-way: rdn and ev ch over 1f out: styd on same pce ins fnl f* **25/1**

0140 5 ½ **Bluella**[22] 7737 4-8-1 47 (vt) GeorgeRooke(7) 7 44
(Robyn Brisland) *chsd ldrs: led 1/2-way: rdn and hdd over 1f out: styd on same pce ins fnl f* **16/1**

6215 6 nk **Atty's Edge**[26] 7568 3-9-7 60 LukeMorris 9 57
(Christopher Mason) *chsd ldrs: rdn over 1f out: styd on same pce fnl f* **6/1**[3]

0305 7 nk **Loulin**[14] 7962 4-8-9 48 (t) JamesSullivan 2 43+
(Ruth Carr) *s.s: pushed along in rr: hdwy over 1f out: no ex ins fnl f (jockey said gelding was slowly away)* **6/1**[3]

0000 8 ½ **Classic Pursuit**[6] 8235 8-9-4 57 (v) SamJames 1 50
(Marjorie Fife) *chsd ldrs: lost pl whn hmpd and stmbld wl over 1f out: n.d after* **15/2**

0000 9 3½ **Cox Bazar (FR)**[20] 7800 5-9-6 62 (t) GabrieleMalune(3) 4 43
(Ivan Furtado) *s.i.s: sn chsng ldrs: wknd fnl f* **12/1**

6004 10 3 **Miaella**[18] 7844 4-9-2 55 (p) JoeyHaynes 10 25
(Chelsea Banham) *chsd ldrs: rdn over 1f out: sn wknd* **16/1**
58.39s (-1.31) **Going Correction** -0.25s/f (Stan) **10** Ran SP% **113.6**
Speed ratings (Par 101): **100,97,97,95,94 93,93,92,86,82**
CSF £37.94 CT £149.40 TOTE £5.50: £1.70, £1.50, £1.60; EX 30.50 Trifecta £130.90.
Owner T T Racing **Bred** Mrs J McMahon & Mickley Stud **Trained** Tadcaster, N Yorks

FOCUS
A modest sprint handicap. The winner has been rated close to his best.

8402 VISIT ATTHERACES.COM MEDIAN AUCTION MAIDEN STKS 1m 13y(F)
6:00 (6:01) (Class 5) 2-Y-O **£3,428** (£1,020; £509; £254) **Stalls** Low

Form RPR
2 1 **Finery**[34] 7304 2-9-0 0 BenCurtis 4 73+
(K R Burke) *w ldrs: led 7f out tl over 4f out: chsd ldr tl led again 2f out: shkn up over 1f out: styd on wl* **1/1**[1]

3 2 1¾ **Capla Cubiste**[13] 7981 2-9-0 0 LukeMorris 6 66
(Sir Mark Prescott Bt) *s.i.s: sn prom: drvn along over 2f out: edgd lft and styd on same pce ins fnl f* **12/1**

502 3 hd **London Calling (IRE)**[27] 7548 2-9-5 71 StevieDonohoe 3 71
(Richard Spencer) *chsd ldrs: rdn over 2f out: styd on same pce ins fnl f* **4/1**[3]

0 4 1¼ **Batalha**[20] 7778 2-9-5 0 PJMcDonald 2 68
(Mark Johnston) *w ldrs: led over 4f out: hdd 2f out: sn rdn: edgd lft and no ex ins fnl f* **14/1**

04 5 4 **Compensate**[39] 7124 2-9-5 0 JosephineGordon 1 59
(Andrew Balding) *s.i.s: pushed along in rr: swtchd rt over 6f out: hdwy over 2f out: sn rdn: styd on same pce fr over 1f out* **33/1**

4432 6 21 **Creativity**[17] 7871 2-9-0 69 TonyHamilton 7 8
(Richard Fahey) *led 1f: chsd ldrs: edgd rt 5f out: rdn and wknd over 2f out (trainer's rep could offer no explanation for the filly's performance)* **7/2**[2]

00 7 3 **Purple Sandpiper**[5] 8257 2-9-5 0 KieranO'Neill 8 6
(Robyn Brisland) *prom: pushed along on outer and lost pl 1/2-way: rdn and wknd over 2f out: sn hung lft (jockey said colt hung right in home straight)* **33/1**

0 8 17 **Titanium Grey**[40] 7067 2-9-5 0 JoeyHaynes 5
(Jedd O'Keeffe) *dwlt: outpcd* **33/1**
1m 41.42s (-2.28) **Going Correction** -0.25s/f (Stan) **8** Ran SP% **115.4**
Speed ratings (Par 95): **101,99,99,97,93 72,69,52**
CSF £15.13 TOTE £1.70: £1.10, £2.70, £1.70; EX 14.50 Trifecta £35.70.
Owner Cheveley Park Stud **Bred** Cheveley Park Stud Ltd **Trained** Middleham Moor, N Yorks

FOCUS
An ordinary juvenile maiden.

8403 SKY SPORTS RACING ON VIRGIN 535 H'CAP 6f 16y(F)
6:30 (6:32) (Class 4) (0-80,81) 3-Y-O+

£5,207 (£1,549; £774; £400; £400; £400) **Stalls** Low

Form RPR
5412 1 **Young John (IRE)**[25] 7621 6-9-7 79 AlistairRawlinson 5 88
(Mike Murphy) *w ldr: rdn to ld wl over 1f out: sn hdd: rallied to ld nr fin* **9/2**[2]

6605 2 shd **Airglow (IRE)**[2] 8342 4-9-3 75 (h) NathanEvans 4 83
(Michael Easterby) *hld up in tch: led over 1f out: sn rdn: hdd nr fin* **10/3**[1]

100 3 4 **Liamba**[11] 8070 4-8-11 69 (v) CamHardie 8 64
(David O'Meara) *chsd ldrs: rdn over 1f out: styd on same pce fnl f* **10/1**

3104 4 ½ **Gullane One (IRE)**[23] 7703 4-8-8 66 (p) RachelRichardson 3 60
(Tim Easterby) *led: rdn and hdd wl over 1f out: no ex ins fnl f* **16/1**

0012 5 4 **Samovar**[5] 8267 4-9-1 73 (b) KieranO'Neill 1 54
(Scott Dixon) *s.i.s: sn prom: rdn over 1f out: edgd rt and wknd fnl f* **13/2**

0260 6 ¾ **Angel Palanas**[236] 929 5-9-2 81 (p) RhonaPindar(7) 10 59
(K R Burke) *chsd ldrs on outer tl wknd 2f out* **14/1**

4252 7 4 **Orange Blossom**[19] 7828 3-8-13 72 BarryMcHugh 6 38
(Richard Fahey) *s.i.s: outpcd (jockey said filly resented the kickback on this occasion)* **11/2**

3060 8 1¾ **Praxidice**[16] 7901 3-8-9 68 (t) BenCurtis 9 28
(K R Burke) *s.i.s: sn outpcd (jockey said filly was slowly away)* **5/1**[3]

The Form Book Flat 2019, Raceform Ltd, Newbury, RG14 5SJ

6040 9 18 **Mutawaffer (IRE)**[12] 8023 3-9-2 75 SamJames 7
(Phillip Makin) *free to post: in tch: outpcd fr over 4f out* 33/1
1m 13.76s (-2.74) **Going Correction** -0.25s/f (Stan)
WFA 3 from 4yo+ 1lb 9 Ran SP% **111.2**
Speed ratings (Par 105): **108,107,102,101,96 95,90,87,63**
CSF £18.76 CT £135.88 TOTE £3.60: £1.20, £1.40, £3.70; EX 24.20 Trifecta £144.40.
Owner Murphy, Cooper & East **Bred** Carpet Lady Partnership **Trained** Westoning, Beds
FOCUS
The feature contest was a fair sprint handicap. The second-favourite won gamely in under standard time. The winner has been rated back to his old best.

8404 JORDAN ROAD SURFACING H'CAP 7f 14y(F)
7:00 (7:03) (Class 6) (0-60,58) 3-Y-O+
£2,781 (£827; £413; £400; £400; £400) Stalls Low

Form RPR
4022 1 **Suitcase 'N' Taxi**[30] 7443 5-9-8 58 DuranFentiman 6 68
(Tim Easterby) *mde all: rdn over 1f out: styd on wl* 6/1
1623 2 2 1/4 **Break The Silence**[5] 8270 5-9-0 57 (b) JonathanFisher(7) 7 61
(Scott Dixon) *s.i.s: sn rcvrd to chse wnr: rdn over 1f out: styd on same pce ins fnl f* 1/1[1]
0025 3 hd **Bee Machine (IRE)**[5] 8266 4-8-10 53 (t) ZakWheatley(7) 8 56
(Declan Carroll) *prom: pushed along 1/2-way: sn outpcd: hdwy over 1f out: styd on* 4/1[2]
2404 4 3/4 **Fly True**[11] 8068 6-9-8 58 NickyMackay 4 60
(Ivan Furtado) *chsd ldrs: rdn over 2f out: no ex wl ins fnl f* 9/2[3]
0605 5 10 **Vicky Cristina (IRE)**[13] 8009 4-8-9 45 (v) KieranO'Neill 3 21
(John Holt) *sn pushed along in rr: outpcd fr over 4f out* 33/1
-000 6 6 **Declamation (IRE)**[40] 7080 9-9-8 58 JoeyHaynes 2 18
(John Butler) *chsd ldrs: rdn 1/2-way: wknd over 2f out* 16/1
7 5 **Mojambo (IRE)**[195] 1669 4-8-9 45 (vt[1]) LukeMorris 9
(Stephen Michael Hanlon, Ire) *s.s: outpcd* 25/1
-000 8 6 **Ocean Spray**[109] 4568 4-8-9 45 (bt[1]) JohnFahy 1
(Eugene Stanford) *s.i.s: outpcd* 100/1
1m 28.22s (-2.08) **Going Correction** -0.25s/f (Stan) 8 Ran SP% **116.1**
Speed ratings (Par 101): **101,98,98,97,85 79,73,66**
CSF £12.56 CT £27.40 TOTE £6.00: £2.00, £1.10, £1.80; EX 14.70 Trifecta £39.90.
Owner Ontoawinner 10 & Partner 3 **Bred** Crossfields Bloodstock Ltd **Trained** Great Habton, N Yorks
FOCUS
A moderate handicap. Straightforward form rated around the second and third.

8405 SOUTHWELL RACECOURSE IRISH NIGHT ON 9TH NOVEMBER H'CAP 1m 13y(F)
7:30 (7:31) (Class 6) (0-60,61) 3-Y-O+
£2,781 (£827; £413; £400; £400; £400) Stalls Low

Form RPR
6255 1 **Jazz Hands (IRE)**[14] 7956 3-8-10 52 (p[1]) SeanDavis(3) 4 60
(Richard Fahey) *s.i.s: outpcd: hdwy u.p over 1f out: r.o to ld wl ins fnl f* 10/1
0031 2 1 3/4 **Atalanta Queen**[11] 8068 4-9-1 51 (b) KieranO'Neill 2 56
(Robyn Brisland) *led: hdd over 5f out: outpcd over 3f out: rallied 2f out: rdn to ld 1f out: hdd and unable qck wl ins fnl f* 4/1[2]
0050 3 1 1/2 **Almokhtaar (USA)**[28] 7514 3-9-7 60 (p[1]) TomEaves 7 61
(Kevin Ryan) *w ldrs: rdn to ld over 1f out: sn hdd: styd on same pce ins fnl f* 14/1
0151 4 3 3/4 **Alpha Tauri (USA)**[228] 1069 13-9-4 61 AledBeech(7) 11 55
(Charles Smith) *s.i.s: hdwy over 4f out: swtchd lft ins fnl f: styd on same pce* 22/1
3353 5 2 1/4 **Move In Faster**[69] 6036 4-9-7 57 (v) PaulMulrennan 5 46
(Michael Dods) *reminders sn after s: prom: led over 5f out: rdn and hdd over 1f out: wknd ins fnl f* 5/2[1]
0050 6 3/4 **Captain Peaky**[100] 4914 6-8-4 45 (b[1]) AndrewBreslin(5) 1 32
(Liam Bailey) *s.i.s: outpcd: styd on ins fnl f: nvr nrr* 50/1
4530 7 3/4 **Harbour City (USA)**[32] 7376 3-9-6 59 PJMcDonald 6 43
(James Tate) *sn pushed along in rr: nvr on terms* 14/1
2056 8 nk **Heatherdown (IRE)**[13] 8001 3-8-12 51 (b[1]) LukeMorris 8 35
(Ian Williams) *prom: sn drvn along: nt clr run and lost pl 5f out: n.d after* 16/1
3600 9 1/2 **Molten Lava (IRE)**[14] 7960 7-9-1 51 (p) RobertHavlin 9 35
(Steve Gollings) *prom: lost pl over 4f out: n.d after* 12/1
4350 10 4 **Port Soif**[32] 7385 5-8-7 50 (p) JonathanFisher(7) 3 25
(Scott Dixon) *chsd ldrs: rdn over 2f out: wknd over 1f out* 14/1
0363 11 4 **Global Exceed**[24] 7652 4-9-8 61 (t) GemmaTutty(3) 10 27
(Karen Tutty) *s.i.s: pushed along in rr: hdwy on outer over 4f out: wknd over 2f out (jockey said gelding was slowly into stride and was never travelling thereafter)* 11/2[3]
1m 42.23s (-1.47) **Going Correction** -0.25s/f (Stan)
WFA 3 from 4yo+ 3lb 11 Ran SP% **112.9**
Speed ratings (Par 101): **97,95,93,90,87 87,86,85,85,81 77**
CSF £47.73 CT £573.55 TOTE £11.50: £2.50, £1.20, £2.50; EX 54.90 Trifecta £345.20.
Owner Mike Browne & Mrs Dee Howe **Bred** Golden Vale Stud **Trained** Musley Bank, N Yorks
FOCUS
A modest handicap. The second helps set the level.

8406 SOUTHWELL RACECOURSE FESTIVE FIXTURES CLASSIFIED STKS 1m 4f 14y(F)
8:00 (8:00) (Class 6) 3-Y-O+
£2,846 (£847; £423; £400; £400; £400) Stalls Low

Form RPR
3042 1 **Risk Mitigation (USA)**[5] 8269 3-9-0 48 (v) BenCurtis 13 54+
(David Evans) *sn prom: rdn over 2f out: styd on to ld wl ins fnl f* 5/2[1]
0 2 1/2 **Cape Agulhas (IRE)**[99] 4958 5-9-1 48 (t) SeamusCronin(5) 12 52
(W J Martin, Ire) *s.s: bhd: racd wd tl swtchd lft over 4f out: hdwy over 3f out: rdn and edgd rt fr over 1f out: led 1f out: hdd wl ins fnl f* 22/1
0503 3 1 1/4 **Keith**[13] 8003 3-8-11 48 (p[1]) MeganNicholls(3) 4 51
(Rod Millman) *hld up in tch: swtchd lft wl over 4f out: hmpd over 1f out: sn rdn: styd on* 14/1
5005 4 1/2 **Milldean Felix (IRE)**[36] 7232 3-9-0 45 (b) LukeMorris 9 51
(Suzi Best) *chsd ldrs: wnt 2nd over 4f out: rdn over 2f out: ev ch over 1f out: styd on same pce ins fnl f* 20/1
0035 5 1/2 **Bonneville (IRE)**[13] 8003 3-9-0 48 (b) PaulMulrennan 10 50
(Rod Millman) *chsd ldr after 1f tl led over 8f out: rdn and hdd 1f out: no ex wl ins fnl f* 7/1[3]
0540 6 9 **Lady Of York**[23] 7685 5-9-6 50 JoeyHaynes 14 35
(Chelsea Banham) *hld up in tch: rdn on outer over 3f out: wknd over 1f out* 13/2[2]
4300 7 10 **Going Native**[17] 7873 4-8-13 50 RhonaPindar(7) 3 20
(Olly Williams) *s.i.s: hdwy over 6f out: hmpd and lost pl wl over 4f out: nt clr run and swtchd rt over 3f out: sn wknd* 16/1
-506 8 5 **Call Me Madam**[11] 8072 4-9-6 46 PJMcDonald 8 13
(James Bethell) *sn pushed along in rr: nvr on terms* 8/1
0050 9 1 **Fanny Chenal**[71] 5987 3-9-0 45 RobertHavlin 6 12
(Jim Boyle) *plld hrd and prom: rdn over 3f out: sn wknd* 20/1
10 16 **Ringo Kid**[10] 8109 6-9-6 49 (t) KieranO'Neill 11
(Mrs Olivia Byrne, Ire) *pushed along in rr: sme hdwy on outer over 5f out: wknd over 4f out* 8/1
2005 11 2 3/4 **French Flyer (IRE)**[28] 7509 4-9-6 45 LewisEdmunds 1
(Rebecca Bastiman) *led over 3f: remained handy tl rdn and wknd over 3f out* 50/1
000 12 2 3/4 **Misread**[62] 6315 3-9-0 40 StevieDonohoe 5
(Geoffrey Deacon) *s.i.s: outpcd* 50/1
13 13 **Loudest Whisper (IRE)**[12] 8041 4-9-6 44 BarryMcHugh 2
(E D Delany, Ire) *chsd ldrs: rdn over 4f out: sn wknd* 8/1
2m 38.02s (-2.98) **Going Correction** -0.25s/f (Stan)
WFA 3 from 4yo+ 6lb 13 Ran SP% **118.1**
Speed ratings (Par 101): **99,98,97,97,97 91,84,81,80,69 68,66,57**
CSF £69.82 TOTE £2.40: £1.10, £6.50, £4.60; EX 67.90 Trifecta £378.10.
Owner Mrs I M Folkes **Bred** Robert B Trussell Jr **Trained** Pandy, Monmouths
■ Stewards' Enquiry : Megan Nicholls two-day ban: interference & careless riding (Nov 4-5)
FOCUS
A moderate middle-distance classified stakes. The 3yo favourite made the most of the 6lb weight-for-age allowance he received from the slow-starting runner-up. The third has been rated in line with his recent turf deep ground selling form.

8407 8TH NOVEMBER 30TH ANNIVERSARY DINNER MAIDEN STKS 6f 16y(F)
8:30 (8:30) (Class 5) 3-Y-O+ £3,428 (£1,020; £509; £254) Stalls Low

Form RPR
0040 1 **Royal Sands (FR)**[37] 7189 3-9-5 68 BarryMcHugh 4 77
(James Given) *a.p: chsd ldr over 4f out tl led over 2f out: rdn over 1f out: styd on wl (trainer said, regarding the apparent improvement in form, the gelding appreciated drop in trip)* 10/1
2222 2 1 1/2 **Marvel**[31] 7417 3-9-2 68 HarrisonShaw(3) 7 71
(Julie Camacho) *a.p: chsd wnr over 1f out: rdn and edgd rt ins fnl f: styd on same pce* 11/4[2]
0302 3 3 3/4 **Tease Maid**[11] 8071 3-9-0 60 (p) PJMcDonald 2 54
(John Quinn) *chsd ldrs: wnt 2nd over 2f out tl rdn over 1f out: no ex ins fnl f* 7/2[3]
0306 4 7 **Henrietta's Dream**[33] 7335 5-9-1 43 (v) KieranO'Neill 1 32
(Robyn Brisland) *s.i.s: outpcd: styd on to go 4th ins fnl f: nvr nrr* 33/1
5 3 **Inn With The Gin** 3-8-7 0 JonathanFisher(7) 8 22
(Scott Dixon) *s.i.s: sn pushed along in rr: hdwy over 4f out: rdn and hung rt over 3f out: wknd 2f out* 33/1
60- 6 1 1/2 **Fox Shinji**[345] 9000 3-9-5 0 SilvestreDeSousa 3 22
(Andrew Balding) *s.i.s: sn swtchd rt and wd: outpcd* 15/8[1]
0400 7 nk **Ventura Glory**[135] 3570 3-9-0 66 (p) BenCurtis 9 16
(Richard Hannon) *chsd ldrs: rdn over 2f out: wknd wl over 1f out* 8/1
8 20 **Henry The Sixth** 3-9-5 0 LukeMorris 5
(Scott Dixon) *led over 3f: sn wknd* 33/1
1m 14.15s (-2.35) **Going Correction** -0.25s/f (Stan)
WFA 3 from 5yo 1lb 8 Ran SP% **112.7**
Speed ratings (Par 103): **105,103,98,88,84 82,82,55**
CSF £36.58 TOTE £10.90: £2.00, £1.50, £1.30; EX 37.20 Trifecta £123.80.
Owner The Cool Silk Partnership **Bred** Mme Geraldine Henochsberg Et Al **Trained** Willoughton, Lincs
FOCUS
An ordinary maiden. The fifth-favourite came home well to register the second-best comparative time on the night. The second has been rated close to form.
T/Plt: £16.80 to a £1 stake. Pool: £87,664.03 - 3,800.06 winning units T/Qpdt: £7.40 to a £1 stake. Pool: £12,041.88 - 1,194.68 winning units **Colin Roberts**

7971 WINDSOR (R-H)
Monday, October 21
OFFICIAL GOING: Heavy (soft in places; 5.8) changing to heavy after race 3 (3.00)
Wind: light, across Weather: overcast

8408 WINDSOR RACECOURSE SUPPORTS RACING TO SCHOOL H'CAP 6f 12y
2:00 (2:02) (Class 6) (0-60,60) 3-Y-O+
£2,781 (£827; £413; £300; £300; £300) Stalls Centre

Form RPR
3004 1 **Arctic Flower (IRE)**[14] 7977 6-8-2 48 AledBeech(7) 13 55
(John Bridger) *chsd ldr tl led 1/2-way: rdn over 1f out: hld on gamely ins fnl f* 5/1[2]
0053 2 nk **Just An Idea (IRE)**[14] 7977 5-8-9 48 (b) HollieDoyle 5 54
(Roger Ingram) *chsd ldrs: clsd to press ldrs 1/2-way: rdn and wandered rt u.p over 1f out: kpt on u.p ins fnl f: wnt 2nd last strides (jockey said gelding lugged right-handed)* 6/1[3]
2030 3 nk **Ricochet (IRE)**[30] 7447 3-8-13 60 Pierre-LouisJamin(7) 14 65
(Tom Ward) *in tch in midfield: clsd to join ldrs over 3f out: rdn over 1f out: kpt on u.p: hld towards fin: lost 2nd last strides* 8/1
5052 4 1 **Field Of Vision (IRE)**[13] 8009 6-8-7 51 (b) WilliamCarver(5) 9 53
(John Flint) *midfield: rdn and outpcd 1/2-way: prog 1f out: styd on ins fnl f: nt rch ldrs* 5/2[1]
P040 5 3 1/2 **Roca Magica**[14] 7961 3-8-8 48 DavidEgan 3 40
(Ed Dunlop) *midfield: effrt over 2f out: sn u.p: plugged on and passed btn rivals ins fnl f: nvr trbld ldrs* 12/1
2600 6 1/2 **Billiebrookedit (IRE)**[32] 7384 4-8-4 46 oh1 (p) JaneElliott(3) 4 36
(Kevin Frost) *in tch in midfield: effrt and hung lft over 2f out: no imp and btn over 1f out: wknd ins fnl f (jockey said gelding lugged left-handed inside the final 2 furlongs)* 16/1
3563 7 1 1/4 **Perfect Symphony (IRE)**[26] 7576 5-9-4 60 PaddyBradley(3) 8 46
(Mark Pattinson) *chsd ldrs: swtchd lft and drvn over 1f out: no ex 1f out: wknd ins fnl f (trainer said gelding was unsuited by the testing conditions and would prefer a faster surface)* 8/1

001 **8** 1 3/4 **Dansepo**[13] 8006 3-9-4 **58**........................ KieranShoemark 11 39
(Adam West) *midfield: rdn over 2f out: no imp u.p and edgd lft over 1f out: wknd fnl f* **12/1**

1200 **9** 4 1/2 **Fantasy Justifier (IRE)**[34] 7299 8-9-3 **56**...............(p) DavidProbert 12 24
(Ronald Harris) *midfield: u.p over 2f out: sn no imp and btn over 1f out: wknd fnl f* **12/1**

0640 **10** 6 **Brockey Rise (IRE)**[35] 7286 4-9-4 **57**.................. EoinWalsh 7 7
(David Evans) *a towards rr: rdn and no hdwy over 2f out: wl bhd fnl f* **25/1**

0000 **11** nk **Alban's Dream**[11] 8071 3-8-11 **54**..................(p[1]) DarraghKeenan(3) 10 3
(Robert Eddery) *led tl 1/2-way: sn dropped out: wknd over 1f out* **66/1**

4540 **12** 3 1/2 **Sally Hope**[13] 8008 3-8-11 **51**.................. HectorCrouch 1
(John Gallagher) *a towards rr: no hdwy u.p over 1f out: wl bhd fnl f* **16/1**

0000 **13** 1 3/4 **Hellofagame**[5] 8263 4-8-2 **46** oh1..................(t[1]) SophieRalston(5) 6
(Richard Price) *uns rdr coming onto crse and galloped loose to post: a bhd* **100/1**

1m 16.38s (4.28) **Going Correction** +0.725s/f (Yiel)
WFA 3 from 4yo+ 1lb **13** Ran SP% **122.9**
Speed ratings (Par 101): **100,99,99,97,93 92,90,88,82,74 74,69,67**
CSF £35.97 CT £252.88 TOTE £6.10: £2.10, £2.00, £3.50; EX 39.70 Trifecta £260.70.
Owner Mr & Mrs K Finch **Bred** B Kennedy **Trained** Liphook, Hants

FOCUS
Rail movements added 39yds to races 4, 5, 6 and 7. There was a fresh strip of ground up the far side of the straight from the intersection to the winning line. Testing conditions for Windsor's final fixture of the year. Hector Crouch and Hollie Doyle both said: "It's heavy ground and hard work." The principals raced prominently in this minor handicap and it was an advantage to race towards the far side. The winner has been rated in line with this year's soft ground form.

8409 VISIT ATTHERACES.COM NOVICE MEDIAN AUCTION STKS 5f 21y
2:30 (2:32) (Class 5) 2-Y-O **£3,428** (£1,020; £509; £254) **Stalls** Centre

Form RPR

4 **1** **Letscrackon (IRE)**[71] 5988 2-9-0 **0**.................. HectorCrouch 9 79+
(Gary Moore) *mde all: pushed along and kicking clr jst over 2f out: wl in command fnl f: comf* **10/1**

2 5 **Agent Shiftwell** 2-9-5 **0**.................. JasonWatson 10 66
(Stuart Williams) *chsd ldrs: rdn and chsd clr wnr over 1f out: kpt on but no ch w wnr (stewards questioned colt's running on testing conditions when declared a non-runner at Great Yarmouth last time on similar ground; trainer said colt was running over 5f instead of 6f, so was happy for him to participate.)* **11/2[3]**

062 **3** 1 1/2 **Brenner Pass**[25] 7627 2-9-2 **69**.................. FinleyMarsh(3) 3 61
(Richard Hughes) *hld up in tch in midfield: edgd lft and nt clrest of runs wl over 1f out: sn swtchd rt and rdn: wnt 3rd ins fnl f: no ch w wnr (trainer's rep said colt was unsuited by the ground and would prefer a faster surface)* **3/1[2]**

6035 **4** 1 1/2 **Shani**[5] 8243 2-8-7 **58**..................(p) AledBeech(7) 6 50
(John Bridger) *chsd wnr: rdn and getting outpcd ent fnl 2f: lost 2nd over 1f out: wknd ins fnl f* **13/2**

5 3/4 **Rocking Reg (IRE)** 2-9-5 **0**.................. JackMitchell 1 54
(Roger Teal) *dwlt: sn rcvrd and in midfield after 1f out: squeezed for room wl over 1f out: sn swtchd lft: no ch w wnr and kpt on same pce ins fnl f* **16/1**

3 **6** 1/2 **Dark Phoenix (IRE)**[7] 8195 2-9-5 **0**.................. SeanLevey 4 51
(Paul Cole) *chsd ldrs: outpcd jst over 2f out: lost pl u.p over 1f out: wknd ins fnl f* **8/1**

7 1 1/4 **Rodin** 2-9-5 **0**.................. DavidProbert 2 46
(Andrew Balding) *s.i.s: racd in last trio: effrt jst over 2f out: no imp whn edgd lft and stmbld over 1f out: n.d* **5/2[1]**

0 **8** 1 **Chisana**[77] 5745 2-9-0 **0**.................. GeorgeWood 8 38
(Chris Wall) *chsd ldrs: rdn over 1f out: sn lost pl: wknd ins fnl f* **50/1**

0306 **9** 1 1/2 **Ask Siri (IRE)**[54] 6604 2-8-11 **45**.................. MitchGodwin(3) 7 32
(John Bridger) *a in rr: rdn 2f out: sn bhd* **50/1**

10 1 1/4 **Vitare (IRE)** 2-9-5 **0**.................. TomMarquand 5 33
(Mick Channon) *s.i.s: rn green and sn pushed along: a bhd (jockey said gelding was slowly away)* **14/1**

1m 2.6s (2.50) **Going Correction** +0.725s/f (Yiel) **10** Ran SP% **119.0**
Speed ratings (Par 95): **109,101,98,96,95 94,92,90,88,86**
CSF £65.49 TOTE £10.40: £2.30, £2.60, £1.40; EX 80.30 Trifecta £451.90.
Owner Mrs Catherine Reed **Bred** Thomas J Murphy **Trained** Lower Beeding, W Sussex

FOCUS
A wide-margin winner of this ordinary event, but it's not form to treat too literally given how the ground was riding. The level is fluid.

8410 ALEX@ALEXDONOHUEPR.CO.UK CLASSIFIED CLAIMING STKS 6f 12y
3:00 (3:02) (Class 5) 3-Y-O+
£3,428 (£1,020; £509; £300; £300; £300) **Stalls** Centre

Form RPR

2225 **1** **Voltaic**[30] 7460 3-8-10 **70**.................. SeanLevey 2 72+
(Paul Cole) *stdd and sltly impeded leaving stalls: in tch in midfield: trckd ldng pair wl over 2f out: rdn and hdwy to ld jst over 1f out: clr and r.o wl ins fnl f* **11/4[2]**

5000 **2** 2 3/4 **Flowing Clarets**[4] 8279 6-7-10 **44**.................. RhiainIngram(5) 1 54
(John Bridger) *taken down early and led to post: chsd ldr: ev ch and rdn 2f out: unable to match pce of wnr 1f out: wl hld 2nd and kpt on same pce fnl 150yds* **14/1**

1304 **3** 2 1/2 **Pettochside**[4] 8285 10-9-5 **72**.................. HollieDoyle 5 65
(John Bridger) *racd keenly: led: rdn over 1f out: sn hdd and no ex: wknd ins fnl f* **15/8[1]**

2600 **4** 5 **Ambient (IRE)**[26] 7587 4-8-11 **70**..................(p) NicolaCurrie 6 42
(Jamie Osborne) *hld up in tch in 5th: outpcd 1/2-way: effrt over 2f out: no imp and wl hld 4th fr over 1f out* **6/1**

0000 **5** 5 **The Right Choice (IRE)**[40] 7085 4-8-1 **63**..................(p) DavidEgan 7 17
(Jamie Osborne) *chsd ldrs tl wl over 2f out: no rspnse to press and btn over 2f out: wknd over 1f out* **4/1[3]**

4255 **6** 3 1/4 **Blaine**[84] 5495 9-8-4 **74**..................(b) AngusVilliers(7) 3 17
(Brian Barr) *sn dropped to rr and rdn: wl bhd fr 1/2-way (jockey said gelding was never travelling; trainer's rep said gelding was unsuited by the ground and would prefer a faster surface)* **8/1**

1m 15.69s (3.59) **Going Correction** +0.725s/f (Yiel)
WFA 3 from 4yo+ 1lb **6** Ran SP% **113.5**
Speed ratings (Par 103): **105,101,98,91,84 80**
CSF £37.31 TOTE £3.50: £1.90, £4.50; EX 39.90 Trifecta £125.30.The winner was claimed by Mr B J Llewellyn for £8,000
Owner The Fairy Story Partnership **Bred** Deepwood Farm Stud **Trained** Whatcombe, Oxon

FOCUS
A moderate claimer, run about 0.7sec slower than the opening Class 6 handicap, and it's form to treat cautiously.

8411 WINDSOR'S GREATEST SHOW FIREWORKS EXTRAVAGANZA H'CAP 1m 2f
3:30 (3:32) (Class 4) (0-85,87) 3-Y-O+
£5,207 (£1,549; £774; £387; £300; £300) **Stalls** Centre

Form RPR

133- **1** **Rajinsky (IRE)**[389] 7700 3-9-0 **80**.................. JaneElliott(3) 6 87+
(Tom Dascombe) *pushed rt leaving stalls: towards rr: rdn 5f out: clsd to chse ldrs over 1f out: pressing ldr whn hung rt 1f out: led ins fnl f: styd on* **7/1**

1004 **2** 1/2 **Regular Income (IRE)**[19] 7829 4-9-2 **80**..................(p) TobyEley(5) 4 86
(Adam West) *midfield: rdn and hdwy to chse ldr wl over 1f out: ev ch 1f out: kpt on u.p but hld towards fin* **5/1[2]**

1221 **3** 1 1/4 **Data Protection**[24] 7663 4-9-10 **83**..................(t) NicolaCurrie 7 87
(William Muir) *chsd ldr: kicking clr w ldr 3f out: led over 2f out: hdd and no ex ins fnl f* **13/2**

03-3 **4** 9 **Royal Big Night (USA)**[12] 8032 3-9-2 **79**.................. JamieSpencer 9 66
(Mark Johnston) *hmpd leaving stalls: hld up in rr: swtchd lft 4f out: hding to far rail over 2f out: no ch w ldng trio: plugged on to pass btn rivals ins fnl f* **14/1**

-450 **5** hd **Mostawaa**[17] 7863 3-9-0 **84**.................. EllieMacKenzie(7) 2 70
(Heather Main) *chsd ldrs: rdn and getting outpcd over 3f out: hung lft and wknd over 1f out (jockey said gelding hung left-handed under pressure)* **10/1**

4260 **6** nk **Sputnik Planum (USA)**[5] 8260 5-9-6 **86**..................(bt[1]) AngusVilliers(7) 3 71
(Michael Appleby) *chsd ldrs: rdn over 3f out: sn struggling and outpcd: wknd over 1f out* **12/1**

4266 **7** 3 1/2 **Autumn War (IRE)**[14] 7974 4-9-10 **83**..................(b[1]) KieranShoemark 1 61
(Charles Hills) *wnt rt leaving stalls and slowly away: hdwy into midfield after 2f: u.p and struggling 3f out: sn btn and wknd over 1f out* **8/1**

0106 **8** 1 **Valence**[16] 7915 3-8-9 **72**..................(p) DavidProbert 8 49
(Ed Dunlop) *bmpd leaving stalls: hld up in last pair: effrt and hding to far rail over 2f out: no imp and wknd over 1f out* **20/1**

6555 **9** nse **Mr Top Hat**[5] 8260 4-10-0 **87**..................(b[1]) JasonWatson 5 62
(David Evans) *led: kicked clr w rival 3f out: hdd over 2f out: lost 2nd and btn wl over 1f out: wknd (trainer could offer no explanation for the gelding's performance)* **7/2[1]**

0-16 **10** 4 1/2 **Blistering Bob**[46] 6909 4-9-3 **79**..................(h) WilliamCox(3) 10 45
(Roger Teal) *taken down early: wnt sharply rt leaving stalls: midfield: lost pl u.p and bhd 2f out: wknd* **11/2[3]**

2m 16.51s (7.51) **Going Correction** +0.725s/f (Yiel)
WFA 3 from 4yo+ 4lb **10** Ran SP% **119.4**
Speed ratings (Par 105): **99,98,97,90,90 90,87,86,86,82**
CSF £43.03 CT £243.38 TOTE £7.60: £3.10, £2.20, £2.50; EX 52.20 Trifecta £682.30.
Owner R S Matharu **Bred** Miss Elaine Marie Smith **Trained** Malpas, Cheshire

FOCUS
Add 39yds. The going was changed to heavy all over before this race, a fair handicap which saw the first three pull clear. The field raced mainly down the centre in the straight. It's been rated around the second.

8412 BEN WOOLLACOTT MEMORIAL H'CAP 1m 31y
4:00 (4:03) (Class 4) (0-85,85) 3-Y-O+
£5,207 (£1,549; £774; £387; £300; £300) **Stalls** Low

Form RPR

5132 **1** **Prince Of Harts**[86] 5412 3-9-5 **83**.................. RobHornby 8 96+
(Rod Millman) *chsd ldrs: clsd to ld over 2f out: clr over 1f out: kpt on and a doing enough ins fnl f: eased towards fin* **9/2[2]**

5153 **2** 1 **Saikung (IRE)**[30] 7463 3-9-1 **79**.................. KieranShoemark 1 88
(Charles Hills) *hld up in last quintet: hdwy over 2f out: rdn and chsd clr wnr over 1f out: kpt on wl ins fnl f: nvr getting to wnr* **20/1**

4430 **3** 6 **Defence Treaty (IRE)**[24] 7653 3-9-1 **79**..................(p) JamieSpencer 12 74
(Richard Fahey) *hld up in last quintet: effrt 2f out: edgd out rt and effrt over 1f out: kpt on ins fnl f: wnt 3rd last strides: no ch w ldrs* **9/1**

4255 **4** hd **Scofflaw**[14] 7975 5-9-4 **79**..................(v) TomMarquand 2 75
(David Evans) *in tch in midfield: effrt over 2f out: chsd ldng pair over 1f out: no imp and wl hld fnl f: lost 3rd last strides* **12/1**

2040 **5** 1 **Dourado (IRE)**[7] 8197 5-9-4 **79**.................. DavidProbert 14 72
(Patrick Chamings) *midfield: effrt over 2f out: no imp u.p over 1f out: plugged on same pce and wl hld ins fnl f* **14/1**

0053 **6** 3/4 **George Of Hearts (FR)**[14] 7975 4-9-2 **77**..................(t) NicolaCurrie 10 69
(George Baker) *s.i.s: hld up towards rr: effrt jst over 2f out: no hdwy u.p over 1f out: wl hld and plugged on same pce fnl f (jockey said gelding was slowly away)* **6/1[3]**

4404 **7** 2 1/2 **Leroy Leroy**[25] 7622 3-9-7 **85**..................(p) SeanLevey 6 70
(Richard Hannon) *t.k.h: chsd ldrs: effrt and ev ch 3f out: chsd clr wnr over 2f out: no imp and lost pl over 1f out: wknd fnl f* **20/1**

6404 **8** 1/2 **Central City (IRE)**[23] 7680 4-8-8 **76**.................. RPWalsh(7) 3 61
(Ian Williams) *s.i.s: hld up in last pair: effrt over 2f out: nvr involved (jockey said gelding was slowly away)* **20/1**

2010 **9** 1 1/2 **Secret Return (IRE)**[14] 7975 6-8-13 **79**.................. RhiainIngram(5) 11 60
(Karen George) *s.i.s: hld up in last pair: shkn up ent fnl 2f: no prog: nvr involved (jockey said mare was slowly away)* **20/1**

2030 **10** 1 3/4 **Los Camachos (IRE)**[14] 7975 4-9-1 **76**.................. HectorCrouch 9 53
(John Gallagher) *chsd ldr: rdn and ev ch 3f out: sn lost pl: bhd ins fnl f* **33/1**

225 **11** 1 **Beauty Of Deira (IRE)**[79] 5690 3-8-12 **76**..................(p[1]) JasonWatson 7 50
(Hugo Palmer) *chsd ldrs: struggling u.p over 2f out: lost pl and wknd over 1f out* **14/1**

22F5 **12** 10 **Alnadir (USA)**[12] 8024 3-9-6 **84**..................(p) JackMitchell 13 35
(Simon Crisford) *led: hdd 3f out and racd along nr stands' rail after: lost pl over 2f out: wl bhd and eased wl ins fnl f* **7/1**

0-10 **13** 2 1/2 **Itsakindamagic**[159] 2739 5-9-7 **82**.................. LiamKeniry 4 28
(Geoffrey Deacon) *t.k.h: chsd ldrs tl 3f out: sn lost pl: wl bhd and eased wl ins fnl f* **66/1**

0461 **R** **Leader Writer (FR)**[14] 7975 7-9-3 **78**..................(p) HayleyTurner 5
(David Elsworth) *ref to r (stewards reviewed start and was satisfied horse had refused to race and deemed to be a runner)* **11/4[1]**

1m 49.86s (5.36) **Going Correction** +0.725s/f (Yiel)
WFA 3 from 4yo+ 3lb **14** Ran SP% **126.1**
Speed ratings (Par 105): **106,105,99,98,97 97,94,94,92,90 89,79,77,**
CSF £101.83 CT £824.78 TOTE £5.40: £2.10, £5.20, £2.90; EX 109.30 Trifecta £592.70.
Owner Perfect Match 2 **Bred** Harts Farm Stud **Trained** Kentisbeare, Devon

FOCUS
Add 39yds. Quite a competitive handicap, although the favourite didn't leave the stalls. With one exception they made for the far side of the course, and the first two finished clear. The level is a bit fluid.

8413 SKY SPORTS RACING ON VIRGIN 535 H'CAP — 1m 31y
4:30 (4:31) (Class 5) (0-70,78) 3-Y-0+
£3,428 (£1,020; £509; £300; £300; £300) Stalls Low

Form — RPR

0524 **1** **Madeleine Bond**[36] 7237 5-9-4 71 .... MarcoGhiani(5) 10 — 79
(Henry Candy) *hld up in midfield: clsd on far rail whn edgd rt and cannoned into rival over 2f out: chsd ldr and swtchd rt over 1f out: drvn to ld ins fnl f: hld on gamely* — 4/1[1]

4012 **2** *nk* **Espresso Freddo (IRE)**[12] 8030 5-9-4 66 ....(v) KieranShoemark 1 — 73
(Robert Stephens) *hld up towards rr: clsd over 2f out: rdn and hdwy to chse ldrs over 1f out: drvn and str chal ins fnl f: kpt on but hld cl home* — 10/1

3124 **3** *nk* **Sootability (IRE)**[31] 7404 3-9-5 70 .... AdamMcNamara 7 — 75
(Richard Fahey) *dwlt: racd in last trio: effrt 3f out: hdwy u.p over 1f out: chsd ldng pair ins fnl f: kpt on wl: nt quite rch ldrs* — 8/1

-002 **4** *3 1/4* **Sir Hamilton (IRE)**[7] 8206 4-9-1 68 ....(p) RayDawson(5) 13 — 67
(Luke McJannet) *sn led: rdn 3f out: drvn over 1f out: hdd ins fnl f: no ex and wknd wl ins fnl f* — 11/1

5232 **5** *shd* **Flying Dragon (FR)**[31] 7404 3-9-6 71 ....(h) RossaRyan 3 — 69
(Richard Hannon) *in tch in midfield: effrt over 2f out: hdwy and drvn to chse ldrs over 1f out: no ex and wknd wl ins fnl f* — 9/1

5311 **6** *1/2* **Stallone (IRE)**[7] 8207 3-9-8 78 6ex ....(v) SeanKirrane(5) 9 — 74
(Richard Spencer) *chsd ldr tl over 4f out: chsd ldr again over 2f out tl over 1f out: no ex and wknd ins fnl f* — 7/1[3]

0023 **7** *1* **Bombastic (IRE)**[27] 7554 4-9-4 71 .... SeamusCronin(5) 6 — 66
(Ed de Giles) *hld up in rr: hdwy towards far side over 2f out: midfield and swtchd rt over 1f out: kpt on but no threat to ldrs fnl f* — 11/1

4031 **8** *5* **Kingson (IRE)**[28] 7512 3-9-6 71 .... JamieSpencer 8 — 53
(Richard Fahey) *hld up towards rr: effrt 3f out: nvr getting on terms: wl hld fnl f: fin 9th: plcd 8th* — 5/1[2]

4200 **9** *1 1/4* **Kendergarten Kop (IRE)**[11] 8070 4-9-2 64 ....(b) DavidProbert 2 — 44
(David Flood) *t.k.h: hld up in midfield: clsd 3f out: no imp whn hung lft and squeezed for room over 1f out: wknd ins fnl f: fin 10th: plcd 9th (jockey said gelding hung left-handed)* — 33/1

6206 **10** *5* **Noble Fox**[27] 7560 3-9-2 67 ....(b[1]) HectorCrouch 14 — 35
(Clive Cox) *in tch in midfield: effrt 3f out: edgd lft and cannoned into wnr over 2f out: lost pl u.p and btn over 1f out: wl bhd and eased ins fnl f: fin 11th: plcd 10th* — 20/1

3400 **11** *8* **Global Express**[21] 7773 3-9-2 67 ....(b[1]) GeraldMosse 12 — 16
(Ed Dunlop) *t.k.h: midfield: hdwy to chse ldrs after 2f: chsd ldr over 4f tl over 2f out: sn lost pl: wl bhd ins fnl f: fin 12th: plcd 11th* — 25/1

0605 **12** *4 1/2* **Here's Two**[27] 7554 6-9-3 68 .... WilliamCox(3) 11 — 8
(Ron Hodges) *t.k.h: chsd ldrs tl 3f out: lost pl: wl bhd and eased ins fnl f: fin 13th: plcd 12th* — 20/1

4134 **13** *6* **Cuttin' Edge (IRE)**[24] 7663 5-9-2 64 .... MartinDwyer 4
(William Muir) *in tch in midfield: rdn 3f out: sn struggling and lost pl: wl bhd ins fnl f: fin 14th: plcd 13th* — 11/1

6200 **D** *nk* **Sir Plato (IRE)**[12] 8031 5-8-11 66 ....(v) AngusVilliers(7) 5 — 60
(Rod Millman) *chsd ldrs: rdn 3f out: no ex u.p over 1f out: wknd ins fnl f: disqualified: rdr failed to weigh in* — 20/1

1m 51.75s (7.25) **Going Correction** +0.725s/f (Yiel) — 14 Ran SP% 125.4
WFA 3 from 4yo+ 3lb
Speed ratings (Par 103): **96,95,95,92,92 91,90,85,84,79 71,66,60,90**
CSF £42.51 CT £327.91 TOTE £4.20: £1.40, £3.30, £3.40; EX 51.50 Trifecta £429.90.
Owner Candy, Pritchard & Thomas **Bred** Hellwood Stud Farm **Trained** Kingston Warren, Oxon
■ Stewards' Enquiry : Angus Villiers three-day ban: failed to weigh-in (Nov 4-6)

FOCUS
Add 39yds. An open handicap in which the field tacked over to the far side in the last couple of furlongs. The second has been rated close to his turf best.

8414 WINDSOR 2020 MEMBERSHIP NOW ON SALE H'CAP (FOR GENTLEMAN AMATEUR RIDERS) — 1m 3f 99y
5:00 (5:04) (Class 6) (0-65,65) 3-Y-0+
£2,682 (£832; £415; £300; £300; £300) Stalls Centre

Form — RPR

0616 **1** **Para Queen (IRE)**[17] 7873 3-10-2 51 .... MrJamesHarding 11 — 63
(Heather Main) *taken down early: in tch in midfield: clsd to chse ldrs 1/2-way: led 5f out: sn clr: 5 l clr and rdn 3f out: styd on and nvr in any danger after* — 8/1

0546 **2** *7* **Spirit Of Angel (IRE)**[13] 7984 3-10-6 62 .... MrGeorgeTregoning(7) 12 — 63
(Marcus Tregoning) *s.i.s: wl off the pce towards rr: rdn and sme prog whn swtchd lft over 2f out: plugged on to chse wnr and edgd rt ins fnl f: nvr a threat* — 7/1[2]

3530 **3** *3 1/2* **Essenaitch (IRE)**[39] 7116 6-10-9 58 ....(v) MrPhilipThomas(5) 10 — 53
(David Evans) *midfield: clsd 5f out: chsd clr wnr over 3f out: no imp: lost wl hld 2nd and rdn over 1f out: plugged on same pce* — 8/1

0051 **4** *1 1/4* **King Athelstan (IRE)**[35] 7271 4-10-10 57 ....(b) MrGeorgeGorman(3) 13 — 50
(Gary Moore) *broke wl: sn settled bk into midfield: chsd ldrs over 3f out: rdn to chse clr wnr over 1f out: no imp and wl btn whn lost 2 pls ins fnl f* — 14/1

500- **5** *1* **Outcrop (IRE)**[19] 5790 5-11-2 65 .... MrRyanHolmes(5) 6 — 56
(Jennie Candlish) *wl off the pce in rr: prog into midfield 4f out: plugged on but nvr involved* — 16/1

4006 **6** *4 1/2* **Country'N'Western (FR)**[12] 8033 7-10-11 60 ...... MrGeorgeEddery(5) 15 — 44
(Robert Eddery) *midfield: effrt in 6th 3f out: no imp and wl hld 2f out: wknd fnl f* — 8/1

0-50 **7** *5* **Bazooka (IRE)**[27] 7558 8-11-0 65 ....(t[1]) MrCiaranJones(7) 9 — 42
(David Flood) *s.i.s: hld up in wl off the pce: rdn 4f out: nvr any ch: plugged on to pass btn rivals fnl f* — 28/1

330- **8** *3 3/4* **Cousin Khee**[190] 9663 12-11-0 65 .... MrWilliamClesham(7) 4 — 36
(Hughie Morrison) *hld up wl off the pce in rr: n.d* — 50/1

3635 **9** *1 3/4* **Highway Robbery**[37] 7202 3-9-9 51 oh5..................(p) MrSamFeilden(7) 5 — 20
(Julia Feilden) *midfield: rdn and lost pl over 4f out: no ch fnl 3f* — 16/1

1140 **10** *2* **Power Home (IRE)**[20] 7790 5-11-1 64 ow2........... MrJeromePower(7) 3 — 31
(Denis Coakley) *led after 1f: hdd 5f out: lost 2nd and over 3f out: sn btn and dropped out: wl bhd fnl f* — 20/1

6350 **11** *1* **Banksy's Art**[13] 7984 4-10-11 60 .... MrJamiePerrett(5) 14 — 23
(Amanda Perrett) *midfield: effrt in 5th 3f out: no imp and sn btn: wknd 2f out* — 15/2[3]

0406 **12** *37* **L'Un Deux Trois (IRE)**[30] 7439 3-10-9 65 .... MrLukeScott(7) 1
(Michael Bell) *chsd ldrs tl 1/2-way: sn lost pl: t.o over 2f out* — 11/1

3610 **13** *4 1/2* **Milan Reef (IRE)**[5] 8247 4-10-8 59 .... MrBradleyRoberts(7) 8
(David Loughnane) *sn led: hdd after 1f: styd w ldr but pushed along: lost pl over 5f out: sn btn and dropped out: t.o* — 9/4[1]

/300 **14** *28* **Onomatopoeia**[27] 7560 5-10-9 60 .... MrNathanMcCann(7) 2
(Camilla Poulton) *chsd ldrs tl 1/2-way: sn dropped out: t.o fnl 3f (jockey said mare was never travelling.)* — 66/1

2m 42.18s (12.48) **Going Correction** +0.725s/f (Yiel)
WFA 3 from 4yo+ 5lb — 14 Ran SP% 126.8
Speed ratings (Par 101): **87,81,79,78,77 74,70,68,66,65 64,37,34,14**
CSF £64.72 CT £480.06 TOTE £10.10: £2.80, £2.60, £2.70; EX 76.30 Trifecta £664.00.
Owner Don Knott And Wetumpka Racing **Bred** Sir E J Loder **Trained** Kingston Lisle, Oxon
■ Thermal was withdrawn. Price at time of withdrawal 50/1. Rule 4 does not apply
■ Stewards' Enquiry : Mr Jerome Power one-day ban: weighing in at more than 2lb overweight (Nov 5); one-day ban: failed to take all reasonable and permissible measures to obtain the best possible placing (Nov 27)

FOCUS
Add 39yds. They finished well strung out in this moderate handicap for amateurs, having gone what appeared to be a brisk initial gallop.
T/Plt: £340.30 to a £1 stake. Pool: £63,776.26 - 136.79 winning units T/Qpdt: £51.00 to a £1 stake. Pool: £6,493.76 - 94.17 winning units **Steve Payne**

8249 KEMPTON (A.W) (R-H)
Tuesday, October 22

OFFICIAL GOING: Polytrack: standard to slow
Wind: virtually nil Weather: dry

8415 BET AT RACINGTV.COM NURSERY H'CAP — 1m (P)
4:55 (4:58) (Class 6) (0-65,65) 2-Y-0
£3,105 (£924; £461; £400; £400; £400) Stalls Low

Form — RPR

0606 **1** **Precision Storm**[24] 7677 2-9-5 63 .... EdwardGreatrex 5 — 69+
(Mark Loughnane) *hld up in tch: swtchd lft and effrt over 2f out: hdwy over 1f out: rdn and r.o wl to ld ins fnl f* — 14/1

3465 **2** *1 3/4* **Red Jasper**[8] 8201 2-9-3 61 ....(v[1]) DavidProbert 2 — 63
(Michael Appleby) *dwlt: sn rcvrd and in tch: swtchd ins and effrt jst over 2f out: hdwy and rdn to ld over 1f out: hdd and one pce ins fnl f* — 4/1[1]

5653 **3** *hd* **Treaty Of Dingle**[17] 7910 2-8-12 56 .... TomMarquand 1 — 58
(Hughie Morrison) *led: sn hdd trckd ldr tl over 4f out: styd handy: effrt over 2f out: drvn and ev ch over 1f out: kpt on same pce ins fnl f* — 6/1[2]

0042 **4** *1 1/2* **Castel Angelo (IRE)**[36] 7275 2-9-2 60 .... CharlesBishop 10 — 58
(Henry Candy) *stdd after s: hld up towards rr: effrt and hdwy on outer over 1f out: kpt on ins fnl f: nvr getting to ldrs* — 7/1[3]

6010 **5** *1/2* **Hermano Bello (FR)**[17] 7910 2-9-0 63........ ThoreHammerHansen(5) 12 — 60
(Richard Hannon) *in tch on outer: effrt over 2f out: kpt on same pce and no imp ins fnl f* — 15/2

540 **6** *3* **Pinatar (IRE)**[20] 7814 2-9-7 65 .... KierenFox 14 — 55
(John Best) *hld up in tch on outer: effrt ent fnl 2f: kpt on ins fnl f: nvr threatened ldrs* — 15/2

035 **7** *1/2* **Liberty Filly**[21] 7787 2-9-0 63 .... ThomasGreatrex(5) 11 — 52
(Roger Charlton) *hld up in tch: struggling u.p over 1f out: kpt on ins fnl f but nvr enough pce to get involved* — 16/1

6002 **8** *hd* **Never Said Nothing (IRE)**[56] 6571 2-9-2 60 .... RobHornby 6 — 48
(Jonathan Portman) *t.k.h: prom: effrt jst over 2f out: unable qck over 1f out: wknd ins fnl f* — 10/1

6063 **9** *1/2* **Mungo's Quest (IRE)**[12] 8058 2-9-0 58 .... HectorCrouch 3 — 45
(Simon Dow) *taken down early: in tch: effrt over 2f out: unable qck over 1f out: wknd ins fnl f* — 14/1

600 **10** *1/2* **Blairlogie**[17] 7911 2-9-0 58 .... CallumShepherd 13 — 44
(Mick Channon) *stdd after s: a towards rr: effrt over 2f out: kpt on but nvr threatened to get on terms* — 40/1

0530 **11** *6* **Pure Purfection (IRE)**[14] 7980 2-8-12 56 .... CharlieBennett 8 — 28
(Jim Boyle) *chsd ldrs: wnt 2nd over 4f out tl 2f out: sn struggling and lost pl over 1f out: wknd* — 66/1

0322 **12** *1 1/4* **Grace Plunkett**[17] 7910 2-8-9 53 ....(b) KieranShoemark 4 — 22
(Richard Spencer) *sn led: hdd and no ex u.p over 1f out: sn wknd* — 8/1

0050 **13** *nk* **Gifted Dreamer (IRE)**[17] 7910 2-7-8 45 ....(p) IsobelFrancis(7) 7 — 14
(Mark Usher) *s.i.s: a bhd* — 66/1

1m 41.89s (2.09) **Going Correction** +0.05s/f (Slow) — 13 Ran SP% 115.2
Speed ratings (Par 93): **91,89,89,87,87 84,83,83,82,82 76,75,74**
CSF £66.38 CT £308.67 TOTE £12.10: £2.90, £1.60, £1.70; EX 110.60 Trifecta £848.60.
Owner Precision Facades Ltd **Bred** Mrs D O Joly **Trained** Rock, Worcs

FOCUS
It paid to be ridden with a bit of patience here.

8416 RACINGTV.COM H'CAP (DIV I) — 1m (P)
5:30 (5:32) (Class 6) (0-55,55) 3-Y-0+
£3,105 (£924; £461; £400; £400; £400) Stalls Low

Form — RPR

6124 **1** **Mabo**[6] 8256 4-9-7 55 ....(b) RossaRyan 6 — 61
(Grace Harris) *wl in tch in midfield: effrt ent fnl 2f: hdwy u.p to ld jst over 1f out: edgd rt and kpt on u.p ins fnl f* — 9/2[2]

3046 **2** *1* **Gerry The Glover (IRE)**[52] 6723 7-9-6 54 ....(v) TomMarquand 4 — 58
(Lee Carter) *hld up in tch towards rr: hdwy u.p and drifting rt over 1f out: chsd wnr 1f out: kpt on* — 7/1

0400 **3** *nk* **A Hundred Echoes**[32] 7420 3-9-1 52 ....(b) JimCrowley 7 — 54
(Roger Varian) *hld up in tch in midfield: effrt 2f out: hdwy u.p and chsd ldng pair 1f out: kpt on* — 9/2[2]

0025 **4** *1 1/2* **Red Cossack (CAN)**[28] 7549 8-8-13 47 ....(b) JoeyHaynes 3 — 47
(Dean Ivory) *sn prom: hdwy to chse ldr after 3f: swtchd lft and effrt 2f out: rdn to ld over 1f out: sn hdd and one pce u.p ins fnl f* — 5/1[3]

4346 **5** *1 3/4* **N Over J**[58] 6507 4-8-13 47 ....(v) JasonWatson 2 — 43
(William Knight) *sn led: rdn over 2f out: hdd and no ex over 1f out: edgd lft and wknd ins fnl f (jockey said gelding hung left-handed under pressure)* — 5/2[1]

4140 **6** *4 1/2* **Harlequin Rose (IRE)**[28] 7549 5-9-5 53 ....(v) LiamKeniry 12 — 38
(Patrick Chamings) *hld up in tch in midfield: effrt towards inner 2f out: 6th and no imp over 1f out: wknd ins fnl f* — 50/1

5225 **7** *1* **Duke Of North (IRE)**[14] 7982 7-8-10 51 ....(p) IsobelFrancis(7) 5 — 34
(Jim Boyle) *dwlt: hld up in rr: effrt on stands side: sn rdn: kpt on: nvr threatened to ldrs (jockey said gelding was slowly away)* — 16/1

5504 **8** *4 ½* **Cheerful**[14] 8009 3-9-2 **53**.. RobHornby 11 25
(Philip McBride) *hld up in tch towards rr: effrt over 2f out: no prog and wl hld over 1f out* **16/1**

4000 **9** *hd* **Moon Artist (FR)**[33] 7376 3-8-9 **46** oh1.......................... CharlieBennett 10 17
(Michael Blanshard) *broke wl: sn restrained and hld up in last quintet: effrt 2f out: no prog and wl btn over 1f out* **66/1**

3305 **10** *shd* **Captain Marmalade (IRE)**[15] 6049 7-8-12 **46** oh1.... FergusSweeney 1 18
(Jimmy Fox) *stdd after s: hld up in last trio: effrt 2f out: no prog and sn wl btn* **25/1**

6630 **11** *½* **Ramblow**[63] 6305 6-8-5 **46** oh1.........................(vt) KeelanBaker(7) 13 17
(Alexandra Dunn) *chsd ldr for 3f: outpcd u.p and btn over 1f out: sn wknd (trainer's rep said mare had a breathing problem)* **66/1**

00-0 **12** *7* **Dr Julius No**[236] 940 5-9-4 **52**..........................(p) ShaneKelly 14 7
(Murty McGrath) *midfield: unable qck and outpcd u.p over 2f out: bhd ins fnl f* **66/1**

1m 40.2s (0.40) **Going Correction** +0.05s/f (Slow)
WFA 3 from 4yo+ 3lb 12 Ran SP% **116.2**
Speed ratings (Par 101): **100,99,98,97,95 90,89,85,85,85 84,77**
CSF £34.24 CT £147.98 TOTE £5.30: £1.70, £2.30, £2.00; EX 41.50 Trifecta £192.30.
Owner Paul & Ann de Weck **Bred** Fernham Farm Ltd **Trained** Shirenewton, Monmouthshire

FOCUS
This was run at a good gallop and the time was 1.57sec quicker than the second division. The third has been rated to his best.

8417 RACINGTV.COM H'CAP (DIV II) 1m (P)
6:00 (6:02) (Class 6) (0-55,54) 3-Y-0+
£3,105 (£924; £461; £400; £400; £400) **Stalls** Low

Form RPR

2000 **1** **Purple Paddy**[70] 6051 4-9-1 **48**.......................... FergusSweeney 4 55
(Jimmy Fox) *stdd after s: t.k.h: hld up in tch towards rr: clsd and nt clr run 2f out: swtchd lft over 1f out: r.o wl u.p ins fnl f: led towards fin* **4/1**[2]

3500 **2** *nk* **Itmakesyouthink**[10] 8123 5-9-7 **54**......................(h) EdwardGreatrex 2 60
(Mark Loughnane) *t.k.h: trckd ldrs: chsd ldr and swtchd lft 2f out: rdn to chal over 1f out: led 1f out: kpt on wl u.p: hdd and no ex towards fin* **12/1**

5053 **3** *1 ¾* **Mister Musicmaster**[37] 7232 10-9-6 **53**................... DavidProbert 11 55
(Ron Hodges) *broke wl: stdd bk and hld up in midfield: nt clr run jst over 2f out: swtchd lft over 1f out: styd on strly ins fnl f: nt rch ldrs* **20/1**

031 **4** *nk* **Pike Corner Cross (IRE)**[5] 8299 7-9-7 **54** 4ex..........(vt) HarryBentley 5 56
(David Evans) *t.k.h: hld up in tch: effrt and rdn to chal over 1f out: no ex ins fnl f: wknd towards fin* **7/4**[1]

5 *1 ¾* **Doogan's Warren (IRE)**[72] 5998 4-8-12 **45**............. TomMarquand 14 44
(John Butler) *stdd after s: t.k.h: hld up in rr: clsd: nt clr run and swtchd 2f out: styd on ins fnl f: nt rch ldrs* **11/2**[3]

0000 **6** *nk* **Solveig's Song**[43] 7028 7-9-4 **51**.............................(p) NicolaCurrie 3 48
(Steve Woodman) *hld up in rr: effrt over 1f out: styd on ins fnl f: nvr trbld ldrs* **20/1**

500 **7** *1 ½* **Vikivaki (USA)**[12] 8071 3-8-13 **54**........................ ThomasGreatrex(5) 9 46
(David Loughnane) *led: drvn and hrd pressed over 1f out: hdd 1f out: wknd ins fnl f* **33/1**

0140 **8** *½* **Haraz (IRE)**[26] 7603 6-8-12 **52**............................. GeorgeRooke(7) 8 44
(Paddy Butler) *t.k.h: chsd ldrs on outer: wnt 2nd over 4f out tl 2f out: outpcd over 1f out: wknd ins fnl f* **66/1**

0500 **9** *1 ¼* **Dukes Meadow**[33] 7374 8-8-7 **45**............................. RhiainIngram(5) 7 34
(Roger Ingram) *t.k.h early: wl in tch in midfield: unable qck u.p over 1f out: wknd ins fnl f* **50/1**

3060 **10** *nk* **Chop Chop (IRE)**[52] 6737 3-9-3 **53**............................ RobHornby 6 41
(Brian Barr) *hld up in tch in midfield: u.p and no imp over 1f out: kpt on same pce ins fnl f* **66/1**

4025 **11** *¾* **Cottingham**[6] 8256 4-8-12 **45**.................................(p) KieranShoemark 12 32
(Kevin Frost) *hld up in rr: nvr involved* **10/1**

0000 **12** *1 ¼* **Confab (USA)**[56] 6569 3-9-2 **52**.............................. CharlesBishop 10 35
(George Baker) *chsd ldr tl over 4f out: rdn 3f out: sn struggling to qckn: wknd over 1f out* **8/1**

0000 **13** *½* **Such Promise**[19] 7838 3-8-6 **45**.............................. JaneElliott(3) 1 27
(Mike Murphy) *t.k.h early: hld up in tch in midfield: effrt to chse ldrs 2f out: unable qck over 1f out: wknd ins fnl f (jockey said gelding ran too free)* **25/1**

2420 **14** *hd* **Flying Sakhee**[20] 7812 6-8-11 **47**..........................(p) MitchGodwin(3) 13 30
(John Bridger) *hld up in midfield on outer: effrt over 2f out: unable qck and no imp over 1f out: wknd ins fnl f* **25/1**

1m 41.77s (1.97) **Going Correction** +0.05s/f (Slow)
WFA 3 from 4yo+ 3lb 14 Ran SP% **124.7**
Speed ratings (Par 101): **92,91,89,89,87 87,86,85,84,84 83,82,81,81**
CSF £48.01 CT £899.56 TOTE £4.50: £1.90, £2.30, £3.70; EX 61.70 Trifecta £279.90.
Owner Mrs Barbara Fuller **Bred** Babs Fuller **Trained** Collingbourne Ducis, Wilts

FOCUS
A bit of a messy early pace and it turned into more of a test of speed in the straight than the first division, the time being 1.57sec slower. The winner has been rated in line with last year's C&D form.

8418 32RED CASINO NOVICE STKS 6f (P)
6:30 (6:33) (Class 5) 2-Y-0 **£3,881** (£1,155; £577; £288) **Stalls** Low

Form RPR

12 **1** **Raaeb (IRE)**[17] 7899 2-9-9 0.. JimCrowley 7 89+
(Saeed bin Suroor) *mde all: pushed along and readily asserted over 1f out: styd on strly ins fnl f: comf* **2/5**[1]

02 **2** *2 ½* **Colouring**[21] 7786 2-8-11 0.. LiamKeniry 4 69
(Ed Walker) *t.k.h: chsd wnr: rdn and unable to match pce of wnr over 1f out: kpt on same pce ins fnl f* **16/1**

10 **3** *1* **Danyah (IRE)**[47] 6891 2-9-9 0.................................(h[1]) KieranShoemark 8 78
(Owen Burrows) *chsd ldrs: rdn and unable qck over 1f out: no threat to wnr and kpt on same pce ins fnl f (vet said colt lost its left hind shoe)* **5/1**[2]

0 **4** *4* **Newton Jack**[159] 2767 2-9-2 0...................................... RobHornby 10 59+
(Stuart Kittow) *hld up towards rr: effrt towards inner and sme hdwy 2f out: no ch w ldrs but kpt on ins fnl f* **125/1**

4 **5** *1 ¼* **Streeton (IRE)**[22] 7769 2-9-2 0...................................... HarryBentley 1 55
(Ralph Beckett) *midfield: 5th and unable qck over 2f out: wl btn over 1f out: plugged on* **8/1**[3]

6 **6** *½* **Almuerzo Loco (IRE)**[19] 7842 2-9-2 0........................ RossaRyan 5 53
(Richard Hannon) *chsd ldrs: rdn over 2f out: unable qck u.p and btn over 1f out: wknd ins fnl f* **12/1**

7 *2 ¾* **Good Time Charlie** 2-9-2 0..................................... HectorCrouch 12 45
(Clive Cox) *wnt lft leaving stalls: sn swtchd rt: rn green and a towards rr: nvr involved* **50/1**

54 **8** *1* **Al Verde**[119] 4214 2-9-2 0.. CharlesBishop 6 42
(Ali Stronge) *wnt lft leaving stalls: hld up in midfield: no prog and wl hld over 2f out: wknd over 1f out* **80/1**

6 **9** *2* **Mackelly (IRE)**[27] 7571 2-9-2 0.................................... ShaneKelly 9 36
(Richard Hughes) *off the pce in midfield: rdn and no hdwy over 2f out: sn btn and wknd over 1f out* **40/1**

00 **10** *6* **Jungle Capers (IRE)**[17] 7899 2-9-2 0.......................... TomMarquand 11 18
(Mick Channon) *towards rr: hung lft and v wd bnd 4f out: wl bhd after (jockey said gelding hung badly left-handed)* **80/1**

11 *2 ½* **Bajan Breeze** 2-9-2 0.. JasonWatson 2 11
(Stuart Williams) *s.i.s: t.k.h and rn green in rr: wknd and hung lft over 1f out* **33/1**

1m 13.16s (0.06) **Going Correction** +0.05s/f (Slow) 11 Ran SP% **123.4**
Speed ratings (Par 95): **101,97,96,91,89 88,85,83,81,73 69**
CSF £10.22 TOTE £1.30: £1.02, £3.90, £1.40; EX 10.20 Trifecta £31.30.
Owner Godolphin **Bred** Shadwell Estate Company Limited **Trained** Newmarket, Suffolk

FOCUS
This proved straightforward enough for the odds-on favourite. A small step up from the winner.

8419 100% PROFIT BOOST AT 32REDSPORT.COM H'CAP 6f (P)
7:00 (7:02) (Class 5) (0-70,70) 3-Y-0+
£3,752 (£1,116; £557; £400; £400; £400) **Stalls** Low

Form RPR

6424 **1** **Turn To Rock (IRE)**[7] 8221 3-9-3 **67**........................(b[1]) HectorCrouch 9 77
(Ed Walker) *hld up in tch towards rr: effrt and hdwy on outer over 1f out: led ins fnl f: sn in command and r.o strly* **5/1**[2]

1310 **2** *2* **Global Hope (IRE)**[32] 7402 4-9-7 **70**.........................(e[1]) ShaneKelly 2 74
(Gay Kelleway) *in tch in midfield: effrt over 2f out: hdwy and swtchd lft over 1f out: kpt on ins fnl f to go 2nd towards fin: no threat to wnr* **3/1**[1]

2000 **3** *1 ¼* **Diamonique**[29] 7511 3-9-6 **70**.................................... ShaneGray 3 70
(Keith Dalgleish) *chsd ldrs: effrt over 1f out: ev ch 1f out: nt match pce of wnr and kpt on same pce ins fnl f: lost 2nd towards fin* **14/1**

3221 **4** *1 ¼* **Urban Highway (IRE)**[51] 6754 3-9-4 **68**..................... TomMarquand 5 64
(Tony Carroll) *hmpd leaving stalls: hld up in tch towards rr: effrt 3f out: hdwy ins fnl f: styd on but no threat to wnr* **10/1**

0000 **5** *hd* **Black Isle Boy (IRE)**[28] 7552 5-9-6 **69**...................... DavidProbert 8 64
(David C Griffiths) *t.k.h: chsd ldr: effrt over 2f out: unable qck and kpt on same pce ins fnl f* **16/1**

320- **6** *nk* **Royal Dynasty**[403] 7255 3-9-5 **69**.............................(h[1]) DanielMuscutt 10 63
(James Fanshawe) *stdd s: t.k.h: hld up in rr: hung rt over 2f out: swtchd rt over 1f out: hdwy and styd on ins fnl f: nvr threatened ldrs* **25/1**

0256 **7** *shd* **Hey Ho Let's Go**[14] 8007 3-8-6 **59**............................(h) WilliamCox(3) 6 53
(Clive Cox) *led: rdn ent fnl 2f: hdd ins fnl f: no ex and sn wknd* **15/2**

34 **8** *½* **Mid Atlantic Storm (IRE)**[7] 8220 3-8-11 **66**......(b[1]) ThomasGreatrex(5) 1 58
(Tom Ward) *dwlt: sn rcvrd and in tch in midfield: unable qck over 1f out: wknd ins fnl f* **6/1**[3]

0620 **9** *2 ¼* **First Link (USA)**[37] 7236 4-9-4 **67**.............................(p[1]) NicolaCurrie 12 52
(Jean-Rene Auvray) *stdd s: t.k.h: hld up towards rr: hdwy into midfield 4f out: rdn and wknd over 1f out* **14/1**

2142 **10** *3* **Desert Fox**[19] 7837 5-9-5 **68**.....................................(p) RossaRyan 11 44
(Mike Murphy) *half-rrd as stalls opened and s.i.s: hld up: swtchd rt and effrt and sme hdwy over 1f out: wknd ins fnl f* **7/1**

3160 **11** *4* **Aquarius (IRE)**[12] 8071 3-8-7 **57**................................ LiamJones 7 20
(Michael Appleby) *taken down early: chsd ldrs: rdn over 2f out: sn struggling and wknd over 1f out* **25/1**

6-60 **12** *1* **Doubly Beautiful (IRE)**[15] 7976 3-9-6 **70**.................(h[1]) RobHornby 4 30
(Ed de Giles) *wnt lft leaving stalls: t.k.h: chsd ldrs: rdn over 2f out: sn struggling and wknd over 1f out* **40/1**

1m 12.34s (-0.76) **Going Correction** +0.05s/f (Slow)
WFA 3 from 4yo+ 1lb 12 Ran SP% **118.7**
Speed ratings (Par 103): **107,104,102,101,100 100,100,99,96,92 87,85**
CSF £19.91 CT £203.05 TOTE £5.10: £1.40, £1.90, £5.40; EX 26.30 Trifecta £351.70.
Owner P K Siu **Bred** Corduff Stud Ltd **Trained** Upper Lambourn, Berks

FOCUS
A modest handicap won in good style. The second has been rated in line with the better view of his form.

8420 32RED H'CAP 6f (P)
7:30 (7:31) (Class 4) (0-85,86) 3-Y-0+
£6,469 (£1,925; £962; £481; £400; £400) **Stalls** Low

Form RPR

-101 **1** **Total Commitment (IRE)**[21] 7789 3-9-7 **85**.................. JasonWatson 5 98+
(Roger Charlton) *edgd rt leaving stalls: chsd ldrs: effrt on inner 2f out: rdn to ld jst over 1f out: styd on wl and in command ins fnl f* **9/4**[2]

1443 **2** *1 ¾* **Thegreatestshowman**[34] 7348 3-9-6 **84**....................... GeorgeWood 7 91
(Amy Murphy) *mounted in chute: chsd ldrs: effrt 2f out: chsd wnr ins fnl f: kpt on but no imp* **25/1**

0013 **3** *¾* **Revolutionise (IRE)**[21] 7789 3-9-2 **80**....................... JimCrowley 4 88+
(Roger Varian) *mounted in chute: impeded s: t.k.h: hld up in tch towards rr: nt clr run 2f tl swtchd lft jst ins fnl f: r.o wl ins fnl f: no threat to wnr* **2/1**[1]

1114 **4** *nk* **Yimou (IRE)**[33] 7397 4-9-9 **86**.................................. JoeyHaynes 6 90
(Dean Ivory) *led: drvn and hdd over 1f out: no ex: kpt on same pce and lost 2 pls ins fnl f* **10/1**

55 **5** *¾* **Lihou**[18] 7868 3-9-5 **83**.. HarryBentley 11 84
(David Evans) *bmpd s: hld up in tch in midfield: effrt ent fnl f: styd on ins fnl f: no threat to ldrs* **16/1**

5-54 **6** *¾* **Sparkalot**[40] 7107 5-9-6 **83**...................................... TomMarquand 3 82
(Simon Dow) *short of room sn after s: in tch in midfield: effrt ent fnl 2f: kpt on same pce ins fnl f* **9/2**[3]

0222 **7** *½* **Iconic Knight (IRE)**[46] 6916 4-9-1 **78**........................ HectorCrouch 10 75
(Ed Walker) *wnt lft leaving stalls: t.k.h: chsd ldr tl unable qck u.p over 1f out: wknd ins fnl f* **12/1**

1110 **8** *1 ¾* **Camachess (IRE)**[122] 4123 3-8-13 **77**......................... RobHornby 9 69
(Philip McBride) *hld up in rr: effrt ent fnl 2f: sme hdwy over 1f out: sn no imp: nvr involved* **66/1**

500 **9** *3 ¾* **Regulator (IRE)**[55] 6588 4-8-5 **71**............................ WilliamCox(3) 12 51
(Alexandra Dunn) *pushed lft leaving stalls: hld up in last pair: effrt on inner 2f out: sn btn and wknd fnl f* **100/1**

0100 **10** *1 ½* **Forseti**[19] 7839 3-8-11 **75**.......................................(h) DavidProbert 1 50
(Michael Appleby) *t.k.h: hld up in tch in midfield: effrt over 1f out: unable qck and wknd ins fnl f* **33/1**

4400 11 5 **Converter (IRE)**[104] 4793 3-8-9 **78**...........................(b[1]) DylanHogan(5) 2 37
(John Butler) *hld up in tch: rdn ent fnl 2f: unable qck over 1f out: wknd fnl f* **66/1**

1m 12.25s (-0.85) **Going Correction** +0.05s/f (Slow)
WFA 3 from 4yo+ 1lb 11 Ran SP% **115.7**
Speed ratings (Par 105): **107,104,103,103,102 101,100,98,93,91 84**
CSF £63.85 CT £130.38 TOTE £3.20: £1.30, £4.80, £1.10; EX 52.50 Trifecta £160.00.
Owner Brook Farm Bloodstock **Bred** Watership Down Stud **Trained** Beckhampton, Wilts

FOCUS
It was an advantage to race handily.

8421 32RED.COM H'CAP 1m 3f 219y(P)
8:00 (8:03) (Class 4) (0-85,87) 3-Y-O+
£6,469 (£1,925; £962; £481; £400; £400) **Stalls** Low

Form RPR

231 1 **All Yours (FR)**[27] 7575 8-9-9 **81**........................ JoeyHaynes 2 91+
(Sean Curran) *trckd ldrs: clsd to press ldr and travelling strly 2f: led over 1f out: rdn and qcknd clr: r.o strly: comf* **5/1**[3]

633 2 2 ½ **Fearless Warrior (FR)**[59] 6454 3-8-12 **76**..............(h[1] w) DavidProbert 7 81
(Eve Johnson Houghton) *chsd ldng trio: effrt ent fnl 2f: chsd ldrs over 1f out: unable to match pce of wnr: kpt on same pce u.p: wnt 2nd last strides* **11/1**

0000 3 hd **Maquisard (FR)**[23] 7729 7-9-8 **80**........................ HectorCrouch 3 84
(Michael Madgwick) *hld up in tch in midfield: effrt and hdwy ent fnl 2f: chsd ldrs over 1f out: no threat to wnr and kpt on same pce ins fnl f: wnt 3rd on post* **66/1**

1030 4 nse **My Boy Sepoy**[32] 7413 4-9-8 **80**........................ JasonWatson 12 84
(Stuart Williams) *in tch in midfield: pushed along 4f out: hdwy u.p over 1f out: chsd clr wnr jst over 1f out: kpt on same pce and no imp ins fnl f: lost 2 pls last strides* **25/1**

6134 5 1 **C'Est No Mour (GER)**[13] 8014 6-9-6 **78**..............(v) TomMarquand 10 80
(Peter Hedger) *hld up in last trio: hdwy and swtchd rt over 1f out: kpt on same pce ins fnl f* **12/1**

-343 6 nk **Pirate King**[115] 4407 4-9-11 **83**........................ StevieDonohoe 4 85
(Charlie Fellowes) *wl in tch in midfield: effrt ent fnl 2f: unable qck 1f out: wknd wl ins fnl f* **11/4**[2]

6232 7 ¾ **City Tour**[20] 7816 3-8-13 **77**........................ CallumShepherd 9 78
(Lydia Richards) *hld up in towards rr: effrt ent fnl f: kpt on ins fnl f: no threat to wnr* **11/1**

2060 8 1 **Al Kout**[67] 6171 5-9-12 **84**........................ RossaRyan 1 83
(Heather Main) *led: rdn and hdd over 1f out: no ex and lost 2nd 1f out: wknd ins fnl f* **7/1**

521 9 2 ¼ **Arabist**[47] 6890 3-9-3 **81**........................ KieranO'Neill 11 77
(John Gosden) *chsd ldr tl rdn and unable qck jst over 2f out: outpcd and btn over 1f out: wknd ins fnl f* **9/4**[1]

4036 10 ¾ **Sophosc (IRE)**[34] 7342 3-9-5 **83**........................ CharlesBishop 13 77
(Joseph Tuite) *stdd s: t.k.h: hld up in rr: effrt over 2f out: nvr trbld ldrs* **20/1**

2026 11 1 ¾ **Fairy Tale (IRE)**[57] 6535 4-10-1 **87**........................ ShaneKelly 14 79
(Gay Kelleway) *stdd s and dropped in bhd: n.d* **20/1**

500- 12 4 **Bear Valley (IRE)**[493] 3868 5-9-10 **82**..............(t) RaulDaSilva 6 67
(Amy Murphy) *hld up towards rr: effrt over 2f out: wknd over 1f out* **66/1**

2m 33.82s (-0.68) **Going Correction** +0.05s/f (Slow)
WFA 3 from 4yo+ 6lb 12 Ran SP% **127.3**
Speed ratings (Par 105): **104,102,102,102,101 101,100,100,98,98 96,94**
CSF £59.66 CT £3298.55 TOTE £5.10: £1.30, £3.10, £19.20; EX 68.30 Trifecta £3659.20.
Owner Power Geneva Ltd **Bred** S C A La Perrigne **Trained** Upper Lambourn, Berks

FOCUS
Not a bad handicap, and a comfortable winner. The fourth has been rated close to form.

8422 32RED ON THE APP STORE H'CAP 1m 2f 219y(P)
8:30 (8:35) (Class 5) (0-70,70) 4-Y-O+
£3,752 (£1,116; £557; £400; £400; £400) **Stalls** Low

Form RPR

1404 1 **Trailboss (IRE)**[17] 7915 4-9-7 **70**..............(b) StevieDonohoe 2 80
(Ed Vaughan) *chsd ldrs: clsd to press ldrs 2f out: rdn to ld over 1f out: clr ins fnl f: kpt on and a doing enough* **4/1**[1]

3510 2 ¾ **Topology**[21] 7790 6-8-12 **61**........................ CharlesBishop 5 69
(Joseph Tuite) *hld up in last trio: clsd and nt clr run 2f: swtchd rt and hdwy over 1f out: chsd clr wnr ins fnl f: r.o wl u.p: nvr quite getting to wnr* **10/1**

4030 3 2 ¾ **Dangerous Ends**[59] 6439 5-9-6 **69**........................ RossaRyan 6 72
(Brett Johnson) *hld up in rr: clsd and nt clr run 2f out: rdn and hdwy over 1f out: kpt on wl ins fnl f: wnt 3rd wl ins fnl f: no threat to ldng pair* **7/1**

0000 4 1 **Margie's Choice (GER)**[14] 7982 4-9-7 **70**..............(bt[1]) LiamKeniry 10 71
(Michael Madgwick) *stdd s: t.k.h: hld up in tch in midfield: rdn and hdwy to chse ldrs over 1f out: kpt on same pce ins fnl f* **80/1**

3304 5 ½ **Highway One (USA)**[22] 7756 5-8-11 **60**........................ NicolaCurrie 12 60
(George Baker) *chsd ldrs tl led 7f out: hdd 5f out: chsd ldr: rdn and ev ch 2f out: led briefly over 1f out: sn hdd and no ex ins fnl f: lost 2 pls wl ins fnl f* **16/1**

0010 6 1 ¼ **Near Kettering**[31] 7439 5-9-0 **66**..............(t) JaneElliott(3) 9 64
(Sam England) *t.k.h: chsd ldrs: rdn and ev ch 2f out tl no ex jst over 1f out: wknd ins fnl f* **9/2**[2]

5421 7 nk **Mullarkey**[21] 7790 5-8-13 **62**..............(t) KierenFox 8 60
(John Best) *t.k.h: hld up in tch in midfield: effrt over 2f out: kpt on ins fnl f: nvr enough pce to get involved* **9/2**[2]

3552 8 3 ¾ **Miss Blondell**[37] 7229 6-9-1 **64**..............(v) KieranO'Neill 14 55
(Marcus Tregoning) *in tch in midfield on outer: rdn over 3f out: unable qck u.p over 2f out: wl hld over 1f out* **10/1**

0500 9 nk **The Warrior (IRE)**[7] 8223 7-8-11 **60**........................ CharlieBennett 13 51
(Lee Carter) *stdd s: hld up in last trio: effrt and n.m.r 2f out: rdn over 1f out: nvr involved* **33/1**

0355 10 ¾ **Sweet Charity**[28] 7560 4-9-2 **65**........................ JasonWatson 1 55
(Denis Coakley) *t.k.h: in tch in midfield: effrt on outer 3f out: unable qck and btn over 1f out: wknd ins fnl f (jockey said filly ran too free)* **5/1**[3]

2114 11 3 ½ **Fair Power (IRE)**[24] 7685 5-8-13 **62**........................ JFEgan 11 46
(John Butler) *t.k.h: hld up in tch in midfield: swtchd lft and hdwy to ld 5f out: rdn and hdd over 1f out: sn outpcd and wknd ins fnl f (jockey said gelding hung right-handed and ran too free)* **25/1**

0230 12 3 ¼ **Simbirsk**[37] 7233 4-9-7 **70**..............(b[1]) TomMarquand 7 48
(John O'Shea) *hld up in tch in midfield: effrt over 2f out: unable qck u.p and btn over 1f out: wknd ins fnl f* **16/1**

5500 13 3 ¾ **Glacier Fox**[108] 4658 4-9-1 **64**........................ ShaneKelly 4 36
(Mark Loughnane) *led tl 7f out: chsd ldrs: rdn over 2f out: sn struggling: wknd over 1f out (jockey said gelding hung left-handed)* **50/1**

2m 21.53s (0.53) **Going Correction** +0.05s/f (Slow) 13 Ran SP% **125.5**
Speed ratings (Par 103): **103,102,100,99,99 98,98,95,95,94 92,89,87**
CSF £46.30 CT £283.76 TOTE £4.80: £2.20, £2.40, £2.30; EX 43.00 Trifecta £304.80.
Owner The Open Range **Bred** Camas Park, Lynch Bages & Summerhill **Trained** Newmarket, Suffolk

FOCUS
A modest affair but the winner did it nicely. The winner has been rated in line with his Doncaster win.
T/Plt: £76.40 to a £1 stake. Pool: £57,898.36 - 552.89 winning units T/Qpdt: £10.70 to a £1 stake. Pool: £12,156.61 - 838.02 winning units **Steve Payne**

8300 NEWCASTLE (A.W) (L-H)
Tuesday, October 22

OFFICIAL GOING: Tapeta: standard
Wind: Breezy, half against in races on the straight course and in over 3f of home straight in races on the Weather: Overcast, dry

8423 BETWAY APPRENTICE H'CAP 1m 4f 98y (Tp)
2:00 (2:02) (Class 6) (0-60,60) 3-Y-O+
£2,781 (£620; £300; £300; £300) **Stalls** High

Form RPR

0-03 1 **Mamdood (IRE)**[7] 8238 5-8-10 **49**..............(vt) ZakWheatley(5) 14 56+
(Stef Keniry) *t.k.h: prom: smooth hdwy to ld over 2f out: rdn ins fnl f: kpt on wl* **6/1**[3]

0562 2 1 ¾ **Yvette**[20] 7817 3-9-2 **59**..............(p) GavinAshton(3) 5 64
(Sir Mark Prescott Bt) *hld up in midfield: stdy hdwy over 3f out: rdn and chsd wnr 2f out: kpt on ins fnl f: jnd for 2nd last stride* **6/4**[1]

0535 2 dht **Majestic Stone (IRE)**[32] 7415 5-9-0 **48**........................ HarryRussell 13 52
(Julie Camacho) *s.s: bhd: hdwy over 2f out: effrt and cl 3rd over 1f out: kpt on fnl f to dead-heat for 2nd last stride* **9/1**

60-0 4 1 ¾ **Imperial Focus (IRE)**[8] 8186 6-9-11 **59**........................ AngusVilliers 3 61
(Simon Waugh) *hld up on ins: stdy hdwy over 2f out: rdn over 1f out: r.o ins fnl f* **100/1**

0024 5 ¾ **Gworn**[7] 8238 9-9-2 **50**........................ AledBeech 1 51
(R Mike Smith) *midfield: drvn and outpcd over 3f out: rallied over 1f out: kpt on fnl f: no imp* **33/1**

6523 6 2 ½ **Elysee Star**[28] 7544 4-8-13 **47**..............(p) TobyEley 4 44
(Mark Walford) *hld up: effrt whn nt clr run briefly over 2f out: effrt over 1f out: one pce fnl f* **14/1**

0060 7 1 ¾ **Cormier (IRE)**[13] 8033 3-9-3 **60**........................ AidenBlakemore(3) 6 55
(Stef Keniry) *t.k.h: chsd ldr to over 3f out: rdn and hung lft 2f out: sn wknd* **25/1**

2132 8 hd **Sulafaat (IRE)**[25] 7650 4-9-4 **55**..............(p) RussellHarris(3) 10 49
(Rebecca Menzies) *t.k.h: prom on ins: nt clr run over 2f out to over 1f out: angled rt and sn no imp (jockey said filly was denied a clear run 1 1/2f out)* **7/2**[2]

0366 9 2 **Life Knowledge (IRE)**[23] 7739 7-8-8 **49**..............(v[1]) OwenPayton(7) 2 40
(Liam Bailey) *dwlt: bhd: rdn along and effrt on outside over 2f out: hung rt over 1f out: sn btn* **25/1**

0500 10 ¾ **Clovenstone**[27] 7581 3-8-12 **55**..............(v[1]) OliverStammers(3) 11 46
(Alistair Whillans) *plld hrd: led to over 2f out: rdn and wknd over 1f out* **66/1**

1355 11 3 ½ **Jan De Heem**[3] 8343 9-9-10 **58**..............(v) RhonaPindar 9 43
(Tina Jackson) *trckd ldrs: wnt 2nd over 3f out: rdn over 2f out: wknd over 1f out* **14/1**

440 12 2 ¼ **Lyford (IRE)**[32] 7415 4-9-2 **53**..............(p) CoreyMadden(3) 7 34
(Alistair Whillans) *midfield on outside: hdwy and prom over 2f out: wknd wl over 1f out* **25/1**

0065 13 nk **Bannockburn (IRE)**[23] 7739 3-8-8 **48**..............(p[1]) EllaMcCain 8 30
(Keith Dalgleish) *bhd: drvn along over 5f out: struggling fr 3f out: nvr on terms* **33/1**

2m 41.7s (0.60) **Going Correction** +0.075s/f (Slow)
WFA 3 from 4yo+ 6lb 13 Ran SP% **119.7**
Speed ratings (Par 101): **101,99,99,98,98 96,95,95,93,93 91,89,89**
WIN: MD 5.70; PL: YV 1.20, MD 1.70, MS 3.10; EX: MD/MS 33.00, MD/YV 10.00; CSF: MD/YV 7.22, MD/MS 27.57; TC: MD/YV/MS 42.12, MD/MS/YV 61.41; TF: MD/MS/YV 107.20, MD/YV/MS 69.60.
Owner Mrs Stef Keniry **Bred** Whitethorn Bloodstock **Trained** Middleham, N Yorks

FOCUS
A modest middle-distance apprentice riders' handicap.

8424 LADBROKES WHERE THE NATION PLAYS EBF NOVICE STKS (PLUS 10 RACE) 7f 14y (Tp)
2:35 (2:36) (Class 4) 2-Y-O **£4,787** (£1,424; £711; £355) **Stalls** Centre

Form RPR

66 1 **Count Of Amazonia (IRE)**[33] 7392 2-9-2 0........................ AndreaAtzeni 5 80
(Richard Hannon) *cl up in centre of gp: led after 2f: mde rest: rdn over 1f out: r.o wl fnl f* **14/1**

2 1 **Khaloosy (IRE)** 2-9-2 0........................ JackMitchell 9 78
(Roger Varian) *prom in centre of gp: effrt and chsd wnr 2f out: kpt on ins fnl f: nt pce to chal* **16/1**

3 3 1 ½ **Grand Bazaar**[47] 6892 2-9-2 0........................ RobertHavlin 13 74
(John Gosden) *dwlt: t.k.h: hld up in centre of gp: shkn up over 2f out: hdwy over 1f out: r.o fnl f: nrst fin* **5/6**[1]

4 4 ½ **Carlos Felix (IRE)**[33] 7392 2-9-2 0........................ JamieSpencer 4 73
(David Simcock) *dwlt: t.k.h: hld up towards far side of gp: drvn over 2f out: kpt on fnl f: nvr able to chal* **3/1**[2]

06 5 3 ½ **Rulers Kingdom (IRE)**[12] 8069 2-9-2 0........................ JoeFanning 2 64
(Mark Johnston) *cl up on far side of gp: rdn over 2f out: outpcd fr over 1f out* **100/1**

6 2 ¼ **Foreshore** 2-9-2 0........................ CliffordLee 10 58
(K R Burke) *prom towards centre of gp: drvn and outpcd over 2f out: n.d after* **25/1**

0 7 1 ¼ **Dreaming Blue**[33] 7361 2-9-2 0........................ TonyHamilton 11 55+
(Richard Fahey) *hld up in centre of gp: rdn and outpcd over 2f out: r.o fnl f: nvr able to chal* **100/1**

12 8 1 **Amaan**[19] 7842 2-9-8 0........................ DaneO'Neill 3 60
(Simon Crisford) *propped leaving stalls: led in centre of gp 2f: chsd wnr to 2f out: sn rdn and wknd* **11/2**[3]

0 **9** *1* **Double D's**[32] [7398] 2-9-2 0........ PaulMulrennan 12 50+
(Michael Dods) *dwlt: hld up on nr side of gp: outpcd over 2f out: n.d* **150/1**

10 *1 1/4* **Doubling Dice** 2-9-2 0........ BenCurtis 7 47
(Hugo Palmer) *dwlt: hld up towards far side of gp: struggling over 2f out: sn btn* **28/1**

11 *8* **Monsaraz** 2-9-2 0........ TomEaves 1 27
(James Given) *hld up on far side of gp: struggling 3f out: sn btn* **200/1**

00 **12** *2 3/4* **Bouncing Bobby (IRE)**[15] [7958] 2-9-2 0........ GrahamLee 14 20
(Michael Dods) *prom on nr side of gp: rdn and struggling 3f out: sn btn* **200/1**

13 *shd* **Phoenix Strike** 2-9-2 0........ AndrewMullen 8 20
(Ben Haslam) *dwlt: bhd on nr side of gp: struggling 3f out: sn btn* **150/1**

1m 27.03s (0.83) **Going Correction** +0.075s/f (Slow) **13** Ran SP% **119.1**
Speed ratings (Par 97): **98,96,95,94,90 88,86,85,84,82 73,70,70**
CSF £206.15 TOTE £12.80: £3.10, £3.60, £1.10; EX 245.30 Trifecta £873.40.
Owner Sheikh Mohammed Obaid Al Maktoum **Bred** Rosetown Bloodstock **Trained** East Everleigh, Wilts

FOCUS
A fairly decent juvenile novice contest won last year by 2019 1m Group 3 Thoroughbred Stakes runner-up Turjomaan. The level is a bit fluid.

8425 BETWAY OPTIONAL CLAIMING H'CAP 6f (Tp)
3:10 (3:11) (Class 2) 4-Y-0+
£18,675 (£5,592; £2,796; £1,398; £699; £351) **Stalls** Centre

Form RPR

4210 **1** **Buridan (FR)**[80] [5664] 4-9-3 **91**........ SeanLevey 6 100
(Richard Hannon) *midfield in centre of gp: rdn 2f out: hdwy to ld wl ins fnl f: kpt on wl cl home* **14/1**

632- **2** *nk* **Warsaw Road (IRE)**[364] [8503] 5-9-0 **88**........ AlistairRawlinson 10 96
(Robert Cowell) *prom in centre of gp: hdwy to ld over 1f out: rdn and hdd wl ins fnl f: kpt on* **14/1**

5000 **3** *1 1/4* **Above The Rest (IRE)**[24] [7697] 8-10-0 **102**........(h) BenCurtis 7 106+
(David Barron) *hld up in centre of gp: rdn and hdwy over 1f out: kpt on fnl f: nrst fin* **11/1**

6005 **4** *nk* **Muscika**[24] [7701] 5-8-6 **87**........(p) AngusVilliers(7) 12 90
(David O'Meara) *t.k.h: led on nr side of gp: rdn and hdd over 1f out: rallied: one pce ins fnl f* **11/1**

2313 **5** *hd* **Saluti (IRE)**[26] [7621] 5-8-7 **81**........ LukeMorris 5 83
(Paul Midgley) *t.k.h: midfield on far side of gp: effrt and rdn whn hmpd over 1f out: kpt on ins fnl f* **28/1**

3030 **6** *shd* **Intisaab**[10] [8127] 8-9-7 **95**........(p) DanielTudhope 14 97
(David O'Meara) *hld up in tch on nr side of gp: effrt and rdn wl over 1f out: r.o same pce ins fnl f* **9/2**[2]

0556 **7** *shd* **Polybius**[33] [7397] 8-9-1 **89**........ JamieSpencer 1 91+
(David Simcock) *missed break: swtchd rt and hld up in centre of gp: swtchd to nr side of gp 1/2-way: nt clr run over 1f out to ins fnl f: shkn up and kpt on wl last 75yds: nrst fin (jockey said gelding denied a clear run continually from 2f out to the final 1/2f)* **50/1**

3520 **8** *nse* **Lucky Lucky Man (IRE)**[32] [7402] 4-8-3 **77**........ JamesSullivan 3 79
(Richard Fahey) *midfield on far side of gp: drvn and outpcd over 2f out: rallied appr fnl f: one pce last 100yds* **28/1**

0026 **9** *shd* **Firmdecisions (IRE)**[31] [7467] 9-8-7 **84**........ RowanScott(3) 8 85
(Nigel Tinkler) *hld up in centre of gp: effrt and swtchd lft over 1f out: no imp ins fnl f* **66/1**

1422 **10** *3/4* **Athollblair Boy (IRE)**[35] [7310] 6-8-5 **84**........ FayeMcManoman(5) 9 83
(Nigel Tinkler) *midfield towards centre of gp: rdn and outpcd over 2f out: rallied over 1f out: no imp ins fnl f* **10/1**

5036 **11** *nk* **Paddy Power (IRE)**[32] [7402] 6-8-2 **79**........ SeanDavis(3) 13 77
(Richard Fahey) *hld up on ins: effrt and rdn over 1f out: no further imp last 100yds* **20/1**

0005 **12** *1* **Tommy G**[21] [7781] 6-8-1 **75**........ JamieGormley 4 70
(Jim Goldie) *cl up on far side of gp: rdn over 2f out: wknd 1f out* **25/1**

0500 **13** *3/4* **Staxton**[10] [8127] 4-9-7 **95**........(p) DavidAllan 2 87
(Tim Easterby) *cl up on far side of gp: drvn along over 2f out: wknd 1f out* **11/4**[1]

5401 **14** *shd* **Equiano Springs**[31] [7467] 5-8-10 **84**........ AndrewMullen 11 76
(Tom Tate) *dwlt: sn cl up on nr side of gp: rdn and ev ch 2f out: wknd appr fnl f (jockey said gelding ran flat)* **15/2**[3]

1m 12.19s (-0.31) **Going Correction** +0.075s/f (Slow) **14** Ran SP% **114.7**
Speed ratings (Par 109): **105,104,102,102,102 102,102,101,101,100 100,99,98,97**
CSF £172.09 CT £2224.07 TOTE £16.30: £4.10, £4.60, £3.50; EX 161.70 Trifecta £2109.50.
Owner Al Shaqab Racing **Bred** S C A La Perrigne **Trained** East Everleigh, Wilts
■ Stewards' Enquiry : David Allan two-day ban: careless riding (Nov 5-6)

FOCUS
A good optional claiming sprint handicap. The winner has been rated right up to his old best, with the second also to his best.

8426 LADBROKES HOME OF THE ODDS BOOST CONDITIONS STKS (PLUS 10 RACE) (AW CHAMPS' FAST-TRACK QUALIFIER) 6f (Tp)
3:45 (3:46) (Class 2) 2-Y-O **£14,555** (£4,331; £2,164; £1,082) **Stalls** Centre

Form RPR

110 **1** **Temple Of Heaven**[125] [3988] 2-9-9 94........(b[1]) SeanLevey 3 104+
(Richard Hannon) *t.k.h: prom: smooth hdwy to ld over 1f out: shkn up and qcknd clr whn hung lft ins fnl f: eased cl home: readily* **4/1**[3]

113 **2** *5* **Desert Safari (IRE)**[17] [7904] 2-9-9 95........ JoeFanning 2 87
(Mark Johnston) *led: rdn: hung lft and hdd over 1f out: kpt on fnl f: no ch w wnr* **13/8**[1]

10 **3** *1* **Aleneva (IRE)**[31] [7432] 2-9-1 0........ PJMcDonald 4 76
(Richard Fahey) *hld up in tch: effrt and rdn 2f out: edgd lft and kpt on ins fnl f: no imp (jockey said filly hung left)* **25/1**

110 **4** *nse* **Macho Time (IRE)**[32] [7409] 2-9-9 86........ CliffordLee 5 84
(K R Burke) *pressed ldr: drvn and outpcd over 1f out: rallied ins fnl f: no imp* **8/1**

5113 **5** *1 3/4* **Hamish Macbeth**[37] [7247] 2-9-9 90........ BenCurtis 1 79
(Hugo Palmer) *cl up: rdn along 2f out: wknd 1f out* **7/4**[2]

1m 12.02s (-0.48) **Going Correction** +0.075s/f (Slow) **5** Ran SP% **109.4**
Speed ratings (Par 101): **106,99,98,97,95**
CSF £10.83 TOTE £4.80: £2.70, £1.40; EX 9.10 Trifecta £44.00.
Owner Rockcliffe Stud **Bred** Highclere Stud & Jake Warren Ltd **Trained** East Everleigh, Wilts

FOCUS
A good quality juvenile conditions contest. The third-favourite clocked a marginally quicker winning time than the previous C&D handicap. The winner has been rated in line with his early season form.

8427 BOMBARDIER CLASSIFIED STKS 1m 5y (Tp)
4:20 (4:21) (Class 5) 3-Y-O+
£3,428 (£1,020; £509; £300; £300; £300) **Stalls** Centre

Form RPR

6265 **1** **First Response**[33] [7378] 4-9-3 74........(t[1]) TonyHamilton 4 81
(Linda Stubbs) *hld up in tch: rdn and hdwy over 1f out: led wl ins fnl f: r.o* **7/1**[3]

1460 **2** *nk* **Geizy Teizy (IRE)**[67] [6170] 3-9-0 74........ BenCurtis 6 79+
(Marco Botti) *stdd s: hld up: smooth hdwy to ld over 1f out: sn rdn and edgd lft: hdd wl ins fnl f: r.o* **7/2**[2]

6162 **3** *1 3/4* **In The Cove (IRE)**[7] [8220] 3-9-0 73........(b) SeanLevey 2 75
(Richard Hannon) *t.k.h: trckd ldrs: drvn along 2f out: effrt appr fnl f: one pce last 100yds* **3/1**[1]

230- **4** *5* **Fortissimo (IRE)**[305] [9669] 3-9-0 73........ JoeFanning 3 64
(Mark Johnston) *pressed ldr: rdn and ev ch briefly wl over 1f out: sn outpcd: n.d after: lost hind shoe (vet said gelding lost left hind shoe)* **18/1**

102 **5** *hd* **Robotique Danseur (FR)**[20] [7822] 3-9-0 75........ PJMcDonald 1 63
(K R Burke) *led at ordinary gallop: rdn and hdd over 1f out: sn outpcd: btn fnl f* **9/1**

1135 **6** *7* **Blindingly (GER)**[20] [7820] 4-9-3 72........(p) PaulMulrennan 5 48
(Ben Haslam) *stdd s: t.k.h in rr: drvn and outpcd over 2f out: sn btn* **15/2**

2236 **7** *4 1/2* **Scheme**[28] [7554] 3-9-0 74........(p) LukeMorris 7 37
(Sir Mark Prescott Bt) *prom: rdn over 2f out: hung lft and wknd over 1f out (jockey said filly weakened quickly 3f out)* **3/1**[1]

1m 41.34s (2.74) **Going Correction** +0.075s/f (Slow)
WFA 3 from 4yo 3lb **7** Ran SP% **111.8**
Speed ratings (Par 103): **89,88,86,81,81 74,70**
CSF £30.12 TOTE £7.70: £3.20, £2.20; EX 38.90 Trifecta £152.20.
Owner D M Smith, P G Shorrock & L Stubbs **Bred** Juddmonte Farms Ltd **Trained** Norton, N Yorks

FOCUS
An ordinary classified stakes. The third-favourite came through to lead off a slow gallop, but couldn't fend off another finisher close home. The winner has been rated in line with his better form this year.

8428 BETWAY HEED YOUR HUNCH H'CAP 6f (Tp)
4:50 (4:51) (Class 4) (0-80,81) 3-Y-O+
£5,207 (£1,549; £774; £387; £300; £300) **Stalls** Centre

Form RPR

360 **1** **Zamjar**[34] [7348] 5-8-12 **77**........ AngusVilliers(7) 3 86
(Robert Cowell) *t.k.h: prom on far side of gp: effrt and rdn over 1f out: led ins fnl f: kpt on wl* **16/1**

6660 **2** *1/2* **Reckless Endeavour (IRE)**[182] [2015] 6-9-5 **77**........ BenCurtis 6 84
(David Barron) *dwlt: bhd in centre of gp: rdn over 2f out: angled lft and hdwy over 1f out: wnt 2nd wl ins fnl f: r.o* **12/1**

4051 **3** *1/2* **John Kirkup**[21] [7777] 4-9-8 **80**........(b) GrahamLee 7 85
(Michael Dods) *t.k.h: cl up in centre of gp: effrt whn nt clr run over 2f out: sn rdn: hdwy over 1f out: one pce wl ins fnl f* **6/1**[3]

2060 **4** *nk* **Tomily (IRE)**[17] [7908] 5-9-9 **81**........(v[1]) DanielTudhope 10 85
(David O'Meara) *hld up on nr side of gp: rdn and effrt 2f out: kpt on ins fnl f: hld towards fin* **9/2**[2]

3344 **5** *1/2* **Kindly**[33] [7380] 6-9-5 **77**........ NathanEvans 11 80
(Michael Easterby) *cl up on nr side of gp: effrt and disp ld over 1f out to ins fnl f: no ex last 50yds* **4/1**[1]

0400 **6** *1 1/4* **Big Les (IRE)**[32] [7402] 4-9-8 **80**........ PJMcDonald 4 79
(Karen McLintock) *led in centre of gp: rdn and hrd pressed fr over 1f out: hdd ins fnl f: sn no ex* **10/1**

000 **7** *1/2* **Galloway Hills**[26] [7621] 4-9-2 **77**........(p) MeganNicholls(3) 9 74
(Phillip Makin) *hld up in centre of gp: rdn over 2f out: effrt and angled rt over 1f out: no imp fnl f* **25/1**

100 **8** *nk* **Dutch Pursuit (IRE)**[53] [6677] 3-9-5 **78**........ PaulMulrennan 2 74
(Michael Dods) *dwlt and wnt lft s: bhd and detached towards nr side of gp: rdn and hdwy over 1f out: no imp ins fnl f (jockey said gelding missed the break)* **14/1**

3001 **9** *1 1/2* **Secretinthepark**[13] [8023] 9-9-7 **79**........(b) JackGarritty 12 70
(Michael Mullineaux) *racd on nr side of gp: w ldr to over 1f out: rdn and wknd ins fnl f* **10/1**

0066 **10** *1 3/4* **Glory Of Paris (IRE)**[28] [7551] 5-9-5 **77**........ LukeMorris 8 63
(Michael Appleby) *taken early to post: cl up on far side of gp: rdn over 2f out: wknd over 1f out* **17/2**

0541 **11** *3* **Axe Axelrod (USA)**[11] [8083] 3-8-7 **66** oh1........(b) AndrewMullen 1 42
(Michael Dods) *hld up on far side of gp: rdn and outpcd over 2f out: hung lft and wknd over 1f out* **17/2**

1m 11.84s (-0.66) **Going Correction** +0.075s/f (Slow)
WFA 3 from 4yo+ 1lb **11** Ran SP% **115.8**
Speed ratings (Par 105): **107,106,105,105,104 102,102,101,99,97 93**
CSF £191.52 CT £1288.91 TOTE £15.30: £3.30, £3.20, £1.90; EX 236.20 Trifecta £1280.10.
Owner Mrs J Morley **Bred** Manor Farm Stud (Rutland) **Trained** Six Mile Bottom, Cambs

FOCUS
A fair handicap. One of the outsiders won well in a good comparative 6f time on the day. The winner has been rated close to his best, and the third close to form.

8429 BETWAY H'CAP 5f (Tp)
5:20 (5:23) (Class 5) (0-70,69) 3-Y-O+
£3,428 (£1,020; £509; £300; £300; £300) **Stalls** Centre

Form RPR

4540 **1** **Tathmeen (IRE)**[13] [8023] 4-9-7 **69**........ SeanLevey 7 75
(Antony Brittain) *hld up in centre of gp: rdn and hdwy over 1f out: led wl ins fnl f: kpt on wl* **11/2**[2]

4215 **2** *nk* **Be Proud (IRE)**[20] [7823] 3-8-13 **61**........ BenRobinson 9 67
(Jim Goldie) *hld up towards rr in centre of gp: rdn and hdwy over 1f out: disp 2nd pl wl ins fnl f: kpt on* **13/2**

2030 **3** *nse* **Leo Minor (USA)**[12] [8063] 5-8-11 **66**........(t) AngusVilliers(7) 13 71
(Robert Cowell) *t.k.h early: prom on nr side of gp: rdn and sltly outpcd over 1f out: rallied and disp 2nd pl wl ins fnl f: r.o* **16/1**

010 **4** *nk* **Hard Solution**[5] [8296] 3-9-5 **67**........ DanielTudhope 4 72
(David O'Meara) *cl up on far side of gp: rdn to ld over 1f out: hdd and no ex wl ins fnl f* **7/1**

-310 **5** *hd* **Buniann (IRE)**[27] [7588] 3-9-7 **69**........ KevinStott 11 73
(Paul Midgley) *midfield on nr side of gp: rdn and hdwy over 1f out: kpt on fnl f: hld towards fin* **6/1**[3]

0065 **6** *1* **Almurr (IRE)**[25] 7656 3-9-2 **67**................................ SeanDavis(3) 5 67
(Phillip Makin) *midfield towards far side of gp: rdn and hdwy over 1f out: one pce wl ins fnl f* **12/1**

00 **7** *nk* **Arnold**[20] 7823 5-8-9 **57**.. LukeMorris 12 57
(Ann Duffield) *hld up on nr side of gp: effrt and rdn over 1f out: no room and ins fnl f: kpt on: no imp (jockey said gelding was denied a clear run inside final furlong)* **20/1**

2320 **8** *nk* **Burtonwood**[42] 7050 7-8-10 **58**.. CliffordLee 2 55
(Julie Camacho) *hld up on far side of gp: rdn over 2f out: hdwy over 1f out: no imp fnl f* **18/1**

4421 **9** *1 1/4* **Swiss Connection**[15] 7959 3-9-3 **65**...................(h) GrahamLee 14 59
(Bryan Smart) *in tch on nr side of gp: effrt and rdn 2f out: wknd ins fnl f* **4/1**[1]

6 **10** *1/2* **Heavenly Rainbow (IRE)**[19] 7855 3-9-3 **65**.................. PhilDennis 10 57
(Michael Herrington) *hld up towards nr side of gp: rdn and edgd lft over 1f out: kpt on fnl f: n.d* **33/1**

0242 **11** *nk* **Mr Greenlight**[7] 8235 4-8-12 **60**..........................(p) DavidAllan 8 50
(Tim Easterby) *cl up in centre of gp: drvn and ev ch over 1f out: wknd ins fnl f* **9/1**

0000 **12** *3/4* **Granny Roz**[12] 8066 5-8-12 **65**................................. PaulaMuir(5) 1 52
(Ray Craggs) *midfield on far side of gp: rdn along 2f out: wknd ins fnl f* **80/1**

3510 **13** *1* **Brandy Station (IRE)**[19] 7855 4-8-9 **64**....................(p) GavinAshton(7) 6 48
(Lisa Williamson) *led in centre of gp: drvn and hdd over 1f out: wknd ins fnl f* **50/1**

0000 **14** *3 1/2* **Point Of Woods**[6] 8263 6-8-9 **57**............................(bt) JamesSullivan 3 28
(Tina Jackson) *dwlt: bhd on far side of gp: rdn over 2f out: hung lft and wknd over 1f out* **66/1**

59.62s (0.12) **Going Correction** +0.075s/f (Slow) **14** Ran SP% **116.7**
Speed ratings (Par 103): **102,101,101,100,100 99,98,98,96,95 94,93,92,86**
CSF £38.24 CT £556.25 TOTE £12.50: £2.40, £2.50, £5.30; EX 38.40 Trifecta £406.40.
Owner Antony Brittain **Bred** Shadwell Estate Company Limited **Trained** Warthill, N Yorks
■ Stewards' Enquiry : Angus Villiers four-day ban: used whip above permitted level (Nov 7-9, 16)

FOCUS
An ordinary sprint handicap and about two lengths covered the first seven home. Ordinary form.
T/Plt: £235.60 to a £1 stake. Pool: £51,714.95 - 160.19 winning units T/Qpdt: £215.70 to a £1 stake. Pool: £5,148.16 - 17.66 winning units **Richard Young**

8201 YARMOUTH (L-H)
Tuesday, October 22

OFFICIAL GOING: Heavy (soft in places; 5.0)
Wind: Light half against Weather: Overcast

8430 WARNERS GUNTON HALL & CORTON LEISURE BREAKS NURSERY H'CAP 6f 3y
1:40 (1:44) (Class 5) (0-75,77) 2-Y-O
£3,428 (£1,020; £509; £300; £300; £300) **Stalls** Centre

Form RPR

0334 **1** **Little Brown Trout**[33] 7391 2-8-13 **72**........................ MarcoGhiani(5) 10 80
(William Stone) *s.i.s: hld up: hdwy over 2f out: led over 1f out: edgd lft ins fnl f: styd on wl* **6/1**[3]

0420 **2** *2 1/4* **Order Of St John**[33] 7391 2-9-2 **70**.........................(v[1]) SilvestreDeSousa 5 71
(John Ryan) *s.i.s: hdwy over 4f out: rdn and edgd rt over 1f out: styd on same pce wl ins fnl f (jockey said colt hung right-handed)* **4/1**[1]

5546 **3** *1 1/4* **Bowling Russian (IRE)**[22] 7754 2-9-0 **68**.......................(p[1]) DavidEgan 1 66
(George Baker) *chsd ldrs: led over 2f out: rdn and hdd over 1f out: styd on same pce ins fnl f* **7/1**

5045 **4** *1* **Global Agreement**[14] 7980 2-8-11 **65**..............................(v[1]) JFEgan 3 60
(Milton Harris) *s.i.s: sn pushed along in rr: rdn over 2f out: hung rt over 1f out: r.o ins fnl f: nvr nrr* **8/1**

1401 **5** *1 1/4* **Dragon Command**[14] 7994 2-9-9 **77**..........................(p) HayleyTurner 4 68
(George Scott) *prom: chsd ldr over 4f out: rdn and ev ch over 1f out: no ex ins fnl f* **8/1**

6534 **6** *1 3/4* **Roman Melody**[12] 8059 2-9-7 **75**.................................. GeraldMosse 6 61
(David Elsworth) *chsd ldrs: sn pushed along: rdn over 2f out: wknd ins fnl f* **11/2**[2]

045 **7** *1/2* **Seven Emirates (IRE)**[18] 7870 2-8-13 **70**.................. HarrisonShaw(3) 2 54
(K R Burke) *chsd ldrs: lost pl over 3f out: rallied over 1f out: wknd ins fnl f* **7/1**

300 **8** *8* **Tyler Durden (IRE)**[37] 7247 2-9-5 **73**.........................(h) StevieDonohoe 8 33
(Richard Spencer) *chsd ldrs: rdn and lost pl over 2f out: wknd over 1f out* **22/1**

2300 **9** *2* **Littleton Hall (IRE)**[22] 7754 2-9-1 **69**........................ KieranO'Neill 9 23
(Mick Channon) *pushed along and prom: rdn over 2f out: wknd over 1f out* **66/1**

0111 **10** *9* **Queens Blade**[34] 7329 2-8-12 **66**..............................(b) DuranFentiman 11
(Tim Easterby) *sn led: hdd over 2f out: wknd over 1f out (trainer's rep said filly was unsuited by testing conditions and would prefer a quicker surface)* **18/1**

060 **11** *5* **Asstech (IRE)**[75] 5856 2-8-12 **69**............................. ConnorMurtagh(3) 7
(Richard Fahey) *s.i.s: pushed along in rr whn nt clr run over 2f out: sn wknd* **16/1**

1m 16.19s (3.59) **Going Correction** +0.55s/f (Yiel) **11** Ran SP% **113.9**
Speed ratings (Par 95): **98,95,93,92,90 88,87,76,74,62 55**
CSF £29.16 CT £174.52 TOTE £7.40: £2.60, £1.50, £2.80; EX 37.00 Trifecta £192.60.
Owner Shane Fairweather & Dr C Scott **Bred** Caroline Scott & Shane Fairweather **Trained** West Wickham, Cambs

FOCUS
The final meeting of Yarmouth's season and it was genuinely soft underfoot, as advertised by the winning time of the first race. This run-of-the-mill nursery looked to be wide open on paper. The runner-up sets the standard.

8431 BRITISH EUROPEAN BREEDERS FUND EBF FILLIES' NOVICE STKS (PLUS 10 RACE) 6f 3y
2:15 (2:16) (Class 4) 2-Y-O
£4,851 (£1,443; £721; £360) **Stalls** Centre

Form RPR

1 **Lady Light** 2-9-0 0.. HayleyTurner 1 86+
(Michael Bell) *hld up: hdwy over 2f out: led and edgd rt over 1f out: r.o wl* **8/1**

544 **2** *4 1/2* **Vintage Polly (IRE)**[14] 7995 2-9-0 70..........................(p[1]) JamesDoyle 8 71
(Hugo Palmer) *chsd ldrs: led over 2f out: rdn and hdd over 1f out: styd on same pce fnl f* **13/2**

05 **3** *1/2* **Ikebana**[25] 7644 2-9-0 0.. DavidEgan 5 70
(Roger Varian) *prom: rdn over 1f out: styd on same pce fnl f* **9/2**[2]

5 **4** *1/2* **Harbour Point**[8] 8202 2-8-11 0................................. TheodoreLadd(3) 7 68
(Michael Appleby) *hld up: plld hrd: swtchd lft and hdwy over 1f out: nt trble ldrs (jockey said filly hung left-handed throughout)* **66/1**

3 **5** *3 1/2* **Made For All (FR)**[25] 7644 2-8-11 0......................... HarrisonShaw(3) 3 58
(K R Burke) *sn led: hdd over 2f out: rdn and edgd rt over 1f out: wknd ins fnl f* **6/5**[1]

6 *1 1/4* **Shymay** 2-9-0 0.. TomQueally 2 54
(George Margarson) *plld hrd prom: rdn over 1f out: wknd ins fnl f* **16/1**

66 **7** *1 1/4* **Don'tyouwantmebaby (IRE)**[21] 7786 2-9-0 0.............. StevieDonohoe 9 50
(Richard Spencer) *hld up: rdn and wknd over 1f out* **33/1**

4 **8** *4 1/2* **Lady Tati (IRE)**[70] 6047 2-9-0 0.............................. SilvestreDeSousa 6 37
(David Simcock) *chsd ldrs: rdn over 2f out: nt clr run and wknd over 1f out (jockey said filly had no more to give and lugged left-handed under pressure)* **6/1**[3]

9 *31* **Molly Shaw** 2-9-0 0...(h[1]) GeorgeWood 4
(Chris Wall) *chsd ldrs: pushed along lost pl 4f out: wknd over 2f out (jockey said filly ran very green; trainer said filly was unsuited by the ground and would prefer a quicker surface)* **25/1**

1m 16.55s (3.95) **Going Correction** +0.55s/f (Yiel) **9** Ran SP% **116.5**
Speed ratings (Par 94): **95,89,88,87,83 81,79,73,32**
CSF £58.39 TOTE £7.00: £2.20, £1.90, £1.50; EX 40.00 Trifecta £303.50.
Owner China Horse Club International Limited **Bred** Whitsbury Manor Stud **Trained** Newmarket, Suffolk

FOCUS
This modest fillies' novice event was run at a solid enough pace. The second helps guide the opening level.

8432 BRITISH STALLION STUDS EBF FILLIES' NOVICE STKS (PLUS 10 RACE) 1m 3y
2:50 (2:51) (Class 4) 2-Y-O
£4,463 (£1,328; £663; £331) **Stalls** Centre

Form RPR

1 **Cabaletta** 2-9-0 0... DavidEgan 9 82+
(Roger Varian) *s.i.s: sn prom: shkn up to ld over 1f out: edgd lft: styd on* **6/1**

2 *1* **Frankly Darling** 2-9-0 0... NickyMackay 1 80+
(John Gosden) *led 2f: chsd ldrs: led again over 2f out: hdd over 1f out: edgd lft: styd on same pce wl ins fnl f* **7/2**[2]

3 *2* **Combine (IRE)** 2-9-0 0... JamesDoyle 2 76
(Hugo Palmer) *hld up: swtchd lft and hdwy over 2f out: ev ch over 1f out: no ex wl ins fnl f* **9/1**

44 **4** *4* **My Poem**[19] 7832 2-9-0 0.. LouisSteward 7 67
(Sir Michael Stoute) *trckd ldrs: nt clr run over 2f out: no ex fnl f* **5/1**[3]

5 *2 1/2* **Float (IRE)** 2-9-0 0... StevieDonohoe 5 62
(David Simcock) *s.i.s: in rr: shkn up over 1f out: styd on ins fnl f: nvr nrr* **14/1**

4 **6** *2 1/4* **Too Big To Fail (IRE)**[13] 8028 2-9-0 0........................... JFEgan 6 57
(Mark Johnston) *chsd ldrs: reminder over 4f out: rdn and hung lft over 2f out: wknd over 1f out* **6/4**[1]

00 **7** *hd* **Pax Britannica (IRE)**[24] 7695 2-9-0 0........................ MartinDwyer 3 56
(David Simcock) *chsd ldrs on outer: shkn up over 1f out: wknd fnl f* **33/1**

0 **8** *3 1/4* **Wendreda**[20] 7826 2-9-0 0... GeraldMosse 8 49
(Mrs Ilka Gansera-Leveque) *prom: led 6f out tl over 2f out: rdn: edgd lft and wknd over 1f out* **50/1**

00 **9** *13* **Havana Princess**[63] 6314 2-9-0 0.................................. RyanTate 4 20
(Dr Jon Scargill) *chsd ldrs: lost pl over 3f out: wknd 2f out* **100/1**

1m 43.89s (5.69) **Going Correction** +0.55s/f (Yiel) **9** Ran SP% **115.7**
Speed ratings (Par 94): **93,92,90,86,83 81,81,77,64**
CSF £27.21 TOTE £5.50: £1.20, £1.50, £2.50; EX 30.90 Trifecta £238.40.
Owner Cheveley Park Stud **Bred** Cheveley Park Stud Ltd **Trained** Newmarket, Suffolk

FOCUS
Usually an informative contest. They kept stands' side and the principals came clear. The opening level is fluid.

8433 COMPARE BOOKMAKERS SITES AT BONUSCODEBETS.CO.UK H'CAP 1m 3f 104y
3:25 (3:25) (Class 5) (0-75,75) 3-Y-O+
£3,428 (£1,020; £509; £300; £300; £300) **Stalls** Low

Form RPR

3623 **1** **Royal Family (FR)**[41] 7081 3-9-5 **75**..............................(t) LouisSteward 1 85
(Amy Murphy) *chsd ldrs: led over 2f out: rdn over 1f out: styd on* **33/1**

1532 **2** *3/4* **Potenza (IRE)**[66] 6232 3-8-13 **69**................................. RyanTate 7 77
(James Eustace) *hld up: hdwy over 3f out: rdn over 1f out: ev ch ins fnl f: kpt on* **4/1**[2]

1064 **3** *5* **Edmond Dantes (IRE)**[52] 6722 3-8-7 **70**.......... Pierre-LouisJamin(7) 13 71+
(David Menuisier) *hld up: hdwy on outer over 6f out: rdn and ev ch over 1f out: wknd wl ins fnl f* **9/1**

0121 **4** *1 3/4* **Harmonise**[30] 6371 5-9-4 **69**...................................... KieranO'Neill 12 66
(Sheena West) *led: hdd over 2f out: wknd ins fnl f* **7/1**[3]

-565 **5** *1 1/2* **Awesomedude**[162] 2697 3-8-7 **63**.........................(vt[1] w) JosephineGordon 2 59
(Mrs Ilka Gansera-Leveque) *hld up: pushed along over 4f out: hdwy u.p over 1f out: nt trble ldrs (vet said gelding lost right fore shoe)* **10/1**

1013 **6** *1/2* **Blowing Dixie**[18] 7872 3-8-11 **67**.................................. JFEgan 9 62
(Jane Chapple-Hyam) *rrd s: sn prom: rdn over 2f out: wknd fnl f* **10/1**

06-3 **7** *1/2* **Westbrook Bertie**[13] 8033 4-9-2 **72**........................... ScottMcCullagh(5) 10 66
(Mick Channon) *hld up in tch: plld hrd: rdn over 1f out: wknd ins fnl f* **4/1**[2]

042 **8** *1 1/4* **Lord Halifax (IRE)**[113] 4459 3-9-2 **72**............................(t[1]) StevieDonohoe 3 65
(Charlie Fellowes) *s.i.s: hld up: rdn over 2f out: edgd lft over 1f out: n.d (jockey said gelding was never travelling)* **7/2**[1]

00 **9** *5* **Great Hall**[37] 7394 9-9-5 **70**.. TomQueally 6 54
(Mick Quinn) *hld up: rdn over 2f out: wknd over 1f out (vet said gelding lost right fore shoe)* **40/1**

4060 **10** *11* **Sheberghan (IRE)**[13] 8014 4-9-9 **74**..........................(p) SilvestreDeSousa 11 42
(Ed Dunlop) *chsd ldr: rdn over 2f out: wknd over 1f out: eased (jockey said gelding stopped quickly; trainer's rep said gelding was unsuited by the testing conditions and would therefore prefer a quicker surface)* **16/1**

3550 **11** *22* **Seeusoon (IRE)**[24] 7683 3-8-11 **67**............................... MartinDwyer 14 3
(Andrew Balding) *mid-div: rdn over 3f out: wknd over 2f out (jockey said gelding stopped quickly)* **20/1**

2m 33.35s (5.55) **Going Correction** +0.55s/f (Yiel) **11** Ran SP% **118.9**
WFA 3 from 4yo+ 5lb
Speed ratings (Par 103): **101,100,96,95,94 94,93,92,89,81 65**
CSF £160.67 CT £1330.49 TOTE £22.30: £5.90, £1.60, £2.80; EX 262.90 Trifecta £1729.20.
Owner Amy Murphy **Bred** E A R L Qatar Bloodstock Ltd **Trained** Newmarket, Suffolk

FOCUS
The first pair drew clear in this modest handicap. The winner has been rated in line with her Chelmsford run two starts back.

8434 JARK (KL) LTD H'CAP 1m 2f 23y
4:00 (4:00) (Class 6) (0-65,65) 3-Y-O+
£2,781 (£827; £413; £300; £300; £300) **Stalls** Low

Form RPR
222 **1** **Bruyere (FR)**[13] 8033 3-9-7 **65**..(h) MartinDwyer 1 71
(Dean Ivory) *chsd ldrs: led wl over 2f out: rdn and hung rt fr over 1f out: styd on u.p* **5/1**[2]
3304 **2** *1* **Carey Street (IRE)**[33] 7363 3-9-7 **65**........................ JosephineGordon 2 69
(John Quinn) *led 3f: chsd ldr tl led again over 4f out: hdd wl over 2f out: rdn over 1f out: styd on* **15/2**
0346 **3** *shd* **Bolt N Brown**[8] 8196 3-9-4 **62**..(vt[1]) DavidEgan 9 66
(Gay Kelleway) *chsd ldrs: outpcd over 2f out: rallied over 1f out: r.o* **7/1**[3]
0004 **4** *nk* **Lynchpin (IRE)**[8] 8205 3-8-2 **51** oh4 ow1..............(b) RayDawson(5) 13 54
(Lydia Pearce) *hld up in tch: rdn over 1f out: styd on* **28/1**
0501 **5** *6* **Mac Ailey**[8] 8205 3-9-0 **58** 6ex.............................. RachelRichardson 15 51
(Tim Easterby) *prom: rdn over 1f out: wknd fnl f* **3/1**[1]
0055 **6** *3/4* **Sociologist (FR)**[13] 8033 4-8-11 **58**........................(p) JonathanFisher(7) 3 48
(Scott Dixon) *chsd ldr: led over 7f out tl over 4f out: rdn over 2f out: wknd over 1f out* **8/1**
2251 **7** *hd* **Hidden Dream (IRE)**[14] 8000 4-8-10 **50** oh2..............(p) KieranO'Neill 12 40
(Christine Dunnett) *chsd ldrs: rdn over 1f out: wknd ins fnl f* **20/1**
2314 **8** *2 3/4* **Catch My Breath**[8] 8186 3-9-4 **65**........................... DarraghKeenan(3) 8 51
(John Ryan) *s.s: hld up: hdwy and swtchd rt over 2f out: rdn and wknd over 1f out (jockey said gelding was slowly away)* **8/1**
0050 **9** *7* **Reformed Character (IRE)**[48] 6860 3-8-6 **50** oh5.......(b) JimmyQuinn 5 23
(Lydia Pearce) *hld up: hdwy over 6f out: rdn over 2f out: wknd over 1f out* **50/1**
5200 **10** *2* **Militry Decoration (IRE)**[13] 8033 4-9-4 **58**........................ RyanTate 11 27
(Dr Jon Scargill) *s.i.s: hld up: rdn over 3f out: wknd over 2f out* **12/1**
3400 **11** *8* **Percy Toplis**[8] 8204 5-8-10 **50** oh3..............................(b) AdrianMcCarthy 6 4
(Christine Dunnett) *s.i.s: a in rr: eased over 1f out* **33/1**
6005 **12** *nk* **Burguillos**[28] 7545 6-9-10 **64**......................................(t) LouisSteward 7 18
(John Butler) *hld up in tch: lost pl 7f out: sme hdwy over 3f out: sn rdn: wknd over 2f out: eased over 1f out* **20/1**
0040 **13** *1* **Global Rock (FR)**[19] 7858 3-9-2 **60**.....................(b[1]) SilvestreDeSousa 14 13
(Ed Dunlop) *hld up: rdn over 3f out: sn wknd and eased (jockey said gelding stopped quickly; trainer's rep said gelding was unsuited by the testing conditions and would prefer a quicker surface.)* **20/1**
0000 **14** *4 1/2* **Bated Beauty (IRE)**[13] 8033 4-9-3 **57**........................... TomQueally 10 1
(John Butler) *s.i.s: a in rr: bhd fnl 6f: eased over 1f out* **66/1**
0000 **15** *4* **Best Haaf**[8] 8205 3-8-9 **56**..(h[1]) TheodoreLadd(3) 16
(Michael Appleby) *s.i.s: sn pushed along in rr: bhd fnl 6f: eased* **40/1**

2m 14.41s (5.61) **Going Correction** +0.55s/f (Yiel)
WFA 3 from 4yo+ 4lb **15 Ran SP% 122.4**
Speed ratings (Par 101): **99,98,98,97,93 92,92,90,84,82 76,76,75,71,68**
CSF £38.33 CT £270.29 TOTE £6.00: £1.90, £2.60, £2.90; EX 41.90 Trifecta £322.00.
Owner Heather & Michael Yarrow **Bred** Merriebelle Irish Farm Ltd **Trained** Radlett, Herts

FOCUS
There was a tight four-way finish in this ordinary handicap. Straightforward, sound late season form.

8435 LAVISH HAIR BEAUTY AESTHETICS H'CAP 6f 3y
4:30 (4:49) (Class 6) (0-65,65) 3-Y-O+
£2,781 (£827; £413; £300; £300; £300) **Stalls** Centre

Form RPR
0040 **1** **Herringswell (FR)**[33] 7374 4-8-0 **46** oh1..................... LauraPearson(7) 9 56+
(Henry Spiller) *hld up: swtchd lft over 3f out: hdwy over 2f out: led over 1f out: rdn clr (trainer's rep said, regarding apparent improvement in form, the filly appreciated the return to Yarmouth having won she previously)* **6/1**
6530 **2** *3 3/4* **Tulloona**[41] 7080 3-9-10 **64**..(w) DavidEgan 2 63
(Tom Clover) *chsd ldrs: nt clr run over 2f out: rdn over 1f out: styd on same pce ins fnl f* **5/1**[3]
2040 **3** *hd* **Phoenix Star (IRE)**[19] 7837 3-9-6 **60**..................(t) SilvestreDeSousa 10 58
(Stuart Williams) *hld up: hdwy on outer over 1f out: sn rdn: styd on same pce ins fnl f* **11/4**[1]
336- **4** *4 1/2* **Drop Kick Murphi (IRE)**[340] 9098 5-8-7 **46** oh1......... AdrianMcCarthy 1 31
(Christine Dunnett) *led 1f: chsd ldrs: rdn and ev ch over 1f out: wknd ins fnl f* **25/1**
0500 **5** *2* **Reshaan (IRE)**[6] 8256 4-8-4 **46** oh1..........................(p) TheodoreLadd(3) 5 25
(Alexandra Dunn) *s.i.s: rcvrd to ld 5f out: hdd over 2f out: wknd fnl f* **7/1**
6550 **6** *nk* **Alabama Dreaming**[7] 8217 3-9-10 **64**........................ HayleyTurner 12 42
(George Scott) *chsd ldrs: led over 2f out: rdn and hdd over 1f out: wknd fnl f* **10/1**
4006 **7** *nk* **Spenny's Lass**[7] 8235 4-8-4 **46** oh1..........................(v) DarraghKeenan(3) 4 23
(John Ryan) *chsd ldrs tl rdn and wknd over 1f out* **7/1**
6453 **8** *10* **Kraka (IRE)**[14] 7986 4-9-7 **60**......................................(p) JimmyQuinn 7 7
(Christine Dunnett) *s.s: a in rr: eased over 1f out* **4/1**[2]

1m 16.11s (3.51) **Going Correction** +0.55s/f (Yiel)
WFA 3 from 4yo+ 1lb **8 Ran SP% 115.6**
Speed ratings (Par 101): **98,93,92,86,84 83,83,69**
CSF £36.33 CT £101.83 TOTE £5.70: £2.10, £1.70, £1.40; EX 39.40 Trifecta £153.60.
Owner The Champagne Poppers **Bred** Brendan Boyle Bloodstock Ltd **Trained** Newmarket, Suffolk
■ Jean Valjean was withdrawn. Price at time of withdrawal 15/2. Rule 4 applies to board prices prior to withdrawal. Deduct 10p in the pound. New market formed.

FOCUS
This weak sprint handicap was delayed by 19mins due to the bizarre situation of Jean Valjean getting loose and then lost in that time. It's been rated a bit cautiously around the second and third.

8436 PETER DUNNETT 21 YEAR MEMORIAL H'CAP 7f 3y
5:00 (5:31) (Class 6) (0-65,63) 3-Y-O+
£2,781 (£827; £413; £300; £300; £300) **Stalls** Centre

Form RPR
1202 **1** **Dutch Story**[8] 8207 3-9-1 **56**..(p) MartinDwyer 8 68
(Amanda Perrett) *w ldrs: led over 4f out: rdn clr fnl f* **10/11**[1]
3000 **2** *8* **Confrerie (IRE)**[14] 7982 4-9-7 **60**........................ JosephineGordon 5 53
(George Baker) *s.i.s: hld up: hdwy u.p over 2f out: styd on to go 2nd wl ins fnl f: no ch w wnr* **22/1**
5550 **3** *1 1/4* **Kodiac Lass (IRE)**[27] 7573 3-9-7 **60**..........................(h[1]) DavidEgan 4 51
(Marco Botti) *sn pushed along in rr: hdwy u.p over 1f out: styd on to go 3rd post* **20/1**
4404 **4** *shd* **Reasoned (IRE)**[8] 8207 3-9-3 **58**...................................(p[1]) RyanTate 7 47
(James Eustace) *led 1f: chsd ldrs: rdn over 1f out: wknd ins fnl f* **12/1**
6056 **5** *1 1/2* **Ocean Temptress**[5] 8279 5-8-3 **47** oh1 ow1..............(b) RayDawson(5) 9 33
(Louise Allan) *led 6f out: hdd over 4f out: rdn and outpcd over 2f out: n.d after* **18/1**
0600 **6** *1* **Soaring Spirits (IRE)**[36] 7273 9-8-8 **52**...........(b) SophieRalston(5) 6 35
(Dean Ivory) *s.i.s: hld up: hdwy over 2f out: rdn over 1f out: wknd fnl f* **28/1**
3605 **7** *1/2* **Agent Of Fortune**[6] 8255 4-9-0 **53**.............................(p) HayleyTurner 3 35
(Christine Dunnett) *sn outpcd: nvr on terms* **7/1**[2]
0604 **8** *1/2* **Spencers Son (IRE)**[8] 8206 3-9-3 **63**......................(b) SeanKirrane(5) 10 43
(Richard Spencer) *prom: rdn over 2f out: wknd over 1f out* **11/1**[3]
0000 **9** *3 3/4* **Bevsboy (IRE)**[6] 8266 5-8-4 **46** oh1.............................. TheodoreLadd(3) 2 18
(Lynn Siddall) *chsd ldrs: rdn over 2f out: wknd over 1f out* **66/1**
0520 **10** *shd* **Princess Florence (IRE)**[8] 8205 3-8-4 **52**............... LauraPearson(7) 11 22
(John Ryan) *hld up: rdn over 2f out: sn wknd* **28/1**
0310 **11** *5* **Hi Ho Silver**[29] 7527 5-9-4 **57**.. GeraldMosse 1 16
(Chris Wall) *s.i.s: sn pushed along in rr: wknd over 2f out: eased over 1f out (jockey said gelding was never travelling; trainer said gelding was unsuited to these testing conditions and would prefer a quicker surface)* **7/1**[2]

1m 28.3s (3.20) **Going Correction** +0.55s/f (Yiel)
WFA 3 from 4yo+ 2lb **11 Ran SP% 116.2**
Speed ratings (Par 101): **103,93,92,92,90 89,88,88,84,83 78**
CSF £30.82 CT £258.88 TOTE £1.70: £1.10, £5.00, £3.30; EX 26.10 Trifecta £289.40.
Owner Mr & Mrs R Scott & & Mrs D Bevan **Bred** Mr & Mrs R & P Scott **Trained** Pulborough, W Sussex

FOCUS
This delayed finale was a soft race and it proved one-way traffic.
T/Plt: £410.20 to a £1 stake. Pool: £57,447.43 - 102.21 winning units T/Qpdt: £43.80 to a £1 stake. Pool: £7,618.63 - 128.51 winning units **Colin Roberts**

8437 - 8444a (Foreign Racing) - See Raceform Interactive

6584
DEAUVILLE (R-H)
Tuesday, October 22

OFFICIAL GOING: Polytrack: standard; turf: heavy

8445a PRIX VULCAIN (LISTED RACE) (3YO) (ROUND COURSE) (TURF) 1m 4f 110y
1:20 3-Y-0 £24,774 (£9,909; £7,432; £4,954; £2,477)

RPR
1 **Palomba (IRE)**[18] 7888 3-8-10 0.. OlivierPeslier 4 108
(C Laffon-Parias, France) **27/10**[2]
2 *8* **Argyron (IRE)**[31] 7478 3-9-0 0.............................. Pierre-CharlesBoudot 1 99
(A Fabre, France) **31/5**
3 *nk* **Visage (IRE)**[30] 3-8-10 0.. CristianDemuro 3 94
(J-C Rouget, France) **49/10**[3]
4 *4* **Scarlet Tufty (FR)**[61] 6385 3-9-0 0.. JulienAuge 6 92
(C Ferland, France) **10/1**
5 *1 1/4* **Qarasu (IRE)**[27] 7565 3-9-0 0.................................... MickaelBarzalona 7 90
(Roger Charlton) *w.w in fnl pair: tk clsr order on outer over 3f out: pushed along and effrt over 2f out: edgd lft u.p: one pce ins fnl f: no ex* **11/10**[1]
6 *15* **Alabaa**[43] 7045 3-9-0 0.. TheoBachelot 8 66
(L Gadbin, France) **18/1**

2m 56.96s (10.56) **6 Ran SP% 119.8**
PARI-MUTUEL (all including 1 euro stake): WIN 3.70; PLACE 1.50, 2.10; SF 9.50.
Owner Wertheimer & Frere **Bred** Wertheimer & Frere **Trained** Chantilly, France

8446a PRIX ZEDDAAN (LISTED RACE) (2YO) (STRAIGHT COURSE) (TURF) 6f
1:55 2-Y-0 £27,027 (£10,810; £8,108; £5,405; £2,702)

RPR
1 **Abama (FR)**[36] 7292 2-8-9 0.. StephanePasquier 5 95
(Y Barberot, France) **22/5**
2 *nk* **Bavaria Baby (FR)**[22] 2-8-9 0.................................... MickaelBarzalona 7 94
(F Chappet, France) **31/10**[2]
3 *3/4* **Gold Step (FR)**[37] 2-8-9 0.. TheoBachelot 6 92
(F Rossi, France) **41/5**
4 *1* **Gifted Ruler**[25] 7645 2-8-13 0.................................... RichardKingscote 1 93
(Tom Dascombe) *prom on nr side rail: pushed along and effrt 2f out: limited rspnse and sn rdn: kpt on ins fnl f: nvr gng pce to threaten* **43/10**[3]
5 *nk* **Lorelei Rock (IRE)**[22] 7775 2-8-9 0..............................(b) CristianDemuro 2 88
(G Botti, France) **10/1**
6 *3 1/2* **Maystar (IRE)**[37] 7247 2-8-13 0..(p) HollieDoyle 4 81
(Archie Watson) *led: tried to qckn over 2f out: hdd 1 1/2f out: grad wknd u.p fr over 1f out: no ex* **8/5**[1]

1m 17.18s (6.18) **6 Ran SP% 120.2**
PARI-MUTUEL (all including 1 euro stake): WIN 5.40; PLACE 1.60, 1.50; SF 9.70.
Owner Malcolm Parrish **Bred** T De La Heronniere & Sarl Jedburgh Stud **Trained** France

8447a PRIX DE VARANVILLE (MAIDEN) (2YO) (STRAIGHT COURSE) (TURF) 6f
2:35 2-Y-0 £12,162 (£4,864; £3,648; £2,432; £1,216)

RPR
1 **Lin Chong**[39] 7160 2-9-2 0.. OlivierPeslier 6 82+
(Paul Cole) *mde virtually all: 2 l clr gng best over 2f out: shkn up ent fnl f: kpt on strly: v readily* **3/1**[2]
2 *3* **Jenufa (FR)** 2-8-13 0.. VincentCheminaud 1 69
(H-A Pantall, France) **51/10**[3]
3 *snk* **Calypso Rose (IRE)**[15] 2-8-13 0.. AlexisBadel 8 69
(H-F Devin, France) **12/1**
4 *1 3/4* **Bentley Mood (IRE)** 2-9-2 0.. CristianDemuro 10 66
(G Botti, France) **10/1**
5 *snk* **Zelote (FR)**[15] 2-9-2 0.............................. Pierre-CharlesBoudot 9 66
(Mme M Bollack-Badel, France) **59/10**
6 *4* **Green Backspin (IRE)**[39] 2-9-2 0.. AntoineHamelin 3 54
(Gavin Hernon, France) **22/1**
7 *1 1/4* **Dalacrown (IRE)** 2-8-8 0.. AurelienLemaitre 5 42
(J-V Toux, France) **17/1**
8 *hd* **Over Attracted (USA)** 2-8-13 0.............................. MickaelBarzalona 2 47
(F Chappet, France) **21/10**[1]
9 *1 3/4* **Agnostic (IRE)**[15] 2-9-2 0.. RonanThomas 4 44
(C Lerner, France) **34/1**

10 5½ **Style Major (FR)**[15] 2-9-2 0 .... JeromeCabre 7 28
(Mlle V Dissaux, France) **42/1**
1m 16.69s (5.69) **10** Ran SP% **120.0**
PARI-MUTUEL (all including 1 euro stake): WIN 4.00; PLACE 1.70, 1.80, 3.00; DF 11.10.
Owner Hurun UK Racing **Bred** Rabbah Bloodstock Limited **Trained** Whatcombe, Oxon

8448a PRIX DE PUTANGES (CLAIMER) (2YO) (ALL-WEATHER TRACK) (POLYTRACK) 1m 1f 110y(P)
3:45 2-Y-O **£12,162** (£4,864; £3,648; £2,432; £1,216)

RPR
1 **Makito** 2-8-9 0 .... JenteMarien(6) 3 77
(C Laffon-Parias, France) **11/5**[1]
2 shd **The First King (IRE)** 2-9-4 0 ....(b[1]) TonyPiccone 10 80
(Paul Cole) *cl up on outer: drvn to keep tabs on ldr over 3f out: responded for press to renew chal over 1f out: kpt on wl ins fnl f: jst hld* **19/5**[3]
3 3½ **Rubiglia (FR)** 2-8-6 0 .... AlexandreChesneau(5) 9 66
(G Botti, France) **33/1**
4 2 **High Charm (FR)**[11] 2-8-3 0 .... MlleAmbreMolins(8) 8 62+
(S Wattel, France) **33/10**[2]
5 1¼ **Mixologist (FR)**[53] 2-8-4 0 .... ClementGuitraud(7) 2 60
(Y Barberot, France) **8/1**
6 1 **Mr Shady (IRE)**[60] 6433 2-8-6 0 ....(p) AlexisPouchin(5) 4 58
(J S Moore) *hld up in fnl trio: pushed along over 2f out: limited rspnse and sn rdn: kpt on same pce ins fnl f: nvr a factor* **79/10**
7 snk **Happy Chrisnat (FR)**[43] 7043 2-9-1 0 ....(p) AntoineHamelin 1 61
(C Plisson, France) **18/1**
8 3 **Secret Player (FR)** 2-8-11 0 .... PierreBazire 7 51
(G Botti, France) **13/1**
9 12 **Got Charm (FR)** 2-8-9 0 ow1 ....(p) SebastienMartino 5 26
(Edouard Monfort, France) **15/1**
1m 59.39s **9** Ran SP% **119.3**
PARI-MUTUEL (all including 1 euro stake): WIN 3.20; PLACE 1.60, 2.20, 7.10; DF 6.40.
Owner Tolmi Racing Sc, Alain Jathiere & Philip Booth **Bred** Stilvi Compagnia Financiera Sa **Trained** Chantilly, France

8449a PRIX D'AMFREVILLE (CLAIMER) (3YO) (STRAIGHT COURSE) (TURF) 6f
4:20 3-Y-O **£10,360** (£4,144; £3,108; £2,072; £1,036)

RPR
1 **Bonarda (FR)**[11] 3-8-11 0 .... MlleCoraliePacaut(4) 9 75
(M Boutin, France) **42/10**[3]
2 nk **Tosen Shauna (IRE)**[19] 3-8-10 0 .... MlleAmbreMolins(9) 6 78
(F Rossi, France) **2/1**[1]
3 snk **Dancing Mountain (IRE)**[38] 3-8-5 0 ....(b) ThomasTrullier(3) 5 67
(P Monfort, France) **14/1**
4 1 **Champion Brogie (IRE)**[22] 7760 3-8-6 0 .... AlexisPouchin(5) 8 67
(J S Moore) *hld up in rr: pushed along and prog fr 2f out: drvn over 1f out: kpt on ins fnl f but nvr gng pce to chal* **28/1**
5 1¼ **Spanish Miss (IRE)**[70] 3-8-8 0 .... GregoryBenoist 7 60
(Mlle A Wattel, France) **53/10**
6 5 **Silver Amerhican (FR)**[10] 3-9-8 0 ....(p) ClementLecoeuvre 2 58
(Matthieu Palussiere, France) **83/10**
7 2 **Mya George (FR)**[81] 3-8-8 0 .... AurelienLemaitre 3 37
(G Doleuze, France) **30/1**
8 nk **Cool Reflection (IRE)**[68] 6108 3-8-9 0 .... MlleFriedaValleSkar(9) 4 46
(Sofie Lanslots, France) **19/1**
9 3 **Matista (IRE)**[65] 6267 3-9-5 0 .... Pierre-CharlesBoudot 1 38
(H-A Pantall, France) **37/10**[2]
1m 16.26s (5.26) **9** Ran SP% **118.8**
PARI-MUTUEL (all including 1 euro stake): WIN 5.20; PLACE 1.60, 1.30, 2.40; DF 5.00.
Owner Diego Fernandez-Ortega & Mme Marie-Carmen Boutin **Bred** S.C.E.A. Des Prairies, B Jeffroy & T Jeffroy **Trained** France

8415 # KEMPTON (A.W) (R-H)
Wednesday, October 23

OFFICIAL GOING: Polytrack: standard to slow
Wind: Virtually nil Weather: Overcast

8450 32RED CASINO H'CAP 5f (P)
4:40 (4:40) (Class 6) (0-55,54) 3-Y-O+
£3,105 (£924; £461; £400; £400; £400) **Stalls** Low

Form RPR
0-40 1 **Miss Gradenko**[7] 8249 3-9-3 **50** .... RaulDaSilva 4 55
(Robert Cowell) *prom in 4th: pushed along to chse ldrs 2f out: rdn 1f out: styd on wl to ld fnl 50yds* **12/1**
2561 2 nk **Katherine Place**[22] 7784 4-9-7 **54** ....(t) RyanTate 9 57+
(Bill Turner) *broke wl and moved over fr wd stall to trck ldr: rdn along to ld over 1f out: drvn and kpt on fnl f: hdd by wnr fnl 50yds* **9/2**[1]
-505 3 hd **Chocco Star (IRE)**[132] 3775 3-9-6 **53** .... JoeyHaynes 6 56
(Chelsea Banham) *dwlt and racd in rr: bmpd along in rr over 2f out: rdn and kpt on strly ins fnl f: nt quite rch ldng pair* **20/1**
1400 4 nk **Knockout Blow**[37] 7274 4-9-7 **54** ....(p) DanielMuscutt 2 55
(John E Long) *pushed along to hold position in midfield: rdn and hdwy between rivals over 1f out: kpt on wl fnl f: nt rch ldrs* **11/2**[3]
0000 5 1¼ **Kibaar**[21] 7824 7-9-3 **50** .... JamesSullivan 8 47
(Ruth Carr) *dwlt and racd in rr: pushed along and wd off home bnd 2f out: rdn and late hdwy fnl f but n.d* **16/1**
0-20 6 ½ **Blackcurrent**[13] 8071 3-9-3 **50** .... DavidNolan 7 46
(Alan Brown) *led: rdn along and hdd over 1f out: wknd fnl f* **8/1**
5303 7 ½ **Edged Out**[20] 7844 9-9-4 **54** .... MitchGodwin(3) 3 47
(Christopher Mason) *prom on inner: swtchd lft off heels and rdn to chse ldrs 2f out: one pce and lost several pls ins fnl f* **5/1**[2]
2320 8 nse **Spot Lite**[38] 7230 4-9-5 **52** ....(p) LukeMorris 1 45
(Rod Millman) *chsd along in midfield to hold position: rdn and no hdwy over 1f out: one pce fnl f* **9/2**[1]
2030 9 1¾ **Arnoul Of Metz**[21] 7824 4-9-4 **51** ....(p) HollieDoyle 10 38
(Henry Spiller) *outpcd in last pair: rdn and detached 2f out: nvr on terms (jockey said gelding hung left-handed)* **7/1**

-300 10 1½ **Catheadans Fiyah**[14] 8018 3-9-2 **49** .... LiamKeniry 5 31
(Martin Bosley) *racd in midfield: effrt whn short of room over 1f out: wknd fnl f* **16/1**
59.91s (-0.59) **Going Correction** -0.025s/f (Stan) **10** Ran SP% **116.2**
Speed ratings (Par 101): **103,102,102,101,99 98,98,98,95,92**
CSF £65.14 CT £1104.91 TOTE £20.60: £5.20, £1.70, £4.20; EX 94.10 Trifecta £2029.40.
Owner Bottisham Heath Stud **Bred** Bottisham Heath Stud **Trained** Six Mile Bottom, Cambs

FOCUS
Just a moderate sprint and a bunched finish.

8451 100% PROFIT BOOST AT 32REDSPORT.COM NOVICE MEDIAN AUCTION STKS 1m 3f 219y(P)
5:10 (5:12) (Class 5) 3-5-Y-O **£3,881** (£1,155; £577; £288) **Stalls** Low

Form RPR
425- 1 **Capla Crusader**[319] 9460 3-9-0 77 .... WilliamCarver(5) 9 70
(Nick Littmoden) *trckd ldr: pushed along and drifted lft over 1f out: rdn and styd on wl to ld ins fnl f: kpt on wl* **8/1**
03 2 ½ **Torbellino**[51] 6811 3-9-0 0 .... KierenFox 2 64
(John Best) *trckd ldng pair: effrt to cl 2 out: rdn along to ld ins fnl f: sn hdd by wnr and no ex (jockey said filly ran too free)* **11/8**[1]
34 3 3 **End Over End**[15] 7999 3-9-0 0 .... HollieDoyle 1 60
(Archie Watson) *led and racd freely: rdn along and hdd ins fnl f: one pce clsng stages* **4/1**[2]
4 nk **Brighton Pier (GER)** 3-9-5 0 .... LukeMorris 6 64+
(Harry Dunlop) *racd in midfield: swtchd lft and pushed along over 2f out: sn rdn and kpt on wl ins fnl f: bttr for run* **14/1**
4 5 2 **Badessa**[44] 7035 3-9-0 0 .... LiamKeniry 5 56
(Andrew Balding) *dwlt and rcvrd to r in midfield: pushed along and outpcd 3f out: sn rdn and no hdwy 2f out: kpt on one pce fnl f* **5/1**[3]
5 6 2½ **Social City**[30] 7525 3-9-5 0 .... JFEgan 8 57
(Tony Carroll) *dwlt and racd in rr: minor hdwy 2f out: rdn and mde sme late hdwy: nvr a factor* **66/1**
0- 7 hd **Border Warrior**[315] 9499 3-9-5 0 .... CharlesBishop 7 57
(Henry Candy) *prom: rdn along and readily outpcd over 2f out: one pce after* **9/1**
8 9 **Hey Gracie** 3-9-0 0 .... RyanTate 11 37
(Mark Usher) *hld up: rdn in rr over 2f out: nvr on terms* **66/1**
60 9 2 **Smart Samba (IRE)**[15] 7999 3-9-5 0 ....(b[1]) TomQueally 10 39
(Chris Wall) *j.lft and racd in rr: a bhd* **66/1**
40 10 16 **Lilly's Legacy**[23] 7772 3-8-11 0 .... MitchGodwin(3) 4 8
(Nikki Evans) *racd in midfield: rdn along and lost pl over 2f out: sn detached* **150/1**
11 shd **Tinkerbird** 3-9-5 0 .... JoeyHaynes 3 13
(Eugene Stanford) *hld up: a bhd* **40/1**
2m 38.9s (4.40) **Going Correction** -0.025s/f (Stan) **11** Ran SP% **114.1**
Speed ratings (Par 103): **84,83,81,81,80 78,78,72,71,60 60**
CSF £18.75 TOTE £5.80: £2.50, £1.10, £2.50; EX 22.30 Trifecta £82.90.
Owner Strawberry Fields Stud **Bred** Strawberry Fields Stud **Trained** Newmarket, Suffolk

FOCUS
A lack of pace throughout and not form that can be rated too highly. It's been rated cautiously.

8452 BET AT RACINGTV.COM NURSERY H'CAP 6f (P)
5:40 (5:43) (Class 6) (0-60,60) 2-Y-O
£3,105 (£924; £461; £400; £400; £400) **Stalls** Low

Form RPR
0042 1 **Jems Bond**[12] 8085 2-9-7 **60** .... DavidNolan 6 62
(Alan Brown) *squeezed s but rcvrd to trck ldr: effrt to cl over 1f out: rdn and kpt on wl to ld ins fnl 50yds whn edgd lft and bmpd rival: a doing enough (jockey said gelding hung left-handed; vet said gelding lost it's left hind shoe)* **9/2**[2]
050 2 nk **Magical Force**[50] 6846 2-9-7 **60** .... RobertHavlin 3 61
(Rod Millman) *settled wl in 4th: hdwy to cl on ldrs over 1f out: rdn and ev ch in bunch fin fnl f: bmpd by wnr whn hld cl home* **6/1**[3]
0405 3 shd **You Don't Own Me (IRE)**[42] 7079 2-9-1 **54** .... LiamKeniry 9 55
(Joseph Tuite) *led: rdn along and hdd over 1f out: rallied wl u.p and kpt on all the way to the line* **12/1**
2243 4 hd **Simply Susan (IRE)**[20] 7833 2-9-5 **58** .... CharlesBishop 2 58
(Eve Johnson Houghton) *trckd ldr: rdn along to ld on inner over 1f out: drvn and hdd by wnr fnl 50yds: no ex fnl strides* **4/1**[1]
6653 5 2¼ **New Jack Swing (IRE)**[74] 5958 2-8-12 **58** ....(p) MarkCrehan(7) 8 51+
(Richard Hannon) *bdly squeezed out at the s and racd in rr: pushed along and wd off home bnd 3f out: rdn and gd late hdwy over 1f out: nvr able to chal (jockey said gelding suffered interference leaving the stalls)* **8/1**
5606 6 2 **Fair Sabra**[22] 7785 2-9-5 **58** .... HollieDoyle 10 45+
(David Elsworth) *hmpd after 100yds and racd in rr: hdwy between rivals over 2f out: rdn and kpt on fr over 1f out but n.d* **14/1**
1265 7 nse **Queenoftheclyde (IRE)**[20] 7853 2-9-5 **58** .... CliffordLee 11 45
(K R Burke) *prom on outer: drvn along and outpcd 2f out: one pce fnl f* **14/1**
5026 8 ½ **Serious Jockin**[15] 7994 2-8-7 **53** .... GeorgeBass(7) 7 39+
(Mick Channon) *bdly squeezed leaving stalls and racd in last: sme late hdwy passed btn rivals* **25/1**
060 9 1 **Loco Dempsey (FR)**[32] 7461 2-8-9 **55** .... LukeCatton(7) 1 38
(Richard Hannon) *racd in midfield: pushed along and lost pl 3f out: sn rdn and no imp 2f out: wknd fnl f* **12/1**
2465 10 1¾ **Call Me Cheers**[11] 8118 2-9-3 **56** ....(v[1]) HarryBentley 5 34
(David Evans) *racd in midfield: rdn and outpcd over 2 out: lost pl and wknd fr over 1f out* **11/1**
3024 11 2¼ **Santorini Sal**[6] 8280 2-9-1 **57** .... MitchGodwin(3) 4 28
(John Bridger) *midfield: niggled along 1/2-way: rdn along and lost pl 2f out: sn wknd* **12/1**
354 12 4 **Lady Phyllis**[29] 7546 2-9-6 **59** .... LukeMorris 12 18+
(Michael Attwater) *restrained into rr of midfield: keen and wd thrght: rdn and readily outpcd 2f out: sn bhd* **14/1**
1m 14.13s (1.03) **Going Correction** -0.025s/f (Stan) **12** Ran SP% **118.8**
Speed ratings (Par 93): **92,91,91,91,88 85,85,84,83,81 78,72**
CSF £31.83 CT £312.00 TOTE £3.50: £1.20, £3.00, £4.10; EX 37.50 Trifecta £276.30.
Owner S Pedersen & Frank Reay **Bred** Norton Grove Stud Ltd **Trained** Yedingham, N Yorks

■ Stewards' Enquiry : David Nolan caution; careless riding

FOCUS
Only one previous winner took their chance in this modest, open nursery. There was a good finish, with those who raced prominently at an advantage and the winner survived a stewards' inquiry. Ordinary form.

8453 32RED ON THE APP STORE EBF FILLIES' NOVICE STKS (PLUS 10 RACE) (DIV I) 7f (P)
6:10 (6:12) (Class 5) 2-Y-O **£3,881** (£1,155; £577; £288) **Stalls** Low

Form RPR
23 **1** **Faakhirah (IRE)**[36] 7304 2-9-0 0 DaneO'Neill 3 78
(Saeed bin Suroor) *racd in midfield: gd hdwy on outer to cl on ldrs 2f out: rdn along to ld appr fnl f: kpt on wl* **5/2**[2]
5 **2** *3/4* **Evening Spirit**[25] 7695 2-9-0 0 HarryBentley 4 76+
(Ralph Beckett) *dwlt sltly: rcvrd into midfield on inner: had to wait for gap between rivals over 1f out: rdn and kpt on to chse wnr ins fnl f: a being hld clsng stages* **10/11**[1]
3 *nk* **Long Haired Lover (IRE)** 2-9-0 0 DanielMuscutt 7 75+
(James Fanshawe) *hld up on inner: hdwy and swtchd lft off inner 2f out: sn rdn and styd on wl ins fnl f: nt rch wnr* **40/1**
12 **4** *3 3/4* **Wren**[81] 5676 2-9-7 0 JasonWatson 5 73
(Roger Charlton) *prom in 4th: effrt on outer 2f out: sn rdn and outpcd over 1f out: one pce fnl f* **3/1**[3]
5 *1/2* **Lottie Marie** 2-9-0 0 LukeMorris 6 64+
(Robert Cowell) *racd in rr: hdwy u.p over 2f out: sn rdn and rn green: gd late hdwy but n.d* **66/1**
0 **6** *nk* **Queen's Favour**[25] 7695 2-9-0 0 TomMarquand 8 63
(Sir Michael Stoute) *trckd ldr tl rdn and outpcd 2f out: lost pl over 1f out: one pce fnl f* **20/1**
60 **7** *1/2* **Lady Codee**[29] 7547 2-9-0 0 RobertHavlin 11 62
(Michael Attwater) *led: rdn along and hdd over 1f out: wknd ins fnl f* **100/1**
0 **8** *nk* **Chosen Star**[43] 7054 2-9-0 0 CliffordLee 2 61
(Michael Bell) *trckd ldrs: niggled along over 2f out: sn rdn and lost pl over 1f out: wknd fnl f* **40/1**
9 *1 1/4* **Ballerina Showgirl** 2-9-0 0 DavidEgan 12 58
(Hugo Palmer) *dwlt and racd in rr: a bhd (jockey said filly was slowly away)* **33/1**
10 *1/2* **Spandavia (IRE)** 2-9-0 0 AdrianMcCarthy 10 57
(Ed Dunlop) *hld up: nvr a factor* **100/1**

1m 26.43s (0.43) **Going Correction** -0.025s/f (Stan) **10** Ran SP% **122.0**
Speed ratings (Par 92): **96,95,94,90,89 89,89,88,87,86**
CSF £5.24 TOTE £4.00: £1.10, £1.10, £7.90; EX 7.50 Trifecta £79.90.
Owner Godolphin **Bred** Shadwell Estate Company Limited **Trained** Newmarket, Suffolk

FOCUS
Not many could be given a realistic chance in the opening division of the juvenile fillies' maiden, but the right horses came clear.

8454 32RED ON THE APP STORE EBF FILLIES' NOVICE STKS (PLUS 10 RACE) (DIV II) 7f (P)
6:40 (6:44) (Class 5) 2-Y-O **£3,881** (£1,155; £577; £288) **Stalls** Low

Form RPR
1 **Little Becky** 2-9-0 0 HollieDoyle 7 78+
(Ed Vaughan) *settled wl in midfield: pushed along on inner over 2f out: rdn and wnt 2nd appr fnl f: styd on wl to ld ins fnl f: kpt on wl* **11/1**
4 **2** *1 1/2* **Sorrel (IRE)**[47] 6928 2-9-0 0 TomMarquand 9 74
(Sir Michael Stoute) *led: rdn along whn pressed over 1f out: kpt on fnl f but no match for wnr whn hdd fnl 100yds* **5/6**[1]
3 *2* **Due Care** 2-9-0 0 JasonWatson 12 69
(Roger Charlton) *j. awkwardly: trckd ldr: rdn and outpcd by ldng pair 1f out: one pce fnl f (jockey said filly hung left-handed in the straight)* **25/1**
0 **4** *3/4* **Island Hideaway**[25] 7695 2-9-0 0 StevieDonohoe 2 67
(David Lanigan) *prom: rdn along and outpcd over 1f out: one pce fnl f* **10/1**
5 *1/2* **Indie Angel (IRE)** 2-9-0 0 RobertHavlin 10 66+
(John Gosden) *midfield on outer: rdn along and sme hdwy 2f out: kpt on fnl f: nt rch ldrs* **8/1**[3]
6 *4* **Narrate** 2-9-0 0 DavidEgan 4 55+
(Hugo Palmer) *hld up: rdn and hdwy appr fnl f: kpt on: n.d* **6/1**[2]
05 **7** *1 3/4* **Sweet Serenade**[70] 6072 2-9-0 0 HarryBentley 8 51
(James Tate) *t.k.h: in tch in midfield: rdn and hung sltly lft 2f out: wknd fnl f (jockey said filly hung left-handed)* **10/1**
0 **8** *1 1/4* **Jaunty**[158] 2840 2-8-9 0 WilliamCarver[(5)] 11 47
(Conrad Allen) *trckd ldrs on outer: rdn along and outpcd 2f out: hung lft over 1f out: wknd fnl f* **50/1**
9 *1 3/4* **Zenaida (IRE)** 2-9-0 0 (h[1]) AdrianMcCarthy 13 43+
(Ed Dunlop) *hld up: nvr on terms* **100/1**
10 *1 1/4* **Lady Eleanor** 2-9-0 0 DanielMuscutt 14 40+
(James Fanshawe) *hld up: nvr on terms* **66/1**
0 **11** *shd* **Folie D'Amour**[25] 7695 2-9-0 0 CharlesBishop 5 39
(Eve Johnson Houghton) *dwlt sltly: racd in midfield: rdn and outpcd over 2f out: sn bhd* **20/1**
12 *1 1/4* **Nikolayeva** 2-9-0 0 (h[1]) LukeMorris 6 36
(Sir Mark Prescott Bt) *racd in midfield and lazy at times: rdn and outpcd 3f out: nvr on terms* **66/1**
13 *1 3/4* **Encashment** 2-9-0 0 TomQueally 1 31
(Alan King) *dwlt and racd in rr: a bhd* **66/1**

1m 26.23s (0.23) **Going Correction** -0.025s/f (Stan) **13** Ran SP% **122.5**
Speed ratings (Par 92): **97,95,93,92,91 87,85,83,81,80 80,78,76**
CSF £20.41 TOTE £14.40: £2.70, £1.10, £6.30; EX 28.60 Trifecta £348.30.
Owner A E Oppenheimer **Bred** Hascombe & Valiant Stud Ltd **Trained** Newmarket, Suffolk

FOCUS
The pace held up once more, a feature of the night, and it was slightly quicker than the first division.

8455 32RED.COM EBF NOVICE STKS 7f (P)
7:10 (7:13) (Class 5) 2-Y-O **£3,881** (£1,155; £577; £288) **Stalls** Low

Form RPR
1 **Satono Japan (JPN)** 2-9-5 0 JasonWatson 10 80+
(Sir Michael Stoute) *racd in rr of midfield and travelled sweetly: effrt to cl on ldrs over 1f out: qcknd up smartly to ld wl ins fnl f: cosily* **14/1**
36 **2** *3/4* **Raatea**[33] 7410 2-9-5 0 DaneO'Neill 12 76
(Marcus Tregoning) *in tch: hdwy u.p to over 1f out: rdn to ld ins fnl f: hdd by wnr clsng stages* **13/2**
0 **3** *1* **Fruition**[54] 6669 2-9-5 0 TomMarquand 2 73
(William Haggas) *led: rdn along and hdd jst ins fnl f: kpt on one pce in battle for 3rd clsng stages* **2/1**[1]
3 **4** *shd* **Lord Neidin**[21] 7814 2-9-5 0 TomQueally 5 73
(Alan King) *trckd ldrs on inner: clsd gng wl 2f out: sn rdn and no imp over 1f out: kpt on one pce clsng stages* **11/2**[3]
5 *3/4* **Creek Horizon** 2-9-5 0 DavidEgan 9 71+
(Saeed bin Suroor) *racd in midfield: rdn along and no imp over 1f out: kpt gng one pce fnl f* **13/2**
6 *1/2* **Magical Morning** 2-9-5 0 RobertHavlin 4 70
(John Gosden) *dwlt and racd in last: pushed along and sme hdwy on inner 2f out: sn rdn: nvr on terms* **9/2**[2]
7 *2 1/4* **Marble Bay (IRE)** 2-9-0 0 CliffordLee 7 59
(David Evans) *racd in midfield: rdn and no imp 2f out: one pce fnl f* **50/1**
8 *1 1/4* **Tippler** 2-9-5 0 HarryBentley 8 60
(Sir Mark Todd) *towards rr of midfield: rdn and outpcd 2f out: one pce fnl f* **66/1**
9 *1 1/4* **Bayar** 2-9-5 0 HectorCrouch 14 57
(Clive Cox) *midfield on outer: hdwy u.p over 2f out: sn rdn and lost pl over 1f out* **20/1**
10 *1* **Estate House (FR)** 2-9-5 0 GeorgeWood 1 54
(James Fanshawe) *racd in midfield on inner: stl gng wl 3f out: rdn and fnd little over 1f out: sn wknd* **14/1**
11 *3/4* **Rocking My Boat (IRE)** 2-9-0 0 WilliamCarver[(5)] 11 52
(Nick Littmoden) *racd in rr: pushed along on outer 3f out: drvn and no imp 2f out: n.d* **66/1**
0 **12** *shd* **Moment Of Peace**[9] 8203 2-9-5 0 AdrianMcCarthy 13 52
(Christine Dunnett) *dwlt and racd in rr: a bhd* **150/1**
0 **13** *1/2* **Bee Magic (IRE)**[18] 7911 2-9-5 0 MartinDwyer 6 50
(William Muir) *racd keenly in tch: rdn and no imp 2f out: sn wknd over 1f out* **66/1**

1m 27.7s (1.70) **Going Correction** -0.025s/f (Stan) **13** Ran SP% **118.8**
Speed ratings (Par 95): **89,88,87,86,86 85,82,81,80,78 78,77,77**
CSF £98.84 TOTE £12.60: £3.20, £2.00, £1.40; EX 97.10 Trifecta £271.30.
Owner Satomi Horse Company Ltd **Bred** Shadai Farm **Trained** Newmarket, Suffolk

FOCUS
No more than a fair novice and slower than the preceding fillies' events, this was still a taking performance from the winner. It's been rated around the balance of the second, third and fourth.

8456 32RED FILLIES' H'CAP 7f (P)
7:40 (7:43) (Class 4) (0-85,82) 3-Y-O+
£6,469 (£1,925; £962; £481; £400; £400) **Stalls** Low

Form RPR
3431 **1** **Kwela**[30] 7514 3-8-12 **76** (p) GeorgiaDobie[(5)] 2 83
(Eve Johnson Houghton) *racd in midfield: hdwy u.p over 1f out: rdn and styd on strly ins fnl f: led post (jockey said filly jumped right leaving the stalls)* **9/2**[3]
0405 **2** *nk* **Javelin**[20] 7843 4-8-12 **69** MartinDwyer 11 76
(William Muir) *led: rdn along and strly pressed by rivals appr fnl f: kpt on wl: hdd by wnr post* **16/1**
2010 **3** *nk* **Lady Of Aran (IRE)**[27] 7613 4-9-10 **81** StevieDonohoe 7 87+
(Charlie Fellowes) *dwlt and racd keenly in rr: hdwy on inner 2f out: swtchd rt over 1f out: sn swtchd lft and kpt on wl fnl f: nt match wnr clsng stages* **4/1**[2]
1000 **4** *nk* **Itizzit**[41] 7128 3-9-4 **77** JasonWatson 8 81
(Hughie Morrison) *trckd ldr: rdn and no imp over 1f out: kpt on one pce fnl f* **20/1**
2103 **5** *3/4* **Visionara**[32] 7471 3-9-7 **80** HollieDoyle 6 82
(Simon Crisford) *prom: rdn along to chse ldrs on inner over 1f out: drvn and no imp fnl f* **11/4**[1]
00- **6** *2 1/4* **Reponse Exacte (FR)**[392] 7690 3-9-9 **82** (h[1] w) HarryBentley 1 78
(Amy Murphy) *dwlt and racd in rr: racd keenly: rdn and mde hdwy over 1f out: nrst fin* **33/1**
0054 **7** *3/4* **Octave (IRE)**[124] 4072 3-9-7 **80** JFEgan 3 74
(Mark Johnston) *in tch: rdn and outpcd over 1f out: r.o one pce ins fnl f* **16/1**
4656 **8** *3/4* **Elysium Dream**[32] 7462 4-9-2 **73** (b) TomMarquand 9 66
(Richard Hannon) *hld up: pushed along 3f out: rdn and no imp 2f out: nvr a factor* **25/1**
1145 **9** *1/2* **Lapidary**[18] 7914 3-9-4 **77** LukeMorris 10 68
(Heather Main) *midfield in tch: rdn along and no imp 2f out: wknd fnl f* **40/1**
3211 **10** *3 1/2* **Crystal Casque**[22] 7788 4-9-0 **76** WilliamCarver[(5)] 5 58
(Rod Millman) *in tch on outer: rdn along and outpcd 2f out: wknd fnl f* **9/2**[3]
0233 **11** *3 1/4* **Chitra**[18] 7914 3-9-6 **79** KieranShoemark 4 51
(Daniel Kubler) *towards rr of midfield: rdn and struggling 2f out: nvr on terms* **12/1**

1m 25.76s (-0.24) **Going Correction** -0.025s/f (Stan)
WFA 3 from 4yo 2lb **11** Ran SP% **116.5**
Speed ratings (Par 102): **100,99,99,98,98 95,94,93,93,89 85**
CSF £68.72 CT £320.52 TOTE £4.30: £1.60, £3.70, £1.70; EX 66.20 Trifecta £321.50.
Owner Mr & Mrs James Blyth Currie **Bred** Exors Of The Late Sir Eric Parker **Trained** Blewbury, Oxon

FOCUS
A fair fillies' handicap, with plenty of recent winning form on offer. It was quicker than the other 7f races, although they were juvenile events. The second has been rated close to her best.

8457 WISE BETTING AT RACINGTV.COM H'CAP 6f (P)
8:10 (8:13) (Class 6) (0-55,60) 3-Y-O+
£3,105 (£924; £461; £400; £400; £400) **Stalls** Low

Form RPR
0400 **1** **Mercers**[6] 8279 5-8-9 **51** (v[1]) GeorgeRooke[(7)] 1 57
(Paddy Butler) *hld up in last: stl last over 2f out: hdwy u.p on inner over 1f out: rdn and styd on wl to ld wl ins fnl f: pushed out (trainer said, regarding the apparent improvement in form, the mare benefitted from the application of a visor and from the jockey having a 7lb claim)* **22/1**
0354 **2** *1* **Independence Day (IRE)**[21] 7824 6-9-2 **51** JoeyHaynes 3 54
(Chelsea Banham) *racd in midfield: hdwy u.p over 1f out: sn rdn and styd on wl fnl f: wnt 2nd post* **11/4**[2]
4301 **3** *nse* **Penarth Pier (IRE)**[7] 8255 3-9-10 **60** 6ex RobertHavlin 8 63+
(Christine Dunnett) *led for 2f: trckd ldrs: effrt to ld again over 1f out: sn rdn and hdd by wnr wl ins fnl f: lost 2nd post* **2/1**[1]
0256 **4** *1 1/2* **Patrick (IRE)**[42] 7065 7-9-6 **55** LukeMorris 5 53
(Paul Midgley) *racd in midfield: rdn and minor hdwy over 1f out: kpt on one pce ins fnl f* **10/1**[3]

4603 **5** *1* **Roaring Rory**[23] 7770 6-9-6 **55**........................ LewisEdmunds 12 50
(Ollie Pears) *hld up: hdwy whn briefly short of room 2f out: sn rcvrd and rdn: styd on wl fnl f* **14/1**

030U **6** *2* **Englishman**[23] 7770 9-9-5 **54**........................(p) PhilipPrince 7 43
(Milton Bradley) *trckd ldrs: clsd gng wl over 1f out: rdn and fnd little: wknd clsng stages* **20/1**

065 **7** *½* **Billyoakes (IRE)**[23] 7770 7-9-6 **55**........................(p) BenRobinson 6 43
(Ollie Pears) *pushed along in rr early: drvn and no imp 2f out: sme late hdwy* **16/1**

4-00 **8** *¾* **Madame Ritz (IRE)**[23] 7770 4-9-3 **52**........................ KieranShoemark 2 38
(Richard Phillips) *hld up: short of room 5f out: hdwy into midfield u.p 2f out: rdn and one pce fnl f* **25/1**

0000 **9** *4½* **Shaffire**[6] 8279 3-9-2 **52**........................(v[1]) CharlesBishop 9 24
(Joseph Tuite) *chsd ldrs on outer: wnt 2nd 4f out: rdn and lost pl over 1f out: wknd fnl f* **50/1**

0350 **10** *1¾* **Mayfair Madame**[14] 8018 3-9-2 **52**........................(b[1]) JasonWatson 10 19
(Stuart Kittow) *prom: rdn along and outpcd 2f out: wknd fnl f* **20/1**

6400 **11** *2½* **Te Amo Te Amo**[141] 3440 3-9-3 **53**........................ TomMarquand 11 12
(Simon Dow) *trckd ldr tl led after 2f: rdn along and hdd over 1f out: lost pl and wknd fnl f* **14/1**

0062 **12** *4½* **Tiger Lyon (USA)**[145] 3320 4-9-3 **55**........................(t) DarraghKeenan(3) 4 1
(John Butler) *racd in tch in midfield: rdn and outpcd 2f out: wknd fnl f* **10/1**[3]

1m 12.67s (-0.43) **Going Correction** -0.025s/f (Stan)
WFA 3 from 4yo+ 1lb **12 Ran SP% 117.1**
Speed ratings (Par 101): **101,99,99,97,96 93,92,91,85,83 80,74**
CSF £76.69 CT £186.00 TOTE £25.80: £5.00, £1.30, £1.60; EX 124.60 Trifecta £397.30.
Owner Homewoodgate Racing Club **Bred** Peter Crate **Trained** East Chiltington, E Sussex

FOCUS
A suicidal pace set it up for the closers in this low-grade affair.
T/Plt: £65.60 to a £1 stake. Pool: £47,962.00 - 533.28 winning units T/Qpdt: £13.20 to a £1 stake. Pool: £6,810.00 - 380.8 winning units **Mark Grantham**

8110 NEWMARKET (R-H)
Wednesday, October 23

OFFICIAL GOING: Soft (good to soft in places; 6.7)
Wind: Light half against Weather: Cloudy

8458 ALLICARE FILLIES' NOVICE MEDIAN AUCTION STKS (PLUS 10 RACE) 7f
1:20 (1:22) (Class 4) 2-Y-O **£4,528** (£1,347; £673; £336) **Stalls** High

Form RPR

0 **1** **Chamade**[53] 6718 2-9-0 0........................(b[1]) RichardKingscote 10 79+
(Ralph Beckett) *str; mde all in centre: rdn and edgd lft over 1f out: edgd rt ins fnl f: styd on: 1st of 16 in gp* **25/1**

2 *½* **Mostly** 2-9-0 0........................ FrankieDettori 8 78+
(John Gosden) *str; looked wl; s.i.s: racd centre: hdwy 6f out: shkn up to chse wnr over 1f out: r.o: 2nd of 16 in gp* **7/4**[1]

06 **3** *4½* **Al Gaiya (FR)**[32] 7461 2-9-0 0........................ SeanLevey 9 67
(Richard Hannon) *racd centre: chsd ldr: rdn over 1f out: styd on same pce: 3rd of 16 in gp* **20/1**

4 *hd* **Astrogem** 2-9-0 0........................ RyanTate 2 66+
(James Eustace) *ly; bit bkward; racd centre: prom: rdn over 2f out: styd on same pce fr over 1f out: 4th of 16 in gp* **100/1**

0 **5** *shd* **Lyrical**[43] 7054 2-9-0 0........................ RobertHavlin 6 66+
(Ed Dunlop) *compact; racd centre: mid-div: pushed along and hdwy over 2f out: r.o: 5th of 16 in gp* **66/1**

6 *1½* **Queen Gamrah** 2-9-0 0........................ JoeFanning 7 62
(Mark Johnston) *racd centre: chsd ldrs: rdn and edgd lft over 1f out: no ex: 6th of 16 in gp* **14/1**

7 *1* **Alchimista** 2-9-0 0........................ CallumShepherd 3 60+
(David Simcock) *str; dwlt: racd centre: in rr: pushed along over 2f out: r.o ins fnl f: nvr nrr: 7th of 16 in gp* **20/1**

8 *hd* **Joanie Stubbs** 2-9-0 0........................ StevieDonohoe 13 59
(Richard Spencer) *athletic; s.i.s and hmpd s: racd centre: hld up: shkn up over 2f out: r.o ins fnl f: nrst fin: 8th of 16 in gp* **33/1**

00 **9** *½* **Isayalittleprayer**[16] 7972 2-9-0 0........................ HectorCrouch 11 58
(Gary Moore) *racd centre: edgd lft s: hld up: rdn over 2f out: styd on ins fnl f: nvr nrr: 9th of 16 in gp* **16/1**

10 *1½* **Calatrava (IRE)** 2-9-0 0........................ HarryBentley 14 54
(Ralph Beckett) *athletic; racd centre: prom: rdn over 2f out: wknd over 1f out: 10th of 16 in gp* **5/1**[2]

11 *½* **Cheese And Wine** 2-9-0 0........................(h[1]) GeorgeWood 1 53
(Chris Wall) *leggy; racd centre: sn pushed along in rr: nvr on terms: 11th of 16 in gp* **40/1**

5 **12** *½* **Easy Desire**[14] 8021 2-9-0 0........................ PaulHanagan 15 52
(Richard Fahey) *workmanlike; s.i.s: racd centre: sn mid-div: rdn over 2f out: wknd over 1f out: 12th of 16 in gp* **16/1**

0 **13** *½* **Bright Spells (IRE)**[29] 7547 2-9-0 0........................ NicolaCurrie 18 50+
(Jamie Osborne) *unfurnished; racd stands' side: chsd ldrs: rdn and hung rt over 1f out: led that gp ins fnl f: no ch w far side: 1st of 4 in gp (jockey said filly hung right-handed under pressure)* **33/1**

00 **14** *3¾* **Lightning Blue**[7] 8258 2-9-0 0........................ SilvestreDeSousa 12 41
(Mick Channon) *athletic; racd centre: hmpd s: sn mid-div: rdn over 2f out: sn wknd: 13th of 16 in gp (jockey said filly hung left-handed and had no more to give)* **66/1**

40 **15** *½* **High Shine**[23] 7755 2-9-0 0........................(h) HayleyTurner 5 40
(Michael Bell) *str; racd centre: s.i.s: rdn over 2f out: a in rr: 14th of 16 in gp* **28/1**

16 *1¼* **Sound Mixer** 2-9-0 0........................(b[1]) JamesDoyle 17 37+
(William Haggas) *str; led stands' side quartet: rdn over 1f out: hdd & wknd ins fnl f: 2nd of 4 in gp* **11/2**[3]

0 **17** *1¼* **Taima**[29] 7547 2-9-0 0........................ LukeMorris 4 33
(Sir Mark Prescott Bt) *str; racd centre: mid-div: drvn along 1/2-way: wknd over 2f out: 15th of 16 in gp* **25/1**

18 *3* **Madame Winner** 2-9-0 0........................ JasonWatson 20 26+
(Stuart Williams) *compact; racd stands' side: s.i.s: outpcd: 3rd of 4 in gp* **25/1**

19 *6* **Dawn View (IRE)** 2-9-0 0........................ GeraldMosse 19 11+
(Stuart Williams) *tall; racd stands' side: s.i.s: hdwy over 5f out: rdn and wknd over 2f out: last of 4 in gp* **25/1**

00 **20** *nk* **Theydon Louboutin**[18] 7899 2-9-0 0........................ AdrianMcCarthy 16 10
(Peter Charalambous) *racd centre: s.i.s: hld up: rdn over 2f out: wkng whn hung lft over 1f out: last of 16 in gp* **200/1**

1m 29.26s (3.86) **Going Correction** +0.525s/f (Yiel) **20 Ran SP% 128.0**
Speed ratings (Par 94): **98,97,92,92,91 90,89,88,88,86 86,85,84,80,80 78,77,73,66,66**
CSF £62.60 TOTE £37.40: £9.30, £1.10, £6.00; EX 99.80 Trifecta £813.00.
Owner Mr and Mrs David Aykroyd **Bred** Mr & Mrs David Aykroyd **Trained** Kimpton, Hants

FOCUS
Stands' side course used. Stalls: far side. Two came clear in this fillies' novice and the much bigger grouping racing centre-field dominated. The level is fluid.

8459 COATES & SEELY BLANC DE BLANCS NOVICE STKS (PLUS 10 RACE) (C&G) (DIV I) 7f
1:55 (1:55) (Class 4) 2-Y-O **£5,175** (£1,540; £769; £384) **Stalls** High

Form RPR

1 **King Leonidas** 2-9-0 0........................ FrankieDettori 2 85+
(John Gosden) *str; stdd s: hld up: hdwy over 2f out: led over 1f out: shkn up ins fnl f: r.o* **13/8**[1]

4 **2** *2* **Evening Sun**[32] 7453 2-9-0 0........................ JasonWatson 5 78
(Roger Charlton) *athletic; trckd ldrs: racd keenly: outpcd over 1f out: r.o ins fnl f (jockey said colt ran green)* **4/1**[2]

5 **3** *½* **Blue Skyline (IRE)**[14] 8012 2-9-0 0........................ GeraldMosse 1 77
(David Elsworth) *str; hld up in tch: led and edgd lft over 1f out: sn hdd: styd on same pce ins fnl f* **16/1**

4 *1* **Mafia Power** 2-9-0 0........................ SilvestreDeSousa 10 74
(Richard Hannon) *athletic; hld up: swtchd rt over 2f out: sn rdn: hdwy over 1f out: styd on* **7/1**

0 **5** *nk* **Huwaiteb**[77] 5809 2-9-0 0........................(h) KieranShoemark 7 74
(Owen Burrows) *compact; led: racd keenly: rdn and hdd over 1f out: styd on same pce ins fnl f* **33/1**

433 **6** *½* **Klopp Of The Kop (IRE)**[47] 6911 2-9-0 **83**........................ HectorCrouch 9 73
(Clive Cox) *chsd ldrs: rdn and ev ch over 1f out: styd on same pce ins fnl f* **8/1**

3 **7** *3¼* **Emaraty Hero**[21] 7821 2-9-0 0........................ JamieSpencer 11 64
(K R Burke) *unfurnished; scope; hdwy over 5f out: rdn and hung lft over 1f out: wknd fnl f* **13/2**[3]

66 **8** *½* **Albert Edward (IRE)**[18] 7899 2-9-0 0........................ MartinDwyer 3 63
(Brian Meehan) *chsd ldr: rdn and ev ch over 1f out: wknd ins fnl f* **25/1**

66 **9** *1¼* **Jack Ryan (IRE)**[68] 6161 2-9-0 0........................ AdrianMcCarthy 6 61
(John Ryan) *s.i.s: hld up: hdwy over 2f out: ev ch whn nt clr run over 1f out: wknd fnl f* **100/1**

10 *½* **Al Zaraqaan** 2-9-0 0........................ JimCrowley 8 59
(William Haggas) *tall; ly; coltish; green; hld up: wknd over 1f out* **14/1**

11 *12* **Lord Warburton (IRE)** 2-9-0 0........................ HayleyTurner 4 29
(Michael Bell) *compact; rn green in rr: wknd over 2f out* **50/1**

1m 29.41s (4.01) **Going Correction** +0.525s/f (Yiel) **11 Ran SP% 117.3**
Speed ratings (Par 97): **98,95,95,94,93 93,89,88,87,86 73**
CSF £7.55 TOTE £2.50: £1.50, £1.20, £4.30; EX 8.70 Trifecta £79.90.
Owner Sheikh Hamdan bin Mohammed Al Maktoum **Bred** Essafinaat Uk Ltd **Trained** Newmarket, Suffolk

FOCUS
The first leg of a decent novice, they raced centre-to-far side. It's been rated towards the lower end of the race average.

8460 COATES & SEELY BLANC DE BLANCS NOVICE STKS (PLUS 10 RACE (C&G) (DIV II) 7f
2:30 (2:31) (Class 4) 2-Y-O **£5,175** (£1,540; £769; £384) **Stalls** High

Form RPR

02 **1** **Tom Collins**[13] 8060 2-9-0 0........................ GeraldMosse 7 84+
(David Elsworth) *str; led early: chsd ldrs: led and edgd lft over 1f out: styd on wl* **9/2**[2]

2 *1¾* **Galsworthy** 2-9-0 0........................ FrankieDettori 3 80+
(John Gosden) *str; hld up: hdwy 1/2-way: ev ch over 1f out: no ex towards fin* **3/1**[1]

3 *½* **Al Aasy (IRE)** 2-9-0 0........................ JimCrowley 10 78+
(William Haggas) *athletic; hld up: hdwy 1/2-way: rdn and edgd rt over 1f out: styd on* **5/1**[3]

4 *¾* **Blackcastle Storm** 2-9-0 0........................ ShaneKelly 2 77
(Richard Hughes) *str; bit bkward; chsd ldrs: led over 2f out: edgd lft and hdd over 1f out: no ex wl ins fnl f* **25/1**

5 *nk* **Formality** 2-9-0 0........................ JamesDoyle 11 76+
(Michael Bell) *str; s.i.s: hld up: hdwy 1/2-way: shkn up over 1f out: kpt on* **8/1**

6 *¾* **Burano Boy (IRE)** 2-9-0 0........................ RobertHavlin 6 74
(Ed Dunlop) *athletic; s.i.s: rn green in rr: hdwy over 2f out: shkn up over 1f out: styd on same pce* **50/1**

7 *3¾* **Bobby The Great** 2-9-0 0........................ FrannyNorton 8 65+
(Mark Johnston) *unfurnished; ly; s.i.s: sn pushed along and prom: nt clr run over 1f out: wknd fnl f* **9/2**[2]

0 **8** *½* **Punctuate (FR)**[14] 8011 2-9-0 0........................ SeanLevey 4 63
(Richard Hannon) *leggy; prom: lost pl 1/2-way: wknd over 1f out* **33/1**

0 **9** *hd* **Blessed (IRE)**[50] 6845 2-9-0 0........................ HarryBentley 1 63
(Henry Candy) *str; prom: racd keenly: ev ch over 2f out: sn rdn: wknd fnl f* **10/1**

10 *2¾* **Angelic Time (IRE)** 2-9-0 0........................ DavidEgan 5 56
(Ed Vaughan) *athletic; relaxed; s.i.s: hld up: hdwy over 2f out: wknd over 1f out* **16/1**

00 **11** *11* **Jadeer (IRE)**[18] 7899 2-9-0 0........................ SilvestreDeSousa 9 28
(Mick Channon) *noisy; free to post: sn led: hdd & wknd over 2f out: eased over 1f out* **33/1**

1m 29.72s (4.32) **Going Correction** +0.525s/f (Yiel) **11 Ran SP% 115.8**
Speed ratings (Par 97): **96,94,93,92,92 91,87,86,86,83 70**
CSF £17.46 TOTE £5.00: £1.80, £1.30, £1.80; EX 23.00 Trifecta £97.90.
Owner J C Smith **Bred** Littleton Stud **Trained** Newmarket, Suffolk

FOCUS
The slower of the two divisions by 0.31secs, but still a race a that should produce some nice winners. It's hard to pin down the level.

8461 COATES & SEELY BRUT RESERVE MAIDEN STKS (PLUS 10 RACE) 1m 2f
3:05 (3:06) (Class 3) 2-Y-O **£6,469** (£1,925; £962; £481) **Stalls** High

Form RPR

1 **Brentford Hope** 2-9-5 0........................ JamieSpencer 8 93+
(Richard Hughes) *str; noisy; green; hld up: hdwy over 3f out: carried rt wl over 1f out: led on bit over 1f out: shkn up and r.o wl: impressive* **8/1**

34 **2** *5* **Princess Bride**[25] 7695 2-9-0 0 HectorCrouch 9 76
(Saeed bin Suroor) *athletic; chsd ldrs: rdn to ld over 1f out: sn hdd: outpcd ins fnl f* **8/1**

02 **3** *½* **Arthurian Fable (IRE)**[18] 7897 2-9-5 0 MartinDwyer 5 80
(Brian Meehan) *athletic; hld up: hdwy over 6f out: rdn over 2f out: styd on same pce fr over 1f out* **13/2**

3 **4** *½* **Grain Of Sense (IRE)**[18] 7897 2-9-5 0 HarryBentley 3 79
(Ralph Beckett) *athletic; s.i.s: sn chsng ldrs: rdn over 1f out: styd on same pce* **5/2**[1]

042 **5** *¾* **Damage Control**[14] 8028 2-9-5 78 WilliamBuick 1 78
(Andrew Balding) *compact; looked wl; led: rdn and hung lft over 2f out: hung rt: lft and hdd over 1f out: no ex ins fnl f* **7/2**[2]

0 **6** *¾* **Quickthorn**[14] 8028 2-9-5 0 RichardKingscote 7 77
(Hughie Morrison) *str; hld up: hdwy 3f out: styd on same pce fr over 1f out* **50/1**

0 **7** *1½* **Baltic Wolve**[28] 7571 2-9-5 0 KieranO'Neill 2 74
(John Gosden) *leggy; hld up in tch: pushed along over 4f out: sn lost pl: swtchd lft over 2f out: rdn and wkng whn hung rt over 1f out* **16/1**

6343 **8** *1* **Herman Hesse**[7] 8244 2-9-5 76 (p[1]) FrankieDettori 10 72
(John Gosden) *str; hld up: hdwy over 2f out: sn rdn: edgd rt and wknd fnl f* **5/1**[3]

63 **9** *4* **Bondi Sands (IRE)**[20] 7834 2-9-5 0 JoeFanning 4 65
(Mark Johnston) *hmpd s: hdwy 8f out: wknd over 1f out* **16/1**

45 **10** *23* **Sea Of Cool (IRE)**[27] 7611 2-9-5 0 (p[1]) GeraldMosse 6 23
(John Ryan) *compact; chsd ldrs: rdn over 2f out: sn wknd* **100/1**

2m 10.65s (5.25) **Going Correction** +0.525s/f (Yiel) **10 Ran SP% 117.7**
Speed ratings (Par 99): **100,96,95,95,94 94,92,92,88,70**
CSF £71.10 TOTE £9.20: £3.20, £2.30, £1.90; EX 74.40 Trifecta £540.80.
Owner Bernardine And Sean Mulryan **Bred** Haras Du Logis St Germain **Trained** Upper Lambourn, Berks

FOCUS
A fair maiden won in taking style by a really promising newcomer.

8462 MATCHBOOK EBF FUTURE STAYERS NURSERY H'CAP (SIRE AND DAM RESTRICTED RACE) 1m 2f
3:40 (3:40) (Class 2) 2-Y-O
£24,900 (£7,456; £3,728; £1,864; £932; £468) **Stalls** High

Form RPR
6612 **1** **Convict**[11] 8124 2-8-11 **85** TomMarquand 5 95+
(William Haggas) *compact; looked wl; hld up: hdwy over 2f out: chsd ldr over 1f out: led ins fnl f: sn clr* **6/5**[1]

1113 **2** *4* **King's Caper**[24] 7726 2-9-7 **95** FrannyNorton 4 95
(Mark Johnston) *chsd ldrs: led over 2f out: rdn and hdd ins fnl f: styd on same pce* **11/1**

0233 **3** *4* **Green Book (FR)**[14] 8029 2-8-1 **75** CamHardie 6 68
(Brian Ellison) *str; hld up: hdwy u.p over 1f out: wknd ins fnl f* **9/2**[3]

1316 **4** *7* **Walkonby**[14] 8029 2-8-0 **74** oh2 DavidEgan 1 54
(Mick Channon) *sltly on toes; hld up: hdwy over 3f out: rdn and ev ch over 2f out: wknd fnl f* **9/1**

531 **5** *8* **Baptism (IRE)**[20] 7834 2-8-12 **86** (p) FrankieDettori 3 52
(John Gosden) *str; looked wl; led: racd freely: hdd over 2f out: hung lft and wknd over 1f out (jockey said colt ran too freely)* **4/1**[2]

1210 **6** *12* **Flylikeaneagle (IRE)**[14] 8029 2-8-9 **83** JoeFanning 2 27
(Mark Johnston) *chsd ldr: carried hd high and ev ch over 2f out: sn wknd: hung lft over 1f out* **11/1**

2m 9.72s (4.32) **Going Correction** +0.525s/f (Yiel) **6 Ran SP% 110.3**
Speed ratings (Par 101): **103,99,96,91,84 75**
CSF £14.91 TOTE £2.00: £1.40, £3.70; EX 11.80 Trifecta £36.40.
Owner B Haggas **Bred** J B Haggas **Trained** Newmarket, Suffolk

FOCUS
They finished well strung out in what looked a useful nursery, with them going an okay pace up front early. The second has been rated to his mark.

8463 AR LEGAL FILLIES' H'CAP 1m
4:10 (4:15) (Class 2) (0-100,94) 3-Y-O+ **£12,938** (£3,850; £1,924; £962) **Stalls** High

Form RPR
1614 **1** **Be More**[54] 6670 3-8-12 **83** WilliamBuick 7 91+
(Andrew Balding) *hld up in tch: shkn up to ld and edgd rt fr over 1f out: sn rdn: styd on (starter said filly was reluctant to enter the stalls; trainer was told that filly could not run until passing a stalls test)* **5/2**[1]

-512 **2** *1* **Lady Bowthorpe**[35] 7341 3-8-10 **81** KieranShoemark 5 86
(William Jarvis) *looked wl; s.i.s: hld up: hdwy over 2f out: shkn up over 1f out: r.o to go 2nd nr fin* **3/1**[2]

1166 **3** *½* **Mubtasimah**[46] 6951 3-9-9 **94** JamesDoyle 2 98
(William Haggas) *chsd ldrs: led over 2f out: rdn and hdd over 1f out: styd on same pce wl ins fnl f* **9/2**[3]

1341 **4** *2½* **Black Lotus**[65] 6289 4-9-4 **86** GeorgeWood 4 85
(Chris Wall) *looked wl; hld up: hdwy over 2f out: shkn up over 1f out: styd on same pce ins fnl f* **5/1**

2310 **5** *5* **Ocean Paradise**[116] 4393 3-8-10 **81** AndreaAtzeni 1 68
(William Knight) *led over 5f: sn rdn: wknd fnl f* **9/1**

6121 **6** *1* **Sufficient**[95] 5187 3-9-2 **87** (h) SeanLevey 3 71
(Rod Millman) *hld up: plld hrd: shkn up over 2f out: nt clr run and wknd over 1f out (jockey said filly lost its action in the dip)* **8/1**

135 **7** *1¾* **Toronado Queen (IRE)**[25] 7681 3-8-7 **78** PaulHanagan 6 58
(Richard Fahey) *workmanlike; chsd ldr tl rdn over 2f out: edgd lft and wknd over 1f out* **20/1**

1m 41.94s (3.54) **Going Correction** +0.525s/f (Yiel)
WFA 3 from 4yo 3lb **7 Ran SP% 114.3**
Speed ratings (Par 96): **103,102,101,99,94 93,91**
CSF £10.21 TOTE £3.40: £1.80, £1.60; EX 9.70 Trifecta £47.20.
Owner Cayton Park Stud Limited **Bred** George Strawbridge **Trained** Kingsclere, Hants

FOCUS
A decent fillies' handicap, there was plenty of pace on and the race set up for the closers. The third has been rated close to her July course win.

8464 MATCHBOOK EBF FUTURE STAYERS NOVICE STKS (PLUS 10 RACE) (SIRE/DAM-RESTRICTED RACE) 1m
4:45 (4:47) (Class 2) 2-Y-O **£10,350** (£3,080; £1,539; £769) **Stalls** High

Form RPR
1 **Trefoil** 2-9-0 0 RichardKingscote 8 77
(Ralph Beckett) *str; looked wl; s.i.s: rcvrd to go prom after 1f: led 6f out: shkn up and edgd lft fr over 2f out: styd on* **8/1**

4 **2** *1¼* **Secret Victory**[15] 7996 2-9-5 0 WilliamBuick 6 79
(Charlie Appleby) *compact; chsd ldrs: ev ch over 2f: rdn and edgd lft over 1f out: styd on* **4/1**[2]

0 **3** *¾* **Sly Minx**[18] 7897 2-9-0 0 SilvestreDeSousa 9 72
(Mick Channon) *athletic; hld up in tch: rdn over 2f out: styd on same pce wl ins fnl f* **10/1**

4 *¾* **Oriental Mystique** 2-9-0 0 JamieSpencer 1 71+
(David Simcock) *str; s.i.s: hld up: hdwy over 1f out: r.o: nt rch ldrs* **20/1**

42 **5** *shd* **Trumpet Man**[32] 7473 2-9-5 0 JoeFanning 7 75
(Mark Johnston) *str; looked wl; led 7f out tl 6f out: remained handy: shkn up over 2f out: styng on same pce whn hung rt towards fin* **3/1**[1]

6 *1¾* **Solar Screen (IRE)** 2-9-5 0 AndreaAtzeni 2 72
(Roger Varian) *ly; prom: rdn over 3f out: styd on same pce fnl f* **9/1**

7 *hd* **English King (FR)** 2-9-5 0 KieranShoemark 5 71
(Ed Walker) *athletic; s.i.s: hdwy over 6f out: shkn up over 2f out: styd on same pce fnl f (jockey said colt ran green)* **18/1**

05 **8** *3¾* **Island Nation (IRE)**[13] 8058 2-9-5 0 NicolaCurrie 4 63
(Heather Main) *racd keenly: led 1f: remained handy: rdn over 2f out: edgd lft over 1f out: wknd fnl f* **100/1**

9 *½* **King's Castle (IRE)** 2-9-5 0 JamesDoyle 10 62+
(William Haggas) *athletic; s.s: bhd: shkn up over 1f out: nvr on terms (jockey said colt was slowly away)* **12/1**

10 *2* **Almighwar** 2-9-5 0 JimCrowley 11 57
(John Gosden) *str; ly; looked wl; s.i.s: hdwy over 6f out: rdn over 2f out: wknd over 1f out* **9/2**[3]

11 *2¾* **Pillars Of Earth** 2-9-5 0 (h[1]) ShaneKelly 13 51
(James Eustace) *str; chsd ldrs: lost pl over 6f out: rdn over 3f out: wknd over 2f out* **100/1**

12 *4* **Nevendon** 2-9-5 0 CallumShepherd 12 43
(Michael Bell) *str; hld up: shkn up and hung lft over 2f out: sn wknd (jockey said colt hung left-handed)* **33/1**

13 *4* **St Just** 2-9-5 0 GeraldMosse 3 34
(William Haggas) *compact; hld up: hdwy over 2f out: wkng whn hung lft over 1f out* **20/1**

1m 43.19s (4.79) **Going Correction** +0.525s/f (Yiel) **13 Ran SP% 120.8**
Speed ratings (Par 101): **97,95,95,94,94 92,92,88,87,85 83,79,75**
CSF £38.67 TOTE £10.90: £3.90, £2.50, £3.50; EX 56.30 Trifecta £447.90.
Owner J H Richmond-Watson **Bred** J H Richmond-Watson **Trained** Kimpton, Hants

FOCUS
In all likelihood a race that will throw plenty of decent 3yo winners. There were a trio of fillies in the race and they claimed three of the first four places.

8465 DISCOVER NEWMARKET NURSERY H'CAP 7f
5:20 (5:22) (Class 5) (0-75,77) 2-Y-O
£4,528 (£1,347; £673; £336; £300; £300) **Stalls** High

Form RPR
4523 **1** **High Flying Bird (FR)**[27] 7620 2-9-6 **74** RichardKingscote 1 78
(Tom Dascombe) *a.p: racd keenly: led and hung lft fr over 1f out: sn rdn: styd on* **10/1**

6146 **2** *1* **Elegant Erin (IRE)**[25] 7696 2-9-7 **75** SeanLevey 8 77
(Richard Hannon) *s.i.s: hld up: hdwy over 1f out: r.o* **10/3**[1]

2210 **3** *½* **Hashtagmetoo (USA)**[25] 7696 2-9-3 **71** NicolaCurrie 5 71
(Jamie Osborne) *hld up in tch: racd keenly: rdn over 1f out: r.o* **10/1**

2403 **4** *hd* **Willa**[39] 7173 2-8-11 **70** ThoreHammerHansen[(5)] 14 70
(Richard Hannon) *hld up: hdwy 1/2-way: rdn and edgd lft over 1f out: r.o* **14/1**

423 **5** *1¼* **North Point**[40] 7154 2-9-7 **75** GeraldMosse 3 72
(David Elsworth) *str; sweating; hld up: hdwy over 2f out: rdn over 1f out: no ex wl ins fnl f* **5/1**[2]

4402 **6** *1* **Light The Fuse (IRE)**[9] 8201 2-8-13 **70** HarrisonShaw[(3)] 9 64
(K R Burke) *prom: rdn over 2f out: styd on same pce fnl f* **5/1**[2]

5555 **7** *2* **Go Well Spicy (IRE)**[7] 8261 2-9-5 **73** SilvestreDeSousa 12 62
(Mick Channon) *s.i.s: hld up: rdn over 2f out: nt trble ldrs* **9/1**[3]

6000 **8** *hd* **Too Shy Shy (IRE)**[62] 6375 2-9-8 **76** (b[1]) KieranO'Neill 4 65
(Richard Spencer) *chsd ldr tl led 3f out: rdn: edgd lft and hdd over 1f out: wknd ins fnl f* **25/1**

603 **9** *nk* **Sir Oliver (IRE)**[44] 7030 2-9-5 **73** ShaneKelly 10 61
(Richard Hughes) *bmpd s: hld up: plld hrd: swtchd lft over 2f out: rdn over 1f out: nt trble ldrs* **12/1**

006 **10** *1¼* **Bad Company**[28] 7570 2-8-11 **65** CharlieBennett 6 50
(Jim Boyle) *led 4f: rdn over 1f out: wknd fnl f* **33/1**

4020 **11** *4* **Zingaro Boy (IRE)**[33] 7419 2-9-6 **74** JamesDoyle 2 57
(Hugo Palmer) *hld up: sme hdwy over 1f out: rdn: hung rt and wknd ins fnl f (jockey said gelding ran keen early)* **10/1**

046 **12** *19* **Desert Palms**[60] 6464 2-9-9 **77** AndreaAtzeni 13 4
(Richard Hannon) *athletic; s.i.s: hdwy over 5f out: rdn over 2f out: wknd and eased over 1f out (trainer's rep said colt had made a noise)* **14/1**

1m 29.68s (4.28) **Going Correction** +0.525s/f (Yiel) **12 Ran SP% 121.5**
Speed ratings (Par 95): **96,94,94,94,92 91,89,88,88,87 82,60**
CSF £44.37 CT £361.55 TOTE £9.50: £2.80, £1.60, £2.80; EX 52.50 Trifecta £538.60.
Owner The High Flying Bird Partnership **Bred** Ra & Je Ferguson Partnership **Trained** Malpas, Cheshire

FOCUS
An ordinary but competitive nursery. Straightforward form.
T/Jkpt: Not Won. T/Plt: £50.80 to a £1 stake. Pool: £53,657.41 - 769.58 winning units T/Qpdt: £17.10 to a £1 stake. Pool: £5,565.08 - 239.46 winning units **Colin Roberts**

8345 WOLVERHAMPTON (A.W) (L-H)
Wednesday, October 23

OFFICIAL GOING: Tapeta: standard
Wind: Faint breeze Weather: Mainly cloudy, quite cool

8466 BETWAY CASINO H'CAP 1m 1f 104y (Tp)
5:25 (5:26) (Class 6) (0-55,55) 4-Y-O+
£2,781 (£827; £413; £400; £400; £400) **Stalls** Low

Form RPR
2200 **1** **Greengage (IRE)**[29] 7544 4-9-1 **54** (h) PhilDennis 12 63+
(Tristan Davidson) *hld up: pushed along and hdwy 2f out: led 1f out: rdn clr fnl f (trainer said, regarding the apparent improvement in form, the filly benefitted from stronger handling on this occasion)* **4/1**[2]

1134 **2** *1¾* **Warning Light**[32] 7474 4-9-1 **54** (tp) JosephineGordon 11 60
(Shaun Keightley) *led: drvn 2f out: rdn and hdd 1f out: kpt on fnl f* **3/1**[1]

2034 **3** *nk* **Red Gunner**[8] 8224 5-8-13 **52** .... EdwardGreatrex 1 57
(Mark Loughnane) *hld up: pushed along 2f out: hdwy over 1f out: rdn into 3rd ent fnl f: one pce* **5/1**

365/ **4** *2* **Mary Le Bow**[1005] 351 8-8-13 **55** ....(t) MeganNicholls(3) 9 56
(Paul George) *hld up: drvn and hdwy over 1f out: rdn into 4th ins fnl f* **50/1**

0256 **5** *nk* **I Think So (IRE)**[20] 7859 4-8-10 **54** ....(b) ThomasGreatrex(5) 13 55
(David Loughnane) *prom: rdn in 2nd 2f out: wknd 1f out* **7/1**

0100 **6** *nk* **Melabi (IRE)**[28] 7578 6-8-9 **48** .... ShaneGray 6 48
(Stella Barclay) *in rr: drvn 1 1/2f out: effrt ent fnl f: rdn and kpt on nr fin* **16/1**

0030 **7** *hd* **Final Attack (IRE)**[6] 8299 8-8-9 **48** ....(p) RobHornby 7 48
(Sarah Hollinshead) *hld up: pushed along 2f out: rdn fnl f: one pce* **16/1**

5100 **8** *1/2* **Pact Of Steel**[20] 7859 4-8-11 **53** ....(t[1]) GabrieleMalune(3) 3 52
(Ivan Furtado) *t.k.h: trckd ldrs: drvn in 3rd 2f out: rdn and wknd 1f out (jockey said colt stopped quickly)* **9/2**[3]

6000 **9** *1* **Arrowzone**[46] 6977 8-8-6 **52** ....(bt w) AledBeech(7) 4 49
(Katy Price) *mid-div: pushed into 4th 2f out: cl up and rdn over 1f out: wknd fnl f* **50/1**

0000 **10** *3/4* **Right About Now (IRE)**[36] 7318 5-8-13 **52** ....(p) DavidAllan 8 48
(Charlie Wallis) *mid-div: pushed along and effrt on outer over 2f out: reminder and wknd over 1f out* **28/1**

5004 **11** *nk* **Edge (IRE)**[29] 7549 8-8-12 **51** ....(b) DavidProbert 2 46
(Bernard Llewellyn) *hld up: drvn 2f out: rdn over 1f out: wknd fnl f* **12/1**

000 **12** *4* **Lucy's Law (IRE)**[28] 7578 5-8-12 **51** ....(p) AndrewMullen 5 38
(Tom Tate) *dwlt: a bhd* **20/1**

2m 0.71s (-0.09) **Going Correction** -0.075s/f (Stan) **12** Ran SP% **123.9**
Speed ratings (Par 101): **66,64,64,62,62 61,61,61,60,59 59,55**
CSF £16.69 CT £63.30 TOTE £8.50: £2.30, £1.20, £2.30; EX 16.10 Trifecta £106.10.
Owner J T Davidson **Bred** Joe And Edel Banahan **Trained** Irthington, Cumbria

FOCUS
A moderate affair. The second has been rated roughly in line with her recent form, and the third fits.

8467 LADBROKES WHERE THE NATION PLAYS MAIDEN FILLIES' STKS 1m 1f 104y (Tp)
5:55 (5:59) (Class 5) 3-Y-O+ **£3,428** (£1,020; £509; £254) **Stalls** Low

Form RPR

42 **1** **Orchidia (IRE)**[106] 4768 3-8-9 0 .... ThomasGreatrex(5) 3 73
(Roger Charlton) *trckd ldrs: hdwy to go 2nd 2f out: led 1 1/2f out: sn rdn: c clr fnl f: comf* **11/10**[1]

5 **2** *2 1/4* **Early Riser (IRE)**[28] 7572 3-9-0 0 .... DavidAllan 9 69
(James Tate) *mid-div: pushed along and hdwy on outer over 2f out: rdn in 4th 1 1/2f out: chsd wnr ent fnl f: r.o but nvr a threat* **5/1**[3]

00 **3** *5* **Storm Approaching**[146] 3247 3-9-0 0 .... JackMitchell 13 58
(James Fanshawe) *led: drvn and hdd 1 1/2f out: sn rdn: wknd fnl f* **20/1**

56 **4** *nk* **Mystic Dragon**[14] 8013 3-9-0 0 .... RossaRyan 5 58
(Mrs Ilka Gansera-Leveque) *mid-div: drvn in 5th 2f out: rdn 1 1/2f out: wnt 4th 1f out: no ex fnl f* **25/1**

5 *hd* **Finespun (IRE)** 3-9-0 0 .... NickyMackay 4 57
(John Gosden) *hld up: plenty to do 2f out: hdwy 1f out: kpt on steadily fnl f: nvr nrr* **15/8**[2]

0 **6** *1* **Fire Island**[20] 7841 3-9-0 0 .... RobHornby 12 55
(Tom Ward) *prom: drvn and lost pl 1 1/2f out: no ex* **66/1**

7 *1 1/4* **Mercury Dime (IRE)** 3-9-0 0 .... JosephineGordon 7 52
(Ed Dunlop) *hld up: drvn 2f out: no imp* **50/1**

5 **8** *1 1/4* **Kiraleah**[21] 7822 3-9-0 0 .... DougieCostello 1 50
(Ivan Furtado) *restless in stalls: mid-div: pushed along 2f out: wknd fnl f* **66/1**

05 **9** *6* **Strictly Legal (IRE)**[37] 7287 3-9-0 0 .... DavidProbert 11 37
(David O'Meara) *hld up: pushed along 2f out: reminder over 1f out: no imp* **66/1**

10 *3 3/4* **Kelis (IRE)** 3-8-11 0 .... JaneElliott(3) 8 29
(Heather Main) *bhd: rdn and lost tch 2f out (jockey said filly ran green)* **20/1**

6- **11** *1 3/4* **Bescaby**[566] 1608 4-9-1 0 .... TheodoreLadd(3) 10 26
(Michael Appleby) *slowly away: bhd: drvn on outer and nt clr run 2f out: rn v wd 1 1/2f out: wknd* **50/1**

50 **12** *18* **Kira's Star**[20] 7841 3-8-9 0 .... RhiainIngram(5) 6
(Richenda Ford) *mid-div: drvn: hung rt and dropped away over 2f out: eased (jockey said filly was slowly away)* **200/1**

2m 0.15s (-0.65) **Going Correction** -0.075s/f (Stan) **12** Ran SP% **121.3**
WFA 3 from 4yo 4lb
Speed ratings (Par 100): **99,97,92,92,92 91,90,89,83,80 78,62**
CSF £6.90 TOTE £1.90: £1.20, £1.30, £5.00; EX 8.30 Trifecta £48.60.
Owner Glentree Pastoral Pty Ltd **Bred** Barronstown Stud **Trained** Beckhampton, Wilts
■ Dolly Clothespeg was withdrawn, price at time of withdrawal 66/1. Rule 4 does not apply.

FOCUS
A good opportunity for the favourite, and she took it comfortably.

8468 BETWAY HEED YOUR HUNCH H'CAP 1m 5f 219y (Tp)
6:25 (6:27) (Class 5) (0-75,76) 3-Y-O+ **£3,428** (£1,020; £509; £400; £400; £400) **Stalls** Low

Form RPR

4331 **1** **Waterfront (IRE)**[32] 7450 3-9-2 **69** .... JackMitchell 8 79
(Simon Crisford) *hld up: tk clsr order 1/2-way: hdwy to ld 2f out: rdn in narrow ld over 1f out: strly pressed fnl f: r.o wl: jst hld on* **2/1**[1]

1433 **2** *shd* **Manton Warrior (IRE)**[20] 7845 3-9-6 **73** ....(t) HayleyTurner 3 82
(Charlie Fellowes) *trckd ldrs: pushed along and hdwy into 3rd 2f out: drvn and wnt 2nd 1 1/2f out: rdn to chal wnr fnl f: r.o wl: jst hld (jockey said gelding hung left-handed)* **10/3**[3]

0453 **3** *3* **Sauchiehall Street (IRE)**[14] 7109 4-9-6 **71** ....(v) ThomasGreatrex(5) 6 76
(Noel Williams) *hld up: drvn over 2f out: reminder and wnt 5th 2f out: sn rdn: wnt 3rd ent fnl f: one pce* **25/1**

1111 **4** *3 1/4* **Trouble Shooter (IRE)**[14] 8019 3-9-4 **71** ....(v) JosephineGordon 1 71
(Shaun Keightley) *hld up: drvn in last 2f out: hdwy on outer over 1f out: kpt on into 4th fnl f* **5/2**[2]

563 **5** *1 3/4* **Bill Cody (IRE)**[42] 7070 4-9-0 **60** .... KevinStott 2 58
(Julie Camacho) *chsd ldrs: drvn in 4th 2f out: rdn over 1f out: wknd fnl f* **16/1**

6330 **6** *1 1/4* **Honfleur (IRE)**[13] 8064 3-9-1 **68** ....(b) DavidProbert 9 64
(Sir Michael Stoute) *prom: led after 6f: sn 5 l clr: much reduced ld over 2f out: sn drvn and hdd: wknd over 1f out* **12/1**

3100 **7** *1/2* **Hope Is High**[25] 7688 6-9-5 **68** .... MeganNicholls(3) 12 64
(John Berry) *hld up on outer: drvn 3f out: rdn over 1f out: no imp* **33/1**

0140 **8** *3/4* **El Borracho (IRE)**[14] 8014 4-9-9 **76** ....(h) LeviWilliams(7) 10 71
(Simon Dow) *dwlt: t.k.h in rr: pushed along and effrt 1 1/2f out: rdn and wknd fnl f* **20/1**

0043 **9** *16* **War Eagle (IRE)**[14] 6849 3-9-1 **68** ....(b[1]) BenCurtis 4 40
(Ian Williams) *led: hdd after 6f: chsd clr ldr: drvn and lost pl over 2f out: sn dropped away* **12/1**

3m 1.14s (0.14) **Going Correction** -0.075s/f (Stan) **9** Ran SP% **117.8**
WFA 3 from 4yo+ 7lb
Speed ratings (Par 103): **96,95,94,92,91 90,90,89,80**
CSF £8.90 CT £126.25 TOTE £3.20: £1.60, £1.20, £6.50; EX 10.00 Trifecta £81.90.
Owner Abdulla Belhabb **Bred** Rabbah Bloodstock Limited **Trained** Newmarket, Suffolk

FOCUS
The first two had a good battle here. The third helps set the level.

8469 BETWAY CLASSIFIED STKS 6f 20y (Tp)
6:55 (6:56) (Class 6) 3-Y-O+ **£2,781** (£827; £413; £400; £400; £400) **Stalls** Low

Form RPR

6660 **1** **Santafiora**[28] 7591 5-9-1 48 .... KevinStott 3 56
(Julie Camacho) *trckd ldrs: hdwy on inner 2f out: drvn to ld ent fnl f: sn rdn: r.o wl* **5/1**[3]

0505 **2** *3/4* **Groupie**[26] 7654 5-9-1 49 .... AndrewMullen 5 54
(Tom Tate) *hld up: pushed along 2f out: rdn and hdwy over 1f out: r.o wl fnl f: tk 2nd fnl 100yds* **10/1**

0253 **3** *3/4* **Eldelbar (SPA)**[16] 7962 5-9-1 49 ....(h) SamJames 1 52
(Geoffrey Harker) *disp ld tl led on own 1/2-way: rdn in narrow ld over 1f out: hdd ent fnl f: no ex* **7/2**[2]

00-0 **4** *1 1/2* **Lottie Deno**[69] 6131 3-9-0 44 ....(t[1]) JackMitchell 13 47
(D J Jeffreys) *bhd: pushed along and hdwy over 1f out: rdn fnl f: r.o: tk 4th last stride* **14/1**

0630 **5** *nse* **Lady Lavinia**[32] 7443 3-9-0 47 .... NathanEvans 7 47
(Michael Easterby) *hld up: drvn 2f out: rdn and hdwy on inner over 1f out: kpt on fnl f: pipped for 4th last stride* **12/1**

3000 **6** *3/4* **Moneta**[11] 8119 3-9-0 49 .... DavidProbert 4 45
(Ronald Harris) *mid-div: pushed along in 5th 2f out: drvn and swtchd over 1f out: rdn fnl f: no ex* **33/1**

0365 **7** *1/2* **Dodgy Bob**[6] 8295 6-9-1 48 ....(v) PhilDennis 2 43
(Michael Mullineaux) *disp ld tl hdd 1/2-way: drvn and lost pl 1 1/2f out: rdn and wknd fnl f* **16/1**

420 **8** *1 3/4* **Cosmic Chatter**[7] 8266 9-9-1 47 ....(p) JackGarritty 10 38
(Ruth Carr) *hld up: drvn 2f out: rdn 1 1/2f out: no imp* **28/1**

0432 **9** *1/2* **Obsession For Gold (IRE)**[11] 8119 3-9-0 49 ......(t) JosephineGordon 9 36
(Mrs Ilka Gansera-Leveque) *t.k.h: chsd ldrs on outer: drvn and lost pl 2f out: no ex (jockey said gelding ran too free)* **3/1**[1]

00 **10** *1* **Dreamboat Annie**[11] 8123 4-8-8 50 .... EllieMacKenzie(7) 6 33
(Mark Usher) *disp ld tl hdd 1/2-way: drvn 2f out: sn rdn and wknd: lost shoe (vet said filly lost it's right-hind shoe)* **25/1**

0304 **11** *1/2* **Mooroverthebridge**[11] 8123 5-9-1 50 ....(b) RossaRyan 11 32
(Grace Harris) *hld up: drvn 2f out: nvr involved* **10/1**

060 **12** *hd* **Juniors Dream (IRE)**[87] 5477 3-8-11 29 ....(t[1]) GabrieleMalune(3) 12 31
(Ivan Furtado) *chsd ldrs on outer: drvn and wknd 2f out* **12/1**

350 **13** *9* **Moudallal**[16] 7976 3-9-0 35 ....(v[1]) HayleyTurner 8 4
(Robert Cowell) *a bhd* **50/1**

1m 13.25s (-1.25) **Going Correction** -0.075s/f (Stan) **13** Ran SP% **122.2**
WFA 3 from 4yo+ 1lb
Speed ratings (Par 101): **105,104,103,101,100 99,99,96,96,94 94,94,82**
CSF £53.79 TOTE £5.90: £1.50, £3.60, £1.40; EX 57.30 Trifecta £270.60.
Owner Judy & Richard Peck & Partner **Bred** Highbury Stud & John Troy **Trained** Norton, N Yorks

FOCUS
A low-grade classified sprint, but a competitive one. The second has been rated to form.

8470 BETWAY H'CAP 5f 21y (Tp)
7:25 (7:25) (Class 4) (0-80,80) 3-Y-O+ **£5,207** (£1,549; £774; £400; £400; £400) **Stalls** Low

Form RPR

5604 **1** **Helvetian**[104] 4835 4-9-7 **80** .... RossaRyan 1 89
(Kevin Frost) *mid-div: hdwy into 4th 2f out: drvn over 1f out: rdn and hdwy ent fnl f: r.o wl to ld 25yds out* **12/1**

3000 **2** *1/2* **Fizzy Feet (IRE)**[4] 8349 3-8-13 **77** .... ThomasGreatrex(5) 5 85
(David Loughnane) *mid-div: drvn in 5th 2f out: rdn over 1f out: hdwy fnl f: r.o wl nr fin: tk 2nd last two strides* **5/1**[2]

5035 **3** *nk* **Canford Bay (IRE)**[14] 8023 5-9-6 **79** .... CamHardie 9 85
(Antony Brittain) *disp ld tl led on own 2f out: pushed along in 1 l ld 1f out: rdn fnl f: hdd 25yds out: no ex* **11/2**[3]

6034 **4** *1 1/2* **Royal Brave (IRE)**[14] 8023 8-9-6 **79** .... DavidAllan 6 80
(Rebecca Bastiman) *hld up: drvn in rr 2f out: rdn over 1f out: r.o fnl f: nvr nrr* **12/1**

2413 **5** *nse* **Secretfact**[23] 7771 6-9-4 **77** .... RobHornby 2 77
(Malcolm Saunders) *slowly away: bhd: hdwy 2f out: drvn over 1f out: rdn fnl f: one pce* **5/1**[2]

6011 **6** *3/4* **Powerful Dream (IRE)**[9] 8194 6-9-0 **73** 5ex ....(p) DavidProbert 10 71
(Ronald Harris) *bhd: drvn over 1f out: rdn and r.o fnl f (jockey said mare was slowly away)* **16/1**

1350 **7** *hd* **Enchanted Linda**[34] 7380 3-9-5 **78** .... PhilDennis 4 76
(Michael Herrington) *disp ld tl hdd 2f out: drvn 1 1/2f out: sn rdn: wknd fnl f* **12/1**

300 **8** *1/2* **Laubali**[32] 7470 4-9-1 **74** ....(p) ShaneGray 8 69
(David O'Meara) *hld up: drvn 1 1/2f out: rdn fnl f: no imp* **25/1**

63 **9** *nk* **Joegogo (IRE)**[35] 7337 4-9-6 **79** ....(v) BenCurtis 3 73
(David Evans) *chsd ldrs: drvn in 3rd 2f out: rdn 1f out: wknd fnl f* **3/1**[1]

2332 **10** *2 1/4* **Show Me The Bubbly**[11] 8117 3-8-8 **74** ....(p) KateLeahy(7) 7 61
(John O'Shea) *bhd: pushed along on outer 2f out: rdn over 1f out: no imp (jockey said filly missed the break and hung right-handed)* **7/1**

02-0 **11** *11* **Golden Circle (IRE)**[135] 3654 3-9-4 **77** .... LouisSteward 11 24
(Patrick Owens) *t.k.h: prom: lost pl over 2f out: sn dropped away* **33/1**

1m 0.08s (-1.82) **Going Correction** -0.075s/f (Stan) **11** Ran SP% **122.0**
Speed ratings (Par 105): **111,110,109,107,107 106,105,104,104,100 83**
CSF £73.73 CT £386.15 TOTE £15.10: £4.10, £2.60, £2.50; EX 89.10 Trifecta £874.20.
Owner Ms Trisha Keane **Bred** Whitsbury Manor Stud **Trained** Newcastle-under-Lyme, Staffs

FOCUS
An open sprint and they finished quite well bunched. The third has been rated close to form.

8471 BOMBARDIER H'CAP 7f 36y (Tp)
7:55 (7:57) (Class 5) (0-70,69) 4-Y-0+
£3,428 (£1,020; £509; £400; £400; £400) Stalls High

Form RPR
2050 1 **Chookie Dunedin**[14] 8023 4-8-12 **66**........................ BenSanderson(5) 6 74
(Keith Dalgleish) *trckd ldrs: drvn in 4th 2f out: rdn and hdwy to ld 1f out: sustained duel w runner-up fnl f: r.o wl: jst prevailed* **7/1**[3]
4303 2 *hd* **Lucky Lodge**[21] 7820 9-9-3 **66**..............................(v) CamHardie 4 73
(Antony Brittain) *prom: 1 l 2nd 2f out: cl up and rdn 1f out: ev ch thrght fnl f: r.o: jst hld* **14/1**
5240 3 *1* **Rock Boy Grey (IRE)**[9] 8199 4-9-2 **65**..............................(t) LiamJones 5 70
(Mark Loughnane) *mid-div: looking for room over 1f out: swtchd and in clr fnl f: sn rdn: r.o* **9/2**[2]
000- 4 *1 1/2* **Holiday Magic (IRE)**[306] 9656 8-9-2 **65**........................ NathanEvans 2 65
(Michael Easterby) *t.k.h: hld up: pushed along and hdwy over 1f out: rdn fnl f: r.o: tk 4th nr fin (jockey said gelding was unable to obtain a desired prominent position)* **11/1**
4143 5 *1/2* **Our Charlie Brown**[9] 8199 5-9-2 **65**..............................(p) PhilDennis 1 64
(Tim Easterby) *trckd ldrs: pushed along and cl up over 1f out: rdn and wknd fnl f* **7/2**[1]
0640 6 *nk* **Born To Finish (IRE)**[30] 7519 6-9-5 **68**........................ RossaRyan 10 66
(Ed de Giles) *hld up: drvn and swtchd to outer over 1f out: rdn fnl f: one pce* **25/1**
2622 7 *1/2* **Seprani**[20] 7843 5-9-2 **68**..............................(h) GabrieleMalune(3) 9 65
(Amy Murphy) *hld up: drvn on outer 1 1/2f out: rdn fnl f: no imp* **11/1**
521 8 *3/4* **Eponina (IRE)**[14] 8031 5-9-1 **67**........................ TheodoreLadd(3) 8 62
(Michael Appleby) *led: pushed along in 1 l ld 2f out: rdn and hdd 1f out: wknd fnl f* **7/1**[3]
1000 9 *1* **Astrospeed (IRE)**[30] 7519 4-9-5 **68**..............................(h) JackMitchell 7 60
(James Fanshawe) *t.k.h: hld up: drvn 1 1/2f out: sn rdn: carried hd to one side ins fnl f: no imp (jockey said gelding ran too free)* **12/1**
153 10 *1/2* **The Groove**[8] 8220 6-9-5 **68**........................ BenCurtis 11 59
(David Evans) *mid-div: pushed along 2f out: rdn over 1f out: wknd fnl f (vet said gelding bled from the nose)* **9/2**[2]
3560 11 *3/4* **Amor Fati (IRE)**[11] 8122 4-9-3 **66**........................ EoinWalsh 3 55
(David Evans) *slowly away: bhd: drvn and rn wd over 2f out: nvr a factor (jockey said gelding was slowly away)* **25/1**

1m 27.55s (-1.25) **Going Correction** -0.075s/f (Stan) **11** Ran SP% **122.3**
Speed ratings (Par 103): **104,103,102,100,100 100,99,98,97,96 96**
CSF £104.66 CT £493.84 TOTE £7.60: £2.40, £3.60, £1.70; EX 95.00 Trifecta £458.60.
Owner Raeburn Brick Limited **Bred** D And J Raeburn **Trained** Carluke, S Lanarks

FOCUS
A modest but competitive handicap. The second has been rated close to his recent best.

8472 BOMBARDIER NOVICE MEDIAN AUCTION STKS 7f 36y (Tp)
8:25 (8:25) (Class 5) 3-5-Y-0 £3,428 (£1,020; £509; £254) Stalls High

Form RPR
4- 1 **The Met**[392] 7669 3-9-5 0........................ DavidAllan 3 79
(James Tate) *prom: pushed along in 1 l 2nd 2f out: drvn to chal 1f out: rdn fnl f: led 1/2f out: pushed out to assert nr fin* **5/6**[1]
04 2 *3/4* **Mohareb**[165] 2634 3-9-5 0........................ AlistairRawlinson 1 77
(Michael Appleby) *led: pushed along in 1 l ld 2f out: sn drvn: rdn over 1f out: hdd 1/2f out: no ex* **4/1**[2]
2565 3 *6* **Gazton**[41] 7126 3-9-5 70........................ DougieCostello 7 61
(Ivan Furtado) *chsd ldrs: drvn in 3rd 2f out: rdn over 1f out: one pce fnl f* **15/2**
6050 4 *3* **Nutopia**[44] 7032 4-9-2 44........................ CamHardie 2 49
(Antony Brittain) *trckd ldrs: drvn in 4th 2f out: sn rdn and wknd* **28/1**
5 *1/2* **Memory Hill (IRE)** 3-9-5 0........................ BenCurtis 8 52
(David Evans) *hld up on outer: pushed along 2f out: sn rdn: no ex (jockey said gelding ran green)* **10/1**
U-00 6 *1 3/4* **Loveatfirstlight (IRE)**[25] 7681 3-9-0 0........................ RobHornby 6 42
(James Unett) *slowly away: bhd: drvn 2f out: rdn over 1f out: no imp (jockey was slow to remove the blindfold explaining that the filly was standing awkwardly against the side of the stalls which made it difficult to remove the blindfold)* **40/1**
0440 7 *nk* **Peters Pudding (IRE)**[183] 2016 3-8-12 58..............(p[1]) GavinAshton(7) 5 46
(Lisa Williamson) *t.k.h: mid-div: drvn 2f out: sn wknd* **50/1**
35 8 *12* **Capla Berry**[44] 7032 3-9-0 0........................ DavidProbert 9 9
(Rae Guest) *hld up: pushed along and nt clr run on inner over 2f out: sn wknd: eased fnl f (jockey said filly ran green)* **5/1**[3]

1m 27.25s (-1.55) **Going Correction** -0.075s/f (Stan)
WFA 3 from 4yo 2lb 8 Ran SP% **119.9**
Speed ratings (Par 103): **105,104,97,93,93 91,90,77**
CSF £4.76 TOTE £1.40: £1.10, £1.20, £1.80; EX 4.10 Trifecta £19.00.
Owner Saeed Manana **Bred** Chippenham Lodge Stud **Trained** Newmarket, Suffolk

FOCUS
This concerned only the front two in the market from the home turn. The second has been rated in line with the better view of his Thirsk run, and the fourth to her C&D best.
T/Plt: £47.80 to a £1 stake. Pool: £66,348.12 - 1,011.80 winning units T/Qpdt: £19.70 to a £1 stake. Pool: £8,998.16 - 336.70 winning units **Keith McHugh**

8473 - 8480a (Foreign Racing) - See Raceform Interactive

8445 DEAUVILLE (R-H)
Wednesday, October 23

OFFICIAL GOING: Polytrack: standard; turf: heavy

8481a PRIX DE KILDARE (MAIDEN) (2YO COLTS & GELDINGS) (ROUND COURSE) (TURF) 1m 2f
11:40 2-Y-0 £12,162 (£4,864; £3,648; £2,432; £1,216)

RPR
1 **Green Spirit (FR)**[20] 2-9-2 0........................ AlexisBadel 6 75
(Mme M Bollack-Badel, France) **7/5**[1]
2 *snk* **Nemean Lion (GER)**[20] 2-9-2 0........................ MickaelBarzalona 2 75
(A Fabre, France) *settled midfield: shkn up and mde prog 2f out: delivered str chal ins fnl f but jst hld* **9/5**[2]
3 *3* **Turkistan Express (FR)**[54] 2-8-13 0........................ RosarioMangione(3) 4 69
(Laurent Loisel, France) **87/10**
4 *1 3/4* **Avremesnil (FR)**[20] 2-9-2 0........................ TonyPiccone 3 66
(J Carayon, France) **14/1**
5 *3/4* **Vigo (FR)** 2-9-2 0........................ TheoBachelot 1 65
(L Gadbin, France) **12/1**
6 *4* **Inca Man (FR)**[15] 7983 2-9-2 0........................ PJMcDonald 5 58
(Paul Cole) *racd towards rr: niggled along over 2f out: nt qckn st: sn wl btn* **48/10**[3]

2m 24.73s (14.53) **6** Ran SP% **119.3**
PARI-MUTUEL (all including 1 euro stake): WIN 2.40; PLACE 1.20, 1.40; SF 5.50.
Owner J C Smith **Bred** J C Smith **Trained** Lamorlaye, France

8482a PRIX DES RESERVOIRS (GROUP 3) (2YO FILLIES) (ROUND COURSE) (TURF) 1m (R)
12:10 2-Y-0 £36,036 (£14,414; £10,810; £7,207; £3,603)

RPR
1 **Pocket Square**[46] 6949 2-8-10 0........................ MickaelBarzalona 2 107+
(Roger Charlton) *trckd ldng pair: wnt 2nd after 3f: shkn up and led 2f out: rdn and kpt on wl fnl f* **53/10**
2 *1 1/2* **Run Wild (GER)**[41] 7120 2-8-10 0........................ Pierre-CharlesBoudot 3 104
(John Gosden) *racd in midfield and keen early: sat in 4th after 3f: smooth prog to chal over a f out: styd on wl u.p fnl f but a hld by the wnr* **21/10**[1]
3 *3* **Scripturale (FR)**[53] 6750 2-8-10 0........................ TonyPiccone 6 97
(M Delcher Sanchez, France) *hld up in fnl pair: pushed along 3f out: styd on to take 3rd 1f out: nvr a threat to ldrs* **23/5**
4 *7* **Ceinture Noire (FR)**[18] 7925 2-8-10 0........................ StephanePasquier 7 82
(R Le Dren Doleuze, France) *hld up at rr: nudged along 3f out: stl last and rdn 2f out: prog into 4th ins fnl f but nvr involved* **9/2**[3]
5 *2 1/2* **Frankel's Storm**[45] 7004 2-8-10 0........................ IoritzMendizabal 5 77
(Mark Johnston) *sn led: 2 l clr after 3f: urged along over 2f out: vigorously drvn whn chal sn after: wknd qckly* **13/1**
6 *1 1/4* **Festive Star**[25] 7724 2-8-10 0........................ CristianDemuro 4 74
(Simon Crisford) *settled rr of midfield: little rspnse whn rdn over 2f out: plugged on one pce* **39/10**[2]
7 *6* **Glengowan (IRE)**[52] 6774 2-8-10 0........................ PJMcDonald 1 61
(Paul Cole) *trckd ldr and keen early: racd in 3rd on inner after 3f: rdn along and sn btn fnl 2 1/2f: eased ins fnl f* **11/1**

1m 52.58s (11.78) **7** Ran SP% **120.1**
PARI-MUTUEL (all including 1 euro stake): WIN 6.30; PLACE 3.10, 1.90; SF 10.90.
Owner K Abdullah **Bred** Juddmonte Farms Ltd **Trained** Beckhampton, Wilts

FOCUS
It's been rated a shade cautiously.

8483a PRIX ISONOMY (LISTED RACE) (2YO) (ROUND COURSE) (TURF) 1m (R)
1:20 2-Y-0 £27,027 (£10,810; £8,108; £5,405; £2,702)

RPR
1 **Tammani**[23] 7774 2-8-13 0........................ Pierre-CharlesBoudot 5 105+
(William Haggas) *mde all: 2 l clr 1/2-way: asked for more ent home st: styd on strly against far side rail: unchal* **33/10**[2]
2 *4* **Celtic Art (FR)**[50] 6832 2-8-13 0........................ PJMcDonald 3 96
(Paul Cole) *racd midfield: occasionally niggled to maintain position: rdn over 2f out and grad began to make hdwy: styd on strly fnl f to take 2nd: nt trble wnr* **42/10**
3 *1 1/2* **Choise Of Raison**[26] 7673 2-8-13 0........................ TonyPiccone 6 93
(F Rossi, France) **39/10**[3]
4 *10* **Karankawa (USA)**[23] 2-8-9 0........................ AlexisBadel 2 67
(H-F Devin, France) **89/10**
5 *1 1/4* **C'Moi Cesar (FR)**[18] 7925 2-8-13 0........................ AurelienLemaitre 1 68
(Laurent Loisel, France) **22/1**
6 *12* **Ketil (USA)**[35] 2-8-13 0........................ StephanePasquier 4 42
(P Bary, France) **7/5**[1]

1m 51.22s (10.42) **6** Ran SP% **119.0**
PARI-MUTUEL (all including 1 euro stake): WIN 4.30; PLACE 1.80, 2.60; SF 17.50.
Owner Prince A A Faisal **Bred** Nawara Stud Company Ltd S A **Trained** Newmarket, Suffolk

8484 - 8492a (Foreign Racing) - See Raceform Interactive

8286 CHELMSFORD (A.W) (L-H)
Thursday, October 24

OFFICIAL GOING: Polytrack: standard
Wind: light, half behind Weather: dry, after a wet day

8493 BET AT TOTESPORT.COM NURSERY H'CAP 1m 2f (P)
5:00 (5:03) (Class 6) (0-60,62) 2-Y-0
£3,105 (£924; £461; £400; £400; £400) Stalls Low

Form RPR
0000 1 **Goddess Of Fire**[37] 7315 2-8-11 **50**..............................(p[1]) AdrianMcCarthy 4 56
(John Ryan) *hld up in tch in midfield: hdwy u.p on inner over 1f out: chal 1f out: led ins fnl f: styd on* **33/1**
5012 2 *1/2* **Sophar Sogood (IRE)**[7] 8286 2-9-3 **56**........................ JFEgan 6 61
(Paul D'Arcy) *rousted along early and reminder after 1f: trckd ldrs on inner after 2f: effrt in 3rd and flashed tail u.p over 2f out: kpt on to chal ins fnl f: hld towards fin* **5/4**[1]
4265 3 *2 1/2* **Chateau Peapod**[24] 7767 2-9-1 **54**........................ BrettDoyle 2 55
(Lydia Pearce) *led: rdn jst over 2f out: hdd ins fnl f: no ex and outpcd towards fin* **16/1**
0004 4 *2 1/4* **Prestigious (IRE)**[7] 8286 2-9-4 **57**..............................(p) AdamMcNamara 11 53
(Archie Watson) *midfield and pushed along early: hdwy to press ldr after 2f: rdn ent fnl 2f: no ex ent fnl f: wknd ins fnl f* **12/1**
6066 5 *1/2* **Pitcher**[52] 6808 2-9-2 **62**........................ MarkCrehan(7) 5 58
(Richard Hannon) *hld up in tch towards rr: effrt 3f out: hdwy over 1f out: kpt on same pce and no imp ins fnl f* **10/1**
2454 6 *1* **Lexington Quest (IRE)**[19] 7910 2-9-7 **60**..............(b) TomMarquand 10 54
(Richard Hannon) *hld up in rr: effrt over 3f out: sme modest hdwy 1f out: nvr trbld ldrs* **8/1**[3]
550 7 *3/4* **Ami Li Bert (IRE)**[20] 7870 2-8-10 **52**........................ TheodoreLadd(3) 3 44
(Michael Appleby) *chsd ldr for 2f: rdn and outpcd whn racd awkwardly over 2f out: wknd fnl f* **16/1**
066 8 *nk* **Master Rocco (IRE)**[54] 6704 2-9-4 **62**........................ RayDawson(5) 9 54
(Jane Chapple-Hyam) *t.k.h: hld up in rr: nt clr run 3f out: effrt over 1f out: nvr trbld ldrs* **10/1**
030 9 *2* **Draw Lots (IRE)**[33] 7437 2-9-1 **59**..............(h[1]) ThomasGreatrex(5) 1 47
(Brian Meehan) *awkward leaving stalls: hld up towards rr and nvr travelling: outpcd over 2f out: wl btn whn wnt lft ins fnl f (jockey said hung badly right-handed)* **10/1**

The Form Book Flat 2019, Raceform Ltd, Newbury, RG14 5SJ

6003 **10** *4* **Big Boris (IRE)**[42] 7111 2-9-5 **58**.......................... BenCurtis 8 39
(David Evans) *t.k.h: chsd ldrs tl settled bk into midfield after 2f: rdn over 3f out: sn struggling: wl btn over 1f out* **6/1**[2]

0000 **11** *30* **Austin Taetious**[19] 7910 2-8-3 **45**..........................(p) GabrieleMalune(3) 7
(Adam West) *chsd ldrs on outer: rdn over 3f out: lost pl: bhd and eased over 1f out: t.o* **16/1**

2m 8.97s (0.37) **Going Correction** -0.125s/f (Stan) **11** Ran SP% **125.4**
Speed ratings (Par 93): **93,92,90,88,88 87,87,86,85,81 57**
CSF £79.82 CT £787.83 TOTE £96.30: £20.80, £1.20, £4.70; EX 150.10 Trifecta £2407.50.
Owner Jon A Thompson **Bred** Miss G Abbey **Trained** Newmarket, Suffolk

■ Stewards' Enquiry : Adrian McCarthy seven-day ban: used whip above the permitted level (Nov 7-9, 16, 18-20)

FOCUS
A moderate staying nursery, run at an uneven pace. Straightforward form. The winner has been credited with 5lb improvement on her first start for a new stable.

8494 TOTEPOOL CASHBACK CLUB AT TOTESPORT.COM EBF NOVICE STKS (PLUS 10 RACE) 7f (P)
5:30 (5:33) (Class 4) 2-Y-O **£6,727** (£2,001; £1,000; £500) **Stalls** Low

Form RPR

32 **1** **Animal Instinct**[20] 7870 2-9-2 0.......................... RyanTate 15 77
(Sir Mark Prescott Bt) *rousted along leaving stalls: led after 1f: mde rest: rdn ent fnl 2f: hld on wl ins fnl f: gamely* **6/1**[2]

33 **2** *½* **Karibana (IRE)**[28] 7611 2-9-2 0.......................... JasonWatson 12 76
(Richard Hughes) *led for 1f: chsd wnr after: effrt ent fnl 2f: kpt on wl u.p: hld towards fin* **6/1**[2]

3 *¾* **Greycoat** 2-9-2 0.......................... GeorgeWood 2 74+
(James Fanshawe) *dwlt and pushed along early: midfield: nt clr run on inner 2f out: swtchd lft and hdwy over 1f out: kpt on wl ins fnl f: wnt 3rd towards fin* **16/1**

5 **4** *½* **Aberffraw**[37] 7316 2-9-2 0.......................... TomMarquand 10 73
(William Haggas) *midfield: 6th and rdn over 2f out: kpt on u.p to chse ldrs and swtchd rt 1f out: chsd ldng pair jst ins fnl f: kpt on same pce and lost 3rd towards fin* **16/1**

00 **5** *1* **Quimerico**[15] 8012 2-9-2 0.......................... KierenFox 1 70
(John Best) *hld up in tch in midfield: 7th and rdn over 2f out: clsd u.p and chsd ldrs 1f out: sn no ex and wknd wl ins fnl f* **50/1**

50 **6** *1* **Abnaa**[19] 7911 2-9-2 0.......................... MartinDwyer 14 68
(Brian Meehan) *bmpd leaving stalls: hld up in rr: hdwy on inner over 1f out: kpt on steadily ins fnl f: nvr trbld ldrs* **33/1**

44 **7** *½* **Perfect Empire**[14] 8069 2-9-2 0.......................... FrannyNorton 8 66
(Mark Johnston) *chsd ldrs: rdn and outpcd whn impeded and swtchd lft over 1f out: edgd lft and wknd ins fnl f* **25/1**

8 *shd* **Lyric Gold** 2-9-2 0.......................... AndreaAtzeni 11 66+
(Richard Hannon) *dwlt: racd in last quartet: effrt over 2f out: swtchd rt 1f out: hdwy and kpt on ins fnl f: nvr trbld ldrs* **9/1**[3]

4 **9** *nk* **Daysaq (IRE)**[19] 7911 2-9-2 0.......................... JimCrowley 7 65+
(Owen Burrows) *t.k.h: trckd ldrs: swtchd rt and effrt over 1f out: fnd little for press and wknd ins fnl f* **5/4**[1]

00 **10** *1¼* **Station To Station**[62] 6424 2-9-2 0.......................... HectorCrouch 6 62
(Clive Cox) *wnt lft leaving stalls: t.k.h: hld up in tch in midfield: shkn up 2f out: unable qck over 1f out: kpt on same pce ins fnl f* **10/1**

11 *1* **El Conquistador (USA)** 2-9-2 0.......................... JosephineGordon 3 59
(Shaun Keightley) *squeezed for room and hmpd leaving stalls: hld up in rr: rdn 3f out: swtchd rt over 1f out: kpt on but no real imp fnl f* **20/1**

2150 **12** *hd* **Modern British Art (IRE)**[35] 7391 2-9-3 80........ ThomasGreatrex(5) 13 65
(Michael Bell) *wnt rt leaving stalls: in tch in midfield: effrt wl over 1f out: sn outpcd and btn: wknd ins fnl f* **25/1**

4 **13** *3½* **Marie's Gem (IRE)**[25] 7733 2-9-2 0.......................... PJMcDonald 9 50
(Mark Johnston) *in tch in midfield: u.p and nt qckning whn hmpd 1f out: wknd fnl f* **16/1**

14 *53* **Howizeegeezer** 2-8-13 0.......................... DarraghKeenan(3) 5
(Charlie Wallis) *s.i.s: sn pushed along in rr: lost tch 3f out: t.o* **50/1**

1m 26.39s (-0.81) **Going Correction** -0.125s/f (Stan) **14** Ran SP% **129.1**
Speed ratings (Par 97): **99,98,97,97,95 94,94,94,93,92 91,90,86,26**
CSF £42.06 TOTE £6.30: £1.70, £1.70, £7.70; EX 36.50 Trifecta £773.10.
Owner G Moore - Osborne House **Bred** Miss K Rausing **Trained** Newmarket, Suffolk

FOCUS
The first pair controlled this modest novice event, with those held up struggling to land a blow. It's been rated around the first two.

8495 EXTRA PLACES AT TOTESPORT.COM H'CAP (DIV I) 7f (P)
6:00 (6:02) (Class 5) (0-75,81) 3-Y-O+
£5,110 (£1,520; £759; £400; £400; £400) **Stalls** Low

Form RPR

4620 **1** **Self Assessment (IRE)**[5] 8342 3-9-5 **73**.......................... BenCurtis 4 83
(K R Burke) *hld up in tch in midfield: swtchd rt and effrt ent fnl 2f: clsd u.p and pressing ldrs 1f out: led wl ins fnl f: styd on wl (trainer rep's said, regarding apparent improvement in form, the gelding benefited from return to an all-weather surface after running on soft ground last time out)* **8/1**[3]

3025 **2** *¾* **Swiss Knight**[23] 7789 4-9-11 **77**..........................(t) JasonWatson 3 86
(Stuart Williams) *trckd ldrs: trying to go between ldrs and nt clrest of runs over 1f out: rdn and ev ch 1f out: drvn to ld 100yds out: sn hdd and one pce* **5/1**[2]

5121 **3** *1* **Futuristic (IRE)**[6] 8304 3-9-13 **81** 6ex.......................... PJMcDonald 6 86
(James Tate) *chsd ldr: rdn and ev ch and hrd drvn over 1f out: no ex and jst outpcd fnl 100yds* **8/11**[1]

6153 **4** *1½* **Final Frontier (IRE)**[9] 8221 6-9-2 **68**.......................... JackGarritty 9 70
(Ruth Carr) *taken down early: led: rdn and hrd pressed over 1f out: hrd drvn 1f out: hdd 100yds: wknd towards fin* **12/1**

5435 **5** *½* **Punjab Mail**[27] 7652 3-9-0 **68**.......................... TomMarquand 7 68
(Ian Williams) *hld up in last trio: swtchd lft and hdwy over 1f out: kpt on ins fnl f: nt rch ldrs* **11/1**

-430 **6** *1* **Swiss Cheer (FR)**[10] 8206 3-9-4 **72**.......................... RobertHavlin 2 69
(Jonathan Portman) *taken down early: hld up in rr: effrt on inner over 1f out: swtchd rt 1f out: kpt on ins fnl f: nvr trbld ldrs* **20/1**

6250 **7** *2¼* **Full Intention**[26] 7684 5-9-1 **67**..........................(p) AdrianMcCarthy 5 59
(Lydia Pearce) *midfield: effrt and drifted rt bnd 2f out: sn no imp and wl hld ins fnl f* **20/1**

1504 **8** *½* **Keepup Kevin**[30] 7540 5-9-7 **73**.......................... CallumShepherd 11 64
(Pam Sly) *hld up in tch in midfield: effrt ent fnl 2f: hdwy on inner over 1f out: no imp ins fnl f: wknd fnl 100yds* **20/1**

2000 **9** *1¾* **Lestrade**[9] 8220 3-9-9 **77**..........................(h) JimCrowley 12 62
(David O'Meara) *mounted in chute and taken down early: stdd and dropped in after s: hld up in rr: c wd and effrt bnd 2f out: sn no imp and wknd ins fnl f* **25/1**

3053 **10** *2* **Penrhos**[62] 6399 3-9-2 **70**..........................(t[1] w) KieranShoemark 8 50
(Charles Hills) *hld up in tch in midfield: effrt over 1f out: sn no imp and wknd ins fnl f* **25/1**

0000 **11** *4½* **Shining Armor**[10] 8181 3-9-7 **75**.......................... DarraghKeenan 10 42
(John Ryan) *chsd ldrs: rdn over 2f out: lost pl and bhd 1f out: eased wl ins fnl f* **28/1**

1m 25.31s (-1.89) **Going Correction** -0.125s/f (Stan)
WFA 3 from 4yo+ 2lb **11** Ran SP% **127.1**
Speed ratings (Par 103): **105,104,103,101,100 99,97,96,94,92 87**
CSF £46.21 CT £66.51 TOTE £8.40: £2.10, £1.70, £1.10; EX 55.40 Trifecta £194.30.
Owner Hold Your Horses Racing & Mrs E Burke **Bred** Joe Bishop Snr **Trained** Middleham Moor, N Yorks

FOCUS
This modest handicap was another race where it paid to be handy. The winner has been rated back to his best, with the second in line with his recent form.

8496 EXTRA PLACES AT TOTESPORT.COM H'CAP (DIV II) 7f (P)
6:30 (6:32) (Class 5) (0-75,77) 3-Y-O+
£5,110 (£1,520; £759; £400; £400; £400) **Stalls** Low

Form RPR

5504 **1** **Human Nature (IRE)**[14] 8063 6-9-5 **72**..........................(t) PJMcDonald 1 83
(Stuart Williams) *broke wl to ld: sn restrained and settled in midfield: effrt to chse ldrs over 1f out: chalng whn bmpd jst ins fnl f: led 100yds out: r.o wl* **7/2**[1]

1060 **2** *1½* **Broughtons Flare (IRE)**[14] 8063 3-8-12 **67**.......................... HayleyTurner 9 73
(Philip McBride) *bmpd leaving stalls: rcvrd to ld 5f out: rdn and wnt sharply rt over 1f out: hung lft u.p jst ins fnl f: hdd and no ex 100yds out* **5/1**[2]

0000 **3** *1* **Florencio**[14] 8062 6-9-10 **77**..........................(p) DougieCostello 10 81
(Jamie Osborne) *sn led: hdd after 2f and chsd ldrs: effrt to chal and pushed rt over 1f out: kpt on same pce ins fnl f* **14/1**

6460 **4** *3* **Red Bravo (IRE)**[9] 8220 3-8-13 **68**..........................(b) KieranShoemark 5 63
(Charles Hills) *hld up in tch towards rr: wd and effrt bnd 2f out: kpt on ins fnl f: nvr trbld ldrs* **14/1**

-460 **5** *hd* **Al Asef**[231] 1061 4-9-7 **74**.......................... CallumShepherd 3 70
(David Simcock) *hld up in tch in rr: effrt towards inner and hdwy over 1f out: nvr getting to ldrs and kpt same pce on ins fnl f* **12/1**

666 **6** *½* **Onebaba (IRE)**[27] 7656 3-9-1 **70**.......................... TomMarquand 2 63
(Tony Carroll) *hld up in tch in last pair: effrt and hdwy towards inner over 1f out: nvr getting to ldr and one pce ins fnl f* **10/1**

05 **7** *hd* **Derry Boy**[146] 3302 3-9-1 **70**.......................... EoinWalsh 4 63
(David Evans) *taken down early and led to post: hld up in tch towards rr: clsd and n.m.r over 1f out: hdwy 1f out: nvr trbld ldrs* **16/1**

0660 **8** *¾* **Glory Of Paris (IRE)**[2] 8428 5-9-3 **77**.......................... MarkCrehan(7) 7 69
(Michael Appleby) *taken down early: awkward and shifted rt leaving stalls: sn rcvrd and chsd ldrs: rdn and unable qck over 1f out: wknd ins fnl f* **5/1**[2]

6446 **9** *3½* **Kamikaze Lord (USA)**[9] 8221 3-9-2 **71**..........................(t) RobertHavlin 12 52
(John Butler) *in tch in midfield: unable qck u.p over 1f out: wknd ins fnl f* **6/1**[3]

3501 **10** *nk* **Rapture (FR)**[21] 7843 3-9-5 **74**.......................... AdamMcNamara 6 54
(Archie Watson) *hld up in tch in midfield: unable qck u.p over 1f out: wknd ins fnl f* **7/1**

3040 **11** *11* **Highland Acclaim (IRE)**[21] 7837 8-9-4 **71**.......................... JasonWatson 11 23
(David O'Meara) *sn prom: chsd ldr over 4f out tl over 2f out: sn lost pl: bhd and eased ins fnl f (jockey said gelding stopped quickly)* **20/1**

1m 25.63s (-1.57) **Going Correction** -0.125s/f (Stan)
WFA 3 from 4yo+ 2lb **11** Ran SP% **123.1**
Speed ratings (Par 103): **103,101,100,96,96 95,95,94,90,90 77**
CSF £21.59 CT £230.67 TOTE £3.80: £1.70, £2.00, £4.70; EX 25.50 Trifecta £263.80.
Owner W Enticknap & B Ralph **Bred** Tally-Ho Stud **Trained** Newmarket, Suffolk

FOCUS
There was a solid pace on in this competitive handicap and the principals came clear. The second has been rated back to the level of his Newmarket win in May.

8497 IRISH LOTTO AT TOTESPORT.COM EBF FILLIES' NOVICE STKS 7f (P)
7:00 (7:00) (Class 4) 3-Y-O+ **£6,727** (£2,001; £1,000; £500) **Stalls** Low

Form RPR

-5 **1** **Farnham**[195] 1740 3-9-0 0.......................... AndreaAtzeni 1 83+
(Roger Varian) *trckd ldng pair: swtchd rt and effrt over 1f out: rdn to chse ldr ins fnl f: styd on wl to ld towards fin* **4/5**[1]

4 **2** *¾* **Moment Of Silence (IRE)**[27] 7655 3-8-11 0.......... GabrieleMalune(3) 7 81+
(Saeed bin Suroor) *chsd ldr: rdn to ld over 1f out: hdd and no ex towards fin* **10/3**[2]

3 *5* **Reims** 3-9-0 0.......................... TomMarquand 4 68
(William Haggas) *dwlt and keen early: hld up in tch: effrt in 4th 2f out: no ex ins fnl f: wknd fnl 100yds: wnt 3rd cl home* **8/1**

-43 **4** *hd* **Almahha**[21] 7841 3-9-0 0.......................... JimCrowley 6 67
(Owen Burrows) *led: rdn and hdd over 1f out: no ex and wknd fnl 100yds: lost 3rd cl home* **9/2**[3]

65 **5** *15* **Petit Bay**[19] 7912 3-9-0 0.......................... NicolaCurrie 5 27
(Sir Mark Todd) *pressed ldrs early: dropped to rr after 1f: rdn and struggling over 2f out: sn outpcd and wl btn over 1f out (jockey said filly hung right-handed in the straight)* **66/1**

6 *1¼* **Feleena's Spell** 3-9-0 0.......................... AdrianMcCarthy 3 23
(Peter Charalambous) *t.k.h and pressed ldrs early: in tch in midfield: rdn and outpcd over 2f out: sn wknd and wl bhd ins fnl f* **50/1**

1m 25.8s (-1.40) **Going Correction** -0.125s/f (Stan) **6** Ran SP% **111.4**
Speed ratings (Par 102): **103,102,96,96,79 77**
CSF £3.69 TOTE £1.50: £1.10, £1.70; EX 3.60 Trifecta £13.40.
Owner Clipper Logistics **Bred** Rabbah Bloodstock Limited **Trained** Newmarket, Suffolk

FOCUS
This fair fillies' novice event was run at just a routine pace, but two very useful sorts pulled clear. It's hard to pin down the level.

8498 BET IN PLAY AT TOTESPORT.COM H'CAP 1m (P)
7:30 (7:33) (Class 4) (0-80,82) 3-Y-O+
£5,530 (£1,645; £616; £400; £400) **Stalls** Low

Form RPR

0315 **1** **Jabalaly (IRE)**[13] 8101 3-9-5 **81**.....................(b) JimCrowley 5 89
(Ed Dunlop) *swtchd lft after s: hld up towards rr: hdwy into midfield 1/2-way: rdn and clsd to chse ldrs 1f out: r.o wl to ld towards fin* **4/1**[1]

2053 **2** *shd* **Balladeer**[21] 7836 3-9-0 **76**..................... HayleyTurner 1 83
(Michael Bell) *chsd ldrs: swtchd out rt and effrt to press ldr over 1f out: drvn and ev ch ins fnl f: kpt on wl: jst hld cl home* **10/1**

1123 **3** *nk* **Dargel (IRE)**[55] 6671 3-9-2 **78**..................... HectorCrouch 8 84
(Clive Cox) *t.k.h: hld up in tch towards rr: rdn and hdwy over 1f out: chsd ldrs and swtchd rt ins fnl f: r.o wl towards fin: nt quite rch ldrs* **12/1**

5050 **3** *dht* **Absolutio (FR)**[27] 7653 3-9-1 **77**.....................(h) BenCurtis 3 83
(K R Burke) *led: rdn wl over 1f out: hrd pressed 1f out: kpt on wl tl hdd and no ex towards fin* **10/1**

0340 **5** *1* **Assembled**[19] 7907 3-8-11 **73**.....................(v[1]) RobertHavlin 14 77
(Hugo Palmer) *stdd s: hld up in rr: clsd on inner: rdn and hdwy to chse ldrs whn swtchd rt ins fnl f: nt clr run and no imp towards fin (jockey said colt was denied a clear run)* **33/1**

1335 **6** *nk* **Light Up Our Stars (IRE)**[41] 7153 3-9-6 **82**..................... TomMarquand 11 85
(Richard Hughes) *hld up in midfield: nt clr run and swtchd rt over 1f out: hdwy ins fnl f: styd on strly fnl 100yds: nt rch ldrs* **20/1**

2136 **7** *2* **Arigato**[47] 6964 4-9-7 **80**.....................(p) JosephineGordon 6 79
(William Jarvis) *chsd ldr tl over 1f out: unable qck u.p: wknd ins fnl f* **10/1**

1400 **8** *hd* **Glengarry**[15] 8024 6-9-7 **80**..................... ShaneGray 15 79
(Keith Dalgleish) *hld up in tch in midfield: effrt over 1f out: unable qck 1f out and kpt on same pce ins fnl f* **33/1**

2461 **9** *nse* **Bardo Contiguo (IRE)**[35] 7364 3-9-0 **76**..................... AndreaAtzeni 4 74
(Roger Varian) *hld up in tch in midfield: nt clrest of runs 2f out: effrt over 1f out: kpt on ins fnl f: no threat to ldrs* **9/2**[2]

5400 **10** *shd* **Freerolling**[12] 8130 4-9-8 **81**.....................(h) KieranShoemark 9 80
(Charlie Fellowes) *stdd s: hld up in last pair: c wd and effrt bnd: lugging lft and no imp over 1f out: styd on ins fnl f: nvr threatened ldrs* **5/1**[3]

2602 **11** *1* **Yusra**[23] 7788 4-9-6 **79**..................... JasonWatson 2 75
(Marco Botti) *chsd ldng trio: rdn over 1f out: struggling to qckn whn nt clrest of runs 1f out: wknd ins fnl f* **12/1**

41 **12** *shd* **Reine De Vitesse (FR)**[21] 7841 3-9-4 **80**..................... JFEgan 7 75
(Jane Chapple-Hyam) *t.k.h: hld up in tch in midfield: effrt u.p over 1f out: no imp 1f out: btn and eased wl ins fnl f* **4/1**[1]

5050 **13** *2 ½* **Battle Of Waterloo (IRE)**[9] 8237 3-8-12 **77**..................... DarraghKeenan(3) 13 66
(John Ryan) *hld up in rr: effrt over 1f out: rdn 1f out: no imp and nvr involved* **33/1**

0266 **14** *11* **Banksea**[15] 8024 6-9-6 **82**.....................(p[1]) ConnorMurtagh(3) 12 47
(Marjorie Fife) *taken down early: t.k.h: midfield on outer: hdwy to chse ldrs 5f out: rdn and struggling ent fnl 2f: losing pl and impeded over 1f out: bhd and eased ins fnl f* **50/1**

1m 38.31s (-1.59) **Going Correction** -0.125s/f (Stan)
WFA 3 from 4yo+ 3lb **14** Ran SP% **133.1**
Speed ratings (Par 105): **102,101,101,101,100 100,98,98,98,97 96,96,94,83**
TC: J/B/D 243.16; J/B/A 157.59; TF: J/B/A 188.80 J/B/D 315.80 CSF £47.83 TOTE £4.90: £2.10, £3.50, £1.60; EX 61.50.
Owner Hamdan Al Maktoum **Bred** Rathbarry Stud & Abbeylands Farm **Trained** Newmarket, Suffolk

FOCUS
An open-looking handicap, run at a sound enough pace. The dead-heating pair help set the level.

8499 DOUBLE DELIGHT HAT-TRICK HEAVEN AT TOTESPORT.COM H'CAP 1m (P)
8:00 (8:04) (Class 6) (0-65,66) 3-Y-O+
£3,105 (£924; £461; £400; £400; £400) **Stalls** Low

Form RPR

3131 **1** **Zefferino**[7] 8291 5-9-8 **66** 5ex.....................(t) GeorgeWood 11 74
(Martin Bosley) *s.i.s: hld up in tch in rr: clsd and swtchd out rt over 1f out: rdn and hdwy to chal 1f out: led wl ins fnl f: r.o wl* **3/1**[1]

0630 **2** *nk* **J'Ouvert (IRE)**[26] 7682 3-8-11 **58**.....................(h) BenCurtis 1 64
(David Evans) *wl in tch in midfield: effrt to chse ldr over 1f out: sn chalng: led ins fnl f: hdd wl ins fnl f: kpt on but hld towards fin* **16/1**

0243 **3** *2* **My Amigo**[7] 8291 6-9-7 **65**.....................(p) PJMcDonald 8 68
(Marjorie Fife) *in tch in midfield: effrt to chse ldrs and hung lft over 1f out: kpt on same pce ins fnl f* **3/1**[1]

2304 **4** *1 ½* **Seraphim**[78] 5807 3-9-2 **63**.....................(t w) AndreaAtzeni 2 61
(Marco Botti) *chsd ldrs tl wnt 2nd over 3f out: rdn to ld 2f out: hdd ins fnl f: no ex and wknd wl ins fnl f* **6/1**[2]

-066 **5** *3 ½* **Arabian King**[70] 6121 3-9-1 **62**..................... GeraldMosse 14 52+
(David Elsworth) *t.k.h: hld up in tch towards rr: hdwy on outer over 2f out: chsd ldrs and hung lft ins fnl f: no imp* **14/1**

060 **6** *4* **Adashelby (IRE)**[29] 7572 3-8-8 **62**..................... LauraPearson(7) 15 43
(John Ryan) *s.i.s: hld up in rr: hdwy over 1f out: sn swtchd rt and kpt on but no threat to ldrs ins fnl f* **33/1**

0643 **7** *2* **Aubretia (IRE)**[16] 7999 3-9-1 **62**.....................(b) TomMarquand 3 38
(Richard Hannon) *wl in tch in midfield: effrt to chse ldrs 2f out: unable qck u.p over 1f out: wknd ins fnl f* **8/1**[3]

0000 **8** *1 ¼* **Subliminal**[54] 6717 4-9-1 **59**.....................(b) JimCrowley 5 34
(Simon Dow) *t.k.h: hld up in tch in midfield: effrt on inner over 1f out: sn no imp: hung lft and wknd ins fnl f (jockey said gelding hung left-handed throughout)* **10/1**

2224 **9** *3 ½* **Miss Icon**[31] 7527 5-9-3 **61**..................... LiamKeniry 9 27
(Patrick Chamings) *hld up in tch in midfield: effrt and squeezed for room over 2f out: sn btn and wknd fnl f* **16/1**

0000 **10** *1 ½* **Gennaro (IRE)**[7] 8291 3-8-8 **58**.....................(b[1]) GabrieleMalune(3) 16 20
(Ivan Furtado) *taken down early: led tl 2f out: sn lost pl and wknd fnl f (jockey said gelding ran too free early and stopped quickly)* **25/1**

2300 **11** *nk* **Midas Girl (FR)**[8] 8254 3-9-4 **65**..................... HectorCrouch 12 26
(Ed Walker) *hld up in tch in midfield: lost pl and wd over 2f out: wl btn over 1f out (jockey said filly moved poorly; vet said filly was struck into on its left hind)* **20/1**

00-1 **12** *1* **Brains (IRE)**[292] 79 3-8-12 **59**..................... NicolaCurrie 4 18
(Jamie Osborne) *hld up in rr: lost tch u.p 4f out: n.d after (jockey said gelding was denied a clear run)* **14/1**

135 **13** *1 ¾* **French Twist**[14] 8070 3-8-10 **62**.....................(p) ThomasGreatrex(5) 6 17
(David Loughnane) *restless in stalls: chsd ldr tl over 3f out: lost pl and bhd 1f out: wknd ins fnl f* **10/1**

1m 38.39s (-1.51) **Going Correction** -0.125s/f (Stan)
WFA 3 from 4yo+ 3lb **13** Ran SP% **130.2**
Speed ratings (Par 101): **102,101,99,98,94 90,88,87,83,82 82,81,79**
CSF £62.72 CT £172.96 TOTE £3.40: £1.60, £7.10, £1.40; EX 92.30 Trifecta £436.60.
Owner John Carey **Bred** Saleh Al Homaizi & Imad Al Sagar **Trained** Chalfont St Giles, Bucks

FOCUS
This ordinary handicap was set up for the closers. The winner has been rated back to his 2018 best, and the second near her best to date.

8500 BUY TICKETS ONLINE AT CHELMSFORDCITYRACECOURSE.COM NOVICE STKS 1m 5f 66y(P)
8:30 (8:33) (Class 5) 3-Y-O+ £5,433 (£1,617; £808; £404) **Stalls** Low

Form RPR

2322 **1** **Pianissimo**[20] 7867 3-9-2 78.....................(b) RobertHavlin 7 83
(John Gosden) *t.k.h: led early: sn hdd and chsd ldr tl shkn up to ld again 2f out: hld on u.p ins fnl f* **6/4**[2]

2 **2** *nk* **Casual Reply**[15] 8013 3-8-11 0..................... JasonWatson 4 77
(Roger Charlton) *trckd ldrs: swtchd rt and effrt to chse wnr over 1f out: drvn and ev ch fnl f: kpt on but a jst hld* **11/8**[1]

3 *8* **Harbour Front** 3-8-11 0..................... SeamusCronin(5) 2 70
(Robyn Brisland) *awkward leaving stalls and v.s.a: hld up in rr: shkn up 2f out: stuck bhd horses over 1f out: hmpd and swtchd rt ins fnl f: r.o to go 3rd last strides: no ch w ldng pair* **50/1**

6-23 **4** *nk* **Persuer**[33] 7451 3-8-11 72..................... CallumShepherd 5 64
(David Simcock) *stdd s: t.k.h: hld up in tch: effrt ent fnl 2f: outpcd in 3rd ent fnl f: wl hld after: lost 3rd last strides* **10/1**

63 **5** *1 ¼* **King's Counsel**[26] 7689 3-9-2 0..................... JosephineGordon 8 67
(Daniel Kubler) *sltly impeded leaving stalls: hld up in tch: clsd on outer 4f out: unable qck and outpcd over 1f out: wknd ins fnl f* **40/1**

0340 **6** *3 ½* **Constraint**[53] 6366 3-8-11 64..................... BenCurtis 6 57
(Andrew Balding) *sn led: rdn over 2f out: hdd 2f out: outpcd and btn over 1f out: wknd fnl f* **28/1**

0- **7** *53* **Tajawoz (USA)**[308] 9635 3-9-2 0.....................(b[1] w) JimCrowley 1
(Owen Burrows) *rn in snatches: chsd ldrs tl 4f out: lost pl: bhd and eased over 1f out: t.o* **6/1**[3]

2m 52.92s (-0.68) **Going Correction** -0.125s/f (Stan)
WFA 3 from 4yo 6lb **7** Ran SP% **113.3**
Speed ratings (Par 103): **97,96,91,91,90 88,56**
CSF £3.82 TOTE £2.10: £1.20, £1.20; EX 4.30 Trifecta £42.20.
Owner The Queen **Bred** Godolphin **Trained** Newmarket, Suffolk

FOCUS
This modest novice event was run at an average pace. The winner has been rated to form, and the second pretty much to her debut run.
T/Plt: £67.10 to a £1 stake. Pool: £30,750.90 - 458.11 winning units T/Qpdt: £6.70 to a £1 stake. Pool: £4,999.26 - 739.53 winning units **Steve Payne**

8466 WOLVERHAMPTON (A.W) (L-H)
Thursday, October 24

OFFICIAL GOING: Tapeta: standard
Wind: virtually nil Weather: overcast with sunny spells

8501 BETWAY H'CAP 5f 21y (Tp)
5:15 (5:18) (Class 6) (0-65,65) 3-Y-O+
£2,781 (£827; £413; £400; £400; £400) **Stalls** Low

Form RPR

0660 **1** **Coronation Cottage**[39] 7230 5-9-2 **60**..................... CharlieBennett 2 68
(Malcolm Saunders) *midfield on inner: swtchd rt off home bnd and effrt to cl on ldrs over 1f out: sn rdn and styd on wl to ld wl ins fnl f: rdn out* **25/1**

0015 **2** *½* **Dark Side Dream**[37] 7320 7-9-2 **65**.....................(p) ThoreHammerHansen(5) 4 71
(Charlie Wallis) *in rr of midfield: pushed along and hdwy appr fnl f: sn swtchd rt: rdn and kpt on strly to go 2nd cl home* **17/2**[3]

6531 **3** *½* **Shepherd's Purse**[7] 8296 7-9-4 **62** 4ex.....................(b) JamesSullivan 1 66
(Ruth Carr) *prom on inner: rdn along to cl and ev ch 1f out: nt pce of wnr clsng stages* **15/8**[1]

6025 **4** *shd* **Aquadabra (IRE)**[10] 8194 4-8-7 **59**..................... AngusVilliers(7) 3 63
(Christopher Mason) *trckd ldr: rdn along to ld v briefly ent fnl f: sn hdd by wnr and no ex clsng stages* **11/1**

031 **5** *1 ¾* **Amor Kethley**[33] 7447 3-9-1 **64**.....................(tp) SeanKirrane(5) 5 64+
(Amy Murphy) *midfield on outer: little keen early: rdn along and outpcd over 1f out: briefly hmpd 1f out: kpt on again fnl f* **11/2**[2]

0400 **6** *hd* **Angel Force (IRE)**[7] 8296 4-9-7 **65**.....................(vt[1]) DavidAllan 8 62
(David C Griffiths) *led: rdn along and hdd appr fnl f: wknd clsng stages* **18/1**

0R00 **7** *½* **Red Invader (IRE)**[14] 8066 9-9-5 **63**..................... JoeyHaynes 10 58
(John Butler) *hld up in last: rdn in rr over 2f out: n.d* **50/1**

5600 **8** *hd* **Kath's Lustre**[26] 7690 4-9-2 **60**.....................(b) ShaneKelly 7 55+
(Richard Hughes) *squeezed s and racd in rr: rdn over 2f out: nvr on terms* **16/1**

000- **9** *1 ¼* **Equally Fast**[311] 9587 7-9-7 **65**.....................(p[1]) DavidProbert 9 55
(Roy Brotherton) *hld up: rdn and outpcd 1/2-way: nvr on terms (jockey said gelding hung left-handed)* **20/1**

1m 0.69s (-1.21) **Going Correction** -0.375s/f (Stan) **9** Ran SP% **90.7**
Speed ratings (Par 101): **94,93,92,92,89 89,88,88,86**
CSF £127.97 CT £279.96 TOTE £33.50: £8.90, £2.00, £1.10; EX 211.00 Trifecta £792.00.
Owner Pat Hancock & Eric Jones **Bred** Eric Jones, Pat Hancock **Trained** Green Ore, Somerset
■ Great Suspense and Longroom were withdrawn. Prices at time of withdrawal 15-2 and 9-2. Rule 4 applies to all bets- deduction 25p in the pound

FOCUS
A modest sprint run at a good gallop.

8502 BOMBARDIER H'CAP 7f 36y (Tp)
5:45 (5:49) (Class 6) (0-55,55) 3-Y-O+
£2,781 (£827; £413; £400; £400; £400) **Stalls** High

Form RPR

1 **Footsteps At Dawn (IRE)**[34] 7423 4-9-5 **53**.....................(tp) LukeMorris 11 60+
(Shane Nolan, Ire) *in rr of midfield: hdwy on outer 2f out: c wdst of all off home bnd and sn rdn to chse ldrs: wnt 2nd appr fnl f: styd on strly to ld cl home* **4/1**[2]

3430 **2** 3/4 **Puchita (IRE)**[17] 7961 4-8-10 **51**....................(p) AngusVilliers(7) 4 56
(Antony Brittain) *j. slowly and racd in rr: hdwy gng wl 2f out: kpt on wl to go 2nd and chse wnr fnl f: a hld* **8/1**

5453 **3** 1 3/4 **Scandinavian Lady (IRE)**[8] 8264 3-9-5 **55**.................... DavidNolan 10 55
(Ivan Furtado) *prom in 4th: effrt to go 2nd 2f out: rdn along to ld appr fnl f: sn hdd by wnr ins fnl f and no ex clsng stages* **11/2**

0005 **4** 1/2 **Capla Demon**[12] 8123 4-9-6 **54**.................... CamHardie 8 54
(Antony Brittain) *racd in midfield: hmpd 4f out: pushed along to hold position 3f out: rdn and minor hdwy over 1f out: kpt on fnl f (vet said a post-race examination revealed gelding had been struck into on its right-hind)* **14/1**

3162 **5** 1 1/2 **Brigand**[12] 8123 4-9-7 **55**.................... JoeyHaynes 2 51
(John Butler) *trckd ldrs on inner: rdn along and ev ch appr fnl f: wknd clsng stages* **5/1**[3]

5441 **6** 1/2 **Sharrabang**[12] 8119 3-9-0 **53**.................... MeganNicholls(3) 3 47
(Stella Barclay) *hld up: effrt on inner over 2f out: sn rdn and no imp over 1f out: one pce fnl f* **3/1**[1]

00 **7** 1 1/4 **Satchville Flyer**[39] 7236 8-9-0 **48**.................... PhilipPrince 7 39
(Milton Bradley) *hld up in last: rdn in rr 2f out: mde sme late hdwy* **40/1**

2303 **8** nk **Tarrzan (IRE)**[38] 7273 3-9-1 **51**.................... RichardKingscote 12 41
(John Gallagher) *chsd ldr tl led 3f out: rdn and hdd appr fnl f: sn wknd (jockey said hung right-handed)* **20/1**

1600 **9** nk **Pocket Warrior**[16] 7986 8-9-3 **51**....................(t) DavidEgan 6 41
(Paul D'Arcy) *midfield on outer: gd hdwy on outside 3f out: rdn and no further imp over 1f out: wknd fnl f* **20/1**

0540 **10** 1 3/4 **Torque Of The Town (IRE)**[69] 6176 3-9-0 **50**.................... PhilDennis 1 35
(Noel Wilson) *racd keenly in midfield: pushed along 2f out: sn rdn and no imp over 1f out: no ex (jockey said gelding ran too free)* **18/1**

-360 **11** 7 **Nananita (IRE)**[227] 1141 3-9-4 **54**....................(t[1]) LiamJones 9 21
(Mark Loughnane) *led: rdn along and hdd 3f out: wknd fr over 1f out* **33/1**

1m 26.97s (-1.83) **Going Correction** -0.375s/f (Stan)
WFA 3 from 4yo+ 2lb **11 Ran SP% 115.0**
Speed ratings (Par 101): **95,94,92,91,89 89,87,87,85 77**
CSF £33.20 CT £178.56 TOTE £4.30: £2.10, £2.40, £1.90; EX 32.00 Trifecta £168.50.
Owner A Martin **Bred** Adrian Martin **Trained** Clane, Co. Kildare

FOCUS
Due to a malfunction that put the starting stalls out of use this race was started by flip start. A decent enough gallop and a couple of closers came through to fill the first two positions. The second has been rated back towards her better form, while the third and fourth fit.

8503 LADBROKES, HOME OF THE ODDS BOOST NOVICE STKS 7f 36y (Tp)
6:15 (6:20) (Class 5) 2-Y-O **£3,428** (£1,020; £509; £254)

Form RPR

3 **1** **Kinsman**[36] 7346 2-9-2 0.................... JamesDoyle 1 77+
(William Haggas) *trckd ldrs on inner: effrt to cl over 1f out: rdn along to ld ent fnl f: styd on wl* **1/2**[1]

33 **2** 1 1/4 **Well Prepared**[14] 8060 2-9-2 0.................... SeanLevey 7 73
(Richard Hannon) *trckd ldr: shkn up 2f out: rdn to chal over 1f out: kpt on but nt pce of wnr clsng stages* **5/1**[3]

3 **3** 3/4 **Abwaaq (USA)**[19] 7911 2-9-2 0.................... DaneO'Neill 6 71
(Simon Crisford) *racd a little freely and led: rdn along and hdd by wnr ent fnl f: no ex* **4/1**[2]

1 **4** nk **San Rafael (IRE)**[19] 7911 2-9-9 0.................... JoeFanning 3 77
(Mark Johnston) *wl in tch: pushed along to chse ldrs 2f out: rdn and outpcd over 1f out: kpt on again clsng stages* **11/2**

5 1 1/4 **Cedar Cage** 2-9-2 0.................... LukeMorris 9 68+
(Sir Mark Prescott Bt) *dwlt and racd in last: niggled along 1/2-way: effrt and hung lft over 1f out: rdn and kpt on fnl f* **50/1**

00 **6** 2 **More Than Love**[29] 7586 2-9-2 0....................(t) DavidAllan 4 62
(Tim Easterby) *in rr of midfield: pushed along and no imp 2f out: kpt on one pce fr over 1f out* **100/1**

0 **7** 9 **Recall It All**[12] 8121 2-9-2 0.................... LewisEdmunds 2 40
(Ivan Furtado) *hld up: rdn and outpcd in rr over 2f out: nvr on terms* **125/1**

8 5 **Gypsy Traveller** 2-8-11 0.................... ThoreHammerHansen(5) 8 27
(Kevin Frost) *s.s: qckly rcvrd into midfield: hdwy on outer 4f out: pushed along and no imp wd 2f out: sn wknd* **50/1**

1m 27.51s (-1.29) **Going Correction** -0.375s/f (Stan) **8 Ran SP% 124.4**
Speed ratings (Par 95): **92,90,89,89,87 85,75,69**
CSF £4.37 TOTE £1.50: £1.10, £1.10, £1.30; EX 4.40 Trifecta £8.40.
Owner Cheveley Park Stud **Bred** Cheveley Park Stud Ltd **Trained** Newmarket, Suffolk

FOCUS
With the stalls out of commission, this race was started by flag. The second has been rated near his debut effort.

8504 LADBROKES "PLAY 1-2-FREE" ON FOOTBALL NOVICE STKS 1m 142y (Tp)
6:45 (6:45) (Class 5) 2-Y-O **£3,428** (£1,020; £509; £254)

Form RPR

0 **1** **Fly Falcon (IRE)**[19] 7897 2-9-5 0.................... SeanLevey 11 78
(Richard Hannon) *prom: wnt 2nd after 2f: led on bit 2f out: sn rdn w 1 l ld appr fnl f: drvn and kpt on wl ins fnl f* **4/1**[2]

62 **2** nk **Buwardy**[16] 7996 2-9-5 0.................... KieranO'Neill 9 77
(John Gosden) *trckd ldr for 2f then remained handy: wnt 2nd and chsd wnr 2f out: sn rdn and kpt on wl fnl f: a being hld by wnr* **3/1**[1]

06 **3** 2 **Heliaebel**[22] 7826 2-9-0 0.................... StevieDonohoe 4 68
(Charlie Fellowes) *settled wl in tch: effrt to cl on inner 2f out: sn rdn and nt pce of ldng pair appr fnl f: kpt on* **16/1**

4 1/2 **French Asset (IRE)** 2-9-5 0.................... DavidProbert 7 72+
(Sir Michael Stoute) *midfield: pushed along over 2f out: rdn and no immediate imp over 1f out: kpt on wl fnl f but nvr a threat* **11/2**[3]

50 **5** 3 1/2 **Visibility (IRE)**[48] 6911 2-9-5 0.................... RobHornby 8 64
(Martyn Meade) *hld up: effrt on outer over 2f out: c wdst of all off home bnd: rdn and minor hdwy ins fnl f* **12/1**

34 **6** 2 1/4 **Ambassador (IRE)**[35] 7361 2-9-5 0.................... TonyHamilton 12 60
(Richard Fahey) *midfield on outer: rdn along and struggling to hold position over 2f out: rdn and lost pl over 1f out: no ex* **22/1**

53 **7** 1 3/4 **Imperial Square (IRE)**[16] 7996 2-9-5 0.................... JoeFanning 2 56
(Mark Johnston) *racd in midfield: effrt on inner over 2f out: rdn and no imp over 1f out: one pce under hands and heels fnl f* **6/1**

066 **8** 2 **Anno Lucis (IRE)**[22] 7821 2-9-5 0.................... LukeMorris 1 52+
(Sir Mark Prescott Bt) *v s.i.s and detached early: rdn and struggling in rr over 2f out: nvr on terms* **80/1**

6 **9** 1 1/2 **Arij (IRE)**[17] 7972 2-9-5 0.................... JackMitchell 6 49
(Simon Crisford) *led: rdn along and hdd 2f out: wknd qckly fr 1f out (jockey said colt stopped quickly)* **4/1**[2]

0 **10** shd **Grouseman**[118] 4324 2-9-5 0.................... ShaneKelly 5 48
(Pam Sly) *racd in midfield: pushed along and outpcd over 2f out: wknd fnl f* **20/1**

1m 46.37s (-3.73) **Going Correction** -0.375s/f (Stan) 2y crse rec **10 Ran SP% 118.6**
Speed ratings (Par 95): **101,100,98,98,95 93,91,90,88,88**
CSF £16.40 TOTE £5.00: £2.10, £1.30, £4.90; EX 18.10 Trifecta £180.20.
Owner Saeed Suhail **Bred** Mrs C R Philipson & Lofts Hall Stud **Trained** East Everleigh, Wilts
■ Stewards' Enquiry : Sean Levey jockey cautioned: careless riding

FOCUS
Flag start. Fair novice form. The second has been rated to his previous start for now.

8505 LADBROKES FOOTBALL ACCA BOOSTY NURSERY H'CAP 1m 142y (Tp)
7:15 (7:15) (Class 4) (0-80,80) 2-Y-O
£4,463 (£1,328; £663; £400; £400; £400)

Form RPR

2020 **1** **Clay Regazzoni**[19] 7904 2-9-3 **76**.................... CallumRodriguez 11 80
(Keith Dalgleish) *hld up: hdwy on rail 2f out: wnt 5th over 1f out: rdn and styd on strly ins fnl f to ld fnl 50yds: all out* **6/1**

5532 **2** hd **Talap**[17] 7971 2-9-4 **77**....................(p) DavidEgan 3 81
(Roger Varian) *midfield: hdwy on outer over 1f out: rdn to chse wnr ins fnl f: jst failed* **11/4**[1]

4345 **3** 1 1/2 **Three Fans (FR)**[17] 7971 2-8-11 **70**....................(v[1]) RichardKingscote 10 71
(Tom Dascombe) *slowly away fr flag s: quick hdwy to ld after 1f: rdn along and hdd 1f out: no ex* **14/1**

054 **4** nse **Abadie**[33] 7445 2-8-8 **67**.................... HollieDoyle 4 68
(Archie Watson) *led for 1f then trckd ldr: rdn along and almost upsides over 1f out: led v briefly 1f out: sn hdd by wnr and wknd fnl 100yds* **12/1**

4100 **5** 3 3/4 **Top Buck (IRE)**[8] 8252 2-9-4 **77**....................(b[1]) HarryBentley 6 70
(Brian Meehan) *prom: rdn along and no imp over 2f out: kpt on one pce fnl f* **12/1**

5533 **6** 2 **Sir Charles Punch**[30] 7539 2-9-4 **77**.................... GrahamLee 1 66
(James Given) *dwlt and r in rr: effrt to cl over 1f out: rdn and no imp fnl f* **12/1**

0343 **7** 1 **Anglo Saxon (IRE)**[16] 7980 2-9-2 **75**.................... StevieDonohoe 2 62
(Charlie Fellowes) *midfield: rdn and outpcd over 2f out: one pce over 1f out: nvr on terms* **5/1**[2]

0104 **8** 2 1/4 **Cheat (IRE)**[8] 8252 2-9-7 **80**.................... SeanLevey 9 62
(Richard Hannon) *hld up: rdn in rr over 2f out: nvr on terms* **11/2**[3]

3224 **9** 22 **Expensive Dirham**[20] 7874 2-9-3 **76**.................... JoeFanning 7 12
(Mark Johnston) *trckd ldrs: rdn along and lost pl over 2f out: sn bhd (trainer's rep could offer no explanation for the filly's performance)* **13/2**

1m 45.76s (-4.34) **Going Correction** -0.375s/f (Stan) 2y crse rec **9 Ran SP% 116.1**
Speed ratings (Par 97): **104,103,102,102,99 97,96,94,74**
CSF £23.00 CT £224.29 TOTE £5.80: £2.60, £1.40, £4.70; EX 22.10 Trifecta £550.00.
Owner Middleham Park Racing XXXVIII & Partner **Bred** M E Wates **Trained** Carluke, S Lanarks

FOCUS
Flag start. There was a good gallop on here and a couple of closers came through to fight out the finish. The winner has been rated back to his debut level.

8506 LADBROKES WHERE THE NATION PLAYS NURSERY H'CAP 5f 21y (Tp)
7:45 (7:45) (Class 5) (0-75,75) 2-Y-O
£3,428 (£1,020; £509; £400; £400; £400)

Form RPR

5532 **1** **Swinley (IRE)**[6] 8315 2-9-3 **71**.................... ShaneKelly 6 78
(Richard Hughes) *broke wl and mde all: rdn whn pressed by rival ent fnl f: kpt on wl: a doing enough* **5/4**[1]

2266 **2** nk **Birkenhead**[93] 5275 2-9-3 **71**....................(v) LewisEdmunds 5 77
(Les Eyre) *chsd wnr: rdn to chal appr fnl f: kpt on: a hld by wnr* **11/1**

5106 **3** 3 1/4 **Port Winston (IRE)**[9] 8219 2-9-6 **74**....................(h) DavidProbert 2 68
(Alan King) *midfield and keen at times: rdn to chse ldrs 2f out: drvn and kpt on one pce for remote 3rd fnl f* **15/2**[2]

1110 **4** nk **Queens Blade**[2] 8430 2-8-12 **66**....................(b) DuranFentiman 8 59
(Tim Easterby) *midfield on outer: pushed along and outpcd 3f out: wdst of all off home bnd: rdn and mde gd late hdwy fnl f: n.d* **14/1**

2326 **5** 1/2 **Airbrush (IRE)**[30] 7556 2-9-0 **68**.................... RossaRyan 3 59
(Richard Hannon) *trckd ldrs on inner: swtchd lft and rdn to chse ldrs over 1f out: one pce fnl f* **9/1**

043 **6** nse **Abbaleka**[22] 7825 2-9-0 **68**.................... AlistairRawlinson 10 59
(Michael Appleby) *hld up: hdwy between rivals 2f out: rdn and sme late hdwy fnl f (jockey said colt was slowly away)* **10/1**

4616 **7** 3/4 **Dreamy Rascal (IRE)**[39] 7234 2-9-0 **68**.................... SeanLevey 1 56
(Richard Hannon) *midfield on inner: stl gng wl 2f out: rdn and fnd little over 1f out: one pce after* **14/1**

1030 **8** 1 3/4 **Silver Start**[19] 7896 2-9-7 **75**.................... HarryBentley 7 57
(Charles Hills) *hld up: hdwy on inner 2f out: rdn and no imp over 1f out: wknd fnl f* **8/1**[3]

023 **9** 1 1/2 **Azteca**[171] 2475 2-9-6 **74**.................... GrahamLee 11 51
(Bryan Smart) *prom on outer: pushed wd on home bnd 3f out: rdn and no imp 2f out: wknd fnl f* **25/1**

2303 **10** 8 **She Looks Like Fun**[36] 7329 2-8-8 **65**....................(v[1]) HarrisonShaw(3) 4 13
(K R Burke) *midfield: drvn along and outpcd 1/2-way: sn lost pl and wknd 2f out* **12/1**

1m 0.31s (-1.59) **Going Correction** -0.375s/f (Stan) **10 Ran SP% 119.6**
Speed ratings (Par 95): **97,96,91,90,90 89,88,85,83,70**
CSF £17.04 CT £80.57 TOTE £2.10: £1.20, £3.90, £2.40; EX 20.40 Trifecta £93.80.
Owner Clarke, Devine, Hughes & Peters **Bred** Hyde Park Stud & Lissglen Bloodstock **Trained** Upper Lambourn, Berks

FOCUS
Flag start. They went a steady early pace and the first two held those positions throughout. The second's previous AW start could be rated this high.

8507 BETWAY HEED YOUR HUNCH H'CAP 1m 1f 104y (Tp)
8:15 (8:17) (Class 5) (0-70,70) 3-Y-O+
£3,428 (£1,020; £509; £400; £400; £400)

Form RPR

3232 **1** **Stormbomber (CAN)**[13] 8087 3-9-2 **70**.................... LukeMorris 12 82
(Ed Walker) *settled wl in midfield: smooth hdwy to go 2nd 2f out: rdn to ld over 1f out: sn clr: rdn out* **2/1**[1]

0423 **2** 2 1/2 **Roving Mission (USA)**[25] 7730 3-9-2 **70**.................... HarryBentley 9 77
(Ralph Beckett) *pushed along to ld after 2f: rdn along and readily brushed aside by wnr over 1f out: kpt on wl in battle for 2nd fnl f* **5/1**[2]

6064 **3** nk **International Law**[35] 7378 5-9-4 **68**.................... CamHardie 7 74
(Antony Brittain) *racd in midfield: effrt to cl 2f out: sn rdn and hdwy to go 3rd 1f out: kpt on fnl f* **9/1**

5503 **4** *1* **Redgrave (IRE)**[32] 7489 5-9-6 **70** .... CharlesBishop 4 74
(Joseph Tuite) *trckd ldrs: pushed along in 5th 2f out: swtchd rt and rdn off home bnd: kpt on one pce fnl f* **7/1**

4535 **5** *1 1/2* **Memphis Bleek**[25] 7730 3-9-2 **70** .... (b) DavidNolan 6 71
(Ivan Furtado) *prom: pushed along and outpcd 2f out: sn rdn and no imp 1f out: one pce fnl f* **14/1**

3641 **6** *1* **Hermocrates (FR)**[16] 7984 3-9-2 **70** .... (b) RossaRyan 11 69
(Richard Hannon) *midfield: rdn and no imp 2f out: drvn and hung lft over 1f out: one pce after (jockey said gelding hung left-handed)* **11/2**[3]

00 **7** *1/2* **He's Our Star (IRE)**[72] 6050 4-9-5 **69** .... HollieDoyle 5 67
(Ali Stronge) *midfield on outer: rdn and no hdwy 2f out: drvn and no imp over 1f out: no ex* **33/1**

3010 **8** *1/2* **Ruby Gates (IRE)**[30] 7560 6-8-13 **68** .... DylanHogan(5) 3 65
(John Butler) *led for 2f then trckd ldr: rdn and lost pl 2f out: wknd fnl f* **22/1**

0-00 **9** *1* **Abel Tasman**[48] 6925 5-9-6 **70** .... DavidProbert 8 64
(Roy Brotherton) *hld up: rdn along in rr over 2f out: nvr a factor* **50/1**

3320 **10** *2* **Elhafei (USA)**[20] 7875 4-9-6 **70** .... AlistairRawlinson 1 60
(Michael Appleby) *almost ref to jump fr flag s: racd in rr: nvr on terms* **7/1**

0015 **11** *8* **Spirit Of Sarwan (IRE)**[10] 8186 5-9-0 **67** .... (v) JaneElliott(3) 2 40
(Stef Keniry) *reluctant to line up: s.v.s: detached early: a bhd (jockey said gelding was reluctant to line up and never travelling thereafter)* **25/1**

2450 **12** *1* **Smiley Bagel (IRE)**[19] 7915 6-8-11 **66** .... KevinLundie(5) 13 37
(Mark Loughnane) *hld up: outpcd and detached over 2f out: a bhd (jockey said gelding ran too free)* **80/1**

1m 56.9s (-3.90) **Going Correction** -0.375s/f (Stan)
WFA 3 from 4yo+ 4lb **12** Ran SP% **121.4**
Speed ratings (Par 103): **102,99,99,98,97 96,95,95,94,92 85,84**
CSF £11.37 CT £76.77 TOTE £2.30: £1.20, £2.00, £3.30; EX 9.90 Trifecta £110.30.
Owner P K Siu **Bred** Josham Farms Limited **Trained** Upper Lambourn, Berks
■ Stewards' Enquiry : Luke Morris cautioned: careless riding

FOCUS
Flag start. A modest handicap won pretty convincingly. The second has been rated in line with his penultimate start.
T/Plt: £9.00 to a £1 stake. Pool: £44,586.26 - 4,901.96 winning units T/Qpdt: £2.80 to a £1 stake. Pool: £5,882.07 - 2092.64 winning units **Mark Grantham**

8481 DEAUVILLE (R-H)
Thursday, October 24
OFFICIAL GOING: Polytrack: standard; turf: heavy

8508a PRIX ARAZI (CONDITIONS) (2YO COLTS & GELDINGS) (ALL-WEATHER TRACK) (POLYTRACK) 7f 110y(P)
11:55 2-Y-O
£15,315 (£5,819; £4,288; £2,450; £1,225; £918)

RPR

1 **Coronado Beach**[58] 6584 2-8-10 0 .... GregoryBenoist 5 83
(Mlle A Wattel, France) **107/10**

2 *nse* **Le Solaire**[17] 2-8-10 0 .... StephanePasquier 1 83
(P Bary, France) **63/10**

3 *nk* **Lauenen (FR)**[24] 2-9-0 0 .... CristianDemuro 9 86
(J-C Rouget, France) **2/1**[1]

4 *hd* **Yoker (FR)**[17] 2-9-0 0 .... MaximeGuyon 6 86
(Mme Pia Brandt, France) **19/5**[2]

5 *1 1/4* **Sky Power (FR)**[24] 2-8-10 0 .... (b) EddyHardouin 3 79
(G Barbedette, France) **24/1**

6 *1 1/4* **Chill Chainnigh (FR)**[20] 7887 2-9-4 0 .... JeromeCabre 2 84
(Y Barberot, France) **68/10**

7 *1 1/4* **Fighting Don (FR)**[45] 7043 2-8-10 0 .... IoritzMendizabal 4 73
(Harry Dunlop) **33/1**

8 *2 1/2* **Motarajel**[44] 2-9-0 .... Pierre-CharlesBoudot 8 71
(F Rohaut, France) *racd towards rr early: prog on outer to sit on heels of ldr by 1/2-way: asked for effrt over 2f out: grad wknd* **39/10**[3]

9 *2* **New Cracker's (IRE)** 2-8-8 0 .... AurelienLemaitre 7 60
(N Caullery, France) **41/1**

1m 28.49s **9** Ran SP% **119.0**
PARI-MUTUEL (all including 1 euro stake): WIN 11.70; PLACE 2.50, 1.90, 1.40; DF 31.90.
Owner Ecurie Pierre Pilarski **Bred** Team Hogdala A.B. **Trained** France

7193 DONCASTER (L-H)
Friday, October 25
OFFICIAL GOING: Soft changing to heavy after race 1 (1.50)
Wind: Moderate against Weather: Heavy cloud and rain

8509 HAGUE PRINT MANAGEMENT NURSERY H'CAP 1m (S)
1:50 (1:54) (Class 3) (0-95,87) 2-Y-O **£6,847** (£2,050; £1,025; £512) Stalls High

Form RPR

0621 **1** **She's A Unicorn**[9] 8259 2-8-5 **74** 6ex .... (v) JaneElliott(3) 4 78
(Tom Dascombe) *hld up: sltly hmpd after 150yds: in rr: pushed along 3f out: hdwy 2f out: rdn to chal over 1f out: drvn ins fnl f: kpt on wl to ld last 50yds* **5/1**

3012 **2** *1/2* **Gold Souk (IRE)**[27] 7699 2-9-7 **87** .... FrannyNorton 2 90
(Mark Johnston) *led and edgd rt to stands' rail after 150yds: set stdy pce: pushed along and clr over 2f out: jnd and rdn over 1f out: drvn and edgd lft ins fnl f: hdd and no ex last 50yds* **4/1**[3]

0231 **3** *19* **Qaaddim (IRE)**[22] 7840 2-9-0 **80** .... (p) AndreaAtzeni 3 41+
(Roger Varian) *t.k.h: hmpd after 150yds: trckd ldng pair: pushed along over 2f out: sn rdn and wknd wl over 1f out* **6/4**[1]

4511 **4** *3/4* **Borsdane Wood**[21] 7871 2-9-3 **83** .... BenCurtis 1 43+
(K R Burke) *trckd ldr: pushed along over 2f out: sn rdn and wknd wl over 1f out* **2/1**[2]

1m 49.72s (9.52) **Going Correction** +1.125s/f (Soft) **4** Ran SP% **110.0**
Speed ratings (Par 99): **97,96,77,76**
CSF £22.55 TOTE £5.60; EX 23.10 Trifecta £39.90.
Owner T Dascombe **Bred** Hall Of Fame Stud **Trained** Malpas, Cheshire
■ Stewards' Enquiry : Franny Norton two-day ban: interference & careless riding (Nov 8-9)

FOCUS
After winning the first - and riding out her claim - Jane Elliott said: "It's very testing and it's going to get worse with this weather." An interesting nursery despite the small field, but only two gave their running. It's been rated cautiously.

8510 BREWSTER PARTNERS BRITISH EBF MAIDEN FILLIES' STKS (PLUS 10 RACE) 1m (S)
2:25 (2:26) (Class 5) 2-Y-O **£3,428** (£1,020; £509; £254) Stalls High

Form RPR

1 **Domino Darling** 2-9-0 0 .... TomMarquand 7 85+
(William Haggas) *in tch: pushed along and hdwy over 2f out: chal over 1f out: sn rdn: styd on wl to ld last 100yds* **10/1**[3]

2 *nk* **Gold Wand (IRE)** 2-9-0 0 .... AndreaAtzeni 2 84+
(Roger Varian) *led: pushed along 2f out: jnd wl over 1f out and sn rdn: drvn and edgd lft ins fnl f: hdd last 100yds: kpt on* **6/4**[1]

3 *4 1/2* **Wonderful Tonight (FR)** 2-9-0 0 .... PJMcDonald 16 74+
(David Menuisier) *towards rr: stdy hdwy 1/2-way: rdn to chse ldrs 2f out: styd on wl fnl f* **25/1**

4 *3/4* **Lady G (IRE)** 2-9-0 0 .... BenCurtis 14 73
(William Haggas) *trckd ldrs: hdwy 3f out: cl up 2f out: rdn and ev ch over 1f out: grad wknd* **7/1**[2]

0 **5** *1 1/2* **Make It Rain (IRE)**[14] 8093 2-9-0 0 .... MartinDwyer 9 69
(Simon Crisford) *trckd ldrs: hdwy and cl up 3f out: chal wl over 1f out: sn rdn and ev ch: drvn and wknd appr fnl f* **7/1**[2]

6 *6* **Arriviste** 2-9-0 0 .... PaulMulrennan 10 56+
(Rae Guest) *stdd s: t.k.h and sn in midfield: hdwy over 2f out: sn rdn along and no imp* **33/1**

7 *1 3/4* **Suestar** 2-9-0 0 .... JimCrowley 11 52+
(David Simcock) *hmpd s and bhd: hdwy 2f out: kpt on appr fnl f* **20/1**

8 *2 1/2* **Viola (IRE)** 2-9-0 0 .... (h[1]) DanielMuscutt 12 47
(James Fanshawe) *nvr bttr than midfield* **16/1**

9 *3* **True Scarlet (IRE)** 2-9-0 0 .... PaulHanagan 13 40
(Ed Walker) *wnt lft s: towards rr: rdn along over 3f out: nvr a factor* **16/1**

0 **10** *4* **Volcano Bay**[23] 7826 2-9-0 0 .... HarryBentley 6 32
(Ismail Mohammed) *prom: cl up 1/2-way: pushed along 3f out: rdn 2f out: sn wknd* **50/1**

11 *1* **Sea Of Shadows** 2-8-9 0 .... GerO'Neill(5) 3 29
(Michael Easterby) *s.i.s and green in rr: hdwy over 3f out: rdn along over 2f out: sn wknd* **66/1**

0 **12** *3/4* **Echo's Love (IRE)**[14] 8093 2-9-0 0 .... RobertHavlin 4 28
(John Gosden) *chsd ldrs: rdn along over 3f out: sn wknd* **12/1**

13 *11* **Hayuplass** 2-9-0 0 .... RachelRichardson 8 3
(Tim Easterby) *chsd ldrs: rdn along over 3f out: sn wknd* **66/1**

14 *3 1/4* **Approximate** 2-9-0 0 .... HayleyTurner 5
(Michael Bell) *in tch: rdn along 1/2-way: sn wknd* **10/1**[3]

0 **15** *13* **Global Orchid (IRE)**[30] 7580 2-9-0 0 .... GeraldMosse 1
(Tom Dascombe) *trckd ldrs: pushed along over 3f out: sn rdn and wknd wl over 2f out* **33/1**

1m 46.69s (6.49) **Going Correction** +1.125s/f (Soft) **15** Ran SP% **122.1**
Speed ratings (Par 92): **111,110,106,105,103 97,96,93,90,86 85,84,73,70,57**
CSF £23.99 TOTE £12.30: £3.00, £1.40, £6.30; EX 36.20 Trifecta £501.30.
Owner A E Oppenheimer **Bred** Hascombe & Valiant Stud Ltd **Trained** Newmarket, Suffolk

FOCUS
The official ground description became heavy before this race, and it was hard work for these inexperienced fillies. The first two pulled nicely clear and the wining time was 3sec quicker than the four-runner nursery.

8511 AQUASPERSIONS GROUP BRITISH EBF MAIDEN STKS 7f 6y
3:00 (3:01) (Class 5) 2-Y-O **£3,428** (£1,020; £509; £254) Stalls High

Form RPR

1 **Magnetised** 2-9-5 0 .... AndreaAtzeni 4 77+
(Roger Varian) *dwlt: sn in tch: trckd ldrs 1/2-way: effrt to chse ldng pair and rdn over 1f out: styd on to chal ins fnl f: kpt on wl to ld towards fin* **7/4**[1]

5 **2** *nk* **Beauty Choice**[16] 8011 2-9-5 0 .... HayleyTurner 5 76
(Charlie Fellowes) *prom: led over 4f out: rdn along 2f out: drvn ent fnl f: hdd and no ex towards fin* **7/1**[3]

3 *1 1/4* **Camahawk** 2-9-5 0 .... DavidAllan 15 73
(Tim Easterby) *trckd ldrs: prom over 4f out: chal over 2f out: sn rdn and ev ch: drvn ent fnl f: kpt on same pce* **25/1**

4 *1 3/4* **Born A King** 2-9-5 0 .... TomMarquand 10 69+
(William Haggas) *hld up towards rr: hdwy wl over 2f out: rdn over 1f out: kpt on fnl f* **11/4**[2]

5 *1/2* **Brunch** 2-9-5 0 .... CallumRodriguez 2 68+
(Michael Dods) *green: dwlt and fly j. s: bhd: hdwy 1/2-way: rdn along to chse ldrs wl over 1f out: kpt on same pce fnl f (jockey said gelding bucked and bronked for several strides after the start)* **16/1**

6 *2 1/4* **Borstal Bull (IRE)** 2-9-5 0 .... ShaneGray 13 62
(Phillip Makin) *dwlt and in rr: hdwy over 2f out: kpt on fnl f* **33/1**

7 *3 1/2* **Grey Eminence** 2-9-5 0 .... BarryMcHugh 9 53
(James Given) *trckd ldrs: hdwy and cl up over 3f out: rdn along 2f out: sn drvn and wknd* **40/1**

8 *3 3/4* **Whosegottheshekles (IRE)** 2-9-0 0 .... FayeMcManoman(5) 12 44
(Nigel Tinkler) *slt ld: hdd over 4f out: cl up: rdn along over 3f out: sn wknd* **66/1**

4 **9** *1/2* **Imperial Command (IRE)**[179] 2205 2-9-5 0 .... FrannyNorton 8 43
(Jonjo O'Neill) *chsd ldrs: rdn along wl over 2f out: sn wknd* **12/1**

0 **10** *1/2* **Bold Suitor**[20] 7911 2-9-5 0 .... PaulHanagan 7 41
(Ed Walker) *hld up: a towards rr* **12/1**

11 *shd* **Emerald Swalk (IRE)** 2-9-5 0 .... RachelRichardson 3 41
(Tim Easterby) *prom: cl up 1/2-way: rdn along wl over 2f out: sn wknd* **40/1**

12 *shd* **Angel On High (IRE)** 2-9-5 0 .... BenCurtis 16 41
(Harry Dunlop) *a in rr (vet said colt lost its left fore shoe)* **12/1**

13 *3 1/2* **Free Cash (IRE)** 2-9-5 0 .... LewisEdmunds 14 32
(Nigel Tinkler) *prom: rdn along bef 1/2-way: sn outpcd* **40/1**

1m 36.33s (9.93) **Going Correction** +1.125s/f (Soft) **13** Ran SP% **120.1**
Speed ratings (Par 95): **88,87,86,84,83 81,77,72,72,71 71,71,67**
CSF £13.79 TOTE £2.50: £1.50, £1.60, £5.40; EX 12.50 Trifecta £200.60.
Owner Sheikh Mohammed Obaid Al Maktoum **Bred** Sheikh Mohammed Obaid Al Maktoum **Trained** Newmarket, Suffolk

FOCUS
Probably just a fair maiden, but a very promising start from the favourite. The field raced down the centre, with the 1-2 both positioned on the far side of the group. It's been rated conservatively for the time being.

8512 VERTEM LEADING THE FIELD H'CAP — 6f 2y
3:35 (3:35) (Class 2) (0-105,97) 3-Y-0+
£12,450 (£3,728; £1,864; £932; £466; £234) Stalls High

Form — RPR

-110 **1** **Bielsa (IRE)**[41] 7193 4-9-4 **93** ... KevinStott 1 109
(Kevin Ryan) *slt ld: hdd narrowly 2f out: rdn to ld again appr fnl f: kpt on strly* 5/1[1]

3251 **2** 2 ¼ **Pendleton**[20] 7894 3-8-13 **89** ... (p) CallumRodriguez 6 98
(Michael Dods) *cl up slt ld 2f out: rdn and hdd appr fnl f: sn drvn and kpt on same pce* 6/1[2]

0400 **3** 4 ½ **Cold Stare (IRE)**[13] 8127 4-9-5 **94** ... (t) HarryBentley 5 90
(David O'Meara) *trckd ldrs: pushed along over 2f out: sn rdn to chse ldng pair: drvn over 1f out: kpt on same pce* 8/1

0223 **4** 1 ½ **Gabrial The Saint (IRE)**[7] 8317 4-9-3 **92** ... (h[1]) PaulHanagan 11 83
(Richard Fahey) *in tch: hdwy 2f out: sn chsng ldrs: rdn along over 1f out: no imp fnl f* 7/1[3]

0030 **5** ¾ **Dalton**[69] 6227 5-8-9 **84** ... (p) RachelRichardson 7 73
(Julie Camacho) *cl up: pushed along over 2f out: sn rdn and grad wknd* 14/1

6205 **6** 1 **Lahore (USA)**[13] 8127 5-9-8 **97** ... PaulMulrennan 3 83
(Phillip Makin) *trckd ldrs: pushed along and hdwy over 2f out: sn rdn: drvn wl over 1f out: sn one pce* 7/1[3]

0106 **7** 3 **Alaadel**[13] 8127 6-9-4 **93** ... (t) GeraldMosse 2 70
(Stuart Williams) *dwlt and towards rr: hdwy over 3f out: sn chsng ldrs: rdn along 2f out: sn wknd* 15/2

5216 **8** 1 **Call Me Ginger**[20] 7894 3-8-11 **87** ... BenRobinson 14 61
(Jim Goldie) *a towards rr* 11/1

0020 **9** 2 **Gunmetal (IRE)**[13] 8127 6-9-8 **97** ... PJMcDonald 10 65
(David Barron) *chsd ldrs: rdn along wl over 2f out: sn wknd* 20/1

6210 **10** 1 ¼ **Bernardo O'Reilly**[13] 8127 5-9-5 **94** ... MartinDwyer 8 58
(Richard Spencer) *awkward s and in rr: swtchd lft and hdwy 1/2-way: rdn along to chse ldrs over 2f out: sn drvn and wknd* 25/1

0551 **11** 12 **Diamond Dougal (IRE)**[27] 7701 4-9-1 **90** ... (v) TomMarquand 9 18
(Mick Channon) *in tch: hdwy to chse ldrs 1/2-way: rdn along over 2f out: sn drvn and wknd* 16/1

0403 **12** 1 **Triggered (IRE)**[48] 6976 3-8-11 **87** ... AndreaAtzeni 12 12
(Ed Walker) *a towards rr* 8/1

1m 17.73s (5.03) **Going Correction** +1.125s/f (Soft)
WFA 3 from 4yo+ 1lb — **12** Ran SP% **119.4**
Speed ratings (Par 109): **111,108,102,100,99 97,93,92,89,88 72,70**
CSF £34.32 CT £240.73 TOTE £5.20: £1.80, £2.00, £2.80; EX 25.50 Trifecta £316.30.
Owner Highbank Stud **Bred** Highbank Stud **Trained** Hambleton, N Yorks

FOCUS
This decent sprint handicap really only ever concerned two. The second has been rated in line with his Ascot win.

8513 VERTEM INVESTING FOR THE FUTURE H'CAP — 1m 6f 115y
4:10 (4:11) (Class 3) (0-90,89) 3-Y-0 £7,561 (£2,263; £1,131; £566; £282) Stalls Low

Form — RPR

2321 **1** **Caravan Of Hope (IRE)**[21] 7867 3-8-12 **80** ... AndreaAtzeni 2 93+
(Hugo Palmer) *hld up in tch: hdwy over 5f out: trckd ldrs over 3f out: cl up 2f out: led 1 1/2f out: sn rdn clr: kpt on wl* 9/4[1]

3446 **2** 3 ¾ **Contrebasse**[13] 8129 4-8-9 **70** oh1 ... (p) DavidAllan 5 76
(Tim Easterby) *trckd ldrs on inner: hdwy over 4f out: swtchd rt and rdn over 2f out: sn chsng ldng pair: drvn to chse wnr ins fnl f: kpt on: no imp* 12/1

6-23 **3** 1 ¾ **River Icon**[13] 8129 7-9-5 **80** ... (p) PaulMulrennan 12 84
(Iain Jardine) *trckd ldrs: hdwy 5f out: led over 2f out: rdn along and hdd 1 1/2f out: sn drvn: kpt on same pce* 28/1

1015 **4** 13 **Overhaugh Street**[27] 7683 6-8-12 **73** ... ShaneGray 9 60
(Ed de Giles) *trckd ldrs on inner: pushed along over 4f out: rdn along and sltly outpcd 3f out: plugged on u.p fnl 2f* 40/1

P-40 **5** 5 **Belisa (IRE)**[20] 7900 5-9-4 **79** ... DougieCostello 3 59
(Ivan Furtado) *chsd clr ldr: hdwy and cl up over 3f out: rdn along over 2f out: sn drvn and wknd* 80/1

2322 **6** 1 ½ **Celestial Force (IRE)**[23] 7830 4-9-9 **84** ... (v) PJMcDonald 1 62
(Tom Dascombe) *led and sn clr: pushed along over 4f out: rdn 3f out: hdd over 2f out: grad wknd* 7/1

2152 **7** 7 **Teodora De Vega (IRE)**[27] 7702 3-8-10 **78** ... HarryBentley 6 49
(Ralph Beckett) *hld up towards rr: hdwy over 5f out: chsd ldrs 3f out: rdn along over 2f out: sn drvn and btn* 9/2[3]

2326 **8** 6 **Funny Man**[21] 7864 3-9-1 **83** ... (b) JimCrowley 10 46
(David O'Meara) *hld up in rr: effrt and sme hdwy 4f out: sn rdn and nvr a factor* 16/1

4235 **9** 31 **Employer (IRE)**[11] 8185 4-9-0 **75** ... BenRobinson 8
(Jim Goldie) *hld up: a in rr* 25/1

/10- **10** 7 **Master Of Irony (IRE)**[515] 3152 7-9-8 **83** ... (p) KevinStott 15
(John Quinn) *dwlt: a in rr* 66/1

124 **11** 47 **Mankayan (IRE)**[32] 7525 3-8-12 **80** ... (p) StevieDonohoe 7
(Charlie Fellowes) *hld up: a towards rr* 14/1

200 **12** 12 **Billy Ray**[13] 8114 4-10-0 **89** ... (v) SilvestreDeSousa 13
(Mick Channon) *dwlt: a in rr* 10/1

1301 **13** 31 **Battle Of Marathon (USA)**[11] 8185 7-9-1 **83** 4ex ... LauraPearson(7) 11
(John Ryan) *hld up in rr: rapid hdwy on outer to chse ldng pair 7f out: wd st and sn wknd (jockey said gelding hung right in the home straight)* 50/1

5661 **14** 62 **Ginistrelli (IRE)**[49] 6924 3-8-11 **79** ... TomMarquand 14
(Ed Walker) *chsd ldrs: rdn along 7f out: sn lost pl and bhd: t.o fnl 4f (trainer's rep could offer no explanation for the gelding's performance)* 4/1[2]

3m 29.97s (18.37) **Going Correction** +1.40s/f (Soft)
WFA 3 from 4yo+ 7lb — **14** Ran SP% **125.2**
Speed ratings (Par 107): **107,105,104,97,94 93,89,86,70,66 41,35,18,**
CSF £32.12 CT £638.55 TOTE £3.40: £1.30, £3.60, £6.30; EX 34.50 Trifecta £539.20.
Owner Dr Ali Ridha **Bred** Oak Hill Stud **Trained** Newmarket, Suffolk

FOCUS
Fairly useful staying form. They were soon strung out as the sixth set a searching pace in the conditions. A pb from the winner, with the second and third close to form.

8514 1ST SECURITY SOLUTIONS H'CAP — 1m 2f 43y
4:45 (4:46) (Class 3) (0-95,93) 3-Y-O £7,762 (£2,310; £1,154; £577) Stalls Low

Form — RPR

2310 **1** **Passion And Glory (IRE)**[47] 6998 3-9-3 **89** ... CallumShepherd 9 100+
(Saeed bin Suroor) *led 3f: trckd ldr: led again 3f out: rdn 2f out: drvn clr over 1f out: hld on wl towards fin* 5/1[2]

3256 **2** *nk* **Dark Lochnagar (USA)**[34] 7436 3-9-0 **86** ... ShaneGray 10 94
(Keith Dalgleish) *chsd ldng pair: hdwy 4f out: cl up 3f out: rdn to chse wnr 2f out: drvn over 1f out: kpt on wl u.p towards fin* 6/1[3]

1640 **3** 7 **Aweedram (IRE)**[105] 4882 3-9-3 **89** ... (h[1]) TomMarquand 4 83
(Alan King) *dwlt and in rr: hdwy 4f out: pushed along to chse ldrs 3f out: rdn along over 2f out: drvn to chse ldng pair and ch wl over 1f out: kpt on same pce appr fnl f* 11/1

6-6 **4** 5 **Princesse Mathilde**[103] 4964 3-9-2 **88** ... HayleyTurner 6 72
(Charlie Fellowes) *trckd ldrs: hdwy 4f out: cl up 3f out: rdn over 2f out: drvn and wknd wl over 1f out* 6/1[3]

2231 **5** 11 **Olympic Conqueror (IRE)**[20] 7907 3-8-7 **79** oh4 ... BarryMcHugh 2 41
(James Fanshawe) *in tch: effrt and sme hdwy 4f out: rdn along 3f out: n.d* 6/1[3]

4512 **6** 9 **Storting**[42] 7153 3-9-0 **86** ... SilvestreDeSousa 1 30
(Mick Channon) *trckd ldr: led after 3f: pushed along over 3f out: sn rdn: hdd & wknd over 2f out (trainer's rep could offer no explanation for the gelding's performance)* 10/3[1]

3303 **7** 62 **Oasis Prince**[26] 7727 3-9-7 **93** ... PJMcDonald 3
(Mark Johnston) *a bhd: t.o fnl 4f* 16/1

421 **8** 25 **Modakhar (IRE)**[33] 7490 3-8-9 **81** ... BenCurtis 8
(K R Burke) *trckd ldrs: pushed along over 5f out: rdn over 4f out: sn outpcd: wl bhd and eased fnl 3f (jockey said gelding ran too free)* 5/1[2]

2m 22.84s (10.54) **Going Correction** +1.40s/f (Soft) — **8** Ran SP% **113.5**
Speed ratings (Par 105): **110,109,104,100,91 84,34,14**
CSF £34.27 CT £312.34 TOTE £4.80: £1.90, £1.70, £3.60; EX 34.90 Trifecta £251.60.
Owner Godolphin **Bred** Godolphin **Trained** Newmarket, Suffolk

FOCUS
A decent handicap, but not form to take too literally given the state of the ground. A pb from the winner, with the second back to form.

8515 AMATEUR JOCKEYS ASSOCIATION AMATEUR RIDERS' H'CAP — 1m 2f 43y
5:15 (5:18) (Class 5) (0-75,75) 3-Y-0+
£3,306 (£1,025; £512; £300; £300; £300) Stalls Low

Form — RPR

0211 **1** **Gamesters Icon**[9] 8247 4-9-11 **65** 5ex ... (tp) MrCaiWilliams(7) 15 83
(Oliver Greenall) *trckd ldrs: hdwy over 4f out: led 3f out: rdn along 2f out: drvn ent fnl f: hld on gamely towards fin* 9/2[1]

5534 **2** ½ **Grazeon Roy**[35] 7405 3-10-1 **69** ... MrAaronAnderson(3) 2 86
(John Quinn) *a.p: effrt 3f out: rdn to chse wnr wl over 1f out: drvn to chal ent fnl f: ev ch tl no ex towards fin* 16/1

2305 **3** 13 **Firewater**[23] 7829 3-9-10 **66** ... (p) MrEireannCagney(5) 9 57
(Richard Fahey) *hld up in midfield: hdwy 4f out: swtchd lft to inner and effrt 3f out: sn cl up and rdn: drvn wl over 1f out: kpt on same pce* 12/1

6000 **4** ½ **Kyoto Star (FR)**[34] 7439 5-9-12 **64** ... (b) MissCharlotteCrane(5) 14 53
(Tim Easterby) *in tch: hdwy over 3f out: sn rdn along to chse ldrs: drvn 2f out: plugged on same pce* 50/1

6311 **5** ½ **Deinonychus**[16] 8033 8-10-9 **70** ... (h) MissSerenaBrotherton 8 58
(Michael Appleby) *hld up: hdwy over 3f out: chsd ldrs 2f out: sn rdn and no imp* 6/1[2]

302 **6** 1 **Railport Dolly**[20] 7907 4-11-0 **75** ... MissJoannaMason 16 61
(David Barron) *trckd ldrs: hdwy over 4f out: chsd wnr 3f out: rdn along over 2f out: sn drvn and grad wknd fr wl over 1f out* 10/1

3561 **7** *nse* **Thorntoun Care**[31] 7544 8-10-4 **70** ... (p) MissAmyCollier(5) 10 56
(Karen Tutty) *dwlt: hld up and bhd: hdwy over 3f out: rdn along over 2f out: plugged on: n.d* 20/1

1562 **8** 4 ½ **Zealous (IRE)**[11] 8186 6-9-7 **61** ... (p) MrConnorWood(7) 12 38
(Alistair Whillans) *bhd: hdwy over 4f out: plugged on fnl 3f: n.d (trainer said gelding was never travelling on the heavy going)* 9/1

1221 **9** 8 **Luna Magic**[11] 8186 5-10-12 **73** 5ex ... MissBrodieHampson 18 34
(Archie Watson) *hld up in tch: hdwy on outer to chse ldrs 3f out: rdn along over 2f out: sn drvn and grad wknd (trainer said mare was unsuited by the heavy going and would prefer a quicker surface)* 15/2[3]

0006 **10** 4 **Majeste**[10] 8238 5-10-0 **61** ... MrJamesHarding 13 14
(Rebecca Bastiman) *hld up: effrt and sme hdwy on outer over 3f out: sn rdn along and n.d* 20/1

3003 **11** 5 **Firby (IRE)**[62] 6456 4-9-13 **67** ... MissRachelTaylor(7) 17 10
(Michael Dods) *a towards rr* 40/1

4020 **12** 8 **Abushamah (IRE)**[24] 7776 8-9-10 **62** ... MissEmilyBullock(5) 19
(Ruth Carr) *t.k.h: chsd ldrs on outer: rdn along over 3f out: sn wknd* 28/1

0554 **13** 2 ¾ **Jupiter Road**[48] 6973 3-10-2 **74** ... (tp) MrJoshuaScott(7) 5
(Nigel Tinkler) *a towards rr* 50/1

5446 **14** 3 ¼ **Earth And Sky (USA)**[78] 5855 3-10-4 **69** ... (p[1] w) MrSimonWalker 11
(George Scott) *a towards rr* 16/1

5400 **15** 9 **Dutch Uncle**[16] 8033 7-10-5 **71** ow1 ... (b) MrCharlesClover(5) 20
(Tom Clover) *led: rdn along over 4f out: hdd over 3f out: sn wknd* 20/1

0034 **16** 2 **Dance King**[20] 7907 9-10-6 **67** ... (tp) MrWilliamEasterby 7
(Tim Easterby) *dwlt: a towards rr* 8/1

4444 **17** 18 **Thomas Cranmer (USA)**[62] 6456 5-10-10 **71** ... MissEmmaTodd 4
(Tina Jackson) *a towards rr* 33/1

3100 **18** 8 **Flood Defence (IRE)**[36] 7366 5-10-0 **64** ... MissSarahBowen(3) 1
(Iain Jardine) *a towards rr* 20/1

6640 **19** 11 **Stringybark Creek**[31] 7540 5-10-6 **74** ... MrBradleyRoberts(7) 3
(David Loughnane) *chsd ldr: pushed along over 4f out: rdn over 3f out: sn wknd* 33/1

2m 26.13s (13.83) **Going Correction** +1.40s/f (Soft)
WFA 3 from 4yo+ 4lb — **19** Ran SP% **128.6**
Speed ratings (Par 103): **100,99,89,88,88 87,87,83,77,74 70,63,61,59,51 50,35,29,20**
CSF £70.70 CT £839.90 TOTE £4.70: £1.60, £5.10, £2.20, £11.10; EX 101.00 Trifecta £1300.40.

Owner Gamesters Partnership **Bred** D V Williams **Trained** Oldcastle Heath, Cheshire

FOCUS
This big-field amateurs' race was run at a pretty strong initial gallop in the worst of the ground, and only two of them truly saw it out. The winner has been rated as backing up her Bath win.
T/Plt: £390.20 to a £1 stake. Pool: £67,603.28 - 126.47 winning units T/Qpdt: £30.90 to a £1 stake. Pool: £8,919.06 - 213.06 winning units **Joe Rowntree**

7453 NEWBURY (L-H)

Friday, October 25

OFFICIAL GOING: Heavy (5.0)

Wind: light, across, strengthening during the afternoon Weather: drizzly rain

8516 ENERGY CHECK EBF MAIDEN STKS (PLUS 10 RACE) 6f 110y

1:10 (1:13) (Class 4) 2-Y-O £4,463 (£1,328; £663; £331) Stalls High

Form RPR

1 **With Respect (IRE)** 2-9-5 0 RichardKingscote 3 85+
(Hughie Morrison) *wnt rt s: hld up in tch in midfield: clsd and travelling wl whn nt clr run 2f out: rdn and hdwy over 1f out: chsd ldr and swtchd rt ins fnl f: r.o wl to ld last strides* 22/1

2 hd **Cold Front** 2-9-5 0 JamesDoyle 11 84+
(William Haggas) *led: travelling strly and wnt 2 l clr over 1f out: rdn ins fnl f: hrd pressed towards fin: hdd last strides* 3/1[1]

3 4 1/2 **Sky Storm** 2-9-0 0 HollieDoyle 9 67
(Hughie Morrison) *chsd ldrs: effrt to chse ldr 2f out: rdn and unable to match pce of wnr over 1f out: lost 2nd and kpt on same pce ins fnl f* 14/1

4 1 3/4 **Risk Taker (IRE)** 2-9-5 0 HectorCrouch 2 67
(Clive Cox) *hld up in tch in midfield: clsd on ldrs whn effrt 2f out: no ex u.p over 1f out: outpcd ins fnl f* 17/2

5 2 3/4 **Grey Fox (IRE)** 2-9-5 0 CharlesBishop 4 60
(Emma Lavelle) *bmpd s: hld up in tch in midfield: rdn over 2f out: sn outpcd and sltly impeded over 1f out: no threat to ldrs but kpt on ins fnl f* 16/1

6 1/2 **Oksana Astankova** 2-9-0 0 KieranO'Neill 12 53
(Mick Channon) *chsd ldrs: effrt ent fnl 2f: unable qck and outpcd over 1f out: wknd ins fnl f* 16/1

7 3/4 **Motamayiz** 2-9-5 0 JackMitchell 20 56+
(Roger Varian) *chsd ldrs: effrt and rdn over 2f out: unable qck and outpcd over 1f out: wknd ins fnl f* 7/1[3]

4 8 1 1/4 **Waddat (IRE)**[130] 3942 2-9-5 0 ShaneKelly 15 53+
(Richard Hughes) *taken down early: chsd ldr tl rdn and edgd lft 2f out: lost pl over 1f out: wknd ins fnl f* 33/1

9 nk **Bullfinch** 2-9-5 0 JasonWatson 18 52+
(Roger Charlton) *t.k.h: hld up in midfield: swtchd rt over 2f out: sn rdn and outpcd: no threat to ldrs but kpt on steadily ins fnl f* 5/1[2]

10 3/4 **Iron Heart** 2-9-5 0 DavidProbert 14 50
(Andrew Balding) *in tch in midfield: effrt over 2f out: sn struggling to qckn and outpcd over 1f out: edgd lft and wl hld ins fnl f* 10/1

11 1 1/4 **Kafee (IRE)** 2-9-5 0 RobHornby 5 47
(Andrew Balding) *chsd ldrs: effrt ent fnl 2f: unable qck and lost pl over 1f out: wknd ins fnl f* 9/1

12 shd **Mabre (IRE)** 2-9-5 0 KieranShoemark 6 46
(David Evans) *hld up towards rr: hdwy 3f out: effrt jst over 2f out: rdn and no imp over 1f out: wknd ins fnl f* 50/1

13 1 1/4 **Egypsyan Crackajak** 2-9-5 0 JFEgan 16 43+
(Dominic Ffrench Davis) *hld up towards rr: rdn over 2f out: sn struggling and outpcd: wl hld over 1f out* 125/1

14 1 1/2 **Springvale Lad** 2-9-0 0 KevinLundie(5) 8 39
(Mark Loughnane) *chsd ldrs: rdn over 2f out: sn struggling and lost pl wl over 1f out: wknd fnl f* 125/1

15 1 **Saracen Star** 2-9-0 0 LukeMorris 7 31
(J S Moore) *hld up in tch in midfield: rdn over 2f out: sn struggling: wl btn over 1f out* 100/1

0 16 1 1/2 **Big Jimbo**[20] 7899 2-9-5 0 RossaRyan 1 32
(Gary Moore) *hld up in tch in midfield: rdn over 2f out: sn struggling and outpcd: wl btn over 1f out* 33/1

17 5 **Saharan Shimmer** 2-8-12 0 AngusVilliers(7) 10 18
(David Menuisier) *dwlt: sn pushed along and hdwy into midfield: lost pl over 3f out: bhd fnl 2f* 40/1

18 nk **Blue Slate (IRE)** 2-9-5 0 LiamKeniry 17 17
(J S Moore) *s.i.s: hld up towards rr: struggling over 2f out: sn wl btn* 125/1

19 2 3/4 **Truffle Mac** 2-9-0 0 CharlieBennett 19 5+
(Hughie Morrison) *hld up towards rr: effrt and rn green over 2f out: sn outpcd and wl btn over 1f out* 50/1

20 1 1/2 **Hurricane Alex** 2-9-5 0 SeanLevey 13 6+
(Richard Hannon) *in tch in midfield: rdn 3f out: sn lost pl: bhd over 1f out* 25/1

1m 26.01s (5.91) **Going Correction** +1.175s/f (Soft) 20 Ran SP% 126.0
Speed ratings (Par 97): **110,109,104,102,99 98,98,96,96,95 94,93,92,90,89 87,82,81,78,76**
CSF £84.41 TOTE £21.20: £5.50, £2.10, £5.00; EX 184.80 Trifecta £1083.00.
Owner Thurloe Thoroughbreds XLVIII **Bred** D Phelan **Trained** East Ilsley, Berks

FOCUS
It was dry overnight but there had been 7mm of rain the previous day and the ground was given as heavy (GoingStick 5.0). Returning after the first, Hector Crouch agreed with the official description and James Doyle said "It's heavy, hard work." The 7f and 5f bends were 1 metre out from the innermost line, adding 4yds to race distances starting in the back straight and the 2m race. The first two finished nicely clear in this maiden. The opening level is fluid.

8517 JOIN HOT TO TROT FOR 2020 NOVICE STKS (PLUS 10 RACE) (DIV I) 1m (S)

1:40 (1:46) (Class 4) 2-Y-O £5,110 (£1,520; £759; £379) Stalls High

Form RPR

1 **Dancing Harry (IRE)** 2-9-2 0 JasonWatson 13 77+
(Roger Charlton) *s.i.s and rn green early: in tch: swtchd rt and effrt over 3f out: hdwy and chsd ldng pair 2f out: swtchd lft over 1f out: styd on wl ins fnl f to ld 50yds out* 16/1

01 2 1 **Sea Voice**[43] 7113 2-9-3 0 ThoreHammerHansen(5) 14 81
(Richard Hannon) *chsd ldr tl led jst over 2f out: rdn over 1f out: drvn ins fnl f: hdd and no ex fnl 50yds (jockey said colt ran green)* 11/1

2 3 nse **Bright Eyed Eagle (IRE)**[30] 7586 2-9-2 0 LukeMorris 10 75
(Ed Walker) *trckd ldrs: wnt 2nd ent fnl 2f: effrt over 1f out: kpt on same pce ins fnl f* 11/8[1]

0 4 15 **Elham Valley (FR)**[18] 7972 2-9-2 0 DavidProbert 5 43
(Andrew Balding) *hld up in tch towards rr of main gp: pushed along over 2f out: sn outpcd and wl hld whn edgd lft over 1f out: plugged on into modest 4th ins fnl f* 16/1

5 9 **Call My Bluff (IRE)** 2-9-2 0 JFEgan 9 24
(Dominic Ffrench Davis) *dwlt: in tch in rr of main gp: effrt over 2f out: sn outpcd and wl btn over 1f out: no ch but plugged on to pass btn rivals ins fnl f* 66/1

26 6 3 **Lost Empire (IRE)**[52] 6845 2-9-2 0 (b) RichardKingscote 4 18
(Harry Dunlop) *t.k.h: led: hung bdly lft and wnt to centre over 5f out: hdd jst over 2f out: sn btn and wknd over 1f out (jockey said gelding ran too free)* 8/1[3]

60 7 7 **Shadow Glen**[35] 7407 2-9-2 0 CharlesBishop 8 3
(Eve Johnson Houghton) *in tch in midfield: effrt and cl enough jst over 2f out: outpcd and btn over 1f out: sn wknd: t.o* 25/1

5 8 nk **Whisper Not**[8] 8287 2-9-2 0 SeanLevey 6 3
(Richard Hannon) *chsd ldrs: effrt over 2f out: sn outpcd: wknd and wl bhd and eased ins fnl f: t.o* 11/4[2]

00 9 4 1/2 **Willy Nilly (IRE)**[37] 7338 2-9-2 0 HectorCrouch 1
(Clive Cox) *in tch in midfield: effrt over 2f out: sn struggling and btn: wknd: t.o* 16/1

5 10 11 **On The Right Track**[34] 7453 2-9-2 0 JoeyHaynes 7
(Mark Usher) *in tch in midfield: rdn and struggling over 2f out: sn btn and wknd: t.o* 50/1

00 11 1 **Jen's Lad (IRE)**[30] 7562 2-9-2 0 RossaRyan 3
(Richard Hannon) *in tch in midfield: rdn over 2f out: sn outpcd and btn: wknd: t.o* 50/1

12 22 **Siempre Rapido** 2-9-2 0 RobHornby 2
(Stuart Kittow) *a in rr: lost tch 3f out: t.o* 40/1

1m 49.86s (9.96) **Going Correction** +1.175s/f (Soft) 12 Ran SP% 117.6
Speed ratings (Par 97): **97,96,95,80,71 68,61,61,57,46 45,23**
CSF £172.15 TOTE £13.70: £3.30, £2.40, £1.10; EX 143.20 Trifecta £200.60.
Owner Fishdance Ltd **Bred** Fishdance **Trained** Beckhampton, Wilts

FOCUS
Quite a test for these 2yos in the ground and they finished well strung out behind the first three. The time was 1.52sec quicker than the second division. It's been rated quite negatively.

8518 JOIN HOT TO TROT FOR 2020 NOVICE STKS (PLUS 10 RACE) (DIV II) 1m (S)

2:15 (2:20) (Class 4) 2-Y-O £5,110 (£1,520; £759; £379) Stalls High

Form RPR

14 1 **Acquitted (IRE)**[35] 7410 2-9-8 0 KieranShoemark 11 87
(Hugo Palmer) *chsd ldr tl pushed into ld over 1f out: sn rdn and over 1 l clr ins fnl f: pushed out and a jst holding on towards fin* 5/1[3]

2 hd **Waleydd** 2-9-2 0 JackMitchell 12 81+
(Roger Varian) *hld up in tch in midfield: effrt and edgd out lft jst over 2f out: rdn to chse wnr over 1f out: no imp and looked hld 100yds out: styd on and clsng towards fin: nvr quite getting to wnr* 7/1

4 3 2 1/4 **Mishriff (IRE)**[11] 8203 2-9-2 0 FrankieDettori 9 77+
(John Gosden) *stdd and wnt lft s: t.k.h: hld up in tch in midfield: clsd: nt clr run and swtchd lft jst over 2f out: bmpd over 1f out: chsd ldrs and swtchd rt ins fnl f: kpt on same pce* 7/4[1]

6 4 1/2 **Favorite Moon (GER)**[16] 8028 2-9-2 0 JamesDoyle 2 75
(William Haggas) *in tch in midfield and furthest fr stands' rail: clsd and effrt to chse ldrs over 1f out: sn rdn: kpt on same pce ins fnl f* 9/2[2]

5 5 **Amir Kabir** 2-9-2 0 JasonWatson 14 64+
(Roger Charlton) *hld up in tch in midfield: clsd over 2f out: hemmed in: trying to switch lft and bumping w rival over 1f out: hung rt and wknd ins fnl f (jockey said gelding hung right-handed in the closing stages)* 20/1

054 6 3 1/2 **Jellystone (IRE)**[23] 7814 2-9-2 76 RobHornby 13 57
(Ralph Beckett) *led: rdn and hdd over 1f out: no ex: wknd and impeded ins fnl f* 12/1

0 7 4 **Mr Rusty (IRE)**[18] 7972 2-9-2 0 RossaRyan 3 49
(Richard Hannon) *hld up in tch in midfield: effrt over 2f out: sn outpcd and btn over 1f out: wknd fnl f* 25/1

8 11 **Relativity (FR)** 2-9-2 0 LukeMorris 4 25
(Harry Dunlop) *chsd ldrs: rdn over 2f out: sn struggling and outpcd: wknd qckly over 1f out* 66/1

9 1 3/4 **Sure I'm Your Man (IRE)** 2-9-2 0 AdamMcNamara 8 22
(Roger Charlton) *hld up in tch towards rr: effrt 3f out: sn struggling and outpcd: wl btn over 1f out: wknd* 10/1

10 1 1/2 **Beat The Heat** 2-9-2 0 CharlieBennett 6 19
(Jim Boyle) *s.i.s: hld up in tch towards rr: struggling 3f out: sn outpcd and wl bhd over 1f out* 100/1

0 11 4 1/2 **Cloud Thunder**[23] 7814 2-9-2 0 RichardKingscote 1 9
(Heather Main) *awkward leaving stalls and s.i.s: hld up in tch in rr: rdn over 3f out: sn struggling: bhd fnl 2f* 40/1

12 1/2 **Winander** 2-9-2 0 KieranO'Neill 10 8
(Stuart Kittow) *hld up in tch towards rr: rdn over 2f out: sn hung lft and btn: wknd* 66/1

13 2 1/2 **Platinum Prince** 2-9-2 0 ShaneKelly 7 3
(Gary Moore) *chsd ldrs tl over 2f out: sn outpcd and wknd qckly over 1f out* 80/1

1m 51.38s (11.48) **Going Correction** +1.175s/f (Soft) 13 Ran SP% 116.8
Speed ratings (Par 97): **89,88,86,86,81 77,73,62,60,59 54,54,51**
CSF £37.04 TOTE £4.90: £1.80, £2.40, £1.20; EX 39.10 Trifecta £167.60.
Owner John Livock & Nat Lacy **Bred** Lannister Holdings **Trained** Newmarket, Suffolk

FOCUS
The slower of the two divisions by 1.52sec and there were more in contention this time.

8519 THATCHAM BUTCHERS FILLIES' H'CAP 1m 2f

2:50 (2:50) (Class 4) (0-85,86) 3-Y-O+ £5,207 (£1,549; £774; £387; £300; £300) Stalls High

Form RPR

4216 1 **Colony Queen**[20] 7900 3-8-8 **69** LukeMorris 8 77
(Steve Gollings) *chsd ldrs: effrt over 2f out: drvn to chse ldr 1f out: styd on ins fnl f: led fnl 50yds* 16/1

2412 2 1/2 **Elegant Love**[18] 7973 3-8-4 **65** HollieDoyle 6 72
(David Evans) *chsd ldr: effrt over 2f out: rdn to ld over 1f out: drvn ins fnl f: hdd and no ex 50yds out* 13/2

3140 3 3 **Fannie By Gaslight**[18] 7974 4-9-4 **75** JamesDoyle 9 75
(Mick Channon) *hld up in tch in midfield: effrt jst over 2f out: rdn over 1f out: kpt on same pce ins fnl f: snatched 3rd last stride* 7/2[2]

3135 4 shd **Junoesque**[41] 7200 5-8-10 **67** (p) CharlieBennett 2 67
(John Gallagher) *led: rdn ent fnl 2f: drvn and hdd over 1f out: no ex and kpt on same pce ins fnl f: lost 3rd last stride* 25/1

1202 5 12 **I'm Available (IRE)**[26] 7728 3-9-11 **86** DavidProbert 3 63
(Andrew Balding) *hld up in tch in midfield: effrt over 2f out: 5th and no imp over 1f out: wknd fnl f (trainer's rep said filly was unsuited by the heavy going over the 1m2f trip and would prefer a quicker surface)* 5/2[1]

3120 6 1/2 **Escape The City**[20] 7895 4-8-10 **74** AngusVilliers(7) 7 49
(Hughie Morrison) *dwlt: sn rcvrd and in tch in midfield: effrt ent fnl 2f: outpcd u.p and btn over 1f out: wknd fnl f* 14/1

21-4 **7** *26* **Lady Adelaide (IRE)**173 2445 3-9-7 **82**........................ JasonWatson 1 6
(Roger Charlton) *mounted in chute: wl in tch in midfield: effrt over 2f out: sn struggling and btn: lost tch over 1f out: t.o and eased ins fnl f (jockey said filly stopped quickly)* **11/2**3

4633 **8** *5* **Regal Banner**30 7583 3-8-10 **71**........................ JackMitchell 5
(Roger Varian) *stdd after s: t.k.h: hld up in last pair: lost tch over 2f out: t.o and eased ins fnl f (jockey said filly was unsuited by the heavy going and would prefer a quicker surface)* **15/2**

2160 **9** *4 1/2* **Alnaseem**20 7895 3-9-0 **80**........................ RayDawson(5) 4
(Luke McJannet) *taken down early: stdd after s: t.k.h: hld up in last pair: lost tch over 2f out: t.o and eased ins fnl f* **25/1**

2m 18.26s (8.56) **Going Correction** +1.15s/f (Soft)
WFA 3 from 4yo+ 4lb **9** Ran SP% **111.5**
Speed ratings (Par 102): **108,107,105,105,95 95,74,70,66**
CSF £110.47 CT £443.36 TOTE £9.80: £3.50, £2.00, £1.50; EX 134.70 Trifecta £1513.30.
Owner David & Ros Chapman **Bred** Mrs J A Cornwell **Trained** Scamblesby, Lincs

FOCUS
Add 4yds. The two at the bottom of the weights fought this out. The winner has been rated in keeping with her Sandown win.

8520 BRITISH EUROPEAN BREEDERS' FUND CONDITIONS STKS (PLUS 10 RACE) 1m 5f 61y
3:25 (3:25) (Class 2) 3-Y-O **£32,345** (£9,625; £4,810; £2,405) **Stalls** High

Form RPR

1121 **1** **Trueshan (FR)**14 8092 3-9-5 103........................ WilliamBuick 3 112
(Alan King) *t.k.h: chsd ldr tl rdn to ld over 2f out: hdd over 1f out: drvn and battled bk to ld 100yds out: styd on strly* **2/1**2

1311 **2** *nk* **Hamish**14 8098 3-9-5 109........................ JamesDoyle 4 111
(William Haggas) *mounted in the chute and taken down early: stdd s: hld up in tch in rr: clsd and upsides wnr travelling strly over 2f out: rdn to ld over 1f out: drvn and edgd lft ins fnl f: hdd 100yds out: a hld after* **4/7**1

1000 **3** *14* **Hiroshima**125 4136 3-9-2 87........................ LukeMorris 1 87
(John Ryan) *t.k.h: trckd ldng pair: rdn over 2f out: sn struggling: outpcd and wl btn 3rd over 1f out* **66/1**

4613 **4** *4 1/2* **Summer Moon**13 8114 3-9-5 100........................ RichardKingscote 2 83
(Mark Johnston) *led tl rdn and hdd over 2f out: sn outpcd and wl btn over 1f out (trainer's rep could offer no explanation for the colt's performance)* **9/1**3

3m 12.56s (18.16) **Going Correction** +1.15s/f (Soft) **4** Ran SP% **108.5**
Speed ratings (Par 107): **90,89,81,78**
CSF £3.55 TOTE £2.60; EX 3.40 Trifecta £20.10.
Owner Barbury Lions 5 **Bred** Didier Blot **Trained** Barbury Castle, Wilts

FOCUS
Add 4yds. A couple of smart 3yos on show here, and both have the potential to do better still in 2020.

8521 ENERGY CHECK H'CAP 7f (S)
4:00 (4:01) (Class 4) (0-85,87) 3-Y-O+
£5,207 (£1,549; £774; £387; £300; £300) **Stalls** High

Form RPR

420 **1** **Molls Memory**29 7613 4-9-7 **85**........................ LiamKeniry 11 94
(Ed Walker) *hld up in tch: clsd to trck ldrs and travelling strly 2f out: effrt to press ldrs over 1f out: drvn and ev ch ins fnl f: led wl ins fnl f: edgd lft and kpt on (vet said filly lost its left hind shoe)* **7/1**3

0444 **2** *1/2* **Dance Diva**14 8101 4-9-6 **84**........................ TonyHamilton 3 91
(Richard Fahey) *chsd ldrs tl rdn to ld 2f out: drvn and hrd pressed ins fnl f: hdd and one pce wl ins fnl f* **8/1**

1534 **3** *1 1/2* **Dream World (IRE)**33 7491 4-8-2 **73**........................ AngusVilliers(7) 6 76
(Michael Appleby) *chsd ldrs: effrt ent fnl 2f: chsd ldr over 1f out: 3rd and kpt on same pce ins fnl f* **9/1**

1332 **4** *5* **Foxy Femme**38 7299 3-8-5 **71** oh2........................ LukeMorris 4 60
(John Gallagher) *hld up in tch: swtchd lft and effrt over 2f out: hdwy u.p over 1f out: chsd ldng trio 1f out: no imp* **20/1**

3003 **5** *3* **Moxy Mares**16 8031 4-8-10 **74**........................(p) LiamJones 14 56
(Mark Loughnane) *hld up in tch in rr: swtchd rt and effrt over 2f out: no ch w ldrs but kpt on to pass btn rivals ins fnl f* **20/1**

3602 **6** *1 3/4* **Dragons Tail (IRE)**27 7678 4-9-4 **82**........................(p) RichardKingscote 17 60
(Tom Dascombe) *in tch in midfield: effrt over 1f out: unable qck and sn btn: wknd ins fnl f* **8/1**

0060 **7** *1* **Jackpot Royale**6 8342 4-9-0 **78**........................ JasonWatson 2 53
(Michael Appleby) *in tch in midfield: clsd and effrt to chse ldrs 2f out: unable qck over 1f out: wknd ins fnl f* **9/2**2

4140 **8** *3/4* **Daddy's Daughter (CAN)**70 6155 4-9-5 **83**........................(h) JoeyHaynes 7 56
(Dean Ivory) *chsd ldr tl led jst over 2f out: sn rdn and hdd: outpcd over 1f out: wknd ins fnl f* **14/1**

2002 **9** *1/2* **John Betjeman**72 6084 3-8-3 **72**........................ WilliamCox(3) 10 43
(Mark Gillard) *chsd ldrs: rdn over 2f out: sn struggling to qckn and lost pl over 1f out: wknd fnl f* **28/1**

3250 **10** *1 1/4* **Scorched Breath**10 8220 3-8-5 **71**........................(h) HollieDoyle 8 39
(Charlie Fellowes) *hld up in tch in rr: effrt over 2f out: nvr threatened to get on terms and wknd ins fnl f* **14/1**

5156 **11** *3/4* **Gambon (GER)**41 7205 3-9-1 **81**........................ CharlesBishop 9 47
(Eve Johnson Houghton) *hld up in tch towards rr: nt clr run ent fnl 2f: no prog over 1f out: wknd ins fnl f* **20/1**

0201 **12** *3/4* **Zeyzoun (FR)**26 7731 5-9-5 **83**........................(h) GeorgeWood 12 48
(Chris Wall) *taken down early: t.k.h: hld up in tch in midfield: clsd over 2f out: rdn ent 2f out: unable qck and btn over 1f out: wknd ins fnl f (trainer said gelding was unsuited by the heavy going, which in his opinion, was particularly testing)* **4/1**1

6203 **13** *3/4* **Mountain Rescue (IRE)**30 7563 7-9-5 **83**........................(p) DavidProbert 5 46
(Michael Attwater) *led tl jst over 2f out: edgd rt and lost pl over 1f out: wknd ins fnl f* **16/1**

0003 **14** *38* **Azor Ahai**116 4444 3-8-6 **72**........................ RobHornby 15
(Chris Gordon) *hld up in tch in rr: effrt over 2f out: sn btn and lost tch: t.o and virtually p.u ins fnl f* **50/1**

2400 **15** *32* **Masham Star (IRE)**15 8062 5-9-9 **87**........................ WilliamBuick 13
(Mark Johnston) *chsd ldrs tl 1/2-way: sn lost pl: t.o and virtually p.u ins fnl f* **28/1**

1m 33.64s (6.64) **Going Correction** +1.175s/f (Soft) **15** Ran SP% **125.3**
WFA 3 from 4yo+ 2lb
Speed ratings (Par 105): **109,108,106,101,97 95,94,93,93,91 90,89,89,45,9**
CSF £58.09 CT £534.64 TOTE £8.90: £2.80, £2.80, £3.60; EX 81.40 Trifecta £1081.60.
Owner Andrew Buxton **Bred** Andrew Buxton **Trained** Upper Lambourn, Berks

FOCUS
The first two travelled best and had it between them inside the last half furlong. It's been rated around the second to this year's form.

8522 CAROLE DOUGLAS REMEMBRANCE H'CAP 6f
4:35 (4:38) (Class 3) (0-90,91) 3-Y-O+ **£7,439** (£2,213; £1,106; £553) **Stalls** High

Form RPR

0035 **1** **Teruntum Star (FR)**6 8340 7-9-7 **90**........................(p) AlistairRawlinson 3 101
(David C Griffiths) *hld up in tch: clsd to trck ldrs and travelling strly over 2f out: rdn to ld over 1f out: in command and r.o wl ins fnl f* **14/1**

4600 **2** *2* **Ice Lord (IRE)**49 6920 7-9-4 **87**........................ JamesDoyle 6 92+
(Chris Wall) *stdd s: hld up in tch in rr: clsd jst over 2f out: effrt and hdwy over 1f out: edgd lft and r.o u.p ins fnl f: wnt 2nd last strides* **16/1**

6110 **3** *nk* **Eye Of The Water (IRE)**49 6913 3-8-12 **82**........................ DavidProbert 2 86
(Ronald Harris) *pressed ldrs tl led 2f out: rdn and hdd over 1f out: kpt on same pce ins fnl f: lost 2nd last strides* **16/1**

2435 **4** *1* **Little Boy Blue**41 7175 4-9-1 **89**........................(h) SeamusCronin(5) 9 89
(Bill Turner) *stdd s: hld up in tch in rr: clsd and shkn up 2f out: chsd ldrs and edgd lft u.p over 1f out: kpt on same pce ins fnl f* **16/1**

0420 **5** *hd* **Gabrial The Devil (IRE)**27 7678 4-9-2 **85**........................ TonyHamilton 5 85
(Richard Fahey) *hld up in tch in midfield: n.m.r over 1f out: rallied and hdwy u.p over 1f out: kpt on same pce ins fnl f* **25/1**

2323 **6** *3/4* **Whelans Way (IRE)**49 6916 3-8-10 **80**........................ WilliamBuick 4 77
(Roger Teal) *stdd s: hld up in tch in rr: clsd over 2f out: rdn and no imp over 1f out: kpt on same pce ins fnl f (jockey said gelding was never travelling)* **5/1**2

5503 **7** *3 1/2* **After John**30 7564 3-8-6 **76** oh1........................ KieranO'Neill 7 62
(Mick Channon) *chsd ldrs tl shuffled bk over 2f out: tried to rally over 1f out: no imp ins fnl f* **10/1**

0006 **8** *3/4* **Jackstar (IRE)**36 7362 3-8-13 **83**........................ RichardKingscote 12 67
(Tom Dascombe) *hld up in tch in midfield: effrt ent fnl 2f: hung lft and no imp over 1f out: wknd ins fnl f* **17/2**

2161 **9** *2* **Atalanta's Boy**30 7564 4-8-12 **81**........................(h) JasonWatson 13 58
(David Menuisier) *chsd ldrs tl led 3f out: hdd 2f out: no ex u.p over 1f out: wknd ins fnl f* **7/2**1

3011 **10** *3 1/2* **Smokey Lane (IRE)**17 8007 5-8-7 **76**........................ LiamJones 8 42
(David Evans) *in tch in midfield: shuffled bk to rr and n.m.r over 2f out: no hdwy u.p over 1f out: wknd ins fnl f (jockey said gelding was never travelling)* **16/1**

6132 **11** *1 3/4* **Sweet Pursuit**30 7564 5-8-7 **76** oh1........................ HollieDoyle 1 37
(Rod Millman) *stdd s: hld up in tch towards rr: hdwy and edgd rt over 2f out: rdn and no imp over 1f out: sn btn and wknd ins fnl f (jockey said mare was never travelling)* **8/1**3

3620 **12** *3 1/2* **Goodnight Girl (IRE)**29 7613 4-9-6 **89**........................ RobHornby 14 38
(Jonathan Portman) *w ldr tl led 4f out: hdd 3f out: sn rdn and struggling: wknd over 1f out (trainer said filly was unsuited by the heavy going and would prefer a quicker surface)* **33/1**

0250 **13** *3 3/4* **Ice Age (IRE)**13 8127 6-9-3 **91**........................ GeorgiaDobie(5) 11 28
(Eve Johnson Houghton) *t.k.h: led tl 4f out: rdn and lost pl over 2f out: wknd over 1f out* **16/1**

4121 **14** *2 1/2* **Young John (IRE)**4 8403 6-9-1 **84** 5ex........................ RossaRyan 15 13
(Mike Murphy) *racd along nr stands' rail: chsd ldrs tl 3f out: sn u.p and lost pl: bhd ins fnl f (trainer said gelding was unsuited by the heavy going and would prefer a quicker surface)* **10/1**

1m 19.66s (6.46) **Going Correction** +1.175s/f (Soft) **14** Ran SP% **121.6**
WFA 3 from 4yo+ 1lb
Speed ratings (Par 107): **103,100,99,98,98 97,92,91,89,84 82,77,72,69**
CSF £223.19 CT £3606.03 TOTE £15.20: £3.80, £4.50, £4.90; EX 156.60 Trifecta £2766.40.
Owner Miss Emma Shepherd **Bred** Petra Bloodstock Agency **Trained** Bawtry, S Yorks

FOCUS
A competitive sprint. The winner has been rated to his best over the past year, with the third to form.

8523 ENERGY CHECK "HANDS AND HEELS" APPRENTICE H'CAP (FINAL) (PART OF RACING EXCELLENCE INITIATIVE) 2m
5:05 (5:05) (Class 5) (0-70,72) 4-Y-O+
£3,428 (£1,020; £509; £300; £300; £300) **Stalls** High

Form RPR

3202 **1** **Cristal Spirit**49 6929 4-10-0 **72**........................(p) GavinAshton 5 78
(George Baker) *chsd ldrs tl wnt 2nd 10f out: led 7f out and sn clr w rival: pushed clr ent fnl 2f: styd on wl* **5/2**2

1033 **2** *5* **Colwood**29 7631 5-9-10 **68**........................ StefanoCherchi 2 69
(Robert Eddery) *chsd ldr tl 10f out: 4th and lost tch w ldrs 7f out: hdwy towards inner 3f out: chsd clr wnr 1f out: kpt on but nvr a threat* **5/1**3

/004 **3** *1 3/4* **Montys Angel (IRE)**9 8246 9-8-2 **49** oh4........................ GeorgeRooke(3) 6 48
(John Bridger) *midfield: lost tch w ldrs 7f out: sme prog towards inner 3f out: kpt on steadily ins fnl f: wnt 3rd nr fin: no threat to wnr* **25/1**

0-04 **4** *nk* **Pumblechook**29 7631 6-10-0 **72**........................(p) SeanKirrane 8 71
(Amy Murphy) *led: hdd 7f out: styd w wnr and sn wnt clr: rdn: nt match pce of wnr and hung rt 2f out: wl hld after and lost 2 pls fnl f* **5/1**3

40/1 **5** *19* **Mr Smith**80 3686 8-8-8 **55**........................(p) LeviWilliams(3) 3 35
(C Byrnes, Ire) *hld up in midfield: hdwy to chse ldng pair and wnt clr 7f out: btn 4f out: wknd (trainer's rep said gelding was unsuited by the heavy ground on this occasion and would prefer less testing conditions)* **11/8**1

64-6 **6** *7* **With Pleasure**15 6849 6-9-10 **68**........................(p) OliverStammers 1 41
(John Flint) *stdd s: hld up in last pair: lost tch 7f out: n.d after* **14/1**

0006 **7** *20* **Duration (IRE)**14 8081 4-8-5 **49**........................(b) ZakWheatley 7 2
(J R Jenkins) *s.i.s: a in rr: lost tch 7f out: t.o* **40/1**

3m 55.48s (16.08) **Going Correction** +1.15s/f (Soft) **7** Ran SP% **117.0**
Speed ratings (Par 103): **105,102,101,101,91 88,78**
CSF £16.08 CT £252.81 TOTE £3.40: £1.70, £2.10; EX 15.00 Trifecta £93.80.
Owner Turf Club 2018 & PJL Racing **Bred** Meon Valley Stud **Trained** Chiddingfold, Surrey

FOCUS
Add 4yds. A modest affair for apprentice riders. It's been rated cautiously.
T/Plt: £156.00 to a £1 stake. Pool: £54,747.72 - 256.07 winning units T/Qpdt: £44.40 to a £1 stake. Pool: £6,084.67 - 101.30 winning units **Steve Payne**

[8423]NEWCASTLE (A.W) (L-H)

Friday, October 25

OFFICIAL GOING: Tapeta: standard

Wind: Breezy, half against in races on the straight course and in over 3f of home straight in race on the Weather: Persistent rain

8524 BETWAY CASINO H'CAP — 2m 56y (Tp)

5:25 (5:26) (Class 4) (0-80,81) 3-Y-O+

£5,072 (£1,518; £759; £400; £400; £400) **Stalls** Low

Form — RPR

2455 **1** **Doctor Cross (IRE)**[13] 8129 5-10-0 **74** DavidNolan 7 — 78
(Richard Fahey) *trckd ldrs: wnt 2nd over 3f out: effrt and led over 1f out: edgd lft ins fnl f: hld on wl cl home* **11/2**[3]

4121 **2** *nk* **Anyonecanhaveitall**[35] 7414 3-9-13 **81** JoeFanning 4 — 84
(Mark Johnston) *led: rdn and hdd over 1f out: rallied and ev ch whn edgd lft ins fnl f: kpt on: hld cl home* **5/4**[1]

6201 **3** *½* **Nataleena (IRE)**[14] 8081 3-8-8 **62** AndrewMullen 5 — 64
(Ben Haslam) *dwlt: hld up in last pl: hdwy over 2f out: effrt and chsd ldrs over 1f out: kpt on ins fnl f* **3/1**[2]

400 **4** *nk* **The Resdev Way**[29] 7631 6-9-13 **73** CliffordLee 3 — 75
(Philip Kirby) *dwlt: t.k.h: hld up: stdy hdwy over 2f out: effrt and rdn over 1f out: kpt on fnl f: hld towards fin* **50/1**

5550 **5** *1 ½* **Flash Point (IRE)**[41] 7209 3-8-13 **67** CamHardie 2 — 67
(Tracy Waggott) *t.k.h: prom: shkn up over 2f out: rdn whn blkd over 1f out: one pce ins fnl f* **12/1**

4223 **6** *shd* **Carbon Dating (IRE)**[32] 7510 7-9-9 **72** RowanScott(3) 6 — 72
(Andrew Hughes, Ire) *t.k.h: hld up in tch: stdy hdwy over 2f out: rdn whn blkd over 1f out: one pce ins fnl f* **10/1**

000 **7** *1 ¾* **Swordbill**[22] 7845 4-9-11 **74** (b[1]) GabrieleMalune(3) 8 — 72
(Ian Williams) *chsd ldr to over 3f out: sn rdn along: outpcd over 1f out: btn fnl f* **16/1**

3m 39.91s (4.91) **Going Correction** +0.275s/f (Slow)
WFA 3 from 4yo+ 8lb — 7 Ran SP% **109.5**
Speed ratings (Par 105): **98,97,97,97,96 96,95**
CSF £11.70 CT £21.28 TOTE £5.70: £2.30, £1.50; EX 16.80 Trifecta £44.70.
Owner Havelock Racing **Bred** Lodge Park Stud **Trained** Musley Bank, N Yorks

FOCUS
A fair staying handicap on newly relayed standard Tapeta on a soggy evening. The third-favourite's winning time was modest from off a steady gallop.

8525 LADBROKES WHERE THE NATION PLAYS EBF FILLIES' NOVICE STKS (PLUS 10 RACE) — 7f 14y (Tp)

6:00 (6:03) (Class 5) 2-Y-O

£3,428 (£1,020; £509; £254) **Stalls** Centre

Form — RPR

1 **Fooraat (IRE)** 2-9-0 0 JamesSullivan 6 — 84+
(Roger Varian) *t.k.h early: prom: shkn up over 2f out: effrt and wnt 2nd over 1f out: led wl ins fnl f: kpt on wl* **5/1**[3]

2 *nk* **Maria Rosa (USA)** 2-9-0 0 RobertHavlin 9 — 84+
(John Gosden) *slowly away: hld up: smooth hdwy on outside over 2f out: led over 1f out: rdn: edgd lft and hdd wl ins fnl f: kpt on* **8/13**[1]

332 **3** *3* **Tulip Fields**[16] 8021 2-9-0 80 JoeFanning 3 — 76
(Mark Johnston) *t.k.h early: led: rdn over 2f out: hung lft and hdd over 1f out: sn outpcd by first two* **4/1**[2]

4 *shd* **Time Voyage (IRE)** 2-9-0 0 AndrewMullen 5 — 76
(John Quinn) *dwlt: plld hrd: hld up: rn green and outpcd over 2f out: rallied ins fnl f: bttr for r* **50/1**

50 **5** *3* **Nibras Shadow (IRE)**[27] 7695 2-8-11 0 GabrieleMalune(3) 7 — 68
(Ismail Mohammed) *trckd ldrs: rdn over 2f out: wknd fnl f* **40/1**

261 **6** *½* **Tadreej**[22] 7832 2-9-7 82 DaneO'Neill 4 — 74
(Saeed bin Suroor) *t.k.h: prom: rdn over 2f out: wknd over 1f out* **4/1**[2]

7 *¾* **Amor De Vega** 2-9-0 0 CamHardie 8 — 65
(Roger Fell) *bmpd s: t.k.h in rr: drvn and outpcd over 2f out: sn btn* **50/1**

8 *18* **Jaggy Nettle (IRE)** 2-8-11 0 RowanScott(3) 2 — 20
(Andrew Hughes, Ire) *slowly away: bhd: rn green and struggling 3f out: sn lost tch* **125/1**

00 **9** *9* **Queen Of Rock (IRE)**[29] 7627 2-9-0 0 CliffordLee 1
(Philip Kirby) *w ldr to over 3f out: rdn and wknd over 2f out: eased whn no ch fnl f* **200/1**

1m 27.9s (1.70) **Going Correction** +0.275s/f (Slow) — 9 Ran SP% **126.2**
Speed ratings (Par 92): **101,100,97,97,93 93,92,71,61**
CSF £9.47 TOTE £7.50: £1.40, £1.10, £1.40; EX 14.20 Trifecta £31.60.
Owner Sheikh Ahmed Al Maktoum **Bred** Godolphin **Trained** Newmarket, Suffolk

FOCUS
A fairly decent juvenile fillies' novice contest won in 2018 by subsequent Ascot Listed winner Duneflower. Two particularly well-bred newcomers came clear of the rest. It's been rated at face value.

8526 LADBROKES HOME OF ODDS BOOST NURSERY H'CAP — 7f 14y (Tp)

6:30 (6:32) (Class 6) (0-55,55) 2-Y-O

£2,781 (£827; £413; £400; £400; £400) **Stalls** Centre

Form — RPR

060 **1** **Ventura Destiny (FR)**[16] 8021 2-8-9 **48** ow2 BenSanderson(5) 5 — 55+
(Keith Dalgleish) *hld up in centre of gp: hdwy over 2f out: rdn to ld ins fnl f: sn clr* **16/1**

0040 **2** *2 ¼* **Camacho Man (IRE)**[15] 8061 2-9-4 **52** JoeFanning 8 — 53
(Jennie Candlish) *wnt rt and bmpd s: midfield in centre of gp: hdwy to ld over 2f out: rdn and edgd lft over 1f out: kpt on same pce* **11/4**[1]

5650 **3** *¾* **Halfacrown (IRE)**[58] 6604 2-8-13 **47** (w) NicolaCurrie 3 — 46
(Jamie Osborne) *hld up on far side of gp: stdy hdwy over 3f out: effrt and rdn 2f out: kpt on same pce ins fnl f* **18/1**

0504 **4** *1 ¼* **Schumli**[25] 7768 2-9-4 **52** DavidNolan 6 — 48
(David O'Meara) *in tch in centre of gp: angled rt and hdwy over 2f out: ev ch wl over 1f out to ent fnl f: sn no ex* **20/1**

0664 **5** *½* **Star Of St Louis (FR)**[22] 7833 2-9-0 **48** (p[1]) RobertHavlin 2 — 43
(Denis Quinn) *hld up: hdwy in centre of gp and chsd ldrs over 2f out: rdn and no ex fnl f* **8/1**[3]

0256 **6** *1* **Indra Dawn (FR)**[29] 7626 2-9-1 **49** (b) AndrewMullen 11 — 43+
(Archie Watson) *midfield on nr side of gp: n.m.r and lost pl over 3f out: rallied over 1f out: kpt on fnl f: nvr able to chal* **8/1**[3]

600 **7** *3 ¼* **Sheung Wan**[15] 8069 2-9-2 **53** SeanDavis(3) 1 — 37
(Richard Fahey) *hld up on far side of gp: hdwy and prom over 2f out: wknd over 1f out* **22/1**

0000 **8** *1 ¾* **Imperial Eagle (IRE)**[25] 7768 2-9-3 **51** PhilDennis 4 — 31
(Lawrence Mullaney) *midfield towards far side of gp: rdn and hung lft over 2f out: wknd over 1f out (jockey said filly hung left throughout)* **33/1**

0050 **9** *2 ¾* **Inductive**[16] 8022 2-9-6 **54** (p) CliffordLee 9 — 28
(Michael Dods) *dwlt and bmpd s: bhd: nt clr run over 2f out: hdwy over 1f out: nvr able to chal* **7/2**[2]

506 **10** *5* **William Thomas (IRE)**[50] 6883 2-9-4 **55** (p[1]) DarraghKeenan(3) 14 — 17
(Robert Eddery) *midfield on nr side of gp: hmpd over 3f out: lost pl over 2f out: sn btn* **12/1**

6616 **11** *5* **Romininthegloamin (IRE)**[25] 7763 2-9-4 **55** RowanScott(3) 10 — 3
(Andrew Hughes, Ire) *bmpd s: sn prom in centre of gp: rdn over 2f out: sn lost pl and struggling* **14/1**

4500 **12** *2 ½* **Yorkshire Grey (IRE)**[39] 7284 2-9-7 **55** (p) TomEaves 12
(Ann Duffield) *wnt lft s: cl up on nr side of gp: n.m.r and lost pl over 2f out: sn struggling* **33/1**

0000 **13** *11* **Sassy Lassy (IRE)**[22] 7833 2-8-12 **46** oh1 (p) DavidEgan 7
(David Loughnane) *led on nr side of gp: rdn and hdd over 2f out: sn wknd* **80/1**

1m 29.22s (3.02) **Going Correction** +0.275s/f (Slow) — 13 Ran SP% **112.8**
Speed ratings (Par 93): **93,90,89,88,87 86,82,80,77,71 66,63,50**
CSF £53.36 CT £814.44 TOTE £17.30: £4.90, £1.40, £5.30; EX 99.10 Trifecta £1710.90.
Owner Middleham Park Racing Cxviii & Partner **Bred** S A S Elevage Du Haras De Bourgeauville **Trained** Carluke, S Lanarks

FOCUS
A moderate nursery. A fractional pb from the second.

8527 LADBROKES FOOTBALL ACCA BOOSTY NURSERY H'CAP — 5f (Tp)

7:00 (7:01) (Class 6) (0-55,55) 2-Y-O

£2,781 (£827; £413; £400; £400; £400) **Stalls** Centre

Form — RPR

005 **1** **Lezardrieux**[38] 7308 2-9-6 **54** SamJames 11 — 60
(Grant Tuer) *in tch in centre of gp: hdwy to ld over 1f out: sn hrd pressed: kpt on wl u.p ins fnl f* **6/1**[2]

5206 **2** *½* **Comeatchoo (IRE)**[26] 7734 2-9-2 **50** (b) DuranFentiman 10 — 54
(Tim Easterby) *in tch nr side of gp: hdwy to dispute ld over 1f out to ins fnl f: hld towards fin* **6/1**[2]

0245 **3** *2 ¾* **Classy Lady**[93] 5295 2-9-2 **53** SeanDavis(3) 12 — 47
(Ollie Pears) *led on nr side of gp: rdn over 2f out: hdd over 1f out: sn one pce* **18/1**

004 **4** *shd* **Aiden's Reward (IRE)**[101] 5026 2-9-4 **52** GrahamLee 4 — 46+
(Ben Haslam) *hld midfield in centre of gp: rdn and sltly outpcd wl over 1f out: r.o ins fnl f: nt pce to chal* **18/1**

0043 **5** *¾* **She's Easyontheeye (IRE)**[22] 7853 2-9-1 **54** FayeMcManoman(5) 14 — 45
(John Quinn) *hld up on nr side of gp: rdn and hdwy over 1f out: kpt on fnl f: nvr able to chal* **7/2**[1]

000 **6** *nk* **Northern Celt (IRE)**[29] 7619 2-8-12 **46** oh1 PhilDennis 3 — 36
(Tim Easterby) *t.k.h: hld up on in tch on far side of gp: hdwy over 2f out: sn rdn: fdd fnl f* **16/1**

0605 **7** *½* **South Light (IRE)**[37] 7329 2-8-13 **47** (t[1]) CamHardie 9 — 35+
(Antony Brittain) *dwlt: bhd in centre of gp: rdn 1/2-way: gd hdwy fnl f: nrst fin* **40/1**

0200 **8** *¾* **Chocoholic**[41] 7208 2-9-4 **52** TomEaves 5 — 38
(Bryan Smart) *cl up on far side of gp: rdn over 2f out: wknd over 1f out* **12/1**

0400 **9** *½* **Sweet Embrace (IRE)**[22] 7833 2-9-1 **49** JamesSullivan 8 — 33
(John Wainwright) *hld up in centre of gp: drvn along over 2f out: no imp fr over 1f out* **28/1**

6000 **10** *nk* **Jazz Style (IRE)**[44] 7079 2-9-7 **55** DavidNolan 6 — 38
(David Brown) *prom in centre of gp: rdn along 1/2-way: wknd over 1f out* **17/2**[3]

605 **11** *1 ¼* **Orange Justice**[15] 8067 2-9-0 **48** DavidEgan 13 — 26
(David Loughnane) *prom on nr side of gp: rdn over 2f out: wknd over 1f out* **12/1**

0066 **12** *nse* **Norton Lad**[38] 7308 2-9-3 **51** (b[1]) JackGarritty 1 — 29
(Tim Easterby) *dwlt: sn in tch on far side of gp: struggling 2f out: sn btn* **12/1**

056 **13** *½* **Krystal Crown (IRE)**[25] 7765 2-9-0 **51** RowanScott(3) 2 — 27
(Andrew Hughes, Ire) *hld up far side of gp: drvn along over 2f out: sn wknd* **16/1**

0540 **14** *2 ½* **Is She The One**[34] 7469 2-8-12 **49** DarraghKeenan(3) 7 — 16
(Denis Quinn) *dwlt: bhd in centre of gp: drvn along 1/2-way: sn struggling* **66/1**

1m 0.82s (1.32) **Going Correction** +0.275s/f (Slow) — 14 Ran SP% **114.1**
Speed ratings (Par 93): **100,99,94,94,93 92,92,90,90,89 87,87,86,82**
CSF £38.95 CT £452.78 TOTE £7.80: £2.90, £2.30, £4.20; EX 45.30 Trifecta £458.00.
Owner D R Tucker **Bred** D R Tucker **Trained** Birkby, N Yorks

FOCUS
A moderate nursery sprint. The two joint-second favourites fought it out from high draws central to near side.

8528 LADBROKES "PLAY 1-2 FREE" ON FOOTBALL NOVICE AUCTION STKS — 1m 5y (Tp)

7:30 (7:33) (Class 6) 2-Y-O

£2,658 (£785; £392) **Stalls** Centre

Form — RPR

0 **1** **Sky Lake (GER)**[31] 7547 2-9-0 0 DavidEgan 4 — 79+
(Marco Botti) *dwlt: hld up: gd hdwy on far side of gp to ld over 1f out: rdn clr fnl f* **18/1**

0 **2** *4 ½* **Nicks Not Wonder**[31] 7555 2-9-5 0 NicolaCurrie 7 — 74
(Jamie Osborne) *stdd s: t.k.h: hld up in centre of gp: swtchd rt and hdwy over 2f out: edgd lft and chsd (clr) wnr ins fnl f: kpt on: no imp* **10/1**

2 **3** *1* **Trinity Girl**[11] 8198 2-9-0 0 JoeFanning 2 — 67
(Mark Johnston) *pressed ldr on far side of gp: led briefly over 1f out: sn rdn and edgd lft: lost 2nd and no ex ins fnl f* **15/8**[1]

4 *1 ½* **Jahrawi (USA)** 2-9-5 0 TomEaves 3 — 69
(Kevin Ryan) *dwlt: hld up in centre of gp: angled rt and hdwy 2f out: pushed along and no imp fnl f* **16/1**

32 **5** *hd* **Hua Mulan (IRE)**[10] 8232 2-9-0 0 CallumRodriguez 5 — 63
(Keith Dalgleish) *towards rr: rdn over 2f out: hdwy on far side over 1f out: no imp fnl f* **9/2**[2]

53 **6** *1 ½* **Untouchable Beauty**[11] 8198 2-9-0 0 RobertHavlin 6 — 60
(Hugo Palmer) *in tch towards far side of gp: shkn up over 1f out: wknd ins fnl f* **10/1**

7 *4 ½* **Spanish Persuader (FR)** 2-9-5 0 FrannyNorton 8 — 55
(Mark Johnston) *dwlt: t.k.h and sn cl up in centre of gp: rdn and outpcd over 2f out: sn btn* **16/1**

0 **8** ½ **Cliffs Of Freedom (IRE)**[36] 7386 2-9-2 0 .... SeanDavis(3) 1 54
(Kevin Thomas Coleman, Ire) *plld hrd: led in centre of gp: rdn and hdd over 1f out: sn wknd* **8/1**[3]

9 6 **Home For Half Past (IRE)** 2-9-5 0 .... DavidNolan 11 41
(David O'Meara) *dwlt: hld up on nr side of gp: hdwy and prom 2f out: edgd lft and sn wknd* **100/1**

4 **10** 2 ¼ **Provocation (IRE)**[29] 7623 2-9-5 0 .... DaneO'Neill 10 36
(Mark Johnston) *dwlt: sn prom on nr side of gp: rdn: edgd lft and wknd fr 2f out* **8/1**[3]

11 15 **Cold War Steve** 2-9-5 0 .... CliffordLee 9 3
(Roger Fell) *in tch on nr side of gp: rdn and struggling over 2f out: sn lost tch: t.o* **40/1**

1m 40.98s (2.38) **Going Correction** +0.275s/f (Slow) **11 Ran SP% 113.8**
Speed ratings (Par 93): **99,94,93,92,91 90,85,85,79,77 62**
CSF £181.03 TOTE £22.10: £4.60, £2.90, £1.20; EX 210.20 Trifecta £1051.80.
Owner Scuderia Archi Romani & Partner **Bred** K Hofmann **Trained** Newmarket, Suffolk

FOCUS
An ordinary juvenile novice contest. One of the relative outsiders won convincingly on her second start. The opening level is fluid.

8529 BOMBARDIER BRITISH HOPPED AMBER BEER NOVICE STKS 1m 5y (Tp)
8:00 (8:02) (Class 5) 3-Y-O+ **£3,428** (£1,020; £509; £254) **Stalls Centre**

Form RPR

31 **1** **Qamka**[134] 3761 3-9-5 0 .... DavidEgan 6 79+
(Roger Varian) *mde all: hrd pressed fr over 2f out: drvn and styd on wl fnl f* **6/4**[2]

2 **2** ¾ **Millicent Fawcett**[196] 1740 3-8-12 0 .... RobertHavlin 1 70+
(John Gosden) *dwlt and wnt lft s: sn swtchd rt and prom: effrt and pressed ldr over 1f out: rdn and one pce last 100yds* **8/13**[1]

43- **3** 1 ¾ **Mosakhar**[310] 9607 3-9-3 0 .... BenRobinson 4 71
(Ollie Pears) *in tch: drvn and outpcd over 2f out: rallied ins fnl f: nt pce to chal* **33/1**[3]

52 **4** 2 ½ **Siena Mia**[46] 7032 4-9-1 0 .... PhilDennis 5 61
(Philip Kirby) *t.k.h: pressed wnr: ev ch over 2f out to over 1f out: rdn and wknd ins fnl f* **40/1**

1m 44.8s (6.20) **Going Correction** +0.275s/f (Slow)
WFA 3 from 4yo 3lb **4 Ran SP% 107.3**
Speed ratings (Par 103): **80,79,77,75**
CSF £2.73 TOTE £2.50; EX 2.30 Trifecta £4.70.
Owner Nurlan Bizakov **Bred** Hesmonds Stud Ltd **Trained** Newmarket, Suffolk

FOCUS
A fair novice contest. The second-favourite won a shade cosily in a modest comparative time. The third and fourth limit the level.

8530 BOMBARDIER GOLDEN BEER H'CAP 1m 5y (Tp)
8:30 (8:31) (Class 7) (0-50,50) 3-Y-O+ **£2,522** (£750; £375; £187) **Stalls Centre**

Form RPR

6023 **1** **Rebel State (IRE)**[7] 8301 6-8-12 **48** .... OwenPayton(7) 5 56
(Jedd O'Keeffe) *hld up in centre of gp: effrt and swtchd to far side over 2f out: led ins fnl f: r.o wl* **9/2**[1]

6265 **2** 1 ¼ **Mr Cool Cash**[18] 7960 7-9-0 **46** ....(t) SeanDavis(3) 11 51
(John Davies) *prom in centre of gp: hdwy to ld over 1f out: rdn and hdd ins fnl f: kpt on same pce* **16/1**

0606 **3** 1 ¾ **Proceeding**[30] 7587 4-9-5 **48** .... CamHardie 9 49
(Tracy Waggott) *towards rr on nr side of gp: drvn and outpcd over 2f out: rallied fnl f: r.o* **11/2**[3]

0003 **4** ½ **The Retriever (IRE)**[18] 7961 4-9-3 **46** .... GrahamLee 12 46
(Micky Hammond) *in tch on nr side of gp: smooth hdwy over 2f out: rdn and ev ch over 1f out: no ex ins fnl f* **5/1**[2]

6002 **5** 1 **Tarnhelm**[10] 8233 4-9-0 **50** .... RhonaPindar(7) 7 48
(Wilf Storey) *missed break: bhd in centre of gp: swtchd to far side and hdwy to ld over 3f out: edgd rt and hdd over 1f out: wknd ins fnl f* **17/2**

0205 **6** 1 **Silk Mill Blue**[7] 8301 5-9-6 **49** ....(p) PhilDennis 4 45
(Richard Whitaker) *hld up in midfield in centre of gp: effrt and rdn 2f out: no imp appr fnl f* **12/1**

4000 **7** nse **Gun Case**[18] 7961 7-9-4 **47** ....(v) DougieCostello 8 43
(Alistair Whillans) *dwlt: hld up in centre of gp: rdn and effrt over 2f out: no imp over 1f out* **10/1**

0000 **8** ¾ **Deeds Not Words (IRE)**[7] 8301 8-9-5 **48** ....(p) FrannyNorton 6 42
(Tracy Waggott) *t.k.h: cl up in centre of gp tl rdn and wknd over 1f out (jockey said gelding ran too free)* **20/1**

6603 **9** 3 ¼ **High Fort (IRE)**[18] 7960 4-9-7 **50** .... CliffordLee 1 37
(Karen McLintock) *led on far side of gp to over 3f out: rdn and wknd over 1f out* **7/1**

6000 **10** 3 ¾ **Mr Sundowner (USA)**[22] 7859 7-9-4 **47** .... TomEaves 2 26
(Michael Herrington) *t.k.h: prom on far side of gp tl rdn and wknd fr 2f out* **11/1**

60-6 **11** nk **Santana Slew**[20] 7912 3-8-11 **48** .... ThomasGreatrex(5) 3 25
(James Given) *cl up on far side of gp: struggling over 2f out: sn btn* **33/1**

0055 **12** 6 **Lord Rob**[18] 7961 8-9-3 **46** .... AndrewMullen 14 11
(David Thompson) *t.k.h: hld up on nr side of gp: struggling over 2f out: sn btn* **40/1**

1m 42.51s (3.91) **Going Correction** +0.275s/f (Slow)
WFA 3 from 4yo+ 3lb **12 Ran SP% 114.4**
Speed ratings (Par 97): **91,89,88,87,86 85,85,84,81,77 77,71**
CSF £72.45 CT £408.99 TOTE £4.90: £1.60, £3.90, £2.40; EX 78.60 Trifecta £322.20.
Owner Jedd O'Keeffe **Bred** B Kennedy **Trained** Middleham Moor, N Yorks

FOCUS
A moderate handicap. Fairly straightforward form.
T/Plt: £102.40 to a £1 stake. Pool: £65,614.23 - 467.38 winning units T/Qpdt: £32.50 to a £1 stake. Pool: £8,741.02 - 198.82 winning units **Richard Young**

8531 - 8545a (Foreign Racing) - See Raceform Interactive

8493
CHELMSFORD (A.W) (L-H)
Saturday, October 26

OFFICIAL GOING: Polytrack: standard
Wind: breezy Weather: overcast with showers

8546 BET TOTEPLACEPOT AT TOTESPORT.COM NOVICE AUCTION STKS 7f (P)
4:50 (4:54) (Class 5) 2-Y-O **£4,204** (£1,251; £625; £312) **Stalls Low**

Form RPR

060 **1** **Forus**[9] 8286 2-9-1 63 .... DougieCostello 1 67
(Jamie Osborne) *trckd ldrs on inner: gd hdwy between rivals to ld over 1f out: rdn and r.o wl fnl f* **9/1**

2 1 ¼ **Trigger Happy (IRE)** 2-8-13 0 .... MeganNicholls(3) 7 65
(Richard Spencer) *dwlt and racd in rr: lazy at times: pushed along and hdwy over 1f out: rdn and ev ch fnl f: kpt on (jockey said colt was slowly away and ran green)* **20/1**

0310 **3** 1 ¼ **Never In Red (IRE)**[8] 8302 2-9-5 72 .... KieranO'Neill 12 65
(Robyn Brisland) *racd freely in tch: rdn along and ev ch appr fnl f: rdn and one pce fnl 100yds* **7/2**[3]

00 **4** hd **Prairie Moppins (USA)**[12] 8198 2-8-5 0 .... ThomasGreatrex(5) 11 55+
(Sylvester Kirk) *hld up: pushed along and outpcd over 2f out: swtchd rt to outer over 1f out: sn rdn and r.o wl fnl f: nrst fin (jockey said filly was denied a clear run)* **50/1**

05 **5** ½ **Burning (IRE)**[18] 7981 2-9-2 0 .... StevieDonohoe 9 60
(Charlie Fellowes) *racd in midfield: rdn and no imp over 1f out: kpt on one pce fnl f* **5/1**

6 1 **High Maintenance** 2-8-10 0 .... ShaneKelly 5 51
(Mark Loughnane) *led: rdn along and hdd over 1f out: wknd fnl f* **33/1**

522 **7** 1 **Lyricist Voice**[25] 7787 2-8-13 72 .... LukeMorris 10 51
(Marco Botti) *midfield on outer: c wd off home bnd: sn rdn and no imp: n.d (trainer could offer no explanation for the colt's performance)* **9/4**[1]

3520 **8** 6 **Freshwater Cliffs**[12] 8201 2-8-12 68 ....(h[1]) FinleyMarsh(3) 3 38
(Richard Hughes) *racd freely and chsd ldrs: rdn along and fnd little over 1f out: wknd fnl f (jockey said colt ran keen early)* **10/3**[2]

00 **9** 3 **Evaporust (IRE)**[9] 8297 2-8-5 0 ....(e[1]) EllieMacKenzie(7) 2 27
(Mark Usher) *hld up: rdn and outpcd 1/2-way: nvr on terms* **33/1**

55 **10** 9 **Billy Button (IRE)**[131] 3942 2-8-13 0 .... JoeyHaynes 8 5
(Dean Ivory) *prom on outer: rdn and lost pl 2f out: wknd over 1f out* **16/1**

00 **11** nk **Scorpio's Dream**[16] 8058 2-8-11 0 .... DarraghKeenan(3) 6 5
(Charlie Wallis) *trckd ldr: pushed along to hold position over 2f out: rdn and lost pl over 1f out: sn bhd* **66/1**

1m 27.52s (0.32) **Going Correction** -0.025s/f (Stan) **11 Ran SP% 122.7**
Speed ratings (Par 95): **97,95,94,93,93 92,91,84,80,70 70**
CSF £177.48 TOTE £10.40: £2.20, £4.10, £1.50; EX 218.10 Trifecta £1254.80.
Owner The 10 For 10 Partnership **Bred** Ed's Stud Ltd **Trained** Upper Lambourn, Berks

FOCUS
A modest novice and a punt was landed.

8547 BET TOTEEXACTA AT TOTESPORT.COM CLASSIFIED STKS 7f (P)
5:25 (5:27) (Class 6) 3-Y-O+
£3,105 (£924; £461; £400; £400; £400) **Stalls Low**

Form RPR

3006 **1** **Quick Monet (IRE)**[32] 7550 6-9-2 46 .... MartinDwyer 7 52
(Shaun Harris) *hld up: stl last gng wl 2f out: swift hdwy on inner over 1f out: rdn to ld jst ins fnl f: kpt on strly* **10/1**

4001 **2** 2 ¼ **So Claire**[9] 8295 3-8-12 51 .... JaneElliott(3) 8 46+
(William Muir) *hld up: wd off home bnd: rdn and hdwy 1f out: drvn and kpt on wl fnl f to go 2nd clsng stages* **12/1**

4P/0 **3** hd **Ultimat Power (IRE)**[10] 8255 5-8-13 44 .... FinleyMarsh(3) 3 46
(Frank Bishop) *trckd ldrs: hdwy u.p over 1f out: rdn and kpt on fnl f: nt rch ldng pair* **33/1**

2523 **4** shd **Prince Rock (IRE)**[30] 7606 4-9-2 47 ....(h) LukeMorris 5 45
(Simon Dow) *rrd s and racd in rr: rdn along on inner and hdwy over 1f out: kpt on wl fnl f but n.d (jockey said gelding reared leaving the stalls and was slowly away as a result)* **8/1**

0500 **5** hd **Salmon Fishing (IRE)**[18] 8000 3-8-9 50 .... SeamusCronin(5) 4 44
(Mohamed Moubarak) *prom: effrt to cl on ldrs 2f out: rdn and kpt on one pce ins fnl f* **5/1**[3]

5 **6** 1 **Doogan's Warren (IRE)**[4] 8417 4-9-2 42 .... HollieDoyle 9 42
(John Butler) *hld up: rdn and no imp 2f out: drvn and kpt on fnl f: n.d* **7/2**[2]

2315 **7** ¾ **Catapult**[10] 8249 4-9-2 48 .... JosephineGordon 1 40+
(Shaun Keightley) *led: rdn along to hold position over 1f out: hdd by wnr jst ins fnl f and wknd clsng stages* **5/2**[1]

6664 **8** ½ **Gulland Rock**[30] 7603 8-8-13 40 .... DarraghKeenan(3) 14 39
(Anthony Carson) *trckd ldr: rdn and no imp 2f out: wknd fnl f* **50/1**

006 **9** 1 **Jane Camille**[19] 7976 3-9-0 40 .... TomQueally 6 35
(Peter Hedger) *hld up: rdn along and outpcd 3f out: nvr on terms* **25/1**

2302 **10** ¾ **Islay Mist**[30] 7604 3-9-0 48 ....(tp) KierenFox 2 33
(Lee Carter) *prom: pushed along 2f out: sn rdn and no imp over 1f out: wknd fnl f* **8/1**

0504 **11** 5 **Caledonian Gold**[21] 7912 6-8-9 43 ....(h) GavinAshton(7) 11 21
(Lisa Williamson) *hld up: a bhd* **50/1**

6046 **12** 3 ¼ **Opera Kiss (IRE)**[38] 7336 3-9-0 42 .... DougieCostello 13 12
(Ivan Furtado) *midfield on outer: wd thrght: rdn and wknd over 1f out* **33/1**

6P04 **13** 4 ½ **Caesonia**[9] 8295 3-9-0 47 ....(b[1]) PJMcDonald 10
(Charles Hills) *trckd ldrs early: rdn along and lost pl 2f out: sn wknd* **16/1**

1m 26.88s (-0.32) **Going Correction** -0.025s/f (Stan)
WFA 3 from 4yo+ 2lb **13 Ran SP% 126.0**
Speed ratings (Par 101): **100,97,97,97,96 95,94,94,93,92 86,82,77**
CSF £125.24 TOTE £10.10: £2.90, £3.70, £11.80; EX 138.20 Trifecta £2588.30.
Owner J Morris **Bred** Ms Nadja Humphreys **Trained** Carburton, Notts

FOCUS
They went a solid gallop in this low-grade affair, and three of the first four came from the four who raced at the back of the field. Limited form.

8548 BET TOTEQUADPOT AT TOTESPORT.COM H'CAP (DIV I) 1m (P)
6:00 (6:02) (Class 5) (0-75,77) 3-Y-O+
£5,175 (£1,540; £769; £400; £400; £400) **Stalls Low**

Form RPR

2410 **1** **Desert Lion**[81] 5782 3-8-10 **72** ....(h[1]) DylanHogan(5) 2 81
(David Simcock) *dwlt and hld up in last: swtchd rt and hdwy between rivals over 1f out: sn rdn to ld ent fnl f: r.o wl (trainer said regarding apparent improvement in form that the gelding benefitted from the return to an all-weather surface on this occasion after running on Soft ground last time out)* **8/1**[3]

6561 **2** 1 ½ **Bobby Biscuit (USA)**[23] 7839 4-9-4 **72** .... JFEgan 1 78
(Roger Varian) *midfield on inner: clsd gng wl 2f out: briefly short of room over 1f out: rdn and kpt on fnl f: nt match wnr clsng stages* **5/6**[1]

-450 **3** ½ **Camelot Rakti (IRE)**[84] 5651 3-9-4 **75** .... PJMcDonald 4 79
(James Tate) *in tch: pushed along over 2f out: sn rdn and hdwy 1f out: kpt on wl fnl f* **9/1**

4355 **4** ½ **Punjab Mail**[2] 8495 3-8-8 **68** .... GabrieleMalune(3) 7 71
(Ian Williams) *slowly away and racd in rr: c wd off home bnd: rdn and hdwy 1f out: nt rch ldrs* **7/1**[2]

6301 **5** nk **Nawar**[128] 4028 4-9-7 **75** ....(t) RobertHavlin 5 78
(Martin Bosley) *led tl 3f out then styd handy: led again over 1f out: rdn and hdd by wnr ins fnl f: no ex* **16/1**

3356 **6** *2* **Bollihope**[15] 8087 7-8-11 **65** JosephineGordon 10 64
(Shaun Keightley) *dwlt and in rr early: hdwy on outer to trck ldrs 5f out: pushed along to ld 3f out: rdn and hdd over 1f out: sn wknd fnl f* **16/1**

2066 **7** *hd* **Al Reeh (IRE)**[28] 7684 5-9-2 **70** (h) LukeMorris 6 68
(Marco Botti) *racd in midfield: rdn and outpcd 2f out: one pce fnl f* **12/1**

3440 **8** *2 3/4* **Creek Island (IRE)**[21] 7906 3-8-6 **68** AndrewBreslin(5) 8 59
(Mark Johnston) *midfield in tch: racd lazily over 2f out: rdn and outpcd over 1f out: wknd fnl f* **16/1**

-323 **9** *1 1/2* **City Of Love**[21] 7912 3-9-3 **74** DanielMuscutt 3 61
(David Lanigan) *midfield on inner: rdn along and no imp 2f out: wknd over 1f out* **25/1**

0613 **10** *1/2* **Take It Down Under**[179] 2256 4-8-13 **67** (t) DavidProbert 11 54
(Amy Murphy) *trckd ldrs: rdn and outpcd 2f out: wknd over 1f out (jockey said gelding hung right-handed)* **20/1**

1m 38.14s (-1.76) **Going Correction** -0.025s/f (Stan)
WFA 3 from 4yo+ 3lb **10** Ran SP% **122.1**
Speed ratings (Par 103): **107,105,105,104,104 102,102,99,97,97**
CSF £15.74 CT £69.33 TOTE £9.60: £2.60, £1.10, £2.90; EX 20.70 Trifecta £172.40.
Owner Qatar Racing Ltd & Partners **Bred** The Sorella Bella Partnership **Trained** Newmarket, Suffolk
■ Stewards' Enquiry : Andrew Breslin caution; careless riding

FOCUS
A fair handicap. The third has been rated to form.

8549 BET TOTEQUADPOT AT TOTESPORT.COM H'CAP (DIV II) 1m (P)

6:30 (6:32) (Class 5) (0-75,76) 3-Y-O+

£5,175 (£1,540; £769; £400; £400; £400) **Stalls** Low

Form RPR

6324 **1** **Glory Awaits (IRE)**[42] 7191 9-9-1 **72** (b) DylanHogan(5) 2 79
(David Simcock) *mde all: shkn up w short ld 2f out: rdn and strly pressed 1f out: kpt on gamely all the way to the line: all out* **5/1**[2]

3004 **2** *nse* **John Clare (IRE)**[32] 7542 3-8-13 **68** LukeMorris 6 74
(Pam Sly) *trckd ldrs: rdn along and clsd into 2nd over 1f out: drvn and kpt on way fnl f: jst failed* **10/1**

6204 **3** *1* **Harbour Vision**[52] 6863 4-9-6 **72** (v) LewisEdmunds 4 77
(Derek Shaw) *settled in midfield: stl gng wl whn briefly denied clr run over 1f out: swtchd rt and rdn ent fnl f: kpt on* **9/2**[1]

5425 **4** *1/2* **Philamundo (IRE)**[9] 8289 4-9-10 **76** (p1) StevieDonohoe 7 79+
(Richard Spencer) *hld up: niggled along 1/2-way: rdn and no imp 2f out: drvn and kpt on fnl f but n.d* **9/2**[1]

6136 **5** *nk* **Universal Effect**[14] 8122 3-9-4 **73** (h) LiamJones 1 75
(Mark Loughnane) *midfield on inner: clsd gng wl over 1f out: sn rdn and ev ch 1f out: one pce fnl f* **5/1**[2]

3002 **6** *1 1/4* **Filles De Fleur**[84] 5651 3-9-3 **72** HollieDoyle 3 71
(George Scott) *hld up and t.k.h: wd off home bnd: rdn and styd on fnl f: nt trble ldrs (jockey said filly ran keen early)* **6/1**[3]

2540 **7** *3* **Carnival Rose**[32] 7554 3-9-4 **73** GeorgeWood 9 65
(James Fanshawe) *in tch and tk little t.k.h: effrt to cl 2f out: rdn and no hdwy over 1f out: wknd fnl f* **9/1**

1350 **8** *nk* **Rambaldi (IRE)**[26] 7773 3-9-0 **69** (t) ShaneKelly 8 60
(Marco Botti) *dwlt and r in rr: wd: hmpd 5f out: rdn and no imp over 1f out: nvr on terms (jockey said gelding hung right-handed throughout)* **12/1**

3365 **9** *2* **Consequences (IRE)**[11] 8220 4-9-7 **73** DavidProbert 10 61
(Ian Williams) *hld up: rdn and outpcd over 1f out: a in rr (jockey said gelding ran too freely)* **16/1**

0000 **10** *nse* **Mr Minerals**[50] 6931 5-8-13 **65** (p) RobertHavlin 5 53
(Alexandra Dunn) *midfield on inner: rdn along and lost pl over 1f out: wknd fnl f* **33/1**

1m 39.5s (-0.40) **Going Correction** -0.025s/f (Stan)
WFA 3 from 4yo+ 3lb **10** Ran SP% **119.6**
Speed ratings (Par 103): **101,100,99,99,99 97,94,94,92,92**
CSF £55.64 CT £244.90 TOTE £6.20: £2.10, £3.20, £2.20; EX 56.10 Trifecta £402.90.
Owner John Cook **Bred** J Fisher **Trained** Newmarket, Suffolk
■ Stewards' Enquiry : Lewis Edmunds two-day ban; careless riding (Nov 9,16)

FOCUS
The pace wasn't as strong in this division (time was 1.36sec slower) and the winner held on out in front. The winner has been rated to his recent best.

8550 BET TOTETRIFECTA AT TOTESPORT.COM H'CAP 6f (P)

7:00 (7:04) (Class 4) (0-80,82) 3-Y-O+

£5,433 (£1,617; £808; £404; £400; £400) **Stalls** Centre

Form RPR

3135 **1** **Spirit Of May**[35] 7467 3-9-4 **78** JackMitchell 9 85
(Roger Teal) *trckd ldrs and travelled wl: rdn along to cl over 1f out: drvn and r.o wl to ld ins fnl f* **20/1**

0646 **2** *nk* **Sandridge Lad (IRE)**[10] 8267 3-8-9 **69** HollieDoyle 13 75
(John Ryan) *dwlt: sn rcvrd arnd field to press ldrs: rdn along to ld 1f out: drvn and hdd by wnr cl home* **50/1**

0353 **3** *nk* **Uncle Jerry**[33] 7519 3-8-13 **73** RobertHavlin 4 78
(Mohamed Moubarak) *midfield: hdwy to chse ldrs over 1f out: rdn and kpt on fnl f* **7/1**

4530 **4** *1/2* **Tommy Taylor (USA)**[15] 8101 5-9-4 **82** ThomasGreatrex(5) 2 85+
(Kevin Ryan) *hld up: stl last 2f out: rdn and picked up wl appr fnl f: kpt on wl: fin on heels of ldrs* **7/2**[2]

2130 **5** *hd* **Restless Rose**[14] 8115 4-9-9 **82** HayleyTurner 8 85+
(Stuart Williams) *midfield: rdn along to make prog on outer over 1f out: drvn and kpt on fnl f: nt rch ldrs* **12/1**

0005 **6** *nk* **Alfie Solomons (IRE)**[38] 7351 3-9-4 **78** (b1) LukeMorris 12 80+
(Richard Spencer) *hld up: rdn along and minor hdwy over 1f out: drvn and kpt on fnl f: n.d* **25/1**

1015 **7** *1* **Fantastic Flyer**[16] 8063 4-9-2 **75** (p) RobHornby 10 74
(Dean Ivory) *trckd ldrs: rdn along and no imp over 1f out: drvn and kpt on one pce fnl f* **14/1**

6243 **8** *2 3/4* **Vee Man Ten**[56] 6715 3-8-9 **72** (h) GabrieleMalune(3) 6 62
(Ivan Furtado) *led: rdn along and hdd 1f out: wknd ins fnl f* **20/1**

2-22 **9** *1/2* **Promote (IRE)**[79] 5868 3-9-5 **79** PJMcDonald 3 67
(James Tate) *dwlt and racd in rr: rdn along and minor hdwy over 1f out: kpt on one pce fnl f (jockey said filly suffered interference when leaving the stalls)* **5/1**[3]

1500 **10** *2 3/4* **You're Cool**[26] 7771 7-9-7 **80** (t) LewisEdmunds 7 59
(John Balding) *hld up: rdn and outpcd in rr 2f out: nvr on terms* **33/1**

0252 **11** *1 1/2* **Swiss Knight**[2] 8495 4-9-4 **77** (t) RossaRyan 1 52
(Stuart Williams) *midfield on inner: shkn up and fnd little over 1f out: wknd fnl f (trainer said that the race came too soon for the gelding)* **2/1**[1]

1306 **12** *shd* **Cent Flying**[16] 8063 4-8-13 **72** (t) MartinDwyer 11 46
(William Muir) *midfield on outer: rdn along and no imp 2f out: sn bhd* **33/1**

2505 **13** *3 3/4* **Good Luck Fox (IRE)**[42] 7178 3-9-1 **75** SilvestreDeSousa 5 37
(Richard Hannon) *midfield: rdn and no imp over 1f out: wknd fnl f* **20/1**

1m 11.43s (-2.27) **Going Correction** -0.025s/f (Stan)
WFA 3 from 4yo+ 1lb **13** Ran SP% **125.1**
Speed ratings (Par 105): **114,113,113,112,112 111,110,106,106,102 100,100,95**
CSF £764.54 CT £7696.92 TOTE £26.90: £4.60, £26.20, £2.00; EX 1917.40 Trifecta £1878.30.
Owner Mrs Carol Borras **Bred** R P Phillips **Trained** Lambourn, Berks

FOCUS
A fair sprint handicap but they finished in a bit of a heap. It's been rated around the winner to the better view of his Chester win.

8551 BET TOTESWINGER AT TOTESPORT.COM H'CAP 1m 6f (P)

7:30 (7:38) (Class 6) (0-55,56) 3-Y-O+

£3,105 (£924; £461; £400; £400; £400) **Stalls** Low

Form RPR

6350 **1** **Homesick Boy (IRE)**[12] 8204 3-8-9 **50** (v) RobertHavlin 16 60+
(Ed Dunlop) *hld up: hdwy into midfield 4f out: short of room whn making hdwy 3f out: rdn w plenty to do over 1f out: styd on strly to ld wl ins fnl f (trainer's rep said regarding apparent improvement in form that the gelding benefited from the step up in trip from 1m3 1/2f to 1m6f)* **14/1**

6631 **2** *2 1/2* **Mongolia**[10] 8269 3-9-1 **56** LukeMorris 7 63
(Michael Appleby) *trckd ldrs: shkn up to chal 2f out: sn rdn to ld over 1f out: drvn and hdd by wnr clsng stages: no ex* **6/1**[3]

5533 **3** *2 1/2* **Ignatius (IRE)**[33] 7520 3-8-11 **52** KierenFox 15 56
(John Best) *led after 2f: rdn along and hdd over 1f out: kpt on u.p ins fnl f in battle for 3rd* **9/2**[1]

2045 **4** *shd* **Falls Creek (USA)**[18] 8000 4-8-12 **46** oh1 (v) DavidProbert 1 47
(Andrew Balding) *midfield: clsd on ldrs gng wl over 2f out: shkn up and no immediate rspnse over 1f out: kpt on one pce fnl f wout troubling ldng pair* **5/1**[2]

2050 **5** *4 1/2* **General Allenby**[76] 5993 5-8-7 **48** (p) GavinAshton(7) 12 44
(Shaun Keightley) *hld up: minor hdwy on outer over 3f out: rdn along and no imp 2f out: kpt on one pce fnl f: n.d* **25/1**

0500 **6** *1/2* **Carvelas (IRE)**[28] 7685 10-9-3 **51** DanielMuscutt 13 46
(J R Jenkins) *hld up: hdwy u.p over 2f out: rdn and minor hdwy fnl f but nvr on terms* **33/1**

0505 **7** *1 1/2* **Vin D'Honneur (IRE)**[64] 6405 3-9-0 **55** (p) CallumShepherd 6 50
(Stuart Williams) *led for 2f then trckd ldr: rdn along and lost pl 2f out: wknd fnl f* **14/1**

0000 **8** *1/2* **Strictly Art (IRE)**[52] 6853 6-9-4 **55** TimClark(3) 8 47
(Alan Bailey) *in tch: rdn along and outpcd 4f out: drvn and plugged on one pce fr over 1f out* **20/1**

0003 **9** *1 3/4* **Blue Beirut (IRE)**[12] 8196 3-8-5 **46** oh1 HollieDoyle 10 38
(William Muir) *midfield: pushed along and no hdwy 3f out: rdn and no imp 2f out: kpt on one pce (jockey said gelding ran in snatches)* **5/1**[2]

05-0 **10** *2 1/4* **Midport (IRE)**[154] 3092 3-8-9 **55** ThomasGreatrex(5) 5 44
(Roger Charlton) *dwlt and racd in rr: niggled along 4f out: rdn and no imp 2f out: nvr a factor* **7/1**

0006 **11** *1/2* **Garrison Law**[18] 7998 3-8-3 **49** (p) PoppyBridgwater(5) 9 37
(David Simcock) *hld up: a bhd* **20/1**

0503 **12** *2* **Pecorino**[18] 7985 3-9-0 **55** (p1) ShaneKelly 2 41
(Richard Hughes) *midfield: pushed along and short of room over 2f out: sn rdn and no imp over 1f out: one pce* **7/1**

0004 **13** *12* **Ruler Of The Nile**[7] 8343 7-8-11 **48** JaneElliott(3) 3 16
(Marjorie Fife) *trckd ldrs: rdn along and outpcd 3f out: lost pl 2f out: sn wknd (jockey said gelding hung right-handed throughout)* **33/1**

5502 **14** *8* **Seventii**[16] 8072 5-9-0 **48** JosephineGordon 14 6
(Robert Eddery) *in tch: pushed along and lost pl 3f out: wknd wl over 1f out* **20/1**

50-0 **15** *4* **Hermosa Vaquera (IRE)**[18] 7985 9-9-2 **50** (p) HectorCrouch 11 3
(Gary Moore) *hld up: a bhd* **50/1**

4020 **16** *17* **Teemlucky**[12] 8200 3-8-12 **53** MartinDwyer 4
(Ian Williams) *midfield: rdn and lost pl over 3f out: eased over 1f out* **20/1**

3m 2.62s (-0.58) **Going Correction** -0.025s/f (Stan)
WFA 3 from 4yo+ 7lb **16** Ran SP% **134.9**
Speed ratings (Par 101): **100,98,97,97,94 94,93,93,92,90 90,89,82,77,75 65**
CSF £95.27 CT £462.65 TOTE £13.70: £3.10, £1.80, £1.60, £1.70; EX 140.60 Trifecta £1369.20.
Owner The Old Etonian Racing Syndicate **Bred** John Gunther **Trained** Newmarket, Suffolk
■ Stewards' Enquiry : Josephine Gordon four-day ban; careless riding (Nov 9,16,18-19)

FOCUS
A moderate staying contest, but it was run at a good gallop and was a proper test. The winner has been rated in keeping with his better recent form, and those close help pin a fairly straightforward level.

8552 BET TOTESCOOP6 AT TOTESPORT.COM NOVICE STKS 1m 2f (P)

8:00 (8:09) (Class 5) 3-Y-O+ **£4,948** (£1,472; £735; £367) **Stalls** Low

Form RPR

6 **1** **Wemyss Ware (IRE)**[9] 8294 3-9-2 0 LouisSteward 5 78+
(Sir Michael Stoute) *trckd ldrs: effrt to chal over 1f out: swtchd let and rdn to ld ins fnl f: kpt on wl* **9/2**[3]

6243 **2** *3/4* **Cheer The Title (IRE)**[56] 6730 4-9-6 78 LukeMorris 3 76
(Tom Clover) *hld up: hdwy on outer over 2f out: rdn along to ld briefly 1f out: sn hdd by wnr and no ex fnl f* **11/4**[2]

2-1 **3** *1/2* **Edinburgh Castle (IRE)**[27] 7730 3-9-9 0 DavidProbert 6 82+
(Andrew Balding) *hld up: short of room 2f out: sn rdn and hdwy between rivals over 1f out: drvn and clsd all the way to the line: nt rch ldng pair (jockey said colt was slowly away)* **10/11**[1]

6 **4** *3/4* **Dawry (IRE)**[23] 7841 3-8-13 0 JaneElliott(3) 9 74
(Heather Main) *trckd ldr: led 3f out: drvn along over 1f out: hdd 1f out: one pce fnl f* **33/1**

020 **5** *4* **Rewrite The Stars (IRE)**[80] 5810 3-8-11 0 PJMcDonald 2 61
(James Tate) *midfield on inner: bmpd along 3f out: pushed along and hung lft over 1f out: one pce fnl f (vet said filly bled from the nose)* **6/1**

30-6 **6** *1 1/2* **Wingreen (IRE)**[115] 4506 3-8-11 74 HectorCrouch 7 58
(Martin Smith) *in rr of midfield: hdwy on outer 5f out: rdn along to chal 2f out: sn outpcd: wknd fnl f* **20/1**

0 **7** *8* **Limalima (IRE)**[42] 7190 3-8-11 0 CallumShepherd 1 42
(Stuart Williams) *midfield: rdn along and outpcd 2f out: wknd over 1f out* **25/1**

0 **8** *nk* **Big Bang**[27] 7730 6-9-6 0 ShelleyBirkett 8 45
(Julia Feilden) *hld up: pushed along 4f out: a in rr* **66/1**

 The Form Book Flat 2019, Raceform Ltd, Newbury, RG14 5SJ

0000 **9** *10* **Daniel Dravot**[16] 8072 3-9-2 39..............................(v[1]) RobHornby 4 26
(Michael Attwater) *led tl 3f out: rdn and lost pl over 2f out: sn bhd* **100/1**

2m 8.23s (-0.37) **Going Correction** -0.025s/f (Stan) **9** Ran SP% **125.5**
WFA 3 from 4yo+ 4lb
Speed ratings (Par 103): **100,99,99,98,95 94,87,87,79**
CSF £18.26 TOTE £6.00: £1.30, £1.20, £1.10; EX 21.00 Trifecta £35.10.
Owner The Queen **Bred** Godolphin **Trained** Newmarket, Suffolk

FOCUS
The early gallop wasn't that strong and the principals finished in a bit of a bunch. Muddling form, but the second and third have been rated close to form for now.

8553 CHRISTMAS PARTIES AT CCR CLASSIFIED STKS 1m 2f (P)
8:30 (8:37) (Class 6) 3-Y-O+

£3,105 (£924; £461; £400; £400; £400) **Stalls** Low

Form RPR

0034 **1** **Dyagilev**[12] 8204 4-9-4 48..............................(b) AdrianMcCarthy 4 54+
(Lydia Pearce) *midfield on inner: swtchd lft and hdwy to chse ldrs 2f out: rdn and clsd over 1f out drifted lft and bmpd rival ins fnl f: sn led and asserted clsng stages (jockey said gelding hung left-handed throughout)* **6/1**[2]

5205 **2** *½* **Waterproof**[9] 8293 3-9-0 48..............................(v[1]) JosephineGordon 2 54
(Shaun Keightley) *midfield: pushed along to go 3rd over 1f out: rdn and ev ch whn bmpd by wnr ent fnl f: kpt on* **6/1**[2]

0402 **3** *1 ½* **Born To Reason (IRE)**[40] 7270 5-9-4 48..............................(b) LukeMorris 10 50
(Alexandra Dunn) *racd in midfield: hdwy 2f out: rdn along to ld over 1f out: drvn and hdd by wnr ins fnl f: no ex* **14/1**

-604 **4** *4 ½* **Gladden (IRE)**[42] 7200 4-9-4 42.............................. DanielMuscutt 13 42
(Lee Carter) *hld up: hdwy u.p into midfield over 1f out: rdn and kpt on fnl f but n.d* **33/1**

0006 **5** *2* **Capricorn Prince**[65] 6367 3-9-0 39.............................. HectorCrouch 3 40
(Gary Moore) *led: rdn along and hdd over 1f out: kpt on one pce fnl f* **9/1**

2460 **6** *½* **Chakrii (IRE)**[18] 8001 3-9-0 50..............................(p) HayleyTurner 15 39
(Henry Spiller) *in rr of midfield: c wd off home bnd: rdn and minor hdwy over 1f out: nrst fin (trainer was informed that the gelding could not run until the day after passing a stalls test)* **8/1**[3]

321 **7** *¾* **Necoleta**[10] 8251 3-9-3 53.............................. LiamKeniry 14 40
(Sylvester Kirk) *dwlt and swtchd lft in rr: bmpd along 3f out: rdn along and no imp over 1f out: plugged on (jockey said filly was never travelling)* **11/4**[1]

05-0 **8** *1* **Skating Away (IRE)**[41] 7236 3-9-0 50..............................(v[1]) RobHornby 7 36
(Joseph Tuite) *in tch in midfield: rdn along on outer over 1f out: kpt on one pce fnl f* **33/1**

0-00 **9** *¾* **Sunshine Coast**[18] 8001 4-9-4 50.............................. EllieMacKenzie 1 33
(Jamie Osborne) *trckd ldrs on inner: rdn and no imp 2f out: wknd 1f out* **12/1**

0000 **10** *4* **Dee Dee Dottie**[10] 8251 3-8-9 39..............................(p[1]) KevinLundie[(5)] 5 27
(Mark Loughnane) *midfield: rdn along and no imp over 1f out: kpt on one pce fnl f* **50/1**

063 **11** *¾* **Tops No**[19] 7973 4-9-4 50.............................. GeorgeWood 8 25
(William Muir) *hld up: rdn and no imp 2f out: nvr on terms* **16/1**

0042 **12** *2 ¼* **Dolly McQueen**[41] 7232 3-9-0 46.............................. HollieDoyle 16 22
(Anthony Carson) *midfield on outer: rdn along and outpcd 2f out: sn lost pl over 1f out* **8/1**[3]

5-00 **13** *4 ½* **Indian Sea**[18] 8000 3-8-9 40.............................. SeamusCronin[(5)] 6 14
(Dr Jon Scargill) *trckd ldr: rdn along and lost pl 2f out: wknd fr over 1f out* **40/1**

0000 **14** *6* **Bader**[10] 8251 3-9-0 48..............................(b) RossaRyan 11 3
(Richard Hannon) *in rr of midfield on outer: rdn 3f out: nvr on terms* **12/1**

0-00 **15** *1 ¼* **Vakilita (IRE)**[163] 2770 3-9-0 37.............................. DavidProbert 9
(Andrew Balding) *hld up: a in rr (jockey said filly was never travelling)* **20/1**

0500 **16** *27* **Piccolo Ramoscello**[28] 7682 6-8-11 10..............................(p) GavinAshton[(7)] 12
(Lisa Williamson) *midfield on outer: rn v wd home bnd 3f out: sn bhd* **66/1**

2m 7.99s (-0.61) **Going Correction** -0.025s/f (Stan) **16** Ran SP% **131.9**
WFA 3 from 4yo+ 4lb
Speed ratings (Par 101): **101,100,99,95,94 93,93,92,91,88 88,86,82,77,76 55**
CSF £43.19 TOTE £6.30: £2.30, £2.00, £4.90; EX 45.80 Trifecta £445.30.
Owner Killarney Glen & Lydia Pearce **Bred** Loderi **Trained** Newmarket, Suffolk

FOCUS
A low-grade classified race. The second and third suggest the form can't be rated much higher.
T/Plt: £1,085.10 to a £1 stake. Pool: £68,706.84 - 46.22 winning units T/Qpdt: £37.50 to a £1 stake. Pool: £15,872.41 - 312.51 winning units **Mark Grantham**

8509 DONCASTER (L-H)
Saturday, October 26

8554 Meeting Abandoned -

8516 NEWBURY (L-H)
Saturday, October 26

8561 Meeting Abandoned -

8569 - 8571a (Foreign Racing) - See Raceform Interactive

8352 LEOPARDSTOWN (L-H)
Saturday, October 26

OFFICIAL GOING: Soft to heavy (heavy in places)

8572a TOTE PROUD SPONSORS OF LEOPARDSTOWN RACECOURSE KNOCKAIRE STKS (LISTED RACE) 7f
3:05 (3:08) 3-Y-O+

£24,981 (£8,045; £3,810; £1,693; £846; £423)

RPR

1 **Psychedelic Funk**[20] 7934 5-9-7 100..............................(b) GaryCarroll 3 103+
(G M Lyons, Ire) *chsd ldrs: 5th 1/2-way: pushed along and impr on inner over 2f out into 2nd: rdn to ld under 2f out: kpt on wl for press ins fnl f* **8/1**

2 *¾* **Thiswaycadeaux (IRE)**[14] 8177 5-9-2 88..............................(v) LeighRoche 5 96
(W McCreery, Ire) *s.i.s and pushed along briefly in rr: pushed along again stl in rr fr 1/2-way: impr on inner into st and wnt 3rd under 2f out: rdn into 2nd 1f out and kpt on wl wout matching wnr clsng stages* **28/1**

3 *1 ¾* **Laughifuwant (IRE)**[25] 7794 4-9-7 101.............................. ColinKeane 1 96
(Gerard Keane, Ire) *broke wl to ld: 1 l clr at 1/2-way: pressed clly into st: drvn and hdd under 2f out: dropped to 3rd 1f out: no imp on ldrs ins fnl f: kpt on same pce* **9/4**[2]

4 *½* **Myth Creation (USA)**[25] 7794 4-9-2 87..............................(t) ShaneCrosse 4 90
(Joseph Patrick O'Brien, Ire) *w.w towards rr: 7th 1/2-way: tk clsr order 2f out: sn rdn in 5th and sme hdwy into 4th ins fnl f where no imp on ldrs: kpt on same pce* **25/1**

5 *¾* **Come September (IRE)**[6] 8367 3-9-0 94.............................. ChrisHayes 8 87
(Gavin Cromwell, Ire) *sn settled bhd ldrs: 4th 1/2-way: pushed along bhd ldrs out wd over 2f out and no imp u.p in 6th ent fnl f: kpt on same pce in 5th wl ins fnl f: nvr trbld ldrs* **16/1**

6 *3* **Amedeo Modigliani (IRE)**[7] 8336 4-9-7 101.........(t) DonnachaO'Brien 6 85
(A P O'Brien, Ire) *w.w towards rr: 6th 1/2-way: pushed along over 2f out and dropped to rr: swtchd lft under 2f out and no imp in 7th over 1f out: kpt on one pce ins fnl f where nt clr run and swtchd lft into mod 6th* **4/1**[3]

7 *½* **Pincheck (IRE)**[14] 8116 5-9-7 109..............................(p[1]) ShaneFoley 2 83
(Mrs John Harrington, Ire) *settled bhd ldrs: 3rd 1/2-way: pushed along bhd ldrs over 2f out: sn rdn and no ex u.p in 4th 1 1/2f out: wknd ins fnl f* **2/1**[1]

8 *5 ½* **Finoah (IRE)**[70] 6207 3-9-5 93..............................(v) DeclanMcDonogh 7 68
(Tom Dascombe) *sn trckd ldr in 2nd: 1 l bhd ldr at 1/2-way: pushed along after 1/2-way and wknd into st: dropped to rr u.p 1 1/2f out: eased ins fnl f* **14/1**

1m 36.41s (6.01) **Going Correction** +1.10s/f (Soft) **8** Ran SP% **115.1**
WFA 3 from 4yo+ 2lb
Speed ratings: **109,108,106,105,104 101,100,94**
CSF £189.62 TOTE £10.50: £2.40, £6.00, £1.20; DF 348.70 Trifecta £1046.70.
Owner Sean Jones **Bred** Mrs J Imray **Trained** Dunsany, Co Meath

FOCUS
An up-to-scratch Listed race that saw a welcome return to form of a formerly smart type. The winner has been rated closer to last year's best.

8573a (Foreign Racing) - See Raceform Interactive

8574a BET WITH THE TOTE AT LEOPARDSTOWN EYREFIELD STKS (GROUP 3) 1m 1f
4:15 (4:18) 2-Y-O

£33,486 (£10,783; £5,108; £2,270; £1,135)

RPR

1 **Degraves (IRE)**[17] 8039 2-9-3 0.............................. ShaneCrosse 5 104+
(Joseph Patrick O'Brien, Ire) *chsd ldrs: 4th over 4f out: gng wl bhd ldrs on outer 3f out: impr nr side gng best to ld over 1f out: rdn clr ins fnl f where edgd lft: reduced advantage nr fin hung sltly and pressed: hld on* **7/2**[2]

2 *½* **Persia (IRE)**[14] 8112 2-9-3 0.............................. SeamieHeffernan 4 103
(A P O'Brien, Ire) *chsd ldrs: 3rd over 4f out: pushed along bhd ldrs into st: rdn in 4th far side under 2f out and clsd u.p into 2nd ins fnl f where sn swtchd rt: kpt on wl to press wnr nr fin: hld* **4/1**[3]

3 *½* **Justifier (IRE)**[22] 7879 2-9-3 106.............................. ColinKeane 2 102
(G M Lyons, Ire) *sn settled in 2nd: over 1 l bhd ldr bef 1/2-way: clsr 2nd fr 1/2-way: led narrowly under 2f out and rdn: hdd over 1f out and sn dropped to 3rd: kpt on wl under hands and heels clsng stages: nt trble wnr* **7/4**[1]

4 *4 ¼* **Franklin Street (IRE)**[6] 8366 2-9-3 90.............................. DeclanMcDonogh 3 94
(Joseph Patrick O'Brien, Ire) *sn led: over 1 l clr bef 1/2-way: reduced advantage fr 1/2-way: drvn and hdd under 2f out: no ex u.p in 4th ins fnl f* **11/2**

5 *2 ¾* **Dawn Rising (IRE)** 2-9-3 0.............................. DonnachaO'Brien 1 88+
(A P O'Brien, Ire) *s.i.s and detached in rr early: sn tk clsr order stl in rr: niggled along briefly after 1/2-way: pushed along 3f out: rdn into st and no imp under 2f out where hung sltly: eased* **5/1**

2m 9.32s (11.52) **Going Correction** +1.50s/f (Heav) **5** Ran SP% **110.6**
Speed ratings: **108,107,107,103,100**
CSF £17.30 TOTE £5.00: £1.70, £2.30; DF 15.50 Trifecta £94.60.
Owner Williams, Gudinski & Ateam Syndicate **Bred** Longueville Bloodstock&matrix Bloodstock **Trained** Owning Hill, Co Kilkenny

FOCUS
Testing conditions for juveniles over this trip but the leader went a sensible gallop early. The winner quickened up smartly in the straight before looking to idle close home. A big step up from the winner, but the third and fourth give the form some validity.

8573 - 8576a (Foreign Racing) - See Raceform Interactive

8539 MOONEE VALLEY (L-H)
Saturday, October 26

OFFICIAL GOING: Turf: good

8577a MCCAFE MOONEE VALLEY GOLD CUP (GROUP 2) (4YO+) (TURF) 1m 4f 110y
5:35 4-Y-O+

£171,823 (£49,723; £24,861; £12,430; £6,906; £5,524)

RPR

1 **Hunting Horn (IRE)**[42] 7219 4-8-11 0..............................(p) RyanMoore 3 107+
(A P O'Brien, Ire) *cl up 1f: settled in midfield: drvn along in 3rd 2f out: led and rdn along 1f out: r.o wl: rdn out* **16/5**[3]

2 *1 ¼* **Mr Quickie (AUS)**[7] 8361 4-8-11 0..............................(b) LukeNolen 1 105
(Phillip Stokes, Australia) **14/5**[1]

3 *nk* **Downdraft (IRE)**[71] 6191 4-8-13 0..............................(t) JohnAllen 7 107
(Joseph Patrick O'Brien, Ire) *settled in 2nd: drvn along to ld under 2f out: sn pressed: hdd and rdn along 1f out: kpt on fnl f* **29/10**[2]

4 *¾* **Humidor (NZ)**[14] 8136 7-8-9 0.............................. DamianLane 5 101+
(Ciaron Maher & David Eustace, Australia) **17/5**

5 *¾* **Ventura Storm (IRE)**[14] 8134 6-9-0 0..............................(b) MarkZahra 2 105
(David A & B Hayes & Tom Dabernig, Australia) **14/1**

6 *3 ¼* **Shraaoh (IRE)**[21] 7931 6-9-2 0..............................(t) NashRawiller 6 102
(Chris Waller, Australia) **30/1**

7 *hd* **Alfarris (FR)**[21] 5-8-9 ....(b) KerrinMcEvoy 4 95
(David A & B Hayes & Tom Dabernig, Australia) *towards rr: effrt over 2f out: no imp: nvr a factor* **20/1**

8 *¾* **Etymology (AUS)**[21] 7-8-13 0..............................(b) BenMelham 8 97
(James Cummings, Australia) *hld up in fnl pair: shkn up turning in: wl hld fnl f* **25/1**

2m 39.48s **8** Ran SP% **117.0**

Owner Mrs John Magnier & Michael Tabor & Derrick Smith **Bred** Lynch-Bages $ Rhinestone Bloodstock **Trained** Cashel, Co Tipperary

FOCUS
The level is set by the fifth, sixth and eighth.

8578a SCHWEPPES CRYSTAL MILE (GROUP 2) (2YO+) (TURF) 1m
6:10 2-Y-0+
£101,104 (£29,834; £14,917; £7,458; £4,143; £3,314)

RPR

1 **Chief Ironside**[14] 8138 4-9-4 0 JamieSpencer 6 109
(David Menuisier) *settled bhd ldrs: gng wl and pushed along to take clsr order under 2f out: rdn along in 3rd 1f out: styd on wl to ld fnl strides* **25/1**

2 *shd* **Cliff's Edge (AUS)**[14] 8138 5-9-4 0 JohnAllen 3 109
(Ciaron Maher & David Eustace, Australia) **9/1**

3 *shd* **Best Of Days**[21] 7930 5-9-4 0 (b) HughBowman 10 109+
(James Cummings, Australia) *settled towards rr: drvn along and hdwy on outer under 2f out: rdn along and continued prog fnl 1/2f: clst fin* **6/1**

4 *½* **Pacodali (IRE)**[14] 6-9-4 0 DeanYendall 7 107
(Lindsey Smith, Australia) **7/1**

5 *shd* **Dreamforce (AUS)**[21] 7930 7-9-4 0 (bt) NashRawiller 4 107
(John P Thompson, Australia) **3/1**[1]

6 *hd* **Sikandarabad (IRE)**[14] 8138 6-9-4 0 (b) MarkZahra 5 107
(David A & B Hayes & Tom Dabernig, Australia) **11/2**[3]

7 *shd* **Debt Agent (NZ)**[21] 7-9-4 0 MichaelRodd 2 106
(Jim Conlan, Australia) **30/1**

8 *½* **Madison County (NZ)**[14] 8138 4-9-3 0 DamianLane 11 104
(Murray Baker & Andrew Forsman, New Zealand) **5/1**[2]

9 *3* **Gailo Chop (FR)**[14] 8136 8-9-4 0 (b[1]) DamienOliver 8 98
(Matthew Williams, Australia) **10/1**

10 *8* **Pounamu (AUS)**[406] 7321 8-9-4 0 CraigAWilliams 9 80
(Michael Kent, Australia) **60/1**

11 *2* **Dream Castle**[14] 8136 5-9-4 0 PatCosgrave 1 75
(Saeed bin Suroor) *trckd ldrs: pushed along and lost position 3f out: wl hld fnl f* **16/1**

1m 35.46s 11 Ran SP% **117.5**

Owner Australian Bloodstock, Coastline Racing Et Al **Bred** W & R Barnett Ltd **Trained** Pulborough, W Sussex

8579a LADBROKES COX PLATE (GROUP 1) (3YO+) (TURF) 1m 2f 44y
6:55 3-Y-0+
£1,685,082 (£414,364; £207,182; £138,121; £110,497; £55,248)

RPR

1 **Lys Gracieux (JPN)**[125] 4158 5-9-0 0 DamianLane 11 121+
(Yoshito Yahagi, Japan) *hld up in rr of midfield: drvn along and gd hdwy on outer 2f out: rdn to chal 110yds out: led 75yds out: r.o strly* **6/4**[1]

2 *1 ½* **Castelvecchio (AUS)**[14] 8142 3-7-11 0 (b) CraigAWilliams 3 116
(Richard Litt, Australia) *midfield: pushed along to ld 2 1/2f out: hrd pressed and rdn 110yds out: hdd 75yds out: no ex* **15/2**[3]

3 *2* **Te Akau Shark (NZ)**[21] 7930 5-9-4 0 (t) OpieBosson 14 117
(Jamie Richards, New Zealand) *towards rr: effrt and hdwy on inner over 2f out: disputing 4th and rdn along 1f out: styd on to go 3rd cl home: rdn out* **16/1**

4 *½* **Magic Wand (IRE)**[42] 7219 4-9-0 0 (p) RyanMoore 2 112
(A P O'Brien, Ire) *cl up: led briefly after 2f: led again over 5f out: pushed along and hdd 3f out: sn rdn: pressed ldr again 2f out: no ex fnl f* **8/1**

5 *hd* **Mystic Journey (AUS)**[21] 7918 4-8-10 0 (b) AnthonyDarmanin 5 108
(Adam Trinder, Australia) *trckd ldrs: tk clsr order under 3f out: sn outpcd and shkn up: kpt on same pce fnl 2f* **13/2**[2]

6 *2 ½* **Kings Will Dream (IRE)**[21] 7918 5-9-4 0 HughBowman 13 111
(Chris Waller, Australia) *towards rr: angled out and drvn along 2f out: rdn along w plenty to do 1f out: styd on wl fnl f: nvr on terms w ldrs* **25/1**

7 *½* **Avilius**[14] 8136 5-9-4 0 KerrinMcEvoy 6 110
(James Cummings, Australia) *midfield on inner: angled off rail and hdwy 3f out: drvn along 2f out: lost position and rdn along 1f out: kpt on same pce* **12/1**

8 *¾* **Harlem**[14] 8136 7-9-4 0 (b) DwayneDunn 1 108
(David A & B Hayes & Tom Dabernig, Australia) *settled in 4th on inner: lost position 3f out: sn drvn along in midfield: rdn and kpt on same pce fnl f* **60/1**

9 *hd* **Black Heart Bart (AUS)**[14] 8136 9-9-4 0 (t) BradRawiller 10 108
(Lindsey Smith, Australia) *led: hdd after 2f: sn led again: hdd over 5f out: led 3f out: hdd 2 1/2f out: shkn up and sn lost position: wknd fnl f* **40/1**

10 *nk* **Cape Of Good Hope (IRE)**[14] 8136 3-8-13 0 MarkZahra 7 107
(David A & B Hayes & Tom Dabernig, Australia) *settled in midfield: pushed along and prog 3f out: rdn and lost position over 1f out: kpt on same pce* **20/1**

11 *shd* **Homesman (USA)**[14] 8136 5-9-4 0 (b) BenMelham 12 107
(Liam Howley, Australia) *towards rr: shkn up and limited hdwy fnl 2f: nvr a factor* **30/1**

12 *2* **Verry Elleegant (NZ)**[21] 4-8-10 0 JamesMcDonald 4 95
(Chris Waller, Australia) *s.i.s: sn in midfield: t.k.h early: pushed along and lost position over 2f out: wl hld fnl f* **20/1**

13 *2* **Kluger (JPN)**[69] 7-9-4 0 TommyBerry 8 99
(Tomokazu Takano, Japan) *settled in 5th: rdn along 3f out: sn lost position: wl hld fnl f* **20/1**

14 *7 ¾* **Danceteria (FR)**[90] 5483 4-9-4 0 JamieSpencer 9 83
(David Menuisier) *in rr of midfield: effrt out wd turning in: no imp and wl hld fnl f* **20/1**

2m 4.21s
WFA 3 from 4yo+ 4lb 14 Ran SP% **120.0**

Owner U Carrot Farm **Bred** Northern Farm **Trained** Japan

FOCUS
No Winx this year, but the Cox Plate again went the way of another classy filly. Magic Wand in fourth rates a solid benchmark.

4680 NANTES (R-H)
Saturday, October 26

OFFICIAL GOING: Turf: heavy

8580a GRAND PRIX DE NANTES (LISTED RACE) (3YO+) (TURF) 1m 4f
12:45 3-Y-0+ **£27,027** (£10,810; £8,108; £5,405; £2,702)

RPR

1 **Mille Et Mille**[21] 7928 9-9-1 0 FranckBlondel 3 103
(C Lerner, France) **7/5**[1]

2 *1 ½* **Smart Whip (FR)**[33] 7536 8-9-1 0 AlexandreRoussel 1 100
(C Lotoux, France) **16/5**[3]

3 *snk* **Moll Davis (IRE)**[38] 7347 3-8-5 0 AugustinMadamet 2 97
(George Scott) *settled in rr: pushed along 2f out: brought to outside: rdn to chal: sn drvn ent fnl f: r.o wl u.p to go 3rd cl to home* **23/5**

4 *hd* **Caravagio (FR)**[54] 6820 6-9-1 0 MathieuAndrouin 5 100
(Alain Couetil, France) **29/10**[2]

5 *17* **Shepton Joa (FR)**[21] 6-8-11 0 TristanBaron 4 68
(N Paysan, France) **44/5**

2m 45.15s (10.15)
WFA 3 from 6yo+ 6lb 5 Ran SP% **119.2**
PARI-MUTUEL (all including 1 euro stake): WIN 2.40; PLACE 1.40, 1.60; SF 5.70.
Owner Alexis Anghert **Bred** Haras De La Perelle **Trained** France

7885 SAINT-CLOUD (L-H)
Saturday, October 26

OFFICIAL GOING: Turf: heavy

8581a PRIX BELLE DE NUIT (GROUP 3) (3YO+ FILLIES & MARES) (TURF) 1m 6f
1:00 3-Y-0+ **£36,036** (£14,414; £10,810; £7,207; £3,603)

RPR

1 **Monica Sheriff**[31] 7566 3-8-10 0 TomMarquand 6 107+
(William Haggas) *a cl up on outer: drvn to chal along stands' rail ins fnl 2f: rdn to ld w 1f to run: styd on u.p: wl on top at fin* **9/10**[1]

2 *1 ¾* **Endorphine (FR)**[62] 4-9-3 0 AnthonyCrastus 4 103
(Hiroo Shimizu, France) *impeded s by rival cutting across: allowed to rcvr bef moving up to trck ldr: led bef 1/2-way: towed field towards stands' side st: pushed along 1 1/2f out: hdd w 1f to rn: kpt on gamely but nt match wnr* **10/1**

3 *5* **Magical Touch**[41] 7249 4-9-3 0 MickaelBarzalona 5 96
(H-A Pantall, France) *wnt sharply lft s and impeded Endorphine: hld up in fnl pair: prog to chse two ldrs over 2f out: kpt on but nt match ldrs fr wl over 1f out* **41/5**

4 *3 ½* **Villa D'Amore (IRE)**[76] 6003 3-8-10 0 Pierre-CharlesBoudot 1 93
(A Fabre, France) *reluctant ldr under tight hold: hdd after 1f and trckd ldrs on inner: niggled along and no imp over 2f out: grad dropped away* **59/10**[3]

5 *20* **Bletilla**[52] 6875 3-8-10 0 MaximeGuyon 2 65
(Mme Pia Brandt, France) *a in fnl pair: pushed along but no imp fr 3f out: lost tch fnl 1 1/2f* **9/1**

6 *20* **Vivid Diamond (IRE)**[21] 7890 3-8-10 0 OlivierPeslier 3 37
(Mark Johnston) *led after 1f: hdd bef 1/2-way but remained cl up: shkn up but nt qckn 2 1/2f fr home: wknd fnl 1 1/2f* **17/5**[2]

3m 19.81s (7.61)
WFA 3 from 4yo 7lb 6 Ran SP% **119.8**
PARI-MUTUEL (all including 1 euro stake): WIN 1.90; PLACE 1.30, 3.50; SF 11.60.
Owner Duke Of Devonshire **Bred** The Duke Of Devonshire **Trained** Newmarket, Suffolk

8582a CRITERIUM DE SAINT-CLOUD (GROUP 1) (2YO COLTS & FILLIES) (TURF) 1m 2f
2:50 2-Y-0 **£128,693** (£51,486; £25,743; £12,860; £6,441)

RPR

1 **Mkfancy (FR)**[29] 7675 2-9-0 0 TheoBachelot 2 109
(Mme Pia Brandt, France) *mde all: drvn whn pressed 2f out: shook off chalr ins fnl 1 1/2f: styd on strly fnl f* **53/10**[3]

2 *3* **Arthur's Kingdom (IRE)**[12] 8208 2-9-0 0 OlivierPeslier 3 104
(A P O'Brien, Ire) *chsd ldr: 3rd and niggled along 3f fr home: outpcd over 2f out: kpt on again fnl f: wnt 2nd fnl 75yds: nt trble wnr* **36/5**

3 *½* **Mythical (FR)**[14] 8111 2-9-0 0 MickaelBarzalona 6 103+
(A P O'Brien, Ire) *a cl up: 3rd and pushed along in st: tried to chal ldr 2f out: shkn off by ldr over 1f out: kpt on but lost 2nd fnl 75yds* **48/10**[2]

4 *3* **Sound Of Cannons**[28] 7691 2-9-0 0 StephanePasquier 7 97
(Brian Meehan) *settled in fnl trio: drvn to cl over 2f out: chal for pls u.p 1 1/2f out: effrt petered out ins fnl f* **61/10**

5 *6* **The Summit (FR)**[26] 7774 2-9-0 0 Pierre-CharlesBoudot 9 87
(H-A Pantall, France) *racd keenly: in rr: rdn and effrt 2f out: sn no further imp: lft bhd fnl f* **13/5**[1]

6 *1 ¾* **Via De Vega (FR)**[38] 7338 2-9-0 0 CristianDemuro 5 83
(Andrew Balding) *racd in fnl trio: last and drvn 2 1/2f out: kpt on past btn horses ins fnl f: nvr in contention* **71/10**

7 *4* **Thunderspeed (FR)**[21] 2-9-0 0 JulienAuge 1 76
(C Ferland, France) *cl up on inner: rdn and nt qckn 2f out: sn wknd* **8/1**

8 *3 ½* **Celtic High King (IRE)**[7] 8353 2-9-0 0 EmmetMcNamara 4 70
(A P O'Brien, Ire) *racd keenly: prom: drvn but no imp over 2f out: wknd last 1 1/2f* **11/1**

2m 20.21s (4.21) 8 Ran SP% **119.0**
PARI-MUTUEL (all including 1 euro stake): WIN 6.30; PLACE 2.10, 2.40, 2.10; DF 22.20.
Owner Abdullah Al Maddah **Bred** Marbat Llc **Trained** France

The Form Book Flat 2019, Raceform Ltd, Newbury, RG14 5SJ

FOCUS
This Group 1 can produce a decent winner, with Fame and Glory (2008) and Waldgeist (2016) two notable recent examples. The winner made all and not many got involved in this with the first three in front rank throughout.

8583a PRIX PERTH (GROUP 3) (3YO+) (TURF) 1m
3:25 3-Y-O+ £36,036 (£14,414; £10,810; £7,207; £3,603)

RPR
1 **Miss O Connor (IRE)**[77] 5949 4-8-11 0............ Pierre-CharlesBoudot 2 108+
(William Haggas) *chsd ldr: led after 1f: mde rest: wnt clr 1/2-way: drvn to repel chalrs over 1f out: rallied gamely fnl f: asserted cl home* **7/5**[1]
2 *1* **Kourkan (FR)**[25] 6-9-1 0 AlexisBadel 6 110
(J-M Beguigne, France) *settled in fnl trio: hdwy 2 1/2f out: drvn to chse ldrs fr 1 1/2f out: ev ch ent fnl f: styd on and tk 2nd cl home* **31/5**[3]
3 *snk* **Plumatic**[178] 2313 5-9-6 0 MaximeGuyon 9 115
(A Fabre, France) *hld up in fnl trio: hdwy 3f out: rdn to chal over 1f out: styd on u.p: no ex cl home and dropped to 3rd* **27/10**[2]
4 *6* **Lilly Kafeine (FR)**[41] 7255 5-8-11 0 CristianDemuro 8 92
(A Schutz, France) *hld up in rr: clsd fr 2 1/2f out: chsd ldng gp over 2f out: plugged on at one pce* **15/1**
5 *3 1/2* **Sun At Work (GER)**[27] 7750 7-9-1 0 EddyHardouin 1 88
(W Haustein, Germany) *led: hdd after 1f: remained in 2nd: pushed along to chse clr ldr 3f out: outpcd by ldrs 1 1/2f out: sn dropped away* **41/1**
6 *nk* **El Rey Brillante (CHI)**[27] 5-9-1 0..............(b) FrankPanicucci 5 87
(I Endaltsev, Czech Republic) *chsd ldrs: 4th and outpcd over 3f out: sn rdn and nt go on w ldrs fnl 1 1/2f* **30/1**
7 *3/4* **Matematica (GER)**[6] 8376 3-8-8 0 ThierryThulliez 4 81
(C Laffon-Parias, France) *prom on inner: drvn and no imp 2 1/2f out: wknd wl over 1f out* **69/10**
8 *8* **Wonnemond (GER)**[34] 7494 6-9-1 0 BayarsaikhanGanbat 7 67
(S Smrczek, Germany) *settled in midfield: 5th but 12 l off pce 3f out: sn rdn and btn* **14/1**
9 *18* **Tifosa (IRE)**[72] 6142 3-8-8 0 TheoBachelot 3 21
(Mme Pia Brandt, France) *towards rr on inner: bhd over 2f out and eased* **14/1**

1m 49.99s (2.49) **9** Ran SP% **120.4**
WFA 3 from 4yo+ 3lb
PARI-MUTUEL (all including 1 euro stake): WIN 2.40; PLACE 1.30, 1.60, 1.50; DF 6.80.
Owner Lael Stable **Bred** Kilnamoragh Stud **Trained** Newmarket, Suffolk

8584a PRIX DE FLORE (GROUP 3) (3YO+ FILLIES & MARES) (TURF) 1m 2f 110y
4:00 3-Y-O+ £36,036 (£14,414; £10,810; £7,207; £3,603)

RPR
1 **Spirit Of Nelson (IRE)**[35] 7477 4-9-0 0 MaximeGuyon 3 110+
(J Reynier, France) *settled in fnl pair: last bhd line of four over 1 1/2f out: smooth prog whn nt clr run and stdd over 1f out: gap sn c and qcknd to ld fnl 150yds: sn clr* **3/1**[2]
2 *3* **Mashael (FR)**[19] 7978 3-8-9 0 VincentCheminaud 4 105
(A Fabre, France) *trckd ldr on outer: 3rd and pushed along 2f fr home: drvn to chal 1 1/2f out: led over 1f out: hdd fnl 150yds: readily outpcd by wnr* **7/10**[1]
3 *2 1/2* **Tosen Gift (IRE)**[22] 7885 4-9-0 0 GregoryBenoist 2 99
(S Kobayashi, France) *led in centre of trck: c stands' side st: shkn up and hdd 2f out: regained ld 1 1/2f out: hdd over 1f out: outpcd and dropped to 4th: kpt on under driving: tk 3rd cl home* **63/10**
4 *snk* **Lanana (FR)**[22] 7885 4-9-0 0 EddyHardouin 5 99
(Robert Collet, France) *sltly awkward leaving stalls: in rr: cl 4th and pushed along wl over 1 1/2f out: sn rdn: outpcd by ldrs ins fnl f: lost 3rd cl home* **54/10**[3]
5 *20* **Jackson Hole (FR)**[19] 3-8-9 0 AntoineHamelin 1 62
(M Rulec, Germany) *racd keenly: chsd ldr on inner: shkn up to ld 2f out: sn rdn: hdd ins fnl 1 1/2f: sn wknd and eased* **15/1**

2m 25.69s (6.09) **5** Ran SP% **119.4**
WFA 3 from 4yo 4lb
PARI-MUTUEL (all including 1 euro stake): WIN 4.00; PLACE 1.40, 1.20; SF 9.70.
Owner Jean-Claude Seroul **Bred** Jean-Claude Seroul **Trained** France

8390 SAN SIRO (R-H)
Saturday, October 26

OFFICIAL GOING: Turf: good

8585a ST LEGER ITALIANO (GROUP 3) (3YO+) (GRANDE COURSE) (TURF) 1m 7f
3:25 3-Y-O+ £29,279 (£12,882; £7,027; £3,513)

RPR
1 **Pretending (ITY)**[937] 6-9-0 0..............(b) FabioBranca 2 104
(A Botti, Italy) *mde all: eased clr 2 1/2f out: v easily* **306/100**[3]
2 *14* **Great Aventura (IRE)**[14] 8153 5-8-10 0 SilvanoMulas 1 83
(Cristiano Davide Fais, Italy) *w.w in rr: clsd u.p over 2f out: wnt 2nd last 150yds: no ch w wnr* **26/1**
3 *2 1/2* **Alkuin (IRE)**[47] 4-9-0 0 AlexanderPietsch 3 84
(Waldemar Hickst, Germany) *racd keenly: trckd ldr: rdn but no match for wnr fr 2 1/2f out: lost 2nd fnl 150yds* **49/100**[1]
4 *3/4* **Caterpillar (IRE)** 4-9-0 0 DarioDiTocco 4 83
(Marco Gasparini, Italy) *hld up next to last: drvn ins fnl 3f but no imp: kpt on ins fnl f: nvr in contention* **10/1**
5 *1/2* **Ormuz (GER)**[111] 4707 3-8-5 0 DarioVargiu 5 83
(Henk Grewe, Germany) *racd keenly: hld up in 3rd: outpcd and pushed along 3f out: dropped to last ins fnl f* **20/7**[2]

3m 19.9s (3.50) **5** Ran SP% **130.5**
WFA 3 from 4yo+ 7lb
PARI-MUTUEL (all including 1 euro stake): WIN 4.07; PLACE 3.07, 8.97; SF 33.64.
Owner Scuderia Effevi SRL **Bred** Societa Agricola Al Deni Srl **Trained** Italy

7250 HANOVER (L-H)
Sunday, October 27

OFFICIAL GOING: Turf: soft to heavy

8586a GROSSER PREIS DER MEHL-MULHENS-STIFTUNG (LISTED RACE) (2YO FILLIES) (TURF) 7f
11:45 2-Y-O £12,612 (£5,855; £2,702; £1,351)

RPR
1 **Paloma Ohe**[119] 2-9-2 0 BauyrzhanMurzabayev 2 93
(Jan Korpas, Germany) **12/1**
2 *nk* **Democracy (GER)** 2-9-2 0 LukasDelozier 3 92
(P Schiergen, Germany) **49/10**[3]
3 *2 1/2* **Lips Eagle (GER)**[28] 7749 2-9-2 0 FilipMinarik 4 86
(Andreas Suborics, Germany) **113/10**
4 *1 1/4* **Tiramisu (GER)** 2-9-2 0 AlexanderPietsch 1 83
(Andreas Suborics, Germany) **127/10**
5 *5 1/2* **Belle Anglaise**[16] 8089 2-9-2 0 MichaelCadeddu 7 69
(Stuart Williams) *hld up in tch: outpcd and drvn over 2 1/2f out: no imp ins fnl 2f: wl hld fnl f* **9/10**[1]
6 *2 3/4* **After Rain Sun (FR)** 2-9-2 0 ClementLecoeuvre 6 62
(Henk Grewe, Germany) **17/5**[2]
7 *7 1/2* **Odina** 2-9-2 0 BayarsaikhanGanbat 5 44
(Mario Hofer, Germany) **223/10**

1m 29.81s **7** Ran SP% **119.7**
PARI-MUTUEL (all including 1 euro stake): WIN 13.00 PLACE: 3.70, 2.70; SF: 25.00.
Owner Heinz Dieter Jarling **Bred** Ellis Stud Partnership & Bellow Hill Stud **Trained** Germany

8587a GROSSER PREIS DES GESTUTS AMMERLAND (GROUP 3) (3YO+ FILLIES & MARES) (TURF) 1m 3f
12:50 3-Y-O+ £28,828 (£10,810; £5,405; £2,702; £1,801)

RPR
1 **Lips Queen (GER)** 3-9-0 0 JozefBojko 4 101
(Eva Fabianova, Germany) *detached in rr: tk clsr order fr wl over 2f out: styd on strly ins fnl 1 1/2f: led fnl 75yds and asserted* **57/1**
2 *1 1/4* **Anna Magnolia (FR)**[28] 5-9-4 0 JulienGuillochon 2 96
(D Moser, Germany) *midfield: outpcd and scrubbed along 2 1/2f out: sn drvn and styd on to ld 1f fr home: began to labour and hdd last 75yds: no ex* **153/10**
3 *3/4* **Atlanta (GER)**[28] 6-9-4 0 RenePiechulek 5 95
(Dr A Bolte, Germany) *fnl trio: pushed along but no imp 3 1/2f out: began to cl whn drvn w 2f to run: styd on u.p to go 3rd last 100yds: nt pce to chal* **57/1**
4 *nk* **All For Rome (GER)** 3-9-0 0 MichaelCadeddu 6 96
(Jean-Pierre Carvalho, Germany) *in rr of main gp: one of four to cross to stands' side st: gd hdwy appr fnl 1 1/2f: styd on strly fnl f: nrest at fin* **91/10**
5 *3/4* **Ismene (GER)**[24] 7862 3-9-0 0 LukasDelozier 11 95
(Jean-Pierre Carvalho, Germany) *w.w towards rr: began to cl fr 3f out: led three others stands' side into st: styd on u.p fnl f: nvr trbld ldrs* **123/10**
6 *2 1/4* **Stex (IRE)**[57] 6747 3-9-0 0 BauyrzhanMurzabayev 9 91
(R Dzubasz, Germany) *trckd ldr: led ins fnl 2f and kicked clr: hrd rdn over 1 1/2f out: struggling whn hdd w 1f to run: sn lft bhd* **27/10**[1]
7 *1 1/4* **Mythica (IRE)**[20] 7978 3-9-0 0 FilipMinarik 7 89
(Jean-Pierre Carvalho, Germany) *led: hdd after 1f: remained prom: rdn and no imp 1 1/2f out: wknd ins fnl f* **10/1**
8 *1 1/2* **Edith (GER)**[70] 5-9-4 0..............(p) ClementLecoeuvre 3 84
(R Dzubasz, Germany) *w.w towards rr: rdn and effrt between horses over 2f out: kpt on u.p but nt pce to trble ldrs* **106/10**
9 *10* **Akua'rella (GER)**[60] 4-9-4 0 WladimirPanov 1 66
(D Moser, Germany) *midfield on inner: drvn to chse ldng gp 2 1/2f out: began to labour w 2f to run: sn wknd* **269/10**
10 *7 1/2* **Akribie (GER)**[35] 7504 3-9-0 0 MartinSeidl 8 55
(Markus Klug, Germany) *led after 1f: hdd ins fnl 2f: sn wknd and eased* **69/10**[3]
11 *18* **Satomi (GER)**[22] 7926 3-9-0 0 MaximPecheur 10 22
(Markus Klug, Germany) *prom: lost pl fr 4f out: wknd fnl 2f: t.o* **19/5**[2]
12 *11* **Eleni (FR)**[28] 4-9-4 0 AlexanderPietsch 12
(Waldemar Hickst, Germany) *midfield on outer: dropped towards rr 3f out: c stands' side st: sn wknd and t.o* **205/10**
13 *26* **In Memory (IRE)**[57] 6747 3-9-0 0 BayarsaikhanGanbat 13
(S Richter, Germany) *pushed along to chse ldrs after 1f: shkn up but began to lose pl 4f out: c stands' side st but t.o: virtually p.u* **186/10**

2m 28.22s **13** Ran SP% **118.6**
WFA 3 from 4yo+ 5lb
PARI-MUTUEL (all including 1 euro stake): WIN 57.70 PLACE: 14.70, 5.30, 10.30; SF: 1000.00.
Owner Rennstall Germanius **Bred** Stall Parthenaue **Trained** Germany

8376 LONGCHAMP (R-H)
Sunday, October 27

OFFICIAL GOING: Turf: heavy

8588a CRITERIUM INTERNATIONAL (GROUP 1) (2YO COLTS & FILLIES) (NEW COURSE: 2ND POST) (TURF) 7f
1:00 2-Y-O £128,693 (£51,486)

RPR
1 **Alson (GER)**[21] 7940 2-9-0 0 FrankieDettori 4 113+
(Jean-Pierre Carvalho, Germany) *sn led on outer: travelling strly and had rival off bridle 3f out: shkn up ins fnl 2f: sn clr: easily* **1/2**[1]
2 *20* **Armory (IRE)**[21] 7940 2-9-0 0 DonnachaO'Brien 2 63+
(A P O'Brien, Ire) *trckd rival on inner: u.p and hrd rdn 3f out: sn btn* **9/10**[2]

1m 28.61s (7.91) **2** Ran SP% **119.3**
PARI-MUTUEL (all including 1 euro stake): WIN 1.50.
Owner Gestut Schlenderhan **Bred** Gestut Schlenderhan **Trained** Germany

FOCUS
An already decimated field was further reduced when Lady Penelope was withdrawn just before the start after getting upset in the stalls. An unsatisfactory edition of this Group 1 with the winner dictating it.

8589a PRIX ROYAL-OAK (GROUP 1) (3YO+) (GRANDE COURSE) (TURF) 1m 7f 110y
2:50 3-Y-O+ £180,171 (£72,081; £36,040; £18,004; £9,018)

RPR

1 **Technician (IRE)**[22] 7927 3-8-10 0...................... Pierre-CharlesBoudot 8 115+
(Martyn Meade) *racd midfield: occasionally nudged along to maintain position: strly drvn over 3f out: delivered to chal 2f out: tk ld over a f out: styd on wl clsng stages* **12/5**[2]

2 1 1/4 **Call The Wind**[22] 7928 5-9-4 0...................... OlivierPeslier 1 112
(F Head, France) *settled jst bhd ldrs: pushed along false st: prog to chal over a f out u.str.p: styd on wl but nt match wnr* **11/5**[1]

3 3 1/2 **Holdthasigreen (FR)**[22] 7928 7-9-4 0...................... TonyPiccone 2 108
(B Audouin, France) *settled in 2nd: tk the ld w 6f to run: asked for more 3f out: hdd over 1f out: kpt on one pce* **14/5**[3]

4 2 1/2 **Lah Ti Dar**[22] 7926 4-9-1 0...................... FrankieDettori 3 102
(John Gosden) *racd promly and tk outrt ld after 2f: hdd w 6f to run: drvn 3f out: wandered u.p in home st: wkng whn sltly short of room over a f out: no ex* **41/10**

5 3/4 **Way To Paris**[22] 7928 6-9-4 0...................... CristianDemuro 4 105
(Andrea Marcialis, France) *hld up: u.p w over 3f to run: no imp home st: kpt on one pce* **9/1**

6 1 1/4 **Iskanderhon (USA)**[22] 7927 3-8-10 0...................... FrankPanicucci 5 105
(I Endaltsev, Czech Republic) *hld up in last: pushed along over 3f out: unable qck: styd on one pce clsng stages* **32/1**

3m 40.13s (18.63)
WFA 3 from 4yo+ 7lb **6** Ran SP% **119.6**
PARI-MUTUEL (all including 1 euro stake): WIN 3.40; PLACE 1.20, 1.10; SF 6.10.
Owner Team Valor 1 **Bred** Barronstown Stud **Trained** Manton, Wilts

FOCUS
An interesting renewal of the Prix Royal Oak with a young pretender outstaying two established French stayers in a war of attrition in deep ground. This was an impressive performance and augurs well for his future as a cup horse in the coming seasons. The race was run at a decent enough pace given the conditions and it suited those with the most abundant stamina.

8590 - 8599a (Foreign Racing) - See Raceform Interactive

GEELONG (L-H)
Wednesday, October 23

OFFICIAL GOING: Turf: good

8600a BET365 GEELONG CUP (GROUP 3 H'CAP) (3YO+) (TURF) 1m 4f
6:00 3-Y-O+
£132,596 (£39,779; £19,889; £9,944; £5,524; £4,419)

RPR

1 **Prince Of Arran**[11] 8134 6-9-2 0...................... MichaelWalker 11 111
(Charlie Fellowes) *trckd ldr: gng wl and tk clsr order under 3f out: shkn up to ld over 1 1/2f out: styd on wl: hld off late chal* **16/5**[1]

2 hd **True Self (IRE)**[60] 6473 6-8-13 0...................... JohnAllen 1 108
(W P Mullins, Ire) *wnt lft s: settled in rr of midfield on inner: angled off rail and hdwy 3f out: in clr and shkn up 1 1/2f out: styd on strly ins fnl f: jst failed* **18/5**[2]

3 1 1/2 **Haky (IRE)**[11] 8134 5-9-0 0...................... LindaMeech 3 106
(J E Hammond, France) **25/1**

4 1/2 **Red Cardinal (IRE)**[33] 7-9-2 0...................... KerrinMcEvoy 10 107
(Kris Lees, Australia) **25/1**

5 hd **Red Galileo**[60] 6473 8-9-1 0...................... PatCosgrave 4 106
(Saeed bin Suroor) *settled bhd ldrs: pushed along and lost position over 4f out: rdn along towards rr of midfield 1 1/2f out: sn styd on again: gd hdwy fnl f wout troubling ldrs* **12/1**

6 1 **Supernova**[18] 4-8-7 0......................(t) DwayneDunn 7 97
(Michael, Wayne & John Hawkes, Australia) **9/2**[3]

7 1 1/4 **Steel Prince (IRE)**[32] 5-9-1 0...................... DamienOliver 8 103
(Anthony Freedman, Australia) **5/1**

8 hd **Grey Lion (IRE)**[18] 7931 7-9-1 0...................... CraigAWilliams 2 102
(Matthew A Smith, Australia) **20/1**

9 shd **Neufbosc (FR)**[18] 7931 4-9-2 0......................(b[1]) LukeCurrie 6 103
(David A & B Hayes & Tom Dabernig, Australia) **30/1**

10 3 1/2 **Dal Harraild**[18] 6-9-1 0......................(b) MarkZahra 5 96
(Ciaron Maher & David Eustace, Australia) **9/1**

11 1 1/4 **Muntahaa (IRE)**[18] 6-9-2 0...................... LukeNolen 9 95
(David A & B Hayes & Tom Dabernig, Australia) *midfield on outer early: settled in 3rd after 2f: tk clsr order and drvn along over 2f out: sn rdn and outpcd: eased whn wl hld fnl 100yds* **100/1**

2m 26.84s **11** Ran SP% **114.8**

Owner Saeed bel Obaida **Bred** Rabbah Bloodstock Limited **Trained** Newmarket, Suffolk

8450 KEMPTON (A.W) (R-H)
Monday, October 28

OFFICIAL GOING: Polytrack: standard to slow
Wind: virtually nil Weather: overcast

8601 32RED CASINO H'CAP 5f (P)
4:25 (4:26) (Class 4) (0-80,80) 3-Y-O+
£6,469 (£1,925; £962; £481; £400; £400) Stalls Low

Form RPR

3240 1 **Mercenary Rose (IRE)**[23] 7894 3-9-3 77......................(b[1]) DavidEgan 9 87
(Paul Cole) *broke fast: crossed to inner and mde all: pushed along and qcknd clr over 1f out: in command and r.o wl ins fnl f* **7/1**

1530 2 2 3/4 **Shining**[27] 7789 3-9-2 76...................... OisinMurphy 4 76
(Jim Boyle) *taken down early: t.k.h: chsd ldrs: effrt over 1f out: no imp on wnr: kpt on and wnt 2nd last stride* **12/1**

6045 3 shd **Benny And The Jets (IRE)**[35] 7524 3-9-6 80...................... RobHornby 7 80
(Sylvester Kirk) *chsd wnr: rdn and unable to match pce of wnr over 1f out: kpt on but no imp ins fnl f: lost 2nd last stride* **13/2**

1641 4 1 1/2 **Enthaar**[40] 7337 4-9-2 76......................(tp) JasonWatson 10 69+
(Stuart Williams) *stdd leaving stalls and dropped in bhd: hld up in last trio: effrt over 1f out: styd on ins fnl f: no threat to wnr* **6/1**[3]

313 5 nk **Wiley Post**[46] 7130 6-9-3 77......................(b) TomMarquand 3 69+
(Tony Carroll) *hld up in last pair: effrt and swtchd lft over 1f out: styd on ins fnl f: styd on ins fnl f: nvr trbld ldrs* **5/1**[1]

0322 6 nk **Foxy Forever (IRE)**[19] 8023 9-9-6 80......................(bt) RobertHavlin 5 71+
(Michael Wigham) *hld up in tch in midfield: effrt over 1f out: keeping on whn nt clrest of runs and swtchd rt ins fnl f: kpt on: no ch w wnr* **11/2**[2]

4135 7 shd **Secretfact**[5] 8470 6-9-3 77...................... JimmyQuinn 6 68
(Malcolm Saunders) *stdd s: midfield on outer: effrt over 1f out: no imp: kpt on same pce ins fnl f: lost 3 pls last strides* **11/1**

6636 8 hd **Manshood (IRE)**[23] 7908 6-9-4 78......................(b) LukeMorris 2 68
(Paul Midgley) *in tch in midfield: rdn over 1f out: unable qck and edgd rt: no threat to wnr and kpt on same pce ins fnl f* **11/2**[2]

0505 9 3 1/2 **Waseem Faris (IRE)**[56] 6809 10-9-5 79......................(t[1]) HollieDoyle 1 56
(Milton Harris) *in tch in midfield: rdn over 1f out: sn struggling and outpcd: wknd ins fnl f* **25/1**

2500 10 3 3/4 **Youkan (IRE)**[12] 8262 4-9-3 77......................(p) BenCurtis 8 41
(Stuart Kittow) *taken down early: hld up in rr: nvr involved* **14/1**

58.96s (-1.54) **Going Correction** -0.125s/f (Stan) **10** Ran SP% **114.1**
Speed ratings (Par 105): **107,102,102,100,99 99,98,98,93,87**
CSF £85.46 CT £583.71 TOTE £8.00: £1.90, £5.00, £2.70; EX 103.60 Trifecta £1331.80.
Owner Frank Stella **Bred** Hr Partnership **Trained** Whatcombe, Oxon

FOCUS
A fair sprint and the winner made all. The 3yos dominated. It's been rated a bit cautiously.

8602 32RED ON THE APP STORE FILLIES' NOVICE STKS (PLUS 10 RACE) 7f (P)
4:55 (5:00) (Class 5) 2-Y-O £3,881 (£1,155; £577; £288) Stalls Low

Form RPR

1 **Jaariyah (USA)** 2-9-0 0...................... DaneO'Neill 12 75+
(Roger Varian) *hld up in tch in midfield: effrt 2f out: pushed along and hdwy over 1f out: rdn and str run to ld ins fnl f: r.o strly* **7/1**[3]

00 2 1 1/4 **Tiritomba (IRE)**[107] 4918 2-9-0 0...................... TomMarquand 10 72
(Richard Hannon) *pressed ldr: effrt and ev ch 2f out: drvn over 1f out: led ins fnl f: sn hdd and unable to match pce of wnr* **25/1**

3 1/2 **Shimmering (IRE)** 2-9-0 0...................... RobertHavlin 9 71+
(John Gosden) *hld up in tch in midfield: effrt 2f out: pushed along and hdwy over 1f out: clsng whn swtchd lft ins fnl f: styd on wl to go 3rd 50yds out: gng on fin* **8/1**

4 1 1/4 **Plath** 2-9-0 0...................... JasonWatson 1 67+
(Sir Michael Stoute) *in tch in midfield: effrt and swtchd to ins and effrt 2f out: rdn and hdwy to chse ldrs 1f out: kpt on same pce ins fnl f* **14/1**

5 1/2 **Flower Of Thunder (IRE)** 2-9-0 0...................... RossaRyan 2 66
(Richard Hannon) *chsd ldrs: effrt to press ldrs 2f out: rdn over 1f out: unable qck 1f out: kpt on same pce ins fnl f* **25/1**

6 nk **Cosmic Princess** 2-9-0 0...................... HollieDoyle 13 65+
(Hughie Morrison) *stdd and swtchd rt after s: bhd: effrt towards inner 2f out: sme hdwy 1f out: clsng and swtchd lft ins fnl f: styd on wl and gng on strly at fin* **33/1**

7 1/2 **Almareekh (USA)** 2-9-0 0...................... JimCrowley 4 64+
(Sir Michael Stoute) *chsd ldrs: effrt over 2f out: unable qck and outpcd over 1f out: wknd ins fnl f* **3/1**[2]

8 nk **Sunshine Fun (USA)** 2-9-0 0...................... OisinMurphy 7 63
(Jamie Osborne) *t.k.h: hld up in midfield: effrt over 2f out: no imp over 1f out: kpt on ins fnl f: no threat to ldrs (jockey said filly ran too free)* **20/1**

00 9 nse **Madame Peltier (IRE)**[25] 7832 2-9-0 0...................... StevieDonohoe 6 63
(Charlie Fellowes) *in tch in midfield: effrt jst over 2f out: unable qck and outpcd over 1f out: no threat to ldrs and kpt on same pce ins fnl f* **66/1**

10 nk **Crispina** 2-9-0 0...................... HarryBentley 3 62
(Ralph Beckett) *t.k.h: led: rdn ent fnl 2f: hdd jst ins fnl f: no ex and wknd wl ins fnl f* **7/4**[1]

60 11 3/4 **Kavadi**[26] 7826 2-9-0 0...................... DavidEgan 14 60
(Hughie Morrison) *stdd and swtchd rt sn after s: hld up towards rr: effrt ent fnl f: no imp: nvr involved* **100/1**

12 nk **Fairmet** 2-9-0 0...................... AndreaAtzeni 8 60
(Marco Botti) *hld up towards rr: effrt over 2f out: no imp: n.d* **66/1**

0 13 4 **Lipslikecherries**[26] 7813 2-9-0 0...................... NicolaCurrie 5 49
(Jamie Osborne) *t.k.h: midfield tl stdd bk towards rr and wd 1/2-way: effrt over 2f out: sn btn* **33/1**

1m 27.53s (1.53) **Going Correction** -0.125s/f (Stan) **13** Ran SP% **114.0**
Speed ratings (Par 92): **86,84,84,82,82 81,81,80,80,80 79,79,74**
CSF £166.94 TOTE £7.00: £2.10, £6.50, £2.70; EX 174.30 Trifecta £1435.70.
Owner Hamdan Al Maktoum **Bred** Shadwell Farm LLC **Trained** Newmarket, Suffolk
■ Bruisa was withdrawn. Price at time of withdrawal 66/1. Rule 4 does not apply

FOCUS
This had the look of a useful fillies' novice and it ought to throw up plenty of winners. The bare form is unlikely to be much better than rated.

8603 MAGICAL FIREWORKS SPECTACULAR HERE ON SATURDAY NURSERY H'CAP 7f (P)
5:30 (5:31) (Class 6) (0-60,60) 2-Y-O
£3,105 (£924; £461; £400; £400; £400) Stalls Low

Form RPR

505 1 **Bavardages (IRE)**[11] 8280 2-9-6 59...................... JoeFanning 5 61
(Mark Johnston) *sn led and mde rest: rdn ent fnl 2f: edgd lft wl over 1f out: kpt finding ex and styd on gamely ins fnl f: all out* **8/1**[2]

450 2 3/4 **Kuwaity**[20] 7981 2-9-6 59......................(b[1]) TomMarquand 4 59
(Mohamed Moubarak) *dwlt: hld up in rr: effrt over 2f out: gd hdwy over 1f out: kpt on wl ins fnl f: wnt 2nd last stride* **10/1**

5003 3 shd **Bryn Du**[19] 8022 2-9-6 59......................(t) OisinMurphy 11 59
(William Haggas) *wnt rt s: sn wl in tch in midfield: clsd to chse ldrs on outer over 3f out: effrt to press ldrs and bmpd over 1f out: ev ch 1f out: kpt on but hld: lost 2nd last stride* **11/8**[1]

6065 4 shd **Divine Connection**[18] 8061 2-9-7 60...................... RobHornby 13 60
(Jonathan Portman) *hld up in midfield: effrt over 2f out: hdwy and edging rt over 1f out: swtchd lft 1f out: kpt on u.p ins fnl f* **9/1**[3]

2300 5 nse **Hiconic**[18] 8061 2-9-4 57...................... LukeMorris 3 57
(Alex Hales) *bustled along leaving stalls: in tch in midfield: effrt 3f out: nt clr run over 2f out: swtchd rt 2f out: drvn to chse ldrs 1f out: edgd lft and kpt on u.p ins fnl f* **14/1**

550 6 3/4 **Mr Kodi (IRE)**[18] 8061 2-9-0 53...................... HarryBentley 1 51
(David Evans) *chsd ldrs: effrt ent fnl 2f: swtchd rt over 1f out: ev ch 1f out: no ex and jst outpcd fnl 100yds* **9/1**[3]

6004 **7** *nk* **Candid (IRE)**[16] 8118 2-8-9 **48**..........................(p) NicolaCurrie 6 45
(Jonathan Portman) *hld up in rr: effrt on inner 2f out: hdwy over 1f out: kpt on but no imp fnl 100yds* **14/1**

500 **8** *1 ¾* **Poetic Lilly**[44] 7203 2-9-0 **53**.......................... JasonWatson 7 45
(David Menuisier) *in tch in midfield: effrt ent fnl 2f: clsd to chse ldrs 1f out: no ex whn sltly impeded jst ins fnl f: wknd towards fin* **20/1**

0040 **9** *1* **Flashy Flyer**[23] 7896 2-8-5 **49**.......................... SophieRalston(5) 12 39
(Dean Ivory) *t.k.h: pressed wnr: rdn and carried lft over 1f out: stl chsng ldrs but struggling to qckn whn short of room 1f out: wknd ins fnl f* **50/1**

0600 **10** *4* **Roman's Empress (IRE)**[33] 7585 2-8-12 **54**...(p[1]) ThomasGreatrex(3) 10 33
(David Loughnane) *bmpd leaving stalls: t.k.h: hld up towards rr: effrt on outer over 2f out: nt threatening to get on terms whn hmpd over 1f out: nvr involved (vet said filly lost right hind shoe)* **33/1**

005 **11** *1* **Loretta Lass**[70] 6281 2-8-11 **50**.......................... DavidProbert 2 27
(Adam West) *hld up towards rr: effrt over 2f out: drifted rt 2f out and sn unable qck: wknd ins fnl f* **25/1**

0504 **12** *9* **Buy Nice Not Twice (IRE)**[46] 7111 2-8-12 **51**.......................... RossaRyan 8 4
(Richard Hannon) *in tch in midfield: rdn over 2f out: sn struggling and losing pl whn hung lft over 1f out: sn wknd* **12/1**

3460 **13** *3 ½* **Sweet Sixteen (GER)**[12] 8259 2-9-6 **59**..........................(b) DanielMuscutt 9 3
(Amy Murphy) *midfield: rdn and lost pl over 2f out: btn whn pushed lft and hmpd over 1f out: bhd fnl f* **25/1**

1m 26.77s (0.77) **Going Correction** -0.125s/f (Stan) 13 Ran SP% **120.7**
Speed ratings (Par 93): **90,89,89,88,88 88,87,85,84,79 78,68,64**
CSF £80.80 CT £182.79 TOTE £6.80: £2.60, £3.40, £1.10; EX 99.90 Trifecta £391.50.
Owner Kingsley Park 11 **Bred** Knocktoran Stud **Trained** Middleham Moor, N Yorks

FOCUS
The main action unfolded centre field in the straight and there was something of a bunched finish. It's been rated as very ordinary form.

8604 FIREWORK TICKETS £7 IN ADVANCE MAIDEN STKS (DIV I) 1m (P)

6:00 (6:02) (Class 5) 2-Y-O £3,881 (£1,155; £577; £288) **Stalls Low**

Form RPR

6 **1** **The Turpinator (IRE)**[19] 8011 2-9-5 0.......................... GeraldMosse 5 79+
(David Elsworth) *hld up in midfield: effrt ent fnl 2f: swtchd lft over 1f out: str run ins fnl f to ld towards fin* **10/1**

0 **2** *½* **Tahitian Prince (FR)**[37] 7453 2-9-5 0.......................... SeanLevey 12 77
(Richard Hannon) *led tl 5f out: styd chsng ldrs: swtchd and effrt over 1f out: sn chalng u.p: led ins fnl f: kpt on wl tl hdd and no ex towards fin* **40/1**

4 **3** *1 ½* **Aquileo (IRE)**[23] 7897 2-9-5 0.......................... AndreaAtzeni 11 74
(Roger Varian) *t.k.h: hld up in tch in midfield: swtchd lft and hdwy to ld 5f out: rdn and hdd 2f out: stl w ldr and led again jst ins fnl f: sn hdd and one pce* **7/4**[1]

04 **4** *nse* **Campari**[45] 7162 2-9-5 0.......................... JasonWatson 1 74
(Roger Charlton) *chsd ldrs: effrt and edgd lft over 1f out: kpt on same pce ins fnl f (jockey said colt hung left-handed in str)* **5/1**[3]

22 **5** *nk* **Zafeer (JPN)**[40] 7346 2-9-5 0.......................... DavidEgan 8 73
(Marco Botti) *mostly chsd ldr: rdn to ld narrowly 2f out: hdd jst ins fnl f: no ex and outpcd fnl 100yds* **8/1**

6 *1 ¾* **Galata Bridge** 2-9-5 0.......................... LouisSteward 10 69
(Sir Michael Stoute) *dwlt and towards rr: sme hdwy into midfield 5f out: rdn and sme hdwy over 1f out: kpt on ins fnl f: nvr trbld ldrs* **16/1**

7 *1* **Nova Roma** 2-9-5 0.......................... RobertHavlin 2 67
(John Gosden) *s.i.s: in rr: effrt jst over 2f out: no threat to ldrs but kpt on ins fnl f* **9/2**[2]

8 *nk* **Back From Dubai (IRE)** 2-9-5 0.......................... CallumShepherd 13 66
(Saeed bin Suroor) *hld up in midfield: effrt ent fnl 2f: no imp over 1f out: wknd ins fnl f* **7/1**

9 *6* **Medika (IRE)** 2-9-0 0.......................... OisinMurphy 7 47
(Andrew Balding) *hld up towards rr: effrt over 2f out: sn struggling and outpcd 2f out: wknd over 1f out* **33/1**

10 *2* **Jersey Grey (FR)** 2-9-5 0.......................... NicolaCurrie 3 48
(Jamie Osborne) *hld up towards rr: n.d* **66/1**

11 *hd* **Sea Bright** 2-9-2 0.......................... PaddyBradley(3) 9 47
(Michael Attwater) *in tch in midfield: rdn over 2f out: sn struggling and outpcd: wknd over 1f out* **100/1**

0 **12** *4 ½* **Ginger Box**[21] 7972 2-9-0 0..........................(p) LukeMorris 4 32
(Karen George) *s.i.s: a bhd* **150/1**

60 **13** *¾* **Toolmaker**[18] 8069 2-9-5 0.......................... DavidProbert 6 35
(David Flood) *t.k.h: chsd ldr tl 5f out: outpcd and hung lft 2f out: sn wknd* **150/1**

1m 40.17s (0.37) **Going Correction** -0.125s/f (Stan) 13 Ran SP% **119.0**
Speed ratings (Par 95): **93,92,91,90,90 88,87,87,81,79 79,74,74**
CSF £359.47 TOTE £13.70: £3.00, £9.90, £1.10; EX 506.00 Trifecta £2288.60.
Owner John Manley **Bred** John Manley **Trained** Newmarket, Suffolk

FOCUS
The first leg of a fair maiden, little got into it from off the pace. The balance of the third, fourth and fifth help set the opening level.

8605 FIREWORK TICKETS £7 IN ADVANCE MAIDEN STKS (DIV II) 1m (P)

6:30 (6:35) (Class 5) 2-Y-O £3,881 (£1,155; £577; £288) **Stalls Low**

Form RPR

6 **1** **Ya Hayati (USA)**[26] 7814 2-9-5 0.......................... WilliamBuick 13 80
(Charlie Appleby) *hdwy to ld after 2f: mde rest: rdn 2f out: sn clr w runner-up: battled on wl u.p ins fnl f* **3/1**[1]

53 **2** *hd* **Cipango**[79] 5940 2-9-5 0.......................... DanielMuscutt 5 80
(Marco Botti) *rousted along leaving stalls: hdwy to chse ldrs after 1f: effrt to press wnr 2f out: sn kicked clr w wnr: sustained chal u.p fnl f: jst hld* **3/1**[1]

3 *3 ½* **Thumur (USA)** 2-9-5 0..........................(w) JimCrowley 1 76+
(Owen Burrows) *s.i.s: hld up in rr of main gp: swtchd rt and nt clr run over 2f out: swtchd rt again and hdwy 2f out: kpt on to chse clr ldng pair ins fnl f: kpt on wl but nvr a threat* **11/2**[2]

4 *3 ½* **Nashy (IRE)** 2-9-5 0.......................... LouisSteward 4 64
(Sir Michael Stoute) *broke wl: sn restrained and hld up in midfield: clsd over 2f out: rdn to chse clr ldng pair over 1f out: no imp and lost 3rd ins fnl f* **8/1**

5 *2* **Pawpaw** 2-9-5 0.......................... HectorCrouch 6 60
(Clive Cox) *s.i.s: towards rr of main gp: shkn up 3f out: effrt over 2f out: no imp and wl hld 6th 1f out: kpt on* **12/1**

633 **6** *½* **Ivor**[143] 3534 2-9-5 78.......................... TomMarquand 8 59
(Richard Hannon) *t.k.h: led tl 6f out: chsd wnr tl edgd lft and outpcd 2f out: lost btn 3rd over 1f out: wknd ins fnl f* **25/1**

6 **7** *nk* **Gibraltar (IRE)**[12] 8257 2-9-5 0.......................... HayleyTurner 11 58
(Michael Bell) *hld up in tch in midfield: effrt over 2f out: sn outpcd and wl hld whn nt clrest of runs ins fnl f* **50/1**

8 *½* **Itsallaboutluck (IRE)** 2-9-2 0.......................... FinleyMarsh(3) 3 57
(Richard Hughes) *chsd ldrs early: steadily lost pl: rdn: outpcd and edgd lft 2f out: sn wl btn* **16/1**

9 *½* **Cemhaan** 2-9-5 0.......................... RobertHavlin 7 56
(John Gosden) *s.i.s: in rr of main gp: hung rt over 2f out: sn swtchd lft and pushed along over 2f out: nvr trbld ldrs (jockey said colt was slowly away and denied a clear run)* **6/1**[3]

10 *2 ½* **Mazekine** 2-9-0 0.......................... KierenFox 10 45
(Roger Ingram) *chsd ldrs: rdn over 2f out: sn outpcd and wknd over 1f out (jockey said filly ran green)* **100/1**

11 *¾* **Lord Chapelfield** 2-9-5 0.......................... GeorgeWood 2 48
(Amy Murphy) *in tch in midfield: rdn over 2f out: struggling and outpcd 2f out: sn wknd* **66/1**

00 **12** *35* **Majestyk Fire (IRE)**[21] 7972 2-8-12 0..........................(t) EllieMacKenzie(7) 12
(David Flood) *rdn leaving stalls: hdwy to chse ldrs after 1f: lost pl and hung lft wl over 2f out: sn wknd: t.o (jockey said colt hung left-handed off bend)* **100/1**

13 *17* **Mack The Knife (IRE)** 2-9-5 0.......................... NicolaCurrie 9
(Jamie Osborne) *sn dropped to rr and outpcd: t.o fnl 3f (jockey said colt ran green; post-race examination failed to reveal any abnormalities)* **20/1**

1m 38.85s (-0.95) **Going Correction** -0.125s/f (Stan) 13 Ran SP% **118.4**
Speed ratings (Par 95): **99,98,95,92,90 89,89,88,88,85 85,50,33**
CSF £10.45 TOTE £3.30: £1.20, £1.30, £2.20; EX 10.90 Trifecta £66.60.
Owner Godolphin **Bred** Godolphin **Trained** Newmarket, Suffolk

FOCUS
This looked a better race than the first division and the time appeared to back up that impression. The opening level is fluid.

8606 32RED.COM H'CAP 1m (P)

7:00 (7:02) (Class 4) (0-85,87) 3-Y-O+
£6,469 (£1,925; £962; £481; £400; £400) **Stalls Low**

Form RPR

-050 **1** **Piece Of History (IRE)**[44] 7188 4-9-9 **87**.......................... OisinMurphy 1 99+
(Saeed bin Suroor) *hld up in tch in midfield: smooth hdwy ent fnl 2f: swtchd lft over 1f out: rdn to ld 1f out: sn in command and r.o wl: comf* **13/8**[1]

4103 **2** *2 ¼* **Corazon Espinado (IRE)**[11] 8289 4-9-6 **84**.......................... TomMarquand 2 89
(Simon Dow) *hld up wl in tch in midfield: effrt and clsd ent fnl 2f: rdn and ev ch over 1f out tl nt match pce of wnr ins fnl f (jockey said colt hung left-handed)* **20/1**

1424 **3** *shd* **Canal Rocks**[40] 7349 3-9-0 **81**.......................... JasonWatson 11 85
(Henry Candy) *chsd ldrs: effrt ent fnl 2f: nt clr run over 1f out tl ent fnl f: kpt on wl ins fnl f: no ch w wnr (jockey said gelding was denied a clear run)* **16/1**

6054 **4** *nk* **Chairmanoftheboard (IRE)**[12] 8253 3-8-12 **84**..... ScottMcCullagh(5) 5 87
(Mick Channon) *hld up towards rr: effrt on inner ent fnl 2f: hdwy to chse ldrs 1f out: kpt on same pce ins fnl f* **12/1**

051- **5** *¾* **Eden Gardens (IRE)**[339] 9227 3-9-1 **82**.......................... JimCrowley 8 83+
(Simon Crisford) *hld up towards rr: effrt over 2f out: kpt on wl ins fnl f: no ch w wnr* **5/1**[2]

3342 **6** *¾* **Reloaded (IRE)**[25] 7856 3-9-4 **85**.......................... HayleyTurner 13 85
(George Scott) *awkward leaving stalls and slowly away: sn swtchd rt and hld up in rr: effrt and hdwy over 1f out: kpt on same pce and no imp ins fnl f* **18/1**

0352 **7** *nse* **I'lletyougonow**[21] 7975 3-8-6 **73**..........................(p) SilvestreDeSousa 3 73
(Mick Channon) *hld up in midfield: nt clr run and swtchd lft over 2f out: kpt on ins fnl f: no threat to ldrs* **14/1**

64-0 **8** *nk* **Easy Tiger**[19] 8016 7-9-7 **85**.......................... LiamKeniry 6 85
(David Weston) *chsd ldr tl rdn to ld 2f out: hdd 1f out: no ex and wknd ins fnl f* **100/1**

5201 **9** *1 ½* **Fennaan (IRE)**[19] 8024 4-9-9 **87**.......................... BenCurtis 10 83
(Phillip Makin) *t.k.h: hld up in rr: effrt ent fnl 2f: no imp and short of room ent fnl f: nvr involved* **8/1**[3]

4306 **10** *½* **Poetic Force (IRE)**[46] 7128 5-9-8 **86**..........................(t) GeorgeDowning 7 81
(Tony Carroll) *mounted in the chute: in tch in midfield: rdn jst over 2f out: unable qck and btn whn nt clr run jst over 1f out: wknd ins fnl f (jockey said gelding was denied a clear run)* **50/1**

5303 **11** *4 ½* **Akvavera**[26] 7815 4-9-7 **85**.......................... HarryBentley 12 70
(Ralph Beckett) *t.k.h: chsd ldrs on outer: chsd ldr over 5f out tl 2f out: sn outpcd u.p and edgd lft over 1f out: wknd fnl f* **8/1**[3]

1236 **12** *nk* **Call Out Loud**[87] 5626 7-9-6 **84**..........................(t) AlistairRawlinson 9 68
(Michael Appleby) *led tl rdn and hdd 2f out: sn outpcd: wknd fnl f* **40/1**

-345 **13** *14* **Kentucky Kingdom (IRE)**[28] 7772 3-8-4 **71**.......................... RaulDaSilva 4 22
(James Evans) *stdd after s: plld hrd and hld up towards rr: swtchd lft and rapid hdwy over 4f out: chsd ldrs over 3f out tl lost pl qckly over 2f out: sn bhd (jockey said gelding ran too free)* **100/1**

1m 37.86s (-1.94) **Going Correction** -0.125s/f (Stan)
WFA 3 from 4yo+ 3lb 13 Ran SP% **113.6**
Speed ratings (Par 105): **104,101,101,101,100 99,99,99,98,97 93,92,78**
CSF £41.36 CT £395.70 TOTE £2.40: £1.10, £5.40, £4.50; EX 23.30 Trifecta £254.20.
Owner Godolphin **Bred** Godolphin **Trained** Newmarket, Suffolk

FOCUS
A fair handicap won in good style by the class of the race. The winner has been rated close to his form here last October, the second to his recent form, and the third and fourth close to their recent marks.

8607 32RED H'CAP 6f (P)

7:30 (7:30) (Class 3) (0-95,95) 3-Y-O+
£9,337 (£2,796; £1,398; £699; £349; £175) **Stalls Low**

Form RPR

0000 **1** **Soldier's Minute**[16] 8127 4-9-7 **95**..........................(h) JoeFanning 3 106
(Keith Dalgleish) *chsd ldrs: effrt ent fnl 2f: clsd u.p jst over 1f out: led and edgd rt jst ins fnl f: hld on wl fnl 100yds* **11/8**[1]

5160 **2** *½* **Beyond Equal**[66] 6396 4-9-0 **88**.......................... RobHornby 4 97
(Stuart Kittow) *t.k.h: hld up towards rr: swtchd rt and effrt ent fnl 2f: hdwy to chse ldrs 1f out: squeezed through to chse wnr ins fnl f: kpt on wl* **22/1**

-304 **3** *3 ¾* **Firelight (FR)**[122] 4340 3-8-13 **88**.......................... OisinMurphy 1 85
(Andrew Balding) *hld up in tch in midfield: effrt ent fnl 2f: jst getting outpcd whn sltly squeezed for room ent fnl 2f: no threat to ldrs but kpt on ins fnl f* **7/1**[3]

4556 **4** *shd* **Jumira Bridge**[44] 7175 5-9-1 **89**.................................(t) SilvestreDeSousa 8 86
(Robert Cowell) *wnt lft leaving stalls: sn rcvrd to chse ldr after 1f tl over 4f out: effrt to chse ldr again over 2f out: clsd over 1f out: lost 2nd and squeezed for room ins fnl f: sn wknd: lost 3rd last stride* **12/1**

2530 **5** *hd* **Count Otto (IRE)**[30] 7697 4-9-0 **88**.........................(h) KieranShoemark 6 84
(Amanda Perrett) *hld up towards rr: effrt ent fnl 2f: n.m.r over 1f out: kpt on wl ins fnl f: no ch w ldng pair* **15/2**

0416 **6** *½* **Moon Trouble (IRE)**[117] 4521 6-9-3 **91**...................... TomMarquand 12 85
(Michael Appleby) *sn led and crossed to inner: rdn ent fnl 2f: hdd jst ins fnl f: no ex and sn wknd* **25/1**

-500 **7** *½* **Mythmaker**[39] 7372 7-9-2 **90**.. GrahamLee 5 83
(Bryan Smart) *chsd ldr early: in tch in midfield after: effrt ent fnl 2f: unable qck over 1f out: wknd ins fnl f* **20/1**

5560 **8** *¾* **Polybius**[6] 8425 8-9-1 **89**.. AndreaAtzeni 10 79
(David Simcock) *short of room leaving stalls: sn swtchd rt and hld up in rr: effrt over 1f out: no imp ins fnl f (vet said gelding bled from nse)* **5/1**[2]

3035 **9** *½* **Concierge (IRE)**[44] 7187 3-8-12 **87**...........................(v) HarryBentley 11 76
(George Scott) *swtchd rt after s: hld up in rr: rdn over 2f out: nvr trbld ldrs* **16/1**

1110 **10** *2¾* **Major Valentine**[37] 7431 7-8-11 **92**.......................... KateLeahy(7) 7 72
(John O'Shea) *midfield: hdwy to chse ldrs over 3f out: rdn and outpcd whn edgd rt over 1f out: wknd ins fnl f* **33/1**

1120 **11** *12* **Drummond Warrior (IRE)**[46] 7121 3-8-12 **87**................... ShaneKelly 9 29
(Pam Sly) *bmpd leaving stalls: rcvrd and hdwy to chse ldr over 4f out tl over 2f out: sn lost pl: bhd ins fnl f* **20/1**

1m 10.91s (-2.19) **Going Correction** -0.125s/f (Stan)
WFA 3 from 4yo+ 1lb **11** Ran SP% **117.3**
Speed ratings (Par 107): **109,108,103,103,102 102,101,100,99,96 80**
CSF £42.96 CT £167.43 TOTE £1.80: £1.20, £5.90, £3.10; EX 26.40 Trifecta £194.40.
Owner Weldspec Glasgow Limited **Bred** Rabbah Bloodstock Limited **Trained** Carluke, S Lanarks
■ Stewards' Enquiry : Joe Fanning two-day ban: careless riding (Nov 16, 18)

FOCUS
A decent sprint. The first two have been rated back to their best.

8608 100% PROFIT BOOST AT 32REDSPORT.COM H'CAP 1m 3f 219y(P)
8:00 (8:02) (Class 4) (0-85,82) 3-Y-O+

£6,469 (£1,925; £962; £481; £400; £400) **Stalls** Low

Form RPR

0003 **1** **Kyllachy Gala**[19] 8014 6-9-5 **80**.................................. GabrieleMalune(3) 2 91+
(Marco Botti) *in tch in midfield: effrt to chse ldr jst over 2f out: rdn to ld over 1f out: styd on wl ins fnl f* **5/1**[2]

6504 **2** *1¾* **He's Amazing (IRE)**[38] 7413 4-9-4 **76**.......................... LukeMorris 3 83+
(Ed Walker) *in tch in midfield: short of room and hmpd over 3f out: hdwy u.p and edgd rt over 1f out: chsd wnr 1f out: kpt on* **8/1**[3]

0000 **3** *2* **Tralee Hills**[23] 7915 5-9-2 **74**..................................(v¹) HayleyTurner 5 78
(Peter Hedger) *stdd s: hld up in rr: hdwy on inner over 2f out: rdn to chse ldrs over 1f out: kpt on same pce ins fnl f* **33/1**

10/0 **4** *½* **Fiesole**[51] 6452 7-9-10 **82**.. SilvestreDeSousa 4 85
(Olly Murphy) *t.k.h: hld up in tch in midfield: nt clr run over 2f out: hmpd and swtchd lft over 1f out: kpt on ins fnl f (jockey said gelding was denied a clear run)* **12/1**

1220 **5** *¾* **Natty Night**[17] 8092 3-8-13 **77**..................................... MartinDwyer 7 79
(William Muir) *sn w ldr tl led after 2f: rdn over 2f out: hdd over 1f out: no ex and outpcd fnl f (jockey said colt ran too free)* **5/2**[1]

0443 **6** *8* **Noble Gift**[51] 6967 9-9-5 **77**.. KierenFox 8 66
(William Knight) *t.k.h: hld up in last trio: swtchd lft and hdwy on outer over 3f out: rdn and chse ldrs and edgd rt 2f out: outpcd over 1f out: sn wknd and eased ins fnl f (jockey said gelding ran too free)* **9/1**

1260 **7** *2* **Allegiant (USA)**[26] 7829 4-9-8 **80**.............................. OisinMurphy 6 66
(Stuart Williams) *wl in tch in midfield: nt clr run and swtchd lft over 2f out: squeezed for room and hmpd over 1f out: edgd rt and wknd ins fnl f* **5/1**[2]

0531 **8** *1¾* **Quintada**[37] 7466 3-9-4 **82**... JoeFanning 1 65
(Mark Johnston) *chsd ldrs tl wnt 2nd over 3f out tl jst over 2f out: sn outpcd and wknd* **9/1**

1324 **9** *1¾* **Stagehand**[37] 7466 3-9-2 **80**..................................... KieranShoemark 10 60
(Charles Hills) *s.i.s: hld up in last pair: effrt 3f out: sn struggling and wl btn over 1f out (jockey said filly was slowly away)* **10/1**

45-0 **10** *26* **Adams Park**[11] 8298 4-9-1 **73**................................ AlistairRawlinson 9 12
(Michael Appleby) *led for 2f: chsd ldr tl over 3f out: sn dropped out: bhd 2f out: t.o* **50/1**

2m 31.09s (-3.41) **Going Correction** -0.125s/f (Stan)
WFA 3 from 4yo+ 6lb **10** Ran SP% **114.7**
Speed ratings (Par 105): **106,104,103,103,102 97,96,94,93,76**
CSF £43.91 CT £1183.28 TOTE £4.90: £1.50, £3.20, £8.40; EX 47.80 Trifecta £756.20.
Owner Excel Racing **Bred** Sc Blueberry S R L **Trained** Newmarket, Suffolk

FOCUS
A decent handicap run at a fair gallop. The third has been rated close to his AW form.
T/Plt: £122.60 to a £1 stake. Pool: £82,322.26 - 490.10 winning units T/Qpdt: £5.00 to a £1 stake. Pool: £18,057.94 - 2,635.51 winning units **Steve Payne**

8002 LEICESTER (R-H)
Monday, October 28
8609 Meeting Abandoned - Waterlogged Track

7902 REDCAR (L-H)
Monday, October 28
8616 Meeting Abandoned - Waterlogged track

8623 - 8630a (Foreign Racing) - See Raceform Interactive

8337 CATTERICK (L-H)
Tuesday, October 29

OFFICIAL GOING: Heavy (soft in places; 5.9)
Wind: Virtually nil Weather: Sunny

8631 BRITISH STALLION STUDS EBF NOVICE STKS 5f
12:30 (12:32) (Class 5) 2-Y-O **£4,140** (£1,232; £615; £307) **Stalls** Low

Form RPR

3252 **1** **Mighty Spirit (IRE)**[45] 7211 2-8-11 91............................ PJMcDonald 6 75
(Richard Fahey) *pressed ldr: pushed into ld appr fnl f: drvn out ins fnl f* **11/10**[1]

23 **2** *nk* **The Bell Conductor (IRE)**[18] 8097 2-9-2 0.................. ShaneGray 9 79
(Phillip Makin) *led narrowly: rdn along and hdd appr fnl f: sn drvn: kpt on but a jst hld* **9/4**[2]

02 **3** *1* **Intrinsic Bond**[31] 7698 2-9-2 0.. CamHardie 2 75
(Tracy Waggott) *chsd ldng pair: rdn over 2f out: drvn over 2f out: kpt on ins fnl f* **16/1**

6 **4** *3¼* **Where's Mick (IRE)**[10] 8337 2-9-2 0.............................. JackGarritty 10 64
(Jedd O'Keeffe) *dwlt: hld up: hdwy and chsd ldng pair 2f out: pushed along over 1f out: one pce ins fnl f* **50/1**

04 **5** *3¾* **Clotherholme (IRE)**[8] 8395 2-9-2 0................................ PaulMulrennan 11 50
(Ann Duffield) *chsd ldng pair: pushed along and lost pl 3f out: sn outpcd: plugged on ins fnl f* **25/1**

6 *3* **Marina Grove (IRE)** 2-8-11 0... DavidAllan 8 34
(Tim Easterby) *hld up: sn pushed along: minor late hdwy: nvr threatened (jockey said filly stumbled approx 2f out)* **22/1**

4010 **7** *1¾* **Rapid Russo**[39] 7399 2-9-6 76.................................... CallumRodriguez 5 37
(Michael Dods) *chsd ldng pair: rdn along over 2f out: edgd lft and wknd over 1f out* **9/2**[3]

00 **8** *2¼* **Staxton Hill**[82] 5856 2-9-2 0.. PaulHanagan 4 25
(Richard Fahey) *chsd ldng pair: lost pl 3f out: wknd over 1f out* **28/1**

0 **9** *2¾* **The Last Bow**[31] 7698 2-8-11 0.................................... JamesSullivan 7 10
(Michael Easterby) *dwlt: a outpcd in rr* **150/1**

00 **10** *3¼* **Pronghorn**[137] 3812 2-9-2 0... NathanEvans 1 3
(Michael Easterby) *midfield on outer: wknd over 1f out* **100/1**

11 *2½* **Jean Mary** 2-8-11 0... TomEaves 3
(Stef Keniry) *a outpcd in rr* **66/1**

1m 1.97s (1.47) **Going Correction** +0.325s/f (Good) **11** Ran SP% **119.2**
Speed ratings (Par 95): **101,100,98,93,87 82,80,76,72,66 62**
CSF £3.50 TOTE £1.70: £1.10, £1.20, £3.40; EX 4.00 Trifecta £16.10.
Owner John Dance **Bred** Mountarmstrong Stud **Trained** Musley Bank, N Yorks

FOCUS
The close of Flat racing for the year at Catterick and, on genuinely heavy ground, not surprisingly the stands' side was the place to be in the home straight. The two market leaders dominated this 2yo sprint and it wasn't a bad winning time.

8632 ALAN BOND MEMORIAL H'CAP 5f
1:00 (1:01) (Class 6) (0-60,62) 3-Y-O+

£3,105 (£924; £461; £300; £300; £300) **Stalls** Low

Form RPR

0040 **1** **Hawk In The Sky**[18] 8083 3-9-5 **58**.................................. PhilDennis 12 66
(Richard Whitaker) *mde all: racd against stands' rail tl rdn and edgd lft appr fnl f: kpt on wl (trainer said, regarding improvement in form, gelding may have appreciated drop in class and return to 5f)* **14/1**

0362 **2** *1¾* **Sambucca Spirit**[13] 8268 3-8-11 **50**............................... KevinStott 9 52
(Paul Midgley) *chsd ldr: rdn 2f out: kpt on* **6/1**[3]

0410 **3** *½* **Astrophysics**[15] 8183 7-9-6 **59**..............................(p) PaulMulrennan 4 58
(Lynn Siddall) *midfield: sn pushed along: hdwy appr fnl f: kpt on* **9/1**

3302 **4** *½* **The Grey Zebedee**[22] 7959 3-9-7 **60**........................(b) DuranFentiman 7 58
(Tim Easterby) *in tch: rdn 2f out: drvn to chse ldr ins fnl f: no ex fnl 110yds* **10/3**[1]

0434 **5** *1½* **Rockley Point**[22] 7962 6-8-7 **46** oh1...........................(b) AndrewMullen 11 38
(Katie Scott) *hld up in midfield: rdn along 3f out: plugged on ins fnl f (trainer said gelding lost left fore shoe)* **15/2**

0500 **6** *¾* **Mightaswellsmile**[34] 7591 5-8-7 **46** oh1............................ CamHardie 10 35
(Ron Barr) *midfield: sn pushed along: nvr threatened* **25/1**

0506 **7** *½* **Economic Crisis (IRE)**[10] 8339 10-9-4 **62**........... FayeMcManoman(5) 8 49
(Alan Berry) *hld up: nvr threatened* **22/1**

0363 **8** *1* **Burmese Blazer (IRE)**[14] 8235 4-9-3 **56**...................(p) BenRobinson 2 40
(Jim Goldie) *hld up: nvr threatened* **5/1**[2]

6301 **9** *1¼* **Trulove**[37] 7488 6-8-11 **50**..(p) JamieGormley 5 29
(John David Riches) *chsd ldr: rdn 2f out: wknd fnl f* **14/1**

0000 **10** *nk* **Adam's Ale**[56] 6826 10-9-4 **60**...............................(p) ConnorMurtagh(3) 3 38
(Marjorie Fife) *chsd ldr towards outer: rdn 2f out: wknd appr fnl f* **20/1**

5006 **11** *1½* **Robbian**[13] 8263 8-8-2 **46** oh1... AledBeech(5) 6 19
(Charles Smith) *a outpcd in rr* **7/1**

0000 **12** *40* **Raise A Billion**[29] 7761 8-8-7 **46** oh1..........................(b¹) JamesSullivan 1
(Alan Berry) *a outpcd in rr* **100/1**

1m 2.61s (2.11) **Going Correction** +0.325s/f (Good) **12** Ran SP% **115.6**
Speed ratings (Par 101): **96,93,92,91,89 88,87,85,83,83 80,16**
CSF £89.55 CT £819.62 TOTE £19.00: £5.80, £2.20, £2.80; EX 158.60 Trifecta £1913.80.
Owner Michael Hawkins **Bred** R C Dollar & Hellwood Stud Farm **Trained** Scarcroft, W Yorks

FOCUS
Few got into this moderate sprint handicap.

8633 MILLBRY HILL H'CAP 1m 4f 13y
1:30 (1:31) (Class 4) (0-85,85) 3-Y-O+

£5,757 (£1,713; £856; £428; £300; £300) **Stalls** Low

Form RPR

3231 **1** **Bo Samraan (IRE)**[8] 8396 3-9-4 **85** 6ex.......................... JoeFanning 6 93
(Mark Johnston) *sn prom: pushed into narrow ld 3f out: drvn and hld on wl in sustained duel w 2nd fnl 2f* **4/5**[1]

2036 **2** *shd* **Jabbaar**[45] 7181 6-9-10 **85**...(p¹) TomEaves 3 92
(Iain Jardine) *hld up in tch: hdwy on outer over 4f out: sn prom: sustained duel w wnr in fnl 2f: styd on wl but a jst hld* **11/2**[3]

3163 **3** *3¼* **First Flight (IRE)**[32] 7663 8-8-11 **72**............................. BenRobinson 5 74
(Brian Ellison) *trckd ldrs: rdn and one pce in 3rd fr over 2f out* **7/1**

1060 **4** *2¼* **Mutamaded (IRE)**[17] 8130 6-9-9 **84**........................... PaulMulrennan 4 82
(Ruth Carr) *hld up in tch: rdn along over 2f out: no imp* **16/1**

/502 **5** *20* **Tamleek (USA)**[15] 8185 5-9-10 **85**.............................(p) DavidNolan 2 51
(David O'Meara) *trckd ldrs: rdn and outpcd 3f out: sn wknd* **20/1**

3101 **6** *6* **Where's Jeff**[52] 6975 4-9-9 **84**.................................. NathanEvans 1 41
(Michael Easterby) *led narrowly: rdn along and hdd 3f out: sn wknd (trainer rep said gelding was unsuited by the Heavy, Soft in places ground on this occasion and would prefer a sounder surface)* **5/1**[2]

2m 50.22s (9.62) **Going Correction** +1.05s/f (Soft)
WFA 3 from 4yo+ 6lb **6** Ran SP% **110.8**
Speed ratings (Par 105): **109,108,106,105,91 87**
CSF £5.46 TOTE £1.50: £1.30, £2.60; EX 5.60 Trifecta £16.50.
Owner Jaber Abdullah **Bred** Sunderland Holdings Inc **Trained** Middleham Moor, N Yorks
■ Stewards' Enquiry : Joe Fanning two-day ban: excessive use of whip (Nov 19-20)

FOCUS
Add 15yds. A fair little handicap. The second has been rated to this year's form.

8634 SARAH LIPSETT'S 60TH BIRTHDAY CELEBRATION H'CAP 7f 6y
2:05 (2:08) (Class 4) (0-85,85) 3-Y-O+

£6,080 (£1,809; £904; £452; £300; £300) **Stalls** Centre

Form RPR

3053 **1** **Zip**[10] 8342 3-8-4 **72**.................................. SeanDavis(3) 2 79
(Richard Fahey) *trckd ldrs: rdn to ld appr fnl f: drvn out* **5/2**[1]

1046 **2** *1* **Breanski**[24] 7906 5-9-1 **85**.............................. OwenPayton(7) 5 90+
(Jedd O'Keeffe) *hld up in rr: pushed along and stl lot to do whn short of room towards stands' rail over 1f out: sn swtchd lft towards outer: r.o wl fnl f: wnt 2nd towards fin (jockey said gelding was denied a clear run approx 2f out)* **5/1**[3]

4120 **3** *nk* **Sparklealot (IRE)**[18] 8101 3-9-6 **85**...........................(p) DougieCostello 3 89
(Ivan Furtado) *led: rdn and hdd appr fnl f: drvn and one pce: lost 2nd towards fin* **7/2**[2]

1060 **4** *½* **Parys Mountain (IRE)**[10] 8342 5-9-1 **78**.........................(t) CamHardie 4 81
(Tim Easterby) *trckd ldrs: rdn along over 2f out: drvn over 1f out: kpt on same pce* **12/1**

0402 **5** *nse* **Magical Effect (IRE)**[10] 8339 7-8-12 **75**...................(p) JamieGormley 6 78
(Ruth Carr) *hld up: rdn and hdwy over 1f out: one pce ins fnl f* **9/1**

1215 **6** *2 ½* **Tukhoom (IRE)**[34] 7563 6-9-6 **83**...................................(v) DavidNolan 1 80
(David O'Meara) *dwlt: hld up in midfield: rdn over 2f out: nvr threatened* **8/1**

0600 **7** *2 ½* **Dark Defender**[18] 8099 6-9-3 **80**...................................(b) DavidAllan 7 70
(Rebecca Bastiman) *trckd ldrs: rdn over 2f out: wknd appr fnl f* **14/1**

3210 **8** *7* **Casement (IRE)**[42] 7312 5-9-4 **81**.............................. AlistairRawlinson 8 53
(Michael Appleby) *prom: rdn along 3f out: wknd over 2f out* **9/1**

1m 33.46s (6.06) **Going Correction** +1.05s/f (Soft)
WFA 3 from 5yo+ 2lb **8** Ran SP% **112.9**
Speed ratings (Par 105): **107,105,105,104,104 102,99,91**
CSF £14.77 CT £42.31 TOTE £4.20: £1.20, £2.00, £1.10; EX 18.90 Trifecta £90.40.
Owner The Knavesmire Partnership **Bred** Worksop Manor Stud **Trained** Musley Bank, N Yorks

FOCUS
Add 15yds. They went hard up front in this fair handicap. The winner has been rated to his best, and the second to this year's form.

8635 40 YEARS OF GO-RACING-IN-YORKSHIRE SEASON TICKETS H'CAP 1m 7f 189y
2:35 (2:37) (Class 5) (0-70,72) 3-Y-O+

£4,075 (£1,212; £606; £303; £300; £300) **Stalls** Centre

Form RPR

/5-2 **1** **Cornerstone Lad**[151] 3294 5-9-9 **65**.............................. GrahamLee 8 77
(Micky Hammond) *trckd ldrs: prom 4f out: led over 2f out: rdn and pressed over 1f out: styd on wl* **4/1**[1]

000 **2** *½* **Rayna's World (IRE)**[31] 7683 4-9-9 **65**.............................. KevinStott 2 76
(Philip Kirby) *hld up: stdy hdwy fr over 5f out: trckd ldrs 3f out: rdn to chal strly over 1f out: drvn ins fnl f: one pce towards fin* **14/1**

6433 **3** *14* **St Andrews (IRE)**[10] 8344 6-8-3 **52**.....................(v) OliverStammers(7) 10 47
(Gillian Boanas) *slowly away: hld up in rr: rdn along over 4f out: plugged on to go poor 3rd fnl 50yds* **15/2**

1146 **4** *2 ¼* **Kensington Art**[27] 7830 3-9-8 **72**.................................(p) TonyHamilton 7 66
(Richard Fahey) *led: rdn and hdd over 2f out: sn wknd* **9/2**[2]

5641 **5** *½* **Miss Ranger (IRE)**[10] 8343 7-8-4 **51**.............................. PaulaMuir(5) 3 42
(Roger Fell) *midfield: racd quite keenly: rdn over 3f out: wknd over 1f out* **15/2**

5645 **6** *1 ½* **Elite Icon**[14] 8238 5-8-9 **51** oh6.................................(v) JamieGormley 4 41
(Jim Goldie) *hld up in midfield: rdn over 3f out: no imp and nvr a threat* **12/1**

0225 **7** *14* **Put The Law On You (IRE)**[18] 8081 4-8-9 **51** oh3..(p) AndrewMullen 12 24
(Alistair Whillans) *midfield on outer: rdn over 4f out: wknd fnl 2f* **5/1**[3]

4644 **8** *11* **Tor**[14] 8236 5-9-13 **69**.................................. JamesSullivan 6 29
(Marjorie Fife) *trckd ldrs: rdn over 3f out: wknd 2f out (jockey said gelding ran flat; post-race examination failed to reveal any abnormalities)* **10/1**

2620 **9** *24* **Urban Spirit (IRE)**[18] 8081 5-8-10 **55**.............................. SeanDavis(3) 11
(Karen McLintock) *prom: rdn over 3f out: sn outpcd and btn: eased and bhd fnl 2f* **16/1**

0606 **10** *6* **Percy (IRE)**[33] 7631 5-10-0 **70**.................................(v[1]) JoeFanning 1
(Frank Bishop) *slowly away: racd keenly and sn prom on outer: wknd qckly 4f out: t.o* **25/1**

005 **11** *20* **Ho Whole Dream (IRE)**[46] 7143 3-9-1 **65**.............................. NathanEvans 9
(Michael Easterby) *midfield: rdn along 5f out: sn struggling: t.o fnl 3f* **16/1**

/00- **12** *3 ¼* **Canny Style**[174] 7782 6-9-11 **67**.................................. TomEaves 5
(Joanne Foster) *hld up: bhd fr 1/2-way* **100/1**

3m 49.97s (13.97) **Going Correction** +1.05s/f (Soft)
WFA 3 from 4yo+ 8lb **12** Ran SP% **118.4**
Speed ratings (Par 103): **107,106,99,98,98 97,90,85,73,70 60,58**
CSF £61.15 CT £409.86 TOTE £5.00: £1.90, £4.50, £2.30; EX 66.00 Trifecta £432.70.
Owner Mrs B M Lofthouse **Bred** Cranford Bloodstock & Overbury Stallions **Trained** Middleham, N Yorks

FOCUS
Add 15yds. The first pair came right away in this ordinary staying handicap. The level is a bit fluid.

8636 RACINGTV.COM H'CAP 5f 212y
3:10 (3:10) (Class 4) (0-85,87) 3-Y-O+

£5,757 (£1,713; £856; £428; £300; £300) **Stalls** Low

Form RPR

4205 **1** **Gabrial The Devil (IRE)**[4] 8522 4-9-8 **85**.............................. PaulHanagan 1 92
(Richard Fahey) *trckd ldrs: rdn and edgd rt appr fnl f: led 1f out: kpt on* **5/1**[3]

0023 **2** *¾* **Jewel Maker (IRE)**[15] 8183 4-8-10 **73**.............................. DavidAllan 10 78
(Tim Easterby) *racd on outer: led narrowly: rdn over 1f out: hdd 1f out: kpt on same pce* **9/1**

032 **3** *shd* **Captain Jameson (IRE)**[10] 8342 4-9-7 **84**...................(v[1]) BenRobinson 9 88
(John Quinn) *midfield: pushed along and hdwy to chse ldrs 2f out: sn rdn: kpt on ins fnl f (jockey said gelding was denied a clear run 2f out)* **9/2**[2]

2561 **4** *nk* **Black Friday**[15] 8181 4-8-10 **76**...................................(p) SeanDavis(3) 5 80
(Karen McLintock) *hld up in midfield: rdn and hdwy on outer over 1f out: kpt on ins fnl f* **5/1**[3]

2100 **5** *1* **Zumurud (IRE)**[60] 6676 4-9-6 **83**.................................. JoeFanning 4 84
(Rebecca Bastiman) *dwlt: hld up: rdn and hdwy over 1f out: sn chsd ldrs: edgd lft and no ex ins fnl f* **18/1**

1244 **6** *shd* **Six Strings**[33] 7607 5-9-4 **81**.................................. AlistairRawlinson 6 81
(Michael Appleby) *trckd ldrs: rdn and bit outpcd over 1f out: plugged on ins fnl f* **16/1**

2053 **7** *nse* **Broken Spear**[10] 8340 3-9-8 **86**...................................(p) BarryMcHugh 8 86
(Tony Coyle) *pressed ldr: rdn whn sltly short of room appr fnl f: no ex ins fnl f (vet said gelding was struck into left fore)* **10/1**

2632 **8** *1 ½* **Dancing Rave**[28] 7777 3-8-9 **73**.................................. ShaneGray 2 69
(David O'Meara) *hld up in rr: sme late hdwy: nvr a threat* **22/1**

061 **9** *1* **Quick Look**[136] 3846 6-9-10 **87**.................................. JamesSullivan 7 80
(Michael Easterby) *dwlt: hld up: nvr threatened* **18/1**

6052 **10** *nk* **Airglow (IRE)**[8] 8403 4-8-10 **73**...................................(h) NathanEvans 3 65
(Michael Easterby) *trckd ldrs: racd keenly: bit short of room 3f out: rdn and wknd appr fnl f* **3/1**[1]

1m 19.11s (5.51) **Going Correction** +1.05s/f (Soft)
WFA 3 from 4yo+ 1lb **10** Ran SP% **116.4**
Speed ratings (Par 105): **105,104,103,103,102 102,101,99,98,98**
CSF £49.33 CT £222.63 TOTE £6.00: £2.30, £3.00, £1.40; EX 48.70 Trifecta £167.90.
Owner Dr Marwan Koukash **Bred** Austin Curran **Trained** Musley Bank, N Yorks
■ Stewards' Enquiry : Paul Hanagan two-day ban: careless riding (Nov 16, 18)

FOCUS
Add 15yds. This fair sprint handicap was run at a solid pace and it saw a tight finish. It's been rated as ordinary form around the first three.

8637 JUMP SEASON STARTS 22ND NOVEMBER H'CAP (DIV I) 5f 212y
3:45 (3:45) (Class 6) (0-55,56) 3-Y-O+

£3,105 (£924; £461; £300; £300; £300) **Stalls** Low

Form RPR

0 **1** **Hummingbird (IRE)**[11] 8306 3-9-1 **53**..................... ThomasGreatrex(3) 4 59
(David Loughnane) *trckd ldrs: drvn over 1f out: led ins fnl f: kpt on (trainer rep said, regarding improvement in form, that filly settled better on this occasion and may have appreciated the return to turf)* **16/1**

6006 **2** *¾* **Billiebrookedit (IRE)**[8] 8408 4-8-12 **46** oh1.........................(p) JaneElliott 2 50
(Kevin Frost) *led: rdn 2f out: hdd ins fnl f: kpt on same pce* **5/1**[2]

6056 **3** *1 ¾* **Moonlit Sands (IRE)**[34] 7590 4-9-7 **55**.................(tp w) BenRobinson 12 54
(Brian Ellison) *chsd ldrs: rdn over 2f out: kpt on ins fnl f* **7/1**

1500 **4** *shd* **Someone Exciting**[22] 7962 6-9-8 **56**.............................. KevinStott 9 54
(David Thompson) *hld up: rdn and hdwy over 1f out: kpt on ins fnl f* **7/1**

1611 **5** *1 ½* **My Valentino (IRE)**[36] 7508 6-9-7 **55**...........................(b) JamesSullivan 11 49+
(Dianne Sayer) *dwlt: hld up in rr: sn pushed along: sme hdwy over 1f out: kpt on ins fnl f: nvr trbld ldrs* **4/1**[1]

0304 **6** *¾* **Alfred The Grey (IRE)**[120] 4434 3-9-3 **52**.....................(p[1]) PaulHanagan 7 43
(Tracy Waggott) *hld up in rr: racd keenly: rdn and hdwy over 1f out: no ex ins fnl f* **8/1**

200 **7** *1 ½* **Cosmic Chatter**[6] 8469 9-9-1 **49**.................................(p) JackGarritty 1 36
(Ruth Carr) *dwlt sltly: sn prom: rdn over 2f out: wknd ins fnl f* **6/1**[3]

4063 **8** *2 ¼* **Isabella Ruby**[17] 8119 4-8-6 **47**.................................(p) GavinAshton(7) 8 27
(Lisa Williamson) *midfield: rdn over 2f out: wknd ins fnl f* **16/1**

0/00 **9** *2* **Jackman**[104] 5043 5-8-12 **46** oh1.................................. BarryMcHugh 10 20
(Lee James) *midfield on outer: rdn over 2f out: wknd over 1f out* **125/1**

0030 **10** *2 ½* **Tilsworth Diamond**[13] 8251 4-8-12 **46** oh1.............................. RossaRyan 3 13
(Mike Murphy) *prom: rdn over 2f out: wknd fnl f* **20/1**

4004 **11** *nse* **Naples Bay**[14] 8234 5-9-4 **52**.................................. PhilDennis 6 19
(Katie Scott) *midfield: rdn over 2f out: wknd over 1f out* **9/1**

1m 20.74s (7.14) **Going Correction** +1.05s/f (Soft)
WFA 3 from 4yo+ 1lb **11** Ran SP% **114.4**
Speed ratings (Par 101): **94,93,90,90,88 87,85,82,79,76 76**
CSF £91.65 CT £630.36 TOTE £20.50: £5.40, £1.70, £2.30; EX 104.90 Trifecta £688.70.
Owner Miss Sarah Hoyland **Bred** Wardstown Stud Ltd **Trained** Tern Hill, Shropshire

FOCUS
Add 15yds. It paid to be handy enough in this moderate sprint handicap.

8638 JUMP SEASON STARTS 22ND NOVEMBER H'CAP (DIV II) 5f 212y
4:15 (4:20) (Class 6) (0-55,55) 3-Y-O+

£3,105 (£924; £461; £300; £300; £300) **Stalls** Low

Form RPR

0000 **1** **Bevsboy (IRE)**[7] 8436 5-8-7 **46** oh1.............................(p) PaulaMuir(5) 10 51
(Lynn Siddall) *hld up: c stands' side st: rdn and hdwy over 1f out: kpt on to ld fnl 50yds (trainer said, regarding improvement in form, gelding may have appreciated drop in trip and the Heavy, Soft in places ground on this occasion)* **50/1**

0063 **2** *nk* **I'll Be Good**[29] 7766 10-8-13 **47**.................................. KevinStott 2 51
(Alan Berry) *chsd ldrs: styd far side st: rdn and ev ch over 1f out: kpt on* **14/1**

1654 **3** *1* **Carlovian**[13] 8263 6-9-4 **52**.................................(v) DougieCostello 8 53
(Mark Walford) *prom: c stands' side st: led over 2f out: sn rdn: pressed appr fnl f: hdd 50yds out: no ex* **11/2**[2]

1600 **4** *1 ½* **Kellington Kitty (USA)**[17] 8123 4-9-3 **51**.........................(p) RossaRyan 4 48
(Mike Murphy) *hld up: c stands' side st: rdn and sme hdwy appr fnl f: kpt on* **11/2**[2]

3612 **5** *½* **Vallarta (IRE)**[13] 8264 9-9-3 **51**.................................. JamesSullivan 3 46
(Ruth Carr) *chsd ldrs: c stands' side st: rdn to chal appr fnl f: no ex fnl 110yds* **5/2**[1]

6000 **6** *6* **Picks Pinta**[12] 8295 8-8-12 **46** oh1.............................(b) JamieGormley 5 23
(John David Riches) *hld up: styd far side st: nvr threatened* **33/1**

0000 **7** *2* **Mitchum**[40] 7389 10-8-12 **46** oh1.................................. BarryMcHugh 11 17
(Ron Barr) *midfield on outer: rdn and sme hdwy 3f out: brought stands' side st: wknd over 1f out* **25/1**

0000 **8** *1* **Furni Factors**[33] 7628 4-8-12 **46**.................................(b) RaulDaSilva 9 14
(Ronald Thompson) *dwlt: hld up: styd far side st: nvr threatened* **50/1**

1100 **9** *hd* **Night Law**[14] 8235 5-9-7 **55**.................................(b) PhilDennis 7 23
(Katie Scott) *midfield: c stands' side st: rdn over 2f out: wknd over 1f out* **17/2**[3]

3002 **10** *3 3/4* **Cuppacoco**[27] 7824 4-9-7 **55**..........(b) JackGarritty 1 11
(Ann Duffield) *sn led: styd far side st: rdn and hdd over 2f out: wknd over 1f out (trainer said filly was unsuited by Heavy, Soft in places ground on this occasion and would prefer a sounder surface)* **11/1**

40-0 **11** *19* **Grandma Tilly**[13] 8242 4-9-7 **55**.......... DavidAllan 6
(Steph Hollinshead) *prom: rdn and lost pl over 3f out: sn wknd: eased and bhd fnl 2f (jockey said filly lost action; post-race examination failed to reveal any abnormalities)* **33/1**

1m 21.8s (8.20) **Going Correction** +1.05s/f (Soft) **11** Ran SP% **98.5**
Speed ratings (Par 101): **87,86,85,83,82 74,71,70,70,65 40**
CSF £415.59 CT £2411.59 TOTE £71.10: £14.30, £2.90, £2.00; EX 592.60 Trifecta £2316.20.
Owner Andrew Longden **Bred** Denise Brennan **Trained** Colton, N Yorks
■ Chickenfortea was withdrawn, price at time of withdrawal 4/1. Rule 4 applies to all bets. Deduction of 20p in the pound.

FOCUS
Add 15yds. There was a 6min delay to this second division of the weak sprint due to well-fancied Chickenfortea bolted prior to loading. The main action developed far side this time.
T/Plt: £45.10 to a £1 stake. Pool: £52,351.57 - 846.36 winning units T/Qpdt: £8.00 to a £1 stake. Pool: £7,129.25 - 653.95 winning units **Andrew Sheret**

8401 SOUTHWELL (L-H)
Tuesday, October 29

OFFICIAL GOING: Fibresand: standard
Wind: Virtually nil Weather: Clear skies

8639 BETWAY APPRENTICE H'CAP 2m 102y(F)
4:45 (4:46) (Class 6) (0-60,61) 3-Y-O+
£2,781 (£827; £413; £400; £400; £400) **Stalls** Low

Form RPR

1215 **1** **Thahab Ifraj (IRE)**[55] 6864 6-9-9 **57**.......... ThoreHammerHansen 8 65
(Alexandra Dunn) *hld up in midfield: trckd ldrs over 5f out: hdwy on inner 3f out: pushed along over 2f out: sn led: rdn clr appr fnl f: kpt on strly* **2/1**[1]

405 **2** *2 1/2* **Shine Baby Shine**[33] 7631 5-9-6 **61**.......... NickBarratt-Atkin(7) 6 66
(Philip Kirby) *hld up in rr: tk clsr order over 6f out: gd hdwy on outer to chse ldrs 3f out: wd st: chal and ev ch 2f out: sn rdn and edgd lft: chsd wnr and drvn over 1f out: no imp* **7/2**[2]

0050 **3** *1/2* **Irish Minister (USA)**[11] 8301 4-9-1 **52**..........(t) TobyEley(3) 9 56
(David Thompson) *hld up in rr: tk clsr order over 4f out: chsd ldrs over 2f out: sn rdn: drvn and kpt on same pce fnl f* **25/1**

32-0 **4** *3 1/4* **Sincerely Resdev**[13] 7390 4-9-0 **48**..........(p) SeamusCronin 3 49
(Philip Kirby) *trckd ldrs: effrt over 4f out: cl up over 3f out: rdn along and wd st: drvn and kpt on same pce fnl 2f* **12/1**

06/6 **5** *1* **Never A Word (USA)**[10] 8347 5-9-7 **58**..........(bt) HarryRussell(3) 7 57
(Oliver Greenall) *prom: cl up 1/2-way: led 5f out: rdn along and wd st: drvn and hdd 2f out: grad wknd* **16/1**

3460 **6** *1/2* **Panatos (FR)**[26] 7860 4-9-9 **60**.......... AngusVilliers(3) 11 59
(Alexandra Dunn) *trckd ldrs: pushed along 4f out: rdn and wd st: drvn over 2f out: sn wknd* **6/1**[3]

3000 **7** *5* **Going Native**[8] 8406 4-8-13 **50**.......... RhonaPindar(3) 5 43
(Olly Williams) *t.k.h: in tch: pushed along over 4f out: rdn and wd st: n.d (jockey said filly ran too free)* **14/1**

0060 **8** *shd* **Duration (IRE)**[4] 8523 4-9-5 **53**..........(b) DylanHogan 10 46
(J R Jenkins) *prom: rdn along over 4f out: wknd over 3f out* **33/1**

-000 **9** *12* **Doctor Jazz (IRE)**[15] 8196 4-9-7 **58**.......... MarkCrehan(3) 4 36
(Michael Appleby) *t.k.h and sn led: pushed along and hdd 5f out: cl up: rdn along 3f out: drvn and wknd over 2f out* **11/1**

5 **10** *54* **Angel Of My Heart (IRE)**[13] 8269 4-9-7 **55**..........(b[1]) GerO'Neill 1
(Michael Easterby) *a in rr: bhd fnl 4f (jockey said filly ran too free)* **16/1**

05-0 **11** *81* **Port Lairge**[191] 508 9-8-12 **46** oh1.......... WilliamCarver 2
(Michael Chapman) *v.s.a: a bhd: t.o fnl 4f* **150/1**

3m 40.54s (-4.96) **Going Correction** -0.325s/f (Stan) **11** Ran SP% **111.7**
Speed ratings (Par 101): **99,97,97,95,95 95,92,92,86,59 19**
CSF £7.85 CT £122.98 TOTE £2.60: £1.20, £1.50, £5.50; EX 9.20 Trifecta £111.80.
Owner The Dunnitalls **Bred** P G Lyons **Trained** West Buckland, Somerset

FOCUS
A moderate handicap in which they went a solid gallop and the principals came from off the pace.

8640 LADBROKES WHERE THE NATION PLAYS FILLIES' NOVICE STKS (PLUS 10 RACE) 6f 16y(F)
5:15 (5:19) (Class 5) 2-Y-O **£3,428** (£1,020; £509; £254) **Stalls** Low

Form RPR

25 **1** **Dark Regard**[90] 5550 2-9-0 0.......... PJMcDonald 5 72+
(Mark Johnston) *trckd ldrs: hdwy on inner 2f out: rdn to ld over 1f out: kpt on strly* **5/2**[1]

53 **2** *3* **Quaint (IRE)**[19] 8067 2-9-0 0.......... CharlieBennett 11 63
(Hughie Morrison) *led: rdn along over 2f out: drvn and hdd over 1f out: kpt on same pce* **14/1**

3 **3** *3/4* **Alex Gracie**[33] 7627 2-8-7 0.......... JonathanFisher(7) 9 61
(Scott Dixon) *prom: rdn along and wd st: cl up over 2f out: sn rdn and ev ch: drvn over 1f out: kpt on same pce* **12/1**

4 *6* **Out For A Duck** 2-8-11 0.......... TheodoreLadd(3) 7 43
(Michael Appleby) *dwlt and sltly hmpd s: green and towards rr: hdwy on outer over 3f out: wd st: sn rdn and styng on whn edgd lft wl over 1f out and again appr fnl f: kpt on same pce (jockey said filly hung left-handed)* **33/1**

5602 **5** *1/2* **Hollaback Girl**[19] 8067 2-9-0 57..........(v) StevieDonohoe 12 41
(Richard Spencer) *chsd ldrs: rdn along over 2f out: drvn wl over 1f out: sn one pce* **20/1**

64 **6** *3/4* **Superiority (IRE)**[11] 8316 2-8-7 0.......... RhonaPindar(7) 4 39
(K R Burke) *towards rr: rdn along and hdwy on inner over 2f out: kpt on appr fnl f: n.d (jockey said filly did not face the kick back)* **9/2**[3]

005 **7** *3* **Love Not Money**[15] 8195 2-8-7 55.......... AngusVilliers(7) 8 30
(Robert Cowell) *cl up: rdn along wl over 2f out: sn drvn and grad wknd* **25/1**

4 **8** *1* **Gmasha**[15] 8202 2-9-0 0.......... LukeMorris 1 27
(Robert Cowell) *towards rr and rdn along on inner over 3f out: sn swtchd rt and wd st: n.d* **20/1**

00 **9** *shd* **Azure World**[85] 5737 2-9-0 0.......... TomEaves 3 27
(Kevin Ryan) *chsd ldrs: rdn along 3f out: sn drvn and wknd* **33/1**

066 **10** *2* **Gina D'Cleaner**[10] 8338 2-9-0 61.......... CallumRodriguez 2 21
(Keith Dalgleish) *in tch: hdwy and wd st: sn wknd* **15/2**

03 **11** *hd* **Secret Diary**[22] 7958 2-9-0 0.......... DanielTudhope 10 20
(Declan Carroll) *a towards rr* **7/2**[2]

0 **12** *8* **Jay Me Lo (IRE)**[118] 4516 2-9-0 0.......... PaulMulrennan 6
(Lawrence Mullaney) *wnt rt and sltly hmpd s: a in rr: bhd and wd st* **66/1**

1m 14.82s (-1.68) **Going Correction** -0.325s/f (Stan) **12** Ran SP% **115.8**
Speed ratings (Par 92): **98,94,93,85,84 83,79,78,77,75 74,64**
CSF £34.61 TOTE £3.10: £1.10, £4.00, £3.50; EX 31.80 Trifecta £208.50.
Owner John Dance **Bred** Brightwalton Bloodstock Ltd **Trained** Middleham Moor, N Yorks

FOCUS
A modest novice and the winner won comfortably.

8641 BETWAY H'CAP 1m 4f 14y(F)
5:45 (5:45) (Class 5) (0-70,71) 3-Y-O+
£3,428 (£1,020; £509; £400; £400; £400) **Stalls** Low

Form RPR

5342 **1** **Grazeon Roy**[4] 8515 3-9-6 **69**.......... PaulMulrennan 3 83+
(John Quinn) *in tch: hdwy over 4f out: chal on outer over 2f out: sn rdn: led 1 1/2f out: drvn clr ent fnl f: kpt on strly* **11/8**[1]

0420 **2** *6* **Say Nothing**[68] 6371 3-9-4 **67**.......... PJMcDonald 7 70
(Hughie Morrison) *trckd ldrs: hdwy over 3f out: rdn to chal 2f out: ev ch: drvn appr fnl f and kpt on same pce* **8/1**

0010 **3** *3 3/4* **Cold Harbour**[11] 8300 4-9-7 **64**..........(t) KieranO'Neill 4 61
(Robyn Brisland) *led 2f: trckd ldng pair: hdwy and cl up over 3f out: led wl over 2f out: sn jnd and rdn: hdd and drvn 1 1/2f out: one pce* **5/1**[3]

6013 **4** *4 1/2* **George Mallory**[37] 7493 3-9-5 **68**.......... TomEaves 8 59
(Kevin Ryan) *prom: led after 2f: pushed along 4f out: rdn over 3f out: hdd wl over 2f out: grad wknd* **8/1**

1450 **5** *1 1/4* **Cuba Ruba**[14] 8238 3-8-8 **57**..........(p) RachelRichardson 9 46
(Tim Easterby) *hld up in rr: hdwy 5f out: rdn along to chse ldrs on outer 3f out: drvn over 2f out: sn wknd* **22/1**

4350 **6** *4 1/2* **Couldn't Could She**[21] 7984 4-9-4 **61**.......... CharlieBennett 6 42
(Adam West) *hld up: hdwy 4f out: in tch and rdn along 3f out: sn drvn and wknd* **66/1**

03-0 **7** *1 1/4* **Clooney**[12] 8294 4-9-1 **65**.......... MorganCole(7) 5 44
(Lydia Pearce) *prom: cl up after 3f: rdn along over 3f out: sn drvn and wknd* **100/1**

0133 **8** *11* **The Dancing Poet**[29] 7773 3-9-8 **71**..........(p) HollieDoyle 1 33
(Ed Vaughan) *chsd ldrs: rdn along 4f out: wknd 3f out (jockey said gelding did not face the kick back)* **7/2**[2]

5415 **9** *99* **Renardeau**[78] 6022 3-9-7 **70**..........(v[1]) CharlesBishop 2
(Ali Stronge) *a in rr: rdn along 1/2-way: sn outpcd and wl bhd fnl 3f (trainer's rep said gelding didn't face the first time visor)* **25/1**

2m 35.63s (-5.37) **Going Correction** -0.325s/f (Stan)
WFA 3 from 4yo 6lb **9** Ran SP% **113.9**
Speed ratings (Par 103): **104,100,97,94,93 90,89,82,16**
CSF £12.79 CT £43.06 TOTE £1.80: £1.20, £2.20, £1.70; EX 12.70 Trifecta £54.00.
Owner J R Rowbottom **Bred** J R Rowbottom **Trained** Settrington, N Yorks

FOCUS
The well-treated winner took this in comfortable fashion.

8642 BOMBARDIER BRITISH HOPPED AMBER BEER H'CAP 1m 13y(F)
6:15 (6:15) (Class 4) (0-80,82) 3-Y-O+
£5,207 (£1,549; £774; £400; £400; £400) **Stalls** Low

Form RPR

2602 **1** **Al Erayg (IRE)**[14] 8237 6-9-3 **76**..........(p) CamHardie 2 86
(Tim Easterby) *slt ld: pushed along over 2f out: rdn clr over 1f out: kpt on strly* **13/2**

0021 **2** *3 1/4* **Hammer Gun (USA)**[40] 7378 6-9-5 **78**..........(v) LewisEdmunds 9 81
(Derek Shaw) *dwlt and towards rr: hdwy and pushed along 3f out: rdn 2f out: chsd ldrs over 1f out: kpt on fnl f* **5/2**[1]

4420 **3** *1/2* **Ollivander (IRE)**[15] 8181 3-8-13 **75**..........(v) DanielTudhope 8 75
(David O'Meara) *prom: effrt on outer 3f out: rdn along 2f out: drvn and edgd lft over 1f out: kpt on same pce* **6/1**[3]

0002 **4** *2 1/2* **Love Your Work (IRE)**[25] 7875 3-8-7 **69**.......... CharlieBennett 6 64
(Adam West) *prom: rdn along and outpcd 3f out: swtchd rt to outer and drvn 2f out: kpt on fnl f* **4/1**[2]

0043 **5** *nk* **Gremoboy**[14] 8233 3-8-4 **66** oh1..........(p) DuranFentiman 1 60
(Tim Easterby) *trckd ldng pair: hdwy over 3f out: rdn along over 2f out: drvn wl over 1f out: one pce* **14/1**

0000 **6** *nk* **Mister Music**[46] 7145 10-9-4 **82**.......... AledBeech(5) 5 76
(Tony Carroll) *dwlt and bhd: hdwy on inner 2f out: sn rdn: kpt on fnl f: n.d* **14/1**

0350 **7** *2 1/2* **Nick Vedder**[13] 8267 5-9-7 **80**.......... PaulMulrennan 3 68
(Robyn Brisland) *sn outpcd in rr: rdn along over 3f out: plugged on fnl 2f (jockey said gelding hung left-handed)* **14/1**

3200 **8** *3* **Elhafei (USA)**[5] 8507 4-8-11 **70**..........(v[1]) AlistairRawlinson 4 52
(Michael Appleby) *cl up: disp ld over 3f out: sn rdn along: drvn and wknd 2f out* **4/1**[2]

9 *61* **Vivax (IRE)**[157] 3107 3-8-7 **69**.......... AndrewMullen 7
(Ruth Carr) *in tch: rdn along and lost pl 1/2-way: sn bhd* **40/1**

1m 39.47s (-4.23) **Going Correction** -0.325s/f (Stan)
WFA 3 from 4yo+ 3lb **9** Ran SP% **118.6**
Speed ratings (Par 105): **108,104,104,101,101 101,98,95,34**
CSF £23.81 CT £106.14 TOTE £7.00: £1.80, £1.30, £2.50; EX 32.50 Trifecta £152.80.
Owner Reality Partnerships III **Bred** The Vallee Des Reves Syndicate **Trained** Great Habton, N Yorks

FOCUS
A nice performance from the winner on his AW debut. The winner has been rated back to his early season form.

8643 BETWAY HEED YOUR HUNCH H'CAP 4f 214y(F)
6:45 (6:46) (Class 6) (0-65,67) 3-Y-O+
£2,781 (£827; £413; £400; £400; £400) **Stalls** Centre

Form RPR

0054 **1** **Filbert Street**[13] 8268 4-8-6 **48**..........(b) LukeMorris 1 55
(Michael Appleby) *racd towards far side: prom: rdn along 2f out: drvn to chal over 1f out: kpt on wl to ld fnl 100yds* **13/2**[3]

6033 **2** *3/4* **Piazon**[8] 8401 8-9-4 **60**..........(be) NathanEvans 5 64
(Julia Brooke) *trckd ldrs centre: cl up 1/2-way: rdn to ld over 1f out: drvn ent fnl f: hdd and no ex fnl 100yds* **5/1**[2]

6656 **3** *1 1/4* **Qaaraat**[27] 7823 4-9-0 **56**..........(p) CamHardie 3 56
(Antony Brittain) *cl up centre: led over 3f out: rdn along 2f out: sn drvn: hdd over 1f out: kpt on same pce* **13/2**[3]

The Form Book Flat 2019, Raceform Ltd, Newbury, RG14 5SJ

40 **4** ½ **Final Legacy**[71] 6277 3-8-3 **45**..HollieDoyle 4 44+
(Derek Shaw) *dwlt and towards rr: detached and swtchd markedly rt to stands' rail after 1f: switch lft towards centre 2f out: gd hdwy over 1f out: rdn and styd on strly fnl f (jockey said filly hung right-handed)* **100/1**

5341 **5** ¾ **Skeetah**[13] 8263 3-9-7 **63**..PaulMulrennan 7 59+
(John Quinn) *trckd ldrs centre: effrt over 2f out and ev ch: drvn wl over 1f out: grad wknd* **10/1**

6362 **6** nk **Arzaak (IRE)**[8] 8401 5-9-5 **61**..............................(b) JosephineGordon 13 55+
(Charlie Wallis) *racd against stands' rail: cl up: rdn along 2f out: drvn and edgd lft over 1f out: grad wknd (jockey said gelding hung left-handed throughout)* **7/1**

2522 **7** nk **Rose Marmara**[49] 7051 6-9-8 **67**..............................(tp) ConnorMurtagh(3) 9 60
(Brian Rothwell) *racd towards stands' side: cl up: rdn along over 2f out: sn drvn and wknd* **16/1**

4006 **8** 1 **Angel Force (IRE)**[5] 8501 4-8-13 **62**..............................(b) AngusVilliers(7) 2 52
(David C Griffiths) *racd towards far side: cl up: rdn along 2f out: sn drvn and wknd over 1f out* **8/1**

3560 **9** 2 **Le Manege Enchante (IRE)**[73] 6220 6-8-4 **46**..............................(v) KieranO'Neill 11 28
(Derek Shaw) *bdly hmpd s: bhd and detached on stands' side: swtchd markedly lft to far rail 1/2-way: n.d (jockey said gelding was hampered at the start by Honey GG unseating its rider)* **12/1**

0510 **10** 1½ **Dahik (IRE)**[35] 7552 4-9-0 **61**..............................(b) GerO'Neill(5) 8 38
(Michael Easterby) *slt ld centre: hdd over 3f out: cl up: rdn 2f out: sn hung rt and wknd* **10/1**

0030 **11** 8 **Purely Prosecco**[33] 7628 3-8-3 **45**..DuranFentiman 6
(Derek Shaw) *chsd ldrs centre: rdn along over 2f out: sn wknd* **80/1**

0350 **U** **Honey Gg**[13] 8263 4-9-6 **62**..DavidNolan 10
(Declan Carroll) *awkward and stmbld bdly s: veered sharply rt and uns rdr* **9/2**[1]

58.78s (-0.92) **Going Correction** -0.325s/f (Stan) **12 Ran SP% 119.1**
Speed ratings (Par 101): **94,92,90,90,88 88,87,86,83,80 67,**
CSF £39.18 CT £224.04 TOTE £8.10: £2.10, £1.90, £2.90; EX 37.30 Trifecta £239.00.
Owner Michael Appleby **Bred** D Curran **Trained** Oakham, Rutland

FOCUS
An ordinary but competitive sprint.

8644 BETWAY LIVE CASINO H'CAP 1m 6f 21y(F)
7:15 (7:15) (Class 6) (0-65,65) 3-Y-O
£2,781 (£827; £413; £400; £400; £400) **Stalls Low**

Form RPR

4240 **1** **Wadacre Galoubet**[20] 8019 3-9-5 **63**..PJMcDonald 8 72
(Mark Johnston) *trckd ldr: cl up 4f out: rdn along to take slt ld 2f out: drvn and hdd narrowly ent fnl f: sn drvn and rallied gamely to ld fnl 75yds (trainer's rep could offer no explanation for the gelding's improved form)* **5/1**[3]

4344 **2** ½ **J Gaye (IRE)**[96] 5344 3-9-7 **65**..LukeMorris 3 73
(Richard Phillips) *trckd ldrs: hdwy over 3f out: cl up 2f out: rdn to chal over 1f out: drvn to take slt ld ent fnl f: hrd drvn and edgd rt ins fnl f: hdd and no ex fnl 75yds* **8/1**

5033 **3** 6 **Keith**[8] 8406 3-8-4 **48**..............................(p) HollieDoyle 4 49
(Rod Millman) *led: pushed along 3f out: sn rdn and hdd 2f out: sn drvn and grad wknd (jockey said gelding hung both ways)* **5/4**[1]

2215 **4** 4 **Royal Dancer**[14] 8224 3-8-6 **55**..WilliamCarver(5) 2 50
(Sylvester Kirk) *trckd ldrs on inner: effrt over 3f out: rdn along and ev ch 2f out: sn drvn and wknd* **4/1**[2]

465 **5** 8 **Sible Hedingham**[54] 6903 3-9-2 **60**..RyanTate 6 45
(James Eustace) *s.i.s and bhd: clsd up w field after 4f: rdn along in rr 5f out: drvn and wknd 3f out (jockey said filly was slowly away)* **25/1**

0000 **6** 2¾ **Holy Hymn (IRE)**[26] 7857 3-8-8 **52**..............................(t) CliffordLee 5 33
(Kevin Frost) *trckd ldrs: pushed along on outer 4f out: rdn 3f out: sn drvn and wknd* **14/1**

050 **7** 10 **Gustave Aitch (FR)**[21] 7999 3-8-9 **53**..KieranO'Neill 1 21
(Sophie Leech) *in rr: rdn along over 4f out: drvn and wknd 3f out* **14/1**

3m 4.34s (-3.96) **Going Correction** -0.325s/f (Stan) **7 Ran SP% 109.4**
Speed ratings (Par 99): **98,97,94,92,87 85,80**
CSF £39.49 CT £71.61 TOTE £5.50: £3.30, £2.70; EX 35.20 Trifecta £99.70.
Owner Wadacre Stud **Bred** Wadacre Stud **Trained** Middleham Moor, N Yorks

FOCUS
The first two had a good battle here.

8645 BOMBARDIER GOLDEN BEER NOVICE STKS 1m 13y(F)
7:45 (7:46) (Class 5) 3-Y-O+
£3,428 (£1,020; £509; £254) **Stalls Low**

Form RPR

20 **1** **Snow Ocean (IRE)**[25] 7875 3-9-2 **69**..............................(h) CliffordLee 6 81
(David Evans) *trckd ldr: hdwy 3f out: sn rdn to chal: led 2f out: drvn clr over 1f out: kpt on strly* **2/1**[2]

4402 **2** 4½ **Oblate**[13] 8270 3-8-11 **60**..............................(p) KieranO'Neill 5 66
(Robyn Brisland) *s.i.s and bhd: hdwy and in tch 1/2-way: rdn along to chse ldrs over 2f out: drvn over 1f out: kpt on fnl f (jockey said filly was slowly away)* **5/1**[3]

1 **3** 1¼ **Healing Power**[12] 8290 3-9-6 **0**..GabrieleMalune(3) 9 75
(Ivan Furtado) *sn led: jnd and pushed along over 2f out: rdn and hdd 2f out sn drvn and kpt on same pce* **5/4**[1]

2 **4** 5 **Cathedral Street (IRE)**[35] 7543 3-8-9 **0**..AidanRedpath(7) 3 56+
(Mark Johnston) *chsd ldrs: n.m.r and outpcd after 2f: sn detached: hdwy on inner 2f out: kpt on fnl f* **10/1**

50 **5** 11 **Never To Forget**[29] 7772 4-9-0 **0**..DylanHogan(5) 7 32
(John Butler) *chsd ldng pair: rdn along 3f out: sn drvn and wknd* **50/1**

600 **6** 1¼ **Freshfield Ferris**[154] 3200 3-8-8 **38**..ConnorMurtagh(3) 1 23
(Brian Rothwell) *in tch: rdn along over 3f out: sn outpcd* **200/1**

0 **7** 8 **Archon**[12] 8294 3-9-2 **0**..PaulMulrennan 2
(Michael Easterby) *t.k.h: in tch: hdwy on inner to chse ldrs over 3f out: sn lost pl and bhd fnl 2f* **20/1**

0 **8** 5 **Troisouni (FR)**[123] 4341 3-8-6 **0**..............................(t w) WilliamCarver(5) 4
(Conrad Allen) *chsd ldrs on outer: rdn along wl over 3f out: sn wknd* **25/1**

0 **9** 74 **Scarlett Sun**[57] 6811 3-9-2 **0**..LukeMorris 8
(George Margarson) *dwlt: green and hung bdly lft s: a in rr: outpcd and wl bhd fr 1/2-way* **33/1**

1m 40.63s (-3.07) **Going Correction** -0.325s/f (Stan) **9 Ran SP% 117.5**
WFA 3 from 4yo 3lb
Speed ratings (Par 103): **102,97,96,91,80 79,71,66,**
CSF £12.03 TOTE £3.00: £1.10, £1.10, £1.10; EX 10.60 Trifecta £21.70.
Owner Shropshire Wolves 3 **Bred** M Enright **Trained** Pandy, Monmouths

FOCUS
Modest novice form. The winner has been rated to his best.

8646 BOMBARDIER "MARCH TO YOUR OWN DRUM" H'CAP 7f 14y(F)
8:15 (8:16) (Class 6) (0-60,63) 3-Y-O+
£2,781 (£827; £413; £400; £400; £400) **Stalls Low**

Form RPR

0221 **1** **Suitcase 'N' Taxi**[8] 8404 5-9-12 **63** 5ex..DuranFentiman 11 71+
(Tim Easterby) *wnt rt s: sn cl up: led over 5f out: pushed along wl over 1f out: rdn ins fnl f: kpt on wl* **13/8**[1]

130 **2** 2¼ **Geography Teacher (IRE)**[53] 6937 3-9-6 **59**..............................(p) RossaRyan 3 60
(R Mike Smith) *towards rr and sn rdn along on inner: hdwy 3f out: rdn to chse ldrs wl over 1f out: kpt on u.p fnl f: tk 2nd nr fin* **20/1**

6232 **3** shd **Break The Silence**[8] 8404 5-8-13 **57**..............................(b) JonathanFisher(7) 6 59
(Scott Dixon) *cl up: effrt over 2f out: sn rdn along: drvn over 1f out: kpt on same pce* **3/1**[2]

0060 **4** 1 **Sooqaan**[26] 7859 8-9-1 **52**..............................(p) CamHardie 4 51
(Antony Brittain) *trckd ldrs: hdwy 3f out: sn chsng ldng pair: rdn 2f out: drvn wl over 1f out: kpt on one pce* **14/1**

0253 **5** ¾ **Bee Machine (IRE)**[8] 8404 4-8-8 **52**..............................(t) ZakWheatley(7) 10 49
(Declan Carroll) *towards rr: hdwy on outer over 3f out: chsd ldrs and rdn along wl over 2f out: drvn and no imp fr over 1f out* **15/2**[3]

4006 **6** 4 **Epona**[13] 8266 3-9-8 **61**..CallumRodriguez 5 47
(Keith Dalgleish) *led: hdd over 5f out: cl up: rdn along over 3f out: drvn over 2f out: sn wknd* **12/1**

0000 **7** ¾ **Longville Lilly**[52] 6977 4-8-8 **45**..............................(b) JosephineGordon 8 30
(Trevor Wall) *swtchd to r wd after 1f: a in rr* **80/1**

0563 **8** nk **Strict (IRE)**[126] 4225 3-9-9 **62**..AlistairRawlinson 9 45
(Michael Appleby) *dwlt: a in rr (jockey said gelding was slowly away and never travelling thereafter)* **8/1**

0060 **9** 1½ **Newstead Abbey**[14] 8233 9-9-6 **57**..TomEaves 7 37
(Rebecca Bastiman) *in tch: rdn along 1/2-way: sn outpcd and bhd* **40/1**

0050 **10** 1½ **Any Smile (IRE)**[15] 8207 3-8-10 **49**..ShelleyBirkett 2 24
(Julia Feilden) *chsd ldrs on inner: rdn along 3f out: drvn 2f out: sn wknd* **33/1**

0400 **11** 15 **The Golden Cue**[13] 8263 4-9-0 **51**..LukeMorris 13
(Steph Hollinshead) *chsd ldrs: rdn along 3f out: sn wknd* **33/1**

1m 28.02s (-2.28) **Going Correction** -0.325s/f (Stan) **11 Ran SP% 114.6**
WFA 3 from 4yo+ 2lb
Speed ratings (Par 101): **100,97,97,96,95 90,89,89,87,86 68**
CSF £41.82 CT £93.76 TOTE £2.70: £1.30, £4.30, £1.10; EX 36.80 Trifecta £101.00.
Owner Ontoawinner 10 & Partner 3 **Bred** Crossfields Bloodstock Ltd **Trained** Great Habton, N Yorks

FOCUS
A modest affair.
T/Plt: £77.10 to a £1 stake. Pool: £89,952.11 - 850.81 winning units T/Qpdt: £29.60 to a £1 stake. Pool: £12,452.46 - 310.5 winning units **Joe Rowntree**

8330

MAISONS-LAFFITTE (R-H)
Tuesday, October 29

OFFICIAL GOING: Turf: heavy

8647a PRIX MIESQUE (GROUP 3) (2YO FILLIES) (TURF) 7f
12:10 2-Y-O
£36,036 (£14,414; £10,810; £7,207; £3,603)

RPR

1 **Dream And Do (IRE)**[28] 2-8-11 0..MaximeGuyon 1 101
(F Rossi, France) *racd keenly: disp ld: hdd after 2f and chsd ldr: shkn up and rallied to regain ld 1 1/2f out: styd on fnl f: drvn out and a holding runner-up* **13/10**[1]

2 nk **Les Hogues (IRE)**[58] 6777 2-8-11 0..CristianDemuro 2 100
(J-C Rouget, France) *hld up in fnl pair: shkn up and hdwy over 1 1/2f out: chsd wnr fnl f: styd on but nvr quite looked like getting there* **23/5**[2]

3 3½ **Yomogi (FR)**[28] 2-8-11 0..TheoBachelot 6 92
(Hiroo Shimizu, France) *disp ld: wnt on after 2f: rdn w 2f to run: hdd 1 1/2f out: one pce fnl f* **21/1**

4 ½ **Wanaway (FR)**[11] 2-8-11 0..............................(b) Pierre-CharlesBoudot 8 90
(P Bary, France) *racd keenly: hld up in midfield on outer: rdn and tried to chal for pls 1 1/2f out: kpt on at one u.p* **77/10**

5 hd **Mageva**[28] 2-8-11 0..StephanePasquier 3 90
(F Chappet, France) *plld hrd: hld up in midfield on inner: sltly outpcd over 1 1/2f out: kpt on again u.p ins fnl f: nvr in contention* **12/1**

6 2 **Afficionado (FR)**[19] 2-8-11 0..MlleCoraliePacaut 7 85
(J-C Rouget, France) *chsd ldrs: nt qckn whn drvn 1 1/2f out: sn btn* **73/10**

7 12 **Sopran Ival (IRE)**[16] 2-8-11 0..GeraldMosse 5 55
(Grizzetti Galoppo SRL, Italy) *towards rr: outpcd and drvn 1/2-way: lost pl 1 1/2f out: eased ins fnl f* **57/10**[3]

8 12 **Ikigai**[34] 7602 2-8-11 0..MickaelBarzalona 4 25
(Mrs Ilka Gansera-Leveque) *racd keenly: hld up in last pair: lost tch after 1/2-way: eased ins fnl f* **14/1**

1m 30.2s (2.20) **8 Ran SP% 118.7**
PARI-MUTUEL (all including 1 euro stake): WIN 2.30; PLACE 1.20, 1.60, 2.70; DF 4.80.
Owner Haras Du Logis Saint Germain **Bred** Haras Du Logis Saint Germain **Trained** France

FOCUS
An ordinary Group 3 race.

8648a PRIX DE SEINE-ET-OISE (GROUP 3) (3YO+) (TURF) 6f
12:50 3-Y-O+
£36,036 (£14,414; £10,810; £7,207; £3,603)

RPR

1 **Trois Mille (FR)**[17] 8141 3-8-13 0..AlexisBadel 15 114
(S Cerulis, France) *led gp of 8 in centre: cl up bhd overall ldrs whn gps converged w 2 1/2f to run: drvn to chal ent fnl 1 1/2f: str run to ld ins fnl f: drvn out* **13/1**

2 1 **Angel Alexander (IRE)**[38] 7433 3-8-13 0..RichardKingscote 6 111
(Tom Dascombe) *chsd ldr stands' side gp of 7: disp overall ld whn gps merged w 2 1/2f to run: wnt on u.p 1 1/2f out: hdd ins fnl f: no ex* **11/2**[2]

3 2 **Ilanga (FR)**[65] 6520 3-8-11 0..AlexandreGavilan 10 103
(D Guillemin, France) *chsd ld centre gp: rdn but nt qckn wl over 1 1/2f out: styd on same pce* **18/1**

4 hd **Comedia Eria (FR)**[17] 8141 7-8-10 0..StephanePasquier 12 100
(P Monfort, France) *chsd ldr centre gp: rdn and no imp over 1 1/2f out: kpt on same pce* **23/1**

5 2 **Red Torch (FR)**[44] 7255 4-9-0 0 Pierre-CharlesBoudot 1 98
(H-A Pantall, France) *towards rr stands' side gp: hdwy on stands' rail over 2f out: nvr nrr* **15/1**

6 nk **Tinto**[25] 7868 3-8-13 0 MaximeGuyon 7 97
(Amanda Perrett) *chsd ldrs early stands' side gp: sn lost pl: last 1/2-way: sn drvn and stmbld sltly over 2f out: sme late prog: n.d* **14/1**

7 snk **Forza Capitano (FR)**[44] 7254 4-9-0 0 VincentCheminaud 9 96
(H-A Pantall, France) *towards rr in centre gp: pushed along and effrt appr fnl 1 1/2f: kpt on at same pce* **11/1**

8 snk **Lady In France**[39] 7401 3-8-9 0 BenCurtis 3 92
(K R Burke) *t.k.h early: prom stands' side gp: w ldrs fr 1/2-way: hdd 1 1/2f out and grad dropped away* **12/1**

9 1 3/4 **Finsbury Square (IRE)**[23] 7943 7-9-0 0 MickaelBarzalona 13 90
(M Delcher Sanchez, France) *chsd ldrs centre gp: nt qckn whn asked fr 2f out: wknd u.p ins fnl f* **17/1**

10 1/2 **Imperial Tango (FR)**[28] 7800 5-8-10 0 RonanThomas 14 84
(A Schutz, France) *dwlt: outpcd in rr: sme prog u.p after 1/2-way: sn btn* **53/1**

11 hd **Archer's Dream (IRE)**[21] 8004 3-8-9 0 GeorgeWood 8 84
(James Fanshawe) *sn swtchd to gp in centre: rdn and effrt wl over 1 1/2f out: sn btn* **15/1**

12 hd **The Right Man**[17] 8141 7-9-0 0 GeraldMosse 5 87
(D Guillemin, France) *outpcd towards rr of centre gp: rdn after 1/2-way: nvr in contention* **33/10**[1]

13 hd **Tertius (FR)**[17] 8141 3-8-13 0 TheoBachelot 11 87
(M Nigge, France) *midfield in centre gp: hrd rdn 2f out: sn btn* **9/1**[3]

14 1 **Bakoel Koffie (IRE)**[17] 8141 5-9-0 0 TonyPiccone 4 83
(M Delcher Sanchez, France) *towards rr stands' side gp: short-lived effrt 2f out: nt given a hrd time once btn* **23/1**

15 2 **Charline Royale (IRE)**[25] 4-8-10 0 CristianDemuro 2 73
(Silvia Amendola, Italy) *led gp of 7 stands' side: jnd 1/2-way: hdd sn after but remained cl up: wknd fnl 1 1/2f* **11/1**

1m 14.96s (1.56)
WFA 3 from 4yo+ 1lb **15** Ran SP% **120.3**
PARI-MUTUEL (all including 1 euro stake): WIN 14.00; PLACE 4.20, 3.00, 6.20; DF 45.20.
Owner Stephan Hoffmeister **Bred** P Boudengen **Trained** France
FOCUS
Th level is set by the second to the fifth.

8601 **KEMPTON (A.W)** (R-H)
Wednesday, October 30
OFFICIAL GOING: Polytrack: standard to slow
Wind: minor cross breeze Weather: Cold, overcast

8649 MAGICAL FIREWORKS HERE ON SATURDAY EVENING CLASSIFIED CLAIMING STKS 6f (P)
4:40 (4:40) (Class 5) 3-Y-O+
£3,752 (£1,116; £557; £400; £400; £400) **Stalls** Low

Form RPR
5230 1 **Swiss Pride (IRE)**[29] 7789 3-8-13 73 (p) AngusVilliers(7) 7 75
(Richard Hughes) *trckd ldr and racd freely: effrt on inner to ld over 1f out: sn rdn and kpt on wl fnl f* **11/8**[1]

3043 2 nk **Pettochside**[9] 8410 10-8-13 70 HollieDoyle 2 66
(John Bridger) *hld up: hdwy on outer 2f out: rdn to chse wnr over 1f out: kpt on fnl f: nt rch wnr* **9/2**[2]

4205 3 1/2 **Steelriver (IRE)**[79] 6027 9-9-3 75 PhilDennis 3 69
(Michael Herrington) *dwlt and racd in last: hdwy into 3rd over 1f out: rdn and kpt on fnl f: nt rch ldng pair (jockey said gelding anticipated the start and was slowly away)* **5/1**[3]

0020 4 2 3/4 **Mujassam**[21] 8031 7-9-3 71 (b) LiamKeniry 5 60
(Sophie Leech) *trckd ldrs: clsd gng wl 2f out: sn rdn and outpcd over 1f out: one pce fnl f* **6/1**

3012 5 1/2 **Pour La Victoire (IRE)**[44] 7268 9-9-3 73 (p) TomMarquand 6 59
(Tony Carroll) *hld up: pushed along and outpcd 1/2-way: nvr able to land a blow* **11/2**

0002 6 1 1/4 **Flowing Clarets**[9] 8410 6-8-8 43 RhiainIngram(5) 4 51
(John Bridger) *led: rdn along and hdd by wnr over 1f out: short of room whn wkng fnl f: no ex (jockey said mare ran too free; vet said mare most it's left fore shoe)* **66/1**

0600 7 7 **Swendab (IRE)**[48] 7112 11-8-6 40 (b) KateLeahy(7) 1 30
(John O'Shea) *prom on inner: rdn and lost pl 2f out: sn bhd* **200/1**

1m 12.36s (-0.74) **Going Correction** -0.05s/f (Stan)
WFA 3 from 6yo+ 1lb **7** Ran SP% **108.6**
Speed ratings (Par 103): **102,101,100,97,96 94,85**
CSF £6.98 TOTE £1.60: £1.20, £2.60; EX 9.60 Trifecta £28.40.
Owner Don Churston & Ray Greatorex **Bred** Edward Lynam & John Cullinan **Trained** Upper Lambourn, Berks
FOCUS
An ordinary claimer on standard to slow Polytrack.

8650 BOOK FIREWORK TICKETS IN ADVANCE FOR £7 NURSERY H'CAP 6f (P)
5:10 (5:10) (Class 5) (0-70,70) 2-Y-O
£3,752 (£1,116; £557; £400; £400; £400) **Stalls** Low

Form RPR
5430 1 **Mitty's Smile (IRE)**[38] 7495 2-9-7 70 (b1) HollieDoyle 4 72
(Archie Watson) *mde all: shkn up to extend ld 2f out: rdn w 2 l ld appr fnl f: kpt on wl: rdn out* **4/1**[1]

615 2 1 1/2 **Miss Thoughtful**[48] 7104 2-9-5 68 NicolaCurrie 5 66
(Jamie Osborne) *prom: taken bk briefly 4f out: rdn and outpcd over 1f out: drvn and kpt on wl to go 2nd wl ins fnl f: no ch w wnr* **20/1**

0552 3 hd **Lilkian**[16] 8195 2-9-2 65 JosephineGordon 2 67+
(Shaun Keightley) *in rr of midfield: hmpd and lost grnd home bnd: pushed along and hdwy between rivals over 1f out: swtchd lft and rdn 1f out: kpt on wl fnl f tl short of room fnl 50yds* **9/2**[2]

4530 4 nk **Twice As Likely**[44] 7276 2-9-3 66 TomMarquand 1 62
(Richard Hughes) *trckd ldrs on inner: rdn along and outpcd by wnr over 1f out: kpt on one pce ins fnl f* **10/1**

5463 5 shd **Bowling Russian (IRE)**[8] 8430 2-9-5 68 (p) CharlesBishop 8 64
(George Baker) *trckd wnr: drvn along to chse wnr over 1f out: kpt on but lost 2 pls clsng stages* **13/2**

0200 6 1/2 **King's View (IRE)**[30] 7754 2-8-11 65 (b1) ThoreHammerHansen(5) 9 59
(Richard Hannon) *midfield: hdwy u.p on outer 2f out: rdn and minor imp 1f out: kpt on fnl f but nvr a danger* **25/1**

3310 7 1 **Colonel Whitehead (IRE)**[30] 7754 2-9-0 70 AngusVilliers(7) 6 61
(Heather Main) *midfield: rdn along and outpcd over 1f out: kpt on one pce fnl f* **9/2**[2]

105 8 1 **Sovereign Beauty (IRE)**[39] 7458 2-9-7 70 LiamKeniry 12 58
(Clive Cox) *hld up: rdn along in rr over 1f out: sme late hdwy passed btn rivals* **20/1**

642 9 3/4 **Qinwan**[41] 7386 2-9-5 68 OisinMurphy 3 54
(Andrew Balding) *midfield and a little keen: bdly short of room leaving bk st: hmpd and taken bk 3f out: rdn and no imp over 1f out: one pce after* **5/1**[3]

1605 10 2 **Bartat**[47] 7156 2-9-1 64 DavidEgan 10 44
(Mick Channon) *in rr of midfield: wd off home bnd: rdn and no imp over 1f out: no ex* **50/1**

6203 11 hd **Sir Gordon**[116] 4652 2-9-3 66 DavidProbert 7 45
(Ralph J Smith) *hld up: rdn in rr 2f out: nvr on terms* **50/1**

4151 12 1 **War Of Clans (IRE)**[58] 6792 2-9-5 68 CliffordLee 11 44
(K R Burke) *prom on outer early: rdn along and lost pl 2f out: sn wknd* **20/1**

1m 13.4s (0.30) **Going Correction** -0.05s/f (Stan) **12** Ran SP% **117.5**
Speed ratings (Par 95): **96,94,93,93,93 92,91,89,88,86 85,84**
CSF £89.08 CT £374.69 TOTE £5.90: £2.60, £4.70, £2.00; EX 75.10 Trifecta £484.40.
Owner M Aziz **Bred** Summerseat Stables Ltd **Trained** Upper Lambourn, W Berks
FOCUS
An ordinary nursery. The dominant winner's time was about a second slower than the previous C&D claimer.

8651 FIREWORKS SPECTACULAR HERE ON SATURDAY EVENING FILLIES' NOVICE AUCTION STKS 1m (P)
5:40 (5:44) (Class 6) 2-Y-O
£3,105 (£924; £461; £230) **Stalls** Low

Form RPR
6 1 **Queen Gamrah**[7] 8458 2-8-11 0 JoeFanning 8 69
(Mark Johnston) *midfield: hdwy to trck ldr after 3f: pushed along to ld 2f out: rdn w 1 l advantage 1f out: kpt on wl* **4/1**[2]

0 2 1 **Licit (IRE)**[20] 8058 2-8-12 0 TomMarquand 2 68+
(Mohamed Moubarak) *dwlt but sn rcvrd into midfield: swtchd rt and effrt 2f out: sn rdn and kpt on wl fnl f: nrst fin* **16/1**

54 3 1/2 **Gonna Dancealot (IRE)**[13] 8287 2-8-13 0 JFEgan 13 68
(Jane Chapple-Hyam) *midfield: drvn along and no immediate imp 2f out: kpt on u.str.p fnl f* **7/1**[3]

4 3/4 **Gazelle** 2-9-0 0 JasonWatson 3 67
(Roger Charlton) *midfield on inner: effrt to chse ldrs 2f out: sn rdn and kpt on one pce fnl f* **8/1**

5 1/2 **Lady Magda** 2-9-0 0 HollieDoyle 7 66
(Jonathan Portman) *in rr of midfield: pushed along over 2f out: rdn and no immediate imp over 1f out: drvn and mde gd late hdwy fnl f* **25/1**

321 6 1 **Rosardo Senorita**[37] 7515 2-9-4 77 DavidProbert 14 68
(Rae Guest) *prom early: rdn and outpcd 2f out: kpt on one pce for press fnl f* **4/1**[2]

05 7 1 3/4 **Chiarodiluna**[51] 7031 2-9-0 0 NicolaCurrie 9 60
(Philip McBride) *taken bk early and racd in rr: rdn 2f out: mde sme late hdwy but n.d* **66/1**

0 8 3/4 **So Special**[53] 6949 2-8-11 0 DavidEgan 6 55
(William Muir) *midfield: rdn along and outpcd over 2f out: wknd over 1f out* **14/1**

00 9 1 **Russian Rumour (IRE)**[37] 7515 2-8-11 0 RobHornby 10 53
(Jonathan Portman) *hld up: stl last over 2f out: nvr on terms* **33/1**

04 10 nk **Berkshire Philly**[16] 8198 2-8-11 0 OisinMurphy 5 52
(Andrew Balding) *in rr of midfield: rdn along and no imp 2f out: one pce fnl f* **12/1**

300 11 1 1/2 **Looks Good (IRE)**[13] 8287 2-8-7 64 (b1) AngusVilliers(7) 11 52
(Richard Hughes) *hld up: a in rr* **50/1**

12 nk **Youneverletmedown (IRE)** 2-9-0 0 CallumRodriguez 4 51
(Keith Dalgleish) *broke smartly and led: rdn along and hdd by wnr 2f out: sn tired and lost pl qckly over 1f out* **7/2**[1]

0 13 21 **Centrifuge (IRE)**[29] 7787 2-8-11 0 CharlesBishop 12
(Michael Blanshard) *midfield: rdn and wd off home bnd: sn lots pl over 2f out: eased fnl f* **150/1**

1m 39.83s (0.03) **Going Correction** -0.05s/f (Stan) **13** Ran SP% **117.0**
Speed ratings (Par 90): **97,96,95,94,94 93,91,90,89,89 87,87,66**
CSF £62.36 TOTE £4.10: £1.10, £4.30, £3.10; EX 68.20 Trifecta £810.80.
Owner Jaber Abdullah **Bred** The National Stud **Trained** Middleham Moor, N Yorks
■ Stewards' Enquiry : J F Egan two-day ban; misuse of whip (Nov 16,18)
FOCUS
A fair fillies' juvenile novice auction contest. One of the joint-second favourites won in game fashion.

8652 32RED CASINO H'CAP 1m (P)
6:10 (6:13) (Class 5) (0-70,70) 3-Y-O+
£3,752 (£1,116; £557; £400; £400; £400) **Stalls** Low

Form RPR
0600 1 **Choral Music**[32] 7684 4-9-3 65 RobHornby 9 72+
(John E Long) *in rr of midfield: hdwy u.p 2f out: briefly short of room over 1f out: swtchd rt and rdn ent fnl f: styd on strly fnl f and led post* **16/1**

4554 2 shd **Crimewave (IRE)**[30] 7773 3-9-3 68 (p) JackMitchell 10 74
(Tom Clover) *trckd ldr: pushed along to ld over 1f out: sn rdn and 2 l clr appr fnl f: drvn and hdd by wnr post* **4/1**[2]

541 3 shd **Takeonefortheteam**[15] 8223 4-9-2 64 LiamJones 2 71
(Mark Loughnane) *midfield: rdn and gd hdwy appr fnl f: drvn and kpt on strly fnl f: jst failed to rch ldng pair* **9/1**

0 4 1/2 **Andaleep (IRE)**[28] 7816 3-9-2 67 LiamKeniry 8 71
(Graeme McPherson) *midfield: drvn and no imp 2f out: kpt on wl for press fnl f but n.d* **20/1**

2600 5 nk **Roman Spinner**[14] 8254 4-9-5 67 (t) DavidProbert 6 72+
(Rae Guest) *hld up: swtchd lft 2f out: effrt whn short of room over 1f out: fnlly in clr and rdn fnl f: styd on v strly clsng stages* **7/2**[1]

0334 6 1/2 **Kings Royal Hussar (FR)**[77] 6075 3-9-2 67 TomMarquand 4 70
(Alan King) *midfield in tch: rdn along and wnt 3rd over 2f out: drvn and kpt on one pce fnl f* **7/1**[3]

005 7 1 **Walkman (IRE)**[49] 7080 3-9-4 69 (t1) MartinDwyer 3 69
(Tim Pinfield) *led: rdn along and hdd over 1f out: wknd fnl f* **8/1**

3055 8 1 **I Can (IRE)**[15] 8221 4-9-6 68 NicolaCurrie 13 67
(Sir Mark Todd) *prom on outer: rdn along and no imp 2 out: kpt on one pce u.p fnl f* **10/1**

0336 9 3 3/4 **Danecase**[15] 8220 6-8-12 67..........(tp) AngusVilliers(7) 12 57
(David Dennis) *midfield on outer: rdn and outpcd over 1f out: one pce fnl f* 25/1

0446 10 2 3/4 **Black Medick**[27] 7843 3-9-3 68.......... DavidEgan 5 51
(Laura Mongan) *hld up: wd off home bnd: sn rdn over 2f out: no imp over 1f out: plugged on* 16/1

050 11 3/4 **Entertaining (IRE)**[18] 8122 3-9-5 70.......... OisinMurphy 11 51
(Richard Hannon) *hld up: pushed along in rr over 2f out: nvr on terms* 14/1

0060 12 1 3/4 **Keeper's Choice (IRE)**[15] 6469 5-9-3 65.......... CharlesBishop 7 43
(Denis Coakley) *midfield on inner: rdn along and lost pl 2f out: sn bhd* 50/1

-500 13 1/2 **Island Glen (USA)**[21] 8025 3-9-2 67.......... JasonWatson 1 43
(Heather Main) *trckd ldrs on inner: rdn along and qckly lost pl over 1f out (jockey said gelding stopped quickly)* 16/1

1m 38.86s (-0.94) **Going Correction** -0.05s/f (Stan)
WFA 3 from 4yo+ 3lb **13 Ran SP% 119.8**
Speed ratings (Par 103): **102,101,101,101,101 100,99,98,94,92 91,89,89**
CSF £77.69 CT £652.24 TOTE £23.30: £4.10, £2.70, £3.20; EX 109.10 Trifecta £439.20.
Owner Mrs A M Sturges **Bred** Farmers Hill Stud **Trained** Brighton, East Sussex
■ Stewards' Enquiry : Jack Mitchell four-day ban; misuse of whip (Nov 16,18-20)

FOCUS
An ordinary handicap. One of the longer-priced contenders got up right on the line and her winning time was about a second quicker than the previous C&D juvenile fillies' novice contest. Sound form, rated around the third and fourth.

8653 32RED ON THE APP STORE NOVICE STKS 7f (P)
6:40 (6:40) (Class 5) 3-Y-O+ £3,881 (£1,155; £577; £288) Stalls Low

Form RPR

60 1 **Ice Cave (IRE)**[162] 2938 3-9-0 0.......... SeanKirrane(5) 5 84+
(Saeed bin Suroor) *racd in midfield: smooth hdwy on outer to chal 2f out: rdn and easily qcknd clr over 1f out: pushed out fnl f: comf* 11/4[2]

62 2 4 **Pentimento**[13] 8290 3-9-5 0.......... KierenFox 7 70+
(John Best) *hld up: rdn and briefly outpcd over 1f out: drvn and kpt on wl fnl f to snatch remote 2nd clsng stages* 5/6[1]

3 1/2 **Prompting** 3-9-5 0.......... EoinWalsh 2 69
(Olly Murphy) *trckd ldrs: shkn up 2f out: rdn on inner and qckly outpcd by wnr over 1f out: kpt on one pce fnl f* 12/1

4 *hd* **Montys Inn (IRE)** 3-9-5 0.......... JohnFahy 1 68
(Richard Hannon) *led: rdn along and hdd by wnr over 1f out: kpt on one pce fnl f* 11/1

0340 5 6 **Molly's Game**[47] 7157 3-9-0 62.......... HayleyTurner 6 47
(David Elsworth) *trckd ldr: rdn and readily outpcd over 1f out: wknd fnl f* 9/1[3]

0 6 5 **Rockstar Max (GER)**[27] 7841 3-9-5 0.......... DougieCostello 4 38
(Denis Coakley) *hld up: rdn and bhd over 1f out: nvr on terms* 33/1

7 2 1/2 **Disturbing Beauty** 3-8-7 0.......... EllieMacKenzie(7) 3 27
(Natalie Lloyd-Beavis) *hld up: a bhd* 150/1

1m 26.91s (0.91) **Going Correction** -0.05s/f (Stan) **7 Ran SP% 110.9**
Speed ratings (Par 103): **92,87,86,86,79 74,71**
CSF £5.00 TOTE £2.40: £2.10, £1.10; EX 5.90 Trifecta £31.10.
Owner Godolphin **Bred** Kenilworth House Stud **Trained** Newmarket, Suffolk

FOCUS
An ordinary 3yo novice contest. The second-favourite quickened up to win well from off an admittedly muddling gallop over 1f out.

8654 32RED.COM H'CAP 1m 7f 218y(P)
7:10 (7:10) (Class 4) (0-85,85) 3-Y-O+ £6,469 (£1,925; £962; £481; £400; £400) Stalls Low

Form RPR

10-2 1 **Astromachia**[43] 7294 4-10-0 85.......... JoeFanning 6 95+
(Amanda Perrett) *wl in tch: quick hdwy to ld 6f out: shkn up and readily asserted 2f out: rdn out fnl f: comf* 11/8[1]

4220 2 3 1/4 **Black Kalanisi (IRE)**[37] 7510 6-9-7 78.......... CharlesBishop 1 82
(Joseph Tuite) *in tch: smooth hdwy 3f out: rdn along and wnt 2nd over 1f out: drvn and jst hld on for 2nd clsng stages* 11/1

0160 3 *hd* **Knight Crusader**[18] 8129 7-9-12 83.......... LiamJones 4 87
(John O'Shea) *midfield: hdwy u.p over 2f out: rdn to cl over 1f out: styd on wl fnl f* 20/1

2340 4 1 3/4 **Seinesational**[18] 8114 4-9-13 84..........(v) JasonWatson 10 86
(William Knight) *trckd ldr tl 6f out: remained prom: rdn along and outpcd over 1f out: one pce fnl f* 7/1[3]

3035 5 3/4 **Age Of Wisdom (IRE)**[55] 6901 6-9-9 80..........(p) TomMarquand 5 81
(Gary Moore) *in rr of midfield: niggled to get clsr 4f out: rdn along and no imp over 1f out: kpt on one pce fnl f* 16/1

3550 6 *nk* **Gavlar**[27] 7845 8-8-13 70.......... CallumShepherd 3 71
(William Knight) *racd in midfield: rdn along and outpcd 2f out: kpt on one pce fnl f* 16/1

0111 7 2 1/4 **Casa Comigo (IRE)**[28] 7818 4-8-11 68.......... KierenFox 8 66+
(John Best) *hld up in last: rdn w plenty to do over 2f out: plugged on* 11/4[2]

1500 8 4 1/2 **Tin Fandango**[27] 7845 4-8-9 66..........(p) JosephineGordon 2 59
(Mark Usher) *led tl 6f out: remained handy: rdn along and lost pl 2f out: wknd fnl f* 33/1

0060 9 3/4 **Nakeeta**[26] 7866 8-9-13 84..........(t) RobertHavlin 11 76
(Linda Jewell) *hld up: rdn in rr 2f out: n.d* 66/1

0110 10 3 **Conkering Hero (IRE)**[27] 7845 5-9-5 76..........(b) RobHornby 9 64
(Joseph Tuite) *hld up and t.k.h: rdn 3f out: nvr on terms* 25/1

3140 11 2 3/4 **Nafaayes (IRE)**[60] 6716 5-8-9 66..........(p) MartinDwyer 7 51
(Jean-Rene Auvray) *racd in midfield: rdn and lost pl over 2f out: sn bhd* 33/1

3m 28.71s (-1.39) **Going Correction** -0.05s/f (Stan) **11 Ran SP% 117.4**
Speed ratings (Par 105): **101,99,99,98,98 97,96,94,94,92 91**
CSF £17.03 CT £218.67 TOTE £1.90: £1.20, £4.00, £6.40; EX 21.80 Trifecta £197.60.
Owner John Connolly & Odile Griffith **Bred** Newsells Park Stud **Trained** Pulborough, W Sussex

FOCUS
A decent staying handicap. The favourite was rushed up to build upon the even gallop down the back straight and outclassed this opposition in the home straight. The form looks sound enough rated around the second, third and fourth.

8655 32RED H'CAP 1m 3f 219y(P)
7:40 (7:41) (Class 2) (0-100,99) 3-Y-O £15,562 (£4,660; £2,330; £1,165) Stalls Low

Form RPR

2122 1 **El Misk**[11] 8350 3-9-7 99.......... RobertHavlin 1 109+
(John Gosden) *trckd ldng pair: wnt 2nd gng wl 2f out: pushed along to ld over 1f out: grad drew clr fnl f: comf* 4/5[1]

2 3 1/4 **Grandmaster Flash (IRE)**[19] 8106 3-8-7 85..........(p) JasonWatson 3 90
(Joseph Patrick O'Brien, Ire) *trckd ldr: effrt rdn along to ld 3f out: hung lft to over 2f out: sn drvn and hdd by wnr over 1f out: kpt on one pce* 4/1[3]

4311 3 11 **Monsieur Lambrays**[25] 7915 3-8-3 81..........(b) DavidEgan 2 68
(Tom Clover) *hld up in last of quartet: rdn and outpcd over 2f out: hung lft to stands' rail over 1f out: plugged on* 10/1

3204 4 3/4 **The Trader (IRE)**[19] 8092 3-8-13 91.......... JoeFanning 4 77
(Mark Johnston) *led: rdn along and hdd 3f out: wknd fr over 1f out* 7/2[2]

2m 32.59s (-1.91) **Going Correction** -0.05s/f (Stan) **4 Ran SP% 106.9**
Speed ratings (Par 107): **104,101,94,94**
CSF £4.17 TOTE £1.40; EX 4.00 Trifecta £9.40.
Owner Sheikh Mohammed Bin Khalifa Al Maktoum **Bred** Essafinaat Ltd **Trained** Newmarket, Suffolk

FOCUS
The feature contest was a good little 3yo middle-distance handicap. Despite the small field the odds-on favourite won readily in one of the quickest comparative times on the night. The second has been rated to his Irish form.

8656 100% PROFIT BOOST AT 32REDSPORT.COM H'CAP 1m 3f 219y(P)
8:10 (8:11) (Class 5) (0-75,77) 3-Y-O+ £3,752 (£1,116; £557; £400; £400; £400) Stalls Low

Form RPR

2352 1 **Sweet Celebration (IRE)**[13] 8298 3-8-5 69.......... StefanoCherchi(7) 9 87
(Marco Botti) *hld up: niggled along in last 3f out: swtchd rt over 2f out: rdn and hdwy into 4th 2f out: rapid hdwy to ld over 1f out: sn clr* 7/1

5660 2 8 **Wimpole Hall**[53] 6967 6-9-10 75..........(b) DavidProbert 6 79
(William Jarvis) *led after 1f and racd keenly: rdn along and hdd by wnr over 1f out: kpt on for remote 2nd fnl f* 10/1

3025 3 1 **Ned Pepper (IRE)**[13] 8298 3-9-1 72.......... TomQueally 7 75
(Alan King) *midfield: pushed along and wd off home bnd 3f out: rdn and no imp 2f out: kpt on again fnl f for remote 3rd* 3/1[2]

4436 4 1 **Noble Gift**[2] 8608 9-9-12 77.......... KierenFox 5 78
(William Knight) *led for 1f then trckd ldr: rdn along to chal 2f out: sn one pce appr fnl f: plugged on* 5/1[3]

6401 5 2 1/2 **Philonikia**[20] 8065 3-9-0 71.......... RobHornby 1 69
(Ralph Beckett) *trckd ldng pair: rdn along and unable qck 2f out: wknd fnl f* 11/4[1]

600 6 11 **Rail Dancer**[89] 5631 7-8-7 65..........(p) GavinAshton(7) 4 44
(Shaun Keightley) *hld up: rdn and outpcd over 2f out: nvr on terms* 33/1

034 7 47 **Fields Of Dreams**[13] 8294 3-9-4 75.......... JasonWatson 2
(Roger Charlton) *midfield ealry: rdn along and lost pl 3f out: sn t.o* 5/1[3]

2m 30.95s (-3.55) **Going Correction** -0.05s/f (Stan)
WFA 3 from 4yo+ 6lb **7 Ran SP% 109.5**
Speed ratings (Par 103): **109,103,103,102,100 93,62**
CSF £65.42 CT £234.00 TOTE £7.30: £3.10, £5.20; EX 66.80 Trifecta £129.20.
Owner Mpr, Ventura Racing 5 & Partner **Bred** Kildaragh Stud & M Downey **Trained** Newmarket, Suffolk

FOCUS
A fair middle-distance handicap. The winner came clear late from off a strong pace to win decisively in a good comparative time. The level is a bit fluid.
T/Plt: £47.50 to a £1 stake. Pool: £49,253.21 - 755.76 winning units T/Qpdt: £13.90 to a £1 stake. Pool: £5,462.15 - 290.40 winning units **Mark Grantham**

8257 NOTTINGHAM (L-H)
Wednesday, October 30

OFFICIAL GOING: Soft (heavy in places; 5.3)
Wind: Moderate half behind Weather: Fine & dry

8657 EBF STALLIONS GOLDEN HORN MAIDEN STKS (PLUS 10 RACE) 1m 75y
12:50 (12:58) (Class 4) 2-Y-O £6,469 (£1,925; £962; £481) Stalls Centre

Form RPR

0 1 **Tremor (IRE)**[42] 7339 2-9-0 0.......... TomQueally 3 73+
(Alan King) *trckd ldrs on inner: hdwy and cl up over 2f out: rdn over 1f out: led ent fnl f: drvn out* 50/1

04 2 *nk* **Junkanoo**[42] 7339 2-9-0 0.......... HectorCrouch 9 72
(Gary Moore) *t.k.h: trckd ldng pair: hdwy on outer over 3f out: cl up over 2f out: rdn to chal over 1f out: ev ch and edgd lft ins fnl f: kpt on towards fin* 11/1

5 3 *shd* **Finely Tuned (IRE)**[28] 7821 2-9-0 0.......... JackMitchell 4 72+
(Simon Crisford) *hld up in midfield: pushed along 4f out: hdwy wl over 2f out: sn chsng ldrs: rdn over 1f out: styd on strly fnl f* 3/1[1]

522 4 2 **Tinnahalla (IRE)**[23] 7972 2-9-0 75.......... NicolaCurrie 8 68
(Jamie Osborne) *t.k.h: led: jnd and rdn along 3f out: hdd over 2f out: sn drvn: kpt on same pce fnl f* 5/1[3]

52 5 1/2 **Jumaira Bay (FR)**[16] 8203 2-9-0 0.......... DavidEgan 10 67
(Roger Varian) *trckd ldr: hdwy and cl up 3f out: led over 2f out: sn rdn: drvn and hdd ent fnl f: grad wknd* 7/2[2]

0 6 7 **Tazaman**[20] 8058 2-9-0 0.......... RossaRyan 6 51
(Kevin Frost) *a towards rr* 150/1

50 7 1 **Danking**[102] 5177 2-8-11 0.......... ThomasGreatrex(3) 7 49
(Alan King) *midfield: effrt and sme hdwy 3f out: rdn along over 2f out: n.d* 66/1

50 8 1 **Thunder King (FR)**[88] 5655 2-8-11 0.......... SeanDavis(3) 2 47
(Amy Murphy) *t.k.h: trckd ldrs: pushed along on inner 3f out: rdn over 2f out: sn wknd* 40/1

9 2 1/4 **Newbolt (IRE)** 2-9-0 0.......... RobHornby 5 42
(Ralph Beckett) *s.i.s: a in rr* 10/1

0 10 1 1/4 **Itojeh**[25] 7902 2-8-9 0.......... GerO'Neill(5) 11 39
(Michael Easterby) *dwlt: a in rr* 250/1

1m 52.95s (6.25) **Going Correction** +0.75s/f (Yiel) **10 Ran SP% 88.3**
Speed ratings (Par 97): **98,97,97,95,95 88,87,86,83,82**
CSF £300.24 TOTE £49.50: £10.60, £2.50, £1.20; EX 431.50 Trifecta £848.20.
Owner Elysees Partnership **Bred** Shake The Moon Partnership **Trained** Barbury Castle, Wilts
■ Bobby The Great was withdrawn. Price at time of withdrawal 11/4. Rule 4 applies to all bets - deduction 25p in the pound.

FOCUS
Inner track and all distances as advertised. This opening 2yo maiden changed complexion before the stalls opened due well-backed Bobby The Great breaking loose. They went a fair pace and stuck to the centre of the home straight, with experience coming to the fore.

8658 MANSIONBET PROUD TO SUPPORT BRITISH RACING H'CAP 1m 75y
1:20 (1:20) (Class 4) (0-85,84) 3-Y-O+
£6,469 (£1,925; £962; £481; £300; £300) **Stalls** Centre

Form RPR
4402 1 **Mustarrid (IRE)**[46] 7212 5-9-10 **84**........ PaulHanagan 5 95+
(Ian Williams) *trckd ldrs: smooth hdwy on inner 3f out: cl up over 2f out: led on bit wl over 1f out: shkn up ent fnl f: sn rdn clr: readily* **11/4**[2]
2110 2 5 **Dubai Acclaim (IRE)**[12] 8305 4-8-12 **75**........(p) SeanDavis(3) 4 74
(Richard Fahey) *dwlt: t.k.h and hld up in rr: hdwy 3f out: cl up wl over 1f out: sn rdn and ev ch: drvn and kpt on same pce fnl f* **4/1**[3]
2333 3 ½ **Al Mureib (IRE)**[94] 5477 3-9-6 **83**........(p[1]) JosephineGordon 3 80
(Saeed bin Suroor) *trckd ldr: hdwy on outer over 3f out: sn cl up: rdn along 2f out and ev ch: drvn appr fnl f and kpt on same pce* **5/2**[1]
2166 4 8 **Oud Metha Bridge (IRE)**[86] 5726 5-8-12 **72**........ ShelleyBirkett 1 51
(Julia Feilden) *trckd ldng pair: hdwy on inner and cl up over 3f out: rdn along and ev ch 2f out: sn drvn and wknd over 1f out* **8/1**
0230 5 shd **Directory**[53] 6964 4-9-4 **78**........ RyanTate 8 57
(James Eustace) *led: rdn along over 3f out: drvn 2f out: sn hdd & wknd* **11/1**
0-50 6 nk **Keswick**[21] 8024 5-9-4 **78**........(t) BenCurtis 7 57
(Heather Main) *hld up in tch: effrt and hdwy on outer 3f out: rdn along over 2f out: sn btn* **11/1**
200- 7 16 **Zlatan (IRE)**[247] 9155 6-9-6 **80**........ RossaRyan 6 22
(Ed de Giles) *hld up in tch: effrt over 3f out: sn rdn and wknd* **14/1**

1m 50.66s (3.96) **Going Correction** +0.75s/f (Yiel)
WFA 3 from 4yo+ 3lb **7 Ran SP% 109.7**
Speed ratings (Par 105): **110,105,104,96,96 96,80**
CSF £12.93 CT £26.80 TOTE £2.30: £2.00, £1.80; EX 16.60 Trifecta £49.60.
Owner A Dale **Bred** John Malone **Trained** Portway, Worcs

FOCUS
This fair handicap rather fell apart from 2f out. The winner has been rated back to his best.

8659 MANSIONBET BEATEN BY A HEAD NURSERY H'CAP 5f 8y
1:50 (1:50) (Class 2) 2-Y-O **£9,703** (£2,887; £1,443; £721) **Stalls** High

Form RPR
3211 1 **Ainsdale**[14] 8261 2-9-5 **89**........ BenCurtis 3 94+
(K R Burke) *trckd ldr: cl up 1/2-way: led wl over 1f out: rdn ins fnl f: readily* **4/6**[1]
460 2 2½ **Zulu Zander (IRE)**[91] 5542 2-8-9 **79**........ PJMcDonald 4 75
(David Evans) *led: jnd 1/2-way and sn pushed along: rdn and hdd wl over 1f out: drvn and kpt on same pce fnl f* **18/1**
2221 3 1¼ **Daily Times**[20] 8067 2-8-8 **78**........(t) NickyMackay 2 70
(John Gosden) *trckd ldrs: hdwy on inner 2f out: rdn over 1f out: sn drvn and no imp* **9/2**[3]
4010 4 4 **Praxeology (IRE)**[25] 7904 2-9-7 **91**........ FrannyNorton 5 68
(Mark Johnston) *cl up on outer: pushed along 1/2-way: sn rdn and wknd wl over 1f out* **10/3**[2]

1m 2.77s (2.57) **Going Correction** +0.75s/f (Yiel) **4 Ran SP% 106.5**
Speed ratings (Par 101): **109,105,103,96**
CSF £11.27 TOTE £1.40; EX 11.80 Trifecta £21.60.
Owner David W Armstrong **Bred** Highfield Farm Llp **Trained** Middleham Moor, N Yorks

FOCUS
A fair little nursery.

8660 DOWNLOAD THE MANSIONBET APP H'CAP 5f 8y
2:20 (2:21) (Class 5) (0-75,76) 3-Y-O+
£3,881 (£1,155; £577; £300; £300; £300) **Stalls** High

Form RPR
4002 1 **Bellevarde (IRE)**[14] 8262 5-9-5 **73**........ BenCurtis 8 81
(Richard Price) *trckd ldrs: hdwy to chal over 1f out: sn rdn: drvn to ld ins fnl f: kpt on* **4/1**[2]
-064 2 1 **Hieronymus**[14] 8242 3-9-2 **70**........(tp) TomQueally 3 75
(Seamus Durack) *dwlt and towards rr: hdwy 2f out: rdn over 1f out: styd on wl fnl f* **16/1**
0400 3 nk **Quench Dolly**[14] 8262 5-9-3 **71**........(b) HectorCrouch 6 74
(John Gallagher) *cl up: chal 2f out and sn ev ch: rdn over 1f out: drvn and kpt on same pce fnl f* **16/1**
1302 4 ¾ **Show Palace**[16] 8183 6-9-8 **76**........(p) ShaneGray 9 77
(Jennie Candlish) *slt ld: rdn along 2f out: drvn jst over 1f out: hdd ins fnl f: kpt on same pce* **5/1**[3]
0220 5 nk **Lydiate Lady**[20] 8066 7-8-7 **61** oh1........ JamesSullivan 5 61
(Eric Alston) *cl up: disp ld 1/2-way: rdn 2f out: sn drvn and kpt on same pce* **17/2**
1065 6 1¾ **Red Pike (IRE)**[20] 8066 8-9-5 **73**........ GrahamLee 2 66
(Bryan Smart) *trckd ldrs: hdwy over 2f out: rdn and ch over 1f out: sn drvn and wknd* **10/1**
1032 7 2 **Aperitif**[28] 7831 3-9-0 **68**........(v[1]) PJMcDonald 1 55
(Michael Bell) *in tch: rdn along 2f out: sn btn* **7/2**[1]
0125 8 7 **Samovar**[9] 8403 4-9-0 **75**........(b) JonathanFisher(7) 7 36
(Scott Dixon) *chsd ldrs: rdn along over 2f out: sn drvn and wknd* **7/1**
050 9 7 **Somewhere Secret**[12] 8304 5-8-13 **67**........(p) NathanEvans 4 3
(Michael Mullineaux) *a in rr* **8/1**

1m 2.21s (2.01) **Going Correction** +0.75s/f (Yiel) **9 Ran SP% 113.9**
Speed ratings (Par 103): **113,111,110,109,109 106,103,92,80**
CSF £63.92 CT £921.20 TOTE £3.70: £1.70, £5.70, £4.20; EX 72.90 Trifecta £619.00.
Owner Barry Veasey **Bred** Tally-Ho Stud **Trained** Ullingswick, H'fords

FOCUS
The early pace came down the middle in this modest sprint handicap. The winner has been rated back to her best.

8661 GAMBLE RESPONSIBLY WITH MANSIONBET H'CAP 1m 6f
2:50 (2:52) (Class 4) (0-85,83) 3-Y-O+
£6,469 (£1,925; £962; £481; £300; £300) **Stalls** Low

Form RPR
0-11 1 **Goshen (FR)**[138] 3809 3-9-4 **80**........ HectorCrouch 4 97+
(Gary Moore) *trckd ldr: hdwy and cl up 4f out: led 3f out: rdn clr wl over 1f out: easily* **11/10**[1]
1613 2 7 **Theatro (IRE)**[54] 6924 3-9-3 **79**........ GrahamLee 3 84
(Jedd O'Keeffe) *hld up in rr: hdwy 4f out: rdn along to chse ldrs over 2f out: drvn over 1f out: kpt on fnl f: no ch w wnr* **11/2**[3]
3052 3 1½ **Buriram (IRE)**[32] 7683 3-9-6 **82**........ RossaRyan 9 85
(Ralph Beckett) *hld up in rr: stdy hdwy 5f out: trckd ldrs over 3f out: rdn along to chse wnr wl over 1f out: sn drvn and kpt on same pce: lost 2nd towards fin* **9/2**[2]
0663 4 2¼ **Handiwork**[28] 7819 9-10-0 **83**........(p) PaulMulrennan 5 81
(Steve Gollings) *in rr: niggled along 7f out: reminders 1/2-way: outpcd and detached over 4f out: plugged on u.p fnl 2f: nvr a factor* **33/1**
002/ 5 3 **Turning Gold**[196] 7550 5-9-10 **79**........ TonyHamilton 1 73
(Nigel Twiston-Davies) *led: jnd and rdn along over 4f out: hdd 3f out: sn drvn: grad wknd fnl 2f* **20/1**
6034 6 6 **Music Seeker (IRE)**[14] 8260 5-9-4 **80**........(t) ZakWheatley(7) 6 65
(Declan Carroll) *trckd ldrs: pushed along over 4f out: rdn over 3f out: sn wknd* **12/1**
1056 7 6 **Goscote**[45] 7239 4-9-1 **70**........ PaulHanagan 2 47
(Henry Candy) *trckd ldng pair on inner: pushed along over 4f out: rdn over 3f out: sn wknd* **16/1**
0304 8 12 **Polish**[28] 7819 4-9-9 **78**........(p) BenCurtis 7 38
(John Gallagher) *chsd ldrs: rdn along over 4f out: sn wknd (jockey said gelding hung left-handed throughout)* **14/1**

3m 12.71s (6.31) **Going Correction** +0.75s/f (Yiel)
WFA 3 from 4yo+ 7lb **8 Ran SP% 109.1**
Speed ratings (Par 105): **112,108,107,105,104 100,97,90**
CSF £6.54 CT £16.55 TOTE £1.80: £1.10, £1.50, £1.60; EX 6.30 Trifecta £20.70.
Owner Steven Packham **Bred** Christophe Toulorge **Trained** Lower Beeding, W Sussex
■ Albert's Back was withdrawn. Price at time of withdrawal 16/1. Rule 4 does not apply

FOCUS
There was a solid early pace on in this fair staying handicap. Decent form. The second and third have been rated close to form.

8662 MANSIONBET BEST ODDS GUARANTEED NOVICE STKS 1m 6f
3:20 (3:20) (Class 4) 3-Y-O+ **£6,469** (£1,925; £962; £481) **Stalls** Low

Form RPR
1 **Lovely Lou Lou**[11] 3-8-6 0........ DarraghKeenan(3) 4 64+
(John Ryan) *trckd ldr: smooth hdwy to ld 4f out: clr 2f out: kpt on strly: v easily* **5/2**[2]
54 2 10 **Paintball Wizard (IRE)**[74] 6216 3-9-0 0........ ShelleyBirkett 1 51
(Julia Feilden) *trckd ldrs: hdwy over 4f out: chsd wnr 3f out: sn rdn: drvn 2f out: plugged on: no ch w wnr* **14/1**[3]
40 3 1½ **Montelimar**[9] 8398 4-8-11 0........ AndrewBreslin(5) 3 42
(Andrew Crook) *trckd ldng pair: pushed along on inner 4f out: rdn 3f out: drvn over 2f out: sn outpcd* **100/1**
-402 4 hd **Visor**[45] 7240 4-9-7 62........(h) HectorCrouch 2 47
(James Fanshawe) *hld up in rr: hdwy over 5f out: chsd ldng pair over 3f out: sn rdn along: drvn over 2f out: sn btn (trainers rep said, regarding the poor performance, gelding was unsuited by the ground on this occasion)* **2/5**[1]
0 5 31 **Indisposed**[61] 6687 3-9-0 0........ BrettDoyle 5 8
(Mrs Ilka Gansera-Leveque) *led: pushed along and jnd over 4f out: sn hdd & wknd* **28/1**

3m 20.8s (14.40) **Going Correction** +0.75s/f (Yiel)
WFA 3 from 4yo 7lb **5 Ran SP% 111.1**
Speed ratings (Par 105): **88,82,81,81,63**
CSF £30.49 TOTE £2.30: £1.20, £5.40; EX 24.90 Trifecta £155.00.
Owner John Ryan Racing Partnership **Bred** Miss Elizabeth Dent **Trained** Newmarket, Suffolk

FOCUS
A weak staying contest, which proved tactical.

8663 MANSIONBET OFFER DEPOSIT LIMITS H'CAP (FOR GENTLEMAN AMATEUR RIDERS) (DIV I) 1m 2f 50y
3:50 (3:50) (Class 6) (0-60,61) 3-Y-O+
£3,119 (£967; £483; £300; £300; £300) **Stalls** Low

Form RPR
0066 1 **Country'N'Western (FR)**[9] 8414 7-11-2 **60**........ MrGeorgeEddery(5) 7 67
(Robert Eddery) *trckd ldrs: hdwy 4f out: chal over 2f out: rdn to ld wl over 1f out: drvn out* **12/1**
0025 2 1 **Telekinetic**[56] 6855 4-10-7 **46**........ MrRossBirkett 2 51
(Julia Feilden) *led: rdn along and wd st to stands' rail: jnd over 2f out: hdd and drvn wl over 1f out: kpt on u.p fnl f* **10/1**
6161 3 2¼ **Para Queen (IRE)**[9] 8414 3-11-0 **57** 6ex........ MrJamesHarding 5 59+
(Heather Main) *s.i.s and bhd: rapid hdwy after 3f to chse ldrs on wd outside: rdn along and wd st: drvn over 2f out: kpt on u.p fr over 1f out (jockey said filly was slowly away)* **10/11**[1]
2520 4 nse **Apache Blaze**[31] 7732 4-11-8 **61**........(p) MrWilliamEasterby 9 62
(Robyn Brisland) *hld up: hdwy over 4f out: chsd ldrs 3f out: rdn over 2f out: swtchd lft and drvn wl over 1f out: plugged on same pce* **8/1**[3]
5303 5 1½ **Essenaitch (IRE)**[9] 8414 6-11-0 **58**........ MrPhilipThomas(5) 8 56
(David Evans) *trckd ldng pair: hdwy 4f out: rdn along 3f out: drvn over 2f out: grad wknd* **6/1**[2]
5504 6 5 **Frankster (FR)**[84] 5816 6-11-4 **57**........(t) MrPatrickMillman 3 46
(Micky Hammond) *hld up towards rr: smooth hdwy over 4f out: cl up over 3f out: sn chsng ldr: rdn along over 2f out: drvn wl over 1f out: sn wknd (jockey said gelding hung right-handed in the straight)* **16/1**
0503 7 8 **Dolly Dupree**[16] 8205 3-9-10 **46**........ MrOliverDaykin(7) 1 22
(Paul D'Arcy) *hld up towards rr: hdwy on inner and in tch over 3f out: sn rdn along and wknd over 2f out* **8/1**[3]
-000 8 2¼ **New Rhythm**[38] 7489 4-10-0 **46** oh1........ MrConnorWood(7) 10 17
(Alistair Whillans) *a towards rr* **80/1**
0100 9 27 **Mime Dance**[34] 7604 8-10-7 **51**........ MrMatthewJohnson(5) 6
(John Butler) *chsd ldrs: rdn along 4f out: sn wknd* **100/1**
3046 10 1¾ **Be Thankful**[78] 6039 4-10-8 **54**........ MrPatrickBerkins(7) 11
(Martin Keighley) *chsd ldrs: rdn along over 4f out: sn wknd* **33/1**

2m 23.09s (9.69) **Going Correction** +0.75s/f (Yiel)
WFA 3 from 4yo+ 4lb **10 Ran SP% 116.7**
Speed ratings (Par 101): **91,90,88,88,87 83,76,74,53,51**
CSF £124.49 CT £218.23 TOTE £15.10: £2.80, £2.90, £1.10; EX 153.60 Trifecta £606.30.
Owner Robert Eddery **Bred** Capital Pur Sang **Trained** Newmarket, Suffolk

The Form Book Flat 2019, Raceform Ltd, Newbury, RG14 5SJ

FOCUS
The ground played a big part in this moderate handicap, confined to amateur riders.

8664 MANSIONBET OFFER DEPOSIT LIMITS H'CAP (FOR GENTLEMAN AMATEUR RIDERS) (DIV II) 1m 2f 50y
4:20 (4:20) (Class 6) (0-60,60) 3-Y-O+

£3,119 (£967; £483; £300; £300; £300) Stalls Low

Form RPR
0055 1 **Born To Please**[14] 8247 5-10-3 49 ....(p) MrCiaranJones(7) 4 59
(Mark Usher) *hld up: hdwy towards inner over 3f out: chsd clr ldr 2f out: sn rdn: styd on wl fnl f to ld last 75yds* 9/1
0556 2 3/4 **Sociologist (FR)**[8] 8434 4-11-5 58 ....(p) MrSimonWalker 2 67
(Scott Dixon) *trckd ldrs: led 7f out: wd st to stands' rail and sn clr: rdn along 2f out: drvn ent fnl f: hdd and no ex last 75yds* 2/1[1]
2000 3 8 **Lily Ash (IRE)**[20] 8068 6-11-0 53 .... MrPatrickMillman 9 47
(Mike Murphy) *trckd ldrs: hdwy in centre 4f out: rdn along over 2f out: drvn wl over 1f out: kpt on same pce* 9/1
6353 4 2 1/4 **Star Ascending (IRE)**[16] 8186 7-10-12 56 ....(p) MrRyanHolmes(5) 6 46
(Jennie Candlish) *hld up in tch: hdwy in centre 4f out: rdn along to chse ldrs over 2f out: sn drvn and one pce* 11/2[2]
000 5 2 1/4 **Jo's Girl (IRE)**[35] 7583 4-10-8 54 .... MrJWaggott(7) 3 40
(Micky Hammond) *awkward s: s.i.s and bhd: wd st to stands' side: rdn over 3f out: kpt on u.p fnl 2f: n.d* 25/1
-040 6 2 **So You Thought (USA)**[130] 4109 5-10-13 57(w) MrEireannCagney(5) 10 40
(Simon West) *led 3f: prom: styd centre home st: rdn along 3f out: drvn 2f out: sn wknd* 11/1
5054 7 1 1/4 **The Brora Pobbles**[29] 7783 4-10-0 46 oh1 .... MrConnorWood(7) 1 26
(Alistair Whillans) *hld up towards rr: hdwy on inner 4f out: chsd ldrs 3f out: sn rdn and no imp* 6/1[3]
3063 8 1 3/4 **Manfadh (IRE)**[27] 7858 4-11-7 60 .... MrAlexEdwards 7 37
(Kevin Frost) *chsd ldrs: rdn along 4f out: wknd 3f out* 7/1
000- 9 39 **If We Can Can**[470] 5049 4-11-0 58 .... MrTDurrell(5) 8
(Olly Williams) *prom: pushed along centre 4f out: rdn 3f out: sn wknd* 66/1
0040 10 22 **Inflexiball**[20] 8072 7-10-7 46 oh1 .... MrJamesHarding 5
(John Mackie) *chsd ldrs on outer: wd st: sn rdn along and wknd (jockey said mare stopped quickly; trainers rep could offer no explanation for the poor performance)* 16/1

2m 22.43s (9.03) **Going Correction** +0.75s/f (Yiel) 10 Ran SP% 115.1
Speed ratings (Par 101): **93,92,86,84,82 80,79,78,47,29**
CSF £26.93 CT £170.67 TOTE £11.10: £2.30, £1.50, £3.10; EX 34.90 Trifecta £370.20.
Owner The Mark Usher Racing Club **Bred** P H Davies **Trained** Upper Lambourn, Berks

FOCUS
The first pair came right away in this second division of the weak amateur riders' handicap.
T/Plt: £108.10 to a £1 stake. Pool: £44,362.35 - 299.57 winning units. T/Qpdt: £18.90 to a £1 stake. Pool: £4,094.12 - 159.61 winning units. **Joe Rowntree**

8501 WOLVERHAMPTON (A.W) (L-H)
Wednesday, October 30

OFFICIAL GOING: Tapeta: standard
Wind: Light against Weather: Cloudy

8665 LADBROKES HOME OF THE ODDS BOOST NURSERY H'CAP 7f 36y (Tp)
4:50 (4:52) (Class 4) (0-80,80) 2-Y-O

£4,463 (£1,328; £663; £400; £400; £400) Stalls High

Form RPR
6016 1 **Blausee (IRE)**[14] 8252 2-9-0 73 .... StevieDonohoe 6 76
(Philip McBride) *hld up: swtchd rt over 1f out: gd hdwy fnl f: str run to ld post* 9/1
4205 2 shd **One Hart (IRE)**[30] 7763 2-9-7 80 .... PJMcDonald 7 83
(Mark Johnston) *led: rdn and edgd rt over 1f out: hdd post* 10/1
5651 3 nk **Good Job Power (IRE)**[64] 6563 2-9-2 75 .... SilvestreDeSousa 2 77
(Richard Hannon) *chsd ldrs: wnt 2nd over 1f out: rdn and ev ch ins fnl f: unable qck nr fin* 7/2[2]
1105 4 3/4 **Nirodha (IRE)**[34] 7620 2-8-12 74 ....(p) SeanDavis(3) 5 74
(Amy Murphy) *prom: rdn over 2f out: edgd lft ins fnl f: styd on* 33/1
1031 5 nk **Mischief Star**[12] 8318 2-9-7 80 .... DavidNolan 12 79
(David O'Meara) *hdwy on outer over 4f out: rdn over 1f out: no ex towards fin* 11/4[1]
0464 6 hd **Richard R H B (IRE)**[14] 8259 2-8-7 66 .... LukeMorris 11 65
(David Loughnane) *hld up: racd keenly: hdwy on outer 1/2-way: rdn over 1f out: hung lft ins fnl f: styd on* 16/1
6340 7 shd **Fantasy Believer (IRE)**[34] 7612 2-9-1 74 .... KieranShoemark 9 73
(Charles Hills) *s.i.s: hld up: r.o ins fnl f: nt rch ldrs (jockey said colt was slowly away)* 8/1[3]
432 8 1 **Anfield Girl (IRE)**[43] 7297 2-8-11 70 .... JaneElliott 1 66
(Tom Dascombe) *s.i.s: hld up: r.o ins fnl f: nt trble ldrs (jockey said filly was slowly away)* 12/1
3355 9 1/2 **Call Me Katie (IRE)**[27] 7832 2-9-4 77 ....(b[1]) KieranO'Neill 4 72
(John Gosden) *s.i.s: hld up: styd on u.p ins fnl f: nt rch ldrs* 11/1
6345 10 1 1/4 **Striding Edge (IRE)**[43] 7315 2-8-9 68 .... FrannyNorton 3 60
(Mark Johnston) *pushed along and prom: rdn over 1f out: no ex ins fnl f* 16/1
2030 11 6 **When Comes Here (IRE)**[48] 7119 2-9-1 77 ....(p[1]) ThomasGreatrex(3) 8 54
(David Loughnane) *racd keenly in 2nd tl shkn up over 1f out: wknd ins fnl f* 12/1

1m 28.34s (-0.46) **Going Correction** -0.10s/f (Stan) 11 Ran SP% 117.5
Speed ratings (Par 97): **98,97,97,96,96 96,96,94,94,92 86**
CSF £95.62 CT £384.43 TOTE £13.40: £2.90, £2.60, £1.50; EX 98.60 Trifecta £721.40.
Owner Maelor Racing **Bred** Robert Allcock **Trained** Newmarket, Suffolk

FOCUS
A competitive nursery and they finished in a bit of a heap, but the winner came from the clouds.

8666 BOMBARDIER BRITISH HOPPED AMBER BEER H'CAP 7f 36y (Tp)
5:20 (5:21) (Class 6) (0-55,59) 3-Y-O+

£2,781 (£827; £413; £400; £400; £400) Stalls High

Form RPR
1 **Shamarouski (IRE)**[106] 5033 3-9-4 54 .... PaulMulrennan 6 61+
(Louise Allan) *chsd ldr tl led over 2f out: shkn up and edgd rt over 1f out: rdn and wandered ins fnl f: r.o wl* 10/3[2]
2056 2 1 3/4 **Silk Mill Blue**[5] 8530 5-9-0 48 ....(p) LewisEdmunds 8 52
(Richard Whitaker) *fly-jmpd s: hld up: hdwy on outer over 2f out: chsd wnr over 1f out: rdn and edgd lft ins fnl f: styd on same pce towards fin* 8/1
4302 3 2 **Puchita (IRE)**[6] 8502 4-9-3 51 .... CamHardie 3 50
(Antony Brittain) *chsd ldrs: rdn and edgd rt over 1f out: styd on same pce wl ins fnl f* 3/1[1]
5002 4 1/2 **Itmakesyouthink**[8] 8417 5-9-6 54 ....(h) ShaneKelly 10 52
(Mark Loughnane) *s.i.s: hld up: racd keenly: swtchd rt over 1f out: rdn and r.o ins fnl f: nt rch ldrs (jockey said gelding anticipated the start and missed the break as a result)* 7/1[3]
0606 5 1 **Darwina**[15] 8234 3-8-10 46 .... JamesSullivan 11 40
(Alistair Whillans) *s.i.s: hdwy on outer over 1f out: styd on ins fnl f: nt rch ldrs* 22/1
0524 6 1 1/2 **Field Of Vision (IRE)**[9] 8408 6-9-3 51 ....(b) LukeMorris 5 43
(John Flint) *prom: rdn 3f out: styd on same pce fr over 1f out* 10/1
5500 7 1/2 **Elusif (IRE)**[18] 8123 4-9-4 52 .... AdrianMcCarthy 4 42
(Shaun Keightley) *hld up: rdn over 1f out: nt trble ldrs* 25/1
646 8 2 **My Law**[22] 8009 3-9-5 55 .... PJMcDonald 9 39
(Jim Boyle) *rrer s and bhd: nvr nrr* 11/1
6050 9 hd **Majdool (IRE)**[12] 8306 6-9-7 55 ....(e) DavidNolan 12 40
(Noel Wilson) *hld up: hdwy on outer over 4f out: rdn over 1f out: wknd wl ins fnl f (jockey said gelding lost it's action in the home straight)* 9/1
0056 10 nk **Kyllachy Castle**[13] 8295 3-8-10 46 oh1 .... TomEaves 1 29
(Lynn Siddall) *hld up in tch: rdn over 1f out: wknd ins fnl f* 12/1
1100 11 10 **Jazz Legend (USA)**[20] 8071 6-9-6 54 .... KieranO'Neill 2 13
(Mandy Rowland) *racd keenly: led 5f: wknd and eased ins fnl f* 33/1

1m 27.93s (-0.87) **Going Correction** -0.10s/f (Stan)
WFA 3 from 4yo+ 2lb 11 Ran SP% 117.9
Speed ratings (Par 101): **100,98,95,95,94 92,91,89,89,88 77**
CSF £29.66 CT £89.08 TOTE £4.40: £3.00, £2.10, £1.20; EX 37.50 Trifecta £150.60.
Owner Miss Louise Allan **Bred** Miss Philippa Proctor Quinn **Trained** Exning, Suffolk

FOCUS
A moderate affair but notable for a punt being landed.

8667 BOMBARDIER GOLDEN BEER H'CAP 1m 142y (Tp)
5:50 (5:50) (Class 6) (0-55,59) 3-Y-O+

£2,781 (£827; £413; £400; £400; £400) Stalls Low

Form RPR
3246 1 **Star Of Valour (IRE)**[16] 8186 4-9-7 55 .... PaulMulrennan 10 61
(Lynn Siddall) *hld up: swtchd wd and hdwy over 1f out: rdn and edgd lft ins fnl f: r.o to ld post* 9/2[3]
3322 2 hd **Troop**[12] 8301 4-9-6 54 ....(p) FrannyNorton 12 60
(Ann Duffield) *chsd ldrs on outer: rdn over 2f out: led ins fnl f: hdd post* 7/2[1]
4453 3 2 1/4 **Four Mile Bridge (IRE)**[13] 8299 3-8-12 53 ....(p) ThomasGreatrex(3) 5 54
(Mark Usher) *prom: lost pl 7f out: hdwy on outer over 1f out: rdn and edgd lft ins fnl f: styd on (jockey said gelding hung badly right)* 4/1[2]
1241 4 2 1/4 **Mabo**[8] 8416 4-9-11 59 5ex ....(b) RossaRyan 2 55
(Grace Harris) *s.i.s: sn rcvrd to chse ldrs: rdn and ev ch ins fnl f: no ex towards fin* 7/1
5000 5 shd **Sumner Beach**[13] 8299 5-9-4 52 .... BenRobinson 6 48
(Brian Ellison) *hld up: hdwy over 1f out: sn rdn and edgd lft: styd on same pce fnl f* 20/1
0004 6 shd **Ebbisham (IRE)**[53] 6977 6-9-2 55 ....(v) TobyEley(5) 13 51
(John Mackie) *s.i.s: pushed along early in rr: hmpd over 7f out: r.o ins fnl f: nvr nrr (jockey said gelding was slowly away)* 14/1
0636 7 3/4 **Sea Shack**[44] 7281 5-8-11 50 ....(t) ScottMcCullagh(5) 1 44
(Julia Feilden) *led: rdn over 1f out: hdd ins fnl f: wknd towards fin* 14/1
4050 8 1/2 **Padura Brave**[14] 8254 3-9-2 54 ....(p) StevieDonohoe 9 47
(Mark Usher) *prom early: sn stdd and lost pl: swtchd lft over 7f out: n.d after* 28/1
4055 9 shd **Steal The Scene (IRE)**[13] 8299 7-9-5 53 ....(tp) PJMcDonald 4 54+
(Kevin Frost) *trckd ldrs: nt clr run fr over 1f out: nt rcvr (jockey said gelding was denied a clear run in the final furlong)* 8/1
0000 10 nk **Arrowzone**[7] 8466 8-8-13 52 ....(t[1]) AledBeech(5) 3 44
(Katy Price) *chsd ldrs: lft 2nd over 4f out: rdn and ev ch 1f out: wknd wl ins fnl f* 50/1
206 11 1 3/4 **Farrdhana**[170] 2677 3-9-3 55 ....(t[1]) BenCurtis 7 44
(Phillip Makin) *s.i.s: hdwy: nt clr run and hung lft over 1f out: sn rdn: wknd wl ins fnl f* 20/1
0541 12 90 **Maisie Moo**[14] 8256 3-9-2 54 .... ShaneKelly 11
(Shaun Keightley) *racd keenly: wnt 2nd 8f out tl sddle slipped and swtchd wd over 4f out: virtually p.u (jockey said saddle slipped)* 12/1

1m 49.07s (-1.03) **Going Correction** -0.10s/f (Stan)
WFA 3 from 4yo+ 4lb 12 Ran SP% 120.0
Speed ratings (Par 101): **100,99,97,95,95 95,94,94,94,94 92,12**
CSF £19.88 CT £70.47 TOTE £6.50: £2.50, £1.10, £3.40; EX 26.50 Trifecta £131.10.
Owner Jimmy Kay **Bred** Darley **Trained** Colton, N Yorks

FOCUS
A moderate handicap but the first two finished clear of the rest.

8668 BETWAY (S) STKS 5f 21y (Tp)
6:20 (6:20) (Class 5) 3-6-Y-O

£3,428 (£1,020; £509; £400; £400; £400) Stalls Low

Form RPR
2266 1 **Tan**[20] 8066 5-9-2 62 .... AlistairRawlinson 1 69
(Michael Appleby) *rrd s: rcvrd to ld over 4f out: rdn over 1f out: r.o* 5/2[2]
4130 2 1 1/2 **More Than Likely**[35] 7568 3-9-1 74 .... ShaneKelly 2 64
(Richard Hughes) *led: hdd over 4f out: chsd ldrs: swtchd rt 1/2-way: chsd wnr 2f out: rdn ins fnl f: no imp* 4/11[1]
50 3 2 1/4 **Celerity (IRE)**[18] 8119 5-8-6 45 ....(v) SeamusCronin(5) 3 51
(Lisa Williamson) *chsd ldrs: carried wd 1/2-way: edgd lft fr over 1f out: styd on same pce fnl f* 33/1
400 4 2 3/4 **Midnight Guest (IRE)**[89] 5629 4-8-11 51 ....(v) RossaRyan 6 41
(David Evans) *hld up: rdn over 1f out: wknd ins fnl f* 28/1[3]
5006 5 nk **Lope De Loop (IRE)**[15] 4764 4-8-11 42 ....(h) CamHardie 7 40
(Aytach Sadik) *chsd wnr 4f out tl rdn 2f out: wknd fnl f (vet said filly lost it's right fore shoe)* 100/1
30-0 6 3/4 **Mocead Cappall**[39] 7468 4-8-6 45 .... TobyEley(5) 4 37
(John Holt) *prom: plld hrd: sn lost pl: n.d after (jockey said filly ran too free)* 50/1

1m 1.27s (-0.63) **Going Correction** -0.10s/f (Stan) 6 Ran SP% 111.2
Speed ratings: **101,98,94,90,90 88**
CSF £3.78 TOTE £2.80: £1.30, £1.10; EX 5.30 Trifecta £9.00.The winner was sold for £7,000.
Owner Stephen Louch **Bred** Whatton Manor Stud **Trained** Oakham, Rutland

FOCUS
An uncompetitive seller.

8669 BETWAY H'CAP — 1m 1f 104y (Tp)
6:50 (6:52) (Class 6) (0-65,65) 3-Y-O+
£2,781 (£827; £413; £400; £400; £400) Stalls Low

Form RPR
4256 1 **First Dance (IRE)**33 7650 5-9-6 62 JamesSullivan 6 69
(Tom Tate) *hld up in tch: shkn up over 1f out carried lft and led wl ins fnl f: r.o: comf* 9/1
012 2 3/4 **Charlie Arthur (IRE)**13 8293 3-8-13 62 FinleyMarsh(3) 2 68
(Richard Hughes) *chsd ldrs: nt clr run over 2f out: rdn and ev ch wl ins fnl f: styd on same pce towards fin* 7/2[1]
1254 3 1 **Billy Roberts (IRE)**41 7379 6-9-6 62 PaulMulrennan 12 66
(Richard Whitaker) *chsd ldr 8f out tl led over 2f out: shkn up and edgd rt over 1f out: rdn and hung lft ins fnl f: sn hung rt and hdd: styd on same pce (jockey said gelding hung both left and right-handed in the home straight)* 9/2[2]
6600 4 hd **Velvet Vision**99 5271 4-9-5 61 LukeMorris 1 65
(Mrs Ilka Gansera-Leveque) *s.i.s: racd keenly and hdwy over 6f out: rdn over 1f out: r.o* 7/1[3]
312 5 1/2 **Enzo (IRE)**53 6977 4-9-7 63 JoeyHaynes 13 65
(John Butler) *s.i.s: hld up: hdwy on outer over 1f out: r.o: nt rch ldrs* 10/1
1150 6 nk **Compass Point**34 7609 4-9-6 62 KieranO'Neill 7 64
(Robyn Brisland) *prom: racd keenly: rdn over 1f out: carried lft and no ex wl ins fnl f* 16/1
-000 7 hd **Mrs Hoo (IRE)**28 7829 3-9-2 65 SeanDavis(3) 3 66
(Richard Fahey) *led early: lost pl over 8f out: pushed along over 5f out: rdn over 2f out: r.o u.p wl ins fnl f* 50/1
0316 8 nk **Maldonado (FR)**36 7544 5-8-12 59 ScottMcCullagh(5) 9 60
(Michael Easterby) *s.i.s: hld up: hdwy on outer over 2f out: rdn over 1f out: hung lft ins fnl f: styd on (jockey said gelding was slowly away and hung left throughout)* 12/1
4044 9 3/4 **Thawry**11 8348 4-9-2 58 CamHardie 10 57
(Antony Brittain) *pushed along early in rr: hld up: running on whn nt clr run ins fnl f: nt trble ldrs* 17/2
0505 10 3/4 **Bell Heather (IRE)**32 7682 6-9-4 63 (p) ThomasGreatrex(3) 11 61
(Patrick Morris) *pushed along early in rr: hdwy over 7f out: rdn over 1f out: no ex ins fnl f* 16/1
550 11 1 **The Grey Goat (IRE)**13 8290 3-9-5 65 AdrianMcCarthy 8 61
(Peter Charalambous) *chsd ldrs: rdn over 2f out: nt clr run and no ex ins fnl f* 20/1
000 12 3 1/2 **High Gloss**21 8013 3-9-3 63 DanielMuscutt 5 52
(James Fanshawe) *s.i.s: hld up: racd keenly: rdn over 1f out: wknd ins fnl f* 18/1
6630 13 1 1/4 **Cheap Jack**216 1385 3-9-2 62 RaulDaSilva 4 49
(Ronald Thompson) *led: rdn and hdd over 2f out: wknd fnl f* 66/1

2m 0.2s (-0.60) **Going Correction** -0.10s/f (Stan)
WFA 3 from 4yo+ 4lb 13 Ran SP% 115.5
Speed ratings (Par 101): **98,97,96,96,95 95,95,95,94,93 92,89,88**
CSF £38.44 CT £162.89 TOTE £11.40: £2.00, £2.20, £2.80; EX 47.90 Trifecta £196.60.
Owner T T Racing **Bred** Mount Coote Stud **Trained** Tadcaster, N Yorks
FOCUS
This was fairly steadily run and turned into a bit of a dash off the home turn.

8670 BETWAY CASINO H'CAP — 1m 4f 51y (Tp)
7:20 (7:21) (Class 6) (0-55,55) 3-Y-O+
£2,781 (£827; £413; £400; £400; £400) Stalls Low

Form RPR
-500 1 **Mrs Ivy**22 8000 3-8-12 52 (b) RossaRyan 8 59
(Ralph Beckett) *pushed along early in rr: hdwy on outer over 2f out: rdn to ld over 1f out: hung rt wl ins fnl f: styd on* 15/2[3]
4400 2 1/2 **Lyford (IRE)**8 8423 4-9-5 53 (p) PJMcDonald 12 58
(Alistair Whillans) *hld up in tch: led 2f out: rdn and hdd over 1f out: ev ch wl ins fnl f: styd on* 12/1
-031 3 1/2 **Mamdood (IRE)**8 8423 5-8-12 49 (vt) MeganNicholls(3) 1 53
(Stef Keniry) *hld up: nt clr run over 3f out: swtchd rt and hdwy over 2f out: rdn over 1f out: r.o* 8/11[1]
1142 4 1 1/4 **About Glory**27 7857 5-9-5 53 (bt) JamieGormley 11 55+
(Iain Jardine) *hld up: hdwy on outer 4f out: rdn over 1f out: styd on same pce ins fnl f* 3/1[2]
0400 5 4 1/2 **Pot Luck**76 6117 3-8-8 48 JaneElliott 7 44
(Sharon Watt) *prom: nt clr run and lost pl over 3f out: rallied over 2f out: rdn over 1f out: hung rt and wknd ins fnl f* 80/1
5600 6 7 **Airplane (IRE)**23 7956 4-9-6 54 TomEaves 10 38
(Paul Collins) *plld hrd and prom: led over 9f out tl over 7f out: led again over 6f out: rdn and hdd 2f out: wknd fnl f* 28/1
6000 7 10 **Raven's Raft (IRE)**11 8348 4-9-6 54 StevieDonohoe 2 22
(David Loughnane) *led: hdd over 9f out: led again over 7f out tl over 6f out: rdn and wknd over 2f out* 12/1
-000 8 1/2 **War Drums**14 8246 5-9-2 55 (p[1]) AndrewBreslin(5) 5 22
(Alexandra Dunn) *s.i.s: a in rr: bhd fnl 5f* 28/1
00-0 9 9 **Bunker Hill Lad**14 8270 4-9-2 50 AlistairRawlinson 4 3
(Michael Appleby) *trckd ldrs: rdn over 3f out: wknd over 2f out (jockey said gelding was never travelling)* 100/1
2000 10 37 **Thecornishbarron (IRE)**26 7873 7-8-13 47 CamHardie 9
(Aytach Sadik) *chsd ldr 2f: remained handy tl rdn over 3f out: sn wknd (jockey said gelding hung left throughout)* 80/1

2m 39.22s (-1.58) **Going Correction** -0.10s/f (Stan)
WFA 3 from 4yo+ 6lb 10 Ran SP% 120.4
Speed ratings (Par 101): **101,100,100,99,96 91,85,84,78,54**
CSF £89.39 CT £144.34 TOTE £8.00: £2.30, £2.40, £1.02; EX 73.30 Trifecta £194.30.
Owner Make A Circle I **Bred** Al-Baha Bloodstock **Trained** Kimpton, Hants
FOCUS
A moderate handicap.

8671 BETWAY HEED YOUR HUNCH NOVICE STKS — 1m 4f 51y (Tp)
7:50 (7:51) (Class 5) 3-Y-O+ £3,428 (£1,020; £509; £254) Stalls Low

Form RPR
5 1 **Bye Bye Lady (FR)**21 8013 3-8-11 0 SilvestreDeSousa 2 75
(Andrew Balding) *chsd ldr: shkn up over 3f out: rdn over 1f out: styd on to ld wl ins fnl f: hung lft towards fin* 3/1[2]
06 2 1 **Raining Fire (IRE)**11 8351 3-9-2 0 (h[1]) DanielMuscutt 4 78
(James Fanshawe) *trckd ldrs: shkn up over 3f out: swtchd lft over 1f out: styd on to go 2nd wl ins fnl f* 6/1[3]
10 3 1 1/4 **Kesia (IRE)**102 5190 3-9-4 0 KieranO'Neill 1 78
(John Gosden) *led: rdn and edgd rt over 1f out: hdd and no ex wl ins fnl f* 1/2[1]
4 19 **Yer Tekkin Mick** 4-9-8 0 AlistairRawlinson 5 45
(Michael Appleby) *hld up in tch: plld hrd: rdn and hung lft over 2f out: sn wknd (jockey said gelding hung left)* 66/1

2m 37.5s (-3.30) **Going Correction** -0.10s/f (Stan)
WFA 3 from 4yo 6lb 4 Ran SP% 107.4
Speed ratings (Par 103): **107,106,105,92**
CSF £17.57 TOTE £3.50; EX 13.80 Trifecta £15.30.
Owner King Power Racing Co Ltd **Bred** Jean-Pierre Dubois **Trained** Kingsclere, Hants
FOCUS
No more than a fair novice. The level is fluid.

8672 BETWAY NOVICE STKS — 5f 21y (Tp)
8:20 (8:21) (Class 5) 3-Y-O+ £3,428 (£1,020; £509; £254) Stalls Low

Form RPR
2043 1 **Great Suspense**14 8268 3-9-5 59 DavidNolan 3 70
(David O'Meara) *prom: chsd ldr 1/2-way: led ins fnl f: hung lft and rdn clr* 13/8[2]
34 2 3 1/4 **Oh So Nice**79 6023 3-9-0 0 BrettDoyle 7 53
(Tony Carroll) *led: rdn and hdd ins fnl f: no ex* 28/1
555- 3 nk **Tomshalfbrother**371 8532 3-9-5 66 LukeMorris 6 57
(Robert Cowell) *hld up: hdwy 2f out: rdn over 1f out: styd on same pce fnl f* 9/2[3]
04 4 1 1/2 **Maqboola (USA)**23 7976 3-9-0 0 ShaneKelly 1 47
(Richard Hughes) *s.i.s: outpcd: swtchd lft and r.o ins fnl f: nvr nrr* 12/1
222 5 1/2 **Vandella (IRE)**119 4496 3-9-0 74 BenCurtis 2 45
(David Evans) *sn outpcd: hdwy on outer over 2f out: rdn over 1f out: no ex* 11/8[1]
05 6 9 **Auntie June**58 6802 3-9-0 0 KieranO'Neill 4 12
(Roy Brotherton) *hung lft: chsd ldr to 1/2-way: rdn and wknd over 1f out* 100/1
604 7 3/4 **Del's Edge**64 6561 3-8-11 25 MitchGodwin(3) 5 10
(Christopher Mason) *s.i.s: outpcd* 100/1

1m 0.69s (-1.21) **Going Correction** -0.10s/f (Stan) 7 Ran SP% 111.5
Speed ratings (Par 103): **105,99,99,96,96 81,80**
CSF £37.01 TOTE £2.50: £1.50, £10.70; EX 34.60 Trifecta £119.80.
Owner Clive Washbourn **Bred** Peter Winkworth **Trained** Upper Helmsley, N Yorks
FOCUS
The well-backed winner got the job done easily enough. The second has been rated in line with her debut form for now.
T/Plt: £18.60 to a £1 stake. Pool: £62,933.39 - 2,469.03 winning units T/Qpdt: £2.90 to a £1 stake. Pool: £7,671.75 - 1,892.84 winning units **Colin Roberts**

8673 - 8688a (Foreign Racing) - See Raceform Interactive

8546 CHELMSFORD (A.W) (L-H)
Thursday, October 31

OFFICIAL GOING: Polytrack: standard
Wind: light, across Weather: dry

8689 BET AT TOTESPORT.COM CLASSIFIED STKS — 7f (P)
4:55 (4:55) (Class 6) 3-Y-O+
£3,105 (£924; £461; £400; £400; £400) Stalls Low

Form RPR
0003 1 **The King's Steed**14 8295 6-9-2 50 (bt) KieranShoemark 6 57
(Shaun Lycett) *wnt lft leaving stalls: mde all: rdn over 1f out: styd on wl ins fnl f* 9/2[2]
0622 2 1 3/4 **Aiguillette**15 8249 3-9-0 48 HollieDoyle 7 51
(Gary Moore) *chsd wnr thrght: effrt over 1f out: sn rdn: edgd rt and kpt on same pce ins fnl f (jockey said gelding hung right-handed throughout)* 7/4[1]
0605 3 1 1/4 **Atwaar**28 7838 3-8-9 44 FayeMcManoman(5) 10 50+
(Charles Smith) *hld up in tch: nt clr run 2f out: swtchd lft and effrt on inner over 1f out: chsd ldng pair ent fnl f: kpt on same pce* 33/1
3500 4 3/4 **Quick Recovery**35 7606 4-9-2 49 CharlieBennett 3 47
(Jim Boyle) *in tch in midfield: effrt ent fnl 2f: edgd lft in 4th and kpt on same pce ins fnl f (jockey said filly hung left-handed under pressure)* 9/1
6006 5 3 **Dalness Express**15 8256 6-8-9 41 (bt) KateLeahy(7) 1 39
(Archie Watson) *trckd ldrs: effrt over 1f out: fnd little and sn btn: wknd ins fnl f* 8/1
0005 6 3/4 **Lily Of Year (FR)**23 8008 4-8-9 45 (p[1]) MichaelPitt(7) 4 38
(Denis Coakley) *taken down early: s.i.s: detached in last: clsd and in tch 1/2-way: effrt over 1f out: no imp* 8/1
2500 7 3 3/4 **Tavener**24 7961 7-9-2 49 (p) AlistairRawlinson 5 28
(David C Griffiths) *wnt lft and hmpd leaving stalls: hld up in rr of main gp: effrt u.p over 1f out: sn no imp and wknd ins fnl f* 12/1
000- 8 1 **Crakadawn**304 9771 3-9-0 39 JoeyHaynes 2 24
(Chelsea Banham) *rrd as stalls opened: t.k.h: hld up wl in tch in midfield: rdn over 2f out: sn struggling and lost pl wl over 1f out: wknd fnl f (jockey said filly reared leaving the stalls)* 20/1
5040 9 4 1/2 **Caledonian Gold**5 8547 6-8-9 43 GavinAshton(7) 8 13
(Lisa Williamson) *taken down early: hld up in tch in midfield: swtchd rt and hdwy 5f out: rdn and lost pl over 2f out: bhd ins fnl f* 66/1
P/03 10 1 1/4 **Ultimat Power (IRE)**5 8547 5-8-11 44 SeamusCronin(5) 9 10
(Frank Bishop) *chsd ldrs: rdn and lost pl over 2f out: wknd and bhd ins fnl f (trainer's rep said the race may have come too soon having run at Chelmsford 5 days ago)* 6/1[3]

1m 26.43s (-0.77) **Going Correction** -0.125s/f (Stan)
WFA 3 from 4yo+ 2lb 10 Ran SP% 117.9
Speed ratings (Par 101): **99,97,95,94,91 90,86,85,79,78**
CSF £12.70 TOTE £4.70: £1.60, £1.10, £9.60; EX 13.90 Trifecta £180.30.
Owner D Gilbert, J Lancaster, G Wills **Bred** Littleton Stud **Trained** Leafield, Oxon
FOCUS
A weak affair dominated by the winner from the front.

8690 TOTEPOOL CASHBACK CLUB AT TOTESPORT.COM CLAIMING STKS — 7f (P)
5:25 (5:27) (Class 6) 3-Y-O+
£3,105 (£924; £461; £400; £400; £400) Stalls Low

Form RPR
0604 1 **Tomily (IRE)**9 8428 5-10-0 81 AdamKirby 2 85
(David O'Meara) *chsd ldr early: styd trcking ldrs: swtchd rt and effrt over 1f out: rdn to ld 1f out: drvn and styd on wl ins fnl f* 4/1[2]

6666 **2** ¾ **Onebaba (IRE)**[7] 8496 3-8-13 70..............................(b¹) MeganNicholls(3) 8 72
(Tony Carroll) *wnt lft and bmpd s: sn rcvrd and chsd ldrs: effrt over 1f out: edgd lft 1f out: kpt edging lft but chsd wnr 100yds out: kpt on (jockey said gelding lugged left-handed inside the final furlong)* **16/1**

3105 **3** ¾ **Love Dreams (IRE)**[21] 8062 5-10-0 87..............................(p) NicolaCurrie 7 81
(Jamie Osborne) *sn chsd ldr: effrt 2f out: rdn and nt qckn over 1f out: kpt on same pce ins fnl f* **6/4¹**

2040 **4** nk **Shady McCoy (USA)**[21] 8062 9-10-0 85.................. StevieDonohoe 6 80
(Ian Williams) *stdd and jostled leaving stalls: hld up in tch: effrt over 1f out: sme hdwy whn nt clr run and swtchd lft 1f out: kpt on ins fnl f* **9/2³**

0400 **5** 1 **Highland Acclaim (IRE)**[7] 8496 8-9-6 71..............(h) KieranShoemark 5 70
(David O'Meara) *led: rdn and edgd lft over 1f out: hdd 1f out: no ex and lost 2nd 100yds out: wknd towards fin* **33/1**

6400 **6** 2¾ **Fuwairt (IRE)**[30] 7789 7-9-3 76.............................. ThomasGreatrex(3) 4 65
(David Loughnane) *stdd and swtchd lft leaving stalls: hld up in tch: effrt on inner whn nt clr run and hmpd over 1f out: sn swtchd rt: no imp fnl f* **8/1**

0500 **7** 1¾ **Mardle**[22] 8024 3-9-8 78..............................(p¹) CliffordLee 3 61
(K R Burke) *in tch in midfield: rdn over 2f out: sn struggling and outpcd: wl hld and plugged on same pce fr over 1f out* **8/1**

0400 **8** 11 **Gold Hunter (IRE)**[17] 8199 9-8-8 63..............................(vt¹) HollieDoyle 1 17+
(Steve Flook) *restless and rrng in stalls: v.s.a and lost many l: grad rcvrd and in tch 1/2-way: swtchd rt and rdn over 2f out: sn struggling: wl bhd fnl f (jockey said gelding was restless in the stalls and was slowly away as a result)* **14/1**

1m 26.72s (-0.48) **Going Correction** -0.125s/f (Stan)
WFA 3 from 5yo+ 2lb **8** Ran SP% **115.9**
Speed ratings (Par 101): **97,96,95,94,93 90,88,76**
CSF £64.36 TOTE £4.40: £1.30, £4.70, £1.20; EX 37.50 Trifecta £209.80.Love Dreams was claimed by Michael Blake for £12,000; Tomily claimed by Mr A. G. Newcombe for £12,000
Owner Thoroughbred British Racing **Bred** D J Anderson **Trained** Upper Helmsley, N Yorks
■ Stewards' Enquiry : Kieran Shoemark cautioned: careless riding

FOCUS
They finished in a bit of a heap in this claimer.

8691 EXTRA PLACES AT TOTESPORT.COM H'CAP 7f (P)
5:55 (5:57) (Class 4) (0-80,80) 3-Y-O+
£5,433 (£1,617; £808; £404; £400; £400) Stalls Low

Form RPR
4550 **1** **Reeves**[51] 7049 3-9-7 80.............................. AlistairRawlinson 6 88
(Robert Cowell) *pressed ldr tl rdn to ld over 1f out: kpt on wl u.p ins fnl f* **7/2²**

3512 **2** ½ **Zafaranah (USA)**[17] 8197 5-9-7 78.............................. AdamKirby 1 85
(Pam Sly) *trckd ldrs: effrt wl over 1f out: chsd wnr 1f out: drvn and pressing wnr ins fnl f: kpt on but a hld* **7/4¹**

4330 **3** 3¾ **Rose Berry**[12] 8349 5-9-7 78..............................(h) SilvestreDeSousa 2 75
(Charlie Wallis) *stdd and flashed tail leaving stalls: hld up in tch in last pair: effrt and nt clr run over 1f out: chsd clr ldng pair ins fnl f: no imp* **8/1**

4254 **4** ¾ **Hunni**[26] 7901 4-8-10 70.............................. ThomasGreatrex(3) 3 65
(Tom Clover) *short of room leaving stalls: in tch in last pair: swtchd lft 5f out: effrt over 1f out: no imp fnl f* **4/1³**

1053 **5** ¾ **Global Destination (IRE)**[32] 7731 3-8-12 71.................. BenCurtis 4 63
(Ed Dunlop) *t.k.h: chsd ldrs: unable qck u.p over 1f out: wknd ins fnl f* **7/1**

0600 **6** 1¾ **Quiet Endeavour (IRE)**[14] 8289 3-9-7 80..............(b) NicolaCurrie 5 67
(George Baker) *sn led: rdn and hdd over 1f out: no ex and wknd ins fnl f* **9/1**

1m 25.44s (-1.76) **Going Correction** -0.125s/f (Stan)
WFA 3 from 4yo+ 2lb **6** Ran SP% **112.2**
Speed ratings (Par 105): **105,104,100,99,98 96**
CSF £10.07 TOTE £3.90: £2.00, £1.70; EX 9.80 Trifecta £59.70.
Owner T W Morley **Bred** Bearstone Stud Ltd **Trained** Six Mile Bottom, Cambs

FOCUS
The first two finished nicely clear in this fair handicap. The second has been rated as backing up her latest effort and this is in line with the better view of her previous form.

8692 IRISH LOTTO AT TOTESPORT.COM H'CAP 1m 2f (P)
6:25 (6:27) (Class 4) (0-80,79) 3-Y-O+
£5,433 (£1,617; £808; £404; £400; £400) Stalls Low

Form RPR
014 **1** **Champs De Reves**[29] 7816 4-9-1 73.................. MeganNicholls(3) 11 80
(Michael Blake) *hld up towards rr: hdwy on outer into midfield 6f out: effrt and hdwy over 1f out: chal 1f out: sn led and kpt on wl* **8/1**

1002 **2** nk **Amjaady (USA)**[35] 7610 3-9-6 79..............................(p¹) AdamKirby 1 85
(David O'Meara) *rousted along leaving stalls: sn prom: trckd ldrs 6f out: effrt on inner over 1f out: ev ch ins fnl f: kpt on wl but hld cl home* **11/4²**

0400 **3** ½ **Seven Clans (IRE)**[22] 8014 7-9-7 76..............................(p¹) BenCurtis 3 81
(Neil Mulholland) *wl in tch in midfield: effrt to chse ldrs over 2f out: ev ch u.p 1f out: kpt on same pce towards fin* **20/1**

4231 **4** 1¾ **Skerryvore**[55] 6940 3-9-5 78.............................. HollieDoyle 7 80
(James Fanshawe) *in tch in midfield: effrt over 2f out: edging lft and no imp 1f out: swtchd rt ins fnl f: kpt on but nvr enough pce to threaten ldrs (jockey said gelding ran in snatches)* **5/2¹**

5650 **5** nk **Cote D'Azur**[47] 7185 6-9-10 79.............................. LewisEdmunds 8 80
(Les Eyre) *stdd s: t.k.h: hld up in tch in midfield: hdwy to chse ldrs 1/2-way: effrt and ev ch over 2f out: rdn to ld over 1f out: hdd ins fnl f: no ex and wknd towards fin* **12/1**

0660 **6** ½ **Grand Inquisitor**[22] 8014 7-9-6 75..............(b) AlistairRawlinson 10 75
(Conor Dore) *swtchd lft after s: t.k.h: hld up towards rr: effrt over 1f out: swtchd rt and styd on wl ins fnl f: nt rch ldrs (jockey said gelding ran keen and hung left-handed)* **33/1**

-133 **7** ½ **Lady Dauphin (IRE)**[43] 7350 3-9-1 74.................. StevieDonohoe 5 73
(Charlie Fellowes) *hld up in tch in last trio: effrt over 1f out: kpt on ins fnl f: nvr getting on terms w ldrs (trainer's rep could offer no explanation for the filly's poor performance)* **10/1**

2043 **8** 2¼ **Harbour Vision**[5] 8549 4-9-3 72..............................(v) TomMarquand 6 67
(Derek Shaw) *taken down early: hld up in tch towards rr: effrt over 1f out: no imp and wl hld ins fnl f* **6/1³**

5430 **9** 1¼ **Global Art**[17] 8197 4-9-10 79.............................. SilvestreDeSousa 9 71
(Ed Dunlop) *chsd ldr after 1f tl led over 3f out: rdn over 2f out: hdd over 1f out: no ex and wknd ins fnl f* **9/1**

4006 **10** 1½ **Cafe Espresso**[14] 8298 3-9-0 73.............................. JoeyHaynes 2 62
(Chelsea Banham) *in tch in midfield: rdn over 3f out: struggling and lost pl over 2f out: towards rr and swtchd rt over 1f out: wknd ins fnl f* **33/1**

-260 **11** 17 **Millions Memories**[100] 5267 3-9-5 78.............................. NicolaCurrie 4 33
(Laura Mongan) *t.k.h: led tl over 3f out: lost pl over 2f out: bhd and eased wl ins fnl f (jockey said gelding stopped quickly)* **25/1**

2m 6.28s (-2.32) **Going Correction** -0.125s/f (Stan)
WFA 3 from 4yo+ 4lb **11** Ran SP% **121.9**
Speed ratings (Par 105): **104,103,103,101,101 101,100,99,98,96 83**
CSF £30.20 CT £437.78 TOTE £9.40: £2.40, £1.60, £7.10; EX 43.60 Trifecta £394.70.
Owner Staverton Owners Group **Bred** Redgate Bstock & Peter Bottowley Bstock **Trained** Trowbridge, Wilts

FOCUS
A competitive handicap and they finished well bunched. The second has been rated to his latest, with the fourth close to his Newcastle win.

8693 BET IN PLAY AT TOTESPORT.COM NOVICE STKS 1m (P)
6:55 (6:58) (Class 5) 3-Y-O+
£4,204 (£1,251; £625; £312) Stalls Low

Form RPR
020 **1** **Extrodinair**[20] 8086 4-9-5 73.............................. BrettDoyle 1 78
(Jane Chapple-Hyam) *mde all: clr and travelling best 2f out: pushed along and drifted rt over 1f out: rdn and styd on ins fnl f* **8/1³**

3 **2** 2 **It Had To Be You**[42] 7373 3-9-2 0.............................. TomMarquand 5 72
(William Haggas) *chsd wnr thrght: effrt over 2f out: hung lft but kpt on u.p for clr 2nd: a hld (jockey said colt hung left-handed throughout)* **4/9¹**

3 11 **Engrave** 3-8-11 0.............................. BenCurtis 6 42+
(Hugo Palmer) *s.i.s and rn green: sn rcvrd and midfield: rdn over 3f out: outpcd u.p over 2f out: wl btn 3rd over 1f out* **10/3²**

6-0 **4** 1¾ **Bescaby**[8] 8467 4-9-0 0.............................. AlistairRawlinson 2 39
(Michael Appleby) *stdd s: t.k.h: hld up in last pair: rdn over 3f out: struggling and outpcd over 2f out: wknd and wl btn over 1f out (jockey said filly ran keen)* **80/1**

5 2¾ **Marmalade Day** 3-8-11 0.............................. JoeyHaynes 4 32
(Gary Moore) *chsd ldrs: rdn over 3f out: outpcd over 2f out wl btn 4th over 1f out: wknd* **20/1**

0 **6** 7 **Berties Mission (USA)**[14] 8290 3-9-2 0..............(h¹) LewisEdmunds 3 21
(Derek Shaw) *stdd s: t.k.h: hld up in last pair: rdn over 3f out: drvn and outpcd over 2f out: lost tch over 1f out (jockey said gelding ran keen)* **50/1**

1m 38.02s (-1.88) **Going Correction** -0.125s/f (Stan)
WFA 3 from 4yo 3lb **6** Ran SP% **111.4**
Speed ratings (Par 103): **104,102,91,89,86 79**
CSF £12.17 TOTE £7.00: £2.10, £1.10; EX 17.20 Trifecta £34.00.
Owner Jakes Family **Bred** B Whitehouse **Trained** Dalham, Suffolk

FOCUS
A bit of a turn-up here based on the betting, but not on form. The winner has been rated in line with the better view of his September form with the runner-up.

8694 DOUBLE DELIGHT HAT-TRICK HEAVEN AT TOTESPORT.COM CLASSIFIED STKS 1m (P)
7:25 (7:30) (Class 6) 3-Y-O+
£3,105 (£924; £461; £400; £400; £400) Stalls Low

Form RPR
3020 **1** **Clipsham Tiger (IRE)**[15] 8251 3-8-7 47..............(h) GeorgeRooke(7) 12 59+
(Michael Appleby) *t.k.h: hld up wl in tch in midfield: rdn and hdwy to chse ldr over 1f out: led 1f out: clr and styd on strly ins fnl f (trainer said, regarding the apparent improvement in form, the gelding benefited from racing with cover on this occasion having raced wide last time out)* **16/1**

0043 **2** 2½ **Rosarno (IRE)**[15] 8251 5-9-3 48..............................(bt) JoeyHaynes 2 54
(Chelsea Banham) *dwlt: sn rcvrd and in tch in midfield: effrt over 2f out: swtchd rt and clsd u.p 1f out: chsd clr wnr ins fnl f: styd on but nvr getting on terms* **3/1¹**

6135 **3** 3¼ **Brother In Arms (IRE)**[45] 7271 5-9-3 49.................. HollieDoyle 8 47
(Tony Carroll) *dwlt: hld up towards rr: nt clr run over 2f out: swtchd lft and effrt over 1f out: hdwy ins fnl f: styd on to go 3rd towards fin: no threat to ldrs* **10/1**

6300 **4** ¾ **Squire**[21] 8068 8-9-0 50..............................(bt) ConnorMurtagh(3) 7 45
(Marjorie Fife) *t.k.h: w ldr tl led after over 1f out: rdn over 1f out: hdd 1f out: wknd u.p ins fnl f* **16/1**

0062 **5** ½ **Emojie**[37] 7549 5-9-3 47..............................(b) BrettDoyle 5 44
(Jane Chapple-Hyam) *reminder sn after s: led for over 1f: chsd ldr tl over 1f out: wknd ins fnl f* **7/2²**

4646 **6** ½ **Optima Petamus**[57] 6545 7-9-3 45..............................(b) BenRobinson 3 43
(Liam Bailey) *hld up in tch in midfield: rdn 3f out: nt clr run over 2f out: effrt over 1f out: unable qck and kpt on same pce ins fnl f* **16/1**

5600 **7** hd **Dutch Artist (IRE)**[14] 8299 7-8-12 45..............(p) FayeMcManoman(5) 10 42
(Nigel Tinkler) *dwlt: hld up in rr of main gp: effrt over 1f out: kpt on ins fnl f: nvr trbld ldrs* **20/1**

0506 **8** 1 **Captain Peaky**[10] 8405 6-9-3 41..............................(p) BenCurtis 4 40
(Liam Bailey) *hld up in tch in midfield: unable qck u.p over 1f out: wl hld ins fnl f* **10/1**

0035 **9** 1¼ **Merdon Castle (IRE)**[37] 7550 7-9-0 46.................. MeganNicholls(3) 6 37
(Michael Blake) *in tch in midfield: effrt over 1f out: unable qck and wl hld ins fnl f* **9/1**

2004 **10** nse **Sir Magnum**[15] 8251 4-9-3 48..............................(b¹) TomMarquand 11 37
(Tony Carroll) *in tch in midfield on outer: rdn over 2f out: no imp and btn over 1f out: wknd ins fnl f* **9/1**

360- **11** 8 **Emilene**[315] 9644 5-9-3 40..............................(t¹) StevieDonohoe 9 19
(John Groucott) *chsd ldrs: rdn over 2f out: unable qck and lost pl over 1f out: wknd fnl f* **50/1**

0000 **12** 9 **Roser Moter (IRE)**[15] 8270 4-9-3 40..............(tp) AlistairRawlinson 14
(Michael Appleby) *t.k.h: hld up in tch in midfield: rdn over 3f out: sn lost pl: bhd and eased over 1f out* **50/1**

-000 **13** 10 **Sunshine Coast**[5] 8553 4-9-3 50.............................. NicolaCurrie 1
(Jamie Osborne) *sn in rr: pushed along 5f out: sn detached and nvr travelling after: wl bhd over 1f out (jockey said gelding was never travelling)* **6/1³**

1m 38.59s (-1.31) **Going Correction** -0.125s/f (Stan)
WFA 3 from 4yo+ 3lb **13** Ran SP% **126.0**
Speed ratings (Par 101): **101,98,95,94,94 93,93,92,91,91 83,74,64**
CSF £66.30 TOTE £26.90: £6.00, £1.40, £3.30; EX 120.20 Trifecta £1024.30.
Owner F Morley **Bred** Mrs Noreen Maher **Trained** Oakham, Rutland

FOCUS
A weak affair won by the only 3yo in the race.

8695 BOOK TICKETS AT CHELMSFORDCITYRACECOURSE.COM NOVICE STKS 6f (P)
7:55 (7:55) (Class 5) 3-Y-O+ £4,948 (£1,472; £735; £367) Stalls Centre

Form RPR
042 1 **Mohareb**[8] 8472 3-9-5 0 AlistairRawlinson 2 77+
(Michael Appleby) *racd keenly: mde all: rdn over 1f out: kpt on u.p and hld on ins fnl f* 4/6[1]
2330 2 ½ **Rhossili Down**[26] 7901 3-9-0 71 KieranShoemark 1 70
(Charles Hills) *chsd wnr: effrt wl over 1f out: pressed wnr thrght fnl f and kpt on ins fnl f: a jst hld* 4/1[2]
3 2¾ **Nigel Nott** 3-9-0 0 DylanHogan[(5)] 5 66
(David Simcock) *stdd after s: hld up in tch in rr: rdn over 2f out: sn outpcd: swtchd rt over 1f out: wnt 3rd ins fnl f: kpt on but no threat to ldrs* 14/1[3]
3 4 6 **Reims**[7] 8497 3-9-0 0 TomMarquand 3 42
(William Haggas) *s.i.s: chsd ldng pair: edgd lft u.p and unable qck over 1f out: wknd ins fnl f* 4/1[2]

1m 12.3s (-1.40) **Going Correction** -0.125s/f (Stan) 4 Ran SP% 106.7
Speed ratings (Par 103): **104,103,99,91**
CSF £3.52 TOTE £1.60; EX 2.70 Trifecta £8.40.
Owner Ian Lawrence **Bred** Crossfields Bloodstock Ltd **Trained** Oakham, Rutland
FOCUS
An ordinary novice. The winner has been rated to his latest.

8696 CCR 2020 MEMBERSHIP AVAILABLE H'CAP 1m 6f (P)
8:25 (8:28) (Class 5) (0-70,72) 3-Y-O+ £5,175 (£1,540; £769; £400; £400; £400) Stalls Low

Form RPR
5010 1 **Fragrant Belle**[28] 7845 3-9-7 70 (h) RossaRyan 1 84
(Ralph Beckett) *hld up in tch in midfield: effrt and rdn to chse ldrs over 2f out: led over 1f out: edgd lft but sn asserted: r.o wl: comf* 5/2[2]
4061 2 5 **Red Secret (CAN)**[17] 8196 3-8-12 61 (b) SilvestreDeSousa 5 68
(Ed Dunlop) *midfield: swtchd rt and hdwy to ld after 2f: rdn over 2f out: hdd over 1f out: sn outpcd and plugged on same pce ins fnl f* 13/8[1]
3525 3 4 **Givepeaceachance**[12] 8347 4-8-12 54 BenCurtis 8 55
(Denis Coakley) *hld up in tch in midfield: effrt in 6th over 2f out: plugged on to go 3rd 150yds out: no threat to ldrs* 8/1
2033 4 3½ **Circle Of Stars (IRE)**[17] 8200 3-9-1 64 StevieDonohoe 2 62
(Charlie Fellowes) *t.k.h: trckd ldrs: effrt to chse ldr over 2f out tl wl over 1f out: edgd rt and wknd 1f out* 6/1[3]
4533 5 2½ **Sauchiehall Street (IRE)**[8] 8468 4-9-12 71 (v) ThomasGreatrex[(3)] 7 64
(Noel Williams) *chsd ldrs early: mainly midfield after: hdwy and rdn to chse ldrs over 2f out: outpcd and btn over 1f out: wknd fnl f* 14/1
3416 6 5 **Potters Lady Jane**[42] 7395 7-10-2 72 (p) KieranShoemark 3 58
(Lucy Wadham) *taken down early: chsd ldr for 2f and again 10f out: rdn and lost pl over 2f out: wknd over 1f out* 16/1
4305 7 2 **Fields Of Fortune**[69] 6419 5-9-8 64 TomMarquand 9 47
(Joseph Tuite) *hmpd leaving stalls: sn swtchd lft: hld up in tch: effrt over 3f out: outpcd and btn over 2f out: wknd over 1f out* 20/1
P560 8 hd **Hurry Kane**[52] 7035 3-8-10 62 (h) MeganNicholls[(3)] 10 47
(Paul George) *hld up in rr: rdn over 3f out: sn struggling: wl btn fnl 2f* 50/1
1214 9 12 **Harmonise**[9] 8433 5-9-13 69 KieranO'Neill 6 35
(Sheena West) *led for 2f: chsd ldr tl 10f out: steadily lost pl: wknd u.p over 1f out* 14/1
620- P **Clemento (IRE)**[432] 5636 5-9-11 67 (p) BenRobinson 11
(John Quinn) *hld up in tch in rr: rdn 4f out: sn btn: t.o and p.u over 1f out (jockey said that he pulled up the gelding as something felt amiss)* 33/1

3m 0.59s (-2.61) **Going Correction** -0.125s/f (Stan)
WFA 3 from 4yo+ 7lb 10 Ran SP% 120.9
Speed ratings (Par 103): **102,99,96,94,93 90,89,89,82,**
CSF £7.11 CT £28.34 TOTE £3.20: £1.30, £1.20, £2.50; EX 8.60 Trifecta £69.00.
Owner Robert Ng **Bred** Robert Ng **Trained** Kimpton, Hants
FOCUS
A modest staying handicap, but the first two are 3yos with the potential to progress. Muddling form, but it's been rated on the positive side, with the third close to her recent effort.
T/Plt: £19.10 to a £1 stake. Pool: £41,750.15 - 2173.02 winning units T/Qpdt: £11.90 to a £1 stake. Pool: £5,330.41 - 444.30 winning units **Steve Payne**

8649 KEMPTON (A.W) (R-H)
Thursday, October 31

OFFICIAL GOING: Polytrack: standard to slow
Wind: virtually nil Weather: cold and overcast

8697 BOOK FIREWORKS TICKETS @THEJOCKEYCLUB.CO.UK/KEMPTON H'CAP 6f (P)
4:40 (4:40) (Class 7) (0-50,49) 3-Y-O+ £2,587 (£770; £384; £192) Stalls Low

Form RPR
4000 1 **Hollander**[29] 7811 5-9-7 49 (bt) RossaRyan 7 55
(Alexandra Dunn) *in tch: rdn along and hdwy to chal appr fnl f: styd on wl for press to ld wl ins fnl f: jst hld on* 11/4[1]
36-4 2 nk **Drop Kick Murphi (IRE)**[9] 8435 5-9-3 45 AdrianMcCarthy 6 50
(Christine Dunnett) *racd in last: pushed along in rr 3f out: rdn and stl last over 1f out: styd on v strly ins fnl f: jst failed to rch wnr* 6/1
0006 3 1¼ **Moneta**[8] 8469 3-9-6 49 (v[1]) DavidProbert 4 50
(Ronald Harris) *racd in midfield: smooth prog on inner to ld over 1f out: sn rdn and hdd by wnr wl ins fnl f: lost 2nd last strides* 11/2[3]
0500 4 ½ **Captain Ryan**[150] 3425 8-9-7 49 LiamKeniry 9 49
(Geoffrey Deacon) *restrained in rr: hdwy into midfield over 2f out: rdn along and wnt 4th over 1f out: kpt on one pce fnl f* 25/1
06-0 5 hd **Illustrious Spirit**[152] 3352 4-9-3 45 (p[1] w) KieranO'Neill 10 44
(Ali Stronge) *led: rdn along and hdd over 1f out: wknd fnl f* 33/1
5000 6 2¾ **Vino Rosso (IRE)**[47] 7172 3-9-4 47 DanielMuscutt 3 38
(Michael Blanshard) *midfield: clsd gng wl 2f out: rdn along to chal appr fnl f: wknd clsng stages* 16/1
5534 7 1 **Jaganory (IRE)**[15] 8249 7-9-1 48 (v) RhiainIngram[(5)] 8 36
(Christopher Mason) *racd in midfield: rdn along and no imp on outer 2f out: one pce fnl f* 6/1
646 8 nk **Penwood (FR)**[19] 8119 4-9-4 46 (b) CharlesBishop 5 33
(Joseph Tuite) *in rr of midfield: minor hdwy whn briefly short of room over 2f out: sn rdn and no imp over 1f out: wknd fnl f* 7/2[2]
0003 9 1¼ **Carla Koala**[15] 8249 3-8-11 47 (p) EllieMacKenzie[(7)] 12 30
(Natalie Lloyd-Beavis) *chsd ldr tl over 1f out: rdn and lost pl appr fnl f: wknd clsng stages (jockey said filly ran too free)* 20/1
0650 10 6 **Diamond Cara**[44] 7319 3-9-2 45 (v) MartinDwyer 2 10
(Stuart Williams) *hld up: nvr on terms* 10/1

1m 13.3s (0.20) **Going Correction** -0.025s/f (Stan)
WFA 3 from 4yo+ 1lb 10 Ran SP% 119.4
Speed ratings (Par 97): **97,96,94,94,94 90,89,88,86,78**
CSF £19.67 CT £87.02 TOTE £3.80: £1.30, £1.70, £2.20; EX 16.80 Trifecta £119.70.
Owner Helium Racing Ltd **Bred** Cheveley Park Stud Ltd **Trained** West Buckland, Somerset
FOCUS
Rock-bottom stuff to start with.

8698 100% PROFIT BOOST AT 32REDSPORT.COM H'CAP 7f (P)
5:10 (5:11) (Class 6) (0-65,65) 3-Y-O £3,105 (£924; £461; £400; £400; £400) Stalls Low

Form RPR
4064 1 **Champion Brogie (IRE)**[9] 8449 3-9-4 62 LiamKeniry 10 68
(J S Moore) *hld up: smooth hdwy between rivals 2f out: rdn and hdwy to chse ldr jst ins fnl f: styd on strly to ld post* 33/1
202 2 nse **Glamorous Crescent**[15] 8255 3-8-10 57 CameronNoble[(3)] 11 63
(Grace Harris) *led: rdn along w 1 l ld appr fnl f: kpt on wl for press ins fnl f: hdd post* 16/1
2012 3 1 **Cauthen (IRE)**[16] 8223 3-9-0 58 (h) RobertHavlin 14 61
(Milton Harris) *restrained in rr: hdwy u.p 2f out: rdn and wnt 3rd appr fnl f: kpt on wl but n.d to front pair* 8/1
06U3 4 1 **Dancing Jo**[31] 7758 3-8-12 61 ScottMcCullagh[(5)] 8 62
(Mick Channon) *midfield in tch: rdn along and unable qck over 1f out: kpt on one pce fnl f* 7/1
2264 5 nk **Classic Star**[23] 8008 3-8-9 60 LukeBacon[(7)] 2 60
(Dean Ivory) *racd in midfield: rn wd off home bnd: sn rdn and minor hdwy over 1f out: kpt on fnl f (jockey said gelding ran too free)* 5/1[2]
0-23 6 nk **A Place To Dream**[49] 7114 3-9-5 63 RossaRyan 13 62
(Mike Murphy) *racd in midfield: rdn and no imp over 1f out: kpt on one pce fnl f* 20/1
3044 7 ½ **Seraphim**[7] 8499 3-9-2 63 (t) GabrieleMalune[(3)] 12 61
(Marco Botti) *trckd ldr early: rdn along to chal 2f out: sn one pce and wknd fnl f* 7/2[1]
3006 8 ½ **Rajman**[36] 7576 3-9-0 58 (h) LukeMorris 4 55
(Tom Clover) *trckd ldrs on inner: drvn along 2f out: wknd fnl f* 10/1
60 9 1 **Heavenly Rainbow (IRE)**[9] 8429 3-9-7 65 PhilDennis 1 59
(Michael Herrington) *midfield on inner: rdn along and no prog 2f out: kpt on one pce ins fnl f* 10/1
0200 10 6 **Recuerdame (USA)**[65] 6569 3-9-5 63 HectorCrouch 5 41
(Simon Dow) *hld up: rn wd off home bnd: sn rdn and fnd little: bhd* 13/2[3]
-200 11 1¾ **Soul Searching**[173] 2630 3-9-4 65 PaddyBradley[(3)] 7 39
(Pat Phelan) *midfield on inner: rdn along and lost pl 2f out: wknd over 1f out* 66/1
0-00 12 15 **Dark Mystique**[22] 8030 3-9-0 58 (t[1]) MartinDwyer 3
(Dean Ivory) *last and detached early: a in rr* 14/1
13 3½ **Ketchup (FR)**[143] 3-9-2 60 CharlesBishop 6
(Ali Stronge) *midfield: rdn and lost pl qckly over 2f out: sn t.o* 50/1

1m 26.0s **Going Correction** -0.025s/f (Stan) 13 Ran SP% 117.7
Speed ratings (Par 99): **99,98,97,96,96 95,95,94,93,86 84,67,63**
CSF £473.56 CT £2822.50 TOTE £29.00: £9.10, £3.50, £2.70; EX 536.20.
Owner Tom Vaughan & Sara Moore **Bred** Ms Mary Ryan **Trained** Upper Lambourn, Berks
FOCUS
A modest 3yo handicap, but a thrilling finish.

8699 32RED ON THE APP STORE NURSERY H'CAP 1m (P)
5:40 (5:43) (Class 5) (0-70,72) 2-Y-O £3,752 (£1,116; £557; £400; £400; £400) Stalls Low

Form RPR
306 1 **Pretty In Grey**[42] 7393 2-8-13 68 StefanoCherchi[(7)] 3 72+
(Marco Botti) *racd in midfield: hdwy on outer 2f out: rdn and quick hdwy to ld wl ins fnl f: won gng away* 5/1[3]
6061 2 1½ **Precision Storm**[9] 8415 2-9-2 69 6ex KevinLundie[(5)] 7 70
(Mark Loughnane) *hld up: hdwy into 4th 2f out: hung lft over 1f out: sn rdn and kpt on wl fnl f: wnt 2nd cl home* 9/2[2]
1140 3 1 **Luna Wish**[37] 7548 2-9-2 64 TomQueally 2 62
(George Margarson) *led: shkn up w 1 l ld over 1f out: rdn and hdd by wnr ins fnl f: no ex and lost 2nd cl home* 8/1
5023 4 ¾ **London Calling (IRE)**[10] 8402 2-9-9 71 CharlesBishop 6 69
(Richard Spencer) *trckd ldrs: rdn along and wnt 2nd 2f out: u.p whn snatched up and hmpd ins fnl f: nt rcvr* 9/4[1]
450 5 ½ **Itmusthavebeenlove (IRE)**[56] 6906 2-9-1 63 HayleyTurner 4 58
(Michael Bell) *hld up in last trio: rdn along and outpcd over 1f out: mde sme late hdwy fnl f* 14/1
3613 6 2 **Gert Lush (IRE)**[44] 7297 2-9-7 69 JackMitchell 11 60
(Roger Teal) *restrained in last: minor hdwy 2f out: sn rdn and no imp 1f out: one pce after* 12/1
440 7 1½ **Costello**[14] 8288 2-9-3 65 RossaRyan 5 52
(Mike Murphy) *s.i.s: sn rcvrd into midfield: rdn along and outpcd over 1f out: n.d* 16/1
252 8 5 **Lola Paige (IRE)**[47] 7203 2-9-10 72 DavidProbert 1 48
(David O'Meara) *trckd ldrs: rdn along to chse ldrs 2f out: wknd ins fnl f* 11/1
565 9 6 **Murraymint (FR)**[33] 7677 2-9-3 65 RobHornby 9 27
(Ralph Beckett) *trckd ldr: rdn along and lost pl over 2f out: sn bhd* 8/1

1m 39.65s (-0.15) **Going Correction** -0.025s/f (Stan) 9 Ran SP% 116.4
Speed ratings (Par 95): **99,97,96,95,95 93,91,86,80**
CSF £28.03 CT £179.32 TOTE £8.40: £3.10, £1.50, £4.10; EX 32.60 Trifecta £197.90.
Owner Scuderia Archi Romani **Bred** Scuderia Archi Romani **Trained** Newmarket, Suffolk
FOCUS
An ordinary nursery, but won by a filly who will prove much better than this grade.

8700 32RED.COM NOVICE AUCTION STKS (PLUS 10 RACE) 7f (P)
6:10 (6:12) (Class 4) 2-Y-O £5,822 (£1,732; £865; £432) Stalls Low

Form RPR
1 **Eevilynn Drew** 2-8-12 0 DarraghKeenan[(3)] 6 71
(Robert Eddery) *midfield in tch: clsd gng wl 2f out: rdn along to ld over 1f out: kpt on wl* 16/1
0 2 ½ **Hurricane Alex**[6] 8516 2-9-1 0 RossaRyan 3 70
(Richard Hannon) *racd in midfield: hdwy u.p 2f out: drvn and kpt on wl ins fnl f: clsd all the way to the line* 5/1[2]

The Form Book Flat 2019, Raceform Ltd, Newbury, RG14 5SJ

3 1 1/4 **Dromara King** 2-9-2 0 .... FinleyMarsh(3) 2 70
(Richard Hughes) *in rr of midfield: rdn and hdwy on inner 2f out: kpt on fnl f but no ch w front pair* **17/2[3]**

0 4 1/2 **Morlaix**[21] 8058 2-9-0 0 .... PoppyBridgwater(5) 10 69
(David Simcock) *hld up in rr: hdwy on inner 2f out: rdn and kpt on one pce ins fnl f* **25/1**

5 1/2 **Uncle Swayze** 2-9-1 0 .... RobHornby 14 64+
(Ralph Beckett) *bmpd s and racd in rr: pushed along in rr 2f out: sn rdn and mde str late hdwy ins fnl f* **11/1**

0 6 1/2 **Secret Smile (IRE)**[12] 8338 2-9-2 0 .... FrannyNorton 13 63
(Mark Johnston) *wnt lft s: sn rcvrd to ld after 2f: rdn along and hdd over 1f out: kpt on one pce fnl f* **20/1**

6 7 1 **Rock Of Redmond (IRE)**[21] 8058 2-8-5 0 .... SophieRalston(5) 12 55
(Dean Ivory) *trckd ldrs: pushed along to chal over 1f out: rdn and wknd fnl f* **40/1**

8 1 **Light Bay** 2-8-10 0 .... DavidProbert 5 52
(Henry Candy) *hld up in rr: rdn and wl bhd 2f out: sme late hdwy* **12/1**

22 9 1/2 **Secret Acquisition**[38] 7515 2-9-0 0 .... DavidEgan 1 55+
(Daniel Kubler) *led for 2f then remained in tch: rdn and no imp over 1f out: one pce fnl f (jockey said he had to take a check on the bend)* **11/10[1]**

0 10 1 **Anno Maximo (GER)**[20] 8100 2-9-5 0 .... CallumShepherd 11 57
(Michael Bell) *in rr of midfield: rdn and outpcd 2f out: n.d* **50/1**

11 nk **Paint It Black** 2-9-5 0 .... LukeMorris 4 57
(Sylvester Kirk) *racd in midfield in tch: rdn along and no imp 2f out: wknd fr over 1f out* **28/1**

0 12 1 3/4 **Various (IRE)**[15] 8250 2-9-5 0 .... CharlesBishop 7 52
(Eve Johnson Houghton) *in rr: wd off home bnd: sn struggling: nvr on terms* **25/1**

44 13 1/2 **Stony Look (IRE)**[21] 8058 2-8-10 0 .... MartinDwyer 8 42
(Andrew Balding) *racd in midfield: rdn along and qckly lost pl 2f out: sn bhd* **11/1**

0 14 2 1/4 **Joanna Vassa**[101] 5250 2-8-5 0 .... RhiainIngram(5) 9 36
(Roger Ingram) *trckd ldr: rdn and lost pl over 1f out: sn bhd* **100/1**

1m 26.92s (0.92) **Going Correction** -0.025s/f (Stan) **14 Ran SP% 126.3**
Speed ratings (Par 97): **93,92,91,90,89 89,88,87,86,85 84,82,82,79**
CSF £93.26 TOTE £26.90: £6.10, £1.80, £3.50; EX 158.80 Trifecta £1608.30.
Owner Graham & Lynn Knight **Bred** Killashee House Limited **Trained** Newmarket, Suffolk

FOCUS
Not a deep novice and the winner wouldn't have been the easiest to find. A few caught the eye, though.

8701 32RED H'CAP (LONDON MIDDLE DISTANCE SERIES QUALIFIER) 1m 2f 219y(P)
6:40 (6:41) (Class 3) (0-95,95) 3-Y-O+

£9,337 (£2,796; £1,398; £699; £349; £175) **Stalls Low**

Form RPR

3125 1 **Just The Man (FR)**[43] 7342 3-8-10 **86** .... HectorCrouch 3 93+
(Clive Cox) *hld up: gd hdwy 2f out: rdn and wnt cl 2nd over 1f out: drvn to ld ins fnl f: styd on wl* **7/2[2]**

311 2 nk **Good Tidings (FR)**[22] 8020 3-8-10 **86** .... RobertHavlin 7 92+
(John Gosden) *in rr of midfield: gng wl w plenty to do 3f out: hdwy 2f out: sn rdn and clsd on ldrs appr fnl f: kpt on wl* **11/8[1]**

1120 3 hd **Geetanjali (IRE)**[26] 7895 4-8-10 **84** ....(v) CameronNoble(3) 8 89
(Michael Bell) *hld up: swtchd rt and rdn 2f out: gd hdwy appr fnl f: styd on strly fnl f: nt rch ldng pair* **40/1**

5005 4 3/4 **Creationist (USA)**[16] 8222 3-9-1 **91** .... JasonWatson 4 95
(Roger Charlton) *dwlt and racd in rr: rdn and stl in rr over 1f out: kpt on wl fnl f wout threatening (jockey said gelding was slowly away)* **7/1**

0056 5 nk **El Ghazwani (IRE)**[33] 7686 4-9-2 **87** ....(t) JackMitchell 1 90
(Hugo Palmer) *trckd ldrs on inner: effrt on inner to ld over 1f out: sn rdn and hdd by wnr ins fnl f: no ex* **10/1**

3511 6 1 3/4 **Cantiniere (USA)**[54] 6981 4-9-5 **90** ....(p) HayleyTurner 6 91
(Saeed bin Suroor) *trckd ldr: rdn along to chal w ev ch over 1f out: sn one pce fnl f* **9/2[3]**

4004 7 1/2 **Exceeding Power**[68] 6437 8-9-2 **87** .... GeorgeWood 2 86
(Martin Bosley) *racd in midfield: pushed along to maintain position 3f out: effrt whn short of room over 1f out: nt rcvr fnl f* **40/1**

651 8 1 3/4 **Lawn Ranger**[68] 6447 4-9-10 **95** .... KierenFox 5 91
(Michael Attwater) *led: shkn up over 2f out: rdn along and hdd over 1f out: wknd fnl f* **20/1**

0500 9 17 **Star Archer**[19] 8130 5-8-8 **84** .... GerO'Neill(5) 9 52
(Michael Easterby) *midfield: pushed along 3f out: rdn and lost pl 2f out: sn bhd* **25/1**

2m 17.6s (-3.40) **Going Correction** -0.025s/f (Stan)
WFA 3 from 4yo+ 5lb **9 Ran SP% 117.6**
Speed ratings (Par 107): **111,110,110,110,109 108,108,106,94**
CSF £8.55 CT £156.01 TOTE £4.30: £1.40, £1.20, £6.00; EX 12.50 Trifecta £105.40.
Owner Paul & Clare Rooney **Bred** Compagnia Generale Srl **Trained** Lambourn, Berks

FOCUS
A good handicap, but although the pace was ordinary and several held a chance passing the furlong pole, the first three came from behind.

8702 32RED CASINO H'CAP 7f (P)
7:10 (7:11) (Class 5) (0-75,76) 3-Y-O+

£3,752 (£1,116; £557; £400; £400; £400) **Stalls Low**

Form RPR

0602 1 **Mendoza (IRE)**[16] 8221 3-9-5 **74** .... RyanTate 4 82
(James Eustace) *trckd ldrs: wnt 2nd gng wl 2f out: rdn along to ld over 1f out: styd on wl* **7/1[3]**

-600 2 1 1/4 **One Cool Daddy (USA)**[136] 3944 4-9-7 **74** .... MartinDwyer 3 80
(Dean Ivory) *racd in midfield: rdn along and wnt 3rd 2f out: kpt on to go 2nd wl ins fnl f* **14/1**

2000 3 3/4 **Kendergarten Kop (IRE)**[10] 8413 4-9-1 **68** ....(bt) DavidProbert 5 72
(David Flood) *hld up: effrt to cl 2f out: swtchd lft over 1f out: sn rdn and gd late hdwy to go 3rd clsng stages* **25/1**

-145 4 1 1/4 **Daring Venture (IRE)**[126] 4288 3-9-5 **74** .... DavidEgan 2 74
(Roger Varian) *led: rdn along and hdd by wnr over 1f out: one pce fnl f* **7/2[2]**

6541 5 3/4 **Dawaaween (IRE)**[15] 8254 3-9-4 **73** .... JimCrowley 8 71
(Owen Burrows) *racd in midfield: hdwy on outer 2f out: sn rdn and no imp 1f out: one pce fnl f (jockey said filly ran too free)* **6/5[1]**

6010 6 3/4 **Sirius Slew**[47] 7189 3-8-12 **70** ....(p) DarraghKeenan(3) 1 66
(Alan Bailey) *hld up: rdn along and no imp 2f out: v minor hdwy fnl f* **25/1**

1550 7 2 1/4 **Gilt Edge**[12] 8349 3-8-10 **70** .... RhiainIngram(5) 9 60
(Christopher Mason) *trckd ldr: rdn along and lost pl over 1f out: wknd fnl f* **50/1**

4106 8 3/4 **Inner Circle (IRE)**[22] 8030 5-9-4 **71** ....(p) LukeMorris 7 59
(Mark Loughnane) *hld up: swtchd rt and rdn to cl 2f out: no imp 1f out: no ex* **50/1**

1024 9 1 3/4 **Fortune And Glory (USA)**[24] 7975 6-9-6 **73** .... CharlesBishop 10 57
(Joseph Tuite) *prom on outer and racd freely: rdn along and lost pl over 1f out: wknd fnl f* **8/1**

0110 10 nk **Soar Above**[100] 5283 4-9-4 **76** .... PoppyBridgwater(5) 6 59
(John Butler) *in rr of midfield: wd off home bnd: sn rdn and nvr competitive* **8/1**

6360 11 nse **Surrey Blaze (IRE)**[67] 6511 4-9-6 **73** .... RobHornby 11 56
(Joseph Tuite) *restrained early: a in rr* **66/1**

1m 24.73s (-1.27) **Going Correction** -0.025s/f (Stan)
WFA 3 from 4yo+ 2lb **11 Ran SP% 122.2**
Speed ratings (Par 103): **106,104,103,102,101 100,98,97,95,94 94**
CSF £97.00 CT £2334.06 TOTE £6.50: £1.40, £5.10, £4.00; EX 107.20 Trifecta £1554.40.
Owner The MacDougall Two **Bred** Gortskagh House Stud & Tally Ho Stud **Trained** Newmarket, Suffolk

FOCUS
An ordinary handicap. A length pb from the winner.

8703 100% PROFIT BOOST AT 32REDSPORT.COM H'CAP 1m 3f 219y(P)
7:40 (7:44) (Class 6) (0-60,60) 3-Y-O+

£3,105 (£924; £461; £400; £400; £400) **Stalls Low**

Form RPR

0400 1 **Ice Canyon**[30] 7790 5-9-9 **60** .... EoinWalsh 6 68
(Kevin Frost) *trckd ldrs: effrt to chse ldr 3f out: rdn to ld 2f out and qckly asserted: drvn out fnl f (trainer could offer no explanation for gelding's improved form)* **14/1**

/606 2 1/2 **Tulane (IRE)**[16] 8224 4-9-4 **55** .... JaneElliott 8 62
(Richard Phillips) *hld up: stl bhd w plenty to do 3f out: rdn and hdwy into 3rd 2f out: drvn and clsd on wnr all the way to the line* **7/2[1]**

5062 3 1 1/2 **Falcon Cliffs (IRE)**[12] 8347 5-9-4 **55** .... RobHornby 1 60
(Tony Carroll) *racd in midfield: hdwy on inner to chse ldrs 2f out: kpt on fnl f: nt rch ldng pair* **4/1[2]**

5200 4 nse **Mobham (IRE)**[87] 5744 4-9-9 **60** .... DanielMuscutt 12 65
(J R Jenkins) *hld up: effrt to cl 2f out: rdn along and hdwy 1f out: kpt on but n.d* **25/1**

36 5 1 1/2 **Zamani (GER)**[14] 8293 3-8-12 **60** .... PoppyBridgwater(5) 7 63
(David Bridgwater) *racd in midfield: rdn and no imp on ldrs 2f out: sn one pce* **13/2[3]**

6000 6 nk **Arlecchino's Arc (IRE)**[23] 8000 4-9-5 **56** ....(v) JasonWatson 2 58
(Mark Usher) *racd in midfield: rdn and briefly wnt 3rd 2f out: wknd fnl f* **10/1**

5040 7 1 3/4 **Sir Gnet (IRE)**[24] 7956 5-9-7 **58** ....(p[1]) RobertHavlin 10 57
(Ed Dunlop) *hld up: pushed along on outer w plenty to do over 2f out: rdn and minor hdwy appr fnl f: one pce fnl f* **11/1**

6000 8 1 1/4 **Albishr (IRE)**[33] 7685 4-9-6 **57** ....(p) HectorCrouch 11 54
(Simon Dow) *led: rdn along and hdd by wnr 2f out: wknd fnl f* **25/1**

4506 9 2 1/2 **Bakht A Rawan (IRE)**[31] 7758 7-9-2 **53** ....(p[1]) JackMitchell 3 46
(Roger Teal) *hld up: hdwy u.p on inner 2f out: rdn and plugged on one pce fnl f* **20/1**

1400 10 1 1/2 **Music Major**[21] 8065 6-9-6 **57** .... LukeMorris 9 48
(Michael Attwater) *racd in midfield: effrt to cl whn briefly denied clr run 2f out: rdn and no imp over 1f out* **25/1**

3000 11 13 **Vanity Vanity (USA)**[120] 4499 4-9-3 **54** .... DavidEgan 13 24
(Denis Coakley) *prom: drvn along and lost pl 3f out: sn bhd* **25/1**

0120 12 11 **Genuine Approval (IRE)**[40] 7474 6-9-6 **60** ....(t) DarraghKeenan(3) 14 12
(John Butler) *hld up: rdn along and t.o 3f out* **25/1**

20-0 13 1 1/2 **Ceyhan**[156] 3209 7-9-9 **60** .... CharlieBennett 5 10
(Barry Brennan) *chsd ldr tl 3f out: sn rdn and lost pl 2f out: bhd* **50/1**

2m 35.02s (0.52) **Going Correction** -0.025s/f (Stan)
WFA 3 from 4yo+ 6lb **13 Ran SP% 105.6**
Speed ratings (Par 101): **97,96,95,95,94 94,93,92,90,89 81,73,72**
CSF £42.96 CT £153.92 TOTE £17.10: £4.30, £1.40, £2.20; EX 77.70 Trifecta £269.00.
Owner Derek & Mrs Marie Dean **Bred** Darley **Trained** Newcastle-under-Lyme, Staffs
■ Y Fyn Duw A Fydd was withdrawn. Price at time of withdrawal 11/2. Rule 4 applies to all bets - deduction 15p in the £.

FOCUS
A moderate handicap.

8704 MAGICAL FIREWORKS SPECTACULAR HERE ON SATURDAY H'CAP 6f (P)
8:10 (8:15) (Class 6) (0-60,60) 3-Y-O+

£3,105 (£924; £461; £400; £400; £400) **Stalls Low**

Form RPR

3020 1 **My Town Chicago (USA)**[20] 8083 4-9-4 **60** .... JackMitchell 6 68
(Kevin Frost) *hld up: gd hdwy on outer into 4th 2f out: sn rdn and qckend up wl to ld ent fnl f: won gng away* **3/1[2]**

3011 2 1 3/4 **Viola Park**[19] 8123 5-9-4 **60** ....(p) DavidProbert 2 63
(Ronald Harris) *prom: drvn along to chse ldrs over 1f out: kpt on wl for press to go 2nd fnl f: no ch w wnr* **11/4[1]**

0503 3 3/4 **The Lacemaker**[16] 8217 5-9-3 **59** ....(p) HayleyTurner 5 60
(Milton Harris) *led: rdn along and hdd over 1f out: kpt battling wl ins fnl f for 3rd* **10/1**

0403 4 nk **Phoenix Star (IRE)**[9] 8435 3-9-3 **60** ....(t) JasonWatson 7 60
(Stuart Williams) *midfield in tch: rdn along to chal over 1f out: drvn and nt pce of wnr clsng stages (jockey said gelding hung right-handed under pressure)* **5/1[3]**

5630 5 1/2 **Perfect Symphony (IRE)**[10] 8408 5-9-1 **60** .... PaddyBradley(3) 8 58
(Mark Pattinson) *chsd ldr tl led briefly over 1f out: sn hdd by wnr ent fnl f: one pce after* **11/2**

3103 6 shd **Miss Gargar**[17] 8194 3-9-2 **59** ....(v) RobertHavlin 4 57
(Harry Dunlop) *racd in midfield: rdn along and no imp over 1f out: one pce fnl f* **14/1**

0525 7 1 **Wild Dancer**[29] 7812 6-9-3 **59** .... DanielMuscutt 12 54
(Patrick Chamings) *hld up: rdn in rr over 1f out: nvr on terms* **16/1**

6340 8 2 3/4 **Pink Iceburg (IRE)**[43] 7337 3-9-3 **60** .... TomQueally 11 47
(Peter Crate) *in rr of midfield: wd of home bnd: sn rdn and bhd* **40/1**

0400 9 shd **Mont Kiara (FR)**[94] 5503 6-8-10 **59** .... LeviWilliams(7) 1 45
(Simon Dow) *j. awkwardly: rcvrd into midfield on inner: rdn and lost pl over 1f out* **14/1**

3600 **10** ¾ **Cookupastorm (IRE)**[52] 7024 3-9-2 **59**.........................(p[1]) EoinWalsh 3 43
(Martin Smith) *a in rr* **66/1**

1m 13.04s (-0.06) **Going Correction** -0.025s/f (Stan)
WFA 3 from 4yo+ 1lb **10** Ran SP% **116.0**
Speed ratings (Par 101): **99,96,95,95,94 94,93,89,89,88**
CSF £11.61 CT £71.74 TOTE £3.70: £1.30, £1.80, £2.60; EX 15.20 Trifecta £80.30.
Owner J T Stimpson **Bred** Godolphin **Trained** Newcastle-under-Lyme, Staffs

FOCUS
A moderate sprint handicap and virtually a classified event with just 1lb covering the whole field.
T/Plt: £6,533.10 to a £1 stake. Pool: £44,752.23 - 6.85 winning units T/Qpdt: £219.80 to a 31 stake. Pool: £7,122.85 - 32.40 winning units **Mark Grantham**

7839 LINGFIELD (L-H)

Thursday, October 31

OFFICIAL GOING: Polytrack: standard to slow
Wind: light breeze Weather: sunny intervals, cool

8705 PLAY 4 TO SCORE AT BETWAY H'CAP — 1m 2f (P)

12:50 (12:52) (Class 5) (0-70,70) 3-Y-0+
£3,428 (£1,020; £509; £300; £300; £300) **Stalls** Low

Form — RPR

0451 **1** **Hindaam (USA)**[35] 7609 3-9-2 **66**.......................... JimCrowley 10 74
(Owen Burrows) *mid-div on outer: hdwy 2f out: rdn to chal 1f out: r.o wl fnl f: led last stride* **10/3**[1]

3440 **2** *nse* **Kvetuschka**[33] 7682 3-9-6 **70**.......................... DavidProbert 8 78
(Peter Chapple-Hyam) *trckd ldrs: drvn to ld 1f out: rdn and strly pressed fnl f: r.o wl: hdd last stride* **22/1**

1263 **3** *nk* **Iron Mike**[14] 8298 3-9-5 **69**..........................(b) JoeFanning 4 76
(Keith Dalgleish) *hld up on outer: hdwy 2f out: drvn over 1f out: rdn and ev ch fnl f: r.o: jst hld by first two* **4/1**[2]

4331 **4** *hd* **Canasta**[28] 7858 3-9-4 **68**.......................... JackMitchell 5 75
(James Fanshawe) *trckd ldrs: drvn on inner over 1f out: rdn fnl f: sn ev ch: no ex nr fin* **4/1**[2]

4415 **5** 3 ½ **The Game Is On**[91] 5580 3-9-2 **66**..........................(p[1]) LukeMorris 6 66
(Sir Mark Prescott Bt) *mid-div: drvn 2f out: rdn over 1f out: kpt on fnl f* **14/1**

2060 **6** ½ **Perfect Grace**[31] 7756 3-9-2 **66**..........................(p) HollieDoyle 13 65
(Archie Watson) *led: drvn 2f out: rdn and hdd 1f out: wknd fnl f* **25/1**

442 **7** *nk* **Exmoor Beast**[23] 7999 3-9-6 **70**.......................... DavidEgan 14 68
(Peter Charalambous) *prom: drvn and lost pl 2f out: rdn and wknd over 1f out* **14/1**

4325 **8** *nk* **Angel's Whisper (IRE)**[28] 7835 4-9-10 **70**..........................(p[1]) TomMarquand 9 66
(Amy Murphy) *prom: drvn and hdwy to chal 2f out: sn rdn and wknd* **8/1**[3]

031 **9** 1 ½ **Dreamboat Dave (IRE)**[23] 8001 3-8-11 **61**.......................... EoinWalsh 1 55
(Sarah Humphrey) *hld up: drvn over 2f out: no imp (jockey said gelding was struck into left hind)* **11/1**

1550 **10** *nse* **Tiar Na Nog (IRE)**[15] 8248 7-9-10 **70**.......................... JasonWatson 2 63
(Denis Coakley) *hld up: drvn 2f out: rdn fnl f: no imp (jockey said mare lipped the heels of Dreamboat Dave when the pace of the race slowed five furlongs out)* **33/1**

3040 **11** *nk* **Tangramm**[22] 8033 7-9-6 **66**..........................(p) RyanTate 7 59
(Dean Ivory) *hld up: drvn over 2f out: rdn over 1f out: nvr a factor* **10/1**

0430 **12** 1 **Jumping Jack (IRE)**[23] 7984 5-9-1 **61**..........................(p) CharlesBishop 3 52
(Chris Gordon) *hld up: drvn and wl bhd fr 2f out (jockey said gelding hung badly left-handed throughout)* **16/1**

0000 **13** ½ **Narjes**[37] 7560 5-8-12 **63**..........................(h) SophieRalston(5) 11 53
(Laura Mongan) *a in rr* **66/1**

2m 5.54s (-1.06) **Going Correction** -0.025s/f (Stan)
WFA 3 from 4yo+ 4lb **13** Ran SP% **123.5**
Speed ratings (Par 103): **103,102,102,102,99 99,99,98,97,97 97,96,96**
CSF £86.81 CT £314.80 TOTE £3.60: £1.40, £7.40, £1.40; EX 96.70 Trifecta £626.90.
Owner Hamdan Al Maktoum **Bred** Shadwell Farm LLC **Trained** Lambourn, Berks

FOCUS
This was run minus the paper favourite but still looked a competitive race for the grade. The first four finished in a heap but finished well clear of the rest. It's been rated at face value for now, with the third to his latest.

8706 LADBROKES / BRITISH STALLION STUDS EBF FILLIES' NOVICE MEDIAN AUCTION STKS (PLUS 10 RACE) — 7f 1y(P)

1:20 (1:27) (Class 5) 2-Y-O **£3,428** (£1,020; £509; £254) **Stalls** Low

Form — RPR

2 **1** **Cranberry**[37] 7547 2-9-0 0.......................... DavidEgan 11 80+
(Richard Hughes) *mde all: pushed along in 2 l ld 2f out: drvn in 3 l ld 1f out: reminder and c further clr fnl f: easily* **15/8**[1]

03 **2** 3 ½ **Paycheck**[37] 7547 2-9-0 0.......................... JimCrowley 5 72+
(David Simcock) *chsd ldrs: drvn in 4th over 1f out: reminders 1f out: r.o into 2nd fnl f: no ch w wnr* **5/2**[2]

25 **3** 1 ½ **Qaseeda**[29] 7813 2-9-0 0.......................... TomMarquand 13 66
(William Haggas) *prom: drvn in 2nd 2f out: reminder over 1f out: no ex and lost 2nd fnl f (jockey said filly hung left-handed in the straight)* **4/1**[3]

4 ½ **Mazikeen** 2-9-0 0.......................... MartinDwyer 10 65+
(Richard Hughes) *hld up: pushed along and hdwy over 1f out: kpt on steadily into 4th wl ins fnl f* **16/1**

5 *nk* **Alianne** 2-9-0 0.......................... LukeMorris 12 64
(Tom Clover) *chsd ldrs: drvn 2f out: lost pl over 1f out: reminder fnl f: one pce* **40/1**

50 **6** *nse* **Summer Valley**[20] 8093 2-9-0 0.......................... LiamKeniry 7 64
(Gary Moore) *mid-div: pushed along 2f out: rdn over 1f out: kpt on fnl f* **66/1**

0 **7** ½ **Amicia**[42] 7393 2-8-11 0.......................... GabrieleMalune(3) 3 62
(Marco Botti) *trckd ldrs: drvn in 3rd 2f out: rdn and wknd fnl f* **16/1**

8 2 ¾ **Tampere (IRE)** 2-9-0 0.......................... CallumShepherd 8 55+
(David Simcock) *slowly away: bhd: last 2f out: pushed along over 1f out: kpt on fnl f (jockey said filly reared as the stalls opened)* **20/1**

9 1 ¾ **Amarsanaa** 2-9-0 0.......................... HectorCrouch 6 51
(Clive Cox) *mid-div: drvn over 2f out: wknd fnl f* **16/1**

00 **10** *nk* **Bright Spells (IRE)**[8] 8458 2-9-0 0.......................... NicolaCurrie 2 49
(Jamie Osborne) *hld up: pushed along and bhd fr 2f out* **33/1**

11 1 **Sparkling Or Still (IRE)** 2-9-0 0..........................(t[1]) DanielMuscutt 9 47
(David Lanigan) *slowly away: a bhd* **25/1**

00 **12** *shd* **Villa Paloma (IRE)**[13] 8302 2-9-0 0.......................... JoeFanning 1 47
(Mark Johnston) *hld up: pushed along 2f out: no imp* **33/1**

1m 26.86s (2.06) **Going Correction** -0.025s/f (Stan) **12** Ran SP% **119.4**
Speed ratings (Par 92): **87,83,81,80,80 80,79,76,74,74 72,72**
CSF £6.02 TOTE £2.60: £1.20, £1.10, £1.40; EX 7.00 Trifecta £15.70.
Owner The Queen **Bred** The Queen **Trained** Upper Lambourn, Berks

FOCUS
Not much to go on in terms of form and it revolved around the top two in the betting, who'd finished second and third in a similar event at Chelmsford last month.

8707 BOMBARDIER BRITISH HOPPED AMBER BEER H'CAP — 7f 1y(P)

1:55 (1:58) (Class 2) (0-105,105) 3-Y-O+ **£11,971** (£3,583; £1,791; £896; £446) **Stalls** Low

Form — RPR

5131 **1** **War Glory (IRE)**[40] 7448 6-9-8 **103**.......................... TomMarquand 10 114
(Richard Hannon) *trckd ldrs: pushed along in 4th 2f out: drvn to chal ent fnl f: rdn to ld 1/2f out: sn pushed clr: comf* **12/1**

6600 **2** 2 ½ **Gifted Master (IRE)**[131] 4095 6-9-10 **105**.......................... JackMitchell 11 110
(Hugo Palmer) *unruly at s: led: pushed along in 1/2 l ld 2f out: rdn over 1f out: hdd 1/2f out: no ex* **16/1**

0003 **3** *hd* **Above The Rest (IRE)**[9] 8425 8-9-7 **102**..........................(h) BenCurtis 7 106
(David Barron) *mid-div on outer: pushed along 2f out: rdn and r.o fnl f: tk 3rd last 50yds* **16/1**

6022 **4** ¾ **Documenting**[40] 7448 6-9-3 **105**.......................... AngusVilliers(7) 4 107+
(Kevin Frost) *t.k.h: mid-div: pushed along 2f out: drvn 1f out: rdn and kpt on into 4th fnl f (jockey said gelding ran too free)* **8/1**

0000 **5** *hd* **Blackheath**[33] 7697 4-8-6 **87**.......................... HollieDoyle 9 88
(Ed Walker) *prom: pushed along in 1/2 l 2nd 2f out: rdn over 1f out: wknd fnl f* **15/2**[3]

3506 **6** 1 ½ **Almufti**[42] 7372 3-8-5 **88**..........................(t) DavidEgan 8 84
(Hugo Palmer) *hld up: drvn 1 1/2f out: rdn fnl f: one pce* **10/1**

-040 **7** *nse* **Mutafani**[103] 5173 4-8-10 **91** ow1..........................(w) RobertHavlin 5 88
(Simon Crisford) *trckd ldrs: drvn in 3rd 2f out: rdn over 1f out: wknd fnl f* **9/1**

1033 **8** *hd* **Revich (IRE)**[27] 7868 3-8-6 **89**.......................... LukeMorris 3 85
(Richard Spencer) *hld up: drvn 2f out: reminder fnl f: no imp* **20/1**

502- **9** 1 ¼ **Silent Echo**[437] 6361 5-9-4 **99**..........................(h) JimCrowley 6 92
(Peter Hedger) *hld up on outer: drvn 1 1/2f out: rdn fnl f: no imp* **25/1**

4101 **10** *nk* **Lethal Lunch**[47] 7188 4-9-2 **97**.......................... AdamKirby 12 90+
(Clive Cox) *hld up: drvn 2f out: sn rdn: no imp (trainer said, regarding gelding's poor run, that he may have been unsuited by the standard to slow going on the track which has had remedial work carried out on it since the last meeting)* **7/2**[2]

0100 **11** *nk* **Major Partnership (IRE)**[54] 6953 4-9-5 **100**.......................... OisinMurphy 2 97
(Saeed bin Suroor) *mid-div on inner: drvn and effrt over 1f out: hmpd ent fnl f: no ch after* **5/2**[1]

1034 **12** *hd* **Charles Molson**[40] 7448 8-9-2 **97**.......................... DanielMuscutt 14 88+
(Patrick Chamings) *hld up: drvn in last 2f out: nvr a factor* **33/1**

0006 **13** 3 ½ **Silent Attack**[21] 8062 6-9-5 **100**.......................... GeorgeDowning 13 82
(Tony Carroll) *slowly away: bhd: drvn over 1f out: rdn and dropped to last ent fnl f* **25/1**

1m 22.53s (-2.27) **Going Correction** -0.025s/f (Stan)
WFA 3 from 4yo+ 2lb **13** Ran SP% **127.6**
Speed ratings (Par 109): **111,108,107,107,106 105,105,104,103,103 102,102,98**
CSF £192.88 CT £3102.05 TOTE £7.70: £2.20, £5.80, £4.70; EX 253.40 Trifecta £3310.00.
Owner Mohamed Saeed Al Shahi **Bred** Pier House Stud **Trained** East Everleigh, Wilts
■ Stewards' Enquiry : Robert Havlin cautioned: careless riding

FOCUS
A competitive handicap on paper was taken apart by the hugely progressive War Glory. The third has been rated to his latest.

8708 LADBROKES HOME OF THE ODDS BOOST EBF FLEUR DE LYS FILLIES' STKS (LISTED RACE) (FAST TRACK QUAL') — 1m 1y(P)

2:30 (2:32) (Class 1) 3-Y-O+ **£22,684** (£8,600; £4,304; £2,144; £1,076; £540) **Stalls** High

1510 **1** **Scentasia**[26] 7895 3-8-11 97.......................... DavidEgan 9 106
(John Gosden) *mid-div on outer: hdwy into cl 2nd 2f out: rdn to ld 1f out: rdn clr fnl f: comf* **10/1**

4330 **2** 2 **Chaleur**[34] 7657 3-8-11 100.......................... RobHornby 3 102
(Ralph Beckett) *trckd ldrs: pushed along in 5th 2f out: rdn and hdwy fnl f: r.o wl into 2nd last few strides* **15/2**[3]

3112 **3** *nk* **She's Got You**[34] 7657 3-8-11 99.......................... RobertHavlin 4 101
(John Gosden) *mid-div on inner: hdwy and drvn in 4th 2f out: rdn in 3rd over 1f out: kpt on fnl f* **7/2**[1]

4546 **4** ½ **Coral Beach (IRE)**[47] 7220 3-8-11 102..........................(t) SeamieHeffernan 6 100
(A P O'Brien, Ire) *mid-div: pushed along and hdwy on outer 2f out: rdn and kpt on into 4th fnl f* **10/1**

6120 **5** *nk* **California Love**[48] 7146 3-8-12 98 ow1.......................... StevieDonohoe 8 100
(Richard Spencer) *led: pushed along in narrow ld 2f out: rdn and hdd 1f out: wknd fnl f* **25/1**

2042 **6** *nk* **Preening**[48] 7146 4-9-0 99.......................... JasonWatson 5 101+
(James Fanshawe) *hld up: drvn and n.m.r 1 1/2f out: rdn fnl f: kpt on (jockey said filly was denied a clear run)* **7/2**[1]

2035 **7** ½ **Crossing The Line**[60] 6770 4-9-0 99.......................... OisinMurphy 7 98
(Andrew Balding) *hld up: racd wd 1 1/2f out: reminder over 1f out: one pce fnl f* **8/1**

0404 **8** *hd* **Solar Gold (IRE)**[20] 8090 4-9-0 98..........................(t[1]) TomMarquand 12 98
(William Haggas) *hld up: pushed along in last 2f out: sn drvn: rdn fnl f: one pce* **10/1**

4353 **9** 1 **Muchly**[26] 7893 3-8-11 98.......................... DavidProbert 10 95
(John Gosden) *hld up: pushed along and effrt on inner 2f out: drvn in 5th 1f out: wknd fnl f* **11/1**

0151 **10** ¾ **Breathtaking Look**[48] 7146 4-9-5 101.......................... JimCrowley 1 99
(Stuart Williams) *trckd ldrs: hdwy into 2nd over 2f out: sn drvn and dropped to 3rd: rdn and wknd over 1f out* **13/2**[2]

2350 **11** ¾ **Rock On Baileys**[26] 7892 4-9-0 97.......................... LewisEdmunds 11 92
(Amy Murphy) *hld up: drvn 1 1/2f out: dropped away fnl f* **66/1**

2-46 **12** 27 **Lucymai**[282] 351 6-9-0 99.......................... MartinDwyer 2 30
(Dean Ivory) *chsd ldr: drvn and lost pl over 2f out: dropped to last over 1f out: eased* **33/1**

1m 35.65s (-2.55) **Going Correction** -0.025s/f (Stan)
WFA 3 from 4yo+ 3lb **12** Ran SP% **124.5**
Speed ratings (Par 108): **111,109,108,108,107 107,107,106,105,105 104,77**
CSF £86.22 TOTE £11.80: £3.40, £3.40, £1.50; EX 109.10 Trifecta £607.00.
Owner Sheikh Juma Dalmook Al Maktoum **Bred** Godolphin **Trained** Newmarket, Suffolk

The Form Book Flat 2019, Raceform Ltd, Newbury, RG14 5SJ

FOCUS
A hugely competitive renewal of this Listed event, in which only 5lb separated the 12 runners. The second and third have been rated to form, while the fifth helps set the level.

8709 LADBROKES "PLAY 1-2-FREE" ON FOOTBALL/BRITISH STALLION STUDS EBF NOVICE STKS — 7f 1y(P)
3:00 (3:02) (Class 5) 2-Y-O £3,428 (£1,020; £509; £254) Stalls Low

Form RPR

00 **1** **King Of Athens (USA)**[75] 6233 2-9-2 0 .... SeamieHeffernan 1 91+
(A P O'Brien, Ire) *mde all: 1 l ld 2f out: drvn 1 1/2f out: pushed clr fnl f: easily* 15/8[2]

4162 **2** *5* **Lexington Rebel (FR)**[40] 7445 2-9-9 87 .... SilvestreDeSousa 2 83
(Richard Hannon) *chsd ldrs: wnt 2nd over 2f out: sn drvn: rdn and chsd wnr ent fnl f: kpt on but sn lft bhd* 6/4[1]

3 *2* **Inhalation** 2-9-2 0 ....(w) StevieDonohoe 5 71+
(Ed Vaughan) *hld up: pushed along and hdwy over 1f out: r.o steadily ins fnl f: tk 3rd nr fin* 20/1

4 *nse* **Convertible (IRE)** 2-9-2 0 .... JackMitchell 6 71
(Hugo Palmer) *hld up on outer: pushed along in 5th 2f out: reminder and wnt 3rd ent fnl f: sn no ex: lost 3rd nr fin* 11/2[3]

00 **5** *6* **Siberian Night (IRE)**[22] 8011 2-9-2 0 .... LukeMorris 4 55
(Ed Walker) *chsd ldrs: drvn in 3rd 2f out: wknd over 1f out (jockey said colt hung left-handed in the straight)* 8/1

60 **6** *½* **Son Of Red (IRE)**[38] 7521 2-9-2 0 .... TomQueally 3 54
(Alan King) *hld up: pushed along 2f out: no imp* 33/1

50 **7** *nse* **Exciting Days (USA)**[119] 4564 2-9-2 0 .... HayleyTurner 7 54
(Robert Cowell) *prom: drvn and lost pl 2f out: sn dropped away* 25/1

8 *4* **Surrey Flame (FR)** 2-9-2 0 .... CharlesBishop 8 43
(Joseph Tuite) *a in rr* 25/1

1m 24.87s (0.07) **Going Correction** -0.025s/f (Stan) 8 Ran SP% **116.7**
Speed ratings (Par 95): **98,92,90,89,83 82,82,77**
CSF £4.91 TOTE £2.30: £1.10, £1.10, £5.70; EX 5.20 Trifecta £30.70.
Owner Smith/Mrs Magnier/Tabor/Flaxman Stables **Bred** Orpendale, Chelston & Wynatt **Trained** Cashel, Co Tipperary

FOCUS
An informative novice and a taking performance from the well bred winner.

8710 LADBROKES FOOTBALL ACCA BOOSTY EBF RIVER EDEN FILLIES' STKS (LISTED RACE) — 1m 5f (P)
3:35 (3:35) (Class 1) 3-Y-O+
£22,684 (£8,600; £4,304; £2,144; £1,076; £540) Stalls Low

Form RPR

3222 **1** **Delphinia (IRE)**[12] 8333 3-8-11 113 .... SeamieHeffernan 4 93+
(A P O'Brien, Ire) *hld up: drvn and plenty to do 1 1/2f out: reminder over 1f out: str run fnl f: led 25yds out: won gng away* 4/6[1]

0414 **2** *¾* **Hameem**[70] 6378 4-9-3 101 .... JimCrowley 6 92
(John Gosden) *hld up: hdwy on outer over 2f out: sn drvn: rdn in 3rd 1f out: ev ch ins fnl f: tk 2nd last stride* 6/1[2]

243 **3** *hd* **Nkosikazi**[26] 7895 4-9-3 90 .... TomMarquand 9 91
(William Haggas) *prom: sn settled in bhd ldrs: drvn 2f out: rdn in 3rd 1f out: kpt on wl fnl f* 14/1

51 **4** *shd* **Expressionism (IRE)**[85] 5810 3-8-11 0 .... OisinMurphy 13 91
(Charlie Appleby) *mid-div: tk clsr order 1/2-way: pushed along and disp ld over 2f out: led over 1f out: rdn fnl f: hdd 25yds out: no ex and lost two pls last stride* 7/1[3]

0320 **5** *¾* **Lady Bergamot (FR)**[33] 7688 5-9-3 88 ....(p[1]) GeorgeWood 7 90
(James Fanshawe) *mid-div: drvn 1 1/2f out: rdn ent fnl f: kpt on nr fin* 66/1

3012 **6** *1 ¼* **Miss Latin (IRE)**[42] 7395 4-9-3 77 .... CallumShepherd 10 88
(David Simcock) *hld up in rr: drvn and hdwy over 1f out: rdn fnl f: one pce* 100/1

6164 **7** *½* **Hyanna**[26] 7895 4-9-3 94 .... GeorgiaDobie 14 87
(Eve Johnson Houghton) *hld up: drvn on outer 2f out: last over 1f out: kpt on past btn rivals ins fnl f* 50/1

60 **8** *¾* **Invitation (IRE)**[11] 8368 3-8-11 84 .... SilvestreDeSousa 3 86
(A P O'Brien, Ire) *led: drvn and hdd over 2f out: sn wknd* 33/1

0563 **9** *¾* **Dance Legend**[15] 8245 4-9-3 94 .... LukeMorris 12 85
(Rae Guest) *trckd ldrs: sn racing in cl 2nd: drvn in share of ld over 2f out: rdn and hdd over 1f out: wknd fnl f* 40/1

3244 **10** *½* **Moteo (IRE)**[33] 7717 4-9-3 99 .... RonanWhelan 2 84
(John M Oxx, Ire) *hld up: drvn 2f out: no imp* 25/1

0644 **11** *1 ¾* **Fresnel**[7] 7668 3-8-11 99 .... BenCurtis 1 84
(Jack W Davison, Ire) *trckd ldrs: drvn and lost pl over 2f out: sn rdn and wknd* 17/2

4466 **12** *¾* **Rasima**[34] 7658 4-9-3 100 ....(p) DavidEgan 8 81
(Roger Varian) *hld up: pushed along over 2f out: nt clr run on inner 1 1/2f out: sn rdn and wknd (jockey said filly was denied a clear run rounding the home bend)* 16/1

2m 43.29s (-2.71) **Going Correction** -0.025s/f (Stan)
WFA 3 from 4yo+ 6lb 12 Ran SP% **123.5**
Speed ratings (Par 108): **107,106,106,106,105 105,104,104,103,103 102,102**
CSF £5.06 TOTE £1.70: £1.10, £1.60, £3.30; EX 6.70 Trifecta £45.60.
Owner Mrs John Magnier & Michael Tabor & Derrick Smith **Bred** Orpendale And Chelston **Trained** Cashel, Co Tipperary

FOCUS
A high-quality edition of this Listed race with recent Group 1 runner-up, Delphinia taking a big drop in class. It was a messy affair but class won the day. The level is set around the third, fifth and eighth.

8711 BOMBARDIER GOLDEN BEER APPRENTICE H'CAP — 7f 1y(P)
4:05 (4:07) (Class 6) (0-65,65) 3-Y-O+
£2,781 (£827; £413; £300; £300; £300) Stalls Low

Form RPR

4604 **1** **Beepeecee**[14] 8291 5-9-2 62 ....(b) AmeliaGlass(5) 6 71
(Thomas Gallagher) *hld up: pushed along and hdwy on outer 1 1/2f out: clsd on ldrs ent fnl f: led 1/2f out: sn clr* 7/1

1304 **2** *2 ¼* **Good Luck Charm**[23] 7982 10-8-13 61 ....(b) RhysClutterbuck(7) 14 64
(Gary Moore) *hld up: pushed along and plenty to do over 1f out: reminder 1f out: r.o wl fnl f: tk 2nd last stride* 20/1

314 **3** *shd* **Fiery Breath**[17] 8199 4-9-6 64 ....(h) StefanoCherchi(3) 13 67
(Robert Eddery) *prom on outer: drvn to ld ent fnl f: reminder and hdd 1/2f out: no ex: lost 2nd last stride* 13/2[3]

5250 **4** *¾* **Chetan**[56] 6904 7-9-0 58 .... MarkCrehan(3) 1 59
(Tony Carroll) *trckd ldr: drvn and hdwy on inner 1 1/2f out: rdn and ev ch 1f out: no ex fnl f* 8/1

5213 **5** *¾* **Vincenzo Coccotti (USA)**[33] 7684 7-8-9 57 ....(p) GeorgeRooke(7) 10 56
(Patrick Chamings) *hld up: drvn 1 1/2f out: swtchd 1f out: kpt on fnl f* 6/1[2]

4212 **6** *nk* **Sonnet Rose (IRE)**[15] 8254 5-9-10 65 ....(bt) WilliamCarver 2 63
(Conrad Allen) *mid-div: pushed along on inner 1 1/2f out: one pce fnl f* 7/2[1]

0041 **6** *dht* **Arctic Flower (IRE)**[10] 8408 6-8-9 53 5ex .... AledBeech(3) 8 51
(John Bridger) *led: reminder in 1/2 l ld 2f out: rdn and hdd ent fnl f: no ex* 16/1

666 **8** *1 ¾* **Altar Boy**[29] 7811 3-9-1 65 .... ShariqMohd(7) 7 57
(Sylvester Kirk) *mid-div on outer: reminder 1 1/2f out: sn rdn: hdwy 1f out: wknd fnl f* 20/1

1056 **9** *¾* **Incentive**[15] 8247 5-9-5 63 ....(p) AngusVilliers(3) 4 54
(Stuart Kittow) *chsd ldr: drvn and lost pl 1 1/2f out: sn rdn and wknd* 16/1

143/ **10** *1 ¾* **Wordismybond**[731] 8473 10-9-6 61 .... ThoreHammerHansen 9 47
(Amanda Perrett) *hld up: pushed along 2f out: rdn over 1f out: no imp* 16/1

3146 **11** *nk* **Napping**[17] 8199 6-9-6 64 .... SeanKirrane(3) 5 56
(Amy Murphy) *mid-div: pushed along 2f out: hmpd ent fnl f: no ch after (jockey said mare was denied a clear run)* 8/1

405 **12** *1 ½* **Hellovasinger**[24] 7976 3-8-3 53 .... TylerHeard(7) 12 33
(Richard Hughes) *hld up: pushed along on inner over 1f out: btn whn hmpd ins fnl f (jockey said gelding was denied a clear run)* 20/1

3000 **13** *1 ¼* **The British Lion (IRE)**[107] 5016 4-9-4 59 .... AndrewBreslin 3 37
(Alexandra Dunn) *hld up: lost tch over 2f out* 33/1

0303 **14** *½* **Freedom And Wheat (IRE)**[15] 8266 3-8-9 59 ....(v) IsobelFrancis(7) 11 35
(Mark Usher) *a in rr (jockey said gelding hung badly left-handed throughout)* 12/1

1m 24.68s (-0.12) **Going Correction** -0.025s/f (Stan)
WFA 3 from 4yo+ 2lb 14 Ran SP% **127.1**
Speed ratings (Par 101): **99,96,96,95,94 94,94,92,91,89 89,87,85,85**
CSF £150.03 CT £999.39 TOTE £7.50: £2.60, £6.00, £2.70; EX 162.50 Trifecta £722.30.
Owner John Reddington **Bred** Equine Origin Ltd **Trained** St Albans, Hertfordshire
■ Stewards' Enquiry : Shariq Mohd two-day ban: careless riding (Nov 16, 18)

FOCUS
A moderate handicap. The first two home came from the rear.
T/Jkpt: Not won. T/Plt: £17.50 to a £1 stake. Pool: £72,442.23 - 3,018.84 winning units. T/Qpdt: £11.10 to a £1 stake. Pool: £7,574.26 - 502.21 winning units. **Keith McHugh**

8524 NEWCASTLE (A.W) (L-H)
Friday, November 1

OFFICIAL GOING: Tapeta: standard
Wind: Light, across

8712 BETWAY APPRENTICE H'CAP — 6f (Tp)
3:45 (3:47) (Class 5) (0-75,76) 3-Y-O+
£3,428 (£1,020; £509; £400; £400; £400) Stalls Centre

Form RPR

3032 **1** **Lucky Lodge**[9] 8471 9-8-13 66 ....(v) HarryRussell 12 76
(Antony Brittain) *in tch on nr side of gp: led and hrd pressed over 1f out: kpt on wl last 100yds* 8/1

426- **2** *1 ¾* **Jonboy**[463] 5383 4-9-5 72 .... DannyRedmond 7 76
(David Brown) *hld up in centre of gp: hdwy and disp ld over 1f out to ins fnl f: rdn and one pce last 100yds* 33/1

0303 **3** *2* **Ricochet (IRE)**[11] 8408 3-8-7 60 .... GabrieleMalune 2 58
(Tom Ward) *cl up on far side of gp: effrt and ev ch over 2f out to over 1f out: one pce ins fnl f* 12/1

-603 **4** *¾* **Global Humor (USA)**[55] 6978 4-8-9 62 ow1 .... BenRobinson 9 58
(Jim Goldie) *s.s: bhd in centre of gp: rdn over 2f out: kpt on fnl f: nvr able to chal (jockey said gelding was slowly away)* 16/1

0000 **5** *nk* **Ower Fly**[14] 8304 6-9-0 67 ....(b) PaulaMuir 11 62
(Ruth Carr) *dwlt: led after 1f on nr side of gp: rdn and hdd over 1f out: no ex ins fnl f* 40/1

4550 **6** *hd* **Daafr (IRE)**[29] 7856 3-9-7 74 .... SeamusCronin 8 68
(Antony Brittain) *t.k.h: cl up in centre of gp: rdn over 2f out: no ex fr over 1f out* 17/2

450- **7** *nse* **Metallic Black**[391] 7983 3-9-9 76 .... SeanDavis 14 70
(Richard Fahey) *hld up on nr side of gp: effrt and rdn over 2f out: no imp over 1f out* 8/1

0003 **8** *1 ½* **Bugler Bob (IRE)**[14] 8304 3-9-3 70 .... MeganNicholls 5 59
(John Quinn) *hld up in centre of gp: rdn over 2f out: no imp over 1f out (jockey said gelding suffered interference 1f out)* 7/1[3]

3332 **9** *1 ½* **Mr Buttons (IRE)**[39] 7514 3-9-3 70 ....(p) CameronNoble 6 54
(Linda Stubbs) *prom towards far side of gp: drvn along 2f out: wknd over 1f out* 7/1[3]

0410 **10** *1 ½* **Penny Pot Lane**[11] 8400 6-8-10 63 ....(p) GavinAshton 4 42
(Richard Whitaker) *in tch on far side of gp: drvn and outpcd over 2f out: sn btn* 28/1

2403 **11** *4 ½* **Kaafy (IRE)**[21] 8083 3-8-9 62 .... RowanScott 13 27
(Grant Tuer) *s.i.s: hld up on nr side of gp: struggling over 2f out: sn btn* 6/1[1]

0441 **12** *1 ¾* **Choosey (IRE)**[29] 7855 4-9-3 70 ....(t) GerO'Neill 1 29
(Michael Easterby) *t.k.h: w ldrs in centre of gp: rdn over 2f out: wknd over 1f out* 22/1

0455 **13** *14* **Ascended (IRE)**[14] 8304 3-9-7 74 .... GeorgiaCox 3
(William Haggas) *s.i.s: bhd on far side of gp: struggling over 2f out: sn btn (jockey said filly was never travelling; vet found the filly to have an irregular heartbeat)* 13/2[2]

1m 11.67s (-0.83) **Going Correction** +0.05s/f (Slow) 13 Ran SP% **112.1**
Speed ratings (Par 103): **107,104,102,101,100 100,100,98,96,94 88,85,67**
CSF £247.73 CT £3194.24 TOTE £8.60: £2.60, £7.30, £4.60; EX 290.10 Trifecta £2747.60.
Owner Antony Brittain **Bred** Mel Brittain **Trained** Warthill, N Yorks

FOCUS
A wide-open apprentice handicap to open proceedings on an historic evening at Newcastle. The early pace was solid but the comfortable success of the fully-exposed winner suggests it's not form to get carried away with. The winner sets the level.

8713 BOMBARDIER GOLDEN BEER H'CAP — 1m 5y (Tp)
4:15 (4:18) (Class 6) (0-65,65) 3-Y-O+
£2,781 (£827; £413; £400; £400; £400) Stalls Centre

Form RPR

3340 **1** **Swansdown**[29] 7835 3-9-5 62 ....(p) BenCurtis 8 73
(William Haggas) *hld up in centre of gp: hdwy whn nt clr run briefly over 1f out: led ins fnl f: kpt on wl* 13/2[2]

0332 **2** *1* **Gottardo (IRE)**[18] 8199 4-9-10 **65** .... HollieDoyle 2 71
(Ed Dunlop) *hld up on far side of gp: rdn over 2f out: hdwy to ld over 1f out: hdd ins fnl f: one pce* **14/1**

2060 **3** *nse* **Newmarket Warrior (IRE)**[21] 8087 8-9-10 **65** ....(p) DavidAllan 14 71
(Iain Jardine) *hld up on nr side of gp: rdn over 2f out: hdwy over 1f out: kpt on fnl f: nt pce to chal* **14/1**

1230 **4** *½* **Termonator**[23] 8025 3-9-6 **63** .... SamJames 6 68
(Grant Tuer) *in tch in centre of gp: effrt and drvn along over 1f out: no ex ins fnl f* **15/2**

3242 **5** *1* **Traveller (FR)**[13] 8345 5-9-2 **57** ....(tp) CamHardie 10 59
(Antony Brittain) *dwlt: sn cl up on nr side of gp: rdn over 2f out: one pce ins fnl f* **6/1**[1]

4156 **6** *1½* **Melgate Majeure**[41] 7452 3-9-5 **62** .... JamesSullivan 12 61
(Michael Easterby) *hld up on nr side of gp: rdn over 2f out: kpt on fnl f: nvr able to chal* **7/1**[3]

4460 **7** *½* **Molly Mai**[41] 7452 3-9-5 **62** .... FrannyNorton 13 60
(Philip McBride) *midfield on nr side of gp: effrt over 2f out: hdwy to chse ldrs over 1f out: no ex ins fnl f* **14/1**

5054 **8** *1½* **Curfewed (IRE)**[66] 6582 3-9-5 **62** ....(p) LukeMorris 9 57
(Tracy Waggott) *cl up on nr side of gp: rdn and led briefly 2f out: wknd ins fnl f* **33/1**

3042 **9** *nse* **Carey Street (IRE)**[10] 8434 3-9-5 **65** .... CameronNoble(3) 5 60
(John Quinn) *led in centre of gp: rdn and hdd 2f out: wknd fnl f* **13/2**[2]

5030 **10** *½* **Beverley Bullet**[30] 7829 6-9-6 **61** ....(p) PhilDennis 3 54
(Lawrence Mullaney) *cl up in centre of gp: drvn and ev ch over 2f out: wknd over 1f out* **12/1**

0-04 **11** *¾* **Imperial Focus (IRE)**[10] 8423 6-9-2 **57** .... PaulHanagan 7 49
(Simon Waugh) *bhd towards far side of gp: rdn over 2f out: sn btn* **22/1**

3630 **12** *3* **Global Exceed**[11] 8405 4-9-3 **61** ....(t) GemmaTutty(3) 1 46
(Karen Tutty) *t.k.h: cl up on far side of gp: drvn over 2f out: wknd over 1f out* **25/1**

0000 **13** *2¾* **Najashee (IRE)**[56] 6940 5-9-2 **62** ....(v) PaulaMuir(5) 4 41
(Roger Fell) *cl up on far side of gp: struggling over 2f out: sn btn (jockey said gelding was slowly away)* **10/1**

1m 39.05s (0.45) **Going Correction** +0.05s/f (Slow)
WFA 3 from 4yo+ 2lb **13 Ran SP% 113.1**
Speed ratings (Par 101): **99,98,97,97,96 94,94,92,92,92 91,88,85**
CSF £86.61 CT £1260.67 TOTE £6.50: £2.50, £2.40, £4.60; EX 68.90 Trifecta £1770.10.
Owner Fittocks Stud **Bred** Fittocks Stud **Trained** Newmarket, Suffolk

FOCUS
A low-grade handicap but the winner looked a cut above this level in overcoming a troubled passage to score decisively.

8714 LADBROKES WHERE THE NATION PLAYS NOVICE STKS (PLUS 10 RACE) 7f 14y (Tp)
4:50 (4:53) (Class 4) 2-Y-0 £4,463 (£1,328; £663; £331) **Stalls Centre**

Form RPR

54 **1** **Aberffraw**[8] 8494 2-9-5 0 .... BenCurtis 5 76+
(William Haggas) *cl up in centre of gp: led 2f out: rdn and kpt on wl fnl f* **7/2**[2]

0 **2** *½* **Kumasi**[70] 6424 2-9-5 0 .... ShaneGray 9 75
(David O'Meara) *hld up on nr side of gp: hdwy to chse ldrs 2f out: sn rdn: wnt 2nd wl ins fnl f: clsng at fin* **15/2**

4423 **3** *1* **Hello Baileys**[55] 6971 2-9-5 77 .... FrannyNorton 10 72
(Mark Johnston) *cl up on nr side of gp: effrt and chsd wnr over 1f out tl lost 2nd wl ins fnl f: no ex* **4/1**[3]

4 *½* **Velma** 2-9-0 0 .... MichaelStainton 4 66
(Chris Fairhurst) *dwlt: hld up on nr side of gp: rdn over 2f out: effrt over 1f out: kpt on fnl f: nvr able to chal* **100/1**

0 **5** *½* **Athabasca (IRE)**[13] 8338 2-9-0 0 .... SamJames 6 65
(Grant Tuer) *led in centre of gp: rdn and hdd 2f out: kpt on same pce fnl f* **66/1**

6 *1¾* **Glaer** 2-9-5 0 .... RobertHavlin 1 65
(John Gosden) *dwlt: hld up on far side of gp: pushed along and effrt whn nt clr run briefly over 1f out: nvr able to chal* **2/1**[1]

0 **7** *1½* **Sports Reporter**[27] 7902 2-9-5 0 .... TonyHamilton 7 62
(Richard Fahey) *hld up in centre of gp: drvn along over 2f out: no imp fr over 1f out* **7/1**

4 **8** *1* **Jackate**[86] 5815 2-9-5 0 .... CamHardie 11 59
(Ollie Pears) *hld up on nr side of gp: drvn and outpcd over 2f out: sme late hdwy: nvr on terms* **33/1**

6 **9** *nse* **Star Prize (IRE)**[15] 8297 2-8-9 0 .... FayeMcManoman(5) 8 54
(Noel Wilson) *chsd ldrs in centre of gp: rdn over 2f out: wknd over 1f out* **200/1**

0 **10** *2½* **Camouflaged (IRE)**[27] 7902 2-9-5 0 .... JoeFanning 3 53
(Mark Johnston) *in tch on far side of gp: rdn over 2f out: wknd over 1f out* **12/1**

0 **11** *6* **Mereside Blue**[51] 7063 2-9-0 0 .... DavidAllan 2 33
(David Barron) *cl up towards far side of gp: struggling over 2f out: sn btn* **50/1**

1m 27.48s (1.28) **Going Correction** +0.05s/f (Slow) **11 Ran SP% 115.4**
Speed ratings (Par 98): **94,93,92,91,91 89,87,86,86,83 76**
CSF £28.79 TOTE £3.80: £1.40, £2.50, £1.30; EX 29.20 Trifecta £145.80.
Owner Dan Hall & Mrs Julie & David R Martin **Bred** Rabbah Bloodstock Limited **Trained** Newmarket, Suffolk

FOCUS
Some powerful stables were represented in this novice race and although the favourite, a newcomer, was disappointing, it looks form to be positive enough about.

8715 BETWAY CASINO H'CAP 5f (Tp)
5:25 (5:25) (Class 5) (0-70,72) 3-Y-0+
£3,428 (£1,020; £509; £400; £400; £400) **Stalls Centre**

Form RPR

6563 **1** **Qaaraat**[3] 8643 4-8-7 **56** ....(p) CamHardie 8 63
(Antony Brittain) *hld up in centre of gp: rdn and hdwy over 1f out: led ins fnl f: hld on wl cl home* **7/1**[3]

2152 **2** *shd* **Be Proud (IRE)**[10] 8429 3-8-12 **61** .... BenRobinson 10 68
(Jim Goldie) *hld up in centre of gp: swtchd lft and hdwy over 1f out: disp ld ins fnl f: hung rt cl home: jst hld* **3/1**[1]

1045 **3** *½* **Landing Night (IRE)**[15] 8296 7-8-13 **65** ....(tp) MeganNicholls(3) 4 70
(Rebecca Menzies) *trckd ldrs in centre of gp: drvn and effrt over 1f out: kpt on fnl f: hld cl home* **9/1**

0033 **4** *shd* **Kyllachy Warrior (IRE)**[22] 8066 3-9-4 **67** .... OisinMurphy 9 72
(Lawrence Mullaney) *prom on nr side of gp: effrt and rdn 2f out: kpt on fnl f: hld towards fin* **4/1**[2]

3125 **5** *shd* **Hassaad**[15] 8285 3-9-7 **70** .... HollieDoyle 2 74
(Archie Watson) *trckd ldrs on far side of gp: effrt and ev ch over 1f out to ins fnl f: one pce whn hmpd cl home* **8/1**

4403 **6** *1* **Longroom**[15] 8296 7-8-13 **62** .... PhilDennis 5 63
(Noel Wilson) *led in centre of gp: drvn over 1f out: hdd ins fnl f: kpt on same pce* **16/1**

0656 **7** *1½* **Almurr (IRE)**[10] 8429 3-9-1 **67** .... SeanDavis(3) 3 62
(Phillip Makin) *bhd on far side of gp: drvn along over 2f out: hdwy over 1f out: no imp fnl f* **14/1**

5100 **8** *nk* **Brandy Station (IRE)**[10] 8429 4-8-8 **64** ....(h) GavinAshton(7) 7 58
(Lisa Williamson) *bhd in centre of gp: drvn over 2f out: kpt on fnl f: nvr able to chal* **80/1**

6640 **9** *1¼* **Henley**[23] 8023 7-9-4 **67** .... BenCurtis 6 57
(Tracy Waggott) *cl up in centre of gp tl rdn and wknd over 1f out* **14/1**

0000 **10** *2* **Superseded (IRE)**[20] 8117 3-8-10 **64** .... DylanHogan(5) 1 47
(John Butler) *hld up on far side of gp: drvn along 1/2-way: nvr able to chal* **66/1**

104 **11** *1* **Hard Solution**[10] 8429 3-9-4 **67** .... ShaneGray 11 46
(David O'Meara) *hld up on nr side of gp: rdn over 2f out: wknd over 1f out* **9/1**

1260 **12** *2¼* **Arishka (IRE)**[32] 7771 3-9-9 **72** .... KieranO'Neill 12 43
(Daniel Kubler) *hld up in tch on nr side of gp: drvn 1/2-way: wknd over 1f out* **20/1**

0200 **13** *12* **Raspberry**[18] 8194 3-9-2 **65** .... DuranFentiman 13
(Olly Williams) *bhd on nr side of gp: drvn and struggling after 2f: lost tch fnl 2f* **50/1**

58.48s (-1.02) **Going Correction** +0.05s/f (Slow) **13 Ran SP% 117.3**
Speed ratings (Par 103): **110,109,109,108,108 107,104,104,102,99 97,93,74**
CSF £27.03 CT £200.23 TOTE £7.80: £2.50, £1.70, £2.30; EX 31.30 Trifecta £212.50.
Owner Antony Brittain **Bred** Cheveley Park Stud Ltd **Trained** Warthill, N Yorks

FOCUS
Competitive enough for the grade and an eventful finish, the fast-finishing winner ending a losing run of 21 in the process. Ordinary form rated around the second to the fifth.

8716 VERTEM FUTURITY TROPHY STKS (GROUP 1) (C&F) 1m 5y (Tp)
6:00 (6:00) (Class 1) 2-Y-0
£113,420 (£43,000; £21,520; £10,720; £5,380; £2,700) **Stalls Centre**

Form RPR

122 **1** **Kameko (USA)**[34] 7691 2-9-1 108 .... OisinMurphy 6 117+
(Andrew Balding) *in tch: smooth hdwy on far side of gp to ld over 1f out: rdn and clr whn drifted (rt) to stands' rail ins fnl f: comf* **11/2**[3]

1 **2** *3¼* **Innisfree (IRE)**[33] 7744 2-9-1 107 .... SeamieHeffernan 4 110
(A P O'Brien, Ire) *in tch on nr side of gp: effrt and pushed along over 2f out: ev ch briefly wl over 1f out: sn chsng wnr: kpt on fnl f: nt pce to chal* **11/1**

0044 **3** *nk* **Year Of The Tiger (IRE)**[20] 8113 2-9-1 108 .... PBBeggy 7 109
(A P O'Brien, Ire) *hld up in centre of gp: rdn and hdwy 2f out: disp 2nd pl thrght fnl f: one pce towards fin* **16/1**

1 **4** *shd* **Mogul**[48] 7217 2-9-1 108 .... DonnachaO'Brien 3 109
(A P O'Brien, Ire) *dwlt: hld up towards rr: hdwy on far side of gp over 2f out: disp 2nd pl thrght fnl f: hld towards fin* **7/2**[2]

1 **5** *2½* **Kinross**[27] 7899 2-9-1 0 .... HarryBentley 8 104
(Ralph Beckett) *dwlt: hld up in centre of gp: pushed along and stdy hdwy over 2f out: effrt and angled rt over 1f out: no imp fnl f* **13/8**[1]

6 *5* **King Of The Throne (USA)**[13] 8353 2-9-1 0 .... PaulHanagan 5 93
(Emmet Mullins, Ire) *bhd on far side of gp: drvn and outpcd 3f out: sme late hdwy: nvr rchd ldrs* **150/1**

1 **7** *½* **Verboten (IRE)**[107] 5059 2-9-1 0 .... RobertHavlin 12 92
(John Gosden) *dwlt and wnt rt s: hld up on nr side of gp: drvn along and outpcd over 2f out: no imp fr over 1f out* **8/1**

1 **8** *2¼* **New World Tapestry (USA)**[35] 7661 2-9-1 0 .... EmmetMcNamara 11 87
(A P O'Brien, Ire) *cl up on nr side of gp: rdn and led briefly 2f out: wknd fnl f* **20/1**

1341 **9** *hd* **Tammani**[9] 8483 2-9-1 97 .... BenCurtis 2 86
(William Haggas) *cl up in centre of gp: effrt and ev ch over 2f out: rdn and wknd over 1f out* **20/1**

365 **10** *10* **Geometrical (IRE)**[13] 8356 2-9-1 103 .... KevinManning 1 64
(J S Bolger, Ire) *midfield on far side of gp: drvn and struggling over 2f out: sn btn* **33/1**

6 **11** *2½* **Royal County Down (IRE)**[48] 7217 2-9-1 92 ....(b) AndreaAtzeni 10 59
(A P O'Brien, Ire) *t.k.h: led at decent gallop: rdn and hdd over 2f out: sn wknd* **50/1**

1m 36.26s (-2.34) **Going Correction** +0.05s/f (Slow) 2y crse rec **11 Ran SP% 116.1**
Speed ratings (Par 110): **113,109,109,109,106 101,101,99,98,88 86**
CSF £59.01 CT £911.74 TOTE £6.50: £2.00, £1.80, £4.80; EX 54.50 Trifecta £483.10.
Owner Qatar Racing Limited **Bred** Calumet Farm **Trained** Kingsclere, Hants

FOCUS
The first Group 1 race to be run on an AW surface in Britain, rescheduled from Doncaster last weekend, and it produced an emphatic display from Kameko, who was providing Andrew Balding and Qatar Racing with a second win in the race following Elm Park's victory in 2014. The pace, set by one of the five Aidan O'Brien-trained runners, was solid. It's been rated around the second, third and fourth.

8717 LADBROKES "PLAY 1-2 FREE" ON FOOTBALL MEDIAN AUCTION MAIDEN STKS (PLUS 10 RACE) 1m 5y (Tp)
6:30 (6:32) (Class 4) 2-Y-0 £4,463 (£1,328; £663; £331) **Stalls Centre**

Form RPR

64 **1** **HMS President (IRE)**[23] 8012 2-9-5 0 .... OisinMurphy 10 81+
(Eve Johnson Houghton) *cl up on nr side of gp: smooth hdwy to ld 2f out: rdn clr fnl f: comf* **5/1**[2]

2 *3* **Mrs Upjohn (FR)** 2-9-0 0 .... HollieDoyle 4 69+
(Archie Watson) *prom on far side of gp: effrt and ev ch briefly 2f out: sn chsng wnr: kpt on same pce fnl f* **14/1**[3]

03 **3** *2* **Genesius (IRE)**[37] 7579 2-9-5 0 .... CallumRodriguez 5 70+
(Julie Camacho) *trckd ldrs in centre of gp: effrt and rdn 2f out: kpt on same pce fnl f* **16/1**

22 **4** *1* **Glenties (USA)**[20] 8121 2-9-5 0 .... JoeFanning 6 68
(Mark Johnston) *led on far side of gp: drvn and hdd 2f out: outpcd fnl f* **4/9**[1]

5 *1½* **Bollin Margaret** 2-9-0 0 .... DavidAllan 2 60
(Tim Easterby) *slowly away: bhd on far side of gp: effrt and rdn over 2f out: no further imp over 1f out* **40/1**

00 **6** *1¼* **Galispeed (FR)**[49] 7154 2-9-5 0 .... AdamMcNamara 1 62
(Archie Watson) *cl up on far side of gp: drvn and ev ch over 2f out: wknd fnl f* **40/1**

7 2 1/2 **Exhalation** 2-9-0 0 FrannyNorton 11 51
(Mark Johnston) *in tch on nr side of gp: drvn and outpcd over 2f out: btn over 1f out* **16/1**

8 2 **Cheshire** 2-9-0 0 KevinStott 3 47
(James Bethell) *slowly away: bhd in centre of gp: drvn along 3f out: nvr rchd ldrs* **28/1**

0 9 3 1/4 **Brasingamanbellamy**[51] 7067 2-9-5 0 JackGarritty 8 45
(Jedd O'Keeffe) *chsd ldr in centre of gp: drvn and outpcd over 2f out: wknd over 1f out* **33/1**

0 10 1 1/2 **Phoenix Strike**[10] 8424 2-9-5 0 AndrewMullen 13 41
(Ben Haslam) *dwlt: t.k.h: hld up in midfield on nr side of gp: struggling over 2f out: sn btn* **125/1**

11 2 3/4 **African Sun (IRE)** 2-9-5 0 BenCurtis 7 35
(Ed Dunlop) *towards rr on nr side of gp: drvn and outpcd over 2f out: sn btn* **22/1**

12 8 **Allerthorpe** 2-9-5 0 (t[1]) CamHardie 14 18
(Brian Rothwell) *hld up on nr side of gp: rdn and struggling 3f out: sn btn* **150/1**

13 2 3/4 **Thriller's Moon** 2-9-5 0 PhilDennis 9 12
(Richard Whitaker) *s.i.s: bhd on nr side of gp: struggling 3f out: sn btn* **50/1**

1m 39.76s (1.16) **Going Correction** +0.05s/f (Slow) **13** Ran SP% **123.4**
Speed ratings (Par 98): **96,93,91,90,88 87,84,82,79,78 75,67,64**
CSF £68.96 TOTE £6.00: £1.10, £3.00, £4.70; EX 60.50 Trifecta £977.50.
Owner HP Racing HMS President **Bred** Skymarc Farm **Trained** Blewbury, Oxon

FOCUS
A fair maiden. The winner continues to improve and scored in emphatic style.

8718 BOMBARDIER "MARCH TO YOUR OWN DRUM" NOVICE STKS 1m 5y (Tp)
7:00 (7:00) (Class 5) 3-Y-O+ £3,428 (£1,020; £509; £254) **Stalls** Centre

Form RPR

1 **Desert Caravan** 3-9-2 0 BenCurtis 4 77+
(William Haggas) *hld up: tk clsr order 1/2-way: cl up 2f out: led 1f out: pushed clr fnl f* **5/2[1]**

42 2 1 1/2 **Bobby Shaft**[207] 1649 3-9-2 0 PaulHanagan 7 72
(Richard Fahey) *t.k.h: trckd ldr: led over 1f out: sn drvn and hdd: no ex fnl f* **5/2[1]**

01 3 1 1/4 **Fortamour (IRE)**[45] 7303 3-9-7 0 GrahamLee 1 74
(Ben Haslam) *hld up: pushed along 2f out: rdn over 1f out: kpt on into 3rd fnl f* **10/3[3]**

3 4 nk **Hill Hollow (IRE)**[21] 8086 3-8-11 0 DylanHogan(5) 2 68
(David Simcock) *t.k.h: hld up: drvn 2f out: rdn over 1f out: one pce fnl f* **3/1[2]**

30 5 1 1/4 **Ideal Destiny**[36] 7630 3-8-11 0 ShaneGray 8 60
(Karen Tutty) *t.k.h: led at modest gallop: qcknd pce bef 1/2-way: drvn and hdd over 1f out: wknd fnl f* **50/1**

06 6 6 **Fire Island**[9] 8467 3-8-11 0 HollieDoyle 6 46
(Tom Ward) *t.k.h: chsd ldr: drvn and lost pl over 2f out: sn dropped away* **28/1**

4 7 2 **Battle Commander**[56] 6941 3-9-2 0 DuranFentiman 3 46
(Olly Williams) *hld up: drvn and lost tch over 2f out* **50/1**

1m 44.84s (6.24) **Going Correction** +0.05s/f (Slow) **7** Ran SP% **112.6**
Speed ratings (Par 103): **70,68,67,66,65 59,57**
CSF £8.74 TOTE £2.80: £2.20, £2.40; EX 7.80 Trifecta £27.00.
Owner The Queen **Bred** The Queen **Trained** Newmarket, Suffolk

FOCUS
What looked an interesting novice on paper was rather spoiled by a pedestrian early pace. The winner looks a nice prospect, though. The fifth has been rated to her shaky debut figure, with the second, third and fourth within lengths of their previous marks.

8719 BOMBARDIER BRITISH HOPPED AMBER BEER H'CAP 7f 14y (Tp)
7:30 (7:30) (Class 5) (0-75,74) 3-Y-O+
£3,428 (£1,020; £509; £400; £400; £400) **Stalls** Centre

Form RPR

1034 1 **Valley Of Fire**[14] 8305 7-9-0 67 (p) LewisEdmunds 9 76
(Les Eyre) *awkward leaving stalls and slowly away: bhd: hdwy 2f out: rdn to ld 1/2f out: sn clr* **11/2[3]**

0440 2 1 1/4 **Vive La Difference (IRE)**[18] 8206 5-8-13 66 (b) DavidAllan 4 72+
(Tim Easterby) *hld up: pushed along and hdwy over 1f out: rdn and r.o wl fnl f: tk 2nd last few strides* **9/1**

1031 3 nk **Castle Quarter (IRE)**[23] 8025 3-9-1 69 (b) TomEaves 7 73+
(Seb Spencer) *mid-div: trckd ldrs gng wl over 1f out: drvn fnl f: r.o to take 3rd last 50yds* **7/2[1]**

6-00 4 3/4 **Silver Dust (IRE)**[43] 7364 3-9-3 71 TonyHamilton 3 73
(Richard Fahey) *mid-div: hdwy 2f out: drvn to ld ent fnl f: rdn and hdd 1/2f out: no ex: lost two pls last 50yds* **20/1**

6454 5 3/4 **Double Martini (IRE)**[23] 8025 3-8-8 67 PaulaMuir(5) 1 67
(Roger Fell) *hld up in rr: hdwy over 1f out: kpt on fnl f* **14/1**

5542 6 1 1/4 **Esprit De Corps**[22] 8070 5-9-0 72 DylanHogan(5) 8 69
(David Barron) *trckd ldrs: hdwy to ld 1 1/2f out: rdn and hdd ent fnl f: no ex* **7/1**

0520 7 nk **Elixsoft (IRE)**[14] 8305 4-9-7 74 (p) BenCurtis 5 71
(Roger Fell) *hld up: rdn over 1f out: one pce fnl f* **12/1**

0200 8 nk **Avenue Of Stars**[21] 8083 6-8-9 62 LukeMorris 12 58
(Karen McLintock) *trckd ldrs: nt clr run and lost pl over 1f out: rdn and kpt on fnl f* **33/1**

6212 9 1 **Harvest Day**[30] 7820 4-9-2 74 (t) GerO'Neill(5) 11 67
(Michael Easterby) *hld up: hdwy on stands' rail over 1f out: drvn fnl f: no ex* **4/1[2]**

1060 10 1 1/2 **Oriental Lilly**[14] 8304 5-9-2 69 BenRobinson 10 58
(Jim Goldie) *hld up: pushed along 2f out: no imp* **12/1**

0300 11 1/2 **Ideal Candy (IRE)**[14] 8305 4-8-13 69 GemmaTutty(3) 13 57
(Karen Tutty) *led: drvn and hdd 1 1/2f out: sn wknd* **28/1**

0000 12 3/4 **Drogon (IRE)**[14] 8304 3-9-2 70 PaulHanagan 6 55
(Jackie Stephen) *trckd ldr: drvn 2f out: wknd 1f out* **50/1**

40/0 13 3 1/2 **Fast And Furious (IRE)**[35] 7656 6-9-2 69 KevinStott 2 45
(James Bethell) *hld up: drvn and dropped to last over 1f out* **40/1**

1m 25.85s (-0.35) **Going Correction** +0.05s/f (Slow)
WFA 3 from 4yo+ 1lb **13** Ran SP% **117.7**
Speed ratings (Par 103): **104,102,102,101,100 99,98,98,97,95 94,94,90**
CSF £50.32 CT £199.30 TOTE £7.20: £2.80, £3.00, £1.90; EX 63.60 Trifecta £322.50.
Owner Billy Parker & Steven Parker **Bred** Bearstone Stud Ltd **Trained** Catwick, N Yorks

FOCUS
A competitive handicap which saw the winner recover well from an awkward start. The winner has been rated up a length on this year's form.

8720 BETWAY HEED YOUR HUNCH H'CAP 5f (Tp)
8:00 (8:02) (Class 6) (0-55,57) 3-Y-O+
£2,781 (£827; £413; £400; £400; £400) **Stalls** Centre

Form RPR

0440 1 **Rangefield Express (IRE)**[30] 7824 3-9-0 48 (b) SamJames 8 54
(Geoffrey Harker) *mde all: drvn in 1 l ld 1f out: rdn and r.o wl fnl f* **22/1**

0050 2 3/4 **Star Cracker (IRE)**[17] 8233 7-8-12 46 oh1 (p) PhilDennis 5 49
(Jim Goldie) *prom: drvn in 1 l 2nd 1f out: rdn fnl f: r.o but a hld* **14/1**

000 3 nk **Arnold**[10] 8429 5-9-9 57 FrannyNorton 1 59
(Ann Duffield) *hld up: pushed along over 1f out: drvn fnl f: kpt on into 3rd nr fin* **11/2[2]**

6606 4 hd **Lord Of The Glen**[25] 7959 4-8-12 46 (v) BenRobinson 13 48
(Jim Goldie) *bhd: drvn and hdwy over 1f out: r.o fnl f: nvr nrr* **13/2**

2564 5 nse **Patrick (IRE)**[9] 8457 7-9-7 55 (p) LukeMorris 2 56
(Paul Midgley) *mid-div: drvn and hdwy 1 1/2f out: rdn fnl f: kpt on* **8/1**

5006 6 1/2 **Mightaswellsmile**[3] 8632 5-8-12 46 oh1 KevinStott 9 46
(Ron Barr) *mid-div: drvn over 1f out: rdn fnl f: one pce* **16/1**

2460 7 1/2 **Guardia Svizzera (IRE)**[16] 8263 5-9-6 54 (h) BenCurtis 12 52
(Roger Fell) *prom: rdn over 1f out: wknd fnl f* **6/1[3]**

0000 8 1 **Encoded (IRE)**[35] 7651 6-8-13 47 ow1 CallumRodriguez 10 41
(Lynn Siddall) *slowly away: bhd: drvn and hdwy over 1f out: rdn fnl f: no ex* **33/1**

3342 9 3/4 **Red Allure**[25] 7962 4-8-13 47 TomEaves 7 40
(Michael Mullineaux) *mid-div: drvn 1 1/2f out: sn rdn: btn whn hmpd ins fnl f* **5/1[1]**

0005 10 1 1/4 **Kibaar**[9] 8450 7-9-2 50 JamesSullivan 11 37
(Ruth Carr) *bhd: pushed along 1 1/2f out: no imp* **10/1**

6120 11 3/4 **One One Seven (IRE)**[30] 7824 3-9-7 55 CamHardie 4 39
(Antony Brittain) *mid-div: drvn and wknd 1f out* **11/1**

0005 12 1/2 **Alisia R (IRE)**[37] 7591 3-8-13 47 (h) LewisEdmunds 3 29
(Les Eyre) *hld up: drvn and no ch fr 2f out* **33/1**

0005 13 1 **Little Miss Lola**[33] 7737 5-8-7 46 oh1 PaulaMuir(5) 6 25
(Lynn Siddall) *mid-div: rdn and lost pl over 1f out: dropped away fnl f* **22/1**

59.21s (-0.29) **Going Correction** +0.05s/f (Slow) **13** Ran SP% **115.3**
Speed ratings (Par 101): **104,102,102,102,101 101,100,98,97,95 94,93,91**
CSF £282.06 CT £1990.72 TOTE £30.20: £8.80, £4.10, £1.50; EX 284.60 Trifecta £2114.80.
Owner Cloud 9 Racing & Phil Harker **Bred** Rangefield Bloodstock **Trained** Thirkleby, N Yorks

FOCUS
An open sprint handicap which saw the winner make all.
T/Plt: £1,401.30 to a £1 stake. Pool: £80,723.05 - 42.05 winning units T/Qpdt: £53.80 to a £1 stake. Pool: £14,034.87 - 192.74 winning units **Richard Young & Keith McHugh**

8458 NEWMARKET (R-H)
Friday, November 1

OFFICIAL GOING: Soft (good to soft in places; 6.2)
Wind: light, half behind Weather: overcast

8721 HEATH COURT HOTEL EBF NOVICE STKS (PLUS 10 RACE) (C&G) (DIV I) 7f
12:00 (12:02) (Class 4) 2-Y-O £5,175 (£1,540; £769; £384) **Stalls** Low

Form RPR

1 **Louganini** 2-9-0 0 JasonWatson 8 84+
(Roger Charlton) *rn green: in tch in midfield: effrt and hdwy to chse ldr 2f out: rdn and clsd to ld jst ins fnl f: styd on strly and drew clr: pushed out* **10/1**

3 2 2 3/4 **Naizagai**[18] 8203 2-9-0 0 DavidEgan 5 77
(Roger Varian) *sn pressing ldr tl led over 3f out: rdn over 2f out: edgd lft over 1f out: hdd jst ins fnl f: no ex and kpt on same pce after (jockey said colt hung left-handed under pressure)* **9/2[2]**

3 3/4 **Celestran** 2-9-0 0 NickyMackay 10 75
(John Gosden) *rn green: s.i.s: t.k.h: hld up towards rr: effrt over 2f out: hdwy to chse ldrs and edging rt over 1f out: kpt on ins fnl f: no threat to wnr* **12/1**

4 5 **Keats (IRE)**[10] 8437 2-9-0 0 AdamKirby 11 63
(A P O'Brien, Ire) *in tch in midfield: effrt 3f out: chsd ldrs and wnt lft 2f out: no imp and hung rt over 1f out: wl hld 4th fnl f* **4/6[1]**

55 5 3 1/4 **Gold Desert**[20] 8128 2-9-0 0 TomMarquand 6 55
(Richard Hannon) *sn led: hdd over 3f out and sn rdn: unable qck and outpcd over 1f out: wknd ins fnl f* **7/1[3]**

0 6 4 1/2 **Lord Warburton (IRE)**[9] 8459 2-9-0 0 CallumShepherd 3 43
(Michael Bell) *hld up wl in tch in midfield: pushed along 3f out: rdn over 2f out and sn outpcd: wknd over 1f out* **100/1**

7 1 1/4 **Prince Percy** 2-9-0 0 HectorCrouch 9 40
(Gary Moore) *hld up in tch in midfield: rdn over 2f out: sn outpcd: wknd over 1f out* **66/1**

00 8 1/2 **Big Jimbo**[7] 8516 2-9-0 0 LiamKeniry 1 39
(Gary Moore) *hld up in tch in last trio: effrt over 2f out: sn struggling and wknd over 1f out* **100/1**

0 9 2 3/4 **Wadi Al Sail (IRE)**[94] 5523 2-9-0 0 DavidProbert 4 32
(Gay Kelleway) *t.k.h: sn w ldrs: pressing ldr and rdn over 2f out: outpcd and lost 2nd wl over 1f out: sn btn and wknd ins fnl f* **25/1**

10 12 **Johnny Utah (IRE)** 2-9-0 0 StevieDonohoe 7
(Richard Spencer) *s.i.s: a towards rr: struggling 3f out: lost tch 2f out* **25/1**

1m 29.58s (4.18) **Going Correction** +0.675s/f (Yiel) **10** Ran SP% **118.6**
Speed ratings (Par 98): **103,99,99,93,89 84,83,82,79,65**
CSF £53.87 TOTE £12.40: £2.80, £1.50, £2.60; EX 51.10 Trifecta £403.40.
Owner Imad Alsagar **Bred** Saleh Al Homaizi & Imad Al Sagar **Trained** Beckhampton, Wilts

FOCUS
Stands' side course. Stalls: far side. Middle rail moved to within 10 metres of the far side rail to provide a fresh running line. Rail positioning on the bend added 7yds to races over 1m2f and further. The going had eased slightly and was now soft, good to soft in places (GoingStick 6.2). Jason Watson said it was nearly heavy. The first division of an interesting novice run in a time 7.28sec outside standard, which suggests the ground was indeed testing.

8722 HEATH COURT HOTEL EBF NOVICE STKS (PLUS 10 RACE) (C&G) (DIV II) 7f
12:30 (12:33) (Class 4) 2-Y-O **£5,175** (£1,540; £769; £384) **Stalls** Low

Form RPR

1 **Tuscan Gaze (IRE)** 2-9-0 0 NickyMackay 3 80+
(John Gosden) *awkward leaving stalls: sn rcvrd to ld: hdd 5f out: styd w ldr tl led again 2f out: sn rdn: styd on wl under mainly hands and heels riding ins fnl f* **9/1**

2 1 **Photograph (IRE)** 2-9-0 0 AndreaAtzeni 4 76
(Richard Hannon) *sn w ldrs: led 5f out tl rdn and hdd 2f out: stl ev ch over 1f out: kpt on but a hld ins fnl f* **7/2**[2]

3 1 **Sky Power (IRE)** 2-9-0 0 SilvestreDeSousa 6 73
(Richard Hannon) *t.k.h: chsd ldrs: effrt and swtchd rt over 1f out: rdn to chse ldng pair ins fnl f: kpt on* **11/2**[3]

4 4 1 3/4 **Casa Loupi**[24] 7981 2-9-0 0 HectorCrouch 1 69
(Gary Moore) *led: sn hdd: styd prom: rdn and pressing ldrs ent fnl 2f: unable qck over 1f out: lost 3rd and kpt on same pce ins fnl f* **33/1**

50 5 4 **Frankly Mr Shankly (GER)**[18] 8203 2-9-0 0 (h) CallumShepherd 2 59
(Michael Bell) *taken down early: stdd and awkward leaving stalls: hld up in tch in midfield: effrt over 2f out: outpcd u.p and btn over 1f out: wknd ins fnl f* **20/1**

6 nk **Nitro Express** 2-9-0 0 JasonWatson 8 58
(Roger Charlton) *s.i.s: hld up in tch towards rr: effrt ent fnl 2f: swtchd rt and no hdwy over 1f out: wknd ins fnl f* **7/2**[2]

53 7 nse **Blue Skyline (IRE)**[9] 8459 2-9-0 0 JimCrowley 9 58
(David Elsworth) *t.k.h: trckd ldrs: effrt ent fnl 2f: no imp: hung rt and btn over 1f out: wknd ins fnl f (vet said gelding lost its right hind shoe)* **5/2**[1]

8 1/2 **Forge Valley Lad** 2-9-0 0 StevieDonohoe 5 57+
(Ed Vaughan) *hld up in rr: effrt ent fnl 2f: no imp and outpcd over 1f out: wl hld ins fnl f* **16/1**

00 9 nse **Uncle Sid**[27] 7896 2-9-0 0 AdrianMcCarthy 10 56
(William Jarvis) *hld up in tch in midfield: effrt over 2f out: outpcd u.p and btn over 1f out: wknd ins fnl f* **66/1**

10 1 1/2 **Caribbean Spice (IRE)** 2-9-0 0 (t[1] w) MartinDwyer 7 53
(Brian Meehan) *hld up in tch: effrt 3f out: unable qck and outpcd 2f out: wknd over 1f out* **25/1**

1m 31.19s (5.79) **Going Correction** +0.675s/f (Yiel) **10** Ran SP% **117.3**
Speed ratings (Par 98): **93,91,90,88,84 83,83,83,83,81**
CSF £39.43 TOTE £6.70: £2.00, £1.10, £1.80; EX 36.20 Trifecta £131.80.
Owner Lady Bamford, Magnier, Smith & Tabor **Bred** Coolmore & Daylesford Stud **Trained** Newmarket, Suffolk

FOCUS
This division was dominated by the newcomers and nothing got into it from off the pace. The winning time was 1.61sec slower than the first leg.

8723 HEATH COURT HOTEL BESTWESTERN.CO.UK CONDITIONS STKS 6f
1:05 (1:08) (Class 3) 2-3-Y-O **£8,715** (£2,609; £1,304; £652; £326) **Stalls** Low

Form RPR

131 1 **Brad The Brief**[32] 7769 2-8-5 89 JaneElliott 7 90
(Tom Dascombe) *racd keenly: chsd ldrs: shkn up and effrt to chal over 1f out: led 1f out and sn hung rt: r.o strly ins fnl f* **9/2**[3]

4123 2 2 1/2 **Jeanie B**[16] 8243 2-8-0 79 ow3 DarraghKeenan(3) 5 81
(Mick Channon) *led: rdn and hdd over 1f out: sn unable qck and outpcd: kpt on same pce ins fnl f: wnt 2nd towards fin* **14/1**

1 3 1/2 **Raasel**[16] 8243 2-8-5 0 MartinDwyer 3 81
(Marcus Tregoning) *stdd s: t.k.h early: hld up in tch: effrt and qcknd to ld over 1f out: hdd 1f out: no ex u.p: wknd wl ins fnl f: lost 2nd towards fin* **6/5**[1]

020 4 3/4 **Kuwait Direction (IRE)**[136] 3949 2-8-5 97 SilvestreDeSousa 2 79
(Richard Hannon) *in tch in rr: clsd and rdn ent fnl 2f: unable qck and no imp over 1f out: kpt on same pce ins fnl f* **3/1**[2]

3341 5 1 3/4 **Little Brown Trout**[10] 8430 2-8-5 72 JosephineGordon 1 74
(William Stone) *t.k.h: pressed ldr tl unable qck and lost pl over 1f out: wknd ins fnl f* **13/2**

1m 14.74s (2.84) **Going Correction** +0.675s/f (Yiel) **5** Ran SP% **108.6**
Speed ratings: **108,104,104,103,100**
CSF £49.72 TOTE £5.10: £2.20, £4.00; EX 33.30 Trifecta £109.60.
Owner Chasemore Farm **Bred** Chasemore Farm **Trained** Malpas, Cheshire

FOCUS
This had gone to a 3yo four times in the past five years, but they didn't bother turning up this time. The winner did it nicely.

8724 IRISH STALLION FARMS EBF "BOSRA SHAM" FILLIES' STKS (LISTED RACE) 6f
1:40 (1:43) (Class 1) 2-Y-O
£17,013 (£6,450; £3,228; £1,608; £807; £405) **Stalls** Low

Form RPR

3102 1 **Mild Illusion (IRE)**[27] 7896 2-9-0 90 JosephineGordon 19 96
(Jonathan Portman) *chsd ldr tl led over 4f out: rdn over 1f out: sn drvn: edgd lft and styd on gamely ins fnl f* **10/1**

1 2 3/4 **Magical Journey (IRE)**[44] 7333 2-9-0 0 PJMcDonald 17 94
(James Tate) *wnt rt and short of room leaving stalls: hld up in tch towards rr: effrt and swtchd lft 2f out: hdwy to chse ldrs and hung rt 1f out: keeping on whn carried lft ins fnl f: chsd wnr towards fin: kpt on* **14/1**

1 3 3/4 **Lady Light**[10] 8431 2-9-0 0 HayleyTurner 12 92
(Michael Bell) *t.k.h: led tl over 4f out: chsd wnr after: rdn over 1f out: sn drvn: kpt on same pce ins fnl f: lost 2nd towards fin* **10/1**

0425 4 3/4 **Keep Busy (IRE)**[27] 7896 2-9-0 82 JFEgan 14 89
(John Quinn) *hld up in tch in midfield: pushed along ent fnl 2f: swtchd lft over 1f out: hdwy ins fnl f: swtchd rt and kpt on wl towards fin* **25/1**

615 5 1 **Stormy Girl (IRE)**[20] 8125 2-9-0 87 ThomasGreatrex 18 86
(David Loughnane) *in tch in midfield: effrt 2f out: kpt on u.p ins fnl f: nvr getting on terms w ldrs* **25/1**

4143 6 1 1/4 **Orlaith (IRE)**[20] 8125 2-9-3 99 PaulMulrennan 3 86+
(Iain Jardine) *chsd ldrs: effrt over 1f out: unable qck and edgd lft 1f out: no ex and wknd ins fnl f* **12/1**

3260 7 1/2 **Aroha (IRE)**[55] 6966 2-9-0 100 JasonWatson 5 81+
(Brian Meehan) *chsd ldrs: effrt 2f out: drvn and swtchd rt 1f out: kpt on same pce and no imp ins fnl f* **14/1**

2 8 nk **Minhaaj (IRE)**[21] 8097 2-9-0 0 JimCrowley 13 80
(William Haggas) *chsd ldrs early: in tch in midfield after: effrt over 1f out: swtchd rt 1f out: kpt on same pce and no imp ins fnl f* **9/1**[3]

9 nk **For The Trees (IRE)**[12] 8365 2-9-0 0 KieranShoemark 16 79
(Mrs John Harrington, Ire) *restless in stalls: chsd ldrs: effrt over 1f out: unable qck u.p over 1f out: wknd ins fnl f* **12/1**

145 10 1 **Final Option**[41] 7432 2-9-0 92 MartinDwyer 4 76+
(William Muir) *hld up in tch: effrt over 2f out: no imp u.p over 1f out: wknd ins fnl f* **16/1**

315 11 shd **Star Alexander**[125] 4387 2-9-0 89 AdamKirby 15 76
(Clive Cox) *in tch: effrt 2f out: drvn and unable qck over 1f out: wknd ins fnl f* **25/1**

2460 12 3 **Precious Moments (IRE)**[19] 8163 2-9-0 0 SilvestreDeSousa 7 67+
(A P O'Brien, Ire) *hld up in tch in midfield: effrt over 1f out: sn drvn and no imp: wknd ins fnl f (trainer's rep said filly did not handle the dip on this occasion)* **11/4**[1]

0522 13 3 1/4 **Divine Spirit**[32] 7775 2-9-0 101 BrettDoyle 2 57+
(Charlie Appleby) *hld up in tch: effrt ent fnl 2f: no imp u.p over 1f out: wknd ins fnl f (trainer's rep could offer no explanation for the filly's performance)* **6/1**[2]

1414 14 2 1/4 **Caspian Queen (IRE)**[34] 7696 2-9-0 85 LouisSteward 1 50+
(Mohamed Moubarak) *in tch in midfield: hdwy to chse ldrs 3f out: rdn and unable qck over 1f out: sn btn and wknd ins fnl f: eased wl ins fnl f* **20/1**

1 15 3 **Brookside Banner (IRE)**[56] 6919 2-9-0 0 TomMarquand 11 41
(Tom Dascombe) *a towards rr: effrt over 2f out: sn struggling and wl btn over 1f out: eased ins fnl f (jockey said filly was never travelling)* **33/1**

215 16 3 3/4 **Hot Touch**[35] 7659 2-9-0 88 JackMitchell 9 30
(Hugo Palmer) *in tch in midfield: effrt over 2f out: sn drvn and struggling: bhd over 1f out: eased ins fnl f (jockey said filly never travelling)* **33/1**

1m 15.05s (3.15) **Going Correction** +0.675s/f (Yiel) **16** Ran SP% **125.9**
Speed ratings (Par 101): **106,105,104,103,101 100,99,98,98,97 97,93,88,85,81 76**
CSF £134.33 TOTE £14.10: £4.90, £4.30, £3.10; EX 184.00 Trifecta £3295.70.
Owner Old Stoic Racing Club **Bred** Marston Stud **Trained** Upper Lambourn, Berks
■ Flaming Princess was withdrawn. Price at time of withdrawal 16/1. Rule 4 does not apply

FOCUS
A big field for this Listed event, but those drawn in the higher stalls very much held sway.

8725 HEATH COURT DINING CLUB H'CAP 1m 2f
2:15 (2:17) (Class 3) (0-95,94) 3-Y-O+ **£9,056** (£2,695; £1,346; £673) **Stalls** Low

Form RPR

3340 1 **Alternative Fact**[34] 7694 4-8-13 **86** SilvestreDeSousa 7 94
(Ed Dunlop) *stdd and swtchd rt after s: hld up in tch: clsd to chse ldrs 4f out: effrt over 2f out: rdn to ld jst over 1f out: kpt on wl ins fnl f* **7/1**[2]

0353 2 1 1/2 **Awake My Soul (IRE)**[11] 8396 10-8-8 **81** BarryMcHugh 1 86
(Tom Tate) *chsd ldr tl 3f out: sn u.p and outpcd whn swtchd lft 2f out: rallied ins fnl f: kpt on to go 2nd towards fin* **14/1**

0351 3 3/4 **Majestic Dawn (IRE)**[16] 8260 3-9-4 **94** DavidEgan 3 98
(Paul Cole) *led: rdn and hrd pressed wl over 2f out: hdd 2f out: unable qck over 1f out: kpt on same pce ins fnl f* **2/1**[1]

3002 4 hd **Cockalorum (IRE)**[20] 8130 4-9-2 **89** (b) PaulMulrennan 10 92
(Roger Fell) *stdd after s: hld up in tch towards rr: effrt over 2f out: hdwy and hung bdly lft over 1f out: kpt on ins fnl f (jockey said gelding hung left-handed under pressure)* **9/1**[3]

0042 5 shd **Regular Income (IRE)**[11] 8411 4-8-7 **80** (p) JimmyQuinn 5 83
(Adam West) *dwlt: hld up in tch: hdwy into midfield 5f out: effrt over 2f out: kpt on ins fnl f* **14/1**

/44 6 1 **Dalgarno (FR)**[176] 2560 6-9-7 **94** JFEgan 12 95
(Jane Chapple-Hyam) *t.k.h: chsd ldrs: hdwy to press ldr wl over 2f out: rdn to ld 2f out: drvn: edgd rt and hdd jst over 1f out: wknd ins fnl f (jockey said gelding hung badly right-handed under pressure)* **25/1**

6003 7 nk **Severance**[72] 6349 3-9-0 **90** (h) TomMarquand 6 90
(Mick Channon) *taken down early: hld up in tch towards rr: effrt over 2f out: rdn and hdwy over 1f out: kpt on ins fnl f: no threat to ldrs* **7/1**[2]

0004 8 1/2 **Badenscoth**[20] 8130 5-9-3 **90** JoeyHaynes 8 89
(Dean Ivory) *t.k.h: hld up in midfield: effrt over 2f out: wandered u.p 1f out: kpt on ins fnl f: no threat to ldrs* **12/1**

4205 9 1/2 **Mordred (IRE)**[33] 7727 3-8-2 **83** ThoreHammerHansen(5) 9 81
(Richard Hannon) *hld up in tch towards rr: effrt and hdwy over 2f out: wandered u.p over 1f out: kpt on same pce and no imp ins fnl f* **25/1**

515 10 4 **Rake's Progress**[11] 8396 5-8-0 **80** oh1 AngusVilliers(7) 4 70
(Heather Main) *in tch in midfield: rdn over 3f out: outpcd u.p 2f out: wl hld and plugged on same pce after* **16/1**

412 11 20 **Zzoro (IRE)**[33] 7727 6-8-8 **81** (t) JasonWatson 13 31
(Amanda Perrett) *in tch in midfield: effrt 3f out: no imp and btn over 1f out: eased ins fnl f* **12/1**

360 12 2 3/4 **Enigmatic (IRE)**[22] 8062 5-8-12 **85** DavidProbert 2 30
(Alan Bailey) *hld up in tch towards rr: effrt 3f out: sn struggling: bhd and eased ins fnl f* **50/1**

2233 13 26 **The Jean Genie**[36] 7610 5-8-9 **82** JackMitchell 11
(William Stone) *taken down early: chsd ldrs: rdn 3f out: sn struggling: bhd and eased over 1f out: t.o* **16/1**

2m 10.44s (5.04) **Going Correction** +0.675s/f (Yiel)
WFA 3 from 4yo+ 3lb **13** Ran SP% **118.5**
Speed ratings (Par 107): **106,104,104,104,103 103,102,102,102,98 82,80,59**
CSF £98.27 CT £269.68 TOTE £8.40: £2.50, £4.60, £1.30; EX 96.00 Trifecta £403.10.
Owner The Alternative Lot **Bred** Rabbah Bloodstock Limited **Trained** Newmarket, Suffolk

FOCUS
Add 7yds to race distance. A decent handicap, but a messy race with the runners finishing spread all over the track. Ordinary form rated around the first three in line with this year's form.

8726 HEATH COURT HOTEL CHRISTMAS H'CAP 2m
2:50 (2:53) (Class 3) (0-95,97) 3-Y-O+ **£9,056** (£2,695; £1,346; £673) **Stalls** Low

Form RPR

-364 1 **Champagne Champ**[41] 7464 7-8-12 **77** (t) DavidEgan 1 84
(Rod Millman) *sn led and mde rest: drvn over 2f out: forged ahd ent fnl f: styd on wl* **3/1**[1]

/100 2 7 **Rainbow Dreamer**[20] 8114 6-10-0 **93** (p) TomMarquand 7 92
(Alan King) *chsd wnr after 2f: rdn and ev ch 3f out: no ex ent fnl f: wknd ins fnl f* **11/2**[3]

0332 3 1/2 **Colwood**[7] 8523 5-8-6 **74** oh6 DarraghKeenan(3) 5 72
(Robert Eddery) *chsd ldrs: rdn over 4f out: outpcd over 2f out: swtchd lft and chsd clr ldng pair over 1f out: kpt on same pce and no ch w wnr* **5/1**[2]

4001 **4** *2 ¾* **Fun Mac (GER)**[11] 8399 8-9-9 **88** 4ex........................(t) PJMcDonald 2 83
(Hughie Morrison) *hld up in tch in last pair: rdn ent fnl 2f: n.m.r over 1f out: no ch w wnr and plugged on same pce fnl f* **3/1**[1]

1200 **5** *½* **Graceful Lady**[20] 8114 6-8-11 **81**.......................... AndrewBreslin(5) 4 75
(Robert Eddery) *stdd s: hld up in tch in rr: effrt and hdwy u.p over 3f out: outpcd u.p 2f out: no threat to wnr and plugged on same pce fnl f* **13/2**

4551 **6** *2* **Doctor Cross (IRE)**[7] 8524 5-8-11 **79** 5ex.............. ConnorMurtagh(3) 6 71
(Richard Fahey) *led early: sn hdd and in tch in midfield: effrt and hdwy to press ldrs 3f out: no ex and outpcd ent fnl 2f: wknd fnl f* **11/2**[3]

3m 40.71s (11.41) **Going Correction** +0.675s/f (Yiel) **6** Ran SP% **110.8**
Speed ratings (Par 107): **98,94,94,92,92 91**
CSF £19.06 TOTE £3.90: £2.30, £3.10; EX 20.50 Trifecta £105.70.
Owner Five Horses Ltd **Bred** Five Horses Ltd **Trained** Kentisbeare, Devon

FOCUS
Add 7yds to race distance. A decent staying handicap and although they went a sensible pace in the conditions, it was still quite a test and the winner bolted up. They stayed against the inside rail up the final straight.

8727 HEATH COURT HOTEL CORPORATE CLIENTS H'CAP 1m 4f
3:25 (3:34) (Class 4) (0-85,87) 3-Y-0+
£6,469 (£1,925; £962; £481; £300; £300) **Stalls** Low

Form RPR

2625 **1** **Point In Time (IRE)**[22] 8064 4-9-3 **76**........................ DavidProbert 3 84
(Mark Usher) *stdd s: hld up in tch in rr: clsd and chsd ldrs 3f out: effrt to chse ldng pair over 2f out: str chal over 1f out: hung rt and led wl ins fnl f: all out (jockey said filly hung right-handed under pressure)* **25/1**

2202 **2** *nk* **Arabic Culture (USA)**[21] 8082 5-9-5 **78**.................... JackMitchell 11 85
(Grant Tuer) *hld up in tch: hdwy to join ldrs and travelling strly 3f out: drvn to ld over 1f out: carried rt and hdd wl ins fnl f: kpt on* **15/2**[3]

4043 **3** *2 ¾* **Top Power (FR)**[25] 7974 3-9-1 **79**.................(h[1]) SilvestreDeSousa 12 82
(Andrew Balding) *chsd ldrs tl wnt 2nd over 4f out: led 3f out: sn rdn: hdd over 1f out: no ex and kpt on same pce ins fnl f* **9/2**[2]

341 **4** *3 ¼* **Fly The Flag**[64] 6633 3-9-2 **80**........................ NickyMackay 4 77+
(John Gosden) *hld up in tch in rr: hdwy and rdn 3f out: no imp and hung lft 1f out: kpt on ins fnl f* **10/1**

3434 **5** *13* **Rotherwick (IRE)**[33] 7729 7-9-6 **79**.......................(t) DavidEgan 7 56
(Paul Cole) *dwlt and pushed along: in rr: hdwy into midfield 7f out: drvn and lost pl 3f out: no ch fnl 2f* **12/1**

4101 **6** *3 ¼* **Frontispiece**[77] 6156 5-10-0 **87**.......................... KieranShoemark 6 58
(Amanda Perrett) *led: rdn and hdd 3f out: sn outpcd and btn 2f out: wknd* **9/1**

2-41 **7** *2 ½* **Chartered**[140] 3800 3-9-7 **85**.......................... RobHornby 10 53
(Ralph Beckett) *hld up in tch in midfield: clsd and rdn to chse ldrs 3f out: sn outpcd and btn 2f out: wknd* **2/1**[1]

1-54 **8** *24* **Persian Sun**[36] 7616 4-9-5 **78**.......................(t) PJMcDonald 2 7
(Stuart Williams) *chsd ldr tl 9f out: styd chsng ldrs: effrt and rdn to chal 3f out: sn outpcd and btn: wknd 2f out: eased: t.o* **8/1**

4040 **9** *9* **Alfredo (IRE)**[28] 7866 7-9-10 **83**.......................(bt) TomQueally 9
(Seamus Durack) *sn chsng ldrs: hdwy to chse ldr 9f out tl lost pl u.p 4f out: bhd 2f out: eased: t.o* **66/1**

60-2 **10** *26* **Jus Pires (USA)**[28] 7872 5-9-10 **83**.......................(t) DavidNolan 5
(Declan Carroll) *hld up in tch: rdn ent fnl 3f: sn outpcd and wl btn 2f out: eased: t.o* **10/1**

/50- **11** *8* **Zack Mayo**[524] 3109 5-10-0 **87**.......................... TomMarquand 1
(Philip McBride) *in tch in midfield: u.p and struggling 3f out: sn bhd and eased: t.o* **33/1**

2m 40.73s (8.23) **Going Correction** +0.675s/f (Yiel)
WFA 3 from 4yo+ 5lb **11** Ran SP% **118.5**
Speed ratings (Par 105): **99,98,96,94,86 83,82,66,60,42 37**
CSF £201.63 CT £1016.79 TOTE £31.50: £5.50, £2.50, £1.90; EX 212.30 Trifecta £1426.90.
Owner Gaf Racing **Bred** John O'Connor **Trained** Upper Lambourn, Berks
■ Amourice was withdrawn. Price at time of withdrawal 14/1. Rule 4 applies to bets placed prior to withdrawal but not to SP bets - deduction 5p in the pound.
■ Stewards' Enquiry : David Probert three-day ban: interference & careless riding (Nov 16, 18-19)

FOCUS
Add 7yds to race distance. A fair handicap run at just an even pace and they came up the centre this time. The front pair got close late on, but the result was allowed to stand. A surprise pb from the winner, and a small pb from the second. The third has been rated close to his recent form.

8728 CHIEF SEAN BRICE 30 YEAR RETIREMENT H'CAP 1m
4:00 (4:06) (Class 3) (0-95,97) 3-Y-0+ **£9,056** (£2,695; £1,346; £673) **Stalls** Low

Form RPR

2251 **1** **Hafeet Alain (IRE)**[21] 8101 3-9-0 **90**........................ BarryMcHugh 8 100
(Adrian Nicholls) *tok t.k.h: led main gp and chsd overall ldr: led overall over 3f out: rdn 2f out: styd on wl ins fnl f* **15/2**

1201 **2** *1* **Ebury**[56] 6914 3-9-3 **93**.......................... JasonWatson 6 100+
(Martyn Meade) *stdd s: hld up in rr: effrt and stl plenty to do over 2f out: hdwy over 1f out: swtchd lft 1f out: styd on wl to go 2nd cl home: nt rch wnr* **7/1**

11 **3** *½* **Severnaya (IRE)**[50] 7114 3-8-12 **88**........................ NickyMackay 12 94
(John Gosden) *swtchd rt s: hld up in tch in midfield: clsd to chse ldrs 3f out: rdn to chse wnr over 1f out: kpt on ins fnl f: a hld and lost 2nd cl home* **9/2**[1]

2111 **4** *1* **Ouzo**[127] 4300 3-9-1 **91**.......................... PJMcDonald 10 95
(Richard Hannon) *in tch in midfield: clsd to chse ldrs 3f out: rdn and chsd wnr 2f out tl over 1f out: kpt on same pce ins fnl f* **5/1**[2]

4155 **5** *¾* **Waarif (IRE)**[13] 8336 6-9-9 **97**.......................... TomMarquand 9 99
(David O'Meara) *chsd ldrs tl wnt 2nd over 3f out: ev ch 3f out: jst outpcd by wnr and lost 2nd over 2f out: no ex u.p and wknd wl ins fnl f* **14/1**

3100 **6** *4 ½* **Hortzadar**[21] 8096 4-9-5 **93**.......................... DavidNolan 4 85
(David O'Meara) *in tch in midfield: clsd to chse ldrs 3f out: sn rdn: no ex u.p over 1f out: wknd ins fnl f* **11/1**

3001 **7** *nk* **Sawwaah**[28] 7863 4-9-3 **91**.......................(b) JimCrowley 13 82
(Owen Burrows) *racd away fr main gp in centre: s.i.s and rousted along early: hdwy into midfield 1/2-way: unable qck and outpcd wl over 2f out: no threat to ldrs after (jockey said gelding was slowly away)* **11/2**[3]

5540 **8** *3* **Battered**[27] 7891 5-9-7 **95**.......................... SilvestreDeSousa 2 79
(Ralph Beckett) *stdd s: t.k.h: hld up towards rr: effrt but no imp whn hung rt u.p over 1f out: wknd ins fnl f* **14/1**

5446 **9** *1 ¼* **Target Zone**[28] 7863 3-8-11 **87**.......................... HayleyTurner 5 68
(David Elsworth) *stdd s: hld up in rr: swtchd lft 6f out: effrt 3f out: no imp u.p and nvr involved (jockey said colt hung left-handed)* **12/1**

114 **10** *3 ½* **Alfred Boucher**[49] 7163 3-8-12 **88**.......................... DavidProbert 3 61
(Henry Candy) *in tch in midfield: effrt to chse ldrs 3f out: no ex: hung lft and btn over 1f out: wknd fnl f* **11/1**

-0P0 **11** *15* **Humbert (IRE)**[21] 8096 5-9-6 **94**.......................(p) AdamKirby 1 33
(David O'Meara) *racd alone nr far rail: overall ldr tl over 3f out: sn u.p and lost pl: wl bhd and virtually p.u ins fnl f* **20/1**

0004 **12** *hd* **Gossiping**[23] 8016 7-9-5 **93**.......................... HectorCrouch 7 31
(Gary Moore) *in tch in midfield: rdn 3f out: sn lost pl: wl bhd and eased ins fnl f (trainer said gelding was unsuited by the ground on this occasion, which in his opinion, was riding loose and would prefer a quicker surface)* **33/1**

1m 41.41s (3.01) **Going Correction** +0.675s/f (Yiel)
WFA 3 from 4yo+ 2lb **12** Ran SP% **119.9**
Speed ratings (Par 107): **111,110,109,108,107 103,102,99,98,95 80,80**
CSF £59.96 CT £272.14 TOTE £7.20: £2.10, £2.20, £3.20; EX 69.70 Trifecta £651.10.
Owner Mohd Al Aassar **Bred** Miss Samantha Jarrom **Trained** Sessay, N Yorks

FOCUS
A decent handicap in which they stretched across the track early, but ended up in the middle. They finished well spread out. Sound form, with the second rated to his Ascot figure.
T/Jkpt: Not Won. T/Plt: £2,421.20 to a £1 stake. Pool: £60,198.39 - 18.15 winning units T/Qpdt: £159.30 to a £1 stake. Pool: £8,515.79 - 39.55 winning units **Steve Payne**

8729 - 8733a (Foreign Racing) - See Raceform Interactive

8673 DUNDALK (A.W) (L-H)
Friday, November 1

OFFICIAL GOING: Polytrack: standard

8734a AL BASTI EQUIWORLD IRISH EBF COOLEY FILLIES STKS (LISTED) (AW CHAMPIONSHIP FAST TRACK QUALIFIER) 1m (P)
7:45 (7:46) 3-Y-0+
£31,891 (£10,270; £4,864; £2,162; £1,081; £540)

RPR

1 **Surrounding (IRE)**[48] 7220 6-9-7 105........................(t) RonanWhelan 6 106+
(M Halford, Ire) *racd in mid-div: travelled wl to chse ldrs 2f out: led gng easily 1f out: sn pushed clr: comf* **10/11**[1]

2 *2 ¾* **Crotchet**[28] 7880 4-9-2 93........................(t) GaryHalpin 5 95
(Joseph Patrick O'Brien, Ire) *racd in mid-div: clsr under 2f out to chse ldrs: wnt 2nd ent fnl f: sn no match for wnr: kpt on same pce in 2nd* **10/1**[3]

3 *1 ½* **Festina Plente**[14] 8325 3-9-0 87........................ NGMcCullagh 10 92
(J P Murtagh, Ire) *racd in rr of mid-div: prog over 1f out: 6th ent fnl f: styd on wl into 3rd fnl 100yds: nvr nrr* **33/1**

4 *2 ¾* **Titanium Sky (IRE)**[12] 8367 3-9-0 93........................ OisinOrr 1 85
(D K Weld, Ire) *chsd ldrs on inner: clsr in 2nd under 2f out: briefly disp over 1f out: sn hdd: no ex in 4th fnl 100yds* **12/1**

5 *nk* **Snapraeceps (IRE)**[12] 8368 3-9-0 100........................ DeclanMcDonogh 2 85
(Joseph Patrick O'Brien, Ire) *chsd ldrs: rdn in mid-div over 2f out: kpt on wl for press ins fnl f: nvr on terms* **10/1**[3]

6 *1 ½* **She's A Babe (IRE)**[14] 8325 3-9-0 84........................ AndrewSlattery 12 81
(Aidan F Fogarty, Ire) *racd towards rr: prog on outer under 2f out: kpt on wl ins fnl f: nvr nrr* **33/1**

7 *nk* **Dancing On A Dream (IRE)**[21] 8104 3-9-0 86.......(b) MarkGallagher 11 80
(Joseph Patrick O'Brien, Ire) *sn trckd ldr in 2nd: rdn in 3rd under 2f out: wknd ent fnl f* **11/1**

8 *nk* **Kaftan**[28] 7880 3-9-0 93........................ ColinKeane 4 80
(G M Lyons, Ire) *trckd early ldrs: sn mid-div: rdn and no imp under 2f out: swtchd lft 1f out: kpt on same pce under hands and heels fnl f* **6/1**[2]

9 *hd* **Harriet's Force (IRE)**[35] 7668 3-9-0 96........................ RobbieColgan 3 79
(Keith Henry Clarke, Ire) *sn led: rdn 2f out: hdd appr fnl f: sn wknd* **14/1**

10 *hd* **Come September (IRE)**[6] 8572 3-9-0 93........................ GaryCarroll 13 79
(Gavin Cromwell, Ire) *trckd early ldr in 2nd: 4th at 1/2-way: rdn and nt qckn under 2f out: sn no ex* **20/1**

11 *shd* **Cnoc An Oir (IRE)**[44] 7347 3-9-0 90........................ ShaneCrosse 9 79
(Joseph Patrick O'Brien, Ire) *racd towards rr: swtchd to inner 2f out: mod late hdwy wout ever threatening* **14/1**

12 *½* **Frosty (IRE)**[12] 8367 3-9-0 97........................(h[1]) KillianHennessy 8 77
(A P O'Brien, Ire) *racd in rr of mid-div: pushed along under 3f out: no imp under 2f out* **14/1**

13 *nk* **Chablis (IRE)**[12] 8368 3-9-0 96........................ RoryCleary 14 77
(A P O'Brien, Ire) *racd in mid-div: rdn and dropped towards rr under 2f out: nvr a factor* **25/1**

14 *½* **Jumellea (IRE)**[12] 8367 3-9-0 94........................(bt) TrevorWhelan 15 76
(Joseph Patrick O'Brien, Ire) *sn outpcd in rr and detached: clsr to join field after 3f: no imp 2f out* **20/1**

1m 36.9s (-1.90) **Going Correction** +0.15s/f (Slow)
WFA 3 from 4yo+ 2lb **14** Ran SP% **140.1**
Speed ratings: **115,112,110,108,107 106,105,105,105,105 105,104,104,103**
CSF £12.97 TOTE £2.10: £1.10, £2.50, £7.60; DF 14.00 Trifecta £350.30.
Owner P E I Newell **Bred** P E I Newell **Trained** Doneany, Co Kildare

FOCUS
Back-to-back wins in this feature contest for Surrounding, who could have been called the winner a long way from home.

8735 - 8736a (Foreign Racing) - See Raceform Interactive

DURTAL (R-H)
Friday, November 1

OFFICIAL GOING: Turf: heavy

8737a PRIX CLAUDE ROUGET (CONDITIONS) (GENTLEMAN AMATEUR RIDERS) (4YO+) (TURF) 1m 3f 110y
1:00 4-Y-0+ **£3,828** (£1,531; £1,148; £765; £382)

RPR

1 **Imago Jasius (FR)**[155] 6-10-8 0 ow2........................ MrGuillaumeViel 5 71
(F Monnier, France)

2 *3 ½* **Eos Quercus (IRE)**[52] 7062 7-10-6 0........................ MrAntoineBesnier 10 63
(N Leenders, France)

3 *4 ½* **Goldy Baby (FR)**[88] 5761 9-10-7 0........................(b[1]) MrDamienArtu 3 57
(N Paysan, France)

4 *2 ½* **Royal Bowl (FR)**[15] 6-10-10 0........................ MrAdrienFoucher 8 56
(F Seguin, France)

5 *5 ½* **Tete Raide (FR)**[139] 4-10-1 0........................ Leo-PaulBrechet(9) 7 47
(B Deniel, France)

6 *5 ½* **Cold Fusion (IRE)**[12] 8373 6-10-2 0........................(p) MrHugoBoutin 2 30
(Dai Williams) *sn towards rr: rdn and short-lived effrt 2f out: nvr in contention*

7 1 **Nicolina (GER)**[19] 4-10-2 0........................ MrFrederickTett 9 29
(Jo Hughes, France)
8 ¾ **Break Fort (FR)**[1221] 8-10-6 0........................ MrThibaudMace 11 31
(Noam Chevalier, France)
9 ¾ **Raspoutin (FR)**[50] 5-9-11 0........................ MrThibaultJourniac(9) 6 30
(P Journiac, France)
10 dist **Burmese Temple (FR)**[1237] 8-10-8 0 ow2......(p) Marc-AndreSebaoun 1
(V Devillars, France)
11 19 **Ibn Medecis (FR)**[359] 4-10-6 0........................ MrYvesCormier-Martin 4
(P-J Fertillet, France)
2m 36.79s 11 Ran

Owner Michel Beuchey **Bred** M Beuchey **Trained** France

8738 - 8744a (Foreign Racing) - See Raceform Interactive

7945 SANTA ANITA (L-H)
Friday, November 1

OFFICIAL GOING: Dirt: fast; turf: firm

8745a BREEDERS' CUP JUVENILE TURF SPRINT (GRADE 2) (2YO) (TURF) 5f
8:12 2-Y-O

£433,070 (£133,858; £70,866; £39,370; £23,622; £7,874)

RPR

1 **Four Wheel Drive (USA)**[26] 2-8-10 0........................(b) IradOrtizJr 9 112
(Wesley A Ward, U.S.A) *mde all: rdn 1 1/2f out: drvn and kpt on wl fnl f* **5/2**[1]
2 ¾ **Chimney Rock (USA)**[26] 2-8-10 0........................(b) JoseLOrtiz 1 109
(Michael J Maker, U.S.A) *trckd ldrs: chsd ldr 2f out: rdn ins fnl 2f: kpt on wl fnl f: no imp on wnr* **14/1**
3 1 ½ **Another Miracle (USA)**[26] 2-8-10 0........................ ManuelFranco 3 104+
(Gary Contessa, U.S.A) *midfield: rdn and styd on fr 1 1/2f out: wnt 3rd ins fnl f: nt gng pce to rch ldrs* **25/1**
4 hd **Kimari (USA)**[26] 2-8-7 0........................ JohnRVelazquez 7 100+
(Wesley A Ward, U.S.A) *towards rr: rdn 2f out: styd on wl fnl f: nrst fin* **11/4**[2]
5 1 **Dr Simpson (FR)**[14] 8328 2-8-7 0........................ RichardKingscote 8 97
(Tom Dascombe) *chsd ldr: dropped to 3rd 2f out: rdn ins fnl 2f: drvn and kpt on same pce fnl f* **28/1**
6 nse **Encoder (USA)**[26] 2-8-10 0........................ FlavienPrat 5 100
(John W Sadler, U.S.A) *towards rr of midfield: rdn ins fnl 2f: kpt on fnl f* **33/1**
7 1 **Dream Shot (IRE)**[14] 8328 2-8-10 0........................ ChrisHayes 4 96
(James Tate) *in tch on outside: rdn over 2f out: wknd steadily fnl f* **28/1**
8 nk **Alligator Alley**[49] 7149 2-8-10 0........................(b¹) WayneLordan 6 95
(Joseph Patrick O'Brien, Ire) *dwlt: towards rr of midfield: rdn 2f out: sme hdwy on inner 1 1/2f out: no further imp fnl f* **10/1**
9 ½ **Cambria (USA)**[55] 2-8-7 0........................(b) TylerGaffalione 12 90
(Wesley A Ward, U.S.A) *hld up in rr: rdn 2f out: same late hdwy: nvr in contention* **20/1**
10 ½ **A'Ali (IRE)**[49] 7149 2-8-10 0........................ FrankieDettori 10 91
(Simon Crisford) *hld up in rr: rdn and no imp fr 2f out: wd into st* **9/2**[3]
11 hd **King Neptune (USA)**[34] 7693 2-8-10 0........................ RyanMoore 11 91
(A P O'Brien, Ire) *towards rr of midfield: rdn ins fnl 2f: wknd steadily fnl f* **20/1**
12 3 **Band Practice (IRE)**[32] 7775 2-8-7 0........................ JamieSpencer 2 77
(Archie Watson) *in tch in midfield: rdn under 2f out: wknd tamely fnl f* **12/1**

55.66s **12 Ran SP% 120.1**
PARI-MUTUEL (all including 2 unit stake): WIN 5.00; PLACE (1-2) 3.40, 8.20; SHOW (1-2-3) 3.00, 5.40, 7.80; SF 46.20.
Owner Breeze Easy LLC **Bred** Glenvale Stud **Trained** North America

FOCUS
A sharp 5f on fast ground, and the pace held up, the winner making all.

8746a BREEDERS' CUP JUVENILE TURF PRESENTED BY COOLMORE (GRADE 1) (2YO COLTS, GELDINGS & RIDGLINGS) (TURF) 1m (T)
8:52 2-Y-O

£433,070 (£133,858; £70,866; £39,370; £23,622; £7,874)

RPR

1 **Structor (USA)**[34] 2-8-10 0........................ JoseLOrtiz 2 109
(Chad C Brown, U.S.A) *midfield on inner: rdn 2f out: styd on strly fnl f: led 50yds out: rdn out* **11/2**[3]
2 ¾ **Billy Batts (USA)**[26] 2-8-10 0........................ PacoLopez 7 107
(Peter Miller, U.S.A) *trckd ldrs: rdn ins fnl 2f: hung lft ins fnl f: drvn to ld 100yds out: hdd 50yds out: kpt on* **66/1**
3 nk **Gear Jockey (USA)**[26] 2-8-10 0........................ TylerGaffalione 8 106
(George R Arnold II, U.S.A) *in tch in midfield: rdn 1 1/2f out: swtchd 1f out: styd on fnl f: nt able to chal* **66/1**
4 ½ **Decorated Invader (USA)**[47] 7266 2-8-10 0........................ IradOrtizJr 4 105
(Christophe Clement, U.S.A) *towards rr: hdwy on wd outside fr 2f out: rdn 1 1/2f out: styd on wl fnl f* **3/1**[2]
5 nk **Arizona (IRE)**[20] 8113 2-8-10 0........................ RyanMoore 11 104
(A P O'Brien, Ire) *hld up towards rr: rdn ins fnl 2f: swtchd to wd outside over 1f out: styd on fnl f: nrst fin* **2/1**[1]
6 nk **Proven Strategies (USA)**[47] 7266 2-8-10 0........................ EdgardJZayas 10 104
(Mark Casse, Canada) *chsd ldr: rdn ins fnl 2f: drvn to press ldr 1 1/2f out: lft in ld 1f out: hdd 100yds out: no ex clsng stages* **80/1**
7 ½ **Fort Myers (USA)**[28] 7879 2-8-10........................ WayneLordan 12 102
(A P O'Brien, Ire) *midfield: rdn 2f out: sltly outpcd 1 1/2f out: bmpd and short of room over 1f out: kpt on fnl f: fin dead-heat 7th: plcd 7th outrt* **18/1**
8 nse **Our Country (USA)**[34] 2-8-10 0........................ JohnRVelazquez 1 102
(George Weaver, U.S.A) *towards rr of midfield: dropped towards rr 2f out: rdn under 2f out: drvn and styd on fnl f: nrst fin: fin 9th: plcd 8th* **12/1**
9 ½ **Andesite (USA)**[34] 2-8-10 0........................ JoelRosario 6 101
(Brad H Cox, U.S.A) *towards rr: v wd ent st: rdn 1 1/2f out: kpt on fr over 1f out: fin 10th: plcd 9th* **16/1**
10 ¾ **War Beast (USA)**[26] 2-8-10 0........................(b) AbelCedillo 9 99
(Doug O'Neill, U.S.A) *in tch: rdn 2f out: wknd over 1f out: fin 11th: plcd 10th* **66/1**
11 1 ¾ **Peace Achieved (USA)**[26] 2-8-10 0........................(b) MiguelMena 3 95
(Mark Casse, Canada) *midfield: rdn under 2f out: hung rt and bmpd rival over 1f out: squeezed out under 1f out: sn btn: fin 12th: plcd 11th* **14/1**
12 nse **Graceful Kitten (USA)**[34] 2-8-10 0........................ HectorlBerrios 5 95
(Amador Merei Sanchez, U.S.A) *led: rdn 1 1/2f out: swvd lft and hit rail 1f out: sn hdd and lost pl: wknd fnl 150yds: fin 13th: plcd 12th* **18/1**
13 13 ¼ **Deviant (CAN)**[26] 2-8-10 0........................(b) DraydenVanDyke 14 65
(Danny Pish, U.S.A) *midfield on outside: hmpd and stmbld 1 1/2f out: sn eased: fin 14th: plcd 13th* **80/1**
D dht **Hit The Road (USA)**[26] 2-8-10........................ FlavienPrat 13 102
(Dan Blacker, U.S.A) *towards rr of midfield: rdn under 2f out: swtchd and hmpd rival 1 1/2f out: kpt on fr over 1f out: fin dead-heat 7th: disqualified* **8/1**

1m 35.11s (1.24) **14 Ran SP% 122.5**
PARI-MUTUEL (all including 2 unit stake): WIN 12.60; PLACE (1-2) 7.20, 33.40; SHOW (1-2-3) 5.20, 18.20, 20.20; SF 518.20.
Owner Jeff Drown & Don Rachel **Bred** Three Chimneys Farm Llc **Trained** USA

FOCUS
The early pace was pretty steady and they finished in a bit of heap.

8747a BREEDERS' CUP JUVENILE FILLIES (GRADE 1) (2YO FILLIES) (MAIN TRACK) (DIRT) 1m 110y(D)
9:32 2-Y-O

£866,141 (£267,716; £141,732; £78,740; £47,244; £15,748)

RPR

1 **British Idiom (USA)**[28] 7884 2-8-10 0........................(b) JavierCastellano 4 112
(Brad H Cox, U.S.A) *midfield: hmpd on bnd after 2f: rdn and stdy hdwy fr over 3f out: chsd ldrs whn drvn 2f out: styd on dourly to ld 150yds out: kpt on wl and maintained narrow advantage* **11/4**[2]
2 nk **Donna Veloce (USA)**[34] 2-8-10 0........................ FlavienPrat 1 112
(Simon Callaghan, U.S.A) *in tch: trckd ldrs gng wl 3f out: rdn to ld 2f out: drvn 1 1/2f out: hdd 150yds out: kpt on gamely* **5/2**[1]
3 1 ¾ **Bast (USA)**[35] 2-8-10 0........................(b) JohnRVelazquez 6 108
(Bob Baffert, U.S.A) *w ldr: led 4f out: rdn and hdd 2f out: kpt on same pce* **4/1**[3]
4 1 ¾ **Perfect Alibi (USA)**[28] 7884 2-8-10 0........................ IradOrtizJr 3 104
(Mark Casse, Canada) *hld up in rr: stdy hdwy fr 1/2-way: rdn 3f out: drvn and kpt on fr 1 1/2f out: nrst fin* **20/1**
5 13 **Wicked Whisper (USA)**[26] 7936 2-8-10 0........................ JoelRosario 7 75
(Steven Asmussen, U.S.A) *prom on outside: rdn and unable qck 2f out: sn wl btn* **4/1**[3]
6 6 ¾ **Lazy Daisy (USA)**[48] 2-8-10 0........................ RafaelBejarano 5 61
(Doug O'Neill, U.S.A) *midfield: dropped to rr 1/2-way: rdn and sme stdy hdwy fr 3 1/2f out: lost tch fr 2f out* **28/1**
7 1 ¾ **Comical (USA)**[35] 2-8-10 0........................ AbelCedillo 9 57
(Doug O'Neill, U.S.A) *midfield: dropped towards rr 1/2-way: struggling and lost tch fr 2f out* **14/1**
8 2 ¼ **K P Dreamin (USA)**[35] 2-8-10 0........................ RubenFuentes 8 52
(Jeff Mullins, U.S.A) *s.s: a in rr* **40/1**
9 15 ½ **Two Sixty (USA)**[34] 2-8-10 0........................ EdgardJZayas 2 18
(Mark Casse, Canada) *led: hdd 4f out: lost pl over 3f out: sn struggling* **25/1**

1m 47.07s (4.65) **9 Ran SP% 116.4**
PARI-MUTUEL (all including 2 unit stake): WIN 7.40; PLACE (1-2) 3.80, 4.00; SHOW (1-2-3) 2.80, 3.00, 3.40; SF 26.00.
Owner Michael Dubb, The Elkstone Group Et Al **Bred** Hargus & Sandra Sexton & Silver Fern Farm Llc **Trained** USA

FOCUS
With a three-way battle for the early lead, they went fast early and finished slowly over a track that was riding dead: 22.71 (2f), 23.31 (4f), 25.91 (6f), 27.72 (1m), 7.42 (line).

8748a BREEDERS' CUP JUVENILE FILLIES TURF (GRADE 1) (2YO FILLIES) (TURF) 1m (T)
10:12 2-Y-O

£433,070 (£133,858; £70,866; £39,370; £23,622; £7,874)

RPR

1 **Sharing (USA)**[41] 2-8-10 0........................ ManuelFranco 11 110
(H Graham Motion, U.S.A) *in tch: rdn to chse ldrs ins fnl 2f: drvn and hung lft over 1f out: styd on strly to ld 100yds out: readily* **16/1**
2 1 ¼ **Daahyeh**[35] 7659 2-8-10 0........................ WilliamBuick 5 107+
(Roger Varian) *in tch in midfield: drvn ins fnl 2f: styd on wl fnl f: wnt 2nd cl home: nt rch wnr* **7/2**[1]
3 nk **Sweet Melania (USA)**[23] 2-8-10 0........................ JoseLOrtiz 12 106
(Todd Pletcher, U.S.A) *chsd ldr: led gng wl ins fnl 2f: rdn 1 1/2f out: hdd 100yds out: no ex and lost 2nd cl home* **6/1**[3]
4 1 **Albigna (IRE)**[26] 7939 2-8-10 0........................ ShaneFoley 9 104+
(Mrs John Harrington, Ire) *hld up towards rr: rdn ins fnl 2f: drvn and styd on wl fr over 1f out: nrst fin* **4/1**[2]
5 1 ½ **Selflessly (USA)**[33] 2-8-10 0........................ JavierCastellano 13 100
(Chad C Brown, U.S.A) *midfield: rdn ins fnl 2f: wd into st: kpt on fnl f* **8/1**
6 ½ **Croughavouke (IRE)**[25] 2-8-10 0........................ FlavienPrat 2 99
(Jeff Mullins, U.S.A) *midfield: rdn and kpt on same pce ins fnl 2f* **66/1**
7 hd **Abscond (USA)**[47] 7267 2-8-10........................ IradOrtizJr 4 99
(Eddie Kenneally, U.S.A) *led: hdd ins fnl 2f: rdn 1 1/2f out: wknd fnl f* **20/1**
8 1 ¼ **Tango (IRE)**[19] 8164 2-8-10 0........................ RyanMoore 8 96
(A P O'Brien, Ire) *midfield: rdn and outpcd under 2f out: sn no imp* **14/1**
9 hd **Shadn (IRE)**[20] 8140 2-8-10 0........................ JamieSpencer 3 95
(Andrew Balding) *towards rr: rdn and no imp fr 2f out* **20/1**
10 hd **Etoile (USA)**[34] 7692 2-8-10 0........................ FrankieDettori 14 95
(A P O'Brien, Ire) *in tch in midfield: tk clsr order 2f out: rdn ins fnl 2f: wknd fnl f* **16/1**
11 1 ¼ **Crystalle (USA)**[33] 2-8-10 0........................ JoelRosario 7 92
(John C Kimmel, U.S.A) *v s.i.s: sn bhd: rdn and no imp fr 2f out: wd into st* **7/1**
12 nk **Fair Maiden (USA)**[47] 7267 2-8-10 0........................(b¹) DraydenVanDyke 10 91
(Eoin Harty, U.S.A) *towards rr of midfield on outside: rdn ins fnl 2f: wknd steadily fnl f* **14/1**
13 1 ¼ **Unforgetable (IRE)**[28] 7879 2-8-10 0........................ WayneLordan 6 88
(Joseph Patrick O'Brien, Ire) *a towards rr* **40/1**
14 1 ¼ **Living In The Past (IRE)**[34] 7692 2-8-10 0........................ DanielTudhope 1 86
(K R Burke) *trckd ldrs: rdn ins fnl 3f: lost pl 2f out: wknd over 1f out* **25/1**

1m 34.59s (0.72) **14 Ran SP% 122.5**
PARI-MUTUEL (all including 2 unit stake): WIN 29.60; PLACE (1-2) 10.60, 5.60; SHOW (1-2-3) 8.40, 3.80, 4.60; SF 160.20.
Owner Eclipse Thoroughbred Partners & Gainesway Stable **Bred** Sagamore Farm **Trained** USA

FOCUS
A nice performance from the winner, who showed a handy turn of foot to settle matters.

8749a TVG BREEDERS' CUP JUVENILE (GRADE 1) (2YO COLTS, GELDINGS & RIDGLINGS) (MAIN TRACK) (DIRT) 1m 110y(D)
11:03 2-Y-O

£866,141 (£267,716; £141,732; £78,740; £47,244; £15,748)

RPR

1 **Storm The Court (USA)**^{34} 7723 2-8-10 0....................(b^{1}) FlavienPrat 4 115
(Peter Eurton, U.S.A) *mde all: rdn whn chal 2f out: drvn and strly pressed thrght fnl f: hld on gamely: all out* **50/1**

2 *nk* **Anneau D'Or (USA)**^{33} 2-8-10 0.......................... JuanJHernandez 7 114
(Blaine D Wright, U.S.A) *trckd ldrs: drvn 3f out: chal on outside 2f out: kpt on wl and pressed wnr thrght fnl f: a jst hld* **28/1**

3 *3¼* **Wrecking Crew (USA)**^{59} 6850 2-8-10 0.........................(b) PacoLopez 2 107
(Peter Miller, U.S.A) *in tch: rdn 2f out: drvn and wnt 3rd over 1f out: kpt on same pce fnl f* **40/1**

4 *4½* **Scabbard (USA)**^{48} 2-8-10 0..................................(b) MikeESmith 5 97
(Eddie Kenneally, U.S.A) *midfield: rdn 3f out: kpt on steadily fr 1 1/2f out* **5/1^{3}**

5 *nk* **Full Flat (USA)**^{20} 2-8-10 0.................................... YutakaTake 8 96
(Hideyuki Mori, Japan) *towards rr of midfield: rdn and no imp fr 2 1/2f out* **80/1**

6 *4¼* **Eight Rings (USA)**^{34} 7723 2-8-10 0........................(b) JohnRVelazquez 6 87
(Bob Baffert, U.S.A) *chsd ldr: rdn 2f out: wknd over 1f out* **7/4^{2}**

7 *1¾* **Shoplifted (USA)**^{34} 7723 2-8-10 0......................... RicardoSantanaJr 3 83
(Steven Asmussen, U.S.A) *a towards rr* **40/1**

8 *7¼* **Dennis' Moment (USA)**^{48} 2-8-10 0.......................... IradOrtizJr 1 67
(Dale Romans, U.S.A) *a in rr* **1/1^{1}**

1m 44.93s (2.51) **8 Ran SP% 114.6**
PARI-MUTUEL (all including 2 unit stake): WIN 93.80; PLACE (1-2) 24.80, 17.60; SHOW (1-2-3) 12.00, 10.40, 12.20; SF 976.40.
Owner Exline-Border Racing LLC, David A Bernsen LLC Et A **Bred** Stepping Stone Farm **Trained** USA

FOCUS
A more sensible early pace than in the Juvenile Fillies, with the winner controlling the tempo, but still a slow finish on this gluey track: 23.49, 23.58, 24.53, 26.39, 6.94. With the exciting Maxfield scratched, the front three in the market underperforming and the winner dictating over this demanding surface, this isn't form to buy into.

8689 CHELMSFORD (A.W) (L-H)
Saturday, November 2

OFFICIAL GOING: Polytrack: standard
Weather: heavy shower during race 2

8750 BET TOTEPLACEPOT AT TOTESPORT.COM NURSERY H'CAP 5f (P)
4:30 (4:30) (Class 6) (0-65,67) 2-Y-O

£3,105 (£924; £461; £400; £400) **Stalls Low**

Form RPR

063 1 **Veleta**^{32} 7786 2-9-7 **63**.. AdamKirby 4 69+
(Clive Cox) *mde all: pushed along 2f out: drvn appr fnl f: kpt on wl* **10/3^{1}**

400 2 *1¾* **Queens Road (IRE)**^{32} 7786 2-8-12 **54**.........................(h^{1}) RyanTate 6 54
(Bill Turner) *prom: rdn over 2f out: kpt on same pce fnl f* **12/1**

0000 3 *¾* **Il Maestro (IRE)**^{30} 7833 2-9-2 **58**.......................... PaulMulrennan 7 55
(John Quinn) *midfield: rdn 2f out: kpt on ins fnl f* **6/1^{3}**

0260 4 *½* **Serious Jockin**^{10} 8452 2-8-9 **51**............................ KieranO'Neill 2 46
(Mick Channon) *dwlt: hld up in midfield: rdn 2f out: kpt on ins fnl f* **5/1^{2}**

130 4 *dht* **Crime Of Passion (IRE)**^{54} 7029 2-9-11 **67**................... NicolaCurrie 11 62
(Jamie Osborne) *dwlt sltly: outpcd in rr tl kpt on fnl f* **8/1**

3546 6 *1¾* **The Blue Bower (IRE)**^{47} 7276 2-9-6 **62**........................ JaneElliott 9 51
(Suzy Smith) *hld up in midfield on outer: rdn and hdwy over 1f out: carried rt to wd outside jst ins fnl f: one pce* **14/1**

000 7 *1¼* **Apache Bay**^{14} 8337 2-9-1 **57**...................................... BenRobinson 1 41
(John Quinn) *trckd ldrs: rdn 2f out: wknd ins fnl f* **6/1^{3}**

063 8 *shd* **Falacho (IRE)**^{25} 7995 2-8-13 **58**........................ ThomasGreatrex$^{(3)}$ 8 42
(David Loughnane) *trckd ldrs on outer: rdn to chal over 1f out: edgd rt and wknd ins fnl f* **10/3^{1}**

6000 9 *2¼* **Red Cinderella**^{51} 7110 2-7-12 **45**........................ RhiainIngram$^{(5)}$ 5 21
(David Evans) *hld up: rdn over 2f out: sn btn* **25/1**

59.9s (-0.30) **Going Correction** -0.175s/f (Stan) **9 Ran SP% 120.7**
Speed ratings (Par 94): **95,92,91,90,90 87,85,85,81**
WIN: 2.90 Veleta; PL: 1.60 Veleta 5.60 Queens Road; EX: 52.20; CSF: 47.84; TC: 237.43 CSF £47.84 CT £237.43 TOTE £2.90: £1.60, £5.60; EX 52.20.
Owner Cheveley Park Stud **Bred** Cheveley Park Stud Ltd **Trained** Lambourn, Berks

FOCUS
A modest nursery on standard Polytrack.

8751 BET TOTEEXACTA AT TOTESPORT.COM NOVICE STKS 7f (P)
5:00 (5:01) (Class 5) 2-Y-O

£4,204 (£1,251; £625; £312) **Stalls Low**

Form RPR

1 **Battle of Liege (USA)**^{45} 7357 2-9-2 0.................... DonnachaO'Brien 9 80
(A P O'Brien, Ire) *hld up in tch on outer: hdwy and trckd ldrs 3f out: pushed along to chal 2f out: drvn into narrow ld ins fnl f: styd on wl to assert towards fin* **9/2^{2}**

5 2 *¾* **Emirates Currency**^{28} 7911 2-9-2 0.......................... HectorCrouch 2 78
(Clive Cox) *trckd ldr on inner: led narrowly over 1f out: sn drvn: hdd narrowly ins fnl f: one pce towards fin* **9/2^{2}**

1 3 *1½* **Desert Peace (USA)**^{24} 8011 2-9-9 0............................ AdamKirby 8 81
(Charlie Appleby) *trckd ldrs: angled rt and n.m.r wl over 1f out: in clr and drvn appr fnl f: styd on same pce ins fnl f* **30/100^{1}**

0 4 *1½* **Cruyff**^{71} 6424 2-9-2 0... StevieDonohoe 6 70
(Richard Spencer) *hld up in tch: rdn along and hdwy on outer 2f out: kpt on same pce ins fnl f* **10/1^{3}**

5 *14* **Mayson Mount** 2-9-2 0.................................... JosephineGordon 10 34
(Shaun Keightley) *s.i.s: sn rcvrd to trck ldrs on outer: chal 3f out: rdn and wknd over 1f out* **50/1**

00 6 *2* **Party Island (IRE)**^{43} 7407 2-8-9 0........................ MichaelPitt$^{(7)}$ 3 28+
(Denis Coakley) *awkward s and rdr lost irons: a towards rr: passed 2 wkng rivals fnl f (jockey said gelding stumbled leaving the stalls causing him to lose his iron)* **33/1**

00 7 *4½* **Theydon Bagel**^{28} 7899 2-8-11 0............................ AdrianMcCarthy 1 12
(Peter Charalambous) *dwlt: hld up in tch on inner: rdn and wknd fnl 2f* **100/1**

00 8 *2½* **The Simple Truth (FR)**^{28} 7899 2-9-2 0................................ JFEgan 5
(John Berry) *led: rdn and hdd over 1f out: wknd* **100/1**

05 9 *4½* **Trouser The Cash (IRE)**^{61} 6793 2-8-8 0................ GabrieleMalune$^{(3)}$ 4 +
(Amy Murphy) *rrd as stalls opened and lft 30 l s: trailed thrght (jockey said filly reared as the stalls opened and was slowly away as a result)* **33/1**

1m 26.62s (-0.58) **Going Correction** -0.175s/f (Stan) **9 Ran SP% 132.2**
Speed ratings (Par 96): **96,95,93,91,75 73,68,65,60**
CSF £28.09 TOTE £5.80: £1.30, £1.20; EX 29.10.
Owner Mrs E M Stockwell **Bred** Mrs E Stockwell **Trained** Cashel, Co Tipperary

FOCUS
A fairly decent staying juvenile novice contest won last year by subsequent Group 3 Bahrain Trophy Stakes winner Spanish Mission. The race took place in driving rain and the odds-on favourite couldn't defy his penalty.

8752 BET TOTEQUADPOT AT TOTESPORT.COM CONDITIONS STKS (PLUS 10 RACE) 1m 2f (P)
5:30 (5:31) (Class 2) 2-Y-O

£9,056 (£2,695; £1,346; £673) **Stalls Low**

Form RPR

52 1 **Persia (IRE)**^{7} 8574 2-9-1 0............................. DonnachaO'Brien 2 104
(A P O'Brien, Ire) *trckd ldr: pushed along over 2f out: drvn over 1f out: led ins fnl f: styd on wl* **4/9^{1}**

5 2 *2¼* **Cormorant (IRE)**^{49} 7217 2-9-1 0........................ SeamieHeffernan 3 98
(A P O'Brien, Ire) *led: rdn over 1f out: drvn and hdd ins fnl f: one pce* **11/4^{2}**

0 3 *8* **Perfect Arch (IRE)**^{21} 8121 2-8-12 0......................... CallumShepherd 5 80
(Saeed bin Suroor) *hld up in tch: rdn along to go 3rd 2f out: no further imp* **12/1^{3}**

2 4 *7* **Warranty (FR)**^{26} 7957 2-8-12 0................................ FrannyNorton 1 66
(Mark Johnston) *trckd ldr: pushed along over 3f out: wknd fnl 2f* **16/1**

2m 6.47s (-2.13) **Going Correction** -0.175s/f (Stan) **4 Ran SP% 109.5**
Speed ratings (Par 102): **101,99,92,87**
CSF £1.98 TOTE £1.20; EX 2.10.
Owner Michael Tabor & Derrick Smith & Mrs John Magnier **Bred** Coolmore **Trained** Cashel, Co Tipperary

FOCUS
A good quality little juvenile conditions contest. The odds-on favourite won easily from his front-running stablemate. It's been rated at face value, with the winner, third and fourth close to their pre-race marks.

8753 BET TOTETRIFECTA AT TOTESPORT.COM (S) STKS 1m 2f (P)
6:00 (6:00) (Class 5) 3-6-Y-O

£4,948 (£1,472; £735; £400; £400; £400) **Stalls Low**

Form RPR

0435 1 **Cash N Carrie (IRE)**^{25} 8001 5-8-8 **44**.................... TheodoreLadd$^{(3)}$ 1 50
(Michael Appleby) *mde all: drvn and strly pressed over 1f out: kpt on ins fnl f* **5/1^{2}**

4000 2 *1¾* **Guvenor's Choice (IRE)**^{19} 8186 4-9-2 **72**...........(t) PaulMulrennan 5 52
(Marjorie Fife) *prom: chal strly over 1f out: drvn and one pce ins fnl f* **5/1^{2}**

2433 3 *1¾* **My Amigo**^{9} 8499 6-9-2 **64**..(p) JaneElliott 3 49
(Marjorie Fife) *trckd ldrs: rdn along 2f out: one pce in 3rd fr over 1f out* **1/1^{1}**

0640 4 *2* **Duke Of Yorkie (IRE)**^{35} 7685 3-8-13 **43**.....................(v^{1}) JimmyQuinn 7 46
(Adam West) *dwlt: hld up: rdn over 2f out: hrd drvn over 1f styd on ins fnl f: nvr a threat* **25/1**

5 *1* **Tiffindell (IRE)** 3-8-5 0.. DarraghKeenan$^{(3)}$ 4 39
(Robert Eddery) *trckd ldrs: rdn along over 2f out: wknd ins fnl f* **8/1^{3}**

6502 6 *1½* **Max Guevara (IRE)**^{25} 8003 3-8-6 **52**...................(b) AngusVilliers$^{(7)}$ 6 41
(William Muir) *midfield: rdn over 2f out: drvn over 1f out: wknd fnl 110yds* **8/1^{3}**

7 *9* **Ethics Boy (FR)** 3-8-13 0.. JFEgan 2 24
(John Berry) *dwlt: a towards rr* **12/1**

6 8 *9* **Feleena's Spell**^{9} 8497 3-8-8 0................................ AdrianMcCarthy 8
(Peter Charalambous) *midfield: rdn over 2f out: sn wknd* **66/1**

2m 7.02s (-1.58) **Going Correction** -0.175s/f (Stan)
WFA 3 from 4yo+ 3lb **8 Ran SP% 118.6**
Speed ratings: **99,97,96,94,93 92,85,78**
CSF £31.34 TOTE £6.40: £1.50, £1.60, £1.10; EX 27.70.There was no bid for the winner.
Owner Mick Appleby Racing **Bred** Declan Phelan **Trained** Oakham, Rutland

FOCUS
An ordinary seller.

8754 BET TOTESWINGER AT TOTESPORT.COM H'CAP 1m 6f (P)
6:30 (6:33) (Class 2) 3-Y-O

£31,125 (£9,320; £4,660; £2,330; £1,165; £585) **Stalls Low**

Form RPR

1202 1 **First In Line**^{22} 8092 3-9-4 **105**.............................. CierenFallon$^{(3)}$ 9 115+
(John Gosden) *midfield: keen early: hdwy on outer 3f out: rdn to ld wl over 1f out: pressed ent fnl f: edgd rt fnl 110yds: drvn all out* **7/4^{1}**

5013 2 *hd* **Holy Kingdom (IRE)**^{22} 8098 3-8-0 **84** oh3...................... LukeMorris 10 93
(Tom Clover) *hld up: rdn and hdwy on outer 2f out: drvn to chal ent fnl f: carried sltly rt by wnr fnl 110yds: styd on wl* **16/1**

3311 3 *1¼* **Tammooz**^{35} 7702 3-8-6 **90**.. DavidEgan 1 97
(Roger Varian) *midfield on inner: rdn and hdwy wl over 1f out: styd on fnl f* **7/1**

-251 4 *2¼* **Ballylemon (IRE)**^{44} 7382 3-8-0 **84** oh2....................... KieranO'Neill 8 88
(Richard Hughes) *dwlt: hld up on inner: angled rt and short of room over 2f out: rdn w plenty to do on outer wl over 1f out: edgd lft and styd on ins fnl f* **3/1^{2}**

1524 5 *4* **I'll Have Another (IRE)**^{29} 7864 3-8-13 **97**.................... FrannyNorton 5 95
(Mark Johnston) *led for 2f: trckd ldrs: rdn along 3f out: wknd over 1f out* **20/1**

1515 6 *nk* **Just Hubert (IRE)**^{29} 7864 3-8-7 **91**............................ NicolaCurrie 7 89
(William Muir) *hld up in rr: rdn over 2f out: nvr a threat* **12/1**

2114 7 *2½* **Emirates Empire (IRE)**^{154} 3337 3-8-6 **90**.................... DavidProbert 6 84
(Michael Bell) *led after 2f: rdn and hdd wl over 1f out: wknd fnl f* **9/1**

0000 8 *18* **Western Australia (IRE)**^{49} 7196 3-9-6 **104**........... DonnachaO'Brien 2 73
(A P O'Brien, Ire) *trckd ldrs: rdn wl over 2f out: wknd over 1f out* **6/1^{3}**

1300 9 *11* **Rochester House (IRE)**^{21} 8114 3-8-9 **93**..................... JoeFanning 3 47
(Mark Johnston) *sn prom: rdn along and already losing pl whn short of room over 2f out: sn wknd* **16/1**

2m 57.13s (-6.07) **Going Correction** -0.175s/f (Stan) **9 Ran SP% 122.4**
Speed ratings (Par 108): **110,109,109,107,105 105,104,93,87**
CSF £35.72 CT £172.01 TOTE £2.50: £1.20, £4.50; EX 29.60.
Owner A E Oppenheimer **Bred** Hascombe And Valiant Studs **Trained** Newmarket, Suffolk
■ Stewards' Enquiry : Cieren Fallon two-day ban: interference & careless riding (Nov 20-21)

FOCUS
The feature contest was a good 3yo staying handicap. The favourite won narrowly and survived a lengthy inquiry. Solid form, rated around the winner, third and fourth.

8755 BET TOTESCOOP6 AT TOTESPORT.COM H'CAP 6f (P)
7:00 (7:01) (Class 5) (0-70,72) 3-Y-O+
£5,175 (£1,540; £769; £400; £400; £400) **Stalls** Centre

Form RPR

6406 1 **Born To Finish (IRE)**[10] 8471 6-9-2 **65**.........................(p) DavidProbert 6 72+
(Ed de Giles) *dwlt: hld up: rdn over 2f out: carried wd on bnd wl over 1f out: drvn and stl plenty to do in dispute of 5th ent fnl f: r.o strly to ld post* **5/1**[2]

3254 2 *hd* **Something Lucky (IRE)**[91] 5647 7-9-6 **69**.................... RobertHavlin 13 75
(Michael Attwater) *sn pressed ldr: rdn 2f out: drvn into narrow ld 1f out: kpt on: hdd post* **20/1**

2460 3 *nk* **Lalania**[26] 7977 4-8-13 **62**.................................... CallumShepherd 5 67
(Stuart Williams) *led narrowly: rdn 2f out: hdd 1f out but remained chalng: kpt on* **7/1**[3]

3231 4 *1 ¾* **Poeta Brasileiro (IRE)**[17] 8264 4-9-1 **67**.........(t) DarraghKeenan(3) 8 66
(David Brown) *trckd ldrs: pushed along to chal ent fnl f: drvn and no ex fnl 110yds* **10/3**[1]

000 5 *¾* **Regulator (IRE)**[11] 8420 4-9-4 **67**.............................. DanielMuscutt 3 64
(Alexandra Dunn) *midfield on inner: pushed along over 2f out: kpt on ins fnl f (jockey said gelding hung left-handed throughout)* **16/1**

2120 6 *1* **Senorita Grande (IRE)**[29] 7869 3-8-12 **61**...............(v) PaulMulrennan 9 55
(John Quinn) *in tch: pushed along to chse ldrs over 2f out: drvn over 1f out: no ex ins fnl f* **5/1**[2]

5156 7 *1* **Good Answer**[61] 6806 3-8-11 **67**............................... AngusVilliers(7) 10 58
(Robert Cowell) *dwlt: hld up: rdn 3f out: nvr a threat* **16/1**

1650 8 *1 ½* **Case Key**[14] 8339 6-9-3 **69**.................................(b) TheodoreLadd(3) 1 55
(Michael Appleby) *chsd ldrs: rdn and outpcd 3f out: no threat after* **11/1**

0450 9 *1 ¾* **Hic Bibi**[19] 8199 4-8-11 **63**.. ThomasGreatrex(3) 4 43
(David Loughnane) *midfield: drvn over 2f out: wknd over 1f out* **5/1**[2]

2540 10 *6* **Kodiline (IRE)**[54] 7028 5-8-11 **60**................................... BenCurtis 11 21
(David Evans) *sn rdn along and a in rr (jockey said gelding was slow into stride and was never travelling thereafter)* **9/1**

0000 11 *7* **In The Red (IRE)**[16] 8289 6-9-7 **70**...............................(p) EoinWalsh 12 9
(Martin Smith) *dwlt: a towards rr* **33/1**

1m 12.05s (-1.65) **Going Correction** -0.175s/f (Stan) **11 Ran SP% 123.4**
Speed ratings (Par 103): **104,103,103,101,100 98,97,95,93,85 75**
CSF £104.90 CT £733.59 TOTE £6.40; EX 119.80.
Owner Crowd Racing Partnership **Bred** B Kennedy & Mrs Ann Marie Kennedy **Trained** Ledbury, H'fords

FOCUS
An ordinary handicap. One of the co-second favourites lived up his name to get up right on the line in a good comparative time on the night. The fourth has been rated in line with his earlier C&D form.

8756 BOOK TICKETS AT CHELMSFORDCITYRACECOURSE.COM H'CAP 1m (P)
7:30 (7:31) (Class 6) (0-60,61) 3-Y-O+
£3,105 (£924; £461; £400; £400; £400) **Stalls** Low

Form RPR

6302 1 **J'Ouvert (IRE)**[9] 8499 3-9-6 **61**...................................(h) BenCurtis 1 70
(David Evans) *trckd ldrs on inner: angled rt 2f out: rdn to chal over 1f out: drvn to ld 1f out: all out* **11/4**[1]

3112 2 *nse* **Parknacilla (IRE)**[16] 8291 3-8-13 **59**.......................(p) DylanHogan(5) 3 68
(Henry Spiller) *dwlt: hld up on inner: angled rt 2f out: rdn and hdwy over 1f out: drvn to chse ldr ins fnl f: kpt on wl* **4/1**[2]

1300 3 *6* **Mochalov**[22] 8083 4-9-4 **60**.. TimClark(3) 4 55
(Jane Chapple-Hyam) *pressed ldr: led over 2f out: drvn over 1f out: hdd 1f out: no ex* **8/1**[3]

0005 4 *1* **Presence Process**[44] 7375 5-9-1 **54**.............................. CharlieBennett 7 47
(Pat Phelan) *trckd ldrs: rdn over 2f out: hung lft and no ex fnl f* **16/1**

2130 5 *2* **Voice Of A Leader (IRE)**[39] 7550 8-9-1 **54**...................... JoeyHaynes 8 42
(Chelsea Banham) *dwlt: sn midfield: rdn 2f out: one pce* **16/1**

0000 6 *1 ¼* **Air Hair Lair (IRE)**[126] 4378 3-9-5 **60**........................... KieranO'Neill 5 45
(Sheena West) *midfield on inner: rdn over 2f out: no imp* **14/1**

3304 7 *2 ¼* **Magic Shuffle (IRE)**[21] 7573 3-9-1 **61**............ ThoreHammerHansen(5) 9 41
(Barry Brennan) *midfield: sn pushed along: drvn over 3f out: sn btn* **20/1**

5544 8 *hd* **Cashel (IRE)**[18] 8223 4-9-3 **59**..................................(p[1]) TheodoreLadd(3) 12 39
(Michael Appleby) *hld up on outside: hung lft thrght: rdn over 2f out: nvr involved (jockey said gelding hung left-handed throughout)* **4/1**[2]

6300 9 *hd* **Ramblow**[11] 8416 6-8-7 **46** oh1.....................................(bt[1]) LukeMorris 11 25
(Alexandra Dunn) *hld up: nvr a threat* **66/1**

6-06 10 *¾* **Havana Sunset**[18] 8223 3-9-1 **56**..................................... RossaRyan 2 33
(Mike Murphy) *led narrowly: rdn and hdd over 2f out: wknd over 1f out* **14/1**

0606 11 *½* **Adashelby (IRE)**[9] 8499 3-9-1 **59**........................... DarraghKeenan(3) 6 35
(John Ryan) *prom: rdn and outpcd over 2f out: wknd over 1f out* **10/1**

5306 12 *hd* **Noble Peace**[19] 8206 6-9-7 **60**..................................(b) DavidProbert 10 36
(Lydia Pearce) *midfield: rdn over 2f out: wknd over 1f out* **10/1**

1m 38.59s (-1.31) **Going Correction** -0.175s/f (Stan)
WFA 3 from 4yo+ 2lb **12 Ran SP% 127.3**
Speed ratings (Par 101): **99,98,92,91,89 88,86,86,86,85 84,84**
CSF £14.44 CT £82.71 TOTE £3.30: £1.30, £1.20, £2.60; EX 13.90.
Owner S W Banks **Bred** Rabbah Bloodstock Limited **Trained** Pandy, Monmouths

FOCUS
A modest handicap. The markets thought the eventual winner, and favourite, had got collared right on the line but it proved not to be the case.

8757 2020 CCR MEMBERSHIP AVAILABLE NOW CLASSIFIED STKS 7f (P)
8:00 (8:01) (Class 6) 3-Y-O+
£3,105 (£924; £461; £400; £400; £400) **Stalls** Low

Form RPR

0236 1 **Garth Rockett**[17] 8255 5-9-1 55.................................(tp) LukeMorris 2 64
(Mike Murphy) *trckd ldrs: pushed along to chal over 1f out: drvn ins fnl f: kpt on to ld towards fin* **7/2**[2]

0362 2 *½* **Letmestopyouthere (IRE)**[37] 7603 5-9-1 51...................(p) HollieDoyle 7 63
(Archie Watson) *pressed ldr: pushed into ld over 2f out: drvn and pressed over 1f out: one pce and hdd towards fin* **7/2**[2]

0061 3 *6* **Quick Monet (IRE)**[7] 8547 6-9-1 52.............................. MartinDwyer 3 47
(Shaun Harris) *s.i.s: hld up: drvn on wd outside over 1f out: wnt poor 3rd ins fnl f: no threat to ldng pair (jockey said gelding was slowly away)* **5/2**[1]

221 4 *1 ¼* **Sweet Forgetme Not (IRE)**[100] 5352 3-8-7 52....(vt) GraceMcEntee(7) 4 43
(Phil McEntee) *hld up: rdn along over 1f out: nvr threatened* **14/1**

3503 5 *shd* **Caribbean Spring (IRE)**[37] 7604 6-9-1 55.......................... JaneElliott 6 44
(George Margarson) *trckd ldrs: rdn over 2f out: outpcd and btn over 1f out* **6/1**

3460 6 *8* **Jupiter**[18] 8223 4-9-1 55..(v) RossaRyan 1 23
(Alexandra Dunn) *led: rdn and hdd over 2f out: sn wknd* **4/1**[3]

1m 25.78s (-1.42) **Going Correction** -0.175s/f (Stan)
WFA 3 from 4yo+ 1lb **6 Ran SP% 114.0**
Speed ratings (Par 101): **101,100,93,92,92 82**
CSF £16.42 TOTE £4.00: £1.90, £1.80; EX 14.90.
Owner Philip Banfield **Bred** P Banfield **Trained** Westoning, Beds

FOCUS
A moderate classified stakes.
T/Plt: £29.90 to a £1 stake. Pool: £47,312.58 - 1,579.57 winning units T/Qpdt: £12.00 to a £1 stake. Pool: £5,750.96 - 476.37 winning units **Andrew Sheret**

8721 NEWMARKET (R-H)
Saturday, November 2

OFFICIAL GOING: Soft (6.8) changing to heavy after race 1 (11.45)
Wind: Strong against Weather: Rain clearing after race 1

8758 PRESTIGE VEHICLES BRITISH EBF FILLIES' NOVICE STKS (PLUS 10 RACE) (DIV I) 7f
11:45 (11:47) (Class 4) 2-Y-O
£5,175 (£1,540; £769; £384) **Stalls** High

Form RPR

1 **Heiress** 2-9-0 0.. RobertHavlin 11 84+
(John Gosden) *a.p: chsd ldr over 2f out: shkn up to ld ins fnl f: r.o wl* **11/2**[2]

2 *3 ½* **Dancin Inthestreet** 2-8-11 0................................. GeorgiaCox(3) 10 76
(William Haggas) *led: shkn up over 1f out: hdd and no ex ins fnl f* **16/1**

3 *1 ¼* **Angel Power** 2-9-0 0...................................... SilvestreDeSousa 12 73
(Roger Varian) *s.i.s: hdwy over 5f out: swtchd rt 2f out: styd on to go 3rd ins fnl f: nt trble ldrs* **5/2**[1]

6 4 *1* **Dusty Dream**[57] 6918 2-9-0 0..................................... TomMarquand 14 70
(William Haggas) *chsd ldr 1f: remained handy: shkn up over 2f out: styd on same pce fnl f* **9/1**

0 5 *¾* **Perfect Sunset**[31] 7813 2-9-0 0.................................. DavidProbert 3 68
(Andrew Balding) *chsd ldr 6f out tl over 2f out: rdn and edgd lft over 1f out: no ex ins fnl f* **33/1**

6 *2* **Grenadine (IRE)** 2-9-0 0...................................... DonnachaO'Brien 2 63
(A P O'Brien, Ire) *hld up: shkn up over 2f out: nt trble ldrs* **6/1**[3]

7 *¾* **Choral Work** 2-8-11 0... CierenFallon(3) 9 61+
(William Haggas) *hld up: pushed along 1/2-way: n.d* **12/1**

8 *nse* **Exhibit (IRE)** 2-9-0 0... AndreaAtzeni 13 61+
(Richard Hannon) *s.i.s: hld up: swtchd rt over 1f out: styd on ins fnl f: nvr nrr* **11/1**

9 *shd* **La Dragontea** 2-9-0 0.. HayleyTurner 8 61
(Michael Bell) *s.i.s: pushed along in rr: hdwy u.p over 1f out: n.d* **25/1**

0 10 *3 ¾* **She Strides On**[138] 3942 2-9-0 0............................ CallumShepherd 5 52
(Mick Channon) *prom: shkn up over 1f out: wknd fnl f* **50/1**

3 11 *1* **Lady Isabel (IRE)**[19] 8202 2-9-0 0.................................... DavidEgan 7 49
(Alan Bailey) *sn pushed along in rr: no ch whn hung rt over 1f out* **8/1**

5 12 *¾* **Ampney Red**[17] 8258 2-9-0 0...................................... HollieDoyle 1 47
(Hughie Morrison) *wnt rt s: sn pushed along and a in rr* **14/1**

0 13 *13* **Madame Winner**[10] 8458 2-9-0 0......................... CallumRodriguez 4 15
(Stuart Williams) *s.i.s: sn pushed along and a in rr* **50/1**

14 *nk* **Current** 2-9-0 0... OisinMurphy 15 14
(Richard Hannon) *prom 5f* **12/1**

1m 32.94s (7.54) **Going Correction** +0.775s/f (Yiel) **14 Ran SP% 126.3**
Speed ratings (Par 95): **87,83,81,80,79 77,76,76,76,71 70,69,55,54**
CSF £92.62 TOTE £5.60: £2.30, £6.00, £1.90; EX 184.40 Trifecta £470.80.
Owner Lordship Stud **Bred** Lordship Stud **Trained** Newmarket, Suffolk

FOCUS
Stands' side course. Stalls: stands' side. The meeting started in rain and there was a stiff breeze towards the stands. A bumper card commencing with the first division of a fillies' novice from which the two 2018 winners both distinguished themselves at Group level this season. They came up the stands' rail, and despite difficult conditions, the first three were all newcomers.

8759 PRESTIGE VEHICLES BRITISH EBF FILLIES' NOVICE STKS (PLUS 10 RACE) (DIV II) 7f
12:20 (12:22) (Class 4) 2-Y-O
£5,175 (£1,540; £769; £384) **Stalls** High

Form RPR

1 **With Thanks (IRE)** 2-8-11 0................................. CierenFallon(3) 13 83+
(William Haggas) *hld up in tch: plld hrd: chsd ldr over 2f out: led 1f out: pushed out* **16/1**

2 2 *¾* **Waliyak (FR)**[22] 8093 2-9-0 0.................................... AndreaAtzeni 1 81
(Roger Varian) *led: shkn up and hdd 1f out: kpt on* **8/11**[1]

05 3 *3 ½* **Lyrical**[10] 8458 2-9-0 0... RobertHavlin 10 72
(Ed Dunlop) *hld up: hdwy over 2f out: shkn up over 1f out: no imp ins fnl f* **33/1**

0 4 *2 ¼* **Some Picture (IRE)**[22] 8093 2-9-0 0....................... SilvestreDeSousa 3 67
(Mick Channon) *s.i.s: hld up: hdwy over 2f out: rdn and hung lft over 1f out: no ex fnl f* **50/1**

5 *hd* **Ice Sprite** 2-9-0 0... TomMarquand 11 66
(William Haggas) *s.i.s: in rr: hdwy over 1f out: hung rt and no ex ins fnl f* **10/1**[3]

6 *5* **Transcript** 2-9-0 0... PJMcDonald 8 54
(James Tate) *s.i.s: pushed along in rr: hdwy over 1f out: wknd fnl f* **8/1**[2]

7 *½* **First Kingdom (IRE)** 2-9-0 0....................................... DavidEgan 2 53
(William Haggas) *chsd ldr 1f: remained handy: rdn over 2f out: edgd lft over 1f out: wknd fnl f* **8/1**[2]

8 *1 ¼* **Little Downs** 2-9-0 0... OisinMurphy 5 49
(Richard Hannon) *s.i.s: hld up: sme hdwy on outer over 1f out: sn wknd* **14/1**

9 *3 ¼* **By My Side (IRE)** 2-9-0 0... HayleyTurner 6 41
(Michael Bell) *mid-div: sn pushed along: lost pl 4f out: n.d after* **14/1**

0 10 *11* **Ragtime Sally**[22] 8093 2-9-0 0.................................. NicolaCurrie 12 14
(Harry Dunlop) *prom: pushed along over 2f out: wknd over 1f out (trainer's rep said filly was unsuited by the heavy going on this occasion)* **33/1**

0 11 *2 ½* **Dramatica (IRE)**[22] 8093 2-9-0 0............................ CallumRodriguez 4 8
(Stuart Williams) *hld up: pushed along 1/2-way: wknd over 1f out* **25/1**

0 12 16 **London (GER)**[19] 8203 2-9-0 0.................................... JosephineGordon 14
(Mrs Ilka Gansera-Leveque) *chsd ldr 6f out tl shkn up over 2f out: sn wknd* **50/1**

1m 31.53s (6.13) **Going Correction** +0.775s/f (Yiel) 12 Ran SP% **122.1**
Speed ratings (Par 95): **96,95,91,88,88 82,82,80,76,64 61,43**
CSF £28.04 TOTE £19.60: £4.50, £1.10, £6.10; EX 45.20 Trifecta £696.40.
Owner Sheikh Rashid Dalmook Al Maktoum **Bred** Mrs E Thompson **Trained** Newmarket, Suffolk

FOCUS
The going was changed to heavy before this contest. The second leg of the fillies' novice was run 1.41sec faster than the first and the first two finished clear. So this might prove to be the better division.

8760 ARIONEO NURSERY H'CAP 1m 1f
12:55 (12:55) (Class 4) (0-85,83) 2-Y-O
£5,175 (£1,540; £769; £384; £300; £300) Stalls High

Form RPR
223 1 **Global Storm (IRE)**[50] 7162 2-9-3 **82**.............................. CierenFallon[(3)] 1 86
(Charlie Appleby) *hld up: hdwy over 2f out: rdn to ld and hung lft fr over 1f out: styd on* **7/2**[1]

210 2 2 **It's Good To Laugh (IRE)**[43] 7410 2-9-7 **83**....................(p[1]) AdamKirby 4 85
(Clive Cox) *pushed along early in rr: drvn along over 3f out: hdwy u.p over 2f out: hung lft over 1f out: ev ch whn hmpd and eased wl ins fnl f* **5/1**[2]

0201 3 1 1/4 **Clay Regazzoni**[9] 8505 2-9-4 **80**.............................. CallumRodriguez 6 78
(Keith Dalgleish) *hld up: hdwy over 2f out: sn edgd lft: nt clr run and lost pl over 1f out: r.o ins fnl f* **5/1**[2]

5525 4 hd **Tantivy**[17] 8244 2-9-1 **77**.. RossaRyan 8 74
(Richard Hannon) *chsd ldr tl rdn over 2f out: hmpd and lost pl wl over 1f out: sn swtchd rt: r.o ins fnl f* **5/1**[2]

645 5 3/4 **Selecto**[59] 6858 2-8-9 **74**................................ ThomasGreatrex[(3)] 2 72
(Roger Charlton) *chsd ldrs: led 2f out: rdn and hdd over 1f out: hmpd and no ex ins fnl f* **11/1**

023 6 1/2 **Eventful**[24] 8021 2-8-11 **73**...(p[1]) BenCurtis 7 70
(Hugo Palmer) *led 7f: sn rdn: n.m.r ins fnl f: wknd towards fin* **20/1**

501 7 1/2 **Tafish (IRE)**[29] 7870 2-9-4 **80**.. ShaneKelly 9 74
(Richard Hughes) *racd alone on stands' side: s.i.s: sn pushed along and up w the pce: edgd rt fr 1/2-way: rdn over 1f out: wknd ins fnl f* **6/1**[3]

520 8 24 **Stars In The Sky**[57] 6926 2-9-2 **78**................................ OisinMurphy 5 24
(William Haggas) *hld up: hdwy over 3f out: wknd over 1f out* **8/1**

5323 9 2 **Rochford (IRE)**[23] 8061 2-8-0 **62** oh1................................(p) KieranO'Neill 3 4
(Henry Spiller) *chsd ldrs: rdn over 3f out: wknd 2f out* **20/1**

1m 58.97s (7.87) **Going Correction** +0.775s/f (Yiel) 9 Ran SP% **115.5**
Speed ratings (Par 98): **96,94,93,92,92 91,91,70,68**
CSF £20.88 CT £85.31 TOTE £4.10: £1.80, £2.10, £1.90; EX 23.30 Trifecta £99.30.
Owner Godolphin **Bred** Grenane House Stud **Trained** Newmarket, Suffolk
■ Stewards' Enquiry : Cieren Fallon three-day ban: careless riding (Nov 16,18,19)

FOCUS
A competitive nursery handicap and quite open betting. The trip was a real test in the conditions and the winner hung into his rivals up the hill.

8761 HAPPY 21ST BIRTHDAY TOM BOWNES H'CAP 1m
1:30 (1:32) (Class 4) (0-80,82) 3-Y-O+
£6,469 (£1,925; £962; £481; £300; £300) Stalls High

Form RPR
0536 1 **George Of Hearts (FR)**[12] 8412 4-9-1 **75**....................(t) CierenFallon[(3)] 6 84
(George Baker) *hld up: hdwy 1/2-way: led over 1f out: sn rdn and edgd lft: styd on* **13/2**[3]

0122 2 1 3/4 **Espresso Freddo (IRE)**[12] 8413 5-8-11 **68**..........(v) KieranShoemark 18 73+
(Robert Stephens) *s.s: hld up: hdwy over 2f out: nt clr run and swtchd rt over 1f out: r.o to go 2nd nr fin: nt rch wnr (jockey said gelding was slowly away)* **5/1**[1]

5241 3 shd **Madeleine Bond**[12] 8413 5-9-4 **75**................................ DavidProbert 16 80
(Henry Candy) *hld up: hdwy 1/2-way: rdn and edgd lft over 1f out: styd on* **6/1**[2]

3300 4 1 1/2 **Sassoon**[100] 5350 3-8-11 **70**..(b[1]) BenCurtis 19 72
(Paul Cole) *chsd ldrs: led over 2f out: rdn and hdd over 1f out: no ex wl ins fnl f* **16/1**

0644 5 3/4 **Villette (IRE)**[24] 8032 5-9-4 **75**.. JoeyHaynes 5 75
(Dean Ivory) *hld up in tch: lost pl over 4f out: hdwy over 2f out: rdn over 1f out: edgd lft and no ex wl ins fnl f* **9/1**

004 6 1 **Shattering (IRE)**[34] 7730 3-8-9 **68**.. DavidEgan 14 66
(Paul Cole) *s.i.s: sn prom: pushed along 1/2-way: rdn and nt clr run over 1f out: swtchd rt: styd on same pce ins fnl f (jockey said gelding was slowly away)* **16/1**

4102 7 2 1/2 **Woodside Wonder**[40] 7512 3-9-5 **78**....................(v) CallumRodriguez 12 71
(Keith Dalgleish) *led 7f out: rdn and hdd over 2f out: wknd fnl f* **16/1**

4033 8 1 **Storm Ahead (IRE)**[19] 8197 6-9-4 **75**................................(b) DavidAllan 10 66
(Tim Easterby) *hld up: styd on u.p fr over 1f out: nt trble ldrs* **12/1**

/0-0 9 1 3/4 **Epic Adventure (FR)**[73] 6350 4-9-1 **72**................................ GeraldMosse 7 59
(Roger Teal) *led 1f: chsd ldrs: rdn over 3f out: nt clr run and lost pl over 2f out: n.d after* **40/1**

6560 10 nse **Elysium Dream**[10] 8456 4-9-0 **71**................................ OisinMurphy 8 58
(Richard Hannon) *chsd ldrs: rdn over 3f out: wknd over 1f out* **25/1**

0004 11 1 **Highlight Reel (IRE)**[19] 8181 4-8-11 **68**................................ JoeFanning 2 53
(Rebecca Bastiman) *hld up: hdwy 1/2-way: wknd fnl f* **11/1**

0252 12 2 1/4 **Hawridge Storm (IRE)**[29] 7865 3-9-5 **78**................................ JFEgan 3 58
(Rod Millman) *s.s: outpcd: nvr nrr* **14/1**

0212 13 1 1/2 **Hammer Gun (USA)**[4] 8642 6-9-1 **72**....................(v) LewisEdmunds 15 49
(Derek Shaw) *s.i.s: hdwy over 4f out: wknd over 2f out (jockey said gelding hung both ways under pressure)* **10/1**

5202 14 1/2 **Robero**[21] 8122 7-8-11 **73**.. TobyEley[(5)] 11 49
(Gay Kelleway) *prom: racd keenly: wknd over 1f out* **16/1**

5221 15 nk **Critical Time**[38] 7583 3-9-4 **77**....................(p[1]) TomMarquand 9 52
(William Haggas) *chsd ldrs: rdn over 3f out: wknd over 1f out (trainer said filly was unsuited by the heavy going on this occasion)* **8/1**

533 16 13 **The Night King**[108] 5060 4-8-12 **69**................................ FrannyNorton 1 17
(Mick Quinn) *s.i.s: outpcd* **25/1**

1m 43.58s (5.18) **Going Correction** +0.775s/f (Yiel)
WFA 3 from 4yo+ 2lb 16 Ran SP% **130.8**
Speed ratings (Par 105): **105,103,103,101,100 99,97,96,94,94 93,91,89,89,89 76**
CSF £41.08 CT £225.67 TOTE £7.20: £2.40, £1.60, £2.30, £5.00; EX 51.80 Trifecta £161.90.
Owner David Howden **Bred** S C E A Haras De Saint Pair **Trained** Chiddingfold, Surrey

FOCUS
A big field for this competitive mile handicap, in which all previous runnings were won by trainers based outside Newmarket. An open betting heat but the winner ended a losing run. The third helps set the level.

8762 HEATH COURT HOTEL HORRIS HILL STKS (GROUP 3) (C&G) 7f
2:05 (2:05) (Class 1) 2-Y-O
£22,684 (£8,600; £4,304; £2,144; £1,076; £540) Stalls High

Form RPR
1 1 **Kenzai Warrior (USA)**[58] 6905 2-9-0 0.............................. JackMitchell 5 102
(Roger Teal) *chsd ldrs: shkn up 1/2-way: rdn and nt clr run over 1f out: r.o u.p to ld nr fin* **13/2**[3]

3533 2 1/2 **Ropey Guest**[21] 8112 2-9-0 99.. TomQueally 13 101
(George Margarson) *hld up: hdwy over 2f out: rdn to ld wl ins fnl f: hdd nr fin* **8/1**

410 3 3/4 **Impressor (IRE)**[42] 7456 2-9-0 93.................................(p[1]) MartinDwyer 1 99
(Marcus Tregoning) *racd alone: led: hung lft fr over 1f out: sn rdn: hdd and unable qck wl ins fnl f* **16/1**

212 4 3 1/4 **Gravity Force**[28] 7902 2-9-0 83.. CliffordLee 3 91
(K R Burke) *prom: rdn over 2f out: hung lft over 1f out: styd on same pce ins fnl f* **20/1**

3201 5 1/2 **Embolden (IRE)**[28] 7902 2-9-0 79.. TonyHamilton 7 90
(Richard Fahey) *prom: rdn over 2f out: sn outpcd: styd on ins fnl f* **33/1**

1151 6 nk **Tomfre**[21] 8110 2-9-0 95.. HarryBentley 8 89
(Ralph Beckett) *hld up: hdwy u.p over 1f out: nt trble ldrs* **4/1**[2]

7 3 1/4 **Hong Kong (USA)**[13] 8363 2-9-0 88..........................(b) SeamieHeffernan 6 81
(A P O'Brien, Ire) *led main gp after 1f: rdn over 1f out: wknd ins fnl f* **12/1**

511 8 5 **Surf Dancer (IRE)**[65] 6632 2-9-0 94.. TomMarquand 9 68
(William Haggas) *hld up: hdwy u.p over 1f out: wknd fnl f (jockey said colt was slowly away)* **9/1**

4141 9 2 1/4 **Aberama Gold**[21] 8125 2-9-0 102.. ShaneGray 12 63
(Keith Dalgleish) *led main gp 1f: chsd ldrs: rdn over 2f out: wknd over 1f out* **9/1**

10 10 **San Pedro (IRE)**[7] 8570 2-9-1 ow1.............................. DonnachaO'Brien 10 39
(A P O'Brien, Ire) *prom: lost pl after 1f: rdn over 2f out: wknd over 1f out (trainer's rep said colt was unsuited by the heavy going on this occasion)* **11/4**[1]

021 11 1 1/4 **Tom Collins**[10] 8460 2-9-0 84.. GeraldMosse 4 35
(David Elsworth) *hld up: pushed along 1/2-way: wknd over 2f out: eased (trainer's rep said the colt was unsuited by the heavy going on this occasion)* **14/1**

1m 28.74s (3.34) **Going Correction** +0.775s/f (Yiel) 11 Ran SP% **119.1**
Speed ratings (Par 106): **111,110,109,105,105 104,101,95,92,81 80**
CSF £58.49 TOTE £8.00: £2.80, £3.00, £4.70; EX 65.20 Trifecta £1069.70.
Owner Mr & Mrs Rae Borras **Bred** John D Gunther **Trained** Lambourn, Berks

FOCUS
This Group 3, rescheduled following Newbury's abandonment the previous weekend, was full of in-form horses, all but three being last-time-out winners. They went a decent pace, as evidenced by the time, which was 2.79secs faster than the quicker of the two earlier maidens, and stamina proved important in the end.

8763 BRITISH STALLION STUDS EBF MONTROSE FILLIES' STKS (LISTED RACE) 1m
2:40 (2:40) (Class 1) 2-Y-O
£17,013 (£6,450; £3,228; £1,608; £807; £405) Stalls High

Form RPR
1 **Born With Pride (IRE)** 2-9-0 0.. TomMarquand 1 101+
(William Haggas) *led 7f out: shkn up over 1f out: r.o* **20/1**

2 nk **Peaceful (IRE)**[23] 8073 2-9-1 ow1.............................. DonnachaO'Brien 4 101+
(A P O'Brien, Ire) *edgd lft s: prom: rdn over 1f out: r.o to go 2nd nr fin* **3/1**[1]

4142 3 1 1/4 **Run Wild (GER)**[10] 8482 2-9-0 105.. HarryBentley 2 98
(John Gosden) *hld up in tch: chsd wnr over 2f out: rdn and ev ch over 1f out: styd on same pce wl ins fnl f* **4/1**[2]

5 4 2 3/4 **Celestial Object (IRE)**[7] 8569 2-9-0 97.. JimCrowley 3 92
(Mrs John Harrington, Ire) *led 1f: chsd wnr tl rdn over 2f out: bo ex fnl f* **6/1**[3]

1 5 2 **Heart Reef (FR)**[57] 6918 2-9-0 0.. OisinMurphy 6 87
(Ralph Beckett) *hld up: rdn over 2f out: sn outpcd: n.d after (jockey said filly ran too free)* **4/1**[2]

213 6 nk **Alpen Rose (IRE)**[51] 7120 2-9-0 103.. AdamKirby 7 86
(Charlie Appleby) *hld up: rdn and outpcd over 2f out: n.d after (trainer's rep could offer no explanation for the performance shown)* **4/1**[2]

0123 7 1/2 **Separate**[22] 8089 2-9-0 98.................................(b) AndreaAtzeni 5 85
(Richard Hannon) *hmpd s: sn prom: rdn over 2f out: wknd over 1f out* **11/1**

1m 43.29s (4.89) **Going Correction** +0.775s/f (Yiel) 7 Ran SP% **112.4**
Speed ratings (Par 101): **106,105,104,101,99 99,98**
CSF £76.48 TOTE £27.20: £8.00, £2.10; EX 122.40 Trifecta £750.10.
Owner Sunderland Holding Inc **Bred** Sunderland Holdings Inc **Trained** Newmarket, Suffolk

FOCUS
The best recent winner of this Listed fillies' contest was the dual Classic winner Blue Bunting. There were several interesting types from major yards here but it fell to the complete outsider, who was making her racecourse debut. The time was only fractionally slower than the earlier older horse handicap.

8764 WEATHERBYS TBA JAMES SEYMOUR STKS (LISTED RACE) 1m 2f
3:15 (3:15) (Class 1) 3-Y-O+ £20,982 (£7,955; £3,981; £1,983; £995) Stalls High

Form RPR
0212 1 **Lord North (IRE)**[14] 8336 3-9-1 112.. RobertHavlin 3 113+
(John Gosden) *chsd ldrs: led 2f out: shkn up and edgd lft over 1f out: r.o* **10/11**[1]

-225 2 2 1/4 **Pablo Escobarr (IRE)**[134] 4049 3-9-1 103....................(t w) TomMarquand 4 108
(William Haggas) *led: hdd 2f out: swtchd rt over 1f out: styd on* **6/1**

1102 3 shd **Indeed**[21] 8116 4-9-4 107.. LiamKeniry 5 107
(Dominic Ffrench Davis) *prom: nt clr run 2f out: rdn over 1f out: styd on* **9/2**[3]

0456 4 6 **Aquarium**[21] 8116 4-9-4 100.. JFEgan 1 95
(Jane Chapple-Hyam) *s.s: hld up: hdwy over 2f out: rdn over 1f out: wknd fnl f* **20/1**

2-31 5 6 **Air Pilot**[38] 7565 10-9-7 114.. HarryBentley 2 86
(Ralph Beckett) *racd wd: w ldrs tl shkn up over 2f out: wknd over 1f out* **7/2**[2]

2m 11.11s (5.71) **Going Correction** +0.775s/f (Yiel)
WFA 3 from 4yo+ 3lb 5 Ran SP% **111.8**
Speed ratings (Par 111): **108,106,106,101,96**
CSF £7.11 TOTE £1.70: £1.30, £2.00; EX 5.70 Trifecta £11.70.

Owner HH Sheikh Zayed bin Mohammed Racing **Bred** Godolphin **Trained** Newmarket, Suffolk

FOCUS

A small field for this Listed race, but an intriguing clash between two progressive 3yos and three seasoned warriors. The younger generation came out best. The winner has been rated to form, and the third to his latest.

8765 PRICE BAILEY BEN MARSHALL STKS (LISTED RACE) 1m

3:45 (3:47) (Class 1) 3-Y-O+

£20,982 (£7,955; £3,981; £1,983; £995; £499) **Stalls High**

Form — RPR

3125 **1** **Roseman (IRE)**[135] 4013 3-9-0 105 .... AndreaAtzeni 2 117
(Roger Varian) *a.p: chsd ldr 5f out: led 2f out: rdn clr ins fnl f* **4/1**[2]

2400 **2** *4 1/2* **Century Dream (IRE)**[14] 8334 5-9-2 112 .... (t) OisinMurphy 4 108
(Simon Crisford) *chsd ldr 3f: remained handy: rdn to chse wnr over 1f out: styd on same pce ins fnl f* **13/8**[1]

0230 **3** *2* **Accidental Agent**[14] 8334 5-9-2 108 .... (p) CharlesBishop 7 104
(Eve Johnson Houghton) *s.s: hld up: hdwy on outer over 1f out: sn rdn: styd on same pce fnl f (jockey said horse was slowly away)* **8/1**[3]

5033 **4** *3 3/4* **Mitchum Swagger**[14] 8336 7-9-2 105 .... HarryBentley 3 96
(Ralph Beckett) *hld up: hdwy over 4f out: rdn over 1f out: wknd fnl f* **4/1**[2]

0050 **5** *2 1/2* **Iconic Choice**[13] 8367 3-8-9 100 .... FrannyNorton 5 86
(Tom Dascombe) *s.i.s: hdwy over 6f out: shkn up over 2f out: wknd over 1f out* **14/1**

1001 **6** *7* **Main Edition (IRE)**[28] 7905 3-9-2 107 .... JoeFanning 1 78
(Mark Johnston) *led 6f: sn rdn: wknd fnl f (trainer's rep could offer no explanation for the performance shown)* **10/1**

0300 **7** *9* **Fox Champion (IRE)**[69] 6508 3-9-7 108 .... SilvestreDeSousa 6 64
(Richard Hannon) *plld hrd and prom: stdd and lost pl over 6f out: shkn up over 2f out: wknd and eased over 1f out (trainer's rep said the colt was unsuited by the heavy going on this occasion)* **10/1**

1m 42.46s (4.06) **Going Correction** +0.775s/f (Yiel)
WFA 3 from 5yo+ 2lb **7 Ran SP% 114.1**
Speed ratings (Par 111): **110,105,103,99,97 90,81**
CSF £10.88 TOTE £4.00: £2.30, £1.40; EX 12.90 Trifecta £58.20.

Owner Sheikh Mohammed Obaid Al Maktoum **Bred** Knocktoran Stud **Trained** Newmarket, Suffolk

FOCUS

Quite a tight little Listed event, and another clash between the 3yos and several battle-hardened older rivals. Again a 3yo came out best and he looks a good prospect. The level is hard to pin down, but the winner has been rated up with the best winners of this race, with the second to his QEII latest.

8766 JIGSAW SPORTS BRANDING H'CAP 7f

4:15 (4:15) (Class 4) (0-85,86) 3-Y-O+

£6,469 (£1,925; £962; £481; £300; £300) **Stalls High**

Form — RPR

0050 **1** **King Of Tonga (IRE)**[22] 8101 3-9-4 **83** .... HarryBentley 7 93
(David O'Meara) *racd centre tl gps merged 4f out: hld up: pushed along and hdwy over 2f out: rdn to ld and hung lft ins fnl f: r.o* **7/1**[3]

3403 **2** *hd* **Material Girl**[28] 7901 3-8-6 **71** .... (v) HollieDoyle 1 80
(Richard Spencer) *racd centre tl gps merged 4f out: chsd ldrs: led over 1f out: sn rdn and hung lft: hdd ins fnl f: r.o* **8/1**

1632 **3** *6* **Swift Approval (IRE)**[34] 7731 7-9-4 **82** .... JimCrowley 4 77
(Stuart Williams) *racd centre tl gps merged 4f out: chsd ldr: led 2f out: rdn and hdd over 1f out: wknd wl ins fnl f* **12/1**

0532 **4** *1 3/4* **Flying Pursuit**[22] 8101 6-9-8 **86** .... (tp) RachelRichardson 3 76
(Tim Easterby) *racd centre tl gps merged 4f out: led that gp: overall ldr 1/2-way: rdn and hdd 2f out: wknd ins fnl f* **8/1**

0042 **5** *1/2* **Howzer Black (IRE)**[32] 7781 3-9-1 **80** .... CallumRodriguez 5 68
(Keith Dalgleish) *racd centre tl gps merged 4f out: s.i.s: hld up: rdn over 2f out: r.o ins fnl f: nvr nrr* **8/1**

4442 **6** *1 3/4* **Dance Diva**[8] 8521 4-9-8 **86** .... TonyHamilton 9 70
(Richard Fahey) *racd centre tl gps merged 4f out: chsd ldrs: rdn over 1f out: wknd fnl f* **5/1**[1]

0205 **7** *1* **Presidential (IRE)**[57] 6922 5-9-7 **85** .... (p) BenCurtis 13 67
(Roger Fell) *racd stands' side tl gps merged 4f out: hld up: hdwy over 1f out: sn rdn: wknd ins fnl f* **6/1**[2]

5014 **8** *1 1/4* **Colonel Frank**[85] 5911 5-8-13 **77** .... JackMitchell 12 56
(Mick Quinn) *racd stands' side tl gps merged 4f out: chsd ldrs: rdn over 1f out: wknd fnl f* **20/1**

0060 **9** *nk* **Stay Classy (IRE)**[37] 7613 3-9-2 **84** .... (v[1]) MeganNicholls(3) 18 61
(Richard Spencer) *racd stands' side tl gps merged 4f out: s.s: hld up: nt clr run over 2f out: rdn and hung rt over 1f out: n.d (jockey said filly was slowly away)* **16/1**

4220 **10** *nk* **Typhoon Ten (IRE)**[74] 6319 3-9-6 **85** .... RossaRyan 16 61
(Richard Hannon) *racd stands' side tl gps merged 4f out: s.i.s: hld up: hdwy over 2f out: rdn and wknd over 1f out* **16/1**

2260 **11** *5* **Chosen World**[19] 8197 5-8-8 **72** .... BarryMcHugh 8 36
(Julie Camacho) *racd centre tl gps merged 4f out: hld up: rdn over 2f out: sn wknd* **16/1**

3460 **12** *3/4* **Custard The Dragon**[138] 3944 6-8-10 **74** .... (v) SilvestreDeSousa 11 36
(John Mackie) *racd stands' side tl gps merged 4f out: s.i.s: hdwy over 4f out: wknd and eased over 1f out* **20/1**

2220 **13** *7* **Iconic Knight (IRE)**[11] 8420 4-8-13 **77** .... OisinMurphy 10 21
(Ed Walker) *racd stands' side tl gps merged 4f out: prom over 5f (jockey said gelding became unbalanced in the dip)* **8/1**

0600 **14** *18* **London Protocol (FR)**[23] 8070 6-8-7 **71** oh4 .... (b) JimmyQuinn 14
(John Mackie) *racd stands' side tl gps merged 4f out: overall ldr to 1/2-way: wknd over 2f out* **33/1**

1m 29.42s (4.02) **Going Correction** +0.775s/f (Yiel)
WFA 3 from 4yo+ 1lb **14 Ran SP% 125.7**
Speed ratings (Par 105): **108,107,100,98,98 96,95,93,93,93 87,86,78,57**
CSF £63.35 CT £490.48 TOTE £7.60: £3.10, £3.50, £2.20; EX 68.40 Trifecta £1310.20.

Owner Middleham Park Racing LXV **Bred** Martyn J McEnery **Trained** Upper Helmsley, N Yorks

FOCUS

The last race of the year at the track, and another really competitive handicap on paper, although it was weakened by five non-runners. The first two came clear. The winner has been rated back to his early season best, with the second running a length pb.

T/Plt: £374.30 to a £1 stake. Pool: £65,232.43 - 127.21 winning units T/Qpdt: £73.30 to a £1 stake. Pool: £6,486.10 - 65.46 winning units **Colin Roberts**

7918 FLEMINGTON (L-H)

Saturday, November 2

OFFICIAL GOING: Turf: good to soft changing to soft after race 3 (2.00)

8767a LEXUS HOTHAM STKS (GROUP 3 H'CAP) (3YO+) (TURF) 1m 4f 110y

2:40 3-Y-O+

£100,276 (£29,834; £14,917; £7,458; £4,143; £3,314)

RPR

1 **Downdraft (IRE)**[7] 8577 4-9-4 0 .... (t) JohnAllen 1 114+
(Joseph Patrick O'Brien, Ire) *prom on inner 3f: trckd ldrs: smooth hdwy to ld over 2f out: drvn along and readily plld clr: won easing down* **9/2**[1]

2 *1 1/2* **Carif (AUS)**[14] 4-8-8 0 ow1 .... JamieKah 4 100
(Peter & Paul Snowden, Australia) **17/2**

3 *4* **Azuro (FR)**[14] 5-8-8 0 .... (tp) DeanYendall 5 94
(Ciaron Maher & David Eustace, Australia) **17/2**

4 *1 1/4* **Sir Charles Road (AUS)**[14] 6-9-1 0 .... (bt) DwayneDunn 8 99
(Lance O'Sullivan & Andrew Scott, New Zealand) **17/2**

5 *1* **The Chosen One (NZ)**[14] 8361 4-9-1 0 .... (b) MarkZahra 3 97
(Murray Baker & Andrew Forsman, New Zealand) **5/1**[2]

6 *2* **Hush Writer (JPN)**[14] 4-9-1 0 .... TimothyClark 10 94
(Gai Waterhouse & Adrian Bott, Australia) **6/1**[3]

7 *3/4* **Wall Of Fire (IRE)**[21] 8134 6-8-7 0 .... (b) JyeMcNeil 2 85
(Ciaron Maher & David Eustace, Australia) **13/1**

8 *hd* **Haky (IRE)**[10] 8600 5-9-1 0 .... LindaMeech 9 92
(J E Hammond, France) **7/1**

9 *12* **Valac (IRE)**[14] 7-8-7 0 .... CraigAWilliams 7 65
(David A & B Hayes & Tom Dabernig, Australia) **25/1**

10 *6* **Patrick Erin (NZ)**[14] 8-9-1 0 .... (b) HughBowman 6 63
(Chris Waller, Australia) **17/2**

2m 38.85s **10 Ran SP% 114.7**

Owner OTI Racing, J Boyd Et Al **Bred** Airlie Stud **Trained** Owning Hill, Co Kilkenny

8768a KENNEDY CANTALA (GROUP 1 H'CAP) (2YO+) (TURF) 1m

5:35 2-Y-O+

£664,364 (£198,895; £99,447; £49,723; £27,624; £22,099)

RPR

1 **Fierce Impact (JPN)**[21] 8138 5-8-11 **0** .... (b) CraigAWilliams 14 108
(Matthew A Smith, Australia) **7/1**[2]

2 *shd* **Fifty Stars (IRE)**[28] 7930 4-8-13 **0** .... (bt) MarkZahra 3 110
(David A & B Hayes & Tom Dabernig, Australia) **9/1**[3]

3 *hd* **Cascadian**[14] 4-8-6 **0** .... DeanYendall 16 102
(James Cummings, Australia) *in rr of midfield: pushed along and hdwy between runners 2f out: rdn along and qckna over 1f out: clsd on ldrs cl home: clst fin* **11/1**

4 *1 1/4* **So Si Bon (AUS)**[21] 8138 6-8-10 **0** .... LukeNolen 12 103
(David A & B Hayes & Tom Dabernig, Australia) **30/1**

5 *1 3/4* **Best Of Days**[7] 8578 5-9-0 **0** .... (b) JamesDoyle 11 103
(James Cummings, Australia) *midfield: pushed along on outer turning in: tk clsr order and rdn along 1 1/2f out: kpt on but nvr on terms w ldrs* **25/1**

6 *shd* **Night's Watch (NZ)**[21] 8138 6-8-10 **0** .... (t) DamienOliver 7 99
(Chris Waller, Australia) **6/1**[1]

7 *3/4* **Life Less Ordinary (IRE)**[14] 7-8-13 **0** .... HughBowman 15 100
(Chris Waller, Australia) **20/1**

8 *3/4* **Streets Of Avalon (AUS)**[14] 8360 5-8-10 **0** .... (bt) ZacSpain 8 96
(Shane Nichols, Australia) **60/1**

9 *hd* **Star Of The Seas (NZ)**[28] 7930 5-8-7 **0** ow1 .... (b) MichaelWalker 4 92
(Chris Waller, Australia) **6/1**[1]

10 *hd* **Sikandarabad (IRE)**[7] 8578 6-8-8 **0** .... (b) JyeMcNeil 9 93
(David A & B Hayes & Tom Dabernig, Australia) **20/1**

11 *nk* **Mahamedeis (AUS)**[21] 8138 5-8-5 **0** .... (bt) BrettPrebble 5 89
(Nick Ryan, Australia) **20/1**

12 *1 1/4* **Rock (AUS)**[28] 7930 4-8-6 **0** .... (vt) TimothyClark 10 87
(Michael, Wayne & John Hawkes, Australia) **9/1**[3]

13 *3 1/4* **Land Of Plenty (AUS)**[14] 8360 6-9-0 **0** .... (vt) BenAllen 1 88
(Peter & Paul Snowden, Australia) **40/1**

14 *12* **Cliff's Edge (AUS)**[7] 8578 5-8-10 **0** .... JohnAllen 2 56
(Ciaron Maher & David Eustace, Australia) **20/1**

15 *hd* **Chief Ironside**[7] 8578 4-8-5 **0** .... StephenBaster 6 51
(David Menuisier) *led after 2f: pushed along and hdd over 2f out: wknd qckly* **13/1**

16 *2 3/4* **Royal Meeting (IRE)**[14] 8360 3-8-13 **0** .... (t) DwayneDunn 13 54
(Saeed bin Suroor) *midfield: rdn along and lost position over 2f out: wl hld fnl 1 1/2f* **11/1**

1m 38.21s
WFA 3 from 4yo+ 2lb **16 Ran SP% 115.1**

Owner Seymour Bloodstock, Denns Racing Et Al **Bred** Keiai Orthopedic Appliance Co Ltd **Trained** Australia

8745 SANTA ANITA (L-H)

Saturday, November 2

OFFICIAL GOING: Dirt: fast; turf: firm

8769a BREEDERS' CUP FILLY & MARE SPRINT (GRADE 1) (3YO+) (MAIN TRACK) (DIRT) 7f (D)

6:55 3-Y-O+

£433,070 (£133,858; £70,866; £39,370; £23,622; £7,874)

RPR

1 **Covfefe (USA)**[42] 3-8-10 0 .... JoelRosario 1 114
(Brad H Cox, U.S.A) *trckd ldrs: rdn to ld 2f out: sn drvn clr: kpt on wl fnl f* **2/1**[1]

2 *3/4* **Bellafina (USA)**[42] 7479 3-8-10 0 .... (b) FlavienPrat 6 112
(Simon Callaghan, U.S.A) *racd keenly: in tch: drvn to chse ldr 1f out: styd on fnl f: nt able to chal* **13/2**[3]

3 7 3/4 **Dawn The Destroyer (USA)**[28] 5-8-12 0 TylerGaffalione 8 93
(Kiaran McLaughlin, U.S.A) *hld up: sn bhd: latched on to main gp 2f out: sn rdn and hdwy: swtchd off rail over 1f out: kpt on fnl f: tk modest 3rd cl home* **18/1**

4 1/2 **Spiced Perfection (USA)**[28] 4-8-12 0 (b) JohnRVelazquez 9 92
(Peter Miller, U.S.A) *in tch on outside: rdn and ev ch ins fnl 2f: wknd fnl f: lost modest 3rd cl home* **11/2**[2]

5 2 1/4 **Danuska's My Girl (USA)**[28] 5-8-12 0 (b) GeovanniFranco 2 86
(Dan Ward, U.S.A) *led: rdn and hdd 2f out: sn wknd* **50/1**

6 1 1/4 **Come Dancing (USA)**[41] 5-8-12 0 JavierCastellano 4 82
(Carlos F Martin, U.S.A) *hld up: rdn and brief effrt over 2f out: wknd over 1f out* **2/1**[1]

7 2 1/4 **Selcourt (USA)**[28] 5-8-12 0 LuisSaez 7 76
(John W Sadler, U.S.A) *in tch in midfield: rdn 3f out: lost pl over 2f out: sn wl btn* **14/1**

8 1 1/2 **Lady Ninja (USA)**[28] 5-8-12 0 (b) DraydenVanDyke 5 72
(Richard Baltas, U.S.A) *hld up: outpcd ins fnl 3f: wknd fnl f* **22/1**

9 15 **Heavenhasmynikki (USA)**[28] 4-8-12 0 (b) RicardoSantanaJr 3 32
(Robert B Hess Jr, U.S.A) *w ldr: rdn and lost pl qckly ins fnl 2f: sn wl btn* **33/1**

1m 22.4s
WFA 3 from 4yo+ 1lb **9** Ran SP% **116.6**
PARI-MUTUEL (all including 2 unit stake): WIN 5.00; PLACE (1-2) 3.60, 5.00; SHOW (1-2-3) 3.00, 3.60, 6.60; SF 20.80.
Owner LNJ Foxwoods **Bred** Alexander-Groves Thoroughbreds **Trained** USA

FOCUS
A fast, contested pace: 22.13, 22.65, 24.80, 12.82.

8770a BREEDERS' CUP TURF SPRINT (GRADE 1) (3YO+) (TURF) 5f
7:33 3-Y-O+
£433,070 (£133,858; £70,866; £39,370; £23,622; £7,874)

RPR

1 **Belvoir Bay**[147] [3615] 6-9-0 0 JavierCastellano 12 119
(Peter Miller, U.S.A) *mde all: rdn and kpt on wl fr over 1f out: unchal* **16/1**

2 1 1/4 **Om (USA)**[126] 7-9-0 0 ManuelFranco 11 114
(Peter Miller, U.S.A) *chsd ldr: rdn ins fnl 2f: kpt on wl fnl f: nt able to chal* **16/1**

3 nse **Shekky Shebaz (USA)**[28] 4-9-0 0 IradOrtizJr 4 114
(Jason Servis, U.S.A) *trckd ldrs: rdn and kpt on wl fr over 1f out: nt able to chal* **13/2**

4 1 3/4 **Stubbins (USA)**[28] 3-8-12 0 (b) FlavienPrat 5 106
(Doug O'Neill, U.S.A) *hld up in rr pair: pushed along whn nt clr run over 1f out: rdn and styd on strly fnl 100yds: nrst fin* **9/1**

5 hd **Pure Sensation (USA)**[61] 8-9-0 0 PacoLopez 2 107
(Christophe Clement, U.S.A) *in tch in midfield: drvn and kpt on same pce fr over 1f out* **9/2**[1]

6 3/4 **Imprimis (USA)**[28] 5-9-0 0 FrankieDettori 3 104
(Joseph Orseno, U.S.A) *towards rr of midfield: rdn 2f out: kpt on steadily fr over 1f out: nvr rchd ldrs* **8/1**

7 nk **Leinster (USA)**[28] 4-9-0 0 (b) TylerGaffalione 7 103
(George R Arnold II, U.S.A) *midfield: rdn ins fnl 2f: drvn and kpt on same pce fr over 1f out* **12/1**

8 1/2 **Stormy Liberal (USA)**[36] 7-9-0 0 JohnRVelazquez 6 101
(Peter Miller, U.S.A) *trckd ldrs: rdn over 1f out: wknd ins fnl f* **12/1**

9 1 1/4 **Final Frontier (USA)**[28] 4-9-0 0 (b) LuisSaez 9 97
(Thomas Albertrani, U.S.A) *midfield: rdn and outpcd ins fnl 2f: sn no imp* **14/1**

10 1/2 **Totally Boss (USA)**[56] 4-9-0 0 JoseLOrtiz 1 95
(George R Arnold II, U.S.A) *in rr pair: rdn and no imp fr 2f out: wd into st* **11/2**[2]

11 hd **Eddie Haskell (USA)**[36] 6-9-0 0 JoelRosario 10 94
(Mark Glatt, U.S.A) *towards rr: awkward on turn ins fnl 2f: sn rdn and no imp* **6/1**[3]

12 2 1/4 **Legends Of War (USA)**[51] 3-8-12 0 RafaelBejarano 8 84
(Doug O'Neill, U.S.A) *in tch in midfield on outside: rdn and outpcd 2f out: wknd over 1f out* **28/1**

54.83s **12** Ran SP% **119.6**
PARI-MUTUEL (all including 2 unit stake): WIN 31.60; PLACE (1-2) 14.40, 13.80; SHOW (1-2-3) 7.60, 9.40, 5.60; SF 267.40.
Owner Gary Barber **Bred** Mrs R D Peacock **Trained** USA

FOCUS
The pace held up here, the winner making every yard. The prominent positioning of her stablemates was helpful in that endeavour, and a new track record was set.

8771a BIG ASS FANS BREEDERS' CUP DIRT MILE (GRADE 1) (3YO+) (MAIN TRACK) (DIRT) 1m (D)
8:10 3-Y-O+
£433,070 (£133,858; £70,866; £39,370; £23,622; £7,874)

RPR

1 **Spun To Run (USA)**[21] 3-8-11 0 (b) IradOrtizJr 3 118
(Juan Carlos Guerrero, U.S.A) *mde all: rdn and hung rt over 1f out: drvn and kpt on strly fnl f* **8/1**[3]

2 2 3/4 **Omaha Beach (USA)**[27] [7945] 3-8-11 0 MikeESmith 5 114+
(Richard E Mandella, U.S.A) *hld up towards rr: rdn and hdwy on wd outside fr 2f out: styd on fnl f: wnt 2nd 75yds out: no imp on wnr* **1/1**[1]

3 1 1/4 **Blue Chipper (USA)**[55] [7010] 4-9-0 0 FlavienPrat 8 110
(Kim Young Kwan, Korea) *chsd ldr: rdn ins fnl 2f: no ex fnl f: lost 2nd 75yds out* **22/1**

4 3 1/4 **Snapper Sinclair (USA)**[63] 4-9-0 0 RicardoSantanaJr 10 103
(Steven Asmussen, U.S.A) *towards rr of midfield: rdn over 2f out: nt clr run over 1f out: drvn and kpt on fr over 1f out* **40/1**

5 1 3/4 **Improbable (USA)**[42] [7480] 3-8-11 0 (b) RafaelBejarano 2 98
(Bob Baffert, U.S.A) *in tch: rdn and outpcd 3f out: wknd steadily fr over 1f out* **9/2**[2]

6 1/2 **Coal Front (USA)**[42] 5-9-0 0 JavierCastellano 7 97
(Todd Pletcher, U.S.A) *midfield: rdn 2f out: short of room and sltly hmpd over 1f out: sn outpcd and no imp* **12/1**

7 1 1/4 **Mr. Money (USA)**[42] [7480] 3-8-11 0 GabrielSaez 4 93
(W Bret Calhoun, U.S.A) *in tch: rdn 3f out: losing pl whn hung lft and hmpd rival over 1f out: sn wknd* **9/1**

8 1 **Diamond Oops (USA)**[28] [7922] 4-9-0 0 (b) JulienRLeparoux 9 92
(Patrick L Biancone, U.S.A) *a towards rr* **12/1**

9 nk **Ambassadorial (USA)**[25] [7997] 5-9-0 0 JamieSpencer 6 91
(Jane Chapple-Hyam) *a towards rr* **50/1**

10 17 **Giant Expectations (USA)**[69] 6-9-0 0 (b) JoseLOrtiz 1 52
(Peter Eurton, U.S.A) *a towards rr: eased fr over 1f out* **20/1**

1m 36.58s
WFA 3 from 4yo+ 2lb **10** Ran SP% **118.2**
PARI-MUTUEL (all including 2 unit stake): WIN 20.20; PLACE (1-2) 7.00, 3.40; SHOW (1-2-3) 4.80, 2.40, 6.00; SF 55.40.
Owner Robert P Donaldson **Bred** Sabana Farm Llc **Trained** North America

FOCUS
This looked competitive beforehand but the winner was allowed an uncontested lead through fast early/slow late splits of 23.05, 23.46, 23.99, 26.08.

8772a MAKER'S MARK BREEDERS' CUP FILLY & MARE TURF (GRADE 1) (3YO+) (TURF) 1m 2f (T)
8:54 3-Y-O+
£866,141 (£267,716; £141,732; £78,740; £47,244; £15,748)

RPR

1 **Iridessa (IRE)**[28] [7898] 3-8-8 0 WayneLordan 1 114
(Joseph Patrick O'Brien, Ire) *chsd clr ldng pair: effrt over 2f out: led and hrd pressed ins fnl f: kpt on gamely u.p cl home* **8/1**[3]

2 nk **Vasilika (USA)**[28] [7920] 5-8-12 0 (b) FlavienPrat 5 113
(Dan Ward, U.S.A) *chsd clr ldr: effrt and rdn over 1f out: pressed wnr and ev ch ins fnl f: r.o wl: jst hld* **15/2**[2]

3 2 1/4 **Sistercharlie (IRE)**[27] [7935] 5-8-12 0 JohnRVelazquez 2 109+
(Chad C Brown, U.S.A) *in tch in chsng gp: effrt and rdn over 2f out: chsd clr ldng pair ins fnl f: r.o: nt pce to chal* **5/6**[1]

4 3/4 **Fanny Logan (IRE)**[22] [8094] 3-8-8 0 (h) FrankieDettori 10 107+
(John Gosden) *hld up in tch: effrt and pushed along whn carried rt bnd over 2f out: drvn and kpt on fnl f: nt pce to chal* **11/1**

5 1 **Just Wonderful (USA)**[28] [7920] 3-8-8 0 RyanMoore 9 105+
(A P O'Brien, Ire) *hld up on ins: pushed along 3f out: hdwy over 1f out: kpt on fnl f: nvr able to chal* **33/1**

6 1 1/2 **Mirth (USA)**[34] [7751] 4-8-12 0 (b) MikeESmith 4 102
(Philip D'Amato, U.S.A) *led: clr after 2f to over 1f out: rdn and hdd ins fnl f: sn wknd* **28/1**

7 nk **Villa Marina**[27] [7942] 3-8-8 0 OlivierPeslier 7 101
(C Laffon-Parias, France) *hld up towards rr: rdn 3f out: no imp fr 2f out* **14/1**

8 1 1/4 **Billesdon Brook**[28] [7898] 4-8-12 0 SeanLevey 3 99
(Richard Hannon) *t.k.h early: dwlt: hld up on ins: rdn whn veered rt bnd 2f out: sn wknd* **10/1**

9 4 1/4 **Mrs Sippy (USA)**[27] [7935] 4-8-12 0 JoelRosario 8 90
(H Graham Motion, U.S.A) *dwlt: bhd: struggling 3f out: nvr on terms* **20/1**

10 1 1/4 **Castle Lady (IRE)**[21] [8139] 3-8-8 0 MickaelBarzalona 6 88
(H-A Pantall, France) *prom in chsng gp: drvn along over 2f out: wknd over 1f out* **18/1**

1m 57.77s (-1.51)
WFA 3 from 4yo+ 3lb **10** Ran SP% **117.9**
PARI-MUTUEL (all including 2 unit stake): WIN 28.40; PLACE (1-2) 11.20, 5.40; SHOW (1-2-3) 5.00, 3.20, 2.20; SF 131.00.
Owner Mrs C C Regalado-Gonzalez **Bred** Whisperview Trading Ltd **Trained** Owning Hill, Co Kilkenny

FOCUS
It didn't pay to be too far off the pace here, the first two leading the pursuit of the clear leader. The winner has been rated to her best.

8773a BREEDERS' CUP SPRINT (GRADE 1) (3YO+) (MAIN TRACK) (DIRT) 6f (D)
9:36 3-Y-O+
£866,141 (£267,716; £141,732; £78,740; £47,244; £15,748)

RPR

1 **Mitole (USA)**[70] [6488] 4-9-0 0 RicardoSantanaJr 4 127
(Steven Asmussen, U.S.A) *prom: hdwy on outside 2f out: drvn and led fnl 50yds: kpt on strly* **7/4**[1]

2 1 1/4 **Shancelot (USA)**[27] [7945] 3-8-12 0 (b) JoseLOrtiz 6 121
(Jorge Navarro, U.S.A) *led at decent gallop: drvn along over 1f out: hdd and no ex fnl 50yds* **15/8**[2]

3 2 1/4 **Whitmore (USA)**[29] 6-9-0 0 (b) FlavienPrat 7 115
(Ronald Moquett, U.S.A) *s.i.s: bhd and sn pushed along: hdwy on outside over 1f out: chsd clr ldng pair ins fnl f: r.o* **22/1**

4 1/2 **Engage (USA)**[29] 4-9-0 0 JohnRVelazquez 5 114
(Steven Asmussen, U.S.A) *hld up bhd ldng gp: rdn over 2f out: kpt on ins fnl f: nvr able to chal* **20/1**

5 1/2 **Firenze Fire (USA)**[35] [7720] 4-9-0 0 IradOrtizJr 3 112
(Jason Servis, U.S.A) *cl up: effrt and wnt 2nd over 2f out to over 1f out: rdn and no ex ins fnl f* **11/1**

6 nse **Hog Creek Hustle (USA)**[29] 3-8-12 0 MikeESmith 2 110
(Vickie L Foley, U.S.A) *s.i.s: bhd and outpcd: hdwy on outside fnl f: nvr rchd ldrs* **25/1**

7 3/4 **Catalina Cruiser (USA)**[69] 5-9-0 0 JoelRosario 1 110
(John W Sadler, U.S.A) *s.i.s: hld up bhd ldng gp: drvn and outpcd over 2f out: btn fnl f* **4/1**[3]

8 4 1/4 **Matera Sky (USA)**[55] 5-9-0 0 YutakaTake 8 96
(Hideyuki Mori, Japan) *chsd ldr to over 2f out: rdn and wknd fnl f* **28/1**

1m 9.0s (0.74) **8** Ran SP% **115.9**
PARI-MUTUEL (all including 2 unit stake): WIN 5.60; PLACE (1-2) 3.20, 3.20; SHOW (1-2-3) 2.60, 2.80, 5.00; SF 15.60.
Owner L William & Corinne Heiligbrodt **Bred** Edward A Cox Jr **Trained** USA

FOCUS
There was no Roy H, who had won the race for the last two years, or Imperial Hint, who was placed in the last two runnings, but still a belting contest. The runner-up set a scorching pace before being overhauled late on: 21.47, 22.57, 24.96.

8774a TVG BREEDERS' CUP MILE (GRADE 1) (3YO+) (TURF) 1m (T)
10:20 3-Y-O+
£866,141 (£267,716; £141,732; £78,740; £47,244; £15,748)

RPR

1 **Uni**[28] [7920] 5-8-11 0 JoelRosario 9 119
(Chad C Brown, U.S.A) *hld up towards rr: gd hdwy on outside over 2f out: led and hrd pressed appr fnl f: asserted fnl 100yds: kpt on strly* **9/2**[2]

2 1 1/2 **Got Stormy (USA)**[49] [7225] 4-8-11 0 TylerGaffalione 5 116
(Mark Casse, Canada) *in tch in chsng gp: hdwy to dispute ld appr fnl f to fnl 100yds: kpt on same pce* **10/3**[1]

3 1 1/4 **Without Parole**[168] 2829 4-9-0 0 ....(b) IradOrtizJr 8 116
(Chad C Brown, U.S.A) *hld up towards rr: drvn along over 2f out: hdwy on outside fnl f: tk 3rd last stride: nrst fin* 7/1[3]

4 nse **Circus Maximus (IRE)**[55] 7007 3-8-11 0 ....(b) RyanMoore 7 115
(A P O'Brien, Ire) *dwlt: sn midfield: effrt and drvn over 2f out: hdwy to chse clr ldng pair ins fnl f: kpt on: no imp and lost 3rd last stride* 10/3[1]

5 1 1/2 **Bowies Hero (USA)**[28] 7922 5-9-0 0 ....(b) FlavienPrat 12 113
(Philip D'Amato, U.S.A) *chsd clr ldng pair: effrt and clsd over 2f out: rdn and fdd ins fnl f* 25/1

6 nk **El Tormenta (CAN)**[49] 7225 4-9-0 0 ....(b) EuricoRosaDaSilva 6 112
(Gail Cox, Canada) *pressed ldr and sn clr of rest: rdn and ev ch over 2f out to over 1f out: fdd ins fnl f* 20/1

7 nse **Hey Gaman**[27] 7944 4-9-0 0 .... FrankieDettori 11 112
(James Tate) *led fr wd draw and swtchd to ins rail after 1f: rdn and hdd appr fnl f: sn outpcd* 16/1

8 1/2 **Space Traveller**[49] 7220 3-8-11 0 .... DanielTudhope 2 110
(Richard Fahey) *hld up towards rr: drvn and outpcd 3f out: sme hdwy fnl f: nvr able to chal* 16/1

9 1/2 **Lord Glitters (FR)**[14] 8334 6-9-0 0 .... JamieSpencer 10 109
(David O'Meara) *s.i.s: hld up: rdn 3f out: hdwy on outside over 1f out: kpt on fnl f: nt pce to chal* 18/1

10 1/2 **True Valour (IRE)**[27] 5-9-0 0 .... DraydenVanDyke 4 108
(Simon Callaghan, U.S.A) *prom in chsng gp: effrt over 1f out: short of room ent fnl f: sn btn* 18/1

11 nk **Trais Fluors**[47] 7293 5-9-0 0 .... WJLee 3 108
(K J Condon, Ire) *dwlt: bhd: rdn and outpcd over 2f out: nvr on terms* 28/1

11 dht **Lucullan (USA)**[19] 5-9-0 0 .... LuisSaez 1 108
(Kiaran McLaughlin, U.S.A) *midfield: effrt against far rail whn nt clr run over 1f out and ent fnl f: sn no imp and eased* 11/1

13 3 1/4 **Next Shares (USA)**[28] 7922 6-9-0 0 ....(b) JohnRVelazquez 13 100
(Richard Baltas, U.S.A) *swtchd lft s: last and detached: nvr on terms* 80/1

1m 32.45s (-1.42)
WFA 3 from 4yo+ 2lb 13 Ran SP% 124.6
PARI-MUTUEL (all including 2 unit stake): WIN 9.20; PLACE (1-2) 4.80, 4.80; SHOW (1-2-3) 3.60, 3.40, 5.60; SF 32.60.
Owner Michael Dubb, Head Of Plains Partners LLC Et Al **Bred** Haras D'Etreham **Trained** USA

FOCUS
The leaders set a good gallop and that allowed the smart winner to show off her trademark late finish.

8775a LONGINES BREEDERS' CUP DISTAFF (GRADE 1) (3YO+ FILLIES & MARES) (MAIN TRACK) (DIRT) 1m 1f (D)
11:00 3-Y-O+

£866,141 (£267,716; £141,732; £78,740; £47,244; £15,748)

RPR

1 **Blue Prize (ARG)**[27] 7938 6-8-12 0 ....(b) JoeBravo 11 120
(Ignacio Correas IV, U.S.A) *hld up towards rr: gd hdwy over 2f out: edgd lft and led ins fnl f: drvn out* 9/1[3]

2 1 1/2 **Midnight Bisou (USA)**[35] 4-8-12 0 .... MikeESmith 4 116+
(Steven Asmussen, U.S.A) *hld up towards rr: rdn and hdwy over 2f out: edgd lft and chsd wnr ins fnl f: r.o: nt pce to chal* 10/11[1]

3 3 1/4 **Serengeti Empress (USA)**[42] 7479 3-8-9 0 .... FlavienPrat 9 111
(Thomas Amoss, U.S.A) *wnt lft s: led: rdn along over 1f out: hdd ins fnl f: sn btn* 12/1

4 1 1/4 **Ollie's Candy (USA)**[34] 4-8-12 0 ....(b) JoelRosario 2 107
(John W Sadler, U.S.A) *chsd ldrs: drvn along over 2f out: wknd fnl f* 20/1

5 1 1/4 **Dunbar Road (USA)**[27] 7938 3-8-9 0 .... JoseLOrtiz 5 105
(Chad C Brown, U.S.A) *hld up towards rr: drvn along over 2f out: no imp fr over 1f out* 11/2[2]

6 6 3/4 **Mo See Cal (USA)**[23] 4-8-12 0 .... PacoLopez 10 90
(Peter Miller, U.S.A) *t.k.h early: chsd ldr 2f: cl up tl rdn and wknd over 1f out* 40/1

7 hd **Wow Cat (CHI)**[35] 5-8-12 0 .... IradOrtizJr 6 90
(Chad C Brown, U.S.A) *n.m.r sn after s: bhd: rdn over 2f out: sme late hdwy: nvr able to chal* 22/1

8 1 1/4 **Street Band (USA)**[42] 7479 3-8-9 0 ....(b) SophieDoyle 3 88
(J Larry Jones, U.S.A) *in tch: drvn along over 2f out: sn wknd* 11/1

9 1 1/4 **Secret Spice (USA)**[34] 4-8-12 0 .... JohnRVelazquez 7 85
(Richard Baltas, U.S.A) *in tch: drvn and struggling over 2f out: btn over 1f out* 14/1

10 6 1/2 **La Force (GER)**[34] 5-8-12 0 ....(p) DraydenVanDyke 8 71
(Patrick Gallagher, U.S.A) *towards rr: drvn and struggling over 2f out: nvr on terms* 80/1

11 5 1/2 **Paradise Woods (USA)**[34] 5-8-12 0 .... AbelCedillo 1 59
(John Shirreffs, U.S.A) *dwlt: sn prom: chsd ldr after 2f to 3f out: sn rdn and wknd qckly* 12/1

1m 50.5s (1.60)
WFA 3 from 4yo+ 3lb 11 Ran SP% 120.9
PARI-MUTUEL (all including 2 unit stake): WIN 19.80; PLACE (1-2) 5.60, 2.80; SHOW (1-2-3) 4.20, 2.20, 6.00; SF 42.20.
Owner Merriebelle Stables LLC **Bred** Bioart S A **Trained** USA

FOCUS
The pace was fast and they finished slowly: 22.98 (2f), 23.70 (4f), 24.15 (6f), 26.31 (1m), 13.36 (line).

8776a LONGINES BREEDERS' CUP TURF (GRADE 1) (3YO+) (HILLSIDE COURSE) (TURF) 1m 4f (T)
11:40 3-Y-O+

£1,732,283 (£535,433; £283,464; £157,480; £94,488; £31,496)

RPR

1 **Bricks And Mortar (USA)**[83] 6001 5-9-0 0 .... IradOrtizJr 9 114
(Chad C Brown, U.S.A) *t.k.h: in tch in midfield: rdn 1 1/2f out: drvn and styd on strly fnl f: led 75yds out: rdn out* 11/8[1]

2 hd **United (USA)**[35] 4-9-0 0 ....(b) FlavienPrat 3 114
(Richard E Mandella, U.S.A) *trckd ldrs: rdn ins 2f out: hung rt ent st: drvn to ld ins fnl f: hdd 75yds out: kpt on* 50/1

3 1 1/4 **Anthony Van Dyck (IRE)**[49] 7219 3-8-10 0 .... RyanMoore 5 114
(A P O'Brien, Ire) *in tch in midfield: rdn 2f out: hdwy on inner on turn into st: chsng ldrs whn nt clr run and stmbld over 1f out: kpt on wl fnl f* 3/1[2]

4 1/2 **Zulu Alpha (USA)**[28] 7916 6-9-0 0 .... JoseLOrtiz 1 111+
(Michael J Maker, U.S.A) *hld up in rr: v wd into st: rdn 1 1/2f out: styd on wl fnl f: nrst fin* 22/1

5 1/2 **Alounak (FR)**[21] 8155 4-9-0 0 .... ClementLecoeuvre 7 110
(Waldemar Hickst, Germany) *towards rr of midfield: rdn 2f out: drvn and hdwy on inner appr fnl f: one pce ins fnl f* 28/1

6 hd **Mount Everest (IRE)**[14] 8358 3-8-10 0 .... WayneLordan 4 112+
(A P O'Brien, Ire) *s.s: towards rr: drvn and styd on fnl f: nrst fin* 18/1

7 nse **Channel Cat (USA)**[28] 7916 4-9-0 0 .... LuisSaez 6 110+
(Todd Pletcher, U.S.A) *towards rr: hung rt on turn over 3f out: rdn over 2f out: pushed wd ent st: drvn and kpt on fr over 1f out* 50/1

8 nk **Arklow (USA)**[28] 7916 5-9-0 0 .... JavierCastellano 11 109
(Brad H Cox, U.S.A) *midfield on outside: rdn over 2f out: pushed wd ent st: kpt on same pce* 14/1

9 1 3/4 **Acclimate (USA)**[35] 5-9-0 0 ....(b) MartinGarcia 2 106
(Philip D'Amato, U.S.A) *led: rdn ins 2f out: hdd 1 1/2f out: wknd fnl 150yds* 66/1

10 nk **Bandua (USA)**[28] 7922 4-9-0 0 .... TylerGaffalione 8 106
(Jack Sisterson, U.S.A) *chsd ldr: w ldr 3f out: rdn ins 2f out: led 1 1/2f out: hdd ins fnl f: sn wknd* 66/1

11 3 3/4 **Old Persian**[49] 7226 4-9-0 0 .... WilliamBuick 10 100
(Charlie Appleby) *midfield: rdn over 2f out: lost pl ins 2f out: sn no imp: wknd ins fnl f* 10/3[3]

12 nk **Channel Maker (CAN)**[28] 7916 5-9-0 0 ....(b) JohnRVelazquez 12 99
(William Mott, U.S.A) *racd keenly: in tch: rdn ins 2f out: lost pl 1 1/2f out: sn btn* 28/1

2m 24.73s (-1.92)
WFA 3 from 4yo+ 5lb 12 Ran SP% 120.3
PARI-MUTUEL (all including 2 unit stake): WIN 4.00; PLACE (1-2) 3.20, 25.60; SHOW (1-2-3) 2.40, 13.00, 4.00; SF 137.20.
Owner Klaravich Stables Inc & William H Lawrence **Bred** George Strawbridge Jr **Trained** USA

FOCUS
This wasn't a true test at the trip. They went a steady gallop and finished in a heap as the race developed into a sprint from the home turn. The fifth and seventh are among those who limit the level of the form.

8769 SANTA ANITA (L-H)
Sunday, November 3

OFFICIAL GOING: Dirt: fast; turf: firm

8777a LONGINES BREEDERS' CUP CLASSIC (GRADE 1) (3YO+) (MAIN TRACK) (DIRT) 1m 2f (D)
12:44 3-Y-O+

£2,598,425 (£803,149; £425,196; £236,220; £141,732; £47,244)

RPR

1 **Vino Rosso (USA)**[36] 7721 4-9-0 0 .... IradOrtizJr 10 128
(Todd Pletcher, U.S.A) *in tch: rdn 3f out: hdwy on outside appr 2f out: chsd ldr whn drvn ins fnl 2f: led ins fnl f: kpt on wl and drew clr fnl 100yds* 4/1[3]

2 4 1/4 **McKinzie (USA)**[35] 7752 4-9-0 0 .... JoelRosario 8 120+
(Bob Baffert, U.S.A) *chsd ldr: checked whn attempting to squeeze through gap on ins after 4f: led 3 1/2f out: rdn ins fnl 2f: hdd ins fnl f: flashed tail and no ex fnl 150yds* 3/1[1]

3 4 1/4 **Higher Power (USA)**[35] 7752 4-9-0 0 ....(b) FlavienPrat 7 111
(John W Sadler, U.S.A) *midfield: rdn over 3f out: kpt on fr 2f out: wnt 3rd over 1f out: no ch w front pair* 10/1

4 2 1/4 **Elate (USA)**[28] 7938 5-8-11 0 .... JoseLOrtiz 6 104
(William Mott, U.S.A) *towards rr: rdn 2f out: styd on fr 1 1/2f out: tk 4th ins fnl f: no threat to ldrs* 8/1

5 4 1/4 **Math Wizard (USA)**[43] 7480 3-8-10 0 .... RicardoSantanaJr 1 98
(Saffie A Joseph Jr, U.S.A) *hld up in rr: rdn and kpt on steadily fr 2f out: n.d* 50/1

6 nk **Seeking The Soul (USA)**[35] 7752 6-9-0 0 .... BrianJosephHernandezJr 2 97
(Dallas Stewart, U.S.A) *towards rr of midfield: rdn over 2f out: kpt on steadily fr 1 1/2f out: n.d* 40/1

7 nse **Code Of Honor (USA)**[36] 7721 3-8-10 0 .... JohnRVelazquez 11 97
(Claude McGaughey III, U.S.A) *towards rr of midfield: rdn and sme hdwy 3f out: wknd 1 1/2f out* 7/2[2]

8 1 1/2 **Yoshida (JPN)**[64] 6753 5-9-0 0 .... MikeESmith 5 94
(William Mott, U.S.A) *hld up towards rr: rdn and no imp fr 2 1/2f out: wd into st* 9/1

9 3 **War Of Will (USA)**[43] 7480 3-8-10 0 ....(b[1]) TylerGaffalione 4 88
(Mark Casse, Canada) *led: hdd 3 1/2f out: rdn 2 1/2f out: wknd 2f out* 22/1

10 2 3/4 **Owendale (USA)**[34] 3-8-10 0 ....(b) JavierCastellano 3 83
(Brad H Cox, U.S.A) *in tch: rdn over 3f out: lost pl appr 2f out: sn struggling* 14/1

P **Mongolian Groom (USA)**[35] 7752 4-9-0 0 ....(b) AbelCedillo 9
(Enebish Ganbat, U.S.A) *trckd ldrs: chsd ldr over 3f out: sn rdn: dropped to 3rd ins fnl 2f: keeping on whn wnt wrong and p.u sharply 1 1/2f out* 14/1

2m 2.8s (2.92)
WFA 3 from 4yo+ 3lb 11 Ran SP% 119.5
PARI-MUTUEL (all including 2 unit stake): WIN 11.20; PLACE (1-2) 5.80, 4.80; SHOW (1-2-3) 4.00, 3.60, 6.00; SF 47.60.
Owner Repole Stable & St Elias Stable **Bred** John D Gunther **Trained** USA

FOCUS
Not a strong Breeders' Cup Classic and they finished strung out, but the winner put up a high-class performance. The splits were 23.09, 24.07, 23.55, 25.64, 26.45 over a demanding surface.

8778 - 8783a (Foreign Racing) - See Raceform Interactive

8363 NAAS (L-H)
Sunday, November 3

OFFICIAL GOING: Heavy

8784a FINALE STKS (LISTED RACE) 1m 3f 180y
3:45 (3:48) 3-Y-O+

£23,918 (£7,702; £3,648; £1,621; £810; £405)

RPR

1 **Warnaq (IRE)**[14] 8368 5-9-0 97 .... RobbieColgan 8 100
(Matthew J Smith, Ire) *mde all: stl gng wl over 2 l clr under 4f out: pushed along over 2f out and sn extended advantage: rdn 1 1/2f out and reduced ld u.p wl ins fnl f: hld on wl* 7/2[2]

2 2 1/4 **Quote**[14] 8368 3-8-10 95..........(t) KillianHennessy 3 100+
(A P O'Brien, Ire) *mid-div: 6th 1/2-way: drvn disputing 4th into st and hdwy: rdn into 2nd 1 1/2f out where hung sltly: kpt on wl u.p ins fnl f to press wnr nr fin: a hld* **12/1**

3 8 1/2 **Solage**[14] 8368 3-8-13 99.......... KevinManning 9 88
(J S Bolger, Ire) *chsd ldrs: 3rd 1/2-way: impr into 2nd over 3f out: sn rdn and no imp on wnr: dropped to 3rd 1 1/2f out: one pce fnl f* **3/1**[1]

4 7 **Perfect Tapatino (FR)**[14] 8370 5-9-5 90.......... DonnachaO'Brien 2 77
(Joseph Patrick O'Brien, Ire) *w.w: 7th 1/2-way: drvn in 7th into st and no imp on ldrs over 2f out where swtchd lft: u.p in 5th under 2f out: wnt mod 4th ins fnl f: kpt on one pce* **13/2**[3]

5 2 **Riven Light (IRE)**[15] 8358 7-9-5 103.......... DeclanMcDonogh 5 74
(W P Mullins, Ire) *mid-div: 5th 1/2-way: drvn disputing 4th into st and no imp on wnr u.p in 4th under 2f out: one pce in mod 5th ins fnl f* **7/2**[2]

6 4 3/4 **Jumellea (IRE)**[2] 8734 3-8-10 94..........(bt) GaryHalpin 4 63
(Joseph Patrick O'Brien, Ire) *w.w towards rr: 9th 1/2-way: drvn in 9th 3f out and no imp u.p 2f out: kpt on one pce in bhd into mod 6th* **8/1**

7 3 1/2 **Invitation (IRE)**[3] 8710 3-8-10 0.......... ColinKeane 10 57
(A P O'Brien, Ire) *sn trckd ldr: 2nd 1/2-way: pushed along in 2nd under 4f out and sn lost pl: rdn bhd ldrs under 3f out and wknd: eased* **25/1**

8 7 1/2 **Lady Stormborn (IRE)**[15] 8359 3-8-10 0.......... AndrewSlattery 1 45
(Andrew Slattery, Ire) *hld up towards rr: last at 1/2-way: pushed along and sme hdwy over 3f out: rdn in 7th and no ex over 2f out: sn wknd* **10/1**

9 7 **Istoria (IRE)**[15] 8358 3-8-10 76..........(b) GaryCarroll 7 34
(Joseph G Murphy, Ire) *cl up early tl sn settled bhd ldrs: short of room and checked on inner in 4th after 2f: 4th 1/2-way: drvn in 5th under 4f out and sn wknd: eased ins fnl f* **66/1**

10 28 **Stivers (ARG)**[50] 7218 6-9-5 100..........(p[1]) OisinOrr 6
(D K Weld, Ire) *towards rr and pushed along briefly early: pushed along in 8th fr 1/2-way and wknd u.p to rr 4f out: eased over 2f out* **25/1**

2m 45.8s
WFA 3 from 5yo+ 5lb **10** Ran SP% **119.9**
CSF £45.38 TOTE £4.70: £1.80, £3.30, £1.40; DF 54.10 Trifecta £219.60.
Owner Kevin John Smith **Bred** J Connolly **Trained** Kilmessan, Co. Meath

FOCUS
The winner has become a last-day specialist at Naas, this was her biggest win to date. The winner has been rated to the better view of her previous form.

8785 - (Foreign Racing) - See Raceform Interactive

2885
CAPANNELLE (R-H)
Sunday, November 3

OFFICIAL GOING: Turf: heavy

8786a PREMIO RIBOT - MEM. LORETO LUCIANI (GROUP 3) (3YO+) (GRANDE COURSE) (TURF) 1m
12:45 3-Y-O+ **£32,882** (£14,468; £7,891; £3,945)

RPR

1 **Out Of Time (ITY)**[14] 8392 3-9-4 0.......... DarioVargiu 5 109
(A Botti, Italy) *w.w in rr: angled out and began to cl 2 1/2f out: str run to ld ent fnl f: drvn clr: readily* **1/2**[1]

2 2 1/2 **Villabate (IRE)**[224] 4-9-4 0..........(t) ClaudioColombi 4 101
(Nicolo Simondi, Italy) *led: sn 3 l clr: drvn 1 1/2f out: hdd ent fnl f: kpt on same pce: nvr trbld to hold on for 2nd* **184/10**

3 5 **Fulminix (ITY)**[126] 4432 4-9-4 0..........(t) AntonioFresu 6 90
(Endo Botti, Italy) *racd keenly: hld up in fnl trio: rdn and no imp over 2f out: kpt on to go 3rd fnl f: n.d* **105/10**

4 1 1/4 **Kronprinz (GER)**[35] 7750 4-9-4 0.......... PierantonioConvertino 2 87
(Pavel Tuma, Czech Republic) *chsd ldr on outer: kpt on at one pce u.p fnl 1 1/2f* **11/5**[2]

5 1/2 **Mission Boy**[14] 8392 3-9-2 0.......... CarloFiocchi 1 85
(A Botti, Italy) *chsd ldr on inner: rdn in pursuit of clr ldr over 2f out: dropped away fnl f* **84/10**[3]

6 17 **Pensiero D'Amore (IRE)**[147] 3-9-2 0.......... FabioBranca 3 46
(A Botti, Italy) *awkward leaving stalls: w.w in fnl trio: rdn and wknd 1 1/2f out: wl btn whn eased late on* **121/10**

1m 38.0s (-1.80)
WFA 3 from 4yo 2lb **6** Ran SP% **130.0**
PARI-MUTUEL (all including 1 euro stake): WIN 1.50; PLACE 1.13, 2.57; DF 10.97.
Owner Scuderia Del Giglio Sardo Srl **Bred** Rz Del Velino Srl **Trained** Italy

8787a PREMIO CARLO & FRANCESCO ALOISI (GROUP 3) (2YO+) (DRITTA COURSE) (TURF) 6f
1:20 2-Y-O+ **£29,279** (£12,882; £7,027; £3,513)

RPR

1 **Nikisophia (IRE)**[30] 3-9-1 0..........(t) GiuseppeErcegovic 7 95
(Maurizio Grassi, Italy) *a.p: drvn to chal 2f out: led 1f out: r.o: drvn out: readily* **109/20**

2 1 **From Me To Me (IRE)**[113] 5-9-4 0..........(t) AntonioFresu 10 95
(Endo Botti, Italy) *midfield: rdn to chse ldng pair 1 1/2f out: styd on fnl f: nvr on terms w wnr* **129/10**

3 1 1/2 **Django (ITY)**[140] 4-9-4 0..........(tp) SalvatoreBasile 9 90
(Riccardo Bandini, Italy) *chsd ldr on outer: drvn to chal 2f out: led 1 1/2f out: hdd 1f out: no ex fnl 100yds* **29/1**

4 2 1/2 **Trust You**[140] 7-9-4 0..........(p) CarloFiocchi 1 82
(Endo Botti, Italy) *towards rr on inner: hdwy 1 1/2f out: kpt on u.p fnl f: nvr able to chal* **758/100**

5 1/2 **The Conqueror (IRE)**[14] 4-9-6 0.......... FabioBranca 4 82
(A Botti, Italy) *midfield on inner: clsd to press ldr 1/2-way: led 2 1/2f out: outpcd and hdd 1 1/2f out: kpt on at one pce* **29/10**[1]

6 1/2 **Ratnaraj (ITY)**[364] 8868 4-9-4 0..........(tp) GianpasqualeFois 3 79
(Ottavio Di Paolo, Italy) *towards rr: sme prog 1/2-way: kpt on u.p fnl f: n.d* **17/4**[3]

7 2 1/4 **Buonasera (IRE)**[14] 4-9-3 0..........(t) MarioSanna 8 71
(P L Giannotti, Italy) *led: hdd 2 1/2f out: grad lft bhd ins fnl 1 1/2f* **39/10**[2]

8 1 **Pensierieparole**[14] 7-9-4 0..........(t) SilvanoMulas 2 68
(Grizzetti Galoppo SRL, Italy) *slow to stride and drvn: in rr: detached and rdn 1/2-way: sme late prog: nvr in contention* **639/100**

9 13 **Toda Joya (IRE)**[140] 5-9-1 0.......... AndreaMezzatesta 8 24
(Giuseppe Renzi, Italy) *racd keenly: hld up in midfield: rdn and wknd over 1 1/2f out* **186/10**

10 3 **Zargun (GER)**[14] 8392 4-9-4 0..........(p) DarioVargiu 6 17
(Henk Grewe, Germany) *chsd ldr: nt qckn whn asked sn after 1/2-way: sn wknd* **11/2**

1m 9.7s (-0.60) **10** Ran SP% **136.8**
PARI-MUTUEL (all including 1 euro stake): WIN 6.45; PLACE 2.57, 3.94, 9.04; DF 60.86.
Owner Fabio Belluccini **Bred** Apache Dream Syndicate **Trained** Italy

8788a PREMIO ROMA (GROUP 2) (3YO+) (GRANDE COURSE) (TURF) 1m 2f
1:55 3-Y-O+ **£105,405** (£46,378; £25,297; £12,648)

RPR

1 **Skalleti (FR)**[29] 7923 4-9-5 0.......... Pierre-CharlesBoudot 4 111
(J Reynier, France) *w.w one fr last: shkn up and tk clsr order 2f out: rdn and styd on strly to ld fnl 150yds: sn asserted: comf* **4/11**[1]

2 2 **Presley (ITY)**[42] 7502 6-9-3 0.......... CristianDemuro 2 105
(A Botti, Italy) *chsd ldr: led after 1f: kicked 3 l clr 2f out: sn rdn: hdd fnl 150yds: no match for wnr* **87/10**

3 2 1/4 **Thunderman (ITY)**[35] 3-9-0 0.......... DarioVargiu 1 101
(A Botti, Italy) *led: hdd after 1f: chsd ldr: rdn and nt go on w ldr 2f out: kpt on at one pce* **21/4**[3]

4 3 **Time To Choose**[42] 7502 6-9-3 0.......... FabioBranca 3 94
(A Botti, Italy) *chsd two clr ldrs: rdn and no imp 2f out: grad dropped away* **19/2**

5 dist **Frozen Juke (IRE)**[168] 2887 3-9-0 0.......... SamueleDiana 5
(Fabio Marchi, Italy) *hld up in rr: rdn and lost tch fr 2 1/2f out: t.o* **71/20**[2]

2m 7.5s (4.20)
WFA 3 from 4yo+ 3lb **5** Ran SP% **131.1**
PARI-MUTUEL (all including 1 euro stake): WIN 1.38; PLACE 1.14, 2.32; DF 5.63.
Owner Jean-Claude Seroul **Bred** Guy Pariente Holding **Trained** France

8789a PREMIO BERARDELLI (GROUP 3) (2YO) (GRANDE COURSE) (TURF) 1m 1f
2:30 2-Y-O **£31,531** (£13,873; £7,567; £3,783)

RPR

1 **Aurelius In Love (IRE)**[14] 2-8-11 0..........(t) ClaudioColombi 9 100
(Luciano Vitabile, Italy) *in rr: shkn up and hdwy 2f out: drvn and styd on strly fnl f: led cl home* **17/5**[3]

2 1/2 **Luigi Pirandello (USA)**[36] 2-8-11 0..........(t) CarloFiocchi 4 99
(Agostino Affe', Italy) *midfield on outer: drvn to chse ldrs over 2f out: sn chalng u.p: led over 1f out: styd on gamely u.p: hdd cl home* **79/10**

3 1/2 **Norohna (FR)**[14] 2-8-8 0.......... SergioUrru 1 95
(Nicolo Simondi, Italy) *chsd clr ldrs: drvn to ld appr 2f out: styd on u.p: hdd over 1f out: rallied gamely* **57/20**[2]

4 1 **Cool And Dry (ITY)**[21] 2-8-11 0.......... DarioVargiu 8 96
(A Botti, Italy) *chsd clr ldrs on outer: cl 3rd and rdn wl over 2f out: styd on u.p: no ex fnl 100yds* **49/20**[1]

5 1 1/4 **Torquato (ITY)** 2-8-11 0..........(b) CristianDemuro 3 94
(A Botti, Italy) *towards rr: rdn to cl 2f out: styd on u.p fnl f: effrt flattened out fnl 100yds* **17/4**

6 8 **Urus**[14] 8390 2-8-11 0..........(t) SilvanoMulas 5 78
(Grizzetti Galoppo SRL, Italy) *prom: outpcd and rdn over 2f out: wl hld fnl 1 1/2* **33/4**

7 6 **Voices From War (IRE)**[14] 2-8-11 0.......... FabioBranca 11 66
(A Botti, Italy) *towards rr: rdn and no real imp 2f out: sn btn* **163/10**

8 5 **Avengers Endgame (IRE)**[7] 2-8-11 0..........(t) MarioSanna 7 56
(Agostino Affe', Italy) *plld hrd: chsd ldr under restraint: wknd u.p over 2f out* **23/1**

9 1/2 **Turbiondo (ITY)**[21] 2-8-11 0..........(bt) SamueleDiana 6 55
(Fabio Marchi, Italy) *led: drvn 2 1/2f out: hdd appr 2f out: wknd fnl 1 1/2f* **22/1**

10 6 **Spirit Noir (IRE)**[28] 2-8-11 0..........(bt) AntonioFresu 2 43
(Sebastiano Guerrieri, Italy) *midfield on inner: wknd u.p ins fnl 2f* **173/10**

11 1 **Elysees Mumtaza (IRE)**[21] 2-8-8 0..........(t) PierantonioConvertino 10 38
(A Peraino, Italy) *racd in fnl pair: drvn but no imp 2 1/2f out: sn wknd* **38/1**

1m 54.0s (-0.70) **11** Ran SP% **141.1**
PARI-MUTUEL (all including 1 euro stake): WIN 4.40; PLACE 1.65, 2.57, 1.59; DF 63.32.
Owner Aurelio Golino **Bred** Thomas G Lennon **Trained** Italy

8790a PREMIO LYDIA TESIO (GROUP 2) (3YO+ FILLIES & MARES) (GRANDE COURSE) (TURF) 1m 2f
3:10 3-Y-O+ **£126,126** (£55,495; £30,270; £15,135)

RPR

1 **Call Me Love**[22] 8153 3-8-11 0.......... FabioBranca 4 107
(A Botti, Italy) *mde all: hrd rdn whn pressed 1 1/2f out: asserted ent fnl f: styd on strly u.p* **6/5**[1]

2 1 1/2 **Moonoon (FR)**[34] 3-8-11 0..........(t) CristianDemuro 1 104
(C Ferland, France) *w.w in fnl trio: tk clsr order 2f out: styd on fnl f: no match for wnr* **3/1**[2]

3 3/4 **Elisa Again**[22] 8153 3-8-11 0..........(tp) AndreaMezzatesta 10 102
(R Biondi, Italy) *chsd ldr: drvn and virtually on terms w ldr 1 1/2f out: outpcd by ldr 1f out: no ex fnl 100yds* **43/5**

4 4 **Binti Al Nar (GER)**[22] 8153 4-9-1 0.......... CarloFiocchi 3 94
(P Schiergen, Germany) *a cl up: rdn but nt qckn 2f out: outpcd by ldrs fnl f* **35/4**

5 3/4 **Lanana (FR)**[8] 8584 4-9-1 0..........(t) EddyHardouin 5 93
(Robert Collet, France) *racd keenly: hld up in fnl trio: clsd u.p over 2f out: no further imp fnl f* **92/10**

6 1 **Waitingfortheday (IRE)**[49] 7242 4-9-1 0..........(p) ShaneCrosse 9 91
(Joseph Patrick O'Brien, Ire) *w.w in midfield on outer: drvn and no imp 2f out: wl hld fnl f* **10/3**[3]

7 2 **Zillione Sun (FR)**[29] 4-9-1 0..........(t) Pierre-CharlesBoudot 2 87
(Mme P Butel & J-L Beaunez, France) *plld hrd: hld up in midfield: rdn and sn btn ins fnl 2f* **159/10**

8 2 1/4 **Romance d'Amour (IRE)**[35] 4-9-1 0..........(t) GianpasqualeFois 6 82
(Ottavio Di Paolo, Italy) *racd keenly: hld up in fnl trio: outpcd in rr 2f out: bhd fnl 1 1/2f* **37/1**

9 8 **Sword Peinture (GER)**[42] 7504 4-9-1 0.......... DarioVargiu 7 66
(Andreas Suborics, Germany) *prom: rdn and wknd fr 2f out* **107/10**

2m 6.0s (2.70)
WFA 3 from 4yo 3lb **9** Ran SP% **141.1**
PARI-MUTUEL (all including 1 euro stake): WIN 2.20; PLACE 1.27, 1.55, 1.57; DF 8.43.
Owner Scuderia Effevi SRL **Bred** Grundy Bloodstock Ltd **Trained** Italy

8791a **PREMIO REQUINTO DIVINO AMORE (LISTED RACE) (2YO) (DRITTA COURSE) (TURF)** **5f**
3:45 2-Y-O **£17,567** (£7,729; £4,216; £2,108)

RPR
1 **Lorelei Rock (IRE)**^{12} 8446 2-8-6 0..........................(b) CristianDemuro 3 94
(G Botti, France) **5/2**^{2}
2 *nse* **Das Rote (IRE)**^{21} 2-8-6 0.......................... SalvatoreSulas 9 94
(Mario Giorgi, Italy) **116/10**
3 *1/2* **Lovely Smile (ITY)**^{36} 2-8-9 0.......................... DarioVargiu 5 95
(A Botti, Italy) **102/10**
4 *1/2* **Agiato** 2-8-9 0..........................(t) SilvanoMulas 2 93
(Grizzetti Galoppo SRL, Italy) **21/10**^{1}
5 *nk* **Miss Rouge (IRE)** 2-8-6 0..........................(t) ChristianDiNapoli 1 89
(Sebastiano Guerrieri, Italy) **58/10**
6 *hd* **Sicilian Focus (IRE)**^{36} 2-8-9 0..........................(t) FabioBranca 4 91
(Sebastiano Guerrieri, Italy) **58/10**
7 *4 1/2* **Penelope Queen**^{21} 2-8-6 0..........................(t) SamueleDiana 10 72
(Agostino Affe', Italy) **8/1**
8 *1 1/4* **Avalon Ena (ITY)**^{21} 2-8-6 0.......................... AntonioFresu 7 68
(Endo Botti, Italy) **238/10**
9 *4* **Lady Lavender (ITY)** 2-8-6 0..........................(t) GiuseppeErcegovic 8 53
(Sebastiano Guerrieri, Italy) **58/10**
10 *7* **Hot Affair**^{68} 6577 2-8-6 0.......................... CarloFiocchi 6 28
(Tom Dascombe) *midfield on outer: lost pl after 1/2-way: wl bhd ins fnl 1 1/2f* **282/100**^{3}

58.2s (-0.90) **10** Ran SP% **163.1**
PARI-MUTUEL (all including 1 euro stake): WIN 2.91; PLACE 1.57, 2.00, 1.62; DF 13.95.
Owner Thomas Whitehead **Bred** P F Kelly & Peter Kelly **Trained** France

5483 MUNICH (L-H)
Sunday, November 3

OFFICIAL GOING: Turf: soft

8792a **GROSSER PREIS VON BAYERN (GROUP 1) (3YO+) (TURF)** **1m 4f**
2:15 3-Y-O+ **£90,090** (£27,027; £13,513; £6,306; £2,702)

RPR
1 **Nancho (GER)**^{14} 8372 4-9-6 0.......................... BayarsaikhanGanbat 9 110
(Gabor Maronka, Hungary) *chsd ldr: drvn to ld appr 2f out: hrd rdn and styd on strly ent fnl 1 1/2f: hld on gamely to rapidly diminishing ld fnl 100yds* **19/5**^{3}
2 *nk* **Manuela De Vega (IRE)**^{50} 7180 3-8-13 0.......................... RobHornby 10 108
(Ralph Beckett) *a cl up: pushed along wl over 2f out: styd on to chse clr ldr appr fnl f: r.o u.p to reel in ldr: nvr quite getting there* **162/10**
3 *nk* **Ashrun (FR)**^{29} 7927 3-9-2 0.......................... TheoBachelot 7 111
(A Wohler, Germany) *a.p on outer: outpcd and drvn over 2f out: styd on wl fnl f: nvr quite on terms* **17/1**
4 *hd* **Antonia De Vega (IRE)**^{15} 8333 3-8-13 0.......................... HarryBentley 6 108
(Ralph Beckett) *w.w towards rr: drvn over 2f out: hdwy u.p towards centre of trck 1 1/2f out: styd on wl fnl f: nrest at fin* **37/10**^{2}
5 *1 1/4* **Donjah (GER)**^{14} 8391 3-8-13 0.......................... AntoineHamelin 1 106
(Henk Grewe, Germany) *w.w in fnl pair: hdwy on ins rail fr 3f out: styd on u.p but nt pce to chal* **5/2**^{1}
6 *1 3/4* **Accon (GER)**^{49} 7249 3-9-2 0.......................... JiriPalik 4 106
(Markus Klug, Germany) *midfield: outpcd and rdn 2f out: styd on u.p to cl 1 1/2f out: effrt petered out fnl 100yds* **35/1**
7 *2* **Wai Key Star (GER)**^{35} 7753 6-9-6 0..........................(b) GeraldMosse 8 101
(Frau S Steinberg, Germany) *racd keenly: hld up in fnl pair: prog u.p 2f out: no further imp fnl f* **144/10**
8 *nk* **Amorella (IRE)**^{42} 7500 4-9-3 0.......................... MartinSeidl 2 97
(Markus Klug, Germany) *towards rr of midfield on inner: nt qckn whn rdn over 2f out: sn btn* **87/10**
9 *1* **Ladykiller (GER)**^{21} 8171 3-9-2 0.......................... BauyrzhanMurzabayev 11 101
(A Wohler, Germany) *sn led: drvn and hdd appr 2f out: grad dropped away fnl 1 1/2f* **81/10**
10 *nk* **Nikkei (GER)**^{35} 7753 4-9-6 0.......................... LukasDelozier 3 98
(P Schiergen, Germany) *prom on inner: drvn to chse ldr 1 1/2f out: wknd fnl f* **38/1**
11 *7* **Guardian Fay (IRE)**^{18} 3-8-13 0.......................... FilipMinarik 5 86
(Jean-Pierre Carvalho, Germany) *towards rr of midfield on outer: no hdwy u.p wl over 2 1/2f out: wknd ins fnl 1 1/2f* **27/1**

2m 41.9s
WFA 3 from 4yo+ 5lb **11** Ran SP% **118.8**
PARI-MUTUEL (all including 1 euro stake): WIN 4.80 PLACE: 3.40, 5.10, 5.40; SF: 23.20.
Owner Intergaj **Bred** H Johanpeter **Trained** Hungary
FOCUS
The first four have been rated to form.

BENDIGO
Wednesday, October 30

OFFICIAL GOING: Turf: good

8803a **JAYCO BENDIGO CUP (GROUP 3 H'CAP) (3YO+) (TURF)** **1m 4f**
5:00 3-Y-O+
£132,596 (£39,779; £19,889; £9,944; £5,524; £4,419)

RPR
1 **Top Of The Range (NZ)**^{14} 6-8-7 **0**..........................(b) WilliamPike 11 96
(Michael Moroney, Australia) **7/1**^{3}
2 *hd* **Brimham Rocks**^{11} 8361 5-8-13 **0**..........................(t) MichaelWalker 8 102
(Chris Waller, Australia) **5/1**^{2}
3 *1* **Hang Man (IRE)**^{18} 8134 5-8-7 **0**.......................... JamesWinks 7 94
(Michael Moroney, Australia) **12/1**
4 *1* **Captain Cook**^{17} 6-8-11 **0**..........................(t) LindaMeech 10 97
(Chris Waller, Australia) **8/1**
5 *shd* **Bondeiger (AUS)**^{13} 8-8-7 **0**.......................... DwayneDunn 2 93
(Ciaron Maher & David Eustace, Australia) **30/1**
6 *shd* **Rupture (AUS)**^{18} 6-8-7 **0**..........................(b) DeanHolland 6 92
(Paul Preusker, Australia) **8/1**
7 *1/2* **Sully (NZ)**^{18} 8134 5-8-8 **0**..........................(bt) BrettPrebble 5 93
(Trent Busuttin & Natalie Young, Australia) **4/1**^{1}
8 *1 1/2* **Super Girl (AUS)**^{7} 5-8-7 **0**.......................... DamienThornton 9 89
(Joshua Julius, Australia) **60/1**
9 *shd* **Sin To Win (NZ)**^{14} 7-8-8 **0** ow1..........................(p) LukeNolen 12 90
(David A & B Hayes & Tom Dabernig, Australia) **20/1**
10 *1/2* **Creedence (AUS)**^{14} 5-8-7 **0**..........................(v) JyeMcNeil 13 88
(David A & B Hayes & Tom Dabernig, Australia) **60/1**
11 *3 1/2* **Angel Of Truth (AUS)**^{11} 8361 4-9-2 **0**.......................... LukeCurrie 3 92
(Gwenda Markwell, Australia) **11/1**
12 *1 1/4* **Single Handed (AUS)**^{13} 5-8-7 **0**.......................... DeclanBates 4 81
(Nick Smart, Australia) **100/1**
13 *4 1/2* **Raheen House (IRE)**^{18} 8134 5-9-2 **0**..........................(p) BrentonAvdulla 14 83
(William Haggas) *settled in fnl pair: pushed along and sme hdwy on outer 4f out: wd turning in and dropped to rr: eased fnl 2f* **7/1**^{3}
14 *1/2* **Volkstok'n'barrell (NZ)**^{17} 8-8-11 **0**.......................... DamienOliver 1 77
(Danny O'Brien, Australia) **12/1**

2m 27.41s **14** Ran SP% **119.9**

Owner Pinecliff Racing, R & C Legh Racing & Gurners Bloo **Bred** Mrs H G & W G Bax **Trained** Australia

MULHEIM (R-H)
Saturday, November 2

OFFICIAL GOING: Turf: soft

8804a **RP GRUPPE 76TH SILBERNES BAND DER RUHR (LISTED RACE) (3YO+) (TURF)** **2m 4f**
12:00 3-Y-O+ **£12,612** (£5,855; £2,702; £1,351)

RPR
1 **The Tiger (GER)** 6-9-2 0.......................... SibylleVogt 8 97
(Frau Anna Schleusner-Fruhriep, Germany) **32/1**
2 *1 3/4* **Khan (GER)**^{13} 8391 5-9-2 0..........................(p) CarlosHenrique 7 95
(Henk Grewe, Germany) **41/10**^{3}
3 *7* **Nacida (GER)**^{20} 8171 5-9-2 0.......................... MaximPecheur 2 88
(Yasmin Almenrader, Germany) **9/5**^{1}
4 *7* **Ajas (FR)**^{394} 5-9-2 0.......................... AnnaPilroth 5 81
(Tobias Hellgren, Sweden) **214/10**
5 *nk* **Quita**^{34} 3-8-4 0.......................... MartinSeidl 4 82
(Waldemar Hickst, Germany) **31/5**
6 *36* **Altra Vita**^{29} 7866 4-8-13 0..........................(p) LukeMorris 1 42
(Sir Mark Prescott Bt) *in tch: lost pl after 1/2-way: wl bhd fr 2f out: t.o* **7/2**^{2}
7 *42* **Wutzelmann (GER)** 9-9-2 0.......................... MiguelLopez 3 3
(Frau Anna Schleusner-Fruhriep, Germany) **162/10**
8 *nk* **Apoleon (GER)**^{84} 9-9-2 0.......................... MichaelCadeddu 10 3
(Frau Anna Schleusner-Fruhriep, Germany) **177/10**
P **Guardian Witch (IRE)**^{372} 4-8-13 0.......................... FilipMinarik 6
(Jean-Pierre Carvalho, Germany) **96/10**

4m 45.53s
WFA 3 from 4yo+ 9lb **9** Ran SP% **119.5**
PARI-MUTUEL (all including 1 euro stake): WIN 32.70 PLACE: 4.60, 1.90, 1.50; SF: 758.70.
Owner Volker Franz Schleusner **Bred** V F Schleusner **Trained** Germany

7722 ROSEHILL
Saturday, November 2

OFFICIAL GOING: Turf: good

8805a **IRON JACK GOLDEN EAGLE (CONDITIONS) (3-4YO) (TURF)** **7f 110y**
5:15 3-4-Y-O
£2,265,193 (£828,729; £414,364; £207,734; £99,447; £55,248)

RPR
1 **Kolding (NZ)**^{28} 7930 4-9-1 0.......................... GlenBoss 4 114
(Chris Waller, Australia) **5/1**^{2}
2 *1/2* **Sunlight (AUS)**^{14} 8362 4-8-10 0.......................... LukeCurrie 15 108
(Tony McEvoy & Calvin McEvoy, Australia) **25/1**
3 *1 1/4* **Mizzy (AUS)**^{21} 4-8-10 0.......................... JasonCollett 6 105
(Anthony Cummings, Australia) **40/1**
4 *shd* **Behemoth (AUS)**^{21} 4-9-1 0.......................... ToddPannell 8 110
(David Jolly, Australia) **100/1**
5 *hd* **Arcadia Queen (AUS)**^{14} 8362 4-8-10 0..........................(t) JamesMcDonald 5 104
(Chris Waller, Australia) **23/10**^{1}
6 *1 3/4* **Beat Le Bon (FR)**^{70} 6443 3-8-13 0.......................... PatDobbs 14 105
(Richard Hannon) *in fnl pair: drvn along on outer 2f out: rdn along and hdwy fnl f: nvr on terms w ldrs* **50/1**
7 *nk* **Military Zone (AUS)**^{21} 4-9-1 0..........................(t) AndrewAdkins 12 104
(Peter & Paul Snowden, Australia) **100/1**
8 *shd* **Jonker (AUS)**^{14} 4-9-1 0.......................... RobbieDolan 2 104
(David Atkins, Australia) **200/1**
9 *shd* **Fasika (AUS)**^{21} 4-8-10 0.......................... RachelKing 11 99
(Joseph Pride, Australia) **13/1**
10 *1 1/2* **Classique Legend (AUS)**^{14} 8362 4-9-1 0.......................... KerrinMcEvoy 1 100
(Les Bridge, Australia) **5/1**^{2}
11 *hd* **Brutal (NZ)**^{14} 4-9-1 0.......................... TommyBerry 16 99
(Michael, Wayne & John Hawkes, Australia) **15/2**
12 *hd* **The Inevitable (AUS)**^{21} 4-9-1 0..........................(b) NashRawiller 3 99
(Scott Brunton, Australia) **11/2**^{3}
13 *3/4* **I Am Superman (IRE)**^{79} 6137 3-8-13 0.......................... LeighRoche 13 97
(M D O'Callaghan, Ire) *in rr of midfield: hdwy to join ldrs 3f out: effrt 2f out: rdn and wknd over 1f out: dropped away fnl f* **100/1**
14 *2 1/4* **Never No More (IRE)**^{49} 7194 3-8-13 0.......................... Pierre-CharlesBoudot 7 91
(A P O'Brien, Ire) *midfield: drvn along under 3f out: kpt on same pce: wknd fnl f* **40/1**
15 *3* **Fun Fact (AUS)**^{147} 4-9-1 0..........................(b) BrandonLerena 10 84
(Bjorn Baker, Australia) **300/1**

16 35 **Gem Song (AUS)**[28] 7930 4-9-1 0 BrentonAvdulla 9
(Kris Lees, Australia) 60/1

1m 28.28s 16 Ran SP% 114.1
WFA 3 from 4yo 1lb

Owner N Morgan **Bred** W Pegg **Trained** Australia

8697 KEMPTON (A.W) (R-H)

Monday, November 4

OFFICIAL GOING: Polytrack: standard to slow
Wind: light, behind Weather: fine

8806 MATCHBOOK BEST VALUE EXCHANGE H'CAP (DIV I) 1m (P)
1:30 (1:30) (Class 5) (0-70,72) 3-Y-O+
£3,752 (£1,116; £557; £300; £300; £300) **Stalls** Low

Form RPR
4460 **1** **Earth And Sky (USA)**[10] 8515 3-9-2 67 HarryBentley 4 76
(George Scott) *chsd ldrs early: sn stdd bk and hld up in tch in midfield: effrt ent fnl 2f: edgd out lft and hdwy u.p over 1f out: styd on wl to ld wl ins fnl f: sn in command* 20/1
6210 **2** 1 3/4 **Orange Suit (IRE)**[33] 7829 4-9-6 69 (b) TomMarquand 6 74
(Ed de Giles) *sn trcking ldrs and t.k.h: effrt to chal and edgd lft 2f out: rdn to ld over 1f out: sn drvn: hdd and nt match pce of wnr wl ins fnl f* 9/2[1]
1040 **3** 3/4 **Run After Genesis (IRE)**[51] 7189 3-9-0 65 RossaRyan 2 68
(Brett Johnson) *hld up in tch in midfield: swtchd rt and hdwy ent fnl 2f: nt clr run: impeded and swtchd rt 2f out: drvn and hdwy to press ldr ent fnl f: styd on same pce ins fnl f (jockey said gelding was denied a clear run)* 10/1
5540 **4** 3/4 **Hackle Setter (USA)**[41] 7542 3-9-2 67 JasonWatson 1 69
(Sylvester Kirk) *in tch in midfield: clsd to chse ldrs and nt clr run 2f out: drvn over 1f out: kpt on same pce ins fnl f* 9/2[1]
5000 **5** 1 1/2 **Ghazan (IRE)**[33] 7812 4-8-9 61 (p) GabrieleMalune(3) 3 59
(Ivan Furtado) *hld up in tch in last trio: effrt and hdwy on inner 2f out: chsd ldrs over 1f out: no imp and one pce ins fnl f* 15/2[2]
0-66 **6** 3/4 **Wingreen (IRE)**[9] 8552 3-9-5 70 GeraldMosse 8 66
(Martin Smith) *hld up in tch towards rr: effrt on outer ent fnl 2f: styd on ins fnl f: nvr trbld ldrs* 25/1
6660 **7** 1 **Kyllachy Dragon (IRE)**[20] 8220 4-9-9 72 (h) RobHornby 7 66
(Mark Rimell) *hld up in tch in last trio: effrt ent fnl 2f: hdwy over 1f out: no imp and kpt on same pce ins fnl f* 25/1
4463 **8** 1/2 **Sheila's Showcase**[23] 8122 3-9-7 72 CharlesBishop 12 65
(Denis Coakley) *chsd ldrs: rdn ent fnl 2f: drvn and unable qck over 1f out: wknd ins fnl f* 8/1[3]
5 **9** 1 3/4 **Dormio**[19] 8242 3-9-2 67 DavidEgan 5 56
(Stuart Kittow) *led: rdn ent fnl 2f: hdd over 1f out: sn outpcd and wknd ins fnl f* 10/1
2140 **10** 1 **Pempie (IRE)**[121] 4671 3-9-6 71 (w) DavidProbert 10 58
(Andrew Balding) *dwlt and pushed along early: in tch in rr: effrt over 2f out: edgd rt u.p and no imp over 1f out: nvr involved (jockey said filly was never travelling)* 8/1[3]
0512 **11** 2 1/4 **Kyllachys Tale (IRE)**[27] 7982 5-9-2 65 JackMitchell 9 46
(Roger Teal) *in tch in midfield: lost pl u.p and bhd over 1f out: wknd ins fnl f* 8/1[3]
610 **12** 1/2 **Baashiq (IRE)**[32] 7839 5-9-7 70 (p) AdamKirby 11 50
(Peter Hiatt) *chsd ldr tl ent fnl 2f: sn struggling and lost pl over 1f out: wknd ins fnl f* 8/1[3]

1m 38.78s (-1.02) **Going Correction** -0.025s/f (Stan) 12 Ran SP% 123.2
WFA 3 from 4yo+ 2lb
Speed ratings (Par 103): **104,102,101,100,99 98,97,97,95,94 92,91**
CSF £109.74 CT £981.12 TOTE £28.00: £7.50, £1.80, £4.10; EX 146.90 Trifecta £2343.00.
Owner Flaxman Stables Ireland Ltd **Bred** Flaxman Holdings Ltd **Trained** Newmarket, Suffolk

FOCUS
The weaker of the two divisions and it threw up a surprise result. The second has been rated to his recent form, and the third to his course form.

8807 MATCHBOOK BEST VALUE EXCHANGE H'CAP (DIV II) 1m (P)
2:00 (2:00) (Class 5) (0-70,72) 3-Y-O+
£3,752 (£1,116; £557; £300; £300; £300) **Stalls** Low

Form RPR
2225 **1** **Delicate Kiss**[32] 7839 5-9-6 72 (b) AledBeech(5) 4 79
(John Bridger) *s.i.s: sn rcvrd and hld up in midfield: effrt and edgd rt 2f out: hdwy over 1f out: wnt between rivals: edgd lft and led wl ins fnl f: r.o wl* 8/1
4461 **2** 1 1/2 **River Dawn**[118] 4754 3-9-4 67 RossaRyan 6 70
(Paul Cole) *chsd ldrs tl chsd clr ldr 4f out: effrt over 2f out: edgd lft wl over 1f out: clsd u.p and ev ch ins fnl f: nudged lft and nt match pce of wnr wl ins fnl f* 5/1[2]
2320 **3** shd **Quarry Beach**[26] 8030 3-9-8 71 (p[1]) DavidProbert 3 74
(Henry Candy) *taken down early: hld up in midfield: clsd u.p over 1f out: chsng ldrs and swtchd lft ins fnl f: kpt on to snatch 3rd last strides* 6/1[3]
0211 **4** nk **Colonel Slade (IRE)**[16] 8345 3-8-13 67 (tp) DannyRedmond(5) 7 69+
(Phillip Makin) *led: wnt clr over 5f out: rdn ent fnl 2f: reduced ld over 1f out: hdd wl ins fnl f: no ex and lost 2 pls cl home* 7/2[1]
2410 **5** 1 **Perfecimperfection (IRE)**[32] 7835 3-9-1 71 StefanoCherchi(7) 8 71
(Marco Botti) *hld up in midfield: hdwy u.p over 1f out: kpt on ins fnl f: nvr getting on terms w ldrs* 13/2
2231 **6** 2 **Gregorian Girl**[40] 7573 3-9-5 68 MartinDwyer 11 63
(Dean Ivory) *midfield: effrt to chse ldrs but ldr stl clr 2f out: shifted rt wl over 1f out: no imp and one pce fnl f* 7/1
2050 **7** 2 1/2 **Mr Mac**[41] 7554 5-9-7 68 (h) CharlesBishop 5 58
(Peter Hedger) *stdd s: t.k.h: hld up in rr: effrt over 2f out: kpt on ins fnl f: nvr trbld ldrs* 33/1
1340 **8** 1 **Cuttin' Edge (IRE)**[14] 8413 5-9-2 63 NicolaCurrie 2 50
(William Muir) *chsd ldr tl 4f out: rdn ent fnl 2f: unable qck and no imp over 1f out: wknd ins fnl f* 9/1
660 **9** shd **Altar Boy**[4] 8711 3-8-9 65 ShariqMohd(7) 9 52
(Sylvester Kirk) *dwlt: hld up in rr: effrt on inner over 2f out: no imp over 1f out: nvr involved* 20/1
2-00 **10** 7 **Winter Gleam (IRE)**[171] 2798 3-9-4 67 JasonWatson 1 38
(William Knight) *mounted in the chute: midfield: unable qck and press and short of room wl over 1f out: sn wknd* 33/1
060 **11** 1 3/4 **Magic Mirror**[131] 4249 6-9-10 71 (p) TomMarquand 10 38
(Mark Rimell) *hld up in rr: effrt over 2f out: no prog: nvr involved* 12/1

1m 38.88s (-0.92) **Going Correction** -0.025s/f (Stan) 11 Ran SP% 118.5
WFA 3 from 5yo+ 2lb
Speed ratings (Par 103): **103,101,101,101,100 98,95,94,94,87 85**
CSF £47.14 CT £259.24 TOTE £8.80: £2.30, £1.40, £2.60; EX 53.10 Trifecta £397.00.
Owner Dbd Partnership **Bred** T Ellison, B Olkowicz And C Speller **Trained** Liphook, Hants

FOCUS
The stronger of the two divisions on paper and likely any of the first four home would have won that division. The gallop was strong, too strong as it turned out, and that enabled the closers to pounce late on. The second and third have been rated close to their marks.

8808 MATCHBOOK/BREEDERS BACKING RACING EBF FILLIES' NOVICE STKS 1m (P)
2:30 (2:35) (Class 5) 3-Y-O+
£5,175 (£1,540; £769; £384) **Stalls** Low

Form RPR
1-3 **1** **Ardiente**[108] 5141 3-9-7 0 StevieDonohoe 7 89+
(Ed Vaughan) *s.i.s: steadily rcvrd and hdwy to ld after 2f: mde rest: shkn up over 1f out: pushed out and r.o wl ins fnl f* 8/13[1]
2 2 **Perfect Winter (IRE)** 3-9-0 0 CallumShepherd 6 76
(Saeed bin Suroor) *led for 2f: chsd wnr tl 4f out: effrt to chse wnr again wl over 1f out: sn drvn: kpt on wl but a hld ins fnl f* 11/4[2]
0- **3** 9 **Al Daiha**[355] 9048 3-9-0 0 (h[1]) TomMarquand 8 56
(Ed Walker) *stdd after s and dropped in bhd: hld up in rr: effrt jst over 2f out: no ch w ldrs but kpt on to go modest 3rd ins fnl f* 10/1
00 **4** 5 **Miss Ditsy (IRE)**[49] 7278 3-9-0 0 RobertHavlin 2 44
(Michael Attwater) *pressed ldrs early: settled bk into midfield: effrt over 2f out: sn outpcd and wl btn over 1f out: plugged on to go modest 4th towards fin* 100/1
03 **5** 3/4 **Levanter (FR)**[35] 7772 3-9-0 0 HarryBentley 5 42
(Harry Dunlop) *chsd ldrs: chsd wnr 4f out tl wl over 1f out: sn outpcd u.p and btn: wknd fnl f* 5/1[3]
6 1/2 **Mahuika** 3-9-0 0 HectorCrouch 1 41
(John Gallagher) *s.i.s: pushed along and rn green in last pair: rdn and outpcd over 2f out: wl btn after: plugged on* 66/1
00- **7** nk **Delcia**[373] 8639 3-9-0 0 CharlesBishop 3 41
(Emma Lavelle) *hld up in tch: rdn over 2f out: sn outpcd and wl btn over 1f out* 40/1
00 **8** 1 **Anything For You**[26] 8013 3-9-0 0 RobHornby 4 38
(Jonathan Portman) *t.k.h: hld up in midfield on outer: effrt over 2f out: sn outpcd and wl btn over 1f out* 25/1

1m 39.6s (-0.20) **Going Correction** -0.025s/f (Stan) 8 Ran SP% 123.1
Speed ratings (Par 100): **100,98,89,84,83 82,82,81**
CSF £2.89 TOTE £1.40: £1.10, £1.10, £2.50; EX 3.00 Trifecta £12.10.
Owner A E Oppenheimer **Bred** Hascombe And Valiant Studs **Trained** Newmarket, Suffolk

FOCUS
Quite an interesting little fillies' novice event in which the front two came a mile clear. The less exposed runner-up looks sure to take some stopping next time. It's been rated around the winner.

8809 MATCHBOOK BETTING PODCAST H'CAP 1m (P)
3:00 (3:04) (Class 4) (0-85,87) 3-Y-O+
£6,469 (£1,925; £962; £481; £300; £300) **Stalls** Low

Form RPR
3-54 **1** **Rangali Island (IRE)**[23] 8122 3-8-11 73 CallumShepherd 3 85+
(David Simcock) *hld up in tch in midfield: effrt ent fnl 2f: rdn and hdwy over 1f out: led ins fnl f: r.o strly and sn clr* 9/2[3]
5460 **2** 2 1/2 **Samphire Coast**[181] 2509 6-9-4 78 (v) LewisEdmunds 8 84
(Derek Shaw) *taken down early: dwlt: hld up in tch in rr: effrt and clsd jst over 2f out: rdn and hdwy over 2f out: kpt on u.p ins fnl f: wnt 2nd last strides: no threat to wnr* 66/1
1233 **3** nk **Dargel (IRE)**[11] 8498 3-9-2 78 AdamKirby 2 83
(Clive Cox) *awkward leaving stalls and nt that wl away: sn pushed along and hdwy into midfield: edgd out lft and effrt to chal 2f out: drvn to ld jst over 1f out: hdd and nt match pce of wnr ins fnl f: lost 2nd last strides* 9/4[1]
3520 **4** 3/4 **Hesslewood (IRE)**[24] 8101 3-9-7 83 JaneElliott 9 87
(James Bethell) *hld up in tch: effrt over 2f out: styd on ins fnl f: no threat to wnr* 14/1
1405 **5** hd **Sezim**[38] 7653 3-9-3 79 RobertHavlin 7 82
(Mohamed Moubarak) *pressed ldr tl rdn to ld 2f out: drvn and hdd ent fnl f: no ex and outpcd ins fnl f* 20/1
4201 **6** 1/2 **Jalaad (IRE)**[38] 7653 4-9-7 86 SeanKirrane(5) 4 88
(Saeed bin Suroor) *chsd ldrs: effrt over 2f out: drvn and unable qck over 1f out: kpt on same pce ins fnl f* 3/1[2]
5400 **7** 1/2 **Al Hayette (USA)**[121] 4667 3-9-11 87 JasonWatson 1 88
(Ismail Mohammed) *trckd ldrs: swtchd lft and effrt wl over 1f out: no imp: keeping on same pce and hld whn swtchd lft again ins fnl f* 33/1
0100 **8** 1 3/4 **Secret Return (IRE)**[14] 8412 6-9-0 79 RhiainIngram(5) 11 76
(Karen George) *stdd after s: t.k.h: hld up in rr: effrt over 2f out: sn swtchd lft: no real imp: nvr involved* 66/1
/3-0 **9** 1/2 **Profound (IRE)**[18] 8294 4-9-3 77 (h[1]) DavidProbert 12 73
(Mark Usher) *stdd after s: hld up in last pair: effrt over 2f out: no hdwy u.p over 1f out: nvr trbld ldrs* 50/1
2106 **10** 1 1/4 **Gallic**[30] 7895 3-9-10 86 TomMarquand 5 79
(Ed Walker) *led tl rdn and hdd 2f out: sn outpcd and wknd ins fnl f* 5/1
1-12 **11** 26 **Diamond Oasis**[196] 1985 3-9-3 79 (h) JackMitchell 6 12
(Hugo Palmer) *chsd ldrs on outer: lost pl over 2f out: bhd and eased fnl f (jockey said filly stopped quickly)* 20/1

1m 37.89s (-1.91) **Going Correction** -0.025s/f (Stan) 11 Ran SP% 114.7
WFA 3 from 4yo+ 2lb
Speed ratings (Par 105): **108,105,105,104,104 103,103,101,101,99 73**
CSF £278.93 CT £843.03 TOTE £4.90: £1.50, £10.60, £1.30; EX 481.20 Trifecta £2420.90.
Owner Jos & Mrs Jane Rodosthenous **Bred** Ballyhampshire Stud Ltd **Trained** Newmarket, Suffolk

The Form Book Flat 2019, Raceform Ltd, Newbury, RG14 5SJ

FOCUS
Quite a competitive contest and they went what looked to the naked eye a reasonable gallop. The winner swept clear in the final furlong and looks one that can hold his own in a higher grade. The level is set around the third, fourth and fifth.

8810 BRITISH EBF MATCHBOOK FUTURE STAYERS MAIDEN STKS (PLUS 10 RACE) (SIRE/DAM-RESTRICTED RACE) 7f (P)
3:30 (3:33) (Class 4) 2-Y-O

£9,960 (£2,982; £1,491; £745; £372; £187) **Stalls** Low

Form RPR
3 **1** **Canagat**[18] 8288 2-9-5 0 DavidEgan 3 80+
(Archie Watson) *t.k.h: led early: trckd ldrs after: swtchd rt and effrt 2f out: rdn to ld over 1f out: kpt on u.p and a doing enough ins fnl f* **13/2**

5 **2** ½ **Code Of Conduct**[45] 7410 2-9-5 0 JasonWatson 4 79+
(Roger Charlton) *hld up in tch in last pair: edgd out lft and effrt over 2f out: hdwy to chse wnr 1f out: edgd rt and grad clsd ins fnl f: nvr quite getting to wnr* **9/4**[2]

02 **3** ½ **Establish**[44] 7458 2-9-5 0 JackMitchell 2 77+
(Roger Varian) *t.k.h: hld up in tch: nt clrest of runs over 2f out: hdwy over 1f out: drvn to chse ldng pair ins fnl f: kpt on but nvr quite getting to wnr (jockey said colt ran too free)* **11/8**[1]

0 **4** 3¾ **Grey Eminence**[10] 8511 2-9-5 0 TomMarquand 6 67
(James Given) *chsd ldrs tl clsd to press ldr 5f out: rdn 2f out: drvn over 1f out: no ex 1f out: outpcd ins fnl f* **66/1**

5 1 **Power Of Time (IRE)** 2-9-5 0 (p[1]) AdamKirby 1 64
(Charlie Appleby) *hld up in tch in last pair: effrt 2f out: no imp and hld whn nt clr run and swtchd lft ins fnl f* **5/1**[3]

50 **6** hd **On The Right Track**[10] 8517 2-9-5 0 (p[1]) DavidProbert 7 64
(Mark Usher) *sn led and crossed to inner: rdn ent fnl 2f: hdd over 1f out: sn no ex and outpcd ins fnl f* **66/1**

0 **7** 4½ **St Just**[12] 8464 2-9-5 0 GeraldMosse 5 52
(William Haggas) *in tch in midfield on outer: lost pl u.p over 1f out: wknd ins fnl f* **20/1**

1m 26.25s (0.25) **Going Correction** -0.025s/f (Stan) **7** Ran SP% **110.6**
Speed ratings (Par 98): **97,96,95,91,90 90,85**
CSF £20.09 TOTE £6.00: £2.60, £1.60; EX 20.30 Trifecta £41.20.
Owner Nurlan Bizakov **Bred** Hesmonds Stud Ltd **Trained** Upper Lambourn, W Berks

FOCUS
A messy race and that did for Establish and Code Of Conduct, the two market leaders. They both still have loads of potential next year. The front three pulled clear in the closing stages.

8811 MATCHBOOK FLOODLIT STKS (LISTED RACE) 1m 3f 219y(P)
4:00 (4:01) (Class 1) 3-Y-O+

£28,355 (£10,750; £5,380; £2,680; £1,345; £675) **Stalls** Low

Form RPR
1-56 **1** **Young Rascal (FR)**[184] 2410 4-9-4 115 TomMarquand 3 117
(William Haggas) *trckd ldrs tl wnt 2nd 4f out: effrt over 2f out: drvn over 1f out: led jst ins fnl f: styd on wl* **4/1**[2]

-562 **2** 3 **Loxley (IRE)**[38] 7662 4-9-4 110 AdamKirby 4 112
(Charlie Appleby) *stdd after s: hld up in last pair: clsd over 3f out: effrt on inner to chse ldng pair 2f out: kpt on same pce ins fnl f: wnt 2nd and no imp fnl 100yds* **5/1**[3]

2431 **3** ½ **Spirit Of Appin**[38] 7658 4-9-2 105 MartinDwyer 2 109
(Brian Meehan) *chsd ldr tl led 5f out: rdn ent fnl 2f: drvn over 1f out: hdd jst ins fnl f: no ex and lost 2nd 100yds out* **7/1**

6 **4** 7 **Last Winter (SAF)**[47] 7340 6-9-4 112 LouisSteward 5 100
(Sir Michael Stoute) *stdd after s: hld up in tch in last pair: effrt over 2f out: no imp: outpcd and wl hld whn hung rt ins fnl f* **25/1**

-413 **5** 3 **Royal Line**[16] 8332 5-9-7 113 RobertHavlin 6 98
(John Gosden) *in tch in midfield: clsd to chse ldrs 4f out: rdn over 2f out: sn outpcd and wl btn over 1f out: eased wl ins fnl f (trainer's rep said horse ran flat)* **5/6**[1]

213 **6** 32 **Mina Vagante**[25] 8064 3-8-8 76 (p[1]) JosephineGordon 1 40
(Hugo Palmer) *led tl 5f out: rdn and lost 2nd 4f out: dropped to rr over 2f out: sn lost tch: t.o* **66/1**

2m 30.64s (-3.86) **Going Correction** -0.025s/f (Stan)
WFA 3 from 4yo+ 5lb **6** Ran SP% **109.1**
Speed ratings (Par 111): **111,109,108,104,102 80**
CSF £22.28 TOTE £4.00: £2.50, £1.40; EX 24.50 Trifecta £64.40.
Owner Bernard Kantor **Bred** Ecurie Peregrine SAS **Trained** Newmarket, Suffolk

FOCUS
A strong Listed race for the time of year and, despite the smallish field, they went a decent gallop. The obvious negative to the form is that the odds-on favourite didn't run his race. The winner has been rated back to something like his best, while the third helps set the level.

8812 MATCHBOOK TIME TO MOVE OVER FILLIES' H'CAP 1m 2f 219y(P)
4:30 (4:31) (Class 4) (0-80,79) 3-Y-O+

£6,469 (£1,925; £962; £481; £300; £300) **Stalls** Low

Form RPR
0641 **1** **Sashenka (GER)**[38] 7650 3-9-3 75 AdamKirby 2 86+
(Sylvester Kirk) *s.i.s: hld up in last pair: clsd: nt clr run and swtchd lft 2f: stl no room: looking to switch and pushed lft over 1f out: str run u.p ins fnl f: led last strides* **7/2**[2]

2231 **2** hd **Maximum Effect**[26] 8013 3-9-7 79 RobertHavlin 9 87+
(John Gosden) *led for 1f: trckd ldrs after tl rdn to ld 2f out: sn kicked 2 l clr: kpt on: hdd last strides* **9/4**[1]

4262 **3** 1½ **Capriolette (IRE)**[19] 8247 4-9-5 73 TomMarquand 4 77
(Ed Walker) *in tch in midfield: effrt ent fnl 2f: drvn to chse ldr over 1f out tl ins fnl f: kpt on same pce* **12/1**

3224 **4** ¾ **Dubious Affair (IRE)**[26] 8013 3-9-2 74 JimmyQuinn 1 78
(Sir Michael Stoute) *hld up in tch towards rr: swtchd rt and hdwy 2f out: chsd ldrs and kpt on same pce ins fnl f* **14/1**

0445 **5** 1 **Voi**[97] 5529 5-9-4 72 (t w) MartinDwyer 3 73
(Conrad Allen) *s.i.s: hld up in rr: clsd on to rr of field 1/2-way: hdwy 2f out: rdn to chse ldrs 1f out: kpt on same pce ins fnl f (jockey said mare was slowly away)* **25/1**

0422 **6** 2 **Miss M (IRE)**[25] 8065 5-8-9 63 DavidEgan 11 61
(William Muir) *chsd ldrs: unable qck u.p and outpcd over 1f out: wknd ins fnl f* **10/1**

0212 **7** 1 **Freckles**[56] 7026 4-9-5 73 (h) HayleyTurner 10 69
(Marcus Tregoning) *chsd ldrs early: restrained and hld up in midfield: effrt ent fnl 2f: impeded and edgd out lft over 1f out: no imp u.p and wl hld fnl f* **12/1**

135 **8** 2¾ **Perfect Number**[18] 8294 3-9-0 75 GabrieleMalune(3) 12 67
(Saeed bin Suroor) *t.k.h: hdwy to ld after 1f: hdd 2f out: sn edgd lft u.p and lost pl: wknd ins fnl f* **8/1**[3]

0004 **9** ½ **Margie's Choice (GER)**[13] 8422 4-9-0 68 (bt) HectorCrouch 5 58
(Michael Madgwick) *hld up in tch on outer: effrt over 2f out: keeping on but nt threatening ldrs whn nudged lft over 1f out: wl hld fnl f* **33/1**

0023 **10** 1¼ **Jamaican Jill**[208] 1688 4-9-4 72 NicolaCurrie 6 60
(William Muir) *midfield: hdwy to chse ldr over 7f out tl 2f out: sn lost pl u.p: wknd fnl f* **12/1**

1225 **11** 6 **Geranium**[26] 8014 4-9-5 73 CharlieBennett 8 51
(Hughie Morrison) *midfield: rdn over 3f out: lost pl and bhd 2f out: wknd* **9/1**

2m 19.66s (-1.34) **Going Correction** -0.025s/f (Stan)
WFA 3 from 4yo+ 4lb **11** Ran SP% **119.7**
Speed ratings (Par 102): **103,102,101,101,100 99,98,96,95,95 90**
CSF £12.00 CT £86.28 TOTE £4.20: £1.40, £1.60, £2.20; EX 14.10 Trifecta £160.40.
Owner N Pickett **Bred** Stiftung Gestut Fahrhof **Trained** Upper Lambourn, Berks
■ Stewards' Enquiry : Gabriele Malune caution: careless riding

FOCUS
Not a bad little fillies' handicap, run at what looked an even enough tempo, and the winner has to be value for more than the winning margin given she was forced to come from much further back than the runner-up. The front two are both 3yos. Ordinary form rated around the third, fifth and sixth.

8813 MATCHBOOK CASINO APPRENTICE H'CAP 1m 2f 219y(P)
5:00 (5:00) (Class 6) (0-65,66) 4-Y-O+

£3,105 (£924; £461; £300; £300; £300) **Stalls** Low

Form RPR
5000 **1** **Bird To Love**[33] 7818 5-8-2 51 oh5 (p) IsobelFrancis(5) 3 57
(Mark Usher) *midfield and pushed along at times: chsd ldrs 4f out: rdn and hdwy to ld 2f out: kpt on wl u.p ins fnl f (trainer said, regarding the improved form shown, the mare benefitted from the drop back in trip on this occasion)* **20/1**

5102 **2** 1½ **Topology**[13] 8422 6-9-0 63 LeviWilliams(5) 8 68
(Joseph Tuite) *stdd and wnt rt leaving stalls: hld up in rr: clsd on inner and nt clr run over 2f out: hdwy over 1f out: pressed wnr ins fnl f: no ex and jst outpcd towards fin* **10/3**[1]

0530 **3** 2¼ **Cheeky Rascal (IRE)**[26] 8033 4-9-7 65 (v) LauraCoughlan 9 64
(Tom Ward) *in tch in midfield: lost pl and dropped to last trio 4f out: swtchd lft 2f out: styd on ins fnl f to go 3rd cl home* **16/1**

0640 **4** ½ **Ahfad**[46] 7375 4-8-2 51 oh6 (b) LouisGaroghan(5) 6 49
(Gary Moore) *dwlt and impeded leaving stalls: hld up in rr: hdwy into midfield 4f out: effrt to chse ldrs 2f out: kpt on same pce ins fnl f* **25/1**

5520 **5** nk **Miss Blondell**[13] 8422 6-9-5 63 StefanoCherchi 5 61
(Marcus Tregoning) *in tch: dropped to rr 4f out: hdwy u.p to chse ldr wl over 1f out: 3rd and outpcd ins fnl f: lost 2 pls cl home* **7/2**[2]

3045 **6** 5 **Highway One (USA)**[13] 8422 5-9-0 58 GavinAshton 10 47
(George Baker) *in tch in midfield on outer: rdn over 2f out: unable qck and btn over 1f out: wknd ins fnl f* **4/1**[3]

0004 **7** 2¾ **The Eagle's Nest (IRE)**[182] 2471 5-9-2 60 (tp w) SeanKirrane 1 44
(Alexandra Dunn) *t.k.h: led tl 7f out: chsd ldr tl led again over 2f out: sn rdn and sn lost pl: wknd fnl f (jockey said gelding hung left-handed throughout)* **14/1**

0045 **8** 2½ **Pilot Wings (IRE)**[16] 8348 4-9-0 58 (tp) HarryRussell 2 37
(David Dennis) *chsd ldrs: rdn over 2f out: sn lost pl: wknd over 1f out* **7/1**

1311 **9** 3¾ **Peace Prevails**[69] 6566 4-9-5 66 (p) AmeliaGlass(3) 4 39
(Jim Boyle) *t.k.h: chsd ldr tl led 7f out tl hdd over 2f out: sn wknd (jockey said filly ran too free)* **11/2**

2m 21.01s (0.01) **Going Correction** -0.025s/f (Stan) **9** Ran SP% **114.3**
Speed ratings (Par 101): **99,97,96,95,95 92,90,88,85**
CSF £85.08 CT £1116.56 TOTE £26.30: £5.20, £1.40, £4.40; EX 125.40 Trifecta £2484.60.
Owner The Mark Usher Racing Club **Bred** Mrs Robert Langton **Trained** Upper Lambourn, Berks

FOCUS
A modest staying event for apprentice riders and they went quite a tempo on the front end. Quite a few of these are unreliable types so this wouldn't be form to get carried away with. The fourth likely limits the form.
T/Plt: £214.20 to a £1 stake. Pool: £57,182.09 - 194.81 winning units T/Qpdt: £15.30 to a £1 stake. Pool: £6,711.01 - 323.42 winning units **Steve Payne**

8712 NEWCASTLE (A.W) (L-H)
Monday, November 4

OFFICIAL GOING: Tapeta: standard
Wind: Breezy, across Weather: Overcast, showers

8814 BETWAY HEED YOUR HUNCH NOVICE STKS 1m 2f 42y (Tp)
4:05 (4:05) (Class 5) 3-Y-O+ **£3,428** (£1,020; £509; £254) **Stalls** High

Form RPR
1 **1** **Tonyx**[52] 7159 3-9-4 0 LiamKeniry 5 67+
(Ed Walker) *plld hrd: led after 1f and maintained stdy gallop: rdn over 1f out: edgd rt and kpt on wl fnl f* **5/6**[1]

2343 **2** 1¼ **Two Bids**[31] 7867 3-9-2 77 BenCurtis 4 62+
(William Haggas) *t.k.h: led at stdy gallop 1f: pressed wnr: effrt and edgd lft over 1f out: kpt on same pce ins fnl f* **11/10**[2]

3 2¾ **Sharp Suited** 4-9-5 0 BenRobinson 6 56+
(Brian Ellison) *s.s: rcvrd to join bk of gp after 1f: hdwy to chse clr ldng pair 2f out: sn rdn and edgd lft: one pce fnl f (jockey said gelding was slowly away)* **22/1**[3]

4 nk **Ska Ridge**[72] 7-9-5 0 (t[1]) CamHardie 2 55
(Rebecca Menzies) *s.i.s: sn chsng ldrs: drvn and outpcd over 2f out: rallied over 1f out: r.o same pce fnl f* **125/1**

4000 **5** 2¾ **Coup De Gold (IRE)**[59] 6940 3-9-2 62 PJMcDonald 3 51
(David Thompson) *plld hrd: prom: effrt and chsd clr ldng pair briefly over 2f out: wknd over 1f out* **33/1**

2m 15.75s (5.35) **Going Correction** +0.125s/f (Slow)
WFA 3 from 4yo+ 3lb **5** Ran SP% **110.3**
Speed ratings (Par 103): **83,82,79,79,77**
CSF £1.99 TOTE £1.70: £1.10, £1.10; EX 2.10 Trifecta £4.30.
Owner Nyx Racing Club **Bred** Springfield Farm Partnership **Trained** Upper Lambourn, Berks

FOCUS
The course had taken 20-25mm of rain since the meeting three evenings previously. Only two were seriously fancied in this opening novice event, and the favourite wasn't too hard pushed to make it two from two. Weak, shaky form.

8815 BOMBARDIER BRITISH HOPPED AMBER BEER NURSERY H'CAP 7f 14y (Tp)
4:40 (4:41) (Class 6) (0-65,67) 2-Y-O

£2,781 (£827; £413; £400; £400; £400) Stalls Centre

Form RPR

306 1 **Castlehill Retreat**[21] 8195 2-9-7 65 PaulMulrennan 3 68
(Ben Haslam) *hld up in centre of gp: hdwy and swtchd to far side of gp over 1f out: led ins fnl f: sn hrd pressed: hld on wl cl home* 13/2[3]

5433 2 nse **Dancing Leopard (IRE)**[24] 8085 2-9-5 63 (v) BenCurtis 2 66
(K R Burke) *in tch on far side of gp: rdn over 2f out: hdwy over 1f out: ev ch ins fnl f: kpt on wl: jst hld* 10/1

2405 3 hd **Bendy Spirit (IRE)**[26] 8022 2-9-9 67 TonyHamilton 11 70
(Richard Fahey) *prom in centre of gp: rdn and sltly outpcd over 1f out: rallied and hung lft ins fnl f: kpt on wl: jst hld* 3/1[1]

056 4 1 **Penmellyn (IRE)**[24] 8084 2-9-4 62 (h) ShaneGray 1 63+
(Phillip Makin) *hld up on far side of gp: hdwy and shkn up over 1f out: keeping on whn n.m.r wl ins fnl f: eased cl home* 14/1

2000 5 1 **Chocoholic**[10] 8527 2-8-5 49 LukeMorris 10 47
(Bryan Smart) *led in centre of gp: rdn and edgd rt over 1f out: hdd ins fnl f: kpt on same pce* 33/1

0000 6 ½ **Fair Warning**[39] 7626 2-8-3 54 LauraPearson(7) 12 50
(Henry Spiller) *dwlt: midfield on nr side of gp: drvn and outpcd over 2f out: rallied over 1f out: kpt on fnl f: no imp: lost front shoe (vet reported gelding lost its left fore shoe)* 18/1

0300 7 ½ **River Of Kings (IRE)**[30] 7904 2-8-10 59 (h) BenSanderson(5) 13 54
(Keith Dalgleish) *hld up on nr side of gp: rdn over 2f out: hdwy over 1f out: no imp ins fnl f* 15/2

065 8 ½ **Rulers Kingdom (IRE)**[13] 8424 2-9-9 67 JoeFanning 7 61
(Mark Johnston) *pressed ldr towards centre of gp: effrt and ch over 1f out: wknd last 100yds* 5/1[2]

0300 9 2½ **Angels Faces (IRE)**[56] 7029 2-9-8 66 SamJames 14 54
(Grant Tuer) *prom on nr side of gp: drvn along over 2f out: wknd over 1f out* 12/1

0050 10 ¾ **Tiltilys Rock (IRE)**[49] 7284 2-8-2 46 ow1 KieranO'Neill 6 32
(Andrew Crook) *towards rr in centre of gp: rdn over 2f out: wknd over 1f out* 100/1

5044 11 nk **Schumli**[10] 8526 2-8-7 51 CamHardie 4 36
(David O'Meara) *dwlt: hld up in centre of gp: drvn along 2f out: sn no imp: btn fnl f* 20/1

046 12 3 **Fansurper (IRE)**[30] 7911 2-9-1 64 PaulaMuir(5) 8 41
(Roger Fell) *midfield in centre of gp: drvn and outpcd over 2f out: btn over 1f out* 18/1

0000 13 3¾ **Gold Venture (IRE)**[35] 7767 2-8-12 56 KevinStott 5 24
(Philip Kirby) *prom on far side: rdn over 2f out: wknd over 1f out* 40/1

1m 27.41s (1.21) **Going Correction** +0.125s/f (Slow) 13 Ran SP% 111.9
Speed ratings (Par 94): **98,97,97,96,95 94,94,93,90,90 89,86,81**
CSF £63.03 CT £239.00 TOTE £6.70: £2.30, £2.40, £1.40; EX 66.50 Trifecta £290.70.
Owner Middleham Park Xx, Mrs C Barclay & J Pak **Bred** Cuadra Africa Sl **Trained** Middleham Moor, N Yorks

■ Stewards' Enquiry : Paul Mulrennan two-day ban: misuse of the whip (Nov 18-19)

FOCUS
A three-way head-bob on the far side of the track determined the outcome of this modest but competitive nursery, after the entire field had initially come down the centre.

8816 LADBROKES HOME OF THE ODDS BOOST NOVICE MEDIAN AUCTION STKS 6f (Tp)
5:15 (5:17) (Class 6) 2-Y-O

£2,781 (£827; £413; £206) Stalls Centre

Form RPR

0323 1 **Asmund (IRE)**[17] 8318 2-9-5 83 (p[1]) BenCurtis 1 71+
(K R Burke) *mde all at ordinary gallop: pushed along over 1f out: kpt on strly fnl f* 4/11[1]

2 1¼ **Tommy De Vito** 2-9-5 0 PJMcDonald 7 67
(Charles Hills) *dwlt: hld up bhd ldng gp: hdwy to press wnr over 1f out: rdn and one pce ins fnl f* 4/1[2]

50 3 1¼ **Grandads Best Girl**[20] 8232 2-9-0 0 BenRobinson 3 58
(Linda Perratt) *trckd ldrs: effrt and rdn 2f out: kpt on same pce ins fnl f* 40/1

000 4 1¾ **Redzone**[80] 6175 2-9-5 58 GrahamLee 8 58
(Bryan Smart) *hld up: pushed along over 2f out: hdwy over 1f out: kpt on fnl f: nt pce to chal* 12/1

00 5 1¾ **Pushover**[38] 7644 2-9-0 0 JasonHart 9 48+
(Steph Hollinshead) *hld up: rdn and outpcd over 2f out: kpt on steadily fnl f: nvr able to chal* 50/1

45 6 ¾ **Lincoln Gamble**[14] 8395 2-9-5 0 TonyHamilton 4 51
(Richard Fahey) *t.k.h: trckd wnr to over 1f out: wknd ins fnl f* 6/1[3]

7 ½ **Anjika (IRE)** 2-8-9 0 PaulaMuir(5) 6 44
(Miss Clare Louise Cannon, Ire) *dwlt: t.k.h: sn cl up: rdn over 2f out: wknd fnl f* 50/1

0 8 12 **Jean Mary**[6] 8631 2-9-0 0 TomEaves 2 8
(Stef Keniry) *t.k.h: hld up: pushed along and struggling over 2f out: sn btn* 66/1

50 9 1¼ **Momentum**[24] 8084 2-9-0 0 CamHardie 5 4
(Antony Brittain) *hld up in tch: rdn over 2f out: wknd over 1f out (jockey said he felt something was amiss with the filly in the closing stages)* 14/1

1m 14.79s (2.29) **Going Correction** +0.125s/f (Slow) 9 Ran SP% 129.8
Speed ratings (Par 94): **89,87,85,83,81 80,79,63,61**
CSF £2.89 TOTE £1.30: £1.02, £1.90, £9.40; EX 3.60 Trifecta £68.60.
Owner Ontoawinner, R Mckeown & E Burke **Bred** Tally-Ho Stud **Trained** Middleham Moor, N Yorks

FOCUS
Job done at last for the hot favourite, obliging at the eighth time of asking. The winner did not need to match the balance of his form to win.

8817 LADBROKES WHERE THE NATION PLAYS NURSERY H'CAP 5f (Tp)
5:45 (5:46) (Class 4) (0-85,85) 2-Y-O

£5,207 (£1,549; £774; £400; £400; £400) Stalls Centre

Form RPR

0120 1 **Reassure**[24] 8095 2-8-12 76 BenCurtis 2 85
(William Haggas) *hld up on far side of gp: rdn and hdwy over 1f out: led ins fnl f: edgd rt: comf* 11/2[2]

230 2 2 **Dazzling Des (IRE)**[24] 8095 2-9-2 80 (p) ShaneGray 7 82
(David O'Meara) *hld up in centre of gp: hdwy and swtchd rt 2f out: chsd wnr ins fnl f: kpt on: nt pce to chal* 25/1

2001 3 1½ **Get Boosting**[17] 8315 2-8-8 77 BenSanderson(5) 9 73
(Keith Dalgleish) *hld up in centre of gp: angled rt and hdwy 2f out: kpt on fnl f: nvr able to chal* 15/2

4411 4 nk **Auckland Lodge (IRE)**[44] 7440 2-9-0 78 AndrewMullen 6 73
(Ben Haslam) *led in centre of gp: rdn 2f out: hdd ins fnl f: kpt on same pce* 14/1

1102 5 ½ **He's A Laddie (IRE)**[46] 7369 2-9-6 84 HollieDoyle 11 78
(Archie Watson) *t.k.h: in tch on nr side of gp: hdwy and ev ch over 1f out to ins fnl f: sn btn* 7/1[3]

3234 6 ½ **Baltic State (IRE)**[58] 6980 2-8-5 74 SeamusCronin(5) 8 66
(Kevin Ryan) *t.k.h: cl up on nr side of gp: rdn over 1f out: wknd ins fnl f* 4/1[1]

6220 7 1½ **Dark Silver (IRE)**[34] 7785 2-8-11 75 LukeMorris 1 61
(Ed Walker) *prom on far side of gp: drvn along over 2f out: wknd over 1f out* 11/1

4134 8 4½ **Strong Power (IRE)**[24] 8097 2-9-5 83 DanielMuscutt 5 53
(George Scott) *prom in centre of gp: drvn along over 2f out: wknd over 1f out* 7/1[3]

1633 9 1 **Proper Beau**[71] 6498 2-9-7 85 (t) GrahamLee 4 52
(Bryan Smart) *t.k.h: in tch towards centre of gp: rdn over 2f out: wknd over 1f out: lost hind shoe (vet reported colt lost its left hind shoe)* 14/1

0201 10 2½ **Holloa**[24] 8085 2-8-3 67 DuranFentiman 10 25
(Tim Easterby) *dwlt: t.k.h: hld up on nr side: rdn over 2f out: wknd over 1f out* 20/1

5215 11 ½ **Balancing Act (IRE)**[44] 7440 2-8-11 75 PJMcDonald 3 31
(Jedd O'Keeffe) *prom on far side of gp tl rdn and wknd over 1f out* 16/1

58.65s (-0.85) **Going Correction** +0.125s/f (Slow) 11 Ran SP% 108.3
Speed ratings (Par 98): **111,107,105,104,104 103,100,93,92,88 87**
CSF £119.56 CT £929.19 TOTE £5.30: £1.90, £5.40, £2.70; EX 112.40 Trifecta £1625.20.
Owner Sheikh Juma Dalmook Al Maktoum **Bred** Rabbah Bloodstock Limited **Trained** Newmarket, Suffolk

FOCUS
A pretty competitive sprint nursery for the evening's feature, and as with the 7f equivalent earlier on the card the winner came from off the pace. The second has been rated to his best.

8818 BOMBARDIER GOLDEN BEER H'CAP 1m 5y (Tp)
6:15 (6:19) (Class 6) (0-65,65) 3-Y-O+

£2,781 (£827; £413; £400; £400; £400) Stalls Centre

Form RPR

6063 1 **Proceeding**[10] 8530 4-8-7 48 LukeMorris 12 55
(Tracy Waggott) *in tch on nr side of gp: rdn and hdwy to ld over 1f out: kpt on wl fnl f* 9/1

6030 2 1¼ **High Fort (IRE)**[10] 8530 4-8-7 48 JamieGormley 6 52
(Karen McLintock) *cl up on nr side of gp: rdn and edgd lft over 2f out: ev ch over 1f out to ins fnl f: kpt on same pce* 14/1

0540 3 nse **Curfewed (IRE)**[3] 8713 3-9-5 62 (p) CamHardie 8 66
(Tracy Waggott) *hld up towards rr in centre of gp: rdn and hdwy 2f out: kpt on ins fnl f* 17/2[3]

3313 4 1½ **Corked (IRE)**[28] 7956 6-9-3 58 PJMcDonald 7 59
(Alistair Whillans) *hld up on far side of gp: rdn over 2f out: gd hdwy fnl f: nrst fin* 5/1[2]

5-F1 5 1½ **Cawthorne Lad**[20] 8234 3-9-0 57 DuranFentiman 5 55
(Tim Easterby) *led in centre of gp: hdd 3f out: sn rdn: outpcd ins fnl f* 9/1

5400 6 shd **Rivas Rob Roy**[56] 7024 4-8-7 48 JoeyHaynes 14 45
(John Gallagher) *hld up on nr side of gp: rdn over 2f out: edgd lft and hdwy over 1f out: no imp fnl f* 28/1

2551 7 1 **Jazz Hands (IRE)**[14] 8405 3-8-13 56 (p) TonyHamilton 4 51
(Richard Fahey) *towards rr towards far side of gp: outpcd over 2f out: rallied ins fnl f: r.o* 10/1

524 8 nk **Siena Mia**[10] 8529 4-9-3 65 NickBarratt-Atkin(7) 3 59
(Philip Kirby) *cl up on far side of gp: led 3f out to over 1f out: rdn and wknd ins fnl f* 50/1

300- 9 1¾ **Boing**[10] 8532 4-9-2 62 (h[1]) PaulaMuir(5) 1 53
(Miss Clare Louise Cannon, Ire) *plld hrd: prom on far side of gp: rdn over 2f out: wknd over 1f out* 50/1

0030 10 shd **Shamaheart (IRE)**[28] 7960 9-8-11 52 (tp) SamJames 9 42
(Geoffrey Harker) *dwlt: hld up in centre of gp: rdn and outpcd over 2f out: sme late hdwy: nvr rchd ldrs* 33/1

610 11 ½ **Top Offer**[40] 7581 10-8-6 47 HollieDoyle 11 36
(Patrick Morris) *hld up on nr side of gp: rdn over 2f out: no further imp fr over 1f out* 16/1

0534 12 ½ **Chinese Spirit (IRE)**[34] 7776 5-9-6 61 DavidNolan 10 49
(Linda Perratt) *hld up on nr side of gp: drvn along over 2f out: nvr able to chal* 18/1

0032 13 2 **Uncle Charlie (IRE)**[17] 8306 5-9-5 60 FrannyNorton 13 44
(Ann Duffield) *t.k.h: hld up in centre of gp: drvn along 2f out: sn wknd (trainer said she felt the gelding may have failed to stay the 1 mile trip on this occasion)* 11/4[1]

5000 14 2 **Clovenstone**[13] 8423 3-8-7 50 (v) AndrewMullen 2 29
(Alistair Whillans) *dwlt: t.k.h and sn cl up in centre of gp: drvn along over 2f out: sn wknd* 50/1

1m 38.74s (0.14) **Going Correction** +0.125s/f (Slow) 14 Ran SP% 113.0
WFA 3 from 4yo+ 2lb
Speed ratings (Par 101): **104,102,102,101,99 99,98,98,96,96 95,95,93,91**
CSF £115.66 CT £1129.81 TOTE £10.70: £3.30, £5.30, £3.10; EX 129.20 Trifecta £760.00.
Owner David Tate **Bred** Ors Bloodstock & Stanley House Stud **Trained** Spennymoor, Co Durham

FOCUS
An ordinary but competitive straight mile event, and a 1-3 for Tracy Waggott. The third has been rated near this year's best.

8819 BOMBARDIER "MARCH TO YOUR OWN DRUM" CLASSIFIED STKS 7f 14y (Tp)
6:45 (6:49) (Class 6) 3-Y-O+

£2,781 (£827; £413; £400; £400; £400) Stalls Centre

Form RPR

5300 1 **With Approval (IRE)**[17] 8301 7-8-12 50 (b) GemmaTutty(3) 5 57
(Karen Tutty) *racd on nr side of gp: mde all: rdn and edgd (rt) to stands' rail over 1f out: drvn and kpt on wl fnl f (trainer's rep said, in regards to the apparent improvement in form, the gelding may have appreciated the drop back in trip and re-application of blinkers on this occasion)* 11/2[2]

2 1 1/2 **Queen Mia (IRE)**[61] 6865 3-9-0 45..............................(t[1]) KevinStott 9 52+
(Declan Carroll) *t.k.h: hld up in centre of gp: hdwy 2f out: chsd wnr ins fnl f: kpt on fin* **18/1**

4050 3 2 1/2 **Lethal Laura**[45] 7404 3-8-9 50.................................. SeamusCronin(5) 7 46
(R Mike Smith) *prom on nr side of gp: rdn and effrt 2f out: kpt on fnl f: nt rch first two* **16/1**

0060 4 1/2 **Hasili Filly**[28] 7962 3-9-0 35.................................. PaulMulrennan 6 45
(Lawrence Mullaney) *prom in centre of gp: effrt and rdn 2f out: kpt on same pce ins fnl f* **33/1**

0004 5 1 1/4 **One Last Hug**[34] 7779 4-8-8 45.................................. CoreyMadden(7) 2 43
(Jim Goldie) *t.k.h: in tch on far side of gp: rdn over 2f out: outpcd over 1f out: n.d after* **7/1[3]**

-060 6 hd **Philyaboots**[70] 4488 3-8-7 46.................................. EllaMcCain(7) 3 41
(Donald McCain) *cl up on far side of gp: edgd (lft) to far rail and rdn wl over 1f out: wknd ins fnl f* **28/1**

0504 7 1/2 **Nutopia**[12] 8472 4-9-1 50.................................. CamHardie 1 41
(Antony Brittain) *fly-jmpd s: hld up on far side of gp: drvn and outpcd over 2f out: rallied ins fnl f: no imp (jockey said filly fly-lept leaving the stalls)* **22/1**

500 8 2 1/4 **Midnight Vixen**[42] 7509 5-9-1 50..............................(v[1]) AndrewMullen 14 35
(Ben Haslam) *t.k.h: hld up on nr side of gp: drvn and outpcd over 2f out: btn over 1f out* **15/2**

0-04 9 nk **Lottie Deno**[12] 8469 3-9-0 44..............................(t) LukeMorris 11 34
(D J Jeffreys) *hld up towards nr side of gp: drvn over 2f out: hung lft and wknd over 1f out* **11/1**

4000 10 6 **Swerved (IRE)**[18] 8293 3-9-0 50.................................. TomEaves 12 19
(Ollie Pears) *stdd towards nr side of gp: t.k.h: hld up: struggling 3f out: sn btn* **33/1**

4000 11 1 **Kroy**[159] 3214 5-9-1 50..............................(p) BenRobinson 10 17
(Ollie Pears) *hld up in centre of gp: drvn along over 2f out: edgd lft and wknd wl over 1f out (jockey said gelding hung left throughout)* **9/2[1]**

0452 12 2 **Searanger (USA)**[18] 8295 6-9-1 50..............................(tp) PJMcDonald 4 12
(Rebecca Menzies) *dwlt: sn prom towards far side of gp: drvn and struggling over 2f out: sn btn (jockey said gelding ran too free)* **9/2[1]**

1m 26.88s (0.68) **Going Correction** +0.125s/f (Slow)
WFA 3 from 4yo+ 1lb 12 Ran SP% **109.2**
Speed ratings (Par 101): **101,99,96,95,94 94,93,91,90,83 82,80**
CSF £86.15 TOTE £5.90: £2.20, £5.10, £4.50; EX 96.50 Trifecta £733.30.
Owner Thoroughbred Homes Ltd **Bred** Yeomanstown Stud **Trained** Osmotherley, N Yorks

FOCUS
A number of the leading fancies disappointed in this classified event. It's been rated around the front three to their better recent form.

8820 BETWAY NOVICE STKS 6f (Tp)
7:15 (7:15) (Class 5) 3-Y-O+ £3,428 (£1,020; £509) **Stalls** Centre

Form RPR

1 1 **Brushwork**[38] 7655 3-9-9 0.................................. BenCurtis 2 76+
(Charles Hills) *mde all: nudged along briefly and qcknd clr over 1f out: v easily* **1/25[1]**

45 2 3 1/4 **Wings Of Dubai (IRE)**[48] 7319 3-8-11 0.................................. KieranO'Neill 3 43
(Ismail Mohammed) *plld hrd: chsd wnr: outpcd whn hung lft over 1f out: kpt on ins fnl f: flattered by proximity to v easy wnr* **20/1[2]**

0050 3 nk **Hunters Step**[69] 6575 3-8-11 45.................................. FayeMcManoman(5) 1 47?
(Noel Wilson) *t.k.h: cl up: drvn and outpcd over 2f out: rallied fnl f: no imp* **66/1[3]**

1m 14.01s (1.51) **Going Correction** +0.125s/f (Slow) 3 Ran SP% **102.4**
Speed ratings (Par 103): **94,89,89**
CSF £1.21 TOTE £1.02; EX 1.10 Trifecta £1.10.
Owner K Abdullah **Bred** Bearstone Stud Ltd **Trained** Lambourn, Berks

FOCUS
As one-sided an affair as you'll see for a while.

8821 BETWAY H'CAP 6f (Tp)
7:45 (7:45) (Class 6) (0-52,52) 3-Y-O+
£2,781 (£827; £413; £400; £400; £400) **Stalls** Centre

Form RPR

0401 1 **Herringswell (FR)**[13] 8435 4-8-13 **52**.................................. LauraPearson(7) 7 62+
(Henry Spiller) *hld up towards far side of gp: smooth hdwy over 2f out: led over 1f out: rdn out fnl f* **14/1**

4345 2 1 3/4 **Rockley Point**[6] 8632 6-9-2 **48**..............................(b) PhilDennis 12 53
(Katie Scott) *prom towards nr side of gp: led over 2f out to over 1f out: kpt on fnl f: nt pce of wnr* **15/2[2]**

4543 3 3/4 **The Bull (IRE)**[38] 7654 4-9-6 **52**..............................(v) AndrewMullen 13 55
(Ben Haslam) *hld up in centre of gp: effrt and angled rt 2f out: kpt on fnl f: nt pce to chal* **7/2[1]**

0060 4 3/4 **Griggy (IRE)**[23] 8119 3-9-6 **52**.................................. LiamKeniry 5 52
(John Butler) *hld up in centre of gp: effrt and rdn 2f out: kpt on same pce ins fnl f* **9/1[3]**

0030 5 1/2 **Extrasolar**[28] 7961 9-9-4 **50**..............................(t) SamJames 2 49
(Geoffrey Harker) *hld up on far side of gp: stdy hdwy over 2f out: rdn over 1f out: outpcd fnl f* **22/1**

3542 6 4 1/2 **Independence Day (IRE)**[12] 8457 6-9-6 **52**.................................. JoeyHaynes 9 37
(Chelsea Banham) *hld up in centre of gp: effrt and rdn over 2f out: no further imp over 1f out* **7/2[1]**

1260 7 1 **Poppy May (IRE)**[145] 3738 5-9-6 **52**.................................. BarryMcHugh 4 34
(James Given) *prom on far side of gp: ev ch over 2f out: rdn and wknd over 1f out* **33/1**

3206 8 1 **Tizwotitiz**[33] 7824 3-9-6 **52**..............................(v) JasonHart 1 31
(Steph Hollinshead) *led on far side of gp: rdn and hdd over 2f out: wknd over 1f out* **25/1**

02 9 nk **Coffeemeanscoffee (IRE)**[79] 6234 4-9-0 **51**........(p) SeamusCronin(5) 6 29
(W J Martin, Ire) *towards rr on nr side of gp: drvn and outpcd over 2f out: n.d after* **14/1**

0025 10 hd **Tarnhelm**[10] 8530 4-8-12 **51**.................................. RhonaPindar(7) 3 29
(Wilf Storey) *s.s and sn t.o in centre of crse: rdn and edgd lft over 3f out: hdwy over 1f out: passed btn horses ins fnl f: nrst fin (jockey said filly was slowly away)* **14/1**

3530 11 1 1/4 **Bithiah (IRE)**[33] 7824 3-9-3 **49**..............................(h) KieranO'Neill 10 23
(Ismail Mohammed) *cl up in centre of gp: drvn along over 2f out: wknd over 1f out* **33/1**

4000 12 1 3/4 **King Of Rooks**[188] 2235 6-9-0 **51**.................................. PoppyBridgwater(5) 14 20
(Henry Spiller) *bhd on nr side of gp: struggling over 3f out: nvr on terms* **28/1**

3030 13 4 **Tarrzan (IRE)**[11] 8502 3-9-4 **50**.................................. PJMcDonald 8 7
(John Gallagher) *prom in centre of crse: drvn over 2f out: wknd qckly over 1f out* **18/1**

3046 14 1 1/4 **Alfred The Grey (IRE)**[6] 8637 3-9-6 **52**.................................. LukeMorris 11 5
(Tracy Waggott) *hld on nr side of gp: rdn and struggling over 2f out: sn btn (jockey said gelding weakened quickly in the final 2 furlongs)* **14/1**

1m 11.97s (-0.53) **Going Correction** +0.125s/f (Slow) 14 Ran SP% **115.7**
Speed ratings (Par 101): **108,105,104,103,103 97,95,94,93,93 92,89,84,82**
CSF £103.79 CT £463.38 TOTE £8.80: £3.10, £2.70, £1.70; EX 112.10 Trifecta £786.10.
Owner The Champagne Poppers **Bred** Brendan Boyle Bloodstock Ltd **Trained** Newmarket, Suffolk

FOCUS
Plenty still in with chances 2f out, but in the end a clear-cut scorer. The winner has been rated back towards her best, and the form could be rated up to 3lb better.
T/Plt: £165.30 to a £1 stake. Pool: £66,247.61 - 292.50 winning units T/Qpdt: £147.00 to a £1 stake. Pool: £12,027.70 - 60.51 winning units **Richard Young**

8806 KEMPTON (A.W) (R-H)
Tuesday, November 5

OFFICIAL GOING: Polytrack: standard to slow
Wind: Light, against Weather: Overcast, light rain

8822 BET AT RACINGTV.COM H'CAP 1m (P)
4:40 (4:42) (Class 6) (0-55,55) 3-Y-O+
£3,105 (£924; £461; £400; £400; £400) **Stalls** Low

Form RPR

0001 1 **Purple Paddy**[14] 8417 4-8-11 **52**.................................. MarkCrehan(7) 1 63+
(Jimmy Fox) *hld up in tch in midfield: effrt and hdwy jst over 2f out: rdn to ld over 1f out: kicked clr w runner-up and sustained duel ins fnl f: edgd lft but kpt on wl* **10/3[1]**

0032 2 hd **Pearl Jam**[20] 8251 3-9-3 **53**..............................(p[1]) TomMarquand 11 64+
(James Fanshawe) *hdwy to chse ldr after 2f: effrt to chal over 1f out: kicked clr w wnr and sustained duel ins fnl f: kpt on wl: jst hld* **9/2[2]**

0000 3 7 **Tebay (IRE)**[136] 4115 4-9-2 **50**.................................. KierenFox 6 45
(John Best) *stdd s: hld up in last pair: effrt 2f out: swtchd lft and hdwy jst over 1f out: kpt on to chse ldng pair ins fnl f: n.d* **5/1[3]**

0533 4 1 1/4 **Mister Musicmaster**[14] 8417 10-9-5 **53**.................................. DavidProbert 13 45
(Ron Hodges) *broke wl: sn restrained and chsd ldrs: effrt jst over 2f out: no imp over 1f out: wl hld and plugged on same pce ins fnl f* **25/1**

4533 5 3 1/2 **Four Mile Bridge (IRE)**[6] 8667 3-9-0 **53**........(v[1]) ThomasGreatrex(3) 10 37
(Mark Usher) *t.k.h: hld up in tch on outer: effrt over 2f out: unable qck and no imp over 1f out: wknd fnl f* **5/1[3]**

620 6 1/2 **Ecstasea (IRE)**[20] 8256 3-9-5 **55**.................................. JFEgan 9 38
(Rae Guest) *led after 1f: hdd and no ex u.p over 1f out: wknd fnl f* **25/1**

4060 7 1/2 **Geneva Spur (USA)**[45] 7472 3-9-5 **55**.................................. JackMitchell 5 37
(Roger Varian) *sn led: hdd after 1f: chsd ldr tl 6f out: styd handy: unable qck u.p over 1f out: sn wknd* **12/1**

0300 8 nk **Rifft (IRE)**[21] 8223 4-9-6 **54**..............................(t) RichardKingscote 4 35
(Lydia Richards) *in tch in midfield: effrt over 2f out: unable qck u.p and no imp over 1f out: wknd fnl f* **14/1**

0006 9 nk **Declamation (IRE)**[15] 8404 9-9-7 **55**.................................. JoeyHaynes 8 35
(John Butler) *hld up in tch in midfield: effrt over 2f out: no imp and n.m.r jst over 1f out: wl hld fnl f (jockey said gelding was denied a clear run 1 1/2f out)* **100/1**

5044 10 nk **Lippy Lady (IRE)**[31] 7909 3-9-1 **51**..............................(h) LukeMorris 12 31
(Paul George) *stdd s: hld up in rr: effrt on outer ent fnl 2f: no imp and nvr trbld ldrs* **25/1**

6550 11 nse **Paddy's Pursuit (IRE)**[42] 7549 3-9-4 **54**.................................. DavidEgan 7 33
(David Loughnane) *hld up towards rr: effrt over 2f out: nvr threatened to get on terms: wl btn fnl f* **16/1**

2120 12 2 3/4 **Lady Morpheus**[61] 6897 3-9-2 **52**.................................. HectorCrouch 14 25
(Gary Moore) *stdd s: t.k.h: hld up towards rr: swtchd lft and effrt over 2f out: no prog over 1f out: wknd fnl f* **33/1**

5026 13 1/2 **Max Guevara (IRE)**[3] 8753 3-9-2 **52**..............................(b) MartinDwyer 2 24
(William Muir) *t.k.h: hld up in tch in midfield: effrt over 2f out: no hdwy u.p over 1f out: wknd fnl f (jockey said gelding raced awkwardly in the early stages)* **16/1**

0006 14 2 3/4 **Solveig's Song**[14] 8417 7-9-2 **50**..............................(p) NicolaCurrie 3 16
(Steve Woodman) *a towards rr: rdn over 2f out: no hdwy and nvr involved (vet said mare had scoped dirty post-race; trainer's rep said mare had a breathing problem)* **25/1**

1m 38.98s (-0.82) **Going Correction** -0.025s/f (Stan)
WFA 3 from 4yo+ 2lb 14 Ran SP% **120.0**
Speed ratings (Par 101): **103,102,95,94,91 90,90,89,89,89 89,86,85,83**
CSF £16.13 CT £77.60 TOTE £3.50: £1.70, £1.80, £2.20; EX 19.10 Trifecta £229.60.
Owner Mrs Barbara Fuller **Bred** Babs Fuller **Trained** Collingbourne Ducis, Wilts

FOCUS
A moderate handicap.

8823 32RED CASINO NOVICE STKS 1m (P)
5:10 (5:12) (Class 5) 2-Y-O £3,881 (£1,155; £577; £288) **Stalls** Low

Form RPR

1 1 **First View (IRE)**[34] 7814 2-9-9 0.................................. HectorCrouch 5 86+
(Saeed bin Suroor) *broke wl: led for over 1f: chsd ldr tl over 4f out: styd handy: swtchd ins and effrt ent fnl 2f: rdn and chal over 1f out: led ins fnl f: styd on strly* **3/1[1]**

3 2 1/2 **First Receiver**[116] 4886 2-9-2 0.................................. LouisSteward 14 77
(Sir Michael Stoute) *chsd ldrs after over 1f: wnt 2nd over 4f out: upsides ldr and travelling strly 2f out: led over 1f out: sn rdn: hdd ins fnl f: styd on wl but jst outpcd fnl 75yds* **10/3[2]**

44 3 1 1/2 **Carlos Felix (IRE)**[14] 8424 2-9-2 0.................................. CallumShepherd 12 74
(David Simcock) *chsd ldrs: effrt ent fnl f: effrt ent fnl 2f: drvn and sltly outpcd over 1f out: kpt on again ins fnl f* **20/1**

4 3/4 **Thibaan (USA)** 2-9-2 0.................................. JimCrowley 2 72+
(Sir Michael Stoute) *broke wl and chsd ldrs early: sn restrained and hld up in midfield: swtchd lft and effrt over 1f out: kpt on ins fnl f* **8/1**

33 5 hd **Grand Bazaar**[14] 8424 2-9-2 0.................................. NickyMackay 7 72
(John Gosden) *hdwy to ld after over 1f: rdn and hrd pressed ent fnl 2f: hdd over 1f out: unable qck and one pce ins fnl f* **4/1[3]**

4 6 nk **Bucephalus (GER)**[25] 8100 2-9-2 0.................................. RichardKingscote 1 71
(Ed Walker) *wl in tch in midfield: effrt ent fnl 2f: kpt on same pce ins fnl f* **8/1**

03 7 3/4 **Zambezi Magic**[27] 8012 2-9-2 0..............................(h) LiamKeniry 8 69
(Clive Cox) *in tch in midfield: effrt over 2f out: outpcd 2f out: kpt on again ins fnl f* **25/1**

8 3 1/2 **Lord Of The Sky** 2-9-2 0.................................. TomMarquand 6 61
(James Tate) *hld up in midfield: rdn over 2f out: outpcd and btn over 1f out: wl hld and one pce ins fnl f* **25/1**

9 1 3/4 **King Of The North (IRE)** 2-9-2 0 RobHornby 10 57
(Jonathan Portman) *hld up in midfield: rdn over 3f out: no imp over 2f out: wl hld and kpt on same pce fr over 1f out* **66/1**

10 nk **Pharoah King (USA)** 2-9-2 0 HarryBentley 13 57
(John Gosden) *s.i.s: pushed along and rn green early: hld up in rr: outpcd over 2f out: wl hld fnl 2f* **10/1**

11 1 1/2 **Swooping Eagle (IRE)** 2-9-2 0 JackMitchell 11 53
(Roger Varian) *sn dropped towards rr and rn green: outpcd over 2f out: wl hld fnl 2f* **66/1**

12 1/2 **Deposit (IRE)** 2-8-11 0 PoppyBridgwater(5) 9 52
(David Simcock) *hld up towards rr: effrt over 2f out: sn outpcd and hung rt 2f out: wl hld after* **100/1**

13 1 3/4 **Grand Canal (IRE)** 2-9-2 0 DavidEgan 4 48
(Tom Clover) *hld up towards rr: effrt over 2f out: sn outpcd and wl btn fnl 2f* **100/1**

14 12 **Sir Dandy** 2-9-2 0 DavidProbert 3 20
(Lucy Wadham) *s.i.s: rn green and a towards rr: rdn over 2f out: sn btn and bhd whn hung lft 1f out* **33/1**

1m 38.42s (-1.38) **Going Correction** -0.025s/f (Stan) **14 Ran SP% 119.8**
Speed ratings (Par 96): **105,104,103,102,102 101,101,97,95,95 93,93,91,79**
CSF £11.93 TOTE £3.90: £1.50, £1.60, £4.80; EX 15.80 Trifecta £161.90.
Owner Godolphin **Bred** Godolphin **Trained** Newmarket, Suffolk

FOCUS
A decent juvenile novice contest. The winning time was slightly quicker than the previous C&D handicap.

8824 CLOSE BROTHERS BUSINESS FINANCE NURSERY H'CAP 1m (P)
5:40 (5:43) (Class 6) (0-60,61) 2-Y-O

£3,105 (£924; £461; £400; £400; £400) **Stalls Low**

Form RPR

05U4 1 **Lafontaine (FR)**[26] 8061 2-8-7 46 DavidEgan 6 49
(Sylvester Kirk) *sn prom: chsd ldr after 3f tl led over 2f out: sn rdn and hld on wl ins fnl f* **9/2[2]**

2653 2 nk **Chateau Peapod**[12] 8493 2-9-1 54 (p1) BrettDoyle 5 56
(Lydia Pearce) *t.k.h: sn prom: chsd ldr after 1f tl 3f out: str chal over 1f out: kpt on wl but a jst hld ins fnl f* **8/1**

0654 3 1/2 **Divine Connection**[8] 8603 2-9-7 60 RobHornby 7 61
(Jonathan Portman) *hld up in tch in midfield: effrt to press ldrs over 1f out: kpt on wl but a jst hld ins fnl f* **11/4[1]**

060 4 2 3/4 **Dazzling Darren (IRE)**[53] 7162 2-8-11 50 (p1) LukeMorris 3 46
(Adam West) *dwlt: hld up in tch: effrt on inner but nt clrest of runs over 2f out: swtchd ins and effrt ent fnl 2f: kpt on ins fnl f: no threat to ldrs (jockey said gelding clipped heels when running free)* **16/1**

3060 5 nk **Ask Siri (IRE)**[15] 8409 2-8-1 45 AledBeech(5) 11 40
(John Bridger) *stdd after s: hld up towards rr: effrt and nt clrest of runs wl over 1f out: hdwy 1f out: styd on wl ins fnl f: no threat to ldrs* **100/1**

6503 6 3/4 **Halfacrown (IRE)**[11] 8526 2-8-8 47 NicolaCurrie 9 40
(Jamie Osborne) *sn dropped to rr: clsng but nt clrest of runs over 2f out: swtchd ins and hdwy 2f out: kpt on ins fnl f: no threat to ldrs* **15/2**

0350 7 2 1/4 **Liberty Filly**[14] 8415 2-9-7 60 JasonWatson 1 48
(Roger Charlton) *hld up in tch in midfield: hdwy to chse ldrs over 3f out: drvn and pressed wnr 2f out: sn outpcd and wknd ins fnl f* **5/1[3]**

5000 8 1 1/2 **Fact Or Fable (IRE)**[75] 6384 2-9-1 61 (p) OwenLewis(7) 12 46
(J S Moore) *stdd after s: shkn up and effrt over 2f out: no imp: nvr involved* **50/1**

0000 9 hd **Red Hottie**[33] 7833 2-8-3 45 TheodoreLadd(3) 8 29
(Michael Appleby) *in tch in midfield on outer: unable qck u.p and btn over 1f out: wknd ins fnl f* **50/1**

004 10 nse **Prairie Moppins (USA)**[10] 8546 2-9-3 59 ThomasGreatrex(3) 4 43
(Sylvester Kirk) *chsd ldr early: sn settled bk and in tch in midfield: u.p and struggling over 2f out: wl hld fnl f* **9/2[2]**

3006 11 3 1/4 **Moontide (IRE)**[36] 7768 2-9-7 60 LiamKeniry 2 37
(J S Moore) *midfield: rdn ent fnl 3f: unable qck and btn over 1f out: wknd fnl f* **20/1**

006 12 hd **Lily Bonnette**[77] 6322 2-8-6 45 (b1) ShelleyBirkett 10 21
(Julia Feilden) *racd keenly: sn led: hdd over 2f out: lost pl u.p over 1f out: wknd fnl f* **66/1**

1m 40.66s (0.86) **Going Correction** -0.025s/f (Stan) **12 Ran SP% 119.6**
Speed ratings (Par 94): **94,93,93,90,90 89,87,85,85,85 82,81**
CSF £39.45 CT £118.82 TOTE £5.70: £1.90, £2.30, £1.60; EX 32.10 Trifecta £116.40.
Owner Homebred Racing **Bred** Glebe Farm Stud **Trained** Upper Lambourn, Berks

FOCUS
A modest nursery. The winning time was notably slower than the previous two C&D contests. Limited form.

8825 WISE BETTING AT RACINGTV.COM NURSERY H'CAP 6f (P)
6:10 (6:12) (Class 6) (0-60,61) 2-Y-O

£3,105 (£924; £461; £400; £400; £400) **Stalls Low**

Form RPR

5300 1 **Sir Rodneyredblood**[33] 7833 2-9-0 50 DavidProbert 10 61
(J R Jenkins) *wnt rt leaving stalls: mde all and travelled strly: clr and rdn over 1f ont: r.o strly: unchal* **11/1**

006 2 4 1/2 **Oasis Song**[18] 8316 2-9-1 51 CharlieBennett 3 49
(Hughie Morrison) *wnt lft leaving stalls: chsd wnr: effrt jst over 2f out: unable to match pce of wnr over 1f out: wl hld ins fnl f: hung on for 2nd cl home* **13/2[3]**

4053 3 hd **You Don't Own Me (IRE)**[13] 8452 2-9-6 56 CharlesBishop 5 53
(Joseph Tuite) *wnt lft leaving stalls: midfield: effrt over 2f out: 3rd and no threat to wnr whn edgd lft ins fnl f: kpt on same pce and pressing for 2nd cl home* **5/2[1]**

0501 4 4 **Last Date**[33] 7833 2-9-11 61 DougieCostello 12 46
(Ivan Furtado) *s.i.s: midfield: effrt over 2f out: 4th and no imp 1f out: wknd and wnt rt ins fnl f* **8/1**

6066 5 1/2 **Fair Sabra**[13] 8452 2-9-6 56 (b1) WilliamCarson 9 39
(David Elsworth) *edgd rt leaving stalls: hld up in midfield: swtchd lft over 2f out: no imp over 1f out: wl hld ins fnl f* **11/1**

6645 6 1 3/4 **Star Of St Louis (FR)**[11] 8526 2-8-11 47 RobHornby 8 25
(Denis Quinn) *edgd rt leaving stalls: chsd ldrs: rdn over 2f out: outpcd and btn over 1f out: wknd ins fnl f* **4/1[2]**

400 7 1/2 **Penny Diamond**[99] 5501 2-8-9 45 MartinDwyer 6 22
(Amanda Perrett) *pushed lft and short of room leaving stalls: hld up in last trio: effrt over 2f out: no imp u.p over 1f out: wknd fnl f* **9/1**

0500 8 hd **Maisie Ellie (IRE)**[33] 7853 2-9-3 53 (t) LukeMorris 7 29
(Paul George) *short of room and hmpd leaving stalls: a towards rr: nvr involved* **66/1**

6050 9 3/4 **Orange Justice**[11] 8527 2-8-10 46 DavidEgan 2 20
(David Loughnane) *chsd ldrs: unable qck and btn over 1f out: wknd ins fnl f* **16/1**

0655 10 3 **Mumsbirthdaygirl (IRE)**[41] 7584 2-8-9 45 NicolaCurrie 1 10
(Mark Loughnane) *hld up in last trio: effrt over 2f out: no hdwy over 1f out: wknd fnl f* **16/1**

1m 12.96s (-0.14) **Going Correction** -0.025s/f (Stan) **10 Ran SP% 112.9**
Speed ratings (Par 94): **99,93,92,87,86 84,83,82,78**
CSF £78.13 CT £240.27 TOTE £11.50: £3.30, £2.20, £1.10; EX 75.70 Trifecta £237.50.
Owner Mrs Claire Goddard **Bred** Worksop Manor Stud **Trained** Royston, Herts
■ Stewards' Enquiry : Charlie Bennett two-day ban; careless riding (Nov 19-20)

FOCUS
Another modest nursery.

8826 32RED.COM H'CAP 6f (P)
6:40 (6:40) (Class 4) (0-80,83) 3-Y-O+

£6,469 (£1,925; £962; £481; £400; £400) **Stalls Low**

Form RPR

00 1 **Last Page**[18] 8317 4-9-8 81 TomMarquand 1 89
(Tony Carroll) *t.k.h: hld up in tch in midfield on inner: effrt ent fnl 2f: pressed ldrs over 1f out: kpt on wl and maintained chal ins fnl f: led last strides* **8/1**

0453 2 nk **Benny And The Jets (IRE)**[8] 8601 3-9-7 80 RobHornby 8 87
(Sylvester Kirk) *wnt rt leaving stalls: chsd ldrs on outer: effrt jst over 2f out: rdn to ld 1f out: kpt on wl u.p ins fnl f: hdd and no ex last strides* **9/2[2]**

5000 3 1 3/4 **Youkan (IRE)**[8] 8601 4-9-4 77 (p) MartinDwyer 4 78
(Stuart Kittow) *taken down early: sn pressing ldr: led 4f out: pushed along ent fnl 2f: rdn and hdd wl over 1f out: kpt on same pce ins fnl f* **25/1**

4030 4 1/2 **Big Lachie**[46] 7402 5-8-8 72 KevinLundie(5) 5 72
(Mark Loughnane) *hld up in tch in last pair: effrt on inner 2f out: kpt on to chse ldrs ins fnl f: one pce and no imp fnl 100yds* **10/1**

0222 5 1 **Excellent George**[40] 7607 7-9-0 80 (t) MarkCrehan(7) 7 77
(Stuart Williams) *in tch in midfield on outer: effrt ent fnl 2f: unable qck and kpt on same pce ins fnl f* **15/2[3]**

5410 6 nse **Velvet Morn (IRE)**[209] 1687 4-8-11 70 JasonWatson 6 66
(William Knight) *in rr: effrt over 2f out: kpt on ins fnl f: nvr trbld ldrs* **16/1**

2401 7 1 1/2 **Mercenary Rose (IRE)**[8] 8601 3-9-10 83 6ex (b) DavidEgan 3 75
(Paul Cole) *t.k.h: led tl 4f out: rdn to ld again wl over 1f out: drvn and hdd 1f out: wknd ins fnl f* **11/10[1]**

0013 8 1 **Spanish Star (IRE)**[19] 8285 4-9-0 73 LiamKeniry 2 61
(Patrick Chamings) *t.k.h: hld up in tch in midfield: unable qck and outpcd over 1f out: wknd ins fnl f* **14/1**

1m 12.33s (-0.77) **Going Correction** -0.025s/f (Stan) **8 Ran SP% 114.2**
Speed ratings (Par 105): **104,103,101,100,99 99,97,95**
CSF £43.60 CT £865.11 TOTE £10.50: £2.20, £1.30, £5.80; EX 48.10 Trifecta £748.80.
Owner Harvey Lawrence Ltd **Bred** Philip Graham Harvey **Trained** Cropthorne, Worcs

FOCUS
A fair handicap. The winning time was notably quicker than the previous C&D nursery. The first two have been rated back to their best.

8827 32RED ON THE APP STORE H'CAP 7f (P)
7:10 (7:10) (Class 4) (0-80,77) 4-Y-O+

£6,469 (£1,925; £962; £481; £400; £400) **Stalls Low**

Form RPR

2500 1 **Full Intention**[12] 8495 5-8-10 66 (p) DavidProbert 4 73
(Lydia Pearce) *hld up in tch in last pair: effrt over 2f out: styd on wl u.p ins fnl f to ld towards fin* **18/1**

2521 2 1/2 **Busby (IRE)**[26] 8063 4-9-7 77 (p) MartinDwyer 5 83
(Conrad Allen) *chsd ldr: effrt ent fnl 2f: sn drvn and kpt on to ld ins fnl f: hdd: edgd lft and no ex towards fin* **2/1[1]**

4-05 3 shd **Reaction Time**[66] 6732 4-9-1 74 (v1) CierenFallon(3) 6 80
(Saeed bin Suroor) *led and edgd rt sn after s: rdn ent fnl 2f: drvn and hdd ins fnl f: kpt on: bmpd towards fin* **5/2[2]**

6600 4 1 3/4 **Glory Of Paris (IRE)**[12] 8496 5-9-4 74 LukeMorris 3 75
(Michael Appleby) *taken down early: t.k.h: hld up wl in tch in midfield: effrt ent fnl 2f: drvn and chsd ldrs over 1f out: kpt on same pce and no imp ins fnl f* **10/1**

0125 5 1 **Pour La Victoire (IRE)**[6] 8649 9-9-3 73 (p) GeorgeDowning 2 71
(Tony Carroll) *hld up in tch in last trio: effrt 2f out: kpt on ins fnl f: nt enough pce to chal* **20/1**

0414 6 1 3/4 **Thechildren'strust (IRE)**[54] 7125 4-8-13 76 RhysClutterbuck(7) 1 70
(Gary Moore) *awkward leaving stalls: t.k.h: sn rcvrd to chse ldrs: rdn and unable qck over 1f out: wknd ins fnl f (jockey said gelding ran too free early on)* **9/2[3]**

5110 7 shd **Inexes**[46] 7402 7-9-5 75 (p) JasonHart 7 68
(Ivan Furtado) *stdd and dropped in bhd after s: hld up in rr: effrt over 2f out: nvr threatened to get on terms and no imp fnl f* **20/1**

1100 8 hd **Soar Above**[5] 8702 4-9-3 76 DarraghKeenan(3) 8 69
(John Butler) *wl in tch in midfield on outer: effrt over 2f out: no imp and outpcd over 1f out: wknd ins fnl f* **17/2**

1m 25.31s (-0.69) **Going Correction** -0.025s/f (Stan) **8 Ran SP% 114.5**
Speed ratings (Par 105): **102,101,101,99,98 96,96,95**
CSF £54.54 CT £124.57 TOTE £22.40: £5.00, £1.10, £1.40; EX 78.80 Trifecta £368.40.
Owner Killarney Glen & Lydia Pearce **Bred** Springcombe Park Stud **Trained** Newmarket, Suffolk
■ Stewards' Enquiry : Cieren Fallon four-day ban; careless riding (Nov 22-23, 26-27)

FOCUS
Another fair handicap. One of the outsiders got up late in the best comparative time on the night. The winner has been rated in line with last winter's C&D form, the second as running close to his best and the third as matching last year's debut run.

8828 100% PROFIT BOOST AT 32REDSPORT.COM H'CAP 1m 7f 218y(P)
7:40 (7:41) (Class 6) (0-65,65) 3-Y-O+

£3,105 (£924; £461; £400; £400; £400) **Stalls Low**

Form RPR

2426 1 **Vibrance**[15] 8398 3-9-7 65 TomMarquand 3 74+
(James Fanshawe) *trckd ldrs tl wnt 2nd ent fnl 2f: rdn to chal ent fnl f: led ins fnl f: r.o wl* **5/2[1]**

00 2 1 1/4 **Devizes (IRE)**[63] 6836 3-8-8 52 (b1) CharlieBennett 11 59
(Pat Phelan) *pushed lft leaving stalls: sn chsng ldr tl led over 8f out: rdn over 2f out: hdd and one pce ins fnl f* **20/1**

2453 3 2 1/2 **Sinndarella (IRE)**[19] 8293 3-8-3 47 (p) RaulDaSilva 1 51
(Sarah Hollinshead) *hld up in tch in midfield: clsd to chse ldrs ent fnl 2f: sn rdn: chsd ldng pair 1f out: kpt on same pce ins fnl f* **8/1**

050 **4** *nse* **War Empress (IRE)**[27] 8013 3-9-5 **63** .... ShelleyBirkett 8 68+
(Julia Feilden) *short of room and hmpd leaving stalls: hld up in rr: clsd and nt clr run jst over 2f out: stl nt clrest of runs but hdwy over 1f out: swtchd rt and r.o wl ins fnl f (jockey said filly was denied a clear run)* **66/1**

4242 **5** *1 3/4* **Volcanique (IRE)**[28] 7998 3-8-2 **46** .... (v) LukeMorris 5 47
(Sir Mark Prescott Bt) *wl in tch in midfield: clsd to chse ldrs 4f out: unable qck u.p over 1f out: wknd ins fnl f* **13/2**[3]

4116 **6** *hd* **Extreme Appeal (IRE)**[168] 1981 7-9-8 **59** .... (p) ShaneKelly 2 58
(Kelly Morgan) *hld up in rr: clsd and effrt on inner 2f out: no imp over 1f out: kpt on same pce ins fnl f* **25/1**

6203 **7** *1 1/4* **Butterfield (IRE)**[17] 8347 6-8-12 **49** .... EoinWalsh 12 47
(Brian Forsey) *wnt rt leaving stalls: in tch in midfield: n.m.r over 2f out: kpt on same pce ins fnl f* **14/1**

0135 **8** *1 1/4* **Sir Canford (IRE)**[78] 6279 3-9-1 **59** .... (p) CharlesBishop 6 57
(Ali Stronge) *chsd ldrs: effrt over 2f out: unable qck u.p and lost pl over 1f out: wknd ins fnl f* **10/1**

0-20 **9** *1/2* **Vlannon**[21] 8224 4-8-13 **50** .... (v) LiamKeniry 4 46
(Michael Madgwick) *s.i.s: hld up in tch: effrt over 2f out: no imp and n.m.r over 1f out: sn swtchd lft and no imp fnl f* **7/1**

0510 **10** *4* **Thresholdofadream (IRE)**[105] 5271 4-9-7 **58** .... JasonWatson 14 49
(Amanda Perrett) *in tch in midfield on outer: effrt ent fnl 2f: sn outpcd and btn over 1f out: wknd ins fnl f* **6/1**[2]

003 **11** *3/4* **Zamoyski**[28] 7998 9-9-9 **60** .... (p) DavidProbert 7 50
(Steve Gollings) *wnt lft leaving stalls: hld up towards rr: hdwy to chse ldrs 11f out: wnt 2nd 6f out tl lost pl u.p ent fnl 2f: wknd over 1f out* **16/1**

3-00 **12** *10* **Clooney**[7] 8641 4-10-0 **65** .... AdrianMcCarthy 10 43
(Lydia Pearce) *hmpd leaving stalls: effrt whn nt clr run and hmpd ent fnl 2f: nt rcvr and n.d after (jockey said gelding was short of room 2f)* **50/1**

0-00 **13** *99* **Incus**[220] 1429 6-8-8 **50** .... SeamusCronin[(5)] 13
(Ed de Giles) *t.k.h: led tl over 8f out: lost 2nd 6f out and dropped out rapidly: sn t.o (vet said gelding had an irregular heartbeat)* **40/1**

3m 30.93s (0.83) **Going Correction** -0.025s/f (Stan)
WFA 3 from 4yo+ 7lb **13** Ran SP% **115.9**
Speed ratings (Par 101): **96,95,94,94,93 93,92,91,91,89 89,84,34**
CSF £60.48 CT £354.72 TOTE £3.50: £1.50, £5.50, £2.70; EX 59.00 Trifecta £597.90.
Owner Cheveley Park Stud **Bred** Brookside Breeders Club **Trained** Newmarket, Suffolk
FOCUS
A modest staying handicap. The favourite won well from just off a muddling gallop. The third and a few more help pin the level.

8829 32RED AMATEUR RIDERS' H'CAP 1m 3f 219y(P)
8:10 (8:10) (Class 4) (0-80,80) 3-Y-0+
£6,239 (£1,935; £967; £484; £400; £400) **Stalls** Low

Form RPR

402- **1** **Sarim (IRE)**[496] 4240 4-10-0 **73** .... MrCaoilinQuinn[(7)] 8 80
(Warren Greatrex) *mostly chsd ldr tl over 2f out: rdn and ev ch over 1f out: led 1f out: hld on wl ins fnl f* **20/1**

0304 **2** *1/2* **My Boy Sepoy**[14] 8421 4-11-0 **80** .... MissSerenaBrotherton 3 86
(Stuart Williams) *chsd ldrs: ct on heels and stmbld after nrly 2f: chsd ldr over 2f out and sn ev ch: rdn over 1f out: kpt on but hld ins fnl f* **7/2**[2]

2106 **3** *1 1/4* **Blue Medici**[27] 8014 5-10-8 **74** .... MissBeckySmith 2 78
(Mark Loughnane) *hdwy to ld after over 1f: sn clr: pressed over 2f out: sn rdn: hdd 1f out: no ex and jst outpcd wl ins fnl f* **5/1**

6131 **4** *1/2* **Long Call**[45] 7465 6-10-8 **77** .... MissSarahBowen[(3)] 6 80
(Tony Carroll) *stdd s: hld up in last pair: effrt on inner over 2f out: chsd ldrs and kpt on ins fnl f* **6/1**

0003 **5** *6* **Tralee Hills**[8] 8608 5-10-8 **74** .... (v) MrSimonWalker 1 68
(Peter Hedger) *hld up in midfield: ct on heels and stmbld after 1 1/2f: effrt on inner ent fnl 2f: no imp over 1f out: wknd ins fnl f* **10/3**[1]

2550 **6** *1* **French Mix (USA)**[56] 7053 5-10-7 **76** .... MissHannahWelch[(3)] 7 68
(Alexandra Dunn) *t.k.h: led for over 1f: midfield after: swtchd lft and effrt over 2f out: sn outpcd and wknd over 1f out* **20/1**

6063 **7** *15* **Ravenous**[19] 7683 8-9-8 **67** .... MrGuyMitchell[(7)] 4 35
(Luke Dace) *chsd ldrs: wd 3f out: sn lost pl: wknd over 1f out* **33/1**

1304 **8** *1/2* **Bird For Life**[33] 7845 5-9-11 **68** .... (p) MrCiaranJones[(5)] 9 35
(Mark Usher) *stdd and dropped in after s: hld up in last pair: effrt wl over 2f out: sn outpcd and wl btn 2f out* **16/1**

0211 **9** *13* **Percy Prosecco**[17] 6681 4-10-4 **70** .... MissBrodieHampson 5 17
(Archie Watson) *hld up in midfield: rdn over 2f out: sn btn and bhd (trainer could offer no explanation for the gelding's performance)* **9/2**[3]

2m 36.63s (2.13) **Going Correction** -0.025s/f (Stan) **9** Ran SP% **112.8**
Speed ratings (Par 105): **91,90,89,89,85 84,74,74,65**
CSF £85.11 CT £412.54 TOTE £25.20: £6.40, £1.60, £1.80; EX 142.10 Trifecta £470.00.
Owner Fitorfat Racing **Bred** Lynch-Bages & Rhinestone Bloodstock **Trained** Upper Lambourn, Berks
■ Stewards' Enquiry : Miss Hannah Welch six-day ban; careless riding (Nov 27, Dec 4, 16, Jan 3, 8, 24)
FOCUS
A fair amateur riders' middle-distance handicap, but quite a rough, messy race due to another muddling gallop. The second has been rated to form, with the third running as well as ever.
T/Plt: £44.80 to a £1 stake. Pool: £81,807.41 - 1,330.98 winning units T/Qpdt: £18.90 to a £1 stake. Pool: £10,885.97 - 425.16 winning units **Steve Payne**

7902 REDCAR (L-H)
Tuesday, November 5
8830 Meeting Abandoned - Waterlogged

8639 SOUTHWELL (L-H)
Tuesday, November 5
OFFICIAL GOING: Fibresand: standard
Wind: Fresh half across Weather: Heavy cloud and rain

8837 BETWAY LIVE CASINO H'CAP 1m 4f 14y(F)
1:00 (1:01) (Class 6) (0-65,63) 3-Y-O
£2,781 (£827; £413; £300; £300; £300) **Stalls** Low

Form RPR

4U26 **1** **Twpsyn (IRE)**[95] 5601 3-9-5 **61** .... (v[1]) BenCurtis 8 74+
(David Evans) *trckd ldrs: hdwy over 3f out: led wl over 2f out: rdn clr over 1f out: styd on strly* **6/1**[3]

2060 **2** *7* **Thunderoad**[17] 8348 3-9-3 **59** .... ShaneKelly 10 62+
(Tony Carroll) *hld up in tch: hdwy to trck ldrs 4f out: effrt over 2f out: rdn to chse wnr wl over 1f out: drvn and no imp fnl f* **8/1**

3 *3 1/4* **Be Fair**[76] 6358 3-9-3 **59** .... GeorgeDowning 5 55
(Tony Carroll) *hld up: hdwy over 4f out: chsd ldrs 3f out: rdn along 2f out: kpt on same pce* **33/1**

3463 **4** *shd* **Bolt N Brown**[14] 8434 3-9-6 **62** .... (t) LukeMorris 7 57
(Gay Kelleway) *hld up towards rr: hdwy 4f out: chsd ldrs 3f out: sn rdn along: drvn and edgd lft 2f out: sn one pce* **7/1**

5 *1 3/4* **Bajan Excell (IRE)**[8] 8630 3-9-7 **63** .... KieranO'Neill 4 56
(Gavin Cromwell, Ire) *hld up towards rr: hdwy over 4f out: sn trcking ldrs: rdn along and outpcd 3f out: kpt on fr over 1f out* **7/2**[2]

4045 **6** *4* **Ideal Grace**[86] 5987 3-8-10 **52** .... (p) RaulDaSilva 9 38
(Brian Barr) *cl up: slt ld over 3f out: rdn along and hdd wl over 2f out: sn drvn and grad wknd* **40/1**

7 *2* **Pretty Fantasy (IRE)**[386] 8286 3-8-4 **46** .... FrannyNorton 6 29
(Gavin Cromwell, Ire) *a towards rr: detached 1/2-way: pushed along over 4f out: rdn over 3f out: nvr a factor (jockey said filly was never travelling)* **13/8**[1]

0600 **8** *2 1/4* **Cormier (IRE)**[14] 8423 3-9-1 **57** .... (h[1]) LiamKeniry 3 36
(Stef Keniry) *led: pushed along over 4f out: rdn and hdd over 3f out: sn wknd* **12/1**

0 **9** *6* **Mia Vittoria**[47] 7375 3-8-8 **57** .... StefanoCherchi[(7)] 2 27
(Amy Murphy) *trckd ldng pair on inner: pushed along over 4f out: rdn over 3f out: sn wknd* **66/1**

6006 **10** *19* **Freshfield Ferris**[7] 8645 3-8-3 **45** .... CamHardie 1
(Brian Rothwell) *chsd ldrs: pushed along 5f out: sn rdn and wknd wl over 3f out* **150/1**

2m 36.87s (-4.13) **Going Correction** -0.30s/f (Stan) **10** Ran SP% **113.4**
Speed ratings (Par 98): **101,96,94,94,92 90,88,87,83,70**
CSF £50.48 CT £1444.17 TOTE £6.40: £1.50, £2.60, £10.10; EX 52.00 Trifecta £1133.40.
Owner Rob Emmanuelle, T Burns & P D Evans **Bred** Rathasker Stud **Trained** Pandy, Monmouths
FOCUS
This weak 3yo handicap proved a lively betting heat, but it was one-way traffic.

8838 BETWAY MAIDEN STKS 1m 4f 14y(F)
1:30 (1:30) (Class 5) 3-Y-O+
£3,428 (£1,020; £509) **Stalls** Low

Form RPR

32 **1** **Goobinator (USA)**[27] 8020 3-9-5 0 .... (h[1]) PaulMulrennan 1 78
(Donald McCain) *mde all: pushed along 3f out: rdn over 2f out: kpt on wl appr fnl f* **5/6**[1]

-252 **2** *6* **Tranquil Storm (IRE)**[50] 7287 4-9-5 69 .... TomEaves 2 62
(Kevin Ryan) *trckd ldng pair: hdwy to trck wnr 5f out: effrt and cl up 3f out: rdn along over 2f out and ev ch: drvn and edgd lft over 1f out: sn one pce* **Evs**[2]

3 *55* **Bella Amoura**[34] 3-9-0 0 .... LiamKeniry 3
(Brian Barr) *t.k.h: trckd wnr: pushed along 1/2-way: rdn 5f out: sn outpcd* **33/1**[3]

2m 36.99s (-4.01) **Going Correction** -0.30s/f (Stan)
WFA 3 from 4yo 5lb **3** Ran SP% **107.5**
Speed ratings (Par 103): **101,97,60**
CSF £2.00 TOTE £1.70; EX 1.50 Trifecta £1.50.
Owner T G Leslie **Bred** Fred W Hertrich III & John D Fielding **Trained** Cholmondeley, Cheshire
FOCUS
This ordinary little maiden was always going to be tactical. The winner has been rated in line with the better view of his previous runs.

8839 BETWAY HEED YOUR HUNCH H'CAP 6f 16y(F)
2:00 (2:03) (Class 6) (0-65,65) 3-Y-O+
£2,781 (£827; £413; £300; £300; £300) **Stalls** Low

Form RPR

1 **Rock Sound (IRE)**[378] 8520 4-9-7 **65** .... DavidNolan 10 85+
(Declan Carroll) *trckd ldrs: smooth hdwy on outer 1/2-way: wd st: chal 2f out: rdn over 1f out: edgd sltly lft and led ent fnl f: kpt on* **7/4**[1]

5000 **2** *4 1/2* **First Excel**[26] 8066 7-9-5 **63** .... (b) LewisEdmunds 14 67
(Roy Bowring) *cl up: led 3f out: wd st: jnd and rdn 2f out: drvn over 1f out: hdd ent fnl f: kpt on same pce* **9/1**

3030 **3** *3/4* **Freedom And Wheat (IRE)**[5] 8711 3-9-1 **59** .... (v) ShaneKelly 3 61
(Mark Usher) *in tch: hdwy wl over 2f out: rdn wl over 1f out: kpt on u.p fnl f* **12/1**

052 **4** *1/2* **Dandy Highwayman (IRE)**[34] 7823 5-9-1 **59** .... (bt) BenRobinson 7 59
(Ollie Pears) *towards rr and sn rdn along: wd st: styd on u.p fr wl over 1f out: nrst fin (jockey said gelding missed the break)* **17/2**[3]

1645 **5** *nse* **Jill Rose**[26] 8071 3-9-1 **59** .... (p) PhilDennis 8 59
(Richard Whitaker) *chsd ldrs: hdwy 3f out: rdn over 2f out: drvn wl over 1f out: kpt on same pce* **16/1**

5000 **6** *hd* **Shellebeau (IRE)**[21] 8217 3-9-4 **62** .... RossaRyan 1 62
(Alexandra Dunn) *towards rr and sn pushed along on inner: hdwy 1/2-way: rdn wl over 2f out: kpt on fnl f* **33/1**

030 **7** *3 1/4* **Remission**[86] 5985 3-8-2 **46** oh1 .... DuranFentiman 6 36
(Derek Shaw) *trckd ldng pair on inner: pushed along 3f out: rdn 2f out: sn drvn and grad wknd* **80/1**

3460 **8** *shd* **Gupta**[29] 7959 3-8-13 **62** .... ThoreHammerHansen[(5)] 13 51
(David Brown) *slt ld: rdn along and hdd 3f out: drvn 2f out: grad wknd (jockey said gelding hung right)* **12/1**

P025 **9** *nk* **Sir Hector (IRE)**[33] 7837 4-8-12 **56** .... WilliamCarson 12 45
(Charlie Wallis) *a towards rr* **7/1**[2]

5011 **10** *1 1/4* **Wild Flower (IRE)**[19] 8279 7-8-8 **52** .... (p) KieranO'Neill 2 37
(Luke McJannet) *in tch on inner: rdn along wl over 2f out: sn drvn and wknd* **14/1**

0504 **11** *2* **North Korea (IRE)**[24] 8119 3-8-2 **46** oh1 .... AndrewMullen 4 25
(Brian Baugh) *towards rr: bhd and wd st* **50/1**

3302 **12** *3/4* **Kodicat (IRE)**[43] 7507 5-8-13 **57** .... (p) KevinStott 5 34
(Kevin Ryan) *towards rr: bhd and wd st: effrt and sme hdwy 2f out: sn rdn and btn* **9/1**

-405 **13** *4* **Zebulon (IRE)**[186] 2379 5-9-5 **63** .... JamesSullivan 11 28
(Ruth Carr) *dwlt: swtchd rt to outer s: a bhd and wd st (jockey said gelding anticipated the start and missed the break as a result)* **22/1**

-650 **14** *15* **Bawtry Lady**[278] 505 3-8-2 **46** oh1 .... (b) HollieDoyle 9
(David C Griffiths) *t.k.h: chsd ldrs: rdn along 3f out: wknd qckly: sn bhd and eased (vet reported filly bled from the nose)* **50/1**

1m 13.49s (-3.01) **Going Correction** -0.30s/f (Stan) course record **14** Ran SP% **119.8**
Speed ratings (Par 101): **108,102,101,100,100 100,95,95,95,93 90,89,84,64**
CSF £16.76 CT £155.90 TOTE £2.60: £1.60, £2.80, £3.30; EX 19.40 Trifecta £224.50.
Owner The Bramblers **Bred** Moyglare Stud Farm Ltd **Trained** Malton, N Yorks

The Form Book Flat 2019, Raceform Ltd, Newbury, RG14 5SJ

FOCUS
They went hard in this modest sprint handicap, resulting in the course record just being lowered.

8840 BETWAY H'CAP — 4f 214y(F)
2:30 (2:32) (Class 6) (0-58,60) 3-Y-O+
£2,781 (£827; £413; £300; £300; £300) **Stalls** Centre

Form — RPR

3150 **1** **Catapult**[10] 8547 4-8-11 **47**....................(p) JosephineGordon 5 54
(Shaun Keightley) *prom centre: hdwy 2f out: rdn to ld over 1f out: drvn and edgd lft jst ins fnl f: kpt on wl* **13/2**

2560 **2** ¾ **Hey Ho Let's Go**[14] 8419 3-9-0 **57**.................... AmeliaGlass(7) 7 61
(Clive Cox) *hld up: hdwy in centre 2f out: chsd ldrs over 1f out: swtchd rt and rdn to chal ins fnl f: rdr dropped whip 100yds out: no imp towards fin* **5/1**[2]

1300 **3** 2 **Decision Maker (IRE)**[86] 5986 5-9-9 **59**.................... KieranO'Neill 4 56
(Roy Bowring) *sn led towards far side: rdn 2f out: hdd over 1f out: drvn and kpt on fnl f* **14/1**

0000 **4** ¾ **Inner Charm**[29] 7959 3-9-3 **53**.................... KevinStott 3 47
(Kevin Ryan) *racd towards far side: chsd ldrs: rdn along and sltly outpcd 2f out: kpt on fnl f* **14/1**

0311 **5** *nk* **Young Tiger**[15] 8401 6-9-9 **59**....................(h) AndrewMullen 11 52
(Tom Tate) *racd towards stands' side: prom: ev ch 2f out: sn rdn: hld whn edgd rt and kpt on same pce ins fnl f* **4/1**[1]

0332 **6** ½ **Piazon**[7] 8643 8-9-3 **60**....................(be) HarryRussell(7) 13 52
(Julia Brooke) *racd nr stands' rail: cl up: rdn along 2f out: drvn over 1f out: grad wknd* **11/2**[3]

-401 **7** 3 ¼ **Miss Gradenko**[13] 8450 3-9-2 **52**.................... RaulDaSilva 12 37
(Robert Cowell) *racd nr stands' rail: cl up: rdn along 2f out: drvn and hld whn n.m.r and sltly hmpd ins fnl f* **14/1**

404 **8** ¾ **Final Legacy**[7] 8643 3-8-9 **45**.................... LewisEdmunds 8 22
(Derek Shaw) *sn swtchd rt to strnds' rail and rdn along in rr: outpcd and detached 1/2-way: hdwy wl over 1f out: kpt on fnl f* **16/1**

4600 **9** *nse* **Guardia Svizzera (IRE)**[4] 8720 5-9-4 **54**....................(h) BenCurtis 9 31
(Roger Fell) *chsd ldrs centre: rdn along 1/2-way: sn outpcd* **7/1**

0005 **10** *nk* **Murqaab**[20] 8264 3-8-10 **53**.................... IzzyClifton(7) 2 29
(John Balding) *chsd ldrs towards far side: rdn along over 2f out: sn wknd* **12/1**

11 2 ½ **Gala N Dandy (IRE)**[74] 6428 4-8-9 **45**....................(p) ShaneKelly 6 12
(S M Duffy, Ire) *cl up centre: rdn along 2f out: sn wknd* **50/1**

0300 **12** ½ **Purely Prosecco**[7] 8643 3-8-9 **45**.................... DuranFentiman 1 10
(Derek Shaw) *swtchd rt towards centre s: sn rdn along in rr: detached fr 1/2-way* **100/1**

57.63s (-2.07) **Going Correction** -0.30s/f (Stan) **12 Ran SP% 114.4**
Speed ratings (Par 101): **104,102,99,98,97 97,91,90,90,90 86,85**
CSF £37.50 CT £439.22 TOTE £8.10: £2.20, £1.80, £5.10; EX 34.40 Trifecta £393.60.
Owner Simon Lockyer **Bred** Owen O'Brien **Trained** Newmarket, Suffolk

FOCUS
Not the worst sprint handicap and two came clear late. It's been rated with feet on the ground.

8841 LADBROKES WHERE THE NATION PLAYS NURSERY H'CAP — 4f 214y(F)
3:00 (3:00) (Class 5) (0-70,67) 2-Y-O
£3,428 (£1,020; £509; £300; £300; £300) **Stalls** Centre

Form — RPR

5523 **1** **Lilkian**[6] 8650 2-9-5 **65**.................... JosephineGordon 2 69
(Shaun Keightley) *trckd ldrs centre: hdwy wl over 1f out: rdn to chal and edgd lft ent fnl f: led 150yds out: sn drvn hung rt and kpt on wl* **7/4**[1]

623 **2** ¾ **Astrozone**[48] 7333 2-9-6 **66**.................... GrahamLee 7 67+
(Bryan Smart) *racd towards stands' side: cl up: rdn to take narrow ld over 1f out: hdd 150yds out: sn drvn and kpt on wl towards fin* **13/2**

0436 **3** 1 ¼ **Abbaleka**[12] 8506 2-9-7 **67**.................... AlistairRawlinson 4 64
(Michael Appleby) *dwlt: sn trcking ldrs centre: swtchd rt and hdwy wl over 1f out: rdn and n.m.r ent fnl f: green and edgd lft last 100yds: kpt on* **11/2**[2]

336 **4** 1 **Lady Nectar (IRE)**[58] 6997 2-9-5 **65**.................... FrannyNorton 3 58
(Ann Duffield) *racd centre: led: rdn along 2f out: drvn and hdd jst over 1f out: kpt on same pce* **10/1**

034 **5** 1 ¼ **Catechism**[21] 8218 2-9-7 **67**.................... KieranShoemark 9 55
(Richard Spencer) *racd towards stands' side: prom: effrt 2f out: sn rdn and kpt on same pce* **9/1**

0630 **6** ½ **Falacho (IRE)**[3] 8750 2-8-12 **58**.................... HollieDoyle 1 45
(David Loughnane) *cl up centre: rdn along wl over 1f out: sn drvn and wknd* **6/1**[3]

304 **7** *hd* **Crime Of Passion (IRE)**[3] 8750 2-9-2 **67** ThoreHammerHansen(5) 8 53+
(Jamie Osborne) *racd nr stands' side: chsd ldrs: rdn along 2f out: sn drvn and btn* **9/1**

5063 **8** 3 **Lili Wen Fach (IRE)**[49] 7296 2-9-4 **64**....................(v) BenCurtis 6 39
(David Evans) *dwlt: sn outpcd and bhd fr 1/2-way* **20/1**

58.32s (-1.38) **Going Correction** -0.30s/f (Stan) **8 Ran SP% 113.2**
Speed ratings (Par 96): **99,97,95,94,92 91,91,86**
CSF £13.16 CT £51.35 TOTE £2.40: £1.20, £1.30, £2.30; EX 13.10 Trifecta £55.00.
Owner D S Lovatt **Bred** Biddestone Stud Ltd **Trained** Newmarket, Suffolk

FOCUS
An ordinary nursery in which the main action was nearer the stands' side.

8842 BOMBARDIER BRITISH HOPPED AMBER BEER MAIDEN STKS — 1m 13y(F)
3:30 (3:33) (Class 5) 3-Y-O+
£3,428 (£1,020; £509; £254) **Stalls** Low

Form — RPR

43-3 **1** **Mosakhar**[11] 8529 3-9-5 78.................... BenRobinson 1 80
(Ollie Pears) *cl up on inner: disp ld 1/2-way: slt ld over 3f out: pushed along 2f out: rdn wl over 1f out: clr ins fnl f: kpt on strly* **9/2**[2]

3-35 **2** 4 **Momtalik (USA)**[50] 2185 4-9-7 71.................... LewisEdmunds 3 71
(Derek Shaw) *trckd ldrs on inner: hdwy over 2f out: rdn wl over 1f out: kpt on u.p fnl f* **10/1**[3]

5 **3** 1 ¼ **Memory Hill (IRE)**[13] 8472 3-9-5 0.................... BenCurtis 2 68
(David Evans) *slt ld: hdd narrowly over 3f out: cl up and rdn over 2f out: drvn and ev ch over 1f out: kpt on same pce fnl f* **16/1**

22 **4** ½ **Millicent Fawcett**[11] 8529 3-9-0 0.................... RobertHavlin 7 62
(John Gosden) *dwlt: trckd ldrs on wd outside: cl up 1/2-way: pushed along and wd st: sn rdn: drvn 2f out: sn btn* **4/11**[1]

-66 **5** 4 ½ **Abwab (IRE)**[27] 8020 3-9-0 0.................... GerO'Neill(5) 4 57
(Michael Easterby) *bhd: rdn along and hdwy over 2f out: plugged on: n.d* **14/1**

06 **6** 3 **Berties Mission (USA)**[5] 8693 3-9-5 0....................(h) DuranFentiman 5 50
(Derek Shaw) *chsd ldrs: rdn along over 3f out: sn wknd* **100/1**

0 **7** 17 **Highland Sun (IRE)**[31] 7912 3-9-0 0.................... JaneElliott 6 6
(Richard Phillips) *a towards rr: outpcd and bhd fnl 3f* **66/1**

1m 41.44s (-2.26) **Going Correction** -0.30s/f (Stan)
WFA 3 from 4yo 2lb **7 Ran SP% 115.6**
Speed ratings (Par 103): **99,95,93,93,88 85,68**
CSF £47.86 TOTE £5.30: £1.80, £3.50; EX 29.10 Trifecta £211.10.
Owner Mrs S D Pearson **Bred** Shadwell Estate Company Limited **Trained** Norton, N Yorks

FOCUS
An uncompetitive maiden. The level is tricky to pin down.

8843 BETWAY AMATEUR RIDERS' H'CAP — 1m 6f 21y(F)
4:05 (4:05) (Class 6) (0-60,62) 3-Y-O+
£2,682 (£832; £415; £300; £300; £300) **Stalls** Low

Form — RPR

0630 **1** **Restive (IRE)**[56] 7053 6-11-5 **62**....................(t) MissSerenaBrotherton 8 76
(Michael Appleby) *hld up in tch: hdwy to trck ldrs 1/2-way: cl up over 5f out: led over 4f out: rdn clr over 2f out: kpt on strly unchal* **11/4**[1]

0504 **2** 11 **Grandscape**[76] 6343 4-11-0 **62**.................... SophieSmith(5) 9 62
(Ed Dunlop) *prom: slt ld 6f out: hdd over 4f out: sn rdn along: chsd wnr and drvn 2f out: kpt on one pce* **6/1**

0333 **3** ¾ **Keith**[7] 8644 3-9-13 **48**....................(p) MrPatrickMillman 1 45
(Rod Millman) *in tch: pushed along to chse ldrs over 4f out: rdn and outpcd fr over 3f out: fin 4th: plcd 3rd* **6/1**

3602 **4** *hd* **Duke Of Yorkshire**[56] 7053 9-11-0 **57**....................(p) MissEmilyEasterby 2 52
(Tim Easterby) *chsd ldrs on inner: pushed along over 5f out: rdn wl over 3f out: sn outpcd and bhd: fin 5th: plcd 4th* **20/1**

5020 **5** 18 **Seventii**[10] 8551 5-9-13 **47**.................... MrGeorgeEddery(5) 4 18
(Robert Eddery) *chsd ldrs: rdn along 6f out: wknd over 4f out and bhd: fin 6th: plcd 5th* **16/1**

0313 **6** ½ **Mamdood (IRE)**[6] 8670 5-10-7 **55**....................(vt) MrEireannCagney(5) 7 25+
(Stef Keniry) *led: hdd 1/2-way: sn rdn along and wknd: bhd fnl 4f: fin 7th: plcd 6th* **4/1**[3]

2-5 **7** 1 ¼ **Viscount Wilson**[40] 7492 4-10-4 **54**....................(bt) MrNiallMoore(7) 5 23
(S M Duffy, Ire) *a in rr: t.o fnl 4f: fin 8th: plcd 7th* **50/1**

0505 **D** 3 ¼ **General Allenby**[10] 8551 5-9-10 **46**....................(p) MissMollyPresland(7) 3 42
(Shaun Keightley) *in rr: pushed along 1/2-way: hdwy 3f out: styd on wl fnl 2f: tk 3rd nr fin: disqualified - rdr weighed in light* **25/1**

0421 **F** **Risk Mitigation (USA)**[15] 8406 3-10-0 **49**....................(b[1]) MissJoannaMason 6
(David Evans) *trckd ldrs: hdwy 5f out: chsd ldng pair whn fell and fatally injured over 3f out* **7/2**[2]

3m 5.45s (-2.85) **Going Correction** -0.30s/f (Stan)
WFA 3 from 4yo+ 6lb **9 Ran SP% 113.9**
Speed ratings (Par 101): **96,89,87,87,77 76,76,87,**
CSF £18.92 CT £90.11 TOTE £3.30: £1.50, £1.60, £2.30; EX 16.40 Trifecta £105.80.
Owner Michael Appleby **Bred** Epona Bloodstock Ltd **Trained** Oakham, Rutland
■ Stewards' Enquiry : Miss Molly Presland four-day ban: failed to weigh-in (TBA)

FOCUS
There was no hanging about in this moderate amateur riders' handicap, which saw drama going into the final bend. The winner has been rated 7lb better than any of his previous runs over the past two years, with the second not too far off his recent form.
T/Plt: £1,003.10 to a £1 stake. Pool: £59,267.78 - 43.13 winning units. T/Qpdt: £111.70 to a £1 stake. Pool: £8,273.02 - 54.76 winning units. **Joe Rowntree**

8767 FLEMINGTON (L-H)
Tuesday, November 5

OFFICIAL GOING: Turf: good to soft

8844a LEXUS MELBOURNE CUP (GROUP 1 H'CAP) (3YO+) (TURF) — 2m
4:00 3-Y-O+
£2,569,060 (£607,734; £303,867; £193,370; £127,071; £88,397)

RPR

1 **Vow And Declare (AUS)**[17] 8361 4-8-3 **0**.................... CraigAWilliams 21 112
(Danny O'Brien, Australia) *w ldrs early: led after 4f: hdd after 4f: a.p on inner: drvn fnl bnd to chse ldr 2f out: sn rdn: sustained chal fnl f: led cl home* **10/1**[3]

2 *nse* **Prince Of Arran**[13] 8600 6-8-7 **0** 2ex.................... MichaelWalker 8 112
(Charlie Fellowes) *w ldrs early: a.p: rdn to chse ldng pair over 1 1/2f out: r.o u.p fnl f: jst missed out: fin 3rd: plcd 2nd* **16/1**

3 *nse* **Il Paradiso (USA)**[52] 7196 3-8-4 **0**....................(b[1]) WayneLordan 17 118
(A P O'Brien, Ire) *hld up towards rr: rdn and hdwy 2f out: r.o wl fnl f: chal between horses but squeezed out late on: fin 4th: plcd 3rd* **14/1**

4 *hd* **Master Of Reality (IRE)**[51] 7246 4-8-10 **0**.................... FrankieDettori 1 115
(Joseph Patrick O'Brien, Ire) *w ldrs: chsd ldr after 2f: remained cl up: led 2 1/2f out: rdn for home 2f out: r.o u.p but moved lft and hdd cl home: fin 2nd: disqualified and plcd 4th* **25/1**

5 ½ **Surprise Baby (NZ)**[31] 5-8-6 **0** 2ex.................... JordanChilds 20 110
(Paul Preusker, Australia) *hld up in fnl pair: hdwy on outer appr fnl 1 1/2f: r.o fnl f: nrest at fin* **11/1**

6 *nk* **Mer De Glace (JPN)**[17] 8361 4-8-11 **0** 2ex....................(b) DamianLane 2 115
(Hisashi Shimizu, Japan) *racd keenly: sn hld up in midfield: lost pl and angled out over 2 1/2f out: sn cut bk ins and began to cl 1 1/2f out: styd on wl fnl f: nvr nrr* **17/2**[2]

7 *hd* **Finche**[17] 8361 5-8-7 **0**.................... KerrinMcEvoy 4 111
(Chris Waller, Australia) *w ldrs early: a.p: sltly outpcd 3f out: rdn but no immediate imp ins fnl 2f: styd on fnl f: run evened out fnl 75yds* **15/2**[1]

8 *hd* **Cross Counter**[51] 7246 4-9-1 **0**.................... WilliamBuick 5 119
(Charlie Appleby) *settled in midfield: styd on u.p ins fnl 2f: nt pce to get on terms: effrt levelled out late on* **12/1**

9 ½ **Steel Prince (IRE)**[13] 8600 5-8-4 **0**.................... BrettPrebble 16 107
(Anthony Freedman, Australia) *racd keenly: hld up in midfield: drvn over 2f out: styd on fnl f: nvr trbld ldrs* **60/1**

10 1 ½ **Magic Wand (IRE)**[10] 8579 4-8-6 **0**.................... RyanMoore 24 107
(A P O'Brien, Ire) *towards rr: hdwy appr 1 1/2f out: styd on fnl f: nt pce to get on terms* **25/1**

11 *hd* **Twilight Payment (IRE)**[51] 7246 6-8-9 **0**....................(tp) HughBowman 19 110
(Joseph Patrick O'Brien, Ire) *prom on outer: led after 4f: hdd 2 1/2f out: kpt on at one pce* **40/1**

12 *shd* **Sound (GER)**[17] 8361 6-8-6 **0**.................... JamesWinks 10 107
(Michael Moroney, Australia) *towards rr of midfield: drvn to stay on over 1 1/2f out: no further imp ins fnl f* **90/1**

13 hd **Constantinople (IRE)**[17] 8361 3-8-4 **0**..........................(p) JoaoMoreira 7 114
(David A & B Hayes & Tom Dabernig, Australia) *midfield on inner: angled out over 3f out: drvn to take clsr order more than 2f out: kpt on fnl f but nvr able to land a blow* **17/2**[2]

14 hd **Mirage Dancer**[17] 8361 5-8-10 **0**..........................(t) BenMelham 13 111
(Trent Busuttin & Natalie Young, Australia) *racd keenly: hld up in midfield: kpt on at same pce fnl 2f: n.d* **50/1**

15 hd **Hunting Horn (IRE)**[10] 8577 4-8-9 **0**..........................(p) SeamieHeffernan 11 109
(A P O'Brien, Ire) *prom: cl 3rd 4f out: sn rdn and no imp fr 3f out: grad lft bhd fnl 1 1/2f* **50/1**

16 1/2 **Raymond Tusk (IRE)**[73] 6473 4-8-7 **0**.......................... JamieSpencer 3 107
(Richard Hannon) *hld up in midfield on inner: styd on u.p to chse ldrs wl over 1f out: no ex ins fnl f and dropped away* **20/1**

17 hd **The Chosen One (NZ)**[3] 8767 4-8-3 **0** 1ex.......................... TimothyClark 18 107
(Murray Baker & Andrew Forsman, New Zealand) *towards rr: sme late hdwy: nvr threatened to get involved* **30/1**

18 1 1/4 **Latrobe (IRE)**[51] 7246 4-8-9 **0**..........................(t) JamesMcDonald 22 107
(Joseph Patrick O'Brien, Ire) *qckly taken ins fr wd draw: towards rr of midfield on inner: rdn and effrt 2f out: nvr in contention* **20/1**

19 shd **Southern France (IRE)**[51] 7246 4-8-10 **0**..........................(t) MarkZahra 14 108
(Ciaron Maher & David Eustace, Australia) *w.w in midfield on outer: rdn and shortlived effrt 2 1/2f out* **25/1**

20 3/4 **Youngstar (AUS)**[17] 5-8-3 **0**..........................(t) TommyBerry 9 100
(Chris Waller, Australia) *w ldrs early: prom: outpcd and rdn ins fnl 2f: sn btn* **30/1**

21 1 **Neufbosc (FR)**[13] 8600 4-8-6 **0**..........................(b) LukeNolen 23 102
(David A & B Hayes & Tom Dabernig, Australia) *racd keenly: hld up in rr: passed btn rivals: nvr in contention* **100/1**

22 nk **Downdraft (IRE)**[3] 8767 4-8-6 **0**..........................(t) JohnAllen 15 102
(Joseph Patrick O'Brien, Ire) *w.w towards rr of midfield: c wdst of all fnl bnd: sn btn* **20/1**

23 2 1/4 **Mustajeer**[17] 8361 6-8-9 **0**.......................... DamienOliver 6 102
(Kris Lees, Australia) *towards rr of midfield: quick prog on outer 4f out: chsd ldrs 2 1/2f out but c wd into st: wknd fnl 2f* **18/1**

24 dist **Rostropovich (IRE)**[17] 8361 4-8-9 **0**..........................(t) DwayneDunn 12
(David A & B Hayes & Tom Dabernig, Australia) *w.w towards rr: rdn 3f out but no imp: sn wknd: t.o* **40/1**

3m 24.76s (5.12) **Going Correction** +0.75s/f (Yiel)
WFA 3 from 4yo+ 7lb **24** Ran SP% **120.5**
Speed ratings: **117,116,116,116,116 116,116,116,116,115 115,115,115,114,114 114,114,113,113,113 112,112,111,E**

Owner G & Mrs S M Corrigan, P J Lanskey Et Al **Bred** P Lanskey **Trained** Australia

FOCUS
On paper this was a cracking edition. However, a sluggish early tempo meant that racing handily was a huge advantage, and it saw a messy finish towards the inside. There were eyecatchers aplenty and the winning time was 8secs off the course record.

8845 - 8846a (Foreign Racing) - See Raceform Interactive

8822

KEMPTON (A.W) (R-H)

Wednesday, November 6

OFFICIAL GOING: Polytrack: standard to slow
Wind: virtually nil Weather: overcast

8847 WISE BETTING AT RACINGTV.COM H'CAP 7f (P)

4:40 (4:40) (Class 6) (0-60,60) 3-Y-O+
£3,105 (£924; £461; £400; £400) **Stalls** Low

Form RPR

-205 1 **Violet's Lads (IRE)**[243] 1075 5-9-7 **60**.......................... JackMitchell 4 67
(Brett Johnson) *hld up in tch in midfield: swtchd lft and effrt over 1f out: rdn to chal 1f out: led 100yds out: r.o wl* **10/1**

0123 2 1 1/4 **Cauthen (IRE)**[6] 8698 3-9-4 **58**..........................(h) HayleyTurner 3 61
(Milton Harris) *t.k.h: hld up in tch in midfield: effrt and hdwy 2f out: drvn to chal ent fnl f: led ins fnl f: sn hdd and outpcd by wnr fnl 100yds* **5/2**[1]

233 3 shd **Silverturnstogold**[29] 7982 4-9-7 **60**..........................(b[1]) TomMarquand 8 63
(Tony Carroll) *in tch in last trio: nt clr run over 2f out: clsd and swtchd rt 2f out: hdwy to chse ldrs 1f out: kpt on ins fnl f* **3/1**[2]

5240 4 3/4 **Maazel (IRE)**[139] 4025 5-9-2 **55**.......................... DanielMuscutt 9 57
(Lee Carter) *hld up in rr: clsd but nt clrest of runs over 1f out: swtchd lft and styd on wl ins fnl f: nt rch ldrs* **25/1**

2433 4 dht **Maid Millie**[55] 7105 3-9-2 **56**..........................(p) LukeMorris 1 57
(Robert Cowell) *chsd ldrs: rdn to ld over 1f out: drvn and hdd ins fnl f: kpt on same pce after* **14/1**

330 6 nk **Harry Beau**[20] 8291 5-9-7 **60**..........................(bt) HollieDoyle 10 61
(David Evans) *led: rdn over 2f out: hdd over 1f out: no ex and wknd ins fnl f* **9/1**

0503 7 1 **Avorisk Et Perils (FR)**[127] 4472 4-9-4 **57**.......................... AdamKirby 11 55
(Gary Moore) *stdd s: chsd ldrs: unable qck u.p over 1f out: kpt on same pce ins fnl f* **20/1**

0222 8 1/2 **Mister Freeze (IRE)**[20] 8279 5-8-13 **52**..........................(vt) LiamKeniry 6 49
(Patrick Chamings) *hld up in last trio: swtchd rt and effrt 2f out: rdn and hdwy over 1f out: no imp ins fnl f* **12/1**

3040 9 2 **Solfeggio (IRE)**[106] 5284 3-9-6 **60**.......................... GeorgeWood 7 51
(Chris Wall) *in tch in midfield: rdn wl over 2f out: unable qck and lost pl over 1f out: kpt on same pce ins fnl f* **5/1**[3]

560- 10 3 **Castelo (IRE)**[439] 6475 3-9-3 **57**.......................... JasonWatson 12 40
(Daniel Kubler) *chsd ldr: rdn over 2f out: lost pl 2f out: wknd ins fnl f* **66/1**

3055 11 4 1/2 **Air Of York (IRE)**[18] 8345 7-9-3 **59**..........................(p) CameronNoble[(3)] 5 31
(Grace Harris) *midfield on outer: rdn over 2f out: sn struggling and outpcd: wknd over 1f out* **14/1**

1000 12 1/2 **Rita's Folly**[46] 7472 3-9-2 **56**.......................... WilliamCarson 2 26
(Anthony Carson) *in tch in midfield: unable qck u.p: lost pl qckly over 1f out: wknd fnl f* **33/1**

1m 25.63s (-0.37) **Going Correction** -0.05s/f (Stan)
WFA 3 from 4yo+ 1lb **12** Ran SP% **123.4**
Speed ratings (Par 101): **100,98,98,97,97 97,96,95,93,89 84,84**
CSF £35.49 CT £100.63 TOTE £13.90: £2.90, £1.10, £1.80; EX 57.50 Trifecta £191.00.
Owner The Savy Group **Bred** James F Hanly **Trained** Epsom, Surrey

FOCUS
The pace was solid from the outset and this looks above-average form for the grade. Straightforward form rated around those close up.

8848 32RED CASINO EBF FILLIES' NOVICE STKS (PLUS 10 RACE) 1m (P)

5:10 (5:13) (Class 5) 2-Y-O **£3,881** (£1,155; £577; £288) **Stalls** Low

Form RPR

4 1 **Oriental Mystique**[14] 8464 2-9-0 0.......................... JimCrowley 7 76+
(David Simcock) *chsd ldr: drvn to chal over 1f out: led jst ins fnl f: styd on strly* **4/1**[2]

3 2 1 1/2 **Declared Interest**[46] 7458 2-9-0 0.......................... RobHornby 5 73
(Ralph Beckett) *chsd ldr: effrt ent fnl 2f: chsd wnr and kpt on same pce u.p fnl 100yds* **9/2**[3]

1 3 nk **Dubai Love**[35] 7826 2-9-7 0.......................... CallumShepherd 6 79
(Saeed bin Suroor) *t.k.h: led: rdn and hrd pressed over 1f out: hdd jst ins fnl f: no ex: lost 2nd and one pce fnl 100yds* **15/8**[1]

4 1 3/4 **Tacitly** 2-9-0 0.......................... DavidEgan 1 68+
(Roger Charlton) *in tch in midfield: effrt 2f out: rdn and chsd ldng trio over 1f out: kpt on but nvr enough pce to get on terms w ldrs* **14/1**

5 1 1/2 **Majestic Noor** 2-9-0 0.......................... RobertHavlin 8 65+
(John Gosden) *in tch in midfield: effrt ent fnl 2f: 5th over 1f out: kpt on but no threat to ldrs ins fnl f* **9/2**[3]

6 2 **Fiveandtwenty** 2-9-0 0.......................... PJMcDonald 4 60
(Mark Johnston) *chsd ldrs: rdn over 2f out: unable qck and outpcd over 1f out: wknd ins fnl f* **33/1**

7 nk **French Polish** 2-9-0 0.......................... TomMarquand 11 60+
(William Haggas) *s.i.s: in rr: effrt over 2f: hdwy over 1f out: no threat to ldrs and kpt on wl ins fnl f (jockey said filly was slowly away)* **20/1**

0 8 2 **Presidential Sweet (ITY)**[28] 8021 2-9-0 0.......................... LukeMorris 12 55
(Marco Botti) *in tch in midfield: pushed along over 3f out: rdn over 2f out: sn struggling and outpcd: wl hld and kpt on same pce fnl f* **50/1**

9 1 **Wand** 2-9-0 0.......................... RichardKingscote 13 53
(Lucy Wadham) *midfield: effrt 2f out: sn outpcd and wl hld over 1f out* **28/1**

10 3 1/2 **Dancing Approach** 2-9-0 0.......................... JasonWatson 3 45
(Roger Charlton) *s.i.s: impeded after 1f: a in rr: outpcd and rdn 2f out: wl hld over 1f out* **20/1**

11 1 **Villanelle** 2-9-0 0.......................... NicolaCurrie 2 42
(Jonathan Portman) *a towards rr: rdn over 2f out: sn struggling and wl hld over 1f out* **66/1**

12 4 1/2 **Josephine Bettany** 2-9-0 0.......................... CharlieBennett 9 32
(Hughie Morrison) *s.i.s and sn towards rr: n.d* **66/1**

13 shd **Ever Amber (IRE)** 2-8-9 0.......................... TylerSaunders[(5)] 10 32
(Jonathan Portman) *rn green: s.i.s and sn dropped to rr: n.d* **100/1**

1m 40.29s (0.49) **Going Correction** -0.05s/f (Stan) **13** Ran SP% **119.7**
Speed ratings (Par 93): **95,93,93,91,89 87,87,85,84,81 80,75,75**
CSF £20.66 TOTE £5.30: £1.60, £1.30, £1.40; EX 26.00 Trifecta £69.10.
Owner Miss K Rausing **Bred** Miss K Rausing **Trained** Newmarket, Suffolk

FOCUS
The trio with experience and the best form dominated this fillies' novice that's worth keeping an eye on, with the bulk of the field bred to do much better next year. The pace was on the steady side. The second and third have been rated near their pre-race figures.

8849 32RED/BRITISH STALLION STUDS EBF FILLIES' NOVICE STKS (PLUS 10 RACE) 7f (P)

5:40 (5:44) (Class 5) 2-Y-O **£3,881** (£1,155; £577; £288) **Stalls** Low

Form RPR

3 1 **Penpal (IRE)**[84] 6072 2-9-0 0.......................... DanielMuscutt 11 73
(James Fanshawe) *chsd ldrs: wnt 2nd over 4f out tl led and travelling strly ent fnl 2f: rdn over 1f out: hdd 1f out: battled bk u.p ins fnl f: led on post* **11/2**[3]

2 nse **Elmetto** 2-9-0 0.......................... HollieDoyle 3 73+
(Hughie Morrison) *t.k.h: chsd ldrs: swtchd ins and effrt 2f out: hdwy u.p to ld 1f out: kpt on u.p: hdd on post* **12/1**

3 1/2 **Must Be An Angel (IRE)** 2-9-0 0..........................(w) TomMarquand 9 72
(Sylvester Kirk) *in tch in midfield: effrt and rn green over 2f out: sn swtchd lft: hdwy u.p over 1f out: styd on wl ins fnl f: nt quite rch ldrs* **50/1**

64 4 3/4 **Royal Nation**[50] 7297 2-8-9 0.......................... SeamusCronin[(5)] 7 70+
(Archie Watson) *t.k.h: hld up in tch in midfield: swtchd rt and pushed along over 1f out: styd on wl ins fnl f: nt quite rch ldrs* **20/1**

40 5 nse **Spinacia (IRE)**[22] 8218 2-9-0 0.......................... CharlesBishop 6 70
(Eve Johnson Houghton) *chsd ldrs: effrt ent fnl 2f: rdn over 1f out: kpt on to chse ldng pair briefly ins fnl f: kpt on but lost 2 pls cl home* **33/1**

02 6 3/4 **Depose**[22] 8218 2-9-0 0..........................(h) JackMitchell 2 68
(Hugo Palmer) *t.k.h: led for over 1f: chsd ldr tl over 4f out: styd pressing ldrs tl unable qck u.p over 1f out: kpt on same pce ins fnl f (jockey said filly ran too free in the early stages)* **5/4**[1]

7 1 **Aswaat** 2-9-0 0.......................... JimCrowley 8 65+
(John Gosden) *dwlt: hld up in midfield: swtchd lft and effrt over 2f out: kpt on wl ins fnl f: no threat to ldrs* **11/4**[2]

8 3 **Widaad** 2-9-0 0.......................... DavidEgan 12 58
(Owen Burrows) *hld up towards rr: effrt ent fnl 2f: pushed along and hdwy over 1f out: no threat to ldrs but kpt on ins fnl f* **14/1**

9 1/2 **Lucky Draw** 2-9-0 0.......................... GeorgeWood 1 57
(Ed de Giles) *midfield: rdn over 2f out: outpcd and btn over 1f out: wknd ins fnl f* **50/1**

10 3 **Dame Denali** 2-9-0 0.......................... WilliamCarson 5 49
(Anthony Carson) *hld up in midfield: rdn over 2f out: sn outpcd and wknd over 1f out* **100/1**

11 1/2 **Celtic Mist (IRE)** 2-9-0 0.......................... JosephineGordon 4 48
(Shaun Keightley) *s.i.s: a in rr: outpcd whn swtchd rt 2f out: n.d (jockey said filly was slowly away)* **100/1**

12 1 **Majestic Endeavour** 2-9-0 0.......................... PJMcDonald 10 45
(Mark Johnston) *a towards rr: effrt over 2f out: no imp over 1f out: nvr involved* **25/1**

13 1 **Dawning (IRE)** 2-9-0 0.......................... RobHornby 14 43+
(Martyn Meade) *wnt lft leaving stalls: a in rr (jockey said filly ran green)* **25/1**

14 2 1/4 **Rhythmic Motion** 2-9-0 0.......................... CharlieBennett 13 37
(Jim Boyle) *wnt lft leaving stalls: hdwy to ld after over 1f out: hdd ent fnl 2f: edgd lft and lost pl over 1f out: sn wknd (jockey said filly hung left-handed throughout)* **100/1**

1m 28.09s (2.09) **Going Correction** -0.05s/f (Stan) **14** Ran SP% **123.1**
Speed ratings (Par 93): **86,85,85,84,84 83,82,79,78,75 74,73,72,69**
CSF £64.64 TOTE £11.50: £1.50, £3.80, £9.00; EX 91.80 Trifecta £3873.00.
Owner Fred Archer Racing - Jannette **Bred** Kilcarn Stud **Trained** Newmarket, Suffolk

FOCUS
A novice to view positively on the whole but it's worth noting that those held up seemed at an advantage, so the closers need marking up. A small step forward from the winner.

8850 32RED ON THE APP STORE NURSERY H'CAP 7f (P)
6:10 (6:12) (Class 4) (0-85,87) 2-Y-O

£6,469 (£1,925; £962; £481; £400; £400) Stalls Low

Form RPR
11 1 **Dance Fever (IRE)**[42] 7570 2-9-11 **87** .... AdamKirby 6 91+
(Clive Cox) *edgd lft leaving stalls: hld up in midfield: effrt over 2f out: drvn and hdwy over 1f out: styd on to ld wl ins fnl f: sn in command* **4/1**[2]

6100 2 1 1/4 **Picture Frame**[39] 7696 2-9-4 **80** .... JosephineGordon 2 81
(Saeed bin Suroor) *in tch in midfield: rdn 3f out: hdwy u.p on inner over 1f out: styd on to ld 100yds: sn hdd and nt match pce of wnr* **7/2**[1]

260 3 shd **Commit No Nuisance (IRE)**[52] 7247 2-8-11 **73** .... DavidEgan 3 73
(William Knight) *edgd lft and bmpd leaving stalls: in rr: rdn over 2f out: styd on strly ins fnl f: snatched 3rd cl home (jockey said colt was slowly away)* **12/1**

321 4 3/4 **Silver Samurai**[20] 8280 2-9-3 **79** .... DanielMuscutt 5 78
(Marco Botti) *t.k.h: hld up in tch in midfield: effrt over 2f out: drvn over 1f out: kpt on ins fnl f* **11/2**

2052 5 1 **One Hart (IRE)**[7] 8665 2-9-4 **80** .... PJMcDonald 1 76
(Mark Johnston) *led: rdn over 1f out: edgd lft 1f out: hdd 100yds: no ex and wknd towards fin* **5/1**[3]

242 6 3/4 **Breath Of Joy**[61] 6928 2-9-4 **80** .... TomMarquand 4 74
(Amy Murphy) *chsd ldr for over 1f: chsd ldrs after: rdn over 2f out: drvn to chse ldr again over 1f out: clsd and pressing ldr whn bmpd 1f out: wknd wl ins fnl f (jockey said filly hung left-handed under pressure)* **11/1**

3516 7 1/2 **Old News**[25] 8110 2-9-4 **83** .... FinleyMarsh(3) 7 76
(Richard Hughes) *hmpd sn after leaving stalls: swtchd lft and hdwy to chse ldr over 5f out: rdn over 2f out: lost 2nd over 1f out: no ex and wknd ins fnl f* **5/1**[3]

1403 8 7 **Banmi (IRE)**[28] 8011 2-8-8 **70** .... HollieDoyle 9 44
(Mohamed Moubarak) *a in rr: n.d (jockey said filly was never travelling)* **33/1**

024 9 nk **Rajguru**[77] 6344 2-8-9 **71** .... LukeMorris 8 45
(Tom Clover) *midfield: rdn over 2f out: sn struggling and wknd over 1f out* **33/1**

1m 24.93s (-1.07) **Going Correction** -0.05s/f (Stan) **9 Ran SP% 112.8**
Speed ratings (Par 98): **104,102,102,101,100 99,99,91,90**
CSF £17.92 CT £150.65 TOTE £5.10: £1.80, £2.00, £4.40; EX 22.20 Trifecta £199.50.
Owner Kennet Valley Thoroughbreds VIII **Bred** Silk Fan Syndicate **Trained** Lambourn, Berks

FOCUS
A useful handicap in which the leaders went off too hard, meaning the race changed complexion around 1f out. The second, third and fourth set a fairly straightforward level.

8851 32RED H'CAP 6f (P)
6:40 (6:45) (Class 2) (0-105,105) 3-Y-O+

£12,450 (£3,728; £1,864; £932; £466; £234) Stalls Low

Form RPR
3534 1 **Show Stealer**[46] 7431 6-8-6 **93** ....(p) CameronNoble(3) 1 102
(Rae Guest) *hld up in tch: clsd on inner over 2f out: rdn to chal ent fnl f: led ins fnl f: r.o wl* **9/1**

0000 2 1 1/4 **Junius Brutus (FR)**[32] 7913 3-8-7 **91** .... SilvestreDeSousa 4 96
(Ralph Beckett) *t.k.h: chsd ldrs: effrt to chal over 1f out: drvn to ld ent fnl f: hdd ins fnl f: kpt on same pce after* **7/1**

3332 3 nse **Lady Dancealot (IRE)**[46] 7467 4-8-2 **86** oh3 .... HayleyTurner 8 91
(David Elsworth) *stdd s: hld up in tch in rr: effrt on outer over 1f out: styd on strly ins fnl f: nvr getting to wnr* **9/1**

0213 4 1 1/4 **Corinthia Knight (IRE)**[19] 8328 4-9-7 **105** .... HollieDoyle 10 106
(Archie Watson) *led for over 1f: chsd ldr: drvn and ev ch over 1f out: no ex and wknd wl ins fnl f* **16/1**

1602 5 1/2 **Beyond Equal**[9] 8607 4-8-4 **88** .... LukeMorris 2 87
(Stuart Kittow) *in tch in midfield: effrt and clsd ent fnl 2f: drvn and pressed ldrs over 1f out: no ex and wknd ins fnl f* **7/2**[1]

6030 6 2 1/2 **Lancelot Du Lac (ITY)**[25] 8127 9-9-2 **100** ....(h) AdamKirby 7 91
(Dean Ivory) *taken down early: hdwy to ld after over 1f: rdn ent fnl 2f: hdd ent fnl f: no ex and wknd ins fnl f* **14/1**

2101 7 shd **Buridan (FR)**[15] 8425 4-8-11 **95** .... TomMarquand 5 86
(Richard Hannon) *hld up in tch: effrt ent fnl 2f: no imp over 1f out: nvr threatened ldrs* **6/1**[3]

2500 8 nk **Pass The Vino (IRE)**[25] 8127 3-8-12 **96** .... DavidEgan 6 86
(Paul D'Arcy) *in tch in midfield: effrt ent fnl 2f: unable qck and no hdwy over 1f out: wknd ins fnl f* **11/2**[2]

0306 9 2 3/4 **Intisaab**[15] 8425 8-8-10 **94** ....(p) JasonWatson 9 75
(David O'Meara) *chsd ldrs on outer: rdn over 2f out: unable qck and lost pl over 1f out: wknd fnl f* **14/1**

1m 10.95s (-2.15) **Going Correction** -0.05s/f (Stan) **9 Ran SP% 103.6**
Speed ratings (Par 109): **112,110,110,108,107 104,104,104,100**
CSF £57.08 CT £429.06 TOTE £9.00: £3.30, £2.40, £2.70; EX 75.40 Trifecta £684.30.
Owner Colin Joseph **Bred** Max Weston **Trained** Newmarket, Suffolk
■ Warsaw Road was withdrawn. Price at time of withdrawal 8/1. Rule 4 applies to all bets - deduction 10p in the £.

FOCUS
A smart sprint handicap which looks like solid form with no obvious hard-luck stories. The second has been rated close to form.

8852 32RED CASINO H'CAP 7f (P)
7:10 (7:12) (Class 4) (0-85,83) 3-Y-O £6,469 (£1,925; £962; £481; £400) Stalls Low

Form RPR
1405 1 **Tipperary Jack (USA)**[70] 6593 3-9-2 **78** .... KierenFox 8 88+
(John Best) *stdd after s: hld up in rr: swtchd ins and hdwy 2f out: clsd and rdn to ld jst ins fnl f: r.o strly and drew clr: readily* **11/2**

5520 2 2 1/4 **Buckingham (IRE)**[34] 7836 3-9-7 **83** .... CharlesBishop 7 86
(Eve Johnson Houghton) *stdd and bmpd leaving stalls: hld up in tch towards rr: effrt over 2f out: swtchd lft and u.p over 1f out: styd on wl ins fnl f: snatched 2nd last stride: no threat to wnr* **5/1**[3]

00-6 3 shd **Reponse Exacte (FR)**[14] 8456 3-9-1 **77** ....(h) TomMarquand 4 80
(Amy Murphy) *in tch in midfield: effrt jst over 2f out: drvn over 1f out: kpt on to chse clr wnr wl ins fnl f: no imp: lost 2nd last stride* **20/1**

0036 4 3/4 **Alhakmah (IRE)**[18] 8349 3-9-3 **79** .... SeanLevey 2 80
(Richard Hannon) *hld up in tch: clsd over 2f out: drvn to chal jst over 1f out tl unable to match pce of wnr jst ins fnl f: lost 2 pls wl ins fnl f* **9/2**[2]

2403 5 nk **Whisper Aloud**[18] 8349 3-8-12 **81** .... Pierre-LouisJamin(7) 6 81+
(Archie Watson) *led: rdn over 2f out: drvn and hrd pressed over 1f out: hdd jst ins fnl f: no ex and sn outpcd: wknd towards fin* **7/1**

0060 5 dht **Jackstar (IRE)**[12] 8522 3-9-4 **80** .... RichardKingscote 9 80
(Tom Dascombe) *in tch towards rr: effrt ent fnl 2f: clsd and nt clrest 1f out: edgd out lft and kpt on ins fnl f: no ch w wnr* **9/4**[1]

5164 7 1 3/4 **Irene May (IRE)**[18] 8349 3-9-4 **80** .... LukeMorris 1 75
(Sylvester Kirk) *chsd ldrs: effrt over 2f out: pressed ldr and hrd drvn and unable qck over 1f out: wknd ins fnl f* **11/1**

1203 8 2 1/4 **Tin Hat (IRE)**[49] 7351 3-9-0 **81** ....(p) GeorgiaDobie(5) 3 70
(Eve Johnson Houghton) *chsd ldr tl over 1f out: wknd ins fnl f* **16/1**

050 9 1/2 **Derry Boy**[13] 8496 3-8-5 **67** .... HollieDoyle 5 55
(David Evans) *in tch in midfield on outer: rdn over 2f out: no ex and outpcd over 1f out: wknd ins fnl f* **8/1**

1m 24.33s (-1.67) **Going Correction** -0.05s/f (Stan) **9 Ran SP% 123.6**
Speed ratings (Par 104): **107,104,104,103,103 103,101,98,97**
CSF £35.68 CT £531.85 TOTE £4.80: £1.60, £3.20, £4.30; EX 64.20 Trifecta £429.80.
Owner Curtis & Tomkins **Bred** Edward A Cox Jr **Trained** Oad Street, Kent

FOCUS
An average 0-85 with the exception of the impressive winner. The pace was even but those patiently ridden came to the fore again. The level is set around the second and third.

8853 32RED H'CAP 1m 3f 219y(P)
7:40 (7:40) (Class 3) (0-95,97) 3-Y-O+

£9,337 (£2,796; £1,398; £699; £349; £175) Stalls Low

Form RPR
0313 1 **Kitaabaat**[39] 7688 4-9-4 **89** ....(h) JimCrowley 2 96
(David Simcock) *stdd s: hld up in rr: clsd over 2f out: effrt u.p on outer over 1f out: styd on wl u.p ins fnl f: carried lft towards fin: led last strides* **3/1**[2]

0000 2 hd **Big Challenge (IRE)**[39] 7688 5-9-0 **88** .... CierenFallon(3) 5 94
(Saeed bin Suroor) *hld up in tch: nt clr run over 2f out: hdwy and switching rt over 1f out: rdn and led ins fnl f: kpt on u.p: hdd last strides* **6/1**[3]

6605 3 nse **Island Brave (IRE)**[74] 6452 5-9-12 **97** .... LukeMorris 4 103
(Heather Main) *hld up in tch: effrt over 2f out: drvn over 1f out: hrd drvn and styd on to chal wl ins fnl f: kpt on but edgd lft towards fin* **6/1**[3]

0115 4 3 1/4 **Sameem (IRE)**[81] 6213 3-9-6 **96** .... PJMcDonald 6 98
(James Tate) *led: rdn ent fnl 2f: drvn over 1f out: hdd ins fnl f: sn btn and wknd wl ins fnl f* **11/8**[1]

0100 5 nk **Jersey Wonder (IRE)**[18] 8350 3-8-11 **87** .... HollieDoyle 7 88
(Jamie Osborne) *chsd ldr: rdn over 2f out: stl ev ch and drvn over 1f out: no ex and wknd ins fnl f* **14/1**

00-6 6 3/4 **To Be Wild (IRE)**[244] 1062 6-9-10 **95** ....(h[1]) AdamKirby 1 94
(Jane Chapple-Hyam) *chsd ldrs: swtchd rt and effrt 2f out: no imp u.p over 1f out: wknd ins fnl f* **10/1**

2m 33.78s (-0.72) **Going Correction** -0.05s/f (Stan)
WFA 3 from 4yo+ 5lb **6 Ran SP% 111.4**
Speed ratings (Par 107): **100,99,99,97,97 96**
CSF £20.39 TOTE £3.30: £1.90, £3.10; EX 19.60 Trifecta £47.80.
Owner Khalifa Dasmal & Partners **Bred** Shadwell Estate Company Limited **Trained** Newmarket, Suffolk
■ Stewards' Enquiry : Luke Morris cautioned: careless riding

FOCUS
This turned into a sprint following a stop-start gallop but the result seems a fair one. The front trio were the only ones to give their running. The third has been rated to form.

8854 RACINGTV.COM H'CAP 1m 3f 219y(P)
8:10 (8:13) (Class 6) (0-55,55) 3-Y-O+

£3,105 (£924; £461; £400; £400; £400) Stalls Low

Form RPR
065 1 **Foresee (GER)**[37] 7759 6-9-3 **48** .... RobHornby 11 55
(Tony Carroll) *chsd ldr after over 1f tl led ent fnl 2f: rdn over 1f out: drvn and hld on wl ins fnl f* **8/1**[3]

0025 2 3/4 **Mistress Nellie**[23] 8204 4-9-3 **48** .... HollieDoyle 3 54
(William Stone) *wl in tch in midfield: effrt 2f out: chsd wnr ent fnl f: pressing wnr and drvn ins fnl f: kpt on but a hld (jockey said filly hung badly right-handed)* **8/1**[3]

0514 3 2 1/4 **Percy's Prince**[35] 7818 3-9-5 **55** ....(p) JimCrowley 1 58
(Amanda Perrett) *hld up in tch in midfield: effrt over 2f out: swtchd lft jst over 1f out: kpt on to chse ldng pair 100yds out: no imp* **11/4**[1]

6050 4 nk **Alramz**[118] 4834 3-9-3 **53** .... DanielMuscutt 7 56
(Lee Carter) *s.i.s: hld up in midfield: swtchd rt and effrt 2f out: hdwy over 1f out: kpt on ins fnl f: no threat to ldrs* **16/1**

0545 5 3/4 **Picture Poet (IRE)**[32] 7909 3-9-3 **53** .... HayleyTurner 8 55
(Henry Spiller) *hld up in last trio: effrt and swtchd lft jst over 2f out: kpt on u.p ins fnl f: nvr trbld ldrs* **12/1**

4023 6 nse **Born To Reason (IRE)**[11] 8553 5-9-3 **48** ....(b) RobertHavlin 4 48
(Alexandra Dunn) *impeded leaving stalls: sn led: hdd after over 1f out: chsd ldrs: effrt 2f out: drvn and no ex 1f out: wknd ins fnl f* **9/1**

5400 7 1/2 **Sweet Nature (IRE)**[22] 8224 4-9-5 **50** ....(p) GeorgeDowning 12 50
(Laura Mongan) *swtchd rt after s: hld up towards rr: pushed along ent fnl 2f: rdn and hdwy over 1f out: nvr trbld ldrs* **66/1**

5443 8 2 **Passing Clouds**[22] 8224 4-9-6 **51** .... KierenFox 5 47
(Michael Attwater) *rousted along leaving stalls: hdwy to ld after over 1f out: rdn and hdd ent fnl 2f: no ex and btn 1f out: wknd ins fnl f* **6/1**[2]

3631 9 hd **Ramatuelle**[51] 7270 3-9-5 **55** ....(b) LukeMorris 2 52
(Laura Mongan) *in tch in midfield: rdn ent fnl 2f: drvn and unable qck over 1f out: wknd ins fnl f* **25/1**

10 3 **Snow Leopard (IRE)**[98] 5567 3-9-1 **51** .... RaulDaSilva 14 43
(Tony Carroll) *stdd and dropped in bhd after s: hld up in rr: rdn over 2f out: no imp and wknd over 1f out* **40/1**

0341 11 5 **Dyagilev**[11] 8553 4-9-7 **52** ....(b) AdrianMcCarthy 6 35
(Lydia Pearce) *stdd bk after s: hld up in midfield: wnt lft and hdwy on outer 4f out: pushed along 2f out: outpcd and btn over 1f out: wknd ins fnl f (jockey said gelding hung left-handed throughout)* **6/1**[2]

0036 12 4 **Famous Dynasty (IRE)**[23] 8204 5-9-3 **48** .... CharlieBennett 13 25
(Michael Blanshard) *hld up towards rr: wd and effrt wl over 2f out: sn btn* **16/1**

0300 13 13 **Dimmesdale**[36] 7790 4-9-5 **50** ....(p[1]) LiamJones 9 6
(John O'Shea) *dwlt and rousted along leaving stalls: hdwy to chse ldrs after 2f: rdn over 3f out: lost pl and bhd 2f out: wknd* **16/1**

2m 33.26s (-1.24) **Going Correction** -0.05s/f (Stan)
WFA 3 from 4yo+ 5lb **13 Ran SP% 120.6**
Speed ratings (Par 101): **102,101,100,99,99 99,98,97,97,95 92,89,80**
CSF £70.47 CT £224.76 TOTE £10.70: £3.20, £3.30, £1.10; EX 74.70 Trifecta £352.50.

Owner Millen & Cooke **Bred** Graf U Grafin V Stauffenberg **Trained** Cropthorne, Worcs

FOCUS

A weak middle-distance handicap that isn't worth dwelling on. The pace was steady and those ridden prominently were seen to advantage. Straightforward form rated around the second.

T/Plt: £690.10 to a £1 stake. Pool: £55,445.99 - 58.65 winning units T/Qpdt: £248.70 to a £1 stake. Pool: £6,272.99 - 18.66 winning units **Steve Payne**

8657 NOTTINGHAM (L-H)

Wednesday, November 6

OFFICIAL GOING: Heavy (soft in places; 4.7)

Wind: Virtually nil Weather: Cloudy but dry

8855 DOWNLOAD THE MANSIONBET APP MAIDEN FILLIES' STKS (PLUS 10 RACE) 1m 75y

12:20 (12:20) (Class 5) 2-Y-O £3,881 (£1,155; £577; £288) Stalls Centre

Form RPR

1 **Moonlight In Paris (IRE)** 2-9-0 0 KieranO'Neill 2 78+
(John Gosden) *hld up in tch on inner: hdwy towards centre 3f out: led wl over 1f out: rdn and edgd markedly rt ins fnl f: hld on wl towards fin* **5/1**

2 *shd* **Sun Bear** 2-9-0 0 RobertHavlin 8 78+
(John Gosden) *hld up towards rr: stdy hdwy nr stands' rail 3f out: trckd ldrs 2f out: rdn over 1f out: styd on to chal ins fnl f: ev ch: jst hld* **7/2**[2]

03 3 *1 3/4* **Warne's Army**[22] 8232 2-9-0 0 FrannyNorton 10 75
(Mark Johnston) *sltly checked sn after s: trckd ldrs: hdwy 4f out: chsd ldr over 2f out: rdn wl over 1f out: kpt on same pce* **14/1**

4 *6* **Our Girl Sheila (IRE)** 2-9-0 0 CliffordLee 4 62
(K R Burke) *hld up towards rr: pushed along and hdwy towards centre 3f out: rdn 2f out: styd on fnl f* **16/1**

5 *2* **Soramond (GER)** 2-9-0 0 KieranShoemark 12 58
(Ed Dunlop) *t.k.h: led: c wd st towards stands' side: pushed along over 2f out: rdn and hdd wl over 1f out: grad wknd* **33/1**

6 *4* **Frankenstella (IRE)** 2-9-0 0 JasonHart 9 49
(John Quinn) *dwlt: green and in rr: pushed along 4f out: rdn 3f out: plugged on fnl 2f* **4/1**[3]

04 7 *4* **Girl From Mars (IRE)**[21] 8258 2-9-0 0 RichardKingscote 11 41
(Tom Dascombe) *in rr: sme hdwy 3f out: rdn along over 2f out: n.d* **25/1**

6 8 *3/4* **Beauty Stone (IRE)**[26] 8093 2-9-0 0 BrettDoyle 5 39
(Charlie Appleby) *awkward s: t.k.h and sn prom: cl up after 3f: pushed along over 3f out: rdn over 2f out: sn wknd (jockey said filly had become unbalanced on the sticky ground on this occasion)* **15/8**[1]

0 9 *nk* **High Moor Flyer**[28] 8021 2-9-0 0 JackGarritty 1 39
(Jedd O'Keeffe) *t.k.h: prom on inner: pushed along 4f out: rdn 3f out: sn wknd* **66/1**

0 10 *16* **Sea Of Shadows**[12] 8510 2-8-9 0 GerO'Neill(5) 7 5
(Michael Easterby) *t.k.h: chsd ldrs: pushed along over 3f out: sn rdn and wknd* **125/1**

00 11 *8* **Volcano Bay**[12] 8510 2-9-0 0 RossaRyan 6
(Ismail Mohammed) *t.k.h: hld up: a towards rr* **80/1**

1m 56.62s (9.92) **Going Correction** +1.20s/f (Soft) **11 Ran SP% 116.5**

Speed ratings (Par 93): **98,97,96,90,88 84,80,79,79,63 55**

CSF £22.11 TOTE £7.50: £2.00, £1.40, £2.70; EX 27.60 Trifecta £166.30.

Owner S Mulryan, Mrs J Magnier, Mrs P Shanahan **Bred** Skymarc Farm **Trained** Newmarket, Suffolk

FOCUS

Inner Track for the final meeting of 2019 and it was obviously hard work underfoot. Rail was set 2yds out on the home bend, adding 6yds to races around the bend. They went just an ordinary pace in this interesting fillies' maiden and ignored the far side off the home turn. It was a 1-2 for John Gosden. Add 6yds. The opening level is fluid.

8856 MANSIONBET BEATEN BY A HEAD NURSERY H'CAP 1m 75y

12:50 (12:50) (Class 5) (0-75,75) 2-Y-O

£3,881 (£1,155; £577; £300; £300; £300) Stalls Centre

Form RPR

635 1 **Hooroo (IRE)**[16] 8394 2-8-8 **62** (p[1]) CliffordLee 2 66
(K R Burke) *cl up: wd st: rdn to ld over 2f out: jnd and drvn over 1f out: hdd narrowly ins fnl f: rallied gamely to ld again nr fin* **5/2**[1]

6211 2 *hd* **She's A Unicorn**[12] 8509 2-9-0 **75** (v) PoppyFielding(7) 8 79
(Tom Dascombe) *trckd ldrs: wd st: hdwy over 2f out: chal over 1f out: rdn to take slt ld ins fnl f: hdd and no ex nr fin* **7/2**[2]

0454 3 *3 1/2* **Global Agreement**[15] 8430 2-8-9 **63** (v) JFEgan 7 59
(Milton Harris) *dwlt and hld up towards rr: hdwy over 3f out: chsd ldrs and rdn 2f out: drvn to chse ldng pair ent fnl f: no imp* **6/1**[3]

0310 4 *8* **Sterling Stamp (IRE)**[20] 8297 2-9-4 **72** (p[1]) RossaRyan 3 50
(Paul Cole) *hld up towards rr: hdwy towards centre 3f out: sn rdn along: plugged on fnl 2f: n.d* **14/1**

450 5 *2 1/4* **Sea Of Cool (IRE)**[14] 8461 2-8-1 **55** ow1 AdrianMcCarthy 5 28
(John Ryan) *a towards rr* **20/1**

0541 6 *hd* **Parikarma (IRE)**[23] 8201 2-9-5 **73** RobertHavlin 6 46
(Ed Dunlop) *trckd ldrs: pushed along over 3f out: rdn wl over 2f out: sn wknd (trainer's rep said filly was unsuited by the heavy ground, which in his opinion, was riding very testing on this occasion and would prefer a sounder surface)* **7/2**[2]

0650 7 *2* **Barry Magoo**[38] 7725 2-8-2 **56** LukeMorris 1 24
(Adam West) *prom: rdn along over 3f out: wknd over 2f out* **28/1**

3451 8 *5* **Isobar Wind (IRE)**[37] 7768 2-8-13 **67** (b) BenCurtis 4 24
(David Evans) *led: rdn along over 3f out: hdd over 2f out: sn drvn and wknd* **9/1**

1m 57.09s (10.39) **Going Correction** +1.20s/f (Soft) **8 Ran SP% 112.2**

Speed ratings (Par 96): **96,95,92,84,82 81,79,74**

CSF £10.84 CT £45.18 TOTE £2.50: £1.10, £2.00, £1.60; EX 12.70 Trifecta £56.70.

Owner Nick Bradley Racing 2 & Mrs E Burke **Bred** Old Carhue Stud **Trained** Middleham Moor, N Yorks

FOCUS

A modest nursery, run at a routine pace, and again the stands' side was favoured. Add 6yds. The first two have been rated in line with their best pre-race figures.

8857 MANSIONBET PROUD TO SUPPORT BRITISH RACING MAIDEN STKS (DIV I) 1m 75y

1:25 (1:27) (Class 5) 2-Y-O £3,881 (£1,155; £577; £288) Stalls Centre

Form RPR

43 1 **Mishriff (IRE)**[12] 8518 2-9-5 0 DavidEgan 6 88+
(John Gosden) *trckd ldrs: smooth hdwy and cl up 3f out: led 2f out: sn clr easily* **5/6**[1]

0 2 *10* **Spanish Persuader (FR)**[12] 8528 2-9-5 0 FrannyNorton 5 65
(Mark Johnston) *cl up on outer: slt ld after 2f: wd st towards stands' rail: pushed along 3f out: rdn and hdd 2f out: sn drvn: kpt on fnl f: no ch w wnr* **14/1**

0 3 *5* **Justified**[21] 8244 2-9-5 0 RichardKingscote 3 55
(Mark Johnston) *slt ld 2f: cl up: rdn along over 2f out: sn drvn and one pce* **6/1**[3]

0 4 *1 1/2* **King's Castle (IRE)**[14] 8464 2-9-5 0 BenCurtis 4 51
(William Haggas) *t.k.h: chsd ldrs: pushed along 3f out: rdn 2f out: sn btn* **2/1**[2]

0 5 *6* **Screeching Dragon (IRE)**[76] 6368 2-9-5 0 (t[1]) RossaRyan 9 39
(Kevin Frost) *in tch: hdwy over 3f out and sn pushed along: rdn wl over 2f out: outpcd* **100/1**

6 *3 1/2* **Zero Limits** 2-8-12 0 StefanoCherchi(7) 1 31
(Marco Botti) *dwlt: a towards rr* **22/1**

7 *1/2* **Donald Llewellyn** 2-9-5 0 HectorCrouch 7 30
(Gary Moore) *trckd ldrs: rdn along over 3f out: sn wknd* **25/1**

0660 8 *7* **Anno Lucis (IRE)**[13] 8504 2-9-5 0 LukeMorris 8 16
(Sir Mark Prescott Bt) *a towards rr* **80/1**

50 9 *2 1/2* **Dangeroffizz (IRE)**[42] 7586 2-9-5 0 DuranFentiman 2 10
(Tim Easterby) *in tch: rdn along 4f out: sn outpcd* **50/1**

10 *27* **Highfield Haven** 2-9-5 0 JasonHart 11
(John Quinn) *a in rr* **50/1**

U **Tindrum** 2-9-5 0 JaneElliott 10
(Heather Main) *wnt bdly rt and uns rdr at the s* **100/1**

1m 56.6s (9.90) **Going Correction** +1.20s/f (Soft) **11 Ran SP% 124.2**

Speed ratings (Par 96): **98,88,83,81,75 72,71,64,62,35**

CSF £16.56 TOTE £1.70: £1.60, £2.70, £1.70; EX 12.90 Trifecta £89.90.

Owner Prince A A Faisal **Bred** Nawara Stud Limited **Trained** Newmarket, Suffolk

FOCUS

This 2yo maiden usually goes to a Pattern-class performer and it proved one-way traffic. Add 6yds. It's been rated cautiously.

8858 MANSIONBET PROUD TO SUPPORT BRITISH RACING MAIDEN STKS (DIV II) 1m 75y

1:55 (1:57) (Class 5) 2-Y-O £3,881 (£1,155; £577; £288) Stalls Centre

Form RPR

32 1 **Salamanca School (FR)**[21] 8244 2-9-5 0 FrannyNorton 10 76+
(Mark Johnston) *chsd ldr: wd st to stands' rail and led over 4f out: pushed clr 2f out: rdn ins fnl f: kpt on (vet said colt had lost its right hind shoe)* **3/1**[2]

2 *1 1/2* **Book Review** 2-9-5 0 RobertHavlin 6 73+
(John Gosden) *dwlt and towards rr: hdwy 3f out and sn pushed along: chsd ldrs and rdn over 1f out: styd on strly fnl f* **7/2**[3]

2 3 *2* **Phoenix Aquilus (IRE)**[21] 8257 2-9-5 0 TomQueally 7 69
(Seamus Durack) *trckd ldrs: hdwy and wd st: chsd wnr 3f out: rdn along wl over 1f out: kpt on same pce* **14/1**

00 4 *nk* **Dreaming Blue**[15] 8424 2-9-5 0 TonyHamilton 11 68
(Richard Fahey) *chsd ldrs: hdwy 3f out: rdn along 2f out: sn drvn and kpt on same pce appr fnl f* **66/1**

00 5 *10* **Edebez (IRE)**[29] 7981 2-9-5 0 JimmyQuinn 5 47
(Seamus Mullins) *towards rr: hdwy 3f out: sn rdn and nvr nr ldrs* **150/1**

4 6 *7* **French Asset (IRE)**[13] 8504 2-9-5 0 LouisSteward 2 32
(Sir Michael Stoute) *in tch: pushed along over 3f out: rdn over 2f out: sn edgd lft and wknd* **9/4**[1]

0 7 *9* **I'm Easy**[32] 7902 2-9-0 0 GerO'Neill(5) 1 13
(Michael Easterby) *dwlt: a bhd* **100/1**

3 8 *14* **Camahawk**[12] 8511 2-9-5 0 DuranFentiman 3
(Tim Easterby) *chsd ldng pair: wd st to stands' rail and sn chsng wnr: rdn along over 3f out: sn wknd (trainer's rep could offer no explanation for the gelding's poor performance)* **5/1**

050 9 *5* **Abenakian (IRE)**[36] 7787 2-9-2 38 (b) TimClark(3) 8
(Jane Chapple-Hyam) *t.k.h: led and sn clr: hung rt and rn wd v wd home turn: hdd over 4f out: sn wknd (jockey said gelding did not handle the bend on this occasion)* **200/1**

10 *1 3/4* **Witch Hunt (IRE)** 2-9-5 0 KieranShoemark 9
(David Menuisier) *dwlt: a bhd* **16/1**

11 *1 1/4* **Critique (IRE)** 2-9-5 0 HectorCrouch 4
(Ed Walker) *midfield: rdn along wl over 3f out: sn wknd* **16/1**

1m 57.12s (10.42) **Going Correction** +1.20s/f (Soft) **11 Ran SP% 116.7**

Speed ratings (Par 96): **95,93,91,91,81 74,65,51,46,44 43**

CSF £13.96 TOTE £3.80: £1.40, £1.40, £3.40; EX 16.10 Trifecta £113.70.

Owner Dr J Walker **Bred** Jean-Francois Gribomont **Trained** Middleham Moor, N Yorks

FOCUS

There was a brisk early pace on here and the race fell apart. It was 2.62sec slower than the preceding division. Add 6yds.

8859 GAMBLE RESPONSIBLY WITH MANSIONBET NURSERY H'CAP 1m 2f 50y

2:30 (2:31) (Class 5) (0-70,67) 2-Y-O £3,881 (£1,155; £577; £300) Stalls Low

Form RPR

5500 1 **Ami Li Bert (IRE)**[13] 8493 2-8-1 **50** TheodoreLadd(3) 2 52
(Michael Appleby) *trckd ldr: pushed along over 2f out: sn rdn: drvn ent fnl f: styd on wl to ld last 50yds* **6/1**

0020 2 *3/4* **Never Said Nothing (IRE)**[15] 8415 2-9-0 **60** AlistairRawlinson 1 61
(Jonathan Portman) *led: wd st to stands' rail pushed along 3f out: rdn 2f out: clr over 1f out: drvn ins fnl f: wknd and hdd last 50yds* **4/1**[3]

0001 3 *2 1/2* **Goddess Of Fire**[13] 8493 2-8-2 **55** (p) LauraPearson(7) 4 51
(John Ryan) *dwlt and in rr: hdwy on outer over 5f out: wd st and sn cl up: rdn along wl over 2f out: kpt on same pce* **7/2**[2]

3153 4 *11* **International Lion**[25] 8124 2-9-7 **67** (p) TonyHamilton 3 43
(Richard Fahey) *chsd ldng pair: pushed along over 4f out: rdn over 3f out: drvn over 2f out: sn btn (trainer's rep could offer no explanation for the colt's poor performance)* **5/6**[1]

2m 28.96s (15.56) **Going Correction** +1.20s/f (Soft) **4 Ran SP% 111.1**

Speed ratings (Par 96): **85,84,82,73**

CSF £26.97 TOTE £5.60; EX 21.90 Trifecta £43.30.

Owner S & R Racing Partnership **Bred** Johnston King **Trained** Oakham, Rutland
FOCUS
An ordinary nursery that served up a proper test. Add 6yds. A token figure has been given.

8860 MANSIONBET BEST ODDS GUARANTEED H'CAP 5f 8y
3:00 (3:01) (Class 4) (0-80,79) 3-Y-0+

£7,762 (£2,310; £1,154; £577; £300; £300) **Stalls** High

Form RPR
0140 **1** **Colonel Frank**[4] 8766 5-9-5 77 FrannyNorton 6 85
(Mick Quinn) *cl up: rdn to ld wl over 1f out: drvn ins fnl f: hld on wl towards fin (trainer said, regarding the apparent improvement in form, the gelding appreciated the drop in trip to 5 furlongs on this occasion)* **10/1**
6103 **2** *nk* **Afandem (IRE)**[21] 8262 5-9-2 79 (p) DannyRedmond(5) 7 86
(Tim Easterby) *dwlt and in rr: swtchd lft and hdwy 2f out: rdn ent fnl f: sn chal and ev ch whn edgd rt ins fnl 100yds: no ex nr fin* **8/1**
0656 **3** *1 ½* **Red Pike (IRE)**[7] 8660 8-9-1 73 GrahamLee 5 75
(Bryan Smart) *cl up: rdn and ev ch over 1f out: drvn ent fnl f: kpt on same pce* **22/1**
3024 **4** *½* **Show Palace**[7] 8660 6-9-4 76 (p) RossaRyan 1 76
(Jennie Candlish) *racd wd towards far side: cl up: rdn and ev ch over 1f out: drvn and kpt on same pce fnl f* **9/2**[1]
0110 **5** *nse* **Smokey Lane (IRE)**[12] 8522 5-9-3 75 CliffordLee 9 75
(David Evans) *in tch: hdwy towards stands' side 2f out: rdn over 1f out: chsd ldrs ins fnl f: kpt on towards fin* **9/1**
0021 **6** *1 ¾* **Bellevarde (IRE)**[7] 8660 5-9-6 78 5ex BenCurtis 4 71
(Richard Price) *prom: rdn along 2f out: drvn and wknd over 1f out* **9/2**[1]
4541 **7** *hd* **Michaels Choice**[20] 8285 3-8-12 70 (b) DavidProbert 2 63
(William Jarvis) *trckd ldrs: rdn along 2f out: sn wknd* **5/1**[2]
0642 **8** *1* **Hieronymus**[7] 8660 3-8-12 70 (vt) TomQueally 3 59
(Seamus Durack) *trckd ldrs: effrt 2f out: sn rdn and btn* **7/1**[3]
20- **9** *8* **Andre Amar (IRE)**[82] 6195 3-9-6 78 PaulMulrennan 8 38
(Robyn Brisland) *dwlt: a in rr* **66/1**
4006 **10** *1 ¼* **Big Les (IRE)**[15] 8428 4-9-6 78 JasonHart 10 34
(Karen McLintock) *racd nr stands' rail: led: pushed along 1/2-way: rdn and hdd wl over 1f out: sn wknd* **7/1**[3]
1m 4.69s (4.49) **Going Correction** +1.20s/f (Soft) **10** Ran SP% **114.1**
Speed ratings (Par 105): **109,108,106,105,105 102,102,100,87,85**
CSF £85.48 CT £1711.21 TOTE £9.60: £2.60, £2.00, £5.80; EX 97.70 Trifecta £1371.30.
Owner Kenny Bruce **Bred** Eliza Park International Pty Ltd **Trained** Newmarket, Suffolk
FOCUS
Competitive stuff. The main action came down the centre. The winner has been rated close to his old best.

8861 MANSIONBET OFFER DEPOSIT H'CAP 5f 8y
3:35 (3:36) (Class 6) (0-65,65) 3-Y-0+

£3,234 (£962; £481; £300; £300; £300) **Stalls** High

Form RPR
2205 **1** **Lydiate Lady**[7] 8660 7-9-2 60 JasonHart 4 66
(Eric Alston) *racd centre: slt ld: pushed along and hdd narrowly over 2f out: rdn to ld again over 1f out: drvn and edgd lft ins fnl f: kpt on wl towards fin* **5/2**[1]
0060 **2** *1 ¼* **Robbian**[8] 8632 8-8-2 51 oh6 AledBeech(5) 3 53
(Charles Smith) *racd centre: trckd ldrs: hdwy wl over 1f out: rdn to chal ins fnl f: ev ch and edgd lft: kpt on same pce towards fin* **12/1**
0020 **3** *5* **Intense Style (IRE)**[27] 8070 7-9-0 61 DarraghKeenan(3) 5 45
(Denis Quinn) *dwlt and sn detached in rr: hdwy wl over 1f out: rdn and kpt on strly fnl f: tk 3rd nr fin (jockey said gelding was slowly away)* **14/1**
2156 **4** *1* **Atty's Edge**[16] 8401 3-8-12 59 MitchGodwin(3) 2 39
(Christopher Mason) *chsd ldrs centre: rdn along and hdwy over 1f out: drvn ent fnl f: lost 3rd towards fin* **9/2**[3]
-003 **5** *6* **Ebitda**[21] 8263 5-9-0 65 JonathanFisher(7) 6 23
(Scott Dixon) *cl up centre: disp ld 1/2-way: led over 2f out: rdn and hdd wl over 1f out: sn drvn and wknd* **11/4**[2]
4103 **6** *2* **Astrophysics**[8] 8632 7-9-1 59 (p) PaulMulrennan 7 10
(Lynn Siddall) *chsd ldrs centre: rdn along 2f out: drvn and wknd over 1f out* **5/1**
2166 **7** *4 ½* **Majorette**[56] 7078 5-9-4 62 EoinWalsh 1
(Brian Barr) *s.i.s: a bhd (jockey said mare had jumped awkwardly leaving the stalls and was slowly away as a result)* **25/1**
5340 **8** *4 ½* **Ginvincible**[21] 8263 3-9-4 62 BarryMcHugh 8
(James Given) *racd alone on stands' rail: cl up: rdn along over 2f out: sn drvn and wknd* **14/1**
1m 5.25s (5.05) **Going Correction** +1.20s/f (Soft) **8** Ran SP% **115.0**
Speed ratings (Par 101): **104,102,94,92,82 79,72,65**
CSF £33.29 CT £237.39 TOTE £2.80: £1.10, £3.50, £3.90; EX 27.80 Trifecta £237.70.
Owner The Scotch Piper Racing **Bred** Catridge Farm Stud **Trained** Longton, Lancs
FOCUS
The ground played a huge part in this moderate sprint handicap. It's been rated cautiously.

8862 AJA LADY RIDERS' H'CAP (FOR LADY AMATEUR RIDERS) 1m 2f 50y
4:05 (4:07) (Class 5) (0-75,75) 3-Y-0+

£3,743 (£1,161; £580; £300; £300; £300) **Stalls** Low

Form RPR
2111 **1** **Gamesters Icon**[12] 8515 4-9-13 72 (tp) MissAliceStevens(5) 6 81
(Oliver Greenall) *trckd ldrs: hdwy to ld over 6f out: pushed along 4f out: rdn and hdd over 2f out: cl up: drvn to ld again jst ins fnl f: edgd lft and kpt on wl towards fin* **2/1**[1]
1000 **2** *¾* **Bombero (IRE)**[21] 8248 5-9-9 68 MissCharlotteCrane(5) 16 75
(Ed de Giles) *prom: trckd wnr 6f out: cl up 4f out: rdn to ld jst over 2f out: hdd jst ins fnl f: sn edgd lft: kpt on* **20/1**
3 *2* **She's A Novelty (IRE)**[132] 4314 4-9-6 65 MissAntoniaPeck(5) 10 68
(Dai Williams) *chsd ldrs: hdwy 3f out: rdn over 2f out: chsd ldng pair over 1f out: kpt on but no imp towards fin* **12/1**
0030 **4** *1* **Firby (IRE)**[12] 8515 4-9-5 66 MissRachelTaylor(7) 12 67
(Michael Dods) *hld up towards rr: hdwy over 3f out: effrt and in tch whn hung lft to far rail 2f out: sn rdn: styd on wl fnl f: nrst fin (jockey said gelding had hung left-handed in the straight)* **33/1**
3204 **5** *½* **Don't Jump George (IRE)**[26] 8086 4-10-4 72 (t) MissAbbieMcCain 2 72
(Shaun Lycett) *dwlt and in rr: hdwy on far side 3f out: chsd ldrs and rdn wl over 1f out: kpt on same pce fnl f* **16/1**
1645 **6** *¾* **Stormingin (IRE)**[46] 7452 6-10-1 74 MissKatyBrooks(5) 1 73
(Gary Moore) *towards rr: hdwy over 4f out: chsd ldrs wl over 2f out: sn rdn and kpt on same pce* **10/1**
053- **7** *5* **Roudrapour (FR)**[334] 8893 4-9-8 65 MissSarahBowen(3) 8 54
(Tony Carroll) *towards rr: hdwy over 4f out: in tch whn sltly hmpd 2f out: sn swtchd rt and rdn: no imp* **10/1**
2210 **8** *hd* **Luna Magic**[12] 8515 5-10-5 73 MissBrodieHampson 14 61
(Archie Watson) *hld up in tch on outer: hdwy 4f out: chsd ldng pair 3f out: rdn over 2f out: sn drvn and grad wknd* **9/1**[3]
3115 **9** *1 ½* **Deinonychus**[12] 8515 8-10-2 70 (p) MissGinaAndrews 5 55
(Michael Appleby) *in tch: effrt and hdwy over 3f out: rdn along and chsd ldrs over 2f out: sn drvn and btn* **9/2**[2]
0/00 **10** *7* **Flight Officer**[16] 8396 8-9-12 73 MissMaisieSharp(7) 4 44
(Michael Easterby) *nvr bttr than midfield* **66/1**
0552 **11** *6* **Bollin Ted**[43] 7544 5-9-10 64 (p) MissEmilyEasterby 15 23
(Tim Easterby) *chsd ldrs: rdn along 3f out: wknd over 2f out* **12/1**
0150 **12** *½* **Spirit Of Sarwan (IRE)**[13] 8507 5-9-12 66 (v) MissBeckySmith 13 24
(Stef Keniry) *dwlt: a in rr* **25/1**
5000 **13** *hd* **Glacier Fox**[15] 8422 4-9-1 62 (p[1]) MissMeganJordan(7) 7 20
(Mark Loughnane) *chsd ldng pair on inner: rdn along over 3f out: sn wknd* **66/1**
05-0 **14** *5* **Novelty Seeker (USA)**[21] 8260 10-10-7 75 MissJoannaMason 9 23
(Michael Easterby) *a towards rr* **20/1**
61-0 **15** *31* **Scrafton**[300] 162 8-9-4 65 MissEmmaWilkinson(7) 11
(Tony Carroll) *midfield: rdn along over 3f out: sn outpcd* **50/1**
00 **16** *¾* **Western Dawn (IRE)**[23] 8181 3-10-0 71 MissSerenaBrotherton 3
(Phillip Makin) *sn led: hdd over 6f out: chsd ldrs: rdn along over 3f out: sn wknd (jockey said gelding had ran too freely)* **25/1**
2m 27.75s (14.35) **Going Correction** +1.20s/f (Soft)
WFA 3 from 4yo+ 3lb **16** Ran SP% **126.1**
Speed ratings (Par 103): **90,89,87,87,86 86,82,81,80,75 70,69,69,65,40 40**
CSF £52.53 CT £415.74 TOTE £2.50: £1.70, £4.40, £1.80, £7.70; EX 45.30 Trifecta £582.60.
Owner Gamesters Partnership **Bred** D V Williams **Trained** Oldcastle Heath, Cheshire
FOCUS
A modest handicap, confined to lady amateur riders, and again the ground found out most. Add 6yds. The winner has been rated in line with her Doncaster win.
T/Plt: £388.40 to a £1 stake. Pool: £35,494.92 - 66.71 winning units. T/Qpdt: £124.50 to a £1 stake. Pool: £3,585.87 - 21.31 winning units. **Joe Rowntree**

8665 WOLVERHAMPTON (A.W) (L-H)
Wednesday, November 6

OFFICIAL GOING: Tapeta: standard
Wind: Light behind Weather: Overcast

8863 BOMBARDIER "MARCH TO YOUR OWN DRUM" H'CAP 1m 142y (Tp)
4:50 (4:50) (Class 6) (0-60,60) 3-Y-0+

£2,781 (£827; £413; £400; £400; £400) **Stalls** Low

Form RPR
1 **Tio Esteban (FR)**[41] 7639 4-8-7 46 oh1 KieranO'Neill 13 56+
(W J Martin, Ire) *s.s: hld up: hdwy on outer over 2f out: rdn to ld ins fnl f: r.o: comf (trainer's rep said, regarding the apparent improvement in form, the gelding had stripped fitter for its reappearance run after a 98 day break and appeared to benefit from the tapeta surface on this occasion)* **3/1**[1]
2565 **2** *2* **I Think So (IRE)**[14] 8466 4-9-0 53 (b) DougieCostello 11 57
(David Loughnane) *chsd ldrs: wnt 2nd over 2f out: led over 1f out: rdn and hdd ins fnl f: styd on same pce* **7/1**
0-30 **3** *nse* **Kybosh (IRE)**[160] 3275 3-8-10 52 JimmyQuinn 10 57
(Michael Appleby) *hld up: hdwy u.p over 1f out: styd on* **14/1**
4206 **4** *1* **Barbarosa (IRE)**[28] 8025 3-9-3 59 (p) PhilDennis 7 62
(Michael Herrington) *prom: rdn over 1f out: styd on same pce wl ins fnl f* **7/2**[2]
0400 **5** *1 ¼* **Is It Off (IRE)**[27] 8068 4-9-4 57 (p) JoeyHaynes 3 56
(Sean Curran) *chsd ldr tl led over 2f out: rdn and hdd over 1f out: no ex ins fnl f* **8/1**
6040 **6** *3* **King Oswald (USA)**[34] 7858 6-9-7 60 (tp) DavidProbert 4 53
(James Unett) *hld up: hdwy over 1f out: sn rdn: no ex ins fnl f* **11/2**[3]
0340 **7** *½* **Zarkavon**[141] 3960 5-8-7 46 oh1 (p) JamesSullivan 8 38
(John Wainwright) *hmpd sn after s: hld up: swtchd lft over 1f out: sn rdn: n.d* **33/1**
-054 **8** *5* **Carlow Boy (IRE)**[76] 6361 3-8-4 46 oh1 (b) JaneElliott 2 28
(Christopher Kellett) *prom: rdn over 2f out: sn wknd* **28/1**
003 **9** *hd* **Medici Moon**[22] 8223 5-9-3 56 (p) ShaneKelly 1 37
(Richard Price) *led: rdn and hdd over 2f out: wknd over 1f out (trainer's rep could offer no explanation for the gelding's poor performance)* **9/1**
6060 **10** *2 ¼* **Transpennine Gold**[32] 7909 3-8-5 47 (p) AndrewMullen 12 24
(Michael Dods) *chsd ldrs: rdn over 2f out: wknd over 1f out* **18/1**
3600 **11** *9* **Johni Boxit**[83] 6121 4-8-11 53 (p w) WilliamCox(3) 5 10
(Brian Barr) *prom: lost pl after 1f: rdn over 3f out: wknd over 2f out* **50/1**
1m 47.75s (-2.35) **Going Correction** -0.175s/f (Stan)
WFA 3 from 4yo+ 3lb **11** Ran SP% **116.5**
Speed ratings (Par 101): **103,101,101,100,99 96,96,91,91,89 81**
CSF £23.74 CT £218.20 TOTE £4.30: £1.60, £2.90, £5.40; EX 25.10 Trifecta £208.80.
Owner W J Martin **Bred** Mme Larissa Kneip & Mlle Sandrine Grevet **Trained** Enniscorthy, Co Wexford
FOCUS
They went a good gallop and it set up for a closer. A minor pb from the winner, but the second and fourth offer perspective.

8864 BOMBARDIER BRITISH HOPPED AMBER BEER CLASSIFIED STKS 7f 36y (Tp)
5:20 (5:21) (Class 6) 3-Y-0+

£2,781 (£827; £413; £400; £400; £400) **Stalls** High

Form RPR
0004 **1** **Ishebayorgrey (IRE)**[19] 8306 7-9-1 55 (h) TomEaves 8 62
(Iain Jardine) *s.i.s: hld up: hdwy over 1f out: nt clr run ins fnl f: r.o to ld nr fin* **7/2**[2]
6400 **2** *nk* **Brockey Rise (IRE)**[16] 8408 4-9-1 55 (b) BenCurtis 2 60
(David Evans) *chsd ldrs: rdn to ld and edgd rt ins fnl f: hdd nr fin* **9/2**[3]
6000 **3** *¾* **Bobby Joe Leg**[18] 8345 5-9-1 55 (v[1]) JamesSullivan 1 58
(Ruth Carr) *s.i.s: hld up: hdwy over 1f out: sn rdn: r.o* **7/1**
/2-0 **4** *nk* **Mercury**[215] 1575 7-9-1 49 (t[1]) DavidProbert 6 58
(Stephen Michael Hanlon, Ire) *chsd ldrs: led over 1f out: rdn and hdd ins fnl f: no ex towards fin* **14/1**
5410 **5** *1 ¼* **Maisie Moo**[7] 8667 3-9-0 54 ShaneKelly 7 54
(Shaun Keightley) *hld up: hdwy on outer over 2f out: rdn over 1f out: edgd lft ins fnl f: styd on same pce* **11/4**[1]

000 **6** *1* **Satchville Flyer**[13] 8502 8-9-1 47........................ PhilipPrince 4 52
(Milton Bradley) *s.i.s: pushed along early in rr: hmpd over 6f out: rdn and hung lft ins fnl f: r.o: nt rch ldrs* **80/1**

0600 **7** *2 1/4* **Chop Chop (IRE)**[15] 8417 3-8-11 51........................ WilliamCox(3) 11 45
(Brian Barr) *s.s: hld up: rdn and swtchd lft ins fnl f: nt trble ldrs (jockey said filly was slowly away and denied a clear run approaching the home turn)* **100/1**

214 **8** *hd* **Sweet Forgetme Not (IRE)**[4] 8757 3-8-7 52......(vt) GraceMcEntee(7) 10 45
(Phil McEntee) *chsd ldrs on outer: led 2f out: hdd over 1f out: wknd wl ins fnl f* **22/1**

01 **9** *4 1/2* **Hummingbird (IRE)**[8] 8637 3-9-6 53........................ DougieCostello 5 40
(David Loughnane) *racd keenly: led: hdd over 5f out: chsd ldr: ev ch over 1f out: wknd and eased ins fnl f (vet said filly had lost its right fore shoe)* **20/1**

1625 **10** *3/4* **Brigand**[13] 8502 4-9-1 55........................(p1) JoeyHaynes 3 33
(John Butler) *s.i.s: hdwy 6f out: rdn and lost pl whn nt clr run over 1f out: wkng whn n.m.r ins fnl f (jockey said gelding ran too free)* **11/2**

4400 **11** *5* **Peters Pudding (IRE)**[14] 8472 3-8-7 55..............(b) GavinAshton(7) 12 19
(Lisa Williamson) *led over 5f out: rdn and hdd 2f out: wknd fnl f* **125/1**

1m 28.04s (-0.76) **Going Correction** -0.175s/f (Stan)
WFA 3 from 4yo+ 1lb **11** Ran SP% **113.8**
Speed ratings (Par 101): **97,96,95,95,94 92,90,90,84,84 78**
CSF £18.15 TOTE £5.60: £2.20, £1.80, £3.00; EX 22.30 Trifecta £161.30.
Owner Iain Jardine Racing Club **Bred** Ms Patricia Walsh **Trained** Carruthers town, D'fries & G'way

FOCUS
An ordinary affair in which they raced well bunched. The second has been rated within 3lb of this year's 7f form.

8865 LADBROKES "PLAY 1-2-FREE" ON FOOTBALL NOVICE STKS 6f 20y (Tp)
5:50 (5:54) (Class 5) 2-Y-O **£3,428** (£1,020; £509; £254) **Stalls** Low

Form RPR

40 **1** **Waddat (IRE)**[12] 8516 2-9-2 0........................ ShaneKelly 6 75
(Richard Hughes) *a.p: chsd ldr over 1f out: rdn to ld ins fnl f: styd on* **8/1**

2 *nk* **Shine On Brendan (IRE)** 2-9-2 0........................ HectorCrouch 12 74
(Clive Cox) *sn prom: shkn up over 3f out: rdn and hung lft fr over 1f out: r.o to go 2nd nr fin* **6/1**

3 *1/2* **Blake's Vision (IRE)** 2-9-2 0........................ FrannyNorton 7 72
(Mark Johnston) *s.i.s: hdwy on outer over 3f out: outpcd over 2f out: r.o ins fnl f: wnt 3rd nr fin* **22/1**

51 **4** *nk* **Moosmee (IRE)**[28] 8026 2-9-6 0........................ GeorgiaCox(3) 11 78
(William Haggas) *plld hrd and prom: swtchd rt over 4f out: sn chsng ldr: shkn up to ld and hung lft over 1f out: hdd ins fnl f: styd on same pce* **5/2**[1]

3 **5** *1* **Gossip**[64] 6846 2-8-11 0........................ BenCurtis 8 65
(Martyn Meade) *trckd ldrs: racd keenly: nt clr run over 1f out: styd on same pce ins fnl f* **3/1**[2]

6 *shd* **Arbiter** 2-9-2 0........................(h1) KieranO'Neill 5 68
(John Gosden) *s.i.s: hld up: plld hrd: hdwy and hung lft fr over 1f out: swtchd rt ent fnl f: r.o (jockey said colt had hung badly left throughout)* **5/1**[3]

6 **7** *1* **Kingmans Spirit (IRE)**[37] 7769 2-8-11 0........................ JasonHart 10 60
(David Loughnane) *led 1f: chsd ldr tl carried rt over 4f out: remained handy on outer: rdn over 1f out: styd on same pce fnl f* **28/1**

03 **8** *2* **I'm Watching You**[20] 8297 2-9-2 0........................ DavidProbert 1 59
(Ronald Harris) *hld up in tch: effrt and nt clr run over 1f out: no ex ins fnl f* **12/1**

0 **9** *5* **Gypsy Traveller**[13] 8503 2-9-2 0........................ RossaRyan 9 44
(Kevin Frost) *led 5f out: hdd and hung lft over 1f out: wknd ins fnl f* **150/1**

0 **10** *2 1/4* **Heer I Am**[28] 8011 2-9-2 0........................(v1) JFEgan 2 37
(Paul George) *s.i.s: a in rr* **66/1**

0 **11** *nk* **Lady Dandy (IRE)**[23] 8198 2-8-12 1 ow1........................ DougieCostello 3 32
(Ivan Furtado) *s.i.s: a in rr* **150/1**

12 *3 3/4* **Dabbersgirl** 2-8-11 0........................ AndrewMullen 4 20
(Brian Baugh) *sn lost pl: bhd 1/2-way* **200/1**

1m 13.85s (-0.65) **Going Correction** -0.175s/f (Stan) **12** Ran SP% **114.4**
Speed ratings (Par 96): **97,96,95,95,94 94,92,90,83,80 80,75**
CSF £51.81 TOTE £7.50: £2.10, £1.60, £4.30; EX 74.90 Trifecta £1287.00.
Owner N Martin **Bred** Tally-Ho Stud **Trained** Upper Lambourn, Berks

FOCUS
There was a bunchy finish to this fair novice. Messy form, and the level is a bit fluid.

8866 BETWAY HEED YOUR HUNCH H'CAP 6f 20y (Tp)
6:25 (6:26) (Class 5) (0-75,75) 3-Y-O+
£3,428 (£1,020; £509; £400; £400; £400) **Stalls** Low

Form RPR

2602 **1** **Bahuta Acha**[30] 7977 4-8-11 65........................ JasonHart 4 72
(David Loughnane) *sn chsng ldr: rdn to ld over 1f out: styd on u.p* **5/1**[2]

2053 **2** *nk* **Steelriver (IRE)**[7] 8649 9-9-7 75........................ PhilDennis 6 81
(Michael Herrington) *trckd ldrs: rdn and ev ch ins fnl f: styd on* **5/1**[2]

0400 **3** *1 1/2* **Spirit Of Wedza (IRE)**[28] 8023 7-8-7 68........................ VictorSantos(7) 1 69
(Julie Camacho) *chsd ldrs: rdn over 1f out: styd on same pce ins fnl f* **16/1**

1420 **4** *2* **Great Shout (IRE)**[19] 8304 3-9-2 70........................(t) KieranShoemark 5 65+
(Amy Murphy) *rrd as stalls opened and s.s: hld up: hmpd 5f out: swtchd rt over 1f out: edgd lft and r.o ins fnl f: nt rch ldrs (jockey said filly had reared as the stalls opened and was slowly away as a result)* **5/1**[2]

4540 **5** *1 1/2* **Silca Mistress**[44] 7519 4-9-5 73........................ HectorCrouch 3 63
(Clive Cox) *sn led: rdn and hdd over 1f out: wknd wl ins fnl f* **7/1**[3]

3000 **6** *3* **Laubali**[14] 8470 4-9-4 72........................(p) DavidProbert 9 52
(David O'Meara) *hld up: hdwy over 1f out: no ex ins fnl f* **9/1**

0050 **7** *4* **Miracle Garden**[100] 5503 7-8-13 67........................(b) KieranO'Neill 7 35
(Roy Brotherton) *led early: chsd ldrs: drvn along 1/2-way: wknd over 1f out* **33/1**

6046 **8** *hd* **Upstaging**[19] 8304 7-9-6 74........................(b) RossaRyan 2 41
(Noel Wilson) *s.i.s: hld up: nvr on terms (jockey said gelding was never travelling)* **8/1**

0224 **9** *3 1/4* **Turanga Leela**[32] 7914 5-9-0 73........................(b) TobyEley(5) 8 30
(John Mackie) *s.i.s: edgd lft 5f out: outpcd (jockey said mare was never travelling and ran flat; trainer said he intended to give the mare a break)* **7/2**[1]

1m 12.75s (-1.75) **Going Correction** -0.175s/f (Stan) **9** Ran SP% **114.7**
Speed ratings (Par 103): **104,103,101,98,96 92,87,87,83**
CSF £29.96 CT £373.24 TOTE £4.70: £1.80, £3.30, £4.30; EX 24.50 Trifecta £209.50.
Owner Lancashire Lads Partnership **Bred** Mrs G S Rees **Trained** Tern Hill, Shropshire
■ Stewards' Enquiry : Toby Eley two-day ban: careless riding (Nov 20-21)

FOCUS
The first two had a good tussle inside the final furlong. The second has been rated close to his spring revival form.

8867 BETWAY H'CAP 5f 21y (Tp)
6:55 (6:55) (Class 3) (0-95,92) 3-Y-O **£7,246** (£2,168; £1,084; £542; £270) **Stalls** Low

Form RPR

0412 **1** **Rocket Action**[46] 7449 3-9-6 91........................(t) TomQueally 2 105
(Robert Cowell) *hld up: hdwy over 1f out: rdn to ld ins fnl f: sn clr: comf* **4/1**[2]

5065 **2** *2 1/4* **Watchable**[19] 8317 9-9-7 92........................(p) DavidNolan 9 98
(David O'Meara) *sn chsng ldr: rdn and carried rt over 1f out: styd on same pce ins fnl f* **14/1**

0203 **3** *hd* **Puds**[45] 7497 4-9-5 90........................ ShaneKelly 6 95
(Richard Hughes) *led early: chsd ldrs: rdn over 1f out: nt clr run ent fnl f: styd on same pce* **6/1**

1144 **4** *nk* **Yimou (IRE)**[15] 8420 4-9-0 85........................ MartinDwyer 1 89
(Dean Ivory) *pushed along to chse ldrs: rdn over 1f out: styd on same pce ins fnl f* **11/4**[1]

1003 **5** *1* **Orvar (IRE)**[26] 8099 6-9-6 91........................ JasonHart 4 92
(Paul Midgley) *prom: lost pl 4f out: hdwy over 1f out: rdn whn nt clr run ins fnl f: styd on same pce* **11/2**[3]

1052 **6** *nk* **Just That Lord**[128] 4458 6-9-1 86........................ JFEgan 8 86
(Michael Attwater) *sn led: rdn and hung rt fr over 1f out: hdd and no ex ins fnl f* **20/1**

4414 **7** *hd* **The Daley Express (IRE)**[26] 8099 5-9-5 90........................ DavidProbert 3 89
(Ronald Harris) *sn pushed along in rr: hdwy over 1f out: no ex ins fnl f* **11/2**[3]

4120 **8** *3 1/4* **Holmeswood**[26] 8099 5-9-5 90........................(p) TomEaves 7 77
(Julie Camacho) *hdwy on outer over 3f out: rdn over 1f out: wknd fnl f* **16/1**

0606 **9** *hd* **Moonraker**[19] 8317 7-9-3 88........................ AlistairRawlinson 5 74
(Michael Appleby) *hld up: hung rt and bhd fr 1/2-way (jockey said gelding had hung right)* **33/1**

59.41s (-2.49) **Going Correction** -0.175s/f (Stan) **9** Ran SP% **112.0**
Speed ratings (Par 107): **112,108,108,107,106 105,105,100,99**
CSF £55.46 CT £329.81 TOTE £4.40: £1.50, £3.00, £2.80; EX 34.70 Trifecta £222.00.
Owner Robert Ng **Bred** Robert Ng **Trained** Six Mile Bottom, Cambs

FOCUS
A decent sprint run at a good pace, and the winner was impressive. A clear pb from the winner, with the second rated in line with his 5f form and the third close to form.

8868 BETWAY CASINO H'CAP 1m 5f 219y (Tp)
7:25 (7:28) (Class 6) (0-65,66) 3-Y-O+
£2,781 (£827; £413; £400; £400; £400) **Stalls** Low

Form RPR

362 **1** **Star Of Athena**[78] 6303 4-9-6 58........................ KieranO'Neill 8 66
(Ali Stronge) *s.i.s: hld up: hdwy on outer over 2f out: led over 1f out: styd on wl* **10/1**

3500 **2** *5* **Brinkleys Katie**[35] 7818 3-7-10 45........................(v) RhiainIngram(5) 5 48
(Paul George) *hld up: plld hrd: hung rt almost thrght: hdwy over 9f out: led on outer over 4f out: rdn and hdd over 1f out: styd on same pce (jockey said filly ran too free and hung badly right)* **25/1**

-000 **3** *1* **Sea Sovereign (IRE)**[27] 8065 6-9-1 60........................ RPWalsh(7) 10 59
(Ian Williams) *prom: lost pl 12f out: hdwy 2f out: sn rdn: styd on u.p* **11/2**[3]

0321 **4** *1 1/2* **Willkommen**[169] 2941 3-9-0 65........................(b) StefanoCherchi(7) 9 64
(Marco Botti) *chsd ldrs: pushed along and outpcd over 3f out: styd on u.p fnl f* **3/1**[1]

6063 **5** *nse* **Ebqaa (IRE)**[39] 7682 5-9-10 62........................(p) DavidProbert 4 59
(James Unett) *hld up: hdwy over 2f out: rdn over 1f out: wknd wl ins fnl f* **7/2**[2]

441 **6** *1* **Minnelli**[50] 7318 3-9-6 64........................ StevieDonohoe 3 62
(Philip McBride) *s.i.s: hld up: hdwy over 2f out: rdn over 1f out: wknd ins fnl f (jockey said filly was never travelling)* **15/2**

3400 **7** *1/2* **Joyceick (FR)**[19] 7033 5-9-8 60........................(b) HectorCrouch 11 55
(Nick Littmoden) *led 1f: chsd ldrs: rdn over 3f out: wknd ins fnl f* **12/1**

0050 **8** *hd* **Uncle Bernie (IRE)**[68] 6681 9-9-3 55........................(p) JamesSullivan 6 50
(Sarah Hollinshead) *s.i.s: hld up: hdwy over 1f out: wknd ins fnl f* **28/1**

4-05 **9** *6* **Tingo In The Tale (IRE)**[31] 2901 10-8-4 45........................(p) WilliamCox(3) 7 31
(Tony Forbes) *s.i.s: hld up: nvr on terms* **50/1**

40-0 **10** *2 1/2* **Last Chance Paddy (USA)**[18] 810 5-8-9 47........................(v1) MartinDwyer 2 29+
(Sarah-Jayne Davies) *prom: chsd ldr 12f out tl led over 9f out: hdd over 6f out: rdn over 2f out: wknd and eased fnl f (jockey said gelding lost its action upon pulling up)* **80/1**

343 **11** *17* **End Over End**[14] 8451 3-9-8 66........................ AdamMcNamara 12 26+
(Archie Watson) *led after 1f tl hdd over 9f out: remained handy tl rdn and wknd over 2f out: eased fnl f (trainer's rep could offer no explanation for the filly's poor performance)* **18/1**

5035 **12** *19* **Bambys Boy**[21] 8246 8-9-5 57........................(t) ShaneKelly 1 +
(Neil Mulholland) *s.i.s: hdwy to go prom after 1f: chsd ldr over 7f out tl led over 6f out: hdd over 4f out: rdn and wknd wl over 2f out: eased (jockey said gelding suffered interference in running)* **11/1**

3m 0.54s (-0.46) **Going Correction** -0.175s/f (Stan)
WFA 3 from 4yo+ 6lb **12** Ran SP% **115.2**
Speed ratings (Par 101): **94,91,90,89,89 89,88,88,85,83 74,63**
CSF £236.01 CT £1510.14 TOTE £11.80: £3.20, £6.50, £2.20; EX 370.90 Trifecta £2069.70.
Owner Tim Dykes & Hugh Doubtfire **Bred** Mrs S A Hunt **Trained** Eastbury, Berks

FOCUS
The lead changed hands several times and that meant the gallop was kept up and the race set up for a closer.

8869 BETWAY CLASSIFIED STKS 1m 4f 51y (Tp)
7:55 (7:55) (Class 6) 3-Y-O+
£2,781 (£827; £413; £400; £400; £400) **Stalls** Low

Form RPR

4510 **1** **Herm (IRE)**[162] 3186 5-9-5 48........................ BenCurtis 5 56
(David Evans) *hld up in tch: shkn up to ld over 1f out: rdn clr* **5/1**[2]

42-0 **2** *2* **Sunhill Lad (IRE)**[81] 3225 4-9-5 49........................(p) AndrewMullen 3 53
(Julia Brooke) *chsd ldrs: wnt 2nd over 3f out tl led over 2f out: rdn: edgd rt and hdd over 1f out: styd on same pce ins fnl f* **7/2**[1]

5006 **3** *2* **Carvelas (IRE)**[11] 8551 10-9-5 50........................ DavidProbert 2 51
(J R Jenkins) *hld up: nt clr run: swtchd rt and hdwy over 1f out: rdn and edgd lft ins fnl f: styd on (jockey said gelding was denied a clear run approaching 2f out)* **9/1**

4006 **4** hd **Ember's Glow**34 7857 5-9-5 48 .... EoinWalsh 4 51
(Mark Loughnane) *hld up in tch: hmpd over 3f out: nt clr run and lost pl over 2f out: nt clr run again wl over 1f out: hdwy and swtchd lft ent fnl f: styd on (jockey said gelding was denied a clear run entering the home straight; vet said the gelding lost its left hind shoe)* **11/2**3

0044 **5** 2 3/4 **Lynchpin (IRE)**15 8434 3-9-0 50 ....(p1) JoeyHaynes 7 46
(Lydia Pearce) *hld up: hdwy over 2f out: rdn over 1f out: no ex ins fnl f* **8/1**

6000 **6** 2 1/4 **Miss Harriett**75 6400 3-9-0 46 ....(w) MartinDwyer 8 42
(Stuart Kittow) *prom: chsd ldr 7f out tl led over 3f out: hdd over 2f out: sn rdn: wknd ins fnl f* **12/1**

0-00 **7** 1/2 **Brilliant Riposte**67 6723 4-8-12 44 .... MichaelPitt(7) 12 40
(Denis Coakley) *s.i.s: bhd: styd on fnl f: nvr on terms* **33/1**

000 **8** 1 1/4 **Noverre Dancer (IRE)**70 6594 3-9-0 41 ....(b1) HectorCrouch 10 39
(Nick Littmoden) *s.i.s: hld up: hdwy on outer over 2f out: sn rdn: wknd fnl f* **17/2**

4005 **9** 1/2 **Pot Luck**7 8670 3-9-0 48 ....(p1) PhilDennis 6 39
(Sharon Watt) *sn led: hdd over 9f out: chsd ldrs: rdn over 2f out: wknd over 1f out* **33/1**

6505 **10** 1 1/2 **Delta Bravo (IRE)**19 7474 3-9-0 49 .... JFEgan 11 36
(J S Moore) *s.i.s: hld up: swtchd rt over 5f out: hdwy on outer over 4f out: rdn over 2f out: wknd over 1f out* **12/1**

0630 **11** 35 **Tops No**11 8553 4-9-5 48 .... JaneElliott 1
(William Muir) *hld up: rdn over 3f out: sn wknd* **40/1**

00-0 **12** 60 **Pukka Tique**18 8351 3-9-0 47 ....(t1) DougieCostello 9
(Ivan Furtado) *pushed along to chse ldrs: led over 9f out tl rdn and hdd over 3f out: sn wknd (jockey said gelding stopped quickly; trainer said the gelding had a breathing problem)* **33/1**

2m 38.7s (-2.10) **Going Correction** -0.175s/f (Stan)
WFA 3 from 4yo+ 5lb **12 Ran SP% 112.6**
Speed ratings (Par 101): **100,98,97,97,95 93,93,92,92,91 68,28**
CSF £20.79 TOTE £4.20: £1.40, £2.40, £3.10; EX 25.60 Trifecta £208.00.
Owner Trevor Gallienne **Bred** Mountarmstrong Stud **Trained** Pandy, Monmouths

FOCUS
A moderate affair.

8870 BETWAY LIVE CASINO H'CAP 1m 1f 104y (Tp)
8:25 (8:26) (Class 6) (0-60,59) 3-Y-O+
£2,781 (£827; £413; £400; £400; £400) **Stalls Low**

Form RPR

0343 **1** **Red Gunner**14 8466 5-9-0 52 .... RossaRyan 13 58
(Mark Loughnane) *hld up: hdwy on outer over 2f out: rdn to ld and hung lft ins fnl f: r.o* **6/1**3

0314 **2** 1 1/4 **Pike Corner Cross (IRE)**15 8417 7-9-1 53 ....(vt) BenCurtis 6 57
(David Evans) *hld up in tch: rdn and ev ch ins fnl f: styd on same pce towards fin* **5/1**2

4463 **3** nk **Quoteline Direct**43 7545 6-9-7 59 ....(h) FrannyNorton 8 62
(Micky Hammond) *hld up: hdwy over 1f out: rdn and edgd lft ins fnl f: r.o* **11/1**

2040 **4** 3/4 **Uncertain Smile (IRE)**35 7817 3-9-1 59 ....(h) WilliamCox(3) 9 62
(Clive Cox) *sn prom: chsd ldr 7f out tl led over 3f out: rdn over 1f out: hdd ins fnl f: no ex towards fin* **8/1**

0000 **5** 2 **Raven's Raft (IRE)**7 8670 4-9-2 54 ....(b1) DougieCostello 7 52
(David Loughnane) *hld up: hdwy over 2f out: nt clr run over 1f out: styd on same pce ins fnl f* **28/1**

3342 **6** 3/4 **Vipin (FR)**18 8348 4-9-4 59 .... GeorgiaCox(3) 2 55
(William Muir) *hld up in tch: racd keenly: shkn up over 1f out: styd on same pce fnl f* **10/3**1

000- **7** 3 1/4 **Louisiana Beat (IRE)**321 9636 3-8-9 50 .... JoeyHaynes 10 41
(Mike Murphy) *s.i.s: hld up: shkn up and hung lft over 1f out: n.d* **80/1**

0521 **8** nk **Archdeacon**159 3299 3-9-3 58 .... KieranO'Neill 3 49
(Dean Ivory) *led early: chsd ldrs: rdn over 2f out: wknd fnl f (jockey said gelding ran too free)* **6/1**3

6001 **9** 9 **Chamomile**32 7909 3-9-4 59 .... KieranShoemark 1 33
(Daniel Kubler) *plld hrd in 2nd 2f: remained handy tl wknd over 1f out (trainer could offer no explanation for filly's poor performance other than she ran too free in the early stages)* **5/1**2

0-00 **10** 3 1/2 **Bunker Hill Lad**7 8670 4-8-12 50 ....(v1) AlistairRawlinson 4 16
(Michael Appleby) *sn led: rdn and hdd over 3f out: wknd over 1f out* **125/1**

0400 **11** 11 **Sherwood Forrester**21 8248 3-8-11 57 ....(h1) RhiainIngram(5) 5 3
(Paul George) *s.i.s: a in rr: bhd fnl 6f (jockey said gelding was never travelling)* **40/1**

1m 58.87s (-1.93) **Going Correction** -0.175s/f (Stan)
WFA 3 from 4yo+ 3lb **11 Ran SP% 112.3**
Speed ratings (Par 101): **101,99,99,98,97 96,93,93,85,82 72**
CSF £33.78 CT £318.34 TOTE £6.80: £2.20, £1.40, £2.60; EX 36.80 Trifecta £251.30.
Owner 2 Counties Racing **Bred** Scea Haras De Saint Pair **Trained** Rock, Worcs

FOCUS
It paid to be ridden with a bit of patience here. Straightforward form.
T/Plt: £9,196.00 to a £1 stake. Pool: £71,174.78 - 5.65 winning units T/Qpdt: £428.50 to a £1 stake. Pool: £10,174.59 - 17.57 winning units **Colin Roberts**

8871 - 8888a (Foreign Racing) - See Raceform Interactive

8750
CHELMSFORD (A.W) (L-H)
Thursday, November 7

OFFICIAL GOING: Polytrack: standard
Wind: virtually nil Weather: light cloud

8889 BET AT TOTESPORT.COM NOVICE STKS 7f (P)
4:25 (4:26) (Class 5) 2-Y-O
£4,204 (£1,251; £625; £312) **Stalls Low**

Form RPR

0 **1** **Bullfinch**13 8516 2-9-2 0 .... JasonWatson 2 81+
(Roger Charlton) *mde virtually all: rdn over 2f out: kicked clr over 1f out: styd on strly ins fnl f: eased towards fin* **9/4**1

5 **2** 2 **Cedar Cage**14 8503 2-9-2 0 .... LukeMorris 9 75
(Sir Mark Prescott Bt) *swtchd lft after s: hdwy over 3f out: nt clr run over 2f out: swtchd rt and effrt over 1f out: hdwy to chse clr wnr and hung lft 1f out: stl hanging but kpt on: nvr getting to wnr (jockey said gelding lugged left-handed under pressure)* **25/1**

60 **3** 2 **Gibraltar (IRE)**10 8605 2-9-2 0 .... HayleyTurner 8 70+
(Michael Bell) *hld up in tch in midfield: swtchd rt and effrt over 1f out: pushed along over 1f out: kpt on wl under hands and heels riding ins fnl f: wnt 3rd towards fin: no threat to ldrs* **50/1**

4 1 1/2 **Choice Of Mine (AUS)** 2-9-2 0 .... AndreaAtzeni 4 66
(Joseph Patrick O'Brien, Ire) *chsd ldrs: effrt to chse clr wnr and edgd rt over 1f out: no imp and lost 2nd 1f out: wknd ins fnl f* **5/2**2

05 **5** 1 **Huwaiteb**15 8459 2-9-2 0 ....(h) DavidProbert 7 63
(Owen Burrows) *taken down early and led to post: chsd wnr for over 1f out: effrt to dispute 2nd but wnr gng clr over 1f out: no imp and sltly squeezed for room 1f out: wknd ins fnl f* **8/1**

50 **6** 2 1/4 **Sweet Reward (IRE)**27 8100 2-9-2 0 .... RobHornby 6 57
(Jonathan Portman) *in tch in midfield: shuffled bk towards rr over 2f out: effrt over 1f out: kpt on but no threat to ldrs ins fnl f* **40/1**

0 **7** 1 **Monsaraz**16 8424 2-9-2 0 .... DavidEgan 5 55
(James Given) *hld up towards rr: effrt and sme hdwy on inner over 1f out: no imp ins fnl f* **100/1**

00 **8** 1 3/4 **Bee Magic (IRE)**15 8455 2-9-2 0 .... HollieDoyle 1 50
(William Muir) *hld up in tch in midfield: swtchd rt and effrt over 1f out: no imp and wl hld ins fnl f* **80/1**

4 **9** 3 1/4 **Reehaam**104 5366 2-8-11 0 .... RobertHavlin 3 37
(John Gosden) *awkward leaving stalls: t.k.h: sn in midfield: sltly impeded over 4f out: lost pl and towards rr 2f out: wknd fnl f* **5/1**3

10 3 **Thebian** 2-9-2 0 .... JimCrowley 11 34+
(John Gosden) *sltly impeded leaving stalls: t.k.h and hdwy to join wnr over 5f out: rdn ent fnl 2f: lost pl and btn over 1f out: wknd fnl f* **7/1**

14 **11** shd **San Rafael (IRE)**14 8503 2-9-9 0 .... FrannyNorton 10 41+
(Mark Johnston) *stmbld bdly and wnt rt leaving stalls: sn rcvrd and in tch in midfield: edgd lft over 4f out: lost pl and towards rr 2f out: wknd fnl f (jockey said colt stumbled leaving the stalls)* **11/1**

1m 25.91s (-1.29) **Going Correction** -0.25s/f (Stan) **11 Ran SP% 118.4**
Speed ratings (Par 96): **97,94,92,90,89 87,85,83,80,76 76**
CSF £65.70 TOTE £2.60: £1.20, £7.60, £14.60; EX 74.80 Trifecta £1079.20.
Owner Exors Of The Late Lady Rothschild **Bred** The Rt Hon Lord Rothschild **Trained** Beckhampton, Wilts

FOCUS
A fair novice.

8890 TOTEPOOL CASHBACK AT TOTESPORT.COM NURSERY H'CAP 6f (P)
4:55 (4:56) (Class 5) (0-75,77) 2-Y-O
£4,787 (£1,424; £711; £400; £400; £400) **Stalls Centre**

Form RPR

2501 **1** **Taste The Nectar (USA)**30 7995 2-9-4 71 ....(p) SilvestreDeSousa 13 73+
(Robert Cowell) *hld up in rr: hdwy and switching rt over 1f out: 7th and stl plenty to do 1f out: lugged lft and clsd ins fnl f: stened and str run to ld last strides* **12/1**

034 **2** nk **Many A Star (IRE)**55 7160 2-9-7 74 .... DavidEgan 3 75
(James Given) *hld up in tch in midfield: clsd on outer ent fnl 2f: clsd and edgd lft ins fnl f: ev ch 100yds out: kpt on (jockey said colt hung left-handed under pressure)* **5/1**2

6030 **3** nse **Sir Oliver (IRE)**15 8465 2-9-4 71 ....(b1) ShaneKelly 8 72+
(Richard Hughes) *plld hrd: sn w ldr tl led 1/2-way: drvn and forged ahd over 1f out: hrd pressed 100yds out: hdd and lost 2 pls last strides* **10/1**

022 **4** 3/4 **Great Image (IRE)**28 8059 2-9-10 77 .... HectorCrouch 2 76
(Saeed bin Suroor) *chsd ldrs: effrt to chse ldr 2f out: kpt on u.p and clsd ins fnl f: ev ch 100yds out: kpt on same pce towards fin* **2/1**1

0422 **5** 1 3/4 **Live In The Moment (IRE)**28 8069 2-9-7 74 .... DavidProbert 7 67
(Adam West) *pressed ldr early: chsd ldrs after: effrt to press ldrs 2f out: sn drvn: no ex ins fnl f: wknd towards fin* **8/1**

4620 **6** 1 3/4 **Shoot To Kill (IRE)**26 8110 2-9-9 76 .... HayleyTurner 1 64
(George Scott) *hld up in tch in midfield: swtchd rt and effrt u.p over 1f out: unable qck and kpt on same pce ins fnl f* **5/1**2

236 **7** 1 3/4 **Harlequin**48 7407 2-9-5 72 .... JimCrowley 14 55
(William Knight) *styd wd early: towards rr: effrt whn impeded over 1f out: edgd lft but kpt on ins fnl f: no threat to ldrs (jockey said colt hung left-handed)* **7/1**3

2210 **8** 4 1/2 **Heer We Go Again**40 7679 2-9-7 74 .... JasonWatson 6 43
(David Evans) *led tl 1/2-way: lost 2nd 2f out and sn lost pl: wknd ins fnl f* **25/1**

606 **9** 1 1/4 **Deverell**20 8319 2-9-4 71 ....(v1) RobertHavlin 10 37
(John Gosden) *hld up in midfield: effrt over 2f out: losing pl whn hmpd over 1f out: sn wknd* **22/1**

033 **10** nk **Alfies Watch**43 7570 2-9-4 71 .... RossaRyan 9 36
(John O'Shea) *hld up towards rr: no imp u.p over 1f out: wknd ins fnl f* **25/1**

2030 **11** 1 **Sir Gordon**8 8650 2-8-13 66 .... CharlesBishop 5 28
(Ralph J Smith) *hld up in last quartet: sme hdwy but stl plenty to do whn edgd rt u.p over 1f out: sn no imp and wknd ins fnl f* **66/1**

2600 **12** 8 **Jim 'N' Tomic (IRE)**31 7971 2-9-4 71 .... JFEgan 4 9
(Dominic Ffrench Davis) *a towards rr: u.p and no rspnse over 1f out: sn wknd* **28/1**

1m 12.65s (-1.05) **Going Correction** -0.25s/f (Stan) **12 Ran SP% 124.0**
Speed ratings (Par 96): **97,96,96,95,93 90,88,82,80,80 79,68**
CSF £70.38 CT £651.76 TOTE £13.10: £3.30, £1.70, £3.00; EX 116.60 Trifecta £1430.60.
Owner T W Morley **Bred** Winstar Farm Llc, B P Walden Jr Et Al **Trained** Six Mile Bottom, Cambs

FOCUS
A tight finish to this nursery, the winner getting up late having hit 1000 for a small amount in running. A minor pb from the third.

8891 EXTRA PLACES AT TOTESPORT.COM FILLIES' NOVICE STKS (PLUS 10 RACE) 6f (P)
5:25 (5:28) (Class 4) 2-Y-O
£6,469 (£1,925; £962; £481) **Stalls Centre**

Form RPR

1 **Silver Machine** 2-9-0 0 .... HollieDoyle 3 80+
(Archie Watson) *edgd rt leaving stalls: in tch in midfield: clsd to chse ldrs and swtchd rt over 1f out: hdwy to ld ins fnl f: r.o strly and drew clr fnl 100yds: readily* **8/1**

25 **2** 3 **Sendacard**57 7063 2-9-0 0 .... TonyHamilton 8 71
(Richard Fahey) *t.k.h: chsd ldrs tl wnt 2nd over 3f out: rdn over 1f out: clsd to press ldng pair 1f out: nt match pce of wnr ins fnl f: kpt on to go 2nd cl home* **16/1**

41 **3** 1/2 **Letscrackon (IRE)**17 8409 2-9-3 0 .... HectorCrouch 4 73
(Gary Moore) *led: rdn ent fnl 2f: hdd ins fnl f: nt match pce of wnr and one pce after: lost 2nd cl home* **11/4**1

4 **4** 3/4 **Kohoof**68 6704 2-9-0 0 .... JimCrowley 9 67
(William Haggas) *in tch in midfield on outer: effrt and drifted rt bnd 2f out: kpt on ins fnl f: no threat to wnr (jockey said filly hung right-handed)* **3/1**2

0 **5** 1 ¼ **Miss Carla (IRE)**[65] 6846 2-9-0 0.. ShaneKelly 2 64+
(Jamie Osborne) *edgd rt leaving stalls: hld up in tch in midfield: nt clr run and edgd lft over 1f out: pushed along and swtchd rt 1f out: edgd lft and kpt on ins fnl f: no threat to ldrs (jockey said filly was denied a clear run)* **20/1**

6 ½ **Endowment** 2-9-0 0.. LiamKeniry 1 62
(Clive Cox) *chsd ldrs: rdn over 3f out: no ex and flashed tail ins fnl f: wknd fnl 100yds* **14/1**

40 **7** 1 ¾ **Urtzi (IRE)**[23] 8218 2-9-0 0.. RobertHavlin 10 57
(Michael Attwater) *hld up in rr: clsd and nt clr run over 1f out: sn swtchd rt and hdwy 1f out: kpt on ins fnl f: nvr trbld ldrs* **40/1**

8 1 ¼ **She's On The Edge (IRE)** 2-9-0 0.. WilliamCarson 5 53
(Anthony Carson) *dwlt and short of room leaving stalls: rn green and pushed along in rr: effrt on inner over 1f out: kpt on but nvr a threat to ldrs* **50/1**

65 **9** nk **Rock Of Fame**[23] 8218 2-9-0 0.. AndreaAtzeni 13 52
(Roger Varian) *swtchd lft after s: hld up in rr: pushed along and clsd whn nt clr run over 1f out: kpt on fnl 100yds: nvr trbld ldrs* **8/1**

06 **10** nse **Tiger Balm**[30] 7995 2-9-0 0.. JackMitchell 6 52
(George Boughey) *hld up off the pce in midfield: no imp over 1f out: wl hld and kpt on same pce ins fnl f* **50/1**

21 **11** 4 **Pepper Bay**[22] 8250 2-9-3 0.. CallumShepherd 12 43
(Michael Bell) *chsd ldrs tl clsd to press ldr over 3f out: lost pl over 1f out: wknd ins fnl f (jockey said filly stopped quickly)* **7/2**[3]

5 **12** 1 **Light Lily**[98] 5590 2-9-0 0.. JFEgan 11 37
(Paul D'Arcy) *s.i.s: off the pce towards rr: rdn and no hdwy over 1f out: wknd ins fnl f* **50/1**

13 1 ¼ **Little Fortune** 2-9-0 0.. DavidProbert 7 33
(Henry Candy) *chsd ldr tl over 3f out: losing pl whn squeezed for room 1f out: wknd ins fnl f* **25/1**

1m 12.21s (-1.49) **Going Correction** -0.25s/f (Stan) **13** Ran SP% **125.6**
Speed ratings (Par 95): **99,95,94,93,91 91,88,87,86,86 81,79,78**
CSF £124.89 TOTE £8.90: £2.70, £4.30, £1.30; EX 118.10 Trifecta £635.20.
Owner Tweenhills Fillies **Bred** Llety Farms **Trained** Upper Lambourn, W Berks

FOCUS
A nice performance from the winner, who was one of four newcomers in the line-up.

8892 IRISH LOTTO AT TOTESPORT.COM H'CAP 1m 2f (P)
5:55 (5:57) (Class 2) (0-105,105) 3-Y-O+ **£12,602** (£3,772; £1,886; £944; £470) **Stalls** Low

Form RPR

-120 **1** **Dubai Warrior**[47] 7478 3-9-7 **103**.. RobertHavlin 5 113
(John Gosden) *chsd ldr tl led over 2f out: rdn over 1f out: kpt on u.p and doing enough towards fin* **6/4**[1]

0114 **2** ½ **Kasbaan**[28] 8062 4-9-4 **97**.. AlistairRawlinson 6 105
(Michael Appleby) *t.k.h: chsd ldrs: effrt to chse wnr jst over 2f out: kpt on and pressing wnr towards fin: a hld* **6/1**[3]

-055 **3** 1 ¾ **Victory Bond**[202] 1921 6-9-4 **100**.. CierenFallon(3) 3 105
(William Haggas) *hld up in last pair: effrt 3f out: hdwy to chse ldng pair and hung lft 1f out: kpt on but nt getting on terms w ldrs ins fnl f* **8/1**

6403 **4** 3 ¾ **Aweedram (IRE)**[13] 8514 3-8-6 **88**..(h) DavidEgan 4 86
(Alan King) *stdd s: hld up in rr: swtchd rt and effrt over 2f out: 4th: hung lft and no imp ins fnl f* **7/1**

1000 **5** 4 ½ **Circus Couture (IRE)**[19] 8336 7-9-1 **94**..(v) JFEgan 1 82
(Jane Chapple-Hyam) *chsd ldrs: rdn over 3f out: outpcd and btn over 1f out: wknd ins fnl f* **25/1**

-625 **6** 12 **Elwazir**[43] 7565 4-9-12 **105**..(h) JimCrowley 2 69
(Owen Burrows) *led tl rdn and hdd over 2f out: sn dropped out and bhd over 1f out: wknd fnl f (jockey said stopped quickly)* **5/2**[2]

2m 3.3s (-5.30) **Going Correction** -0.25s/f (Stan)
WFA 3 from 4yo+ 3lb **6** Ran SP% **110.3**
Speed ratings (Par 109): **111,110,109,106,102 93**
CSF £10.61 TOTE £2.20: £1.40, £2.70; EX 9.40 Trifecta £40.10.
Owner Sheikh Mohammed Bin Khalifa Al Maktoum **Bred** Essafinaat Ltd **Trained** Newmarket, Suffolk

FOCUS
A good handicap but the early pace wasn't that strong. The third has been rated in line with his recent form.

8893 BET IN PLAY AT TOTESPORT.COM H'CAP 7f (P)
6:25 (6:27) (Class 4) (0-85,87) 3-Y-O+
£5,530 (£1,645; £822; £411; £400; £400) **Stalls** Low

Form RPR

1062 **1** **Boy In The Bar**[55] 7164 8-9-5 **82**..(v) DavidProbert 3 90
(Ian Williams) *t.k.h early: hld up in tch: effrt over 1f out: r.o wl u.p to ld towards fin* **5/1**[3]

0544 **2** ½ **Martineo**[61] 6968 4-9-1 **78**..(p[1]) LukeMorris 2 85
(John Butler) *stdd after s: in tch: clsd to trck ldrs over 2f out: rdn to chal over 1f out: drvn to ld ins fnl f: hdd and no ex towards fin* **4/1**[1]

2615 **3** ¾ **Envisaging (IRE)**[61] 6968 5-9-5 **82**..(t) GeorgeWood 5 87
(James Fanshawe) *stdd after s: hld up in tch towards rr: effrt on outer over 1f out: clsd to chse ldrs and rdn ins fnl f: kpt on* **9/2**[2]

1046 **4** 1 **Unabated (IRE)**[29] 8015 5-9-10 **87**.. JFEgan 1 89
(Jane Chapple-Hyam) *t.k.h: sn w ldr tl led on inner over 3f out: rdn over 1f out: hdd and no ex ins fnl f: wknd towards fin* **6/1**

000 **5** 2 ½ **Zap**[27] 8096 4-9-7 **84**.. TonyHamilton 7 80
(Richard Fahey) *swtchd lft after s: hld up in tch in rr: effrt on inner over 1f out: no imp u.p ins fnl f* **7/1**

2200 **6** 2 ¼ **Atletico (IRE)**[21] 8289 7-9-0 **77**.. JasonWatson 8 66
(David Evans) *swtchd lft after s: hld up in tch towards rr: effrt and hung lft over 1f out: no imp and wl hld ins fnl f* **8/1**

1203 **7** ½ **Sparklealot (IRE)**[9] 8634 3-9-7 **85**..(p) DougieCostello 4 72
(Ivan Furtado) *led tl over 3f out: rdn over 2f out: lost pl over 1f out: wknd ins fnl f* **4/1**[1]

/50- **8** 1 ¾ **Omran**[363] 8987 5-9-9 **86**..(t w) FrannyNorton 6 69
(Michael Wigham) *chsd ldrs tl outpcd over 1f out: wknd ins fnl f (jockey said gelding hung right-handed)* **20/1**

1m 24.27s (-2.93) **Going Correction** -0.25s/f (Stan)
WFA 3 from 4yo+ 1lb **8** Ran SP% **117.5**
Speed ratings (Par 105): **106,105,104,103,100 98,97,95**
CSF £26.08 CT £97.38 TOTE £6.10: £1.90, £1.60, £1.60; EX 27.60 Trifecta £131.10.
Owner Allwins Stables **Bred** Brinkley Stud S R L **Trained** Portway, Worcs

FOCUS
An open handicap. It's been rated as straightforward form, with the second to his 7f best.

8894 DOUBLE DELIGHT HAT-TRICK HEAVEN AT TOTESPORT.COM NOVICE STKS 7f (P)
6:55 (6:55) (Class 5) 3-Y-O+ **£4,948** (£1,472; £735; £367) **Stalls** Low

Form RPR

0-1 **1** **The Gill Brothers**[43] 7572 3-9-9 0..(t) SeanLevey 4 88+
(Stuart Williams) *t.k.h: hld up and trckd ldng pair: swtchd rt and effrt over 1f out: rdn and clsd under hands and heels to ld ins fnl f: sn clr: comf* **8/11**[1]

0-0 **2** 2 ¼ **Qaabil (IRE)**[216] 3-9-2 72.. JimCrowley 5 75
(William Haggas) *chsd ldr: rdn and ev ch over 1f out: drvn to ld 1f out: hdd ins fnl f: sn outpcd and eased towards fin* **9/4**[2]

01 **3** 6 **Cockney Hill**[264] 753 3-9-9 0.. CharlesBishop 2 66
(Joseph Tuite) *led: pushed along ent fnl 2f: rdn and hdd 1f out: wknd ins fnl f* **7/1**[3]

56 **4** ¾ **Dor's Diamond**[191] 2236 3-8-11 0..(h) SophieRalston(5) 1 57
(Dean Ivory) *in tch in 4th: rdn over 2f out: outpcd and hung lft over 1f out: wl hld and plugged on same pce ins fnl f* **20/1**

5 14 **Just A Touch (IRE)** 3-8-11 0.. DavidEgan 3 14
(Jane Chapple-Hyam) *v.s.a: green and broncing leaving stalls: nvr rcvrd and nvr involved (jockey said filly was slowly away and bronked for several strides)* **25/1**

1m 26.29s (-0.91) **Going Correction** -0.25s/f (Stan) **5** Ran SP% **109.8**
Speed ratings (Par 103): **95,92,85,84,68**
CSF £2.55 TOTE £1.40: £1.10, £1.30; EX 2.60 Trifecta £7.60.
Owner The Gill Brothers **Bred** P A & M J Reditt & Catridge Stud **Trained** Newmarket, Suffolk

FOCUS
The winner defied his penalty easily enough despite racing keenly. The winner has been rated in line with his Kempton win, and the fourth close to his previous runs.

8895 BUY TICKETS ONLINE AT CHELMSFORDCITYRACECOURSE.COM H'CAP 5f (P)
7:25 (7:26) (Class 5) (0-75,77) 3-Y-O+
£5,110 (£1,520; £759; £400; £400; £400) **Stalls** Low

Form RPR

3213 **1** **Spirited Guest**[26] 8117 3-9-6 **74**.. TomQueally 10 83+
(George Margarson) *chsd ldrs on outer: swtchd rt and effrt over 1f out: str run to chal 100yds out: r.o wl to ld last strides* **9/2**[2]

120- **2** hd **Nampara**[435] 6680 4-8-9 **63**.. JFEgan 7 71
(Paul D'Arcy) *chsd ldrs: effrt to chal over 1f out: drvn to ld 1f out: kpt on u.p: hdd last strides* **25/1**

30 **3** 1 ½ **Joegogo (IRE)**[15] 8470 4-9-9 **77**.. JasonWatson 2 80
(David Evans) *in tch in midfield: effrt on inner over 1f out: chsd ldrs u.p 1f out: kpt on same pce ins fnl f: wnt 3rd on post* **7/2**[1]

54 **4** nse **Kodiac Express (IRE)**[80] 6288 4-9-1 **69**.. DanielMuscutt 1 72
(Mike Murphy) *led: rdn over 1f out: hdd 1f out: no ex 100yds out: wknd cl home and lost 3rd on post* **7/1**[3]

35 **5** ½ **Three Little Birds**[53] 7230 4-8-11 **72**.. StefanoCherchi(7) 8 73
(Sylvester Kirk) *in tch in midfield: effrt over 1f out: chsd ldrs and edgd lft 100yds out: no imp towards fin* **7/1**[3]

5401 **6** 1 **Tathmeen (IRE)**[16] 8429 4-9-3 **71**.. CamHardie 3 69
(Antony Brittain) *t.k.h: hld up in tch: effrt towards inner over 1f out: chsd ldrs 1f out: rdn and no imp 100yds out* **9/2**[2]

6356 **7** 1 ¾ **Harrogate (IRE)**[21] 8285 4-9-7 **75**..(b) CharlieBennett 9 68
(Jim Boyle) *chsd ldr tl unable qck over 1f out: wknd ins fnl f* **14/1**

3320 **8** 3 ½ **Show Me The Bubbly**[15] 8470 3-8-13 **74**.. KateLeahy(7) 6 55
(John O'Shea) *short of room sn after s: hld up in rr and swtchd wd: no hdwy over 1f out: wknd ins fnl f* **8/1**

5302 **9** nk **Shining**[10] 8601 3-9-8 **76**.. JackMitchell 11 56
(Jim Boyle) *wnt rt leaving stalls: swtchd lft and hld up in rr: effrt over 1f out: nvr threatened ldrs and wl hld whn bdly hmpd 50yds out* **8/1**

3040 **10** 1 ¾ **Time To Reason (IRE)**[105] 5352 6-8-10 **64**..(p) DavidEgan 4 39
(Charlie Wallis) *broke okay but sn restrained and hld up in rr: effrt over 1f out: swtchd rt 1f out: no imp and wl hld whn bdly hmpd and rdr lost irons 50yds out* **20/1**

1000 **F** **Brandy Station (IRE)**[6] 8715 4-8-1 **62**..(h) GavinAshton(7) 5 60
(Lisa Williamson) *hld up in tch in midfield: effrt over 1f out: chsd ldrs 1f out: no imp ins fnl f and hld whn short of room: clipped heels and fell 50yds* **16/1**

58.95s (-1.25) **Going Correction** -0.25s/f (Stan) **11** Ran SP% **127.0**
Speed ratings (Par 103): **100,99,97,97,96 94,92,86,85,83**
CSF £118.98 CT £460.52 TOTE £4.90: £1.80, £7.90, £1.50; EX 124.50 Trifecta £769.20.
Owner John Guest Racing **Bred** Crossfields Bloodstock Ltd **Trained** Newmarket, Suffolk
■ Stewards' Enquiry : Stefano Cherchi 12-day ban: interference & careless riding (Nov 21-30, Dec 2-5)

FOCUS
An ordinary handicap, but the winner is better than the bare result indicates. The second has been rated as good as ever.

8896 BUY YOUR 2020 CCR MEMBERSHIP NOW H'CAP 6f (P)
7:55 (7:56) (Class 6) (0-60,60) 3-Y-O+
£3,105 (£924; £461; £400; £400; £400) **Stalls** Centre

Form RPR

6000 **1** **Kath's Lustre**[14] 8501 4-8-9 **57**..(b) GeorgeRooke(7) 10 64
(Richard Hughes) *in tch in midfield: clsd to chse ldrs and swtchd lft over 1f out: chal u.p 1f out: led 100yds out: hld on wl cl home* **12/1**

P206 **2** hd **Catheadans Fury**[23] 8217 5-9-3 **58**..(t) GeorgeWood 5 64
(Martin Bosley) *hmpd leaving stalls: hld up in tch in midfield: swtchd lft and effrt over 1f out: drvn and str chal wl ins fnl f: kpt on but hld cl home* **7/1**[3]

3002 **3** ¾ **Halle's Harbour**[29] 8018 3-9-2 **57**..(v) LukeMorris 7 61
(Paul George) *hmpd leaving stalls: t.k.h: hld up in tch: swtchd rt and effrt over 1f out: hung lft u.p but hdwy ins fnl f: kpt on wl* **10/1**

4034 **4** nk **Phoenix Star (IRE)**[7] 8704 3-9-4 **59**..(t) SilvestreDeSousa 2 64+
(Stuart Williams) *hmpd leaving stalls: hld up in tch in midfield on inner: nt clr run 2f out: swtchd rt over 1f out: hung lft 1f out: swtchd lft and styd on wl fnl 100yds: nt rch ldrs (jockey said gelding was denied a clear run)* **9/4**[1]

0050 **5** nse **Bernie's Boy**[47] 7446 6-8-9 **57**..(tp) GraceMcEntee(7) 9 60
(Phil McEntee) *chsd ldrs: rdn to ld over 1f out: hdd 100yds out: no ex and jst outpcd towards fin* **40/1**

5033 **6** 1 **The Lacemaker**[7] 8704 5-9-4 **59**...............................(p) HayleyTurner 1 59
(Milton Harris) *wnt bdly rt leaving stalls: led for 1f: chsd ldr: ev ch u.p over 1f out: no ex ins fnl f: wknd towards fin* **6/1**[2]

000 **7** nk **Flora Tristan**[114] 5030 4-9-1 **59**.........................(t[1]) GabrieleMalune(3) 3 58
(Ivan Furtado) *taken down early: hmpd leaving stalls: hld up towards rr: effrt on outer over 1f out: kpt on wl fnl 100yds: nvr trbld ldrs (jockey said filly suffered interference shortly after the start)* **12/1**

6550 **8** ½ **Mutabaahy (IRE)**[27] 8083 4-9-5 **60**.............................. CamHardie 14 58
(Antony Brittain) *t.k.h: hld up in tch: effrt over 1f out: carried lft and no imp ins fnl f: kpt on same pce fnl 100yds* **7/1**[3]

5251 **9** nk **Terri Rules (IRE)**[29] 8018 4-9-2 **57**.............................. DanielMuscutt 8 54
(Lee Carter) *restless in stalls: broke wl: restrained and t.k.h in midfield: effrt to press ldrs over 1f out: no ex and wknd ins fnl f* **8/1**

0250 **10** ½ **Sepahi**[27] 8083 3-8-11 **59**..............................(p) LauraPearson(7) 11 54
(Henry Spiller) *dwlt: hld up in rr: effrt over 1f out: kpt on but nvr threatened ldrs* **25/1**

0050 **11** 3¼ **Your Choice**[22] 8254 4-9-2 **57**..............................(v) JackMitchell 6 43
(Laura Mongan) *hmpd leaving stalls: in tch in midfield: rdn 3f out: outpcd over 1f out: wl hld ins fnl f* **11/1**

0220 **12** 10 **Brogans Bay (IRE)**[35] 7844 4-9-2 **57**.............................. JFEgan 12 13
(Simon Dow) *dashed up to ld after 1f: rdn and hdd over 1f out: sn lost pl: wknd fnl f (jockey said filly stopped quickly)* **25/1**

1m 12.21s (-1.49) **Going Correction** -0.25s/f (Stan) **12** Ran SP% **124.1**
Speed ratings (Par 101): **99,98,97,97,97 95,95,94,94,93 89,76**
CSF £96.30 CT £904.73 TOTE £14.50: £3.70, £2.40, £3.20; EX 107.00 Trifecta £2296.80.
Owner Merv Cox **Bred** Merv Cox **Trained** Upper Lambourn, Berks

FOCUS
They finished in a heap in this moderate sprint handicap. The second and third help pin the level.
T/Plt: £102.10 to a £1 stake. Pool: £35,294.58 - 345.57 winning units T/Qpdt: £8.70 to a £1 stake. Pool: £5,377.99 - 614.02 winning units **Steve Payne**

8837 SOUTHWELL (L-H)

Thursday, November 7

OFFICIAL GOING: Fibresand: standard
Wind: Virtually nil Weather: Heavy cloud and rain

8897 LADBROKES FOOTBALL ACCA BOOSTY NURSERY H'CAP 7f 14y(F)

4:40 (4:41) (Class 6) (0-55,57) 2-Y-O

£2,781 (£827; £413; £400; £400; £400) **Stalls** Low

Form RPR

0601 **1** **Ventura Destiny (FR)**[13] 8526 2-9-2 **54**.................... BenSanderson(5) 6 64+
(Keith Dalgleish) *in tch: pushed along over 4f out: gd hdwy on inner to trck ldrs 3f out: chal over 2f out: rdn to ld wl over 1f out: styd on strly* **3/1**[1]

4440 **2** 5 **Red Maharani**[29] 8022 2-9-10 **57**.............................. BarryMcHugh 2 54
(James Given) *wnt rt s: cl up: slt ld over 3f out: rdn wl over 2f out: hdd wl over 1f out: sn drvn and kpt on: no ch w wnr* **12/1**

0040 **3** ¾ **Comvida (IRE)**[17] 8394 2-9-4 **51**..........................(b) RichardKingscote 9 45
(Hugo Palmer) *prom: cl up 3f out: sn rdn and ev ch: drvn wl over 1f out: kpt on same pce* **7/2**[2]

506 **4** 2¼ **Mr Kodi (IRE)**[10] 8603 2-9-6 **53**.............................. BenCurtis 1 41
(David Evans) *slt ld on inner: pushed along and hdd over 3f out: rdn along wl over 2f out: drvn wl over 1f out: grad wknd* **3/1**[1]

5000 **5** 1¼ **The Works (IRE)**[43] 7582 2-8-12 **45**.............................. PaulMulrennan 4 30
(Declan Carroll) *rrd and hmpd s: in rr and sn swtchd rt to wd outside: hdwy and wd st: sn rdn and plugged on fnl 2f (jockey said filly reared leaving the stalls and was slowly away)* **16/1**

0000 **6** nk **Jazz Style (IRE)**[13] 8527 2-9-0 **52**.................... ThoreHammerHansen(5) 5 36
(David Brown) *wnt lft s: a towards rr* **13/2**[3]

0600 **7** 15 **Es Que Pearl (IRE)**[98] 5576 2-9-1 **48**.............................. PJMcDonald 8
(Rod Millman) *trckd ldrs on outer: effrt and pushed along 3f out: wd st: sn rdn and wknd* **33/1**

0600 **8** ½ **Hootenanny (IRE)**[30] 7980 2-9-7 **54**.............................. KieranShoemark 7
(Adam West) *a in rr* **25/1**

5060 **9** 3¼ **William Thomas (IRE)**[13] 8526 2-9-2 **52**.................(t[1]) GabrieleMalune(3) 3
(Robert Eddery) *hmpd s: a in rr* **20/1**

1m 28.44s (-1.86) **Going Correction** -0.425s/f (Stan) **9** Ran SP% **110.7**
Speed ratings (Par 94): **93,87,86,83,82 82,64,64,60**
CSF £36.64 CT £124.03 TOTE £2.30: £1.10, £2.00, £1.70; EX 15.60 Trifecta £102.10.
Owner Middleham Park Racing Cxviii & Partner **Bred** S A S Elevage Du Haras De Bourgeauville **Trained** Carluke, S Lanarks

FOCUS
Despite a lack of market confidence, the favourite took the opener easily.

8898 BETWAY HEED YOUR HUNCH CLASSIFIED STKS 4f 214y(F)

5:10 (5:11) (Class 6) 3-Y-O+

£2,781 (£827; £413; £400; £400; £400) **Stalls** Centre

Form RPR

3050 **1** **Loulin**[17] 8401 4-9-0 47..............................(t) JamesSullivan 9 54
(Ruth Carr) *cl up centre: rdn to ld wl over 1f out: drvn ins fnl f: hld on wl towards fin* **10/1**[3]

-206 **2** nk **Blackcurrent**[15] 8450 3-9-2 50 ow2.............................. DavidNolan 5 55
(Alan Brown) *prom centre: cl up over 2f out: rdn over 1f out: ev ch ins fnl f: sn drvn and kpt on same pce towards fin* **17/2**[2]

3622 **3** nk **Sambucca Spirit**[9] 8632 3-9-0 50.............................. KevinStott 6 52
(Paul Midgley) *sn trcking ldrs centre: hdwy 2f out: rdn to chal over 1f out: drvn and ev ch ins fnl f: kpt on same pce towards fin* **1/1**[1]

4000 **4** 1¼ **Alba Del Sole (IRE)**[26] 8119 4-9-0 50..................(p) RichardKingscote 12 47
(Charlie Wallis) *racd centre: towards rr: rdn along 1/2-way: hdwy wl over 1f out: kpt on wl fnl f* **20/1**

5600 **5** 1 **Le Manege Enchante (IRE)**[9] 8643 6-9-0 46........(v) LewisEdmunds 10 44
(Derek Shaw) *racd towards stands' side: outpcd and bhd 1/2-way: rdn and hdwy wl over 1f out: kpt on wl fnl f* **20/1**

0541 **6** ¾ **Filbert Street**[9] 8643 4-9-5 48..............................(b) KieranO'Neill 14 46+
(Roy Brotherton) *racd towards stands' rail: chsd ldr: rdn along 2f out: sn drvn and kpt on same pce* **10/1**[3]

7 ¾ **Bonnie Park (IRE)**[15] 8475 4-9-0 36..............................(t) ShaneGray 2 38
(Matthew J Smith, Ire) *racd towards far side: chsd ldrs: rdn along 2f out: sn drvn and one pce* **14/1**

1405 **8** hd **Bluella**[17] 8401 4-8-9 46..............................(bt) SeamusCronin(5) 11 38
(Robyn Brisland) *racd towards stands' side: led: rdn along 2f out: sn hdd & wknd* **14/1**

0 **9** 2½ **Gala N Dandy (IRE)**[2] 8840 4-8-7 36..............................(p) GearoidBrouder(7) 4 29
(S M Duffy, Ire) *chsd ldrs centre: rdn along 2f out: sn wknd* **50/1**

3234 **10** shd **Thornaby Princess**[39] 7737 8-9-0 48..............................(p) TomEaves 8 28
(Jason Ward) *racd centre: a in rr* **33/1**

0-06 **11** 1½ **Mocead Cappall**[8] 8668 4-8-9 45..............................(t[1]) TobyEley(5) 1 23
(John Holt) *racd far side: chsd ldrs: rdn along 2f out: sn wknd (jockey said filly hung left-handed)* **100/1**

-000 **12** 2½ **Madame Ritz (IRE)**[15] 8457 4-9-0 50.............................. JoeFanning 3 14
(Richard Phillips) *awkward s: racd towards far side: a towards rr* **12/1**

60 **13** 1¼ **Mysusy (IRE)**[47] 7468 3-9-0 46..............................(b) BenCurtis 13 9
(Robert Cowell) *racd nr stands' rail: in tch: rdn along bef 1/2-way: sn wknd* **50/1**

50-3 **14** 2¼ **Dollywaggon Pike**[82] 6199 5-9-0 42.............................. RaulDaSilva 7
(J R Jenkins) *chsd ldrs centre: rdn along over 2f out: sn drvn and wknd (jockey said mare was never travelling)* **80/1**

57.9s (-1.80) **Going Correction** -0.425s/f (Stan) **14** Ran SP% **118.3**
Speed ratings (Par 101): **97,96,96,94,92 91,90,89,85,85 83,79,77,73**
CSF £85.71 TOTE £11.40: £3.00, £2.40, £1.10; EX 104.50 Trifecta £218.40.
Owner George Murray **Bred** Rabbah Bloodstock Limited **Trained** Huby, N Yorks

FOCUS
A moderate sprint handicap. The winner has been rated to his best over the past two years.

8899 LADBROKES WHERE THE NATION PLAYS NOVICE STKS 4f 214y(F)

5:40 (5:42) (Class 5) 2-Y-O

£3,428 (£1,020; £509; £254) **Stalls** Centre

Form RPR

232 **1** **The Bell Conductor (IRE)**[9] 8631 2-9-2 0.............................. BenCurtis 5 74
(Phillip Makin) *mde most centre: rdn wl over 1f out: drvn ins fnl f: kpt on wl towards fin* **10/11**[1]

1 **2** 1¼ **Auchterarder (IRE)**[177] 2706 2-9-4 0.............................. JoeFanning 3 72+
(Mark Johnston) *dwlt and hmpd s: sn swtchd lft towards far rail: chsd ldrs: hdwy 2f out: rdn over 1f out: ev ch and drvn ins fnl f: edgd lft and kpt on same pce towards fin* **5/1**[3]

41 **3** ½ **Royal Context (IRE)**[42] 7627 2-9-9 0.............................. PaulMulrennan 6 75
(Michael Dods) *wnt lft s: trckd ldrs centre: cl up 1/2-way: rdn to chal wl over 1f out: ev ch: drvn ins fnl f: kpt on same pce towards fin* **4/1**[2]

5250 **4** 3 **Navajo Dawn (IRE)**[97] 5618 2-8-6 60.............................. SeamusCronin(5) 9 52
(Robyn Brisland) *stdd s: sn outpcd and bhd towards stands' side: rdn along and hdwy wl over 1f out: kpt on fnl f: nrst fin* **40/1**

0 **5** ½ **Mews House**[117] 4937 2-8-11 0.............................. ThoreHammerHansen(5) 7 55
(David Brown) *racd towards stands' side: chsd ldrs: rdn along 2f out: sn edgd lft and one pce* **50/1**

52 **6** 1½ **Rathagan**[36] 7825 2-8-13 0.............................. FinleyMarsh(3) 2 50
(Richard Hughes) *cl up centre: rdn along 2f out: sn drvn and wknd* **8/1**

7 nk **Ilsereno** 2-8-11 0.............................. JamesSullivan 4 44
(Scott Dixon) *hmpd s: sn swtchd lft and cl up towards far side: rdn along over 2f out: wknd wl over 1f out (vet said filly had finished lame on its right fore)* **20/1**

05 **8** hd **Quiet Word (FR)**[22] 8250 2-8-11 0.............................. AdamMcNamara 1 43
(Archie Watson) *cl up centre: rdn along over 2f out: sn drvn and wknd over 1f out* **16/1**

40 **9** ¾ **Evora Knights**[27] 8097 2-8-11 0.............................. GerO'Neill(5) 8 45
(Michael Easterby) *sn rdn along and outpcd in rr: bhd 1/2-way: sme late hdwy* **66/1**

57.61s (-2.09) **Going Correction** -0.425s/f (Stan) 2y crse rec **9** Ran SP% **116.7**
Speed ratings (Par 96): **99,97,96,91,90 88,87,87,86**
CSF £5.71 TOTE £1.50: £1.10, £2.40, £1.20; EX 6.50 Trifecta £15.30.
Owner Mrs Wendy Burdett **Bred** Denis B McCarthy **Trained** Easingwold, N Yorks

FOCUS
This only concerned three in the final stages. The market leader beat the two previous winners in the field. It's been rated as limited form, with the third seemingly to his pre-race mark.

8900 BETWAY SUPPORTING RESPONSIBLE GAMBLING H'CAP 4f 214y(F)

6:10 (6:12) (Class 4) (0-85,85) 3-Y-O+

£5,207 (£1,549; £774; £400; £400; £400) **Stalls** Centre

Form RPR

441 **1** **Hareem Queen (IRE)**[22] 8268 3-9-0 **78**.............................. PJMcDonald 1 93+
(K R Burke) *cl up: led wl over 1f out: rdn clr ent fnl f: v readily* **2/1**[1]

3400 **2** 2¾ **Free Love**[19] 8340 3-9-3 **84**.............................. TheodoreLadd(3) 7 89
(Michael Appleby) *chsd ldrs: rdn along 2f out: drvn over 1f out: kpt on fnl f* **8/1**

1410 **3** ¾ **Crosse Fire**[22] 8267 7-9-5 **83**..............................(b) KieranO'Neill 6 85
(Scott Dixon) *dwlt: sn cl up: rdn along 2f out: drvn over 1f out: kpt on wl u.p fnl f* **7/1**

0000 **4** nse **Erissimus Maximus (FR)**[22] 8262 5-9-2 **80**.......... RichardKingscote 2 82
(Robert Cowell) *wnt rt s: in tch: pushed along and outpcd 3f out: rdn over 2f out: hdwy over 1f out: kpt on fnl f: nrst fin* **10/3**[2]

5060 **5** nk **Yousini**[47] 7431 3-9-7 **85**..............................(v) TomEaves 4 86
(Kevin Ryan) *hmpd s: sn swtchd lft towards far side and hdwy to chse ldrs after 1f: rdn along 2f out: drvn over 1f out: kpt on same pce fnl f* **5/1**[3]

5000 **6** 1 **Machree (IRE)**[19] 8349 4-9-2 **80**.............................. PaulMulrennan 8 77
(Declan Carroll) *sn led: rdn along and hdd over 1f out: wknd fnl f* **14/1**

0604 **7** 2 **Peggie Sue**[22] 8262 4-9-3 **81**.............................. KieranShoemark 9 71
(Adam West) *racd towards stands' side: chsd ldrs: rdn along over 2f out: sn wknd* **16/1**

-005 **8** 10 **Rapid Applause**[44] 7541 7-9-1 **84**.............................. GerO'Neill(5) 5 38
(Michael Easterby) *towards rr: rdn along and outpcd after 1f: bhd and eased over 1f out* **33/1**

56.97s (-2.73) **Going Correction** -0.425s/f (Stan) **8** Ran SP% **112.2**
Speed ratings (Par 105): **104,99,98,98,97 96,93,77**
CSF £18.11 CT £92.36 TOTE £1.90: £1.10, £2.90, £2.00; EX 18.50 Trifecta £80.10.
Owner John Dance **Bred** Corduff Stud **Trained** Middleham Moor, N Yorks

FOCUS
This went to the unexposed 3yo in among some far more experienced performers. The second has been rated in line with her best, and the third close to form.

8901 BETWAY CLASSIFIED STKS 6f 16y(F)

6:40 (6:43) (Class 6) 3-Y-O+

£2,781 (£827; £413; £400; £400; £400) **Stalls** Low

Form RPR

6053 **1** **Atwaar**[7] 8689 3-8-9 44.............................. FayeMcManoman(5) 1 52
(Charles Smith) *hld up towards rr: hdwy on inner 3f out: rdn to chse ldrs wl over 1f out: led jst ins fnl f: kpt on wl* **10/1**

5052 **2** 1¾ **Groupie**[15] 8469 5-9-0 50.............................. AndrewMullen 2 50
(Tom Tate) *chsd ldrs: rdn 2f out: n.m.r and swtchd lft over 1f out: keeping on whn nt clr run ins fnl f: swtchd rt and drvn: fin strly* **4/1**[2]

The Form Book Flat 2019, Raceform Ltd, Newbury, RG14 5SJ

0000 **3** shd **Hellofagame**[17] 8408 4-8-9 25.....(t) SeamusCronin(5) 8 46
(Richard Price) *cl up: rdn along over 2f out: drvn and ev ch over 1f out: k*
66/1

5060 **4** ½ **Tilsworth Rose**[49] 7371 5-9-0 43.....(b) RaulDaSilva 13 45
(J R Jenkins) *prom: led 4f out: rdn along over 2f out: drvn over 1f out: hdd jst ins fnl f: kpt on same pce*
28/1

5005 **5** nk **Reshaan (IRE)**[16] 8435 4-8-9 40.....(b[1]) ThoreHammerHansen(5) 11 44
(Alexandra Dunn) *rdn along and outpcd in rr: bhd and wd st: hdwy nr stands' rail 2f out: kpt on u.p fnl f*
15/2

0654 **6** 1¾ **Tadaany (IRE)**[17] 8401 7-9-0 47.....(v) JackGarritty 4 39
(Ruth Carr) *slt ld on inner: hdd 4f out: chsd ldrs: rdn along 2f out: sn drvn and kpt on same pce*
6/1[3]

0632 **7** ½ **I'll Be Good**[9] 8638 10-9-0 47..... KevinStott 9 37
(Alan Berry) *prom: cl up 3f out: rdn along over 2f out: drvn and wknd over 1f out*
10/1

0653 **8** 1¾ **Meshardal (GER)**[140] 4037 9-9-0 47.....(p w) JamesSullivan 3 32
(Ruth Carr) *chsd ldrs: rdn along 2f out: sn drvn and wknd*
10/1

9 1 **Baile Ghilibert (IRE)**[772] 7497 7-8-11 39..... TheodoreLadd(3) 12 29
(Michael Appleby) *hld up towards rr: wd st: sn rdn along: n.d*
5/2[1]

/000 **10** 2¼ **Jackman**[9] 8637 5-9-0 34.....(b[1]) BarryMcHugh 6 22
(Lee James) *sn rdn along and outpcd: a in rr: wd st and bhd fnl 2f* **66/1**

0200 **11** 3½ **Kyllukey**[164] 3143 6-9-0 46..... BenCurtis 7 12
(Charlie Wallis) *nvr bttr than midfield*
20/1

500 **12** 3½ **Cominginonmonday (IRE)**[131] 4367 4-9-0 46..... KieranO'Neill 5
(Robyn Brisland) *a towards rr*
22/1

1m 13.97s (-2.53) **Going Correction** -0.425s/f (Stan) 12 Ran SP% 117.4
Speed ratings (Par 101): **99,96,96,95,95 93,92,90,88,85 81,76**
CSF £46.85 TOTE £15.70: £2.80, £2.20, £35.10; EX 49.10 Trifecta £2492.60.
Owner M Smeed **Bred** Shadwell Estate Company Limited **Trained** Temple Bruer, Lincs

■ Countess Matilda was withdrawn. Price at time of withdrawal 14-1. Rule 4 applies to bets struck prior to withdrawal but not to SP bets - dedcution 5p in the pound. New market formed.

■ Stewards' Enquiry : Jack Garritty three-day ban: interference & careless riding (Nov 21-23)
Seamus Cronin 10-day ban: failing to ride out (Nov 21-23, 26-30, Dec 2-3)

FOCUS
The run of the third, who had an official mark of 25, confirms this as being really moderate form.

8902 BOMBARDIER GOLDEN BEER H'CAP 1m 13y(F)
7:10 (7:11) (Class 5) (0-75,81) 3-Y-O+

£3,428 (£1,020; £509; £400; £400; £400) **Stalls** Low

Form RPR

3- **1** **Fancy Footings (IRE)**[69] 6694 3-9-6 **74**..... RichardKingscote 1 85
(Tom Dascombe) *trckd ldrs on inner: hdwy 3f out: sn chsng ldr: rdn to ld 1 1/2f out: styd on strly*
14/1

3564 **2** 3¼ **Fieldsman (USA)**[66] 6795 7-8-8 **67**..... LauraCoughlan(7) 12 71
(Tony Carroll) *hld up: hdwy on outer 3f out: chsd ldrs wl over 1f out: sn rdn: chsd wnr ins fnl f: no imp towards fin*
40/1

4203 **3** 1¼ **Ollivander (IRE)**[9] 8642 3-9-7 **75**.....(v) DavidNolan 2 76
(David O'Meara) *led: rdn along over 2f out: rdn and hdd 1 1/2f out: sn drvn and kpt on same pce fnl f*
12/1

4311 **4** nk **Makambe (IRE)**[34] 7875 4-9-5 **71**.....(p) JoeyHaynes 9 71+
(Chelsea Banham) *towards rr: pushed along 3f out: rdn and hdwy over 2f out: drvn over 1f out: styd on fnl f*
7/2[2]

6021 **5** 1¼ **Al Erayg (IRE)**[9] 8642 6-10-1 **81** 5ex.....(p) DavidAllan 3 79
(Tim Easterby) *trckd ldrs: pushed along over 3f out: rdn along over 2f out: drvn wl over 1f out: sn one pce*
13/8[1]

0026 **6** ½ **Filles De Fleur**[12] 8549 3-9-4 **72**.....(p[1]) PaulMulrennan 7 68
(George Scott) *t.k.h: trckd ldrs: hdwy over 2f out: rdn wl over 1f out: wknd fnl f*
25/1

0001 **7** 2 **Bond Angel**[22] 8270 4-8-13 **65**..... BenCurtis 5 57
(David Evans) *in rr: sme hdwy on inner over 2f out: rdn along wl over 1f out: no imp (jockey said filly suffered interference in running)*
9/1[3]

0035 **8** 4½ **Moxy Mares**[13] 8521 4-9-2 **73**.....(p) KevinLundie(5) 4 54
(Mark Loughnane) *in tch on inner: pushed along 3f out: rdn over 2f out: sn drvn and n.d*
20/1

260 **9** 1¼ **Sylviacliffs (FR)**[149] 3685 3-8-4 **65**.....(p) RhonaPindar(7) 11 44
(K R Burke) *trckd ldrs: hdwy on outer 3f out: rdn along 2f out: sn drvn and wknd over 1f out*
40/1

5152 **10** ½ **Muqarred (USA)**[22] 8266 7-8-13 **65**.....(b) ShaneGray 6 42
(Karen Tutty) *cl up: pushed along over 3f out: rdn wl over 2f out: sn wknd*
9/1[3]

2250 **11** 4 **Dashing Poet**[104] 5373 5-8-12 **64**..... PJMcDonald 8 32
(Heather Main) *awkward and dwlt s: sn swtchd rt to wd outside: a bhd (jockey said mare was slowly away)*
14/1

1m 39.08s (-4.62) **Going Correction** -0.425s/f (Stan)
WFA 3 from 4yo+ 2lb 11 Ran SP% 114.8
Speed ratings (Par 103): **106,102,101,101,99 99,97,92,91,91 87**
CSF £476.62 CT £6797.52 TOTE £10.70: £3.20, £10.70, £3.30; EX 362.70 Trifecta £2199.20.
Owner Andrew Brown & Gemma Brown **Bred** William Joseph Martin **Trained** Malpas, Cheshire

FOCUS
Just an ordinary event for the level, with the market leaders running below expectations. The second has been rated to last year's C&D form.

8903 BOMBARDIER "MARCH TO YOUR OWN DRUM" H'CAP 1m 13y(F)
7:40 (7:42) (Class 6) (0-60,62) 3-Y-O+

£2,781 (£827; £413; £400; £400; £400) **Stalls** Low

Form RPR

0122 **1** **Charlie Arthur (IRE)**[8] 8669 3-9-6 **62**..... FinleyMarsh(3) 5 72+
(Richard Hughes) *dwlt: hdwy to trck ldrs on outer after 2f: cl up 1/2-way: led over 2f out: rdn wl over 1f out: drvn clr ent fnl f: sn edgd lft and kpt on wl*
3/1[1]

302 **2** 3¾ **Geography Teacher (IRE)**[9] 8646 3-9-6 **59**.....(b[1]) RossaRyan 3 60
(R Mike Smith) *trckd ldrs: smooth hdwy 3f out: sn cl up: chal 2f out: sn rdn and ev ch: drvn ent fnl f and kpt on same pce*
6/1[3]

3000 **3** 1¼ **Amber Rock (USA)**[24] 8205 3-8-6 **45**.....(tp) JoeFanning 2 44
(Les Eyre) *t.k.h: hld up in rr: hdwy whn hmpd over 3f out and wnt wd home turn: chsd ldrs and hung lft to inner 2f out: sn rdn: styd on appr fnl f: nrst fin*
8/1

1514 **4** hd **Alpha Tauri (USA)**[17] 8405 13-9-5 **61**..... AledBeech(5) 6 59
(Charles Smith) *in tch: pushed along to chse ldrs over 3f out: rdn over 2f out: drvn wl over 1f out: kpt on same pce fnl f*
14/1

0605 **5** 6 **God Has Given**[23] 8223 3-9-5 **58**.....(t) DavidNolan 7 42
(Ivan Furtado) *hld up in rr: hdwy over 3f out: chsd ldrs over 2f out: sn rdn and no imp*
12/1

0312 **6** ¾ **Atalanta Queen**[17] 8405 4-9-1 **52**.....(b) KieranO'Neill 11 35
(Robyn Brisland) *cl up: led over 4f out: rdn along over 3f out: hdd over 2f out: sn drvn and wknd*
7/2[2]

3420 **7** 6 **Osmosis**[24] 8205 3-9-7 **60**..... BenCurtis 1 29
(Jason Ward) *trckd ldrs on inner: pushed along 3f out: rdn over 2f out: sn wknd*
9/1

0004 **8** nk **The Gingerbreadman**[22] 8266 4-8-3 **45**..... PaulaMuir(5) 10 13
(Chris Fairhurst) *dwlt: sn chsng ldrs on outer: rdn along 3f out: sn wknd*
20/1

3000 **9** 15 **Closer Than Close**[24] 8205 3-9-6 **59**.....(b[1]) PJMcDonald 8
(Jonathan Portman) *slt ld: hdd over 4f out: rdn along and lost pl over 3f out: sn bhd*
6/1[3]

1m 40.11s (-3.59) **Going Correction** -0.425s/f (Stan)
WFA 3 from 4yo+ 2lb 9 Ran SP% 116.0
Speed ratings (Par 101): **100,96,95,94,88 88,82,81,66**
CSF £21.43 CT £130.70 TOTE £2.60: £1.50, £1.40, £2.10; EX 21.60 Trifecta £202.00.
Owner L Turland And A Smith **Bred** Rathbarry Stud **Trained** Upper Lambourn, Berks

FOCUS
Three-year-olds filled the first three positions in this modest event. The second has been rated as running at least as well as of late, but the third raises doubts it's worth more than this.

8904 BETWAY LIVE CASINO H'CAP 1m 4f 14y(F)
8:10 (8:11) (Class 6) (0-60,61) 4-Y-O+

£2,781 (£827; £413; £400; £400; £400) **Stalls** Low

Form RPR

4211 **1** **Blyton Lass**[28] 8072 4-9-3 **55**..... BarryMcHugh 1 61
(James Given) *trckd ldrs on inner: smooth hdwy over 3f out: led 2f out: sn rdn: drvn ins fnl f: hld on wl towards fin*
5/2[1]

0000 **2** nk **Going Native**[9] 8639 4-8-5 **50**..... RhonaPindar(7) 8 56
(Olly Williams) *hld up in rr: hdwy on inner 3f out: chsd ldrs 2f out: effrt whn nt clr run and swtchd lft wl over 1f out: sn rdn and chal ent fnl f: sn drvn and ev ch tl no ex towards fin*
16/1

0000 **3** 3½ **Doctor Jazz (IRE)**[9] 8639 4-8-13 **58**..... MarkCrehan(7) 9 58
(Michael Appleby) *led: pushed along 4f out: rdn over 3f out: hdd 2f out: drvn over 1f out: wknd fnl f*
16/1

5204 **4** hd **Apache Blaze**[8] 8663 4-9-4 **61**..... SeamusCronin(5) 2 61
(Robyn Brisland) *hld up towards rr: hdwy 3f out: chsd ldrs and rdn 2f out: sn drvn and kpt on same pce*
4/1[2]

0544 **5** 8 **Tyrsal (IRE)**[34] 7873 8-8-7 **45**.....(p) JosephineGordon 4 32
(Shaun Keightley) *hld up: effrt and hdwy over 3f out: rdn along over 2f out: sn btn*
10/1

5-66 **6** shd **Lilypad (IRE)**[19] 3708 4-9-7 **59**..... BenCurtis 5 46
(Amy Murphy) *prom: pushed along 1/2-way: rdn along and wknd over 3f out*
10/1

0245 **7** 2 **Gworn**[16] 8423 9-8-10 **48**..... PJMcDonald 7 32
(R Mike Smith) *prom: cl up over 7f out: rdn along over 3f out: drvn wl over 2f out: sn wknd*
4/1[2]

6-00 **8** 3¼ **Finisher (USA)**[23] 8224 4-9-0 **55**.....(b[1]) TimClark(3) 6 34
(Mark Gillard) *t.k.h: trckd ldrs: chsd ldng pair over 4f out: rdn along 3f out: sn drvn and wknd*
7/1[3]

0400 **9** 99 **Bold Statement (IRE)**[39] 7732 4-8-2 **45**.....(b[1]) PaulaMuir(5) 3
(Alan Berry) *dwlt and reminders s: sn outpcd and bhd: t.o fnl 4f (jockey said gelding was never travelling; vet said a post-race examination revealed the gelding finished lame on its right-fore)*
50/1

2m 35.86s (-5.14) **Going Correction** -0.425s/f (Stan) 9 Ran SP% 113.0
Speed ratings (Par 101): **100,99,97,97,92 91,90,88,22**
CSF £44.48 CT £524.24 TOTE £2.50: £1.40, £3.50, £3.30; EX 37.40 Trifecta £246.80.
Owner Andy Clarke **Bred** Mrs V J Lovelace **Trained** Willoughton, Lincs

FOCUS
A modest middle-distance contest.
T/Plt: £86.70 to a £1 stake. Pool: £65,752.66 - 553.20 winning unit T/Qpdt: £48.70 to a £1 stake. Pool: 7,313.32 - 111.06 winning units **Joe Rowntree**

8905 - 8911a (Foreign Racing) - See Raceform Interactive

8889
CHELMSFORD (A.W) (L-H)
Friday, November 8

OFFICIAL GOING: Polytrack: standard
Wind: light, half against Weather: rain early, then dry

8912 TOTEPOOL CASHBACK AT TOTESPORT.COM NOVICE STKS (PLUS 10 RACE) 6f (P)
5:25 (5:27) (Class 4) 2-Y-O **£5,822** (£1,732; £865; £432) **Stalls** Centre

Form RPR

523 **1** **Ottoman Court**[84] 6154 2-9-5 90.....(p) WilliamBuick 8 91+
(Charlie Appleby) *mde all: rdn clr over 1f out: in n.d and r.o strly ins fnl f*
6/4[2]

2 **2** 6 **King Ragnar**[49] 7406 2-9-5 0..... AndreaAtzeni 5 71
(Roger Varian) *in tch in midfield: effrt 2f out: rdn over 1f out: chsd clr wnr 1f out: no imp*
11/10[1]

5 **3** 4½ **Creek Horizon**[16] 8455 2-9-5 0..... CallumShepherd 6 58
(Saeed bin Suroor) *chsd ldrs: effrt to chse wnr 2f out: unable qck u.p and lost btn 2nd 1f out: wknd ins fnl f*
5/1[3]

0 **4** ½ **Tyger Bay**[23] 8250 2-8-12 0.....(t) GavinAshton(7) 1 56
(Shaun Keightley) *midfield: nudged along over 1f out: sn outpcd and no ch w wnr 1f out: kpt on to go modest 4th 100yds out (jockey said regarding running and ridding that his instructions were to jump off and get colt settled into a nice rhythm, to sit as handy as possible in the home straight and to keep both hands on the reins. The trainer stated that the ride accorded wit*
50/1

45 **5** 2¾ **Streeton (IRE)**[17] 8418 2-9-5 0.....(b[1]) HarryBentley 9 48
(Ralph Beckett) *restless in stalls: dwlt and swtchd lft after s: rdn wl over 1f out: sn outpcd and wl btn 1f out*
20/1

0 **6** ½ **Rains Of Castamere**[31] 7981 2-9-0 0..... ScottMcCullagh(5) 2 46
(Mick Channon) *chsd wnr tl 2f out: sn outpcd and btn: wknd fnl f (jockey said that the bit slipped through the gelding's mouth)*
33/1

7 ½ **Casaruan** 2-8-12 0..... MarkCrehan(7) 4 45
(Michael Appleby) *s.i.s: outpcd and shkn up wl over 1f out: sn wl btn* **80/1**

00 **8** 1¼ **Joanna Vassa**[8] 8700 2-9-0 0..... HollieDoyle 7 36
(Roger Ingram) *t.k.h: hld up in midfield on outer: rdn and lost pl over 2f out: wknd over 1f out*
100/1

06 **9** *1* **Lethal Blast**[88] 8028 2-8-9 0.............................(t[1] w) RhiainIngram(5) 3 33
(Karen George) *t.k.h: hld up in rr: outpcd and pushed along 2f out: sn wknd* **100/1**

1m 11.76s (-1.94) **Going Correction** -0.175s/f (Stan) **9** Ran SP% **117.2**
Speed ratings (Par 98): **105,97,91,90,86 86,85,83,82**
CSF £3.44 TOTE £2.00: £1.10, £1.10, £1.20; EX 3.50 Trifecta £7.50.
Owner Godolphin **Bred** Godolphin **Trained** Newmarket, Suffolk

FOCUS
An uneventful novice in which the all-the-way winner proved a cut above. Some of those further back will improve in time. The likes of the fourth are the key to the form, but the winner thrashed these and could be value for a few lengths better than rated.

8913 EXTRA PLACES AT TOTESPORT.COM FILLIES' NOVICE STKS (PLUS 10 RACE) 7f (P)

5:55 (5:59) (Class 4) 2-Y-O **£5,822** (£1,732; £865; £432) **Stalls** Low

Form RPR

1232 **1** **Jeanie B**[7] 8723 2-8-13 80.............................. ScottMcCullagh(5) 12 81
(Mick Channon) *chsd ldrs tl hdwy to chse ldr after 2f: rdn to ld over 1f out: hld on wl u.p ins fnl f* **7/1**[2]

2 *nk* **Franconia** 2-9-0 0.............................. RobertHavlin 9 76+
(John Gosden) *chsd ldrs: effrt over 2f out: rdn and clsd to press wnr 1f out: maintained chal ins fnl f: kpt on wl but hld towards fin* **9/4**[1]

6 **3** *1 1/4* **Folk Dance**[41] 7695 2-9-0 0.............................. JamieSpencer 2 73+
(David Simcock) *hld up in tch in midfield: swtchd wd bnd 2f out: effrt over 1f out: lugged lft ins fnl f: kpt on to go 3rd last strides: nvr getting to ldrs* **9/4**[1]

06 **4** *hd* **Secret Smile (IRE)**[8] 8700 2-9-0 0.............................. RichardKingscote 8 72
(Mark Johnston) *chsd ldr for 2f: styd chsng ldrs: effrt 2f out: drvn and pressing ldrs 1f out: no ex 100yds out: outpcd towards fin and lost 3rd last strides* **20/1**

5 *4 1/2* **Far Rockaway** 2-9-0 0..............................(h[1]) TomMarquand 5 61+
(William Haggas) *towards rr: rdn over 2f out: hdwy ent fnl f: kpt on wl to pass btn horses ins fnl f: nvr trbld ldrs* **11/1**

43 **6** *hd* **Grace And Virtue (IRE)**[21] 8316 2-9-0 0.............................. TonyHamilton 4 60
(Richard Fahey) *in tch in midfield: rdn and struggling to qckn ent fnl 2f: sn outpcd: wl hld and plugged on same pce ins fnl f* **20/1**

0 **7** *1 3/4* **Queen Of Clubs**[94] 5772 2-9-0 0..............................(w) JasonWatson 13 56
(Roger Charlton) *led: rdn jst over 2f out: hdd over 1f out: sn outpcd and wknd ins fnl f* **40/1**

00 **8** *1/2* **Chosen Star**[16] 8453 2-9-0 0.............................. CallumShepherd 1 54
(Michael Bell) *midfield: rdn over 2f out: sn outpcd: wl hld and kpt on same pce ins fnl f* **50/1**

0 **9** *3/4* **Fleet Street**[59] 7054 2-9-0 0.............................. NickyMackay 16 52
(John Gosden) *swtchd lft after s: in tch in midfield: rdn over 2f out: sn struggling and outpcd: wknd fnl f* **7/1**[2]

0 **10** *hd* **Alpine Mistral (IRE)**[25] 8198 2-9-0 0.............................. ShaneKelly 15 52
(Shaun Keightley) *swtchd lft after s: hld up in midfield: shkn up 2f out: rdn over 1f out: no imp and edgd lft 1f out: wl hld and kpt on same pce ins fnl f* **66/1**

11 *nk* **Charming Rose** 2-9-0 0.............................. KieranO'Neill 10 51
(John Gosden) *hld up towards rr: rdn over 3f out: kpt on but no imp: nvr involved* **10/1**[3]

0 **12** *4 1/2* **Spandavia (IRE)**[16] 8453 2-9-0 0.............................. HollieDoyle 11 39
(Ed Dunlop) *t.k.h: hld up towards rr: rdn and outpcd over 2f out: wl hld over 1f out* **50/1**

0 **13** *2 1/4* **Truffle Mac**[14] 8516 2-9-0 0.............................. CharlieBennett 3 34
(Hughie Morrison) *s.i.s: off the pce in midfield: effrt ent fnl 2f: sn struggling and outpcd: wknd fnl f* **25/1**

0 **14** *1 1/4* **Nikolayeva**[16] 8454 2-9-0 0..............................(h) LukeMorris 14 30
(Sir Mark Prescott Bt) *dwlt: rn green and sn rousted along: a in rr: rdn over 2f out: sn outpcd and wl btn over 1f out* **100/1**

15 *1/2* **Brazen Sheila** 2-8-8 0 ow1.............................. MarkCrehan(7) 7 30
(Michael Appleby) *led most of the way to s: awkward leaving stalls and slowly away: a in rr: rdn and detached last over 3f out: no ch after* **100/1**

1m 25.16s (-2.04) **Going Correction** -0.175s/f (Stan) **15** Ran SP% **127.2**
Speed ratings (Par 95): **104,103,102,102,96 96,94,94,93,92 92,87,84,83,82**
CSF £22.60 TOTE £9.20: £2.20, £1.10, £1.30; EX 34.60 Trifecta £74.80.
Owner Bastian Family **Bred** E & R Bastian **Trained** West Ilsley, Berks

FOCUS
An interesting fillies' novice in which those ridden prominently dominated and the winner's experience counted for plenty, so those closing late are worth marking up.

8914 BET TOTEEXACTA AT TOTESPORT.COM NOVICE STKS (PLUS 10 RACE) 1m (P)

6:25 (6:29) (Class 4) 2-Y-O **£5,822** (£1,732; £865; £432) **Stalls** Low

Form RPR

0 **1** **Stepney Causeway**[119] 4886 2-9-5 0.............................. CallumShepherd 13 75
(Michael Bell) *chsd ldrs: hdwy to press ldr after 2f: rdn and ev ch over 1f out: drvn to ld 1f out: edgd rt ins fnl f: all out cl home: hld on* **40/1**

4 **2** *hd* **Al Qaqaa (USA)**[34] 7899 2-9-5 0.............................. TomMarquand 2 75+
(William Haggas) *broke wl: sn restrained and wl in tch in midfield: effrt and rdn ent fnl 2f: drvn and clsd to chse ldrs ins fnl f: swtchd rt and chsd wnr towards fin: r.o: jst hld* **8/13**[1]

40 **3** *1 1/4* **Provocation (IRE)**[14] 8528 2-9-0 0.............................. AndrewBreslin(5) 12 72
(Mark Johnston) *hdwy to ld over 6f out: rdn ent fnl 2f: drvn over 1f out: hdd 1f out: no ex and wknd towards fin* **66/1**

0 **4** *nse* **Spanish Kiss**[37] 7814 2-9-5 0.............................. HollieDoyle 10 72
(William Knight) *t.k.h: chsd ldrs: effrt over 1f out: keeping on same pce and hld whn bmpd towards fin (jockey said colt hung right-handed throughout)* **16/1**

0 **5** *4 1/2* **Sure I'm Your Man (IRE)**[14] 8518 2-9-5 0.............................. JasonWatson 6 62
(Roger Charlton) *in tch in midfield: rdn over 2f out: sn struggling to qckn and outpcd over 1f out: wl hld and kpt on same pce ins fnl f* **16/1**

6 *1/2* **Colonize** 2-9-5 0.............................. DavidEgan 5 61+
(John Gosden) *s.i.s: hld up in last quintet: effrt over 2f out: swtchd rt and kpt on ins fnl f: nvr trbld ldrs (jockey said colt was slowly away)* **9/2**[2]

7 *1 1/4* **Alkhat** 2-9-5 0.............................. RobertHavlin 7 58
(John Gosden) *led for over 1f: chsd ldrs: rdn over 1f out: unable qck and wknd ins fnl f* **7/1**[3]

8 *1 3/4* **You Owe Me** 2-9-5 0.............................. RichardKingscote 4 54
(Mark Johnston) *rn green: towards rr: rdn over 2f out: hung lft and no imp over 1f out: nvr trbld ldrs (jockey said colt ran green)* **16/1**

00 **9** *1/2* **Bee Able (USA)**[37] 7814 2-9-0 0.............................. HarryBentley 9 47
(Ralph Beckett) *dwlt: a towards rr: rdn and outpcd over 2f out: n.d after* **33/1**

10 *shd* **Been Bobbied (IRE)** 2-9-5 0.............................. KieranO'Neill 1 52
(Richard Fahey) *t.k.h: in tch in midfield: effrt and clsd over 2f out: no imp over 1f out: hung rt 1f out and wknd ins fnl f (jockey said colt ran keen)* **33/1**

11 *1 1/4* **Good Try** 2-9-0 0.............................. StevieDonohoe 11 44
(Michael Bell) *dwlt: midfield: rdn over 2f out: sn outpcd and btn over 1f out: wknd ins fnl f* **66/1**

0 **12** *1 3/4* **African Sun (IRE)**[7] 8717 2-9-5 0.............................. KieranShoemark 8 45
(Ed Dunlop) *dwlt: a towards rr: effrt over 1f out: no imp and wknd ins fnl f* **100/1**

0 **13** *12* **Spring To Mind**[32] 7972 2-9-0 0.............................. RobHornby 3 13
(Ralph Beckett) *broke wl enough and chsd ldrs early: steadily lost pl: bhd over 1f out* **40/1**

1m 39.62s (-0.28) **Going Correction** -0.175s/f (Stan) **13** Ran SP% **125.0**
Speed ratings (Par 98): **94,93,92,92,88 87,86,84,84,83 82,80,68**
CSF £67.81 TOTE £47.20: £9.80, £1.10, £16.00; EX 136.60 Trifecta £1819.40.
Owner W J and T C O Gredley **Bred** Laundry Cottage Stud Farm **Trained** Newmarket, Suffolk

FOCUS
An informative novice in which, once again, a prominent position proved crucial, so any late headway needs marking up. The bare form has been rated as ordinary, with the time slow.

8915 BUY YOUR 2020 CCR MEMBERSHIP NOW H'CAP 1m (P)

6:55 (6:59) (Class 6) (0-52,53) 3-Y-O+ **£3,315** (£986; £493; £300; £300; £300) **Stalls** Low

Form RPR

2504 **1** **Caledonia Laird**[36] 7859 8-9-7 52..............................(e) HollieDoyle 3 58
(Gay Kelleway) *in tch in midfield: nt clr run over 2f out: gap opened and hdwy to chal over 1f out: hung rt but maintained chal to ld cl home (jockey said gelding hung badly right-handed)* **7/1**

5004 **2** *shd* **Quick Recovery**[8] 8689 4-9-2 47.............................. CharlieBennett 2 53
(Jim Boyle) *chsd ldrs: rdn to ld wl over 1f out: sustained duel w wnr fnl f: kpt on u.p: hdd cl home* **11/1**

5035 **3** *3/4* **Caribbean Spring (IRE)**[6] 8757 6-9-3 53.............................. GeorgiaDobie(5) 10 57
(George Margarson) *in tch in midfield: effrt over 1f out: kpt on ins fnl f: wnt 3rd towards fin: nt rch ldrs* **6/1**[3]

0432 **4** *1 3/4* **Rosarno (IRE)**[8] 8694 5-9-5 50..............................(bt) JoeyHaynes 7 50
(Chelsea Banham) *in tch in midfield: effrt on outer 2f out: drvn and ev ch over 1f out: no ex 100yds out and wknd towards fin* **5/2**[1]

0000 **5** *nk* **Lady Carduros (IRE)**[74] 6529 5-9-1 46 oh1..............................(p[1]) LiamJones 8 45
(Michael Appleby) *towards rr and pushed along at times: nt clr run over 1f out: hdwy u.p 1f out: styd on ins fnl f: nt rch ldrs* **66/1**

3000 **6** *1/2* **Ramblow**[6] 8756 6-8-8 46 oh1..............................(bt) KeelanBaker(7) 12 45
(Alexandra Dunn) *reluctant to go to post and led to post: s.i.s: hld up in rr: clsd and nt clr run over 1f out: styd on u.p ins fnl f: nt rch ldrs (jockey said mare was slowly away and was denied a clear run)* **100/1**

4000 **7** *3 1/4* **Jailbreak (IRE)**[64] 6885 3-8-13 46 oh1.............................. RobertHavlin 13 37
(Conrad Allen) *stdd s: hld up in rr: effrt on inner over 1f out: nvr getting on terms but kpt on ins fnl f* **25/1**

0012 **8** *nse* **So Claire**[13] 8547 3-9-4 51.............................. JaneElliott 9 42
(William Muir) *hld up towards rr: forced v wd and effrt bnd 2f out: kpt on ins fnl f: nvr trbld ldrs* **11/1**

3004 **9** *shd* **Squire**[8] 8694 8-9-4 49..............................(bt) TomMarquand 14 39
(Marjorie Fife) *dwlt: styd wd early: in tch in midfield: effrt and drvn over 1f out: unable qck and wknd ins fnl f* **10/1**

0260 **10** *1/2* **Clement (IRE)**[21] 8301 9-9-6 51..............................(p) LukeMorris 1 40
(Marjorie Fife) *in tch in midfield: effrt over 1f out: sn drvn and unable qck: wknd ins fnl f* **16/1**

0031 **11** *1 1/2* **The King's Steed**[8] 8689 6-9-8 53..............................(bt) KieranShoemark 4 39
(Shaun Lycett) *chsd ldrs: squeezed for room wl over 1f out: sn lost pl and wknd fnl f (jockey said gelding lugged right-handed)* **3/1**[2]

6600 **12** *4* **Iris's Spirit**[23] 8256 3-8-13 46 oh1.............................. RobHornby 5 23
(Tony Carroll) *pushed along in midfield on outer: lost pl u.p over 1f out: wknd fnl f* **40/1**

0565 **13** *nk* **Ocean Temptress**[17] 8436 5-8-10 46 oh1..............................(b) RayDawson(5) 11 22
(Louise Allan) *rousted along leaving stalls: sn led: drvn ent fnl 3f: hdd wl over 1f out: sn dropped out and wknd fnl f* **50/1**

0000 **14** *2* **Arrowzone**[9] 8667 8-9-4 49..............................(bt) ShaneKelly 6 20
(Katy Price) *led early: sn hdd and chsd ldrs tl wl over 1f out: sn lost pl and wknd fnl f* **33/1**

1m 38.84s (-1.06) **Going Correction** -0.175s/f (Stan)
WFA 3 from 4yo+ 2lb **14** Ran SP% **125.7**
Speed ratings (Par 101): **98,97,97,95,95 94,91,91,91,90 89,85,84,82**
CSF £81.85 CT £516.66 TOTE £7.60: £1.70, £3.50, £2.70; EX 42.90 Trifecta £286.70.
Owner Isla & Colin Cage **Bred** Mrs I M Cage And Mr C J Cage **Trained** Exning, Suffolk

FOCUS
A well-run race which looks solid form for the grade. Straightforward form.

8916 BET AT TOTESPORT.COM H'CAP 1m 5f 66y(P)

7:25 (7:26) (Class 6) (0-55,56) 3-Y-O+ **£3,338** (£993; £496; £300; £300; £300) **Stalls** Low

Form RPR

0623 **1** **Falcon Cliffs (IRE)**[8] 8703 5-9-10 55.............................. TomMarquand 12 62
(Tony Carroll) *pushed along early: racd in rr: rdn: hdwy and swtchd rt 2f out: styd on u.p to ld ins fnl f: sn clr* **3/1**[1]

2154 **2** *2 1/2* **Royal Dancer**[10] 8644 3-9-2 52.............................. JasonWatson 2 57
(Sylvester Kirk) *hld up in tch in midfield: effrt on inner over 1f out: drvn to ld and edgd rt jst over 1f out: hdd and one pce ins fnl f* **10/3**[2]

0035 **3** *1 1/2* **Millie May**[31] 7985 5-9-1 46 oh1.............................. HollieDoyle 4 47
(Jimmy Fox) *short of room and pushed along leaving stalls: racd in last pair: clsd and pushed rt bnd 2f out: hdwy u.p over 1f out: kpt on ins fnl f (jockey said mare suffered interference when leaving the stalls)* **20/1**

0006 **4** *nk* **Affair**[31] 7985 5-9-1 46..............................(t[1]) CharlieBennett 11 47
(Hughie Morrison) *midfield: effrt over 2f out: clsd u.p to press ldrs 1f out: hung lft and no ex ins fnl f* **25/1**

0053 **5** *nk* **Miss Swift**[22] 8292 3-8-3 46 oh1.............................. StefanoCherchi(7) 5 48
(Marcus Tregoning) *hld up in tch: nt clr run over 2f out: swtchd lft and hdwy u.p over 1f out: swtchd rt and no imp ins fnl f* **10/1**

3000 **6** *2 1/4* **Guaracha**[25] 8196 8-8-8 46 oh1..............................(v) KeelanBaker(7) 10 44
(Alexandra Dunn) *t.k.h: hld up towards rr: clsd whn nt clr run and swtchd rt over 1f out: swtchd rt again 1f out: kpt on ins fnl f: nvr trbld ldrs (jockey said gelding was denied a clear run)* **50/1**

4630 **7** *nk* **Demophon**[37] 7818 5-9-1 46 oh1..............................(w) RaulDaSilva 1 43
(Steve Flook) *in tch in midfield: effrt ent fnl 3f: unable qck over 1f out: wknd ins fnl f* **10/1**

5406 **8** *2 ½* **Lady Of York**[18] 8406 5-9-3 **48**.......................(t) JoeyHaynes 9 41
(Chelsea Banham) *chsd ldrs tl hdwy to chse ldr over 8f out: led 6f out tl hdd jst over 1f out: no ex and wknd ins fnl f* **7/1**[3]

0400 **9** *3* **Sir Gnet (IRE)**[8] 8703 5-9-11 **56**....................... RobertHavlin 8 45
(Ed Dunlop) *hld up in midfield: hdwy to chse ldr over 3f out: drvn over 1f out: sn btn and wknd ins fnl f* **8/1**

5050 **10** *2 ½* **Vin D'Honneur (IRE)**[13] 8551 3-9-5 **55**..............(tp) CallumShepherd 7 42
(Stuart Williams) *chsd ldrs: bmpd 4f out: rdn over 2f out: unable qck over 1f out: wknd ins fnl f* **14/1**

0230 **11** *3* **Beechwood James (FR)**[55] 7202 3-9-1 **51**....................... LukeMorris 14 34
(Michael Appleby) *dropped in after s: t.k.h: hld up towards rr: no imp u.p over 2f out: wl hld over 1f out: wknd ins fnl f* **14/1**

3056 **12** *2* **Miss Green Dream**[48] 7450 3-8-10 **46** oh1..............(p) ShelleyBirkett 3 26
(Julia Feilden) *chsd ldrs early: in tch in midfield after: nt clrest of runs jst over 2f out: lost pl and btn whn impeded over 1f out: wknd ins fnl f* **33/1**

0000 **13** *20* **Argent Bleu**[50] 7376 4-8-10 **46** oh1....................... RhiainIngram(5) 6
(Roger Ingram) *chsd ldr tl over 8f out: styd chsng ldrs tl lost pl over 1f out: t.o ins fnl f* **66/1**

0066 **14** *42* **Lady Elysia**[55] 7202 3-9-0 **50**.......................(v[1]) ShaneKelly 13
(Harry Dunlop) *led tl 6f out: stl chsng ldr whn swtchd rt and rdn 4f out: sn lost pl: virtually p.u fnl f: t.o (jockey said filly stopped quickly)* **14/1**

2m 52.21s (-1.39) **Going Correction** -0.175s/f (Stan)
WFA 3 from 4yo+ 5lb **14** Ran SP% **124.9**
Speed ratings (Par 101): **97,95,94,94,94 92,92,91,89,87 85,84,72,46**
CSF £12.59 CT £178.92 TOTE £4.10: £2.10, £2.30, £6.00; EX 15.00 Trifecta £171.20.
Owner A A Byrne & Mark Wellbelove **Bred** Gerry Smith **Trained** Cropthorne, Worcs

FOCUS
A low-grade staying handicap in which the prominent racers pressed on too soon, setting it up for the closers. The second, third and fourth set a straightforward level.

8917 BUY TICKETS ONLINE AT CHELMSFORDRACECOURSE.COM H'CAP 6f (P)
7:55 (7:56) (Class 6) (0-57,59) 3-Y-O+
£3,315 (£986; £493; £300; £300; £300) **Stalls** Centre

Form RPR

5 **1** **Split Down South**[48] 7447 3-9-2 **59**....................... GraceMcEntee(7) 6 68
(Phil McEntee) *dwlt and edgd rt leaving stalls: pushed along early: rcvrd to chse ldrs after 2f: rdn to ld over 1f out: hld on wl towards fin* **14/1**

4512 **2** *nk* **Broughton Excels**[36] 7838 4-9-7 **57**....................... StevieDonohoe 1 65
(Stuart Williams) *hld up in tch: swtchd rt ent fnl 2f: hdwy on outer over 1f out: chsd wnr ins fnl f: kpt on wl towards fin: nvr quite getting to wnr* **6/4**[1]

0110 **3** *2 ¾* **Wild Flower (IRE)**[3] 8839 7-9-2 **52**..............(p) KieranO'Neill 5 52
(Luke McJannet) *led: edgd rt: rdn and hdd over 1f out: wknd ins fnl f* **9/1**

5046 **4** *hd* **Pearl Spectre (USA)**[46] 7527 8-9-6 **56**..............(v) CallumShepherd 10 55
(Phil McEntee) *styd wd early: in tch in rr: effrt over 2f out: kpt on ins fnl f: nt rch ldrs* **12/1**

603 **5** *1* **At Your Service**[37] 7823 5-9-8 **58**....................... JoeyHaynes 2 54
(Chelsea Banham) *hld up in rr: effrt over 2f out: edgd lft and hdwy 1f out: kpt on ins fnl f: nvr trbld ldrs* **7/2**[2]

000 **6** *hd* **Dreamboat Annie**[16] 8469 4-8-12 **48**..............(p) JasonWatson 9 44
(Mark Usher) *chsd ldrs early: in tch in midfield after: effrt and drvn to chse ldrs again over 1f out: unable qck and wknd ins fnl f* **14/1**

4004 **7** *¾* **Knockout Blow**[16] 8450 4-9-4 **54**..............(p) HectorCrouch 3 47
(John E Long) *in tch in midfield: carried rt bnd 2f out: no imp and kpt on same pce fr over 1f out: nvr trbld ldrs* **12/1**

1666 **8** *1* **Bond Street Beau**[92] 5870 4-9-8 **58**....................... TomMarquand 4 48
(Philip McBride) *chsd ldrs: effrt over 1f out: unable qck and wknd ins fnl f* **7/1**[3]

1600 **9** *¾* **Aquarius (IRE)**[17] 8419 3-9-6 **56**....................... LiamJones 8 44
(Michael Appleby) *taken down early: midfield: hdwy to chse ldr over 4f out: jostled and unable qck over 1f out: wknd ins fnl f* **25/1**

1m 12.54s (-1.16) **Going Correction** -0.175s/f (Stan) **9** Ran SP% **117.3**
Speed ratings (Par 101): **100,99,95,95,94 94,93,91,90**
CSF £36.04 CT £214.03 TOTE £10.60: £2.60, £1.20, £2.60; EX 33.20 Trifecta £345.20.
Owner Trevor Johnson **Bred** Mike Smith **Trained** Newmarket, Suffolk

FOCUS
Form to be positive in the context of this grade given the front pair pulled clear. The pace was on the steady side for a sprint, meaning it was hard to make up ground.
T/Plt: £20.60 to a £1 stake. Pool: £55,466.36 - 1,962.14 winning units T/Qpdt: £19.60 to a £1 stake. Pool: £5,055.83 - 190.10 winning units **Steve Payne**

8814 NEWCASTLE (A.W) (L-H)
Friday, November 8

OFFICIAL GOING: Tapeta: standard
Wind: Light, half against Weather: Dry

8918 BOMBARDIER BRITISH HOPPED AMBER BEER H'CAP 1m 5y (Tp)
4:35 (4:37) (Class 4) (0-85,85) 3-Y-O+
£5,207 (£1,549; £774; £400; £400; £400) **Stalls** Centre

Form RPR

0050 **1** **My Target (IRE)**[25] 8197 8-9-0 **77**....................... PJMcDonald 7 85
(Michael Wigham) *t.k.h: hld up in centre of gp: stdy hdwy over 1f out: rdn ins fnl f: kpt on wl to ld cl home* **25/1**

6505 **2** *shd* **Cote D'Azur**[8] 8692 6-9-2 **79**....................... LewisEdmunds 2 86
(Les Eyre) *dwlt: sn prom in centre of gp: hdwy to ld over 1f out: kpt on fnl f: hdd cl home* **22/1**

31-0 **3** *hd* **Little Jo**[41] 7694 5-9-6 **83**..............(p) BenRobinson 6 89
(Brian Ellison) *dwlt: hld up on far side: hdwy whn nt clr run over 1f out: kpt on wl fnl f to take 3rd cl home: nrst fin (jockey said gelding had missed the break)* **17/2**

-002 **4** *½* **La Rav (IRE)**[21] 8305 5-8-12 **75**....................... NathanEvans 5 80
(Michael Easterby) *t.k.h: hld up on far side of gp: hdwy over 2f out: effrt and rdn over 1f out: kpt on same pce ins fnl f* **4/1**[1]

4210 **5** *nk* **Modakhar (IRE)**[14] 8514 3-9-2 **81**....................... BenCurtis 9 85
(K R Burke) *hld up towards nr side of gp: hdwy and prom over 2f out: rdn and one pce ins fnl f* **15/2**

5223 **6** *hd* **Star Shield**[34] 7906 4-9-8 **85**....................... DavidNolan 14 89
(David O'Meara) *hld up in centre of gp: effrt and angled rt over 1f out: rdn and kpt on ins fnl f: no imp* **11/2**[2]

2651 **7** *½* **First Response**[17] 8427 4-9-0 **77**..............(t) TomEaves 11 80
(Linda Stubbs) *hld up on nr side of gp: rdn over 2f out: no further imp ins fnl f* **11/1**

0200 **8** *2 ½* **Poet's Dawn**[27] 8130 4-9-6 **83**....................... DavidAllan 1 80
(Tim Easterby) *prom on far side of gp: drvn over 2f out: wknd over 1f out* **25/1**

6002 **9** *shd* **Tangled (IRE)**[30] 8024 4-9-1 **81**..............(h) GemmaTutty(3) 8 78
(Karen Tutty) *plld hrd in midfield in centre of gp: rdn and outpcd 2f out: kpt on fnl f: no imp* **6/1**[3]

0603 **10** *8* **Saisons D'Or (IRE)**[30] 8024 4-8-8 **78**....................... OwenPayton(7) 3 56
(Jedd O'Keeffe) *cl up in centre of gp: drvn over 2f out: wknd over 1f out* **11/1**

2100 **11** *1 ¼* **Queen's Sargent (FR)**[28] 8101 4-9-4 **81**....................... ShaneGray 10 56
(Kevin Ryan) *cl up on nr side of gp: led over 2f out to over 1f out: wknd fnl f* **20/1**

2360 **12** *½* **Call Out Loud**[11] 8606 7-9-7 **84**....................... AlistairRawlinson 4 58
(Michael Appleby) *led on far side of gp to over 2f out: wknd wl over 1f out* **80/1**

031 **13** *nk* **Willy Sewell**[244] 1102 6-8-13 **79**....................... TheodoreLadd(3) 12 53
(Michael Appleby) *hld up on nr side: drvn along 3f out: wknd over 1f out* **50/1**

0P00 **P** **Rey Loopy (IRE)**[30] 8024 5-9-6 **83**....................... PaulMulrennan 13
(Ben Haslam) *dwlt and swtchd (lft) to r on far side of gp: struggling over 3f out: sn p.u: dismntd over 1f out: b.b.v (vet said gelding had bled from the nose)* **33/1**

1m 38.1s (-0.50) **Going Correction** +0.075s/f (Slow)
WFA 3 from 4yo+ 2lb **14** Ran SP% **111.6**
Speed ratings (Par 105): **105,104,104,104,103 103,103,100,100,92 91,90,90,**
CSF £439.67 CT £4909.04 TOTE £24.60: £5.20, £6.60, £2.50; EX 537.20 Trifecta £2785.30.
Owner G Linder,M Wigham,J Williams,A Dearden **Bred** Darley **Trained** Newmarket, Suffolk

FOCUS
A wide-open handicap run at a solid gallop, setting things up for the closers. They finished in a bit of a heap. Sound form, with the second close to this year's best and the fourth close to his recent C&D run.

8919 LADBROKES HOME OF THE ODDS BOOST NOVICE AUCTION STKS 7f 14y (Tp)
5:05 (5:07) (Class 6) 2-Y-O
£2,781 (£827; £413; £206) **Stalls** Centre

Form RPR

5 **1** **Brunch**[14] 8511 2-8-12 0....................... CallumRodriguez 1 74+
(Michael Dods) *t.k.h: in tch on far side of gp: hdwy to chse ldr over 1f out: rdn to ld ins fnl f: sn clr: eased cl home* **7/2**[2]

64 **2** *2 ½* **Where's Mick (IRE)**[10] 8631 2-9-0 0....................... JackGarritty 8 70
(Jedd O'Keeffe) *dwlt: sn cl up in centre of gp: led gng wl over 2f: rdn and over 2 l clr over 1f out: hdd ins fnl f: one pce* **9/1**

3 *1 ¼* **Martin's Brig (IRE)** 2-9-0 0....................... PaulMulrennan 10 67
(Iain Jardine) *hld up: stdy hdwy on nr side of gp over 2f out: effrt and disp 2nd pl briefly over 1f out: one pce ins fnl f* **6/1**

23 **4** *3* **Trinity Girl**[14] 8528 2-8-7 0....................... JoeFanning 7 52
(Mark Johnston) *dwlt: angled (rt) to nr side of gp after 2f: in tch: rdn over 2f out: outpcd fr over 1f out* **5/2**[1]

00 **5** *3 ½* **Glencoe Boy (IRE)**[36] 7842 2-8-9 0....................... EllieMacKenzie(7) 9 53
(David Flood) *t.k.h: led in centre of gp: rdn and hdd over 2f out: wknd fnl f* **25/1**

0 **6** *hd* **Home For Half Past (IRE)**[14] 8528 2-8-12 0....................... CamHardie 12 48
(David O'Meara) *hld up in centre of gp: stdy hdwy over 2f out: rdn and no further imp over 1f out* **100/1**

661 **7** *¾* **Wadi Al Salaam (IRE)**[21] 8302 2-9-6 74....................... DuranFentiman 3 54
(Tim Easterby) *prom on far side of gp: rdn over 2f out: wknd over 1f out* **4/1**[3]

00 **8** *1 ¼* **Anno Maximo (GER)**[8] 8700 2-9-1 0....................... CliffordLee 6 46
(Michael Bell) *midfield in centre of gp: rdn over 2f out: wknd over 1f out* **50/1**

0 **9** *nk* **Marengo Sally (IRE)**[151] 3652 2-8-8 0....................... AndrewMullen 4 38
(Ben Haslam) *t.k.h: hld up in centre of gp: drvn along over 2f out: wknd over 1f out (jockey said filly suffered interference in running)* **100/1**

05 **10** *1* **Class Clown (IRE)**[29] 8069 2-8-12 0....................... BenRobinson 5 40
(David Barron) *prom towards far side of gp: rdn over 2f out: wknd wl over 1f out (jockey said gelding ran too free.)* **25/1**

0 **11** *1 ¼* **Hayuplass**[14] 8510 2-8-9 0....................... DavidAllan 2 34
(Tim Easterby) *hld up on far side of gp: struggling over 2f out: sn btn* **50/1**

0 **12** *5* **Free Cash (IRE)**[14] 8511 2-8-11 0....................... FayeMcManoman(5) 14 28
(Nigel Tinkler) *hld up on nr side of gp: drvn and struggling over 2f out: nvr on terms* **200/1**

13 *hd* **Malizia** 2-8-5 0....................... SeanDavis(3) 13 20
(Amy Murphy) *hld up on nr side of gp: drvn and outpcd over 2f out: sn btn* **50/1**

00 **14** *20* **Charmore**[21] 8302 2-8-6 0....................... ShaneGray 11
(Ann Duffield) *t.k.h: hld up in centre of gp: struggling over 2f out: lost tch and eased over 1f out* **250/1**

1m 26.75s (0.55) **Going Correction** +0.075s/f (Slow) **14** Ran SP% **111.5**
Speed ratings (Par 94): **99,96,94,91,87 87,86,84,84,83 81,76,75,53**
CSF £30.16 TOTE £4.30: £1.50, £2.20, £2.30; EX 31.40 Trifecta £188.50.
Owner Mrs F Denniff **Bred** Denniff Farms Ltd **Trained** Denton, Co Durham

FOCUS
Those that had run didn't set a particularly high standard and most of these are likely to be handicap projects in the long term. Whether the winner can prove better than a handicapper in time remains to be seen but he looks a horse with a big engine. The opening level is fluid.

8920 LADBROKES WHERE THE NATION PLAYS FILLIES' NOVICE STKS 6f (Tp)
5:35 (5:36) (Class 5) 3-Y-O+
£3,428 (£1,020; £509; £254) **Stalls** Centre

Form RPR

3426 **1** **Society Guest (IRE)**[22] 8290 3-9-0 65..............(v) BenCurtis 3 64
(Mick Channon) *dwlt: sn pressed ldr: led over 1f out: rdn out fnl f* **11/4**[2]

20-6 **2** *1 ¼* **Royal Dynasty**[17] 8419 3-9-0 67..............(h) DanielMuscutt 5 60
(James Fanshawe) *t.k.h: prom: effrt and pressed wnr over 1f out: rdn and one pce last 100yds* **3/1**[3]

000 **3** *4 ½* **Kemmeridge Bay**[40] 7737 3-9-0 44....................... SamJames 4 46?
(Grant Tuer) *led to over 1f out: drvn and outpcd fnl f* **33/1**

4 *4 ½* **Milagre Da Vida (IRE)** 3-9-0 0....................... PJMcDonald 6 32+
(K R Burke) *dwlt: hld up in tch: rdn and rn green over 2f out: no imp whn hmpd over 1f out (jockey said filly suffered interference in running)* **10/11**[1]

0 **5** *11* **Abbi Dab**[260] 831 3-9-0 0....................... AlistairRawlinson 1
(Michael Appleby) *dwlt: t.k.h: in tch: outpcd whn veered rt over 1f out: sn wknd* **66/1**

1m 13.65s (1.15) **Going Correction** +0.075s/f (Slow) **5** Ran SP% **108.5**
Speed ratings (Par 100): **95,93,87,81,66**
CSF £10.90 TOTE £3.70: £1.50, £2.00; EX 8.60 Trifecta £37.70.

Owner John Guest Racing **Bred** Tally-Ho Stud **Trained** West Ilsley, Berks

FOCUS

A pretty weak novice event won by an exposed 65-rated performer. The third sets the level for now based on her 2yo form here.

8921 BETWAY SUPPORTING RESPONSIBLE GAMBLING WEEK H'CAP 6f (Tp)

6:05 (6:07) (Class 4) (0-85,83) 3-Y-O+

£5,207 (£1,549; £774; £400; £400; £400) **Stalls** Centre

Form				RPR
0360	1		**Paddy Power (IRE)**[17] 8425 6-8-12 **77** .... ConnorMurtagh(3) 1 (Richard Fahey) *midfield on far side of gp: hdwy 2f out: rdn to ld ins fnl f: kpt on wl (jockey said gelding hung right-handed)* **22/1**	85
1651	2	1/2	**Magical Spirit (IRE)**[42] 7656 3-9-5 **81** .... KevinStott 5 (Kevin Ryan) *led on far side of gp: rdn 2f out: hdd ins fnl f: kpt on: hld cl home* **6/1**[3]	88
2242	3	1/2	**Epeius (IRE)**[21] 8304 6-8-12 **74** .... AndrewMullen 3 (Ben Haslam) *dwlt: hld up on far side of gp: stdy hdwy over 1f out: kpt on fnl f: nrst fin* **16/1**	79
6602	4	nk	**Reckless Endeavour (IRE)**[17] 8428 6-9-2 **78** .... BenRobinson 8 (David Barron) *dwlt: hld up in centre of gp: drvn and outpcd over 2f out: rallied ins fnl f: kpt on wl towards fin (jockey said gelding was denied a clear run inside the final furlong)* **17/2**	82+
1330	5	hd	**Kupa River (IRE)**[147] 3813 5-8-12 **79** ....(h) PaulaMuir(5) 13 (Roger Fell) *t.k.h: hld up on nr side of gp: rdn and hdwy 2f out: one pce ins fnl f* **40/1**	82
0260	6	shd	**Firmdecisions (IRE)**[17] 8425 9-9-4 **83** .... RowanScott(3) 2 (Nigel Tinkler) *bhd on far side of gp: drvn over 2f out: hdwy over 1f out: r.o ins fnl f: nt pce to chal* **33/1**	86
0400	7	nk	**Shallow Hal**[49] 7402 3-9-7 **83** ....(p[1] w) BenCurtis 12 (K R Burke) *prom in centre of gp: drvn along 2f out: one pce ins fnl f* **11/2**[2]	85
0344	8	1/2	**Royal Brave (IRE)**[16] 8470 8-9-2 **78** .... NathanEvans 14 (Rebecca Bastiman) *hld up: effrt and rdn on nr side of gp 2f out: no imp ins fnl f* **40/1**	79
0513	9	shd	**John Kirkup**[17] 8428 4-9-4 **80** ....(b) CallumRodriguez 6 (Michael Dods) *cl up in centre of gp: drvn over 2f out: wknd ins fnl f* **4/1**[1]	80
2446	10	1/2	**Six Strings**[10] 8636 5-9-2 **81** .... TheodoreLadd(3) 7 (Michael Appleby) *dwlt: bhd on nr side of gp: rdn and outpcd over 2f out: rallied fnl f: kpt on: no imp* **10/1**	80
122	11	shd	**Astro Jakk (IRE)**[188] 2397 3-9-4 **80** .... PJMcDonald 9 (K R Burke) *hld up in centre of gp: effrt whn nt clr run over 1f out: n.m.r ins fnl f: sn n.d* **11/2**[2]	78+
000	12	nk	**Galloway Hills**[17] 8428 4-8-10 **75** ....(p) SeanDavis(3) 4 (Phillip Makin) *cl up on far side of gp: drvn over 2f out: wknd over 1f out (jockey said gelding suffered interference in running)* **33/1**	72
1100	13	1	**Camachess (IRE)**[17] 8420 3-8-13 **75** .... PhilDennis 10 (Philip McBride) *dwlt: towards rr in centre of gp: drvn over 2f out: wknd over 1f out* **40/1**	69
3021	14	2 1/2	**East Street Revue**[62] 6972 6-9-0 **76** ....(b) DavidAllan 11 (Tim Easterby) *prom on nr side of gp: drvn along over 2f out: wknd over 1f out (trainer's rep said gelding weakened quickly in the final furlong; vet revealed the gelding to be displaying a prolonged recovery)* **22/1**	62

1m 12.2s (-0.30) **Going Correction** +0.075s/f (Slow) **14 Ran SP% 112.4**

Speed ratings (Par 105): **105,104,103,103,103 102,102,101,101,101 100,100,99,95**

CSF £132.85 CT £1416.85 TOTE £21.90: £5.60, £1.60, £4.70; EX 219.70 Trifecta £3172.30.

Owner M Scaife & R A Fahey **Bred** Yeguada De Milagro Sa **Trained** Musley Bank, N Yorks

FOCUS

An open sprint handicap but the field bunched tightly down the middle of the track and that meant trouble in running for a few. Sound form, with the third helping to set the level.

8922 BOMBARDIER GOLDEN BEER H'CAP 1m 5y (Tp)

6:35 (6:38) (Class 6) (0-55,55) 3-Y-O+

£2,781 (£827; £413; £400; £400; £400) **Stalls** Centre

Form				RPR
0631	1		**Proceeding**[4] 8818 4-9-5 **53** 5ex .... JoeFanning 9 (Tracy Waggott) *prom in centre of gp: hdwy to ld over 1f out: rdn and r.o wl fnl f* **7/5**[1]	61+
2566	2	1	**Ritchie Star (IRE)**[19] 7578 3-9-3 **53** .... AndrewMullen 4 (Ben Haslam) *prom on far side of gp: rdn over 2f out: chsd wnr ins fnl f: r.o* **22/1**	59
3222	3	1	**Troop**[9] 8667 4-9-3 **54** ....(b[1]) SeanDavis(3) 14 (Ann Duffield) *midfield on nr side of gp: rdn and outpcd 3f out: rallied and prom over 1f out: edgd lft: kpt on ins fnl f: no imp* **10/3**[2]	58
6246	4	1/2	**Spark Of War (IRE)**[19] 7509 4-9-4 **52** ....(v) CallumRodriguez 2 (Keith Dalgleish) *hld up on far side of gp: rdn over 2f out: hdwy over 1f out: r.o ins fnl f* **12/1**	55
0250	5	1 1/4	**Tarnhelm**[4] 8821 4-8-10 **51** ....(h) RhonaPindar(7) 1 (Wilf Storey) *dwlt: angled rt and hld up in centre of gp: swtchd to nr side of gp 3f out: hdwy and prom over 1f out: edgd lft and no ex ins fnl f* **33/1**	51
5050	6	nk	**Lucky Violet (IRE)**[73] 6573 7-9-1 **49** ....(h) JamieGormley 3 (Linda Perratt) *t.k.h: led at ordinary gallop on far side of gp: rdn and hdd over 1f out: wknd ins fnl f (trainer said that the gelding had been struck into on its right fore heel; jockey said mare ran too free)* **40/1**	48
0231	7	3/4	**Rebel State (IRE)**[14] 8530 6-8-13 **54** .... OwenPayton(7) 13 (Jedd O'Keeffe) *hld up towards nr side of gp: rdn over 2f out: effrt over 1f out: no imp fnl f* **10/1**[3]	52
3023	8	3/4	**Puchita (IRE)**[9] 8666 4-9-5 **53** ....(p) CamHardie 7 (Antony Brittain) *hld up in centre of gp: hdwy whn nt clr run over 2f out to over 1f out: rdn and no imp fnl f (jockey said filly was denied a clear run inside the final two furlongs and hung right-handed in the closing stages)* **25/1**	49
1301	9	4 1/2	**Lukoutoldmakezebak**[42] 7654 6-9-4 **55** ....(p) HarrisonShaw(3) 6 (David Thompson) *prom in centre of gp: drvn over 2f out: wknd wl over 1f out* **12/1**	41
0005	10	nse	**Sumner Beach**[9] 8667 5-9-4 **52** .... BenRobinson 8 (Brian Ellison) *hld up towards rr in centre of gp: rdn over 2f out: wknd over 1f out* **10/1**[3]	38
-000	11	3 1/2	**Amood (IRE)**[21] 8301 8-9-1 **52** ....(b[1]) RowanScott(3) 11 (Simon West) *dwlt: in tch on nr side of gp: effrt and edgd lft over 2f out: wknd over 1f out* **40/1**	30
6-06	12	3/4	**It's Never Enough**[23] 8269 5-9-7 **55** ....(h) LucyAlexander 12 (James Ewart) *cl up on nr side of gp tl rdn and wknd over 2f out* **40/1**	32

1m 40.3s (1.70) **Going Correction** +0.075s/f (Slow) **12 Ran SP% 116.8**

WFA 3 from 4yo+ 2lb

Speed ratings (Par 101): **94,93,92,91,90 89,89,88,83,83 80,79**

CSF £43.07 CT £90.05 TOTE £2.70: £1.60, £5.60, £1.30; EX 34.50 Trifecta £146.80.

Owner David Tate **Bred** Ors Bloodstock & Stanley House Stud **Trained** Spennymoor, Co Durham

FOCUS

A weak handicap, weaker than the one Proceeding won here earlier in the week, and he made no mistake under the penalty. The second and third help set a straightforward level.

8923 BOMBARDIER 'MARCH TO YOUR OWN DRUM' H'CAP 7f 14y (Tp)

7:05 (7:12) (Class 6) (0-65,68) 3-Y-O+

£2,781 (£827; £413; £400; £400; £400) **Stalls** Centre

Form				RPR
2100	1		**Etikaal**[73] 6572 5-9-1 **59** .... SamJames 6 (Grant Tuer) *dwlt: hld up on far side of gp: angled rt and hdwy over 1f out: rdn to ld ins fnl f: kpt on strly (trainer said regarding apparent improvement in from that the gelding had benefitted from a 73 day break)* **14/1**	69
3013	2	1 1/2	**Gavi Di Gavi (IRE)**[37] 7812 4-9-3 **61** .... TomQueally 7 (Alan King) *hld up in centre of gp: effrt and angled rt over 1f out: kpt on wl fnl f to take 2nd last stride* **11/4**[2]	67
3401	3	hd	**Swansdown**[7] 8713 3-9-9 **68** 6ex ....(p) BenCurtis 4 (William Haggas) *hld up in midfield in centre of gp: rdn and hdwy over 1f out: ev ch briefly ins fnl f: sn chsng ldr: no ex and lost 2nd last stride* **2/1**[1]	73
0010	4	3/4	**I Know How (IRE)**[28] 8083 4-9-2 **60** ....(b) KevinStott 13 (Julie Camacho) *prom towards centre of gp: rdn and led over 2f out: hdd and edgd lft ins fnl f: sn no ex* **16/1**	64
2403	5	3/4	**Rock Boy Grey (IRE)**[16] 8471 4-9-7 **65** ....(t) AndrewMullen 2 (Mark Loughnane) *t.k.h: cl up on far side of gp: effrt and ev ch over 1f out to ins fnl f: sn edgd rt: checked and outpcd* **11/2**[3]	67
0000	6	3 1/2	**Tagur (IRE)**[50] 7363 5-8-10 **61** ....(v) HarriettLees(7) 14 (Kevin Ryan) *led on nr side of gp: rdn and hdd over 2f out: wknd over 1f out* **50/1**	54
0300	7	1/2	**Beverley Bullet**[7] 8713 6-9-0 **61** ....(p) HarrisonShaw(3) 5 (Lawrence Mullaney) *cl up in centre of gp: rdn over 2f out: wknd over 1f out* **9/1**	53
3134	8	1 3/4	**Round The Island**[23] 8264 6-9-0 **58** .... PhilDennis 8 (Richard Whitaker) *dwlt: sn in tch towards nr side of gp: led and edgd lft over 2f out: wknd fnl f* **28/1**	46
0400	9	1/2	**Scots Sonnet**[109] 5239 5-9-3 **61** ....(h w) BenRobinson 11 (Jim Goldie) *hld up on nr side of gp: drvn and outpcd over 2f out: shortlived effrt over 1f out: sn btn* **18/1**	47
6600	10	3/4	**Dancing Speed (IRE)**[121] 4784 3-9-0 **59** ....(w) PJMcDonald 10 (Marjorie Fife) *cl up in centre of gp: rdn over 2f out: wknd over 1f out* **80/1**	43
-011	11	3	**Mi Capricho (IRE)**[179] 2682 4-9-3 **61** .... CallumRodriguez 3 (Keith Dalgleish) *hld up towards far side of gp: drvn over 2f out: wknd over 1f out* **22/1**	38
6300	12	nse	**Global Exceed**[7] 8713 4-8-13 **60** ....(t[1]) GemmaTutty(3) 1 (Karen Tutty) *t.k.h: hld up on far side of gp: drvn over 2f out: wknd over 1f out* **22/1**	37
4-05	13	1	**Dream Mount (IRE)**[261] 801 4-9-1 **59** ....(p[1]) PaulMulrennan 12 (Julie Camacho) *midfield on nr side of gp: drvn over 2f out: wknd over 1f out* **28/1**	33

1m 26.63s (0.43) **Going Correction** +0.075s/f (Slow) **13 Ran SP% 122.0**

WFA 3 from 4yo+ 1lb

Speed ratings (Par 101): **100,98,98,97,96 92,91,89,89,88 84,84,83**

CSF £50.32 CT £115.90 TOTE £16.00: £4.00, £1.50, £1.40; EX 76.90 Trifecta £364.70.

Owner Moment of Madness **Bred** Shadwell Estate Company Limited **Trained** Birkby, N Yorks

FOCUS

Modest stuff but the right horses were in and about the frame.

8924 LADBROKES 'PLAY 1-2 FREE' ON FOOTBALL FILLIES' H'CAP 6f (Tp)

7:35 (7:39) (Class 5) (0-70,72) 3-Y-O+

£3,428 (£1,020; £509; £400; £400; £400) **Stalls** Centre

Form				RPR
3000	1		**Summer Daydream (IRE)**[20] 8342 3-9-10 **72** ....(p) CallumRodriguez 6 (Keith Dalgleish) *hld up in midfield towards centre of gp: hdwy to ld appr fnl f: rdn and hung lft ins fnl f: kpt on wl (trainer's rep could offer no explanation for the filly's improved form other than she may be suited by the switch to the all weather)* **17/2**	82
0600	2	1/2	**Oriental Lilly**[7] 8719 5-9-0 **69** ....(p) CoreyMadden(7) 4 (Jim Goldie) *dwlt: hld up in centre of gp: hdwy over 1f out: effrt and chsd wnr ins fnl f: r.o* **17/2**	76
5111	3	1 1/4	**Queen Of Kalahari**[29] 8071 4-9-1 **63** ....(p) LewisEdmunds 1 (Les Eyre) *t.k.h: led in centre of gp: rdn and hdd over 1f out: no ex and lost 2nd ins fnl f* **11/2**[2]	66
1660	4	1 1/2	**Klopp**[114] 5056 3-9-3 **65** ....(h) CamHardie 11 (Antony Brittain) *hld up on nr side of gp: effrt and hdwy whn n.m.r briefly over 1f out: rdn and no imp fnl f (jockey said filly was denied a clear run approaching the final furlong)* **14/1**	63
6556	5	shd	**Porcelain Girl (IRE)**[63] 6930 3-9-6 **68** .... CliffordLee 2 (Michael Bell) *prom on far side of gp: drvn along over 2f out: outpcd fr over 1f out* **6/1**[3]	66
4100	6	nk	**Penny Pot Lane**[7] 8712 6-9-1 **63** ....(b[1]) PhilDennis 7 (Richard Whitaker) *cl up on nr side of gp: rdn and led briefly over 1f out: wknd ins fnl f* **10/1**	60
3403	7	1/2	**Chloellie**[23] 8254 4-9-5 **67** .... DanielMuscutt 8 (J R Jenkins) *hld up towards rr in centre of gp: drvn and outpcd over 2f out: rallied ins fnl f: r.o* **7/2**[1]	62
656	8	1/2	**Pinarella (FR)**[28] 8083 3-9-0 **62** ....(p) PaulMulrennan 10 (Ben Haslam) *hld up on nr side of gp: rdn and outpcd over 2f out: n.d after* **10/1**	56
0000	9	1/2	**Granny Roz**[17] 8429 5-8-8 **61** .... PaulaMuir(5) 5 (Ray Craggs) *t.k.h: cl up in centre of gp: drvn along 2f out: wknd fnl f* **40/1**	53
5265	10	3 1/4	**Strawberryandcream**[39] 7762 4-9-0 **62** .... PJMcDonald 12 (James Bethell) *slowly away: bhd on nr side of gp: struggling over 2f out: sn btn* **10/1**	44
500	11	3/4	**Calima Calling (IRE)**[22] 8294 3-8-7 **58** .... TheodoreLadd(3) 3 (Michael Appleby) *prom on far side of gp: drvn along over 2f out: wknd over 1f out* **33/1**	37
0006	12	nk	**Uponastar (IRE)**[28] 8086 3-8-2 **50** oh2 .... AndrewMullen 9 (Ben Haslam) *slowly away: bhd towards nr side of gp: outpcd 1/2-way: nvr on terms* **66/1**	28

1m 12.45s (-0.05) **Going Correction** +0.075s/f (Slow) **12 Ran SP% 113.8**

Speed ratings (Par 100): **103,102,100,98,98 98,97,96,96,91 90,90**

CSF £74.73 CT £439.68 TOTE £10.00: £3.80, £2.70, £2.00; EX 69.50 Trifecta £386.30.

Owner Ronnie Docherty **Bred** Flaxman Stables Ire & Scuderia Vittadini **Trained** Carluke, S Lanarks

FOCUS
Not many in-form candidates in here, including the winner, but the drop in class proved the catalyst for a return to form. The second has been rated to her best since her April win here, while the third has been rated close to her recent Southwell form.

8925 BETWAY H'CAP 5f (Tp)
8:05 (8:07) (Class 6) (0-60,60) 3-Y-O+

£2,781 (£827; £413; £400; £400; £400) **Stalls** Centre

Form RPR

0521 **1** **Jeffrey Harris**[32] 7962 4-8-9 **55** CoreyMadden(7) 1 63
(Jim Goldie) *hld up: gd hdwy on far side of gp over 1f out: led ins fnl f: edgd rt: r.o wl* **11/1**

3200 **2** 1/2 **Burtonwood**[17] 8429 7-9-3 **56** CallumRodriguez 12 62
(Julie Camacho) *hld up on nr side of gp: effrt and rdn over 1f out: chsd wnr ins fnl f: kpt on fin* **5/1**[2]

0014 **3** *hd* **Gleaming Arch**[32] 7959 5-9-5 **58** KevinStott 11 63
(Fred Watson) *bmpd s: bhd on nr side of gp: rdn and hdwy 2f out: kpt on fnl f: nrst fin (jockey said gelding suffered interference leaving the stalls)* **7/2**[1]

0305 **4** 1 1/2 **Extrasolar**[4] 8821 9-8-11 **50** (tp) SamJames 14 50
(Geoffrey Harker) *chsd ldrs on nr side of gp: effrt and rdn over 1f out: one pce ins fnl f* **9/1**

6543 **5** *nk* **Carlovian**[10] 8638 6-8-13 **52** (p) DougieCostello 6 51
(Mark Walford) *prom on far side of gp: drvn and outpcd over 1f out: kpt on ins fnl f* **22/1**

0050 **6** 1/2 **Kibaar**[7] 8720 7-8-10 **49** TomEaves 13 46
(Ruth Carr) *stdd s: t.k.h: hld up on nr side of gp: rdn and effrt wl over 1f out: sn edgd lft: one pce ins fnl f* **28/1**

6000 **7** *shd* **Guardia Svizzera (IRE)**[3] 8840 5-9-1 **54** (h) BenCurtis 10 51
(Roger Fell) *led on nr side of gp: edgd lft over 2f out: rdn and hdd ins fnl f: sn no ex* **8/1**[3]

0550 **8** 3/4 **Amelia R (IRE)**[29] 8071 3-8-11 **55** PaulaMuir(5) 3 49
(Ray Craggs) *midfield towards far side of gp: drvn along over 2f out: no imp over 1f out (jockey said filly was denied a clear run 2f out)* **22/1**

4600 **9** 1/2 **Everkyllachy (IRE)**[52] 7307 5-9-0 **56** SeanDavis(3) 9 48
(Karen McLintock) *hld up on nr side of gp: stdy hdwy 1/2-way: effrt over 1f out: keeping on same pce whn n.m.r ins fnl f* **25/1**

3024 **10** *shd* **The Grey Zebedee**[10] 8632 3-9-7 **60** (b) DuranFentiman 7 52
(Tim Easterby) *cl up in centre of gp: rdn over 2f out: wknd ins fnl f* **5/1**[2]

6125 **11** *hd* **Vallarta (IRE)**[10] 8638 9-8-12 **51** JamesSullivan 5 42
(Ruth Carr) *hld up in centre of gp: rdn wl over 1f out: sn no imp: btn fnl f* **25/1**

26-0 **12** 2 **Mable Lee (IRE)**[155] 3503 4-9-7 **60** GrahamLee 4 44
(Bryan Smart) *midfield towards far side of gp: outpcd whn n.m.r briefly over 2f out: n.d after* **28/1**

0563 **13** 3/4 **Moonlit Sands (IRE)**[10] 8637 4-9-2 **55** (tp) BenRobinson 2 36
(Brian Ellison) *midfield on far side of gp: drvn along over 2f out: wknd over 1f out* **22/1**

0040 **14** 2 3/4 **Tomahawk Ridge (IRE)**[44] 7588 3-9-6 **59** PJMcDonald 8 30
(John Gallagher) *midfield in centre of gp: pushed along and outpcd 2f out: sn wknd* **28/1**

59.55s (0.05) **Going Correction** +0.075s/f (Slow) **14 Ran SP% 116.1**
Speed ratings (Par 101): **102,101,100,98,98 97,97,95,95,94 94,91,90,85**
CSF £54.82 CT £238.60 TOTE £9.30: £2.70, £2.30, £2.30; EX 72.30 Trifecta £371.10.
Owner Mrs & Exors The Late Philip C Smith **Bred** Philip C Smith & Mrs Joyce W Smith **Trained** Uplawmoor, E Renfrews

FOCUS
They went quick here and that teed things up nicely for the closers. Straightforward form for the grade.
T/Jkpt: Not Won. T/Plt: £242.80 to a £1 stake. Pool: £76,197.76 - 229.03 winning units T/Qpdt: £16.40 to a £1 stake. Pool: £9,394.35 - 423.35 winning units **Richard Young**

8926 - 8934a (Foreign Racing) - See Raceform Interactive

8509 DONCASTER (L-H)
Saturday, November 9

8935 Meeting Abandoned - Waterlogged Course

8897 SOUTHWELL (L-H)
Saturday, November 9

OFFICIAL GOING: Fibresand: standard
Wind: Fresh against Weather: Cloudy

8942 BOMBARDIER BRITISH HOPPED AMBER BEER CLASSIFIED STKS 1m 13y(F)
4:40 (4:42) (Class 6) 3-Y-O+

£2,781 (£827; £413; £400; £400; £400) **Stalls** Low

Form RPR

0201 **1** **Clipsham Tiger (IRE)**[9] 8694 3-8-12 55 (h) GeorgeRooke(7) 6 69+
(Michael Appleby) *trckd ldrs: led wl over 2f out: pushed clr fr over 1f out* **11/8**[1]

0000 **2** 10 **Jagerbond**[61] 7024 3-8-9 43 (e[1]) AndrewBreslin(5) 12 41
(Andrew Crook) *s.i.s: outpcd: hdwy over 1f out: styd on to go 2nd wl ins fnl f: no ch w wnr* **50/1**

6360 **3** 1 1/4 **Sea Shack**[10] 8667 5-8-11 49 (tp) DylanHogan(5) 3 38
(Julia Feilden) *led 1f: led again over 5f out: hdd wl over 2f out: sn rdn: wknd fnl f* **13/2**[2]

0000 **4** 1 **Face Like Thunder**[26] 8207 4-9-2 48 (be) DannyBrock 5 36
(John Butler) *sn pushed along in rr: hdwy over 3f out: rdn: edgd rt and wknd over 1f out* **33/1**

6000 **5** *hd* **Dutch Artist (IRE)**[9] 8694 7-8-11 45 FayeMcManoman(5) 1 35
(Nigel Tinkler) *s.s: outpcd: nt clr run over 1f out: sn swtchd rt and hung rt: nvr nrr (jockey said gelding was never travelling)* **16/1**

5644 **6** 3 3/4 **You Little Beauty**[143] 4003 3-9-0 44 LukeMorris 8 27
(Ann Duffield) *chsd ldrs: rdn over 4f out: wknd 2f out* **33/1**

6000 **7** *hd* **Molten Lava (IRE)**[19] 8405 7-9-2 50 (p) PJMcDonald 11 26
(Steve Gollings) *s.i.s: hdwy over 6f out: lost pl over 4f out: sn rdn: n.d after* **7/1**[3]

3064 **8** 2 **Henrietta's Dream**[19] 8407 5-9-2 43 (p) KieranO'Neill 9 22
(Robyn Brisland) *in tch and sn pushed along: lost pl over 4f out: n.d after* **12/1**

5025 **9** 4 1/2 **Limerick Lord (IRE)**[61] 7028 7-9-2 48 (p) ShelleyBirkett 10 11
(Julia Feilden) *chsd ldrs: rdn over 2f out: wknd wl over 1f out (jockey said gelding had no more to give)* **8/1**

5020 **10** 2 1/4 **Prince Consort (IRE)**[23] 8295 4-9-2 48 (b) TomEaves 14 6
(John Wainwright) *prom: lost pl over 5f out: n.d after* **50/1**

0060 **11** 3/4 **Jane Camille**[14] 8547 3-9-0 40 TomQueally 13 4
(Peter Hedger) *bhd fnl 5f* **40/1**

-000 **12** 1 3/4 **Stainforth Swagger**[76] 6502 3-9-0 43 (e[1]) RaulDaSilva 2
(Ronald Thompson) *sn drvn along to chse ldrs: wknd 2f out (jockey said gelding stopped quickly; trainer said gelding did not stay the 1 mile trip on the fibresand surface)* **66/1**

3500 **13** 20 **Port Soif**[19] 8405 5-8-9 47 (p) JonathanFisher(7) 7
(Scott Dixon) *w ldr: led 7f out tl over 5f out: rdn and wknd over 2f out* **12/1**

0400 **P** **Little Choosey**[30] 8068 9-9-2 43 (vt) JFEgan 4
(Roy Bowring) *prom: lost pl 5f out: sn rdn: p.u over 2f out: dismntd: lame* **100/1**

1m 40.36s (-3.34) **Going Correction** -0.275s/f (Stan)
WFA 3 from 4yo+ 2lb **14 Ran SP% 115.0**
Speed ratings (Par 101): **105,95,93,92,92 88,88,86,82,79 79,77,57,**
CSF £103.43 TOTE £2.30: £1.10, £12.50, £2.40; EX 65.00 Trifecta £407.90.
Owner F Morley **Bred** Mrs Noreen Maher **Trained** Oakham, Rutland

FOCUS
The track was harrowed the day before and again during the morning to a depth of four inches, in the hope of making it ride slightly less quick than it has been recently. However the times suggested the track was still on the fast side. They seemed to go a good gallop and were soon stretched out, with the winner thoroughly dominant in a weak race.

8943 BETWAY SUPPORTING RESPONSIBLE GAMBLING H'CAP 4f 214y(F)
5:10 (5:12) (Class 5) (0-73,74) 3-Y-O+

£3,428 (£1,020; £509; £400; £400; £400) **Stalls** Centre

Form RPR

0625 **1** **Zapper Cass (FR)**[24] 8263 6-9-4 **70** (be[1]) AlistairRawlinson 2 82
(Michael Appleby) *s.i.s: sn pushed along: hdwy 1/2-way: rdn to ld over 1f out: edgd rt ins fnl f: r.o u.p* **7/1**

1250 **2** 1 1/4 **Samovar**[10] 8660 4-9-7 **73** (b) KieranO'Neill 4 80
(Scott Dixon) *s.i.s: sn chsng ldrs: rdn and ev ch over 1f out: styd on same pce wl ins fnl f* **8/1**

0210 **3** 1 1/4 **Requited (IRE)**[24] 8242 3-9-4 **70** CharlieBennett 1 73
(Hughie Morrison) *sn led: hdd 3f out: rdn and ev ch over 1f out: styd on same pce ins fnl f* **15/8**[1]

0401 **4** 1/2 **Royal Sands (FR)**[19] 8407 3-9-6 **72** BarryMcHugh 7 73
(James Given) *pushed along early towards rr: hdwy 1/2-way: rdn and edgd lft over 1f out: no ex ins fnl f* **11/4**[2]

0446 **5** 3 **Private Matter**[45] 7564 5-9-4 **70** (p[1] w) JackMitchell 5 60
(Amy Murphy) *s.i.s: hdwy over 3f out: rdn 1/2-way: wknd fnl f* **11/2**[3]

0035 **6** 1 3/4 **Ebitda**[3] 8861 5-8-6 **65** (p[1]) JonathanFisher(7) 3 49
(Scott Dixon) *w ldr tl led 3f out: rdn and hdd over 1f out: wknd ins fnl f* **22/1**

2500 **7** 2 1/4 **Eternal Sun**[165] 3206 4-9-5 **74** (t[1]) GabrieleMalune(3) 6 50
(Ivan Furtado) *s.i.s: in rr and pushed along 1/2-way: hung lft fr over 1f out: nvr on terms (jockey said filly fly leapt leaving the stalls and was slowly into stride as a result)* **22/1**

58.39s (-1.31) **Going Correction** -0.275s/f (Stan) **7 Ran SP% 109.1**
Speed ratings (Par 103): **99,97,95,94,89 86,83**
CSF £54.38 TOTE £6.00: £2.60, £3.50; EX 28.90 Trifecta £110.50.
Owner Stephen Louch **Bred** Arunas Cicenas **Trained** Oakham, Rutland

FOCUS
Just an ordinary sprint handicap.

8944 BETWAY MEDIAN AUCTION MAIDEN STKS 1m 3f 23y(F)
5:40 (5:42) (Class 5) 3-5-Y-O **£3,428** (£1,020; £509; £254) **Stalls** Low

Form RPR

0420 **1** **Dolly McQueen**[14] 8553 3-9-0 46 WilliamCarson 7 63+
(Anthony Carson) *trckd ldrs: racd keenly: nt clr run and swtchd rt wl over 2f out: led 2f: wnt readily clr fr over 1f out: easily (trainer said filly could never get competitive from a wide draw in its last run and appeared to benefit for the first time run on fibresand in a less competitive race)* **7/1**[3]

56 **2** 7 **Social City**[17] 8451 3-9-5 0 JFEgan 1 54
(Tony Carroll) *broke wl enough: sn pushed along and lost pl: hdwy on outer over 3f out: rdn over 2f out: styd on same pce fr over 1f out: wnt 2nd ins fnl f* **15/2**

55-3 **3** 2 **Ormesher**[25] 7643 4-9-2 61 EllaMcCain(7) 3 50
(Donald McCain) *pushed along to chse ldr: led 9f out: rdn and hung rt over 2f out: sn hdd: wknd ins fnl f (jockey said gelding hung right-handed)* **3/1**[2]

030 **4** 2 3/4 **Mirabelle Plum (IRE)**[117] 5004 3-9-0 48 KieranO'Neill 5 41
(Robyn Brisland) *led: hdd 9f out: chsd ldr: rdn and ev ch over 2f out: wknd fnl f* **25/1**

000 **5** 2 1/2 **Goldfox Grey**[91] 5969 3-9-5 47 (h[1]) TomEaves 4 42
(Robyn Brisland) *s.i.s: hld up: hdwy over 2f out: rdn and wknd over 1f out: hung rt ins fnl f* **20/1**

6 **6** 7 **Sandy Street**[75] 6544 3-9-5 0 JackGarritty 8 30
(Donald McCain) *s.i.s: sn prom: rdn over 2f out: wknd over 1f out* **14/1**

0006 **7** 31 **Gloryella**[73] 6612 3-8-11 30 (b[1]) ConnorMurtagh(3) 2
(Brian Rothwell) *chsd ldrs: lost pl over 8f out: in rr and swtchd rt over 6f out: sn wknd* **100/1**

8 30 **Lexington Flair (FR)** 4-9-9 0 BenCurtis 6
(Hugo Palmer) *s.i.s: hdwy 8f out: rdn over 4f out: wknd over 3f out: b.b.v (vet said gelding bled from the nose)* **1/1**[1]

2m 24.76s (-3.24) **Going Correction** -0.275s/f (Stan)
WFA 3 from 4yo 4lb **8 Ran SP% 115.5**
Speed ratings (Par 103): **100,94,93,91,89 84,62,40**
CSF £56.56 TOTE £6.90: £1.80, £1.70, £1.40; EX 35.60 Trifecta £139.20.
Owner Rita's Racing **Bred** Minster Stud **Trained** Newmarket, Suffolk

FOCUS
Weak maiden form.

8945 BETWAY LIVE CASINO H'CAP 2m 102y(F)
6:10 (6:12) (Class 5) (0-75,73) 3-Y-O+

£3,428 (£1,020; £509; £400; £400; £400) **Stalls** Low

Form RPR

4463 **1** **Bodacious Name (IRE)**[25] 8236 5-9-7 **66** JasonHart 8 72
(John Quinn) *hld up: hdwy 11f out: nt clr run over 2f out: sn swtchd rt: r.o u.p to ld towards fin* **15/2**

052 **2** *nk* **Shine Baby Shine**[11] 8639 5-8-9 **61**........................ NickBarratt-Atkin(7) 6 66
(Philip Kirby) *s.i.s: hld up: racd wd: hdwy on outer over 3f out: rdn to ld over 2f out: edgd rt ins fnl f: hdd towards fin* **7/1**[3]

4004 **3** *½* **The Resdev Way**[15] 8524 6-10-0 **73**........................ CliffordLee 1 77
(Philip Kirby) *s.i.s: hld up: hdwy over 2f out: rdn to chse wnr over 1f out: ev ch ins fnl f: unable qck nr fin* **22/1**

-044 **4** *4½* **Pumblechook**[15] 8523 6-9-12 **71**........................(p) BenCurtis 4 70
(Amy Murphy) *chsd ldrs: wnt 2nd 10f out: rdn and ev ch over 2f out: no ex ins fnl f* **7/1**[3]

2401 **5** *3¼* **Wadacre Galoubet**[11] 8644 3-9-2 **68**........................ PJMcDonald 2 65
(Mark Johnston) *led after 1f: hdd over 2f out: wknd fnl f* **9/4**[1]

330 **6** *nk* **Echo (IRE)**[62] 7001 4-9-13 **72**........................(p¹) JackGarritty 5 66
(Jedd O'Keeffe) *prom: rdn over 3f out: outpcd fr over 2f out* **8/1**

4524 **7** *½* **Tigray (USA)**[22] 8321 3-9-4 **73**........................ TheodoreLadd(3) 3 69
(Michael Appleby) *led 1f: chsd ldr tl 10f out: lost pl over 8f out: rdn on outer over 3f out: no imp fnl 2f* **3/1**[2]

056- **8** *13* **Caged Lightning (IRE)**[506] 4031 9-9-7 **66**........................(p) LukeMorris 7 44
(Steve Gollings) *hld up: hdwy over 8f out: rdn over 3f out: sn wknd* **25/1**

3m 40.73s (-4.77) **Going Correction** -0.275s/f (Stan) 8 Ran SP% **111.8**
WFA 3 from 4yo+ 7lb
Speed ratings (Par 103): **100,99,99,97,95 95,95,88**
CSF £55.82 CT £1086.20 TOTE £7.90: £2.00, £1.80, £4.70; EX 64.70 Trifecta £448.90.
Owner JJ Quinn Racing Ltd **Bred** Jude Doherty **Trained** Settrington, N Yorks

FOCUS
This staying handicap wasn't run at a solid gallop and turned into something of a sprint.

8946 BETWAY HEED YOUR HUNCH H'CAP 6f 16y(F)

6:40 (6:47) (Class 5) (0-75,74) 4-Y-0+

£3,428 (£1,020; £509; £400; £400; £400) **Stalls** Low

Form RPR

5426 **1** **Esprit De Corps**[8] 8719 5-9-4 **71**........................(p) BenCurtis 7 79
(David Barron) *hld up: hdwy over 2f out: rdn to ld ins fnl f: r.o* **2/1**[1]

2314 **2** *¾* **Poeta Brasileiro (IRE)**[7] 8755 4-8-9 **67**........(t) ThoreHammerHansen(5) 4 73
(David Brown) *chsd ldrs: rdn to ld over 1f out: hdd ins fnl f: styd on same pce nr fin* **9/4**[2]

1003 **3** *½* **Liamba**[19] 8403 4-9-0 **67**........................(v) CamHardie 5 71
(David O'Meara) *prom: pushed along over 4f out: rdn and ev ch over 1f out: styd on same pce wl ins fnl f* **6/1**[3]

0000 **4** *3¼* **Rock Of Estonia (IRE)**[25] 8220 4-9-6 **73**........................ LukeMorris 2 67
(Michael Squance) *led: hdd over 4f out: remained w ldr: rdn over 2f out: ev ch over 1f out: no ex ins fnl f* **18/1**

5220 **5** *½* **Rose Marmara**[11] 8643 6-8-10 **66**........................(tp) ConnorMurtagh(3) 1 58
(Brian Rothwell) *w ldr tl led over 4f out: rdn and hdd over 1f out: no ex ins fnl f* **33/1**

0005 **6** *3½* **Ower Fly**[8] 8712 6-8-10 **63**........................(v¹) JamesSullivan 9 44
(Ruth Carr) *sn pushed along in rr: rdn over 2f out: nvr on terms* **10/1**

0606 **7** *1½* **Mama Africa (IRE)**[33] 7977 5-8-11 **67**........................(p) WilliamCox(3) 6 43
(John Flint) *sn pushed along in rr: sme hdwy u.p 2f out: wknd fnl f* **33/1**

5600 **8** *4½* **Amor Fati (IRE)**[17] 8471 4-8-4 **64**........................ LauraPearson(7) 10 26
(David Evans) *s.s: a wl bhd (jockey said gelding was reluctant to race and very slowly away)* **16/1**

2050 **R** **Gnaad (IRE)**[38] 7828 5-9-7 **74**........................ JoeyHaynes 3
(Alan Bailey) *rrd s: ref to r* **8/1**

1m 13.97s (-2.53) **Going Correction** -0.275s/f (Stan) 9 Ran SP% **115.6**
Speed ratings (Par 103): **105,104,103,99,98 93,91,85,**
CSF £6.65 CT £20.72 TOTE £2.80: £1.10, £1.40, £1.30; EX 7.50 Trifecta £29.00.
Owner Laurence O'Kane **Bred** David Jamison & Gordon Roddick **Trained** Maunby, N Yorks
■ Rolladice was withdrawn. Price at time of withdrawal 10/1. Rule 4 applies to board prices prior to withdrawal - deduction 5p in the pound. New market formed

FOCUS
This was delayed and the runners were reloaded after Rolladice (withdrawn) broke out of the stalls. Modest sprinting form, but the time was fractionally inside the standard.

8947 BETWAY NOVICE STKS 4f 214y(F)

7:10 (7:11) (Class 5) 3-Y-0+ **£3,428** (£1,020; £509; £254) **Stalls** Centre

Form RPR

2 **1** **Sommer Katze (FR)**[32] 8006 3-9-5 0........................ DavidNolan 1 64
(Declan Carroll) *mde all: pushed clr fnl f: comf* **1/5**[1]

0 **2** *8* **Jeans Maite**[133] 4367 3-9-0 0........................(h¹) JFEgan 2 30
(Roy Bowring) *dwlt: racd keenly: hdwy 4f out: chsd wnr 1/2-way: sn rdn and edgd lft: outpcd and edgd rt fnl f* **12/1**[3]

0 **3** *7* **Henry The Sixth**[19] 8407 3-8-12 0........................ JonathanFisher(7) 4 10
(Scott Dixon) *sn w wnr ldr tl over 3f out: rdn and lost 2nd 1/2-way: wknd over 1f out* **10/1**[2]

-0 **4** *1½* **Arthur Shelby**[53] 7303 3-9-5 0........................ PhilDennis 3 5
(David C Griffiths) *prom: pushed along and lost pl 4f out: sn bhd* **10/1**[2]

58.08s (-1.62) **Going Correction** -0.275s/f (Stan) 4 Ran SP% **109.2**
Speed ratings (Par 103): **101,88,77,74**
CSF £3.61 TOTE £1.10; EX 3.50 Trifecta £6.20.
Owner F Gillespie **Bred** Debra Hooper **Trained** Malton, N Yorks

FOCUS
A seriously uncompetitive novice event.

8948 BETWAY H'CAP 1m 4f 14y(F)

7:40 (7:40) (Class 4) (0-85,88) 3-Y-0+

£5,207 (£1,549; £774; £400; £400; £400) **Stalls** Low

Form RPR

3421 **1** **Grazeon Roy**[11] 8641 3-9-0 **78**........................ JasonHart 1 92
(John Quinn) *a.p: chsd ldr 3f out: shkn up to ld and edgd rt wl ins fnl f: r.o* **6/5**[1]

2311 **2** *1¼* **Bo Samraan (IRE)**[11] 8633 3-9-10 **88**........................ JoeFanning 2 100
(Mark Johnston) *led: shkn and edgd rt over 1f out: sn rdn: hdd and unable qck wl ins fnl f* **2/1**[2]

0103 **3** *11* **Cold Harbour**[11] 8641 4-8-7 **66** oh2........................(t) KieranO'Neill 3 59
(Robyn Brisland) *chsd ldrs: swtchd rt over 3f out: rdn and edgd lft over 2f out: wknd over 1f out* **10/1**[3]

6136 **4** *4* **Lopes Dancer (IRE)**[19] 8396 7-9-4 **77**........................ BenRobinson 4 64
(Brian Ellison) *s.i.s: sn prom on outer: rdn over 3f out: wknd wl over 1f out* **12/1**

5345 **5** *4½* **Azari**[182] 2613 7-9-1 **79**........................(b) ThoreHammerHansen(5) 5 58
(Alexandra Dunn) *s.i.s: outpcd (jockey said gelding was never travelling)* **18/1**

1233 **6** *¾* **Wanaasah**[65] 6888 3-8-12 **76**........................ DavidEgan 6 55
(David Loughnane) *w ldr tl rdn over 3f out: wknd wl over 1f out* **12/1**

2m 34.67s (-6.33) **Going Correction** -0.275s/f (Stan) 6 Ran SP% **108.5**
WFA 3 from 4yo+ 5lb
Speed ratings (Par 105): **110,109,101,99,96 95**
CSF £3.45 TOTE £1.90: £1.10, £1.60; EX 4.20 Trifecta £14.40.
Owner J R Rowbottom **Bred** J R Rowbottom **Trained** Settrington, N Yorks

FOCUS
They went what appeared to be a good gallop in this fairly decent handicap and the first two finished nicely clear.

8949 BOMBARDIER GOLDEN BEER H'CAP 7f 14y(F)

8:10 (8:13) (Class 6) (0-60,60) 3-Y-0+

£2,781 (£827; £413; £400; £400; £400) **Stalls** Low

Form RPR

2535 **1** **Bee Machine (IRE)**[11] 8646 4-8-7 **52**........................(t) ZakWheatley(7) 11 59
(Declan Carroll) *prom: nt clr run and lost pl over 4f out: hdwy over 2f out: rdn to ld and edgd lft over 1f out: r.o* **8/1**

5236 **2** *1* **Elysee Star**[18] 8423 4-8-8 **46**........................(p) LukeMorris 4 50
(Mark Walford) *chsd ldrs: drvn along over 3f out: ev ch over 1f out: styd on same pce towards fin* **25/1**

2220 **3** *nk* **Mister Freeze (IRE)**[3] 8847 5-9-0 **52**........................(vt) LiamKeniry 5 56
(Patrick Chamings) *prom: nt clr run and lost pl 6f out: rdn over 3f out: hdwy over 1f out: r.o ins fnl f: nt rch ldrs* **5/1**[2]

2323 **4** *1½* **Break The Silence**[11] 8646 5-8-12 **57**........................(b) JonathanFisher(7) 12 57
(Scott Dixon) *s.i.s: hdwy over 5f out: rdn and ev ch over 1f out: styd on same pce ins fnl f* **4/1**[1]

6640 **5** *2¾* **Gulland Rock**[14] 8547 8-8-7 **45**........................ WilliamCarson 6 38
(Anthony Carson) *led: rdn and hdd over 1f out: no ex ins fnl f* **33/1**

0330 **6** *1¼* **Abie's Hollow**[24] 8270 3-9-6 **59**........................ DougieCostello 10 47
(Tony Coyle) *hld up: swtchd rt over 5f out: hdwy and hung lft over 1f out: nt rch ldrs* **10/1**

4044 **7** *1¾* **Fly True**[19] 8404 6-9-5 **57**........................ NickyMackay 13 42
(Ivan Furtado) *hdwy on outer over 5f out: rdn over 1f out: wknd fnl f* **17/2**

505 **8** *1¼* **Ginger Max**[24] 8268 3-9-5 **58**........................ DavidNolan 7 39
(Richard Fahey) *chsd ldrs: rdn and ev ch over 2f out: wknd fnl f* **9/1**

5400 **9** *nk* **Kodiline (IRE)**[7] 8755 5-8-13 **58**........................ CameronIles(7) 14 39
(David Evans) *s.i.s: rdn over 2f out: nvr nrr* **28/1**

5630 **10** *7* **Strict (IRE)**[11] 8646 3-9-7 **60**........................(p) AlistairRawlinson 2 22
(Michael Appleby) *s.i.s: outpcd* **16/1**

-456 **11** *4* **Disruptor (FR)**[73] 6602 3-9-3 **56**........................ DavidEgan 1 7
(David Evans) *s.i.s: outpcd* **14/1**

3023 **12** *3* **Tease Maid**[19] 8407 3-9-7 **60**........................(p) JasonHart 9 3
(John Quinn) *chsd ldrs: lost pl over 4f out: rdn 1/2-way: wknd over 2f out (jockey said filly had become uncharacteristically upset in the stalls due to the unruly behaviour of the runner drawn on its inside)* **15/2**[3]

040 **13** *22* **Pecheurs De Perles (IRE)**[26] 8207 5-8-7 **45**........................ JoeyHaynes 3
(John Butler) *chsd ldrs: pushed along and lost pl over 4f out: wknd 1/2-way* **66/1**

1m 27.78s (-2.52) **Going Correction** -0.275s/f (Stan) 13 Ran SP% **113.4**
WFA 3 from 4yo+ 1lb
Speed ratings (Par 101): **103,101,101,99,96 95,93,91,91,83 78,75,50**
CSF £181.21 CT £984.35 TOTE £8.50: £2.70, £4.00, £2.10; EX 188.10 Trifecta £943.40.
Owner Mrs Sarah Bryan **Bred** Drumlin Bloodstock **Trained** Malton, N Yorks
■ Rock In Society was withdrawn. Price at time of withdrawal 14/1. Rule 4 applies to all bets - deduction 5p in the pound.

FOCUS
They went what appeared to be a decent gallop in this very modest handicap. The winner has been rated to his best form over the past 12 months.
T/Plt: £67.70 to a £1 stake. Pool: £87,852.50 - 946.42 winning units T/Qpdt: £6.30 to a £1 stake. Pool: £12,012.84 - 1,407.35 winning units **Colin Roberts**

8950 - 8951a (Foreign Racing) - See Raceform Interactive

8905 FLEMINGTON (L-H)

Saturday, November 9

OFFICIAL GOING: Turf: good

8952a SEPPELT MACKINNON STKS (GROUP 1) (3YO+) (TURF) 1m 2f

5:55 3-Y-0+

£665,745 (£198,895; £99,447; £49,723; £27,624; £22,099)

RPR

1 **Magic Wand (IRE)**[4] 8844 4-9-0 0........................(p) RyanMoore 9 108
(A P O'Brien, Ire) *prom: pushed along to chse ldng pair over 2f out: drvn to dispute ld over 1f out: led jst ins fnl f: kpt on strly u.p* **19/5**[2]

2 *1* **Melody Belle (NZ)**[7] 5-9-0 0........................(bt) OpieBosson 15 106+
(Jamie Richards, New Zealand) **14/5**[1]

3 *shd* **Hartnell**[21] 8361 8-9-4 0........................ HughBowman 13 109
(James Cummings, Australia) *cl up: prog to join ldr 3f out: asked to qckn over 2f out: sn rdn: unable to match pce of eventual wnr ins fnl f: lost 2nd fnl strides* **9/1**

4 *hd* **Life Less Ordinary (IRE)**[7] 8768 7-9-4 0........................ NashRawiller 4 109
(Chris Waller, Australia) **40/1**

5 *2* **Fifty Stars (IRE)**[7] 8768 4-9-4 0........................(bt) JyeMcNeil 10 105
(David A & B Hayes & Tom Dabernig, Australia) **15/1**

6 *hd* **Kings Will Dream (IRE)**[14] 8579 5-9-4 0........................ JamesMcDonald 12 105
(Chris Waller, Australia) **6/1**[3]

7 *1½* **Suzuka Devious (JPN)**[28] 8136 8-9-4 0........................ MichaelDee 16 102
(Mitsuru Hashida, Japan) **60/1**

8 *½* **Kluger (JPN)**[14] 8579 7-9-4 0........................ KerrinMcEvoy 8 101
(Tomokazu Takano, Japan) **17/1**

9 *shd* **Humidor (NZ)**[14] 8577 7-9-4 0........................ DamianLane 11 100
(Ciaron Maher & David Eustace, Australia) **11/1**

10 *¾* **Aristia (AUS)**[7] 4-8-13 0........................(t) CraigAWilliams 5 94
(Mathew Ellerton & Simon Zahra, Australia) **19/1**

11 *½* **Gailo Chop (FR)**[14] 8578 8-9-4 0........................(b) JohnAllen 14 98
(Matthew Williams, Australia) **50/1**

12 *hd* **Harlem**[14] 8579 7-9-4 0........................(b) JamieKah 3 98
(David A & B Hayes & Tom Dabernig, Australia) **30/1**

13 *hd* **Night's Watch (NZ)**[7] 8768 6-9-4 0........................(t) DamienOliver 1 97
(Chris Waller, Australia) **30/1**

14 *4¼* **So Si Bon (AUS)**[7] 8768 6-9-4 0........................ LukeNolen 7 89
(David A & B Hayes & Tom Dabernig, Australia) **50/1**

15 1 1/2 **Debt Agent (NZ)**14 8578 7-9-4 0 MichaelRodd 6 86
(Jim Conlan, Australia) **40/1**
16 1 **Cape Of Good Hope (IRE)**14 8579 3-9-1 0 MarkZahra 2 85
(David A & B Hayes & Tom Dabernig, Australia) *midfield on inner: asked for effrt over 2f out: limited rspnse and sn rdn: no imp and wknd fr over 1 1/2f out: eased clsng stages* **20/1**
2m 1.82s
WFA 3 from 4yo+ 3lb **16** Ran **SP% 118.2**

Owner Michael Tabor & Derrick Smith & Mrs John Magnier **Bred** Ecurie Des Monceaux & Skymarc Farm Inc **Trained** Cashel, Co Tipperary

8953 - 8963a (Foreign Racing) - See Raceform Interactive

2163 KREFELD (R-H)
Sunday, November 10
OFFICIAL GOING: Turf: soft

8964a HERZOG VON RATIBOR-RENNEN (GROUP 3) (2YO) (TURF) 1m 110y
12:50 2-Y-O £28,828 (£10,810; £5,405; £2,702; £1,801)

RPR
1 **Wonderful Moon (GER)**35 7937 2-9-2 0 AndraschStarke 1 115+
(Henk Grewe, Germany) *prom: led 3f out: sn drvn along: stretched clr: v easily* **6/4**1
2 12 **Schwesterherz (FR)**21 8371 2-8-13 0 BauyrzhanMurzabayev 3 86
(Henk Grewe, Germany) *mid-div: shkn up 2f out: sn wnt 2nd and outpcd by ldr: kpt on but nvr trbld wnr* **165/10**
3 3 1/4 **Near Poet (GER)** 2-9-2 0 CarlosHenrique 4 82
(Markus Klug, Germany) *towards rr: drvn along 2f out: styd on for mod 3rd: drvn out* **94/10**
4 1 1/4 **Tickle Me Green (GER)**21 8371 2-8-13 0 MaximPecheur 5 77
(Markus Klug, Germany) *t.k.h cl up early: settled in midfield after 2f: shkn up 2f out: kpt on* **29/10**3
5 4 1/2 **Inaugural (GER)** 2-9-2 0 LukasDelozier 7 70
(P Schiergen, Germany) *mid-div: effrt 2f out: plugged on same pce* **28/1**
6 shd **No Limit Credit (GER)**22 2-8-13 0 ClementLecoeuvre 8 67
(Andreas Suborics, Germany) *hld up towards rr early: tk clsr order 1/2-way: effrt 2f out: no imp and dropped away fnl f* **13/5**2
7 1 3/4 **Nona (GER)**21 8371 2-8-13 0 MichaelCadeddu 2 63
(Mario Hofer, Germany) *led 2f: trckd ldrs: shkn up and lost position 2f out: wl hld fnl f* **31/1**
8 3/4 **Prince Oliver (FR)** 2-9-2 0 WladimirPanov 6 64
(M Figge, Germany) *awkward s: in rr and pushed along early: led after 2f: hdd 3f out: effrt and hung rt 3f out: sn btn* **242/10**
1m 49.84s (3.24) **8** Ran **SP% 119.3**
PARI-MUTUEL (all including 1 euro stake): WIN 2.50 PLACE: 1.30, 3.10, 3.20; SF: 13.90.
Owner Stall Wasserfreunde **Bred** Gestut Goerlsdorf **Trained** Germany

8965 - (Foreign Racing) - See Raceform Interactive

8845 SAINT-CLOUD (L-H)
Saturday, November 9
OFFICIAL GOING: Turf: heavy

8966a PRIX BARON HENRY DE MONTESQUIEU (CLAIMER) (4YO+) (GENTLEMAN RIDERS) (TURF) 1m 7f
12:15 4-Y-O+ £8,108 (£3,243; £2,432; £1,621; £810)

RPR
1 **Cutty Pie (IRE)**24 5-10-6 (p) MrAlexisLemer 5 75
(J Phelippon, France) **11/5**2
2 10 **Calcite (FR)**14 8-10-2 0 (b) MrPatrickMillman 2 59
(G Mousnier, France) **13/1**
3 6 **Tres Solid (FR)**14 8-10-10 0 (p) MrGuillaumeViel 1 60
(M Boutin, France) **19/10**1
4 7 **Argus (IRE)**45 7575 7-10-6 0 MrMAGalligan 3 47
(Alexandra Dunn) *prom on outer: struggling to go pce and pushed along over 2 1/2f out: sn rdn: no imp and wl btn over 1 1/2f out: kpt on same pce* **36/5**
5 dist **Brave Impact**430 8-10-10 0 AlbertoCarrassiDelVillar 6
(Mme J-F Bernard, France) **18/5**3
6 dist **Jenilat Pearl (FR)**211 4-10-2 0 PabloLabordeFernandez 4
(J Phelippon, France) **69/10**
3m 55.48s **6** Ran **SP% 119.5**
PARI-MUTUEL (all including 1 euro stake): WIN 3.20; PLACE 1.90, 3.20; SF 31.10.
Owner Ecurie Foret Jaune **Bred** Robert Nahas **Trained** France

8967 - 8968a (Foreign Racing) - See Raceform Interactive

7979 TOULOUSE
Monday, November 11
OFFICIAL GOING: Turf: heavy

8969a PRIX FILLE DE L'AIR (GROUP 3) (3YO+ FILLIES & MARES) (TURF) 1m 2f 110y
2:50 3-Y-O+ £36,036 (£14,414; £10,810; £7,207; £3,603)

RPR
1 **Ambition**35 7979 3-8-9 0 MickaelBarzalona 1 103
(X Thomas-Demeaulte, France) *prom on inner: drvn to squeeze between rivals over 1 1/2f out: chal ldr jst ins fnl f: led fnl 75yds: kpt on strly* **69/10**
2 1 1/4 **Vespera (IRE)**6 4-8-13 0 Pierre-CharlesBoudot 8 100
(F-H Graffard, France) *w.w in rr: prog on outer to r cl up over 1/2-way: pushed along and effrt over 2f out: rdn over 1f out: kpt on but nt match pce of wnr ins fnl f* **73/10**
3 1/2 **Tosen Gift (IRE)**16 8584 4-8-13 0 CristianDemuro 3 99
(S Kobayashi, France) *led after 1f: asked to qckn 2f out: sn rdn: jnd jst ins fnl f: hdd fnl 75yds: no ex towards fin* **59/10**3
4 1/2 **Made To Lead (FR)**22 8377 4-8-13 0 (p) JeromeClaudic 4 98
(Laurent Loisel, France) *cl up on outer: lost position but remained prom over 1/2-way: asked for effrt over 2f out: rdn 1 1/2f out: kpt on but nvr pce to chal* **21/1**
5 1 1/4 **Tresorerie (FR)**35 7979 4-8-13 0 JulienAuge 9 96
(C Ferland, France) *midfield on inner: pushed along over 2f out: rdn 1 1/2f out: unable qck: kpt on same pce ins fnl f* **14/1**
6 1 1/4 **Spirit Of Nelson (IRE)**16 8584 4-9-5 0 MaximeGuyon 6 99
(J Reynier, France) *hld up in fnl pair: dropped to last over 1/2-way: swtchd off rail and drvn 2f out: limited rspnse: kpt on same pce fr over 1f out: nvr threatened* **8/5**1
7 4 1/2 **Likala (FR)**66 6946 3-8-9 0 Jean-BernardEyquem 5 86
(J-C Rouget, France) *a towards rr: asked for effrt on outer over 2f out: rdn over 1f out: sn hld and allowed to fin in own time* **13/5**2
8 snk **Palmyre (FR)**38 7885 4-8-13 0 VincentCheminaud 2 84
(H-F Devin, France) *in midfield: dropped to fnl trio and struggling to go pce over 2f out: btn over 1f out: allowed to fin in own time* **37/1**
2m 18.9s
WFA 3 from 4yo 3lb **8** Ran **SP% 119.3**
PARI-MUTUEL (all including 1 euro stake): WIN 7.90; PLACE 2.30, 2.30, 2.20; DF 22.00.
Owner James Rowsell & Steve Ashley **Bred** Ashbrittle Stud & M H Dixon **Trained** France

8879 CHANTILLY (R-H)
Tuesday, November 12
OFFICIAL GOING: Polytrack: standard; turf: heavy

8970a PRIX YACOWLEF (LISTED RACE) (2YO) (TURF) 5f 110y
1:42 2-Y-O £27,027 (£10,810; £8,108; £5,405; £2,702)

RPR
1 **Keep Busy (IRE)**11 8724 2-8-9 0 IoritzMendizabal 2 96
(John Quinn) *racd in 2nd of stands' side trio: shkn up after 1/2-way: hdwy to chal 2f out: strly drvn to ld ins fnl f: styd on wl to get on top nr fin* **131/10**
2 3/4 **Bavaria Baby (FR)**21 8446 2-8-9 0 MickaelBarzalona 3 94
(F Chappet, France) **53/10**3
3 2 **Ernesto De La Cruz (FR)**41 2-8-13 0 TonyPiccone 1 91
(Andrea Marcialis, France) **10/1**
4 snk **Wanaway (FR)**14 8647 2-8-9 0 (b) MaximeGuyon 9 86
(P Bary, France) **44/5**
5 3 **Lady Penelope (IRE)**31 8140 2-8-9 0 TheoBachelot 6 77
(Joseph Patrick O'Brien, Ire) *broke alertly and led main body of field: pushed along whn chal at 1/2-way: hdd 2f out and strly drvn: grad fdd fnl f* **37/10**2
6 5 **Gold Step (FR)**21 8446 2-8-9 0 GeraldMosse 7 60
(F Rossi, France) **14/1**
7 2 1/2 **Spartan Fighter**31 8140 2-8-13 0 Pierre-CharlesBoudot 4 61
(Declan Carroll) *hld up in tch: travelled wl 1/2-way: pushed along to get clsr over 2f out: sn u.p and began to weaken: eased ins fnl f* **74/10**
8 5 **Nina Bailarina**45 7692 2-8-9 0 ShaneKelly 5 35
(Ed Walker) *prom: urged along bef 1/2-way: strly rdn over 2f out to remain on heels of ldrs: sn no ex: eased ins fnl f* **12/5**1
9 6 **Autumnal (FR)**25 8330 2-8-9 0 DamienBoche 10 15
(L Gadbin, France) **39/1**
10 11 **Lorelei Rock (IRE)**9 8791 2-8-13 0 (b) CristianDemuro 8
(G Botti, France) **17/1**
1m 11.8s (7.30) **10** Ran **SP% 119.6**
PARI-MUTUEL (all including 1 euro stake): WIN 14.10; PLACE 4.10, 2.30, 3.50; DF 42.10.
Owner Altitude Racing **Bred** Hackcanter Ltd & Mr P Gleeson **Trained** Settrington, N Yorks
FOCUS
It's been rated fairly negatively, with the second in line with her previous form.

8171- 8179a (Foreign Racing) - See Raceform Interactive

8010 LYON PARILLY (R-H)
Wednesday, November 13
OFFICIAL GOING: Turf: heavy

8980a PRIX DU GRAND CAMP (LISTED RACE) (3YO+) (TURF) 1m 4f
1:42 3-Y-O+ £23,423 (£9,369; £7,027; £4,684; £2,342)

RPR
1 **Pontille (FR)**44 4-9-0 0 (p) AurelienLemaitre 11 107
(Elias Mikhalides, France) **172/10**
2 6 1/2 **Good Question (FR)**36 8010 4-9-6 0 MaximeGuyon 2 103
(C Escuder, France) **13/2**2
3 2 1/2 **Forever Yours (FR)**28 4-9-0 0 (p) TheoBachelot 8 93
(S Wattel, France) **13/2**2
4 1/2 **Jacksun (FR)**36 5-9-3 0 (b) AntoineHamelin 4 95
(M Figge, Germany) **14/1**
5 nk **Fabulous Las Vegas (FR)**45 4-9-3 0 FranckBlondel 6 95
(Krzysztof Ziemianski, Poland) **38/1**
6 2 **Royal Family (FR)**22 8433 3-8-8 0 IoritzMendizabal 5 89
(Amy Murphy) *disp early ld: settled jst bhd ldrs after 2f: niggled appr entrnce to home st: sn strly drvn and began to weaken: no ex ins fnl f* **14/1**
7 nk **Jizellita (FR)**156 4-9-0 0 MickaelBerto 9 88
(A De Royer-Dupre, France) **27/1**
8 6 1/2 **Dalvini (FR)**220 4-9-3 0 StephanePasquier 7 81
(A De Royer-Dupre, France) **11/1**
9 3/4 **Boulevard (IRE)**66 7008 4-9-3 0 OlivierPeslier 10 79
(Charley Rossi, France) **68/10**3
10 dist **Argyron (IRE)**22 8445 3-8-11 0 VincentCheminaud 1
(A Fabre, France) **36/5**
11 dist **Silverwave (FR)**24 8378 7-9-6 0 MickaelBarzalona 3
(F Vermeulen, France) **19/10**1
2m 47.31s (13.80)
WFA 3 from 4yo+ 5lb **11** Ran **SP% 119.5**
PARI-MUTUEL (all including 1 euro stake): WIN 18.20; PLACE 4.70, 2.50, 2.80; DF 45.70.
Owner Ecurie De Montlahuc, Mme Lucile Falque & Laurent B **Bred** J-C Seroul **Trained** France

8981 - (Foreign Racing) - See Raceform Interactive

7561 **FONTAINEBLEAU**

Thursday, November 14

OFFICIAL GOING: Turf: heavy

8982a PRIX CONTESSINA (CONDITIONS) (3YO+) (TURF) 6f
12:25 3-Y-O+

£15,765 (£5,990; £4,414; £2,522; £1,261; £945)

RPR

1 **Red Torch (FR)**16 8648 4-9-6 0 Pierre-CharlesBoudot 3 98
(H-A Pantall, France) 2/1[1]

2 ½ **Ecolo (FR)**7 3-9-0 0 MaximeGuyon 2 90
(C Laffon-Parias, France) 51/10[3]

3 hd **Viscount Barfield**18 6-9-3 0 TheoBachelot 4 93
(Mme Pia Brandt, France) 78/10

4 hd **Fighting Irish (IRE)**117 5188 4-9-0 0 (p) CristianDemuro 5 89
(Harry Dunlop) *rdn fr the stalls to take early advantage: sn passed and settled in 2nd bhd clr ldr: pushed along to try and reduce deficit over 1f out: hdwy to chal wl ins fnl 1f: kpt on same pce clsng stages* 21/1

5 ½ **Bakoel Koffie (IRE)**16 8648 5-9-6 0 (b[1]) TonyPiccone 1 94
(M Delcher Sanchez, France) 48/10[2]

6 6 **Tudo Bem (FR)**34 3-9-3 0 MickaelBarzalona 7 71
(M Boutin, France) 66/10

7 snk **McQueen (FR)**18 7-9-6 0 AntoineHamelin 10 74
(Yasmin Almenrader, Germany) 17/1

8 7 **Shining Emerald**18 8-9-6 0 BauyrzhanMurzabayev 6 51
(A Wohler, Germany) 25/1

9 nk **Henrytheaeroplane (USA)**418 7578 7-9-0 0 (p) JanVerner 8 44
(Z Koplik, Czech Republic) 26/1

10 9 **Alba Power (IRE)**88 4-9-0 0 (b) StephanePasquier 9 16
(F Chappet, France) 87/10

1m 12.01s 10 Ran SP% 119.4
PARI-MUTUEL (all including 1 euro stake): WIN 3.00; PLACE 1.50, 1.90, 2.40; DF 8.80.
Owner Sandro V Gianella **Bred** Appapays Racing Club **Trained** France

8983a PRIX CERES (LISTED RACE) (3YO FILLIES) (TURF) 7f
1:42 3-Y-O £24,774 (£9,909; £7,432; £4,954; £2,477)

RPR

1 **Invitational**33 8115 3-9-2 0 StephanePasquier 17 96
(Roger Varian) *broke wl fr wd draw: chsd ldrs: smooth hdwy to get clsr w 3f to run: pushed along over 2f out: strly drvn to deliver chal 1f out: styd on wl ins fnl 100yds to ld cl home* 69/10[3]

2 snk **Grace Spirit**25 8376 3-9-2 0 AntoineHamelin 3 96
(A De Royer-Dupre, France) 16/1

3 shd **Orchid Star**25 8376 3-9-2 0 MickaelBarzalona 2 96
(Charlie Appleby) *broke wl and sn led but a pressed: stl travelling comf over 3f out: rdn whn jnd for ld over 2f out: battled tenaciously to regain outrt advantage ins fnl 1f: began to tire fnl 100yds: ct cl home* 21/10[1]

4 ¾ **Tosen Shauna (IRE)**23 8449 3-9-2 0 TheoBachelot 11 94
(M Rulec, Germany) 19/1

5 snk **Gypsy Spirit**33 8115 3-9-2 0 MaximeGuyon 14 93
(Tom Clover) *midfield: briefly bmpd along at 1/2-way: pushed along over 2f out: hdwy u.p to chal 1f out: kpt on wl clsng stages but nt quite rch ldrs* 7/1

6 1½ **Air De Valse (FR)**33 3-9-2 0 CristianDemuro 5 89
(Mme C Barande-Barbe, France) 51/10[2]

7 ½ **Simona (FR)**9 8845 3-9-2 0 (b) JeromeMoutard 6 88
(F-H Graffard, France) 43/1

8 ½ **Villalar (FR)**198 3-9-2 0 OlivierPeslier 12 87
(C Laffon-Parias, France) 16/1

9 3 **Green Siren (FR)**35 3-9-2 0 ClementLecoeuvre 16 78
(Mme M Bollack-Badel, France) 42/1

10 3½ **Bowled Over (IRE)**25 8377 3-9-2 0 StephaneBreux 10 69
(F-H Graffard, France) 47/1

11 4 **Waldblumchen (GER)**25 8376 3-9-2 0 GregoryBenoist 7 58
(G Botti, France) 29/1

12 1¾ **Tencaratrubieslace (FR)**49 3-9-2 0 TonyPiccone 8 53
(M Delcher Sanchez, France) 33/1

13 3½ **K Club (IRE)**18 3-9-2 0 EddyHardouin 13 44
(J Hirschberger, Germany) 16/1

14 1 **Parousia**14 3-9-2 0 VincentCheminaud 4 41
(H-A Pantall, France) 15/1

15 3 **Lady Aria**33 8115 3-9-2 0 JasonWatson 9 33
(Michael Bell) *fraction slow to break: hld up in rr: stl towards bk and bhd wall of horses at 1/2-way: plld wdst of all and rdn along over 2f out: failed to respond to press and sn wknd: eased ins fnl f* 25/1

1m 31.19s 15 Ran SP% 119.5
PARI-MUTUEL (all including 1 euro stake): WIN 7.90; PLACE 2.50, 3.70, 1.70; DF 50.30.
Owner Ziad A Galadari **Bred** Galadari Sons Stud Company Limited **Trained** Newmarket, Suffolk

8994 - 8997a (Foreign Racing) - See Raceform Interactive

8705 **LINGFIELD** (L-H)

Saturday, November 16

OFFICIAL GOING: Polytrack: standard

Wind: virtually nil Weather: overcast

8998 BOMBARDIER "MARCH TO YOUR OWN DRUM" H'CAP 1m 1y(P)
11:55 (11:56) (Class 6) (0-55,55) 3-Y-O+

£2,781 (£827; £413; £300; £300; £300) Stalls High

Form RPR

5030 1 **Avorisk Et Perils (FR)**10 8847 4-9-9 55 HectorCrouch 11 65+
(Gary Moore) *hld up: effrt to make quick hdwy between rivals into 4th 2f out: sn rdn and qcknd up to ld 1f out: rdn out* 9/2[1]

460 2 2¾ **My Law**17 8666 3-9-5 53 (p[1]) AdamKirby 8 56
(Jim Boyle) *racd in midfield on outer: hdwy u.p 2f out: sn rdn and chal ldr over 1f out: drvn and kpt on fnl f but nt match pce of wnr* 8/1

0464 3 2 **Pearl Spectre (USA)**8 8917 8-9-1 54 (p) GraceMcEntee(7) 5 53
(Phil McEntee) *led: drvn along over 1f out: hdd by wnr 1f out: kpt on one pce* 13/2[3]

5334 4 ½ **Mister Musicmaster**11 8822 10-9-6 52 DavidProbert 6 51
(Ron Hodges) *anticipated s: sn in midfield: pushed along whn short of room 2f out: sn rdn and kpt on wl again fnl f* 13/2[3]

2250 5 2¾ **Duke Of North (IRE)**25 8416 7-8-11 50 (p) IsobelFrancis(7) 9 43
(Jim Boyle) *hld up: dropped to last 1/2-way: prog into midfield whn hmpd off home bnd: sn rdn and kpt on one pce (jockey said gelding was denied a clear run)* 12/1

0416 6 1¾ **Arctic Flower (IRE)**16 8711 6-8-13 50 AledBeech(5) 10 38
(John Bridger) *chsd ldrs: rdn and outpcd over 1f out: kpt on one pce fnl f* 9/1

006 7 2¼ **Maryellen**68 7032 3-9-7 55 (p[1]) LukeMorris 12 36
(Alan Bailey) *in tch early: rdn along to hold position 3f out: drvn and no imp over 1f out: no further hdwy* 25/1

064 8 nk **Annakonda (IRE)**85 6388 3-9-2 50 BrettDoyle 7 31
(Peter Chapple-Hyam) *racd in midfield: effrt whn short of room 2f out: sn rdn and kpt on one pce fr over 1f out* 16/1

6000 9 nse **Chop Chop (IRE)**10 8864 3-9-3 51 StevieDonohoe 3 32
(Brian Barr) *racd in rr of midfield: rdn and dropped to last over 2f out: nvr a factor* 40/1

0042 10 2 **Quick Recovery**8 8915 4-9-3 49 CharlieBennett 1 26
(Jim Boyle) *midfield early: pushed along and lost pl over 2f out: sn bhd (jockey said filly ran flat)* 9/2[1]

0404 11 hd **Fitzy**83 6502 3-9-6 54 (p) JasonWatson 4 30
(Paddy Butler) *dwlt bdly and racd in last: effrt into midfield 1/2-way: sn rdn and lost pl again 2f out (jockey said gelding was slowly away)* 25/1

1000 12 8 **Pact Of Steel**24 8466 4-9-3 52 (t) GabrieleMalune(3) 2 10
(Ivan Furtado) *trckd ldr on inner: rdn along and lost pl 2f out: eased fnl f (jockey said colt stopped quickly. trainer said colt had a breathing problem)* 5/1[2]

1m 38.07s (-0.13) **Going Correction** +0.05s/f (Slow) 12 Ran SP% 124.5
WFA 3 from 4yo+ 2lb
Speed ratings (Par 101): **102,99,97,96,94 92,90,89,89,87 87,79**
CSF £42.12 CT £245.43 TOTE £6.10: £2.30, £2.10, £2.60; EX 60.80 Trifecta £272.20.
Owner Dedman Properties **Bred** Miss Isabelle Mauger **Trained** Lower Beeding, W Sussex

FOCUS
A low-grade opener to a cracking card and it saw the winner land some good support in decisive fashion.

8999 LADBROKES HOME OF THE ODDS BOOST / EBF NOVICE STKS 1m 1y(P)
12:25 (12:28) (Class 5) 2-Y-O £3,428 (£1,020; £509; £254) Stalls High

Form RPR

03 1 **Fruition**24 8455 2-9-5 0 Pierre-CharlesBoudot 2 75
(William Haggas) *trckd ldrs: pushed along and outpcd by front pair 2f out: rdn 1f out: kpt on strly between rivals under mostly hands and heels to ld post* 5/1[3]

3 2 shd **Hibernian Warrior (USA)**50 7661 2-9-5 0 JFEgan 5 75
(Roger Varian) *wnt to post early: led: rdn along and strly pressed 1f out: rallied wl u.p fnl f: hdd post* 13/8[1]

4 3 ½ **Zeimaam (IRE)**30 8288 2-9-5 0 KieranShoemark 10 74+
(Owen Burrows) *racd in midfield: rdn along and outpcd 2f out: drvn and kpt on strly ins fnl f: nrst fin* 15/2

4 nk **Katzoff (IRE)** 2-9-5 0 (h[1]) RossaRyan 11 73
(Richard Hannon) *trckd ldr: rdn upsides to chal appr fnl f: drvn and lost 2 pls clsng stages* 25/1

5 ½ **Arabian Warrior** 2-9-5 0 CallumShepherd 7 72
(Saeed bin Suroor) *racd in midfield: green at times: niggled along 1/2-way: c wd off home bnd: sn rdn and kpt on one pce fnl f* 5/2[2]

4 6 nse **Blackcastle Storm**24 8460 2-9-5 0 ShaneKelly 1 72
(Richard Hughes) *prom: rdn along and outpcd 2f out: no imp on ldrs 1f out: kpt on same pce* 12/1

7 1 **Zoran** 2-9-5 0 (t[1]) JackMitchell 9 70+
(Hugo Palmer) *dwlt and racd in rr: effrt into midfield over 1f out: rdn and late hdwy fnl f* 16/1

8 3½ **Sulochana (IRE)** 2-9-0 0 CharlieBennett 8 57
(Hughie Morrison) *hld up: a in rr* 50/1

9 2½ **Nafaas** 2-9-5 0 JasonWatson 3 56
(Roger Charlton) *in rr of midfield: rdn along and outpcd 2f out: nvr on terms* 20/1

10 7 **Ower Bush Mills** 2-9-5 0 JohnFahy 6 40
(Richard Hannon) *dwlt and racd in last: rdn in rr 2f out: nvr on terms* 50/1

11 7 **Yukon Thunder** 2-9-0 0 TobyEley(5) 4 24
(Steph Hollinshead) *midfield early: rdn and lost pl over 2f out: sn bhd* 66/1

12 11 **Girl Of Dreams** 2-8-11 0 MitchGodwin(3) 12
(Nikki Evans) *hld up: effrt to cl into midfield 3f out: sn lost pl and bhd 2f out* 66/1

1m 38.46s (0.26) **Going Correction** +0.05s/f (Slow) 12 Ran SP% 124.2
Speed ratings (Par 96): **100,99,99,99,98 98,97,94,91,84 77,66**
CSF £13.59 TOTE £6.40: £2.50, £1.20, £1.50; EX 15.80 Trifecta £99.00.
Owner The Queen **Bred** The Queen **Trained** Newmarket, Suffolk

FOCUS
An interesting novice event which produced a thrilling finish. There was a stop-start tempo which saw the runner-up to maximum effect.

9000 BOMBARDIER GOLDEN BEER H'CAP 1m 1y(P)
1:00 (1:01) (Class 2) (0-105,102) 3-Y-£01,971 (£3,583; £1,791; £896; £446) Stalls High

Form RPR

2111 1 **Alrajaa**32 8222 3-9-6 100 JimCrowley 4 113+
(John Gosden) *trckd ldr: pushed along to ld off home bnd over 1f out: rdn and sn clr appr fnl f: pushed out: comf* 8/11[1]

0300 2 3¼ **So Beloved**28 8336 9-9-4 96 AdamKirby 7 102
(David O'Meara) *hld up: rdn and hdwy between rivals 2f out: wnt 3rd appr fnl f: kpt on to go 2nd fnl f: no ch w wnr* 6/1[2]

0150 3 ¾ **Goring (GER)**161 3581 7-9-8 100 (v) CharlesBishop 3 105
(Eve Johnson Houghton) *prom: rdn along to chse wnr over 1f out: drvn and no imp 1f out: kpt on but lost 2nd ins fnl f* 20/1

4-36 4 ¾ **Wait Forever (IRE)**160 3643 4-9-3 102 StefanoCherchi(7) 5 105
(Marco Botti) *hld up: hdwy between rivals u.p 2f out: effrt whn short of room appr fnl f: trapped on heels and rdn once in clr fnl 100yds* 16/1

6054 5 ¾ **Bubble And Squeak**27 8377 4-8-11 89 JasonWatson 6 90
(Sylvester Kirk) *hld up: hdwy u.p 2f out: rdn and kpt on wl fnl f but n.d* 20/1

3313 6 1 **Alemaratalyoum (IRE)**36 8096 5-9-5 97 (t) RichardKingscote 10 96
(Stuart Williams) *midfield in tch: drvn along and no imp 2f out: plugged on one pce after* 13/2[3]

1560 **7** ½ **Universal Gleam**[42] [7906] 4-8-12 **90** JoeFanning 2 91
(Keith Dalgleish) *racd in midfield: u.p whn hmpd over 1f out: rdn once in clr but nt rcvr* **11/1**

2002 **8** 1¼ **Ptarmigan Ridge**[71] [6920] 5-8-3 **88** GeorgeRooke(7) 9 83
(Richard Hughes) *racd in midfield: rdn on inner 2f out: drvn and no hdwy over 1f out: nvr on terms* **14/1**

0000 **9** ½ **Apex King (IRE)**[31] [8253] 5-8-0 **85** IsobelFrancis(7) 1 79
(Mark Usher) *led: rdn along and readily hdd by wnr off home bnd: sn wknd over 1f out* **40/1**

0340 **10** ¾ **Charles Molson**[16] [8707] 8-9-4 **96** DanielMuscutt 8 88
(Patrick Chamings) *dwlt bdly but sn rcvrd into midfield: rdn along and lost pl over 1f out: wknd fnl f (jockey said gelding was slowly away)* **33/1**

1m 36.49s (-1.71) **Going Correction** +0.05s/f (Slow)
WFA 3 from 4yo+ 2lb **10** Ran SP% **121.3**
Speed ratings (Par 109): **110,106,106,105,104 103,103,101,101,100**
CSF £5.40 CT £53.74 TOTE £1.50: £1.10, £1.70, £4.50; EX 5.60 Trifecta £47.70.
Owner Hamdan Al Maktoum **Bred** Shadwell Estate Company Limited **Trained** Newmarket, Suffolk

FOCUS
A good quality handicap, albeit low on unexposed improvers, and a performance of some authority from the one 3yo in the line up. He produced a smart performance, with the second close to his latter turf form.

9001 BETWAY MEDIAN AUCTION MAIDEN STKS 6f 1y(P)
1:35 (1:35) (Class 6) 3-5-Y-O **£2,781** (£827; £413; £206) **Stalls** Low

Form RPR

0405 **1** **Sarsaparilla Kit**[140] [4396] 3-9-0 52 RichardKingscote 7 54
(Stuart Williams) *trckd ldr: shkn up to chal over 1f out: rdn along to ld ent fnl f: kpt on wl* **4/1**[2]

5530 **2** 1 **Ghost Buy (FR)**[31] [8264] 3-9-5 55 (t[1]) AdamKirby 1 56
(Ivan Furtado) *led and t.k.h early: rdn along and hdd by wnr ent fnl f: kpt on one pce after* **4/1**[2]

5 **3** hd **Alvaro**[30] [8290] 3-9-5 0 ChrisHayes 5 55+
(Michael Wigham) *s.i.s and racd in rr: hdwy on outer and forced wd off home bnd: sn rdn and hung lft in bhd wnr over 1f out: kpt on fnl f* **4/7**[1]

0600 **4** 1 **Swiper (IRE)**[70] [6983] 3-8-12 51 (bt[1]) KateLeahy(7) 6 52
(John O'Shea) *hld up: hdwy on outer over 2f out: sn rdn and no imp over 1f out: one pce after* **20/1**[3]

60-0 **5** 1¾ **Emilene**[16] [8694] 5-9-0 39 (t) StevieDonohoe 2 42
(John Groucott) *hld up: rdn and outpcd over 1f out: one pce after* **33/1**

0400 **6** 2¼ **Tilsworth Prisca**[93] [6131] 4-9-0 29 (h) DannyBrock 4 35
(J R Jenkins) *trckd ldrs early: pushed along over 2f out: sn rdn and no imp over 1f out: wknd fnl f* **66/1**

1m 13.61s (1.71) **Going Correction** +0.05s/f (Slow) **6** Ran SP% **112.8**
Speed ratings (Par 101): **90,88,88,87,84 81**
CSF £19.50 TOTE £4.40: £1.40, £1.80; EX 17.60 Trifecta £22.00.
Owner J W Parry & Partner **Bred** Cincinnati Kit Partnership **Trained** Newmarket, Suffolk

FOCUS
Very low-grade fare with the winner coming into the race with a BHA mark of just 52.

9002 BRITISH STALLION STUDS EBF GILLIES FILLIES' STKS (LISTED RACE) 1m 2f (P)
2:10 (2:11) (Class 1) 3-Y-O+
£21,266 (£8,062; £4,035; £2,010; £1,008; £506) **Stalls** Low

Form RPR

5101 **1** **Scentasia**[16] [8708] 3-9-2 104 FrankieDettori 6 107+
(John Gosden) *broke wl and settled in 5th: smooth hdwy into 2nd over 2f out: pushed along to ld over 1f out: sn rdn and qcknd 3 l clr 1f out: kpt up to work fnl f* **11/8**[1]

0- **2** 1¾ **Velma Valento (FR)**[24] 4-9-2 90 (t[1]) Pierre-CharlesBoudot 3 99
(C Ferland, France) *racd in midfield: hdwy on inner 2f out: rdn and wnt 2nd ins fnl f: kpt on wl but no ch w wnr* **14/1**

5115 **3** ½ **Ojooba**[50] [7662] 3-8-13 95 JimCrowley 11 98+
(Owen Burrows) *in rr of midfield: effrt to cl on ldrs whn wd off home bnd: sn rdn and hdwy 1f out: kpt on wl fnl f* **9/1**

-002 **4** ¾ **Crotchet**[15] [8734] 4-9-2 92 (t) DanielMuscutt 10 97
(Joseph Patrick O'Brien, Ire) *prom: rdn along and outpcd over 1f out: kpt on one pce fnl f* **25/1**

5230 **5** ¾ **Simply Beautiful (IRE)**[27] [8368] 3-8-13 103 SeamieHeffernan 12 95+
(A P O'Brien, Ire) *hld up in last pair: rdn and hdwy on outer over 1f out: mde gd late hdwy but nvr a factor* **9/1**

13/2 **6** ¾ **Magic Lily**[43] [7885] 4-9-2 107 JasonWatson 14 94
(Charlie Appleby) *j.rt and pushed along to go prom: wnt 2nd after 3f out: led over 2f out: sn rdn and hdd by wnr over 1f out: wknd fnl f* **5/1**[2]

52 **7** hd **Quote**[13] [8784] 3-8-13 99 (t) WayneLordan 13 93
(A P O'Brien, Ire) *hld up in last pair: hdwy between rivals over 1f out: rdn and kpt on wl fnl f but n.d* **16/1**

0152 **8** 1 **Hulcote**[31] [8245] 4-9-2 94 AdamKirby 4 91
(Clive Cox) *in rr of midfield: rdn and no imp 2f out: kpt on one pce fnl f* **16/1**

0265 **9** 1¼ **Snapraeceps (IRE)**[15] [8734] 3-8-13 100 JoeFanning 8 89
(Joseph Patrick O'Brien, Ire) *racd in midfield: hdwy on outer 2f out: sn rdn and no imp over 1f out: one pce after* **25/1**

0500 **10** 1 **Sh Boom**[50] [7657] 3-8-13 95 (b) LukeMorris 5 87
(Peter Chapple-Hyam) *racd in midfield: hdwy u.p over 2f out: effrt to cl whn short of room over 1f out: sn rdn and nt rcvr* **33/1**

2666 **11** 3¾ **Contrive (IRE)**[98] [5949] 4-9-2 93 JackMitchell 1 79
(Roger Varian) *trckd ldr: rdn along and lost pl 2f out: wknd fnl f* **40/1**

1211 **12** 1½ **Eva Maria**[42] [7895] 3-8-13 92 CallumShepherd 7 76
(Richard Fahey) *hld up: rdn and struggling 2f out: nvr on terms (jockey said filly hung left-handed)* **8/1**[3]

5400 **13** 7 **Bella Ragazza**[48] [7750] 4-9-2 95 RichardKingscote 2 62
(Hughie Morrison) *racd in midfield: rdn along and lost pl 2f out: sn bhd* **40/1**

1420 **14** 6 **Maid For Life**[59] [7347] 3-8-13 95 (h) KieranShoemark 9 50
(Charlie Fellowes) *led: rdn along and hdd over 2f out: wknd over 1f out (jockey said filly moved poorly. trainer further added the filly was feeling the effects of a long season)* **25/1**

2m 3.73s (-2.87) **Going Correction** +0.05s/f (Slow)
WFA 3 from 4yo 3lb **14** Ran SP% **127.7**
Speed ratings (Par 108): **113,111,111,110,110 109,109,108,107,106 103,102,96,92**
CSF £23.37 TOTE £2.10: £1.30, £3.70, £3.20; EX 20.80 Trifecta £151.30.
Owner Sheikh Juma Dalmook Al Maktoum **Bred** Godolphin **Trained** Newmarket, Suffolk

FOCUS
A Listed race saved from the abandoned Doncaster fixture last weekend and a strong renewal, the winner providing a double on the card for John Gosden. The form seems sound with the third and fourth close to their marks, and the fifth and sixth both need their efforts upgrading.

9003 BETWAY CHURCHILL STKS (LISTED RACE) (FAST TRACK QUALIFIER) 1m 2f (P)
2:45 (2:45) (Class 1) 3-Y-O+
£20,982 (£7,955; £3,981; £1,983; £995; £499) **Stalls** Low

Form RPR

6-02 **1** **Crossed Baton**[82] [6536] 4-9-2 100 (t[1]) FrankieDettori 5 109
(John Gosden) *j. awkwardly and racd in rr: hdwy to cl on ldrs 2f out: rdn and gd hdwy to ld appr fnl f: won gng away* **9/4**[2]

1212 **2** 2 **Kuwait Currency (USA)**[32] [8222] 3-8-13 100 (t) JimCrowley 4 105
(Richard Hannon) *settled wl in midfield: hdwy gng wl 2f out: rdn to ld over 1f out: sn pressed and hdd by wnr appr fnl f: kpt on* **11/4**[3]

6423 **3** 2½ **Pactolus (IRE)**[37] [8062] 8-9-2 102 (t) RichardKingscote 6 100
(Stuart Williams) *midfield early: dropped to last 4f out: rdn on outer and no imp 2f out: wnt 3rd appr fnl f: kpt on but no match for front pair* **8/1**

4131 **4** 3¾ **Caradoc (IRE)**[56] [7457] 4-9-2 100 KieranShoemark 7 93
(Ed Walker) *pushed up to be prom early: wnt 2nd after 2f out: rdn along and readily outpcd over 1f out: wknd fnl f (jockey said gelding hung left-handed throughout)* **6/4**[1]

0103 **5** 1¾ **Mr Scaramanga**[82] [6537] 5-9-2 87 AdamKirby 1 89
(Simon Dow) *led: rdn along and hdd over 1f out: wknd fnl f* **25/1**

1600 **6** 1¼ **Petite Jack**[86] [3992] 6-9-2 98 LukeMorris 2 87
(Neil King) *midfield: rdn along and hung lft to rail over 1f out: sn wknd fnl f* **25/1**

2m 4.04s (-2.56) **Going Correction** +0.05s/f (Slow)
WFA 3 from 4yo+ 3lb **6** Ran SP% **116.2**
Speed ratings (Par 111): **112,110,108,105,104 103**
CSF £9.35 TOTE £3.20: £1.60, £1.80; EX 9.20 Trifecta £37.60.
Owner K Abdullah **Bred** Juddmonte Farms Ltd **Trained** Newmarket, Suffolk

FOCUS
The absence of Lord North robbed this Listed prize of much of its lustre but it didn't prevent John Gosden from completing a treble on the afternoon. Crossed Baton was back to his best with the runner-up to form.

9004 BETWAY GOLDEN ROSE STKS (LISTED RACE) (FAST TRACK QUALIFIER) 6f 1y(P)
3:15 (3:19) (Class 1) 3-Y-O+
£20,982 (£7,955; £3,981; £1,983; £995; £499) **Stalls** Low

Form RPR

1615 **1** **Judicial (IRE)**[56] [7454] 7-9-6 107 CallumRodriguez 12 114
(Julie Camacho) *hld up fr wd draw: last over 2f out: c wd off home bnd: sn rdn and rapid hdwy on outer 1f out: kpt on strly to win gng away fnl f* **20/1**

2116 **2** 1¾ **Tinto**[18] [8648] 3-9-3 100 JimCrowley 4 105
(Amanda Perrett) *hld up: hdwy on inner u.p over 1f out: rdn and wnt 3rd 1f out: kpt on wl but no match for wnr* **9/1**

0001 **3** 1 **Soldier's Minute**[19] [8607] 4-9-3 101 (h) JoeFanning 2 102
(Keith Dalgleish) *prom: clsd gng wl 2f out: rdn to chal and ev ch appr fnl f: nt match wnr clsng stages* **10/3**[1]

3205 **4** nse **Stake Acclaim (IRE)**[42] [7889] 7-9-3 104 FrankieDettori 3 102
(Dean Ivory) *racd in midfield: gd hdwy to chal over 1f out: sn rdn and led briefly ent fnl f: no ex whn hdd by wnr and lost 3 pls fnl f* **11/1**

0112 **5** 1½ **Royal Birth**[38] [8015] 8-9-3 102 (t) RichardKingscote 7 97
(Stuart Williams) *in tch: pushed along on outer 2f out: sn rdn and unable qck over 1f out: kpt on one pce* **12/1**

2134 **6** shd **Corinthia Knight (IRE)**[10] [8851] 4-9-3 104 LukeMorris 11 97
(Archie Watson) *in rr of midfield: rdn and outpcd 2f out: sn drvn and minor hdwy appr fnl f: kpt on* **20/1**

0010 **7** nk **Leodis Dream (IRE)**[29] [8328] 3-9-3 104 AdamKirby 6 96
(David O'Meara) *led: rdn along and hdd ent fnl f: wknd clsng stages* **10/1**

6002 **8** nk **Gifted Master (IRE)**[16] [8707] 6-9-3 105 (b) JackMitchell 8 95
(Hugo Palmer) *reluctant to post: walked to s: trckd ldr: rdn whn wd off home bnd: wknd fnl f* **7/2**[2]

5165 **9** ½ **Maygold**[35] [8141] 4-8-12 97 LiamKeniry 9 88
(Ed Walker) *dwlt and racd in rr: a bhd* **25/1**

0033 **10** shd **Above The Rest (IRE)**[16] [8707] 8-9-3 102 (h) CliffordLee 5 93
(David Barron) *midfield: pushed along and outpcd 2f out: sn rdn and no imp fnl f* **8/1**

5341 **11** 1½ **Show Stealer**[10] [8851] 6-8-12 98 (p) CameronNoble 1 83
(Rae Guest) *hld up in rr: nvr on terms* **7/1**[3]

/040 **12** ½ **Beckford**[49] [7713] 4-9-3 99 ChrisHayes 10 86
(Gordon Elliott, Ire) *midfield: rdn and lost pl over 1f out: sn bhd* **14/1**

1m 10.46s (-1.44) **Going Correction** +0.05s/f (Slow) **12** Ran SP% **124.1**
Speed ratings (Par 111): **111,108,107,107,105 105,104,104,103,103 101,100**
CSF £193.68 TOTE £25.80: £4.70, £2.80, £1.90; EX 235.90 Trifecta £2151.80.
Owner Elite Racing Club **Bred** Elite Racing Club **Trained** Norton, N Yorks

FOCUS
A good field for this Listed sprint, run at a good pace, and the winner came with a flourish to win impressively. He's rated better than ever.

9005 BETWAY H'CAP 1m 4f (P)
3:45 (3:47) (Class 6) (0-60,64) 3-Y-O+
£2,781 (£827; £413; £300; £300; £300) **Stalls** Low

Form RPR

2344 **1** **Shifting Gold (IRE)**[39] [7984] 3-8-12 **60** Pierre-LouisJamin(7) 15 71+
(William Knight) *hld up in last: hdwy on outer into 6th off home bnd: sn rdn and rapid hdwy to ld jst ins fnl f: won gng away* **9/1**

2004 **2** 3½ **Mobham (IRE)**[16] [8703] 4-9-10 **60** DanielMuscutt 6 64
(J R Jenkins) *hld up: hdwy u.p on outer over 1f out: sn rdn and wnt 3rd ent fnl f: kpt on and tk remote 2nd clsng stages* **10/1**

4000 **3** ½ **Music Major**[16] [8703] 6-9-6 **56** CallumShepherd 3 60
(Michael Attwater) *racd in midfield: clsd on ldrs 2f out: rdn to ld briefly over 1f out: sn hdd by wnr ins fnl f: lost 2nd last strides* **25/1**

0602 **4** ¾ **Thunderoad**[11] [8837] 3-9-3 **58** ShaneKelly 9 61
(Tony Carroll) *racd in rr of midfield: rdn along and no imp 2f out: sn drvn and kpt on wl fnl f but n.d* **7/1**[2]

621 **5** ½ **Star Of Athena**[10] [8868] 4-10-0 **64** JimCrowley 11 66
(Ali Stronge) *in rr of midfield: hdwy on outer over 2f out: sn rdn and hung lft over 1f out: kpt on fnl f* **11/8**[1]

2225 **6** ½ **Hammy End (IRE)**[31] 8248 3-9-5 **60**...........(h) LewisEdmunds 7 62
(William Muir) *in rr of midfield: rdn and outpcd 2f out: drvn and mde sme late hdwy fnl f* **8/1**[3]

0000 **7** ½ **Vanity Vanity (USA)**[16] 8703 4-9-0 **50**........... LukeMorris 8 50
(Denis Coakley) *hld up: bmpd along 2f out: sn drvn and no imp over 1f out: plugged on* **16/1**

2000 **8** ½ **Attain**[187] 2698 10-8-9 **52**........... KateLeahy(7) 10 51+
(Archie Watson) *prom: rdn along and outpcd over 1f out: wknd fnl f* **33/1**

6055 **9** *nk* **God Has Given**[9] 8903 3-8-8 **56**...........(t) JonathanFisher(7) 4 56
(Ivan Furtado) *racd in midfield: rdn and no imp on ldrs over 1f out: kpt on one pce* **16/1**

0000 **10** ¾ **Albishr (IRE)**[16] 8703 4-9-4 **54**...........(p) AdamKirby 14 52+
(Simon Dow) *led for 4f then trckd new ldr: rdn along and led again briefly over 1f out: sn hdd & wknd fnl f* **14/1**

500 **11** *hd* **Gibraltarian (IRE)**[75] 6811 3-9-1 **56**........... CharlieBennett 5 54
(Jim Boyle) *trckd ldrs early: rdn along and lost pl 2f out: wknd fnl f* **20/1**

3500 **12** *1* **Banksy's Art**[26] 8414 4-9-9 **59**........... KieranShoemark 2 55
(Amanda Perrett) *in rr of midfield: rdn along and outpcd over 2f out: n.d* **14/1**

0006 **13** *1* **Air Hair Lair (IRE)**[14] 8756 3-9-2 **57**........... LiamJones 1 52
(Sheena West) *hld up: rdn on inner 2f out: nvr able to land a blow* **25/1**

5034 **14** *hd* **Taurean Dancer (IRE)**[17] 6853 4-9-9 **59**...........(p) StevieDonohoe 16 53+
(Roger Teal) *prom early: led after 4f tl rdn and hdd over 1f out: sn lost pl and wknd fnl f* **12/1**

0-00 **15** *7* **Betsalottie**[267] 859 6-8-13 **54**...........(p) AledBeech(5) 12 36
(John Bridger) *midfield early: rdn and lost pl over 2f out: sn detached* **50/1**

2m 34.55s (1.55) **Going Correction** +0.05s/f (Slow)
WFA 3 from 4yo+ 5lb **15 Ran SP% 135.0**
Speed ratings (Par 101): **96,93,93,92,92 92,91,91,91,90 90,90,89,89,84**
CSF £101.51 CT £2244.89 TOTE £10.70: £3.10, £3.20, £8.10; EX 103.70 Trifecta £2023.10.
Owner Mrs Joanna Farrant & Partner **Bred** Airlie Stud **Trained** Angmering, W Sussex

FOCUS
A big field for the finale but a one-sided contest as things panned out, the winner relishing the step up to 1m4f. The form could be rated slightly higher.
T/Plt: £40.10 to a £1 stake. Pool: £66,915.23 - 1,216.16 winning units T/Qpdt: £13.50 to a £1 stake. Pool: £6,391.02 - 348.38 winning units **Mark Grantham**

8863 WOLVERHAMPTON (A.W) (L-H)
Saturday, November 16

OFFICIAL GOING: Tapeta: standard
Wind: Almost nil Weather: Dry

9006 BOMBARDIER GOLDEN BEER H'CAP — 1m 142y (Tp)
4:15 (4:16) (Class 6) (0-65,65) 3-Y-O+
£2,781 (£827; £413; £400; £400; £400) **Stalls Low**

Form — RPR

5000 **1** **Roller**[52] 7587 6-9-6 **62**...........(p) DougieCostello 1 72
(Mark Loughnane) *dwlt s: towards rr on inner: stdy hdwy whn nt clr run over 2f out: rdn and hdwy over 1f out: led ins fnl f: kpt on* **33/1**

2461 **2** 1¾ **Star Of Valour (IRE)**[17] 8667 4-9-2 **58**........... JackGarritty 7 64
(Lynn Siddall) *prom: hdwy and wnt 2nd over 2f out: rdn to ld over 1f out: sn edgd lft: hdd ins fnl f: kpt on* **11/4**[1]

3322 **3** 1½ **Gottardo (IRE)**[15] 8713 4-9-9 **65**........... CharlesBishop 6 68
(Ed Dunlop) *hld up in rr: stdy hdwy gng easily over 2f out: rdn on outer over 1f out: wnt 3rd ins fnl f: kpt on* **7/1**

1200 **4** *hd* **Scoffsman**[33] 8199 4-9-5 **61**...........(h[1]) RossaRyan 9 64
(Kevin Frost) *dwlt s: swtchd lft early: in rr: rdn and hdwy on inner over 1f out: r.o fnl f: nrst fin (jockey said gelding was slowly away)* **11/2**[3]

0606 **5** ½ **Perfect Grace**[16] 8705 3-9-5 **64**...........(b[1]) DanielTudhope 13 66
(Archie Watson) *t.k.h: led: rdn and hdd over 1f out: sn edgd lft: no ex ins fnl f* **15/2**

5433 **6** ½ **Ballet Red (FR)**[145] 4179 3-9-5 **64**...........(w) HectorCrouch 3 65
(Harry Dunlop) *midfield: pushed along and hdwy over 2f out: rdn and no imp fnl f* **16/1**

0000 **7** ¾ **Weloof (FR)**[74] 6839 5-9-7 **63**........... AndrewMullen 2 62
(John Butler) *t.k.h: hld up in midfield: stdy hdwy whn bit short of room over 2f out: rdn and hung lft over 1f out: sn no imp (jockey said gelding was denied a clear run)* **3/1**[2]

0005 **8** ¾ **Ghazan (IRE)**[12] 8806 4-9-0 **59**...........(v[1]) GabrieleMalune(3) 8 57
(Ivan Furtado) *hld up in rr: pushed along 2f out: sme hdwy on outer ins fnl f: n.d (jockey said gelding jumped awkwardly leaving the stalls)* **11/1**

-000 **9** *4* **Deleyll**[44] 7858 5-9-4 **60**........... CamHardie 11 49
(John Butler) *dwlt s: in rr: shkn up and outpcd 2f out: sn btn* **25/1**

4000 **10** 1½ **Gold Hunter (IRE)**[16] 8690 9-9-6 **62**........... RaulDaSilva 4 48
(Steve Flook) *t.k.h: cl up: rdn over 1f out: sn wknd* **66/1**

0200 **11** 1½ **Thornaby Nash**[43] 7875 8-9-9 **65**...........(b) TomEaves 5 48
(Jason Ward) *chsd ldr: rdn and lost 2nd over 2f out: wknd over 1f out* **66/1**

350 **12** 1½ **French Twist**[23] 8499 3-9-0 **62**...........(p) ThomasGreatrex(3) 12 42
(David Loughnane) *t.k.h: midfield on outer: struggling over 2f out: sn wknd* **16/1**

332- **13** *12* **Canadian George (FR)**[29] 8082 4-9-9 **65**...........(p) ShaneGray 10 19
(Jennie Candlish) *trckd ldrs on outer: rdn and struggling over 2f out: sn btn* **33/1**

1m 47.4s (-2.70) **Going Correction** -0.275s/f (Stan)
WFA 3 from 4yo+ 3lb **13 Ran SP% 124.1**
Speed ratings (Par 101): **101,99,98,97,97 97,96,95,92,90 89,88,77**
CSF £124.44 CT £780.19 TOTE £61.90: £13.60, £1.40, £1.90; EX 349.00 Trifecta £1490.70.
Owner Over The Moon Racing **Bred** Juddmonte Farms Ltd **Trained** Rock, Worcs

FOCUS
A modest affair. The winner is rated in line with his fairly recent form.

9007 LADBROKES FOOTBALL ACCA BOOSTY EBF NOVICE STKS — 1m 1f 104y (Tp)
4:45 (4:47) (Class 5) 2-Y-O **£3,428** (£1,020; £509; £254) **Stalls Low**

Form — RPR

3 **1** **Celestran**[15] 8721 2-9-5 **0**........... NickyMackay 2 75+
(John Gosden) *midfield on inner: shkn up and hdwy 2f out: rdn to ld ins fnl f: kpt on wl towards fin: comf* **9/4**[1]

2 ½ **Kipps (IRE)** 2-9-5 **0**........... DavidProbert 5 74+
(Hughie Morrison) *hld up in midfield: stdy hdwy whn short of room over 2f out: shkn up and hdwy over 1f out: kpt on fnl f: wnt 2nd towards fin: eyecatcher* **13/2**

64 **3** ½ **Favorite Moon (GER)**[22] 8518 2-9-5 **0**........... DanielTudhope 9 73
(William Haggas) *pressed ldr: rdn over 2f out: led over 1f out: hdd ins fnl f: no ex towards fin* **7/2**[3]

4 ½ **Pride Of America (FR)** 2-9-5 **0**........... CharlesBishop 3 73
(Harry Dunlop) *dwlt s: hld up in rr: hdwy whn nt clr run over 1f out: short of room and swtchd lft ins fnl f: kpt on towards fin (jockey said colt was denied a clear run)* **50/1**

53 **5** *hd* **Finely Tuned (IRE)**[17] 8657 2-9-5 **0**........... TomEaves 6 72
(Simon Crisford) *trckd ldrs: rdn over 2f out: rallied over 1f out: no ex ins fnl f* **10/1**

04 **6** 3¾ **Batalha**[26] 8402 2-9-5 **0**........... AndrewMullen 8 65
(Mark Johnston) *t.k.h: led: rdn and hdd over 1f out: wknd ins fnl f* **33/1**

00 **7** *nk* **Grinling (IRE)**[47] 7755 2-9-5 **0**........... RossaRyan 7 64
(Richard Hannon) *hld up in rr: shkn up and stdy hdwy over 2f out: pushed along and edgd lft over 1f out: no imp fnl f* **50/1**

2 **8** *3* **Poet's Mind (USA)**[29] 8319 2-9-5 **0**........... BrettDoyle 11 58
(Charlie Appleby) *t.k.h: prom: rdn over 2f out: wknd over 1f out* **11/4**[2]

00 **9** *7* **Savanna Gold (IRE)**[28] 8346 2-9-5 **0**........... RobHornby 4 45
(Hugo Palmer) *s.i.s: sn pushed along in rr: rdn and outpcd 3f out: sn btn* **50/1**

3 **10** *14* **My Vision**[28] 8346 2-9-5 **0**........... HectorCrouch 12 18
(Saeed bin Suroor) *cl up on outer: rdn over 3f out: wknd over 2f out: btn and eased fnl f* **11/1**

11 *11* **Avis Bay** 2-8-7 **0**........... NickBarratt-Atkin(7) 10
(Philip Kirby) *lost many l s: racd in last: struggling 3f out: sn lost tch: t.o* **100/1**

1m 58.93s (-1.87) **Going Correction** -0.275s/f (Stan) **11 Ran SP% 120.2**
Speed ratings (Par 96): **97,96,96,95,95 92,91,89,83,70 60**
CSF £17.78 TOTE £3.30: £1.60, £2.10, £1.40; EX 22.00 Trifecta £83.10.
Owner Cheveley Park Stud **Bred** Cheveley Park Stud Ltd **Trained** Newmarket, Suffolk

FOCUS
The early gallop wasn't hectic and there was a bit of a bunched finish to this fairly interesting novice.

9008 LADBROKES WHERE THE NATION PLAYS EBF NOVICE STKS (PLUS 10 RACE) — 6f 20y (Tp)
5:15 (5:16) (Class 4) 2-Y-O **£4,463** (£1,328; £663; £331) **Stalls Low**

Form — RPR

32 **1** **River Nymph**[57] 7407 2-9-5 **0**........... HectorCrouch 9 80+
(Clive Cox) *t.k.h: trckd ldrs: rdn over 1f out: edgd lft and led ins fnl f: kpt on wl towards fin* **4/7**[1]

2 ¾ **Prince Caspian** 2-9-5 **0**........... RossaRyan 8 78
(Richard Hannon) *led: rdn over 1f out: hdd ins fnl f: sn rallied: no ex towards fin* **14/1**

3 *2* **Kilconquhar** 2-9-5 **0**........... ShaneGray 4 72
(David O'Meara) *t.k.h: prom: shkn up and rn green over 1f out: wnt 3rd ins fnl f: nt rch ldrs* **50/1**

0 **4** 1¼ **Rodin**[26] 8409 2-9-5 **0**........... DavidProbert 13 68
(Andrew Balding) *disp ld to over 2f out: rdn and outpcd fnl f* **8/1**[3]

5 1½ **Queen's Course (IRE)** 2-9-0 **0**........... DanielTudhope 10 59+
(William Haggas) *midfield on outer: stdy hdwy over 2f out: shkn up and edgd lft over 1f out: no imp fnl f* **5/1**[2]

04 **6** *1* **Newton Jack**[25] 8418 2-9-2 **0**........... FinleyMarsh(3) 6 61
(Stuart Kittow) *t.k.h: prom: rdn and outpcd 2f out: no imp fnl f* **25/1**

7 *nk* **Giovanni Tiepolo** 2-9-2 **0**........... ThomasGreatrex(3) 3 60
(Henry Candy) *towards rr on inner: bit short of room over 3f out: rdn over 2f out: no imp over 1f out* **50/1**

8 2½ **The Weed Machine (IRE)** 2-9-5 **0**........... AndrewMullen 2 52
(Mark Johnston) *s.i.s: rn green in rr: rdn and outpcd 3f out: n.d* **16/1**

0 **9** 3¼ **Dabbersgirl**[10] 8865 2-9-0 **0**........... TomEaves 5 37
(Brian Baugh) *towards rr: rdn and struggling over 2f out: sn btn* **200/1**

5 **10** ¾ **Park Lane Dancer (IRE)**[38] 8026 2-9-5 **0**........... BenRobinson 7 40
(John Quinn) *s.i.s: in rr: rdn and struggling 3f out: sn btn (jockey said gelding was slowly away)* **28/1**

P **Viaduct** 2-9-5 **0**........... RobHornby 1
(Martyn Meade) *dwlt s: p.u after 1f: lost action (jockey said he felt it prudent to pull up after 1½f as he felt the colt lost its action and felt wrong behind)* **14/1**

1m 13.44s (-1.06) **Going Correction** -0.275s/f (Stan) **11 Ran SP% 122.4**
Speed ratings (Par 98): **96,95,92,90,88 87,86,83,79,78**
CSF £11.13 TOTE £1.50: £1.10, £2.70, £10.60; EX 9.60 Trifecta £218.90.
Owner Trevor Fox **Bred** T H S Fox **Trained** Lambourn, Berks

FOCUS
Few got into this, the front four dominating throughout.

9009 LADBROKES, HOME OF THE ODDS BOOST NURSERY H'CAP — 7f 36y (Tp)
5:45 (5:48) (Class 6) (0-60,64) 2-Y-O
£2,781 (£827; £413; £400; £400; £400) **Stalls High**

Form — RPR

0440 **1** **Schumli**[12] 8815 2-8-6 **48**...........(t[1]) HarrisonShaw(3) 8 52
(David O'Meara) *t.k.h: pressed ldr: led 2f out: sn rdn: kpt on wl fnl f (trainer said, regarding the apparent improvement in form, the filly benefited from the application of a first time tongue tie and being ridden more prominently)* **10/1**

0533 **2** ½ **You Don't Own Me (IRE)**[11] 8825 2-9-3 **56**...........(b[1]) CharlesBishop 4 59
(Joseph Tuite) *t.k.h: led: rdn and hdd 2f out: sn rallied: no ex ins fnl 110yds* **9/2**[3]

0056 **3** *1* **Captain Corelli (IRE)**[36] 8085 2-9-6 **59**........... TomEaves 11 59+
(Julie Camacho) *dwlt s: hld up in rr: rdn 2f out: hdwy and wnt 3rd ins fnl f: kpt on towards fin* **7/1**

0402 **4** *shd* **Camacho Man (IRE)**[22] 8526 2-9-0 **53**........... DougieCostello 7 53+
(Jennie Candlish) *dwlt s: pushed along over 3f out: hdwy 2f out: rdn and r.o ins fnl f: nvr able to chal* **3/1**[2]

0000 **5** ½ **Fact Or Fable (IRE)**[11] 8824 2-9-4 **57**...........(p) JasonWatson 12 56
(J S Moore) *t.k.h: prom: rdn and edgd lft over 2f out: no ex fnl f (jockey said gelding hung left-handed)* **20/1**

600 **6** *nk* **Cappella Fella (IRE)**[68] 7030 2-8-10 **49**........... DavidProbert 1 47
(Sarah Hollinshead) *hld up in rr: nt clr run over 2f out: rdn and hdwy over 1f out: no imp fnl f* **18/1**

0400 **7** ¾ **Butterfly Pose (IRE)**[67] 7056 2-8-8 **50**...........(p) ThomasGreatrex(3) 10 46
(J S Moore) *in rr: rdn over 2f out: hdwy on outer over 1f out: no imp ins fnl f* **33/1**

5500 **8** 4½ **Parker's Boy**[61] 7275 2-9-2 **55**........... RobHornby 6 40
(Brian Barr) *t.k.h: cl up: rdn over 2f out: wknd over 1f out* **28/1**

0000 **9** *3* **Gold Venture (IRE)**[12] 8815 2-8-13 **52**........... RossaRyan 2 29
(Philip Kirby) *chsd ldrs: rdn over 2f out: wknd over 1f out* **33/1**

6011 **10** *4* **Ventura Destiny (FR)**[9] 8897 2-9-6 **64**...................... BenSanderson(5) 5 31
(Keith Dalgleish) *towards rr: rdn on outer over 2f out: sn btn (trainer's rep could offer no explanation for the filly's performance other than the rider reported that she was never travelling and the filly's handicap mark had risen significantly following recent wins)* **9/4**[1]

1m 28.41s (-0.39) **Going Correction** -0.275s/f (Stan) **10** Ran SP% **114.9**
Speed ratings (Par 94): **91,90,89,89,88 88,87,82,78,74**
CSF £49.06 CT £300.70 TOTE £10.60: £2.80, £1.60, £2.20; EX 60.40 Trifecta £268.10.
Owner D O'Meara **Bred** Whitsbury Manor Stud **Trained** Upper Helmsley, N Yorks
■ Serious Jockin was withdrawn. Price at time of withdrawal 11/1. Rule 4 applies to all bets - deduction 5p in the pound.

FOCUS
The front two quickened into the straight and poached a decisive advantage over those trying to close from behind.

9010 LADBROKES "PLAY 1-2-FREE" ON FOOTBALL FILLIES' CONDITIONS STKS 7f 36y (Tp)
6:15 (6:16) (Class 3) 3-Y-0+ **£7,439** (£2,213; £1,106; £553) **Stalls** High

Form RPR
42 **1** **Moment Of Silence (IRE)**[23] 8497 3-8-11 0........... GabrieleMalune(3) 3 93
(Saeed bin Suroor) *t.k.h: prom: hdwy and wnt 2nd over 1f out: rdn to ld ins fnl f: kpt on wl* **7/2**[2]

2200 **2** *1 ½* **Emily Goldfinch**[84] 6453 6-8-8 91..................(p) GraceMcEntee(7) 1 90
(Phil McEntee) *led: rdn and qcknd 2f out: hdd ins fnl f: sn no ex* **28/1**

0041 **3** *1* **Dutch Treat**[42] 7901 3-9-0 89.. DavidProbert 2 86
(Andrew Balding) *dwlt s: sn pushed along in rr: rdn and outpcd over 2f out: rallied and wnt 3rd ins fnl f: kpt on: nrst fin* **5/1**[3]

6325 **4** *1 ¾* **Canton Queen (IRE)**[42] 7901 3-9-0 91.......................... RossaRyan 4 82
(Richard Hannon) *t.k.h: prom: rdn and hdwy on outer over 1f out: no imp fnl f* **6/4**[1]

131 **5** *½* **Dizzy G (IRE)**[28] 8349 4-9-1 82.............................. CliffordLee 6 81
(K R Burke) *t.k.h: pressed ldr to over 2f out: sn rdn: wknd fnl f* **11/2**

2431 **6** *19* **Betsey Trotter (IRE)**[42] 7914 4-9-1 90...................(p) DanielTudhope 5 30
(David O'Meara) *prom on outer: rdn and outpcd over 2f out: lost tch over 1f out: sn eased (jockey said filly ran flat)* **5/1**[3]

1m 25.69s (-3.11) **Going Correction** -0.275s/f (Stan)
WFA 3 from 4yo+ 1lb **6** Ran SP% **114.4**
Speed ratings (Par 104): **106,104,103,101,100 78**
CSF £75.35 TOTE £3.60: £2.70, £5.00; EX 52.90 Trifecta £311.20.
Owner Godolphin **Bred** Springbank Way Stud **Trained** Newmarket, Suffolk

FOCUS
Quite a competitive little heat, but not an easy race to assess with the favourite disappointing. The runner-up is the key.

9011 BETWAY MAIDEN STKS 1m 1f 104y (Tp)
6:45 (6:46) (Class 5) 3-Y-0+ **£3,428** (£1,020; £509; £254) **Stalls** Low

Form RPR
03 **1** **Classic Design (IRE)**[28] 8351 3-9-5 0.......................... JackMitchell 9 82+
(Simon Crisford) *trckd ldrs: led gng easily 2f out: sn rdn clr: kpt on strly fnl f: eased towards fin (vet said gelding had a trickle of blood from its right nostril)* **5/2**[2]

64 **2** *2 ½* **Dawry (IRE)**[21] 8552 3-9-5 0.. JaneElliott 1 74
(Heather Main) *prom: rdn over 2f out: wnt 2nd over 1f out: kpt on fnl f: no match for wnr* **10/1**

5 **3** *2 ½* **Finespun (IRE)**[24] 8467 3-9-0 0.............................. NickyMackay 6 64
(John Gosden) *prom: rdn and outpcd over 2f out: rallied fnl f: nt rch ldrs* **11/4**[3]

2226 **4** *¾* **Loving Glance**[59] 7341 3-9-0 83.............................. DanielTudhope 5 62
(Martyn Meade) *pressed ldr: led gng easily over 3f out: rdn and hdd 2f out: sn lost 2nd: btn fnl f* **1/1**[1]

0 **5** *3 ¼* **Mercury Dime (IRE)**[24] 8467 3-9-0 0.......................... CharlesBishop 4 55
(Ed Dunlop) *prom: short of room and outpcd over 2f out: rdn and no imp fr over 1f out* **40/1**

00 **6** *6* **Gms Princess**[30] 8294 3-9-0 0.................................... RaulDaSilva 7 43
(Sarah Hollinshead) *in rr: pushed along over 3f out: sme hdwy over 1f out: n.d* **200/1**

7 *3* **Courteva**[40] 4-9-3 0.. RobHornby 13 36
(Richard Price) *midfield: rdn and outpcd 3f out: sn btn* **100/1**

40 **8** *1 ¾* **Battle Commander**[15] 8718 3-9-5 0............................ CamHardie 3 38
(Olly Williams) *midfield on inner: rdn 3f out: sn wknd* **80/1**

00 **9** *7* **Just A Minute**[197] 2361 4-9-0 0........................ MitchGodwin(3) 11 18
(Steph Hollinshead) *ducked rt s: led: hdd over 3f out: sn rdn: wknd fr 2f out* **100/1**

0 **10** *5* **Pour Joie**[201] 2208 4-9-8 0....................................... DavidProbert 8 13
(Ian Williams) *dwlt s: plld hrd: in rr: rdn and struggling over 3f out: sn wknd (jockey said gelding hung left-handed)* **20/1**

11 *nk* **Enchanted Island (IRE)**[27] 4-9-3 0.......................... DougieCostello 12 7
(Nick Kent) *slowly away: in rr: rdn and struggling 4f out: sn btn (jockey said filly was slowly away)* **150/1**

0 **12** *30* **Ingleby George**[133] 4636 5-9-8 0.................................... TomEaves 2
(Jason Ward) *slowly away: in rr on inner: reminders 1/2-way: wknd 3f out: sn lost tch: t.o* **100/1**

1m 58.17s (-2.63) **Going Correction** -0.275s/f (Stan)
WFA 3 from 4yo+ 3lb **12** Ran SP% **126.9**
Speed ratings (Par 103): **100,97,95,94,92 86,84,82,76,71 71,44**
CSF £28.97 TOTE £3.70: £1.30, £3.10, £1.40; EX 31.70 Trifecta £103.80.
Owner Sheikh Marwan Al Maktoum **Bred** Godolphin **Trained** Newmarket, Suffolk

FOCUS
They finished well strung out in this maiden, which lacked depth. The form is taken at face value, with the winner progressing again.

9012 BETWAY H'CAP 1m 4f 51y (Tp)
7:15 (7:17) (Class 5) (0-75,75) 3-Y-0+
£3,428 (£1,020; £509; £400; £400; £400) **Stalls** Low

Form RPR
32-4 **1** **Cuillin (USA)**[163] 434 4-9-4 **69**................................ RobHornby 8 76
(Noel Williams) *hld up in midfield: hrd rdn and hdwy fr over 1f out: led and hrd pressed ins fnl f: kpt on wl towards fin* **25/1**

5256 **2** *hd* **Guandi (USA)**[145] 4188 3-9-1 **71**......................... RichardKingscote 2 77
(Tom Dascombe) *cl up: rdn and edgd lft over 1f out: disp ld ins fnl f: jst hld* **9/2**[3]

3321 **3** *2 ¾* **Forbidden Dance**[33] 8200 3-8-13 **69**......................(p[1]) DanielTudhope 1 71
(Hughie Morrison) *led: hdd after 3f: sn pressed ldr: rdn and led again 2f out: hdd ins fnl f: sn no ex* **2/1**[2]

4266 **4** *nk* **Baladio (IRE)**[77] 6733 3-9-2 **72**.............................. AndrewMullen 10 74
(John Mackie) *hld up in rr: pushed along 3f out: hdwy over 1f out: kpt on fnl f: nrst fin* **66/1**

3300 **5** *hd* **Dream Magic (IRE)**[107] 5570 5-8-8 **66**.......................... MolliePhillips(7) 7 67
(Mark Loughnane) *midfield on inner: hdwy whn short of room and swtchd rt over 1f out: kpt on ins fnl f: nvr able to chal* **50/1**

0630 **6** *3 ¾* **Ravenous**[11] 8829 8-8-11 **65**.............................. TheodoreLadd(3) 5 60
(Luke Dace) *towards rr: rdn 3f out: no imp fr 2f out* **50/1**

55-5 **7** *1* **Gift Of Raaj (IRE)**[29] 8300 4-9-4 **69**.........................(t[1]) DougieCostello 4 63
(Ivan Furtado) *dwlt s: hld up in rr: short of room over 2f out: sn rdn: no imp fr over 1f out* **25/1**

2633 **8** *1 ½* **Iron Mike**[16] 8705 3-8-13 **69**......................(p[1]) CallumRodriguez 9 60
(Keith Dalgleish) *t.k.h: cl up: led after 3f: rdn and hdd 2f out: wknd fnl f (trainer's rep could offer no explanation for the gelding's performance)* **11/8**[1]

3-00 **9** *¾* **Profound (IRE)**[12] 8809 4-9-9 **74**............................(h) DavidProbert 12 64
(Mark Usher) *in rr: rdn 2f out: sn hung lft and no imp* **25/1**

6606 **10** *8* **Grand Inquisitor**[16] 8692 7-9-10 **75**..........................(b) TomEaves 11 52
(Conor Dore) *hld up in rr: hdwy and prom 4f out: rdn and wknd fr 2f out* **28/1**

11 *1 ¼* **Raihaan (IRE)**[203] 3-9-5 **75**.................................... JasonWatson 6 50
(Ed Dunlop) *trckd ldrs: rdn over 2f out: wknd over 1f out* **14/1**

2m 35.98s (-4.82) **Going Correction** -0.275s/f (Stan)
WFA 3 from 4yo+ 5lb **11** Ran SP% **120.7**
Speed ratings (Par 103): **105,104,103,102,102 100,99,98,98,92 91**
CSF £131.49 CT £339.15 TOTE £32.10: £5.70, £1.60, £1.10; EX 226.20 Trifecta £1055.90.
Owner Noel Williams **Bred** John Ryan & Charles J Cummings **Trained** Blewbury, Oxon

FOCUS
The early pace was disputed and didn't settle down until they headed out on the final circuit. It played into the hands of a closer. There was little depth to the race and the market 1-2 were both disappointing. It's rated as ordinary form around the winner.

9013 BETWAY HEED YOUR HUNCH H'CAP 5f 21y (Tp)
7:45 (7:46) (Class 5) (0-70,75) 3-Y-0+
£3,428 (£1,020; £509; £400; £400; £400) **Stalls** Low

Form RPR
1545 **1** **Lethal Angel**[28] 8349 4-9-7 **70**..............................(p) RichardKingscote 8 76
(Stuart Williams) *cl up: wnt 2nd after 2f: rdn 2f out: kpt on wl fnl f: led fnl strides* **9/4**[1]

355 **2** *shd* **Three Little Birds**[9] 8895 4-9-4 **70**..................... ThomasGreatrex(3) 11 77+
(Sylvester Kirk) *swtchd lft early: hld up in rr: shkn up whn hmpd over 1f out: sn swtchd rt: rdn and kpt on wl fnl f: wnt 2nd fnl strides* **7/1**

6601 **3** *nse* **Coronation Cottage**[23] 8501 5-9-1 **64**..................... CharlieBennett 3 69
(Malcolm Saunders) *led: rdn 2f out: kpt on fnl f: hdd towards fin* **16/1**

0152 **4** *shd* **Dark Side Dream**[23] 8501 7-8-13 **67**...........(p) ThoreHammerHansen(5) 6 72
(Charlie Wallis) *towards rr: pushed along and hdwy on outer over 1f out: kpt on wl fnl f: jst hld* **14/1**

5313 **5** *nk* **Shepherd's Purse**[23] 8501 7-9-0 **63**..........................(b) JackGarritty 5 67
(Ruth Carr) *t.k.h: prom: short of room over 2f out: rdn over 1f out: kpt on fnl f* **8/1**

4036 **6** *½* **Longroom**[15] 8715 7-8-11 **60**.. DavidProbert 2 62
(Noel Wilson) *cl up: rdn over 1f out: no ex ins fnl f* **13/2**[3]

6251 **7** *shd* **Zapper Cass (FR)**[7] 8943 6-9-12 **75**..........................(be) LukeMorris 4 76
(Michael Appleby) *dwlt s: towards rr: hdwy 2f out: sn rdn: no imp fnl 110yds* **9/2**[2]

3200 **8** *2 ¼* **Princely**[31] 8242 4-8-13 **62**.. RossaRyan 1 55
(Tony Newcombe) *towards rr: rdn and edgd lft over 1f out: sn no imp* **8/1**

3106 **9** *1 ½* **Red Stripes (USA)**[30] 8296 7-9-0 **63**...........................(b) AndrewMullen 9 51
(Lisa Williamson) *pressed ldr: lost 2nd after 2f: rdn over 2f out: wknd over 1f out* **33/1**

2661 **10** *1 ½* **Tan**[17] 8668 5-9-0 **63**.. CamHardie 7 46
(Lisa Williamson) *midfield on outer: rdn over 2f out: edgd lft and wknd over 1f out* **25/1**

0405 **11** *1* **Creek Harbour (IRE)**[44] 7855 4-8-13 **67**..................... TobyEley(5) 10 46
(Milton Bradley) *dwlt s: racd in last: struggling 1/2-way: sn wknd (jockey said gelding was slowly into stride)* **20/1**

1m 0.01s (-1.89) **Going Correction** -0.275s/f (Stan) **11** Ran SP% **121.1**
Speed ratings (Par 103): **104,103,103,103,103 102,102,98,96,93 92**
CSF £18.46 CT £214.71 TOTE £2.90: £1.40, £2.10, £5.10; EX 21.80 Trifecta £223.40.
Owner The Secretly Hopeful Partnership **Bred** Park Farm Racing **Trained** Newmarket, Suffolk

FOCUS
A blanket finish to this modest sprint handicap. A small pb from the winner but the runner-up was unlucky.
T/Plt: £184.90 to a £1 stake. Pool: £87,055.88 - 343.60 winning units T/Qpdt: £34.20 to a £1 stake. Pool: £11,103.74 - 240.12 winning units **Richard Young**

4228 LE CROISE-LAROCHE
Saturday, November 16

OFFICIAL GOING: Turf: heavy

9014a GRAND PRIX DE LA VILLE DE MARCQ-EN-BAROEUL (CONDITIONS) (4YO+) (TURF) 1m 1f
3:42 4-Y-0+
£20,270 (£7,702; £5,675; £3,243; £1,621; £1,216)

RPR
1 **Monty (FR)**[51] 4-9-0 0... MickaelBerto 8 98
(A De Royer-Dupre, France) **31/5**

2 *1 ¾* **Mount Pelion (IRE)**[27] 8379 4-9-6 0................. MickaelBarzalona 5 100
(A Fabre, France) *a.p: cl 3rd travelling wl 1/2-way: led wl over 2f out: sn drvn and r.o: began to labour wl ins fnl f: hdd fnl 100yds: no ex* **21/10**[1]

3 *2 ½* **Hout Bay (FR)**[97] 6-9-3 0..................................(p) LukasDelozier 6 92
(Mario Hofer, Germany) **12/1**

4 *2* **Vilaro (FR)**[20] 6-9-0 0.. CristianDemuro 9 85
(D Smaga, France) **37/10**[2]

5 *¾* **Trouble Of Course (FR)**[31] 5-9-0 0.......................... MaximeGuyon 13 83
(Mme Pia Brandt, France) **12/1**

6 *2 ½* **Maximum Aurelius (FR)**[461] 6-9-0 0......................... StephaneBreux 7 78
(F-H Graffard, France) **36/1**

7 *nk* **Lijian (GER)**[25] 5-9-0 0... MiguelLopez 4 77
(J Hirschberger, Germany) **11/1**

8 *12* **A Head Ahead (GER)**[37] 5-9-0 0..........................(b) CyrilleStefan 3 52
(S Smrczek, Germany) **39/1**

9 2 **Glen Shiel**[28] 8336 5-9-3 0................................ AdamMcNamara 10 51
(Archie Watson) *midfield: drvn along over 2f out but no real imp: wknd fnl f: nvr trbld ldrs* **51/10**[3]

10 1 ¼ **Copper Baked (FR)**[11] 5-8-10 0...........................(p) SebastienMaillot 1 41
(L Rovisse, France) **102/1**

11 1 ½ **Alinaro (GER)**[126] 4-9-6 0................................ MaximPecheur 11 48
(H Blume, Germany) **32/1**

12 30 **El Rey Brillante (CHI)**[21] 8583 5-9-0 0...........................(b) FrankPanicucci 12
(I Endaltsev, Czech Republic) **71/1**

13 5 ½ **Miss Australia (FR)**[17] 7-8-10 0...........................(b) LudovicBoisseau 2
(Guillaume Courbot, France) **104/1**

1m 55.2s **13 Ran SP% 119.1**

PARI-MUTUEL (all including 1 euro stake): WIN 7.20; PLACE 2.30, 1.60, 3.00; DF 9.70.

Owner The Duke Of Bedford **Bred** Ducse De Bedford **Trained** Chantilly, France

SANDOWN (AUS) (L-H)

Saturday, November 16

OFFICIAL GOING: Turf: good

9015a KEVIN HEFFERNAN STKS (GROUP 3) (2YO+) (TURF) 6f 110y

4:25 2-Y-O+

£53,453 (£15,911; £7,955; £3,977; £2,209; £1,767)

RPR

1 **Teleplay (AUS)**[11] 5-9-0 0................................ BenMelham 5 109
(Mick Price & Michael Kent Jnr, Australia) **9/1**

2 nse **Home Of The Brave (IRE)**[14] 7-9-4 0................................ DamianLane 4 113
(James Cummings, Australia) *racd in 2nd: effrt 2f out: chal fnl 75yds: jst lost out in hd bobbing fin* **7/5**[1]

3 hd **Hey Doc (AUS)**[427] 6-9-4 0................................ LukeCurrie 3 112
(Tony McEvoy & Calvin McEvoy, Australia) **5/1**[3]

4 ½ **D'bai (IRE)**[210] 1974 5-9-4 0...........................(bt) JamesDoyle 8 111
(Charlie Appleby) *towards rr: shkn up 2f out: hdwy ins fnl f: clst fin: rdn out* **19/5**[2]

5 hd **Odeon (NZ)**[210] 6-9-4 0...........................(t) LindaMeech 2 110
(Mathew Ellerton & Simon Zahra, Australia) **16/1**

6 shd **Ringerdingding (AUS)**[161] 4-9-4 0...........................(bt) MarkZahra 6 110
(Anthony Freedman, Australia) **15/1**

7 3 ½ **Order Of Command (AUS)**[14] 5-9-4 0...........................(b) CraigAWilliams 1 100
(Danny O'Brien, Australia) **7/1**

8 hd **Levendi (AUS)**[588] 1676 5-9-4 0................................ JyeMcNeil 7 99
(Peter Gelagotis, Australia) **40/1**

1m 17.26s **8 Ran SP% 116.2**

Owner Dynamic Syndications Racing, Mrs B J Zions Et Al **Bred** P Burke **Trained** Australia

9016a THE BIG SCREEN COMPANY ECLIPSE STKS (GROUP 3 H'CAP) (2YO+) (TURF) 1m 1f

6:55 2-Y-O+

£53,453 (£15,911; £7,955; £3,977; £2,209; £1,767)

RPR

1 **Pacodali (IRE)**[21] 8578 6-9-4 0................................ DeanYendall 8 109
(Lindsey Smith, Australia) **11/2**[3]

2 1 ¾ **Setting Sail**[82] 6536 4-8-11 0................................ JamesDoyle 2 98
(Charlie Appleby) *led after 1f: pressed and shkn up over 1 1/2f out: hdd over 1f out: kpt on fnl f* **21/20**[1]

3 2 ½ **Exasperate (AUS)**[384] 5-8-7 0...........................(v) BeauMertens 5 89
(Matthew Brown, Australia) **50/1**

4 hd **Savaheat (NZ)**[9] 5-8-7 0...........................(b) MichaelDee 11 89
(Mick Price & Michael Kent Jnr, Australia) **12/1**

5 1 ¼ **Mr Money Bags (AUS)**[9] 5-8-7 0...........................(v) JyeMcNeil 1 86
(Robbie Griffiths, Australia) **17/2**

6 ¾ **Danon Roman (JPN)**[371] 5-8-7 0...........................(bt) DamienThornton 9 84
(Anthony Freedman, Australia) **20/1**

7 1 ½ **Plein Ciel (GER)**[11] 6-9-0 0...........................(bt) CraigAWilliams 10 88
(Anthony Freedman, Australia) **5/1**[2]

8 ¾ **Main Stage (NZ)**[9] 5-8-7 0...........................(bt) BarendVorster 6 80
(Trent Busuttin & Natalie Young, Australia) **30/1**

9 ¾ **Mr Clarify (NZ)**[30] 7-8-7 0...........................(bt) PatrickMoloney 3 78
(Wayne Walters, Australia) **150/1**

10 shd **Moss 'N' Dale (NZ)**[11] 7-9-1 0...........................(t) JackMartin 7 86
(Peter Gelagotis, Australia) **25/1**

11 1 ½ **Zouy's Comet (AUS)**[189] 4-8-7 0...........................(b) LindaMeech 4 75
(Richard Laming, Australia) **40/1**

1m 51.56s **11 Ran SP% 115.9**

Owner S G McPeake & Mrs K McPeake **Bred** The Manjri Stud Farm PVT Ltd **Trained** Australia

9017 - 9027a (Foreign Racing) - See Raceform Interactive

8942

SOUTHWELL (L-H)

Monday, November 18

OFFICIAL GOING: Fibresand: standard

Wind: light, behind Weather: clear and cold

9028 BOMBARDIER BRITISH HOPPED AMBER BEER H'CAP 1m 13y(F)

4:15 (4:16) (Class 6) (0-60,62) 3-Y-O+

£2,781 (£827; £413; £400; £400; £400) **Stalls** Low

Form RPR

2011 1 **Clipsham Tiger (IRE)**[9] 8942 3-9-0 62...........................(h) GeorgeRooke(7) 9 71
(Michael Appleby) *chsd ldrs: rdn to take 2nd 3f out: led jst over 2f out: pushed out and r.o ins fnl f* **10/11**[1]

0625 2 1 ½ **Emojie**[18] 8694 5-8-3 47...........................(p[1]) RayDawson(5) 7 54
(Jane Chapple-Hyam) *chsd ldrs: led wl over 3f out: rdn and hdd jst over 2f out: kpt on u.p fnl f but nt pce of wnr* **14/1**

3 1 ½ **Crimson King (IRE)**[53] 7640 3-9-1 59................................ TimClark(3) 4 61
(Michael Appleby) *hdwy over 3f out: carried hd high and hung lft fr over 2f out: chsd ldrs over 1f out: nvr able to chal (jockey said gelding was slowly into stride)* **10/1**[3]

0002 4 3 **Jagerbond**[9] 8942 3-8-0 46 oh1...........................(e) AndrewBreslin(5) 2 41
(Andrew Crook) *pushed along and sn bhd: hdwy ent fnl 2f: styd on: nt rch ldrs: eased fnl 75yds* **25/1**

4643 5 1 ¾ **Pearl Spectre (USA)**[2] 8998 8-8-8 54...........................(be[1]) GraceMcEntee(7) 11 46
(Phil McEntee) *sn pushed along in midfield: hdwy u.p 2f out: kpt on ins fnl f: nvr able to trble ldrs* **6/1**[2]

6 1 ½ **Meryems Way (IRE)**[48] 7796 3-9-2 57...........................(p) ShaneGray 10 45
(Patrick Martin, Ire) *in tch: rdn over 4f out: one pce fnl 2f* **16/1**

5144 7 ¾ **Alpha Tauri (USA)**[11] 8903 13-9-2 60................................ AledBeech(5) 12 47
(Charles Smith) *handy: rdn over 3f out: unable qck u.p over 2f out: outpcd after* **16/1**

50 8 ¾ **Angel Of My Heart (IRE)**[20] 8639 4-8-11 50...........................(b) BenRobinson 3 35
(Michael Easterby) *in tch on inner: rdn and outpcd 3f out: no imp after* **66/1**

4022 9 3 ¼ **Oblate**[20] 8645 3-9-5 60...........................(p) PaulMulrennan 5 37
(Robyn Brisland) *completely missed break: in midfield after 2f: impr to chse ldrs 4f out: rdn over 2f out: wknd over 1f out (jockey said filly was slowly away)* **6/1**[2]

0000 10 3 ½ **Longville Lilly**[20] 8646 4-8-7 46 oh1...........................(b) AndrewMullen 6 16
(Trevor Wall) *midfield: lost pl and outpcd after 2f: bhd after* **100/1**

066 11 4 **Berties Mission (USA)**[13] 8842 3-9-0 55...........................(h) JasonHart 14 15
(Derek Shaw) *wnt to post early: sluggish s: racd on outer: nvr bttr than midfield: lost pl and outpcd 1/2-way: n.d after (jockey said gelding missed the break)* **66/1**

0050 12 6 **Rosin Box (IRE)**[31] 8301 6-8-8 47................................ WilliamCarson 13
(Tristan Davidson) *in tch: lost pl after 2f: sn outpcd: bhd fr 1/2-way* **33/1**

1400 13 2 ¼ **Echo Of Lightning**[35] 8199 9-9-9 62...........................(p) BenCurtis 8 4
(Roger Fell) *led: hdd wl over 3f out: sn drvn: wknd over 2f out* **50/1**

1m 41.57s (-2.13) **Going Correction** -0.25s/f (Stan)

WFA 3 from 4yo+ 2lb **13 Ran SP% 121.2**

Speed ratings (Par 101): **100,98,97,94,92 90,90,89,86,82 78,72,70**

CSF £15.80 CT £91.70 TOTE £1.80: £1.10, £3.20, £2.50; EX 17.10 Trifecta £126.90.

Owner F Morley **Bred** Mrs Noreen Maher **Trained** Oakham, Rutland

FOCUS

A moderate handicap and a one-sided betting market which proved to be spot-on.

9029 LADBROKES WHERE THE NATION PLAYS NOVICE AUCTION STKS 7f 14y(F)

4:45 (4:46) (Class 5) 2-Y-O

£3,428 (£1,020; £509; £254) **Stalls** Low

Form RPR

3 1 **Blake's Vision (IRE)**[12] 8865 2-8-12 0................................ JasonHart 6 75
(Mark Johnston) *w ldr: led narrowly over 2f out: sn hdd: continued to chal: kpt on gamely to regain slender ld towards fin* **7/4**[1]

0 2 shd **Curtiz**[79] 6718 2-8-8 0................................ CharlieBennett 4 71
(Hughie Morrison) *in tch: effrt over 2f out: sn led narrowly: a hrd pressed: hdd but kpt on towards fin* **13/2**

4332 3 2 **Dancing Leopard (IRE)**[14] 8815 2-8-5 66...........................(v) AndrewMullen 2 63
(K R Burke) *in rr: rdn along thrght: hdwy over 2f out: chalng wl over 1f out: edgd lft sn after: no ex fnl 75yds* **5/2**[2]

00 4 7 **Brass Clankers**[30] 8337 2-8-8 0................................ JamesSullivan 7 47
(Robyn Brisland) *broke wl: prom: lost pl after 2f: u.p and outpcd over 3f out: kpt on ins fnl f but n.d* **14/1**

1 5 ¾ **Come On My Son**[132] 4766 2-9-4 0................................ KevinLundie(5) 9 60
(Mark Loughnane) *racd on outer towards rr: pushed along and hdwy over 3f out: rdn and outpcd whn hung lft over 2f out: plugged on but n.d fnl f* **4/1**[3]

0 6 nk **Cold War Steve**[24] 8528 2-8-12 0................................ CallumRodriguez 3 49
(Roger Fell) *in tch: effrt to chse ldrs over 2f out: wknd over 1f out* **33/1**

36 7 8 **Gracie's Girl**[207] 2052 2-8-5 0................................ LukeMorris 5 21
(Michael Appleby) *sn led: rdn and hdd over 2f out: wknd over 1f out* **25/1**

00 8 3 ¼ **Ochre Riu (IRE)**[45] 7870 2-8-8 0................................ ShaneGray 8 15
(Ivan Furtado) *racd keenly: handy and wd: rdn over 2f out: sn wknd* **66/1**

1m 28.83s (-1.47) **Going Correction** -0.25s/f (Stan) **8 Ran SP% 113.2**

Speed ratings (Par 96): **98,97,95,87,86 86,77,73**

CSF £13.51 TOTE £2.20: £1.30, £1.70, £1.10; EX 11.50 Trifecta £29.30.

Owner Kingsley Park 13 **Bred** Rathbarry Stud **Trained** Middleham Moor, N Yorks

FOCUS

A modest novice auction in which the first three pulled a long way clear.

9030 BETWAY HEED YOUR HUNCH H'CAP 4f 214y(F)

5:15 (5:17) (Class 4) (0-85,85) 3-Y-O+

£5,207 (£1,549; £774; £400; £400; £400) **Stalls** Centre

Form RPR

6000 1 **Tawny Port**[44] 7894 5-9-5 83................................ RichardKingscote 3 92
(Stuart Williams) *midfield: hdwy over 1f out: led ins fnl f: r.o wl towards fin* **7/2**[1]

2502 2 1 ½ **Samovar**[9] 8943 4-8-10 74...........................(b) LukeMorris 1 78
(Scott Dixon) *chsd ldrs: sn pushed along: rdn over 2f out: ev ch ins fnl f: nt pce of wnr towards fin* **12/1**

0353 3 nk **Canford Bay (IRE)**[26] 8470 5-9-2 80................................ CamHardie 2 83
(Antony Brittain) *a.p: chalng over 2f out: led wl over 1f out: hdd ins fnl f: styd on same pce fnl 75yds* **13/2**[3]

4103 4 ½ **Crosse Fire**[11] 8900 7-8-11 82...........................(b) JonathanFisher(7) 7 83
(Scott Dixon) *a.p: rdn over 2f out: ev ch wl over 1f out: kpt on same pce u.p ins fnl f (jockey said gelding hung right)* **12/1**

2100 5 ¾ **Fantasy Keeper**[33] 8262 5-8-13 84................................ GeorgeRooke(7) 6 82
(Michael Appleby) *in tch: lost pl over 3f out: sn pushed along to go pce: hdwy ent fnl f: kpt on: nvr able to chal* **11/2**[2]

3500 6 nk **Nick Vedder**[20] 8642 5-9-0 78................................ PaulMulrennan 10 75
(Robyn Brisland) *missed break: sn swtchd lft: bhd: drifted lft 3f out: hdwy for press ins fnl f: styd on: nrst fin* **25/1**

3500 7 ¾ **Enchanted Linda**[26] 8470 3-8-12 76...........................(h) JasonHart 4 70
(Michael Herrington) *wnt to post early: led: rdn over 2f out: hdd wl over 1f out: wknd ins fnl f* **16/1**

1032 8 shd **Afandem (IRE)**[12] 8860 5-9-2 80...........................(p) DavidAllan 12 74
(Tim Easterby) *pushed along towards rr: nt clr run and swtchd lft over 2f out: hdwy u.p over 1f out: kpt on ins fnl f: nvr able to trble ldrs* **10/1**

6060 9 1 ¼ **Moonraker**[12] 8867 7-9-7 85................................ CharlesBishop 8 74
(Michael Appleby) *wnt to post early: chsd ldrs: rdn over 2f out: outpcd over 1f out: one pce fnl f* **8/1**

0004 10 2 ¼ **Erissimus Maximus (FR)**[11] 8900 5-8-8 79................................ AngusVilliers(7) 9 60
(Robert Cowell) *chsd ldrs: rdn over 2f out: sn lost pl: wknd ent fnl 2f (jockey said gelding hung right under pressure)* **10/1**

0-66 11 1 ¼ **Isle Of Innisfree (USA)**[93] 6225 3-9-1 79...........................(vt[1] w) BenCurtis 11 56
(Paul D'Arcy) *wnt to post early: n.m.r s: towards rr: drifted lft after 1f: outpcd over 2f out: nvr a threat* **25/1**

4002 **12** 1 **Free Love**[11] 8900 3-9-3 **84** .... TheodoreLadd(3) 13 57
(Michael Appleby) *midfield: rdn over 2f out: sn wknd* **10/1**

20-0 **13** 1 **Andre Amar (IRE)**[12] 8860 3-8-11 **75** .... TomEaves 5 45
(Robyn Brisland) *missed break: a in rr-div: sn outpcd* **80/1**

58.52s (-1.18) **Going Correction** -0.25s/f (Stan) **13** Ran SP% **119.5**
Speed ratings (Par 105): **99,96,96,95,94 93,92,92,90,86 84,83,81**
CSF £46.33 CT £224.48 TOTE £4.50: £2.00, £3.40, £2.10; EX 44.20 Trifecta £263.20.
Owner Mrs J Morley **Bred** Mrs D O'Brien **Trained** Newmarket, Suffolk

FOCUS
A fair sprint handicap and again the market got it right. The draw played its part with the first three starting from stalls 3, 1 and 2.

9031 LADBROKES HOME OF THE ODDS BOOST NURSERY H'CAP 6f 16y(F)
5:45 (5:49) (Class 5) (0-75,77) 2-Y-O
£3,339 (£999; £499; £400; £400; £400) Stalls Low

Form RPR

251 **1** **Dark Regard**[20] 8640 2-9-4 **72** .... JasonHart 14 81+
(Mark Johnston) *mde all: rdn over 1f out: r.o to draw clr ins fnl f: comf* **9/4**[1]

340 **2** 3 ¼ **Havana Dawn**[70] 7029 2-9-0 **68** ....(p) PaulMulrennan 10 67
(Phillip Makin) *in tch: effrt to chse ldrs over 2f out: kpt on to take 2nd fnl 150yds: no imp and nt pce of wnr* **40/1**

0420 **3** ¾ **Baileys In Bloom (FR)**[121] 5185 2-9-5 **73** .... BarryMcHugh 12 70
(Richard Fahey) *chsd ldrs: rdn to chse wnr over 2f out: no imp: lost 2nd fnl 150yds: styd on same pce* **20/1**

2320 **4** 1 ¾ **We're Reunited (IRE)**[51] 7679 2-9-7 **75** .... CharlesBishop 7 67
(Ronald Harris) *w wnr tl rdn over 2f out: kpt on same pce u.p after* **8/1**

2542 **5** hd **Good Earth (IRE)**[53] 7619 2-9-7 **75** .... NicolaCurrie 8 66
(Jamie Osborne) *sltly worse than midfield: pushed along and hdwy over 2f out: styd on ins fnl f: nt trble ldrs* **15/2**

5231 **6** 1 ½ **Lilkian**[13] 8841 2-9-1 **69** .... TomEaves 2 56
(Shaun Keightley) *midfield: rdn and hdwy over 2f out: edgd lft and no imp over 1f out: one pce ins fnl f* **9/2**[2]

5550 **7** ½ **Go Well Spicy (IRE)**[26] 8465 2-9-2 **70** .... DougieCostello 1 55
(Tim Fitzgerald) *midfield: pushed along over 4f out: hdwy over 2f out: edgd rt u.p ins fnl f: kpt on but no imp* **33/1**

4363 **8** 4 ½ **Abbaleka**[13] 8841 2-8-12 **66** .... LukeMorris 13 38
(Michael Appleby) *s.i.s: pushed along in midfield: swtchd lft over 2f out: one pce and nvr able to trble ldrs* **16/1**

5100 **9** 1 ¼ **Wentworth Amigo (IRE)**[108] 5612 2-9-9 **77** ....(t[1]) CallumShepherd 3 45
(Jamie Osborne) *chsd ldrs: rdn over 3f out: outpcd over 2f out: wknd ins fnl f* **16/1**

3446 **10** ½ **Little Ted**[35] 8201 2-8-4 **58** ....(bt) CamHardie 4 24
(Tim Easterby) *towards rr: pushed along and outpcd over 4f out: nvr a threat* **8/1**

346 **11** 2 ¼ **Dark Optimist (IRE)**[65] 7182 2-9-6 **74** ....(h) CliffordLee 9 34
(David Evans) *little worse than midfield: rdn and outpcd over 3f out: nvr a threat* **66/1**

2433 **12** nk **Hot Heels**[31] 8315 2-9-8 **76** .... RichardKingscote 6 35
(Tom Dascombe) *chsd ldrs tl rdn and wknd over 2f out* **13/2**[3]

5442 **13** 7 **Vintage Polly (IRE)**[27] 8431 2-9-2 **70** ....(p) BenCurtis 5 8
(Hugo Palmer) *s.i.s: a outpcd and bhd* **20/1**

000 **14** 1 ¾ **Bal Mal (FR)**[58] 7437 2-8-2 **56** .... JamesSullivan 11
(John Quinn) *towards rr: nvr gng pce: bhd fnl f* **50/1**

1m 14.85s (-1.65) **Going Correction** -0.25s/f (Stan) **14** Ran SP% **126.4**
Speed ratings (Par 96): **101,96,95,93,93 91,90,84,82,82 79,78,69,67**
CSF £129.93 CT £1215.46 TOTE £3.60: £1.50, £10.10, £4.70; EX 124.50 Trifecta £3313.00.
Owner John Dance **Bred** Brightwalton Bloodstock Ltd **Trained** Middleham Moor, N Yorks

FOCUS
An ordinary nursery and not many got into it, with the high draws coming to the fore this time. The favourite bolted up under a positive ride.

9032 BOMBARDIER GOLDEN BEER NOVICE STKS 7f 14y(F)
6:15 (6:17) (Class 5) 3-Y-O+ £3,428 (£1,020; £509; £254) Stalls Low

Form RPR

3263 **1** **Gleeful**[62] 7298 3-8-13 67 ....(v[1]) DanielTudhope 3 71
(David O'Meara) *racd keenly: hld up: angled out and hdwy over 2f out: rdn over 1f out: r.o ins fnl f: led post* **3/1**[2]

422 **2** shd **Bobby Shaft**[17] 8718 3-9-4 74 .... BarryMcHugh 9 76
(Richard Fahey) *chsd ldr: rdn to ld ent fnl 2f: abt 2 l clr ins fnl f: all out towards fin: ct post* **1/1**[1]

40 **3** 7 **Six Til Twelve (IRE)**[32] 8290 3-8-11 0 .... GavinAshton(7) 6 58
(Robyn Brisland) *racd keenly: led: rdn and hdd ent fnl 2f: no ex fnl 100yds* **14/1**

53 **4** 5 **Memory Hill (IRE)**[13] 8842 3-9-4 0 .... BenCurtis 1 45
(David Evans) *chsd ldrs: rdn and outpcd 2f out: no imp after* **5/1**[3]

5 **5** 2 **Inn With The Gin**[28] 8407 3-8-13 0 .... LukeMorris 5 35
(Scott Dixon) *midfield: rdn 4f out: outpcd over 3f out: plugged on but n.d fnl f* **50/1**

6 1 ¼ **Feel The Thunder** 3-8-11 0 .... JonathanFisher(7) 8 37
(Scott Dixon) *in tch: effrt whn chsng ldrs over 2f out: wknd over 1f out* **33/1**

0600 **7** nk **Geneva Spur (USA)**[13] 8822 3-8-13 52 .... RossaRyan 4 31
(Roger Varian) *chsd ldrs: rdn over 2f out: wknd over 1f out* **9/1**

5 **8** nk **Just A Touch (IRE)**[11] 8894 3-8-8 0 .... RayDawson(5) 2 30
(Jane Chapple-Hyam) *bhd: outpcd over 3f out: nvr involved* **66/1**

62 **9** 15 **Thornaby Spirit (IRE)**[58] 7442 4-9-5 0 .... TomEaves 7
(Jason Ward) *hld up bhd: outpcd over 3f out: fin wl bhd* **25/1**

1m 28.06s (-2.24) **Going Correction** -0.25s/f (Stan)
WFA 3 from 4yo 1lb **9** Ran SP% **118.6**
Speed ratings (Par 103): **102,101,93,88,85 84,84,83,66**
CSF £6.41 TOTE £3.60: £1.50, £1.10, £2.70; EX 7.10 Trifecta £38.80.
Owner Cheveley Park Stud **Bred** Cheveley Park Stud Ltd **Trained** Upper Helmsley, N Yorks

FOCUS
An uncompetitive novice event, but a dramatic finish.

9033 BETWAY CASINO H'CAP 1m 4f 14y(F)
6:45 (6:48) (Class 5) (0-70,72) 3-Y-O+
£3,428 (£1,020; £509; £400; £400; £400) Stalls Low

Form RPR

0136 **1** **Blowing Dixie**[27] 8433 3-9-3 **65** .... RichardKingscote 3 84+
(Jane Chapple-Hyam) *hld up: hdwy over 3f out: led gng wl 2f out: stormed clr 1f out: easily* **11/8**[1]

3442 **2** 7 **J Gaye (IRE)**[20] 8644 3-9-2 **69** .... GeorgiaDobie(5) 8 74
(Richard Phillips) *hld up: rdn and hdwy over 2f out: kpt on to take 2nd fnl 150yds: no ch w wnr (jockey said filly hung left)* **15/2**

2000 **3** 1 **Princess Harley (IRE)**[41] 7998 4-9-3 **60** ....(p) CharlesBishop 5 63
(Mick Quinn) *broke wl: trckd ldrs after 3f: rdn to ld briefly over 2f out: unable to go w wnr over 1f out: lost 2nd fnl 150yds: one pce* **33/1**

1033 **4** 11 **Cold Harbour**[9] 8948 4-9-7 **64** ....(t) TomEaves 7 50
(Robyn Brisland) *hld up: hdwy 7f out: rdn 3f out: chsd ldrs over 2f out: no imp* **10/1**

1000 **5** 1 ½ **Pioneering (IRE)**[31] 8300 5-9-10 **67** .... PaulMulrennan 6 50
(Roger Fell) *sn led: rdn and hdd over 2f out: wknd over 1f out* **40/1**

6330 **6** ½ **Contingency Fee**[62] 7318 4-8-13 **63** ....(p) GraceMcEntee(7) 1 46
(Phil McEntee) *pushed along to go prom: rdn and wknd over 2f out* **33/1**

6301 **7** nk **Restive (IRE)**[13] 8843 6-10-1 **72** ....(t) LukeMorris 4 54
(Michael Appleby) *midfield: hdwy after 4f: drvn and wknd over 2f out* **7/1**[3]

U261 **8** 3 **Twpsyn (IRE)**[13] 8837 3-9-6 **68** ....(v) BenCurtis 9 45
(David Evans) *midfield: hdwy over 4f out: drvn over 3f out: sn outpcd: wknd over 1f out (jockey reported that when dismounting after the winning post, he noticed that the blinkers on the gelding had dislodged and were covering one eye)* **3/1**[2]

1-00 **9** 10 **Scrafton**[12] 8862 8-9-1 **65** .... ElishaWhittington(7) 11 26
(Tony Carroll) *hld up: pushed along over 6f out: nvr a threat* **100/1**

-000 **10** 28 **Compatriot (IRE)**[55] 7545 5-9-10 **67** ....(p) CallumRodriguez 10
(Roger Fell) *prom tl rdn and wknd 4f out* **40/1**

00-0 **11** 20 **If We Can Can**[19] 8664 4-8-13 **56** .... CamHardie 12
(Olly Williams) *drvn along and a bhd: t.o* **100/1**

0661 **12** 8 **Country'N'Western (FR)**[19] 8663 7-9-8 **65** ....(t[1]) WilliamCarson 2
(Robert Eddery) *prom: dropped to midfield after 3f: lost pl over 6f out: eased whn wl bhd fnl 2f: b.b.v (vet reported gelding bled from the nose)* **14/1**

2m 36.08s (-4.92) **Going Correction** -0.25s/f (Stan)
WFA 3 from 4yo+ 5lb **12** Ran SP% **119.9**
Speed ratings (Par 103): **106,101,100,93,92 92,91,89,83,64 51,45**
CSF £12.36 CT £242.22 TOTE £2.20: £1.10, £3.60, £7.50; EX 12.60 Trifecta £267.80.
Owner Mohammed Alenezi **Bred** Merry Fox Stud Limited **Trained** Dalham, Suffolk

FOCUS
A modest handicap and they finished well spread out, with the favourite taking the race apart.

9034 #BETYOURWAY AT BETWAY H'CAP 4f 214y(F)
7:15 (7:19) (Class 7) (0-50,50) 3-Y-O+ £2,264 (£673; £336; £168) Stalls Centre

Form RPR

0063 **1** **Moneta**[18] 8697 3-9-6 **49** ....(b) CharlesBishop 3 55
(Ronald Harris) *mde all: rdn over 1f out: r.o ins fnl f* **10/1**

0604 **2** 1 ¼ **Tilsworth Rose**[11] 8901 5-9-2 **45** ....(b) RaulDaSilva 1 47
(J R Jenkins) *prom: rdn over 2f out: chsd wnr over 1f out: kpt on ins fnl f but no imp* **7/2**[1]

0050 **3** 1 ½ **Alisia R (IRE)**[17] 8720 3-9-3 **46** .... JasonHart 14 42
(Les Eyre) *in tch: rdn over 2f out: styd on towards fin: nvr able to mount serious chal* **18/1**

5340 **4** ½ **Jaganory (IRE)**[18] 8697 7-8-11 **47** ....(v) AngusVilliers(7) 8 41
(Christopher Mason) *towards rr: sn pushed along: hdwy ent fnl f: styd on wl: gng on towards fin* **10/1**

-550 **5** hd **Maerchengarten**[33] 8249 3-9-4 **47** .... RossaRyan 13 41
(Ed de Giles) *in tch: rdn over 2f out: kpt on ins fnl f: nvr able to chal: run flattened out fnl strides* **33/1**

0004 **6** 1 ½ **Alba Del Sole (IRE)**[11] 8898 4-9-6 **49** ....(p) RichardKingscote 12 37
(Charlie Wallis) *chsd ldrs: rdn over 2f out: sn outpcd: one pce fnl f* **11/2**[2]

4050 **7** 1 **Bluella**[11] 8898 4-9-3 **46** ....(bt) TomEaves 10 31
(Robyn Brisland) *prom: rdn 2f out: unable qck over 1f out: wknd wl ins fnl f* **12/1**

5300 **8** hd **Bithiah (IRE)**[14] 8821 3-9-1 **47** .... GabrieleMalune(3) 6 31
(Ismail Mohammed) *prom: rdn 2f out: unable qck over 1f out: wknd wl ins fnl f* **7/1**

003 **9** 1 **Kemmeridge Bay**[10] 8920 3-9-2 **45** .... SamJames 7 25
(Grant Tuer) *midfield: rdn over 2f out: nvr a threat* **12/1**

6546 **10** shd **Tadaany (IRE)**[11] 8901 7-9-2 **45** ....(v) JamesSullivan 9 25
(Ruth Carr) *outpcd and bhd: edgd rt after 1f: nvr involved* **6/1**[3]

5405 **11** 1 ¼ **Newgate Angel**[138] 4508 3-9-2 **45** ....(p) AndrewMullen 11 20
(Tony Coyle) *midfield: rdn over 2f out: wknd over 1f out* **40/1**

0-00 **12** ¾ **Juan Horsepower**[49] 7770 5-9-7 **50** ....(b) DannyBrock 5 23
(Denis Quinn) *towards rr: sn outpcd: hung lft over 1f out: nvr a threat* **50/1**

3300 **13** nse **Tina Teaspoon**[103] 5822 5-9-2 **45** ....(h) CamHardie 4 18
(Derek Shaw) *chsd ldrs: rdn over 1f out: sn outpcd: wknd ins fnl f* **80/1**

542 **14** 7 **Nifty Niece (IRE)**[82] 6590 5-9-4 **47** .... LukeMorris 2
(Ann Duffield) *midfield: outpcd 3f out: eased whn bhd fnl f* **25/1**

58.86s (-0.84) **Going Correction** -0.25s/f (Stan) **14** Ran SP% **115.6**
Speed ratings (Par 97): **96,94,91,90,90 88,86,86,84,84 82,81,81,69**
CSF £41.50 CT £648.31 TOTE £9.90: £2.50, £1.40, £6.00; EX 43.40 Trifecta £844.30.
Owner Wayne Clifford **Bred** Whatton Manor Stud **Trained** Earlswood, Monmouths

FOCUS
A rock-bottom sprint handicap and again the draw played its part, with the first two up with the pace throughout from their low stalls.

9035 BOMBARDIER "MARCH TO YOUR OWN DRUM" ALL-WEATHER "HANDS AND HEELS" APPRENTICE H'CAP 7f 14y(F)
7:45 (7:49) (Class 6) (0-60,62) 3-Y-O+
£2,781 (£827; £413; £400; £400; £400) Stalls Low

Form RPR

2333 **1** **Silverturnstogold**[12] 8847 4-9-12 **60** ....(b) ElishaWhittington 2 69
(Tony Carroll) *in tch: effrt to ld narrowly over 1f out: strly pressed ins fnl f: kpt on to do enough towards fin* **6/1**

51 **2** hd **Split Down South**[10] 8917 3-9-13 **62** .... GraceMcEntee 9 69
(Phil McEntee) *sn led: pushed along over 2f out: hdd narrowly over 1f out: continued to chal: kpt on: jst hld* **7/2**[1]

2362 **3** 3 ½ **Elysee Star**[9] 8949 4-8-13 **47** ....(p) AidenBlakemore 3 46
(Mark Walford) *led early: lost pl after 2f: dropped bhd ldrs: outpcd over 2f out: styd on fnl 100yds: no imp on front two* **9/2**[2]

0604 **4** 1 **Sooqaan**[20] 8646 8-9-3 **51** ....(p) RussellHarris 6 47
(Antony Brittain) *w ldr: pushed along and ev ch 2f out: unable qck over 1f out: no ex fnl 100yds* **6/1**

0006 **5** ½ **Tagur (IRE)**[10] 8923 5-9-5 **58** ....(v) HarriettLees(5) 8 53
(Kevin Ryan) *towards rr: hdwy 2f out: kpt on ins fnl f: nvr able to trble ldrs* **5/1**[3]

0055 **6** ½ **Reshaan (IRE)**[11] 8901 4-8-12 **46** oh1.............................(b) LukeCatton 5 40
(Alexandra Dunn) *prom early: sn lost pl: dropped to midfield after 2f: outpcd 3f out: kpt on one pce ins fnl f (jockey said gelding hung right throughout)* **20/1**

7 ¾ **Ebony Belle (IRE)**[39] 8076 3-8-11 **46** oh1.............................(b[1]) KateLeahy 4 37
(Patrick Martin, Ire) *in rr: pushed along over 2f out: sn swtchd rt: kpt on ins fnl f: nvr able to get involved* **40/1**

3306 **8** 1¾ **Abie's Hollow**[9] 8949 3-9-9 **58**.............................(p) ZakWheatley 7 44
(Tony Coyle) *trckd ldrs: pushed along over 2f out: wknd over 1f out* **7/1**

0 **9** 8 **Baile Ghilibert (IRE)**[11] 8901 7-8-12 **46** oh1..........(p[1]) GeorgeRooke 10 12
(Michael Appleby) *prom: pushed along over 2f out: sn wknd* **20/1**

5030 **10** 2½ **Prince Of Time**[34] 8233 7-8-12 **46** oh1.............................(p) OliverStammers 1 6
(Stella Barclay) *sn pushed along towards rr: nvr a threat* **33/1**

0006 **11** 11 **Shellebeau (IRE)**[13] 8839 3-9-6 **60**.............................KeelanBaker(5) 11
(Alexandra Dunn) *restless in stalls: a struggling and bhd (jockey said his saddle slipped. vet reported filly finished lame on its right fore)* **16/1**

1m 28.47s (-1.83) **Going Correction** -0.25s/f (Stan) 11 Ran SP% **118.9**
WFA 3 from 4yo+ 1lb
Speed ratings (Par 101): **100,99,95,94,94 93,92,90,81,78 66**
CSF £26.36 CT £107.39 TOTE £7.00: £2.20, £2.10, £1.40; EX 28.90 Trifecta £89.20.
Owner A A Byrne **Bred** Anthony Byrne **Trained** Cropthorne, Worcs

FOCUS
A moderate apprentice handicap to end with, but quite a battle between the first two.
T/Plt: £16.00 to a £1 stake. Pool: £97,869.21 - 4,455.78 winning units T/Qpdt: £12.50 to a £1 stake. Pool: £13,812.15 - 815.44 winning units **Darren Owen**

9006 WOLVERHAMPTON (A.W) (L-H)
Monday, November 18

OFFICIAL GOING: Tapeta: standard

9036 LADBROKES FOOTBALL ACCA BOOSTY NOVICE STKS 5f 21y (Tp)
12:50 (12:54) (Class 5) 2-Y-O £3,428 (£1,020; £509; £254) Stalls Low

Form RPR

12 **1** **Auchterarder (IRE)**[11] 8899 2-9-5 0.............................JasonHart 4 84
(Mark Johnston) *mde all: 2 l ahd whn nudged along 2f out: rdn fr over 1f out: r.o* **5/2**[2]

5 **2** 4 **Rocking Reg (IRE)**[28] 8409 2-9-3 0.............................JasonWatson 10 68
(Roger Teal) *cl up: pushed along 3f out: kpt on but no match for wnr (jockey said colt ran green)* **10/1**[3]

20 **3** 1 **Minhaaj (IRE)**[17] 8724 2-8-12 0.............................JimCrowley 3 59+
(William Haggas) *bit short of room and midfield into first turn: nt clr run tl rdn over 1f out: kpt on but mde no imp* **4/6**[1]

6 **4** 5 **Marina Grove (IRE)**[20] 8631 2-8-12 0.............................DavidAllan 8 41+
(Tim Easterby) *dwlt s: towards rr: rdn 3f out: kpt on but nvr able to chal* **33/1**

5 ½ **Tattletime (USA)** 2-8-9 0.............................ThomasGreatrex(3) 11 39
(David Loughnane) *walked to post: rushed up early: prom abt three wd: rdn 3f out: outpcd fr 2f out* **100/1**

6 ½ **Cliff Wind** 2-8-12 0.............................LukeMorris 9 37
(Sir Mark Prescott Bt) *chsd ldrs: racd awkwardly: cajoled along 3f out: mde no imp* **40/1**

05 **7** nse **Mews House**[11] 8899 2-8-12 0.............................ThoreHammerHansen(5) 5 42
(David Brown) *midfield abt three wd: rdn 3f out: mde no imp* **25/1**

0 **8** nk **Alioski**[89] 6336 2-9-3 0.............................TomEaves 6 41
(Kevin Ryan) *towards rr: outpcd and pushed along over 3f out: racd extremely wd home turn: kpt on but mde no imp* **14/1**

00 **9** ¾ **Knockacurra (IRE)**[32] 8297 2-9-3 0.............................(t[1]) ShaneKelly 2 38
(Mark Loughnane) *trckd ldr: rdn and wknd fr 2f out* **100/1**

10 1¼ **Skyllachy** 2-9-3 0.............................StevieDonohoe 7 34
(Mark Usher) *s.i.s: racd in last: sn outpcd: sme hdwy fnl f* **66/1**

0 **11** ¾ **Littlemissattitude**[41] 7995 2-8-12 0.............................KierenFox 1 26
(Derek Shaw) *s.i.s: a towards rr* **250/1**

59.76s (-2.14) **Going Correction** -0.30s/f (Stan) 11 Ran SP% **117.4**
Speed ratings (Par 96): **105,98,97,89,88 87,87,86,85,83 82**
CSF £26.29 TOTE £3.30: £1.10, £2.10, £1.10; EX 26.70 Trifecta £41.30.
Owner Kingsley Park 11 **Bred** Newstead Breeding **Trained** Middleham Moor, N Yorks

FOCUS
The first two raced 1-2 throughout and the third, not best placed, was below form, but the winner is useful.

9037 LADBROKES WHERE THE NATION PLAYS NURSERY H'CAP 1m 142y (Tp)
1:20 (1:21) (Class 6) (0-60,59) 2-Y-O
£2,781 (£827; £413; £300; £300; £300) Stalls Low

Form RPR

6533 **1** **Treaty Of Dingle**[27] 8415 2-9-6 **58**.............................JasonWatson 11 66
(Hughie Morrison) *prom: hdwy on outer to ld over 2f out: rdn and edgd lft over 1f out: wnt clr ins fnl f: eased towards fin* **5/2**[1]

5U41 **2** 2¾ **Lafontaine (FR)**[13] 8824 2-8-9 **50**.............................ThomasGreatrex(3) 9 50
(Sylvester Kirk) *led: hdd after 1f: sn trckd ldr: shkn up and ev ch over 2f out: sn rdn: no ex ins fnl f: jst hld 2nd* **11/2**[3]

0604 **3** nse **Dazzling Darren (IRE)**[13] 8824 2-8-11 **49**.............................(p) LukeMorris 7 49
(Adam West) *t.k.h: trckd ldrs: nt clr run over 2f out: rdn and edgd lft over 1f out: kpt on ins fnl f* **8/1**

040 **4** 4 **Berkshire Philly**[19] 8651 2-9-7 **59**.............................RobHornby 2 51
(Andrew Balding) *bmpd s: midfield on inner: shkn up and swtchd rt over 2f out: rdn and no imp over 1f out* **8/1**

0006 **5** 2½ **Jazz Style (IRE)**[11] 8897 2-8-7 **50** ow2.............................ThoreHammerHansen(5) 5 36
(David Brown) *bmpd s: towards rr: pushed along and hdwy on outer over 2f out: sn rdn: hung lft and wknd over 1f out* **11/1**

3000 **6** 7 **River Of Kings (IRE)**[14] 8815 2-9-1 **58**.............................(h) BenSanderson(5) 6 30
(Keith Dalgleish) *s.i.s: hld up in rr: rdn 4f out: wknd over 2f out* **4/1**[2]

040 **7** 1¼ **No Can Do**[84] 6532 2-9-7 **59**.............................(t) NicolaCurrie 10 28
(Jamie Osborne) *hld up in rr: pushed along and outpcd 3f out: sn btn (jockey said colt was never travelling)* **12/1**

0000 **8** 2¼ **Speed Dating (FR)**[32] 8286 2-8-13 **51**.............................(v) KierenFox 1 15
(Derek Shaw) *t.k.h: led after 1f: rdn and hdd over 2f out: sn wknd (jockey said gelding ran too freely and hung both ways)* **11/1**

1m 48.4s (-1.70) **Going Correction** -0.30s/f (Stan) 8 Ran SP% **110.5**
Speed ratings (Par 94): **95,92,92,88,86 80,79,77**
CSF £15.16 CT £87.89 TOTE £2.80: £1.50, £2.30, £1.10; EX 13.00 Trifecta £52.20.
Owner The Tod Partnership **Bred** Lord Margadale **Trained** East Ilsley, Berks

FOCUS
Not much to dwell on in a moderate nursery. An ordinary gallop picked up when the winner went on at the top of the home straight and those held up were at a disadvantage.

9038 BOMBARDIER GOLDEN BEER NOVICE STKS 1m 142y (Tp)
1:50 (1:53) (Class 5) 3-Y-O+ £3,428 (£1,020; £509; £254) Stalls Low

Form RPR

1 **1** **Desert Caravan**[17] 8718 3-9-9 0.............................BenCurtis 6 85+
(William Haggas) *dwlt s: chsd ldrs: rdn and led over 1f out: kpt on wl: a doing jst enough* **5/6**[1]

2 ½ **White Mountain** 3-8-11 0.............................HectorCrouch 1 72+
(Saeed bin Suroor) *t.k.h: led: nudged along 3f out: hrd rdn home st: hdd over 1f out: kpt on fnl f: no ex fnl strides* **11/4**[2]

3 3¾ **Bridgewater Bay (IRE)** 3-9-2 0.............................AdamKirby 7 68
(Jane Chapple-Hyam) *midfield: hdwy over 3f out: wnt 3rd bef st: kpt on but rn green fnl f: no match for first two* **25/1**

4 5 **Bustaan (USA)** 3-8-11 0.............................KieranShoemark 4 52
(Owen Burrows) *cl up on outer early: sn midfield: rdn 3f out: kpt on: n.d* **5/1**[3]

5 3 **Just Magic** 3-9-2 0.............................DavidAllan 5 50
(Tim Easterby) *s.i.s: hld up in last: rdn and sme hdwy 3f out: n.d* **66/1**

00 **6** 2½ **Highland Sun (IRE)**[13] 8842 3-8-11 0.............................JaneElliott 8 39
(Richard Phillips) *a towards rr: rdn 4f out: mde no imp* **150/1**

0 **7** ½ **Kelis (IRE)**[26] 8467 3-8-11 0.............................LukeMorris 2 38
(Heather Main) *chsd ldrs: rdn after 3f: reminders under 4f out: wknd grad fr 3f out* **66/1**

24 **8** ¾ **Cathedral Street (IRE)**[20] 8645 3-8-9 0.............................OliverStammers(7) 3 41
(Mark Johnston) *cl up: rdn and wknd qckly fr under 3f out* **10/1**

1m 46.46s (-3.64) **Going Correction** -0.30s/f (Stan) 8 Ran SP% **114.5**
Speed ratings (Par 103): **104,103,100,95,93 90,90,89**
CSF £3.27 TOTE £1.50: £1.10, £1.20, £4.60; EX 3.30 Trifecta £23.60.
Owner The Queen **Bred** The Queen **Trained** Newmarket, Suffolk

FOCUS
Ordinary novice form.

9039 BOMBARDIER BRITISH HOPPED AMBER BEER H'CAP 7f 36y (Tp)
2:20 (2:23) (Class 6) (0-55,55) 3-Y-O+
£2,781 (£827; £413; £300; £300; £300) Stalls High

Form RPR

0550 **1** **Steal The Scene (IRE)**[19] 8667 7-9-3 **53**.............................(t) RossaRyan 8 63
(Kevin Frost) *cl up: 2 l 2nd whn shkn up 2f out: rdn and hung lft ins fnl f: kpt on wl to ld towards fin* **9/2**[2]

4044 **2** ½ **Reasoned (IRE)**[27] 8436 3-9-4 **55**.............................ShaneKelly 9 63
(James Eustace) *led: pushed along and 2 l ahd 2f out: rdn and kpt on fnl f: hdd and no ex towards fin* **10/1**

0230 **3** 3½ **Puchita (IRE)**[10] 8922 4-9-2 **52**.............................(p) CamHardie 12 52
(Antony Brittain) *hld up in rr: stl plenty to do whn rdn 2f out: wnt 3rd ins fnl f: no match for first two* **20/1**

4334 **4** nk **Maid Millie**[12] 8847 3-9-4 **55**.............................(p) LukeMorris 3 53
(Robert Cowell) *dwlt s: sn midfield: rdn and outpcd over 3f out: rallied over 2f out: kpt on fnl f: mde no imp* **10/1**

0040 **5** ½ **Elena Osorio (IRE)**[81] 6643 3-9-3 **54**.............................HectorCrouch 1 52
(Ed Walker) *hld up in rr: short of room over 2f out: rdn and hdwy over 1f out: nvr able to chal* **4/1**[1]

0003 **6** ½ **Bobby Joe Leg**[12] 8864 5-9-4 **54**.............................(v) JamesSullivan 7 51
(Ruth Carr) *dwlt s: t.k.h: sn prom: rdn 2f out: hung lft and outpcd fr 1f out* **9/1**

0600 **7** 1 **Newstead Abbey**[20] 8646 9-9-4 **54**.............................(p) TomEaves 6 48
(Rebecca Bastiman) *prom: rdn over 2f out: wknd ins fnl f (vet reported gelding lost its left-fore shoe)* **40/1**

0310 **8** 1¾ **The King's Steed**[10] 8915 6-9-3 **53**.............................(bt) KieranShoemark 11 43
(Shaun Lycett) *t.k.h: chsd ldr to over 2f out: rdn and wknd over 1f out* **10/1**

6000 **9** shd **Aquarius (IRE)**[10] 8917 3-9-3 **54**.............................(p) LiamJones 4 43
(Michael Appleby) *t.k.h: towards rr: bit short of room over 3f out: rdn and outpcd over 2f out: sn btn* **40/1**

4-10 **10** nse **Miss Bates**[285] 624 5-9-4 **54**.............................DavidAllan 5 44
(Ann Duffield) *slowly away: in rr: struggling 3f out: sn btn* **22/1**

4002 **11** 2¾ **Brockey Rise (IRE)**[12] 8864 4-9-5 **55**.............................(b) CliffordLee 10 38
(David Evans) *midfield on outer: rdn and lost position over 2f out: sn wknd* **15/2**

3001 **12** nk **With Approval (IRE)**[14] 8819 7-9-0 **53**.............................(b) GemmaTutty(3) 2 35
(Karen Tutty) *t.k.h: midfield on inner: pushed along and struggling over 2f out: sn btn (trainer's rep said the gelding may have been unsuited by being unable to dominate)* **13/2**[3]

1m 27.17s (-1.63) **Going Correction** -0.30s/f (Stan) 12 Ran SP% **114.5**
WFA 3 from 4yo+ 1lb
Speed ratings (Par 101): **97,96,92,92,91 90,89,87,87,87 84,84**
CSF £44.84 CT £802.88 TOTE £5.20: £2.00, £3.30, £4.00; EX 54.10 Trifecta £684.70.
Owner Curzon House Partnership & Friends **Bred** Shane Doyle **Trained** Newcastle-under-Lyme, Staffs

FOCUS
A low-grade handicap in which an ordinary gallop increased turning for home.

9040 BETWAY LIVE CASINO H'CAP 1m 1f 104y (Tp)
2:50 (2:50) (Class 6) (0-60,60) 3-Y-O+
£2,781 (£827; £413; £300; £300; £300) Stalls Low

Form RPR

2001 **1** **Greengage (IRE)**[26] 8466 4-9-6 **59**.............................(h) PhilDennis 3 66+
(Tristan Davidson) *midfield: nt clr run 2f out: rdn and qcknd to ld ins fnl f: comf* **11/4**[1]

2064 **2** 1 **Barbarosa (IRE)**[12] 8863 3-9-2 **58**.............................TomEaves 8 63
(Michael Herrington) *t.k.h: prom: led 2f out: rdn and hdd ins fnl f: kpt on* **6/1**[3]

2425 **3** hd **Traveller (FR)**[17] 8713 5-9-4 **57**.............................(vt) CamHardie 1 62
(Antony Brittain) *towards rr of midfield: rdn and hdwy fr over 1f out: kpt on wl* **8/1**

0400 **4** nse **Solfeggio (IRE)**[12] 8847 3-9-2 **58**.............................GeorgeWood 6 63
(Chris Wall) *t.k.h: chsd ldrs: rdn over 1f out: kpt on fnl f* **12/1**

3426 **5** 1 **Vipin (FR)**[12] 8870 4-9-6 **59**.............................GrahamLee 9 62
(William Muir) *sn led: hdd 2f out: rdn over 1f out: wknd ins fnl f* **5/1**[2]

304 **6** ¾ **Triple Nickle (IRE)**[33] 8247 3-9-4 **60**.............................(p) DanielMuscutt 7 61
(Bernard Llewellyn) *midfield: rdn 2f out: kpt on ins fnl f* **20/1**

The Form Book Flat 2019, Raceform Ltd, Newbury, RG14 5SJ

0046 **7** 1 3/4 **Ebbisham (IRE)**[19] 8667 6-8-11 **55**....(v) TobyEley(5) 11 53
(John Mackie) *s.i.s: towards rr of midfield: rdn over 1f out: no imp ins fnl f (jockey said gelding was slowly away)* **16/1**

1300 **8** *hd* **La Sioux (IRE)**[50] 7738 5-9-2 **58**.... SeanDavis(3) 10 55
(Richard Fahey) *upset in stalls: chsd ldrs: rdn 2f out: wknd over 1f out* **28/1**

0404 **9** 3/4 **Uncertain Smile (IRE)**[12] 8870 3-8-13 **58**....(h) WilliamCox(3) 13 54
(Clive Cox) *t.k.h: cl up but abt three wd: rdn and wknd fr 2f out (jockey said filly hung right-handed off the home bend)* **13/2**

0450 **10** 5 **Pilot Wings (IRE)**[14] 8813 4-9-3 **56**....(tp) KieranShoemark 12 42
(David Dennis) *hld up in rr: rdn and wknd fr over 2f out: btn whn hung lft over 1f out* **16/1**

0030 **11** 16 **Medici Moon**[12] 8863 5-9-3 **56**....(p) StevieDonohoe 4 11
(Richard Price) *towards rr: pushed along 3f out: wknd fr 2f out* **28/1**

1m 59.69s (-1.11) **Going Correction** -0.30s/f (Stan)
WFA 3 from 4yo+ 3lb **11** Ran SP% **113.2**
Speed ratings (Par 101): **92,91,90,90,90 89,87,87,86,82 68**
CSF £17.43 CT £114.14 TOTE £3.10: £1.40, £1.70, £2.40; EX 19.50 Trifecta £80.40.
Owner J T Davidson **Bred** Joe And Edel Banahan **Trained** Irthington, Cumbria

FOCUS
No great pace on here and it was an advantage to be handy.

9041 BETWAY H'CAP 1m 1f 104y (Tp)
3:20 (3:20) (Class 3) (0-95,96) 3-Y-0+ **£7,439** (£2,213; £1,106; £553) **Stalls** Low

Form RPR

0330 **1** **Storm Ahead (IRE)**[16] 8761 6-8-8 **74**....(b) PhilDennis 5 83
(Tim Easterby) *hld up in rr: gd hdwy 2f out: sn rdn: swtchd lft and led ins fnl f: kpt on wl towards fin* **28/1**

2160 **2** 3/4 **Furzig**[37] 8130 4-9-5 **88**.... SeanDavis(3) 4 95
(Richard Fahey) *prom: rdn and hdwy over 1f out: wnt 2nd ins fnl f: kpt on towards fin* **13/2**[2]

2225 **3** 2 **Michele Strogoff**[46] 7836 6-9-5 **85**.... JaneElliott 8 88
(Michael Appleby) *led: rdn 2f out: hdd ins fnl f: sn no ex* **16/1**

421 **4** *nk* **Sandret (IRE)**[66] 7153 3-9-8 **91**.... GrahamLee 13 94+
(Ben Haslam) *hld up in rr: pushed along and hdwy whn hung lft over 1f out: shkn up and kpt on ins fnl f: nrst fin (jockey said gelding hung left handed in the home straight)* **11/2**[1]

2554 **5** *nk* **Scofflaw**[28] 8412 5-8-4 **77**....(v) LauraPearson(7) 1 79
(David Evans) *towards rr on inner: rdn and hdwy over 1f out: kpt on fnl f: nvr able to chal* **28/1**

5550 **6** 1/2 **Mr Top Hat**[28] 8411 4-8-12 **85**.... CameronIles(7) 2 86
(David Evans) *cl up: rdn over 2f out: wnt 2nd fr 1f out: outpcd ins fnl f* **28/1**

0505 **7** *nk* **King's Slipper**[51] 7686 4-9-7 **87**.... AdamKirby 11 87
(Clive Cox) *plld hrd: midfield: rdn and hdwy on outer over 1f out: hung lft and no imp ins fnl f* **13/2**[2]

1601 **8** 1 1/4 **Kaser (IRE)**[35] 8197 4-9-0 **83**.... ThomasGreatrex(3) 9 81
(David Loughnane) *hld up in rr: rdn over 2f out: hung lft over 1f out: hdwy ins fnl f: nvr able to chal* **15/2**

2025 **9** 3/4 **I'm Available (IRE)**[24] 8519 3-9-3 **86**.... RobHornby 6 82
(Andrew Balding) *prom: rdn over 2f out: outpcd whn short of room ins fnl f: sn btn* **7/1**[3]

0416 **10** 3 3/4 **Original Choice (IRE)**[53] 7616 5-9-11 **96**...(v) ThoreHammerHansen(5) 3 84
(Nick Littmoden) *dwlt s: sn midfield on inner: rdn 2f out: wknd fr 1f out* **14/1**

2213 **11** *nk* **Data Protection**[28] 8411 4-9-3 **83**....(t) JasonWatson 7 71
(William Muir) *t.k.h: chsd ldr to over 1f out: sn rdn: wknd ins fnl f (jockey said gelding hung right-handed throughout)* **9/1**

5130 **12** 12 **Siglo Six**[34] 8222 3-9-5 **88**....(h) KieranShoemark 10 50
(Hugo Palmer) *slowly away: sn prom on outer: rdn 3f out: sn struggling: lost tch over 1f out: eased whn btn fnl f (jockey said colt was slowly away)* **16/1**

15-0 **13** 22 **Alfurat River**[89] 6347 3-9-4 **87**.... CallumShepherd 12 3
(Saeed bin Suroor) *towards rr on outer: rdn and outpcd over 3f out: lost tch fr 2f out: sn eased (jockey said gelding moved poorly throughout)* **13/2**[2]

1m 55.91s (-4.89) **Going Correction** -0.30s/f (Stan) course record
WFA 3 from 4yo+ 3lb **13** Ran SP% **118.4**
Speed ratings (Par 107): **109,108,106,106,106 105,105,104,103,100 99,89,69**
CSF £196.70 CT £3005.79 TOTE £41.10: £8.70, £1.70, £5.00; EX 313.30 Trifecta £1176.90.
Owner Ambrose Turnbull **Bred** Victor Stud And Brendan Cummins **Trained** Great Habton, N Yorks

FOCUS
A few of those at single-figure odds disappointed, but this useful contest was run at a reasonable gallop, and the form should prove reliable.

9042 BETWAY APPRENTICE H'CAP 1m 4f 51y (Tp)
3:50 (3:50) (Class 6) (0-55,55) 3-Y-0+
£2,781 (£827; £413; £300; £300; £300) **Stalls** Low

Form RPR

0651 **1** **Foresee (GER)**[12] 8854 6-9-4 **52**.... SeanDavis 1 59
(Tony Carroll) *t.k.h: led: hdd after 1f: pushed along over 2f out: led over 1f out: rdn out ins fnl f* **7/1**[3]

-345 **2** 1 1/2 **Estrela Star (IRE)**[84] 6531 3-8-13 **55**....(b[1]) BenSanderson(3) 10 61
(Ali Stronge) *dwlt s: sn midfield: rdn and hdwy but racd wd fr over 2f out: kpt on ins fnl f: no match for wnr* **7/1**[3]

1542 **3** 2 **Royal Dancer**[10] 8916 3-9-0 **53**.... ThomasGreatrex 8 55
(Sylvester Kirk) *cl up: rdn and hdwy fr over 2f out: no imp ins fnl f* **4/1**[2]

2034 **4** *shd* **Yasir (USA)**[30] 8347 11-8-11 **52**.... KateLeahy(7) 6 53
(Sophie Leech) *s.i.s: towards rr: short of room 3f out: rdn and hdwy fr 2f out: kpt on (jockey said gelding was slowly away)* **11/1**

002/ **5** 1 3/4 **Ingleby Mackenzie**[21] 7671 5-9-1 **52**....(tp) ThoreHammerHansen(3) 3 50
(Eoin Doyle, Ire) *t.k.h: led after 1f: rdn over 2f out: hdd over 1f out: wknd ins fnl f* **11/4**[1]

02 **6** 1 **Cape Agulhas (IRE)**[12] 8877 5-9-0 **48**....(t) GabrieleMalune 2 45
(W J Martin, Ire) *t.k.h: midfield: short of room and hmpd 4f out: rdn over 2f out: no ex fr 1f out* **10/1**

0 **7** 3/4 **Ringo Kid**[28] 8406 6-8-11 **48**....(t) PaulaMuir(3) 7 44
(Mrs Olivia Byrne, Ire) *prom but abt three wd: pressed ldr over 2f out: rdn and wknd fr over 1f out* **16/1**

0500 **8** *hd* **Padura Brave**[19] 8667 3-8-13 **52**....(h[1]) WilliamCox 12 48
(Mark Usher) *towards rr: rdn and carried rt fr 3f out: racd wd home turn: wknd fr over 1f out* **33/1**

6006 **9** 3 3/4 **Airplane (IRE)**[19] 8670 4-8-10 **51**.... OliverStammers(7) 9 40
(Paul Collins) *towards rr of midfield: rdn and no rspnse fr 2f out* **40/1**

0005 **10** 2 1/2 **Raven's Raft (IRE)**[12] 8870 4-9-4 **52**....(p) JaneElliott 11 37
(David Loughnane) *towards rr: rdn over 4f out: no imp fr 3f out (jockey said filly stopped quickly)* **22/1**

0001 **11** *nk* **Bird To Love**[14] 8813 5-9-0 **55**....(p) IsobelFrancis(7) 5 40
(Mark Usher) *midfield: nt clr run fr over 2f out: swtchd rt over 1f out: no imp fr over 1f out (jockey said mare was denied a clear run for some distance approaching the home bend)* **8/1**

660/ **12** 10 **Marju's Quest (IRE)**[15] 8647 9-9-7 **55**.... FinleyMarsh 4 24
(Adrian Wintle) *prom: pushed along and wknd over 3f out (jockey said gelding stopped quickly)* **100/1**

2m 36.63s (-4.17) **Going Correction** -0.30s/f (Stan)
WFA 3 from 4yo+ 5lb **12** Ran SP% **116.8**
Speed ratings (Par 101): **101,100,98,98,97 96,96,96,93,91 91,85**
CSF £52.93 CT £224.41 TOTE £6.10: £2.00, £2.70, £1.70; EX 58.00 Trifecta £283.30.
Owner Millen & Cooke **Bred** Graf U Grafin V Stauffenberg **Trained** Cropthorne, Worcs

FOCUS
An ordinary handicap.
T/Jkpt: Not Won. T/Plt: £34.20 to a £1 stake. Pool: £76,058.45 - 1,621.50 winning units. T/Qpdt: £27.80 to a £1 stake. Pool: £7,187.70 - 190.86 winning units. **Raceform**

8912 CHELMSFORD (A.W) (L-H)
Tuesday, November 19

OFFICIAL GOING: Polytrack: standard
Wind: Virtually nil Weather: Overcast

9043 BET TOTEPLACEPOT AT TOTESPORT.COM NOVICE STKS 6f (P)
4:15 (4:16) (Class 5) 2-Y-0 **£4,204** (£1,251; £625; £312) **Stalls** Centre

Form RPR

5 **1** **Story Of Light (IRE)**[187] 2780 2-9-2 0....(h[1]) JamesDoyle 1 85+
(Charlie Appleby) *dwlt: settled in tch: pushed along to go 2nd appr fnl f: qcknd up wl to ld ins fnl f and sn in command* **8/11**[1]

34 **2** 2 3/4 **Irish Acclaim (IRE)**[134] 4734 2-9-2 0.... LiamKeniry 7 76
(Clive Cox) *racd in midfield: effrt to cl on ldrs over 1f out: rdn and kpt on wl fnl f: wnt 2nd fnl strides* **20/1**

3231 **3** *shd* **Asmund (IRE)**[15] 8816 2-9-6 83....(p) CliffordLee 4 80
(K R Burke) *led: rdn along w 1 l ld over 1f out: hdd by wnr ins fnl f: no ex whn lost 2nd fnl strides* **8/1**

0204 **4** 3/4 **Kuwait Direction (IRE)**[18] 8723 2-9-2 94.... RossaRyan 2 74
(Richard Hannon) *trckd ldrs: rdn and no imp over 1f out: kpt on one pce ins fnl f* **4/1**[2]

5 4 1/2 **Yukon Mission (IRE)** 2-8-11 0.... JasonHart 6 55
(John Quinn) *hld up: hdwy u.p 2f out: rdn over 1f out: no further imp fnl f* **33/1**

0 **6** *nk* **Motamayiz**[25] 8516 2-9-2 0.... DanielMuscutt 8 59
(Roger Varian) *racd in midfield: bmpd along 1/2-way: rdn and no imp over 1f out: wknd fnl f* **9/2**[3]

0210 **7** 2 3/4 **Lincoln Blue**[109] 5624 2-9-6 80.... TimClark(3) 12 58
(Jane Chapple-Hyam) *dwlt and racd in rr: rdn along over 2f out: nvr on terms (jockey said colt was restless in the stalls)* **50/1**

6 **8** *nk* **Boom Boom Boom**[36] 8202 2-9-2 0....(t) RichardKingscote 11 50
(Stuart Williams) *racd in midfield: rdn and no imp 2f out: wknd fnl f* **33/1**

0 **9** 1 1/4 **Casaruan**[11] 8912 2-8-13 0.... TheodoreLadd(3) 3 46
(Michael Appleby) *trckd ldr and racd keenly: rdn along and outpcd over 1f out: wknd fnl f* **100/1**

60 **10** 4 1/2 **Mackelly (IRE)**[28] 8418 2-9-2 0.... ShaneKelly 5 33
(Richard Hughes) *hld up: pushed along and no imp 2f out: nvr on terms* **66/1**

11 *nk* **Bank Holiday (IRE)** 2-8-8 0.... SeanDavis(3) 10 27
(Richard Fahey) *hld up: a bhd* **50/1**

1m 12.11s (-1.59) **Going Correction** -0.25s/f (Stan) **11** Ran SP% **124.2**
Speed ratings (Par 96): **100,96,96,95,89 88,85,84,83,77 76**
CSF £24.40 TOTE £1.50: £1.10, £4.50; EX 18.30 Trifecta £59.70.
Owner Godolphin **Bred** Godolphin **Trained** Newmarket, Suffolk

FOCUS
The track had been lightly decompacted and gallop master finished to two inches for raceday. The long-absent Godolphin-trained favourite answered most questions of him in this opening sprint novice.

9044 BET TOTEEXACTA AT TOTESPORT.COM NURSERY H'CAP 1m 2f (P)
4:45 (4:47) (Class 4) (0-85,80) 2-Y-0 **£4,948** (£1,472; £735; £400; £400) **Stalls** Low

Form RPR

063 **1** **Summeronsevenhills (USA)**[40] 8069 2-8-11 **70**....(b[1]) ShaneKelly 2 82+
(Richard Hughes) *settled wl in midfield: clsd into 2nd gng wl over 2f out: pushed along to ld over 1f: sn clr: easily* **11/8**[1]

2112 **2** 6 **She's A Unicorn**[13] 8856 2-9-5 **78**....(v) RichardKingscote 3 77
(Tom Dascombe) *hld up in last pair: pushed along and outpcd over 2f out: wd off home bnd: sn rdn and r.o to take remote 2nd cl home* **10/1**

1403 **3** 3/4 **Luna Wish**[19] 8699 2-8-5 **64**.... JoeFanning 1 62
(George Margarson) *led: rdn along and hdd by wnr over 1f out: wknd fnl f* **6/1**

0361 **4** 2 **Good Reason**[33] 8286 2-9-4 **80**.... GabrieleMalune(3) 5 74
(Saeed bin Suroor) *hld up: effrt on inner 2f out: sn rdn and no imp over 1f out: wknd fnl f* **3/1**[2]

5254 **5** 8 **Tantivy**[17] 8760 2-9-4 **77**.... JamesDoyle 4 56
(Richard Hannon) *t.k.h to post: trckd ldr: drvn along to hold position 3f out: wknd fr 2f out (trainer's rep said colt boiled over in the preliminaries)* **7/2**[3]

2m 5.53s (-3.07) **Going Correction** -0.25s/f (Stan) **5** Ran SP% **112.7**
Speed ratings (Par 98): **102,97,96,95,88**
CSF £15.66 TOTE £2.00: £1.30; EX 16.20 Trifecta £44.80.
Owner Frank Deely And John McGarry **Bred** George E Bates Trustee **Trained** Upper Lambourn, Berks

FOCUS
All very straightforward for the well-backed favourite in this small-field nursery.

9045 BET TOTEQUADPOT AT TOTESPORT.COM NURSERY H'CAP 1m (P)
5:15 (5:17) (Class 6) (0-60,62) 2-Y-0
£3,105 (£924; £461; £400; £400; £400) **Stalls** Low

Form RPR

5051 **1** **Bavardages (IRE)**[22] 8603 2-9-9 **62**.... JoeFanning 5 68
(Mark Johnston) *mde all: shkn up to extend advantage over 1f out: sn clr and in command fnl f: comf* **9/4**[1]

5036 **2** 3 1/4 **Halfacrown (IRE)**14 8824 2-8-7 **46** NickyMackay 3 45
(Jamie Osborne) *dwlt and racd in rr: pushed along and outpcd 2f out: rdn and hdwy over 1f out: styd on wl fnl f but no ch w wnr* **6/1**3

6532 **3** 1/2 **Chateau Peapod**14 8824 2-9-4 **57** (p) BrettDoyle 4 55
(Lydia Pearce) *trckd ldrs: rdn along to chse wnr over 1f out: sn one pce: lost 2nd cl home* **6/1**3

6543 **4** nse **Divine Connection**14 8824 2-9-4 **62** TylerSaunders(5) 10 60
(Jonathan Portman) *racd in midfield: effrt on outer over 2f out: sn rdn and hung lft over 1f out: kpt on wl fnl f but continued to hang lft* **7/1**

4505 **5** 1 3/4 **Sea Of Cool (IRE)**13 8856 2-8-8 **50** (p) DarraghKeenan(3) 12 44
(John Ryan) *prom on outer: rdn along to chse ldrs over 1f out: kpt on one pce fnl f* **16/1**

0040 **6** 1 **Prairie Moppins (USA)**14 8824 2-9-0 **56** ThomasGreatrex(3) 1 47
(Sylvester Kirk) *racd in midfield: rdn and no immediate imp 2f out: kpt on one pce fr over 1f out* **14/1**

6406 **7** 3/4 **Boy George**45 7910 2-9-2 **55** LiamKeniry 7 45
(Dominic Ffrench Davis) *racd in midfield: niggled along 3f out: rdn and unable qck over 1f out: gng bkwards whn hmpd fnl f: nt rcvr* **14/1**

3230 **8** 1 **Rochford (IRE)**17 8760 2-9-7 **60** (p) RichardKingscote 8 47
(Henry Spiller) *trckd wnr: rdn and outpcd 2f out: sn drvn and lost pl over 1f out: no ex* **4/1**2

0600 **9** 1 1/2 **Sooty's Return (IRE)**57 7516 2-8-6 **45** TheodoreLadd 6 29
(J S Moore) *hld up: hdwy u.p over 1f out: plugged on but n.d (jockey said gelding hung left-handed throughout)* **50/1**

0600 **10** 1/2 **Loco Dempsey (FR)**27 8452 2-8-8 **52** ThoreHammerHansen(5) 2 35
(Richard Hannon) *dwlt and racd in rr: nvr on terms (jockey said filly was never travelling)* **14/1**

0050 **11** 2 1/4 **Loretta Lass**22 8603 2-8-7 **46** LiamJones 9 24
(Adam West) *dwlt and racd in rr: a bhd (jockey said filly was slowly away)* **50/1**

6060 **12** 3 1/4 **Dark Side Division**45 7910 2-8-2 **48** (p) LauraPearson(7) 13 18
(John Ryan) *racd in midfield: rdn along and outpcd over 2f out: sn bhd* **33/1**

1m 39.62s (-0.28) **Going Correction** -0.25s/f (Stan) **12 Ran SP% 124.6**
Speed ratings (Par 94): **91,87,87,87,85 84,83,82,81,80 78,75**
CSF £16.68 CT £75.44 TOTE £2.70: £1.20, £2.40, £1.90; EX 17.80 Trifecta £98.30.
Owner Kingsley Park 11 **Bred** Knocktoran Stud **Trained** Middleham Moor, N Yorks
■ Stewards' Enquiry : Tyler Saunders two-day ban: interference & careless riding (Dec 3-4)

FOCUS
A moderate mile nursery, and the winner looks far too good for this grade now.

9046 BET TOTETRIFECTA AT TOTESPORT.COM EBF FILLIES' NOVICE STKS (PLUS 10 RACE) 1m (P)
5:45 (5:49) (Class 3) 2-Y-O
£9,055 (£2,694; £1,346; £673) **Stalls Low**

Form RPR

1 **Fantail** 2-9-0 0 JoeFanning 8 80
(Simon Crisford) *mde all: shkn up over 1f out: rdn ent fnl f and sn asserted: cosily* **25/1**

04 **2** 2 1/2 **Island Hideaway**27 8454 2-9-0 0 LiamKeniry 5 74
(David Lanigan) *trckd wnr: rdn along to chal over 1f out: drvn and unable to match wnr fnl f* **20/1**

2 **3** 1 3/4 **Rideson**47 7832 2-9-0 0 KieranShoemark 3 70+
(Roger Varian) *midfield in tch: effrt amongst rivals over 1f out: sn rdn and kpt on fnl f: too much to do* **4/7**1

4 1 1/4 **Assayer (IRE)** 2-8-11 0 SeanDavis(3) 1 67
(Richard Fahey) *trckd ldrs: pushed along and outpcd 2f out: rdn and no imp on ldng pair over 1f out: kpt on one pce fnl f* **20/1**

5 2 1/4 **Wannabe Betsy (IRE)** 2-8-11 0 ThomasGreatrex(3) 7 62
(William Jarvis) *racd in midfield: rdn and minor hdwy over 1f out: kpt on fnl f* **66/1**

6 nk **Agreed** 2-9-0 0 NickyMackay 9 61+
(John Gosden) *towards rr of midfield: effrt whn n.m.r 2f out: rdn and no imp over 1f out: kpt on under hands and heels fnl f* **14/1**

7 3/4 **Lisbet** 2-9-0 0 (h1) ShaneKelly 4 60+
(John Gosden) *hld up: rdn and prog over 1f out: kpt on fnl f but n.d* **12/1**3

8 1/2 **Marcela De Vega** 2-9-0 0 RichardKingscote 12 60
(Ralph Beckett) *dwlt and racd in rr: hdwy whn short of room over 1f out: swtchd rt and rdn 1f out: nvr able to land a blow* **9/2**2

5 **9** 1/2 **Flower Of Thunder (IRE)**22 8602 2-9-0 0 RossaRyan 11 57
(Richard Hannon) *trckd wnr: pushed along and lost pl over 2f out: rdn and no imp over 1f out: wknd fnl f* **33/1**

10 nk **Surprise Encounter** 2-8-9 0 DylanHogan(5) 14 57
(David Simcock) *midfield on outer: rdn along and no imp over 1f out: one pce fnl f* **50/1**

40 **11** 1/2 **Reehaam**12 8889 2-9-0 0 DanielMuscutt 15 56
(John Gosden) *prom and keen early: pushed along 2f out: sn rdn and no imp over 1f out: one pce fnl f* **50/1**

0 **12** 1 3/4 **Cheese And Wine**27 8458 2-9-0 0 GeorgeWood 16 52
(Chris Wall) *midfield on outer: effrt whn short of room over 1f out: sn rdn and no imp 1f out: no ex* **50/1**

2 **13** 6 **Magic Dust**34 8258 2-8-7 0 StefanoCherchi(7) 10 38
(Marco Botti) *prom on outer and keen early: rdn along and lost pl 2f out: consistently hung lft over 1f out: wknd fnl f* **12/1**3

4 **14** 5 **Out For A Duck**21 8640 2-8-11 0 TheodoreLadd(3) 2 26
(Michael Appleby) *hld up: wd in rr off 3f out: a bhd (jockey said filly did not face the kickback on this occasion)* **25/1**

1m 38.53s (-1.37) **Going Correction** -0.25s/f (Stan) **14 Ran SP% 131.4**
Speed ratings (Par 97): **96,93,91,90,88 87,87,86,86,85 85,83,77,72**
CSF £447.91 TOTE £55.30: £8.20, £4.30, £1.10; EX 1536.20 Trifecta £3594.20.
Owner Highclere T'Bred Racing - Claire Lomas **Bred** The Hon R J Arculli **Trained** Newmarket, Suffolk

FOCUS
The evening's feature, and a winning time over 1.1 seconds quicker than the preceding Class 6 nursery.

9047 BET TOTESWINGER AT TOTESPORT.COM H'CAP 1m (P)
6:15 (6:18) (Class 5) (0-70,70) 3-Y-O+
£5,110 (£1,520; £759; £400; £400; £400) **Stalls Low**

Form RPR

4306 **1** **Swiss Cheer (FR)**26 8495 3-9-4 **69** (h) RobHornby 5 84+
(Jonathan Portman) *hld up and travelled strly: c wd off home bnd and effrt to cl: gd prog but hung lft over 1f out: sn rdn along to ld ins fnl f: won gng away* **12/1**

0635 **2** 2 1/2 **Squelch**36 8206 3-9-5 **70** ShaneKelly 8 77
(Rae Guest) *trckd ldr: rdn along to chal over 1f out: kpt on wl fnl f but no match for wnr clsng stages* **14/1**

2114 **3** nk **Colonel Slade (IRE)**15 8807 3-9-2 **67** (tp) BenCurtis 11 73
(Phillip Makin) *led after 1f: rdn along and strly pressed by rival over 1f out: drvn and hdd by wnr ins fnl f: lost 2nd clsng stages* **7/2**1

4440 **4** 3 **Bint Dandy (IRE)**34 8254 8-9-3 **66** (b) RichardKingscote 3 66
(Charlie Wallis) *trckd ldng pair: rdn and no imp over 1f out: one pce fnl f* **20/1**

5542 **5** 1/2 **Crimewave (IRE)**20 8652 3-9-1 **69** (p) SeanDavis(3) 14 67
(Tom Clover) *in rr of midfield: bmpd along 1/2-way: hdwy u.p over 1f out: rdn and kpt on wl fnl f but n.d* **12/1**

500 **6** 1/2 **Entertaining (IRE)**20 8652 3-9-1 **66** (b1) RossaRyan 1 63
(Richard Hannon) *midfield on inner: drvn along 2f out: minor hdwy over 1f out: kpt on one pce fnl f* **16/1**

0462 **7** 1 **Undercolours (IRE)**80 6733 3-8-11 **69** StefanoCherchi(7) 7 64
(Marco Botti) *racd in midfield on inner: lost pl 2f out: rdn along and minor hdwy 1f out: kpt on* **18/1**

6041 **8** 1 **Beepeecee**19 8711 5-9-1 **67** (b) DarraghKeenan(3) 2 61
(Thomas Gallagher) *racd in midfield: short of room and clipped heels after 2f: stl gng ok 2f out: sn rdn and minor hdwy over 1f out: wknd fnl f* **9/1**

1311 **9** 1 **Zefferino**26 8499 5-9-7 **70** (t) GeorgeWood 12 61
(Martin Bosley) *dwlt: racd in rr: nvr on terms (jockey said gelding was slowly away)* **5/1**3

2100 **10** 1 **Global Wonder (IRE)**20 1065 4-9-5 **68** DougieCostello 9 57
(Suzi Best) *hld up: nvr on terms (jockey said gelding was slowly away)* **50/1**

0042 **11** 3/4 **John Clare (IRE)**24 8549 3-9-5 **70** LukeMorris 4 56
(Pam Sly) *racd in midfield and v keen early: rdn along and no imp 2f out: wknd over 1f out (jockey said gelding ran too freely)* **9/2**2

1160 **12** 2 **Lagenda**36 8186 6-9-0 **63** JasonHart 13 46
(Liam Bailey) *racd in midfield in tch: rdn along 2f out: wknd fr over 1f out* **33/1**

2600 **13** 3/4 **Chosen World**17 8766 5-9-7 **70** CallumRodriguez 15 51
(Julie Camacho) *restrained and racd in rr: nvr on terms* **11/1**

35-0 **14** 1 **Flaunt It (IRE)**36 8206 3-8-7 **63** RayDawson(5) 6 41
(Jane Chapple-Hyam) *led for 1f then trckd ldrs: rdn along and lost pl over 1f out: sn bhd* **25/1**

1222 **15** 5 **Espresso Freddo (IRE)**17 8761 5-9-7 **70** (v) KieranShoemark 10 37
(Robert Stephens) *racd in midfield: rdn and no imp 2f out: wknd over 1f out* **12/1**

1m 36.96s (-2.94) **Going Correction** -0.25s/f (Stan)
WFA 3 from 4yo+ 2lb **15 Ran SP% 129.8**
Speed ratings (Par 103): **104,101,101,98,97 97,96,95,94,93 92,90,89,88,83**
CSF £175.44 CT £743.84 TOTE £12.30: £4.10, £5.70, £1.80; EX 217.20 Trifecta £2130.00.
Owner Whitcoombe Park Racing **Bred** Mme Heather Murat & Mr Sebastien Murat **Trained** Upper Lambourn, Berks
■ Stewards' Enquiry : Ben Curtis five-day ban: interference & careless riding (Dec 3-7)

FOCUS
Just a fair to middling handicap, but much the quickest of the three 1m events on the card.

9048 BET TOTESCOOP6 AT TOTESPORT.COM H'CAP 7f (P)
6:45 (6:48) (Class 5) (0-75,75) 3-Y-O+
£5,110 (£1,520; £759; £400; £400; £400) **Stalls Low**

Form RPR

4000 **1** **Strawberry Jack**103 5839 3-9-6 **75** (vt) BenCurtis 6 86
(George Scott) *hmpd s and racd in rr: hdwy between rivals 2f out: rdn along and gd hdwy to ld ent fnl f: drvn out* **20/1**

6004 **2** 2 **Glory Of Paris (IRE)**14 8827 5-8-13 **72** (p) MarkCrehan(5) 2 79
(Michael Appleby) *midfield on inner: effrt to cl over 1f out: rdn and wnt 2nd ent fnl f: nt match wnr clsng stages* **6/1**2

4605 **3** 1 1/2 **Al Asef**26 8496 4-8-12 **71** DylanHogan(5) 8 74
(David Simcock) *in rr of midfield and racd freely: hdwy u.p over 1f out: rdn and kpt on wl to go 3rd ins fnl f: no ch w wnr* **12/1**

0441 **4** 1 **Knowing Glance (IRE)**98 6037 4-8-12 **69** (h) SeanDavis(3) 14 69
(Richard Fahey) *trckd ldr: rdn along and outpcd over 1f out: swtchd rt off heels 1f out: kpt on again fnl f* **16/1**

0602 **5** 3/4 **Broughtons Flare (IRE)**26 8496 3-8-13 **68** JoeFanning 4 65
(Philip McBride) *racd in midfield: effrt to cl on ldrs 2f out: carried wd off bnd: sn rdn and no imp over 1f out: kpt on (jockey said gelding hung left-handed)* **11/4**1

1351 **6** 3/4 **Captain Dion**31 8339 6-9-4 **75** (b) GabrieleMalune(3) 10 71
(Ivan Furtado) *led: rdn along and hdd ent fnl f: wknd clsng stages* **9/1**

1454 **7** 1/2 **Daring Venture (IRE)**19 8702 3-9-4 **73** (h1) RossaRyan 12 66
(Roger Varian) *midfield in tch: pushed along 2f out: sn rdn and carried rt by rival appr fnl f: one pce after* **6/1**2

4061 **8** nk **Born To Finish (IRE)**17 8755 6-8-11 **68** (p) ThomasGreatrex(3) 9 62
(Ed de Giles) *s.i.s: pushed along in rr 3f out: rdn and sme minor hdwy fnl f* **10/1**

4401 **9** 1 1/4 **Secondo (FR)**36 8199 9-8-13 **67** (v) RichardKingscote 3 57
(Robert Stephens) *racd in midfield: rdn in rr and wl off pce 2f out: sme late hdwy fnl f* **12/1**

2126 **10** 4 **Sonnet Rose (IRE)**19 8711 5-8-10 **64** (bt) NickyMackay 15 43
(Conrad Allen) *midfield: effrt on outer 3f out: sn rdn and no imp over 1f out: wknd fnl f (jockey said mare had no more to give)* **16/1**

0415 **11** 1/2 **Redemptive**34 8254 3-8-11 **66** (p1) LukeMorris 11 43
(John Butler) *trckd ldrs on inner: rdn and outpcd 2f out: wknd over 1f out* **25/1**

1000 **12** 4 1/2 **Forseti**28 8420 3-9-0 **72** (h) TheodoreLadd(3) 5 37
(Michael Appleby) *snatched up leaving stalls and sn wl bhd: nvr on terms (jockey said gelding hung right-handed)* **25/1**

0150 **13** 2 3/4 **Blessed To Empress (IRE)**33 8291 4-8-12 **66** NicolaCurrie 1 25
(Amy Murphy) *s.i.s: pushed along and lost pl early: nvr on terms (jockey said filly was never travelling)* **25/1**

3620 **U** **Fighting Temeraire (IRE)**35 8221 6-9-6 **74** AdamKirby 7
(Dean Ivory) *stmbld leaving stalls and uns rdr* **8/1**3

1m 24.78s (-2.42) **Going Correction** -0.25s/f (Stan)
WFA 3 from 4yo+ 1lb **14 Ran SP% 128.9**
Speed ratings (Par 103): **103,100,99,97,97 96,95,95,93,89 88,83,80,**
CSF £139.54 CT £1571.66 TOTE £30.70: £7.50, £2.30, £4.70; EX 153.80 Trifecta £2002.70.
Owner Jack Stephenson **Bred** Whitsbury Manor Stud **Trained** Newmarket, Suffolk

The Form Book Flat 2019, Raceform Ltd, Newbury, RG14 5SJ

FOCUS
A modest but well-stocked 7f event, in which the winner arguably rates value for further.

9049 CHRISTMAS PARTY NIGHTS H'CAP 1m 6f (P)
7:15 (7:16) (Class 6) (0-65,66) 3-Y-O+
£3,105 (£924; £461; £400; £400; £400) Stalls Low

Form				RPR
1244	1		**Affluence (IRE)**[20] 8196 4-10-1 66 ....(p) HectorCrouch 7 (Martin Smith) *hld up: clsd on ldrs gng wl 2f out waited for gap to appear between rivals over 1f out: sn rdn and qcknd up to ld ins fnl f: rdn out* 5/2[1]	71
3501	2	¾	**Homesick Boy (IRE)**[24] 8551 3-9-1 58 ....(v) JasonWatson 6 (Ed Dunlop) *t.k.h in midfield: hdwy on inner 3f out: effrt to cl whn short of room over 1f out: sn swtchd lft and rdn to chal 1f out: kpt on but readily outpcd by wnr fnl f (jockey said gelding ran too freely)* 4/1[2]	65
0-02	3	1 ¼	**Que Quieres (USA)**[33] 8292 3-8-5 48 .... LukeMorris 9 (Simon Dow) *hld up: waited for gap to appear on inner 2f out: rdn along whn briefly short of room 1f out: kpt on fnl f* 12/1	52
5635	4	nk	**Bill Cody (IRE)**[27] 8468 4-9-7 58 .... CallumRodriguez 1 (Julie Camacho) *led at a stdy pce: shkn up w short ld over 1f out: rdn along and hdd by wnr ins fnl f: wknd clsng stages* 5/1[3]	60
5333	5	¾	**Ignatius (IRE)**[24] 8551 3-8-8 51 .... JoeyHaynes 8 (John Best) *midfield in tch: effrt on outer to cl 2f out: rdn along to chal and ev ch appr fnl f: no ex clsng stages* 5/1[3]	54
1166	6	nk	**Extreme Appeal (IRE)**[14] 8828 7-9-0 58 ....(v) LauraPearson(7) 11 (Kelly Morgan) *hld up on outer: pushed along on outer 2f out: sn rdn and kpt on one pce fr over 1f out* 20/1	59
2300	7	nse	**Sea Of Mystery (IRE)**[31] 8341 6-9-7 63 ....(t) MarkCrehan(5) 5 (Michael Appleby) *midfield: drvn along and outpcd 3f out: kpt on one pce fr over 1f out* 14/1	64
1630	8	nk	**Heron (USA)**[40] 8065 5-10-0 65 ....(p) DanielMuscutt 2 (Brett Johnson) *trckd ldrs: pushed along and no imp over 1f out: rdn whn denied clr run 1f out: one pce after* 8/1	65
3500	9	1 ¾	**Konigin**[31] 8347 4-9-6 57 ....(tp) NicolaCurrie 10 (John Berry) *trckd ldr: shkn up to chal 2f out: sn rdn and lost pl 1f out: no ex* 16/1	55
0126	10	10	**Olaf**[45] 7909 3-8-10 53 ....(b[1]) BenCurtis 4 (George Boughey) *in rr of midfield: rdn along and lost pl over 1f out: sn bhd* 16/1	40

3m 2.05s (-1.15) **Going Correction** -0.25s/f (Stan)
WFA 3 from 4yo+ 6lb 10 Ran SP% 123.9
Speed ratings (Par 101): **93,92,91,91,91 91,91,90,89,84**
CSF £13.23 CT £106.38 TOTE £2.90: £1.40, £1.60, £3.50; EX 12.60 Trifecta £115.60.
Owner The Affluence Partnership **Bred** Mrs Michelle Smith **Trained** Newmarket, Suffolk

FOCUS
No pace on at all until after halfway, such that most still held chances 2f out.

9050 CELEBRATE NOVEMBER'S HERO RICHARD SHEPHERD H'CAP 1m 2f (P)
7:45 (7:50) (Class 4) (0-80,82) 3-Y-O+
£5,530 (£1,645; £822; £411; £400; £400) Stalls Low

Form				RPR
6602	1		**Wimpole Hall**[20] 8656 6-8-11 74 ....(p) GaiaBoni(7) 4 (William Jarvis) *midfield on inner: hdwy to chse ldrs 2f out: swtchd lft between rivals and rdn to ld ent fnl f: kpt on wl* 20/1	82
3120	2	¾	**Torochica**[45] 7895 3-9-7 80 .... KierenFox 9 (John Best) *hld up: hdwy on inner over 1f out: rdn and styd on strly fnl f: nt rch wnr* 12/1	86
0022	3	shd	**Amjaady (USA)**[19] 8692 3-9-7 80 ....(v[1]) AdamKirby 2 (David O'Meara) *led: rdn along and hdd ent fnl f: no ex clsng stages* 4/1[2]	86
51-5	4	shd	**Eden Gardens (IRE)**[22] 8606 3-9-9 82 .... JoeFanning 6 (Simon Crisford) *trckd ldr: rdn along to chal over 1f out: ev ch whn one pce fnl f* 7/2[1]	88
-506	5	¾	**Keswick**[20] 8658 5-8-13 76 ....(t) EllieMacKenzie(7) 3 (Heather Main) *racd in midfield: hdwy u.p over 1f out: rdn along to chal ent fnl f: one pce fnl f (jockey said gelding ran too freely)* 25/1	80
1-40	6	¾	**Lady Adelaide (IRE)**[25] 8519 3-9-7 80 ....(t[1]) JasonWatson 8 (Roger Charlton) *hld up: effrt to cl over 1f out: sn rdn and no imp fnl f* 14/1	83
6510	7	shd	**First Response**[11] 8918 4-9-7 77 ....(t) TomEaves 12 (Linda Stubbs) *hld up: pushed along to cl on ldrs over 1f out: sn rdn and no imp fnl f* 16/1	80
04	8	½	**Andaleep (IRE)**[20] 8652 3-8-5 67 .... TheodoreLadd(3) 7 (Graeme McPherson) *trckd ldr: rdn along and unable qck over 1f out: drvn and hung lft 1f out: one pce after* 12/1	69
3652	9	1	**Gallatin**[47] 7835 3-8-10 69 .... NicolaCurrie 5 (Andrew Balding) *racd in rr: rdn and minor hdwy over 1f out: nvr on terms* 10/1	69
4345	10	nk	**Rotherwick (IRE)**[18] 8727 7-9-4 77 ....(b) SeanDavis(3) 1 (Paul Cole) *trckd ldrs early: rdn along and lost pl 2f out: sn bhd (vet said gelding was struck into behind)* 20/1	76
2050	11	¾	**Mordred (IRE)**[18] 8725 3-9-3 81 ....(h[1]) ThoreHammerHansen(5) 10 (Richard Hannon) *racd in midfield in tch: effrt to cl on ldrs over 1f out: sn rdn and no imp fnl f* 8/1	79
4003	12	2 ½	**Double Reflection**[41] 8027 4-9-0 70 .... LukeMorris 11 (Michael Appleby) *racd in midfield: rdn and lost pl over 1f out: wknd fnl f (vet said filly finished with a wound on its left hind fetlock)* 25/1	63
0623	13	4	**Lunar Deity**[77] 6844 10-8-9 72 .... GraceMcEntee(7) 14 (Stuart Williams) *hld up: a in rr* 50/1	57
2312	14	2	**Maximum Effect**[15] 8812 3-9-7 80 .... NickyMackay 13 (John Gosden) *prom: effrt to go cl on outer after 2f: rdn along and lost pl over 1f out: sn bhd (trainer's rep said the jockey had to make too much use of the filly early from a wide draw)* 9/2[3]	61

2m 4.38s (-4.22) **Going Correction** -0.25s/f (Stan)
WFA 3 from 4yo+ 3lb 14 Ran SP% 127.7
Speed ratings (Par 105): **106,105,105,105,104 104,103,103,102,102 101,99,96,95**
CSF £242.45 CT £1179.30 TOTE £27.70: £5.80, £4.00, £1.70; EX 362.30 Trifecta £2331.50.
Owner William Jarvis **Bred** R F And S D Knipe **Trained** Newmarket, Suffolk

FOCUS
This appeared to be fairly generously run, but, as with the preceding contest, there were any number still holding chances turning in.
T/Plt: £88.20 to a £1 stake. Pool: £64,582.88 - 534.25 winning units T/Qpdt: £27.40 to a £1 stake. Pool: £10,673.37 - 287.44 winning units **Mark Grantham**

8847

KEMPTON (A.W) (R-H)
Tuesday, November 19

OFFICIAL GOING: Polytrack: standard to slow

9051 MATCHBOOK BEST VALUE EXCHANGE NOVICE STKS 1m 3f 219y(P)
1:20 (1:21) (Class 5) 3-Y-O+
£3,881 (£1,155; £577; £288) Stalls Low

Form				RPR
21	1		**Dubai Future**[120] 5254 3-9-9 0 .... CallumShepherd 1 (Saeed bin Suroor) *travelled strly: cl up on inner: led 2f out: wnt wl clr over 1f out: eased towards fin: comf* 1/1[1]	99+
60	2	4	**Ela Katrina**[136] 4641 3-8-11 0 .... KieranShoemark 2 (Roger Varian) *midfield on inner: hdwy fr 3f out: rdn over 1f out: kpt on (jockey said his saddle slipped)* 25/1	78
12-	3	½	**Beauvais (IRE)**[513] 4157 4-10-0 0 .... GeorgeWood 6 (Saeed bin Suroor) *cl up on outer: outpcd 3f out: rdn over 1f out: no ex fnl 110yds* 5/1[3]	90
0344	4	10	**King Power**[29] 8398 3-8-11 74 .... RobHornby 8 (Andrew Balding) *prom on outer: rdn 4f out: swtchd rt and no imp 2f out: wknd ins fnl f* 12/1	62
22	5	11	**Casual Reply**[26] 8500 3-8-11 0 .... JasonWatson 5 (Roger Charlton) *sn led: rdn under 3f out: hdd 2f out: wknd qckly over 1f out (jockey said filly stopped quickly)* 2/1[2]	44
0	6	9	**Tinkerbird**[27] 8451 3-9-2 0 .... JoeyHaynes 4 (Eugene Stanford) *stdd s: hld up in rr: reminder early: rdn 3f out: fnd little and wknd fr 2f out (jockey said colt hung left-handed throughout)* 150/1	35
0-0	7	1 ¾	**Border Warrior**[27] 8451 3-9-2 0 .... CharlesBishop 3 (Henry Candy) *rn in snatches: in rr: outpcd and no rspnse 3f out: wknd over 2f out (jockey said gelding was never travelling)* 100/1	32

2m 32.51s (-1.99) **Going Correction** +0.025s/f (Slow)
WFA 3 from 4yo 5lb 7 Ran SP% 113.2
Speed ratings (Par 103): **107,104,104,97,90 84,82**
CSF £26.35 TOTE £1.60: £1.40, £5.70; EX 26.90 Trifecta £82.80.
Owner Godolphin **Bred** Godolphin **Trained** Newmarket, Suffolk

FOCUS
This looked interesting on paper and there was a fair enough pace on, but the winner proved a class apart.

9052 BRITISH EBF MATCHBOOK FUTURE STAYERS NOVICE STKS (PLUS 10 RACE) (SIRE AND DAM RESTRICTED RACE) 1m (P)
1:50 (1:59) (Class 4) 2-Y-O
£10,350 (£3,080; £1,539; £769) Stalls Low

Form				RPR
3	1		**Hukum (IRE)**[59] 7453 2-9-2 0 .... JimCrowley 3 (Owen Burrows) *midfield: short of room over 4f out: pushed along and hdwy fr 3f out: kpt on strly fr 2f out: led towards fin* 11/4[2]	83
1	2	1	**Laser Show (IRE)**[137] 4611 2-9-9 0 .... HectorCrouch 5 (Saeed bin Suroor) *trckd ldr: pushed along and led 2f out: hdd towards fin* 6/4[1]	88
34	3	4 ½	**Lord Neidin**[27] 8455 2-9-2 0 .... TomQueally 11 (Alan King) *led after 1f: hdd 2f out: rdn and wknd over 1f out* 25/1	71
	4	4 ½	**Pyramid Place (IRE)** 2-9-2 0 .... TomMarquand 4 (John Gosden) *in rr: pushed along over 3f out: hdwy fr 2f out: kpt on: nrst fin* 16/1	60+
0	5	½	**Aljalela (FR)**[35] 8218 2-8-11 0 .... RossaRyan 7 (Richard Hannon) *chsd ldrs: rdn 1/2-way: no ex fr over 1f out* 40/1	54
2	6	¾	**Book Review**[13] 8858 2-9-2 0 .... KieranShoemark 8 (John Gosden) *towards rr: pushed along 3f out: rdn and hdwy fr over 2f out: nt clr run ins fnl f: kpt on (jockey said colt was slowly away)* 3/1[3]	58
5	7	nse	**Lady Magda**[20] 8651 2-8-11 0 .... HollieDoyle 14 (Jonathan Portman) *towards rr: nt clr run over 3f out: rdn over 2f out: kpt on fr over 1f out* 50/1	52
0	8	½	**Deposit (IRE)**[14] 8823 2-9-2 0 .... LukeMorris 9 (David Simcock) *midfield: pushed along over 2f out: no imp fr 1f out* 66/1	56
0	9	1 ¼	**Approximate**[25] 8510 2-8-11 0 .... CallumShepherd 6 (Michael Bell) *t.k.h: midfield: pushed along over 2f out: wknd fr over 1f out* 66/1	48
	10	1	**Billhilly (GER)** 2-9-2 0 .... CharlesBishop 12 (Eve Johnson Houghton) *t.k.h: chsd ldrs: rdn over 2f out: wknd over 1f out* 66/1	51
	11	½	**Cozone** 2-9-2 0 .... JasonWatson 13 (Amanda Perrett) *midfield: sme hdwy fr 4f out: rdn over 2f out: wknd over 1f out* 16/1	50
	12	4 ½	**Stagiaire** 2-8-11 0 .... RobHornby 2 (Ralph Beckett) *cl up but cajoled along: pushed along and wknd fr over 4f out* 33/1	34
	13	2 ¾	**Rodrigo Diaz** 2-9-2 0 .... StevieDonohoe 10 (David Simcock) *towards rr: pushed along over 3f out: mde no imp* 100/1	33
	14	69	**Gloriano (IRE)** 2-9-2 0 .... GeorgeWood 1 (Paul Webber) *slowly away: plld hrd: swtchd lft and racd wd: wnt 2nd after 3f: rdn and outpcd whn hung lft 4f out: wkng whn hung bdly lft 3f out: sn lost tch: t.o (jockey said colt ran too free)* 100/1	

1m 39.33s (-0.47) **Going Correction** +0.025s/f (Slow) 14 Ran SP% 121.1
Speed ratings (Par 98): **103,102,97,93,92 91,91,91,89,88 88,83,81,12**
CSF £6.92 TOTE £3.00: £1.10, £1.20, £4.90; EX 8.00 Trifecta £73.60.
Owner Hamdan Al Maktoum **Bred** Shadwell Estate Company Limited **Trained** Lambourn, Berks

FOCUS
A good performance from the winner to run down the favourite.

9053 MATCHBOOK BETTING PODCAST H'CAP 1m (P)
2:20 (2:29) (Class 3) (0-95,95) 3-Y-O+
£9,337 (£2,796; £1,398; £699; £349; £175) Stalls Low

Form				RPR
111/	1		**Entangling (IRE)**[727] 8893 5-9-2 85 .... WilliamCarson 4 (David Elsworth) *midfield: gd hdwy over 2f out: mde str chal fnl f: led towards fin: all out* 50/1	95
0411	2	½	**Bear Force One**[59] 7460 3-9-5 90 .... JasonWatson 10 (Roger Teal) *s.i.s: trckd ldrs after 1f: rdn but hdwy 2f out: led over 1f out: hdd towards fin: jst hld* 6/1[3]	98
0006	3	1 ¼	**Glendevon (USA)**[76] 6861 4-8-9 85 .... AngusVilliers(7) 8 (Richard Hughes) *t.k.h: cl up: niggled along 3f out: rdn 2f out: hdwy over 1f out: kpt on* 11/1	91

1132 **4** *nk* **Montatham**[36] 8184 3-9-4 **89**.......... JimCrowley 1 93
(William Haggas) *midfield: hdwy over 2f out: rdn and outpcd over 1f out: kpt on wl fnl 110yds* **9/4**[1]

1114 **5** *1* **Ouzo**[18] 8728 3-9-6 **91**.......... TomMarquand 9 93
(Richard Hannon) *cl up on outer: led 4f out: nudged along 2f out: hdd over 1f out: wknd fnl 110yds* **7/2**[2]

4602 **6** *1/2* **Samphire Coast**[15] 8809 6-8-9 **78**.......... (v) LukeMorris 3 80
(Derek Shaw) *awkward s: midfield after 1f: sme hdwy on inner over 2f out: rdn over 1f out: styd on: nvr able to chal* **33/1**

3054 **7** *3/4* **Glenn Coco**[59] 7462 5-9-6 **89**.......... (t) CallumRodriguez 6 89
(Stuart Williams) *prom on inner: rdn 2f out: no ex fr 1f out* **16/1**

1202 **8** *3/4* **Pinnata (IRE)**[40] 8062 5-9-12 **95**.......... (t) RobHornby 14 93
(Stuart Williams) *stdd s: hdwy on outer 4f out: rdn over 2f out: kpt on ins fnl f: nvr able to chal* **12/1**

0166 **9** *1 1/2* **Young Fire (FR)**[39] 8096 4-9-5 **88**.......... RossaRyan 5 83
(David O'Meara) *hld up in midfield: niggled along 3f out: minor hdwy 2f out: rdn over 1f out: no ex fnl 110yds* **8/1**

6000 **10** *1/2* **Golden Wolf (IRE)**[34] 8253 5-8-9 **78**.......... BrettDoyle 2 72
(Tony Carroll) *s.i.s: hld up in rr: outpcd 2f out: styng on ins fnl f: nvr able to chal* **100/1**

0P00 **11** *nk* **Humbert (IRE)**[18] 8728 5-9-9 **92**.......... (p) AdamKirby 7 85
(David O'Meara) *sn led: hdd 4f out: rdn over 2f out: wknd fr 1f out* **20/1**

1500 **12** *2* **Gentle Look**[41] 8016 3-9-2 **87**.......... CallumShepherd 11 75
(Saeed bin Suroor) *hld up in rr: outpcd 3f out: rdn 2f out: no ex fr over 1f out: wknd fnl 110yds* **25/1**

2520 **13** *1/2* **Masked Identity**[77] 6841 4-8-6 **82**.......... GavinAshton(7) 12 69
(Shaun Keightley) *hld up in rr: rdn and no imp fr over 2f out* **50/1**

410- **14** *11* **Bobby Wheeler (IRE)**[634] 858 6-8-12 **88**.......... ImogenCarter(7) 13 50
(Clive Cox) *prom: rdn and wknd qckly fr over 3f out* **66/1**

1m 37.77s (-2.03) **Going Correction** +0.025s/f (Slow)
WFA 3 from 4yo+ 2lb **14** Ran SP% **118.2**
Speed ratings (Par 107): **111,110,109,108,107 107,106,105,104,103 103,101,101,90**
CSF £315.45 CT £3671.17 TOTE £63.60: £13.00, £2.30, £3.40; EX 561.40 Trifecta £3459.50.
Owner Ben CM Wong **Bred** Sweetmans Bloodstock **Trained** Newmarket, Suffolk

FOCUS
There was a ten minute delay to this good-quality handicap. The first pair came clear late on.

9054 MATCHBOOK TIME TO MOVE OVER H'CAP 7f (P)
2:50 (2:57) (Class 4) (0-80,79) 3-Y-0+
£6,469 (£1,925; £962; £481; £300; £300) **Stalls Low**

Form RPR

6400 **1** **Stringybark Creek**[25] 8515 5-9-1 **72**.......... HollieDoyle 11 80
(David Loughnane) *mde all: rdn over 1f out: kpt on wl (trainer said, regarding the improved form shown, the gelding benefitted from stronger handling on this occasion)* **25/1**

4311 **2** *1/2* **Kwela**[27] 8456 3-9-2 **79**.......... (p) GeorgiaDobie(5) 7 85
(Eve Johnson Houghton) *t.k.h: midfield: rdn and hdwy fr 2f out: wnt 2nd ins fnl f: styd on towards fin* **13/2**[3]

5200 **3** *1/2* **Haddaf (IRE)**[59] 7467 4-9-5 **76**.......... (t) JimCrowley 5 82
(Stuart Williams) *midfield: hdwy over 2f out: rdn and kpt on fr over 1f out: briefly wnt 2nd ins fnl f: kpt on towards fin* **12/1**

1035 **4** *1 1/4* **Visionara**[27] 8456 3-9-7 **79**.......... CallumShepherd 4 80
(Simon Crisford) *chsd ldrs: bit short of room 2f out: rdn over 1f out: kpt on towards fin* **7/1**

6002 **5** *hd* **One Cool Daddy (USA)**[19] 8702 4-9-4 **75**.......... JoeyHaynes 1 77
(Dean Ivory) *hld up in midfield: rdn over 2f out: nt clr run over 1f out: styd on ins fnl f* **3/1**[1]

4006 **6** *1/2* **Fuwairt (IRE)**[19] 8690 7-8-13 **73**.......... ThomasGreatrex(3) 13 73
(David Loughnane) *s.i.s: swtchd rt and hld up in rr: pushed along and gd hdwy fr over 2f out: wknd ins fnl f* **50/1**

6021 **7** *nk* **Mendoza (IRE)**[19] 8702 3-9-6 **78**.......... LukeMorris 14 77
(James Eustace) *chsd ldr: rdn 2f out: wknd ins fnl f* **9/1**

0430 **8** *hd* **Harbour Vision**[19] 8692 4-9-1 **72**.......... (v) KierenFox 2 71
(Derek Shaw) *towards rr: rdn over 2f out: kpt on ins fnl f* **9/1**

6201 **9** *3 1/2* **Self Assessment (IRE)**[26] 8495 3-9-6 **78**.......... BenCurtis 6 67
(K R Burke) *in tch w ldrs: rdn over 2f out: wknd over 1f out* **5/1**[2]

5622 **10** *3/4* **Gold At Midnight**[62] 7351 3-9-6 **78**.......... TomMarquand 9 65
(William Muir) *towards rr of midfield and abt three wd: rdn 3f out: no imp fr 2f out* **10/1**

6600 **11** *shd* **Kyllachy Dragon (IRE)**[15] 8806 4-8-12 **69**.......... (h) JasonWatson 10 56
(Mark Rimell) *midfield and abt three wd: rdn and wknd over 2f out* **25/1**

3600 **12** *4 1/2* **Surrey Blaze (IRE)**[19] 8702 4-9-0 **71**.......... CharlesBishop 12 46
(Joseph Tuite) *towards rr: rdn and no rspnse over 2f out* **100/1**

104P **P** **Nahham (IRE)**[136] 4643 4-9-6 **77**.......... HectorCrouch 3
(Alexandra Dunn) *sweating: t.k.h: cl up: pushed along and outpcd over 3f out: lost position and eased over 2f out: sn p.u: burst blood vessel (vet reported gelding bled from the nose)* **33/1**

1m 25.51s (-0.49) **Going Correction** +0.025s/f (Slow)
WFA 3 from 4yo+ 1lb **13** Ran SP% **117.9**
Speed ratings (Par 105): **103,102,101,100,100 99,99,99,95,94 94,88,**
CSF £172.89 CT £2074.65 TOTE £38.20: £8.50, £2.10, £3.70; EX 253.10 Trifecta £1821.00.
Owner Miss Sarah Hoyland **Bred** Whatton Manor Stud **Trained** Tern Hill, Shropshire

FOCUS
The winner controlled the pace out in front and held them all off in a bit of a bunched finish.

9055 MATCHBOOK LONDON MIDDLE DISTANCE SERIES FINAL H'CAP 2m 2f 219y(P)
3:20 (3:27) (Class 2) 3-Y-0+
£43,575 (£13,048; £6,524; £3,262; £1,631; £819) **Stalls Low**

Form RPR

2311 **1** **All Yours (FR)**[28] 8421 8-8-12 **86**.......... JoeyHaynes 8 93
(Sean Curran) *travelled strly: trckd ldrs on inner: hrd rdn over 1f out: led ins fnl 110yds: a doing jst enough* **8/1**

0054 **2** *hd* **Creationist (USA)**[19] 8701 3-8-13 **91**.......... JasonWatson 3 98
(Roger Charlton) *t.k.h: trckd ldrs: wnt 3rd after 3f: rdn 2f out: led narrowly over 1f out: hdd fnl 110yds: jst failed (jockey said gelding hung right-handed under pressure)* **4/1**[1]

3112 **3** *hd* **Good Tidings (FR)**[19] 8701 3-8-10 **88**.......... (v[1]) KieranShoemark 2 94+
(John Gosden) *racd freely: s.i.s: midfield after 1f: gd hdwy fr 3f out: nt clr run swtchd rt 2f out: kpt on strly ins fnl f: jst hld (jockey said colt was slowly away and ran too free)* **5/1**[2]

4130 **4** *1* **Emirates Knight (IRE)**[39] 8098 3-8-9 **87**.......... BenCurtis 6 92
(Roger Varian) *led: rdn 2f out: hdd over 1f out: styd on ins fnl f* **8/1**

3000 **5** *1* **Cosmeapolitan**[12] 2832 6-9-5 **93**.......... TomMarquand 9 96+
(Alan King) *midfield: outpcd 3f out: rallied 2f out: kpt on wl ins fnl f* **33/1**

6510 **6** *3/4* **Lawn Ranger**[19] 8701 4-9-5 **93**.......... KierenFox 7 95
(Michael Attwater) *midfield: sme hdwy 3f out: rdn 2f out: no ex ins fnl f* **40/1**

0031 **7** *3/4* **Kyllachy Gala**[22] 8608 6-8-9 **83**.......... LukeMorris 11 83
(Marco Botti) *midfield on inner: outpcd 2f out: rdn over 1f out: kpt on* **10/1**

3131 **8** *hd* **Kitaabaat**[13] 8853 4-9-3 **91**.......... (h) JimCrowley 12 91+
(David Simcock) *stdd s: hld up in last: nudged along over 2f out: styng on fr over 1f out: too much to do* **12/1**

6053 **9** *1/2* **Island Brave (IRE)**[13] 8853 5-9-3 **98**.......... AngusVilliers(7) 5 97
(Heather Main) *cl up: disp ld 1/2-way: rdn over 2f out: wknd ins fnl f* **10/1**

4332 **10** *nk* **Escapability (IRE)**[23] 7974 4-8-6 **80**.......... (p) NicolaCurrie 1 79
(Alan King) *prom on inner: outpcd fr over 2f out: no ex fr 1f out: wknd fnl 110yds* **25/1**

1261 **11** *2 1/2* **The Pinto Kid (FR)**[52] 7688 4-9-2 **90**.......... (t) GeorgeWood 14 85
(James Fanshawe) *hld up in rr: shkn up over 2f out: sme hdwy over 1f out: no ex fnl 110yds* **12/1**

120 **12** *1 3/4* **Zzoro (IRE)**[18] 8725 6-8-6 **80**.......... (t) HollieDoyle 4 72
(Amanda Perrett) *prom: lost position 4f out: kpt on fr 2f out: no ex ins fnl f* **33/1**

1251 **13** *2* **Just The Man (FR)**[19] 8701 3-8-11 **89**.......... HectorCrouch 10 77
(Clive Cox) *hld up in rr: rdn 3f out: no imp fr over 2f out: wknd ins fnl f* **7/1**[3]

4260 **14** *11* **Fire Fighting (IRE)**[150] 4102 8-9-5 **93**.......... AdamKirby 13 62
(Mark Johnston) *in rr on outer: midfield after 3f: rdn 5f out: brief hdwy over 3f out: wknd qckly over 2f out* **66/1**

2m 21.48s (0.48) **Going Correction** +0.025s/f (Slow)
WFA 3 from 4yo+ 4lb **14** Ran SP% **118.6**
Speed ratings (Par 109): **99,98,98,97,97 96,96,96,95,95 93,92,90,82**
CSF £37.67 CT £180.41 TOTE £9.70: £2.50, £1.70, £2.00; EX 49.60 Trifecta £318.00.
Owner Power Geneva Ltd **Bred** S C A La Perrigne **Trained** Upper Lambourn, Berks

FOCUS
Racing handily was a must in this decent handicap.

9056 GET SWITCHED ON WITH MATCHBOOK H'CAP 1m 7f 218y(P)
3:50 (3:57) (Class 4) (0-85,86) 3-Y-0+
£6,469 (£1,925; £962; £481; £300; £300) **Stalls Low**

Form RPR

3221 **1** **Pianissimo**[26] 8500 3-9-4 **81**.......... (b) WilliamCarson 2 88
(Anthony Carson) *midfield: pushed along and hdwy over 2f out: wnt 2nd fnl f: rdn to ld towards fin* **20/1**

1005 **2** *nk* **Jersey Wonder (IRE)**[13] 8853 3-9-9 **86**.......... TomMarquand 3 92
(Jamie Osborne) *led: pushed along and qcknd over 2f out: rdn over 1f out: hdd towards fin* **14/1**

1110 **3** *nk* **Casa Comigo (IRE)**[20] 8654 4-8-12 **68**.......... KierenFox 11 73
(John Best) *chsd ldr: rdn over 1f out: kpt on* **7/1**[3]

6251 **4** *1/2* **Point In Time (IRE)**[18] 8727 4-9-10 **80**.......... JasonWatson 9 84
(Mark Usher) *t.k.h: towards rr: pushed along and gd hdwy fr over 2f out: kpt on ins fnl f* **9/1**

3410 **5** *1* **Western Duke (IRE)**[88] 6420 5-10-2 **86**.......... JimCrowley 5 89
(Ian Williams) *towards rr of midfield: rdn over 2f out: styd on ins fnl f* **9/1**

3436 **6** *1 3/4* **Pirate King**[28] 8421 4-9-12 **82**.......... StevieDonohoe 7 83
(Charlie Fellowes) *midfield: swtchd lft over 2f out: rdn and kpt on fr over 1f out* **7/2**[2]

0003 **7** *1 1/2* **Maquisard (FR)**[28] 8421 7-9-10 **80**.......... HectorCrouch 8 79
(Michael Madgwick) *hld up in rr: rdn over 2f out: nt clr run and hmpd over 1f out: nt rcvr* **20/1**

3214 **8** *nk* **Past Master**[61] 7394 6-9-12 **82**.......... AdamKirby 1 81
(Henry Candy) *cl up: rdn over 2f out: wknd over 1f out* **2/1**[1]

3010 **9** *7* **Battle Of Marathon (USA)**[25] 8513 7-9-9 **79**.......... LukeMorris 10 69
(John Ryan) *in rr: hdwy and prom but abt three wd 4f out: hung rt fr 3f out: rdn and wknd fr 2f out* **33/1**

4442 **10** *hd* **Rydan (IRE)**[68] 7127 8-10-0 **84**.......... (v) TomQueally 6 74
(Gary Moore) *towards rr of midfield: pushed along and wknd over 2f out* **20/1**

3455 **11** *12* **Azari**[10] 8948 7-9-9 **79**.......... (p) HollieDoyle 4 55
(Alexandra Dunn) *prom: pushed along over 3f out: wknd over 2f out* **66/1**

3m 32.07s (1.97) **Going Correction** +0.025s/f (Slow)
WFA 3 from 4yo+ 7lb **11** Ran SP% **113.4**
Speed ratings (Par 105): **96,95,95,95,94 94,93,93,89,89 83**
CSF £246.78 CT £2150.11 TOTE £17.10: £4.50, £3.90, £2.40; EX 288.10 Trifecta £2001.90.
Owner Chris Butler **Bred** Godolphin **Trained** Newmarket, Suffolk

FOCUS
They finished in a bit of a heap here, the early gallop having been fairly pedestrian, and the long-time leader almost held on.

9057 MATCHBOOK CASINO H'CAP 6f (P)
4:25 (4:28) (Class 4) (0-85,84) 3-Y-0+
£6,469 (£1,925; £962; £481; £300; £300) **Stalls Low**

Form RPR

4240 **1** **Ginger Fox**[41] 8017 3-8-5 **75**.......... (p) JonathanFisher(7) 8 84
(David Loughnane) *midfield on inner: shkn up and hdwy over 1f out: rdn to ld ins fnl f: kpt on wl towards fin* **8/1**

1423 **2** *nk* **Hart Stopper**[68] 7121 5-9-4 **81**.......... (t) CallumShepherd 11 89
(Stuart Williams) *swtchd rt: hld up in rr: pushed along over 2f out: hdwy and briefly led ins fnl f: kpt on towards fin: jst hld* **20/1**

4532 **3** *2 1/2* **Benny And The Jets (IRE)**[14] 8826 3-9-0 **82**.......... PoppyBridgwater(5) 5 82+
(Sylvester Kirk) *t.k.h: disp ld: led 1/2-way: rdn over 1f out: no ex ins fnl f: jst hld 3rd* **9/4**[2]

1305 **4** *shd* **Restless Rose**[24] 8550 4-9-5 **82**.......... JimCrowley 9 82
(Stuart Williams) *hld up in rr: rdn and hdwy on outer over 1f out: kpt on fnl f: nvr able to chal* **5/1**[3]

6041 **5** *3/4* **Helvetian**[27] 8470 4-9-2 **84**.......... (t[1]) TobyEley(5) 4 81
(Kevin Frost) *dwlt s: sn prom: rdn and hdwy over 1f out: no ex ins fnl f (jockey said gelding was never travelling)* **14/1**

601 **6** *nk* **Ice Cave (IRE)**[20] 8653 3-9-7 **84**.......... JasonWatson 7 80
(Saeed bin Suroor) *midfield: pushed along over 2f out: rdn and hdwy over 1f out: no ex ins fnl f* **2/1**[1]

6261 **7** *2 3/4* **Red Alert**[79] 6756 5-9-7 **84**.......... (p) TomMarquand 2 72
(Tony Carroll) *prom: rdn over 2f out: wknd fr 1f out* **20/1**

3226 **8** *1 3/4* **Foxy Forever (IRE)**[22] 8601 9-9-3 **80**.......... (t[1]) CharlesBishop 6 62
(Michael Wigham) *cl up on outer: rdn over 2f out: wknd ins fnl f* **25/1**

5050 **9** *5* **Waseem Faris (IRE)**[22] 8601 10-8-13 **76**.......... HollieDoyle 1 42
(Milton Harris) *led: hdd 1/2-way: sn pressed ldr: rdn over 2f out: wknd over 1f out* **50/1**

The Form Book Flat 2019, Raceform Ltd, Newbury, RG14 5SJ

50-0 **10** *8* **Omran**[12] 8893 5-9-6 **83**......................................(t) StevieDonohoe 10 23
(Michael Wigham) *dwlt s: racd in last: struggling 1/2-way: sn btn* **50/1**

1m 11.88s (-1.22) **Going Correction** +0.025s/f (Slow) **10** Ran SP% **115.8**
Speed ratings (Par 105): **109,108,105,105,104 103,100,97,91,80**
CSF £152.64 CT £489.36 TOTE £8.70: £1.90, £3.30, £1.40; EX 143.40 Trifecta £905.80.
Owner Shughal Mela Racing **Bred** Denford Stud Ltd **Trained** Tern Hill, Shropshire

FOCUS
Mainly exposed performers in a useful handicap. The contested lead helped to tee things up for the closers late on.
T/Jkpt: Not won. T/Plt: £186.00 to a £1 stake. Pool: £68,575.53 - 269.07 winning units. T/Qpdt: £98.60 to a £1 stake. Pool: £7,821.82 - 58.65 winning units. **Raceform**

8970 CHANTILLY (R-H)
Tuesday, November 19

OFFICIAL GOING: Polytrack: standard; turf: heavy

9058a PRIX MAGDELENE (MAIDEN) (3YO) (ALL-WEATHER TRACK) (POLYTRACK) 1m (P)
1:25 3-Y-O **£11,261** (£4,504; £3,378; £2,252; £1,126)

RPR

1 **Rey Pelayo (FR)**[19] 3-9-2 0.............................. TonyPiccone 9 82
(F Chappet, France) **68/10**

2 *3/4* **Septems (FR)**[12] 3-8-7 0.............................. MlleAudeDuporte(9) 5 80
(Mme J Hendriks, Holland) **23/5**[2]

3 *snk* **Glaciate**[33] 3-8-13 0.............................. MaximeGuyon 2 77
(P Bary, France) **17/5**[1]

4 *1/2* **Masetto (FR)**[103] 3-9-2 0.............................. TheoBachelot 16 79
(M Nigge, France) **53/10**[3]

5 *nk* **Caja Primera (GER)**[72] 3-8-13 0..............................(p) JulienGuillochon 1 75
(H-A Pantall, France) **16/1**

6 *1 1/4* **Lucky You (FR)**[35] 3-8-4 0.............................. MlleFriedaValleSkar(9) 4 72
(C Lerner, France) **15/1**

7 *1 1/2* **Melissa (FR)**[56] 7561 3-8-5 0.............................. MlleCoraliePacaut(3) 13 63
(Ivan Furtado) *broke on terms fr wd draw: proged to ld after 2f and sn grabbed rail: pushed along over 2f out: chal and hdd 1f out: wknd fnl 100yds* **62/1**

8 *1/2* **Cardino (FR)**[12] 3-8-11 0.............................. AntoineHamelin 10 65
(Carmen Bocskai, Germany) **11/2**

9 *1/2* **Glorious Emaraty (FR)**[12] 3-9-2 0.............................. MickaelForest 11 69
(Mme G Rarick, France) **26/1**

10 *hd* **Mirage Vert (FR)**[262] 3-8-11 0.............................. EmmanuelEtienne 8 64
(S Wattel, France) **83/1**

11 *nk* **Nathaniella**[7] 3-8-5 0.............................. AlexandreChesneau(3) 3 60
(Mme M-C Chaalon, France) **97/1**

12 *nk* **Drosay (FR)**[12] 3-8-11 0.............................. FabienLefebvre 12 62
(Georgios Alimpinisis, France) **99/1**

13 *1 1/4* **Ridgy (FR)**[190] 3-8-5 0.............................. MlleZoePfeil(3) 7 56
(Gerard Aidant, France) **126/1**

14 *3/4* **Blackalfa (FR)**[14] 3-8-3 0.............................. QuentinPerrette(5) 6 55
(Laurent Loisel, France) **76/1**

15 *2* **Galiva (FR)** 3-8-8 0.............................. AurelienLemaitre 14 50
(Mlle Y Vollmer, France) **58/1**

16 *1 1/2* **Mubarmaj (FR)**[33] 3-9-2 0.............................. CristianDemuro 15 55
(E J O'Neill, France) **9/1**

1m 39.15s **16** Ran SP% **119.1**
PARI-MUTUEL (all including 1 euro stake): WIN 7.80; PLACE 2.30, 1.80, 1.70; DF 16.30.
Owner Haras D'Etreham **Bred** Haras D'Etreham **Trained** France

9059a PRIX HEROD (LISTED RACE) (2YO) (TURF) 7f
2:00 2-Y-O **£27,027** (£10,810; £8,108; £5,405; £2,702)

RPR

1 **Milltown Star**[38] 8110 2-8-13 0.............................. GeraldMosse 6 96
(Mick Channon) *midfield: travelling strly under restraint at 1/2-way: shkn up ent home st: prog to ld over 2f out: fnd more whn strly chal w 1f to run: styd on wl clsng stages and a holding runner-up* **73/10**

2 *1/2* **Ellerslie Lace (FR)**[30] 2-8-9 0.............................. VincentCheminaud 3 91
(M Delzangles, France) **27/1**

3 *1 1/4* **Choise Of Raison**[27] 8483 2-8-13 0..............................(p) TonyPiccone 4 92
(F Rossi, France) **41/10**[3]

4 *1 3/4* **Kraquante**[30] 2-8-9 0.............................. MickaelBarzalona 8 83
(F Chappet, France) **26/5**

5 *snk* **Private Romance (IRE)**[19] 2-8-9 0.............................. StephanePasquier 7 83
(N Clement, France) **36/5**

6 *7* **Chrysalism (IRE)**[24] 8571 2-8-9 0.............................. MaximeGuyon 5 65
(Joseph Patrick O'Brien, Ire) *racd towards rr: nudged along early on to maintain position: pushed along 3f out: edgd rt whn drvn and had to be plld off heels over 2f out: one pce clsng stages* **13/1**

7 *9* **Afraid Of Nothing**[51] 7725 2-8-9 0.............................. TheoBachelot 9 43
(Ralph Beckett) *sn led: 2 l advantage at 1/2-way: pushed along over 2f out: wknd qckly whn hdd over 1f out: eased fnl 100yds* **7/2**[1]

8 *2 1/2* **Mangkhut (FR)**[10] 2-8-13 0.............................. CristianDemuro 2 41
(Andrea Marcialis, France) **39/10**[2]

9 *3* **Cobra Eye**[38] 8125 2-8-13 0.............................. IoritzMendizabal 1 33
(John Quinn) *racd keenly in 2nd: hld together 3f out: sn pushed along and no ex: qckly btn and eased fnl f* **18/1**

1m 32.37s (6.27) **9** Ran SP% **118.6**
PARI-MUTUEL (all including 1 euro stake): WIN 8.30; PLACE 2.80, 5.50, 1.60; DF 129.10.
Owner Hunscote Stud Limited And Partner **Bred** Hunscote Stud **Trained** West Ilsley, Berks

9051 KEMPTON (A.W) (R-H)
Wednesday, November 20

OFFICIAL GOING: Polytrack: standard to slow
Wind: virtually nil Weather: partly cloudy

9060 CLOSE BROTHERS BUSINESS FINANCE NURSERY H'CAP 7f (P)
4:10 (4:11) (Class 6) (0-65,65) 2-Y-O
£3,234 (£962; £481; £400; £400; £400) **Stalls** Low

Form RPR

3041 **1** **Speed Merchant (IRE)**[39] 8118 2-9-5 **63**..............................(p) AlistairRawlinson 14 68
(Michael Appleby) *mde all: wnt clr 4f out: rdn 2f out: tiring fnl 100yds but a gng to hold on* **14/1**

0564 **2** *3/4* **Penmellyn (IRE)**[16] 8815 2-9-5 **63**..............................(h) ShaneGray 2 66
(Phillip Makin) *wl in tch in midfield: effrt over 2f out: chsd clr wnr 1f out: styd on and clsng fnl 100yds: nvr quite getting to wnr* **7/2**[2]

030 **3** *1 3/4* **Secret Diary**[22] 8640 2-9-3 **61**.............................. KieranShoemark 10 59
(Declan Carroll) *hdwy to chse wnr over 4f out: effrt over 2f out: no imp over 1f out: 3rd and kpt on ins fnl f: nvr enough pce to rch wnr* **33/1**

5064 **4** *3/4* **Burniston Rocks**[37] 8201 2-9-7 **65**..............................(b[1]) TomMarquand 3 62
(Ed Vaughan) *dwlt: towards rr: hdwy into midfield and rdn over 2f out: kpt on u.p ins fnl f: nvr enough pce to rch ldrs* **5/2**[1]

0650 **5** *3/4* **Rulers Kingdom (IRE)**[16] 8815 2-9-7 **65**.............................. JamesDoyle 8 60
(Mark Johnston) *chsd ldrs: rdn over 2f out: unable qck and no imp over 1f out: kpt on steadily wout threatening ldrs ins fnl f* **7/1**[3]

0005 **6** *1* **Jochi Khan (USA)**[48] 7833 2-8-3 **47**..............................(b[1]) HollieDoyle 5 39
(Mohamed Moubarak) *short of room leaving stalls: t.k.h: towards rr: effrt on inner jst over 2f out: drvn and sme hdwy over 1f out: kpt on but no threat to ldrs ins fnl f (jockey said gelding ran too free)* **16/1**

0502 **7** *1/2* **Magical Force**[28] 8452 2-9-4 **62**.............................. RobHornby 7 53
(Rod Millman) *in tch in midfield: effrt over 2f out: unable qck and no imp over 1f out: wl hld and kpt on same pce ins fnl f* **9/1**

3000 **8** *nk* **Angels Faces (IRE)**[16] 8815 2-9-4 **62**.............................. SamJames 6 52
(Grant Tuer) *chsd wnr tl over 4f out: styd prom in chsng gp: unable qck u.p over 1f out: wknd ins fnl f* **16/1**

6010 **9** *3/4* **Constitutional (IRE)**[56] 7582 2-9-5 **63**.............................. CliffordLee 4 51
(K R Burke) *hld up towards rr: effrt over 2f out: sme prog over 1f out: n.d* **12/1**

0613 **10** *2 1/4* **Chromium**[43] 7994 2-9-3 **61**.............................. NicolaCurrie 13 43
(Michael Attwater) *a towards rr: nvr involved* **25/1**

0206 **11** *1 3/4* **Moondance**[43] 7980 2-9-5 **63**.............................. HectorCrouch 9 41
(Gary Moore) *towards rr: rdn over 2f out: sn btn* **33/1**

562 **12** *4* **Utopian Lad (IRE)**[41] 8061 2-9-7 **65**..............................(p) JaneElliott 12 32
(Tom Dascombe) *midfield: rdn over 2f out: sn lost pl: bhd ins fnl f (trainer's rep said gelding had a breathing problem)* **7/1**[3]

1m 26.4s (0.40) **Going Correction** -0.075s/f (Stan) **12** Ran SP% **121.6**
Speed ratings (Par 94): **94,93,91,90,89 88,87,87,86,83 81,77**
CSF £63.21 CT £1646.40 TOTE £8.60: £2.20, £1.50, £12.00; EX 54.40 Trifecta £758.70.
Owner Slipstream Racing **Bred** J McAteer & L McAteer **Trained** Oakham, Rutland

FOCUS
A modest nursery in which the winner made all.

9061 BET @RACINGTV.COM NURSERY H'CAP 6f (P)
4:40 (4:40) (Class 6) (0-60,60) 2-Y-O
£3,234 (£962; £481; £400; £400; £400) **Stalls** Low

Form RPR

5332 **1** **You Don't Own Me (IRE)**[4] 9009 2-9-3 **56**..............................(b) CharlesBishop 1 64
(Joseph Tuite) *chsd ldrs: effrt u.p to chal over 1f out: drvn to ld 1f out: styd on wl* **4/1**[3]

5466 **2** *1 3/4* **The Blue Bower (IRE)**[18] 8750 2-9-6 **59**.............................. JaneElliott 9 62
(Suzy Smith) *stdd after s and swtchd rt: hld up towards rr: effrt 2f out: hdwy to chse ldrs 1f out: chsd wnr 100yds out: no imp towards fin* **50/1**

000 **3** *1 1/2* **Ivadream**[61] 7406 2-9-7 **60**.............................. JasonWatson 12 58+
(Roger Charlton) *stdd and dropped in bhd after s: hld up in rr: hdwy over 1f out: styd on wl ins fnl f: snatched 3rd last stride: nvr trbld ldrs* **16/1**

2062 **4** *shd* **Comeatchoo (IRE)**[26] 8527 2-8-8 **54**.............................. GraceMcEntee(7) 3 52
(Phil McEntee) *led: rdn ent fnl 2f: hdd 1f out: no ex: lost 2nd 100yds out: wknd towards fin and lost 3rd last stride* **16/1**

0051 **5** *1 1/4* **Lezardrieux**[26] 8527 2-9-7 **60**.............................. SamJames 5 54
(Grant Tuer) *in tch in midfield: edgd out lft and effrt over 1f out: kpt on ins fnl f: nvr trbld ldrs* **8/1**

0024 **6** *1/2* **Rebel Redemption**[56] 7584 2-9-7 **60**..............................(p) JasonHart 7 53
(John Quinn) *t.k.h: chsd ldr tl 2f out: unable qck u.p and no imp in 3rd 1f out: wknd fnl 100yds* **10/3**[2]

060 **7** *1 1/2* **Scallywagtail (IRE)**[43] 7981 2-9-0 **53**.............................. HectorCrouch 2 41
(Gary Moore) *awkward leaving stalls: sn rcvrd and in tch in midfield: effrt jst over 2f out: unable qck and wknd ins fnl f* **16/1**

5060 **8** *1 1/4* **Birkie Queen (IRE)**[110] 5630 2-9-0 **53**.............................. LiamKeniry 10 37
(J S Moore) *hld up in tch in midfield: no imp u.p over 1f out: nvr trbld ldrs* **80/1**

3001 **9** *1 1/4* **Sir Rodneyredblood**[15] 8825 2-9-6 **59**.............................. DavidProbert 6 40+
(J R Jenkins) *chsd ldrs: short of room briefly ent fnl 2f: unable qck u.p and btn over 1f out: wknd ins fnl f* **9/4**[1]

0003 **10** *1/2* **Il Maestro (IRE)**[18] 8750 2-9-4 **57**.............................. AdamKirby 4 36
(John Quinn) *in tch in midfield: swtchd lft and effrt over 2f out: no imp: wl hld fnl f* **12/1**

0050 **11** *4 1/2* **Love Not Money**[22] 8640 2-8-10 **54**.............................. AledBeech(5) 11 20
(John Bridger) *swtchd rt after s: hld up in rr: rdn and no hdwy over 2f out: wl btn over 1f out* **66/1**

6005 **12** *16* **Calbuco**[64] 7296 2-9-1 **54**.............................. RobHornby 8
(Rod Millman) *wdm: midfield: lost pl and towards rr 3f out: wknd over 1f out* **50/1**

1m 12.84s (-0.26) **Going Correction** -0.075s/f (Stan) **12** Ran SP% **116.9**
Speed ratings (Par 94): **98,95,93,93,91 91,89,87,85,85 79,57**
CSF £195.86 CT £2934.51 TOTE £4.80: £1.60, £6.30, £4.40; EX 175.40 Trifecta £3646.00.
Owner Klein, Forbes and Partner **Bred** Mount Coote Stud & Highfort Stud **Trained** Lambourn, Berks

FOCUS
An ordinary nursery.

9062 32RED CASINO FILLIES' NOVICE AUCTION STKS (PLUS 10 RACE) 6f (P)
5:10 (5:15) (Class 5) 2-Y-O £3,881 (£1,155; £577; £288) Stalls Low

Form RPR

2 **1** **Cry Havoc (IRE)**[35] 8250 2-8-12 0........................RobHornby 5 80+
(Rae Guest) *wl in tch in midfield: effrt to chse ldrs over 1f out: rdn to chse ldr 1f out: led wl ins fnl f: r.o strly: gng away at fin* **11/10**[1]

2 1 1/4 **Lapses Linguae (FR)**[31] 8364 2-9-0 0........................(t) JamesDoyle 1 78
(Emmet Mullins, Ire) *chsd ldrs tl clsd to join ldr 2f out: rdn to ld over 1f out: hdd and no ex wl ins fnl f* **13/8**[2]

3 3 3/4 **Broughton Sunpearl** 2-8-11 0........................JoeyHaynes 9 64+
(Tom Clover) *stdd after s: hld up in tch in midfield: effrt and rn green over 2f out: nt clr run over 1f out: hdwy 1f out: chsd clr ldng pair wl ins fnl f: nvr getting on terms: eased cl home* **66/1**

4 1 1/2 **New Arrival (IRE)** 2-8-11 0........................CallumShepherd 10 59+
(James Tate) *swtchd rt after s: hld up in last trio: effrt ent fnl 2f: hdwy ins fnl f: kpt on wl fnl 100yds: nvr trbld ldrs* **25/1**

4 **5** 1/2 **Gazelle**[21] 8651 2-9-0 0........................JasonWatson 7 61
(Roger Charlton) *restless in stalls: led: rdn and hrd pressed 2f out: hdd over 1f out: 3rd and outpcd 1f out: wknd and lost 2 pls wl ins fnl f* **6/1**[3]

0 **6** 1/2 **Celtic Mist (IRE)**[14] 8849 2-8-13 0........................JosephineGordon 2 58
(Shaun Keightley) *in tch in midfield: rdn over 2f out: no imp over 1f out: no threat to ldrs and kpt on same pce ins fnl f* **80/1**

6 **7** 2 1/4 **High Maintenance**[25] 8546 2-8-13 0........................ShaneKelly 6 52
(Mark Loughnane) *chsd ldrs: rdn ent fnl 2f: unable qck and outpcd over 1f out: wknd ins fnl f* **25/1**

8 2 3/4 **Catherine Bay** 2-8-12 0........................DavidProbert 3 42
(Henry Candy) *wl in tch in midfield: effrt on inner ent fnl 2f: sn struggling and outpcd over 1f out: wknd ins fnl f* **25/1**

0 **9** 1/2 **May Happen**[35] 8250 2-8-11 0........................NicolaCurrie 12 40
(Jamie Osborne) *wd: midfield tl dropped towards rr and rdn over 2f out: bhd over 1f out* **66/1**

0 **10** hd **Little Floozie**[49] 7813 2-8-12 0........................WilliamCarson 11 40
(Brett Johnson) *pressed ldr tl 2f out: unable qck and lost pl over 1f out: wknd ins fnl f* **100/1**

11 1/2 **Don't Tell Claire** 2-9-0 0........................HollieDoyle 8 41
(Daniel Kubler) *a in rr: nvr involved* **40/1**

12 1 1/2 **Cath The Great (IRE)** 2-8-12 0........................HectorCrouch 4 34
(Gary Moore) *s.i.s: rn green and a towards rr* **33/1**

1m 13.28s (0.18) **Going Correction** -0.075s/f (Stan) 12 Ran SP% **122.1**
Speed ratings (Par 93): **95,93,88,86,85 85,82,78,77,77 76,74**
CSF £2.88 TOTE £1.90: £1.10, £1.10, £15.40; EX 3.70 Trifecta £93.60.
Owner The Musketeers **Bred** Coseda Ltd **Trained** Newmarket, Suffolk

FOCUS
In line with market expectations, this developed into a match from a furlong out.

9063 100% PROFIT BOOST AT 32REDSPORT.COM NOVICE MEDIAN AUCTION STKS 1m (P)
5:40 (5:46) (Class 6) 2-Y-O £3,234 (£962; £481; £240) Stalls Low

Form RPR

1 **Eastern Sheriff** 2-9-3 0........................JamesDoyle 3 81+
(Hugo Palmer) *wl in tch in midfield: clsd and swtchd rt over 1f out: rdn and str chal 1f out: led ins fnl f: r.o strly and gng away at fin* **8/1**[3]

02 **2** 2 **Hurricane Alex**[20] 8700 2-9-3 0........................TomMarquand 12 76
(Richard Hannon) *chsd ldrs: effrt and ev ch 2f out: drvn over 1f out: led 1f out: hdd ins fnl f: nt match pce of wnr towards fin* **9/1**

21 **3** hd **Cranberry**[20] 8706 2-8-12 0........................AngusVilliers(7) 1 78
(Richard Hughes) *led: rdn 2f out: drvn and hdd 1f out: kpt on same pce ins fnl f* **10/11**[1]

32 **4** 2 1/4 **Capla Cubiste**[30] 8402 2-8-12 0........................JaneElliott 9 66
(Sir Mark Prescott Bt) *chsd ldrs: effrt to press ldr 2f out: hung rt and unable qck over 1f out: wknd ins fnl f* **11/2**[2]

04 **5** 3/4 **Morlaix**[20] 8700 2-8-12 0........................PoppyBridgwater(5) 8 69
(David Simcock) *in tch in midfield: effrt ent fnl 2f: unable qck and kpt on same pce ins fnl f* **16/1**

04 **6** 4 **Golden Cygnet**[98] 6072 2-8-12 0........................RobHornby 14 55
(Ralph Beckett) *t.k.h: chsd ldr tl 2f out: unable qck and lost pl over 1f out: wknd ins fnl f* **40/1**

7 2 1/2 **Alveda** 2-8-12 0........................DavidProbert 2 49
(George Margarson) *in tch in midfield: rdn wl over 2f out: unable qck and outpcd 2f out: wknd ins fnl f* **50/1**

8 3/4 **Scarlet Ruby** 2-8-12 0........................JasonWatson 4 47
(Roger Charlton) *s.i.s: rn green in rr: sme prog over 1f out: nvr trbld ldrs* **16/1**

9 1 **Arietta** 2-8-12 0........................NicolaCurrie 11 45
(Jonathan Portman) *midfield: outpcd wl over 2f out: no imp and btn whn rn green and edgd rt over 1f out: wknd ins fnl f* **66/1**

10 1 1/2 **Vertice (IRE)** 2-8-5 0........................StefanoCherchi(7) 7 42
(Marco Botti) *a towards rr: rdn and outpcd over 2f out: wl hld fnl 2f* **50/1**

11 shd **Royal Astronomer** 2-9-3 0........................GeraldMosse 6 46
(Hughie Morrison) *dwlt: a towards rr: outpcd over 2f out: n.d after* **25/1**

12 hd **Brown Eyed Girl** 2-8-12 0........................KieranO'Neill 5 41
(Mick Channon) *pushed along at times and rn green towards rr: rdn and outpcd over 2f out: wl btn over 1f out* **66/1**

13 4 1/2 **Cinnabar** 2-8-9 0........................ThomasGreatrex(3) 10 31
(Roger Charlton) *s.i.s: a towards rr: wl btn fnl 2f (jockey said filly was slowly away)* **66/1**

03 **14** 20 **Justified**[14] 8857 2-9-3 0........................AdamKirby 13
(Mark Johnston) *chsd ldrs tl lost pl qckly 3f out: wl bhd fnl f: t.o (jockey said colt stopped quickly)* **20/1**

1m 39.84s (0.04) **Going Correction** -0.075s/f (Stan) 14 Ran SP% **120.1**
Speed ratings (Par 94): **96,94,93,91,90 86,84,83,82,81 80,80,76,56**
CSF £72.91 TOTE £11.40: £2.60, £2.50, £1.10; EX 64.00 Trifecta £162.30.
Owner Isa Salman **Bred** Sheikh Isa Salman Al Khalifa **Trained** Newmarket, Suffolk

FOCUS
A fair novice.

9064 BRITISH STALLION STUDS EBF HYDE STKS (LISTED RACE) (AW CHAMPIONSHIPS FAST-TRACK QUALIFIER) 1m (P)
6:10 (6:16) (Class 1) 3-Y-O+ £25,519 (£9,675; £4,842; £2,412; £1,210; £607) Stalls Low

Form RPR

1300 **1** **Set Piece**[115] 5480 3-9-0 99........................(bt w) JamesDoyle 12 112
(Hugo Palmer) *hld up in last quartet: edgd out lft and effrt over 2f out: hdwy u.p over 1f out: chsd clr ldr 1f out: r.o wl to ld last stride* **16/1**

-521 **2** shd **Khuzaam (USA)**[35] 8253 3-9-0 103........................JimCrowley 8 112+
(Roger Varian) *led: rdn and qcknd clr wl over 1f out: drvn 1f out: kpt on but grad worn down and hdd last stride* **5/6**[1]

2303 **3** 2 **Accidental Agent**[18] 8765 5-9-2 107........................(p) CharlesBishop 1 108
(Eve Johnson Houghton) *hld up in last quartet: swtchd lft and effrt ent fnl 2f: hdwy u.p 1f out: chsd ldng pair 100yds out: kpt on wl but nvr getting to ldrs* **12/1**

0426 **4** 3 1/2 **Preening**[20] 8708 4-8-11 99........................DavidProbert 5 95
(James Fanshawe) *hld up in tch in midfield: swtchd rt and effrt on inner 2f out: no imp over 1f out: wknd ins fnl f* **9/1**[3]

6601 **5** nse **Via Serendipity**[41] 8062 5-9-2 108........................(t) AdamKirby 3 100
(Stuart Williams) *chsd ldr: swtchd lft and effrt to chse ldr ent fnl 2f: unable to match pce of wnr over 1f out: lost 2nd 1f out and wknd ins fnl f* **15/2**[2]

-100 **6** 3/4 **Dandhu**[46] 7893 3-9-0 105........................GeraldMosse 9 97
(David Elsworth) *hld up in last quartet: effrt over 2f out: no imp tl kpt on ins fnl f: no threat to ldrs* **14/1**

0-20 **7** 1/2 **Librisa Breeze**[32] 8331 7-9-2 113........................JoeyHaynes 6 97
(Dean Ivory) *hld up in tch in midfield: effrt ent fnl 2f: unable qck and outpcd over 1f out: wl hld ins fnl f* **25/1**

0350 **8** 1/2 **Lush Life (IRE)**[47] 7863 4-8-11 89........................(bt) NicolaCurrie 4 91
(Jamie Osborne) *hld up in rr: effrt over 2f out: sme modest late hdwy: nvr trbld ldrs* **100/1**

5013 **9** 2 **Oh This Is Us (IRE)**[40] 8090 6-9-2 110........................TomMarquand 2 91
(Richard Hannon) *in tch in midfield: effrt to chse ldrs 2f out: unable qck u.p and outpcd over 1f out: wknd ins fnl f* **12/1**

104 **10** 1/2 **Makzeem**[46] 7905 6-9-2 103........................(t) JasonWatson 14 90
(Roger Charlton) *chsd ldrs: unable qck u.p and outpcd over 1f out: wknd ins fnl f* **66/1**

1311 **11** 4 **War Glory (IRE)**[20] 8707 6-9-2 109........................HollieDoyle 10 81
(Richard Hannon) *chsd ldr tl unable qck u.p and lost 2nd ent fnl 2f: lost pl over 1f out: wknd ins fnl f* **12/1**

-500 **12** 10 **Flaming Spear (IRE)**[32] 8336 7-9-2 105........................BenCurtis 7 58
(Dean Ivory) *t.k.h: hld up in tch in midfield: rdn over 2f out: sn lost pl and bhd over 1f out* **25/1**

1m 36.27s (-3.53) **Going Correction** -0.075s/f (Stan)
WFA 3 from 4yo+ 2lb 12 Ran SP% **122.1**
Speed ratings (Par 111): **114,113,111,108,108 107,107,106,104,104 100,90**
CSF £30.08 TOTE £16.90: £3.70, £1.30, £3.00; EX 42.60 Trifecta £326.60.
Owner K Abdullah **Bred** Juddmonte Farms (east) Ltd **Trained** Newmarket, Suffolk

FOCUS
A good race, and the first two have more to offer on the AW.

9065 32RED H'CAP 1m 7f 218y(P)
6:40 (6:43) (Class 2) (0-105,97) 3-Y-O+ £15,562 (£4,660; £2,330; £1,165; £582; £292) Stalls Low

Form RPR

0003 **1** **Reshoun (FR)**[74] 6958 5-9-11 **94**........................(p) JimCrowley 8 100
(Ian Williams) *wl in tch in rr: rdn 4f out: reminders over 3f out: chsd ldng trio u.p over 1f out: styd on wl to ld wl ins fnl f* **13/2**[3]

6620 **2** 3/4 **Busy Street**[94] 6255 7-9-3 **93**........................AngusVilliers(7) 7 98
(Michael Appleby) *t.k.h: trckd ldrs: effrt to chal ent fnl 2f: drvn and led narrowly over 1f out: hdd ins fnl f: kpt on: nt quite match pce of wnr towards fin (jockey said gelding ran too free)* **14/1**

0-66 **3** hd **To Be Wild (IRE)**[14] 8853 6-9-9 **92**........................(h) AdamKirby 3 97
(Jane Chapple-Hyam) *trckd ldrs: rdn over 2f out: drvn and ev ch over 1f out: led ins fnl f: hdd and no ex wl ins fnl f* **25/1**

4133 **4** 2 3/4 **Infrastructure**[91] 6355 4-9-11 **94**........................RobHornby 9 96
(Martyn Meade) *sn chsng ldr tl rdn to ld over 2f out: hdd over 1f out: no ex and outpcd ins fnl f* **6/1**[2]

2R33 **5** 4 1/2 **Platitude**[47] 7866 6-10-0 **97**........................KieranShoemark 1 93
(Amanda Perrett) *hld up wl in tch: swtchd ins and effrt ent fnl 2f: unable qck: edgd rt and outpcd over 1f out: wknd fnl f (jockey said gelding hung right-handed)* **20/1**

2514 **6** 2 1/4 **Ballylemon (IRE)**[18] 8754 3-7-13 **82**........................GeorgeRooke(7) 4 77
(Richard Hughes) *t.k.h: in tch: rdn ent fnl 2f: sn outpcd and btn: wknd fnl f (jockey said gelding ran too free)* **4/6**[1]

3000 **7** 36 **Rochester House (IRE)**[18] 8754 3-9-0 **90**........................JamesDoyle 5 42
(Mark Johnston) *led tl rdn and hdd over 2f out: sn lost pl: bhd and eased ent fnl f: t.o (jockey said gelding ran too free)* **12/1**

3m 27.69s (-2.41) **Going Correction** -0.075s/f (Stan)
WFA 3 from 4yo+ 7lb 7 Ran SP% **110.6**
Speed ratings (Par 109): **103,102,102,101,98 97,79**
CSF £81.02 CT £2010.63 TOTE £7.60: £2.50, £4.50; EX 77.30 Trifecta £427.70.
Owner Ian Williams **Bred** S C E A Haras De Son Altesse L'Aga Khan **Trained** Portway, Worcs

FOCUS
A messy race that was run at a steady gallop and turned into a sprint from the home turn. They finished in a bit of a heap.

9066 32RED.COM H'CAP 1m 3f 219y(P)
7:10 (7:13) (Class 4) (0-85,85) 3-Y-O+ £6,469 (£1,925; £962; £481; £400; £400) Stalls Low

Form RPR

332 **1** **Fearless Warrior (FR)**[29] 8421 3-8-10 **76**........................(h) HollieDoyle 1 84
(Eve Johnson Houghton) *led: sn hdd and trckd ldng pair after 2f: swtchd lft and effrt ent fnl 2f: rdn to ld over 1f out: sustained duel w runner-up fnl f: hld on gamely* **4/1**[2]

1323 **2** nk **Sir Prize**[33] 8321 4-9-2 **77**........................JoeyHaynes 2 84
(Dean Ivory) *hld up in tch in midfield: effrt on inner ent fnl 2f: drvn and ev ch over 1f out: sustained effrt and duelled w wnr fnl f: a jst hld* **5/1**[3]

-301 **3** 3 1/2 **Purdey's Gift**[34] 8298 3-8-12 **78**........................DavidProbert 4 79
(Andrew Balding) *impeded and swtchd rt after s: hld up in last pair: nt clr run over 2f out: swtchd lft and effrt ent fnl f: chsd clr ldng pair 100yds: nvr getting on terms* **5/4**[1]

-540 **4** 2½ **Persian Sun**[19] 8727 4-9-0 **75**........................(t) JamesDoyle 7 72
(Stuart Williams) sn led: drvn and hdd over 1f out: 3rd and no ex 1f out: wknd ins fnl f **10/1**

0-20 **5** 2 **Jus Pires (USA)**[19] 8727 5-9-7 **82**........................(t) AdamKirby 3 76
(Declan Carroll) in tch in midfield: effrt over 2f out: unable qck over 1f out: wknd ins fnl f **6/1**

6-64 **6** 7 **Princesse Mathilde**[26] 8514 3-9-5 **85**........................ KieranShoemark 6 68
(Charlie Fellowes) hld up in tch in last pair: effrt jst over 2f out: sn struggling and outpcd: wknd over 1f out **16/1**

1500 **7** 2½ **Ilhabela Fact**[182] 2969 5-9-4 **79**........................ TomMarquand 8 58
(Tony Carroll) chsd ldr 10f out tl ent fnl 2f: sn lost pl and wknd fnl f **16/1**

2m 32.98s (-1.52) **Going Correction** -0.075s/f (Stan)
WFA 3 from 4yo+ 5lb **7 Ran SP% 116.3**
Speed ratings (Par 105): **102,101,99,97,96 91,90**
CSF £24.87 CT £38.26 TOTE £4.00: £1.70, £1.90; EX 15.70 Trifecta £42.90.
Owner H Frost **Bred** Rashit Shaykhutdinov **Trained** Blewbury, Oxon
■ Stewards' Enquiry : Joey Haynes three-day ban: careless riding (Dec 4-6)

FOCUS
The first two finished nicely clear.

9067 32RED ON THE APP STORE H'CAP 1m 2f 219y(P)
7:40 (7:42) (Class 5) (0-70,70) 3-Y-O+
£3,752 (£1,116; £557; £400; £400; £400) **Stalls Low**

Form RPR

5321 **1** **Guroor**[34] 8293 3-8-10 **69**........................ StefanoCherchi(7) 11 79+
(Marco Botti) t.k.h early: hld up in tch in midfield: edgd out lft and effrt over 1f out: str run to ld ins fnl f: sn in command and r.o strly: readily **2/1**[1]

0040 **2** 2 **Margie's Choice (GER)**[16] 8812 4-9-3 **65**..............(bt) HectorCrouch 14 71
(Michael Madgwick) chsd ldrs: effrt ent fnl 2f: drvn over 1f out: chsd wnr ins fnl f: no imp **25/1**

5303 **3** ½ **Cheeky Rascal (IRE)**[16] 8813 4-8-9 **64**..................(v) LauraCoughlan(7) 8 69
(Tom Ward) chsd ldr tl 2f out: unable qck u.p over 1f out: kpt on again ins fnl f **16/1**

0303 **4** ½ **Dangerous Ends**[29] 8422 5-9-1 **68**........................(p) RayDawson(5) 3 72
(Brett Johnson) restrained sn after s: hld up in tch in midfield: swtchd rt and effrt to chal over 1f out: led ins fnl f: sn hdd and no ex **7/1**

600 **5** ½ **Magic Mirror**[16] 8807 6-9-7 **69**........................(p) RobHornby 4 72
(Mark Rimell) chsd ldrs: effrt on inner 2f out: drvn to ld over 1f out: hdd ins fnl f: no ex fnl 100yds **25/1**

5323 **6** 2 **Slade King (IRE)**[63] 7342 3-9-4 **70**........................ TomQueally 6 71
(Gary Moore) led: hdd and unable qck u.p over 1f out: wknd ins fnl f **7/2**[2]

1400 **7** nse **Pempie (IRE)**[16] 8806 3-9-3 **69**........................(t[1]) DavidProbert 12 70
(Andrew Balding) hld up in tch in midfield: effrt over 2f out: kpt on ins fnl f: no threat to wnr **16/1**

1022 **8** hd **Topology**[16] 8813 6-8-9 **64**........................ LeviWilliams(7) 9 64
(Joseph Tuite) hld up in tch in last quartet: effrt over 2f out: kpt on ins fnl f: nvr trbld ldrs **10/1**

000 **9** 1 **He's Our Star (IRE)**[27] 8507 4-9-5 **67**........................ TomMarquand 10 65
(Ali Stronge) stdd s: hld up towards rr: effrt and hdwy ent fnl 2f: drvn over 1f out: no imp ins fnl f **25/1**

006 **10** nk **Rail Dancer**[21] 8656 7-8-9 **64**........................(p) GavinAshton(7) 1 61
(Shaun Keightley) t.k.h: hld up in tch in midfield: effrt on inner ent fnl 2f: no ex u.p over 1f out: wknd ins fnl f **25/1**

0130 **11** 2½ **Bug Boy (IRE)**[46] 7915 3-8-11 **68**........................(p) RhiainIngram(5) 7 62
(Paul George) taken down early: stdd s: a in rr: nvr involved **20/1**

0-30 **12** 2¼ **Peckinpah (IRE)**[200] 2407 3-9-4 **70**........................ NicolaCurrie 5 60
(Alan King) stdd s: t.k.h in rr: nvr involved **13/2**[3]

2m 23.51s (2.51) **Going Correction** -0.075s/f (Stan)
WFA 3 from 4yo+ 4lb **12 Ran SP% 122.4**
Speed ratings (Par 103): **87,85,85,84,84 83,82,82,82,81 80,78**
CSF £67.62 CT £820.85 TOTE £3.30: £2.90, £5.60, £3.10; EX 55.30 Trifecta £568.70.
Owner Fabfive **Bred** Essafinaat Ltd **Trained** Newmarket, Suffolk

FOCUS
The favourite is improving and proved too good for these at the weights.
T/Plt: £137.80 to a £1 stake. Pool: £75,424.41 - 399.29 winning units T/Qpdt: £10.20 to a £1 stake. Pool: £13,962.18 - 1,010.70 winning units **Steve Payne**

9068 - 9084a (Foreign Racing) - See Raceform Interactive

9043

CHELMSFORD (A.W) (L-H)
Thursday, November 21

OFFICIAL GOING: Polytrack: standard
Wind: light, half behind Weather: cloudy

9085 BET AT TOTESPORT.COM NOVICE MEDIAN AUCTION STKS 7f (P)
4:25 (4:25) (Class 5) 2-Y-O **£4,204** (£1,251; £625; £312) **Stalls Low**

Form RPR

1 **The Perfect Crown (IRE)** 2-9-5 0........................ HollieDoyle 12 92+
(Archie Watson) t.k.h: chsd ldrs tl wnt 2nd over 5f out: rdn to ld over 1f out: r.o v strly: v readily **2/1**[1]

2 8 **Corvair (IRE)** 2-9-5 0........................ AdamKirby 4 71+
(Simon Crisford) led after almost 1f: rdn and hdd over 1f out: sn outpcd and wknd ins fnl f **5/2**[2]

44 **3** ¾ **Kohoof**[14] 8891 2-9-0 0........................ LiamJones 3 64
(William Haggas) t.k.h: chsd ldrs: outpcd u.p over 1f out: hung rt 1f out: plugged on same pce ins fnl f **9/1**

3 **4** 2½ **Inhalation**[21] 8709 2-9-5 0........................ KieranShoemark 5 63
(Ed Vaughan) hld up in tch in midfield: effrt wl over 1f out: sn outpcd: no ch w wnr and plugged on same pce ins fnl f **9/2**[3]

04 **5** 1 **Tyger Bay**[13] 8912 2-9-5 0........................(t) JosephineGordon 13 60+
(Shaun Keightley) hld up in rr of main gp: swtchd rt and pushed along wl over 1f out: kpt on ins fnl f: nvr trbld ldrs **33/1**

3 **6** 1½ **Due Care**[29] 8454 2-8-11 0........................ ThomasGreatrex(3) 9 51
(Roger Charlton) t.k.h: wl in tch in midfield: clsd to chse ldrs 4f out: rdn 2f out: sn outpcd and btn: wknd ins fnl f **7/1**

7 nk **Front Of Line** 2-9-0 0........................ GeorgeWood 11 50
(Chris Wall) rn green in rr: effrt and hung lft over 1f out: nvr on terms but kpt on ins fnl f (jockey said filly ran green) **33/1**

0 **8** 1¼ **Rocking My Boat (IRE)**[29] 8455 2-9-5 0........................ RobHornby 10 52
(Nick Littmoden) led for almost 1f out: chsd ldrs tl 2f out: wknd over 1f out **50/1**

0 **9** ¾ **Colada Cove (IRE)**[33] 8346 2-9-5 0........................(t[1]) CharlesBishop 8 50
(Tom Ward) impeded sn after s: a towards rr after **66/1**

4 **10** 3½ **Plath**[24] 8602 2-9-0 0........................ DavidProbert 6 36
(Sir Michael Stoute) t.k.h: hld up in tch in midfield: rdn 2f out: sn lost pl and wl btn over 1f out **8/1**

0 **11** 6 **Sea Bright**[24] 8604 2-9-5 0........................ WilliamCarson 1 25
(Michael Attwater) sn pushed along in midfield: lost pl and bhd over 1f out: wknd **66/1**

0 **12** 4½ **Rhythmic Motion**[15] 8849 2-9-0 0........................ CharlieBennett 7 9
(Jim Boyle) s.i.s: a outpcd in rr: lame (jockey said filly was never travelling) **100/1**

1m 25.36s (-1.84) **Going Correction** -0.225s/f (Stan) **12 Ran SP% 125.5**
Speed ratings (Par 96): **101,91,91,88,87 85,84,83,82,78 71,66**
CSF £7.40 TOTE £2.70: £1.20, £1.30, £2.70; EX 9.00 Trifecta £42.30.
Owner Sheikh Hamed Dalmook Al Maktoum **Bred** Mrs O M E McKeever **Trained** Upper Lambourn, W Berks

FOCUS
A very useful performance from the winner and some encouraging signs in behind make this a novice to take a positive view of. The opening couple of furlongs were a bit messy and few got involved form the back.

9086 TOTEPOOL CASHBACK CLUB AT TOTESPORT.COM CLAIMING STKS 1m (P)
5:00 (5:01) (Class 6) 3-Y-O+
£3,105 (£924; £461; £400; £400; £400) **Stalls Low**

Form RPR

1256 **1** **Unforgiving Minute**[198] 2514 8-9-3 **83**........................ AdamKirby 4 77+
(Sean Curran) t.k.h: trckd ldrs: wnt 2nd over 4f out: rdn to ld over 1f out: r.o wl and asserted ins fnl f: eased towards fin **3/1**[2]

6304 **2** 1½ **Azzeccagarbugli (IRE)**[43] 8017 6-8-9 **78**..............(p) GeorgeRooke(7) 6 72
(Mike Murphy) t.k.h: led after over 1f: rdn and hdd over 1f out: no ex and outpcd fnl 100yds **7/4**[1]

3003 **3** 2 **Mochalov**[19] 8756 4-8-9 **59**........................ RayDawson(5) 3 65
(Jane Chapple-Hyam) led for over 1f: chsd ldrs after: effrt 2f out: unable qck and kpt on same pce ins fnl f **10/1**[3]

0404 **4** 2¾ **Shady McCoy (USA)**[21] 8690 9-8-8 **83**........................ AngusVilliers(7) 1 60
(Ian Williams) s.i.s: t.k.h: hld up in tch in last pair: effrt 2f out: sn outpcd and wl hld 4th fr over 1f out (jockey said gelding was slowly away) **7/4**[1]

4/65 **5** 2¼ **First Voyage (IRE)**[43] 8032 6-9-2 **70**........................(t[1]) AlistairRawlinson 5 56
(Michael Appleby) t.k.h: hld up in tch: pushed along wl over 1f out: sn btn: burst blood vessel (vet said gelding bled from the nose) **20/1**

0200 **6** 7 **Song Of Summer**[102] 5981 4-8-6 **44**..................(tp) JosephineGordon 2 29
(Phil McEntee) t.k.h: hld up in tch: outpcd 2f out: sn bhd **66/1**

1m 40.29s (0.39) **Going Correction** -0.225s/f (Stan) **6 Ran SP% 113.1**
Speed ratings (Par 101): **89,87,85,82,80 73**
CSF £8.83 TOTE £3.40: £1.60, £1.50; EX 10.40 Trifecta £31.33.
Owner Power Geneva Ltd **Bred** Equine Breeding Limited **Trained** Upper Lambourn, Berks

FOCUS
An uneventful, steadily run claimer that few got into.

9087 EXTRA PLACES AT TOTESPORT.COM H'CAP 2m (P)
5:30 (5:31) (Class 6) (0-65,65) 3-Y-O+
£3,105 (£924; £461; £400; £400; £400) **Stalls Low**

Form RPR

6002 **1** **Noble Behest**[38] 8196 5-9-7 **65**........................(p) RPWalsh(7) 7 71+
(Ian Williams) t.k.h: hld up in rr early: hdwy on outer to chse ldr after 4f: led over 3f out: hld on wl u.p fr over 1f out: rdn out **7/2**[2]

5122 **2** ¾ **Land Of Winter (FR)**[36] 8246 3-9-6 **64**........................ DavidProbert 9 71
(Rae Guest) chsd ldrs tl wnt 2nd 3f out: drvn and ev ch 1f out: no ex and hld towards fin **1/1**[1]

3024 **3** 2¼ **Ban Shoof**[35] 6566 6-9-13 **64**........................(b) HectorCrouch 4 66
(Gary Moore) hld up in tch in rr: hdwy on outer to chse ldrs over 2f out: edgd lft u.p and one pce ins fnl f **7/1**[3]

5250 **4** ½ **Lazarus (IRE)**[28] 7558 5-8-10 **47**........................(bt[1]) BarryMcHugh 1 49
(Amy Murphy) wl in tch in midfield: effrt to chse ldrs over 2f out: edgd lft u.p over 1f out: kpt on same pce ins fnl f **20/1**

5053 **5** 8 **General Allenby**[16] 8843 5-8-9 **46**........................(p) JosephineGordon 8 38
(Shaun Keightley) in tch in rr: pushed along over 7f out: rdn over 6f out: rdn and outpcd over 2f out: no ch but plugged on to pass btn horses ins fnl f **14/1**

0535 **6** ¾ **Miss Swift**[13] 8916 3-8-2 **46** oh1........................ RaulDaSilva 5 39
(Marcus Tregoning) chsd ldr tl 4f out: chsd ldrs tl short of room and shuffled bk over 2f out: tried to rally u.p over 1f out: no imp: wknd ins fnl f **11/1**

0006 **7** 1 **Guaracha**[13] 8916 8-8-2 **46** oh1........................(v) KeelanBaker(7) 3 36
(Alexandra Dunn) t.k.h: hld up in tch in midfield: clsd and effrt over 2f out: outpcd u.p over 1f out: wknd ins fnl f **33/1**

4002 **8** 2¼ **Lyford (IRE)**[22] 8670 4-9-4 **55**........................(p) TomQueally 2 42
(Alistair Whillans) hld up in tch in midfield: clsd and n.m.r over 2f out: no imp u.p over 1f out: wknd ins fnl f **16/1**

5455 **9** 17 **Picture Poet (IRE)**[15] 8854 3-8-1 **52**........................ LauraPearson(7) 6 21
(Henry Spiller) sn towards rr: lost tch 4f out **20/1**

2300 **10** 15 **Beechwood James (FR)**[13] 8916 3-8-3 **50**........(v[1]) TheodoreLadd(3) 10
(Michael Appleby) t.k.h: led tl over 3f out: losing pl whn hmpd over 2f out: bhd over 1f out: eased: t.o (jockey said colt ran too freely and stopped quickly) **33/1**

3m 28.5s (-1.50) **Going Correction** -0.225s/f (Stan)
WFA 3 from 4yo+ 7lb **10 Ran SP% 121.0**
Speed ratings (Par 101): **94,93,92,92,88 87,87,86,77,70**
CSF £7.28 CT £22.70 TOTE £3.90: £1.30, £1.10, £1.60; EX 8.30 Trifecta £33.60.
Owner A C Elliott **Bred** Mr & Mrs A E Pakenham **Trained** Portway, Worcs

FOCUS
A fair staying handicap that looks strong form for the grade. The pace lifted at the end of the back straight but it proved hard to make up ground from the rear.

9088 IRISH LOTTO AT TOTESPORT.COM H'CAP 6f (P)
6:00 (6:02) (Class 2) (0-105,102) 3-Y-O+ **£12,938** (£3,850; £1,924; £962) **Stalls Centre**

Form RPR

3323 **1** **Lady Dancealot (IRE)**[15] 8851 4-8-6 **87**........................ HollieDoyle 10 98
(David Elsworth) stdd after s: hld up in rr: swtchd rt and hdwy over 1f out: str run to ld ins fnl f: r.o wl **5/1**[3]

0500 **2** 1¼ **Gracious John (IRE)**[68] 7183 6-8-7 **88**........................ JosephineGordon 12 95
(Ian Williams) hld up in tch: swtchd rt and effrt over 1f out: hdwy ins fnl f: r.o wl to go 2nd towards fin: nvr getting to wnr **25/1**

2342 **3** ½ **Heath Charnock**[68] 7187 3-8-5 **86**........................ KieranO'Neill 5 91
(Michael Dods) led tl over 3f out: styd pressing ldrs: rdn to ld again over 1f out: hdd and one pce ins fnl f: lost 2nd towards fin **5/2**[1]

0210 **4** hd **Mokaatil**[75] 6953 4-7-11 **85**........................(p) RPWalsh(7) 7 89
(Ian Williams) chsd ldrs: pushed along and clsd to press ldrs 2f out: hung lft over 1f out: drvn and ev ch 1f out: no ex and outpcd wl ins fnl f **25/1**

1125 **5** *nk* **Royal Birth**[5] 9004 8-9-7 **102**....................(t) AdamKirby 13 105
(Stuart Williams) *hld up in tch in midfield: effrt over 1f out: kpt on same pce u.p ins fnl f* **8/1**

0306 **6** *2 ¼* **Lancelot Du Lac (ITY)**[15] 8851 9-9-2 **97**.................... JoeyHaynes 4 93
(Dean Ivory) *taken down early: chsd ldrs: nt clr run 2f out: gap opened and rdn to chal ent fnl f: no ex ins fnl f: wknd wl ins fnl f* **10/1**

0330 **7** *½* **Revich (IRE)**[21] 8707 3-8-7 **88**....................(p[1]) GeorgeWood 6 83
(Richard Spencer) *sn rousted along and nvr travelling wl: hdwy u.p 1f out: kpt on ins fnl f: nvr trbld ldrs* **12/1**

3500 **8** *1* **Rock On Baileys**[21] 8708 4-9-0 **95**....................(b) BarryMcHugh 2 86+
(Amy Murphy) *awkward leaving stalls: hld up in midfield: nt clr run and hmpd over 1f out: nvr enough room after and no hdwy* **10/1**

0300 **9** *1 ½* **Verne Castle**[182] 3021 6-8-8 **89**....................(h) LiamJones 1 76
(Michael Wigham) *chsd ldrs on inner: effrt to press ldrs and edgd rt over 1f out: no ex 1f out: wknd ins fnl f* **50/1**

5600 **10** *shd* **Polybius**[24] 8607 8-8-8 **89**.................... CallumShepherd 8 75
(David Simcock) *stdd s: hld up in tch towards rr: effrt over 1f out: no imp u.p ins fnl f: wknd towards fin: burst blood vessel (vet said gelding bled from the nose)* **20/1**

166 **11** *1* **Moon Trouble (IRE)**[24] 8607 6-8-1 **89**.................... AngusVilliers(7) 3 72
(Michael Appleby) *taken down early: w ldrs tl rdn to ld ent fnl 2f: edgd lft: bmpd and hdd over 1f out: wknd ins fnl f* **9/2**[2]

6003 **12** *hd* **Merhoob (IRE)**[38] 8182 7-8-13 **97**.................... DarraghKeenan(3) 9 79+
(John Ryan) *hld up in tch: clsd on inner: nt clr run and hmpd over 1f out: nvr enough room after and no hdwy (jockey said gelding was denied a clear run)* **14/1**

0041 **13** *¾* **Shamshon (IRE)**[59] 7524 8-8-8 **89**.................... DavidProbert 11 69
(Stuart Williams) *chsd ldrs on outer: led over 3f out tl ent fnl 2f: lost pl over 1f out: wknd ins fnl f* **25/1**

1m 11.13s (-2.57) **Going Correction** -0.225s/f (Stan) **13 Ran SP% 125.3**
Speed ratings (Par 109): **108,106,105,105,105 102,101,100,98,97 96,96,95**
CSF £135.97 CT £405.89 TOTE £6.10: £2.00, £7.10, £1.30; EX 152.80 Trifecta £846.50.
Owner Kevin Quinn **Bred** P J B O'Callaghan **Trained** Newmarket, Suffolk

FOCUS
The pace collapsed in the straight and several towards the inside met trouble, so this form might not prove all that strong.

9089 BET IN PLAY AT TOTESPORT.COM H'CAP — 6f (P)
6:30 (6:32) (Class 6) (0-65,65) 3-Y-O+
£3,105 (£924; £461; £400; £400; £400) **Stalls Centre**

Form — RPR

512 **1** **Split Down South**[3] 9035 3-8-11 **62**.................... GraceMcEntee(7) 7 71
(Phil McEntee) *hld up in midfield: clsd and rdn 2f out: swtchd rt and hdwy over 1f out: led ins fnl f: r.o wl* **11/4**[1]

5122 **2** *1 ¾* **Broughton Excels**[13] 8917 4-9-1 **59**.................... RobHornby 4 63
(Stuart Williams) *stdd s: hld up in tch towards rr: clsd and swtchd rt over 1f out: edgd lft but styd on ins fnl f: wnt 2nd towards fin: nvr getting to wnr* **10/3**[2]

0440 **3** *¾* **Seraphim**[21] 8698 3-9-2 **60**....................(bt[1]) DavidProbert 3 62
(Marco Botti) *chsd ldrs: wnt 2nd over 3f out tl lft in ld 3f out: rdn over 1f out: hdd ins fnl f: no ex and one pce fnl 100yds: lost 2nd towards fin* **7/1**

1414 **4** *1 ¾* **Holdenhurst**[37] 8217 4-9-6 **64**.................... AdamKirby 6 60
(Bill Turner) *chsd ldrs: lft pressing ldr 3f out: rdn and ev ch 2f out: drvn ent fnl 2f: no ex and one pce ins fnl f* **6/1**[3]

4261 **5** *1 ¼* **Society Guest (IRE)**[13] 8920 3-9-7 **65**....................(v) CallumShepherd 8 58
(Mick Channon) *in tch in midfield: clsd to chse ldrs and swtchd lft over 1f out: sn rdn and unable qck: wknd ins fnl f* **12/1**

0315 **6** *1 ½* **Amor Kethley**[28] 8501 3-9-5 **63**....................(tp) RaulDaSilva 12 51
(Amy Murphy) *chsd ldr for over 1f out: drvn and unable qck over 1f out: wknd ins fnl f* **20/1**

0301 **7** *½* **Kingsley Klarion (IRE)**[49] 7837 6-9-2 **63**.................... DarraghKeenan(3) 2 50
(John Butler) *hld up towards rr: swtchd rt and effrt over 1f out: rdn 1f out: kpt on same pce ins fnl f* **7/1**

6444 **8** *¾* **Global Melody**[157] 3936 4-9-7 **65**....................(p) JosephineGordon 14 49
(Phil McEntee) *midfield on outer: effrt and swtchd lft over 1f out: no imp and wl hld ins fnl f* **22/1**

0060 **9** *1 ¼* **Angel Force (IRE)**[23] 8643 4-9-1 **59**....................(h) LiamKeniry 13 40
(David C Griffiths) *t.k.h: chsd ldrs: unable qck u.p over 2f out: lost pl over 1f out: wknd ins fnl f* **50/1**

0050 **10** *7* **George Dryden (IRE)**[54] 7690 7-9-6 **64**.................... DannyBrock 5 24
(Denis Quinn) *taken down early: stdd s: a bhd* **33/1**

1251 **11** *3 ½* **Lordsbridge Boy**[37] 8217 3-9-2 **65**.................... SophieRalston(5) 10 14
(Dean Ivory) *hung rt thrght: led: wd and hdd bnd 3f out: lost pl and racing on far rail in home st: sn bhd (jockey said gelding hung badly right-handed)* **8/1**

1m 11.62s (-2.08) **Going Correction** -0.225s/f (Stan) **11 Ran SP% 121.8**
Speed ratings (Par 101): **104,101,100,98,96 94,94,93,91,82 77**
CSF £11.78 CT £60.08 TOTE £3.30: £1.50, £1.40, £2.20; EX 11.00 Trifecta £71.60.
Owner Trevor Johnson **Bred** Mike Smith **Trained** Newmarket, Suffolk

FOCUS
A modest sprint handicap with no hard-luck stories. The form looks solid.

9090 DOUBLE DELIGHT HAT-TRICK HEAVEN AT TOTESPORT.COM H'CAP — 1m 2f (P)
7:00 (7:05) (Class 6) (0-55,55) 3-Y-O+
£3,105 (£924; £461; £400; £400; £400) **Stalls Low**

Form — RPR

3431 **1** **Red Gunner**[15] 8870 5-9-7 **55**.................... AdamKirby 2 66
(Mark Loughnane) *hld up in tch in midfield: clsd to trck ldr and travelling strly over 1f out: shkn up to ld 1f out: sn rdn clr: r.o wl: readily* **6/1**[2]

0006 **2** *4 ½* **Arlecchino's Arc (IRE)**[21] 8703 4-9-7 **55**....................(v) DavidProbert 13 57
(Mark Usher) *chsd ldr for 2f: styd chsng ldrs tl clsd to ld and travelling wl ent fnl 2f: rdn over 1f out: hdd 1f out: no match for wnr fnl f* **10/1**

3410 **3** *hd* **Dyagilev**[15] 8854 4-9-4 **52**....................(b) AdrianMcCarthy 8 54
(Lydia Pearce) *hld up towards rr: nt clr run over 2f out: swtchd rt and hdwy over 1f out: kpt on ins fnl f: no threat to wnr* **8/1**[3]

210 **4** *nk* **Necoleta**[26] 8553 3-9-2 **53**.................... LiamKeniry 4 56
(Sylvester Kirk) *midfield: effrt ent fnl 2f: swtchd rt 1f out: kpt on ins fnl f: no threat to wnr* **9/1**

0000 **5** *½* **Clovenstone**[17] 8818 3-8-3 **47**.................... OliverStammers(7) 3 49
(Alistair Whillans) *t.k.h early: hld up in tch: edgd out rt and effrt over 1f out: kpt on same pce and no threat to wnr ins fnl f* **20/1**

05 **6** *3* **Dolphin Village (IRE)**[225] 1680 9-8-12 **46**....................(h) JoeyHaynes 7 41
(Shaun Harris) *hld up towards rr: effrt on inner ent fnl 2f: swtchd rt over 1f out: no imp u.p ins fnl f* **33/1**

4351 **7** *¾* **Cash N Carrie (IRE)**[19] 8753 5-8-11 **48**.................... TheodoreLadd(3) 12 41
(Michael Appleby) *led tl over 4f out: drvn over 1f out: 3rd and no ex 1f out: wknd ins fnl f* **9/1**

0003 **8** *½* **Tebay (IRE)**[16] 8822 4-9-2 **50**.................... KierenFox 14 42
(John Best) *hld up towards rr: nt clr run over 2f out: swtchd rt ins fnl f: nvr trbld ldrs* **5/1**[1]

5041 **9** *1 ½* **Caledonia Laird**[13] 8915 8-9-7 **55**....................(e) HollieDoyle 9 45
(Gay Kelleway) *stdd s: hld up in rr: effrt on inner over 1f out: nvr threatened to get on terms: wl hld ins fnl f* **14/1**

5040 **10** *1 ½* **Cheerful**[30] 8416 3-8-11 **48**....................(p[1]) LiamJones 15 36
(Michael Squance) *hld up towards rr: shkn up 2f out: rdn over 1f out: no hdwy and wl hld ins fnl f* **33/1**

206 **11** *1 ¾* **Ecstasea (IRE)**[16] 8822 3-8-9 **53**.................... AngusVilliers(7) 1 37
(Rae Guest) *chsd ldrs: rdn jst over 3f out: unable qck and outpcd over 1f out: wkng whn sltly impeded ins fnl f* **14/1**

60-6 **12** *1 ½* **George Junior**[52] 7772 3-8-6 **46**.................... ThomasGreatrex(3) 6 28
(Ed Walker) *t.k.h: chsd ldrs for 2f: settled bk into midfield: swtchd rt and effrt bnd 2f out: no prog and wknd ins fnl f (jockey said gelding hung badly left-handed throughout)* **20/1**

000 **13** *1 ½* **Anything For You**[17] 8808 3-9-1 **52**.................... RobHornby 11 31
(Jonathan Portman) *hld up in midfield on outer: effrt ent fnl 2f: sn struggling and lost pl: wknd fnl f* **25/1**

0236 **14** *1 ¼* **Born To Reason (IRE)**[15] 8854 5-9-0 **48**....................(b) CallumShepherd 10 23
(Alexandra Dunn) *chsd ldrs: rdn over 2f out: unable qck and lost pl over 1f out: wknd ins fnl f* **12/1**

1342 **F** **Warning Light**[29] 8466 4-9-6 **54**.................... JosephineGordon 16
(Shaun Keightley) *styd wd early: hdwy to chse ldr after 2f: led over 4f out: rdn and hdd ent fnl 2f: wkng whn lost action and fell ins fnl f: fatally injured* **5/1**[1]

2m 5.76s (-2.84) **Going Correction** -0.225s/f (Stan)
WFA 3 from 4yo+ 3lb **15 Ran SP% 128.1**
Speed ratings (Par 101): **102,98,98,98,97 95,94,94,93,91 90,89,88,87,**
CSF £64.04 CT £498.11 TOTE £6.10: £2.00, £3.80, £2.80; EX 89.90 Trifecta £408.90.
Owner 2 Counties Racing **Bred** Scea Haras De Saint Pair **Trained** Rock, Worcs

FOCUS
A strongly run, moderate handicap in which an in-form pair filled the first two positions.

9091 CHRISTMAS PARTY NIGHTS AT CCR NOVICE STKS — 1m 2f (P)
7:30 (7:35) (Class 5) 3-Y-O+
£4,948 (£1,472; £735; £367) **Stalls Low**

Form — RPR

45 **1** **Mons Star (IRE)**[197] 2524 3-9-2 0....................(p[1]) HectorCrouch 2 89
(Saeed bin Suroor) *mde all: gng best and gng clr 2f out: r.o wl and in command whn reminder ins fnl f: easily* **1/6**[1]

3 **2** *8* **Engrave**[21] 8693 3-8-11 0....................(p[1]) DavidProbert 8 68
(Hugo Palmer) *sn chsng wnr: rdn over 2f out: sn struggling and outpcd over 1f out: wl hld and one pce fnl f* **8/1**[3]

040 **3** *15* **Sea It My Way (IRE)**[59] 7518 3-9-2 66....................(t[1]) GeorgeWood 1 43
(James Fanshawe) *chsd ldng pair over 7f out: rdn 3f out: sn struggling and outpcd: wknd fnl f* **5/1**[2]

6 **4** *4* **The Rocket Park (IRE)**[69] 7159 6-9-5 0.................... HowardCheng 3 34
(John Berry) *dwlt: hld up in last pair: rdn over 3f out: sn struggling and outpcd: wl hld 4th over 1f out* **20/1**

00 **5** *4 ½* **Big Bang**[26] 8552 6-9-5 0....................(h[1]) ShelleyBirkett 5 25
(Julia Feilden) *hld up in last pair: swtchd rt 4f out: sn struggling: outpcd wl over 2f out: bhd over 1f out* **66/1**

6 **6** *½* **Byron Green (IRE)**[77] 6887 7-9-2 0.................... DarraghKeenan(3) 7 24
(Thomas Gallagher) *t.k.h: chsd ldrs for 2f: in tch in midfield after: rdn over 3f out: sn struggling: bhd over 1f out* **50/1**

2m 4.17s (-4.43) **Going Correction** -0.225s/f (Stan)
WFA 3 from 6yo+ 3lb **6 Ran SP% 121.7**
Speed ratings (Par 103): **108,101,89,86,82 82**
CSF £3.14 TOTE £1.10: £1.20, £1.80; EX 3.30 Trifecta £5.90.
Owner Godolphin **Bred** Brucetown Farms Ltd **Trained** Newmarket, Suffolk

FOCUS
Something of a non-contest with the winner being a cut above. There was no promise behind the front two.

9092 LASER'S MINI BUS DASH H'CAP — 5f (P)
8:00 (8:03) (Class 6) (0-65,65) 3-Y-O+
£3,105 (£924; £461; £400; £400; £400) **Stalls Low**

Form — RPR

4603 **1** **Lalania**[19] 8755 4-9-5 **63**.................... CallumShepherd 5 73
(Stuart Williams) *chsd ldrs: effrt ent fnl 2f: chsd ldr 1f out: kpt on wl to ld wl ins fnl f: rdn out* **3/1**[2]

3500 **2** *1* **Roundabout Magic (IRE)**[44] 7986 5-8-6 **57**.................... LeviWilliams(7) 7 63+
(Simon Dow) *stdd and short of room leaving stalls: hld up in last pair: hdwy and swtchd rt 1f out: r.o wl to go 2nd towards fin: nt rch wnr* **25/1**

6610 **3** *¾* **Tan**[5] 9013 5-9-5 **63**.................... CharlesBishop 4 67
(Lisa Williamson) *led: rdn over 1f out: drvn ins fnl f: hdd and no ex wl ins fnl f: lost 2nd towards fin* **6/1**

0 **4** *2 ¼* **Nautical Haven**[102] 5990 5-9-2 **60**.................... DougieCostello 9 56
(Suzi Best) *s.i.s: bhd: effrt over 1f out: swtchd rt and r.o wl ins fnl f: nvr trbld ldrs (jockey said gelding was slowly away)* **20/1**

0400 **5** *¾* **Time To Reason (IRE)**[14] 8895 6-9-4 **62**....................(p) HectorCrouch 8 55
(Charlie Wallis) *chsd ldr: rdn over 2f out: unable qck and lost 2nd 1f out: wknd wl ins fnl f* **33/1**

20-2 **6** *nse* **Nampara**[14] 8895 4-9-7 **65**.................... WilliamCarson 1 58
(Paul D'Arcy) *in tch in midfield: effrt over 1f out: rdn and no imp ins fnl f* **2/1**[1]

6660 **7** *½* **Bond Street Beau**[13] 8917 4-8-12 **56**.................... RobHornby 3 47
(Philip McBride) *towards rr: effrt ent fnl 2f: swtchd rt over 1f out: kpt on ins fnl f: nvr trbld ldrs* **11/1**

1060 **8** *1 ¾* **Red Stripes (USA)**[5] 9013 7-8-12 **63**....................(b) GavinAshton(7) 6 48
(Lisa Williamson) *midfield: effrt wl over 1f out: sn hung lft and no imp: wl hld ins fnl f* **4/1**[3]

0000 **9** *nk* **Superseded (IRE)**[20] 8715 3-8-13 **62**....................(p[1]) DylanHogan(5) 2 46
(John Butler) *chsd ldrs: unable qck u.p over 1f out: wknd ins fnl f* **16/1**

0530 **10** *1 ¼* **Fareeq**[61] 7446 5-9-2 **60**....................(bt w) DavidProbert 12 39
(Charlie Wallis) *hld up in rr: swtchd rt and effrt u.p over 1f out: no hdwy: nvr involved* **33/1**

4600 **11** *3 ¼* **Gupta**[16] 8839 3-9-2 **60**.................... DarraghKeenan 10 27
(David Brown) *midfield on outer: rdn over 1f out: sn struggling and outpcd: edgd lft and wknd ins fnl f: sddle slipped (jockey said his saddle slipped)* **25/1**

59.16s (-1.04) **Going Correction** -0.225s/f (Stan) **11 Ran SP% 125.2**
Speed ratings (Par 101): **99,97,96,92,91 91,90,87,87,85 80**
CSF £86.30 CT £441.66 TOTE £3.90: £1.20, £7.00, £1.90; EX 111.60 Trifecta £941.80.

Owner Mrs A Shone **Bred** Mrs A Shone **Trained** Newmarket, Suffolk

FOCUS

A modest sprint handicap run at a good pace and there's no reason to doubt the form.

T/Plt: £19.50 to a £1 stake. Pool: £59,330.95 - 3032.15 winning units T/Qpdt: £8.70 to a £1 stake. Pool: £9,476.80 - 1087.26 winning units **Steve Payne**

8918 NEWCASTLE (A.W) (L-H)

Thursday, November 21

OFFICIAL GOING: Tapeta: standard to slow

Wind: Fresh, half behind in races on the straight course and in over 3f of home straight in races on the r Weather: Overcast, dry

9093 BETWAY LIVE CASINO H'CAP — 1m 4f 98y (Tp)

1:20 (1:20) (Class 6) (0-65,65) 3-Y-O+

£2,781 (£827; £413; £300; £300; £300) **Stalls** High

Form				RPR
5462	1		**Spirit Of Angel (IRE)**[31] 8414 3-9-2 **62** BenCurtis 4 (Marcus Tregoning) *hld up in rr: hdwy gng easily 3f out: pushed along and led over 1f out: r.o wl* **7/2**[1]	72+
3063	2	6	**Glorious Dane**[43] 8019 3-9-4 **64** DougieCostello 12 (Mark Walford) *t.k.h: midfield: rdn and led 2f out: hdd over 1f out: no match for wnr* **20/1**	65
4024	3	*hd*	**Visor**[22] 8662 4-9-7 **62** (h) TomMarquand 7 (James Fanshawe) *dwlt s: in rr: rdn and styd on fr 3f out: nvr able to chal* **7/1**	62
1613	4	1 ½	**Para Queen (IRE)**[22] 8663 3-9-2 **62** JaneElliott 11 (Heather Main) *slowly away: in rr: rdn and styd on fr 4f out: n.d (jockey said filly was slowly away)* **10/1**	60
313/	5	*shd*	**Taopix**[1010] 727 7-9-10 **65** JasonHart 9 (Karen McLintock) *t.k.h: towards rr of midfield: pushed along and sme hdwy fr 3f out: n.d* **9/1**	62
3541	6	*nk*	**Kaizer**[26] 7739 4-9-5 **60** AndrewMullen 1 (Alistair Whillans) *t.k.h: midfield: niggled along and hdwy fr 4f out: cl up whn rdn 2f out: wknd fr over 1f out* **13/2**[3]	57
2226	7	3	**Mr Carbonator**[120] 5301 4-9-2 **64** NickBarratt-Atkin(7) 14 (Philip Kirby) *racd wd: midfield: rdn over 3f out: mde no imp* **28/1**	56
5505	8	3 ¾	**Flash Point (IRE)**[27] 8524 3-9-5 **65** CamHardie 2 (Tracy Waggott) *led at stdy pce tl hdd and cl up after 3f: pushed along over 3f out: wknd fr 2f out* **12/1**	53
416	9	6	**Minnelli**[15] 8868 3-9-1 **64** SeanDavis(3) 3 (Philip McBride) *dwlt s: towards rr: bit short of room on inner early: nvr gng wl* **33/1**	43
6004	10	*nk*	**Velvet Vision**[22] 8669 4-9-6 **61** PaulMulrennan 10 (Mrs Ilka Gansera-Leveque) *slowly away: t.k.h: abt three wd and prom after 1f: led after 3f: 3 l ahd and gng easily 3f out: hdd whn pushed along and fnd nthing 2f out (vet said filly scoped dirty post-race)* **6/1**[2]	38
3430	11	*nk*	**Eesha's Smile (IRE)**[41] 8087 3-8-12 **65** (h[1]) JonathanFisher(7) 5 (Ivan Furtado) *midfield: pushed along 3f out: mde no imp* **40/1**	43
2420	12	22	**Duke Of Alba (IRE)**[48] 7873 4-9-7 **62** JoeFanning 8 (John Mackie) *t.k.h: prom: pushed along and fnd little 3f out: eased fnl f (jockey said gelding ran flat)* **6/1**[2]	6
10-6	13	13	**Gripper**[15] 8236 4-9-10 **65** (p) GrahamLee 13 (Lucinda Russell) *hung lft thrght: prom: pushed along and wknd grad fr 4f out: eased fnl f (jockey said gelding hung left throughout)* **150/1**	
0	14	59	**Vivax (IRE)**[23] 8642 3-9-5 **65** JamesSullivan 6 (Ruth Carr) *uns rdr in preliminaries: t.k.h: prom: pushed along and wknd fr 4f out: eased fr 3f out (jockey said gelding moved poorly)* **100/1**	

2m 41.9s (0.80) **Going Correction** +0.025s/f (Slow)

WFA 3 from 4yo+ 5lb — **14** Ran SP% **118.7**

Speed ratings (Par 101): **98,94,93,92,92 92,90,88,84,83 83,69,60,21**

CSF £80.73 CT £473.79 TOTE £2.90: £1.10, £5.90, £2.50; EX 67.10 Trifecta £416.60.

Owner Owenstown Stud & M P N Tregoning **Bred** Owenstown Stud **Trained** Whitsbury, Hants

FOCUS

A modest middle-distance handicap. A mid-race injection of pace brought those ridden more patiently to the fore.

9094 BETWAY HEED YOUR HUNCH H'CAP — 1m 4f 98y (Tp)

1:55 (1:55) (Class 2) (0-105,101) 3-Y-O+ £13,584 (£4,042; £2,020; £1,010) **Stalls** High

Form				RPR
0512	1		**Francis Xavier (IRE)**[56] 7622 5-9-8 **99** CliffordLee 5 (Kevin Frost) *t.k.h: pressed ldr: shkn up to ld over 2f out: rdn over 1f out: kpt on strly fnl f* **12/1**	106
0111	2	¾	**Paths Of Glory**[33] 8350 4-9-5 **96** (t) JackMitchell 3 (Hugo Palmer) *prom: smooth hdwy and trckd wnr 2f out: sn rdn: kpt on fnl f: hld towards fin* **11/8**[1]	102
-600	3	*nk*	**Sir Chauvelin**[190] 2742 7-9-10 **101** BenRobinson 1 (Jim Goldie) *stdd s: hld up in last: shkn up over 2f out: rdn and hdwy over 1f out: kpt on strly fnl 110yds: nrst fin* **50/1**	106
0132	4	*shd*	**Spanish Archer (FR)**[44] 8005 4-9-7 **98** (h) DanielMuscutt 7 (James Fanshawe) *towards rr: stdy hdwy over 2f out: rdn over 1f out: kpt on ins fnl f: nrst fin* **11/2**[3]	103
11-1	5	¾	**Deja (FR)**[141] 4504 4-9-9 **100** PaulMulrennan 6 (Peter Chapple-Hyam) *t.k.h: towards rr on inner: rdn and hdwy over 1f out: sn edgd lft: no ex ins fnl f* **5/2**[2]	104
0403	6	6	**Archi's Affaire**[54] 7702 5-8-10 **87** AndrewMullen 2 (Michael Dods) *t.k.h: trckd ldrs: rdn over 2f out: wknd fr 1f out* **28/1**	81
3066	7	3 ¾	**Lunar Jet**[76] 6923 5-9-1 **92** JoeFanning 8 (John Mackie) *t.k.h: midfield on outer: stdy hdwy over 2f out: shkn up and edgd lft over 1f out: sn wknd* **22/1**	80
266P	8	2 ¾	**Seafarer (IRE)**[149] 4224 5-8-12 **89** (b) BenCurtis 4 (Marcus Tregoning) *led at stdy pce: rdn and hdd over 2f out: wknd over 1f out* **10/1**	73

2m 44.91s (3.81) **Going Correction** +0.025s/f (Slow) — **8** Ran SP% **112.6**

Speed ratings (Par 109): **88,87,87,87,86 82,80,78**

CSF £28.23 CT £816.22 TOTE £11.20: £2.50, £1.10, £8.40; EX 34.50 Trifecta £420.80.

Owner Curzon House Partnership **Bred** Rockhart Trading Ltd **Trained** Newcastle-under-Lyme, Staffs

FOCUS

The feature contest was a good middle-distance handicap. The winner held on gamely in a sprint finish and his winning time was notably slower than the preceding lower-class C&D handicap.

9095 LADBROKES HOME OF THE ODDS BOOST EBF MAIDEN STKS (PLUS 10 RACE) — 1m 2f 42y (Tp)

2:25 (2:29) (Class 4) 2-Y-O — £6,469 (£1,925; £962; £481) **Stalls** High

Form				RPR
0	1		**English King (FR)**[29] 8464 2-9-5 0 TomMarquand 10 (Ed Walker) *hld up in rr: stdy hdwy gng easily over 2f out: shkn up over 1f out: led fnl 110yds: sn pushed out: readily* **13/2**	87+
2	2	1 ¾	**Waleydd**[27] 8518 2-9-5 0 JackMitchell 13 (Roger Varian) *t.k.h: cl up: led gng easily over 2f out: rdn and hrd pressed over 1f out: hdd fnl 110yds: no match for wnr* **11/10**[1]	83
2	3	2 ½	**Galsworthy**[29] 8460 2-9-5 0 NickyMackay 8 (John Gosden) *t.k.h: prom: smooth hdwy over 2f out: rdn and disp ld over 1f out: no ex ins fnl f* **9/4**[2]	79
43	4	3 ¾	**Sun Cuisine (USA)**[82] 6708 2-9-5 0 (b) KevinStott 4 (Charlie Appleby) *t.k.h: midfield: smooth hdwy and cl up over 2f out: rdn and wknd fr 1f out* **6/1**[3]	72
	5	6	**Night Bear** 2-9-5 0 PaulMulrennan 11 (Ed Vaughan) *s.i.s: hld up in last: rdn and rn green 3f out: rallied over 1f out: nvr able to chal* **50/1**	61+
63	6	2	**Three Dragons**[45] 7957 2-9-5 0 AndrewMullen 6 (Ben Haslam) *t.k.h: towards rr: pushed along over 2f out: sme hdwy over 1f out: mde no imp* **125/1**	58
0	7	1 ¼	**Clever Trick**[105] 5848 2-9-5 0 TomEaves 3 (Kevin Ryan) *prom: rdn and outpcd 3f out: no imp fr 2f out* **150/1**	55
0	8	½	**You Owe Me**[13] 8914 2-9-5 0 JasonHart 14 (Mark Johnston) *led: rdn and hdd over 2f out: wknd over 1f out* **66/1**	54
02	9	2 ¼	**Spanish Persuader (FR)**[15] 8857 2-9-5 0 JoeFanning 1 (Mark Johnston) *had to be re-shod: cl up and: outpcd over 2f out: sn btn* **33/1**	50
4	10	1 ½	**Despoina (IRE)**[57] 7579 2-9-0 0 GrahamLee 12 (Jedd O'Keeffe) *t.k.h: midfield on inner: rdn over 2f out: sn wknd* **33/1**	43
0	11	1 ¼	**Allerthorpe**[20] 8717 2-9-2 0 (t) ConnorMurtagh(3) 5 (Brian Rothwell) *hld up in rr: rdn and struggling 3f out: sn wknd* **250/1**	45
00	12	72	**Fiannoglaigh (IRE)**[41] 8100 2-9-0 0 CamHardie 2 (Rebecca Menzies) *in rr: rdn and struggling 3f out: sn btn* **250/1**	

2m 11.23s (0.83) **Going Correction** +0.025s/f (Slow) — **12** Ran SP% **117.6**

Speed ratings (Par 98): **97,95,93,90,85 84,83,82,81,79 78,21**

CSF £13.95 TOTE £7.30: £2.60, £1.10, £1.20; EX 17.90 Trifecta £46.60.

Owner B E Nielsen **Bred** S A S U Ecurie Des Monceaux Et Al **Trained** Upper Lambourn, Berks

FOCUS

A fairly decent staying juvenile maiden won by the subsequent Group 3 winner Moonlight Spirit in 2018. The gallop was slightly muddling.

9096 PLAY 4 TO SCORE AT BETWAY H'CAP — 1m 2f 42y (Tp)

3:00 (3:00) (Class 4) (0-85,84) 3-Y-O+

£5,207 (£1,549; £774; £387; £300; £300) **Stalls** High

Form				RPR
342	1		**Big Daddy Kane**[33] 8351 3-8-8 **74** JasonWatson 7 (Marco Botti) *t.k.h: hld up in rr: smooth hdwy over 2f out: rdn to ld over 1f out: pushed out ins fnl f: comf* **15/2**	87+
2022	2	2 ¼	**Arabic Culture (USA)**[20] 8727 5-9-4 **81** SamJames 1 (Grant Tuer) *midfield on inner: stdy hdwy over 2f out: shkn up whn bit short of room over 1f out: sn rdn: chsd wnr ins fnl f: kpt on* **9/2**[3]	88
2314	3	1 ½	**Skerryvore**[21] 8692 3-8-12 **78** TomMarquand 9 (James Fanshawe) *t.k.h: pressed ldr: rdn over 2f out: lost 2nd over 1f out: no ex ins fnl f* **4/1**[2]	82
33-1	4	¾	**Rajinsky (IRE)**[31] 8411 3-9-3 **83** (p[1]) JaneElliott 4 (Tom Dascombe) *s.i.s: hld up in rr: rdn over 2f out: kpt on fnl f: nrst fin* **7/2**[1]	86
2211	5	*hd*	**Home Before Dusk**[34] 8305 4-9-2 **84** (p) BenSanderson(5) 8 (Keith Dalgleish) *hld up in rr: stdy hdwy gng easily over 2f out: rdn over 1f out: no ex ins fnl f* **11/2**	86
0-50	6	3	**Paddyplex**[41] 8082 6-9-3 **80** JasonHart 3 (Karen McLintock) *t.k.h: trckd ldrs: rdn over 2f out: wknd fnl 110yds* **33/1**	76
6460	7	1 ½	**Madeeh**[54] 7680 3-8-5 **71** (t w) PhilDennis 6 (Philip Kirby) *midfield: rdn over 2f out: wknd over 1f out* **50/1**	64
026	8	1 ¼	**Railport Dolly**[27] 8515 4-8-11 **74** JoeFanning 2 (David Barron) *t.k.h: led: rdn and hdd over 1f out: wknd fr 1f out* **11/1**	65
4003	9	*nk*	**Seven Clans (IRE)**[21] 8692 7-8-10 **76** (p) GemmaTutty(3) 10 (Karen Tutty) *t.k.h: midfield on outer: pushed along and outpcd over 2f out: sn btn* **33/1**	66
4505	10	3 ¼	**Mostawaa**[31] 8411 3-9-2 **82** (p[1]) BenCurtis 5 (Heather Main) *chsd ldrs: rdn over 2f out: wknd over 1f out* **8/1**	66

2m 10.33s (-0.07) **Going Correction** +0.025s/f (Slow)

WFA 3 from 4yo+ 3lb — **10** Ran SP% **114.8**

Speed ratings (Par 105): **101,99,98,97,97 94,93,92,92,89**

CSF £40.05 CT £155.02 TOTE £5.40: £1.80, £1.70, £1.40; EX 40.40 Trifecta £254.40.

Owner K Sohi & Partners **Bred** Miss K Rausing **Trained** Newmarket, Suffolk

FOCUS

A decent handicap.

9097 LADBROKES WHERE THE NATION PLAYS FILLIES' NOVICE AUCTION STKS — 7f 14y (Tp)

3:30 (3:33) (Class 6) 2-Y-O — £2,781 (£827; £413; £206) **Stalls** Centre

Form				RPR
61	1		**Queen Gamrah**[22] 8651 2-9-7 0 JoeFanning 7 (Mark Johnston) *t.k.h: mde all: shkn up and qcknd over 1f out: sn clr: kpt on strly fnl f: unchal* **5/2**[2]	86+
4	2	3	**Time Voyage (IRE)**[27] 8525 2-9-0 0 JasonHart 4 (John Quinn) *trckd ldrs: pushed along 2f out: wnt 2nd fnl 110yds: no match for wnr* **5/4**[1]	72
4	3	1	**Velma**[20] 8714 2-8-9 0 PaulaMuir(5) 1 (Chris Fairhurst) *dwlt s: towards rr: stdy hdwy and prom over 2f out: rdn and outpcd over 1f out: rallied ins fnl f: kpt on: nvr able to chal* **9/1**	69
	4	¾	**River Song (IRE)** 2-9-0 0 AdamMcNamara 9 (Archie Watson) *swvd rt s: trckd wnr: rdn 2f out: lost 2nd ins fnl f: sn no ex* **18/1**	67
3323	5	3	**Dancing Leopard (IRE)**[3] 9029 2-9-0 66 (p[1]) CliffordLee 8 (K R Burke) *midfield: rdn over 2f out: outpcd fnl f* **4/1**[3]	60
	6	10	**Summerbridge (IRE)** 2-9-0 0 JaneElliott 3 (James Bethell) *t.k.h: prom: rdn and hung lft over 2f out: sn wknd* **33/1**	35

00 7 1 1/4 **Cindy Looper**31 8395 2-9-0 0 PhilDennis 6 32
(Richard Whitaker) *towards rr: rdn and outpcd over 2f out: sn wknd* **80/1**

8 1 3/4 **Welsh Back** 2-8-11 0 CameronNoble(3) 5 27
(Michael Bell) *in rr: rdn over 3f out: wknd over 2f out* **28/1**

0 9 1 1/4 **Dark Discretion**38 8198 2-9-0 0 JackMitchell 10 24
(Kevin Frost) *dwlt s: in rr: rdn over 3f out: wknd over 2f out* **200/1**

00 10 7 **Lady Dandy (IRE)**15 8865 2-9-0 0 TomEaves 2
(Ivan Furtado) *t.k.h: hld up in rr: rdn over 2f out: sn wknd* **200/1**

1m 27.25s (1.05) **Going Correction** +0.025s/f (Slow) **10 Ran SP% 116.9**
Speed ratings (Par 91): **95,91,90,89,86 74,73,71,69,61**
CSF £5.93 TOTE £2.80: £1.10, £1.30, £2.00; EX 7.70 Trifecta £33.10.
Owner Jaber Abdullah **Bred** The National Stud **Trained** Middleham Moor, N Yorks

FOCUS
A fair juvenile fillies' novice contest.

9098 BETWAY H'CAP 5f (Tp)
4:05 (4:06) (Class 3) (0-95,97) 3-Y-O- **£7,876** (£2,357; £1,178; £590; £293) **Stalls** Centre

Form RPR

0652 1 **Watchable**15 8867 9-9-4 **92** (p) ShaneGray 6 103
(David O'Meara) *mde all: in centre of gp: rdn and hrd pressed over 1f out: kpt on strly fnl 110yds* **22/1**

1005 2 1/2 **Good Effort (IRE)**47 7892 4-9-9 **97** (p) BenCurtis 7 106
(Ismail Mohammed) *cl up on nr side of gp: rdn and chalng over 1f out: r.o ins fnl f: no ex towards fin* **10/3**3

1132 3 hd **Harry's Bar**54 7687 4-9-3 **91** TomMarquand 11 99
(James Fanshawe) *prom in centre of gp: rdn 2f out: kpt on ins fnl f* **3/1**2

0000 4 1 3/4 **Abel Handy (IRE)**49 7856 4-8-9 **83** (t) JamesSullivan 2 85
(Declan Carroll) *cl up on far side of gp: rdn 2f out: no ex ins fnl f* **28/1**

505 5 1/2 **Savalas (IRE)**41 8099 4-8-9 **86** SeanDavis(3) 1 86
(Robert Cowell) *s.i.s: sn midfield on far side of gp: rdn 1/2-way: no ex ins fnl f* **33/1**

-350 6 1 1/4 **Red Impression**62 7401 3-9-5 **93** (t1) JasonWatson 10 89
(Roger Charlton) *dwlt s: in rr: sn swtchd lft and on far side of gp: rdn and hdwy 1/2-way: no imp fnl f* **9/4**1

2054 7 1 **Fendale**125 5154 7-8-10 **84** GrahamLee 5 76
(Bryan Smart) *prom in centre of gp: rdn 1/2-way: outpcd over 1f out* **14/1**

34 8 nk **Primo's Comet**110 5661 4-8-7 **81** oh1 PhilDennis 12 72
(Jim Goldie) *hld up in last in centre of gp: pushed along and hdwy over 1f out: nvr able to chal* **14/1**

5564 9 1 1/2 **Jumira Bridge**24 8607 5-9-0 **88** (t) CallumRodriguez 4 74
(Robert Cowell) *dwlt s: in rr on far side of gp: rdn 1/2-way: no imp over 1f out* **14/1**

0010 10 2 **Secretinthepark**30 8428 9-8-7 **81** oh2 (b) AndrewMullen 8 60
(Michael Mullineaux) *awkward s: in rr on nr side of gp: rdn and struggling 1/2-way: sn btn (jockey said gelding missed the break)* **100/1**

6140 11 1 1/2 **Princes Des Sables**74 6999 3-9-7 **95** TomEaves 9 68
(Kevin Ryan) *dwlt s: sn midfield on nr side of gp: rdn 1/2-way: wknd over 1f out* **20/1**

57.95s (-1.55) **Going Correction** +0.025s/f (Slow) **11 Ran SP% 115.3**
Speed ratings (Par 107): **113,112,111,109,108 106,104,104,101,98 96**
CSF £88.91 CT £297.17 TOTE £20.30: £3.60, £1.30, £1.40; EX 113.10 Trifecta £589.60.
Owner Hambleton Xxxix P Bamford Roses Partners **Bred** Cheveley Park Stud Ltd **Trained** Upper Helmsley, N Yorks

FOCUS
A good sprint handicap. One of the relative outsiders went one better than last year in just under standard time.

9099 LADBROKES "PLAY 1-2-FREE" ON FOOTBALL EBF NOVICE STKS (PLUS 10 RACE) 5f (Tp)
4:35 (4:35) (Class 4) 2-Y-O **£4,787** (£1,424; £711; £355) **Stalls** Centre

Form RPR

3100 1 **Colonel Whitehead (IRE)**22 8650 2-8-12 68 EllieMacKenzie(7) 9 78
(Heather Main) *prom in centre of gp: rdn and hdwy over 1f out: led fnl 110yds: kpt on wl* **11/1**

210 2 1/2 **Pepper Bay**14 8891 2-8-11 77 CameronNoble(3) 10 71
(Michael Bell) *cl up in centre of gp: rdn to ld over 1f out: sn edgd lft: hdd fnl 110yds: hld towards fin* **12/1**

2 3 1 3/4 **Agent Shiftwell**31 8409 2-9-2 0 CallumRodriguez 12 67
(Stuart Williams) *cl up on nr side of gp: rdn and ev ch over 1f out: edgd rt and no ex ins fnl f* **5/2**1

0 4 nk **Sound Mixer**29 8458 2-8-11 0 TomMarquand 6 61
(William Haggas) *in rr: bit short of room after 1f: sn outpcd: hdwy on nr side of gp over 1f out: kpt on ins fnl f: nrst fin* **8/1**

0 5 3/4 **Gowanlad**33 8337 2-9-2 0 PhilDennis 8 63
(Philip Kirby) *in rr: outpcd after 2f: rdn and hdwy on nr side of gp 2f out: kpt on fnl f: nvr able to chal* **66/1**

42 6 1 1/2 **Baileys Blues (FR)**38 8202 2-9-2 0 JoeFanning 11 58
(Mark Johnston) *led in centre of gp: rdn and hdd over 1f out: edgd lft and outpcd ins fnl f* **11/2**2

21 7 1 **Felicia Blue**33 8337 2-8-11 0 SeanDavis(3) 5 52
(Richard Fahey) *towards rr in centre of gp: rdn 1/2-way: hdwy and edgd rt over 1f out: no imp fnl f* **6/1**3

25 8 3/4 **Leoch**33 8337 2-9-2 0 KevinStott 2 51
(Kevin Ryan) *prom on far side of gp: rdn 2f out: sn outpcd* **8/1**

0 9 1 **Only Alone (IRE)**64 7333 2-8-11 0 GrahamLee 4 43
(Jedd O'Keeffe) *midfield on far side of gp: pushed along and outpcd 1/2-way: btn over 1f out* **33/1**

2213 10 1 **Daily Times**22 8659 2-9-3 77 (t) NickyMackay 1 45
(John Gosden) *towards rr on far side of gp: stdy hdwy 1/2-way: rdn and wknd over 1f out (jockey said filly ran flat)* **7/1**

11 6 **Chocolaat Heer** 2-9-2 0 JasonHart 3 23
(John Quinn) *slowly away: sn detached and no ch* **50/1**

59.04s (-0.46) **Going Correction** +0.025s/f (Slow) **11 Ran SP% 115.4**
Speed ratings (Par 98): **104,103,100,99,98 96,94,93,91,90 80**
CSF £131.42 TOTE £19.80: £3.50, £3.70, £1.50; EX 134.00 Trifecta £552.40.
Owner Andrew Tuck And Wetumpka Racing **Bred** Wood Hall Stud **Trained** Kingston Lisle, Oxon

FOCUS
A fair juvenile novice sprint in which the first three horses home raced prominently.
T/Plt: £18.50 to a £1 stake. Pool: £66,516.43 - 2,615.28 winning units T/Qpdt: £3.60 to a £1 stake. Pool: £8,533.89 - 1,724.88 winning units **Raceform**

9100 - 9105a (Foreign Racing) - See Raceform Interactive

9093
NEWCASTLE (A.W) (L-H)
Friday, November 22

OFFICIAL GOING: Tapeta: standard
Wind: Breezy, half behind Weather: Dry

9106 BETWAY "HANDS AND HEELS" APPRENTICE H'CAP (RACING EXCELLENCE AWT HANDS AND HEELS SERIES) 6f (Tp)
3:30 (3:32) (Class 5) (0-70,71) 3-Y-O+
£3,428 (£1,020; £509; £400; £400; £400) **Stalls** Centre

Form RPR

6034 1 **Global Humor (USA)**21 8712 4-9-1 **59** CoreyMadden 6 67
(Jim Goldie) *dwlt s: t.k.h: hld up in rr in centre of gp: smooth hdwy and swtchd rt over 1f out: pushed along and kpt on fnl f: led towards fin* **15/2**

1255 2 nk **Hassaad**21 8715 3-9-12 **70** KateLeahy 11 77
(Archie Watson) *cl up on nr side of gp: pushed along and led over 1f out: kpt on fnl f: hdd towards fin* **5/1**2

0321 3 3/4 **Lucky Lodge**21 8712 9-9-13 **71** (v) OliverStammers 7 76
(Antony Brittain) *prom in centre of gp: shkn up and hdwy over 1f out: kpt on fnl f: hld towards fin* **7/2**1

6320 4 1 1/2 **Dancing Rave**24 8636 3-9-10 **71** GeorgeBass(3) 2 71
(David O'Meara) *hld up in rr on far side of gp: pushed along and hdwy over 1f out: no ex fnl 110yds* **14/1**

3602 5 4 **It Must Be Faith**36 8296 9-8-11 **60** (p) ErikaParkinson(5) 10 47
(Michael Appleby) *led at fast pce on nr side of gp: pushed along and hdd over 1f out: wknd ins fnl f* **18/1**

2660 6 nk **Tobeeornottobee**35 8306 3-8-8 **57** JessicaAnderson(5) 12 43
(Declan Carroll) *prom on nr side of gp: pushed along over 2f out: wknd fnl f* **13/2**

600 7 hd **Heavenly Rainbow (IRE)**22 8698 3-9-3 **61** AidenBlakemore 8 47
(Michael Herrington) *t.k.h: prom in centre of gp: shkn up over 1f out: sn wknd* **18/1**

5506 8 nk **Daafr (IRE)**21 8712 3-9-13 **71** (h1) RussellHarris 5 56
(Antony Brittain) *towards rr in centre of gp: pushed along over 2f out: hdwy over 1f out: no imp fnl f* **8/1**

0066 9 5 **Epona**24 8646 3-8-9 **58** NickBarratt-Atkin(5) 9 27
(Keith Dalgleish) *t.k.h: cl up in centre of gp: pushed along and edgd lft 1/2-way: sn wknd* **22/1**

4000 10 1/2 **Dirchill (IRE)**35 8306 5-8-12 **56** oh1 (b) ElishaWhittington 4 23
(David Thompson) *towards rr on far side of gp: hdwy and edgd lft over 2f out: sn pushed along: wknd over 1f out* **25/1**

3033 11 1 3/4 **Ricochet (IRE)**21 8712 3-8-11 **60** (v1) EmmaTaff(5) 1 22
(Tom Ward) *bhd on far side of gp: hung lft and struggling over 2f out: sn btn* **6/1**3

1m 12.64s (0.14) **Going Correction** +0.075s/f (Slow) **11 Ran SP% 114.8**
Speed ratings (Par 103): **102,101,100,98,93 92,92,92,85,84 82**
CSF £43.70 CT £157.91 TOTE £8.10: £2.10, £1.90, £1.40; EX 51.00 Trifecta £209.20.
Owner Johnnie Delta Racing **Bred** Russell L Reineman Stable, Inc **Trained** Uplawmoor, E Renfrews

FOCUS
The going was standard. Stalls - Straight: centre. 1m2f/1m4f: outside. 2m: inside. An ordinary apprentice handicap. The winner swooped late under a competent ride.

9107 LADBROKES WHERE THE NATION PLAYS NOVICE STKS 6f (Tp)
4:00 (4:04) (Class 5) 2-Y-O **£3,428** (£1,020; £509; £254) **Stalls** Centre

Form RPR

22 1 **King Ragnar**14 8912 2-9-5 0 JackMitchell 12 77
(Roger Varian) *prom on nr side of gp: rdn and wnt 2nd over 1f out: led fnl 110yds: kpt on strly* **11/8**2

2 1/2 **Glen Force (IRE)** 2-9-5 0 DanielMuscutt 11 76+
(Sir Mark Prescott Bt) *carried lft s: towards rr on nr side of gp: pushed along and hdwy over 1f out: wnt 2nd towards fin* **20/1**

3 3/4 **Frozen Ocean (FR)** 2-9-5 0 CallumShepherd 2 73
(Saeed bin Suroor) *prom on far side of gp: swtchd rt after 2f: rdn to ld over 1f out: sn edgd rt: hdd fnl 110yds: no ex and lost 2nd towards fin* **5/4**1

4 3/4 **Anjah (IRE)** 2-9-5 0 PaulMulrennan 3 71+
(Simon Crisford) *prom on far side of gp: pushed along and outpcd 2f out: rallied fnl f: nrst fin* **7/1**3

5 hd **Muritz** 2-9-0 0 JasonHart 10 65+
(John Quinn) *ducked lft s: in rr on nr side of gp: rdn and outpcd over 2f out: rallied fnl f: nvr able to chal* **66/1**

33 6 3 **Lairig Ghru**42 8084 2-9-5 0 AndrewMullen 14 61
(Micky Hammond) *led on nr side of gp: rdn and hdd over 1f out: wknd fnl f* **16/1**

04 7 1 1/2 **Slingshot**42 8084 2-9-0 0 (h) GrahamLee 8 52
(Bryan Smart) *prom on far side of gp: rdn over 2f out: wknd over 1f out* **28/1**

8 shd **Brazen Bolt** 2-9-5 0 BenRobinson 9 57
(John Quinn) *dwlt s: sn towards rr in centre of gp: rdn over 2f out: no imp over 1f out: btn fnl f* **150/1**

9 1 **Indian Road (IRE)** 2-9-5 0 JoeFanning 5 54
(Mark Johnston) *disp ld on far side of gp: pushed along 2f out: wknd fnl f* **14/1**

10 3 **Golden Sandbanks** 2-9-5 0 JamieGormley 1 45
(Iain Jardine) *slowly away: in rr on far side of gp: pushed along and hdwy fnl f: n.d (jockey said colt was slowly away)* **100/1**

11 1 3/4 **Outofthegloom** 2-8-11 0 ConnorMurtagh(3) 13 34
(Brian Rothwell) *cl up on nr side of gp: rdn over 2f out: wknd over 1f out* **250/1**

12 nse **On Display** 2-9-5 0 TomEaves 7 39
(Nigel Tinkler) *towards rr on far side of gp: rdn and outpcd over 2f out: wknd over 1f out* **80/1**

13 15 **Carlton Bella** 2-9-5 0 JamesSullivan 4
(Michael Easterby) *slowly away: in rr on nr side of gp: rdn and struggling 1/2-way: sn btn* **125/1**

1m 12.83s (0.33) **Going Correction** +0.075s/f (Slow) **13 Ran SP% 125.4**
Speed ratings (Par 96): **100,99,98,97,97 93,91,90,89,85 83,83,63**
CSF £37.15 TOTE £2.30: £1.10, £4.70, £1.10; EX 31.90 Trifecta £84.40.
Owner Sheikh Mana Bin Mohammed Al Maktoum **Bred** J Bernstein & R Haim **Trained** Newmarket, Suffolk

FOCUS
Some nicely-bred juveniles fought out this novice event and it should throw up a few winners.

9108 BETWAY HEED YOUR HUNCH H'CAP 5f (Tp)

4:30 (4:32) (Class 5) (0-75,77) 3-Y-0+

£3,428 (£1,020; £509; £400; £400; £400) **Stalls** Centre

Form RPR

0060 **1** **Big Les (IRE)**[16] 8860 4-9-7 **75** JasonHart 6 84
(Karen McLintock) *disp ld on far side of gp: rdn to ld over 1f out: sn edgd rt: kpt on strly fnl f (trainer said regarding apparent improvement in form that the gelding may have appreciated the sounder tapeta surface on this occasion following the Heavy ground at Nottingham)* **14/1**

0304 **2** ¾ **Commander Han (FR)**[36] 8289 4-9-9 **77** (t[1]) CallumRodriguez 4 83+
(Stuart Williams) *hld up in rr in centre of gp: stdy hdwy gng easily 2f out: rdn and kpt on wl fnl f: wnt 2nd towards fin* **7/2**[2]

0453 **3** 1 **Landing Night (IRE)**[21] 8715 7-8-11 **65** (tp) CliffordLee 1 68
(Rebecca Menzies) *towards rr on far side of gp: shkn up and hdwy over 1f out: rdn and briefly wnt 2nd ins fnl f: no ex towards fin* **25/1**

1522 **4** nse **Be Proud (IRE)**[21] 8715 3-8-8 **62** BenRobinson 2 65
(Jim Goldie) *towards rr on nr side of gp: rdn over 2f out: hdwy over 1f out: kpt on fnl f: nrst fin* **5/1**[3]

26-2 **5** ½ **Jonboy**[21] 8712 4-9-5 **73** BenCurtis 10 74
(David Brown) *disp ld on nr side of gp: rdn over 1f out: no ex ins fnl f* **2/1**[1]

4016 **6** ½ **Tathmeen (IRE)**[15] 8895 4-9-3 **71** CamHardie 3 70
(Antony Brittain) *dwlt s: hld up in rr on far side of gp: rdn and hdwy over 1f out: no imp ins fnl f* **14/1**

3135 **7** 1 **Shepherd's Purse**[6] 9013 7-8-9 **63** (b) JamesSullivan 5 58
(Ruth Carr) *t.k.h: prom on far side of gp: rdn over 1f out: no ex ins fnl f* **18/1**

253 **8** 1 **Followthesteps (IRE)**[169] 3504 4-9-8 **76** (h[1]) DougieCostello 9 68
(Ivan Furtado) *blindfold off late: slowly away: bhd on nr side of gp: rdn after 2f: sme hdwy fnl f: nvr able to chal (jockey said he was slow to remove the blindfold resulting in his horse being slow to start)* **16/1**

1000 **9** nk **Camachess (IRE)**[14] 8921 3-9-5 **73** ShaneKelly 11 64
(Philip McBride) *prom on nr side of gp: rdn over 2f out: wknd ins fnl f* **40/1**

3120 **10** shd **Gowanbuster**[186] 2893 4-9-6 **74** (t) PaulMulrennan 7 64
(Susan Corbett) *slt ld in centre of gp: rdn and hdd over 1f out: sn wknd (vet said gelding had been struck into right hind)* **11/1**

1006 **11** 2 **Penny Pot Lane**[14] 8924 6-8-7 **61** oh1 (b) PhilDennis 8 44
(Richard Whitaker) *prom in centre of gp: rdn 1/2-way: wknd over 1f out* **33/1**

58.97s (-0.53) **Going Correction** +0.075s/f (Slow) **11 Ran SP% 114.3**
Speed ratings (Par 103): **107,105,104,104,103 102,100,99,98,98 95**
CSF £59.88 CT £1247.39 TOTE £15.80: £4.40, £1.70, £5.20; EX 74.50 Trifecta £979.10.
Owner Stockdale Racing **Bred** Corrin Stud **Trained** Ingoe, Northumberland

FOCUS
A fair sprint handicap which saw the winner grind it out under a positive ride.

9109 BOMBARDIER BRITISH HOPPED AMBER BEER H'CAP 1m 5y (Tp)

5:00 (5:01) (Class 5) (0-75,75) 3-Y-0+

£3,428 (£1,020; £509; £400; £400; £400) **Stalls** Centre

Form RPR

0103 **1** **Anif (IRE)**[83] 6733 5-9-5 **71** TomEaves 5 79
(Michael Herrington) *midfield on far side of gp: pushed along and hdwy over 2f out: led over 1f out: rdn and kpt on wl fnl f* **16/1**

352 **2** 1 **Ascot Week (USA)**[64] 7364 5-9-5 **71** (v) JasonHart 4 77
(John Quinn) *midfield on far side of gp: hdwy and prom 2f out: rdn and kpt on fnl f: wnt 2nd towards fin* **8/1**[3]

2500 **3** nk **Merweb (IRE)**[59] 7554 4-9-5 **71** (p[1]) JackMitchell 3 76
(Heather Main) *cl up in centre of gp: rdn over 2f out: hdwy and briefly led over 1f out: kpt on fnl f: lost 2nd towards fin* **5/1**[2]

1510 **4** ½ **Insurplus (IRE)**[42] 8087 6-9-5 **71** BenRobinson 12 75
(Jim Goldie) *towards rr on nr side of gp: pushed along over 2f out: hdwy over 1f out: rdn and kpt on ins fnl f* **14/1**

3060 **5** ¾ **Amber Spark (IRE)**[35] 8305 3-9-5 **73** BarryMcHugh 2 74
(Richard Fahey) *slowly away: in rr in centre of gp: rdn over 2f out: kpt on fnl f: nvr able to chal* **18/1**

3000 **6** nse **Ideal Candy (IRE)**[21] 8719 4-8-12 **67** (h) GemmaTutty(3) 6 69
(Karen Tutty) *led on far side of gp: sn clr: rdn over 2f out: hdd over 1f out: no ex ins fnl f* **50/1**

0411 **7** ¾ **Perfect Swiss**[35] 8301 3-9-0 **68** CamHardie 1 68
(Tim Easterby) *hld up in rr on far side of gp: rdn over 2f out: hdwy over 1f out: no imp ins fnl f (trainer was informed that the gelding could not run until the day after passing a stalls test)* **3/1**[1]

520 **8** ¾ **Lady Alavesa**[37] 8247 4-9-4 **70** PhilDennis 11 69
(Michael Herrington) *rrd s: hld up in rr in centre of gp: rdn and hdwy over 1f out: no imp ins fnl f* **10/1**

5200 **9** 2 ¼ **Elixsoft (IRE)**[21] 8719 4-9-6 **72** (p) BenCurtis 13 66
(Roger Fell) *hld up in rr on nr side of gp: rdn and hdwy over 1f out: nvr able to chal* **12/1**

30-4 **10** 1 ¼ **Fortissimo (IRE)**[31] 8427 3-9-2 **70** JoeFanning 14 60
(Mark Johnston) *prom on nr side of gp: rdn and ev ch over 1f out: wknd ins fnl f* **11/1**

1025 **11** 1 ¾ **Robotique Danseur (FR)**[31] 8427 3-9-7 **75** (p[1]) CliffordLee 8 61
(K R Burke) *cl up in centre of gp: rdn and ev ch over 1f out: wknd ins fnl f* **20/1**

4056 **12** 4 ½ **Detachment**[34] 8341 6-9-3 **69** GrahamLee 10 45
(Shaun Harris) *in rr on nr side of gp: rdn and struggling over 2f out: sn btn* **66/1**

-605 **13** 1 ½ **Najib (IRE)**[39] 8181 3-9-2 **70** PaulMulrennan 7 42
(Roger Fell) *midfield in centre of gp: rdn and outpcd over 2f out: btn over 1f out* **33/1**

0040 **14** 1 **Highlight Reel (IRE)**[20] 8761 4-8-13 **68** TheodoreLadd(3) 9 39
(Rebecca Bastiman) *dwlt s: bhd on far side of gp: struggling and hung lft over 2f out: sn wknd* **18/1**

1m 39.82s (1.22) **Going Correction** +0.075s/f (Slow) **14 Ran SP% 113.9**
WFA 3 from 4yo+ 2lb
Speed ratings (Par 103): **96,95,94,94,93 93,92,91,89,88 86,82,80,79**
CSF £126.51 CT £547.93 TOTE £27.50: £4.50, £2.10, £2.20; EX 113.80 Trifecta £981.70.
Owner Stuart Herrington & Peter Forster **Bred** Shadwell Estate Company Limited **Trained** Cold Kirby, N Yorks

FOCUS
Not many got into this. The winner was always well placed and that proved decisive.

9110 LADBROKES HOME OF THE ODDS BOOST NURSERY H'CAP 1m 5y (Tp)

5:30 (5:31) (Class 5) (0-75,76) 2-Y-0

£3,428 (£1,020; £509; £400; £400; £400) **Stalls** Centre

Form RPR

0310 **1** **Island Storm (IRE)**[44] 8029 2-9-7 **74** JackMitchell 7 78+
(Heather Main) *mde all: set slow pce: rdn over 1f out: kpt on strly fnl f: unchal* **9/4**[2]

0030 **2** 2 **Genever Dragon (IRE)**[32] 8394 2-9-5 **72** (p) JaneElliott 6 72
(Tom Dascombe) *chsd wnr: pushed along 2f out: kpt on fnl f: no match for wnr* **5/1**[3]

3061 **3** ½ **Castlehill Retreat**[18] 8815 2-9-2 **69** PaulMulrennan 4 68
(Ben Haslam) *stdd s: hld up in rr: rdn and hdwy over 1f out: no ex fnl 110yds* **15/8**[1]

045 **4** 2 ½ **Brainchild**[35] 8316 2-8-13 **66** CallumRodriguez 1 59
(Keith Dalgleish) *towards rr: rdn and hdwy over 1f out: no imp fnl f* **12/1**

5335 **5** ½ **Sky Vega (IRE)**[53] 7754 2-9-6 **73** (t[1]) TomMarquand 3 65
(Tom Ward) *prom: pushed along and hdwy: rdn and wknd ins fnl f* **11/2**

0065 **6** 1 ¼ **Jazz Style (IRE)**[4] 9037 2-8-0 **53** oh5 CamHardie 2 42
(David Brown) *t.k.h: hld up in last: rdn and outpcd over 2f out: no imp fr over 1f out (jockey said gelding ran too free)* **50/1**

1500 **7** 5 **Big City**[49] 7871 2-9-3 **70** (p[1]) BenCurtis 5 48
(Roger Fell) *dwlt s: sn cl up: rdn over 2f out: wknd over 1f out* **33/1**

1m 44.25s (5.65) **Going Correction** +0.075s/f (Slow) **7 Ran SP% 110.2**
Speed ratings (Par 96): **74,72,71,69,68 67,62**
CSF £12.84 CT £21.92 TOTE £3.10: £1.80, £3.20; EX 13.50 Trifecta £40.40.
Owner Donald Kerr & Wetumpka Racing **Bred** Roy W Tector **Trained** Kingston Lisle, Oxon

FOCUS
A run-of-the-mill nursery controlled by the winner, who was allowed to set a moderate early gallop before quickening the pace after halfway.

9111 BOMBARDIER GOLDEN BEER H'CAP 7f 14y (Tp)

6:00 (6:00) (Class 7) (0-50,50) 3-Y-0+ £2,264 (£673; £336; £168) **Stalls** Centre

Form RPR

4006 **1** **Rivas Rob Roy**[18] 8818 4-9-2 **47** (b[1]) BenCurtis 11 55
(John Gallagher) *cl up on nr side of gp: led over 2f out: rdn and clr whn edgd lft over 1f out: kpt on strly fnl f: unchal* **9/2**[2]

0506 **2** 4 ½ **Lucky Violet (IRE)**[14] 8922 7-9-4 **49** (h) BenRobinson 9 46
(Linda Perratt) *stdd s: hld up in rr on nr side of gp: rdn over 2f out: hdwy and wnt 2nd over 1f out: no match for wnr* **9/1**

4353 **3** nk **Snooker Jim**[45] 8008 4-9-2 **47** (tp) JackMitchell 10 43
(Steph Hollinshead) *prom on far side of gp: rdn and outpcd over 1f out: rallied and wnt 3rd ins fnl f: mde no imp* **8/1**

0000 **4** 1 **Amood (IRE)**[14] 8922 8-9-4 **49** (b) AndrewMullen 8 43
(Simon West) *dwlt s: t.k.h: hld up in rr on far side of gp: rdn and hdwy over 1f out: kpt on fnl f: nrst fin* **33/1**

2 **5** ½ **Queen Mia (IRE)**[18] 8819 3-9-3 **49** (t) TomEaves 5 40
(Declan Carroll) *prom in centre of gp: pushed along 2f out: sn outpcd: rallied and edgd rt ins fnl f: sn no imp* **12/1**

0440 **6** ½ **Relight My Fire**[56] 7654 9-9-2 **47** (bt) JamesSullivan 1 38
(Tim Easterby) *t.k.h: led: hdd over 2f out: rallied over 1f out: no ex ins fnl f* **66/1**

0562 **7** shd **Silk Mill Blue**[23] 8666 5-9-4 **49** (p) PhilDennis 14 40
(Richard Whitaker) *midfield on nr side of gp: rdn and hdwy 2f out: no ex ins fnl f* **8/1**

2533 **8** ½ **Eldelbar (SPA)**[30] 8469 5-9-4 **49** (h) SamJames 3 39
(Geoffrey Harker) *plld hrd: cl up on far side of gp: rdn and ev ch over 2f out: outpcd fnl f* **10/3**[1]

5004 **9** ½ **Someone Exciting**[24] 8637 6-9-4 **49** CallumRodriguez 7 37
(David Thompson) *dwlt s: in rr on far side of gp: pushed along and hdwy 2f out: rdn and no imp fnl f* **20/1**

0460 **10** 2 ¼ **Alfred The Grey (IRE)**[18] 8821 3-9-3 **49** JasonHart 2 31
(Tracy Waggott) *t.k.h: cl up in centre of gp: rdn and ev ch over 2f out: wknd over 1f out* **20/1**

5040 **11** ¾ **Nutopia**[18] 8819 4-9-3 **48** CamHardie 13 29
(Antony Brittain) *rrd s: bhd in centre of gp: rdn and outpcd over 2f out: btn over 1f out* **28/1**

2600 **12** 1 ¼ **Clement (IRE)**[14] 8915 9-9-5 **50** (p) JaneElliott 12 28
(Marjorie Fife) *dwlt s: t.k.h: in rr on nr side of gp: sn stmbld: rdn and outpcd over 2f out: sn btn* **40/1**

0062 **13** 3 ¼ **Joyful Star**[46] 7961 9-9-2 **47** JackGarritty 6 17
(Fred Watson) *towards rr in centre of gp: rdn and outpcd over 2f out: sn btn (jockey said gelding ran flat; trainer said gelding was found to have bruised ribs and a high temperature on the morning after the race)* **7/1**[3]

1m 27.22s (1.02) **Going Correction** +0.075s/f (Slow)
WFA 3 from 4yo+ 1lb **13 Ran SP% 113.5**
Speed ratings (Par 97): **97,91,91,90,89 89,89,88,87,85 84,83,79**
CSF £38.15 CT £312.15 TOTE £5.00: £1.90, £3.20, £3.10; EX 44.40 Trifecta £227.30.
Owner T J F Smith **Bred** D Hefin Jones **Trained** Chastleton, Oxon

FOCUS
Another race run at a moderate early gallop. Wearing blinkers for the first time, the winner settled matters in a few strides.

9112 BETWAY NOVICE STKS 6f (Tp)

6:30 (6:31) (Class 5) 3-Y-0+ £3,428 (£1,020; £509; £254) **Stalls** Centre

Form RPR

3302 **1** **Rhossili Down**[22] 8695 3-9-0 71 (p[1]) BenCurtis 5 66
(Charles Hills) *t.k.h: pressed ldr: led and hung lft over 1f out: sn rdn: kpt on wl fnl 110yds* **1/3**[1]

2 1 ½ **Redesdale Rebel** 3-9-5 0 PaulMulrennan 4 65
(Susan Corbett) *t.k.h: led: edgd lft and hdd over 1f out: sn rallied and ev ch: no ex fnl 110yds* **33/1**

00 **3** hd **Loretta (IRE)**[97] 6206 3-9-0 0 CallumRodriguez 1 60
(Julie Camacho) *ducked lft s: hld up in last: rdn and outpcd over 2f out: rallied over 1f out: kpt on: nrst fin* **8/1**[3]

3230 **4** 8 **City Of Love**[27] 8548 3-9-0 72 (p[1]) ShaneKelly 2 34
(David Lanigan) *chsd ldrs: rdn over 2f out: wknd over 1f out* **10/3**[2]

5 13 **Sixties Coed** 4-9-0 0 (t[1]) FayeMcManoman(5) 3
(Nigel Tinkler) *slowly away: sn prom: rdn and outpcd 1/2-way: lost tch fr 2f out* **40/1**

1m 12.57s (0.07) **Going Correction** +0.075s/f (Slow) **5 Ran SP% 114.6**
Speed ratings (Par 103): **102,100,99,89,71**
CSF £15.89 TOTE £1.50: £1.10, £3.30; EX 8.20 Trifecta £46.40.
Owner D J Deer **Bred** D J And Mrs Deer **Trained** Lambourn, Berks

FOCUS
A weak novice. The long odds-on favourite took her time to get by the pacesetting runner-up.

9113 BETWAY H'CAP 6f (Tp)
7:00 (7:01) (Class 5) (0-70,70) 3-Y-0+
£3,428 (£1,020; £509; £400; £400; £400) Stalls Centre

Form RPR
4000 1 **Wasntexpectingthat**[34] 8342 3-9-2 65 BarryMcHugh 14 76+
(Richard Fahey) *hld up in rr on nr side of gp: smooth hdwy 2f out: shkn up to ld fr 1f out: sn edgd lft: rdn and kpt on wl fnl 110yds (trainer said regarding apparent improvement in form that the gelding may have appreciated the drop in class on this occasion)* 10/1[3]
4104 2 1 ¾ **Kenny The Captain (IRE)**[34] 8339 8-9-2 65 JasonHart 5 71
(Tim Easterby) *led on far side of gp: rdn 2f out: hdd fr 1f out: sn rallied: no ex fnl 110yds* 10/1[3]
6560 3 1 ¾ **Almurr (IRE)**[21] 8715 3-9-2 65 BenCurtis 8 66
(Phillip Makin) *cl up on nr side of gp: rdn and ev ch over 1f out: no ex fnl 110yds* 7/1[2]
5240 4 2 **Siena Mia**[18] 8818 4-8-13 62 PhilDennis 1 57
(Philip Kirby) *prom on far side of gp: rdn 2f out: outpcd ins fnl f* 28/1
6604 5 shd **Klopp**[14] 8924 3-9-1 64 (h) CamHardie 12 58
(Antony Brittain) *midfield on nr side of gp: rdn and hdwy 2f out: no imp ins fnl f* 20/1
6002 6 nse **Oriental Lilly**[14] 8924 5-9-0 70 (p) CoreyMadden(7) 13 64
(Jim Goldie) *dwlt s: hld up in rr on nr side of gp: rdn and hdwy over 1f out: kpt on fnl f: nvr able to chal* 7/1[2]
6045 7 hd **Socru (IRE)**[51] 7828 3-9-5 68 (h) PaulMulrennan 3 62
(Michael Easterby) *chsd ldrs in centre of gp: rdn and outpcd over 1f out: no imp fnl f* 11/1
4220 8 2 ¼ **Zoravan (USA)**[35] 8305 6-8-12 66 (p) BenSanderson(5) 4 53
(Keith Dalgleish) *slowly away: in rr on far side of gp: rdn and edgd lft over 1f out: nvr able to chal* 16/1
0400 9 nk **Lightning Charlie**[43] 8063 7-9-4 67 JamieGormley 9 53
(Iain Jardine) *hld up in rr on far side of gp: rdn and outpcd 2f out: sn btn* 14/1
2300 10 1 ¼ **Mount Wellington (IRE)**[196] 2580 4-8-13 62 (t[1]) CallumRodriguez 6 44
(Stuart Williams) *pressed ldr: rdn and lost 2nd over 2f out: wknd over 1f out* 9/4[1]
6004 11 hd **Kommander Kirkup**[282] 705 8-9-1 64 TomEaves 11 46
(Michael Herrington) *hld up in rr in centre of gp: pushed along and sme hdwy over 1f out: btn ins fnl f* 125/1
1363 12 ¾ **Bedtime Bella (IRE)**[64] 7383 3-9-4 70 (v) TheodoreLadd(3) 10 49
(Michael Appleby) *in rr in centre of gp: rdn over 2f out: wknd over 1f out (jockey said regarding running and riding that his instructions were to get cover as the filly had ran too freely on her recent starts, and finish as best he could. He added that after getting cover he didn't have a clear run through the middle part of* 20/1
005 13 1 ¾ **Black Isle Boy (IRE)**[31] 8419 5-9-4 67 (v[1]) CliffordLee 2 41
(David C Griffiths) *cl up on far side of gp: rdn over 2f out: wknd over 1f out* 20/1
63/5 14 2 **Star Citizen**[34] 8339 7-8-13 62 ShaneGray 7 30
(Fred Watson) *midfield in centre of gp: rdn and struggling over 2f out: sn wknd* 50/1

1m 11.87s (-0.63) **Going Correction** +0.075s/f (Slow) 14 Ran SP% 115.3
Speed ratings (Par 103): **107,104,102,99,99 99,99,96,95,94 93,92,90,87**
CSF £92.68 CT £771.50 TOTE £14.30: £4.00, £3.00, £1.90; EX 105.00 Trifecta £695.90.
Owner The Good Bad Ugly And Deaf **Bred** Mr & Mrs A & D Flannigan **Trained** Musley Bank, N Yorks

FOCUS
A competitive handicap on paper, but the winner scored in fine style on his AW debut.
T/Plt: £89.80 to a £1 stake. Pool: £77,545.58 - 630.28 winning units. T/Qpdt: £64.80 to a £1 stake. Pool: £9,184.64 - 104.74 winning units. **Richard Young**

9114 - 9122a (Foreign Racing) - See Raceform Interactive

8966 SAINT-CLOUD (L-H)
Friday, November 22

OFFICIAL GOING: Turf: heavy

9123a PRIX PHARSALE (MAIDEN) (2YO FILLIES) (TURF) 1m 2f
11:15 2-Y-0 £12,162 (£4,864; £3,648; £2,432; £1,216)

RPR
1 **Wonderful Tonight (FR)**[28] 8510 2-9-2 0 OlivierPeslier 11 79
(David Menuisier) *cl up: prog to dispute ld over 2f out: sn led: shkn up and asked to qckn over 1 1/2f out: chal ins fnl f: kpt on u.p: jst hld on* 9/5[1]
2 shd **Karlarina (FR)**[29] 2-9-2 0 TheoBachelot 6 79
(M Nigge, France) 7/2[2]
3 3 **Circe (FR)**[50] 2-9-2 0 MickaelBarzalona 3 73
(J-M Beguigne, France) 7/2[2]
4 2 ½ **Eliaure (FR)** 2-9-2 0 EddyHardouin 10 69
(N Leenders, France) 21/1
5 2 **Birdie Hop (FR)**[36] 2-8-10 0 QuentinPerrette(6) 9 65
(F Belmont, France) 19/1
6 3 **Liberte Absolue (FR)** 2-8-4 0 MohammedLyesTabti(7) 8 55
(C Lerner, France) 40/1
7 2 ½ **Diamond Cruz (FR)** 2-8-11 0 MickaelBerto 1 50
(S Dehez, France) 57/1
8 2 **Soundproof (FR)** 2-8-6 0 AlexisPouchin(5) 5 47
(Mme M Bollack-Badel, France) 49/1
9 7 **Valtice Du Berlais (FR)** 2-8-11 0 AurelienLemaitre 7 34
(Robert Collet, France) 54/1
10 8 **Wing Dancer (FR)** 2-8-11 0 ClementLecoeuvre 13 20
(Mme M Bollack-Badel, France) 15/1
11 nk **Repentir** 2-8-8 0 MlleMarylineEon(3) 4 19
(Mme M Bollack-Badel, France) 31/1
12 1 ¾ **Diamonds Forever (FR)**[22] 2-9-2 0 (b[1]) MaximeGuyon 2 21
(L Gadbin, France) 10/1[3]
13 2 ½ **Peristera (IRE)** 2-9-2 0 AntoineHamelin 12 17
(Gavin Hernon, France) 27/1

2m 33.34s (17.34) 13 Ran SP% 119.7
PARI-MUTUEL (all including 1 euro stake): WIN 2.80; PLACE 1.20, 1.30, 1.30; DF 5.20.
Owner Christopher Wright **Bred** S A R L Ecurie La Cauviniere **Trained** Pulborough, W Sussex

9124a PRIX TANTIEME (LISTED RACE) (3YO+) (TURF) 1m
1:58 3-Y-0+ £23,423 (£9,369; £7,027; £4,684; £2,342)

RPR
1 **History Writer (IRE)**[33] 8379 4-9-1 0 TonyPiccone 8 103+
(David Menuisier) *hld up in fnl trio: pushed along on nr side rail over 2 1/2f out: prog fr 2f out: rdn to ld narrowly over 1f out: kpt on wl ins fnl f* 216/10
2 1 ¼ **Mitchum Swagger**[20] 8765 7-9-1 0 MickaelBarzalona 3 101+
(Ralph Beckett) *midfield on inner: pushed along and prog fr 2 1/2f out: rdn to chal over 1 1/2f out: ev ch over 1f out: nt match pce of eventual wnr ins fnl f* 74/10
3 3 **Folie De Louise (FR)**[17] 8845 5-8-11 0 AntoineHamelin 9 90
(Carmen Bocskai, Germany) 11/1
4 nk **Recover Me (FR)**[32] 4-8-11 0 CristianDemuro 11 89
(J-C Rouget, France) 20/1
5 1 ¼ **Qualisaga (FR)**[17] 8845 5-9-4 0 EddyHardouin 4 93
(Carina Fey, France) 29/10[2]
6 1 ¼ **Sugar Daddy (GER)**[33] 5-9-1 0 ThoreHammerHansen 6 87
(Lennart Hammer-Hansen, Germany) 25/1
7 hd **Larno (FR)**[9] 5-9-1 0 HugoJourniac 7 87
(M Boutin, France) 17/1
8 nk **Kourkan (FR)**[27] 8583 6-9-1 0 OlivierPeslier 5 86
(J-M Beguigne, France) 9/5[1]
9 dist **Infanta Isabella**[91] 6406 5-8-11 0 TheoBachelot 1
(George Baker) *prom on inner: struggling to go pce and lost position 2 1/2f out: sn wknd: eased over 1f out* 15/1
10 8 **Kingstar (FR)**[205] 4-9-1 0 MaximeGuyon 10
(Mme Pia Brandt, France) 73/10[3]
11 5 ½ **King Platin (FR)**[31] 7-9-1 0 ThomasTrullier 2
(Mme C Barande-Barbe, France) 55/1

1m 57.68s (10.18) 11 Ran SP% 120.3
PARI-MUTUEL (all including 1 euro stake): WIN 22.60; PLACE 6.40, 2.90, 3.50; DF 62.10.
Owner Clive Washbourn & Partner **Bred** Kildaragh Stud **Trained** Pulborough, W Sussex

SAKHIR
Friday, November 22

OFFICIAL GOING: Turf: good

9125a BAHRAIN INTERNATIONAL TROPHY (CONDITIONS) (3YO+) (TURF) 1m 2f
1:30 3-Y-0+ £250,000 (£125,000; £62,500; £37,500; £25,000)

RPR
1 **Royal Julius (IRE)**[61] 7504 6-9-2 0 StephanePasquier 11 107
(J Reynier, France) 12/1
2 ¾ **Turgenev**[65] 7340 3-8-13 0 (p) RobertHavlin 3 107
(John Gosden) *midfield in main gp: prog fr over 2f out: asked for effrt over 1 1/2f out: drvn to chse clr ldr ent fnl f: r.o strly: nt quite pce to match eventual wnr cl home* 5/2[1]
3 hd **Rustang (FR)**[413] 7958 4-9-2 0 GeraldMosse 12 105
(Allan Smith, Bahrain) 22/1
4 shd **Afaak**[55] 7694 5-9-2 0 JimCrowley 9 105
(Charles Hills) *towards rr of midfield: sltly outpcd 3f out: pushed along over 2f out: rdn over 1f out: responded for press ins fnl f: r.o strly: nt quite pce to chal* 11/1
5 hd **Intellogent (IRE)**[33] 8378 4-9-2 0 (p) Pierre-CharlesBoudot 6 105
(F Chappet, France) 9/1
6 ¾ **Pivoine (IRE)**[41] 8155 5-9-2 0 (b) SilvestreDeSousa 13 103
(Andrew Balding) *hld up in fnl pair: nudged along at times: pushed along over 3f out: rdn and prog fr 1 1/2f out: r.o wl ins fnl f: nvr cl enough to land a blow* 3/1[2]
7 ¾ **Coolagh Forest (IRE)**[34] 8336 3-8-13 0 JFEgan 8 103
(Paul D'Arcy) *prom in main gp: pushed along and effrt over 2f out: sn rdn: unable qck: kpt on same pce ins fnl f* 18/1
8 ½ **Aquarium**[20] 8764 4-9-2 0 RichardKingscote 4 101
(Jane Chapple-Hyam) *racd towards rr of midfield: pushed along and effrt over 2f out: limited rspnse: rdn over 1f out: kpt on ins fnl f but nvr threatened* 25/1
9 ½ **Thorkhill Star (IRE)**[595] 7-9-2 0 JamesDoyle 2 100
(Allan Smith, Bahrain) 11/1
10 2 ½ **Proposed**[307] 329 7-9-2 0 BrettDoyle 14 95
(Jaber Ramadhan, Bahrain) 66/1
11 nse **Sword Peinture (GER)**[19] 8790 4-8-11 0 FilipMinarik 7 89
(Andreas Suborics, Germany) 28/1
12 nk **Vale Do Sol (IRE)**[293] 572 7-9-2 0 AdriedeVries 1 94
(Hesham Al Haddad, Bahrain) 40/1
13 5 **Mountain Angel (IRE)**[48] 7923 5-9-2 0 AndreaAtzeni 5 84
(Roger Varian) *prom in main gp: asked for effrt over 2f out: sn lost position: grad wknd u.p fr 1 1/2f out* 9/2[3]

2m 0.41s
WFA 3 from 4yo+ 3lb 13 Ran SP% 126.9

Owner Jean-Jacques Biarese **Bred** Old Carhue Stud **Trained** France

8998 LINGFIELD (L-H)
Saturday, November 23

OFFICIAL GOING: Polytrack: standard
Wind: virtually nil Weather: overcast

9126 LADBROKES WHERE THE NATION PLAYS FILLIES' H'CAP 1m 1y(P)
12:10 (12:10) (Class 4) (0-85,82) 3-Y-0+
£5,207 (£1,549; £580; £300; £300) Stalls High

Form RPR
0600 1 **Stay Classy (IRE)**[21] 8766 3-9-3 82 (p[1]) AngusVilliers(7) 5 87
(Richard Spencer) *dwlt and awkward leaving stalls: hld up in tch: hdwy to chse ldrs and pushed along 2f out: swtchd lft over 1f out: rdn and r.o wl to ld towards fin* 14/1

The Form Book Flat 2019, Raceform Ltd, Newbury, RG14 5SJ

5122 **2** *nk* **Zafaranah (USA)**[23] 8691 5-9-10 **80**.................... AdamKirby 2 85
(Pam Sly) *broke wl restrained and hld up in tch in midfield: effrt ent fnl 2f: drvn and ev ch 1f out: led 100yds out: hdd and no ex towards fin* **6/1**

2251 **3** *hd* **Delicate Kiss**[19] 8807 5-9-1 **76**....................(b) AledBeech(5) 3 81
(John Bridger) *awkward leaving stalls and bustled along: in tch towards rr: effrt over 1f out: swtchd rt and r.o strly fnl 100yds: nt quite rch ldrs* **9/2**[2]

3520 **3** *dht* **I'lletyougonow**[26] 8606 3-9-0 **72**....................(p) TomMarquand 1 76
(Mick Channon) *in tch in midfield: swtchd rt and effrt ent fnl 2f: drvn over 1f out: hdwy u.p ins fnl f: r.o strly fnl 100yds: nt quite rch ldrs* **8/1**

6200 **5** *nk* **First Link (USA)**[32] 8419 4-8-6 **65**.................... ThomasGreatrex(3) 10 69+
(Jean-Rene Auvray) *t.k.h: hld up in tch towards rr: effrt bnd 2f out: hdwy u.p ins fnl f: styd on strly towards fin: nt rch ldrs* **8/1**

0004 **6** *2* **Itizzit**[31] 8456 3-9-5 **77**.................... JasonWatson 9 76
(Hughie Morrison) *chsd ldrs: effrt to ld 2f out: sn drvn and stl hrd pressed: hdd 100yds out: no ex and wknd wl ins fnl f* **4/1**[1]

1400 **7** *nk* **Daddy's Daughter (CAN)**[29] 8521 4-9-10 **80**....................(h) MartinDwyer 6 79
(Dean Ivory) *taken down early: sn led: rdn and hdd 2f out: stl ev ch u.p tl no ex ins fnl f: wknd wl ins fnl f* **11/2**[3]

1000 **8** *1 ½* **Secret Return (IRE)**[19] 8809 6-9-3 **78**.................... RhiainIngram(5) 8 73
(Karen George) *hld up in tch in midfield: effrt over 1f out: nt clr run 1f out: switching lft and rt ins fnl f: nvr trbld ldrs* **25/1**

2410 **9** *nk* **Song Of The Isles (IRE)**[63] 7460 3-9-2 **74**.................... JaneElliott 7 68
(Heather Main) *chsd ldr: rdn ent fnl 2f: unable qck over 1f out: wknd ins fnl f* **16/1**

1532 **10** *1 ½* **Saikung (IRE)**[33] 8412 3-9-9 **81**.................... KieranShoemark 4 71+
(Charles Hills) *in tch in midfield: effrt over 1f out: no imp whn squeezed for room and hmpd over 1f out: wl hld ins fnl f* **6/1**

1m 37.96s (-0.24) **Going Correction** +0.05s/f (Slow)
WFA 3 from 4yo+ 2lb **10 Ran SP% 120.8**
Speed ratings (Par 102): **103,102,102,102,102 100,99,98,98,96**
WIN: 21.00 Stay Classy; PL: 4.50 Stay Classy 1.20 Zafaranah 1.00 Delicate Kiss 1.40 I'lletyougonow; EX: 96.30; CSF: 99.04; TC: 367.75 225.06; TF: 150.60 402.30 CSF £99.04 CT £225.06 TOTE £21.00: £4.50, £1.20, £1.00; EX 96.30 Trifecta £150.60.
Owner Balasuriya,CookCunningham,Gowing,Spencer **Bred** Northern Bloodstock Agency Ltd **Trained** Newmarket, Suffolk

FOCUS
All race distances as advertised on standard going. A competitive fillies' handicap produced a blanket finish.

9127 LADBROKES HOME OF THE ODDS BOOST (S) STKS 1m 1y(P)

12:45 (12:48) (Class 6) 2-Y-O

£2,781 (£827; £413; £300; £300; £300) **Stalls** High

Form RPR

06 **1** **Rains Of Castamere**[15] 8912 2-8-12 0.................... TomMarquand 8 61+
(Mick Channon) *hld up in rr: effrt over 1f out: hdwy u.p 1f out: chal ins fnl f: r.o wl to ld last strides* **9/4**[2]

0 **2** *hd* **Saracen Star**[29] 8516 2-8-4 0.................... TheodoreLadd(3) 7 56+
(J S Moore) *short of room leaving stalls: hld up in last trio: rdn and hdwy over 1f out: chal and rdr dropped whip jst ins fnl f: sn led: rn green in front but kpt on: hdd last strides* **12/1**

00 **3** *6* **Xquisite (IRE)**[123] 5286 2-8-0 0.................... LauraCoughlan(7) 10 42
(J S Moore) *s.i.s and swtchd lft after s: hld up in rr: effrt u.p and hdwy on inner over 1f out: no ch w ldng pair: snatched modest 3rd on post* **33/1**

0 **4** *nse* **Blue Slate (IRE)**[29] 8516 2-8-12 0....................(p[1]) LiamKeniry 5 47
(J S Moore) *midfield: effrt over 2f out: sme hdwy u.p over 1f out: no ch w ldng pair ins fnl f: wnt modest 3rd wl ins fnl f tl lost 3rd on post* **20/1**

0406 **5** *1 ¼* **Prairie Moppins (USA)**[4] 9045 2-8-7 56.................... JosephineGordon 2 39
(Sylvester Kirk) *chsd ldr tl 5f out: styd chsng ldrs tl chsd clr ldr again 2f out tl 1f out: wknd ins fnl f* **8/1**[3]

0400 **6** *¾* **No Can Do**[5] 9037 2-8-12 59....................(t[1]) NicolaCurrie 6 42
(Jamie Osborne) *hld up in tch in midfield: effrt 2f out: rdn and fnd little over 1f out: wknd ins fnl f* **12/1**

4510 **7** *hd* **Isobar Wind (IRE)**[17] 8856 2-9-5 65....................(b) AdamKirby 9 49
(David Evans) *led: rdn and kicked clr 2f out: drvn and drifted rt over 1f out: hdd ins fnl f: sn wknd* **6/4**[1]

6000 **8** *¾* **Hootenanny (IRE)**[16] 8897 2-8-5 50.................... LeviWilliams(7) 1 40
(Adam West) *hld up in midfield: effrt over 1f out: no imp and wl hld ins fnl f* **50/1**

6000 **9** *5* **Jim 'N' Tomic (IRE)**[16] 8890 2-8-12 66....................(b[1]) CallumShepherd 3 28
(Dominic Ffrench Davis) *chsd ldrs: rdn and effrt ent fnl 2f: no imp over 1f out: wknd ins fnl f* **12/1**

00 **10** *7* **Mr Bowjangles**[143] 4517 2-8-12 0....................(h[1]) ShaneKelly 4 12
(Gay Kelleway) *chsd ldrs: wnt 2nd 5f out tl 2f out: sn lost pl: bhd fnl f (vet said gelding lost left hind shoe)* **16/1**

1m 39.63s (1.43) **Going Correction** +0.05s/f (Slow) **10 Ran SP% 120.5**
Speed ratings (Par 94): **94,93,87,87,86 85,85,84,79,72**
CSF £30.23 TOTE £3.10: £1.40, £3.20, £7.70; EX 32.60 Trifecta £402.40.There was no bid for the winner.
Owner M Channon **Bred** Mike Channon Bloodstock Limited **Trained** West Ilsley, Berks

FOCUS
A tight seller won like the first by the closers.

9128 BOMBARDIER "MARCH TO YOUR OWN DRUM" H'CAP 7f 1y(P)

1:20 (1:22) (Class 6) (0-60,62) 3-Y-O+

£2,781 (£827; £413; £300; £300; £300) **Stalls** Low

Form RPR

2361 **1** **Garth Rockett**[21] 8757 5-9-2 **57**....................(tp) ShaneKelly 10 64
(Mike Murphy) *taken down early: wl in tch in midfield: clsd to press ldr 2f out: rdn over 1f out: drvn ins fnl f: led 75yds out: styd on* **4/1**[2]

0-60 **2** *¾* **Hit The Beat**[280] 759 4-8-11 **59**.................... AmeliaGlass(7) 14 64
(Clive Cox) *in tch in midfield: effrt to chse ldrs 1f out: kpt on wl ins fnl f: wnt 2nd towards fin: nvr getting to wnr* **50/1**

0301 **3** *½* **Avorisk Et Perils (FR)**[7] 8998 4-9-7 **62**.................... HectorCrouch 9 66+
(Gary Moore) *hld up in tch in midfield: nt clr run ent fnl 2f: swtchd rt over 1f out: styd on wl ins fnl f: wnt 3rd last strides: nvr getting to wnr* **7/4**[1]

0336 **4** *hd* **The Lacemaker**[16] 8896 5-8-13 **57**....................(p) DarraghKeenan(3) 12 60
(Milton Harris) *chsd ldrs tl wnt 2nd 5f out: led over 2f out: rdn and kicked clr w wnr over 1f out: hdd 75yds out: no ex and lost 2 pls towards fin* **20/1**

000 **5** *1 ½* **Flora Tristan**[16] 8896 4-8-13 **57**....................(t) GabrieleMalune(3) 6 56
(Ivan Furtado) *taken down early: hld up in last quartet: effrt and sme hdwy over 1f out: kpt on ins fnl f: nvr threatened ldrs* **25/1**

1340 **6** *nk* **Round The Island**[15] 8923 6-9-2 **57**....................(p) PhilDennis 3 56
(Richard Whitaker) *chsd ldrs: effrt ent fnl 2f: rdn and unable qck 1f out: one pce ins fnl f* **16/1**

5 **7** *1 ¾* **Papa Delta**[39] 8217 5-9-4 **59**.................... DavidProbert 13 53
(Tony Carroll) *stdd after s: hld up in tch towards rr: effrt 2f out: kpt on ins fnl f: nvr trbld ldrs* **9/2**[3]

2000 **8** *1* **Recuerdame (USA)**[23] 8698 3-9-4 **60**.................... AdamKirby 2 50
(Simon Dow) *hld up in tch in midfield on inner: nt clr run and shuffled bk ent fnl 2f: swtchd rt over 1f out: no threat to ldrs but kpt on ins fnl f* **10/1**

4536 **9** *1* **Rockesbury**[134] 4875 4-9-0 **58**.................... ThomasGreatrex(3) 4 47
(David Loughnane) *led tl over 2f out: unable qck over 1f out: wknd ins fnl f* **11/1**

6140 **10** *shd* **Kennocha (IRE)**[46] 7982 3-9-3 **59**....................(tp) TomMarquand 1 47
(Amy Murphy) *chsd ldr for 2f: lost pl and midfield over 2f out: rdn and no hdwy over 1f out: wknd fnl f* **10/1**

0000 **11** *½* **The British Lion (IRE)**[23] 8711 4-8-11 **57**(v) ThoreHammerHansen(5) 11 44
(Alexandra Dunn) *hld up in last pair: effrt on outer over 1f out: sn hung lft and no hdwy: nvr involved* **33/1**

2000 **12** *12* **Soul Searching**[23] 8698 3-9-4 **60**....................(p[1]) CharlieBennett 5 15
(Pat Phelan) *in tch in midfield: struggling over 2f out: rdn and lost tch over 1f out: wl bhd ins fnl f* **66/1**

405 **13** *3* **Potters Question**[179] 3184 3-9-4 **60**.................... GeorgeWood 7 7
(Amy Murphy) *a towards rr: rdn 3f out: wl bhd ins fnl f* **33/1**

1m 24.62s (-0.18) **Going Correction** +0.05s/f (Slow)
WFA 3 from 4yo+ 1lb **13 Ran SP% 124.9**
Speed ratings (Par 101): **103,102,101,101,99 99,97,96,95,94 94,80,77**
CSF £213.63 CT £484.60 TOTE £4.70: £1.70, £11.10, £1.40; EX 304.50 Trifecta £1217.30.
Owner Philip Banfield **Bred** P Banfield **Trained** Westoning, Beds

FOCUS
A open 7f handicap where they haven't gone too fast for the first time today.

9129 BOMBARDIER GOLDEN BEER CONDITIONS STKS 7f 1y(P)

1:55 (1:56) (Class 3) 3-Y-O+ **£7,246** (£2,168; £1,084; £542; £270) **Stalls** Low

Form RPR

0224 **1** **Documenting**[23] 8707 6-9-0 105.................... JackMitchell 6 105+
(Kevin Frost) *chsd ldng pair: shkn up over 1f out: qcknd and hdwy to ld ins fnl f: r.o wl: comf* **10/11**[1]

6103 **2** *2 ¾* **Turn 'n Twirl (USA)**[45] 8016 3-8-8 88.................... CallumShepherd 3 92
(Simon Crisford) *chsd ldr: rdn and hdwy to ld ent fnl f: hdd ins fnl f: sn brushed aside by wnr and wl btn: hung on for 2nd cl home* **7/1**[3]

02-0 **3** *hd* **Silent Echo**[23] 8707 5-9-0 97....................(h) TomMarquand 4 97+
(Peter Hedger) *hld up in rr: effrt wl over 1f out: hung lft over 1f out: styd on wl ins fnl f: no ch w wnr* **10/1**

3002 **4** *½* **So Beloved**[7] 9000 9-9-2 99 ow2.................... AdamKirby 5 98
(David O'Meara) *in tch in midfield: effrt wl over 1f out: kpt on u.p ins fnl f: nvr any ch w wnr* **5/2**[2]

0000 **5** *4* **Apex King (IRE)**[7] 9000 5-9-0 82.................... KieranShoemark 1 85
(Mark Usher) *in tch in midfield: rdn and unable qck over 1f out: wknd ins fnl f* **40/1**

2002 **6** *¾* **Emily Goldfinch**[7] 9010 6-8-2 91....................(p) GraceMcEntee(7) 7 78
(Phil McEntee) *led: rdn over 1f out: sn hdd and no ex: wknd fnl f* **25/1**

3043 **7** *2 ¼* **Firelight (FR)**[26] 8607 3-8-8 86....................(h[1]) DavidProbert 2 71
(Andrew Balding) *t.k.h: hld up in tch in last trio: swtchd lft and effrt over 1f out: no hdwy and wknd ins fnl f* **20/1**

1m 23.95s (-0.85) **Going Correction** +0.05s/f (Slow)
WFA 3 from 5yo+ 1lb **7 Ran SP% 113.6**
Speed ratings (Par 107): **106,102,102,102,97 96,94**
CSF £7.95 TOTE £1.60: £1.10, £2.70; EX 8.00 Trifecta £30.90.
Owner Kevin Frost Racing Club & M A Humphreys **Bred** Millsec Limited **Trained** Newcastle-under-Lyme, Staffs

FOCUS
A clear favourite for this conditions race and he landed the odds without fuss.

9130 LADBROKES "PLAY 1-2-FREE" ON FOOTBALL/EBF STALLIONS NOVICE STKS 6f 1y(P)

2:30 (2:33) (Class 5) 2-Y-O **£3,428** (£1,020; £509; £254) **Stalls** Low

Form RPR

2 **1** **Dancin Inthestreet**[21] 8758 2-9-0 0.................... TomMarquand 9 79
(William Haggas) *sn led and mde rest: rdn and kicked clr over 1f out: kpt on and a doing enough ins fnl f* **3/1**[2]

2 *1 ¼* **Lexington Dash (FR)** 2-9-0 0.................... ThoreHammerHansen(5) 3 80+
(Richard Hannon) *chsd wnr: rdn and unable to match pce of wnr over 1f out: kpt on ins fnl f: nvr quite getting bk on terms* **7/1**[3]

P **3** *4* **Viaduct**[7] 9008 2-9-5 0.................... RobHornby 4 68
(Martyn Meade) *chsd ldrs: rdn over 1f out: sn outpcd: chsd clr ldng pair 1f out: one pce and no imp ins fnl f* **20/1**

4 *1 ¼* **Coto Donana** 2-9-0 0.................... KieranShoemark 7 60+
(Ed Vaughan) *dwlt and short of room leaving stalls: hld up in rr: effrt and wd bnd wl over 1f out: hdwy 1f out: styd on ins fnl f: nvr trbld ldrs (jockey said filly was slowly away)* **8/1**

4 **5** *½* **Risk Taker (IRE)**[29] 8516 2-9-5 0.................... AdamKirby 2 63+
(Clive Cox) *in tch in midfield: effrt jst over 2f out: unable qck and outpcd over 1f out: wl hld and plugged on same pce ins fnl f* **1/1**[1]

0 **6** *2 ½* **Forge Valley Lad**[22] 8722 2-9-5 0.................... DavidProbert 10 56
(Ed Vaughan) *t.k.h: hld up towards rr: effrt over 1f out: wl hld and kpt on same pce ins fnl f* **20/1**

7 *nse* **Limaro Prospect (IRE)** 2-9-5 0.................... JaneElliott 1 55
(Sir Mark Prescott Bt) *t.k.h: hld up wl in tch in midfield: rdn and outpcd over 1f out: wknd ins fnl f* **33/1**

8 *1* **Calamity May** 2-8-11 0.................... TheodoreLadd(3) 5 47
(Luke Dace) *midfield: short of room and sltly hmpd 5f out: effrt over 1f out: sn outpcd and wknd ins fnl f* **66/1**

0 **9** *nk* **Saffron Lane**[45] 8012 2-9-0 0.................... GeorgeWood 8 46
(Harry Dunlop) *chsd ldrs: rdn and struggling to qckn ent fnl 2f: sn outpcd and wknd ins fnl f* **50/1**

10 *1* **Mr Terry (IRE)** 2-9-5 0.................... NicolaCurrie 11 48
(Jamie Osborne) *wnt rt leaving stalls: rn green and a in rr (jockey said colt ran green early on)* **33/1**

6 **11** *1 ½* **Step To The Beat**[44] 8060 2-9-5 0.................... HectorCrouch 6 44
(Clive Cox) *in tch in midfield: rdn and struggling to qckn ent fnl 2f: lost pl over 1f out: wknd ins fnl f* **16/1**

1m 12.51s (0.61) **Going Correction** +0.05s/f (Slow) **11 Ran SP% 123.4**
Speed ratings (Par 96): **97,95,90,88,87 84,84,82,82,81 79**
CSF £23.53 TOTE £3.30: £1.30, £1.70, £5.30; EX 22.10 Trifecta £203.50.
Owner Christopher Wright **Bred** Stratford Place Stud **Trained** Newmarket, Suffolk

FOCUS
A couple of decent prospects dominated this novice stakes.

9131 BETWAY H'CAP 5f 6y(P)
3:05 (3:08) (Class 4) (0-85,85) 3-Y-O+
£5,207 (£1,549; £774; £387; £300; £300) Stalls High

Form RPR
4432 1 **Thegreatestshowman**32 8420 3-9-7 85 GeorgeWood 10 92
(Amy Murphy) *stdd and dropped in after s: hld up in rr: effrt over 1f out: hdwy and rdn to chal 100yds out: r.o wl to ld cl home* 4/1²
0002 2 hd **Fizzy Feet (IRE)**31 8470 3-8-12 79 ThomasGreatrex(3) 3 85
(David Loughnane) *chsd ldrs for 1f: wl in tch in midfield after: rdn and hdwy over 1f out: led wl ins fnl f: hdd and no ex cl home* 7/1
0526 3 nk **Just That Lord**17 8867 6-9-7 85 KieranShoemark 4 90
(Michael Attwater) *awkward as stalls opened and slowly away: hld up towards rr: rdn and hdwy on inner over 1f out: ev ch 100yds out: kpt on* 8/1
303 4 2 **Joegogo (IRE)**16 8895 4-8-12 76 DavidProbert 6 74
(David Evans) *chsd ldrs tl hdwy to join ldr wl over 3f out: led 2f out: sn rdn: hdd wl ins fnl f: wknd towards fin* 10/1
3021 5 hd **Doc Sportello (IRE)**38 8242 7-9-4 82 TomQueally 9 79
(Tony Carroll) *hld up in last pair: effrt and swtchd lft over 1f out: nt clr run and swtchd rt wl ins fnl f: kpt on towards fin: nvr trbld ldrs* 12/1
1300 6 ½ **Green Door (IRE)**38 8262 8-8-5 76 (v) GraceMcEntee(7) 8 71
(Robert Cowell) *pushed along leaving stalls: sn pressed ldrs and t.k.h: rdn over 1f out: unable qck and outpcd ins fnl f: btn whn nt clr run and swtchd rt cl home* 20/1
1350 7 nk **Secretfact**26 8601 6-8-12 76 (p) CharlieBennett 5 70
(Malcolm Saunders) *hld up in tch in midfield: effrt over 1f out: kpt on same pce ins fnl f* 14/1
4010 8 ½ **Mercenary Rose (IRE)**18 8826 3-9-5 83 (p¹) HectorCrouch 1 75
(Paul Cole) *sn led: hdd 2f out: stl ev ch u.p tl no ex 100yds out: wknd towards fin* 3/1¹
0114 9 ½ **Harry Hurricane**38 8267 7-9-6 84 (p) AdamKirby 2 82+
(George Baker) *wl in tch in midfield: chsd ldrs over 1f out: nt clr run and stuck bhd a wall of horses fnl f: nvr any ch to cl (jockey said gelding was denied a clear run for a sustained period in the straight)* 9/2³
3020 10 1¾ **Shining**16 8895 7-8-5 74 RhiainIngram(5) 7 58
(Jim Boyle) *chsd ldrs: short of room and dropped to midfield after 1f: rdn and struggling to qckn 2f out: wknd fnl f* 33/1

58.72s (-0.08) **Going Correction** +0.05s/f (Slow) 10 Ran SP% 117.9
Speed ratings (Par 105): **102,101,101,98,97 96,96,95,94,92**
CSF £32.67 CT £220.63 TOTE £4.60: £2.50, £2.20, £2.30; EX 31.10 Trifecta £311.90.
Owner Amy Murphy **Bred** Biddestone Stud Ltd **Trained** Newmarket, Suffolk

FOCUS
A tight class 4 over the minimum and the winner swooped late in a tight finish.

9132 BETWAY HEED YOUR HUNCH H'CAP 1m 2f (P)
3:35 (3:37) (Class 6) (0-65,67) 3-Y-O+
£2,781 (£827; £413; £300; £300; £300) Stalls Low

Form RPR
3640 1 **Helian (IRE)**72 7116 3-9-4 65 KieranShoemark 7 71
(Ed Dunlop) *in tch in midfield: effrt to chal and hung lft ent fnl f: led jst ins fnl f: battled on and hld on wl fnl 100yds* 13/2
2060 2 nk **Noble Fox**33 8413 3-9-4 65 (b) AdamKirby 1 70
(Clive Cox) *chsd ldrs: effrt to chal 1f out: sustained duel w wnr fr jst ins fnl f: kpt on u.p: a jst hld* 5/1³
634 3 2¼ **Savitar (IRE)**38 8270 4-9-4 62 (p) CallumShepherd 3 62
(Lee Carter) *in tch in midfield: effrt in cl 5th 2f out: chsd ldrs 1f out: outpcd and swtchd rt 100yds out: kpt on same pce after* 8/1
0000 4 hd **Narjes**23 8705 5-9-3 61 (h) HectorCrouch 2 61
(Laura Mongan) *dwlt and rousted along leaving stalls: sn rcvrd and in tch in midfield: effrt 2f out: kpt on same pce u.p ins fnl f* 25/1
005 5 1½ **Regulator (IRE)**21 8755 4-9-6 64 LiamKeniry 5 64
(Alexandra Dunn) *hld up in midfield: effrt and clsd over 1f out: chsd ldrs on inner but nowhere to go ins fnl f: forced to switch rt arnd many rivals 100yds out: nt rcvr but kpt on towards fin* 25/1
6540 6 ½ **Last Enchantment (IRE)**53 7790 4-9-5 63 (t) ShaneKelly 10 59
(Neil Mulholland) *chsd ldr: rdn and ev ch 2f out tl no ex ins fnl f: wknd towards fin* 33/1
3441 7 ¾ **Shifting Gold (IRE)**7 9005 3-8-13 67 Pierre-LouisJamin(7) 11 63+
(William Knight) *hld up in rr: effrt on outer bnd 2f out: styd on ins fnl f: nvr trbld ldrs* 11/4¹
0-06 8 1½ **Admodum (USA)**107 5842 6-8-13 60 (p) DarraghKeenan(3) 9 52
(John Butler) *t.k.h: hld up in rr: effrt and nt clr run wl over 1f out: swtchd rt and pushed along over 1f out: styd on ins fnl f: nvr trble ldrs (An enquiry was held into the running and riding of the gelding. The rider and the trainer's rep were interviewed and shown recordings of the race. The Vet reported that an initial post-race examination of the gelding failed to reveal any abnormalities.* 20/1
1240 9 hd **Misu Pete**61 7527 7-8-10 61 (p) IsobelFrancis(7) 12 53
(Mark Usher) *t.k.h: hld up in tch in midfield on outer: rdn and outpcd jst over 2f out: wl hld and one pce fr over 1f out* 33/1
2543 10 nk **Billy Roberts (IRE)**24 8669 6-9-4 62 PhilDennis 4 54
(Richard Whitaker) *taken down early: led: rdn and hrd pressed ent fnl 2f: hdd jst ins fnl f: sn btn and wknd fnl 100yds* 4/1²
360 11 5 **Maroc**38 8248 6-9-5 63 (p) DavidProbert 8 46
(Nikki Evans) *chsd ldrs: rdn and losing pl over 2f out: wknd over 1f out* 33/1
66 12 hd **Ariette Du Rue (USA)**63 7472 3-9-2 63 (p¹) NicolaCurrie 6 46
(Ed Vaughan) *hld up towards rr: effrt whn nt clr run wl over 1f out: squeezed between rivals over 1f out: no imp* 14/1
5205 13 hd **Miss Blondell**19 8813 6-8-11 62 AngusVilliers(7) 13 44
(Marcus Tregoning) *stdd and swtchd lft after s: nvr involved* 7/1
0050 14 4½ **Burguillos**16 8434 6-9-4 62 (tp) WilliamCarson 14 36
(John Butler) *taken down early: stdd and wnt rt leaving stalls: hld up towards rr: effrt 2f out: sn btn and wknd fnl f* 50/1

2m 7.53s (0.93) **Going Correction** +0.05s/f (Slow)
WFA 3 from 4yo+ 3lb 14 Ran SP% 130.2
Speed ratings (Par 101): **98,97,95,95,94 94,93,92,92,92 88,87,87,84**
CSF £39.44 CT £279.40 TOTE £7.60: £2.40, £2.20, £3.00; EX 45.30 Trifecta £322.10.
Owner Ms Helian Jianru & Yin Yue **Bred** Kildaragh Stud **Trained** Newmarket, Suffolk

FOCUS
A lowly, class 6 but two 3yos fought out the finish.
T/Plt: £64.40 to a £1 stake. Pool: £58,190.28 - 659.13 winning units T/Qpdt: £10.20 to a £1 stake. Pool: £4,457.91 - 323.22 winning units **Steve Payne**

9036 WOLVERHAMPTON (A.W) (L-H)
Saturday, November 23

OFFICIAL GOING: Tapeta: standard

9133 BETWAY HEED YOUR HUNCH H'CAP 6f 20y (Tp)
4:10 (4:11) (Class 6) (0-55,55) 3-Y-O+
£2,781 (£827; £413; £400; £400; £400) Stalls Low

Form RPR
0000 1 **Aquarius (IRE)**5 9039 3-9-4 54 AlistairRawlinson 4 63
(Michael Appleby) *prom: swtchd rt and hdwy over 1f out: rdn to ld ins fnl f: won gng away* 10/1
4330 2 2 **Mansfield**52 7823 6-9-5 55 DougieCostello 6 58
(Stella Barclay) *midfield: hdwy gng easily 2f out: rdn and chsd wnr ins fnl f: kpt on* 7/1³
3344 3 nk **Maid Millie**5 9039 3-9-5 55 (v) HayleyTurner 7 57
(Robert Cowell) *t.k.h: led: rdn and hung rt over 1f out: hdd ins fnl f: sn no ex* 4/1²
0060 4 hd **Watheer**38 8270 4-9-0 55 PaulaMuir(5) 5 57
(Roger Fell) *s.i.s: hld up in rr: shkn up over 2f out: rdn and hdwy over 1f out: kpt on fnl f: nrst fin* 8/1
0650 5 ½ **Billyoakes (IRE)**31 8457 7-9-4 54 (b¹) BenRobinson 13 54
(Ollie Pears) *trckd ldrs: rdn over 1f out: no ex ins fnl f* 16/1
6601 6 ¾ **Santafiora**31 8469 5-9-2 52 CallumRodriguez 10 50
(Julie Camacho) *t.k.h: disp ld: rdn 2f out: no ex ins fnl f* 7/2¹
1200 7 ½ **One One Seven (IRE)**22 8720 3-9-3 53 CamHardie 11 49
(Antony Brittain) *midfield: rdn over 2f out: no imp fnl f* 14/1
0060 8 1 **Declamation (IRE)**18 8822 9-9-3 53 JoeyHaynes 12 46
(John Butler) *s.i.s: hld up in rr: shkn up 2f out: sme hdwy fnl f: n.d* 33/1
6035 9 shd **Roaring Rory**31 8457 6-9-4 54 (p) ShaneGray 8 47
(Ollie Pears) *s.i.s: in rr: rdn over 2f out: no imp fnl f* 7/1³
60-0 10 5 **Castelo (IRE)**17 8847 3-9-4 54 JasonWatson 2 32
(Daniel Kubler) *midfield on inner: rdn over 2f out: wknd over 1f out* 25/1
110 11 1¼ **Krazy Paving**214 2013 7-9-5 55 (p) EoinWalsh 1 29
(Olly Murphy) *dwlt s: in rr: struggling over 2f out: sn btn* 20/1
1-25 12 1¾ **Distant Applause (IRE)**303 383 4-9-3 53 BenCurtis 3 22
(Dominic Ffrench Davis) *trckd ldrs: rdn over 2f out: wknd over 1f out* 15/2

1m 13.47s (-1.03) **Going Correction** -0.20s/f (Stan) 12 Ran SP% 123.3
Speed ratings (Par 101): **98,95,94,94,94 93,92,91,90,84 82,80**
CSF £79.76 CT £335.72 TOTE £10.70: £3.60, £2.50, £2.10; EX 90.80 Trifecta £442.20.
Owner C L Bacon **Bred** Michael Downey & Roalso Ltd **Trained** Oakham, Rutland

FOCUS
The going was standard. Stalls - 7f: outside; remainder: inside. A modest sprint handicap which produced an authoritative winner.

9134 #BETYOURWAY AT BETWAY H'CAP 1m 5f 219y (Tp)
4:40 (4:40) (Class 5) (0-75,75) 3-Y-O+
£3,428 (£1,020; £509; £400; £400; £400) Stalls Low

Form RPR
001 1 **Inteldream**75 7035 3-9-1 68 DanielMuscutt 9 75+
(Marco Botti) *towards rr: rdn over 3f out: gd hdwy and hung lft over 1f out: led ins fnl f: kpt on* 5/6¹
544 2 1 **Clap Your Hands**186 2925 3-8-12 70 PoppyBridgwater(5) 4 75+
(David Simcock) *s.i.s: sn midfield: short of room and lost grnd over 2f out: rdn and hdwy over 1f out: kpt on fnl f: wnt 2nd fnl stride* 11/2³
-005 3 nse **Dance To Paris**134 4881 4-9-12 73 (b) HayleyTurner 8 77
(Lucy Wadham) *prom: hdwy and wnt 2nd over 2f out: rdn to ld over 1f out: hdd ins fnl f: lost 2nd fnl stride* 9/2²
5-00 4 2¾ **Adams Park**26 8608 4-9-8 69 (v) AlistairRawlinson 1 69
(Michael Appleby) *cl up: wnt 2nd 1/2-way: led 3f out: rdn and hdd over 1f out: no ex ins fnl f* 16/1
2323 5 1½ **Lafilia (GER)**116 5513 4-8-13 60 (b) KieranO'Neill 10 57
(Giuseppe Fierro) *t.k.h: cl up: rdn 2f out: outpcd fnl f* 22/1
-040 6 ¾ **Amanto (GER)**36 6303 9-9-4 65 (vt¹) CharlesBishop 3 61
(Ali Stronge) *dwlt s: hld up in rr: pushed along 3f out: hdwy and hung lft over 1f out: sn no imp* 18/1
0060 7 10 **Cafe Espresso**23 8692 3-9-3 70 JoeyHaynes 7 51
(Chelsea Banham) *s.i.s: in rr: rdn 3f out: sn wknd* 18/1
0000 8 14 **Compatriot (IRE)**5 9033 5-9-6 67 (p) BenCurtis 6 25
(Roger Fell) *t.k.h: led at stdy pce: hdd 3f out: sn rdn and wknd* 12/1

3m 4.65s (3.65) **Going Correction** -0.20s/f (Stan)
WFA 3 from 4yo+ 6lb 8 Ran SP% 116.6
Speed ratings (Par 103): **81,80,80,78,77 77,71,63**
CSF £6.01 CT £13.95 TOTE £1.70: £1.10, £1.90, £1.20; EX 7.60 Trifecta £20.60.
Owner Fabfive **Bred** Ed's Stud Ltd **Trained** Newmarket, Suffolk

FOCUS
An ordinary handicap, but the winner ground it out well and looks a promising stayer.

9135 PLAY 4 TO SCORE AT BETWAY H'CAP 5f 21y (Tp)
5:10 (5:11) (Class 5) (0-70,70) 3-Y-O+
£3,428 (£1,020; £509; £400; £400; £400) Stalls Low

Form RPR
552 1 **Three Little Birds**7 9013 4-9-7 70 BenCurtis 5 80
(Sylvester Kirk) *prom: shkn up and hdwy over 1f out: led ins fnl f: sn pushed out: comf* 5/4¹
5631 2 1½ **Qaaraat**22 8715 4-8-9 58 (p) CamHardie 10 62
(Antony Brittain) *hld up in rr: hdwy whn shkn up and edgd rt over 1f out: kpt on fnl f: wnt 2nd towards fin: no match for wnr* 13/2²
120 3 nk **Toni's A Star**46 7986 7-8-6 62 ElishaWhittington(7) 11 65
(Tony Carroll) *trckd ldrs: shkn up and hdwy over 1f out: briefly wnt 2nd ins fnl f: sn edgd lft: no ex towards fin* 20/1
100 4 nse **Awsaaf**42 8117 4-9-6 69 (h) CharlesBishop 6 71
(Michael Wigham) *dwlt s: hld up in rr on outer: stdy hdwy 1/2-way: rdn and edgd lft over 1f out: kpt on fnl f: nrst fin* 12/1
012P 5 1 **Look Surprised**82 6809 6-9-7 70 JasonWatson 2 72+
(Roger Teal) *hld up in rr on inner: hdwy whn bit short of room over 1f out: keeping on whn bdly hmpd ins fnl f: nt rcvr* 7/1³
6040 6 ¾ **Autumn Splendour (IRE)**46 7986 3-8-8 57 (b¹) RaulDaSilva 4 53
(Milton Bradley) *dwlt s: in rr: rdn 1/2-way: edgd lft and kpt on ins fnl f: nvr able to chal* 28/1
1036 7 1¾ **Miss Gargar**23 8704 3-8-8 57 (b¹) JoeFanning 7 47
(Harry Dunlop) *hld up in rr: rdn on outer over 1f out: no imp fnl f* 14/1

544 **8** *1 ¼* **Kodiac Express (IRE)**[16] 8895 4-9-5 **68**........................ DanielMuscutt 9 53
(Mike Murphy) *led at fast pce: hdd 2f out: wknd fr 1f out* **7/1**[3]

5224 **9** *1 ½* **Glamorous Rocket (IRE)**[70] 7178 4-9-3 **69**........................ MitchGodwin(3) 8 49
(Christopher Mason) *disp ld: led 2f out: rdn and hdd ins fnl f: sn wknd* **16/1**

03 **10** *¾* **Celerity (IRE)**[24] 8668 5-8-7 **56** oh11........................(p) KieranO'Neill 1 33
(Lisa Williamson) *prom on inner: rdn and struggling over 2f out: sn btn* **80/1**

1040 **11** *shd* **Hard Solution**[22] 8715 3-9-4 **67**........................ ShaneGray 3 44
(David O'Meara) *prom: bit short of room over 2f out: rdn and wknd over 1f out* **10/1**

1m 0.58s (-1.32) **Going Correction** -0.20s/f (Stan) **11** Ran SP% **121.6**
Speed ratings (Par 103): **102,99,99,99,97 96,93,91,89,87 87**
CSF £9.78 CT £120.57 TOTE £1.90: £1.10, £1.80, £5.30; EX 11.40 Trifecta £111.60.
Owner Miss Amanda Rawding **Bred** T J Cooper **Trained** Upper Lambourn, Berks

FOCUS
A routine sprint handicap which saw the winner score cosily.

9136 LADBROKES WHERE THE NATION PLAYS EBF NOVICE STKS 1m 142y (Tp)
5:40 (5:41) (Class 5) 2-Y-O £3,428 (£1,020; £509; £254) **Stalls** Low

Form RPR

2 **1** **Khaloosy (IRE)**[32] 8424 2-9-5 0........................ JackMitchell 5 86+
(Roger Varian) *travelled strly: trckd ldrs: smooth hdwy over 1f out: led gng easily ins fnl f: sn shkn up and wnt clr: eased towards fin: impressive* **5/4**[1]

2 *4 ½* **Summit Reach** 2-9-5 0........................ RobHornby 2 73
(Ralph Beckett) *pressed ldr: chalng 3f out: rdn and led over 1f out: hdd ins fnl f: kpt on: no match for wnr* **16/1**

46 **3** *¾* **Red Missile (IRE)**[71] 7154 2-9-5 0........................ TomMarquand 7 71+
(William Haggas) *hld up in rr: rdn and hdwy over 1f out: sn hung lft: kpt on fnl f: nrst fin* **11/1**[3]

4 *½* **Dollar Bid** 2-9-5 0........................ HollieDoyle 4 70
(Sir Michael Stoute) *t.k.h: midfield: stdy hdwy and prom 3f out: rdn and drifted lft over 1f out: no imp ins fnl f* **11/1**[3]

5 *1 ¾* **Superior Moment (IRE)** 2-9-5 0........................ BenCurtis 6 66
(Tom Clover) *dwlt s: swtchd lft early: towards rr on inner: shkn up whn short of room over 2f out: pushed along and edgd lft over 1f out: sn no imp* **66/1**

2 **6** *1 ¼* **King Of Arms**[35] 8346 2-9-5 0........................ KieranO'Neill 1 64
(John Gosden) *t.k.h: led: hrd pressed 3f out: rdn and hdd over 1f out: wknd ins fnl f* **6/4**[2]

7 *3* **Shumba (USA)** 2-9-5 0........................ HayleyTurner 8 57
(David Simcock) *hld up in rr: shkn up whn bit short of room over 3f out: rdn and no imp fr 2f out* **25/1**

5 **8** *2 ½* **Pawpaw**[26] 8605 2-9-5 0........................ JasonWatson 3 52
(Clive Cox) *prom: rdn over 2f out: wknd over 1f out* **16/1**

40 **9** *7* **Marie's Gem (IRE)**[30] 8494 2-9-5 0........................ JoeFanning 10 37
(Mark Johnston) *s.i.s: racd in last: pushed along and outpcd over 3f out: sn btn* **50/1**

40 **10** *7* **Jackate**[22] 8714 2-9-5 0........................ CamHardie 13 23
(Ollie Pears) *towards rr on outer: rdn and struggling over 3f out: sn btn* **100/1**

1m 47.79s (-2.31) **Going Correction** -0.20s/f (Stan) **10** Ran SP% **121.2**
Speed ratings (Par 96): **102,98,97,96,95 94,91,89,83,76**
CSF £24.51 TOTE £2.00: £1.10, £3.00, £2.80; EX 26.30 Trifecta £168.80.
Owner Hamdan Al Maktoum **Bred** Shadwell Estate Company Limited **Trained** Newmarket, Suffolk

FOCUS
Some nicely-bred juveniles on show, but the winner was in a different league to his rivals.

9137 LADBROKES HOME OF THE ODDS BOOST NURSERY H'CAP 7f 36y (Tp)
6:10 (6:11) (Class 5) (0-75,77) 2-Y-O £3,428 (£1,020; £509; £400; £400; £400) **Stalls** High

Form RPR

4646 **1** **Richard R H B (IRE)**[24] 8665 2-8-11 **65**........................ ShaneGray 9 69
(David Loughnane) *cl up on outer: rdn to over 1f out: sn hrd pressed: kpt on wl fnl f: gamely* **9/1**

4053 **2** *hd* **Bendy Spirit (IRE)**[19] 8815 2-8-13 **70**........................ SeanDavis(3) 5 73
(Richard Fahey) *trckd ldrs: rdn and disp ld fr 1f out: kpt on: jst hld* **7/1**

054 **3** *1* **Triple Spear**[45] 8026 2-8-10 **67**........................ TheodoreLadd(3) 4 68
(Michael Appleby) *t.k.h: led: rdn and hdd over 1f out: sn rallied: kpt on fnl 110yds* **12/1**

4 *1 ½* **Holy Eleanor (IRE)**[66] 7353 2-8-13 **67**........................ HollieDoyle 8 64
(Archie Watson) *dwlt s: t.k.h: sn midfield: rdn 2f out: kpt on fnl f: nt rch ldrs* **4/1**[1]

006 **5** *shd* **Galispeed (FR)**[22] 8717 2-8-12 **66**........................ AdamMcNamara 12 63
(Archie Watson) *dwlt s: in rr: rdn and hdwy on outer over 1f out: kpt on fnl f: nrst fin* **25/1**

5321 **6** *½* **Danny Ocean (IRE)**[52] 7827 2-9-9 **77**........................(p) BenCurtis 7 72
(K R Burke) *hld up in rr: rdn over 2f out: hdwy on outer over 1f out: kpt on fnl f: mde no imp* **5/1**[3]

3453 **7** *½* **Three Fans (FR)**[30] 8505 2-9-2 **70**........................(v) JaneElliott 10 64
(Tom Dascombe) *midfield on outer: rdn over 2f out: edgd lft over 1f out: sn no imp* **9/2**[2]

6653 **8** *¾* **Clegane**[45] 8026 2-9-2 **70**........................ TomMarquand 3 65+
(Ed Walker) *towards rr on inner: short of room 1/2-way: sn lost grnd: rdn over 1f out: nvr able to chal* **6/1**

3550 **9** *2* **Call Me Katie (IRE)**[24] 8665 2-9-7 **75**........................(b) NickyMackay 2 62
(John Gosden) *prom on inner: short of room and lost grnd 2f out: sn rdn and wknd* **16/1**

335 **10** *1 ¾* **Wailea Nights (IRE)**[59] 7569 2-8-12 **66**........................ JasonWatson 6 49
(Marco Botti) *dwlt s: in rr: pushed along but no imp whn short of room over 1f out: sn btn* **16/1**

1054 **11** *5* **Nirodha (IRE)**[24] 8665 2-9-6 **74**........................(v[1]) JasonHart 1 44
(Amy Murphy) *disp ld: rdn 2f out: sn wknd* **14/1**

1m 26.77s (-2.03) **Going Correction** -0.20s/f (Stan) 2y crse rec **11** Ran SP% **121.6**
Speed ratings (Par 96): **103,102,101,99,99 99,98,97,95,93 87**
CSF £73.19 CT £788.32 TOTE £12.70: £3.50, £2.40, £3.10; EX 81.40 Trifecta £858.90.
Owner Peter R Ball & Gentech Products Ltd **Bred** Mr And Mrs P McEnery **Trained** Tern Hill, Shropshire

FOCUS
A fair nursery in which it paid to race close to the pace.

9138 BETWAY CLAIMING STKS 1m 1f 104y (Tp)
6:40 (6:40) (Class 5) 3-Y-O+ £3,428 (£1,020; £509; £400; £400; £400) **Stalls** Low

Form RPR

5545 **1** **Scofflaw**[5] 9041 5-8-13 77........................(v) LauraPearson(7) 6 84
(David Evans) *t.k.h: midfield: hdwy on outer over 2f out: led over 1f out: pushed out fnl f: comf* **3/1**[1]

1633 **2** *1* **First Flight (IRE)**[25] 8633 8-8-10 71........................ BenRobinson 4 72
(Brian Ellison) *dwlt s: hld up in rr: stdy hdwy on outer over 2f out: rdn and edgd lft over 1f out: wnt 2nd ins fnl f: kpt on* **3/1**[1]

3052 **3** *nk* **Indomeneo**[49] 7903 4-8-12 73........................ SeanDavis(3) 2 77
(Richard Fahey) *prom: bit short of room over 2f out: rdn and hdwy over 1f out: kpt on ins fnl f* **8/1**

324 **4** *½* **Little India (FR)**[99] 6186 3-8-12 75........................ BenCurtis 1 76
(K R Burke) *t.k.h: led: hdd after 1f: sn trckd ldr: rdn and ev ch over 1f out: no ex ins fnl 110yds* **13/2**[3]

2562 **5** *3 ¼* **Guandi (USA)**[7] 9012 3-9-3 74........................(v[1]) JaneElliott 11 74
(Tom Dascombe) *cl up: led after 1f: rdn and hdd over 1f out: wknd fr 1f out* **4/1**[2]

-000 **6** *7* **Profound (IRE)**[7] 9012 4-9-4 68........................(p[1]) JasonWatson 7 59
(Mark Usher) *t.k.h: midfield on outer: rdn 3f out: sn outpcd: wkng whn hung lft over 1f out* **16/1**

0010 **7** *3 ¾* **Bond Angel**[16] 8902 4-8-7 65........................ HollieDoyle 5 43
(David Evans) *t.k.h: prom on inner: pushed along and outpcd whn hmpd over 2f out: sn wknd* **16/1**

5 **8** *7* **Tiffindell (IRE)**[21] 8753 3-8-3 0........................ AndrewBreslin(5) 12 32
(Robert Eddery) *in rr: rdn and struggling 4f out: sn btn* **66/1**

0460 **9** *2 ½* **Opera Kiss (IRE)**[28] 8547 3-7-12 40........................(p[1]) KieranSchofield(5) 8 22
(Ivan Furtado) *t.k.h: cl up: rdn and lost position over 2f out: sn wknd* **100/1**

5025 **P** **Tamleek (USA)**[25] 8633 5-9-7 80........................(p) CamHardie 10
(David O'Meara) *dwlt s: hld up in rr: p.u qckly 4f out: fatally injured* **10/1**

0046 **P** **Shattering (IRE)**[21] 8761 3-8-12 66........................ CameronNoble(3) 3
(Paul Cole) *hld up in rr: p.u qckly 4f out: fatally injured* **16/1**

1m 58.72s (-2.08) **Going Correction** -0.20s/f (Stan)
WFA 3 from 4yo+ 3lb **11** Ran SP% **123.7**
Speed ratings (Par 103): **101,100,99,99,96 90,86,80,78,,**
CSF £12.38 TOTE £3.50: £1.50, £1.50, £2.70; EX 15.10 Trifecta £72.40.First Flight was claimed by Mr A. G. Newcombe for £4,000
Owner John Abbey & Emma Evans **Bred** Mrs M E Slade **Trained** Pandy, Monmouths

FOCUS
A fair claimer which saw the winner register his fifth success of the year.

9139 BETWAY CLASSIFIED STKS 1m 1f 104y (Tp)
7:10 (7:24) (Class 6) 3-Y-O+ £2,781 (£827; £413; £400; £400; £400) **Stalls** Low

Form RPR

2360 **1** **Born To Reason (IRE)**[2] 9090 5-9-3 48........................(b) DanielMuscutt 6 58
(Alexandra Dunn) *trckd ldrs: led gng easily over 1f out: sn rdn clr: unchal* **5/1**[3]

0340 **2** *3* **Klipperty Klopp**[36] 8301 3-9-0 50........................ CamHardie 11 52
(Antony Brittain) *prom: rdn and outpcd over 2f out: rallied and wnt 2nd ins fnl f: no match for wnr* **12/1**

0-00 **3** *nk* **Relative Ease**[207] 2249 3-8-7 50........................ SophieReed(7) 5 52
(J S Moore) *midfield: shkn up and hdwy over 1f out: sn edgd lft: wnt 3rd ins fnl f: nrst fin* **50/1**

1353 **4** *¾* **Brother In Arms (IRE)**[23] 8694 5-9-0 49........................ SeanDavis(3) 13 50
(Tony Carroll) *t.k.h: hld up in rr: rdn and hdwy on outer over 1f out: sn edgd lft: kpt on ins fnl f: nvr able to chal* **12/1**

0255 **5** *2 ¼* **Cat Royale (IRE)**[38] 8251 6-9-3 48........................(b) DannyBrock 7 46
(John Butler) *pressed ldr: led over 2f out: rdn and hdd over 1f out: wknd ins fnl f* **17/2**

0252 **6** *3 ½* **Mistress Nellie**[17] 8854 4-9-3 50........................(t[1]) HollieDoyle 2 39
(William Stone) *towards rr: shkn up over 2f out: sme hdwy over 1f out: sn no imp* **5/2**[1]

5060 **7** *9* **Bakht A Rawan (IRE)**[23] 8703 7-9-3 50........................(p) JackMitchell 10 21
(Roger Teal) *hld up in rr: rdn over 2f out: nt rch ldrs* **6/1**

00 **8** *2 ½* **Drumshanbo Destiny (FR)**[90] 6505 3-9-0 46........................ CharlesBishop 9 16
(Ronald Harris) *s.i.s: in rr: rdn and struggling over 2f out: sn btn* **25/1**

0024 **9** *3* **Golden Deal (IRE)**[46] 8000 4-9-3 48........................ JoeFanning 8 11
(Richard Phillips) *t.k.h: led: pushed along and hdd over 2f out: wknd qckly over 1f out* **3/1**[2]

0060 **10** *4 ½* **Storm Girl**[163] 3764 3-9-0 47........................ MartinDwyer 3
(Sarah-Jayne Davies) *slowly away: in rr: struggling 3f out: sn btn* **80/1**

0456 **11** *3* **Ideal Grace**[18] 8837 3-9-0 50........................(p) RobHornby 4
(Brian Barr) *t.k.h: cl up: rdn over 3f out: wknd over 2f out* **25/1**

050 **12** *nse* **Strictly Legal (IRE)**[31] 8467 3-9-0 40........................ ShaneGray 1
(David O'Meara) *midfield on inner: rdn and struggling 3f out: sn btn* **50/1**

1m 59.21s (-1.59) **Going Correction** -0.20s/f (Stan)
WFA 3 from 4yo+ 3lb **12** Ran SP% **123.3**
Speed ratings (Par 101): **99,96,96,95,93 90,82,80,77,73 70,70**
CSF £63.14 TOTE £4.80: £2.10, £3.30, £15.40; EX 66.50 Trifecta £2416.70.
Owner West Buckland Bloodstock Ltd **Bred** Christopher Glynn **Trained** West Buckland, Somerset

FOCUS
Not the strongest of races. The winner was always well placed and scored in good style.

9140 BOMBARDIER "MARCH TO YOUR OWN DRUM" H'CAP 7f 36y (Tp)
7:40 (7:51) (Class 5) (0-70,70) 3-Y-O+ £3,428 (£1,020; £509; £400; £400; £400) **Stalls** High

Form RPR

0000 **1** **Inaam (IRE)**[73] 7080 6-9-2 **67**........................ JoeyHaynes 8 79
(John Butler) *dwlt s: hld up in rr: smooth hdwy over 2f out: shkn up and led over 1f out: edgd lft and qcknd clr ins fnl f: readily* **11/4**[1]

6662 **2** *2 ½* **Onebaba (IRE)**[23] 8690 3-9-4 70........................(b) HollieDoyle 2 74
(Tony Carroll) *dwlt s: in rr: rdn and hdwy over 1f out: kpt on fnl f: no match for wnr* **10/1**

4414 **3** *nk* **Knowing Glance (IRE)**[4] 9048 4-9-1 **69**........................(h) SeanDavis(3) 7 73
(Richard Fahey) *prom: rdn and hdwy over 1f out: kpt on ins fnl f* **6/1**[3]

6021 **4** *hd* **Bahuta Acha**[17] 8866 4-8-13 **67**........................ ThomasGreatrex(3) 5 71
(David Loughnane) *cl up on outer: rdn and ev ch over 1f out: sn chsd wnr: lost 2nd and no ex ins fnl f* **7/1**

0501 **5** 1 1/2 **Chookie Dunedin**[31] 8471 4-8-12 **68** .... BenSanderson(5) 9 68
(Keith Dalgleish) *towards rr on outer: rdn 2f out: kpt on fnl f: nvr able to chal* **6/1**[3]

4204 **6** 3/4 **Great Shout (IRE)**[17] 8866 3-9-3 **69** ....(t) GeorgeWood 3 66
(Amy Murphy) *cl up on inner: rdn and ev ch over 1f out: wknd ins fnl f* **11/1**

0441 **7** 1/2 **Al Suil Eile (FR)**[61] 7523 3-9-2 **68** .... JasonHart 11 63
(John Quinn) *t.k.h: prom on outer: rdn and outpcd 2f out: edgd lft and btn ins fnl f* **16/1**

2530 **8** 1 1/4 **Puerto Banus**[52] 7816 3-8-10 **69** .... RPWalsh(7) 10 61
(Ian Williams) *dwlt s: racd in last: pushed along briefly and stdy hdwy fnl f: n.d* **16/1**

4063 **9** 2 **Bay Of Naples (IRE)**[137] 4762 3-9-4 **70** .... TomEaves 4 56
(Michael Herrington) *midfield on inner: rdn 2f out: sn wknd* **16/1**

4005 **10** 2 1/2 **Highland Acclaim (IRE)**[23] 8690 8-9-2 **67** ....(h) ShaneGray 12 48
(David O'Meara) *t.k.h: led: rdn and hdd over 1f out: sn wknd* **40/1**

4052 **11** *nk* **Javelin**[31] 8456 4-9-5 **70** .... MartinDwyer 1 50
(William Muir) *hld up in rr: rdn over 2f out: n.d* **11/2**[2]

2331 **12** 1/2 **De Little Engine (IRE)**[68] 7273 5-9-4 **69** ....(p) DanielMuscutt 6 48
(Alexandra Dunn) *pressed ldr: pushed along over 2f out: wknd over 1f out* **20/1**

1m 26.87s (-1.93) **Going Correction** -0.20s/f (Stan)
WFA 3 from 4yo+ 1lb 12 Ran SP% **125.4**
Speed ratings (Par 103): **103,100,99,99,97 97,96,95,92,89 89,88**
CSF £33.87 CT £164.95 TOTE £5.00: £2.20, £3.30, £2.50; EX 50.60 Trifecta £273.90.
Owner Power Geneva Ltd **Bred** John Doyle **Trained** Newmarket, Suffolk

FOCUS
What looked a competitive handicap was dominated by the gambled-on winner.
T/Plt: £73.20 to a £1 stake. Pool: £82,080.40 - 818.29 winning units T/Qpdt: £20.60 to a £1 stake. Pool: £7,978.31 - 286.16 winning units **Richard Young**

9141 - 9152a (Foreign Racing) - See Raceform Interactive

8599 TOKYO (L-H)
Sunday, November 24

OFFICIAL GOING: Turf: yielding

9153a JAPAN CUP IN ASSOCIATION WITH LONGINES - DEEP IMPACT MEMORIAL (GRADE 1) (3YO+) (TURF) 1m 4f
6:40 3-Y-0+ **£2,167,824** (£864,521; £539,510; £321,750; £214,500)

RPR

1 **Suave Richard (JPN)**[28] 8599 5-9-0 0........(p) OisinMurphy 5 121
(Yasushi Shono, Japan) **41/10**[3]

2 3/4 **Curren Bouquetd'or (JPN)**[42] 8172 3-8-5 0........ AkihideTsumura 1 117
(Sakae Kunieda, Japan) **19/2**

3 1 1/2 **Wagnerian (JPN)**[28] 8599 4-9-0 0........ YugaKawada 2 118
(Yasuo Tomomichi, Japan) **33/10**[2]

4 1 3/4 **Makahiki (JPN)**[28] 8599 6-9-0 0........(p) YutakaTake 14 115
(Yasuo Tomomichi, Japan) **49/1**

5 *nk* **You Can Smile (JPN)**[28] 8599 4-9-0 0........ YasunariIwata 6 115
(Yasuo Tomomichi, Japan) **26/5**

6 *nk* **Daiwa Cagney (JPN)**[34] 5-9-0 0........(b) ShuIshibashi 7 114
(Takanori Kikuzawa, Japan) **120/1**

7 1 1/2 **Etario (JPN)**[49] 4-9-0 0........(b) NorihiroYokoyama 13 112
(Yasuo Tomomichi, Japan) **228/10**

8 1 1/4 **Muito Obrigado (JPN)**[21] 5-9-0 0........ Christophe-PatriceLemaire 4 110
(Koichi Tsunoda, Japan) **144/10**

9 *nk* **Cheval Grand (JPN)**[95] 6354 7-9-0 0........ ChristopheSoumillon 11 109
(Yasuo Tomomichi, Japan) **19/1**

10 1 1/2 **Look Twice (JPN)**[21] 6-9-0 0........ FrankieDettori 9 107
(Hideaki Fujiwara, Japan) **144/10**

11 5 **Rey De Oro (JPN)**[63] 5-9-0 0........ WilliamBuick 8 99
(Kazuo Fujisawa, Japan) **16/5**[1]

12 5 **Win Tenderness (JPN)**[21] 6-9-0 0........ HironobuTanabe 3 91
(Haruki Sugiyama, Japan) **246/1**

13 1 1/2 **Jinambo (JPN)**[84] 4-9-0 0........ RyanMoore 15 88
(Noriyuki Hori, Japan) **33/1**

14 *nk* **Danburite (JPN)**[49] 5-9-0 0........ FumaMatsuwaka 10 88
(Hidetaka Otonashi, Japan) **30/1**

15 3 1/2 **Taisei Trail (JPN)**[21] 4-9-0 0........ MircoDemuro 12 82
(Yoshito Yahagi, Japan) **57/1**

2m 25.9s (0.40) 15 Ran SP% **125.6**
WFA 3 from 4yo+ 5lb
PARI-MUTUEL (all including 100 jpy stake): WIN 510; SHOW 180, 280, 170; DF 2900; SF 4810.
Owner NICKS Co Ltd **Bred** Northern Racing **Trained** Japan

9085 CHELMSFORD (A.W) (L-H)
Monday, November 25

OFFICIAL GOING: Polytrack: standard
Wind: Virtually nil Weather: overcast

9154 EXTRA PLACES AT TOTESPORT.COM NOVICE STKS (PLUS 10 RACE) 1m 2f (P)
3:25 (3:30) (Class 4) 2-Y-O **£5,045** (£1,501; £750; £375) **Stalls Low**

Form RPR

6 **1** **Colonize**[17] 8914 2-9-2 0........ JimCrowley 5 76+
(John Gosden) *trckd ldrs: effrt to chal on outer over 2f out: rdn along to ld over 1f out: hung rt and green u.p clsng stages: a holding on* **4/1**[2]

5 **2** 1/2 **Far Rockaway**[17] 8913 2-8-11 0........(h) TomMarquand 7 70+
(William Haggas) *in tch on inner: pushed along 2f out: swtchd rt and rdn to chse wnr over 1f out: carried rt whn clsng by wnr fnl 100yds* **5/2**[1]

0 **3** 1/2 **Pharoah King (USA)**[20] 8823 2-9-2 0........ KieranO'Neill 12 74+
(John Gosden) *racd in midfield: effrt to chse ldrs 2f out: sn rdn and kpt on wl ent fnl f: carried rt by ldng pair clsng stages* **12/1**

6 **4** 4 1/2 **Fiveandtwenty**[19] 8848 2-8-11 0........ JoeFanning 6 61
(Mark Johnston) *led: rdn along and hdd by wnr over 1f out: kpt on one pce fnl f* **16/1**

5 3/4 **I Spied** 2-9-2 0........ PJMcDonald 8 65
(Mark Johnston) *midfield on inner: hdwy between rivals 2f out: sn rdn over 1f out: rn green but kpt on wl fnl f* **33/1**

0 **6** *nk* **King Of The North (IRE)**[20] 8823 2-9-2 0........ RobHornby 9 64
(Jonathan Portman) *trckd ldr: rdn and lost pl over 1f out: one pce fnl f* **25/1**

26 **7** *nk* **Book Review**[6] 9052 2-9-2 0........ RobertHavlin 4 64+
(John Gosden) *s.i.s: in rr: pushed along and no hdwy over 2f out: rdn and mde sme late hdwy fnl f* **5/2**[1]

8 2 1/2 **A Star Above** 2-9-2 0........ JamesDoyle 10 59
(William Haggas) *racd in midfield: rdn along and no imp 2f out: kpt on one pce under mostly hands and heels fnl f* **6/1**[3]

0660 **9** 3 1/4 **Master Rocco (IRE)**[32] 8493 2-9-2 60........ RichardKingscote 2 53
(Jane Chapple-Hyam) *trckd ldrs: rdn along and outpcd over 1f out: wknd fnl f* **25/1**

0 **10** 3/4 **Jersey Grey (FR)**[28] 8604 2-9-2 0........ CallumShepherd 3 52
(Jamie Osborne) *racd in midfield: pushed along over 3f out: rdn and lost pl 2f out: n.d* **50/1**

11 *nse* **Table Mountain** 2-8-11 0........ DavidProbert 13 47
(Andrew Balding) *j.rt: sn swtchd to rail in rr: rdn in rr 3f out: nvr a factor* **33/1**

01 **12** 18 **Spantik**[86] 6718 2-9-7 0........ AndreaAtzeni 11 24
(Roger Fell) *hld up: a bhd* **20/1**

0 **13** 1 1/2 **Mack The Knife (IRE)**[28] 8605 2-9-2 0........(b[1]) NicolaCurrie 1 17
(Jamie Osborne) *hld up: rdn and detached over 3f out (jockey said colt was never travelling)* **50/1**

2m 7.31s (-1.29) **Going Correction** -0.15s/f (Stan) 13 Ran SP% **127.3**
Speed ratings (Par 98): **99,98,98,94,94 93,93,91,88,88 88,73,72**
CSF £14.38 TOTE £4.90: £1.70, £1.30, £2.80; EX 23.60 Trifecta £194.40.
Owner Prince A A Faisal **Bred** Nawara Stud Limited **Trained** Newmarket, Suffolk

FOCUS
A few potentially interesting juveniles in here but very little got into it. There was a lengthy stewards' enquiry but it was always unlikely that the result would be reversed given the winning margin. It's been rated slightly cautiously.

9155 TOTEPOOL CASHBACK CLUB AT TOTESPORT.COM NOVICE STKS (PLUS 10 RACE) (DIV I) 1m (P)
4:00 (4:02) (Class 4) 2-Y-O **£5,045** (£1,501; £750; £375) **Stalls Low**

Form RPR

0 **1** **Newbolt (IRE)**[26] 8657 2-9-5 0........ RobHornby 5 78+
(Ralph Beckett) *trckd ldrs: swtchd rt and effrt to chse ldr over 1f out: rdn to ld ins fnl f: kpt on wl* **16/1**

6 **2** 1 1/4 **School Of Thought**[39] 8287 2-9-5 0........ PJMcDonald 7 75
(James Tate) *trckd ldr: pushed along to ld over 1f out: sn rdn and strly pressed by wnr: hdd wl ins fnl f: no ex* **5/2**[1]

65 **3** 1 1/4 **Diyari (IRE)**[76] 7055 2-9-5 0........ RobertHavlin 8 72
(John Gosden) *led: rdn along and hdd over 1f out: kpt on one pce fnl f* **10/3**[2]

0 **4** 2 3/4 **Dawn View (IRE)**[33] 8458 2-9-0 0........ RichardKingscote 2 61
(Stuart Williams) *racd in midfield: hdwy into 5th 2f out: sn rdn and kpt on fnl f but n.d* **25/1**

5 2 1/2 **Al Salt (IRE)** 2-9-5 0........ JimCrowley 14 60+
(William Haggas) *in tch on outer: pushed along to go 3rd 2f out: sn rdn and unable qck over 1f out: wknd fnl f* **7/2**[3]

403 **6** 1 1/4 **Provocation (IRE)**[17] 8914 2-9-0 77........ AndrewBreslin(5) 3 57
(Mark Johnston) *in rr of midfield: effrt to cl over 2f out: rdn and no imp over 1f out: kpt on one pce fnl f* **6/1**

7 6 **Logan Roy** 2-9-5 0........ DavidProbert 1 43
(Andrew Balding) *hld up: rdn along in rr over 2f out: plugged on fnl f* **20/1**

00 **8** 3/4 **Arabescato**[73] 7162 2-9-5 0........ CallumShepherd 10 42
(Nick Littmoden) *hld up: rdn in last 2f out: passed btn horses fnl f* **50/1**

05 **9** *nse* **Sure I'm Your Man (IRE)**[17] 8914 2-9-5 0........ JasonWatson 12 41
(Roger Charlton) *slowly away: hld up: rdn in rr 2f out: hmpd whn trying to make minor hdwy over 1f out: nvr on terms (jockey said colt was denied a clear run)* **16/1**

0 **10** 3/4 **Dame Denali**[19] 8849 2-9-0 0........ WilliamCarson 13 35
(Anthony Carson) *hld up: rdn in rr 2f out: nvr on terms* **100/1**

0 **11** *nse* **Estate House (FR)**[33] 8455 2-9-5 0........ GeorgeWood 4 40
(James Fanshawe) *midfield in tch: rdn along and lost pl 2f out: wknd over 1f out (jockey said colt ran green)* **12/1**

0 **12** *nse* **Lord Chapelfield**[28] 8605 2-9-5 0........ JackMitchell 6 39
(Amy Murphy) *racd in midfield on outer: rdn and outpcd 3f out: sn drvn along and lost pl over 1f out* **66/1**

1m 39.81s (-0.09) **Going Correction** -0.15s/f (Stan) 12 Ran SP% **120.7**
Speed ratings (Par 98): **94,92,91,88,86 85,79,78,78,77 77,77**
CSF £55.33 TOTE £20.70: £5.00, £1.30, £1.40; EX 85.00 Trifecta £388.60.
Owner Manor Farm Partnership **Bred** A D G Oldrey & G C Hartigan **Trained** Kimpton, Hants

FOCUS
Probably no more than an ordinary novice and it was run in a slower time than the second division.

9156 TOTEPOOL CASHBACK CLUB AT TOTESPORT.COM NOVICE STKS (PLUS 10 RACE) (DIV II) 1m (P)
4:30 (4:32) (Class 4) 2-Y-O **£5,045** (£1,501; £750; £375) **Stalls Low**

Form RPR

1 **Montather (IRE)** 2-9-5 0........ JimCrowley 6 84+
(Roger Varian) *midfield in tch: hdwy to chse ldr over 1f out: rdn and clsd ent fnl f: kpt on wl to ld cl home* **8/11**[1]

5 **2** 3/4 **Majestic Noor**[19] 8848 2-9-0 0........ RobertHavlin 11 77
(John Gosden) *trckd ldr: effrt to ld over 1f out: rdn along and strly pressed by wnr ent fnl f: hdd and no ex clsng stages* **6/1**[3]

5 **3** 3 1/2 **Power Of Time (IRE)**[21] 8810 2-9-5 0........(p) JamesDoyle 5 74
(Charlie Appleby) *trckd ldrs early: rdn along and wnt 2nd over 1f out: dropped to 3rd and kpt on one pce fnl f* **5/1**[2]

0 **4** 3 1/4 **Lord Of The Sky**[20] 8823 2-9-5 0........ PJMcDonald 7 66
(James Tate) *racd in midfield on inner: rdn along and no imp over 1f out: kpt on one pce fnl f* **5/1**[2]

00 **5** 6 **Ragtime Sally**[23] 8759 2-9-0 0........ JasonWatson 13 48
(Harry Dunlop) *midfield on outer: drvn along and lost pl 2f out: one pce fnl f* **33/1**

6 *hd* **Lord P** 2-9-0 0........ ThoreHammerHansen(5) 4 52
(Richard Hannon) *led: rdn along and hdd over 1f out: wknd fnl f* **22/1**

0 **7** 2 1/4 **Grand Canal (IRE)**[20] 8823 2-9-5 0........ JackMitchell 10 47
(Tom Clover) *hld up: rdn and minor hdwy over 1f out: sme late hdwy under hands and heels fnl f* **66/1**

00 **8** 1 3/4 **African Sun (IRE)**[17] 8914 2-9-5 0........ AdrianMcCarthy 12 43
(Ed Dunlop) *in rr of midfield: pushed along and no imp 2f out: sn rdn and no hdwy over 1f out: plugged on* **100/1**

00 **9** *4 1/2* **Colada Cove (IRE)**[4] 9085 2-9-5 0 ....(t) DavidProbert 3 33
(Tom Ward) *prom on inner: rdn along and lost pl over 2f out: wknd fnl f* **100/1**

0 **10** *8* **Mazekine**[28] 8605 2-8-9 0 .... RhiainIngram(5) 8 9
(Roger Ingram) *hld up: a in rr* **100/1**

11 *2 1/4* **Cuban** 2-9-5 0 .... EoinWalsh 9 9
(Christine Dunnett) *hld up: a bhd* **100/1**

12 *1/2* **Pedal Power** 2-9-5 0 .... RobHornby 1 8
(Andrew Balding) *hld up: rdn in rr over 3f out: nvr on terms* **20/1**

1m 38.43s (-1.47) **Going Correction** -0.15s/f (Stan) **12** Ran SP% **123.0**
Speed ratings (Par 98): **101,100,96,93,87 87,85,83,78,70 68,68**
CSF £5.71 TOTE £1.60: £1.20, £1.30, £1.30; EX 6.70 Trifecta £22.80.
Owner Hamdan Al Maktoum **Bred** Shadwell Estate Company Limited **Trained** Newmarket, Suffolk

FOCUS
An extremely well-backed winner of this novice and he could be well above average. His winning time was 1.5sec quicker than the first division.

9157 DOUBLE DELIGHT HAT-TRICK HEAVEN AT TOTESPORT.COM H'CAP 1m (P)
5:00 (5:02) (Class 6) (0-52,53) 3-Y-0+
£4,140 (£1,232; £615; £307; £300; £300) **Stalls Low**

Form RPR

-000 **1** **Kerrera**[179] 3252 6-8-12 **46** .... SophieRalston(5) 6 51+
(Dean Ivory) *in rr of midfield: dropped to last but stl gng wl 2f out: hdwy between rivals to cl over 1f out: swtchd rt and rdn fnl 100yds: clsd rapidly to ld post* **12/1**

6435 **2** *nse* **Pearl Spectre (USA)**[7] 9028 8-9-10 **53** ....(v) CallumShepherd 16 58
(Phil McEntee) *midfield on outer: rdn along to chse ldrs over 1f out: led ins fnl f: no ex whn hdd by wnr post* **9/2**[2]

00 **3** *1 1/2* **Margaret J**[101] 6153 3-8-7 **45** ....(p) GraceMcEntee(7) 7 46
(Phil McEntee) *hld up: rdn along and hdwy on outer over 1f out: kpt on wl fnl f* **25/1**

1560 **4** *nk* **Cristal Pallas Cat (IRE)**[40] 8255 4-8-12 **46** .... RhiainIngram(5) 13 47
(Roger Ingram) *led: rdn along and strly pressed over 1f out: hdd ins fnl f and no ex clsng stages* **10/1**

5000 **5** *1 3/4* **Dukes Meadow**[34] 8417 8-8-9 **45** .... LeviWilliams(7) 15 42
(Roger Ingram) *hld up: hdwy u.p on outer over 1f out: kpt on one pce fnl f but n.d* **33/1**

-056 **6** *2* **Theydon Spirit**[209] 2234 4-9-2 **45** .... GeorgeWood 5 37
(Peter Charalambous) *chsd ldr and disp at times: rdn along and lost pl ent fnl f: no ex* **9/2**[2]

1305 **7** *1 3/4* **Voice Of A Leader (IRE)**[23] 8756 8-9-10 **53** .... JoeyHaynes 2 41
(Chelsea Banham) *dwlt and racd in rr: rdn along to cl over 1f out: swtchd rt and kpt on wl fnl f but n.d (jockey said gelding jumped awkwardly leaving the stalls and was slowly away as a result)* **7/1**[3]

56 **8** *1/2* **Doogan's Warren (IRE)**[30] 8547 4-8-13 **45** .... DarraghKeenan(3) 4 32
(John Butler) *trckd ldrs: rdn along and no imp over 1f out: wknd fnl f* **11/4**[1]

6055 **9** *nse* **Vicky Cristina (IRE)**[35] 8404 4-9-2 **45** ....(v) KieranO'Neill 1 32
(John Holt) *chsd ldrs: rdn along over 2f out: wknd over 1f out* **25/1**

0450 **10** *1 1/2* **Invincible One (IRE)**[98] 6284 3-9-1 **46** ....(p) TomMarquand 10 28
(Sylvester Kirk) *hld up: nvr on terms* **8/1**

00-0 **11** *1* **Delcia**[21] 8808 3-9-4 **49** .... CharlesBishop 9 29
(Emma Lavelle) *racd in midfield: rdn and wknd over 1f out: sn bhd* **25/1**

4000 **12** *nse* **Langley Vale**[91] 6529 10-9-2 **45** .... JackMitchell 11 26
(Roger Teal) *chsd ldrs on outer: drvn along and no imp 2f out: lost pl and wknd over 1f out* **16/1**

1m 40.07s (0.17) **Going Correction** -0.15s/f (Stan)
WFA 3 from 4yo+ 2lb **12** Ran SP% **123.8**
Speed ratings (Par 101): **93,92,91,91,89 87,85,85,85,83 82,82**
CSF £65.62 CT £1384.59 TOTE £15.20: £3.60, £1.80, £7.90; EX 102.80 Trifecta £1506.90.
Owner Mrs Gwen Thomas **Bred** Millsec Limited **Trained** Radlett, Herts

FOCUS
Very little solid recent form on office and the sort of race that would throw up a different result every time it was run, so not form to get excited about. The winner was matched at the Betfair ceiling price of 1000 in running.

9158 BET AT TOTESPORT.COM FILLIES' NOVICE STKS (PLUS 10 RACE) (DIV I) 7f (P)
5:30 (5:31) (Class 4) 2-Y-O **£5,045** (£1,501; £750; £375) **Stalls Low**

Form RPR

0 **1** **Exhibit (IRE)**[23] 8758 2-9-0 0 .... JamesDoyle 9 77+
(Richard Hannon) *broke wl: mde all: shkn up w short ld over 1f out: rdn and extended advantage fnl f: comf* **7/1**[3]

0 **2** *2 1/2* **Etheric**[40] 8250 2-9-0 0 .... ShaneKelly 5 71
(Marco Botti) *trckd ldrs: swtchd rt and rdn to chse wnr over 1f out: kpt on one pce fnl f (vet said filly finished lame right fore)* **33/1**

52 **3** *3/4* **Evening Spirit**[33] 8453 2-9-0 0 .... RichardKingscote 10 69
(Ralph Beckett) *trckd ldrs on outer: effrt to cl on outer 2f out: rdn and no immediate imp over 1f out: kpt on one pce fnl f* **11/10**[1]

5 **4** *1 3/4* **Indie Angel (IRE)**[33] 8454 2-9-0 0 .... RobertHavlin 7 64+
(John Gosden) *dwlt and racd in rr: hdwy into midfield 1/2-way: rdn along on outer and no imp over 1f out: kpt on one pce fnl f* **15/8**[2]

00 **5** *2* **Spandavia (IRE)**[17] 8913 2-9-0 0 .... HollieDoyle 12 59
(Ed Dunlop) *chsd ldr: rdn along and lost pl over 1f out: wknd fnl f* **33/1**

50 **6** *1 3/4* **Ampney Red**[23] 8758 2-9-0 0 .... TomMarquand 3 54
(Hughie Morrison) *hld up: pushed along and no hdwy 2f out: sn rdn and no imp over 1f out: plugged on* **14/1**

0 **7** *1* **Good Try**[17] 8914 2-9-0 0 .... HayleyTurner 2 52
(Michael Bell) *hld up: rdn in rr over 1f out: kpt on one pce fnl f* **25/1**

06 **8** *1 1/4* **Cesifire (IRE)**[47] 8026 2-9-0 0 .... NicolaCurrie 4 49
(Adam West) *hld up in last: rdn along on outer over 1f out: no imp fnl f* **33/1**

9 *2* **Storm At Dawn (IRE)** 2-9-0 0 .... KieranO'Neill 1 43
(Ismail Mohammed) *in rr of midfield on inner: rdn along and no imp over 1f out: wknd fnl f* **25/1**

0 **10** *13* **Last Days Of May**[39] 8287 2-9-0 0 .... AdrianMcCarthy 6 10
(Christine Dunnett) *midfield: rdn along and lost pl over 2f out: sn bhd* **100/1**

1m 26.8s (-0.40) **Going Correction** -0.15s/f (Stan) **10** Ran SP% **119.1**
Speed ratings (Par 95): **96,93,92,90,88 86,84,83,81,66**
CSF £206.12 TOTE £6.60: £1.60, £5.50, £1.10; EX 165.80 Trifecta £435.80.
Owner Denford Stud **Bred** Denford Stud Ltd **Trained** East Everleigh, Wilts

FOCUS
Not much depth to this fillies' event and, with the market leaders underperforming to varying degrees, this probably won't be a race that throws up loads of future winners.

9159 BET AT TOTESPORT.COM FILLIES' NOVICE STKS (PLUS 10 RACE) (DIV II) 7f (P)
6:00 (6:03) (Class 4) 2-Y-O **£5,045** (£1,501; £750; £375) **Stalls Low**

Form RPR

0 **1** **Dawning (IRE)**[19] 8849 2-9-0 0 .... RobHornby 3 74+
(Martyn Meade) *dwlt sltly: racd in midfield: rdn along on outer over 1f out: drvn and styd on strly fnl f: led fnl strides* **33/1**

0 **2** *1/2* **Al Dawodiya (IRE)**[116] 5588 2-9-0 0 .... JamesDoyle 10 73+
(Richard Hannon) *led: stl gng wl 2f out: shkn up over 1f out: sn rdn ent fnl f: hdd fnl strides* **2/1**[1]

0 **3** *3/4* **Lady Eleanor**[33] 8454 2-9-0 0 .... DanielMuscutt 6 72
(James Fanshawe) *dwlt and racd in rr: pushed along to cl on ldrs over 1f out: rdn and short of room 1f out: r.o once in clr* **20/1**

4 *nk* **Clinician** 2-9-0 0 .... KieranShoemark 2 70
(Sir Michael Stoute) *trckd ldrs: pushed along to hold position 2f out: rdn and no imp 1f out: kpt on one pce fnl f* **6/1**

00 **5** *1* **Fleet Street**[17] 8913 2-9-0 0 .... RobertHavlin 1 67
(John Gosden) *racd in midfield in tch: effrt to cl over 1f out: rdn and kpt on one pce fnl f* **8/1**

3 **6** *1 1/2* **Must Be An Angel (IRE)**[19] 8849 2-9-0 0 .... TomMarquand 12 63
(Sylvester Kirk) *trckd ldr and racd freely: pushed along to hold position 2f out: rdn and wknd fnl f* **7/2**[2]

064 **7** *nk* **Secret Smile (IRE)**[17] 8913 2-9-0 75 .... JoeFanning 4 63
(Mark Johnston) *trckd ldrs: wnt 2nd and rdn to chse ldr over 1f out: wknd and lost several pls ins fnl f* **5/1**[3]

00 **8** *5* **Queen Of Clubs**[17] 8913 2-9-0 0 .... JasonWatson 8 50
(Roger Charlton) *midfield: rdn along and no imp over 1f out: wknd fnl f* **20/1**

00 **9** *3* **Truffle Mac**[17] 8913 2-9-0 0 .... CharlieBennett 5 42
(Hughie Morrison) *hld up: pushed along and no hdwy 2f out: sn bhd* **66/1**

10 *hd* **September Power (IRE)** 2-9-0 0 .... AndreaAtzeni 11 41
(Roger Varian) *dwlt and racd in rr: nvr on terms (jockey said filly was slowly away)* **9/1**

60 **11** *8* **Princess Siyouni (IRE)**[58] 7695 2-9-0 0 .... CharlesBishop 9 21
(Mick Quinn) *midfield on outer: pushed along and no imp on outer 2f out: rdn and wknd over 1f out* **50/1**

00 **12** *1/2* **Kates Star**[68] 7346 2-9-0 0 .... AdrianMcCarthy 7 19
(Christine Dunnett) *midfield on outer: pushed along and lost pl qckly 4f out: sn bhd* **100/1**

1m 26.42s (-0.78) **Going Correction** -0.15s/f (Stan) **12** Ran SP% **124.5**
Speed ratings (Par 95): **98,97,96,96,95 93,93,87,83,83 74,73**
CSF £100.23 TOTE £90.40: £14.60, £1.20, £5.60; EX 278.90 Trifecta £2254.20.
Owner Mrs Paul Shanahan 1 **Bred** Overbury Stallions Ltd **Trained** Manton, Wilts

FOCUS
Probably stronger than the first division and they clocked a slightly quicker time.

9160 BET IN PLAY AT TOTESPORT.COM H'CAP 7f (P)
6:30 (6:31) (Class 6) (0-52,52) 3-Y-O+
£4,140 (£1,232; £615; £307; £300; £300) **Stalls Low**

Form RPR

0531 **1** **Atwaar**[18] 8901 3-8-13 **50** .... FayeMcManoman(5) 8 56
(Charles Smith) *midfield in tch: effrt to cl on outer over 1f out: rdn to ld ent fnl f: r.o wl* **10/1**

5234 **2** *1/2* **Prince Rock (IRE)**[30] 8547 4-9-1 **46** .... TomMarquand 4 52
(Simon Dow) *midfield on inner: gng keenly whn short of room over 2f out: swtchd lft to rail and rdn over 1f out: styd on wl: nt rch wnr* **11/4**[1]

/030 **3** *hd* **Ultimat Power (IRE)**[25] 8689 5-8-10 **46** .... SeamusCronin(5) 10 51
(Frank Bishop) *hld up: swtchd rt to outer and hdwy over 1f out: rdn and styd on wl fnl f: too much to do* **25/1**

6-42 **4** *1/2* **Drop Kick Murphi (IRE)**[25] 8697 5-9-3 **48** .... AdrianMcCarthy 5 52
(Christine Dunnett) *chsd ldr: pushed along to ld over 2f out: drvn along and hdd ent fnl f: kpt on* **11/1**

0405 **5** *1/2* **Roca Magica**[35] 8408 3-9-1 **47** ....(p[1]) RobertHavlin 1 49
(Ed Dunlop) *racd in midfield on inner: effrt to cl whn briefly short of room over 1f out: rdn and keeping on fnl f whn snatched up nr line* **10/1**

2060 **6** *nk* **My Lady Claire**[48] 7982 3-9-5 **51** ....(p) DavidProbert 2 52
(Patrick Chamings) *racd in midfield: rdn along and no immediate imp over 1f out: kpt on one pce fnl f* **14/1**

0254 **7** *1/2* **Red Cossack (CAN)**[34] 8416 8-8-10 **46** ....(p) SophieRalston(5) 3 48
(Dean Ivory) *chsd ldrs: stl gng wl whn denied a clr run over 1f out: rdn once in clr 1f out and no imp clsng stages (jockey said gelding ran too free)* **5/1**[2]

0522 **8** *1 1/4* **Groupie**[18] 8901 5-9-5 **50** .... JamesSullivan 12 48
(Tom Tate) *in rr of midfield: niggled along 3f out: pushed along and nt clr run over 1f out: nt rcvr fnl f (jockey said mare was denied a clear run)* **7/1**[3]

0613 **9** *1 1/4* **Quick Monet (IRE)**[23] 8757 6-9-4 **52** .... DarraghKeenan(3) 15 46
(Shaun Harris) *hld up: stl in rr gng wl 2f out: swtchd rt and rdn over 1f out: kpt on fnl f but nvr on terms* **8/1**

0006 **10** *1* **Dreamboat Annie**[17] 8917 4-9-1 **46** ....(p) JasonWatson 13 37
(Mark Usher) *hld up: effrt to cl whn denied a clr run over 1f out: swtchd lft and rdn 1f out: one pce fnl f* **20/1**

0000 **11** *3/4* **Madame Ritz (IRE)**[18] 8898 4-9-2 **47** .... JoeFanning 14 36
(Richard Phillips) *trckd ldrs on outer: rdn along to chse ldr 2f out tl qckly lost pl 1f out: wknd clsng stages* **33/1**

0330 **12** *2 3/4* **Navarra Princess (IRE)**[170] 3592 4-9-1 **46** oh1 ....(t) HayleyTurner 9 28
(Don Cantillon) *midfield on outer: c wd off home bnd 2f out: sn rdn and minor hdwy over 1f out: wknd fnl f* **16/1**

452 **13** *15* **Wings Of Dubai (IRE)**[21] 8820 3-9-3 **49** .... KieranO'Neill 11
(Ismail Mohammed) *led: rdn along and hdd over 2f out: lost pl qckly over 1f out (jockey said filly hung left-handed in the straight)* **16/1**

2006 **14** *9* **Song Of Summer**[4] 9086 4-8-8 **46** oh1 ....(tp) GraceMcEntee(7) 16
(Phil McEntee) *hld up: rdn and detached 3f out: a in rr* **50/1**

1m 26.17s (-1.03) **Going Correction** -0.15s/f (Stan)
WFA 3 from 4yo+ 1lb **14** Ran SP% **125.4**
Speed ratings (Par 101): **99,98,98,97,97 96,96,94,93,92 91,88,71,60**
CSF £37.73 CT £708.94 TOTE £9.20: £3.60, £1.40, £7.70; EX 60.30 Trifecta £910.20.
Owner M Smeed **Bred** Shadwell Estate Company Limited **Trained** Temple Bruer, Lincs
■ Miaella was withdrawn. Price at time of withdrawal 20/1. Rule 4 does not apply.

FOCUS
A wide-open contest in which one or two didn't get the smoothest of passages, but the winner is 3yo on the up now, albeit at a modest level. Ordinary form.

9161 IRISH LOTTO AT TOTESPORT.COM H'CAP 6f (P)
7:00 (7:00) (Class 6) (0-52,52) 3-Y-O+
£4,140 (£1,232; £615; £307; £300; £300) **Stalls** Centre

Form RPR
0000 **1** **Guardia Svizzera (IRE)**[17] 8925 5-8-13 **52**.........(h) PaulaMuir(5) 5 58+
(Roger Fell) *trckd ldrs: shkn up to cl over 1f out: swtchd lft and rdn along to ld ent fnl f: drifted rt u.p clsng stages but kpt on wl* **12/1**

0000 **2** ¾ **Holy Tiber (IRE)**[58] 7684 4-9-3 **51**.........(b) JoeyHaynes 2 55
(Chelsea Banham) *hld up in rr: rdn w lots to do in rr 2f out: c wd off bnd: drvn and styd on strly clsng stages: nt rch wnr* **10/1**

0604 **3** ½ **Griggy (IRE)**[21] 8821 3-9-3 **51**.........(p[1]) CharlesBishop 11 54
(Sean Curran) *trckd ldrs: effrt to cl on outer over 1f out: rdn along to chal and ev ch 1f out: kpt on* **9/2**[2]

1501 **4** 2 **Catapult**[20] 8840 4-9-3 **51**.........(p) JosephineGordon 8 48
(Shaun Keightley) *chsd ldr: pushed along to ld over 1f out: sn drvn and hdd ent fnl f: no ex clsng stages* **4/1**[1]

4051 **5** 2¼ **Sarsaparilla Kit**[9] 9001 3-9-4 **52**......... RichardKingscote 7 42
(Stuart Williams) *led: rdn along and hdd over 1f out: wknd clsng stages* **7/1**[3]

400 **6** ½ **Valley Belle (IRE)**[65] 7447 3-9-4 **52**......... CallumShepherd 1 40
(Phil McEntee) *racd in midfield: rdn along and no imp over 1f out: kpt on one pce fnl f* **10/1**

4000 **7** 1¾ **Te Amo Te Amo**[33] 8457 3-9-2 **50**......... TomMarquand 13 33
(Simon Dow) *hld up in last: hdwy whn short of room 2f out: sn rdn and kpt on wl fnl f: n.d* **25/1**

2600 **8** ¾ **Poppy May (IRE)**[21] 8821 5-9-2 **50**......... BarryMcHugh 3 31
(James Given) *in rr of midfield: effrt whn short of room 2f out: sn rdn and no imp over 1f out: kpt on one pce fnl f* **10/1**

140 **9** 1 **Sweet Forgetme Not (IRE)**[19] 8864 3-8-10 **51**..(vt) GraceMcEntee(7) 10 29
(Phil McEntee) *midfield on outer: rdn along to and no imp over 1f out: one pce after* **20/1**

-300 **10** ¾ **Invisible Storm**[157] 4074 4-9-2 **50**.........(b) HectorCrouch 6 26
(William Stone) *chsd ldrs: rdn along and lost pl over 1f out: wknd fnl f* **12/1**

-000 **11** 2¼ **Juan Horsepower**[7] 9034 5-9-2 **50**.........(b) DannyBrock 12 19
(Denis Quinn) *hld up: v wd off home bnd: a bhd* **50/1**

3600 **12** 2 **Nananita (IRE)**[32] 8502 3-9-4 **52**......... LiamJones 9 15
(Mark Loughnane) *hld up: wd off home bnd: sn rdn and no imp: wknd fnl f* **25/1**

430 **13** 16 **Sagittarian Wind**[40] 8255 3-9-4 **52**......... HollieDoyle 14
(Archie Watson) *midfield on outer: drvn along and lost pl 2f out: sn bhd (jockey said filly stopped quickly)* **7/1**[3]

4050 **14** 74 **Hellovasinger**[25] 8711 3-9-3 **51**......... ShaneKelly 4
(Richard Hughes) *midfield on inner: rdn along and lost pl over 2f out: hmpd whn wkng 2f out: nt persevered w* **14/1**

1m 12.55s (-1.15) **Going Correction** -0.15s/f (Stan) **14** Ran SP% **126.9**
Speed ratings (Par 101): **101,100,99,96,93 93,90,89,88,87 84,81,60,**
CSF £128.50 CT £655.92 TOTE £11.30: £3.20, £3.80, £2.00; EX 130.10 Trifecta £915.20.
Owner Mpr, Ventura Racing 7 & Partner **Bred** W J Kennedy **Trained** Nawton, N Yorks
■ Stewards' Enquiry : Callum Shepherd seven-day ban; careless riding (Dec 9th-16th)

FOCUS
They went a strong gallop in this wide-open handicap and the winner was never far off the speed.
T/Plt: £75.70 to a £1 stake. Pool: £49,609.19 - 655.07 winning units T/Qpdt: £24.00 to a £1 stake. Pool: £5,079.56 - 211.37 winning units **Mark Grantham**

9133 WOLVERHAMPTON (A.W) (L-H)
Tuesday, November 26

OFFICIAL GOING: Tapeta: standard
Wind: Fresh behind Weather: Overcast

9162 LADBROKES "PLAY 1-2-FREE" ON FOOTBALL NURSERY H'CAP 6f 20y (Tp)
3:50 (3:53) (Class 4) (0-85,84) 2-Y-O
£4,463 (£1,328; £663; £400; £400; £400) **Stalls** Low

Form RPR
2511 **1** **Dark Regard**[8] 9031 2-9-1 **78** 6ex......... PJMcDonald 7 81
(Mark Johnston) *chsd ldrs: rdn to ld and hung lft ins fnl f: styd on* **7/2**[1]

122 **2** shd **Apollinaire**[164] 3841 2-9-4 **81**......... RobHornby 9 84+
(Ralph Beckett) *pushed along early in rr: nt clr run and swtchd rt ins fnl f: rdn and r.o wl to go 2nd post: nt rch wnr* **9/1**[3]

0010 **3** hd **Moon Of Love (IRE)**[59] 7692 2-9-4 **81**......... BarryMcHugh 12 83+
(Richard Fahey) *hld up: hdwy over 1f out: nt clr run and swtchd lft ins fnl f: sn rdn: r.o* **11/1**

6160 **4** 1¼ **Winning Streak**[45] 8110 2-9-4 **81**.........(t) JasonWatson 11 81+
(Stuart Williams) *prom: lost pl after 1f: hdwy and nt clr run over 1f out: r.o: nt trble ldrs (jockey said colt was denied a clear run just inside the final furlong)* **11/1**

0013 **5** 1 **Get Boosting**[22] 8817 2-9-0 **77**......... JoeFanning 6 72
(Keith Dalgleish) *s.i.s: hdwy over 4f out: rdn and edgd lft ins fnl f: styd on same pce* **11/2**[2]

1060 **6** 2 **Ocasio Cortez (IRE)**[72] 7247 2-9-4 **81**......... TomMarquand 10 70
(Richard Hannon) *led early: chsd ldrs: rdn over 2f out: styd on same pce fnl f* **25/1**

602 **7** ¾ **Zulu Zander (IRE)**[27] 8659 2-9-2 **79**......... CliffordLee 8 66
(David Evans) *sn chsng ldr: rdn and ev ch 1f out: carried lft and wknd wl ins fnl f* **50/1**

2302 **8** ¾ **Dazzling Des (IRE)**[22] 8817 2-9-4 **81**.........(p) ShaneGray 5 67
(David O'Meara) *hld up in tch: rdn and nt clr run over 1f out: wknd wl ins fnl f* **22/1**

3415 **9** nse **Little Brown Trout**[25] 8723 2-9-1 **78**......... HollieDoyle 4 70
(William Stone) *s.i.s: hld up: hdwy and nt clr run fr over 1f out tl swtchd rt wl ins fnl f: nt trble ldrs (jockey said gelding was denied a clear run for some distance in the home straight until approaching half a furlong out)* **9/1**[3]

0342 **10** ½ **Many A Star (IRE)**[19] 8890 2-9-0 **77**......... ShaneKelly 2 60
(James Given) *sn led: shkn up: hung lft and hdd ins fnl f: nt clr run sn after and wknd* **9/1**[3]

1201 **11** 1 **Reassure**[22] 8817 2-9-7 **84**......... JamesDoyle 3 64
(William Haggas) *hld up in tch: racd keenly: shkn up and nt clr run over 1f out tl ins fnl f: no ch after (jockey said filly was denied a clear run for some distance from approaching the final furlong)* **11/2**[2]

2212 **12** ½ **Audio**[42] 8219 2-9-2 **84**.........(t) ThoreHammerHansen(5) 1 66
(Richard Hannon) *prom: rdn over 1f out: styng on same pce whn nt clr run ins fnl f: hmpd and snatched up sn after (jockey said gelding was denied a clear run approaching half a furlong)* **18/1**

055 **13** 9 **Great Dame (IRE)**[93] 6498 2-9-0 **84**......... AngusVilliers(7) 13 36
(David O'Meara) *s.i.s: outpcd (jockey said filly was slowly away and did not face kickback)* **150/1**

1m 13.35s (-1.15) **Going Correction** -0.225s/f (Stan) **13** Ran SP% **115.7**
Speed ratings (Par 98): **98,97,97,95,94 91,90,89,89,89 87,87,75**
CSF £32.95 CT £314.47 TOTE £4.30: £2.00, £3.30, £3.50; EX 34.20 Trifecta £346.20.
Owner John Dance **Bred** Brightwalton Bloodstock Ltd **Trained** Middleham Moor, N Yorks
■ Stewards' Enquiry : P J McDonald two-day ban: careless riding (29th Nov & 10th Dec)

FOCUS
They went a solid gallop in this nursery and a few met trouble in running as they tried to close from behind. A good race for the time of year.

9163 LADBROKES FOOTBALL ACCA BOOSTY FILLIES' NOVICE STKS (PLUS 10 RACE) 1m 142y (Tp)
4:20 (4:25) (Class 5) 2-Y-O
£3,428 (£1,020; £509; £254) **Stalls** Low

Form RPR
22 **1** **Waliyak (FR)**[24] 8759 2-9-0 0......... JackMitchell 8 81+
(Roger Varian) *mde all: shkn up over 1f out: pushed clr fnl f: comf* **10/11**[1]

6 **2** 3¼ **Kepala**[54] 7832 2-9-0 0......... CharlesBishop 1 72+
(Eve Johnson Houghton) *chsd ldrs: shkn up to chse wnr over 1f out: no imp ins fnl f* **33/1**

3 1¼ **Lightness (IRE)** 2-9-0 0......... RobertHavlin 5 69+
(John Gosden) *prom: shkn up over 3f out: outpcd over 1f out: styd on to go 3rd wl ins fnl f* **9/1**

0 **4** 1¾ **Dancing Approach**[20] 8848 2-9-0 0......... JasonWatson 2 66
(Roger Charlton) *chsd wnr: shkn up over 2f out: lost 2nd over 1f out: wknd ins fnl f* **125/1**

5 3½ **Red Poppy** 2-9-0 0......... JamesDoyle 4 58
(William Haggas) *prom: pushed along over 3f out: wknd over 1f out* **3/1**[2]

0 **6** shd **La Foglietta**[46] 8100 2-9-0 0......... RichardKingscote 12 58
(Ralph Beckett) *s.s: rn green in rr: r.o ins fnl f: nvr nrr (jockey said filly was slowly away)* **15/2**[3]

7 1¾ **Aqrab (IRE)** 2-9-0 0......... TomMarquand 11 54
(Roger Varian) *s.i.s: hld up: pushed along over 2f out: nvr on terms* **16/1**

8 nk **Stand Free** 2-9-0 0.........(h[1]) JamesSullivan 9 54
(Suzzanne France) *hld up: shkn up over 2f out: nvr on terms* **200/1**

9 1½ **Schmoozie (IRE)** 2-9-0 0......... NicolaCurrie 6 51
(Jonathan Portman) *sn pushed along and rn green in rr: n.d* **100/1**

10 ¾ **Nablawyh (IRE)** 2-9-0 0......... KieranO'Neill 10 49
(Ismail Mohammed) *s.i.s: sn prom: rdn on outer over 2f out: wknd over 1f out (jockey said filly ran greenly)* **125/1**

0 **11** 43 **New Tune**[124] 5342 2-9-0 0.........(b[1]) RobHornby 3
(Ralph Beckett) *s.i.s: sn pushed along in rr: reminders 7f out: wknd 1/2-way* **33/1**

1m 49.22s (-0.88) **Going Correction** -0.225s/f (Stan) **11** Ran SP% **114.0**
Speed ratings (Par 93): **94,91,90,88,85 85,83,83,82,81 43**
CSF £45.15 TOTE £1.80: £1.10, £4.60, £2.30; EX 29.10 Trifecta £100.60.
Owner Fawzi Abdulla Nass **Bred** S De Moratalla Et Al **Trained** Newmarket, Suffolk
■ Dima was withdrawn. Price at time of withdrawal 33/1. Rule 4 does not apply.

FOCUS
This proved straightforward for the odds-on favourite. The opening level is ordinary.

9164 LADBROKES WHERE THE NATION PLAYS NURSERY H'CAP 7f 36y (Tp)
4:50 (4:54) (Class 6) (0-60,64) 2-Y-O
£2,781 (£827; £413; £400; £400; £400) **Stalls** High

Form RPR
5650 **1** **Maurice Dancer**[46] 8085 2-9-7 **60**......... PaulMulrennan 4 65
(Julie Camacho) *a.p: chsd ldr over 2f out: led over 1f out: rdn and edgd rt ins fnl f: jst hld on* **12/1**

000 **2** shd **Beat The Breeze**[141] 4734 2-8-11 **50**......... JFEgan 3 55
(Simon Dow) *s.i.s: hld up: racd keenly: swtchd rt and hdwy over 1f out: rdn and ev ch ins fnl f: edgd rt nr fin: styd on* **16/1**

4460 **3** 1¼ **Little Ted**[8] 9031 2-9-5 **58**.........(bt) JamesSullivan 10 60
(Tim Easterby) *s.s: pushed along early in rr: hdwy on outer over 1f out: rdn and hung rt ins fnl f: styd on* **11/2**[2]

3321 **4** 1¾ **You Don't Own Me (IRE)**[6] 9061 2-9-4 **64** 6ex(b) Pierre-LouisJamin(7) 1 62
(Joseph Tuite) *prom: racd keenly: lost pl over 5f out: rdn over 1f out: r.o ins fnl f* **13/2**[3]

4024 **5** 2¼ **Camacho Man (IRE)**[10] 9009 2-9-0 **53**......... JoeFanning 8 45
(Jennie Candlish) *s.i.s: hdwy over 5f out: shkn up on outer over 2f out: no ex fnl f* **5/2**[1]

0044 **6** 1¾ **Aiden's Reward (IRE)**[32] 8527 2-8-11 **50**......... GrahamLee 2 38
(Ben Haslam) *chsd ldrs: rdn 1/2-way: nt clr run and wknd ins fnl f* **11/1**

064 **7** ½ **Mr Kodi (IRE)**[19] 8897 2-8-12 **51**......... HollieDoyle 7 37
(David Evans) *chsd ldr tl over 5f out: remained handy: rdn over 2f out: wknd ins fnl f* **15/2**

4401 **8** 3 **Schumli**[10] 9009 2-8-12 **51**.........(t) CamHardie 9 30
(David O'Meara) *sn chsng ldrs: led over 4f out: rdn and hdd over 1f out: wknd ins fnl f (regarding the apparent improvement in form, trainer said rider had to make too much use of the filly early from a wide draw on this occasion)* **12/1**

000 **9** 3¾ **Bee Magic (IRE)**[19] 8889 2-9-2 **55**......... MartinDwyer 5 25
(William Muir) *s.i.s: pushed along early in rr: hmpd over 5f out: rdn and hung lft fr over 1f out: nvr on terms* **12/1**

6606 **10** 1½ **Secret Identity**[71] 7283 2-9-7 **60**......... PhilDennis 6 26
(Michael Mullineaux) *led: hdd over 4f out: chsd ldr tl over 2f out: rdn and wknd over 1f out* **100/1**

5323 **11** 40 **Enjoy The Moment**[85] 6792 2-9-7 **60**......... BarryMcHugh 11
(Adrian Nicholls) *s.i.s: hld up: hung rt fr 1/2-way: sn wknd (jockey said filly lost its action)* **22/1**

1m 28.51s (-0.29) **Going Correction** -0.225s/f (Stan) **11** Ran SP% **111.7**
Speed ratings (Par 94): **92,91,90,88,85 83,83,79,75,73 28**
CSF £179.39 CT £1177.99 TOTE £13.70: £3.70, £4.90, £2.10; EX 235.20 Trifecta £2380.60.
Owner Elite Racing Club **Bred** Elite Racing Club **Trained** Norton, N Yorks

FOCUS
An ordinary nursery. The second has been rated near his debut level.

9165 BOMBARDIER BRITISH HOPPED AMBER BEER NOVICE STKS 7f 36y (Tp)
5:20 (5:23) (Class 5) 3-Y-O+ **£3,428** (£1,020; £509; £254) **Stalls** High

Form RPR

2264 **1** **Loving Glance**[10] 9011 3-9-0 79 RichardKingscote 6 79
(Martyn Meade) *pushed along to chse ldrs: rdn to ld over 1f out: edgd lft ins fnl f: r.o wl* **13/8**[1]

3 **2** *4* **Prompting**[27] 8653 3-9-5 0 JamesDoyle 4 73
(Olly Murphy) *hld up: hdwy over 2f out: styd on to go 2nd wl ins fnl f: no ch w wnr* **9/2**[3]

344 **3** *1 1/2* **Karisoke**[49] 8006 3-9-5 71 JackMitchell 9 69
(Simon Crisford) *racd keenly in 2nd tl led 2f out: rdn: edgd lft and hdd over 1f out: no ex ins fnl f* **2/1**[2]

0-3 **4** *9* **Al Daiha**[22] 8808 3-9-0 0 (h) HectorCrouch 2 40
(Ed Walker) *s.i.s: sn prom: pushed along 1/2-way: rdn and hung lft fr over 2f out: wknd over 1f out* **16/1**

34 **5** *2 1/2* **Reims**[26] 8695 3-9-0 0 TomMarquand 1 33
(William Haggas) *sn led: hdd 2f out: hung lft over 1f out: wknd fnl f* **12/1**

53 **6** *1 1/4* **Alvaro**[10] 9001 3-9-5 0 CharlesBishop 8 35
(Michael Wigham) *s.i.s: sn pushed along in rr: nvr nrr* **11/1**

0-05 **7** *nk* **Emilene**[10] 9001 5-8-8 39 (t) GeorgeRooke(7) 3 30
(John Groucott) *chsd ldrs: rdn and wknd over 1f out* **150/1**

06 **8** *1 3/4* **Rockstar Max (GER)**[27] 8653 3-9-5 0 DougieCostello 5 29
(Denis Coakley) *s.i.s: hld up: shkn up over 2f out: nvr nr to chal* **150/1**

00 **9** *18* **Troisouni (FR)**[28] 8645 3-9-0 0 (t[1]) MartinDwyer 7
(Conrad Allen) *hld up: wknd over 2f out* **100/1**

1m 26.41s (-2.39) **Going Correction** -0.225s/f (Stan)
WFA 3 from 5yo 1lb **9 Ran SP% 113.8**
Speed ratings (Par 103): **104,99,97,87,84 83,82,80,60**
CSF £9.38 TOTE £2.20: £1.10, £1.50, £1.10; EX 8.20 Trifecta £18.80.
Owner Lordship Stud 1 **Bred** Lordship Stud **Trained** Manton, Wilts

FOCUS
A well-run novice and they finished strung out. The second has been rated in line with the better view of his debut run.

9166 BETWAY H'CAP 5f 21y (Tp)
5:50 (5:50) (Class 2) (0-105,103) 3-Y-O+
£11,827 (£3,541; £1,770; £885; £442; £222) **Stalls** Low

Form RPR

4121 **1** **Rocket Action**[20] 8867 3-9-3 99 (t) TomQueally 3 109+
(Robert Cowell) *hld up: hdwy over 1f out: rdn to ld ins fnl f: r.o u.p* **5/2**[1]

1346 **2** *hd* **Corinthia Knight (IRE)**[10] 9004 4-9-7 103 HollieDoyle 7 111
(Archie Watson) *pushed along to chse ldrs: rdn and ev ch fnl f: r.o* **6/1**

1255 **3** *1 1/4* **Royal Birth**[5] 9088 8-9-5 101 (t) PJMcDonald 5 105
(Stuart Williams) *prom: hung rt 1/2-way: rdn over 1f out: r.o* **5/1**[3]

4321 **4** *nk* **Thegreatestshowman**[3] 9131 3-8-9 91 6ex GeorgeWood 2 93
(Amy Murphy) *hld up: pushed along 1/2-way: hdwy and nt clr run over 1f out: r.o* **9/2**[2]

3005 **5** *hd* **Kick On Kick On**[101] 6208 4-8-7 89 MartinDwyer 6 91
(Ian Williams) *s.i.s: hld up: rdn over 1f out: r.o ins fnl f: nt rch ldrs* **25/1**

3533 **6** *1 1/2* **Canford Bay (IRE)**[8] 9030 5-7-11 84 oh4 KieranSchofield(5) 8 80
(Antony Brittain) *racd freely: sn w ldr: led 1/2-way: rdn and hdd ins fnl f: no ex* **12/1**

0100 **7** *1* **Leodis Dream (IRE)**[10] 9004 3-9-7 103 DavidProbert 4 96
(David O'Meara) *led to 1/2-way: rdn and ev ch 1f out: no ex ins fnl f* **9/2**[2]

56-1 **8** *4* **Tanasoq (IRE)**[238] 1501 6-9-2 98 GrahamLee 1 76
(Paul Midgley) *s.i.s: hld up: outpcd fr 1/2-way* **50/1**

59.65s (-2.25) **Going Correction** -0.225s/f (Stan) **8 Ran SP% 109.4**
Speed ratings (Par 109): **109,108,106,106,105 103,101,95**
CSF £16.22 CT £62.13 TOTE £2.70: £1.40, £2.00, £1.40; EX 16.60 Trifecta £70.20.
Owner Robert Ng **Bred** Robert Ng **Trained** Six Mile Bottom, Cambs

FOCUS
A good sprint handicap run at a decent gallop, and the winner did it well once again. The second has been rated close to his old best.

9167 BETWAY HEED YOUR HUNCH H'CAP 1m 4f 51y (Tp)
6:20 (6:20) (Class 4) (0-80,82) 3-Y-O+
£5,207 (£1,549; £774; £400; £400; £400) **Stalls** Low

Form RPR

1063 **1** **Blue Medici**[21] 8829 5-9-6 74 RichardKingscote 1 82
(Mark Loughnane) *chsd ldr tl led 2f out: rdn and edgd lft fr over 1f out: styd on u.p* **7/1**

2205 **2** *1 1/4* **Natty Night**[29] 8608 3-9-3 76 MartinDwyer 2 82
(William Muir) *led: racd freely: hdd 2f out: rdn over 1f out: nt clr run and swtchd rt wl ins fnl f: kpt on* **15/8**[1]

1550 **3** *1 1/4* **The Throstles**[60] 7663 4-9-8 76 (p) JackMitchell 7 80
(Kevin Frost) *hdwy over 10f out: rdn over 1f out: styd on* **8/1**

2061 **4** *1/2* **Htilominlo**[110] 5840 3-9-7 80 (t) TomMarquand 3 83
(Sylvester Kirk) *s.i.s: hdwy over 2f out: rdn over 1f out: styd on: nt trble ldrs* **9/2**[3]

0/04 **5** *1* **Fiesole**[29] 8608 7-10-0 82 JamesDoyle 5 84
(Olly Murphy) *prom: plld hrd: stdd and lost pl after 1f: hdwy over 3f out: rdn and hung lft over 1f out: swtchd rt ins fnl f: styd on same pce* **3/1**[2]

4-00 **6** *29* **Liva (IRE)**[122] 5423 4-9-0 68 LiamKeniry 4 23
(Stef Keniry) *chsd ldrs: rdn over 4f out: wknd over 2f out* **18/1**

0310 **7** *21* **Willy Sewell**[18] 8918 6-9-6 77 TheodoreLadd(3) 6
(Michael Appleby) *hld up: pushed along on outer over 4f out: wknd over 2f out (jockey said gelding hung right-handed and lost its action)* **40/1**

2m 37.03s (-3.77) **Going Correction** -0.225s/f (Stan)
WFA 3 from 4yo+ 5lb **7 Ran SP% 109.3**
Speed ratings (Par 105): **103,102,101,101,100 81,67**
CSF £18.75 TOTE £5.90: £2.20, £1.50; EX 21.30 Trifecta £97.90.
Owner Laurence Bellman **Bred** Kirtlington Stud Ltd **Trained** Rock, Worcs

FOCUS
Few got into this. It's been rated around the second to form and the third to this year's form.

9168 BETWAY LIVE CASINO H'CAP 1m 4f 51y (Tp)
6:50 (6:51) (Class 6) (0-60,60) 3-Y-O+
£2,781 (£827; £413; £400; £400; £400) **Stalls** Low

Form RPR

3144 **1** **Hooflepuff (IRE)**[40] 8293 3-9-3 59 (p) BenRobinson 7 66+
(Brian Ellison) *chsd ldrs: led over 2f out: rdn over 1f out: styd on* **9/2**[2]

210- **2** *nk* **Henry Croft**[413] 8071 6-9-9 60 TomMarquand 11 66
(Tony Carroll) *hld up: hdwy on outer over 2f out: rdn to chse wnr ins fnl f: styd on* **14/1**

5000 **3** *1 1/2* **Enmeshing**[41] 8248 6-9-2 53 DanielMuscutt 6 56
(Alexandra Dunn) *s.i.s: hld up: nt clr run over 2f out: swtchd rt and hdwy over 1f out: sn rdn: edgd lft ins fnl f: styd on* **9/1**

3610 **4** *1 1/4* **Good Impression**[57] 7759 4-9-5 56 (p) HollieDoyle 10 57
(Dai Burchell) *hld up in tch: shkn up on outer to chse wnr over 2f out: rdn over 1f out: lost 2nd and no ex ins fnl f* **12/1**

6062 **5** *3/4* **Tulane (IRE)**[26] 8703 4-9-6 57 (t[1]) JaneElliott 5 57
(Richard Phillips) *hld up: hdwy over 1f out: nt rch ldrs* **3/1**[1]

20-0 **6** *1/2* **Calvinist**[34] 2344 6-9-1 57 (p) TobyEley(5) 8 56
(Kevin Frost) *hld up: pushed along over 3f out: hdwy on outer over 1f out: nt rch ldrs* **20/1**

1350 **7** *1 1/4* **Sir Canford (IRE)**[21] 8828 3-9-2 58 (p) CharlesBishop 3 56
(Ali Stronge) *led 1f: chsd ldrs: nt clr run: hmpd and lost pl over 2f out: nt rcvr (jockey said gelding hung left-handed)* **10/1**

3130 **8** *6* **Mamdood (IRE)**[21] 8843 5-9-3 54 (vt) LiamKeniry 1 42
(Stef Keniry) *prom: rdn over 1f out: wknd fnl f* **8/1**

0460 **9** *1 1/4* **Ebbisham (IRE)**[8] 9040 6-9-4 55 (v) JasonHart 2 41
(John Mackie) *s.i.s: hld up: nvr nrr* **22/1**

1200 **10** *5* **Genuine Approval (IRE)**[26] 8703 6-9-5 59 (t) DarraghKeenan(3) 4 37
(John Butler) *hld up: nvr on terms* **40/1**

3250 **11** *2 3/4* **Chinese Alphabet**[54] 7858 3-9-4 60 (v) AlistairRawlinson 9 34
(Michael Appleby) *led after 1f: rdn and hdd 2f out: wknd over 1f out* **5/1**[3]

4000 **12** *5* **Viking Prince (IRE)**[74] 7141 3-9-3 59 GrahamLee 12 25
(Patrick Morris) *s.i.s: rcvrd to chse ldr over 10f out: rdn: hung lft and lost 2nd over 2f out: hmpd and wknd sn after* **80/1**

2m 37.54s (-3.26) **Going Correction** -0.225s/f (Stan)
WFA 3 from 4yo+ 5lb **12 Ran SP% 117.2**
Speed ratings (Par 101): **101,100,99,98,98 98,97,93,92,89 87,83**
CSF £62.16 CT £547.98 TOTE £6.00: £1.90, £3.80, £3.20; EX 65.40 Trifecta £779.60.
Owner Keith Brown **Bred** Old Carhue Stud **Trained** Norton, N Yorks
■ Stewards' Enquiry : Hollie Doyle two-day ban: careless riding (Dec 10-11)

FOCUS
A moderate affair. Straightforward form rated around the front pair to their recent best.

9169 #BETYOURWAY AT BETWAY H'CAP 5f 21y (Tp)
7:20 (7:21) (Class 6) (0-55,55) 3-Y-O+
£2,781 (£827; £413; £400; £400; £400) **Stalls** Low

Form RPR

5612 **1** **Katherine Place**[34] 8450 4-9-5 55 (t) EoinWalsh 2 61
(Bill Turner) *chsd ldr 4f out: led over 2f out: rdn over 1f out: styd on* **7/1**

30U6 **2** *1* **Englishman**[34] 8457 9-9-2 52 (b[1]) PhilipPrince 5 54
(Milton Bradley) *chsd ldrs: rdn ins fnl f: r.o* **14/1**

005 **3** *hd* **Harry's Ridge (IRE)**[176] 3416 4-9-3 53 JasonHart 1 55+
(Eric Alston) *s.i.s: in rr and reminder sn after s: swtchd rt over 1f out: sn hung lft: hdwy: nt clr run and swtchd rt ins fnl f: r.o wl: nt rch ldrs* **3/1**[1]

6021 **4** *nse* **Twilighting**[41] 8249 3-9-3 53 NicolaCurrie 3 55
(Henry Candy) *s.i.s: hld up: hdwy and nt clr run fr over 1f out tl wl ins fnl f: r.o wl towards fin: nt rch ldrs (jockey said filly was denied a clear run for some distance in the home straight)* **4/1**[2]

0631 **5** *hd* **Moneta**[8] 9034 3-9-5 55 6ex (b) DavidProbert 10 56
(Ronald Harris) *hld up: hdwy over 1f out: sn rdn: r.o* **11/1**

342 **6** *hd* **Oh So Nice**[27] 8672 3-9-3 53 TomMarquand 8 53
(Tony Carroll) *rrd s: hld up: hdwy over 1f out: sn rdn: r.o (jockey said filly reared as stalls opened)* **11/2**[3]

0000 **7** *3* **Jorvik Prince**[140] 4763 5-9-2 52 (p) PaulMulrennan 4 41
(Julia Brooke) *pushed along to chse ldrs: rdn over 1f out: no ex ins fnl f* **8/1**

3030 **8** *2 1/4* **Edged Out**[34] 8450 9-9-0 53 MitchGodwin(3) 6 34
(Christopher Mason) *led: hdd over 2f out: rdn over 1f out: wknd wl ins fnl f* **33/1**

0620 **9** *1 3/4* **Tiger Lyon (USA)**[34] 8457 4-9-4 54 (t) JoeyHaynes 9 29
(John Butler) *hld up: pushed along over 3f out: wknd ins fnl f* **14/1**

2200 **10** *8* **Brogans Bay (IRE)**[19] 8896 4-9-5 55 JFEgan 7 1
(Simon Dow) *pushed along to chse ldrs: rdn 1/2-way: wknd and eased over 1f out (trainer's rep said filly had a breathing problem)* **16/1**

1m 1.11s (-0.79) **Going Correction** -0.225s/f (Stan) **10 Ran SP% 114.5**
Speed ratings (Par 101): **97,95,95,95,94 94,89,85,83,70**
CSF £97.91 CT £355.56 TOTE £7.00: £2.00, £2.70, £2.20; EX 99.90 Trifecta £426.20.
Owner Ansells Of Watford **Bred** The Hon Mrs R Pease **Trained** Sigwells, Somerset

FOCUS
A competitive sprint and they finished in a heap in behind the winner. Limited form which can't be rated any higher.
T/Jkpt: Not won. T/Plt: £58.40 to a £1 stake. Pool: £97,777.69 - 1,221.69 winning units T/Qpdt: £20.30 to a £1 stake. Pool: £11,989.75 - 436.97 winning units **Colin Roberts**

8508 DEAUVILLE (R-H)
Tuesday, November 26
OFFICIAL GOING: Polytrack: standard

9170a PRIX PETITE ETOILE (LISTED RACE) (3YO FILLIES) (ALL-WEATHER TRACK) (POLYTRACK) 1m 1f 110y(P)
2:00 3-Y-O **£24,774** (£9,909; £7,432; £4,954; £2,477)

RPR

1 **Glance**[86] 6775 3-9-2 0 (b[1]) TheoBachelot 11 97
(Ralph Beckett) *hld up in rr: stl towards bk at 1/2-way: hdwy on the outer appr home turn: rdn to chal 2f out: stl several l to find ent fnl 1f but began to pick up: styd on wl u.p to ld cl home* **41/5**[3]

2 *nk* **Gwendola**[21] 8845 3-9-2 0 MaximeGuyon 4 96
(C Laffon-Parias, France) **13/2**[2]

3 *shd* **Brassica (IRE)**[62] 7589 3-9-2 0 Jean-BernardEyquem 7 96
(Sir Mark Prescott Bt) *midfield: sltly crowded 3f out and niggled: pushed along and looking for room 2f out: swtchd ins fnl 1f and began to make hdwy: styd on strly fnl 100yds* **10/1**

4 *1/2* **Nuala (FR)**[37] 8376 3-9-2 0 Pierre-CharlesBoudot 1 95
(A Fabre, France) **13/2**[2]

5 *hd* **Ridaa (IRE)**[46] 3-9-2 0 VincentCheminaud 9 94
(J E Hammond, France) *prom: pushed along to take outrt ld after 2f: shkn up ent home st: strly drvn whn hdd over 1f out: kpt on* **14/1**

6 *nk* **Qamka**[32] 8529 3-9-2 0 TonyPiccone 8 94
(Roger Varian) *chsd ldrs under restraint early: in tch in 5th at 1/2-way: drvn to try and chal 3f out: nt qckn and one pce clsng stages* **10/1**

7 *1/2* **Ebony (FR)**[50] 7978 3-9-2 0 CristianDemuro 5 93
(J-C Rouget, France) **33/10**[1]

8 *nse* **Freedom Rising (GER)**[26] 3-9-2 0 MlleAnnaVanDenTroost 15 93
(Yasmin Almenrader, Germany) **70/1**

9 *shd* **Ardiente**[22] 8808 3-9-2 0 AntoineHamelin 14 93
(Ed Vaughan) *hld up in tch: prog on outside to sit promly after 2f: narrow 2nd at 1/2-way: pushed along 2f out: prog to ld over 1f out: began to drift lft u.p and sn hdd: wknd clsng stages* **11/1**

10 *1 1/4* **Gharabeel (FR)**[34] 3-9-2 0 Francois-XavierBertras 10 90
(F Rohaut, France) **31/1**

11 *1/2* **Ababeel (FR)**[66] 3-9-2 0 (p) StephanePasquier 16 89
(N Clement, France) **24/1**

12 *snk* **Okarina Dream (FR)**[10] 3-9-2 0 EddyHardouin 12 89
(H De Nicolay, France) **49/1**

13 *7* **Terra Dina (FR)**[50] 7978 3-9-2 0 MickaelBarzalona 13 75
(H-F Devin, France) **20/1**

14 *4* **Turea**[20] 8879 3-9-2 0 (p) AurelienLemaitre 2 67
(L Gadbin, France) **18/1**

15 *1 1/4* **Sakura Zensen (FR)**[14] 3-9-2 0 (b) GregoryBenoist 6 64
(Hiroo Shimizu, France) **62/1**

16 *4* **Hermiona (USA)**[19] 3-9-2 0 IoritzMendizabal 3 56
(F Chappet, France) **26/1**

1m 56.02s **16** Ran SP% **119.8**
PARI-MUTUEL (all including 1 euro stake): WIN 9.20; PLACE 3.20, 2.70, 4.20; DF 32.70.
Owner J H Richmond-Watson **Bred** Lawn Stud **Trained** Kimpton, Hants

FOCUS
They finished in a but of a heap here.

9060 **KEMPTON (A.W)** (R-H)
Wednesday, November 27

OFFICIAL GOING: Polytrack: standard to slow
Wind: light, across Weather: cloudy, showers

9171 BET AT RACINGTV.COM NOVICE STKS 6f (P)
4:10 (4:10) (Class 5) 3-Y-O+ **£3,881** (£1,155; £577; £288) **Stalls** Low

Form RPR

64- **1** **Venture (IRE)**[400] 8496 3-9-2 0 TomMarquand 3 78
(Tom Ward) *trckd ldrs on inner: rdn jst over 2f out: hdwy u.p to ld jst over 1f out: drvn and styd on strly ins fnl f* **16/1**

1-0 **2** *3 1/4* **Thrilla In Manila**[53] 7892 3-9-9 0 AdamKirby 4 75
(Richard Spencer) *led: rdn jst over 2f out: hdd jst over 1f out: unable qck and nt match pce of wnr ins fnl f* **7/4**[2]

05 **3** *1 1/2* **Treble Clef**[202] 2555 4-9-2 0 CallumShepherd 2 63
(Lee Carter) *midfield: rdn over 2f out: no imp over 1f out: kpt on to go 3rd fnl 100yds: no threat to wnr* **50/1**

4 **4** *1 1/2* **Montys Inn (IRE)**[28] 8653 3-9-2 0 JohnFahy 1 58
(Richard Hannon) *awkward leaving stalls: hld up in rr: effrt on inner 2f out: swtchd rt and drvn over 1f out: swtchd lft and kpt on ins fnl f: no threat to ldrs* **5/1**[3]

6420 **5** *nk* **Hieronymus**[21] 8860 3-9-2 70 (vt) TomQueally 7 57
(Seamus Durack) *chsd ldr tl unable qck u.p over 1f out: wknd and lost 2 pls fnl 100yds* **7/1**

0-4 **6** *hd* **Fujaira King (USA)**[40] 8329 3-9-2 72 (t[1]) JamesDoyle 5 56
(Stuart Williams) *midfield: short of room after 1f: effrt ent fnl 2f: drvn over 1f out: kpt on same pce and swtchd rt ins fnl f* **5/4**[1]

000 **7** *1 1/4* **Winalotwithalittle (IRE)**[99] 6315 3-8-11 16 KierenFox 8 47
(J R Jenkins) *dropped in sn after s: t.k.h: hld up in rr: effrt 2f out: kpt on ins fnl f: nvr trbld ldrs* **66/1**

0 **8** *7* **Purple Tommy**[213] 2140 3-8-10 1 ow1 LukeCatton(7) 9 31
(Jimmy Fox) *a towards rr: hung lft bnd 4f: lost tch over 1f out* **100/1**

9 *24* **Laurentia (IRE)** 3-8-6 0 SophieRalston(5) 6
(Dean Ivory) *chsd ldrs tl over 2f out: sn lost pl: wl bhd ins fnl f: t.o* **33/1**

1m 12.51s (-0.59) **Going Correction** +0.025s/f (Slow) **9** Ran SP% **123.2**
Speed ratings (Par 103): **104,99,97,95,95 95,93,84,52**
CSF £47.52 TOTE £12.90: £2.20, £1.10, £13.40; EX 65.80 Trifecta £1268.90.
Owner Tom Ward **Bred** M C Bloodstock Ltd & Cbs Bloodstock **Trained** Upper Lambourn, Berks

FOCUS
The market had this ordinary novice pegged as a two-horse race but there was a bit of a turn up.

9172 32RED CASINO NURSERY H'CAP 1m (P)
4:40 (4:42) (Class 5) (0-75,76) 2-Y-O
£3,881 (£1,155; £577; £400; £400; £400) **Stalls** Low

Form RPR

3400 **1** **Fantasy Believer (IRE)**[28] 8665 2-9-7 74 KieranShoemark 6 83
(Charles Hills) *wnt lft and pushed along leaving stalls: sn led and mde rest: rdn 2f out: drvn over 1f out: styd on and hld on wl ins fnl f* **4/1**[2]

644 **2** *1* **Royal Nation**[21] 8849 2-9-4 71 HollieDoyle 2 78
(Archie Watson) *chsd ldrs: swtchd ins and effrt ent fnl 2f: chsd wnr u.p wl over 1f out: kpt on wl but a hld ins fnl f* **7/1**

002 **3** *1 1/4* **Tiritomba (IRE)**[30] 8602 2-9-6 73 JamesDoyle 5 77
(Richard Hannon) *led early: sn hdd and chsd ldr tl over 4f out: rdn ent fnl 2f: 3rd and kpt on same pce u.p ins fnl f* **5/1**[3]

5220 **4** *6* **Lyricist Voice**[32] 8546 2-9-4 71 (t[1]) AndreaAtzeni 12 61+
(Marco Botti) *sn in rr and bustled along: hdwy u.p to pass btn horses over 1f out: chsd clr ldng trio fnl f: no imp* **8/1**

606 **5** *1 1/4* **Son Of Red (IRE)**[27] 8709 2-8-11 64 TomMarquand 1 51
(Alan King) *in tch in midfield: swtchd lft and effrt over 2f out: unable qck u.p over 1f out: wl hld ins fnl f* **16/1**

543 **6** *1/2* **Can't Stop Now (IRE)**[108] 5980 2-9-7 74 (h[1]) AdamKirby 9 60
(Clive Cox) *sn dropped towards rr: swtchd lft and effrt over 2f out: drvn 2f out: nvr threatened to get on terms: plugged on ins fnl f* **10/3**[1]

0050 **7** *1/2* **Brown Eyes Blue (IRE)**[159] 4075 2-8-7 60 JFEgan 7 45
(J S Moore) *hmpd leaving stalls and sn towards rr: rdn 3f out: modest prog ins fnl f: nvr trbld ldrs* **66/1**

4652 **8** *3* **Red Jasper**[36] 8415 2-8-10 63 (v) DavidProbert 10 41
(Michael Appleby) *midfield: effrt and nt clrest of runs over 2f out: sn struggling: wknd over 1f out* **8/1**

4635 **9** *1 1/4* **Bowling Russian (IRE)**[28] 8650 2-9-0 67 (p) CharlesBishop 4 42
(George Baker) *t.k.h: hld up in midfield: swtchd lft and hdwy on outer 1/2-way: rdn and briefly chsd ldrs 2f out: sn outpcd and wknd* **8/1**

000 **10** *9* **Power Of Love**[63] 7571 2-8-0 53 oh8 RaulDaSilva 3 8
(George Baker) *midfield tl lost pl and wd 3f out: sn rdn and btn: wknd 2f out* **66/1**

320 **11** *5* **Magic Twist (USA)**[76] 7113 2-8-13 71 AndrewBreslin(5) 8 14
(Mark Johnston) *t.k.h: chsd ldrs tl hdwy to chse wnr over 4f out: rdn and lost pl over 2f out: sn wknd* **33/1**

1m 39.94s (0.14) **Going Correction** +0.025s/f (Slow) **11** Ran SP% **117.4**
Speed ratings (Par 96): **100,99,97,91,90 90,89,86,85,76 71**
CSF £31.92 CT £142.83 TOTE £4.90: £2.30, £2.30, £2.50; EX 32.20 Trifecta £158.80.
Owner The Fantasy Believer Syndicate **Bred** Rathasker Stud **Trained** Lambourn, Berks

FOCUS
Probably a fair nursery and the first three came clear.

9173 JOIN RACING TV NOW H'CAP 1m (P)
5:10 (5:12) (Class 5) (0-75,77) 3-Y-O+
£3,752 (£1,116; £557; £400; £400; £400) **Stalls** Low

Form RPR

4601 **1** **Earth And Sky (USA)**[23] 8806 3-9-2 72 BenCurtis 4 81+
(George Scott) *hld up in midfield: effrt over 2f out: rdn and hdwy to ld jst over 1f out: r.o wl* **9/4**[1]

005 **2** *1 1/2* **Magic Mirror**[7] 9067 6-9-1 69 (p) RobHornby 5 76
(Mark Rimell) *hld up in tch in midfield: swtchd rt and effrt jst over 2f out: hdwy u.p to chse ldrs over 1f out: chsd wnr and kpt on same pce ins fnl f* **12/1**

622 **3** *3/4* **Pentimento**[28] 8653 3-9-4 74 KierenFox 2 78
(John Best) *midfield: effrt to chse ldr wl over 1f out: ev ch briefly jst over 1f out: kpt on same pce and one pce ins fnl f* **5/1**[2]

0240 **4** *2* **Fortune And Glory (USA)**[27] 8702 6-9-3 71 CharlesBishop 12 72
(Joseph Tuite) *in rr: effrt ent fnl 2f: hdwy over 1f out: kpt on ins fnl f: nt rch ldrs* **16/1**

4001 **5** *1* **Stringybark Creek**[8] 9054 5-9-6 77 5ex ThomasGreatrex(3) 11 75
(David Loughnane) *in tch in midfield: effrt ent fnl 2f: hdwy between rivals over 1f out: kpt on ins fnl f: nvr enough pce to chal* **8/1**[3]

4146 **6** *1* **Thechildren'strust (IRE)**[22] 8827 4-9-7 75 HectorCrouch 1 71
(Gary Moore) *led: rdn over 2f out: hdd jst over 1f out: wknd ins fnl f* **10/1**

0005 **7** *4* **Sing Out Loud (IRE)**[16] 7125 4-9-4 72 LiamKeniry 13 59
(Michael Madgwick) *hld up in rr: nt clr run and hmpd on inner over 2f out: sme late hdwy: nvr involved* **50/1**

3015 **8** *1 3/4* **Nawar**[32] 8548 4-9-7 75 (t) GeorgeWood 9 58
(Martin Bosley) *chsd ldrs: rdn over 2f out: unable qck and outpcd over 1f out: wknd ins fnl f* **12/1**

1623 **9** *1 1/4* **In The Cove (IRE)**[36] 8427 3-8-11 74 (b) LukeCatton(7) 14 53
(Richard Hannon) *chsd ldr over 6f out tl unable qck and lost pl wl over 1f out: wknd fnl f* **12/1**

1664 **10** *1 3/4* **Oud Metha Bridge (IRE)**[28] 8658 5-9-7 75 ShelleyBirkett 7 51
(Julia Feilden) *sn dropped to rr: effrt: whn nt clr run and hmpd over 2f out: nvr trbld ldrs* **16/1**

1365 **11** *1* **Universal Effect**[32] 8549 3-9-2 72 (h) AdamKirby 3 45
(Mark Loughnane) *chsd ldrs: rdn over 2f out: no ex and outpcd over 1f out: sn wknd* **8/1**[3]

2600 **12** *3 1/4* **Millions Memories**[27] 8692 3-9-5 75 DavidProbert 8 40
(Laura Mongan) *midfield: rdn over 3f out: swtchd lft and hung rt over 2f out: no prog and wl hld over 1f out* **66/1**

020 **13** *21* **Wild Animal**[153] 4304 3-9-2 72 ShaneKelly 6
(Murty McGrath) *chsd ldr for over 1f: steadily lost pl: wl bhd and eased ins fnl f* **33/1**

3-55 **14** *43* **Tofan**[39] 8351 4-9-4 72 (t) DanielMuscutt 10
(Marco Botti) *mainly midfield: edgd out lft and rdn over 2f out: lost pl qckly: wl bhd and eased ins fnl f: t.o (vet said colt bled from the nose)* **10/1**

1m 38.78s (-1.02) **Going Correction** +0.025s/f (Slow)
WFA 3 from 4yo+ 2lb **14** Ran SP% **129.1**
Speed ratings (Par 103): **106,104,103,101,100 99,95,94,92,91 90,86,65,22**
CSF £34.03 CT £129.00 TOTE £3.00: £1.40, £4.00, £1.90; EX 40.30 Trifecta £239.30.
Owner Flaxman Stables Ireland Ltd **Bred** Flaxman Holdings Ltd **Trained** Newmarket, Suffolk

FOCUS
A run-of-the-mill class 5 handicap notable for the confidence behind the winner.

9174 100% PROFIT BOOST AT 32REDSPORT.COM NOVICE STKS 7f (P)
5:40 (5:43) (Class 5) 2-Y-O **£3,881** (£1,155; £577; £288) **Stalls** Low

Form RPR

1 **1** **Boccaccio (IRE)**[181] 3274 2-9-9 0 JamesDoyle 5 87+
(Charlie Appleby) *t.k.h: led for 2f: chsd ldr tl rdn to last again over 1f out: r.o strly ins fnl f: readily* **4/9**[1]

03 **2** *3 1/4* **Juan Les Pins**[48] 8059 2-9-2 0 TomMarquand 1 72
(Ed Walker) *t.k.h: trckd ldrs: effrt 2f out: rdn over 1f out: chsd wnr jst ins fnl f: no imp* **6/1**[3]

3 *1/2* **One Idea** 2-9-2 0 AndreaAtzeni 6 70
(Simon Crisford) *t.k.h: chsd wnr for 2f: effrt to press ldrs again 2f out: no ch w wnr and kpt on same pce ins fnl f* **4/1**[2]

3 **4** *3/4* **Jalwan (USA)**[98] 6344 2-9-2 0 RobertHavlin 8 68
(John Butler) *dwlt: sn rcvrd and in tch in midfield: swtchd lft and hdwy to ld after 2f: rdn and hdd over 1f out: sn outpcd: kpt on same pce ins fnl f* **25/1**

5 *1/2* **Union (IRE)** 2-9-2 0 JackMitchell 14 67+
(Roger Varian) *hld up towards rr: effrt ent fnl 2f: hdwy over 1f out: styd on strly ins fnl f: no ch w wnr* **33/1**

6 *1* **Biggles** 2-9-2 0 AdamKirby 11 64
(Ralph Beckett) *wnt lft leaving stalls: sn rcvrd to chse ldrs and t.k.h: chsd ldrs: rdn ent fnl 2f: outpcd over 1f out: wknd ins fnl f* **33/1**

44 **7** *5* **Casa Loupi**[26] 8722 2-9-2 0 HectorCrouch 9 51
(Gary Moore) *dwlt and short of room leaving stalls: in tch in midfield: rdn ent fnl 2f: sn outpcd and btn over 1f out* **50/1**

8 *1/2* **Choreograph** 2-9-2 0 (t[1] w) JasonWatson 2 50+
(Roger Charlton) *s.i.s: off the pce towards rr: effrt over 2f out: edgd rt and hdwy over 1f out: kpt on ins fnl f: nvr trbld ldrs* **25/1**

9 *1 1/2* **Within Reach** 2-8-11 0 RobHornby 13 41+
(Ralph Beckett) *dwlt and hmpd leaving stalls: off the pce towards rr: hmpd again after 1f: effrt over 2f out: sme hdwy over 1f out: nvr trbld ldrs* **33/1**

10 *1* **Hong Kong Dragon** 2-9-2 0 BenCurtis 3 44
(George Scott) *midfield: rdn over 2f out: sn outpcd and wl hld over 1f out: wknd* **66/1**

11 *1 1/2* **Dolla Dolla Bill (IRE)** 2-9-2 0 HollieDoyle 10 40
(Richard Hannon) *edgd rt leaving stalls: midfield: rdn ent fnl 2f: sn struggling and wknd* **33/1**

03 **12** *8* **Amazon Princess**[67] 7469 2-8-12 1 ow1 CallumShepherd 7 15
(Tony Newcombe) *midfield: jinked lft after 1f: rdn over 2f out: sn outpcd and btn* **100/1**

13 *4* **Buzztothemoon** 2-9-2 0 DanielMuscutt 4 9
(Marco Botti) *sn in last and nvr travelled wl: nvr on terms* **66/1**

14 *4 ½* **Mercurist** 2-9-2 0 LiamKeniry 12
(Rod Millman) *dwlt and hmpd leaving stalls: a towards rr: wknd jst over 2f out* **100/1**

1m 26.23s (0.23) **Going Correction** +0.025s/f (Slow) **14** Ran SP% **129.9**
Speed ratings (Par 96): **99,95,94,93,93 92,86,85,84,83 81,72,67,62**
CSF £3.81 TOTE £1.40: £1.10, £1.70, £1.50; EX 4.60 Trifecta £12.10.
Owner Godolphin **Bred** Andrew Rosen **Trained** Newmarket, Suffolk

FOCUS
This novice played out almost exactly how the market suggested, with a taking performance from the winner, justifying favouritism.

9175 32RED NURSERY H'CAP — 7f (P)
6:10 (6:10) (Class 3) (0-90,89) 2-Y-O **£9,337** (£2,796; £1,398; £699; £349) **Stalls** Low

Form RPR

4050 **1** **Bella Brazil (IRE)**[65] 7522 2-8-0 **68** oh5 HollieDoyle 5 72
(Mrs John Harrington, Ire) *hld up in tch in last pair: effrt 2f out: hung rt and swtchd lft 1f out: str run to ld wl ins fnl f: sn clr* **8/1**

0242 **2** *2* **Baadirr**[42] 8265 2-8-12 **80** TomMarquand 1 79
(William Haggas) *chsd ldrs: effrt on inner 2f out: ev ch u.p over 1f out: led ins fnl f: hdd and nt match pce of wnr wl ins fnl f* **7/4**[1]

1401 **3** *nk* **Lethal Talent**[44] 8198 2-8-7 **80** TylerSaunders(5) 2 78
(Jonathan Portman) *t.k.h: chsd ldr: pushed along 2f out: lost 2nd over 1f out but stl pressing ldrs ins fnl f: one pce fnl 100yds* **5/1**[3]

2110 **4** *1 ¾* **Fuwayrit (IRE)**[60] 7679 2-9-7 **89** JoeFanning 6 82
(Mark Johnston) *led and set stdy gallop: rdn over 1f out: hdd and no ex u.p ins fnl f: wknd towards fin* **2/1**[2]

5011 **5** *½* **Taste The Nectar (USA)**[20] 8890 2-8-7 **75** (p) JasonWatson 3 67
(Robert Cowell) *dwlt: hld up in last pair: effrt ent fnl 2f: unable qck over 1f out: hld and kpt on same pce ins fnl f* **7/1**

1m 26.25s (0.25) **Going Correction** +0.025s/f (Slow) **5** Ran SP% **110.0**
Speed ratings (Par 100): **99,96,96,94,93**
CSF £22.43 TOTE £12.30: £4.30, £1.60; EX 19.60 Trifecta £67.30.
Owner P D Savill **Bred** Cottage Lodge Stud **Trained** Moone, Co Kildare

FOCUS
A disappointing turnout and, for a class 3, this should be treated with a degree of caution.

9176 32RED ON THE APP STORE H'CAP — 7f (P)
6:40 (6:41) (Class 4) (0-80,81) 3-Y-O+
£6,469 (£1,925; £962; £481; £400; £400) **Stalls** Low

Form RPR

5212 **1** **Busby (IRE)**[22] 8827 4-9-6 **78** (p) MartinDwyer 13 87
(Conrad Allen) *trckd ldrs: smooth hdwy to cl and rdn to ld over 1f out: r.o and a doing enough ins fnl f* **6/1**[3]

0001 **2** *¾* **Strawberry Jack**[8] 9048 3-9-8 **81** 6ex (vt) BenCurtis 8 87
(George Scott) *dwlt: midfield: effrt ent fnl 2f: hdwy u.p 1f out: chse wnr ins fnl f: kpt on but a hld (jockey said gelding was slowly away)* **6/1**[3]

5001 **3** *nk* **Full Intention**[22] 8827 5-8-10 **68** (p) DavidProbert 10 74
(Simon Pearce) *chsd ldrs: rdn 2f out: drvn to chse wnr ent fnl f: 3rd and kpt on same pce fnl 100yds* **11/2**[2]

2003 **4** *1 ¼* **Haddaf (IRE)**[8] 9054 4-9-4 **76** JamesDoyle 7 79
(Stuart Williams) *in tch in midfield: effrt ent fnl 2f: drvn ent fnl f: kpt on same pce ins fnl f* **9/2**[1]

4460 **5** *2 ½* **Six Strings**[19] 8921 5-9-0 **79** (p) AngusVilliers(7) 12 75+
(Michael Appleby) *s.i.s and pushed along early: hld up towards rr: r.oto heels over 3f out: effrt over 2f out: hdwy ins fnl f: kpt on but nvr getting on terms w ldrs* **20/1**

0364 **6** *1 ¾* **Alhakmah (IRE)**[21] 8852 3-9-5 **78** JoeFanning 9 68
(Richard Hannon) *t.k.h: hld up towards rr of main gp on outer: swtchd lft and effrt over 1f out: no imp and kpt on same pce fnl f* **9/1**

4106 **7** *½* **Velvet Morn (IRE)**[22] 8826 4-8-10 **68** AndreaAtzeni 6 58
(William Knight) *midfield: swtchd lft and effrt over 2f out: no imp over 1f out: wl hld and one pce ins fnl f* **16/1**

0066 **8** *½* **Fuwairt (IRE)**[8] 9054 7-8-12 **73** CameronNoble(3) 2 61
(David Loughnane) *swtchd rt after s: in rr: swtchd lft and effrt over 2f out: kpt on ins fnl f: nvr trbld ldrs* **11/2**[2]

4400 **9** *1 ¾* **Baltic Prince (IRE)**[49] 8017 9-9-0 **72** TomMarquand 1 56
(Tony Carroll) *led: hdd and unable to match pce of wnr over 1f out: sn lost 2nd and wknd ins fnl f* **25/1**

3105 **10** *½* **Ocean Paradise**[35] 8463 3-9-5 **78** (h) JasonWatson 4 59
(William Knight) *chsd ldr: rdn over 2f out: sn struggling to qckn and lost pl over 1f out: wknd ins fnl f* **10/1**

4-00 **11** *1* **Easy Tiger**[30] 8606 7-9-9 **81** LiamKeniry 5 61
(David Weston) *chsd ldrs: effrt on inner 2f out: unable qck u.p over 1f out: wknd ins fnl f* **20/1**

0024 **12** *2* **Sir Hamilton (IRE)**[37] 8413 4-9-6 **78** (p) AdamKirby 3 52
(Luke McJannet) *s.i.s: nvr travelling wl and a bhd (jockey said gelding hung badly left-handed)* **12/1**

1m 25.33s (-0.67) **Going Correction** +0.025s/f (Slow)
WFA 3 from 4yo+ 1lb **12** Ran SP% **123.6**
Speed ratings (Par 105): **104,103,102,101,98 96,95,95,93,92 91,89**
CSF £42.58 CT £216.35 TOTE £6.40: £2.40, £2.60, £2.50; EX 37.50 Trifecta £241.50.
Owner John C Davies **Bred** J C Davies **Trained** Newmarket, Suffolk

FOCUS
Straightforward form with the right horses coming to the fore.

9177 32RED.COM H'CAP — 1m 2f 219y(P)
7:10 (7:11) (Class 4) (0-85,85) 3-Y-O+
£6,469 (£1,925; £962; £481; £400; £400) **Stalls** Low

Form RPR

6224 **1** **Queen Constantine (GER)**[67] 7452 3-8-3 **75** (h) GaiaBoni(7) 1 83
(William Jarvis) *t.k.h: chsd ldrs: effrt to chal over 1f out: rdn to ld ins fnl f: kpt on wl* **8/1**

0040 **2** *nk* **Exceeding Power**[27] 8701 8-9-10 **85** GeorgeWood 7 92
(Martin Bosley) *led: rdn over 2f out: drvn and hrd pressed over 1f out: rdr dropped rein and hdd ins fnl f: kpt on but hld towards fin* **16/1**

1202 **3** *1 ¼* **Torochica**[8] 9050 3-9-1 **80** KierenFox 9 85
(John Best) *chsd ldrs: effrt over 2f out: ev ch and drvn whn whipped knocked out of rdrs hand ent fnl f: jst outpcd fnl 100yds* **3/1**[2]

6333 **4** *¾* **Ocala**[59] 7729 4-9-10 **85** DavidProbert 4 89
(Andrew Balding) *in tch in midfield: rdn and unable qck over 1f out: kpt on ins fnl f: nt enough pce to chal* **9/2**[3]

5054 **5** *shd* **Family Fortunes**[63] 7567 5-9-9 **84** TomMarquand 6 87
(Michael Madgwick) *stdd s: hld up in rr: hdwy u.p over 1f out: kpt on ins fnl f: nvr getting to ldrs* **8/1**

4455 **6** *1 ¼* **Voi**[23] 8812 5-8-3 **71** (t) AngusVilliers(7) 5 72
(Conrad Allen) *midfield: effrt over 2f out: no imp u.p over 1f out: hld and one pce ins fnl f* **16/1**

311 **7** *1 ½* **Contrast (IRE)**[64] 7560 5-8-10 **71** oh2 (b) CamHardie 3 70
(Michael Easterby) *t.k.h: chsd ldng trio: rdn over 2f out: unable qck and outpcd over 1f out: wknd ins fnl f (jockey said gelding ran too free)* **14/1**

50-0 **8** *5* **Zack Mayo**[26] 8727 5-9-8 **83** (p) RobHornby 8 73
(Philip McBride) *hld up in last trio: rdn over 2f out: sn outpcd and bhd over 1f out* **33/1**

02-1 **9** *hd* **Sarim (IRE)**[22] 8829 4-8-12 **76** ThomasGreatrex(3) 2 66
(Warren Greatrex) *hld up in last trio: effrt over 2f out: no imp u.p over 1f out: wknd fnl f (trainers rep said race may have come too soon for the gelding having won 22 days previously following a lay off of 496 days)* **11/4**[1]

2m 23.12s (2.12) **Going Correction** +0.025s/f (Slow)
WFA 3 from 4yo+ 4lb **9** Ran SP% **113.4**
Speed ratings (Par 105): **93,92,91,91,91 90,89,85,85**
CSF £122.88 CT £468.58 TOTE £8.80: £2.40, £2.40, £1.40; EX 175.80 Trifecta £1110.50.
Owner Kevin Hickman **Bred** Stiftung Gestut Fahrhof **Trained** Newmarket, Suffolk

FOCUS
There was no great pace on in what looked to be a fair handicap.

9178 WATCH MORE WITH RACING TV EXTRA H'CAP — 1m 3f 219y(P)
7:40 (7:40) (Class 5) (0-80,79) 3-Y-O **£3,752** (£1,116; £557; £400; £400) **Stalls** Low

Form RPR

3521 **1** **Sweet Celebration (IRE)**[28] 8656 3-8-13 **78** GraceMcEntee(7) 3 86+
(Marco Botti) *in tch in rr: clsd to chse ldrs and swtchd rt over 1f out: rdn to ld 1f out: pushed along: kpt on and doing enough ins fnl f* **2/1**[2]

2320 **2** *½* **City Tour**[36] 8421 3-9-4 **76** RichardKingscote 4 83
(Lydia Richards) *chsd ldr for 2f: styd wl in tch: rdn to chal 2f out: hung rt over 1f out: stl lugging rt and kpt on ins fnl f* **7/2**[3]

6411 **3** *shd* **Sashenka (GER)**[23] 8812 3-9-7 **79** LiamKeniry 5 86
(Sylvester Kirk) *stdd s: hdwy to chse ldr after 2f: rdn to ld 2f out: hdd 1f out: kpt on but no ex whn squeezed for room towards fin* **6/4**[1]

04-3 **4** *9* **Dalakina (IRE)**[277] 884 3-8-11 **69** HollieDoyle 1 61
(David Weston) *t.k.h: led tl 2f out: sn outpcd and btn: wknd fnl f* **25/1**

25-1 **5** *14* **Capla Crusader**[35] 8451 3-9-5 **77** CallumShepherd 2 47
(Nick Littmoden) *in tch: rdn over 3f out: outpcd and btn over 1f out: bhd and eased ins fnl f* **8/1**

2m 34.62s (0.12) **Going Correction** +0.025s/f (Slow) **5** Ran SP% **110.5**
Speed ratings (Par 102): **100,99,99,93,84**
CSF £9.33 TOTE £2.90: £1.40, £1.90; EX 9.00 Trifecta £15.30.
Owner Mpr, Ventura Racing 5 & Partner **Bred** Kildaragh Stud & M Downey **Trained** Newmarket, Suffolk

FOCUS
Just the five but three of those came here off the back of a win, so a fair enough race for the grade.
T/Plt: £47.10 to a £1 stake. Pool: £89,963.36 - 1,392.89 winning units T/Qpdt: £10.40 to a £1 stake. Pool: £13,439.04 - 952.30 winning units **Steve Payne**

9028 SOUTHWELL (L-H)
Wednesday, November 27

OFFICIAL GOING: Fibresand: standard

9179 LADBROKES HOME OF THE ODDS BOOST NURSERY H'CAP — 1m 13y(F)
12:20 (12:21) (Class 6) (0-60,62) 2-Y-O
£2,781 (£827; £413; £300; £300; £300) **Stalls** Low

Form RPR

0000 **1** **Speed Dating (FR)**[9] 9037 2-9-1 **51** (v) JasonHart 6 56
(Derek Shaw) *in rr: reminders after 1f: pushed along and hdwy over 3f out: rdn over 1f out: kpt on ins fnl f: led towards fin* **14/1**

0202 **2** *1* **Never Said Nothing (IRE)**[21] 8859 2-9-12 **62** (p[1]) AlistairRawlinson 9 61
(Jonathan Portman) *disp ld: pushed along over 3f out: rdn and wknd grad fr over 1f out: fin 3rd: plcd 2nd* **9/2**[2]

0056 **3** *4* **Jochi Khan (USA)**[7] 9060 2-8-11 **47** (v[1]) RobertHavlin 5 37
(Mohamed Moubarak) *in rr: niggled along after 1f: pushed along over 3f out: styd on but n.d: fin 4th: plcd 3rd* **8/1**

5001 **4** *shd* **Ami Li Bert (IRE)**[21] 8859 2-9-0 **53** TheodoreLadd(3) 8 43
(Michael Appleby) *in rr: pushed along and swtchd lft after 1f: sme hdwy on inner 3f out: styd on but nt rch ldrs: fin 5th: plcd 4th* **7/1**

0030 **5** *2 ¼* **Big Boris (IRE)**[34] 8493 2-9-7 **57** CliffordLee 10 41
(David Evans) *cl up on outer: pushed along over 3f out: rdn and kpt on fr over 2f out: n.d: fin 6th: plcd 5th* **9/1**

4402 **6** *6* **Red Maharani**[20] 8897 2-9-7 **57** BarryMcHugh 3 28
(James Given) *midfield: niggled along after 2f: hdwy and cl up 3f out: rdn and wknd fr over 2f out: fin 7th: plcd 6th* **11/1**

0005 **7** *4 ½* **The Works (IRE)**[20] 8897 2-8-9 **45** TomEaves 4 5
(Declan Carroll) *trckd ldrs: pushed along on outer over 3f out: rdn and kpt on fr 2f out: fin 8th: plcd 7th* **33/1**

000 **8** *14* **Bright Spells (IRE)**[27] 8706 2-9-7 **57** NicolaCurrie 11
(Jamie Osborne) *in rr on outer: pushed along over 3f out: kpt on but n.d: fin 9th: plcd 8th* **20/1**

6500 **9** *1 ¼* **Barry Magoo**[21] 8856 2-9-1 **51** CharlieBennett 1
(Adam West) *trckd ldr: pushed along and lost position over 4f out: dropped to last 3f out: mde no imp: fin 10th: plcd 9th* **40/1**

0403 **10** *9* **Comvida (IRE)**[20] 8897 2-9-0 **50** (b) JackMitchell 2
(Hugo Palmer) *cl up: rdn and lost position 4f out: wknd grad fr 3f out: eased fnl f: fin 11th: plcd 10th (trainers rep could offer no explanation for the poor performance)* **5/1**[3]

5055 **D** *1 ¾* **Sea Of Cool (IRE)**[8] 9045 2-8-11 **50** (p) DarraghKeenan(3) 7 50
(John Ryan) *disp ld: pushed along 3f out: led narrowly over 1f out: kpt on ins fnl f: hdd towards fin: fin 2nd: disqualified: weighed in light* **4/1**[1]

1m 42.24s (-1.46) **Going Correction** -0.30s/f (Stan) **11** Ran SP% **113.6**
Speed ratings (Par 94): **95,92,88,88,85 79,75,61,60,51 93**
CSF £72.01 CT £544.89 TOTE £15.60: £4.90, £1.90, £3.10; EX 80.80 Trifecta £887.30.
Owner Mrs Lyndsey Shaw **Bred** S A R L Ecurie Haras De Beauvoir **Trained** Sproxton, Leics

FOCUS
The first two home in this moderate event were trying Fibresand for the first time, and improved for the switch. However, the second past the post was demoted to last when the jockey weighed in light. It's been rated as limited form, with the second in line with his heavy ground 1m2f run.

9180 BOMBARDIER GOLDEN BEER H'CAP 1m 13y(F)
12:50 (12:53) (Class 5) (0-70,73) 3-Y-O+
£3,428 (£1,020; £509; £300; £300; £300) **Stalls Low**

Form RPR
3331 1 **Silverturnstogold**[9] 9035 4-8-7 **60**.....................(b) ElishaWhittington(7) 6 72
(Tony Carroll) *chsd ldrs: rdn to ld 2f out: kpt on wl: comf* **5/2**[1]

3114 2 2 1/2 **Makambe (IRE)**[20] 8902 4-9-11 **71**.............................(p) JoeyHaynes 11 77
(Chelsea Banham) *midfield: rdn fr 4f out: hdwy and chsd ldrs 2f out: wnt 2nd ins fnl f: kpt on* **9/2**[2]

3234 3 1 1/2 **Break The Silence**[18] 8949 5-8-11 **57**.....................(b) BarryMcHugh 7 60
(Scott Dixon) *prom: pressed ldr 3f out: rdn over 2f out: edgd lft fr over 1f out: wknd ins fnl f* **10/1**

4-00 4 2 1/4 **Dove Divine (FR)**[42] 8254 3-9-4 **66**.............................. RobertHavlin 12 62
(Hughie Morrison) *chsd ldrs: rdn and outpcd 3f out: kpt on ins fnl f* **11/1**

0400 5 hd **Jem Scuttle (USA)**[49] 8025 3-9-4 **66**.............................(t) TomEaves 9 62
(Declan Carroll) *cl up but racd wd: pushed along and pressed ldrs over 2f out: rdn and wandered arnd fr over 1f out: wknd ins fnl f* **16/1**

0100 6 1/2 **Bond Angel**[4] 9138 4-8-12 **65**.............................. LauraPearson(7) 8 61
(David Evans) *towards rr: pushed along and racd extremely wd fr 4f out: sme hdwy fr 2f out: rdn over 1f out: styd on* **9/1**[3]

0024 7 4 **Love Your Work (IRE)**[29] 8642 3-9-7 **69**..................... CharlieBennett 13 55
(Adam West) *led: pushed along and hdd 2f out: rdn and wknd over 1f out* **9/1**[3]

1566 8 3 3/4 **Melgate Majeure**[26] 8713 3-8-13 **61**............................ JamesSullivan 1 38
(Michael Easterby) *midfield: reminders after 1f: rdn and outpcd after 3f: towards rr 3f out: n.d* **14/1**

-352 9 1 1/4 **Momtalik (USA)**[22] 8842 4-9-11 **71**.............................. JasonHart 10 46
(Derek Shaw) *s.i.s: towards rr of midfield abt three wd: reminder over 4f out: rdn and no imp fr over 2f out* **20/1**

1520 10 1 1/2 **Muqarred (USA)**[20] 8902 7-9-2 **65**.....................(b) GemmaTutty(3) 2 37
(Karen Tutty) *cl up: pushed along and wknd fr over 3f out* **20/1**

6423 11 2 3/4 **Thorn**[49] 8030 3-9-6 **68**...(h) KieranO'Neill 4 32
(Peter Hiatt) *towards rr: swtchd rt and racd wd fr 4f out: wknd fr 3f out* **11/1**

1m 40.65s (-3.05) **Going Correction** -0.30s/f (Stan)
WFA 3 from 4yo+ 2lb 11 Ran SP% **114.6**
Speed ratings (Par 103): **103,100,99,96,96 96,92,88,87,85 82**
CSF £12.47 CT £93.36 TOTE £3.00: £1.90, £1.02, £2.90; EX 10.30 Trifecta £46.70.
Owner A A Byrne **Bred** Anthony Byrne **Trained** Cropthorne, Worcs

FOCUS
A modest affair but the winner is improving. The second has been rated to his recent best, while the third helps set the level.

9181 LADBROKES "PLAY 1-2-FREE" ON FOOTBALL EBF NOVICE STKS 7f 14y(F)
1:25 (1:26) (Class 5) 2-Y-O **£3,428** (£1,020; £509; £254) **Stalls Low**

Form RPR
52 1 **Cedar Cage**[20] 8889 2-9-5 0.............................. DanielMuscutt 3 78+
(Sir Mark Prescott Bt) *trckd ldr: pushed along to ld 2f out: rdn and wnt clr fr 1f out: eased towards fin: comf* **5/2**[1]

0 2 3 1/2 **Itsallaboutluck (IRE)**[30] 8605 2-9-2 0........................ FinleyMarsh(3) 13 66
(Richard Hughes) *cl up on outer: pushed along and hung lft 2f out: kpt on wl ins fnl f (jockey said gelding hung left-handed in the home straight)* **10/1**

06 3 4 **Cold War Steve**[9] 9029 2-9-5 0.............................. CallumRodriguez 4 56
(Roger Fell) *prom: gng okay whn nudged along 3f out: rdn and wknd fr 1f out* **80/1**

6 4 nk **Arbiter**[21] 8865 2-9-5 0...(h) KieranO'Neill 5 55
(John Gosden) *t.k.h: hld up in rr: hdwy into midfield after 3f: pushed along and hung lft over 2f out: styd on ins fnl f* **11/4**[2]

33 5 1/2 **Alex Gracie**[29] 8640 2-8-7 0.............................. JonathanFisher(7) 11 48
(Scott Dixon) *cl up: rdn over 1f out: wknd ins fnl f* **14/1**

6 6 1 1/2 **Foreshore**[36] 8424 2-9-5 0.............................. CliffordLee 12 50+
(K R Burke) *trckd ldr: pushed along and outpcd fr over 3f out: n.d* **4/1**[3]

54 7 1 3/4 **Harbour Point**[36] 8431 2-8-11 0.............................. TheodoreLadd(3) 1 40
(Michael Appleby) *sn led: hdd 2f out: rdn and wknd grad fr over 1f out* **40/1**

0 8 1 1/4 **Mabre (IRE)**[33] 8516 2-9-5 0.............................. CamHardie 10 42
(David Evans) *dwlt s: in rr: pushed along after 1f: abt seven wd and stl plenty to do home turn: kpt on wl fr over 3f out (jockey said colt ran green)* **20/1**

9 3/4 **Whitehaven (FR)** 2-9-5 0.............................. CharlieBennett 2 40
(Hughie Morrison) *prom: pushed along over 3f out: wknd grad fr 2f out* **25/1**

10 3 1/2 **Potencia (IRE)** 2-9-0 0.............................. TomEaves 14 26
(Declan Carroll) *trckd ldr: pushed along and lost position 5f out: mde no imp* **100/1**

50 11 2 1/2 **Bulldozer (IRE)**[37] 8395 2-9-5 0.............................. AlistairRawlinson 6 24
(Michael Appleby) *in rr: swtchd sharply rt after 1f: outpcd and pushed along on outer after 2f: got wl bhd 4f out: rdn and sme hdwy fr 3f out* **100/1**

04 12 1 **Grey Eminence**[23] 8810 2-9-5 0.............................. RichardKingscote 9 22
(James Given) *trckd ldr: outpcd and lost position 5f out: sn wknd* **9/1**

00 13 8 **Monsaraz**[20] 8889 2-9-5 0.............................. JasonHart 8
(James Given) *trckd ldr: lost position 5f out: outpcd over 4f out: n.d* **50/1**

0 14 1 3/4 **Thriller's Moon**[26] 8717 2-9-5 0.............................. PhilDennis 7
(Richard Whitaker) *prom: outpcd and lost position 5f out: rdn and wknd fr over 3f out* **150/1**

1m 28.45s (-1.85) **Going Correction** -0.30s/f (Stan) 14 Ran SP% **117.9**
Speed ratings (Par 96): **98,94,89,89,88 86,84,83,82,78 75,74,65,63**
CSF £26.42 TOTE £4.10: £1.10, £3.30, £13.70; EX 32.30 Trifecta £1303.10.
Owner Paddy Barrett **Bred** P E Barrett **Trained** Newmarket, Suffolk

FOCUS
Quite a few were struggling early but the winner was much the best of these.

9182 BETWAY CLASSIFIED CLAIMING STKS 6f 16y(F)
2:00 (2:02) (Class 5) 3-Y-O+
£3,428 (£1,020; £509; £300; £300; £300) **Stalls Low**

Form RPR
3630 1 **Bedtime Bella (IRE)**[5] 9113 3-8-10 70.....................(v) AngusVilliers(7) 1 72
(Michael Appleby) *towards rr: pushed along 4f out: rdn and hdwy over 2f out: led ins fnl 110yds: kpt on wl* **6/1**

0005 2 1/2 **The Right Choice (IRE)**[37] 8410 4-9-1 70.....................(b) JackMitchell 6 69
(James Ferguson) *towards rr of midfield: pushed along over 3f out: rdn and kpt on wl fr 2f out: wnt 2nd towards fin* **7/2**[2]

0334 3 nk **Kyllachy Warrior (IRE)**[26] 8715 3-9-5 67.............................. PhilDennis 4 72
(Lawrence Mullaney) *led: rdn over 1f out: no ex and hdd ins fnl 110yds* **7/2**[2]

0164 4 1 1/2 **Falcao (IRE)**[203] 2532 7-8-10 56.............................. DarraghKeenan(3) 3 61
(John Butler) *chsd ldrs: rdn 2f out: kpt on but no imp ins fnl f* **20/1**

004 5 nse **Awsaaf**[4] 9135 4-9-5 69...(h) RichardKingscote 2 67
(Michael Wigham) *midfield: rdn and hdwy over 2f out: wnt 2nd over 1f out: wknd ins fnl f* **9/4**[1]

0450 6 6 **Robsdelight (IRE)**[44] 8206 4-9-3 67.............................(b[1]) JasonHart 8 47
(Gay Kelleway) *t.k.h: pressed ldr: rdn and wknd over 2f out* **5/1**[3]

0602 7 8 **Robbian**[21] 8861 8-8-7 39.. AledBeech(5) 5 18
(Charles Smith) *s.i.s: in rr: pushed along over 4f out: n.d* **50/1**

0065 8 1 3/4 **Lope De Loop (IRE)**[28] 8668 4-9-0 42.............................(h) CamHardie 7 15
(Aytach Sadik) *cl up: outpcd 4f out: rdn and wknd over 3f out (vet said filly lost it's left-fore shoe)* **100/1**

1m 14.37s (-2.13) **Going Correction** -0.30s/f (Stan) 8 Ran SP% **113.9**
Speed ratings (Par 103): **102,101,100,98,98 90,80,77**
CSF £26.81 TOTE £6.60: £2.10, £1.30, £1.20; EX 29.90 Trifecta £101.50.There were no claims from this race.
Owner Rod In Pickle Partnership **Bred** Gce Farm Ltd **Trained** Oakham, Rutland

FOCUS
There were a few in with a chance inside the last but eventually it was the highest rated pair in the line-up who came through to fill the first two places.

9183 BOMBARDIER "MARCH TO YOUR OWN DRUM" H'CAP 7f 14y(F)
2:30 (2:31) (Class 4) (0-85,87) 3-Y-O+
£5,207 (£1,549; £774; £387; £300; £300) **Stalls Low**

Form RPR
2211 1 **Suitcase 'N' Taxi**[29] 8646 5-8-7 **70** oh1.............................. DuranFentiman 3 79
(Tim Easterby) *mde all: pushed along 3f out: rdn and kpt on wl fr over 1f out: jst hld on* **12/1**

1210 2 hd **Young John (IRE)**[33] 8522 6-9-5 **82**.............................. AlistairRawlinson 1 90
(Mike Murphy) *trckd ldr: pushed along over 3f out: rdn and kpt on fr over 1f out: jst hld* **9/1**

3-1 3 2 1/2 **Fancy Footings (IRE)**[20] 8902 3-9-4 **82**..................... RichardKingscote 9 82
(Tom Dascombe) *midfield: rdn 2f out: kpt on wl fr over 1f out: wnt 3rd fnl strides* **13/8**[1]

2606 4 nk **Angel Palanas**[37] 8403 5-9-2 **79**...(p) CliffordLee 7 79
(K R Burke) *cl up: pushed along 4f out: rdn 2f out: wknd grad ins fnl f: lost 3rd fnl strides* **10/1**

0006 5 3/4 **Mister Music**[29] 8642 10-8-9 **79**.............................. ElishaWhittington(7) 2 77
(Tony Carroll) *s.i.s: got bhd after 2f: pushed along 4f out: hdwy over 2f out: kpt on fr over 1f out: nvr able to chal (jockey said gelding was slowly away)* **16/1**

4600 6 3 **Custard The Dragon**[25] 8766 6-9-1 **78**..............................(v) JasonHart 6 68
(John Mackie) *s.i.s: in rr: pushed along on outer 4f out: rdn and brief hdwy 2f out: wknd ins fnl f* **9/1**

5100 7 2 1/4 **Wahoo**[47] 8096 4-9-10 **87**.. CallumRodriguez 4 71
(Michael Dods) *s.i.s: midfield: rdn and lost position over 3f out* **11/2**[2]

1005 8 3/4 **Fantasy Keeper**[9] 9030 5-9-0 **84**.............................. AngusVilliers(7) 8 66
(Michael Appleby) *midfield: pushed along and dropped to rr fr over 3f out* **17/2**[3]

3445 9 2 **Kindly**[36] 8428 6-8-13 **76**...(e[1]) JamesSullivan 5 53
(Michael Easterby) *trckd ldr: pushed along over 3f out: rdn and wknd grad fr 2f out* **20/1**

1m 26.96s (-3.34) **Going Correction** -0.30s/f (Stan)
WFA 3 from 4yo+ 1lb 9 Ran SP% **111.4**
Speed ratings (Par 105): **107,106,103,103,102 99,96,95,93**
CSF £108.84 CT £264.41 TOTE £7.70: £2.40, £2.70, £1.20; EX 44.20 Trifecta £129.10.
Owner Ontoawinner 10 & Partner 3 **Bred** Crossfields Bloodstock Ltd **Trained** Great Habton, N Yorks

FOCUS
A good race for the level, and the pace was sound from the outset. The winner has been rated close to his old best, and the second rated in line with his old best.

9184 BETWAY HEED YOUR HUNCH H'CAP 1m 6f 21y(F)
3:05 (3:05) (Class 5) (0-75,75) 3-Y-O+ **£3,428** (£1,020; £509; £300; £300; £300) **Stalls Low**

Form RPR
2304 1 **Argus (IRE)**[18] 8966 7-9-11 **75**.............................(t[1]) RichardKingscote 4 83
(Alexandra Dunn) *trckd ldrs: cl up and gng easily 3f out: rdn over 1f out: led ins fnl f: jst did enough* **9/4**[1]

2112 2 nk **Tynecastle Park**[226] 1815 6-8-13 **66**.............................. DarraghKeenan(3) 5 73
(Robert Eddery) *rushed up and disp ld: led over 4f out: pushed along and hrd pressed fr 3f out: kpt on but hdd ins fnl f: jst hld* **3/1**[2]

5240 3 4 **Tigray (USA)**[18] 8945 3-9-2 **72**.............................(p) AlistairRawlinson 3 74
(Michael Appleby) *in rr early: sn trckd ldrs: pushed along and chalng 3f out: no ex fr over 1f out* **10/3**[3]

0043 4 19 **The Resdev Way**[18] 8945 6-9-9 **73**.............................. CliffordLee 1 48
(Philip Kirby) *slowly away: in rr: pushed along 3f out: sn wknd* **13/2**

0444 5 12 **Pumblechook**[18] 8945 6-9-5 **69**.............................(b[1]) JasonHart 2 27
(Amy Murphy) *disp ld: rdn and lost position over 4f out: t.o* **11/2**

3m 2.87s (-5.43) **Going Correction** -0.30s/f (Stan)
WFA 3 from 6yo+ 6lb 5 Ran SP% **107.6**
Speed ratings (Par 103): **103,102,100,89,82**
CSF £8.73 TOTE £3.20: £1.60, £1.40; EX 8.20 Trifecta £26.60.
Owner Helium Racing Ltd **Bred** Grangecon Stud **Trained** West Buckland, Somerset

FOCUS
A fair staying handicap. The second has been rated as running as well as ever.

9185 BETWAY AMATEUR RIDERS' H'CAP 6f 16y(F)
3:40 (3:41) (Class 6) (0-65,65) 3-Y-0+

£2,682 (£832; £415; £300; £300; £300) Stalls Low

Form RPR

3143 1 **Fiery Breath**[27] 8711 4-10-8 64 (h) MrGeorgeEddery(5) 4 71
(Robert Eddery) *trckd ldr: rdn over 1f out: led ins fnl f: pushed out towards fin* 4/1[1]

1250 2 3/4 **Vallarta (IRE)**[19] 8925 9-9-8 50 MissEmilyBullock(5) 8 55
(Ruth Carr) *led: rdn over 1f out: hdd ins fnl f: kpt on* 14/1

4440 3 nk **Global Melody**[6] 9089 4-10-7 65 (v) MissKatieWebb(7) 14 69
(Phil McEntee) *cl up but racd wd: pushed along over 1f out: kpt on towards fin* 11/1

3622 4 3 **Letmestopyouthere (IRE)**[25] 8757 5-10-4 55(p) MissBrodieHampson 3 52
(Archie Watson) *in rr: short of room over 3f out: rdn and hdwy fr 2f out: kpt on ins fnl f* 5/1[2]

0230 5 1/2 **Tease Maid**[18] 8949 3-10-4 58 (p) MrAaronAnderson(3) 10 51
(John Quinn) *midfield: rdn and sme hdwy 2f out: wknd fr 1f out* 20/1

3060 6 1/2 **Fair Alibi**[68] 7418 3-11-0 65 MrPatrickMillman 7 57
(Tom Tate) *t.k.h: prom: lost position 4f out: rdn and hdwy fr 2f out: wknd fr 1f out* 4/1[1]

0532 7 2 1/2 **Just An Idea (IRE)**[37] 8408 5-9-5 49 (b) MissCamillaSwift(7) 1 33
(Roger Ingram) *midfield: pushed along and chsd ldrs 3f out: rdn and wknd fr 2f out* 7/1[3]

0353 8 1/2 **Caribbean Spring (IRE)**[19] 8915 6-9-11 53. MissRosieMargarson(5) 12 36+
(George Margarson) *in rr and racd extremely wd: pushed along over 2f out: kpt on* 16/1

6060 9 1 1/4 **Mama Africa (IRE)**[18] 8946 5-10-7 63 (p) MissImogenMathias(5) 5 42
(John Flint) *midfield: bit short of room and lost position over 4f out: rdn and no ex fr 2f out* 33/1

5435 10 1 1/2 **Carlovian**[19] 8925 6-10-0 51 (b) MissAmieWaugh 2 26
(Mark Walford) *t.k.h: midfield: rdn and wknd over 1f out* 14/1

0430 11 1 **Letsbe Avenue (IRE)**[41] 8291 4-10-6 64 (b) MrCharlieSprake(7) 9 36
(Bill Turner) *midfield: hmpd and dropped to rr over 4f out: rdn and no imp over 2f out* 20/1

3500 12 1/2 **Little Miss Muffin**[100] 6273 3-10-2 53 MissBeckySmith 13 23
(Sam England) *chsd ldr: lost position over 2f out: rdn and wknd over 1f out* 50/1

2340 13 2 **Thornaby Princess**[20] 8898 8-9-5 49 ow2 (p) MrAndrewMcBride(7) 6 13
(Jason Ward) *s.i.s: towards rr: pushed along but no rspnse over 2f out* 66/1

0004 P **Inner Charm**[22] 8840 3-10-0 51 MissJoannaMason 11
(Kevin Ryan) *hld up in rr: carried rt and racd wd over 4f out: p.u qckly over 2f out* 14/1

1m 15.41s (-1.09) **Going Correction** -0.30s/f (Stan) 14 Ran SP% 119.3
Speed ratings (Par 101): **95,94,93,89,88 88,84,84,82,80 79,78,75,**
CSF £57.76 CT £594.93 TOTE £4.30: £1.40, £4.00, £4.00; EX 57.00 Trifecta £692.70.
Owner Edwin S Phillips **Bred** S Clarke, G Parsons & A Wideson **Trained** Newmarket, Suffolk

FOCUS
The early gallop wasn't that strong and it paid to be handy. The winner has been rated back to his best.
T/Plt: £24.90 to a £1 stake. Pool: £54,901.53 - 1,603.96 winning units T/Qpdt: £7.00 to a £1 stake. Pool: £5,995.31 - 621.67 winning units **Raceform**

9186 - 9194a (Foreign Racing) - See Raceform Interactive

9154 CHELMSFORD (A.W) (L-H)
Thursday, November 28

OFFICIAL GOING: Polytrack: standard
Wind: virtually nil Weather: showers

9195 BET TOTEPLACEPOT AT TOTESPORT.COM NOVICE STKS 6f (P)
4:00 (4:01) (Class 5) 2-Y-0 £4,204 (£1,251; £625; £312) Stalls Centre

Form RPR

1 **Its A Given** 2-8-11 0 JasonWatson 14 71+
(Roger Charlton) *midfield: rn green and hung bnd 3f out: swtchd rt and hdwy over 1f out: led jst ins fnl f: stl green and wnt lft u.p: kpt on wl* 8/1[3]

5 2 1/2 **Batchelor Boy (IRE)**[157] 4184 2-9-2 0 DanielMuscutt 4 74
(Marco Botti) *midfield: effrt and hdwy u.p over 1f out: ev ch ins fnl f: kpt on wl* 3/1[2]

06 3 1/2 **Vandad (IRE)**[42] 8288 2-9-2 0 (t[1]) JasonHart 7 73
(Mohamed Moubarak) *midfield: swtchd rt and effrt over 1f out: hdwy to chal jst ins fnl f: intimidated and edgd lft after: kpt on* 14/1

4 1/2 **Notforalongtime** 2-9-2 0 AdamKirby 5 71+
(Clive Cox) *s.i.s and rdn along thrght: towards rr: hdwy into midfield after 2f: hdwy and swtchd rt 1f out: styd on strly fnl 100yds: nt rch ldrs* 16/1

56 5 2 1/4 **Millionaire Waltz**[68] 7453 2-9-2 0 BenCurtis 12 64
(Paul Cole) *chsd ldrs: effrt 2f out: drvn and ev ch 1f out: unable qck and wknd fnl 100yds* 14/1

00 6 1/2 **Sports Reporter**[27] 8714 2-9-2 0 BarryMcHugh 1 63
(Richard Fahey) *trckd ldrs on inner: effrt over 1f out: drvn and pressed ldrs 1f out: sn no ex and wknd ins fnl f* 11/1

514 7 1/2 **Moosmee (IRE)**[22] 8865 2-9-6 82 GeorgiaCox(3) 2 68
(William Haggas) *led: rdn over 1f out: hdd jst ins fnl f: sn outpcd and wknd ins fnl f (jockey said colt ran flat)* 7/4[1]

60 8 nk **Kelinda Dice**[111] 5906 2-8-11 0 ShaneKelly 3 55
(Mick Quinn) *midfield: clsd on inner to chse ldrs: nt clr run and swtchd rt ins fnl f: no imp towards fin* 66/1

06 9 2 1/4 **Motamayiz**[9] 9043 2-9-2 0 MartinDwyer 11 54
(Roger Varian) *dwlt and hmpd leaving stall: rdn along in rr: swtchd rt over 1f out: kpt on ins fnl f: nvr trbld ldrs* 9/1

50 10 3/4 **Light Lily**[21] 8891 2-8-11 0 JFEgan 13 46
(Paul D'Arcy) *swtchd lft after s: midfield: pushed along over 2f out: no imp over 1f out: kpt on same pce fnl f* 66/1

00 11 1 1/2 **Casaruan**[9] 9043 2-9-2 0 DougieCostello 6 47
(Michael Appleby) *chsd ldrs: pushed along and hung lft over 1f out: unable qck and wknd ins fnl f* 100/1

3 12 1/2 **Kilconquhar**[12] 9008 2-9-2 0 ShaneGray 9 45
(David O'Meara) *wnt rt leaving stalls: chsd ldr tl 2f: lost pl u.p over 1f out: wknd ins fnl f* 10/1

60 13 1 3/4 **Boom Boom Boom**[9] 9043 2-9-2 0 (t) HayleyTurner 8 40
(Stuart Williams) *sn towards rr: n.d* 33/1

36 14 1/2 **Dark Phoenix (IRE)**[38] 8409 2-9-2 0 GrahamLee 10 39
(Paul Cole) *towards rr: rdn and no rspnse over 1f out: sn wl btn* 33/1

1m 12.15s (-1.55) **Going Correction** -0.225s/f (Stan) 14 Ran SP% 129.0
Speed ratings (Par 96): **101,100,99,99,96 95,94,94,91,90 88,87,85,84**
CSF £34.02 TOTE £12.20: £2.80, £1.50, £4.10; EX 54.00 Trifecta £634.60.
Owner K Abdullah **Bred** Juddmonte Farms Ltd **Trained** Beckhampton, Wilts

FOCUS
The favourite was disappointing but a debutante scored with something in hand in this novice and there was also plenty of promise from another newcomer in fourth.

9196 BET TOTEEXACTA AT TOTESPORT.COM NURSERY H'CAP 6f (P)
4:30 (4:31) (Class 6) (0-65,69) 2-Y-0

£3,105 (£924; £461; £400; £400; £400) Stalls Centre

Form RPR

5014 1 **Last Date**[23] 8825 2-9-3 61 DougieCostello 6 64
(Ivan Furtado) *midfield: effrt u.p over 1f out: clsd u.p ins fnl f: kpt on to ld towards fin (trainer said, regarding the apparent improvement in form, the gelding appreciated the return to Chelmsford where it has previously won over 6f)* 16/1

640 2 hd **Diamonds And Rust**[63] 7627 2-9-3 61 (h[1]) ShaneKelly 3 63
(Bill Turner) *wnt lft s: chsd ldng trio: effrt over 1f out: clsd u.p and swtchd rt ins fnl f: ev ch wl ins fnl f: kpt on* 33/1

4662 3 hd **The Blue Bower (IRE)**[8] 9061 2-9-1 59 JaneElliott 7 61
(Suzy Smith) *racd in last quartet: swtchd rt and effrt u.p over 1f out: hdwy ins fnl f: ev ch towards fin: kpt on* 10/1

0003 4 nk **Ivadream**[8] 9061 2-9-2 60 JasonWatson 5 61
(Roger Charlton) *midfield: rdn and hdwy over 1f out: kpt on wl ins fnl f: gng on wl at fin: nt quite rch ldrs* 7/2[2]

555 5 1/2 **Pretty Lady (IRE)**[48] 8084 2-9-3 61 JasonHart 9 60
(Mark Johnston) *led: rdn and kicked clr over 1f out: tired ins fnl f: hdd towards fin: sn wknd* 16/1

0411 6 1/2 **Speed Merchant (IRE)**[8] 9060 2-9-11 69 6ex (p) AlistairRawlinson 8 67+
(Michael Appleby) *chsd ldrs tl wnt 2nd ent fnl 2f: outpcd u.p over 1f out: kpt on and chsng ldrs ins fnl f: one pce towards fin* 13/8[1]

0004 7 1 **Redzone**[24] 8816 2-9-3 61 GrahamLee 4 56
(Bryan Smart) *racd in last pair: effrt over 1f out: sn rdn: kpt on ins fnl f: nt rch ldrs* 14/1

050 8 shd **Sweet Serenade**[36] 8454 2-9-4 62 AdamKirby 1 62+
(James Tate) *wnt lft leaving stalls: in rr: rdn and hdwy over 1f out: clsng and keeping on wl whn swtchd lft and nt clr run 100yds out: nowhere to go after and eased (jockey said filly was denied a clear run)* 8/1[3]

0665 9 2 **Constanzia**[51] 7994 2-9-6 64 (p[1]) NicolaCurrie 2 53
(Jamie Osborne) *racd in last quartet: effrt on inner over 1f out: rdn and kpt on ins fnl f: nt rch ldrs* 12/1

0345 10 hd **Catechism**[23] 8841 2-9-7 65 BenCurtis 12 53
(Richard Spencer) *midfield: rdn over 2f out: unable qck and no imp over 1f out: wknd ins fnl f* 14/1

6420 11 6 **Qinwan**[29] 8650 2-9-7 65 MartinDwyer 11 35
(Andrew Balding) *bustled along leaving stalls: sn chsng ldr: lost 2nd ent fnl 2f: sn outpcd and bhd ins fnl f* 16/1

1m 12.51s (-1.19) **Going Correction** -0.225s/f (Stan) 11 Ran SP% 122.1
Speed ratings (Par 94): **98,97,97,97,96 95,94,94,91,91 83**
CSF £458.56 CT £5454.97 TOTE £17.80: £4.40, £21.20, £2.50; EX 1495.70 Trifecta £2759.40.
Owner Eamon Spain **Bred** Eamon Patrick Spain **Trained** Wiseton, Nottinghamshire

FOCUS
The leader went off hard in this sprint nursery and it set up for the closers.

9197 MATCHBOOK EBF FUTURE STAYERS' NOVICE STKS (PLUS 10 RACE) (MATCHBOOK/EBF SIRE/DAM-RESTRICTED) 7f (P)
5:00 (5:04) (Class 3) 2-Y-0 £10,350 (£3,080; £1,539; £769) Stalls Low

Form RPR

2230 1 **Great Ambassador**[77] 7119 2-9-5 87 (t[1]) RichardKingscote 5 85+
(Ralph Beckett) *chsd ldr for over 1f: styd chsng ldrs: effrt to chal over 1f out: rdn to ld ins fnl f: r.o strly and drew clr fnl 100yds* 4/6[1]

2 3 1/2 **Morning Shadow** 2-9-0 0 JasonHart 10 71
(Mark Johnston) *led: rdn over 1f out: hdd ins fnl f: sn outpcd and no ch w wnr: hld on to 2nd cl home* 33/1

6 3 nk **Arriviste**[34] 8510 2-9-0 0 DavidProbert 4 70
(Rae Guest) *t.k.h: hld up in tch in midfield: effrt over 1f out: no ch w wnr but kpt on ins fnl f* 14/1

4 shd **Dublin Pharaoh (USA)** 2-9-5 0 JFEgan 3 75+
(Roger Varian) *restless in stalls: in tch in midfield: swtchd rt 2f out: rdn and swtchd lft 1f out: no ch w wnr but kpt on ins fnl f* 2/1[2]

02 5 1/2 **Kumasi**[27] 8714 2-9-5 0 AdamKirby 8 74
(David O'Meara) *chsd ldrs: wnt 2nd over 5f out tl unable qck and lost 2nd over 1f out: no ch w wnr and kpt on same pce ins fnl f* 8/1[3]

6 7 **Seventeen O Four (IRE)** 2-9-5 0 HayleyTurner 6 55
(Michael Bell) *chsd ldng trio: outpcd: rdn and edgd lft over 1f out: wknd fnl f* 33/1

0 7 shd **Billhilly (GER)**[9] 9052 2-9-5 0 CharlesBishop 7 55
(Eve Johnson Houghton) *t.k.h: hld up in tch in midfield: rdn wl over 1f out: sn outpcd and wknd fnl f* 50/1

8 nk **Alphabetical** 2-9-5 0 LukeMorris 9 54
(Sir Mark Prescott Bt) *sn in rr: rdn over 3f out: wknd fnl f* 50/1

0 9 1 **Sparkling Or Still (IRE)**[28] 8706 2-9-0 0 ShaneKelly 2 47
(David Lanigan) *short of room sn after s: hld up in last trio: effrt over 1f out: sn rdn and no hdwy: wknd fnl f* 100/1

10 1 3/4 **Talking About You** 2-9-0 0 BenCurtis 1 42
(Mick Channon) *short of room and dropped to last trio sn after s: nvr danger after* 50/1

1m 26.38s (-0.82) **Going Correction** -0.225s/f (Stan) 10 Ran SP% 123.9
Speed ratings (Par 100): **95,91,90,90,89 81,81,81,80,78**
CSF £40.27 TOTE £1.40: £1.10, £4.40, £3.30; EX 29.60 Trifecta £171.50.
Owner J C Smith **Bred** Littleton Stud **Trained** Kimpton, Hants

FOCUS
The hot favourite trounced his rivals in this novice event.

9198 BET TOTEQUADPOT AT TOTESPORT.COM H'CAP 7f (P)
5:30 (5:35) (Class 2) (0-105,103) 3-Y-0+

£12,450 (£3,728; £1,864; £932; £466; £234) Stalls Low

Form RPR

5501 1 **Reeves**[28] 8691 3-8-6 84 HollieDoyle 7 94
(Robert Cowell) *chsd ldr: rdn to ld ent fnl 2f: edgd lft u.p and styd on strly ins fnl f* 5/2[2]

0060 **2** 2 1/4 **Silent Attack**[28] 8707 6-9-7 **98** JasonWatson 6 103
(Tony Carroll) *chsd ldrs: effrt 2f out: drvn jst over 1f out: kpt on same pce u.p ins fnl f: wnt 2nd last stride* **10/1**

0030 **3** shd **Merhoob (IRE)**[7] 9088 7-9-6 **97** LukeMorris 5 102
(John Ryan) *chsd ldrs on inner: swtchd out rt and effrt to chse wnr over 1f out: nt match pce of wnr and one pce ins fnl f: lost 2nd last stride* **10/1**

6000 **4** nk **Keyser Soze (IRE)**[54] 7891 5-9-12 **103** AdamKirby 2 107+
(Richard Spencer) *s.i.s: hld up in rr: clsd and nt clr run over 1f out: gap opened and rdn 1f out: swtchd lft and hdwy to chse ldrs 100yds: kpt on: no ch w wnr (jockey said gelding was denied a clear run)* **2/1**[1]

3136 **5** 2 3/4 **Alemaratalyoum (IRE)**[12] 9000 5-9-6 **97** (t) RichardKingscote 8 93
(Stuart Williams) *in tch in midfield: edgd out rt and effrt over 1f out: no imp and kpt on same pce ins fnl f* **5/1**[3]

-460 **6** 1 1/4 **Lucymai**[28] 8708 6-9-6 **97** JoeyHaynes 1 90
(Dean Ivory) *in tch: effrt over 1f out: no imp and wl hld whn n.m.r ins fnl f* **12/1**

2060 **7** 1 1/4 **Muntadab (IRE)**[45] 8184 7-9-8 **99** BenCurtis 3 89
(Roger Fell) *sn led: rdn and hdd ent fnl 2f: no ex and outpcd over 1f out: wknd ins fnl f* **20/1**

5530 **8** shd **Jack's Point**[50] 8016 3-9-1 **93** MartinDwyer 9 81
(William Muir) *t.k.h: hld up in tch: effrt over 1f out: no imp: nvr trbld ldrs* **20/1**

410 **9** 1 3/4 **De Vegas Kid (IRE)**[43] 8253 5-8-5 **85** DarraghKeenan(3) 4 70
(Tony Carroll) *stdd after s: t.k.h: hld up in tch: swtchd rt and effrt bnd 2f out: sn struggling: wknd fnl f (jockey said gelding ran too free)* **16/1**

1m 23.69s (-3.51) **Going Correction** -0.225s/f (Stan)
WFA 3 from 5yo+ 1lb **9 Ran SP% 119.9**
Speed ratings (Par 109): **111,108,108,107,104 103,101,101,99**
CSF £29.19 CT £214.03 TOTE £3.10: £1.20, £3.10, £2.90; EX 32.40 Trifecta £187.30.
Owner T W Morley **Bred** Bearstone Stud Ltd **Trained** Six Mile Bottom, Cambs

FOCUS
A useful handicap and the winner completed a double in good style under a prominent ride. It's been rated around the second.

9199 BET TOTETRIFECTA AT TOTESPORT.COM H'CAP 1m (P)
6:00 (6:05) (Class 4) (0-80,82) 3-Y-O+
£5,530 (£1,645; £822; £411; £400; £400) **Stalls Low**

Form RPR

6026 **1** **Samphire Coast**[9] 9053 6-9-5 **78** (v) BenCurtis 10 86
(Derek Shaw) *dwlt and pushed along leaving stalls: in rr: swtchd wd and effrt bnd 2f out: styd on wl ins fnl f: led last strides* **6/1**[2]

4300 **2** nk **Global Art**[28] 8692 4-9-4 **77** (b) PJMcDonald 6 84
(Ed Dunlop) *hld up in last quartet: effrt and rdn over 1f out: styd on wl ins fnl f: led cl home: hdd last strides* **10/1**

4602 **3** 1/2 **Geizy Teizy (IRE)**[37] 8427 3-9-1 **76** DanielMuscutt 5 81
(Marco Botti) *in tch in midfield: nt clrest of runs over 1f out: swtchd lft and effrt to chse ldrs 1f out: ev ch wl ins fnl f: kpt on* **6/1**[2]

2305 **4** nk **Directory**[29] 8658 4-9-5 **78** LukeMorris 2 83
(James Eustace) *t.k.h: chsd ldrs tl wnt 2nd wl over 1f out: sn drvn: kpt on u.p to ld wl ins fnl f: hdd and no ex cl home* **14/1**

0201 **5** 1 **Extrodinair**[28] 8693 4-8-10 **74** RayDawson(5) 13 77+
(Jane Chapple-Hyam) *led: rdn and kicked clr over 1f out: tired ins fnl f: hdd wl ins fnl f: wknd towards fin* **14/1**

5052 **6** shd **Cote D'Azur**[20] 8918 6-9-7 **80** LewisEdmunds 1 83
(Les Eyre) *broke wl: sn restrained and hld up in midfield: effrt to chse ldrs u.p 1f out: kpt on same pce ins fnl f* **10/3**[1]

4055 **7** 3/4 **Sezim**[24] 8809 3-9-3 **78** (vt[1]) RobertHavlin 3 78
(Mohamed Moubarak) *t.k.h: hld up in last quartet: effrt on inner over 1f out: chsd ldrs and kpt on same pce fnl 100yds* **8/1**

0-63 **8** 1/2 **Reponse Exacte (FR)**[22] 8852 3-9-2 **77** (h) GeorgeWood 8 76
(Amy Murphy) *midfield: effrt over 1f out: hung lft and kpt on same pce ins fnl f* **20/1**

4550 **9** 1 **Royal Welcome**[95] 6518 3-8-6 **67** JasonWatson 12 64
(James Tate) *sn chsd ldr: rdn and lost 2nd wl over 1f out: wknd ins fnl f* **25/1**

5000 **10** 1/2 **Star Archer**[28] 8701 5-9-4 **82** GerO'Neill(5) 7 79
(Michael Easterby) *midfield: effrt and unable qck over 1f out: wknd ins fnl f* **33/1**

0- **11** 1/2 **Peruvian Lily (FR)**[98] 6380 3-8-5 **69** TheodoreLadd(3) 4 69+
(Michael Appleby) *midfield tl lost pl 4f out: hung lft: short of room and hmpd wl over 2f out: bhd and pushed along over 1f out: swtchd rt and kpt on ins fnl f: no threat to ldrs (jockey said filly hung badly left-handed throughout)* **6/1**[2]

4254 **12** 4 **Philamundo (IRE)**[33] 8549 4-9-2 **75** (b) KieranShoemark 9 61
(Richard Spencer) *s.i.s: bhd: wd and effrt 2f: nvr involved (trainer could offer no explanation for the gelding's performance, other than when asked for an effort, he found very little)* **7/1**[3]

1m 37.18s (-2.72) **Going Correction** -0.225s/f (Stan)
WFA 3 from 4yo+ 2lb **12 Ran SP% 123.5**
Speed ratings (Par 105): **104,103,103,102,101 101,101,100,99,99 98,94**
CSF £66.07 CT £390.19 TOTE £7.00: £2.10, £3.60, £2.20; EX 72.40 Trifecta £553.20.
Owner Paddy Barrett **Bred** P E Barrett **Trained** Sproxton, Leics
■ Stewards' Enquiry : Luke Morris two-day ban: used whip above shoulder height (Dec 12-13)

FOCUS
They went a good pace and there was an exciting finish in this handicap. The first two have been rated back to something like their best.

9200 BET TOTESWINGER AT TOTESPORT.COM H'CAP 1m (P)
6:30 (6:32) (Class 3) (0-95,96) 3-Y-O+ **£9,703** (£2,887; £1,443; £721) **Stalls Low**

Form RPR

-450 **1** **Another Touch**[61] 7694 6-9-7 **92** BarryMcHugh 3 100
(Richard Fahey) *in tch towards rr: effrt over 1f out: swtchd lft and hdwy to chse ldrs ins fnl f: r.o wl to ld towards fin* **7/1**

0400 **2** 3/4 **Mutafani**[28] 8707 4-9-4 **89** JackMitchell 6 95
(Simon Crisford) *led tl over 5f out: chsd ldr: rdn to ld again jst over 1f out: kpt on tl hdd and no ex towards fin* **9/2**[3]

0-11 **3** hd **The Gill Brothers**[21] 8894 3-9-0 **87** (t) DanielMuscutt 5 92
(Stuart Williams) *t.k.h: in tch in midfield: effrt over 1f out: chsd ldrs and swtchd rt 1f out: kpt on ins fnl f* **7/2**[2]

1032 **4** 1 1/4 **Corazon Espinado (IRE)**[31] 8606 4-8-13 **84** LukeMorris 10 87
(Simon Dow) *t.k.h: chsd ldr tl led over 5f out: rdn over 1f out: sn hdd: no ex and wknd wl ins fnl f* **20/1**

2300 **5** 3/4 **Smile A Mile (IRE)**[61] 7694 3-9-5 **92** JasonHart 7 92
(Mark Johnston) *dwlt: in rr: last and rdn over 3f out: hdwy and swtchd rt 1f out: kpt on wl ins fnl f: nt rch ldrs* **25/1**

1150 **6** 1/2 **Casanova**[41] 8320 3-9-9 **96** RobertHavlin 1 95
(John Gosden) *t.k.h: in tch in midfield: effrt on inner over 1f out: no imp ins fnl f (jockey said gelding ran too free)* **9/4**[1]

1410 **7** nse **Star Of Southwold (FR)**[61] 7686 4-9-8 **96** TheodoreLadd(3) 11 96
(Michael Appleby) *midfield on outer: rdn ent fnl 2f: no imp over 1f out: kpt on same pce ins fnl f* **9/2**[3]

2360 **8** nk **Trevithick**[154] 4292 4-9-4 **89** GrahamLee 4 88
(Bryan Smart) *chsd ldrs: rdn and unable qck over 1f out: outpcd ins fnl f* **33/1**

3500 **9** 3 **Lush Life (IRE)**[8] 9064 4-9-4 **89** (bt) NicolaCurrie 8 81
(Jamie Osborne) *s.i.s: in rr: effrt and wd 2f out: hung lft over 1f out: wknd ins fnl f* **16/1**

1m 37.51s (-2.39) **Going Correction** -0.225s/f (Stan)
WFA 3 from 4yo+ 2lb **9 Ran SP% 119.3**
Speed ratings (Par 107): **102,101,101,99,99 98,98,98,95**
CSF £38.88 CT £131.60 TOTE £8.60: £2.10, £1.70, £1.70; EX 49.70 Trifecta £323.70.
Owner Nicholas Wrigley & Kevin Hart **Bred** Shadwell Estate Company Limited **Trained** Musley Bank, N Yorks

FOCUS
A well-handicapped runner rallied well to justify support in this handicap. The second has been rated to form, and the fourth close to form.

9201 HAVENS HOSPICE H'CAP 1m 5f 66y(P)
7:00 (7:02) (Class 6) (0-65,68) 3-Y-O
£3,105 (£924; £461; £400; £400; £400) **Stalls Low**

Form RPR

-023 **1** **Que Quieres (USA)**[9] 9049 3-8-7 **48** LukeMorris 2 55
(Simon Dow) *dwlt: hld up in rr of main gp: clsd to trck ldrs and nt clr run 2f out: rdn to ld over 1f out: styd on and drvn out* **7/2**[2]

0500 **2** 3/4 **Ezzrah**[78] 7070 3-8-13 **54** KieranShoemark 4 60
(Charlie Fellowes) *in rr: clsd and rdn to chse ldrs 2f out: hung lft over 1f out: kpt on ins fnl f: wnt 2nd last strides* **6/1**[3]

3021 **3** nk **Cheng Gong**[45] 8204 3-8-10 **51** JackMitchell 9 57
(Tom Clover) *t.k.h early: w ldrs tl midfield after 3f: rdn over 7f out and reminder 6f out: rdn to ld over 1f out: sn hdd and kpt on same pce ins fnl f: lost 2nd last strides* **11/8**[1]

4122 **4** 3 1/2 **Elegant Love**[34] 8519 3-9-12 **67** DavidProbert 10 68
(David Evans) *in tch in midfield: clsd to chse ldrs and nt clr run over 1f out: swtchd lft and drvn 1f out: no ex and wknd ins fnl f* **7/1**

4201 **5** 4 **Dolly McQueen**[19] 8944 3-9-4 **59** WilliamCarson 5 54
(Anthony Carson) *in tch in midfield: clsd to trck ldrs over 2f out: nt clrest of runs 2f out: effrt over 1f out: fnd little and wknd ins fnl f* **12/1**

6350 **6** 3 **Highway Robbery**[38] 8414 3-8-5 **46** (p) ShelleyBirkett 11 37
(Julia Feilden) *racd wd early: chsd ldrs: wnt 2nd over 3f out: rdn to ld wl over 1f out: no ex and wknd ins fnl f* **14/1**

6404 **7** 20 **Duke Of Yorkie (IRE)**[26] 8753 3-8-4 **45** (v) MartinDwyer 8 8
(Adam West) *t.k.h: led for 2f: chsd ldr tl led again 4f out: rdn and hdd wl over 1f out: no ex and btn 1f out: sn eased* **33/1**

3000 **8** 9 **Beechwood James (FR)**[7] 9087 3-8-9 **50** (b[1]) JasonWatson 1
(Michael Appleby) *t.k.h: hld up in tch: rdn over 2f out: sn struggling: wl btn and eased fnl f: t.o* **22/1**

-665 **9** 20 **Suakin (IRE)**[185] 3153 3-9-12 **67** (b) RobertHavlin 3
(John Gosden) *w ldr tl led after 2f: hdd 4f out: sn lost pl: t.o and virtually p.u fnl 2f: burst blood vessel (vet said filly had bled from the nose)* **12/1**

2m 51.91s (-1.69) **Going Correction** -0.225s/f (Stan) **9 Ran SP% 120.5**
Speed ratings (Par 98): **96,95,95,93,90 88,76,71,58**
CSF £26.13 CT £42.52 TOTE £4.30: £1.30, £2.10, £1.10; EX 32.70 Trifecta £138.40.
Owner Robert Moss **Bred** Stonestreet Thoroughbred Holdings LLC **Trained** Epsom, Surrey

FOCUS
The three market leaders pulled clear in this handicap.

9202 FLUID BUSINESS COACHING H'CAP 1m 2f (P)
7:30 (7:33) (Class 5) (0-75,75) 3-Y-O+
£5,110 (£1,520; £759; £400; £400; £400) **Stalls Low**

Form RPR

010 **1** **Lucky Turn (IRE)**[49] 8064 3-9-4 **73** HayleyTurner 3 84+
(Michael Bell) *wl in tch in midfield: clsd to trck ldrs over 2f out: rdn to ld over 1f out: clr ins fnl f: r.o wl* **7/1**[3]

2244 **2** 2 **Dubious Affair (IRE)**[24] 8812 3-9-3 **72** (v) KieranShoemark 11 78
(Sir Michael Stoute) *hld up in tch in midfield: hdwy: nt clr run and swtchd lft over 1f out: kpt on ins fnl f: wnt 2nd towards fin: no threat to wnr* **12/1**

0230 **3** 1 **Toro Dorado**[51] 7982 3-9-0 **69** PJMcDonald 7 73
(Ed Dunlop) *hld up in tch in midfield: nt clr run and swtchd lft over 1f out: rdn to chse wnr 1f out: kpt on but no imp: lost 2nd towards fin* **14/1**

0300 **4** 1 **Windsor Cross (IRE)**[67] 7489 4-8-10 **65** ConnorMurtagh(3) 9 67
(Richard Fahey) *in tch in midfield: effrt ent fnl 2f: unable qck over 1f out: kpt on same pce ins fnl f* **33/1**

2000 **5** 1/2 **Elixsoft (IRE)**[6] 9109 4-9-1 **72** PaulaMuir(5) 13 73
(Roger Fell) *t.k.h: hld up in midfield: rdn and hdwy over 1f out: kpt on ins fnl f: nvr trbld ldrs* **33/1**

0310 **6** 1 1/4 **Dreamboat Dave (IRE)**[28] 8705 3-8-6 **61** KieranO'Neill 16 60
(Sarah Humphrey) *chsd ldr over 8f out: rdn and ev ch briefly over 1f out: unable qck u.p 1f out: wknd wl ins fnl f* **16/1**

2221 **7** nk **Bruyere (FR)**[37] 8434 3-8-13 **68** (h) MartinDwyer 6 66+
(Dean Ivory) *stdd s: hld up in last quartet: hdwy over 1f out: nt clr run and hmpd 1f out: swtchd rt and kpt on ins fnl f: nvr trbld ldrs (jockey said filly was slowly away and denied a clear run)* **10/1**

0340 **8** 1 3/4 **Fields Of Dreams**[29] 8656 3-9-6 **75** JasonWatson 15 69
(Roger Charlton) *hld up in last quartet: swtchd rt and effrt wl over 1f out: sme prog 1f out: nvr trbld ldrs* **33/1**

3021 **9** 1 3/4 **J'Ouvert (IRE)**[26] 8756 3-8-12 **67** (h) BenCurtis 14 58
(David Evans) *t.k.h: hld up in tch in midfield: effrt over 1f out: fnd little and hung lft 1f out: sn wknd* **14/1**

3250 **10** hd **Angel's Whisper (IRE)**[28] 8705 4-9-2 **68** (p) DavidProbert 12 59
(Amy Murphy) *swtchd lft after s: hld up in rr: swtchd rt and effrt over 1f out: no imp: nvr trbld ldrs* **20/1**

330 **11** 2 1/2 **The Night King**[26] 8761 4-9-3 **69** ShaneKelly 10 54
(Mick Quinn) *midfield: rdn and struggling 3f out: lost pl over 1f out: wknd ins fnl f* **20/1**

4232 **12** 1 3/4 **Roving Mission (USA)**[35] 8507 3-9-1 **70** RichardKingscote 4 52
(Ralph Beckett) *t.k.h: led: rdn and hdd over 1f out: sn outpcd and wknd ins fnl f* **5/1**[2]

2161 **13** *2 1/4* **Sandy Steve**[57] 7817 3-8-12 **67** .... CallumShepherd 5 58+
(Stuart Williams) *chsd ldr for over 1f: styd chsng ldrs: rdn and hung rt bnd 3f out: lost pl over 1f out: btn and eased ins fnl f (jockey said gelding hung right-handed throughout)* **13/8**[1]

000 **14** *2* **Rakematiz**[77] 7125 5-9-1 **72** .... RayDawson(5) 2 45
(Brett Johnson) *hld up in midfield: rdn over 1f out: no hdwy and wknd ins fnl f* **33/1**

6060 **15** *2 1/2* **Grand Inquisitor**[12] 9012 7-9-7 **73** ....(b) AlistairRawlinson 1 41
(Conor Dore) *chsd ldrs: rdn over 2f out: racd awkwardly and lost pl over 1f out: sn wknd (jockey said gelding stopped quickly)* **33/1**

0266 **16** *16* **Filles De Fleur**[21] 8902 3-8-9 **71** .... AlexJary(7) 8 8
(George Scott) *t.k.h: hld up in rr: sddle slipped over 6f out: lost tch 3f out: t.o (jockey said his saddle slipped)* **33/1**

2m 4.9s (-3.70) **Going Correction** -0.225s/f (Stan)
WFA 3 from 4yo+ 3lb **16** Ran SP% **130.4**
Speed ratings (Par 103): **105,103,102,101,101 100,100,98,97,97 95,93,92,90,88 75**
CSF £85.54 CT £1142.87 TOTE £8.00: £2.00, £2.30, £3.10, £7.00; EX 85.10 Trifecta £1915.50.
Owner Mrs I Corbani **Bred** Rockhart Trading Ltd **Trained** Newmarket, Suffolk

FOCUS
The two market leaders were disappointing but the winner forged clear and has resumed her progress. The second and third have been rated to form.
T/Plt: £1,674.00 to a £1 stake. Pool: £56,849.61 - 33.96 winning units. T/Qpdt: £41.30 to a £1 stake. Pool: £5,115.81 - 123.65 winning units. **Steve Payne**

9126
LINGFIELD (L-H)
Thursday, November 28

OFFICIAL GOING: Polytrack: standard

9203 BETWAY H'CAP 6f 1y(P)
12:10 (12:11) (Class 4) (0-80,80) 3-Y-O+
£5,207 (£1,549; £774; £387; £300; £300) **Stalls** Low

Form RPR

0421 **1** **Mohareb**[28] 8695 3-9-6 **79** .... AlistairRawlinson 12 89+
(Michael Appleby) *cl up on outer: led over 1f out: rdn out fnl f: comf* **9/2**[2]

135 **2** *1* **Wiley Post**[31] 8601 6-9-4 **77** ....(b) HollieDoyle 8 83
(Tony Carroll) *t.k.h: hld up in rr: pushed along and hdwy on outer over 1f out: wnt 2nd ins fnl f: r.o* **8/1**

2131 **3** *1/2* **Spirited Guest**[21] 8895 3-9-4 **77** .... TomQueally 6 81
(George Margarson) *stmbld s: midfield on outer: rdn and hdwy over 1f out: kpt on fnl f: no ex towards fin (trainer said gelding stumbled leaving the stalls; vet said gelding suffered an over-reach on his right-fore)* **9/4**[1]

1006 **4** *1 1/4* **Sonja Henie (IRE)**[50] 8023 3-8-13 **79** .... JonathanFisher(7) 4 79
(David Loughnane) *midfield: rdn 2f out: kpt on fnl f: nrst fin* **8/1**

050R **5** *hd* **Gnaad (IRE)**[19] 8946 5-8-12 **74** .... DarraghKeenan(3) 11 74
(Alan Bailey) *dwlt s: swtchd lft early: hld up in rr early: rdn and hdwy over 1f out: kpt on fnl 110yds: nt pce to chal* **33/1**

4540 **6** *hd* **Daring Venture (IRE)**[9] 9048 3-9-0 **73** .... JackMitchell 9 72
(Roger Varian) *hld up in last: stl plenty to do and pushed along 2f out: rdn and kpt on fnl f: mde no imp* **11/2**[3]

2330 **7** *hd* **Chitra**[36] 8456 3-9-5 **78** .... RichardKingscote 10 76
(Daniel Kubler) *led: rdn and hdd over 1f out: lost 2nd ins fnl f: wknd towards fin* **20/1**

3034 **8** *2* **Joegogo (IRE)**[5] 9131 4-9-3 **76** .... DavidProbert 5 68
(David Evans) *prom: rdn over 2f out: wknd ins fnl f* **10/1**

0500 **9** *nk* **Oberyn Martell**[126] 5335 3-9-2 **75** .... CharlesBishop 7 66
(Eve Johnson Houghton) *towards rr: rdn 2f out: pushed along and no imp fnl f* **25/1**

3-00 **10** *hd* **Ghost Queen**[271] 997 3-8-11 **77** .... GaiaBoni(7) 2 67
(William Jarvis) *s.i.s: in rr on inner: rdn over 2f out: wknd over 1f out* **33/1**

0010 **11** *nk* **Spring Romance (IRE)**[125] 5395 4-9-2 **75** .... JoeyHaynes 1 65
(Dean Ivory) *pressed ldrs on inner: rdn over 2f out: wknd fnl f* **8/1**

-500 **12** *11* **Laith Alareen**[43] 8267 4-9-7 **80** ....(t) DougieCostello 3 34
(Ivan Furtado) *disp ld to over 2f out: rdn and wknd over 1f out* **50/1**

1m 10.55s (-1.35) **Going Correction** -0.05s/f (Stan) **12** Ran SP% **123.2**
Speed ratings (Par 105): **107,105,105,103,103 102,102,99,99,99 98,84**
CSF £39.58 CT £106.10 TOTE £5.60: £2.00, £2.40, £1.30; EX 41.60 Trifecta £178.30.
Owner Ian Lawrence **Bred** Crossfields Bloodstock Ltd **Trained** Oakham, Rutland

FOCUS
A fair handicap. The second has been rated to this year's form.

9204 PLAY 4 TO SCORE AT BETWAY H'CAP 1m 7f 169y(P)
12:45 (12:46) (Class 6) (0-65,71) 3-Y-O+
£2,781 (£827; £413; £300; £300; £300) **Stalls** Low

Form RPR

0114 **1** **Giving Back**[20] 7558 5-10-1 **66** ....(v) DavidProbert 7 72
(Alan King) *hld up in midfield: stdy hdwy over 2f out: rdn over 1f out: styd on fnl f: led fnl stride* **7/1**

4000 **2** *nse* **Sweet Nature (IRE)**[22] 8854 4-8-10 **47** ....(p) LukeMorris 8 53
(Laura Mongan) *hld up in midfield: stdy hdwy and prom 4f out: wnt 2nd over 2f out: rdn and led ins fnl f: sn edgd lft: hdd fnl stride* **20/1**

1400 **3** *1/2* **Nafaayes (IRE)**[14] 8654 5-9-11 **62** ....(p) HollieDoyle 9 67
(Jean-Rene Auvray) *prom: rdn and led over 2f out: hdd ins fnl f: sn rallied: no ex towards fin* **4/1**[1]

2441 **4** *1/2* **Affluence (IRE)**[9] 9049 4-9-13 **71** 5ex..........................(p) JacobClark(7) 11 76
(Martin Smith) *hld up in rr: rdn and hdwy 2f out: kpt on fnl f: nrst fin* **5/1**[3]

5100 **5** *3* **Thresholdofadream (IRE)**[23] 8828 4-9-7 **58** .... JoeFanning 5 59
(Amanda Perrett) *midfield on inner: stdy hdwy gng easily whn nt clr run over 2f out: shkn up and hdwy over 1f out: no ex fnl 110yds* **6/1**

0220 **6** *2 1/4* **Continuum**[45] 8196 10-10-1 **66** ....(v) TomQueally 4 64
(Peter Hedger) *slowly away: hld up in rr: pushed along and hdwy over 1f out: kpt on fnl f: nt pce to chal* **11/1**

-000 **7** *1* **Betsalottie**[12] 9005 6-8-12 **49** ....(p) KieranO'Neill 13 46
(John Bridger) *slowly away: swtchd lft early: hld up in rr early: pushed along and outpcd 3f out: rallied over 1f out: kpt on: nt pce to chal* **50/1**

5143 **8** *1 1/4* **Percy's Prince**[22] 8854 3-8-11 **55** ....(p) KieranShoemark 10 53
(Amanda Perrett) *led after 1f: ducked rt on turn after 6f: rdn and hdd over 2f out: rdn and wknd fnl f* **11/2**

5645 **9** *nse* **Dancing Lilly**[65] 7558 4-8-9 **46** .... WilliamCarson 1 42
(Debbie Hughes) *t.k.h: led: hdd after 1f: sn pressed ldr: rdn and ev ch over 2f out: wknd over 1f out* **20/1**

0003 **10** *6* **Sea Sovereign (IRE)**[22] 8868 6-9-3 **59** .... RPWalsh(5) 3 47
(Ian Williams) *prom: dropped to midfield after 5f: rdn and outpcd on outer over 2f out: sn btn (trainers rep said, regards the poor performance, the gelding may have been unsuited by the track which, in his opinion, may be too sharp; jockey said gelding hung right-handed)* **9/2**[2]

6430 **11** *2 1/2* **Lady Natasha (IRE)**[74] 7231 6-8-4 **46** oh1..........(t) SophieRalston(5) 12 31
(James Grassick) *t.k.h: hld up in rr: rdn and outpcd over 4f out: n.d* **50/1**

/00- **12** *3 1/4* **Phoenix Dawn**[411] 6656 5-9-12 **63** ....(t) LiamKeniry 6 45
(Louise Allan) *trckd ldrs: rdn 4f out: wknd over 2f out* **40/1**

3m 28.76s (3.06) **Going Correction** -0.05s/f (Stan)
WFA 3 from 4yo+ 7lb **12** Ran SP% **121.2**
Speed ratings (Par 101): **90,89,89,89,87 86,86,85,85,82 81,79**
CSF £144.86 CT £641.45 TOTE £5.30: £2.40, £5.90, £1.80; EX 157.60 Trifecta £1603.60.
Owner Pitchall Stud Partnership & Mrs Pat Toye **Bred** Pitchall Stud **Trained** Barbury Castle, Wilts

FOCUS
A modest staying handicap.

9205 LADBROKES HOME OF THE ODDS BOOST NURSERY H'CAP 5f 6y(P)
1:20 (1:21) (Class 5) (0-75,75) 2-Y-O
£3,428 (£1,020; £509; £300; £300; £300) **Stalls** High

Form RPR

2662 **1** **Birkenhead**[35] 8506 2-9-7 **75** ....(p[1]) LewisEdmunds 9 78
(Les Eyre) *prom on outer: rdn and hdwy over 1f out: led ins fnl f: kpt on wl* **6/1**[3]

022 **2** *1/2* **Colouring**[37] 8418 2-9-4 **72** .... HectorCrouch 6 73
(Ed Walker) *midfield on outer: rdn and hdwy over 1f out: kpt on fnl f: wnt 2nd towards fin* **9/2**[2]

2100 **3** *1/2* **Heer We Go Again**[21] 8890 2-9-3 **71** ....(v) DavidProbert 7 70
(David Evans) *t.k.h: hld up in last: pushed along over 2f out: kpt on wl fnl f: wnt 3rd fnl stride (jockey said colt ran too free early)* **20/1**

0300 **4** *nse* **Silver Start**[35] 8506 2-9-4 **72** .... KieranShoemark 1 71
(Charles Hills) *led at fast pce: rdn 2f out: hdd ins fnl f: no ex and lost two pls towards fin* **25/1**

240 **5** *3/4* **Chasanda**[58] 7785 2-8-10 **71** ....(h) LauraPearson(7) 5 68
(David Evans) *chsd ldr: rdn over 2f out: lost 2nd over 1f out: no ex ins fnl 110yds* **33/1**

6650 **6** *shd* **Wilfy**[51] 7980 2-9-2 **70** .... LiamKeniry 10 67
(Sylvester Kirk) *hld up in rr: shkn up over 1f out: bit short of room ins fnl 110yds: r.o (jockey said gelding was denied a clear run)* **16/1**

526 **7** *1/2* **Rathagan**[21] 8899 2-8-10 **67** .... FinleyMarsh(3) 4 61
(Richard Hughes) *t.k.h: prom: rdn over 1f out: no ex ins fnl f* **8/1**

1445 **8** *1* **Champagne Supanova (IRE)**[44] 8219 2-8-9 **70**...(b[1]) AngusVilliers(7) 8 61
(Richard Spencer) *towards rr: rdn and hdwy over 1f out: outpcd fnl 110yds (jockey said gelding hung left-handed)* **10/1**

2306 **9** *1* **Seraphinite (IRE)**[41] 8315 2-9-6 **74** ....(p[1]) NicolaCurrie 3 65
(Jamie Osborne) *hld up in rr: pushed along over 1f out: keeping on whn repeatedly short of room ins fnl f: n.d* **14/1**

1001 **10** *1 1/4* **Colonel Whitehead (IRE)**[7] 9099 2-8-13 **74** 6ex...... EllieMacKenzie(7) 2 57
(Heather Main) *towards rr on inner: pushed along whn hmpd on turn over 1f out: sn btn* **11/8**[1]

58.9s (0.10) **Going Correction** -0.05s/f (Stan) **10** Ran SP% **118.9**
Speed ratings (Par 96): **97,96,95,95,94 93,93,91,89,87**
CSF £33.07 CT £515.96 TOTE £6.80: £1.90, £1.40, £4.00; EX 31.20 Trifecta £252.50.
Owner Sunpak Racing **Bred** Mike Channon Bloodstock Limited **Trained** Catwick, N Yorks

FOCUS
A fair nursery.

9206 BETWAY HEED YOUR HUNCH H'CAP 1m 2f (P)
1:55 (1:55) (Class 3) (0-95,93) 3-Y-O **£7,246** (£2,168; £1,084; £542; £270) **Stalls** Low

Form RPR

5600 **1** **Universal Gleam**[12] 9000 4-9-3 **89** .... CallumRodriguez 5 97+
(Keith Dalgleish) *towards rr: stdy hdwy gng easily over 2f out: nt clr run over 1f out: rdn to ld ins fnl f: sn edgd rt: sn pushed out: comf* **5/1**[2]

1506 **2** *1 1/4* **Time Change**[71] 7347 4-9-4 **90** ....(b[1]) RichardKingscote 7 95
(Ralph Beckett) *s.i.s: hld up in last: pushed along over 2f out: rdn whn short of room and swtchd lft over 1f out: wnt 2nd ins fnl 110yds: no match for wnr* **9/1**

1035 **3** *nk* **Mr Scaramanga**[12] 9003 5-9-1 **87** .... LukeMorris 2 91
(Simon Dow) *t.k.h: trckd ldrs: rdn to ld over 1f out: hdd ins fnl f: no ex and lost 2nd ins fnl 110yds* **16/1**

3-10 **4** *2* **Sky Defender**[194] 2828 3-8-10 **85** .... JoeFanning 6 85
(Mark Johnston) *s.i.s: hld up in rr on outer: hdwy and prom over 1f out: rdn and no ex whn edgd lft ins fnl f* **13/2**

2253 **5** *2 1/4* **Michele Strogoff**[10] 9041 6-8-13 **85** .... AlistairRawlinson 3 80
(Michael Appleby) *t.k.h: led: rdn and hdd 2f out: rallied and ev ch over 1f out: wknd ins fnl 110yds (jockey said gelding ran too free)* **6/1**[3]

0565 **6** *1 1/4* **El Ghazwani (IRE)**[28] 8701 4-9-0 **86** ....(t) JackMitchell 8 79
(Hugo Palmer) *cl up: wnt 2nd 1/2-way: rdn and led 2f out: hdd over 1f out: wknd ins fnl 110yds (vet said colt had been struck into on his right-hind)* **6/4**[1]

5106 **7** *1 3/4* **Lawn Ranger**[9] 9055 4-9-7 **93** .... KierenFox 1 82
(Michael Attwater) *pressed ldr to 1/2-way: sn cl up: rdn and wknd over 2f out* **7/1**

0155 **8** *nk* **Stamford Raffles**[63] 7616 6-9-1 **90** .... DarraghKeenan(3) 4 79
(Jane Chapple-Hyam) *in tch w ldrs: short of room and dropped to rr over 2f out: rdn and wknd over 1f out* **25/1**

2m 2.85s (-3.75) **Going Correction** -0.05s/f (Stan)
WFA 3 from 4yo+ 3lb **8** Ran SP% **116.5**
Speed ratings (Par 107): **113,112,111,110,108 107,105,105**
CSF £49.57 CT £672.14 TOTE £7.10: £1.80, £2.00, £2.70; EX 56.50 Trifecta £768.30.
Owner Weldspec Glasgow Limited **Bred** Mrs D O'Brien **Trained** Carluke, S Lanarks

FOCUS
The feature contest was a fairly good handicap won by the smart Franklin D in 2015. It's been rated around the well-placed third to his non-claim best over the past year.

9207 BETWAY H'CAP 1m 2f (P)
2:25 (2:26) (Class 6) (0-55,60) 3-Y-O+
£2,781 (£827; £413; £300; £300; £300) **Stalls** Low

Form RPR

0462 **1** **Gerry The Glover (IRE)**[37] 8416 7-9-6 **55** ....(p) CallumShepherd 2 63
(Lee Carter) *slowly away: midfield on inner: stdy hdwy and prom 3f out: wnt 2nd and rdn 2f out: led ins fnl f: kpt on towards fin* **16/1**

6511 **2** *nk* **Foresee (GER)**[10] 9042 6-9-3 **52** .... RobHornby 4 59
(Tony Carroll) *t.k.h: led: hdd after 1f: sn pressed ldr: led again over 2f out: rdn and hdd ins fnl f: sn rallied: kpt on towards fin* **7/4**[1]

4000 **3** *1* **Sir Gnet (IRE)**[20] 8916 5-9-6 **55**..............................(b1) KieranShoemark 6 61
(Ed Dunlop) *t.k.h: hld up in rr: nt clr run 4f out: rdn and hdwy on outer over 1f out: wnt 3rd ins fnl f: kpt on towards fin* **12/1**

4311 **4** *2 3/4* **Red Gunner**[7] 9090 5-9-6 **60** 5ex.............................. KevinLundie(5) 10 60
(Mark Loughnane) *t.k.h: hld up in rr: hdwy over 2f out: sn rdn: wnt 4th ins fnl f: sn no imp* **11/4[2]**

3142 **5** *1/2* **Pike Corner Cross (IRE)**[22] 8870 7-8-11 **53**.........(vt) LauraPearson(7) 3 52
(David Evans) *t.k.h: led after 1f: rdn and hdd over 2f out: outpcd ins fnl f* **14/1**

0054 **6** *2 1/2* **Presence Process**[26] 8756 5-9-3 **52**.............................. CharlieBennett 1 47
(Pat Phelan) *cl up: rdn over 2f out: wknd fnl f* **14/1**

066 **7** *1 1/4* **Fire Island**[27] 8718 3-9-3 **55**.............................. HollieDoyle 12 49
(Tom Ward) *t.k.h: prom: dropped to midfield after 2f: pushed along and hdwy over 2f out: wknd fr 1f out* **8/1**

6310 **8** *1 1/2* **Ramatuelle**[22] 8854 3-9-3 **55**.............................. LukeMorris 7 45
(Laura Mongan) *in rr: rdn 4f out: edgd lft and no imp fr 2f out* **33/1**

2464 **9** *nk* **Spark Of War (IRE)**[20] 8922 4-9-2 **51**..............(v) CallumRodriguez 13 40
(Keith Dalgleish) *hld up in rr on outer: outpcd and hung lft over 2f out: sme hdwy on inner over 1f out: rdn and btn fnl f* **11/2[3]**

6000 **10** *1 1/2* **Johni Boxit**[22] 8863 4-8-13 **51**..............................(v) FinleyMarsh(3) 5 37
(Brian Barr) *trckd ldrs: rdn 3f out: wknd over 1f out: sn eased (jockey said gelding moved poorly)* **66/1**

3344 **11** *6* **Mister Musicmaster**[12] 8998 10-9-2 **51**.............................. DavidProbert 8 26
(Ron Hodges) *in rr on inner: rdn 4f out: wknd fr 3f out* **20/1**

505 **12** *hd* **Never To Forget**[30] 8645 4-9-1 **55**.............................. DylanHogan(5) 9 29
(John Butler) *s.i.s: in rr: rdn and struggling over 3f out: sn wknd* **50/1**

3000 **13** *99* **Onomatopoeia**[38] 8414 5-9-6 **55**.............................. CharlesBishop 14
(Camilla Poulton) *midfield on outer: rdn and struggling fr 4f out: lost tch fr over 2f out: t.o (vet said mare was lame on it's right-fore leg)* **66/1**

2m 5.62s (-0.98) **Going Correction** -0.05s/f (Stan)
WFA 3 from 4yo+ 3lb **13 Ran SP% 129.1**
Speed ratings (Par 101): **101,100,99,97,97 95,94,93,92,91 86,86,7**
CSF £46.64 CT £387.20 TOTE £15.90: £3.60, £1.20, £3.80; EX 63.00 Trifecta £726.30.
Owner John Joseph Smith **Bred** Aidan Fogarty **Trained** Epsom, Surrey

FOCUS
A modest handicap.

9208 LADBROKES WHERE THE NATION PLAYS EBF NOVICE STKS 1m 1y(P)
3:00 (3:02) (Class 5) 2-Y-O **£3,428** (£1,020; £509; £254) **Stalls** High

Form RPR

34 **1** **Transition**[56] 7842 2-9-5 0.............................. JoeFanning 1 78
(Amanda Perrett) *mde all: pushed along and increased tempo 2f out: rdn and reduced ld ins fnl 110yds: kpt on towards fin* **4/1[2]**

32 **2** *1/2* **Naizagai**[27] 8721 2-9-5 0.............................. JackMitchell 2 77
(Roger Varian) *cl up: wnt 2nd 2f out: sn edgd lft: rdn and kpt on wl ins fnl 110yds* **4/5[1]**

3 *2 1/4* **Line Of Enquiry** 2-9-5 0.............................. PJMcDonald 12 72
(James Tate) *trckd wnr: pushed along and lost 2nd 2f out: kpt on ins fnl f: no match for first two* **10/1**

4 *3/4* **Jazz Party** 2-9-5 0.............................. KieranO'Neill 3 70
(Paul Cole) *prom: rdn over 1f out: kpt on ins fnl f: nt pce to chal* **33/1**

0 **5** *1/2* **Glorious Caesar**[84] 6905 2-9-5 0.............................. HectorCrouch 10 69+
(Ed Walker) *midfield on outer: rdn and outpcd over 2f out: rallied on outer ins fnl f: kpt on: nrst fin* **25/1**

5 **6** *nk* **Grey Fox (IRE)**[34] 8516 2-9-5 0.............................. CharlesBishop 6 68
(Emma Lavelle) *in tch w ldrs: rdn and outpcd 2f out: rallied over 1f out: no imp fnl f* **8/1[3]**

04 **7** *1/2* **Sefton Warrior**[40] 8346 2-9-5 0.............................. RobHornby 5 67
(Richard Spencer) *cl up on outer: rdn 2f out: edgd lft and no ex ins fnl f* **16/1**

8 *3/4* **Moomba (IRE)** 2-9-5 0.............................. RobertHavlin 7 65
(Amanda Perrett) *towards rr on inner: pushed along and outpcd over 2f out: rallying whn short of room ins fnl f: sn no imp* **20/1**

9 *12* **Pleasure Garden (USA)** 2-9-5 0.............................. LukeMorris 9 38
(Sir Mark Prescott Bt) *s.i.s: in rr: rdn and outpcd 3f out: sn struggling* **20/1**

10 *5* **Sparrow Hawk** 2-9-0 0.............................. CallumShepherd 4 21
(J S Moore) *s.i.s: bhd: rdn and outpcd 3f out: btn fr 2f out* **100/1**

11 *2 3/4* **Beggarman** 2-9-5 0.............................. LiamKeniry 11 20
(J S Moore) *slowly away: in rr and rn green: outpcd and hung lft over 3f out: sn btn* **100/1**

0 **12** *2* **Sir Dandy**[23] 8823 2-9-5 0.............................. JosephineGordon 8 15
(Lucy Wadham) *towards rr: pushed along 3f out: wknd over 2f out* **33/1**

1m 37.71s (-0.49) **Going Correction** -0.05s/f (Stan) **12 Ran SP% 122.9**
Speed ratings (Par 96): **100,99,97,96,96 95,95,94,82,77 74,72**
CSF £7.30 TOTE £4.60: £1.10, £1.40, £2.40; EX 9.90 Trifecta £50.60.
Owner K Abdullah **Bred** John Gunther **Trained** Pulborough, W Sussex

FOCUS
A fair juvenile novice contest.

9209 BOMBARDIER GOLDEN BEER APPRENTICE H'CAP 1m 1y(P)
3:30 (3:32) (Class 6) (0-60,59) 3-Y-O+ **£2,781** (£827; £413; £300; £300; £300) **Stalls** High

Form RPR

5450 **1** **Huddle**[86] 6844 3-8-13 **57**.............................. Pierre-LouisJamin(5) 10 63
(William Knight) *hld up in rr: rdn over 1f out: gd hdwy to ld ins fnl 110yds: kpt on wl* **8/1**

5000 **2** *nk* **The Warrior (IRE)**[37] 8422 7-9-7 **58**.............................. PaddyBradley 7 64
(Lee Carter) *midfield on inner: pushed along and hdwy on inner whn bit short of room over 1f out: rdn and ev ch ins fnl 110yds: jst hld* **8/1**

0000 **3** *1/2* **Subliminal**[35] 8499 4-9-6 **57**..............................(b) ThoreHammerHansen 2 63
(Simon Dow) *in tch w ldrs: shkn up and cl up 2f out: short of room and hmpd over 1f out: rallied ins fnl f: wnt 3rd towards fin* **4/1[1]**

0-10 **4** *1 1/4* **Brains (IRE)**[35] 8499 3-9-1 **59**..............................(b) AngusVilliers(5) 11 61+
(Jamie Osborne) *t.k.h: led: hdd whn hmpd over 2f out: hung lft and led again fr 1f out: hdd and no ex ins fnl 110yds (jockey said gelding hung left-handed under pressure)* **7/1[3]**

2505 **5** *2 1/4* **Duke Of North (IRE)**[12] 8998 7-8-5 **49**..............................(b1) IsobelFrancis(7) 8 46+
(Jim Boyle) *dwlt s: plld hrd: in rr: hdwy and prom bef 1/2-way: led over 2f out: sn edgd lft: hdd fr 1f out: wknd towards fin (jockey said gelding ran too free and hung left-handed)* **14/1**

4000 **6** *1/2* **Kodiline (IRE)**[19] 8949 5-8-12 **56**..............................(v) LauraPearson(7) 5 52
(David Evans) *blindfold off late and lost many l s: plld hrd: in rr: hdwy on outer 1/2-way: racd wd and outpcd on turn over 1f out: kpt on ins fnl f: mde no imp (jockey was slow to remove the blindfold, explaining that it had become stuck in the bridle when first attempting to remove it, at which point the gelding put his head down meaning she was slow to remove it on the second attempt)* **12/1**

2135 **7** *nk* **Vincenzo Coccotti (USA)**[28] 8711 7-8-12 **56**.........(p) GeorgeRooke(7) 3 51
(Patrick Chamings) *t.k.h: cl up: rdn over 2f out: no ex ins fnl f* **13/2[2]**

6000 **8** *1* **Cookupastorm (IRE)**[28] 8704 3-8-9 **55**..............................(t1) JacobClark(7) 6 47
(Martin Smith) *t.k.h: in rr: pushed along 2f out: sme hdwy ins fnl f: n.d* **66/1**

5000 **9** *1/2* **Calima Calling (IRE)**[20] 8924 3-9-2 **55**..............................(p1) CameronNoble 12 46
(Michael Appleby) *hld up in rr: stdy hdwy on outer over 2f out: sn pushed along: no imp over 1f out* **66/1**

4602 **10** *nk* **My Law**[12] 8998 3-8-8 **54**..............................(p) LukeCatton(7) 1 44
(Jim Boyle) *cl up on inner: rdn and outpcd over 2f out: btn fnl f* **7/1[3]**

2504 **11** *1 1/4* **Chetan**[28] 8711 7-9-1 **57**.............................. TobyEley(5) 9 45
(Tony Carroll) *prom on outer: rdn 3f out: wknd fr 2f out* **4/1[1]**

-000 **12** *1 3/4* **Sweet Jemima (USA)**[171] 3650 3-9-0 **58**..............................(w) GeorgiaDobie(5) 4 41
(William Muir) *in rr on inner: rdn over 3f out: struggling fr 2f out* **16/1**

1m 38.5s (0.30) **Going Correction** -0.05s/f (Stan)
WFA 3 from 4yo+ 2lb **12 Ran SP% 123.8**
Speed ratings (Par 101): **96,95,95,93,91 91,90,89,89,89 87,86**
CSF £73.92 CT £304.12 TOTE £10.00: £3.00, £3.40, £2.40; EX 93.40 Trifecta £573.20.
Owner Mr & Mrs N Welby **Bred** Mr & Mrs N Welby **Trained** Angmering, W Sussex

FOCUS
A modest apprentice riders' handicap.
T/Plt: £125.60 to a £1 stake. Pool: £54,459.88 - 316.47 winning units. T/Qpdt: £23.70 to a £1 stake. Pool: £6,320.68 - 196.86 winning units. **Raceform**

9170 DEAUVILLE (R-H)
Thursday, November 28

OFFICIAL GOING: Polytrack: standard

9210a PRIX LYPHARD (LISTED RACE) (3YO+) (ALL-WEATHER TRACK) (POLYTRACK) 1m 1f 110y(P)
12:50 3-Y-O+ **£23,423** (£9,369; £7,027; £4,684; £2,342)

RPR

1 **Dalgarno (FR)**[27] 8725 6-9-0 0.............................. StephanePasquier 13 98
(Jane Chapple-Hyam) *settled towards rr: shkn up 2f out: gd hdwy ins fnl f: led fnl 50yds* **247/10**

2 *snk* **Carlton Choice (IRE)**[32] 5-9-0 0..............................(p) Jean-BernardEyquem 8 98
(Laurent Loisel, France) **31/1**

3 *1 1/4* **Folamour**[179] 3389 4-9-3 0.............................. MaximeGuyon 12 98
(A Fabre, France) **84/10**

4 *shd* **Rolando (IRE)**[39] 8372 5-9-3 0.............................. MickaelBarzalona 9 98
(A Wohler, Germany) **31/5[2]**

5 *shd* **Century Dream (IRE)**[26] 8765 5-9-0 0.............................. Pierre-CharlesBoudot 11 95
(Simon Crisford) *prom early: led after 3 1/2f: wnt 2 l clr and drvn along 2f out: rdn 1f out: hdd 50yds out: no ex and dropped away* **12/5[1]**

6 *shd* **Pump Pump Palace (FR)**[51] 8010 6-9-0 0.............................. TheoBachelot 3 95
(J-P Gauvin, France) **10/1**

7 *3/4* **Stellar Mass (IRE)**[55] 7888 6-9-0 0.............................. EddyHardouin 4 93
(Carina Fey, France) **39/1**

8 *nk* **Chasselay (FR)**[37] 5-9-0 0..............................(b) MickaelBerto 7 92
(S Dehez, France) **10/1**

9 *1 1/4* **Ficelle Du Houley (FR)**[82] 6992 4-8-10 0.............................. GregoryBenoist 5 86
(Y Barberot, France) **25/1**

10 *1* **Roc Angel (FR)**[109] 5-9-0 0.............................. TonyPiccone 14 88
(F Chappet, France) **16/1**

11 *snk* **Wonnemond (GER)**[33] 8583 6-9-0 0.............................. BayarsaikhanGanbat 10 87
(S Smrczek, Germany) **49/1**

12 *1* **Nkosikazi**[28] 8710 4-8-10 0.............................. TomMarquand 2 81
(William Haggas) *led: hdd after 3 1/2f: drvn along in 2nd 3f out: rdn and wknd fnl 1 /2f* **10/1**

13 *nse* **Air Dance (FR)**[61] 3-8-11 0.............................. CristianDemuro 1 86
(J-C Rouget, France) **68/10[3]**

14 *12* **Replenish (FR)**[68] 6-9-0 0.............................. VincentCheminaud 6 61
(S Cerulis, France) **25/1**

1m 53.82s **14 Ran SP% 119.1**
WFA 3 from 4yo+ 3lb
PARI-MUTUEL (all including 1 euro stake): WIN 25.70; PLACE 7.00, 9.00, 3.90; DF 191.70.
Owner Ms Fiona Carmichael **Bred** Viktor Timoshenko **Trained** Dalham, Suffolk

9171 KEMPTON (A.W) (R-H)
Friday, November 29

OFFICIAL GOING: Polytrack: standard to slow
Wind: virtually nil Weather: dry, chilly

9211 BET AT RACINGTV.COM FILLIES' NOVICE MEDIAN AUCTION STKS 7f (P)
4:30 (4:38) (Class 6) 2-Y-O **£3,234** (£962; £481; £240) **Stalls** Low

Form RPR

1 **Queen Of All** 2-8-11 0.............................. FinleyMarsh(3) 8 75+
(Richard Hughes) *trckd ldrs: swtchd lft and effrt wl over 1f out: sn rdn: hdwy 1f out: led 75yds out: styd on strly: gng away at fin* **14/1**

2 *2* **Buy Me Back** 2-9-0 0.............................. HollieDoyle 5 70+
(Archie Watson) *led: rdn wl over 1f out: hdd 75yds out: no ex and sn outpcd* **8/13[1]**

0 **3** *2 1/4* **Amarsanaa**[29] 8706 2-9-0 0.............................. HectorCrouch 11 64
(Clive Cox) *chsd ldr: rdn over 2f out: unable qck u.p ent fnl f: lost 2nd and outpcd ins fnl f* **25/1**

4 *1/2* **Punting (IRE)** 2-9-0 0.............................. JimCrowley 3 63+
(Richard Hughes) *midfield: swtchd lft and effrt over 2f out: no imp tl hdwy ins fnl f: kpt on fnl 100yds: nvr enough pce to chal* **10/1[3]**

0 **5** *nk* **Marble Bay (IRE)**[37] 8455 2-9-0 0.............................. CliffordLee 7 62
(David Evans) *chsd ldrs: rdn over 2f out: drvn and unable qck ent fnl f: outpcd ins fnl f* **16/1**

6 **6** ½ **Shymay**[38] 8431 2-9-0 0 .... TomQueally 14 60
(George Margarson) *chsd ldrs on outer: effrt ent fnl 2f: unable qck and rn green over 1f out: outpcd ins fnl f* **20/1**

7 5 **Midnight Drift** 2-9-0 0 .... LiamKeniry 12 47
(Clive Cox) *midfield: pushed along ent fnl 3f: unable qck u.p and outpcd 2f out: wl hld after (trainer was informed that the filly could not run until the day after passing a stalls test)* **14/1**

0 **8** 1½ **Lucky Draw**[23] 8849 2-9-0 0 .... (h[1]) CallumShepherd 2 43
(Ed de Giles) *a towards rr: rdn over 2f out: outpcd 2f out and wl hld after* **33/1**

9 2¼ **Crazy Love** 2-9-0 0 .... CharlesBishop 9 37
(Mick Channon) *s.i.s: hdwy into midfield after 2f: rdn over 2f out: sn outpcd: wknd over 1f out* **33/1**

10 3¼ **Rosa Gold** 2-9-0 0 .... RobHornby 13 28
(Rae Guest) *a towards rr: pushed along 4f out: wknd 2f out* **8/1**[2]

0 **11** 2¾ **Welsh Back**[8] 9097 2-8-7 0 .... JoeBradnam(7) 10 21
(Michael Bell) *midfield: wd bnd 3f out: rdn and outpcd over 2f out: wknd over 1f out* **100/1**

12 7 **Adrued (IRE)** 2-9-0 0 .... JoeyHaynes 4 2
(Mark Usher) *s.i.s: a bhd* **100/1**

1m 27.87s (1.87) **Going Correction** +0.025s/f (Slow) **12** Ran SP% **117.8**
Speed ratings (Par 91): **90,87,85,84,84 83,77,76,73,69 66,58**
CSF £21.90 TOTE £16.40: £2.80, £1.10, £5.30; EX 34.10 Trifecta £477.90.
Owner Jaber Abdullah **Bred** Rabbah Bloodstock Limited **Trained** Upper Lambourn, Berks
■ Pretty Packet was withdrawn. Price at time of withdrawal 33/1. Rule 4 does not apply.

FOCUS
The market was only interested in one horse, but there was a turn-up.

9212 32RED ON THE APP STORE NURSERY H'CAP 1m (P)
5:00 (5:06) (Class 6) (0-65,64) 2-Y-O

£3,234 (£962; £481; £400; £400; £400) **Stalls** Low

Form RPR

2060 **1** **Moondance**[9] 9060 2-9-6 **63** .... (b[1]) HectorCrouch 5 65
(Gary Moore) *towards rr: effrt and edgd rt 2f out: rdn and hdwy over 1f out: styd on wl u.p ins fnl f: led cl home* **20/1**

005 **2** hd **Siberian Night (IRE)**[29] 8709 2-9-6 **63** .... LukeMorris 11 65+
(Ed Walker) *s.i.s: towards rr: nt clr run and swtchd rt ent fnl 2f: rdn and hdwy on inner over 1f out: led ins fnl f: rn green and hung lft in front: drvn and hdd cl home* **7/2**[1]

0605 **3** ¾ **Ask Siri (IRE)**[24] 8824 2-7-13 **47** ow2 .... AledBeech(5) 2 47
(John Bridger) *midfield: swtchd lft and effrt over 2f out: hdwy u.p over 1f out: ev ch ins fnl f: keeping on same pce and hld whn squeezed for room cl home* **16/1**

000 **4** 1 **Bee Able (USA)**[21] 8914 2-9-5 **62** .... TomMarquand 6 61
(Ralph Beckett) *s.i.s and rdn thrght: towards rr: hdwy u.p ent fnl f: clsng and swtchd lft ins fnl f: chsng ldrs whn nt clr run and hmpd towards fin* **13/2**

0030 **5** 1 **Broughtons Compass**[74] 7277 2-8-2 **45** .... HollieDoyle 7 411
(Mark Hoad) *sn chsng ldr: rdn and ev ch 2f out: led over 1f out: hdd ins fnl f: no ex and wknd towards fin* **6/1**

6106 **6** shd **Twittering (IRE)**[48] 8118 2-9-4 **61** .... (p[1]) NicolaCurrie 3 56
(Oliver Signy) *t.k.h: chsd ldrs early: stdd bk and hld up in midfield: effrt to chse ldrs 2f out: no ex ins fnl f: outpcd fnl 100yds* **8/1**

4000 **7** hd **Penny Diamond**[24] 8825 2-7-11 **45** .... SophieRalston(5) 8 40
(Amanda Perrett) *midfield: rdn over 2f out: no imp and outpcd over 1f out: rallied and kpt on ins fnl f: no threat to ldrs* **50/1**

3000 **8** hd **Looks Good (IRE)**[30] 8651 2-8-12 **58** .... (b) FinleyMarsh(3) 9 52
(Richard Hughes) *stdd after s: in rr: pushed along over 3f out: sme hdwy 1f out: kpt on ins fnl f: nvr trbld ldrs* **16/1**

0500 **9** 1½ **Love Not Money**[9] 9061 2-8-10 **56** ow2 .... MitchGodwin(3) 10 47
(John Bridger) *chsd ldr early: styd prom: rdn and outpcd over 1f out: wknd ins fnl f* **66/1**

4033 **10** 4 **Luna Wish**[10] 9044 2-9-7 **64** .... TomQueally 13 45
(George Margarson) *led: rdn and hdd over 1f out: wknd and impeded ins fnl f* **9/2**[2]

033 **11** 1½ **Annie Quickstep (IRE)**[74] 7269 2-9-5 **62** .... RobHornby 14 40
(Jonathan Portman) *nt that wl away: hdwy to chse ldrs after 2f: rdn over 2f out: lost pl over 1f out: sn wknd* **25/1**

506 **12** 8 **On The Right Track**[25] 8810 2-9-3 **60** .... (p) JoeyHaynes 12 20
(Mark Usher) *midfield on outer: rdn over 2f out: sn struggling and wknd over 1f out* **11/2**[3]

1m 40.61s (0.81) **Going Correction** +0.025s/f (Slow) **12** Ran SP% **118.3**
Speed ratings (Par 94): **96,95,95,94,93 92,92,92,91,87 85,77**
CSF £86.78 CT £1197.25 TOTE £30.50: £7.70, £1.60, £5.20; EX 203.60 Trifecta £2836.60.
Owner Shark Bay Racing Syndicate **Bred** Shark Bay Racing 1 **Trained** Lower Beeding, W Sussex
■ Stewards' Enquiry : Luke Morris two-day ban; careless riding (Dec 14, 16)

FOCUS
The pace picked up a fair way out here and that set things up for the closers.

9213 100% PROFIT BOOST AT 32REDSPORT.COM MAIDEN STKS 1m (P)
5:30 (5:35) (Class 5) 3-4-Y-O **£3,881** (£1,155; £577; £288) **Stalls** Low

Form RPR

1 **Godhead** 3-9-5 0 .... NickyMackay 9 80+
(John Gosden) *chsd ldr for 2f: styd chsng ldr: effrt and qcknd to ld 2f out: sn rdn: hld on wl ins fnl f* **8/1**

3-2 **2** nk **Sheriffmuir (USA)**[57] 7841 3-9-5 0 .... (p) RobertHavlin 10 79+
(John Gosden) *taken down early: hld up in tch in midfield: effrt and swtchd lft ent fnl 2f: hdwy jst over 1f out: wnt 2nd and pressing wnr ins fnl f: kpt on but a jst hld* **13/8**[1]

3 2 **Pledge Of Honour** 3-9-5 0 .... JoeyHaynes 8 75
(Dean Ivory) *s.i.s: sn in tch in midfield: effrt: rn green and edgd rt over 1f out: hdwy ins fnl f: kpt on wl to snatch 3rd last strides: no threat to ldrs* **33/1**

0-02 **4** nk **Qaabil (IRE)**[22] 8894 3-9-5 72 .... JimCrowley 13 74
(William Haggas) *chsd ldrs: effrt to chal 2f out: unable to match pce of wnr over 1f out: wknd and lost 2 pls ins fnl f* **5/1**[3]

42 **5** 3¼ **Qatar Queen (IRE)**[86] 6862 3-9-0 0 .... TomMarquand 7 62
(James Fanshawe) *t.k.h: led: rdn and hdd 2f out: outpcd and btn over 1f out: wknd ins fnl f* **5/2**[2]

00 **6** 1 **Melburnian**[100] 6345 3-9-0 0 .... RayDawson(5) 11 64
(Jane Chapple-Hyam) *midfield and rdn early: hdwy to chse ldr after 2f: rdn over 2f out: outpcd and btn over 1f out: wknd ins fnl f* **66/1**

7 hd **Brenbar (USA)** 3-9-5 0 .... JFEgan 3 64
(Roger Varian) *midfield: effrt over 2f out: no imp over 1f out and wl hld fnl f* **5/1**[3]

0 **8** 1¾ **Orion's Shore (IRE)**[41] 8351 3-9-5 0 .... (t[1]) NicolaCurrie 5 60
(Jamie Osborne) *s.i.s: bhd: swtchd rt and effrt over 2f out: nvr trbld ldrs* **100/1**

0006 **9** ¾ **Birthday Girl (IRE)**[106] 6116 4-9-2 38 .... (t) HollieDoyle 4 54?
(Amanda Perrett) *chsd ldrs: rdn over 2f out: struggling and outpcd over 1f out: wknd fnl f* **100/1**

50 **10** 8 **Tiffindell (IRE)**[6] 9138 3-8-11 0 .... DarraghKeenan(3) 2 35
(Robert Eddery) *midfield: rdn over 2f out: sn btn and wknd over 1f out* **150/1**

3 **11** ½ **Bella Amoura**[24] 8838 3-9-0 0 .... LiamKeniry 12 33
(Brian Barr) *stdd s: t.k.h: hld up in rr: n.d* **150/1**

12 6 **Into Debt** 3-9-5 0 .... CharlieBennett 6 25
(Camilla Poulton) *sn towards rr: last and lost tch 1/2-way* **66/1**

1m 39.18s (-0.62) **Going Correction** +0.025s/f (Slow)
WFA 3 from 4yo 2lb **12** Ran SP% **121.3**
Speed ratings (Par 103): **104,103,101,101,98 97,96,95,94,86 85,79**
CSF £21.93 TOTE £9.30: £1.90, £1.10, £9.30; EX 27.50 Trifecta £625.40.
Owner Martin Hughes & Michael Kerr-Dineen **Bred** Whitsbury Manor Stud And Mrs M E Slade **Trained** Newmarket, Suffolk

FOCUS
A fair maiden won by one of the four newcomers in the line-up. The level is a bit shaky with the well placed sixth and ninth running above expectations, but the second has been rated in line with his previous form.

9214 32RED H'CAP 6f (P)
6:00 (6:05) (Class 3) (0-90,89) 3-Y-O+

£9,337 (£2,796; £1,398; £699; £349; £175) **Stalls** Low

Form RPR

6000 **1** **Polybius**[8] 9088 8-9-7 **89** .... CallumShepherd 8 97
(David Simcock) *stdd s: hld up in rr: clsd and swtchd rt over 1f out: rdn and hdwy to ld ins fnl f: r.o wl: rdn out* **20/1**

0040 **2** ½ **Dunkerron**[41] 8350 3-9-7 **89** .... CharlesBishop 3 95
(Joseph Tuite) *midfield: swtchd lft and effrt over 2f out: hdwy u.p 1f out: r.o wl ins fnl f: wnt 2nd cl home: nt quite rch wnr* **12/1**

3234 **3** ½ **Prince Of Rome (IRE)**[76] 7187 3-8-12 **87** .... TylerHeard(7) 5 92
(Richard Hughes) *led: rdn and hrd pressed over 1f out: hdd ins fnl f: kpt on but no ex towards fin: lost 2nd cl home* **16/1**

-546 **4** shd **Sparkalot**[38] 8420 5-9-0 **82** .... LukeMorris 2 86
(Simon Dow) *midfield: swtchd rt and hdwy over 1f out: sn rdn: styd on wl ins fnl f: nt quite rch ldrs* **11/4**[1]

6323 **5** 1 **Swift Approval (IRE)**[27] 8766 7-9-0 **82** .... JimCrowley 4 83
(Stuart Williams) *chsd ldrs: wnt 2nd 2f out and sn rdn to chal: no ex 100yds out and wknd towards fin* **9/2**[2]

1514 **6** nse **Second Collection**[123] 5504 3-9-2 **84** .... (h) HollieDoyle 10 85
(Tony Carroll) *stdd s: hld up in rr: swtchd lft and effrt 2f out: styd on ins fnl f: nt rch ldrs* **12/1**

0030 **7** ¾ **Spoof**[55] 7894 4-9-5 **87** .... (h) KieranShoemark 1 86
(Charles Hills) *taken down early: t.k.h: hld up in tch in midfield on inner: effrt and swtchd rt 2f out: hdwy to chse ldrs over 1f out: no ex and wknd ins fnl f (jockey said gelding ran too free early on)* **10/1**

4540 **8** hd **Suzi's Connoisseur**[58] 7828 8-8-10 **83** .... (b) RayDawson(5) 11 81
(Jane Chapple-Hyam) *hld up in tch in midfield: rdn over 1f out: kpt on ins fnl f: nt enough pce to rch ldrs* **20/1**

55 **9** 2 **Lihou**[38] 8420 3-9-0 **82** .... TomQueally 6 74
(David Evans) *hld up towards rr: swtchd rt and hdwy 2f out: chsd ldrs 1f out: no ex and wknd ins fnl f* **7/1**[3]

001 **10** 2 **Last Page**[24] 8826 4-9-2 **84** .... TomMarquand 12 70
(Tony Carroll) *rousted along leaving stalls: sn w ldr and crossed to inner: lost 2nd 2f out and lost pl over 1f out: wknd ins fnl f* **12/1**

315 **11** ½ **Dizzy G (IRE)**[13] 9010 4-9-0 **82** .... CliffordLee 7 67
(K R Burke) *mounted in chute: midfield: rdn over 2f out: lost pl and btn over 1f out: wknd ins fnl f* **8/1**

103- **12** 1 **So Brave**[454] 6798 3-9-2 **84** .... RobHornby 9 66
(Eve Johnson Houghton) *midfield: rdn over 2f out: sn struggling and lost pl over 1f out: bhd ins fnl f* **40/1**

1m 11.63s (-1.47) **Going Correction** +0.025s/f (Slow) **12** Ran SP% **118.5**
Speed ratings (Par 107): **110,109,108,108,107 107,106,105,103,100 99,98**
CSF £236.76 CT £3957.91 TOTE £20.20: £4.80, £4.50, £4.90; EX 483.20 Trifecta £3743.30.
Owner Amo Racing Ltd & Partners **Bred** Niarchos Family **Trained** Newmarket, Suffolk

FOCUS
A competitive sprint handicap. The second has been rated in line with this year's form.

9215 32RED.COM H'CAP 1m 7f 218y(P)
6:30 (6:32) (Class 4) (0-85,86) 3-Y-O+

£6,469 (£1,925; £962; £481; £400; £400) **Stalls** Low

Form RPR

4261 **1** **Vibrance**[24] 8828 3-8-9 **70** .... HollieDoyle 2 82+
(James Fanshawe) *chsd ldng pair: swtchd lft and effrt over 2f out: hdwy and rdn to ld over 1f out: clr and styd on wl ins fnl f* **13/8**[1]

1103 **2** 2¼ **Casa Comigo (IRE)**[10] 9056 4-9-0 **68** .... KierenFox 4 75
(John Best) *t.k.h: hld up in tch in midfield: effrt over 2f out: hdwy and rdn to chse wnr ent fnl f: kpt on but no imp* **4/1**[3]

0446 **3** 3 **Dono Di Dio**[50] 8064 4-9-10 **78** .... (b) LiamKeniry 8 81
(Michael Madgwick) *t.k.h: hld up in last pair: clsd on inner jst over 2f out: swtchd lft and rdn over 1f out: chsd ldng pair ins fnl f: no imp* **20/1**

4366 **4** 8 **Pirate King**[10] 9056 4-10-0 **82** .... StevieDonohoe 3 76
(Charlie Fellowes) *midfield: hdwy to chse ldr 1/2-way: rdn and chal over 2f out: led 2f out: hdd over 1f out: sn outpcd: wknd ins fnl f* **7/2**[2]

1402 **5** 3 **Cotton Club (IRE)**[45] 7819 8-9-12 **80** .... JackMitchell 7 70
(George Boughey) *chsd ldr tl 1/2-way: dropped to midfield: rdn 4f out: outpcd over 2f out: wl btn fnl 2f* **33/1**

1100 **6** ½ **Conkering Hero (IRE)**[30] 8654 5-9-0 **75** .... LeviWilliams(7) 6 65
(Joseph Tuite) *midfield: dropped to last pair 1/2-way: rdn and outpcd over 2f out: n.d after* **33/1**

0052 **7** 4½ **Jersey Wonder (IRE)**[10] 9056 3-9-11 **86** .... TomMarquand 1 72
(Jamie Osborne) *led: rdn and hrd pressed over 2f out: hdd over 1f out: lost pl u.p over 1f out: wknd fnl f* **4/1**[3]

00-0 **8** 14 **Bear Valley (IRE)**[22] 8421 5-9-11 **79** .... (t) GeorgeWood 5 46
(Amy Murphy) *v.s.a and early reminder: clsd and in tch after 3f: hdwy into midfield 1/2-way: rdn over 2f out: sn lost pl and btn (jockey said gelding was very slowly away)* **50/1**

3m 28.45s (-1.65) **Going Correction** +0.025s/f (Slow)
WFA 3 from 4yo+ 7lb **8** Ran SP% **112.9**
Speed ratings (Par 105): **105,103,102,98,96 96,94,87**
CSF £7.94 CT £88.66 TOTE £2.20: £1.10, £1.40, £3.40; EX 8.20 Trifecta £54.70.
Owner Cheveley Park Stud **Bred** Brookside Breeders Club **Trained** Newmarket, Suffolk
■ Stewards' Enquiry : Hollie Doyle four-day ban; misuse of whip (Dec 13-14, 16, 18)

FOCUS
They didn't go much of a gallop in this staying handicap. Muddling form. The third has been rated in line with her non-claim best for the time being.

9216 JOIN RACING TV NOW H'CAP 1m 2f 219y(P)
7:00 (7:03) (Class 6) (0-60,60) 3-Y-O
£3,105 (£924; £461; £400; £400; £400) Stalls Low

Form RPR
6616 1 **Lord Howard (IRE)**[46] 8205 3-8-5 51 ....(v) GeorgeBass(7) 5 57
(Mick Channon) *midfield: lost pl and in last trio 3f out: rdn over 2f out: hdwy and swtchd lft jst over 1f out: str run to ld wl ins fnl f: sn in command* 9/1
5306 2 2 **Toybox**[43] 8291 3-9-7 60 .... RobHornby 11 62
(Jonathan Portman) *hld up in midfield: effrt over 2f out: rdn and hdwy to chal 1f out: led ins fnl f: hdd and nt gng pce of wnr wl ins fnl f* 6/1[3]
562 3 3/4 **Social City**[20] 8944 3-9-6 59 .... JFEgan 8 60
(Tony Carroll) *w ldr early: chsd ldrs after: rdn over 3f out: hdwy u.p and ev ch ins fnl f: one pce fnl 75yds* 10/1
330 4 1 **Just Once**[63] 7643 3-9-5 58 ....(p1) DanielMuscutt 12 57
(Mrs Ilka Gansera-Leveque) *swtchd rt after s: t.k.h: hld up in midfield: swtchd rt and effrt ent fnl 2f: chsd ldrs 1f out: kpt on same pce ins fnl f (jockey said filly ran too free)* 10/1
0050 5 nk **Miss Pollyanna (IRE)**[58] 7817 3-8-11 50 ....(h) RobertHavlin 1 49
(Roger Ingram) *stdd and dropped in bhd after s: hld up in rr: clsd and nt clr run over 1f out: swtchd lft ent fnl f: styd on wl ins fnl f: nt rch ldrs* 33/1
00-0 6 hd **Louisiana Beat (IRE)**[23] 8870 3-8-9 48 .... HollieDoyle 6 46
(Mike Murphy) *t.k.h: chsd ldrs: swtchd rt and effrt 2f out: ev ch u.p 1f out: no ex and wknd ins fnl f* 25/1
5423 7 3/4 **Royal Dancer**[11] 9042 3-9-0 53 .... TomMarquand 9 50
(Sylvester Kirk) *hld up in midfield: hdwy to press ldr 5f out: rdn and ev ch ent fnl 2f: drvn to ld 1f out: sn hdd & wknd fnl 100yds* 5/1[2]
4634 8 1 1/4 **Bolt N Brown**[24] 8837 3-9-7 60 ....(vt) LukeMorris 14 55
(Gay Kelleway) *t.k.h: hld up wl in tch in midfield: rdn over 3f out: stl chsng ldrs and hrd rdn over 1f out: no ex and wknd ins fnl f* 9/2[1]
0642 9 1/2 **Barbarosa (IRE)**[11] 9040 3-9-5 58 .... PhilDennis 13 52
(Michael Herrington) *rrd as stalls opened and s.i.s: hld up in last quartet: hdwy into midfield 4f out: effrt 2f out: edging rt and no hdwy over 1f out: wknd ins fnl f (jockey said gelding reared as the stalls opened)* 5/1[2]
5002 10 1/2 **Brinkleys Katie**[23] 8868 3-8-2 46 oh1 ....(v) RhiainIngram(5) 2 39
(Paul George) *t.k.h: hld up towards rr: rapid hdwy to press ldrs 4f out: rdn ent fnl 2f: lost pl: edgd rt and short of room over 1f out: wknd fnl f (jockey said filly ran too free and hung right-handed under pressure)* 8/1
5000 11 1/2 **Savoy Brown**[74] 7280 3-8-7 46 oh1 .... JohnFahy 7 38
(Michael Attwater) *t.k.h: led tl 8f out: chsd ldr tl 5f out: chsd ldrs after: rdn over 1f out: no ex and wknd ins fnl f* 20/1
5000 12 nk **Gibraltarian (IRE)**[13] 9005 3-9-1 54 ....(p1) CharlieBennett 10 46
(Jim Boyle) *w ldrs tl led 8f out: rdn ent fnl 2f: hdd 1f out: wknd ins fnl f* 25/1
0000 13 5 **Jailbreak (IRE)**[21] 8915 3-8-7 46 oh1 ....(p1) JosephineGordon 3 29
(Conrad Allen) *midfield: effrt on inner 2f out: no imp and lost pl over 1f out: wknd fnl f* 33/1
0000 14 3 3/4 **Chutzpah (IRE)**[181] 3348 3-8-7 46 ....(t) JoeyHaynes 4 22
(Mark Hoad) *a towards rr: n.d* 66/1
2m 24.54s (3.54) **Going Correction** +0.025s/f (Slow) 14 Ran SP% 124.9
Speed ratings (Par 98): **88,86,86,85,85 84,84,83,83,82 82,82,78,75**
CSF £59.95 CT £569.17 TOTE £10.50: £3.40, £2.10, £2.90; EX 73.90 Trifecta £699.50.
Owner M Channon **Bred** Mount Coote Stud **Trained** West Ilsley, Berks
FOCUS
The early pace was steady but it increased on the turn in and the winner closed from a fair way back.

9217 EVERY RACE LIVE ON RACING TV H'CAP 7f (P)
7:30 (7:33) (Class 6) (0-65,68) 3-Y-O+
£3,105 (£924; £461; £400; £400; £400) Stalls Low

Form RPR
00-4 1 **Holiday Magic (IRE)**[37] 8471 8-9-4 62 .... TomMarquand 2 69
(Lee Carter) *mde all: rdn 2f out: battled on gamely u.p ins fnl f: rdn out* 4/1[1]
4035 2 1/2 **Rock Boy Grey (IRE)**[21] 8923 4-9-6 64 ....(t1) LukeMorris 1 70
(Mark Loughnane) *chsd ldrs: wnt 2nd on inner 2f out: rdn to chal over 1f out: hrd drvn and hld fnl 100yds* 6/1[3]
5121 3 nk **Split Down South**[8] 9089 3-9-2 68 6ex .... GraceMcEntee(7) 8 72+
(Phil McEntee) *hld up in midfield on outer: hdwy to press ldrs 4f out: rdn and ev ch over 1f out: kpt on ins fnl f: unable qck towards fin* 4/1[1]
2051 4 3/4 **Violet's Lads (IRE)**[23] 8847 5-9-5 63 .... JackMitchell 6 66
(Brett Johnson) *hld up in last trio: nt clr run over 2f out: swtchd lft and hdwy over 1f out: styd on wl ins fnl f: nt rch ldrs* 5/1[2]
0641 5 nse **Champion Brogie (IRE)**[29] 8698 3-9-6 65 .... LiamKeniry 12 67
(J S Moore) *swtchd rt after s: hld up in midfield: effrt and hdwy on inner 2f out: chsd ldrs u.p 1f out: edgd lft and kpt on same pce ins fnl f* 20/1
1260 6 1 1/4 **Sonnet Rose (IRE)**[10] 9048 5-8-13 64 ....(bt) AngusVilliers(7) 11 64
(Conrad Allen) *bmpd s: in tch in midfield: rdn and hdwy to chse ldrs over 1f out: kpt on same pce ins fnl f* 16/1
0-62 7 nk **Royal Dynasty**[21] 8920 3-9-3 62 ....(h) DanielMuscutt 5 60
(James Fanshawe) *in tch in midfield: nt clrest of runs over 2f out: effrt over 1f out: kpt on same pce ins fnl f* 11/1
3013 8 1 1/4 **Penarth Pier (IRE)**[37] 8457 3-9-2 61 .... RobertHavlin 10 56
(Christine Dunnett) *wnt lft and bmpd rival leaving stalls: t.k.h: midfield on outer: effrt over 2f out: unable qck over 1f out: kpt on same pce ins fnl f* 10/1
6000 9 1 3/4 **Amor Fati (IRE)**[20] 8946 4-8-13 64 .... CameronIles(7) 13 55
(David Evans) *stdd: impeded and dropped in bhd after s: hld up in rr: swtchd lft and effrt 2f out: styd on ins fnl f: nvr trbld ldrs* 66/1
1554 10 1/2 **Swissal (IRE)**[106] 6116 4-9-4 62 ....(p) BenCurtis 4 52
(David Dennis) *midfield: effrt 2f out: no imp u.p 1f out: wknd ins fnl f* 10/1
0435 11 1/2 **Bullington Boy (FR)**[46] 8207 3-9-4 63 .... JFEgan 9 50
(Jane Chapple-Hyam) *t.k.h: hld up in midfield: effrt over 2f out: no imp u.p over 1f out: wl hld ins fnl f* 10/1
0500 12 nse **Miracle Garden**[23] 8866 7-9-7 65 ....(p) RobHornby 3 53
(Roy Brotherton) *chsd wnr tl 2f out: lost pl over 1f out: wknd ins fnl f* 50/1
-406 13 2 1/4 **Tanqeeb**[53] 7975 3-8-13 65 .... JoshuaThorman(7) 7 46
(Ian Williams) *in rr: hung lft bnd 4f out: n.d* 33/1
1m 26.43s (0.43) **Going Correction** +0.025s/f (Slow) 13 Ran SP% 123.6
WFA 3 from 4yo+ 1lb
Speed ratings (Par 101): **98,97,97,96,96 94,94,92,90,90 89,89,87**
CSF £27.97 CT £109.57 TOTE £6.10: £2.40, £2.60, £1.40; EX 38.70 Trifecta £226.40.
Owner The Emily Charlotte Partnership **Bred** Mrs Ann Fortune **Trained** Epsom, Surrey
■ Stewards' Enquiry : Liam Keniry three-day ban; careless riding (Dec 13-14, 16)
FOCUS
A modest affair and the pace was controlled by the winner.

9218 32RED CASINO H'CAP 6f (P)
8:00 (8:01) (Class 5) (0-70,70) 3-Y-O
£3,752 (£1,116; £557; £400; £400; £400) Stalls Low

Form RPR
0344 1 **Phoenix Star (IRE)**[22] 8896 3-8-9 58 ....(t1) BenCurtis 3 65
(Stuart Williams) *bmpd leaving stalls: in tch in midfield: rdn and hdwy over 1f out: str chal ins fnl f: led wl ins fnl f: r.o wl* 6/1
560 2 1/2 **Good Answer**[27] 8755 3-8-9 65 .... AngusVilliers(7) 4 70
(Robert Cowell) *towards rr: hdwy on inner 2f out: ev ch u.p ins fnl f: kpt on wl* 25/1
2012 3 nse **True Belief (IRE)**[45] 8217 3-9-3 66 ....(h) JackMitchell 8 71
(Brett Johnson) *swtchd rt after s: hld up towards rr: rdn and gd hdwy over 1f out: ev ch 1f out: led ins fnl f: sn hdd: kpt on wl* 8/1
2510 4 nk **Lordsbridge Boy**[8] 9089 3-9-2 65 .... JoeyHaynes 5 69+
(Dean Ivory) *bmpd leaving stalls: sn led: rdn 2f out: drvn and hdd ins fnl f: kpt on but no ex cl home* 4/1[2]
0030 5 3 1/2 **Bugler Bob (IRE)**[28] 8712 3-9-7 70 .... JasonHart 7 63
(John Quinn) *midfield: n.m.r over 1f out: kpt on same pce u.p ins fnl f* 10/1
5034 6 3/4 **Devils Roc**[44] 8254 3-9-6 69 .... RobHornby 1 59
(Jonathan Portman) *chsd ldrs: drvn to chse ldr but unable qck over 1f out: wknd ins fnl f* 11/2[3]
5500 7 1 3/4 **Gilt Edge**[29] 8702 3-9-2 68 .... MitchGodwin(3) 11 53
(Christopher Mason) *bhd and rdn 1/2-way: edgd rt and hdwy ent fnl f: kpt on: nvr trbld ldrs* 33/1
004 8 2 1/4 **Moveonup (IRE)**[101] 6325 3-8-13 62 .... LukeMorris 6 40
(Gay Kelleway) *chsd ldrs: shkn up 2f out: drvn and unable qck over 1f out: wknd ins fnl f* 25/1
2144 9 nse **Knockabout Queen**[43] 8296 3-9-4 67 .... KierenFox 12 44
(Tony Carroll) *hld up in tch in last quartet: rdn over 2f out: no imp over 1f out and wl hld ins fnl f* 25/1
2600 10 1 **Arishka (IRE)**[28] 8715 3-9-6 69 ....(b1) LiamKeniry 9 43
(Daniel Kubler) *chsd ldr tl over 1f out: lost pl and btn 1f out: wknd ins fnl f* 50/1
2552 11 7 **Hassaad**[7] 9106 3-9-7 70 .... HollieDoyle 10 22+
(Archie Watson) *chsd ldrs on outer: rdn over 2f out: lost pl qckly and btn over 1f out: bhd ins fnl f (jockey said filly stopped quickly)* 7/4[1]
1m 12.04s (-1.06) **Going Correction** +0.025s/f (Slow) 11 Ran SP% 122.7
Speed ratings (Par 102): **108,107,107,106,102 101,98,95,95,94 85**
CSF £153.25 CT £1243.74 TOTE £7.70: £2.20, £5.40, £1.80; EX 133.60 Trifecta £2046.80.
Owner Flying High Syndicate **Bred** Caroline, Mark & Stephanie Hanly **Trained** Newmarket, Suffolk
FOCUS
A modest sprint run at a good gallop. It's been rated around the third and fourth's previous C&D form.
T/Plt: £569.00 to a £1 stake. Pool: £92,871.40 - 119.13 winning units. T/Qpdt: £143.60 to a £1 stake. Pool: £12,358.34 - 63.68 winning units. **Steve Payne**

9179 SOUTHWELL (L-H)
Friday, November 29

OFFICIAL GOING: Fibresand: standard
Wind: Virtually nil Weather: Fine & dry

9219 BETWAY H'CAP 4f 214y(F)
12:55 (12:56) (Class 6) (0-65,64) 3-Y-O+
£2,781 (£827; £413; £300; £300; £300) Stalls Centre

Form RPR
3115 1 **Young Tiger**[24] 8840 6-9-2 59 ....(h) AndrewMullen 2 69
(Tom Tate) *t.k.h: hld up towards far side: swtchd rt and hdwy 1/2-way: sn chsng ldrs: rdn to chal over 1f out: drvn: edgd lft and led ins fnl f: kpt on wl towards fin* 4/1[2]
350U 2 1 3/4 **Honey Gg**[31] 8643 4-9-5 62 .... PaulMulrennan 3 66
(Declan Carroll) *racd towards far side: cl up: rdn to ld 1 1/2f out: drvn ent fnl f: sn hdd and kpt on same pce* 10/3[1]
3415 3 1 1/2 **Skeetah**[31] 8643 3-9-6 63 .... JasonHart 1 61
(John Quinn) *racd towards far side: cl up: rdn to take slt ld 2f out: sn hdd and drvn: kpt on same pce fnl f* 6/1[3]
0501 4 3/4 **Loulin**[22] 8898 4-8-8 51 ....(t) JamesSullivan 10 47+
(Ruth Carr) *awkward s: cl up towards stands' side: slt ld 3f out: rdn along over 2f out: sn hdd and drvn: grad wknd* 15/2
0600 5 hd **Red Stripes (USA)**[8] 9092 7-8-12 62 ....(b) Pierre-LouisJamin(7) 7 57
(Lisa Williamson) *racd towards stands' side: prom: led after 1f: hdd 3f out: cl up and rdn over 2f out: drvn over 1f out: grad wknd* 10/1
6025 6 2 1/2 **It Must Be Faith**[7] 9106 9-8-10 60 ....(p) ErikaParkinson(7) 4 46
(Michael Appleby) *in tch centre: lost pl and detached bef 1/2-way: hdwy 2f out: styd on wl fnl f: nrst fin (jockey said gelding hung right-handed and did not face the kickback)* 16/1
3326 7 1 1/4 **Piazon**[24] 8840 8-9-4 61 ....(be) GrahamLee 8 42
(Julia Brooke) *dwlt and towards rr centre: rdn along and hdwy 2f out: kpt on fnl f: n.d* 11/1
6000 8 hd **Gupta**[8] 9092 3-9-3 60 ....(t1) CamHardie 9 41
(David Brown) *racd towards stands' side: prom: rdn along over 2f out: sn drvn and wknd* 40/1
3003 9 3/4 **Decision Maker (IRE)**[24] 8840 5-9-1 58 .... LewisEdmunds 13 36+
(Roy Bowring) *racd nr stands' rail: led 1f: cl up: rdn along over 2f out: sn drvn and wknd* 10/1
0356 10 3 **Ebitda**[20] 8943 5-8-10 60 ....(b1) JonathanFisher(7) 6 27
(Scott Dixon) *chsd ldrs centre: rdn along 2f out: sn wknd* 25/1
6103 11 2 **Tan**[8] 9092 5-9-4 61 ....(b1) DavidProbert 5 21
(Lisa Williamson) *chsd ldrs: rdn along over 2f out: sn wknd* 14/1
0500 12 6 **George Dryden (IRE)**[8] 9089 7-9-7 64 .... DannyBrock 11
(Denis Quinn) *s.i.s and a bhd* 100/1
57.73s (-1.97) **Going Correction** -0.30s/f (Stan) 12 Ran SP% 115.5
Speed ratings (Par 101): **103,100,97,96,96 92,90,89,88,83 80,71**
CSF £16.95 CT £76.65 TOTE £4.10: £1.60, £1.70, £2.50; EX 21.30 Trifecta £90.50.
Owner T T Racing **Bred** Mrs J McMahon & Mickley Stud **Trained** Tadcaster, N Yorks
■ Stewards' Enquiry : Jonathan Fisher one-day ban: weighing in at 2 lbs overweight (Dec 13)

FOCUS
A modest sprint handicap. The first three horses home were drawn low with the race developing centrally.

9220 BOMBARDIER BRITISH HOPPED AMBER BEER (S) H'CAP 7f 14y(F)
1:30 (1:31) (Class 6) (0-55,53) 3-6-Y-O

£2,781 (£827; £413; £300; £300; £300) **Stalls** Low

Form RPR

4-43 **1** **Al Batal**[42] 8327 6-9-6 **52**.. BarryMcHugh 6 58
(Adrian Nicholls) *trckd ldrs: hdwy and cl up 1/2-way: led 3f out: rdn wl over 1f out: strly pressed and drvn ins fnl f: hld on wl towards fin* **3/1**[2]

0556 **2** *hd* **Reshaan (IRE)**[11] 9035 4-8-8 **45**..................(b) ThoreHammerHansen(5) 7 50
(Alexandra Dunn) *hld up: hdwy 1/2-way: chsd ldrs over 2f out: rdn to chal over 1f out: drvn and ev ch ins fnl f: no ex towards fin* **15/2**[3]

3603 **3** *1 1/2* **Sea Shack**[20] 8942 5-8-10 **47**..............................(tp) DylanHogan(5) 11 49
(Julia Feilden) *trckd ldrs: hdwy on outer 3f out: sn cl up: rdn along on outer to chal wl over 1f out: ev ch tl drvn and kpt on same pce fnl f* **8/1**

200 **4** *nk* **Crazy Spin**[44] 8270 3-9-4 **51**..............................(p) CallumRodriguez 1 51
(Ivan Furtado) *prom on inner: pushed along 3f out: rdn over 2f out: drvn wl over 1f out: kpt on same pce (vet said filly had a wound on its left fore)* **20/1**

0005 **5** *1* **Lady Carduros (IRE)**[21] 8915 5-8-6 **45**..................(p) AngusVilliers(7) 5 43
(Michael Appleby) *dwlt and in rr: hdwy on inner 2f out: sn rdn: styd on fnl f (jockey said mare hung left-handed)* **25/1**

3623 **6** *nk* **Elysee Star**[11] 9035 4-9-1 **47**..(p) JasonHart 10 44
(Mark Walford) *chsd ldrs: rdn along and outpcd 1/2-way: plugged on u.p fnl 2f: n.d* **2/1**[1]

6-00 **7** *shd* **Palazzo**[134] 5099 3-9-0 **47**..(t[1]) GrahamLee 8 43
(Bryan Smart) *dwlt and in rr: sn swtchd wd and bhd: rdn along 1/2-way: hdwy over 2f out: kpt on fnl f: nrst fin* **25/1**

46 **8** *1/2* **Dixieland (IRE)**[42] 8301 3-9-4 **51**................................ DanielTudhope 12 46
(Marjorie Fife) *in tch: hdwy on outer to chse ldrs 1/2-way: rdn along 2f out: grad wknd* **9/1**

0000 **9** *hd* **Mountain Of Stars**[44] 8269 4-8-8 **45**................(p) FayeMcManoman(5) 3 40
(Suzzanne France) *in rr: effrt and sme hdwy 2f out: sn rdn and n.d* **100/1**

0045 **10** *5* **One Last Hug**[25] 8819 4-8-6 **45**................................ CoreyMadden(7) 9 27
(Jim Goldie) *a towards rr* **12/1**

0604 **11** *6* **Hasili Filly**[25] 8819 3-8-12 **45**.. CamHardie 2 11
(Lawrence Mullaney) *chsd ldrs: rdn along 3f out: sn wknd* **33/1**

5000 **12** *7* **Cominginonmonday (IRE)**[22] 8901 4-8-13 **45**................. KieranO'Neill 4
(Robyn Brisland) *a towards rr* **100/1**

0000 **13** *1 1/2* **Staplegrove (IRE)**[41] 8345 4-9-7 **53**......................(b[1]) DougieCostello 13
(Stella Barclay) *qckly away and led: rdn along and jnd over 3f out: sn hdd & wknd (jockey said gelding stopped quickly)* **8/1**

1m 29.06s (-1.24) **Going Correction** -0.30s/f (Stan)
WFA 3 from 4yo+ 1lb **13 Ran SP% 127.4**
Speed ratings: **95,94,93,92,91 91,91,90,90,84 77,69,68**
CSF £26.15 CT £173.96 TOTE £4.00: £1.50, £2.30, £2.70; EX 27.60 Trifecta £176.30.There was no bid for the winner.
Owner M Goggin **Bred** Wood Hall Stud **Trained** Sessay, N Yorks
■ Stewards' Enquiry : Dylan Hogan two-day ban: used whip above the permitted level (Dec 13-14)

FOCUS
A moderate selling handicap.

9221 BETWAY LIVE CASINO H'CAP 1m 4f 14y(F)
2:00 (2:01) (Class 5) (0-75,76) 4-Y-0+

£3,428 (£1,020; £509; £300; £300; £300) **Stalls** Low

Form RPR

3306 **1** **Contingency Fee**[11] 9033 4-8-5 **63**..............................(p) GraceMcEntee(7) 6 72
(Phil McEntee) *cl up: led 1/2-way: rdn over 2f out: clr over 1f out: kpt on strly (trainer said, regarding the apparent improvement in form, the gelding was able to gain an easy lead from a wide draw and was able to dominate in a small field)* **10/1**

3010 **2** *5* **Restive (IRE)**[11] 9033 6-9-7 **72**..............................(t) AlistairRawlinson 2 73
(Michael Appleby) *hld up towards rr: hdwy 4f out: trckd ldng pair over 2f out: rdn to chse wnr wl over 1f out: drvn and no imp fnl f (jockey said gelding hung left-handed throughout)* **11/4**[1]

5562 **3** *6* **Sociologist (FR)**[30] 8664 4-8-9 **60**..............................(p) BarryMcHugh 3 51
(Scott Dixon) *trckd ldng pair: hdwy to chse wnr over 3f out: rdn wl over 2f out: drvn wl over 1f out: kpt on one pce* **7/2**[2]

656- **4** *1 1/2* **L'Inganno Felice (FR)**[41] 1408 9-9-11 **76**.......................... PaulMulrennan 1 65
(Iain Jardine) *t.k.h: trckd ldrs on inner: swtchd rt and effrt 4f out: rdn along to chse ldrs 3f out: sn drvn and one pce* **9/2**[3]

2044 **5** *1* **Apache Blaze**[22] 8904 4-8-8 **59**.. KieranO'Neill 5 46
(Robyn Brisland) *hld up in rr: sme hdwy over 3f out: rdn along over 2f out: n.d (jockey said filly hung left-handed throughout)* **5/1**

1150 **6** *12* **Deinonychus**[23] 8862 8-9-1 **69**..............................(h) TheodoreLadd(3) 7 37
(Michael Appleby) *trckd ldrs: pushed along on outer over 4f out: rdn over 3f out: sn outpcd* **7/1**

0003 **7** *3* **Doctor Jazz (IRE)**[22] 8904 4-8-7 **58** oh2........................... RaulDaSilva 4 21
(Michael Appleby) *led: pushed along and hdd 1/2-way: rdn over 4f out: drvn over 3f out and sn wknd* **12/1**

2m 36.63s (-4.37) **Going Correction** -0.30s/f (Stan) **7 Ran SP% 113.0**
Speed ratings (Par 103): **102,98,94,93,93 85,83**
CSF £36.79 TOTE £11.50: £4.00, £1.90; EX 39.30 Trifecta £204.80.
Owner M Hall **Bred** Whitwell Bloodstock **Trained** Newmarket, Suffolk

FOCUS
A fair middle-distance handicap. A clear pb from the winner.

9222 BETWAY EBF BUCCANEER CONDITIONS STKS 1m 4f 14y(F)
2:35 (2:35) (Class 3) 3-Y-0+ **£9,337** (£2,796; £1,398; £699) **Stalls** Low

Form RPR

3112 **1** **Bo Samraan (IRE)**[20] 8948 3-8-12 92................................ JoeFanning 3 97+
(Mark Johnston) *mde all: pushed along over 2f out: rdn and clr ent fnl f: readily* **8/15**[1]

0362 **2** *1 3/4* **Jabbaar**[31] 8633 6-9-3 87..(p) TomEaves 4 91
(Iain Jardine) *hld up: hdwy 3f out: rdn to chse wnr wl over 1f out: drvn and no imp fnl f* **9/1**

6202 **3** *1 3/4* **Busy Street**[9] 9065 7-9-3 93.. AngusVilliers(7) 2 95
(Michael Appleby) *trckd ldng pair: pushed along and hdwy on inner over 3f out: rdn to chal wl over 2f out: drvn wl over 1f out: kpt on same pce* **4/1**[2]

-004 **4** *17* **Sevenna Star (IRE)**[64] 7615 4-9-3 97..........................(t) PaulMulrennan 1 61
(John Ryan) *sn trcking wnr: cl up over 7f out: pushed along over 4f out: rdn over 3f out: drvn and wknd over 2f out* **8/1**[3]

2m 36.47s (-4.53) **Going Correction** -0.30s/f (Stan)
WFA 3 from 4yo+ 5lb **4 Ran SP% 106.3**
Speed ratings (Par 107): **103,101,100,89**
CSF £5.52 TOTE £1.60; EX 4.30 Trifecta £5.40.
Owner Jaber Abdullah **Bred** Sunderland Holdings Inc **Trained** Middleham Moor, N Yorks

FOCUS
The feature race was a good little middle-distance conditions contest. The strong favourite won with authority. His winning time was slightly quicker than the previous C&D handicap from off his own initially modest gallop. It's been rated around the second.

9223 BETWAY HEED YOUR HUNCH H'CAP 6f 16y(F)
3:10 (3:11) (Class 5) (0-70,70) 4-Y-0+

£3,428 (£1,020; £509; £300; £300; £300) **Stalls** Low

Form RPR

1113 **1** **Queen Of Kalahari**[21] 8924 4-9-0 **63**..............................(p) LewisEdmunds 2 72
(Les Eyre) *trckd ldr on inner: cl up 3f out: rdn to take slt ld appr fnl f: kpt on strly* **11/4**[1]

4465 **2** *1 1/4* **Private Matter**[20] 8943 5-9-4 **67**..(p) JasonHart 4 72
(Amy Murphy) *trckd ldng pair: hdwy on outer and cl up 3f out: rdn 2f out: ev ch: drvn ins fnl f: kpt on* **7/1**[3]

0002 **3** *4* **First Excel**[24] 8839 7-9-0 **63**..............................(b) AlistairRawlinson 8 55
(Roy Bowring) *led: jnd and rdn 3f out: drvn over 1f out: hdd appr fnl f: grad wknd* **5/1**[2]

5210 **4** *1/2* **Eponina (IRE)**[37] 8471 5-9-1 **67**................................ TheodoreLadd(3) 3 58
(Michael Appleby) *in tch: pushed along and hdwy on outer over 2f out: rdn wl over 1f out: kpt on u.p fnl f* **8/1**

0004 **5** *shd* **Rock Of Estonia (IRE)**[20] 8946 4-9-2 **70**.................. DylanHogan(5) 7 60
(Michael Squance) *chsd ldrs: rdn along wl over 2f out: drvn wl over 1f out: kpt on same pce* **8/1**

0341 **6** *1/2* **Global Humor (USA)**[7] 9106 4-8-3 **59**...................... CoreyMadden(7) 5 48
(Jim Goldie) *s.i.s and bhd: tk clsr order 1/2-way: rdn over 2f out: drvn over 1f out: no imp (jockey said gelding was slowly away)* **11/4**[1]

2002 **7** *1* **Burtonwood**[21] 8925 7-8-9 **58**.. BarryMcHugh 1 43
(Julie Camacho) *trckd ldrs on inner: pushed along 3f out: rdn over 2f out: sn wknd* **11/1**

1m 14.29s (-2.21) **Going Correction** -0.30s/f (Stan) **7 Ran SP% 113.1**
Speed ratings (Par 103): **102,100,95,94,94 93,92**
CSF £22.08 CT £89.87 TOTE £3.70: £1.60, £3.90; EX 22.00 Trifecta £102.80.
Owner Les Eyre Racing Partnership I **Bred** Minster Stud **Trained** Catwick, N Yorks

FOCUS
A modest handicap. The winner has been rated close to her old best.

9224 BOMBARDIER GOLDEN BEER H'CAP 7f 14y(F)
3:45 (3:47) (Class 5) (0-70,74) 4-Y-0+

£3,428 (£1,020; £509; £300; £300; £300) **Stalls** Low

Form RPR

3311 **1** **Silverturnstogold**[2] 9180 4-8-10 **65** 5ex.............(b) ElishaWhittington(7) 4 72
(Tony Carroll) *trckd ldng pair on inner: hdwy 3f out: styd cl to inner rail home st: cl up over 2f out: rdn to ld 1 1/2f out: kpt on strly fnl f* **13/8**[1]

2343 **2** *1* **Break The Silence**[2] 9180 5-8-9 **57**..............................(b) BarryMcHugh 1 61
(Scott Dixon) *cl up: slt ld 1/2-way: rdn along in centre over 2f out: hdd 1 1/2f out: sn drvn: kpt on* **4/1**[2]

3142 **3** *2 1/4* **Poeta Brasileiro (IRE)**[20] 8946 4-9-1 **68**.....(t) ThoreHammerHansen(5) 6 66
(Henry Spiller) *trckd ldrs: hdwy 3f out: rdn along over 2f out: drvn and edgd lft over 1f out: kpt on same pce* **9/1**

0033 **4** *1* **Liamba**[20] 8946 4-9-5 **67**..(v) DanielTudhope 7 62
(David O'Meara) *slt ld: hdd 1/2-way: cl up in centre over 2f out: sn rdn: drvn wl over 1f out: grad wknd* **5/1**[3]

5343 **5** *5* **Dream World (IRE)**[35] 8521 4-9-10 **72**................(p[1]) AlistairRawlinson 2 54
(Michael Appleby) *chsd ldrs: rdn along 3f out: drvn over 2f out: no hdwy* **14/1**

1506 **6** *3/4* **Compass Point**[30] 8669 4-8-13 **61**.. KieranO'Neill 5 41
(Robyn Brisland) *dwlt and swtchd wd sn after s: hdwy to chse ldrs on outer over 3f out: rdn along wl over 2f out: sn drvn and wknd* **16/1**

4300 **7** *6* **Harbour Vision**[10] 9054 4-9-10 **72**..............................(v) LewisEdmunds 3 36
(Derek Shaw) *a in rr* **8/1**

1m 27.09s (-3.21) **Going Correction** -0.30s/f (Stan) **7 Ran SP% 108.4**
Speed ratings (Par 103): **106,104,102,101,95 94,87**
CSF £7.17 CT £35.85 TOTE £2.10: £1.10, £2.70; EX 8.10 Trifecta £30.20.
Owner A A Byrne **Bred** Anthony Byrne **Trained** Cropthorne, Worcs

FOCUS
An ordinary handicap. The second has been rated to his recent best.

9225 BOMBARDIER "MARCH TO YOUR OWN DRUM" H'CAP 1m 13y(F)
4:15 (4:18) (Class 6) (0-55,55) 3-Y-0+

£2,781 (£827; £413; £300; £300; £300) **Stalls** Low

Form RPR

0460 **1** **Motahassen (IRE)**[58] 7830 5-9-7 **54**..............................(t) PaulMulrennan 6 66+
(Declan Carroll) *trckd ldrs: smooth hdwy 3f out: led 1 1/2f out: sn rdn clr: readily* **11/1**

0034 **2** *7* **The Retriever (IRE)**[35] 8530 4-8-12 **45**................................ GrahamLee 12 41
(Micky Hammond) *cl up: effrt to ld wl over 2f out: sn jnd and rdn: hdd 1 1/2f out: kpt on: no ch w wnr* **6/1**[3]

0004 **3** *3 1/4* **Face Like Thunder**[20] 8942 4-9-0 **47**..............................(be) DannyBrock 9 36
(John Butler) *dwlt and in rr: sn pushed along: hdwy into midfield 1/2-way: wd st: rdn over 2f out: styd on wl fnl f* **25/1**

6044 **4** *1 1/2* **Sooqaan**[11] 9035 8-9-4 **51**..(p) CamHardie 5 36
(Antony Brittain) *trckd ldrs: hdwy 3f out: rdn along over 2f out: drvn wl over 1f out: one pce* **8/1**

2203 **5** *nk* **Mister Freeze (IRE)**[20] 8949 5-9-5 **52**..............................(vt) DavidProbert 2 36
(Patrick Chamings) *in tch: hdwy to chse ldrs and pushed along over 3f out: rdn over 2f out: sn drvn and no imp (jockey said gelding was never travelling)* **7/2**[1]

6060 **6** *2 1/2* **Adashelby (IRE)**[27] 8756 3-9-6 **55**.. KieranO'Neill 10 33
(John Ryan) *sn slt ld: pushed along over 3f out: rdn and hdd wl over 2f out: drvn and wknd wl over 1f out* **20/1**

6006 **7** *3 1/4* **Azets**[113] 5864 3-9-3 **55**.. PaddyBradley(3) 3 25
(Jane Chapple-Hyam) *chsd ldrs: rdn along 3f out: sn drvn and wknd* **8/1**

5662 **8** *6* **Ritchie Star (IRE)**[21] 8922 3-9-6 **55**..............................(p[1]) AndrewMullen 4 11
(Ben Haslam) *in tch: rdn along 3f out: sn wknd* **4/1**[2]

-062 **9** *hd* **Odds On Oli**[170] 3720 4-9-4 **54**.. ConnorMurtagh(3) 7 11
(Richard Fahey) *a towards rr* **11/1**

-000 **10** 3½ **Candesta (USA)**[259] 1214 9-9-1 **53**.............................. DylanHogan(5) 1 2
(Julia Feilden) *a towards rr (jockey said gelding hung right-handed in the straight)* **40/1**
0660 **11** 4 **Berties Mission (USA)**[11] 9028 3-9-6 **55**..................(t[1]) LewisEdmunds 11
(Derek Shaw) *a towards rr* **66/1**
5505 **12** 1¼ **Maerchengarten**[11] 9034 3-8-12 **47**.............................. JaneElliott 14
(Ed de Giles) *prom on outer: chsd ldng pair 1/2-way: rdn along over 3f out: sn wknd* **40/1**
0250 **13** 2¼ **Limerick Lord (IRE)**[20] 8942 7-9-0 **47**......................(p) ShelleyBirkett 13
(Julia Feilden) *chsd ldrs on outer rdn along and wd st: sn wknd* **20/1**
0005 **14** 2 **Goldfox Grey**[20] 8944 3-8-12 **47**..............................(h) TomEaves 8
(Robyn Brisland) *chsd ldrs: rdn along over 3f out: sn wknd* **33/1**

1m 40.43s (-3.27) **Going Correction** -0.30s/f (Stan)
WFA 3 from 4yo+ 2lb **14** Ran SP% **118.1**
Speed ratings (Par 101): **104,97,93,92,91 89,86,80,80,76 72,71,69,67**
CSF £68.63 CT £1667.01 TOTE £13.40: £3.80, £2.20, £8.80; EX 91.70 Trifecta £1577.10.
Owner Mrs Sarah Bryan **Bred** Diomed Bloodstock Ltd **Trained** Malton, N Yorks

FOCUS
A moderate handicap. A career best from the winner.
T/Plt: £84.20 to a £1 stake. Pool: £66,326.08 - 574.93 winning units T/Qpdt: £10.60 to a £1 stake. Pool: £5,211.16 - 362.96 winning units **Joe Rowntree**

9226 - 9241a (Foreign Racing) - See Raceform Interactive

9203
LINGFIELD (L-H)
Saturday, November 30

OFFICIAL GOING: Polytrack: standard
Weather: Fine

9242 LADBROKES HOME OF THE ODDS BOOST NOVICE MEDIAN AUCTION STKS 7f 1y(P)
11:25 (11:28) (Class 5) 2-Y-O **£4,140** (£1,232; £615; £307) **Stalls** Low

Form RPR
0302 **1** **Odyssey Girl (IRE)**[44] 8297 2-8-12 **78**.............. AngusVilliers(7) 8 77
(Richard Spencer) *chsd ldrs: rdn to ld ins fnl f: r.o* **6/1**
0532 **2** ½ **Bendy Spirit (IRE)**[7] 9137 2-9-3 **73**.............................. PaulMulrennan 6 74
(Richard Fahey) *led 6f out: rdn and hdd ins fnl f: styd on* **7/4**[1]
224 **3** 1¼ **Fanzone (IRE)**[116] 5780 2-9-3 **81**.............................. HollieDoyle 7 70
(Archie Watson) *pushed along and prom: chsd ldr 6f out: rdn over 2f out: lost 2nd 1f out: styd on same pce wl ins fnl f* **5/1**[3]
00 **4** 2½ **Blessed (IRE)**[38] 8460 2-9-3 **0**.............................. DavidProbert 5 64+
(Henry Candy) *hld up in tch: plld hrd: rdn and hung lft over 1f out: styd on same pce ins fnl f* **9/1**
0 **5** 1 **Prince Percy**[29] 8721 2-9-3 **0**.............................. LiamKeniry 11 61
(Gary Moore) *hld up: hdwy and hung lft over 1f out: sn rdn: nt rch ldrs* **25/1**
00 **6** 1¾ **Nikolayeva**[22] 8913 2-8-12 **0**.............................. LukeMorris 4 52+
(Sir Mark Prescott Bt) *s.i.s: hld up: shkn up over 3f out: r.o ins fnl f: nvr nrr* **66/1**
4233 **7** *nse* **Hello Baileys**[29] 8714 2-9-3 **75**.............................. JasonHart 9 57
(Mark Johnston) *led 1f: chsd ldrs: rdn over 1f out: styd on same pce* **7/2**[2]
00 **8** *shd* **Amicia**[30] 8706 2-8-5 **0**.............................. GraceMcEntee(7) 13 51
(Marco Botti) *s.i.s: hld up: styd on fr over 1f out: nvr trbld ldrs* **25/1**
0 **9** 1 **Hong Kong Dragon**[3] 9174 2-8-10 **0**.............................. AlexJary(7) 12 54+
(George Scott) *hld up: racd wd: hung rt over 2f out: nvr on terms* **50/1**
00 **10** 2 **Lord Chapelfield**[5] 9155 2-9-3 **0**.............................. JackMitchell 10 49
(Amy Murphy) *hld up: shkn up over 2f out: n.d* **66/1**
06 **11** ½ **Celtic Mist (IRE)**[10] 9062 2-8-12 **0**.............................. JosephineGordon 2 44
(Shaun Keightley) *s.i.s: sn mid-div: nt clr run and lost pl over 2f out: n.d after* **50/1**
0 **12** 7 **Tidal Racer**[51] 8059 2-9-3 **0**.............................. HectorCrouch 1 29
(Clive Cox) *s.i.s: a in rr* **8/1**
00 **13** 2¼ **May Happen**[10] 9062 2-8-12 **0**.............................. NicolaCurrie 3 18
(Jamie Osborne) *chsd ldrs over 4f* **66/1**
00 **14** 2¼ **Heer I Am**[24] 8865 2-9-3 **0**..............................(v) JFEgan 14 17
(Paul George) *s.i.s: racd keenly: hdwy on outer 5f out: rdn and wknd over 2f out (jockey said colt hung right-handed throughout)* **66/1**

1m 23.91s (-0.89) **Going Correction** -0.05s/f (Stan) **14** Ran SP% **128.2**
Speed ratings (Par 96): **103,102,101,98,97 95,94,94,93,91 90,82,80,77**
CSF £17.36 TOTE £5.70: £1.70, £1.10, £2.00; EX 17.90 Trifecta £60.70.
Owner Mrs Emma Cunningham **Bred** Guy O'Callaghan **Trained** Newmarket, Suffolk

FOCUS
Not a particularly deep novice event with the winner rated 78 and conceding weight all round. The first three home filled those positions throughout. It's been rated around the first two.

9243 LADBROKES WHERE THE NATION PLAYS MAIDEN AUCTION STKS 1m 1y(P)
11:55 (11:59) (Class 5) 2-Y-O **£4,140** (£1,232; £615; £307) **Stalls** High

Form RPR
32 **1** **Urban Hero (IRE)**[71] 7416 2-9-4 **0**..............................(b[1]) HollieDoyle 1 75
(Archie Watson) *prom and sn pushed along: chsd ldr over 2f out: sn hung rt: shkn up to ld over 1f out: rdn clr* **8/13**[1]
0266 **2** 5 **Mr Shady (IRE)**[39] 8448 2-9-4 **0**..............................(p) LiamKeniry 2 64
(J S Moore) *s.i.s: sn prom: nt clr run and swtchd rt over 2f out: rdn over 1f out: styd on to go 2nd nr fin* **9/2**[2]
0 **3** ½ **Ever Amber (IRE)**[24] 8848 2-8-12 **0**.............................. RobHornby 6 56
(Jonathan Portman) *hld up: hdwy over 1f out: styd on to go 3rd nr fin* **50/1**
0 **4** *nk* **Platinum Prince**[36] 8518 2-9-2 **0**.............................. HectorCrouch 9 60
(Gary Moore) *prom: chsd ldr 6f out tl led over 2f out: sn rdn: hdd over 1f out: no ex ins fnl f* **16/1**
0 **5** 1½ **Dancing Girl (FR)**[68] 7515 2-9-0 **0**.............................. GeorgeWood 8 54
(Harry Dunlop) *chsd ldrs: outpcd over 2f out: styd on ins fnl f* **33/1**
5 **6** *nk* **Soramond (GER)**[24] 8855 2-8-12 **0**.............................. KieranShoemark 4 52
(Ed Dunlop) *s.i.s: in rr: hung lft and styd on fr over 1f out: nvr on terms (jockey said filly was slowly away and hung left-handed in the straight)* **7/1**[3]
0 **7** *hd* **Beggarman**[2] 9208 2-9-2 **0**.............................. JFEgan 5 55
(J S Moore) *hld up in tch: reminders over 4f out: styd on same pce fr over 1f out* **50/1**
50 **8** ¾ **Doctor Nuno**[71] 7406 2-9-4 **0**.............................. DougieCostello 10 55
(Mark Loughnane) *stdd s: hld up: hmpd over 3f out: styd on ins fnl f: nvr nrr* **16/1**
6 **9** 2¼ **Stealth Command**[60] 7787 2-9-2 **0**.............................. TomQueally 3 48
(Murty McGrath) *hld up: swtchd rt over 3f out: rdn and lost pl over 2f out* **16/1**
5 **10** 21 **Golden Times (SWI)**[167] 3881 2-8-12 **0**.............................. JasonHart 7
(Mark Johnston) *led over 5f: sn wknd* **10/1**

1m 37.77s (-0.43) **Going Correction** -0.05s/f (Stan) **10** Ran SP% **126.2**
Speed ratings (Par 96): **100,95,94,94,92 92,92,91,89,68**
CSF £4.18 TOTE £1.20: £1.10, £1.50, £12.00; EX 4.20 Trifecta £113.80.
Owner Clipper Logistics **Bred** Newtown Anner Stud **Trained** Upper Lambourn, W Berks

FOCUS
A weak maiden, even for the time of year, and Urban Hero came home alone despite not setting a particularly high standard with his RPR of 81.

9244 BOMBARDIER GOLDEN BEER H'CAP 1m 1y(P)
12:30 (12:33) (Class 5) (0-69,70) 3-Y-O+ **£4,140** (£1,232; £615; £307; £300; £300) **Stalls** High

Form RPR
6005 **1** **Roman Spinner**[31] 8652 4-9-5 **67**..............................(t) RobHornby 5 78
(Rae Guest) *pushed along early in rr: racd wd turning for home: hdwy and hung lft 1f out: str run on to ld wl ins fnl f: comf* **9/2**[1]
5300 **2** 1¾ **Puerto Banus**[7] 9140 3-9-0 **69**.............................. RPWalsh(5) 4 75
(Ian Williams) *s.i.s: hld up: hdwy on outer over 2f out: rdn and ev ch wl ins fnl f: styd on* **6/1**[2]
5413 **3** ½ **Takeonefortheteam**[31] 8652 4-9-3 **65**.............................. DougieCostello 12 71
(Mark Loughnane) *stdd s: sn swtchd lft: hld up: nt clr run and r.o ins fnl f: wnt 3rd towards fin* **8/1**
6440 **4** ¾ **Jack Berry House**[65] 7609 3-9-1 **65**..............................(t[1] w) JackMitchell 10 68
(George Boughey) *led: rdn over 1f out: hdd and unable qck wl ins fnl f* **8/1**
236 **5** 1¾ **A Place To Dream**[30] 8698 3-8-11 **61**.............................. JosephineGordon 7 60
(Mike Murphy) *hld up in tch: outpcd over 2f out: styng on whn hmpd wl ins fnl f* **14/1**
4460 **6** ¾ **Black Medick**[31] 8652 3-9-3 **67**.............................. HectorCrouch 8 64
(Laura Mongan) *chsd ldrs: rdn over 1f out: no ex ins fnl f* **20/1**
3110 **7** ½ **Zefferino**[11] 9047 5-9-8 **70**..............................(t) GeorgeWood 2 67
(Martin Bosley) *s.i.s: hld up: hdwy over 1f out: no ex ins fnl f* **6/1**[2]
4150 **8** 2½ **Redemptive**[11] 9048 3-9-1 **65**.............................. LukeMorris 3 55
(Phil McEntee) *sn chsng ldrs: wnt 2nd over 2f out: rdn and hung lft over 1f out: wknd wl ins fnl f* **20/1**
12-0 **9** 1¼ **Red Armour**[140] 4922 3-9-3 **67**.............................. KieranO'Neill 6 55
(Luke McJannet) *chsd ldr over 5f out: wknd fnl f* **25/1**
3310 **10** *nk* **De Little Engine (IRE)**[7] 9140 5-9-7 **69**.............................. RobertHavlin 9 57
(Alexandra Dunn) *hld up: shkn up over 1f out: n.d* **25/1**
004 **11** 3¾ **Sassoon**[28] 8761 3-9-5 **69**..............................(b) DavidProbert 1 47
(Paul Cole) *hld up in tch: pushed along 1/2-way: rdn over 2f out: wknd fnl f* **9/2**[1]
2500 **12** 2 **Scorched Breath**[36] 8521 3-9-4 **68**..............................(h) StevieDonohoe 11 42
(Charlie Fellowes) *hld up: rdn over 3f out: nvr on terms (trainer's rep could offer no explanation for the gelding's performance)* **13/2**[3]

1m 36.84s (-1.36) **Going Correction** -0.05s/f (Stan)
WFA 3 from 4yo+ 2lb **12** Ran SP% **124.4**
Speed ratings (Par 103): **104,102,101,101,99 98,98,95,94,93 90,88**
CSF £30.96 CT £217.28 TOTE £3.50: £1.30, £2.00, £2.80; EX 43.30 Trifecta £299.90.
Owner Reprobates Too **Bred** Ashbrittle Stud **Trained** Newmarket, Suffolk

FOCUS
Not many in-form contenders in this modest handicap but they went a decent gallop and plenty still had a chance off the home turn. The third helps set the level.

9245 BETWAY H'CAP 6f 1y(P)
1:05 (1:10) (Class 5) (0-73,75) 3-Y-O+ **£4,140** (£1,232; £615; £307; £300; £300) **Stalls** Low

Form RPR
1333 **1** **Luis Vaz De Torres (IRE)**[79] 7128 7-9-6 **71**.............. PaulMulrennan 7 79
(Richard Fahey) *chsd ldrs: rdn and r.o to ld wl ins fnl f* **9/2**[2]
0-02 **2** *nk* **Aloysius Lilius (IRE)**[15] 8985 3-9-1 **66**..............................(p) LiamKeniry 5 73
(Gerard O'Leary, Ire) *a.p: chsd ldr 1/2-way: led 1f out: rdn and hdd wl ins fnl f* **7/1**
5506 **3** ¾ **Alicia Darcy (IRE)**[56] 7914 3-9-5 **70**..............................(b) AdamMcNamara 9 75+
(Archie Watson) *s.i.s: in rr: r.o ins fnl f: nt rch ldrs (jockey said filly was slowly away)* **25/1**
2542 **4** 1 **Something Lucky (IRE)**[28] 8755 7-9-6 **71**.............................. RobertHavlin 11 72
(Michael Attwater) *hld up: hdwy over 1f out: styd on same pce wl ins fnl f* **14/1**
3156 **5** *nk* **Amor Kethley**[9] 9089 3-8-8 **62**..............................(vt[1]) GabrieleMalune(3) 3 62
(Amy Murphy) *hld up: hdwy over 1f out: nt clr run sn after: styd on same pce wl ins fnl f* **16/1**
1431 **6** 1¾ **Fiery Breath**[3] 9185 4-9-4 **69** 5ex..............................(h) WilliamCarson 10 64
(Robert Eddery) *sn prom: swtchd lft over 5f out: nt clr run wl over 1f out: sn rdn: no ex wl ins fnl f* **11/4**[1]
3455 **7** ½ **Grey Galleon (USA)**[99] 6401 5-8-9 **67**..............................(b[1]) AmeliaGlass(7) 1 60
(Clive Cox) *hld up: r.o ins fnl f: nt trble ldrs* **9/1**
3516 **8** ¾ **Captain Dion**[11] 9048 6-9-10 **75**..............................(b) LukeMorris 4 66
(Ivan Furtado) *led: rdn and hdd 1f out: sn edgd rt and no ex* **6/1**[3]
0200 **9** *nk* **Shining**[7] 9131 3-9-7 **72**.............................. CharlieBennett 8 62
(Jim Boyle) *prom: rdn over 1f out: lost pl over 2f out: n.d after (vet said filly had been struck into on its right hind)* **40/1**
-106 **10** 1¾ **Briyouni (FR)**[143] 4786 6-9-1 **66**.............................. RobHornby 2 50
(Ralph Beckett) *s.i.s: nvr on terms* **16/1**
6462 **11** *nk* **Sandridge Lad (IRE)**[35] 8550 3-9-6 **71**.............................. StevieDonohoe 6 54
(John Ryan) *chsd ldr to 1/2-way: rdn over 1f out: wknd fnl f* **7/1**

1m 10.66s (-1.24) **Going Correction** -0.05s/f (Stan) **11** Ran SP% **118.9**
Speed ratings (Par 103): **106,105,104,103,102 100,99,98,98,96 95**
CSF £36.58 CT £716.67 TOTE £5.40: £2.00, £2.50, £9.50; EX 42.70 Trifecta £989.10.
Owner Lets Go Racing 1 **Bred** Peter Molony **Trained** Musley Bank, N Yorks

FOCUS
Reasonably competitive for the grade and they went what appeared an even gallop. The second has been rated to his 3yo form.

9246 #BETYOURWAY AT BETWAY H'CAP (DIV I) 6f 1y(P)
1:40 (1:44) (Class 6) (0-59,58) 3-Y-O+ **£3,169** (£943; £471; £300; £300; £300) **Stalls** Low

Form RPR
3364 **1** **The Lacemaker**[7] 9128 5-9-2 **56**..............................(p) DarraghKeenan(3) 7 63
(Milton Harris) *trckd ldrs: wnt 2nd over 4f out: led over 2f out: rdn out* **4/1**[2]
5144 **2** 1½ **Dandilion (IRE)**[52] 8018 6-9-1 **52**.............................. NicolaCurrie 9 55+
(Alex Hales) *wnt rt s: hld up: rn wd 2f out: rdn and r.o ins fnl f: wnt 2nd nr fin: no ch w wnr (jockey said mare jumped right leaving the stalls)* **12/1**

2510 **3** *nk* **Terri Rules (IRE)**[23] 8896 4-9-6 **57**.................................. DanielMuscutt 1 59
(Lee Carter) *stdd s: hld up: hdwy over 1f out: r.o* **9/1**

50 **4** *nk* **Papa Delta**[7] 9128 5-9-7 **58**.................................. DavidProbert 4 59
(Tony Carroll) *chsd ldrs: rdn over 1f out: styd on same pce wl ins fnl f* **6/4**[1]

0023 **5** *hd* **Halle's Harbour**[23] 8896 3-9-6 **57**..................................(v) LukeMorris 2 57
(Paul George) *hld up: hdwy on outer over 3f out: rdn over 1f out: styd on same pce wl ins fnl f* **9/1**

0000 **6** *3/4* **Te Amo Te Amo**[5] 9161 3-8-13 **50**..................................(h[1]) HectorCrouch 8 48
(Simon Dow) *hld up: r.o ins fnl f: nvr nrr* **8/1**[3]

0406 **7** *2 1/4* **Autumn Splendour (IRE)**[7] 9135 3-9-4 **55**..................(b) RaulDaSilva 5 46
(Milton Bradley) *chsd ldr tl over 4f out: remained handy: rdn over 1f out: no ex ins fnl f* **12/1**

0001 **8** *2 1/2* **Hollander**[30] 8697 5-9-2 **53**..................................(bt) RobertHavlin 3 37
(Alexandra Dunn) *s.i.s: hld up: nvr on terms (jockey said gelding was slightly slow away and unsuited by being unable to race prominently on this occasion)* **10/1**

0026 **9** *3* **Flowing Clarets**[31] 8649 6-8-4 **46**.................................. RhiainIngram(5) 6 21
(Roger Ingram) *sn led: racd freely: hdd over 2f out: wknd fnl f (jockey said mare ran too free)* **33/1**

1m 11.7s (-0.20) **Going Correction** -0.05s/f (Stan) **9** Ran SP% **118.5**
Speed ratings (Par 101): **99,97,96,96,95 94,91,88,84**
CSF £52.22 CT £416.31 TOTE £4.40: £1.70, £3.40, £3.20; EX 54.50 Trifecta £320.70.
Owner Mrs Dawn Scott **Bred** S A R L Srl **Trained** Warminster, Wiltshire

FOCUS
A weak handicap won by a decisive move by Darragh Keenan around the home turn.

9247 #BETYOURWAY AT BETWAY H'CAP (DIV II) 6f 1y(P)
2:15 (2:19) (Class 6) (0-59,57) 3-Y-O+
£3,169 (£943; £471; £300; £300; £300) **Stalls** Low

Form RPR
0040 **1** **Knockout Blow**[22] 8917 4-9-3 **53**..................................(p) HectorCrouch 6 60
(John E Long) *s.i.s: hld up: hdwy on outer 2f out: rdn to ld ins fnl f: r.o* **4/1**[2]

5200 **2** *1 3/4* **Porto Ferro (IRE)**[45] 8242 5-9-4 **54**..................................(t) KieranO'Neill 3 56
(John Bridger) *chsd ldrs: rdn to ld over 1f out: hdd ins fnl f: styd on same pce* **10/3**[1]

6042 **3** *1 3/4* **Tilsworth Rose**[12] 9034 5-8-11 **47**..................................(b) RaulDaSilva 5 44
(J R Jenkins) *chsd ldr 1f: remained handy: nt clr run over 2f out: rdn over 1f out: styd on same pce ins fnl f* **7/1**

1103 **4** *3/4* **Wild Flower (IRE)**[22] 8917 7-9-1 **51**..................................(p) EoinWalsh 7 45
(Luke McJannet) *chsd ldr 5f out: rdn and ev ch over 1f out: no ex ins fnl f* **6/1**

50-U **5** *4 1/2* **Temple Road (IRE)**[323] 179 11-9-7 **57**..................................(bt) PhilipPrince 9 38
(Milton Bradley) *s.s: hdwy over 1f out: wknd ins fnl f* **25/1**

0600 **6** *3/4* **Angel Force (IRE)**[9] 9089 4-9-7 **57**..................................(p) TomQueally 4 36
(David C Griffiths) *led: rdn and hdd over 1f out: wknd ins fnl f* **5/1**[3]

0140 **7** *shd* **Kinglami**[66] 7576 10-9-7 **57**..................................(p) LukeMorris 1 35
(John O'Shea) *chsd ldrs: pushed along 1/2-way: wknd fnl f* **9/1**

4636 **8** *4 1/2* **Canimar**[223] 1969 4-8-2 **45**..................................(p) GavinAshton(7) 2 10
(Shaun Keightley) *hld up: plld hrd: hdwy over 1f out: nt clr run and eased ins fnl f (jockey said filly hung badly left-handed and was difficult to steer)* **6/1**

1m 11.76s (-0.14) **Going Correction** -0.05s/f (Stan) **8** Ran SP% **114.7**
Speed ratings (Par 101): **98,95,93,92,86 85,85,79**
CSF £17.82 CT £89.31 TOTE £5.30: £1.60, £1.30, £2.50; EX 22.00 Trifecta £98.70.
Owner Mrs S Colville **Bred** Christopher & Annabelle Mason **Trained** Brighton, East Sussex

FOCUS
A weak handicap won by an inconsistent 53-rated gelding, so hardly form to get excited about. They did at least go a decent clip. The winner has been rated in line with his best to date for John Long.

9248 BOMBARDIER BRITISH HOPPED AMBER BEER H'CAP (DIV I) 7f 1y(P)
2:50 (2:53) (Class 6) (0-57,56) 3-Y-O+
£3,169 (£943; £471; £300; £300; £300) **Stalls** Low

Form RPR
4000 **1** **Mont Kiara (FR)**[30] 8704 6-9-7 **56**.................................. LukeMorris 4 62
(Simon Dow) *hld up: swtchd rt and hdwy over 1f out: rdn and r.o to ld nr fin* **11/1**

6250 **2** *3/4* **Brigand**[24] 8864 4-9-6 **55**.................................. JoeyHaynes 3 59
(John Butler) *led 1f: chsd ldr tl led again 2f out: rdn over 1f out: hdd nr fin* **11/2**

0005 **3** *nk* **Flora Tristan**[7] 9128 4-9-6 **55**..................................(t) LiamKeniry 8 58
(Ivan Furtado) *s.i.s: hld up: plld hrd: hdwy over 1f out: r.o (jockey said filly ran too free)* **4/1**[3]

4 *2* **Newgirlintown (IRE)**[29] 8732 3-9-1 **51**..................(p[1]) StevieDonohoe 6 48
(Gerard O'Leary, Ire) *prom: shkn up and hung lft fr over 1f out: styd on same pce ins fnl f* **5/2**[1]

0000 **5** *1 1/4* **The British Lion (IRE)**[7] 9128 4-9-5 **54**..................(v) RobertHavlin 11 49
(Alexandra Dunn) *chsd ldrs: rdn and hung lft over 1f out: no ex ins fnl f* **12/1**

4322 **6** *3/4* **Red Skye Delight (IRE)**[67] 7550 3-9-2 **52**..................(p[1]) KieranO'Neill 2 44
(Luke McJannet) *led 6f out: rdn and hdd 2f out: wknd ins fnl f* **11/4**[2]

6004 **7** *2 1/4* **Swiper (IRE)**[14] 9001 3-8-7 **50**..................................(bt) KateLeahy(7) 1 36
(John O'Shea) *chsd ldrs: rdn and nt clr run over 1f out: wknd ins fnl f* **25/1**

0000 **8** *1 1/4* **Tintern Spirit (IRE)**[59] 7812 3-8-9 **45**..................(t w) RaulDaSilva 7 28
(Milton Bradley) *prom: stdd and lost pl 6f out: rdn over 1f out: wknd fnl f* **100/1**

00-0 **9** *7* **River Cafe (IRE)**[318] 257 4-8-9 **47**.................................. MitchGodwin(3) 10 13
(John Bridger) *hld up: a in rr: wknd over 2f out* **33/1**

-500 **10** *6* **Runaiocht (IRE)**[269] 1032 9-8-6 **46**.................................. RPWalsh(5) 5
(Brian Forsey) *s.s: a in rr: wknd over 2f out (jockey said gelding was slowly away)* **33/1**

1m 24.64s (-0.16) **Going Correction** -0.05s/f (Stan)
WFA 3 from 4yo+ 1lb **10** Ran SP% **117.4**
Speed ratings (Par 101): **98,97,96,94,93 92,89,88,80,73**
CSF £68.79 CT £296.01 TOTE £13.00: £2.60, £2.10, £1.30; EX 67.60 Trifecta £256.50.
Owner J C G Chua **Bred** Guy Pariente Holding Sprl **Trained** Epsom, Surrey
■ Stewards' Enquiry : Mitch Godwin one-day ban: weighing in 2lbs overweight (Dec 14)

FOCUS
Typically uncompetitive. The second and third help pin a straightforward level.

9249 BOMBARDIER BRITISH HOPPED AMBER BEER H'CAP (DIV II) 7f 1y(P)
3:25 (3:28) (Class 6) (0-57,57) 3-Y-O+
£3,169 (£943; £471; £300; £300; £300) **Stalls** Low

Form RPR
2342 **1** **Prince Rock (IRE)**[5] 9160 4-8-11 **46**.................................. LukeMorris 9 56
(Simon Dow) *s.i.s: hld up: swtchd rt and hdwy 2f out: rdn to ld and hung lft ins fnl f: r.o wl* **11/4**[2]

2404 **2** *3* **Maazel (IRE)**[24] 8847 5-9-6 **55**.................................. DanielMuscutt 10 58
(Lee Carter) *s.i.s: hld up: hdwy and nt clr run over 1f out: carried lft ins fnl f: styd on same pce* **4/1**[3]

500 **3** *3/4* **Your Choice**[23] 8896 4-9-5 **54**..................................(b[1]) HectorCrouch 6 54
(Laura Mongan) *prom: racd keenly: rdn to ld 1f out: sn hung lft and hdd: styd on same pce* **16/1**

4352 **4** *nk* **Pearl Spectre (USA)**[5] 9157 8-8-10 **52**..................(p) GraceMcEntee(7) 3 51
(Phil McEntee) *chsd ldrs: led over 1f out: hdd 1f out: styd on same pce* **9/4**[1]

064 **5** *nk* **Painted Dream**[51] 8071 3-9-7 **57**.................................. TomQueally 4 54
(George Margarson) *s.i.s: hld up: r.o ins fnl f: nt trble ldrs* **8/1**

4200 **6** *1/2* **Flying Sakhee**[39] 8417 6-8-10 **45**..................................(p) KieranO'Neill 2 42
(John Bridger) *chsd ldrs: nt clr run over 2f out: rdn whn hmpd over 1f out: styd on same pce* **25/1**

1400 **7** *1* **Haraz (IRE)**[39] 8417 6-8-8 **50**.................................. GeorgeRooke(7) 8 44
(Paddy Butler) *hld up: hung rt over 2f out: nvr on terms* **33/1**

006 **8** *1/2* **Satchville Flyer**[24] 8864 8-8-12 **47**.................................. RaulDaSilva 5 40
(Milton Bradley) *hld up: hdwy over 1f out: wknd ins fnl f* **25/1**

6405 **9** *3/4* **Gulland Rock**[21] 8949 8-8-10 **45**.................................. WilliamCarson 7 36
(Anthony Carson) *chsd ldr tl led 2f out: rdn and hdd over 1f out: wknd ins fnl f* **12/1**

4166 **10** *1 3/4* **Arctic Flower (IRE)**[14] 8998 6-8-9 **49**.................................. AledBeech(5) 1 35
(John Bridger) *sn led: hdd 2f out: wknd fnl f* **14/1**

1m 24.4s (-0.40) **Going Correction** -0.05s/f (Stan)
WFA 3 from 4yo+ 1lb **10** Ran SP% **119.4**
Speed ratings (Par 101): **100,96,95,95,95 94,93,92,91,89**
CSF £14.35 CT £150.75 TOTE £3.30: £1.70, £1.40, £4.20; EX 15.80 Trifecta £139.50.
Owner Mark McAllister **Bred** Thomas Heatrick **Trained** Epsom, Surrey
■ Stewards' Enquiry : William Carson two-day ban: interference & careless riding (Dec 14, 16)

FOCUS
Weak fare but a rewarding success for the connections of Prince Rock who has hit the crossbar time after time but this was finally to be his day. The third suggests this is a sensible starting point for the ratings.
T/Plt: £66.20 to a £1 stake. Pool: £52,757.35 - 581.59 winning units T/Qpdt: £33.80 to a £1 stake. Pool: £4,556.45 - 99.60 winning units **Colin Roberts**

9162 WOLVERHAMPTON (A.W) (L-H)
Saturday, November 30

OFFICIAL GOING: Tapeta: standard
Wind: Almost nil Weather: Misty

9250 LADBROKES, HOME OF THE ODDS BOOST NURSERY H'CAP 1m 1f 104y (Tp)
4:50 (4:52) (Class 5) (0-75,72) 2-Y-O
£3,428 (£1,020; £509; £400; £400; £400) **Stalls** Low

Form RPR
0040 **1** **Locked N' Loaded**[67] 7548 2-9-3 **68**.................................. BarryMcHugh 4 75+
(Tim Fitzgerald) *prom: led over 1f out: styd on wl* **25/1**

0236 **2** *2 3/4* **Eventful**[28] 8760 2-9-7 **72**..................................(b[1]) JackMitchell 5 74
(Hugo Palmer) *hld up: hdwy on outer over 2f out: rdn to chse wnr and edgd lft ins fnl f: styd on same pce* **15/2**

0013 **3** *1/2* **Goddess Of Fire**[24] 8859 2-8-4 **55**..................................(p) AdrianMcCarthy 7 57+
(John Ryan) *hld up: hdwy: nt clr run and swtchd rt over 1f out: r.o to go 3rd post: nt rch ldrs (jockey said filly was denied a clear run approaching the final furlong)* **25/1**

603 **4** *hd* **Gibraltar (IRE)**[23] 8889 2-9-5 **70**.................................. CallumShepherd 3 70
(Michael Bell) *sn prom: shkn up over 3f out: rdn and nt clr run over 1f out: styd on same pce ins fnl f* **5/4**[1]

5331 **5** *5* **Treaty Of Dingle**[12] 9037 2-8-13 **64**.................................. TomMarquand 8 55
(Hughie Morrison) *sn chsng ldrs: wnt 2nd over 5f out tl led over 2f out: rdn and hdd over 1f out: wknd ins fnl f* **4/1**[2]

0302 **6** *nk* **Genever Dragon (IRE)**[8] 9110 2-9-7 **72**..................(p) RichardKingscote 1 62
(Tom Dascombe) *led: hdd 7f out: chsd ldr tl over 5f out: hung lft fr over 3f out: rdn over 1f out: wknd ins fnl f* **6/1**[3]

0044 **7** *3 1/4* **Prestigious (IRE)**[37] 8493 2-8-4 **55**..................................(p) HollieDoyle 2 39
(Archie Watson) *w ldr: led 7f out tl over 2f out: sn rdn: wknd fnl f* **16/1**

045 **8** *1* **Got The T Shirt**[43] 8302 2-9-3 **68**.................................. CallumRodriguez 6 50
(Keith Dalgleish) *s.i.s: hld up: rdn: hung lft and wknd over 1f out* **13/2**

1m 58.95s (-1.85) **Going Correction** -0.225s/f (Stan) **8** Ran SP% **117.4**
Speed ratings (Par 96): **99,96,96,95,91 91,88,87**
CSF £202.79 CT £4707.66 TOTE £31.20: £5.70, £2.50, £3.90; EX 226.10 Trifecta £1661.40.
Owner Star Sports Bloodstock **Bred** Nick Bradley Bloodstock **Trained** Norton, N Yorks

FOCUS
A modest nursery. Straightforward, limited form.

9251 LADBROKES WHERE THE NATION PLAYS NOVICE STKS 5f 21y (Tp)
5:20 (5:23) (Class 5) 2-Y-O £3,428 (£1,020; £509; £254) **Stalls** Low

Form RPR
23 **1** **Agent Shiftwell**[9] 9099 2-9-3 0.................................. PJMcDonald 7 73
(Stuart Williams) *mde all: racd freely: rdn out* **4/5**[1]

34 **2** *1/2* **Autumn Trail**[66] 7569 2-8-12 0.................................. JFEgan 8 66
(Rae Guest) *a.p: chsd wnr 1/2-way: rdn over 1f out: r.o* **12/1**

34 **3** *2 1/4* **East Of Eden (IRE)**[113] 5906 2-8-12 0..................................(h[1]) JackMitchell 11 58
(Hugo Palmer) *s.i.s: hld up: pushed along and hdwy 1/2-way: styd on to go 3rd wl ins fnl f* **5/1**[2]

10 **4** *1 1/4* **Rosa (IRE)**[50] 8097 2-9-2 0.................................. ConnorMurtagh(3) 6 61
(Richard Fahey) *chsd wnr to 1/2-way: rdn over 1f out: no ex ins fnl f* **11/2**[3]

5 **5** *1* **Lady Melody (IRE)**[166] 3927 2-8-12 0..................................(h[1]) ShaneGray 1 50
(David O'Meara) *hld up in tch: plld hrd: nt clr run over 3f out: shkn up over 1f out: styd on same pce fnl f* **12/1**

00 **6** *shd* **Gypsy Traveller**[24] 8865 2-9-3 0.................................. CliffordLee 5 55
(Kevin Frost) *hld up: hdwy and swtchd lft over 1f out: styd on same pce fnl f* **50/1**

The Form Book Flat 2019, Raceform Ltd, Newbury, RG14 5SJ

64 **7** 2 **Marina Grove (IRE)**[12] 9036 2-8-12 0 DuranFentiman 3 42
(Tim Easterby) *hld up: shkn up 1/2-way: nvr on terms* 33/1

5 **8** nse **Tattletime (USA)**[12] 9036 2-8-9 0 (t[1]) ThomasGreatrex(3) 10 42
(David Loughnane) *chsd ldrs: pushed along 1/2-way: wknd fnl f* 50/1

0 **9** 1/2 **Chocolaat Heer**[9] 9099 2-9-3 0 JasonHart 2 45
(John Quinn) *s.i.s: hld up: n.d* 100/1

10 1 **Bring The Money (IRE)** 2-9-3 0 CallumShepherd 9 42
(Mick Channon) *s.i.s: outpcd (jockey said gelding hung right-handed throughout)* 14/1

11 2 3/4 **Dreamboat Girl (IRE)** 2-8-12 0 ShaneKelly 4 27
(Rae Guest) *s.i.s: outpcd (jockey said filly was slowly away)* 25/1

1m 0.71s (-1.19) **Going Correction** -0.225s/f (Stan) 11 Ran SP% **121.4**
Speed ratings (Par 96): **100,99,95,93,92 91,88,88,87,86 81**
CSF £12.53 TOTE £1.60: £1.10, £2.80, £1.60; EX 11.10 Trifecta £40.80.
Owner J W Parry **Bred** J W Parry **Trained** Newmarket, Suffolk

FOCUS
An ordinary novice.

9252 LADBROKES "PLAY 1-2-FREE" ON FOOTBALL EBF NOVICE STKS (PLUS 10 RACE) 7f 36y (Tp)
5:50 (5:57) (Class 4) 2-Y-O £4,851 (£1,443; £721; £360) Stalls High

Form RPR

0 **1** **Angelic Time (IRE)**[38] 8460 2-9-5 0 HollieDoyle 3 77+
(Ed Vaughan) *chsd ldrs: swtchd rt over 1f out: hung lft and led ins fnl f: rdn out* 4/1[2]

6 **2** 1/2 **Borstal Bull (IRE)**[36] 8511 2-9-5 0 BenCurtis 9 75
(Phillip Makin) *hld up: racd keenly: hdwy and hung lft over 1f out: swtchd rt ins fnl f: r.o: nt rch wnr* 9/1

52 **3** 1 1/4 **Emirates Currency**[28] 8751 2-9-5 0 AdamKirby 4 72
(Clive Cox) *sn led: rdn over 1f out: hdd ins fnl f: styd on same pce* 11/10[1]

4 shd **Amazing News** 2-9-5 0 (h[1]) CallumShepherd 1 72
(George Scott) *hld up: hdwy and hung rt over 2f out: ev ch ins fnl f: styd on same pce (jockey said gelding hung right-handed throughout)* 20/1

66 **5** 3 1/4 **Foreshore**[3] 9181 2-8-12 0 RhonaPindar(7) 2 64
(K R Burke) *racd keenly: w ldr 1f: remained handy: shkn up over 1f out: no ex ins fnl f* 12/1

4 **6** hd **Striking Approach**[99] 6409 2-9-2 0 ThomasGreatrex(3) 7 63
(Roger Charlton) *chsd ldrs: hung rt over 2f out: rdn over 1f out: styd on same pce* 9/2[3]

0 **7** 2 1/2 **The Weed Machine (IRE)**[14] 9008 2-9-5 0 JasonHart 11 57
(Mark Johnston) *chsd ldr over 5f out tl rdn over 1f out: wknd ins fnl f* 25/1

8 3 1/2 **Extra Shot (IRE)** 2-8-7 0 CameronIles(7) 12 43
(David Evans) *s.i.s: hld up: n.d* 100/1

9 1 1/4 **Lethal Shadow** 2-9-5 0 (t[1]) ShaneKelly 8 45
(Marco Botti) *s.s: rn green in rr: no ch whn hung lft over 1f out* 22/1

10 7 **Skirrid Mountain (IRE)** 2-9-0 0 CliffordLee 10 23
(David Evans) *s.i.s: outpcd (jockey said filly ran green)* 80/1

1m 27.72s (-1.08) **Going Correction** -0.225s/f (Stan) 10 Ran SP% **118.7**
Speed ratings (Par 98): **97,96,95,94,91 90,88,84,82,74**
CSF £37.39 TOTE £4.80: £1.60, £2.50, £1.10; EX 38.10 Trifecta £92.70.
Owner Phoenix Thoroughbred Limited **Bred** BEC Bloodstock **Trained** Newmarket, Suffolk

FOCUS
A fair novice.

9253 BOMBARDIER BRITISH HOPPED AMBER BEER H'CAP 7f 36y (Tp)
6:20 (6:25) (Class 6) (0-60,60) 3-Y-O+ £2,781 (£827; £413; £400; £400; £400) Stalls High

Form RPR

2500 **1** **Sepahi**[23] 8896 3-9-2 57 (b[1]) BenCurtis 8 65
(Henry Spiller) *s.i.s: hld up: hdwy on outer over 1f out: rdn: hung lft and r.o to ld towards fin* 25/1

0442 **2** 3/4 **Reasoned (IRE)**[12] 9039 3-9-3 58 ShaneKelly 3 64
(James Eustace) *chsd ldr: shkn up to ld ins fnl f: sn rdn: hdd towards fin* 9/2[2]

5360 **3** 1 1/4 **Rockesbury**[7] 9128 4-8-13 56 (p) ThomasGreatrex(3) 10 60
(David Loughnane) *led: pushed along 1/2-way: rdn over 2f out: hdd ins fnl f: styd on same pce* 17/2[3]

0041 **4** nk **Ishebayorgrey (IRE)**[24] 8864 7-9-3 57 TomEaves 7 60
(Iain Jardine) *trckd ldrs: racd keenly: rdn over 1f out: styd on same pce ins fnl f* 7/2[1]

2000 **5** 3/4 **Avenue Of Stars**[29] 8719 6-9-6 60 JasonHart 5 61
(Karen McLintock) *s.i.s: hdwy over 1f out: r.o: nt rch ldrs* 9/1

0550 **6** nk **Air Of York (IRE)**[24] 8847 7-9-3 57 (p) HollieDoyle 4 58
(Grace Harris) *hld up in tch: rdn over 1f out: styd on same pce ins fnl f* 18/1

1620 **7** hd **Peachey Carnehan**[43] 8306 5-9-4 58 (v) JamesSullivan 1 58
(Michael Mullineaux) *hld up: nt clr run over 1f out: r.o ins fnl f: nvr nrr* 12/1

-F15 **8** hd **Cawthorne Lad**[26] 8818 3-9-2 57 DuranFentiman 2 56
(Tim Easterby) *chsd ldrs: rdn over 1f out: styd on same pce ins fnl f* 9/2[2]

0112 **9** hd **Viola Park**[30] 8704 5-9-6 60 (p) DavidProbert 12 59
(Ronald Harris) *hld up in tch: swtchd rt over 1f out: rdn: hung lft and no ex ins fnl f* 9/1

050 **10** 1 1/4 **Bell Heather (IRE)**[31] 8669 6-9-6 60 (p) BarryMcHugh 11 59
(Patrick Morris) *hld up: effrt and nt clr run ins fnl f: nt trble ldrs (jockey said mare was denied a clear run inside the final furlong)* 18/1

0056 **11** 2 1/2 **Ower Fly**[21] 8946 6-9-5 59 (v) CallumRodriguez 6 49
(Ruth Carr) *s.i.s: hld up: a in rr* 10/1

1m 27.44s (-1.36) **Going Correction** -0.225s/f (Stan)
WFA 3 from 4yo+ 1lb 11 Ran SP% **120.3**
Speed ratings (Par 101): **98,97,95,95,94 94,93,93,93,92 89**
CSF £137.41 CT £1089.25 TOTE £35.20: £7.00, £1.80, £3.60; EX 205.60 Trifecta £2807.20.
Owner Birdie Racing Club **Bred** Mr & Mrs I Wilson **Trained** Newmarket, Suffolk

FOCUS
Not that many got involved in this modest affair, and the winner did well to close from off the pace. The winner has been rated in line with this year's better efforts.

9254 BOMBARDIER GOLDEN BEER H'CAP 7f 36y (Tp)
6:50 (6:52) (Class 3) (0-95,93) 3-Y-O £7,246 (£2,168; £1,084; £542; £270) Stalls High

Form RPR

0121 **1** **Power Link (USA)**[43] 8317 3-9-6 92 (p) PJMcDonald 4 100+
(James Tate) *hld up: hdwy 4f out: shkn up to ld and edgd lft ins fnl f: rdn out* 13/8[1]

1660 **2** 1/2 **Young Fire (FR)**[11] 9053 4-9-2 87 (v[1]) DavidProbert 3 94
(David O'Meara) *s.i.s: hld up: hdwy 1f out: rdn to chse wnr and edgd lft wl ins fnl f: r.o* 13/2

332 **3** 1 1/4 **Baby Steps**[43] 8317 3-8-9 81 BenCurtis 6 84
(David Loughnane) *led 6f out: shkn up and qcknd over 2f out: rdn and hung rt over 1f out: sn hdd: styd on same pce ins fnl f* 11/2[3]

0540 **4** 1/2 **Glenn Coco**[11] 9053 5-9-2 87 (t) CallumShepherd 1 89
(Stuart Williams) *led 1f: chsd ldrs: rdn to ld over 1f out: hdd ins fnl f: no ex towards fin* 7/2[2]

5140 **5** 1/2 **Finoah (IRE)**[35] 8572 3-9-7 93 (v) RichardKingscote 2 93
(Tom Dascombe) *chsd ldrs: lost pl 4f out: hdwy on inner over 1f out: sn rdn: styd on same pce ins fnl f* 11/2[3]

1020 **6** 1 3/4 **Woodside Wonder**[28] 8761 3-8-13 85 (v) CallumRodriguez 5 80
(Keith Dalgleish) *prom: chsd ldr 5f out tl rdn over 1f out: no ex fnl f* 12/1

1m 26.11s (-2.69) **Going Correction** -0.225s/f (Stan)
WFA 3 from 4yo+ 1lb 6 Ran SP% **112.1**
Speed ratings (Par 107): **106,105,104,103,102 100**
CSF £12.69 TOTE £2.50: £1.70, £2.10; EX 14.90 Trifecta £70.70.
Owner Sheikh Rashid Dalmook Al Maktoum **Bred** SF Bloodstock LLC **Trained** Newmarket, Suffolk

FOCUS
Not a bad handicap, and the winner keeps progressing. The second has been rated to his turf form.

9255 BOMBARDIER "MARCH TO YOUR OWN DRUM" H'CAP 1m 142y (Tp)
7:20 (7:21) (Class 4) (0-85,86) 3-Y-O+ £5,207 (£1,549; £774; £400; £400; £400) Stalls Low

Form RPR

061 **1** **Sea Fox (IRE)**[49] 8122 5-8-13 76 CliffordLee 5 85
(David Evans) *prom: racd keenly: pushed along over 3f out: rdn to ld and hung rt wl ins fnl f: styd on* 15/2

3146 **2** 1/2 **Mickey (IRE)**[58] 7856 6-9-3 80 (v) RichardKingscote 4 88
(Tom Dascombe) *chsd ldr: led over 1f out: rdn and hdd whn hmpd wl ins fnl f: styd on* 8/1

6010 **3** 1 1/4 **Kaser (IRE)**[12] 9041 4-9-3 83 ThomasGreatrex(3) 8 88
(David Loughnane) *hld up: hdwy and nt clr run over 1f out: sn rdn: r.o* 4/1[2]

40-0 **4** 1/2 **Pastime**[234] 1694 5-8-13 76 JackMitchell 10 80+
(Kevin Frost) *hld up: shkn up over 1f out: rdn and r.o ins fnl f: nt rch ldrs* 12/1

0501 **5** hd **My Target (IRE)**[22] 8918 8-9-2 79 PJMcDonald 7 82
(Michael Wigham) *hld up: hdwy over 1f out: r.o* 14/1

5506 **6** 3/4 **Mr Top Hat**[12] 9041 4-9-0 84 (b) CameronIles(7) 9 86
(David Evans) *led: rdn and hdd over 1f out: styd on same pce ins fnl f* 9/1

0463 **7** 1 **Rectory Road**[46] 8222 3-9-3 83 (h) DavidProbert 1 82
(Ronald Harris) *hld up in tch: racd keenly: nt clr run over 2f out: rdn over 1f out: styd on same pce ins fnl f* 7/1[3]

5202 **8** 1/2 **Buckingham (IRE)**[24] 8852 3-9-3 83 CharlesBishop 11 81
(Eve Johnson Houghton) *s.i.s: swtchd lft sn after s: nt clr run and swtchd lft over 1f out: r.o ins fnl f: nvr nrr* 12/1

4000 **9** 1 1/2 **Al Hayette (USA)**[26] 8809 3-9-4 84 BenCurtis 3 79
(Ismail Mohammed) *chsd ldrs: rdn over 2f out: wknd ins fnl f (jockey said filly hung right-handed off the bend)* 20/1

10 1 1/2 **The Game Of Life**[43] 8322 4-9-3 80 TomEaves 2 71
(Michael Herrington) *hld up: nvr on terms* 20/1

5066 **11** 2 **Almufti**[30] 8707 3-9-6 86 (t) TomMarquand 6 73
(Hugo Palmer) *chsd ldrs on outer: rdn over 2f out: wknd over 1f out (jockey said gelding hung right-handed throughout)* 3/1[1]

1m 47.13s (-2.97) **Going Correction** -0.225s/f (Stan)
WFA 3 from 4yo+ 3lb 11 Ran SP% **122.0**
Speed ratings (Par 105): **104,103,102,102,101 101,100,99,98,97 95**
CSF £68.87 CT £276.65 TOTE £7.50: £2.30, £2.70, £2.00; EX 54.10 Trifecta £601.90.
Owner Eric Griffiths & P D Evans **Bred** Tally-Ho Stud **Trained** Pandy, Monmouths
■ Stewards' Enquiry : Clifford Lee two-day ban: interference & careless riding (Dec 14, 16)

FOCUS
A competitive heat. The second has been rated in line with this year's form.

9256 BETWAY HEED YOUR HUNCH H'CAP 1m 1f 104y (Tp)
7:50 (7:55) (Class 6) (0-65,65) 3-Y-O+ £2,781 (£827; £413; £400; £400; £400) Stalls Low

Form RPR

4155 **1** **The Game Is On**[30] 8705 3-9-4 65 (p) LukeMorris 11 71
(Sir Mark Prescott Bt) *led after 1f: drvn along over 2f out: jst hld on* 15/2

0011 **2** shd **Greengage (IRE)**[12] 9040 4-9-4 62 (h) PhilDennis 12 68+
(Tristan Davidson) *hld up in tch: shkn up over 1f out: rdn to chse wnr ins fnl f: r.o* 7/2[2]

125 **3** 1 **Enzo (IRE)**[31] 8669 4-9-5 63 JoeyHaynes 13 67
(John Butler) *prom: chsd wnr 1/2-way: rdn over 1f out: styd on same pce ins fnl f* 6/1[3]

0000 **4** 1 1/2 **Mrs Hoo (IRE)**[31] 8669 3-8-13 63 ConnorMurtagh(3) 7 64
(Richard Fahey) *led 1f: chsd wnr to 1/2-way: remained handy: rdn over 1f out: no ex ins fnl f* 20/1

500 **5** 1 **Derry Boy**[24] 8852 3-9-3 64 BenCurtis 5 63
(David Evans) *s.i.s: hld up: hdwy over 1f out: sn rdn: styd on same pce ins fnl f* 8/1

0000 **6** 1 **Chiavari (IRE)**[100] 6362 5-9-4 62 (w) HollieDoyle 2 59
(Alexandra Dunn) *edgd rt s: hld up: rdn over 1f out: r.o ins fnl f: nvr nrr* 40/1

2400 **7** hd **Beatbybeatbybeat**[52] 8033 6-9-4 62 (v) CamHardie 4 59
(Antony Brittain) *hld up: effrt on outer over 1f out: nt rch ldrs (starter reported that the mare was reluctant to enter the stalls; trainer's rep was informed that the mare could not run until the day after passing a stalls test)* 14/1

4040 **8** shd **Dark Devil (IRE)**[59] 7829 6-9-2 60 (p) BarryMcHugh 9 57
(Patrick Morris) *s.i.s: hld up: styd on ins fnl f: nvr nrr* 25/1

0603 **9** shd **Newmarket Warrior (IRE)**[29] 8713 8-9-7 65 (p) KieranO'Neill 3 62
(Iain Jardine) *sn chsng ldrs: pushed along over 3f out: rdn over 1f out: no ex ins fnl f* 16/1

6100 **10** nk **Creative Talent (IRE)**[75] 7270 7-9-3 61 TomMarquand 1 57
(Tony Carroll) *dwlt: hld up: shkn up over 2f out: hung lft over 1f out: r.o towards fin (jockey said gelding hung left-handed)* 20/1

0000 **11** hd **Mr Minerals**[35] 8549 5-9-2 60 (tp) DanielMuscutt 10 56
(Alexandra Dunn) *prom: rdn over 2f out: wknd ins fnl f* 50/1

0400 **12** 1 **Tangramm**[30] 8705 7-9-1 64 (t[1]) SophieRalston(5) 6 58
(Dean Ivory) *hld up: nvr on terms* 10/1

2004 **R** **Scoffsman**[14] 9006 4-9-3 61 (h) RichardKingscote 8
(Kevin Frost) *ref to r* 3/1[1]

2m 1.7s (0.90) **Going Correction** -0.225s/f (Stan)
WFA 3 from 4yo+ 3lb 13 Ran SP% **123.8**
Speed ratings (Par 101): **87,86,86,84,83 82,82,82,82,82 82,81,**
CSF £33.05 CT £175.66 TOTE £10.50: £3.10, £1.40, £2.20; EX 46.30 Trifecta £396.10.

Owner Timothy J Rooney **Bred** Mrs Ann Greenwood **Trained** Newmarket, Suffolk
FOCUS
This was run at a steady gallop and suited those towards the head of affairs.

9257 BETWAY H'CAP — 5f 21y (Tp)
8:20 (8:23) (Class 5) (0-75,80) 3-Y-O+
£3,428 (£1,020; £509; £400; £400; £400) **Stalls** Low

Form				RPR
0601	**1**		**Big Les (IRE)**[8] 9108 4-9-12 **80**.......... JasonHart 4	90
			(Karen McLintock) *mde all: rdn over 1f out: styd on* **3/1**[1]
0532	**2**	3/4	**Steelriver (IRE)**[24] 8866 9-9-1 **76**.......... AngusVilliers(7) 3	83
			(Michael Herrington) *trckd ldrs: racd keenly: rdn to chse wnr and hung lft wl ins fnl f: r.o (jockey said gelding hung left-handed in the straight)* **13/2**[3]
0166	**3**	nk	**Tathmeen (IRE)**[8] 9108 4-9-2 **70**.......... CamHardie 6	76
			(Antony Brittain) *s.i.s: hld up: racd keenly: hdwy over 1f out: r.o* **7/1**
0340	**4**	2	**Joegogo (IRE)**[2] 9203 4-9-7 **75**.......... BenCurtis 1	74
			(David Evans) *sn given reminders to chse wnr: rdn 1/2-way: lost 2nd ins fnl f: styd on same pce* **4/1**[2]
0116	**5**	1/2	**Powerful Dream (IRE)**[38] 8470 6-9-4 **72**..........(p) DavidProbert 8	69
			(Ronald Harris) *hld up: hdwy over 1f out: r.o: nt rch ldrs* **16/1**
0000	**6**	3/4	**Dynamo Walt (IRE)**[183] 3303 8-9-4 **72**.......... LewisEdmunds 2	66
			(Derek Shaw) *trckd ldrs: rdn over 1f out: no ex ins fnl f* **25/1**
440	**7**	1 1/2	**Kodiac Express (IRE)**[7] 9135 4-8-12 **69** ow3....... ConnorMurtagh(3) 10	58
			(Mike Murphy) *trckd ldrs on outer: racd freely: rdn over 1f out: sn outpcd* **12/1**
2400	**8**	hd	**Aguerooo (IRE)**[187] 3147 6-8-13 **67**..........(tp) RichardKingscote 5	55
			(Charlie Wallis) *hld up: sme hdwy over 1f out: no ex ins fnl f* **33/1**
1366	**9**	1 1/2	**Indian Raj**[78] 7161 5-9-5 **73**..........(t) PJMcDonald 9	56
			(Stuart Williams) *s.i.s: nvr on terms* **3/1**[1]
030	**10**	2	**Celerity (IRE)**[7] 9135 5-8-2 **61** oh16..........(p) SophieRalston(5) 7	37
			(Lisa Williamson) *hld up: a in rr* **100/1**
2340	**11**	1/2	**Cappananty Con**[138] 5000 5-9-6 **74**.......... LukeMorris 11	48
			(Charlie Wallis) *s.i.s: hdwy on outer over 3f out: wknd wl over 1f out: eased fnl f* **25/1**

1m 0.29s (-1.61) **Going Correction** -0.225s/f (Stan) **11 Ran SP% 121.0**
Speed ratings (Par 103): **103,101,101,98,97 96,93,93,91,87 87**
CSF £23.16 CT £130.05 TOTE £4.50: £1.80, £1.50, £2.50; EX 18.60 Trifecta £147.50.
Owner Stockdale Racing **Bred** Corrin Stud **Trained** Ingoe, Northumberland
FOCUS
This was dominated from the front by the winner, who set a pace to suit himself. The winner has been rated back to his best, and the third to his recent form.
T/Plt: £338.70 to a £1 stake. Pool: £115,992.96 - 249.93 winning units. T/Qpdt: £20.10 to a £1 stake. Pool: £17,794.53 - 652.14 winning units. **Colin Roberts**

9258 - 9271a (Foreign Racing) - See Raceform Interactive

9250 WOLVERHAMPTON (A.W) (L-H)
Monday, December 2

OFFICIAL GOING: Tapeta: standard
Wind: Light behind Weather: Cloudy

9272 BETWAY HEED YOUR HUNCH H'CAP — 5f 21y (Tp)
3:45 (3:45) (Class 6) (0-55,57) 3-Y-O+
£2,781 (£827; £413; £400; £400; £400) **Stalls** Low

Form				RPR
0250	**1**		**Sir Hector (IRE)**[27] 8839 4-9-5 **54**.......... WilliamCarson 8	60
			(Charlie Wallis) *prom: chsd ldr and edgd lft over 1f out: rdn to ld and hung rt ins fnl f: styd on: fin 1st: disqualified and plcd 2nd: awrdd r on appeal* **9/2**[1]
6000	**2**	shd	**Everkyllachy (IRE)**[24] 8925 5-9-5 **54**..........(p) BenCurtis 4	60
			(Karen McLintock) *hld up: hdwy over 1f out: rdn and ev ch whn carried rt wl ins fnl f: r.o: fin 2nd: awrdd the r: plcd 2nd following appeal* **6/1**[3]
5053	**3**	1 1/4	**Chocco Star (IRE)**[40] 8450 3-9-5 **54**.......... JoeyHaynes 6	55
			(Chelsea Banham) *s.i.s: hld up: pushed along 1/2-way: hdwy over 1f out: running on whn hmpd wl ins fnl f (jockey said filly was slowly away)* **10/1**
6043	**4**	1 1/2	**Griggy (IRE)**[7] 9161 3-9-2 **51**..........(b[1]) LukeMorris 11	47
			(Sean Curran) *s.i.s: hld up: pushed along and hdwy over 1f out: nt rch ldrs* **9/2**[1]
0001	**5**	hd	**Guardia Svizzera (IRE)**[7] 9161 5-9-3 **57** 5ex..........(h) PaulaMuir(5) 7	52
			(Roger Fell) *hld up: swtchd rt 2f out: r.o ins fnl f: nt rch ldrs* **11/2**[2]
4010	**6**	1	**Miss Gradenko**[27] 8840 3-9-3 **52**..........(p[1]) RaulDaSilva 2	43
			(Robert Cowell) *chsd ldrs: pushed along 1/2-way: rdn over 1f out: styd on same pce ins fnl f* **11/1**
3426	**7**	3/4	**Oh So Nice**[6] 9169 3-9-4 **53**.......... TomMarquand 5	42+
			(Tony Carroll) *led: rdn over 1f out: edgd rt and hdd ins fnl f: no ex (vet said filly lost its right fore shoe)* **6/1**[3]
4060	**8**	3/4	**Autumn Splendour (IRE)**[2] 9246 3-9-6 **55**..........(b) PhilipPrince 9	41
			(Milton Bradley) *hld up: pushed along 1/2-way: nt clr run over 1f out: n.d* **14/1**
6065	**9**	1	**Brother Bentley**[93] 6737 3-9-2 **51**..........(p) DavidProbert 3	33
			(Ronald Harris) *hld up: pushed along 1/2-way: nvr on terms* **14/1**
0400	**10**	2 1/2	**Normal Equilibrium**[47] 8264 9-9-5 **54**.......... TomEaves 1	27
			(Ivan Furtado) *hld up: hdwy over 1f out: sn rdn and hung lft: wknd ins fnl f* **25/1**
0000	**11**	1 1/2	**Jorvik Prince**[6] 9169 5-9-3 **52**..........(b) PaulMulrennan 10	20+
			(Julia Brooke) *chsd ldr tl rdn over 1f out: wkng whn nt clr run ins fnl f* **16/1**

1m 0.25s (-1.65) **Going Correction** -0.10s/f (Stan) **11 Ran SP% 120.8**
Speed ratings (Par 101): **109,108,106,104,104 102,101,100,98,94 92**
CSF £34.15 CT £272.76 TOTE £7.60: £2.20, £2.80, £2.40; EX 30.30 Trifecta £454.40.
Owner A L Barnes **Bred** Tally-Ho Stud **Trained** Ardleigh, Essex
■ Stewards' Enquiry : William Carson two-day ban: careless riding (Dec 18-19)
FOCUS
The going was standard. Stalls: 7f outside; remainder inside. A modest sprint handicap which produced a thrilling finish and saw the first two placings reversed.

9273 BETWAY LIVE CASINO H'CAP — 1m 1f 104y (Tp)
4:15 (4:16) (Class 5) (0-75,75) 3-Y-O+
£3,428 (£1,020; £509; £400; £400; £400) **Stalls** Low

Form				RPR
201	**1**		**Snow Ocean (IRE)**[34] 8645 3-9-7 **75**..........(h) CliffordLee 4	84
			(David Evans) *hld up: racd keenly: hdwy over 1f out: rdn to ld wl ins fnl f: r.o* **8/1**
0523	**2**	1 1/2	**Indomeneo**[9] 9138 4-9-4 **73**.......... ConnorMurtagh(3) 11	79
			(Richard Fahey) *chsd ldrs: rdn to ld and hung lft ins fnl f: sn hdd: styd on same pce (jockey said gelding hung left in the home straight)* **11/1**
5425	**3**	1/2	**Crimewave (IRE)**[13] 9047 3-9-1 **69**..........(v[1]) JackMitchell 6	74
			(Tom Clover) *prom: nt clr run over 1f out: rdn and ev ch ins fnl f: styd on same pce towards fin* **10/3**[2]
1346	**4**	2 1/4	**Eesha My Flower (USA)**[96] 6595 3-8-7 **68**..........(p) JonathanFisher(7) 2	68
			(Marco Botti) *prom: edgd lft over 8f out: sn lost pl: hdwy over 1f out: rdn and swtchd rt ins fnl f: styd on* **40/1**
2623	**5**	nk	**Capriolette (IRE)**[28] 8812 4-9-6 **72**.......... TomMarquand 10	72
			(Ed Walker) *sn chsng ldr: rdn to ld and edgd lft over 1f out: hdd ins fnl f: no ex wl ins fnl f* **13/2**[3]
0425	**6**	hd	**Fares Poet (IRE)**[49] 8197 3-9-6 **74**..........(h) DanielMuscutt 7	73
			(Marco Botti) *chsd ldrs: rdn over 1f out: styd on same pce ins fnl f* **7/1**
2561	**7**	1 1/2	**First Dance (IRE)**[33] 8669 5-9-1 **67**.......... JamesSullivan 12	63
			(Tom Tate) *hld up: shkn up over 1f out: styd on ins fnl f: nvr nrr* **14/1**
2315	**8**	3/4	**Olympic Conqueror (IRE)**[38] 8514 3-9-5 **73**.......... BarryMcHugh 13	67
			(James Fanshawe) *s.i.s: hld up: hdwy on outer over 3f out: rdn over 1f out: edgd lft and wknd ins fnl f* **3/1**[1]
6545	**9**	1 1/2	**Casting Spells**[66] 7643 3-9-0 **68**.......... PJMcDonald 8	59
			(Tom Dascombe) *led: rdn and hdd over 1f out: hmpd sn after: wknd ins fnl f* **20/1**
50-0	**10**	hd	**Boychick (IRE)**[146] 1988 6-8-9 **66**.......... KevinLundie(5) 9	57
			(Mark Loughnane) *hld up: shkn up over 2f out: n.d* **66/1**
2136	**11**	2 1/4	**Classic Charm**[54] 8031 4-9-5 **71**.......... JoeyHaynes 5	57
			(Dean Ivory) *s.i.s: swtchd rt over 1f out: n.d* **20/1**
2102	**12**	1/2	**Orange Suit (IRE)**[28] 8806 4-9-4 **70**..........(b) DavidProbert 1	55
			(Ed de Giles) *awkward s: sn prom: hmpd and lost pl over 8f out: n.d after* **8/1**
33-0	**13**	28	**Saxo Jack (FR)**[137] 5086 9-9-3 **69**..........(t) CallumShepherd 3
			(Sophie Leech) *s.i.s: a in rr: rdn and wknd over 2f out* **50/1**

1m 58.19s (-2.61) **Going Correction** -0.10s/f (Stan)
WFA 3 from 4yo+ 2lb **13 Ran SP% 126.6**
Speed ratings (Par 103): **107,105,105,103,102 102,101,100,99,99 97,96,71**
CSF £93.40 CT £360.77 TOTE £9.90: £2.80, £3.70, £1.70; EX 112.40 Trifecta £588.10.
Owner Shropshire Wolves 3 **Bred** M Enright **Trained** Pandy, Monmouths
■ Stewards' Enquiry : Jack Mitchell two-day ban: misuse of the whip (Dec 16, 18)
Jonathan Fisher two-day ban: careless riding (Dec 16, 18)
FOCUS
A run of the mill handicap, but the winner did it nicely and is progressive.

9274 BETWAY H'CAP — 1m 4f 51y (Tp)
4:45 (4:45) (Class 4) (0-85,84) 3-Y-O+ **£5,207** (£1,549; £774; £400; £400) **Stalls** Low

Form				RPR
0222	**1**		**Arabic Culture (USA)**[11] 9096 5-9-9 **82**.......... SamJames 5	89
			(Grant Tuer) *prom: shkn up on outer over 2f out: rdn over 1f out: styd on to ld post* **5/4**[1]
61	**2**	nse	**Matewan (IRE)**[119] 5743 4-9-2 **75**..........(p) PJMcDonald 4	82
			(Ian Williams) *chsd ldr: led over 2f out: rdn over 1f out: hdd post* **4/1**[3]
0402	**3**	3/4	**Singing Sheriff**[54] 8014 4-9-3 **76**.......... LiamKeniry 1	82
			(Ed Walker) *trckd ldrs: racd keenly: flashed tail at times: nt clr run over 2f out: rdn: edgd lft and ev ch ins fnl f: unable qck towards fin* **9/4**[2]
4310	**4**	1 3/4	**Gabrials Boy**[86] 6955 3-9-4 **84**.......... ConnorMurtagh(3) 2	87
			(Richard Fahey) *hld up: racd keenly: shkn up over 2f out: rdn: hung lft and hdwy over 1f out: nt pce to chal* **8/1**
5145	**5**	11	**Production**[43] 5417 3-9-2 **79**.......... DavidProbert 3	65
			(Alan King) *led: rdn and hdd over 2f out: wknd fnl f* **9/1**

2m 40.2s (-0.60) **Going Correction** -0.10s/f (Stan)
WFA 3 from 4yo+ 4lb **5 Ran SP% 116.3**
Speed ratings (Par 105): **98,97,97,96,88**
CSF £7.21 TOTE £1.90: £1.40, £1.50; EX 7.10 Trifecta £14.60.
Owner Grant Tuer & Ng Racing **Bred** Darley **Trained** Birkby, N Yorks
FOCUS
What looked a moderate early gallop set this up for a tight finish. The winner has developed into a course specialist.

9275 BETWAY CASINO H'CAP — 1m 5f 219y (Tp)
5:15 (5:18) (Class 6) (0-60,60) 3-Y-O+
£2,781 (£827; £413; £400; £400; £400) **Stalls** Low

Form				RPR
5101	**1**		**Herm (IRE)**[26] 8869 5-9-6 **56**.......... BenCurtis 13	61+
			(David Evans) *hld up in tch: swtchd rt over 1f out: rdn to ld ins fnl f: styd on* **8/1**
0-06	**2**	nk	**Calvinist**[6] 9168 6-9-7 **57**.......... JaneElliott 7	62
			(Kevin Frost) *led early: chsd ldrs: pushed along over 3f out: led over 1f out: rdn and hdd ins fnl f: styd on* **6/1**[3]
3452	**3**	1 1/4	**Estrela Star (IRE)**[14] 9042 3-9-2 **57**..........(b) TomMarquand 2	63+
			(Ali Stronge) *hld up: shkn up over 2f out: hdwy: nt clr run and swtchd rt over 1f out: r.o to go 3rd nr fin* **3/1**[1]
0454	**4**	nk	**Falls Creek (USA)**[37] 8551 4-8-10 **46** oh1..........(v) DavidProbert 9	49
			(Andrew Balding) *hld up: racd keenly: swtchd rt over 1f out: hdwy sn after: rdn and edgd lft ins fnl f: styd on (jockey said gelding ran too free)* **13/2**
4533	**5**	nk	**Sinndarella (IRE)**[27] 8828 3-8-5 **46**..........(p) RaulDaSilva 4	50
			(Sarah Hollinshead) *chsd ldr tl over 12f out: remained handy: rdn and ev ch over 1f out: styd on same pce ins fnl f* **7/1**
5012	**6**	1	**Homesick Boy (IRE)**[13] 9049 3-8-12 **60**..........(v) AngusVilliers(7) 10	63
			(Ed Dunlop) *s.i.s: pushed along early in rr: rdn over 1f out: nt clr run: swtchd lft and r.o ins fnl f: nt rch ldrs (jockey said gelding ran too free)* **4/1**[2]
0550	**7**	1/2	**God Has Given**[16] 9005 3-8-6 **54**..........(t) JonathanFisher(7) 12	56
			(Ivan Furtado) *prom: chsd ldr over 12f out: led over 2f out: rdn and hdd over 1f out: no ex ins fnl f (jockey said gelding ran too free)* **16/1**
0020	**8**	1/2	**Lyford (IRE)**[11] 9087 4-9-4 **54**..........(p) PJMcDonald 5	53
			(Alistair Whillans) *s.i.s: hld up: sme hdwy whn carried lft ins fnl f: nt trble ldrs (jockey said gelding missed the break)* **9/1**
000-	**9**	1	**Bob Maxwell (IRE)**[56] 8053 5-9-10 **60**.......... LukeMorris 6	58
			(Robin Dickin) *prom: rdn over 2f out: no ex fnl f* **66/1**
3235	**10**	3	**Lafilia (GER)**[9] 9134 4-9-4 **59**.......... TobyEley(5) 11	53
			(Giuseppe Fierro) *s.i.s: hld up: rdn over 4f out: a in rr* **40/1**
5/00	**11**	4 1/2	**Cross Step (USA)**[12] 9070 5-9-5 **60**..........(p) MarkCrehan(5) 1	48
			(C Moore, Ire) *s.i.s: pushed along and sn rcvrd to ld: racd keenly: rdn and hdd over 2f out: wknd ins fnl f* **20/1**

3m 2.89s (1.89) **Going Correction** -0.10s/f (Stan)
WFA 3 from 4yo+ 5lb **11 Ran SP% 120.8**
Speed ratings (Par 101): **90,89,89,88,88 88,87,87,87,85 82**
CSF £56.18 CT £180.60 TOTE £9.70: £2.60, £2.30, £1.50; EX 77.00 Trifecta £408.30.
Owner Trevor Gallienne **Bred** Mountarmstrong Stud **Trained** Pandy, Monmouths

FOCUS
Quite a lot were involved at the business end of this stamina test which suggests they did not go the greatest of gallops.

9276 ALL WEATHER CHAMPIONSHIP SEASON 7 NOVICE MEDIAN AUCTION STKS — 7f 36y (Tp)

5:45 (5:50) (Class 6) 3-5-Y-O — £2,781 (£827; £413; £206) Stalls High

Form RPR

1 **Sherpa Trail (USA)** 3-9-5 0 .... LukeMorris 8 65+
(Ed Walker) *chsd ldrs: wnt 2nd over 4f out: shkn up to ld and rn green over 1f out: rdn out* 15/8[1]

3450 2 ¾ **Kentucky Kingdom (IRE)**[35] 8606 3-9-5 67 .... DougieCostello 10 63
(James Evans) *hld up: plld hrd: hdwy 3f out: rdn to chse wnr ins fnl f: styd on* 7/1[3]

5 3 1 ¼ **Just Magic**[14] 9038 3-9-5 0 .... DuranFentiman 1 60
(Tim Easterby) *prom: rdn over 1f out: styd on* 8/1

0630 4 ½ **Isabella Ruby**[34] 8637 4-8-7 46 ....(h) GavinAshton(7) 2 54
(Lisa Williamson) *s.i.s: hld up: swtchd rt over 1f out: r.o wl ins fnl f: nt rch ldrs* 9/1

00- 5 2 **Duke Debonair (IRE)**[382] 9065 3-9-5 0 .... NicolaCurrie 5 54
(Jamie Osborne) *hmpd s: hld up: r.o ins fnl f: nt trble ldrs* 20/1

5302 6 1 ¼ **Ghost Buy (FR)**[16] 9001 3-9-5 54 ....(bt[1]) TomEaves 4 51
(Ivan Furtado) *led: rdn and hdd over 1f out: wknd wl ins fnl f* 7/2[2]

4000 7 ½ **Peters Pudding (IRE)**[26] 8864 3-9-5 53 ....(p) KieranO'Neill 7 49
(Lisa Williamson) *chsd ldr tl over 4f out: remained handy: rdn over 1f out: wknd ins fnl f* 28/1

0000 8 1 **Andies Armies**[65] 7681 3-8-12 38 ....(p) ElishaWhittington(7) 9 47
(Lisa Williamson) *s.s: rdn over 1f out: nvr nrr* 66/1

-600 9 nk **Doubly Beautiful (IRE)**[41] 8419 3-9-5 65 ....(h) CallumShepherd 11 46
(Ed de Giles) *hld up: plld hrd: rdn over 2f out: nt trble ldrs* 9/1

5056 10 12 **Disey's Edge**[47] 8249 3-8-11 47 ....(p) MitchGodwin(3) 3 11
(Christopher Mason) *in rr and pushed along 5f out: rdn over 1f out: sn wknd* 20/1

0060 11 7 **Freshfield Ferris**[27] 8837 3-8-11 35 ....(b[1]) ConnorMurtagh(3) 6
(Brian Rothwell) *edgd lft s: sn mid-div: pushed along 1/2-way: hung rt and wknd over 2f out* 100/1

1m 28.21s (-0.59) **Going Correction** -0.10s/f (Stan) 11 Ran SP% 116.1
Speed ratings (Par 101): **99,98,96,96,93 92,91,90,90,76 68**
CSF £14.31 TOTE £2.40: £1.20, £2.00, £2.50; EX 15.70 Trifecta £96.10.
Owner Mrs T Walker **Bred** James Moloney & Patrick Moloney **Trained** Upper Lambourn, Berks

FOCUS
A modest maiden which was won by the only newcomer.

9277 ALL WEATHER CHAMPIONSHIP SEASON 7 H'CAP — 7f 36y (Tp)

6:15 (6:17) (Class 6) (0-60,60) 3-Y-O+ — £2,781 (£827; £413; £400; £400; £400) Stalls High

Form RPR

3000 1 **Mount Wellington (IRE)**[10] 9113 4-9-5 59 ....(t[1]) PJMcDonald 5 67+
(Stuart Williams) *hld up: hdwy 2f out: r.o to ld wl ins fnl f: rdn out* 4/1[2]

6024 2 nk **Elzaam's Dream (IRE)**[55] 8007 3-9-2 56 ....(h) DavidProbert 8 63
(Ronald Harris) *s.i.s: hld up: pushed along 1/2-way: hdwy over 1f out: chsd wnr wl ins fnl f: r.o* 14/1

0145 3 2 **Ubla (IRE)**[49] 8199 6-9-6 60 ....(e) LukeMorris 6 62
(Gay Kelleway) *prom: racd keenly: rdn over 1f out: styd on same pce ins fnl f* 10/1

4403 4 hd **Seraphim**[11] 9089 3-8-13 60 ....(bt) GraceMcEntee(7) 12 62
(Marco Botti) *chsd ldr tl led over 2f out: rdn and hung lft over 1f out: hdd and no ex wl ins fnl f* 6/1

6200 5 ½ **Peachey Carnehan**[2] 9253 5-9-4 58 ....(v) JamesSullivan 9 59
(Michael Mullineaux) *s.i.s: hld up: edgd lft and r.o ins fnl f: nt rch ldrs* 8/1

0050 6 2 **Ghazan (IRE)**[16] 9006 4-9-3 57 .... TomMarquand 3 53
(Ivan Furtado) *trckd ldrs: shkn up over 1f out: no ex ins fnl f* 5/1[3]

5-4 7 2 **Iron Ryan (FR)**[61] 7823 7-9-3 57 .... KieranO'Neill 1 48
(Lee Smyth, Ire) *edgd lft s: hld up: rdn over 1f out: nt trble ldrs* 16/1

0061 8 ¾ **Rivas Rob Roy**[10] 9111 4-9-2 56 ....(b) BenCurtis 4 45
(John Gallagher) *sn led: hdd over 2f out: nt clr run over 1f out: wknd ins fnl f (trainer's rep said gelding ran too free in the early stages and may have been unsuited by the sharp track on this occasion, having won on the straight track at Newcastle last time)* 11/4[1]

3406 9 20 **Round The Island**[9] 9128 6-9-2 56 ....(b) PhilDennis 10
(Richard Whitaker) *hld up: plld hrd: hung rt thrght: hdwy on outer over 4f out: wknd over 2f out (jockey said gelding hung right throughout)* 12/1

1m 26.92s (-1.88) **Going Correction** -0.10s/f (Stan) 9 Ran SP% 118.1
Speed ratings (Par 101): **106,105,103,103,102 100,98,97,74**
CSF £59.32 CT £529.31 TOTE £4.80: £1.90, £4.00, £2.60; EX 47.30 Trifecta £290.30.
Owner GG Thoroughbreds IX **Bred** Alan O'Flynn **Trained** Newmarket, Suffolk

FOCUS
Not the strongest of handicaps. The winner stepped up markedly on a disappointing stable debut.

9278 LADBROKES FOOTBALL ACCA BOOSTY EBF FILLIES' H'CAP — 1m 142y (Tp)

6:45 (6:45) (Class 2) (0-105,87) 3-Y-O+ — £11,827 (£3,541; £1,770; £885; £442; £222) Stalls Low

Form RPR

0545 1 **Bubble And Squeak**[16] 9000 4-9-12 87 .... BenCurtis 6 95+
(Sylvester Kirk) *hld up: hdwy on outer over 2f out: rdn to chse wnr and hung lft ins fnl f: r.o to ld nr fin: comf* 9/4[2]

6001 2 ½ **Stay Classy (IRE)**[9] 9126 3-8-13 83 ....(p) AngusVilliers(7) 2 89
(Richard Spencer) *s.i.s: sn chsng ldrs: led over 1f out: sn rdn: hdd nr fin* 5/1[3]

0260 3 2 **Railport Dolly**[11] 9096 4-8-11 72 ....(h) LiamKeniry 1 73
(David Barron) *led: rdn and hdd over 1f out: styd on same pce ins fnl f* 8/1

6200 4 nk **Innamorare (IRE)**[24] 8931 4-9-8 83 .... PJMcDonald 4 84+
(Gavin Cromwell, Ire) *broke wl: sn stdd and lost pl: hld up: nt clr run over 2f out: rdn and r.o ins fnl f: nrst fin* 15/8[1]

0-0 5 1 ¼ **Peruvian Lily (FR)**[4] 9199 3-8-6 69 .... LukeMorris 5 67
(Michael Appleby) *prom: hung lft almost thrght: rdn over 1f out: no ex fnl f (jockey said filly hung left throughout)* 8/1

0100 6 1 ½ **Ruby Gates (IRE)**[39] 8507 6-8-4 68 oh2 .... DarraghKeenan(3) 7 62
(John Butler) *s.i.s: hdwy on outer 7f out: rdn over 1f out: edgd lft and wknd ins fnl f* 16/1

055- 7 17 **Cupboard Love**[444] 7251 3-9-1 78 .... JoeFanning 3 33
(Mark Johnston) *w ldr 6f: wknd wl over 1f out* 14/1

1m 47.99s (-2.11) **Going Correction** -0.10s/f (Stan) 7 Ran SP% 117.0
WFA 3 from 4yo+ 2lb
Speed ratings (Par 96): **105,104,102,102,101 100,84**
CSF £14.59 TOTE £3.00: £1.70, £2.70; EX 13.60 Trifecta £66.20.
Owner Chris Wright,Holly Wright,Chloe Forsyth **Bred** Stratford Place Stud **Trained** Upper Lambourn, Berks

FOCUS
A quite valuable handicap which developed into a bit of a dash from over 2f out.

9279 BETWAY APPRENTICE H'CAP — 1m 1f 104y (Tp)

7:15 (7:17) (Class 6) (0-60,62) 3-Y-O — £2,781 (£827; £413; £400; £400; £400) Stalls Low

Form RPR

3046 1 **Triple Nickle (IRE)**[14] 9040 3-9-5 58 ....(p) PoppyBridgwater 7 63
(Bernard Llewellyn) *chsd ldrs: led over 1f out: rdn and hung rt ins fnl f: styd on* 14/1

4336 2 ¾ **Ballet Red (FR)**[16] 9006 3-9-6 62 .... ElishaWhittington(3) 3 66
(Harry Dunlop) *chsd ldrs: nt clr run over 2f out: rdn over 1f out: r.o* 6/1[3]

00-0 3 nk **Usanecolt (IRE)**[325] 183 3-8-11 53 .... GavinAshton(3) 11 56
(Jamie Osborne) *hld up: hdwy on outer over 1f out: r.o to go 3rd post: nt rch ldrs* 20/1

4035 4 nse **Elena**[60] 7858 3-9-5 61 .... TylerSaunders(3) 4 64
(Charles Hills) *hld up: racd keenly: hdwy on outer over 2f out: chsd wnr over 1f out: sn rdn: styd on* 13/2

4422 5 ¾ **Impressionable**[46] 8299 3-9-1 57 .... GeorgiaDobie(3) 13 58
(William Muir) *s.i.s: hld up: rn wd turning for home: rdn and r.o wl ins fnl f: nt rch ldrs* 9/2[2]

6300 6 ½ **Strict (IRE)**[23] 8949 3-9-2 58 ....(p) AngusVilliers(3) 9 59
(Michael Appleby) *s.i.s: hld up: hung rt over 2f out: rdn over 1f out: r.o: nt trble ldrs (jockey said gelding hung right in the home straight)* 16/1

4563 7 ¾ **Storm Eleanor**[44] 8345 3-9-6 59 .... DylanHogan 10 58
(Hughie Morrison) *hld up: hdwy on outer 3f out: rdn over 1f out: styd on same pce ins fnl f* 7/2[1]

0000 8 ½ **Daniel Dravot**[37] 8552 3-8-4 46 oh1 ....(p[1]) AledBeech(3) 8 44
(Michael Attwater) *hld up: hdwy over 2f out: rdn over 1f out: styd on same pce ins fnl f* 40/1

6034 9 1 **Star Talent (IRE)**[49] 8200 3-9-4 60 ....(v[1]) TobyEley(3) 12 56
(Gay Kelleway) *s.i.s: hld up: rdn and hung lft fr over 1f out: nvr nrr (jockey said gelding hung left in the home straight)* 13/2

0005 10 1 **Clovenstone**[11] 9090 3-8-3 47 .... OliverStammers(5) 1 41
(Alistair Whillans) *prom: racd keenly: nt clr run and lost pl over 2f out: rdn over 1f out: no ex fnl f* 10/1

003 11 1 ¾ **Margaret J**[7] 9157 3-8-2 46 oh1 ....(p) GraceMcEntee(5) 2 37
(Phil McEntee) *chsd ldr tl led 2f out: hdd over 1f out: wknd ins fnl f* 14/1

0560 12 3 ¼ **Miss Green Dream**[24] 8916 3-8-7 46 oh1 .....(b[1]) ThoreHammerHansen 6 31
(Julia Feilden) *led over 7f: wknd fnl f* 20/1

1m 59.07s (-1.73) **Going Correction** -0.10s/f (Stan) 12 Ran SP% 121.6
Speed ratings (Par 98): **103,102,102,102,101 100,100,99,98,98 96,93**
CSF £96.03 CT £1710.95 TOTE £14.20: £3.50, £2.60, £8.70; EX 108.90 Trifecta £3748.90.
Owner Alex James & B J Llewellyn **Bred** George Kent **Trained** Fochriw, Caerphilly

FOCUS
Plenty of runners, but a weak handicap. The winner was scoring at the 11th attempt.
T/Plt: £132.20 to a £1 stake. Pool: £128,175.79 - 707.38 winning units T/Qpdt: £16.70 to a £1 stake. Pool: £18,469.42 - 816.95 winning units **Colin Roberts**

9210 DEAUVILLE (R-H)

Monday, December 2

OFFICIAL GOING: Polytrack: standard

9280a PRIX DE MORICAUD (CLAIMER) (3YO) (ALL-WEATHER TRACK) (POLYTRACK) — 7f 110y(P)

11:25 3-Y-O — £7,657 (£3,063; £2,297; £1,531; £765)

RPR

1 **Ricochet (IRE)**[10] 9106 3-8-11 0 .... IoritzMendizabal 1 62
(Tom Ward) *t.k.h: led at brisk pce: 5 l clr 3f out: drvn 2f out: drifted lft u.p ins fnl f: reduced ld clsng stages but a holding on* 84/10

2 ¾ **Infox (FR)**[13] 3-9-1 0 .... TheoBachelot 3 64
(Guillaume Courbot, France) 16/5[2]

3 nse **Carambole (GER)**[13] 3-8-11 0 .... YoannRousset 5 60
(Julien Morel, France) 71/1

4 snk **La Regle Du Jeu (FR)**[13] 3-8-8 0 ....(p) ClementGuitraud(8) 6 65
(Y Barberot, France) 12/1

5 1 **Dame Gladys**[445] 7198 3-8-11 0 .... FabienLefebvre 4 57
(E Zahariev, Germany) 26/1

6 1 ¼ **Fantastic Glory (FR)**[34] 3-8-11 0 .... ThomasTrullier(4) 14 58
(A De Watrigant, France) 56/10[3]

7 1 ½ **Dancing Mountain (IRE)**[13] 3-8-11 0 ....(b) MaximeGuyon 8 50
(P Monfort, France) 27/10[1]

8 2 **Mantega (FR)**[27] 3-9-2 0 .... JulienGuillochon 11 50
(H-A Pantall, France) 12/1

9 5 **Million Dreams (FR)**[193] 3028 3-8-8 0 ....(b) AntoineHamelin 12 30
(Laurent Loisel, France) 42/1

10 1 ½ **Duende**[25] 3-8-9 0 .... QuentinPerrette(6) 2 33
(Mlle L Kneip, France) 8/1

11 1 ½ **What Secret (IRE)**[152] 3-8-11 0 ....(p) SebastienMaillot 9 25
(C Boutin, France) 44/1

12 ¾ **Tagda**[534] 3855 3-8-4 0 .... JeremieMonteiro(4) 7 20
(Mlle M Henry, France) 126/1

13 1 ¼ **Black And Blue (FR)**[104] 6328 3-8-8 0 .... EddyHardouin 15 17
(Mario Hofer, Germany) 21/1

14 2 ½ **Grey Rasko (FR)**[212] 3-8-8 0 .... MlleAlisonMassin(3) 13 14
(Edouard Thueux, France) 147/1

1m 27.96s 14 Ran SP% 118.8
PARI-MUTUEL (all including 1 euro stake): WIN 9.40; PLACE 2.80, 2.10, 12.60; DF 18.90.
Owner Beswick Bros B/S, T Ward & W Bird **Bred** Ballylinch Stud **Trained** Upper Lambourn, Berks

9281a PRIX DE BONNERIE (CLAIMER) (3YO) (ALL-WEATHER TRACK) (POLYTRACK) 1m 1f 110y(P)

11:55 3-Y-O £9,009 (£3,603; £2,702; £1,801; £900)

RPR

1 **Hallalulu**[65] 7702 3-9-1 0 StephaneLaurent 11 83
(S Cerulis, France) **29/1**

2 3 ½ **Balgees Time (FR)**[121] 5695 3-8-11 0 Pierre-LouisJamin 4 72
(Tom Ward) *rdn fr stalls: midfield: impr to chse ldrs 4f out: short of room over 2f out: swtchd rt and hdwy u.p over 1f out: kpt on wl* **17/1**

3 nse **Makda (FR)**[58] 3-8-5 0 MlleLucieOger(3) 2 69
(J Boisnard, France) **19/1**

4 nk **Parafection (IRE)**[158] 3-9-4 0 MarcNobili 7 78
(C Ferland, France) **11/10**[1]

5 nse **Anecdotic (USA)**[20] 3-9-4 0 (p) AntonioPolli 13 78
(I Endaltsev, Czech Republic) **18/1**

6 1 ¾ **Delachance (FR)**[112] 6013 3-9-4 0 RichardJuteau 14 75
(P Monfort, France) **87/10**[3]

7 ½ **Jaidaa**[158] 4284 3-8-11 0 BenjaminHubert 8 67
(P Monfort, France) **94/1**

8 2 **Bertrimont (FR)** 3-8-8 0 MlleLauraGrosso(3) 10 63
(E Zahariev, Germany) **28/1**

9 ½ **Pray (GER)**[10] 3-9-1 0 MathieuPelletan 15 66
(Andreas Suborics, Germany) **44/1**

10 nk **Marylin (FR)**[32] 3-9-1 0 FrankPanicucci 9 65
(S Cerulis, France) **26/5**[2]

11 1 **Jetcologne (GER)**[20] 3-8-11 0 AxelBaron 1 59
(Miss V Haigh, France) **100/1**

12 nk **Run Ashore (FR)**[20] 3-9-2 0 (b) GlenBraem 3 64
(M Nigge, France) **10/1**

13 2 ½ **Nathaniella**[13] 9058 3-8-8 0 MlleAlisonMassin(3) 6 54
(Mme M-C Chaalon, France) **129/1**

14 nse **Lollipop Lady**[13] 3-8-5 0 (b) MlleAudeDuporte(3) 16 50
(Mme M-C Chaalon, France) **87/1**

15 14 **Grace Of Cliffs (FR)**[117] 3-8-8 (b) AntoineCoutier 5 16
(A De Watrigant, France) **10/1**

1m 55.53s **15** Ran **SP% 121.0**
PARI-MUTUEL (all including 1 euro stake): WIN 30.10; PLACE 10.70, 4.80, 7.20; DF 203.20.
Owner C R Hirst **Bred** Aston Mullins Stud **Trained** France

[9272]WOLVERHAMPTON (A.W) (L-H)

Tuesday, December 3

OFFICIAL GOING: Tapeta: standard
Wind: Almost nil Weather: Fine

9282 BOMBARDIER GOLDEN BEER CLASSIFIED STKS 1m 142y (Tp)

3:45 (3:45) (Class 6) 3-Y-O+
£2,781 (£827; £413; £400; £400; £400) **Stalls Low**

Form RPR

006 1 **Seaforth (IRE)**[117] 5837 7-8-13 47 FinleyMarsh(3) 9 57
(Adrian Wintle) *s.i.s: hld up: hdwy on outer over 1f out: rdn to ld and hung lft ins fnl f: r.o wl* **25/1**

0040 2 3 **Sir Magnum**[33] 8694 4-9-2 46 (h[1]) HollieDoyle 13 50
(Tony Carroll) *pushed along on outer to go prom after 1f: chsd ldr over 6f out: rdn to ld over 1f out: hdd and no ex ins fnl f* **5/1**[3]

25 3 ¾ **Queen Mia (IRE)**[11] 9111 3-9-0 48 (t) TomEaves 6 48
(Declan Carroll) *hld up in tch: rdn over 1f out: styd on same pce ins fnl f* **7/1**

0200 4 ½ **Prince Consort (IRE)**[24] 8942 4-9-2 47 (p) PaulMulrennan 7 47
(John Wainwright) *chsd ldrs: lost pl 7f out: hdwy over 1f out: styd on* **40/1**

0-60 5 ½ **George Junior**[12] 9090 3-9-0 44 (b[1]) LiamKeniry 5 46
(Ed Walker) *mid-div: pushed along over 3f out: styd on ins fnl f: nvr trbld ldrs* **20/1**

0000 6 nk **Molten Lava (IRE)**[24] 8942 7-9-2 47 (p) RobertHavlin 3 45
(Steve Gollings) *led: hdd 7f out: chsd ldrs: nt clr run and swtchd rt over 1f out: nt clr run and swtchd lft ins fnl f: styd on same pce (jockey said gelding was denied a clear run rounding the home turn and in the early part of the home straight)* **9/1**

0503 7 ¾ **Lethal Laura**[29] 8819 3-9-0 48 PJMcDonald 11 44
(Kevin Frost) *mid-div: hdwy on outer over 6f out: rdn and edgd lft over 1f out: no ex ins fnl f* **9/2**[2]

5620 8 ½ **Silk Mill Blue**[11] 9111 5-9-2 49 (p) PhilDennis 4 43
(Richard Whitaker) *chsd ldrs: rdn over 2f out: wknd wl ins fnl f* **10/1**

0302 9 hd **High Fort (IRE)**[29] 8818 4-9-2 48 JasonHart 1 42
(Karen McLintock) *s.i.s: hld up: rdn and swtchd rt ins fnl f: nvr on terms (jockey said gelding missed the break and was also denied a clear run in the concluding stages, which meant he was therefore unable to ride out for eighth place)* **2/1**[1]

6-04 10 1 ¼ **Bescaby**[33] 8693 4-9-2 45 (p[1]) AlistairRawlinson 12 40
(Michael Appleby) *s.i.s: a in rr (jockey said filly missed the break)* **25/1**

5000 11 2 ¼ **Nabvutika (IRE)**[56] 8001 3-9-0 48 TomQueally 2 35
(John Butler) *prom: rdn over 1f out: wknd ins fnl f* **14/1**

0100 12 ¾ **Valentine Mist (IRE)**[79] 7232 7-8-11 47 SophieRalston(5) 10 33
(James Grassick) *sn prom: led 7f out: rdn and hdd over 1f out: wknd ins fnl f* **66/1**

1m 48.66s (-1.44) **Going Correction** -0.15s/f (Stan)
WFA 3 from 4yo+ 2lb **12** Ran **SP% 122.8**
Speed ratings (Par 101): **100,97,96,96,95 95,94,94,94,93 91,90**
CSF £144.90 TOTE £35.50: £6.50, £1.80, £2.40; EX 233.10 Trifecta £2081.10.
Owner Wintle Racing Club **Bred** W Maxwell Ervine **Trained** Westbury-On-Severn, Gloucs

FOCUS
A low-grade affair but won in good style.

9283 BOMBARDIER "MARCH TO YOUR DRUM" CLAIMING STKS 7f 36y (Tp)

4:15 (4:18) (Class 6) 3-Y-O+
£2,781 (£827; £413; £400; £400; £400) **Stalls High**

Form RPR

2561 1 **Unforgiving Minute**[12] 9086 8-9-12 83 JamesDoyle 11 81+
(Sean Curran) *a.p: chsd ldr over 2f out: led over 1f out: rdn and edgd lft ins fnl f: styd on* **9/4**[1]

3042 2 ½ **Azzeccagarbugli (IRE)**[12] 9086 6-9-4 77 (v[1]) JosephineGordon 5 72
(Mike Murphy) *bmpd s: hld up: shkn up on outer over 2f out: hdwy over 1f out: rdn and r.o to go 2nd nr fin: nt rch wnr* **9/2**[2]

2156 3 nk **Tukhoom (IRE)**[35] 8634 6-9-7 82 (b) AngusVilliers(7) 9 81
(David O'Meara) *wnt lft s: hld up: hdwy over 1f out: swtchd lft ins fnl f: sn rdn: r.o* **9/2**[2]

0660 4 ½ **Fuwairt (IRE)**[6] 9176 7-8-7 71 CameronNoble(3) 10 62
(David Loughnane) *hld up: rdn and r.o ins fnl f: wnt 4th nr fin: nt rch ldrs* **11/2**[3]

2006 5 ½ **Atletico (IRE)**[26] 8893 7-9-8 75 (b) HollieDoyle 8 73
(David Evans) *hmpd s: hld up: nt clr run: swtchd rt and r.o ins fnl f: nt rch ldrs* **6/1**

2006 6 ½ **Smugglers Creek (IRE)**[62] 7820 5-9-3 66 (p) PaulMulrennan 12 66
(Iain Jardine) *pushed along to ld over 6f out: rdn: hung rt and hdd over 1f out: no ex wl ins fnl f* **25/1**

4044 7 ½ **Shady McCoy (USA)**[12] 9086 9-9-4 80 PJMcDonald 4 66
(Ian Williams) *s.i.s: hld up: shkn up and hdwy over 1f out: carried lft ins fnl f: nt trble ldrs* **16/1**

0050 8 4 **Highland Acclaim (IRE)**[10] 9140 8-8-8 65 (h) DavidProbert 7 46
(David O'Meara) *hmpd s: chsd ldr over 6f out tl shkn up over 2f out: edgd lft and wknd ins fnl f* **25/1**

5040 9 3 ¾ **North Korea (IRE)**[28] 8839 3-8-1 42 KieranO'Neill 3 30
(Brian Baugh) *prom: rdn over 1f out: hung lft and wknd fnl f* **100/1**

6000 10 ½ **Newstead Abbey**[15] 9039 9-8-2 51 (p) TheodoreLadd(3) 2 32
(Rebecca Bastiman) *led early: chsd ldrs: rdn and wknd over 1f out* **50/1**

4600 11 8 **Opera Kiss (IRE)**[10] 9138 3-7-13 40 KieranSchofield(5) 6 11+
(Ivan Furtado) *s.i.s and edgd rt s: shkn up over 2f out: nvr on terms* **100/1**

/4-0 12 6 **Phoenix Lightning (IRE)**[19] 5754 4-9-0 34 (p) TomQueally 1 6
(Kevin Bishop) *s.i.s: sn pushed along and a in rr* **150/1**

1m 26.68s (-2.12) **Going Correction** -0.15s/f (Stan) **12** Ran **SP% 115.0**
Speed ratings (Par 101): **106,105,105,104,103 103,102,98,93,93 84,77**
CSF £11.35 TOTE £2.90: £1.30, £1.70, £1.50; EX 12.70 Trifecta £42.60.
Owner Power Geneva Ltd **Bred** Equine Breeding Limited **Trained** Upper Lambourn, Berks

FOCUS
A solidly run claimer.

9284 LADBROKES WHERE THE NATION PLAYS FILLIES' NOVICE STKS (PLUS 10 RACE) 7f 36y (Tp)

4:45 (4:47) (Class 5) 2-Y-O £3,428 (£1,020; £509; £254) **Stalls High**

Form RPR

54 1 **Noble Dawn (GER)**[67] 7644 2-9-0 0 PJMcDonald 2 73+
(Ivan Furtado) *chsd ldrs: wnt 2nd over 2f out: led over 1f out: edgd lft and rdn clr ins fnl f* **5/1**[2]

2 2 ½ **Dubai Quality (IRE)** 2-9-0 0 CallumShepherd 4 67
(Saeed bin Suroor) *hld up: hdwy 1/2-way: shkn up and edgd rt over 1f out: styd on to go 2nd wl ins fnl f* **4/9**[1]

3 ½ **True Believer (IRE)** 2-9-0 0 JasonHart 7 65
(Mark Johnston) *led: rdn and hdd over 1f out: styd on same pce ins fnl f* **9/1**[3]

4 3 ¾ **Full Secret (IRE)** 2-9-0 0 BarryMcHugh 9 56+
(Richard Fahey) *s.i.s: hld up: hdwy and edgd lft over 1f out: nvr nrr* **20/1**

5 2 **Knapsack (IRE)** 2-9-0 0 HectorCrouch 8 51
(Clive Cox) *chsd ldr: pushed along 1/2-way: lost 2nd over 2f out: wknd fnl f* **16/1**

6 1 **Goldie Hawk** 2-9-0 0 GeorgeWood 1 49
(Chris Wall) *hld up: shkn up over 2f out: nvr on terms* **33/1**

7 ½ **Tamao** 2-9-0 0 (h[1]) DavidProbert 6 47+
(Andrew Balding) *s.s: hld up: swtchd lft over 1f out: n.d (jockey said filly was slowly away)* **25/1**

0 8 ½ **Diamond Cottage**[69] 7571 2-9-0 0 CharlieBennett 3 46
(Malcolm Saunders) *prom: rdn over 2f out: wknd over 1f out* **66/1**

9 ½ **Diamond Jill (IRE)** 2-9-0 0 JamesSullivan 11 45
(Sarah Hollinshead) *chsd ldrs on outer: shkn up over 2f out: wknd over 1f out* **100/1**

10 8 **Elixir Sky** 2-9-0 0 JackMitchell 12 25
(Kevin Frost) *s.s: hung lft over 2f out: n.d (jockey said filly ran green)* **100/1**

6 11 7 **Voice Of Dubawi**[56] 7981 2-9-0 0 MartinDwyer 5 7
(Paul Webber) *rrd s: hdwy 6f out: pushed along 1/2-way: wknd over 2f out* **25/1**

1m 27.82s (-0.98) **Going Correction** -0.15s/f (Stan) **11** Ran **SP% 120.7**
Speed ratings (Par 93): **99,96,95,91,89 87,87,86,86,77 69**
CSF £7.40 TOTE £5.50: £1.20, £1.10, £1.80; EX 10.40 Trifecta £37.20.
Owner John Marriott **Bred** Stiftung Gestut Fahrhof **Trained** Wiseton, Nottinghamshire

FOCUS
No more than a fair novice.

9285 BETWAY APPRENTICE H'CAP 1m 1f 104y (Tp)

5:15 (5:15) (Class 4) (0-85,85) 4-Y-O+
£5,207 (£1,549; £774; £400; £400; £400) **Stalls Low**

Form RPR

0643 1 **International Law**[40] 8507 5-8-7 71 oh3 AngusVilliers 2 77
(Antony Brittain) *s.i.s: hld up: hdwy over 1f out: swtchd lft ins fnl f: rdn and r.o to ld post* **8/1**

3301 2 nse **Storm Ahead (IRE)**[15] 9041 6-9-1 79 (b) EllaMcCain 6 85
(Tim Easterby) *chsd ldr 1f: remained handy: led over 1f out: rdn ins fnl f: hdd post* **9/4**[2]

5065 3 ¾ **Keswick**[14] 9050 5-8-11 75 (t) GeorgiaDobie 5 79
(Heather Main) *s.i.s: hld up: hdwy on outer over 1f out: sn rdn: r.o* **6/1**[3]

2535 4 hd **Michele Strogoff**[5] 9206 6-9-7 85 MarkCrehan 4 89
(Michael Appleby) *led: rdn and hdd over 1f out: styd on* **7/4**[1]

5503 5 1 ½ **The Throstles**[7] 9167 4-8-12 76 (p) TobyEley 1 76
(Kevin Frost) *chsd ldrs: rdn over 1f out: styd on same pce ins fnl f* **8/1**

4000 6 nk **Masham Star (IRE)**[39] 8521 5-9-4 85 OliverStammers(3) 3 85
(Mark Johnston) *chsd ldr after 1f tl shkn up over 1f out: styd on same pce ins fnl f (vet said gelding was found to be lame on his left-hind)* **12/1**

1m 59.33s (-1.47) **Going Correction** -0.15s/f (Stan) **6** Ran **SP% 111.3**
Speed ratings (Par 105): **100,99,99,99,97 97**
CSF £25.93 TOTE £9.00: £3.90, £1.60; EX 32.30 Trifecta £181.70.
Owner John And Tony Jarvis And Partner **Bred** Ed's Stud Ltd **Trained** Warthill, N Yorks

The Form Book Flat 2019, Raceform Ltd, Newbury, RG14 5SJ

FOCUS
The pace picked up down the back and that played into the hands of the closers, although they finished in a heap.

9286 BETWAY HEED YOUR HUNCH H'CAP 5f 21y (Tp)
5:45 (5:45) (Class 4) (0-80,82) 3-Y-O+

£5,207 (£1,549; £774; £400; £400; £400) **Stalls Low**

Form RPR

0050 **1** **Lomu (IRE)**[65] 7736 5-9-6 **79** .... PaulMulrennan 2 93
(Iain Jardine) *sn chsng ldrs: nt clr run wl over 1f out: led ins fnl f: rdn clr* **16/1**

5336 **2** *3* **Canford Bay (IRE)**[7] 9166 5-9-7 **80** .... CamHardie 5 83
(Antony Brittain) *trckd ldrs: racd keenly: rdn over 1f out: edgd rt and styd on same pce ins fnl f* **4/1**[2]

0022 **3** *nse* **Fizzy Feet (IRE)**[10] 9131 3-9-7 **80** .... HollieDoyle 6 83+
(David Loughnane) *prom: lost pl 4f out: sn pushed along: rdn and r.o wl ins fnl f: wnt 3rd nr fin (jockey said filly was outpaced in the early stages of the race)* **7/2**[1]

0004 **4** *½* **Abel Handy (IRE)**[12] 9098 4-9-7 **82** .... (t) DavidNolan 3 83
(Declan Carroll) *led to 1/2-way: led again over 1f out: rdn and hdd ins fnl f: no ex towards fin* **4/1**[2]

6005 **5** *½* **Red Stripes (USA)**[4] 9219 7-8-0 **66** oh5 .... (b) ElishaWhittington(7) 4 65
(Lisa Williamson) *pushed along to join ldr: led 1/2-way: rdn and hdd over 1f out: no ex wl ins fnl f* **40/1**

3500 **6** *¾* **Secretfact**[10] 9131 6-9-1 **74** .... (p) CharlieBennett 7 71
(Malcolm Saunders) *hld up: hdwy 1/2-way: rdn over 1f out: styd on same pce ins fnl f* **14/1**

2225 **7** *½* **Excellent George**[28] 8826 7-9-6 **79** .... (t) PJMcDonald 9 74
(Stuart Williams) *hld up: rn wd turning for home: nvr on terms* **7/1**

2510 **8** *hd* **Zapper Cass (FR)**[17] 9013 6-9-2 **75** .... (be) AlistairRawlinson 1 69
(Michael Appleby) *s.i.s: nt clr run 1/2-way: nvr on terms* **10/1**

521 **9** *nk* **Three Little Birds**[10] 9135 4-8-13 **75** .... ThomasGreatrex(3) 10 68
(Sylvester Kirk) *hld up: rn wd turning for home: n.d* **13/2**[3]

4116 **10** *3 ¼* **Union Rose**[76] 7337 7-9-8 **81** .... (v) DavidProbert 8 62
(Ronald Harris) *sn pushed along and prom: lost pl 1/2-way: wknd over 1f out* **16/1**

59.33s (-2.57) **Going Correction** -0.15s/f (Stan) course record **10 Ran SP% 118.0**
Speed ratings (Par 105): **114,109,109,108,107 106,105,105,104,99**
CSF £80.08 CT £283.45 TOTE £16.60: £4.60, £2.10, £1.10; EX 75.90 Trifecta £402.70.
Owner Steve Macdonald **Bred** Michael G Daly **Trained** Carrutherstown, D'fries & G'way

FOCUS
This looked a competitive heat, but the winner impressed in shaving 0.06sec off the course record.

9287 BETWAY CLASSIFIED STKS 6f 20y (Tp)
6:15 (6:17) (Class 6) 3-Y-O+

£2,781 (£827; £413; £400; £400; £400) **Stalls Low**

Form RPR

2000 **1** **One One Seven (IRE)**[10] 9133 3-9-0 **52** .... CamHardie 3 59
(Antony Brittain) *broke wl: lost pl after 1f: hdwy 2f out: led over 1f out: rdn and edgd rt ins fnl f: styd on* **10/1**

0020 **2** *1* **Brockey Rise (IRE)**[15] 9039 4-9-0 **54** .... (v) DavidProbert 4 59
(David Evans) *led early: chsd ldrs: shkn up: nt clr run and swtchd lft over 1f out: rdn ins fnl f: r.o* **11/2**[2]

3302 **3** *nk* **Mansfield**[10] 9133 6-9-0 **55** .... DougieCostello 9 55
(Stella Barclay) *s.i.s: hld up: swtchd rt and hdwy over 1f out: rdn and edgd lft ins fnl f: r.o* **6/1**[3]

3026 **4** *½* **Ghost Buy (FR)**[1] 9276 3-9-0 **54** .... (bt) PJMcDonald 13 54
(Ivan Furtado) *hld up: hdwy: nt clr run and swtchd lft over 1f out: shkn up ins fnl f: r.o* **10/1**

6505 **5** *3* **Billyoakes (IRE)**[10] 9133 7-9-0 **53** .... (b) BenRobinson 6 45
(Ollie Pears) *prom: shkn up and swtchd rt over 1f out: rdn and hung lft ins fnl f: styd on* **8/1**

0053 **6** *¾* **Flora Tristan**[3] 9248 4-9-0 **55** .... (t) LiamKeniry 1 42
(Ivan Furtado) *s.i.s: hdwy 5f out: swtchd rt over 1f out: rdn and no ex ins fnl f* **6/1**[3]

6606 **7** *nk* **Tobeeornottobee**[11] 9106 3-9-0 **55** .... TomEaves 2 41
(Declan Carroll) *s.i.s: sn pushed along and prom: led over 4f out: rdn and hdd over 1f out: hung rt and wknd ins fnl f* **5/1**[1]

0606 **8** *1 ¼* **Philyaboots**[29] 8819 3-8-7 **45** .... EllaMcCain(7) 10 38
(Donald McCain) *sn led: hdd over 4f out: remained w ldr tl rdn over 1f out: nt clr run and wknd ins fnl f* **28/1**

6600 **9** *1 ½* **Bond Street Beau**[12] 9092 4-9-0 **54** .... KieranO'Neill 5 33
(Philip McBride) *pushed along and prom: rdn over 2f out: wknd ins fnl f* **12/1**

056 **10** *nk* **Auntie June**[34] 8672 3-9-0 **26** .... CallumShepherd 7 32
(Roy Brotherton) *hld up: pushed along 1/2-way: sme hdwy u.p over 1f out: wknd ins fnl f* **100/1**

0360 **11** *1 ¾* **Miss Gargar**[10] 9135 3-9-0 **55** .... (v) RobertHavlin 11 27
(Harry Dunlop) *hld up: shkn up over 1f out: n.d* **20/1**

1100 **12** *2 ¾* **Krazy Paving**[10] 9133 7-9-0 **54** .... (p) EoinWalsh 12 19
(Olly Murphy) *awkward s: sn prom: rdn over 3f out: wknd over 2f out* **50/1**

0000 **13** *¾* **Our Man In Havana**[225] 1986 4-9-0 **55** .... HollieDoyle 8 17
(Tony Carroll) *broke wl: racd freely: sn stdd and lost pl: n.d after (jockey said gelding lost its action; vet said the gelding was found to be lame on his left-hind and had also sustained a wound to his outside fetlock)* **11/2**[2]

1m 13.08s (-1.42) **Going Correction** -0.15s/f (Stan) **13 Ran SP% 124.2**
Speed ratings (Par 101): **103,101,101,100,96 95,95,93,91,91 88,85,84**
CSF £65.05 TOTE £12.20: £3.40, £3.10, £1.90; EX 96.90 Trifecta £612.90.
Owner John And Tony Jarvis And Partner **Bred** Lynch Bages, Camas Park & Summerhill B/S **Trained** Warthill, N Yorks
■ Stewards' Enquiry : Liam Keniry caution: careless riding

FOCUS
An ordinary sprint run at a good gallop that suited those closing from behind.

9288 BETWAY H'CAP 1m 5f 219y (Tp)
6:45 (6:50) (Class 4) (0-85,86) 3-Y-O+

£5,207 (£1,549; £774; £400; £400; £400) **Stalls Low**

Form RPR

3-14 **1** **Rajinsky (IRE)**[12] 9096 3-9-7 **82** .... RichardKingscote 8 94+
(Tom Dascombe) *s.i.s: sn prom: shkn up over 2f out: rdn to ld over 1f out: styd on* **1/1**[1]

0100 **2** *½* **Battle Of Marathon (USA)**[14] 9056 7-9-4 **77** .... DarraghKeenan(3) 5 86
(John Ryan) *s.i.s: hld up: hdwy on outer over 2f out: rdn to ld wl over 1f out: sn hdd: styd on* **11/1**

0053 **3** *1 ½* **Dance To Paris**[10] 9134 4-9-5 **75** .... (b) JackMitchell 1 82
(Lucy Wadham) *hld up in tch: swtchd rt over 2f out: rdn and swtchd lft ins fnl f: styd on same pce towards fin* **10/1**[3]

2336 **4** *3* **Wanaasah**[24] 8948 3-9-0 **75** .... HollieDoyle 6 78
(David Loughnane) *led: rdn and hdd wl over 1f out: no ex ins fnl f* **5/1**[2]

6450 **5** *¾* **Manjaam (IRE)**[45] 8350 6-9-1 **78** .... (p) JonathanFisher(7) 2 80
(Ian Williams) *s.i.s: hld up: rdn over 2f out: nt trble ldrs* **11/1**

5322 **6** *2* **Diodorus (IRE)**[95] 6674 5-9-2 **72** .... (p) JasonHart 10 71
(Karen McLintock) *chsd ldr after 1f tl rdn over 2f out: wknd ins fnl f* **12/1**

4430 **7** *11* **Cry Wolf**[108] 6218 6-9-9 **79** .... DanielMuscutt 9 62
(Alexandra Dunn) *chsd ldr 1f: remained handy: rdn over 2f out: wknd over 1f out* **33/1**

2000 **8** *3* **Billy Ray**[39] 8513 4-10-2 **86** .... DougieCostello 7 65
(Sam England) *s.i.s: a in rr: rdn and wknd over 3f out (jockey said gelding was slowly away)* **20/1**

3m 0.73s (-0.27) **Going Correction** -0.15s/f (Stan)
WFA 3 from 4yo+ 5lb **8 Ran SP% 107.8**
Speed ratings (Par 105): **94,93,92,91,90 89,83,81**
CSF £11.35 CT £57.96 TOTE £1.70: £1.10, £3.00, £2.90; EX 9.30 Trifecta £55.80.
Owner R S Matharu **Bred** Miss Elaine Marie Smith **Trained** Malpas, Cheshire
■ Weather Front was withdrawn. Price at time of withdrawal 20/1. Rule 4 does not apply.

FOCUS
This was won in workmanlike fashion but the unexposed winner is open to improvement over staying trips.

9289 BETWAY LIVE CASINO CLASSIFIED STKS 1m 4f 51y (Tp)
7:15 (7:18) (Class 6) 3-Y-O+

£2,781 (£827; £413; £400; £400; £400) **Stalls Low**

Form RPR

0064 **1** **Ember's Glow**[27] 8869 5-9-4 **49** .... DougieCostello 6 54
(Mark Loughnane) *trckd ldrs: rdn to ld ins fnl f: edgd lft: styd on wl* **7/2**[3]

6044 **2** *1 ¼* **Gladden (IRE)**[38] 8553 4-9-4 **42** .... DanielMuscutt 4 52
(Lee Carter) *hld up in tch: lost pl over 5f out: hdwy over 2f out: rdn and ev ch ins fnl f: styng on same pce whn edgd lft towards fin* **14/1**

5352 **3** *½* **Majestic Stone (IRE)**[42] 8423 5-9-4 **49** .... JasonHart 5 51
(Julie Camacho) *s.i.s: hld up: hdwy over 5f out: rdn over 1f out: styd on (jockey said gelding was slowly away)* **3/1**[2]

1006 **4** *hd* **Melabi (IRE)**[41] 8466 6-9-4 **47** .... ShaneGray 1 51
(Stella Barclay) *hld up in tch: rdn and ev ch ins fnl f: styd on same pce towards fin* **25/1**

3402 **5** *nk* **Klipperty Klopp**[10] 9139 3-9-0 **50** .... CamHardie 3 51
(Antony Brittain) *led: rdn over 1f out: edgd rt and hdd ins fnl f: styng on same pce whn nt clr run towards fin (jockey said gelding was denied a clear run in the closing stages)* **8/1**

0 **6** *2 ¾* **Snow Leopard (IRE)**[27] 8854 3-9-0 **50** .... RaulDaSilva 10 47
(Tony Carroll) *hld up: pushed along 4f out: hdwy u.p over 1f out: styd on same pce ins fnl f* **14/1**

0252 **7** *½* **Telekinetic**[34] 8663 4-9-4 **47** .... HollieDoyle 7 45
(Tony Carroll) *chsd ldr after 1f: rdn over 2f out: no ex ins fnl f* **11/4**[1]

2000 **8** *4 ½* **Bumblekite**[59] 7909 3-9-0 **47** .... DavidProbert 8 39
(Steph Hollinshead) *hld up: hdwy u.p over 1f out: wknd ins fnl f* **50/1**

620 **9** *½* **Brecqhou Island**[156] 4426 4-9-1 **49** .... (w) PaddyBradley(3) 11 37
(Mark Pattinson) *hld up: rdn over 2f out: wknd over 1f out* **33/1**

6404 **10** *16* **Ahfad**[29] 8813 4-9-4 **48** .... (b) HectorCrouch 9 12
(Gary Moore) *prom: racd keenly: rdn on outer over 2f out: sn wknd (jockey said gelding ran too freely)* **9/1**

2m 40.43s (-0.37) **Going Correction** -0.15s/f (Stan)
WFA 3 from 4yo+ 4lb **10 Ran SP% 117.1**
Speed ratings (Par 101): **95,94,93,93,93 91,91,88,88,77**
CSF £50.49 TOTE £4.60: £1.30, £5.00, £1.10; EX 59.50 Trifecta £196.60.
Owner Trevor Johnson **Bred** Darley **Trained** Rock, Worcs

FOCUS
A low-grade classified race, and not form to get excited about.
T/Jkpt: Not won. T/Plt: £68.90 to a £1 stake. Pool: £92,573.55 - 979.94 winning units T/Qpdt: £10.80 to a £1 stake. Pool: £17,209.73 - 1,172.79 winning units **Colin Roberts**

9290 - 9297a (Foreign Racing) - See Raceform Interactive

9211
KEMPTON (A.W) (R-H)
Wednesday, December 4

OFFICIAL GOING: Polytrack: standard to slow
Wind: virtually nil Weather: dry, foggy from race 5

9298 ALL-WEATHER RACING INFORMATION AT SANDFORM.CO.UK H'CAP 7f (P)
3:40 (3:43) (Class 6) (0-55,55) 3-Y-O+

£3,105 (£924; £461; £400; £400; £400) **Stalls Low**

Form RPR

0060 **1** **Rajman**[34] 8698 3-9-7 **55** .... (h) DavidProbert 6 61
(Tom Clover) *in tch in midfield: effrt over 2f out: rdn and hdwy over 1f out: led 1f out: hld on wl ins fnl f* **6/1**[2]

4560 **2** *nk* **Disruptor (FR)**[25] 8949 3-9-5 **53** .... (v[1]) TomMarquand 5 58
(David Evans) *chsd ldrs and t.k.h: hdwy u.p and ev ch 1f out: kpt on wl: a jst hld* **20/1**

-424 **3** *1 ¼* **Drop Kick Murphi (IRE)**[9] 9160 5-9-0 **48** .... AdrianMcCarthy 11 51+
(Christine Dunnett) *rrd as stalls opened and slowly away: hld up in rr: rdn and hdwy whn nt clr run ent fnl f: rdn and hdwy to chse ldng pair 100yds out: kpt on (jockey said gelding reared as the stalls opened and was subsequently slowly away and denied a clear run)* **8/1**[3]

0010 **4** *1 ½* **Hollander**[4] 9246 5-9-5 **53** .... (bt) RobertHavlin 12 51
(Alexandra Dunn) *led and crossed to inner: rdn wl over 1f out: hdd 1f out: no ex and wknd fnl 100yds* **16/1**

6000 **5** *shd* **Geneva Spur (USA)**[16] 9032 3-9-2 **50** .... (b[1]) JackMitchell 1 47
(Roger Varian) *trckd ldrs on inner: rdn 2f out: unable qck u.p over 1f out: wknd fnl 100yds* **9/1**

2106 **6** *nk* **Captain Sedgwick (IRE)**[53] 8123 5-9-0 **48** .... JaneElliott 7 45
(John Spearing) *chsd ldr: rdn over 2f out: unable qck u.p over 1f out: n.m.r and wknd fnl 100yds (jockey said mare suffered interference in the final furlong)* **20/1**

060 **7** *½* **Satchville Flyer**[4] 9249 8-8-13 **47** .... (p) PhilipPrince 3 42
(Milton Bradley) *hld up in tch in midfield: swtchd and effrt on inner 2f out: drvn and unable qck over 1f out: wknd ins fnl f* **20/1**

The Form Book Flat 2019, Raceform Ltd, Newbury, RG14 5SJ

4042 **8** ½ **Maazel (IRE)**[4] 9249 5-9-7 **55** DanielMuscutt 8 51+
(Lee Carter) *hld up in tch in midfield: effrt and clsd to chse ldrs whn nt clr run jst over 1f out: squeezed for room 1f out: nt rcvr and kpt on same pce ins fnl f (jockey said gelding was denied a clear run)* **5/4**[1]

0040 **9** ½ **Miaella**[44] 8401 4-9-4 **52** JoeyHaynes 14 45
(Chelsea Banham) *taken down early: in tch in midfield: rdn over 2f out: drvn over 1f out: kpt on same pce ins fnl f* **20/1**

2006 **10** 1 ½ **Flying Sakhee**[4] 9249 6-8-12 **46** oh1 (p) KieranO'Neill 13 35
(John Bridger) *s.i.s: hld up in tch in last pair: swtchd lft and effrt ent fnl 2f: nvr threatened to get on terms* **20/1**

06-0 **11** 19 **Bird Of Wonder**[177] 3661 4-8-11 **52** EmmaTaff(7) 9
(Henry Candy) *wd thrght: midfield: rdn over 2f out: sn outpcd and wl bhd ins fnl f* **12/1**

1m 25.86s (-0.14) **Going Correction** -0.05s/f (Stan) **11 Ran SP% 117.2**
Speed ratings (Par 101): **98,97,96,94,94 94,93,92,92,90 68**
CSF £122.80 CT £976.27 TOTE £5.50: £1.60, £6.60, £1.80; EX 124.70 Trifecta £1692.20.
Owner R S Matharu **Bred** Highclere Stud & Jake Warren Ltd **Trained** Newmarket, Suffolk

FOCUS
A muddling, low-grade affair in which several were hampered as the front pair made the best of their way home down the outside, so it's not reliable form.

9299 BRITISH STALLIONS STUDS EBF NOVICE STKS 6f (P)
4:10 (4:12) (Class 5) 2-Y-O **£3,881** (£1,155; £577; £288) **Stalls** Low

Form RPR

1 **Brunel Charm** 2-9-2 0 FinleyMarsh(3) 11 82+
(Richard Hughes) *wnt lft leaving stalls and s.i.s: hdwy on outer to chse ldr over 4f out: rdn and sltly outpcd 2f out: sn rallied and chal ent fnl f: led 150yds out: r.o wl* **25/1**

02 **2** ¾ **Al Dawodiya (IRE)**[9] 9159 2-9-0 0 JimCrowley 1 75
(Richard Hannon) *t.k.h: led and dictated stdy gallop: rdn and kicked 2 l clr 2f out: hrd pressed ent fnl f: hdd 150yds out: kpt on same pce after* **6/4**[1]

3 2 ½ **Never Dark** 2-9-5 0 DavidProbert 2 72
(Andrew Balding) *trckd ldrs on inner: effrt 2f out: 3rd and kpt on same pce ins fnl f* **9/4**[2]

04 **4** 2 **Sound Mixer**[13] 9099 2-9-0 0 (b) JamesDoyle 4 61
(William Haggas) *midfield: effrt over 2f out: chsd ldng trio and styd on same pce ins fnl f* **5/1**[3]

5 1 ¼ **Mount Mogan** 2-9-5 0 HectorCrouch 8 62
(Ed Walker) *hld up in last trio: rdn ent fnl 2f: swtchd lft jst over 2f out: hdwy over 1f out: kpt on ins fnl f: nvr trbld ldrs* **66/1**

00 **6** hd **Saffron Lane**[11] 9130 2-9-0 0 GeorgeWood 12 56
(Harry Dunlop) *chsd ldr tl over 4f out: styd chsng ldrs: rdn over 2f out: struggling and outpcd wl over 1f out: wl hld and kpt on same pce fnl f* **66/1**

00 **7** 3 **Sacred Legacy (IRE)**[55] 8059 2-9-5 0 (h) KieranO'Neill 6 51
(Ronald Harris) *hld up in last trio: effrt and hung rt over 2f out: sn outpcd and wl hld over 1f out (jockey said colt hung right-handed in the straight)* **33/1**

3 **8** nse **Ayr Harbour**[62] 7842 2-9-5 0 AlistairRawlinson 10 51
(Michael Appleby) *midfield: rdn and rn green over 2f out: sn outpcd and wl hld over 1f out* **5/1**[3]

0 **9** ¾ **Surrey Flame (FR)**[34] 8709 2-9-5 0 LiamKeniry 5 49
(Joseph Tuite) *in tch in midfield: rdn and no imp over 1f out: wknd ins fnl f* **66/1**

10 ½ **Sena** 2-9-0 0 TomMarquand 7 42
(William Haggas) *s.i.s: hld up in last trio: swtchd rt and effrt on inner 2f out: sme hdwy over 1f out but nvr getting on terms: wknd ins fnl f (jockey said filly was slowly away)* **25/1**

1m 12.76s (-0.34) **Going Correction** -0.05s/f (Stan) **10 Ran SP% 119.2**
Speed ratings (Par 96): **100,99,95,93,91 91,87,87,86,85**
CSF £63.15 TOTE £34.20: £5.20, £1.10, £1.30; EX 85.60 Trifecta £429.00.
Owner J Langridge & R Lane **Bred** Jupiter Bloodstock Ltd **Trained** Upper Lambourn, Berks

FOCUS
Nothing much got into this sprint novice and the form looks nothing out of the ordinary.

9300 32RED ON THE APP STORE NURSERY H'CAP 6f (P)
4:40 (4:41) (Class 5) (0-75,75) 2-Y-O **£3,881** (£1,155; £577; £400; £400; £400) **Stalls** Low

Form RPR

401 **1** **Waddat (IRE)**[28] 8865 2-9-7 **75** ShaneKelly 3 79+
(Richard Hughes) *taken down early: t.k.h: mde all: edgd rt over 1f out: sn rdn: drvn ins fnl f: hrd pressed towards fin: hld on wl* **7/2**[2]

054 **2** nk **Honore Daumier (IRE)**[89] 6912 2-9-6 **74** AdamKirby 10 77+
(Henry Candy) *s.i.s and swtchd rt sn after s: hld up in rr: sltly impeded and rdn over 2f out: swtchd lft 2f out: rdn and gd hdwy over 1f out: str chal towards fin: hld last strides* **14/1**

2234 **3** 2 **River Cam**[47] 8302 2-9-1 **69** PJMcDonald 6 66
(James Tate) *in tch in midfield: nt clrest of runs 2f out: swtchd lft and rdn over 1f out: kpt on wl ins fnl f: snatched 3rd last stride: nvr getting to ldrs* **10/1**

026 **4** shd **Depose**[28] 8849 2-9-7 **75** JamesDoyle 1 74
(Hugo Palmer) *in tch in midfield: effrt to chse wnr 2f out: pressing wnr on inner whn squeezed for room and forced to swtchd lft over 1f out: kpt on same pce after: lost 2 pls ins fnl f* **3/1**[1]

6506 **5** 1 **Wilfy**[6] 9205 2-9-2 **70** LiamKeniry 11 64
(Sylvester Kirk) *stdd and swtchd rt after s: swtchd rt and effrt on inner ent fnl 2f: rdn and nt clr run over 1f out: trying to switch lft but nvr much room and one pce ins fnl f (jockey said gelding was denied a clear run)* **14/1**

3204 **6** 1 ¾ **We're Reunited (IRE)**[16] 9031 2-9-5 **73** DavidProbert 12 62+
(Ronald Harris) *hdwy on outer to chse ldrs over 4f out: rdn ent fnl 2f: drvn and unable qck over 1f out: short of room and wknd ins fnl f* **12/1**

532 **7** 2 ½ **Quaint (IRE)**[36] 8640 2-8-11 **65** RichardKingscote 4 46
(Hughie Morrison) *t.k.h: chsd wnr tl over 4f out: chsd ldrs after tl drvn and unable qck over 1f out: wknd ins fnl f* **7/1**

3400 **8** hd **Amnaa**[65] 7768 2-8-7 **61** KieranO'Neill 5 41
(John Bridger) *in tch in midfield on outer: rdn jst over 2f out: drvn and unable qck over 1f out: wknd ins fnl f (vet said filly lost it's right hind shoe)* **66/1**

6152 **9** hd **Miss Thoughtful**[35] 8650 2-9-0 **68** NicolaCurrie 8 48
(Jamie Osborne) *nudged rt leaving stalls: hdwy to chse wnr over 4f out: rdn and lost 2nd 2f out: unable qck over 1f out: btn whn squeezed for room ins fnl f: sn wknd (jockey said filly suffered interference in the final furlong)* **20/1**

0243 **10** ¾ **Royal Council (IRE)**[71] 7556 2-9-2 **70** LukeMorris 9 48
(Michael Appleby) *edgd rt leaving stalls: in tch in midfield: swtchd lft and effrt over 2f out: no imp u.p over 1f out: wl hld ins fnl f* **20/1**

4301 **11** ½ **Mitty's Smile (IRE)**[35] 8650 2-9-6 **74** (b) HollieDoyle 7 50+
(Archie Watson) *bmpd leaving stalls: hld up in tch towards rr: effrt 2f out: n.m.r and no imp over 1f out: wl btn fnl f (jockey said filly suffered interference leaving the stalls)* **6/1**[3]

110 **12** hd **Lets Go Lucky**[47] 8318 2-9-6 **74** TomMarquand 2 50
(David Evans) *s.i.s: sn rcvrd and in tch in midfield: effrt ent fnl 2f: bmpd over 1f out: sn btn and wknd ins fnl f* **20/1**

1m 12.52s (-0.58) **Going Correction** -0.05s/f (Stan) **12 Ran SP% 119.9**
Speed ratings (Par 96): **101,100,97,97,96 94,90,90,90,89 88,88**
CSF £49.48 CT £463.65 TOTE £4.30: £1.90, £4.30, £3.20; EX 74.20 Trifecta £637.40.
Owner N Martin **Bred** Tally-Ho Stud **Trained** Upper Lambourn, Berks
■ Stewards' Enquiry : Shane Kelly caution; careless riding

FOCUS
A fair, well-run race in which the front pair adopted contrasting tactics and there wasn't much trouble in running, so it's a fair result.

9301 32RED.COM H'CAP 6f (P)
5:10 (5:12) (Class 2) (0-105,101) 3-Y-O+ **£15,562** (£4,660; £2,330; £1,165; £582; £292) **Stalls** Low

Form RPR

1323 **1** **Harry's Bar**[13] 9098 4-8-12 **92** TomMarquand 4 102
(James Fanshawe) *hld up in tch in midfield: nt clrest of runs 2f out: rdn and hdwy between rivals over 1f out: drvn to ld ins fnl f: r.o strly* **4/1**[2]

1010 **2** 1 **Lethal Lunch**[34] 8707 4-9-3 **97** AdamKirby 3 104
(Clive Cox) *trckd ldrs on inner: effrt ent fnl 2f: drvn and ev ch 1f out: chsd wnr and kpt on same pce ins fnl f* **3/1**[1]

2-03 **3** nk **Silent Echo**[11] 9129 5-9-1 **95** JimCrowley 9 101
(Peter Hedger) *bmpd leaving stalls: t.k.h: hld up in last pair: effrt over 1f out: hdwy 1f out: r.o wl ins fnl f: nt rch ldrs* **8/1**

2553 **4** ½ **Royal Birth**[8] 9166 8-9-7 **101** (t) PJMcDonald 8 105
(Stuart Williams) *wnt lft and bmpd rivals leaving stalls: sn led: rdn 2f out: hdd ins fnl f: no ex and outpcd fnl 100yds* **20/1**

0001 **5** nk **Polybius**[5] 9214 8-8-11 **91** 4ex CallumShepherd 1 94
(David Simcock) *hld up in tch in midfield: hdwy on inner and rdn to chse ldrs 1f out: kpt on same pce ins fnl f* **10/1**

3231 **6** ¾ **Lady Dancealot (IRE)**[13] 9088 4-8-12 **92** HollieDoyle 6 93+
(David Elsworth) *squeezed for room leaving stalls: t.k.h: hld up in rr: effrt over 2f out: swtchd lft and stl plenty to do over 1f out: r.o wl ins fnl f: nvr trbld ldrs (jockey said filly ran too free)* **3/1**[1]

0001 **7** ¾ **Tawny Port**[16] 9030 5-8-2 **89** AngusVilliers(7) 5 88
(Stuart Williams) *stdd: edgd lft and bmpd rival s: hld up in tch: effrt 2f out: no imp and kpt on same pce ins fnl f (jockey said gelding suffered interference leaving the stalls)* **16/1**

5323 **8** shd **Benny And The Jets (IRE)**[15] 9057 3-8-2 **82** FrannyNorton 7 80
(Sylvester Kirk) *in tch in midfield: unable qck u.p over 1f out: wknd ins fnl f* **7/1**[3]

0410 **9** 1 ½ **Shamshon (IRE)**[13] 9088 8-8-7 **87** RaulDaSilva 12 81
(Stuart Williams) *chsd ldr tl unable qck u.p and lost pl over 1f out: wknd ins fnl f* **66/1**

5000 **10** 5 **Rock On Baileys**[13] 9088 4-9-1 **95** (b) BarryMcHugh 10 86
(Amy Murphy) *edgd rt and bmpd leaving stalls: hdwy to chse ldrs over 4f out: unable qck over 1f out: btn whn short of room and hmpd 1f out: sn wknd (jockey said filly hung right-handed)* **33/1**

1m 11.77s (-1.33) **Going Correction** -0.05s/f (Stan) **10 Ran SP% 117.8**
Speed ratings (Par 109): **106,104,104,103,103 102,101,101,99,92**
CSF £16.33 CT £94.80 TOTE £5.00: £1.60, £1.60, £2.60; EX 22.60 Trifecta £142.40.
Owner Jan and Peter Hopper **Bred** Jan & Peter Hopper **Trained** Newmarket, Suffolk

FOCUS
The result has a solid look to it but the modest gallop acted against those held up, so there's a couple of performances worth marking up.

9302 32RED WILD FLOWER STKS (LISTED RACE) 1m 3f 219y(P)
5:40 (5:42) (Class 1) 3-Y-O+ **£25,519** (£9,675; £4,842; £2,412; £1,210; £607) **Stalls** Low

Form RPR

2252 **1** **Pablo Escobarr (IRE)**[32] 8764 3-9-2 107 (t) TomMarquand 1 113
(William Haggas) *led for over 1f: styd chsng ldrs tl swtchd lft and drvn to ld over 1f out: hrd pressed and sustained duel w runner-up fnl f: hld on gamely u.p* **9/2**[2]

5622 **2** nk **Loxley (IRE)**[30] 8811 4-9-6 109 (p[1]) JamesDoyle 8 112
(Charlie Appleby) *stdd and dropped in bhd after s: hld up in tch in last trio: weaved through and clsd to chse wnr over 1f out: effrt to chal 1f out: sn drvn and sustained duel w wnr fnl f: kpt on but hld cl home* **9/4**[1]

4142 **3** 4 **Hameem**[34] 8710 4-9-1 100 JimCrowley 2 101
(John Gosden) *awkward leaving stalls and s.i.s: effrt ent fnl 2f: weaved through and hdwy on inner over 1f out: kpt on ins fnl f: snatched 3rd last strides: no threat to ldrs (jockey said filly anticipated the start, knocking it's head on the gate and was subsequently slowly away)* **11/2**[3]

1450 **4** hd **Collide**[145] 4884 4-9-6 98 (t w) JackMitchell 3 105
(Hugo Palmer) *midfield: nt clrest of runs over 2f out: rdn and hdwy between rivals over 1f out: 3rd and outpcd by ldng pair ins fnl f: lost 3rd last strides* **11/2**[3]

1520 **5** ¾ **Hulcote**[18] 9002 4-9-1 94 HectorCrouch 4 99
(Clive Cox) *taken down early and led to s: hld up in tch in midfield: effrt on outer over 2f outer: drvn over 1f out: kpt on same pce ins fnl f* **25/1**

-033 **6** 1 **Mildenberger**[201] 2807 4-9-6 109 JoeFanning 5 102
(Mark Johnston) *in tch in midfield: unable qck over 1f out: wknd ins fnl f* **13/2**

4013 **7** 1 ¾ **Weekender**[68] 7662 5-9-6 112 RobertHavlin 6 100
(John Gosden) *chsd ldr 8f out: drvn: unable qck and lost 2nd over 1f out: wknd ins fnl f* **11/2**[3]

4161 **8** 11 **Hermosura**[55] 8064 3-8-11 77 (v) RichardKingscote 7 78
(Ralph Beckett) *hdwy to ld over 10f out: hdd and lost pl qckly u.p over 1f out: wknd fnl f* **50/1**

2m 29.99s (-4.51) **Going Correction** -0.05s/f (Stan)
WFA 3 from 4yo+ 4lb **8 Ran SP% 114.2**
Speed ratings (Par 111): **113,112,110,110,109 108,107,100**
CSF £15.03 TOTE £5.30: £2.00, £1.10, £1.70; EX 17.10 Trifecta £72.50.
Owner Hussain Alabbas Lootah **Bred** R Scarborough & Carradale **Trained** Newmarket, Suffolk

FOCUS
Smart efforts from the front pair, who pulled clear off a steady pace, but there were some disappointments in behind, so there's not much depth to the form. The fourth helps to set the standard.

9303 32RED CASINO H'CAP — 1m 3f 219y(P)
6:10 (6:14) (Class 5) (0-75,76) 3-Y-O+

£3,752 (£1,116; £557; £400; £400; £400) Stalls Low

Form — RPR

0420 **1** **Lord Halifax (IRE)**[43] 8433 3-9-1 **70**.......................... KieranShoemark 7 84+
(Charlie Fellowes) *chsd ldr for 2f: styd chsng ldrs tl rdn to ld jst over 2f out: drvn clr over 1f out: styd on strly: readily* **11/2**

4100 **2** *5* **Torolight**[38] 4769 3-8-7 **69**.......................... AngusVilliers(7) 12 73
(Nicky Henderson) *hld up in rr of main gp: rdn and hdwy on inner over 1f out: kpt on to chse clr wnr wl ins fnl f: nvr a threat* **10/1**

5000 **3** *3/4* **Ilhabela Fact**[14] 9066 5-9-11 **76**.......................... TomMarquand 8 79
(Tony Carroll) *chsd ldrs on outer: chsd ldr over 8f out tl unable to match pce of wnr in 2nd over 1f out: kpt on same pce and lost 2nd wl ins fnl f* **9/1**

112/ **4** *1/2* **Wolfcatcherjack (IRE)**[813] 7019 5-9-10 **75**..................(t[1]) LukeMorris 14 77
(Nick Gifford) *hld up towards rr of main gp: rdn and hdwy over 1f out: kpt on ins fnl f: no threat to wnr* **33/1**

6323 **5** *1* **Debbonair (IRE)**[47] 8300 3-8-13 **68**..........................(b) JackMitchell 2 69
(Hugo Palmer) *midfield: rdn ent fnl 2f: unable qck u.p over 1f out: wl hld and plugged on same pce ins fnl f* **3/1[1]**

2-41 **6** *hd* **Cuillin (USA)**[18] 9012 4-9-8 **73**.......................... AdamKirby 5 73
(Noel Williams) *midfield: effrt over 2f out: kpt on ins fnl f: no ch w wnr* **5/1[3]**

/02- **7** *1 1/2* **Jamacho**[41] 2252 5-9-2 **67**..........................(h) LiamKeniry 3 65
(Charlie Longsdon) *led after over 1f: rdn and hdd jst over 2f out: outpcd and btn over 1f out: wknd ins fnl f* **50/1**

4-36 **8** *3/4* **Royal Star**[220] 2142 3-9-7 **76**.......................... JamesDoyle 4 73
(Roger Charlton) *midfield: effrt on inner 2f out: no imp u.p 1f out: wknd ins fnl f* **9/2[2]**

1000 **9** *1* **New Agenda**[45] 3633 7-9-7 **72**.......................... RobertHavlin 1 67
(Paul Webber) *led for over 1f: chsd ldrs after: rdn and unable qck 2f out: sn outpcd and wknd ins fnl f* **33/1**

6306 **10** *1/2* **Ravenous**[18] 9012 8-8-9 **63**.......................... TheodoreLadd(3) 6 57
(Luke Dace) *swtchd rt and pushed along leaving stalls: midfield: no imp u.p over 1f out: wknd ins fnl f* **40/1**

3033 **11** *1 1/2* **Cheeky Rascal (IRE)**[14] 9067 4-8-5 **63**..........(v) LauraCoughlan(7) 13 55
(Tom Ward) *midfield on outer: rdn over 2f out: unable qck and outpcd over 1f out: wknd ins fnl f* **16/1**

2200 **12** *1* **Hackbridge**[23] 5311 4-9-5 **73**..........................(v) PaddyBradley(3) 10 63
(Pat Phelan) *hld up in rr: nvr involved* **20/1**

0600 **13** *1* **Cafe Espresso**[11] 9134 3-8-13 **68**.......................... JoeyHaynes 9 57
(Chelsea Banham) *towards rr of main gp: rdn over 2f out: sn struggling and wknd wl over 1f out* **100/1**

0060 **14** *3* **Rail Dancer**[14] 9067 7-8-4 **62**..........................(p) GavinAshton(7) 11 46
(Shaun Keightley) *hld up in rr: nvr involved* **33/1**

2m 34.09s (-0.41) **Going Correction** -0.05s/f (Stan)
WFA 3 from 4yo+ 4lb — **14 Ran SP% 119.2**
Speed ratings (Par 103): **99,95,95,94,94 94,93,92,91,91 90,89,89,87**
CSF £55.21 CT £493.79 TOTE £6.60: £2.40, £3.30, £3.10; EX 62.60 Trifecta £467.80.
Owner Never So Bold - Aquino **Bred** Mrs T Mahon **Trained** Newmarket, Suffolk

FOCUS
A fair handicap dominated by an improver. There was no obvious bias.

9304 100% PROFIT BOOST AT 32REDSPORT.COM H'CAP — 1m (P)
6:40 (6:44) (Class 4) (0-80,81) 3-Y-O+

£6,469 (£1,925; £962; £481; £400; £400) Stalls Low

Form — RPR

-252 **1** **Normal Norman**[50] 8236 5-9-1 **76**.......................... DarraghKeenan(3) 6 83+
(John Ryan) *sn stdd bk: t.k.h: hld up in rr: swtchd lft and effrt 2f out: str run u.p ins fnl f to ld towards fin* **8/1[3]**

5003 **2** *1* **Merweb (IRE)**[12] 9109 4-8-13 **71**..........................(p) JackMitchell 8 76
(Heather Main) *led: rdn 2f out: hrd pressed and drvn ins fnl f: kpt on wl tl hdd and nt match pce of wnr towards fin* **16/1**

5451 **3** *nk* **Scofflaw**[11] 9138 5-9-9 **81**..........................(b) TomMarquand 1 85
(David Evans) *trckd ldrs on inner: effrt to chse ldr over 1f out: drvn and ev ch ins fnl f: kpt on wl but unable to match pce of wnr towards fin* **11/1**

112 **4** *1/2* **Lethal Missile (IRE)**[151] 4662 3-9-7 **80**.......................... AdamKirby 7 83
(Clive Cox) *in tch in midfield: rdn over 2f out: kpt on u.p ins fnl f* **8/1[3]**

2513 **5** *1/2* **Delicate Kiss**[11] 9126 5-8-13 **76**..........................(b) AledBeech(5) 10 78
(John Bridger) *dwlt: steadily rcvrd and pressed ldr over 5f out tl over 1f out: unable qck u.p: outpcd ins fnl f* **14/1**

0042 **6** *hd* **Glory Of Paris (IRE)**[15] 9048 5-9-1 **73**..........................(p) LukeMorris 2 75
(Michael Appleby) *dwlt: sn rcvrd and t.k.h in midfield: effrt ent fnl 2f: hrd drvn and unable qck over 1f out* **16/1**

0405 **7** *shd* **Dourado (IRE)**[44] 8412 5-9-4 **76**.......................... DavidProbert 3 77
(Patrick Chamings) *in tch in midfield: effrt over 1f out: unable qck u.p 1f out: kpt on same pce ins fnl f* **14/1**

0025 **8** *1/2* **One Cool Daddy (USA)**[15] 9054 4-9-2 **74**.......................... JimCrowley 4 74
(Dean Ivory) *in tch in midfield: effrt on inner ent fnl 2f: rdn and hdwy to chse ldrs 1f out: no imp ins fnl f: kpt on same pce ins fnl f* **5/1[2]**

-541 **9** *3* **Rangali Island (IRE)**[30] 8809 3-9-7 **80**.......................... CallumShepherd 5 73
(David Simcock) *hld up in tch towards rr: effrt over 2f out: no imp over 1f out: wknd ins fnl f* **11/8[1]**

006- **10** *18* **Frank Bridge**[357] 9506 6-9-0 **72**.......................... RobertHavlin 9 24
(Alexandra Dunn) *chsd ldr tl over 5f out: rdn and losing pl whn n.m.r 2f out: sn btn and bhd* **100/1**

1m 38.36s (-1.44) **Going Correction** -0.05s/f (Stan)
WFA 3 from 4yo+ 1lb — **10 Ran SP% 115.4**
Speed ratings (Par 105): **105,104,103,103,102 102,102,101,98,80**
CSF £125.72 CT £1452.39 TOTE £8.60: £2.30, £4.90, £2.90; EX 126.80 Trifecta £723.90.
Owner Gerry McGladery **Bred** E I Mack **Trained** Newmarket, Suffolk

FOCUS
A fair handicap in which a couple of the market leaders disappointed. All bar the winner found it difficult to make ground from rear.

9305 RACINGTV.COM H'CAP — 1m (P)
7:10 (7:13) (Class 6) (0-60,60) 3-Y-O+

£3,105 (£924; £461; £400; £400; £400) Stalls Low

Form — RPR

-104 **1** **Brains (IRE)**[6] 9209 3-9-6 **59**..........................(b) NicolaCurrie 3 70
(Jamie Osborne) *sn led: hdd over 2f out: led again wl over 1f out and sn rdn clr: r.o strly ins fnl f* **10/1**

3 **2** *2 1/4* **Crimson King (IRE)**[16] 9028 3-9-6 **59**..........................(v[1]) AlistairRawlinson 7 65+
(Michael Appleby) *dwlt: short of room and pushed along early: towards rr: hdwy on inner over 1f out: chsd clr wnr ins fnl f: no imp (jockey said gelding suffered interference at the start)* **4/1[1]**

0405 **3** *1 1/4* **Elena Osorio (IRE)**[16] 9039 3-9-1 **54**.......................... HectorCrouch 8 57
(Ed Walker) *in tch in midfield: effrt over 2f out: drvn and chsd clr wnr 1f out: no imp and lost 2nd ins fnl f* **10/1**

4265 **4** *1 1/2* **Vipin (FR)**[16] 9040 4-9-5 **57**.......................... MartinDwyer 5 57
(William Muir) *t.k.h: chsd ldrs tl wnt 2nd after 3f: led over 2f out: rdn and hdd wl over 1f out: sn outpcd and lost 2nd 1f out: wknd ins fnl f* **7/1[3]**

0002 **5** *nk* **The Warrior (IRE)**[6] 9209 7-9-3 **58**.......................... PaddyBradley(3) 12 57
(Lee Carter) *hld up towards rr: effrt and hdwy over 1f out: kpt on u.p ins fnl f: nvr trbld ldrs* **10/1**

0011 **6** *nk* **Purple Paddy**[29] 8822 4-9-2 **59**.......................... MarkCrehan(5) 9 57
(Jimmy Fox) *dwlt: sn rcvrd and in tch in midfield: hdwy on outer over 2f out: rdn and unable qck wl over 1f out: wl hld ins fnl f* **9/2[2]**

6U34 **7** *3* **Dancing Jo**[34] 8698 3-9-7 **60**.......................... TomMarquand 2 51
(Mick Channon) *in tch in midfield: rdn jst over 2f out: unable qck and outpcd over 1f out: wknd ins fnl f* **8/1**

2414 **8** *1* **Mabo**[35] 8667 4-9-6 **58**..........................(b) LukeMorris 6 47
(Grace Harris) *in tch in midfield: effrt 2f out: unable qck and btn 1f out: sn wknd* **14/1**

001- **9** *1/2* **Connemera Queen**[234] 1792 6-9-6 **58**.......................... JoeyHaynes 4 46
(John Butler) *towards rr: rdn over 2f out: nvr threatened ldrs (jockey said gelding suffered interference at the start)* **33/1**

0000 **10** *1/2* **Recuerdame (USA)**[11] 9128 3-9-4 **57**.......................... HollieDoyle 1 44
(Simon Dow) *led: sn hdd and chsd wnr tl 5f out: lost pl u.p over 1f out: wknd ins fnl f (jockey said gelding hung left-handed under pressure)* **8/1**

0024 **11** *1* **Itmakesyouthink**[35] 8666 5-9-5 **57**..........................(h) ShaneKelly 13 41
(Mark Loughnane) *stdd after s: hld up towards rr: effrt 2f out: no imp and sn btn (jockey said gelding ran too free)* **25/1**

4105 **12** *1/2* **Maisie Moo**[28] 8864 3-9-1 **54**.......................... JosephineGordon 10 37
(Shaun Keightley) *chsd ldrs: rdn ent fnl 2f: lost pl u.p over 1f out: wknd ins fnl f* **25/1**

-000 **13** *nk* **Seeing Red (IRE)**[121] 5730 3-9-3 **56**..........................(w) RobertHavlin 11 39
(Amanda Perrett) *stdd after s: hld up in rr: effrt ent fnl 2f: no prog and wl hld over 1f out* **40/1**

3000 **14** *13* **Rifft (IRE)**[29] 8822 4-8-12 **50**..........................(t) RichardKingscote 14
(Lydia Richards) *midfield early: lost pl and towards rr 1/2-way: rdn over 2f out: sn btn and bhd* **50/1**

1m 39.5s (-0.30) **Going Correction** -0.05s/f (Stan)
WFA 3 from 4yo+ 1lb — **14 Ran SP% 121.9**
Speed ratings (Par 101): **99,96,95,94,93 93,90,89,88,88 87,86,86,73**
CSF £48.04 CT £425.48 TOTE £12.10: £3.90, £2.10, £3.40; EX 69.50 Trifecta £1067.30.
Owner The Judges & Partner **Bred** Kilnamoragh Stud **Trained** Upper Lambourn, Berks

FOCUS
A modest handicap in which there was no obvious pace bias.
T/Jkpt: Not Won. T/Plt: £159.40 to a £1 stake. Pool: £90,213.19 - 413.09 winning units T/Qpdt: £25.00 to a £1 stake. Pool: £13,753.35 - 405.97 winning units **Steve Payne**

9242 LINGFIELD (L-H)
Wednesday, December 4

OFFICIAL GOING: Polytrack: standard

9306 BOMBARDIER GOLDEN BEER H'CAP — 7f 1y(P)
12:10 (12:11) (Class 5) (0-70,70) 3-Y-O+

£3,428 (£1,020; £509; £300; £300; £300) Stalls Low

Form — RPR

0410 **1** **Beepeecee**[15] 9047 5-8-11 **67**..........................(b) AmeliaGlass(7) 11 76
(Thomas Gallagher) *midfield and racd wd: pushed along and hdwy fr 2f out: led ins fnl f: kpt on wl* **8/1**

0610 **2** *1 3/4* **Born To Finish (IRE)**[15] 9048 6-9-5 **68**..........................(p) DavidProbert 5 72
(Ed de Giles) *midfield: rdn and hdwy over 1f out: wnt 2nd towards fin* **8/1**

4404 **3** *nk* **Bint Dandy (IRE)**[15] 9047 8-9-1 **64**..........................(b) RichardKingscote 1 67
(Charlie Wallis) *trckd ldrs: rdn and led over 1f out: hdd & wknd ins fnl f* **12/1**

1-20 **4** *nk* **Para Mio (IRE)**[226] 1988 4-9-5 **68**.......................... TomQueally 9 70+
(Seamus Durack) *s.i.s: hld up in last: racd wd and hdwy fr 2f out: rdn over 1f out: styd on ins fnl f* **20/1**

066 **5** *2 1/4* **Real Estate (IRE)**[62] 7837 4-9-3 **66**..........................(p) CallumShepherd 4 62
(Michael Attwater) *midfield: pushed along over 1f out: nt clr run ins fnl f: styd on towards fin* **14/1**

4612 **6** *nk* **River Dawn**[30] 8807 3-9-4 **67**.......................... HectorCrouch 10 62
(Paul Cole) *swvd rt s: rcvrd to ld after 1f: pushed along over 2f out: hdd & wknd over 1f out* **4/1[2]**

102 **7** *hd* **Global Hope (IRE)**[43] 8419 4-9-7 **70**.......................... LukeMorris 2 65
(Gay Kelleway) *midfield: rdn and hdwy 2f out: wknd ins fnl f* **7/2[1]**

1000 **8** *2 1/4* **Global Wonder (IRE)**[15] 9047 4-9-3 **66**..........................(v) DougieCostello 6 55
(Suzi Best) *s.i.s: towards rr: reminders 4f out: rdn 2f out: sme hdwy over 1f out: kpt on* **50/1**

6025 **9** *nse* **Broughtons Flare (IRE)**[15] 9048 3-9-5 **68**.......................... StevieDonohoe 8 57
(Philip McBride) *chsd ldrs and racd wd: rdn and wknd over 1f out* **9/2[3]**

3120 **10** *1 1/2* **Fancy Flyer**[72] 7514 3-9-0 **70**.......................... LukeBacon(7) 12 55
(Dean Ivory) *t.k.h: pressed ldr: rdn and wknd over 1f out* **20/1**

0230 **11** *1* **Bombastic (IRE)**[44] 8413 4-9-7 **70**.......................... JoeyHaynes 13 52
(John Butler) *hld up in rr: rdn and no imp over 2f out* **8/1**

0030 **12** *1/2* **Azor Ahai**[40] 8521 3-9-7 **70**.......................... TomEaves 3 51
(Chris Gordon) *midfield: rdn and wknd over 2f out* **40/1**

The Form Book Flat 2019, Raceform Ltd, Newbury, RG14 5SJ

4300 **13** *1 1/4* **Eesha's Smile (IRE)**[13] 9093 3-8-7 **63**...................... JonathanFisher(7) 7 40
(Ivan Furtado) *chsd ldrs: rdn and wknd over 2f out* **33/1**

1m 23.64s (-1.16) **Going Correction** -0.10s/f (Stan) **13** Ran SP% **125.0**
Speed ratings (Par 103): **102,100,99,99,96 96,96,93,93,91 90,90,88**
CSF £69.73 CT £808.48 TOTE £8.40: £2.90, £2.90, £2.60; EX 98.60 Trifecta £630.10.
Owner John Reddington **Bred** Equine Origin Ltd **Trained** St Albans, Hertfordshire

FOCUS
A competitive 0-70 handicap with a few unexposed types.

9307 LADBROKES WHERE THE NATION PLAYS NURSERY H'CAP 7f 1y(P)
12:40 (12:42) (Class 6) (0-65,67) 2-Y-O

£2,781 (£827; £413; £300; £300; £300) **Stalls** Low

Form RPR
5500 **1** **Go Well Spicy (IRE)**[16] 9031 2-9-9 **67**...................... DougieCostello 10 69
(Tim Fitzgerald) *trckd ldr: hdwy over 1f out: rdn and r.o wl ins fnl f: led fnl strides* **16/1**
4 **2** *shd* **Holy Eleanor (IRE)**[11] 9137 2-9-8 **66**...................... HollieDoyle 1 68
(Archie Watson) *sn led: rdn and edgd rt fr over 1f out: kpt on wl ins fnl f: hdd fnl strides* **7/2**[1]
0500 **3** *nk* **Ruby Power (IRE)**[72] 7522 2-9-8 **66**...................... JamesDoyle 6 67
(Richard Hannon) *trckd ldr: pushed along over 1f out: kpt on wl ins fnl f* **16/1**
556 **4** *nk* **Barking Mad**[55] 8059 2-9-6 **64**...................... TomMarquand 9 64
(David Evans) *t.k.h: in rr: hdwy on outer fr over 1f out: r.o wl ins fnl f: nt rch ldrs* **7/1**
0246 **5** *nk* **Rebel Redemption**[14] 9061 2-9-0 **58**...................... (p) JasonHart 7 57
(John Quinn) *swvd rt s: prom: pushed along over 3f out: rdn and kpt on wl ins fnl f* **8/1**
6505 **6** *hd* **Rulers Kingdom (IRE)**[14] 9060 2-9-5 **63**...................... JoeFanning 5 62
(Mark Johnston) *midfield: hdwy on outer fr over 1f out: kpt on but edgd lft ins fnl f* **9/2**[2]
0005 **6** *dht* **Fact Or Fable (IRE)**[18] 9009 2-8-13 **57**...................... (p) LiamKeniry 2 56
(J S Moore) *midfield: hdwy and swtchd lft fr 1f out: rdn ins fnl f: wknd towards fin* **20/1**
046 **8** *1* **Itwouldberudenotto**[47] 8302 2-9-5 **63**...................... BarryMcHugh 4 59
(Richard Fahey) *in rr: pushed along fr over 1f out: swtchd lft and kpt on ins fnl f* **7/1**
6130 **9** *1* **Chromium**[14] 9060 2-9-0 **58**...................... (p) LukeMorris 12 51
(Michael Attwater) *cl up: pushed along 2f out: rdn and wknd ins fnl f* **33/1**
3630 **10** *nk* **Abbaleka**[16] 9031 2-9-7 **65**...................... AlistairRawlinson 3 58
(Michael Appleby) *towards rr of midfield: pushed along fr over 1f out: no ex fnl f* **10/1**
5004 **11** *1/2* **Numinous (IRE)**[81] 7174 2-8-2 **46**...................... KieranO'Neill 11 37
(Henry Candy) *cl up: pushed along over 2f out: hung lft and wknd fr 1f out* **25/1**
0644 **12** *3/4* **Burniston Rocks**[14] 9060 2-9-7 **65**...................... (b) StevieDonohoe 8 54
(Ed Vaughan) *dwlt s: hld up in last: niggled along early: nt clr run 2f out: nudged out fr 1f out* **6/1**[3]

1m 24.86s (0.06) **Going Correction** -0.10s/f (Stan) **12** Ran SP% **123.2**
Speed ratings (Par 94): **95,94,94,94,93 93,93,92,91,91 90,89**
WIN: 20.40 Go Well Spicy; PL: 5.30 Go Well Spicy 3.80 Ruby Power 1.40 Holy Eleanor; EX: 103.70; CSF: 72.69; TC: 965.64; TF: 1235.60 CSF £72.69 CT £965.64 TOTE £20.40: £5.30, £1.40, £3.80; EX 103.70 Trifecta £1235.60.
Owner M J Pimlott **Bred** Grangemore Stud **Trained** Norton, N Yorks

FOCUS
A low-grade nursery and it produced a bunched finish.

9308 BOMBARDIER BRITISH HOPPED AMBER BEER H'CAP 7f 1y(P)
1:10 (1:11) (Class 3) (0-90,92) 3-Y-O+ **£7,246** (£2,168; £1,084; £542; £270) **Stalls** Low

Form RPR
2200 **1** **Typhoon Ten (IRE)**[32] 8766 3-9-5 **83**...................... JamesDoyle 5 95
(Richard Hannon) *towards rr of midfield: rdn 2f out: gd hdwy over 1f out: led ins fnl f: kpt on wl* **9/2**[2]
3060 **2** *2 1/4* **Intisaab**[28] 8851 8-10-0 **92**...................... (tp) DavidProbert 9 98
(David O'Meara) *towards rr: rdn 2f out: gd hdwy fr 1f out: wnt 2nd towards fin* **7/1**
3300 **3** *1* **Revich (IRE)**[13] 9088 3-9-0 **85**...................... (p) AngusVilliers(7) 2 88
(Richard Spencer) *midfield: pushed along 2f out: hdwy over 1f out: kpt on ins fnl f* **5/1**[3]
0431 **4** *nk* **Sir Titan**[74] 7462 5-9-5 **83**...................... TomMarquand 4 85
(Tony Carroll) *led: increased tempo over 2f out: rdn over 1f out: hdd & wknd ins fnl f* **8/1**
0323 **5** *nk* **Captain Jameson (IRE)**[36] 8636 4-9-6 **84**...................... (v) JasonHart 6 86
(John Quinn) *t.k.h: chsd ldrs: pushed along 2f out: no ex fr 1f out* **11/2**
3323 **6** *2 1/2* **Baby Steps**[4] 9254 3-9-0 **81**...................... ThomasGreatrex(3) 3 76
(David Loughnane) *cl up: rdn 2f out: wknd ins fnl f* **7/2**[1]
0005 **7** *1 1/2* **Apex King (IRE)**[11] 9129 5-9-4 **82**...................... KieranShoemark 10 73
(Mark Usher) *chsd ldr: rdn over 2f out: wknd over 1f out* **14/1**
4-55 **8** *nk* **Barrington (IRE)**[62] 7856 5-8-13 **77**...................... AlistairRawlinson 8 67
(Michael Appleby) *s.i.s: towards rr: pushed along 2f out: n.d* **10/1**
216- **9** *hd* **Pride Of Angels**[511] 4811 6-9-1 **79**...................... HectorCrouch 7 68
(Gary Moore) *towards rr of midfield: nudged along over 1f out: nvr nr to chal* **28/1**
10-0 **10** *hd* **Bobby Wheeler (IRE)**[15] 9053 6-9-0 **85**...................... AmeliaGlass(7) 1 74
(Clive Cox) *midfield: rdn 2f out: wknd fr 1f out* **25/1**

1m 23.16s (-1.64) **Going Correction** -0.10s/f (Stan) **10** Ran SP% **119.1**
Speed ratings (Par 107): **105,102,101,100,100 97,96,95,95,95**
CSF £36.97 CT £170.16 TOTE £5.10: £2.10, £2.30, £1.90; EX 38.90 Trifecta £233.40.
Owner Des Anderson **Bred** D J Anderson **Trained** East Everleigh, Wilts

FOCUS
A good quality handicap run at a decent clip throughout. There were no hard luck stories.

9309 BETWAY CASINO H'CAP 1m 2f (P)
1:45 (1:45) (Class 2) (0-105,103) 3-Y-O+ **£11,971** (£3,583; £1,791; £896; £446) **Stalls** Low

Form RPR
0553 **1** **Victory Bond**[27] 8892 6-9-9 **100**...................... JamesDoyle 10 108
(William Haggas) *cl up: pushed along fr 1f out: rdn to ld ins fnl f: edgd rt towards fin* **4/1**[2]
4233 **2** *3/4* **Pactolus (IRE)**[18] 9003 8-9-10 **101**...................... (t) RichardKingscote 3 107
(Stuart Williams) *midfield: pushed along fr over 1f out: rdn and kpt on wl ins fnl f: wnt 2nd fnl strides* **14/1**
1142 **3** *shd* **Kasbaan**[27] 8892 4-9-8 **99**...................... AlistairRawlinson 6 105
(Michael Appleby) *t.k.h: trckd ldr: pushed along fr over 1f out: rdn and kpt on fnl 110yds: hmpd towards fin (jockey said gelding ran too free)* **3/1**[1]
11/1 **4** *1/2* **Entangling (IRE)**[15] 9053 5-8-12 **89**...................... WilliamCarson 4 94
(David Elsworth) *cl up: rdn to ld fr 1f out: edgd rt and hdd ins fnl f: wknd ins fnl 110yds* **7/1**
2122 **5** *3/4* **Kuwait Currency (USA)**[18] 9003 3-9-10 **103**...................... (t) TomMarquand 11 106
(Richard Hannon) *hld up in rr: pushed along and hdwy fr over 1f out: rdn and styd on ins fnl f: nt rch ldrs* **8/1**
1602 **6** *1/2* **Furzig**[16] 9041 4-9-0 **91**...................... BarryMcHugh 1 93
(Richard Fahey) *trckd ldr: pushed along 2f out: keeping on whn bit short of room ins fnl f* **5/1**[3]
0005 **7** *hd* **Circus Couture (IRE)**[27] 8892 7-8-8 **90**...................... RayDawson(5) 9 92
(Jane Chapple-Hyam) *hld up in rr: pushed along 2f out: swtchd rt and r.o ins fnl f: nt rch ldrs* **50/1**
5240 **8** *1* **Glen Shiel**[18] 9014 5-9-7 **98**...................... HollieDoyle 5 98
(Archie Watson) *sn led: rdn and hdd fr 1f out: wknd ins fnl f* **11/1**
4021 **9** *1/2* **Mustarrid (IRE)**[35] 8658 5-9-3 **94**...................... DavidProbert 8 93
(Ian Williams) *s.i.s: midfield: pushed along fr over 1f out: rdn whn edgd rt ins fnl f (jockey said gelding was slowly away)* **12/1**
1503 **10** *shd* **Goring (GER)**[18] 9000 7-9-4 **100**...................... (v) GeorgiaDobie(5) 2 99
(Eve Johnson Houghton) *t.k.h: towards rr of midfield ins fnl f: pushed along on outer 2f out: n.d* **20/1**
2415 **11** *4 1/2* **Mythical Madness**[201] 2808 8-9-5 **96**...................... LukeMorris 7 86
(Simon Dow) *in rr: hdwy on outer fr over 2f out: rdn and wknd ins fnl f* **33/1**

2m 3.51s (-3.09) **Going Correction** -0.10s/f (Stan)
WFA 3 from 4yo+ 2lb **11** Ran SP% **117.6**
Speed ratings (Par 109): **108,107,107,106,106 105,105,104,104,104 100**
CSF £57.47 CT £192.43 TOTE £4.10: £1.20, £3.20, £1.60; EX 71.80 Trifecta £262.30.
Owner Bloomsbury Stud **Bred** Bloomsbury Stud **Trained** Newmarket, Suffolk

FOCUS
A strong line-up for this middle-distance handicap.

9310 BETWAY H'CAP 1m 4f (P)
2:15 (2:18) (Class 6) (0-60,60) 3-Y-O+

£2,781 (£827; £413; £300; £300; £300) **Stalls** Low

Form RPR
3 **1** **Be Fair**[29] 8837 3-9-3 **57**...................... TomMarquand 5 65+
(Tony Carroll) *dwlt s: midfield: rdn 3f out: gd hdwy on inner home turn: led over 1f out: kpt on wl ins fnl f* **11/1**
2526 **2** *1 3/4* **Mistress Nellie**[11] 9139 4-9-0 **50**...................... HollieDoyle 9 54
(William Stone) *t.k.h: midfield: swtchd lft and hdwy over 2f out: sn rdn: kpt on wl ins fnl f* **8/1**
0360 **3** *3/4* **Famous Dynasty (IRE)**[28] 8854 5-8-10 **46** oh1...................... DavidProbert 11 49
(Michael Blanshard) *bmpd s: in rr: gng okay but bit short of room 3f out: rdn and kpt on wl fr 2f out: no ex fnl 110yds* **14/1**
3431 **4** *3/4* **Banta Bay**[50] 8224 5-9-3 **53**...................... JosephineGordon 15 55
(John Best) *in rr: rdn 3f out: racd wd home turn: kpt on fr over 1f out: hung lft ins fnl f: wnt 4th fnl stride* **5/1**[3]
0456 **5** *shd* **Highway One (USA)**[30] 8813 5-9-6 **56**...................... NicolaCurrie 7 57
(George Baker) *trckd ldr: hung lft and rdn home turn: lost 2nd over 1f out: no ex ins fnl f* **14/1**
0003 **6** *1* **Music Major**[18] 9005 6-9-6 **56**...................... CallumShepherd 12 56
(Michael Attwater) *towards rr: rdn and sme hdwy whn bmpd under 3f out: kpt on fr 1f out: no ex towards fin* **11/1**
0514 **7** *2* **King Athelstan (IRE)**[44] 8414 4-9-7 **57**...................... (b) HectorCrouch 2 54
(Gary Moore) *midfield on inner: rdn and bit short of room fr under 3f out: kpt on fr 2f out: nt pce to chal* **7/1**
5445 **8** *1/2* **Tyrsal (IRE)**[27] 8904 8-8-3 **46** oh1...................... (v) GavinAshton(7) 1 42
(Shaun Keightley) *towards rr: gng okay but short of room fr 3f out: pushed along home turn: wl hld but keeping on whn hmpd ins fnl f: nvr nr to chal* **50/1**
3335 **9** *2 3/4* **Ignatius (IRE)**[15] 9049 3-8-10 **50**...................... KierenFox 16 42
(John Best) *rdn early: led after 1f: rdn over 2f out: hdd over 1f out: wknd ins fnl f* **7/2**[1]
0004 **10** *2 3/4* **Narjes**[11] 9132 5-9-10 **60**...................... (h) LukeMorris 14 47
(Laura Mongan) *s.i.s: in rr: rdn on outer 3f out: swtchd lft and kpt on fr over 1f out: nt pce to chal* **16/1**
0040 **11** *nse* **Petra's Pony (IRE)**[249] 1431 4-8-10 **46** oh1...................... MartinDwyer 13 33
(Brian Meehan) *t.k.h: chsd ldrs: rdn under 3f out: wknd fr under 2f out* **25/1**
/000 **12** *nse* **Cross Step (USA)**[2] 9275 5-9-5 **60**...................... (p) MarkCrehan(5) 10 47
(C Moore, Ire) *t.k.h: midfield on outer: hdwy over 3f out: rdn over 2f out: racd wd home turn: wknd over 1f out* **33/1**
2050 **13** *5* **Sea's Aria (IRE)**[98] 6601 8-8-5 **46** oh1...................... AledBeech(5) 4 25
(Mark Hoad) *rdn early: a towards rr: rdn and no rspnse under 3f out: nvr on terms* **50/1**
5001 **14** *1 1/2* **Mrs Ivy**[35] 8670 3-9-2 **56**...................... (b) RichardKingscote 6 33
(Ralph Beckett) *chsd ldrs on inner: rdn over 3f out: wkng whn bit short of room 2f out* **9/2**[2]
0000 **15** *12* **Glacier Fox**[28] 8862 4-9-5 **60**...................... (p) KevinLundie(5) 8 17
(Mark Loughnane) *chsd ldrs: rdn 4f out: wknd fr 3f out* **66/1**
0500 **16** *21* **Burguillos**[11] 9132 6-9-8 **58**...................... (h) KieranO'Neill 3
(John Butler) *trckd ldr on inner: rdn 5f out: wknd qckly fr 3f out* **33/1**

2m 30.4s (-2.60) **Going Correction** -0.10s/f (Stan)
WFA 3 from 4yo+ 4lb **16** Ran SP% **131.7**
Speed ratings (Par 101): **104,102,102,101,101 101,99,99,97,95 95,95,92,91,83 69**
CSF £99.82 CT £1284.69 TOTE £14.40: £4.00, £2.60, £4.00, £1.40; EX 125.20 Trifecta £2940.40.
Owner Surefire Racing & Partner **Bred** James Ortega Bloodstock Ltd **Trained** Cropthorne, Worcs

FOCUS
A run-of-the-mill handicap but an unexposed runner came to the fore.

9311 LADBROKES HOME OF THE ODDS BOOST EBF FILLIES' NOVICE STKS (PLUS 10 RACE) 1m 1y(P)
2:50 (2:56) (Class 5) 2-Y-O **£3,428** (£1,020; £509; £254) **Stalls** High

Form RPR
30 **1** **Merryweather**[70] 7562 2-9-0 0...................... AlistairRawlinson 10 76+
(Michael Appleby) *mde virtually all: rdn and r.o ins fnl f: jst hld on* **22/1**
2 **2** *nk* **Mrs Upjohn (FR)**[33] 8717 2-9-0 0...................... HollieDoyle 2 75+
(Archie Watson) *trckd ldr: pushed along 2f out: rdn and r.o wl ins fnl f: jst hld* **3/1**[2]
6 **3** *2 1/2* **Transcript**[32] 8759 2-9-0 0...................... PJMcDonald 4 69
(James Tate) *t.k.h: trckd ldr: pushed along and hung lft over 1f out: kpt on wl ins fnl f* **13/2**[3]
4 **4** *3/4* **Tacitly**[28] 8848 2-9-0 0...................... AdamMcNamara 1 68
(Roger Charlton) *s.i.s: sn midfield: pushed along and hdwy fr over 1f out: styd on ins fnl f (jockey said filly hung left-handed throughout)* **13/8**[1]

5 **5** 2 **Alianne**[34] 8706 2-9-0 0................................ LukeMorris 8 63
(Tom Clover) *cl up: pressed ldr 2f out: pushed along fr over 1f out: wknd ins fnl f* **25/1**

0 **6** ½ **Wand**[28] 8848 2-9-0 0................................ RichardKingscote 9 62
(Lucy Wadham) *t.k.h: midfield: pushed along 2f out: nudged along ins fnl f: eyecatcher* **20/1**

02 **7** 1¼ **Saracen Star**[11] 9127 2-9-0 0................................ LiamKeniry 6 59
(J S Moore) *in rr: pushed along 2f out: rdn and no ex ins fnl f* **33/1**

8 3¾ **Late Romance** 2-9-0 0................................ JamesDoyle 3 50
(Charlie Appleby) *towards rr of midfield: niggled along 5f out: pushed along 2f out: mde no imp* **3/1**[2]

9 ½ **I Hear Thunder (FR)** 2-9-0 0................................ CallumShepherd 5 49
(James Tate) *dwlt s: t.k.h: in rr: gng okay 3f out: nudged along fr over 1f out: nvr on terms (jockey said filly was slowly away)* **50/1**

0 **10** 1¼ **Encashment**[42] 8454 2-9-0 0................................ TomQueally 7 46
(Alan King) *s.i.s: t.k.h: in rr: pushed along 3f out: mde no imp* **100/1**

1m 38.49s (0.29) **Going Correction** -0.10s/f (Stan) **10 Ran SP% 120.3**
Speed ratings (Par 93): **94,93,91,90,88 87,86,82,82,81**
CSF £85.75 TOTE £20.00: £3.90, £1.30, £1.60; EX 89.50 Trifecta £472.40.
Owner The Horse Watchers **Bred** Hall Of Fame Stud **Trained** Oakham, Rutland
■ Up The Aisle was withdrawn. Price at time of withdrawal 100/1. Rule 4 does not apply.

FOCUS
A tight finish for this novice event and it paid to sit handy.

9312 BETWAY AMATEUR RIDERS' H'CAP 1m 7f 169y(P)
3:20 (3:27) (Class 6) (0-55,55) 3-Y-O+
£2,682 (£832; £415; £300; £300; £300) **Stalls Low**

Form RPR

0500 **1** **Uncle Bernie (IRE)**[28] 8868 9-10-4 **52**................(p) MrSeanHawkins(7) 1 59
(Sarah Hollinshead) *slowly away: hld up in rr: hdwy fr over 4f out: chsd ldrs 3f out: wnt 2nd 2f out: pushed along and led towards fin* **20/1**

0344 **2** ½ **Yasir (USA)**[16] 9042 11-10-10 **51**................ MissSerenaBrotherton 12 57
(Sophie Leech) *s.i.s: towards rr: hdwy and cl up after 8f: led 5f out: rdn over 1f out: hdd towards fin* **11/4**[1]

000 **3** 5 **Finisher (USA)**[27] 8904 4-10-4 **50**................(t[1]) MrFergusGillard(5) 11 50
(Mark Gillard) *midfield: rdn 3f out: hdwy over 2f out: kpt on ins fnl f* **20/1**

0535 **4** 1½ **General Allenby**[13] 9087 5-9-12 **46** oh1.....(v[1]) MissJenniferPahlman(7) 3 45
(Shaun Keightley) *midfield: outpcd and cajoled along over 8f out: outpcd over 4f out: swtchd rt and gng okay but nt clr run over 3f out: pushed along over 1f out: styd on ins fnl f* **10/1**

2046 **5** 1¾ **Earthly (USA)**[71] 7553 5-10-1 **47**..............(tp) MissJessicaLlewellyn(5) 13 44
(Bernard Llewellyn) *towards rr: pushed along over 4f out: hdwy over 2f out: kpt on ins fnl f* **4/1**[2]

0000 **6** 2 **Attain**[18] 9005 10-10-9 **50**................ MissBrodieHampson 10 44
(Archie Watson) *s.i.s: towards rr: hdwy and cl up after 8f: wnt 2nd 5f out: pushed along and wknd over 2f out* **7/1**

0065 **7** ½ **Capricorn Prince**[39] 8553 3-9-8 **46** oh1..........(b[1]) MissKatyBrooks(5) 5 42
(Gary Moore) *trckd ldrs: short of room and lost position over 4f out: towards rr over 3f out: nt clr run fr over 2f out: kpt on fr 1f out* **6/1**[3]

6/04 **8** 4½ **Saga Sprint (IRE)**[106] 6324 6-10-0 **46** oh1............ MrAlexChadwick(5) 4 34
(J R Jenkins) *midfield: sme hdwy fr 6f out: rdn and wknd over 3f out* **20/1**

0060 **9** ½ **Guaracha**[13] 9087 8-10-5 **46** oh1................(v) MrSimonWalker 7 34
(Alexandra Dunn) *midfield: hdwy and chsd ldrs 5f out: rdn 4f out: wknd over 2f out* **9/1**

0-00 **10** 15 **Scottsdale**[22] 1463 6-9-12 **46**................ MissLaurenSanders(7) 9 16
(Peter Winks) *s.i.s: t.k.h: towards rr: swtchd rt and racd wd over 4f out: pushed along and no rspnse over 3f out* **20/1**

0000 **11** 4½ **Punkawallah**[13] 7474 5-10-7 **55**................(b[1]) MrTambyWelch(7) 6 19
(Alexandra Dunn) *led: hdd 5f out: rdn and wknd over 4f out* **10/1**

/066 **12** 6 **UAE Soldier (USA)**[15] 7604 4-10-0 **46** oh1...... MissMichelleBryant(5) 14 3
(Paddy Butler) *chsd ldrs: outpcd over 4f out: pushed along and no rspnse over 3f out* **40/1**

6660 **13** shd **Just Right**[79] 7271 4-10-0 **46** oh1................(p) MissImogenMathias(5) 8 3
(John Flint) *pressed ldr: wknd qckly fr 5f out: rdn and no rspnse fr 4f out* **25/1**

3m 25.13s (-0.57) **Going Correction** -0.10s/f (Stan)
WFA 3 from 4yo+ 6lb **13 Ran SP% 127.0**
Speed ratings (Par 101): **97,96,94,93,92 91,91,89,88,81 79,76,76**
CSF £73.09 CT £1191.24 TOTE £26.20: £6.50, £1.70, £7.50; EX 123.80 Trifecta £1436.70.
Owner Miss Sarah Hollinshead **Bred** Roundhill Stud & Gleadhill House Stud Ltd **Trained** Upper Longdon, Staffs

FOCUS
They went off far too quickly in this amateur riders' handicap, so the hold-up horses came to the fore.
T/Plt: £867.30 to a £1 stake. Pool: £79,842.96 - 67.20 winning units T/Qpdt: £58.60 to a £1 stake. Pool: £11,967.78 - 150.94 winning units

9313 - 9321a (Foreign Racing) - See Raceform Interactive

9298 KEMPTON (A.W) (R-H)
Thursday, December 5

OFFICIAL GOING: Polytrack: standard to slow
Wind: light, across Weather: overcast

9322 BET AT RACINGTV.COM NOVICE AUCTION STKS 6f (P)
4:00 (4:02) (Class 5) 2-Y-O **£3,881** (£1,155; £577; £288) **Stalls Low**

Form RPR

4252 **1** **Amarillo Star (IRE)**[50] 8243 2-9-2 87................ KieranShoemark 6 87+
(Charlie Fellowes) *trckd ldr tl rdn to ld ent fnl 2f: sn qcknd clr: r.o wl: comf* **1/4**[1]

110 **2** 5 **Littledidyouknow (IRE)**[188] 3333 2-9-8 82................(b) LukeMorris 4 77
(Archie Watson) *wnt lft leaving stalls: in tch: rdn over 2f out: unable qck and outpcd 2f out: drvn over 1f out: kpt to chse clr wnr wl ins fnl f: no ch: fin lame (vet said filly was lame on its left hind)* **4/1**[2]

606 **3** 1½ **Baileys Freedom**[219] 2228 2-9-0 66................ KieranO'Neill 1 65
(John Bridger) *led: rdn over 2f out: sn hdd and outpcd: lost wl btn 2nd wl ins fnl f* **33/1**

0040 **4** 4½ **Candid (IRE)**[38] 8603 2-8-6 47................(p) TheodoreLadd(3) 3 46
(Jonathan Portman) *trckd ldng pair: rdn 2f out: sn outpcd and wl btn over 1f out: wknd fnl f* **14/1**[3]

5 14 **Criseyde** 2-8-8 0................................ JohnFahy 5 3
(Sylvester Kirk) *sltly impeded leaving stalls: rn v green and t.k.h: sn bhd (jockey said filly ran green and awkwardly rounding the bend)* **20/1**

1m 12.37s (-0.73) **Going Correction** -0.025s/f (Stan) **5 Ran SP% 114.4**
Speed ratings (Par 96): **103,96,94,88,69**
CSF £1.84 TOTE £1.30: £1.10, £1.40; EX 1.90 Trifecta £10.80.
Owner Lady De Ramsey **Bred** Kenneth Purcell **Trained** Newmarket, Suffolk

FOCUS
A one-sided novice that's not really worth dwelling on.

9323 RACINGTV.COM MAIDEN STKS (DIV I) 7f (P)
4:35 (4:35) (Class 5) 2-Y-O **£3,881** (£1,155; £577; £288) **Stalls Low**

Form RPR

0 **1** **Sky Commander (IRE)**[191] 3194 2-9-5 0................ JamesDoyle 3 90+
(James Tate) *trckd ldrs: effrt and clsd on inner ent fnl 2f: rdn to ld: rn green and hung lft over 1f out: r.o strly and drew clr fnl f: v readily* **5/4**[1]

4 **2** 7 **Katzoff (IRE)**[19] 8999 2-9-5 0................(h) JimCrowley 8 71
(Richard Hannon) *in tch in midfield: effrt to chal 2f out: chsd wnr and drvn over 1f out: sn outpcd and kpt on same pce ins fnl f* **5/2**[2]

0 **3** nk **Iron Heart**[41] 8516 2-9-5 0................ LiamKeniry 6 70+
(Andrew Balding) *in tch in midfield: effrt on inner over 2f out: rdn over 1f out: no ch w wnr but kpt on ins fnl f: pressing for 2nd cl home* **4/1**[3]

64 **4** 2½ **Arbiter**[8] 9181 2-9-5 0................(h) KieranO'Neill 7 64
(John Gosden) *taken down early: wnt lft leaving stalls: t.k.h: hld up towards rr: swtchd lft and hdwy after 2f: led over 4f out: rdn and hdd over 1f out: sn outpcd and wknd ins fnl f (jockey said colt ran too free)* **13/2**

00 **5** ¾ **St Just**[31] 8810 2-9-2 0................ GeorgiaCox(3) 9 62
(William Haggas) *in tch towards rr: pushed along over 3f out: rdn over 1f out: no ch w wnr but kpt on steadily ins fnl f* **50/1**

6 1¼ **Golden Fountain (IRE)** 2-9-5 0................ JasonHart 2 58
(Mark Johnston) *led tl over 4f out: chsd ldr: rdn and ev ch 2f out: sn outpcd and btn: wknd ins fnl f* **14/1**

0 **7** 2½ **September Power (IRE)**[10] 9159 2-9-0 0................ JackMitchell 4 46
(Roger Varian) *rn green in rr: rdn over 2f out: no imp and wl hld whn swtchd rt over 1f out* **25/1**

5000 **8** 4½ **Love Not Money**[6] 9212 2-8-11 48................ MitchGodwin(3) 5 34
(John Bridger) *chsd ldr tl over 4f out: chsd ldrs after tl rdn over 2f out: sn lost pl: wknd over 1f out* **66/1**

0 **9** 18 **Girl Of Dreams**[19] 8999 2-8-7 0................ KateLeahy(7) 1
(Nikki Evans) *short of room sn after s: a in rr: rdn over 2f out: sn struggling and lost tch 2f out: t.o (jockey said filly became marginally tight for room shortly after leaving the stalls and subsequently lost its action)* **150/1**

1m 25.21s (-0.79) **Going Correction** -0.025s/f (Stan) **9 Ran SP% 121.0**
Speed ratings (Par 96): **103,95,94,91,90 89,86,81,60**
CSF £4.78 TOTE £2.10: £1.10, £1.10, £1.80; EX 6.00 Trifecta £18.20.
Owner Saeed Manana **Bred** Sheikhnizar Anwar Abulijadayel **Trained** Newmarket, Suffolk

FOCUS
Just a fair novice with the exception of the emphatic winner but there was some late promise in behind from those still learning.

9324 RACINGTV.COM MAIDEN STKS (DIV II) 7f (P)
5:10 (5:11) (Class 5) 2-Y-O **£3,881** (£1,155; £577; £288) **Stalls Low**

Form RPR

4430 **1** **Phuket Power (IRE)**[76] 7419 2-9-5 76................ RichardKingscote 9 73
(Tom Dascombe) *wnt rt leaving stalls: led after 1f: mde rest: rdn ent fnl 2f: drvn ins fnl f: all out and jst lasting home towards fin* **11/4**[2]

5 **2** hd **Lottie Marie**[43] 8453 2-9-0 0................ JimCrowley 8 67
(Robert Cowell) *mainly 2nd: rdn ent fnl 2f: no imp tl kpt on u.p fnl 100yds: grad clsng towards fin: nvr quite getting to wnr* **6/1**

P3 **3** nk **Viaduct**[12] 9130 2-9-5 0................ KieranShoemark 3 72
(Martyn Meade) *led for 1f: chsd ldrs after: effrt on inner jst over 2f out: no imp tl grad clsd and kpt on and towards fin: nvr quite getting to wnr* **5/2**[1]

4 2½ **Disco Fever** 2-9-0 0................ RobertHavlin 5 60+
(John Gosden) *dwlt and pushed lft leaving stalls: in tch in last trio: shkn up over 2f out: rdn and hdwy over 1f out: chsd ldng trio 100yds out: kpt on but nvr a threat* **9/2**[3]

00 **5** ½ **Bold Suitor**[41] 8511 2-9-5 0................ HectorCrouch 7 64
(Ed Walker) *wnt rt and bmpd rivals leaving stalls: midfield: shkn up over 2f out: rdn over 1f out: kpt on same pce ins fnl f* **8/1**

0 **6** 1½ **Dolla Dolla Bill (IRE)**[8] 9174 2-9-5 0................ JamesDoyle 2 60
(Richard Hannon) *in tch in midfield: effrt ent fnl 2f: no imp over 1f out: wknd wl ins fnl f* **11/1**

0 **7** 9 **Alphabetical**[7] 9197 2-9-5 0................ LukeMorris 6 35
(Sir Mark Prescott Bt) *bmpd and pushed rt leaving stalls: in rr: shkn up over 2f out: sn struggling and outpcd: wknd over 1f out* **20/1**

00 **8** 1½ **Good Try**[10] 9158 2-9-0 0................ CallumShepherd 4 26
(Michael Bell) *chsd ldng trio: rdn over 2f out: lost pl qckly over 1f out: sn bhd* **33/1**

00 **9** 6 **Dabbersgirl**[19] 9008 2-9-0 0................ LiamKeniry 1 10
(Brian Baugh) *in tch in last trio: effrt ent fnl 2f: sn rdn and outpcd: wknd over 1f out* **100/1**

1m 27.01s (1.01) **Going Correction** -0.025s/f (Stan) **9 Ran SP% 115.8**
Speed ratings (Par 96): **93,92,92,89,89 87,77,75,68**
CSF £19.42 TOTE £3.40: £1.70, £1.70, £1.50; EX 24.70 Trifecta £67.10.
Owner King Power Racing Co Ltd **Bred** Herbertstown House Stud **Trained** Malpas, Cheshire

FOCUS
Unlike the first division, this was steadily run and there were no standout performances.

9325 RACING TV PROFITS RETURNED TO RACING MAIDEN STKS (DIV I) 1m (P)
5:40 (5:46) (Class 5) 2-Y-O **£3,881** (£1,155; £577; £288) **Stalls Low**

Form RPR

42 **1** **Itkaann (IRE)**[129] 5493 2-9-5 0................ KieranShoemark 7 81+
(Owen Burrows) *led for 1f: chsd ldr tl rdn to ld again over 2f out: wnt clr over 1f out: r.o strly: v readily* **3/1**[2]

0 **2** 5 **Shumba (USA)**[12] 9136 2-9-0 0................ DylanHogan(5) 8 67
(David Simcock) *chsd ldrs: effrt to chse wnr 2f out: no imp: wl hld but kpt on to hold 2nd ins fnl f (jockey said colt hung right-handed in the straight)* **25/1**

0 **3** ¾ **Swooping Eagle (IRE)**[30] 8823 2-9-5 0................ JackMitchell 5 65
(Roger Varian) *in tch in midfield: effrt over 2f out: chsd ldng pair over 1f out: no ch w wnr but kpt on steadily ins fnl f* **6/1**[3]

06 **4** 1 **King Of The North (IRE)**[10] 9154 2-9-5 0................ HectorCrouch 10 63
(Jonathan Portman) *dwlt and rousted along leaving stalls: in tch in midfield: rdn ent fnl 2f: outpcd 2f out: no ch w wnr but kpt on again ins fnl f* **12/1**

5 ¾ **Orczy (IRE)** 2-9-5 0................ JimCrowley 13 61+
(Richard Hannon) *styd wd early: towards rr: rdn over 2f out: sme hdwy 1f out: kpt on ins fnl f: no ch w wnr* **8/1**

4 **6** 1 **Pyramid Place (IRE)**[16] 9052 2-9-5 0................ RobertHavlin 1 59
(John Gosden) *pushed along leaving stalls: chsd ldrs: rdn ent fnl 2f: sn outpcd and btn 4th 1f out: plugged on same pce after* **9/4**[1]

0 **7** 2 3/4 **Royal Astronomer**[15] 9063 2-9-5 0 RichardKingscote 3 53
(Hughie Morrison) *broke wl: sn restrained: in tch in midfield: rdn over 2f out: sn struggling and outpcd: wknd over 1f out* **20/1**

04 **8** 3 1/2 **Blue Slate (IRE)**[12] 9127 2-9-5 0 LiamKeniry 12 45
(J S Moore) *hld up in tch in midfield: rdn and reminder over 2f out: sn struggling and outpcd: wknd over 1f out* **100/1**

0 **9** 1/2 **Ower Bush Mills**[19] 8999 2-9-5 0 JohnFahy 9 43
(Richard Hannon) *dwlt: a towards rr: rdn over 2f out: sn btn* **66/1**

0 **10** 1 3/4 **Pleasure Garden (USA)**[7] 9208 2-9-5 0 LukeMorris 6 39
(Sir Mark Prescott Bt) *awkward leaving stalls and s.i.s: a towards rr: rdn over 2f out: sn struggling and outpcd: wknd over 1f out* **66/1**

64 **11** 1/2 **Fiveandtwenty**[10] 9154 2-9-0 0 JasonHart 4 33
(Mark Johnston) *led after 1f: rdn and hdd over 2f out: sn struggling and wknd over 1f out* **10/1**

12 2 3/4 **Faramman** 2-9-5 0 KieranO'Neill 11 32
(John Gosden) *dwlt: a bhd* **8/1**

1m 39.76s (-0.04) **Going Correction** -0.025s/f (Stan) 12 Ran SP% **121.6**
Speed ratings (Par 96): **99,94,93,92,91 90,87,84,83,82 81,78**
CSF £85.55 TOTE £3.80: £1.60, £6.50, £2.50; EX 76.50 Trifecta £419.80.
Owner Sheikh Ahmed Al Maktoum **Bred** Hyde Park Stud **Trained** Lambourn, Berks

FOCUS
Most lacked pace and/or experience, so this isn't a strong novice acknowledging the winner created a good impression. The time was faster than the second division.

9326 RACING TV PROFITS RETURNED TO RACING MAIDEN STKS (DIV II) 1m (P)

6:15 (6:19) (Class 5) 2-Y-O **£3,881** (£1,155; £577; £288) **Stalls** Low

Form RPR

05 **1** **Make It Rain (IRE)**[41] 8510 2-9-0 0 JamesDoyle 5 76+
(Simon Crisford) *trckd ldrs: shkn up and qcknd to ld over 1f out: sn in command and r.o strly ins fnl f: v readily (jockey said filly ran too free)* **7/2**[3]

5 **2** 3 3/4 **Believe In Love (IRE)**[145] 4918 2-9-0 0 JackMitchell 11 64
(Roger Varian) *hld up in tch in midfield: effrt over 2f out: swtchd lft and hdwy over 1f out: styd on to chse clr wnr fnl 75yds: no threat to wnr* **8/1**

00 **3** 1 **You Owe Me**[14] 9095 2-9-5 0 JasonHart 3 67
(Mark Johnston) *chsd ldrs: effrt on inner ent fnl 2f: nt match pce of wnr over 1f out: rdr dropped reins: edgd lft and chsd clr wnr briefly ins fnl f: 3rd and kpt on same pce fnl 75yds* **66/1**

4 1/2 **Win O'Clock** 2-9-5 0 AdamMcNamara 9 68+
(Roger Charlton) *hld up in rr: swtchd rt: effrt and hdwy on inner over 1f out: flashing tail but styd on wl ins fnl f: no threat to wnr (jockey said colt was slowly away)* **20/1**

5 1/2 **Indigo Lake** 2-9-5 0 RobertHavlin 4 68+
(John Gosden) *dwlt and rn green early: towards rr: effrt ent fnl 2f: hdwy but no ch w wnr whn nt clr run and swtchd ins fnl f: kpt on* **9/4**[1]

0R **6** 1/2 **Great Fengshui (IRE)**[104] 6402 2-9-5 0 JohnFahy 8 64
(Richard Hannon) *sn led: rdn and hdd over 1f out: sn outpcd and wknd ins fnl f* **40/1**

0 **7** 1/2 **Critique (IRE)**[29] 8858 2-9-5 0 HectorCrouch 7 62
(Ed Walker) *in tch in midfield: effrt ent fnl 2f: sn hung rt and unable qck: no ch w wnr and kpt on same pce fnl f* **50/1**

8 nk **Seadance** 2-9-0 0 ThoreHammerHansen(5) 2 62
(Richard Hannon) *in tch in midfield: effrt 2f out: unable qck u.p over 1f out: wl hld and kpt on same pce ins fnl f* **20/1**

00 **9** 1 **Deposit (IRE)**[16] 9052 2-9-0 0 DylanHogan(5) 1 59
(David Simcock) *hld up in tch towards rr: effrt 2f out: no imp and kpt on same pce: nvr involved* **25/1**

10 1 **To Nathaniel** 2-9-5 0 KieranO'Neill 6 57
(John Gosden) *rn green in rr: nvr involved* **11/4**[2]

11 5 **Ayyaamy (IRE)** 2-9-5 0 (b[1]) JimCrowley 12 46
(Owen Burrows) *broke wl: sn led and pressed ldr: lost pl qckly u.p over 1f out: wknd ins fnl f* **10/1**

0 **12** 22 **Buzztothemoon**[8] 9174 2-9-5 0 (b[1]) LukeMorris 10
(Marco Botti) *midfield on outer: rdn over 2f out: drvn and wknd over 1f out* **100/1**

1m 41.81s (2.01) **Going Correction** -0.025s/f (Stan) 12 Ran SP% **120.1**
Speed ratings (Par 96): **88,84,83,82,82 81,81,80,79,78 73,51**
CSF £29.73 TOTE £4.70: £1.60, £2.00, £10.30; EX 28.10 Trifecta £1985.20.
Owner Sheikh Marwan Al Maktoum **Bred** Rabbah Bloodstock Limited **Trained** Newmarket, Suffolk

FOCUS
They went no pace and the Gosden-trained newcomers were too inexperienced to compete, so this isn't form to view positively despite the impressive winner.

9327 WISE BETTING AT RACINGTV.COM MAIDEN FILLIES' STKS (PLUS 10 RACE) 1m (P)

6:45 (6:52) (Class 5) 2-Y-O **£3,881** (£1,155; £577; £288) **Stalls** Low

Form RPR

1 **Delta's Royalty (IRE)** 2-9-0 0 JackMitchell 1 76+
(Roger Varian) *midfield: rdn over 3f out: clsd and swtchd rt 2f out: rdn and hdwy to ld ins fnl f: rn green and hung lft whn hitting the front: styd on* **4/6**[1]

34 **2** 3/4 **Samille (IRE)**[47] 8338 2-9-0 0 CallumShepherd 9 73
(Amy Murphy) *in tch in midfield: effrt 2f out: hdwy u.p to chal 1f out: led ins fnl f: sn hdd: bmpd and no ex towards fin* **33/1**

0 **3** 2 1/2 **Fairmet**[38] 8602 2-9-0 0 LukeMorris 3 67
(Marco Botti) *chsd ldrs: effrt 2f out: sn swtchd rt and drvn to chal over 1f out: sltly impeded: edgd lft and outpcd ins fnl f* **66/1**

0 **4** 3/4 **Aswaat**[29] 8849 2-9-0 0 JimCrowley 13 66
(John Gosden) *chsd ldrs: effrt to chal 2f out: rdn to ld over 1f out: hdd ins fnl f: impeded and edgd lft: outpcd fnl 100yds* **7/2**[2]

0 **5** 2 1/4 **Charming Rose**[27] 8913 2-9-0 0 RobertHavlin 12 60
(John Gosden) *w ldr tl led over 6f out: rdn and hrd pressed 2f out: hdd over 1f out: keeping on same pce whn squeezed for room and hmpd ins fnl f* **9/1**

0 **6** nk **Arietta**[15] 9063 2-8-9 0 TylerSaunders(5) 14 60
(Jonathan Portman) *in tch in midfield: effrt 2f out: unable qck over 1f out: swtchd rt and kpt on same pce ins fnl f* **100/1**

0 **7** 7 **Stagiaire**[16] 9052 2-9-0 0 RichardKingscote 7 44
(Ralph Beckett) *midfield: rdn over 3f out: lost pl over 2f out: no ch after* **50/1**

0 **8** 1 1/4 **Lisbet**[16] 9046 2-9-0 0 (h) KieranO'Neill 5 41
(John Gosden) *dwlt: rn green towards rr: hdwy into midfield 1/2-way: rdn and racd awkwardly: sn outpcd and wl btn 2f out* **8/1**[3]

2 **9** 2 1/2 **Morning Shadow**[7] 9197 2-9-0 0 JasonHart 8 35
(Mark Johnston) *led for over 1f: chsd ldr tl rdn and lost 2nd 2f out: lost pl qckly over 1f out: fdd fnl f* **10/1**

0 **10** nse **Scarlet Ruby**[15] 9063 2-9-0 0 AdamMcNamara 4 35
(Roger Charlton) *pushed along towards rr: rdn over 2f out: outpcd and swtchd rt 2f out: n.d after* **40/1**

11 1/2 **Appletart (IRE)** 2-9-0 0 HectorCrouch 10 34
(Ed Walker) *midfield on outer: rdn: outpcd and edgd rt over 2f out: sn wl btn* **50/1**

0 **12** nk **Villanelle**[29] 8848 2-8-11 0 TheodoreLadd(3) 6 33
(Jonathan Portman) *s.i.s: a in rr* **100/1**

0 **13** 6 **Midnight Welcome**[76] 7407 2-9-0 0 KierenFox 2 19
(Patrick Chamings) *dwlt: a in rr* **100/1**

0 **14** 2 1/2 **Cath The Great (IRE)**[15] 9062 2-9-0 0 LiamKeniry 11 13
(Gary Moore) *stdd after s: rdn over 2f out: sn outpcd and wknd 2f out* **100/1**

1m 39.45s (-0.35) **Going Correction** -0.025s/f (Stan) 14 Ran SP% **127.2**
Speed ratings (Par 93): **100,99,96,96,93 93,86,85,82,82 82,81,75,73**
CSF £42.13 TOTE £1.60: £1.10, £5.70, £11.30; EX 30.80 Trifecta £950.10.
Owner Benjamin Leon Jr **Bred** Besilu Stables LLC **Trained** Newmarket, Suffolk
■ Stewards' Enquiry : Jack Mitchell three-day ban; careless riding (Dec 19-21)

FOCUS
The winner looks to have a bright future but it's just fair form otherwise. The pace was even.

9328 RACING TV NURSERY H'CAP 1m (P)

7:15 (7:19) (Class 4) (0-85,80) 2-Y-O **£5,045** (£1,501; £750; £375; £300) **Stalls** Low

Form RPR

0052 **1** **Siberian Night (IRE)**[6] 9212 2-8-5 **64** LukeMorris 1 69+
(Ed Walker) *dwlt: in tch: effrt 2f out: hdwy u.p over 1f out: led ins fnl f: styd on wl and gng away at fin* **2/1**[2]

2422 **2** 2 **Baadirr**[8] 9175 2-9-7 **80** JamesDoyle 3 80
(William Haggas) *led: rdn 2f out: drvn and hdd ins fnl f: no ex and outpcd towards fin* **7/4**[1]

022 **3** 2 **Hurricane Alex**[15] 9063 2-8-13 **77** ThoreHammerHansen(5) 5 72
(Richard Hannon) *chsd ldr: effrt jst over 2f out: 3rd and unable qck whn edgd rt 1f out: wknd ins fnl f* **4/1**[3]

005 **4** 1 1/4 **Fleet Street**[10] 9159 2-9-1 **74** RobertHavlin 2 67
(John Gosden) *trckd ldrs: effrt ent fnl 2f: unable qck over 1f out: wknd ins fnl f* **8/1**

6520 **5** 17 **Red Jasper**[8] 9172 2-8-2 **64** (b[1]) TheodoreLadd(3) 4 17+
(Michael Appleby) *v.s.a: a last: clsd and in tch 5f out: rdn over 2f out: sn btn and wknd over 1f out (jockey said gelding was very slowly away losing considerable ground at the start; trainer's rep said that the gelding did not face the first-time blinkers)* **10/1**

1m 40.8s (1.00) **Going Correction** -0.025s/f (Stan) 5 Ran SP% **109.9**
Speed ratings (Par 98): **94,92,90,88,71**
CSF £5.88 TOTE £2.40: £1.20, £1.30; EX 5.20 Trifecta £15.80.
Owner Dubai Thoroughbred Racing **Bred** Morera Partnership **Trained** Upper Lambourn, Berks

FOCUS
A fair nursery in which the only progressive sort was readily on top. The pace was steady but didn't affect the result.

9329 RACINGTV.COM H'CAP 7f (P)

7:45 (7:45) (Class 5) (0-78,78) 3-Y-O+
£3,816 (£1,135; £567; £300; £300; £300) **Stalls** Low

Form RPR

6415 **1** **Champion Brogie (IRE)**[6] 9217 3-8-8 **65** LukeMorris 7 72
(J S Moore) *hld up in tch in midfield: effrt 2f out: rdn and clsd over 1f out: ev ch ins fnl f: led wl ins fnl f: styd on* **11/1**

6011 **2** 1/2 **Earth And Sky (USA)**[8] 9173 3-9-7 **78** JamesDoyle 6 83
(George Scott) *chsd ldr: effrt 2f out: drvn over 1f out: drvn and ev ch ins fnl f: kpt on: nt quite match pce of wnr towards fin* **6/5**[1]

0015 **3** 1/2 **Stringybark Creek**[8] 9173 5-9-1 **75** ThomasGreatrex(3) 5 79
(David Loughnane) *led: rdn ent fnl 2f: drvn over 1f out: hdd and one pce wl ins fnl f* **7/2**[2]

5000 **4** 1 **Scorched Breath**[5] 9244 3-8-3 **65** (t) AledBeech(5) 4 66
(Charlie Fellowes) *trckd ldrs: effrt 2f out: kpt on same pce ins fnl f* **12/1**

6053 **5** 1 1/2 **Al Asef**[16] 9048 4-8-8 **70** DylanHogan(5) 9 67
(David Simcock) *stdd s: t.k.h: hld up in tch in last trio: effrt over 2f out: kpt on ins fnl f: nt rch ldrs* **8/1**

0421 **6** 1/2 **Little Palaver**[51] 8221 7-8-10 **74** (p) ImogenCarter(7) 2 70
(Clive Cox) *in tch in midfield: effrt 2f out: pushed along and unable qck over 1f out: kpt on same pce ins fnl f* **6/1**[3]

000 **7** 2 **Dutch Pursuit (IRE)**[44] 8428 3-9-5 **76** RichardKingscote 8 67
(Rebecca Menzies) *stdd and dropped in bhd after s: hld up in rr: effrt over 2f out: no real imp: nvr trbld ldrs* **25/1**

4120 **8** 6 **Act Of Magic (IRE)**[133] 5354 3-8-7 **64** KieranO'Neill 1 38
(Luke McJannet) *hld up in tch in last trio: effrt over 2f out: sn btn and wknd over 1f out* **33/1**

1m 26.74s (0.74) **Going Correction** -0.025s/f (Stan) 8 Ran SP% **115.9**
Speed ratings (Par 103): **94,93,92,91,90 89,87,80**
CSF £25.10 CT £59.08 TOTE £9.70: £2.30, £1.20, £1.50; EX 30.90 Trifecta £98.80.
Owner Tom Vaughan & Sara Moore **Bred** Ms Mary Ryan **Trained** Upper Lambourn, Berks

FOCUS
A fair handicap run at a steady tempo.
T/Plt: £23.30 to a £1 stake. Pool: £56,222.33 - 1760.21 winning units T/Qpdt: £30.20 to a £1 stake. Pool: £5,998.07 - 146.88 winning units **Steve Payne**

9219 SOUTHWELL (L-H)

Thursday, December 5

OFFICIAL GOING: Fibresand: standard
Wind: Fairly strong, across Weather: Dry

9330 LADBROKES WHERE THE NATION PLAYS NURSERY H'CAP 6f 16y(F)

4:15 (4:20) (Class 6) (0-60,58) 2-Y-O
£2,781 (£827; £413; £400; £400; £400) **Stalls** Low

Form RPR

050 **1** **Class Clown (IRE)**[27] 8919 2-9-4 **55** HollieDoyle 13 65
(David Barron) *towards rr on outer: shkn up and hdwy into midfield over 4f out: stdy hdwy over 2f out: rdn and hung lft over 1f out: sn ev ch: kpt on wl fnl f: led towards fin* **4/1**[1]

0564 **2** *hd* **Jochi Khan (USA)**[8] 9179 2-8-9 **46**..........................(v) RaulDaSilva 5 55
(Mohamed Moubarak) *cl up: short of room and lost position after 1f: sn rdn midfield on inner: shkn up and hdwy over 2f out: led and edgd rt over 1f out: sn rdn and hrd pressed: kpt on fnl f: hdd towards fin* **6/1**[3]

0005 **3** *6* **Chocoholic**[31] 8815 2-8-11 **48**.............................. GrahamLee 10 39
(Bryan Smart) *cl up on outer: rdn 2f out: sn hung lft and outpcd: rallied ins fnl f: wnt modest 3rd towards fin: no match for first two* **6/1**[3]

000 **4** *hd* **Queen Of Rock (IRE)**[41] 8525 2-8-8 **45**.............................. PhilDennis 12 35
(Philip Kirby) *disp ld on outer: led 1/2-way: rdn and hdd over 1f out: outpcd fnl f: lost 3rd towards fin* **100/1**

2453 **5** *nk* **Classy Lady**[41] 8527 2-9-0 **51**.............................. BenRobinson 6 41
(Ollie Pears) *cl up on inner: rdn over 2f out: outpcd fnl f* **16/1**

0640 **6** *¾* **Mr Kodi (IRE)**[9] 9164 2-9-0 **51**..............................(b[1]) CliffordLee 7 38
(David Evans) *prom: rdn over 2f out: outpcd and edgd lft over 1f out: no imp fnl f* **5/1**[2]

0000 **7** *4* **Gold Venture (IRE)**[19] 9009 2-8-4 **48**..............(t[1]) NickBarratt-Atkin(7) 8 23
(Philip Kirby) *towards rr: rdn after 2f: sn struggling: sme hdwy fnl f: mde no imp* **66/1**

0624 **8** *1¾* **Comeatchoo (IRE)**[15] 9061 2-8-10 **54**.............................. GraceMcEntee(7) 9 24
(Phil McEntee) *led: hdd but cl up 1/2-way: rdn 2f out: sn wknd* **6/1**[3]

6550 **9** *2* **Mumsbirthdaygirl (IRE)**[30] 8825 2-8-8 **45**.............................. AndrewMullen 3 9
(Mark Loughnane) *in rr and outpcd: rdn and struggling bef 1/2-way: nvr on terms* **66/1**

5000 **10** *2¼* **Parker's Boy**[19] 9009 2-8-13 **50**.............................. EoinWalsh 4 7
(Brian Barr) *s.i.s: in rr and rdn after 2f: sn struggling: btn over 2f out: eased whn no ch fnl f (jockey said gelding was never travelling; trainer's rep said that gelding did not face the kick back)* **33/1**

0062 **11** *¾* **Oasis Song**[30] 8825 2-9-0 **51**.............................. CharlieBennett 2 6
(Hughie Morrison) *in tch w ldrs on inner: short of room and lost grnd after 2f: rdn and outpcd over 3f out: btn whn hung lft 2f out (jockey said filly suffered interference shortly after the start)* **6/1**[3]

6504 **12** *8* **Full Spectrum (IRE)**[94] 6799 2-9-2 **58**..............................(p) RhiainIngram(5) 1
(Paul George) *short of room and dropped to last on inner after 1f: sn rdn and outpcd: no ch whn hung lft fr over 2f out (jockey said filly was never travelling and hung left-handed; trainer said that filly did not face the kick back; vet revealed the filly to be slightly lame on its left-fore)* **40/1**

1m 17.16s (0.66) **Going Correction** -0.10s/f (Stan) **12** Ran SP% **109.0**
Speed ratings (Par 94): **91,90,82,82,82 81,75,73,70,67 66,56**
CSF £24.74 CT £128.45 TOTE £4.70: £1.80, £1.80, £2.50; EX 26.60 Trifecta £141.70.
Owner Miss N J Barron **Bred** Joli Racing **Trained** Maunby, N Yorks
■ Lethal Blast was withdrawn. Price at time of withdrawal 20/1. Rule 4 does not apply.

FOCUS
A modest nursery.

9331 BOMBARDIER GOLDEN BEER H'CAP 1m 13y(F)
4:50 (4:50) (Class 5) (0-70,69) 3-Y-O+
£3,428 (£1,020; £509; £400; £400; £400) **Stalls Low**

Form RPR

5510 **1** **Jazz Hands (IRE)**[31] 8818 3-8-7 **56**..............................(p) BarryMcHugh 7 65
(Richard Fahey) *in tch w ldrs on outer: hdwy and pressed ldr 1/2-way: rdn and led over 1f out: sn edgd lft: kpt on wl fnl 110yds* **7/1**[3]

0065 **2** *nk* **Tagur (IRE)**[17] 9035 5-8-8 **56**..............................(v) JosephineGordon 3 64
(Kevin Ryan) *led: rdn and hdd over 1f out: sn rallied and ev ch: kpt on fnl f: no ex towards fin* **14/1**

4601 **3** *7* **Motahassen (IRE)**[6] 9225 5-8-11 **59** 5ex..............................(t) PaulMulrennan 1 51
(Declan Carroll) *prom: rdn 2f out: sn outpcd: rallied and wnt modest 3rd ins fnl 110yds: no match for first two* **4/5**[1]

0111 **4** *1¼* **Clipsham Tiger (IRE)**[17] 9028 3-8-12 **68**..............................(h) GeorgeRooke(7) 6 57
(Michael Appleby) *plld hrd: trckd ldr: lost 2nd but cl up 1/2-way: rdn over 2f out: edgd lft and outpcd over 1f out: btn and lost 3rd ins fnl 110yds* **5/2**[2]

0- **5** *12* **Natty Dresser (IRE)**[400] 8750 4-8-13 **61**.............................. WilliamCarson 5 23
(Debbie Hughes) *t.k.h: cl up: lost grnd after 2f: rdn and outpcd 1/2-way: sn wknd* **50/1**

1060 **6** *1* **Inner Circle (IRE)**[35] 8702 5-9-2 **69**.............................. KevinLundie(5) 2 28
(Mark Loughnane) *s.i.s: in rr on inner: swtchd rt and hdwy over 3f out: sn rdn: wknd fr 2f out* **40/1**

1m 41.47s (-2.23) **Going Correction** -0.10s/f (Stan)
WFA 3 from 4yo+ 1lb **6** Ran SP% **107.7**
Speed ratings (Par 103): **107,106,99,98,86 85**
CSF £80.32 TOTE £8.00: £2.90, £4.80; EX 53.90 Trifecta £223.10.
Owner Mike Browne & Mrs Dee Howe **Bred** Golden Vale Stud **Trained** Musley Bank, N Yorks

FOCUS
An ordinary handicap. The front two were well placed to dominate something of a sprint finish from the top of the straight.

9332 BETWAY NOVICE STKS 6f 16y(F)
5:25 (5:26) (Class 5) 3-Y-O+ **£3,428** (£1,020; £509; £254) **Stalls Low**

Form RPR

21 **1** **Sommer Katze (FR)**[26] 8947 3-9-9 0.............................. DavidNolan 6 80
(Declan Carroll) *travelled strly: cl up: led 2f out: sn shkn up and wnt clr: eased towards fin: readily* **11/8**[1]

4 **2** *4½* **Milagre Da Vida (IRE)**[27] 8920 3-8-11 0.............................. PJMcDonald 7 54
(K R Burke) *s.i.s: t.k.h: sn in tch w ldrs on outer: hdwy and cl up over 3f out: rdn 2f out: sn edgd lft: wnt 2nd over 1f out: no match for wnr* **10/1**[3]

403 **3** *3* **Six Til Twelve (IRE)**[17] 9032 3-9-2 62.............................. HollieDoyle 4 49
(Robyn Brisland) *t.k.h: led after 1f: rdn and hdd 2f out: lost 2nd over 1f out: btn ins fnl f* **9/2**[2]

0003 **4** *nk* **Hellofagame**[28] 8901 4-8-11 45..............................(t) SeamusCronin(5) 8 48
(Richard Price) *led: swtchd lft early: hdd but prom after 1f: rdn over 2f out: outpcd whn edgd lft over 1f out: sn btn* **33/1**

2 **5** *1¼* **Redesdale Rebel**[13] 9112 3-9-2 0.............................. PaulMulrennan 1 44
(Susan Corbett) *bhd and outpcd: swtchd rt over 4f out: rdn 1/2-way: hdwy and drifted lft 2f out: sn no imp* **9/2**[2]

55 **6** *3¼* **Inn With The Gin**[17] 9032 3-8-11 0..............................(p[1]) JamesSullivan 3 29
(Scott Dixon) *in tch w ldrs: rdn 1/2-way: wknd fr 2f out* **50/1**

7 *2¾* **Mr Millarcky** 3-9-2 0.............................. DavidProbert 2 25
(Rae Guest) *slowly away: outpcd in rr: pushed along and struggling over 3f out: nvr on terms* **10/1**[3]

30 **8** *12* **Alameery**[84] 7114 3-9-2 0.............................. BarryMcHugh 5
(Adrian Nicholls) *s.i.s: in rr on outer: sme hdwy 1/2-way: rdn and wknd fr 2f out* **11/1**

03 **9** *2¾* **Henry The Sixth**[26] 8947 3-8-9 0.............................. JonathanFisher(7) 9
(Scott Dixon) *t.k.h: cl up: disp ld over 4f out: rdn over 2f out: hung lft and wknd qckly fr 2f out (jockey said colt ran too free)* **150/1**

1m 15.35s (-1.15) **Going Correction** -0.10s/f (Stan) **9** Ran SP% **110.5**
Speed ratings (Par 103): **103,97,93,92,90 86,82,66,63**
CSF £15.34 TOTE £2.40: £1.20, £1.90, £1.20; EX 16.20 Trifecta £50.40.
Owner F Gillespie **Bred** Debra Hooper **Trained** Malton, N Yorks
■ Stewards' Enquiry : Seamus Cronin one-day ban; failure to ride to draw (Dec 19)

FOCUS
An ordinary novice contest. The eased-down favourite's winning time was notably quicker than the earlier C&D nursery.

9333 PLAY 4 TO SCORE AT BETWAY H'CAP 1m 4f 14y(F)
6:00 (6:01) (Class 5) (0-70,68) 3-Y-O+
£3,428 (£1,020; £509; £400; £400; £400) **Stalls Low**

Form RPR

442 **1** **Angel Lane (FR)**[70] 7630 3-9-1 **63**.............................. CliffordLee 5 76
(K R Burke) *trckd ldrs: wnt 2nd after 4f: led gng easily 3f out: rdn and edgd rt over 1f out: sn wnt clr: kpt on strly fnl f* **8/1**

5623 **2** *3¾* **Sociologist (FR)**[6] 9221 4-8-9 **60**..............................(p) JonathanFisher(7) 6 66
(Scott Dixon) *t.k.h: led: hdd 3f out: sn rdn and rallied: edgd rt and kpt on fnl f: no match for wnr* **11/2**[2]

0003 **3** *1¼* **Princess Harley (IRE)**[17] 9033 4-9-1 **59**..............................(p) FrannyNorton 4 63
(Mick Quinn) *t.k.h: prom: stdy hdwy gng easily over 3f out: rdn over 2f out: no ex ins fnl f* **3/1**[1]

3061 **4** *6* **Contingency Fee**[6] 9221 4-9-2 **67** 5ex..............................(p) GraceMcEntee(7) 3 61
(Phil McEntee) *t.k.h: towards rr: hdwy on outer and cl up after 4f: rdn 3f out: wknd fr over 1f out* **3/1**[1]

2260 **5** *4½* **Mr Carbonator**[14] 9093 4-9-3 **61**.............................. PhilDennis 8 48
(Philip Kirby) *hld up in rr on outer: rdn 5f out: outpcd over 3f out: btn fr 2f out* **6/1**[3]

0030 **6** *4* **Double Reflection**[16] 9050 4-9-10 **68**.............................. AlistairRawlinson 1 49
(Michael Appleby) *t.k.h: pressed ldr: lost 2nd but prom after 4f: rdn over 4f out: sn struggling: btn over 2f out (vet said filly had been struck into on its right-fore)* **14/1**

4606 **7** *1½* **Panatos (FR)**[37] 8639 4-9-1 **59**.............................. DanielMuscutt 7 37
(Alexandra Dunn) *dwlt s: in tch w ldrs on outer: rdn and lost grnd after 2f: struggling over 4f out: sn btn* **9/1**

0002 **8** *20* **Going Native**[28] 8904 4-8-3 **54** oh2.............................. RhonaPindar(7) 2
(Olly Williams) *awkward s: in rr on inner: rdn and outpcd over 4f out: lost tch over 3f out: t.o (trainer said that the filly had found the grade of race too competitive on this occasion)* **14/1**

2m 38.73s (-2.27) **Going Correction** -0.10s/f (Stan)
WFA 3 from 4yo 4lb **8** Ran SP% **114.1**
Speed ratings (Par 103): **103,100,99,95,92 90,89,75**
CSF £51.00 CT £162.09 TOTE £7.40: £2.50, £2.30, £1.30; EX 43.90 Trifecta £292.90.
Owner Miss Anna Sundstrom **Bred** Mlle Moa Sundstrom & Mlle Lillie Drion **Trained** Middleham Moor, N Yorks

FOCUS
An ordinary middle-distance handicap.

9334 BETWAY H'CAP 6f 16y(F)
6:30 (6:32) (Class 4) (0-80,82) 3-Y-O+
£5,207 (£1,549; £774; £400; £400; £400) **Stalls Low**

Form RPR

5022 **1** **Samovar**[17] 9030 4-9-2 **75**..............................(b) JamesSullivan 10 83
(Scott Dixon) *led: swtchd lft early: hdd but cl up after 1f: rdn and led again 2f out: sn hrd pressed: kpt on fnl f: gamely* **33/1**

1 **2** *nk* **Rock Sound (IRE)**[30] 8839 4-9-2 **75**.............................. PaulMulrennan 12 82
(Declan Carroll) *t.k.h: cl up: led after 1f: rdn and hdd 2f out: sn rallied and ev ch: kpt on fnl f: no ex towards fin* **6/4**[1]

1105 **3** *¾* **Smokey Lane (IRE)**[29] 8860 5-9-1 **74**..............................(b) CliffordLee 6 79
(David Evans) *prom: rdn and hdwy over 2f out: hung lft over 1f out: wnt 3rd ins fnl 110yds: kpt on* **25/1**

4 *1* **Asdaa (IRE)**[182] 3520 3-9-9 **82**.............................. JoeFanning 3 84
(Mark Johnston) *prom: rdn 3f out: hdwy and hung lft over 1f out: no ex fnl 110yds* **10/1**

1034 **5** *1½* **Crosse Fire**[17] 9030 7-9-1 **81**..............................(b) JonathanFisher(7) 14 78
(Scott Dixon) *cl up on outer: ev ch 1/2-way: rdn 2f out: no ex fnl f* **25/1**

4261 **6** *hd* **Esprit De Corps**[26] 8946 5-9-1 **74**..............................(p) HollieDoyle 7 70
(David Barron) *in rr: shkn up over 3f out: rdn and hdwy 2f out: kpt on fnl f: nt pce to chal* **6/1**[2]

6-25 **7** *7* **Jonboy**[13] 9108 4-9-0 **73**.............................. GrahamLee 4 47
(David Brown) *t.k.h: hld up in rr: rdn and hung lft 2f out: sn wknd* **16/1**

1220 **8** *1½* **Astro Jakk (IRE)**[27] 8921 3-9-7 **80**.............................. PJMcDonald 9 49
(K R Burke) *midfield on outer: rdn and outpcd over 2f out: sn hung lft: btn over 1f out* **7/1**[3]

4014 **9** *1* **Royal Sands (FR)**[26] 8943 3-8-13 **72**.............................. BarryMcHugh 2 38
(James Given) *in rr on inner: rdn over 3f out: edgd lft 2f out: sn btn* **10/1**

5130 **10** *½* **John Kirkup**[27] 8921 4-9-7 **80**..............................(b) CallumRodriguez 11 44
(Michael Dods) *towards rr on outer: rdn and struggling over 2f out: sn btn* **11/1**

0520 **11** *1* **Airglow (IRE)**[37] 8636 4-8-13 **77**..............................(h) GerO'Neill(5) 1 38
(Michael Easterby) *in rr on inner: rdn and struggling 1/2-way: sn btn* **11/1**

0-00 **12** *2¼* **Andre Amar (IRE)**[17] 9030 3-8-11 **70**.............................. DavidProbert 8 24
(Robyn Brisland) *s.i.s: outpcd and bhd: struggling 1/2-way: sn btn (jockey said gelding was slowly away)* **150/1**

0020 **13** *18* **Peggy's Angel**[208] 2637 4-8-7 **69**.............................. HarrisonShaw(3) 13
(Stef Keniry) *in rr on outer: rdn and hung rt 1/2-way: sn struggling: lost tch fr 2f out: t.o (jockey said filly hung right-handed throughout)* **100/1**

1m 15.58s (-0.92) **Going Correction** -0.10s/f (Stan) **13** Ran SP% **119.8**
Speed ratings (Par 105): **102,101,100,99,97 97,87,85,84,83 82,79,55**
CSF £81.44 CT £1419.64 TOTE £31.20: £7.70, £1.10, £7.70; EX 193.40 Trifecta £3333.30.
Owner P J Dixon, Chrystal Maze & Ashley Severn **Bred** Paul Dixon & Crystal Maze Partnership **Trained** Babworth, Notts

FOCUS
The feature contest was a fair handicap in which it paid to race prominent to an even gallop.

9335 BETWAY HEED YOUR HUNCH H'CAP 4f 214y(F)
7:00 (7:04) (Class 6) (0-60,62) 3-Y-O+
£2,781 (£827; £413; £400; £400; £400) **Stalls Centre**

Form RPR

0365 **1** **Amazing Amaya**[279] 973 4-8-7 **46** oh1..............................(h) CamHardie 1 52
(Derek Shaw) *in rr on far side of gp: hdwy over 3f out: rdn and cl up over 1f out: kpt on wl fnl f: led fnl stride* **50/1**

5014 **2** *nse* **Loulin**[6] 9219 4-8-12 **51**....................(t) JamesSullivan 3 57
(Ruth Carr) *s.i.s: in rr on far side of gp: hdwy over 3f out: rdn and led over 1f out: kpt on fnl f: hdd fnl stride* **7/2**[2]

40/1 **3** *2 ¼* **Eesha Says (IRE)**[70] 7628 4-8-7 **53**.................... ElishaWhittington(7) 4 51
(Tony Carroll) *cl up on far side of gp: led over 2f out: rdn and hung lft over 1f out: sn hdd: no ex fnl 110yds (jockey said filly hung left-handed throughout)* **12/1**

3626 **4** *2 ¾* **Arzaak (IRE)**[37] 8643 5-9-7 **60**....................(b) PJMcDonald 7 48+
(Charlie Wallis) *cl up in centre of gp: rdn 1/2-way: outpcd fr over 1f out* **7/1**[3]

5014 **5** *2 ½* **Catapult**[10] 9161 4-8-12 **51**....................(p) JosephineGordon 9 30+
(Shaun Keightley) *in rr in centre of gp: rdn and outpcd after 2f: kpt on fnl f: nt pce to chal* **7/2**[2]

0050 **6** *¾* **Pearl Noir**[77] 7389 9-8-4 **46** oh1....................(b) DarraghKeenan(3) 5 22
(Scott Dixon) *prom on far side of gp: rdn and outpcd 1/2-way: btn over 1f out* **50/1**

50U2 **7** *1 ½* **Honey Gg**[6] 9219 4-9-9 **62**.................... DavidNolan 8 33+
(Declan Carroll) *disp ld in centre of gp to 1/2-way: sn rdn: wknd fnl f* **10/3**[1]

6315 **8** *¾* **Moneta**[9] 9169 3-9-2 **55**....................(b) DavidProbert 10 23+
(Ronald Harris) *led on nr side of gp: rdn and hdd over 2f out: wknd over 1f out* **14/1**

4401 **9** *1* **Rangefield Express (IRE)**[34] 8720 3-8-12 **51**....................(b) SamJames 13 15+
(Geoffrey Harker) *in rr on nr side of gp: rdn and struggling bef 1/2-way: sn btn* **20/1**

0256 **10** *2 ¼* **It Must Be Faith**[6] 9219 9-9-6 **59**....................(p) JaneElliott 14 15+
(Michael Appleby) *got wl bhd on nr side of gp: rdn and struggling bef 1/2-way: nvr on terms* **16/1**

0000 **11** *4 ½* **Classic Pursuit**[45] 8401 8-9-1 **54**....................(p) HollieDoyle 6
(Marjorie Fife) *rrd s and blindfold off late: lost many l s: wl bhd in centre of gp: no ch fr over 2f out (jockey said that the gelding had reared high and sat back in the stalls simultaneously as the starter had shouted for the blinds off, causing her to lose her balance and be slow to remove the blindfold)* **20/1**

3560 **12** *4* **Ebitda**[6] 9219 5-9-0 **60**....................(b) JonathanFisher(7) 11
(Scott Dixon) *cl up on nr side of gp: rdn 1/2-way: sn wknd* **50/1**

58.5s (-1.20) **Going Correction** -0.10s/f (Stan) **12 Ran SP% 115.7**
Speed ratings (Par 101): **105,104,101,96,92 91,89,88,86,82 75,69**
CSF £207.55 CT £1675.30 TOTE £28.30: £5.50, £1.80, £3.90; EX 481.20 Trifecta £2615.60.
Owner Paddy Barrett **Bred** P E Barrett **Trained** Sproxton, Leics

FOCUS
A modest sprint handicap. The first three horses home were drawn low and the race developed central to far side.

9336 BETWAY LIVE CASINO H'CAP 1m 6f 21y(F)
7:30 (7:33) (Class 6) (0-65,66) 3-Y-O+

£2,781 (£827; £413; £400; £400; £400) **Stalls Low**

Form RPR

1122 **1** **Tynecastle Park**[8] 9184 6-9-7 **66**.................... SelmaGrage(7) 5 73
(Robert Eddery) *mde virtually all: nudged along fr 2f out: wnt clr fnl f: kpt on wl* **5/1**[1]

0334 **2** *2 ½* **Cold Harbour**[17] 9033 4-9-10 **62**....................(t) DavidProbert 3 66
(Robyn Brisland) *midfield: smooth hdwy and cl up over 3f out: shkn up and wnt 2nd over 2f out: sn rdn: kpt on fnl f: no match for wnr* **7/1**[3]

2-06 **3** *¾* **Earl Of Bunnacurry (IRE)**[20] 8988 5-9-4 **56**.................... CliffordLee 8 59
(Gavin Cromwell, Ire) *cl up: rdn 3f out: edgd lft ins fnl f: kpt on* **5/1**[1]

6354 **4** *1 ½* **Bill Cody (IRE)**[16] 9049 4-9-6 **58**.................... CallumRodriguez 2 59
(Julie Camacho) *disp ld to 3f out: sn rdn: outpcd and edgd rt over 1f out: no ex fnl f* **8/1**

3000 **5** *¾* **Sea Of Mystery (IRE)**[16] 9049 6-9-9 **61**....................(bt) AlistairRawlinson 11 61
(Michael Appleby) *midfield: pushed along 4f out: rdn and outpcd whn hung lft 2f out: no imp fnl f* **7/1**[3]

6300 **6** *2* **Heron (USA)**[16] 9049 5-9-12 **64**....................(p) DanielMuscutt 10 61
(Brett Johnson) *hld up in rr: rdn and outpcd over 4f out: no imp fr 2f out* **5/1**[1]

1666 **7** *21* **Extreme Appeal (IRE)**[16] 9049 7-9-5 **57**....................(be[1]) GrahamLee 6 27
(Kelly Morgan) *s.i.s: in rr on outer: hdwy 4f out: sn pushed along: wknd over 2f out: t.o* **20/1**

6450 **8** *8* **Dancing Lilly**[7] 9204 4-8-8 **46**.................... WilliamCarson 7 6
(Debbie Hughes) *prom on inner: rdn and outpcd 1/2-way: sn lost position: struggling fr 5f out: t.o* **28/1**

5000 **9** *7* **Konigin**[16] 9049 4-9-2 **54**....................(b[1]) NicolaCurrie 9 4
(John Berry) *s.i.s: hdwy and prom on outer after 3f: rdn and struggling 4f out: sn wknd: eased whn no ch over 1f out: t.o (jockey said filly stopped quickly)* **16/1**

2151 **10** *dist* **Thahab Ifraj (IRE)**[37] 8639 6-9-10 **62**.................... JoeFanning 4
(Alexandra Dunn) *in rr: rdn and struggling after 6f: sn lost tch: completely t.o (trainer's rep could offer no explanation for the gelding's performance other than a report from the rider that the gelding was never travelling)* **6/1**[2]

403 **11** *dist* **Montelimar**[20] 8662 4-8-8 **51**.................... AndrewBreslin(5) 1
(Andrew Crook) *in tch w ldrs on inner: lost grnd after 3f: rdn and struggling after 6f: sn lost tch: completely t.o (jockey said filly moved poorly; vet revealed the filly to have bled from the nose)* **100/1**

3m 6.49s (-1.81) **Going Correction** -0.10s/f (Stan) **11 Ran SP% 115.5**
Speed ratings (Par 101): **101,99,99,98,97 96,84,80,76,**
CSF £38.38 CT £184.07 TOTE £4.90: £2.00, £2.50, £1.40; EX 44.70 Trifecta £168.00.
Owner Robert Eddery **Bred** Fittocks Stud Ltd & Arrow Farm Stud **Trained** Newmarket, Suffolk

FOCUS
An ordinary staying handicap.

9337 BOMBARDIER BRITISH HOPPED AMBER BEER H'CAP 7f 14y(F)
8:00 (8:05) (Class 6) (0-65,66) 3-Y-O+

£2,781 (£827; £413; £400; £400; £400) **Stalls Low**

Form RPR

5351 **1** **Bee Machine (IRE)**[26] 8949 4-8-5 **55**....................(t) ZakWheatley(7) 5 64+
(Declan Carroll) *t.k.h: in tch w ldrs: bit short of room over 4f out: rdn 3f out: sn outpcd: rallied and led over 1f out: pushed out fnl f: comf* **7/1**[2]

3432 **2** *1* **Break The Silence**[6] 9224 5-8-7 **57**....................(b) JonathanFisher(7) 2 63
(Scott Dixon) *led: rdn 3f out: hdd over 1f out: sn rallied: kpt on fnl f: no match for wnr* **13/8**[1]

4530 **3** *4 ½* **Kraka (IRE)**[44] 8435 4-9-4 **66**....................(p) KevinLundie(5) 8 60
(Christine Dunnett) *in tch w ldrs on outer: rdn and outpcd over 2f out: hung lft and hdwy over 1f out: wnt 3rd ins fnl f: no match for first two* **20/1**

4403 **4** *nse* **Global Melody**[8] 9185 4-8-13 **63**....................(v) GraceMcEntee(7) 6 57
(Phil McEntee) *cl up: ev ch gng easily over 1f out: sn rdn and hung rt: no ex fnl f* **7/1**[2]

-050 **5** *1 ¼* **Dream Mount (IRE)**[27] 8923 4-8-13 **56**....................(e[1]) PaulMulrennan 7 46
(Julie Camacho) *cl up on outer: rdn over 2f out: carried rt and outpcd over 1f out: wknd ins fnl f* **25/1**

600 **6** *hd* **Sylviacliffs (FR)**[28] 8902 3-9-0 **64**....................(p) RhonaPindar(7) 11 54
(K R Burke) *s.i.s: in rr and outpcd: rdn and hdwy 2f out: no imp fnl f* **25/1**

0005 **7** *½* **Pioneering (IRE)**[17] 9033 5-9-4 **66**.................... PaulaMuir(5) 9 54
(Roger Fell) *in tch w ldrs on outer: rdn and outpcd over 4f out: rallied over 1f out: nt pce to chal (jockey said gelding hung right-handed)* **8/1**

3022 **8** *3 ¼* **Geography Teacher (IRE)**[28] 8903 3-9-2 **59**....................(b) PJMcDonald 12 39
(R Mike Smith) *s.i.s: bhd and outpcd: rdn 3f out: no imp fr 2f out (jockey said gelding was slowly away)* **15/2**[3]

0024 **9** *6* **Jagerbond**[17] 9028 3-8-2 **50** oh5....................(e) AndrewBreslin(5) 1 13
(Andrew Crook) *s.i.s: wl bhd on inner: nvr on terms* **40/1**

1440 **10** *6* **Alpha Tauri (USA)**[17] 9028 13-9-2 **59**.................... BenRobinson 3 6
(Charles Smith) *in rr on inner: rdn and struggling 1/2-way: sn btn (jockey said gelding was never travelling)* **12/1**

050 **11** *nse* **Black Isle Boy (IRE)**[13] 9113 5-9-6 **63**.................... DavidProbert 4 10
(David C Griffiths) *cl up: rdn 1/2-way: wknd over 2f out* **25/1**

12 *1* **Espoir Et Bonheur (IRE)**[44] 8444 3-8-8 **51**....................(t) NicolaCurrie 13
(Gavin Cromwell, Ire) *s.i.s: in rr on outer: rdn and struggling fr over 3f out: nvr on terms* **25/1**

1m 29.51s (-0.79) **Going Correction** -0.10s/f (Stan) **12 Ran SP% 116.2**
Speed ratings (Par 101): **100,98,93,93,92 92,91,87,80,74 73,72**
CSF £16.60 CT £225.02 TOTE £7.80: £2.40, £1.10, £5.50; EX 21.10 Trifecta £258.10.
Owner Mrs Sarah Bryan **Bred** Drumlin Bloodstock **Trained** Malton, N Yorks

FOCUS
An ordinary handicap.

T/Plt: £601.80 to a £1 stake. Pool: £79,927.68 - 96.94 winning units. T/Qpdt: £18.00 to a £1 stake. Pool: £12,081.36 - 493.98 winning units. **Richard Young**

9338 - 9344a (Foreign Racing) - See Raceform Interactive

9106

NEWCASTLE (A.W) (L-H)
Friday, December 6

OFFICIAL GOING: Tapeta: standard
Wind: Breezy, half against on straight course and in over 3f of home straight in races on round course Weather: Dry

9345 PLAY 4 TO SCORE BETWAY H'CAP 1m 4f 98y (Tp)
3:15 (3:15) (Class 6) (0-60,65) 3-Y-O+

£2,781 (£827; £413; £400; £400; £400) **Stalls High**

Form RPR

1320 **1** **Sulafaat (IRE)**[45] 8423 4-9-0 **55**....................(p) RussellHarris(7) 6 61
(Rebecca Menzies) *towards rr: smooth hdwy on outer 3f out: rdn to ld over 1f out: edgd lft and hrd pressed ins fnl f: kpt on wl fnl 110yds: gamely* **14/1**

0560 **2** *hd* **Accessor (IRE)**[71] 7609 4-9-2 **50**....................(p[1]) FrannyNorton 12 56
(Michael Wigham) *t.k.h: in tch w ldrs: stdy hdwy 3f out: hrd rdn over 1f out: sn outpcd: rallied ins fnl f: wnt 2nd towards fin: jst hld* **3/1**[1]

4640 **3** *nk* **Spark Of War (IRE)**[8] 9207 4-9-3 **51**....................(v) JoeFanning 8 56
(Keith Dalgleish) *hld up in rr: stdy hdwy gng easily on outer over 2f out: rdn over 1f out: kpt on fnl f: wnt 3rd towards fin* **15/2**[3]

1441 **4** *nse* **Hooflepuff (IRE)**[10] 9168 3-9-13 **65** 6ex....................(p) BenRobinson 11 71
(Brian Ellison) *cl up: led gng easily over 2f out: rdn and hdd over 1f out: rallied and ev ch ins fnl f: no ex and lost two pls towards fin* **7/2**[2]

0440 **5** *1 ¼* **Thawry**[37] 8669 4-9-9 **57**.................... CamHardie 7 60
(Antony Brittain) *hld up in rr: stdy hdwy gng easily whn nt clr run over 2f out: rdn and swtchd rt over 1f out: kpt on fnl f: nrst fin (jockey said gelding was denied a clear run approaching 2f out)* **8/1**

-640 **6** *2* **Clayton Hall (IRE)**[137] 4690 6-8-11 **45**....................(p) GrahamLee 5 45
(John Wainwright) *towards rr: stdy hdwy whn bit short of room over 2f out: sn rdn: kpt on fnl f: mde no imp (vet said revealed the gelding to be lame on its left-fore)* **100/1**

-040 **7** *½* **Imperial Focus (IRE)**[35] 8713 6-9-7 **55**.................... PhilDennis 13 55
(Simon Waugh) *midfield on outer: smooth hdwy over 2f out: rdn over 1f out: no ex ins fnl f* **22/1**

5550 **8** *½* **Nearly There**[52] 8238 6-9-1 **52**....................(t) SeanDavis(3) 4 51
(Wilf Storey) *midfield: short of room over 2f out: sn rdn: outpcd fnl f* **20/1**

1300 **9** *nk* **Mamdood (IRE)**[10] 9168 5-9-3 **54**....................(t) HarrisonShaw(3) 10 52
(Stef Keniry) *t.k.h: in rr: hdwy and swtchd lft over 2f out: sn rdn: no imp fr over 1f out* **8/1**

10 *7* **High Glory (FR)**[16] 9068 3-8-3 **46**.................... PaulaMuir(5) 1 35
(J F Levins, Ire) *midfield on inner: rdn 3f out: wknd fr 2f out* **14/1**

2-02 **11** *1 ½* **Sunhill Lad (IRE)**[30] 8869 4-9-4 **52**....................(b) AndrewMullen 14 38
(Julia Brooke) *prom on outer: rdn and lost position over 2f out: sn btn (jockey said gelding stopped quickly)* **16/1**

0000 **12** *11* **Anchises**[60] 7956 4-9-6 **54**.................... CliffordLee 3 23
(Rebecca Menzies) *led: rdn and hdd over 2f out: wknd over 1f out* **66/1**

2450 **13** *6* **Gworn**[29] 8904 9-8-8 **47**.................... AledBeech(5) 2 7
(R Mike Smith) *t.k.h: cl up: rdn over 3f out: wknd over 2f out* **33/1**

56 **14** *5* **Dolphin Village (IRE)**[15] 9090 9-8-11 **45**....................(h) LewisEdmunds 9
(Shaun Harris) *lost many l s: in rr: rdn and struggling over 3f out: sn wknd* **40/1**

2m 41.8s (0.70) **Going Correction** +0.40s/f (Slow)
WFA 3 from 4yo+ 4lb **14 Ran SP% 117.4**
Speed ratings (Par 101): **113,112,112,112,111 110,110,109,109,104 103,96,92,89**
CSF £51.35 CT £350.83 TOTE £13.00: £3.70, £1.50, £2.80; EX 83.20 Trifecta £607.30.
Owner A Lister **Bred** Shadwell Estate Company Limited **Trained** Mordon, Durham
■ Stewards' Enquiry : Franny Norton ten-day ban; excessive use of whip (Dec 20, 21, 26-30)

FOCUS
The going was standard. Stalls - 2m: inside. 1m2f/1m4f: outside. Straight course: centre. An ordinary middle-distance handicap which saw most of the fancied horses involved in a tight finish.

9346 LADBROKES WHERE THE NATION PLAYS NURSERY H'CAP 1m 5y (Tp)
3:50 (3:50) (Class 6) (0-60,62) 2-Y-O

£2,781 (£827; £413; £400; £400; £400) **Stalls Centre**

Form RPR

060 **1** **Copperlight (IRE)**[49] 8302 2-9-7 **58**....................(p[1]) AndrewMullen 1 65
(Ben Haslam) *mde all: set stdy pce: rdn 2f out: kpt on strly fnl 110yds: unchal* **28/1**

0006 **2** 2 ½ **Fair Warning**[32] 8815 2-8-8 **52**........ LauraPearson(7) 3 53
(Henry Spiller) *prom: rdn over 2f out: hdwy and wnt 2nd over 1f out: no ex fnl 110yds* **11/2**[2]

0100 **3** 3 ½ **Constitutional (IRE)**[16] 9060 2-9-8 **62**........ HarrisonShaw(3) 9 55
(K R Burke) *ducked rt s: t.k.h: hld up in rr: rdn and hdwy on outer over 1f out: wnt 3rd ins fnl f: sn edgd lft and no imp* **6/1**[3]

066 **4** nk **Pearl Stream**[58] 8022 2-9-4 **55**........ CallumRodriguez 8 48
(Michael Dods) *dwlt s: hld up in rr: rdn and outpcd over 2f out: kpt on fnl 110yds: nt pce to chal* **13/2**

0303 **5** 1 ½ **Secret Diary**[16] 9060 2-9-10 **61**........ DanielTudhope 6 50
(Declan Carroll) *t.k.h: trckd wnr: rdn over 2f out: lost 2nd and outpcd over 1f out: btn fnl f* **2/1**[1]

4010 **6** 1 ¼ **Schumli**[10] 9164 2-9-2 **53**........(t) CamHardie 7 40
(David O'Meara) *in tch w ldrs: rdn over 2f out: wknd over 1f out* **22/1**

6043 **7** nk **Dazzling Darren (IRE)**[18] 9037 2-8-12 **49**........(p) LukeMorris 2 35
(Adam West) *t.k.h: cl up: rdn over 2f out: wknd over 1f out* **11/2**[2]

0001 **8** 3 **Speed Dating (FR)**[9] 9179 2-9-4 **55** 6ex........(v) LewisEdmunds 4 34
(Derek Shaw) *t.k.h: in tch w ldrs: rdn over 2f out: wknd over 1f out* **15/2**

1m 44.11s (5.51) **Going Correction** +0.40s/f (Slow) 8 Ran SP% **111.3**
Speed ratings (Par 94): **88,85,82,81,80 78,78,75**
CSF £164.79 CT £1049.72 TOTE £27.60: £7.10, £2.30, £2.30; EX 205.10 Trifecta £1214.60.
Owner R Brinkley & R Catling **Bred** Fortbarrington Stud **Trained** Middleham Moor, N Yorks

FOCUS
Quite an open nursery on paper, but the unexposed winner dominated.

9347 LADBROKES HOME OF THE ODDS BOOST/BRITISH STALLION STUDS EBF NOVICE STKS 6f (Tp)
4:25 (4:28) (Class 5) 2-Y-O **£4,787** (£1,424; £711; £355) **Stalls** Centre

Form RPR

65 **1** **Dulas (IRE)**[74] 7521 2-9-2 0........ KieranShoemark 11 83+
(Charles Hills) *t.k.h: mde virtually all: on nr side of gp: rdn clr fr 2f out: edgd rt ins fnl f: eased towards fin: unchal* **11/4**[2]

2 2 ¼ **Nehaall** 2-8-11 0........ JackMitchell 10 70+
(Roger Varian) *prom in centre of gp: hdwy and chsd wnr over 2f out: kpt on fnl 110yds: no match for wnr* **7/1**[3]

2 **3** 2 ¾ **Glen Force (IRE)**[14] 9107 2-9-2 0........ LukeMorris 5 67
(Sir Mark Prescott Bt) *midfield in centre of gp: rdn and outpcd over 2f out: rallied over 1f out: wnt 3rd ins fnl 110yds: nrst fin* **1/1**[1]

5 **4** nk **Queen's Course (IRE)**[20] 9008 2-8-13 ow2........ DanielTudhope 2 63
(William Haggas) *midfield on far side of gp: pushed along and hdwy over 2f out: wnt 3rd over 1f out: rdn and no ex fnl 110yds* **10/1**

3216 **5** ½ **Danny Ocean (IRE)**[13] 9137 2-9-6 76........(p) HarrisonShaw(3) 14 72
(K R Burke) *in rr on nr side of gp: rdn and hdwy 2f out: no imp fnl 110yds* **7/1**[3]

00 **6** 4 **Hayuplass**[28] 8919 2-8-11 0........ DuranFentiman 7 48
(Tim Easterby) *towards rr in centre of gp: pushed along whn bit short of room over 2f out: rallied over 1f out: sn no imp: btn ins fnl f* **250/1**

7 ½ **Jorgie (FR)** 2-9-2 0........ PaulMulrennan 4 51
(Iain Jardine) *dwlt s: hld up in rr on far side of gp: shkn up 2f out: sn no imp: btn fnl f* **100/1**

0 **8** 3 ¾ **On Display**[14] 9107 2-9-2 0........(t[1]) TomEaves 13 40
(Nigel Tinkler) *towards rr on nr side of gp: shkn up whn nt clr run and swtchd rt over 1f out: sn no imp: btn fnl f* **150/1**

3 **9** nk **Savage Beauty (IRE)**[48] 8338 2-8-8 0........ SeanDavis(3) 9 34
(Richard Fahey) *chsd wnr in centre of gp: rdn and lost position over 2f out: wknd over 1f out* **22/1**

10 nk **Quiet Night (IRE)** 2-8-11 0........ RobertHavlin 8 33
(Charles Hills) *in rr in centre of gp: rdn and outpcd over 2f out: btn over 1f out* **66/1**

50 **11** 1 ¼ **Park Lane Dancer (IRE)**[20] 9008 2-9-2 0........ JasonHart 1 34
(John Quinn) *in rr on far side of gp: struggling 3f out: sn btn* **80/1**

05 **12** 3 **Sea Ewe**[52] 8232 2-8-11 0........ JamesSullivan 12 20
(Alistair Whillans) *cl up on nr side of gp: rdn over 2f out: wknd over 1f out* **250/1**

00 **13** 1 **Jean Mary**[32] 8816 2-8-11 0........ ShaneGray 6 17
(Stef Keniry) *cl up on far side of gp: rdn and struggling over 2f out: sn wknd* **250/1**

1m 14.72s (2.22) **Going Correction** +0.40s/f (Slow) 13 Ran SP% **120.7**
Speed ratings (Par 96): **101,98,94,93,93 87,87,82,81,81 79,75,74**
CSF £22.61 TOTE £4.30: £1.40, £1.90, £1.10; EX 23.50 Trifecta £54.50.
Owner Julie Martin & David R Martin & Partner **Bred** Kildaragh Stud **Trained** Lambourn, Berks

FOCUS
A fair novice in which there were some nice types on show. The winner may turn out to be quite useful.

9348 BETWAY H'CAP 6f (Tp)
5:00 (5:03) (Class 3) (0-90,90) 3-Y-O+ **£7,698** (£2,290; £1,144; £572) **Stalls** Centre

Form RPR

11 **1** **Brushwork**[32] 8820 3-9-2 **85**........ KieranShoemark 3 94
(Charles Hills) *cl up on far side of gp: rdn to ld over 1f out: kpt on wl fnl 110yds: gamely* **13/2**[3]

0540 **2** ½ **Fendale**[15] 9098 7-8-13 **82**........ GrahamLee 1 89
(Bryan Smart) *towards rr on far side of gp: rdn and hdwy over 1f out: wnt 2nd ins fnl 110yds: kpt on* **40/1**

3304 **3** nse **El Hombre**[49] 8317 5-9-7 **90**........ JoeFanning 7 97
(Keith Dalgleish) *hld up in rr on far side of gp: short of room over 2f out: rdn and gd hdwy over 1f out: kpt on fnl f* **8/1**

3423 **4** nk **Heath Charnock**[15] 9088 3-9-3 **86**........ CallumRodriguez 11 92
(Michael Dods) *midfield on nr side of gp: stdy hdwy and cl up over 2f out: sn rdn and edgd lft: kpt on fnl f: hld towards fin* **3/1**[1]

3042 **5** 2 **Commander Han (FR)**[14] 9108 4-8-11 **80**........(t) PJMcDonald 12 80
(Stuart Williams) *towards rr in centre of gp: rdn and hdwy over 1f out: swtchd lft ins fnl f: kpt on: nt pce to chal* **7/2**[2]

4000 **6** ½ **Shallow Hal**[28] 8921 3-8-13 **82**........(p) CliffordLee 10 80
(K R Burke) *cl up on nr side of gp: rdn and ev ch over 1f out: no ex fnl 110yds* **14/1**

3305 **7** ½ **Kupa River (IRE)**[28] 8921 5-8-4 **78**........(h) PaulaMuir(5) 13 74
(Roger Fell) *midfield on nr side of gp: rdn over 2f out: hdwy over 1f out: no imp fnl f* **25/1**

0425 **8** ¾ **Howzer Black (IRE)**[34] 8766 3-8-11 **80**........(p) ShaneGray 14 74
(Keith Dalgleish) *hld up in rr on nr side of gp: rdn over 2f out: kpt on ins fnl 110yds: nt pce to chal* **25/1**

0660 **9** ½ **Glenamoy Lad**[76] 7431 5-9-6 **89**........(t) FrannyNorton 5 81
(Michael Wigham) *hld up in rr on far side of gp: rdn 2f out: kpt on fnl f: mde no imp (trainer was informed that the gelding could not run until the day after passing a stalls test)* **8/1**

4-54 **10** shd **Glorious Charmer**[179] 3659 3-8-10 **79**........ TomEaves 6 71
(Michael Herrington) *dwlt s: short of room early: t.k.h: in rr in centre of gp: repeatedly short of room fr 2f out: rdn and no imp fnl 110yds (jockey said gelding was continually denied a clear run from approaching the final furlong)* **100/1**

40 **11** nk **Primo's Comet**[15] 9098 4-8-10 **79**........ PhilDennis 9 70
(Jim Goldie) *t.k.h: prom in centre of gp: rdn over 1f out: wknd fnl f* **22/1**

0215 **12** ½ **Doc Sportello (IRE)**[13] 9131 7-8-9 **81**........ SeanDavis(3) 2 71
(Tony Carroll) *midfield on far side of gp: rdn over 2f out: hung lft over 1f out: sn wknd* **25/1**

6011 **13** 3 **Big Les (IRE)**[6] 9257 4-9-2 **85** 5ex........ JasonHart 8 65
(Karen McLintock) *led in centre of gp: rdn and hdd over 1f out: sn wknd* **10/1**

5614 **14** 3 **Black Friday**[38] 8636 4-8-7 **76**........(p) LukeMorris 4 46
(Karen McLintock) *midfield in centre of gp: rdn and outpcd over 2f out: sn hung lft: wknd over 1f out* **28/1**

1m 13.07s (0.57) **Going Correction** +0.40s/f (Slow) 14 Ran SP% **121.3**
Speed ratings (Par 107): **112,111,111,110,108 107,106,105,105,105 104,104,100,96**
CSF £253.36 CT £2170.79 TOTE £4.30: £1.60, £12.40, £3.40; EX 201.70 Trifecta £2557.90.
Owner K Abdullah **Bred** Bearstone Stud Ltd **Trained** Lambourn, Berks

FOCUS
A competitive sprint handicap which went to the least experienced member of the field. The form looks solid.

9349 BOMBARDIER BRITISH HOPPED AMBER BEER CLASSIFIED CLAIMING STKS 1m 5y (Tp)
5:30 (5:30) (Class 5) 3-Y-O+
£3,428 (£1,020; £509; £400; £400; £400) **Stalls** Centre

Form RPR

4402 **1** **Vive La Difference (IRE)**[35] 8719 5-9-7 66........(b) DuranFentiman 6 74
(Tim Easterby) *dwlt s: towards rr: hdwy over 2f out: rdn and led over 1f out: kpt on wl fnl 110yds* **6/1**[3]

3204 **2** ½ **Dancing Rave**[14] 9106 3-9-6 70........ DanielTudhope 1 73+
(David O'Meara) *hld up in rr: hdwy whn nt clr run and swtchd lft over 1f out: sn rdn: wnt 2nd ins fnl 110yds: kpt on* **8/1**

5104 **3** ¾ **Insurplus (IRE)**[14] 9109 6-9-6 70........ BenRobinson 9 70
(Jim Goldie) *midfield: rdn and hdwy 2f out: briefly wnt 2nd ins fnl f: no ex towards fin* **7/2**[1]

0240 **4** 2 **Love Your Work (IRE)**[9] 9180 3-9-9 69........(p) LukeMorris 8 70
(Adam West) *t.k.h: led: wnt clr after 2f: rdn and reduced ld 2f out: hdd over 1f out: no ex fnl 110yds* **17/2**

5 ½ **Calonne (IRE)**[47] 8369 3-9-4 70........ DavidNolan 2 64
(J F Levins, Ire) *towards rr: shkn up and stdy hdwy on outer over 1f out: no imp fnl f* **7/1**

0000 **6** nk **Forseti**[17] 9048 3-9-8 68........(h) AlistairRawlinson 5 67
(Michael Appleby) *dwlt s: t.k.h: in rr: pushed along and hdwy 2f out: rdn and outpcd fnl f (jockey said gelding ran too free)* **33/1**

4410 **7** nk **Al Suil Eile (FR)**[13] 9140 3-9-6 67........ JasonHart 4 64
(John Quinn) *prom: wnt 2nd 3f out: rdn and lost position over 1f out: btn ins fnl f* **8/1**

4620 **8** 1 ¼ **Undercolours (IRE)**[17] 9047 3-8-11 67........ StefanoCherchi(7) 10 60
(Marco Botti) *chsd clr ldr: lost 2nd 3f out: rdn and wknd over 1f out* **11/2**[2]

6622 **9** 6 **Onebaba (IRE)**[13] 9140 3-9-3 70........(b) SeanDavis(3) 3 48
(Tony Carroll) *t.k.h: prom: rdn over 2f out: wknd over 1f out* **7/1**

6065 **10** 9 **Darwina**[37] 8666 3-9-0 45........ JamesSullivan 7 23
(Alistair Whillans) *in rr on outer: rdn and struggling 3f out: sn wknd* **100/1**

1m 42.89s (4.29) **Going Correction** +0.40s/f (Slow)
WFA 3 from 5yo+ 1lb 10 Ran SP% **113.6**
Speed ratings (Par 103): **94,93,92,90,90 89,89,88,82,73**
CSF £51.80 TOTE £4.90: £1.70, £2.80, £1.50; EX 34.90 Trifecta £156.90.
Owner Ryedale Partners No 5 **Bred** Haras D'Etreham **Trained** Great Habton, N Yorks

FOCUS
Quite an interesting claimer which saw the winner end a long, losing sequence.

9350 BOMBARDIER GOLDEN BEER NOVICE STKS 1m 5y (Tp)
6:00 (6:00) (Class 5) 3-Y-O+ **£3,428** (£1,020; £509; £254) **Stalls** Centre

Form RPR

1 **Yuri Gagarin** 3-9-4 0........ RobertHavlin 1 72+
(John Gosden) *disp ld: rdn to ld over 1f out: wnt clr fnl 110yds: comf* **2/5**[1]

642 **2** 2 ¾ **Dawry (IRE)**[20] 9011 3-9-4 73........ LukeMorris 5 65+
(Heather Main) *t.k.h: led: rdn and hdd over 1f out: no ch w wnr fnl 110yds* **9/4**[2]

5 **3** 1 ¼ **Bobba Tee**[71] 7630 7-9-5 0........ CamHardie 9 62
(Lawrence Mullaney) *prom: rdn and outpcd 2f out: rallied ins fnl f: no match for first two* **50/1**

4 3 ¼ **Drums Of War (IRE)**[29] 7-9-5 0........(p) GrahamLee 6 54
(Chris Grant) *slowly away: hld up in rr: rdn and outpcd over 2f out: sme hdwy and wnt 4th ins fnl f: mde no imp* **66/1**

5 2 ½ **Deputy Star** 3-9-4 0........ PaulMulrennan 8 48
(Ben Haslam) *t.k.h: hld up in rr: rdn and outpcd whn edgd lft over 1f out: btn fnl f* **28/1**

6 ½ **Sea Me Win (IRE)**[33] 6-8-12 0........ HarryRussell(7) 4 47
(Brian Ellison) *t.k.h: prom: rdn over 2f out: wknd over 1f out* **16/1**[3]

5 **7** 13 **Sixties Coed**[14] 9112 4-9-5 0........(t) TomEaves 7 16
(Nigel Tinkler) *t.k.h: prom: rdn and outpcd over 2f out: sn struggling: lost tch over 1f out: t.o* **80/1**

1m 45.39s (6.79) **Going Correction** +0.40s/f (Slow)
WFA 3 from 4yo+ 1lb 7 Ran SP% **116.2**
Speed ratings (Par 103): **82,79,78,74,72 71,58**
CSF £1.62 TOTE £1.30: £1.10, £1.50; EX 1.90 Trifecta £13.70.
Owner Godolphin **Bred** Genesis Green Stud Ltd And Thurso Ltd **Trained** Newmarket, Suffolk

FOCUS
A weak maiden which proved quite easy pickings for the successful debutant.

9351 BOMBARDIER "MARCH TO YOUR OWN DRUM" H'CAP 7f 14y (Tp)
6:30 (6:33) (Class 5) (0-75,75) 3-Y-O+
£3,428 (£1,020; £509; £400; £400; £400) **Stalls** Centre

Form RPR

0341 **1** **Valley Of Fire**[35] 8719 7-9-2 **70**........(p) LewisEdmunds 14 85
(Les Eyre) *hld up in rr on nr side of gp: bit short of room over 2f out: gd hdwy to ld over 1f out: sn rdn clr: readily* **7/1**[2]

0024 **2** 3 ¾ **La Rav (IRE)**[28] 8918 5-9-2 **75**........ GerO'Neill(5) 10 80
(Michael Easterby) *hld up in rr in centre of gp: bit short of room over 2f out: rdn and wnt 2nd fnl f: kpt on: no match for wnr* **7/4**[1]

6000 3 3 3/4 **Chosen World**[17] 9047 5-9-0 68..................................(p) BarryMcHugh 11 63
(Julie Camacho) *hld up in rr in centre of gp: stdy hdwy whn bit short of room over 2f out: rdn and wnt 3rd ins fnl f: no match for first two* **11/1**

4545 4 nk **Double Martini (IRE)**[35] 8719 3-8-6 65.............................. PaulaMuir(5) 3 59
(Roger Fell) *dwlt s: t.k.h: midfield in centre of gp: hdwy and cl up over 2f out: rdn over 1f out: sn outpcd: rallied ins fnl f: mde no imp (jockey said colt was briefly denied a clear run approaching 2f out)* **12/1**

0450 5 1 3/4 **Socru (IRE)**[14] 9113 3-8-12 66.. PaulMulrennan 8 55
(Michael Easterby) *prom on nr side of gp: hdwy to chal over 2f out: rdn and wknd fnl f* **14/1**

5601 6 1 **Kentuckyconnection (USA)**[65] 7820 6-8-11 70...... BenSanderson(5) 7 57
(Bryan Smart) *dwlt s: in rr on far side of gp: rdn and hdwy 2f out: no imp fnl f* **10/1**[3]

3435 7 1 1/4 **Dream World (IRE)**[7] 9224 4-9-4 72........................(p) AlistairRawlinson 9 55
(Michael Appleby) *midfield on nr side of gp: rdn and outpcd over 2f out: no imp fr over 1f out* **22/1**

0000 8 1 1/2 **Arcavallo (IRE)**[53] 8181 4-9-0 68.. GrahamLee 6 47
(Michael Dods) *t.k.h: midfield in centre of gp: hdwy to ld over 2f out: rdn and hdd over 1f out: wknd ins fnl f* **40/1**

4143 9 1/2 **Knowing Glance (IRE)**[13] 9140 4-8-12 69...................(h) SeanDavis(3) 5 47
(Richard Fahey) *t.k.h: pressed ldr in centre of gp: rdn to chal over 2f out: wknd over 1f out* **10/1**[3]

0006 10 1 **Ideal Candy (IRE)**[14] 9109 4-8-11 65.................................. ShaneGray 2 40
(Karen Tutty) *led on far side of gp: rdn and hdd over 2f out: wknd over 1f out* **40/1**

5060 11 1 1/4 **Daafr (IRE)**[14] 9106 3-9-0 68..(p) CamHardie 4 40
(Antony Brittain) *prom on far side of gp: stdy hdwy and cl up over 2f out: rdn and wknd over 1f out* **33/1**

12 8 **Edessann (IRE)**[186] 3439 3-9-6 74.................................. TomEaves 1 24
(Michael Herrington) *t.k.h: hld up in rr on far side of gp: pushed along over 1f out: sn wknd* **40/1**

4100 13 9 **Song Of The Isles (IRE)**[13] 9126 3-9-4 72...............(p[1]) JackMitchell 12
(Heather Main) *t.k.h: midfield on nr side of gp: rdn and struggling 3f out: sn wknd* **28/1**

0001 14 3 1/4 **Summer Daydream (IRE)**[28] 8924 3-9-7 75.......(p) CallumRodriguez 13
(Keith Dalgleish) *in rr on nr side of gp: edgd rt and outpcd over 2f out: sn btn* **12/1**

1m 28.12s (1.92) **Going Correction** +0.40s/f (Slow) **14** Ran SP% **115.5**
Speed ratings (Par 103): **105,100,96,96,94 92,91,89,89,88 86,77,67,63**
CSF £17.32 CT £128.53 TOTE £7.40: £2.80, £1.20, £3.20; EX 28.60 Trifecta £199.80.
Owner Billy Parker & Steven Parker **Bred** Bearstone Stud Ltd **Trained** Catwick, N Yorks

FOCUS
Not the strongest of handicaps, as evidenced by the distances separating the first three. The winner is an admirable sort, however.

9352 BETWAY HEED YOUR HUNCH H'CAP 6f (Tp)
7:00 (7:04) (Class 6) (0-60,60) 3-Y-O+

£2,781 (£827; £413; £400; £400; £400) **Stalls** Centre

Form RPR

4011 1 **Herringswell (FR)**[32] 8821 4-8-11 58.......................... LauraPearson(7) 12 73
(Henry Spiller) *in tch w ldrs on nr side of gp: rdn and hdwy to ld over 1f out: clr whn edgd lft ins fnl f: kpt on strly* **8/1**

0104 2 2 1/2 **I Know How (IRE)**[28] 8923 4-9-5 59......................(b) CallumRodriguez 8 66
(Julie Camacho) *cl up on nr side of gp: hdwy and led over 2f out: rdn and hdd over 1f out: sn edgd lft: no ch w wnr fnl f* **4/1**[1]

0215 3 1 **Billy Wedge**[49] 8306 4-9-2 56... BarryMcHugh 4 60
(Tracy Waggott) *dwlt s: swtchd rt early: in rr on nr side of gp: rdn and hdwy over 1f out: wnt 3rd ins fnl f: kpt on: nrst fin* **11/2**[3]

4-14 4 1 1/4 **Eleuthera**[66] 7777 7-9-6 60.......................................(t) DavidNolan 13 60
(J F Levins, Ire) *hld up in rr in centre of gp: smooth hdwy over 2f out: cl up and rdn over 1f out: no ex ins fnl f* **14/1**

5211 5 1 1/2 **Jeffrey Harris**[28] 8925 4-9-5 59...................................... DanielTudhope 6 55
(Jim Goldie) *dwlt s: in rr on far side of gp: hdwy and prom over 1f out: sn rdn: wknd grad ins fnl f* **15/2**

0040 6 nse **Kommander Kirkup**[14] 9113 8-9-6 60................................ PhilDennis 3 56
(Michael Herrington) *stdd s: swtchd rt early: in rr on nr side of gp early: rdn and hdwy over 1f out: no imp ins fnl f* **80/1**

1222 7 1 1/2 **Broughton Excels**[15] 9089 4-9-6 60.............................. PJMcDonald 11 51
(Stuart Williams) *dwlt s: bmpd early: hld up in rr in centre of gp: shkn up and stdy hdwy over 1f out: rdn and wknd fnl 110yds* **9/2**[2]

0001 8 2 3/4 **Aquarius (IRE)**[13] 9133 3-9-5 59.............................. AlistairRawlinson 14 42
(Michael Appleby) *midfield in centre of gp: rdn and outpcd over 2f out: btn over 1f out* **20/1**

6-00 9 1/2 **Mable Lee (IRE)**[28] 8925 4-9-3 57.................................... GrahamLee 2 38
(Bryan Smart) *disp ld on far side of gp: rdn over 2f out: wknd over 1f out* **100/1**

0320 10 1 3/4 **Uncle Charlie (IRE)**[32] 8818 5-9-6 60............................ FrannyNorton 7 36
(Ann Duffield) *towards rr on far side of gp: shkn up whn bit short of room 2f out: sn wknd (jockey said the gelding was denied a clear run approximately 2f out)* **10/1**

0240 11 1/2 **The Grey Zebedee**[28] 8925 3-9-5 59...................(p) DuranFentiman 1 34
(Tim Easterby) *prom on far side of gp: rdn over 2f out: wknd over 1f out* **28/1**

5500 12 hd **Mutabaahy (IRE)**[29] 8896 4-9-3 57..............................(h) CamHardie 5 31
(Antony Brittain) *prom on far side of gp: rdn over 2f out: wknd over 1f out* **9/1**

5100 13 12 **Dahik (IRE)**[38] 8643 4-9-6 60....................................(b) JamesSullivan 9
(Michael Easterby) *plld hrd: led in centre of gp: rdn and hdd over 2f out: sn wknd: eased whn no ch ins fnl f* **50/1**

0110 14 6 **Mi Capricho (IRE)**[28] 8923 4-9-6 60................................... JoeFanning 10
(Keith Dalgleish) *midfield in centre of gp: rdn over 2f out: wknd over 1f out: eased whn no ch ins fnl f* **40/1**

1m 13.9s (1.40) **Going Correction** +0.40s/f (Slow) **14** Ran SP% **117.0**
Speed ratings (Par 101): **106,102,101,99,97 97,95,91,91,88 88,88,72,64**
CSF £36.95 CT £199.67 TOTE £9.20: £2.50, £2.00, £2.80; EX 58.80 Trifecta £369.60.
Owner The Champagne Poppers **Bred** Brendan Boyle Bloodstock Ltd **Trained** Newmarket, Suffolk

FOCUS
Not many got into this sprint handicap which produced a decisive winner who was completing a hat-trick.
T/Plt: £132.60 to a £1 stake. Pool: £76,636.89 - 421.88 winning units. T/Qpdt: £7.00 to a £1 stake. Pool: £14,279.69 - 1,508.59 winning units. **Richard Young**

9353 - 9360a (Foreign Racing) - See Raceform Interactive

9282 WOLVERHAMPTON (A.W) (L-H)
Saturday, December 7

OFFICIAL GOING: Tapeta: standard
Wind: Fresh behind Weather: Overcast

9361 BOMBARDIER BRITISH HOPPED AMBER BEER H'CAP 1m 142y (Tp)
4:50 (4:52) (Class 6) (0-65,65) 3-Y-O+

£2,781 (£827; £413; £400; £400; £400) **Stalls** Low

Form RPR

4612 1 **Star Of Valour (IRE)**[21] 9006 4-9-3 61.......................... PaulMulrennan 8 71+
(Lynn Siddall) *hld up: hdwy on outer over 2f out: led and hung lft ins fnl f: r.o wl* **11/4**[1]

6000 2 3 3/4 **Kyllachy Dragon (IRE)**[18] 9054 4-9-7 65...................... DavidProbert 13 67
(Mark Rimell) *prom: chsd ldr 7f out: led 2f out: rdn and hdd ins fnl f: no ex* **50/1**

0000 3 1/2 **He's Our Star (IRE)**[17] 9067 4-9-5 63.......................... TomMarquand 4 64
(Ali Stronge) *prom: rdn and hung lft over 1f out: styd on same pce ins fnl f* **16/1**

035 4 3/4 **Levanter (FR)**[33] 8808 3-9-4 64.................................... HollieDoyle 11 63
(Harry Dunlop) *edgd rt s: hld up: hung lft over 1f out: r.o ins fnl f: nt rch ldrs* **40/1**

5140 5 nk **Clem A**[72] 7609 3-9-4 64.. LukeMorris 5 63
(Alan Bailey) *s.i.s: hld up: rdn and hung lft over 1f out: r.o ins fnl f: nvr nrr* **25/1**

0000 6 1/2 **Weloof (FR)**[21] 9006 5-9-4 62.. AdamKirby 2 60
(John Butler) *led early: chsd ldrs: swtchd rt and hrd rdn fr over 1f out: no ex wl ins fnl f* **11/2**[3]

1600 7 nk **Lagenda**[18] 9047 6-9-3 61..(p) JasonHart 6 58
(Liam Bailey) *chsd ldrs: rdn over 2f out: styd on same pce fr over 1f out* **40/1**

1302 8 nk **Dreamseller (IRE)**[53] 8234 3-9-1 61..............................(p) PhilDennis 9 57
(Tim Easterby) *s.i.s: hld up: styd on ins fnl f: nvr nrr* **8/1**

0132 9 1 1/2 **Gavi Di Gavi (IRE)**[29] 8923 4-9-4 62............................ TomQueally 1 55
(Alan King) *hld up in tch: rdn over 1f out: wknd ins fnl f* **9/2**[2]

0006 10 nse **Profound (IRE)**[14] 9138 4-8-12 63..........................(p) EllieMacKenzie(7) 7 56
(Mark Usher) *hld up: rdn over 1f out: nvr on terms* **20/1**

500 11 3/4 **French Twist**[21] 9006 3-8-12 61......................(b[1]) ThomasGreatrex(3) 10 53
(David Loughnane) *hld up: nvr on terms* **40/1**

4133 12 2 1/4 **Takeoneforthe team**[7] 9244 4-9-7 65............................ DougieCostello 12 52
(Mark Loughnane) *s.i.s and hmpd s: hld up: shkn up over 1f out: wknd fnl f* **12/1**

6650 13 2 1/4 **Decoration Of War (IRE)**[249] 1511 4-9-7 65........... AlistairRawlinson 3 47
(Michael Appleby) *led 8f out: hdd 2f out: wknd fnl f* **11/4**[1]

1m 48.65s (-1.45) **Going Correction** -0.05s/f (Stan)
WFA 3 from 4yo+ 2lb **13** Ran SP% **129.5**
Speed ratings (Par 101): **104,100,100,99,99 98,98,98,96,96 96,94,92**
CSF £188.93 CT £2052.90 TOTE £3.40: £1.50, £12.20, £4.30; EX 99.30 Trifecta £1399.80.
Owner Jimmy Kay **Bred** Darley **Trained** Colton, N Yorks

FOCUS
A modest handicap.

9362 BETWAY LIVE CASINO H'CAP 1m 1f 104y (Tp)
5:20 (5:22) (Class 6) (0-60,59) 4-Y-O+

£2,781 (£827; £413; £400; £400; £400) **Stalls** Low

Form RPR

00 1 **Sunshineandbubbles**[154] 4658 6-9-1 53.......................... JoeFanning 5 60+
(David Evans) *chsd ldrs: wnt 2nd over 1f out: led ins fnl f: rdn out* **8/1**

3510 2 1 3/4 **Cash N Carrie (IRE)**[16] 9090 5-8-7 48...................... TheodoreLadd(3) 4 52
(Michael Appleby) *sn pushed along to ld: hdd over 8f out: chsd ldrs: rdn over 1f out: styd on* **7/1**

0121 3 shd **Muraaqeb**[113] 6153 5-9-3 55..(p) DavidProbert 13 58
(Milton Bradley) *sn pushed along and prom: stdd into mid-div 7f out: hdwy over 3f out: shkn up and hung lft ins fnl f: styd on* **11/1**

6466 4 1 1/4 **Optima Petamus**[12] 8694 7-8-7 45..............................(v) PhilDennis 7 46
(Liam Bailey) *hld up: hdwy on outer over 2f out: rdn over 1f out: r.o: nt rch ldrs* **16/1**

5 nk **Zayriyan (IRE)**[91] 6867 4-9-5 57.................................(v[1]) TomMarquand 6 57
(Ali Stronge) *prom: chsd ldr 7f out: led over 2f out: rdn over 1f out: hdd and no ex ins fnl f* **8/1**

1425 6 hd **Pike Corner Cross (IRE)**[9] 9207 7-8-8 53...............(vt) CameronIles(7) 2 53
(David Evans) *hld up in tch: n.m.r over 8f out: swtchd rt over 1f out: styd on* **6/1**[3]

0040 7 1 **The Eagle's Nest (IRE)**[33] 8813 5-9-4 56.....................(t) RobertHavlin 11 54
(Alexandra Dunn) *hld up: pushed along on outer over 1f out: r.o ins fnl f: nvr nrr* **14/1**

65/4 8 1/2 **Mary Le Bow**[45] 8466 8-9-2 54..(t) LukeMorris 8 51
(Paul George) *hld up: rdn on outer over 1f out: nt trble ldrs* **14/1**

0300 9 3/4 **Final Attack (IRE)**[45] 8466 8-8-8 46..........................(p) JamesSullivan 1 42
(Sarah Hollinshead) *s.i.s: sn pushed along: reminders after 1f: rdn over 1f out: nvr on terms* **14/1**

5066 10 shd **Compass Point**[8] 9224 4-9-7 59...................................... KieranO'Neill 3 54
(Robyn Brisland) *prom: lost pl after 1f: pushed along over 2f out: rdn over 1f out: no imp fnl f* **4/1**[1]

050 11 1 **Sweet Marmalade (IRE)**[23] 5728 4-9-0 59...........(p) HarryRussell(7) 10 52
(Brian Ellison) *s.i.s: nvr on terms* **40/1**

3601 12 4 1/2 **Born To Reason (IRE)**[14] 9139 5-9-3 55..................(b) DanielMuscutt 12 40
(Alexandra Dunn) *led after 1f: shkn up and hdd over 2f out: wknd fnl f* **5/1**[2]

2m 0.37s (-0.43) **Going Correction** -0.05s/f (Stan) **12** Ran SP% **122.3**
Speed ratings (Par 101): **99,97,97,96,95 95,94,94,93,93 92,88**
CSF £65.19 CT £632.10 TOTE £8.30: £3.10, £1.90, £2.90; EX 69.10 Trifecta £1059.10.
Owner Amazing Racing **Bred** Mickley Stud **Trained** Pandy, Monmouths

FOCUS
An ordinary handicap but it was run at a good gallop.

9363 LADBROKES HOME OF THE ODDS BOOST EBF NOVICE STKS 1m 142y (Tp)
5:50 (5:52) (Class 5) 2-Y-O **£3,428** (£1,020; £509; £254) **Stalls** Low

Form RPR

1 **Waldkonig** 2-9-5 0.. RobertHavlin 6 94+
(John Gosden) *trckd ldrs: hung rt fr over 2f out: led sn after: shkn up and qcknd clr over 1f out: eased towards fin: impressive* **6/4**[1]

0 2 9 **Zoran**[21] 8999 2-9-5 0...(t) JamesDoyle 3 71
(Hugo Palmer) *chsd ldrs: rdn over 1f out: sn outpcd* **9/4**[2]

The Form Book Flat 2019, Raceform Ltd, Newbury, RG14 5SJ

3 ½ **Socially Shady** 2-9-5 0 CliffordLee 8 70+
(K R Burke) *prom: rdn over 2f out: outpcd over 1f out: wnt 3rd nr fin* **20/1**

0540 4 1 **Fighting Don (FR)**[44] 8508 2-9-5 0 LukeMorris 5 68
(Harry Dunlop) *sn led: shkn up and hdd over 2f out: rdn over 1f out: no ex fnl f* **16/1**

5 5 2 ½ **Call My Bluff (IRE)**[43] 8517 2-9-5 0 LiamKeniry 1 63
(Dominic Ffrench Davis) *hld up in tch: rdn and edgd lft over 1f out: wknd fnl f* **50/1**

43 6 nse **Zeimaam (IRE)**[21] 8999 2-9-5 0 KieranShoemark 13 62
(Owen Burrows) *sn prom: chsd ldr 7f out: shkn up and ev ch over 2f out: rdn and edgd lft over 1f out: wknd ins fnl f* **3/1**[3]

7 1 **Vischio (IRE)** 2-9-0 0 CharlieBennett 7 55
(Jonathan Portman) *hld up: shkn up over 1f out: nvr on terms* **66/1**

8 4 **Pablo Hernandez** 2-9-5 0 AdamKirby 4 52
(David O'Meara) *s.i.s: nvr nrr* **12/1**

00 9 1 ½ **Jersey Grey (FR)**[12] 9154 2-9-5 0 DavidProbert 2 49
(Jamie Osborne) *hld up: nvr on terms* **100/1**

00 10 3 ¾ **Handful Of Gold (IRE)**[96] 6800 2-9-0 0 TomQueally 11 36
(Kevin Bishop) *hld up: n.d* **200/1**

00 11 ¾ **Mack The Knife (IRE)**[12] 9154 2-9-5 0 NicolaCurrie 12 39
(Jamie Osborne) *s.i.s: a in rr* **100/1**

1m 50.71s (0.61) **Going Correction** -0.05s/f (Stan) **11** Ran SP% **120.0**
Speed ratings (Par 96): **95,87,86,85,83 83,82,78,77,74 73**
CSF £5.06 TOTE £2.60: £1.10, £1.20, £4.20; EX 5.50 Trifecta £44.80.
Owner Gestut Ammerland & Newsells Park Stud **Bred** Newsells Park & Ammerland Gmbh & Co Kg **Trained** Newmarket, Suffolk

FOCUS
They went steady early on and the race developed into a sprint. The well-bred winner proved different class and the runner-up has been rated similarly to his debut.

9364 LADBROKES "PLAY 1-2-FREE" ON FOOTBALL CONDITIONS STKS (PLUS 10 RACE) (AW CHAMPS FAST TRACK QUAL') 6f 20y (Tp)
6:20 (6:20) (Class 2) 2-Y-O **£8,821** (£2,640; £1,320; £660; £329) **Stalls** Low

2126 1 **Maystar (IRE)**[46] 8446 2-9-2 91 HollieDoyle 7 91
(Archie Watson) *led to 1/2-way: led again 2f out: sn rdn: styd on* **8/1**

0135 2 ¾ **Get Boosting**[11] 9162 2-9-2 77 JoeFanning 3 88
(Keith Dalgleish) *chsd ldrs: shkn up and hung lft over 1f out: swtchd rt ins fnl f: sn rdn: r.o* **20/1**

121 3 ¾ **Auchterarder (IRE)**[19] 9036 2-8-11 87 JasonHart 9 84+
(Mark Johnston) *hld up in tch on outer: shkn up: edgd lft and clipped heels over 2f out: rdn and hung lft ins fnl f: r.o* **9/2**[2]

121 4 hd **Raaeb (IRE)**[46] 8418 2-9-2 91 JimCrowley 1 85
(Saeed bin Suroor) *chsd ldrs: rdn to chse wnr over 1f out tl styd on same pce wl ins fnl f* **5/6**[1]

21 5 2 **Dancin Inthestreet**[14] 9130 2-8-11 0 TomMarquand 8 74
(William Haggas) *chsd ldrs: rdn over 1f out: carried lft and styd on same pce ins fnl f* **15/2**[3]

4 6 nse **Kondratiev Wave (IRE)**[55] 8164 2-9-2 86 JamesDoyle 2 79
(Tony Carroll) *pushed along in rr: hdwy over 1f out: nt trble ldrs* **16/1**

2100 7 hd **Lincoln Blue**[18] 9043 2-9-2 78 RichardKingscote 6 79
(Jane Chapple-Hyam) *hld up: swtchd rt ins fnl f: r.o towards fin: nvr nrr* **66/1**

1622 8 ¾ **Lexington Rebel (FR)**[37] 8709 2-9-2 85 CliffordLee 4 77
(Richard Hannon) *s.i.s: running on whn nt clr run wl ins fnl f: nt trble ldrs* **14/1**

3110 9 1 ¼ **Stone Soldier**[57] 8095 2-9-2 85 BarryMcHugh 11 73
(James Given) *chsd ldr 5f out: led 1/2-way: hdd 2f out: sn rdn: wknd ins fnl f* **16/1**

21 10 2 ¼ **Zim Baby**[180] 3644 2-8-11 0 LukeMorris 10 61
(Paul George) *hld up: swtchd rt wl over 1f out: n.d* **50/1**

1m 13.66s (-0.84) **Going Correction** -0.05s/f (Stan) **10** Ran SP% **122.3**
Speed ratings (Par 102): **103,102,101,100,98 98,97,96,95,92**
CSF £155.65 TOTE £9.20: £2.40, £3.80, £1.60; EX 180.00 Trifecta £681.50.
Owner Hambleton Racing Ltd XXXVI **Bred** Ballinvana House Stud **Trained** Upper Lambourn, W Berks

FOCUS
A tighter race on the ratings than the market might have suggested.

9365 BETWAY HEED YOUR HUNCH H'CAP 6f 20y (Tp)
6:50 (6:51) (Class 5) (0-70,70) 3-Y-O+ **£3,428** (£1,020; £509; £400; £400; £400) **Stalls** Low

Form RPR

5015 1 **Chookie Dunedin**[14] 9140 4-9-0 68 BenSanderson(5) 9 77
(Keith Dalgleish) *hld up: hdwy over 1f out: rdn and edgd lft ins fnl f: r.o to ld nr fin* **9/2**[2]

0214 2 nk **Bahuta Acha**[14] 9140 4-9-4 67 JasonHart 6 75
(David Loughnane) *led 1f: chsd ldrs: swtchd rt and wnt 2nd over 1f out: rdn to ld ins fnl f: edgd rt: hdd nr fin* **11/4**[1]

1530 3 2 ¾ **The Groove**[45] 8471 6-8-10 66 CameronIles(7) 3 65
(David Evans) *broke wl: sn lost pl: swtchd rt 1/2-way: shkn up on outer over 2f out: r.o ins fnl f: wnt 3rd post: nt rch ldrs* **14/1**

4533 4 shd **Landing Night (IRE)**[15] 9108 7-9-2 65 (tp) CliffordLee 13 64
(Rebecca Menzies) *prom: chsd ldr over 3f out: led over 2f out: rdn and hdd ins fnl f: styd on same pce* **20/1**

1524 5 nk **Dark Side Dream**[21] 9013 7-8-13 67 (p) ThoreHammerHansen(5) 2 65
(Charlie Wallis) *chsd ldrs: rdn whn hmpd over 1f out: styd on same pce ins fnl f* **14/1**

4003 6 ½ **Spirit Of Wedza (IRE)**[31] 8866 7-8-11 67 VictorSantos(7) 11 63
(Julie Camacho) *pushed along and hdwy to chse ldrs over 5f out: then racd keenly: rdn and hung lft over 1f out: no ex ins fnl f* **20/1**

1420 7 2 ½ **Desert Fox**[46] 8419 5-9-4 67 (p) ShaneKelly 1 55
(Mike Murphy) *s.i.s: hld up: plld hrd: nt clr run wl over 1f out: nvr nrr* **14/1**

2103 8 2 ¼ **Requited (IRE)**[28] 8943 3-9-7 70 CharlieBennett 12 51
(Hughie Morrison) *led 5f out: hdd over 2f out: wknd ins fnl f* **16/1**

0201 9 ¾ **My Town Chicago (USA)**[37] 8704 4-9-2 65 JackMitchell 4 44
(Kevin Frost) *hld up in tch: plld hrd: rdn whn hmpd over 1f out: wknd ins fnl f* **9/2**[2]

5063 10 ½ **Alicia Darcy (IRE)**[7] 9245 3-9-7 70 (b) AdamMcNamara 7 55
(Archie Watson) *s.i.s: nvr on terms* **12/1**

045 11 ½ **Awsaaf**[10] 9182 4-9-5 68 (h) FrannyNorton 10 44
(Michael Wigham) *s.i.s: a in rr* **14/1**

0006 12 8 **Laubali**[31] 8866 4-9-6 69 (p) AdamKirby 8 19
(David O'Meara) *prom: hmpd and lost pl over 5f out: effrt on outer over 2f out: wknd over 1f out* **17/2**[3]

1m 13.62s (-0.88) **Going Correction** -0.05s/f (Stan) **12** Ran SP% **123.3**
Speed ratings (Par 103): **103,102,98,98,98 97,94,91,90,89 89,78**
CSF £17.99 CT £165.48 TOTE £6.20: £2.10, £1.40, £4.80; EX 19.10 Trifecta £253.30.
Owner Raeburn Brick Limited **Bred** D And J Raeburn **Trained** Carluke, S Lanarks

FOCUS
A modest sprint handicap.

9366 BETWAY H'CAP 1m 4f 51y (Tp)
7:20 (7:20) (Class 2) (0-105,103) 3-Y-O+ **£11,827** (£3,541; £1,770; £885; £442; £222) **Stalls** Low

Form RPR

1043 1 **Getchagetchagetcha**[60] 8005 3-9-3 98 (p) AdamKirby 4 105
(Clive Cox) *hld up: racd keenly: hdwy over 1f out: rdn and r.o to ld wl ins fnl f* **11/2**

2023 2 ¾ **Busy Street**[8] 9222 7-9-2 93 AlistairRawlinson 7 98
(Michael Appleby) *a.p: chsd ldr over 1f out: sn rdn: styd on* **14/1**

1112 3 ¾ **Paths Of Glory**[16] 9094 4-9-7 98 (t) JamesDoyle 3 102
(Hugo Palmer) *s.s: hdwy to chse ldr over 9f out: led 3f out: rdn over 1f out: hdd and unable qck wl ins fnl f* **6/4**[1]

2600 4 1 **Fire Fighting (IRE)**[18] 9055 8-8-13 90 JasonHart 1 92
(Mark Johnston) *hld up: rdn over 2f out: r.o ins fnl f: nt rch ldrs* **40/1**

0530 5 nse **Island Brave (IRE)**[18] 9055 5-9-7 98 LukeMorris 2 100
(Heather Main) *hld up: drvn along over 2f out: r.o ins fnl f: nt rch ldrs* **8/1**

3111 6 nk **All Yours (FR)**[18] 9055 8-8-12 89 JoeyHaynes 5 91
(Sean Curran) *chsd ldrs: rdn over 1f out: styd on same pce ins fnl f* **7/2**[2]

5121 7 10 **Francis Xavier (IRE)**[16] 9094 5-9-12 103 CliffordLee 6 89
(Kevin Frost) *led 9f: wknd fnl f* **9/2**[3]

0660 8 1 ½ **Lunar Jet**[16] 9094 5-8-8 90 TobyEley(5) 8 73
(John Mackie) *s.i.s: hld up: racd keenly: shkn up over 2f out: sn outpcd* **40/1**

2m 39.08s (-1.72) **Going Correction** -0.05s/f (Stan) **8** Ran SP% **118.4**
WFA 3 from 4yo+ 4lb
Speed ratings (Par 109): **103,102,102,101,101 101,94,93**
CSF £79.47 CT £171.16 TOTE £6.50: £2.00, £3.10, £1.10; EX 63.50 Trifecta £228.40.
Owner Paul & Clare Rooney **Bred** Mrs James Wigan **Trained** Lambourn, Berks

FOCUS
A decent handicap won in good style by the youngster of the field.

9367 PLAY 4 TO SCORE AT BETWAY H'CAP 1m 4f 51y (Tp)
7:50 (7:50) (Class 6) (0-65,68) 3-Y-O+ **£2,781** (£827; £413; £400; £400; £400) **Stalls** Low

Form RPR

3005 1 **Dream Magic (IRE)**[21] 9012 5-9-10 65 RichardKingscote 10 77
(Mark Loughnane) *s.i.s: hld up: hdwy 2f out: led over 1f out: rdn clr: comf* **3/1**[1]

0546 2 4 ½ **Fayetta**[93] 6901 3-9-6 65 HollieDoyle 8 70
(David Loughnane) *chsd ldr tl led over 2f out: rdn and hdd over 1f out: styd on same pce ins fnl f* **9/2**[3]

5000 3 nk **Dragon Mountain**[26] 7872 4-9-10 65 JoeFanning 9 69
(Keith Dalgleish) *chsd ldrs: rdn over 1f out: styd on same pce fnl f* **7/1**

5406 4 2 **Last Enchantment (IRE)**[14] 9132 4-9-6 61 (t) AdamKirby 7 62
(Neil Mulholland) *hld up in tch: lost pl over 9f out: pushed along and hdwy over 2f out: rdn over 1f out: no ex ins fnl f* **20/1**

0464 5 ¾ **Straitouttacompton**[59] 8019 3-9-4 63 (t w) DougieCostello 1 64
(Ivan Furtado) *prom: rdn over 2f out: no ex fnl f* **13/2**

0241 6 hd **Miss Elsa**[49] 8348 3-8-11 61 GeorgiaDobie(5) 12 61
(Eve Johnson Houghton) *s.i.s: hld up: plld hrd: nt clr run and swtchd rt over 3f out: sn lost pl: rdn over 1f out: styd on ins fnl f* **4/1**[2]

1400 7 shd **Power Home (IRE)**[47] 8414 5-9-9 64 TomQueally 5 63
(Denis Coakley) *sn led: hdd over 2f out: rdn and ev ch over 1f out: wknd ins fnl f* **20/1**

0304 8 1 **Hidden Depths (IRE)**[14] 7790 4-9-8 63 (bt) ShaneKelly 3 61
(Neil Mulholland) *hld up: hdwy over 2f out: rdn over 1f out: wknd fnl f* **12/1**

3050 9 3 ¼ **Fields Of Fortune**[37] 8696 5-9-6 61 TomMarquand 2 53
(Joseph Tuite) *hld up: rdn over 2f out: n.d* **14/1**

0000 10 6 **Amor Fati (IRE)**[8] 9217 4-9-0 62 LauraPearson(7) 4 45
(David Evans) *s.s: hld up: wknd over 2f out* **12/1**

-000 11 12 **Scrafton**[19] 9033 8-9-0 62 ElishaWhittington(7) 11 26
(Tony Carroll) *plld hrd and prom on outer: rdn over 3f out: wknd wl over 2f out* **25/1**

2m 39.44s (-1.36) **Going Correction** -0.05s/f (Stan) **11** Ran SP% **124.4**
WFA 3 from 4yo+ 4lb
Speed ratings (Par 101): **102,99,98,97,96 96,96,96,93,89 81**
CSF £16.93 CT £91.81 TOTE £3.80: £1.50, £2.10, £2.60; EX 20.90 Trifecta £124.00.
Owner Ben Parish & Clare Loughnane **Bred** Paul V Jackson & Janet P Jackson **Trained** Rock, Worcs

FOCUS
An ordinary handicap.

9368 BETWAY NOVICE STKS 1m 4f 51y (Tp)
8:20 (8:20) (Class 5) 3-Y-O+ **£3,428** (£1,020; £509; £254) **Stalls** Low

Form RPR

4 1 **Brighton Pier (GER)**[45] 8451 3-9-2 0 LukeMorris 8 76
(Harry Dunlop) *chsd ldrs: wnt 2nd over 4f out: led over 2f out: rdn and edgd lft over 1f out: drvn out* **6/1**[3]

3 2 1 ½ **Sharp Suited**[33] 8814 4-9-6 0 BenRobinson 3 73
(Brian Ellison) *hld up: hdwy 4f out: chsd wnr: nt clr run and swtchd rt over 1f out: styd on* **16/1**

1 3 7 **Lovely Lou Lou**[38] 8662 3-9-1 0 DarraghKeenan(3) 5 65
(John Ryan) *prom: rdn over 1f out: no ex fnl f* **7/2**[2]

4 7 **Princess T**[17] 4-9-1 0 ShaneKelly 4 46
(Neil Mulholland) *s.i.s: hld up: styd on appr fnl f: nvr nrr* **33/1**

2/ 5 2 **Silverbook**[758] 8704 4-9-6 0 JamesDoyle 2 47
(Charlie Appleby) *led 1f: racd freely: led again 8f out: shkn up and hdd over 2f out: wknd over 1f out* **1/3**[1]

00 6 3 ¼ **Kelis (IRE)**[19] 9038 3-8-11 0 JackMitchell 6 38
(Heather Main) *hld up: rdn over 3f out: n.d* **100/1**

0 7 1 **Royal Born (IRE)**[269] 1182 3-8-11 0 SeamusCronin(5) 11 42
(Richard Price) *hld up: nvr on terms* **100/1**

0 8 ¾ **Courteva**[21] 9011 4-9-1 0 HollieDoyle 7 34
(Richard Price) *hld up: rdn and hung lft over 1f out: n.d* **66/1**

9 ¾ **Dreadnoughtus** 3-8-13 0 TheodoreLadd(3) 9 39
(Michael Appleby) *s.i.s: hdwy over 3f out: wknd 2f out* **20/1**

006 10 39 **Highland Sun (IRE)**[19] 9038 3-8-11 40 JaneElliott 10
(Richard Phillips) *led after 1f: hdd 8f out: wknd 3f out* **100/1**

11 75 **Ruler Of Natives**[25] 3-9-2 0 KieranO'Neill 1
(Robyn Brisland) *prom: pushed along 8f out: wknd over 5f out* **100/1**

2m 39.64s (-1.16) **Going Correction** -0.05s/f (Stan)
WFA 3 from 4yo 4lb **11** Ran SP% **130.6**
Speed ratings (Par 103): **101,100,95,90,89 87,86,86,85,59 9**
CSF £97.06 TOTE £11.50: £2.10, £3.10, £2.00; EX 90.10 Trifecta £220.20.
Owner Mrs Susan Roy **Bred** Frau Cl U A Rom **Trained** Lambourn, Berks

FOCUS
They finished well strung out in this novice, in which the hot favourite gave himself little chance.
T/Plt: £216.50 to a £1 stake. Pool: £97,946.82 - 330.16 winning units. T/Qpdt: £16.00 to a £1 stake. Pool: £16,004.50 - 739.96 winning units. **Colin Roberts**

9369 - 9375a (Foreign Racing) - See Raceform Interactive

9262 SHA TIN (R-H)
Sunday, December 8

OFFICIAL GOING: Turf: good

9376a LONGINES HONG KONG VASE (GROUP 1) (3YO+) (COURSE A) (TURF) 1m 4f
5:40 3-Y-O+ **£1,141,141** (£440,440; £230,230; £120,120; £70,070)

RPR

1 **Glory Vase (JPN)**[63] 4-9-0 0 JoaoMoreira 7 122
(Tomohito Ozeki, Japan) *t.k.h: hld up in midfield: stdy hdwy 3f out: effrt and swtchd rt 2f out: rdn to ld over 1f out: edgd rt and qcknd clr ins fnl f: impressive* **36/5**[3]

2 3 ½ **Lucky Lilac (JPN)**[28] 8965 4-8-10 0 (h) ChristopheSoumillon 1 112
(Mikio Matsunaga, Japan) *hld up towards rr: stdy hdwy on outside over 2f out: rdn to press ldrs over 1f out: wnt 2nd ins fnl f: kpt on: no ch w wnr* **89/10**

3 nk **Exultant (IRE)**[21] 9024 5-9-0 0 (t) ZacPurton 14 116+
(A S Cruz, Hong Kong) *led at ordinary gallop: rdn and hdd over 1f out: rallied: kpt on same pce ins fnl f* **4/5**[1]

4 ½ **Deirdre (JPN)**[50] 8335 5-8-10 0 OisinMurphy 2 111
(Mitsuru Hashida, Japan) *hld up in rr: hdwy on outside bnd over 2f out: rdn and kpt on fnl f: nt pce to chal* **18/1**

5 2 ¼ **Called To The Bar (IRE)**[91] 7008 5-9-0 0 (t) MaximeGuyon 4 111
(Mme Pia Brandt, France) *hld up: stdy hdwy over 2f out: hung rt and hdwy wl over 1f out: kpt on fnl f: nvr able to chal* **83/1**

6 ¾ **Ho Ho Khan (NZ)**[21] 9024 5-9-0 0 (b¹) CYHo 5 110
(D J Hall, Hong Kong) *hld up towards rr: rdn along over 2f out: nt clr run and swtchd lft over 1f out: kpt on fnl f: nvr rchd ldrs* **38/1**

7 nk **True Self (IRE)**[29] 8950 6-8-10 0 KerrinMcEvoy 6 105
(W P Mullins, Ire) *t.k.h early: hld up on ins: nt clr run over 2f out: rdn wl over 1f out: sn no imp* **76/1**

8 3 **Southern Legend (AUS)**[21] 9024 7-9-0 0 (v) AlbertoSanna 9 105
(C Fownes, Hong Kong) *cl up: drvn along over 2f out: wknd over 1f out* **27/1**

9 1 ¾ **Young Rascal (FR)**[34] 8811 4-9-0 0 FrankieDettori 10 102
(William Haggas) *s.i.s: sn rdn in rr: hdwy into midfield after 2f: short of room and lost grnd whn stmbld 3f out: sn pushed along: btn over 1f out* **64/1**

10 ½ **Eagle Way (AUS)**[21] 9024 7-9-0 0 (bt) JamesMcDonald 3 101
(John Moore, Hong Kong) *hld up on ins: pushed along over 2f out: sn outpcd: btn over 1f out* **48/1**

11 1 **Prince Of Arran**[33] 8844 6-9-0 0 MichaelWalker 8 99
(Charlie Fellowes) *in tch on ins: rdn along over 2f out: wknd over 1f out* **48/1**

12 ½ **Anthony Van Dyck (IRE)**[36] 8776 3-8-9 0 (b¹) RyanMoore 12 99
(A P O'Brien, Ire) *chsd ldr: rdn 3f out: wknd fr 2f out* **22/5**[2]

13 ½ **Aspetar (FR)**[77] 7500 4-9-0 0 JasonWatson 11 98
(Roger Charlton) *plld hrd early: cl up: effrt on outside over 2f out: wknd over 1f out* **42/1**

14 3 ¾ **Mount Everest (IRE)**[36] 8776 3-8-9 0 WayneLordan 13 92
(A P O'Brien, Ire) *in tch on outside: drvn and outpcd over 3f out: wknd over 2f out* **37/1**

2m 24.77s (-3.43)
WFA 3 from 4yo+ 4lb **14** Ran SP% **120.8**
PARI-MUTUEL (all including 10 hkd stake): WIN 82.00; PLACE 20.00, 25.00, 11.00; DF 336.00.
Owner Silk Racing Co Ltd **Bred** Lake Villa Farm **Trained** Japan

FOCUS
A solid-looking field lined up for the Vase, and Japanese-trained horses filled three of the first four places.

9377a LONGINES HONG KONG SPRINT (GROUP 1) (3YO+) (COURSE A) (TURF) 6f
6:20 3-Y-O+ **£1,141,141** (£440,440; £230,230; £120,120; £70,070)

RPR

1 **Beat The Clock (AUS)**[21] 9025 6-9-0 0 (t) JoaoMoreira 3 123
(J Size, Hong Kong) *hld up in midfield on ins: effrt and rdn 2f out: hdwy to ld last 50yds: drvn out* **11/2**[3]

2 nk **Hot King Prawn (AUS)**[21] 9025 5-9-0 0 KarisTeetan 1 122
(J Size, Hong Kong) *cl up: effrt and rdn 2f out: kpt on wl fnl f: wnt 2nd cl home: jst hld* **42/10**[2]

3 shd **Aethero (AUS)**[21] 9025 3-8-5 0 ZacPurton 8 120
(John Moore, Hong Kong) *t.k.h: led and sn crossed to ins rail: shkn up and qcknd over 1f out: rdn and hdd last 50yds: hld cl home* **1/2**[1]

4 ½ **Mr Stunning (AUS)**[21] 9025 7-9-0 0 HughBowman 2 120
(F C Lor, Hong Kong) *pressed ldr: rdn along over 1f out: hdd and no ex wl ins fnl f* **23/1**

5 ½ **Full Of Beauty (AUS)**[21] 9025 5-9-0 0 CYHo 4 119
(J Size, Hong Kong) *hld up towards rr: drvn along 2f out: kpt on fnl f: nvr able to chal* **22/1**

6 nk **Wishful Thinker (AUS)**[21] 9025 6-9-0 0 (b) ChristopheSoumillon 7 118
(Richard Gibson, Hong Kong) *dwlt: hld up on ins: rdn and hdwy over 1f out: kpt on fnl f: nvr able to chal* **130/1**

7 ½ **D B Pin (NZ)**[21] 9025 7-9-0 0 RyanMoore 11 116
(J Size, Hong Kong) *sn bhd and pushed along: rdn along over 2f out: kpt on fnl f: nrst fin* **53/1**

8 ½ **Danon Smash (JPN)**[70] 4-9-0 0 FrankieDettori 6 114
(Takayuki Yasuda, Japan) *hld up on outside: drvn and outpcd 2f out: kpt on fnl f: nvr able to chal* **27/1**

9 ¾ **Seasons Bloom (AUS)**[49] 8382 7-9-0 0 (t) GrantVanNiekerk 12 112
(C S Shum, Hong Kong) *s.i.s: bhd: rdn along over 2f out: sme hdwy fnl f: n.d* **25/1**

10 ½ **Rattan (NZ)**[49] 8382 6-9-0 0 (b) ChadSchofield 5 110
(Richard Gibson, Hong Kong) *prom: drvn along over 2f out: wknd over 1f out* **47/1**

11 1 ¼ **Ivictory (AUS)**[21] 9025 6-9-0 0 (t) AlbertoSanna 9 106
(J Size, Hong Kong) *midfield on outside: rdn along over 2f out: wknd over 1f out* **250/1**

12 1 ½ **Regency Legend (NZ)**[21] 9025 4-9-0 0 (t) SilvestreDeSousa 10 102
(C S Shum, Hong Kong) *prom: drvn along over 2f out: wknd over 1f out* **97/1**

1m 8.12s **12** Ran SP% **123.3**
PARI-MUTUEL (all including 10 hkd stake): WIN 65.00; PLACE 14.50, 16.50, 11.00; DF 146.00.
Owner Merrick Chung Wai Lik **Bred** Miss J Henderson **Trained** Hong Kong

FOCUS
There was a little bit of a shock in the sprint, that featured no European interest. It produced a thrilling finish, with trainer John Size having the first two home.

9379a LONGINES HONG KONG MILE (GROUP 1) (3YO+) (COURSE A) (TURF) 1m
7:30 3-Y-O+ **£1,426,426** (£550,550; £287,787; £150,150; £87,587)

RPR

1 **Admire Mars (JPN)**[50] 3-8-13 0 ChristopheSoumillon 4 119
(Yasuo Tomomichi, Japan) *in tch in midfield: stdy hdwy fr over 2f out: rdn 2f out: led 150yds out: kpt on wl: drvn out* **26/1**

2 ½ **Waikuku (IRE)**[21] 9023 4-9-0 0 JoaoMoreira 10 118
(J Size, Hong Kong) *hld up towards rr: wd into st: rdn over 2f out: styd on fr 1 1/2f out: ev ch 150yds out: kpt on wl: hld fnl 50yds* **29/10**[2]

3 1 ¼ **Beauty Generation (NZ)**[21] 9023 7-9-0 0 (bt) ZacPurton 5 115
(John Moore, Hong Kong) *chsd ldr: led over 2f out: rdn 1 1/2f out: drvn ins fnl f: hdd 150yds out: no ex clsng stages* **19/10**[1]

4 nk **Normcore (JPN)**[50] 4-8-10 0 Christophe-PatriceLemaire 9 110
(Kiyoshi Hagiwara, Japan) *midfield on outside: rdn and kpt on fr 1 1/2f out: nt gng pce to chal* **13/1**

5 nk **Persian Knight (JPN)**[21] 9017 5-9-0 0 (bt) OisinMurphy 6 113
(Yasutoshi Ikee, Japan) *s.s: racd keenly towards rr of midfield: nt clr run fr 2f out tl rdn 1 1/2f out: kpt on fnl f: nt gng pce to chal* **63/1**

6 shd **Citron Spirit (IRE)**[21] 9023 7-9-0 0 (h) CYHo 8 113
(P F Yiu, Hong Kong) *hld up towards rr: rdn over 2f out: styd on ins fnl f* **123/1**

7 1 **Indy Champ (JPN)**[21] 9017 4-9-0 0 DamianLane 3 111
(Hidetaka Otonashi, Japan) *hld up towards rr of midfield: nt clr run fr 2f out tl swtchd to inner 1f out: rdn and kpt on fnl 150yds: too much to do* **19/10**[1]

8 1 **Zaaki**[72] 7660 4-9-0 0 RyanMoore 2 108
(Sir Michael Stoute) *in tch: rdn under 2f out: wknd steadily fnl f* **129/1**

9 shd **Ka Ying Star**[21] 9023 4-9-0 0 (tp) KarisTeetan 1 108
(A S Cruz, Hong Kong) *led: rdn and hdd over 2f out: drvn over 1f out: wknd fnl 150yds* **69/10**[3]

10 3 ¾ **Simply Brilliant**[21] 9023 5-9-0 0 (p) AlexisBadel 7 100
(F C Lor, Hong Kong) *t.k.h: trckd ldrs on outside: prom 2 1/2f out: rdn and lost pl 2f out: sn btn* **98/1**

1m 33.25s (-1.45)
WFA 3 from 4yo+ 1lb **10** Ran SP% **122.3**
PARI-MUTUEL (all including 10 hkd stake): WIN 272.00; PLACE 53.50, 13.50, 13.00; DF 417.50.
Owner Riichi Kondo **Bred** Northern Farm **Trained** Japan

FOCUS
An interesting running of this mile event, which saw a Japanese 3yo win in good style.

9380a LONGINES HONG KONG CUP (GROUP 1) (3YO+) (COURSE A) (TURF) 1m 2f
8:10 3-Y-O+ **£1,597,597** (£616,616; £322,322; £168,168; £98,098)

RPR

1 **Win Bright (JPN)**[42] 8599 5-9-0 0 MasamiMatsuoka 8 118
(Yoshihiro Hatakeyama, Japan) *in tch: drvn 2f out: led 150yds out: kpt on wl: pressed cl home: jst hld on* **22/5**[2]

2 shd **Magic Wand (IRE)**[29] 8952 4-8-10 0 (p) RyanMoore 2 114+
(A P O'Brien, Ire) *in tch: trckd ldrs 3 1/2f out: pushed along fr 2f out but nt clr run tl swtchd and rdn 1 1/2f out: drvn and styd on wl fnl f: pressed wnr cl home: jst hld* **49/10**[3]

3 ½ **Rise High (FR)**[21] 9024 5-9-0 0 CYHo 3 117
(C Fownes, Hong Kong) *midfield: dropped towards rr of midfield 1/2-way: gd hdwy on outside fr 3f out: chsd ldrs whn rdn 2f out: led narrowly 1f out: hdd 150yds out: kpt on wl* **11/5**[1]

4 1 ¼ **Furore (NZ)**[21] 9024 5-9-0 0 (b) HughBowman 1 115
(F C Lor, Hong Kong) *towards rr of midfield: rdn 2f out: nt clr run and hmpd 1 1/2f out: swtchd towards outside 1f out: drvn and styd on ins fnl f* **11/5**[1]

5 ½ **Edisa (USA)**[49] 8378 3-8-7 0 StephanePasquier 4 110
(A De Royer-Dupre, France) *towards rr: rdn 2f out: drvn and kpt on wl fnl f: nt gng pce to chal* **10/1**

6 ½ **Glorious Forever**[21] 9024 5-9-0 0 (bt) ZacPurton 5 113
(F C Lor, Hong Kong) *chsd ldr: rdn 2f out: led narrowly over 1f out: hdd 1f out: wknd fnl 100yds* **44/5**

7 ¾ **Dark Dream (AUS)**[21] 9024 5-9-0 0 (b¹) DamianLane 7 111
(F C Lor, Hong Kong) *towards rr: rdn 2f out: keeping on steadily whn nt clr run 100yds out: coasted home* **40/1**

8 3 ½ **Time Warp**[21] 9024 6-9-0 0 (t) KarisTeetan 6 104
(A S Cruz, Hong Kong) *led: rdn 2f out: hdd over 1f out: wknd fnl f* **38/1**

2m 0.52s (-0.88)
WFA 3 from 4yo+ 2lb **8** Ran SP% **122.3**
PARI-MUTUEL (all including 10 hkd stake): WIN 54.00; PLACE 17.00, 17.00, 14.00; DF 166.50.
Owner Win Co Ltd **Bred** Cosmo View Farm **Trained** Japan

FOCUS
This didn't look a particularly strong running of this contest, but it did see a third Japanese winner of the four major races on the card.

9378, 9381a-9382a (Foreign Racing) - See Raceform Interactive

9306 **LINGFIELD** (L-H)

Monday, December 9

OFFICIAL GOING: Polytrack: standard

Wind: Quite fresh and gusty, against Weather: Fine

9383 LADBROKES HOME OF THE ODDS BOOST MAIDEN FILLIES' STKS (PLUS 10 RACE) 1m 1y(P)

12:00 (12:01) (Class 5) 2-Y-O £3,881 (£1,155; £577; £288) **Stalls** High

Form RPR

042 1 **Island Hideaway**[20] 9046 2-9-0 75 ShaneKelly 1 75
(David Lanigan) *trckd ldrs: led 2f out: sn rdn: kpt on* **15/8**[1]

6 2 3/4 **Agreed**[20] 9046 2-9-0 0 RobertHavlin 4 73
(John Gosden) *s.i.s: towards rr: hdwy 1/2-way: rdn over 2f out: sn chsd ldrs: wnt 2nd towards fin* **5/2**[2]

0 3 1 1/4 **Schmoozie (IRE)**[13] 9163 2-9-0 0 JosephineGordon 10 70
(Jonathan Portman) *trckd ldr: led over 3f out: rdn and hdd 2f out: kpt on: lost 2nd towards fin* **50/1**

0 4 2 1/2 **Aqrab (IRE)**[13] 9163 2-9-0 0 JackMitchell 5 65
(Roger Varian) *midfield: rdn and lost grnd 1/2-way: hdwy over 2f out: styd on: nt pce to chal* **12/1**

5 5 **Night Time Girl** 2-9-0 0 RichardKingscote 2 53
(Ismail Mohammed) *chsd ldrs: rdn 2f out: wknd fr 1f out* **16/1**

6 14 **Peace Treaty (IRE)** 2-9-0 0 FrannyNorton 7 21
(Mark Johnston) *rn green: a towards rr: reminder over 4f out: minor hdwy fnl f* **14/1**

40 7 3/4 **Out For A Duck**[20] 9046 2-8-11 0 TheodoreLadd(3) 8 19
(Michael Appleby) *s.i.s: a towards rr: hmpd 1/2-way* **66/1**

0 8 3 1/2 **Sulochana (IRE)**[23] 8999 2-9-0 0 TomMarquand 6 11
(Hughie Morrison) *led: rdn and hdd over 3f out: wknd over 2f out* **12/1**

60 9 11 **Beauty Stone (IRE)**[33] 8855 2-9-0 0 JamesDoyle 3
(Charlie Appleby) *midfield: rdn over 4f out: sn dropped to rr: no ch fr 3f out (jockey said filly was never travelling)* **11/4**[3]

1m 38.0s (-0.20) **Going Correction** -0.05s/f (Stan) 9 Ran SP% **121.4**

Speed ratings (Par 93): **99,98,97,94,89 75,74,71,60**

CSF £7.17 TOTE £2.90: £1.20, £1.20, £11.40; EX 8.60 Trifecta £199.60.

Owner Saif Ali **Bred** Meon Valley Stud **Trained** Newmarket, Suffolk

FOCUS

Probably just fair fillies' form, rated around the winner. The time was 2.8sec outside standard, with a gusty headwind not helping.

9384 BOMBARDIER "MARCH TO YOUR OWN DRUM" CLASSIFIED STKS 1m 1y(P)

12:30 (12:31) (Class 6) 3-Y-O+

£2,781 (£827; £413; £300; £300; £300) **Stalls** High

Form RPR

6050 1 **Agent Of Fortune**[48] 8436 4-9-1 50 (p) HectorCrouch 9 60+
(Gary Moore) *hld up in rr: gd hdwy abt five wd fr 2f out: rdn and led over 1f out: r.o wl fnl 110yds: readily* **7/4**[1]

0000 2 1/2 **Shaffire**[47] 8457 3-9-0 49 (h) RichardKingscote 12 58+
(Harry Whittington) *hld up in rr: smooth hdwy fr 2f out: rdn over 1f out: kpt on strly ins fnl 110yds* **25/1**

4000 3 3 1/4 **Haraz (IRE)**[9] 9249 6-8-8 48 GeorgeRooke(7) 5 50
(Paddy Butler) *midfield: hdwy 2f out: shkn up over 1f out: rdn ins fnl f: kpt on* **33/1**

5055 4 1/2 **Duke Of North (IRE)**[11] 9209 7-9-1 48 CharlieBennett 3 49
(Jim Boyle) *s.i.s: prom after 1f: gng okay 2f out: rdn over 1f out: wknd fnl 110yds* **12/1**

2555 5 2 **Cat Royale (IRE)**[16] 9139 6-8-10 46 (b) DylanHogan(5) 4 45
(John Butler) *cl up: shkn up and led 2f out: rdn and hdd over 1f out: wknd fnl 110yds* **6/1**[3]

3533 6 8 **Snooker Jim**[17] 9111 4-9-1 46 (tp) JackMitchell 10 26
(Steph Hollinshead) *prom on outer: disp ld 3f out: rdn 2f out: wknd qckly over 1f out* **9/2**[2]

0004 7 hd **Keep It Country Tv**[91] 7027 3-8-12 50 ow1 PaddyBradley(3) 11 27
(Pat Phelan) *awkward s: rushed up on outer sn after s: led after 1f: rdn and hdd fr 2f out: wknd qckly over 1f out* **8/1**

0006 8 3/4 **Te Amo Te Amo**[9] 9246 3-9-0 48 (h) TomMarquand 7 24
(Simon Dow) *s.i.s: hld up in rr: rdn and no imp over 2f out: wknd over 1f out* **8/1**

P040 9 2 **Caesonia**[44] 8547 3-9-0 45 (p) DavidProbert 1 19
(Charles Hills) *stdd s: hld up in rr: rdn over 2f out: wknd over 1f out* **33/1**

0000 10 1 1/4 **Juan Horsepower**[14] 9161 5-8-12 46 DarraghKeenan(3) 2 17
(Denis Quinn) *led: hdd after 1f: rdn over 3f out: wknd qckly ins fnl f* **66/1**

0060 11 3 **Birthday Girl (IRE)**[10] 9213 4-9-1 45 (t) HollieDoyle 6 10
(Amanda Perrett) *t.k.h: midfield: rdn after 4f: no ex 2f out: wknd over 1f out* **20/1**

6006 12 2 1/4 **Soaring Spirits (IRE)**[48] 8436 9-8-10 49 (v) SophieRalston(5) 8 4
(Dean Ivory) *midfield abt three wd: niggled along over 3f out: rdn fr 2f out: keeping on whn hmpd home turn: grad lost position (jockey said gelding hung right-handed off the bend)* **14/1**

1m 37.32s (-0.88) **Going Correction** -0.05s/f (Stan) 12 Ran SP% **121.4**

WFA 3 from 4yo+ 1lb

Speed ratings (Par 101): **102,101,98,97,95 87,87,86,84,83 80,78**

CSF £61.38 TOTE £2.70: £1.20, £7.50, £8.60; EX 41.50 Trifecta £1365.50.

Owner Foreign Legion **Bred** Barton Stud **Trained** Lower Beeding, W Sussex

FOCUS

This weak classified event was run to suit the closers and two came clear. Both were having their first starts for new yards.

9385 LADBROKES WHERE THE NATION PLAYS / EBF NOVICE STKS (PLUS 10 RACE) 7f 1y(P)

1:00 (1:02) (Class 4) 2-Y-O £4,463 (£1,328; £663; £331) **Stalls** Low

Form RPR

2 1 **Harrison Point (FR)**[124] 5809 2-9-2 0 HollieDoyle 7 80+
(Archie Watson) *led: hdd and cl up after 1f: led again 2f out: rdn out (jockey said colt hung both ways in the straight)* **11/4**[2]

51 2 1 1/4 **Story Of Light (IRE)**[20] 9043 2-9-8 0 (h) JamesDoyle 3 83
(Charlie Appleby) *prom: rdn 2f out: wnt 2nd ins fnl 110yds: r.o* **4/7**[1]

00 3 1/2 **The Weed Machine (IRE)**[9] 9252 2-9-2 0 FrannyNorton 10 76
(Mark Johnston) *t.k.h: led after 1f: rdn and hdd 2f out: nt clr run and swtchd rt ins fnl f: lost 2nd ins fnl 110yds* **40/1**

4 2 1/2 **Top Secret** 2-9-2 0 AdamKirby 1 69+
(Clive Cox) *midfield: rdn 2f out: styd on: wnt 4th towards fin* **8/1**[3]

0 5 nk **Shoot The Moon (IRE)**[82] 7346 2-9-2 0 (h[1]) AdrianMcCarthy 5 68
(William Jarvis) *t.k.h: chsd ldrs: rdn under 2f out: wknd grad fnl f* **10/1**

0 6 3 1/2 **Giovanni Tiepolo**[23] 9008 2-9-2 0 DavidProbert 8 59+
(Henry Candy) *t.k.h: midfield: hung rt home turn: sn shkn up: styd on fnl f* **25/1**

7 7 **Kalimotxo** 2-8-4 0 Pierre-LouisJamin(7) 4 35
(William Knight) *towards rr: shkn up 3f out: mde no imp* **66/1**

8 2 1/4 **Note Bleu** 2-9-2 0 HectorCrouch 9 34
(Gary Moore) *a towards rr* **66/1**

9 3/4 **Magnificat (IRE)** 2-9-2 0 TomQueally 2 32
(Alan King) *towards rr: pushed along over 2f out: reminder over 1f out: mde no imp* **33/1**

0 10 1 1/4 **Calamity May**[16] 9130 2-8-8 0 TheodoreLadd(3) 6 23
(Luke Dace) *a towards rr: pushed along over 4f out: mde no imp* **66/1**

1m 24.72s (-0.08) **Going Correction** -0.05s/f (Stan) 10 Ran SP% **124.2**

Speed ratings (Par 98): **98,96,96,93,92 88,80,78,77,75**

CSF £4.87 TOTE £3.30: £1.10, £1.10, £7.90; EX 4.70 Trifecta £45.20.

Owner China Horse Club International Limited **Bred** China Horse Club International Ltd **Trained** Upper Lambourn, W Berks

■ Stewards' Enquiry : Hollie Doyle caution: careless riding

FOCUS

The pace held up and this is fairly useful novice form.

9386 BETYOURWAY AT BETWAY H'CAP 6f 1y(P)

1:30 (1:32) (Class 6) (0-65,65) 3-Y-O+

£2,781 (£827; £413; £300; £300; £300) **Stalls** Low

Form RPR

3641 1 **The Lacemaker**[9] 9246 5-8-13 60 (t[1]) DarraghKeenan(3) 5 66
(Milton Harris) *travelled strly: cl up: led over 2f out: rdn fnl f: r.o wl fnl 110yds: jst hld on* **3/1**[1]

310 2 nk **Daring Guest (IRE)**[122] 5889 5-8-11 62 (t) AngusVilliers(7) 3 67
(Tom Clover) *prom on inner: shkn up over 1f out: kpt on strly fnl 110yds: jst hld* **4/1**[2]

0001 3 1 3/4 **Kath's Lustre**[32] 8896 4-8-9 60 (b) GeorgeRooke(7) 12 60
(Richard Hughes) *racd freely: prom: pushed along over 1f out: rdn ins fnl f: no ex fnl 110yds* **11/2**[3]

4000 4 1/2 **Aguerooo (IRE)**[9] 9257 6-9-7 65 (tp) RichardKingscote 10 63+
(Charlie Wallis) *t.k.h: midfield: rdn over 1f out: kpt on fnl 110yds* **10/1**

3010 5 hd **Kingsley Klarion (IRE)**[18] 9089 6-9-4 62 JoeyHaynes 1 60+
(John Butler) *midfield on inner: rdn and outpcd fr 2f out: kpt on ins fnl f* **10/1**

5300 6 3/4 **Fareeq**[18] 9092 5-9-0 58 (bt) DavidProbert 9 54
(Charlie Wallis) *hld up in rr: pushed along and outpcd fr 2f out: rdn fnl f: nt pce to chal* **33/1**

1060 7 3/4 **Velvet Morn (IRE)**[12] 9176 4-9-0 65 Pierre-LouisJamin(7) 7 58+
(William Knight) *squeezed out s: in rr: rdn and outpcd 3f out: swtchd rt 2f out: styd on ins fnl f: nt rch ldrs: eyecatcher (vet said filly lost its right fore shoe)* **7/1**

1460 8 shd **Napping**[39] 8711 6-9-2 63 GabrieleMalune(3) 8 56
(Amy Murphy) *swvd lft s: t.k.h: midfield: rdn and outpcd over 1f out: kpt on ins fnl f (jockey said mare jumped awkwardly from the stalls)* **8/1**

4050 9 shd **Creek Harbour (IRE)**[23] 9013 4-9-0 65 StefanoCherchi(7) 2 58
(Milton Bradley) *sn led: hdd over 2f out: rdn over 1f out: wknd ins fnl f* **8/1**

040 10 1 1/4 **Moveonup (IRE)**[10] 9218 3-8-10 59 TobyEley(5) 11 48
(Gay Kelleway) *hld up in rr: rdn and outpcd 2f out: swtchd lft over 1f out: no ex fnl 110yds (jockey said gelding was slowly away)* **25/1**

5000 11 3 3/4 **George Dryden (IRE)**[10] 9219 7-9-1 59 CharlieBennett 6 37
(Denis Quinn) *trckd ldrs on outer: rdn and fnd little fr 2f out: wknd qckly over 1f out* **66/1**

1660 12 17 **Majorette**[33] 8861 5-9-3 61 (b[1]) TomQueally 4
(Brian Barr) *t.k.h: hld up in rr: rdn and no imp 3f out: t.o* **33/1**

1m 12.22s (0.32) **Going Correction** -0.05s/f (Stan) 12 Ran SP% **124.5**

Speed ratings (Par 101): **95,94,92,91,91 90,89,89,89,87 82,59**

CSF £15.07 CT £67.29 TOTE £3.80: £1.60, £1.70, £2.30; EX 17.50 Trifecta £54.60.

Owner Mrs Dawn Scott **Bred** S A R L Srl **Trained** Warminster, Wiltshire

FOCUS

They went just an ordinary pace in this moderate sprint handicap.

9387 BETWAY HEED YOUR HUNCH H'CAP 6f 1y(P)

2:00 (2:01) (Class 4) (0-80,80) 3-Y-O+

£5,207 (£1,549; £774; £387; £300; £300) **Stalls** Low

Form RPR

0223 1 **Fizzy Feet (IRE)**[6] 9286 3-9-6 80 RichardKingscote 5 89
(David Loughnane) *trckd ldrs: rdn over 1f out: led ins fnl 110yds: comf* **3/1**[2]

3-35 2 1 **Kamra (USA)**[291] 832 5-9-3 77 (b) AlistairRawlinson 6 83
(Michael Appleby) *trckd ldr: rdn and led 2f out: hdd ins fnl 110yds: kpt on* **10/1**

2301 3 1 3/4 **Swiss Pride (IRE)**[40] 8649 3-8-9 76 (p) AngusVilliers(7) 1 76
(Richard Hughes) *trckd ldrs: rdn over 1f out: sn disputing 2nd: wknd grad ins fnl f* **9/2**

4035 4 nk **Whisper Aloud**[33] 8852 3-8-13 80 Pierre-LouisJamin(7) 3 79
(Archie Watson) *s.i.s: in rr: pushed along over 2f out: reminder over 1f out: r.o: nt rch ldrs* **4/1**[3]

0056 5 5 **Alfie Solomons (IRE)**[44] 8550 3-9-3 77 RobertHavlin 2 60
(Amanda Perrett) *s.i.s: in rr: rdn over 2f out: mde no imp (trainer's rep could offer no explanation for the epoor form shown other than it was gelding's first run for trainer and, having run in head gear with previous trainer, they wanted to try running gelding without any head gear)* **2/1**[1]

6220 6 2 **Gold At Midnight**[20] 9054 3-9-3 77 (p) TomMarquand 4 54
(William Muir) *led: rdn and hdd 2f out: wknd fnl f* **16/1**

1m 10.81s (-1.09) **Going Correction** -0.05s/f (Stan) 6 Ran SP% **111.5**

Speed ratings (Par 105): **105,103,101,100,94 91**

CSF £30.26 TOTE £3.60: £1.60, £4.20; EX 16.10 Trifecta £81.60.

Owner D Lowe & S Hoyland **Bred** Tipper House Stud J Troy & R Levitt **Trained** Tern Hill, Shropshire

FOCUS
Fair sprint form. The winner has been on the upgrade recently.

9388 BETWAY CASINO H'CAP — 1m 2f (P)
2:30 (2:31) (Class 3) (0-90,89) 3-Y-O+ **£7,246** (£2,168; £1,084; £542; £270) **Stalls** Low

Form RPR

2510 **1** **Just The Man (FR)**[20] 9055 3-9-5 **89** AdamKirby 8 97
(Clive Cox) *hld up in last: niggled along sn after s: gd hdwy on outer over 2f out: rdn over 1f out: led fnl 110yds: jst did enough* **15/8**[1]

2330 **2** *1* **The Jean Genie**[38] 8725 5-9-0 **82** HollieDoyle 4 87
(William Stone) *midfield: rdn fr over 2f out: hdwy over 1f out: led fnl f: hdd fnl 110yds: kpt on* **9/1**

P000 **3** *nse* **Humbert (IRE)**[20] 9053 5-9-7 **89** (t[1]) DavidProbert 7 94
(David O'Meara) *hld up in rr: sme hdwy 2f out: rdn and outpcd over 1f out: kpt on wl fnl 110yds* **10/1**

5354 **4** *3/4* **Michele Strogoff**[6] 9285 6-9-2 **84** AlistairRawlinson 2 87
(Michael Appleby) *cl up: shkn up and led over 1f out: hdd fnl f: wknd towards fin* **6/1**[3]

0550 **5** *hd* **Sezim**[11] 9199 3-8-6 **76** (t[1]) RaulDaSilva 5 80
(Mohamed Moubarak) *prom: rdn and outpcd 2f out: kpt on ins fnl f* **16/1**

6021 **6** *3 1/2* **Wimpole Hall**[20] 9050 6-8-1 **76** (p) GaiaBoni[(7)] 3 72
(William Jarvis) *s.i.s: midfield after 1f: rdn and no imp fr 2f out: wknd over 1f out* **7/1**

-104 **7** *1* **Sky Defender**[11] 9206 3-9-0 **84** FrannyNorton 1 79
(Mark Johnston) *t.k.h: led: rdn and hdd over 1f out: wknd qckly fnl 110yds* **3/1**[2]

2m 3.71s (-2.89) **Going Correction** -0.05s/f (Stan)
WFA 3 from 5yo+ 2lb **7 Ran SP% 111.5**
Speed ratings (Par 107): **109,108,108,107,107 104,103**
CSF £18.55 CT £128.61 TOTE £2.70: £1.70, £4.10; EX 19.20 Trifecta £80.60.
Owner Paul & Clare Rooney **Bred** Compagnia Generale Srl **Trained** Lambourn, Berks

FOCUS
This fair handicap was run at an uneven pace and it produced a tight finish. It's rated as ordinary form around the runner-up.

9389 BETWAY H'CAP — 5f 6y(P)
3:00 (3:00) (Class 2) (0-105,103) 3-Y-O+ **£11,971** (£3,583; £1,791; £896; £446) **Stalls** High

Form RPR

6521 **1** **Watchable**[18] 9098 9-8-13 **95** (p) ShaneGray 4 103
(David O'Meara) *dwlt s: hld up in bhd ldrs: rdn 2f out: r.o wl fnl f: edgd lft and led towards fin* **11/2**[3]

2343 **2** *1 1/4* **Prince Of Rome (IRE)**[10] 9214 3-8-5 **87** FrannyNorton 1 91
(Richard Hughes) *chsd ldrs: rdn and led ins fnl f: hdd towards fin* **7/2**[1]

2054 **3** *1 3/4* **Stake Acclaim (IRE)**[23] 9004 7-9-7 **103** AdamKirby 3 100
(Dean Ivory) *prom: rdn 2f out: bit short of room ins fnl f: wnt 3rd fnl strides* **9/2**[2]

5263 **4** *nse* **Just That Lord**[16] 9131 6-8-3 **85** HollieDoyle 5 82
(Michael Attwater) *cl up: led 2f out: sn rdn: hdd and no ex ins fnl f: lost 3rd fnl strides* **11/2**[3]

3214 **5** *3/4* **Thegreatestshowman**[13] 9166 3-8-6 **88** GeorgeWood 7 82
(Amy Murphy) *hld up in rr: hdwy and chsd ldrs over 1f out: wknd grad ins fnl f* **11/2**[3]

660 **6** *1/2* **Moon Trouble (IRE)**[18] 9088 6-8-2 **87** SeanDavis[(3)] 2 80
(Michael Appleby) *led: hdd 2f out: sn rdn: wknd ins fnl f* **16/1**

5002 **7** *7* **Gracious John (IRE)**[18] 9088 6-8-7 **89** JosephineGordon 6 56
(Ian Williams) *racd in last: niggled along after 2f: bhd fr 3f out (jockey said gelding was never travelling)* **7/2**[1]

57.82s (-0.98) **Going Correction** -0.05s/f (Stan) **7 Ran SP% 114.7**
Speed ratings (Par 109): **105,103,100,100,98 98,86**
CSF £25.12 CT £93.58 TOTE £5.20: £2.80, £1.80; EX 22.80 Trifecta £138.30.
Owner Hambleton Xxxix P Bamford Roses Partners **Bred** Cheveley Park Stud Ltd **Trained** Upper Helmsley, N Yorks

FOCUS
A good sprint handicap, run at what appeared a decent clip and in a time 0.72sec outside the standard. This rates up with the winner's best form since 2016.

9390 BETWAY LIVE CASINO H'CAP — 5f 6y(P)
3:30 (3:31) (Class 5) (0-75,76) 3-Y-O+
£3,428 (£1,020; £509; £300; £300; £300) **Stalls** High

Form RPR

3300 **1** **Chitra**[11] 9203 3-9-8 **76** RichardKingscote 4 83
(Daniel Kubler) *sn led: hdd after 1f: rdn over 1f out: led again fnl 110yds: jst did enough* **9/2**[3]

5424 **2** *shd* **Something Lucky (IRE)**[9] 9245 7-9-2 **70** RobertHavlin 7 76
(Michael Attwater) *hld up in rr: gd hdwy fr 2f out: shkn up fr over 1f out: ev ch fr over 1f out: jst failed* **6/1**

3006 **3** *hd* **Green Door (IRE)**[16] 9131 8-8-13 **74** (v) AngusVilliers[(7)] 3 79
(Robert Cowell) *midfield: hdwy 2f out: shkn up over 1f out: rdn ins fnl f: kpt on strly fnl 110yds: jst hld* **4/1**[2]

5210 **4** *1/2* **Three Little Birds**[6] 9286 4-9-7 **75** TomMarquand 2 78
(Sylvester Kirk) *prom on inner: shkn up and outpcd 2f out: rallied over 1f out: no ex towards fin* **3/1**[1]

6013 **5** *1 1/2* **Coronation Cottage**[23] 9013 5-8-10 **64** CharlieBennett 8 62
(Malcolm Saunders) *racd freely: cl up: led after 1f: shkn up over 1f out: rdn and hdd fnl 110yds: wknd towards fin* **10/1**

5100 **6** *1 1/4* **Zapper Cass (FR)**[6] 9286 6-9-7 **75** (be) AlistairRawlinson 5 69
(Michael Appleby) *s.i.s: in rr: sme hdwy on outer 3f out: rdn 2f out: nt pce to chal* **9/2**[3]

0300 **7** *2* **Celerity (IRE)**[9] 9257 5-8-2 **61** oh16 (v) SophieRalston[(5)] 6 47
(Lisa Williamson) *prom on outer: rdn and outpcd 2f out: wknd over 1f out* **100/1**

2240 **8** *1* **Glamorous Rocket (IRE)**[16] 9135 4-8-10 **67** MitchGodwin[(3)] 1 50
(Christopher Mason) *t.k.h: hld up in rr: rdn and no imp over 2f out: wknd fnl f* **20/1**

0040 **9** *2* **Warrior's Valley**[81] 7387 4-9-1 **69** (tp) JosephineGordon 9 45
(David C Griffiths) *t.k.h: cl up: rdn 2f out: wknd qckly fr 1f out* **12/1**

58.29s (-0.51) **Going Correction** -0.05s/f (Stan) **9 Ran SP% 118.2**
Speed ratings (Par 103): **102,101,101,100,98 96,93,91,88**
CSF £32.48 CT £118.72 TOTE £5.70: £1.80, £2.20, £2.20; EX 37.70 Trifecta £185.40.
Owner Mr & Mrs G Middlebrook **Bred** Mr & Mrs G Middlebrook **Trained** Lambourn, Berks
■ Stewards' Enquiry : Angus Villiers three-day ban: careless riding (Dec 26-28)

FOCUS
There was no hanging around in this modest sprint handicap and it saw a cracking finish. The game winner's rated to her best.
T/Plt: £19.60 to a £1 stake. Pool: £70,135.45 - 2,607.59 winning units T/Qpdt: £8.10 to a £1 stake. Pool: £8,694.67 - 793.46 winning units **Raceform**

9345 NEWCASTLE (A.W) (L-H)
Monday, December 9

OFFICIAL GOING: Tapeta: standard
Wind: Moderate against Weather: Fine & dry

9391 BETWAY HEED YOUR HUNCH H'CAP — 1m 2f 42y (Tp)
3:10 (3:13) (Class 6) (0-60,62) 3-Y-O+
£2,781 (£827; £413; £400; £400; £400) **Stalls** High

Form RPR

3134 **1** **Corked (IRE)**[35] 8818 6-9-6 **58** PJMcDonald 5 64
(Alistair Whillans) *trckd ldrs: hdwy 3f out: rdn to chse ldr ins fnl f: sn drvn: kpt on wl to ld nr line* **11/2**[3]

3201 **2** *nk* **Sulafaat (IRE)**[3] 9345 4-9-1 **60** 5ex (p) RussellHarris[(7)] 1 65
(Rebecca Menzies) *trckd ldrs: hdwy 3f out: effrt on inner to chal over 2f out: rdn to ld wl over 1f out: drvn ins fnl f: hdd nr line* **9/4**[1]

2555 **3** *1 1/4* **Kodi Koh (IRE)**[75] 7578 4-8-8 **46** AndrewMullen 6 49
(Simon West) *t.k.h: hld up in rr: hdwy 3f out: rdn to chse ldrs wl over 1f out: drvn and edgd rt ins fnl f: kpt on wl towards fin* **16/1**

5403 **4** *3/4* **Curfewed (IRE)**[35] 8818 3-9-8 **62** (p) LukeMorris 12 65
(Tracy Waggott) *trckd ldrs: hdwy 4f out: sn prom: rdn along 2f out: sn ev ch: drvn appr fnl f: kpt on same pce* **13/2**

4004 **5** *nk* **Solfeggio (IRE)**[21] 9040 3-9-3 **57** BenCurtis 10 59
(Chris Wall) *led: pushed along 3f out: jnd and rdn jst over 2f out: hdd and drvn wl over 1f out: kpt on same pce fnl f* **10/3**[2]

5060 **6** *1 1/4* **Bahkit (IRE)**[63] 7956 5-9-5 **57** PaulMulrennan 13 56
(Philip Kirby) *prom: trckd ldr 1/2-way: rdn along over 2f out: drvn over 1f out: sn one pce* **11/1**

0053 **7** *nk* **Somewhat Sisyphean**[122] 5915 3-8-7 **47** DuranFentiman 8 47
(Wilf Storey) *t.k.h: hld up in rr: hdwy over 3f out: effrt on inner 2f out: sn rdn: kpt on fnl f (jockey said gelding ran too free)* **20/1**

0240 **8** *shd* **Jagerbond**[4] 9337 3-8-0 **45** (e) AndrewBreslin[(5)] 11 44
(Andrew Crook) *t.k.h: hld up: a towards rr* **33/1**

0450 **9** *nk* **One Last Hug**[10] 9220 4-8-7 **45** PhilDennis 4 43
(Jim Goldie) *a towards rr* **14/1**

4633 **10** *1 1/2* **Quoteline Direct**[17] 8870 6-9-6 **58** (h) GrahamLee 14 53
(Micky Hammond) *hld up towards rr: hdwy on outer over 3f out: rdn to chse ldrs 2f out: sn drvn and btn* **7/1**

6000 **11** *4 1/2* **Bigbadboy (IRE)**[76] 7544 6-8-7 **45** (p[1]) BenRobinson 3 32
(Clive Mulhall) *trckd ldr: pushed along 3f out: rdn over 2f out: drvn wl over 1f out: sn wknd (jockey said gelding hung left-handed)* **25/1**

3400 **12** *1/2* **Zarkavon**[33] 8863 5-8-7 **45** (p) JamesSullivan 2 31
(John Wainwright) *midfield: pushed along over 3f out: sn rdn and wknd over 2f out* **40/1**

0006 **13** *1* **False Id**[63] 7956 6-9-7 **59** (v) JasonHart 7 43
(Fred Watson) *dwlt: t.k.h: a towards rr* **16/1**

2m 12.06s (1.66) **Going Correction** +0.10s/f (Slow)
WFA 3 from 4yo+ 2lb **13 Ran SP% 135.8**
Speed ratings (Par 101): **97,96,95,95,94 93,93,93,93,92 88,88,87**
CSF £20.20 CT £210.05 TOTE £6.20: £1.70, £1.30, £4.90; EX 26.10 Trifecta £339.40.
Owner Shmelt For Gold **Bred** Lisieux Stud **Trained** Newmill-On-Slitrig, Borders

FOCUS
There was a headwind. An ordinary affair with a slow finish.

9392 LADBROKES WHERE THE NATION PLAYS MAIDEN STKS — 6f (Tp)
3:45 (3:48) (Class 5) 2-Y-O **£3,428** (£1,020; £509; £254) **Stalls** Centre

Form

1 **Splendidly** 2-9-5 0 BenCurtis 11 74+
(K R Burke) *hld up towards rr: hdwy 1/2-way: trckd ldrs and n.m.r wl over 1f out: hdwy ent fnl f: sn rdn and qcknd wl to ld nr fin* **16/1**

2 **2** *nk* **Corvair (IRE)**[18] 9085 2-9-5 0 GrahamLee 8 73
(Simon Crisford) *trckd ldrs: hdwy 1/2-way: sn cl up: led 2f out: rdn jst over 1f out: drvn ins fnl f: hdd and no ex nr fin* **4/1**[3]

642 **3** *hd* **Where's Mick (IRE)**[31] 8919 2-9-5 72 PJMcDonald 2 72
(Jedd O'Keeffe) *trckd ldrs: hdwy 2f out: rdn to chal over 1f out: drvn and ev ch ins fnl f: nt qckn towards fin* **7/2**[2]

2 **4** *2* **Lexington Dash (FR)**[16] 9130 2-9-0 0 ThoreHammerHansen[(5)] 9 66
(Richard Hannon) *trckd ldrs: effrt whn n.m.r wl over 1f out: sn rdn: kpt on same pce* **5/6**[1]

5 *nse* **Tomorrow's Dream (FR)** 2-9-0 0 DanielTudhope 7 61+
(William Haggas) *hld up towards rr: hdwy nr stands' rail over 2f out: rdn to chse ldng pair jst over 1f out: kpt on same pce fnl f* **5/1**

6 *4* **Dream Game** 2-9-0 0 PaulMulrennan 5 49
(Ben Haslam) *hld up in rr: hdwy over 2f out: rdn along over 1f out: kpt on: nvr nr ldrs* **50/1**

00 **7** *hd* **Alioski**[21] 9036 2-9-5 0 TomEaves 6 53
(Kevin Ryan) *towards rr: pushed along 1/2-way: rdn over 2f out: plugged on fnl f: n.d* **50/1**

50 **8** *nk* **Tattletime (USA)**[9] 9251 2-9-0 0 (t) SamJames 12 47
(David Loughnane) *prom: rdn along over 2f out: sn drvn and wknd* **66/1**

9 *hd* **Full Speight (USA)** 2-9-5 0 LukeMorris 10 52
(Sir Mark Prescott Bt) *cl up: slt ld over 2f out: sn rdn and hdd: drvn and wknd wl over 1f out* **20/1**

0 **10** *3* **Bank Holiday (IRE)**[20] 9043 2-8-11 0 ConnorMurtagh[(3)] 1 38
(Richard Fahey) *a in rr* **100/1**

000 **11** *1 1/2* **Castashadow**[68] 7821 2-9-5 33 CallumRodriguez 3 38
(Alan Brown) *a in rr* **250/1**

0 **12** *1 1/4* **Indian Road (IRE)**[17] 9107 2-9-5 0 JasonHart 4 35
(Mark Johnston) *slt ld: rdn along 1/2-way: sn hdd & wknd* **25/1**

1m 13.03s (0.53) **Going Correction** +0.10s/f (Slow) **12 Ran SP% 134.7**
Speed ratings (Par 96): **100,99,99,96,96 91,91,90,90,86 84,82**
CSF £87.60 TOTE £17.90: £4.10, £1.50, £1.40; EX 100.70 Trifecta £553.10.
Owner J Laughton & Mrs E Burke **Bred** Cheveley Park Stud Ltd **Trained** Middleham Moor, N Yorks

FOCUS
There was a tight finish to this maiden.

9393 LADBROKES HOME OF THE ODDS BOOST NOVICE STKS — 5f (Tp)
4:15 (4:19) (Class 5) 2-Y-O **£3,428** (£1,020; £509; £254) **Stalls** Centre

Form RPR

203 **1** **Minhaaj (IRE)**[21] 9036 2-8-12 82 BenCurtis 3 74+
(William Haggas) *trckd ldrs: smooth hdwy to ld wl over 1f out: jnd and shkn up ent fnl f: sn rdn and kpt on strly* **8/13**[1]

05 **2** 1 1/4 **Gowanlad**[18] 9099 2-9-3 0 .... PhilDennis 1 75
(Philip Kirby) *hld up in tch: hdwy over 2f out: rdn to chal ent fnl f: sn drvn and kpt on same pce* **12/1**

2 **3** 2 1/4 **Lapses Linguae (FR)**[19] 9062 2-8-12 0 .... JasonHart 9 61
(Emmet Mullins, Ire) *t.k.h: cl up: pushed along 2f out: rdn wl over 1f out: kpt on same pce fnl f* **3/1**[2]

0 **4** nk **Ilsereno**[32] 8899 2-8-5 0 .... JonathanFisher(7) 4 60
(Scott Dixon) *cl up: rdn along wl over 1f out: kpt on same pce* **20/1**

6632 **5** hd **Shammah (IRE)**[115] 6158 2-9-5 79 .... PJMcDonald 6 67
(Richard Hannon) *led: rdn along 2f out: sn hdd and grad wknd* **5/1**[3]

00 **6** 3/4 **Littlemissattitude**[21] 9036 2-8-12 0 .... LewisEdmunds 2 57
(Derek Shaw) *towards rr: hdwy over 2f out: rdn to chse ldrs over 1f out: keeping on whn n.m.r wl ins fnl f* **200/1**

6 **7** 1 1/2 **Cliff Wind**[21] 9036 2-8-12 0 .... LukeMorris 7 52
(Sir Mark Prescott Bt) *wnt rt s: chsd ldrs: rdn along over 2f out: sn wknd* **33/1**

0 **8** 3 1/2 **Outofthegloom**[17] 9107 2-8-12 0 .... CamHardie 5 39
(Brian Rothwell) *chsd ldrs: rdn along 1/2-way: sn wknd* **250/1**

9 8 **Katelli (IRE)** 2-9-0 0 .... ConnorMurtagh(3) 8 15
(Richard Fahey) *dwlt: rn green and hung bdly lft sn after s: a wl bhd (jockey said gelding was slowly away losing many lengths and swerved severely to the left during the early stages)* **14/1**

1m 0.17s (0.67) **Going Correction** +0.10s/f (Slow) **9** Ran SP% **126.5**
Speed ratings (Par 96): **98,96,92,91,91 90,88,82,69**
CSF £12.08 TOTE £1.70: £1.10, £3.10, £1.10; EX 14.30 Trifecta £38.90.
Owner Hamdan Al Maktoum **Bred** Shadwell Estate Company Limited **Trained** Newmarket, Suffolk

FOCUS
No more than a fair novice, with little depth.

9394 LADBROKES "PLAY 1-2 FREE" ON FOOTBALL NURSERY H'CAP 5f (Tp)
4:45 (4:50) (Class 6) (0-60,62) 2-Y-O

£2,781 (£827; £413; £400; £400; £400) **Stalls** Centre

Form RPR

0515 **1** **Lezardrieux**[19] 9061 2-9-7 60 .... SamJames 7 62
(Grant Tuer) *slt ld: hdd briefly 3f out: led again jst over 2f out: rdn over 1f out: drvn ins fnl f: kpt on gamely* **5/2**[1]

0500 **2** 1/2 **Tiltilys Rock (IRE)**[35] 8815 2-8-1 45 .... AndrewBreslin(5) 12 45
(Andrew Crook) *towards rr: hdwy over 2f out: rdn to chse ldrs over 1f out: styd on wl fnl f* **66/1**

510 **3** shd **A Go Go**[52] 8315 2-9-2 55 .... CliffordLee 3 55
(David Evans) *in tch: hdwy 2f out: rdn over 1f out: kpt on wl fnl f* **14/1**

050 **4** hd **Mews House**[21] 9036 2-9-4 62 .... ThoreHammerHansen(5) 10 61
(David Brown) *cl up: rdn along 2f out: drvn ent fnl f: kpt on same pce (jockey said colt hung left handed in the final 2f.)* **6/1**

006 **5** 1/2 **The Grey Bay (IRE)**[60] 8067 2-9-2 55 .... JasonHart 11 52
(Julie Camacho) *t.k.h: trckd ldrs: hdwy 2f out: rdn and edgd lft over 1f out: kpt on fnl f* **5/1**[3]

6 3/4 **Smart Project (IRE)**[38] 8729 2-9-3 56 .... AndrewMullen 4 50
(Adrian Nicholls) *prom: cl up 1/2-way: rdn along over 1f out: drvn and ev ch ent fnl f: grad wknd* **7/1**

2504 **7** 1/2 **Navajo Dawn (IRE)**[32] 8899 2-9-7 60 .... TomEaves 5 53
(Robyn Brisland) *in rr: rdn along over 2f out: kpt on fnl f: nrst fin* **10/1**

000 **8** 1/2 **Apples Acre (IRE)**[79] 7437 2-8-6 45 ....(p[1]) LukeMorris 6 36
(Ben Haslam) *towards rr: rdn along 2f out: kpt on fnl f (jockey said filly suffered interference 1 1/2f out.)* **18/1**

0000 **9** 1 1/4 **Newsical**[59] 8085 2-9-1 54 ....(w) DougieCostello 9 40
(Mark Walford) *chsd ldrs towards stands' side: pushed along 1/2-way: sn rdn and wknd* **20/1**

050 **10** 5 **Quiet Word (FR)**[32] 8899 2-8-13 52 ....(t[1]) BenCurtis 8 20
(Archie Watson) *cl up: narrow ld 3f out: hdd over 2f out and sn rdn along: wknd and hld whn hmpd over 1f out (jockey said filly suffered interference 1 1/2f out)* **9/2**[2]

6240 **11** 1 **Comeatchoo (IRE)**[4] 9330 2-8-8 54 .... GraceMcEntee(7) 1 19
(Phil McEntee) *in tch: pushed along 2f out: sn rdn and wknd over 1f out* **9/1**

000 **12** 1/2 **Pacific Coast**[161] 4433 2-8-6 45 .... CamHardie 2 8
(Antony Brittain) *a towards rr: outpcd and bhd fnl 2f* **28/1**

1m 0.41s (0.91) **Going Correction** +0.10s/f (Slow) **12** Ran SP% **130.9**
Speed ratings (Par 94): **96,95,95,94,93 92,91,91,89,81 79,78**
CSF £245.21 CT £2129.30 TOTE £3.10: £1.50, £15.60, £3.90; EX 161.70 Trifecta £4239.00.
Owner D R Tucker **Bred** D R Tucker **Trained** Birkby, N Yorks
■ Stewards' Enquiry : Sam James two-day ban: misuse of the whip (Dec 26,27)

FOCUS
A moderate nursery and limited form in a tight finish.

9395 BOMBARDIER BRITISH HOPPED AMBER BEER H'CAP 1m 5y (Tp)
5:15 (5:19) (Class 6) (0-60,60) 3-Y-O+

£2,781 (£827; £413; £400; £400; £400) **Stalls** Centre

Form RPR

3020 **1** **High Fort (IRE)**[6] 9282 4-8-9 48 .... BenCurtis 2 57
(Karen McLintock) *trckd ldrs: hdwy 1/2-way: led over 2f out: rdn clr over 1f out: kpt on strly* **4/1**[3]

0635 **2** 2 1/2 **Mr Strutter (IRE)**[54] 8270 5-9-6 59 .... TomEaves 1 63
(Ronald Thompson) *hld up and bhd: swtchd rt to stands' rail 3f out: hdwy 2f out: rdn to chse wnr over 1f out: drvn and no imp fnl f* **14/1**

6311 **3** 3 1/4 **Proceeding**[31] 8922 4-9-5 58 .... LukeMorris 11 54
(Tracy Waggott) *hld up in midfield: hdwy over 2f out: effrt and n.m.r wl over 1f out: sn rdn: drvn and kpt on fnl f* **5/2**[1]

0000 **4** 1 3/4 **Turquoise Friendly**[115] 6176 3-9-2 56 ....(t) PaulMulrennan 7 49
(Michael Easterby) *t.k.h: hld up and bhd: hdwy 3f out: effrt and n.m.r 2f out: swtchd lft and rdn over 1f out: kpt on fnl f (jockey said gelding was denied a clear run 2f out and again approaching the final furlong)* **25/1**

004 **5** shd **Blazing Dreams (IRE)**[54] 7581 3-9-5 59 ....(p) AndrewMullen 8 51
(Ben Haslam) *sn trcking ldr: pushed along over 2f out: rdn wl over 1f out: grad wknd* **5/1**

5340 **6** 1 3/4 **Chinese Spirit (IRE)**[35] 8818 5-9-7 60 .... PJMcDonald 4 48
(Linda Perratt) *trckd ldrs: effrt 3f out: rdn along over 2f out: drvn and wknd over 1f out* **14/1**

0540 **7** shd **The Brora Pobbles**[40] 8664 4-8-7 46 oh1 .... BarryMcHugh 10 34
(Alistair Whillans) *in tch: pushed along 3f out: rdn over 2f out: sn wknd* **20/1**

0003 **8** hd **Amber Rock (USA)**[32] 8903 3-8-6 46 oh1 ....(tp) JaneElliott 12 34
(Les Eyre) *trckd ldrs: pushed along 3f out: rdn over 2f out: sn drvn and wknd* **13/2**

4253 **9** 1 **Traveller (FR)**[21] 9040 5-8-12 56 ....(vt) KieranSchofield(5) 13 42
(Antony Brittain) *hld up in tch: hdwy 3f out: rdn along 2f out: sn drvn and wknd (trainer's rep said gelding resented the visor on this occasion)* **3/1**[2]

0600 **10** 1 1/4 **Rock Warbler (IRE)**[126] 5723 6-8-7 46 oh1 .... PhilDennis 9 29
(Michael Mullineaux) *a in rr* **33/1**

2000 **11** 4 **Thornaby Nash**[23] 9006 8-9-7 60 ....(b) JasonHart 6 34
(Jason Ward) *in tch: rdn along over 2f out: wknd wl over 1f out* **25/1**

-006 **12** 2 **Hey Jazzy Lady (IRE)**[83] 7303 3-8-1 46 oh1 .... PaulaMuir(5) 5 16
(Andrew Crook) *in tch: rdn along 3f out: sn wknd* **66/1**

0030 **13** 7 **Margaret J**[7] 9279 3-8-6 46 oh1 ....(p) DuranFentiman 14
(Phil McEntee) *a towards rr: rdn along over 3f out: sn bhd* **33/1**

0000 **14** 1 1/4 **Mitchum**[41] 8638 10-8-7 46 oh1 .... CamHardie 3
(Ron Barr) *led: rdn along and hdd over 2f out: sn wknd* **200/1**

1m 40.5s (1.90) **Going Correction** +0.10s/f (Slow)
WFA 3 from 4yo+ 1lb **14** Ran SP% **137.2**
Speed ratings (Par 101): **94,91,88,86,86 84,84,84,83,82 78,76,69,67**
CSF £64.10 CT £184.20 TOTE £5.60: £2.20, £4.40, £1.40; EX 97.70 Trifecta £340.00.
Owner Ian Clements & Don Eddy **Bred** Patrick Cassidy **Trained** Ingoe, Northumberland

FOCUS
They were quite well strung out here, the winner finishing well on top. The form's rated around the runner-up.

9396 BOMBARDIER GOLDEN BEER H'CAP 7f 14y (Tp)
5:45 (5:50) (Class 6) (0-60,60) 3-Y-O+

£2,781 (£827; £413; £400; £400; £400) **Stalls** Centre

Form RPR

2153 **1** **Billy Wedge**[3] 9352 4-9-3 56 .... BarryMcHugh 12 66
(Tracy Waggott) *hld up in rr: smooth hdwy nr stands' rail 2f out: rdn to ld ent fnl f: kpt on strly* **1/1**[1]

2505 **2** 2 1/4 **Tarnhelm**[31] 8922 4-8-4 50 .... RhonaPindar(7) 3 54
(Wilf Storey) *hld up towards rr: hdwy on outer 3f out: chsd ldrs wl over 1f out: sn rdn: drvn and kpt on same pce fnl f* **22/1**

0010 **3** 3/4 **With Approval (IRE)**[21] 9039 7-8-10 52 ....(b) GemmaTutty(3) 7 55
(Karen Tutty) *led: rdn along 2f out: hdd ent fnl f: sn drvn and kpt on same pce* **14/1**[3]

2650 **4** shd **Strawberryandcream**[31] 8924 4-9-7 60 .... PJMcDonald 11 62
(James Bethell) *hld up towards rr: hdwy 3f out: chsd ldrs and rdn over 1f out: drvn and kpt on same pce fnl f* **25/1**

0036 **5** 1 1/2 **Bobby Joe Leg**[21] 9039 5-8-13 52 ....(v) JamesSullivan 6 51
(Ruth Carr) *trckd ldrs: rdn along and outpcd 2f out: kpt on u.p fnl f* **14/1**[3]

0005 **6** 1/2 **Avenue Of Stars**[9] 9253 6-9-5 58 .... BenCurtis 8 55
(Karen McLintock) *trckd ldrs towards stands' side: pushed along over 2f out: rdn wl over 1f out: sn drvn and wknd* **9/2**[2]

0004 **7** hd **Amood (IRE)**[17] 9111 8-8-9 48 ....(b) AndrewMullen 5 45
(Simon West) *dwlt and bhd: rdn along 3f out: kpt on fnl 2f (jockey said gelding missed the break)* **33/1**

2404 **8** 2 3/4 **Siena Mia**[17] 9113 4-9-7 60 .... PhilDennis 9 50
(Philip Kirby) *chsd ldrs towards stands' side: rdn along over 2f out: drvn wl over 1f out: grad wknd* **14/1**[3]

560 **9** 1 1/4 **Pinarella (FR)**[31] 8924 3-9-4 60 .... HarrisonShaw(3) 1 47
(Ben Haslam) *prom: rdn along 3f out: wknd over 2f out* **20/1**

5062 **10** nse **Lucky Violet (IRE)**[17] 9111 7-8-10 49 ....(h) BenRobinson 2 36
(Linda Perratt) *chsd ldrs: rdn along wl over 2f out: sn wknd* **20/1**

0342 **11** 1/2 **The Retriever (IRE)**[10] 9225 4-8-7 46 oh1 .... LukeMorris 14 31
(Micky Hammond) *chsd ldrs nr stands' rail: rdn along over 2f out: sn drvn and btn* **9/2**[2]

5503 **12** nse **Kodiac Lass (IRE)**[48] 8436 3-9-7 60 .... JasonHart 4 45
(Katie Scott) *a towards rr* **33/1**

0650 **13** nse **Darwina**[3] 9349 3-8-2 46 oh1 .... PaulaMuir(5) 13 31
(Alistair Whillans) *dwlt: a towards rr* **50/1**

5500 **14** 1 3/4 **Amelia R (IRE)**[31] 8925 3-9-0 53 .... TomEaves 10 34
(Ray Craggs) *racd towards stands' side: prom: rdn along wl over 2f out: sn wknd* **33/1**

1m 26.99s (0.79) **Going Correction** +0.10s/f (Slow) **14** Ran SP% **134.9**
Speed ratings (Par 101): **99,96,95,95,93 93,92,89,88,88 87,87,87,85**
CSF £38.04 CT £265.25 TOTE £2.20: £1.10, £4.60, £5.10; EX 38.70 Trifecta £562.90.
Owner David Tate **Bred** David Tate **Trained** Spennymoor, Co Durham

FOCUS
This proved straightforward enough for the short-priced favourite, who matched his career high.

9397 BETWAY H'CAP 6f (Tp)
6:15 (6:17) (Class 6) (0-65,67) 3-Y-O+

£2,781 (£827; £413; £400; £400; £400) **Stalls** Centre

Form RPR

1001 **1** **Etikaal**[31] 8923 5-9-6 64 .... SamJames 7 73+
(Grant Tuer) *hld up towards rr: hdwy 3f out: chsd ldrs and swtchd lft over 1f out: sn rdn to chal: kpt on wl to ld fnl 110yds* **2/1**[1]

4050 **2** 1 1/2 **Zebulon (IRE)**[34] 8839 5-9-3 61 .... JamesSullivan 8 66
(Ruth Carr) *trckd ldrs: hdwy 2f out: rdn over 1f out: ev ch ent fnl f: sn drvn: kpt on same pce fnl 100yds* **16/1**

6045 **3** 1/2 **Klopp**[17] 9113 3-9-4 62 ....(h) CamHardie 11 65+
(Antony Brittain) *trckd ldrs: smooth hdwy over 2f out: led wl over 1f out: sn rdn: hdd ins fnl f: kpt on same pce (jockey said filly hung right-handed throughout)* **8/1**

4000 **4** 1/2 **Lightning Charlie**[17] 9113 7-9-6 64 .... PaulMulrennan 12 66
(Iain Jardine) *hld up towards rr: hdwy 2f out: rdn over 1f out: kpt on fnl f* **10/1**

533- **5** 1 3/4 **I'll Be Brief**[355] 9612 3-9-5 63 .... CallumRodriguez 6 59
(Julie Camacho) *hld up: hdwy 3f out: rdn along and n.m.r wl over 1f out: kpt on fnl f* **12/1**

3416 **6** 3/4 **Global Humor (USA)**[10] 9223 4-8-11 62 .... CoreyMadden(7) 13 56
(Jim Goldie) *dwlt and towards rr: hdwy over 2f out: rdn to chse ldrs wl over 1f out: sn drvn and no imp* **4/1**[3]

5603 **7** 1 **Almurr (IRE)**[17] 9113 3-9-6 64 .... BenCurtis 1 55
(Phillip Makin) *trckd ldr: rdn along 3f out: wknd 2f out* **10/3**[2]

5050 **8** 8 **Maerchengarten**[10] 9225 3-8-7 51 oh6 .... JaneElliott 14 18
(Ed de Giles) *in tch towards stands' side: rdn along 3f out: sn drvn and wknd* **50/1**

0000 **9** 1/2 **Granny Roz**[31] 8924 5-9-0 58 .... PJMcDonald 10 24
(Ray Craggs) *chsd ldng pair: rdn along wl over 2f out: sn wknd* **20/1**

206 **10** 5 **Equidae**[69] 7776 4-9-6 64 ....(t) TomEaves 2 15
(Iain Jardine) *chsd ldrs: pushed along 3f out: rdn over 2f out: sn wknd* **14/1**

4210 **11** *nk* **Super Florence (IRE)**[73] 7651 4-8-13 **57**...................... BarryMcHugh 9 7
(Adrian Nicholls) *t.k.h: led: rdn along over 2f out: hdd wl over 1f out: sn wknd* **25/1**

1m 12.7s (0.20) **Going Correction** +0.10s/f (Slow) **11** Ran SP% **127.4**
Speed ratings (Par 101): **102,100,99,98,96 95,94,83,82,76 75**
CSF £41.51 CT £234.41 TOTE £3.10: £1.50, £4.60, £2.30; EX 42.20 Trifecta £259.30.
Owner Moment of Madness **Bred** Shadwell Estate Company Limited **Trained** Birkby, N Yorks

FOCUS
They went a good early gallop and it was an advantage to be held up.

9398 BETWAY LIVE CASINO CLASSIFIED STKS 5f (Tp)

6:45 (6:46) (Class 6) 3-Y-O+

£2,781 (£827; £413; £400; £400; £400) **Stalls** Centre

Form RPR

3452 **1** **Rockley Point**[35] 8821 6-9-0 49...(b) JasonHart 1 55
(Katie Scott) *mde virtually all: rdn clr over 1f out: kpt on strly* **9/4**[1]

6064 **2** *3/4* **Lord Of The Glen**[38] 8720 4-8-7 46.........................(v) CoreyMadden(7) 2 52
(Jim Goldie) *hld up towards rr: hdwy over 2f out: rdn over 1f out: kpt on wl fnl f* **13/2**[3]

3420 **3** *2 1/4* **Red Allure**[38] 8720 4-9-0 47.. TomEaves 12 44
(Michael Mullineaux) *cl up: rdn along 2f out: drvn over 1f out: kpt on u.p fnl f* **13/2**[3]

0506 **4** *hd* **Kibaar**[31] 8925 7-9-0 47.. JamesSullivan 3 43
(Ruth Carr) *rrd and awkward s: sn chsng ldrs: hdwy to chse wnr 1/2-way: rdn along over 1f out: drvn ent fnl f: grad wknd (jockey said gelding reared in the stalls)* **16/1**

6005 **5** *1/2* **Le Manege Enchante (IRE)**[32] 8898 6-9-0 46........(v) LewisEdmunds 9 42
(Derek Shaw) *towards rr: hdwy 1/2-way: rdn along to chse ldrs whn sltly hmpd over 1f out: kpt on fnl f* **10/1**

-304 **6** *hd* **Poppy In The Wind**[318] 411 7-9-0 50............................(v) LukeMorris 6 41
(Alan Brown) *hld up: hdwy in centre 2f out: nt clr run and swtchd rt over 1f out: sn rdn: kpt on same pce fnl f* **12/1**

0040 **7** *nse* **Someone Exciting**[17] 9111 6-8-11 47......................... HarrisonShaw(3) 5 41
(David Thompson) *towards rr: hdwy over 2f out: rdn wl over 1f out: kpt on fnl f* **14/1**

0066 **8** *1* **Mightaswellsmile**[38] 8720 5-9-0 44...................................... CamHardie 8 37
(Ron Barr) *chsd ldrs: rdn along 2f out: hld whn hmpd over 1f out (jockey said mare suffered interference approaching the final furlong)* **25/1**

0502 **9** *nk* **Star Cracker (IRE)**[38] 8720 7-9-0 46...........................(p) PhilDennis 4 36
(Jim Goldie) *chsd ldrs: rdn along over 2f out: sn wknd* **10/1**

3054 **10** *hd* **Extrasolar**[31] 8925 9-9-0 48...(t) SamJames 14 35
(Geoffrey Harker) *chsd ldrs: rdn along 2f out: hld whn hmpd over 1f out* **6/1**[2]

4006 **11** *nk* **Valley Belle (IRE)**[14] 9161 3-9-0 50..................................(v) BenCurtis 7 34
(Phil McEntee) *chsd ldrs: rdn along over 2f out: sn wknd* **10/1**

5000 **12** *1 1/4* **Little Miss Muffin**[12] 9185 3-9-0 50................................(p[1]) JaneElliott 10 30
(Sam England) *a towards rr* **40/1**

0000 **13** *3/4* **Encoded (IRE)**[38] 8720 6-8-9 45.................................. PaulaMuir(5) 13 27
(Lynn Siddall) *dwlt: a in rr (trainer said mare had not travelled well on the surface on this occasion, and morning after race was found to be very stiff)* **25/1**

400 **14** *1 1/2* **Sweet Forgetme Not (IRE)**[14] 9161 3-8-7 48.....(v) GraceMcEntee(7) 11 22
(Phil McEntee) *dwlt: a in rr* **12/1**

59.59s (0.09) **Going Correction** +0.10s/f (Slow) **14** Ran SP% **137.1**
Speed ratings (Par 101): **103,101,98,97,97 96,96,95,94,94 93,91,90,88**
CSF £18.74 TOTE £3.00: £1.50, £2.80, £2.80; EX 21.00 Trifecta £127.90.
Owner The Vintage Flyers **Bred** Newsells Park Stud **Trained** Galasheils, Scottish Borders

FOCUS
A pretty weak classified race.
T/Jkpt: £14,750.10 to a £1 stake. Pool: £36,875.26 - 2.5 winning units T/Plt: £20.80 to a £1 stake. Pool: £95,161.41 - 3,328.31 winning units T/Qpdt: £4.20 to a £1 stake. Pool: £14,047.31 - 2,446.14 winning units **Joe Rowntree**

9361 WOLVERHAMPTON (A.W) (L-H)

Tuesday, December 10

OFFICIAL GOING: Tapeta: standard
Wind: Strong behind Weather: Raining

9399 LADBROKES FOOTBALL ACCA BOOSTY NURSERY H'CAP 1m 1f 104y (Tp)

3:45 (3:45) (Class 6) (0-60,62) 2-Y-O

£2,781 (£827; £413; £400; £400; £400) **Stalls** Low

Form RPR

0133 **1** **Goddess Of Fire**[10] 9250 2-9-2 **55**..........................(p) AdrianMcCarthy 7 60+
(John Ryan) *hld up: hdwy on outer over 2f out: led over 1f out: pushed out* **7/2**[2]

0015 **2** *1 3/4* **Ami Li Bert (IRE)**[13] 9179 2-9-0 **53**.. BenCurtis 9 53
(Michael Appleby) *chsd ldr over 8f out: led 3f out: rdn and hdd over 1f out: sn edgd lft: styd on same pce ins fnl f (jockey said colt hung left-handed in the home straight)* **13/2**

0362 **3** *hd* **Halfacrown (IRE)**[21] 9045 2-8-9 **48**....................................... ShaneFoley 4 48
(Jamie Osborne) *hld up in tch: rdn over 1f out: styd on* **8/1**

6600 **4** *1 1/2* **Master Rocco (IRE)**[15] 9154 2-9-2 **60**............................ RayDawson(5) 1 57
(Jane Chapple-Hyam) *pushed along to chse ldrs: shkn up over 1f out: styd on same pce ins fnl f* **12/1**

0245 **5** *nse* **Camacho Man (IRE)**[14] 9164 2-9-2 **55**....................... RichardKingscote 2 52
(Jennie Candlish) *trckd ldrs: nt clr run over 2f out: shkn up over 1f out: styd on same pce ins fnl f* **11/2**[3]

000 **6** *1/2* **Arabescato**[15] 9155 2-8-10 **56**...................................... AngusVilliers(7) 8 52
(Nick Littmoden) *swtchd lft after s and sn pushed along in rr: rdn over 2f out: hung lft and styd on ins fnl f: nt trble ldrs* **10/1**

4060 **7** *hd* **Boy George**[21] 9045 2-8-12 **51**... LukeMorris 5 46
(Dominic Ffrench Davis) *trckd ldrs: racd keenly: rdn and ev ch over 1f out: no ex ins fnl f* **16/1**

6006 **8** *7* **Cappella Fella (IRE)**[24] 9009 2-8-9 **48**............................. DavidProbert 3 30
(Sarah Hollinshead) *hld up: nt clr run over 2f out: sme hdwy over 1f out: rdn: edgd rt and wknd fnl f* **20/1**

0500 **9** *3 1/2* **Brown Eyes Blue (IRE)**[13] 9172 2-9-2 **55**..................(p[1]) LiamKeniry 10 30
(J S Moore) *hld up: pushed along 5f out: a in rr: wknd over 2f out* **50/1**

4065 **10** *nk* **Prairie Moppins (USA)**[17] 9127 2-8-10 **52**............... ThomasGreatrex(3) 11 27
(Sylvester Kirk) *s.i.s: hld up: shkn up on outer over 2f out: sn wknd* **33/1**

2023 **11** *12* **Never Said Nothing (IRE)**[13] 9179 2-9-9 **62**........(p) AlistairRawlinson 6 14
(Jonathan Portman) *led: plld hrd: hdd 3f out: wknd over 1f out (jockey said gelding ran too freely)* **3/1**[1]

2m 1.45s (0.65) **Going Correction** -0.10s/f (Stan) **11** Ran SP% **119.4**
Speed ratings (Par 94): **93,91,91,89,89 89,89,83,79,79 69**
CSF £26.59 CT £173.47 TOTE £4.30: £1.40, £2.50, £2.70; EX 25.60 Trifecta £144.20.
Owner M M Foulger **Bred** Miss G Abbey **Trained** Newmarket, Suffolk

FOCUS
A moderate handicap, but the winner did it well and looks ahead of her mark.

9400 LADBROKES WHERE THE NATION PLAYS FILLIES' NOVICE STKS 1m 142y (Tp)

4:15 (4:17) (Class 5) 3-Y-O+

£3,428 (£1,020; £509; £254) **Stalls** Low

Form RPR

224 **1** **Millicent Fawcett**[35] 8842 3-9-0 78.................................... RobertHavlin 3 80+
(John Gosden) *chsd ldrs: shkn up to ld over 1f out: pushed clr and edgd lft fnl f* **9/4**[2]

6462 **2** *7* **Love Explodes**[71] 7772 3-9-0 67............................... RichardKingscote 4 64
(Ed Vaughan) *chsd ldrs: shkn up to chse wnr over 1f out: sn edgd rt and outpcd* **15/8**[1]

42 **3** *2 1/4* **Regal Lilly (IRE)**[182] 3680 3-9-0 0.................................. TomMarquand 9 59+
(David Simcock) *s.i.s: pushed along early in rr: rdn and edgd lft over 1f out: styd on to go 3rd post: nvr nrr* **9/2**[3]

4 **4** *nk* **Bustaan (USA)**[22] 9038 3-9-0 0................................... KieranShoemark 2 59
(Owen Burrows) *led: shkn up over 2f out: hdd over 1f out: wknd ins fnl f* **5/1**

0000 **5** *nse* **Another Approach (FR)**[77] 7550 3-9-0 41.............................. LukeMorris 7 58
(David Loughnane) *chsd ldr over 7f out: rdn and ev ch over 1f out: wknd ins fnl f* **66/1**

3 **6** *1/2* **War Princess (IRE)**[169] 4189 3-9-0 0.................................. DavidProbert 6 57+
(Alan King) *pushed along early in rr: nt clr run over 2f out: styd on ins fnl f: nvr nrr (jockey said filly was denied a clear run approaching the home straight)* **15/2**

7 *12* **Droichead Atha (IRE)**[32] 8927 4-9-2 0............................... ShaneFoley 5 32
(Donal Kinsella, Ire) *hld up: rdn over 2f out: sn wknd* **200/1**

8 *1 1/4* **Rgeebee** 3-9-0 0... ShaneGray 1 29
(David O'Meara) *pushed along early towards rr: sme hdwy over 3f out: wknd over 2f out* **50/1**

1m 47.6s (-2.50) **Going Correction** -0.10s/f (Stan)
WFA 3 from 4yo 2lb **8** Ran SP% **116.1**
Speed ratings (Par 100): **107,100,98,98,98 98,87,86**
CSF £7.03 TOTE £2.50: £1.20, £1.10, £1.60; EX 7.10 Trifecta £23.30.
Owner Ms Rachel D S Hood **Bred** Rachel D S Hood **Trained** Newmarket, Suffolk

FOCUS
This was run at a good gallop and they finished well strung out.

9401 LADBROKES, HOME OF THE ODDS BOOST NURSERY H'CAP 6f 20y (Tp)

4:45 (4:48) (Class 5) (0-75,77) 2-Y-O

£3,428 (£1,020; £509; £400; £400; £400) **Stalls** Low

Form RPR

0222 **1** **Colouring**[12] 9205 2-9-6 **74**.. LukeMorris 8 76
(Ed Walker) *chsd ldrs: lost pl 5f out: hdwy over 3f out: rdn over 1f out: edgd lft and r.o to ld wl ins fnl f* **5/1**[3]

0115 **2** *shd* **Taste The Nectar (USA)**[13] 9175 2-9-0 **75**............(p) AngusVilliers(7) 10 76
(Robert Cowell) *prom: sn pushed along and lost pl: rdn over 1f out: hung lft and r.o ins fnl f: jst failed* **7/1**

0543 **3** *3/4* **Triple Spear**[17] 9137 2-8-11 **68**.................................. TheodoreLadd(3) 11 67
(Michael Appleby) *sn led: hdd over 3f out: rdn to ld over 1f out: hdd wl ins fnl f* **3/1**[1]

3402 **4** *nse* **Havana Dawn**[22] 9031 2-9-0 **68**..(p) BenCurtis 2 67
(Phillip Makin) *s.s: bhd: rdn over 4f out: hung lft and r.o ins fnl f: nt rch ldrs (jockey said filly reared as the stalls opened and as a result missed the break)* **4/1**[2]

5211 **5** *3* **Requiems Dream (IRE)**[146] 5037 2-9-9 **77**.................... FrannyNorton 5 67
(Mark Johnston) *prom: rdn over 2f out: no ex ins fnl f* **25/1**

060 **6** *hd* **Rapidash**[88] 7160 2-8-8 **67**.................................... ThoreHammerHansen(5) 6 56
(Richard Hannon) *hld up: pushed along over 3f out: nt trble ldrs* **11/1**

1003 **7** *hd* **Heer We Go Again**[12] 9205 2-9-3 **71**................................ JoeyHaynes 4 60
(David Evans) *chsd ldrs: led over 3f out: rdn and hdd over 1f out: no ex ins fnl f* **8/1**

1510 **8** *1* **War Of Clans (IRE)**[41] 8650 2-8-9 **66**...................... HarrisonShaw(3) 1 52
(K R Burke) *chsd ldrs: rdn over 2f out: carried lft and no ex ins fnl f* **16/1**

406 **9** *2 1/4* **Dorchester Dom (IRE)**[140] 5280 2-9-1 **69**......................... LiamKeniry 7 48
(Nigel Twiston-Davies) *hld up: pushed along 1/2-way: rdn and hung lft over 1f out: nt trble ldrs* **33/1**

3010 **10** *32* **Mitty's Smile (IRE)**[6] 9300 2-9-6 **74**........................(b) AdamMcNamara 9
(Archie Watson) *chsd ldrs: rdn and lost pl over 3f out: wknd over 2f out (jockey said filly was never travelling and stopped quickly)* **16/1**

1m 14.61s (0.11) **Going Correction** -0.10s/f (Stan) **10** Ran SP% **112.2**
Speed ratings (Par 96): **95,94,93,93,89 89,89,87,84,42**
CSF £38.25 CT £114.57 TOTE £4.80: £1.60, £2.10, £1.70; EX 43.30 Trifecta £163.00.
Owner Mainline Racing **Bred** Whitsbury Manor Stud **Trained** Upper Lambourn, Berks

FOCUS
They went a good gallop here and that suited those ridden with patience.

9402 BETWAY H'CAP 6f 20y (Tp)

5:15 (5:19) (Class 5) (0-75,77) 3-Y-O+

£3,428 (£1,020; £509; £400; £400; £400) **Stalls** Low

Form RPR

-022 **1** **Aloysius Lilius (IRE)**[10] 9245 3-9-0 **68**........................(p) ShaneFoley 10 78
(Gerard O'Leary, Ire) *trckd ldrs: racd keenly: chsd ldr and nt clr run over 1f out: shkn up to ld ins fnl f: rdn out* **13/2**[2]

2142 **2** *1 1/4* **Bahuta Acha**[3] 9365 4-8-13 **67**.. LukeMorris 9 73
(David Loughnane) *s.i.s: hld up: pushed along and hdwy over 1f out: rdn to chse wnr wl ins fnl f: r.o* **6/4**[1]

0304 **3** *nk* **Big Lachie**[35] 8826 5-9-3 **71**.. WilliamCarson 3 76+
(Mark Loughnane) *hld up: plld hrd: nt clr run over 1f out: edgd lft and r.o ins fnl f: wnt 3rd post: nt rch ldrs (jockey said gelding ran too freely)* **12/1**

3213 **4** *hd* **Lucky Lodge**[18] 9106 9-9-3 **71**...............................(v) CamHardie 1 75
(Antony Brittain) *prom: rdn over 2f out: nt clr run over 1f out: styd on (jockey said gelding was denied a clear run approximately 1f out)* **8/1**[3]

5322 **5** *1/2* **Steelriver (IRE)**[10] 9257 9-9-2 **77**.............................. AngusVilliers(7) 11 80
(Michael Herrington) *hld up: hdwy and nt clr run over 1f out: r.o: nt rch ldrs* **9/1**

0003 **6** *2 1/4* **Diamonique**[49] 8419 3-9-1 **69** CallumRodriguez 8 65
(Keith Dalgleish) *chsd ldr: rdn over 2f out: lost 2nd over 1f out: wknd wl ins fnl f* **10/1**

12P5 **7** *hd* **Look Surprised**[17] 9135 6-9-2 **70** TomMarquand 2 65
(Roger Teal) *hld up: hdwy over 2f out: nt clr run over 1f out: styd on same pce ins fnl f* **22/1**

6060 **8** *shd* **Beryl The Petal (IRE)**[52] 8342 3-9-5 **76** (v) HarrisonShaw(3) 7 71
(David O'Meara) *hld up in tch: lost pl over 3f out: effrt and nt clr run over 1f out: n.d after* **28/1**

0006 **9** *1/2* **Sword Exceed (GER)**[108] 6440 5-9-7 **75** KieranO'Neill 6 68
(Ivan Furtado) *led: rdn and edgd lft over 1f out: hdd ins fnl f: wknd towards fin* **16/1**

1440 **10** *1 1/4* **Knockabout Queen**[11] 9218 3-8-9 **63** DavidProbert 4 52
(Tony Carroll) *s.i.s: hld up: hdwy over 1f out: wknd ins fnl f* **33/1**

0-56 **11** *2* **Revolutionary Man (IRE)**[63] 8006 4-9-4 **72** (t) RichardKingscote 5 55
(Mark Loughnane) *s.i.s: shkn up over 1f out: nvr on terms* **20/1**

1030 **12** *hd* **Tan**[11] 9219 5-8-0 **61** ElishaWhittington(7) 13 43
(Lisa Williamson) *chsd ldrs: rdn over 2f out: wknd fnl f* **100/1**

13 *2 1/2* **Clashaniska (IRE)**[102] 5836 3-9-1 **69** FrannyNorton 12 43
(Tony Carroll) *hld up: racd wd: effrt on outer over 2f out: wknd wl over 1f out* **18/1**

1m 13.66s (-0.84) **Going Correction** -0.10s/f (Stan) **13** Ran SP% **118.9**
Speed ratings (Par 103): **101,99,98,98,98 95,94,94,93,92 89,89,86**
CSF £15.47 CT £122.77 TOTE £7.20: £2.50, £1.20, £2.50; EX 19.30 Trifecta £174.00.
Owner Lance Bloodstock Limited **Bred** Maurice Burns **Trained** Kildare, Co. Kildare

FOCUS
They went a steady early gallop in this fair sprint handicap.

9403 BOMBARDIER GOLDEN BEER (S) H'CAP 1m 142y (Tp)
5:45 (5:49) (Class 6) (0-55,57) 3-6-Y-0
£2,781 (£827; £413; £400; £400; £400) **Stalls** Low

Form RPR

6010 **1** **Born To Reason (IRE)**[3] 9362 5-9-7 **55** (b) DanielMuscutt 4 62
(Alexandra Dunn) *a.p: chsd ldr over 2f out: hmpd and led over 1f out: sn rdn: all out* **10/1**

0406 **2** *nse* **Lawyersgunsn'money**[97] 6855 4-9-5 **53** (p) TomMarquand 8 60+
(Roger Teal) *hld up: hdwy and hung lft over 1f out: rdn to chse wnr wl ins fnl f: r.o* **6/1**

5602 **3** *3* **Disruptor (FR)**[6] 9298 3-9-3 **53** (v) BenCurtis 5 53
(David Evans) *led over 7f out: rdn: hung rt and hdd over 1f out: no ex wl ins fnl f* **3/1**[2]

0055 **4** *2 1/2* **Lady Carduros (IRE)**[11] 9220 5-8-5 **46** oh1 AngusVilliers(7) 3 41
(Michael Appleby) *prom: sn pushed along and lost pl: hdwy u.p over 1f out: styd on to go 4th nr fin* **25/1**

0/ **5** *1/2* **Feisty Katerina (IRE)**[7] 9291 4-8-10 **47** (t) SeanDavis(3) 2 41
(Gerard O'Leary, Ire) *sn led: hdd over 7f out: chsd ldrs: rdn over 1f out: wknd wl ins fnl f (jockey said filly hung right-handed in the home straight)* **22/1**

4 **6** *hd* **Newgirlintown (IRE)**[10] 9248 3-8-13 **49** (p) ShaneFoley 7 43
(Gerard O'Leary, Ire) *hld up: pushed along and hdwy over 3f out: rdn over 1f out: edgd lft and styd on same pce* **9/2**[3]

4005 **7** *3/4* **Is It Off (IRE)**[34] 8863 4-9-7 **55** (bt[1]) JoeyHaynes 1 47
(Sean Curran) *trckd ldrs: racd keenly: hung lft and rdn over 2f out: wknd ins fnl f (jockey said gelding hung left-handed throughout)* **10/1**

2654 **8** *nk* **Vipin (FR)**[6] 9305 4-9-2 **57** Pierre-LouisJamin(7) 13 48
(William Muir) *hdwy to go prom 7f out: shkn up on outer over 2f out: edgd lft and wknd fnl f* **11/4**[1]

0060 **9** *1 1/2* **Maryellen**[24] 8998 3-9-3 **53** (p) LukeMorris 12 41
(Alan Bailey) *hld up: nvr on terms* **50/1**

0006 **10** *1 3/4* **Ramblow**[32] 8915 6-8-5 **46** oh1 (vt) KeelanBaker(7) 6 30
(Alexandra Dunn) *s.i.s: plld hrd and sn hld up in tch: lost pl whn nt clr run over 3f out: wknd wl over 1f out* **80/1**

0500 **11** *2 3/4* **Conqueress (IRE)**[117] 6131 5-8-12 **46** oh1 (p) DavidProbert 10 24
(Simon Pearce) *sn prom: chsd ldr over 4f out tl rdn over 2f out: wknd over 1f out* **66/1**

005 **12** *1* **Big Bang**[19] 9091 6-9-0 **48** (h) ShelleyBirkett 11 24
(Julia Feilden) *s.i.s: hld up: a in rr* **66/1**

030- **13** *30* **Go Annie Go**[364] 9489 3-9-2 **52** LiamKeniry 9
(Mandy Rowland) *chsd ldr over 7f out tl rdn over 4f out: wkng whn n.m.r over 3f out (jockey said filly stopped quickly)* **100/1**

1m 48.65s (-1.45) **Going Correction** -0.10s/f (Stan)
WFA 3 from 4yo+ 2lb **13** Ran SP% **117.7**
Speed ratings: **102,101,99,97,96 96,95,95,94,92 90,89,62**
CSF £65.33 CT £227.57 TOTE £9.90: £3.00, £2.50, £1.40; EX 79.30 Trifecta £367.50.There was no bid for the winner
Owner West Buckland Bloodstock Ltd **Bred** Christopher Glynn **Trained** West Buckland, Somerset

FOCUS
A fairly competitive heat, albeit low grade, and there was a tight finish.

9404 BOMBARDIER "MARCH TO YOUR OWN DRUM" H'CAP 7f 36y (Tp)
6:15 (6:18) (Class 4) (0-85,89) 3-Y-0+
£5,207 (£1,549; £774; £400; £400; £400) **Stalls** High

Form RPR

36-0 **1** **Fastar (IRE)**[52] 8355 5-8-13 **76** ShaneFoley 4 85
(Gerard O'Leary, Ire) *hld up: hdwy over 1f out: rdn and r.o to ld wl ins fnl f* **10/1**

2440 **2** *1/2* **Fuente**[70] 7781 3-9-0 **77** CallumRodriguez 9 85
(Keith Dalgleish) *sn prom: chsd ldr over 4f out: led over 2f out: rdn and hdd wl ins fnl f* **12/1**

4211 **3** *shd* **Mohareb**[12] 9203 3-9-7 **84** AlistairRawlinson 7 91
(Michael Appleby) *hld up in tch: plld hrd: rdn and edgd lft ins fnl f: r.o* **3/1**[1]

0621 **4** *2 1/4* **Boy In The Bar**[33] 8893 8-9-7 **84** (v) DavidProbert 8 85
(Ian Williams) *chsd ldr over 2f: remained handy: rdn over 1f out: styd on same pce ins fnl f* **12/1**

2641 **5** *3 1/4* **Loving Glance**[14] 9165 3-9-2 **79** TomMarquand 3 72
(Martyn Meade) *chsd ldrs: rdn over 1f out: wknd ins fnl f* **5/1**[2]

1563 **6** *nk* **Tukhoom (IRE)**[7] 9283 6-8-12 **82** (v) AngusVilliers(7) 2 74
(David O'Meara) *s.s: bhd: rdn and hung lft over 1f out: nt trble ldrs (jockey said gelding anticipated the start and was very slowly away)* **6/1**[3]

5-13 **7** *nk* **Kodiac Pride**[172] 4065 3-9-5 **82** LukeMorris 6 73
(Sir Mark Prescott Bt) *hld up: plld hrd: hung rt fr 1/2-way: nt clr run over 2f out: nvr on terms* **25/1**

000 **8** *1 1/4* **Reflektor (IRE)**[53] 8317 6-9-5 **82** RichardKingscote 1 70
(Tom Dascombe) *led over 4f: wknd fnl f* **14/1**

2001 **9** *nk* **Typhoon Ten (IRE)**[6] 9308 3-9-5 **89** 6ex LukeCatton(7) 5 76
(Richard Hannon) *hld up: plld hrd: rdn and hung rt over 1f out: nvr on terms (jockey said gelding ran too freely)* **3/1**[1]

1m 27.45s (-1.35) **Going Correction** -0.10s/f (Stan) **9** Ran SP% **115.9**
Speed ratings (Par 105): **103,102,102,99,96 95,95,93,93**
CSF £122.18 CT £452.65 TOTE £8.10: £2.50, £4.00, £1.40; EX 115.30 Trifecta £490.20.
Owner Lance Bloodstock Limited **Bred** Ringfort Stud **Trained** Kildare, Co. Kildare

FOCUS
Not a bad handicap, and there are positives to be taken from the performances of each of the first three home. The runner-up is the key to the form.

9405 BETWAY APPRENTICE H'CAP 2m 120y (Tp)
6:45 (6:46) (Class 5) (0-75,77) 3-Y-0+
£3,428 (£1,020; £509; £400; £400; £400) **Stalls** Low

Form RPR

0021 **1** **Noble Behest**[19] 9087 5-9-6 **69** (p) AngusVilliers(5) 9 79
(Ian Williams) *led at stdy pce tl hdd over 4f out: chsd ldr: rdn over 1f out: styd on to ld wl ins fnl f* **9/4**[1]

1002 **2** *hd* **Battle Of Marathon (USA)**[7] 9288 7-9-12 **77** GraceMcEntee(7) 6 86
(John Ryan) *s.i.s: hld up: hdwy and hung rt fr over 5f out: led over 4f out: rdn and hdd wl ins fnl f: styd on (jockey said gelding hung badly right-handed)* **4/1**[3]

66-4 **3** *8* **In Demand (IRE)**[182] 3686 4-9-7 **65** ThomasGreatrex 8 67
(Roger Charlton) *s.i.s: hld up: styd on to go 3rd wl ins fnl f: nt trble ldrs* **7/2**[2]

0030 **4** *3/4* **Doctor Jazz (IRE)**[11] 9221 4-8-11 **55** (vt[1]) TheodoreLadd 1 54
(Michael Appleby) *s.i.s: hld up: racd keenly: hmpd 15f out: lost pl 4f out: hdwy over 1f out: sn rdn: hung rt and wknd ins fnl f* **66/1**

5404 **5** *1/2* **Persian Sun**[20] 9066 4-9-9 **72** (p[1]) MarkCrehan(5) 7 70
(Stuart Williams) *chsd ldr over 3f: remained handy: rdn over 2f out: hung rt and wknd ins fnl f* **8/1**

130/ **6** *2 1/2* **Solstalla**[17] 7173 7-9-4 **65** SeamusCronin(3) 4 60
(David Weston) *broke wl: sn stdd and lost pl: hld up: hdwy on outer over 2f out: sn rdn: wknd over 1f out* **66/1**

1103 **7** *3/4* **Rubenesque (IRE)**[50] 8399 7-10-0 **77** (t) TobyEley(5) 2 71
(Tristan Davidson) *s.s: hld up: hmpd 15f out: hdwy over 3f out: rdn: hung lft and wknd over 1f out (jockey said mare was slowly away)* **12/1**

310- **8** *2 1/2* **Wemyss Point**[241] 3679 7-9-7 **72** (p w) NickBarratt-Atkin(7) 5 63
(Philip Kirby) *chsd ldrs: rdn over 3f out: wknd over 1f out* **20/1**

-111 **9** *10* **Grey Mist**[214] 2591 5-9-12 **70** (h) SeanDavis 3 49
(Karen McLintock) *prom: chsd ldr 13f out tl over 4f out: rdn over 3f out: wknd over 1f out (Integrity Department of the British Horseracing Authority inquired into running and riding with trainer and jockey interviewed over the phone; their explanations were noted and the information forwarded to the Head Office of the British Horseracing Auth* **11/2**

3m 44.16s (4.86) **Going Correction** -0.10s/f (Stan) **9** Ran SP% **114.9**
Speed ratings (Par 103): **84,83,80,79,79 78,78,76,72**
CSF £11.16 CT £29.44 TOTE £3.00: £1.40, £1.80, £1.70; EX 9.90 Trifecta £38.80.
Owner A C Elliott **Bred** Mr & Mrs A E Pakenham **Trained** Portway, Worcs

■ Stewards' Enquiry : Angus Villiers two-day ban: using the whip above the permitted level from 1 1/4f out (Dec 29-30)

FOCUS
The pace was a steady one most of the way before the runner-up picked things up down the back straight the final time. He and the winner had a good battle from the turn in.

9406 BETWAY HEED YOUR HUNCH H'CAP 5f 21y (Tp)
7:15 (7:20) (Class 6) (0-60,60) 3-Y-0+
£2,781 (£827; £413; £400; £400; £400) **Stalls** Low

Form RPR

5000 **1** **Mutabaahy (IRE)**[4] 9352 4-8-11 **57** AngusVilliers(7) 7 66
(Antony Brittain) *trckd ldrs: plld hrd: rdn to ld wl ins fnl f: r.o (trainer's rep said gelding had benefited from the return to Wolverhampton where the gelding had performed well previously)* **3/1**[2]

2501 **2** *3/4* **Sir Hector (IRE)**[8] 9272 4-9-1 **54** WilliamCarson 1 60
(Charlie Wallis) *pushed along early in rr: swtchd rt and hdwy over 1f out: rdn and ev ch wl ins fnl f: unable qck towards fin* **9/4**[1]

2062 **3** *2* **Blackcurrent**[33] 8898 3-8-13 **52** LukeMorris 10 51
(Alan Brown) *led: rdn over 1f out: hung lft and hdd wl ins fnl f: styd on same pce* **20/1**

0U62 **4** *1 1/2* **Englishman**[14] 9169 9-8-13 **52** (b) PhilipPrince 4 46
(Milton Bradley) *prom: rdn over 1f out: styd on same pce fnl f* **14/1**

035 **5** *3/4* **At Your Service**[32] 8917 5-9-3 **56** JoeyHaynes 6 47
(Chelsea Banham) *s.i.s: hld up: r.o ins fnl f: nt trble ldrs* **9/1**

6006 **6** *shd* **Angel Force (IRE)**[10] 9247 4-8-12 **54** (p) TheodoreLadd(3) 5 45
(David C Griffiths) *prom: chsd ldr over 3f out: rdn over 1f out: lost 2nd ins fnl f: wknd towards fin* **33/1**

6312 **7** *1/2* **Qaaraat**[17] 9135 4-9-5 **58** (p) CamHardie 9 47
(Antony Brittain) *hld up: hmpd over 1f out: r.o ins fnl f: nt trble ldrs* **7/1**[3]

2560 **8** *2 1/2* **It Must Be Faith**[5] 9335 9-9-6 **59** (p) JaneElliott 11 39
(Michael Appleby) *dwlt: a in rr* **18/1**

0055 **9** *hd* **Red Stripes (USA)**[7] 9286 7-9-2 **60** (b) SeamusCronin(5) 8 39
(Lisa Williamson) *chsd ldrs: rdn 1/2-way: wknd ins fnl f* **7/1**[3]

0000 **10** *3/4* **Superseded (IRE)**[19] 9092 3-9-1 **59** (p) DylanHogan(5) 3 35
(John Butler) *pushed along to chse ldrs: rdn over 1f out: wknd ins fnl f* **33/1**

1m 0.23s (-1.67) **Going Correction** -0.10s/f (Stan) **10** Ran SP% **113.3**
Speed ratings (Par 101): **109,107,104,102,101 100,100,96,95,94**
CSF £9.56 CT £109.37 TOTE £3.90: £1.40, £1.20, £5.60; EX 9.70 Trifecta £170.70.
Owner Antony Brittain **Bred** Shadwell Estate Company Limited **Trained** Warthill, N Yorks

■ Stewards' Enquiry : William Carson three-day ban: careless riding (Dec 26-28)

FOCUS
A bit of a gamble was landed in this moderate sprint handicap.

T/Jkpt: Not won. T/Plt: £37.50 to a £1 stake. Pool: £104,945.33 - 2,040.79 winning units T/Qpdt: £11.20 to a £1 stake. Pool: £13,237.41 - 871.44 winning units **Colin Roberts**

[9195]CHELMSFORD (A.W) (L-H)

Wednesday, December 11

OFFICIAL GOING: Polytrack: standard

Weather: Partly cloudy

9407 BET TOTEPLACEPOT AT TOTESPORT.COM NURSERY H'CAP 6f (P)

3:25 (3:29) (Class 6) (0-60,62) 2-Y-O

£3,816 (£1,135; £567; £400; £400; £400) **Stalls** Centre

Form				RPR
2465 **1**		**Rebel Redemption**[7] 9307 2-9-5 **58**.....................(v[1]) JasonHart 5	65
(John Quinn) *a.p: chsd ldr 4f out: rdn to ld wl ins fnl f: r.o* **9/4**[1]

000 **2** ¾ **Jungle Capers (IRE)**[50] 8418 2-8-6 **45**..................... KieranO'Neill 1 — 50
(Mick Channon) *wnt lft s: sn chsng ldrs: rdn to ld over 1f out: edgd rt and hdd wl ins fnl f* **6/1**[3]

0010 **3** 2 ¾ **Sir Rodneyredblood**[21] 9061 2-9-4 **57**..................... LewisEdmunds 2 — 54
(J R Jenkins) *led: rdn and hdd over 1f out: no ex ins fnl f* **11/4**[2]

400 **4** 1 **Urtzi (IRE)**[34] 8891 2-9-8 **61**..................... WilliamCarson 3 — 55
(Michael Attwater) *hld up in tch: racd keenly: rdn and flashed tail ins fnl f: styd on same pce* **11/1**

0500 **5** nk **Sweet Serenade**[13] 9196 2-9-9 **62**..................... PaulMulrennan 8 — 56
(James Tate) *prom: shkn up and nt clr run over 1f out: styd on same pce ins fnl f* **6/1**[3]

600 **6** 1 ½ **Kelinda Dice**[13] 9195 2-9-2 **55**..................... FrannyNorton 4 — 43
(Mick Quinn) *s.i.s and hmpd s: hld up: swtchd lft over 1f out: styd on ins fnl f: nt trble ldrs (jockey said filly suffered interference when leaving the stalls)* **14/1**

000 **7** 2 ¼ **May Happen**[11] 9242 2-8-6 **45**..................... JamesSullivan 10 — 27
(Jamie Osborne) *hld up: rdn over 2f out: nt trble ldrs* **40/1**

3540 **8** 2 **Lady Phyllis**[49] 8452 2-8-12 **56**..................... SeamusCronin(5) 13 — 32
(Michael Attwater) *hld up: pushed along 1/2-way: nvr on terms* **22/1**

4020 **9** 1 ¾ **Red Maharani**[14] 9179 2-9-2 **55**..................... BarryMcHugh 9 — 25
(James Given) *hld up in tch: rdn over 2f out: wknd over 1f out* **20/1**

060 **10** 3 ¼ **Celtic Mist (IRE)**[11] 9242 2-9-5 **58**..................... JosephineGordon 14 — 19
(Shaun Keightley) *hld up: pushed along 1/2-way: a in rr* **25/1**

0000 **11** 1 **Hot Hot Hot**[54] 8315 2-8-6 **45**..................... CamHardie 6
(Tony Carroll) *chsd ldr 2f: remained handy: rdn over 2f out: wknd over 1f out* **33/1**

1m 13.44s (-0.26) **Going Correction** +0.025s/f (Slow) **11** Ran SP% **119.3**

Speed ratings (Par 94): **102,101,97,96,95 93,90,87,85,81 79**

CSF £15.23 CT £39.41 TOTE £3.00: £1.40, £2.60, £1.40; EX 18.20.

Owner The Jam Partnership **Bred** Matthew Eves **Trained** Settrington, N Yorks

FOCUS

A moderate nursery that looks solid form, the main protagonists always to the fore.

9408 BET TOTEEXACTA AT TOTESPORT.COM MEDIAN AUCTION MAIDEN STKS (PLUS 10 RACE) 1m (P)

3:55 (4:01) (Class 4) 2-Y-O **£4,463** (£1,328; £663; £331) **Stalls** Low

Form — RPR

4 **1** **Mazikeen**[41] 8706 2-8-11 **0**..................... FinleyMarsh(3) 8 — 71
(Richard Hughes) *led: hdd over 6f out: chsd ldr tl led again 3f out: shkn up and edgd lft over 1f out: styd on wl* **5/2**[2]

3 **2** 2 ½ **Martin's Brig (IRE)**[33] 8919 2-9-5 **0**..................... PaulMulrennan 1 — 70
(Iain Jardine) *trckd ldrs: rdn to chse wnr over 1f out: nt clr run and swtchd rt sn after: styd on same pce ins fnl f* **13/8**[1]

3 ¾ **Beechwood Jim Bob (IRE)** 2-9-5 **0**..................... FrannyNorton 6 — 68
(Mark Johnston) *chsd ldrs: shkn up and hung lft over 1f out: styd on ins fnl f* **8/1**

00 **4** shd **Sparkling Or Still (IRE)**[13] 9197 2-9-0 **0**..................... JosephineGordon 2 — 63
(David Lanigan) *s.i.s: hld up: hdwy and hung lft over 1f out: swtchd rt ins fnl f: styd on: nt rch ldrs* **80/1**

5 ¾ **Alborkan (FR)** 2-9-5 **0**..................... HectorCrouch 4 — 66+
(Amy Murphy) *s.i.s: hld up: swtchd rt 1/2-way: hdwy on outer over 3f out: rdn over 1f out: edgd lft and no ex ins fnl f* **20/1**

0 **6** 3 ½ **Rosa Gold**[12] 9211 2-9-0 **0**..................... RaulDaSilva 9 — 53
(Rae Guest) *mid-div: pushed along 3f out: rdn: hung lft and styd on ins fnl f: nt trble ldrs* **40/1**

6 **7** ½ **Indigo Times (IRE)**[78] 7555 2-9-0 **0**..................... DylanHogan(5) 11 — 57
(David Simcock) *hld up in tch: rdn over 2f out: wknd over 1f out* **12/1**

6 **8** 2 ¼ **Flash To Bang**[214] 2610 2-9-5 **0**.....................(h[1]) JasonHart 3 — 52
(Ivan Furtado) *s.s: hld up: swtchd rt over 3f out: rdn and wknd over 1f out* **7/2**[3]

9 2 **Hoorayforthegrey** 2-9-5 **0**..................... KieranO'Neill 10 — 47
(Robyn Brisland) *s.i.s: sn chsng ldrs: led over 6f out: hdd 3f out: rdn over 2f out: wknd fnl f* **50/1**

00 **10** 4 ½ **Welsh Back**[12] 9211 2-8-11 **0**..................... CameronNoble(3) 5 — 32
(Michael Bell) *broke wl: sn lost pl: no ch whn rdn and hung lft over 1f out* **100/1**

1m 43.13s (3.23) **Going Correction** +0.025s/f (Slow) **10** Ran SP% **119.1**

Speed ratings (Par 98): **84,81,80,80,79 76,75,73,71,67**

CSF £6.93 TOTE £3.60: £1.10, £1.20, £2.50; EX 7.80.

Owner Mrs J Bloomfield **Bred** Norris Bloodstock Ltd **Trained** Upper Lambourn, Berks

FOCUS

Nothing out of the ordinary in this maiden but there was some potential on show. The pace was steady for the most part.

9409 BET TOTEQUADPOT AT TOTESPORT.COM MAIDEN FILLIES' STKS (PLUS 10 RACE) 7f (P)

4:25 (4:29) (Class 4) 2-Y-O **£4,463** (£1,328; £663; £331) **Stalls** Low

Form — RPR

63 **1** **Arriviste**[13] 9197 2-9-0 **0**..................... PaulMulrennan 5 — 75
(Rae Guest) *trckd ldrs: racd keenly: wnt 2nd over 1f out: shkn up to ld ins fnl f: r.o wl: comf* **3/1**[2]

3 **2** 2 **True Believer (IRE)**[8] 9284 2-9-0 **0**..................... FrannyNorton 2 — 70
(Mark Johnston) *led: shkn up and hdd ins fnl f: styd on same pce* **11/4**[1]

3 nk **African Dream** 2-9-0 **0**..................... KieranO'Neill 4 — 69+
(John Gosden) *s.i.s: hld up: shkn up and swtchd rt over 2f out: hdwy over 1f out: r.o: nt rch ldrs* **11/4**[1]

5 **4** 1 ½ **Muritz**[19] 9107 2-9-0 **0**..................... JasonHart 1 — 65
(John Quinn) *chsd ldrs: rdn over 1f out: styd on same pce ins fnl f* **5/1**[3]

03 **5** 3 **Amarsanaa**[12] 9211 2-9-0 **0**..................... HectorCrouch 3 — 57
(Clive Cox) *chsd ldr tl rdn and hung lft over 1f out: wknd wl ins fnl f* **11/1**

60 **6** 1 ¼ **Kingmans Spirit (IRE)**[35] 8865 2-8-11 **0**..................... ThomasGreatrex(3) 8 — 53+
(David Loughnane) *hld up: nt clr run and swtchd rt over 1f out: nt trble ldrs* **25/1**

7 2 ¾ **Fantasy Lover (IRE)** 2-9-0 **0**..................... LewisEdmunds 9 — 46
(Michael Appleby) *s.i.s: hld up: hdwy over 1f out: wknd ins fnl f* **50/1**

02 **8** 2 ½ **Magnificia (IRE)**[134] 5527 2-9-0 **0**..................... AdrianMcCarthy 7 — 39
(Ed Dunlop) *s.i.s and edgd rt s: hld up: rdn on outer and wknd over 1f out* **16/1**

0 **9** 6 **Tamao**[8] 9284 2-9-0 **0**.....................(h) JosephineGordon 6 — 23
(Andrew Balding) *s.i.s: pushed along on outer over 2f out: wknd over 1f out* **40/1**

1m 27.19s (-0.01) **Going Correction** +0.025s/f (Slow) **9** Ran SP% **117.5**

Speed ratings (Par 95): **101,98,98,96,93 91,88,85,78**

CSF £11.78 TOTE £4.00: £1.40, £1.30, £1.40; EX 15.00.

Owner Miss K Rausing **Bred** Miss K Rausing **Trained** Newmarket, Suffolk

■ Trouser The Cash was withdrawn. Price at time of withdrawal 100/1. Rule 4 does not apply.

FOCUS

Just fair form on show in this fillies maiden but it's form to be positive about in terms of potential. Again, it proved hard to make up ground from rear.

9410 BET TOTETRIFECTA AT TOTESPORT.COM CLASSIFIED STKS 7f (P)

4:55 (4:59) (Class 6) 3-Y-O+

£3,816 (£1,135; £567; £400; £400; £400) **Stalls** Low

Form — RPR

0501 **1** **Agent Of Fortune**[2] 9384 4-9-5 **50**..................... HectorCrouch 8 — 58+
(Gary Moore) *s.i.s: hld up: carried rt wl over 1f out: r.o u.p ins fnl f to ld nr fin* **4/5**[1]

004 **2** ½ **Crazy Spin**[12] 9220 3-9-0 **50**.....................(p) JasonHart 2 — 52
(Ivan Furtado) *led: rdn and edgd rt over 1f out: hdd nr fin* **10/1**[3]

0004 **3** ¾ **Sherella**[56] 8255 3-9-0 **43**..................... LewisEdmunds 1 — 50
(J R Jenkins) *a.p: rdn over 1f out: hung rt ins fnl f: styd on* **16/1**

5562 **4** 1 ¾ **Reshaan (IRE)**[12] 9220 4-9-0 **47**.....................(b) FrannyNorton 4 — 46
(Alexandra Dunn) *hld up: hdwy over 1f out: sn rdn: hung rt and styd on same pce ins fnl f (jockey said gelding suffered interference when leaving the stalls)* **7/1**[2]

0566 **5** hd **Theydon Spirit**[16] 9157 4-8-7 **43**..................... GavinAshton(7) 7 — 45
(Peter Charalambous) *chsd ldrs: rdn over 1f out: no ex wl ins fnl f* **12/1**

5000 **6** 1 ¼ **Elusif (IRE)**[42] 8666 4-9-0 **50**..................... JosephineGordon 3 — 42
(Shaun Keightley) *prom: lost pl 5f out: hdwy over 1f out: no ex ins fnl f (jockey said gelding jumped right-handed leaving the stalls)* **7/1**[2]

1034 **7** 4 **Wild Flower (IRE)**[11] 9247 7-9-0 **50**.....................(p) KieranO'Neill 9 — 31
(Luke McJannet) *chsd ldr: wnt upsides over 5f out tl rdn over 2f out: wknd ins fnl f* **16/1**

000 **8** ¾ **Hurricane Heidi**[186] 3598 3-9-0 **30**..................... CamHardie 11 — 29
(Derek Shaw) *s.i.s: outpcd* **100/1**

4055 **9** 8 **Roca Magica**[16] 9160 3-9-0 **46**.....................(b[1]) PaulMulrennan 10 — 9
(Ed Dunlop) *s.i.s: plld hrd: hdwy over 5f out: wknd over 1f out* **10/1**

5030 **10** 1 **Lethal Laura**[8] 9282 3-9-0 **48**..................... JaneElliott 12 — 6
(Kevin Frost) *s.i.s: hdwy on outer 6f out: hung rt over 2f out: sn wknd (jockey said filly hung right-handed in the home straight)* **20/1**

1m 27.29s (0.09) **Going Correction** +0.025s/f (Slow) **10** Ran SP% **122.5**

Speed ratings (Par 101): **100,99,98,96,96 94,90,89,80,79**

CSF £10.96 TOTE £1.60: £1.10, £2.60, £4.90; EX 10.30.

Owner Foreign Legion **Bred** Barton Stud **Trained** Lower Beeding, W Sussex

FOCUS

This looks better than your average 0-50 event given the front pair are in top form. The winner was the only one to make ground from off a modest pace.

9411 BET TOTESWINGER AT TOTESPORT.COM H'CAP 5f (P)

5:25 (5:30) (Class 6) (0-52,51) 3-Y-O+

£3,816 (£1,135; £567; £400; £400; £400) **Stalls** Low

Form — RPR

0142 **1** **Loulin**[6] 9335 4-9-7 **51**.....................(t) JamesSullivan 12 — 58+
(Ruth Carr) *chsd ldrs on outer: wnt 2nd over 1f out: shkn up to ld ins fnl f: r.o: comf* **7/4**[1]

0515 **2** 1 ¼ **Sarsaparilla Kit**[16] 9161 3-9-2 **51**..................... MarkCrehan(5) 1 — 52
(Stuart Williams) *led: rdn over 1f out: hdd ins fnl f: styd on same pce* **3/1**[2]

2000 **3** nk **Sugar Plum Fairy**[88] 7172 4-9-1 **45**.....................(h[1]) FrannyNorton 2 — 44
(Tony Carroll) *s.i.s: hld up: hdwy over 1f out: r.o to go 3rd post* **12/1**

4060 **4** hd **Sing Bertie (IRE)**[76] 7628 3-9-1 **45**..................... PaulMulrennan 7 — 44
(Derek Shaw) *s.i.s: pushed along and hdwy over 3f out: rdn over 1f out: styd on same pce wl ins fnl f* **20/1**

0344 **5** nk **Storm Lightning**[69] 7838 10-9-1 **45**..................... EoinWalsh 6 — 43
(Kevin Frost) *prom: pushed along over 3f out: rdn over 1f out: r.o* **8/1**

2000 **6** 1 ½ **Kyllukey**[34] 8901 6-9-1 **45**..................... JasonHart 8 — 37
(Charlie Wallis) *hld up: racd keenly: rdn over 1f out: nt trble ldrs* **14/1**

3000 **7** hd **Invisible Storm**[16] 9161 4-9-3 **47**.....................(b) HectorCrouch 3 — 39
(William Stone) *chsd ldr tl rdn over 1f out: no ex ins fnl f* **6/1**[3]

0060 **8** ½ **Spenny's Lass**[50] 8435 4-8-12 **45**.....................(v) DarraghKeenan(3) 9 — 35
(John Ryan) *edgd rt s: pushed along to chse ldrs: lost pl 1/2-way: styd on same pce fnl f over 1f out* **10/1**

3000 **9** 2 ½ **Tina Teaspoon**[23] 9034 5-9-1 **45**.....................(h) CamHardie 5 — 26
(Derek Shaw) *hld up: rdn over 1f out: nvr on terms* **66/1**

1m 0.45s (0.25) **Going Correction** +0.025s/f (Slow) **9** Ran SP% **116.5**

Speed ratings (Par 101): **99,97,96,96,95 93,93,92,88**

CSF £6.98 CT £46.66 TOTE £2.30: £1.10, £1.40, £3.30; EX 7.60.

Owner George Murray **Bred** Rabbah Bloodstock Limited **Trained** Huby, N Yorks

■ Ask The Guru was withdrawn. Price at time of withdrawal 33/1. Rule 4 does not apply.

FOCUS

A very moderate sprint handicap in which few got involved.

9412 BET TOTESCOOP6 AT TOTESPORT.COM H'CAP 1m 5f 66y(P)

5:55 (5:58) (Class 6) (0-62,64) 3-Y-O+

£3,816 (£1,135; £567; £400; £400; £400) **Stalls** Low

Form — RPR

4334 **1** **Sibylline**[55] 8292 3-8-3 **50**..................... PoppyBridgwater(5) 8 — 56
(David Simcock) *hld up: hdwy over 4f out: hung lft fr over 2f out: nt clr run over 1f out: sn rdn: styd on to ld wl ins fnl f* **9/1**

0000 **2** ¾ **Zarrar (IRE)**[64] 7998 4-9-7 **59**.....................(bt) PaulMulrennan 6 — 62
(Rae Guest) *led after 1f: clr over 9f out tl over 3f out: rdn and edgd rt over 1f out: hdd wl ins fnl f* **7/1**[3]

3342 **3** 5 **Cold Harbour**[6] 9336 4-9-10 **62**.....................(t) KieranO'Neill 5 — 58
(Robyn Brisland) *hld up: hdwy over 4f out: chsd ldr over 3f out: rdn over 1f out: no ex ins fnl f* **9/2**[2]

0231 4 2 1/4 **Que Quieres (USA)**[13] 9201 3-8-10 52 LukeMorris 2 46
(Simon Dow) *led 1f: chsd ldrs: wnt 2nd over 6f out tl over 3f out: rdn over 2f out: no ex fnl f* 7/4[1]

6215 5 3/4 **Star Of Athena**[25] 9005 4-9-9 64 FinleyMarsh(3) 4 55
(Ali Stronge) *stdd s: hld up: hdwy u.p and hung lft over 1f out: nt trble ldrs (jockey said filly was slowly away)* 9/2[2]

3060 6 2 1/4 **Normandy Blue**[53] 8347 4-8-8 46 oh1 (b[1]) FrannyNorton 1 34
(Luke McJannet) *hld up in tch: hmpd over 3f out: rdn over 1f out: wknd fnl f* 12/1

0050 7 83 **Sleepdancer (IRE)**[70] 7192 3-8-1 46 oh1 (bt[1]) DarraghKeenan(3) 3
(John Ryan) *hld up in tch: rdn and lost pl over 5f out: sn bhd (jockey said the saddle slipped and the gelding also hung left-handed)* 40/1

4544 P **Falls Creek (USA)**[9] 9275 4-8-8 46 oh1 (v) JosephineGordon 7
(Andrew Balding) *chsd ldr after 2f tl over 6f out: rdn and lost pl over 4f out: sn bhd: p.u over 1f out (trainers rep said filly stopped quickly)* 10/1

2m 53.85s (0.25) **Going Correction** +0.025s/f (Slow) 8 Ran SP% **114.4**
WFA 3 from 4yo 4lb
Speed ratings (Par 101): **100,99,96,95,94 93,42,**
CSF £69.76 CT £322.23 TOTE £9.80: £1.80, £2.70, £1.70; EX 87.70.
Owner Miss K Rausing **Bred** Miss K Rausing **Trained** Newmarket, Suffolk
■ Stewards' Enquiry : Poppy Bridgwater two-day ban; misuse of whip (Dec 26-27)

FOCUS
A good pace had the bulk of the field in trouble a long way out and the first two were the only ones to really see things out.
T/Jkpt: £5,000.00 to a £1 stake. Pool: £10,000.00 - 2.0 winning units T/Plt: £16.10 to a £1 stake. Pool: £55,366.29 - 2,496.31 winning units T/Qpdt: £11.10 to a £1 stake. Pool: £7,058.66 - 469.60 winning units **Colin Roberts**

9322 **KEMPTON (A.W)** (R-H)
Wednesday, December 11

OFFICIAL GOING: Polytrack: standard to slow
Weather: Overcast, possible showers

9413 RACINGTV.COM NOVICE STKS 6f (P)
3:40 (3:40) (Class 5) 2-Y-O £3,881 (£1,155; £577; £288) Stalls Low

Form RPR

21 1 **Ivatheengine (IRE)**[198] 3165 2-9-6 0 JimCrowley 12 85
(Paul Cole) *broke wl fr wd draw to trck ldr: shkn up to ld over 1f out: rdn and drew steadily clr fnl f* 4/1[2]

2 2 3 **Shine On Brendan (IRE)**[35] 8865 2-9-2 0 AdamKirby 3 72
(Clive Cox) *led: rdn along and hdd by wnr over 1f out: kpt on one pce fnl f* 10/11[1]

3 1 **Snowball Jackson** 2-9-2 0 JamesDoyle 9 69+
(Richard Hannon) *trckd ldrs on outer: rdn and outpcd by front pair 2f out: kpt on one pce fnl f* 12/1

4 2 1/2 **Bimble (IRE)** 2-8-11 0 HollieDoyle 11 57+
(Henry Candy) *hld up in last: effrt and hdwy between rivals 2f out: n.m.r ent fnl f: kpt on wl under hands and heels once in the clr* 25/1

5 nse **Fuchsia** 2-8-11 0 GeorgeWood 7 56
(James Fanshawe) *trckd ldrs: rdn along and no imp 2f out: kpt on one pce fnl f* 25/1

6 nk **Lily Like** 2-8-11 0 DavidProbert 8 55
(Andrew Balding) *slow into stride and racd in rr: minor hdwy u.p 2f out: kpt on fnl f but n.d* 14/1

0 7 3/4 **Up To Speed**[140] 5317 2-8-11 0 PJMcDonald 4 53
(James Tate) *trckd ldrs and racd freely: rdn and unable qck over 1f out: one pce fnl f (jockey said filly ran too free)* 11/2[3]

0 8 hd **Skyllachy**[23] 9036 2-9-2 0 JasonWatson 1 58
(Mark Usher) *prom on inner: shkn up and outpcd 2f out: sn rdn and no imp over 1f out: one pce after* 50/1

0 9 1/2 **Sena**[7] 9299 2-8-11 0 TomMarquand 2 51
(William Haggas) *racd in midfield: rdn and no hdwy over 1f out: no prog fnl f* 40/1

0 10 1/2 **Limaro Prospect (IRE)**[18] 9130 2-9-2 0 LukeMorris 10 55
(Sir Mark Prescott Bt) *midfield on outer: rdn along and outpcd over 1f out: wknd fnl f* 50/1

0 11 1 1/2 **Mercurist**[14] 9174 2-9-2 0 RichardKingscote 5 50
(Rod Millman) *hld up: rdn in rr 2f out: nvr on terms* 100/1

00 12 1/2 **Hong Kong Dragon**[11] 9242 2-8-9 0 AlexJary(7) 6 49
(George Scott) *hld up: sdle slipped sn after s: sn no ch (jockey said saddle slipped)* 66/1

1m 13.1s **Going Correction** -0.075s/f (Stan) 12 Ran SP% **118.7**
Speed ratings (Par 96): **97,93,91,88,88 87,86,86,85,85 83,82**
CSF £7.61 TOTE £4.90: £1.30, £1.10, £2.60; EX 10.60 Trifecta £50.80.
Owner Frank Stella **Bred** D Byrne **Trained** Whatcombe, Oxon

FOCUS
Not many got involved in this opening juvenile sprint novice, with pace holding up. The winner might be a bit better than rated.

9414 32RED ON THE APP STORE NURSERY H'CAP 7f (P)
4:10 (4:10) (Class 5) (0-75,76) 2-Y-O £3,881 (£1,155; £577; £400; £400; £400) Stalls Low

Form RPR

025 1 **Maysong**[142] 5234 2-9-5 73 PJMcDonald 7 82+
(Ed Dunlop) *restrained in rr: rapid hdwy between rivals 2f out: rdn to ld ent fnl f: rdn clr* 12/1

0240 2 3 **Rajguru**[35] 8850 2-9-1 69 DavidProbert 4 70
(Tom Clover) *racd in midfield: hdwy u.p over 1f out: rdn and kpt on wl to go 2nd wl ins fnl f* 14/1

6442 3 nk **Broken Rifle**[85] 7296 2-9-0 75 (p) AngusVilliers(7) 3 75
(Ivan Furtado) *dwlt but sn t.k.h: chsd ldrs: rdn along and unable qck over 1f out: kpt on one pce fnl f* 7/1[3]

2165 4 1 1/2 **Danny Ocean (IRE)**[5] 9347 2-9-8 76 (p) BenCurtis 8 73
(K R Burke) *prom on outer: rdn along and outpcd 2f out: kpt on again ins fnl f but n.d* 7/2[2]

5020 5 2 **Magical Force**[21] 9060 2-8-8 62 JasonWatson 6 53
(Rod Millman) *led: rdn along and strly pressed over 1f out: hdd ent fnl f and wknd clsng stages* 14/1

2330 6 3/4 **Hello Baileys**[11] 9242 2-9-6 74 (b[1]) AdamKirby 9 63
(Mark Johnston) *trckd ldr: rdn along to chal 2f out: wkng whn short of room 1f out: nt rcvr* 12/1

3355 7 nk **Sky Vega (IRE)**[19] 9110 2-9-2 70 (t[1]) TomMarquand 1 58
(Tom Ward) *hld up: effrt to cl 2f out: rdn and wknd 1f out* 8/1

443 8 6 **Kohoof**[20] 9085 2-9-1 69 JimCrowley 2 42
(William Haggas) *trckd ldrs on inner: rdn and fnd little over 1f out: sn wknd (jockey said filly hung right-handed throughout; trainers rep could offer no explanation for the poor performance)* 5/2[1]

5003 9 6 **Ruby Power (IRE)**[7] 9307 2-8-7 66 ThoreHammerHansen(5) 5 23
(Richard Hannon) *hld up: rdn along and no imp 2f out: sn bhd (trainers rep could offer no explanation for the poor performance)* 8/1

1m 25.86s (-0.14) **Going Correction** -0.075s/f (Stan) 9 Ran SP% **114.2**
Speed ratings (Par 96): **97,93,93,91,89 88,88,81,74**
CSF £162.92 CT £1270.21 TOTE £12.00: £3.50, £3.30, £2.30; EX 143.60 Trifecta £2116.00.
Owner Wilmshurst & Attenborough **Bred** Tareq Al Mazeedi **Trained** Newmarket, Suffolk

FOCUS
A run-of-the-mill nursery, but an emphatic winner.

9415 BRITISH STALLION STUDS EBF NOVICE STKS 1m (P)
4:40 (4:43) (Class 5) 2-Y-O £3,881 (£1,155; £577; £288) Stalls Low

Form RPR

1 **Starcat** 2-9-5 0 PJMcDonald 1 86+
(Hughie Morrison) *midfield on inner: hdwy to chse ldrs 2f out: swtchd rt between rivals and rdn to chal over 1f out: drvn to ld fnl 100yds* 9/1[3]

2 3/4 **Eastern World (IRE)** 2-9-5 0 JamesDoyle 6 84
(Charlie Appleby) *trckd ldrs: rdn to chal and ev ch over 1f out: kpt on to snatch 2nd last strides* 10/11[1]

3 hd **Kuramata (IRE)** 2-9-5 0 KieranShoemark 12 84
(John Gosden) *dwlt but sn rcvrd to trck ldr after 2f: rdn along to ld over 1f out: drvn and hdd fnl 100yds: lost 2nd post* 33/1

4 5 **Prince of Eagles (IRE)** 2-9-5 0 DanielMuscutt 5 72
(David Lanigan) *trckd ldrs: rdn and outpcd over 1f out: kpt on one pce fnl f* 25/1

2 5 2 **Summit Reach**[18] 9136 2-9-5 0 RichardKingscote 2 68
(Ralph Beckett) *led: rdn along and hdd over 1f out: wknd fnl f* 11/4[2]

6 3 1/2 **Life Matters (USA)** 2-9-5 0 ShaneKelly 3 60
(Richard Hughes) *racd in midfield: rdn and no imp 2f out: n.d* 25/1

0 7 3 **Logan Roy**[16] 9155 2-9-5 0 LiamKeniry 8 53
(Andrew Balding) *racd in midfield: rdn and lost grnd over 2f out: nvr on terms* 100/1

6 8 1 1/4 **Lord P**[16] 9156 2-9-5 0 JohnFahy 9 50
(Richard Hannon) *racd in midfield: rdn and minor hdwy over 1f out: no further hdwy fnl f* 50/1

9 1 1/2 **Halfwaytothemoon (IRE)** 2-9-0 0 RobertHavlin 4 41+
(John Gosden) *dwlt and squeezed for room early: racd in rr and rn green at times: minor hdwy over 1f out: nvr on terms* 12/1

10 1 **Khatm** 2-9-5 0 JimCrowley 14 44+
(Saeed bin Suroor) *hld up: rdn in rr 1/2-way: a bhd* 12/1

0 11 nse **Rodrigo Diaz**[22] 9052 2-9-5 0 TomMarquand 11 44
(David Simcock) *hld up: a in rr* 150/1

12 3/4 **Signal Twenty Nine** 2-9-5 0 HollieDoyle 10 42
(William Knight) *hld up and racd keenly: hung lft at times: nvr on terms (jockey said gelding was unsteerable)* 100/1

13 3/4 **Quarry Bay (IRE)** 2-8-12 0 Pierre-LouisJamin(7) 13 41
(William Knight) *midfield on outer: rdn along and lost pl 3f out: sn bhd* 100/1

1m 38.29s (-1.51) **Going Correction** -0.075s/f (Stan) 13 Ran SP% **120.7**
Speed ratings (Par 96): **104,103,103,98,96 92,89,88,86,85 85,85,84**
CSF £17.25 TOTE £9.90: £2.40, £1.10, £5.80; EX 24.90 Trifecta £498.60.
Owner Michael Kerr-Dineen & Martin Hughes **Bred** Qatar Bloodstock & Newsells Park Stud **Trained** East Ilsley, Berks

FOCUS
A fair-looking mile novice event, and a taking winner gave PJ McDonald a rapid-fire double. Three pulled clear and the form is rated positively.

9416 100% PROFIT BOOST AT 32REDSPORT.COM NOVICE STKS 1m (P)
5:10 (5:13) (Class 5) 3-Y-O+ £3,881 (£1,155; £577; £288) Stalls Low

Form RPR

3 1 **Bridgewater Bay (IRE)**[23] 9038 3-9-4 0 AdamKirby 5 79
(Jane Chapple-Hyam) *mde all: rdn and edgd lft over 1f out: drvn and a doing enough fnl f: front pair wl clr* 5/2[2]

3-22 2 1 1/2 **Sheriffmuir (USA)**[12] 9213 3-9-4 77 (p) RobertHavlin 8 76
(John Gosden) *dwlt: rcvrd to trck wnr after 2f: rdn along to chal over 1f out: hung rt and sltly awkward 1f out: one pce after* 4/11[1]

60 3 9 **Emerald Fox**[174] 4022 4-9-0 0 DavidProbert 1 50
(Patrick Chamings) *trckd ldr: rdn along and readily lft bhd by front pair 2f out: plugged on for remote 3rd* 20/1

50 4 3 1/4 **Kiraleah**[49] 8467 3-8-13 0 DougieCostello 3 42
(Ivan Furtado) *hld up: minor hdwy u.p 2f out: kpt on for remote 4th fnl f* 50/1

00 5 4 1/2 **Pour Joie**[25] 9011 4-9-5 0 PJMcDonald 7 37
(Ian Williams) *slowly away: racd in rr: sme minor hdwy but nvr a factor (jockey said gelding hung left-handed)* 25/1

6 1 **Everymananemperor** 3-9-4 0 GeorgeWood 4 35
(James Fanshawe) *dwlt and racd in rr: rdn over 2f out: nvr on terms* 4/1[3]

00 7 7 **Purple Tommy**[14] 9171 3-8-11 0 LukeCatton(7) 6 19
(Jimmy Fox) *trckd ldrs: rdn along and hung rt over 2f out: sn wl bhd* 100/1

0 8 13 **Dandy Lass (IRE)**[205] 2919 3-8-13 0 LiamKeniry 2
(Richard Phillips) *trckd ldrs: rdn along and lost pl over 2f out: sn bhd* 50/1

1m 38.61s (-1.19) **Going Correction** -0.075s/f (Stan) 8 Ran SP% **135.4**
WFA 3 from 4yo 1lb
Speed ratings (Par 103): **102,100,91,88,83 82,75,62**
CSF £4.54 TOTE £3.90: £1.10, £1.02, £5.10; EX 5.90 Trifecta £33.80.
Owner Suzanne & Nigel Williams **Bred** Tower Place Bloodstock **Trained** Dalham, Suffolk
■ Orion's Shore was withdrawn. Rule 4 does not apply.

FOCUS
Very little strength in depth to this mile novice, and a winning time 0.32 seconds slower than the preceding juvenile contest.

9417 32RED.COM FILLIES' H'CAP 1m (P)
5:40 (5:41) (Class 4) (0-85,83) 3-Y-O+ £6,469 (£1,925; £962; £481; £400; £400) Stalls Low

Form RPR

0051 1 **Roman Spinner**[11] 9244 4-9-1 72 (t) DavidProbert 2 80
(Rae Guest) *trckd ldrs: hdwy to chse ldr 2f out: led briefly over 1f out: rallied wl u.p to ld again fnl 50yds* 4/1[2]

5320 2 nk **Saikung (IRE)**[18] 9126 3-9-9 81 KieranShoemark 4 88
(Charles Hills) *hld up: hdwy u.p over 1f out: rdn to ld ent fnl f: drvn and hdd by wnr fnl 50yds* 25/1

3024 **3** 1 **Never Be Enough**[16] 6656 4-9-12 **83**........................ CallumRodriguez 6 88
(Keith Dalgleish) *dwlt and hld up: rdn and sme hdwy 2f out: kpt on wl for press to go 3rd ins fnl f: nrst fin* **14/1**

5203 **4** ½ **I'lletyougonow**[18] 9126 3-9-0 **72**..................................(p) TomMarquand 3 76
(Mick Channon) *midfield: rdn and outpcd 2f out: kpt on one pce fnl f* **13/2**

0112 **5** 1 **Earth And Sky (USA)**[6] 9329 3-9-6 **78**........................ JamesDoyle 1 79
(George Scott) *j. as stalls opened: sn rcvrd to ld: rdn along and hdd over 1f out: wknd fnl f* **11/10**[1]

6023 **6** 7 **Geizy Teizy (IRE)**[13] 9199 3-8-12 **77**..................... StefanoCherchi(7) 5 62
(Marco Botti) *trckd ldrs: rdn and lost pl over 1f out: sn bhd* **5/1**[3]

1m 39.71s (-0.09) **Going Correction** -0.075s/f (Stan)
WFA 3 from 4yo 1lb **6** Ran SP% **108.1**
Speed ratings (Par 102): **97,96,95,95,94 87**
CSF £72.04 TOTE £4.50: £1.90, £5.60; EX 89.10 Trifecta £628.80.
Owner Reprobates Too **Bred** Ashbrittle Stud **Trained** Newmarket, Suffolk

FOCUS
The slowest of the three consecutive 1m races on the card by over a second, but a fair contest and a fourth Kempton success for the winner.

9418 32RED CASINO H'CAP 1m 2f 219y(P)
6:10 (6:11) (Class 4) (0-85,85) 3-Y-0+
£6,469 (£1,925; £962; £481; £400; £400) **Stalls** Low

Form RPR

3202 **1** **City Tour**[14] 9178 3-8-9 **76**..(b[1]) RobertHavlin 6 83
(Lydia Richards) *hld up: stdy hdwy over 2f out: rdn and styd on strly to ld fnl 100yds: kpt on wl* **10/1**

3042 **2** ¾ **My Boy Sepoy**[36] 8829 4-9-4 **82**........................... PJMcDonald 7 88
(Stuart Williams) *midfield in tch: hdwy to chal gng wl over 1f out: led narrowly 1f out: sn hdd by wnr and no ex clsng stages* **10/1**

4113 **3** nk **Sashenka (GER)**[14] 9178 3-8-12 **79**........................ LiamKeniry 8 85
(Sylvester Kirk) *hld up: stl plenty to do in rr 2f out: rdn and hdwy 1f out: kpt on wl fnl f: nrst fin* **10/1**

-406 **4** 1 **Lady Adelaide (IRE)**[22] 9050 3-8-11 **78**.......................(t) JasonWatson 1 82
(Roger Charlton) *trckd ldrs: rdn along to chal and ev ch over 1f out: unable to sustain effrt fnl f* **8/1**

0310 **5** nk **Kyllachy Gala**[22] 9055 6-8-12 **83**........................ GraceMcEntee(7) 5 86
(Marco Botti) *midfield on inner: clsd gng wl 2f out whn short of room: swtchd rt and rdn over 1f out: kpt on one pce fnl f* **6/1**[3]

4556 **6** hd **Voi**[14] 9177 5-8-4 **71** oh1..................................(t) GabrieleMalune(3) 4 74
(Conrad Allen) *hld up wl off pce: rdn and no imp 2f out: drvn and kpt on wl fnl f but n.d* **25/1**

3321 **7** 1 **Fearless Warrior (FR)**[21] 9066 3-9-0 **81**.......................(h) HollieDoyle 2 82
(Eve Johnson Houghton) *trckd ldr: rdn along to ld briefly 2f out: sn drvn and lost pl: no ex fnl f* **11/4**[1]

0063 **8** 2¼ **Glendevon (USA)**[22] 9053 4-9-0 **85**........................ AngusVilliers(7) 3 83
(Richard Hughes) *led and racd freely: rdn along and hdd over 1f out: sn wknd* **4/1**[2]

2241 **9** 10 **Queen Constantine (GER)**[14] 9177 3-8-4 **78**...............(h) GaiaBoni(7) 9 59
(William Jarvis) *blind c off late and dwlt bdly: sn in midfield on outer: wd off home bnd: rdn and lost pl over 1f out: sn bhd (jockey was slow to remove the blindfold, explaining that the filly ducked it's head just as the gates opening pulling the blind from her hands and causing her to become unbalanced)* **11/1**

10 nk **Mouriyani (USA)**[142] 5261 3-7-12 **72**........................ LauraCoughlan(7) 11 53
(Tom Ward) *hld up: detached 4f out: nvr on terms* **50/1**

3100 **11** 58 **Willy Sewell**[15] 9167 6-8-9 **73**.............................. BenCurtis 10
(Michael Appleby) *chsd ldr after 2f tl 4f out: rdn and lost pl 3f out: sn bhd* **66/1**

2m 17.96s (-3.04) **Going Correction** -0.075s/f (Stan)
WFA 3 from 4yo+ 3lb **11** Ran SP% **115.0**
Speed ratings (Par 105): **108,107,107,106,106 106,105,103,96,96 54**
CSF £102.04 CT £1027.26 TOTE £11.60: £3.10, £2.90, £3.00; EX 97.10 Trifecta £870.10.
Owner Mrs Judy Seal **Bred** Jointsense Limited **Trained** Funtington, W Sussex

FOCUS
A bunch finish for this fair middle-distance handicap, in which the first-time headgear likely made the difference.

9419 32RED H'CAP 1m 7f 218y(P)
6:40 (6:41) (Class 3) (0-95,95) 3-Y-0+
£9,337 (£2,796; £1,398; £699; £349; £175) **Stalls** Low

Form RPR

1002 **1** **Rainbow Dreamer**[40] 8726 6-9-11 **92**.......................(p) TomMarquand 5 103
(Alan King) *trckd ldrs: swtchd lft and rdn to chse ldr 2f out: drvn along to ld wl ins fnl f: kpt on wl* **12/1**

0-21 **2** 2 **Astromachia**[42] 8654 4-9-10 **91**........................... JimCrowley 7 100
(Amanda Perrett) *trckd ldr: effrt to press ldr 5f out: pushed along to ld 4f out: pressed on wl over 2f out: rdn and hdd by wnr ins fnl f: one pce after* **5/4**[1]

1116 **3** 2½ **All Yours (FR)**[4] 9366 8-9-8 **89**........................... AdamKirby 1 95
(Sean Curran) *racd in midfield: swtchd rt and rdn to chse ldrs over 1f out: kpt on one pce fnl f* **11/4**[2]

105 **4** 4½ **Western Duke (IRE)**[22] 9056 5-9-5 **86**..................... PJMcDonald 4 86
(Ian Williams) *in tch: effrt to chse ldrs 2f out: rdn and no imp over 1f out: one pce fnl f* **14/1**

0355 **5** 1 **Age Of Wisdom (IRE)**[20] 8654 6-8-12 **79**...................(p) DavidProbert 8 78
(Gary Moore) *hld up: pushed along over 3f out: rdn and minor hdwy on outer over 1f out: kpt on* **25/1**

4-42 **6** nk **Smart Champion**[81] 7464 4-9-6 **87**............................(h) JamesDoyle 3 86
(David Simcock) *hld up: pushed along and wd off home bnd over 2f out: rdn and no imp over 1f out: plugged on* **7/1**[3]

4505 **7** ½ **Manjaam (IRE)**[8] 9288 6-8-4 **78**............................(p) JonathanFisher(7) 6 76
(Ian Williams) *racd in midfield: outpcd on outer 3f out: sn rdn and no imp 2f out: one pce after* **33/1**

R335 **8** 5 **Platitude**[21] 9065 6-10-0 **95**................................(h[1]) KieranShoemark 2 87
(Amanda Perrett) *hld up: pushed along in rr over 2f out: nvr on terms* **25/1**

0560 **9** 17 **Cosmelli (ITY)**[53] 8350 6-9-11 **92**..........................(b) DanielMuscutt 9 64
(Gay Kelleway) *led and racd freely: rdn along and hdd over 4f out: rdn and lost pl 3f out: sn bhd* **33/1**

3m 26.06s (-4.04) **Going Correction** -0.075s/f (Stan) **9** Ran SP% **111.5**
Speed ratings (Par 107): **107,106,104,102,102 101,101,99,90**
CSF £25.72 CT £53.72 TOTE £12.70: £2.80, £1.10, £1.50; EX 33.10 Trifecta £143.10.
Owner The Maple Street Partnership **Bred** Rabbah Bloodstock Limited **Trained** Barbury Castle, Wilts

FOCUS
A decent stayers' handicap for the feature, but the pace didn't appear to lift until deep into the back straight on the final circuit. A pb from the winner with the next two running as well as ever in defeat.

9420 WILLIAM MCLUSKEY MEMORIAL H'CAP 7f (P)
7:10 (7:12) (Class 6) (0-60,64) 3-Y-0+
£3,105 (£924; £461; £400; £400; £400) **Stalls** Low

Form RPR

3-20 **1** **Calin's Lad**[184] 3657 4-9-7 **60**.............................. BenCurtis 4 67+
(Michael Appleby) *hld up: hdwy u.p over 1f out: rdn and gd hdwy to ld wl ins fnl f: won gng away* **9/2**[2]

1453 **2** 1¼ **Ubla (IRE)**[9] 9277 6-9-7 **60**..................................(e) TomMarquand 8 64
(Gay Kelleway) *racd in midfield: rdn along to chse ldrs over 1f out: drvn to ld briefly ins fnl f: sn hdd by wnr and no ex* **9/1**

3611 **3** ½ **Garth Rockett**[18] 9128 5-9-7 **60**............................(tp) ShaneKelly 5 62
(Mike Murphy) *midfield on inner: effrt to cl over 1f out: rdn along and ev ch 1f out: kpt on* **6/1**[3]

1041 **4** ½ **Brains (IRE)**[7] 9305 3-9-4 **64** 6ex.........................(b) AngusVilliers(7) 13 65+
(Jamie Osborne) *trckd ldr: hung lft and dropped to 3rd 3f out: clsd wl and rdn to chal over 1f out: sn hung bdly lft ent fnl f and no ex (jockey said gelding hung both ways)* **11/4**[1]

1120 **5** shd **Viola Park**[11] 9253 5-9-7 **60**.................................(p) DavidProbert 7 61
(Ronald Harris) *in tch in midfield: rdn along and outpcd 2f out: r.o again ins fnl f* **14/1**

-602 **6** ½ **Hit The Beat**[18] 9128 4-9-0 **60**............................ AmeliaGlass(7) 2 60
(Clive Cox) *midfield on inner: clsd on ldrs 2f out: rdn along and unable qck 1f out: kpt on one pce fnl f* **10/1**

5540 **7** hd **Swissal (IRE)**[12] 9217 4-9-7 **60**...............................(v[1]) DougieCostello 3 59
(David Dennis) *chsd ldr: pushed along to ld 2f out: rdn along and hdd ins fnl f: no ex* **20/1**

006 **8** 1½ **Fly The Nest (IRE)**[105] 6598 3-9-7 **60**.......................... KieranShoemark 9 55
(Tony Carroll) *led: rdn along and hdd 2f out: wknd over 1f out* **20/1**

0-00 **9** ¾ **Martin King**[83] 7373 3-9-3 **56**............................... AdamKirby 6 49
(John Butler) *hld up: pushed along in rr over 2f out: sme late hdwy but nvr on terms* **25/1**

0001 **10** nk **Mont Kiara (FR)**[11] 9248 6-9-6 **59**............................ HollieDoyle 1 51
(Simon Dow) *restrained in rr: rdn and minor hdwy over 2f out: wknd fnl f* **8/1**

0645 **11** nk **Lyrical Ballad (IRE)**[107] 6555 3-9-7 **60**.....................(p) LiamKeniry 11 52
(Neil Mulholland) *hld up: pushed along in rr 3f out: nvr on terms* **66/1**

645 **12** 1½ **Painted Dream**[11] 9249 3-9-2 **55**............................ TomQueally 10 43
(George Margarson) *racd in midfield: rdn along and lost pl over 2f out: sn bhd* **25/1**

0104 **13** 2¼ **Hollander**[7] 9298 5-9-0 **53**...................................(bt) DanielMuscutt 12 35
(Alexandra Dunn) *blindfold c off late and dwlt as a result: a in rr* **40/1**

6305 **14** ½ **Perfect Symphony (IRE)**[41] 8704 5-9-2 **58**............... PaddyBradley(3) 14 39
(Mark Pattinson) *hld up: a bhd* **40/1**

1m 25.76s (-0.24) **Going Correction** -0.075s/f (Stan) **14** Ran SP% **119.6**
Speed ratings (Par 101): **98,96,96,95,95 94,94,92,91,91 91,89,86,86**
CSF £40.47 CT £249.29 TOTE £5.10: £2.00, £3.10, £2.00; EX 43.30 Trifecta £220.80.
Owner Lycett Racing 100 Club **Bred** Al-Baha Bloodstock **Trained** Oakham, Rutland

FOCUS
Most of the right horses came to the fore in this finale, won in a time 0.1 seconds quicker than the earlier nursery.
T/Plt: £241.80 to a £1 stake. Pool: £63,641.08 - 192.12 winning units T/Qpdt: £35.10 to a £1 stake. Pool: £8,069.82 - 169.76 winning units **Mark Grantham**

9383 LINGFIELD (L-H)
Wednesday, December 11

OFFICIAL GOING: Polytrack: standard
Wind: Virtually nil Weather: Showers

9421 BETWAY HEED YOUR HUNCH H'CAP 1m 4f (P)
12:10 (12:10) (Class 5) (0-75,76) 3-Y-0+
£3,428 (£1,020; £509; £300; £300; £300) **Stalls** Low

Form RPR

4150 **1** **Renardeau**[43] 8641 3-9-1 **70**.................................(p) TomMarquand 6 79
(Ali Stronge) *in tch in midfield: effrt to chse ldrs 2f out: rdn to chal over 1f out: led ins fnl f: styd on wl: rdn out* **25/1**

12 **2** ¾ **Matewan (IRE)**[9] 9274 4-9-10 **75**...........................(p) JimCrowley 2 83
(Ian Williams) *in tch in midfield: clsd to join ldr and travelling wl over 2f out: led 2f out: sn rdn: hdd and one pce ins fnl f* **5/2**[2]

4201 **3** ¾ **Lord Halifax (IRE)**[7] 9303 3-9-7 **76** 6ex.................... KieranShoemark 1 83
(Charlie Fellowes) *in tch in midfield: rdn over 2f out: swtchd rt and chsd ldrs on outer bnd 2f out: hung lft over 1f out: kpt on fnl 100yds: nt quite enough pce to chal* **4/5**[1]

1130 **4** 2 **Glutnforpunishment**[94] 5778 3-8-8 **70**..................... AngusVilliers(7) 3 74
(Nick Littmoden) *pushed along and led for 1f: chsd ldrs: effrt over 2f out: unable qck over 1f out: kpt on same pce ins fnl f* **7/1**[3]

5500 **5** 8 **Tiar Na Nog (IRE)**[41] 8705 7-9-4 **69**........................ JasonWatson 4 60
(Denis Coakley) *hld up in tch in last pair: effrt over 2f out: no imp and wl hld fnl f* **25/1**

4000 **6** 3 **Pempie (IRE)**[21] 9067 3-8-11 **66**............................(t) DavidProbert 8 52
(Andrew Balding) *hdwy to chse ldr 10f out: led over 2f out: rdn and hdd 2f out: sn lost pl and wknd fnl f* **16/1**

33 **7** 2½ **Gawdawpalin (IRE)**[169] 4220 6-9-2 **67**........................ BenCurtis 5 49
(Sylvester Kirk) *stdd and dropped in bhd after s: hld up in rr: effrt over 2f out: no imp and wl hld whn edgd lft 1f out: fin lame (vet said gelding was lame on it's right-fore leg)* **10/1**

4-34 **8** 4½ **Dalakina (IRE)**[14] 9178 3-8-12 **67**............................ LiamKeniry 7 43
(David Weston) *hdwy to ld after 1f: rdn and hdd over 2f out: sn outpcd and btn: bhd fnl f* **66/1**

2m 30.34s (-2.66) **Going Correction** -0.075s/f (Stan)
WFA 3 from 4yo+ 4lb **8** Ran SP% **120.8**
Speed ratings (Par 103): **105,104,104,102,97 95,93,90**
CSF £90.97 CT £116.00 TOTE £31.60: £4.90, £1.40, £1.10; EX 137.40 Trifecta £310.70.
Owner Laurence Bellman **Bred** Litex Commerce **Trained** Eastbury, Berks

The Form Book Flat 2019, Raceform Ltd, Newbury, RG14 5SJ

FOCUS
A bit of a turn-up here, with the well-treated pair seen off by a 25-1 shot. The winner posted a clear pb.

9422 BOMBARDIER BRITISH HOPPED AMBER BEER H'CAP — 1m 1y(P)
12:40 (12:41) (Class 4) (0-80,79) 3-Y-O+
£5,207 (£1,549; £774; £387; £300; £300) Stalls High

Form				RPR
3400	1		**Fields Of Dreams**[13] 9202 3-8-13 **72** .... JasonWatson 7 (Roger Charlton) *hld up in tch: effrt and hdwy on outer bnd 2f out: edgd lft u.p over 1f out: str chal ins fnl f: r.o wl to ld towards fin* **12/1**	81
1466	2	shd	**Thechildren'strust (IRE)**[14] 9173 4-9-1 **73** .... HectorCrouch 4 (Gary Moore) *t.k.h early: in tch in midfield: rdn: hdwy to chse ldr and swtchd rt over 1f out: led jst ins fnl f: sn hrd pressed: hdd and no ex towards fin* **7/1**	81
5015	3	2 ¾	**My Target (IRE)**[11] 9255 8-9-7 **79** .... FrannyNorton 6 (Michael Wigham) *stdd s: hld up in tch towards rr: nt clrest of runs jst over 2f out: effrt 2f out: kpt on ins fnl f: snatched 3rd on post: no threat to ldrs* **7/2**[1]	81
0426	4	nse	**Glory Of Paris (IRE)**[7] 9304 5-9-1 **73** ....(p) LukeMorris 2 (Michael Appleby) *taken down early: t.k.h: chsd ldrs: effrt over 2f out: bmpd 1f out: kpt on same pce ins fnl f* **8/1**	75
0-04	5	nse	**Pastime**[11] 9255 5-9-4 **76** .... JackMitchell 3 (Kevin Frost) *t.k.h: chsd ldrs: effrt on outer 2f out: hdwy and pushed lft 1f out: kpt on same pce ins fnl f (jockey said gelding was never travelling)* **13/2**[3]	77
410	6	1 ¾	**Reine De Vitesse (FR)**[48] 8498 3-9-0 **78** .... RayDawson(5) 8 (Jane Chapple-Hyam) *hld up in tch: effrt 2f out: kpt on ins fnl f: nvr trbld ldrs* **7/2**[1]	75
-000	7	¾	**Easy Tiger**[14] 9176 7-9-7 **79** ....(p) LiamKeniry 11 (David Weston) *chsd ldr: rdn over 2f out: lost 2nd and struggling to qckn whn bmpd 1f out: short of room and wknd ins fnl f* **33/1**	75
1050	8	¾	**Ocean Paradise**[14] 9176 3-9-1 **74** ....(h) JimCrowley 12 (William Knight) *taken down early: stdd and dropped in bhd after s: hld up in rr: effrt 2f out: nvr trbld ldrs* **16/1**	68
0241	9	nk	**Engrossed (IRE)**[121] 6026 3-9-4 **77** .... BenCurtis 10 (Martyn Meade) *hld up in tch in last trio: effrt 2f out: nvr trbld ldrs* **5/1**[2]	70
0000	10	1	**In The Red (IRE)**[39] 8755 6-8-11 **69** ....(b) TomMarquand 5 (Martin Smith) *led: rdn ent fnl 2f: hdd jst ins fnl f: sn wknd* **25/1**	60

1m 36.62s (-1.58) **Going Correction** -0.075s/f (Stan) **10 Ran SP% 118.4**
WFA 3 from 4yo+ 1lb
Speed ratings (Par 105): **104,103,101,101,101 99,98,97,97,96**
CSF £94.83 CT £362.48 TOTE £12.90: £4.20, £2.20, £1.80; EX 86.80 Trifecta £460.10.
Owner Frank McAleavy **Bred** Meon Valley Stud **Trained** Beckhampton, Wilts
■ Stewards' Enquiry : Jason Watson two-day ban; careless riding (Dec 26-29)

FOCUS
The early gallop wasn't that strong but it really picked up heading to the turn in.

9423 BOMBARDIER GOLDEN BEER (S) H'CAP — 7f 1y(P)
1:10 (1:10) (Class 6) (0-65,65) 3-Y-O+
£2,781 (£827; £413; £300; £300; £300) Stalls Low

Form				RPR
0006	1		**Kodiline (IRE)**[13] 9209 5-8-11 **55** ....(v) CliffordLee 5 (David Evans) *in tch in midfield: hdwy to chse ldrs over 2f out: c to centre and effrt over 1f out: styd on to ld wl ins fnl f: sn in command* **11/4**[2]	61
0060	2	2	**Dreamboat Annie**[16] 9160 4-8-2 **46** oh1 .... HollieDoyle 6 (Mark Usher) *chsd ldrs tl wnt 2nd 3f out: drvn and pressed ldr over 1f out: led ins fnl f: hdd and nt match pce of wnr wl ins fnl f* **6/1**	47
0000	3	1 ¼	**Gold Hunter (IRE)**[25] 9006 9-9-2 **60** ....(tp) RaulDaSilva 9 (Steve Flook) *dropped in after s: hld up in rr of main gp: clsd and carried lft over 2f out: chsd ldrs and drvn over 1f out: swtchd rt and kpt on same pce ins fnl f* **12/1**	58
0500	4	½	**Highland Acclaim (IRE)**[8] 9283 8-9-7 **65** ....(h) DavidProbert 4 (David O'Meara) *led: rdn 2f out: hdd ins fnl f: no ex and wknd wl ins fnl f* **9/4**[1]	61
006	5	4	**Sylviacliffs (FR)**[6] 9337 3-9-6 **64** ....(p) BenCurtis 2 (K R Burke) *chsd ldrs: rdn and edgd lft over 2f out: outpcd and btn over 1f out: wknd ins fnl f* **9/2**[3]	50
6655	6	1 ½	**Pharoh Jake**[55] 8279 11-7-12 **47** oh1 ow1 .... AledBeech(5) 1 (John Bridger) *hld up in tch: effrt ent fnl 2f: no imp and wl hld fnl f (jockey said gelding ran too free)* **20/1**	29
4040	7	2 ¼	**Fitzy**[25] 8998 3-8-2 **53** ....(p) GeorgeRooke(7) 8 (Paddy Butler) *v.s.a: n.d (jockey said gelding was very slowly away)* **25/1**	29
3020	8	1 ¼	**Islay Mist**[46] 8547 3-8-2 **51** ow3 ....(tp) GeorgiaDobie(5) 7 (Lee Carter) *wd thrght: midfield tl lost pl over 2f out: wl btn over 1f out* **8/1**	24
0-65	9	15	**Isla Skye (IRE)**[161] 4496 3-7-13 **46** oh1 .... DarraghKeenan(3) 3 (Barry Brennan) *chsd ldr tl 3f out: rdn and losing pl whn short of room and hmpd over 2f out: bhd fnl 2f* **66/1**	

1m 24.23s (-0.57) **Going Correction** -0.075s/f (Stan) **9 Ran SP% 118.8**
Speed ratings (Par 101): **100,97,96,95,91 89,86,85,68**
CSF £19.95 CT £175.04 TOTE £3.00: £1.50, £1.40, £3.10; EX 20.60 Trifecta £179.00.The wimmer was bought in for £5,000.
Owner K McCabe **Bred** Miss Aoife Boland **Trained** Pandy, Monmouths
■ Stewards' Enquiry : Ben Curtis three-day ban; careless riding (Dec 26-28)

FOCUS
An ordinary affair.

9424 LADBROKES HOME OF THE ODDS BOOST FILLIES' H'CAP — 7f 1y(P)
1:40 (1:41) (Class 3) (0-90,90) 3-Y-O £7,246 (£2,168; £1,084; £542; £270) Stalls Low

Form				RPR
0012	1		**Stay Classy (IRE)**[9] 9278 3-8-7 **83** ....(p) AngusVilliers(7) 4 (Richard Spencer) *in tch in midfield: effrt ent fnl f: rdn and qcknd to ld ins fnl f: sn clr: readily* **4/1**[3]	94
0103	2	2 ½	**Lady Of Aran (IRE)**[49] 8456 4-8-12 **81** .... KieranShoemark 6 (Charlie Fellowes) *hld up in tch in last trio: effrt and drifted rt wl over 1f out: styd on ins fnl f: snatched 2nd last stride: no ch w wnr* **11/4**[2]	85
0354	3	shd	**Visionara**[22] 9054 3-8-9 **78** .... JackMitchell 3 (Simon Crisford) *taken down early: chsd ldr: effrt wl over 1f out: ev ch u.p 1f out: led ins fnl f: sn hdd and nt match pce of wnr: lost 2nd last stride* **5/2**[1]	82
3112	4	hd	**Kwela**[22] 9054 3-8-7 **81** ....(p) GeorgiaDobie(5) 2 (Eve Johnson Houghton) *t.k.h: trckd ldrs: effrt over 1f out: pressed ldrs 1f out: nt match pce of wnr and kpt on same pce ins fnl f* **6/1**	84
2005	5	2	**First Link (USA)**[18] 9126 4-8-2 **71** oh6 .... HollieDoyle 7 (Jean-Rene Auvray) *stdd s: t.k.h: hld up in tch in rr: effrt wl over 1f out: kpt on ins fnl f: nvr trbld ldrs* **5/1**	69
-120	6	hd	**Diamond Oasis**[37] 8809 3-8-10 **79** ....(h) BenCurtis 5 (Hugo Palmer) *mounted in the chute: hld up in tch: effrt on inner wl over 1f out: chsd ldrs and kpt on same pce ins fnl f* **20/1**	76
0026	7	2 ½	**Emily Goldfinch**[18] 9129 6-9-0 **90** ....(p) GraceMcEntee(7) 1 (Phil McEntee) *broke fast: led: rdn ent fnl 2f: hdd ins fnl f: sn wknd* **20/1**	81

1m 23.43s (-1.37) **Going Correction** -0.075s/f (Stan) **7 Ran SP% 115.7**
Speed ratings (Par 104): **104,101,101,100,98 98,95**
CSF £15.84 TOTE £3.70: £2.70, £2.30; EX 16.60 Trifecta £37.40.
Owner Balasuriya,CookCunningham,Gowing,Spencer **Bred** Northern Bloodstock Agency Ltd **Trained** Newmarket, Suffolk

FOCUS
A nice performance from the winner, who has been transformed by the switch to AW racing.

9425 BETWAY NOVICE STKS — 1m 2f (P)
2:10 (2:14) (Class 5) 3-Y-O+ £3,428 (£1,020; £509; £254) Stalls Low

Form				RPR
2442	1		**Dubious Affair (IRE)**[13] 9202 3-8-12 **74** ....(v) KieranShoemark 3 (Sir Michael Stoute) *chsd ldrs tl wnt 2nd 8f out: rdn ent fnl 2f: clsd u.p to ld 100yds out: styd on* **15/8**[2]	69
05	2	1 ½	**Mercury Dime (IRE)**[25] 9011 3-8-12 **0** .... DavidProbert 10 (Ed Dunlop) *chsd ldng trio: effrt to chse ldng pair 2f out: kpt on but nt pce to chal: wnt 2nd last strides* **16/1**	66
23	3	nk	**Merry Vale**[166] 4326 3-8-12 **0** .... RobertHavlin 7 (John Gosden) *chsd ldr tl led after 1f: rdn over 1f out: drvn and hdd 100yds out: no ex and sn btn: lost 2nd last strides* **7/4**[1]	65
	4	2 ½	**Lep** 3-9-0 **0** .... PaddyBradley(3) 9 (Michael Attwater) *t.k.h: hld up in tch in midfield: effrt jst over 2f out: 4th and kpt on same pce fr over 1f out* **50/1**	65
	5	3 ½	**Opportunist** 3-9-3 **0** .... BenCurtis 5 (Martyn Meade) *s.i.s: midfield: rdn and outpcd over 2f out: no threat to ldrs but kpt on steadily ins fnl f (jockey said colt was never travelling)* **5/2**[3]	58
50	6	1	**Just A Touch (IRE)**[23] 9032 3-8-7 **0** .... RayDawson(5) 6 (Jane Chapple-Hyam) *midfield: 6th and outpcd 2f out: no threat to ldrs after: plugged on ins fnl f* **66/1**	51
	7	shd	**Polar Cloud** 3-9-3 **0** ....(b[1]) LukeMorris 1 (Heather Main) *s.i.s: a towards rr: rdn 4f out: outpcd over 2f out: n.d after: plugged on ins fnl f* **20/1**	56
0	8	1 ¼	**Laurentia (IRE)**[14] 9171 3-8-7 **0** .... SophieRalston(5) 4 (Dean Ivory) *t.k.h: led for 1f: chsd ldrs 8f out tl 2f out: sn outpcd u.p: wknd ins fnl f* **25/1**	49
5	9	nk	**Marmalade Day**[41] 8693 3-8-5 **0** .... LouisGaroghan(7) 2 (Gary Moore) *stdd s: t.k.h: hld up in last trio: effrt over 2f out: no imp and wl hld whn swtchd rt 1f out (jockey said filly was denied a clear run on the home bend)* **66/1**	48
66	10	4 ½	**Byron Green (IRE)**[20] 9091 7-9-2 **0** .... DarraghKeenan(3) 8 (Thomas Gallagher) *s.i.s: a bhd: rdn over 3f out: sn edgd lft and outpcd: wl bhd over 1f out (jockey said gelding was slowly away)* **66/1**	43

2m 5.12s (-1.48) **Going Correction** -0.075s/f (Stan) **10 Ran SP% 120.6**
WFA 3 from 7yo 2lb
Speed ratings (Par 103): **102,100,100,98,95 94,94,93,93,90**
CSF £28.71 TOTE £2.40: £1.20, £2.30, £1.10; EX 41.80 Trifecta £114.10.
Owner Mohamed Obaida **Bred** Rabbah Bloodstock Limited **Trained** Newmarket, Suffolk
■ Stewards' Enquiry : Ray Dawson caution; careless riding

FOCUS
No more than fair novice form.

9426 BETWAY H'CAP — 1m 2f (P)
2:40 (2:44) (Class 6) (0-65,66) 3-Y-O+
£2,781 (£827; £413; £300; £300; £300) Stalls Low

Form				RPR
2416	1		**Miss Elsa**[4] 9367 3-8-12 **61** .... GeorgiaDobie(5) 12 (Eve Johnson Houghton) *hld up in rr of main gp: swtchd rt: effrt and stl plenty to do over 1f out: str run u.p ins fnl f to ld towards fin: sn in command* **6/1**[3]	68
0036	2	1	**Music Major**[7] 9310 6-9-0 **56** .... RobertHavlin 8 (Michael Attwater) *bmpd s: in tch in midfield: nt clrest of runs ent fnl 2f: swtchd rt and effrt over 1f out: hdwy u.p 1f out: led 75yds out: sn hdd and nt match pce of wnr towards fin* **8/1**	60
0003	3	hd	**Subliminal**[13] 9209 4-9-2 **58** ....(b) BenCurtis 7 (Simon Dow) *nudged rt leaving stalls: hld up towards rr of main gp: clsd and nt clr run 2f out: swtchd rt over 1f out: hdwy 1f out: styd on wl ins fnl f* **2/1**[1]	62
6630	4	1 ½	**Settle Petal**[78] 7560 5-9-4 **63** .... PaddyBradley(3) 11 (Pat Phelan) *in tch in midfield on outer: effrt over 1f out: rdn and kpt on ins fnl f* **16/1**	64
0354	5	shd	**Elena**[9] 9279 3-9-3 **61** ....(p[1]) KieranShoemark 6 (Charles Hills) *wnt rt leaving stalls: t.k.h: chsd ldrs: effrt to press ldrs 2f out: ev ch u.p 1f out: chsd ldr briefly 100yds out: no ex and wknd towards fin* **10/1**	63
3362	6	nk	**Ballet Red (FR)**[9] 9279 3-8-11 **62** .... ElishaWhittington(7) 5 (Harry Dunlop) *chsd ldr: rdn and ev ch 2f out: drvn to ld 1f out: hdd 75yds out: no ex and wknd towards fin* **8/1**	63
0-34	7	½	**Al Daiha**[15] 9165 3-9-4 **62** .... LiamKeniry 10 (Ed Walker) *s.i.s: hld up in rr of main gp: clsd and swtchd rt 2f out: swtchd lft and hdwy over 1f out: rdn: swtchd rt and styd on ins fnl f: nvr trbld ldrs* **16/1**	62
0000	8	¾	**Global Wonder (IRE)**[7] 9306 4-9-10 **66** ....(b[1]) DougieCostello 4 (Suzi Best) *midfield: clsd and nt clr run ent fnl 2f: swtchd lft 2f out: rdn over 1f out: nt qckn and kpt on same pce ins fnl f* **20/1**	65
4606	9	3	**Black Medick**[11] 9244 3-9-7 **65** .... GeorgeDowning 1 (Laura Mongan) *led: rdn 2f out: drvn and hdd 1f out: wknd ins fnl f* **20/1**	58
343	10	nk	**Savitar (IRE)**[18] 9132 4-9-6 **62** ....(p) DanielMuscutt 9 (Lee Carter) *midfield: hdwy on outer to chse ldrs 1/2-way: rdn and unable qck over 1f out: wknd ins fnl f* **4/1**[2]	53
0650	11	2 ¾	**Stay In The Light**[166] 4346 4-8-2 **49** oh4 ....(w) RhiainIngram(5) 13 (Roger Ingram) *v.s.a: nvr involved (jockey said filly was slowly away)* **66/1**	35
0-00	12	2 ¾	**River Cafe (IRE)**[11] 9248 4-8-2 **49** oh4 .... AledBeech(5) 3 (John Bridger) *chsd ldrs: rdn over 2f out: short of room and hmpd bnd 2f out: nt rcvr and sn wknd* **50/1**	32

2m 5.48s (-1.12) **Going Correction** -0.075s/f (Stan) **12 Ran SP% 123.7**
WFA 3 from 4yo+ 2lb
Speed ratings (Par 101): **101,100,100,98,98 98,98,97,95,94 92,90**
CSF £53.80 CT £132.78 TOTE £7.00: £2.20, £2.40, £1.60; EX 50.60 Trifecta £168.90.
Owner Eden Racing Club **Bred** Eve Johnson Houghton **Trained** Blewbury, Oxon

FOCUS
A competitive handicap. The pace picked up a fair way out and that suited those held up.

9427 BOMBARDIER "MARCH TO YOUR OWN DRUM" "HANDS AND HEELS" APPRENTICE H'CAP (RE APPRENTICE SERIES) 1m 1y(P)
3:10 (3:13) (Class 6) (0-65,67) 3-Y-0+
£2,781 (£827; £413; £300; £300; £300) **Stalls** High

Form RPR
3060 1 **Noble Peace**[39] 8756 6-9-1 **57**.....................(t[1]) MorganCole(3) 2 71+
(Simon Pearce) *chsd ldrs: effrt to ld on inner over 1f out: clr and r.o wl ins fnl f: comf (trainer said, regards the apparent improvement in form, gelding benefitted from the application of a first-time tongue tie and a return to Lingfield where the gelding had won before)* **11/2[2]**
6065 2 5 **Perfect Grace**[25] 9006 3-9-9 **63**.....................(bt) KateLeahy 7 65
(Archie Watson) *led: rdn ent fnl 2f: hdd over 1f out: sn outpcd by wnr: kpt on same pce to hold 2nd ins fnl f* **10/1**
2020 3 1 1/4 **Duchess Of Avon**[64] 7982 4-9-5 **61**..................... RhysClutterbuck(3) 4 60
(Gary Moore) *in tch in midfield: effrt in 4th 2f out: kpt on steadily ins fnl f: no threat to wnr* **11/1**
3223 4 1 1/4 **Gottardo (IRE)**[25] 9006 4-9-9 **65**..................... SophieSmith(3) 1 61
(Ed Dunlop) *trckd ldrs on inner: swtchd rt and chsd ldr over 2f out: rdn and outpcd in 3rd over 1f out: wknd ins fnl f* **7/2[1]**
5303 5 4 **The Groove**[4] 9365 6-9-8 **66**..................... CameronIles(5) 6 53
(David Evans) *hld up in midfield: effrt 2f out: sn outpcd and wl btn fnl f* **7/2[1]**
6256 6 5 **Elsie Violet (IRE)**[79] 7526 3-9-3 **60**..................... SelmaGrage(3) 3 36
(Robert Eddery) *chsd ldr tl over 2f out: 4th and outpcd 2f out: sn btn and wknd fnl f* **12/1**
2400 7 1/2 **Misu Pete**[18] 9132 7-9-8 **61**.....................(p) IsobelFrancis 11 35
(Mark Usher) *wd thrght: a towards rr: rdn over 2f out: sn btn (jockey said gelding ran flat)* **25/1**
6662 8 3/4 **Comeonfeeltheforce (IRE)**[77] 7573 3-9-13 **67**.....................(t) LukeCatton 9 40
(Lee Carter) *a towards rr: rdn ent fnl 2f: no prog: n.d* **12/1**
3524 9 hd **Pearl Spectre (USA)**[11] 9249 8-9-1 **54**.....................(v) GraceMcEntee 8 26
(Phil McEntee) *midfield: lost pl and carried wd bnd 2f out: wl btn after* **8/1[3]**
4501 10 3/4 **Huddle**[13] 9209 3-9-6 **60**..................... GeorgeRooke 5 30
(William Knight) *hld up towards rr: effrt and swtchd rt bnd 2f out: no prog and sn btn: wknd* **11/2[2]**

1m 36.61s (-1.59) **Going Correction** -0.075s/f (Stan)
WFA 3 from 4yo+ 1lb **10 Ran SP% 123.0**
Speed ratings (Par 101): **104,99,97,96,92 87,87,86,86,85**
CSF £62.79 CT £614.74 TOTE £5.80: £2.30, £3.70, £3.90; EX 62.00 Trifecta £427.90.
Owner Killarney Glen **Bred** The Pocock Family **Trained** Newmarket, Suffolk

FOCUS
An ordinary 'hands and heels' contest. The winner matched this year's best.
T/Plt: £31.50 to a £1 stake. Pool: £57,940.45 - 1,338.99 winning units. T/Qpdt: £8.80 to a £1 stake. Pool: £6,189.75 - 514.88 winning units. **Steve Payne**

9428 - 9436a (Foreign Racing) - See Raceform Interactive

9407 CHELMSFORD (A.W) (L-H)
Thursday, December 12

OFFICIAL GOING: Polytrack: standard
Weather: Overcast with heavy showers

9437 BET AT TOTESPORT.COM EBF FILLIES' NOVICE STKS (PLUS 10 RACE) 1m (P)
3:50 (3:55) (Class 4) 2-Y-0 **£5,530** (£1,645; £822; £411) **Stalls** Low

Form RPR
54 1 **Indie Angel (IRE)**[17] 9158 2-9-0 0..................... RobertHavlin 2 74
(John Gosden) *mde all: shkn up whn pressed over 1f out: rdn and kpt on wl fnl f: a jst doing enough* **11/4[2]**
0 2 nk **True Scarlet (IRE)**[48] 8510 2-9-0 0..................... HectorCrouch 1 73
(Ed Walker) *trckd ldng pair: effrt to cl on front pair over 1f out: rdn and kpt on wl to go 2nd ins fnl f: clsd all the way to the line* **6/1[3]**
3 hd **Symbol Of Love** 2-9-0 0..................... JamesDoyle 5 73
(Charlie Appleby) *trckd ldr: rdn to chse wnr over 1f out: keeping on same pce fnl f: lost 2nd cl home* **5/4[1]**
04 4 4 **Dancing Approach**[16] 9163 2-9-0 0..................... JasonWatson 8 64
(Roger Charlton) *trckd ldrs: pushed along over 2f out: rdn and edgd lft over 1f out: kpt on one pce fnl f* **22/1**
5 1/2 **Foronceinmylife (IRE)** 2-9-0 0..................... TomMarquand 11 63
(Jamie Osborne) *racd in midfield: rdn along and no imp over 2f out: hdwy into 5th over 1f out: one pce fnl f* **66/1**
0 6 3/4 **Surprise Encounter**[23] 9046 2-9-0 0..................... BenCurtis 4 61
(David Simcock) *midfield on inner: niggled along 3f out: rdn and no imp over 1f out: one pce fnl f (jockey said filly stumbled leaving the stalls)* **8/1**
7 7 **Lake Lucerne (USA)** 2-9-0 0..................... KieranO'Neill 10 45
(John Gosden) *dwlt bdly and racd in rr: rdn along in rr over 2f out: mde sme late hdwy (jockey said filly was slowly away and ran green)* **14/1**
8 1 3/4 **Maximize** 2-9-0 0..................... JackMitchell 3 41
(Peter Chapple-Hyam) *v.s.a and racd in last: drvn along in rr 2f out: nvr on terms* **33/1**
56 9 1 **Soramond (GER)**[12] 9243 2-9-0 0..................... KieranShoemark 12 38
(Ed Dunlop) *in rr of midfield: minor hdwy on outer over 2f out: wknd fnl f* **66/1**
00 10 6 **Encashment**[8] 9311 2-9-0 0..................... TomQueally 6 25
(Alan King) *midfield in tch: rdn along and outpcd over 2f out: wknd over 1f out* **50/1**
11 1 **Aventuriere** 2-9-0 0..................... PJMcDonald 9 22
(Mark Johnston) *in rr of midfield: rdn along and green 3f out: nvr on terms* **20/1**
05 12 8 **Mums The Law**[79] 7547 2-8-9 0..................... RayDawson(5) 7
(Jane Chapple-Hyam) *midfield on outer: rdn along and lost pl over 2f out: sn bhd* **50/1**

1m 41.14s (1.24) **Going Correction** 0.0s/f (Stan) **12 Ran SP% 122.1**
Speed ratings (Par 95): **93,92,92,88,88 87,80,78,77,71 70,62**
CSF £19.17 TOTE £3.40: £1.20, £1.50, £1.10; EX 21.60 Trifecta £61.30.
Owner Cheveley Park Stud **Bred** Ringfort Stud & P Hancock **Trained** Newmarket, Suffolk

FOCUS
A modest fillies' novice in which nothing got in a blow from off the pace.

9438 TOTEPOOL CASHBACK CLUB AT TOTESPORT.COM NURSERY H'CAP 7f (P)
4:20 (4:23) (Class 6) (0-60,62) 2-Y-0
£3,105 (£924; £461; £400; £400; £400) **Stalls** Low

Form RPR
005 1 **Surrajah (IRE)**[118] 6147 2-8-10 **48**.....................(t[1]) DavidProbert 4 53+
(Tom Clover) *j. awkwardly: racd in midfield: swtchd rt and rdn and clsd on ldrs over 1f out: styd on wl to ld fnl 100yds despite hanging lft* **9/4[1]**
060 2 1 **Cesifire (IRE)**[17] 9158 2-9-3 **55**..................... PJMcDonald 10 56
(Adam West) *midfield on outer: hdwy to trck ldr 4f out: rdn along to ld over 1f out: drvn and hdd by wnr ins fnl f whn edging lft: no ex* **12/1**
5035 3 3/4 **Leg It Lenny (IRE)**[111] 6387 2-9-10 **62**.....................(t[1]) TomQueally 3 61
(Robert Cowell) *midfield on inner: hdwy to chse ldrs 2f out: sn rdn and wnt 3rd over 1f out: no imp on front pair fnl f* **9/2[3]**
050 4 1 1/2 **Sea Willow**[84] 7393 2-8-12 **53**.....................(h[1]) GabrieleMalune(3) 5 49+
(Henry Spiller) *hld up: stl lots to do 2f out: rdn along and swtchd rt over 1f out: kpt on v strly clsng stages to snatch 4th cl home* **25/1**
500 5 1/2 **Light Lily**[14] 9195 2-8-9 **47**..................... JFEgan 1 41
(Paul D'Arcy) *trckd ldrs: rdn along and lost pl over 1f out: one pce fnl f* **8/1**
6456 6 1 3/4 **Star Of St Louis (FR)**[37] 8825 2-8-8 **46**.....................(v[1]) KieranO'Neill 12 36
(Denis Quinn) *led after 1f: rdn along and hdd over 1f out: wknd fnl f* **8/1**
000 7 5 **Heleta**[72] 7786 2-8-13 **54**..................... DarraghKeenan(3) 7 31
(Peter Hedger) *hld up: drvn along in rr over 2f out: nvr on terms* **18/1**
3300 8 2 **Jane Victoria**[101] 6799 2-8-13 **51**.....................(p[1]) EoinWalsh 2 23
(Luke McJannet) *led for 1f then settled in midfield in tch: rdn and outpcd over 2f out: wknd over 1f out* **20/1**
0050 9 nk **The Works (IRE)**[15] 9179 2-8-4 **45**.....................(b[1]) SeanDavis(3) 11 16
(Declan Carroll) *dwlt: midfield on outer and racd freely: wd 3f out: rdn and no imp over 2f out: lost pl and wknd over 1f out* **33/1**
1066 10 2 1/4 **Twittering (IRE)**[13] 9212 2-9-2 **59**.....................(p) GeorgiaDobie(5) 6 24
(Oliver Signy) *in rr of midfield: rdn along and dropped to last over 1f out: sn bhd (jockey said colt stopped quickly)* **11/4[2]**

1m 28.87s (1.67) **Going Correction** 0.0s/f (Stan) **10 Ran SP% 122.3**
Speed ratings (Par 94): **90,88,88,86,85 83,78,75,75,72**
CSF £31.97 CT £121.95 TOTE £3.30: £1.60, £3.20, £1.90; EX 38.00 Trifecta £202.70.
Owner Raj Matharu & Suresh Sivagnanam **Bred** Camas Park & Lynch Bages **Trained** Newmarket, Suffolk

FOCUS
Low grade stuff but one or two have the potential to end up in a better grade than this, not least the winner.

9439 EXTRA PLACES AT TOTESPORT.COM H'CAP 7f (P)
4:50 (4:53) (Class 7) (0-50,51) 3-Y-0+ **£2,911** (£866; £432; £216) **Stalls** Low

Form RPR
5320 1 **Just An Idea (IRE)**[15] 9185 5-9-0 **48**.....................(b) RhiainIngram(5) 4 56
(Roger Ingram) *midfield in tch: hdwy to chse ldng pair over 2f out: rdn along and qcknd up wl to ld over 1f out: r.o wl fnl f* **14/1**
05/0 2 2 **Captain Power (IRE)**[43] 8679 7-9-6 **49**..................... AdamKirby 6 52
(Gordon Elliott, Ire) *in rr of midfield: hdwy u.p over 1f out: swtchd lft to rail and drvn to go 2nd ent fnl f: kpt on wl* **9/4[1]**
1200 3 1/2 **Lady Morpheus**[37] 8822 3-9-7 **50**..................... HectorCrouch 3 52
(Gary Moore) *racd in midfield: bmpd along over 2f out: rdn along to chse ldrs over 1f out: hung lft u.p 1f out: kpt on fnl f* **14/1**
0606 4 1/2 **My Lady Claire**[17] 9160 3-9-6 **49**.....................(v[1]) DavidProbert 8 49
(Patrick Chamings) *in rr of midfield: effrt to cl 2f out: swtchd rt and rdn over 1f out: kpt on wl fnl f: nrst fin* **8/1**
3226 5 1 3/4 **Red Skye Delight (IRE)**[12] 9248 3-9-8 **51**..................... KieranO'Neill 13 47
(Luke McJannet) *chsd ldr: pushed along to ld 2f out: sn rdn and hdd by wnr over 1f out: wknd fnl f* **10/1**
4243 6 1 **Drop Kick Murphi (IRE)**[8] 9298 5-9-5 **48**..................... AdrianMcCarthy 10 41
(Christine Dunnett) *dwlt and racd in rr: hdwy between rivals 2f out: rdn on outer over 1f out: kpt on fnl f but n.d* **9/2[3]**
0005 7 1/2 **Geneva Spur (USA)**[8] 9298 3-9-0 **50**.....................(b) AngusVilliers(7) 7 42
(Roger Varian) *chsd ldrs: rdn along and no imp over 2f out: swtchd rt whn u.p fnl f: no ex* **14/1**
0600 8 1 1/4 **Satchville Flyer**[8] 9298 8-9-2 **45**.....................(p) PhilipPrince 12 34
(Milton Bradley) *hld up: rdn and outpcd over 2f out: nvr on terms* **33/1**
360 9 1 **Canimar**[12] 9247 4-9-2 **45**.....................(v) JosephineGordon 9 31
(Shaun Keightley) *led: rdn along and hdd 2f out: wkng whn short of room ins fnl f* **50/1**
600 10 1 3/4 **Forgotten Girl**[56] 8290 3-9-2 **45**..................... EoinWalsh 2 26
(Christine Dunnett) *hld up: a bhd (jockey said filly was never travelling)* **50/1**
0000 11 1/2 **Supreme Dream**[85] 7335 3-9-2 **45**.....................(w) LewisEdmunds 5 25
(Shaun Harris) *hld up: rdn and minor hdwy 2f out: n.d* **50/1**
4320 12 4 1/2 **Obsession For Gold (IRE)**[50] 8469 3-9-6 **49**.........(t) TomMarquand 14 17
(Mrs Ilka Gansera-Leveque) *racd keenly in midfield: shuffled bk over 3f out: rdn and no imp 2f out: btn whn hmpd over 1f out* **4/1[2]**
5624 13 7 **Reshaan (IRE)**[1] 9410 4-8-13 **47**.....................(b) ThoreHammerHansen(5) 11
(Alexandra Dunn) *chsd ldrs: rdn along and lost pl 2f out: sn bhd* **7/1**
00-0 14 17 **Crakadawn**[42] 8689 3-9-2 **45**.....................(p[1]) JoeyHaynes 15
(Chelsea Banham) *dwlt but sn rcvrd to chse ldrs: hung rt and lost pl qckly over 2f out: sn bhd (jockey said filly hung right-handed)* **50/1**

1m 27.04s (-0.16) **Going Correction** 0.0s/f (Stan) **14 Ran SP% 132.4**
Speed ratings (Par 97): **100,97,97,96,94 93,92,91,90,88 87,82,74,55**
CSF £49.36 CT £410.99 TOTE £15.40: £3.70, £1.70, £4.20; EX 74.20 Trifecta £818.50.
Owner Miss Camilla Swift **Bred** John T Heffernan **Trained** Epsom, Surrey

FOCUS
A desperately weak race won by an exposed 5yo.

9440 IRISH LOTTO AT TOTESPORT.COM H'CAP 1m (P)
5:20 (5:22) (Class 2) (0-110,110) 3-Y-0+ **£12,938** (£3,850; £1,924; £962) **Stalls** Low

Form RPR
1061 1 **Assimilation (IRE)**[70] 7856 3-8-4 **86** oh1..................... KieranO'Neill 3 93
(Ed Walker) *midfield on outer: pushed along and briefly outpcd 2f out: rdn and hdwy over 1f out: led ins fnl f: r.o wl* **10/1**
-113 2 1/2 **The Gill Brothers**[14] 9200 3-8-6 **88**.....................(t) JFEgan 8 94
(Stuart Williams) *restrained in rr and plld hrd: smooth hdwy on inner over 1f out: rdn and wnt 2nd ins fnl f: kpt on wl* **9/2[2]**

0602 **3** nk **Silent Attack**[14] 9198 6-9-3 **98**........................... JasonWatson 5 103
(Tony Carroll) *trckd ldr: rdn along to chal over 1f out: led ins fnl f: sn hdd by wnr and no ex: lost 2nd cl home* **5/1**[3]

32-1 **4** ¾ **Fox Power (IRE)**[237] 1926 3-9-4 **100**........................ JamesDoyle 4 103
(Richard Hannon) *led: shkn up to qckn tempo 2f out: rdn along and strly pressed over 1f out: hdd ins fnl f and no ex* **11/4**[1]

5462 **5** ½ **Firmament**[62] 8096 7-9-2 **97**..............................(p) AdamKirby 6 99
(David O'Meara) *midfield in tch: rdn along and no imp 2f out: kpt on one pce fnl f* **7/1**

0261 **6** 1 **Samphire Coast**[14] 9199 6-8-2 **86** oh5..................(v) DarraghKeenan(3) 2 86
(Derek Shaw) *trckd ldrs on inner: rdn along and no imp over 1f out: wknd fnl f* **14/1**

-364 **7** nse **Wait Forever (IRE)**[26] 9000 4-9-0 **102**.................... StefanoCherchi(7) 7 102
(Marco Botti) *hld up: effrt to cl on outer over 1f out: sn rdn and no imp: n.d* **10/1**

-200 **8** 2¼ **Librisa Breeze**[22] 9064 7-10-1 **110**............................ JoeyHaynes 1 105
(Dean Ivory) *hld up: pushed along 2f out: sn rdn and no hdwy: wknd fnl f* **6/1**

1m 38.81s (-1.09) **Going Correction** 0.0s/f (Stan)
WFA 3 from 4yo+ 1lb **8** Ran SP% **113.1**
Speed ratings (Par 109): **105,104,104,103,102 101,101,99**
CSF £53.25 CT £255.88 TOTE £10.20: £3.40, £1.60, £2.00; EX 62.90 Trifecta £350.90.
Owner Dubai Thoroughbred Racing **Bred** Rathbarry Stud **Trained** Upper Lambourn, Berks

FOCUS
A really good quality handicap that wasn't run at a particularly strong gallop. They finished in a bit of a heap which is never a good sign in terms of value of the form.

9441 BET IN PLAY AT TOTESPORT.COM H'CAP 6f (P)
5:50 (5:51) (Class 4) (0-85,84) 3-Y-O+
£5,530 (£1,645; £822; £411; £400; £400) **Stalls** Centre

Form RPR

1351 **1** **Spirit Of May**[47] 8550 3-9-4 **81**........................... JackMitchell 10 94
(Roger Teal) *broke wl and mde all: shkn up 2f out: sn rdn and grad extended advantage ent fnl f: r.o wl* **7/2**[2]

4620 **2** 3¼ **Sandridge Lad (IRE)**[12] 9245 3-8-4 **70**..................... DarraghKeenan(3) 3 73
(John Ryan) *trckd ldrs: effrt to chse ldr 2f out: sn drvn and no imp on wnr 1f out: kpt on one pce fnl f* **8/1**

0133 **3** 1½ **Revolutionise (IRE)**[51] 8420 3-9-3 **80**.....................(t[1]) PJMcDonald 4 78
(Stuart Williams) *in rr of midfield: hdwy into 5th 2f out: rdn and kpt on to go 3rd wl ins fnl f* **4/1**[3]

5400 **4** 1¾ **Suzi's Connoisseur**[13] 9214 8-9-4 **81**.........................(b) JFEgan 5 74
(Jane Chapple-Hyam) *midfield in tch: rdn along to chse ldrs over 1f out: wknd fnl f* **10/1**

2610 **5** nse **Red Alert**[23] 9057 5-9-7 **84**.. JasonWatson 6 76
(Tony Carroll) *hld up: minor hdwy u.p over 1f out: kpt on but n.d (jockey said gelding hung left-handed)* **16/1**

2102 **6** ½ **Young John (IRE)**[15] 9183 6-9-7 **84**........................ JosephineGordon 2 75
(Mike Murphy) *dwlt and hmpd s: hld up: rdn and sme late hdwy fnl f but n.d (jockey said gelding missed the break)* **6/1**

5442 **7** 2¼ **Martineo**[35] 8893 4-9-2 **79**.. JoeyHaynes 8 63
(John Butler) *hld up in rr: a bhd* **3/1**[1]

0-00 **8** 3½ **Omran**[23] 9057 5-9-1 **78**.......................................(t) HectorCrouch 1 50
(Michael Wigham) *midfield on inner: pushed along and no imp 2f out: rdn and wknd over 1f out (jockey said gelding was denied a clear run)* **25/1**

013 **9** 2¼ **Cockney Hill**[35] 8894 3-9-0 **77**.................................. TomMarquand 7 42
(Joseph Tuite) *chsd wnr: rdn along and lost pl 2f out: sn bhd* **16/1**

1m 12.07s (-1.63) **Going Correction** 0.0s/f (Stan) **9** Ran SP% **117.3**
Speed ratings (Par 105): **110,105,103,101,101 100,97,92,89**
CSF £32.22 CT £118.06 TOTE £5.40: £1.60, £2.90, £1.40; EX 32.00 Trifecta £157.20.
Owner Mrs Carol Borras **Bred** R P Phillips **Trained** Lambourn, Berks

FOCUS
Not many of these came into this in form but Spirit Of May did and he bossed this from the word go.

9442 DOUBLE DELIGHT HAT-TRICK HEAVEN AT TOTESPORT.COM MEDIAN AUCTION MAIDEN STKS 1m 5f 66y(P)
6:20 (6:20) (Class 6) 3-5-Y-O **£3,105** (£924; £461; £230) **Stalls** Low

Form RPR

5442 **1** **Clap Your Hands**[19] 9134 3-9-0 72...................... PoppyBridgwater(5) 5 54+
(David Simcock) *hld up: smooth hdwy 2f out: rdn to chse ldr over 1f out: r.o wl to ld fnl strides* **2/9**[1]

605 **2** nk **Hidden Pearl**[125] 5880 3-8-9 59............................ SophieRalston(5) 3 49+
(John Berry) *trckd ldr and racd freely: pushed along to ld 2f out: drvn and edgd lft ent fnl f: hdd by wnr fnl strides* **6/1**[2]

0406 **3** 3¾ **Maykir**[80] 7520 3-9-5 40.. AdrianMcCarthy 1 45
(J R Jenkins) *racd in last pair: rdn and outpcd over 1f out: swtchd rt and kpt on fnl f: no match for front pair* **33/1**

0000 **4** 2¼ **Jailbreak (IRE)**[13] 9216 3-9-5 42..........................(p) JosephineGordon 4 42
(Conrad Allen) *led at a v stdy pce: qcknd tempo 5f out: rdn along and hdd 2f out: wknd fnl f* **18/1**

P **5** 1 **Bonsai Bay**[73] 7772 4-9-9 0.................................. GeorgeDowning 2 38
(Ian Williams) *racd in last: rdn along in last 5f out: nvr able to get on terms* **8/1**[3]

3m 3.23s (9.63) **Going Correction** 0.0s/f (Stan)
WFA 3 from 4yo 4lb **5** Ran SP% **115.4**
Speed ratings (Par 101): **70,69,67,66,65**
CSF £2.49 TOTE £1.10: £1.10, £1.90; EX 3.40 Trifecta £12.80.
Owner Twenty Stars Partnership **Bred** Rabbah Bloodstock Limited **Trained** Newmarket, Suffolk

FOCUS
A very weak maiden which was run at a very steady early gallop. The finish was fought out by the highest-rated pair.

9443 BUY YOUR 2020 MEMBERSHIP NOW H'CAP 1m 2f (P)
6:50 (6:55) (Class 5) (0-70,71) 3-Y-O+
£5,175 (£1,540; £769; £400; £400; £400) **Stalls** Low

Form RPR

-060 **1** **Admodum (USA)**[19] 9132 6-8-8 **60**.......................(p) DarraghKeenan(3) 2 70+
(John Butler) *trckd ldrs on inner: pushed along and stdy hdwy to ld over 1f out: steadily rdn clr ins fnl f: comf* **7/2**[2]

3106 **2** 2½ **Dreamboat Dave (IRE)**[14] 9202 3-8-9 **60**...................... KieranO'Neill 8 65
(Sarah Humphrey) *midfield on outer: pushed along and forced wd off home bnd 2f out: rdn and hung lft ent fnl f: styd on wl into 2nd clsng stages: no ch w wnr (jockey said gelding hung left-handed in the home straight)* **7/1**

0602 **3** nk **Noble Fox**[19] 9132 3-9-3 **68**..(b) AdamKirby 6 72
(Clive Cox) *hld up: effrt into midfield on outer 2f out: rdn and kpt on wl to go 3rd wl ins fnl f* **5/1**[3]

1134 **4** ½ **Lucky's Dream**[140] 5338 4-9-6 **69**.............................. JasonWatson 9 75+
(Ian Williams) *midfield and travelled strly: prog whn hmpd over 2f out: hdwy and gng wl on the bit over 1f out: swtchd rt and rdn ent fnl f: hmpd immediately and all ch gone: nt rcvr (jockey said gelding ran too freely and was denied a clear run)* **10/1**

0630 **5** nk **Bay Of Naples (IRE)**[19] 9140 3-9-2 **67**............................ TomEaves 7 70
(Michael Herrington) *trckd ldr: rdn along to hold position 2f out: drvn and ev ch over 1f out: no ex fnl f* **33/1**

3314 **6** nk **Canasta**[42] 8705 3-9-3 **68**.. JackMitchell 5 70
(James Fanshawe) *prom on heels of ldrs: pushed along into 4th 2f out: rdn and unable qck over 1f out: no ex fnl f* **5/2**[1]

2045 **7** 3 **Don't Jump George (IRE)**[36] 8862 4-9-8 **71**..........(t) KieranShoemark 3 67
(Shaun Lycett) *led: shkn up w short ld 2f out: rdn along and hdd by wnr over 1f out: wknd fnl f* **14/1**

040 **8** ½ **Andaleep (IRE)**[23] 9050 3-9-2 **67**.................................... BenCurtis 14 62
(Graeme McPherson) *chsd ldrs on outer: rdn along and unable qck over 1f out: wknd fnl f* **8/1**

3300 **9** 1½ **The Night King**[14] 9202 4-9-4 **67**..............................(p) TomQueally 1 59
(Mick Quinn) *rdn along and reminders in rr after 1f: drvn and struggling 2f out: mde sme late hdwy passed btn rivals* **20/1**

050 **10** ¾ **Albanderi**[127] 5810 3-8-10 **61**......................................(w) DavidProbert 16 52
(Andrew Balding) *hld up: drvn along and no imp over 1f out: nvr on terms* **25/1**

26-0 **11** ½ **Zoffany Bay (IRE)**[46] 6200 5-9-5 **68**.....................(v[1]) TomMarquand 12 58
(Ali Stronge) *midfield on outer: pushed along 3f out: rdn and lost pl over 1f out: sn wknd* **33/1**

6000 **12** nse **Surrey Blaze (IRE)**[23] 9054 4-9-6 **69**........................ PJMcDonald 11 59
(Joseph Tuite) *midfield on inner: rdn along and no imp over 1f out: one pce fnl f* **20/1**

3520 **13** 2 **Momtalik (USA)**[15] 9180 4-9-7 **70**.............................. LewisEdmunds 4 56
(Derek Shaw) *racd in midfield: rdn along and struggling 2f out: sn bhd* **33/1**

6332 **14** 2¾ **First Flight (IRE)**[19] 9138 8-9-7 **70**............................ EoinWalsh 15 50
(Tony Newcombe) *dwlt and racd in rr: nvr on terms (jockey said gelding jumped awkwardly leaving the stalls)* **28/1**

2m 7.02s (-1.58) **Going Correction** 0.0s/f (Stan)
WFA 3 from 4yo+ 2lb **14** Ran SP% **132.5**
Speed ratings (Par 103): **106,104,103,103,103 102,100,100,98,98 97,97,96,94**
CSF £28.92 CT £129.17 TOTE £4.50: £1.80, £2.80, £1.80; EX 38.80 Trifecta £292.80.
Owner A Campbell **Bred** J S Bolger **Trained** Newmarket, Suffolk

FOCUS
Ordinary stuff but it provided the stage for a good old fashioned gamble and Admodum's backers never really had too much to worry about.

9444 CELEBRATE DECEMBER'S HERO SAMANTHA HUTCHINGS H'CAP 1m 2f (P)
7:20 (7:24) (Class 6) (0-55,55) 3-Y-O+
£3,105 (£924; £461; £400; £400; £400) **Stalls** Low

Form RPR

0062 **1** **Arlecchino's Arc (IRE)**[21] 9090 4-9-7 **55**..................(v) JasonWatson 6 62
(Mark Usher) *trckd ldr: pushed along to ld 2f out: drvn along w 1 l ld ent fnl f: r.o wl* **4/1**[3]

1213 **2** 1½ **Muraaqeb**[5] 9362 5-9-7 **55**.......................................(p) DavidProbert 5 59
(Milton Bradley) *midfield in tch: wnt 4th 2f out: rdn and continually hung lft ent fnl f: r.o but nt rch wnr (jockey said gelding hung left-handed)* **7/2**[2]

3534 **3** 1½ **Brother In Arms (IRE)**[19] 9139 5-9-1 **49**........................ TomMarquand 7 50
(Tony Carroll) *midfield on inner: drvn along 2f out: kpt on wl for press fnl f: no match for front pair* **10/1**

4450 **4** 1 **Tyrsal (IRE)**[8] 9310 8-8-12 **46** oh1..........................(v) JosephineGordon 12 45
(Shaun Keightley) *midfield on outer: rdn along and outpcd over 2f out: mde late hdwy on the outer fnl f but n.d* **14/1**

5102 **5** ½ **Cash N Carrie (IRE)**[5] 9362 5-8-11 **48**.................. TheodoreLadd(3) 4 46
(Michael Appleby) *led: rdn along and hdd 2f out: wknd fnl f* **5/1**

202 **6** 1¾ **Seaquinn**[65] 8000 4-8-12 **46** oh1.................................. KierenFox 1 41
(John Best) *trckd ldrs on inner: rdn along and no imp over 1f out: wknd fnl f* **7/1**

4103 **7** 2¾ **Dyagilev**[21] 9090 4-9-4 **52**...................................(b) AdrianMcCarthy 8 42
(Simon Pearce) *hld up: nvr on terms (jockey said gelding hung left-handed)* **5/2**[1]

3050 **8** 3¾ **Voice Of A Leader (IRE)**[17] 9157 8-9-4 **52**.................... JoeyHaynes 11 35
(Chelsea Banham) *restrained in rr: rdn and no hdwy 2f out: a bhd* **33/1**

4050 **9** 14 **Potters Question**[19] 9128 3-9-2 **55**.......................... GabrieleMalune(3) 13 12
(Amy Murphy) *restless at s: dwlt bdly and racd in rr: nvr on terms* **50/1**

0206 **10** 3¾ **Seventii**[37] 8843 5-8-5 **46** oh1.................................. SelmaGrage(7) 9
(Robert Eddery) *midfield on outer: lost pl qckly 4f out: sn detached* **33/1**

2m 7.06s (-1.54) **Going Correction** 0.0s/f (Stan)
WFA 3 from 4yo+ 2lb **10** Ran SP% **123.6**
Speed ratings (Par 101): **106,104,103,102,102 101,98,95,84,81**
CSF £19.48 CT £136.49 TOTE £5.00: £1.60, £1.60, £2.40; EX 22.80 Trifecta £159.30.
Owner K Senior **Bred** Mrs Eithne Hamilton **Trained** Upper Lambourn, Berks

FOCUS
A weak handicap in which very few got into contention.
T/Plt: £16.40 to a £1 stake. Pool: £36,194.23 - 2203.14 winning units T/Qpdt: £11.40 to a £1 stake. Pool: £4,068.10 - 354.32 winning units **Mark Grantham**

9399 WOLVERHAMPTON (A.W) (L-H)
Thursday, December 12

OFFICIAL GOING: Tapeta: standard
Wind: Light behind Weather: Rain clearing after race 3

9445 BETWAY CLASSIFIED STKS 6f 20y (Tp)
3:35 (3:37) (Class 6) 3-Y-O+
£3,816 (£1,135; £567; £400; £400; £400) **Stalls** Low

Form RPR

6304 **1** **Isabella Ruby**[10] 9276 4-8-7 46.............................(h) GavinAshton(7) 10 54
(Lisa Williamson) *hld up: hdwy over 1f out: r.o to ld nr fin* **7/1**[2]

300 **2** ½ **Sagittarian Wind**[17] 9161 3-9-0 50..........................(t[1]) HollieDoyle 5 53
(Archie Watson) *a.p: rdn to ld ins fnl f: hdd nr fin* **7/2**[1]

6000 **3** ¾ **Poppy May (IRE)**[17] 9161 5-9-0 48............................ FrannyNorton 12 51
(James Given) *hld up: nt clr run over 2f out: hdwy over 1f out: r.o* **10/1**

00 **4** 1 1/2 **Alaskan Bay (IRE)**[142] 5264 4-8-11 48 CameronNoble(3) 11 46
(Rae Guest) *led early: chsd ldrs: rdn over 1f out: styd on same pce ins fnl f* **16/1**

0400 **5** nk **Cuban Spirit**[56] 8295 4-9-0 49 DanielMuscutt 4 45
(Lee Carter) *plld hrd and prom: wnt 2nd over 3f out: rdn to ld over 1f out: hdd ins fnl f: no ex towards fin (jockey said gelding hung right-handed from half way)* **10/1**

0060 **6** 1/2 **Valley Belle (IRE)**[3] 9398 3-8-7 50 (t[1]) GraceMcEntee(7) 8 43
(Phil McEntee) *s.i.s: sn pushed along in rr: hdwy on outer over 1f out: sn rdn: r.o ins fnl f: nt rch ldrs* **15/2**[3]

6000 **7** nk **Rock Warbler (IRE)**[3] 9395 6-9-0 44 (e) JamesSullivan 6 42
(Michael Mullineaux) *hld up: pushed along 1/2-way: hdwy over 1f out: r.o: nt trble ldrs* **8/1**

3650 **8** 1 3/4 **Dodgy Bob**[50] 8469 6-9-0 46 (v) PhilDennis 3 37
(Michael Mullineaux) *sn pushed along to go prom: rdn over 1f out: no ex ins fnl f* **15/2**[3]

6-05 **9** hd **Illustrious Spirit**[42] 8697 4-9-0 44 (p) PaulMulrennan 7 37
(Ali Stronge) *sn led: rdn and hdd over 1f out: wknd ins fnl f* **7/1**[2]

-006 **10** 1/2 **Loveatfirstlight (IRE)**[50] 8472 3-9-0 48 (p[1]) ShaneKelly 1 35
(James Unett) *s.i.s: rdn over 1f out: n.d (jockey said filly missed the break)* **25/1**

6-00 **11** 1 3/4 **Savannah Beau**[77] 7628 7-8-7 45 JonathanFisher(7) 2 31
(Scott Dixon) *plld hrd in 2nd tl nt clr run over 3f out: rdn over 1f out: wknd ins fnl f* **50/1**

6000 **12** 3/4 **Nananita (IRE)**[17] 9161 3-9-0 49 DougieCostello 13 28
(Mark Loughnane) *hld up: rdn over 2f out: n.d* **50/1**

0560 **13** 7 **Auntie June**[9] 9287 3-9-0 26 LiamKeniry 9 7
(Roy Brotherton) *s.i.s: a in rr: bhd whn hung rt over 2f out* **100/1**

1m 13.61s (-0.89) **Going Correction** -0.125s/f (Stan) 13 Ran SP% 114.7
Speed ratings (Par 101): **100,99,98,96,95 95,94,92,92,91 89,88,78**
CSF £29.69 TOTE £5.30: £1.80, £1.40, £2.70; EX 30.70 Trifecta £167.00.
Owner Wb Fat Boar Racing **Bred** Killashee House Limited **Trained** Taporley, Wrexham
■ Stewards' Enquiry : Paul Mulrennan caution; careless riding

FOCUS
A modest, well-run sprint handicap with no hard-luck stories.

9446 BETWAY LIVE CASINO H'CAP 1m 1f 104y (Tp)
4:05 (4:06) (Class 6) (0-52,54) 3-Y-O+
£3,816 (£1,135; £567; £400; £400; £400) Stalls Low

Form RPR

0 **1** **Mojambo (IRE)**[52] 8404 4-9-2 45 (t[1]) FrannyNorton 6 52
(Stephen Michael Hanlon, Ire) *hld up: hdwy over 1f out: rdn and r.o to ld nr fin (trainers rep said, regards the apparent improvement in form, filly may have appreciated the Tapeta surface on this occasion)* **50/1**

5555 **2** hd **Cat Royale (IRE)**[3] 9384 6-9-3 46 (b) DannyBrock 12 53
(John Butler) *led over 8f out: sn hdd: chsd ldr who wnt clr over 6f out: tk clsr order 3f out: led over 2f out: rdn over 1f out: hdd nr fin* **7/2**[2]

-303 **3** 1 1/4 **Kybosh (IRE)**[36] 8863 3-9-7 52 AlistairRawlinson 4 56
(Michael Appleby) *sn led: hdd over 8f out: chsd ldrs: pushed along over 3f out: rdn to chse ldr and edgd lft ins fnl f: styd on* **2/1**[1]

0064 **4** 1 1/4 **Melabi (IRE)**[9] 9289 6-9-4 47 DougieCostello 3 49
(Stella Barclay) *led early: sn lost pl: hdwy over 2f out: nt clr run over 1f out: swtchd lft ins fnl f: styd on (jockey said gelding was denied a clear run inside the final furlong)* **12/1**

2104 **5** 3/4 **Necoleta**[21] 9090 3-9-8 53 LiamKeniry 13 53
(Sylvester Kirk) *chsd ldrs: rdn to go 2nd 2f out tl no ex ins fnl f* **6/1**[3]

5000 **6** 1/2 **Padura Brave**[24] 9042 3-9-5 50 (h) DanielMuscutt 10 49
(Mark Usher) *hld up: hdwy over 1f out: nt rch ldrs* **10/1**

2565 **7** 1 3/4 **Sea Tea Dea**[84] 7374 5-9-2 45 HollieDoyle 7 41
(Adrian Wintle) *hld up: hdwy over 4f out: rdn on outer over 2f out: no ex ins fnl f* **16/1**

0000 **8** nk **Bumblekite**[9] 9289 3-9-2 47 JasonHart 11 43
(Steph Hollinshead) *hld up: styd on fr over 1f out: nvr nrr* **100/1**

0000 **9** 5 **Andies Armies**[10] 9276 3-8-7 45 (p) ElishaWhittington(7) 8 31
(Lisa Williamson) *hld up: nvr on terms* **100/1**

0000 **10** 2 1/4 **Anchises**[6] 9345 4-9-4 54 RussellHarris(7) 2 36
(Rebecca Menzies) *s.i.s: sn pushed along and prom: led and plld hrd 8f out: clr over 6f out tl 3f out: hdd over 2f out: wknd fnl f* **33/1**

002- **11** 9 **Gunner Moyne**[618] 1565 7-9-3 46 (vt w) JamesSullivan 1 11
(Emma Owen) *prom: rdn over 3f out: wknd 2f out* **66/1**

0 **12** 1 **Fascinating Spirit (IRE)**[55] 8327 4-9-2 45 (t) JaneElliott 9 8
(Marjorie Fife) *s.s: a in rr (jockey said filly fly leapt upon leaving the stalls and as a result was slowly away)* **20/1**

-605 **13** 4 1/2 **George Junior**[9] 9282 3-9-0 45 (b) ShaneKelly 5
(Ed Walker) *hld up: shkn up over 2f out: no ch whn hung lft and eased over 1f out* **10/1**

1m 59.82s (-0.98) **Going Correction** -0.125s/f (Stan)
WFA 3 from 4yo+ 2lb 13 Ran SP% 114.7
Speed ratings (Par 101): **99,98,97,96,95 95,93,93,89,87 79,78,74**
CSF £207.45 CT £531.98 TOTE £59.80: £12.40, £1.90, £1.20; EX 303.40 Trifecta £2178.30.
Owner Stephen Michael Hanlon **Bred** Old Carhue & Graeng Bloodstock **Trained** Suncroft, Co. Kildare

FOCUS
They went a sound gallop and this should prove solid form relative to most low-grade handicaps.

9447 BETWAY HEED YOUR HUNCH H'CAP 2m 120y (Tp)
4:35 (4:37) (Class 6) (0-60,62) 3-Y-O+
£3,816 (£1,135; £567; £400; £400; £400) Stalls Low

Form RPR

6231 **1** **Falcon Cliffs (IRE)**[34] 8916 5-9-10 60 HollieDoyle 5 66
(Tony Carroll) *s.s: hld up: hdwy over 2f out: rdn over 1f out: styd on u.p to ld nr fin* **5/4**[1]

/13- **2** 1/2 **Master Burbidge**[33] 1568 8-9-10 60 (p) LiamKeniry 4 65
(Neil Mulholland) *a.p: rdn to ld over 1f out: edgd lft ins fnl f: hdd nr fin* **15/2**

0406 **3** 2 1/4 **Amanto (GER)**[19] 9134 9-9-7 62 (vt) DylanHogan(5) 3 65
(Ali Stronge) *led at stdy pce after 1f: qcknd over 4f out: rdn and hdd over 1f out: no ex wl ins fnl f* **14/1**

2030 **4** 1/2 **Butterfield (IRE)**[37] 8828 6-8-10 49 ThomasGreatrex(3) 8 51
(Brian Forsey) *hld up in tch: pushed along over 4f out: rdn on outer over 2f out: edgd lft and styd on same pce ins fnl f* **5/1**[3]

3442 **5** 1 1/4 **Yasir (USA)**[8] 9312 11-9-1 51 ShaneKelly 2 52
(Sophie Leech) *s.i.s: sn prom: wnt 2nd over 13f out tl over 11f out: remained handy: wnt 2nd again over 8f out: pushed along over 2f out: lost 2nd over 1f out: no ex ins fnl f* **9/2**[2]

0000 **6** 8 **Prancing Oscar (IRE)**[36] 3224 5-9-4 54 (p) AndrewMullen 9 45
(Ben Haslam) *hld up: racd keenly: pushed along over 4f out: wknd over 2f out* **7/1**

4000 **7** 8 **Ezanak (IRE)**[39] 8019 6-9-12 62 (p) PaulMulrennan 6 43
(John Wainwright) *hld up: rdn and wknd over 3f out* **66/1**

346- **8** 9 **Booborowie (IRE)**[375] 8613 6-8-12 55 GeorgeRooke(7) 1 26
(Mandy Rowland) *led at stdy pce 1f: chsd ldr tl over 13f out: wnt 2nd again over 11f out tl over 8f out: remained handy: rdn over 3f out: wknd over 2f out* **66/1**

3m 46.23s (6.93) **Going Correction** -0.125s/f (Stan)
WFA 3 from 5yo+ 6lb 8 Ran SP% 113.2
Speed ratings (Par 101): **78,77,76,76,75 72,68,64**
CSF £11.32 CT £86.18 TOTE £2.30: £1.10, £1.40, £3.40; EX 11.70 Trifecta £64.20.
Owner A A Byrne & Mark Wellbelove **Bred** Gerry Smith **Trained** Cropthorne, Worcs

FOCUS
They crawled round for the most part, so this wasn't a true test of stamina. The front pair deserve extra credit for pulling comfortably clear.

9448 LADBROKES FOOTBALL ACCA BOOSTY MAIDEN AUCTION STKS (PLUS 10 RACE) 7f 36y (Tp)
5:05 (5:06) (Class 4) 2-Y-O
£5,110 (£1,520; £759; £379) Stalls High

Form RPR

565 **1** **Millionaire Waltz**[14] 9195 2-9-2 75 (t[1]) ThomasGreatrex(3) 8 79
(Paul Cole) *hld up: hdwy on outer over 4f out: rdn to ld and hung lft wl ins fnl f: r.o* **4/1**[3]

42 **2** 2 1/4 **Holy Eleanor (IRE)**[8] 9307 2-9-0 66 (p[1]) HollieDoyle 9 68
(Archie Watson) *sn chsng ldr: rdn over 2f out: styd on same pce ins fnl f* **5/2**[2]

0640 **3** shd **Secret Smile (IRE)**[17] 9159 2-9-0 74 JasonHart 1 68
(Mark Johnston) *chsd ldrs: rdn over 1f out: led ins fnl f: sn hdd: no ex towards fin* **13/2**

34 **4** nk **Jalwan (USA)**[15] 9174 2-9-5 0 DanielMuscutt 3 72
(John Butler) *led: rdn and hdd ins fnl f: no ex towards fin* **9/4**[1]

60 **5** 7 **High Maintenance**[22] 9062 2-8-9 0 KevinLundie(5) 7 49
(Mark Loughnane) *hld up: hdwy over 4f out: rdn over 1f out: wknd fnl f* **66/1**

50 **6** 3/4 **Golden Times (SWI)**[12] 9243 2-9-0 0 FrannyNorton 6 47
(Mark Johnston) *hld up: edgd lft 1/2-way: shkn up over 2f out: nvr on terms* **80/1**

0 **7** 1 **Paint It Black**[42] 8700 2-9-5 0 ShaneKelly 2 49
(Sylvester Kirk) *hld up in tch: rdn over 2f out: wknd over 1f out* **18/1**

8 7 **Rich Girl (IRE)** 2-9-0 0 LiamKeniry 5 26
(Sylvester Kirk) *in rr: pushed along over 4f out: bhd fr 1/2-way* **40/1**

0 **9** 16 **Whitehaven (FR)**[15] 9181 2-9-5 0 CharlieBennett 4
(Hughie Morrison) *chsd ldrs: hung lft and lost pl over 4f out: nt clr run 1/2-way: sn wknd (jockey said gelding hung left-handed throughout; vet said gelding lost his left-fore shoe)* **18/1**

1m 27.25s (-1.55) **Going Correction** -0.125s/f (Stan) 9 Ran SP% 108.4
Speed ratings (Par 98): **103,100,100,99,91 91,89,81,63**
CSF £12.80 TOTE £3.70: £1.50, £1.10, £2.40; EX 14.20 Trifecta £53.50.
Owner P F I Cole Ltd **Bred** Allseasons Bloodstock **Trained** Whatcombe, Oxon

FOCUS
A maiden auction in which it was hard to make up ground and, with the exception of the winner, there's very little potential.

9449 LADBROKES PLAY 1-2-FREE ON FOOTBALL NURSERY H'CAP 1m 142y (Tp)
5:35 (5:35) (Class 6) (0-60,64) 2-Y-O
£3,816 (£1,135; £567; £400; £400; £400) Stalls Low

Form RPR

1331 **1** **Goddess Of Fire**[2] 9399 2-9-3 61 6ex (p) GraceMcEntee(7) 2 72+
(John Ryan) *chsd ldr tl led over 2f out: pushed clr fr over 1f out: easily* **11/10**[1]

0601 **2** 5 **Copperlight (IRE)**[6] 9346 2-9-13 64 6ex (p) AndrewMullen 3 63
(Ben Haslam) *led 6f: rdn over 1f out: edgd lft and no ex fnl f* **5/2**[2]

5000 **3** nse **Brown Eyes Blue (IRE)**[2] 9399 2-8-11 55 (p) LauraCoughlan(7) 1 54
(J S Moore) *chsd ldrs: rdn over 1f out: styd on same pce* **33/1**

0056 **4** 7 **Fact Or Fable (IRE)**[8] 9307 2-9-6 57 LiamKeniry 9 41
(J S Moore) *hld up: racd keenly: hdwy on outer over 2f out: rdn and hung lft over 1f out: wknd ins fnl f* **15/2**[3]

000 **5** 5 **Dream Isle (IRE)**[174] 4075 2-9-0 51 JasonHart 8 25
(Steph Hollinshead) *hld up: pushed along over 3f out: wknd over 2f out* **33/1**

0000 **6** 1/2 **Looks Good (IRE)**[13] 9212 2-9-3 54 (p[1]) ShaneKelly 6 27
(Richard Hughes) *chsd ldrs: rdn over 2f out: sn wknd* **12/1**

000 **7** 3/4 **Villa Paloma (IRE)**[42] 8706 2-9-0 51 FrannyNorton 7 22
(Mark Johnston) *hld up: pushed along over 5f out: wknd over 3f out* **16/1**

1m 49.3s (-0.80) **Going Correction** -0.125s/f (Stan) 7 Ran SP% 107.4
Speed ratings (Par 94): **98,93,93,87,82 82,81**
CSF £3.34 CT £35.67 TOTE £2.00: £1.10, £1.80; EX 4.30 Trifecta £29.00.
Owner M M Foulger **Bred** Miss G Abbey **Trained** Newmarket, Suffolk

FOCUS
A very one-sided nursery run at a reasonable pace.

9450 BOMBARDIER "MARCH TO YOUR OWN DRUM" H'CAP 1m 142y (Tp)
6:05 (6:05) (Class 6) (0-52,53) 3-Y-O+
£3,816 (£1,135; £567; £400; £400; £400) Stalls Low

Form RPR

1 **Beau Geste (IRE)**[146] 5162 3-8-13 46 HollieDoyle 10 54+
(Tony Carroll) *chsd ldrs: rdn and hung lft fr over 1f out: styd on to ld nr fin* **11/2**

044 **2** 3/4 **Maqboola (USA)**[43] 8672 3-9-5 52 ShaneKelly 12 58
(Richard Hughes) *led 8f out: rdn over 1f out: hdd nr fin* **9/2**[2]

0005 **3** 1 1/4 **The British Lion (IRE)**[12] 9248 4-9-6 51 (v) CharlieBennett 8 55
(Alexandra Dunn) *chsd ldr tl over 5f out: remained handy: wnt 2nd again over 2f out: rdn over 1f out: no ex wl ins fnl f* **20/1**

0-00 **4** 2 **Castelo (IRE)**[19] 9133 3-9-3 50 (p[1]) JasonHart 9 50
(Daniel Kubler) *prom: chsd ldr over 5f out tl rdn over 2f out: edgd rt and no ex fnl f* **66/1**

0061 **5** 1/2 **Seaforth (IRE)**[9] 9282 7-9-3 51 4ex FinleyMarsh(3) 13 50
(Adrian Wintle) *s.i.s: swtchd lft sn after s: hld up: swtchd rt over 1f out: r.o ins fnl f: too much to do* **5/1**[3]

2004 **6** 1/2 **Prince Consort (IRE)**[9] 9282 4-9-2 47 (p) PaulMulrennan 2 45
(John Wainwright) *led early: sn lost pl: shkn up over 2f out: swtchd rt and hdwy over 1f out: nt clr run ins fnl f: nt trble ldrs* **20/1**

5652 **7** 1/2 **I Think So (IRE)**[36] 8863 4-9-5 **53**.....................(b) ThomasGreatrex(3) 7 49
(David Loughnane) *hld up in tch: rdn over 2f out: no ex fnl f* **5/2**[1]

5/00 **8** nse **Muzaawel**[262] 1331 4-9-7 **52**.............................. BorjaFayosMartin 6 48
(Ralph J Smith) *s.s: hld up: hrd rdn fr over 1f out: nt rch ldrs* **20/1**

3300 **9** nk **Navarra Princess (IRE)**[17] 9160 4-9-1 **46** oh1..............(t) LiamKeniry 5 42
(Don Cantillon) *hld up: rdn over 1f out: nt trble ldrs* **22/1**

6050 **10** 3 1/4 **Rebecke (IRE)**[119] 6107 3-9-2 **49**.............................. DanielMuscutt 1 38
(Lee Carter) *s.i.s: hld up: plld hrd: hdwy over 1f out: wknd fnl f (jockey said filly ran too freely)* **100/1**

2-04 **11** 1/2 **Mercury**[36] 8864 7-9-2 **52**.............................(tp) DylanHogan(5) 3 40
(Stephen Michael Hanlon, Ire) *chsd ldrs: rdn over 2f out: wknd fnl f* **7/1**

4500 **12** 1 1/2 **Invincible One (IRE)**[17] 9157 3-8-13 **46** oh1.................. FrannyNorton 4 31
(Sylvester Kirk) *hld up: pushed along over 3f out: n.d (jockey said gelding ran too freely)* **16/1**

00 **13** 4 **Baile Ghilibert (IRE)**[24] 9035 7-9-1 **46** oh1.........(p) AlistairRawlinson 11 22
(Michael Appleby) *hld up: wknd over 2f out* **40/1**

1m 48.82s (-1.28) **Going Correction** -0.125s/f (Stan)
WFA 3 from 4yo+ 2lb **13** Ran SP% **120.7**
Speed ratings (Par 101): **100,99,98,96,96 95,95,95,94,91 91,90,86**
CSF £28.28 CT £472.06 TOTE £5.00: £1.70, £2.60, £5.10; EX 37.30 Trifecta £525.30.
Owner A W Carroll **Bred** Highfort Stud **Trained** Cropthorne, Worcs

FOCUS
A modest handicap in which it proved hard to make up ground from behind.
T/Plt: £19.00 to a £1 stake. Pool: £51,362.43 - 2,702.10 winning units T/Qpdt: £7.80 to a 31 stake. Pool: £5,627.35 - 714.25 winning units **Colin Roberts**

9437 **CHELMSFORD (A.W)** (L-H)
Friday, December 13

OFFICIAL GOING: Polytrack: standard
Weather: Overcast

9451 BET TOTEPLACEPOT AT TOTESPORT.COM EBF NOVICE STKS (PLUS 10 RACE) 7f (P)
4:00 (4:00) (Class 4) 2-Y-O **£6,727** (£2,001; £1,000; £500) **Stalls** Low

Form RPR

4 **1** **Notforalongtime**[15] 9195 2-9-2 0.............................. AdamKirby 4 75+
(Clive Cox) *trckd ldr: nudged along to ld ent fnl f: edgd sltly lft u.p but sn rdn and wl in command* **4/7**[1]

1 **2** 3 1/4 **Eevilynn Drew**[43] 8700 2-9-3 0.............................. DarraghKeenan(3) 5 71
(Robert Eddery) *led: rdn along and hdd by wnr ent fnl f: one pce clsng stages* **9/4**[2]

00 **3** 1 1/4 **Union Spirit**[129] 5774 2-9-2 0.............................. RobertHavlin 1 63+
(Peter Chapple-Hyam) *trckd ldng pair: pushed along and outpcd 2f out: sn rdn and kpt on one pce fnl f* **18/1**

0 **4** 3/4 **Astroman**[174] 4117 2-9-2 0.............................. ShaneKelly 2 61
(James Eustace) *midfield: effrt to cl over 2f out: sn rdn and kpt on steadily fnl f* **20/1**

5 nk **Showmolina** 2-9-2 0.............................. DanielMuscutt 7 61
(David Lanigan) *dwlt and racd in rr: rdn and rn a little green over 2f out: kpt on and minor hdwy fnl f* **8/1**[3]

6 **6** 1 1/4 **Seventeen O Four (IRE)**[15] 9197 2-9-2 0.............................. DavidProbert 3 57
(Michael Bell) *prom: rdn along and outpcd over 1f out: wknd fnl f (vet said gelding lost its right hind shoe)* **12/1**

00 **7** 4 1/2 **Dame Denali**[18] 9155 2-8-11 0.............................. WilliamCarson 8 41
(Anthony Carson) *hld up: rdn and no imp 2f out: nvr on terms* **66/1**

8 9 **The Cherokee Kid (IRE)** 2-8-9 0.............................. LauraPearson(7) 6 22
(David Evans) *hld up: green and outpcd 1/2-way: rdn and no imp over 2f out: sn wknd* **20/1**

1m 28.51s (1.31) **Going Correction** -0.075s/f (Stan) **8** Ran SP% **129.5**
Speed ratings (Par 98): **89,85,83,83,82 81,76,65**
CSF £2.52 TOTE £1.50: £1.10, £1.10, £2.70; EX 2.90 Trifecta £15.70.
Owner Paul & Clare Rooney **Bred** Mr & Mrs Paul & Clare Rooney **Trained** Lambourn, Berks

FOCUS
They went steady and it was an advantage to be handy. The time was slow and it was a modest race in all probability.

9452 MATCHBOOK EBF FUTURE STAYERS' NOVICE STKS (PLUS 10 RACE) (SIRE AND DAM RESTRICTED RACE) 1m (P)
4:30 (4:31) (Class 3) 2-Y-O **£10,350** (£3,080; £1,539; £769) **Stalls** Low

Form RPR

1 **Hypothetical (IRE)** 2-9-5 0.............................. RobertHavlin 2 82+
(John Gosden) *hld up on inner: waited for gap to appear bhd rivals over 1f out: rdn and qcknd up to ld 1f out: sn clr* **7/4**[2]

2 5 **London Arch** 2-9-5 0.............................. KieranShoemark 3 71
(Charlie Fellowes) *trckd ldrs: niggled along over 2f out: rdn along and wnt 2nd ent fnl f: kpt on* **20/1**

4 **3** 1 1/4 **In The Night (IRE)**[56] 8319 2-9-5 0.............................. AdamKirby 1 68
(Charlie Appleby) *trckd ldrs on inner: swtchd rt and effrt to chal over 1f out: sn rdn and one pce fnl f* **6/4**[1]

4 nk **Mystic River (IRE)** 2-9-5 0.............................. ShaneKelly 6 67+
(James Ferguson) *dwlt sltly and racd in rr: rdn along and briefly outpcd over 1f out: kpt on fnl f* **33/1**

0 **5** nse **Marcela De Vega**[24] 9046 2-9-0 0.............................. BenCurtis 5 62
(Ralph Beckett) *trckd ldr: rdn along to ld briefly over 1f out: sn hdd by wnr and wknd fnl f* **6/1**[3]

0 **6** 3 1/4 **Bobby The Great**[51] 8460 2-9-5 0.............................. FrannyNorton 4 60
(Mark Johnston) *led: rdn along and hdd over 1f out: wknd qckly fnl f* **7/1**

1m 40.38s (0.48) **Going Correction** -0.075s/f (Stan) **6** Ran SP% **110.9**
Speed ratings (Par 100): **94,89,87,87,87 84**
CSF £31.32 TOTE £2.20: £1.20, £8.40; EX 26.40 Trifecta £83.60.
Owner Sheikh Hamdan bin Mohammed Al Maktoum **Bred** Knocktoran Stud **Trained** Newmarket, Suffolk

FOCUS
Probably a decent novice race, and the winner put up a good performance to distance the rest from the furlong marker. It's tricky to pin the standard in behind.

9453 BET TOTEEXACTA AT TOTESPORT.COM H'CAP 1m (P)
5:00 (5:01) (Class 5) (0-70,70) 3-Y-O+ **£5,110** (£1,520; £759; £400; £400; £400) **Stalls** Low

Form RPR

3406 **1** **Coviglia (IRE)**[85] 7364 5-9-1 **64**.............................. JamesSullivan 4 72
(Jacqueline Coward) *in rr of midfield: hdwy u.p on outer over 2f out: rdn and clsd on ldrs over 1f out: styd on wl to ld wl ins fnl f* **12/1**

4420 **2** 1 **Exmoor Beast**[43] 8705 3-9-4 **68**.............................. PaulMulrennan 12 74
(Peter Charalambous) *trckd ldr: effrt to ld 3f out: rdn along and strly pressed over 1f out: hdd by wnr and no ex ins fnl f* **14/1**

2303 **3** 1/2 **Toro Dorado**[15] 9202 3-9-5 **69**.............................. RobertHavlin 15 74+
(Ed Dunlop) *restrained in rr: short of room over 6f out: hdwy between rivals over 1f out: swtchd lft to rail and rdn ent fnl f: styd on wl to go 3rd cl home* **12/1**

4013 **4** 1/2 **Swansdown**[35] 8923 3-9-4 **68**.............................(p) TomMarquand 9 71
(William Haggas) *Chased ldrs: rdn along to chse ldr over 1f out: one pce and lost two pls fnl f* **7/1**[3]

0001 **5** 1 1/4 **Roller**[27] 9006 6-9-6 **69**.............................(p) DougieCostello 5 70
(Mark Loughnane) *hld up in rr: hdwy u.p on outer over 1f out: rdn and kpt on wl fnl f but n.d* **10/1**

3000 **6** 1/2 **Harbour Vision**[14] 9224 4-9-7 **70**.............................. JasonHart 2 69
(Derek Shaw) *prom: rdn along and unable qck over 1f out: kpt on one pce fnl f* **9/2**[1]

6604 **7** hd **Fuwairt (IRE)**[10] 9283 7-9-7 **70**.............................. DanielMuscutt 10 69
(Lee Carter) *hld up on inner: effrt to cl and swtchd rt 2f out: rdn and minor hdwy over 1f out: kpt on (vet said gelding lost its left hind shoe)* **20/1**

6102 **8** shd **Born To Finish (IRE)**[9] 9306 6-9-5 **68**.............................(p) DavidProbert 11 67
(Ed de Giles) *hld up: rdn and minor hdwy over 1f out: nvr on terms (jockey said gelding was denied a clear run)* **16/1**

4550 **9** 2 **Grey Galleon (USA)**[13] 9245 5-9-2 **65**.............................(p) AdamKirby 13 59
(Clive Cox) *hld up in rr: nvr on terms* **16/1**

1114 **10** 1/2 **Clipsham Tiger (IRE)**[8] 9331 3-8-11 **68**.....................(h) GeorgeRooke(7) 1 61
(Michael Appleby) *trckd ldrs on inner and racd keenly: swtchd lft and effrt against rail over 1f out: sn rdn and wknd fnl f* **5/1**[2]

3554 **11** 2 1/4 **Punjab Mail**[48] 8548 3-9-3 **67**.............................(t[1]) BarryMcHugh 6 55
(Tim Fitzgerald) *dwlt and racd in rr: nvr on terms* **5/1**[2]

6001 **12** 1 **Choral Music**[44] 8652 4-9-4 **67**.............................. FrannyNorton 14 52
(John E Long) *hld up and a bhd* **14/1**

/43- **13** 2 3/4 **Swiss Vinnare**[665] 742 5-9-0 **70**.............................(h) GraceMcEntee(7) 7 49
(Phil McEntee) *midfield and racd keenly: hdwy onto heels of ldrs over 2f out: sn rdn and lost pl over 1f out: wknd sn after* **33/1**

0500 **14** 1 1/4 **Mr Mac**[39] 8807 5-9-0 **66**.............................. DarraghKeenan(3) 8 42
(Peter Hedger) *hld up: a in rr* **25/1**

0210 **15** 10 **J'Ouvert (IRE)**[15] 9202 3-9-3 **67**.............................(h) BenCurtis 16 20
(David Evans) *trckd ldrs on outer: niggled along to hold position over 2f out: rdn along and wknd over 1f out: sn bhd (trainer's rep could offer no explanation for the filly's performance)* **12/1**

0200 **16** 3/4 **Wild Animal**[16] 9173 3-9-6 **70**.............................. ShaneKelly 3 22
(Murty McGrath) *led: rdn along and hdd 3f out: sn wknd and bhd* **50/1**

1m 39.33s (-0.57) **Going Correction** -0.075s/f (Stan)
WFA 3 from 4yo+ 1lb **16** Ran SP% **134.8**
Speed ratings (Par 103): **99,98,97,97,95 95,95,94,92,92 90,89,86,85,75 74**
CSF £181.41 CT £2181.63 TOTE £11.70: £3.30, £3.60, £2.90, £2.20; EX 334.50 Trifecta £3795.70.
Owner John Blackburn Racing **Bred** Tullamaine Castle Stud And Partners **Trained** Dalby, North Yorks

■ Stewards' Enquiry : Grace McEntee three-day ban; careless riding (Dec 27-29)

FOCUS
They didn't go a great gallop early on in this modest handicap. The winner was close to his best.

9454 WEATHERBYS TBA H'CAP 1m 6f (P)
5:30 (5:31) (Class 2) (0-105,97) 3-Y-O **£32,345** (£9,625; £4,810; £2,405) **Stalls** Low

Form RPR

2211 **1** **Pianissimo**[24] 9056 3-8-7 **83**.............................(b) WilliamCarson 2 94
(Anthony Carson) *hld up: hdwy gng wl 2f out: effrt to chse ldr over 1f out: sn drvn and styd on wl to ld post* **16/1**

2 **2** nse **Grandmaster Flash (IRE)**[14] 9227 3-8-13 **89**......... DeclanMcDonogh 6 100
(Joseph Patrick O'Brien, Ire) *in rr of midfield: gd hdwy 2f out: effrt to ld over 1f out: sn drvn and strly pressed by wnr ins fnl f: hdd post* **4/1**[2]

1210 **3** 6 **Deal A Dollar**[63] 8098 3-9-7 **97**.............................. TomMarquand 9 100
(David Simcock) *dwlt and racd in rr: pushed along to cl over 1f out: sn rdn and kpt on for remote 3rd ins fnl f* **11/1**

0542 **4** 1 3/4 **Creationist (USA)**[24] 9055 3-9-3 **93**.............................. JasonWatson 3 94
(Roger Charlton) *midfield on inner: pushed along to chse ldrs 2f out: sn rdn and kpt on one pce fnl f* **5/1**

1361 **5** 5 **Blowing Dixie**[25] 9033 3-7-12 **79** ow3.............................. RayDawson(5) 8 73
(Jane Chapple-Hyam) *trckd ldrs: pushed along to ld 3f out: rdn and hdd over 1f out: wknd fnl f* **20/1**

5211 **6** 1/2 **Sweet Celebration (IRE)**[16] 9178 3-7-13 **82** ow2......... GraceMcEntee(7) 4 75
(Marco Botti) *hld up: effrt to cl on outside over 2f out: sn rdn and no imp over 1f out: wknd fnl f* **14/1**

1121 **7** 8 **Bo Samraan (IRE)**[14] 9222 3-9-2 **92**.............................. FrannyNorton 5 74
(Mark Johnston) *trckd ldrs: rdn along and outpcd over 1f out: wknd fnl f* **6/1**

5146 **8** 28 **Ballylemon (IRE)**[23] 9065 3-8-6 **82**.............................. KieranO'Neill 1 24
(Richard Hughes) *led for 2f: remained handy and led again 4f out: rdn and hdd 3f out: lost pl qckly and sn bhd* **9/2**[3]

1123 **9** 26 **Good Tidings (FR)**[24] 9055 3-9-0 **90**.............................(v) RobertHavlin 7
(John Gosden) *cl up tl led after 2f: reminders and racing lazily 5f out: rdn whn hdd and lost pl qckly 4f out: sn t.o (jockey said colt stopped quickly; trainer could offer no explanation for the colt's performance)* **10/3**[1]

2m 58.54s (-4.66) **Going Correction** -0.075s/f (Stan) **9** Ran SP% **117.9**
Speed ratings (Par 108): **110,109,106,105,102 102,97,81,66**
CSF £80.66 CT £753.88 TOTE £15.00: £4.50, £1.50, £2.90; EX 79.30 Trifecta £428.40.
Owner Chris Butler **Bred** Godolphin **Trained** Newmarket, Suffolk

FOCUS
A good 3yo handicap with plenty of recent winning form, and a race that set up nicely for the closers.

9455 BET TOTETRIFECTA AT TOTESPORT.COM H'CAP 7f (P)
6:00 (6:03) (Class 5) (0-75,75) 3-Y-O+ **£3,428** (£1,020; £509; £400; £400; £400) **Stalls** Low

Form RPR

620U **1** **Fighting Temeraire (IRE)**[24] 9048 6-9-6 **74**.............................. AdamKirby 7 83
(Dean Ivory) *dwlt and pushed along into midfield: hdwy between rivals 2f out: swtchd rt and rdn to chse clr ldr ent fnl f: styd on strly to ld post* **10/1**

2015 **2** nk **Extrodinair**[15] 9199 4-9-1 **74**.............................. RayDawson(5) 13 82
(Jane Chapple-Hyam) *led at a gd pce after 2f: shkn up and readily extended advantage to 5 l over 1f out: rdn and stride shortened fnl f: no ex whn hdd by wnr post* **8/1**

0034 **3** nse **Haddaf (IRE)**[16] 9176 4-9-7 **75**.............................(p) JasonWatson 5 83
(Stuart Williams) *midfield: smooth hdwy 2f out: sn rdn and clsd on ldr 1f out: kpt on wl fnl f but nt match wnr* **10/3**[1]

0013 **4** 1 ¾ **Full Intention**[16] 9176 5-9-1 **69**....(p) DavidProbert 11 72
(Simon Pearce) *midfield on outer: rdn and unable qck over 1f out: kpt on one pce fnl f* **9/2[2]**

1213 **5** 1 ¼ **Split Down South**[14] 9217 3-8-8 **69**.... GraceMcEntee(7) 15 69
(Phil McEntee) *chsd ldrs: rdn to chse ldr 2f out tl over 1f out: sn one pce fnl f* **7/1[3]**

2606 **6** 1 ½ **Sonnet Rose (IRE)**[14] 9217 5-8-6 **63**....(bt) GabrieleMalune(3) 14 59
(Conrad Allen) *trckd ldrs: rdn along and unable qck over 1f out: wknd fnl f* **25/1**

4005 **7** ½ **Jem Scuttle (USA)**[16] 9180 3-8-10 **64**....(t) JasonHart 4 59
(Declan Carroll) *led briefly and then sat in midfield on inner: drvn along and racd awkwardly over 1f out: swtchd lft and one pce fnl f* **7/1[3]**

0065 **8** 1 ¼ **Atletico (IRE)**[10] 9283 7-9-0 **75**....(b) LauraPearson(7) 8 66
(David Evans) *hld up: hdwy u.p on wd outside over 2f out: wd off home bnd: sn rdn and no hdwy over 1f out: wknd sn after* **12/1**

644 **9** ½ **Plunger**[56] 8305 4-9-7 **75**.... JoeyHaynes 9 65
(John Butler) *dwlt bdly and racd in last: drvn in rr 2f out: sme minor late hdwy (jockey said he was slow to remove the blindfold)* **10/1**

5400 **10** 5 **Carnival Rose**[48] 8549 3-9-4 **72**....(h[1]) DanielMuscutt 16 48
(James Fanshawe) *hld up: pushed along and struggling 3f out: wd off home bnd: nvr on terms (jockey said filly hung right-handed from half way)* **25/1**

2420 **11** *nk* **Sweet And Dandy (IRE)**[200] 3146 4-9-1 **69**.... KieranO'Neill 3 44
(Luke McJannet) *in rr of midfield: hdwy between rivals 2f out: swtchd rt and effrt over 1f out: wknd fnl f* **25/1**

0520 **12** 4 ½ **Javelin**[20] 9140 4-9-2 **70**....(p) TomMarquand 6 33
(William Muir) *midfield on inner: drvn along and lost pl over 2f out: sn bhd* **14/1**

-660 **13** 8 **Isle Of Innisfree (USA)**[25] 9030 3-9-6 **74**.... JFEgan 2 16
(Paul D'Arcy) *in rr of midfield on inner: rdn and struggling 2f out: nvr on terms (trainer said colt had a breathing problem)* **25/1**

060- **14** 1 ½ **Theydon Boxer**[563] 3197 4-8-8 **62**.... GeorgeWood 10
(Peter Charalambous) *chsd ldr tl drvn and lost pl 2f out: wknd qckly over 1f out: bhd* **50/1**

1m 24.83s (-2.37) **Going Correction** -0.075s/f (Stan) **14** Ran SP% **127.3**
Speed ratings (Par 103): **110,109,109,107,106 104,103,102,101,96 95,90,81,79**
CSF £87.65 CT £342.14 TOTE £10.90: £3.00, £2.90, £1.50; EX 108.60 Trifecta £551.70.
Owner Michael & Heather Yarrow **Bred** Hot Ticket Partnership **Trained** Radlett, Herts

FOCUS
A fair handicap. The winner stepped up on this year's turf form.

9456 BET TOTESWINGER AT TOTESPORT.COM H'CAP 1m (P)
6:30 (6:32) (Class 6) (0-55,54) 3-Y-O+

£2,781 (£827; £413; £400; £400; £400) **Stalls** Low

Form RPR

3100 **1** **The King's Steed**[25] 9039 6-9-5 **52**....(bt) AdamKirby 2 58
(Shaun Lycett) *mde all: shkn up over 2f out: rdn and extended advantage over 1f out: edgd lft u.p clsng stages: comf* **7/1**

0060 **2** 2 ¾ **Azets**[14] 9225 3-8-13 **52**.... RayDawson(5) 12 52
(Jane Chapple-Hyam) *chsd wnr: drvn along and unable to cl on wnr over 1f out: kpt on one pce fnl f* **14/1**

0000 **3** 1 ¾ **Bated Beauty (IRE)**[52] 8434 4-9-5 **52**.... TomQueally 6 48
(John Butler) *midfield in tch: rdn on outer and unable qck over 1f out: kpt on one pce to go 3rd wl ins fnl f* **5/2[1]**

0006 **4** *nse* **Molten Lava (IRE)**[10] 9282 7-9-0 **47**....(p) RobertHavlin 1 43
(Steve Gollings) *trckd ldrs on inner: rdn along to chse ldrs over 1f out: one pce fnl f: lost 3rd cl home* **8/1**

0005 **5** ½ **Dukes Meadow**[18] 9157 8-8-7 **45**.... RhiainIngram(5) 8 39
(Roger Ingram) *hld up: rdn in rr 2f out: kpt on fnl f but n.d (jockey said gelding was denied a clear run)* **33/1**

0001 **6** ¾ **Kerrera**[18] 9157 6-8-10 **48**.... SophieRalston(5) 7 41
(Dean Ivory) *in rr of midfield on inner: rdn and minor hdwy over 1f out: no imp fnl f* **5/1[3]**

4256 **7** 2 **Pike Corner Cross (IRE)**[6] 9362 7-9-6 **53**....(vt) BenCurtis 9 41
(David Evans) *racd in midfield: minor hdwy u.p over 1f out: one pce fnl f* **4/1[2]**

0006 **8** *hd* **Lacan (IRE)**[60] 8207 8-9-4 **54**.... CameronNoble(3) 4 42
(Michael Bell) *dwlt and racd freely in rr: hdwy on outer over 3f out: wd off home bnd: sn rdn: hung lft and wknd over 1f out* **4/1[2]**

0000 **9** 2 ½ **Moon Artist (FR)**[52] 8416 3-8-11 **45**.... DavidProbert 5 27
(Michael Blanshard) *racd in midfield: rdn along over 1f out: wknd fnl f* **33/1**

0000 **10** 6 **Mazmerize**[58] 8251 3-8-11 **45**....(v) AdrianMcCarthy 11 13
(Christine Dunnett) *hld up: a in rr* **66/1**

1m 39.35s (-0.55) **Going Correction** -0.075s/f (Stan)
WFA 3 from 4yo+ 1lb **10** Ran SP% **122.9**
Speed ratings (Par 101): **99,96,94,94,93 93,91,91,88,82**
CSF £102.90 CT £326.90 TOTE £7.80: £2.00, £4.20, £1.60; EX 70.90 Trifecta £523.60.
Owner D Gilbert, J Lancaster, G Wills **Bred** Littleton Stud **Trained** Leafield, Oxon

FOCUS
Low-grade fare, and with the pace holding up very few got competitive. The winner was well treated on early-season form.

9457 BOOK TICKETS AT CHELMSFORDCITYRACECOURSE.COM H'CAP 6f (P)
7:00 (7:03) (Class 7) (0-50,51) 3-Y-O+ £2,911 (£866; £432; £108) **Stalls** Centre

Form RPR

0434 **1** **Griggy (IRE)**[11] 9272 3-9-8 **51**....(b) AdamKirby 10 58
(Sean Curran) *hld up: smooth hdwy to cl on ldrs over 1f out: sn rdn and qcknd up wl to ld ent fnl f: r.o wl* **15/8[1]**

6530 **2** 2 **Meshardal (GER)**[36] 8901 9-9-2 **45**....(p) JamesSullivan 3 46
(Ruth Carr) *chsd ldr: pushed along to chal 2f out: sn rdn and ev ch appr fnl f: nt match wnr clsng stages* **8/1[3]**

0000 **3** *nk* **Madame Ritz (IRE)**[18] 9160 4-9-2 **45**.... RobertHavlin 4 45
(Richard Phillips) *dwlt and racd in rr: keen at times: rdn and mde late hdwy but n.d* **12/1**

0423 **4** *shd* **Tilsworth Rose**[13] 9247 5-9-4 **47**....(b) RaulDaSilva 7 47
(J R Jenkins) *led: rdn along to maintain short ld over 1f out: drvn and hdd ent fnl f: no ex fnl 100yds* **12/1**

0006 **4** *dht* **Kyllukey**[2] 9411 6-9-2 **45**.... FrannyNorton 2 45
(Charlie Wallis) *trckd ldrs on inner and racd freely: rdn along to chal over 1f out: one pce fnl f* **8/1[3]**

5/02 **6** *nk* **Captain Power (IRE)**[1] 9439 7-9-3 **49**.... SeanDavis(3) 6 48
(Gordon Elliott, Ire) *racd in midfield in tch: rdn along and drifted lft over 1f out: kpt on one pce fnl f* **9/4[2]**

0046 **7** 1 ¼ **Alba Del Sole (IRE)**[25] 9034 4-9-4 **47**....(p) JasonHart 13 42
(Charlie Wallis) *hld up in rr: rdn and minor hdwy over 1f out: nvr on terms* **16/1**

0600 **8** 6 **Spenny's Lass**[2] 9411 4-8-13 **45**....(p) DarraghKeenan(3) 14 22
(John Ryan) *chsd ldrs on outer: rdn along and lost pl over 1f out: sn bhd* **11/1**

0300 **P** **Plum Duff**[58] 8249 3-9-2 **45**.... DavidProbert 1
(Michael Blanshard) *hld up: pushed along over 2f out: lost action eased and p.u over 1f out (jockey said filly lost its action)* **25/1**

1m 12.73s (-0.97) **Going Correction** -0.075s/f (Stan) **9** Ran SP% **121.2**
Speed ratings (Par 97): **103,100,99,99,99 99,97,89,**
CSF £19.05 CT £149.88 TOTE £2.60: £1.10, £1.90, £3.10; EX 19.10 Trifecta £175.00.
Owner Power Geneva Ltd **Bred** Holburn Trust Co **Trained** Upper Lambourn, Berks
■ Stewards' Enquiry : Raul Da Silva three-day ban; careless riding (Dec 27-29)

FOCUS
This weak race was won by the only one in the line-up rated in the 50s. Limited form behind him.

9458 MERRY CHRISTMAS TO ALL OUR CUSTOMERS H'CAP 5f (P)
7:30 (7:32) (Class 4) (0-85,87) 3-Y-O+

£5,530 (£1,645; £822; £411; £400; £400) **Stalls** Low

Form RPR

3434 **1** **Acclaim The Nation (IRE)**[74] 7771 6-9-6 **84**....(p) JasonHart 5 95
(Eric Alston) *broke wl and mde all: shkn up w short ld over 1f out: sn rdn and kpt on wl fnl f: all out to hold on clsng stages* **3/1[1]**

055 **2** *hd* **Savalas (IRE)**[22] 9098 4-9-6 **84**.... AdamKirby 2 94
(Robert Cowell) *dwlt and racd in rr: rdn along and outpcd over 1f out: swtchd rt: drvn and c w a str run fnl f: jst failed to rch wnr* **3/1[1]**

3112 **3** 2 ½ **Grisons (FR)**[80] 7552 3-8-6 **73**.... SeanDavis(3) 4 74
(Robert Cowell) *trckd ldrs: rdn and hung immediately lft over 1f out: kpt on one pce fnl f (vet said colt bled from the nose)* **11/1**

0006 **4** ½ **Dynamo Walt (IRE)**[13] 9257 8-8-4 **71** oh1.... DarraghKeenan(3) 3 70
(Derek Shaw) *trckd ldrs on inner: rdn along and no imp over 1f out: kpt gng one pce fnl f* **25/1**

6414 **5** ½ **Enthaar**[46] 8601 4-8-12 **76**....(tp) JasonWatson 7 73
(Stuart Williams) *midfield on outer: pushed along 1/2-way: rdn and unable qck over 1f out: one pce after* **7/1[3]**

0006 **6** *nk* **Machree (IRE)**[36] 8900 4-9-0 **78**.... PaulMulrennan 8 74
(Declan Carroll) *chsd wnr: rdn and no imp over 1f out: lost 2nd wl ins fnl f and wknd clsng stages* **14/1**

3000 **7** 1 ½ **Verne Castle**[22] 9088 6-9-9 **87**....(h) FrannyNorton 6 78
(Michael Wigham) *hld up: effrt to cl on ldrs over 1f out: wknd fnl f* **7/1[3]**

2634 **8** ½ **Just That Lord**[4] 9389 6-9-7 **85**.... RobertHavlin 9 74
(Michael Attwater) *hld up: rdn along and outpcd 1/2-way: nvr on terms* **8/1**

0415 **9** 1 ¼ **Helvetian**[24] 9057 4-9-6 **84**.... BenCurtis 1 69
(Kevin Frost) *midfield on inner: rdn and minor hdwy over 1f out: wknd fnl f* **4/1[2]**

58.74s (-1.46) **Going Correction** -0.075s/f (Stan) **9** Ran SP% **125.0**
Speed ratings (Par 105): **108,107,103,102,102 101,99,98,96**
CSF £13.07 CT £92.10 TOTE £4.00: £1.50, £1.40, £3.20; EX 14.50 Trifecta £118.00.
Owner Con Harrington **Bred** Con Harrington **Trained** Longton, Lancs

FOCUS
An open sprint handicap and a tight finish, the winner just holding the runner-up's late swoop.
T/Plt: £388.80 to a £1 stake. Pool: £47,721.36 - 122.73 winning units T/Qpdt: £185.90 to a £1 stake. Pool: £8,072.18 - 43.40 winning units **Mark Grantham**

9459 - 9466a (Foreign Racing) - See Raceform Interactive

9391
NEWCASTLE (A.W) (L-H)
Saturday, December 14

OFFICIAL GOING: Tapeta: standard
Wind: Fairly strong, half against Weather: Overcast, dry

9467 BETWAY HEED YOUR HUNCH H'CAP 2m 56y (Tp)
12:15 (12:17) (Class 6) (0-65,67) 3-Y-O+

£2,781 (£827; £413; £300; £300; £300) **Stalls** Low

Form RPR

0000 **1** **Bravantina**[204] 3057 4-8-8 **45**....(t) CamHardie 14 51
(Mark Walford) *t.k.h: prom: rdn over 2f out: hdwy to ld over 1f out: kpt on wl fnl f* **100/1**

5060 **2** ¾ **Call Me Madam**[54] 8406 4-8-8 **45**.... JaneElliott 9 50
(James Bethell) *pressed ldr: lost 2nd but cl up 6f out: rdn and disp ld over 1f out: kpt on fnl f: jst hld 2nd* **40/1**

0522 **3** *nse* **Shine Baby Shine**[35] 8945 5-9-3 **61**.... NickBarratt-Atkin(7) 13 66
(Philip Kirby) *hld up in rr: hdwy 3f out: chsd ldrs and rdn over 1f out: kpt on fnl f* **12/1**

2013 **4** 2 ¼ **Nataleena (IRE)**[50] 8524 3-9-5 **62**.... AndrewMullen 6 66
(Ben Haslam) *t.k.h: hld up in rr on inner: rdn over 2f out: hdwy over 1f out: kpt on fnl f: nt pce to chal* **7/2[2]**

5002 **5** ¾ **Ezzrah**[16] 9201 3-9-0 **57**.... KieranShoemark 5 60
(Charlie Fellowes) *trckd ldrs: rdn and outpcd over 2f out: sn edgd lft: rallied over 1f out: no ex fnl 110yds* **3/1[1]**

0040 **6** 1 ½ **Major Snugfit**[17] 8200 3-9-0 **62**....(p) GerO'Neill(5) 7 64
(Michael Easterby) *t.k.h: midfield: pushed along and outpcd over 3f out: rallied 2f out: rdn and no imp ins fnl f* **16/1**

0500 **7** *shd* **Needs To Be Seen (FR)**[19] 7368 4-10-2 **67**.... BenRobinson 8 68
(Jim Goldie) *stdd s: hld up in rr: stdy hdwy 3f out: rdn and swtchd lft 2f out: no imp fnl f* **25/1**

0005 **8** *nk* **Coup De Gold (IRE)**[40] 8814 3-9-5 **62**.... JasonHart 1 63
(David Thompson) *dwlt s: t.k.h: hld up in rr: hdwy and wnt 2nd 6f out: led over 3f out: rdn and hdd over 1f out: wknd fnl 110yds (jockey said gelding ran too free)* **100/1**

0504 **9** 4 **War Empress (IRE)**[39] 8828 3-9-5 **62**.... ShelleyBirkett 3 58
(Julia Feilden) *midfield on inner: rdn over 2f out: wknd over 1f out* **11/1**

/0-1 **10** 1 ¼ **Yamato (IRE)**[56] 8347 6-9-2 **56**....(t) SeanDavis(3) 12 49
(John C McConnell, Ire) *towards rr: rdn 4f out: sn outpcd: rallied over 2f out: wknd over 1f out (jockey said gelding ran flat)* **5/1**

6134 **11** 4 ½ **Para Queen (IRE)**[23] 9093 3-8-11 **61**.... EllieMacKenzie(7) 10 50
(Heather Main) *dwlt s: midfield: rdn and hdwy over 2f out: wknd over 1f out* **9/2[3]**

6440 **12** 3 ¼ **Tor**[46] 8635 5-10-2 **67**.... PaulMulrennan 2 51
(Marjorie Fife) *led: rdn and hdd over 3f out: wknd over 1f out* **80/1**

-060 **13** *8* **Mercer's Troop (IRE)**[49] 5728 4-9-7 63........................ BenSanderson(5) 4 37
(Alistair Whillans) *towards rr on inner: dropped to rr over 5f out: rdn and hung lft over 3f out: sn wknd* **50/1**

3m 40.14s (5.14) **Going Correction** +0.25s/f (Slow)
WFA 3 from 4yo+ 6lb **13 Ran SP% 115.4**
Speed ratings (Par 101): **97,96,96,95,95 94,94,94,92,91 89,87,83**
CSF £2219.77 CT £40844.28 TOTE £91.70: £13.50, £9.30, £1.80; EX 1721.60.
Owner Nunstainton Racing Club & Partner **Bred** Christopher T Dawson **Trained** Sherriff Hutton, N Yorks

FOCUS
The going was standard.\n\x\x Stalls - 2m: inside; 1m2f/1m4f outside: straight course: centre\n\x\x An ordinary stayers' handicap which produced a shock winner. They did not seem to go a great gallop.

9468 BETWAY CONDITIONS STKS (ALL-WEATHER CHAMPIONSHIPS FAST-TRACK QUALIFIER) 2m 56y (Tp)

12:50 (12:52) (Class 2) 3-Y-O+ **£13,584** (£4,042; £2,020; £505) **Stalls** Low

Form RPR

3040 **1** **Raymond Tusk (IRE)**[39] 8844 4-9-3 113........................ TomMarquand 3 108
(Richard Hannon) *trckd ldr: led gng easily over 2f out: rdn and hrd pressed over 1f out: carried lft ins fnl f: kpt on wl fnl f: gamely* **11/4**[1]

5-00 **2** *½* **Funny Kid (USA)**[70] 7928 6-9-6 103........................(t) JulienAuge 6 110
(C Ferland, France) *towards rr: smooth hdwy over 2f out: rdn and disp ld fr over 1f out: edgd lft ins fnl f: kpt on: jst hld* **12/1**

0336 **3** *1 ¼* **Mildenberger**[10] 9302 4-9-3 108........................ FrannyNorton 8 106
(Mark Johnston) *led: rdn and hdd over 2f out: outpcd over 1f out: rallied ins fnl f: kpt on towards fin: no match for first two* **3/1**[2]

2000 **4** *2 ¼* **Dubawi Fifty**[63] 8114 6-9-3 97........................(v) LukeMorris 7 103
(Karen McLintock) *prom: rdn over 2f out: edgd lft over 1f out: no ex ins fnl f* **13/2**

6003 **4** *dht* **Sir Chauvelin**[23] 9094 7-9-3 102........................ BenRobinson 4 103
(Jim Goldie) *stdd s: hld up in last: rdn and swtchd rt 2f out: kpt on fnl f: mde no imp* **10/1**

1334 **6** *2 ¼* **Infrastructure**[24] 9065 4-9-3 93........................ BenCurtis 1 100
(Martyn Meade) *t.k.h: in tch w ldrs: smooth hdwy over 2f out: rdn over 1f out: sn wknd* **9/1**

-663 **7** *11* **To Be Wild (IRE)**[24] 9065 6-9-3 92........................ PaulMulrennan 2 87
(Jane Chapple-Hyam) *t.k.h: cl up: rdn over 2f out: wknd over 1f out* **40/1**

1105 **8** *1 ½* **Carnwennan (IRE)**[115] 6355 4-9-3 94........................ KieranShoemark 5 85
(Charlie Fellowes) *hld up in rr: rdn and outpcd 3f out: sn wknd* **11/2**[3]

3m 32.72s (-2.28) **Going Correction** +0.25s/f (Slow) **8 Ran SP% 109.6**
Speed ratings (Par 109): **115,114,114,113,113 111,106,105**
CSF £32.78 TOTE £3.20: £1.30, £1.80, £1.60; EX 23.40 Trifecta £72.30.
Owner Middleham Park Racing XXXI & K Sohi **Bred** Lynch-Bages & Rhinestone Bloodstock **Trained** East Everleigh, Wilts

FOCUS
A stirring finish to this AW Championships Fast-Track qualifier. The classy winner showed battling qualities to prevail.

9469 BETWAY NOVICE STKS 1m 4f 98y (Tp)

1:25 (1:30) (Class 5) 3-Y-O+ **£3,428** (£1,020; £509; £254) **Stalls** High

Form RPR

32 **1** **Sharp Suited**[7] 9368 4-9-6 0........................ BenRobinson 7 67+
(Brian Ellison) *prom: stdy hdwy over 2f out: rdn and disp ld fr over 1f out: led ins fnl 110yds: jst prevailed* **7/4**[2]

53 **2** *nse* **Finespun (IRE)**[28] 9011 3-8-11 0........................ RobertHavlin 4 63+
(John Gosden) *t.k.h: trckd ldrs: led gng easily over 2f out: sn hrd pressed: rdn and hdd ins fnl 110yds: sn rallied: jst failed* **13/8**[1]

2-3 **3** *½* **Ice Pyramid (IRE)**[346] 18 4-9-6 0........................ BenCurtis 11 67+
(Philip Kirby) *carried rt s: hld up in rr: smooth hdwy over 2f out: rdn and disp ld fr over 1f out: kpt on fnl f: hld towards fin* **8/1**

3 **4** *1* **Harbour Front**[51] 8500 3-8-11 0........................ SeamusCronin(5) 10 66
(Robyn Brisland) *ducked rt s: midfield: pushed along whn nt clr run over 2f out: swtchd rt and rdn 2f out: kpt on fnl f: nt pce to chal* **11/2**[3]

006 **5** *1 ¼* **Melburnian**[15] 9213 3-8-11 63........................ RayDawson(5) 9 64
(Jane Chapple-Hyam) *pressed ldr: rdn and ev ch over 2f out: no ex ins fnl f* **16/1**

53 **6** *2* **Bobba Tee**[8] 9350 7-9-6 0........................ CamHardie 5 60
(Lawrence Mullaney) *midfield on inner: stdy hdwy gng easily over 2f out: rdn over 1f out: outpcd ins fnl f* **33/1**

4 **7** *1 ¾* **Drums Of War (IRE)**[8] 9350 7-9-6 0........................(p) GrahamLee 2 57
(Chris Grant) *hld up in rr: pushed along 3f out: hdwy over 1f out: kpt on fnl f: nt pce to chal* **100/1**

45 **8** *2* **Gabriel Oak**[59] 6890 3-9-2 0........................(t[1] w) PaulMulrennan 3 55
(Donald McCain) *hld up in rr on inner: rdn and outpcd over 3f out: no imp fr 2f out* **22/1**

4 **9** *7* **Ska Ridge**[40] 8814 7-9-3 0........................(tp) HarrisonShaw(3) 6 43
(Rebecca Menzies) *led: rdn and hdd over 2f out: wknd over 1f out* **50/1**

10 *14* **Mount Barina** 4-8-12 0........................ SeanDavis(3) 1 15
(John Davies) *slowly away: in rr: rdn and struggling 4f out: edgd lft and btn 2f out* **100/1**

400 **11** *12* **Battle Commander**[28] 9011 3-8-13 59........................ DarraghKeenan(3) 8 2
(Olly Williams) *dwlt s: in tch w ldrs: rdn and lost grnd qckly over 2f out: sn btn* **150/1**

2m 45.28s (4.18) **Going Correction** +0.25s/f (Slow) **11 Ran SP% 118.7**
WFA 3 from 4yo+ 4lb
Speed ratings (Par 103): **96,95,95,94,94 92,91,90,85,76 68**
CSF £4.86 TOTE £3.00: £1.30, £1.10, £2.20; EX 4.50 Trifecta £21.60.
Owner D Gilbert, M Lawrence, A Bruce **Bred** Sheikh Mohammed Obaid Al Maktoum **Trained** Norton, N Yorks

FOCUS
A fair novice in which the game winner took another step forward.

9470 BETWAY CLASSIFIED STKS 1m 4f 98y (Tp)

2:00 (2:06) (Class 6) 3-Y-O+ **£2,781** (£827; £413; £300; £300; £300) **Stalls** High

Form RPR

4664 **1** **Optima Petamus**[7] 9362 7-9-4 45........................(p) BenRobinson 9 51
(Liam Bailey) *towards rr: stdy hdwy gng easily over 3f out: rdn and led over 1f out: kpt on fnl 110yds: jst hld on* **14/1**

0406 **2** *shd* **Calevade (IRE)**[68] 7960 3-9-0 48........................ PaulMulrennan 12 52
(Ben Haslam) *t.k.h: hld up in rr: rdn over 2f out: hdwy over 1f out: wnt 2nd fnl 110yds: kpt on wl towards fin: jst hld* **4/1**[2]

5400 **3** *2 ½* **The Brora Pobbles**[5] 9395 4-9-4 44........................ BarryMcHugh 4 47
(Alistair Whillans) *hld up in rr: shkn up and hdwy over 2f out: rdn over 1f out: wnt 3rd ins fnl 110yds: no match for first two* **14/1**

23-4 **4** *2* **Traditional Dancer (IRE)**[55] 208 7-9-4 46........................(b) LukeMorris 6 44
(Iain Jardine) *dwlt s: hld up in rr: smooth hdwy over 2f out: sn rdn: outpcd over 1f out: rallied fnl 110yds: wnt 4th towards fin* **10/1**

3660 **5** *½* **Life Knowledge (IRE)**[53] 8423 7-9-4 47........................(b) BenCurtis 7 43
(Liam Bailey) *dwlt s: midfield: hdwy on outer and disp ld over 2f out: rdn and briefly led over 1f out: no ex fnl 110yds* **12/1**

4500 **6** *¾* **Gworn**[8] 9345 9-9-4 45........................ RobertHavlin 8 42
(R Mike Smith) *cl up: led gng easily over 2f out: rdn and hdd over 1f out: outpcd ins fnl f* **22/1**

3523 **7** *1 ¾* **Majestic Stone (IRE)**[11] 9289 5-9-4 48........................ JasonHart 11 40
(Julie Camacho) *slowly away: in rr: rdn and sme hdwy over 2f out: kpt on fnl f: nt pce to chal (jockey said gelding was slowly away and hung right in the home straight)* **7/2**[1]

2053 **8** *1* **Das Kapital**[61] 8204 4-9-4 47........................(p) FrannyNorton 1 38
(John Berry) *midfield on inner: rdn 3f out: no imp fr 2f out* **5/1**[3]

4025 **9** *5* **Klipperty Klopp**[11] 9289 3-9-0 49........................ CamHardie 3 32
(Antony Brittain) *prom: rdn over 2f out: wknd over 1f out* **11/1**

0060 **10** *11* **Airplane (IRE)**[26] 9042 4-9-1 45........................ ConorMcGovern(3) 2 14
(Paul Collins) *led: rdn and hdd over 2f out: sn wknd* **28/1**

460 **11** *13* **Dixieland (IRE)**[15] 9220 3-9-0 49........................(p[1]) DanielTudhope 13
(Marjorie Fife) *t.k.h: pressed ldr: lost 2nd and rdn over 3f out: wknd over 2f out: t.o* **14/1**

0000 **12** *13* **Initial Approach (IRE)**[161] 4628 3-9-0 40........................ GrahamLee 10
(Alan Brown) *t.k.h: midfield: rdn and struggling over 3f out: sn wknd: t.o* **125/1**

0-00 **13** *29* **If We Can Can**[26] 9033 4-9-1 50........................(b) DarraghKeenan(3) 5
(Olly Williams) *cl up: rdn and lost position over 3f out: sn wknd: t.o* **100/1**

2m 43.22s (2.12) **Going Correction** +0.25s/f (Slow)
WFA 3 from 4yo+ 4lb **13 Ran SP% 113.6**
Speed ratings (Par 101): **102,101,100,98,98 98,96,96,92,85 76,68,48**
CSF £64.44 TOTE £16.40: £4.20, £1.40, £4.70; EX 94.90 Trifecta £1381.10.
Owner Mrs C M Clarke, Foulrice Park Racing Ltd **Bred** Richard Moses Bloodstock **Trained** Middleham, N Yorks

FOCUS
Moderate fare. The winner hung on in a desperate finish.

9471 LADBROKES WHERE THE NATION PLAYS EBF NOVICE STKS 1m 5y (Tp)

2:35 (2:40) (Class 5) 2-Y-O **£3,428** (£1,020; £509; £254) **Stalls** Centre

Form RPR

1 **Desert Flyer** 2-9-0 0........................ RobertHavlin 3 72+
(John Gosden) *cl up in centre of gp: swtchd rt 1/2-way: led against nr rail 2f out: pushed out fnl f: comf* **11/4**[2]

2 *¾* **Spectrum Of Light (IRE)** 2-9-5 0........................ KieranShoemark 13 75
(Charlie Appleby) *midfield on nr side of gp: pushed along and hdwy 2f out: wnt 2nd ins fnl 110yds: kpt on towards fin* **9/1**

4 **3** *½* **Dublin Pharaoh (USA)**[16] 9197 2-9-5 0........................ JackMitchell 9 74
(Roger Varian) *dwlt s: hld up in rr on far side of gp: smooth hdwy over 2f out: rdn and trckd wnr over 1f out: sn edgd rt: lost 2nd but kpt on ins fnl 110yds: no ex towards fin* **11/10**[1]

4 *½* **Cable Speed (IRE)** 2-9-5 0........................ BenCurtis 7 73
(Charles Hills) *hmpd sn after s: midfield in centre of gp: rdn 2f out: kpt on fnl f: nrst fin* **11/1**

5 *½* **Salsada (IRE)** 2-9-0 0........................ GrahamLee 5 67
(Jedd O'Keeffe) *cl up on nr side of gp: rdn over 2f out: kpt on ins fnl f* **80/1**

6 *1 ¾* **Liberation Point (IRE)** 2-9-5 0........................ DanielTudhope 10 68+
(Richard Fahey) *dwlt s: hld up in rr on nr side of gp: shkn up and hdwy over 1f out: bit short of room ins fnl f: kpt on towards fin: eyecatcher* **17/2**[3]

7 *¾* **Innovation** 2-9-0 0........................ KieranO'Neill 12 61
(John Gosden) *dwlt s: hld up in rr on far side of gp: pushed along over 2f out: hdwy over 1f out: no imp fnl f* **18/1**

00 **8** *½* **Jay Me Lo (IRE)**[46] 8640 2-9-0 0........................ CamHardie 8 60
(Lawrence Mullaney) *cl up on nr side of gp: rdn over 2f out: outpcd fnl f* **250/1**

9 *1* **Celestial Wood (IRE)** 2-9-0 0........................ BenSanderson(5) 4 63
(Keith Dalgleish) *slowly away: carried lft after 1f: sn prom on far side of gp: rdn 2f out: wknd fnl f* **100/1**

10 *3 ¼* **Ancyre (FR)** 2-8-7 0........................ RhonaPindar(7) 2 50
(K R Burke) *t.k.h: led on far side of gp: rdn and hdd 2f out: wknd ins fnl f* **80/1**

0 **11** *7* **Potencia (IRE)**[17] 9181 2-9-0 0........................ PaulMulrennan 6 34
(Declan Carroll) *plld hrd: jinked rt sn after s: cl up in centre of gp: swtchd lft after 1f: rdn over 2f out: wknd over 1f out* **150/1**

0 **12** *shd* **Onedin (IRE)**[98] 6971 2-9-5 0........................ ShaneGray 1 39
(Kevin Ryan) *dwlt s: t.k.h: prom on far side of gp: rdn over 2f out: wknd over 1f out* **80/1**

13 *24* **Harbour Mist (IRE)** 2-9-5 0........................ JasonHart 11
(Tim Easterby) *hmpd sn after s: in rr in centre of gp sn after s: rdn and struggling 1/2-way: sn lost tch: t.o* **100/1**

1m 47.37s (8.77) **Going Correction** +0.25s/f (Slow) **13 Ran SP% 115.2**
Speed ratings (Par 96): **66,65,64,64,63 62,61,60,59,56 49,49,25**
CSF £26.84 TOTE £3.70: £1.50, £2.10, £1.10; EX 25.30 Trifecta £59.80.
Owner The Queen **Bred** Godolphin **Trained** Newmarket, Suffolk

FOCUS
An interesting novice which contained some nicely-bred sorts. The winner could be useful.

9472 BOMBARDIER BRITSH HOPPED AMBER BEER H'CAP 7f 14y (Tp)

3:10 (3:12) (Class 2) (0-105,105) 3-Y£13,232 (£3,960; £1,980; £991; £493) **Stalls** Centre

Form RPR

0330 **1** **Above The Rest (IRE)**[28] 9004 8-9-3 101........................(h) BenCurtis 9 110
(David Barron) *in tch w ldrs on nr side of gp: smooth hdwy to ld over 1f out: sn hrd pressed and rdn: kpt on strly fnl 110yds* **3/1**[1]

4115 **2** *1 ¼* **Aljari**[81] 7551 3-8-4 88........................ LukeMorris 3 94
(Marco Botti) *dwlt s: hld up in rr: hdwy on far side of gp over 2f out: rdn to chal over 1f out: kpt on fnl 110yds: no match for wnr* **6/1**

5350 **3** *1* **Raydiance**[70] 7891 4-8-7 94 ow3........................ HarrisonShaw(3) 8 97
(K R Burke) *cl up in centre of gp: led over 2f out: rdn and hdd over 1f out: sn rallied: no ex fnl 110yds* **13/2**

0602 **4** *2 ¼* **Intisaab**[10] 9308 8-8-8 92........................(tp) ShaneGray 1 89
(David O'Meara) *s.i.s: hld up in rr in centre of gp: rdn and hdwy over 1f out: kpt on fnl f: mde no imp* **14/1**

2000 **5** *shd* **Straight Right (FR)**[175] 4095 5-9-2 **100**..........................(h) GrahamLee 7 97
(Andrew Balding) *t.k.h: prom in centre of gp: rdn over 1f out: no ex ins fnl 110yds* **11/2**[3]

001- **6** *nk* **Caballero (IRE)**[427] 8189 3-8-3 **87**.............................. AndrewMullen 5 83
(Keith Dalgleish) *dwlt s: hld up in rr in centre of gp: pushed along over 2f out: hdwy and hung lft over 1f out: no imp fnl f* **33/1**

1405 **7** *5* **Finoah (IRE)**[14] 9254 3-8-8 **92**..............................(v) JaneElliott 4 74
(Tom Dascombe) *prom in centre of gp: rdn over 2f out: wknd over 1f out (jockey said gelding was denied a clear run 1 1/2f out)* **18/1**

5220 **8** *2 1/4* **Arctic Sound**[56] 8336 3-9-7 **105**.............................. FrannyNorton 2 81
(Mark Johnston) *cl up on far side of gp: rdn over 2f out: wknd over 1f out* **14/1**

0600 **9** *1/2* **Muntadab (IRE)**[16] 9198 7-8-11 **95**.............................. PaulMulrennan 6 70
(Roger Fell) *led on far side of gp: rdn and hdd fr over 2f out: wknd over 1f out* **50/1**

2020 **10** *1* **Pinnata (IRE)**[25] 9053 5-8-10 **94**..............................(t) JasonHart 10 66
(Stuart Williams) *t.k.h: cl up on nr side of gp: rdn over 2f out: wknd over 1f out* **7/2**[2]

1m 25.81s (-0.39) **Going Correction** +0.25s/f (Slow) **10** Ran SP% **113.7**
Speed ratings (Par 109): **112,110,109,106,106 106,100,98,97,96**
CSF £20.67 CT £109.09 TOTE £4.00: £1.50, £2.10, £2.40; EX 22.00 Trifecta £154.10.
Owner Laurence O'Kane **Bred** J C Carr **Trained** Maunby, N Yorks

FOCUS
A decent handicap won in good style by a horse who enjoys racing on Tapeta.

9473 BETWAY H'CAP 5f (Tp)
3:45 (3:47) (Class 6) (0-65,67) 3-Y-O+
£2,781 (£827; £413; £300; £300; £300) **Stalls** Centre

Form RPR

5224 **1** **Be Proud (IRE)**[22] 9108 3-9-4 **62**.............................. DanielTudhope 9 71
(Jim Goldie) *towards rr on nr side of gp: pushed along and hdwy over 1f out: rdn and led fnl 110yds: kpt on wl* **10/3**[1]

1151 **2** *1* **Young Tiger**[15] 9219 6-9-7 **65**..............................(h) AndrewMullen 12 70
(Tom Tate) *dwlt s: in rr on nr side of gp: rdn and hdwy over 1f out: wnt 2nd towards fin* **12/1**

0001 **3** *1/2* **Mutabaahy (IRE)**[4] 9406 4-8-10 **59** 5ex.................. SeamusCronin(5) 3 63
(Antony Brittain) *hld up in rr on far side of gp: hdwy 1/2-way: rdn to ld over 1f out: edgd rt and hdd fnl 110yds: no ex and lost 2nd towards fin* **4/1**[2]

5334 **4** *1 1/2* **Landing Night (IRE)**[7] 9365 7-9-6 **64**..............................(tp) BenCurtis 6 62
(Rebecca Menzies) *hld up in rr in centre of gp: pushed along and hdwy over 1f out: wnt 4th fnl 110yds: sn no imp (jockey said gelding hung left)* **6/1**[3]

0020 **5** *1/2* **Burtonwood**[15] 9223 7-8-13 **57**.............................. PaulMulrennan 5 53
(Julie Camacho) *cl up in centre of gp: rdn 2f out: no ex ins fnl f* **20/1**

3260 **6** *nk* **Piazon**[15] 9219 8-8-13 **60**..............................(be) HarrisonShaw(3) 7 55
(Julia Brooke) *led in centre of gp: rdn 2f out: hdd over 1f out: no ex ins fnl f* **50/1**

0600 **7** *nk* **Jan Van Hoof (IRE)**[174] 4149 8-9-7 **65**.............................. BarryMcHugh 4 59
(Michael Herrington) *hld up in rr in centre of gp: swtchd rt 1/2-way: rdn and hdwy fnl f: nt pce to chal* **25/1**

3120 **8** *nk* **Qaaraat**[4] 9406 4-9-0 **58**..............................(p) CamHardie 8 51
(Antony Brittain) *midfield in centre of gp: stdy hdwy 1/2-way: rdn over 1f out: outpcd fnl f* **7/1**

6000 **9** *2 1/2* **Arishka (IRE)**[15] 9218 3-9-7 **65**..............................(b) KieranO'Neill 13 49
(Daniel Kubler) *cl up on nr side of gp: rdn 1/2-way: wknd over 1f out* **33/1**

0000 **10** *1 1/2* **Peters Pudding (IRE)**[12] 9276 3-7-13 **50**..............................(v) GavinAshton(7) 10 29
(Lisa Williamson) *in rr on nr side of gp: hung lft and struggling 1/2-way: nvr on terms* **150/1**

4210 **11** *nk* **Swiss Connection**[53] 8429 3-9-7 **65**..............................(h) GrahamLee 1 43
(Bryan Smart) *cl up on far side of gp: rdn 1/2-way: wknd over 1f out* **14/1**

4521 **12** *2 1/4* **Rockley Point**[5] 9398 6-8-10 **54** 5ex..............................(b) JasonHart 2 24
(Katie Scott) *cl up on far side of gp: rdn 1/2-way: wknd over 1f out (jockey said gelding ran flat)* **13/2**

59.53s (0.03) **Going Correction** +0.25s/f (Slow) **12** Ran SP% **111.7**
Speed ratings (Par 101): **109,107,106,104,103 102,102,101,97,95 95,91**
CSF £39.11 CT £162.89 TOTE £3.50: £1.40, £3.10, £2.00; EX 32.40 Trifecta £135.20.
Owner Gregg And O Shea **Bred** John Lyons **Trained** Uplawmoor, E Renfrews

FOCUS
An open-looking sprint but a comfortable winner.
T/Plt: £659.30 to a £1 stake. Pool: £55,275.30 - 61.20 winning units T/Qpdt: £12.20 to a £1 stake. Pool: £6,817.81 - 413.02 winning units **Richard Young**

9445 WOLVERHAMPTON (A.W) (L-H)
Saturday, December 14

OFFICIAL GOING: Tapeta: standard
Wind: Fresh behind Weather: Showers

9474 LADBROKES "PLAY 1-2-FREE" ON FOOTBALL MAIDEN AUCTION STKS 5f 21y (Tp)
4:50 (4:51) (Class 5) 2-Y-O
£3,428 (£1,020; £509; £254) **Stalls** Low

Form RPR

5433 **1** **Triple Spear**[4] 9401 2-8-13 68.............................. AngusVilliers(5) 4 69
(Michael Appleby) *chsd ldr: hung rt 1/2-way: rdn to ld and edgd lft over 1f out: r.o* **7/4**[2]

52 **2** *2* **Rocking Reg (IRE)**[26] 9036 2-9-5 0.............................. JimCrowley 2 63
(Roger Teal) *led: rdn and hdd over 1f out: styd on same pce ins fnl f* **11/8**[1]

0 **3** *hd* **Bring The Money (IRE)**[14] 9251 2-9-5 0.............................. DavidProbert 3 62
(Mick Channon) *chsd ldrs: hung rt 1/2-way: rdn over 1f out: r.o* **33/1**

4 *1* **Viva Voce (IRE)** 2-9-3 0.............................. HollieDoyle 6 56+
(David Barron) *s.i.s: hld up: r.o ins fnl f: nt rch ldrs* **20/1**

5 *1 1/2* **Dress Circle** 2-8-13 0.............................. PJMcDonald 5 47
(James Tate) *s.i.s: pushed along early in rr: shkn up over 1f out: styd on same pce fnl f* **4/1**[3]

6 *4* **The Kyllachy Touch** 2-9-3 0.............................. LewisEdmunds 1 37
(Derek Shaw) *trckd ldrs: plld hrd: rdn and edgd lft over 1f out: wknd ins fnl f* **125/1**

1m 1.7s (-0.20) **Going Correction** -0.125s/f (Stan) **6** Ran SP% **107.0**
Speed ratings (Par 96): **96,92,92,90,88 82**
CSF £4.01 TOTE £2.40: £1.40, £1.10; EX 4.30 Trifecta £28.90.
Owner Minster Developments **Bred** Whitsbury Manor Stud **Trained** Oakham, Rutland

FOCUS
An ordinary 2yo maiden.

9475 BOMBARDIER BRITISH HOPPED AMBER BEER MAIDEN STKS 7f 36y (Tp)
5:20 (5:23) (Class 5) 3-Y-O+
£3,428 (£1,020; £509; £254) **Stalls** High

Form RPR

1 **Motawaafeq (FR)**[88] 3-9-5 77.............................. AlistairRawlinson 10 74+
(Michael Appleby) *s.s: pushed along early in rr: racd keenly on outer over 5f out: hung rt over 2f out: hdwy over 1f out: rdn and r.o to ld nr fin* **5/1**[2]

2- **2** *1/2* **Badayel (IRE)**[378] 9355 3-9-5 0..............................(p[1]) PJMcDonald 9 73
(Ivan Furtado) *s.i.s: hdwy over 5f out: shkn up to ld over 1f out: sn rdn and hung lft: hdd nr fin* **5/1**[2]

3 *nk* **Monya (IRE)** 3-9-0 0.............................. JimCrowley 2 67+
(Charles Hills) *s.s: hld up: racd keenly: swtchd rt over 2f out: r.o ins fnl f: wnt 3rd nr fin* **5/4**[1]

0 **4** *nk* **Brenbar (USA)**[15] 9213 3-9-5 0.............................. JFEgan 5 71
(Roger Varian) *plld hrd and prom: rdn and hung rt over 1f out: r.o* **6/1**[3]

5 *nk* **Zhukovsky (IRE)** 3-9-5 0.............................. RichardKingscote 6 70+
(Ismail Mohammed) *hld up: nt clr run over 1f out: r.o ins fnl f* **14/1**

44 **6** *2* **Montys Inn (IRE)**[17] 9171 3-9-5 0.............................. JohnFahy 4 65
(Richard Hannon) *led: rdn and hdd over 1f out: no ex ins fnl f (jockey said gelding hung right-handed throughout)* **14/1**

53 **7** *2* **Just Magic**[12] 9276 3-9-5 0.............................. DuranFentiman 3 60
(Tim Easterby) *chsd ldr tl shkn up over 1f out: wknd ins fnl f* **25/1**

534 **8** *nk* **Memory Hill (IRE)**[26] 9032 3-9-5 68.............................. CliffordLee 8 59
(David Evans) *prom: rdn over 1f out: wknd ins fnl f* **22/1**

0 **9** *1* **Mr Millarcky**[9] 9332 3-9-5 0.............................. DavidProbert 1 56
(Rae Guest) *hld up: sme hdwy over 1f out: wknd ins fnl f (jockey said gelding hung left-handed throughout)* **40/1**

4006 **10** *10* **Tilsworth Prisca**[28] 9001 4-9-0 29..............................(h) RaulDaSilva 7 24
(J R Jenkins) *chsd ldrs: lost pl 1/2-way: sn rdn: wknd 2f out* **200/1**

1m 28.06s (-0.74) **Going Correction** -0.125s/f (Stan) **10** Ran SP% **116.5**
Speed ratings (Par 103): **99,98,98,97,97 95,92,92,91,79**
CSF £29.24 TOTE £6.10: £1.70, £1.90, £1.10; EX 27.00 Trifecta £94.40.
Owner Middleham Park Racing II **Bred** Duchess Henrietta De Bedford **Trained** Oakham, Rutland

FOCUS
Not a bad 3yo maiden and it saw a tight finish.

9476 BOMBARDIER GOLDEN BEER H'CAP 7f 36y (Tp)
5:50 (5:54) (Class 4) (0-80,80) 3-Y-O+
£5,207 (£1,549; £774; £400; £400; £400) **Stalls** High

Form RPR

0605 **1** **Jackstar (IRE)**[38] 8852 3-9-6 **79**.............................. RichardKingscote 8 89
(Tom Dascombe) *mde virtually all: rdn over 1f out: edgd rt sn after: styd on u.p* **13/8**[1]

2401 **2** *1* **Ginger Fox**[25] 9057 3-9-1 **79**..............................(p) AngusVilliers(5) 4 86
(David Loughnane) *s.i.s: racd keenly and sn hld up in tch: rdn and edgd lft over 1f out: r.o to go 2nd wl ins fnl f: nt rch wnr* **4/1**[2]

6024 **3** *3/4* **Reckless Endeavour (IRE)**[36] 8921 6-9-5 **78**.................. HollieDoyle 9 83
(David Barron) *hld up: nt clr run and swtchd rt over 1f out: r.o wl ins fnl f: wnt 3rd nr fin* **10/1**[3]

-550 **4** *nk* **Barrington (IRE)**[10] 9308 5-9-2 **75**..............................(v) AlistairRawlinson 12 79
(Michael Appleby) *chsd wnr: rdn over 1f out: styd on same pce wl ins fnl f* **40/1**

1222 **5** *hd* **Zafaranah (USA)**[21] 9126 5-9-7 **80**.............................. ShaneKelly 3 84
(Pam Sly) *chsd ldrs: rdn over 1f out: styd on same pce wl ins fnl f (trainer was informed that the mare could not run until the day after passing a stalls test)* **12/1**

4250 **6** *3/4* **Howzer Black (IRE)**[8] 9348 3-9-6 **79**..............................(p) CallumRodriguez 1 81
(Keith Dalgleish) *s.i.s: sn hld up in tch: rdn over 1f out: styd on same pce ins fnl f* **10/1**[3]

3050 **7** *1* **Kupa River (IRE)**[8] 9348 5-8-12 **76**..............................(h) PaulaMuir(5) 11 75
(Roger Fell) *s.s: hld up: plld hrd: nt clr run over 1f out: styd on ins fnl f: nt trble ldrs* **20/1**

5041 **8** *3/4* **Human Nature (IRE)**[51] 8496 6-9-4 **77**..............................(t) PJMcDonald 5 74
(Stuart Williams) *plld hrd and prom: shkn up over 1f out: edgd lft and no ex ins fnl f* **12/1**

2010 **9** *hd* **Self Assessment (IRE)**[25] 9054 3-9-5 **78**.............................. CliffordLee 7 74
(K R Burke) *s.i.s: hld up: carried lft over 1f out: nt clr run ins fnl f: nt trble ldrs (jockey said gelding was denied a clear run inside the final furlong)* **16/1**

10 *3 1/2* **Merricourt (IRE)**[45] 8674 3-9-5 **78**.............................. TomMarquand 10 65
(Iain Jardine) *sn prom: rdn over 2f out: edgd lft and wknd ins fnl f* **14/1**

0 **11** *1 1/4* **The Game Of Life**[14] 9255 4-9-5 **78**.............................. TomEaves 6 62
(Michael Herrington) *dwlt: hld up: rdn over 1f out: n.d* **33/1**

5006 **12** *7* **Nick Vedder**[26] 9030 5-9-4 **77**.............................. EoinWalsh 2 42
(Robyn Brisland) *s.i.s: hld up: a in rr* **50/1**

1m 26.53s (-2.27) **Going Correction** -0.125s/f (Stan) **12** Ran SP% **116.3**
Speed ratings (Par 105): **107,105,105,104,104 103,102,101,101,97 95,87**
CSF £6.90 CT £49.39 TOTE £2.60: £1.20, £1.70, £1.90; EX 9.80 Trifecta £64.50.
Owner Mrs Caroline Ingram **Bred** Skymarc Farm **Trained** Malpas, Cheshire

FOCUS
This fair handicap was run at a sound pace and it's reliable AW form.

9477 BETWAY HEED YOUR HUNCH H'CAP 6f 20y (Tp)
6:20 (6:22) (Class 6) (0-60,60) 3-Y-O+
£1,804; £413; £400; £400; £400 **Stalls** Low

Form RPR

4034 **1** **Seraphim**[12] 9277 3-9-6 **59**..............................(bt) DanielMuscutt 5 66
(Marco Botti) *trckd ldrs: led over 1f out: sn rdn and edgd lft: jnd post* **7/2**[2]

5600 **1** *dht* **It Must Be Faith**[4] 9406 9-8-11 **57**..............................(p) ErikaParkinson(7) 2 64
(Michael Appleby) *plld hrd and prom: shkn up over 1f out: r.o to join wnr post (trainer said regarding apparent improvement in form appreciated the return to 6 furlongs from 5 furlongs and that the gelding appeared to jump better on this occasion)* **18/1**

3441 **3** *2 3/4* **Phoenix Star (IRE)**[15] 9218 3-9-7 **60**..............................(t) PJMcDonald 9 59
(Stuart Williams) *hld up: pushed along 1/2-way: r.o ins fnl f: nt rch ldrs* **9/4**[1]

5000 **4** *3/4* **Miracle Garden**[15] 9217 7-9-7 **60**..............................(b) TomMarquand 3 57
(Roy Brotherton) *chsd ldrs: rdn over 1f out: styd on same pce ins fnl f* **22/1**

1540 **5** *nse* **Dubai Elegance**[80] 7590 5-9-1 **54**..............................(p) LewisEdmunds 10 50
(Derek Shaw) *s.i.s: hld up: rdn and r.o ins fnl f: nt rch ldrs* **33/1**

The Form Book Flat 2019, Raceform Ltd, Newbury, RG14 5SJ

2005 **6** *hd* **Peachey Carnehan**12 9277 5-9-4 **57**..........................(v) JamesSullivan 8 53
(Michael Mullineaux) *hld up: swtchd rt over 1f out: r.o ins fnl f: nt rch ldrs* **15/2**3

1300 **7** *1* **Tawaafoq**75 7757 5-9-3 **56**..........................(h w) HollieDoyle 11 49
(Adrian Wintle) *chsd ldrs: led over 1f out: sn rdn and hdd: no ex ins fnl f* **25/1**

0202 **8** ½ **Brockey Rise (IRE)**11 9287 4-8-9 **55**..........................(b) LauraPearson(7) 6 46
(David Evans) *chsd ldrs: rdn over 1f out: no ex ins fnl f* **8/1**

6000 **9** *nse* **Heavenly Rainbow (IRE)**22 9106 3-9-5 **58**.......................... PhilDennis 1 49
(Michael Herrington) *s.i.s: hld up: hdwy over 1f out: nt clr run ins fnl f: no ex* **10/1**

4005 **10** *1¾* **Time To Reason (IRE)**23 9092 6-9-7 **60**..........................(p) CliffordLee 4 46
(Charlie Wallis) *led: racd freely: rdn and hdd over 1f out: wknd ins fnl f* **12/1**

6050 **11** *nk* **No More Regrets (IRE)**99 6945 3-9-5 **58**.......................... CallumRodriguez 7 43
(Patrick Morris) *s.i.s: nvr on terms* **25/1**

0015 **12** ½ **Guardia Svizzera (IRE)**12 9272 5-8-11 **55**..........................(h) PaulaMuir(5) 13 38
(Roger Fell) *s.i.s: hld up: plld hrd: hdwy on outer over 3f out: wknd fnl f (jockey said gelding ran too freely)* **20/1**

1m 13.4s (-1.10) **Going Correction** -0.125s/f (Stan) **12** Ran SP% **117.7**
Speed ratings (Par 101): **102,102,98,97,97 97,95,95,94,92 92,91**WIN: 2.00 Seraphim, 10.10 lt Must Be Faith; PL: 1.20 Phoenix Star, 1.60 Seraphim, 4.90 lt Must Be Faith; EX: S&IMBF 31.40, IMBF&S 54.30; CSF: S&IMBF 28.84, IMBF&S 37.09; TC: S&IMBF&PS 87.65, IMBF&S&PS 103.21; TF: S&IMBF&PS 61.60, IMBF&S&PS 231.60 CSF £28.84 CT £8727 TOTE £Owner: £Excel Racing & Partner, £Bred, £Glebe Farm Stud, £TrainedNewmarket, Suffolk.
Owner Mick Appleby Racing **Bred** Matthew Sharkey & Newsells Park Stud Ltd **Trained** Oakham, Rutland

FOCUS
This moderate sprint handicap was run at an ordinary pace and the first pair couldn't be separated at the finish.

9478 BETWAY H'CAP 6f 20y (Tp)
6:50 (6:52) (Class 2) (0-105,105) 3-Y-O+ **£11,971** (£3,583; £1,791; £896; £446) **Stalls** Low

Form RPR

5011 **1** **Reeves**16 9198 3-8-3 **90**.......................... SeanDavis(3) 4 99+
(Robert Cowell) *prom: lost pl over 4f out: hdwy over 1f out: rdn to ld and edgd lft wl ins fnl f: r.o* **4/1**2

0401 **2** ½ **Desert Doctor (IRE)**86 7372 4-8-11 **95**.......................... TomMarquand 2 103
(Ed Walker) *hld up: hdwy over 1f out: rdn: edgd lft and r.o to go 2nd wl ins fnl f: nt rch wnr* **5/1**3

0013 **3** ½ **Soldier's Minute**28 9004 4-9-1 **99**..........................(h) CallumRodriguez 9 105
(Keith Dalgleish) *plld hrd and prom: rdn ins fnl f: r.o* **7/2**1

1011 **4** ¾ **Total Commitment (IRE)**53 8420 3-8-3 **92**.......................... AngusVilliers(5) 8 96
(Peter Hedger) *led: hdd over 3f out: led again over 3f out: rdn: edgd lft and hdd wl ins fnl f: styd on same pce* **13/2**

0303 **5** *nk* **Merhoob (IRE)**16 9198 7-8-13 **97**.......................... LukeMorris 1 100
(John Ryan) *hld up: hdwy and nt clr run over 1f out: r.o: nt rch ldrs* **8/1**

3066 **6** *3* **Lancelot Du Lac (ITY)**23 9088 9-8-10 **94**.......................... ShaneKelly 6 87
(Dean Ivory) *trckd ldrs: rdn and cl up whn hmpd and eased ins fnl f* **22/1**

3462 **7** ½ **Corinthia Knight (IRE)**18 9166 4-9-7 **105**.......................... HollieDoyle 10 96
(Archie Watson) *racd keenly: wnt 2nd over 5f out tl led over 3f out: hdd over 2f out: wknd ins fnl f* **7/1**

2104 **8** *1¾* **Mokaatil**23 9088 4-8-2 **86** oh1..........................(p) JamesSullivan 7 72
(Ian Williams) *hld up: plld hrd: hdwy on outer over 4f out: edgd lft and wknd over 1f out* **16/1**

1m 12.3s (-2.20) **Going Correction** -0.125s/f (Stan) **8** Ran SP% **106.1**
Speed ratings (Par 109): **109,108,107,106,106 102,101,99**
CSF £20.62 CT £61.18 TOTE £4.90: £1.40, £1.10, £1.60; EX 20.40 Trifecta £72.30.
Owner T W Morley **Bred** Bearstone Stud Ltd **Trained** Six Mile Bottom, Cambs

■ Warsaw Road (11-1) was withdrawn. Rule 4 applies to all bets struck prior to withdrawal, but not to SP bets. Deduction - 5p in the pound. New market formed

■ Stewards' Enquiry : Angus Villiers three-day ban; careless riding (Dec 31, Jan 1-2)

FOCUS
A decent sprint handicap, but one run at a modest pace.

9479 #BETYOURWAY AT BETWAY H'CAP 1m 1f 104y (Tp)
7:20 (7:21) (Class 6) (0-60,63) 3-Y-O+ **£2,781** (£827; £413; £400; £400; £400) **Stalls** Low

Form RPR

1140 **1** **Fair Power (IRE)**53 8422 5-9-8 **61**.......................... LukeMorris 7 69
(John Butler) *hld up: racd keenly: hdwy on outer over 1f out: rdn to ld and hung lft ins fnl f: r.o* **11/1**

01 **2** *1* **Mojambo (IRE)**2 9446 4-8-11 **50** 5ex..........................(tp) HollieDoyle 8 56
(Stephen Michael Hanlon, Ire) *hld up in tch: shkn up and qcknd to ld over 1f out: rdn: edgd rt and hdd wl ins fnl f: styd on same pce* **7/1**

001 **3** *1* **Sunshineandbubbles**7 9362 6-9-3 **56**.......................... CliffordLee 6 60
(David Evans) *chsd ldrs: rdn over 1f out: styd on same pce ins fnl f* **4/1**2

0000 **4** *1* **Deleyll**28 9006 5-9-4 **57**.......................... JoeyHaynes 1 59
(John Butler) *s.i.s: hld up: pushed along over 2f out: rdn and r.o ins fnl f: nt trble ldrs* **25/1**

3033 **5** *hd* **Kybosh (IRE)**2 9446 3-8-6 **52**.......................... AngusVilliers(5) 9 54
(Michael Appleby) *hld up: shkn up over 2f out: rdn: edgd lft and r.o ins fnl f: nt rch ldrs* **11/4**1

0400 **6** *1¼* **The Eagle's Nest (IRE)**7 9362 5-9-1 **54**..........................(t) DanielMuscutt 2 54
(Alexandra Dunn) *chsd ldrs: rdn and ev ch over 1f out: no ex ins fnl f* **16/1**

0004 **7** *shd* **Mrs Hoo (IRE)**14 9256 3-9-4 **62**.......................... SeanDavis(3) 5 61
(Richard Fahey) *chsd ldr: rdn and ev ch over 1f out: no ex ins fnl f* **16/1**

6420 **8** *shd* **Barbarosa (IRE)**15 9216 3-9-2 **57**.......................... TomEaves 4 56
(Michael Herrington) *sn led: rdn and hdd over 1f out: no ex ins fnl f* **9/1**

0003 **9** ¾ **Sir Gnet (IRE)**16 9207 5-9-4 **57**..........................(b) TomMarquand 3 55
(Ed Dunlop) *s.i.s: hld up: rdn over 1f out: nvr on terms* **13/2**3

0016 **10** *3¼* **Set Point Charlie (IRE)**107 6643 3-9-5 **60**..........................(vt1) TomQueally 10 52
(Seamus Durack) *s.i.s: hld up: racd wd: n.d* **20/1**

1m 59.83s (-0.97) **Going Correction** -0.125s/f (Stan) **10** Ran SP% **111.2**
WFA 3 from 4yo+ 2lb
Speed ratings (Par 101): **99,98,97,96,96 95,94,94,94,91**
CSF £81.50 CT £352.79 TOTE £12.40: £4.20, £1.90, £1.60; EX 106.00 Trifecta £543.30.
Owner N N Holmes **Bred** Pitrizzia Partnership **Trained** Newmarket, Suffolk

FOCUS
Fair form for the class.

9480 BETWAY CASINO H'CAP 1m 1f 104y (Tp)
7:50 (7:52) (Class 4) (0-85,84) 3-Y-O+ **£5,207** (£1,549; £774; £400; £400; £400) **Stalls** Low

Form RPR

2115 **1** **Home Before Dusk**23 9096 4-9-7 **84**..........................(p) CallumRodriguez 11 93
(Keith Dalgleish) *hld up: hdwy and nt clr run over 1f out: rdn and r.o to ld wl ins fnl f* **9/1**

3421 **2** *1* **Big Daddy Kane**23 9096 3-9-1 **80**.......................... DanielMuscutt 9 87
(Marco Botti) *s.i.s: hld up: nt clr run over 2f out: hdwy to ld over 1f out: rdn: edgd rt and hdd wl ins fnl f* **6/4**1

3012 **3** *1* **Storm Ahead (IRE)**11 9285 6-9-3 **80**..........................(b) PhilDennis 1 85
(Tim Easterby) *hld up: hdwy over 3f out: nt clr run over 1f out: sn rdn: r.o* **8/1**3

0653 **4** ½ **Keswick**11 9285 5-8-12 **75**..........................(bt1) LukeMorris 8 79
(Heather Main) *hld up: swtchd rt and hdwy over 1f out: sn rdn: r.o* **20/1**

3002 **5** *nk* **Global Art**16 9199 4-9-2 **79**..........................(b) PJMcDonald 5 82
(Ed Dunlop) *s.i.s: hld up: rdn and nt clr run over 1f out: r.o ins fnl f: nvr nrr* **16/1**

5505 **6** *1¼* **Sezim**5 9388 3-8-11 **76**..........................(t) TomMarquand 4 77
(Mohamed Moubarak) *led after 1f: rdn: edgd rt and hdd over 1f out: no ex ins fnl f* **9/1**

244 **7** *hd* **Little India (FR)**21 9138 3-8-7 **72**..........................(p1) HollieDoyle 10 72
(K R Burke) *sn prom: chsd ldr 7f out tl over 3f out: wnt 2nd again over 2f out tl rdn over 1f out: no ex ins fnl f* **12/1**

611 **8** *2½* **Sea Fox (IRE)**14 9255 5-9-2 **79**.......................... CliffordLee 7 74
(David Evans) *hld up: hdwy on outer 5f out: chsd ldr over 3f out tl rdn over 2f out: wknd ins fnl f* **6/1**2

3-13 **9** *shd* **Fancy Footings (IRE)**17 9183 3-9-3 **82**.......................... AlistairRawlinson 2 77
(Tom Dascombe) *w ldr 1f: hmpd over 7f out: lost pl 5f out: n.d after (jockey said gelding hung right-handed throughout)* **9/1**

4040 **10** *3¼* **Street Poet (IRE)**63 8122 6-8-9 **72**.......................... TomEaves 6 60
(Michael Herrington) *chsd ldrs: shkn up over 1f out: wknd fnl f* **40/1**

4000 **11** *5* **Daddy's Daughter (CAN)**21 9126 4-9-1 **78**..........................(h) ShaneKelly 3 55
(Dean Ivory) *plld hrd: led 1f: remained handy: shkn up over 1f out: wknd fnl f* **33/1**

1m 58.38s (-2.42) **Going Correction** -0.125s/f (Stan)
WFA 3 from 4yo+ 2lb **11** Ran SP% **119.1**
Speed ratings (Par 105): **105,104,103,102,102 101,101,99,98,96 91**
CSF £22.70 CT £119.55 TOTE £11.10: £4.00, £1.10, £2.80; EX 36.60 Trifecta £192.30.
Owner G R Leckie **Bred** G L S Partnership **Trained** Carluke, S Lanarks

FOCUS
A good handicap, run at an uneven pace.

9481 BETWAY LIVE CASINO H'CAP 1m 4f 51y (Tp)
8:20 (8:20) (Class 6) (0-55,55) 3-Y-O+ **£2,781** (£827; £413; £400; £400; £400) **Stalls** Low

Form RPR

0003 **1** **Enmeshing**18 9168 6-9-5 **53**..........................(p) DanielMuscutt 7 60
(Alexandra Dunn) *hld up in tch: rdn to ld and hung lft fr over 1f out: styd on u.p* **11/2**3

0213 **2** *1¼* **Cheng Gong**16 9201 3-9-1 **53**..........................(b1) JackMitchell 3 59
(Tom Clover) *led: shkn up over 3f out: rdn and hdd over 1f out: hmpd ins fnl f: styd on same pce* **13/8**1

1000 **3** *1¾* **Valentine Mist (IRE)**11 9282 7-8-12 **46**.......................... TomMarquand 4 49
(James Grassick) *chsd ldr 2f: remained handy: rdn and ev ch whn hung lft over 1f out: hmpd ins fnl f: no ex* **80/1**

3000 **4** *1¾* **Final Attack (IRE)**7 9362 8-8-12 **46** oh1..........................(p) JamesSullivan 5 45
(Sarah Hollinshead) *hld up: nt clr run over 2f out: hdwy over 1f out: nt rch ldrs* **20/1**

0641 **5** ½ **Ember's Glow**11 9289 5-9-2 **50**.......................... DougieCostello 6 49
(Mark Loughnane) *hld up: hdwy over 1f out: nt rch ldrs* **6/1**

0000 **6** *nk* **Gibraltarian (IRE)**15 9216 3-8-12 **50**..........................(p) CharlieBennett 10 49
(Jim Boyle) *hld up: swtchd rt over 2f out: r.o ins fnl f: nvr nrr* **40/1**

-000 **7** ½ **Sexy Secret**88 7318 8-8-12 **46** oh1..........................(v) DavidProbert 1 43
(Simon Pearce) *prom: rdn over 2f out: styd on same pce fr over 1f out* **33/1**

006 **8** ½ **Gms Princess**28 9011 3-8-10 **48**.......................... RaulDaSilva 11 46
(Sarah Hollinshead) *hld up: hdwy u.p over 1f out: nt trble ldrs* **50/1**

0-06 **9** *1* **Louisiana Beat (IRE)**15 9216 3-8-9 **47**.......................... HollieDoyle 12 43
(Mike Murphy) *prom: chsd ldr 10f out: rdn and ev ch over 1f out: nt clr run sn after: wknd ins fnl f* **22/1**

6161 **10** *12* **Lord Howard (IRE)**15 9216 3-8-10 **55**..........................(v) GeorgeBass(7) 2 32
(Mick Channon) *s.i.s: hld up: rdn over 3f out: n.d (jockey said gelding was never travelling)* **10/3**2

0240 **11** *4* **Golden Deal (IRE)**21 9139 4-8-13 **47**.......................... LukeMorris 8 16
(Richard Phillips) *hld up: plld hrd: swtchd rt and hdwy 8f out: rdn and wknd over 2f out (jockey said filly ran too freely)* **25/1**

6104 **12** *1½* **Good Impression**18 9168 4-9-7 **55**..........................(p) AlistairRawlinson 9 22
(Dai Burchell) *chsd ldrs: rdn over 3f out: wknd over 2f out* **8/1**

2m 39.21s (-1.59) **Going Correction** -0.125s/f (Stan)
WFA 3 from 4yo+ 4lb **12** Ran SP% **123.5**
Speed ratings (Par 101): **100,99,98,96,96 96,95,95,94,86 84,83**
CSF £14.52 CT £684.28 TOTE £6.70: £1.80, £1.20, £16.80; EX 16.10 Trifecta £2307.40.
Owner The Crafty Six & W B B **Bred** Compagnia Generale Srl **Trained** West Buckland, Somerset

■ Stewards' Enquiry : Daniel Muscutt two-day ban; careless riding (Dec 28-29)

FOCUS
This was competitive enough for the grade. It was run at just an ordinary pace.
T/Plt: £13.30 to a £1 stake. Pool: £94,249.28 - 5,150.17 winning units T/Qpdt: £5.90 to a £1 stake. Pool: £11,978.80 - 1,482.30 winning units **Colin Roberts**

9482 - (Foreign Racing) - See Raceform Interactive

9280 DEAUVILLE (R-H)

Saturday, December 14

OFFICIAL GOING: Polytrack: standard

9483a PRIX FLYING WATER (CONDITIONS) (4YO+) (ALL-WEATHER TRACK) (POLYTRACK) 6f 110y(P)

2:32 4-Y-O+

£9,459 (£3,594; £2,648; £1,513; £756; £567)

RPR

1 **Good Effort (IRE)**[23] 9098 4-9-4 0 ....(p) TheoBachelot 5 107
(Ismail Mohammed) *pushed along early: led after 1 1/2f: mde rest: rdn and wnt clr wl over 1f out: styd on strly* **49/10**[3]

2 4 **Degrisement (FR)**[84] 5-9-4 0 ....(b) AnthonyCrastus 8 95
(J Reynier, France) **13/1**

3 1 1/4 **Alfieri (FR)**[207] 2955 6-8-11 0 ....(b) MlleMarieVelon(9) 3 93
(J-P Gauvin, France) **49/10**[3]

4 1/2 **Deemster (IRE)**[13] 4-9-4 0 .... MickaelBarzalona 7 90
(A Fabre, France) *chsd ldrs: pushed along 3f out: rdn to chal ldng pair over 2f out: kpt on same pce u.p* **21/10**[1]

5 1 1/2 **George The Prince (FR)**[46] 5-9-6 0 ....(b) AurelienLemaitre 6 88
(G Doleuze, France) **12/1**

6 1 1/4 **Gymkhana**[126] 5951 6-9-0 0 .... FabienLefebvre 11 78
(P De Chevigny, France) **22/1**

7 hd **Fighting Irish (IRE)**[30] 8982 4-9-0 0 ....(p) CristianDemuro 4 77
(Harry Dunlop) *midfield: drvn to cl over 2f out: sn no further imp u.p: plugged on one pce* **48/10**[2]

8 1 1/2 **Cheikeljack (FR)**[230] 6-8-8 0 .... AlexisPouchin(6) 2 73
(C Boutin, France) **49/1**

9 snk **Time To Fly (FR)**[108] 4-9-1 0 .... HugoBesnier(5) 9 79
(M Seror, France) **36/1**

10 2 **On The Sea**[230] 5-8-8 0 .... JeremieMonteiro(6) 13 67
(N Caullery, France) **70/1**

11 shd **Beau Massagot (FR)**[164] 4-8-13 0 .... LukaRousseau(5) 14 70
(Vaclav Luka Jr, Czech Republic) **76/1**

12 12 **Nelkan (IRE)**[195] 4-8-10 0 .... TristanBaron 1 28
(H-A Pantall, France) **64/1**

13 4 1/2 **Prestbury Park (USA)**[54] 8400 4-8-13 0 .... RosarioMangione(3) 10 21
(Sofie Lanslots, France) **81/1**

14 snk **Monsieur Mel**[442] 7725 5-8-13 0 .... DelphineSantiago(3) 12 20
(Andre Hermans, Belgium) **13/1**

1m 14.92s **14 Ran SP% 119.9**
PARI-MUTUEL (all including 1 euro stake): WIN 5.90; PLACE 2.10, 3.20, 2.20; DF 30.80.
Owner Abdulla Al Mansoori **Bred** Rabbah Bloodstock Limited **Trained** Newmarket, Suffolk

9484- 9495a (Foreign Racing) - See Raceform Interactive

9474 WOLVERHAMPTON (A.W) (L-H)

Monday, December 16

OFFICIAL GOING: Tapeta: standard
Wind: Light behind Weather: Cloudy

9496 BETWAY AMATEUR RIDERS' H'CAP 1m 1f 104y (Tp)

4:05 (4:06) (Class 5) (0-75,75) 3-Y-O+

£3,306 (£1,025; £512; £400; £400; £400) **Stalls Low**

Form RPR

5035 1 **The Throstles**[13] 9285 4-10-13 **74** ....(p) MrAlexEdwards 13 84
(Kevin Frost) *a.p: shkn up to ld ins fnl f: r.o* **8/1**

2100 2 2 **Luna Magic**[40] 8862 5-10-11 **72** .... MissBrodieHampson 4 78
(Archie Watson) *led 1f: remained handy: chsd ldr over 3f out: led over 1f out: sn rdn: hdd ins fnl f: styd on same pce* **3/1**[1]

3534 3 3 1/4 **Star Ascending (IRE)**[47] 8664 7-10-4 **70** ....(p) MrRyanHolmes(5) 12 69
(Jennie Candlish) *s.i.s: hld up: rdn and hdwy whn rdr dropped whip over 1f out: r.o to go 3rd nr fin: nt rch ldrs* **16/1**

0300 4 1 1/2 **Los Camachos (IRE)**[56] 8412 4-10-7 **75** .... MissZoeHarris(7) 11 71
(John Gallagher) *led over 8f out: clr over 6f out tl 5f out: hdd over 1f out: no ex ins fnl f* **25/1**

440 5 1/2 **Little India (FR)**[2] 9480 3-10-2 **72** ....(p) MrAndrewMcBride(7) 3 67
(K R Burke) *chsd ldr 6f: rdn over 1f out: no ex ins fnl f* **10/1**

2603 6 1/2 **Railport Dolly**[14] 9278 4-10-10 **71** ....(h) MissJoannaMason 2 65
(David Barron) *hld up: pushed along and hdwy over 2f out: rdn over 1f out: no ex ins fnl f* **7/2**[2]

0102 7 1 1/4 **Restive (IRE)**[17] 9221 6-10-10 **71** ....(t) MissSerenaBrotherton 8 62
(Michael Appleby) *hld up: hung lft fr over 2f out: nt trble ldrs* **7/1**[3]

3500 8 1/2 **Zabeel Star (IRE)**[80] 7653 7-10-6 **70** ....(p w) MrAaronAnderson(3) 5 60
(Karen McLintock) *s.s: hld up: nvr nrr (jockey said gelding was slowly away)* **7/1**[3]

5556 9 3 1/4 **Running Cloud (IRE)**[82] 7575 4-10-4 **72** .... MissMeganJordan(7) 7 55
(Mark Loughnane) *s.s: rdn and hung lft ins fnl f: nvr on terms (jockey said gelding was slowly away)* **22/1**

6230 10 3/4 **Lunar Deity**[27] 9050 10-10-2 **70** .... MissJuliaEngstrom(7) 6 52
(Stuart Williams) *hld up: a in rr* **40/1**

5506 11 2 1/4 **French Mix (USA)**[4] 8829 5-10-6 **74** .... MrTambyWelch(7) 1 51
(Alexandra Dunn) *chsd ldrs: rdn over 2f out: wknd over 1f out* **33/1**

0240 12 20 **Sir Hamilton (IRE)**[19] 9176 4-10-7 **73** ....(p) MrGeorgeEddery(5) 10 8
(Alan Bailey) *hld up in tch: lost pl over 3f out: wknd over 2f out: sddle slipped (jockey said saddle slipped)* **12/1**

1m 58.21s (-2.59) **Going Correction** -0.125s/f (Stan)
WFA 3 from 4yo+ 2lb **12 Ran SP% 119.6**
Speed ratings (Par 103): **106,104,101,100,99 99,98,97,94,94 92,74**
CSF £31.24 CT £386.90 TOTE £8.90: £2.80, £1.40, £5.30; EX 42.20 Trifecta £551.10.
Owner Kevin Frost Racing Club & Trisha Keane **Bred** Aislabie Bloodstock Ltd **Trained** Newcastle-under-Lyme, Staffs

FOCUS
A number of previous course winners in this competitive amateur riders' handicap and one of those came out on top. Only three mattered from the home turn. The second has been rated to this year's improved turf form.

9497 BETWAY (S) STKS 2m 120y (Tp)

4:40 (4:40) (Class 6) 3-5-Y-O

£2,781 (£827; £413; £400; £400; £400) **Stalls Low**

Form RPR

0304 1 **Doctor Jazz (IRE)**[6] 9405 4-9-5 55 ....(vt) BenCurtis 3 54+
(Michael Appleby) *s.s: rcvrd to go prom after 1f: chsd ldr over 2f out: led over 1f out: rdn out* **7/2**[2]

3040 2 1/2 **Hidden Depths (IRE)**[9] 9367 4-9-5 61 ....(bt) ShaneKelly 1 52+
(Neil Mulholland) *stdd s: hld up: racd keenly: hdwy over 2f out: chsd wnr over 1f out: sn rdn: styd on* **9/4**[1]

0020 3 nk **Brinkleys Katie**[17] 9216 3-8-8 45 ....(p) FrannyNorton 8 49+
(Paul George) *hld up: plld hrd: hdwy over 1f out: r.o: nt rch ldrs (jockey said filly ran too freely in the early stages and was denied a clear run rounding the fianl bend)* **7/2**[2]

6300 4 4 1/2 **Demophon**[38] 8916 5-9-5 44 ....(t) RaulDaSilva 6 47
(Steve Flook) *pushed along to ld: hdd over 14f out: chsd ldr tl led again over 5f out: rdn over 2f out: hdd over 1f out: no ex ins fnl f* **9/1**

6/65 5 12 **Never A Word (USA)**[48] 8639 5-9-5 56 ....(tp) RobertHavlin 7 32
(Alexandra Dunn) *chsd ldrs: shkn up whn nt clr run and lost pl over 2f out: wknd over 1f out* **13/2**[3]

6060 6 3 3/4 **Panatos (FR)**[11] 9333 4-9-9 58 .... DanielMuscutt 2 32
(Alexandra Dunn) *chsd ldr tl led over 14f out: hdd over 5f out: chsd ldr tl rdn over 2f out: wknd over 1f out* **7/1**

-050 7 9 **Handsome Bob (IRE)**[11] 1235 4-9-5 64 ....(v) JFEgan 5 17
(Neil King) *hld up: pushed along 7f out: rdn on outer over 2f out: wknd over 1f out: eased* **28/1**

3m 42.94s (3.64) **Going Correction** -0.125s/f (Stan)
WFA 3 from 4yo+ 6lb **7 Ran SP% 114.5**
Speed ratings (Par 101): **86,85,85,83,77 76,71**
CSF £11.86 TOTE £4.20: £2.30, £1.50; EX 13.60 Trifecta £38.40.There was no bid for the winner.
Owner The Horse Watchers & Matthew Taylor **Bred** Dr Jim Moore **Trained** Oakham, Rutland

FOCUS
A seller for stayers in which two stood out judged on official ratings, but both had questions to answer. The three market leaders drew clear in the straight. The third and fourth highlight the limitations of the form.

9498 BETWAY H'CAP 6f 20y (Tp)

5:10 (5:12) (Class 5) (0-70,70) 3-Y-O+

£3,428 (£1,020; £509; £400; £400; £400) **Stalls Low**

Form RPR

0665 1 **Real Estate (IRE)**[12] 9306 4-9-2 **65** ....(p) RobertHavlin 6 74
(Michael Attwater) *hld up: swtchd lft and hdwy over 1f out: rdn to ld ins fnl f: r.o* **10/1**[3]

6202 2 1 **Sandridge Lad (IRE)**[4] 9441 3-9-4 **70** .... DarraghKeenan(3) 12 76
(John Ryan) *chsd ldr tl led over 2f out: rdn and hdd ins fnl f: styd on same pce* **7/1**[2]

0123 3 3/4 **True Belief (IRE)**[17] 9218 3-9-3 **66** ....(h) DanielMuscutt 9 70
(Brett Johnson) *s.i.s: hld up: hdwy over 1f out: styd on u.p* **12/1**

5303 4 hd **Kraka (IRE)**[11] 9337 4-9-2 **65** ....(p) KieranO'Neill 13 68
(Christine Dunnett) *prom: racd keenly: rdn and edgd lft ins fnl f: styd on (jockey said gelding hung left-handed in the home straight)* **18/1**

0-26 5 nk **Nampara**[25] 9092 4-9-1 **64** .... JFEgan 8 66
(Paul D'Arcy) *chsd ldrs: swtchd rt over 1f out: sn rdn: styd on* **25/1**

5500 6 1/2 **Tabaahy**[188] 3706 4-9-6 **69** .... DanielTudhope 4 69
(David O'Meara) *hld up: hdwy over 1f out: styd on* **7/1**[2]

4500 7 nk **Hic Bibi**[44] 8755 4-8-13 **62** .... BenCurtis 1 61
(David Loughnane) *chsd ldrs: rdn and hung lft over 1f out: styd on same pce ins fnl f* **16/1**

6005 8 1 **Nezar (IRE)**[107] 6717 8-9-2 **70** .... SophieRalston(5) 3 66
(Dean Ivory) *hld up: racd keenly: nt clr run fr over 2f out tl swtchd rt over 1f out: r.o: nt rch ldrs (jockey said gelding was denied a clear run)* **33/1**

1422 9 1 **Bahuta Acha**[6] 9402 4-9-7 **70** .... PJMcDonald 5 63
(David Loughnane) *s.i.s: hdwy over 4f out: rdn on outer over 2f out: no ex ins fnl f (jockey said gelding was slowly away)* **6/4**[1]

0100 10 1 1/4 **Spirit Power**[70] 7959 4-9-1 **64** .... JasonHart 11 53
(Eric Alston) *led over 3f: edgd rt and wknd ins fnl f* **66/1**

0000 11 nse **The Establishment**[84] 7519 4-9-2 **65** ....(h) EoinWalsh 10 54
(John Butler) *s.s: bhd and pushed along 1/2-way: n.d (jockey said gelding was also never travelling)* **33/1**

602 12 1 **Good Answer**[17] 9218 3-9-2 **65** .... AlistairRawlinson 2 51
(Robert Cowell) *s.i.s: pushed along and hdwy 5f out: rdn over 2f out: wknd fnl f (jockey said gelding was never travelling)* **10/1**[3]

0450 13 2 1/4 **Awsaaf**[9] 9365 4-9-3 **66** ....(h) FrannyNorton 7 44
(Michael Wigham) *sn pushed along in rr: n.d* **20/1**

1m 12.78s (-1.72) **Going Correction** -0.125s/f (Stan) **13 Ran SP% 118.0**
Speed ratings (Par 103): **106,104,103,103,103 102,101,100,99,97 97,96,93**
CSF £73.09 CT £884.63 TOTE £13.00: £2.70, £2.40, £2.70; EX 96.30 Trifecta £1042.50.
Owner Christian Main **Bred** Rabbah Bloodstock Limited **Trained** Epsom, Surrey

FOCUS
A maximum field contested this modest sprint handicap, but only three seemed to matter in the betting. However, the next in the betting came off best. The second and third have been rated to their recent level.

9499 LADBROKES WHERE THE NATION PLAYS NURSERY H'CAP 5f 21y (Tp)

5:40 (5:40) (Class 5) (0-75,77) 2-Y-O

£3,428 (£1,020; £509; £400; £400; £400) **Stalls Low**

Form RPR

0030 1 **Heer We Go Again**[6] 9401 2-9-6 **71** ....(v) JoeyHaynes 1 76
(David Evans) *mde all: rdn out* **7/1**

5065 2 2 1/4 **Wilfy**[12] 9300 2-9-3 **68** .... LiamKeniry 6 68+
(Sylvester Kirk) *prom: hmpd and lost pl sn after s: hdwy 1/2-way: rdn over 1f out: r.o to go 2nd post* **5/1**[3]

6232 3 nse **Astrozone**[41] 8841 2-9-2 **67** .... GrahamLee 5 64
(Bryan Smart) *chsd ldrs: rdn over 1f out: edgd lft ins fnl f: styd on* **15/2**

6020 4 1/2 **Zulu Zander (IRE)**[20] 9162 2-9-12 **77** .... BenCurtis 4 72
(David Evans) *s.i.s: nt clr run and swtchd rt over 1f out: r.o: nt rch ldrs* **4/1**[2]

4203 5 nk **Baileys In Bloom (FR)**[28] 9031 2-9-4 **72** .... SeanDavis(3) 9 66
(Richard Fahey) *prom: lost pl 4f out: hdwy over 1f out: styd on* **12/1**

The Form Book Flat 2019, Raceform Ltd, Newbury, RG14 5SJ

0000 6 *hd* **Newsical**[7] 9394 2-8-3 54 KieranO'Neill 2 47
(Mark Walford) *pushed along to chse ldrs: rdn over 1f out: no ex ins fnl f* 25/1

5321 7 *1* **Augustus Caesar (USA)**[83] 7556 2-9-12 77 DanielTudhope 3 67
(David O'Meara) *chsd wnr: rdn over 1f out: lost 2nd ins fnl f: wknd towards fin* 2/1[1]

4206 8 *4 1/2* **Feelinlikeasomeone**[17] 9228 2-8-10 68 (b[1]) VanessaMaye(7) 8 41
(Jack W Davison, Ire) *s.i.s and edgd rt s: outpcd* 33/1

3004 9 *8* **Silver Start**[18] 9205 2-9-7 72 KieranShoemark 7 17
(Charles Hills) *chsd ldrs over 3f* 18/1

1m 0.79s (-1.11) **Going Correction** -0.125s/f (Stan) 9 Ran SP% 114.0
Speed ratings (Par 96): **103,99,99,98,98 97,96,88,76**
CSF £41.30 CT £272.05 TOTE £8.90: £3.30, £1.90, £1.60; EX 47.30 Trifecta £302.40.
Owner Power Geneva Ltd & Partner **Bred** Dalwhinnie Bloodstock **Trained** Pandy, Monmouths
■ Stewards' Enquiry : Sean Davis two-day ban: careless riding (Dec 30-31)

FOCUS
A fair nursery handicap over the minimum trip and, as in the previous years, a low draw proved important, with the winner making all from the inside stall.

9500 LADBROKES HOME OF THE ODDS BOOST EBF NOVICE MEDIAN AUCTION STKS (PLUS 10 RACE) 1m 1f 104y (Tp)
6:10 (6:11) (Class 4) 2-Y-O £4,851 (£1,443; £721; £360) Stalls Low

Form RPR

4 1 **Punting (IRE)**[17] 9211 2-8-11 0 ShaneKelly 11 69+
(Richard Hughes) *chsd ldr after 1f: led 2f out: shkn up over 1f out: edgd lft ins fnl f: r.o: comf* 12/1

00 2 *1 1/4* **Royal Astronomer**[11] 9325 2-9-2 0 PJMcDonald 3 67
(Hughie Morrison) *hld up: plld hrd: hdwy over 2f out: hung lft fr over 1f out: chsd wnr ins fnl f: r.o* 16/1

3 *3/4* **Captain St Lucifer** 2-9-2 0 TomEaves 6 65
(Ivan Furtado) *s.i.s: hld up: hdwy over 1f out: hung lft ins fnl f: nt rch ldrs* 80/1

0 4 *1 3/4* **Cinnabar**[26] 9063 2-8-11 0 (h[1]) JasonWatson 2 57
(Roger Charlton) *hld up in tch: rdn over 2f out: styd on same pce fr over 1f out* 40/1

5 5 *3/4* **Uncle Swayze**[46] 8700 2-9-2 0 RobHornby 4 60
(Ralph Beckett) *led over 7f: no ex ins fnl f* 11/8[1]

15 6 *1* **Come On My Son**[28] 9029 2-9-9 0 DanielTudhope 12 65
(Mark Loughnane) *hld up: reminder over 2f out: styd on ins fnl f: nvr on terms* 8/1[3]

010 7 *1/2* **Spantik**[21] 9154 2-9-9 78 BenCurtis 1 64
(Roger Fell) *chsd ldrs: rdn over 1f out: wknd ins fnl f* 14/1

8 *3/4* **Soldier On Parade** 2-9-2 0 DanielMuscutt 5 56
(Amy Murphy) *s.i.s: hdwy over 7f out: rdn over 2f out: wknd fnl f* 20/1

6 9 *1 1/4* **Manap**[177] 4114 2-9-2 0 AdamMcNamara 8 53
(Archie Watson) *pushed along to chse ldrs: lost pl over 6f out: rdn over 3f out: wkng whn hung lft fnl f* 11/2[2]

0 10 *1 1/4* **Springvale Lad**[52] 8516 2-8-11 0 KevinLundie(5) 10 51
(Mark Loughnane) *pushed along early in rr: nvr on terms* 18/1

0 11 *nse* **Vertice (IRE)**[26] 9063 2-8-4 0 StefanoCherchi(7) 9 46
(Marco Botti) *chsd ldrs: rdn over 3f out: wknd over 1f out (jockey said filly ran green)* 28/1

6 12 *23* **Zero Limits**[40] 8857 2-8-9 0 GraceMcEntee(7) 7 6
(Marco Botti) *s.i.s: outpcd* 11/1

2m 0.39s (-0.41) **Going Correction** -0.125s/f (Stan) 12 Ran SP% 114.3
Speed ratings (Par 98): **96,94,94,92,92 91,90,90,88,87 87,67**
CSF £175.04 TOTE £10.20: £2.40, £4.90, £15.80; EX 156.90 Trifecta £3972.40.
Owner M H Dixon **Bred** M H Dixon **Trained** Upper Lambourn, Berks

FOCUS
Several major yards represented in this juvenile auction maiden, but the winner was a big drifter beforehand. It's been rated cautiously.

9501 LADBROKES "PLAY 1-2-FREE" ON FOOTBALL CLAIMING STKS 1m 142y (Tp)
6:40 (6:41) (Class 5) 2-Y-O £3,428 (£1,020; £509; £400; £400; £400) Stalls Low

Form RPR

5100 1 **Isobar Wind (IRE)**[23] 9127 2-8-13 64 (v) PJMcDonald 6 65
(David Evans) *trckd ldrs: shkn up to ld and edgd lft ins fnl f: pushed out* 5/1

5434 2 *1* **Divine Connection**[27] 9045 2-8-10 62 JosephineGordon 4 60
(Jonathan Portman) *a.p: chsd ldr over 6f out: rdn to ld ins fnl f: sn edgd lft and hdd: styd on same pce towards fin* 5/2[1]

006 3 *1 1/2* **Nikolayeva**[16] 9242 2-8-2 0 (p[1]) JaneElliott 2 49+
(Sir Mark Prescott Bt) *trckd ldrs: racd keenly: outpcd 3f out: rallied and swtchd lft ins fnl f: styd on* 11/4[2]

05 4 *1/2* **Dancing Girl (FR)**[16] 9243 2-8-8 0 GeorgeWood 3 54
(Harry Dunlop) *chsd ldrs: rdn over 2f out: styng on same pce whn nt clr run wl ins fnl f* 20/1

0106 5 *1 1/4* **Schumli**[10] 9346 2-8-2 51 (t) CamHardie 8 45
(David O'Meara) *led: rdn over 1f out: hdd and no ex ins fnl f* 14/1

003 6 *1 1/2* **Xquisite (IRE)**[23] 9127 2-7-11 0 LauraCoughlan(7) 7 44
(J S Moore) *s.i.s: hld up: rdn over 2f out: styd on ins fnl f: nt trble ldrs* 28/1

0 7 *1 3/4* **Depardieu**[17] 9231 2-8-9 0 BenCurtis 1 45
(M C Grassick, Ire) *s.i.s: hld up: shkn up over 2f out: nvr on terms* 3/1[3]

0 8 *11* **Adrued (IRE)**[17] 9211 2-7-7 0 IsobelFrancis(7) 5 13
(Mark Usher) *s.i.s: a in rr: rdn over 3f out: sn wknd* 125/1

1m 51.63s (1.53) **Going Correction** -0.125s/f (Stan) 8 Ran SP% 112.6
Speed ratings (Par 96): **88,87,85,85,84 82,81,71**
CSF £17.29 TOTE £5.60: £1.70, £1.30, £1.30; EX 18.00 Trifecta £69.70.Dancing Girl was claimed by Mr T J Fitzgerald for £8,000. Nikolayeva was claimed by Mr James Couldwell for £5,000
Owner E R Griffiths **Bred** Eric Griffiths **Trained** Pandy, Monmouths

FOCUS
The first of three races over the mile was a moderate juvenile claimer and the finish was dominated by those with most experience. Straightforward form.

9502 BOMBARDIER BRITISH HOPPED AMBER BEER NOVICE STKS 1m 142y (Tp)
7:10 (7:11) (Class 5) 3-Y-O+ £3,428 (£1,020; £509; £254) Stalls Low

Form RPR

4-1 1 **The Met**[54] 8472 3-9-7 0 PJMcDonald 1 85
(David Loughnane) *chsd ldr tl led over 2f out: shkn up over 1f out: rdn ins fnl f: styd on gamely* 7/2[2]

1 2 *nk* **Godhead**[17] 9213 3-9-9 0 RobertHavlin 4 86
(John Gosden) *trckd keenly: chsd wnr over 1f out: rdn and ev ch whn hit over hd by rivals whip ins fnl f: styd on* 4/7[1]

3 3 *2 3/4* **Pledge Of Honour**[17] 9213 3-9-2 0 JoeyHaynes 6 73
(Dean Ivory) *s.s: hdwy on outer over 4f out: rdn and edgd lft over 1f out: styd on same pce ins fnl f (jockey said gelding was slowly away)* 15/2

-360 4 *22* **Royal Star**[12] 9303 3-8-11 74 JasonWatson 3 17
(Roger Charlton) *led: rdn: hung rt and hdd over 2f out: wknd over 1f out (jockey said filly hung badly right-handed throughout)* 7/1[3]

0 5 *1/2* **Lethal Look**[107] 6732 3-9-2 0 (t[1] w) RobHornby 2 21
(Sarah Hollinshead) *broke wl: sn stdd and lost pl: hld up: wknd over 2f out* 200/1

1m 47.99s (-2.11) **Going Correction** -0.125s/f (Stan) 5 Ran SP% 110.6
Speed ratings (Par 103): **104,103,101,81,81**
CSF £6.00 TOTE £3.60: £1.70, £1.10; EX 7.80 Trifecta £14.80.
Owner K Sohi **Bred** Chippenham Lodge Stud **Trained** Tern Hill, Shropshire

FOCUS
An interesting 3yo novice featuring two previous winners and they fought out a close finish. The second has been rated as progressing from his Kempton win.

9503 BOMBARDIER GOLDEN BEER H'CAP 1m 142y (Tp)
7:40 (7:42) (Class 6) (0-60,65) 3-Y-O+ £2,781 (£827; £413; £400; £400; £400) Stalls Low

Form RPR

5501 1 **Steal The Scene (IRE)**[28] 9039 7-9-5 58 (tp) TomQueally 6 69
(Kevin Frost) *trckd ldrs: led over 1f out: sn rdn and edgd lft: styd on wl* 12/1[2]

0303 2 *2 1/4* **Freedom And Wheat (IRE)**[41] 8839 3-9-2 57 JaneElliott 4 63
(Michael Blake) *hld up: hdwy over 2f out: rdn to chse wnr and hung lft fnl f: styd on same pce* 8/1[1]

166 3 *3 1/4* **Lappet (IRE)**[47] 8674 4-9-4 57 KieranO'Neill 9 56
(Gavin Cromwell, Ire) *led after 1f: hdd 7f out: chsd ldr tl led again over 2f out: hdd over 1f out: no ex ins fnl f* 12/1[2]

4550 4 *1/2* **Your Mothers' Eyes**[81] 7603 3-9-4 59 (p) JoeyHaynes 10 57
(Alan Bailey) *hld up: rdn over 1f out: r.o ins fnl f: nvr nrr (jockey said colt hung right-handed on the bend)* 25/1

5000 5 *1/2* **Burguillos**[12] 9310 6-9-0 56 (e[1]) DarraghKeenan(3) 7 53
(John Butler) *broke wl: sn stdd and lost pl: hld up: styd on fr over 1f out: nt trble ldrs* 25/1

0300 6 *1/2* **Medici Moon**[28] 9040 5-9-2 55 (t[1]) RobHornby 1 51
(Richard Price) *hld up: hdwy 2f out: nt clr run and swtchd rt over 1f out: sn rdn: styd on same pce* 33/1

6000 7 *1 1/2* **Lagenda**[9] 9361 6-9-6 59 JasonHart 2 52
(Liam Bailey) *led 1f: chsd ldrs: rdn over 1f out: wknd ins fnl f* 12/1[2]

0620 8 *1/2* **Odds On Oli**[17] 9225 4-8-10 52 ConnorMurtagh(3) 8 44
(Richard Fahey) *s.i.s: in rr: rdn and swtchd lft over 1f out: n.d* 20/1[3]

0000 9 *shd* **Arlecchino's Leap**[58] 8345 7-8-10 56 IsobelFrancis(7) 3 48
(Mark Usher) *pushed along to chse ldrs: led 7f out: shkn up and hdd over 2f out: wknd ins fnl f (jockey said gelding hung right-handed throughout)* 25/1

2365 10 *3/4* **A Place To Dream**[16] 9244 3-9-5 60 JosephineGordon 11 50
(Mike Murphy) *hld up in tch: rdn over 3f out: wknd over 1f out* 8/1[1]

3000 11 *11* **Eesha's Smile (IRE)**[12] 9306 3-9-5 60 (p) PJMcDonald 13 27
(Ivan Furtado) *chsd ldrs: rdn over 2f out: wknd over 1f out* 22/1

1m 47.8s (-2.30) **Going Correction** -0.125s/f (Stan)
WFA 3 from 4yo+ 2lb 11 Ran SP% 68.9
Speed ratings (Par 101): **105,103,100,99,99 98,97,97,96,96 86**
CSF £25.84 CT £159.39 TOTE £6.00: £2.10, £1.90, £2.40; EX 38.40 Trifecta £169.00.
Owner Curzon House Partnership & Friends **Bred** Shane Doyle **Trained** Newcastle-under-Lyme, Staffs
■ Calin's Lad was withdrawn. Price at time of withdrawal 5/6F. Rule 4 applies to all bets - deduction 50p in the pound.

FOCUS
This moderate handicap was a one-horse race according to the betting, but the favourite Calin's Lad reared up in the stalls and was withdrawn, which left an open contest and a big deduction from all bets. The winner has been rated back towards this year's best, with the second in line with his recent form.
T/Jkpt: Not Won. T/Plt: £254.40 to a £1 stake. Pool: £100,906.52 - 289.48 winning units T/Qpdt: £50.60 to a £1 stake. Pool: £14,786.28 - 215.90 winning units **Colin Roberts**

9482 DEAUVILLE (R-H)
Monday, December 16

OFFICIAL GOING: Polytrack: standard

9504a PRIX DU MESNIL-DURAND (CLAIMER) (3YO) (ALL-WEATHER TRACK) (POLYTRACK) 7f 110y(P)
11:10 3-Y-O £9,009 (£3,603; £2,702; £1,801; £900)

RPR

1 **Bob The King**[14] 3-9-2 0 (b) RosarioMangione 9 73
(F Rossi, France) 66/10

2 *3/4* **Mister Vancouver (FR)**[27] 3-9-5 0 (b) QuentinGervais 6 74
(Y Barberot, France) 13/5[1]

3 *1/2* **Okarina Dream (FR)**[20] 9170 3-9-5 0 BertrandFlandrin 3 73
(H De Nicolay, France) 22/5[3]

4 *1/2* **Nickos (GER)**[423] 8402 3-8-11 0 (p) AntoineCoutier 2 64
(S Smrczek, Germany) 20/1

5 *snk* **Glenorchy (IRE)**[95] 3-9-2 0 (b) FrankPanicucci 1 68
(Mme Pia Brandt, France) 17/5[2]

6 *3/4* **Drosay (FR)**[27] 9058 3-9-1 0 EmmanuelEtienne 13 65
(Georgios Alimpinisis, France) 62/1

7 *shd* **Dancing Mountain (IRE)**[14] 9280 3-8-8 0 (b) BenjaminHubert 7 58
(P Monfort, France) 12/1

8 *shd* **Mantega (FR)**[14] 9280 3-8-8 0 LukaRousseau 4 58
(H-A Pantall, France) 18/1

9 *1/2* **Dream Life (FR)**[14] 3-9-1 0 AxelBaron 8 64
(J-P Dubois, France) 10/1

10 *snk* **Stade Velodrome (FR)**[14] 3-8-11 0 MlleLauraGrosso(4) 5 63
(J Bourgeais, France) 24/1

11 *3/4* **Melissa (FR)**[27] 9058 3-8-8 AdrienMoreau 12 54
(Ivan Furtado) *led: asked to qckn over 2 1/2f out: chal 2f out: hdd ent fnl f: wknd u.p clsng stages* 62/1

12 ½ **On The Edge (FR)**[19] 3-8-5 0 .... MlleLucieOger(3) 11 53
(Mme A Rosa, France) **29/1**
13 7 **Tagda**[14] 9280 3-8-8 0 .... BenjaminMarie 10 36
(Mlle M Henry, France) **92/1**
1m 28.58s **13** Ran SP% **120.6**
PARI-MUTUEL (all including 1 euro stake): WIN 7.60; PLACE 2.00, 1.50, 1.90; DF 10.40.
Owner Abdelhafidh Dridi **Bred** Mme Mt Mimouni **Trained** France

9421 LINGFIELD (L-H)
Wednesday, December 18

OFFICIAL GOING: Polytrack: standard
Wind: LIGHT, ACROSS Weather: FINE

9505 BOMBARDIER "MARCH TO YOUR OWN DRUM" H'CAP 7f 1y(P)
12:10 (12:11) (Class 6) (0-55,60) 3-Y-O+
£2,781 (£827; £413; £300; £300; £300) Stalls Low

Form RPR

0000 1 **Axel Jacklin**[109] 6731 3-9-5 **53** .... (b) JoeyHaynes 3 61
(Chelsea Banham) *chsd ldr: shkn up 2f out: rdn to ld and edgd lft over 1f out: all out cl home: a jst holding on (regarding the improvement in form, trainer said gelding had benefitted from the reapplication of blinkers and a return to Lingfield where he had run well previously)* **10/1**

006 2 *nk* **Elusif (IRE)**[7] 9410 4-9-2 **50** .... (v) JosephineGordon 9 57
(Shaun Keightley) *off the pce in midfield: effrt ent fnl 2f: hdwy u.p 1f out: chsd ldrs 100yds out: wnt 2nd towards fin and gaining cl home: nvr quite getting to wnr* **10/1**

3421 3 ½ **Prince Rock (IRE)**[18] 9249 4-9-4 **52** .... LukeMorris 2 58
(Simon Dow) *chsd ldng pair: clsd and effrt 2f out: drvn and chsd wnr jst ins fnl f: kpt on and grad clsd but nvr quite getting to wnr: lost 2nd towards fin* **4/1**[1]

1350 4 2 **Vincenzo Coccotti (USA)**[20] 9209 7-9-4 **55** .... (p) FinleyMarsh(3) 6 56
(Patrick Chamings) *off the pce in midfield: effrt: hdwy and swtchd rt over 1f out: hdwy to chse ldrs 100yds out: kpt on: nvr getting to ldrs* **7/1**

0554 5 1 ¼ **Duke Of North (IRE)**[9] 9384 7-9-0 **48** .... (b) CharlieBennett 14 46
(Jim Boyle) *s.i.s: wl off the pce in midfield: rdn and hdwy ent fnl f: styd on wl fnl 100yds: nvr trbld ldrs* **16/1**

0000 6 ¾ **Juan Horsepower**[9] 9384 5-8-12 **46** .... (p) DannyBrock 8 42
(Denis Quinn) *chsd ldng trio: rdn over 2f out: unable qck over 1f out: flashed tail u.p and wknd ins fnl f* **50/1**

0420 7 1 ½ **Maazel (IRE)**[14] 9298 5-9-7 **55** .... DanielMuscutt 1 47
(Lee Carter) *off the pce in midfield: effrt over 1f out: kpt on same pce ins fnl f: nvr trbld ldrs* **6/1**[3]

2502 8 1 ¾ **Brigand**[18] 9248 4-9-7 **55** .... AdamKirby 12 42
(John Butler) *stdd s: off the pce in midfield: effrt over 1f out: rdn and kpt on same pce ins fnl f* **9/2**[2]

0600 9 *nk* **Grandee Daisy**[112] 6598 3-8-12 **53** .... GeorgeRooke(7) 13 39
(Michael Appleby) *stdd s and dropped in bhd: wl off the pce in rr: effrt on inner over 1f out: styd on ins fnl f: nvr trbld ldrs* **20/1**

5003 10 *nk* **Your Choice**[18] 9249 4-9-4 **52** .... (b) GeorgeDowning 7 38
(Laura Mongan) *led and set str gallop: rdn: hdd and bmpd over 1f out: lost 2nd and wknd jst ins fnl f* **25/1**

0060 11 4 **Soaring Spirits (IRE)**[9] 9384 9-8-8 **49** .... (p) LukeBacon(7) 5 24
(Dean Ivory) *s.i.s: wl off the pce in last trio: nvr involved* **33/1**

0061 12 ¾ **Kodiline (IRE)**[7] 9423 5-9-12 **60** 5ex .... TomQueally 4 33
(David Evans) *stdd after s: a wl off the pce in last trio: no ch whn rn v wd bnd 2f out* **9/2**[2]

1m 23.77s (-1.03) **Going Correction** -0.10s/f (Stan) **12** Ran SP% **120.7**
Speed ratings (Par 101): **101,100,100,97,96 95,93,91,91,91 86,85**
CSF £103.55 CT £479.07 TOTE £15.10: £4.10, £2.70, £1.80; EX 181.70 Trifecta £720.70.
Owner A Searle **Bred** Godolphin **Trained** Cowlinge, Suffolk
■ Stewards' Enquiry : Danny Brock four-day ban: used whip with arm above shoulder height (Jan 1st-4th)

FOCUS
A run-of-the-mill 7f handicap which saw a late gamble landed. They appeared to go quick enough early. The third has been rated in line with his recent win here.

9506 LADBROKES WHERE THE NATION PLAYS EBF FILLIES' NOVICE STKS (PLUS 10 RACE) 7f 1y(P)
12:40 (12:44) (Class 5) 2-Y-O £3,428 (£1,020; £509; £254) Stalls Low

Form RPR

4 1 **Disco Fever**[13] 9324 2-9-0 0 .... RobertHavlin 6 85+
(John Gosden) *chsd ldr tl led after 1f: shkn up and qcknd ent fnl 2f: reminder and clr 1f out: r.o v strly: v readily* **6/4**[1]

0 2 5 **Zenaida (IRE)**[56] 8454 2-9-0 0 .... KieranShoemark 9 72
(Ed Dunlop) *chsd wnr after 2f: rdn and qckning w wnr ent fnl 2f: unable to match wnr over 1f out: kpt on same pce ins fnl f* **20/1**

36 3 2 ¾ **Must Be An Angel (IRE)**[23] 9159 2-9-0 0 .... JamesDoyle 11 68+
(Sylvester Kirk) *hld up in midfield: effrt and swtchd rt bnd 2f out: rdn and hdwy whn lugged lft 1f out: chsd ldng pair wl ins fnl f: kpt on wl but no ch w wnr* **2/1**[2]

4 1 ½ **Rudaina** 2-9-0 0 .... JasonWatson 7 61+
(Amy Murphy) *trckd ldrs: rdn and unable qck ent fnl 2f: chsd ldng pair and no imp ins fnl f: lost 3rd wl ins fnl f* **16/1**

4 5 2 **Perfect Outing**[134] 5775 2-9-0 0 .... HectorCrouch 3 56+
(Clive Cox) *hld up in tch in midfield: effrt jst over 2f out: sn outpcd: no ch w wnr and kpt on same pce ins fnl f* **8/1**[3]

05 6 *shd* **Marble Bay (IRE)**[19] 9211 2-9-0 0 .... TomQueally 4 55
(David Evans) *led for 1f: styd chsng ldrs tl rdn and outpcd 2f out: lost 3rd and wknd ins fnl f* **33/1**

03 7 *shd* **Ever Amber (IRE)**[18] 9243 2-9-0 0 .... RobHornby 2 55
(Jonathan Portman) *hld up in midfield: effrt jst over 2f out: sn outpcd: no ch w wnr and kpt on same pce ins fnl f* **16/1**

5 8 1 **Criseyde**[13] 9322 2-9-0 0 .... LiamKeniry 8 53
(Sylvester Kirk) *stdd after s: hld up in midfield: effrt on inner over 1f out: kpt on same pce and no ch w wnr whn nt clrest of runs ins fnl f (jockey said filly was denied a clear run)* **66/1**

0 9 1 ¾ **Wonderful Effort (IRE)**[137] 5646 2-9-0 0 .... LukeMorris 13 48
(Ed Vaughan) *s.i.s: hld up towards rr: effrt 2f out: n.d* **25/1**

0 10 2 ½ **Talking About You**[20] 9197 2-9-0 0 .... CharlesBishop 5 42
(Mick Channon) *s.i.s and rousted along early: towards rr: rdn over 1f out: n.d* **66/1**

3 11 1 ½ **Broughton Sunpearl**[28] 9062 2-9-0 0 .... JoeyHaynes 10 38
(Tom Clover) *t.k.h: hld up in midfield: impeded and carried wd bnd 2f out: n.d after (jockey said filly ran too free)* **8/1**[3]

12 1 ¾ **Mistry Girl** 2-8-9 0 .... TobyEley(5) 14 33+
(John Holt) *v.s.a: clsd on to rr of field 4f out: rdn jst over 2f out: sn outpcd and btn (jockey said filly was slowly away)* **66/1**

0 13 1 **Brazen Sheila**[40] 8913 2-8-11 0 .... DarraghKeenan(3) 12 31
(Anthony Carson) *styd wd: in tch in midfield: rdn and hung rt bnd 2f out: lost pl and bhd after (jockey said filly hung right-handed on the bend)* **100/1**

0 14 1 ¼ **Golden Slumbers**[190] 3689 2-9-0 0 .... EoinWalsh 1 27
(Bill Turner) *broke wl: t.k.h: grad settled bk and towards rr 1/2-way: rdn ent fnl 2f: sn wl btn (jockey said filly ran too free)* **100/1**

1m 24.51s (-0.29) **Going Correction** -0.10s/f (Stan) **14** Ran SP% **125.3**
Speed ratings (Par 93): **97,91,88,86,84 84,83,82,80,77 76,74,73,71**
CSF £41.56 TOTE £2.10: £1.20, £5.40, £1.10; EX 32.30 Trifecta £112.80.
Owner Lady Bamford **Bred** Litex Commerce **Trained** Newmarket, Suffolk

FOCUS
A straightforward task for the favourite in the fillies' novice event.

9507 BETWAY HEED YOUR HUNCH H'CAP 6f 1y(P)
1:10 (1:12) (Class 6) (0-60,60) 3-Y-O+
£2,781 (£827; £413; £300; £300; £300) Stalls Low

Form RPR

0401 1 **Knockout Blow**[18] 9247 4-9-4 **57** .... (p) HectorCrouch 12 64
(John E Long) *hld up in tch towards rr: effrt jst over 1f out: rdn and hdwy over 1f out: clsd u.p to ld wl ins fnl f: styd on* **6/1**[2]

505 2 ¾ **Bernie's Boy**[41] 8896 6-8-10 **56** .... (tp) GraceMcEntee(7) 10 61
(Phil McEntee) *hld up in midfield: clsd to press ldrs 2f out: rdn and ev ch over 1f out: led jst ins fnl f: hdd and one pce wl ins fnl f* **10/1**

520- 3 *nk* **Little Miss Lilly**[352] 9776 4-9-4 **57** .... (v) AdamKirby 9 61
(Clive Cox) *wl in tch in midfield: effrt and rdn to chse ldrs ent fnl f: pressed ldrs ins fnl f: unable qck towards fin* **16/1**

0602 4 1 **Dreamboat Annie**[7] 9423 4-8-0 **46** oh1 .... IsobelFrancis(7) 11 47
(Mark Usher) *midfield on outer: effrt and wd bnd 2f out: hdwy ins fnl f: kpt on wl fnl 100yds: nt rch ldrs (jockey said filly hung left-handed throughout)* **16/1**

500 5 *nk* **Black Isle Boy (IRE)**[13] 9337 5-9-7 **60** .... DavidProbert 8 60
(David C Griffiths) *stdd s and sn swtchd lft: t.k.h: hld up in tch in last trio: effrt and hung lft over 1f out: swtchd rt and styd on ins fnl f: nt rch ldrs* **8/1**

062 6 *nk* **Catheadans Fury**[41] 8896 5-9-7 **60** .... (t) GeorgeWood 7 60
(Martin Bosley) *t.k.h: hld up in tch in last trio: nt clrest of runs ent fnl 2f: hdwy over 1f out: swtchd rt and kpt on ins fnl f: n.m.r towards fin* **7/1**[3]

3050 7 *nk* **Perfect Symphony (IRE)**[7] 9420 5-9-5 **58** .... (p) LukeMorris 6 59
(Mark Pattinson) *wnt rt leaving stalls: chsd ldrs: edgd out rt and clsd over 2f out: rdn to ld over 1f out: hdd jst ins fnl f: no ex and outpcd whn short of room and snatched up wl ins fnl f* **9/1**

4001 8 1 ¼ **Mercers**[56] 8457 5-8-9 **55** .... (b) GeorgeRooke(7) 4 53
(Paddy Butler) *in tch in midfield: effrt over 1f out: edging lft and sme hdwy ins fnl f: keeping on same pce and hld whn short of room and snatched up wl ins fnl f* **20/1**

2002 9 1 ¾ **Porto Ferro (IRE)**[18] 9247 5-9-1 **54** .... (t) KieranO'Neill 1 43
(John Bridger) *led: rdn and hdd over 1f out: losing pl whn short of room and snatched up ins fnl f: eased after* **9/1**

3000 10 ½ **Celerity (IRE)**[9] 9390 5-8-0 **46** oh1 .... (p) GavinAshton(7) 5 34
(Lisa Williamson) *chsd ldr tl ent fnl 2f: lost pl and wknd ins fnl f* **50/1**

2220 11 ½ **Broughton Excels**[12] 9352 4-9-6 **59** .... RobHornby 2 45
(Stuart Williams) *chsd ldrs: rdn 2f out: unable qck over 1f out: wknd ins fnl f* **2/1**[1]

1m 11.48s (-0.42) **Going Correction** -0.10s/f (Stan) **11** Ran SP% **118.8**
Speed ratings (Par 101): **98,97,96,95,94 94,94,92,90,89 88**
CSF £65.45 CT £660.67 TOTE £7.10: £2.30, £3.20, £4.40; EX 87.70 Trifecta £2020.10.
Owner Mrs S Colville **Bred** Christopher & Annabelle Mason **Trained** Brighton, East Sussex
■ Stewards' Enquiry : George Rooke three-day ban: careless riding (Jan 1-3)

FOCUS
A low grade handicap. They came late and fast down the straight. The winner has been rated pretty much to his best.

9508 BETWAY CLASSIFIED STKS 6f 1y(P)
1:45 (1:46) (Class 6) 3-Y-O+
£2,781 (£827; £413; £300; £300; £300) Stalls Low

Form RPR

4341 1 **Griggy (IRE)**[5] 9457 3-9-6 50 .... (b) AdamKirby 10 58+
(Sean Curran) *hld up in midfield: swtchd rt and effrt over 1f out: hdwy u.p ins fnl f: str run to ld towards fin* **4/5**[1]

050 2 1 **Illustrious Spirit**[6] 9445 4-9-0 44 .... (t[1]) JasonWatson 4 49
(Ali Stronge) *mounted in chute: chsd ldr tl led 4f out: rdn over 1f out: 2 l clr and drvn 1f out: hdd and no ex towards fin* **14/1**

0400 3 ¾ **Miaella**[14] 9298 4-9-0 50 .... (p) JoeyHaynes 8 47
(Chelsea Banham) *taken down early: chsd ldrs: effrt 2f out: hdwy u.p ins fnl f: chsd ldrs and kpt on same pce wl ins fnl f* **8/1**[3]

5152 4 1 ½ **Sarsaparilla Kit**[7] 9411 3-8-9 50 .... MarkCrehan(5) 5 42
(Stuart Williams) *sn led: hdd 4f out: chsd ldr after: unable qck u.p over 1f out: lost 2nd and kpt on same pce ins fnl f* **8/1**[3]

002 5 ½ **Sagittarian Wind**[6] 9445 3-9-0 50 .... (bt[1]) LukeMorris 6 43
(Archie Watson) *chsd ldrs: nt clrest of runs over 1f out: drvn and kpt on ins fnl f* **7/1**[2]

0460 6 *nk* **Alba Del Sole (IRE)**[5] 9457 4-9-0 47 .... (p) RobertHavlin 9 40
(Charlie Wallis) *s.i.s: t.k.h: hld up in rr: swtchd rt and hdwy over 1f out: kpt on same pce ins fnl f (jockey said filly was slowly away and denied a clear run)* **16/1**

-060 7 *hd* **Jonnysimpson (IRE)**[154] 5046 4-9-0 48 .... CallumShepherd 3 39
(Lee Carter) *hld up in midfield: effrt over 1f out: kpt on same pce ins fnl f* **33/1**

0000 8 ½ **Invisible Storm**[7] 9411 4-9-0 47 .... HectorCrouch 12 38
(William Stone) *chsd ldrs on outer: rdn 2f out: unable qck ent fnl f: wknd ins fnl f* **16/1**

2505 9 *nse* **Starchant**[78] 7784 3-9-0 46 .... (p) KieranO'Neill 2 38
(John Bridger) *t.k.h: hld up in tch in last trio: effrt and switching rt over 1f out: kpt on ins fnl f: nvr involved* **20/1**

0000 10 1 ½ **Peters Pudding (IRE)**[4] 9473 3-8-7 50 .... (v) GavinAshton(7) 1 33
(Lisa Williamson) *broke wl chsd ldrs: unable qck over 1f out: wknd ins fnl f* **25/1**

5000 **11** ½ **Tavener**[48] 8689 7-9-0 47...(tp) DavidProbert 11 32
(David C Griffiths) *s.i.s: t.k.h: hld up in last trio: swtchd rt and effrt over 1f out: no imp (jockey said gelding was slowly away; vet said gelding lost left-fore shoe)* **16/1**

1m 11.8s (-0.10) **Going Correction** -0.10s/f (Stan) 11 Ran SP% **126.1**
Speed ratings (Par 101): **96,94,93,91,91 90,90,89,89,87 86**
CSF £15.63 TOTE £1.70: £1.10, £3.60, £2.70; EX 17.20 Trifecta £111.90.
Owner Power Geneva Ltd **Bred** Holburn Trust Co **Trained** Upper Lambourn, Berks

FOCUS
Poor fare but an in-form horse came to the front.

9509 LADBROKES HOME OF THE ODDS BOOST EBF NOVICE STKS 1m 1y(P)
2:15 (2:18) (Class 5) 2-Y-O £3,428 (£1,020; £509; £254) **Stalls High**

Form RPR
3 **1** **Shimmering (IRE)**[51] 8602 2-9-0 0... RobertHavlin 10 70
(John Gosden) *sn led and edgd across to inner: pushed along and qcknd ent fnl 2f: in command and styd on wl ins fnl f: comf* **7/4**[1]

5 **2** 1¼ **Orczy (IRE)**[13] 9325 2-9-5 0... JasonWatson 3 72
(Richard Hannon) *chsd wnr for over 1f out: chsd ldrs: effrt to chse wnr again ent fnl f: kpt on but a hld* **6/1**[3]

26 **3** ½ **King Of Arms**[25] 9136 2-9-5 0... KieranO'Neill 9 71
(John Gosden) *hld up in midfield: effrt: hdwy and hanging lft over 1f out: kpt on wl ins fnl f: wnt 3rd fnl 50yds: nvr getting to wnr* **7/2**[2]

4 1 **Longsider (IRE)** 2-9-5 0... ShaneKelly 1 69
(David Lanigan) *in tch in midfield: effrt wl over 1f out: 3rd and unable qck over 1f out: kpt on same pce ins fnl f* **33/1**

5 hd **Sheila (IRE)** 2-9-0 0... JamesDoyle 12 65+
(Hugo Palmer) *hld up in rr: effrt over 1f out: rdn and styd on wl ins fnl f: no threat to wnr* **16/1**

03 **6** 1¾ **Swooping Eagle (IRE)**[13] 9325 2-9-5 0... DanielMuscutt 6 64
(Roger Varian) *broke wl: sn hdd: chsd ldrs: unable qck over 1f out: wknd ins fnl f* **8/1**

05 **7** nk **Glorious Caesar**[20] 9208 2-9-5 0... LiamKeniry 11 64+
(Ed Walker) *stdd s: t.k.h: hld up in last trio: effrt over 1f out: no threat to wnr and kpt on same pce ins fnl f* **14/1**

50 **8** hd **Pawpaw**[25] 9136 2-9-5 0... AdamKirby 5 63
(Clive Cox) *hld up in midfield: reminder 4f out: rdn over 1f out: no threat to wnr and kpt on same pce ins fnl f* **25/1**

9 5 **Haida Gwaii (IRE)** 2-9-0 0... KieranShoemark 7 47
(Charles Hills) *chsd ldrs: wnt 2nd after over 1f tl ent fnl 2f: lost pl u.p over 1f out: wknd ins fnl f* **33/1**

00 **10** 6 **Critique (IRE)**[13] 9326 2-9-5 0... HectorCrouch 8 38
(Ed Walker) *a towards rr: outpcd jst over 2f out: wl btn over 1f out* **66/1**

00 **11** 1 **Pleasure Garden (USA)**[13] 9325 2-9-5 0... LukeMorris 4 35
(Sir Mark Prescott Bt) *rousted along leaving stalls: in tch in last trio: rdn over 2f out: sn outpcd and wl btn over 1f out* **100/1**

5 **U** **Superior Moment (IRE)**[25] 9136 2-9-5 0... DavidProbert 2
(Tom Clover) *rrd bdly as stalls opened: wnt lft and uns rdr leaving stalls* **6/1**[3]

1m 37.48s (-0.72) **Going Correction** -0.10s/f (Stan) 12 Ran SP% **123.0**
Speed ratings (Par 96): **99,97,97,96,96 94,94,93,88,82 81,**
CSF £12.80 TOTE £2.50: £1.30, £2.10, £1.30; EX 16.20 Trifecta £63.70.
Owner Lord Lloyd-Webber **Bred** Watership Down Stud **Trained** Newmarket, Suffolk

FOCUS
Many didn't get into this novice stakes as the favourite dictated matters from the start. The ratings could be out a little either way.

9510 BETWAY H'CAP 1m 2f (P)
2:50 (2:50) (Class 4) (0-85,85) 3-Y-O+
£5,207 (£1,549; £774; £387; £300; £300) **Stalls Low**

Form RPR
5656 **1** **El Ghazwani (IRE)**[20] 9206 4-9-7 85...(t) JamesDoyle 5 94
(Hugo Palmer) *hld up in tch in midfield: nt clrest of runs ent fnl 2f: swtchd rt and effrt over 1f out: qcknd between rivals to ld ins fnl f: r.o strly* **2/1**[1]

0153 **2** 1¼ **My Target (IRE)**[7] 9422 8-9-1 79... CharlesBishop 3 85
(Michael Wigham) *in tch in midfield: effrt to chse ldrs on outer bnd 2f out: ev ch ins fnl f: chsd wnr and kpt on same pce fnl 75yds* **8/1**

6235 **3** ¾ **Capriolette (IRE)**[16] 9273 4-8-7 71... LukeMorris 10 76
(Ed Walker) *stdd s: hld up in tch in last trio: effrt and hung lft over 1f out: stl hanging but hdwy ins fnl f: swtchd rt and styd on to go 3rd towards fin* **8/1**

0545 **4** ¾ **Family Fortunes**[21] 9177 5-9-5 83... LiamKeniry 2 86
(Michael Madgwick) *in tch in midfield: hdwy and drvn to chse ldrs 1f out: kpt on same pce ins fnl f* **6/1**[3]

3544 **5** ½ **Michele Strogoff**[9] 9388 6-9-3 84... TheodoreLadd(3) 6 86
(Michael Appleby) *taken down early: led: hrd pressed ent fnl 2f: rdn over 1f out: hdd and no ex ins fnl f* **8/1**

1020 **6** ½ **Orange Suit (IRE)**[16] 9273 4-8-7 71 oh1...(b) DavidProbert 9 72
(Ed de Giles) *t.k.h: chsd ldrs: clsd to chse ldr over 2f out: rdn and ev ch 2f out tl no ex ins fnl f* **16/1**

-630 **7** 1¼ **Reponse Exacte (FR)**[20] 9199 3-8-10 76...(h) GeorgeWood 7 76
(Amy Murphy) *hld up in tch in last trio: effrt 2f out: no hdwy under press over 1f out: swtchd rt and kpt on same pce ins fnl f* **25/1**

2023 **8** ¾ **Torochica**[21] 9177 3-9-0 80... KierenFox 1 78
(John Best) *chsd ldr tl over 8f out: chsd ldrs after: effrt ent fnl 2f: unable qck over 1f out: wknd ins fnl f* **7/1**

35/2 **9** 7 **Baltic Eagle (GER)**[45] 5-9-0 78... MartinDwyer 4 61
(Alan Bailey) *a in rr: struggling u.p and rn v wd bnd 2f out: nvr on terms* **33/1**

3302 **10** 5 **The Jean Genie**[9] 9388 5-9-4 82... AdamKirby 8 55
(William Stone) *mounted in chute and taken down early: hdwy to chse ldr over 8f out: rdn and lost pl over 2f out: bhd and wknd over 1f out: fin lame (jockey said mare stopped quickly)* **9/2**[2]

2m 3.13s (-3.47) **Going Correction** -0.10s/f (Stan)
WFA 3 from 4yo+ 2lb 10 Ran SP% **124.3**
Speed ratings (Par 105): **109,108,107,106,106 106,105,104,98,94**
CSF £20.62 CT £114.21 TOTE £3.00: £1.40, £3.00, £1.90; EX 23.50 Trifecta £157.90.
Owner Hamad Rashed Bin Ghedayer **Bred** Longueville Bloodstock **Trained** Newmarket, Suffolk

FOCUS
A competitive 0-85 handicap and the race developed down the centre of the straight. The winner has been rated close to his best, with the second and third to their recent form.

9511 BETWAY APPRENTICE H'CAP 1m 4f (P)
3:20 (3:21) (Class 5) (0-75,76) 3-Y-O+ **£3,428** (£1,020; £509; £300; £300) **Stalls Low**

Form RPR
1501 **1** **Renardeau**[7] 9421 3-9-9 76 6ex...(p) DylanHogan 4 83
(Ali Stronge) *hld up in tch in last pair: effrt ent fnl 2f: hdwy u.p 1f out: led ins fnl f: r.o wl* **6/5**[1]

3211 **2** 1½ **Guroor**[28] 9067 3-9-5 75... StefanoCherchi(3) 2 79
(Marco Botti) *t.k.h: trckd ldr tl 5f out: edgd out rt and effrt 2f out: rdn to ld 1f out: hdd and one pce ins fnl f* **6/4**[2]

0614 **3** ¾ **Contingency Fee**[13] 9333 4-9-2 68...(p) GraceMcEntee(3) 3 70
(Phil McEntee) *led: rdn ent fnl 2f: hdd 1f out: kpt on same pce ins fnl f* **12/1**

2206 **4** ¾ **Continuum**[20] 9204 10-9-2 65...(v) PoppyBridgwater 1 66
(Peter Hedger) *t.k.h: hld up in tch in last pair: shkn up over 2f out: no imp over 1f out: kpt on ins fnl f: nvr enough pce to chal* **10/1**[3]

-004 **5** shd **Adams Park**[25] 9134 4-9-2 68...(v) MarkCrehan(3) 5 69
(Michael Appleby) *chsd ldrs: wnt 2nd 5f out tl 1f out: unable qck: hld and one pce ins fnl f* **10/1**[3]

2m 32.8s (-0.20) **Going Correction** -0.10s/f (Stan)
WFA 3 from 4yo+ 4lb 5 Ran SP% **111.3**
Speed ratings (Par 103): **96,95,94,94,93**
CSF £3.32 TOTE £2.00: £1.20, £1.20; EX 3.70 Trifecta £13.60.
Owner Laurence Bellman **Bred** Litex Commerce **Trained** Eastbury, Berks

FOCUS
A muddling pace for this apprentice handicap. The race only developed 4f from home and there wasn't much between them at the finish. Another pb from the winner, with the second rated to form.
T/Plt: £42.70 to a £1 stake. Pool: £56,923.81 - 971.69 winning units T/Qpdt: £20.30 to a £1 stake. Pool: £5,538.09 - 201.30 winning units **Steve Payne**

9467 NEWCASTLE (A.W) (L-H)
Wednesday, December 18

OFFICIAL GOING: Tapeta: standard
Wind: Fresh, half behind Weather: Cold, dry

9512 BOMBARDIER BRITISH HOPPED AMBER BEER H'CAP 1m 5y (Tp)
3:45 (3:48) (Class 5) (0-75,74) 3-Y-O+
£3,428 (£1,020; £509; £400; £400; £400) **Stalls Centre**

Form RPR
4021 **1** **Vive La Difference (IRE)**[12] 9349 5-9-3 70...(b) DuranFentiman 7 79
(Tim Easterby) *taken down early: slowly away: towards rr on nr side of gp: rdn over 2f out: hdwy over 1f out: led ins fnl 110yds: kpt on wl* **8/1**[3]

3606 **2** ¾ **Papa Stour (USA)**[130] 5945 4-9-4 71...(t[1]) PJMcDonald 10 79
(Stuart Williams) *cl up on nr side of gp: led gng easily over 2f out: rdn over 1f out: hdd ins fnl 110yds: hld towards fin* **10/1**

1060 **3** 2 **Champagne Rules**[143] 5473 8-9-3 70... PhilDennis 2 73
(Sharon Watt) *s.i.s: t.k.h: hld up in rr: pushed along over 2f out: hdwy on nr side of gp over 1f out: sn chsd ldrs: rdn and no ex ins fnl 110yds* **80/1**

2042 **4** 2½ **Dancing Rave**[12] 9349 3-9-2 70... DanielTudhope 8 66
(David O'Meara) *t.k.h: in rr in centre of gp: bit short of room over 2f out: rdn and hdwy over 1f out: kpt on fnl f: nrst fin* **11/1**

1043 **5** nk **Insurplus (IRE)**[12] 9349 6-9-3 70... CallumRodriguez 12 67
(Jim Goldie) *hld up in rr in centre of gp: rdn 2f out: swtchd lft ins fnl f: kpt on: nt pce to chal* **7/1**[2]

5612 **6** nse **Bobby Biscuit (USA)**[53] 8548 4-9-6 73... JFEgan 4 69
(Roger Varian) *t.k.h: prom on far side of gp: rdn and outpcd over 2f out: rallied over 1f out: no ex ins fnl f (trainer's rep said gelding had a breathing problem)* **5/2**[1]

-600 **7** 1¾ **Thaayer**[158] 4907 4-9-6 73...(w) TomEaves 11 65
(Michael Herrington) *t.k.h: prom on nr side of gp: rdn and edgd lft over 1f out: outpcd fnl f* **8/1**[3]

3200 **8** 1¼ **Coolagh Magic**[70] 8025 3-9-3 74... ConorMcGovern(3) 6 63
(Seb Spencer) *led in centre of gp: rdn and hdd over 2f out: wknd fnl f* **40/1**

6640 **9** 2¼ **Oud Metha Bridge (IRE)**[21] 9173 5-9-3 73... SeanDavis(3) 13 57
(Julia Feilden) *midfield on nr side of gp: rdn over 2f out: sn outpcd: btn fnl f* **18/1**

0306 **10** ½ **Destroyer**[61] 8305 6-8-12 65... JamesSullivan 5 48
(Tom Tate) *cl up on far side of gp: rdn over 2f out: wknd over 1f out* **12/1**

503/ **11** ½ **Reaver (IRE)**[376] 9456 6-9-7 74... ShaneGray 14 56
(John Hodge) *towards rr on nr side of gp: rdn and outpcd over 2f out: btn over 1f out* **66/1**

522 **12** hd **Ascot Week (USA)**[26] 9109 5-9-5 72...(v) JasonHart 1 54
(John Quinn) *midfield on far side of gp: rdn and outpcd over 2f out: sn wknd (stewards inquired into gelding's performance: trainer's rep said gelding may have been unsuited by not being able to get cover on this occasion; explanation was noted)* **9/1**

0000 **13** shd **Dutch Pursuit (IRE)**[13] 9329 3-9-5 73... TomMarquand 3 53
(Rebecca Menzies) *towards rr on far side of gp: rdn over 2f out: sn struggling* **33/1**

-000 **14** ¾ **Mango Chutney**[134] 5770 6-9-0 67... SamJames 9 47
(John Davies) *midfield in centre of gp: rdn over 2f out: sn struggling* **50/1**

1m 36.76s (-1.84) **Going Correction** -0.20s/f (Stan)
WFA 3 from 4yo+ 1lb 14 Ran SP% **113.7**
Speed ratings (Par 103): **101,100,98,95,95 95,93,92,90,89 89,88,88,88**
CSF £78.56 CT £5933.47 TOTE £8.00: £2.40, £3.00, £14.20; EX 99.00 Trifecta £4351.60.
Owner Ryedale Partners No 5 **Bred** Haras D'Etreham **Trained** Great Habton, N Yorks
■ Stewards' Enquiry : Callum Rodriguez two-day ban: careless riding (Jan 1-2)

FOCUS
The track was riding fast. They went a good gallop here and that suited those ridden with patience. The third has been rated close to his best.

9513 LADBROKES WHERE THE NATION PLAYS NURSERY H'CAP 1m 5y (Tp)
4:15 (4:17) (Class 5) (0-75,75) 2-Y-O
£3,428 (£1,020; £509; £400; £400; £400) **Stalls Centre**

Form RPR
6442 **1** **Royal Nation**[21] 9172 2-9-0 75... Pierre-LouisJamin(7) 4 80+
(Archie Watson) *mde all: set stdy pce: rdn and increased tempo over 2f out: kpt on wl fnl f: unchal* **11/2**[3]

5642 **2** 2 1/2 **Penmellyn (IRE)**[28] 9060 2-8-13 **67**...........................(h) PaulMulrennan 5 67
(Phillip Makin) *dwlt s: towards rr: stdy hdwy 1/2-way: rdn and wnt 2nd 2f out: kpt on fnl f: no match for wnr* **7/2**[2]

0460 **3** 1 1/2 **Itwouldberudenotto**[14] 9307 2-8-5 **62**........................ SeanDavis(3) 6 58
(Richard Fahey) *hld up in rr: rdn over 2f out: hdwy over 1f out: wnt 3rd ins fnl 110yds: kpt on: nrst fin* **16/1**

4104 **4** 1/2 **Breguet Boy (IRE)**[58] 8394 2-9-3 **71**........................ CallumRodriguez 7 66
(Keith Dalgleish) *cl up: rdn and outpcd over 2f out: rallied over 1f out: no ex fnl 110yds* **11/4**[1]

665 **5** 6 **Foreshore**[18] 9252 2-8-13 **67**.. CliffordLee 3 49
(K R Burke) *chsd wnr to over 2f out: sn rdn and outpcd: btn over 1f out* **17/2**

3026 **6** 1 3/4 **Genever Dragon (IRE)**[18] 9250 2-9-3 **71**...................(v[1]) JaneElliott 9 49
(Tom Dascombe) *chsd ldrs: rdn over 2f out: sn outpcd and hung lft: wknd over 1f out* **17/2**

5056 **7** 3 **Rulers Kingdom (IRE)**[14] 9307 2-8-9 **63**.................. FrannyNorton 1 34
(Mark Johnston) *anticipated s: s.i.s: in rr: rdn and outpcd 3f out: sn btn (jockey said colt anticipated the start, hit its head on the stalls and as a result was slowly away)* **10/1**

636 **8** 1/2 **Three Dragons**[27] 9095 2-8-9 **63**...........................(p[1]) AndrewMullen 2 33
(Ben Haslam) *chsd ldrs: rdn and struggling over 2f out: sn wknd* **10/1**

5000 **9** 26 **Big City**[26] 9110 2-8-11 **65**.. BenCurtis 8
(Roger Fell) *in rr: pushed along and struggling 3f out: lost tch fr 2f out: t.o* **66/1**

1m 38.66s (0.06) **Going Correction** -0.20s/f (Stan) **9** Ran SP% **110.9**
Speed ratings (Par 96): **91,88,87,86,80 78,75,75,49**
CSF £23.53 CT £274.37 TOTE £4.20: £1.50, £1.70, £4.60; EX 15.90 Trifecta £179.40.
Owner Newsells Park Stud **Bred** Newsells Park Stud **Trained** Upper Lambourn, W Berks

FOCUS
The winner dominated from the off. The second has been rated as backing up her latest effort.

9514 LADBROKES HOME OF THE ODDS BOOST NOVICE MEDIAN AUCTION STKS 6f (Tp)
4:45 (4:46) (Class 6) 2-Y-O £2,781 (£827; £310) **Stalls** Centre

Form RPR

1 **1** **Splendidly**[9] 9392 2-9-9 0.. BenCurtis 2 87+
(K R Burke) *cl up: rdn and outpcd over 2f out: rallied over 1f out: led ins fnl f: sn rdn clr: eased towards fin* **15/8**[1]

426 **2** 2 1/2 **Baileys Blues (FR)**[27] 9099 2-9-2 74........................ FrannyNorton 1 70
(Mark Johnston) *t.k.h: led: rdn and hrd pressed over 1f out: hdd ins fnl f: kpt on: jst hld 2nd* **11/1**

5322 **3** hd **Bendy Spirit (IRE)**[18] 9242 2-8-13 73...........................(p) SeanDavis(3) 3 69
(Richard Fahey) *cl up: rdn and ev ch over 1f out: kpt on ins fnl f* **3/1**[2]

2 **3** dht **Buy Me Back**[19] 9211 2-8-11 0........................ AdamMcNamara 9 64
(Archie Watson) *cl up: rdn and ev ch over 1f out: kpt on ins fnl f* **12/1**

5 2 **Cock A Hoop (IRE)** 2-8-11 0........................ PaulMulrennan 6 58+
(Ben Haslam) *slowly away: swvd lft sn after s: hld up in last: shkn up over 1f out: stdy hdwy ins fnl f: nvr nr to chal* **40/1**

6 3/4 **Ventura Rascal** 2-9-2 0.. ShaneGray 8 61+
(Kevin Ryan) *in tch w ldrs: rdn over 2f out: no imp fr over 1f out* **33/1**

30 **7** 3/4 **Kilconquhar**[20] 9195 2-9-2 0........................ DanielTudhope 5 59
(David O'Meara) *swvd rt s: plld hrd: in rr: rdn over 2f out: sn outpcd: btn fnl f* **10/1**[3]

0 **8** 1/2 **Katelli (IRE)**[9] 9393 2-8-13 0........................ ConnorMurtagh(3) 7 57
(Richard Fahey) *in tch w ldrs: rdn over 2f out: outpcd fr over 1f out* **150/1**

9 1 1/2 **Xian Express (IRE)**[56] 8473 2-9-2 82........................ AlistairRawlinson 4 53
(Michael Appleby) *prom: rdn and outpcd over 2f out: hung lft and wknd over 1f out* **3/1**[2]

1m 11.12s (-1.38) **Going Correction** -0.20s/f (Stan) **9** Ran SP% **115.9**
Speed ratings (Par 94): **101,97,97,97,94 93,92,92,90**
WIN: 2.80 Splendidly; PL: 1.10 Splendidly 3.10 Baileys Blues 0.60 Bendy Spirit 1.50 Buy Me Back; EX: 21.00; CSF: 24.53; TF: 27.70 60.20 CSF £24.53 TOTE £2.80: £1.10, £3.10, £0.60; EX 21.00 Trifecta £27.70.
Owner J Laughton & Mrs E Burke **Bred** Cheveley Park Stud Ltd **Trained** Middleham Moor, N Yorks

FOCUS
A nice performance from the winner, who took a while to get on top but eventually did it well under his penalty. The time and those in behind the winner raise a concern or two about the level of the form.

9515 LADBROKES "PLAY 1-2 FREE" ON FOOTBALL NURSERY H'CAP 6f (Tp)
5:15 (5:20) (Class 5) (0-70,69) 2-Y-O £3,428 (£1,020; £509; £400; £400; £400) **Stalls** Centre

Form RPR

060 **1** **Proclaimer**[119] 6337 2-9-3 **65**........................ JasonHart 13 67+
(Julie Camacho) *hld up in rr on nr side of gp: rdn 2f out: gd hdwy fnl f: led towards fin: jst prevailed* **15/2**[3]

2 nse **Ballyare**[47] 8729 2-9-3 **65**...........................(t[1]) TomEaves 9 67+
(Lucinda Russell) *dwlt s: in rr in centre of gp: swtchd rt and rdn 2f out: gd hdwy fnl f: disp ld towards fin: jst failed* **22/1**

3 nk **Gold Brocade (IRE)**[42] 8873 2-9-4 **66**........................ BenCurtis 10 67
(Michael Appleby) *cl up on nr side of gp: led over 2f out: sn rdn and hrd pressed: kpt on fnl f: hdd and lost two pls towards fin* **11/2**[2]

2343 **4** nk **River Cam**[14] 9300 2-9-7 **69**...........................(p[1]) PJMcDonald 4 69
(James Tate) *t.k.h: led in centre of gp: hdd but disp ld fr over 2f out: rdn and kpt on fnl f: no ex towards fin* **11/2**[2]

0040 **5** 1 **Redzone**[20] 9196 2-8-11 **59**........................ GrahamLee 7 56
(Bryan Smart) *cl up in centre of gp: rdn and outpcd over 1f out: rallied fnl 110yds: kpt on towards fin (jockey said gelding was denied a clear run shortly before the line)* **12/1**

4024 **6** nk **Havana Dawn**[8] 9401 2-9-6 **68**...........................(b[1]) DanielTudhope 2 64
(Phillip Makin) *cl up on far side of gp: rdn over 2f out: no ex fnl 110yds* **11/2**[2]

0613 **7** 2 1/4 **Castlehill Retreat**[26] 9110 2-9-7 **69**........................ PaulMulrennan 3 58
(Ben Haslam) *dwlt s: towards rr on far side of gp: rdn and outpcd over 2f out: rallied over 1f out: sn no imp* **9/2**[1]

0454 **8** 3/4 **Brainchild**[26] 9110 2-8-11 **64**........................ BenSanderson(5) 1 51
(Keith Dalgleish) *in rr on far side of gp: rdn over 2f out: no imp over 1f out* **40/1**

0450 **9** 1/2 **Got The T Shirt**[18] 9250 2-9-4 **66**........................ CallumRodriguez 8 52
(Keith Dalgleish) *towards rr in centre of gp: rdn 3f out: sn outpcd: no imp fr over 1f out* **10/1**

045 **10** 1/2 **Clotherholme (IRE)**[50] 8631 2-9-2 **64**........................ AndrewMullen 12 48
(Ann Duffield) *in rr in centre of gp: rdn over 2f out: sn outpcd: n.d* **12/1**

000 **11** nk **Queen Moya (IRE)**[161] 4778 2-7-10 **51** oh3 ow3........................ IzzyClifton(7) 11 34
(Nigel Tinkler) *t.k.h: prom on nr side of gp: rdn 2f out: sn wknd* **150/1**

4535 **12** 10 **Classy Lady**[13] 9330 2-8-1 **49**........................ JamesSullivan 14 2
(Ollie Pears) *midfield on far side of gp: rdn over 2f out: sn wknd* **28/1**

3200 **13** 4 **Magic Twist (USA)**[21] 9172 2-9-7 **69**........................ FrannyNorton 5 10
(Mark Johnston) *cl up on far side of gp: rdn and lost position over 2f out: sn wknd* **66/1**

0600 **14** 65 **Asstech (IRE)**[57] 8430 2-9-1 **66**........................ SeanDavis(3) 6
(Richard Fahey) *hung lft thrght: in rr in centre of gp: rdn and struggling over 3f out: lost tch 2f out: sn eased (vet said gelding was found to be coughing post-race)* **33/1**

1m 10.96s (-1.54) **Going Correction** -0.20s/f (Stan) **14** Ran SP% **115.9**
Speed ratings (Par 96): **102,101,101,101,99 99,96,95,94,94 93,80,75,**
CSF £168.39 CT £978.99 TOTE £9.20: £3.10, £8.70, £2.10; EX 231.50 Trifecta £1178.70.
Owner Owners Group 033 **Bred** Cheveley Park Stud Ltd **Trained** Norton, N Yorks

FOCUS
This race changed complexion dramatically inside the last, the leaders being overhauled late in the piece. It's been rated around the second and third, with those in behind fitting.

9516 BOMBARDIER GOLDEN BEER H'CAP 7f 14y (Tp)
5:45 (5:51) (Class 6) (0-55,55) 3-Y-O+ £2,781 (£827; £413; £400; £400; £400) **Stalls** Centre

Form RPR

6500 **1** **Dodgy Bob**[6] 9445 6-8-12 **46**...........................(v) PhilDennis 4 53
(Michael Mullineaux) *mde all: rdn on nr side of gp over 2f out: kpt on wl fnl f* **50/1**

06/- **2** nk **Waitaki (IRE)**[47] 8733 6-9-6 **54**........................ BarryMcHugh 9 60
(James Given) *chsd wnr in centre of gp thrght: rdn over 2f out: kpt on fnl f: hld towards fin* **9/1**

0040 **3** 1 1/2 **Amood (IRE)**[9] 9396 8-9-0 **48**...........................(b) JasonHart 14 51
(Simon West) *hld up in rr in centre of gp: stdy hdwy over 2f out: rdn over 1f out: kpt on fnl 110yds: wnt 3rd towards fin* **20/1**

4350 **4** shd **Midnight In Havana**[64] 8233 3-9-7 **55**........................ GrahamLee 8 57
(Bryan Smart) *cl up on far side of gp: rdn over 2f out: kpt on fnl f: no ex and lost 3rd towards fin* **4/1**[1]

6620 **5** 2 1/2 **Ritchie Star (IRE)**[19] 9225 3-9-7 **55**........................ AndrewMullen 11 51
(Ben Haslam) *dwlt s: midfield on nr side of gp: stdy hdwy after 2f: rdn over 2f out: outpcd ins fnl f* **13/2**[2]

5052 **6** hd **Tarnhelm**[9] 9396 4-8-9 **50**........................ RhonaPindar(7) 5 49
(Wilf Storey) *slowly away: in rr in centre of gp: swtchd rt over 3f out: rdn and hdwy over 1f out: no imp whn bit short of room ins fnl f (jockey said filly was denied a clear run in the final furlong)* **11/1**

0503 **7** nk **Hunters Step**[44] 8820 3-8-7 **46** oh1........................ FayeMcManoman(5) 7 41
(Nigel Tinkler) *in tch w ldrs in centre of gp: rdn over 2f out: outpcd fnl f* **28/1**

0103 **8** 1 1/4 **With Approval (IRE)**[9] 9396 7-9-1 **52**...........................(b) GemmaTutty(3) 2 44
(Karen Tutty) *cl up on far side of gp: rdn 3f out: wknd over 1f out* **10/1**

6033 **9** 3 1/4 **Sea Shack**[19] 9220 5-8-10 **47**...........................(tp) SeanDavis(3) 12 31
(Julia Feilden) *prom on nr side of gp: rdn 3f out: wknd over 1f out* **28/1**

0604 **10** 1 1/4 **Watheer**[25] 9133 4-9-1 **54**........................ PaulaMuir(5) 3 34
(Roger Fell) *dwlt s: in rr on far side of gp: rdn 3f out: sn no imp: btn over 1f out* **12/1**

0400 **11** nk **Picture Your Dream**[184] 3921 4-9-2 **53**........................ ConorMcGovern(3) 10 33
(Seb Spencer) *in rr on nr side of gp: rdn 3f out: wknd fr 2f out* **22/1**

-000 **12** 5 **Pageant Master (IRE)**[188] 3780 3-9-4 **52**...........................(w) AlistairRawlinson 1 19
(Michael Appleby) *dwlt s: t.k.h: midfield on far side of gp: rdn and struggling over 2f out: sn lost position and btn (vet said gelding lost its left hind shoe)* **7/1**[3]

2000 **13** 1 **Don't Be Surprised**[72] 7960 4-9-2 **50**...........................(p) TomEaves 6 15
(Seb Spencer) *t.k.h: towards rr on far side of gp: rdn and struggling 3f out: sn wknd* **11/1**

3030 **14** 1 1/4 **I Am Dandy (IRE)**[182] 4002 4-9-1 **49**...........................(w) PaulMulrennan 13 11
(James Ewart) *in tch w ldrs on nr side of gp: rdn and struggling over 2f out: btn whn drifted lft over 1f out* **18/1**

1m 25.25s (-0.95) **Going Correction** -0.20s/f (Stan) **14** Ran SP% **112.5**
Speed ratings (Par 101): **97,96,94,94,91 91,91,89,86,84 84,78,77,76**
CSF £409.42 CT £9258.41 TOTE £19.20: £9.40, £3.80, £5.00; EX 315.90 Trifecta £2845.10.
Owner Michael Mullineaux **Bred** Whatton Manor Stud & Robert Cornelius **Trained** Alpraham, Cheshire

FOCUS
A moderate affair in which the pace held up.

9517 BOMBARDIER "MARCH TO YOUR OWN DRUM" H'CAP 7f 14y (Tp)
6:15 (6:19) (Class 4) (0-85,86) 3-Y-O+ £5,207 (£1,549; £774; £400; £400; £400) **Stalls** Centre

Form RPR

1552 **1** **Northernpowerhouse**[70] 8025 3-9-0 **78**...........................(p) GrahamLee 6 88
(Bryan Smart) *prom: shkn up to ld over 1f out: rdn and edgd rt ins fnl f: kpt on wl* **8/1**

2113 **2** 1/2 **Mohareb**[8] 9404 3-9-6 **84**........................ AlistairRawlinson 8 92
(Michael Appleby) *dwlt s: t.k.h: prom: led over 2f out: rdn and hdd over 1f out: kpt on fnl 110yds: hld towards fin* **2/1**[1]

4 **3** 3/4 **Asdaa (IRE)**[13] 9334 3-9-3 **81**........................ JoeFanning 7 87
(Mark Johnston) *led: rdn and hdd over 2f out: sn rallied: kpt on fnl 110yds* **7/1**

013 **4** 3/4 **Fortamour (IRE)**[47] 8718 3-8-12 **76**........................ PaulMulrennan 2 80
(Ben Haslam) *midfield on outer: rdn over 2f out: kpt on fnl 110yds* **16/1**

3030 **5** hd **Merchant Of Venice**[165] 4639 4-9-6 **84**........................ TomMarquand 3 87
(James Fanshawe) *dwlt s: in rr: rdn and outpcd over 2f out: rallied over 1f out: kpt on fnl f: nt pce to chal* **13/2**[3]

6006 **6** 1 3/4 **Custard The Dragon**[21] 9183 6-8-11 **75**...........................(p) AndrewMullen 12 74
(John Mackie) *in rr: rdn and hdwy over 2f out: no imp fr over 1f out* **25/1**

0206 **7** 3 1/2 **Woodside Wonder**[18] 9254 3-9-4 **82**...........................(v) CallumRodriguez 1 71
(Keith Dalgleish) *cl up: rdn over 2f out: wknd over 1f out* **22/1**

1-03 **8** 2 1/4 **Little Jo**[40] 8918 5-8-13 **84**...........................(p) HarryRussell(7) 10 67
(Brian Ellison) *prom: rdn over 2f out: wknd over 1f out* **7/2**[2]

-540 **9** 1 3/4 **Glorious Charmer**[12] 9348 3-9-0 **78**........................ TomEaves 4 56
(Michael Herrington) *dwlt s: t.k.h: in rr: rdn and struggling over 2f out: sn wknd* **66/1**

2260 **10** nk **Donncha (IRE)**[68] 8096 8-9-7 **85**........................ DavidNolan 5 63
(Seb Spencer) *in rr: rdn and outpcd 3f out: btn fr 2f out* **22/1**

0636 **11** 1 3/4 **Zylan (IRE)**[85] 7540 7-9-8 **86**........................ BenCurtis 9 59
(Roger Fell) *prom: rdn and struggling over 2f out: sn btn* **66/1**

1m 24.1s (-2.10) **Going Correction** -0.20s/f (Stan) course record **11** Ran SP% **113.9**
Speed ratings (Par 105): **104,103,102,101,101 99,95,92,90,90 88**
CSF £22.36 CT £117.66 TOTE £8.00: £2.30, £1.40, £1.70; EX 30.30 Trifecta £193.30.
Owner Michael Moses & Terry Moses **Bred** Bearstone Stud Ltd **Trained** Hambleton, N Yorks

The Form Book Flat 2019, Raceform Ltd, Newbury, RG14 5SJ

FOCUS
Not a bad handicap, and the winner looks improved since getting on the AW. He lowered the course record by 0.38sec. Another pb from the winner, and a small pb from the second. The fifth has been rated 3lb off his best.

9518 BETWAY CASINO H'CAP — 6f (Tp)
6:45 (6:47) (Class 6) (0-60,61) 3-Y-O+
£2,676 (£801; £400; £400; £400; £400) Stalls Centre

Form				RPR
1042	1		**I Know How (IRE)**[12] 9352 4-9-7 59 ....(b) CallumRodriguez 8 *(Julie Camacho) cl up: rdn to ld over 1f out: kpt on strly fnl f* **15/8**[1]	68
0502	2	1 ½	**Zebulon (IRE)**[9] 9397 5-9-9 61 .... JamesSullivan 11 *(Ruth Carr) hld up in rr: rdn and hdwy 2f out: wnt 2nd fnl 110yds: kpt on: no match for wnr* **9/2**[2]	66
0642	3	shd	**Lord Of The Glen**[9] 9398 4-8-8 46 .... DuranFentiman 9 *(Jim Goldie) t.k.h: cl up: rdn and chsd wnr over 1f out: lost 2nd fnl 110yds: kpt on* **11/1**	50
414	4	1	**Ishebayorgrey (IRE)**[18] 9253 7-9-4 56 .... TomEaves 5 *(Iain Jardine) t.k.h: hld up in rr: pushed along and hdwy over 1f out: kpt on fnl f: nvr nr to chal* **10/1**	57
0406	5	hd	**Kommander Kirkup**[12] 9352 8-9-6 58 .... PhilDennis 1 *(Michael Herrington) hld up in rr: rdn over 1f out: kpt on fnl f: mde no imp* **25/1**	59
0056	6	½	**Avenue Of Stars**[9] 9396 6-9-6 58 ....(p) BenCurtis 2 *(Karen McLintock) racd wd: in tch w ldrs: rdn over 2f out: kpt on fnl f: nt pce to chal* **8/1**[3]	57
5302	7	¾	**Meshardal (GER)**[5] 9457 9-8-7 45 ....(p) AndrewMullen 6 *(Ruth Carr) midfield: rdn and outpcd over 2f out: rallied 1f out: sn no imp* **12/1**	42
4203	8	2	**Red Allure**[9] 9398 4-8-9 47 .... JaneElliott 3 *(Michael Mullineaux) racd wd: cl up: rdn over 2f out: wknd fnl f* **20/1**	38
0150	9	¾	**Guardia Svizzera (IRE)**[4] 9477 5-9-3 55 ....(h) DanielTudhope 7 *(Roger Fell) led: rdn and hdd over 1f out: wknd ins fnl f* **10/1**	44
3046	10	2 ¾	**Poppy In The Wind**[9] 9398 7-8-12 50 ....(v) TomMarquand 10 *(Alan Brown) dwlt s: towards rr: rdn and struggling over 2f out: sn btn* **28/1**	30
2000	11	7	**Pushkin Museum (IRE)**[138] 5632 8-9-9 61 .... PJMcDonald 4 *(John Butler) trckd ldrs: rdn over 2f out: sn struggling* **80/1**	20

1m 11.17s (-1.33) **Going Correction** -0.20s/f (Stan) 11 Ran SP% **111.6**
Speed ratings (Par 101): **100,98,97,96,96 95,94,91,90,87 77**
CSF £8.52 CT £67.81 TOTE £2.30: £1.50, £1.40, £1.70; EX 12.20 Trifecta £58.60.
Owner Judy & Richard Peck & Partner **Bred** Miss Sarah Thompson **Trained** Norton, N Yorks

FOCUS
A moderate sprint handicap and straightforward form.

9519 #BETYOURWAY AT BETWAY H'CAP — 6f (Tp)
7:15 (7:17) (Class 5) (0-75,75) 3-Y-O+
£3,428 (£1,020; £509; £400; £400; £400) Stalls Centre

Form				RPR
0001	1		**Wasntexpectingthat**[26] 9113 3-9-3 71 .... BarryMcHugh 8 *(Richard Fahey) hld up in rr in centre of gp: hdwy whn repeatedly short of room over 1f out: pushed along and swtchd rt ins fnl f: qcknd to ld towards fin: comf* **11/4**[2]	84+
5520	2	1 ¼	**Hassaad**[19] 9218 3-9-4 72 .... AdamMcNamara 10 *(Archie Watson) t.k.h: led in centre of gp: rdn and hrd pressed fr 2f out: kpt on fnl 110yds: hdd and no ex towards fin* **22/1**	79
0026	3	½	**Oriental Lilly**[26] 9113 5-9-2 70 ....(p) DanielTudhope 5 *(Jim Goldie) dwlt s: in rr on far side of gp: rdn and hdwy over 1f out: kpt on fnl f: wnt 3rd towards fin* **14/1**	75
0210	4	nk	**East Street Revue**[40] 8921 6-9-5 73 ....(b) DuranFentiman 4 *(Tim Easterby) cl up on far side of gp: rdn and ev ch fr 2f out: kpt on fnl f: no ex and lost two pls towards fin* **40/1**	77
0305	5	½	**Bugler Bob (IRE)**[19] 9218 3-9-0 68 ....(v) JasonHart 11 *(John Quinn) cl up in centre of gp: rdn over 2f out: kpt on fnl f: no ex ins fnl 110yds* **16/1**	71
2423	6	½	**Epeius (IRE)**[40] 8921 6-9-6 74 ....(v) AndrewMullen 7 *(Ben Haslam) ducked lft s: in rr in centre of gp: rdn and hdwy over 1f out: keeping on whn nt clr run towards fin* **9/1**	75
0343	7	½	**Haddaf (IRE)**[5] 9455 4-9-7 75 ....(p) PJMcDonald 12 *(Stuart Williams) cl up on nr side of gp: rdn 2f out: no ex ins fnl f* **2/1**[1]	75
0630	8	1 ¼	**Alicia Darcy (IRE)**[11] 9365 3-8-9 70 ....(b) KateLeahy[(7)] 9 *(Archie Watson) towards rr in centre of gp: pushed along over 2f out: hdwy whn bit short of room over 1f out: sn no imp* **50/1**	66
530	9	2 ¼	**Followthesteps (IRE)**[26] 9108 4-9-7 75 ....(p[1]) DavidNolan 1 *(Ivan Furtado) midfield on far side of gp: rdn over 2f out: wknd over 1f out* **12/1**	63
-250	10	1 ½	**Jonboy**[13] 9334 4-9-1 72 .... HarrisonShaw[(3)] 13 *(David Brown) t.k.h: prom on nr side of gp: rdn over 2f out: wknd over 1f out* **6/1**[3]	56
3304	11	2	**Yes You (IRE)**[79] 7762 5-9-2 70 .... GrahamLee 14 *(Bryan Smart) midfield on nr side of gp: rdn and struggling over 2f out: sn btn* **40/1**	47
0	12	6	**Edessann (IRE)**[12] 9351 3-9-2 70 .... TomEaves 3 *(Michael Herrington) stdd s: hld up in rr in centre of gp: rdn over 2f out: sn wknd* **80/1**	28
55-0	13	3 ¾	**Cupboard Love**[16] 9278 3-9-7 75 .... JoeFanning 2 *(Mark Johnston) cl up on far side of gp: rdn and struggling over 2f out: sn wknd* **100/1**	21

1m 10.35s (-2.15) **Going Correction** -0.20s/f (Stan) 13 Ran SP% **117.9**
Speed ratings (Par 103): **106,104,103,103,102 101,101,99,96,94 91,83,78**
CSF £70.85 CT £735.75 TOTE £3.70: £1.30, £6.00, £4.00; EX 56.30 Trifecta £454.00.
Owner The Good Bad Ugly And Deaf **Bred** Mr & Mrs A & D Flannigan **Trained** Musley Bank, N Yorks

FOCUS
An impressive performance from the winner, who looks improved for being switched to the AW. He's been rated back to his best, and the form looks sound rated around the second and third.
T/Plt: £1099.90 to a £1 stake. Pool: £83,640.09 - 55.51 winning units T/Qpdt: £74.90 to a £1 stake. Pool: £13,263.10 - 131.01 winning units **Richard Young**

9520 - 9536a (Foreign Racing) - See Raceform Interactive

9014 LE CROISE-LAROCHE
Wednesday, December 18

OFFICIAL GOING: Turf: heavy

9537a PRIX DE CLOTURE (CLAIMER) (4YO+) (TURF) — 1m 4f 110y
5:15 4-Y-O+
£7,657 (£3,063; £2,297; £1,531; £765)

			RPR
1		**Gipsy Song (FR)**[43] 4-8-5 0 ....(b) MlleSophieChuette[(3)] 10 *(M Delzangles, France)* **19/5**[3]	85
2	¾	**Attentionadventure**[53] 8-9-11 0 ....(p) MarcNobili 13 *(J Phelippon, France)* **11/5**[1]	100
3	8	**King Nonantais (FR)**[29] 7-8-13 0 ....(b) MlleLauraGrosso[(3)] 4 *(Andreas Suborics, Germany)* **12/1**	79
4	1	**Argus (IRE)**[21] 9184 7-8-11 0 .... BertrandFlandrin 6 *(Alexandra Dunn) mid-div: travelling wl in rr of ldng gp at 1/2-way: urged clsr 4f out: strly drvn over 3f out: kpt on clsng stages: nt pce to chal* **29/1**	72
5	1 ¾	**Thrones Game (FR)**[457] 5691 6-8-13 0 .... FrankPanicucci 15 *(Yannick Fouin, France)* **18/5**[2]	71
6	3 ½	**All Prince (GER)**[29] 4-8-11 0 ....(b) RosarioMangione 2 *(R Rohne, Germany)* **23/1**	64
7	nk	**Hexis (IRE)**[39] 5-9-2 0 ....(b) EmmanuelEtienne 11 *(Guillaume Courbot, France)* **10/1**	68
8	3	**Zeyzoun (FR)**[54] 8521 5-8-11 0 .... QuentinGervais 7 *(Alexandra Dunn) racd v keenly: chsd ldrs: smooth hdwy into chalng position 3f out: pushed along over 2f out: sn wknd* **61/1**	58
9	5	**Movie Star (GER)**[64] 8224 4-8-8 0 .... AdrienMoreau 8 *(C J M Wolters, Holland)* **117/1**	47
10	3 ½	**Motym (FR)**[202] 4-8-11 0 .... HugoLebouc 9 *(Mme V Seignoux, France)* **94/1**	45
11	6	**Cutty Pie (IRE)**[6] 5-8-13 0 .... JenteMarien 12 *(J Phelippon, France)* **17/1**	37
12	¾	**Glorious Warrior (IRE)** 4-8-13 0 .... LiubovGrigorieva[(3)] 3 *(Caroline Fuchs, Germany)* **36/1**	39
13	20	**Just Because**[191] 7-8-11 0 .... BenjaminMarie 14 *(M Bouckaert, Belgium)* **81/1**	2
14	dist	**Marina Marshall (FR)**[779] 5-8-8 0 .... MiguelLopez 5 *(Frau Doris Ursula Smith, Germany)* **164/1**	
15	6	**Zafiro (FR)**[63] 7-8-11 0 ....(p) AntoineCoutier 1 *(D De Waele, France)* **12/1**	

2m 51.8s 15 Ran SP% **119.4**
PARI-MUTUEL (all including 1 euro stake): WIN 4.80; PLACE 1.90, 1.70, 2.70; DF 6.20.
Owner Alain Louis-Dreyfus **Bred** A Louis-Dreyfus **Trained** France

9538a PRIX DE L'ARBRE DE NOEL (CLAIMER) (3YO) (TURF) — 5f 110y
6:45 3-Y-O
£6,756 (£2,702; £2,027; £1,351; £675)

			RPR
1		**Vaerya**[622] 3-8-8 0 .... AntoineCoutier 7 *(Frau C Barsig, Germany)* **93/10**	54
2	1	**Madison Vanzales (FR)**[13] 3-9-0 0 ....(p) MlleCoraliePacaut[(3)] 11 *(M Boutin, France)* **18/5**[2]	60
3	1 ½	**Hello Is You (FR)**[68] 3-8-11 0 .... StephenHellyn 4 *(Mme J Hendriks, Holland)* **38/1**	49
4	snk	**Realityhacking (FR)**[16] 3-8-13 0 ....(b) MlleMickaelleMichel[(3)] 5 *(F Chappet, France)* **67/10**[3]	53
5	¾	**Hit The Track Jack**[109] 3-8-6 0 .... JeremieMonteiro[(5)] 9 *(D De Waele, France)* **11/1**	46
6	3 ½	**What Secret (IRE)**[16] 9280 3-8-4 0 .... HugoMouesan[(7)] 8 *(C Boutin, France)* **40/1**	34
7	1 ¼	**Ghost Buy (FR)**[15] 9287 3-8-11 0 ....(p) AntoineHamelin 2 *(Ivan Furtado) outpcd towards inner: mid-div and hrd rdn by 1/2-way: wknd fnl f* **18/5**[2]	30
8	1	**Ricochet (IRE)**[16] 9280 3-8-10 0 ....(b) AlexisPouchin[(6)] 6 *(C Boutin, France)* **23/10**[1]	32
9	3	**Soft Icing**[132] 3-8-5 0 .... MlleSanneDeCeulaer[(3)] 1 *(Niels Lantsoght, Belgium)* **73/1**	14
10	3 ½	**Imotep (FR)**[25] 3-8-8 0 ....(p) MlleFriedaValleSkar[(9)] 3 *(M Boutin, France)* **12/1**	11

1m 10.9s 10 Ran SP% **118.9**
PARI-MUTUEL (all including 1 euro stake): WIN 10.30; PLACE 2.60, 1.90, 6.30; DF 20.30.
Owner Steffen Molks **Bred** Cuadra Africa **Trained** Germany

9330 SOUTHWELL (L-H)
Thursday, December 19

OFFICIAL GOING: Fibresand: standard
Wind: Moderate across Weather: Cloudy, heavy rain after Race 4

9539 BETWAY H'CAP — 4f 214y(F)
1:30 (1:31) (Class 6) (0-60,59) 3-Y-O+
£2,781 (£827; £413; £300; £300; £300) Stalls Centre

Form				RPR
2400	1		**The Grey Zebedee**[13] 9352 3-9-5 57 ....(b) DuranFentiman 11 *(Tim Easterby) awkward s and rr towards stands' rail: pushed along 4f out: rdn along 1/2-way: hdwy on stands' rail over 1f out: styd on strly ins fnl f: led nr line (trainers rep said, regards the apparent improvement in form, gelding was suited by the drop back to five furlongs and the re-application of blinkers)* **14/1**	64
0/13	2	nk	**Eesha Says (IRE)**[14] 9335 4-8-8 53 .... ElishaWhittington[(7)] 2 *(Tony Carroll) racd towards centre: prom: led 2f out: sn rdn and edgd lft over 1f out: hung lft u.p ins fnl f: hdd nr line* **3/1**[1]	59
3651	3	¾	**Amazing Amaya**[14] 9335 4-8-12 50 ....(h) CamHardie 3 *(Derek Shaw) trckd ldrs centre: pushed along and hdwy 2f out: rdn over 1f out: ev ch ent fnl f: sn drvn and edgd lft: kpt on* **10/3**[2]	53
5602	4	nk	**Hey Ho Let's Go**[44] 8840 3-9-7 59 .... RobertHavlin 1 *(Mark Hoad) racd towards far side: trckd ldrs: hdwy and cl up 2f out: rdn to chal whn nt clr run and hmpd on far rail ins fnl f: swtchd rt and kpt on same pce towards fin* **13/2**[3]	64

0623 **5** *2 1/4* **Blackcurrent**[9] 9406 3-9-0 **52**.. LukeMorris 13 46
(Alan Brown) *racd stands' side: prom: rdn along 2f out: sn drvn and kpt on same pce* **8/1**

0506 **6** *nk* **Pearl Noir**[14] 9335 9-8-2 **45**.................................(b) KieranSchofield(5) 14 38
(Scott Dixon) *racd nr stands' rail: prom: rdn along 2f out: drvn over 1f out: kpt on same pce* **40/1**

600 **7** *hd* **Canimar**[7] 9439 4-8-7 **45**..(v) JosephineGordon 6 37
(Shaun Keightley) *bhd centre: detached and rdn along 1/2-way: hdwy over 1f out: swtchd lft ent fnl f: styd on wl towards far side fnl f: nrst fin (jockey said filly hung left-handed)* **25/1**

0030 **8** *nse* **Decision Maker (IRE)**[20] 9219 5-9-4 **56**..............(p[1]) LewisEdmunds 10 48
(Roy Bowring) *chsd ldrs centre: cl up 1/2-way: rdn along over 1f out: sn drvn and grad wknd fnl f* **8/1**

-000 **9** *1 1/4* **Mable Lee (IRE)**[13] 9352 4-9-2 **54**.............................. GrahamLee 9 42
(Bryan Smart) *chsd ldrs centre: rdn along 1/2-way: wknd wl over 1f out* **33/1**

0000 **10** *1* **Classic Pursuit**[14] 9335 8-9-0 **52**..............................(v) SamJames 4 36
(Marjorie Fife) *dwlt and swtchd lft s: a towards rr far side* **20/1**

0403 **11** *3 1/4* **Champagne Mondays**[76] 7869 3-8-7 **45**....................(b) KieranO'Neill 8 17
(Scott Dixon) *racd centre: slt ld: rdn along 1/2-way: hdd 2f out: sn drvn and wknd* **12/1**

12 *nk* **Espirit D'escalier (IRE)**[202] 3327 3-8-12 **55**................ DylanHogan(5) 7 26
(J F Levins, Ire) *prom centre: rdn along over 2f out: sn drvn and wknd* **25/1**

0000 **13** *1/2* **Little Miss Muffin**[10] 9398 3-8-12 **50**...............................(p) JaneElliott 5 19
(Sam England) *racd towards far side: a towards rr* **100/1**

1m 0.22s (0.52) **Going Correction** 0.0s/f (Stan) **13** Ran SP% **116.8**
Speed ratings (Par 101): **95,94,93,92,89 88,88,88,86,84 79,79,78**
CSF £50.97 CT £183.79 TOTE £16.10: £4.60, £1.40, £1.50; EX 71.50 Trifecta £256.90.
Owner The Geordie Boys & Partner **Bred** D R Botterill **Trained** Great Habton, N Yorks
■ Stewards' Enquiry : Elisha Whittington three-day ban; careless riding (Jan 2-4)

FOCUS
The first pair were unusually separated by the width of the track in this moderate sprint handicap. It's been rated as straightforward form, with the winner within 2lb of his best and the second and third finding a fraction on their recent form.

9540 BETWAY NOVICE STKS 4f 214y(F)

2:00 (2:00) (Class 5) 3-Y-O+ **£3,428** (£1,020; £509; £254) **Stalls** Centre

Form RPR

464- **1** **My Excelsa (IRE)**[29] 9074 3-9-0 68.. JasonHart 3 70
(J F Levins, Ire) *slt ld towards centre: rdn along wl over 1f out: drvn and edgd rt ins fnl f: kpt on strly towards fin* **5/2**[2]

0-46 **2** *1 1/4* **Fujaira King (USA)**[22] 9171 3-9-5 70......................(t) AlistairRawlinson 1 71
(Stuart Williams) *racd centre: trckd ldrs: pushed along over 2f out: sn cl up: rdn to chal and ev ch ent fnl f: sn drvn: edgd lft and kpt on one pce* **11/10**[1]

55-3 **3** *3 1/2* **Tomshalfbrother**[50] 8672 3-9-5 63.................................(p[1]) LukeMorris 5 58
(Robert Cowell) *cl up: rdn over 2f out: drvn wl over 1f out: grad wknd fnl f* **13/2**

4 *1 3/4* **Wondrous Scene (IRE)**[57] 8477 3-9-0 68.......................... DavidProbert 2 47
(K J Condon, Ire) *trckd ldrs: pushed along 1/2-way: rdn wl over 1f out: sn one pce* **5/1**[3]

02 **5** *2 1/2* **Jeans Maite**[40] 8947 3-9-0 0..(h) LewisEdmunds 6 38
(Roy Bowring) *dwlt: sn trcking ldng pair: cl up nr stands' rail 1/2-way: rdn along wl over 1f out: sn wknd* **25/1**

59.62s (-0.08) **Going Correction** 0.0s/f (Stan) **5** Ran SP% **110.0**
Speed ratings (Par 103): **100,98,92,89,85**
CSF £5.66 TOTE £3.70: £1.60, £1.10; EX 5.20 Trifecta £14.00.
Owner David Spratt **Bred** Lynch Bages,Edgeridge Ltd& Glenvale Stud **Trained** The Curragh, Co Kildare

FOCUS
Another race on the straight track with the winner nearer the stands' side. Modest form. A small pb from the winner, with the second rated close to form.

9541 LADBROKES HOME OF THE ODDS BOOST NURSERY H'CAP 6f 16y(F)

2:30 (2:32) (Class 5) (0-70,71) 2-Y-O

£3,428 (£1,020; £509; £300; £300; £300) **Stalls** Low

Form RPR

4116 **1** **Speed Merchant (IRE)**[21] 9196 2-9-7 **69**..............(p) AlistairRawlinson 3 75+
(Michael Appleby) *trckd ldrs: effrt 2f out: sn n.m.r and hmpd wl over 1f out: sn rdn and chal ins fnl f: led last 110yds: kpt on wl* **5/2**[2]

1003 **2** *1 1/4* **Constitutional (IRE)**[13] 9346 2-8-10 **61**.................... HarrisonShaw(3) 7 63
(K R Burke) *trckd ldrs: clsd up on outer 1/2-way: rdn to ld over 1f out: drvn and jnd jst ins fnl f: hdd last 110yds: kpt on same pce* **10/1**

040 **3** *1 1/4* **Slingshot**[27] 9107 2-9-1 **63**..(e[1]) GrahamLee 8 61
(Bryan Smart) *hld up in tch: hdwy 2f out: rdn over 1f out: styd on fnl f* **9/1**

5260 **4** *nse* **Rathagan**[21] 9205 2-9-0 **65**.. FinleyMarsh(3) 1 63
(Richard Hughes) *cl up on inner: effrt to chal over 2f out: sn rdn and edgd rt wl over 1f drvn and wknd ent fnl f* **15/2**

0504 **5** *1/2* **Mews House**[10] 9394 2-9-0 **62**.. BenCurtis 2 59
(David Brown) *slt ld: pushed along over 2f out: sn jnd and rdn: drvn and edgd lft wl over 1f out: sn hdd and grad wknd (jockey said colt hung left-handed in the home straight)* **5/1**[3]

3244 **6** *2 3/4* **Maybellene (IRE)**[66] 8180 2-9-0 **62**................................ CamHardie 4 50
(Alan Berry) *a in rr* **50/1**

2046 **7** *shd* **We're Reunited (IRE)**[15] 9300 2-9-9 **71**...................... DavidProbert 5 59
(Ronald Harris) *trckd ldng pair: cl up 3f out: rdn along over 2f out: sn drvn and btn (trainers rep said, regards the poor performance, colt resented the kickback)* **2/1**[1]

1m 16.7s (0.20) **Going Correction** 0.0s/f (Stan) **7** Ran SP% **111.4**
Speed ratings (Par 96): **98,96,94,94,93 90,90**
CSF £25.50 CT £186.26 TOTE £2.80: £1.50, £4.30; EX 18.30 Trifecta £176.80.
Owner Slipstream Racing **Bred** J McAteer & L McAteer **Trained** Oakham, Rutland

FOCUS
A run-of-the-mill nursery, run at an average pace. It's been rated as straightforward form.

9542 BETWAY HEED YOUR HUNCH H'CAP 1m 3f 23y(F)

3:00 (3:01) (Class 6) (0-65,66) 3-Y-O+

£2,781 (£827; £413; £300; £300; £300) **Stalls** Low

Form RPR

5042 **1** **Grandscape**[44] 8843 4-9-0 **60**.. SophieSmith(7) 12 68
(Ed Dunlop) *dwlt and hld up towards rr: stdy hdwy on inner 5f out: n.m.r over 3f out: trckd ldrs 2f out: rdn to chal ent fnl f: kpt on wl to ld last 50yds* **7/1**

6232 **2** *nk* **Sociologist (FR)**[14] 9333 4-8-13 **59**.......................(p) JonathanFisher(7) 2 67
(Scott Dixon) *in tch: hdwy 1/2-way: led over 4f out: rdn wl over 1f out: drvn jst ins fnl f: hdd and no ex last 50yds* **5/1**[2]

2500 **3** *1 1/2* **Chinese Alphabet**[23] 9168 3-9-2 **58**......................(b[1]) AlistairRawlinson 1 64
(Michael Appleby) *in rr: hdwy and wd st: rdn along stands' side 2f out: styd on to chse ldng pair ins fnl f: nrst fin* **16/1**

0000 **4** *nk* **Mousebird (IRE)**[144] 5473 3-9-6 **62**............................ CharlieBennett 5 68
(Hughie Morrison) *prom: pushed along 4f out: rdn 3f out: chsd ldr 2f out: sn drvn and kpt on same pce* **28/1**

0000 **5** *1/2* **Beechwood James (FR)**[21] 9201 3-8-7 **49** oh4..............(v) JaneElliott 9 54
(Michael Appleby) *chsd ldrs: reminders 5f out: rdn along 3f out: chsd ldr 2f out: sn drvn and kpt on same pce* **50/1**

0400 **6** *2* **Imperial Focus (IRE)**[13] 9345 6-9-0 **53**............................ PhilDennis 7 54
(Simon Waugh) *led tl 3f: prom: rdn along on inner 3f out: sn chsng ldr: drvn wl over 1f out: sn one pce* **11/1**

5462 **7** *3 1/4* **Fayetta**[12] 9367 3-9-7 **63**..(b) DavidProbert 8 59
(David Loughnane) *prom: led after 3f: pushed along and hdd over 4f out: rdn over 3f out: drvn over 2f out: sn wknd* **8/1**

1224 **8** *5* **Elegant Love**[21] 9201 3-9-10 **66**.. BenCurtis 3 54
(David Evans) *midfield: rdn along over 4f out: wd st and sn outpcd* **5/1**[2]

2015 **9** *1/2* **Dolly McQueen**[21] 9201 3-9-3 **59**................................ WilliamCarson 4 47
(Anthony Carson) *in tch: rdn along over 4f out: sn wknd* **13/2**[3]

0243 **10** *1* **Visor**[28] 9093 4-9-9 **62**..(h) NicolaCurrie 10 47
(James Fanshawe) *a towards rr* **4/1**[1]

3564 **11** *25* **Harbour Quay**[206] 3150 5-9-8 **61**.......................................(p) LiamKeniry 11 6
(Patrick Chamings) *chsd ldng pair: rdn along over 3f out: wknd over 2f out* **16/1**

3-00 **12** *5* **Saxo Jack (FR)**[17] 9273 9-9-10 **63**..................................(tp) GrahamLee 6
(Sophie Leech) *dwlt: a in rr: bhd fr 1/2-way: t.o fnl 3f* **66/1**

2m 27.86s (-0.14) **Going Correction** 0.0s/f (Stan)
WFA 3 from 4yo+ 3lb **12** Ran SP% **117.3**
Speed ratings (Par 101): **100,99,98,98,98 96,94,90,90,89 71,67**
CSF £41.02 CT £546.49 TOTE £8.80: £2.30, £1.80, £5.10; EX 57.20 Trifecta £757.30.
Owner Mrs C L Smith **Bred** Laundry Cottage Stud Farm **Trained** Newmarket, Suffolk

FOCUS
This moderate handicap looked wide open. It was run at a fair enough pace. The winner has been rated in line with his better AW form.

9543 PLAY 4 TO SCORE AT BETWAY H'CAP 1m 4f 14y(F)

3:30 (3:33) (Class 4) (0-80,82) 3-Y-O+

£5,207 (£1,549; £774; £387; £300; £300) **Stalls** Low

Form RPR

1 **Rasaasy (IRE)**[215] 3-8-13 **73**.. WilliamCarson 2 81
(Anthony Carson) *towards rr: pushed along over 3f out: rdn and hdwy in centre 2f out: chsd ldng pair over 1f out: styd on strly fnl f to ld nr fin* **20/1**

0030 **2** *3/4* **Seven Clans (IRE)**[28] 9096 7-9-3 **76**............................ GemmaTutty(3) 7 83
(Karen Tutty) *hld up in rr: hdwy over 4f out: chsd ldrs on outer over 2f out: rdn to chse ldr over 1f out: drvn ins fnl f: kpt on wl towards fin* **25/1**

4421 **3** *nk* **Angel Lane (FR)**[14] 9333 3-8-8 **68**.................................. CliffordLee 6 75+
(K R Burke) *t.k.h: trckd ldng pair on outer: smooth hdwy to ld over 3f out and wd st: shkn up wl over 1f out: rdn and hung rt to stands' rail: 1f out: drvn ins fnl f: hdd & wknd towards fin* **6/5**[1]

2304 **4** *9* **Grenadier Guard (IRE)**[120] 6340 3-9-4 **78**...................... FrannyNorton 4 71
(Mark Johnston) *midfield: pushed along 4f out: rdn along 3f out: drvn over 2f out: sn one pce* **7/2**[3]

145- **5** *3 3/4* **Al Kherb**[242] 7697 4-9-12 **82**.. JasonHart 8 68
(John Quinn) *hld up in tch: hdwy to chse ldrs 3f out: rdn along 2f out: sn wknd* **10/1**

-643 **6** *7* **Divine Gift (IRE)**[174] 4327 3-9-7 **81**.................................. BenCurtis 5 57
(Iain Jardine) *led 1 1/2f: cl up: pushed along over 3f out: rdn wl over 2f out: sn drvn and wknd* **3/1**[2]

4550 **7** *9* **Azari**[30] 9056 7-9-9 **79**...(b) RobertHavlin 1 40
(Alexandra Dunn) *cl up: led after 1 1/2f: pushed along and hdd over 3f out: sn rdn and wknd over 2f out* **25/1**

4005 **8** *32* **Temur Khan**[200] 3377 4-9-10 **80**................................ GeorgeDowning 3
(Tony Carroll) *chsd ldrs: rdn along over 4f out: sn lost pl and bhd (jockey said gelding stopped quickly)* **25/1**

2m 39.24s (-1.76) **Going Correction** 0.0s/f (Stan)
WFA 3 from 4yo+ 4lb **8** Ran SP% **118.1**
Speed ratings (Par 105): **105,104,104,98,95 91,85,63**
CSF £395.25 CT £1058.48 TOTE £28.70: £3.80, £5.40, £1.10; EX 345.20 Trifecta £3113.70.
Owner Chris Butler **Bred** Al Asayl Bloodstock Ltd **Trained** Newmarket, Suffolk

FOCUS
The feature handicap was run at a modest pace, but it's fair form with the principals coming clear. The second has been rated close to his old best.

9544 BOMBARDIER BRITISH HOPPED AMBER BEER CLASSIFIED STKS 1m 13y(F)

4:00 (4:02) (Class 6) 3-Y-O+

£2,781 (£827; £413; £300; £300; £300) **Stalls** Low

Form RPR

042 **1** **Crazy Spin**[8] 9410 3-9-0 50..(p) JasonHart 6 56
(Ivan Furtado) *slt ld: hdd 1/2-way: cl up: effrt 2f out and sn rdn: led ent fnl f: sn drvn and kpt on wl* **9/2**[2]

6252 **2** *1 1/2* **Emojie**[31] 9028 5-8-10 48......................................(p) RayDawson(5) 12 54
(Jane Chapple-Hyam) *prom: cl up over 3f out: rdn to ld 2f out: jnd and drvn over 1f out: hdd ent fnl f: kpt on* **15/8**[1]

0043 **3** *2 1/2* **Face Like Thunder**[20] 9225 4-9-1 46............................(be) DannyBrock 9 48
(John Butler) *dwlt and towards rr: hdwy into midfield 1/2-way: rdn along to chse ldrs over 2f out: swtchd rt and drvn wl over 1f out: kpt on u.p fnl f* **10/1**

-000 **4** *2* **Palazzo**[20] 9220 3-9-0 45..(t[1]) GrahamLee 10 42
(Bryan Smart) *dwlt and towards rr: hdwy 3f out: sn rdn along and wd st: chsd ldrs wl over 1f out: kpt on fnl f* **16/1**

6236 **5** *2 1/2* **Elysee Star**[20] 9220 4-9-1 46.......................................(p) AndrewMullen 3 37
(Mark Walford) *towards rr: hdwy on inner over 3f out: rdn wl over 2f out: kpt on u.p fnl f* **10/1**

0 **6** *1 1/2* **High Glory (FR)**[13] 9345 3-9-0 44................................ PaulMulrennan 2 33
(J F Levins, Ire) *in rr and swtchd wd after 1f: bhd and wd st: hdwy 2f out: styd on fnl f: n.d* **12/1**

253 **7** *1 3/4* **Queen Mia (IRE)**[16] 9282 3-8-7 47.............................(t) ZakWheatley(7) 11 29
(Declan Carroll) *midfield: effrt over 3f out: sn rdn and n.d* **8/1**[3]

-060 **8** *1/2* **Je M'En Fiche**[184] 3965 3-9-0 49.................................... LiamKeniry 14 28
(Patrick Chamings) *chsd ldrs: rdn along over 2f out: sn edgd lft and wknd* **66/1**

0444 **9** *1 ¼* **Sooqaan**[20] 9225 8-9-1 49 ....(p) CamHardie 1 26
(Antony Brittain) *cl up on inner: led 1/2-way: rdn along 3f out: hdd 2f out: sn drvn and wknd (jockey said gelding hung right-handed under pressure)* **8/1**[3]

0000 **10** *nk* **Candesta (USA)**[20] 9225 9-8-10 50 .... DylanHogan(5) 8 25
(Julia Feilden) *bhd and wd st: rdn along and hdwy nr stands' rail 2f out: drvn over 1f out: n.d* **12/1**

0040 **11** *10* **Lovely Acclamation (IRE)**[112] 6643 5-9-1 43 ....(p) WilliamCarson 13 2
(Debbie Hughes) *chsd ldrs on wd outside: rdn along over 3f out: sn wknd* **33/1**

00 **12** *1 ½* **Fascinating Spirit (IRE)**[7] 9446 4-9-1 44 ....(vt) SamJames 5
(Marjorie Fife) *chsd ldrs: rdn along over 3f out: wknd over 2f out* **40/1**

0000 **13** *11* **Jazzameer**[63] 8295 4-9-1 31 .... DuranFentiman 7
(Debbie Hughes) *chsd ldrs: rdn along and lost pl 1/2-way: sn bhd* **100/1**

1m 43.26s (-0.44) **Going Correction** 0.0s/f (Stan) 13 Ran SP% **122.5**
WFA 3 from 4yo+ 1lb
Speed ratings (Par 101): **102,100,98,96,93 92,90,89,88,88 78,76,65**
CSF £13.44 CT £86.41 TOTE £5.00: £1.60, £1.30, £3.70; EX 13.80 Trifecta £100.30.
Owner The Giggle Factor Partnership **Bred** Mrs A Shone **Trained** Wiseton, Nottinghamshire
■ Stewards' Enquiry : William Carson caution; entered incorrect stall

FOCUS
A weak handicap, run at a brisk pace and only two mattered inside the final furlong. A minor pb from the winner, with the second rated in line with his latest.

9545 BETWAY LIVE CASINO H'CAP 6f 16y(F)
4:30 (4:31) (Class 6) (0-65,66) 3-Y-0+
£2,781 (£827; £413; £300; £300; £300) **Stalls** Low

Form RPR

0334 **1** **Liamba**[20] 9224 4-9-8 **66** ....(v) DavidNolan 4 74
(David O'Meara) *trckd ldrs: swtchd lft and hdwy 2f out: sn chal: rdn to ld jst over 1f out: drvn and edgd rt ins fnl f: jst hld on* **13/8**[1]

4034 **2** *hd* **Global Melody**[14] 9337 4-9-1 **64** ....(vt) DylanHogan(5) 3 71
(Phil McEntee) *hld up in rr: hdwy wl over 2f out: chsd ldrs towards stands' side over 1f out: rdn ent fnl f: styd on wl: jst hld* **4/1**[2]

0004 **3** *1 ¼* **Lightning Charlie**[10] 9397 7-9-6 **64** .... PaulMulrennan 5 68
(Iain Jardine) *hld up towards rr: hdwy and wd st: effrt nr stands' rail 2f out: sn rdn: kpt on fnl f* **9/2**[3]

6030 **4** *1 ¼* **Almurr (IRE)**[10] 9397 3-9-6 **64** .... SamJames 7 64
(Phillip Makin) *slt ld: hdd 4f out: cl up: rdn over 2f out: drvn over 1f out: kpt on same pce* **5/1**

1435 **5** *nk* **Our Charlie Brown**[57] 8471 5-9-7 **65** ....(p) PhilDennis 6 64
(David C Griffiths) *cl up: led 4f out: rdn along over 2f out: drvn and hdd over 1f out: grad wknd* **14/1**

4600 **6** *2* **Napping**[10] 9386 6-9-2 **63** .... GabrieleMalune(3) 1 56
(Amy Murphy) *trckd ldng pair on inner: hdwy and cl up over 2f out: sn rdn: drvn and wknd over 1f out* **20/1**

4502 **7** *¾* **Kentucky Kingdom (IRE)**[17] 9276 3-9-2 **60** .... GrahamLee 2 51
(James Evans) *chsd ldrs on inner: rdn along 3f out: sn drvn and wknd* **14/1**

R000 **8** *8* **Red Invader (IRE)**[56] 8501 9-9-4 **62** .... JoeyHaynes 8 29
(John Butler) *chsd ldrs: hdwy and cl up over 3f out: rdn wl over 2f out: sn drvn and wknd* **40/1**

1m 15.6s (-0.90) **Going Correction** 0.0s/f (Stan) 8 Ran SP% **113.5**
Speed ratings (Par 101): **106,105,104,102,102 99,98,87**
CSF £8.02 CT £23.40 TOTE £2.70: £1.10, £1.80, £1.50; EX 9.20 Trifecta £29.70.
Owner Diamond Racing Ltd **Bred** Thoroughbreds For The Future Ltd **Trained** Upper Helmsley, N Yorks
■ Stewards' Enquiry : Dylan Hogan two-day ban; misuse of whip (Jan 2-3)

FOCUS
The pace took time to warm up in this tight-looking handicap. The second has been rated close to his best.
T/Plt: £20.50 to a £1 stake. Pool: £65,799.84 - 2,334.36 winning units. T/Qpdt: £12.10 to a £1 stake. Pool: £5,906.58 - 361.18 winning units. **Joe Rowntree**

9496 WOLVERHAMPTON (A.W) (L-H)
Thursday, December 19

OFFICIAL GOING: Tapeta: standard
Wind: Light behind Weather: Showers

9546 LADBROKES HOME OF THE ODDS BOOST NURSERY H'CAP 1m 1f 104y (Tp)
4:50 (4:54) (Class 4) (0-85,82) 2-Y-0
£4,463 (£1,328; £663; £400; £400; £400) **Stalls** Low

Form RPR

0631 **1** **Summeronsevenhills (USA)**[30] 9044 2-9-7 **82** ....(b) ShaneKelly 6 92
(Richard Hughes) *s.i.s: hdwy over 4f out: led over 1f out: drvn out* **9/4**[1]

0401 **2** *2 ¾* **Locked N' Loaded**[19] 9250 2-9-0 **75** .... BarryMcHugh 4 80
(Tim Fitzgerald) *a.p: chsd ldr 7f out tl led over 2f out: rdn and hdd over 1f out: styd on same pce ins fnl f* **4/1**[2]

3223 **3** *1 ¾* **Arabian Moon**[73] 7971 2-9-3 **78** .... RichardKingscote 3 79
(Ralph Beckett) *sn pushed along in rr: hdwy and hung lft over 1f out: swtchd rt ins fnl f: nt trble ldrs* **5/1**

3311 **4** *7* **Goddess Of Fire**[7] 9449 2-8-3 **67** 12ex....(p) DarraghKeenan(3) 5 55
(John Ryan) *prom on outer: chsd ldr 2f out tl over 1f out: wknd ins fnl f* **9/2**[3]

321 **5** *14* **Urban Hero (IRE)**[19] 9243 2-9-1 **76** ....(b) DanielTudhope 2 38
(Archie Watson) *led: rdn and hdd over 2f out: wknd and eased over 1f out (stewards inquiry into performance; trainer's rep said gelding was unsuited by being taken on for the lead on this occasion)* **11/2**

3101 **6** *31* **Island Storm (IRE)**[27] 9110 2-9-3 **78** .... LukeMorris 1
(Heather Main) *w ldr 2f: remained handy: drvn along over 4f out: wknd over 2f out: eased (stewards inquiry into performance; jockey said colt stopped quickly; trainer's rep could offer no explanation other than colt has had a long season and they now intend to give the colt a break.)* **20/1**

1m 59.23s (-1.57) **Going Correction** -0.025s/f (Stan) 6 Ran SP% **105.8**
Speed ratings (Par 98): **105,102,101,94,82 54**
CSF £9.94 TOTE £1.80: £1.40, £1.60; EX 10.80 Trifecta £39.40.
Owner Frank Deely And John McGarry **Bred** George E Bates Trustee **Trained** Upper Lambourn, Berks

FOCUS
A competitive nursery as five of the six runners had won their previous races. The pace was fair, they finished well strung out and the form should prove reliable.

9547 LADBROKES WHERE THE NATION PLAYS FILLIES' NOVICE STKS (PLUS 10 RACE) 7f 36y (Tp)
5:25 (5:29) (Class 5) 3-Y-0
£3,428 (£1,020; £509; £254) **Stalls** High

Form RPR

1 **I Love You Baby** 3-9-0 0 .... LukeMorris 1 70
(Michael Appleby) *led early: chsd ldr: shkn up to ld over 1f out: sn edgd lft: drvn out* **33/1**

425 **2** *nk* **Qatar Queen (IRE)**[20] 9213 3-9-0 72 .... DanielMuscutt 6 69
(James Fanshawe) *plld hrd and prom: shkn up over 2f out: rdn to chse wnr ins fnl f: r.o* **4/7**[1]

6530 **3** *6* **Friday Fizz (IRE)**[89] 7472 3-9-0 57 ....(h[1]) RichardKingscote 3 53
(Mark Loughnane) *sn led: rdn: hung rt and hdd over 1f out: wknd wl ins fnl f* **9/1**[3]

003 **4** *2 ¼* **Loretta (IRE)**[27] 9112 3-9-0 60 .... CallumRodriguez 5 47
(Julie Camacho) *chsd ldrs: shkn up over 1f out: wknd ins fnl f* **5/2**[2]

5 *18* **Wildmountainthyme** 3-8-11 0 .... FinleyMarsh(3) 4
(Stella Barclay) *s.i.s: outpcd: hdwy on outer over 3f out: wknd over 2f out (jockey said filly ran green throughout)* **100/1**

1m 29.36s (0.56) **Going Correction** -0.025s/f (Stan) 5 Ran SP% **106.2**
Speed ratings (Par 99): **95,94,87,85,64**
CSF £50.76 TOTE £18.20: £3.90, £1.10; EX 19.40 Trifecta £122.00.
Owner Craig & Laura Buckingham **Bred** North Bradon Stud **Trained** Oakham, Rutland

FOCUS
This looked an ordinary novice for three-year-old fillies with none of the five having won a race and two dominating the market. The pace was decent.

9548 BOMBARDIER "MARCH TO YOUR OWN DRUM" H'CAP 7f 36y (Tp)
6:00 (6:00) (Class 6) (0-60,61) 3-Y-0
£2,781 (£827; £413; £400; £400; £400) **Stalls** High

Form RPR

4422 **1** **Reasoned (IRE)**[19] 9253 3-9-7 **60** .... ShaneKelly 8 67
(James Eustace) *chsd ldr over 6f out tl led over 1f out: sn rdn and edgd lft: hung rt wl ins fnl f: styd on* **7/2**[2]

000 **2** *nk* **French Twist**[12] 9361 3-9-3 **59** ....(b) ThomasGreatrex(3) 6 65
(David Loughnane) *hld up: nt clr run over 2f out: hdwy over 1f out: rdn to chse wnr and edgd rt wl ins fnl f: r.o* **16/1**

242 **3** *½* **Elzaam's Dream (IRE)**[17] 9277 3-9-5 **58** ....(h) DavidProbert 5 63
(Ronald Harris) *s.i.s: hld up: swtchd rt and pushed along over 2f out: rdn over 1f out: r.o ins fnl f: nt rch ldrs* **3/1**[1]

4 *nk* **Latent Heat (IRE)**[109] 6767 3-9-7 **60** .... RobHornby 11 64
(Tony Carroll) *s.i.s: hld up: hdwy over 1f out: rdn and hmpd ins fnl f: styng on whn hmpd again wl ins fnl f* **14/1**

5001 **5** *½* **Sepahi**[19] 9253 3-9-1 **61** ....(b) GraceMcEntee(7) 10 64
(Henry Spiller) *s.i.s: hld up: hdwy over 1f out: rdn and hung lft ins fnl f: styng on whn hmpd wl ins fnl f* **7/1**

0130 **6** *2 ¼* **Penarth Pier (IRE)**[20] 9217 3-9-8 **61** .... RobertHavlin 4 58
(Christine Dunnett) *led: rdn and hdd over 1f out: no ex wl ins fnl f* **5/1**[3]

6500 **7** *1 ½* **Darwina**[10] 9396 3-8-7 **46** oh1 .... JamesSullivan 12 40
(Alistair Whillans) *sn prom: rdn over 2f out: styd on same pce fr over 1f out* **80/1**

0400 **8** *¾* **Moveonup (IRE)**[10] 9386 3-9-6 **59** ....(p) LukeMorris 9 51
(Gay Kelleway) *racd keenly: prom: wnt 2nd 5f out tl shkn up 2f out: wknd ins fnl f (jockey said gelding ran too free)* **25/1**

4350 **9** *hd* **Bullington Boy (FR)**[20] 9217 3-9-4 **60** .... DarraghKeenan(3) 1 51
(Jane Chapple-Hyam) *hld up: nt clr run 1/2-way: nvr on terms (jockey said gelding was denied a clear run between the 4f and 3f markers behind a weakening filly)* **6/1**

0000 **10** *½* **Andies Armies**[7] 9446 3-8-0 **46** oh1 ....(p) GavinAshton(7) 7 36
(Lisa Williamson) *hld up in tch: racd keenly: rdn over 1f out: wknd ins fnl f* **100/1**

4416 **11** *6* **Sharrabang**[56] 8502 3-8-11 **53** ow1 .... FinleyMarsh(3) 2 28
(Stella Barclay) *prom: rdn over 2f out: wknd over 1f out (jockey said gelding stopped quickly)* **8/1**

0000 **12** *34* **Calima Calling (IRE)**[21] 9209 3-8-13 **52** ....(p[1]) AlistairRawlinson 3
(Michael Appleby) *mid-div: pushed along and wknd 1/2-way* **50/1**

1m 28.66s (-0.14) **Going Correction** -0.025s/f (Stan) 12 Ran SP% **122.4**
Speed ratings (Par 98): **99,98,98,97,97 94,92,92,91,91 84,45**
CSF £59.30 CT £192.78 TOTE £4.20: £1.80, £5.00, £1.20; EX 54.30 Trifecta £363.70.
Owner Park Lodge Racing **Bred** Diomed Bloodstock Ltd **Trained** Newmarket, Suffolk
■ Stewards' Enquiry : Thomas Greatrex two-day ban: careless riding (Jan 2-3)

FOCUS
A 0-60 handicap for three-year-olds. Most were exposed, the pace was ordinary and the form is unlikely to prove anything special. The likes of the third and a few close up behind help confirm the level.

9549 BETWAY H'CAP 6f 20y (Tp)
6:30 (6:31) (Class 4) (0-85,85) 3-Y-0+
£5,207 (£1,549; £774; £400; £400; £400) **Stalls** Low

Form RPR

3420 **1** **Katheefa (USA)**[121] 6319 5-9-4 **82** .... JamesSullivan 10 90
(Ruth Carr) *s.i.s: hld up: hdwy over 1f out: r.o to ld nr fin* **28/1**

3600 **2** *hd* **Storm Over (IRE)**[59] 8400 5-9-4 **82** .... BenCurtis 6 89
(Phillip Makin) *s.i.s: rcvrd to chse ldrs after 1f: rdn to ld ins fnl f: hdd nr fin* **9/2**[2]

000 **3** *nk* **Double Up**[146] 5395 8-9-4 **82** ....(t[1]) RobertHavlin 5 88
(Ian Williams) *s.i.s: hld up: racd keenly: swtchd rt and hdwy over 1f out: sn rdn: r.o* **40/1**

1040 **4** *2 ¼* **Mokaatil**[5] 9478 4-9-7 **85** ....(p) MartinDwyer 9 84
(Ian Williams) *broke wl: sn lost pl: racd wd fr 1/2-way: shkn up over 1f out: r.o ins fnl f: nt trble ldrs* **14/1**

0300 **5** *nk* **Spoof**[20] 9214 4-9-7 **85** ....(h) KieranShoemark 12 83
(Charles Hills) *hld up: racd keenly: swtchd rt over 1f out: r.o ins fnl f: nvr nrr (vet said gelding lost its right hind shoe)* **16/1**

3054 **6** *1* **Restless Rose**[30] 9057 4-9-3 **81** .... RichardKingscote 13 76
(Stuart Williams) *sn chsng ldrs: led 4f out tl hdd 2f out: rdn and ev ch ins fnl f: wknd towards fin* **13/2**[3]

03-0 **7** *nk* **So Brave**[20] 9214 3-9-2 **80** .... CharlesBishop 2 74
(Eve Johnson Houghton) *led 2f: led again 2f out: rdn: edgd rt and hdd ins fnl f: wknd towards fin* **50/1**

-352 **8** *nk* **Kamra (USA)**10 9387 5-8-13 **77**.............................(b) AlistairRawlinson 8 70
(Michael Appleby) *chsd ldrs: nt clr run and lost pl over 3f out: hdwy over 1f out: no ex ins fnl f* **7/2**1

0354 **9** *4* **Whisper Aloud**10 9387 3-9-2 **80**.............................. DanielTudhope 7 60
(Archie Watson) *chsd ldrs: rdn over 2f out: wknd ins fnl f* **7/2**1

2012 **10** *1* **With Caution (IRE)**61 8349 3-9-6 **84**.............................. ShaneKelly 4 61
(James Eustace) *s.i.s and hmpd s: shkn up over 1f out: nvr on terms (jockey said filly was slowly away)* **12/1**

0110 **11** *10* **Big Les (IRE)**13 9348 4-9-6 **84**.............................. LukeMorris 3 29
(Karen McLintock) *chsd ldrs: drvn along over 3f out: wknd and eased fnl f (jockey said gelding stopped quickly; trainer's rep said gelding may benefit from a break)* **14/1**

1103 **12** *2 3/4* **Eye Of The Water (IRE)**55 8522 3-9-4 **82**.................... DavidProbert 11 18
(Ronald Harris) *sn prom: edgd lft over 3f out: pushed along over 2f out: sn wknd: eased fnl f (stewards inquiry into performance; trainer said jockey had to make too much use of the gelding early from a wide draw on this occasion)* **18/1**

1m 13.64s (-0.86) **Going Correction** -0.025s/f (Stan) **12 Ran SP% 116.0**
Speed ratings (Par 105): **104,103,103,100,99 98,98,97,92,91 77,74**
CSF £145.84 CT £5138.01 TOTE £25.90: £7.50, £2.00, £11.40; EX 257.10 Trifecta £3735.80.
Owner Michael Hill **Bred** Shadwell Farm LLC **Trained** Huby, N Yorks
■ Stewards' Enquiry : Robert Havlin two-day ban: misuse of the whip (Jan 2-3)

FOCUS
No more than a fair 0-85 6f handicap with mainly exposed sorts and with only half a length covering the first three home the form is unlikely to prove strong. The pace was decent but it collapsed in the final furlong leaving the closers to fight out the finish.

9550 BETWAY HEED YOUR HUNCH H'CAP — 5f 21y (Tp)
7:00 (7:01) (Class 4) (0-80,80) 4-Y-O+

£5,207 (£1,549; £774; £400; £400; £400) **Stalls** Low

Form RPR

0064 **1** **Dynamo Walt (IRE)**6 9458 8-8-11 **70**.............................. LewisEdmunds 7 81
(Derek Shaw) *hld up: hdwy over 1f out: led ins fnl f: rdn out* **14/1**

2260 **2** *1 1/4* **Foxy Forever (IRE)**30 9057 9-9-6 **79**..........................(bt) FrannyNorton 8 85
(Michael Wigham) *trckd ldrs: plld hrd: ev ch ins fnl f: sn rdn and edgd lft: styd on same pce* **10/1**

1663 **3** *nse* **Tathmeen (IRE)**19 9257 4-8-11 **70**.............................. CallumRodriguez 9 76
(Antony Brittain) *s.i.s: hld up: hdwy and hung lft fr over 1f out: nt clr run ins fnl f: r.o* **3/1**1

3362 **4** *1 1/4* **Canford Bay (IRE)**16 9286 5-9-7 **80**..........................(h1) CamHardie 3 81+
(Antony Brittain) *hmpd s: hld up: nt clr run and r.o ins fnl f: nt rch ldrs (jockey said gelding was hampered at the start and was also denied a clear run inside the final furlong)* **7/2**2

1160 **5** *3/4* **Union Rose**16 9286 7-9-7 **80**..........................(v) DavidProbert 6 79
(Ronald Harris) *led 3f: led again over 1f out: rdn and hdd ins fnl f: hmpd sn after: styd on same pce* **16/1**

2250 **6** *1/2* **Excellent George**16 9286 7-9-4 **77**..........................(t) PJMcDonald 5 74
(Stuart Williams) *chsd ldrs: rdn over 1f out: nt clr run ins fnl f: styd on same pce* **6/1**3

5046 **7** *1/2* **Boom The Groom (IRE)**142 5524 8-9-7 **80**.................... RobHornby 1 75
(Tony Carroll) *stmbld s: sn prom: nt clr run and lost pl after 1f: hdwy over 1f out: nt clr run ins fnl f: styd on same pce* **6/1**3

0063 **8** *1/2* **Green Door (IRE)**10 9390 8-8-8 **74**....................(v) GraceMcEntee(7) 11 67
(Robert Cowell) *chsd ldr 4f out: led 2f out: rdn and hdd over 1f out: wknd wl ins fnl f* **18/1**

1006 **9** *3/4* **Zapper Cass (FR)**10 9390 6-9-1 **74**..........................(be) BenCurtis 10 65
(Michael Appleby) *pushed along to chse ldrs on outer: rdn over 1f out: wknd ins fnl f* **10/1**

0300 **10** *nse* **Tan**9 9402 5-8-0 **66** oh5.............................. GavinAshton(7) 4 56
(Lisa Williamson) *edgd lft s: hld up: racd keenly: hmpd over 4f out: swtchd rt 1/2-way: rdn wl over 1f: sn outpcd (jockey said gelding jumped awkwardly from the stalls)* **66/1**

1m 0.46s (-1.44) **Going Correction** -0.025s/f (Stan) **10 Ran SP% 113.3**
Speed ratings (Par 105): **110,108,107,105,104 103,103,102,101,101**
CSF £141.86 CT £533.72 TOTE £12.50: £3.70, £2.80, £1.50; EX 139.50 Trifecta £933.60.
Owner Derek Shaw **Bred** Dan Major **Trained** Sproxton, Leics
■ Stewards' Enquiry : Franny Norton caution: careless riding

FOCUS
This was quite a competitive 5f handicap featuring several horses with good records here. The pace was respectable. Straightforward form, with the second and third rated to their recent form.

9551 PLAY 4 TO SCORE AT BETWAY H'CAP — 6f 20y (Tp)
7:30 (7:32) (Class 6) (0-55,55) 4-Y-O+

£2,781 (£827; £413; £400; £400; £400) **Stalls** Low

Form RPR

5405 **1** **Dubai Elegance**5 9477 5-9-5 **54**..........................(p) LewisEdmunds 11 61
(Derek Shaw) *hld up: nt clr run and swtchd lft ins fnl f: str run to ld nr fin* **10/1**

2303 **2** *nk* **Puchita (IRE)**31 9039 4-9-3 **52**..........................(p) CamHardie 8 58
(Antony Brittain) *chsd ldrs: led and edgd rt over 1f out: rdn ins fnl f: hdd nr fin (jockey said filly hung right under pressure)* **10/1**

1442 **3** *1 1/4* **Dandilion (IRE)**19 9246 6-9-3 **52**.............................. LukeMorris 1 54
(Alex Hales) *hld up in tch: rdn to chse ldr ins fnl f styd on same pce towards fin* **11/1**

5055 **4** *3/4* **Billyoakes (IRE)**16 9287 7-9-3 **52**..........................(p) ShaneKelly 10 52
(Ollie Pears) *prom: chsd ldr over 3f out: led 2f out: rdn and hdd over 1f out: styd on same pce wl ins fnl f* **25/1**

0000 **5** *nk* **Our Man In Havana**16 9287 4-9-6 **55**.............................. RobHornby 3 54
(Tony Carroll) *chsd ldrs: rdn over 1f out: styd on same pce wl ins fnl f* **16/1**

3023 **6** *1 1/4* **Mansfield**16 9287 6-9-6 **55**.............................. RobertHavlin 4 50
(Stella Barclay) *s.i.s: hld up: hdwy over 1f out: no ex ins fnl f* **3/1**1

2020 **7** *3/4* **Brockey Rise (IRE)**5 9477 4-9-6 **55**..........................(v) BenCurtis 6 48
(David Evans) *led early: chsd ldrs: pushed along on outer over 2f out: no ex ins fnl f* **4/1**2

6016 **8** *1/2* **Santafiora**26 9133 5-9-2 **51**.............................. CallumRodriguez 2 43
(Julie Camacho) *racd keenly: sn prom: rdn and nt clr run over 1f out: no ex ins fnl f* **9/2**3

0350 **9** *1* **Roaring Rory**26 9133 6-9-3 **52**.............................. PJMcDonald 9 41
(Ollie Pears) *s.i.s: outpcd: hdwy over 1f out: no ex ins fnl f* **8/1**

1000 **10** *nk* **Krazy Paving**16 9287 7-9-2 **51**..........................(p) EoinWalsh 7 39
(Olly Murphy) *sn led: rdn and hdd 2f out: wknd ins fnl f* **50/1**

5416 **11** *nk* **Filbert Street**42 8898 4-9-4 **53**..........................(b) DavidProbert 5 40
(Roy Brotherton) *hld up: rdn over 1f out: n.d (jockey said gelding was slowly away)* **33/1**

1m 14.17s (-0.33) **Going Correction** -0.025s/f (Stan) **11 Ran SP% 115.4**
Speed ratings (Par 101): **101,100,98,97,97 95,94,94,92,92 92**
CSF £102.01 CT £1139.42 TOTE £10.60: £3.40, £2.60, £2.80; EX 111.80 Trifecta £1793.00.
Owner Million Dreams Racing 1 **Bred** Glebe Stud & J F Dean **Trained** Sproxton, Leics

FOCUS
Exposed sorts in this 0-55 handicap over 6f in which the pace was ordinary though the winner came from some way back.

9552 BETWAY LIVE CASINO H'CAP — 1m 1f 104y (Tp)
8:00 (8:01) (Class 6) (0-55,60) 3-Y-O+

£2,781 (£827; £413; £400; £400; £400) **Stalls** Low

Form RPR

1045 **1** **Necoleta**7 9446 3-9-3 **53**..........................(p1) LiamKeniry 2 63
(Sylvester Kirk) *pushed along and prom: lost pl 8f out: shkn up 1/2-way: hdwy on outer over 1f out: rdn to ld ins fnl f: r.o wl* **7/1**

2560 **2** *3 3/4* **Pike Corner Cross (IRE)**6 9456 7-9-4 **52**..........................(vt) BenCurtis 8 55
(David Evans) *hld up in tch: shkn up on outer over 2f out: rdn and ev ch ins fnl f: styd on same pce* **5/1**3

0101 **3** *1* **Born To Reason (IRE)**9 9403 5-9-12 **60** 5ex..........(b) DanielMuscutt 1 61
(Alexandra Dunn) *led 1f: hmpd and lost pl over 7f out: hdwy over 1f out: ev ch ins fnl f: sn hung rt and rdn: styd on same pce* **10/1**

0-03 **4** *1 3/4* **Usanecolt (IRE)**17 9279 3-9-3 **53**.............................. NicolaCurrie 5 51
(Jamie Osborne) *hld up: hdwy: nt clr run and swtchd lft over 1f out: sn rdn: styd on same pce ins fnl f* **5/1**3

0050 **5** *2* **Clovenstone**17 9279 3-8-10 **46**.............................. CamHardie 10 40
(Alistair Whillans) *s.i.s: pushed along and hdwy over 7f out: chsd ldr over 4f out: rdn to ld over 1f out: hdd & wknd ins fnl f* **20/1**

4053 **6** *3/4* **Elena Osorio (IRE)**15 9305 3-9-4 **54**..........................(b1) LukeMorris 7 47
(Ed Walker) *trckd ldrs: racd keenly: rdn over 1f out: wknd ins fnl f* **9/2**2

3000 **7** *hd* **Mamdood (IRE)**13 9345 5-9-5 **53**..........................(vt) ShaneKelly 11 45
(Stef Keniry) *led after 1f: rdn and hdd over 1f out: wknd ins fnl f* **12/1**

2132 **8** *hd* **Muraaqeb**7 9444 5-9-7 **55**..........................(p) DavidProbert 4 47
(Milton Bradley) *hld up in tch: rdn over 3f out: wknd ins fnl f (jockey said gelding had no more to give; trainer's rep added the race may have come too soon for the gelding following its run 7 days ago)* **4/1**1

0402 **9** *2 3/4* **Sir Magnum**16 9282 4-8-13 **47**..........................(h) RobHornby 9 34
(Tony Carroll) *prom: pushed along over 4f out: rdn and wknd over 1f out* **9/1**

10 *3 1/2* **But I Like It (IRE)**27 9115 3-9-1 **54**....................(vt) DarraghKeenan(3) 13 34
(Fergal Birrane, Ire) *pushed along to go prom over 7f out: rdn whn hmpd and wknd 1f out* **40/1**

6300 **11** *43* **Mr Frankie**283 1146 8-8-5 **46** oh1..........................(p) SiobhanRutledge(7) 6
(Alan Phillips) *s.i.s: hld up: wknd 4f out* **40/1**

2m 0.23s (-0.57) **Going Correction** -0.025s/f (Stan)
WFA 3 from 4yo+ 2lb **11 Ran SP% 120.4**
Speed ratings (Par 101): **101,97,96,95,93 92,92,92,89,86 48**
CSF £42.27 CT £354.88 TOTE £8.00: £2.60, £2.80, £3.30; EX 45.00 Trifecta £318.60.
Owner Miss A Jones **Bred** Saleh Al Homaizi & Imad Al Sagar **Trained** Upper Lambourn, Berks

FOCUS
A modest 0-55 handicap run at an ordinary gallop but with a decisive winner.

9553 BETWAY CASINO H'CAP — 1m 5f 219y (Tp)
8:30 (8:32) (Class 6) (0-55,60) 4-Y-O+

£2,781 (£827; £413; £400; £400; £400) **Stalls** Low

Form RPR

0304 **1** **Butterfield (IRE)**7 9447 6-9-1 **49**.............................. EoinWalsh 11 56
(Brian Forsey) *a.p: chsd ldr over 3f out: led over 2f out: sn rdn: all out* **17/2**

0625 **2** *nk* **Tulane (IRE)**23 9168 4-9-8 **56**..........................(t) LukeMorris 3 63
(Richard Phillips) *chsd ldrs: rdn to chse wnr over 1f out: styd on u.p* **7/2**2

3041 **3** *1 3/4* **Doctor Jazz (IRE)**3 9497 4-9-12 **60** 5ex..........................(vt) BenCurtis 9 64
(Michael Appleby) *hld up in tch: shkn up and hung lft fr over 2f out: rdn over 1f out: styd on same pce wl ins fnl f* **5/1**3

0200 **4** *6* **Lyford (IRE)**17 9275 4-9-5 **53**..........................(p) PJMcDonald 7 48
(Alistair Whillans) *sn chsng ldr: led over 3f out tl over 2f out: sn rdn: wknd ins fnl f* **8/1**

0006 **5** *3 1/2* **Attain**15 9312 10-8-7 **48**.............................. KateLeahy(7) 10 38
(Archie Watson) *s.i.s: hld up: rdn over 2f out: nvr on terms (jockey said gelding was slowly away)* **33/1**

0465 **6** *1 1/4* **Earthly (USA)**15 9312 5-8-7 **46**..........................(bt) PoppyBridgwater(5) 1 34
(Bernard Llewellyn) *hld up: n.d* **25/1**

0031 **7** *2 1/4* **Enmeshing**5 9481 6-9-10 **58** 5ex..........................(p) DanielMuscutt 5 43
(Alexandra Dunn) *led early: sn stdd to trck ldrs: pushed along and swtchd rt over 3f out: rdn and wknd over 1f out (jockey said gelding stopped quickly)* **2/1**1

00-0 **8** *5* **Fool To Cry (IRE)**139 2695 6-9-0 **48**..........................(p) AndrewMullen 2 26
(Johnny Farrelly) *hld up: n.d* **16/1**

/60- **9** *1 1/4* **Wedding Photo (USA)**20 9230 5-8-12 **46** oh1.................... ShaneGray 8 22
(Peter Fahey, Ire) *s.s: a in rr* **20/1**

0400 **10** *32* **Petra's Pony (IRE)**15 9310 4-8-12 **46** oh1.................... MartinDwyer 4
(Brian Meehan) *sn led: clr over 7f out tl hdd over 3f out: hmpd and wknd sn after* **20/1**

-000 **11** *19* **Unsuspected Girl (IRE)**34 1519 6-8-12 **46** oh1..........(t) DavidProbert 6
(Milton Bradley) *hld up: a in rr: rdn and wknd over 3f out* **66/1**

3m 4.27s (3.27) **Going Correction** -0.025s/f (Stan) **11 Ran SP% 117.5**
Speed ratings (Par 101): **89,88,87,84,82 81,80,77,76,58 47**
CSF £35.95 CT £168.37 TOTE £9.50: £2.60, £1.10, £2.00; EX 49.00 Trifecta £252.40.
Owner Alan Stevens & Brian Forsey **Bred** Lynch Bages Ltd **Trained** Ash Priors, Somerset
■ Stewards' Enquiry : Eoin Walsh two-day ban: misuse of the whip (Jan 2-3)

FOCUS
A 1m6f 0-55 handicap featuring exposed and mainly hard-to-win with sorts. The pace was ordinary and five went clear when it developed into a bit of a sprint up the straight.
T/Plt: £347.50 to a £1 stake. Pool: £104,850.57 - 220.25 winning units T/Qpdt: £121.80 to a £1 stake. Pool: £15,402.77 - 93.53 winning units **Colin Roberts**

9554 - 9558a (Foreign Racing) - See Raceform Interactive

9539 SOUTHWELL (L-H)

Friday, December 20

OFFICIAL GOING: Fibresand: standard (racing abandoned after race 4 (3.20) due to a waterlogged track)

Wind: Virtually nil Weather: Heavy rain

9559 BOMBARDIER GOLDEN BEER H'CAP — 7f 14y(F)

1:35 (1:36) (Class 5) (0-70,70) 3-Y-O+

£3,428 (£1,020; £509; £300; £300; £300) **Stalls** Low

Form				RPR
4652 **1** Private Matter[21] 9223 5-9-6 **69**......(p) JackMitchell 8 78
(Amy Murphy) *mde all: rdn wl over 1f out: drvn ins fnl f: hld on wl* **7/1[3]**

4100 **2** ½ **Al Suil Eile (FR)**[14] 9349 3-9-2 **65**...... JasonHart 9 73
(John Quinn) *cl up: rdn to chal wl over 1f out: drvn and ev ch ins fnl f: no ex towards fin* **16/1**

0052 **3** 3 ½ **The Right Choice (IRE)**[23] 9182 4-8-12 **68**......(b) GeorgeRooke(7) 1 66
(James Ferguson) *prom on inner: effrt over 2f out: rdn wl over 1f out: drvn and kpt on same pce fnl f* **9/1**

6301 **4** *nse* **Bedtime Bella (IRE)**[23] 9182 3-9-7 **70**......(v) BenCurtis 2 68
(Michael Appleby) *awkward s: sn chsng ldrs: rdn along over 2f out: drvn over 1f out: kpt on same pce fnl f (jockey said filly fly leapt leaving the stalls)* **10/1**

5642 **5** 1 ¼ **Fieldsman (USA)**[43] 8902 7-8-11 **67**...... LauraCoughlan(7) 6 62
(Tony Carroll) *chsd ldrs: rdn along wl over 2f out: drvn wl over 1f out: grad wknd* **8/1**

631 **6** 1 ¾ **Gleeful**[32] 9032 3-9-7 **70**......(v) DanielTudhope 4 60
(David O'Meara) *hld up towards rr: hdwy and wd st: pushed along over 2f out: rdn wl over 1f out: kpt on: n.d* **9/1**

3511 **7** *nk* **Bee Machine (IRE)**[15] 9337 4-8-3 **59**......(t) ZakWheatley(7) 3 48
(Declan Carroll) *towards rr: pushed along 1/2-way: hdwy over 2f out: sn rdn and kpt on: n.d* **6/1[2]**

-004 **8** ½ **Silver Dust (IRE)**[49] 8719 3-9-6 **69**...... BarryMcHugh 10 57
(Richard Fahey) *dwlt and in rr: hdwy 3f out: rdn along 2f out: kpt on: n.d* **11/2[1]**

0045 **9** 1 **Rock Of Estonia (IRE)**[21] 9223 4-9-4 **67**......(p[1]) LukeMorris 12 52
(Michael Squance) *towards rr: pushed along and wd st: rdn over 2f out: no hdwy* **22/1**

5200 **10** *nse* **Momtalik (USA)**[8] 9443 4-9-7 **70**...... LewisEdmunds 7 55
(Derek Shaw) *in rr and rdn along bef 1/2-way: nvr a factor* **33/1**

2300 **11** 1 ½ **Bombastic (IRE)**[16] 9306 4-9-5 **68**...... JoeyHaynes 14 49
(John Butler) *racd wd: a in rr* **33/1**

4505 **12** *hd* **Socru (IRE)**[14] 9351 3-8-10 **64**...... GerO'Neill(5) 5 44
(Michael Easterby) *in tch on inner: rdn along 3f out: sn wknd* **10/1**

0004 **13** 6 **Scorched Breath**[15] 9329 3-8-10 **64**......(vt[1]) AledBeech(5) 13 28
(Charlie Fellowes) *chsd ldrs on outer: rdn along 3f out: sn drvn and wknd* **14/1**

0065 **14** 1 **Sylviacliffs (FR)**[9] 9423 3-8-13 **62**......(p) CliffordLee 11 23
(K R Burke) *prom: pushed along 1/2-way: rdn 3f out: sn drvn and wknd* **22/1**

1m 26.69s (-3.61) **Going Correction** -0.30s/f (Stan) **14** Ran SP% **118.6**
Speed ratings (Par 103): **108,107,103,103,101 99,99,99,97,97 96,95,89,87**
CSF £106.79 CT £1041.43 TOTE £7.70: £3.00, £6.10, £3.40; EX 128.30 Trifecta £1316.30.
Owner Paul Foster & Friends 2 **Bred** Cheveley Park Stud Ltd **Trained** Newmarket, Suffolk

FOCUS
A fair 7f handicap with several coming into it in decent form. It was a strange race for it was run at a decent clip, but very few featured and the first five were the first five throughout so it is hard to know what the form is worth.

9560 BETWAY (S) H'CAP — 2m 102y(F)

2:10 (2:11) (Class 6) (0-60,62) 3-Y-O+

£2,781 (£827; £413; £300; £300; £300) **Stalls** Low

Form RPR
0005 **1** **Sea Of Mystery (IRE)**[15] 9336 6-9-10 **60**......(be) AlistairRawlinson 3 68+
(Michael Appleby) *hld up towards rr: smooth hdwy 4f out: cl up on outer 3f out: led 2f out: rdn clr over 1f out: kpt on strly* **11/8[1]**

0503 **2** 3 ½ **Irish Minister (USA)**[24] 8639 4-8-10 **51**......(t) TobyEley(5) 8 54
(David Thompson) *dwlt and in rr: hdwy 4f out: pushed along over 2f out: rdn wl over 1f out: chsd wnr ent fnl f: sn drvn and no imp* **7/2[2]**

0606 **3** 2 ¾ **Panatos (FR)**[4] 9497 4-9-8 **58**...... CamHardie 7 58
(Alexandra Dunn) *trckd ldrs: hdwy 4f out: pushed along to chal wl over 2f out: sn rdn: drvn wl over 1f out: kpt on same pce* **12/1**

/655 **4** 1 ½ **Never A Word (USA)**[4] 9497 5-9-6 **56**......(bt) DanielMuscutt 6 54
(Alexandra Dunn) *trckd ldrs on inner: effrt 3f out: rdn along and ch 2f out: sn drvn and one pce* **11/1**

5354 **5** 1 **General Allenby**[16] 9312 5-8-3 **46** oh1......(p) GavinAshton(7) 1 43
(Shaun Keightley) *a in rr* **4/1[3]**

0000 **6** 13 **Scrafton**[13] 9367 8-9-10 **60**...... GeorgeDowning 4 41
(Tony Carroll) *cl up: led 6f out: rdn along 3f out: hdd 2f out: sn drvn and wknd* **12/1**

0000 **7** 43 **Ezanak (IRE)**[8] 9447 6-9-12 **62**......(p) PaulMulrennan 5
(John Wainwright) *prom: pushed along on outer 6f out: rdn along wl over 3f out: sn outpcd and bhd* **40/1**

0500 **8** 92 **Sleepdancer (IRE)**[9] 9412 3-8-1 **46** oh1......(t) DarraghKeenan(3) 2
(John Ryan) *led: pushed along and hdd 6f out: rdn 5 out: sn lost pl and bhd: t.o fnl 3f (jockey said gelding stopped quickly)* **25/1**

3m 41.17s (-4.33) **Going Correction** -0.30s/f (Stan)
WFA 3 from 4yo+ 6lb **8** Ran SP% **114.3**
Speed ratings (Par 101): **98,96,94,94,93 87,65,19**
CSF £6.21 CT £38.38 TOTE £2.30: £1.30, £1.40, £2.20; EX 7.40 Trifecta £41.40.There was no bid for the winner.
Owner Frank McAleavy **Bred** Sunderland Holdings Inc **Trained** Oakham, Rutland

FOCUS
A modest seller with most of the runners having poor strike rates. It was run at a moderate gallop and the form is likely to be weak. The winner is rated in line with this year's better form.

9561 BOMBARDIER "MARCH ON YOUR OWN DRUM" H'CAP — 1m 13y(F)

2:45 (2:46) (Class 4) (0-80,82) 3-Y-O+

£5,207 (£1,549; £774; £387; £300; £300) **Stalls** Low

Form RPR
3054 **1** **Directory**[22] 9199 4-9-6 **78**...... LukeMorris 1 86
(James Eustace) *trckd ldrs: hdwy 3f out: rdn to ld 2f out: sn edgd rt: drvn ent fnl f: kpt on wl* **5/1[2]**

5636 **2** 1 ¼ **Tukhoom (IRE)**[10] 9404 6-9-10 **82**......(b) DanielTudhope 9 87
(David O'Meara) *trckd ldrs on outer: hdwy 3f out: effrt 2f out: sn chsng wnr: rdn over 1f out: drvn ins fnl f: no imp towards fin* **6/1[3]**

1142 **3** 1 ½ **Makambe (IRE)**[23] 9180 4-9-1 **73**......(p) JoeyHaynes 4 75
(Chelsea Banham) *broke wl: restrained and hld up towards rr: pushed along and hdwy 3f out: rdn over 2f out: drvn wl over 1f out: kpt on fnl f* **3/1[1]**

2616 **4** *shd* **Samphire Coast**[8] 9440 6-9-9 **81**......(v) BenCurtis 3 82
(Derek Shaw) *in rr: pushed along over 3f out: rdn wl over 2f out: kpt on fnl f* **3/1[1]**

4264 **5** 2 **Glory Of Paris (IRE)**[9] 9422 5-9-1 **73**......(h[1]) AlistairRawlinson 5 70
(Michael Appleby) *trckd ldng pair: hdwy 3f out: sn cl up: rdn and ev ch 2f out: drvn over 1f out: grad wknd* **8/1**

6064 **6** 1 ¾ **Angel Palanas**[23] 9183 5-9-2 **77**......(p) HarrisonShaw(3) 8 70
(K R Burke) *cl up: led over 4f out: rdn along 3f out: hdd 2f out: sn drvn and wknd* **8/1**

0422 **7** 2 ¾ **Azzeccagarbugli (IRE)**[17] 9283 6-8-12 **75**......(v) KevinLundie(5) 2 61
(Mike Murphy) *chsd ldrs: rdn along 3f out: sn drvn and wknd over 2f out* **10/1**

0300 **8** 4 ½ **Azor Ahai**[16] 9306 3-8-7 **66**...... KieranO'Neill 6 41
(Chris Gordon) *slt ld: pushed along and hdd over 4f out: rdn over 3f out: sn wknd* **66/1**

1-00 **9** 34 **Artois**[61] 4639 3-9-7 **80**...... DanielMuscutt 7
(Alexandra Dunn) *chsd ldrs: rdn along 1/2-way: sn lost pl and bhd* **50/1**

1m 40.92s (-2.78) **Going Correction** -0.30s/f (Stan)
WFA 3 from 4yo+ 1lb **9** Ran SP% **115.7**
Speed ratings (Par 105): **101,99,98,98,96 94,91,87,53**
CSF £35.10 CT £105.90 TOTE £5.90: £1.70, £1.90, £1.50; EX 42.50 Trifecta £233.40.
Owner Blue Peter Racing 16 **Bred** Juddmonte Farms Ltd **Trained** Newmarket, Suffolk

FOCUS
This wasn't the most competitive of 0-80 handicaps though the pace was fair. The first two both raced well towards the stand side.

9562 BETWAY HEED YOUR HUNCH H'CAP — 4f 214y(F)

3:20 (3:20) (Class 3) (0-90,89) 3-Y-O+

£7,470 (£2,236; £1,118; £559; £279; £140) **Stalls** Centre

Form RPR
0010 **1** **Tawny Port**[16] 9301 5-9-7 **89**...... DanielTudhope 2 104
(Stuart Williams) *hld up: hdwy 2f out: rdn over 1f out: qcknd to chal ent fnl f: kpt on strly to ld last 100yds* **15/8[1]**

4411 **2** ½ **Hareem Queen (IRE)**[43] 8900 3-9-5 **87**...... PJMcDonald 3 100
(K R Burke) *slt ld centre: pushed along 2f out: rdn over 1f out: jnd and drvn ent fnl f: hdd and no ex last 100yds* **9/4[2]**

0221 **3** 1 ½ **Samovar**[15] 9334 4-8-11 **79**......(b) JamesSullivan 1 87
(Scott Dixon) *cl up centre: rdn along 2f out: drvn over 1f out: kpt on same pce fnl f* **11/2[3]**

0600 **4** ½ **Moonraker**[32] 9030 7-9-1 **83**...... AlistairRawlinson 7 89
(Michael Appleby) *racd nr stands' rail: cl up: rdn along 2f out: drvn over 1f out: kpt on same pce fnl f* **16/1**

0050 **5** 1 **Foolaad**[70] 8099 8-9-6 **88**......(t) LewisEdmunds 4 90
(Roy Bowring) *cl up centre: rdn along 2f out: sn drvn and wknd over 1f out* **13/2**

6606 **6** 4 **Moon Trouble (IRE)**[11] 9389 6-9-5 **87**...... BenCurtis 5 75
(Michael Appleby) *racd towards stands' side: chsd ldrs: rdn along 2f out: sn wknd* **17/2**

56.99s (-2.71) **Going Correction** -0.30s/f (Stan) **6** Ran SP% **110.7**
Speed ratings (Par 107): **109,108,105,105,103 97**
CSF £6.14 TOTE £2.80: £1.70, £1.40; EX 7.60 Trifecta £22.70.
Owner Mrs J Morley **Bred** Mrs D O'Brien **Trained** Newmarket, Suffolk

FOCUS
An interesting 5f handicap with a lightly-raced filly chasing a hat-trick up against some experienced AW sprinters. The first three were the three lowest drawn horses and may have had an edge.

9563 BETWAY CASINO H'CAP — 2m 2f 98y(F)

(3:50) (Class 5) (0-75,) 3-Y-O+

£

9564 BOMBARDIER BRITISH HOPPED AMBER BEER H'CAP — 7f 14y(F)

(4:20) (Class 6) (0-55,) 3-Y-O+

£

9565 BOMBARDIER H'CAP — 1m 13y(F)

(4:50) (Class 6) (0-65,) 3-Y-O+

£

T/Plt: £8.70 to a £1 stake. Pool: £75,717.69 - 6,321.80 winning units T/Qpdt: £1.50 to a £1 stake. Pool: £7,892.28 - 3,655.18 winning units **Joe Rowntree**

9546 WOLVERHAMPTON (A.W) (L-H)

Friday, December 20

OFFICIAL GOING: Tapeta: standard

Wind: Light behind Weather: Overcast

9566 BOMBARDIER "MARCH TO YOUR OWN DRUM" H'CAP — 7f 36y (Tp)

5:00 (5:01) (Class 6) (0-60,65) 4-Y-O+

£2,781 (£827; £413; £400; £400; £400) **Stalls** High

Form RPR
5011 **1** **Steal The Scene (IRE)**[4] 9503 7-9-9 **62** 4ex......(tp) JasonWatson 9 68
(Kevin Frost) *sn prom: chsd ldr 1/2-way: rdn over 2f out: led over 1f out: edgd lft ins fnl f: jst hld on* **5/2[1]**

1205 **2** *shd* **Viola Park**[9] 9420 5-9-7 **60**....(p) DavidProbert 6 66
(Ronald Harris) *hld up: hdwy 1/2-way: rdn and hung lft fr over 1f out: r.o* **10/1**

201 **3** *hd* **Calin's Lad**[9] 9420 4-9-9 **65** 5ex.... TheodoreLadd(3) 2 70+
(Michael Appleby) *chsd ldr 1f: remained handy: racd keenly: shkn up and swtchd rt ins fnl f: r.o (jockey said gelding was denied a clear run approaching the final furlong)* **11/4**[2]

3603 **4** *1 ½* **Rockesbury**[20] 9253 4-8-13 **55**....(p) ThomasGreatrex(3) 4 57
(David Loughnane) *led: hdd over 4f out: chsd ldr to 1/2-way: rdn and hung lft over 1f out: styd on* **9/1**

3336 **5** *¾* **Sarasota (IRE)**[17] 6304 4-9-4 **57**.... CharlesBishop 11 57
(Paul George) *hld up: nt clr run over 1f out: swtchd rt and r.o ins fnl f: nt rch ldrs (jockey said filly was denied a clear run for some distance approaching the final furlong)* **66/1**

10 **6** *¾* **Magwadiri (IRE)**[79] 7811 5-9-6 **59**.... AndrewMullen 3 57
(Mark Loughnane) *s.i.s: hld up: racd keenly: shkn up over 1f out: r.o ins fnl f: nt rch ldrs* **80/1**

0056 **7** *½* **Peachey Carnehan**[6] 9477 5-9-4 **57**....(v) PhilDennis 7 54
(Michael Mullineaux) *hld up: rdn over 1f out: r.o towards fin: nvr nrr* **12/1**

1001 **8** *½* **The King's Steed**[7] 9456 6-9-4 **57** 5ex....(bt) AdamKirby 8 52
(Shaun Lycett) *chsd ldr 6f out: led over 4f out: rdn and hdd over 1f out: no ex ins fnl f* **6/1**[3]

060- **9** *1* **Roman Warrior**[49] 8733 4-8-12 **54**....(v) GabrieleMalune(3) 5 47
(Fergal Birrane, Ire) *chsd ldrs: rdn over 1f out: wknd wl ins fnl f* **8/1**

01-0 **10** *1 ¼* **Connemera Queen**[16] 9305 6-9-5 **58**....(p) RobertHavlin 10 48
(John Butler) *hld up: pushed along 1/2-way: nvr on terms* **40/1**

1m 28.6s (-0.20) **Going Correction** -0.125s/f (Stan) **10** Ran SP% **112.6**
Speed ratings (Par 101): **96,95,95,93,93 92,91,91,89,88**
CSF £27.06 CT £73.24 TOTE £3.20: £1.30, £2.80, £1.50; EX 27.70 Trifecta £109.50.
Owner Curzon House Partnership & Friends **Bred** Shane Doyle **Trained** Newcastle-under-Lyme, Staffs
FOCUS
A modest handicap.

9567 LADBROKES WHERE THE NATION PLAYS NOVICE STKS 7f 36y (Tp)
5:30 (5:32) (Class 5) 2-Y-O £3,428 (£1,020; £509; £254) **Stalls** High

Form RPR

4 **1** **Amazing News**[20] 9252 2-9-2 0.... CallumShepherd 2 79+
(George Scott) *wnt rt s: mde all: rdn clr and edgd lft fnl f: eased nr fin* **5/2**[1]

30 **2** *4 ½* **Ayr Harbour**[16] 9299 2-8-13 0.... TheodoreLadd(3) 9 68
(Michael Appleby) *hld up in tch: plld hrd: lost pl 5f out: pushed along on outer over 2f out: rdn and edgd lft fr over 1f out: r.o ins fnl f: wnt 2nd nr fin: no ch w wnr* **18/1**

0 **3** *nk* **Bayar**[58] 8455 2-9-2 0.... AdamKirby 8 67
(Clive Cox) *s.i.s and hmpd s: hdwy over 5f out: rdn to chse wnr and hung lft fnl f: styd on same pce* **4/1**[3]

00 **4** *2 ¼* **September Power (IRE)**[15] 9323 2-8-11 0.... JackMitchell 4 56
(Roger Varian) *s.i.s: hld up: pushed along over 2f out: r.o ins fnl f: nvr nrr* **40/1**

3 **5** *2* **Global Esteem (IRE)**[101] 7055 2-9-2 0....(h) LukeMorris 6 56
(Gay Kelleway) *wnt rt s: plld hrd and prom: wnt 2nd over 5f out tl shkn up over 2f out: hung lft and wknd ins fnl f* **3/1**[2]

0 **6** *1 ¼* **Lethal Shadow**[20] 9252 2-9-2 0....(t[1]) DanielMuscutt 7 53+
(Marco Botti) *s.i.s and hmpd s: hdwy 1/2-way: rdn over 1f out: wknd fnl f (jockey said gelding hung left in the home straight)* **33/1**

65 **7** *2 ½* **Where Next Jo**[137] 5745 2-8-4 0.... LauraPearson(7) 5 42
(David Evans) *chsd ldrs: lost pl 1/2-way: wknd over 1f out* **100/1**

8 *1 ¾* **Brodick** 2-8-4 0.... RhonaPindar(7) 12 38
(K R Burke) *s.i.s: nvr nrr (jockey said filly was slowly away and ran green)* **50/1**

9 *½* **Cool To Be A Cat (FR)** 2-9-2 0.... JasonWatson 1 41
(Ian Williams) *chsd wnr tl over 5f out: remained handy: wnt 2nd again over 2f out: shkn up over 1f out: wknd ins fnl f* **20/1**

10 *6* **Rock Of Pensax (IRE)** 2-9-2 0.... AndrewMullen 11 26
(Mark Loughnane) *s.i.s: a in rr* **100/1**

0 **11** *1 ¾* **The Cherokee Kid (IRE)**[7] 9451 2-8-9 0.... CameronIles(7) 3 22
(David Evans) *s.i.s and hmpd s: a in rr* **125/1**

31 **12** *13* **Blake's Vision (IRE)**[32] 9029 2-9-6 0.... DavidProbert 10
(Mark Johnston) *sn chsng ldrs on outer: shkn up 3f out: wknd over 2f out (trainer's rep could offer no explanation for colt's performance)* **4/1**[3]

1m 28.2s (-0.60) **Going Correction** -0.125s/f (Stan) **12** Ran SP% **113.7**
Speed ratings (Par 96): **98,92,92,89,87 86,83,81,80,73 71,57**
CSF £45.24 TOTE £3.20: £1.50, £3.70, £1.70; EX 40.70 Trifecta £180.60.
Owner W J and T C O Gredley **Bred** Stetchworth & Middle Park Studs Ltd **Trained** Newmarket, Suffolk
FOCUS
This proved fairly straightforward for the favourite. The form is a bit fluid.

9568 LADBROKES FOOTBALL ACCA BOOSTY NURSERY H'CAP 7f 36y (Tp)
6:00 (6:03) (Class 5) (0-70,71) 2-Y-O
£3,428 (£1,020; £509; £400; £400; £400) **Stalls** High

Form RPR

3350 **1** **Wailea Nights (IRE)**[27] 9137 2-9-1 **63**.... JasonWatson 7 67
(Marco Botti) *hld up: hdwy on outer over 1f out: rdn to ld ins fnl f: r.o wl (trainer said filly benefited from a trouble free run on this occasion)* **16/1**

564 **2** *1 ½* **Barking Mad**[16] 9307 2-9-3 **65**.... AdamKirby 9 65
(David Evans) *hld up: racd keenly: swtchd rt and hdwy over 1f out: rdn and ev ch ins fnl f: edgd lft and styd on same pce towards fin* **4/1**[2]

6461 **3** *2 ½* **Richard R H B (IRE)**[27] 9137 2-9-7 **69**.... ShaneGray 3 63
(David Loughnane) *chsd ldrs: pushed along over 2f out: rdn to ld briefly 1f out: no ex ins fnl f* **6/4**[1]

4603 **4** *2 ¼* **Little Ted**[24] 9164 2-8-11 **59**....(bt) RobHornby 5 47
(Tim Easterby) *chsd ldrs: rdn and ev ch 1f out: wknd ins fnl f* **9/2**[3]

422 **5** *1 ¼* **Holy Eleanor (IRE)**[8] 9448 2-9-6 **68**....(p) LukeMorris 8 53
(Archie Watson) *w ldr tl led over 2f out: rdn: edgd rt and hdd 1f out: wknd ins fnl f* **6/1**

600 **6** *¾* **Lady Codee**[58] 8453 2-9-1 **63**.... RobertHavlin 4 46
(Michael Attwater) *s.i.s: hdwy over 1f out: wknd ins fnl f* **66/1**

000 **7** *shd* **Amicia**[20] 9242 2-9-0 **62**.... DanielMuscutt 1 45
(Marco Botti) *prom: pushed along 1/2-way: rdn and ev ch over 1f out: wknd ins fnl f* **20/1**

5120 **8** *13* **Interrupted Dream**[65] 8259 2-9-4 **66**.... DavidProbert 2 17
(Gay Kelleway) *led over 4f: wknd fnl f (vet said gelding finished lame on its left hind)* **18/1**

1m 28.31s (-0.49) **Going Correction** -0.125s/f (Stan) **8** Ran SP% **109.9**
Speed ratings (Par 96): **97,95,92,89,88 87,87,72**
CSF £72.80 CT £146.01 TOTE £15.00: £3.30, £1.80, £1.10; EX 70.00 Trifecta £237.30.
Owner Khalid Bin Ali Al Khalifa **Bred** Sheikh Khalid Bin Ali Al Khalifa **Trained** Newmarket, Suffolk
FOCUS
A competitive nursery and there was a bit of a turn-up. The winner is basically rated in line with his best pre-race form.

9569 LADBROKES "PLAY 1-2-FREE" ON FOOTBALL NOVICE STKS 6f 20y (Tp)
6:30 (6:33) (Class 5) 2-Y-O £3,428 (£1,020; £509; £254) **Stalls** Low

Form RPR

52 **1** **Batchelor Boy (IRE)**[22] 9195 2-9-2 0.... DanielMuscutt 1 75
(Marco Botti) *mde virtually all: shkn up over 1f out: rdn out* **5/4**[1]

06 **2** *1 ¼* **Lakeview (IRE)**[246] 1893 2-9-2 0.... DavidProbert 2 71
(David Loughnane) *sn chsng wnr: rdn over 1f out: styd on same pce towards fin* **66/1**

3 *nk* **Vormir (IRE)**[63] 8324 2-8-13 0.... GabrieleMalune(3) 8 70
(Fergal Birrane, Ire) *chsd ldrs: rdn over 1f out: r.o to go 3rd nr fin* **20/1**

223 **4** *nk* **Spreadsheet (IRE)**[98] 7160 2-9-2 **85**....(h[1]) CharlieBennett 5 69
(Jim Boyle) *trckd ldrs: rdn and edgd rt ins fnl f: kpt on* **11/2**

00 **5** *3 ¼* **Diamond Cottage**[17] 9284 2-8-11 0.... RobertHavlin 6 55
(Malcolm Saunders) *hld up in tch: shkn up over 1f out: nt trble ldrs* **100/1**

34 **6** *½* **Inhalation**[29] 9085 2-9-2 0.... PJMcDonald 10 58
(Ed Vaughan) *hld up on outer: racd keenly: shkn up over 1f out: nvr trbld ldrs* **4/1**[3]

00 **7** *½* **Limaro Prospect (IRE)**[9] 9413 2-9-2 0.... LukeMorris 4 57+
(Sir Mark Prescott Bt) *hld up in tch: rdn and hung lft over 1f out: wknd ins fnl f (jockey said colt hung left under pressure)* **50/1**

00 **8** *1 ¾* **Sena**[9] 9413 2-8-11 0.... HowardCheng 9 46
(William Haggas) *hld up: nvr on terms* **100/1**

9 *3* **Vape** 2-9-2 0.... RobHornby 7 42
(Ralph Beckett) *s.i.s: a in rr (jockey said colt ran green)* **3/1**[2]

0 **10** *10* **Elixir Sky**[17] 9284 2-8-11 0.... JaneElliott 3 7
(Kevin Frost) *s.s: in rr and pushed along over 3f out: rdn and wknd over 1f out* **125/1**

1m 14.2s (-0.30) **Going Correction** -0.125s/f (Stan) **10** Ran SP% **115.8**
Speed ratings (Par 96): **97,95,94,94,90 89,88,86,82,69**
CSF £117.47 TOTE £1.90: £1.10, £6.70, £3.70; EX 118.30 Trifecta £1439.90.
Owner Middleham Park Racing Cxx & Partner 1 **Bred** C M Farrell **Trained** Newmarket, Suffolk
FOCUS
Few got into this, those at the front dominating throughout in another race where pace held up.

9570 #BETYOURWAY AT BETWAY H'CAP 1m 5f 219y (Tp)
7:00 (7:01) (Class 5) (0-75,76) 3-Y-O+
£3,428 (£1,020; £509; £400; £400; £400) **Stalls** Low

Form RPR

0533 **1** **Dance To Paris**[17] 9288 4-9-12 **75**....(b) JackMitchell 10 84
(Lucy Wadham) *chsd ldrs: wnt 2nd 4f out: shkn up to ld over 2f out: rdn out* **3/1**[2]

0230 **2** *¾* **Iconic Belle**[25] 7301 5-9-4 **74**.... NickBarratt-Atkin(7) 2 82
(Philip Kirby) *s.i.s: hld up: hdwy over 5f out: chsd wnr over 1f out: styd on* **80/1**

5 **3** *4 ½* **Flat To The Max (FR)**[111] 6745 4-9-13 **76**.... DougieCostello 1 78
(Tim Fitzgerald) *s.i.s: hmpd and stmbld over 13f out: hld up: nt clr run over 2f out: hdwy over 1f out: sn rdn and flashed tail: r.o to go 3rd nr fin: nt rch ldrs* **22/1**

152 **4** *shd* **Mauricio (IRE)**[106] 6896 5-9-6 **69**....(p) CamHardie 9 71
(Stella Barclay) *s.i.s: hld up: hdwy over 1f out: styd on: nt rch ldrs* **50/1**

5050 **5** *hd* **Manjaam (IRE)**[9] 9419 6-9-13 **76**....(p) PJMcDonald 6 77
(Ian Williams) *s.i.s: pushed along: swtchd rt and hdwy to ld over 12f out: hdd over 2f out: sn rdn: no ex ins fnl f* **5/2**[1]

0003 **6** *5* **Dragon Mountain**[13] 9367 4-9-0 **63**.... CallumRodriguez 12 57
(Keith Dalgleish) *led: hdd over 12f out: chsd ldr tl over 9f out: remained handy: rdn over 2f out: wknd over 1f out (vet said gelding lost its left fore shoe)* **7/2**[3]

4025 **7** *½* **Rosie Royale (IRE)**[96] 7231 7-9-0 **63**.... JasonWatson 5 57
(Roger Teal) *chsd ldrs: lost pl 12f out: rdn over 2f out: n.d after* **20/1**

4445 **8** *1* **Pumblechook**[23] 9184 6-9-2 **65**.... AndrewMullen 4 57
(Iain Jardine) *prom: hmpd and lost pl sn after s: n.d after* **15/2**

60/3 **9** *nse* **California Lad**[56] 8537 6-8-11 **63**....(vt) GabrieleMalune(3) 3 55
(Fergal Birrane, Ire) *s.i.s: hld up: rdn over 2f out: n.d* **20/1**

0306 **10** *1 ¾* **Double Reflection**[15] 9333 4-9-3 **66**.... LukeMorris 11 56
(Michael Appleby) *chsd ldrs: wnt 2nd over 9f out tl 4 out: sn rdn: wknd over 1f out* **33/1**

3540 **11** *1* **Archippos**[125] 6210 6-9-7 **70**.... PhilDennis 13 58
(Michael Herrington) *prom: pushed along 5f out: wknd 2f out* **18/1**

3m 2.13s (1.13) **Going Correction** -0.125s/f (Stan) **11** Ran SP% **112.8**
Speed ratings (Par 103): **91,90,88,87,87 84,84,84,84,83 82**
CSF £239.97 CT £4372.01 TOTE £3.90: £1.60, £10.50, £5.40; EX 119.10 Trifecta £2464.00.
Owner The Calculated Speculators **Bred** D Curran **Trained** Newmarket, Suffolk
■ Stewards' Enquiry : Jason Watson four-day ban; careless riding (Jan 3-6)
FOCUS
A fair staying handicap.

9571 BETWAY H'CAP 5f 21y (Tp)
7:30 (7:34) (Class 2) (0-105,105) 3-Y£01,971 (£3,583; £1,791; £896; £446) **Stalls** Low

Form RPR

0501 **1** **Lomu (IRE)**[17] 9286 5-8-3 **87**.... AndrewMullen 2 97
(Iain Jardine) *s.i.s: hld up: plld hrd: hdwy and nt clr run over 1f out: nt clr run: shkn up and qcknd to ld wl ins fnl f: r.o* **7/2**[1]

5534 **2** *1* **Royal Birth**[16] 9301 8-9-2 **100**....(t) JasonWatson 3 106
(Stuart Williams) *hld up: swtchd rt 1/2-way: rdn over 1f out: r.o u.p ins fnl f: wnt 2nd towards fin (jockey said gelding hung right under pressure)* **6/1**

3043 **3** *¾* **El Hombre**[14] 9348 5-8-7 **91**.... ShaneGray 9 95
(Keith Dalgleish) *s.i.s: hld up: nt clr run and swtchd rt ins fnl f: r.o to go 3rd post: nt rch ldrs* **13/2**

4341 **4** *shd* **Acclaim The Nation (IRE)**[7] 9458 6-8-5 **89** 5ex....(p) PhilDennis 1 92
(Eric Alston) *led: rdn and hdd over 1f out: ev ch wl ins fnl f: styd on same pce towards fin* **4/1**[2]

0002 **5** *nk* **Junius Brutus (FR)**[44] 8851 3-8-8 **92**.... RobHornby 4 94
(Ralph Beckett) *chsd ldrs: rdn over 1f out: styd on* **8/1**

4620 **6** *½* **Corinthia Knight (IRE)**[6] 9478 4-9-7 **105**.... LukeMorris 6 105
(Archie Watson) *chsd ldrs: pushed along 1/2-way: rdn over 1f out: styd on same pce ins fnl f* **8/1**

4140 **7** *nk* **The Daley Express (IRE)**[44] 8867 5-8-5 **89**.... KieranO'Neill 5 88
(Ronald Harris) *chsd ldr tl led over 1f out: rdn: edgd lft and hdd wl ins fnl f: no ex* **18/1**

552 8 1 ½ **Savalas (IRE)**[7] 9458 4-8-2 **86** oh2 CamHardie 7 80
(Robert Cowell) *sn pushed along in rr: carried rt 1/2-way: rdn over 1f out: n.d* **9/2**[3]

59.75s (-2.15) **Going Correction** -0.125s/f (Stan) **8** Ran SP% **115.5**
Speed ratings (Par 109): **112,110,109,109,108 107,107,104**
CSF £25.04 CT £131.02 TOTE £4.80: £2.00, £2.20, £1.70; EX 32.80 Trifecta £190.50.
Owner Steve Macdonald **Bred** Michael G Daly **Trained** Carruthertown, D'fries & G'way

FOCUS
A decent sprint handicap run at a good pace and won by a 5yo who has returned to the top of his game for his new trainer.

9572 BETWAY LIVE CASINO H'CAP 5f 21y (Tp)
8:00 (8:00) (Class 6) (0-55,59) 3-Y-O+

£2,781 (£827; £413; £400; £400; £400) **Stalls** Low

Form RPR
0013 1 **Mutabaahy (IRE)**[6] 9473 4-9-11 **59** 5ex CamHardie 5 70
(Antony Brittain) *trckd ldrs: shkn up to ld over 1f out: rdn out* **2/1**[1]
5012 2 2 **Sir Hector (IRE)**[10] 9406 4-9-7 **55** LukeMorris 9 59
(Charlie Wallis) *sn pushed along towards rr: reminders over 3f out: hdwy over 1f out: r.o u.p to go 2nd wl ins fnl f: nt rch wnr* **3/1**[2]
0053 3 1 **Harry's Ridge (IRE)**[24] 9169 4-9-5 **53** JasonHart 1 53
(Eric Alston) *restless in stalls: pushed along to chse ldrs: wnt 2nd 1/2-way: rdn and ev ch over 1f out: styd on same pce ins fnl f* **2/1**[1]
3443 4 1 **Maid Millie**[27] 9133 3-9-1 **54** (h[1]) RayDawson(5) 11 51
(Jane Chapple-Hyam) *s.i.s: pushed along in rr: edgd lft and r.o ins fnl f: nvr nrr* **12/1**[3]
4010 5 2 **Rangefield Express (IRE)**[15] 9335 3-9-3 **51** (b) SamJames 7 40
(Geoffrey Harker) *chsd ldrs: rdn over 1f out: wknd ins fnl f* **20/1**
5064 6 nse **Kibaar**[11] 9398 7-8-13 **47** TomEaves 6 36
(Ruth Carr) *restless in stalls: hld up: hmpd over 3f out: nvr on terms* **25/1**
0600 7 2 **Autumn Splendour (IRE)**[18] 9272 3-9-4 **52** (b) DavidProbert 10 34
(Milton Bradley) *dwlt: in rr whn hmpd over 3f out: nvr on terms* **33/1**
0300 8 2 ½ **Edged Out**[24] 9169 9-9-0 **51** (p) MitchGodwin(3) 4 24
(Christopher Mason) *led: rdn and hdd over 1f out: wknd ins fnl f* **66/1**
0106 9 7 **Miss Gradenko**[18] 9272 3-9-3 **51** (p) PJMcDonald 3
(Robert Cowell) *w ldr tl over 3f out: pushed along 1/2-way: wknd over 1f out* **14/1**

1m 0.67s (-1.23) **Going Correction** -0.125s/f (Stan) **9** Ran SP% **119.1**
Speed ratings (Par 101): **104,100,99,97,94 94,91,87,75**
CSF £8.25 CT £13.30 TOTE £2.70: £1.20, £1.40, £1.40; EX 8.60 Trifecta £22.10.
Owner Antony Brittain **Bred** Shadwell Estate Company Limited **Trained** Warthill, N Yorks

FOCUS
An ordinary sprint handicap run at a strong pace, and a good effort for the grade from the winner.

9573 BETWAY PLAY 4 TO SCORE AT BETWAY H'CAP 1m 1f 104y (Tp)
8:30 (8:31) (Class 6) (0-65,66) 3-Y-O

£2,781 (£827; £413; £400; £400; £400) **Stalls** Low

Form RPR
1405 1 **Clem A**[13] 9361 3-9-6 **63** JackMitchell 5 70
(Alan Bailey) *trckd ldrs: racd keenly: wnt 2nd 7f out: led over 4f out: shkn up and edgd rt over 1f out: sn rdn and flashed tail: hung lft ins fnl f: styd on* **9/2**[1]
-340 2 2 ½ **Al Daiha**[9] 9426 3-9-5 **62** LukeMorris 7 63
(Ed Walker) *hld up: pushed along and hdwy over 2f out: rdn to go 2nd and hung lft ins fnl f: nt rch wnr* **9/1**
6200 3 2 **Undercolours (IRE)**[14] 9349 3-9-0 **64** (b[1]) StefanoCherchi(7) 8 61
(Marco Botti) *led over 8f out: hdd over 4f out: rdn over 1f out: no ex ins fnl f* **6/1**[2]
564 4 nk **Mystic Dragon**[58] 8467 3-9-3 **60** DanielMuscutt 3 57
(Mrs Ilka Gansera-Leveque) *hld up: swtchd rt and hdwy over 1f out: nt rch ldrs* **16/1**
0354 5 4 **Levanter (FR)**[13] 9361 3-9-6 **63** DavidProbert 10 52
(Harry Dunlop) *hld up: shkn up on outer over 2f out: hung lft fr over 1f out: nvr trbld ldrs* **10/1**
0 6 nk **But I Like It (IRE)**[1] 9552 3-8-8 **54** (vt) DarraghKeenan(3) 4 43
(Fergal Birrane, Ire) *prom: rdn over 1f out: wknd ins fnl f* **40/1**
0-40 7 1 ¼ **Fortissimo (IRE)**[28] 9109 3-9-9 **66** PJMcDonald 2 52
(Mark Johnston) *s.i.s: pushed along to go prom 8f out: hmpd sn after: lost pl over 3f out: n.d after* **9/2**[1]
U340 8 3 ½ **Dancing Jo**[16] 9305 3-9-2 **59** CharlesBishop 1 39
(Mick Channon) *led 1f: chsd ldrs: rdn and wknd over 2f out* **12/1**
0461 9 1 **Triple Nickle (IRE)**[18] 9279 3-8-13 **61** (p) PoppyBridgwater(5) 6 39
(Bernard Llewellyn) *prom: rdn over 3f out: wknd over 2f out* **9/2**[1]
4225 10 3 ¼ **Impressionable**[18] 9279 3-9-0 **57** JaneElliott 9 29
(William Muir) *s.i.s: hld up: hung rt thrght: lost tch fnl 4f (jockey said filly hung badly right and was unsteerable)* **8/1**[3]

2m 0.43s (-0.37) **Going Correction** -0.125s/f (Stan) **10** Ran SP% **115.0**
Speed ratings (Par 98): **96,93,92,91,88 87,86,83,82,79**
CSF £44.92 CT £244.53 TOTE £4.80: £1.90, £3.00, £2.10; EX 47.30 Trifecta £267.40.
Owner The Skills People Group Ltd **Bred** Charley Knoll Partnership **Trained** Newmarket, Suffolk

FOCUS
They didn't go much of a gallop and it paid to be fairly handy.
T/Plt: £44.50 to a £1 stake. Pool: £96,116.95 - 1,574.68 winning units T/Qpdt: £14.30 to a £1 stake. Pool: £11,387.05 - 588.66 winning units **Colin Roberts**

9574 - 9581a (Foreign Racing) - See Raceform Interactive

892 DOHA
Friday, December 20

OFFICIAL GOING: Turf: good

9582a AL RAYYAN STKS (CONDITIONS) (2YO) (TURF) 7f (T)
3:45 2-Y-O £44,881 (£17,322; £8,661; £4,724; £3,149)

RPR
1 **Maystar (IRE)**[13] 9364 2-9-2 0 HollieDoyle 5 97
(Archie Watson) *chsd ldr: drvn along to ld over 1f out: rdn along fnl f: r.o wl*
2 ¾ **Think Big (IRE)**[22] 2-9-2 0 TomLukasek 4 95
(G E Mikhalides, France) *settled bhd ldrs: tk clsr order 1 1/2f out: rdn along to chal ent fnl f: kpt on wl but a hld: rdn out*
3 2 **Happy Bere (FR)**[77] 7887 2-9-2 0 (tp) OlivierPeslier 13 90
(A De Watrigant, France)
4 1 ½ **Flash Henry**[22] 2-9-2 0 (bt) HarryBentley 3 86
(Mohammed Jassim Ghazali, Qatar)
5 nk **Hamish Macbeth**[59] 8426 2-9-2 0 JamesDoyle 12 85+
(Hugo Palmer) *towards rr: asked for effrt and hdwy on outer 2f out: rdn along and kpt on fnl 1 1/2f: nvr on terms w ldrs*
6 2 **Hector Loza**[86] 7602 2-9-2 0 TomMarquand 8 80
(Simon Dow) *midfield: shkn up 2f out: kpt on same pce*
7 nk **Return To Senders (IRE)**[22] 2-9-2 0 (b) J-PGuillambert 7 79
(Jassim Mohammed Ghazali, Qatar)
8 1 ½ **Chattanooga Boy (IRE)**[189] 3812 2-9-2 0 IvanRossi 14 75
(Ahmed Kobeissi, Qatar)
9 1 ½ **Sound Machine (GER)**[62] 2-8-11 0 AndraschStarke 9 66
(Mario Hofer, Germany)
10 ¾ **Mount Fuji (IRE)**[112] 6690 2-9-2 0 (h) RyanCuratolo 6 69
(Debbie Mountain, Qatar)
11 1 ¾ **Fuwayrit (IRE)**[23] 9175 2-9-2 0 SilvestreDeSousa 1 64
(Mark Johnston) *led 100yds: chsd ldrs: lost position 2f out: sn wknd*
12 1 **Skip The Queue (IRE)**[22] 2-9-2 0 (b) AnasAlSeyabi 11 61
(H Al Jehani, Qatar)
13 13 **Wa'ad**[22] 2-8-11 0 RonanThomas 10 21
(H Al Ramzani, Qatar)
14 7 **Six Gun**[22] 2-9-2 0 (b) TheoBachelot 2 7
(Jassim Mohammed Ghazali, Qatar)

1m 21.81s **14** Ran
.
Owner Hambleton Racing Ltd XXXVI **Bred** Ballinvana House Stud **Trained** Upper Lambourn, W Berks

FOCUS
Quite a valuable prize. The winner's Wolverhampton success could perhaps have been rated to this level. Winning rider Hollie Doyle said: "It was quick ground, but they'd had quite a lot of rain and so there was no jar."

9505 LINGFIELD (L-H)
Saturday, December 21

OFFICIAL GOING: Polytrack: standard
Wind: Light behind Weather: Showers

9583 BETWAY CASINO H'CAP 5f 6y(P)
11:45 (11:45) (Class 6) (0-60,59) 3-Y-O+

£2,781 (£827; £413; £300; £300; £300) **Stalls** High

Form RPR
4660 1 **George Thomas**[66] 8263 3-8-12 **57** SelmaGrage(7) 7 64
(Robert Eddery) *a.p: chsd ldr over 3f out: led ins fnl f: pushed out* **16/1**
6121 2 1 **Katherine Place**[25] 9169 4-9-6 **58** (t) EoinWalsh 1 61
(Bill Turner) *pushed along to chse ldrs then racd keenly: rdn over 1f out: led ins fnl f: sn hdd: styd on same pce towards fin (jockey said filly ran too free and hung right-handed in the back straight)* **3/1**[2]
5002 3 ½ **Roundabout Magic (IRE)**[30] 9092 5-9-6 **58** TomMarquand 6 63
(Simon Dow) *s.i.s: hld up: pushed along and hdwy over 1f out: nt clr run and swtchd rt ins fnl f: r.o (jockey said horse was denied a clear run)* **9/4**[1]
5103 4 nse **Terri Rules (IRE)**[21] 9246 4-9-4 **56** DanielMuscutt 5 57
(Lee Carter) *restless in stalls: prom: lost pl after 1f: pushed along 1/2-way: hdwy over 1f out: sn rdn: r.o* **5/1**[3]
3400 5 ½ **Pink Iceburg (IRE)**[51] 8704 3-9-0 **57** RhiainIngram(5) 8 57
(Peter Crate) *chsd ldrs on outer: outpcd wl over 1f out: r.o ins fnl f* **16/1**
6556 6 nk **Pharoh Jake**[10] 9423 11-8-2 **45** AledBeech(5) 3 44
(John Bridger) *chsd ldrs: pushed along 1/2-way: styd on* **25/1**
3006 7 nse **Fareeq**[12] 9386 5-9-4 **56** (bt) DavidProbert 4 54
(Charlie Wallis) *s.i.s: hld up: rdn over 1f out: r.o ins fnl f: nt rch ldrs (jockey said gelding was slowly away)* **7/1**
5050 8 shd **Starchant**[3] 9508 3-8-8 **46** (b[1]) KieranO'Neill 9 44
(John Bridger) *s.i.s: hld up: rdn over 1f out: r.o ins fnl f: nt trble ldrs* **10/1**
0066 9 shd **Angel Force (IRE)**[11] 9406 4-8-11 **52** (p) TheodoreLadd(3) 10 50
(David C Griffiths) *sn led: rdn over 1f out: hdd and no ex ins fnl f* **10/1**

58.23s (-0.57) **Going Correction** -0.075s/f (Stan) **9** Ran SP% **118.7**
Speed ratings (Par 101): **101,99,98,98,97 97,97,97,96**
CSF £65.65 CT £156.49 TOTE £17.60: £4.80, £1.50, £1.10; EX 98.70 Trifecta £467.10.
Owner Robert Eddery **Bred** Fraser & Nell Kent **Trained** Newmarket, Suffolk

FOCUS
A moderate sprint but won by a 3yo open to improvement. Straightforward form.

9584 BETWAY HEED YOUR HUNCH H'CAP 5f 6y(P)
12:20 (12:20) (Class 5) (0-75,77) 3-Y-O£3,428 (£1,020; £509; £300; £300) **Stalls** High

Form RPR
3001 1 **Chitra**[12] 9390 3-9-9 **77** RichardKingscote 8 85
(Daniel Kubler) *chsd ldr: rdn to ld ins fnl f: r.o* **1/1**[1]
6031 2 ¾ **Lalania**[30] 9092 4-8-13 **67** HollieDoyle 7 72
(William Stone) *s.i.s: outpcd: rdn and r.o ins fnl f: wnt 2nd towards fin: nt rch wnr* **15/8**[2]
3400 3 ½ **Cappananty Con**[21] 9257 5-9-4 **72** LukeMorris 1 76
(Charlie Wallis) *chsd ldrs: rdn over 1f out: styd on* **12/1**
0400 4 hd **Warrior's Valley**[12] 9390 4-8-13 **67** (tp) AlistairRawlinson 2 70
(David C Griffiths) *led: racd freely: rdn and hdd ins fnl f: styd on same pce* **6/1**[3]
-000 5 ¾ **Andre Amar (IRE)**[16] 9334 3-8-11 **65** KieranO'Neill 4 65
(Robyn Brisland) *dwlt: hld up: r.o ins fnl f: nt trble ldrs* **16/1**

57.86s (-0.94) **Going Correction** -0.075s/f (Stan) **5** Ran SP% **112.6**
Speed ratings (Par 103): **104,102,102,101,100**
CSF £3.23 TOTE £1.60: £1.10, £1.50; EX 2.90 Trifecta £10.30.
Owner Mr & Mrs G Middlebrook **Bred** Mr & Mrs G Middlebrook **Trained** Lambourn, Berks

FOCUS
They finished quite well bunched at the line, but it proved straightforward enough for the favourite.

9585 LADBROKES WHERE THE NATION PLAYS EBF NOVICE AUCTION STKS 1m 1y(P)
12:55 (12:58) (Class 5) 2-Y-O £3,428 (£1,020; £509; £254) **Stalls** High

Form RPR
2 1 **Rhubarb Bikini (IRE)**[65] 8287 2-9-2 0 (p[1]) HollieDoyle 3 76+
(Archie Watson) *pushed along to ld over 7f out: shkn up over 2f out: rdn out* **1/1**[1]
12 2 1 ¼ **Eevilynn Drew**[8] 9451 2-9-4 0 DylanHogan(5) 5 80
(Robert Eddery) *a.p: rdn to chse wnr over 1f out: styd on (jockey said colt hung left-handed)* **16/1**
32 3 1 ½ **Take Me To The Sky**[113] 6684 2-9-2 0 (w) RobertHavlin 2 70
(Ed Dunlop) *chsd ldrs: rdn over 1f out: styd on same pce ins fnl f* **4/1**[2]

4 ¾ **Made In Italy (IRE)** 2-8-4 0 StefanoCherchi(7) 11 63+
(Marco Botti) *hld up: hdwy over 2f out: rdn over 1f out: styd on* 33/1

42 5 1 ¼ **Time Voyage (IRE)**[30] 9097 2-8-11 0 JasonHart 10 60
(John Quinn) *chsd ldrs: pushed along 1/2-way: outpcd over 1f out: kpt on ins fnl f* 9/2[3]

04 6 1 **Platinum Prince**[21] 9243 2-9-2 0 HectorCrouch 1 63
(Gary Moore) *led early: remained handy: rdn over 2f out: styd on same pce fr over 1f out* 25/1

0 7 ¾ **I Hear Thunder (FR)**[17] 9311 2-8-11 0 TomMarquand 9 56+
(James Tate) *s.i.s: hld up: shkn up over 2f out: nt trble ldrs* 33/1

2 8 hd **Dashing Roger**[74] 7981 2-9-2 0 RichardKingscote 6 61
(William Stone) *chsd wnr over 6f out tl rdn over 1f out: wknd ins fnl f* 7/1

9 nk **Mickey Drippin (IRE)** 2-9-2 0 RobHornby 12 60+
(Noel Williams) *s.i.s: rn green in rr: styd on ins fnl f: nvr nrr* 25/1

10 5 **Strange Brew** 2-8-11 0 KierenFox 7 43
(Michael Attwater) *s.i.s: nvr on terms (vet said filly lost her left-fore shoe)* 22/1

11 8 **Forked Lightning** 2-9-2 0 LiamKeniry 4 30
(Dominic Ffrench Davis) *s.i.s: sn pushed along in rr: wknd over 2f out* 33/1

0 12 3 ¼ **Rich Girl (IRE)**[9] 9448 2-8-8 0 ThomasGreatrex(3) 8 18
(Sylvester Kirk) *hld up: rdn and wknd over 2f out* 66/1

1m 38.19s (-0.01) **Going Correction** -0.075s/f (Stan) 12 Ran SP% **128.9**
Speed ratings (Par 96): **97,95,94,93,92 91,90,90,90,85 77,73**
CSF £22.15 TOTE £1.90: £1.20, £3.00, £1.50; EX 20.10 Trifecta £83.90.
Owner Saxon Thoroughbreds **Bred** M Enright **Trained** Upper Lambourn, W Berks

FOCUS
Just fair novice form, but the pace held up and some meaningful figures were posted down the field.

9586 LADBROKES HOME OF THE ODDS BOOST/IRISH EBF FILLIES' CONDITIONS STKS 7f 1y(P)

1:30 (1:30) (Class 3) 3-Y-O+ **£9,766** (£2,923; £1,461; £731) **Stalls** Low

Form RPR

0000 1 **Rock On Baileys**[17] 9301 4-9-0 92 (b) LewisEdmunds 2 89
(Amy Murphy) *chsd ldrs: wnt 2nd over 2f out: rdn to ld ins fnl f: r.o* 11/4[3]

4606 2 1 ¼ **Lucymai**[23] 9198 6-9-0 95 (e[1]) JoeyHaynes 3 86
(Dean Ivory) *hld up: hdwy 2f out: r.o to go 2nd nr fin: nt rch wnr* 6/4[1]

3543 3 ½ **Visionara**[10] 9424 3-9-0 78 (p[1]) CallumShepherd 1 84
(Simon Crisford) *led: rdn over 1f out: hdd ins fnl f: styd on same pce* 7/4[2]

6066 4 26 **Sonnet Rose (IRE)**[8] 9455 5-9-0 62 (bt) MartinDwyer 5 14
(Conrad Allen) *racd keenly in 2nd tl shkn up over 2f out: wknd over 1f out* 18/1

1m 23.43s (-1.37) **Going Correction** -0.075s/f (Stan) 4 Ran SP% **108.3**
Speed ratings (Par 104): **104,102,102,72**
CSF £7.27 TOTE £3.50; EX 7.20 Trifecta £7.70.
Owner G R Bailey Ltd (Baileys Horse Feeds) **Bred** Petches Farm Ltd **Trained** Newmarket, Suffolk

FOCUS
Not a strong conditions race.

9587 BETWAY QUEBEC STKS (LISTED RACE) 1m 2f (P)

2:00 (2:01) (Class 1) 3-Y-O+ **£20,982** (£7,955; £3,981; £1,983; £995) **Stalls** Low

Form RPR

1201 1 **Dubai Warrior**[44] 8892 3-9-6 107 RobertHavlin 4 111
(John Gosden) *chsd ldr tl shkn up to ld over 2f out: sn edgd rt: rdn clr fnl f* 8/11[1]

1326 2 3 ¾ **Court House (IRE)**[246] 1921 4-9-8 107 KieranO'Neill 1 102
(John Gosden) *trckd ldrs: racd keenly: outpcd 2f out: styd on to go 2nd wl ins fnl f* 14/1

4461 3 nk **Dalgarno (FR)**[23] 9210 6-9-11 100 AdamKirby 5 104
(Jane Chapple-Hyam) *hld up: hdwy over 1f out: sn rdn: styd on to go 3rd wl ins fnl f* 8/1

5531 4 1 ¼ **Victory Bond**[17] 9309 6-9-8 102 JamesDoyle 3 99
(William Haggas) *hld up in tch: shkn up and outpcd 2f out: n.d after* 4/1[2]

1423 5 2 ½ **Kasbaan**[17] 9309 4-9-8 99 AlistairRawlinson 2 94
(Michael Appleby) *led: shkn up and hdd over 2f out: rdn over 1f out: wknd wl ins fnl f* 6/1[3]

2m 2.13s (-4.47) **Going Correction** -0.075s/f (Stan)
WFA 3 from 4yo+ 2lb 5 Ran SP% **110.0**
Speed ratings (Par 111): **114,111,110,109,107**
CSF £11.80 TOTE £1.60: £1.10, £2.80; EX 7.20 Trifecta £65.20.
Owner Sheikh Mohammed Bin Khalifa Al Maktoum **Bred** Essafinaat Ltd **Trained** Newmarket, Suffolk

FOCUS
A smart performance from the winner, who looks a leading contender for the big AW prizes this winter.

9588 BETWAY H'CAP 1m 4f (P)

2:35 (2:35) (Class 2) (0-105,99) 3-Y-O£11,971 (£3,583; £1,791; £896; £446) **Stalls** Low

Form RPR

1/14 1 **Entangling (IRE)**[17] 9309 5-9-0 89 WilliamCarson 5 98
(David Elsworth) *hld up in tch: nt clr run over 2f out: sn swtchd rt: rdn to ld over 1f out: jst hld on* 7/4[1]

0050 2 nk **Circus Couture (IRE)**[17] 9309 7-8-9 89 RayDawson(5) 8 97
(Jane Chapple-Hyam) *prom: lost pl over 9f out: swtchd rt wl over 1f out: gd hdwy fnl f: r.o wl* 14/1

6006 3 ¾ **Petite Jack**[35] 9003 6-9-8 97 (b) JamesDoyle 7 103
(Neil King) *hld up: gd hdwy and hung lft fnl f: running on whn nt clr run towards fin* 12/1

0403 4 2 ½ **Scarlet Dragon**[7] 7408 6-9-10 99 (h) TomMarquand 3 101
(Alan King) *s.i.s: hld up: hdwy and nt clr run over 1f out: styd on to go 4th nr fin* 5/1[3]

0232 5 ½ **Busy Street**[14] 9366 7-9-5 94 AlistairRawlinson 2 96
(Michael Appleby) *led over 2f: chsd ldr: rdn over 3f out: styd on same pce ins fnl f* 13/2

66P0 6 1 **Seafarer (IRE)**[30] 9094 5-8-11 86 (v) MartinDwyer 4 86
(Marcus Tregoning) *hld up: hdwy over 1f out: sn rdn: styd on same pce ins fnl f* 16/1

5205 7 1 **Hulcote**[17] 9302 4-9-5 94 AdamKirby 6 92
(Clive Cox) *s.i.s: hdwy to ld over 9f out: rdn over 2f out: hdd over 1f out: wknd wl ins fnl f* 4/1[2]

4150 8 3 ½ **Mythical Madness**[17] 9309 8-9-1 95 (v) ThoreHammerHansen(5) 1 88
(Simon Dow) *w ldr over 2f: remained handy: rdn over 2f out: wknd ins fnl f* 33/1

6004 9 ½ **Fire Fighting (IRE)**[14] 9366 8-9-0 89 JasonHart 9 81
(Mark Johnston) *pushed along to chse ldrs on outer: rdn over 4f out: carried rt wl over 1f out: hmpd and wknd ent fnl f* 12/1

2m 29.8s (-3.20) **Going Correction** -0.075s/f (Stan) 9 Ran SP% **117.2**
Speed ratings (Par 109): **107,106,106,104,104 103,102,100,100**
CSF £30.10 CT £233.97 TOTE £2.50: £1.40, £3.80, £3.50; EX 23.40 Trifecta £194.10.
Owner Ben CM Wong **Bred** Sweetmans Bloodstock **Trained** Newmarket, Suffolk

FOCUS
A decent handicap won in good style and by a winner who has more to offer on the AW.

9589 BETWAY LIVE CASINO H'CAP 1m 4f (P)

3:10 (3:10) (Class 6) (0-60,60) 3-Y-O+

£2,781 (£827; £413; £300; £300; £300) **Stalls** Low

Form RPR

5140 1 **King Athelstan (IRE)**[17] 9310 4-9-6 56 (b) HectorCrouch 3 63
(Gary Moore) *led 1f: chsd ldrs: rdn to ld wl ins fnl f: styd on* 8/1

0042 2 ½ **Mobham (IRE)**[35] 9005 4-9-10 60 DanielMuscutt 4 66
(J R Jenkins) *s.i.s: hld up: hdwy over 2f out: rdn and ev ch wl ins fnl f: styd on* 6/1[3]

5262 3 1 ½ **Mistress Nellie**[17] 9310 4-9-1 51 HollieDoyle 12 55
(William Stone) *a.p: chsd ldr 10f out: rdn to ld over 1f out: hdd wl ins fnl f: styd on same pce* 11/2[2]

4314 4 ¾ **Banta Bay**[17] 9310 5-9-3 53 JosephineGordon 6 56
(John Best) *chsd ldrs: rdn over 1f out: styd on* 5/1[1]

3062 5 1 ¼ **Toybox**[22] 9216 3-9-6 60 RobHornby 10 62
(Jonathan Portman) *hld up: hdwy over 1f out: r.o* 10/1

4430 6 hd **Passing Clouds**[45] 8854 4-9-0 50 KierenFox 7 50
(Michael Attwater) *led after 1f: hung rt over 9f out: reminders over 7f out: rdn and hdd over 1f out: no ex ins fnl f* 20/1

5064 7 1 ¾ **Mr Fox**[140] 5679 3-9-4 58 CallumShepherd 8 56
(Michael Attwater) *hld up: hdwy over 1f out: nt trble ldrs* 25/1

043- 8 ½ **Billy Star**[387] 9318 4-8-11 47 LiamKeniry 2 44
(Jimmy Fox) *s.i.s: hld up: rdn over 2f out: r.o ins fnl f: nvr nrr* 25/1

6340 9 nse **Bolt N Brown**[22] 9216 3-9-4 58 (v) TomMarquand 1 56
(Gay Kelleway) *prom: rdn over 2f out: wknd ins fnl f* 8/1

0-00 10 2 ¼ **Border Warrior**[32] 9051 3-9-5 59 AdamKirby 14 53
(Henry Candy) *sn chsng ldrs on outer: rdn over 3f out: wknd fnl f* 18/1

5210 11 ¾ **Archdeacon**[45] 8870 3-9-4 58 KieranO'Neill 5 51
(Dean Ivory) *hld up in tch: plld hrd: shkn up and hung lft over 2f out: wknd over 1f out (jockey said gelding ran too free)* 12/1

415- 12 3 ¾ **Bright Saffron**[373] 7302 4-9-9 59 (p) LukeMorris 11 45
(Clare Hobson) *s.i.s: sn pushed along in rr: hrd drvn fr 1/2-way: sme hdwy u.p on outer over 3f out: wknd over 2f out* 50/1

560- 13 1 ¾ **Y Fyn Duw A Fydd**[424] 8500 4-9-6 56 DavidProbert 13 39
(Alan King) *hld up: hdwy on outer over 5f out: rdn and wknd over 2f out* 14/1

5602 14 ½ **Accessor (IRE)**[15] 9345 4-9-1 51 (p) CharlesBishop 15 33
(Michael Wigham) *s.i.s: swtchd lft sn after s: n.d (jockey said gelding was never travelling)* 6/1[3]

0505 15 nk **Miss Pollyanna (IRE)**[22] 9216 3-8-10 50 (h) RobertHavlin 9 33
(Roger Ingram) *hld up: nvr on terms* 25/1

0442 16 2 **Gladden (IRE)**[18] 9289 4-8-9 48 ThomasGreatrex(3) 16 27
(Lee Carter) *s.i.s: hld up: a in rr* 25/1

2m 32.53s (-0.47) **Going Correction** -0.075s/f (Stan)
WFA 3 from 4yo+ 4lb 16 Ran SP% **133.7**
Speed ratings (Par 101): **98,97,96,96,95 95,94,93,93,92 91,89,88,87,87 86**
CSF £56.06 CT £303.69 TOTE £10.30: £2.60, £2.20, £1.70, £1.50; EX 68.60 Trifecta £381.90.
Owner Caplin & Sheridan **Bred** M J Rozenbroek **Trained** Lower Beeding, W Sussex

FOCUS
A competitive but modest affair.
T/Plt: £28.30 to a £1 stake. Pool: £60,785.15 - 1,563.50 winning units T/Qpdt: £17.50 to a £1 stake. Pool: £5,267.18 - 221.98 winning units **Colin Roberts**

9582 DOHA

Saturday, December 21

OFFICIAL GOING: Turf: good

9590a QATAR DERBY (LOCAL GROUP 2) (3YO COLTS & GELDINGS) (TURF) 1m 2f (T)

1:15 3-Y-O **£61,158** (£23,605; £11,802; £6,437; £4,291)

RPR

1 **Pedro Cara (FR)**[105] 6994 3-9-2 0 TonyPiccone 14 104
(M Delcher Sanchez, France) *hld up towards rr: sme hdwy on outside 1/2-way: rdn and gd hdwy fr under 2f out: drvn fnl f: styd on wl to ld 50yds out: readily*

2 1 ¼ **Bangkok (IRE)**[119] 6470 3-9-2 0 (t) SilvestreDeSousa 1 102
(Andrew Balding) *t.k.h in midfield: rdn 2f out: drvn and styd on strly fr over 1f out: led 100yds out: hdd 50yds out: no ex clsng stages*

3 1 ¼ **Al Gazi (IRE)**[23] 3-9-2 0 (t) AnasAlSeyabi 15 99
(Ibrahim Al Malki, Qatar) *hld up towards rr on outside: stdy hdwy into midfield 1/2-way: rdn and styd on wl fr 2f out: short of room fnl 100yds but squeezed through gap to snatch 3rd last stride*

4 nse **Venedegar (IRE)**[6] 3-9-2 0 AlexanderReznikov 6 99
(H Al Ramzani, Qatar) *hld up towards rr: rdn 2f out: styd on strly fnl f: nrst fin*

5 shd **Alwaab (FR)**[91] 7478 3-9-2 0 TheoBachelot 5 99
(F Chappet, France) *in tch in midfield: rdn 2f out: sn chsng ldr: drvn and led ins fnl f: hdd 100yds out: sn no ex*

6 shd **Seeyoubyme (FR)**[17] 3-9-2 0 RyanCuratolo 12 99
(Debbie Mountain, Qatar) *w ldr: rdn to ld 2f out: hdd ins fnl f: no ex fnl 100yds*

7 shd **Markhor (IRE)**[23] 3-9-2 0 (t) LucaManiezzi 7 98
(S Ibido, Qatar) *hld up towards rr: rdn 2f out: styd on wl fnl f: nt clr run fnl 75yds*

8 2 ¾ **Admiral Rous (IRE)**[188] 3903 3-9-2 0 HarryBentley 13 93
(Jassim Mohammed Ghazali, Qatar) *midfield: rdn and hdwy fr over 2f out: wknd ins fnl f*

9 hd **Arabic Channel (USA)**[23] 3-9-2 0 (b) TomLukasek 10 92
(H Al Ramzani, Qatar) *midfield: rdn and effrt 2f out: wknd steadily fnl f*

10 ¾ **Zamharer**[6] 3-9-2 0 J-PGuillambert 9 91
(Mohammed Jassim Ghazali, Qatar) *led: rdn 2 1/2f out: hdd 2f out: drvn fnl f: wkng whn hmpd 100yds out*

11 shd **Dunkirk Harbour (USA)**23 3-9-2 0..........(b) IvanRossi 8 91
(Debbie Mountain, Qatar) *in tch on outside: rdn over 2f out: wknd over 1f out*
12 1/2 **Ernest Aldrich**23 3-9-2 0.......... EduardoPedroza 2 90
(Ibrahim Al Malki, Qatar) *towards rr of midfield: rdn and no imp fr 2f out*
13 3/4 **Say Good Buy (GER)**31 3-9-2 0.......... AndraschStarke 4 88
(Henk Grewe, Germany) *trckd ldrs: rdn 2f out: wknd qckly ins fnl f*
14 10 1/2 **Old Glory (IRE)**141 5609 3-9-2 0.......... RonanThomas 11 67
(H Al Ramzani, Qatar) *a towards rr*
15 4 1/4 **Oklahoma Dancer (USA)**5 3-9-2 0....... AlMoatasembinSaidAlBalush 3 59
(A Selvaratnam, Oman) *a towards rr*
16 5 3/4 **Noble Ancestry**51 3-9-2 0..........(p) MarcoCasamento 16 47
(Jassim Mohammed Ghazali, Qatar) *midfield: lost pl 3f out: sn struggling*
2m 4.66s **16 Ran**

Owner H H Sheikh Mohammed Bin Khalifa Al Thani **Bred** Sas Regnier & O Lesage **Trained** France

FOCUS
A very valuable event.

9591 - 9602a (Foreign Racing) - See Raceform Interactive

9504 DEAUVILLE (R-H)
Sunday, December 22

OFFICIAL GOING: Polytrack: standard

9603a PRIX MISS SATAMIXA - FONDS EUROPEEN DE L'ELEVAGE (LISTED RACE) (3YO+ FILLIES & MARES) (ALL-WEATHER) 7f 110y(P)
2:32 3-Y-O+ £23,423 (£9,369; £7,027; £4,684; £2,342)

RPR
1 **Preening**32 9064 4-8-11 0.......... AurelienLemaitre 13 97
(James Fanshawe) *chsd ldrs on outer: shkn up over 2f out: r.o to ld ins fnl f: kpt on wl* 37/10[1]
2 3/4 **California Love**52 8708 3-8-11 0.......... TomMarquand 2 95
(Richard Spencer) *chsd ldrs between horses: rdn over 2f out: r.o: wnt 2nd clsng stages* 18/1
3 snk **Crotchet**36 9002 4-8-11 0.......... CristianDemuro 9 95
(Joseph Patrick O'Brien, Ire) *trckd ldr: disp ld whn shkn up over 2f out: hdd ent fnl f: no ex* 84/10
4 shd **Jazz Melodie (FR)**31 5-8-11 0.......... FabienLefebvre 11 95
(P De Chevigny, France) 12/1
5 nse **Dream Of Words (IRE)**56 4-8-11 0.......... EddyHardouin 7 94
(J C Cerqueira Germano, Spain) 98/1
6 snk **Dieulefit (IRE)**28 4-8-11 0.......... AntoineHamelin 6 94
(J C Cerqueira Germano, Spain) 81/1
7 3/4 **Testa (IRE)**26 3-8-11 0.......... TheoBachelot 14 92
(S Wattel, France) 69/10
8 nk **Simona (FR)**38 8983 3-8-11 0..........(b) JeromeMoutard 4 91
(F-H Graffard, France) 52/1
9 hd **Heavenly Holly (IRE)**93 7401 4-8-11 0.......... JackMitchell 5 91
(Hugo Palmer) *chsd ldrs on inner: rdn over 2f out: wknd fnl f* 26/1
10 1 1/2 **Zavrinka (FR)**56 4-8-11 0.......... StephanePasquier 3 87
(V Sartori, France) 9/2[2]
11 6 **Jet Setteuse (FR)**63 8376 3-8-11 0.......... GregoryBenoist 15 72
(F Rohaut, France) 10/1
12 2 1/2 **Golden Rajsa (FR)**79 7885 5-8-11 0..........(b) TonyPiccone 10 66
(Pauline Menges, France) 14/1
13 snk **Bella Bolide (FR)**116 5-8-11 0.......... AnthonyCrastus 8 66
(M Brasme, France) 88/1
14 hd **Dutch Treat**36 9010 3-8-11 0.......... DavidProbert 12 65
(Andrew Balding) *racd keenly in rr: rdn over 2f out: n.d* 32/1
15 1 **Nuala (FR)**26 9170 3-8-11 0.......... VincentCheminaud 1 63
(A Fabre, France) 54/10[3]
1m 28.45s **15 Ran SP% 119.1**
PARI-MUTUEL (all including 1 euro stake): WIN 4.70; PLACE 2.40, 5.60, 3.30; DF 35.60.
Owner Cheveley Park Stud **Bred** Cheveley Park Stud Ltd **Trained** Newmarket, Suffolk

9604 - (Foreign Racing) - See Raceform Interactive

9058 CHANTILLY (R-H)
Monday, December 23

OFFICIAL GOING: Polytrack: standard

9605a PRIX DU CARREFOUR DES MARCHANDS DE NAVETS (CLAIMER) (2YO) (ALL-WEATHER TRACK) (POLYTRACK) 6f 110y(P)
11:40 2-Y-O £9,009 (£3,603; £2,702; £1,801; £900)

RPR
1 **Najm**20 2-9-2 0..........(b) MarcNobili 2 77
(F Rossi, France) 29/10[2]
2 3 1/2 **Hernan**44 2-9-1 0.......... MlleZoePfeil(3) 13 69
(Andrea Marcialis, France) 69/10[3]
3 hd **Killing Zoe (FR)**70 2-9-1 0.......... JulesMobian 1 66
(D Guillemin, France) 7/1
4 hd **Sky Vega (IRE)**12 9414 2-9-1 0..........(b1) Pierre-LouisJamin 4 65
(Tom Ward) *rousted along early: midfield: prog on inner 3f out: styd on same pce fnl 2f* 10/1
5 hd **Praise You (IRE)**64 8363 2-8-11 0.......... AdrienMoreau 6 61+
(Tom Ward) *settled towards rr: rdn and nt clr run 2f out: swtchd ins 1 1/2f out: styd on strly fnl 50yds: nvr nrr* 56/1
6 snk **Sneaky**15 2-8-8 0.......... JenteMarien 14 57
(T Van Den Troost, Belgium) 87/1
7 nk **Hard Rock (FR)**21 2-8-11 0.......... BertrandFlandrin 12 59
(Louis Baudron, France) 106/1
8 hd **Es Vedra (FR)**22 2-8-8 0.......... MlleLauraGrosso(3) 5 59
(N Clement, France) 50/1
9 1 1/4 **Esta Bonita (IRE)**21 2-8-8 0.......... LukaRousseau 7 52
(H-A Pantall, France) 11/1
10 1/2 **Lalacelle (FR)**21 2-8-13 0.......... StephaneLaurent 15 56
(S Cerulis, France) 20/1
11 nse **Moonlight Shadow**187 2-8-11 0.......... MlleSophieChuette(4) 10 58
(N Caullery, France) 71/1
12 3/4 **Wasachop (FR)**15 2-8-11 0.......... MlleMarleneMeyer(4) 9 56
(Jane Soubagne, France) 23/10[1]

13 nse **Two Hearts**15 2-8-11 0..........(p) BenjaminHubert 11 51
(P Monfort, France) 14/1
14 1 1/2 **American Lily (FR)**10 2-8-8 0..........(b1) RosarioMangione 3 44
(L Rovisse, France) 52/1
1m 17.74s **14 Ran SP% 119.0**
PARI-MUTUEL (all including 1 euro stake): WIN 3.90; PLACE 1.50, 2.10, 2.10; DF 9.70.
Owner Mme Janina Burger **Bred** Malih L Al Basti **Trained** France

9566 WOLVERHAMPTON (A.W) (L-H)
Thursday, December 26

OFFICIAL GOING: Tapeta: standard
Wind: faint breeze Weather: cool and damp

9606 BOMBARDIER BRITISH HOPPED AMBER BEER H'CAP 7f 36y (Tp)
1:40 (1:42) (Class 5) (0-75,75) 3-Y-O+
£3,428 (£1,020; £509; £300; £300; £300) **Stalls High**

Form RPR
4323 1 **Ghaith**70 8290 4-9-1 72..........(e1) ThomasGreatrex(3) 6 87
(David Loughnane) *led tl hdd after 1f: pushed into ld over 2f out: reminder 2f out: rdn in clr ld over 1f out: in command and pushed out fnl f: easily* 7/2[1]
1000 2 5 **Soar Above**51 8827 4-9-7 75.......... LewisEdmunds 7 76
(John Butler) *chsd ldrs: drvn on outer 2f out: rdn over 1f out: kpt on into 2nd fnl f: no ch w wnr* 8/1
2020 3 3/4 **Robero**54 8761 7-9-5 73..........(e) DavidProbert 12 72
(Gay Kelleway) *mid-div: pushed along 2f out: hdwy into 3rd over 1f out: sn rdn: kpt on fnl f* 4/1[2]
1053 4 1/2 **Smokey Lane (IRE)**21 9334 5-9-0 75..........(v) LauraPearson(7) 8 73
(David Evans) *mid-div: pushed along and lost pl over 2f out: swtchd to outer 1 1/2f out: rdn over 1f out: kpt on into 4th fnl f* 9/1
4000 5 shd **Baltic Prince (IRE)**29 9176 9-8-9 70.......... ElishaWhittington(7) 9 67
(Tony Carroll) *prom: led after 1f: hdd and rdn over 2f out: no ex fr over 1f out* 16/1
0015 6 2 1/2 **Roller**13 9453 6-9-0 68..........(p) DougieCostello 1 59
(Mark Loughnane) *t.k.h: chsd ldrs: pushed along in 3rd 2f out: sn lost pl: wknd fnl f* 6/1[3]
0600 7 2 1/4 **Beryl The Petal (IRE)**16 9402 3-9-3 74..........(v) HarrisonShaw(3) 10 59
(David O'Meara) *hld up: drvn over 2f out: reminders over 1f out and ins fnl f: no imp* 14/1
00 8 1 3/4 **The Game Of Life**12 9476 4-9-7 75.......... TomEaves 11 55
(Michael Herrington) *hld up: drvn over 2f out: no imp* 25/1
05-0 9 4 **Waqaas**274 1357 5-9-0 75.......... EllieMacKenzie(7) 5 44
(Mark Usher) *reluctant to load: hld up: drvn over 2f out: wl bhd fr 2f out (jockey said gelding hung right-handed turning into home straight)* 33/1
1m 27.24s (-1.56) **Going Correction** -0.175s/f (Stan) **9 Ran SP% 97.0**
Speed ratings (Par 103): **101,95,94,93,93 90,88,86,81**
CSF £20.52 CT £52.25 TOTE £2.70: £1.10, £2.90, £1.70; EX 24.00 Trifecta £60.10.
Owner Miss Sarah Hoyland **Bred** Watership Down Stud **Trained** Tern Hill, Shropshire
■ Knowing Glance was withdrawn. Price at time of withdrawal 3/1F. Rule 4 applies to all bets - deduction 25p in the pound.

FOCUS
An ordinary class 5 handicap but it was won by the least exposed runner in the line-up. The form could be rated a length or so higher.

9607 LADBROKES WHERE THE NATION PLAYS EBF NOVICE STKS 5f 21y (Tp)
2:15 (2:15) (Class 5) 2-Y-O £3,428 (£1,020; £509; £254) **Stalls Low**

Form RPR
1 **It'Smabirthday (IRE)** 2-9-2 0.......... HollieDoyle 2 80+
(Archie Watson) *mid-div: pushed along and hdwy on outer 1 1/2f out: chal ent fnl f: rdn to ld fnl 100yds: pushed clr nr fin* 2/1[2]
1352 2 1 **Get Boosting**19 9364 2-9-9 89.......... RichardKingscote 11 83
(Keith Dalgleish) *chsd ldrs: hdwy on outer 1 1/2f out: pushed along to ld ent fnl f: sn rdn: hdd fnl 100yds: no ex (jockey said gelding hung left-handed in home straight)* 5/6[1]
3 1/2 **Ladyleys Beluga** 2-8-11 0.......... CliffordLee 5 74+
(K R Burke) *hld up: pushed along 2f out: hdwy whn nt clr run over 1f out: in clr ins fnl f and sn wnt 3rd: r.o wl and clsng on first two late on* 15/2[3]
0 4 5 **Full Speight (USA)**17 9392 2-9-2 0.......... LukeMorris 9 57
(Sir Mark Prescott Bt) *disp ld: drvn and hdd 2f out: led 1 1/2f out: hdd ent fnl f: sn wknd* 14/1
55 5 hd **Lady Melody (IRE)**26 9251 2-8-11 0..........(h) ShaneGray 4 51
(David O'Meara) *disp ld: led 2f out: drvn and hdd 1 1/2f out: wknd fnl f* 16/1
000 6 1/2 **Hong Kong Dragon**15 9413 2-9-2 55.......... JackMitchell 3 54
(George Scott) *bhd: drvn over 1f out: kpt on past btn rivals fnl f* 25/1
06 7 1/2 **Dolla Dolla Bill (IRE)**21 9324 2-9-2 0.......... DavidProbert 1 52
(Richard Hannon) *mid-div: pushed along in 5th 2f out: chsng ldrs whn reminder over 1f out: wknd fnl f* 14/1
00 8 1 **Chocolaat Heer**26 9251 2-9-2 0.......... DougieCostello 6 49
(John Quinn) *hld up: drvn over 2f out: no imp* 66/1
0000 9 1 3/4 **Parker's Boy**21 9330 2-9-2 46..........(b1) KieranO'Neill 10 42
(Brian Barr) *chsd ldrs: rdn in 4th and looking hld whn hmpd over 1f out: no ch after* 150/1
6 10 2 **The Kyllachy Touch**12 9474 2-9-2 0.......... LewisEdmunds 7 35
(Derek Shaw) *a bhd* 100/1
1m 0.8s (-1.10) **Going Correction** -0.175s/f (Stan) **10 Ran SP% 125.9**
Speed ratings (Par 96): **101,99,98,90,90 89,88,87,84,81**
CSF £4.34 TOTE £3.00: £1.10, £1.10, £2.30; EX 5.10 Trifecta £17.70.
Owner A M B Watson **Bred** Pat Grogan **Trained** Upper Lambourn, W Berks
■ Stewards' Enquiry : Clifford Lee four-day ban: careless riding (Jan 9-12)
Luke Morris caution: careless riding

FOCUS
Not a very deep novice event so not a great surprise that it was plundered by an Archie Watson newcomer. The appeared to go a brisk gallop from the outset and the front three came clear.

9608 LADBROKES HOME OF THE ODDS BOOST NURSERY H'CAP 1m 142y (Tp)
2:50 (2:50) (Class 4) (0-85,85) 2-Y-O

£4,662 (£1,395; £697; £349; £300; £300) **Stalls** Low

Form RPR

4012 **1** **Locked N' Loaded**[7] 9546 2-8-11 **75**.............................. BarryMcHugh 5 80+
(Tim Fitzgerald) *mid-div: hdwy on outer 2f out: drvn to chal over 1f out: reminder and led ent fnl f: responded wl to gain upper hand on runner-up: pushed out nr nr fin* **1/1**[1]

611 **2** 3/4 **Queen Gamrah**[35] 9097 2-9-6 **84**.............................. RichardKingscote 6 87+
(Mark Johnston) *prom: drvn in 1 l 2nd 2f out: rdn to ld over 1f out: hdd ent fnl f: kpt on wl but nt pce of wnr* **4/1**[2]

3400 **3** 2 3/4 **Lexington Warfare (IRE)**[102] 7247 2-8-4 **68**..........(w) DuranFentiman 7 66
(Richard Fahey) *hld up: hdwy 2f out: rdn over 1f out: kpt on into 3rd fnl f* **16/1**

4222 **4** 1 1/2 **Baadirr**[21] 9328 2-8-13 **80**..............................(p[1]) GeorgiaCox(3) 4 75
(William Haggas) *led: drvn in 1 l ld 2f out: hdd and rdn over 1f out: wknd fnl f* **9/1**

0544 **5** 1/2 **Abadie**[63] 8505 2-8-3 **67**.............................. CamHardie 8 60
(David Loughnane) *hld up: pushed along 2f out: reminder 1f out: no imp* **8/1**[3]

4113 **6** shd **Lady Red Moon**[93] 7548 2-8-5 **76**.............................. StefanoCherchi(7) 3 69
(Marco Botti) *hld up: pushed along 2f out: rdn and effrt over 1f out: no ex fnl f* **8/1**[3]

6220 **7** 5 **Lexington Rebel (FR)**[19] 9364 2-9-2 **85**........ ThoreHammerHansen(5) 1 68
(Richard Hannon) *trckd ldrs: rdn and lost pl 2f out: wknd fnl f* **11/1**

0606 **8** 5 **Ocasio Cortez (IRE)**[30] 9162 2-9-1 **79**.............................. DavidProbert 2 51
(Richard Hannon) *mid-div: rdn and lost pl over 2f out: dropped to last 1f out* **25/1**

1m 48.27s (-1.83) **Going Correction** -0.175s/f (Stan) 8 Ran SP% **120.3**
Speed ratings (Par 98): **101,100,97,96,96 96,91,87**
CSF £5.56 CT £41.52 TOTE £2.00: £1.10, £1.70, £4.50; EX 6.50 Trifecta £67.00.
Owner Star Sports Bloodstock **Bred** Nick Bradley Bloodstock **Trained** Norton, N Yorks

FOCUS
Reasonably competitive on paper but the market screamed Locked N' Loaded and he justified the support. The front two are both on the up.

9609 #BETYOURWAY AT BETWAY H'CAP 1m 1f 104y (Tp)
3:25 (3:25) (Class 6) (0-60,60) 3-Y-O+

£2,781 (£827; £413; £300; £300; £300) **Stalls** Low

Form RPR

6200 **1** **Odds On Oli**[10] 9503 4-8-13 **52**.............................. BarryMcHugh 8 59
(Richard Fahey) *chsd ldrs: pushed along and hdwy 2f out: drvn to ld over 1f out: r.o wl fnl f (trainers rep could off no explanation for geldings improved performance other than he stripped fitter for his two recent runs after a break of 170 days)* **12/1**

1000 **2** 1/2 **Creative Talent (IRE)**[26] 9256 7-9-7 **60**.................... RichardKingscote 3 66+
(Tony Carroll) *hld up: pushed along and hdwy 1 1/2f out: rdn and str run fnl f: tk 2nd fnl 25yds* **7/1**[3]

0003 **3** 1/2 **Valentine Mist (IRE)**[12] 9481 7-8-2 **46**.............................. SophieRalston(5) 9 51
(James Grassick) *mid-div: pushed along on outer 2f out: hdwy over 1f out: rdn to chal wnr ins fnl f: wknd and lost 2nd fnl 25yds* **40/1**

3304 **4** 1 1/4 **Just Once**[27] 9216 3-9-2 **57**.............................. LukeMorris 4 60
(Mrs Ilka Gansera-Leveque) *hld up: pushed along and hdwy on inner 1 1/2f out: rdn in 4th fnl f: kpt on* **10/1**

0451 **5** 3/4 **Necoleta**[7] 9552 3-9-3 **58** 6ex..............................(p) LiamKeniry 6 59
(Sylvester Kirk) *hld up: reminder 3f out: pushed along on outer over 2f out: rdn and effrt over 1f out: one pce fnl f (jockey said filly was never travelling)* **9/4**[1]

0615 **6** 1/2 **Seaforth (IRE)**[14] 9450 7-8-11 **53**.............................. FinleyMarsh(3) 13 53
(Adrian Wintle) *hld up: pushed along and effrt over 1f out: drvn and kpt on fnl f* **10/1**

0013 **7** 3/4 **Sunshineandbubbles**[12] 9479 6-9-3 **56**.............................. CliffordLee 11 55
(David Evans) *prom: rdn 2f out: wknd over 1f out* **4/1**[2]

0000 **8** 1 **Longville Lilly**[38] 9028 4-8-7 **46** oh1..............................(b) CamHardie 7 43
(Trevor Wall) *hld up: pushed along 2f out: rdn fnl f: no imp (jockey said filly was slowly away)* **100/1**

0500 **9** nk **Bell Heather (IRE)**[26] 9253 6-9-5 **58**..............................(p) HollieDoyle 1 54
(Patrick Morris) *chsd ldrs: drvn 2f out: rdn and wknd fnl f* **10/1**

0406 **10** 1/2 **King Oswald (USA)**[50] 8863 6-9-5 **58**..............................(tp) DavidProbert 5 53
(James Unett) *mid-div: drvn 2f out: sn rdn and wknd* **11/1**

0000 **11** 1 1/2 **Amor Fati (IRE)**[19] 9367 4-9-0 **60**.............................. LauraPearson(7) 10 52
(David Evans) *hld up: pushed along over 1f out: no imp (jockey said gelding was slowly away)* **16/1**

0400 **12** shd **Dark Devil (IRE)**[26] 9256 6-9-7 **60**..............................(p) ShaneGray 12 52
(Patrick Morris) *hld up on outer: drvn over 1f out: no imp* **20/1**

0005 **13** 3 1/4 **Another Approach (FR)**[16] 9400 3-8-6 **47** oh1 ow1.............. JFEgan 2 33
(David Loughnane) *led: drvn in 1/2 l ld 2f out: hdd and reminder over 1f out: wknd fnl f* **16/1**

1m 59.52s (-1.28) **Going Correction** -0.175s/f (Stan)
WFA 3 from 4yo+ 2lb 13 Ran SP% **126.5**
Speed ratings (Par 101): **98,97,97,96,95 94,94,93,93,92 91,91,88**
CSF £98.07 CT £3307.80 TOTE £16.10: £4.00, £2.70, £8.70; EX 175.90 Trifecta £2467.40.
Owner Richard Fahey Ebor Racing Club Ltd **Bred** Worksop Manor Stud **Trained** Musley Bank, N Yorks

FOCUS
Reasonably competitive for the grade and a whole host of these had their chance off the home turn. The second has been rated as running marginally his best race on the Flat for three years.

9610 BETWAY H'CAP 1m 1f 104y (Tp)
3:55 (3:55) (Class 2) (0-105,101) 3-Y-O+

£12,450 (£3,728; £1,864; £932; £466; £234) **Stalls** Low

Form RPR

4041 **1** **Felix**[91] 7618 3-8-11 **88**..............................(t) DavidProbert 4 97
(Marco Botti) *chsd ldrs: pushed along in 3rd 2f out: sn drvn: rdn and hdwy to chal fnl f: led 100yds out: pushed clr nr fin* **6/1**[3]

2332 **2** 1 **Pactolus (IRE)**[22] 9309 8-9-12 **101**..............................(t) RichardKingscote 5 108
(Stuart Williams) *prom: pushed along in 1 l 2nd 2f out: rdn over 1f out: led 1/2f out: sn hdd and no ex* **5/4**[1]

4100 **3** 2 **Star Of Southwold (FR)**[28] 9200 4-8-13 **95**.............. GeorgeRooke(7) 6 98
(Michael Appleby) *led: pushed along in 1 l ld 2f out: rdn in 1 l ld ent fnl f: hdd 1/2f out: no ex* **9/4**[2]

3033 **4** 5 **Nonios (IRE)**[141] 5796 7-8-13 **93**..............................(h) DylanHogan(5) 1 85
(David Simcock) *slowly away: hld up: hdwy into 4th 2f out: drvn over 1f out: wknd fnl f* **14/1**

3005 **5** 1 1/2 **Smile A Mile (IRE)**[28] 9200 3-9-0 **91**.............................. JFEgan 7 80
(Mark Johnston) *chsd ldrs: drvn on outer 3f out: lost pl 2f out: sn rdn and wknd* **8/1**

6600 **6** 1/2 **Lunar Jet**[19] 9366 5-8-8 **88**.............................. TobyEley(5) 2 76
(John Mackie) *chsd ldrs: pushed along and lost pl 2f out: rdn and no ex fr over 1f out* **20/1**

1000 **7** 22 **Borodin (IRE)**[12] 7434 4-9-3 **92**.............................. CamHardie 3 34
(Sam England) *hld up: drvn in rr 3f out: lost tch 2f out* **33/1**

1m 58.87s (-1.93) **Going Correction** -0.175s/f (Stan)
WFA 3 from 4yo+ 2lb 7 Ran SP% **115.0**
Speed ratings (Par 109): **101,100,98,93,92 92,72**
CSF £14.14 TOTE £6.40: £2.00, £1.20; EX 13.30 Trifecta £40.10.
Owner K Sohi & Partner **Bred** Fittocks Stud **Trained** Newmarket, Suffolk

FOCUS
A good quality race but not a strong 0-105 given only one of these was rated within 10lb of the ceiling. It was won by one of the two three-year-olds. The winner has been rated in line with his best.

9611 BETWAY HEED YOUR HUNCH H'CAP 1m 4f 51y (Tp)
4:25 (4:26) (Class 5) (0-75,77) 3-Y-O+

£3,428 (£1,020; £509; £300; £300; £300) **Stalls** Low

Form RPR

4421 **1** **Clap Your Hands**[14] 9442 3-9-0 **72**.............................. JackMitchell 11 88+
(David Simcock) *hld up: pushed along and hdwy 2f out: drvn in 3rd over 1f out: led 1f out: c wl clr fnl f: easily* **9/1**

5011 **2** 9 **Renardeau**[8] 9511 3-8-12 **75**..............................(p) DylanHogan(5) 9 77
(Ali Stronge) *mid-div: drvn into 4 l 2nd 2f out: sn rdn: chal over 1f out: 2nd ent fnl f: kpt on but no ch w easy wnr* **5/2**[1]

6560 **3** nk **Uther Pendragon (IRE)**[8] 7756 4-9-0 **68**..............................(p) LiamKeniry 5 69
(J S Moore) *hld up: pushed along 2f out: drvn and effrt 1 1/2f out: rdn over 1f out: styd on fnl f: tk 3rd fnl 50yds* **12/1**

0051 **4** 1 1/4 **Dream Magic (IRE)**[19] 9367 5-8-9 **70**.............................. MolliePhillips(7) 8 69
(Mark Loughnane) *t.k.h: trckd ldrs: hdwy on outer 2f out: reminder over 1f out: one pce fnl f* **9/1**

0-00 **5** 1/2 **Zack Mayo**[29] 9177 5-9-9 **77**..............................(b[1]) RichardKingscote 10 75
(Philip McBride) *prom: led gng wl over 2f out: sn pushed into 4 l ld: rdn and reduced ld 1 1/2f out: hdd 1f out: wknd fnl f* **9/1**

0302 **6** 2 3/4 **Seven Clans (IRE)**[7] 9543 7-9-5 **76**.............................. GemmaTutty(3) 6 69
(Karen Tutty) *hld up in rr: drvn and effrt 1 1/2f out: reminder and kpt on past btn rivals fr over 1f out (jockey said gelding was slowly away)* **9/2**[2]

6-00 **7** 5 **Zoffany Bay (IRE)**[14] 9443 5-8-13 **67**..............................(v) KieranO'Neill 1 52
(Ali Stronge) *trckd ldrs: drvn 3f out: nt clr run over 2f out: rdn 1 1/2f out: no ex (jockey said gelding ran too freely)* **40/1**

0000 **8** 8 **Golden Wolf (IRE)**[37] 9053 5-9-7 **75**.............................. HollieDoyle 7 48
(Tony Carroll) *t.k.h: hdwy to take clsr order 1/2-way: drvn and lost pl 2f out: sn rdn and wknd (jockey said gelding ran too freely)* **6/1**[3]

3060 **9** 2 1/4 **Double Reflection**[6] 9570 4-8-12 **66**..............................(p[1]) LukeMorris 12 35
(Michael Appleby) *hld up: drvn over 2f out: no imp* **33/1**

4620 **10** 2 **Fayetta**[7] 9542 3-8-5 **63**..............................(p) CamHardie 2 30
(David Loughnane) *led 2f: remained prom: drvn and lost pl 1/2-way: sn rdn and dropped away* **8/1**

0006 **11** 2 3/4 **Cherries At Dawn (IRE)**[73] 8200 4-8-8 **62**.............................. JFEgan 4 23
(Dominic Ffrench Davis) *prom: led after 2f: hdd and drvn over 2f out: sn wknd (jockey said filly hung right-handed)* **20/1**

0143 **12** 30 **Soloist (IRE)**[67] 7650 3-9-0 **72**..............................(b) DavidProbert 3
(Alexandra Dunn) *hld up: drvn and dropped to last 5f out: wl bhd fr 2f out (jockey said filly hung left-handed and stopped quickly)* **40/1**

2m 34.77s (-6.03) **Going Correction** -0.175s/f (Stan)
WFA 3 from 4yo+ 4lb 12 Ran SP% **122.4**
Speed ratings (Par 103): **113,107,106,105,105 103,100,95,93,92 90,70**
CSF £31.77 CT £282.71 TOTE £8.00: £2.40, £1.40, £4.00; EX 30.60 Trifecta £905.10.
Owner Twenty Stars Partnership **Bred** Rabbah Bloodstock Limited **Trained** Newmarket, Suffolk

FOCUS
This looked reasonably competitive on paper but it was taken apart by Clap Your Hands, who absolutely bolted up. They looked to go quite hard early before the pace slackened mid-race. The winner has been rated as a big improver.

9612 BETWAY CONDITIONS STKS 6f 20y (Tp)
4:55 (4:55) (Class 2) 3-Y-O+

£12,450 (£3,728; £1,864; £932; £466; £234) **Stalls** Low

Form RPR

2440 **1** **Summerghand (IRE)**[75] 8127 5-9-3 100.............................. ShaneGray 1 98
(David O'Meara) *hld up: hdwy in bhd ldrs over 1f out: rdn to chal ins fnl f: r.o wl to ld fnl 25yds* **11/2**

2241 **2** 1/2 **Documenting**[33] 9129 6-9-3 105.............................. JackMitchell 4 96
(Kevin Frost) *led: jnd after 2f: narrow ld 2f out: drvn in 1 l ld 1f out: sn rdn: kpt on fnl f: hdd fnl 25yds* **11/10**[1]

6206 **3** 1 3/4 **Corinthia Knight (IRE)**[6] 9571 4-9-3 104.............................. HollieDoyle 5 91
(Archie Watson) *prom: chsd ldrs 3f out: pushed along in 4th 2f out: rdn over 1f out: kpt on to secure 3rd fnl f* **4/1**[2]

3236 **4** hd **Baby Steps**[22] 9308 3-9-3 80.............................. LukeMorris 6 90
(David Loughnane) *prom: disp ld after 2f: hdd and drvn 2f out: rdn and one pce fr over 1f out* **20/1**

3035 **5** nk **Merhoob (IRE)**[12] 9478 7-9-3 96.............................. LiamKeniry 2 89
(John Ryan) *slowly away: hld up: pushed along 2f out: drvn on outer over 1f out: rdn fnl f: no imp* **8/1**

5342 **6** 1/2 **Royal Birth**[6] 9571 8-9-3 100..............................(t) RichardKingscote 3 87
(Stuart Williams) *chsd ldrs: pushed along in 3rd 2f out: rdn over 1f out: wknd fnl f* **9/2**[3]

1m 12.24s (-2.26) **Going Correction** -0.175s/f (Stan) 6 Ran SP% **117.1**
Speed ratings (Par 109): **108,107,105,104,104 103**
CSF £12.74 TOTE £7.60: £2.60, £1.30; EX 14.80 Trifecta £57.20.
Owner Hamad Rashed Bin Ghedayer **Bred** Airlie Stud **Trained** Upper Helmsley, N Yorks

FOCUS
This good quality conditions event was run at a decent gallop, which enabled Summerghand to come from last to first. The fourth, who has been rated in line with the better view of his October C&D form, is the key to the form.

T/Plt: £37.80 to a £1 stake. Pool: £63,629.69 - 1,225.74 winning units T/Qpdt: £37.60 to a £1 stake. Pool: £5,079.52 - 99.73 winning units **Keith McHugh**

9611-9621a (Foreign Racing) - See Raceform Interactive

9606 WOLVERHAMPTON (A.W) (L-H)

Friday, December 27

OFFICIAL GOING: Tapeta: standard

Wind: Light behind Weather: Overcast

9622 BETWAY CASINO H'CAP 6f 20y (Tp)

1:50 (1:50) (Class 6) (0-65,65) 3-Y-O+

£2,781 (£827; £413; £300; £300; £300) Stalls Low

Form RPR

0352 1 **Rock Boy Grey (IRE)**[28] 9217 4-9-4 65..........(tp) LukeMorris 3 78+
(Mark Loughnane) *s.i.s: hdwy over 3f out: shkn up to chse ldr and hung lft fr over 1f out: rdn to ld ins fnl f: r.o wl* 3/1[1]

0036 2 2 1/2 **Spirit Of Wedza (IRE)**[20] 9365 7-8-11 65.......... VictorSantos(7) 6 70
(Julie Camacho) *sn led: rdn and hdd ins fnl f: styd on same pce* 10/1

3344 3 2 **Landing Night (IRE)**[13] 9473 7-9-2 63..........(tp) JasonHart 5 62
(Rebecca Menzies) *a.p: chsd ldr over 2f out tl rdn and swtchd lft over 1f out: no ex ins fnl f* 11/1

102 4 hd **Daring Guest (IRE)**[18] 9386 5-8-11 65..........(t) StefanoCherchi(7) 1 64
(Tom Clover) *prom: nt clr run and lost pl over 4f out: hdwy and nt clr run over 1f out: r.o towards fin* 13/2[3]

3035 5 hd **The Groove**[16] 9427 6-8-10 64.......... CameronIles(7) 7 62
(David Evans) *chsd ldrs: pushed along on outer over 2f out: hung lft and styd on same pce ins fnl f* 12/1

2010 6 hd **My Town Chicago (USA)**[20] 9365 4-9-4 65.......... JackMitchell 4 62
(Kevin Frost) *s.i.s: racd keenly and sn prom: rdn and nt clr run over 1f out: styd on same pce ins fnl f (jockey said gelding ran too free)* 6/1[2]

3034 7 1/2 **Kraka (IRE)**[11] 9498 4-9-4 65..........(p) KieranO'Neill 11 61
(Christine Dunnett) *broke wl: sn lost pl: rdn and hung lft fr over 1f out: nt trble ldrs* 13/2[3]

0342 8 1 1/2 **Global Melody**[8] 9545 4-8-12 64..........(vt) DylanHogan(5) 2 55
(Phil McEntee) *in tch: sn pushed along and lost pl: n.d after* 13/2[3]

0060 9 1 3/4 **Laubali**[20] 9365 4-9-4 65..........(p) TomMarquand 10 51
(David O'Meara) *hld up: rdn over 1f out: n.d* 28/1

6411 10 1 1/2 **The Lacemaker**[18] 9386 5-9-0 64..........(tp) DarraghKeenan(3) 8 45
(Milton Harris) *chsd ldrs on outer: wnt 2nd over 4f out tl over 2f out: wknd ins fnl f (jockey said mare ran flat)* 16/1

1m 12.82s (-1.68) **Going Correction** -0.175s/f (Stan) 10 Ran SP% **113.7**

Speed ratings (Par 101): **104,100,98,97,97 97,96,94,92,90**

CSF £33.22 CT £288.17 TOTE £3.40: £1.40, £2.80, £3.10; EX 38.70 Trifecta £413.00.

Owner The Likely Lads **Bred** Yeomanstown Stud **Trained** Rock, Worcs

■ Stewards' Enquiry : Jason Hart caution; careless riding

FOCUS

A modest opener but, although the gallop seemed respectable, very few were able to figure. A pb from the winner, and he could be rated higher through the placed horses.

9623 LADBROKES "PLAY 1-2-FREE" ON FOOTBALL FILLIES' NOVICE STKS (PLUS 10 RACE) 6f 20y (Tp)

2:25 (2:27) (Class 5) 2-Y-O

£3,428 (£1,020; £509; £254) Stalls Low

Form RPR

5 1 **Tomorrow's Dream (FR)**[18] 9392 2-9-0 0.......... TomMarquand 9 75+
(William Haggas) *chsd ldr tl led wl over 1f out: rdn out* 10/3[2]

2 1 1/2 **Mountain Brave** 2-9-0 0.......... JackMitchell 4 70
(Mark Johnston) *chsd ldrs: rdn and edgd lft ins fnl f: styd on same pce* 33/1

5 3 1/2 **Yukon Mission (IRE)**[38] 9043 2-9-0 0.......... JasonHart 6 69
(John Quinn) *prom on outer: rdn over 1f out: styd on same pce ins fnl f* 11/1

4 1/2 **Anna Maria** 2-9-0 0.......... BarryMcHugh 10 67
(Richard Fahey) *s.i.s: hld up: racd keenly: hdwy on outer over 2f out: shkn up over 1f out: styd on same pce ins fnl f* 18/1

10 5 1 **Never In Paris (IRE)**[160] 5185 2-9-7 0.......... HollieDoyle 3 71+
(K R Burke) *s.i.s: hld up: swtchd rt and hdwy over 1f out: rdn and hung rt ins fnl f: r.o* 7/4[1]

6 6 nse **Endowment**[50] 8891 2-9-0 0.......... HectorCrouch 8 64
(Clive Cox) *hld up in tch: outpcd over 2f out: hdwy and carried rt over 1f out: r.o* 8/1

32 7 1 **True Believer (IRE)**[16] 9409 2-9-0 0.......... RichardKingscote 5 61
(Mark Johnston) *chsd ldrs: rdn over 1f out: no ex ins fnl f* 7/2[3]

8 2 **Come On Linda** 2-8-9 0.......... GerO'Neill(5) 11 55
(Michael Easterby) *s.i.s: rdn over 1f out: nvr on terms* 150/1

60 9 2 1/2 **Cliff Wind**[18] 9393 2-9-0 0.......... LukeMorris 1 48
(Sir Mark Prescott Bt) *s.i.s: hld up: plld hrd: racd wd fr 1/2-way: shkn up over 1f out: nvr on terms* 66/1

5 10 2 1/4 **Dress Circle**[13] 9474 2-9-0 0.......... CallumShepherd 7 41
(James Tate) *sn led: rdn and hdd wl over 1f out: wknd ins fnl f* 33/1

000 11 1 1/2 **Dabbersgirl**[22] 9324 2-9-0 41.......... LiamKeniry 13 36
(Brian Baugh) *prom: lost pl over 5f out: shkn up over 2f out: sn wknd* 250/1

00 12 nk **Walls Have Ears (IRE)**[76] 8121 2-9-0 0.......... DougieCostello 2 35
(Ivan Furtado) *s.i.s: a in rr: wknd over 2f out* 100/1

1m 14.75s (0.25) **Going Correction** -0.175s/f (Stan) 12 Ran SP% **115.8**

Speed ratings (Par 93): **91,89,88,87,86 86,84,82,78,75 73,73**

CSF £114.21 TOTE £4.10: £1.40, £6.30, £2.50; EX 134.90 Trifecta £814.80.

Owner Apple Tree Stud **Bred** Appletree Stud **Trained** Newmarket, Suffolk

■ Stewards' Enquiry : Hollie Doyle caution; careless riding

FOCUS

A fair novice event for fillies. However, the gallop was an ordinary one and those up with the pace held the edge. The form will take a while to settle.

9624 LADBROKES FOOTBALL ACCA BOOSTY NOVICE STKS 1m 142y (Tp)

3:00 (3:06) (Class 5) 2-Y-O

£3,428 (£1,020; £509; £254) Stalls Low

Form RPR

4 1 **Pride Of America (FR)**[41] 9007 2-9-5 0.......... LukeMorris 12 84+
(Harry Dunlop) *sn prom: racd keenly and wnt 2nd over 6f out: led over 2f out: pushed clr fr over 1f out: rdn and hung lft ins fnl f: eased towards fin* 7/1

52 2 5 **Far Rockaway**[32] 9154 2-9-0 0..........(h) TomMarquand 6 69
(William Haggas) *prom: lost pl over 6f out: hdwy over 1f out: r.o to go 2nd wl ins fnl f: no ch w wnr* 5/1[3]

03 3 1/2 **Schmoozie (IRE)**[18] 9383 2-9-0 0.......... RobHornby 2 67
(Jonathan Portman) *hld up in tch: shkn up over 2f out: r.o to go 3rd nr fin* 28/1

4 1/2 **Tolmount** 2-9-5 0.......... KieranShoemark 9 71
(Charlie Appleby) *chsd ldrs: shkn up over 2f out: rdn and hung lft fr over 1f out: no ex ins fnl f (jockey said colt ran green)* 9/2[2]

3 5 2 1/2 **Socially Shady**[20] 9363 2-9-5 0.......... CliffordLee 4 66
(K R Burke) *hdwy over 6f out: rdn over 2f out: wknd fnl f* 16/1

2 6 hd **Cottonopolis**[141] 5838 2-9-5 0.......... RichardKingscote 1 66
(Mark Johnston) *chsd ldrs: rdn over 2f out: wknd fnl f* 20/1

7 3/4 **Tenbury Wells (USA)** 2-9-5 0.......... RobertHavlin 8 70+
(John Gosden) *dwlt: in rr: shkn up over 1f out: styng on whn nt clr run ins fnl f: nvr on terms (jockey said colt missed the break)* 11/10[1]

4 8 nk **Mystic River (IRE)**[14] 9452 2-9-5 0.......... HectorCrouch 7 64
(James Ferguson) *stdd s: hld up: rdn and hung lft over 1f out: nvr on terms* 20/1

9 hd **Mr Dib Dab (FR)** 2-9-5 0.......... AndrewMullen 10 63
(Mark Loughnane) *s.i.s: racd keenly and hdwy on outer 1/2-way: rdn over 3f out: outpcd fr over 2f out* 100/1

10 3/4 **Star Approach (IRE)** 2-9-2 0.......... GabrieleMalune(3) 11 66+
(Ismail Mohammed) *s.i.s: in rr: shkn up over 1f out: nvr nrr* 50/1

0 11 hd **Seadance**[22] 9326 2-9-0 0.......... ThoreHammerHansen(5) 3 61
(Richard Hannon) *sn led: hdd over 2f out: wknd fnl f* 66/1

0 12 20 **Carlton Bella**[35] 9107 2-9-0 0.......... GerO'Neill(5) 5 19
(Michael Easterby) *mid-div: lost pl over 6f out: wknd over 2f out* 250/1

1m 48.41s (-1.69) **Going Correction** -0.175s/f (Stan) 12 Ran SP% **118.7**

Speed ratings (Par 96): **100,95,95,94,92 92,91,91,91,90 90,72**

CSF £39.81 TOTE £7.90: £1.90, £1.40, £6.30; EX 50.70 Trifecta £501.90.

Owner Haven't A Pot, D Macauliffe & Anoj Don **Bred** Laurent Dulong & Yannick Dulong **Trained** Lambourn, Berks

FOCUS

The well-backed market leader disappointed but still a useful effort from the winner and he should hold his own in stronger company. The gallop was fair.

9625 LADBROKES HOME OF THE ODDS BOOST EBF FILLIES' H'CAP 1m 142y (Tp)

3:40 (3:44) (Class 2) (0-105,94) 3-Y-O+

£16,807 (£5,032; £2,516; £1,258; £629; £315) Stalls Low

Form RPR

0236 1 **Geizy Teizy (IRE)**[16] 9417 3-8-4 76..........(p[1]) HollieDoyle 6 82
(Marco Botti) *s.i.s: hld up: hdwy over 1f out: rdn to ld wl ins fnl f: r.o (trainers rep said, regards the apparent improvement in form, filly appreciated the change of tactics by being held up and coming from off the pace on this occasion)* 5/1[3]

5451 2 nk **Bubble And Squeak**[25] 9278 4-9-6 90.......... RobHornby 7 95
(Sylvester Kirk) *hld up: pushed along and hdwy 2f out: sn swtchd rt: rdn to ld and hung lft wl ins fnl f: sn hdd: r.o* 5/2[1]

0121 3 1 **Stay Classy (IRE)**[16] 9424 3-8-12 89..........(p) AngusVilliers(5) 3 92
(Richard Spencer) *hld up: hdwy over 3f out: led over 1f out: rdn and hdd wl ins fnl f: styd on same pce* 7/2[2]

3650 4 1 1/2 **Universal Effect**[30] 9173 3-8-3 75 oh4.......... AndrewMullen 5 75
(Mark Loughnane) *awkward s: plld hrd and sn prom: wnt 2nd over 7f out: led over 6f out: sn clr: c bk to the field over 2f out: rdn: hung rt and hdd over 1f out: styd on same pce ins fnl f* 25/1

1310 5 1 1/4 **Solar Heights (IRE)**[106] 7106 3-9-8 94..........(v) TomMarquand 4 91
(James Tate) *led 2f: chsd ldr who sn wnt clr: shkn up and tk clsr order over 2f out: rdn and ev ch over 1f out: no ex wl ins fnl f* 5/2[1]

4350 6 4 1/2 **Dream World (IRE)**[21] 9351 4-7-12 75 oh6..........(p) GeorgeRooke(7) 1 61
(Michael Appleby) *hld up: rdn over 2f out: nt trble ldrs* 28/1

-120 7 5 **Yimkin (IRE)**[225] 2760 3-8-3 75.......... LukeMorris 2 50
(Marco Botti) *trckd ldrs: racd keenly: rdn over 2f out: wknd over 1f out* 12/1

1m 48.13s (-1.97) **Going Correction** -0.175s/f (Stan)

WFA 3 from 4yo 2lb 7 Ran SP% **111.0**

Speed ratings (Par 96): **101,100,99,98,97 93,88**

CSF £16.84 TOTE £5.90: £3.30, £2.00; EX 21.50 Trifecta £73.50.

Owner Nick Bradley Racing 30 & Sohi & Partner **Bred** Anne Hallinan & John O' Connor **Trained** Newmarket, Suffolk

FOCUS

A reasonable fillies handicap in which a steady gallop picked up after a quarter of a mile.

9626 BETWAY LIVE CASINO H'CAP 1m 5f 219y (Tp)

4:10 (4:14) (Class 6) (0-65,65) 3-Y-O+

£2,781 (£827; £413; £300; £300; £300) Stalls Low

Form RPR

4000 1 **Power Home (IRE)**[20] 9367 5-9-9 62.......... CharlesBishop 7 68
(Denis Coakley) *sn prom: racd keenly: wnt 2nd over 9f out: rdn to ld over 1f out: styd on* 16/1

-062 2 1/2 **Calvinist**[25] 9275 6-9-5 58.......... JaneElliott 2 63
(Kevin Frost) *trckd ldrs: plld hrd: led after 1f tl over 11f out: remained handy: rdn over 1f out: r.o to go 2nd nr fin* 9/2[3]

02-0 3 nk **Jamacho**[23] 9303 5-9-12 65..........(h) LiamKeniry 9 70
(Charlie Longsdon) *plld hrd and prom: led at stdy pce over 11f out tl shkn up over 3f out: rdn and hdd over 1f out: styd on (jockey said gelding ran too free)* 40/1

2155 4 1 **Star Of Athena**[16] 9412 4-9-9 62.......... TomMarquand 3 65+
(Ali Stronge) *s.i.s: hdwy 12f out: pushed along over 2f out: rdn and hung lft fr over 1f out: r.o* 3/1[1]

0250 5 1 1/2 **Rosie Royale (IRE)**[7] 9570 7-9-10 63.......... JackMitchell 1 64
(Roger Teal) *led 1f: chsd ldrs: rdn over 2f out: styd on same pce fnl f* 25/1

3214 6 1 1/2 **Willkommen**[51] 8868 3-9-0 65..........(b) StefanoCherchi(7) 4 66
(Marco Botti) *trckd ldrs: plld hrd: outpcd over 3f out: rallied over 1f out: no imp ins fnl f* 4/1[2]

0635 7 1 1/4 **Ebqaa (IRE)**[51] 8868 5-9-8 61..........(p) DavidProbert 10 59
(James Unett) *s.i.s: hld up: r.o ins fnl f: nvr nrr (jockey said mare was slowly away)* 8/1

32-0 8 1 1/4 **Canadian George (FR)**[41] 9006 4-9-9 62..........(t[1]) JamesSullivan 12 58
(Jennie Candlish) *hld up: shkn up over 1f out: nt trble ldrs* 50/1

-006 9 3/4 **Liva (IRE)**[31] 9167 4-9-10 63.......... TomEaves 8 58
(Stef Keniry) *hld up: rdn over 1f out: n.d* 33/1

6052 10 3/4 **Hidden Pearl**[15] 9442 3-8-10 59.......... SophieRalston(5) 11 55+
(John Berry) *hld up: plld hrd: swtchd rt over 5f out: hung lft fr over 1f out: n.d* 25/1

56-0 11 1/2 **Caged Lightning (IRE)**[48] 8945 9-9-8 61..........(p) LukeMorris 13 54
(Steve Gollings) *hld up: nvr on terms* 40/1

1011 12 3/4 **Herm (IRE)**[25] 9275 5-9-6 59.......... CliffordLee 6 51
(David Evans) *trckd ldrs: racd keenly: shkn up on outer over 2f out: wknd fnl f (jockey said gelding ran too free)* 9/2[3]

400/ **13** *10* **Fennann**[1034] 721 8-8-8 **52**..............................(p) FayeMcManoman(5) 5 30
(Frank Bishop) *s.s: a in rr: wknd over 2f out* **150/1**

3m 6.64s (5.64) **Going Correction** -0.175s/f (Stan)
WFA 3 from 4yo+ 5lb **13** Ran SP% **116.5**
Speed ratings (Par 101): **76,75,75,74,74 73,72,71,71,70 70,70,64**
CSF £80.52 CT £2850.96 TOTE £15.20: £3.30, £1.90, £10.70; EX 103.20 Trifecta £1468.40.

Owner Poachers' Dozen **Bred** C Farrell **Trained** West Ilsley, Berks

FOCUS
Mainly exposed performers in a modest handicap. A steady gallop picked up on the approach to the home straight and those held up were at a disadvantage. The fourth has been rated back in line with her better recent form.

9627 BETWAY HEED YOUR HUNCH H'CAP 5f 21y (Tp)

4:40 (4:41) (Class 6) (0-65,67) 3-Y-O+

£2,781 (£827; £413; £300; £300; £300) **Stalls** Low

Form RPR

4650 **1** **Becker**[275] 1364 4-9-4 **61**.............................. AlistairRawlinson 3 69+
(Robert Cowell) *s.i.s: outpcd: swtchd rt over 1f out: gd hdwy fnl f: r.o to ld nr fin* **11/4**[2]

0500 **2** *1/2* **Creek Harbour (IRE)**[18] 9386 4-9-5 **62**.............................. DavidProbert 6 68
(Milton Bradley) *prom: nt clr run and lost pl over 3f out: hdwy 1/2-way: rdn to ld wl ins fnl f: hdd nr fin* **20/1**

0450 **3** *hd* **Rock Of Estonia (IRE)**[7] 9559 4-9-10 **67**..............................(p) LukeMorris 4 72
(Michael Squance) *pushed along in rr: drvn along and hdwy over 1f out: r.o* **10/1**

0341 **4** *3/4* **Seraphim**[13] 9477 3-9-5 **62**..............................(bt) DanielMuscutt 7 65
(Marco Botti) *prom: lost pl after 1f: hdwy over 1f out: sn rdn: styd on* **5/2**[1]

0550 **5** *1* **Red Stripes (USA)**[17] 9406 7-9-1 **58**..............................(b) HollieDoyle 1 57+
(Lisa Williamson) *disp ld: rdn over 1f out: hdd and unable qck wl ins fnl f* **8/1**[3]

0220 **6** *3/4* **Teepee Time**[76] 8117 6-8-7 **50** oh5..............................(b) PhilDennis 2 46
(Michael Mullineaux) *trckd ldrs: lost pl 3f out: hdwy over 1f out: styng on whn nt clr run ins fnl f: no ch after* **50/1**

0660 **7** *hd* **Angel Force (IRE)**[6] 9583 4-8-6 **52**..............................(p) TheodoreLadd(3) 5 48
(David C Griffiths) *racd freely: disp ld: rdn over 1f out: hdd and no ex wl ins fnl f* **25/1**

4156 **8** *1 1/2* **Precious Plum**[74] 8194 5-9-7 **64**..............................(p) RichardKingscote 8 54
(Charlie Wallis) *trckd ldrs: rdn over 1f out: no ex ins fnl f* **14/1**

3000 **9** *2 1/2* **Tan**[8] 9550 5-9-2 **59**.............................. CharlesBishop 10 40
(Lisa Williamson) *s.i.s: hdwy to chse ldrs 4f out: rdn over 1f out: sn wknd* **40/1**

5245 **10** *3/4* **Dark Side Dream**[20] 9365 7-9-4 **66**..........(p) ThoreHammerHansen(5) 11 45
(Charlie Wallis) *hld up on outer: hung rt 2f out: nvr on terms* **17/2**

052 **11** *4* **Bernie's Boy**[9] 9507 6-8-8 **56**..............................(tp) DylanHogan(5) 9 20
(Phil McEntee) *prom: rdn 1/2-way: wknd over 1f out: eased fnl f (trainers rep said gelding ran flat)* **9/1**

1m 0.86s (-1.04) **Going Correction** -0.175s/f (Stan) **11** Ran SP% **115.6**
Speed ratings (Par 101): **101,100,99,98,97 95,95,93,89,87 81**
CSF £61.18 CT £484.47 TOTE £4.00: £1.70, £5.60, £3.00; EX 66.80 Trifecta £530.20.

Owner Mrs Morley, R Penney & A Rix **Bred** Maywood Stud **Trained** Six Mile Bottom, Cambs

FOCUS
A modest handicap in which a strong gallop teed things up for the finishers.

9628 BETWAY H'CAP 1m 1f 104y (Tp)

5:10 (5:11) (Class 4) (0-85,83) 3-Y-O+

£5,207 (£1,549; £774; £387; £300; £300) **Stalls** Low

Form RPR

0103 **1** **Kaser (IRE)**[27] 9255 4-9-7 **83**.............................. RichardKingscote 1 90
(David Loughnane) *s.i.s: hld up: gd hdwy fnl f: rdn and swtchd lft wl ins fnl f: qcknd to ld nr fin* **5/1**[3]

5100 **2** *nk* **First Response**[38] 9050 4-9-0 **76**..............................(t) TomEaves 7 82
(Linda Stubbs) *hld up: hdwy over 2f out: rdn to ld and edgd lft wl ins fnl f: hdd nr fin* **14/1**

-112 **3** *1/2* **Red Bond (IRE)**[271] 1462 3-9-1 **79**.............................. TomMarquand 9 84
(Keith Dalgleish) *led after 1f: rdn over 1f out: hdd wl ins fnl f* **12/1**

2011 **4** *1/2* **Snow Ocean (IRE)**[25] 9273 3-9-2 **80**..............................(h) CliffordLee 8 84
(David Evans) *prom: racd keenly: rdn and edgd lft over 1f out: styd on same pce towards fin* **11/4**[1]

3104 **5** *hd* **Gabrials Boy**[25] 9274 3-9-1 **82**.............................. ConnorMurtagh(3) 10 86
(Richard Fahey) *s.i.s: hld up: plld hrd: shkn up over 1f out: hung lft: r.o and nt clr run ins fnl f: nt rch ldrs* **20/1**

031 **6** *1/2* **Classic Design (IRE)**[41] 9011 3-9-1 **79**.............................. JackMitchell 11 82
(Simon Crisford) *chsd ldr after 1f: rdn and ev ch over 1f out: no ex wl ins fnl f* **7/2**[2]

0123 **7** *nse* **Storm Ahead (IRE)**[13] 9480 6-9-4 **80**..............................(b) PhilDennis 4 83
(Tim Easterby) *hld up: hdwy over 1f out: rdn and nt clr run wl ins fnl f: styd on same pce* **13/2**

4513 **8** *nk* **Scofflaw**[23] 9304 5-8-12 **81**..............................(v) LauraPearson(7) 2 83
(David Evans) *hld up: hdwy over 1f out: styd on same pce wl ins fnl f* **16/1**

-506 **9** *4 1/2* **Paddyplex**[36] 9096 6-9-0 **76**..............................(p) JasonHart 3 69
(Tristan Davidson) *chsd ldrs: rdn over 2f out: wknd fnl f* **11/1**

0400 **10** *8* **Street Poet (IRE)**[13] 9480 6-8-9 **71**.............................. JamesSullivan 6 47
(Michael Herrington) *led 1f: chsd ldrs: rdn over 2f out: sn wknd* **50/1**

1 **11** *1 3/4* **Motawaafeq (FR)**[13] 9475 3-8-13 **77**.............................. AlistairRawlinson 5 49
(Michael Appleby) *hld up: hdwy on outer over 4f out: hung rt over 2f out: sn wknd (jockey said colt hung right)* **11/1**

1m 56.9s (-3.90) **Going Correction** -0.175s/f (Stan)
WFA 3 from 4yo+ 2lb **11** Ran SP% **122.5**
Speed ratings (Par 105): **110,109,109,108,108 108,108,107,103,96 95**
CSF £76.23 CT £815.28 TOTE £6.50: £2.10, £4.10, £2.60; EX 77.00 Trifecta £990.90.

Owner Lowe, Lewis And Hoyland **Bred** Irish National Stud **Trained** Tern Hill, Shropshire

FOCUS
A useful-looking handicap in which an ordinary gallop picked up on the approach to the home turn. The first eight finished in a bit of a heap.

T/Plt: £2,245.50 to a £1 stake. Pool: £71,548.47 - 23.26 winning units. T/Qpdt: £201.70 to a £1 stake. Pool: £9,041.81 - 33.17 winning units. **Colin Roberts**

9583 LINGFIELD (L-H)

Saturday, December 28

OFFICIAL GOING: Polytrack: standard
Wind: virtually nil Weather: overcast

9629 BOMBARDIER GOLDEN BEER H'CAP 7f 1y(P)

11:55 (11:56) (Class 6) (0-60,60) 3-Y-O+

£2,781 (£827; £413; £300; £300; £300) **Stalls** Low

Form RPR

442 **1** **Maqboola (USA)**[16] 9450 3-9-1 **54**.............................. ShaneKelly 1 62+
(Richard Hughes) *trckd ldrs: effrt on inner ent fnl f: pushed along to ld 100yds out: r.o wl* **6/1**[3]

0010 **2** *1* **Mont Kiara (FR)**[17] 9420 6-9-6 **59**.............................. LukeMorris 10 64
(Simon Dow) *t.k.h: chsd ldrs on outer: effrt and hung lft over 1f out: swtchd rt ins fnl f: styd on u.p to chse wnr towards fin: kpt on* **16/1**

6026 **3** *1/2* **Hit The Beat**[17] 9420 4-8-13 **59**.............................. AmeliaGlass(7) 14 63
(Clive Cox) *t.k.h: chsd ldr: pushed along to ld 1f out: hdd 100yds out: kpt on same pce and lost 2nd towards fin* **8/1**

5400 **4** *1* **Swissal (IRE)**[17] 9420 4-9-5 **58**..............................(v) DougieCostello 7 60
(David Dennis) *hld up towards rr of main gp: rdn over 2f out: hdwy and swtchd lft ent fnl f: clsd and nt clrest of runs ins fnl f: swtchd rt and kpt on towards fin: bled fr nose (vet said gelding bled from nse)* **14/1**

0601 **5** *nse* **Rajman**[24] 9298 3-9-5 **58**..............................(h) DavidProbert 9 59
(Tom Clover) *in tch in midfield: effrt in 6th ent fnl 2f: kpt on u.p ins fnl f: nvr quite enough pce to rch ldrs* **17/2**

6113 **6** *1 1/4* **Garth Rockett**[17] 9420 5-9-7 **60**..............................(tp) MartinDwyer 11 58
(Mike Murphy) *taken down early: led and crossed to inner: rdn and hdd 1f out: sn drvn: no ex whn sltly impeded wl ins fnl f: wknd towards fin* **7/2**[2]

0610 **7** *1/2* **Rivas Rob Roy**[26] 9277 4-9-3 **56**..............................(b) HectorCrouch 2 52
(John Gallagher) *t.k.h early: chsd ldrs: effrt over 1f out: sn drvn: kpt on same pce ins fnl f* **10/1**

0003 **8** *3/4* **Gold Hunter (IRE)**[17] 9423 9-9-5 **58**..............................(tp) JosephineGordon 8 52
(Steve Flook) *hld up towards rr of main gp: rdn over 2f out: kpt on u.p ins fnl f: nvr getting to ldrs* **25/1**

0033 **9** *2* **Mochalov**[37] 9086 4-9-6 **59**.............................. AdamKirby 12 59+
(Jane Chapple-Hyam) *hld up towards rr of main gp: hdwy whn carried lft and hmpd 1f out: nt rcvr: swtchd rt and nt pushed after* **11/4**[1]

4606 **10** *2 1/4* **Jupiter**[56] 8757 4-9-0 **53**..............................(p) RobertHavlin 6 36
(Alexandra Dunn) *hld up in rr of main gp: pushed along over 1f out: no hdwy: nvr involved* **33/1**

0/30 **11** *2 1/4* **Sixth Of June**[73] 8256 5-8-2 **46** oh1.............................. SophieRalston(5) 13 24
(Simon Earle) *stdd and dropped in bhd after s: in rr: wl detached and pushed along 1/2-way: sme hdwy ins fnl f: nvr involved* **50/1**

0002 **12** *1 3/4* **French Twist**[9] 9548 3-9-4 **60**..............................(b) ThomasGreatrex(3) 3 33
(David Loughnane) *in tch in midfield: pushed along and nudged rail ent fnl 2f: keeping on same pce whn squeezed for room and hmpd jst ins fnl f: eased after* **10/1**

34P5 **13** *3* **Cromwell**[135] 6111 3-9-0 **53**.............................. DanielMuscutt 4 18
(Alexandra Dunn) *hld up in rr of main gp: rdn and no hdwy over 1f out: wknd fnl f* **25/1**

1m 23.7s (-1.10) **Going Correction** -0.175s/f (Stan) **13** Ran SP% **128.1**
Speed ratings (Par 101): **99,97,97,96,96 94,94,93,90,88 85,83,80**
CSF £101.57 CT £820.53 TOTE £6.40: £2.60, £5.00, £2.20; EX 85.10 Trifecta £477.60.

Owner Thames Boys **Bred** Shadwell Farm LLC **Trained** Upper Lambourn, Berks

■ Stewards' Enquiry : Dougie Costello four-day ban: careless riding (Jan 11-14)

FOCUS
The Polytrack was standard ahead of the opener and featured several recent winners, though it went to the most unexposed runner. It paid to race prominently. The third is among those who help pin the straightforward level.

9630 LADBROKES "PLAY 1-2-FREE" ON FOOTBALL NURSERY H'CAP 7f 1y(P)

12:25 (12:27) (Class 6) (0-60,60) 2-Y-O

£2,781 (£827; £413; £300; £300; £300) **Stalls** Low

Form RPR

0330 **1** **Annie Quickstep (IRE)**[29] 9212 2-9-4 **57**.............................. RobHornby 11 59
(Jonathan Portman) *hld up in tch in midfield: effrt in 4th 2f out: drvn 1f out: styd on wl u.p fnl 100yds to ld last strides* **33/1**

4004 **2** *hd* **Urtzi (IRE)**[17] 9407 2-9-6 **59**.............................. WilliamCarson 12 60
(Michael Attwater) *rousted along leaving stalls: hdwy to ld over 4f out: rdn over 1f out: drvn and hdd ins fnl f: stl ev ch and kpt on u.p* **20/1**

0600 **3** *nse* **Boy George**[18] 9399 2-8-10 **49**.............................. HollieDoyle 1 50
(Dominic Ffrench Davis) *hld up in tch in last quartet: hdwy and swtchd rt over 1f out: hdwy between horses and drvn to ld ins fnl f: hdd and lost 2 pls last strides* **4/1**[3]

0002 **4** *3/4* **Beat The Breeze**[32] 9164 2-9-1 **54**.............................. JFEgan 6 53
(Simon Dow) *midfield: rdn over 2f out: drvn 2f out: no imp tl hdwy u.p 100yds out: kpt on wl towards fin* **5/2**[1]

360 **5** *3/4* **Dark Phoenix (IRE)**[30] 9195 2-9-2 **60**........(t[1]) ThoreHammerHansen(5) 5 57
(Paul Cole) *hld up in tch in last quartet: effrt 2f out: kpt on wl ins fnl f: nt rch ldrs* **8/1**

0600 **6** *nk* **Birkie Queen (IRE)**[38] 9061 2-8-11 **50**.............................. LiamKeniry 10 47
(J S Moore) *chsd ldrs: wnt 2nd over 3f out tl unable qck 1f out: unable qck whn hmpd 100yds out: one pce after (jockey said filly was denied clear run)* **50/1**

0051 **7** *hd* **Surrajah (IRE)**[16] 9438 2-9-0 **53**..............................(t) DavidProbert 2 49
(Tom Clover) *t.k.h: hld up in tch in rr: swtchd rt over 2f out: effrt 2f out: kpt on ins fnl f: nt rch ldrs (jockey said colt ran too free)* **3/1**[2]

1300 **8** *hd* **Chromium**[24] 9307 2-9-2 **55**..............................(p) LukeMorris 3 51
(Michael Attwater) *midfield: rdn over 2f out: drvn and ev ch 1f out: no ex 100yds out: wknd towards fin* **14/1**

602 **9** *1 3/4* **Cesifire (IRE)**[16] 9438 2-9-5 **58**.............................. RobertHavlin 7 49
(Adam West) *chsd ldrs: rdn over 2f out: drvn over 1f out: no ex and wknd ins fnl f: eased towards fin* **12/1**

0564 **10** *6* **Fact Or Fable (IRE)**[16] 9449 2-8-10 **56**..............................(p) SophieReed(7) 13 31
(J S Moore) *s.i.s: hld up in tch in rr on outer: hdwy into midfield 2f out: rdn and unable qck over 1f out: sn btn and wknd ins fnl f* **16/1**

000 **11** *99* **Queen Of Clubs**[33] 9159 2-9-4 **60**.......................... ThomasGreatrex(3) 4
(Roger Charlton) *led tl over 4f out: hit rail and lost pl qckly over 3f: sn bhd: virtually p.u fnl 2f: t.o (jockey said filly lost action approx 3f out, but after easing the filly down she seemed to be moving better so he allowed her to canter home quietly; post-race examination failed to reveal any abnormalities)* **14/1**

1m 25.15s (0.35) **Going Correction** -0.175s/f (Stan) **11** Ran SP% **121.3**
Speed ratings (Par 94): **91,90,90,89,89 88,88,88,86,79**
CSF £569.87 CT £3277.26 TOTE £40.60: £8.80, £5.80, £2.00; EX 461.30.
Owner Mark & Connie Burton **Bred** Ringfort Stud **Trained** Upper Lambourn, Berks

FOCUS
An open nursery and they finished in a heap. It's been rated as modest form.

9631 LADBROKES HOME OF THE ODDS BOOST EBF NOVICE STKS 7f 1y(P)
1:00 (1:03) (Class 5) 2-Y-O **£3,428** (£1,020; £509; £254) **Stalls** Low

Form RPR

22 **1** **Corvair (IRE)**[19] 9392 2-9-2 0.. JackMitchell 2 85+
(Simon Crisford) *broke wl: mde all: rdn and qcknd clr over 1f out: r.o strly: easily* **5/2**[1]

2 *4 1/2* **Mutalahef (IRE)** 2-9-2 0.. MartinDwyer 3 74+
(Marcus Tregoning) *dwlt: sn rcvrd and chsd ldrs: rdn ent fnl 2f: unable to match pce of wnr over 1f out: chsd clr wnr ins fnl f: kpt on but no threat* **9/2**[3]

4 **3** *1 3/4* **Top Secret**[19] 9385 2-9-2 0.. HectorCrouch 10 69+
(Clive Cox) *pushed along leaving stalls: midfield: hdwy and effrt ent fnl 2f: wnt 3rd ins fnl f: styd on: no ch w wnr* **8/1**

1 **4** *3/4* **Brunel Charm**[24] 9299 2-9-6 0.. FinleyMarsh(3) 13 74+
(Richard Hughes) *midfield: effrt and swtchd rt over 1f out: kpt on ins fnl f: no ch w wnr* **11/4**[2]

2 **5** *1 1/4* **Prince Caspian**[42] 9008 2-9-2 0.. TomMarquand 4 64
(Richard Hannon) *sn pressing wnr: rdn ent fnl 2f: unable to match pce of wnr over 1f out: wl hld whn lost 2nd and wknd ins fnl f* **9/2**[3]

6 *3* **Careful Thought** 2-8-11 0.. JasonHart 6 51
(Mark Johnston) *pushed along leaving stalls: midfield: pushed along 4f out: outpcd jst over 2f out: no ch after* **25/1**

50 **7** *1* **Trecco Bay**[74] 8218 2-8-11 0.. WilliamCarson 12 48+
(David Elsworth) *impeded sn after s: hld up in last pair: outpcd over 2f out: wd bnd 2f out: sme late hdwy: nvr trbld ldrs* **40/1**

0 **8** *3/4* **Rodney Le Roc**[212] 3257 2-9-2 0.. JoeyHaynes 1 51
(John Best) *chsd ldng pair: rdn ent fnl 2f: sn outpcd: wknd fnl f* **66/1**

60 **9** *hd* **Rock Of Redmond (IRE)**[58] 8700 2-8-6 0.............. SophieRalston(5) 7 46+
(Dean Ivory) *restrained after s: t.k.h: hld up in last quartet: outpcd over 2f out: no ch over 1f out* **66/1**

6 **10** *1/2* **Life Matters (USA)**[17] 9415 2-9-2 0.. ShaneKelly 8 50+
(Richard Hughes) *hld up in last quartet: outpcd over 2f out: no ch over 1f out* **14/1**

0 **11** *hd* **Crazy Love**[29] 9211 2-8-11 0.. CallumShepherd 5 44
(Mick Channon) *stdd s: t.k.h: hld up in last pair: outpcd over 2f out: no ch over 1f out* **33/1**

12 *15* **Francisco Pizarro (IRE)** 2-9-2 0.. RobertHavlin 9 10
(Adam West) *chsd ldrs: hung rt 4f out: lost pl: wl bhd fnl f* **66/1**

1m 23.34s (-1.46) **Going Correction** -0.175s/f (Stan) **12** Ran SP% **123.1**
Speed ratings (Par 96): **101,95,93,93,91 88,87,86,85,85 85,67**
CSF £14.21 TOTE £3.30: £1.70, £2.10, £2.50; EX 15.20 Trifecta £79.50.
Owner Sheikh Juma Dalmook Al Maktoum **Bred** Mubarak Al Naemi **Trained** Newmarket, Suffolk
■ Vape was withdrawn. Price at time of withdrawal 20/1. Rule 4 does not apply.
■ Stewards' Enquiry : Finley Marsh two-day ban: careless riding (Jan 11, 12)

FOCUS
A fair novice in which the winner pulled clear having led throughout. It was run in a 0.36s faster time than the opening handicap for older horses. It's tricky to pin the level.

9632 BETWAY H'CAP 6f 1y(P)
1:35 (1:40) (Class 5) (0-75,75) 3-Y-O+
£3,428 (£1,020; £509; £300; £300; £300) **Stalls** Low

Form RPR

6651 **1** **Real Estate (IRE)**[12] 9498 4-9-1 **69**..............................(p) RobertHavlin 3 78
(Michael Attwater) *midfield: clsd to chse ldrs 2f out: swtchd rt and effrt over 1f out: rdn to ld 1f out: r.o wl* **5/1**[2]

6300 **2** *1* **Alicia Darcy (IRE)**[10] 9519 3-9-0 **68**..............................(b) HollieDoyle 2 74
(Archie Watson) *off the pce in midfield: clsd over 2f out: rdn to chse ldrs 1f out: chsd wnr ins fnl f: kpt on* **8/1**

2354 **3** *nk* **Shake Me Handy**[117] 6806 4-8-13 **67**.............................. JackMitchell 12 72
(Roger Teal) *off the pce in midfield: clsd over 2f out: swtchd rt over 1f out: hdwy u.p to go 3rd ins fnl f: kpt on wl: bled fr nose (vet said gelding bled from nse)* **12/1**

50R5 **4** *2 1/2* **Gnaad (IRE)**[30] 9203 5-9-2 **73**.............................. DarraghKeenan(3) 9 70
(Alan Bailey) *off the pce in midfield: clsd over 2f out: wd and lost pl bnd 2f out: kpt on u.p ins fnl f: nvr threatened ldrs* **12/1**

1123 **5** *nk* **Grisons (FR)**[15] 9458 3-9-4 **72**.............................. RichardKingscote 10 68
(Robert Cowell) *chsd ldr: rdn ent fnl 2f: no ex and lost 2nd ins fnl f: wknd wl ins fnl f* **4/1**[1]

0100 **6** *3/4* **Spring Romance (IRE)**[30] 9203 4-9-6 **74**.............................. JoeyHaynes 6 68
(Dean Ivory) *chsd ldrs: clsd over 2f out: chsng ldrs whn short of room and hmpd 1f out: swtchd rt and no imp after (jockey said gelding was denied a clear run)* **12/1**

3043 **7** *3/4* **Big Lachie**[18] 9402 5-9-3 **71**.............................. WilliamCarson 11 62
(Mark Loughnane) *off the pce in last pair: swtchd rt and hdwy ins fnl f: nvr trbld ldrs* **12/1**

0565 **8** *shd* **Alfie Solomons (IRE)**[19] 9387 3-9-7 **75**..............................(b) MartinDwyer 4 66
(Amanda Perrett) *stdd s: hld up off the pce in rr: hdwy 1f out: kpt on ins fnl f: nvr trbld ldrs* **7/1**[3]

4205 **9** *1 3/4* **Hieronymus**[31] 9171 3-9-0 **68**.............................. NicolaCurrie 5 53
(George Baker) *sn off the pce in last trio: rdn over 3f out: nvr trbld ldrs (jockey said gelding was outpaced early)* **5/1**[2]

5000 **10** *1 1/2* **Oberyn Martell**[30] 9203 3-9-4 **72**.............................. CharlesBishop 8 53
(Eve Johnson Houghton) *chsd ldrs: rdn and struggling 2f out: wknd fnl f* **16/1**

6600 **11** *1* **Isle Of Innisfree (USA)**[15] 9455 3-9-1 **69**..............................(t) JFEgan 7 46
(Paul D'Arcy) *taken down early: led: rdn and hdd 1f out: sn wknd* **33/1**

1m 10.17s (-1.73) **Going Correction** -0.175s/f (Stan) **11** Ran SP% **116.5**
Speed ratings (Par 103): **104,102,102,98,98 97,96,96,94,92 90**
CSF £42.48 CT £404.92 TOTE £5.70: £2.00, £2.70, £3.60; EX 49.00 Trifecta £973.90.
Owner Christian Main **Bred** Rabbah Bloodstock Limited **Trained** Epsom, Surrey
■ Lalania was withdrawn. Price at time of withdrawal 14/1. Rule 4 applies to all bets - deduction 5p in the pound.

FOCUS
An average sprint handicap for the grade, though they went a blazing gallop and the winner came from behind. The second helps set the level.

9633 BETWAY CASINO H'CAP 1m 4f (P)
2:10 (2:12) (Class 4) (0-85,85) 3-Y-O+
£5,207 (£1,549; £774; £387; £300; £300) **Stalls** Low

Form RPR

3664 **1** **Pirate King**[29] 9215 4-9-5 **80**.............................. KieranShoemark 2 89+
(Charlie Fellowes) *midfield: swtchd rt and hdwy over 1f out: rdn and str run to ld ins fnl f: sn in command* **6/1**[3]

0022 **2** *1 1/4* **Battle Of Marathon (USA)**[18] 9405 7-9-2 **80**........ DarraghKeenan(3) 10 86
(John Ryan) *stdd and dropped in bhd after s: hld up in rr: clsd and nt clrest of runs over 2f out: hdwy 1f out: r.o wl to go 2nd last strides: nvr getting to wnr* **14/1**

2221 **3** *nk* **Arabic Culture (USA)**[26] 9274 5-9-10 **85**.............................. SamJames 8 90
(Grant Tuer) *in tch in midfield: clsd to press ldng pair and rdn 2f out: ev ch 1f out: kpt on same pce ins fnl f* **5/1**[2]

1045 **4** *1/2* **Yellow Tiger (FR)**[70] 8350 3-9-2 **81**..............................(p) DavidProbert 5 85
(Ian Williams) *chsd ldrs: short of room over 9f out: drvn ent fnl f: kpt on same pce fnl 100yds* **7/1**

4113 **5** *nk* **Emenem**[126] 6437 5-9-3 **83**.............................. ThoreHammerHansen(5) 6 87
(Simon Dow) *chsd ldr tl led over 3f out: rdn ent fnl 2f: drvn and hrd pressed over 1f out: hdd ins fnl f: no ex and wknd towards fin* **14/1**

6P06 **6** *1* **Seafarer (IRE)**[7] 9588 5-9-8 **83**..............................(v) MartinDwyer 11 85
(Marcus Tregoning) *midfield: hdwy to chse ldrs 9f out: nt clrest of runs 2f out: swtchd rt over 1f out: kpt on same pce ins fnl f* **16/1**

12-0 **7** *2 1/2* **Calling The Wind (IRE)**[210] 3358 3-9-1 **80**..............................(b) ShaneKelly 7 78
(Richard Hughes) *midfield: hdwy to chse ldrs over 4f out: chsd ldr over 3f out tl unable qck 1f out: wknd ins fnl f* **33/1**

3232 **8** *hd* **Sir Prize**[38] 9066 4-9-6 **81**.............................. AdamKirby 12 79
(Dean Ivory) *midfield: effrt jst over 2f out: kpt on same pce and no imp ins fnl f: eased towards fin* **4/1**[1]

0631 **9** *1/2* **Blue Medici**[32] 9167 5-9-3 **78**.............................. RichardKingscote 13 75
(Mark Loughnane) *s.i.s: hld up towards rr: effrt on inner over 1f out: nvr getting on terms and one pce ins fnl f (jockey said gelding was slowly away)* **9/1**

3615 **10** *1/2* **Blowing Dixie**[15] 9454 3-8-11 **76**.............................. JFEgan 1 72
(Jane Chapple-Hyam) *midfield: rdn jst over 2f out: no imp over 1f out: wknd ins fnl f* **8/1**

032 **11** *1 1/4* **Torbellino**[66] 8451 3-8-6 **71**.............................. HollieDoyle 14 65
(John Best) *stdd s: t.k.h: hld up towards rr: effrt bnd 2f out: no imp: nvr involved* **25/1**

4300 **12** *1 1/2* **Cry Wolf**[25] 9288 6-9-3 **78**.............................. DanielMuscutt 15 70
(Alexandra Dunn) *stdd s: hld up in rr: nvr involved* **50/1**

/14- **13** *13* **Petit Palais**[51] 7760 4-9-5 **80**..............................(b) CharlesBishop 4 51
(Tom George) *t.k.h: led tl over 3f out: losing pl whn hmpd over 2f out: bhd over 1f out* **16/1**

14 *43* **Honorable (FR)**[25] 4-9-2 **77**..............................(p) HectorCrouch 3
(Gary Moore) *in tch in midfield: rdn and lost pl over 4f out: lost tch 3f out: eased: t.o (jockey said gelding was never travelling)* **25/1**

0614 **P** **Htilominlo**[32] 9167 3-8-13 **78**..............................(t) LukeMorris 9
(Sylvester Kirk) *pushed along leaving stalls: midfield: eased and p.u after 2f: dismntd (jockey said colt lost action; post-race examination revealed colt lame left-hind)* **14/1**

2m 28.36s (-4.64) **Going Correction** -0.175s/f (Stan)
WFA 3 from 4yo+ 4lb **15** Ran SP% **128.9**
Speed ratings (Par 105): **108,107,106,106,106 105,104,103,103,103 102,101,92,64,**
CSF £90.21 CT £468.15 TOTE £8.20: £2.70, £4.30, £2.30; EX 123.70 Trifecta £712.10.
Owner Daniel Macauliffe & Anoj Don **Bred** Mrs P M Ignarski **Trained** Newmarket, Suffolk

FOCUS
Some good recent form on offer for this open handicap where they went a good gallop. The winner has been rated back to his best, and the second in line with his recent form.

9634 LADBROKES WHERE THE NATION PLAYS NOVICE STKS 1m 2f (P)
2:45 (2:49) (Class 5) 2-Y-O **£3,428** (£1,020; £509; £254) **Stalls** Low

Form RPR

2 **1** **Kipps (IRE)**[42] 9007 2-9-5 0.. DavidProbert 12 78+
(Hughie Morrison) *in tch in midfield: clsd to chse ldrs 4f out: rdn and kicked clr w ldr 2f out: led ins fnl f: r.o wl* **11/10**[1]

2 *nk* **First Winter (IRE)** 2-9-5 0.. AdamKirby 2 77+
(Charlie Appleby) *dwlt and rousted along early: towards rr: hdwy into midfield 5f out: rdn and hdwy on outer to ld over 2f out: kicked clr w wnr 2f out: rn green and edgd lft over 1f out: hdd ins fnl f: kpt on* **5/1**[3]

0 **3** *5* **A Star Above**[33] 9154 2-9-5 0.. TomMarquand 8 69+
(William Haggas) *chsd ldrs: effrt jst over 2f out: swtchd rt and chsd clr ldng pair over 1f out: no imp and kpt on same pce ins fnl f* **15/2**

0 **4** *3/4* **Angel On High (IRE)**[64] 8511 2-9-5 0.. LukeMorris 6 67
(Harry Dunlop) *hld up in tch towards rr: hdwy over 3f out: 5th and rdn ent fnl 2f: sn outpcd by ldng pair: kpt on same pce ins fnl f* **33/1**

5 **5** *1* **Indigo Lake**[23] 9326 2-9-5 0.. RobertHavlin 11 67+
(John Gosden) *dwlt: hdwy to chse ldr after 2f: led 3f out: sn hdd and outpcd whn impeded 2f out: wl hld 1f out* **9/2**[2]

5 **6** *shd* **Night Bear**[37] 9095 2-9-5 0.. KieranShoemark 7 64
(Ed Vaughan) *s.i.s: t.k.h: hld up in rr: effrt whn hung rt and wd bnd 2f out: kpt on ins fnl f: nvr trbld ldrs* **25/1**

02 **7** *nk* **Itsallaboutluck (IRE)**[31] 9181 2-9-2 0.. FinleyMarsh(3) 5 64+
(Richard Hughes) *hld up towards rr: effrt on inner over 1f out: switching rt 1f out and then bk lft ins fnl f: kpt on: nvr trbld ldrs* **14/1**

3 **8** *1/2* **Miraz (IRE)**[77] 8121 2-9-5 0.. RichardKingscote 13 63
(Richard Hannon) *led tl 3f out: sn rdn and struggling: wknd over 1f out* **17/2**

6 **9** *3 1/2* **Cafe Milano**[120] 6684 2-9-0 0.. ThoreHammerHansen(5) 10 56
(Simon Dow) *s.i.s: rn green in rr: rdn over 2f out: n.d but kpt on and swtchd rt ins fnl f* **66/1**

5 **10** *1* **Night Time Girl**[19] 9383 2-8-11 0.. GabrieleMalune(3) 3 51
(Ismail Mohammed) *chsd ldr for 2f: styd chsng ldrs tl nt clr run and shuffled bk over 2f out: swtchd rt 2f out: no imp and wl hld after* **33/1**

0 **11** *hd* **Soldier On Parade**[12] 9500 2-9-5 0.. DanielMuscutt 1 55
(Amy Murphy) *midfield: effrt over 2f out: short of room and hmpd 2f out: no prog and wl hld after* **66/1**

12 *3/4* **Sharney** 2-9-0 0.. HollieDoyle 4 48
(Archie Watson) *midfield: rdn over 2f out: sn outpcd: wl btn over 1f out* **25/1**

13 1 1/2 **Night Of Fashion (IRE)** 2-9-0 0.. RobHornby 9 45
(Ralph Beckett) *rn green in rr: rdn and carried rt bnd 2f out: nvr involved*
50/1
2m 5.1s (-1.50) **Going Correction** -0.175s/f (Stan) **13** Ran SP% **129.9**
Speed ratings (Par 96): **99,98,94,94,93 93,93,92,89,89 88,88,87**
CSF £7.16 TOTE £2.00: £1.20, £1.90, £2.90; EX 10.10 Trifecta £45.00.
Owner M Kerr-Dineen, M Hughes & W Eason **Bred** Rockhart Trading Ltd **Trained** East Ilsley, Berks
FOCUS
Some promising types on show for this novice in which the first two came clear.

9635 BOMBARDIER BRITISH HOPPED AMBER BEER NOVICE STKS 1m 1y(P)
3:20 (3:24) (Class 5) 3-Y-0+ **£3,428** (£1,020; £509; £254) **Stalls** High

Form RPR
1 **Emraan (IRE)** 3-9-2 0.. RichardKingscote 3 77
(Ian Williams) *uns rdr on way to post but sn ct: midfield: effrt to chse ldrs and nt clr run 2f out: swtchd lft and hdwy on inner over 1f out: led jst ins fnl f: sn clr and r.o strly: readily* **16/1**

50 2 3 3/4 **Marmalade Day**[17] [9425] 3-8-11 0.................................... HectorCrouch 8 64
(Gary Moore) *pushed along and outpcd early: clsd on to rr of field 5f out: rdn wl over 2f out: swtchd rt over 1f out: styd on ins fnl f: wnt 2nd last strides: no ch w wnr* **66/1**

31 3 nk **Bridgewater Bay (IRE)**[17] [9416] 3-9-9 0............................ AdamKirby 2 75
(Jane Chapple-Hyam) *sn led: rdn wl over 2f out: drvn over 1f out: hdd jst ins fnl f: sn outpcd and btn: lost 2nd last strides* **10/11**[1]

0 4 nk **Smoke On The Water**[225] [2802] 3-9-2 0............................. KieranShoemark 6 67
(Charlie Fellowes) *hld up in tch: effrt jst over 2f out: swtchd lft and kpt on ins fnl f: no ch w wnr* **7/4**[2]

-41 5 nk **Albadr (USA)**[130] [6315] 3-9-9 0.. DanielMuscutt 5 74
(Roger Ingram) *dwlt and pushed along leaving stalls: hdwy to press ldr over 6f out: rdn and ev ch ent fnl 2f tl nt match pce of wnr jst ins fnl f: kpt on same pce after* **15/2**[3]

36 6 1 **War Princess (IRE)**[18] [9400] 3-8-11 0................................ DavidProbert 4 59
(Alan King) *chsd ldrs on outer: rdn ent fnl 2f: sn outpcd: wknd ins fnl f* **12/1**

7 1/2 **Nearly Perfection (IRE)**[38] 3-8-11 0.................................. HollieDoyle 9 58
(Alan King) *s.i.s: outpcd in last trio early: clsd and in tch 5f out: unable qck 2f out: wl hld: edgd lft and one pce ins fnl f* **10/1**

0 8 4 **Into Debt**[29] [9213] 3-9-2 0.. JFEgan 7 54?
(Camilla Poulton) *sn outpcd in rr: clsd and in tch 5f out: rdn and outpcd over 2f out: wl btn over 1f out* **50/1**

00 9 3/4 **Laurentia (IRE)**[17] [9425] 3-8-6 0................................... SophieRalston(5) 1 47
(Dean Ivory) *broke wl: restrained bk to chse ldrs and t.k.h: rdn and lost pl ent fnl 2f: wknd over 1f out* **66/1**

1m 36.87s (-1.33) **Going Correction** -0.175s/f (Stan) **9** Ran SP% **128.1**
Speed ratings (Par 103): **99,95,94,94,94 93,92,88,88**
CSF £727.10 TOTE £20.50: £3.30, £10.10, £1.10; EX 1319.90 Trifecta £5156.30.
Owner T Green **Bred** Shadwell Estate Company Limited **Trained** Portway, Worcs
FOCUS
An intriguing clash between the first two in the market, though the jolly got involved in a duel up front, leaving the door open for a big-priced winner to pick him off. The race is hard to rate, with doubts over the form horses.
T/Plt: £358.10 to a £1 stake. Pool: £76,118.57 - 155.13 winning units T/Qpdt: £20.70 to a £1 stake. Pool: £9,143.90 - 326.42 winning units **Steve Payne**

9636 - 9656a (Foreign Racing) - See Raceform Interactive

8777 SANTA ANITA (L-H)
Saturday, December 28

OFFICIAL GOING: Dirt: fast; turf: good

9637a AMERICAN OAKS (GRADE 1) (3YO FILLIES) (TURF) 1m 2f (T)
9:44 3-Y-0
£141,732 (£47,244; £28,346; £14,173; £4,724; £276)

RPR
1 **Lady Prancealot (IRE)**[71] 3-8-12 0.. JoeBravo 5 104
(Richard Baltas, U.S.A) *settled toward rr of midfield: shkn up over 3 1/2f out and hdwy: drvn along over 1f out: drvn to the ld between horses and disp pce ins fnl f and styd on wl u.p* **8/5**[1]

2 1/2 **Mucho Unusual (USA)**[27] [9261] 3-8-12 0............................ JoelRosario 3 103
(Tim Yakteen, U.S.A) *hmpd s: settled to trck ldg pair: shkn up nr over 3 1/2f out: angled three wd over 1 1/2f out and drvn: disp pce fnl f: styd on u.p but narrowly denied* **3/1**[3]

3 1 1/2 **Pretty Point (USA)**[42] 3-8-12 0.. MikeESmith 6 100
(Patrick Gallagher, U.S.A) *settled in rr: pushed along nr 2f out: shifted outside nr over 1 1/2f out and drvn to make hdwy: r.o u.p and nrst fin* **248/10**

4 3/4 **Giza Goddess (USA)**[27] [9261] 3-8-12 0............................ VictorEspinoza 7 99
(John Shirreffs, U.S.A) *settled toward rr of midfield: gradual hdwy to midfield 5f out: rowed along over 2 1/2f out: bmpd appr fnl f: drvn and kpt on u.p* **29/10**[2]

5 1 3/4 **Apache Princess (USA)**[13] 3-8-12 0.............................. JavierCastellano 2 95
(J Keith Desormeaux, U.S.A) *settled in midfield: slt hdwy to chse ldg pair over 4f out: pushed along appr 3f out: drvn over 2f out: styd on at same pce u.p fnl 110yds* **89/10**

6 nk **Vibrance (USA)**[28] 3-8-12 0.. AbelCedillo 8 94
(Michael McCarthy, U.S.A) *trckd ldr while t.k.h early: plld out to dispute pce over 4f out: inherited brief ld over 1 1/2f out and drvn to keep it: hdd ins fnl f and wknd* **13/2**

7 2 1/4 **K P Slickem (USA)**[63] 3-8-12 0.....................................(b) JorgelVelez 4 90
(Jeff Mullins, U.S.A) *settled in last pair: drvn along over 3f out: drvn 1 1/2f out and no imp* **61/1**

8 3 3/4 **So Much Happy (USA)**[49] 3-8-12 0........................(b) TiagoJosuePereira 1 82
(George Papaprodromou, U.S.A) *t.k.h to early ld: jnd fr outside over 4f out and disp pce: drvn along 2f out: lost pl over 1 1/2f out: t.o fnl f* **49/1**

2m 1.7s (2.42) **8** Ran SP% **120.0**
PARI-MUTUEL (all including 2 unit stake): WIN 5.20; PLACE (1-2) 3.00, 4.00; SHOW (1-2-3) 2.40, 3.20, 5.80; SF 15.20.
Owner Jules Iavarone, Michael Iavarone & Jerry McClanaha **Bred** Tally-Ho Stud **Trained** North America

9638a LA BREA STKS (GRADE 1) (3YO FILLIES) (MAIN TRACK) (DIRT) 7f (D)
10:18 3-Y-0
£141,732 (£47,244; £28,346; £14,173; £4,724; £276)

RPR
1 **Hard Not To Love (CAN)**[63] 3-8-8 0...................................... MikeESmith 7 113
(John Shirreffs, U.S.A) *settled in rr: pushed along over 3 1/2f out and rapid hdwy outside: in 3rd over 2f out: drvn 1 1/2f out: r.o u.p: led 110yds out and drew clr* **116/10**

2 2 1/4 **Bellafina (USA)**[56] [8769] 3-8-10 0..............................(b) VictorEspinoza 5 109
(Simon Callaghan, U.S.A) *pushed up to ld: pushed along over 3f out: drvn over 2f out while disputing pce w rival to her outside: led again 1f out: styd on u.p but hdd and no ch w wnr in fnl 110yds* **3/5**[1]

3 1 **Mother Mother (USA)**[239] 3-8-8 0.................................(b) JoelRosario 9 104
(Bob Baffert, U.S.A) *trckd ldr: hdwy to press ldr fr over 3 1/2f out: disp pce fr over 2f out: drvn along 1 1/2f out: kpt on u.p but outpcd* **63/10**[3]

4 4 1/2 **First Star (USA)**[70] 3-8-8 0.. DraydenVanDyke 1 92
(Ronald W Ellis, U.S.A) *settled towards rr of midfield: pushed along for hdwy to midfield over 4f out: drvn along over 2 1/2f out: kpt on at same pce u.p* **63/10**[3]

5 1 **Bell's The One (USA)**[70] 3-8-10 0................................. JavierCastellano 6 91
(Neil L Pessin, U.S.A) *settled in rr: pushed along and hdwy over 3f out: hdwy to 3rd position wl bhd ldng pair over 2 1/2f out: drvn over 2f out and grad outpcd by ldrs* **54/10**[2]

6 3 1/2 **Del Mar May (USA)**[35] 3-8-8 0... JoeBravo 2 80
(Richard Baltas, U.S.A) *hld up in midfield: drvn along over 4f out and sn no imp* **54/1**

7 3/4 **Stirred (USA)**[56] 3-8-8 0..(b) GeovanniFranco 4 78
(Michael McCarthy, U.S.A) *settled midfield: pushed along over 3f out: sn relegated to last and no imp* **93/1**

8 10 **Motion Emotion (USA)**[31] 3-8-8 0...................................... MarioGutierrez 8 51
(Richard Baltas, U.S.A) *settled midfield: drvn along over 3f out: no hdwy and relegated towards rr over 2f out: drvn nr 1 1/2f out and wknd* **37/1**

9 6 3/4 **Free Cover (USA)**[70] 3-8-8 0.. AbelCedillo 3 32
(Andrew Lerner, U.S.A) *trckd ldng pair: pushed along whn beginning to lose grnd over 3 1/2f out and outpcd* **53/1**

1m 22.17s **9** Ran SP% **120.8**
PARI-MUTUEL (all including 2 unit stake): WIN 25.20; PLACE (1-2) 6.60, 2.40; SHOW (1-2-3) 4.20, 2.10, 3.60; SF 61.40.
Owner West Point Thoroughbreds, Mercedes Stables LLC Et **Bred** Anderson Farms (Ontario) Inc **Trained** USA

9639a MALIBU STKS (GRADE 1) (3YO) (MAIN TRACK) (DIRT) 7f (D)
11:26 3-Y-0 **£141,732** (£47,244; £28,346; £14,173; £4,724)

RPR
1 **Omaha Beach (USA)**[56] [8771] 3-8-12 0.................................. MikeESmith 5 118
(Richard E Mandella, U.S.A) *settled toward rr in 4th position: gng wl and hdwy fr 3 1/2f out: led over 3f out: drew clr on bridle fnl f and r.o wl* **2/5**[1]

2 2 3/4 **Roadster (USA)**[35] 3-8-10 0..(b) JoelRosario 4 109
(Bob Baffert, U.S.A) *settled last: pushed along over 3 1/2f out: hdwy over 2 1/2f out: rowed along nr 1 1/2f out: drvn fnl f and styd on u.p: no ch w wnr* **9/1**[3]

3 2 1/4 **Manny Wah (USA)**[33] 3-8-8 0.....................................(b) ChanningHill 3 101
(Bob Baffert, U.S.A) *away wl but settled to trck ldng pair: shkn up between horses over 3f out: drvn along appr 2f out: no ch w wnr fnl f: kpt on u.p but lost 2nd 110yds out* **206/10**

4 4 3/4 **Complexity (USA)**[38] 3-8-8 0.. JavierCastellano 2 88
(Chad C Brown, U.S.A) *t.k.h: pushed along nr 3f out: drvn appr fnl f: grad outpcd by ldrs* **12/5**[2]

5 18 **Much Better (USA)**[27] 3-8-8 0.....................................(b) FlavienPrat 1 40
(Bob Baffert, U.S.A) *t.k.h: led: hdd over 3f out and sn t.o* **207/10**

1m 22.33s **5** Ran SP% **120.1**
PARI-MUTUEL (all including 2 unit stake): WIN 2.80; PLACE (1-2) 2.10, 3.60; SHOW (1-2-3) 2.10, 3.00, 3.80; SF 9.20.
Owner Fox Hill Farms Inc **Bred** Charming Syndicate **Trained** USA

9559 SOUTHWELL (L-H)
Sunday, December 29

OFFICIAL GOING: Fibresand: standard
Wind: Moderate across Weather: Fine & dry

9640 LADBROKES WHERE THE NATION PLAYS NURSERY H'CAP 1m 13y(F)
12:05 (12:07) (Class 6) (0-65,65) 2-Y-O
£2,781 (£827; £413; £400; £400; £400) **Stalls** Low

Form RPR
364 1 **Perregrin**[213] [3265] 2-9-0 **58**.. JasonHart 5 62
(Mark Johnston) *trckd ldrs: hdwy and cl up 3f out: chal on outer 2f out: rdn to ld over 1f out: drvn ins fnl f: hld on wl towards fin* **10/3**[2]

0010 2 shd **Speed Dating (FR)**[23] [9346] 2-8-12 **56**..........................(v) LewisEdmunds 8 60
(Derek Shaw) *trckd ldrs: hdwy 3f out: rdn along 2f out: styd on wl to chse wnr ins fnl f: sn drvn to chal and ev ch: no ex nr fin* **3/1**[1]

3235 3 2 **Dancing Leopard (IRE)**[38] [9097] 2-9-4 **65**............... HarrisonShaw(3) 3 64
(K R Burke) *in rr: swtchd rt towards outer and pushed along after 3f: rdn and hdwy over 2f out: drvn to chse ldrs over 1f out: kpt on fnl f (jockey said filly was never travelling)* **4/1**[3]

004 4 1/2 **Brass Clankers**[41] [9029] 2-8-13 **57**................................ KieranO'Neill 2 55
(Robyn Brisland) *trckd ldng pair: pushed along 4f out: rdn along and sltly outpcd over 3f out: drvn along on inner over 2f out: kpt on appr fnl f* **7/1**

546 5 1 3/4 **Gweedore**[101] [7361] 2-9-7 **65**... BenCurtis 7 59
(Katie Scott) *cl up: led wl over 2f out and sn rdn: jnd and drvn 2f out: hdd over 1f out: wknd ent fnl f* **8/1**

0600 6 1 3/4 **Pull Harder Con**[94] [7627] 2-8-10 **54**................................ TomEaves 4 44
(Robyn Brisland) *dwlt: in tch: pushed along and hdwy over 3f out: chsd ldrs and rdn over 2f out: drvn wl over 1f out: edgd lft and no imp fnl f* **25/1**

4030 7 4 1/2 **Comvida (IRE)**[32] [9179] 2-8-4 **48**...(v[1]) LukeMorris 6 28
(Hugo Palmer) *slt ld: rdn along 3f out: sn hdd: drvn and wknd wl over 1f out* **12/1**

The Form Book Flat 2019, Raceform Ltd, Newbury, RG14 5SJ

400 8 *19* **Noddy Shuffle**[158] 5294 2-8-10 **54**.................................... JamesSullivan 1
(Michael Easterby) *chsd ldrs on inner: rdn along and lost pl bef 1/2-way: sn bhd* **12/1**

1m 44.31s (0.61) **Going Correction** -0.05s/f (Stan) **8** Ran SP% **110.9**
Speed ratings (Par 94): **94,93,91,91,89 87,83,64**
CSF £12.89 CT £38.06 TOTE £2.70: £1.60, £1.30, £1.90; EX 17.40 Trifecta £42.50.
Owner Bearstone Stud Limited **Bred** Bearstone Stud **Trained** Middleham Moor, N Yorks
■ Stewards' Enquiry : Lewis Edmunds two-day ban: used whip above the permitted level (Jan 12-13)

FOCUS
Overcast, with a fresh breeze. Competitive enough for the very modest grade and a tight finish ensured off a slow pace. The two market leaders came down the stands' side.

9641 LADBROKES HOME OF THE ODDS BOOST NOVICE MEDIAN AUCTION STKS 4f 214y(F)
12:40 (12:45) (Class 5) 2-Y-O £3,428 (£1,020; £509; £254) **Stalls** Centre

Form RPR

2323 1 **Astrozone**[13] 9499 2-9-0 66.................................... LukeMorris 3 67
(Bryan Smart) *racd towards far side: mde all: rdn along and edgd rt to centre over 1f out: drvn and edgd rt ins fnl f: kpt on wl towards fin* **7/4**[1]

0 2 *3/4* **Xian Express (IRE)**[11] 9514 2-9-5 79..............................(b) BenCurtis 2 69
(Michael Appleby) *racd towards far side: cl up: rdn along to chal wl over 1f out: drvn and ev ch ins fnl f: edgd rt and no ex last 50yds* **7/4**[1]

66 3 *1 3/4* **Shymay**[30] 9211 2-9-0 0.................................... DavidProbert 7 58+
(George Margarson) *racd nr stands' rail: chsd ldrs: rdn along and sltly outpcd over 2f out: kpt on u.p fnl f* **13/2**[3]

4 *2 3/4* **Due A Diamond** 2-9-0 0.................................... LewisEdmunds 4 48
(Derek Shaw) *green and towards rr in centre: rdn along 2f out: styd on fr over 1f out (jockey said filly hung left-handed throughout)* **25/1**

0000 5 *nk* **Castashadow**[20] 9392 2-9-5 44..............................(b[1]) TomEaves 6 52
(Alan Brown) *racd towards stands' side: prom: rdn along 2f out: sn drvn and wknd appr fnl f* **66/1**

335 6 *2* **Alex Gracie**[32] 9181 2-8-7 62.................................... JonathanFisher(7) 5 40
(Scott Dixon) *awkward s: in tch centre: hdwy to chse ldrs 1/2-way: sn rdn and wknd wl over 1f out (jockey said filly stumbled when leaving the stalls)* **5/1**[2]

00 7 *5* **Girl Of Dreams**[24] 9323 2-8-9 0.................................... SophieRalston(5) 1 22
(Nikki Evans) *racd far side: chsd ldrs: rdn along 1/2-way: sn outpcd and bhd* **150/1**

59.54s (-0.16) **Going Correction** -0.05s/f (Stan) **7** Ran SP% **108.7**
Speed ratings (Par 96): **99,97,95,90,90 86,78**
CSF £4.27 TOTE £2.90: £1.40, £1.10; EX 5.40 Trifecta £13.30.
Owner Crossfields Racing **Bred** Crossfields Bloodstock Ltd **Trained** Hambleton, N Yorks

FOCUS
A novice sprint lacking depth. The two market leaders came to the fore.

9642 BOMBARDIER BRITISH HOPPED AMBER BEER H'CAP 1m 13y(F)
1:15 (1:18) (Class 5) (0-75,74) 3-Y-O+
£3,428 (£1,020; £509; £400; £400; £400) **Stalls** Low

Form RPR

0203 1 **Robero**[3] 9606 7-9-1 **73**..............................(e) TobyEley(5) 8 82
(Gay Kelleway) *trckd ldrs: hdwy and cl up 3f out: led 2f out: rdn over 1f out: kpt on wl fnl f* **9/2**[2]

0005 2 *1* **Elixsoft (IRE)**[31] 9202 4-9-0 **70**.................................... GemmaTutty(3) 2 76
(Karen Tutty) *trckd ldrs: hdwy 3f out: rdn to chse wnr over 1f out: drvn ins fnl f: kpt on* **33/1**

0006 3 *1/2* **Forseti**[23] 9349 3-8-12 **66**..............................(h) AlistairRawlinson 7 70
(Michael Appleby) *dwlt: t.k.h and in tch: wd st: hdwy 2f out: rdn wl over 1f out: kpt on fnl f: nrst fin* **16/1**

32 4 *3 1/4* **Crimson King (IRE)**[25] 9305 3-8-8 **62**..............................(v) BenCurtis 1 58
(Michael Appleby) *trckd ldrs on inner: hdwy 3f out: rdn along wl over 1f out: carried hd high and drvn appr fnl f: kpt on one pce (jockey said gelding hung left-handed in the home straight)* **15/8**[1]

2033 5 *1* **Ollivander (IRE)**[52] 8902 3-9-3 **74**..............................(v) HarrisonShaw(3) 3 68
(David O'Meara) *cl up: slt ld 5f out: rdn along 3f out: hdd 2f out: sn drvn and grad wknd* **13/2**[3]

0206 6 *2 1/2* **Orange Suit (IRE)**[11] 9510 4-9-2 **69**..............................(b) DavidProbert 5 58
(Ed de Giles) *in tch: hdwy 3f out: rdn over 2f out: sn drvn and no imp* **9/2**[2]

4040 7 *3 1/4* **Central City (IRE)**[69] 8412 4-9-7 **74**.................................... MartinDwyer 4 56
(Ian Williams) *trckd ldrs: pushed along wl over 3f out: sn rdn and btn over 2f out* **14/1**

6440 8 *13* **Plunger**[16] 9455 4-9-7 **74**.................................... JoeyHaynes 6 26
(John Butler) *slt ld: hdd 5f out: cl up: rdn along over 3f out: sn wknd (jockey said gelding hung right-handed on the home bend)* **10/1**

43-0 9 *1 1/4* **Swiss Vinnare**[16] 9453 5-8-8 **68**..............................(h) GraceMcEntee(7) 9 17
(Phil McEntee) *in tch on outer: rdn along and wd st: sn outpcd and bhd (jockey said gelding hung badly right-handed)* **33/1**

1m 42.17s (-1.53) **Going Correction** -0.05s/f (Stan)
WFA 3 from 4yo+ 1lb **9** Ran SP% **112.0**
Speed ratings (Par 103): **105,104,103,100,99 96,93,80,79**
CSF £127.38 CT £2153.20 TOTE £4.90: £1.40, £6.10, £4.80; EX 134.50 Trifecta £1287.50.
Owner John Farley And Gay Kelleway **Bred** Mrs P C Burton & Mr R J Lampard **Trained** Exning, Suffolk

FOCUS
A modest handicap and the winner did it comfortably. The winner has been rated to the best of his 2019 form.

9643 BETWAY CLASSIFIED STKS 6f 16y(F)
1:50 (1:53) (Class 6) 2-Y-O+
£2,781 (£827; £413; £400; £400; £400) **Stalls** Low

Form RPR

500 1 **Tattletime (USA)**[20] 9392 2-8-7 52..............................(t[1]) PhilDennis 5 56
(David Loughnane) *hld up: hdwy on inner over 3f out: cl up 2f out: rdn to ld over 1f out: drvn ins fnl f: kpt on wl towards fin* **7/1**[3]

5311 2 *1/2* **Atwaar**[34] 9160 3-9-5 53.................................... FayeMcManoman(5) 7 58
(Charles Smith) *hld up: hdwy 3f out: chsd ldrs 2f out: cl up and rdn jst over 1f out: ev ch ins fnl f: kpt on same pce towards fin (vet said filly was struck into on its left hind)* **15/8**[1]

360 3 *1 1/2* **Gracie's Girl**[41] 9029 2-8-7 55.................................... BenCurtis 2 50
(Michael Appleby) *trckd ldrs: hdwy over 2f out: rdn wl over 1f out: drvn and edgd rt ins fnl f: kpt on* **12/1**

0053 4 *1* **Chocoholic**[24] 9330 2-8-7 48.................................... LukeMorris 1 47
(Bryan Smart) *sn led: rdn along wl over 2f out: sn hdd and drvn: kpt on same pce* **9/2**[2]

0050 5 *1* **Murqaab**[54] 8840 3-9-10 51..............................(p) LewisEdmunds 3 48
(John Balding) *cl up: slt ld 2f out: sn rdn: hdd and drvn jst over 1f out: sn wknd* **14/1**

0000 6 *3/4* **Rock Warbler (IRE)**[17] 9445 6-9-10 42..............................(e) JamesSullivan 8 45
(Michael Mullineaux) *chsd ldrs: rdn along wl over 2f out: sn one pce* **10/1**

4000 7 *8* **Butterfly Pose (IRE)**[43] 9009 2-8-0 46..............................(p) GeorgeRooke(7) 6 17
(J S Moore) *n.m.r s: towards rr: wd st: sn rdn along and n.d* **16/1**

4030 8 *5* **Champagne Mondays**[10] 9539 3-9-3 42..............(b) JonathanFisher(7) 9 6
(Scott Dixon) *chsd ldng pair on outer: cl up and wd st: rdn along over 2f out: sn drvn and wknd* **8/1**

1065 9 *nk* **Schumli**[13] 9501 2-8-7 50..............................(t[1]) CamHardie 4 1
(David O'Meara) *chsd ldrs: pushed along over 3f out: rdn wl over 1f out: sn drvn and wknd* **14/1**

1m 17.09s (0.59) **Going Correction** -0.05s/f (Stan) **9** Ran SP% **112.6**
Speed ratings: **94,93,91,90,88 87,77,70,69**
CSF £19.88 TOTE £8.30: £2.60, £1.10, £2.60; EX 26.80 Trifecta £351.60.
Owner The Something Syndicate & Partner **Bred** Deborah R Hancock **Trained** Tern Hill, Shropshire

FOCUS
A very modest race and the pace was genuine enough for the grade.

9644 BOMBARDIER "MARCH ON YOUR DRUM" NOVICE STKS 7f 14y(F)
2:25 (2:27) (Class 5) 3-Y-O+ £3,428 (£1,020; £509; £254) **Stalls** Low

Form RPR

01 1 **Parallel World (IRE)**[252] 1970 3-9-4 0.................................... HarrisonShaw(3) 2 82
(K R Burke) *cl up: slt ld 3f out: rdn clr jst over 1f out: styd on strly: readily* **2/1**[1]

42 2 *3 3/4* **Milagre Da Vida (IRE)**[24] 9332 3-8-11 0.................................... CliffordLee 3 61
(K R Burke) *slt ld: pushed along 1/2-way: hdd narrowly 3f out: sn rdn: drvn wl over 1f out: kpt on: no ch w wnr* **3/1**[2]

1 3 *1/2* **I Love You Baby**[10] 9547 3-9-4 0.................................... LukeMorris 1 67
(Michael Appleby) *trckd ldrs on inner: hdwy 3f out: sn pushed along: rdn 2f out: drvn over 1f out: kpt on u.p fnl f* **6/1**

435 4 *4* **Happy Face (IRE)**[131] 6315 3-8-11 69.................................... DavidProbert 8 49
(Joseph Tuite) *in tch: pushed along and hdwy 3f out: rdn over 2f out: plugged on u.p fr wl over 1f out: n.d* **9/2**[3]

60 5 *3 3/4* **Shamrad (FR)**[300] 1019 3-9-2 0.................................... MartinDwyer 5 44
(Ian Williams) *dwlt and sn pushed along in rr: outpcd and detached 1/2-way: wl bhd and wd st: hdwy nr stands' side 2f out: kpt on fnl f: n.d* **50/1**

06 6 *1 1/4* **Lambristo (IRE)**[172] 4774 3-9-2 0..............................(b[1]) KieranO'Neill 7 40
(J S Moore) *in tch on outer: rdn along and wd st: drvn over 2f out: sn wknd* **100/1**

6 7 *3 1/2* **Feel The Thunder**[41] 9032 3-8-9 0.................................... JonathanFisher(7) 6 31
(Scott Dixon) *chsd ldrs: rdn along over 3f out: drvn over 2f out: sn wknd* **33/1**

8 *10* **Motawaazy**[420] 8857 3-9-2 0.................................... JasonHart 4
(Roger Fell) *chsd ldrs: rdn along bef 1/2-way: sn outpcd and bhd fr wl over 2f out* **9/2**[3]

1m 29.72s (-0.58) **Going Correction** -0.05s/f (Stan) **8** Ran SP% **114.9**
Speed ratings (Par 103): **101,96,96,91,87 85,81,70**
CSF £8.20 TOTE £3.20: £1.40, £1.10, £1.90; EX 8.00 Trifecta £32.10.
Owner Ontoawinner 14 & Mrs E Burke **Bred** Tally-Ho Stud **Trained** Middleham Moor, N Yorks

FOCUS
Few got into this novice which lacked depth and the winner did it well. They finished strung out. Fair form.

9645 BETWAY H'CAP 4f 214y(F)
3:00 (3:04) (Class 4) (0-85,87) 3-Y-O+
£5,207 (£1,549; £774; £400; £400; £400) **Stalls** Centre

Form RPR

6004 1 **Moonraker**[9] 9562 7-9-7 **81**.................................... BenCurtis 4 92
(Michael Appleby) *prom centre: led over 3f out: rdn ent fnl f: kpt on strly* **9/4**[1]

4500 2 *2* **Awsaaf**[13] 9498 4-8-3 **63**..............................(h) JimmyQuinn 3 67
(Michael Wigham) *trckd ldrs centre: hdwy 2f out: rdn to chse wnr ins fnl f: ev ch briefly tl drvn and kpt on same pce fnl 120yds* **12/1**

1512 3 *2 1/2* **Young Tiger**[15] 9473 6-8-7 **67**..............................(h) AndrewMullen 6 62
(Tom Tate) *stdd s: trckd ldrs centre: hdwy 2f out: rdn to chse wnr appr fnl f: sn one pce* **7/2**[2]

0060 4 *1* **Nick Vedder**[15] 9476 5-9-0 **74**.................................... EoinWalsh 2 65
(Robyn Brisland) *towards rr centre: rdn along: outpcd and detached 1/2-way: styd on fr over 1f out: n.d (jockey said gelding was never travelling)* **10/1**

2213 5 *1 1/2* **Samovar**[9] 9562 4-9-5 **79**..............................(b) JamesSullivan 7 65
(Scott Dixon) *dwlt: sn chsng ldrs nr stands' rail: rdn along 2f out: sn btn (jockey said gelding missed the break)* **4/1**[3]

0260 6 *2 1/2* **Emily Goldfinch**[18] 9424 6-9-6 **87**..............................(p) GraceMcEntee(7) 8 64
(Phil McEntee) *qckly away and led towards stands' side: hdd over 3f out: rdn along 2f out: sn wknd* **28/1**

59.07s (-0.63) **Going Correction** -0.05s/f (Stan) **6** Ran SP% **93.2**
Speed ratings (Par 105): **103,99,95,94,91 87**
CSF £18.97 CT £43.61 TOTE £1.90: £1.30, £4.40; EX 19.40 Trifecta £87.90.
Owner The Kettlelites **Bred** Stratford Place Stud **Trained** Oakham, Rutland
■ Jonboy was withdrawn. Price at time of withdrawal 4/1. Rule 4 applies to all bets - deduction 20p in the pound.

FOCUS
A handicap with little depth and as is often the case in sprints here, the one who broke quickly was not for catching.

9646 BETWAY HEED YOUR HUNCH H'CAP 1m 4f 14y(F)
3:35 (3:36) (Class 6) (0-60,62) 3-Y-O+
£2,781 (£827; £413; £400; £400; £400) **Stalls** Low

Form RPR

0033 1 **Princess Harley (IRE)**[24] 9333 4-9-5 **58**..............................(p) CharlesBishop 10 64
(Mick Quinn) *trckd ldng pair: effrt 3f out: pushed along and sltly outpcd over 2f out: rdn and styng on whn n.m.r and swtchd rt over 1f out: sn drvn and styd on wl to ld nr line* **5/1**[3]

3423 2 *hd* **Cold Harbour**[18] 9412 4-9-9 **62**..............................(t) KieranO'Neill 7 68
(Robyn Brisland) *hld up towards rr: stdy hdwy 4f out: chsd ldrs 3f out: rdn to chse clr ldr over 1f out: led ent fnl f: hdd nr line (vet said gelding lost its left-fore shoe)* **7/2**[1]

0020 3 *2* **Going Native**[24] 9333 4-8-6 **52**.................................... RhonaPindar(7) 9 54
(Olly Williams) *cl up: led over 3f out: rdn clr over 2f out: drvn and hdd ent fnl f: kpt on same pce* **33/1**

2322 **4** 3 **Sociologist (FR)**[10] 9542 4-9-0 **60**.........................(p) JonathanFisher(7) 6 58
(Scott Dixon) *led: pushed along 4f out: rdn and hdd over 3f out: drvn 2f out: kpt on one pce* **5/1**[3]
5003 **5** 4 **Chinese Alphabet**[10] 9542 3-9-0 **57**.....................(b) AlistairRawlinson 4 49
(Michael Appleby) *dwlt and towards rr: hdwy 5f out: in tch and rdn along over 3f out: drvn over 2f out: sn no imp (jockey said gelding was slowly away)* **5/1**[3]
4504 **6** 3 ½ **Tyrsal (IRE)**[17] 9444 8-8-7 **46** oh1..........................(v) JosephineGordon 3 32
(Shaun Keightley) *dwlt and towards rr tl styd on fnl 3f: nvr nr ldrs* **25/1**
0340 **7** ¾ **Star Talent (IRE)**[27] 9279 3-9-1 **58**.........................(e) LukeMorris 1 43
(Gay Kelleway) *chsd ldrs: rdn along over 3f out: sn drvn and plugged on one pce* **20/1**
0304 **8** ¾ **Mirabelle Plum (IRE)**[50] 8944 3-7-11 **47**.................. GeorgeRooke(7) 8 31
(Robyn Brisland) *a in rr* **33/1**
9 6 **Shelter (IRE)**[26] 9290 3-8-12 **55**...................................(p[1]) BenCurtis 11 30
(A J McNamara, Ire) *chsd ldrs: rdn along over 4f out: drvn over 3f out and sn wknd* **10/1**
-063 **10** 24 **Earl Of Bunnacurry (IRE)**[24] 9336 5-9-3 **56**................. CliffordLee 5
(Kevin Frost) *chsd ldrs on inner: pushed along over 5f out: rdn along and lost pl over 4f out: sn bhd (trainer said gelding was fractious in the stalls and was never travelling thereafter)* **4/1**[2]

2m 37.9s (-3.10) **Going Correction** -0.05s/f (Stan)
WFA 3 from 4yo+ 4lb **10** Ran SP% **115.8**
Speed ratings (Par 101): **108,107,106,104,101 99,99,98,94,78**
CSF £21.64 CT £511.90 TOTE £6.00: £1.90, £1.90, £9.20; EX 21.80 Trifecta £384.30.
Owner Kenny Bruce **Bred** D C Egan & Corduff Bloodstock **Trained** Newmarket, Suffolk

FOCUS
A low-grade handicap run at a decent pace and the lead changed hands three times in the final furlong. The first three drew a little way clear.
T/Plt: £20.30 to a £1 stake. Pool: £57,797.13 - 2,076.85 winning units T/Qpdt: £15.50 to a £1 stake. Pool: £6,042.16 - 287.5 winning units **Joe Rowntree**

[9629]LINGFIELD (L-H)
Monday, December 30

OFFICIAL GOING: Polytrack: standard
Wind: virtually nil Weather: fine

9657 BOMBARDIER GOLDEN BEER H'CAP 1m 1y(P)
12:05 (12:05) (Class 6) (0-60,60) 3-Y-O+
£2,781 (£827; £413; £300; £300; £300) **Stalls** High

Form RPR
5011 **1** **Agent Of Fortune**[19] 9410 4-9-4 **57**..............................(p) HectorCrouch 4 66+
(Gary Moore) *hld up in midfield: swtchd rt and effrt over 1f out: hdwy u.p to chse ldr jst fnl f: r.o wl to ld wl ins fnl f* **3/1**[1]
0006 **2** 2 **Weloof (FR)**[23] 9361 5-9-7 **60**....................................... JoeyHaynes 11 64
(John Butler) *chsd ldrs: rdn and hdwy to ld ent fnl f: hdd and no ex wl ins fnl f* **5/1**[3]
3500 **3** 2 **Bullington Boy (FR)**[11] 9548 3-8-13 **58**.................. RayDawson(5) 7 56
(Jane Chapple-Hyam) *broke wl: restrained: t.k.h in midfield: effrt towards inner over 1f out: chsd ldng pair jst ins fnl f: no imp* **7/1**
0002 **4** 1 **Shaffire**[21] 9384 3-9-1 **55**...(h) RichardKingscote 8 51+
(Harry Whittington) *hld up in last trio: effrt whn carried rt and wd bnd 2f out: pushed along and styd on wl ins fnl f: no threat to ldrs* **15/2**
4062 **5** 2 ½ **Lawyersgunsn'money**[20] 9403 4-9-4 **57**.....................(p) TomMarquand 5 48
(Roger Teal) *midfield: effrt: swtchd rt and wd bnd 2f out: no imp u.p over 1f out* **7/2**[2]
5010 **6** nk **Huddle**[19] 9427 3-8-13 **60**....................................(v[1]) Pierre-LouisJamin(7) 3 50
(William Knight) *s.i.s: hld up in rr: effrt ent fnl 2f: kpt on ins fnl f: nvr trbld ldrs* **20/1**
06 **7** ½ **Magwadiri (IRE)**[10] 9566 5-8-13 **57**........................... KevinLundie(5) 9 47
(Mark Loughnane) *chsd ldrs: rdn ent fnl 2f: outpcd and btn over 1f out: wknd ins fnl f* **50/1**
5504 **8** ½ **Your Mothers' Eyes**[14] 9503 3-9-3 **57**......................(p) DavidProbert 12 44+
(Alan Bailey) *led and crossed to inner: hdd after over 1f: chsd ldr: rdn and ev ch ent fnl 2f tl no ex 1f out: wknd ins fnl f* **14/1**
0610 **9** nse **Kodiline (IRE)**[12] 9505 5-9-6 **59**..............................(v) CliffordLee 2 47
(David Evans) *a in rr: no hdwy u.p over 1f out: n.d* **16/1**
0033 **10** 2 ¾ **Subliminal**[19] 9426 4-9-5 **58**......................................(b) LukeMorris 1 40+
(Simon Dow) *chsd ldr tl led after over 1f: rdn 2f out: hrd drvn over 1f out: sn hdd & wknd ins fnl f* **6/1**

1m 35.45s (-2.75) **Going Correction** -0.175s/f (Stan)
WFA 3 from 4yo+ 1lb **10** Ran SP% **121.7**
Speed ratings (Par 101): **106,104,102,101,98 98,97,97,97,94**
CSF £19.19 CT £102.77 TOTE £4.60: £1.30, £2.10, £2.50; EX 26.50 Trifecta £145.20.
Owner Foreign Legion **Bred** Barton Stud **Trained** Lower Beeding, W Sussex

FOCUS
A moderate handicap to start in which the two leaders went off far too quick.

9658 BOMBARDIER BRITISH HOPPED AMBER BEER H'CAP 1m 1y(P)
12:35 (12:36) (Class 4) (0-85,83) 3-Y-O+
£5,207 (£1,549; £774; £387; £300; £300) **Stalls** High

Form RPR
0660 **1** **Almufti**[30] 9255 3-9-6 **82**...(t) JackMitchell 8 91+
(Hugo Palmer) *hld up in last trio: nt clr run ent fnl 2f: swtchd rt over 1f out: hdwy and chsd clr ldr ins fnl f: r.o strly to ld fnl 50yds: sn in command (trainers rep said, regards the apparent improvement in form, gelding appreciated being ridden with more cover on this occasion have raced wide last time out)* **7/2**[1]
5135 **2** 1 ¼ **Delicate Kiss**[26] 9304 5-8-10 **76**...............................(b) AledBeech(5) 10 82
(John Bridger) *t.k.h: pressed ldr tl rdn to ld and drifted rt bnd 2f out: drvn and forged clr 1f out: hdd and no ex fnl 50yds* **9/1**
2060 **3** nse **Candelisa (IRE)**[108] 7142 6-8-13 **77**......................(t) ThomasGreatrex(3) 9 83+
(David Loughnane) *hld up in last trio: wd bnd 4f out: swtchd rt: effrt and v wd bnd 2f out: hdwy 1f out: r.o strly fnl 100yds: nvr getting to wnr (vet said gelding had blood in his mouth after biting his tongue)* **16/1**
4662 **4** 1 ¾ **Thechildren'strust (IRE)**[19] 9422 4-9-2 **77**.................. HectorCrouch 3 79
(Gary Moore) *t.k.h: in tch in midfield: effrt ent fnl 2f: kpt on u.p ins fnl f: nvr enough pce to rch ldrs* **6/1**[2]
0511 **5** hd **Roman Spinner**[19] 9417 4-9-0 **75**.................................(t) RobHornby 5 76
(Rae Guest) *hld up in tch in midfield: effrt towards inner and hdwy over 1f out: chsd ldrs ins fnl f: kpt on but no real imp* **13/2**[3]
150 **6** hd **Nawar**[33] 9173 4-8-13 **74**...(t) RobertHavlin 2 75
(Martin Bosley) *in tch in midfield: clsd to chse ldrs and rdn 2f out: unable qck over 1f out: kpt on same pce ins fnl f* **12/1**
3202 **7** 2 **Saikung (IRE)**[19] 9417 3-9-7 **83**.............................. KieranShoemark 7 78+
(Charles Hills) *rdr struggled to remove hood and v.s.a: grad rcvrd and tagged on to rr of field 4f out: effrt over 1f out: kpt on ins fnl f: nvr trbld ldrs (jockey was slow to remove the blindfold resulting in the filly to be slowly away. Jockey explained that the blindfold became caught on the bridle on his first attempt and required a second attempt to remove it)* **16/1**
0153 **8** 1 ½ **Stringybark Creek**[25] 9329 5-9-0 **75**............................. HollieDoyle 6 68
(David Loughnane) *led: rdn and hdd 2f out: stl ev ch tl no ex 1f out: wknd ins fnl f* **13/2**[3]
1462 **9** 1 ¼ **Mickey (IRE)**[30] 9255 6-9-6 **81**.............................(v) RichardKingscote 1 71
(Tom Dascombe) *chsd ldrs: effrt ent fnl 2f: unable qck over 1f out: wknd ins fnl f (trainers rep could offer no explanation for the poor performance)* **6/1**[2]
110 **10** 1 ¼ **Sea Fox (IRE)**[16] 9480 5-9-3 **78**..................................... CliffordLee 4 65
(David Evans) *chsd ldr: pushed along over 3f out: rdn over 2f out: lost pl bnd 2f out: bhd ins fnl f (trainers rep said gelding was never travelling)* **7/1**

1m 35.45s (-2.75) **Going Correction** -0.175s/f (Stan)
WFA 3 from 4yo+ 1lb **10** Ran SP% **119.4**
Speed ratings (Par 105): **106,104,104,102,102 102,100,99,97,96**
CSF £36.87 CT £364.37 TOTE £4.00: £2.10, £2.70, £4.70; EX 38.10 Trifecta £411.60.
Owner Al Shaqab Racing **Bred** Brookside Stud & Highclere Stud **Trained** Newmarket, Suffolk

FOCUS
A fair handicap, though the early pace didn't look that strong. Sound form rated around the reliable runner-up.

9659 BOMBARDIER "MARCH TO YOUR OWN DRUM" H'CAP 7f 1y(P)
1:05 (1:06) (Class 6) (0-55,60) 3-Y-O+
£2,781 (£827; £413; £300; £300; £300) **Stalls** Low

Form RPR
4213 **1** **Prince Rock (IRE)**[12] 9505 4-9-4 **52**................................... LukeMorris 4 58
(Simon Dow) *dwlt: sn in midfield: effrt ent fnl 2f: hdwy over 1f out: str run u.p to chse ldr 100yds out: led towards fin: rdn out* **7/2**[1]
0550 **2** ½ **Roca Magica**[19] 9410 3-8-12 **46** oh1.............................. RobertHavlin 10 51
(Ed Dunlop) *stdd s and t.k.h early: hld up in last quartet: effrt and hdwy over 1f out: r.o strly ins fnl f: wnt 2nd cl home: nvr quite getting to wnr* **20/1**
6023 **3** ¾ **Disruptor (FR)**[20] 9403 3-9-7 **55**....................................(v) CliffordLee 2 58
(David Evans) *led and set str gallop: rdn and kicked 4 l clr 2f out: drvn 1f out: hdd and no ex towards fin* **13/2**
0446 **4** ¾ **Come On Bear (IRE)**[174] 4753 4-8-12 **46** oh1.................. DavidProbert 6 47
(Alan Bailey) *hld up towards rr: effrt arnd bnd 2f out: styd on ins fnl f: nt rch ldrs* **16/1**
6020 **5** shd **My Law**[32] 9209 3-9-0 **53**.. RhiainIngram(5) 3 54
(Jim Boyle) *midfield early: dropped towards rr 5f out: effrt and swtchd rt over 1f out: hdwy 1f out: kpt on ins fnl f: nvr trbld ldrs* **16/1**
3504 **6** nk **Vincenzo Coccotti (USA)**[12] 9505 7-9-6 **54**...........(p) HectorCrouch 11 54
(Patrick Chamings) *midfield: effrt ent fnl 2f: hdwy u.p to chse clr ldr ent fnl f: kpt on u.p but lost 4 pls wl ins fnl f* **7/1**
0503 **7** 1 ¼ **Alisia R (IRE)**[42] 9034 3-8-12 **46**.................................. LewisEdmunds 8 43
(Les Eyre) *chsd ldrs: swtchd lft and unable qck over 1f out: kpt on same pce ins fnl f* **33/1**
062 **8** nk **Elusif (IRE)**[12] 9505 4-9-4 **52**...................................... MartinDwyer 1 48
(Shaun Keightley) *towards rr tl dropped to last and short of room 5f out: effrt on inner over 1f out: nvr getting on terms and kpt on same pce ins fnl f* **6/1**
0600 **9** 3 ¼ **Declamation (IRE)**[37] 9133 9-9-5 **53**............................... JoeyHaynes 5 41
(John Butler) *midfield: rdn wl over 2f out: swtchd rt and no imp over 1f out: wknd ins fnl f* **5/1**[3]
5 **10** 2 ¼ **Zayriyan (IRE)**[23] 9362 4-9-7 **55**.............................(vt) TomMarquand 12 37
(Ali Stronge) *chsd ldrs: effrt ent fnl 2f: sn drvn and unable qck over 1f out: wknd ins fnl f* **9/2**[2]
0040 **11** 2 ½ **Keep It Country Tv**[21] 9384 3-9-0 **48**......................... CharlieBennett 9 23
(Pat Phelan) *mounted in chute: midfield: pushed along 3f out: sn struggling and lost pl bnd 2f out: bhd after* **16/1**
0530 **12** 1 ½ **Yfenni (IRE)**[112] 7024 3-8-12 **46** oh1............................... HollieDoyle 14 17
(Milton Bradley) *chsd ldr: rdn and unable qck whn edgd rt bnd 2f out: sn lost pl: wknd fnl f* **66/1**

1m 23.28s (-1.52) **Going Correction** -0.175s/f (Stan) **12** Ran SP% **124.0**
Speed ratings (Par 101): **101,100,99,98,98 98,96,96,92,90 87,85**
CSF £81.86 CT £459.47 TOTE £3.60: £1.50, £6.20, £2.20; EX 85.90 Trifecta £540.90.
Owner Mark McAllister **Bred** Thomas Heatrick **Trained** Epsom, Surrey

FOCUS
A moderate handicap weakened further by the absence of Saturday's C&D winner Maqboola. It proved to be a race of changing fortunes. The winner has been rated as running to his recent level.

9660 BETWAY H'CAP 6f 1y(P)
1:40 (1:40) (Class 3) (0-95,96) 3-Y-O **£7,246** (£2,168; £1,084; £542; £270) **Stalls** Low

Form RPR
2316 **1** **Lady Dancealot (IRE)**[26] 9301 4-9-7 **92**........................ HayleyTurner 8 101
(David Elsworth) *stdd s: hld up in tch in last trio: shkn up over 1f out: rdn and hdwy 1f out: chsd wnr ins fnl f: r.o strly to ld last strides* **5/1**[3]
3432 **2** hd **Prince Of Rome (IRE)**[21] 9389 3-8-8 **86**.....................(p) TylerHeard(7) 5 94
(Richard Hughes) *led: pushed along and fnd ex over 1f out: kpt on ins fnl f: hdd last strides* **7/1**
0355 **3** 1 ½ **Merhoob (IRE)**[4] 9612 7-9-8 **96**.............................. DarraghKeenan(3) 3 99
(John Ryan) *chsd ldrs: effrt ent fnl 2f: drvn and chsd ldr 1f out tl ins fnl f: kpt on same pce* **4/1**[1]
2231 **4** nse **Fizzy Feet (IRE)**[21] 9387 3-8-13 **84**........................ RichardKingscote 1 90+
(David Loughnane) *anticipated s: in tch in midfield: effrt: nt clr run and trying to switch rt over 1f out: eventually swtchd rt and r.o wl towards fin: nt rch ldrs (jockey said filly was denied a clear run)* **9/2**[2]
4004 **5** shd **Suzi's Connoisseur**[18] 9441 8-8-3 **79**.........................(b) RayDawson(5) 4 82
(Jane Chapple-Hyam) *midfield: rdn ent fnl 2f: no imp tl styd on u.p fnl 100yds: nt enough pce to rch ldrs* **20/1**
0402 **6** 1 **Dunkerron**[31] 9214 3-9-5 **90**... CharlesBishop 9 90
(Joseph Tuite) *midfield: rdn ent fnl 2f: sn drvn: styd on wl ins fnl f: nvr trbld ldrs: bled fr nose (vet said gelding bled from the nose)* **8/1**
5305 **7** ½ **Count Otto (IRE)**[63] 8607 4-9-2 **87**.................................(h) MartinDwyer 2 85
(Amanda Perrett) *chsd ldrs: effrt over 1f out: unable qck ins fnl f: wknd towards fin* **6/1**

6024 **8** *shd* **Intisaab**[16] 9472 8-9-6 91..............................(tp) DavidProbert 10 89
(David O'Meara) *restless in stalls: dwlt: hld up in last pair: swtchd rt and effrt wl over 1f out: kpt on ins fnl f: nvr trbld ldrs* **8/1**

3005 **9** *3/4* **Spoof**[11] 9549 4-8-13 84..............................(h) KieranShoemark 12 79
(Charles Hills) *hld up in last pair: effrt over 1f out: kpt on but no real imp ins fnl f* **16/1**

1660 **10** *3/4* **Charming Kid**[198] 3865 3-9-5 90.............................. JoeyHaynes 7 83
(Dean Ivory) *chsd ldr: pressing ldr and rdn 2f out: unable to match pce of ldr and lost 2nd 1f out: wknd ins fnl f* **20/1**

1m 9.78s (-2.12) **Going Correction** -0.175s/f (Stan) **10 Ran SP% 119.3**
Speed ratings (Par 107): **107,106,104,104,104 103,102,102,101,100**
CSF £40.95 CT £152.75 TOTE £4.80: £1.60, £2.40, £1.70; EX 29.30 Trifecta £105.60.
Owner Kevin Quinn **Bred** P J B O'Callaghan **Trained** Newmarket, Suffolk

FOCUS
A warm sprint handicap and a thrilling finish. They went quick which suited the winner. The third, fourth and fifth have been rated close to their recent form.

9661 LADBROKES WHERE THE NATION PLAYS NURSERY H'CAP 6f 1y(P)
2:10 (2:10) (Class 4) (0-85,85) 2-Y-O
£4,463 (£1,328; £663; £331; £300; £300) **Stalls Low**

Form RPR

4150 **1** **Little Brown Trout**[34] 9162 2-9-0 78.............................. HollieDoyle 3 82
(William Stone) *dwlt: hld up in tch towards rr: hdwy to chse ldrs and swtchd lft 1f out: sn chalng: led ins fnl f: r.o wl* **6/1**

46 **2** *1/2* **Kondratiev Wave (IRE)**[23] 9364 2-9-7 85.............................. TomMarquand 8 88
(Tony Carroll) *rousted along early: chsd ldr after 1f: rdn ent fnl 2f: kpt on u.p and ev ch ins fnl f: chsd wnr and kpt on same pce towards fin* **7/1**

3020 **3** *1* **Dazzling Des (IRE)**[34] 9162 2-9-3 81..............................(p) KieranShoemark 1 81
(David O'Meara) *s.i.s: hld up in tch in rr: effrt ent fnl 2f: hdwy on inner over 1f out: drvn and led ins fnl f: sn hdd: no ex and outpcd towards fin* **14/1**

210 **4** *1 3/4* **Zim Baby**[23] 9364 2-8-11 75.............................. LukeMorris 5 69
(Paul George) *dwlt: pushed along early: hld up in last trio: effrt over 1f out: styd on ins fnl f: nvr trbld ldrs* **20/1**

4262 **5** *nk* **Baileys Blues (FR)**[12] 9514 2-8-10 74.............................. JackMitchell 4 67
(Mark Johnston) *led: rdn 2f out: edgd rt 1f out: hdd and no ex ins fnl f: wknd towards fin* **9/2[3]**

062 **6** *2* **Lakeview (IRE)**[10] 9569 2-8-7 71.............................. DavidProbert 6 58
(David Loughnane) *chsd ldrs: unable qck over 1f out: wknd ins fnl f* **12/1**

1604 **7** *1* **Winning Streak**[34] 9162 2-9-3 81..............................(t) RichardKingscote 7 65
(Stuart Williams) *midfield: wd: rdn and lost pl bnd 2f out: no threat to ldrs after (trainers rep said colt was unsuited by the track)* **15/8[1]**

6621 **8** *nse* **Birkenhead**[32] 9205 2-9-2 80.............................. LewisEdmunds 2 64+
(Les Eyre) *t.k.h: trckd ldrs: struggling to qckn u.p whn impeded 1f out: wknd ins fnl f (jockey said gelding ran too free)* **4/1[2]**

1m 10.73s (-1.17) **Going Correction** -0.175s/f (Stan) **8 Ran SP% 118.9**
Speed ratings (Par 98): **100,99,98,95,95 92,91,91**
CSF £49.05 CT £574.08 TOTE £6.60: £2.00, £2.10, £3.80; EX 57.50 Trifecta £444.90.
Owner Shane Fairweather & Dr C Scott **Bred** Caroline Scott & Shane Fairweather **Trained** West Wickham, Cambs

FOCUS
A fair nursery. The winner has been rated in line with his better turf form, and the third near his best.

9662 BETWAY NOVICE STKS 1m 2f (P)
2:45 (2:45) (Class 5) 3-Y-O+ **£3,428** (£1,020; £509; £254) **Stalls Low**

Form RPR

4202 **1** **Exmoor Beast**[17] 9453 3-9-3 69.............................. PaulMulrennan 2 76
(Peter Charalambous) *mde all: pressed and pushed along 2f out: sn rdn and fnd ex over 1f out: drvn ins fnl f: pressed wl ins fnl f: a jst holding on: rdn out* **13/8[1]**

2 *shd* **Thai Terrier (USA)** 3-9-3 0.............................. RichardKingscote 5 75+
(Mark Johnston) *in tch in midfield: effrt in 5th 2f out: hdwy on inner over 1f out: chsd wnr ins fnl f: kpt on wl towards fin: jst hld* **7/2[2]**

4 **3** *5* **Lep**[19] 9425 3-9-0 0.............................. PaddyBradley(3) 1 65
(Michael Attwater) *t.k.h: chsd ldr for 2f: styd chsng ldrs tl wnt 2nd again 3f out: ev ch and rdn 2f out: outpcd over 1f out: btn whn lost 2nd and no ex jst ins fnl f (jockey said gelding ran too free)* **14/1**

052 **4** *1/2* **Mercury Dime (IRE)**[19] 9425 3-8-12 71.............................. RobertHavlin 3 59
(Ed Dunlop) *chsd ldrs: wnt 2nd briefly 8f out: kpt chsng ldrs: rdn ent fnl 2f: unable qck: wl hld and kpt on same pce ins fnl f* **4/1[3]**

5650 **5** *3/4* **Greek Kodiac (IRE)**[100] 7462 3-9-3 67.............................. CharlesBishop 7 63
(Mick Quinn) *in tch in midfield: hdwy to chse ldrs over 2f out: rdn 2f out: unable qck and wl hld fnl f* **11/1**

4306 **6** *8* **Passing Clouds**[9] 9589 4-9-5 48.............................. LukeMorris 6 46
(Michael Attwater) *rousted along: hdwy on outer to chse wnr over 7f out: drvn 4f out: lost 2nd 3f out and sn struggling: wl btn over 1f out* **25/1**

7 *3/4* **Jolyon** 3-9-3 0.............................. LiamKeniry 8 45
(Michael Scudamore) *s.i.s and dropped in bhd: effrt over 2f out: sn struggling and outpcd: wl btn over 1f out* **33/1**

13 **8** *27* **Lovely Lou Lou**[23] 9368 3-9-2 0.............................. DarraghKeenan(3) 4
(John Ryan) *hld up in tch: rdn 4f out: sn struggling: lost tch over 2f out: t.o (jockey said filly stopped quickly; trainer said filly was unsuited by the track)* **6/1**

2m 4.4s (-2.20) **Going Correction** -0.175s/f (Stan) **8 Ran SP% 116.4**
WFA 3 from 4yo 2lb
Speed ratings (Par 103): **101,100,96,96,95 89,88,67**
CSF £7.56 TOTE £2.20: £1.10, £1.50, £3.60; EX 7.70 Trifecta £73.10.
Owner GG Thoroughbreds V **Bred** Strawberry Fields Stud **Trained** Newmarket, Suffolk

FOCUS
An ordinary older-horse novice in which previous experience may have made the difference. It's been rated around the winner to his recent form and the third to his shaky C&D latest.

9663 BETWAY HEED YOUR HUNCH H'CAP 1m 2f (P)
3:20 (3:20) (Class 6) (0-65,65) 3-Y-O+
£2,781 (£827; £413; £300; £300; £300) **Stalls Low**

Form RPR

1006 **1** **Bond Angel**[33] 9180 4-9-6 64.............................. CliffordLee 2 69
(David Evans) *wl in tch in midfield: swtchd rt and effrt u.p over 1f out: styd on wl u.p ins fnl f: led last strides* **25/1**

0330 **2** *hd* **Cheeky Rascal (IRE)**[26] 9303 4-9-3 61..............................(v) TomMarquand 14 66
(Tom Ward) *hdwy to chse ldr over 8f out: rdn and ev ch ent fnl 2f: sustained effrt u.p: led cl home: hdd last strides* **7/1**

253 **3** *hd* **Enzo (IRE)**[30] 9256 4-9-5 63.............................. JoeyHaynes 3 67
(John Butler) *sn led: pressed 2f out: rdn over 1f out: kpt on wl u.p tl hdd and lost 2 pls cl home* **11/1**

1062 **4** *nk* **Dreamboat Dave (IRE)**[18] 9443 3-9-1 61.............................. EoinWalsh 11 66
(Sarah Humphrey) *pushed along to ld: sn hdd and chsd ldrs fr over 8f out: rdn and pressed ldrs 2f out: sustained chal ins fnl f: no ex cl home* **13/2**

0006 **5** *1/2* **Chiavari (IRE)**[30] 9256 5-9-4 62.............................. DanielMuscutt 7 65+
(Alexandra Dunn) *hld up in midfield: pushed along 2f out: nt clr run over 1f out: swtchd rt 1f out: rdn and styd on wl fnl 100yds* **33/1**

0403 **6** *3/4* **Run After Genesis (IRE)**[56] 8806 3-9-5 65..............................(p[1]) JackMitchell 4 67
(Brett Johnson) *t.k.h: in tch in midfield: effrt over 1f out: sn drvn and unable qck: kpt on ins fnl f (jockey said gelding ran too free in the early stages)* **11/2[3]**

1401 **7** *nk* **Fair Power (IRE)**[16] 9479 5-9-7 65.............................. LukeMorris 1 66
(John Butler) *trckd ldrs: effrt 2f out: nt clr run and swtchd rt over 1f out: unable qck and kpt on same pce u.p ins fnl f (jockey said gelding was denied a clear run)* **8/1**

4161 **8** *hd* **Miss Elsa**[19] 9426 3-8-12 63.............................. GeorgiaDobie(5) 13 64+
(Eve Johnson Houghton) *stdd and dropped in bhd after s: effrt wl over 1f out: hdwy 1f out: styd on ins fnl f: nvr trbld ldrs* **4/1[1]**

0003 **9** *hd* **He's Our Star (IRE)**[23] 9361 4-9-4 62.............................. HollieDoyle 6 62+
(Ali Stronge) *racd in last trio: rdn and switching rt over 2f out: styd on ins fnl f: nvr trbld ldrs* **5/1[2]**

0000 **10** *nk* **Global Wonder (IRE)**[19] 9426 4-9-6 64.............................. DougieCostello 10 63
(Suzi Best) *chsd ldrs early: sn stdd bk and in tch in midfield: effrt over 2f out: kpt on ins fnl f: nt rch ldrs* **20/1**

5000 **11** *1/2* **Mr Mac**[17] 9453 5-9-5 63..............................(p) CharlesBishop 12 61+
(Peter Hedger) *mounted in chute: s.i.s and swtchd sharply lft after s: hld up towards rr: effrt 2f out: styd on ins fnl f: nvr trbld ldrs* **25/1**

2100 **12** *1 1/4* **Archdeacon**[9] 9589 3-8-7 58..............................(p) SophieRalston(5) 9 55+
(Dean Ivory) *dwlt: t.k.h: hld up in last pair: effrt on inner over 1f out: nvr involved (jockey said gelding was slowly away)* **12/1**

6304 **13** *nse* **Settle Petal**[19] 9426 5-9-5 63.............................. CharlieBennett 5 59
(Pat Phelan) *mounted in chute: towards rr on outer: rdn over 2f out: no prog: nvr involved* **12/1**

2m 7.04s (0.44) **Going Correction** -0.175s/f (Stan) **13 Ran SP% 128.1**
WFA 3 from 4yo+ 2lb
Speed ratings (Par 101): **91,90,90,90,90 89,89,89,88,88 88,87,87**
CSF £197.35 CT £2089.33 TOTE £39.00: £9.30, £3.10, £2.90; EX 261.10 Trifecta £4966.30.
Owner M W Lawrence **Bred** R C Bond **Trained** Pandy, Monmouths

FOCUS
A modest handicap to end. Despite the big field, they went no pace early and the fact the race was won by a miler and those up with the pace from the start were still there at the finish shows how slowly they went. Straightforward form rated around the principals.
T/Plt: £283.00 to a £1 stake. Pool: £86,514.25 - 223.15 winning units T/Qpdt: £51.20 to a £1 stake. Pool: £11,403.54 - 164.74 winning units **Steve Payne**

9657 LINGFIELD (L-H)
Tuesday, December 31

OFFICIAL GOING: Polytrack: standard
Wind: virtually nil Weather: overcast

9664 BETWAY CASINO H'CAP 5f 6y(P)
12:00 (12:00) (Class 6) (0-60,60) 3-Y-O+
£2,781 (£827; £413; £300; £300; £300) **Stalls High**

Form RPR

0023 **1** **Roundabout Magic (IRE)**[10] 9583 5-9-5 58.............................. HollieDoyle 2 65
(Simon Dow) *hld up towards rr: hdwy: nt clr run and swtchd rt over 1f out: rdn to chse clr ldr ins fnl f: r.o strly to ld 50yds out: pushed out* **15/8[1]**

1034 **2** *3/4* **Terri Rules (IRE)**[10] 9583 4-9-3 56.............................. DanielMuscutt 9 60
(Lee Carter) *rrd as stalls opened and slowly away: hld up in rr: effrt on inner over 1f out: drvn 1f out: chsd ldrs ins fnl f: styd on wl to go 2nd last strides (jockey said filly reared as stalls opened)* **8/1**

2161 **3** *nk* **Man Of The Sea (IRE)**[127] 6553 3-9-7 60..............................(tp) BenCurtis 3 63
(Neil Mulholland) *taken down early: rousted along leaving stalls: chsd ldrs: unable qck u.p over 1f out: rallied ins fnl f: styd on wl towards fin* **5/1[2]**

0060 **4** *nse* **Fareeq**[10] 9583 5-9-2 55..............................(bt) RichardKingscote 5 58
(Charlie Wallis) *sn dropped towards rr: clsd and nt clr run over 1f out: hdwy 1f out: r.o strly ins fnl f: nt rch ldrs* **5/1[2]**

4260 **5** *hd* **Oh So Nice**[29] 9272 3-8-13 52.............................. TomMarquand 6 54+
(Tony Carroll) *led: rdn and kicked clr over 1f out: stl clr ins fnl f: hdd 50yds out: no ex and wknd cl home: bled fr nose (vet said filly had bled from the nose)* **11/2[3]**

0000 **6** *3/4* **Superseded (IRE)**[21] 9406 3-9-4 57.............................. LukeMorris 10 57
(John Butler) *chsd ldr: rdn and unable qck over 1f out: drvn 1f out: kpt on same pce after* **16/1**

5566 **7** *3/4* **Pharoh Jake**[10] 9583 11-8-0 46 oh1.............................. GeorgeRooke(7) 7 43
(John Bridger) *towards rr: bhd and nt clr run over 1f out: hdwy ins fnl f: styd on fnl 100yds: nvr trbld ldrs* **25/1**

0600 **8** *hd* **Waneen (IRE)**[89] 7838 6-8-7 46 oh1.............................. JoeyHaynes 1 42
(John Butler) *nt that wl away: hdwy and trckd ldrs on inner after 1f: shkn up over 2f out: unable qck over 1f out: kpt on same pce ins fnl f* **20/1**

460 **9** *4* **Ask The Guru**[89] 7844 9-8-7 46 oh1..............................(b) NicolaCurrie 8 28
(Michael Attwater) *chsd ldrs on outer: wd and lost pl bnd 2f out: n.d after* **50/1**

0500 **10** *1 1/2* **Starchant**[10] 9583 3-8-7 46 oh1..............................(b) KieranO'Neill 4 22
(John Bridger) *rousted along leaving stalls: t.k.h: in tch in midfield: rdn ent fnl 2f: outpcd and lost pl over 1f out: bhd ins fnl f* **16/1**

58.83s (0.03) **Going Correction** -0.075s/f (Stan) **10 Ran SP% 116.9**
Speed ratings (Par 101): **96,94,94,94,93 92,91,91,84,82**
CSF £17.44 CT £77.94 TOTE £2.50: £1.10, £2.90, £2.20; EX 18.10 Trifecta £58.20.
Owner Six Mile Hill Racing **Bred** T F Lacy **Trained** Epsom, Surrey

FOCUS
The hold-up horses came to the fore here. Straightforward, ordinary form.

9665 LADBROKES WHERE THE NATION PLAYS NURSERY H'CAP 1m 1y(P)
12:35 (12:35) (Class 5) (0-75,75) 2-Y-O
£3,428 (£1,020; £509; £300; £300; £300) **Stalls High**

Form RPR

005 **1** **St Just**[26] 9323 2-8-13 67.............................. TomMarquand 4 73+
(William Haggas) *wl in tch in midfield: effrt 2f out: hdwy u.p to chse ldr ent fnl f: styd on strly to ld ins fnl f: sn in command* **7/2[2]**

0421 **2** 1 3/4 **Island Hideaway**[22] 9383 2-9-7 **75**.................... ShaneKelly 5 77
(David Lanigan) *chsd ldr after 2f: rdn to ld over 1f out: drvn and hdd ins fnl f: no ex and outpcd towards fin* **11/8**[1]

000 **3** 1 1/4 **Queen Of Silca**[89] 7832 2-8-8 **62**.................... NicolaCurrie 7 61
(Mick Channon) *stdd after s and dropped in bhd: effrt 2f out: sme hdwy and swtchd rt 1f out: kpt on ins fnl f: wnt 3rd last strides* **16/1**

062 **4** nk **Today Power (IRE)**[110] 7111 2-8-7 **61**.................... HollieDoyle 1 59
(Richard Hannon) *mounted in chute and taken down early: t.k.h: chsd ldr for 2f: chsd ldrs: effrt 2f out: pressing ldrs ent fnl f: unable qck and outpcd fnl 150yds* **11/2**

1161 **5** 1 **Speed Merchant (IRE)**[12] 9541 2-9-5 **73**..............(p) AlistairRawlinson 6 69
(Michael Appleby) *hld up in last pair: effrt ent fnl 2f: no imp tl kpt on ins fnl f: nvr enough pce to chal* **9/2**[3]

6403 **6** 2 3/4 **Secret Smile (IRE)**[19] 9448 2-9-3 **71**.................... JasonHart 3 61
(Mark Johnston) *broke wl: led: rdn: hung lft and hdd over 1f out: sn btn and wknd ins fnl f* **12/1**

020 **7** shd **Saracen Star**[27] 9311 2-8-4 **58**.................... LukeMorris 2 48
(J S Moore) *dwlt and rousted along early: a in rr: rdn over 2f out: no prog* **25/1**

1m 36.58s (-1.62) **Going Correction** -0.075s/f (Stan) 7 Ran SP% **115.3**
Speed ratings (Par 96): **105,103,102,101,100 97,97**
CSF £8.89 TOTE £4.40: £2.20, £1.30; EX 10.50 Trifecta £86.70.
Owner G Smith-Bernal **Bred** Saleh Al Homaizi & Imad Al Sagar **Trained** Newmarket, Suffolk

FOCUS
A fair nursery.

9666 BOMBARDIER BRITISH HOPPED AMBER BEER H'CAP 1m 1y(P)
1:05 (1:05) (Class 2) (0-105,103) 3-Y-O+ £11,971 (£3,583; £1,791; £896; £446) Stalls High

Form RPR

4501 **1** **Another Touch**[33] 9200 6-9-2 **95**.................... BarryMcHugh 5 106
(Richard Fahey) *hld up in midfield: clsd and on outer bnd 2f out: rdn and effrt over 1f out: drvn to chse ldr ins fnl f: r.o wl to ld 50yds: sn in command and eased towards fin* **11/4**[2]

5030 **2** 2 **Goring (GER)**[27] 9309 7-9-6 **99**....................(v) CharlesBishop 4 105
(Eve Johnson Houghton) *midfield: clsd over 2f out: effrt over 1f out: pushed into ld 1f out: sn rdn: hdd 50yds: no ex and sn btn* **9/1**

1225 **3** 1 **Kuwait Currency (USA)**[27] 9309 3-9-9 **103**..........(t) RichardKingscote 6 106
(Richard Hannon) *chsd clr ldr: clsd over 2f out: rdn to ld over 1f out: hdd and drvn 1f out: kpt on same pce ins fnl f* **2/1**[1]

5445 **4** 2 3/4 **Michele Strogoff**[13] 9510 6-8-2 **84** oh2.................... TheodoreLadd(3) 3 81
(Michael Appleby) *taken down early: led: wnt clr after 2f: rdn over 2f out: hdd over 1f out: no ex and wknd ins fnl f* **12/1**

0353 **5** 1/2 **Mr Scaramanga**[33] 9206 5-8-8 **87**.................... LukeMorris 2 83
(Simon Dow) *chsd ldrs: clsd over 2f out: drifted rt and unable qck over 1f out: wl hld and kpt on same pce ins fnl f* **8/1**

0050 **6** 1 3/4 **Apex King (IRE)**[27] 9308 5-8-5 **84** oh4.................... HollieDoyle 7 76
(Mark Usher) *rdr struggling to remove hood: wnt rt leaving stalls and slowly away: t.k.h: effrt over 2f out: nvr threatened to get on terms and edgd lft ins fnl f (jockey, who was slow to remove blindfold, said gelding ducked head just before gates opened pulling blind from her hands and leaving her without a good grip on the blind)* **20/1**

500 **P** **Sanaadh**[81] 8096 6-8-10 **89**....................(t) BenCurtis 1
(Michael Wigham) *s.i.s: hld up in last pair: effrt over 2f out: no imp: eased over 1f out: p.u and dismntd ins fnl f (trainer said gelding had a breathing problem)* **7/2**[3]

1m 34.46s (-3.74) **Going Correction** -0.075s/f (Stan)
WFA 3 from 5yo+ 1lb 7 Ran SP% **115.8**
Speed ratings (Par 109): **115,113,112,109,108 107,**
CSF £27.81 TOTE £3.60: £2.10, £3.40; EX 25.60 Trifecta £66.00.
Owner Nicholas Wrigley & Kevin Hart **Bred** Shadwell Estate Company Limited **Trained** Musley Bank, N Yorks

FOCUS
A good handicap run at a strong pace that suited those held up. The winner has been rated back to his best and the second to his November C&D form.

9667 BETWAY H'CAP 1m 4f (P)
1:40 (1:40) (Class 3) (0-95,94) 3-Y-O+ £7,246 (£2,168; £1,084; £542; £270) Stalls Low

Form RPR

6026 **1** **Furzig**[27] 9309 4-9-4 **91**.................... ConnorMurtagh(3) 4 98
(Richard Fahey) *t.k.h: wl in tch in midfield: effrt ent fnl 2f: drvn and chal 1f out: r.o wl under hands and heels riding fnl 100yds to ld last strides* **5/1**[2]

4160 **2** nk **Original Choice (IRE)**[43] 9041 5-9-10 **94**....................(p) HollieDoyle 7 100
(Nick Littmoden) *chsd ldr tl pushed into ld 2f out: rdn over 1f out: kpt on u.p ins fnl f: hdd last strides* **20/1**

/141 **3** nse **Entangling (IRE)**[10] 9588 5-9-8 **92**.................... WilliamCarson 6 98+
(David Elsworth) *hld up in tch in last pair: effrt ent fnl 2f: wd bnd 2f out: clsd to chse ldrs and drvn ins fnl f: styd on wl towards fin* **2/1**[1]

0402 **4** 2 1/2 **Exceeding Power**[34] 9177 8-9-2 **86**.................... TomMarquand 2 88
(Martin Bosley) *chsd ldrs: effrt jst over 2f out: rdn and pressed ldrs 1f out tl no ex ins fnl f: wknd towards fin* **14/1**[3]

5101 **5** 1/2 **Just The Man (FR)**[22] 9388 3-9-4 **92**.................... AdamKirby 3 93
(Clive Cox) *t.k.h: hld up in tch in midfield: effrt and nt clrest of runs ent fnl 2f: swtchd rt over 1f out: kpt on ins fnl f: no threat to ldrs* **2/1**[1]

1210 **6** 3 **Bo Samraan (IRE)**[18] 9454 3-9-4 **92**.................... JasonHart 5 88
(Mark Johnston) *led: hdd and rdn 2f out: outpcd ent fnl f: sn wknd* **5/1**[2]

0 **7** 2 **Thematic (USA)**[122] 3-8-12 **86**.................... LiamKeniry 1 79
(Dominic Ffrench Davis) *t.k.h: hld up in tch in last pair: effrt 2f out: no imp and outpcd over 1f out: wknd fnl f* **33/1**

2m 33.31s (0.31) **Going Correction** -0.075s/f (Stan)
WFA 3 from 4yo+ 4lb 7 Ran SP% **114.4**
Speed ratings (Par 107): **96,95,95,94,93 91,90**
CSF £88.92 TOTE £6.60: £1.90, £9.40; EX 97.40 Trifecta £233.40.
Owner Mr & Mrs P Ashton **Bred** Mr & Mrs P Ashton **Trained** Musley Bank, N Yorks

FOCUS
This was steadily run and there was a tight finish between the first three. Muddling form, but the runner-up has been rated to this year's best for now.

9668 LADBROKES HOME OF THE ODDS BOOST NOVICE MEDIAN AUCTION STKS 7f 1y(P)
2:10 (2:12) (Class 6) 2-Y-O £2,781 (£827; £413; £206) Stalls Low

Form RPR

1 **Ajax Tavern** 2-9-5 0.................... TomMarquand 14 77+
(Richard Hannon) *pushed along early: styd wd tl hdwy to ld and crossed to inner over 2f out: rdn: rn green and racd awkwardly bnd 2f out: high hd carriage but fnd ex to go clr over 1f out: r.o strly ins fnl f* **8/1**[3]

5 **2** 3 1/4 **Alborkan (FR)**[20] 9408 2-9-5 0.................... LewisEdmunds 6 69
(Amy Murphy) *hld up in tch in midfield: swtchd lft and effrt over 1f out: rdn to chse clr ldr ent fnl f: kpt on but no imp* **10/1**

4 **3** 1 3/4 **New Arrival (IRE)**[41] 9062 2-9-0 0.................... JasonHart 4 59
(James Tate) *led for over 1f: chsd ldrs after: wnt 2nd again and rdn wl over 1f out: sn hung rt: flashed tail u.p and lost 2nd: wl hld and kpt on same pce ins fnl f* **7/2**[1]

20 **4** nk **Dashing Roger**[10] 9585 2-9-5 0.................... RichardKingscote 5 64
(William Stone) *chsd ldrs: nt clrest of runs ent fnl 2f: effrt over 1f out: no threat to ldr and kpt on same pce ins fnl f* **5/1**[2]

5 2 **Sepia Belle** 2-8-11 0.................... GabrieleMalune(3) 7 53
(Amy Murphy) *in tch in midfield: pushed along and effrt whn carried wd bnd 2f out: no ch after but rallied and kpt on ins fnl f* **18/1**

06 **6** 1/2 **Arietta**[26] 9327 2-9-0 0.................... RobHornby 1 52
(Jonathan Portman) *in tch in midfield: effrt on inner over 1f out: sn rdn and no imp: wl hld and plugged on same pce ins fnl f* **8/1**[3]

0 **7** hd **Good Time Charlie**[70] 8418 2-9-5 0.................... AdamKirby 8 57+
(Clive Cox) *dwlt and pushed along early: hld up in rr: rdn and sme prog over 1f out: no real imp ins fnl f: nvr trbld ldrs* **7/2**[1]

60 **8** 1 **Indigo Times (IRE)**[20] 9408 2-9-0 0.................... DylanHogan(5) 3 54+
(David Simcock) *stdd bk to rr after s: effrt over 1f out: hdwy into midfield 1f out: no real imp ins fnl f: nvr trbld ldrs* **20/1**

0 **9** nk **Kalimotxo**[22] 9385 2-9-0 0.................... CallumShepherd 13 48
(William Knight) *hld up in tch towards rr: pushed along and hdwy into midfield whn swtchd lft 1f out: no imp ins fnl f* **66/1**

00 **10** 1 1/4 **Various (IRE)**[61] 8700 2-9-5 0.................... CharlesBishop 11 50
(Eve Johnson Houghton) *wd: in tch in midfield: hdwy to chse ldrs 4f out: hung rt and lost pl bnd 2f out: n.d after* **33/1**

0 **11** nse **Brown Eyed Girl**[41] 9063 2-9-0 0.................... KieranO'Neill 12 45
(Mick Channon) *t.k.h: mostly 2nd tl wl over 1f out: sn outpcd u.p: wknd ins fnl f* **25/1**

6 **12** 4 **Golden Fountain (IRE)**[26] 9323 2-9-0 0.................... AndrewBreslin(5) 10 39
(Mark Johnston) *midfield on outer: lost pl qckly ent fnl 2f: bhd over 1f out* **8/1**[3]

13 4 **Coconut Sugar (IRE)** 2-9-0 0.................... LukeMorris 2 24
(Robert Cowell) *s.i.s: a towards rr* **25/1**

1m 25.04s (0.24) **Going Correction** -0.075s/f (Stan) **13** Ran SP% **125.7**
Speed ratings (Par 94): **95,91,89,88,86 86,85,84,84,82 82,78,73**
CSF £84.79 TOTE £8.60: £2.70, £2.70, £1.80; EX 60.20 Trifecta £258.60.
Owner Christopher Wright & Miss Emily Asprey **Bred** Stratford Place Stud & Willow Bloodstock **Trained** East Everleigh, Wilts

FOCUS
An ordinary novice, but won by a useful-looking newcomer. Ordinary form in behind the winner.

9669 BOMBARDIER GOLDEN BEER H'CAP 7f 1y(P)
2:45 (2:45) (Class 4) (0-85,87) 3-Y-O+
£5,207 (£1,549; £774; £387; £300; £300) Stalls Low

Form RPR

1132 **1** **Mohareb**[13] 9517 3-9-8 **86**.................... AlistairRawlinson 3 96
(Michael Appleby) *chsd ldrs: effrt and clsd over 1f out: rdn to ld ins fnl f: r.o wl and asserted towards fin* **11/4**[1]

0324 **2** 1 **Corazon Espinado (IRE)**[33] 9200 4-9-6 **84**.................... TomMarquand 10 91
(Simon Dow) *led for over 1f: chsd ldr after tl rdn and hdwy to ld over 1f out: drvn and hdd ins fnl f: no ex and jst outpcd towards fin* **7/1**[3]

252 **3** 2 3/4 **Ultimate Avenue (IRE)**[167] 5061 5-9-2 **85**..........(h) DylanHogan(5) 11 85
(David Simcock) *stdd and dropped in bhd after s: hld up in rr: swtchd lft and effrt over 1f out: rdn and styd on ins fnl f: snatched 3rd on post: nvr trbld ldrs* **25/1**

6051 **4** nse **Jackstar (IRE)**[17] 9476 3-9-5 **83**.................... RichardKingscote 4 82
(Tom Dascombe) *chsd ldr tl led after over 1f: rdn and hdd over 1f out: no ex and wknd ins fnl f* **11/4**[1]

3331 **5** nk **Luis Vaz De Torres (IRE)**[31] 9245 7-8-7 **74**.................... ConnorMurtagh(3) 6 73
(Richard Fahey) *midfield: effrt ent fnl 2f: rdn and no imp over 1f out: kpt on same pce ins fnl f* **16/1**

600 **6** nk **Eljaddaaf (IRE)**[83] 8016 8-9-4 **87**.................... SophieRalston(5) 2 85
(Dean Ivory) *t.k.h: midfield: effrt wl over 1f out: no imp and kpt on same pce ins fnl f* **33/1**

4151 **7** 1/2 **Champion Brogie (IRE)**[26] 9329 3-8-7 **71** oh4.................... HollieDoyle 1 67
(J S Moore) *dwlt: hld up towards rr: effrt and hdwy over 1f out: kpt on ins fnl f: nvr trbld ldrs* **25/1**

4051 **8** 3/4 **Tipperary Jack (USA)**[55] 8852 3-9-5 **83**.................... AdamKirby 8 77
(John Best) *t.k.h: hld up in tch in midfield: effrt whn nudged rt and bmpd 2f out: no imp over 1f out: kpt on same pce ins fnl f* **7/2**[2]

0350 **9** hd **Concierge (IRE)**[64] 8607 3-9-7 **85**.................... BenCurtis 9 79
(David Loughnane) *midfield on outer: rdn and edgd lft ent fnl 2f: no imp over 1f out: kpt on same pce ins fnl f* **14/1**

-130 **10** shd **Kodiac Pride**[21] 9404 3-9-2 **80**.................... LukeMorris 7 74
(Sir Mark Prescott Bt) *midfield: effrt: edgd rt ent fnl 2f: no imp over 1f out: wl hld and one pce ins fnl f* **20/1**

4420 **11** nk **Martineo**[19] 9441 4-9-1 **79**.................... JoeyHaynes 5 72
(John Butler) *hld up in last trio: effrt 2f out: nvr involved* **20/1**

1m 22.7s (-2.10) **Going Correction** -0.075s/f (Stan) **11** Ran SP% **120.8**
Speed ratings (Par 105): **109,107,104,104,104 103,103,102,102,102 101**
CSF £21.48 CT £415.19 TOTE £3.50: £2.40, £2.00, £5.80; EX 18.90 Trifecta £250.40.
Owner Ian Lawrence **Bred** Crossfields Bloodstock Ltd **Trained** Oakham, Rutland

FOCUS
Few got into this, the first two and fourth racing in the first three places throughout. The second has been rated to his best.

9670 BETWAY HEED YOUR HUNCH H'CAP 6f 1y(P)
3:20 (3:21) (Class 6) (0-60,60) 3-Y-O+
£2,781 (£827; £413; £300; £300; £300) Stalls Low

Form RPR

-620 **1** **Royal Dynasty**[32] 9217 3-9-7 **60**.................... TomMarquand 12 68
(Mohamed Moubarak) *wnt rt leaving stalls: hdwy to ld over 5f out: rdn and kicked clr over 1f out: r.o strly ins fnl f* **13/2**[3]

20-3 **2** 1 1/4 **Little Miss Lilly**[13] 9507 4-8-11 **57**....................(v) AmeliaGlass(7) 6 61
(Clive Cox) *in tch in midfield: effrt over 1f out: hdwy and rdn to chse wnr 100yds out: kpt on but nvr getting on terms* **7/1**

0500 **3** 1 1/4 **Perfect Symphony (IRE)**[13] 9507 5-9-4 **57**..................(p) LukeMorris 11 57
(Mark Pattinson) *led for almost 1f: chsd wnr after: rdn ent fnl 2f: unable to match pce of wnr over 1f out: kpt on same pce and lost 2nd 100yds out* **10/1**

4011 **4** ½ **Knockout Blow**13 9507 4-9-7 **60**..............................(p) HectorCrouch 5 59+
(John E Long) *midfield on outer: effrt ent fnl 2f: styd on ins fnl f: no threat to wnr* **11/4**1

0010 **5** *shd* **Mercers**13 9507 5-8-9 **55**..............................(v) GraceMcEntee(7) 4 53
(Paddy Butler) *mounted in chute and taken down early: t.k.h: chsd ldrs: effrt 2f out: unable qck over 1f out: kpt on same pce ins fnl f* **14/1**

1644 **6** *shd* **Falcao (IRE)**34 9182 7-9-3 **56**.............................. JoeyHaynes 9 54
(John Butler) *chsd ldrs: unable qck over 1f out: wl hld and one pce ins fnl f* **10/1**

626 **7** ¾ **Catheadans Fury**13 9507 5-9-6 **59**..............................(t) AdamKirby 7 55+
(Martin Bosley) *hld up in last trio: effrt and wd bnd 2f out: kpt on ins fnl f: nvr trbld ldrs* **7/2**2

0020 **8** ¾ **Porto Ferro (IRE)**13 9507 5-9-0 **53**..............................(t) KieranO'Neill 2 47+
(John Bridger) *hld up in last quartet: nt clrst of runs 2f out: swtchd rt and effrt wl over 1f out: no imp* **12/1**

3000 **9** ½ **Tawaafoq**17 9477 5-8-12 **54**..............................(h) FinleyMarsh(3) 1 46
(Adrian Wintle) *wnt rt leaving stalls: t.k.h: hld up in tch in midfield: effrt and swtchd rt over 1f: no imp fnl f (jockey said gelding jumped right leaving stalls)* **11/1**

00R- **10** *hd* **Bahamian Heights**467 7456 8-9-0 **60**..............................(v1) JonathanFisher(7) 10 52+
(Emma Owen) *taken down early and led to s: dropped in bhd after s: hld up in rr: effrt over 1f out: nvr involved* **25/1**

000- **11** ½ **Major Assault**453 7938 6-8-9 **48**.............................. WilliamCarson 3 38+
(Debbie Hughes) *hld up in last trio: nt clr run 2f out: nvr involved* **25/1**

1m 11.87s (-0.03) **Going Correction** -0.075s/f (Stan) **11** Ran SP% **123.3**
Speed ratings (Par 101): **97,95,93,93,92 92,91,90,90,89 89**
CSF £54.22 CT £469.06 TOTE £6.90: £2.40, £2.40, £3.20; EX 46.10 Trifecta £429.30.
Owner David Fremel **Bred** The Millisecond Partnership **Trained** Newmarket, Suffolk

FOCUS
Repeating tactics successful earlier on in the 2yo novice, Tom Marquand again got to the front from the widest stall and made the rest of the running, completing a treble on the card in the process. Straightforward form, with the winner rated back to her best.
T/Plt: £292.70 to a £1 stake. Pool: £79,339.42 - 197.81 winning units T/Qpdt: £102.40 to a £1 stake. Pool: £8,708.95 - 62.92 winning units **Steve Payne**

Index to meetings Flat 2019

† Abandoned
* All-Weather
(M) Mixed meeting

INDEX TO FLAT RACING

Horses are shown in alphabetical order; the trainer's name follows the name of the horse. The figures to the right are current master ratings for all-weather and turf; the all-weather rating is preceded by the letter 'a'.Underneath the horse's name is its age, colour and sex in abbreviated format e.g. 6 b g indicates the horse is six-years-old, bay in colour, and a gelding.The descriptive details are followed by the race numbers of the races in which it has taken part in chronological order; a superscript figure indicates its finishing position in that race (brackets indicate it was the winner of the race). Bold figure represents performance with highest RPR. A diamond represents a race in which the horse's performance is deemed especially noteworthy.

A. A. Azula's Arch (USA)
Kevin Attard a89 95
4 b m Arch(USA) Song Of Solomon (USA) (Unbridled's Song (USA))
8154a[9]

A'Ali (IRE) *Simon Crisford* 112
2 b c Society Rock(IRE) Motion Lass (Motivator)
3477[2] (4012)◆ (5228a) 6264a[5] (7149) 8745a[10]

Aaliya *Amy Murphy* a68 64
4 b m Invincible Spirit(IRE) Rappel (Royal Applause)
439[10]

Aarhus (FR) *J-P Dubois* 74
2 b c Bated Breath Sanada (IRE) (Priolo (USA))
5642a[7]

Aasheq (IRE) *Tim Easterby* a78 102
6 b g Dubawi(IRE) Beach Bunny (IRE) (High Chaparral (IRE))
(1664) 2033[3] 2574[3]◆ 4935[8]◆

Ababeel (FR) *N Clement* a89 69
3 b f Dansili Light Up My Life (IRE) (Zamindar (USA))
9170a[11]

Abadan *Henk Grewe* a71 98
5 gr m Samum(GER) Adalea (Dalakhani (IRE))
2666a[6] 6263a[10] 7249a[12]

Abadie *David Loughnane* a68 60
2 b g Muhaarar Sacre Coeur (Compton Place)
2869[9] 6640[5] 7445[4] 8505[4] 9608[5]

Abama (FR) *Y Barberot* 95
2 b f Alhebayeb(IRE) Iffraja (IRE) (Iffraaj)
7292a[5] (8446a)

Aban (IRE) *Henk Grewe* 57
2 ch c Outstrip Tazyeen (Tamayuz)
4228a[6] 5600a[3]

Abanica *Amanda Perrett* a66 66
3 b f Iffraaj Abated (Dansili)
2212[3] 2730[8] 4507[6]

Abate *Adrian Nicholls* a48 77
3 br c Bated Breath Red Kyte (Hawk Wing (USA))
1665[4] 2590[2] 3159[3] 3416[2] (4010) 4368[7] 4908[4] 5791[6] 8262[6]

Abbaleka *Michael Appleby* a64 65
2 b c Equiano(FR) Megaleka (Misu Bond (IRE))
6548[7] 7316[4] 7825[3] 8506[6] 8841[3] 9031[8] 9307[10]

Abbey Wharf (IRE) *Nigel Tinkler* 67
2 ch f Slade Power(IRE) Faraajh (IRE) (Iffraaj)
4125[8] 5456[2] 6457[7] 7902[6]

Abbi Dab *Michael Appleby*
3 b f Equiano(FR) Megaleka (Misu Bond (IRE))
831[8] 8920[5]

Abbotside *James Bethell* a64 66
2 b g Mukhadram Gregoria (IRE) (Holy Roman Emperor (IRE))
5433[6] 5856[6] 6497[3]

Abel Handy (IRE) *Declan Carroll* a85 98
4 b g Arcano(IRE) Belle Isle (Pastoral Pursuits)
1892[4] (2368) 2775[14] 3097[17] 3375[6] 4359[2] 5420[10] 6714[9] 7077[9] 7856[12] 9098[4]◆ 9286[4]

Abe Lincoln (USA) *Jeremy Noseda* a98 57
6 b h Discreet Cat(USA) Truly Blushed (USA) (Yes It's True (USA))
368[6] 565[5] 2808[10]

Abel Tasman *Roy Brotherton* a64 65
5 b g Mount Nelson Helena Molony (IRE) (Sadler's Wells (USA))
272[12] 6925[7] 8507[9]

Abenaki *Sheena West* a46 49
3 gr g Gregorian(IRE) Blakeshall Rose (Tobougg (IRE))
1041[2] 1332[11] 2343[9]

Abenakian (IRE)
Jane Chapple-Hyam a35 29
2 b g Dylan Thomas(IRE) Till Dawn (IRE) (Kheleyf (USA))
5314[15] 5823[5] 7787[11] 8858[9]

Aberama Gold *Keith Dalgleish* 102
2 b c Heeraat(IRE) Nigella (Band On The Run)
3998[6] 4098[3] (4631) 5390[4]◆ 5668[4] (7399) 7904[4] (8125) 8762[9]

Aberffraw *William Haggas* a76 55
2 ch c Exceed And Excel(AUS) Nahab (Selkirk (USA))
7316[5] 8494[4] (8714)◆

Abie's Hollow *Tony Coyle* a61 66
3 b g Harbour Watch(IRE) Cesseras (IRE) (Cape Cross (IRE))
2933[8] 3569[3] 4080[14] 5020[10] 5695[3] 6101[12] 6176[5] 6679[7] 7384[3] 7764[3] 8270[7] 8949[6] 9035[8]

Abiona (GER) *Frau S Steinberg* 86
4 rg m Jukebox Jury(IRE) Ars Nova (GER) (Soldier Hollow)
2002a[5] 6992a[9]

Able Grace (IRE) *Clive Cox* a59
2 b f No Nay Never(USA) Sanadaat (Green Desert (USA))
8218[7]

Able Jack *P J F Murphy* a79 72
6 b g Iffraaj Solva (Singspiel (IRE))
56[6] 557[7] 1213[10] 1544[3] 2064[9] 3147[11] 7089a[9]

Able Kane *Rod Millman* 71
2 b g Due Diligence(USA) Sugar Beet (Beat Hollow)
3165[5] 3694[3] (7538)

Abnaa *Brian Meehan* a68 60
2 b g Dark Angel(IRE) Along Came Casey (IRE) (Oratorio (IRE))
7407[5] 7911[8] 8494[6]

Aborigene (FR) *Louis Baudron* a56 65
3 b g George Vancouver(USA) Around Me (IRE) (Johannesburg (USA))
1741a[6]

About Glory *Iain Jardine* a59 56
5 b g Nayef(USA) Lemon Rock (Green Desert (USA))
2373[11] 3181[7] 3705[11] 4435[11] (6855) (7232)◆ 7578[4] 7857[2] 8670[4]

Abouttimeyoutoldme
Alistair Whillans 25
5 ch g Mastercraftsman(IRE) Mary Boleyn (IRE) (King's Best (USA))
4636[6] 5277[13] 6939[9]

Above (FR) *Archie Watson* a95 99
2 b c Anjaal Broken Applause (IRE) (Acclamation)
(3491)◆ 5082[2] (5615) (6184) 6746a[3] 7879a[6]

Above N Beyond *A bin Harmash* a86 101
6 ch g Exceed And Excel(AUS) Hill Welcome (Most Welcome)
52a[8]◆ 515a[2] 847a[2] 960a[4]

Above The Rest (IRE) *David Barron* a110 108
8 b g Excellent Art Aspasias Tizzy (USA) (Tiznow (USA))
50a[4] 170a[7] (1103)◆ 1922[8] 2609[24] 2844[7]◆ 3863[19] 4380[5] 5711a[16] 7164[9] 7697[7] 8425[3] 8707[3] 9004[10] (9472)◆

Abr Al Hudood (JPN) *Hugo Palmer* a70 67
3 b f Deep Impact(JPN) Amanee (AUS) (Pivotal)
2518[3] 4768[3] 5627[6] 6558[4]

Abrantes (SPA)
G Arizkorreta Elosegui 106
6 b g Caradak(IRE) Abril (FR) (Anabaa (USA))
170a[2]◆

Abscond (USA) *Eddie Kenneally* 99
2 b f Blame(USA) Solitary Life (USA) (Grand Slam (USA))
(7267a) 8748a[7]

Absolute Dream (IRE)
Richard Fahey a65 73
3 ch g Dream Ahead(USA) Absolute Diamond (Monsieur Bond (IRE))
1424[12] 4895[8] 5786[5] 6373[3] 7049[4] 7418[7] 7764[5]

Absolutio (FR) *K R Burke* a83 87
3 b g Kendargent(FR) La Joie (FR) (Montjeu (IRE))
(1646) 2395[3] 3859[4] 4607[5] 5749[7] 6677[5] 7653[11] 8498[3]

Abstemious *Kevin Ryan* 90
2 b g Mukhadram So Refined (IRE) (Cape Cross (IRE))
4937[2] (5456) 6422[12] 8097[6]

Abstraction (IRE)
Miss Natalia Lupini a87 86
9 b h Majestic Missile(IRE) Bronze Queen (IRE) (Invincible Spirit (IRE))
6986a[6]

Abuja (IRE) *Michael Madgwick* 51
3 b f Society Rock(IRE) Liscoa (IRE) (Foxhound (USA))
5429[3] 5957[9] 6797[3]

Abundancia (FR) *D Guillemin* a65
2 b f Dabirsim(FR) Udana (IRE) (Dubawi (IRE))
6584a[5]

Abushamah (IRE) *Ruth Carr* a63 65
8 b g Nayef(USA) Adaala (USA) (Sahm (USA))
1511[4] 1769[8] 2076[3] (2478) 3214[2] (3744) 3957[2] 4634[5] 4982[6] 5560[6] 6103[4] 6582[7] 7545[2] 7776[7] 8515[12]

Abwaaq (USA) *Simon Crisford* a71
2 b g More Than Ready(USA) Hijaab (USA) (Tiznow (USA))
7911[3] 8503[3]

Abwab (IRE) *Michael Easterby* a57 43
3 b g Teofilo(IRE) Alaia (IRE) (Sinndar (IRE))
4732[6] 8020[6] 8842[5]

Acadian Angel (IRE)
Steph Hollinshead a65 59
5 b m Dark Angel(IRE) Bon Ton Roulet (Hawk Wing (USA))
1648[6] 1850[6] 2585[7] 3473[15] 4232[8]

Acapello (IRE) *Bent Olsen* 76
2 b g Cappella Sansevero Maya De La Luz (Selkirk (USA))
7495a[3]

Accelerate (USA) *John W Sadler* a128
6 ch h Lookin At Lucky(USA) Issues (USA) (Awesome Again (CAN))
445a[3]

Accessor (IRE) *Michael Wigham* a56 69
4 b g Exceed And Excel(AUS) Amarette (GER) (Monsun (GER))
1848[10] 3321[7] 4792[11] 5311[8] 6115[5] 6939[6] 7609[11] 9345[2]◆ 9589[14]

Accidental Agent
Eve Johnson Houghton a108 115
5 b g Delegator Roodle (Xaar)
2829[3]◆ 3948[RR] 4900[4] 5543[8] 6122[2] 6467[3] 8334[11] 8765[3] 9064[3]

Acclaim The Nation (IRE)
Eric Alston a95 91
6 b g Acclamation Dani Ridge (IRE) (Indian Ridge (IRE))
163[2] (471) 1915[2] 2589[2] 3097[18] 4894[3] 5420[4] 6208[3] 7771[4] (9458) 9571[4]

Acclamatio (IRE) *A J Martin* a54 75
5 b g Acclamation Incitatus Girl (IRE) (Galileo (IRE))
5712a[16] 6576[3]

Acclimate (USA) *Philip D'Amato* 109
5 b g Acclamation(USA) Knows No Bounds (USA) (Boundary (USA))
8776a[9]

Accommodate (IRE)
Sir Michael Stoute a81 73
3 b f Acclamation Malaspina (IRE) (Whipper (USA))
2809[15] 4023[7]

Accomplice *Michael Blanshard* a70 63
5 b m Sakhee's Secret Witness (Efisio)
175[5] 386[2] 828[2] 1175[7] 1378[6] 2277[5] 2585[3] 3038[8] 3533[3] 4235[3] 4870[7] 5675[3] 6334[4] 6643[3] 7237[5] 7374[6]

Accon (GER) *Markus Klug* 109
3 b c Camelot Anaita (GER) (Dubawi (IRE))
2310a[5] (3385a) 4707a[3] 5719a[2] 6771a[5] 7249a[7] 8792a[6]

Accredited *David Flood* a64 47
3 b f Archipenko(USA) Saltpetre (IRE) (Selkirk (USA))
4372[8]

Ace Cheetah (USA) *J R Jenkins* a61
5 b g Kitten's Joy(USA) Imagistic (USA) (Deputy Minister (CAN))
696[5] 921[4] 5311[9] 6077[14]

Ace Combat *Michael Madgwick* a67 60
4 b g Shamardal(USA) Require (Montjeu (IRE))
1292[9] 1826[6] 3545[11]

Ace Korea (USA) *Peter Wolsley* a56
4 b h Smiling Tiger(USA) Queen Rolex (USA) (Broken Vow (USA))
50a[7] 729a[10] 7010a[12]

Ace Master *Roy Bowring* a56 45
11 ch g Ballet Master(USA) Ace Maite (Komaite (USA))
1553[11] 2693[9]

Aces (IRE) *Ian Williams* 99
7 b g Dark Angel(IRE) Cute Ass (IRE) (Fath (USA))
2572[4] 3069[7] 3602[9] 3863[16] (4319) 5312[4]

Achaeus (GER) *Ed Dunlop* a62 36
3 b g Tertullian(USA) Anatola (GER) (Tiger Hill (IRE))
1033[9] 1510[6] 3311[12] 4568[10]

Achianna (USA) *Rod Millman* 45
4 ch m Gemologist(USA) Adoradancer (USA) (Danzig Connection (USA))
80[12] 256[9]

Achillea (FR) *M Le Forestier* a72 66
6 b m Dylan Thomas(IRE) Afya (Oasis Dream)
1491a[4]

Achille Des Aigles (FR)
Mme C Barande-Barbe a74 74
5 ch g Siyouni(FR) Kiva Des Aigles (FR) (Enrique)
6267a[10]

Acker Bilk (IRE) *Ronald Harris* a57 32
5 ch g Rip Van Winkle(IRE) Portentous (Selkirk (USA))
2124[8] 2516[7] 3700[11]

Acquire *Richard Hannon* 60
2 b f Due Diligence(USA) Diapason (IRE) (Mull Of Kintyre (USA))
5132[12] 6906[10] 7896[8]

Acquitted (IRE) *Hugo Palmer* a78 87
2 b c Night Of Thunder(IRE) Blameless (IRE) (Authorized (IRE))
(6926) 7410[4] (8518)

Acqume (AUS) *Toby Edmonds* 88
4 ch m Sepoy(AUS) Acquired (NZ) (O'Reilly (NZ))
3097[15]

Across The Sea *James Tate* a81 79
3 b f Dubawi(IRE) Alsindi (IRE) (Acclamation)
2635[4] 3293[7] 4303[7] 4844[2] 5056[3] (7105)

Acrux *L Rovisse* a81 74
6 b g Dansili Ikat (IRE) (Pivotal)
(115a)

Actee (IRE) *R Le Dren Doleuze* 69
2 b f Youmzain(IRE) Ravage (Verglas (IRE))
4533a[5]

Acting (NZ)
Trent Busuttin & Natalie Young 102
2 br f Savabeel(AUS) Hollywood (NZ) (Pins (AUS))
8135a[5]

Action Pauliene (FR) *K Borgel* 74
4 b h Tin Horse(IRE) Ninka (FR) (Linamix (FR))
3140a[8]

Active Spirit (IRE) *Doug Watson*
8 ch g Pivotal Local Spirit (USA) (Lion Cavern (USA))
172a[10]

Activius (IRE) *Brian Meehan* a37 56
2 b g Baltic King Miss Megs (IRE) (Croco Rouge (IRE))
3008[6] 3542[6] 6368[13] 6837[8] 7111[10] 7626[9]

Act Of God *E J O'Grady* a73 77
4 b g Camelot Adja (IRE) (Rock Of Gibraltar (IRE))
5508a[9] 7216a[7]

Act Of Magic (IRE) *Luke McJannet* a44 60
3 b g Magician(IRE) Davanti (IRE) (Danehill Dancer (IRE))
319[5] 829[8] 1549[2] (2262) 2734[4] (3256) 3348[2] 5354[9] 9329[8]

Adabeyaat *J-C Rouget* 72
2 b f Oasis Dream Mashoora (IRE) (Barathea (IRE))
6774a[8]

Adam's Ale *Marjorie Fife* a15 54
10 b g Ishiguru(USA) Aqua (Mister Baileys)
4434[5] 5038[7] 5723[10] 6339[7] 6826[10] 8632[10]

Adams Park *Michael Appleby* a69 70
4 b g Mastercraftsman(IRE) Ile Deserte (Green Desert (USA))
8298[7] 8608[10] 9134[4]◆ 9511[5]

Adam Tiler (USA) *Robert Cowell* a51 66
3 b g Justin Phillip(USA) Moneygrabber (USA) (Awesome Again (CAN))
1728[8]

Adashelby (IRE) *John Ryan* a49 50
3 gr f Zebedee Abby Cadabby (IRE) (Jeremy (USA))
5627[9] 7190[6] 7572[7] 8499[6] 8756[11] 9225[6]

Addeybb (IRE) *William Haggas* a115 122
5 ch g Pivotal Bush Cat (USA) (Kingmambo (USA))
2573[4] (3953) 5455[2] (5950)◆ 8335[2]

Addicted Love (FR) *F Foucher* a69 65
3 b f Lope De Vega(IRE) Pride Dancer (IRE) (Fasliyev (USA))
2090a[8] 4357a[2]

Addicted To You (IRE)
Mark Johnston a102 84
5 ch g Medicean Adalawa (IRE) (Barathea (IRE))
82[8] 349[8] 704[7] 1172[3] 1524[2] 2080[7] 2578[12]

Addis Ababa (IRE) *David O'Meara* a91 95
4 ch g Declaration Of War(USA) Song Of My Heart (IRE) (Footstepsinthesand)
1719[3] 2186[2] 2748[12] 3180[2] 3811[2] 4144[4] 4730[5] 6998[3] 7589[2] (7782) 8130[7]

Adehaine (IRE) *N Caullery* 32
2 b c Morpheus Little Red Minx (IRE) (Red Clubs (IRE))
1657a[15]

Adelante (FR) *George Baker* a81 94
3 ch f Zoffany(IRE) Make Up (Kyllachy)
217a[3] 509a[4] 993a[2] 1516[4] (1985) 2285[2] 4621a[4] 5666[8] 6769a[10]

A Delight (FR) *Matthieu Palussiere* a65 51
3 b f George Vancouver(USA) Gulf Stream Lady (IRE) (Cadeaux Genereux)
217a[7]

Adelinda (IRE) *A Botti* a53 96
2 b f Zebedee Feels So Close (IRE) (High Chaparral (IRE))
4172a[9]

Adena Star (IRE) *Jonathan Portman* a65 10
3 b f Big Bad Bob(IRE) Silicon Star (FR) (Starborough)
1359[10] 3354[13]

Adesias (FR) *J-C Rouget* a78 83
3 b f George Vancouver(USA) Kel Away (FR) (Keltos (FR))
(3526a)

Adiator *Seb Spencer* a24 60
11 b m Needwood Blade Retaliator (Rudimentary (USA))
45[7] 2709[15]

Adirondack (IRE) *F Chappet* a60 5
3 b g Kodiac Kikonga (Danehill Dancer (IRE))
2090a[13] 3066a[15]

Adler (GER) *Markus Klug* 104
5 ch h Adlerflug(GER) Azalee (GER) (Lando (GER))
2666a[4]

Ad Libitum *Roger Fell* a83 71
4 b g Elusive Quality(USA) Sarmad (USA) (Dynaformer (USA))
2636[7] 3095[13] 3568[7] 4370[7] 4724[7] 5122[3] 5556[4] 6180[9] 6663[3] (6939)◆ 7301[2] 7816[10] 8298[9]

Admirable Art (IRE) *Tony Carroll* a54 49
9 b g Excellent Art Demi Voix (Halling (USA))
132[2] 530[7] 594[13] 1026[12]

Admiral Anson *Michael Appleby* a21 22
5 br g Bahri(USA) Bromeigan (Mtoto)
155[14] 595[12]

Admirality *Roger Fell* a96 100
5 b g Mount Nelson Dialma (USA) (Songandaprayer (USA))
(2844) 3589[8] 3863[2] 4654[3] 4921[3] 5120[4] 5413[5] 6706[8] 7222a[5] 7431[6]

Admiral Rooke (IRE)
Michael Appleby a61 47
4 b g Rock Of Gibraltar(IRE) Qenaa (Royal Applause)
23[6] 243[11] 882[2] 1021[10] 1215[6] 1339[10] 1554[6] 1595[2] 1716[5] (1883) 2066[5] 2318[9]

Admiral Rous (IRE)
Jassim Mohammed Ghazali a90 103
3 b c Henrythenavigator(USA) Bulrushes (Byron)
893a[4] 3903a[3] 9590a[8]

Admirals Bay (GER)
Andrew Balding a49 63
3 b g Mount Nelson Astragal (Shamardal (USA))
2354[9] 2795[14] (3275) 3765[3] 4484[5]

Admiral Spice (IRE) *Sophie Leech* a56 47
4 gr g Lethal Force(IRE) Rustam (Dansili)
910[9]

Admiral Thrawn (IRE)
Andrea Marcialis a85 78
4 b g Most Improved(IRE) Lathaat (Dubai Destination (USA))
992a[7] 2391a[8]

Admiralty Pier (USA)
Barbara J Minshall a92 103
4 ch g English Channel(USA) Full Steam Ahead (USA) (Kitten's Joy (USA))
7225a[7]

Admire Fuji (IRE) *D De Waele* a74 79
9 b h Oasis Dream Sun Bittern (USA) (Seeking The Gold (USA))
7861a[3]

Admire Mars (JPN)
Yasuo Tomomichi 119
3 ch c Daiwa Major(JPN) Via Medici (IRE) (Medicean)
(9379a)

Admission Office (USA)
Brian A Lynch 105
4 b h Point Of Entry(USA) Miss Chapin (USA) (Royal Academy (USA))
7922a[11]

Admodum (USA) *John Butler* a70 57
6 ch g Majestic Warrior(USA) Unbridled Treasure (USA) (Unbridled's Song (USA))
5151[7] 5842[6] 9132[8] (9443)

Adonijah *Henry Candy* 91
3 b c Sea The Stars(IRE) Meeznah (USA) (Dynaformer (USA))
5384[2]◆ 6216[5]

Adonis Blue (IRE) *Roger Charlton* 39
2 b g Helmet(AUS) Blue Butterfly (Kyllachy)
7338[11]

Adorable (IRE) *William Haggas* 84
4 b m Kodiac Caffe Latte (IRE) (Seattle Dancer (USA))
2608[8] 3318[11]

Adorian (FR) *S Smrczek* 67
3 b c Slickly(FR) Anastra (GER) (Seattle Dancer (USA))
4959a[7]

Adrued (IRE) *Mark Usher* a13
2 b f Battle Of Marengo(IRE) Pandoras Secret (IRE) (Monashee Mountain (USA))
9211[12] 9501[8]

Ad Valorem Queen (IRE) *J R Jenkins* a55 45
4 b m Dandy Man(IRE) Herful Schnerful (Jeremy (USA))
1393[9] 1683[4]◆ 4615[10] 5302[12] 6051[14]

Adventureman *Ruth Carr* a61 53
7 b g Kyllachy Constitute (USA) (Gone West (USA))
912[11] 1231[11] 1398[11] 1722[2] 2012[3] 2596[10] 2944[10] 3730[4] 4293[6] 4728[11] 5247[14] 5787[12]

Advertise *Martyn Meade* 121
3 b c Showcasing Furbelow (Pivotal)
2411[15] (4050) 4923[2] (5716a) 8331[7]

Ad Vitam (IRE) *Suzzanne France* a49 48
11 ch g Ad Valorem(USA) Love Sonnet (Singspiel (IRE))
64[5] 3413[14] 5559[3] 7591[13]

Aegean Legend *John Bridger* a25 69
4 b g Mayson Aegean Mystery (Dr Fong (USA))
2483[12] 4116[9] 5675[8] 7204[8]

Aegean Mist *John Bridger* a35 52
3 ch f Mayson Aegean Shadow (Sakhee (USA))
2008[7] 2489[8] 3258[7] 3801[8] 4185[9] 6018[6] 6286[7] 6401[6]

Aegeus (IRE) *Paddy Butler* a32 40
6 b g Shamardal(USA) Magna Graecia (IRE) (Warning)
404[10]

Aegeus (USA) *Amanda Perrett* a73 73
3 b g First Defence(USA) Supposition (Dansili)
2280[2] 2932[3] 5955[2] (8086)

Aeolus *Ruth Carr* a82 93
8 b g Araafa(IRE) Bright Moll (Mind Games)
1421[8] 1763[4] 2396[9] 2844[6] 3589[11] 5120[6] 5488[8] 6014[6]

Aerolithe (JPN) *Takanori Kikuzawa* 115
5 gr m Kurofune(USA) Asterix (JPN) (Neo Universe (JPN))
444a[9]

Aethero (AUS) *John Moore* 124
2 ch g Sebring(AUS) Pinocchio (AUS) (Encosta De Lago (AUS))
9377a[3]

Afaak *Charles Hills* 113
5 b g Oasis Dream Ghanaati (USA) (Giant's Causeway (USA))
(3987) 4935[5] 5610[12] 7694[18] 9125a[4]

Afandem (IRE) *Tim Easterby* a74 86
5 b g Vale Of York(IRE) Al Mahmeyah (Teofilo (IRE))
1760[5] 1976[4] 2709[12] 2876[12] (3291) 3550[8] 4307[3] 4632[2] 4821[2] 5244[5] (6057) 7077[6] (7736) 7828[10] 8262[3] 8860[2] 9030[8]

Affair *Hughie Morrison* a59 60
5 b m Sakhee's Secret Supatov (USA) (Johannesburg (USA))
38[7] 363[11] 2733[4] 3444[6] 5029[7] 6115[9] 7202[11] 7985[6] 8916[4]

Afficionado (FR) *J-C Rouget* 85
2 b f Cable Bay(IRE) Affolante (USA) (Whywhywhy (USA))
8647a[6]

Affluence (IRE) *Martin Smith* a76 73
4 b g Thewayyouare(USA) Castalian Spring (IRE) (Oasis Dream)
207[4] 436[3] 593[2] 695[2] (1078) 2111[4] 2617[8] 4220[11] (4568) (5106) 5744[2] 6830[4]◆ 8196[4] (9049) 9204[4]

Affogato (FR) *J-C Rouget* 75
3 b c Siyouni(FR) Almilea (GER) (Galileo (IRE))
5644a[5]

A Fine Romance (FR) *Mme Pia Brandt* 81
3 b f Reliable Man A Beautiful Mind (GER) (Winged Love (IRE))
2759a[5] (7061a)

Afleet Destiny (USA) *Uriah St Lewis* a95
3 b f Hard Spun(USA) Afleet Lover (USA) (Northern Afleet (USA))
7479a[8]

Afraid Of Nothing *Ralph Beckett* 87
2 b f Charm Spirit(IRE) Lady Dragon (IRE) (Galileo (IRE))
5774[6] 6697[2]◆ (7124) (7725) 9059a[7]

African Blessing *John Best* a64 68
6 ch g Mount Nelson Bella Beguine (Komaite (USA))
(37) 159[2] 430[8] 857[4] 1038[5]

African Dream *John Gosden* a69
2 b f Oasis Dream Alsindi (IRE) (Acclamation)
9409[3]◆

African Jazz (IRE) *Charlie Appleby* a95 97
4 b g Cape Cross(IRE) Monday Show (USA) (Maria's Mon (USA))
5443[5] 6171[8]

African Ride *Simon Crisford* a109 112
5 b h Candy Ride(ARG) Paiota Falls (USA) (Kris S (USA))
171a[5] 513a[3] (957a) (Dead)

African Showgirl *Eve Johnson Houghton* a48 48
6 ch m Showcasing Georgie The Fourth (IRE) (Cadeaux Genereux)
155[7] (6555a) 6758[7] 7232[4]

African Sun (IRE) *Ed Dunlop* a45
2 b c Teofilo(IRE) Castle Cross (IRE) (Cape Cross (IRE))
8717[11] 8914[12] 9156[8]

African Swift (USA) *Mark Johnston* a75 70
2 ch f Distorted Humor(USA) Sahara Wind (USA) (A.P. Indy (USA))
5588[4] 6072[2] 6424[5] 6965[4] 7548[4] 8303[2]

Afro Blue (IRE) *Richard Hannon* 76
2 b c Oasis Dream Najraan (Cadeaux Genereux)
5908[3] 6424[11]

Afsane (FR) *S Smrczek* a65 87
6 b m Siyouni(FR) La Barquera (Nayef (USA))
3288a[9]

Afterallthat (IRE) *Richard Fahey*
2 b c Anjaal Zahenda (Exceed And Excel (AUS))
3812[15]

After John *Mick Channon* 81
3 b g Dutch Art Rosacara (Green Desert (USA))
2139[3]◆ 2794[2] (3058) 3599[8] 5773[5] 6225[5] 6913[10] 7564[3] 8522[7]

After Rain Sun (FR) *Henk Grewe* 73
2 ch f Prince Gibraltar(FR) Belle Chasse (Kyllachy)
8586a[6]

Agar's Plough *Michael Easterby* a74 74
4 ch g Dutch Art Cloud's End (Dubawi (IRE))
1660[5] 2056[2] 4446[9] 7363[6] 8186[10]

Agent Basterfield (IRE) *Andrew Balding* a73 83
3 b g Raven's Pass(USA) Maridiyna (IRE) (Sinndar (IRE))
1481[2] 2021[2] (2229) 3692[2] 4559[4] 5089[3] 5840[3]

Agente Segreto (IRE) *Nicolo Simondi* 98
3 gr c Mastercraftsman(IRE) Adamantina (Diktat)
2887a[5]

Agent Gibbs *John O'Shea* a77 70
7 ch g Bertolini(USA) Armada Grove (Fleetwood (IRE))
61[5] 246[10] 457[7] 1482[8] 2279[5] 2468[2] 2718[4] 4370[3] 5425[4] 7790[6]

Agent Of Fortune *Gary Moore* a68 58
4 ch m Kheleyf(USA) Royal Bloom (IRE) (Royal Applause)
1338[7] 2261[4] 3146[6] 4567[9] 4807[4] 5531[3] 6327[6] 7374[8] 8255[5]◆ 8436[7] (9384) (9410)◆ (9657)

Agent Shiftwell *Stuart Williams* a73 66
2 b c Equiano(FR) Holley Shiftwell (Bahamian Bounty)
8409[2] 9099[3] (9251)

Agent Smith (IRE) *K R Burke* a32 51
3 b g Morpheus Sand N Sea (IRE) (Desert Story (IRE))
228[11] 319[10]

Age Of Chivalry (NZ) *Mathew Ellerton & Simon Zahra* 105
3 b g He's Remarkable(NZ) Onyx (NZ) (Kaapstad (NZ))
8138a[3]

Age Of Wisdom (IRE) *Gary Moore* a90 76
6 ch g Pivotal Learned Friend (GER) (Seeking The Gold (USA))
1144[2] (3044) 3693[3] 5540[19] 6448[3] 6901[5] 8654[5] 9419[5]

Aggression (ITY) *G Botti* 68
2 b f Arcano(IRE) Torrian (IRE) (Intikhab (USA))
(5713a) 6873a[7]

Aghast *Kevin Ryan* a47 66
3 b f Bated Breath Classic Vision (Classic Cliche (IRE))
(2197) 2937[3] 4080[8] 5147[5] 5985[10] 6680[10] 7632[8]

Agiato *Grizzetti Galoppo SRL* 93
2 ch c Bated Breath Rosa Del Dubai (IRE) (Dubai Destination (USA))
8791a[4]

Agilmente (FR) *L Gadbin* a55 70
2 ch f Rio De La Plata(USA) La Jalousie (FR) (Muhtathir)
(2890a)

Agincourt (IRE) *David O'Meara* a92 102
4 b m Declaration Of War(USA) El Diamante (FR) (Royal Applause)
2097[2]◆ (2809) 3494[2] 4072[2] 4758[3] 6379[2] (7657)

Agitare (IRE) *J S Bolger* 104
2 ch c Teofilo(IRE) Sway Me Now (USA) (Speightstown (USA))
7217a[3]

Agnes (FR) *Mlle J Soudan* a81 100
3 b f Planteur(IRE) Agenda (IRE) (Sadler's Wells (USA))
2312a[4]

Agnostic (IRE) *C Lerner* 45
2 b c Kendargent(FR) Siderante (FR) (Siyouni (FR))
8447a[9]

A Go Go *David Evans* a55 50
2 b f Heeraat(IRE) Gagajulu (Al Hareb (USA))
3350[5] 5294[6] 5577[7] 7234[5] (7853)◆ 8315[7] 9394[3]

Agrapart (FR) *Nick Williams* 84
8 bb g Martaline Afragha (IRE) (Darshaan)
(2571) 5897[3]

Agravain *Tim Easterby* 73
3 b g Camelot Pivotal Lady (Pivotal)
2336[7] 2712[9] (2913) (3219) 4034[4] (4587) 4729[5] 5974[2] 6459[3] 7209[3] 8098[14]

Agreeable (IRE) *Conrad Allen* a26
2 b f Camacho Raas (USA) (Iffraaj)
7515[12]

Agreed *John Gosden* a73
2 b f Gleneagles(IRE) Intrigued (Darshaan)
9046[6] 9383[2]

Agrotera (IRE) *Ed Walker* a106 103
4 ch m Mastercraftsman(IRE) Lombatina (FR) (King's Best (USA))
(1941) 3986[11]

Agua De Valencia (FR) *J-P Gauvin* a83 83
5 b m Approve(IRE) Madonna Lily (IRE) (Daylami (IRE))
2675a[4]

Aguerooo (IRE) *Charlie Wallis* a75 63
6 b g Monsieur Bond(IRE) Vision Of Peace (IRE) (Invincible Spirit (IRE))
144[6] (314) (439) 790[7] 982[6] 1016[2] 1393[4] 1597[7] 3147[12] 9257[8] 9386[4]

Ahdab (IRE) *Ed Dunlop* a49
2 b c Shamardal(USA) Habaayib (Royal Applause)
7571[7]◆

A Head Ahead (GER) *S Smrczek* a68 83
5 b h Makfi Allegro Vivace (FR) (Muhtathir)
(4747a) 9014a[8]

Ahfad *Gary Moore* a50 52
4 br g Dick Turpin(IRE) Big Moza (Pastoral Pursuits)
207[7] 485[4] 940[2] 1032[5] 1683[3] 3348[12] 3687[6] 6049[4] 7375[9] 8813[4] 9289[10]

Ahlan Bil Zain (FR) *M Halford* a91 86
5 b g Elusive City(USA) Fall View (Pivotal)
3062a[9]

Ahorsewithnoname *Brian Ellison* 87
4 b m Cacique(IRE) Sea Of Galilee (Galileo (IRE))
3553[3] (6274) (7287)

Ah Pass *S Gouyette* a15 55
3 b f Sayif(IRE) Timeless Elegance (IRE) (Invincible Spirit (IRE))
6789a[7]

A Hundred Echoes *Roger Varian* a54 54
3 b g Kyllachy Kapsiliat (IRE) (Cape Cross (IRE))
1570[9] 2794[11] 6283[4] 6945[8] 7420[10] 8416[3]

Ahundrednotout *John James Feane* a74 62
5 ch g Mount Nelson Forest Express (AUS) (Kaaptive Edition (NZ))
347[7] 2329[4]

Aide Memoire (IRE) *Neil King* 40
3 b f Rip Van Winkle(IRE) Bessichka (Exceed And Excel (AUS))
1740[17] 2802[11] 4073[7]

Aiden's Reward (IRE) *Ben Haslam* a46 49
2 b g Dandy Man(IRE) Bonne (Namid)
3703[9] 4237[7] 5026[4] 8527[4] 9164[6]

Aigiarne (IRE) *Clive Cox* a61 64
3 b f Helmet(AUS) Golden Shine (Royal Applause)
795[5] 2018[11] 4180[3]

Aigle Teen (FR) *S Dehez* 81
4 bb g Mesnil Des Aigles(FR) Ever Teene (FR) (Even Top (IRE))
1245a[12]

Aiguiere D'Argent (FR) *N Clement* a67 69
2 ch g Excelebration(IRE) Plaisanciere (FR) (Astronomer Royal (USA))
7675a[5]

Aiguillette *Gary Moore* a51 43
3 b g Epaulette(AUS) Lucky Dice (Perugino (USA))
2140[7] 2790[11] 6897[11] 7371[6] 7606[2] 8249[2] 8689[2]

Aim Power (IRE) *Richard Hannon* 91
3 gr f Zebedee Montefino (IRE) (Shamardal (USA))
2934[4] 4052[9] 4922[8] 6220[13] 6908[6]

Ainne *Sylvester Kirk* a55 57
4 ch m Cityscape Ayun (USA) (Swain (IRE))
348[6] 462[9] 940[8] 1339[9] (1732) 1958[9] 2240[15] 3142[11] 4247[9]

Ainsdale *K R Burke* 94
2 b c Mayson Bruni Heinke (IRE) (Dutch Art)
4719[4] 5815[2] 6337[3] 7182[2]◆ (8095) (8261)◆ (8659)

Airbrush (IRE) *Richard Hannon* a65 69
2 b f Camacho Cover Girl (IRE) (Common Grounds)
4337[3] 4790[7] 5317[5] 5800[2] 6557[3] 7227[2] 7556[6] 8506[5]

Aircraft Carrier (IRE) *John Ryan* a109 98
4 b g Declaration Of War(USA) Strategy (Machiavellian (USA))
(238)◆ 1062[4] 1917[6] 2807[8] 4382[14] 5928[5] 6355[17] 6452[6] 7464[8] 8129[12]

Air Dance (FR) *J-C Rouget* a86 88
3 b c So You Think(NZ) Spring Morning (FR) (Ashkalani (IRE))
(3675a) 9210a[13]

Air De Valse (FR) *Mme C Barande-Barbe* a90 90
3 ch f Mesnil Des Aigles(FR) Air Bag (FR) (Poliglote)
8983a[6]

Air Force Amy *Mick Channon* a73 80
3 ch f Sixties Icon Madame Hoi (IRE) (Hawk Wing (USA))
1077[2] 2141[7] 2612[7] 6039[2] 6304[4] (7625) 7835[4]

Air Force Jet *Joseph Patrick O'Brien* 104
2 b c Charm Spirit(IRE) Wind Fire (USA) (Distorted Humor (USA))
4012[13] 4580a[2] 5542[7] 6190a[6] 6690a[10]

Airglow (IRE) *Michael Easterby* a83 77
4 b g Invincible Spirit(IRE) Pearl Grey (Gone West (USA))
5670[7] 6227[4] 6549[6] 6921[6] 7402[22] 8342[5] 8403[2] 8636[10] 9334[11]

Air Hair Lair (IRE) *Sheena West* a52 67
3 ch g Zebedee Blond Beauty (USA) (Theatrical (IRE))
1754[7] 2210[5] 2795[12] 3170[8] 3651[11] 4092[17] 4378[13] 8756[6] 9005[13]

Air Of York (IRE) *Grace Harris* a58 66
7 b g Vale Of York(IRE) State Secret (Green Desert (USA))
31[7] 315[11] (2339) 3089[3] 3575[8] 4181[8] 4479[5] 5579[3] 6084[7] 6844[5] 8345[5] 8847[11] 9253[6]

Air Pilot *Ralph Beckett* 115
10 b g Zamindar(USA) Countess Sybil (IRE) (Dr Devious (IRE))
1244a[3] (7565) 8764[5]

Airplane (IRE) *Paul Collins* a40 69
4 b g Pour Moi(IRE) Abyssinie (IRE) (Danehill Dancer (IRE))
1848[11] 2202[8] 3054[3] 3334[7] 4601[6] 5029[6] 5301[5] 5513[6] 7492[11] 7956[14] 8670[6] 9042[9] 9470[10]

Air Raid *Jedd O'Keeffe* a77 106
4 b g Raven's Pass(USA) Siren Sound (Singspiel (IRE))
2526[7] (3503) (3722)◆ 4379[11] (5120)◆ 5664[22] 8127[17]

Airshow *Michael Appleby* a92 79
4 ch g Showcasing Belle Des Airs (IRE) (Dr Fong (USA))
1847[3] 2824[17] 5649[4] 6319[6]

Airton *David Pipe* a83 83
6 b g Champs Elysees Fly In Style (Hernando (FR))
3091[5]

Airwaves *Martyn Meade* a75 64
3 b f Monsieur Bond(IRE) Forever Bond (Danetime (IRE))
2024[6] 2510[12] 5813[8]

Aisa Dream (IRE) *V Fazio* 92
2 b f Society Rock(IRE) Turuqaat (Fantastic Light (USA))
4172a[5]

Aiseolas (IRE) *Gavin Hernon* 75
4 b m Vocalised(USA) Lavender Blue (Galileo (IRE))
1073a[6] 1578a[4]

Aislabie (FR) *Jason Ward* a29 26
6 gr g Soldier Of Fortune(IRE) Someries (FR) (Kendor (FR))
2185[10] 2819[12]

Aiya (IRE) *Tim Easterby* a76 80
4 ch g Declaration Of War(USA) Flamingo Sea (USA) (Woodman (USA))
2370[4] 3161[2] 3514[5] 3845[7] 5667[8] 6580[5] 6975[9] (7379)

Ajas (FR) *Tobias Hellgren* 81
5 b g No Risk At All(FR) Seraglio (IRE) (Singspiel (IRE))
8804a[4]

Ajax Tavern *Richard Hannon* a77
2 b g Canford Cliffs(IRE) Gimme Some Lovin (IRE) (Desert Style (IRE))
(9668)◆

Ajman Prince (IRE) *Alistair Whillans* a83 49
6 b g Manduro(GER) Jumaireyah (Fairy King (USA))
124[2]

Ajmany (IRE) *J-M Baudrelle* a74 74
9 b g Kheleyf(USA) Passarelle (USA) (In The Wings)
4748a[8]

Ajrar *Richard Hannon* a68 79
3 ch f Nayef(USA) Barnezet (GR) (Invincible Spirit (IRE))
2268[6] 3193[5] 4072[8] 4582[4]

Ajwad *R Bouresly* a62 107
6 b h Rock Of Gibraltar(IRE) Afrodita (IRE) (Montjeu (IRE))
196a[11] 1111a[5]

Akamanto (IRE) *R Mike Smith* a75 86
5 b g Cape Cross(IRE) Allofus (IRE) (Celtic Swing)
1503[3]

Akavit (IRE) *Ed de Giles* a72 62
7 b g Vale Of York(IRE) Along Came Molly (Dr Fong (USA))
700[5] 1144[6] 1663[7] 2936[8] 4251[4] 4483[3]

Akinathor Game (FR) *G Botti* a67 48
4 b h George Vancouver(USA) Akita (USA) (Giant's Causeway (USA))
76a[3]

Akribie (GER) *Markus Klug* 103
3 bb f Reliable Man Aussicht (GER) (Haafhd)
(3639a) 5720a[5] 6771a[6] 7504a[5] 8587a[10]

Aktau *Roger Varian* 97
3 b g Teofilo(IRE) Rare Ransom (Oasis Dream)
1956[3] 2581[4] 3263[2] (5614)

Akua'rella (GER) *D Moser* 98
4 b m Shamardal(USA) Akua'Ba (IRE) (Sadler's Wells (USA))
3288a[3] 4461a[8] 8587a[9]

Akvavera *Ralph Beckett* a97 95
4 ch m Leroidesanimaux(BRZ) Akdarena (Hernando (FR))
2404[7] 3342[7] 4393[5] 5708[3] 7106[7] 7815[3]◆ 8606[11]

Akwaan (IRE) *Simon Crisford* a68 87
3 b g Camacho Saytara (IRE) (Nayef (USA))
2355[3] 3093[3] (4071) (4565) 4919[5]

Akyo (FR) *M Boutin* a70 67
2 b c Rajsaman(FR) Beynotown (Authorized (IRE))
7799a[5]

Alaadel *Stuart Williams* a73 99
6 ch g Dubawi(IRE) Infallible (Pivotal)
3770[2]◆ 6227[11] (6920) 7894[13] 8127[6] 8512[7]

Al Aakif (IRE) *William Haggas* 95
2 b c Acclamation Vastitas (IRE) (Green Desert (USA))
(3371) (4401)◆ 5134[3]

Al Aasy (IRE) *William Haggas* 78
2 b c Sea The Stars(IRE) Kitcara (Shamardal (USA))
8460[3]◆

Alabaa *L Gadbin* 97
3 b c Motivator Absolutly Me (FR) (Anabaa Blue)
1347a[8] 3031a[4] 8445a[6]

Alabama Dreaming *George Scott* a66 67
3 gr f Foxwedge(AUS) Sweet Alabama (Johannesburg (USA))
2938[6] 3651[6] 7189[5] 7811[5] 8217[8] 8435[6]

Alabama Whitman *Richard Spencer* 94
2 b f Ivawood(IRE) Mutoon (IRE) (Erhaab (USA))
3165[2]◆ 4048[4] (4819) 5469a[5] 7659[7]

Alabanza *Keith Dalgleish* a27 76
4 b g Big Bad Bob(IRE) Tahfeez (IRE) (Alhaarth (IRE))
3222[7]

Alabaster *Sir Mark Prescott Bt* a77 79
5 gr g Archipenko(USA) Alvarita (Selkirk (USA))
184[7] 480[5] 799[5] 991[3] 1172[5] 1330[2] 1840[3] 2239[3] 3145[3] 4019[3] 4308[2]

Alacovia (FR) *S Cerulis* a71 83
5 b m Motivator Pomonia (FR) (Anabaa (USA))
5510a[9] 7536a[5]

Alacritas *David Simcock* a66 60
4 gr m Leroidesanimaux(BRZ) Albaraka (Selkirk (USA))
616[6] 2695[7]

Aladaala (IRE) *William Haggas* a76 63
3 b f Dansili Alshadhia (IRE) (Marju (IRE))
4592[3]◆ 5451[6]

Alameery *Adrian Nicholls* a54 13
3 b c Kingman Zacheta (Polish Precedent (USA))
6283[3] 7114[7] 9332[8]

Al Anaab (FR) *Lucinda Egerton* a42 44
3 b f Style Vendome(FR) Lucky For Me (USA) (King Of Kings (IRE))
1359[8] 1543[7] 2909[7] 3598[7]

Alandalos *Charles Hills* a61 78
3 b f Invincible Spirit(IRE) Ghanaati (USA) (Giant's Causeway (USA))
1834[3] 4305[4]◆ 5349[2] 5779[4] (6559) 7341[4]

Alargedram (IRE) *Alan King* a69 66
2 ch g Lope De Vega(IRE) Myrica (Dansili)
6640[9] 7473[4]◆ 7972[4]

Al Asef *David Simcock* a74 66
4 br g Kyllachy Hot Reply (Notnowcato)
254[4] 797[6] 1061[10] 8496[5] 9048[3]◆ 9329[5]

Alash Orda *Roger Varian* 76
2 b f Kodiac Albanka (USA) (Giant's Causeway (USA))
6906[2]◆

Alaskan Bay (IRE) *Rae Guest* a60 48
4 b m Kodiac Party Appeal (USA) (Mr Greeley (USA))
118[2] 298[6] 1883[8] 3001[8] 4074[9] 5264[8] 9445[4]

Alate (IRE) *Sir Mark Prescott Bt* a50
3 b f Holy Roman Emperor(IRE) Alleviate (IRE) (Indian Ridge (IRE))
245[4]

Alatia (IRE) *Jo Hughes* a29 86
3 b g Moohaajim(IRE) Hatria (IRE) (Royal Applause)
289[11]

A La Voile *Sir Michael Stoute* 70
2 b f Invincible Spirit(IRE) All At Sea (Sea The Stars (IRE))
5684[5]◆

Alba Del Sole (IRE) *Charlie Wallis* a47 45
4 b m Dandy Man(IRE) Winterwell (USA) (First Defence (USA))
233[7] 928[5] 1368[6]◆ 2081[7] 3020[4] 4248[8] 6682[4] 7770[8] 8018[12] 8119[8] 8898[4] 9034[6] 9457[7] 9508[6]

Albadr (USA) *Roger Ingram* a85 68
3 b g The Factor(USA) Shawahid (USA) (A.P. Indy (USA))
2764[4] (6315)◆ 9635[5]

Albanderi *Andrew Balding* a52 55
3 bb f Kingman Hazel Lavery (IRE) (Excellent Art)
3495[11] 4600[5] 5810[7] 9443[10]

Albanita *Sir Mark Prescott Bt* a79 80
3 gr f Sea The Moon(GER) Alba Stella (Nashwan (USA))
5605[3] 5954[3] 6323[3] 6661[3] 7229[3] 8120[6]

Alban's Dream *Robert Eddery* a61 42
3 rg f Lethal Force(IRE) Piping Dream (IRE) (Approve (IRE))
235[3] 605[8] 6168[9] 6685[9] 8071[13] 8408[11]

Alba Power (IRE) *F Chappet* a89 106
4 b g Fast Company(IRE) Shehila (IRE) (Zamindar (USA))
(2648a) 8982a[10]

Al Barg (IRE) *Richard Hannon* a89 82
4 b g Acclamation Miss Hawai (FR) (Peintre Celebre (USA))
2116[7] 2551[3] 3149[6] 4546[5]

Al Batal *Adrian Nicholls* a58 59
6 b g Pastoral Pursuits Flam (Singspiel (IRE))
419a[4] 7088a[3] (9220)

Al Battar (IRE) *Ed Vaughan* a73 85
3 b c Dubawi(IRE) Giofra (Dansili)
4423[2]

Alben Spirit *Richard Fahey* 77
2 b g Camacho Priti Fabulous (IRE) (Invincible Spirit (IRE))
6622[4]◆ 6997[3] (7619)

Alberobello (FR)
M Delcher Sanchez a75 51
6 b g Fuisse(FR) Ashkiyra (FR) (Marju (IRE))
4860a[8]

Alberone (IRE) *Bent Olsen* 90
5 b h Born To Sea(IRE) Tara's Wells (IRE) (Sadler's Wells (USA))
4419a[9]

Albert Boy (IRE) *Scott Dixon* a43 64
6 ch g Falco(USA) Trumbaka (IRE) (In The Wings)
2819[2] 3155[2] 4009[3] 4601[7] 5106[10] 5743[7] 6550[5] 6828[7]

Albert Edward (IRE) *Brian Meehan* 64
2 b g Zebedee Edwardian Era (Bering)
7406[6] 7899[6] 8459[8]

Albert Finney *John Gosden* a82 88
3 b g Kingman Gertrude Bell (Sinndar (IRE))
(486) 826[3] 1233[3] (1396) 1823[2] 3262[3] 4553[4]

Albiceleste (FR) *C Lerner* a20
3 ch g Olympic Glory(IRE) Celeste (FR) (Muhtathir)
421a[2]

Albigna (IRE) *Mrs John Harrington* 112
2 ch f Zoffany(IRE) Freedonia (Selkirk (USA))
(4352a) 7244a[6] (7939a) 8748a[4]

Albishr (IRE) *Simon Dow* a54 64
4 rg g Clodovil(IRE) Casual Remark (IRE) (Trans Island)
699[8] 5574[6] 6050[9] 7080[9] 7685[13] 8703[8] 9005[10]

Alborkan (FR) *Amy Murphy* a69
2 b c Joshua Tree(IRE) Plaine Monceau (FR) (One Cool Cat (USA))
9408[5] 9668[2]

Album (IRE) *Martyn Meade* 71
2 gr c Clodovil(IRE) Michael's Song (IRE) (Refuse To Bend (IRE))
1733[6] 1910[2]

Albuquerque (IRE) *A P O'Brien* a85 85
3 b c Galileo(IRE) Looking Back (IRE) (Stravinsky (USA))
1049a[8]

Alcama Doloise (FR) *A Bonin* a76 73
4 gr m Youmzain(IRE) Fiammella (IRE) (Verglas (IRE))
6031a[14]

Alcanar (USA) *Tony Carroll* a59 57
6 ch g Teofilo(IRE) Badalona (Cape Cross (IRE))
59[10] 504[6]

Alcance (FR) *Clive Cox* a28 50
2 ch f Slade Power(IRE) Wanting (IRE) (Acclamation)
5988[10] 6300[7] 7995[7]

Alchimista *David Simcock* 60
2 b f Archipenko(USA) Alta Moda (Sadler's Wells (USA))
8458[7]

Al Daayen (FR) *Conrad Allen* a61 52
3 gr f Joshua Tree(IRE) Get The Ring (FR) (Linamix (FR))
472[5] 739[3] 930[3] 1166[5] 1332[3] 1593[6] 1935[4] 2262[10] (5004) 5679[8] 6186[9]

Al Dabaran *Charlie Appleby* 106
2 b c Dubawi(IRE) Bright Beacon (Manduro (GER))
(4388)◆ (5415) 7005a[3] 7774a[2]

Al Daiha *Ed Walker* a63
3 ch f Olympic Glory(IRE) Alpen Glen (Halling (USA))
8808[3] 9165[4] 9426[7] 9573[2]

Alda'iya (USA) *Doug Watson* a66 40
3 b g Afleet Alex(USA) Splendid Fortune (USA) (Giant's Causeway (USA))
394a[13] 1742a[12]

Al Dawodiya (IRE) *Richard Hannon* a75 48
2 b f Gutaifan(IRE) Lillebonne (FR) (Danehill Dancer (IRE))
5588[14] 9159[2] 9299[2]

Aldente *Andrew Balding* 57
3 gr f Archipenko(USA) Albacocca (With Approval (CAN))
2932[4]

Aldreth *Michael Easterby* a88 84
8 b g Champs Elysees Rowan Flower (IRE) (Ashkalani (IRE))
2748[10] 3816[15] 4404[2]◆

Aldrich Bay (IRE) *William Knight* 49
2 b g Xtension(IRE) Sail With The Wind (Saddlers' Hall (IRE))
4388[6] 5314[6] 6161[10]

Aleatoric (IRE) *Martin Smith*
3 b g Dylan Thomas(IRE) Castalian Spring (IRE) (Oasis Dream)
1754[13] 2566[7] 4258[7]

Aleef (IRE) *K J Condon* a83 87
6 b g Kodiac Okba (USA) (Diesis)
7085a[3]

Aleeka (USA) *David O'Meara* a69 54
3 b f Distorted Humor(USA) Vapour (Galileo (IRE))
442[4]

Alegia (FR) *S Eveno* 24
4 ch m Execute(FR) Princesse Violette (FR) (Lando (GER))
2675a[11]

Aleko *E Charpy* a77 73
6 b h Cape Cross(IRE) Monnavanna (IRE) (Machiavellian (USA))
197a[3]

Alemagna *David Simcock* a81 86
3 b f Sea The Moon(GER) Alta Moda (Sadler's Wells (USA))
5148[4] 5810[3] (6509) 6955[11] 7895[7]

Alemaratalyoum (IRE)
Stuart Williams a96 103
5 ch g Lope De Vega(IRE) Heart Of Ice (IRE) (Montjeu (IRE))
1829[11] 2609[16] 3318[4] 4921[15] 5413[18] 5965[5] 6711[2]◆ 6922[4] 7372[3] 7551[3] (7563) 8096[3] 9000[6] 9198[5]

Aleneva (IRE) *Richard Fahey* a76 76
2 b f Kodiac Peace Palace (Archipenko (USA))
(3506) 7432[9] 8426[3]

Al Erayg (IRE) *Tim Easterby* a86 82
6 b g Oasis Dream Vallee Des Reves (USA) (Kingmambo (USA))
2572[5] 2844[5]◆ 4240[10] 4654[8] 5246[6] 5488[5] 5948[2] 6179[2] 6626[6] 7907[8] 8237[2] (8642)◆ 8902[5]

Ale Tango (FR) *G Botti* a67 58
3 b c Myboycharlie(IRE) Driving Miswaki (USA) (Miswaki (USA))
216a[4]

Alets (FR) *J Reynier* a60 56
4 ch m Maiguri(FR) Atabaska (FR) (Ashkalani (IRE))
1449a[12]

Alexana *William Haggas* 90
4 b m Al Kazeem Dolores (Danehill (USA))
3096[6] 5190[10]

Alexander James (IRE) *Iain Jardine* a91 104
3 b g Camelot Plying (USA) (Hard Spun (USA))
(2192)◆ 2634[3]◆ 3499[3] 5693[14]

Alexandrakollontai (IRE)
Alistair Whillans a82 62
9 b m Amadeus Wolf Story (Observatory (USA))
951[4] 1273[10] 1401[7] 1850[4] 2911[10] 3223[6] 5117[8] 5844[8] 6327[7] 6627[10] 7288[8] 7526[10]

Alexandria *Charlie Fellowes* a14 46
4 gr m Oasis Dream Amarillo Starlight (IRE) (Dalakhani (IRE))
2507[7] 4787[13] 5675[5]

Alex Gracie *Scott Dixon* a61
2 b f Fountain Of Youth(IRE) Kyllarney (Kyllachy)
7627[3]◆ 8640[3] 9181[5] 9641[6]

Alexis Carrington (IRE) *John Quinn* a63 66
4 b m Mastercraftsman(IRE) Cozzene's Angel (USA) (Cozzene (USA))
160[4] 482[9]

Alezan *Eve Johnson Houghton* a53 19
2 ch f Dawn Approach(IRE) Sarinda (Dubawi (IRE))
7412[7] 8060[5]

Alfaatik *John Gosden* a79 97
3 b g Sea The Stars(IRE) Biz Bar (Tobougg (IRE))
2084[5] 3042[7]

Alfa Dawn (IRE) *Phillip Makin* a58 71
3 b f No Nay Never(USA) Aitch (IRE) (Alhaarth (IRE))
4761[3]◆ 5156[5] 5556[9] 6101[2] 6679[9] 7288[9]

Al Fajir Mukbile (IRE)
Ismail Mohammed a68 82
3 br c Dawn Approach(IRE) Sparkling Smile (IRE) (Cape Cross (IRE))
168a[7] 511a[9] 956a[11]

Alfa McGuire (IRE) *Phillip Makin* a81 81
4 b g Lord Shanakill(USA) Watsdaplan (IRE) (Verglas (IRE))
1644[9] 2186[4] 2479[7] 3973[7] 4383[7] (4982) 6179[8] 6734[5] 7289[7] 8122[11]

Alfarqad (USA) *Owen Burrows* a91 78
4 bb g War Front(USA) Love And Pride (USA) (A.P. Indy (USA))
(7551)◆

Alfarris (FR)
David A & B Hayes & Tom Dabern a84 95
5 b g Shamardal(USA) Rose Et Noire (IRE) (Dansili)
8577a[7]

Alfieri (FR) *J-P Gauvin* a93 90
6 b g Naaqoos Jolie Et Belle (FR) (Oratorio (IRE))
2955a[2] 9483a[3]

Alfie's Angel (IRE) *Milton Bradley* a33 46
5 b g Dark Angel(IRE) Penolva (IRE) (Galileo (IRE))
2122[10] 2717[8] 3543[8] 4181[16] 4481[14] 4765[10] 6107[5] 6363[5] 6703[7] 7986[12]

Alfie Solomons (IRE)
Amanda Perrett a80 83
3 b g Acclamation Vastitas (IRE) (Green Desert (USA))
1851[9] 2810[4] 4122[4] 4847[8] 5589[14] 6476[7] 7351[5] 8550[6] 9387[5] 9632[8]

Alfies Watch *John O'Shea* a67 69
2 br g Harbour Watch(IRE) Shes Minnie (Bertolini (USA))
6079[9] 6852[3] 7570[3] 8890[10]

Alfirak *Damian Joseph English* a73 73
5 ch g Tamayuz Bahja (USA) (Seeking The Gold (USA))
7089a[4]

Alfolk (AUS) *M F De Kock* a69 72
4 b g Lonhro(AUS) Alteza Real (AUS) (Exceed And Excel (AUS))
49a[9] 393a[7] 640a[9]

Alfred Boucher *Henry Candy* a79 93
3 gr g Aussie Rules(USA) Policy Term (IRE) (Authorized (IRE))
1665[3] 3465[6] (4377) (5140) (6081)◆ 7163[4] 8728[10]

Alfredo (IRE) *Seamus Durack* a98 95
7 ch g Arcano(IRE) Western Sky (Barathea (IRE))
238[4] 5928[10] 6929[4] 7866[11] 8727[9]

Alfredo Arcano (IRE)
David Marnane a105 98
5 b g Arcano(IRE) Cheherazad (IRE) (Elusive City (USA))
170a[4] 639a[7] 843a[6] 1919[4] 7241a[20] 8328a[5]

Alfred Richardson *John Davies* a94 94
5 ch g Dapper Vera Richardson (IRE) (Dutch Art)
1502[10] (5200) 5693[4] 6543[2] 6998[14] 7430[5] 8096[13]

Alfred The Grey (IRE)
Tracy Waggott a61 43
3 gr g Alhebayeb(IRE) Roseska (USA) (Include (USA))
612[11] 1084[7] 1486[3]◆ 1979[10] 2152[5] 2897[7] 3516[3] 3921[10] 4434[4] 8637[6] 8821[14] 9111[10]

Alfurat River *Saeed bin Suroor* a78 83
3 b g Dubawi(IRE) Suez (Green Desert (USA))
6347[10] 9041[13]

Algaffaal (USA) *Brian Ellison* a83 79
4 ch g Speightstown(USA) Rockcide (USA) (Personal Flag (USA))
1723[5] (2242)◆ 3450[7] 4240[3]◆ 4902[3]◆ 5445[7] 6460[5] 6940[2]◆

Al Gaiya (FR) *Richard Hannon* 67
2 b f Olympic Glory(IRE) Lathah (IRE) (High Chaparral (IRE))
6949[8] 7461[6] 8458[3]

Al Gazi (IRE) *Ibrahim Al Malki* 99
3 b c Havana Gold(IRE) Rock Lily (Rock Of Gibraltar (IRE))
9590a[3]

Algo Rhythm *D J Bunyan* 54
4 ch m Fast Company(IRE) Bronze Star (Mark Of Esteem (IRE))
1309a[8]

Alhaazm *Sir Michael Stoute* a82 85
3 b g Cape Cross(IRE) Asheerah (Shamardal (USA))
1956[4] 2796[2] 3585[3] 4760[3] 6129[2] 6909[5] 8197[4]◆

Al Hadeer (USA) *William Haggas* 87
3 b g War Front(USA) Storybook (UAE) (Halling (USA))
1852[2]◆ 2438[2] 4258[8]

Alhakmah (IRE) *Richard Hannon* a83 81
3 b f No Nay Never(USA) Hureya (USA) (Woodman (USA))
2340[2] (2623) 3075[12] 4023[10] 8017[3] 8349[6] 8852[4] 9176[6]

Al Hamdany (IRE) *Marco Botti* a101 100
5 b g Kodiac Easy Times (Nayef (USA))
1681[2] 1927[5] 3005[5] 3466[8] 4504[3] 5437[5] 8350[6]

Al Hayette (USA) *Ismail Mohammed* a88 81
3 ch f Union Rags(USA) Water Of Life (USA) (Hennessy (USA))
(48a) 510a[10] 845a[5] 1110a[4] 1443a[12] 4667[7] 8809[7] 9255[9]

Alhazm (FR) *A De Mieulle* a84 98
4 b h Acclamation Mikkwa (USA) (Elusive Quality (USA))
894a[10]

Al Hilalee *Charlie Appleby* 106
3 b c Dubawi(IRE) Ambivalent (IRE) (Authorized (IRE))
2411[16] 2833[3] (3904a)

Alianne *Tom Clover* a64
2 b f Worthadd(IRE) Alboretta (Hernando (FR))
8706[5] 9311[5]

Alibaba *Julia Feilden* a31 71
2 b g Lawman(FR) Fantasy In Blue (Galileo (IRE))
3644[11] 5992[4] 6497[2] 7874[5] 8201[7]

Alicia Darcy (IRE) *Archie Watson* a75 80
3 b f Sir Prancealot(IRE) Ballet Of Doha (IRE) (Zebedee)
753[3] 966[5] 1475[4] 2098[14] 2708[6] 3887[5] 4457[2] (4755) (5044)◆ (5308) 5813[7] 5989[3] 6108[2] (6301) 6533[6] 6756[5] 7115[7] 7268[4] 7380[5] 7514[5] 7760[7] 7914[6] 9245[3]◆ 9365[10] 9519[8] 9632[2]

Aliento *Michael Dods* a56 69
4 ch m Bated Breath Scarlet Royal (Red Ransom (USA))
(3414) 4785[3] 5616[6] 7289[11] 7583[7]

Alignak *Sir Michael Stoute* a84 89
3 gr c Sea The Moon(GER) Albanova (Alzao (USA))
2769[2] 6641[3] (7518)◆

Alimnia (FR) *F-H Graffard* 96
3 b f Dubawi(IRE) Alpine Rose (FR) (Linamix (FR))
1626a[4] 3676a[4]

Alinaro (GER) *H Blume* 97
4 b g Soldier Hollow Alisar (GER) (Oasis Dream)
1793a[6] 9014a[11]

Alioski *Kevin Ryan* a53 54
2 b g Kodiac Luluti (IRE) (Kheleyf (USA))
6336[7] 9036[8] 9392[7]

Alisia R (IRE) *Les Eyre* a43 49
3 b f Holy Roman Emperor(IRE) Shamrock Lady (IRE) (Orpen (USA))
2713[12] 3191[5] (4508) 5278[11] 5750[7] 6126[7] 7591[5] 8720[12] 9034[3] 9659[7]

Alison (SWE) *H-J Groschel* 39
2 b f Areion(GER) Caesarina (Hernando (FR))
8371a[10]

Ali Spirit (IRE) *Elias Mikhalides* a69 66
6 b h Invincible Spirit(IRE) Citron Presse (USA) (Lemon Drop Kid (USA))
2955a[8] 4532a[5]

Alix James *Iain Jardine* 73
2 b g Acclamation Tout Va Bien (IRE) (Verglas (IRE))
4238[2]◆ 4976[2] 6337[2] 6622[6] 7399[10] 7679[3] (8232)

Alizee (AUS) *James Cummings* 112
4 b m Sepoy(AUS) Essaouira (AUS) (Exceed And Excel (AUS))
8362a[7]

Alizes (FR) *Harry Dunlop* a19
2 b f Hurricane Run(IRE) Hungry Heart (IRE) (Hawk Wing (USA))
7555[12]

Aljady (FR) *Richard Fahey* 100
4 b g Bated Breath No Truth (IRE) (Galileo (IRE))
2743[3]◆ 3863[15] 5546[10] 6711[7] 7435[5]

Aljalela (FR) *Richard Hannon* a58
2 b f Golden Horn Shahah (Motivator)
8218[9] 9052[5]

Aljari *Marco Botti* a94 60
3 b c Quality Road(USA) Rhagori (Exceed And Excel (AUS))
3019[4] (5057) (6388) 7551[5] 9472[2]◆

Al Jawhra (IRE) *Tim Easterby* 56
2 b f Holy Roman Emperor(IRE) Mango Mischief (IRE) (Desert King (IRE))
6697[6] 7330[4]◆ 8338[8]

Al Jellaby *Clive Cox* a95 93
4 b g Exceed And Excel(AUS) Dolphina (USA) (Kingmambo (USA))
56[3] 441[5] 1413[3] 2095[3] 2563[7] 4450[4] 5383[2] 6347[3] 6841[2] 7694[13]

Aljunood (IRE) *John Norton* a62 78
5 br g Bated Breath Ataraxy (Zamindar (USA))
64[3] 315[12] 349[3] 599[11] 2631[11] 3939[10] 4349[10] 5850[6]

Alkaamel *William Haggas* a72 77
3 b g Havana Gold(IRE) Grace And Glory (IRE) (Montjeu (IRE))
(134)◆ (409)◆ (885) 1485[2]◆ 1897[2] 2414[2] 3341[3]◆ 4882[13]

Alkaid (FR) *Gianluca Bietolini* a70 81
2 b g Sommerabend Mahyara (FR) (Lomitas)
(2757a) 5116a[10]

Alkaraama (USA) *Sir Michael Stoute* a97 102
3 b c War Front(USA) Agreeable Miss (USA) (Speightstown (USA))
2094[3]◆ (2938) 3972[3] (4638) (5266)◆ 6953[2] 7431[7]

Alkawthar (USA) *Mme Pia Brandt* a88 85
3 ch f Data Link(USA) Wish On (USA) (Grand Slam (USA))
1489a[4] 2091a[2] 3713a[4]

Al Khabeer *Simon Crisford* 61
2 gr g Lope De Vega(IRE) Partita (Montjeu (IRE))
7897[10]

Alkhadra *Paul Midgley*
3 b g Mawatheeq(USA) Rainbow's Destiny (Dubai Destination (USA))
5477[12]

Alkhat *John Gosden* a58
2 b c Oasis Dream Yasmeen (Sea The Stars (IRE))
8914[7]

Al Kherb *John Quinn* a68 68
4 b g Al Kazeem Perfect Spirit (IRE) (Invincible Spirit (IRE))
9543[5]

Al Kout *Heather Main* a91 88
5 gr g Oasis Dream Honorlina (FR) (Linamix (FR))
(1425) 3466[9] 3847[7] 4505[2] 5183[16] 5928[6] 6171[7] 8421[8]

Alkuin (IRE) *Waldemar Hickst* 84
4 b g Maxios Almerita (GER) (Medicean)
8585a[3]

All About Maddy *Paul W Flynn* a49 49
3 ch f Arcano(IRE) Elraabeya (CAN) (Seeking The Gold (USA))
4915[6]◆

Alla Mahlak (USA) *R Bouresly* a66 61
3 ch c Kitten's Joy(USA) Lead Me On (USA) (Broken Vow (USA))
394a[11] 727a[6]

All Back To Mine *Joseph Tuite* a30 69
3 ch f Dutch Art Exotic Isle (Exceed And Excel (AUS))
2281[2] **(3045)** 3801[9] 4478[4]

Allegiant (USA) *Stuart Williams* a66 89
4 b g City Zip(USA) Preferential (Dansili)
2207[2] 3192[3] 3806[13] 4548[2]◆ 5089[2] 5571[2] 6021[3] **(6165)** 6535[2] 7127[6] 7829[13] 8608[7]

Allegio (IRE) *Denis Gerard Hogan* a58 89
6 b g Galileo(IRE) Song Of My Heart (IRE) (Footstepsinthesand)
5535a[17] 7794a[13]

Allen A Dale (IRE) *Richard Fahey* a70 66
3 br g Kyllachy Wood Chorus (Singspiel (IRE))
4207[6] 6373[10]

Allerthorpe *Brian Rothwell* a45
2 b g Casamento(IRE) Shirocco Passion (Shirocco (GER))
8717[12] 9095[11]

Allez Henri (IRE)
D & P Prod'Homme a87 82
8 b g Footstepsinthesand Macotte (FR) (Nicolotte)
682a[11]

Allez Kal (IRE) *James M Barcoe* 66
8 b m Kalanisi(IRE) Reynard's Glen (IRE) (Old Vic)
1309a[7]

Allez Sophia (IRE)
Eve Johnson Houghton 79
2 b f Kingman Allez Alaia (IRE) (Pivotal)
2020[4]◆ 4233[2] 5317[3] 6800[3] **(7227)**

All For Rome (GER)
Jean-Pierre Carvalho 96
3 b f Holy Roman Emperor(IRE) All An Star (Galileo (IRE))
8587a[4]

All Grace (FR) *A Fabre* 99
3 b f Kingman Agathe Rare (IRE) (Sadler's Wells (USA))
5470a[5] 6775a[5] 7477a[6]

Allhallowtide (IRE) *Claes Bjorling* a48 65
2 b f Hallowed Crown(AUS) Lisfannon (Bahamian Bounty)
(3212) 7495a[8]

Alliance A Vary (FR) *M Brasme* 73
4 b m Authorized(IRE) Moderna (FR) (Okawango (USA))
1245a[5]

Allieyf *William Haggas* a76 81
4 b g New Approach(IRE) Sajjhaa (King's Best (USA))
968[2] 1331[2]◆ 1771[7]

Alligator *Tony Carroll* a49 44
5 ch g Sepoy(AUS) See You Later (Emarati (USA))
166[4] 357[7] 809[3] 1093[4] 1368[11]

Alligator Alley
Joseph Patrick O'Brien 104
2 b c Kingman Overturned (Cape Cross (IRE))
5542[2]◆ (6474) 7149[6] 8745a[8]

Alligator Blood (AUS)
David Vandyke 111
2 b g All Too Hard(AUS) Lake Superior (AUS) (Encosta De Lago (AUS))
8137a[2]

Alliseeisnibras (IRE)
Ismail Mohammed a53 71
3 b f Slade Power(IRE) Needles And Pins (IRE) (Fasliyev (USA))
2938[5] 3421[2]◆ 4116[7] 5050[4] 6286[10] 7320[6] 8217[11]

Allleedsaren'Twe *Robyn Brisland* a44 50
4 b g Havana Gold(IRE) Minnola (Royal Applause)
792[12] 1026[7] 1158[11] 1520[10] 3497[6] 3769[5]

Allmankind *Michael Bell* a83 89
3 b g Sea The Moon(GER) Wemyss Bay (Sadler's Wells (USA))
2558[6] 4882[14]

All My Love (IRE) *Pam Sly* a76 79
7 b m Lord Shanakill(USA) Afilla (Dansili)
469[5] 8027[4]

Allnite (IRE) *Marjorie Fife* a53 51
4 b g Arcano(IRE) Paint The Town (IRE) (Sadler's Wells (USA))
40[10]

Allocated (IRE) *John Butler* a65 39
3 b g Alhebayeb(IRE) Fickle Feelings (IRE) (Nayef (USA))
4459[6] 6345[4] 6687[5] 7192[8] 7984[11]

Allocator (FR) *Richard Hannon* a78 64
3 b g Kendargent(FR) Vezina (FR) (Bering)
299[3] 1221[3] 1417[7] 1928[4] 6083[6] 6463[6] 6722[6] 7229[6]

Allofmelovesallofu
Ken Cunningham-Brown a43 56
5 ch g Sakhee's Secret La Palma (Sinndar (IRE))
3348[8] 4232[4]

All Or Nothin (IRE) *Paddy Butler* a28 58
10 b g Majestic Missile(IRE) Lady Peculiar (CAN) (Sunshine Forever (USA))
139[9] 2066[11]

All Points West *Sir Mark Prescott Bt* a76 65
3 b g Speightstown(USA) Albamara (Galileo (IRE))
7625[2] 7915[2] 8298[8]

All Prince (GER) *R Rohne* a59 64
4 b g Wiesenpfad(FR) All Saints (GER) (Goofalik (USA))
9537a[6]

All Revved Up (IRE) *C Boutin* 69
2 gr c Rio De La Plata(USA) Rive Neuve (FR) (Enrique)
4949a[5] 5713a[10] 6384a[6]

All Right *Henry Candy* a10 61
3 b f Intello(GER) Alice Alleyne (IRE) (Oasis Dream)
1652[8] 2771[11] 3445[12] 4485[4] 5049[2] (5867)◆ 6643[2] 7385[9]

All Set To Go (IRE) *Kevin Frost* a92 94
8 gr g Verglas(IRE) Firecrest (IRE) (Darshaan)
2126[4] 2801[2]

Allsfineandandy (IRE) *Lynn Siddall* 31
3 b g Dandy Man(IRE) Swish Dancer (IRE) (Whipper (USA))
3292[6] 4731[12] 5554[10] 6204[16] 6624[6]

Alltami (IRE) *Steph Hollinshead* a14
3 b g Lethal Force(IRE) Peace Talks (Pivotal)
4358[14] 6941[7]

All The King's Men (IRE)
A P O'Brien a100 105
3 bb c No Nay Never(USA) Chaibia (IRE) (Peintre Celebre (USA))
1434a[14] 2880a[8] 5207a[8]

All This Time (GER) *F Rossi* a81 91
4 b m Dabirsim(FR) Amazing Bounty (FR) (Tertullian (USA))
3136a[16]

Allucination *C Laffon-Parias* 79
2 b f Lope De Vega(IRE) Desertiste (Green Desert (USA))
6774a[3]

Allux Boy (IRE) *Nigel Tinkler* a69 61
5 b g Iffraaj Ms Victoria (IRE) (Fasliyev (USA))
1841[6] (2513) 3163[4] 3473[4] 4002[4] 4460[2] **(5003)** 5245[6] 5899[6] 6937[11] 7074[16]

All Yours (FR) *Sean Curran* a95 74
8 ch g Halling(USA) Fontaine Riant (FR) (Josr Algarhoud (IRE))
5578[2] 6732[3] (7575) (8421) (9055) 9366[6] 9419[3]

All You Wish *Andrew Balding* a83 32
2 b c Showcasing Moment Of Time (Rainbow Quest (USA))
6845[12] **(7571)**◆

Al Madhar (FR) *Richard Hannon* 88
2 b c Siyouni(FR) Phiz (GER) (Galileo (IRE))
(4886)

Almahha *Owen Burrows* a67
3 b f Sea The Moon(GER) Anqooda (USA) (Oasis Dream)
7190[4] 7841[3] 8497[4]

Alma Linda *Sir Mark Prescott Bt* a84
3 gr f Invincible Spirit(IRE) Alvarita (Selkirk (USA))
3431[5] 4768[6] (5651) 5941[3] 6186[3] 6596[2] (6931) 7279[2]

Almanaara (IRE) *Doug Watson* a99 100
6 gr h Shamardal(USA) Midnight Angel (Machiavellian (USA))
280a[6] 729a[5]◆ 842a[3]

Almania (IRE) *Sir Michael Stoute* 102
3 b g Australia Sent From Heaven (IRE) (Footstepsinthesand)
2777[8] 4017[5] 4901[4] 5583[5] 6471[6]◆ 7864[3]

Almareekh (USA)
Sir Michael Stoute a64
2 bb f War Front(USA) Orate (USA) (A.P. Indy (USA))
8602[7]

Almashriq (USA) *John Gosden* a91 86
3 b c War Front(USA) Theyskens' Theory (USA) (Bernardini (USA))
1888[4] 3003[2] 4882[8] 5383[4]

Al Messila *Richard Hannon* a87 86
3 b f Toronado(IRE) Rose Blossom (Pastoral Pursuits)
2251[4] 2760[2] 3041[4] (4285) (5030) 5525[7] 6282[2] 7341[7]

Almighwar *John Gosden* 57
2 b c Dubawi(IRE) Taghrooda (Sea The Stars (IRE))
8464[10]

Alminoor (IRE) *Mark Johnston* 83
2 b g Kodiac Aravonian (Night Shift (USA))
1499[2]◆ **(1812)**

Al Moataz (IRE) *Marco Botti* a78 82
3 b g Rock Of Gibraltar(IRE) Amwaj (IRE) (Dubawi (IRE))
1352[6] 5592[2] 6316[4] 7189[2] 7519[6] **(8030)**

Al Mohalhal (IRE) *R Al Jehani* a71 81
6 b g Acclamation Secret Question (USA) (Rahy (USA))
869a[10]

Almokhtaar (USA) *Kevin Ryan* a65 56
3 b g War Front(USA) Fascinating (USA) (Smart Strike (CAN))
2321[7] 2795[13] 4179[5] 7514[7] 8405[3]

Almond Eye (JPN) *Sakae Kunieda* 121
4 b m Lord Kanaloa(JPN) Fusaichi Pandora (JPN) (Sunday Silence (USA))
(1445a)

Almoreb (IRE) *A R Al Rayhi* a87 93
5 b g Raven's Pass(USA) Macadamia (IRE) (Classic Cliche (IRE))
1322a[2] 1748a[2]

Almoror *C Ferland* a92 107
7 b g Rip Van Winkle(IRE) Totem (USA) (Mizzen Mast (USA))
4418a[5]

Al Mortajaz (FR) *Adrian Nicholls* a30 30
3 b g Camacho Danse En Soiree (USA) (Cat Thief (USA))
168a[15] 570a[13] 2200[13] 2587[U] 3158[9]

Almost Midnight *David Simcock* a82 103
3 b g Siyouni(FR) Late Night (GER) (Groom Dancer (USA))
(358) 949[2] (2845)◆ 3984[7] 5370[2]◆ 5909[6] 7408[5]

Almuerzo Loco (IRE)
Richard Hannon a60
2 gr g Zebedee Chica Loca (FR) (American Post)
7842[6] 8418[6]

Al Muffrih (IRE) *William Haggas* 100
4 b g Sea The Stars(IRE) Scarlet And Gold (IRE) (Peintre Celebre (USA))
2408[5] **(3160)** 4646[17]

Almufti *Hugo Palmer* a91 91
3 b g Toronado(IRE) Green Tern (ITY) (Miswaki Tern (USA))
1888[3] 2412[5] 4847[16] 7372[6] 8707[6] 9255[11] **(9658)**

Al Mureib (IRE) *Saeed bin Suroor* a84 89
3 ch g Dubawi(IRE) Lava Flow (IRE) (Dalakhani (IRE))
2364[2] 3011[2] 3648[3] 4830[3] 5477[3] 8658[3]

Almurr (IRE) *Phillip Makin* a73 60
3 b g Dandy Man(IRE) Passion Planet (IRE) (Medicean)
4294[5]◆ 4649[11] 5691[7] 6260[7] 6591[11] 7311[6] 7656[5] 8429[6] 8715[7] 9113[3] 9397[7] 9545[4]

Almushref (USA) *M Al Mheiri* a88 74
4 ch g Smart Strike(CAN) Music Room (USA) (Unbridled's Song (USA))
1322a[7]

Al Muthanna (IRE) *William Haggas* 42
2 ch g Lope De Vega(IRE) Saraha (Dansili)
5865[6]

Alnadir (USA) *Simon Crisford* a80 89
3 ch g Noble Mission Sarah's Secret (USA) (Leroidesanimaux (BRZ))
4188[2] 4739[4] 5605[2] 5841[2] 6390[F] 8024[5] 8412[12]

Al Nafoorah *Michael Wigham* a68 60
5 b m Bated Breath Cat O' Nine Tails (Motivator)
7250a[9] 7788[5]

Al Namir (IRE) *Richard Hannon* 80
2 b c Shamardal(USA) Rayaheen (Nayef (USA))
3274[3] 4069[2] 5059[3]

Alnaseem *Luke McJannet* 85
3 ch f Shamardal(USA) Arwaah (IRE) (Dalakhani (IRE))
1740[13] 4405[3] 5193[2] **(5688)** 6408[6] 7895[10] 8519[9]

Alnasherat *Sir Michael Stoute* a84 77
3 b c Kingman Split Trois (FR) (Dubawi (IRE))
1723[4] **(2008)**

Alocasia *H-F Devin* 100
2 b f Kingman Portodora (USA) (Kingmambo (USA))
5469a[2] **(7602a)** 8140a[5]

Aloe Vera *Ralph Beckett* 96
3 b f Invincible Spirit(IRE) Almiranta (Galileo (IRE))
(2354)◆ **(3012)**◆

Alonso Cano (IRE) *Jo Hughes* a64 64
4 b g High Chaparral(IRE) Awjila (Oasis Dream)
232[7] 2266a[10] 2782a[10]

Alotabottle *Kevin Ryan* a64 89
3 ch g Mukhadram Lady Tabitha (IRE) (Tamayuz)
4212[10] (5575)◆ (5771)◆ 6176[2] **(7068)**◆

Alounak (FR) *Waldemar Hickst* 110
4 b h Camelot Awe Struck (Rail Link)
2455a[4] 3386a[4] 4427a[6] 5483a[4] 6007a[5] **(6487a)** 8155a[2] 8776a[5]

Aloysius Lilius (IRE) *Gerard O'Leary* a78 73
3 b g Gregorian(IRE) Nafa (IRE) (Shamardal (USA))
1691[10] 2121[2] 9245[2] **(9402)**◆

Al Ozzdi *Roger Fell* a69 53
4 b g Acclamation Zibeling (IRE) (Cape Cross (IRE))
2785[9] 3214[11] (3430) 3704[12] 7418[2] 7652[6] 8199[10]

Alpasu (IRE) *Adrian Nicholls* a49 70
3 gr g Dalakhani(IRE) St Roch (IRE) (Danehill (USA))
358[3] 858[2] 1221[4] 1365[6] 3474[6] 3931[10] 5792[6] 6012[3] 7290[4] 8196[9]

Alpen Rose (IRE) *Charlie Appleby* 103
2 b f Sea The Stars(IRE) Valais Girl (Holy Roman Emperor (IRE))
5139[2]◆ (6205)◆ 7120[3] 8763[6]

Alphabetical *Sir Mark Prescott Bt* a54
2 gr c Archipenko(USA) Albanova (Alzao (USA))
9197[8] 9324[7]

Alpha Delphini *Bryan Smart* 117
8 b g Captain Gerrard(IRE) Easy To Imagine (USA) (Cozzene (USA))
3084[2]◆

Alpha Tauri (USA) *Charles Smith* a65 58
13 b g Aldebaran(USA) Seven Moons (JPN) (Sunday Silence (USA))
6[8] (590) 830[5] **(1069)** 8405[4] 8903[4] 9028[7] 9337[10]

Alpine Mistral (IRE)
Shaun Keightley a52
2 b f Gale Force Ten Snowtime (IRE) (Galileo (IRE))
8198[8] 8913[10]

Alpine Peak (USA)
Miss Natalia Lupini a47 40
4 gr g Mizzen Mast(USA) Affectionately (Galileo (IRE))
7857[11]

Alpine Star (IRE)
Mrs John Harrington 107
2 ch f Sea The Moon(GER) Alpha Lupi (IRE) (Rahy (USA))
(6429a)

Alpinista *Sir Mark Prescott Bt* 98
2 gr f Frankel Alwilda (Hernando (FR))
(5088)◆ 6444[6] 7006a[4]

Alqaab *Ruth Carr* a68 62
4 gr g Swiss Spirit Skiing (Sakhee's Secret)
1598[4] 2377[5] 2841[12] 3291[9] 4829[5] 5202[7] 5918[7] 6462[3] 7307[9] 7770[9]

Al Qahwa (IRE) *David O'Meara* a23 51
6 b g Fast Company(IRE) Cappuccino (IRE) (Mujadil (USA))
6676[16]

Al Qaqaa (USA) *William Haggas* a75 72
2 b c War Front(USA) Pin Up (IRE) (Lookin At Lucky (USA))
7899[4] 8914[2]◆

Alqifaar (USA) *Owen Burrows* a67
2 rg f The Factor(USA) Atayeb (USA) (Rahy (USA))
5733[5]

Alrajaa *John Gosden* a113 84
3 b g Dubawi(IRE) Ethaara (Green Desert (USA))
6119[2]◆ (6802) (7836)◆ (8222) **(9000)**◆

Alramz *Lee Carter* a56 50
3 b g Intello(GER) Rewaaya (IRE) (Authorized (IRE))
1396[6] 2011[7] 3809[5] 4834[12] 8854[4]

Al Rasmah (IRE) *Richard Fahey* 85
2 b f Iffraaj Oeuvre D'Art (IRE) (Marju (IRE))
(6713)◆ 7432[8]

Al Raya *Simon Crisford* 104
2 b f Siyouni(FR) Fig Roll (Bahamian Bounty)
3469[2]◆ 3983[5] 4610[4] (5681) 6157[2] **(6791a)**

Al Reeh (IRE) *Marco Botti* a80 42
5 br g Invincible Spirit(IRE) Dffra (IRE) (Refuse To Bend (IRE))
54[2] 4067[10] 5651[6] 7684[6] 8548[7]

Alright Sunshine (IRE)
Keith Dalgleish 107
4 b g Casamento(IRE) Miss Gibraltar (Rock Of Gibraltar (IRE))
(2323) 3482[3] 4055[2] (4988) (5902)◆ 6958[2] **(7403)**

Al Rufaa (FR) *John Gosden* a67 82
2 b c Kingman Clarmina (IRE) (Cape Cross (IRE))
7842[5] **(8128)**

Alsafa *Brian Meehan* 27
3 b c Dark Angel(IRE) Jamaayel (Shamardal (USA))
3648[10]

Al Salt (IRE) *William Haggas* a60
2 b c Mukhadram Estedaama (IRE) (Marju (IRE))
9155[5]

Al Seel Legacy's (USA)
Doug Watson a73
3 gr c Uncaptured(CAN) Legacy's Silver (USA) (Robyn Dancer (USA))
169a[3] 394a[9]

Alshahhad (IRE) *H Al Alawi* a19
4 b g Dubawi(IRE) Enfijaar (IRE) (Invincible Spirit (IRE))
634a[8]

Al Shamkhah (USA) *S bin Ghadayer* a74
3 bb f Dialed In(USA) Prime The Pump (USA) (Unbridled's Song (USA))
48a[6]◆ 510a[7]◆ 845a[6] 1110a[5]

Alson (GER) *Jean-Pierre Carvalho* 113
2 b c Areion(GER) Assisi (GER) (Galileo (IRE))
(6746a) 7940a[2] **(8588a)**

Al Suhail *Charlie Appleby* 112
2 b c Dubawi(IRE) Shirocco Star (Shirocco (GER))
4886[2]◆ (6127)◆ 6727[3] 8112[2]◆

Al Suil Eile (FR) *John Quinn* a73 74
3 gr g Alhebayeb(IRE) Visual Element (USA) (Distant View (USA))
1462[7] 3249[8] 3970[9] 6204[4] 6823[4] (7523) 9140[7] 9349[7] 9559[2]

Alsukar *Dean Ivory* 37
2 b f Brazen Beau(AUS) Three Sugars (AUS) (Starcraft (NZ))
5992[11] 6592[11]

Alsvinder *Philip Kirby* a63 82
6 b h Footstepsinthesand Notting Hill (BRZ) (Jules (USA))
(203) 382[9] (762) 1105[5] (1274) 1919[9] 2368[12] 4364[11] 4880[9] 5298[2] 5691[11] 6826[2] 7624[8]

Altair (IRE) *Joseph Patrick O'Brien* a70 88
3 ch f Australia Eccentricity (USA) (Kingmambo (USA))
2157a[5] 4014[11] 7668a[P]

Altaira *Tony Carroll* a49 52
8 b g Dubawi(IRE) Peach Pearl (Invincible Spirit (IRE))
58[9] 479[10] 941[11] 1362[5] 3348[9] **(4475)** 4991[P] (Dead)

Altar Boy *Sylvester Kirk* a69
3 b c Mukhadram Royal Whisper (Royal Applause)
90[7] 442[3] 966[3] 1677[6] 2773[6] 7811[6] 8711[8] 8807[9]

Alternative Fact *Ed Dunlop* a24 94
4 b g Dalakhani(IRE) O Fourlunda (Halling (USA))
1422[15] 2095[12] 3857[3] 5192[3] 5564[4] 7694[9] **(8725)**

Alter Poseidon (GER)
Andrea Marcialis a74 60
3 b c Poseidon Adventure(IRE) Alte Klasse (GER) (Royal Academy (USA))
5641a[2]

Althib *Denis Gerard Hogan* a49 56
5 b g Dansili Great Heavens (Galileo (IRE))
2682[5]

Althiqa *Charlie Appleby* 83
2 b f Dark Angel(IRE) Mistrusting (IRE) (Shamardal (USA))
(2840)◆

Altra Vita *Sir Mark Prescott Bt* a94 91
4 b m Animal Kingdom(USA) Alma Mater (Sadler's Wells (USA))
3096[8] 5404a[6] 7866[5] 8804a[6]

Altropasso *A Giorgi* 72
3 ch f Helmet(AUS) Quintrell (Royal Applause)
2390a[2]

Aluqair (IRE) *Simon Crisford* a83 86
3 b g Kodiac Morethanafeeling (IRE) (Verglas (IRE))
4196[2] 4590[3] 5336[2] (6119) 6803[6] 7462[2] 7836[4] 8289[8]

Alvaro *Michael Wigham* a65
3 b g Archipenko(USA) Aloha (With Approval (CAN))
8290[5]◆ 9001[3] 9165[6]

Alveda *George Margarson* a49
2 b f Archipenko(USA) Alizadora (Zilzal (USA))
9063[7]

Al Verde *Ali Stronge* a42 55
2 ch g Al Kazeem Greenery (IRE) (Green Desert (USA))
3695[5] 4214[4] 8418[8]

Alvilda (USA) *A Fabre* 64
3 b f War Front(USA) Long View (IRE) (Galileo (IRE))
3712a[4]

Alwaab (FR) *F Chappet* 101
3 b c Toronado(IRE) Lady Gorgeous (Compton Place)
(6005a) 7478a[5] 9590a[5]

Alwaatn Sound (IRE) *Kevin Ryan* 63
2 b c Shamardal(USA) Lady Of The Desert (USA) (Rahy (USA))
4275[3]

Al Wafi (IRE) *A R Al Rayhi* a49 61
3 b c Helmet(AUS) Zarabaya (IRE) (Doyoun)
634a[4]

Always A Drama (IRE) *Charles Hills* a82 82
4 b m Red Jazz(USA) Desert Drama (IRE) (Green Desert (USA))
178[3] (759) **(824)** 3427[5] 4560[5] **(5251)**

Always Amazing *Robyn Brisland* a56 53
5 ch g Kyllachy Amazed (Clantime)
42[5] 236[2]◆ 383[9] 759[8] 882[3] 1016[8] 1162[5] 1767[3] 1883[2] 3001[2] 3320[4] 3772[6] 3975[6] 4765[4] 5147[8] 6682[8] 7371[4] 7869[5]

Alwaysandforever (IRE) *Gavin Hernon* a98 103
5 b m Teofilo(IRE) Deep Winter (Pivotal)
682a[15]

Always Dreaming (GER) *Waldemar Hickst* 70
2 gr f Holy Roman Emperor(IRE) Alakhania (IRE) (Dalakhani (IRE))
8393a[7]

Always Fearless (IRE) *Richard Hannon* a77 76
2 ch g Camacho Zenella (Kyllachy)
4324[9] 5177[3] 5550[4] 5956[3] 6416[2] 6965[3] (8288)

Alwaysmining (USA) *Kelly Rubley* a85
3 bb g Stay Thirsty(USA) What Will Be (USA) (Anees (USA))
2856a[11]

Always Resolute *Ian Williams* a73 85
8 b g Refuse To Bend(IRE) Mad Annie (USA) (Anabaa (USA))
2578[3] 3481[2] 4381[7] (5457)

Alwisaam (IRE) *Ed Dunlop*
3 gr g Dark Angel(IRE) Jo Bo Bo (IRE) (Whipper (USA))
6732[11]

Alyx Vance *Lydia Pearce* 53
3 bl f Big Bad Bob(IRE) Casino Dancer (Danehill Dancer (IRE))
3836[3] 4219[5] 4754[6] 5063[9]

Al Zaraqaan *William Haggas* 59
2 br c Golden Horn Asheerah (Shamardal (USA))
8459[10]

Alzire (FR) *J-C Rouget* 105
3 b f Shamardal(USA) Purely Priceless (IRE) (Galileo (IRE))
3677a[8] 5470a[4] (7360a)

Amaan *Simon Crisford* a80 79
2 b g Dawn Approach(IRE) Qareenah (USA) (Arch (USA))
(7055) 7842[2] 8424[8]

Amade (IRE) *G Botti* a112 108
5 b g Casamento(IRE) Sheba Five (USA) (Five Star Day (USA))
(82)◆ (1062) 1917[2] (3561a)

Amadeus (IRE) *Gavin Cromwell* a63 53
4 gr g Fastnet Rock(AUS) Alegra (Galileo (IRE))
1163[9] 1196[2]

Amadeus Grey (IRE) *Tim Easterby* a76 85
3 gr g Zebedee Benedicte (IRE) (Galileo (IRE))
1646[6] 1945[7] 2811[8] 3471[4] (3683)◆ 4107[3] 4723[3] 5198[4] 5394[9] 6258[4]

Amadeus Wolfe Tone (IRE) *Carina Fey* a60 74
10 b g Amadeus Wolf Slieve (Selkirk (USA))
(3715a) (4960a)

Amalita (GER) *Jean-Pierre Carvalho* 74
2 b f Motivator Amalua (GER) (Tiger Hill (IRE))
7749a[6]

Amanaat (IRE) *Denis Gerard Hogan* a92 89
6 b g Exceed And Excel(AUS) Pietra Dura (Cadeaux Genereux)
748a[4]

Amanto (GER) *Ali Stronge* a65 64
9 b g Medicean Amore (GER) (Lando (GER))
3633[8] 5571[4] 6303[9] 9134[6] 9447[3]

Amaranth (IRE) *Simon Dow* a24
6 b g New Approach(IRE) Kitty Kiernan (Pivotal)
1551[2] 6441[11]

Amarena (FR) *S Kobayashi* 100
3 b f Soldier Hollow Amouage (GER) (Tiger Hill (IRE))
3905a[15]

Amaretto *Jim Boyle* a64 65
4 b g Kyllachy Dan Loose Daughter (Sakhee (USA))
(1297) 1826[11] 2732[2] 3766[2] 5087[2] 5570[5] 6469[5]

Amarillo Star (IRE) *Charlie Fellowes* a87 87
2 ch c Society Rock(IRE) Neutrina (IRE) (Hector Protector (USA))
2610[4] 6911[2] 7904[5] 8243[2] (9322)

Amarone (GER) *Eva Fabianova* 90
4 b m Santiago(GER) Amateis (GER) (Tiger Hill (IRE))
8171a[6]

Amarsanaa *Clive Cox* a64
2 gr f Dream Ahead(USA) Nullarbor Sky (IRE) (Aussie Rules (USA))
8706[9] 9211[3] 9409[5]

Amatriciana (FR) *Carina Fey* a52 86
3 ch f Leroidesanimaux(BRZ) Anna Of Russia (GER) (Acatenango (GER))
7499a[8] 8376a[12]

Amaysmont *Richard Fahey* 87
2 b g Mayson Montjen (IRE) (Montjeu (IRE))
(6337)◆ 7733[2]

Amazing Alba *Alistair Whillans* 63
3 ch f Helmet(AUS) Silcasue (Selkirk (USA))
1954[5] 2477[5] 3376[3] 4276[6] 4508[3] 5276[2]◆ 5904[3] 6277[6] 6608[2] 6936[10]

Amazing Amaya *Derek Shaw* a53 47
4 b m New Approach(IRE) Faslen (USA) (Fasliyev (USA))
1291[2] 322[3] 478[6] 973[5]◆ (9335) 9539[3]

Amazing Grazing (IRE) *Rebecca Bastiman* a81 74
5 b g Intense Focus(USA) North Light Rose (USA) (North Light (IRE))
2[5] 278[2] 496[5] 907[2] 1342[4] 2368[3] 2508[7] 3056[6] 3504[8] 4059[4] 4632[8] 4912[2]◆ 4977[3] 5330[5] 6591[3] 7065[5] 7777[3] 8266[7]

Amazing Lips (IRE) *S Kobayashi* 100
4 b m Camelot Athenaire (IRE) (Duke Of Marmalade (IRE))
1627a[9]

Amazing News *George Scott* a79
2 ch g Toronado(IRE) Angelic Air (Oasis Dream)
9252[4] (9567)

Amazing Red (IRE) *Ed Dunlop* a101 106
6 b g Teofilo(IRE) Artisia (IRE) (Peintre Celebre (USA))
1017[4]◆ 1267[3] 1693[2] 2269[7] 3078[3] 3600[15] (6145a) 7498a[7] 8375a[6]

Amazon Princess *Tony Newcombe* a54 32
2 b f War Command(USA) Last Lahar (Sixties Icon)
2275[7] 7469[3] 9174[12]

Amazour (IRE) *Ismail Mohammed* a89 89
7 b g Azamour(IRE) Choose Me (IRE) (Choisir (AUS))
52a[7] 640a[13]

Ambassador (IRE) *Richard Fahey* a60 67
2 b g Invincible Spirit(IRE) Natural Bloom (IRE) (Galileo (IRE))
6664[3]◆ 7361[4] 8504[6]

Ambassadorial (USA) *Jane Chapple-Hyam* a109 91
5 b g Elusive Quality(USA) Tactfully (IRE) (Discreet Cat (USA))
(3991) 4921[11] 5546[17] 6150[3] 7011a[3] 7997[3] 8771a[9]

Amber *Peter Niven* a22
3 ch f Dunaden(FR) Secret Virtue (Iceman)
103[9] 804[5]

Amberine *Malcolm Saunders* a38 48
5 b m Equiano(FR) Crimson Fern (IRE) (Titus Livius (FR))
2728[3] 3036[4] 6329[8] 7172[8] 8256[11]

Amber Island (IRE) *Charlie Appleby* 78
2 b f Exceed And Excel(AUS) Raphinae (Dubawi (IRE))
5684[3] 6322[2] (7054) 7696[15]

Amber Jet (IRE) *John Mackie* a30 24
3 b f Dream Ahead(USA) Star Jet (IRE) (Teofilo (IRE))
4597[6] 6187[7]

Amber Road (IRE) *Richard Hannon* 52
2 ch f Anjaal Trading Places (Dansili)
1821[8] 2761[15]

Amber Rock (USA) *Les Eyre* a44 43
3 b g Australia Amber Isle (USA) (First Defence (USA))
1417[14] 4038[3] 4998[9] 7873[7] 8205[7] 8903[3] 9395[8]

Ambersand (IRE) *Richard Fahey* a10 68
3 b f Footstepsinthesand Miss Sally (IRE) (Danetime (IRE))
3707[2]◆ 4358[8] 7129[5] 7875[14]

Amber Spark (IRE) *Richard Fahey* a74 81
3 b f Fast Company(IRE) Shehila (IRE) (Zamindar (USA))
3336[2] (4007) 4930[3] 5458[6] 5931[10] 6541[3] 6893[3] 7366[8] 7901[6] 8305[11] 9109[5]

Amber Star (IRE) *David O'Meara* 68
3 b f Lope De Vega(IRE) Natural Bloom (IRE) (Galileo (IRE))
3974[4] 4520[4] (4818) 5695[10]

Ambiance (IRE) *Roy Arne Kvisla* a65 99
8 b g Camacho Thawrah (IRE) (Green Desert (USA))
4534a[2] 7497a[2]

Ambient (IRE) *Jamie Osborne* a39 45
4 b g Born To Sea(IRE) Undulant Way (Hurricane Run (IRE))
34[5] 294[3] 429[5] 962[3] 1169[2] 1695[3] 2273[2] 3305[10] 3743[2] 4607[6] 7087a[9] 7587[7] 8410[4]

Ambition *X Thomas-Demeaulte* a83 103
3 ch f Dubawi(IRE) Talent (New Approach (IRE))
(8969a)

Ambitious Icarus *Richard Guest* a41 52
10 b g Striking Ambition Nesting Box (Grand Lodge (USA))
2632[4] 3213[12] 3452[5]

Ambling (IRE) *John Gosden* a89 77
3 b f Lope De Vega(IRE) Royale Danehill (IRE) (Danehill (USA))
2838[3] 4841[8] 5311[2] (6114)◆

Ambyfaeirvine (IRE) *Ivan Furtado* a53 68
2 b c Epaulette(AUS) Corryvreckan (IRE) (Night Shift (USA))
1968[4] 2191[5] 2820[7] (4756) 5146[3] 5296[4] 6372[14] 7140[6] 7827[12] 8259[2] 8394[7]

Amedeo Modigliani (IRE) *A P O'Brien* 100
4 b h Galileo(IRE) Gooseberry Fool (Danehill Dancer (IRE))
1309a[3] 1531a[4] 7794a[4] 8336[14] 8572a[6]

Amelia R (IRE) *Ray Craggs* a49 67
3 b f Zoffany(IRE) Xaloc (IRE) (Shirocco (GER))
3204[13] 3684[8] (5147) 5659[7] 6277[5] 6547[5] 8071[8] 8925[8] 9396[14]

America First (IRE) *Michael Dods* a40 59
2 gr g Le Havre(IRE) Aglaia (IRE) (Invincible Spirit (IRE))
5212[6] 5848[7] 6664[7]

American Dreamer *Jamie Osborne* a28 2
2 b g Fountain Of Youth(IRE) Say A Prayer (Indesatchel (IRE))
5780[13] 7386[6] 7627[11]

American Endeavour (USA) *Marco Botti* a78 34
4 ch m Distorted Humor(USA) Crazy Party (USA) (A.P. Indy (USA))
(814) 1387[7]

American Graffiti (FR) *Charlie Appleby* a86 97
3 ch g Pivotal Adventure Seeker (FR) (Bering)
156[2]◆ 472[2] (804) (4068) 4863[3]

American Guru (USA) *Michael J Doyle* 68
5 b h Unbridled's Song(USA) Camargue (USA) (Mineshaft (USA))
7225a[11]

American Lady (IRE) *J A Stack* a30 93
2 b f Starspangledbanner(AUS) Show Me Off (Showcasing)
2491a[4] 2881a[4] 3983[21] 4580a[4] 6157[6] 7400[9]

American Lily (FR) *L Rovisse* a44 53
2 b f American Devil(FR) Miss Vinga (FR) (High Rock (IRE))
9605a[14]

American Saint (FR) *N Paysan* a66 68
4 b g American Post Sainte Glace (FR) (Grape Tree Road)
(5762a)

Amethyst (FR) *C Escuder* 64
3 ch f Lord Of England(GER) Blue Note (GER) (Okawango (USA))
3526a[3] 5165a[7]

Amicia *Marco Botti* a62 55
2 ch f Camacho Fiancee (IRE) (Pivotal)
7393[10] 8706[7] 9242[8] 9568[7]

Am I Dreaming (IRE) *Adam West* 35
2 b f Make Believe Queen Jock (USA) (Repent (USA))
6532[8] 7023[6]

Amilcar (IRE) *H-A Pantall* 109
3 b c Wootton Bassett Drosia (IRE) (King's Best (USA))
1707a[3]

Ami Li Bert (IRE) *Michael Appleby* a53 52
2 ch c Dragon Pulse(IRE) Taalluf (USA) (Hansel (USA))
6934[5] 7388[5] 7870[9] 8493[7] (8859) 9179[4] 9399[2]

Amiral Chop (FR) *C Boutin* a29 55
4 ch h Deportivo Lonsome Drive (FR) (Domedriver (IRE))
2170a[16] 2647a[13]

Amir Kabir *Roger Charlton* 64
2 b g Mukhadram Victory Garden (New Approach (IRE))
8518[5]

Amiro (GER) *M Figge* 98
3 b c Lord Of England(GER) Amajara (Dalakhani (IRE))
2310a[4] 4707a[14] 6771a[7]

Amitie Waltz (FR) *Richard Hughes* a88 80
7 b g Sinndar(IRE) Lia Waltz (FR) (Linamix (FR))
184[2] 704[4]◆ (980)

Amity Island *Ollie Pears* a53 56
4 ch g Harbour Watch(IRE) Mylington Light (Mount Nelson)
6[5] 590[5] 1390[11] 1958[7] 2587[2] 3447[10] 4005[6] 5024[3] 5518[7] 6578[2] (7336) 7544[9]

Amjaady (USA) *David O'Meara* a86 84
3 b g War Front(USA) Prize Catch (USA) (A.P. Indy (USA))
2765[8] (3647) 4671[7] 6961[15] 7610[2] 8692[2] 9050[3]

Amliba *David O'Meara* a54
3 b f Mayson Hisaronu (IRE) (Stravinsky (USA))
1[5] 186[4] 406[9] 906[7] 2190[4]

Ammobaby (FR) *H De Nicolay* a77 77
2 ch f Planteur(IRE) Ponte Di Legno (FR) (Sinndar (IRE))
1657a[3] 2757a[2] 6384a[4]

Amnaa *John Bridger* a46 60
2 b f Bungle Inthejungle She Mystifies (Indesatchel (IRE))
1812[4] 2051[3] 3196[7] (3812) 4387[7] 5171[6] 5630[3] 5968[4] 7469[8] 7768[7] 9300[8]

A Momentofmadness *Charles Hills* a84 103
6 b g Elnadim(USA) Royal Blush (Royal Applause)
1946[7] 2576[3] 3097[16] 3582[10] 5524[9] 6351[6] 7193[2]

Amood (IRE) *Simon West* a51 41
8 ch g Elnadim(USA) Amanah (USA) (Mr Prospector (USA))
6627[12] 7581[12] 8301[9] 8922[11] 9111[4] 9396[7] 9516[3]

Amor De Vega *Roger Fell* a65
2 b f Lope De Vega(IRE) Hypocoristique (IRE) (High Chaparral (IRE))
8525[7]

Amorella (IRE) *Markus Klug* 108
4 b m Nathaniel(IRE) Anaita (GER) (Dubawi (IRE))
4622a[3] 5719a[5] (6747a) 7500a[2] 8792a[8]

Amor Fati (IRE) *David Evans* a65 76
4 b g Zoffany(IRE) Roman Love (IRE) (Perugino (USA))
(159) 180[3] 379[2] 465[4] 624[5] (792) 1060[7] (1215)◆ 1378[2] (1836) (2504a) 3002[9] 5080[2] (5373)◆ 5881[2] 6414[3] 6904[5] 7378[6] 8122[13] 8471[11] 8946[8] 9217[9] 9367[10] 9609[11]

Amor Kethley *Amy Murphy* a67 56
3 b f Swiss Spirit Nellie Ellis (IRE) (Compton Place)
78[11] 313[3] 550[2] 813[2] 1340a[3] 1842a[9] 2870[7] 4378[14] 7172[3] (7447) 8501[5] 9089[6] 9245[5]

Amorously (IRE) *Richard Hannon* a77 81
3 b f Australia Know Me Love Me (IRE) (Danehill Dancer (IRE))
2253[4] 2582[9] (3154) 3779[6] 4424[3] 5349[4] 5813[3] (6362) (6856) 7176[4] 8289[11]

Amourice (IRE) *Jane Chapple-Hyam* a69 85
4 b m Authorized(IRE) Amancaya (GER) (Dai Jin)
1559[10] 2399[5] 3016[4] 7900[8]

Amourie *Ray Craggs* a55 26
3 ch f Haafhd Tour D'Amour (IRE) (Fruits Of Love (USA))
20[6] 211[9] 1721[11] 3246[9] 4039[8] 5851[12]

Ampeson *Richard John O'Brien* 74
2 b g Mayson Surprise (IRE) (Anabaa Blue)
2491a[7]

Amphitrite (AUS) *David A & B Hayes & Tom Dabern* 103
3 bb f Sebring(AUS) Ocean Dream (AUS) (Redoute's Choice (AUS))
8138a[15]

Ample Plenty *David Simcock* a57 55
3 ch f Dawn Approach(IRE) Silent Serenade (Bertolini (USA))
437[5] 5358[5] 5941[8] 6600[4]

Amplification (USA) *Michael Dods* a77 84
4 b g Lonhro(AUS) Our Drama Queen (IRE) (Danehill Dancer (IRE))
1977[2]◆

Amplify (IRE) *Brian Meehan* a84 95
3 b g Acclamation Obsara (Observatory (USA))
312[3] 1035[6] 1665[2] 2078[5] (3090) (4422) 5589[12] 6148[5] (6332)◆ 6476[6] 6954[14] 7913[9]

Ampney Red *Hughie Morrison* a64 55
2 ch f Mukhadram Golden Delicious (Cadeaux Genereux)
8258[5] 8758[12] 9158[6]

Amy Blair *Stef Keniry* 46
6 b g Captain Gerrard(IRE) Shalad'Or (Golden Heights)
1527[12] 3720[7] 4005[4] 4916[10] 5787[15]

Amy Kane *Jimmy Fox* a41 36
5 b m Excelebration(IRE) Be Free (Selkirk (USA))
288[7] 602[12] 940[12] 1362[11] 2231[10]

Anachronist (FR) *Isidro Vergara* 67
5 b g Soldier Hollow Acacalia (GER) (Ransom O'War (USA))
6523a[9]

Ana Gold (FR) *Laurent Loisel* a74 76
3 b f Champs Elysees Ana Style (FR) (Anabaa Blue)
216a[2]

Ananya *Peter Chapple-Hyam* 99
2 ch f Sepoy(AUS) Whatizzit (Galileo (IRE))
4295[3] (5189) 5964[5] 7120[5] 8091[7]

Anapurna *John Gosden* a86 113
3 b f Frankel Dash To The Top (Montjeu (IRE))
(474) (2618)◆ (3316) 7252a[7]◆ (7926a) 8333[11]

Anastarsia (IRE) *John Gosden* a79 74
2 b f Sea The Stars(IRE) Aniseed (IRE) (Dalakhani (IRE))
6949[4] (7579) 8091[8]

Anchises *Rebecca Menzies* a36 43
4 b g Choisir(AUS) Afrodita (IRE) (Montjeu (IRE))
1418[16] 2104[10] 2785[3] 3567[9] 4130[7] 5518[9] 6628[13] 7956[13] 9345[12] 9446[10]

Ancient Astronaut *Karl Thornton* a56 54
6 b g Kodiac Tatora (Selkirk (USA))
1026[8] 5935[6]

Ancient City (FR) *C Theodorakis* a57 62
4 b g Zoffany(IRE) Happy Town (FR) (Anabaa (USA))
2955a[12]

Ancient Spirit (GER) *J S Bolger* 108
4 b h Invincible Spirit(IRE) Assisi (GER) (Galileo (IRE))
5112a[3] 6137a[6] 7220a[9]

Ancona (IRE) *Andreas Suborics* 93
2 ch f Amaron Amazone (GER) (Adlerflug (GER))
7004a[5] 7724a[2] 8393a[4]

Ancyre (FR) *K R Burke* a50
2 gr f Silver Frost(IRE) Alexia Fedorovna (USA) (Steinlen)
9471[10]

Andaleep (IRE) *Graeme McPherson* a71 73
3 b g Siyouni(FR) Oriental Magic (GER) (Doyen (IRE))
7816[8] 8652[4] 9050[8] 9443[8]

Andalusite *John Gallagher* a47 72
6 br m Equiano(FR) Kammaan (Diktat)
104[6] 2929[9] 3539[2] 3967[9]

Anda Muchacho (IRE) *Nicolo Simondi* 112
5 b h Helmet(AUS) Montefino (IRE) (Shamardal (USA))
2886a[2] (3643a) (7502a) 8392a[2]

Andesite (USA) *Brad H Cox* 105
2 rg c The Factor(USA) Ahh (USA) (Saint Liam (USA))
8746a[9]

Andies Armies *Lisa Williamson* a47 33
3 b g Piccolo Shaymee's Girl (Wizard King)
2357[10] 3319[7] 3775[9] 4909[7] 5176[8] 5847[7] 6181[10] 6638[7] 7681[8] 9276[8] 9446[9] 9548[10]

Andok (IRE) *Richard Fahey* a69 72
5 b g Elzaam(AUS) My Causeway Dream (IRE) (Giant's Causeway (USA))
1418[15] 1949[3] 2335[2]

Andoro (GER) *R Dzubasz* 106
3 b c Jukebox Jury(IRE) Andarta (GER) (Platini (GER))
3674a[9] 4707a[8] 6007a[6]

Andre Amar (IRE) *Robyn Brisland* a65 65
3 b g Dandy Man(IRE) Heaven's Vault (IRE) (Hernando (FR))
8860[9] 9030[13] 9334[12] 9584[5]

And The New (IRE) *Johnny Farrelly* a47 69
8 b g Kalanisi(IRE) Wheredidthemoneygo (IRE) (Anshan)
1771[10] 2192[11] 2999[4] 3571[3]◆

And Yet She Moves (IRE) *Adam West*
3 ch f Roderic O'Connor(IRE) Ms Cromby (IRE) (Arakan (USA))
4377[7] 5678[9]

Anecdotic (USA) *I Endaltsev* a78 79
3 b c Anodin(IRE) Flash Dance (IRE) (Zamindar (USA))
9281a[5]

Aneedh *Clive Mulhall* a11 14
9 b g Lucky Story(USA) Seed Al Maha (USA) (Seeking The Gold (USA))
3960[9]

A New Dawn (IRE) *Joseph Patrick O'Brien* 104
2 ch f Zoffany(IRE) Simply A Star (IRE) (Giant's Causeway (USA))
4352a[10] 6689a[3] 7742a[2] 8165a[2]

An Fear Ciuin (IRE) *R Mike Smith* a53 58
8 b g Galileo(IRE) Potion (Pivotal)
3361[9] 6576[7]

Anfield Girl (IRE) *Tom Dascombe* a66 72
2 b f Starspangledbanner(AUS) Grivele (IRE) (El Prado (IRE))
3506[4] 4605[3] 7297[2] 8665[8]

Angela (FR) *Miss V Haigh* a55 66
2 b f Wootton Bassett Angel Of Harlem (FR) (Holy Roman Emperor (IRE))
4533a[6] 7925a[13]

Angel Alexander (IRE) *Tom Dascombe* a86 111
3 gr g Dark Angel(IRE) Majestic Alexander (IRE) (Bushranger (IRE))
2522[8] (3659) (3844)◆ 4359[5] 5154[2] (5420) 5705[8] 6714[3] (7433) 8648a[2]

Angel Black (IRE) *Shaun Keightley* a44
3 b c Dark Angel(IRE) Basandere (FR) (Green Tune (USA))
554[7] 913[8] 1094[10] 1353[8] 7520[7] 8081[8]

Angel Dundee *Michael Appleby* a8
3 ch f Dunaden(FR) Angel Cake (IRE) (Dark Angel (IRE))
9131[2] 5004[9]

Angel Eyes *John David Riches* a55 54
4 b m Piccolo Miacarla (Forzando)
811[5] 1020[5] 1402[2]◆ 2324[2] 4765[6] 5278[9] 5558[12] 6574[13]

Angel Force (IRE) *David C Griffiths* a62 55
4 ch m Lethal Force(IRE) Indian Angel (Indian Ridge (IRE))
2079^{11} 2576^{6} 3868^{14} 7588^{9} 8194^{4} 8263^{11} 8296^{8} 8501^{6} 8643^{8} 9089^{9} 9247^{6} 9406^{6} 9583^{9} 9627^{7}◆

Angel Gabrial (IRE) *Patrick Morris* a62 69
10 b g Hurricane Run(IRE) Causeway Song (USA) (Giant's Causeway (USA))
318^{4} 469^{8} 1022^{9} 2217^{6} 2695^{2} 3334^{3} (3481) 4126^{2} (4363) 5423^{3} 5897^{5} 6716^{8} 7683^{13}

Angel Grey (IRE) *Andrew Balding* 83
2 gr f Gutaifan(IRE) Violet's Gift (IRE) (Cadeaux Genereux)
4840^{6} 5381^{4} (5988) 6833^{3} 7896^{18}

Angelica (FR) *Laura Lemiere*
3 ch f Kendargent(FR) Avola (FR) (Galileo (IRE))
2954a^{10}

Angelical Eve (IRE) *Dai Williams* a53 40
5 gr m Dark Angel(IRE) First Lady (IRE) (Indian Ridge (IRE))
1731^{11} 2585^{5} 2972^{7} 4116^{10} 4424^{11} 4658^{5} 5025^{9} 5376^{4} 7009a^{5} 7501a^{12}

Angelic Light (IRE)
M D O'Callaghan 87
3 gr f Dark Angel(IRE) Delia Eria (IRE) (Zamindar (USA))
1434a^{5} 2605a^{10} 5923a^{8}

Angelic Time (IRE) *Ed Vaughan* a77 56
2 gr c Dark Angel(IRE) Danetime Out (IRE) (Danetime (IRE))
8460^{10} (9252)

Angel Islington (IRE)
Andrew Balding a70 91
4 gr m Dark Angel(IRE) Doregan (IRE) (Bahhare (USA))
2774^{U} 2971^{10} 4028^{6} 4473^{4}

Angel Lane (FR) *K R Burke* a83 63
3 gr f Rajsaman(FR) Angel Rose (IRE) (Definite Article)
4405^{4} 6701^{4} 7630^{2} (9333) 9543^{3}

Angel Mead *Joseph Tuite* a68 77
3 b f Archipenko(USA) Red Sovereign (Danzig Connection (USA))
5448^{2} 6346^{6} 7115^{6}

Angelo Dream (FR) *Mlle B Dahm* a58 83
6 gr g Palace Episode(USA) Angel Mara (FR) (Ange Gabriel (FR))
(7536a)

Angel Of Delight (IRE)
Hugo Palmer a79 79
2 gr f Dark Angel(IRE) Ventura Mist (Pastoral Pursuits)
3441^{4} (5684) 6444^{7} 8303^{3}

Angel Of My Heart (IRE)
Michael Easterby a48 40
4 ch m Farhh Angel's Tears (Seeking The Gold (USA))
8269^{5}◆ 8639^{10} 9028^{8}

Angel Of The North (IRE)
Robin Dickin a30 33
4 gr m Dark Angel(IRE) Kay Es Jay (FR) (Xaar)
6173^{8} 6681^{12} 6760^{6} 7545^{9}

Angel Of Truth (AUS)
Gwenda Markwell 111
3 bb g Animal Kingdom(USA) Scarletini (AUS) (Bernardini (USA))
8361a^{15} 8803a^{11}

Angel On High (IRE) *Harry Dunlop* a67 41
2 b c Dark Angel(IRE) Angel Of The Gwaun (IRE) (Sadler's Wells (USA))
8511^{12} 9634^{4}

Angel Palanas *K R Burke* a88 66
5 b g Mayson Scottish Exile (IRE) (Ashkalani (IRE))
4^{7} 44^{2} 832^{6} 929^{7} 8403^{6} 9183^{4} 9561^{6}

Angel Power *Roger Varian* 73
2 b f Lope De Vega(IRE) Burning Rules (IRE) (Aussie Rules (USA))
8758^{3}◆

Angels *J P Murtagh* a78 78
4 gb m Dark Angel(IRE) Magic Eye (IRE) (Nayef (USA))
8367a^{12}

Angel's Acclaim (IRE) *Kevin Ryan* a66 62
5 gr m Dark Angel(IRE) Miss Otis (Danetime (IRE))
6^{2} 387^{4}

Angel Sarah (IRE) *Richard Fahey* 34
3 b f Dark Angel(IRE) Padma (Three Valleys (USA))
2337^{8} 3271^{12} 4210^{7}

Angels Chant *Jim Boyle* 52
3 b f Gregorian(IRE) Divine Pamina (IRE) (Dark Angel (IRE))
4452^{14} 5955^{7} 6903^{4}

Angels Faces (IRE) *Grant Tuer* a54 68
2 b f Gutaifan(IRE) Worthington (IRE) (Kodiac)
3244^{7} 5895^{3} 6337^{9} 7029^{7} 8815^{9} 9060^{8}

Angel's Hideaway (IRE)
John Gosden 109
3 gr f Dark Angel(IRE) The Hermitage (IRE) (Kheleyf (USA))
1832^{3} 2443^{4} 3317^{4} 4092^{3} 5608^{9} 6508^{10} 7146^{11}

Angels Tread *David Simcock* a64
2 b f Kitten's Joy(USA) Mistaken Love (USA) (Bernardini (USA))
5733^{7} 6928^{10}

Angel's Whisper (IRE) *Amy Murphy* a74 75
4 gr m Dark Angel(IRE) Tasheyaat (Sakhee (USA))
1355^{5} 2261^{3} 3279^{3} (4336)◆ 5144^{4} 6538^{3} 7344^{2} 7835^{5} 8705^{8} 9202^{10}

Anglesey Penny *J R Jenkins* a51 35
3 ch f Captain Gerrard(IRE) Magic By Bell (Reel Buddy (USA))
90^{8} 341^{11} 1514^{4} 3887^{7} 4376^{13}

Anglo Saxson (IRE)
Charlie Fellowes a62 73
2 ch g Starspangledbanner(AUS) Obligada (IRE) (Beat Hollow)
4886^{14} 6757^{3}◆ 7346^{4} 7980^{3} 8505^{7}

Aniel (FR) *Simone Brogi* a75 70
3 ch c Planteur(IRE) Angel Of Harlem (FR) (Holy Roman Emperor (IRE))
(6328a)

Anif (IRE) *Michael Herrington* a79 78
5 b g Cape Cross(IRE) Cadenza (FR) (Dansili)
315^{6} (603) 835^{4} (1343) 2994^{3} 3541^{2} 4561^{3} 4838^{7} (5216) 5725^{7} 6733^{3} (9109)

Animalinhereyes (IRE)
Mme G Rarick a41
4 b m Rip Van Winkle(IRE) Velvet Ribbon (IRE) (Duke Of Marmalade (IRE))
992a^{12}

Animal Instinct *Sir Mark Prescott Bt* a78
2 ch c Leroidesanimaux(BRZ) Alea Iacta (Invincible Spirit (IRE))
7445^{3}◆ 7870^{2} (8494)

Anima Rock (FR)
Jassim Mohammed Ghazali 106
4 b h Shamalgan(FR) Carnet De Bal (Kingsalsa (USA))
(892a)

Animated Hero *Rebecca Menzies* a33
6 b g Sakhee's Secret Society (IRE) (Barathea (IRE))
40^{9}

Anjah (IRE) *Simon Crisford* a71
2 b g Kodiac Terhaab (USA) (Elusive Quality (USA))
9107^{4}◆

Anjika (IRE)
Miss Clare Louise Cannon a44
2 b f Anjaal Gabriellina Klon (IRE) (Ashkalani (IRE))
8816^{7}

Annabelle Fritton (IRE)
Robyn Brisland a43
4 b m Arcano(IRE) Alexander Duchess (IRE) (Desert Prince (IRE))
1351^{8} 2195^{7}

Annabelle Rock (IRE)
Adrian McGuinness a77 68
3 ch f Dandy Man(IRE) She's A Queen (IRE) (Peintre Celebre (USA))
342^{5}

Anna Bunina (FR) *Jedd O'Keeffe* a57 93
3 b f Poet's Voice Russian Society (Darshaan)
(1980) 2597^{8} 3478^{2} 4322^{2} (4585) (6230) 7379^{2} (8341)

Anna Fallow *Ronald Thompson*
2 b f Music Master Beyond The Rainbow (Mind Games)
1416^{F} (Dead)

Anna Jammeela *Lucy Wadham* a64 57
4 b m Big Bad Bob(IRE) All Annalena (IRE) (Dubai Destination (USA))
387^{2}

Annakonda (IRE)
Peter Chapple-Hyam a49 43
3 b f Morpheus Royal Esteem (Mark Of Esteem (IRE))
4592^{10} 5141^{6} 6388^{4} 8998^{8}

Anna Magnolia (FR) *D Moser* 96
5 b m Makfi Anna Simona (GER) (Slip Anchor)
8587a^{2}

Anna Maria *Richard Fahey* a67
2 b f Invincible Spirit(IRE) Nannina (Medicean)
9623^{4}◆

Anna Nerium *Richard Hannon* a90 110
4 ch m Dubawi(IRE) Anna Oleanda (IRE) (Old Vic)
1941^{8} 2404^{2} (3342) 3986^{6} 5369^{5} 6508^{9} 7660^{6}

Anna Of Sussex (IRE)
Sylvester Kirk a47 78
2 b f Daaher(CAN) Balqaa (USA) (Invasor (ARG))
(5838) 7120^{9} 7412^{6} 8198^{7}

Anna Pivola (GER) *Markus Klug* 96
3 ch f Pivotal Queen's Hall (Singspiel (IRE))
3639a^{4} 4683a^{2}

Anna's Fast (USA) *Wesley A Ward* a90 79
2 b f Fast Anna(USA) True Will (USA) (Yes It's True (USA))
3983^{16}

Anneau D'Or (USA) *Blaine D Wright* a114 90
2 b c Medaglia d'Oro(USA) Walk Close (USA) (Tapit (USA))
8749a^{2}

Annecy *David Simcock* a78
3 b f Swiss Spirit Atheera (IRE) (Shamardal (USA))
698^{8} 1985^{7}

Annexation (FR) *Ed Dunlop* a60 67
3 b c Wootton Bassett Scarlet Sonnet (IRE) (Invincible Spirit (IRE))
3090^{5} 4116^{5} 4421^{4} 5237^{3}◆ 5431^{3} 7204^{6} 7609^{5} 8223^{10}

Annie De Vega *Ralph Beckett* 70
2 ch f Lope De Vega(IRE) Annie's Fortune (IRE) (Montjeu (IRE))
8028^{3}

Annie Fior (IRE) *B A Murphy* a65 97
5 ch m Finsceal Fior(IRE) Annamanamoux (USA) (Leroidesanimaux (BRZ))
808^{4} 1197^{8} 2879a^{6} 3062a^{5} 5075a^{7} 5223a^{3} 6090a^{11} 6692a^{12}

Anniemation (IRE) *Stella Barclay* a62 74
2 b g Acclamation Cafetiere (Iffraaj)
4317^{5} (5273)◆ 5992^{3} 6942^{5}

Annie Quickstep (IRE)
Jonathan Portman a59 57
2 b f Epaulette(AUS) Ragtime Dancer (Medicean)
5745^{7} 6527^{3} 7269^{3} 9212^{11} (9630)

Anno Lucis (IRE)
Sir Mark Prescott Bt a52 16
2 gr g Mastercraftsman(IRE) Summer's Eve (Singspiel (IRE))
7388^{6} 7579^{6} 7821^{6}◆ 8504^{8} 8857^{8}

Anno Maximo (GER) *Michael Bell* a57 6
2 b g Maxios Queen's Hall (Singspiel (IRE))
8100^{11} 8700^{10} 8919^{8}

Anobar (FR) *Andrea Marcialis* 77
2 b f Anodin(IRE) Gribatune (FR) (Green Tune (USA))
4533a^{4}

Anodor (FR) *F Head* 102
3 ch c Anodin(IRE) Decize (FR) (Kentucky Dynamite (USA))
2668a^{7} 3903a^{7}

Anonymous Blonde *David Evans* a2 53
3 b f Toronado(IRE) Angus Newz (Compton Place)
2277^{12} 2995^{6}

Anonymous John (IRE)
Dominic Ffrench Davis a80 77
7 gr g Baltic King Helibel (IRE) (Pivotal)
2531^{0} 347^{6}

Another Angel (IRE) *Antony Brittain* a84 79
5 b g Dark Angel(IRE) Kermana (IRE) (Selkirk (USA))
131^{6} (278) 498^{4} (610) 791^{3} 953^{3} (1082)◆ 1547^{8} 1929^{3} 2421^{8} 3056^{5} 3868^{20} 4103^{4} 6261^{8}

Another Approach (FR)
David Loughnane a58 43
3 b f Dawn Approach(IRE) Marmoom Flower (IRE) (Cape Cross (IRE))
1174^{8} 1593^{4} 2341^{7} 3418^{8} 5249^{9} 6202^{8} 7081^{7} 7550^{10} 9400^{5} 9609^{13}

Another Batt (IRE) *Richard Hughes* a94 97
4 ch g Windsor Knot(IRE) Mrs Batt (IRE) (Medecis)
(52a) 397a^{8} 639a^{4}◆ 843a^{5} 1415^{6} 1753^{14} 2572^{12} 5413^{8} 5930^{9} 6391^{5} 6950^{6} 7494a^{7}

Another Boy *Ralph Beckett* a52 62
6 ch g Paco Boy(IRE) Kurtanella (Pastoral Pursuits)
2483^{11} 3575^{7} 4226^{9} 5351^{7} (6084) 8009^{10}

Another Dressin (IRE)
Garvan Donnelly a46 50
4 ch m Born To Sea(IRE) Main Opinion (IRE) (Ivan Denisovich (IRE))
4690^{13}

Another Go (IRE) *Ralph J Smith* a67 67
6 gr g Strategic Prince Golden Rose (GER) (Winged Love (IRE))
2468^{9} (Dead)

Another Lincolnday
Rebecca Menzies a48 58
8 ch g Desideratum Another Paris (Paris House)
3272^{4} 4126^{6} 4510^{12} 7873^{10} 8081^{9}

Another Miracle (USA)
Gary Contessa 104
2 b c American Pharoah(USA) Retraceable (CAN) (Medaglia d'Oro (USA))
8745a^{3}

Another Planet (FR)
Matthieu Palussiere 79
2 ch c Cockney Rebel(IRE) Flute Divine (Royal Applause)
4679a^{8} 5763a^{2} 6196a^{2}

Another Reason (IRE) *Olly Murphy* a67 43
3 b g Thewayyouare(USA) Ballet School (IRE) (Sadler's Wells (USA))
855^{7} 1510^{2} (1770)

Another Situation (USA)
John Mackie a6 39
4 ch m Trappe Shot(USA) Return The Jewel (USA) (Broken Vow (USA))
1967^{13} 2215^{12}

Another Touch *Richard Fahey* a106 97
6 b g Arcano(IRE) Alsalwa (IRE) (Nayef (USA))
4935^{4} 7434^{5}◆ 7694^{26} (9200) (9666)

Anothertwistafate (USA)
Blaine D Wright a105
3 bb c Scat Daddy(USA) Imprecation (USA) (First Defence (USA))
2856a^{10}

Antagonize *Bryan Smart* a47 52
3 b g Epaulette(AUS) Hakuraa (IRE) (Elnadim (USA))
1926^{11} 6623^{5}

Anthony Van Dyck (IRE)
A P O'Brien 119
3 b c Galileo(IRE) Believe'N'Succeed (AUS) (Exceed And Excel (AUS))
(2619) (3345) 4414a^{2} 5414^{10} 7219a^{3} 8776a^{3} 9376a^{12}

Antico Lady (IRE) *Brian Ellison* a73 74
3 b f Dandy Man(IRE) Former Drama (USA) (Dynaformer (USA))
1389^{5} 2016^{3} 2531^{2} (2943) (3271) 4071^{2} 4329^{5} 5394^{6}

Antidote (IRE) *Richard Hughes* a60 50
3 gr g Dark Angel(IRE) Mood Indigo (IRE) (Indian Ridge (IRE))
1423^{9} 1825^{10} 4179^{8} 4998^{4} 5648^{3} 6400^{15} 6843^{6}

Antigua Biwi (IRE) *M Rolland* a44 74
3 b c Lord Of England(GER) Lexi The Princess (IRE) (Holy Roman Emperor (IRE))
2953a^{9} 3526a^{7}

Antiguan Rock *H Al Alawi* a54 62
4 ch g Rock Of Gibraltar(IRE) Totally Millie (Pivotal)
634a^{5}

Antilles (USA) *A P O'Brien* a108 97
3 b c War Front(USA) Wonder Of Wonders (USA) (Kingmambo (USA))
1713^{2} 2492a^{10} 3063a^{4} 4017^{11} 7668a^{3}

Antimo *A Al Shemaili* a63 63
6 b g Dubawi(IRE) Anna Palariva (IRE) (Caerleon (USA))
1742a^{4}

Antisana *H-A Pantall* 65
4 ch m Dubawi(IRE) Lava Flow (IRE) (Dalakhani (IRE))
1908a^{4}

Anton Dolin (IRE)
Michael Mullineaux a34 36
11 ch g Danehill Dancer(IRE) Ski For Gold (Shirley Heights)
185^{7}

Antonella *T J Martins Novais* 105
5 b m Dream Ahead(USA) Al Janadeirya (Oasis Dream)
5471a^{7}

Antonia Clara *P Monfort* a69 64
3 b f Lope De Vega(IRE) Anna Sophia (USA) (Oasis Dream)
408^{6} 720^{2} 990^{2} 1285^{7} 1476^{3} 1687^{5} 2063^{3} 3713a^{5}

Antonia De Vega (IRE)
Ralph Beckett 108
3 b f Lope De Vega(IRE) Witches Brew (IRE) (Duke Of Marmalade (IRE))
(3762) 8333^{6} 8792a^{4}

Anycity (IRE) *Michael Wigham* a81
3 b g Zoffany(IRE) Loquacity (Diktat)
55^{3} 955a^{2}

Anyonecanhaveitall *Mark Johnston* a27 35
3 ch f Showcasing Generous Heart (Sakhee's Secret)
6823^{6} 7417^{6}

Anyonecanhaveitall *Mark Johnston* a85 83
3 b g Nathaniel(IRE) Floriade (IRE) (Invincible Spirit (IRE))
3197^{3} 3474^{3} 3931^{5} (5975)◆ 6115^{3} 6459^{4} (6901) 7209^{2} (7414) 8524^{2}

Any Smile (IRE) *Julia Feilden* a45 55
3 b f Zoffany(IRE) Bahja (USA) (Seeking The Gold (USA))
556^{4} 795^{3} 2340^{17} 3154^{7} 4316^{7} 4807^{8} 6734^{9} 7608^{5} 8207^{9} 8646^{10}

Anything For You
Jonathan Portman a54
3 b f Dutch Art Station House (IRE) (Galileo (IRE))
7373^{7} 8013^{10} 8808^{9} 9090^{13}

Anythingispossible *Ivan Furtado*
3 b f Born To Sea(IRE) Be Amazing (IRE) (Refuse To Bend (IRE))
1816^{14}

Anythingtoday (IRE) *David O'Meara* a101 102
5 b g Zoffany(IRE) Corking (IRE) (Montjeu (IRE))
1896^{4} 2419^{12} 2873^{4} 3514^{2} (4386) (4890) 5370^{6} 6420^{14} 6923^{5} 7434^{3} 8130^{8}

Anythingyouwantobe *W P Browne* a66 63
3 b f Kingman Clenor (IRE) (Oratorio (IRE))
7486^{10}

Apache Bay *John Quinn* a41 53
2 b f Equiano(FR) Corn Rigs (Exceed And Excel (AUS))
2248^{9} 7377^{7} 8337^{7} 8750^{7}

Apache Blaze *Robyn Brisland* a68 68
4 b m Champs Elysees Polar Circle (USA) (Royal Academy (USA))
272^{8} 536^{2} 793^{5} 1065^{14} 1418^{2} 1688^{7} 2512^{2} 3449^{5} 3939^{3} 5025^{2} 5728^{5} 6324^{2} 7732^{7} 8663^{4} 8904^{4} 9221^{5}

Apache Princess (USA)
J Keith Desormeaux a96 101
3 b f Unusual Heat(USA) Puskita (USA) (Indian Charlie (USA))
9637a^{5}

Apachito *Kevin Frost* 19
2 b g Fountain Of Youth(IRE) Apache Glory (USA) (Cherokee Run (USA))
3371^{8} 6368^{15}

Apadanah (GER) *Waldemar Hickst* 96
3 bb f Holy Roman Emperor(IRE) Amazone (GER) (Adlerflug (GER))
2426a^{6} 4171a^{4} 5720a^{10} 6747a^{9}

Aperitif *Michael Bell* 72
3 b f Pivotal Swiss Dream (Oasis Dream)
1740^{9} 2736^{4}◆ 3302^{8} (3801) (5181)◆ 5659^{9} 6120^{3} 7831^{2} 8660^{7}

Apex King (IRE) *Mark Usher* a85 95
5 b g Kodiac Rainbowskia (FR) (Rainbow Quest (USA))
(205)◆ 880^{2} 1103^{6} 1181^{3} 1414^{7} 2402^{4} (3009) 3581^{7} 4299^{3} 5192^{7} 5546^{13} 5711a^{15} 8253^{9} 9000^{9} 9129^{5} 9308^{7} 9666^{6}

Apex Predator (IRE)
Seamus Durack a62 61
4 b g Acclamation Key Girl (IRE) (Key Of Luck (USA))
(58) 321^{2} 736^{7} 910^{3} 1548^{9} 2127^{5} 2970^{11}

Aphaea *Michael Easterby* a78 58
4 b m Farhh Wood Chorus (Singspiel (IRE))
(2351)◆ 2528^{2} 2591^{9}

A Place To Dream *Mike Murphy* a62 62
3 b g Compton Place Phantasmagoria (Fraam)
6198^{2} 7114^{3} 8698^{6} 9244^{5} 9503^{10}

Aplomb (IRE) *William Haggas* a73 102
3 b g Lope De Vega(IRE) Mickleberry (IRE) (Desert Style (IRE))
1924^{4} 2567^{2}◆ 3357^{4} (3935)◆ 4847^{6} (5983)◆ 6222^{4} 7868^{2} 8127^{21}

Apoleon (GER)
Frau Anna Schleusner-Fruhriep 87
9 br g Ogatonango(GER) Abisou (GER) (Goofalik (USA))
8804a^{8}

Apollinaire *Ralph Beckett* a84 81
2 b c Poet's Voice Affaire De Coeur (Dalakhani (IRE))
(2394) 2761^{2} 3841^{2} 9162^{2}

Apollo Flight (FR) *L Gadbin* a89 101
4 b g Rock Of Gibraltar(IRE) Absolutly Me (FR) (Anabaa Blue)
(2266a) 5926a^{5} 6820a^{3}

Apotheose (FR) *Andrea Marcialis* a60 54
3 b f Clodovil(IRE) Apostrophe (IRE) (Barathea (IRE))
6061a^{3}

Apparate *Roger Varian* 97
3 b c Dubawi(IRE) Appearance (Galileo (IRE))
2099^{5} (2764) 4256^{3}◆ 4924^{2} (6952)◆ 8092^{10}

Appeared *David Simcock* a83 101
7 b g Dubawi(IRE) Appearance (Galileo (IRE))
47a^{4} 281a^{4} 730a^{12}

Appelina (DEN) *Wido Neuroth* 100
6 ch m Appel Au Maitre(FR) Wings Of A Dove (Hernando (FR))
6524a^{3} (7496a)

Applecross (IRE) *Michael Bell* 79
2 b f Sir Prancealot(IRE) Champion Tipster (Pursuit Of Love)
(3033)◆ 3983^{22}

Apples Acre (IRE) *Ben Haslam* a38 31
2 ch f No Nay Never(USA) Matron (Bahamian Bounty)
3419^{9} 6943^{11} 7437^{8} 9394^{8}

Appletart (IRE) *Ed Walker* a34
2 b f Nathaniel(IRE) Gertrude Gray (IRE) (Hurricane Run (IRE))
9327[11]

Appointed *Tim Easterby* a76 84
5 b m Delegator Celestial Harmony (Polish Precedent (USA))
1896[9] 2104[7] 3095[4] 3816[4] (4009) 4241[5] 5201[3] 5458[3] 5982[7] 6230[4] 7702[10] 8341[12]

Approaching Menace *Amy Murphy* a45 49
4 b m Cityscape Candle (Dansili)
2283[7] 2974[8]

Approbare (IRE) *Ross O'Sullivan* a55 70
7 b g Approve(IRE) Tabrina (IRE) (Fasliyev (USA))
7087a[3]

Approve The Dream (IRE)
Julia Feilden a49 59
3 ch g Approve(IRE) Jacquotte (IRE) (Alhaarth (IRE))
1678[9] 2262[2] 3780[5] 4477[3] 5867[4] 6130[11] 6983[8] 7204[3]

Approximate *Michael Bell* a48
2 b f Dubawi(IRE) Estimate (IRE) (Monsun (GER))
8510[14] 9052[9]

April Angel (FR) *P Capelle* a52 61
5 b m Spirit One(FR) Lady Verde (FR) (Meshaheer (USA))
7505a[12]

Aprilios (FR) *Georgios Alimpinisis* a73 77
7 gr g Desert Style(IRE) Allegria (FR) (Verglas (IRE))
4747a[15]

April Wine *Clive Cox* a53 57
3 b f Charm Spirit(IRE) Nandiga (USA) (Bernardini (USA))
380[7] 841[5] 1171[11]

Apron Strings *Michael Attwater* a49
3 b f Mayson Royal Ivy (Mujtahid (USA))
752[6] 918[10] 1515[4] 1726[3]

Apterix (FR) *Brian Ellison* a65 83
9 b g Day Flight Ohe Les Aulmes (FR) (Lute Antique (FR))
1719[6] 1949[2] (2326) (2636)◆ 3073[6] 3862[13]

Aqabah (USA) *Charlie Appleby* a94 73
4 gr g Exchange Rate(USA) Fast Tip (USA) (Najran (USA))
515a[14] 842a[6]

Aql (IRE) *Brian Meehan* 20
3 b g Exceed And Excel(AUS) Pearl Sea (IRE) (Elusive City (USA))
1755[9]

Aqqadeer (USA) *R Bouresly* a24
3 ch f Noble Mission Striking Example (USA) (Empire Maker (USA))
48a[12]

Aqrab (IRE) *Roger Varian* a65
2 br f Dawn Approach(IRE) Aljaaziah (Medaglia d'Oro (USA))
9163[7] 9383[4]

Aquadabra (IRE)
Christopher Mason a63 59
4 b m Born To Sea(IRE) Amazing Win (IRE) (Marju (IRE))
2473[5] 2728[8] 3036[9] 4182[2] 4481[4] (4765) (5084) 5449[3] (6285) 6639[6] 7172[9] 7844[2] 8194[5] 8501[4]

Aqua Libre *Tony Carroll* a65 44
6 b m Aqlaam Be Free (Selkirk (USA))
175[8] 348[2] 814[7] 911[4] 1231[2] 1426[7] 1836[2] 2231[9] 3038[11]

Aquarium *Jane Chapple-Hyam* a107 109
4 ch h Leroidesanimaux(BRZ) Caribana (Hernando (FR))
396a[9] 637a[11] 961a[8] 1101[5]◆ 1415[16] 1545[2] 2033[2] 2408[8] (2574)◆ 3346[10] 4053[7] 4646[15] 4935[12] 5519[10] 5613[4] 5909[5] 8116[8] 8764[4] 9125a[8]

Aquarius (IRE) *Michael Appleby* a63 60
3 b f Charm Spirit(IRE) Puzzled (IRE) (Peintre Celebre (USA))
2904[12] 3420[4] 3742[6] 4183[8] 4436[6] 4754[5] 5377[6] 5622[3] (5890) 7446[6] 8071[7] 8419[11] 8917[9] 9039[9] (9133)◆ 9352[8]

Aquarius Miracle *George Scott* a9
3 ch g Iffraaj Aquatinta (GER) (Samum (GER))
251[13] 1212[9]

Aquascape (IRE) *Harry Dunlop* a72
2 br g Montmartre(FR) Water Feature (Dansili)
7555[4] 8287[3]

Aquileo (IRE) *Roger Varian* a74 76
2 b c Gleneagles(IRE) Nobilis (Rock Of Gibraltar (IRE))
7897[4] 8604[3]

Aquilina *F Rossi* a40 57
3 gr f Kendargent(FR) Letthemusictakeus (IRE) (Holy Roman Emperor (IRE))
1658a[7]

Aquilino (FR) *A Fabre* 68
3 ch g Le Havre(IRE) Asulayana (Sulamani (IRE))
2519a[7]

Aquitaine (IRE) *P Bary* 73
2 ch f Australia Divine Music (IRE) (Gold Away (IRE))
6774a[7]

Arabellas Fortune *Stef Keniry*
4 b m Haafhd Finellas Fortune (Elmaamul (USA))
7287[6]

Arabescato *Nick Littmoden* a52 52
2 ch g Outstrip Cat Hunter (One Cool Cat (USA))
6154[9] 7162[11] 9155[8] 9399[6]

Arabian Dream *Ralph Beckett* 38
2 b f Oasis Dream Arabesque (Zafonic (USA))
5772[13] 6287[7] 6846[11]

Arabian Jazz (IRE) *Michael Bell* a53 80
4 b m Red Jazz(USA) Queen Of Rap (IRE) (Alhaarth (IRE))
4438[4]◆ 4902[5]◆ 6201[9] 6825[4] 7471[7]

Arabian King *David Elsworth* a52 45
3 ch g New Approach(IRE) Barshiba (IRE) (Barathea (IRE))
4120[11] 5477[6] 6121[6] 8499[5]

Arabian Moon *Ralph Beckett* a79 81
2 b g Al Kazeem Midnight Dance (IRE) (Danehill Dancer (IRE))
5493[3]◆ 6040[2] 7151[2] 7971[3] 9546[3]

Arabian Oasis *Lydia Pearce*
7 b g Oasis Dream Love Divine (Diesis)
8298[11]

Arabian Warrior *Saeed bin Suroor* a72
2 b c Dubawi(IRE) Siyaadah (Shamardal (USA))
8999[5]

Arabic Channel (USA)
H Al Ramzani 92
3 b c English Channel(USA) Mahogany Lane (USA) (A.P. Indy (USA))
893a[6] 9590a[9]

Arabic Culture (USA) *Grant Tuer* a90 85
5 b g Lonhro(AUS) Kydd Gloves (USA) (Dubai Millennium)
(181) 507[6] 784[4] (1024) 1183[2] (1508) 7003[7] 8082[2] 8727[2] 9096[2] (9274)◆ 9633[3]

Arabist *John Gosden* a77 86
3 b g Invincible Spirit(IRE) Highest (Dynaformer (USA))
2795[5] 6216[2] (6890) 8421[9]

A Racing Beauty (GER)
Henk Grewe 63
2 rg f Mastercraftsman(IRE) Anabasis (GER) (High Chaparral (IRE))
8371a[8]

Araifjan *Richard Fahey* 68
2 ch c Kyllachy Light Hearted (Green Desert (USA))
4984[7] 5913[4] 7333[4]

Araka Li (IRE) *Tim Easterby* 70
2 b g Havana Gold(IRE) Stylos Ecossais (Aqlaam)
4125[6] 4826[14] 6970[4] 7585[8]

Aramhes (FR) *Carla O'Halloran* 93
3 gr c Kendargent(FR) Anjella (GER) (Monsun (GER))
(2758a)

Arapaho (FR) *A Fabre* 95
2 b c Lope De Vega(IRE) Alzubra (Dansili)
6002a[2]

Arasugar (IRE) *Seamus Mullins* 59
2 b f Arakan(USA) Bahri Sugar (IRE) (Bahri (USA))
1416[5] 1833[5] 2338[7]

Arbalet (IRE) *Hugo Palmer* a95 108
4 gr g Dark Angel(IRE) Miss Beatrix (IRE) (Danehill Dancer (IRE))
1412[5] 2615[6] 3891[4] 4397[4] 5413[11] 6376[12] 6950[8] 7188[6]

Arbequina (IRE) *Mlle Y Vollmer* a66 59
3 b f Toronado(IRE) Dansilady (IRE) (Dansili)
6063a[6]

Arbiter *John Gosden* a68
2 gr c Kingman Approach (Darshaan)
8865[6] 9181[4] 9323[4]

Arbuckle *Michael Madgwick* a53 33
3 b g Heeraat(IRE) Attlongglast (Groom Dancer (USA))
2341[12] 3418[11] 4834[9] 5987[15]

Arcadian Rocks (IRE)
Mick Channon a48 69
3 b g Society Rock(IRE) Spirit Of Success (Invincible Spirit (IRE))
287[5] 401[6]

Arcadia Queen (AUS) *Chris Waller* 104
3 b f Pierro(AUS) Arcadia (AUS) (Redoute's Choice (AUS))
8362a[11] 8805a[5]

Arcadienne *Ralph Beckett* a59 38
3 ch f Leroidesanimaux(BRZ) Archduchess (Archipenko (USA))
2518[7] 3445[7] 4177[7] 5054[4] 6039[9] 6279[13]

Arcanada (IRE) *Tom Dascombe* a113 91
6 ch g Arcano(IRE) Bond Deal (IRE) (Pivotal)
601[5] 1103[4] 1922[9] 2832[12] 3069[9] 3867[10] (4108) 4607[7] 5991[2] 6711[10] 7142[4] 7678[3] 8184[7]

Arcavallo (IRE) *Michael Dods* a47 76
4 ch g Arcano(IRE) Pashmina (IRE) (Barathea (IRE))
3971[9] 4625[5] 5180[6] 5476[9] 6972[15] 7289[10] 8181[9] 9351[8]

Archaeology *Jedd O'Keeffe* a79 87
3 b g Charm Spirit(IRE) Shuttle Mission (Sadler's Wells (USA))
1857[2] (2395) 3683[4] 4325[5] 6425[13] 6913[2]◆ 7123[3] 7653[8] 8396[4]

Archdeacon *Dean Ivory* a59 51
3 b g Archipenko(USA) Akdarena (Hernando (FR))
802[4] 1066[9] 1358[9] 1725[5] 2517[2] (3299)◆ 8870[8] 9589[11] 9663[12]

Archer's Arrow (USA)
A bin Harmash a58 64
5 b g Lonhro(AUS) Midnight Music (IRE) (Dubawi (IRE))
97a[12]

Archer's Dream (IRE)
James Fanshawe 103
3 b f Dream Ahead(USA) Badr Al Badoor (IRE) (Acclamation)
(2077)◆ (2736)◆ (3891) 4891[9] 7073[7] (8004) 8648a[11]

Archie (IRE) *Brian Barr* a78 80
7 b g Fast Company(IRE) Winnifred (Green Desert (USA))
158[5] 364[9] 886[8] 2365[9]

Archie Bear *Mark H Tompkins*
2 b g Swiss Spirit Wolumla (IRE) (Royal Applause)
3812[17]

Archie Perkins (IRE) *Nigel Tinkler* a65 89
4 b g Arcano(IRE) Sidney Girl (Azamour (IRE))
2374[4] (3161) (3568) 3811[3] 4209[3] (4892) 6067[2] 6998[9]

Archies Lad *R Mike Smith* a38 52
3 b g Lawman(FR) Stirring Ballad (Compton Place)
1972[5] 2711[9] (3191) 4280[8] 6610[8] 6937[7] 7207[11] 7405[9] 7489[6] 8233[6]

Archie's Sister *Philip Kirby* a51 43
3 b f Archipenko(USA) Sparkling Clear (Efisio)
5742[8] 6660[5] 7314[7] 8072[4] 8344[7]

Archie Stevens *Clare Ellam* a61 48
9 b g Pastoral Pursuits Miss Wells (IRE) (Sadler's Wells (USA))
834[12]

Archimedes (IRE) *David C Griffiths* a72 73
6 b g Invincible Spirit(IRE) Waveband (Exceed And Excel (AUS))
42[6] (129) (279) 411[U] 498[2] 610[9] 707[2] 743[2] 970[8] 3206[13] 4027[3] 4213[4] 4478[3] 4494[8] 6321[2] (6503) 6699[5] (6936) 7077[17] 7334[2] 7855[8] 8023[12]

Archimento *William Knight* a89 86
6 ch g Archipenko(USA) Caribana (Hernando (FR))
1425[7] 1943[6] 3044[5] 3861[7] 4543[5] 5321[2]

Archippos *Michael Herrington* a66 73
6 b g Archipenko(USA) Sparkling Clear (Efisio)
2185[3] 2577[3] 4333[5] 5179[4] 6210[7] 9570[11]

Archi's Affaire *Michael Dods* a81 90
5 ch g Archipenko(USA) Affaire D'Amour (Hernando (FR))
3862[9] 5818[4] 6657[9] 7702[3] 9094[6]

Archive (FR) *Brian Ellison* a37 41
9 b g Sulamani(IRE) Royale Dorothy (FR) (Smadoun (FR))
124[6] 948[4] (1666) (1848) (2185) 3095[11] 4383[9]

Arch Moon *Michael Dods* 85
2 b g Sea The Moon(GER) Archduchess (Archipenko (USA))
6226[4] 7361[2] 8100[2]◆

Arch My Boy *Martin Smith* a85 84
5 b g Archipenko(USA) Fairy Slipper (Singspiel (IRE))
238[5]

Archon *Michael Easterby* a64
3 ch g Lope De Vega(IRE) Date With Destiny (IRE) (George Washington (IRE))
8294[7] 8645[7]

Arctic Chief *Richard Phillips* a70
9 b g Sleeping Indian Neiges Eternelles (FR) (Exit To Nowhere (USA))
242[4]

Arctic Fire (GER) *Denis W Cullen* 97
10 b g Soldier Hollow Adelma (GER) (Sternkoenig (IRE))
3952[6] 5508a[18]

Arctic Flower (IRE) *John Bridger* a51 56
6 gr m Roderic O'Connor(IRE) Just In Love (FR) (Highest Honor (FR))
3592[4] 3687[7] 4227[9] 5677[2] 6084[3] 6897[3] 7282[13] 7731[8] 7977[4] (8408) 8717[6] 8998[6] 9249[10]

Arctic Fox *Richard Fahey* a69 89
3 ch f Mastercraftsman(IRE) Aurora Borealis (IRE) (Montjeu (IRE))
2251[6] (2765) (3099) (3862) 4644[6] 5687[6] 6696[6]

Arctic Ocean (IRE)
Sir Michael Stoute a67 83
3 b f Camelot Hurricane Emma (USA) (Mr Greeley (USA))
2253[8] 3153[3] (3955) (4599) 5332[3]

Arctic Sea *Paul Cole* a77 78
5 bb g Oasis Dream Rainbow Dancing (Rainbow Quest (USA))
1479[3] 1659[2] 2005[5] 2797[11] 3539[5] (4737) 5858[8] 5993[6] 6804[2] (7233)

Arctic Sound *Mark Johnston* a105 109
3 b c Poet's Voice Polar Circle (USA) (Royal Academy (USA))
1830[5] 2889a[2] 7997[2] 8336[15] 9472[8]

Arctic Spirit *Ed Dunlop* a63 72
3 b f Intello(GER) Tahirah (Green Desert (USA))
1567[5] 2689[3] 4424[8] 7343[7] 7835[10]

Ardamir (FR) *Laura Mongan* a70 55
7 b g Deportivo Kiss And Cry (FR) (Nikos)
84[10] 4791[12] 5047[7]

Ardenlee Star (USA) *Richard Fahey* 83
2 b c Elusive Quality(USA) Bohemian Dance (IRE) (Dansili)
(3702) 4091[13]

Ardhoomey (IRE) *G M Lyons* a87 100
7 b g Dark Angel(IRE) Moy Joy (IRE) (Orpen (USA))
2221a[4] 3103a[4] 3818a[3] 4313a[11] 5205a[7] 6648a[8] 7241a[8]

Ardiente *Ed Vaughan* a93 87
3 b f Australia Hoyam (Royal Applause)
5141[3] (8808) 9170a[9]

Ardimento (IRE) *Rod Millman* a64 47
3 b g Roderic O'Connor(IRE) Begin The Beguine (IRE) (Peintre Celebre (USA))
251[5]◆ 534[4] 1033[8] 2582[8] 3947[7] 5677[8]

Arecibo (FR) *David O'Meara* a85 107
4 b g Invincible Spirit(IRE) Oceanique (USA) (Forest Wildcat (USA))
2117[9] 2743[16] 4379[8] (4722) 4987[2] 5371[2] 5664[13] 6351[3] 6960[2] 7193[4] 7433[8] 7889[2] 8340[10]

Areehaa (IRE) *Sir Michael Stoute* 83
2 b f Kingman Ashaaqah (IRE) (Dansili)
6846[2]

Areen Heart (FR) *David O'Meara* a98 90
5 b g Exceed And Excel(AUS) Reine Zao (FR) (Alzao (USA))
176[2] 351[3] 623[5] 856[3] 1143[2] 1388[2] 1919[5] 2061[2] 3043[6] 3347[7] 3991[5] 5434[9] 5945[5]

Arel Nova (FR) *M Delcher Sanchez* 66
2 b c Havana Gold(IRE) Elzebieta (IRE) (Monsun (GER))
6776a[10]

Argent Bleu *Roger Ingram* a37
4 b g Steele Tango(USA) Silver Marizah (IRE) (Manduro (GER))
1519[9] 3006[15] 6885[11] 7376[8] 8916[13]

Argon *Noel Wilson* a40 11
4 b g Kyllachy Cool Question (Polar Falcon (USA))
129[7] 3227[11]

Argus (IRE) *Alexandra Dunn* a85 80
7 b g Rip Van Winkle(IRE) Steel Princess (IRE) (Danehill (USA))
29[7] (833)◆ 1159[2] 3861[3] 7575[7] 8966a[4] (9184) 9537a[4]

Argyle (IRE) *Gary Moore* a64 65
6 gr g Lawman(FR) All Hallows (IRE) (Dalakhani (IRE))
369[3] 731[3]

Argyron (IRE) *A Fabre* 99
3 ch g Iffraaj Alkania (Dalakhani (IRE))
1347a[3] 3789a[5] 7478a[6] 8445a[2] 8980a[10]

Aria Rose *Harry Whittington* a48 60
4 b g Cityscape Leelu (Largesse)
2970[6] 4308[3] 5499[2] 6077[7]

Arietta *Jonathan Portman* a60
2 b f Casamento(IRE) Air Biscuit (IRE) (Galileo (IRE))
9063[9] 9327[8] 9668[6]

Ariette Du Rue (USA) *Ed Vaughan* a60 52
3 b f Street Sense(USA) Fastbridled (USA) (Unbridled's Song (USA))
1742a[6] 7472[6] 9132[12]

Arigato *William Jarvis* a80 87
4 b g Poet's Voice Xtrasensory (Royal Applause)
2803[6] 3313[7]◆ 4249[4] 4837[2] (5383) 6516[3] 6964[6] 8498[7]

Arij (IRE) *Simon Crisford* a49 66
2 b g Charm Spirit(IRE) Aquarelliste (FR) (Danehill (USA))
7972[6] 8504[9]

Arise (FR) *M Delzangles* 84
3 b c Makfi Sundancer (Hernando (FR))
(6062a)

Arishka (IRE) *Daniel Kubler* a71 76
3 b f Dandy Man(IRE) Symbol Of Peace (IRE) (Desert Sun)
406[2] 550[9] (1275)◆ (1954) 2489[2] 3159[6] 7771[10] 8715[12] 9218[10] 9473[9]

Aristia (AUS)
Mathew Ellerton & Simon Zahra 106
3 b f Lonhro(AUS) Nakaaya (AUS) (Tiger Hill (IRE))
8952a[10]

Aristocracy *John O'Shea* 3
8 b g Royal Applause Pure Speculation (Salse (USA))
2718[11]

Aristocratic Lady (IRE)
Simon Crisford 74
3 b f Invincible Spirit(IRE) Dubai Queen (USA) (Kingmambo (USA))
1855[4] 2366[2]

Arizona (IRE) *A P O'Brien* 117
2 b c No Nay Never(USA) Lady Ederle (USA) (English Channel (USA))
(3949) 6264a[4] 7245a[3] 8113[2] 8746a[5]

Arklow (USA) *Brad H Cox* a96 113
5 b h Arch(USA) Unbridled Empire (USA) (Empire Maker (USA))
2646a[2] 3561a[2] 8776a[8]

Arlecchino's Arc (IRE) *Mark Usher* a62 51
4 ch g Arcano(IRE) Sir Cecil's Girl (IRE) (Thunder Gulch (USA))
58[2] 363[7] 736[3] (983) (1546) 3006[6] 3633[10] 4232[12] 8000[8] 8703[6] 9090[2] (9444)

Arlecchino's Leap *Mark Usher* a65 62
7 br g Kheleyf(USA) Donna Giovanna (Mozart (IRE))
914[5] 1164[11] 1511[5] 2124[5] 2596[4]◆ 3002[5] 4194[5] 5309[7] 5807[9] 7084[9] 8345[8] 9503[9]

Arletta Star *Tim Easterby* 75
3 b f Bated Breath Winfred Jo (Bahamian Bounty)
1894[4]◆ 2371[5] 2896[2] 3202[7] (3923) 4831[2] 5030[3] (5419) 5844[4]

Armandihan (IRE) *Kevin Ryan* a80 86
5 b g Zoffany(IRE) Flying Flag (IRE) (Entrepreneur)
1461[11] 1761[9] 2748[2] 3222[8] 4241[8] 4892[11]

Armed (IRE) *Phillip Makin* a69 68
4 b g Invincible Spirit(IRE) Ange Bleu (USA) (Alleged (USA))
1771[6] 3095[8] 5970[9] 6700[10] 7305[4]◆ 8087[8]

Armen Basc (FR) *A Junk* 69
3 b g Top Trip Crystale Basc (FR) (Martaline)
7291a[6]

Armorial (FR) *Enrique Leon Penate* a62 83
4 b h Maxios Blue Fern (USA) (Woodman (USA))
4418a[9]

Armory (IRE) *A P O'Brien* 111
2 b c Galileo(IRE) After (IRE) (Danehill Dancer (IRE))
(5362a) (6430a) 7245a[2] 7940a[3] 8588a[2]

Arms Of The Angel (GER)
Mark Johnston a66 66
3 ch f Jukebox Jury(IRE) Ange Doree (FR) (Sinyar (IRE))
3926[8] 4005[5] 4587[3]◆ 4834[2] 4983[P]

Arnold *Ann Duffield* a66 65
5 b g Equiano(FR) Azurinta (IRE) (Azamour (IRE))
2433[10] 3452[2] 5094[10] 5515[4] 6503[8] 7823[10] 8429[7]◆ 8720[3]

Arnoul Of Metz *Henry Spiller* a60 60
4 b g Kyllachy Appointee (IRE) (Exceed And Excel (AUS))
1820[11] 2678[2] 3144[3] 4182[5] 4765[2] 6126[10] 7214[3] 7824[10] 8450[9]

Arod (IRE) *David Simcock* a100 114
8 b h Teofilo(IRE) My Personal Space (USA) (Rahy (USA))
51a[16] 395a[9]

Arogo *Kevin Ryan* 54
3 b g Iffraaj Chocolate Hills (FR) (Exceed And Excel (AUS))
2635[12] 4149[8] 5486[6] 7367[14]

Aroha (IRE) *Brian Meehan* a80 102
2 b f Kodiac Surrey Storm (Montjeu (IRE))
2138[4] 2767[2] 3033[4] 4048[3] 5411[2] 6264a[6] 6966[7] 8724[7]

Arranmore *J S Bolger* 84
2 b g Oasis Dream Ceisteach (IRE) (New Approach (IRE))
6690a[11] 8164a[8]

Arretez La Musique (FR) *J-L Bara* a3
4 gr g Kendargent(FR) Marie De Blois (IRE) (Barathea (IRE))
76a[13]

Arriba Arriba (IRE)
Rebecca Menzies 72
2 ch c Outstrip Lady Atlas (Dutch Art)
3477[5] 4509[3] 6254[2] 6822[6] (7046)

Arriba De Toda (IRE) *Brian Ellison* a48 52
3 b g Gale Force Ten Luxuria (IRE) (Kheleyf (USA))
228[2] 585[8] 612[7] 1084[6] 1957[11] 2325[5] 4129[6] 4518[3] 5272[5] 5389[3] 5842[2] 6569[4]

Arriviste *Rae Guest* a75 56
2 b f Sea The Moon(GER) Apparatchika (Archipenko (USA))
8510[6] 9197[3] (9409)◆

Arroway (USA) *S bin Ghadayer* a80 71
4 ch h Kitten's Joy(USA) Shinyshots (USA) (Orientate (USA))
1001[7] 1322a[10]

Arrowtown *Michael Easterby* a75 98
7 b m Rail Link Protectress (Hector Protector (USA))
6958[9] 7403[8] 8129[4] 8399[2]

Arrowzone *Katy Price* a49 62
8 b g Iffraaj Donna Giovanna (Mozart (IRE))
120[3] (348) 465[5] 1015[11] 1836[6] 5497[7] 6731[11] 6977[9] 8466[9] 8667[10] 8915[14]

Ar Saoirse *Clare Hobson* a49 43
4 b g Pastoral Pursuits Tindomiel (Bertolini (USA))
2527[10] 3143[5] 3320[5] 3961[5] 4500[5] 7606[11] 7838[12]

Artair (IRE) *Michael Bell* a77 75
3 b g Kodiac Bonnie Lesley (IRE) (Iffraaj)
(142)

Artarmon (IRE) *Michael Bell* a94 94
4 b g So You Think(NZ) Aljumar (IRE) (Marju (IRE))
1947[14] 2801[10] (4505) 4899[6]

Art Collection (FR)
Andrew Hollinshead a95 87
6 b g Shakespearean(IRE) Renascent Rahy (Rahy (USA))
2648a[4] 5715a[10]

Art Du Val *Charlie Appleby* 106
3 b g No Nay Never(USA) Aquarelle Rare (Rainbow Quest (USA))
(727a) (4428a) 5609[7]

Art Echo *John Mackie* a63 61
6 b g Art Connoisseur(IRE) Madhaaq (IRE) (Medicean)
1563[7] 2076[13] 3781[7] 4455[3] 5282[4] 7604[4]

Arthalot (IRE) *Karen George* 63
2 b g Camelot Annina (IRE) (Singspiel (IRE))
7235[7] 7972[10] 8244[6]

Arthurian Fable (IRE)
Brian Meehan 84
2 ch c Sea The Stars(IRE) Abstain (Araafa (IRE))
7338[10] 7897[2] 8461[3]

Arthurian Fame (IRE)
Joseph Patrick O'Brien a86 101
4 b g Camelot Wishing (Danehill Dancer (IRE))
4053[9]

Arthur Kitt *Tom Dascombe* 108
3 b c Camelot Ceiling Kitty (Red Clubs (IRE))
2031[5] 2523[6] 3646[2] 4013[6] 5484a[6]

Arthur Pendragon (IRE)
Brian Meehan a54 76
3 b c Camelot First Of Many (Darshaan)
1558[4] 1898[3] 3699[7] 4327[5] 4862[5] 5426[2] 6030[10] 6642[3] 8246[11]

Arthur's Court (IRE) *Hugo Palmer* a72 81
2 b g Camelot Logjam (IRE) (Royal Academy (USA))
2973[7] 4117[4] 5212[3] (6020) 6942[4] 7612[9]

Arthur Shelby *David C Griffiths* a25
3 ch g Arakan(USA) Ambonnay (Ashkalani (IRE))
7303[7] 8947[4]

Arthur's Kingdom (IRE) *A P O'Brien* 104
2 b c Camelot Madeira Mist (IRE) (Grand Lodge (USA))
8582a[2]

Arthurs Secret *Sandy Thomson* a67 71
9 ch g Sakhee's Secret Angry Bark (USA) (Woodman (USA))
8236[5]

Artic Nel *Ian Williams* a36 52
5 ch m Haafhd Artic Bliss (Fraam)
2283[10] 3769[2] 4435[5] 5029[3] 5435[9] 5596[7]

Artificier (USA) *Alain Couetil* a80 85
7 ch h Lemon Drop Kid(USA) Quiet Royal (USA) (Royal Academy (USA))
7536a[12]

Artistic Language *Brian Meehan* 76
3 b g Archipenko(USA) Kiswahili (Selkirk (USA))
1645[6] 2096[7] 3295[2] 3604[4] 5385[2]

Artistic Rifles (IRE) *Charles Hills* a73 89
3 b c War Command(USA) Chatham Islands (USA) (Elusive Quality (USA))
2510[3] (2821) (3340) 3858[6] 4851[7] 5666[10]

Artistic Streak *Donald McCain* 66
3 b f New Approach(IRE) Artisti (Cape Cross (IRE))
1828[3] 2524[8] 3264[6] 4602[7] 6101[7] 6624[4]

Art Of Almost (USA)
Roger L Attfield 104
3 bb f Dansili Reimpose (USA) (First Defence (USA))
6993a[7]

Art Of Diplomacy *Michael Easterby* a62 73
3 b g Archipenko(USA) Rowlestone Express (Rail Link)
405[5]◆ 6544[4] (7493) 8098[13]

Art Of Swing (IRE) *Lee Carter* a56 52
7 b g Excellent Art Shahmina (IRE) (Danehill (USA))
619[11] 923[11] 1506[6] 1680[10]

Art Of Unity *John James Feane* a72 76
4 ch g Mazameer(IRE) Vintage Steps (IRE) (Bahamian Bounty)
(4911)◆

Artois *Alexandra Dunn* a43 49
3 gr g Mizzen Mast(USA) Intercontinental (Danehill (USA))
4076[7] 4639[12] 9561[9]

Artplace (IRE) *F Rossi* a70 52
9 b g Teofilo(IRE) Ginostra (Oasis Dream)
4532a[9]

Art Power (IRE) *Tim Easterby* a65 93
2 gr c Dark Angel(IRE) Evening Time (IRE) (Keltos (FR))
6943[3]◆ (8097)◆

Art Song (USA) *Charlie Appleby* a81 91
3 b g Scat Daddy(USA) Practice (USA) (Smart Strike (CAN))
5627[4]

Arty Campbell (IRE)
Bernard Llewellyn a67 75
9 b g Dylan Thomas(IRE) Kincob (USA) (Kingmambo (USA))
2578[8] 4146[7] 4483[5] 5047[5] 5496[2] 6105[6] (6366) 7033[7]

Arusha (FR) *P Decouz* a81 94
4 gr m Zanzibari(USA) Downland (USA) (El Prado (IRE))
1627a[11]

Arvensis *Hughie Morrison* a34
3 b f Sir Percy Raindrop (Primo Dominie)
1236[10] 1677[9] 2009[8]

Aryaaf (IRE) *Simon Crisford* a62 73
2 b f Kodiac Pivotal Era (Pivotal)
4006[4] 4583[4] 5794[2] (6557)◆ 6980[9] 8315[5]

Arzaak (IRE) *Charlie Wallis* a77 61
5 br g Casamento(IRE) Dixieland Kiss (USA) (Dixie Union (USA))
981[6] 1194[6] 1547[7] 2227[6] 4374[8] 5027[6] 5532[U] 6562[6] 7274[3] 7690[6] 8401[2] 8643[6] 9335[4]

Asad (IRE) *Simon Crisford* 76
3 ch c Lope De Vega(IRE) Venus De Milo (IRE) (Duke Of Marmalade (IRE))
2120[3]

Ascended (IRE) *William Haggas* a83 67
3 gr f Dark Angel(IRE) Mamma Morton (IRE) (Elnadim (USA))
(3431) 4119[4] 5573[7] 7206[4] 8025[5] 8304[5] 8712[13]

Ascension *Roger Varian* a83 86
2 gr c Dark Angel(IRE) Making Eyes (IRE) (Dansili)
5131[11] (6078) (6943)◆ 8110[4]

Ascot Angel (FR) *Jane Soubagne* a53 88
5 b g Dark Angel(IRE) Lady Ascot (IRE) (Excellent Art)
(2226a) 4860a[2] 5643a[10]

Ascot Day (FR) *Bernard Llewellyn* a61 77
5 ch g Soave(GER) Allez Hongkong (GER) (Sakhee (USA))
1463[11] 1826[5] 2353[3] (2720) 3155[3] 3571[2] 3847[8] (6104) 6511[4] 7294[5] 7683[11] 8248[6]

Ascot Dreamer *David Brown* a62 64
3 ch f Kyllachy Skirrid (Halling (USA))
834[7] 1081[4]◆ 1337[3] 1384[2] (1982) 2293[4] 2870[2] 3202[4] 4328[10] 4519[12] 5330[10] 5857[7] 6897[5] 7286[16]

Ascot Week (USA) *John Quinn* a77 77
5 br g Lonhro(AUS) Millenia (Unfuwain (USA))
1660[4] 2244[4] 2512[10] 3177[2] (4728) 5087[7] 5560[3] 7074[5] 7364[2] 9109[2] 9512[12]

Ascraeus *Andrew Balding* 61
2 b f Poet's Voice Sciacca (IRE) (Royal Applause)
6906[9] 7826[5]

Asdaa (IRE) *Mark Johnston* a90 85
3 b g Dutch Art Danseuse De Reve (IRE) (Invincible Spirit (IRE))
9334[4]◆ 9517[3]

Asensio *Mohamed Moubarak* a57 63
3 b g Sepoy(AUS) Wind Surf (USA) (Lil's Lad (USA))
4121[8] 4806[5] 5552[9] 6279[4] 6635[7] 7290[7] 7817[14]

Asfurasagira (IRE) *Owen Burrows* 56
2 ch f Night Of Thunder(IRE) Oriental Melody (IRE) (Sakhee (USA))
3194[4]◆

Ashazuri *Jonathan Portman* a70 78
5 b m Dick Turpin(IRE) Shesha Bear (Tobougg (IRE))
(2230) 2612[5] (3264) 4548[3]◆ (5091) 5571[9] 6535[5] 7026[6] 8014[8]

Ashington *John Quinn* a69 89
4 b g Canford Cliffs(IRE) Kadoma (Danehill Dancer (IRE))
1927[11] 2786[5] 3600[6] 5966[7]

Ashpan Sam *David W Drinkwater* a55 88
10 b g Firebreak Sweet Patoopie (Indian Ridge (IRE))
3347[14] 4545[3] 4835[2]

Ashrun (FR) *A Wohler* a57 111
3 b c Authorized(IRE) Ashantee (GER) (Areion (GER))
(5718a) 6771a[8] 7927a[5] 8792a[3]

Ashtara (USA) *A De Royer-Dupre* 98
3 b f Gio Ponti(USA) Ashiyla (FR) (Rock Of Gibraltar (IRE))
4416a[5]

Ashwagandha (FR) *K Borgel* a47 42
3 gr f Palace Episode(USA) Et Pourtant (FR) (Linamix (FR))
955a[7]

Asian Angel (IRE) *Mark Johnston* a94 90
3 b g Dark Angel(IRE) Chiang Mai (IRE) (Sadler's Wells (USA))
3647[2]◆ (4057)◆ 4187[3] 5149[4] 5240[2] 5614[10] 5931[6] 6255[4] 6842[3]◆ 7577[2] (7872) 8350[7]

Ask Me Not (IRE) *F Vermeulen* a79 82
2 ch c Anjaal Dangerous Duo (IRE) (Intikhab (USA))
(1709a) 5116a[11]

Asknotwhat (IRE) *Tom Gretton* a45 55
8 ch g Dylan Thomas(IRE) Princess Roseburg (USA) (Johannesburg (USA))
2970[9] 3205[P]

Ask Siri (IRE) *John Bridger* a47 36
2 br f Clodovil(IRE) Coy (IRE) (Danehill (USA))
2362[5] 2918[12] 4798[8] 5313[3] 5958[10] 6604[6] 8409[9] 8824[5] 9212[3]

Ask The Guru *Michael Attwater* a46 44
9 b g Ishiguru(USA) Tharwa (IRE) (Last Tycoon)
286[6] 986[7] 2924[5] 4027[10] 5884[4] 6285[6] 7844[8] 9664[9]

Asmund (IRE) *K R Burke* a81 80
2 b g Zebedee Suffer Her (IRE) (Whipper (USA))
3810[2] 4237[2] 4910[2] 5612[7] 7399[3] 8026[2] 8318[3] (8816) 9043[3]

Asoof *Saeed bin Suroor* a70 101
4 b m Dubawi(IRE) Lady's Purse (Doyen (IRE))
283a[2] 728a[4] 7075[4]

Aspen Belle (IRE) *Patrick Martin* 86
6 b m Roderic O'Connor(IRE) Silk City (IRE) (Barathea (IRE))
6986a[7]

Aspetar (FR) *Roger Charlton* 117
4 b g Al Kazeem Bella Qatara (IRE) (Dansili)
1750[2] 2428a[5] (3389a) 4430a[4] (7500a) 9376a[13]

Aspettatemi (ITY) *D Grilli* 100
5 ch h Red Rocks(IRE) Fly Queen (Dashing Blade)
3643a[5]

Aspiration (IRE) *Martyn Meade* 63
2 b f Footstepsinthesand Van De Cappelle (IRE) (Pivotal)
6906[7]

Aspire Tower (IRE) *Steve Gollings* a90 91
3 b g Born To Sea(IRE) Red Planet (Pivotal)
2446[5] 3358[3] 4063[3] 5121[3]◆ 5931[3]

Aspiring Diva *Mohamed Moubarak* a23 42
3 b f Sepoy(AUS) Spritzeria (Bigstone (IRE))
5808[12] 6169[6] 6811[8]

Assayer (IRE) *Richard Fahey* a67
2 b f Galileo(IRE) Fix (NZ) (Iffraaj)
9046[4]

Assembled *Hugo Palmer* a77 78
3 gr g Iffraaj Bezique (Cape Cross (IRE))
2507[3] 3306[4] (4189) 4902[9] 5445[3] 6129[4] 7907[9] 8498[5]

Assembly Of Truth (IRE)
David Evans a64 50
3 b f Shamardal(USA) Flame Of Gibraltar (IRE) (Rock Of Gibraltar (IRE))
6638[6]

Assier *Simone Brogi* 76
2 b c Invincible Spirit(IRE) Gameday (Zamindar (USA))
(5759a) 6251a[6]

Assimilation (IRE) *Ed Walker* a93 75
3 b g Xtension(IRE) Park Glen (IRE) (Tagula (IRE))
359[2] 733[2] 1212[2]◆ 1345[2] 3051[4] 4338[8] (5002) 5777[3] 6318[6] (7856)◆ (9440)

Assiro *R Biondi* 109
4 b h Declaration Of War(USA) T'As D'Beaux Yeux (Red Ransom (USA))
(2885a) (4173a)

Asstech (IRE) *Richard Fahey* a54 69
2 b g Ivawood(IRE) Beyond Belief (IRE) (Sadler's Wells (USA))
3265[7] 5125[6]◆ 5856[8] 8430[11] 9515[14]

Assurance (IRE) *J S Bolger* a76 91
2 b f Teofilo(IRE) Gearanai (USA) (Toccet (USA))
7244a[9]

A Star Above *William Haggas* a69
2 b c Sea The Stars(IRE) Loveisallyouneed (IRE) (Sadler's Wells (USA))
9154[8] 9634[3]

Asterios (FR) *M Delzangles* 84
3 bl g Maxios Asteria (FR) (Orpen (USA))
(3712a)

Astonished (IRE) *James Tate* a89 62
4 ch m Sea The Stars(IRE) An Saincheann (IRE) (Dylan Thomas (IRE))
1400[3] 1941[14] 2966[4] 3880[8] (4643)

Astraea *Michael Easterby* a66 58
4 b m Cityscape Rapid Revalation (USA) (Bianconi (USA))
279[6] 926[7] 1021[12] 1505[4] 2215[10] 5722[14] 5857[8] 6277[7] 6503[10] 7051[U]

Astral Girl *Hughie Morrison* a59 57
3 ch f Intello(GER) Celestial Girl (Dubai Destination (USA))
3495[12] 4022[10] 5048[4] 6636[6] 7573[3] (Dead)

Astrogem *James Eustace* 66
2 b f Equiano(FR) Astromancer (USA) (Silver Hawk (USA))
8458[4]

Astro Jakk (IRE) *K R Burke* a91 83
3 b g Zoffany(IRE) By The Edge (IRE) (Shinko Forest (IRE))
(1427)◆ 1862[2] 2397[2] 8921[11] 9334[8]

Astrojewel *Mark H Tompkins* a63 23
4 b m Havana Gold(IRE) Astrolibra (Sakhee (USA))
830[14] 1368[14] 2256[12]

Astrologer *David O'Meara* a77 93
3 ch f Intello(GER) Starscope (Selkirk (USA))
1838[2] 2236[3] (2713) (3552) 4242[11] 4980[3] 5459[6] (6408) 6974[3] 7463[4]

Astrologist (IRE) *Olly Murphy* a74 55
4 b g Sea The Stars(IRE) Jumooh (Monsun (GER))
552[3]◆

Astromachia *Amanda Perrett* a100 92
4 b g Sea The Stars(IRE) Fontley (Sadler's Wells (USA))
7294[2] (8654)◆ 9419[2]

Astroman *James Eustace* a61 30
2 b c Garswood Mega (IRE) (Petardia)
4117[7] 9451[4]

Astromerry *Mark H Tompkins* a26 20
3 br f Farhh Astrodonna (Carnival Dancer)
358[8]

Astronomer (IRE) *M F De Kock* a102 114
4 b h Galileo(IRE) Like A Dame (Danehill (USA))
514a[11] 730a[14]

Astrophysics *Lynn Siddall* a62 66
7 ch g Paco Boy(IRE) Jodrell Bank (IRE) (Observatory (USA))
28[7] 277[3] 2876[7] 3227[4] 4037[8] 4212[3] 5478[4] 5722[11] 5952[3] 6659[8] 7588[4] (7737) 8183[8] 8632[3] 8861[6]

Astrosamantha (FR) *A Giorgi* 45
2 gr f Kendargent(FR) Pam Pam (FR) (King's Best (USA))
3562a[10]

Astrosparkle *Mark H Tompkins* a32
3 b f Dunaden(FR) Astrodiva (Where Or When (IRE))
403[7] 858[7]

Astrospeed (IRE) *James Fanshawe* a76 60
4 ch g Choisir(AUS) Angel Stevens (IRE) (Hawk Wing (USA))
(243) (944)◆ 1560[8] 6350[7] 7519[11] 8471[9]

Astrozone *Bryan Smart* a67 66
2 ch f Fast Company(IRE) Rhal (IRE) (Rahy (USA))
6096[6] 6585[2]◆ 7333[3] 8841[2]◆ 9499[3] (9641)

Astute Boy (IRE) *R Mike Smith* a60 61
5 b g Arcano(IRE) Spa (Sadler's Wells (USA))
7436[12] 8236[9]

A Sure Welcome *John Spearing* a80 86
5 b g Pastoral Pursuits Croeso Bach (Bertolini (USA))
(187) 317[2]◆ 471[3] 790[5] 907[3]◆ (1023) 1342[10] 2107[5] 2515[3] (3576)◆ 4213[2] 5318[8] 5606[4] (6110) 6525[2] 6916[13]

Aswaat *John Gosden* a66
2 b f Muhaarar Hedaaya (IRE) (Indian Ridge (IRE))
8849[7] 9327[4]

Atalanta Breeze *Marcus Tregoning* a46 59
3 b f Champs Elysees Craighall (Dubawi (IRE))
(7025) 7817[8]

Atalanta Queen *Robyn Brisland* a57 55
4 b m Canford Cliffs(IRE) Champagne Aerial (IRE) (Night Shift (USA))
53[9] 809[13] 1060[12] (1527) (2298) 3208[2] 3730[3] 4115[6] 6173[7] 6546[9] 7385[3] (8068) 8405[2] 8903[6]

Atalanta's Boy *David Menuisier* 89
4 b g Paco Boy(IRE) Affirmatively (Diktat)
1649[4] 2076[6] (3014) (5330) 6109[6] (7564) 8522[9]

Ateescomponent (IRE)
David Barron a52 58
3 b g Shirocco(GER) Hula Ballew (Weldnaas (USA))
2713[11] 3200[6] 3926[10] 4990[10] 5915[11]

Athabasca (IRE) *Grant Tuer* a65 53
2 b f Nathaniel(IRE) Sibaya (Exceed And Excel (AUS))
8338[9] 8714[5]

Athassel *David Evans* a58 55
10 ch g Dalakhani(IRE) Hope Island (IRE) (Titus Livius (FR))
53[5] 365[10]◆ 484[12] 719[6]

Atheeb *Sir Michael Stoute* a80 80
2 b c Muhaarar Lady Francesca (Montjeu (IRE))
4069[6] 5172[2] (5848) 7429[6] 8252[3]◆

Athmad (IRE) *Brian Meehan* 86
3 b g Olympic Glory(IRE) Black Mascara (IRE) (Authorized (IRE))
3599[10] 4360[5] 4669[6] 5140[4] 5776[6] 6671[4] 7782[10]

Athollblair Boy (IRE) *Nigel Tinkler* a87 89
6 ch g Frozen Power(IRE) Elixell (IRE) (Exceed And Excel (AUS))
24[3] (214) 407[3] 786[2] 952[3] 1487[3]◆ 1977[4] 2416[3] 2824[4] 4103[3] (4365) 5058[4] 7121[2]◆ 7310[2] 8425[10]

A Thread Of Blue (USA)
Kiaran McLaughlin 105
3 bb c Hard Spun(USA) Enthused (USA) (Seeking The Gold (USA))
6994a[4]

Atlanta (GER) *Dr A Bolte* 95
6 b m Sholokhov(IRE) Altstadt (GER) (Alkalde (GER))
6747a[6] 8587a[3]

Atlantica (FR) *Stephane Chevalier* 68
2 b f Palace Episode(USA) Arrivederla (IRE) (Acclamation)
3562a[3] 5713a[4]

Atlantic City (IRE) *Sylvester Kirk* a22
3 b g Battle Of Marengo(IRE) Autumn Tide (IRE) (Jeremy (USA))
1019[10]

Atlantic Crossing (IRE) *Paul Cole* 65
2 b c Mukhadram Ghizlaan (USA) (Seeking The Gold (USA))
3419[5]◆

Atlantic King (GER) *Kevin Bishop*
6 b g King's Best(USA) Atlantic High (Nashwan (USA))
3571[12]

Atlas (IRE) *Denis Gerard Hogan* a80 81
6 b g Acclamation Sheer Bliss (IRE) (Sadler's Wells (USA))
5537a[5]

Atletico (IRE) *David Evans* a84 75
7 b g Kodiac Queenofthefairies (Pivotal)
127[10] 382[8] 588[9] 762[6] 909[6] 1097[10] 1294[8] 1561[6] 1881[8] 2203[2] 2847[3] 3214[3] 3496[2] 4523[4] 5020[2] 5283[6] 5945[8] 6518[2] 6968[2] 7386[2] 7678[12] 8289[7] 8893[6] 9283[5] 9455[8]

Atmospheric *Clive Cox* 75
2 b f Night Of Thunder(IRE) Havergate (Dansili)
3076[3] 4254[3] 5189[9] 6369[6]

Atocha (FR) *M Delcher Sanchez* 69
2 b c Dream Ahead(USA) Azalee (IRE) (Peintre Celebre (USA))
8330a[5]

Atom Hearth Mother (IRE) *A Botti* 102
3 b c Rock Of Gibraltar(IRE) Altezza Reale (King's Best (USA))
2887a[11]

Atomic Jack *George Baker* a75 75
4 b g Nathaniel(IRE) Indigo River (IRE) (Kodiac)
(619)◆ 731[2] 991[2] 1330[5] 3044[7] (3693) 4791[6] 5047[2] 6105[4]

At Peace (IRE) *John Quinn* 49
3 b f Australia Cherrington (IRE) (Lope De Vega (IRE))
3247[6]◆ 3707[9] 4277[5]

Attain *Archie Watson* a62 59
10 b g Dansili Achieve (Rainbow Quest (USA))
262[3]◆ 404[2] 859[9] 965[4] 1183[9] 1333[5] 1463[14] 1498[3] 1710[2] 1983[11] 2233[9] 2698[9] 9005[8] 9312[6] 9553[5]

Attainment *James Tate* a97 79
3 ch g Exceed And Excel(AUS) Wahylah (IRE) (Shamardal (USA))
1685[2]◆ 1846[3] 3465[9] 4338[6] (5267) 6076[4] (6440) (7191) 7815[7] 8320[10]

Attentionadventure *J Phelippon* a66 100
8 b g Poseidon Adventure(IRE) Akilinda (GER) (Monsun (GER))
(7860a) 9537a[2]

Attention Seaker *Tim Easterby* 73
9 b m Bollin Eric Pay Attention (Revoque (IRE))
2591[10] 3294[3] 3653[11] 3886[5] 5487[4]

Attirance (FR) *N Clement* 78
3 gr f Slickly(FR) Gracieuse (IRE) (Muhtathir)
2265a[4]

Attorney General *Ed Vaughan* 71
3 b g Dream Ahead(USA) Avodale (IRE) (Lawman (FR))
2900[5] 4010[2] (4800)

Atty Persse (IRE)
Enrique Leon Penate a74 91
5 b g Frankel Dorcas Lane (Norse Dancer (IRE))
4418a[12] 6145a[3] 8375a[9]

Atty's Edge *Christopher Mason* a57 64
3 b g Coach House(IRE) Belle's Edge (Danehill Dancer (IRE))
2772[12] 4874[8] 5799[6] 6365[2] (7112) 7568[5] 8401[6] 8861[4]

Atwaar *Charles Smith* a58 51
3 b f Slade Power(IRE) Musharakaat (IRE) (Iffraaj)
388[4] 831[6] 1863[5] 2708[9] 3319[6] 7628[8] 7838[5] 8689[3] (8901) (9160) 9643[2]◆

At War (IRE) *Thomas Cooper* a75 70
2 b g War Command(USA) La Vita E Bella (IRE) (Definite Article)
5710a[8]

Atyaaf *Derek Shaw* a61 61
4 b g Invincible Spirit(IRE) Eshaadeh (USA) (Storm Cat (USA))
27[9] 597[5] (848) 1210[3] 1335[8] 1716[3] 1987[3] 2632[16] 4132[4]◆ 4307[5] 5018[2] 5629[10] 5986[5] (6099) 6699[7]

At Your Service *Chelsea Banham* a57 68
5 b g Frankel Crystal Gaze (IRE) (Rainbow Quest (USA))
(383) 1265[9] 1590[6] 2846[11] 7823[3] 8917[5] 9406[5]

Aubevoye (FR) *J-C Rouget* a101 105
4 b h Le Havre(IRE) Keira (FR) (Turtle Bowl (IRE))
682a[6] 5926a[7]

Aubretia (IRE) *Richard Hannon* a59 73
3 ch f Poet's Voice Abilene (Samum (GER))
4119[2] 4828[5] 5307[6] 5779[13] 6569[6] 7272[4] 7999[3] 8499[7]

Auchterarder (IRE) *Mark Johnston* a84 80
2 b f Gleneagles(IRE) Crossover (Cape Cross (IRE))
(2706)◆ 8899[2] (9036) 9364[3]◆

Auckland Lodge (IRE) *Ben Haslam* a73 78
2 ch f Dandy Man(IRE) Proud Maria (IRE) (Medicean)
3997[5] (4237) 4889[4] 6032[4] (6822) (7440) 8817[4]

Audarya (FR) *James Fanshawe* a80 101
3 b f Wootton Bassett Green Bananas (FR) (Green Tune (USA))
2583[2] 3277[2] (4076) 5458[5] (6406) 7360a[2]

Audible (USA) *Todd Pletcher* a120
4 b h Into Mischief(USA) Blue Devil Bel (USA) (Gilded Time (USA))
445a[5] 1447a[5]

Audio *Richard Hannon* a83 77
2 b g Equiano(FR) Naayla (IRE) (Invincible Spirit (IRE))
1937[3] 2228[3] 2716[3] 3039[4] 4798[3] 5185[10] (5602) 6029[2] 6852[2] (7369) 8219[2] 9162[12]

Augustine (FR) *Louis Baudron* a63 89
2 b f Elusive City(USA) Augusta Lucilla (USA) (Mr Greeley (USA))
5116a[5]

Augustus Caesar (USA)
David O'Meara a77 62
2 ch c Speightstown(USA) Endless Light (Pivotal)
5197[5] 5472[3] 6548[2]◆ (7556) 9499[7]

Auld Boy (USA) *J S Moore*
3 bb g Speightstown(USA) Ilikecandy (USA) (Malibu Moon (USA))
5057[13]

Auntie June *Roy Brotherton* a32
3 ch f Piccolo Basle (Trade Fair)
6119[8] 6802[5] 8672[6] 9287[10] 9445[13]

Aurelius In Love (IRE)
Luciano Vitabile 100
2 gr c Alhebayeb(IRE) Harranda (IRE) (Red Ransom (USA))
(8789a)

Aurum (IRE) *Charlie Appleby* 74
4 b h Exceed And Excel(AUS) Rachelle (IRE) (Mark Of Esteem (IRE))
52a[12] 847a[15]

Aussie Breeze *Tom George* a53 53
3 ch f Australia Terre Du Vent (FR) (Kutub (IRE))
5378[4] 6367[2]◆ 6982[6] 8081[2]

Aussie Lyrics (FR) *Mrs C Gilbert* a60 67
9 gr g Aussie Rules(USA) Operam (Kris)
4686a[4] (6010a) 6554a[3]

Aussie Showstopper (FR)
Richard Hughes a75 86
2 b c Showcasing Aristotelicienne (IRE) (Acclamation)
(4246) 4610[6] 5542[P] (Dead)

Aussie Valentine (IRE)
Adrian McGuinness a94 92
8 b g Aussie Rules(USA) Love Valentine (IRE) (Fruits Of Love (USA))
1308a[18] 5535a[10] 6693a[18]

Aussie View (IRE)
George Margarson a68 82
3 b f Australia Dingle View (IRE) (Mujadil (USA))
2399[4] 5749[5] 6410[5]

Aust Ferry *Eve Johnson Houghton* a49 58
2 b f Avonbridge Spennymoor (IRE) (Exceed And Excel (AUS))
3441[7] 3835[7] 4557[7]◆ 5313[7]

Austin Taetious *Adam West* a40
2 b g Archipenko(USA) Akdarena (Hernando (FR))
3274[P] 3644[15] 4832[P] 6185[7] 6927[9] 7516[12] 7910[7] 8493[11]

Australis (IRE) *Roger Varian* a86 82
3 b g Australia Quiet Down (USA) (Quiet American (USA))
1824[10] 2505[2] 2875[5] 4803[2]◆ 5452[4] 6224[2] (7108) 8120[2]◆

Austrian School (IRE)
Mark Johnston a112 114
4 b h Teofilo(IRE) Swiss Roll (IRE) (Entrepreneur)
(1947) 2575[9] 3024[3] 3864[4]◆ 4382[9] 7615[2]

Authorative (IRE) *Anthony McCann* a12 17
9 b g Refuse To Bend(IRE) Reasonably Devout (CAN) (St Jovite (USA))
8347[13]

Author's Dream *William Knight* a85 77
6 gr g Authorized(IRE) Spring Dream (IRE) (Kalanisi (IRE))
5812[4]◆

Autocrat (FR) *E Libaud* a69 76
5 ch g Vision D'Etat(FR) Abyaan (IRE) (Ela-Mana-Mou)
1245a[9]

Autretot (FR) *David O'Meara* a88 82
4 b g Youmzain(IRE) Great Queen (FR) (King's Best (USA))
2057[4] 2842[5] 3161[3] (4333) 4689[8] 5436[4] 7577[3] 8082[6]

Autumn (FR) *Henk Grewe* 79
2 b c Outstrip Abandagold (IRE) (Orpen (USA))
1448a[7]

Autumnal (FR) *L Gadbin* 70
2 b f Sidestep(AUS) Winter Robin (Three Valleys (USA))
(8330a) 8970a[9]

Autumn Flight (IRE) *Tim Easterby* 82
3 b g Dandy Man(IRE) Swallow Falls (IRE) (Lake Coniston (IRE))
2121[6] 3159[3] 3590[7] 4280[4] 4603[4] 4912[7] 5619[5] 6070[6] 6338[2] (7065) 7486[2] (7766) 8400[13]

Autumn Leaves *Michael Appleby*
4 b m Helmet(AUS) Jadwiga (Pivotal)
81[7] 256[5]

Autumn Pride (IRE) *Mark Johnston* a41 58
3 b c Teofilo(IRE) Rahiyah (USA) (Rahy (USA))
949[3] 1268[2] 1689[2] 2229[4]

Autumn Splendour (IRE)
Milton Bradley a72 62
3 b g Dandy Man(IRE) Harvest Joy (IRE) (Daggers Drawn (USA))
1729[10] 2274[7] 3659[6] 5581[4] 5990[8] 6110[6] 7157[8] 7757[4] 7986[10] 9135[6] 9246[7] 9272[8] 9572[7]

Autumn Trail *Rae Guest* a66 63
2 b f Sixties Icon Boleyna (USA) (Officer (USA))
5547[3] 7569[4] 9251[2]

Autumn War (IRE) *Charles Hills* a90 91
4 ch g Declaration Of War(USA) Autumn Leaves (FR) (Muhtathir)
2095[4] 2606[5] 4250[4] 5174[2] 6895[6] 7974[6] 8411[7]

Auxerre (IRE) *Charlie Appleby* a106 114
4 b g Iffraaj Roscoff (IRE) (Daylami (IRE))
(1415)◆ (Dead)

Auxilia (IRE) *G M Lyons* 99
2 b f Free Eagle(IRE) Ipsa Loquitur (Unfuwain (USA))
8165a[3]

Auxiliary *Liam Bailey* a68 76
6 b g Fast Company(IRE) Lady Xara (IRE) (Xaar)
3500[2]◆ (3816) 4404[7] 5739[6] 6038[3] 6658[9]

Auzebosc (FR) *S Cerulis* a83 78
4 gr g Champs Elysees Akoyama (Peintre Celebre (USA))
6095a[6]

Avalon Ena (ITY) *Endo Botti* a61 68
2 b f Le Vie Infinite(IRE) Avalon Air (ITY) (Blu Air Force (IRE))
8791a[8]

Avanzata *Henry Candy* 47
2 b f Al Kazeem Avessia (Averti (IRE))
6846[5]

Avengers Endgame (IRE)
Agostino Affe' 75
2 b c Battle Of Marengo(IRE) Kiss And Don'Tell (USA) (Rahy (USA))
8789a[8]

Aventuriere *Mark Johnston* a60
2 b f Archipenko(USA) Lady Jane Digby (Oasis Dream)
9437[11]

Avenue Foch *James Fanshawe* a70 65
3 b g Champs Elysees Kindu (Pivotal)
3373[7]◆ 4459[5] 6030[3] 7192[2] 8065[3]

Avenue Of Stars *Karen McLintock* a65 71
6 b g Makfi Clifton Dancer (Fraam)
214[3] (356) 788[4] 2247[5] 3221[2] 3503[6] 4335[8] 4912[3] 5821[8] 7065[2]◆ 7507[7] 8083[13] 8719[8] 9253[5] 9396[6] 9518[6]

Aviateur (FR) *A Kleinkorres* 101
4 b h Intense Focus(USA) Attachante (IRE) (Teofilo (IRE))
1708a[4] 3287a[7]

Aviatress (IRE) *A De Royer-Dupre* a72 101
3 gr f Shamardal(USA) Manerbe (USA) (Unbridled's Song (USA))
3677a[5] 4621a[7] 6910a[5] (8376a)

Avie's Mesa (CAN) *Josie Carroll* a94 100
5 bb h Sky Mesa(USA) Avie's Empire (USA) (Empire Maker (USA))
5484a[5]

Avilius *James Cummings* a88 114
5 br g Pivotal Alessandria (Sunday Silence (USA))
8136a[4] 8579a[7]

Avis Bay *Philip Kirby*
2 br f Cable Bay(IRE) Dos Lunas (IRE) (Galileo (IRE))
9007[11]

Avon Green *Joseph Tuite* a56 47
4 b m Avonbridge Greenery (IRE) (Green Desert (USA))
179[7] 824[5] 1266[4] 1687[9] 1883[11] 2153[9] 4026[3] 4765[5]

Avorisk Et Perils (FR) *Gary Moore* a66 62
4 b m No Risk At All(FR) Pierre Azuree (FR) (Le Glorieux)
2771[14] 3080[5] 3546[7] 4472[3] 8847[7] (8998)◆ 9128[3]◆

Avremesnil (FR) *J Carayon* a66 66
2 b c Dansili Could It Be (IRE) (Galileo (IRE))
8481a[4]

Awa Bomba *Tony Carroll* a79 59
3 b g Heeraat(IRE) Nut (IRE) (Fasliyev (USA))
620[10] 1167[3] (1430)◆ 5308[5] 6058[5] 6598[3] 7632[5] (8070) (8266)

Awake In Asia *Charlie Wallis* a61 70
3 ch g Dragon Pulse(IRE) Gladiatrix (Compton Place)
235[11] 605[4] 906[3]◆ 4563[9] 5044[6] 6285[9] 7557[4] 7844[5]

Awake My Soul (IRE) *Tom Tate* a51 88
10 ch g Teofilo(IRE) Field Of Hope (IRE) (Selkirk (USA))
2095[9] 3726[5] 5657[8] 6923[7] 7589[10] 7622[3] 8130[5] 8396[3] 8725[2]

Awarded *Robert Cowell* a54 53
3 b f Swiss Spirit Royal Award (Cadeaux Genereux)
2592[7] 3148[3] 4192[5] 5064[8] 6321[8]

Award Scheme *William Haggas* 79
2 b f Siyouni(FR) Queen's Prize (Dansili)
4918[3]

A Wave Of The Sea (IRE)
Joseph Patrick O'Brien a71 87
3 b g Born To Sea(IRE) Je T'Adore (IRE) (Montjeu (IRE))
4136a[6]

Away He Goes (IRE)
Ismail Mohammed 98
3 b c Farhh Island Babe (USA) (Kingmambo (USA))
4073[2] (4842) (5384)◆

Awe *William Haggas* a83 96
3 b c Bated Breath On Her Way (Medicean)
2570[2]◆ 3082[8]◆ (3599) 4016[4]◆

Aweedram (IRE) *Alan King* a86 95
3 ch g Mukhadram Invitee (Medicean)
(1857) (2569) 3082[6] 4347[4] 4882[12] 8514[3] 8892[4]

Aweemaweh (IRE) *Mick Channon* 63
2 ch c Bungle Inthejungle Grotta Del Fauno (IRE) (Galileo (IRE))
6078[4] 6330[7]

Awesomedude
Mrs Ilka Gansera-Leveque a63 61
3 ch c Australia Millevini (IRE) (Hawk Wing (USA))
1241a[5] 1643[6] 2697[5] 8433[5]

Awesome Gal (IRE)
Sir Mark Prescott Bt a24 39
5 b m Galileo(IRE) Always Awesome (USA) (Awesome Again (CAN))
185[8] 607[9]

Awesome Gary *Tony Carroll* 67
2 gr g Outstrip Queen Of Heaven (USA) (Mr Greeley (USA))
4992[11] 6464[7] 7023[2] 7980[2]

Awesome Rock (IRE)
Roger Ingram a15 9
10 ch g Rock Of Gibraltar(IRE) Dangerous Diva (IRE) (Royal Academy (USA))
4594[11] 5802[10]

Awesometank *William Haggas* a104 109
4 b m Intense Focus(USA) Janey Muddles (IRE) (Lawman (FR))
(2404) 3334[2] 4900[7] 5978a[2] 7225a[10] 7920a[6]

Awsaaf *Michael Wigham* a71 77
4 b g Swiss Spirit Atheera (IRE) (Shamardal (USA))
1590[7] 2206[4] (3320) (3425) (6562) 7230[11] 8117[8]◆ 9135[4]◆ 9182[5] 9365[11] 9498[13] 9645[2]

Axana (GER) *A Wohler* 106
3 b f Soldier Hollow Achinora (Sleeping Indian)
3119a[2] (4461a)

Axcelerator (IRE) *C Ferland* 85
3 b c Excelebration(IRE) Noble Hachy (Kyllachy)
6252a[5]

Axe Axelrod (USA) *Michael Dods* a70 64
3 b g Street Sense(USA) Please Sign In (USA) (Doc's Leader (USA))
1846[9] 3307[8] 4080[13] 4288[3]◆ 4982[9] 6961[7] 7472[5] 7652[4] (8083) 8428[11]

Axel Jacklin *Chelsea Banham* a61 66
3 b g Iffraaj Reroute (IRE) (Acclamation)
65[4] 140[4] 274[2] (401) 1178[6] 1337[9] 2024[7] 2529[8] 2798[12] 3354[12] 6731[12] (9505)

Axelrod (USA) *S bin Ghadayer* a115
4 b h Warrior's Reward(USA) Volatile Vickie (USA) (Elusive Quality (USA))
1112a[10] 1447a[9]

Aydon Castle (IRE) *A Fabre* a93 93
4 b h Teofilo(IRE) Northern Melody (IRE) (Singspiel (IRE))
2266a[2]

Aye Aye Skipper (IRE)
Ken Cunningham-Brown a45 50
9 b g Captain Marvelous(IRE) Queenfisher (Scottish Reel I (IRE))
2277[4] 3038[10] 4473[10] 6121[7]

Ayeth (FR) *A Fabre* a65 65
3 b g Zoffany(IRE) Crystal Reef (King's Best (USA))
868a[7]

Ayguemorte (FR) *P-L Guerin* a57 57
6 b g Vertigineux(FR) Aiguille Du Midi (FR) (Fly To The Stars)
3711a[5]

Ayounor (FR) *T Mace* a71 60
4 b g Siyouni(FR) Clarte D'Or (FR) (Kendor (FR))
1391a[5]

Ayr Harbour *Michael Appleby* a71
2 b c Harbour Watch(IRE) Sorella Bella (IRE) (Clodovil (IRE))
7842[3] 9299[8] 9567[2]

Ayr Poet *Jim Goldie* 22
4 b g Poet's Voice Jabbara (IRE) (Kingmambo (USA))
3247[13] 3680[9] 4055[10]

Aysar (IRE) *Ed Dunlop* a64 57
2 b g Sir Prancealot(IRE) Yajala (Fasliyev (USA))
4384[6] 5624[9] 6943[4]

Ayutthaya (IRE) *Kevin Ryan* 98
4 ch g Lope De Vega(IRE) Pivotal Role (Pivotal)
1664[8] 1896[7] 2563[2] 3605[3] 4144[5] 5149[2] 5489[7] 6231[4] (6923) (7622) 8130[10]

Ayyaamy (IRE) *Owen Burrows* a46
2 b g Sir Prancealot(IRE) Araajmh (USA) (Street Cry (IRE))
9326[11]

Azano *John Gosden* 107
3 b g Oasis Dream Azanara (IRE) (Hurricane Run (IRE))
1830[3] 2411[11] 2834[2] (3903a) 4705a[11] 7194[5]

Azari *Alexandra Dunn* a86 67
7 b g Azamour(IRE) Atasari (IRE) (Whipper (USA))
(162) (231) 704[5] 799[3] 2577[4] 2613[5] 8948[5] 9056[11] 9543[7]

Azets *Jane Chapple-Hyam* a53 50
3 b g Dubawi(IRE) Nashmiah (IRE) (Elusive City (USA))
1094[3]◆ 1264[6] 2021[7] 2406[4] 3034[6] 3797[7] 4788[9] 5864[6] 9225[7] 9456[2]

Azila (FR) *D K Weld* 84
2 b f Dark Angel(IRE) Azama (IRE) (Sea The Stars (IRE))
6689a[5]

Azor Ahai *Chris Gordon* a51 75
3 b g Sixties Icon Good Morning Lady (Compton Place)
1360[7] 1846[2] 2114[11] 3307[10] 4124[8] 4444[3] 8521[14] 9306[12] 9561[8]

Azteca *Bryan Smart* a51 72
2 b f Fountain Of Youth(IRE) Irrational (Kyllachy)
1642[10] 2051[2] 2475[3] 8506[9]

Aztec Warrior (GER)
Jean-Pierre Carvalho a83 76
4 b g Soldier Hollow Atanua (GER) (Monsun (GER))
6790a[6]

Azure World *Kevin Ryan* a27 43
2 b f Free Eagle(IRE) Acquifer (Oasis Dream)
4517[8] 5737[7] 8640[9]

Azuro (FR)
Ciaron Maher & David Eustace a88 98
5 b g Myboycharlie(IRE) Anthropologie (IRE) (Okawango (USA))
8767a[3]

Azzeccagarbugli (IRE)
Mike Murphy a84 72
6 b g Kodiac Consultant Stylist (IRE) (Desert Style (IRE))
212[2] 3027[8] 3857[12] 6397[6] 6863[3]◆ 7164[8] 8017[4] 9086[2] 9283[2] 9561[7]

Azzurro Cobalto (ITY)
Nicolo Simondi 104
4 b g Aussie Rules(USA) Taurakina (Selkirk (USA))
2885a[2]

Baadirr *William Haggas* a80 77
2 b c Showcasing Belatorio (IRE) (Oratorio (IRE))
7292[7] 3760[2] 4596[4] 8265[2] 9175[2] 9328[2] 9608[4]

Baahi (GER) *J E Hammond* 50
3 ch c Iffraaj Boccassini (GER) (Artan (IRE))
1489a[8]

Baalbek (USA) *Owen Burrows* a53 75
3 b g Elusive Quality(USA) Nasmatt (Danehill (USA))
3019[2]◆ 3648[4]◆ 6370[9]

Baaqiah *Roger Varian* a65
3 b f Teofilo(IRE) Qawaafy (USA) (Street Cry (IRE))
5810[5] 6438[7]

Baaqy (IRE) *John Gosden* 80
2 b f Iffraaj Natalisa (IRE) (Green Desert (USA))
4918[6] 7695[2]

Baasem (USA) *Owen Burrows* a60 98
3 ch g New Approach(IRE) Ausus (USA) (Invasor (ARG))
2354[7] 3195[6] (4795) (5654) 6952[7]

Baasha *Ed Dunlop* a69 40
4 b g Havana Gold(IRE) Tawaasul (Haafhd)
(39) 362[4] 722[7] 911[7] 1333[6] 1653[10] 2111[16]

Baashiq (IRE) *Peter Hiatt* a71 74
5 b g New Approach(IRE) Fatanah (IRE) (Green Desert (USA))
911[5] 942[2] 1176[2] 1355[7] 4615[4] 5151[4] (5807) 6160[7] 6839[6] (7272) 7839[8] 8806[12]

Baba Boom (IRE) *J P Murtagh* 90
4 ch g Thewayyouare(USA) Voom Voom (IRE) (Bahamian Bounty)
5508a[6]

Baba Ghanouj (IRE) *Ed Walker* a80 86
3 b f Sea The Stars(IRE) Lombatina (FR) (King's Best (USA))
2268[7] 2768[2] 4930[4] 5383[3]◆ 6155[8] 6729[5] 7395[5]

Babar (FR) *E Lyon* a80 89
4 b g Motivator Bargouzine (USA) (Stravinsky (USA))
3136a[3]

Babbo's Boy (IRE) *Michael Bell* a98 93
3 gr g Mastercraftsman(IRE) Bunood (IRE) (Sadler's Wells (USA))
1898[2]◆ (2258) (2905) 4017[15] 4924[6] 7574[2] 8092[18]

Babel's Book (FR) *Edouard Monfort* a72 40
6 b g Iffraaj Ponentina (FR) (Lando (GER))
1245a[16]

Babouska *John Flint* a10
5 b m Monsieur Bond(IRE) Prices Lane (Gentleman's Deal (IRE))
8200[11]

Babyfact *Malcolm Saunders* a63 71
8 b m Piccolo Pennyspider (IRE) (Redback)
2729[8] 3577[9]

Baby Gal *Roger Ingram* a50 62
5 b m Royal Applause Our Gal (Kyllachy)
263[7] 365[2] 531[2] 594[10] 2287[8] 3144[9]

Baby Maureb (IRE) *Tony Coyle* 58
3 br f Canford Cliffs(IRE) Almost Blue (USA) (Mr Greeley (USA))
1970[5]

Baby Steps *David Loughnane* a90 84
3 b g Paco Boy(IRE) Stepping Out (IRE) (Tagula (IRE))
1691[7] 2149[5] 3307[12] 4185[2] 4908[3] (5281) 5821[2] 6465[3] 7183[3]◆ 8317[2] 9254[3] 9308[6] 9612[4]

Bacacarat (IRE) *Andrew Balding* a89 77
4 b g Raven's Pass(USA) Mathuna (IRE) (Tagula (IRE))
1461[8] 2064[5] (2966) 3581[10] 8062[13]

Baccara Rose (GER) *S Smrczek* 98
4 bb m Liang Kay(GER) Baccara Of Spain (GER) (Medicus (GER))
7499a[11]

Bacchalot (IRE) *Richard Hannon* a64 63
2 b f Sir Prancealot(IRE) Bacchanalia (IRE) (Blues Traveller (IRE))
2248[8] 2996[4] 3405[3] 3990[4] 5185[13] 5576[6] 6071[3] 6416[3] 7767[2] 8061[7]
Bacchus *Brian Meehan* 85
5 ch g Kheleyf(USA) Rumbled (Halling (USA))
4095[22] 7433[22]
Backcountry *Annette Stjernstrand* a18 93
7 b g Oasis Dream Winter Sunrise (Pivotal)
6523a[5] 7497a[6]
Back From Dubai (IRE)
Saeed bin Suroor a66
2 b g Exceed And Excel(AUS) Emirates Rewards (Dubawi (IRE))
8604[8]
Backstreet Girl (IRE) *Roger Varian* a66 62
3 b f Shamardal(USA) Beyond Desire (Invincible Spirit (IRE))
4651[4] 5828[7]
Back To Brussels (IRE) *J A Stack* 88
2 ch f Starspangledbanner(AUS) Big Boned (USA) (Street Sense (USA))
4048[10] 6690a[12]
Bacon's Rebellion *Ed de Giles* a24
3 b g Nathaniel(IRE) Linda (FR) (Tamayuz)
1019[9]
Bad Attitude *Luke McJannet* 46
2 b c Canford Cliffs(IRE) Cry Freedom (IRE) (Acclamation)
5676[9] 6054[6] 6161[11]
Badayel (IRE) *Ivan Furtado* a73
3 ch g Havana Gold(IRE) Raggiante (IRE) (Rock Of Gibraltar (IRE))
9475[2]
Bad Company *Jim Boyle* a58 63
2 b g Fast Company(IRE) Clearing (Sleeping Indian)
4544[8] 6807[7] 7570[6] 8465[10]
Badenscoth *Dean Ivory* a89 97
5 b g Foxwedge(AUS) Twice Upon A Time (Primo Dominie)
34[10] 429[8] 9424◆ (1169) (1566) 2516[5]◆ (3004) (3806) 4613[10] 5929[10] 7694[10] 8130[4] 8725[8]
Bader *Richard Hannon* a58 57
3 b g Elusive City(USA) Golbahar (IRE) (Holy Roman Emperor (IRE))
1824[11] 3256[12] 3593[7] (4991) 5293[6] 5653[3] 5803[4] 6202[9] 7232[9] 7909[10] 8251[9] 8553[14]
Badessa *Andrew Balding* a56
3 b f Dunaden(FR) Le Badie (IRE) (Spectrum (IRE))
7035[4] 8451[5]
Badger Berry *Nick Littmoden* a29 29
3 b g Epaulette(AUS) Snow Shoes (Sri Pekan (USA))
7371[11] 8295[9]
Badia (FR) *Edouard Monfort* a72 77
5 b m Siyouni(FR) Baldamelle (FR) (Dansili)
(5035a)
Bad Rabbit (IRE) *David Loughnane* 65
2 b g Iffraaj Bint Nayef (IRE) (Nayef (USA))
3047[7] 4324[4] 4897[5] 5980[4] 6416[5]
Badri *Charles Hills* a64 67
2 b c Dark Angel(IRE) Penny Drops (Invincible Spirit (IRE))
6449[6] 8059[5]
Baengmunbaekdap (USA)
Kim Young Kwan a79
4 bb h Tapizar(USA) Shining Victory (USA) (Victory Gallop (CAN))
7011a[7]
Bagatino *Declan Carroll* 14
3 b g Poet's Voice Harlequin Girl (Where Or When (IRE))
2094[15] 2845[9] 3684[12] 3969[12] 4212[14] 4582[9]
Bagel (FR) *J E Hammond* a87 93
5 b g Slickly(FR) Crumpett (IRE) (Montjeu (IRE))
2429a[11]
Baghdad (FR) *Mark Johnston* a106 114
4 b h Frankel Funny Girl (IRE) (Darshaan)
1927[3] (2440) (4053) 4848[5] 5613[3] 6473[17]
Baguera De Vaige (FR) *O Regley* a40 69
4 b m Monitor Closely(IRE) Unity Mag (FR) (Poliglote)
1073a[12]
Bahama Moon (IRE) *Jonjo O'Neill* a32 59
7 b g Lope De Vega(IRE) Bahama Bay (GER) (Dansili)
2577[7] 3192[6]
Bahamian Heights *Emma Owen* a52 56
8 b g Bahamian Bounty Tahirah (Green Desert (USA))
9670[10]
Bahamian Sunrise *John Gallagher* a59 65
7 ch g Bahamian Bounty Tagula Sunrise (IRE) (Tagula (IRE))
1496[11] 2030[7] 2484[6] 2824[13] 3856[8] 4230[14] 7161[4] 7757[8] 8279[4]
Bahango (IRE) *Patrick Morris* a54 38
7 b g Bahamian Bounty Last Tango (IRE) (Lion Cavern (USA))
25[5] 882[8] 1402[5] 1987[2] 2295[6] 3320[3]
Bahkit (IRE) *Philip Kirby* a62 67
5 b g Intikhab(USA) Pink Moon (IRE) (Namid)
102[7] 1647[2] 2244[5] 4333[7] 5096[6] 7956[11] 9391[6]
Bahlwan *Denis Gerard Hogan* a58 65
4 b g Bahamian Bounty Vive Les Rouges (Acclamation)
(2324) 2678[4]
Bahuta Acha *David Loughnane* a75 69
4 b g Captain Gerrard(IRE) Rosein (Komaite (USA))
1899[10] 2997[9] 4207[12] 4552[8] 5038[2] 5551[2] 5952[6] 5986[7] 7977[2] (8866) 9140[4] 9365[2] 9402[2] 9498[9]
Baie De Somme (FR) *P Monfort* 20
2 gr f Literato(FR) Wanate (IRE) (Shamardal (USA))
3714a[9]
Bailarico (IRE) *Warren Greatrex* 80
6 b g Dubawi(IRE) Baila Me (GER) (Samum (GER))
1663[3] 2080[4] 2936[2] 3635[3] 5540[8] 6716[6]

Baile An Roba (IRE) *Kieran P Cotter* a40 28
6 gr g Zebedee Hilarys First (Chevalier (IRE))
7086a[8]
Baile Ghilibert (IRE)
Michael Appleby a29 58
7 b g Majestic Missile(IRE) Reddening (Blushing Flame (USA))
8901[9] 9035[9] 9450[13]
Baileys Blues (FR) *Mark Johnston* a70 79
2 ch c Supplicant Indiana Blues (Indian Ridge (IRE))
7825[4] 8202[2] 9099[6] 9514[2] 9661[5]
Baileys Coquette (FR) *J-V Toux* a80 52
3 b f Elusive City(USA) Jolie Et Belle (FR) (Oratorio (IRE))
5408a[9]
Baileys Courage (FR) *J-V Toux* 79
2 b f Charm Spirit(IRE) Khelwa (FR) (Traditionally (USA))
1657a[9] 7775a[4]
Baileys Freedom *John Bridger* a65 61
2 b g Muhaarar Baileys Jubilee (Bahamian Bounty)
1499[6] 1759[7] 2228[6] 9322[3]
Baileys In Bloom (FR)
Richard Fahey a70 73
2 b f Supplicant Golbahar (IRE) (Holy Roman Emperor (IRE))
(2052) 2805[8] 3927[4] 4780[2] 5185[18] 9031[3] 9499[5]
Baileys Prayer (FR) *Richard Fahey* 42
2 b g Supplicant My Inspiration (IRE) (Invincible Spirit (IRE))
2115[9] 3156[6] 3644[13] 6571[5] 7283[7]
Bailly *G M Lyons* a70 89
3 b f Charm Spirit(IRE) Czarna Roza (Polish Precedent (USA))
2605a[11] 5325a[16]
Bainne Dubh *Bill Turner* a41 66
2 br f Coach House(IRE) Piste (Falbrav (IRE))
1493[5] 1759[4] 2138[3] 2918[5]
Bajan Breeze *Stuart Williams* a11
2 gr g Lethal Force(IRE) Semaphore (Zamindar (USA))
8418[11]
Bajan Excell (IRE) *Gavin Cromwell* a56 66
3 ch g Helmet(AUS) Bajan Belle (IRE) (Efisio)
8837[5]
Bakht A Rawan (IRE) *Roger Teal* a46 57
7 b g Rip Van Winkle(IRE) Foolish Ambition (GER) (Danehill Dancer (IRE))
3541[10] 4426[13] 5446[4] 6123[5] 6643[11] 7758[6] 8703[9] 9139[7]
Bakoel Koffie (IRE)
M Delcher Sanchez a108 109
5 b h Naaqoos Diamond Square (FR) (Dyhim Diamond (IRE))
2667a[7] 7010a[15] 8141a[8] 8648a[14] 8982a[5]
Baladio (IRE) *John Mackie* a74 73
3 ch f Iffraaj Balamana (FR) (Sinndar (IRE))
4636[4] 5477[2] 6034[6] 6733[6] 9012[4]
Balance Of Power *John Quinn* a82 79
3 b g Slade Power(IRE) Classic Falcon (IRE) (Dubawi (IRE))
885[2]
Balancing Act (IRE) *Jedd O'Keeffe* a52 74
2 ch f No Nay Never(USA) My Lass (Elmaamul (USA))
3451[6] 3968[5] 4984[2] (5913) 7440[5] 8817[11]
Balata Bay *Donald McCain* a79 69
3 b c Kyllachy Cumana Bay (Dansili)
1285[3] (1516)◆ 2364[6] 2942[9] 3261[6] 3638[3] 4226[3] 4562[8] 5373[2] 5813[5] 6418[4] 7204[5] 7523[3] 8025[13]
Bal De Rio (FR) *Brian Ellison* a87 85
6 b g Vertigineux(FR) Baldoranic (FR) (Panoramic)
2781[3]
Baldwin (IRE) *Kevin Ryan* a36 57
3 b g Moohaajim(IRE) Cheherazad (IRE) (Elusive City (USA))
2477[4] 4010[8] 4519[13] 4731[6]
Balgair *Tom Clover* a74 91
5 ch g Foxwedge(AUS) Glencal (Compton Place)
(2739) 4300[2] 4851[8] 5383[5] 6516[4] 7350[4] 8101[16]
Balgees Time (FR) *Tom Ward* a72 68
3 b f Dabirsim(FR) Cindy Bould (High Chaparral (IRE))
(2265a) 5124[6] 5695[6] 9281a[2]
Balladeer *Michael Bell* a83 82
3 b g Poet's Voice Diamond Run (Hurricane Run (IRE))
(1480) 2035[3] 2766[3] 2942[10] 3647[7] 5394[2] 6129[8] 6501[5] 7836[3] 8498[2]
Ballard Down (IRE) *David Pipe* a90 96
6 b g Canford Cliffs(IRE) Mackenzie's Friend (Selkirk (USA))
212[3] 441[3] 805[9] 1232[8] 2187[6] (2514) (3423) 4020[6]
Ballerina Showgirl *Hugo Palmer* a58
2 ch f Showcasing Katalea (Mr Greeley (USA))
8453[9]
Ballesteros *Emma Owen* a30 60
10 ch g Tomba Flamenco Dancer (Mark Of Esteem (IRE))
161[11] 2206[14] 3425[10]
Ballet Red (FR) *Harry Dunlop* a66 68
3 ch f Rio De La Plata(USA) Beriosova (FR) (Starborough)
1351[5] 2719[4] 3034[3]◆ 4179[3] 9006[6] 9279[2]◆ 9426[6]
Ballet Russe (IRE) *A Fabre* 98
3 b c Camelot Seatone (USA) (Mizzen Mast (USA))
1450a[2] 3120a[5]
Ballistic (IRE) *David Loughnane* a88 74
3 b g Kodiac Pale Orchid (IRE) (Invincible Spirit (IRE))
140[3] (360)◆ (1104)◆
Ballyare *Lucinda Russell* a67 63
2 b c Hot Streak(IRE) Saddlers Bend (IRE) (Refuse To Bend (IRE))
9515[2]
Ballylemon (IRE) *Richard Hughes* a88 88
3 b g Champs Elysees Athreyaa (Singspiel (IRE))
1568[2] 2796[5] (7382) 8754[4] 9065[6] 9454[8]

Ballymount *Michael Easterby* a73 72
4 ch g Cityscape Symphony Star (IRE) (Amadeus Wolf)
4281[3] 4875[7] 5899[7] 6627[5] 7069[7] 7474[6]
Ballynanty (IRE) *N W Alexander* a104 77
7 gr g Yeats(IRE) Reina Blanca (Darshaan)
3361[6] 8236[10]
Ballyquin (IRE) *Andrew Balding* a85 86
4 b h Acclamation Something Mon (USA) (Maria's Mon (USA))
(178) 564[3] (1061) 1160[6] 2611[2] 4123[2] 5661[21] 6396[7]
Bal Mal (FR) *John Quinn* 51
2 b g The Wow Signal(IRE) Nigwah (FR) (Montjeu (IRE))
5294[8] 6336[11] 7437[7] 9031[14]
Balmoral Castle *Jonathan Portman* a41 78
10 b g Royal Applause Mimiteh (USA) (Maria's Mon (USA))
2691[3] 3541[11] 4561[10] 7125[3]
Baltic Baron (IRE) *David O'Meara* a3 104
4 b g Shamardal(USA) Born Wild (GER) (Sadler's Wells (USA))
3472[2] 3857[2] 4292[9] 5398[2] 5610[5] 6376[11] 7198[3] 7694[14]
Baltic Eagle (GER) *Alan Bailey* a61 93
5 ch g Adlerflug(GER) Baltic Gift (Cadeaux Genereux)
4419a[2] 9510[9]
Baltic Prince (IRE) *Tony Carroll* a84 79
9 b g Baltic King Brunswick (Warning)
3040[9] 4875[12] 5804[4] 5839[4] 7145[9] 8017[12] 9176[9] 9606[5]
Baltic Song (IRE) *John Gosden* a85 91
3 b c Sea The Stars(IRE) Born Wild (GER) (Sadler's Wells (USA))
(858) 5634[3] 6597[4] 8002[2]
Baltic State (IRE) *Kevin Ryan* a70 73
2 b g Dandy Man(IRE) Estonia (Exceed And Excel (AUS))
4719[3] 5388[2] 5913[3] 6980[4] 8817[6]
Baltic Wolve *John Gosden* a34 74
2 b g Australia Baltic Comtesse (FR) (Lope De Vega (IRE))
7571[10] 8461[7]
Balzac *Ed Walker* 56
2 b g Lope De Vega(IRE) Miss You Too (Montjeu (IRE))
7339[5]
Bamako Du Chatelet (FR)
Ian Williams a73 70
8 gr g Voix Du Nord(FR) Royale Du Chatelet (FR) (Sleeping Car (FR))
88[5] 469F
Bambajee (FR) *Tim Pinfield* a48 52
6 b m Rock Of Gibraltar(IRE) Heaven's Dream (IRE) (Oasis Dream)
1958[2]
Bambino Lola *Adam West* a80 98
4 b m Helmet(AUS) Lifetime Romance (IRE) (Mozart (IRE))
4127[3]◆
Bambys Boy *Neil Mulholland* a46 57
8 b g Lucarno(USA) Bamby (IRE) (Glacial Storm (USA))
2354[12] 3464[11] 3946[5] 5269[10] 6400[3] 8246[5] 8868[12]
Banditry (IRE) *Ian Williams* a107 101
7 b g Iffraaj Badalona (Cape Cross (IRE))
1753[24] 2033[11] 3168[3] 4395[4]
Band Practice (IRE) *Archie Watson* 105
2 ch f Society Rock(IRE) Grand Zafeen (Zafeen (FR))
5681[2]◆ 6096[9] (6800)◆ (7211) (7775a) 8745a[12]
Bandua (USA) *Jack Sisterson* a100 109
4 gr h The Factor(USA) If Angels Sang (USA) (Seattle Slew (USA))
6001a[3] 7922a[8] 8776a[10]
Bangkok (IRE) *Andrew Balding* 113
3 b c Australia Tanaghum (Darshaan)
(1417) (2084) 3345[12] 4049[2] 5455[5] 6470[2] 9590a[2]
Banish (USA) *Tom George* a75
6 b g Smart Strike(CAN) Beyond Our Reach (IRE) (Danehill Dancer (IRE))
5796[4] 6804[5] 8014[14]
Bankawi *Michael Easterby* 53
2 b f Coach House(IRE) Whitby (IRE) (Dubawi (IRE))
1642[9] 2747[11] 3477[6] 3927[9] (5296) 6969[9] 8259[6]
Bank Holiday (IRE) *Richard Fahey* a38
2 ch f Ruler Of The World(IRE) Banco Suivi (IRE) (Nashwan (USA))
9043[11] 9392[10]
Banksea *Marjorie Fife* a87 89
6 b g Lawman(FR) Stars In Your Eyes (Galileo (IRE))
2574[9] 4097[9] 4692[6] 6460[11] 6863[2] 7153[6] 8024[6] 8498[14]
Banksy's Art *Amanda Perrett* a55 65
4 b g Sixties Icon Outside Art (Excellent Art)
(2998) 3251[4] 3537[4] 4220[2] 4569[6] 5337[3] 5993[5] 7984[8] 8414[11] 9005[12]
Banmi (IRE) *Mohamed Moubarak* a74 5
2 b f Kodiac Fingal Nights (IRE) (Night Shift (USA))
2840[13] 3990[3] 4502[3] (6146) 6632[4] 7548[8] 8011[3] 8850[8]
Bannister (FR) *Tom George* 66
2 b g Olympic Glory(IRE) Amou Daria (FR) (Kendor (FR))
7972[4]◆
Bannockburn (IRE) *Keith Dalgleish* a52 49
3 b g Battle Of Marengo(IRE) Misrepresent (USA) (Distorted Humor (USA))
1236[11] 1336[8] 1570[10] 6550[9] 6610[6] 7739[5] 8423[13]
Ban Shoof *Gary Moore* a71 66
6 b g Shirocco(GER) Pasithea (IRE) (Celtic Swing)
3541[8] 4795[3] 5425[7] 6115[2] 6566[4] 9087[3]
Banta Bay *John Best* a57 56
5 b g Kheleyf(USA) Atnab (USA) (Riverman (USA))
59[3] 363[5] 549[2] 721[2] 947[4] 1548[6] (3017) 4661[11] 5029[14] 6115[4] 6599[3] 7202[4] 7558[3] (8224) 9310[4] 9589[4]

Baptism (IRE) *John Gosden* a80 71
2 ch c Sea The Stars(IRE) Holy Salt (Holy Roman Emperor (IRE))
5908[5] 6564[3] (7834) 8462[5]
Baraajeel *Owen Burrows* a62
3 b g Kodiac Madany (IRE) (Acclamation)
2598[5]
Baracca Rocks *K R Burke* a50 48
2 b f Society Rock(IRE) Fortune Hunter (FR) (High Chaparral (IRE))
5590[3] 6793[4] 7063[8] 7469[5] 8118[7]
Barakatle *P Bary* 76
2 gr c Poet's Voice Baraket Fayrouz (FR) (Barathea (IRE))
5642a[6]
Barasti Dancer (IRE) *K R Burke* a42 73
3 gr g Helmet(AUS) My Girl Lisa (USA) (With Approval (CAN))
1104[7] 1656[10] (2285) 2897[2] 3249[4]◆ 3885[10] 4239[12]
Baratin (FR) *T Castanheira* 90
2 gr c Tin Horse(IRE) Barouna (FR) (Kouroun (FR))
5642a[3]
Baraweez (IRE) *Brian Ellison* a88 97
9 b g Cape Cross(IRE) Aquarelle Bleue (Sadler's Wells (USA))
2419[14] 2572[3] 3069[6] 4934[5] 5535a[15]
Barbados (IRE) *A P O'Brien* 105
3 b c Galileo(IRE) Sumora (IRE) (Danehill (USA))
3984[2] 4845[4] 7216a[17]
Barbara Villiers *David Evans* a62 47
4 b m Champs Elysees Frances Stuart (IRE) (King's Best (USA))
459[5] 724[7] 814[9]
Barbarella (IRE) *Kevin Ryan* 74
2 b f Hot Streak(IRE) Acid (Clodovil (IRE))
2747[7] 3968[3] 5547[2] 6375[13] 7399[9]
Barbarosa (IRE) *Michael Herrington* a63 64
3 br g Holy Roman Emperor(IRE) Snow Scene (IRE) (Singspiel (IRE))
2035[8] 2630[9] 3018[5] 4288[8] 5002[4] 5517[7] 6024[4] 6540[2] 6945[9] 8025[6] 8863[4] 9040[2] 9216[9] 9479[8]
Barbelo (IRE) *Richard Spencer* a68
2 rg f Dark Angel(IRE) Skehana (IRE) (Mukaddamah (USA))
8316[7]
Barbie O'Conor *Donal Kinsella* a52 44
4 ch m Roderic O'Connor(IRE) Barbsiz (IRE) (Elnadim (USA))
7090a[5]
Barbie's Fox (AUS) *Louise Bonella* 97
2 bb f Foxwedge(AUS) So Barbie Says (AUS) (Kenvain (AUS))
8135a[9]
Barbill (IRE) *Mick Channon* a84 100
3 b g Zebedee Fiuise (IRE) (Montjeu (IRE))
806[4]◆ 1780a[6] 2826[4] 3621a[10] 3865[13] 4847[5] 5184[5] 5932[6] 7433[21] 7868[8]
Barboukha *Luke Dace* a17
2 b f Swiss Spirit Brooksby (Diktat)
6846[14] 7842[11]
Barb's Prince (IRE) *Ian Williams* a5 49
3 b g Casamento(IRE) Bibury (Royal Applause)
2995[11] 3373[9] 4484[4] 5242[3] 5974[9] 7192[9]
Barca (USA) *Marcus Tregoning* a65 59
5 b g War Front(USA) Magnificent Honour (USA) (A.P. Indy (USA))
701[11] 1015[6] 2279[4] 2970[2] 4220[5] 5271[4] (5891) 6864[3] 7553[3] 7818[6]
Bardo Contiguo (IRE) *Roger Varian* a74 78
3 b g Lope De Vega(IRE) Jillnextdoor (IRE) (Henrythenavigator (USA))
2518[2] 3067[4] 4121[6] (7364) 8498[9]
Bare All (IRE) *K R Burke* a39 64
2 b f Dark Angel(IRE) Bear Cheek (IRE) (Kodiac)
1642[3] 1893[4] 2840[10]
Bareed (USA) *Linda Perratt* a47 45
4 ch g Kitten's Joy(USA) Sweet Harp (USA) (Aragorn (IRE))
2328[9] 2964[5] 4725[12] 4978[5] 5238[8] 6572[12] 7780[12]
Barend Boy *Richard John O'Brien* a60 51
3 b g Oasis Dream Scarborough Fair (Pivotal)
1306a[13]
Barenne (FR) *N Leenders* 5
3 b g Tin Horse(IRE) Lourinha (FR) (Loup Solitaire (USA))
7476a[9]
Barking Mad *David Evans* a65 63
2 b g Due Diligence(USA) Jules (IRE) (Danehill (USA))
6330[5] 6899[5] 8059[6] 9307[4] 9568[2]
Barney Bullet (IRE) *Noel Wilson* a31 46
4 b g Havana Gold(IRE) Lalinde (Tiger Hill (IRE))
4078[11] 4512[4] 4915[5] 5100[6] 5787[10] 6545[3] 7544[10]
Barney Roy *Charlie Appleby* 116
5 b g Excelebration(IRE) Alina (IRE) (Galileo (IRE))
2271[2] (3030a) 3948[8]
Barnsdale *Steph Hollinshead* a40 39
6 b g Stimulation(IRE) Seren Teg (Timeless Times (USA))
118[5] 244[11]
Barodar (FR) *T Lemer* a79 73
4 ch h Tin Horse(IRE) Barouda (FR) (My Risk (FR))
1449a[8] 2226a[14]
Baron Bolt *Paul Cole* a100 111
6 br g Kheleyf(USA) Scarlet Royal (Red Ransom (USA))
2062[5] 2916[6] 4095[24] 5664[26] 6847[4] 7701[8]
Baron Run *K R Burke* a63 76
9 ch g Bertolini(USA) Bhima (Polar Falcon (USA))
233[3] 410[13] 705[2] (829) 1197[3] 1369[3] 1526[4] 2297[2] 2631[10]
Baroot *M F De Kock* a82 106
7 ch g Dubawi(IRE) Time Honoured (Sadler's Wells (USA))
(173a) 515a[7] 637a[3] 961a[6]
Barossa Bal (IRE) *Henry Spiller*
3 b f Delegator Anamarka (Mark Of Esteem (IRE))
5057[11]

Barossa Red (IRE) *Andrew Balding* a79 89
3 ch g Tamayuz I Hearyou Knocking (IRE) (Danehill Dancer (IRE))
229[2] 827[4] 1166[2] 1550[2] (5947) 6961[2]

Barrier Reef (IRE) *Tim Vaughan* a48 48
4 b g Galileo(IRE) Honour Bright (IRE) (Danehill (USA))
1989[9] 2128[10] 2970[4]

Barrington (IRE) *Michael Appleby* a83 96
5 b g Casamento(IRE) Mia Divina (Exceed And Excel (AUS))
164[5] 7856[5] 9308[8] 9476[4]

Barristan The Bold *Tom Dascombe* a98 100
3 b g Excelebration(IRE) Cradle Of Life (IRE) (Notnowcato)
2559[3]◆ 3082[5] 4016[18] 4360[2] (5434)◆ 5963[4] 6711[3]◆ 8184[5]

Barritus *George Baker* a69 69
4 b g Exceed And Excel(AUS) Flambeau (Oasis Dream)
178[2]◆ 2397[6] 2929[3]◆ 3406[4]

Bar Room Bore (IRE) *Fergal Birrane* 70
3 b g Big Bad Bob(IRE) Alayna (IRE) (Cape Cross (IRE))
5599a[9]

Barrsbrook *Gary Moore* a69 69
5 b g Doyen(IRE) Sayrianna (Sayaarr (USA))
295[3] 1183[4] 3537[7] 5309[8] 6121[8] (7028) 7270[5]

Barry Magoo *Adam West* 56
2 b g Epaulette(AUS) Azamoura (Azamour (IRE))
1733[7] 2288[7] 3312[6] 6403[5] 7725[7] 8856[7] 9179[9]

Barsanti (IRE) *Roger Varian* a96 114
7 b g Champs Elysees Silver Star (Zafonic (USA))
2607[3] 3077[3] 4390[3] 6473[5] 7148[4]

Bartaba (FR) *A Fabre* a38 105
4 b m Deep Impact(JPN) Baahama (IRE) (Anabaa (USA))
3123a[6] 5718a[8]

Bartat *Mick Channon* a54 65
2 b f Heeraat(IRE) Pacches (IRE) (Clodovil (IRE))
1513[4] 1833[4] 2275[3] 4799[4] 5340[3] (5800) 5958[6] 6369[7] 7156[5] 8650[10]

Bartholomeu Dias *Charles Hills* a103 93
4 b g Mount Nelson Lady Francesca (Montjeu (IRE))
1596[2] (1927) 4382[4] 5662[10] 6355[16] 7147[4] 7686[4]

Bartholomew J (IRE) *Lydia Pearce* a63 73
5 ch g Fast Company(IRE) Mana (IRE) (Motivator)
3192[7] 4308[4] 4569[5] 6323[4] 6812[4] 8065[12]

Bartimaeus (IRE) *Denis Coakley* a68 61
3 b g Nathaniel(IRE) Zora Seas (IRE) (Marju (IRE))
2139[9] 3594[3] 4769[5] 6022[4]

Barton Mills *Michael Easterby* a51 60
4 b g Iffraaj Balladonia (Primo Dominie)
3216[5] 3868[21] 4369[9] 5770[6] 6703[6] 7050[6]

Barwick *Mrs A Malzard* a71 74
11 b g Beat Hollow Tenpence (Bob Back (USA))
2502a[2] 3640a[9]

Barys *Archie Watson* a97 97
3 b c Kodiac Balatoma (IRE) (Mr Greeley (USA))
(683a) 1049a[7] 1713[6] 2163a[6] 3108a[7]

Baryshnikov *Ed Walker* a73 81
3 ch g Mastercraftsman(IRE) Tara Moon (Pivotal)
3011[6] 4188[3] 4865[4] 5776[4] 7773[6]

Basateen (IRE) *Doug Watson* 109
7 ch g Teofilo(IRE) Tasha's Dream (USA) (Woodman (USA))
47a[5]

Bashful Boy (IRE)
John James Feane a72 72
3 b g Magician(IRE) Bacheliere (USA) (Include (USA))
7490[3]

Bashiba (IRE) *Nigel Tinkler* a12 71
8 ch g Iffraaj Nightswimmer (IRE) (Noverre (USA))
1929[12] 2079[9] 2421[5]◆ 2841[13] 4100[8] 4829[3] 5169[4] 5750[4] 6699[14] (6932) 7588[12]

Basildon *Brian Ellison* a57 47
4 b g Champs Elysees Casual (Nayef (USA))
1643[11] 2347[2] 2713[10] 3209[5] 3448[7]◆ 5435[5]

Basilisk (USA) *Roger Charlton* a59 63
3 ch g Speightstown(USA) Treat Gently (Cape Cross (IRE))
2128[9] 3019[5] (6643)◆ 7573[6]

Bassmatchi (FR) *C Boutin* a53 62
2 b g Zoffany(IRE) Tafiya (Bahri (USA))
7925a[12]

Bast (USA) *Bob Baffert* a108
2 b f Uncle Mo(USA) Laffina (USA) (Arch (USA))
8747a[3]

Bataar (IRE) *Richard Fahey* a68 74
3 b g Acclamation Elusive Laurence (IRE) (Lawman (FR))
1723[6] 2371[4] 2766[8] 3354[2]

Batalha *Mark Johnston* a68 44
2 b g Henrythenavigator(USA) Lamentation (Singspiel (IRE))
7778[8] 8402[4] 9007[6]

Batbayar *A Fabre* a52 61
3 b g Intello(GER) Bayargal (USA) (Bernstein (USA))
1198a[7]

Batchelor Boy (IRE) *Marco Botti* a75 68
2 ch c Footstepsinthesand Kathoe (IRE) (Fayruz)
4184[5] 9195[2] (9569)

Bated Beauty (IRE) *John Butler* a59 65
4 ch m Bated Breath Benedicte (IRE) (Galileo (IRE))
2919[9] 3463[12] 4194[11] 6412[7] 8033[13] 8434[14] 9456[3]

Batellik (IRE) *A Peraino* 36
2 b c Epaulette(AUS) Innclassic (IRE) (Stravinsky (USA))
4172a[10]

Battaash (IRE) *Charles Hills* 129
5 b g Dark Angel(IRE) Anna Law (IRE) (Lawman (FR))
(3084)◆ 3950[2] (5611) (6423) 7943a[14]

Battalion (IRE) *Jamie Osborne* a89 89
9 b g Authorized(IRE) Zigarra (Halling (USA))
1106[4]

Battered *Ralph Beckett* a104 102
5 b g Foxwedge(AUS) Swan Wings (Bahamian Bounty)
351[4]◆ 800[5] 7152[5]◆ 7697[4] 7891[17] 8728[8]

Battle Commander *Olly Williams* a65
3 b g Avonbridge Antica Medusa (Tiger Hill (IRE))
6941[4] 8718[7] 9011[8] 9469[11]

Battle Of Issus (IRE)
David Menuisier a34 68
4 b g Declaration Of War(USA) Athenian Way (IRE) (Barathea (IRE))
2738[11] (3500) (3940)

Battle of Liege (USA) *A P O'Brien* a80 58
2 b c War Front(USA) Liscanna (IRE) (Sadler's Wells (USA))
(8751)

Battle Of Marathon (USA)
John Ryan a90 81
7 b g War Front(USA) Sayedah (IRE) (Darshaan)
87[6] 240[5] 440[3] 1917[9] 2126[7] 2620[6] 3361[7] 4118[4] 4308[5] 4569[2] 5625[4] 6573[8] (6933) 7436[3] 7866[9] (8185) 8513[13] 9056[9] 9288[2] 9405[2] 9633[2]

Battle of Paradise (USA)
Sir Mark Prescott Bt a77
3 b g Declaration Of War(USA) Garden of Eden (USA) (Curlin (USA))
251[2]◆ 804[2] (6887) 8092[19]

Battle Of Pembroke (USA)
David Simcock a62 63
3 b g Declaration Of War(USA) Beauty O' Gwaun (IRE) (Rainbow Quest (USA))
949[4] 1165[10] 3198[4] 4345[8]

Battle Of Toro (IRE) *A Fabre* 100
3 gr c New Approach(IRE) Galician (Redoute's Choice (AUS))
3789a[2] 5717a[4]

Battle Of Waterloo (IRE)
John Ryan a81 84
3 b g Big Bad Bob(IRE) Anything (IRE) (Rock Of Gibraltar (IRE))
1713[9] 1888[7] 2364[4]◆ 3357[7] 4124[7] 4565[5] (5270) 5619[2] 6410[4] 6935[5] 7213[9] 7663[5] 8237[12] 8498[13]

Battle Of Wills (IRE) *James Tate* a75 96
3 b c Lawman(FR) Maidin Maith (IRE) (Montjeu (IRE))
2765[4] (3373) 4034[2] 4549[4] (5201) 6156[6] 7302[5]

Battle Of Yarmouk (IRE)
Kevin Ryan a68 43
3 ch c Lope De Vega(IRE) Spesialta (Indian Ridge (IRE))
1195[3] 1550[3] 3517[8] 5238[10]

Batts Rock (IRE) *Gordon Elliott* a88 96
6 b g Fastnet Rock(AUS) Be My Queen (IRE) (Sadler's Wells (USA))
3952[8]

Batwan (FR) *P Sogorb* a83 108
4 gr g Kendargent(FR) Matwan (FR) (Indian Rocket)
2667a[2]

Bavardages (IRE) *Mark Johnston* a68 47
2 b c Dream Ahead(USA) Petits Potins (IRE) (Verglas (IRE))
7627[5]◆ 7896[26] 8280[5] (8603) (9045)◆

Bavaria Baby (FR) *F Chappet* 94
2 b f Dabirsim(FR) Baiadera (GER) (Tertullian (USA))
4947a[4] 8446a[2] 8970a[2]

Bawaader (IRE) *Ed Dunlop* a66
4 gr g Dark Angel(IRE) Aspen Falls (IRE) (Elnadim (USA))
827[6] 1102[5] 2550[5] 3147[13]

Bawaasil *Doug Watson* a80 83
4 b g Oasis Dream Hedaaya (IRE) (Indian Ridge (IRE))
1748a[12]

Bawtry Lady *David C Griffiths* a46 23
3 b f Epaulette(AUS) Precious Secret (IRE) (Fusaichi Pegasus (USA))
228[6] 388[5] 505[7] 8839[14]

Bayaanaat *Peter Hiatt* 47
3 ch g Dawn Approach(IRE) Khothry (IRE) (Marju (IRE))
2210[12]◆ 2715[7] 3947[11]

Bayar *Clive Cox* a73
2 b c Bated Breath So Belle (Singspiel (IRE))
8455[9] 9567[3]

Bayards Cove *Stuart Kittow* a41 44
4 b m Harbour Watch(IRE) Acicula (IRE) (Night Shift (USA))
3036[3] 3771[7] 4494[5]◆ 4873[4] 5806[8] 6844[9]

Baydar *Ivan Furtado* a74 79
6 b g Rock Of Gibraltar(IRE) Splashdown (Falbrav (IRE))
980[7] 1172[6] 1518[9] 2092[14] 2578[6] 3361[2] 3861[8] 6348[4] 7370[6]

Bay Dude *Brett Johnson* a8 42
4 b g Sulamani(IRE) Sky Calling (Bal Harbour)
3017[10] 4111[11] 5310[12]

Bay Filly Rolla *Michael Dods* 67
2 b f Showcasing Memoria (Teofilo (IRE))
5243[8] 6096[4]

Baylagan (FR) *Mme G Rarick* a60 78
3 b g Toronado(IRE) Al Waghaa (FR) (Muhtathir)
3878a[3] 4229a[3] 5408a[5] 7138a[5]

Bayni Baynak (FR) *Elias Mikhalides* 33
3 ch f Anodin(IRE) Belova (IRE) (Soviet Star (USA))
6789a[8]

Bay Of Naples (IRE)
Michael Herrington a70 72
3 b g Exceed And Excel(AUS) Copperbeech (IRE) (Red Ransom (USA))
500[4] (733) (913) 1104[5] 2035[9] 2529[4] 3580[7] 4316[6] 4762[3] 9140[9] 9443[5]

Bay Of Poets (IRE) *Charlie Appleby* a83 110
5 b g Lope De Vega(IRE) Bristol Bay (IRE) (Montjeu (IRE))
51a[5] 395a[8]

Bayoun (FR) *T Lerner* a110 107
6 gr g Kouroun(FR) Baenia (FR) (Verglas (IRE))
3030a[2]

Bayroot (IRE) *Roger Varian* a102 101
3 b c Exceed And Excel(AUS) Alwarga (USA) (Street Sense (USA))
1926[3]◆ 4305[2]◆ 4919[3] 5666[7] 7198[2]

Bayshore Freeway (IRE)
Mark Johnston a107 105
4 b m Declaration Of War(USA) Thewaytosanjose (IRE) (Fasliyev (USA))
1914[2] (2278) (2680) 3096[3] (3995)◆ (4145)

Bayston Hill *Mark Usher* a76 76
5 br g Big Bad Bob(IRE) Jessica Ennis (USA) (English Channel (USA))
86[4] 876[8] 1343[3] (1482) 3022[10] 4235[11] 5086[5] 5570[3] 6439[2]

Bay Watch (IRE)
Tracey Barfoot-Saunt a62 73
5 b g Harbour Watch(IRE) Karuga (Kyllachy)
(5289) (5449)◆ (5678) 7230[6] 7760[4]

Bazooka (IRE) *David Flood* a63 71
8 b g Camacho Janadam (IRE) (Mukaddamah (USA))
4661[5] 7558[8] 8414[7]

Bazzat (IRE) *C Moore* a50 38
6 ch g Roderic O'Connor(IRE) Compradore (Mujtahid (USA))
1837[7]

Bbob Alula *Bill Turner* a48 79
4 ch g Showcasing Island Rhapsody (Bahamian Bounty)
2232[2]◆ 2977[6] 4226[14] 4926[8] 5677[3] 6084[10]

Beach Break *Donald McCain* a45 55
5 b g Cacique(IRE) Wemyss Bay (Sadler's Wells (USA))
2577[6] 3511[12]

Beachcomber (USA) *S Seemar* a79
5 b g Bernardini(USA) Magnificent Song (USA) (Unbridled's Song (USA))
196a[4]

Beadlam (IRE) *Roger Fell* a58 58
6 ch m Frozen Power(IRE) Pivotal Role (Pivotal)
120[11]

Be Ahead *E J O'Neill* a74 77
2 b f Dream Ahead(USA) High Spice (USA) (Songandaprayer (USA))
7044a[3] (8195)

Bealach (IRE)
Eve Johnson Houghton 73
2 b c New Approach(IRE) Samya (Invincible Spirit (IRE))
3760[4] 5131[5] 7235[9]

Beama (FR) *P Monfort* a79 81
6 b m Elusive City(USA) High Will (FR) (High Chaparral (IRE))
115a[7]

Beaming *Peter Hiatt* a42 48
5 b m Shamardal(USA) Connecting (Singspiel (IRE))
118[10] 718[9]

Beam Me Up (GER) *Markus Klug* 95
3 bb c Sea The Moon(GER) Bezzaaf (Machiavellian (USA))
2310a[6] 4707a[12]

Bear Force One *Roger Teal* a98 95
3 b g Swiss Spirit Shesha Bear (Tobougg (IRE))
3696[8] 4452[4] (6594) (7460)◆ 9053[2]

Bear Valley (IRE) *Amy Murphy* a67 77
5 b g Manduro(GER) Shane (GER) (Kornado)
8421[12] 9215[8]

Bea Ryan (IRE) *Declan Carroll* 61
4 b m Dream Ahead(USA) Kimola (IRE) (King's Theatre (IRE))
2909[8] 3707[4] 5770[4]◆ 7779[11]

Beatboxer (USA) *John Gosden* 104
3 bb g Scat Daddy(USA) Thmoruplathlesupay (USA) (Unbridled's Song (USA))
2413[4] (3082) 4016[15] 5963[5]

Beatbybeatbybeat *Antony Brittain* a68 72
6 ch m Poet's Voice Beat As One (Medicean)
951[5] 1169[10] 1343[8] 1688[5] 3057[6] 3267[2] 3547[4] 7526[7] 8033[9] 9256[7]

Beat Le Bon (FR) *Richard Hannon* a87 113
3 b c Wootton Bassett Frida La Blonde (FR) (Elusive City (USA))
(1180) 1736[8] 2412[4]◆ (3075)◆ (4650) (5610) 6443[5] 8805a[6]

Beatrix Enchante *Ruth Carr* 41
3 b f Phoenix Reach(IRE) Bailadeira (Intikhab (USA))
5969[8]

Beat The Bank *Andrew Balding* a85 120
5 b g Paco Boy(IRE) Tiana (Diktat)
(2085) 2829[11] 3948[2] (4900) (Dead)

Beat The Breeze *Simon Dow* a55 41
2 gr c Outstrip Tranquil Flight (Oasis Dream)
3491[9] 4030[7] 4734[8] 9164[2] 9630[4]

Beat The Clock (AUS) *J Size* 123
5 b g Hinchinbrook(AUS) Flion Fenena (AUS) (Lion Hunter (AUS))
(9377a)

Beat The Heat *Jim Boyle* 19
2 b g Hot Streak(IRE) Touriga (Cape Cross (IRE))
8518[10]

Beat The Judge (IRE) *Gary Moore* 62
4 b g Canford Cliffs(IRE) Charmingly (USA) (King Of Kings (IRE))
7567[6]

Beaufort (IRE) *Michael Dods* a65 65
3 b g Zoffany(IRE) Change Course (Sadler's Wells (USA))
2711[5] 3249[5]◆ 3926[7] 5784[11] 6180[6] 6660[3] (7415) 8343[6]

Beau Geste (IRE) *Tony Carroll* a54 43
3 b g Lilbourne Lad(IRE) Valbonne (IRE) (Refuse To Bend (IRE))
(9450)◆

Beau Knight *Alexandra Dunn* a53 63
7 b g Sir Percy Nicola Bella (IRE) (Sadler's Wells (USA))
700[9] 2014[6] 2593[8] 4594[4] (5271) 5891[6]

Beau Massagot (FR) *Vaclav Luka Jr* a76 74
4 ch g Panis(USA) In Memory (FR) (Chimes Band (USA))
9483a[11]

Beaupreau *T Van Den Troost* a68 74
7 b h Mr. Sidney(USA) Kathy's Rocket (USA) (Gold Legend (USA))
6434a[10]

Beau Satchel *Adrian McGuinness* a61 63
9 b g Indesatchel(IRE) Sweet Patoopie (Indian Ridge (IRE))
63[3]

Beautiful Artist (USA)
Robyn Brisland
4 b m Lonhro(AUS) She's A Beauty (USA) (Storm Cat (USA))
1216[10] 2349[12]

Beautiful Gesture *K R Burke* a70 68
3 ch f Shamardal(USA) Viola Da Braccio (IRE) (Vettori (IRE))
1764[3] 2198[5] 3683[6] 5031[3]◆ 5941[2] 6678[5]

Beautrix *Michael Dods* a47 43
2 b f Brazen Beau(AUS) Dartrix (Dutch Art)
2840[9] 3244[9] 3812[9] 4756[13] 5196[3] 5630[4] 5968[9] 6182[9]

Beauty Choice *Charlie Fellowes* a67 76
2 b g Bated Breath Modesty's Way (USA) (Giant's Causeway (USA))
8011[5] 8511[2]

Beauty Filly *William Haggas* a98 105
4 b m Invincible Spirit(IRE) Miss Delila (USA) (Malibu Moon (USA))
2670a[8] (3632)◆ (4905)◆ 6706[10] 7893[5] 8115[7]

Beauty Generation (NZ)
John Moore 128
6 b g Road To Rock(AUS) Stylish Bel (AUS) (Bel Esprit (AUS))
9379a[3]

Beauty Of Deira (IRE) *Hugo Palmer* a77 77
3 ch f Pivotal Phillipina (Medicean)
3761[2] 4592[2] 5690[5] 8412[11]

Beauty Salon *James Fanshawe* a71 45
4 b m Dutch Art Albisola (IRE) (Montjeu (IRE))
135[4] 793[3] (968)

Beauty Stone (IRE) *Charlie Appleby* 68
2 b f Australia Za'hara (IRE) (Raven's Pass (USA))
8093[6] 8855[8] 9383[9]

Beauvais (IRE) *Saeed bin Suroor* a90 86
4 ch h New Approach(IRE) Marie De Medici (USA) (Medicean)
9051[3]

Beau Warrior (IRE)
Adrian McGuinness a89 77
3 b f Declaration Of War(USA) Sign From Heaven (IRE) (Raven's Pass (USA))
2319[6] 2661a[9]

Be A Wave *Gerald Geisler* a61 64
4 br m Bated Breath Soundwave (Prince Sabo)
2956a[4]

Be Bold *Rebecca Bastiman* a49 58
7 ch g Assertive Marysienka (Primo Dominie)
132[5] 530[2] 594[11] 1353[4] 1967[6] 2328[5] 2682[6] 3721[4] (4512) 4916[6] 5100[2] 5816[2] 5933[2] 6572[3] 6655[4] 7508[3] 7780[3] 8234[3]

Becker *Robert Cowell* a71 70
4 b g Delegator Mosa Mine (Exceed And Excel (AUS))
36[4] 317[6] 759[5] 1364[8] (9627)

Beckford *Gordon Elliott* a86 102
4 b h Bated Breath Whirly Dancer (Danehill Dancer (IRE))
2880a[7] 5923a[4] 7713a[7] 9004[12]

Beckwith Place (IRE)
Tracey Collins a72 90
4 b g Mastercraftsman(IRE) Sweet Afton (IRE) (Mujadil (USA))
5537a[2]

Becky Sharp *Jim Boyle* a62 56
4 b m Foxwedge(AUS) Perfect Practice (Medicean)
1679[10] 2283[8] 3017[4] (4287) 5106[3] 5744[4] 6333[6] 7759[10]

Becky The Thatcher
Micky Hammond 73
6 b m Mastercraftsman(IRE) Fairmont (IRE) (Kingmambo (USA))
(4146)

Becquagold (FR) *O Trigodet* a93 106
3 b c Orpen(USA) Berangele (FR) (Medaaly)
(217a)

Bedouin's Story *Saeed bin Suroor* a107 105
4 b g Farhh Time Crystal (IRE) (Sadler's Wells (USA))
285a[3]◆ 515a[4] 847a[5] 960a[6]◆ 1889[6] 3450[2] 4292[5] (5453) 7106[2] 7891[6]

Bedtime Bella (IRE)
Michael Appleby a72 74
3 b f Slade Power(IRE) Slope (Acclamation)
1598[8] 2332[7] 2590[3] 3189[5] 3709[2] 4519[3] 5297[2] (5669) (6033)◆ 6338[3] 7165[6] 7383[3] 9113[12] (9182) 9559[4]

Bee Able (USA) *Ralph Beckett* a67
2 b f Noble Mission Bee Brave (Rail Link)
7555[11] 7814[7] 8914[9] 9212[4]

Beechwood Izzy (IRE)
Keith Dalgleish a51 65
3 b f Dandy Man(IRE) Rugged Up (IRE) (Marju (IRE))
1504[11] 2960[6] 4632[9] 5235[6] 5786[7] 6547[4] 7050[10] 7405[10] 8235[11]

Beechwood James (FR)
Michael Appleby a54 48
3 b c Sunday Break(JPN) Mururoa (FR) (Great Journey (JPN))
1550[7] 4735[3] 5548[7] 6046[2] 6552[3] 7202[12] 8916[11] 9087[10] 9201[8] 9542[5]

Beechwood Jim Bob (IRE)
Mark Johnston a68
2 bl c Footstepsinthesand Clodovina (IRE) (Rock Of Gibraltar (IRE))
9408[3]

Beechwood Jude (FR)
Keith Dalgleish a50 79
3 b g War Command(USA) Ponte Sanangelo (FR) (Authorized (IRE))
2096[2]◆ 2811[9] 3358[6] (3926) 6038[2] 6340[5] 7436[4]◆ (8236)

Beehaar *John Gosden* a61
3 bb f Dark Angel(IRE) Umneeyatee (AUS) (Encosta De Lago (AUS))
380[6] 614[F] (Dead)

Bee Machine (IRE) *Declan Carroll* a64 59
4 b g Footstepsinthesand Lady Royale (Monsieur Bond (IRE))
233[2] 590[3] 829[9] 2631[5] 3208[5] (3970) 6276[9] 6546[11] 7384[7] 7869[2] 8266[5] 8404[3] 8646[5] (8949) (9337) 9559[7]

Bee Magic (IRE) *William Muir* a58
2 b g Zebedee Star Port (Observatory (USA))
7911[10] 8455[13] 8889[8] 9164[9]

Been Bobbied (IRE) *Richard Fahey* a55
2 b c Intello(GER) Roxelana (FR) (Red Ransom (USA))
8914[10]

Beepeecee *Thomas Gallagher* a76 68
5 b g Henrythenavigator(USA) Roedean (IRE) (Oratorio (IRE))
33[4] 1037[4] 1265[6] 1675[8] 8291[4] (8711) 9047[8] (9306)

Beer With The Boys *Mick Channon* a61 70
4 b g Nathaniel(IRE) Bathilde (IRE) (Generous (IRE))
4614[6] 5179[6] 5604[4] 6042[6] 6448[5] 6796[6] 7233[3] 7790[3]◆ 7984[13] 8248[2]

Beeswax (FR) *Gavin Hernon* a76 47
3 gr g Excelebration(IRE) Aifa (Johann Quatz (FR))
421a[3] 1347a[12]

Beethoven's Gal *Richard Fahey* a72 52
3 b f Iffraaj Apasionata Sonata (USA) (Affirmed (USA))
6259[4] 7213[12]

Be Fair *Tony Carroll* a70 55
3 b g Kyllachy Going For Gold (Barathea (IRE))
8837[3] (9310)

Beg For Mercy *Michael Attwater* a48 45
3 b g Heeraat(IRE) Plead (FR) (Bering)
438[6] 2926[5] 3410[8] 3989[12]

Beggarman *J S Moore* a63
2 ch g Toronado(IRE) Let's Dance (IRE) (Danehill Dancer (IRE))
9208[11] 9243[7]

Beguiling Charm (IRE) *Ed Walker* a75 75
3 b f Charm Spirit(IRE) Bryanstown (IRE) (Galileo (IRE))
1828[8] 3154[2] 3478[3] 4336[4] (5307) 6129[7] 6672[5] 7915[3]

Behavioral Bias (USA) *S Seemar* a102
5 ch g Shackleford(USA) Rosie Dooley (USA) (Trempolino (USA))
425a[3] 726a[5] 1112a[8]

Behemoth (AUS) *David Jolly* 110
3 b g All Too Hard(AUS) Penny Banger (AUS) (Zedrich (AUS))
8805a[4]

Beignet (IRE) *Linda Perratt* a61 58
2 b f Canford Cliffs(IRE) Cake (IRE) (Acclamation)
1931[2] 2248[4] 3371[4] 3634[4] 4448[3] 5010[3] 5279[2] 5562[6] 6182[6] 6799[6] 7734[5]

Being Alive *A Botti* 102
3 ch g Champs Elysees Pursuit Of Life (Pursuit Of Love)
4173a[4]

Be Kool (IRE) *Brian Ellison* a82 80
6 b g Approve(IRE) Accounting (Sillery (USA))
3356[2] 3867[13] 5283[3] 6935[3] (7587) 8237[11]

Belabour *Kevin Frost* a70 65
6 b g Bernardini(USA) Criticism (Machiavellian (USA))
(100)◆ 457[8] 782[12] 946[8] 1463[5] 4036[9] 4825[6] 5528[11]

Belated Breath *Hughie Morrison* a85 99
4 ch m Bated Breath Daffydowndilly (Oasis Dream)
2687[3] (3164) 3994[12] 5143[3] 5504[3] 6229[16] (6908) 7613[8]

Beleaguerment (IRE)
Archie Watson a74 66
3 bb g Kodiac Blockade (IRE) (Kheleyf (USA))
83[3] 142[2] 261[4] 838[5] 1028a[3] 1219[5] 1557[2]

Believe In Love (IRE) *Roger Varian* a64 73
2 b f Make Believe Topka (FR) (Kahyasi (IRE))
4918[5] 9326[2]◆

Be Like Me (IRE) *Marco Botti* a91 88
3 b f Helmet(AUS) Bint Malyana (IRE) (Bahamian Bounty)
1729[9] 2008[2] 3068[2] 4340[2] 4904[8] 5736[2]

Belisa (IRE) *Ivan Furtado* a67 65
5 ch m Lope De Vega(IRE) Fleche Brisee (USA) (Dynaformer (USA))
6661[4] 7900[12] 8513[5]

Bella Amoura *Brian Barr* a33
3 b f Nathaniel(IRE) Dream Wild (Oasis Dream)
8838[3] 9213[11]

Bella Bolide (FR) *M Brasme* a83 94
5 ch m Rock Of Gibraltar(IRE) Bellona (IRE) (Bering)
2167a[9] 5229a[6] 9603a[13]

Bella Brazil (IRE)
Mrs John Harrington a72 65
2 b f Clodovil(IRE) Daanaat (IRE) (Kheleyf (USA))
2783[4]◆ (3196) 3564[5] 4780[4] 5683[8] 6372[5] 7522[7] (9175)

Belladone Spirit (IRE)
J-M Baudrelle 80
3 b f Charm Spirit(IRE) Morning Bride (IRE) (Danehill Dancer (IRE))
1512a[8] 2091a[6] 2392a[5]

Bella Figlia *Ollie Pears* 48
2 bl f Brazen Beau(AUS) Powerfulstorm (Bertolini (USA))
6064[7] 7538[6]

Bellafina (USA) *Simon Callaghan* a112
3 b f Quality Road(USA) Akron Moon (CAN) (Malibu Moon (USA))
7479a[4] 8769a[2] 9638a[2]

Bella Ragazza *Hughie Morrison* a62 100
4 gr m Dutch Art Sell Out (Act One)
2608[5] 3342[4] 3986[16] 7750a[7] 9002[13]

Bella Vita *Eve Johnson Houghton* 101
3 gr f Aussie Rules(USA) Garabelle (IRE) (Galileo (IRE))
(2361) (2768) (3698) (4864)◆ 5682[2] 6378[5]

Belle Anglaise *Stuart Williams* a81 95
2 b f Cable Bay(IRE) Belle Allemande (CAN) (Royal Academy (USA))
5988[6]◆ (6793) (7547) 8089[5] 8586a[5]

Belle Bayeux *Mark H Tompkins*
3 b f Epaulette(AUS) Trew Class (Inchinor)
2941[9]

Belle Impression (FR) *Mlle L Kneip* a63 61
2 b f Penny's Picnic(IRE) Becbec (FR) (Slickly (FR))
2890a[3]

Bellepower (IRE)
John James Feane a59 57
3 ch f Slade Power(IRE) Indian Belle (IRE) (Indian Ridge (IRE))
341[7] 2325[2] 5096[4]

Belle Rousse *Sir Mark Prescott Bt* a19
2 ch f Archipenko(USA) Jolie Blonde (Sir Percy)
7386[5] 7605[10] 8121[10]

Bellevarde (IRE) *Richard Price* a79 81
5 b m Kodiac Pearl Mountain (IRE) (Pearl Of Love (IRE))
(2) 165[4] 1597[6] (1822) 2687[7] 3201[7] 3576[6] 4105[6] 4880[2] 5420[7] 5989[4] 6921[4] 7183[11] 7828[8] 8262[2] (8660) 8860[6]

Belle Voci *Stella Barclay*
2 gr f Hellvelyn Oricano (Arcano (IRE))
7377[10] 8337[11]

Bell Heather (IRE) *Patrick Morris* a68 70
6 b m Iffraaj Burren Rose (USA) (Storm Cat (USA))
67[8] 344[7] 814[6] (1387) 2106[2] 3843[3] 4318[3] 4875[3] 5419[8] 5709[5] 7145[14] 7682[5] 8669[10] 9253[10] 9609[9]

Bellick *John C McConnell* a70 58
4 b g Mayson Jane Jubilee (IRE) (Mister Baileys)
7086a[6]

Bell Rock *Andrew Balding* 102
3 b g Kingman Liberally (IRE) (Statue Of Liberty (USA))
3026[6] 3951[10] 4850[6]

Bell's The One (USA) *Neil L Pessin* a101
3 b f Majesticperfection(USA) Street Mate (USA) (Street Cry (IRE))
9638a[5]

Belvelly Boy (IRE) *David O'Meara* 58
3 b g Showcasing Freedom Pass (USA) (Gulch (USA))
4489[3]

Belvoir Bay *Peter Miller* a108 119
6 b m Equiano(FR) Path Of Peace (Rock Of Gibraltar (IRE))
1442a[2] (8770a)

Be More *Andrew Balding* 91
3 b f Shamardal(USA) Pearl Dance (USA) (Nureyev (USA))
2507[2] (3546) 4898[6] (5422) 6670[4] (8463)

Bempton Cliffs (IRE) *Tony Coyle* a40
4 gr g Canford Cliffs(IRE) Grand Lili (Linamix (FR))
18[5]

Be My Best (GER) *T Potters* 88
5 b m Areion(GER) Best Tune (King's Best (USA))
6769a[7]

Be My Day (FR) *F Chappet* a43 76
2 b c Zebedee Gloomy Sunday (FR) (Singspiel (IRE))
7043a[2]

Be My Prince (GER) *Frau S Weis* a75 70
5 ch g Areion(GER) Boucheron (GER) (Turfkonig (GER))
(6434a)

Be My Sea (IRE) *Tony Carroll* a74 74
8 b g Sea The Stars(IRE) Bitooh (Diktat)
3693[6] 6055[3] 7830[7]

Be My Sheriff (GER) *Henk Grewe* a97 113
5 bb h Lawman(FR) Bezzaaf (Machiavellian (USA))
2455a[2] 6487a[2] 7862a[3] 8372a[3]

Benadalid *Chris Fairhurst* a76 88
4 b g Assertive Gambatte (One Cool Cat (USA))
1761[4] 2748[15] 3514[3] 4241[13] 4730[4] (5174) 5694[6] 6067[3] (6580) 7153[4] 8130[11]

Benaras (USA) *Roger Fell* a48 43
4 b m Gio Ponti(USA) Brocatelle (Green Desert (USA))
210[11] 624[3]

Benbatl *Saeed bin Suroor* 124
5 b h Dubawi(IRE) Nahrain (Selkirk (USA))
(7660) 8334[16]

Bendy Spirit (IRE) *Richard Fahey* a83 67
2 b g Helmet(AUS) Parakopi (IRE) (Green Desert (USA))
1416[9] 1812[2] 2191[4] 7247a[15] 8022[5]◆ 8815[3] 9137[2]◆ 9242[2] 9514[3]

Bendzonic (IRE)
Denis Gerard Hogan 52
3 ch f Helmet(AUS) Bendzoldan (IRE) (Refuse To Bend (IRE))
3197[9]

Bene Bene (FR) *M Boutin* a53 52
2 b g Zanzibari(USA) Boulba D'Alben (FR) (Dark Angel (IRE))
1657a[8] 7043a[9]

Bengal Bay *William Haggas* 72
2 b c Cable Bay(IRE) Basque Beauty (Nayef (USA))
6911[5]

Bengali Boys (IRE) *Tony Carroll* a54 78
4 gr g Clodovil(IRE) Caherassdotcom (Compton Place)
127[6] 1274[6] 2625[5] 3509[8] 4303[11] 6220[14] 6547[9] 6839[12] 7632[12] 7828[15]

Benjamin Thomas (IRE)
John Quinn a57 78
5 b g Mayson Strudel (IRE) (Spectrum (IRE))
1158[3]◆ 1378[7]

Benji *Richard Fahey* a59 20
3 b c Magician(IRE) Penny Sixpence (FR) (Kheleyf (USA))
20[7] 274[6] 3969[11] 4606[7]

Ben Lilly (IRE) *Ralph Beckett* a55
2 b g Gleneagles(IRE) Aristocratic Lady (USA) (Kris S (USA))
6112[4] 7473[6]

Benny And The Jets (IRE)
Sylvester Kirk a87 87
3 ch g Showcasing Orange Pip (Bold Edge)
(27) 2624[6] (2937) 4420[6] 4847[18] 6809[4] 7524[5] 8601[3] 8826[2] 9057[3] 9301[8]

Benoordenhout (IRE) *T Le Brocq* a45 40
8 br g Footstepsinthesand Tara Too (IRE) (Danetime (IRE))
2672a[4] 3640a[8] 4686a[8] 6009a[6]

Bentley Mood (IRE) *G Botti* a74 66
2 b c Kodiac Got To Dance (Selkirk (USA))
8447a[4]

Bentley Wood *Mick Channon* 77
2 b c Sixties Icon Dozen (FR) (Mastercraftsman (IRE))
7067[2] 7586[4] 7755[8]

Ben Vrackie *John Gosden* a100 113
4 b h Frankel Kinnaird (IRE) (Dr Devious (IRE))
4053[2]◆ 4884[13] 6473[7] 7180[4]

Be Perfect (USA) *Ruth Carr* a62 74
10 b g Street Cry(IRE) Binya (GER) (Royal Solo (IRE))
1159[10] 1508[7] 1848[3] 2185[7] 2636[5] 3415[7] 4036[3] (4274) 4543[3] (5043) 5621[5] 6278[3] 7053[12] 7439[5]

Be Prepared *Simon Crisford* 87
2 b c Due Diligence(USA) Chicklade (Firebreak)
2931[3] (4302)◆ 4832[2] 7698[3] 8110[7]

Be Proud (IRE) *Jim Goldie* a71 62
3 b g Roderic O'Connor(IRE) Agnista (IRE) (Iffraaj)
2325[8] 4488[6] 4916[2]◆ 7210[2] 7307[4]◆ 7405[2] (7651) 7823[5] 8429[2] 8715[2] 9108[4] (9473)◆

Bequest *Ron Hodges* a63 68
3 b f Equiano(FR) Bandanna (Bandmaster (USA))
367[3]◆ 1020[3] 1287[4] 1687[3] 2276[2] 2474[4] 4457[11]

Beresford (IRE) *Richard Fahey* a55
3 b c Arcano(IRE) Carrauntoohil (IRE) (Marju (IRE))
405[7] 785[10] 930[8]

Berghain (IRE) *J Hirschberger* 104
6 ch h Medicean Basilea Gold (GER) (Monsun (GER))
2666a[7]

Beringer *Alan King* a74 109
4 b g Sea The Stars(IRE) Edaraat (USA) (Rahy (USA))
1415[3]◆ (1889) 2778[5] 3987[13] 4613[2] 5519[5] 6475[12] 7694[2]

Berkshire Boy (IRE) *H Al Alawi* a82 83
5 b g Elzaam(AUS) Circuit City (IRE) (Exit To Nowhere (USA))
197a[4]

Berkshire Philly *Andrew Balding* a55
2 ch f Roderic O'Connor(IRE) Berkshire Beauty (Aqlaam)
7787[8] 8198[4] 8651[10] 9037[4]◆

Berkshire Rocco (FR)
Andrew Balding 98
2 ch c Sir Percy Sunny Again (Shirocco (GER))
4897[4]◆ 5665[4]◆ (6710)◆ 8111[3]

Berkshire Savvy *Andrew Balding* a77 77
2 b g Mukhadram Zubova (Dubawi (IRE))
5563[4] 5992[2] (6684) 7612[5]

Berlin Tango *Andrew Balding* 101
2 b c Dansili Fantasia (Sadler's Wells (USA))
4925[5] (5493) 6417[3] 7150[3]

Berlusca (IRE) *David Loughnane* a67 70
10 b g Holy Roman Emperor(IRE) Shemanikha (FR) (Sendawar (IRE))
102[8] 344[9] 603[6]

Bermuda Schwartz *Richard Hughes* a78 77
2 gr g Outstrip Almaviva (IRE) (Grand Lodge (USA))
4558[7]◆ 5088[2] 5374[6] 6718[5] (7874)

Bernardo O'Reilly *Richard Spencer* 100
5 b g Intikhab(USA) Baldovina (Tale Of The Cat (USA))
3589[6] 5658[2] (6396) 8127[11] 8512[10]

Bernie's Boy *Phil McEntee* a61 56
6 b g Lilbourne Lad(IRE) Stoney Cove (IRE) (Needwood Blade)
91[4] 177[2] 247[5] 254[2] 610[7] 981[7] 1766[11] 6132[7] 6605[8] 6798[5] 7446[8] 8896[5] 9507[2] 9627[11]

Berrahri (IRE) *John Best* a90 89
8 b g Bahri(USA) Band Of Colour (IRE) (Spectrum (IRE))
292[3] 592a[3] (694a) (780a) 1096[4] 1588[5] 2400[2] 3073[3] 3545[3] (4112) (4928) 5423[6] 6448[2] (7127)◆ 7688[4]

Bertie Moon *Barry Leavy* a36 48
9 b g Bertolini(USA) Fleeting Moon (Fleetwood (IRE))
40[5] 1861[8] 2196[10] 3428[6]

Berties Mission (USA) *Derek Shaw* a50
3 b g Noble Mission Invigor (USA) (Medaglia d'Oro (USA))
8290[12] 8693[6] 8842[6] 9028[11] 9225[11]

Bertie's Princess (IRE)
Nigel Tinkler a30 68
2 b f Lawman(FR) Hana Delight (Sakhee (USA))
5152[7] 5514[3]◆ 6064[2] 6458[3] 7331[2] 7539[6] 8085[13]

Bertiewhittle *David Barron* a69 67
11 ch g Bahamian Bounty Minette (Bishop Of Cashel)
3813[19]

Bertog *John Mackie* 68
4 ch g Sepoy(AUS) Lucky Token (IRE) (Key Of Luck (USA))
3179[7] 4108[10]

Bertrimont (FR) *E Zahariev* a63
3 gr c Rajsaman(FR) La Barbacane (FR) (Excellent Art)
9281a[8]

Beryl The Petal (IRE)
David O'Meara a71 85
3 b f Dandy Man(IRE) Pinewoods Lily (IRE) (Indian Ridge (IRE))
65[2] 274[3] 461[3] 798[5] 2904[2] 3189[3] 3569[2] 4080[2] (4444)◆ (4781) 5157[4] 5724[6] 6609[8] 7049[6] 8342[11] 9402[8] 9606[7]

Bescaby *Michael Appleby* a40
4 b m Helmet(AUS) Tidal (Bin Ajwaad (IRE))
8467[11] 8693[4] 9282[10]

Beshaayir *William Haggas* a88 112
4 b m Iffraaj Bahia Breeze (Mister Baileys)
(3105a) 4885[5] 5479a[9]

Best Address (USA)
Amanda Perrett 36
2 b f City Zip(USA) Preferential (Dansili)
6906[12]

Best Evening (FR)
Andreas Suborics 70
2 gr f Sommerabend Best Dreaming (GER) (Big Shuffle (USA))
5713a[6]

Best Haaf *Michael Appleby* 59
3 b g Haafhd Beyeh (IRE) (King's Best (USA))
1562[12] 2023[13] 2764[8] 8205[12] 8434[15]

Best Of Days *James Cummings* a100 110
5 b g Azamour(IRE) Baisse (High Chaparral (IRE))
8578a[3] 8768a[5]

Best On Stage (GER) *P Schiergen* 92
3 b f Pastorius(GER) Best Moving (GER) (Reset (AUS))
2137a[4] 3119a[4] 4461a[5] 7250a[2]

Best Solution (IRE)
Saeed bin Suroor a110 119
5 b h Kodiac Al Andalyya (USA) (Kingmambo (USA))
6962[7] 7500a[5]

Betancourt (IRE) *Stef Keniry* a60 59
9 ch g Refuse To Bend(IRE) Orinoco (IRE) (Darshaan)
185[2] 810[5] 1718[14] 4435[6] 4661[7] 5001[8]

Be Thankful *Martin Keighley* a58 63
4 ch m Helmet(AUS) Be Joyful (IRE) (Teofilo (IRE))
18[4] 248[3] 2994[5] 3691[3] 4287[10] 5652[4] 6039[6] 8663[10]

Be The Mam (FR) *N Leenders* a61 51
2 b c Soul City(IRE) Kamate (FR) (Early March)
6386a[5]

Be Together *Charles Hills* a32
3 ch f Showcasing Love And Cherish (IRE) (Excellent Art)
1740[19] 5057[10] 6074[10] 8255[14]

Betsalottie *John Bridger* a64 65
6 gr g Aqlaam Si Belle (IRE) (Dalakhani (IRE))
619[9] 859[11] 9005[15] 9204[7]

Betsey Trotter (IRE) *David O'Meara* a93 92
4 b m Camacho Inourthoughts (IRE) (Desert Style (IRE))
3201[9] 3706[11] 4438[5] (5038)◆ (5315) (5972) 6581[2] 6908[4] 7380[3] (7914) 9010[6]

Better Than Ever (IRE) *Marco Botti* a70 70
3 b g Mainsail Better Chance (IRE) (Shamardal (USA))
2128[4] 3306[3] 3690[2] 5424[3] 6393[8] 6840[7] 7858[2]

Better The Devil (USA)
Archie Watson a61 79
2 b g Daredevil(USA) Hen Reception (USA) (Henny Hughes (USA))
(3717)◆ 3988[21] 4802[3] 5729[4]

Betty F *Jeremy Noseda* a75 99
4 ch m Frankel Instance (Invincible Spirit (IRE))
1891[6] 2621[6]

Betty Grable (IRE) *Wilf Storey* a53 65
5 b m Delegator Danella (IRE) (Platini (GER))
(210) 2241[2] (2964) (3224) 4633[2] 5239[2] 5787[2] (6628) 6828[5] 7441[2]

Betty's Heart (IRE) *John Best* a47 50
3 b f Camacho Sheer Delight (IRE) (Marju (IRE))
3319[4] 5044[5]

Bettys Hope *Rod Millman* a76 88
2 b f Anjaal Miss Poppy (Averti (IRE))
1513[2] 1843[2] 2191[2] (2996) (4637) (5185) 6542[5] 7896[9]

Between Hills (IRE)
Mrs John Harrington 95
2 b f Hot Streak(IRE) Breedj (IRE) (Acclamation)
5206a[4]

Beverley Bullet *Lawrence Mullaney* a65 70
6 b g Makfi Don't Tell Mary (IRE) (Starcraft (NZ))
1197[5] 1367[10] 1660[8] 3216[4] 3502[8] 3567[2] 3811[4] 3922[4] 4446[3] 4892[8] (5438) 5726[5] 6341[12] 6665[3] 7829[9] 8713[10] 8923[7]

Bevsboy (IRE) *Lynn Siddall* a29 51
5 b g Elzaam(AUS) Eurolink Sundance (Night Shift (USA))
3681[10] 4130[8] 4630[8] 5918[8] 6036[13] 7389[10] 8266[8] 8436[9] (8638)

Beyond Equal *Stuart Kittow* a97 98
4 b g Kheleyf(USA) Samasana (IRE) (Redback)
1654[7] 2393[4] 3347[10] 3770[5] (4236)◆ 4609[6] 6396[9] 8607[2] 8851[5]

Beyond My Dreams (IRE)
F Vermeulen a71 76
4 b h Dream Ahead(USA) Street Romance (USA) (Street Cry (IRE))
2226a[11] 3136a[14] 6267a[12]

Beyond Reason (IRE)
Charlie Appleby a68 93
3 b f Australia No Explaining (IRE) (Azamour (IRE))
4667[4] 5608[12]

Beyond The Clouds *Kevin Ryan* a83 86
6 ch g Peintre Celebre(USA) Evening (Mark Of Esteem (IRE))
3958[3] 4760[5] (5742) 6657[8] 7436[9] 8082[4]

Beyond The Fringe (IRE)
Phil McEntee a40
4 b m Kodiac April (IRE) (Rock Of Gibraltar (IRE))
206[6] 431[7]

Bezzas Lad (IRE) *Phillip Makin* a64 65
2 b g Society Rock(IRE) Red Rosanna (Bertolini (USA))
1758[9] 2184[2] 2706[3] 4624[6] 5703[6] 6032[5] 6980[5]◆ 7469[2]

B Fifty Two (IRE) *Marjorie Fife* a62 70
10 br g Dark Angel(IRE) Petite Maxine (Sharpo)
1818[9] 2294[11] 2876[5] 3203[11] 3716[4]◆ 3928[5] 3975[2] 4276[3] 4434[3] 4694[4] 4721[5] 4824[3] 5299[5] 5722[8] (5768) 6017[2] 6174[3] 6273[2] 6680[2] (6826) 7050[3] 7367[13] 7511[7] 7703[2] 8183[6] 8339[3]

Bhangra *Robert Cowell* a26 67
3 br f Showcasing Soundwave (Prince Sabo)
(6023) 6557[6]
Bharani Star (GER)
Peter Chapple-Hyam 72
2 ch f Sea The Stars(IRE) Bay Of Islands (FR) (Dubawi (IRE))
6949[5] 7461[4]
Bhodi (IRE) *Kevin Frost* a64 62
4 b g Dark Angel(IRE) Modesty's Way (USA) (Giant's Causeway (USA))
2629[7] 3567[15] 4194[6] 5807[3]◆ 6210[6] 7060[3]
Bibbidibobbidiboo (IRE)
Ann Duffield a75 74
4 b m Red Jazz(USA) Provence (Averti (IRE))
2379[7] 2899[6] 3567[13] 4438[3] 4784[2] 5517[14]
Bibi Voice (FR) *N Caullery* a59 60
4 b m Poet's Voice Blue Best (ITY) (Mujahid (USA))
7136a[12]
Bid Adieu (IRE) *Guillaume Courbot* a89 101
5 b g Pour Moi(IRE) Thoughtless Moment (IRE) (Pivotal)
3879a[12]
Bidding War *Michael Appleby* a60 57
4 ch m Champs Elysees Locharia (Wolfhound (USA))
64[6] 348[11] 697[4]◆ 4130[5] 4831[3] 5652[10] 6131[9] 7281[10]
Bielsa (IRE) *Kevin Ryan* 109
4 b g Invincible Spirit(IRE) Bourbon Ball (USA) (Peintre Celebre (USA))
(2823) (6676) 7193[15] (8512)
Big Amigo (IRE) *Ken Wingrove* a55 51
6 b g Bahamian Bounty Goldamour (IRE) (Fasliyev (USA))
467[9] 1158[8] 1339[8]
Big Baby Bull (IRE)
Richard Hannon a77 91
3 ch c Tagula(IRE) Grotta Del Fauno (IRE) (Galileo (IRE))
2088[5] 2616[5]
Bigbadboy (IRE) *Clive Mulhall* a44 50
6 b g Big Bad Bob(IRE) Elegantly (IRE) (Rock Of Gibraltar (IRE))
208[9] 3447[11] 3959[2] 5248[6] 5787[11] 6502[8] 7544[8] 9391[11]
Big Bad Lol (IRE) *Ed Walker* a64 60
5 b g Big Bad Bob(IRE) Indienne (IRE) (Indian Ridge (IRE))
180[2] 348[3] 760[5] 1231[5]
Big Bang *Julia Feilden* a30
2 ch g Observatory(USA) Bavarica (Dansili)
7730[7] 8552[8] 9097[5] 9403[12]
Big Boots (IRE) *Waldemar Hickst* a90 101
3 br c Society Rock(IRE) Dairy Herd (IRE) (Footstepsinthesand)
(1028a) (1340a) 6006a[3] 6519a[3]
Big Boris (IRE) *David Evans* a41 58
2 b g Baltic King Cayambe (IRE) (Selkirk (USA))
5992[6] 6395[10] 6640[8] 7111[3]◆ 8493[10] 9179[5]
Big Boss Man (FR) *Cedric Rossi* 83
2 bl c Big Bad Bob(IRE) Kitty Hawk (Danehill Dancer (IRE))
5286a[3] 5759a[2] 7673a[7]
Big Brothers Pride (FR) *F Rohaut* a79 111
3 b f Invincible Spirit(IRE) Polygreen (FR) (Green Tune (USA))
1199a[8] (1780a) 5611[8] 6520a[7]
Big Challenge (IRE)
Saeed bin Suroor a94 88
5 ch g Sea The Stars(IRE) Something Mon (USA) (Maria's Mon (USA))
47a[8] 284a[8] 513a[11] 7688[10] 8853[2]
Big City *Roger Fell* a48 75
2 b g Zoffany(IRE) Anipa (Sea The Stars (IRE))
3194[11] (3767) 4750[5] 7399[14] 7871[8] 9110[7] 9513[9]
Big Country (IRE) *Michael Appleby* a112 106
6 b g High Chaparral(IRE) Mount Eliza (IRE) (Danehill (USA))
565[2] 879[4] 1420[9] 6466[5] 7076[4] 7365[3] 8126[5]
Bigdabog *Stella Barclay* a23 53
4 b g Sayif(IRE) Alice's Girl (Galileo (IRE))
5248[10] 6180[13] 6663[11] 8081[11]
Big Daddy Kane *Marco Botti* a87
3 b g Sea The Moon(GER) Soft Morning (Pivotal)
2375[3] 7572[4] 8351[2] (9096)◆ 9480[2]
Big Duke (IRE) *Kris Lees* a72 109
7 b g Raven's Pass(USA) Hazarayna (Polish Precedent (USA))
1784a[10] 8361a[18]
Biggles *Ralph Beckett* a64
2 b c Zoffany(IRE) At A Clip (Green Desert (USA))
9174[6]
Bighearted *Michael Bell* a75 97
3 ch f Farhh Bianca Nera (Salse (USA))
1676[3] 2236[4] (2919) (4147) (4626) 7347[2] 7978a[2]
Big Ian *Alan Jones* a39 48
3 b g Archipenko(USA) Whispering Wind (IRE) (Sunshine Street (USA))
3204[11] 5580[6] 6098[6]
Big Impact *Luke McJannet* 65
2 b c Lethal Force(IRE) Valandraud (IRE) (College Chapel)
5381[6] 6330[4]
Big Jimbo *Gary Moore* 39
2 ch c Helmet(AUS) Big Moza (Pastoral Pursuits)
7899[10] 8516[16] 8721[8]
Big Kitten (USA) *William Haggas* a101 96
4 ch g Kitten's Joy(USA) Queen Martha (USA) (Rahy (USA))
1927[10] 2320[2] 3466[2] 4395[5] 4935[6] 5929[7]
Big Lachie *Mark Loughnane* a76 79
5 b g Camacho Ryan's Quest (IRE) (Mukaddamah (USA))
1496[6] 1822[9] 2107[4] 2804[9] 3838[2] (4230) 4478[2] 4775[2] 5503[7] 5882[4] 6203[4] 6916[9] 7230[3]◆ 7402[7] 8826[4] 9402[3] 9632[7]
Big Les (IRE) *Karen McLintock* a90 85
4 b g Big Bad Bob(IRE) Love Match (Danehill Dancer (IRE))
952[9] 5476[4] 6581[8] 7402[11] 8428[6] 8860[10] (9108) (9257) 9348[13] 9549[11]

Bigmouth (FR) *M Le Forestier* a64 55
3 b f Rajsaman(FR) Little Jaw (Footstepsinthesand)
2265a[2]
Big Reaction *X Thomas-Demeaulte* 82
2 b f Zoffany(IRE) Follow A Star (IRE) (Galileo (IRE))
6777a[7]
Bigshotte *Luke Dace* a62 41
4 b g Champs Elysees Humility (Polar Falcon (USA))
2215[3]◆ 2738[9] 4594[14] 5807[7] 6116[11]
Big Sigh (IRE) *John Mackie* a64 70
5 ch g Raven's Pass(USA) Sospira (Cape Cross (IRE))
1341[P]
Big Storm Coming *John Quinn* a74 86
9 b g Indesatchel(IRE) Amber Valley (Foxhound (USA))
2116[14] 2584[8] 3268[8] 3563[8] 4365[9] (4833)◆ (5090) 5416[6] 7128[4]
Big Time Dancer (IRE)
Jennie Candlish 62
6 b g Zoffany(IRE) Final Opinion (IRE) (King's Theatre (IRE))
3334[4] 4126[8]
Big Time Maybe (IRE)
Michael Attwater a78 67
4 b g Dandy Man(IRE) Divine Design (IRE) (Barathea (IRE))
314[4]◆ 468[3] 823[2] 1023[3] (1590) 1767[8] 2515[2] (3206) 3961[6] 4593[2] 5318[3] 5793[2] (6299) 7274[5] 7757[6]
Bigz Belief (IRE) *Matthew J Smith* 61
2 b c Make Believe Manaka (FR) (Falco (USA))
5710a[13]
Bila Shak (USA) *Fawzi Abdulla Nass* a68 77
3 b c Scat Daddy(USA) Dancing Trieste (USA) (Old Trieste (USA))
394a[12] (570a) 727a[2]
Billabong Cat (FR) *F Vermeulen* a90 96
4 b h Siyouni(FR) Lunacat (FR) (One Cool Cat (USA))
(1449a) 3140a[4]
Bill Cody (IRE) *Julie Camacho* a63 64
4 b g Declaration Of War(USA) Call This Cat (IRE) (One Cool Cat (USA))
2636[8] 3816[19] 5179[9] 6055[5] 6674[6] 7070[3] 8468[5] 9049[4] 9336[4]
Billesdon *Michael Madgwick* 12
2 ch g Cappella Sansevero Meebo (IRE) (Captain Rio)
5427[7] 5879[5] 6899[8]
Billesdon Brook *Richard Hannon* a105 116
4 ch m Champs Elysees Coplow (Manduro (GER))
2441[3] 2829[9] (3994)◆ 4758[2] (5608) (7898) 8772a[8]
Billhilly (GER)
Eve Johnson Houghton a55
2 b c Sea The Stars(IRE) Boccassini (GER) (Artan (IRE))
9052[10] 9197[7]
Billie Beane *Dr Jon Scargill* a58 41
4 b m Sir Percy Torver (Lake Coniston (IRE))
243[4] (3687) 4349[8] 5941[4] 7376[2] 8001[4]
Billiebrookedit (IRE) *Kevin Frost* a41 50
4 ch g Dragon Pulse(IRE) Klang (IRE) (Night Shift (USA))
2012[10] 2595[9] 4481[2] 6051[6] 6275[8] 7384[13] 8408[6] 8637[2]
Bill Neigh *John Ryan* 91
2 ch c Mustajeeb Dance Away (Pivotal)
(3355) 3988[12] (4509) 4610[7] 5275[2]◆ 5707[2] 6356[14]
Bill The Butcher (IRE)
Richard Spencer a82 68
2 ch c Starspangledbanner(AUS) Laurelita (IRE) (High Chaparral (IRE))
6464[5] 7103[3] (8069)
Billy Batts (USA) *Peter Miller* 107
2 bb r City Zip(USA) Down To Hearth (USA) (Giant's Causeway (USA))
8746a[2]
Billy Button (IRE) *Dean Ivory* a60 59
2 b c Coach House(IRE) Ojai (IRE) (Big Bad Bob (IRE))
3141[5] 3942[5] 8546[10]
Billy Dylan (IRE) *David O'Meara* a73 81
4 b g Excelebration(IRE) It's True (IRE) (Kheleyf (USA))
1847[6] 2421[13] 2940[5] 4364[5] 4514[5] 5042[6] 5515[3] 5819[7] 6699[15] 7353[6] 8066[11]
Billyfairplay (IRE)
John James Feane a83 51
5 b g Dark Angel(IRE) Nurture (IRE) (Bachelor Duke (USA))
307a[3] 748a[3]
Billy No Mates (IRE) *Michael Dods* 86
3 b g Clodovil(IRE) Sabaidee (IRE) (Beat Hollow)
2075[5] 3862[4] 5127[5] 5973[6] 6975[6] 7702[4] 8341[8]
Billyoakes (IRE) *Ollie Pears* a60 60
7 b g Kodiac Reality Check (IRE) (Sri Pekan (USA))
383[4] 483[5] 596[5] 1179[8] 1328[11] 1595[4] 2013[3] (3144) 4025[4] 5559[15] 7389[6] 7770[5] 8457[7] 9133[5] 9287[5] 9551[4]
Billy Ray *Sam England* a65 96
4 b g Sixties Icon Fiumicino (Danehill Dancer (IRE))
2571[6] 3600[5] 5183[2] 5928[9] 8114[30] 8513[12] 9288[8]
Billy Roberts (IRE)
Richard Whitaker a68 75
6 b g Multiplex Mi Amor (IRE) (Alzao (USA))
886[2] 1659[10] 2902[2] 4194[4] (4627) 5198[2] 5474[5] 7379[4] 8669[3] 9132[10]
Billy Ruskin *Kevin Ryan* a69 55
4 b g Bahamian Bounty Fluffy (Efisio)
2345[8]
Billy Star *Jimmy Fox* a45
4 b g Sixties Icon Appreciative (Cockney Rebel (IRE))
9589[8]

Billy Wedge *Tracy Waggott* a66 59
4 b g Arabian Gleam Misu Billy (Misu Bond (IRE))
2203[12] 3413[8] 3969[2]◆ 5438[10] 6275[9] 7289[14] 7654[2]◆ (7961)◆ 8306[5] 9352[3] (9396)
Bimble (IRE) *Henry Candy* a57
2 b f Acclamation Cape Violet (IRE) (Cape Cross (IRE))
9413[4]◆
Bin Battuta *Saeed bin Suroor* a114 106
5 ch g Dubawi(IRE) Land Of Dreams (Cadeaux Genereux)
(47a)◆ 398a[3] 958a[3] (7686)◆ 8332[9]
Bin Daahir *Charles Hills* a71 57
4 b g Exceed And Excel(AUS) Beach Frolic (Nayef (USA))
1392[8]
Binmar's Sexy Lexy (CAN)
Stuart Kittow a24 43
3 b f Sligo Bay(IRE) Little Scarlet (USA) (Strawberry Road (AUS))
5451[9] 6290[14] 6641[7] 8224[11]
Bint Dandy (IRE) *Charlie Wallis* a73 73
8 b m Dandy Man(IRE) Ceol Loch Aoidh (IRE) (Medecis)
2977[5] 4424[10] 5061[3] 5827[4] 6518[5] 6795[2] 7022[4] 7608[4] 7843[4] 8254[10] 9047[4] 9306[3]
Binti Al Nar (GER) *P Schiergen* 95
4 ch m Areion(GER) Best Moving (GER) (Reset (AUS))
7503a[5] 8153a[3] 8790a[4]
Bint Soghaan *Richard Hannon* a70 88
3 b f Dark Angel(IRE) Deyaar (USA) (Storm Cat (USA))
4178[2] 4597[4] (5138)◆ 5605[4] 6454[2] 7342[7]
Binyon *David Barron* a62 28
2 b g Poet's Voice Pretty Majestic (IRE) (Invincible Spirit (IRE))
7902[13] 8302[7]
Biometric *Ralph Beckett* 104
3 b c Bated Breath Bionic (Zafonic (USA))
(2140) (2790) 3351[2] (4016)◆ 5609[8] 6425[5] 8336[10]
Bionic Woman (IRE) *A Fabre* 102
2 b f Lope De Vega(IRE) Burning Heights (GER) (Montjeu (IRE))
7939a[4]
Biotic *Rod Millman* a68 79
8 b g Aqlaam Bramaputra (IRE) (Choisir (AUS))
1727[8] 2273[8] 2797[5] 3192[5] (4615) 5136[P] 6729[9] 7465[5]◆
Birch Grove (IRE) *David Simcock* a76 102
4 b m Galileo(IRE) Danehurst (Danehill (USA))
1569[3] 2214[3]◆ 2737[2] (3169) 4390[4] 4864[2]◆ (5510a)
Birdcage Walk *Hugo Palmer* a79 87
3 b f Sea The Moon(GER) Baisse (High Chaparral (IRE))
2488[2] 2919[2] (3773)◆ (5253) 6172[4] 6709[4]
Bird For Life *Mark Usher* a70 45
5 b m Delegator Birdolini (Bertolini (USA))
84[6] 363[2] 560[4] 731[5] 947[5] (1361) 2217[5] 4251[2] (5053)◆ 5631[3] 6400[14] 7845[4] 8829[8]
Birdie Bowers (IRE) *Michael Dods* 75
2 b g Bungle Inthejungle Shamiya (IRE) (Acclamation)
1843[3]◆ 2415[9] 3717[5]
Birdie Hop (FR) *F Belmont* 67
2 b f Muhtathir Toile De Soie (FR) (Peintre Celebre (USA))
9123a[5]
Bird Of Wonder *Henry Candy* a37 54
4 gr g Hellvelyn Phoenix Rising (Dr Fong (USA))
3661[8] 9298[11]
Bird On The Branch (FR)
Mme J Hendriks 1
4 gr m Rajsaman(FR) Lisselan Firefly (IRE) (Monashee Mountain (USA))
4960a[11]
Bird To Love *Mark Usher* a57 51
5 b m Delegator Bird Over (Bold Edge)
3664[9] 4503[7] 5499[3] 6039[5] 6843[7] 7390[7] 7818[9] (8813) 9042[11]
Birkenhead *Les Eyre* a78 69
2 b g Captain Gerrard(IRE) Vilnius (Imperial Dancer)
1416[6] 1493[2] (1843) 2115[3] 2586[2] 3212[2] 3997[6] 5275[6] 8506[2] (9205) 9661[8]
Birkie Queen (IRE) *J S Moore* a47 50
2 br f Gutaifan(IRE) The Oldladysays No (IRE) (Perugino (USA))
2138[7] 2565[6] 2918[7] 3714a[5] 4075[10] 5340[6] 5630[7] 9061[8] 9630[6]
Birthday Girl (IRE) *Amanda Perrett* a42 24
4 b m Excelebration(IRE) Street Style (IRE) (Rock Of Gibraltar (IRE))
3187[13] 4219[11] 4776[7] 6116[6] 9213[9] 9384[11]
Birthright *Richard Hannon* 76
4 b g Mawatheeq(USA) Pooka's Daughter (IRE) (Eagle Eyed (USA))
4929[3]◆
Biscuit Queen *Brian Ellison* a39 43
3 br f Harbour Watch(IRE) Ginger Cookie (Bold Edge)
1430[6] 1722[8] 2190[5] 3204[5] 3569[6] 4439[5] 4518[16]
Bithiah (IRE) *Ismail Mohammed* a53 28
3 b f Exceed And Excel(AUS) Sharqawiyah (Dubawi (IRE))
6561[3] 6944[5] 7417[3] 7824[13] 8821[11] 9034[8]
Bit Of A Quirke *Mark Walford* 77
6 ch g Monsieur Bond(IRE) Silk (IRE) (Machiavellian (USA))
1666[3] 1848[6] 2290[3] 3046[4] 3568[2] 3845[2] (4209) 4907[4] 5474[9] 7185[10] 7907[7]
Bizerta (FR) *A Fabre* a72 77
3 ch c Le Havre(IRE) Blue Blue Sea (Galileo (IRE))
1198a[2]
Biz Markee (IRE) *Roger Fell* a64 51
3 b g Slade Power(IRE) Heart's Desire (IRE) (Royal Applause)
32[3]◆ 614[5] 1066[11] 3415[5] 3931[8] 4210[5] 4587[6] 5555[3]

Black Abbey (FR) *Gavin Hernon* a58 55
3 bl g Hannouma(IRE) Alta Stima (IRE) (Raven's Pass (USA))
6094a[6]
Blackalfa (FR) *Laurent Loisel* a55 22
3 b f Alexandros Moody Blues (GER) (Big Shuffle (USA))
9058a[14]
Black And Blue (FR) *Mario Hofer* a64
3 b f Denon(USA) Britney (FR) (Kheleyf (USA))
6328a[4] 9280a[13]
Black Caspian (IRE) *Kevin Ryan* 79
2 b c Dark Angel(IRE) Catch The Sea (IRE) (Barathea (IRE))
3866[12] 5845[2] 6622[13]
Blackcastle Storm *Richard Hughes* a72 77
2 bl c Showcasing How High The Sky (IRE) (Danehill Dancer (IRE))
8460[4]◆ 8999[6]
Black Cat (FR) *Mlle A Wattel* a61 76
4 b g Elusive City(USA) Queen Of Deauville (FR) (Diableneyev (USA))
992a[11] 5643a[14]
Black Comedy (FR)
Richard Hannon 76
2 b c Le Havre(IRE) Vassaria (IRE) (Rock Of Gibraltar (IRE))
6640[2] 7055[2]
Black Corton (FR) *Paul Nicholls* 87
8 br g Laverock(IRE) Pour Le Meilleur (FR) (Video Rock (FR))
4096[8]
Blackcurrent *Alan Brown* a55 49
3 b g Kuroshio(AUS) Mamounia (IRE) (Green Desert (USA))
7628[2] 8071[10] 8450[6] 8898[2]◆ 9406[3] 9539[5]
Black Friday *Karen McLintock* a69 82
4 b g Equiano(FR) The Clan Macdonald (Intikhab (USA))
5000[8] 5616[3] 6037[2] 6665[5] 7418[6] (8181) 8636[4] 9348[14]
Black Granite (IRE)
Jassim Mohammed Ghazali a93 101
7 b g Dark Angel(IRE) Glisten (Oasis Dream)
869a[2]
Black Hambleton *Bryan Smart* a57 59
6 b g Dick Turpin(IRE) Duena (Grand Lodge (USA))
37[4] 738[7] 969[4] 2681[12] 7961[10]
Black Heart Bart (AUS)
Lindsey Smith 112
8 b g Blackfriars(AUS) Sister Theresa (AUS) (At Talaq (USA))
8136a[2] 8579a[9]
Blackheath *Ed Walker* a88 96
4 b g Excelebration(IRE) Da's Wish (IRE) (Sadler's Wells (USA))
1829[6] 2484[2] 3318[7] (4654)◆ 5546[7] 6376[10] 6950[9] 7697[8] 8707[5]
Black Isle Boy (IRE)
David C Griffiths a64 61
5 b g Elzaam(AUS) Shadow Mountain (Selkirk (USA))
2201[9] 2824[16] 3868[16] 4365[11] 7311[7] 7552[9] 8419[5] 9113[13] 9337[11] 9507[5]
Black Kalanisi (IRE) *Joseph Tuite* a82 82
6 b g Kalanisi(IRE) Blackthorne Winter (IRE) (Old Vic)
4066[5] 5268[8] 5451[4] (5840)◆ 7003[2]◆ 7510[7] 8654[2]
Black Kraken *Ben Haslam* a49 30
3 b g Battle Of Marengo(IRE) Stereo Love (FR) (Champs Elysees)
949[7] 1417[16] 1764[13]
Black Label *Karl Thornton* a60 61
8 b g Medicean Black Belt Shopper (IRE) (Desert Prince (IRE))
1572a[3] 5939[4]
Black Lace *Steve Woodman* a45 50
4 b m Showcasing Ivory Lace (Atraf)
202[7] 6120[8]
Blacklooks (IRE)
Joseph Patrick O'Brien a52 75
4 b g Society Rock(IRE) Mosaique Beauty (IRE) (Sadler's Wells (USA))
886[10] 1025[9] 2297[7] 4333[9] 7089a[8]
Black Lotus *Chris Wall* a83 90
4 b m Declaration Of War(USA) Ravensburg (Raven's Pass (USA))
2252[3] (2822) 3338[3] 4007[4] (6289) 8463[4]
Black Magic Woman (IRE)
Jack W Davison a78 97
3 br f Camacho Big Swifty (IRE) (Intikhab (USA))
1306a[2] 1601a[12] 2746[12] 4954a[8] 6235a[2] 7222a[2] 7934a[6]
Black Medick *Laura Mongan* a68 73
3 gr f Dark Angel(IRE) Penny's Gift (Tobougg (IRE))
(140) 320[4] 966[6] 2339[17] 3146[5]◆ 3468[5] (4453) 5350[5] 5651[9] 6567[4] 7129[4] 7843[6] 8652[10] 9244[6] 9426[9]
Black Noah *Johnny Farrelly* a71 71
4 br g Big Bad Bob(IRE) Frequently (Dansili)
1159[13] 1840[7] 2696[10]
Blackpearlsecrete (FR) *S Cerulis* a56 52
3 bb g George Vancouver(USA) Snow Spirit (Verglas (IRE))
2311a[3]
Black Salt *David Barron* a87 77
5 b g Equiano(FR) Marine Girl (Shamardal (USA))
165[3] 407[5] 832[9] 1760[2] 2788[3] 4149[3] 4632[5]
Black Star Dancing (USA)
Keith Dalgleish a39 63
2 b g Lemon Drop Kid(USA) Beautiful Cat (USA) (Kitten's Joy (USA))
7067[5] 7361[7] 7821[7]
Blackstone Cliff (IRE)
Adrian Murray a50 54
3 b g Canford Cliffs(IRE) D'Addario (IRE) (Galileo (IRE))
(4487)

Black Truffle (FR) *Mark Usher* a51 37
9 b g Kyllachy Some Diva (Dr Fong (USA))
161^8 263^4 (531) 701^{10} 1553^6 1731^7 3007^8 3476^{13} 3989^8 4501^8 6045^7

Blaine *Brian Barr* a56 82
9 ch g Avonbridge Lauren Louise (Tagula (IRE))
2611^8 3347^{11} 3636^4 4236^2 4495^5 5495^5 8410^6

Blair House (IRE) *Charlie Appleby* 117
6 ch g Pivotal Patroness (Dubawi (IRE))
395a^4 1115a^{10}

Blairlogie *Mick Channon* a60 57
2 b g Roderic O'Connor(IRE) Desert Morning (IRE) (Pivotal)
7113^6 7453^9 7911^9 8415^{10}

Blairmayne (IRE)
Miss Natalia Lupini a63 87
6 b g Zebedee Amended (Beat Hollow)
5205a^6 7241a^5

Blakeney Point *Roger Charlton* a99 109
6 b g Sir Percy Cartoon (Danehill Dancer (IRE))
1750^8 2742^{15} 5909^4 6355^{10} 6958^6 7408^4

Blake's Vision (IRE) *Mark Johnston* a75
2 b c Slade Power(IRE) Shirley Blake (IRE) (Acclamation)
8865^3◆ (9029) 9567^{12}

Blame Culture (USA)
George Margarson a86 69
4 b g Blame(USA) Pearl In The Sand (IRE) (Footstepsinthesand)
(117) 350^3 526^2 (812) 1036^7 2065^4 2273^{15} 2978^5 5283^2◆ 5945^7 6863^5 7856^8

Blame It On Sally (IRE)
Sir Mark Prescott Bt a81 79
3 b g Canford Cliffs(IRE) Sliding Scale (Sadler's Wells (USA))
(4834)◆ 5452^2 5798^3 (6405) (6597) 7414^2

Blame Me Forever (USA)
Don Cantillon a68
4 b m Blame(USA) Empress Josephine (USA) (Empire Maker (USA))
404^7 616^8 2351^5

Blame Roberta (USA)
Robert Cowell a81 89
3 b f Blame(USA) Royal Parisian (Royal Applause)
1913^4 2319^9 4101^{10} 5596^7 6148^7

Blanchefleur (IRE) *Richard Hannon* a76 78
4 b m Camelot Portrait Of A Lady (IRE) (Peintre Celebre (USA))
1932^5

Blank Canvas *Keith Dalgleish* 62
3 b f Swiss Spirit Verasina (USA) (Woodman (USA))
4827^8 5336^3 5669^2 6033^6 6575^7 6937^{14} 7367^{16}

Blastofmagic *Adrian Brendan Joyce* a55 52
5 gr g Hellvelyn Elegant Pursuit (Pastoral Pursuits)
6936^5 7214^4

Blast Onepiece (JPN)
Masahiro Otake 123
4 b h Harbinger Tsurumaru Onepiece (JPN) (King Kamehameha (JPN))
7941a^{11}

Blausee (IRE) *Philip McBride* a76 74
2 b f Swiss Spirit Fire Line (Firebreak)
2836^5 3578^2 4366^2 5189^6 6221^7 (7315) 8252^6 (8665)

Blazed (IRE) *Ed Vaughan* a77 84
5 gr g Dark Angel(IRE) Sudden Blaze (IRE) (Soviet Star (USA))
962^6 1329^{14} 2365^4 2824^{14}

Blaze Of Hearts (IRE) *Dean Ivory* a81 82
6 b g Canford Cliffs(IRE) Shesthebiscuit (Diktat)
54^5

Blazing Dreams (IRE) *Ben Haslam* a64 63
3 b g Morpheus Pure Folly (IRE) (Machiavellian (USA))
612^3 (1486)◆ (1721) 1980^3 3570^8 5852^7 7581^4 9395^5

Blazing Saddles *Ralph Beckett* 81
4 b g High Chaparral(IRE) Desert Sage (Selkirk (USA))
2092^{11} 2763^4 3349^2 4112^2 4543^{10}

Blazon *Kim Bailey* a73
6 b g Dansili Zante (Zafonic (USA))
(84) (318)◆ (946)◆ 1524^5 3467^4 4791^5

Blenheim Palace (IRE) *A P O'Brien* a103 107
3 ch c Galileo(IRE) Meow (IRE) (Storm Cat (USA))
2662a^2 3390a^{14} 4411a^2 5874a^4 7218a^3 (7668a)

Blessed (IRE) *Henry Candy* a64 63
2 b c Canford Cliffs(IRE) Bless You (Bahamian Bounty)
6845^7 8460^9 9242^4

Blessed To Empress (IRE)
Amy Murphy a68 65
4 b m Holy Roman Emperor(IRE) Blessing Box (Bahamian Bounty)
315^2 701^7 1231^6 1378^8 1933^2 (2286) 2929^7 4472^8 5051^2 6116^7 (6703) 6795^5 8291^{12} 9048^{13}

Bless Him (IRE) *David Simcock* a95 110
5 b g Sea The Stars(IRE) Happy Land (IRE) (Refuse To Bend (IRE))
2778^7◆ 3581^4 4399^2 5519^{12} (6516) (6915)

Bletilla *Mme Pia Brandt* 97
3 b f Galileo(IRE) Belle De Crecy (IRE) (Rock Of Gibraltar (IRE))
8581a^5

Bleu Astral (FR) *Mme G Rarick* a54 70
7 b g Astronomer Royal(USA) Passion Bleue (In The Wings)
1245a^{10}

Bleu Et Noir *Tim Vaughan* a74 62
8 b g Enrique Gastina (FR) (Pistolet Bleu (IRE))
2124^7 2720^7

Bleu Marine (IRE) *A Fabre* a76 95
3 b c Dark Angel(IRE) Blue Picture (IRE) (Peintre Celebre (USA))
3675a^2

Blindingly (GER) *Ben Haslam* a78 76
4 br g Shamardal(USA) Boccassini (GER) (Artan (IRE))
608^2◆ 9713◆ 1849^2 2246^7 3567^{16} 4820^3 (5918) (7418) 7703^3 7820^5 8427^6

Blissful (IRE) *A P O'Brien* 97
2 b f Galileo(IRE) Massarra (Danehill (USA))
4352a^7 (7215a) 7659^6

Blissful Beauty (FR) *Gavin Hernon* 94
3 b f Olympic Glory(IRE) Blissful Beat (Beat Hollow)
4964a^4 6775a^8

Blistering Barney (IRE)
Christopher Kellett a63 40
3 b g Sir Prancealot(IRE) Eternal View (IRE) (Pivotal)
5098^3 6823^5 7303^3 8086^5

Blistering Bob *Roger Teal* a82 86
4 b g Big Bad Bob(IRE) Kristalette (IRE) (Leporello (IRE))
(6083) 6909^6 8411^{10}

Blistering Dancer (IRE)
Tony Carroll a47 48
9 b g Moss Vale(IRE) Datura (Darshaan)
42^8 166^6 478^4 1368^9 2532^{12}

Blitzle *Ollie Pears* a70 64
2 gr f Toronado(IRE) Kept Under Wraps (IRE) (Clodovil (IRE))
2476^5 2840^3 3927^7 (4778) (5279) 6011^4

Blizzard *Ralph Beckett* 99
4 b m Medicean Moretta Blanche (Dansili)
3863^{14} 5608^7◆ 6646a^9 7893^6

Blocking Bet (FR) *M Boutin* a66 62
4 gr g Tin Horse(IRE) Claire (IRE) (Polish Precedent (USA))
2647a^5

Blonde Warrior (IRE) *Hugo Palmer* a80 92
3 ch g Zoffany(IRE) Dame Blanche (IRE) (Be My Guest (USA))
1736^{14} 2414^7 4348^3 5685^6 7187^7

Blood Eagle (IRE) *Andrew Balding* a78 72
3 b c Sea The Stars(IRE) Directa Princess (GER) (Dubai Destination (USA))
156^5◆ 1221^2 (1509) 1911^5 2796^9 3647^4 4321^5 7773^2

Bloody Love (IRE) *Endo Botti* 93
3 b c Rip Van Winkle(IRE) Princess Desire (IRE) (Danehill (USA))
2888a^6

Blowing Dixie *Jane Chapple-Hyam* a84 62
3 b g Dubawi(IRE) Time Control (Sadler's Wells (USA))
2343^7 2913^5 3528^5 6153^4 (6550)◆ 7192^7 (7629) 7872^3 8433^6 (9033) 9454^5 9633^{10}

Blown By Wind *Mark Johnston* a89 106
3 b c Invincible Spirit(IRE) Discourse (USA) (Street Cry (IRE))
3151^2 3599^2 3865^9 4360^9 4847^{15} 5666^{11} 6150^7 6841^5 (8184)◆

Blue Battalion *John Gallagher* 37
3 ch g Cityscape Hollybell (Beveled (USA))
8006^5

Blue Beirut (IRE) *William Muir* a57 42
3 b g Lilbourne Lad(IRE) Ornellaia (IRE) (Mujadil (USA))
1182^6 1419^6 1771^8 3938^6 4769^{10} 5249^{13} 7450^7 8196^3 8551^9

Bluebell Time (IRE)
Malcolm Saunders a58 58
3 br f Coach House(IRE) Matterofact (IRE) (Bold Fact (USA))
1909^2 2276^4 2939^8 6197^3 6851^2 7112^7

Blue Candy *Ivan Furtado* a40
4 b g Bahamian Bounty Sally Can Wait (Sakhee (USA))
249^8 429^9 835^{12}

Blue Chipper (USA)
Kim Young Kwan a110
4 b g Tiznow(USA) Dixie City (USA) (Dixie Union (USA))
(7010a) 8771a^3

Blue De Vega (GER) *Robert Cowell* a94 95
6 b g Lope De Vega(IRE) Burning Heights (GER) (Montjeu (IRE))
1734^2 1938^8 2403^4 2910^5 3344^3 3662^4 4331^9 4896^7◆ 5504^7 5661^{17} (6149) 6534^5 6954^2 7348^5 7894^7

Blue Diamond (FR) *S Smrczek* a77 77
7 b g King's Best(USA) Ripley (GER) (Platini (GER))
1073a^{13}

Blue Gardenia (IRE) *David O'Meara* 100
3 gr f Mastercraftsman(IRE) Alegra (Galileo (IRE))
2745^5 3316^9 5190^5 5682^5 6446^4 7137a^5 7658^9

Blue Harmony *Michael Blake* a51 39
4 b m Bahamian Bounty Fascination Street (IRE) (Mujadil (USA))
80^{11} 485^2 718^3 2513^{11}

Blue Hills (FR) *J Reynier* a69 77
5 b m Myboycharlie(IRE) Acentela (IRE) (Shirocco (GER))
6651a^6

Blue Laureate *Ian Williams* a70 97
4 b g Poet's Voice Powder Blue (Daylami (IRE))
2606^2 3078^5 3655^7 5368^3 5928^8 6355^{15} (7239) 7464^3

Blue Laurel *Richard Hughes* a11
3 b g Showcasing Powder Blue (Daylami (IRE))
5268^{10} 6505^{10}

Bluella *Robyn Brisland* a54 43
4 b m Equiano(FR) Mata Hari Blue (Monsieur Bond (IRE))
604^5 811^4 926^3 1162^{10} 1402^{12} 3518^{10} 3933^2 4182^7 5765^7 6168^7 (6551) 7628^4 7737^{13} 8401^5 8898^8 9034^7

Blue Lyte *Nigel Tinkler* 23
2 b f Sir Percy Sparkling Clear (Efisio)
5017^6 6064^{13} 6497^8

Blue Mariposa (FR)
Mme E Siavy-Julien
4 b m Blu Constellation(ITY) Tektea (FR) (Teofilo (IRE))
4860a^9

Blue Medici *Mark Loughnane* a82 79
5 b g Medicean Bluebelle (Generous (IRE))
3046^9 4426^2◆ (4658) (5338) 5850^2 (6511) 7003^{14} 8014^6 8829^3 (9167) 9633^9

Blue Mist *Roger Charlton* a101 103
4 ch g Makfi Namaskar (Dansili)
2609^6 4097^{11} 5413^3◆ 6706^6

Blue Point (IRE) *Charlie Appleby* 127
5 b h Shamardal(USA) Scarlett Rose (Royal Applause)
(725a)◆ (1111a) (1442a) (3950) (4094)◆

Blue Prize (ARG) *Ignacio Correas IV* a120
5 ch m Pure Prize(USA) Blues For Sale (ARG) (Not For Sale (ARG))
(8775a)

Blue Rambler *Tony Carroll* a52 85
9 b g Monsun(GER) La Nuit Rose (FR) (Rainbow Quest (USA))
2398^2 3044^{11}

Blue Rocks *Lisa Williamson* a57 49
5 b g Indesatchel(IRE) Mabinia (IRE) (Cape Cross (IRE))
479^9 793^8 914^9 1078^5 1390^{12} 1837^{10}

Blue Skimmer (IRE) *Alastair Ralph* a49 47
7 b g Arcano(IRE) Cattiva Generosa (Cadeaux Genereux)
181^4 321^8

Blue Skyline (IRE) *David Elsworth* a64 77
2 ch g Footstepsinthesand Ballerina Blue (IRE) (High Chaparral (IRE))
8012^5 8459^3 8722^7

Blue Slate (IRE) *J S Moore* a47 17
2 gr g Alhebayeb(IRE) Hallbeck (Halling (USA))
8516^{18} 9127^4 9325^8

Blue Suede (IRE) *R K Watson* a48 47
5 b m Requinto(IRE) Shoooz (IRE) (Soviet Star (USA))
279^7

Blue Tango (GER) *M Munch* a70 78
4 gr h Zebedee Beatify (IRE) (Big Bad Bob (IRE))
2956a^7 6267a^7 7601a^3

Bluetta *Robyn Brisland* a28
3 b f Heeraat(IRE) Mata Hari Blue (Monsieur Bond (IRE))
4010^{10} 6551^3 7032^{11}

Blue Uluru (IRE) *G M Lyons* a96 105
4 b m Choisir(AUS) Lady Of Beauty (USA) (Coronado's Quest (USA))
6986a^3 7454^7 8328a^6

Blue Venture *Tony Carroll* a57 56
2 b f Bated Breath Blue Goddess (IRE) (Blues Traveller (IRE))
4448^7 4993^8◆ 6047^2 6799^2◆ 7110^3 7853^2

Blue Whisper *S Donohoe* a62 54
4 ch g Bated Breath Vivid Blue (Haafhd)
2964^{12} 3720^3 5099^5 5933^6

Blury (ITY) *Andrea Marcialis* 62
3 b g Olympic Glory(IRE) Marablu (IRE) (Invincible Spirit (IRE))
1842a^8 2392a^2 3066a^6

Blushing Bere (FR) *E Leenders* a60 67
8 b g Hurricane Cat(USA) Niska (USA) (Smart Strike (CAN))
46a^{13}

Blyton *Luke Comer* a73 81
3 b c Kodiac Minwah (IRE) (Oasis Dream)
2221a^9 7241a^{21}

Blyton Lass *James Given* a61 55
4 ch m Havana Gold(IRE) Cesseras (IRE) (Cape Cross (IRE))
465^3 792^5 984^4 1546^5 2234^4 3142^7 (4518) 5248^4 6502^2 (6982) (8072) (8904)

Boardman *P Bary* a64 90
3 b c Kingman Nimble Thimble (USA) (Mizzen Mast (USA))
4428a^3

Boasty (IRE) *Charlie Fellowes* a66 65
2 b g Sir Prancealot(IRE) Caffe Latte (IRE) (Seattle Dancer (USA))
3257^{11} 3579^5 6449^7 7155^7

Boatrace (IRE) *David Evans* a50 51
4 ch g Camacho Shamarlane (Shamardal (USA))
62^8 602^7 695^9

Bobba Tee *Lawrence Mullaney* a62
7 b g Rail Link Trompette (USA) (Bahri (USA))
7630^5 9350^3 9469^6

Bobby Biscuit (USA) *Roger Varian* a78 13
4 b g Scat Daddy(USA) Poupee Flash (USA) (Elusive Quality (USA))
54^6 292^5◆ 473^6 (7839) 8548^2 9512^6

Bobby Jean (IRE)
Miss Tara Lee Cogan a39 59
8 b m Jeremy(USA) Madam's View (IRE) (Entrepreneur)
3223^3

Bobby Joe Leg *Ruth Carr* a64 47
5 ch g Pastoral Pursuits China Cherub (Inchinor)
22^5 356^2 496^2 609^3 1016^5 1766^5 6174^6 6665^8 7418^{11} 8345^7 8864^3 9039^6 9396^5

Bobby K (IRE) *Simon Crisford* a94 93
4 br g Dabirsim(FR) Shanjia (GER) (Soldier Hollow)
2187^4 2563^P 3338^5 4386^9

Bobby's Charm (USA) *Scott Dixon* a57 60
4 b g Shanghai Bobby(USA) Magic Charm (USA) (Horse Greeley (USA))
3207^9 5330^{10} 7050^{12}

Bobby Shaft *Richard Fahey* a76 69
3 b g Garswood She Mystifies (Indesatchel (IRE))
1346^4 1649^2 8718^2◆ 9032^2

Bobby The Great *Mark Johnston* a60 65
2 b c Frankel Riberac (Efisio)
8460^7 9452^6

Bobby Wheeler (IRE) *Clive Cox* a74 77
6 b g Pivotal Regal Rose (Danehill (USA))
9053^{14} 9308^{10}

Bobesh *Stepanka Myskova* 48
3 gr c Sea The Moon(GER) Batik (IRE) (Peintre Celebre (USA))
1347a^{11}

Bob Maxwell (IRE) *Robin Dickin* a58 54
5 b g Big Bad Bob(IRE) Catching Stars (IRE) (Halling (USA))
9275^9

Bob's Girl *Michael Mullineaux* a45 52
4 b m Big Bad Bob(IRE) Linda (FR) (Tamayuz)
2481^4 2714^{11} 3217^4 4285^7 4633^{12} 5020^7 (5248) 5725^{11} 6499^{12} 7335^{10} 8299^{10}

Bob's Oss (IRE) *Alan Berry* 61
2 b g Anjaal Prisca (Holy Roman Emperor (IRE))
2415^{12} 2906^3 3220^6 4652^5 5196^9 5703^4 6272^2 6653^{11} 7140^{10} 7679^{10}

Bob The King *F Rossi* a73 72
3 ch c Zoffany(IRE) Crystal Curling (IRE) (Peintre Celebre (USA))
(9504a)

Bobydargent (FR) *J-P Gauvin* a93 77
3 gr c Kendargent(FR) Maybe (GER) (Dashing Blade)
1347a^9

Boccaccio (IRE) *Charlie Appleby* a87 81
2 b c Dubawi(IRE) J Wonder (USA) (Footstepsinthesand)
(3274) (9174)◆

Bochart *S Seemar* a101 78
6 ch g Dubawi(IRE) Camlet (Green Desert (USA))
(97a) 513a^{10} 842a^5 957a^2

Bockos Amber (IRE) *Roger Teal* a36 57
2 ch f Kyllachy Goldcrest (Assertive)
4448^9 5772^{12} 6442^8 7234^9 7853^9

Bodacious Name (IRE) *John Quinn* a72 72
5 b g Famous Name Nice Wee Girl (IRE) (Clodovil (IRE))
1971^5 2626^4◆ 3294^4 3653^6 8236^3◆ (8945)

Bodexpress (USA)
Gustavo Delgado a112
3 b c Bodemeister(USA) Pied A Terre (CAN) (City Zip (USA))
2425a^{13} 2856a^U

Bodyline (IRE) *Sir Mark Prescott Bt* 80
2 b c Australia Eurirs (FR) (Indian Ridge (IRE))
5212^5 (5572)◆ 6528^2◆

Boerhan *William Haggas* a96 97
3 b g Sea The Stars(IRE) Greenisland (IRE) (Fasliyev (USA))
1831^3 2553^4 4845^7 5931^8

Boffo (IRE) *Ian Williams*
4 b g Intello(GER) Claxon (Caerleon (USA))
1365^8 1826^{14}

Bogardus (IRE) *Liam Bailey* a54 57
8 b g Dalakhani(IRE) Sugar Mint (IRE) (High Chaparral (IRE))
2436^9 3046^{12} 4510^7 5029^{12} 5905^6 7314^5

Bohemian Rapsody (FR)
E D'Andigne a18 35
9 b g Jarn Marion La Coquine (FR) (Al Nasr (FR))
7501a^6

Bohemien (IRE) *Joeri Goossens* a69 70
6 b g Acclamation Blagueuse (IRE) (Statue Of Liberty (USA))
2956a^{14}

Boing *Miss Clare Louise Cannon* a53 18
4 b g Bated Breath Lomapamar (Nashwan (USA))
8818^9

Bois D'Argile *C Plisson* 26
2 ch c Hot Streak(IRE) Bestfootforward (Motivator)
6485a^8

Boite (IRE) *Warren Greatrex*
9 b g Authorized(IRE) Albiatra (USA) (Dixieland Band (USA))
2606^7

Boitron (FR) *Richard Hannon* 107
3 b c Le Havre(IRE) Bellifiore (FR) (Verglas (IRE))
1752^5 2162a^9 2953a^5

Bokan (FR) *Wido Neuroth* a82 92
7 b g Soldier Of Fortune(IRE) Paree (IRE) (Desert Prince (IRE))
4419a^4 7498a^{11}

Bokra Fil Mishmish (FR)
G Guillermo a39 61
5 b m Manduro(GER) Street Lightning (FR) (Best Of The Bests (IRE))
(7501a)

Bold Approach (IRE) *J S Bolger* a103 94
3 b c Dawn Approach(IRE) Excuse Me (USA) (Distorted Humor (USA))
3063a^6

Bold Rex (SAF) *M F De Kock* 93
5 b g Bold Silvano(SAF) Rexana (SAF) (National Assembly (CAN))
173a^{10} 515a^{12} 637a^9 1748a^{10}

Bold Show *Richard Fahey* a48 58
3 b g Showcasing Bold Bidder (Indesatchel (IRE))
2624^7◆ 2895^4 3510^{10} 5147^{10} 5847^2 6529^{11} 7581^7 8068^{13}

Bold Spirit *Declan Carroll* a77 78
8 b g Invincible Spirit(IRE) Far Shores (USA) (Distant View (USA))
236^6◆

Bold Statement (IRE) *Alan Berry* a44 38
4 b g Arcano(IRE) Kylemore (IRE) (Sadler's Wells (USA))
5709^{11} 6012^5 6343^{12} 6545^8 6824^4 6896^7 7732^{10} 8904^9

Bold Suitor *Ed Walker* a64 41
2 b c Brazen Beau(AUS) Samasana (IRE) (Redback)
7911^7 8511^{10} 9324^5

Bolero Dei Grif (ITY) *G Botti* a70 77
2 b c Sakhee's Secret Pesach (IRE) (Indian Danehill (IRE))
5642a^2

Bolleville (IRE) *J-C Rouget* 106
3 b f Camelot Brasileira (Dubai Destination (USA))
6003a^7

Bollihope *Shaun Keightley* a74 69
7 ch g Medicean Hazy Dancer (Oasis Dream)
(120) 241^2 722^4 5820^3 6839^3 7610^5 8087^6 8548^6

Bollin Joan *Tim Easterby* 79
4 b m Mount Nelson Bollin Greta (Mtoto)
2629^8 3057^5 3568^9 (4371) 4627^5 5039^2◆ (5332) 5849^5 6456^9 7003^6 7366^4 (7441)

Bollin Margaret *Tim Easterby* a60
2 b f Fountain Of Youth(IRE) Bollin Greta (Mtoto)
8717^5◆

Bollin Ted *Tim Easterby* a58 68
5 b g Haafhd Bollin Greta (Mtoto)
3217[3] 4054[7] 4658[7] 5024[2] (5245) 5518[4] 5725[8] 6103[5] 6343[5] 7544[2] 8862[11]

Bolt N Brown *Gay Kelleway* a68 71
3 b f Phoenix Reach(IRE) Beat Seven (Beat Hollow)
66[3] 259[3] 1351[3] 2914[9] 3741[2] 4110[7] 6722[3] 7650[4] 8196[6] 8434[3] 8837[4] 9216[8] 9589[9]

Boma Green *Jeremy Noseda* 79
2 bb c Iffraaj Dubai Cyclone (USA) (Bernardini (USA))
2780[3]◆

Bombastic (IRE) *John Butler* a76 75
4 ch g Raven's Pass(USA) Star Of The West (Galileo (IRE))
3305[9] 4226[16] 7125[2]◆ 7554[3] 8413[7] 9306[11] 9559[11]

Bombero (IRE) *Ed de Giles* a65 75
5 b g Dragon Pulse(IRE) Mathool (IRE) (Alhaarth (IRE))
(3925) 4792[8] 7643[7] 8248[9] 8862[2]

Bombetta (FR) *Rosine Bouckhuyt* a53 57
4 b m George Vancouver(USA) Salvia (FR) (Septieme Ciel (USA))
4532a[11]

Bomb Proof (IRE) *Jeremy Noseda* 95
2 br c Society Rock(IRE) Chantaleen (FR) (Falco (USA))
(2747)

Bombyx *James Fanshawe* 102
4 ch g Sir Percy Bombazine (IRE) (Generous (IRE))
3025[5] 3646[3] 4646[13]

Bonaparte Sizing (FR)
J Bertran De Balanda 84
5 b g Voix Du Nord(FR) Royale Des Bordes (FR) (Lavirco (GER))
6095a[5]

Bonarda (FR) *M Boutin* a74 82
3 b f Style Vendome(FR) Sloane De Borepair (FR) (Sevres Rose (IRE))
(5165a) (8449a)

Bond Angel *David Evans* a70 70
4 gr m Monsieur Bond(IRE) Angel Grigio (Dark Angel (IRE))
(6) 232[3]◆ 507[2] 830[3] 1175[4] 1369[4] 1653[7] (1859) 2193[2] 2297[3] 5080[4] 5446[5] 6160[8] 6362[7] 7084[7] 7875[9] (8270) 8902[7] 9138[7] 9180[6] (9663)

Bondeiger (AUS)
Ciaron Maher & David Eustace 93
7 bb h War Pass(USA) Debutante Robe (JPN) (Admire Vega (JPN))
8803a[5]

Bondi Sands (IRE) *Mark Johnston* a69 69
2 b g Australia Thai Haku (IRE) (Oasis Dream)
7562[6] 7834[3] 8461[9]

Bond's Boy *Richard Fahey* 84
2 ch g Monsieur Bond(IRE) Blades Girl (Bertolini (USA))
(6457) 7896[3]

Bond Street Beau *Philip McBride* a64 58
4 ch g Dandy Man(IRE) Loveleaves (Polar Falcon (USA))
759[4] 857[6] (919) 1565[6] 3144[6] 5870[6] 8917[8] 9092[7] 9287[9]

Bonfire Heart (FR) *R Le Gal* a76 64
7 b g Falco(USA) Arlecchina (GER) (Mtoto)
7676a[7]

Bongiorno (IRE) *W McCreery* 96
4 b m High Chaparral(IRE) Capistrano Day (USA) (Diesis)
1620a[8] 8245[5]

Bonneville (IRE) *Rod Millman* a55 53
3 b g Champs Elysees Aspasi (Dalakhani (IRE))
258[5] 537[1] 765[4] 931[4] 1174[7] 1332[2]◆ 1555[2] 2343[2] 2530[3] 3528[6] 3888[12] 6805[7] 7295[3] 8003[5] 8406[5]

Bonnie Park (IRE) *Matthew J Smith* a38 48
4 b m Sir Prancealot(IRE) Abbey Park (USA) (Known Fact (USA))
8898[7]

Bonnoeil (FR) *Jane Soubagne* 91
3 gr f Rajsaman(FR) Akoyama (Peintre Celebre (USA))
2029a[5]

Bonny Blue *Rod Millman* 58
3 b f Harbour Watch(IRE) Bonnie Grey (Hellvelyn)
3090[9] 3574[4] 4180[12] 4496[3] 5016[5]

Bonsai Bay *Ian Williams* a38
4 b g Multiplex Bonsai (IRE) (Woodman (USA))
7772[P] 9442[5]

Bonus *Jim Boyle* a52 48
2 b g Roderic O'Connor(IRE) Spring Clean (FR) (Danehill (USA))
6669[12] 7124[7] 8060[7]

Booborowie (IRE) *Mandy Rowland* a26 46
6 bb g Big Bad Bob(IRE) Rejuvenation (IRE) (Singspiel (IRE))
9447[8]

Bookieboy (FR) *Yannick Fouin* 23
3 bb g Silver Frost(IRE) Diolefine (FR) (Elusive City (USA))
2519a[10]

Book Of Dreams (IRE)
Michael Appleby a97 96
4 b g Dream Ahead(USA) Moonbi Ridge (IRE) (Definite Article)
89[5] 255[5] (764)

Book Review *John Gosden* a64 73
2 ch g Dubawi(IRE) Criticism (Machiavellian (USA))
8858[2]◆ 9052[6] 9154[7]

Boom Boom Boom *Stuart Williams* a50 51
2 ch g Raven's Pass(USA) Futureland (Echo Of Light)
8202[6] 9043[8] 9195[13]

Boomer *Tom Dascombe* 108
2 b f Kingman Wall Of Sound (Singspiel (IRE))
4551[4] (5342)◆ (6444) 7120[2] 8091[5]

Boom The Groom (IRE)
Tony Carroll a93 88
8 b g Kodiac Ecco Mi (IRE) (Priolo (USA))
127[7] 551[3] (837) 987[6]◆ 2030[8] 2589[5] 3344[8] 3893[5] 4406[13] 5291[4] 5524[6] 9550[7]

Boorowa *Ali Stronge* a41 56
3 b f Dunaden(FR) Sleep Dance (Sleeping Indian)
2772[5]◆ 3258[4] 4180[7] 5498[10] 6181[9]

Boosala (IRE) *William Haggas* 91
2 b c Dawn Approach(IRE) Zoowraa (Azamour (IRE))
(3943)◆ (5396)

Boots And Spurs *Scott Dixon* a57 68
10 b g Oasis Dream Arctic Char (Polar Falcon (USA))
45[12] 232[8]

Bopedro (FR) *J S Bolger* 104
3 b c Pedro The Great(USA) Breizh Touch (FR) (Country Reel (USA))
7222a[4]

Borak (IRE) *Bernard Llewellyn* a64 72
7 b g Kodiac Right After Moyne (IRE) (Imperial Ballet (IRE))
4231[9] 5993[8] 6333[4]

Borderforce (FR) *George Baker* a59 79
6 b g American Post Miss Vic (USA) (Proud Citizen (USA))
2105[7] 3168[4]

Border Warrior *Henry Candy* a57
3 b g Sir Percy Cheviot Heights (Intikhab (USA))
8451[7] 9051[7] 9589[10]

Boreas (IRE) *A Fabre* 82
3 b c Galileo(IRE) Dawning (USA) (War Chant (USA))
1450a[5]

Borelli (IRE) *J P Murtagh* 78
2 gr c Alhebayeb(IRE) Clodilla (IRE) (Clodovil (IRE))
5710a[9]

Born A King *William Haggas* 69
2 b c Frankel Fairwater (USA) (Empire Maker (USA))
8511[4]

Born Fighting (IRE) *Andrew Hughes* 28
3 b c The Carbon Unit(USA) Devine Countenance (IRE) (Danehill Dancer (IRE))
2325[7] 4276[11]

Born For Fun (IRE) *Ali Stronge* 40
2 b g Born To Sea(IRE) Pearl Bell (IRE) (Camacho)
4839[9] 5288[5] 5794[5]

Born In Thorne *Ivan Furtado* a37 60
6 b m Haafhd Royal Nashkova (Mujahid (USA))
913[10] 2244[14]

Born Leader (FR) *Hughie Morrison* a58 61
3 ch f Nathaniel(IRE) Chieftess (IRE) (Mr Greeley (USA))
1738[7] 2087[11] 2795[11] 3593[3] 4372[2] 5175[5] 5987[2] 6400[10]

Born To Destroy *Richard Spencer* a80 77
2 b g Camacho Sahafh (USA) (Rock Hard Ten (USA))
2767[4] 3088[3] 4344[2] 5612[3]◆ 6356[9] 6963[3] 8265[3]

Born To Finish (IRE) *Ed de Giles* a72 68
6 b g Dark Angel(IRE) Music Pearl (IRE) (Oratorio (IRE))
2483[4] 3014[6] 3188[6] 5000[7] 5123[6] 7273[4] 7519[7] 8471[6] (8755) 9048[8] 9306[2] 9453[8]

Born To Frolic (IRE)
Debbie Hughes a59 59
4 b g Born To Sea(IRE) Desert Frolic (IRE) (Persian Bold (IRE))
2720[3] 5378[5] 7116[4] 7857[10]

Born To Please *Mark Usher* a48 59
5 b m Stimulation(IRE) Heart Felt (Beat Hollow)
2685[8] 6042[9] 6896[5] 8247[5] (8664)

Born To Reason (IRE)
Alexandra Dunn a62 52
5 b g Born To Sea(IRE) Laureldean Lady (IRE) (Statue Of Liberty (USA))
155[5] 288[5] 1520[4] 1841[4] 2346[4] 3682[2] (5802) 6049[7] 6303[4] 6599[11] 7270[2] 8553[3] 8854[6] 9090[14] (9139)◆ 9362[12] (9403) 9552[3]

Born To Spend (IRE)
Samuel Farrell
4 ch m Born To Sea(IRE) Banco Suivi (IRE) (Nashwan (USA))
3691[6]

Born With Pride (IRE)
William Haggas 101
2 b f Born To Sea(IRE) Jumooh (Monsun (GER))
(8763)◆

Borodin (IRE) *Sam England* a34 101
4 b g High Chaparral(IRE) Songbird (IRE) (Danehill Dancer (IRE))
1753[3] 2419[4]◆ 3315[7] (4035) 5489[8] 6657[7] 7434[9] 9610[7]

Borsdane Wood *K R Burke* a83 69
2 b c Invincible Spirit(IRE) Highleaf (Pivotal)
6228[4] 6970[5] (7388) (7871) 8509[4]

Borstal Bull (IRE) *Phillip Makin* a75 62
2 ro g Hot Streak(IRE) Acquaint (IRE) (Verglas (IRE))
8511[6]◆ 9252[2]◆

Boru's Brook (IRE) *Emma Owen* a33 34
11 b g Brian Boru Collybrook Lady (IRE) (Mandalus (IRE))
40[6] 589[9]

Bo Samraan (IRE) *Mark Johnston* a100 93
3 b c Sea The Stars(IRE) Sassenach (IRE) (Night Shift (USA))
1696[3] 1928[3] 2524[2] 2845[3] (8396) (8633) 8948[2] (9222)◆ 9454[7] 9667[6]

Bosconero (IRE) *A R Al Rayhi* a76 69
3 ch g Teofilo(IRE) Midget (Invincible Spirit (IRE))
168a[11] 570a[4] 727a[10]

Bosham *Michael Easterby* a81 58
9 b g Shamardal(USA) Awwal Malika (USA) (Kingmambo (USA))
1211[7] 1547[4]◆ 2053[9]

Bosquentin (FR) *S Cerulis* a76 77
4 b g Rajsaman(FR) Scapegrace (IRE) (Cape Cross (IRE))
6521a[4]

Bossipop *Tim Easterby* a74 90
6 ch g Assertive Opopmil (IRE) (Pips Pride)
(1895) 2910[4] 3480[8] 3846[13] 4279[6] 4880[4] (4987) 5266[8] 5740[8] 6227[9] 6339[8] 6714[2]◆ 7183[6] 7701[7] 8099[10]

Boss Power (IRE)
Sir Michael Stoute 61
2 b c Frankel La Vinchina (GER) (Oasis Dream)
6127[4]

Boston George (IRE)
Keith Dalgleish a79 90
3 b g Raven's Pass(USA) Her Own Kind (JPN) (Dubai Millennium)
2506[2] 4981[5] 5488[3] 6425[6] 7430[9]

Boston Girl (IRE) *Ed Dunlop* a39 47
2 gr f Zebedee Morethanafeeling (IRE) (Verglas (IRE))
3578[7] 3934[3] 4344[6] 5912[4] 7111[8]

Bostonian *Shaun Lycett* a39 52
9 b g Dubawi(IRE) Bolshaya (Cadeaux Genereux)
6419[7] 7116[8] 8204[11]

Bosun's Chair *Tim Easterby* 48
2 ch c Harbour Watch(IRE) Pledge Of Honour (FR) (Zoffany (IRE))
2706[10] 2907[7] 3954[11] 4756[11] 7283[9] 7538[7]

Bo Taifan (IRE) *Richard Hughes* a17
2 gr c Gutaifan(IRE) Scarlet Rosefinch (Cockney Rebel (IRE))
8250[11]

Bottom Bay *Michael Bell* 72
2 b c Oasis Dream Coconut Kreek (Pivotal)
7055[4] 7972[3]

Bouclier (IRE) *James Unett* a63 64
9 ch g Zamindar(USA) Bastet (IRE) (Giant's Causeway (USA))
463[11] 1338[5] 2215[6] 7581[14]

Boudica Bay (IRE) *Eric Alston* a49 66
4 b m Rip Van Winkle(IRE) White Shift (IRE) (Night Shift (USA))
1765[15] 2295[4] (2678)◆ 3213[10] 4307[4] 4555[6] (5276)◆ (5620) 6178[5] 6829[6] 7736[2] 8183[4]

Boulevard (IRE) *Charley Rossi* a87 101
4 ch h Galileo(IRE) Walzerkoenigin (USA) (Kingmambo (USA))
3123a[7] 7008a[3] 8980a[9]

Boulevard Beauty (IRE)
Tim Easterby 32
2 b f Champs Elysees Astral Weeks (Sea The Stars (IRE))
5387[11] 5895[8] 6458[6]

Bouncing Bobby (IRE)
Michael Dods a36 57
2 b g Raven's Pass(USA) Silicon Star (FR) (Starborough)
7361[11] 7958[10] 8424[12]

Boundary Lane *Julie Camacho* 89
4 ch m Mayson Dea Caelestis (FR) (Dream Well (FR))
(2079) 2839[4] 3201[4] 3509[2] 4105[2] 4359[3] 4932[8]

Bound For Heaven *K R Burke* a54 72
2 b f Gleneagles(IRE) Sugar Mill (Oasis Dream)
7580[7] (8338)

Bound For Nowhere (USA)
Wesley A Ward 114
5 b h The Factor(USA) Fancy Deed (USA) (Alydeed (CAN))
4094[13]

Boundless *E J O'Neill*
2 b c Kyllachy Zawiyah (Invincible Spirit (IRE))
6584a[10]

Boundsy (IRE) *Richard Fahey* a67 73
5 ch g Dandy Man(IRE) Chiba (UAE) (Timber Country (USA))
1767[7] 2122[7] 2580[5] 3227[2] 3504[13]

Bounty Pursuit *Michael Blake* a77 80
7 b g Pastoral Pursuits Poyle Dee Dee (Oasis Dream)
2339[16] 2971[5] 4226[5] 4453[10] 5446[2] (6085) (6363) 6904[4] (7299) 8221[11]

Bourbon Resolution (USA)
Ian R Wilkes a109 96
4 bb h New Year's Day(USA) Vindicated Ghost (USA) (Vindication (USA))
5484a[7]

Bourbon War (USA) *Mark Hennig* a110 94
3 b c Tapit(USA) My Conquestadory (USA) (Artie Schiller (USA))
2856a[8] 3620a[10]

Boutan *Grace Harris* a28 49
6 gr m Tobougg(IRE) High Tan (High Chaparral (IRE))
6400[5]

Boutonniere (USA) *Andrew Balding* a77 76
3 b g Istan(USA) Asscher Rose (USA) (Dynaformer (USA))
403[3] (1182)◆ 1845[4] 2470[5] 7610[4]

Bowerman *Adrian McGuinness* a109 100
5 b g Dutch Art Jamboretta (IRE) (Danehill (USA))
1694[3] (2187) 4292[7] 7934a[9]

Bowies Hero (USA) *Philip D'Amato* 113
5 b h Artie Schiller(USA) Remembered (USA) (Sky Mesa (USA))
(7922a) 8774a[5]

Bowled Over (IRE) *F-H Graffard* 96
3 b f Kingman Spin (IRE) (Galileo (IRE))
7360a[11] 8377a[6] 8983a[10]

Bowling Russian (IRE)
George Baker a64 70
2 b g Lope De Vega(IRE) Minute Limit (IRE) (Pivotal)
4184[10] 4992[5] 5523[5] 6403[4] 7754[6] 8430[3] 8650[5] 9172[9]

Bowson Fred *Michael Easterby* a87 79
7 b g Monsieur Bond(IRE) Bow Bridge (Bertolini (USA))
353[2] 1899[4] 2421[2]◆ 2910[10] 4375[2] 4880[10] 5691[5] 6178[4] 6699[4] 7077[8] 7588[6] 8023[7]

Box And Cox *Stef Keniry* a38 48
4 br g Harbour Watch(IRE) Rosa Luxemburg (Needwood Blade)
479[12] 969[7]

Boxatricks (IRE) *Julia Feilden* a56 50
4 b g Arakan(USA) Million To One (IRE) (Titus Livius (FR))
1175[3] 1675[5] 2256[5] 2972[11] 3744[3] 4336[8] 5981[6]

Boychick (IRE) *Mark Loughnane* a57 57
6 b g Holy Roman Emperor(IRE) Al Saqiya (USA) (Woodman (USA))
1988[8] 9273[10]

Boycie *Adrian Wintle* a60 56
6 b g Paco Boy(IRE) Eve (Rainbow Quest (USA))
85[9] 479[7] 789[2] 923[10] 3571[8] 4111[8]

Boy George *Dominic Ffrench Davis* a51 56
2 b g Equiano(FR) If I Were A Boy (IRE) (Invincible Spirit (IRE))
3491[11] 4734[6] 5339[4] 6071[12] 7910[6] 9045[7] 9399[7] 9630[3]

Boy In The Bar *Ian Williams* a90 87
8 ch g Dutch Art Lipsia (IRE) (Dubai Destination (USA))
1459[16] 2107[15] 2393[8] 3079[2] (4103) 5661[8] 5942[6] 7164[2] (8893) 9404[4]

Brad The Brief *Tom Dascombe* a82 90
2 b c Dutch Art Kenzadargent (FR) (Kendargent (FR))
(6330)◆ 7071[3]◆ (7769)◆ (8723)◆

Brahma Kamal *Keith Dalgleish* a35 50
3 b g Equiano(FR) Midnight Flower (IRE) (Haafhd)
785[9] 2327[2] 2683[7] 3417[6] 4508[4]

Brainchild *Keith Dalgleish* a61 59
2 gr f Dark Angel(IRE) Impressible (Oasis Dream)
6064[8] 6577[4] 8316[5] 9110[4] 9515[8]

Brains (IRE) *Jamie Osborne* a70
3 b g Dandy Man(IRE) Pure Jazz (IRE) (Marju (IRE))
(79) 8499[12] 9209[4] (9305) 9420[4]

Brainwave (FR) *J-M Baudrelle*
2 ch f Zanzibari(USA) Breakneck (FR) (Chichi Creasy (FR))
5759a[11]

Brambledown *Gary Moore* 63
3 b g Canford Cliffs(IRE) Pretty Flemingo (IRE) (Danehill Dancer (IRE))
5428[4] 5955[4] 6302[6]

Brancaster (IRE) *David Elsworth* a65 75
5 ch g Casamento(IRE) Makheelah (Dansili)
2793[15] 3700[6] 4257[7] 6055[7] 6535[4] 6896[6]

Brand New Day (IRE)
Matthieu Palussiere 92
2 b f Epaulette(AUS) Blue Saphire (Acclamation)
(1448a) 3983[23] 5116a[4] 5976a[4]

Brando *Kevin Ryan* 119
7 ch g Pivotal Argent Du Bois (USA) (Silver Hawk (USA))
1853[3] 2744[7] (3501) 4923[7] 5716a[2] 6959[4] 8331[4]

Brandon (FR) *G Botti* a58 32
3 b g Showcasing Be Released (IRE) (Three Valleys (USA))
360[2] 554[5] 798[7] 1028a[7] 6328a[10]

Brandy James (GER)
Harry Whittington a52 53
4 b g Motivator Bold Classic (USA) (Pembroke (USA))
1815[4] 2528[7]

Brandy Spirit *Michael Easterby* a76 78
3 b g Charm Spirit(IRE) B Berry Brandy (USA) (Event Of The Year (USA))
2147[3] 2895[2] 5394[4] 5741[9] 6734[3] 7301[6]

Brandy Station (IRE)
Lisa Williamson a70 70
4 b g Fast Company(IRE) Kardyls Hope (IRE) (Fath (USA))
317[10] 2576[4] 3021[7] 3509[11] 4364[7] 4555[7] 5180[4] 5582[3] 5952[5] (6639) 7855[10] 8429[13] 8715[8] 8895[F]

Brasca *Ralph Beckett* a95 86
3 ch g Nathaniel(IRE) Regalline (IRE) (Green Desert (USA))
(2999) 4063[5] 4862[4] 6171[5] (6888)◆ 7108[2]

Brasingamanbellamy *Jedd O'Keeffe* a45 21
2 b g Black Sam Bellamy(IRE) Brasingaman Hifive (High Estate)
7067[12] 8717[9]

Brass (FR) *Paul Webber* 46
3 b f Linngari(IRE) Silver Pivotal (IRE) (Pivotal)
1738[6] 4842[10] 6438[6] 7202[13]

Brass Clankers *Robyn Brisland* a55
2 b c Helmet(AUS) Millsini (Rossini (USA))
7627[7] 8337[10] 9029[4] 9640[4]

Brassica (IRE) *Sir Mark Prescott Bt* a96 95
3 b f Australia Lasilia (IRE) (Acclamation)
7347[3]◆ 7589[5] 9170a[3]

Bravantina *Mark Walford* a51 35
4 b m Trans Island Falbrina (IRE) (Falbrav (IRE))
968[6] 1102[8] 1400[9] 2202[13] 3057[9] (9467)◆

Bravazo (USA) *D Wayne Lukas* a117
4 bb h Awesome Again(CAN) Tiz O' Gold (USA) (Cee's Tizzy (USA))
445a[4]

Brave Impact *Mme J-F Bernard*
8 b g Montjeu(IRE) Bellona (IRE) (Bering)
8966a[5]

Brave Shiina (FR) *Hiroo Shimizu* a68 66
2 b g Bated Breath Gospel Mind (FR) (Nayef (USA))
7675a[6]

Brave Smash (JPN) *Kris Lees* 121
6 b h Tosen Phantom(JPN) Tosen Smash (JPN) (Tokai Teio (JPN))
1442a[8]

Bravo Faisal (IRE) *Richard Fahey* a81 84
2 b c Kodiac Israar (Machiavellian (USA))
2108[6] 3047[3] 3335[5] (5853) 6942[2]◆ (7072) 8110[11]

Bravo Sierra *A Fabre* 98
3 b f Siyouni(FR) Kilo Alpha (King's Best (USA))
1780a[8] 3174a[2] 7255a[8] 8115[3]

Bravo Zolo (IRE) *Charlie Appleby* a44 110
7 b g Rip Van Winkle(IRE) Set Fire (IRE) (Bertolini (USA))
397a[3]

Brawler (IRE) *Denis Gerard Hogan* 76
4 b g Teofilo(IRE) Red Avis (Exceed And Excel (AUS))
5508a[11]

Brawny *Charles Hills* a42 62
3 b g Dark Angel(IRE) Natty Bumppo (IRE) (Kheleyf (USA))
2630[8] 3805[6] 4286[4] 4660[5]

Brazen Bolt *John Quinn* a57
2 b g Brazen Beau(AUS) Gladys' Gal (Tobougg (IRE))
9107[8]

Brazen Point *Tim Easterby* 68
2 b c Brazen Beau(AUS) Point Of Control (Pivotal)
6622[9] 7619[4] 8026[8]

Brazen Safa *Michael Bell* a76 71
2 b f Brazen Beau(AUS) Insaaf (Averti (IRE))
1821[5] (2228) 2968[3] 3689[4] 5189[8] 6369[5] 7980[7]

Brazen Sheila *Anthony Carson* a31
2 b f Brazen Beau(AUS) Sail Home (Mizzen Mast (USA))
8913[15] 9506[13]

Brazos (USA) *John Joseph Murphy* 100
5 b g Rock Of Gibraltar(IRE) Les Fazzani (IRE) (Intikhab (USA))
2158a[6] 5508a[17]

Break Cover *James Eustace* a49 41
2 ch g Casamento(IRE) Brushing (Medicean)
3098[8] 4282[8] 8288[7]

Break Down (FR) *P Chevillard* 53
3 bb f Sunday Break(JPN) Daliaway (FR) (Daliapour (IRE))
3139a[9]

Breakfast Time *Archie Watson* a49 21
3 b f Nathaniel(IRE) Eventfull Meet (IRE) (Dalakhani (IRE))
133[9] 370[9] 556[13] 5987[11] 6552[6]

Break Fort (FR) *Noam Chevalier* a49 56
8 b g Sunday Break(JPN) Helguera (FR) (Hamas (IRE))
8737a[8]

Breaking Records (IRE)
Hugo Palmer a92 87
4 b g Kodiac Querulous (USA) (Raven's Pass (USA))
19[6] 1290[8] 4123[11]

Break Of Day *William Haggas* a49 57
3 b f Shamardal(USA) Dawn Glory (Oasis Dream)
2762[12] 3080[7] 3603[12] 4642[7] 5249[10] (5957) 6130[3] 6569[9]

Break The Rules *Martin Smith* a71 76
3 br f Aussie Rules(USA) Fairy Slipper (Singspiel (IRE))
(1077) 5148[8] 5623[5] 6720[4] 6849[2]

Break The Silence *Scott Dixon* a64 55
5 b g Rip Van Winkle(IRE) In A Silent Way (IRE) (Desert Prince (IRE))
45[4] 233[5] 507[4] 590[7] 829[4]◆ 1069[3] 1163[3] 2631[3] 3325[10] 3939[7] 4346[10] (6546) (7384) 7875[6] 8068[2] 8270[3] 8404[2] 8646[3] 8949[4] 9180[3] 9224[2] 9337[2]

Breanski *Jedd O'Keeffe* a89 92
5 b g Delegator Jubilee (Selkirk (USA))
2844[9] 3313[10] 3813[5]◆ 4867[3] (4902) 5434[6] (6207) 6950[13] 7312[4] 7906[6] 8634[2]◆

Breathable *Tim Easterby* 79
4 b g Bated Breath Cassique Lady (IRE) (Langfuhr (CAN))
2479[4] 3095[10] 3925[6] (5473) (5728) 6218[6]

Breathalyze (FR) *Tom Dascombe* 87
2 b g Bated Breath Laber Ildut (IRE) (Whipper (USA))
4324[3] (5704) 6710[2]◆ (7139)

Breath Caught *David Simcock* a87 95
4 b g Bated Breath Double Crossed (Caerleon (USA))
3346[8] 4863[4] 6452[3] 6917[7] 7394[7] 7686[7]

Breathless Times *Stuart Williams* a97 83
4 b g Bated Breath Bea Menace (USA) (Mizzen Mast (USA))
805[5] 1916[7] 2551[4] 7188[11] 7697[10]◆

Breath Of Air *Charles Hills* 92
3 b g Bated Breath Western Appeal (USA) (Gone West (USA))
1851[5] 2746[15] 5173[3] 5666[5] 6396[6] 7059[5]

Breath Of Fire (FR) *Mme Pia Brandt* a76 87
4 ch g Intello(GER) Breath Of Love (USA) (Mutakddim (USA))
(3140a)

Breathoffreshair *Richard Guest* a49 35
5 b g Bated Breath Stormy Weather (Nashwan (USA))
277[11] 410[7] 502[7] 788[7] 2013[12] 3304[7] 4376[8] 5857[12] 7420[2] 7606[9] 7961[6]

Breath Of Joy *Amy Murphy* a77 58
2 b f Kodiac Island Dreams (USA) (Giant's Causeway (USA))
4790[2] 6159[4] 6928[2] 8850[6]

Breath Of Spring (IRE) *Marco Botti* a60 53
3 br g Bated Breath Welcome Spring (IRE) (Lawman (FR))
5650[9] 7319[4]

Breathtaking Look *Stuart Williams* a99 105
4 b m Bated Breath Love Your Looks (Iffraaj)
2809[3] (4072) 4887[7] (5441)◆ 6379[5] (7146) 8708[10]

Breck's Selection (FR)
Mark Johnston a67 61
2 b g War Command(USA) Shiver Stream (IRE) (Cape Cross (IRE))
4456[3]◆ 4766[6] 5273[7] 6372[12] 7173[2] 8022[13]

Brecqhou Island *Mark Pattinson* a51 51
4 b g Pastoral Pursuits Lihou Island (Beveled (USA))
435[8] 942[11] 1683[6] 3592[6] 3744[2] 4426[12] 9289[9]

Breden (IRE) *Linda Jewell* a101 106
9 b g Shamardal(USA) Perfect Touch (USA) (Miswaki (USA))
205[2] 800[4] 1101[2] 1415[3] 1889[5] (2832) 4666[11] 5930[7] 6391[7]

Bredenbury (IRE) *David Simcock* 88
2 ch f Night Of Thunder(IRE) Areyaam (USA) (Elusive Quality (USA))
3776[2] (4214) 4836[3] 5683[3]

Breezing *Sylvester Kirk* a36
3 b f Garswood Presto Levanter (Rock Of Gibraltar (IRE))
476[14] 1174[10] 1494[4]

Breguet Boy (IRE) *Keith Dalgleish* a66 71
2 br g Requinto(IRE) Holly Hawk (IRE) (Dubai Destination (USA))
6585[4] 6822[5] 7046[4] (7585) 8124[7] 8394[4] 9513[4]

Breguet Man (IRE) *Keith Dalgleish* a66 70
2 b c Ivawood(IRE) Real Magic (IRE) (Pour Moi (IRE))
2892[9] 3841[3] 4206[3] 4878[2] 5296[2] 5853[3] 6579[4]

Brenbar (USA) *Roger Varian* a71
3 bb c Scat Daddy(USA) Pretty Elusive (USA) (Elusive Quality (USA))
9213[7] 9475[4]

Brendan (IRE) *Jim Goldie* a54 42
6 b g Elnadim(USA) My (King's Best (USA))
2189[4] 2958[11] 4059[12] 4694[8] 4978[8] 5235[12] 5491[7]

Brendan Brackan (IRE) *G M Lyons* a87 93
10 b g Big Bad Bob(IRE) Abeyr (Unfuwain (USA))
5597a[15]

Brenner Pass *Richard Hughes* a68 61
2 b c Raven's Pass(USA) Bold Bidder (Indesatchel (IRE))
6845[10] 7160[6]◆ 7627[2]◆ 8409[3]

Brentford Hope *Richard Hughes* 93
2 b c Camelot Miss Raven (IRE) (Raven's Pass (USA))
(8461)◆

Breton Rock (IRE) *David Simcock* 108
9 b g Bahamian Bounty Anna's Rock (IRE) (Rock Of Gibraltar (IRE))
2688[3] 3588[7] 4389[5] 5521[9] 6508[5] 7194[3] 7905[5]

Brexitmeansbrexit *Richard Hannon* a73 80
4 b m Helmet(AUS) Lady Scarlett (Woodman (USA))
346[8] 603[2] (965)

Briac (FR) *Tim Vaughan* a40 36
8 b g Kapgarde(FR) Jarwin Do (FR) (Grand Tresor (FR))
3941[13]

Brian Epstein (IRE) *Richard Hannon* a82 98
3 b c Dark Angel(IRE) Jewel In The Sand (IRE) (Bluebird (USA))
1857[5] 2414[4] 2821[2] (3357)

Brian Ryan *Wido Neuroth* a80 102
4 b g Finjaan Touching (IRE) (Kheleyf (USA))
1391a[3] (1631a) (2955a) (3907a) 6523a[3] 7497a[12]

Brian The Snail (IRE)
Richard Fahey a94 95
5 gr g Zebedee Sweet Irish (Shamardal (USA))
1413[12] 1944[6] 2572[11] 2843[5] (3309) 3770[6] 4379[5] 4896[5] 5454[12] 5661[15] 6227[13] 6581[3] 6714[10]

Briardale (IRE) *James Bethell* a65 77
7 b g Arcano(IRE) Marine City (JPN) (Carnegie (IRE))
(3046) 4057[7] 5198[7] 7379[8] 8300[6]

Brick By Brick (IRE)
Mrs John Harrington 83
4 b g Big Bad Bob(IRE) Pivka (Pivotal)
5205a[19]

Bricklebrit *Rae Guest* a43 45
3 ch f Sir Percy Blush's Gift (Cadeaux Genereux)
3003[14] 3690[4] 5268[9] 6636[7] 8204[12]

Bricks And Mortar (USA)
Chad C Brown 119
5 bb h Giant's Causeway(USA) Beyond The Waves (USA) (Ocean Crest (USA))
(444a) (6001a) (8776a)

Bridge Battlango (IRE)
Pierpaolo Sbariggia 90
3 b f Battle Of Marengo(IRE) Fashion Central (Dubawi (IRE))
2161a[7]

Bridge Of Sighs *Steph Hollinshead* a45 45
7 ch g Avonbridge Ashantiana (Ashkalani (IRE))
241[10]

Bridgewater Bay (IRE)
Jane Chapple-Hyam a79
3 ch g Footstepsinthesand Mexican Milly (IRE) (Noverre (USA))
9038[3] (9416) 9635[3]

Bridlemere Court (IRE)
David Elsworth a49 35
3 b f Tamayuz Lovers Peace (IRE) (Oratorio (IRE))
296[8] 401[5]

Bridport (IRE) *Stepanka Myskova* a46 62
4 b g High Chaparral(IRE) Enharmonic (USA) (E Dubai (USA))
1349a[9]

Brigadier *Robert Cowell* a66 62
3 ch g Sepoy(AUS) Nasheej (USA) (Swain (IRE))
752[3] 1139[4] 1598[2] 3339[3] 4081[6] 4591[4]

Brigadoon *Michael Appleby* a71 68
12 b g Compton Place Briggsmaid (Elegant Air)
481[8] 1341[P]

Brigand *John Butler* a60 46
4 b g Dick Turpin(IRE) Juncea (Elnadim (USA))
45[11] 1653[15] 2076[12] 2740[6] 3989[3] (4589) 7282[6] 8123[2] 8502[5] 8864[10] 9248[2] 9505[8]

Brigantine (FR) *C Escuder* 61
3 ch f Cima De Triomphe(IRE) The Lucky Go Girl (GER) (Dr Devious (IRE))
6063a[4]

Brigham Young *Ed Walker* a84
4 br g Street Cry(IRE) Bible Belt (IRE) (Big Bad Bob (IRE))
4879[P] 6076[3] 6968[8] 7470[6]

Bright Eyed Eagle (IRE) *Ed Walker* 75
2 ch c Gleneagles(IRE) Euphrasia (IRE) (Windsor Knot (IRE))
7586[2]◆ 8517[3]

Brighton Pier (GER) *Harry Dunlop* a76
3 ch g Farhh Bearlita (GER) (Lomitas)
8451[4] (9368)

Bright Red (IRE) *Richard Hannon* 37
2 b g Red Jazz(USA) Ceylon Round (FR) (Royal Applause)
5500[7] 6079[11]

Bright Saffron *Clare Hobson* a45 58
4 ch m Champs Elysees Mercy Pecksniff (Shamardal (USA))
9589[12]

Bright Spells (IRE) *Jamie Osborne* a49 50
2 b f Dragon Pulse(IRE) Fillothewisp (Teofilo (IRE))
7547[11] 8458[13] 8706[10] 9179[8]

Bright Valentine *Richard Spencer* 71
2 b f Showcasing Melbourne Memories (Sleeping Indian)
5550[2] 6079[6]

Brilliant Riposte *Denis Coakley* a40 32
4 b g Rip Van Winkle(IRE) Waldena (USA) (Storm Cat (USA))
5310[7] 6723[11] 8869[7]

Brilliant Vanguard (IRE)
Kevin Ryan a68 66
6 b g Fast Company(IRE) Alyska (IRE) (Owington)
1948[6]

Brimham Rocks *Chris Waller* a67 102
5 b g Fastnet Rock(AUS) Colima (IRE) (Authorized (IRE))
1784a[20] 8361a[14] 8803a[2]

Bringitonboris (USA)
Keith Dalgleish 52
2 rg g Distorted Humor(USA) Miss Fontana (USA) (Classic Account (USA))
7623[5]

Bringthehousedown (IRE)
Ron Hodges a30 22
5 b g Royal Applause Raskutani (Dansili)
1095[8]

Bring The Money (IRE)
Mick Channon a62
2 b g Anjaal Princess Banu (Oasis Dream)
9251[10] 9474[3]

Bring Us Paradise *Tony Carroll* a32 86
3 b g Zoffany(IRE) Paradise Way (Elusive Quality (USA))
3638[2]◆ (3964) (5351) 5947[3] (7129)

Brinkleys Katie *Paul George* a49 46
3 ch f New Approach(IRE) Opera Gloves (IRE) (Dalakhani (IRE))
765[9] 1039[2] 2343[5] 2901[3] 3418[5] 4400[11] 7818[8] 8868[2] 9216[10] 9497[3]

Bristano *M G Mintchev* 106
3 b g Dansili Briseida (Pivotal)
(5719a) 7500a[9]

Bristol Missile (USA) *Richard Price* a73 71
5 bb g Kitten's Joy(USA) Dearest Girl (IRE) (Galileo (IRE))
(2106)◆ 2797[17] 3575[5] 3937[5] 4926[7] 5593[8]

British Idiom (USA) *Brad H Cox* a112
2 ch f Flashback(USA) Rose And Shine (CAN) (Mr Sekiguchi (USA))
(8747a)

Brittanic (IRE) *David Simcock* a80 73
5 ch g Excelebration(IRE) Fountain Of Peace (USA) (Kris S (USA))
157[4] 350[5] 922[8] 1213[5] 1566[6] 4569[4] 5086[3] 5811[3] 6512[4] 7109[2] 7553[4] 8065[5]

Briyouni (FR) *Ralph Beckett* a73 85
6 b g Siyouni(FR) Brianza (USA) (Thunder Gulch (USA))
(138) 355[8] 4786[6] 9245[10]

Broad Appeal *Jonathan Portman* a69 74
5 ch g Medicean Shy Appeal (IRE) (Barathea (IRE))
1826[2] (3155) 3941[4]◆ 4426[3] 5316[2] (5993) 6830[3]

Broadbeach (IRE) *David Simcock* 84
2 b f Dandy Man(IRE) Coincidently (Acclamation)
6407[2]

Broadcast (USA) *S Seemar* a39 52
4 ch g Distorted Humor(USA) Announce (Selkirk (USA))
957a[10] 1748a[14]

Broadhaven Dream (IRE)
Ronald Harris a21 68
3 b g Dream Ahead(USA) Queen Grace (IRE) (Choisir (AUS))
2938[10] 3351[4] 3839[5] (4182) 5375[2] (5603)

Broad Street *D K Weld* 106
4 b h Sea The Stars(IRE) Bracing Breeze (Dansili)
5874a[3] 7218a[7]

Broadway Queen (IRE)
Luke W Comer a36 32
4 br m Kargali(IRE) Paksiyma (FR) (Dalakhani (IRE))
7087a[10]

Brockagh Cailin *J S Moore* a63 62
4 b m Helmet(AUS) Step Softly (Golan (IRE))
54[4] 250[5] 2277[6] 2585[6] (3038) 3533[8] 4235[9] 4499[6] 5795[8] 6796[7] 7060[10]

Brockey Rise (IRE) *David Evans* a60 61
4 ch g Zebedee Age Of Diplomacy (Araafa (IRE))
37[6] (263) (402) 467[5] 857[3] 1021[8] (1595) 1820[3] 2503a[5] 3413[2] 5632[7] 6605[6] 6639[4] 7286[14] 8408[10] 8864[2] 9039[11] 9287[2] 9477[8] 9551[7]

Broctune Red *Gillian Boanas* a32 52
4 ch g Haafhd Fairlie (Halling (USA))
2127[6] 3224[4] 4002[6] 4513[P]

Broderie *H-A Pantall* a101 105
4 gr m Pivotal Woven Lace (Hard Spun (USA))
1708a[11] 3907a[3] 5230a[5] 7750a[3] 8379a[7]

Brodick *K R Burke* a38
2 b f Teofilo(IRE) Bedecked (IRE) (Holy Roman Emperor (IRE))
9567[8]

Brogans Bay (IRE) *Simon Dow* a62 45
4 b m Born To Sea(IRE) Sister Sylvia (Fantastic Light (USA))
141[5] 365[13] 520[3] 3036[12] 3425[2] (4027) 4501[7] 5046[6] 6285[8] 6682[2] 7557[2] 7844[9] 8896[12] 9169[10]

Brokeback Mountain (FR)
Y Barberot a74 95
4 b g Le Havre(IRE) Beaumont (FR) (Trempolino (USA))
6820a[4]

Broken Rifle *Ivan Furtado* a75 72
2 b g Havana Gold(IRE) Peace Concluded (Bertolini (USA))
3335[6] 4295[4] 5082[4] 7296[2] 9414[3]

Broken Spear *Tony Coyle* a89 92
3 b g Pastoral Pursuits My Pretty Girl (Arakan (USA))
1692[3] 3844[3] 6735[6] 6960[8] 7700[2] 8099[7]◆ 8182[5] 8340[3] 8636[7]

Broken Wings (IRE) *Keith Dalgleish* a66 75
4 b m Canford Cliffs(IRE) Moss Top (IRE) (Moss Vale (IRE))
6[4] 233[13] 356[11]

Brokopondo (IRE)
Miss Clare Louise Cannon a59 48
7 b g Bushranger(IRE) Saramacca (IRE) (Kahyasi (IRE))
272[7]

Bromance *Peter Niven* a49 54
6 b g Showcasing Romantic Destiny (Dubai Destination (USA))
5851[8] 6663[9]

Bromley Cross (IRE) *Emilie Varin* a27 17
6 ch g Dandy Man(IRE) Marianne's Dancer (IRE) (Bold Fact (USA))
115a[14]

Bronze Beau *Linda Stubbs* a37 61
12 ch g Compton Place Bella Cantata (Singspiel (IRE))
2433[7] 2789[2] 3227[6] 3975[5] 4132[12] 4563[2] 5094[5] 5822[2] 6168[6] 6574[10] 7487[3]

Bronze River *Andrew Balding* a84 77
2 b g Archipenko(USA) Avon Lady (Avonbridge)
(6314)◆ 7174[2] (8287)

Brooklyn Boy *Harry Dunlop* a61 63
3 b g Camelot Tan Tan (King's Best (USA))
2017[3] 3418[14] 4843[3] 6849[5] 7240[14]

Brook On Fifth (IRE)
Joseph Patrick O'Brien 89
2 b f Champs Elysees Slieve (Selkirk (USA))
6689a[4]

Brookside Banner (IRE)
Tom Dascombe 79
2 ch f Starspangledbanner(AUS) Akrivi (IRE) (Tobougg (IRE))
(6919) 8724[15]

Broome (IRE) *A P O'Brien* 117
3 b c Australia Sweepstake (IRE) (Acclamation)
(1603a) (2662a) 3345[4] 4414a[6]

Brother Bentley *Ronald Harris* a51 58
3 gr g Hellvelyn Lady Mango (IRE) (Bahamian Bounty)
605[10] 906[5] 1650[4] 2221[8] (2357) 2474[5] 2995[10] 3650[13] 4180[6] 4481[17] 6181[6] 6737[5] 9272[9]

Brother In Arms (IRE) *Tony Carroll* a50 55
5 b g Kodiac Cool Cousin (IRE) (Distant Relative)
26[3] 244[9] 357[4] 599[6] 848[10] 2514[7] 3187[2] 3966[11] 4473[5] 5806[6] (6507) 6760[3] 7271[5] 8694[3] 9139[4]◆ 9444[3]

Brotherly Company (IRE)
Joanne Foster
7 b g Fast Company(IRE) Good Lady (IRE) (Barathea (IRE))
6674[8]

Brother McGonagall *Tim Easterby* a47 87
5 b r Equiano(FR) Anatase (Danehill (USA))
1644[13] 1977[6] 3305[6] (3567) 4240[9] 4490[4] 5155[5] 5693[6] 5970[8] 6961[3] (7212) 8024[9]

Broughton Excels *Stuart Williams* a65 49
4 b g Kyllachy Excello (Exceed And Excel (AUS))
5822[4] 6510[5] (7606) 7838[2] 8917[2]◆ 9089[2]◆ 9352[7] 9507[11]

Broughtons Admiral *Alastair Ralph* a66 65
5 b g Born To Sea(IRE) Chanter (Lomitas)
1235[3]

Broughtons Bear (IRE)
Stuart Williams a47 49
3 b g Kodiac Though (IRE) (Dansili)
1387[9] 1886[11] 2506[8] 5054[5] 5987[14]

Broughtons Compass *Mark Hoad* a46 40
2 b g Henrythenavigator(USA) Sayrianna (Sayaarr (USA))
3257[13] 4030[5] 4925[10] 6071[7] 6435[3] 7277[7] 9212[5]

Broughtons Flare (IRE)
Philip McBride a73 73
3 ch g Rip Van Winkle(IRE) Purple Glow (IRE) (Orientate (USA))
1219[7] 1516[9] (2798) 4338[7] 6631[6]◆ 8063[7] 8496[2] 9048[5] 9306[9]

Broughtons Gold *Tom Clover* a72 70
2 b g Lethal Force(IRE) Broughtons Jewel (IRE) (Bahri (USA))
2761[4] (8058)◆

Broughton Sunpearl *Tom Clover* a64
2 b f Swiss Spirit Sunpearl (Compton Place)
9062[3] 9506[11]

Brown Eyed Girl *Mick Channon* a45
2 b f Sixties Icon Fading Away (Fraam)
9063[12] 9668[11]

Brown Eyes Blue (IRE) *J S Moore* a54 56
2 b f Epaulette(AUS) Union City Blues (IRE) (Encosta De Lago (AUS))
1556[10] 2205[9] 3562a[5] 4075[11] 9172[7] 9399[9] 9449[3]

Brown Honey *Ismail Mohammed* a72 74
3 b f Farhh Bronwen (IRE) (King's Best (USA))
6559[2]◆ 7347[15] 8013[3]

Brown Velvet *Mrs C Gilbert* a31 35
7 b m Kodiac Silkenveil (IRE) (Indian Ridge (IRE))
2004a[U] 2673a[5] 3174a[5] 4684a[3] 5233[6] (6009a) 6555a[2]

Bruisa *Richard Hannon* 36
2 ch f Sepoy(AUS) Coplow (Manduro (GER))
7407[8]

Brunch *Michael Dods* a74 68
2 b g Harbour Watch(IRE) Granola (Makfi)
8511[5] (8919)

Brundtland (IRE) *Charlie Appleby* 116
4 b h Dubawi(IRE) Future Generation (IRE) (Hurricane Run (IRE))
958a[P] (Dead)

Brunel Charm *Richard Hughes* a85
2 b c Charm Spirit(IRE) Manyara (Manduro (GER))
(9299) 9631[4]

Brunelle (IRE) *G M Lyons* a84 93
2 b f Kodiac Velvetina (IRE) (Barathea (IRE))
6690a[6] (7876a)

Brunel's Boy *Mick Channon*
2 b g Dutch Art Hot Secret (Sakhee's Secret)
2610[7]

Brushwork *Charles Hills* a94
3 b g Kyllachy Miss Elegance (Mind Games)
(7655)◆ (8820) (9348)◆

Brutal (NZ)
Michael, Wayne & John Hawkes 117
3 br c O'Reilly(NZ) Alberton Princess (NZ) (Golan (IRE))
8805a[11]
Brutalab *Tim Easterby* 62
3 b g Epaulette(AUS) Kahalah (IRE) (Darshaan)
2094[10] 2590[10] 2823[7] 3270[3] 3926[3] 4487[4] 5023[2] 5248[8] 5814[3] **(6499)** 7290[6] **(7545)**
Brute Force *Daniel Kubler* a51
3 ch g Paco Boy(IRE) Free Falling (Selkirk (USA))
6315[8]
Bruyere (FR) *Dean Ivory* a66 71
3 b f Exceed And Excel(AUS) Pale Mimosa (IRE) (Singspiel (IRE))
4225[4] 5593[2]◆ 6123[2]◆ 8033[2] **(8434)** *9202*[7]
Bryn Du *William Haggas* a60 53
2 b c Ivawood(IRE) Caption (Motivator)
5591[5] 6287[5] *7030*[7] 7585[12] ***8022***[3] *8603*[3]
Bubbelah (IRE) *David Simcock* a62 49
3 b g Zoffany(IRE) Sanadaat (Green Desert (USA))
798[2] *1140*[7] ***1480***[6] 2337[6]
Bubble And Squeak *Sylvester Kirk* a95 96
4 b m Mastercraftsman(IRE) Comeback Queen (Nayef (USA))
1753[12] 2230[3] **(2608)** *3581*[11] 5187[4] 5545[7] **5926a**[4] **6992a**[6] 7499a[10] 7895[5] 8377a[4] *9000*[5] *(9278)*◆ *9625*[2]
Bubbly *Mark Loughnane* a67 62
4 b m Excelebration(IRE) Baralinka (IRE) (Barathea (IRE))
33[5] ***202***[4] 1850[8]
Bubbly Splash (IRE) *David O'Meara* 70
2 b c Lawman(FR) Brunch Bellini (FR) (Peintre Celebre (USA))
3717[3] **4802**[2]
Buccaneers Vault (IRE)
Paul Midgley a87 81
7 gr g Aussie Rules(USA) Heaven's Vault (IRE) (Hernando (FR))
1457[5] 1977[7] 2437[5] **3309**[2] 3868[10] 4369[6] 4649[8] 5040[6] 5551[7] 6220[5] 6581[5] (6680) (7311) *7656*[3]
Bucephalus (GER) *Ed Walker* a71 80
2 b c Soldier Hollow Batya (IRE) (Whipper (USA))
8100[4] *8823*[6]
Buckhurst (IRE)
Joseph Patrick O'Brien 115
3 b c Australia Artful (IRE) (Green Desert (USA))
2662a[5] 3063a[2] (4411a) **(6192a)** 7218a[2]
Buckingham (IRE)
Eve Johnson Houghton a87 86
3 gr g Clodovil(IRE) Lizzy's Township (USA) (Delaware Township (USA))
1685[4] (2364) 2825[4] *3465*[8] ***4643***[2] 5319[6] *6076*[5] *6440*[5] 7128[2] *7836*[7] *8852*[2] *9255*[8]
Buckland Beau *Charlie Fellowes* a73 71
8 b g Rock Of Gibraltar(IRE) Heavenly Whisper (IRE) (Halling (USA))
1659[4]◆ **2256**[2]
Buckland Boy (IRE)
Charlie Fellowes a74 77
4 b g Bated Breath Rancho Montoya (IRE) (High Chaparral (IRE))
(2202) 2793[9]◆ **(3973)** 5179[8] 6224[RR] *7575*[P]
Buckman Tavern (FR)
Sir Mark Prescott Bt a86 86
3 b g Pastorius(GER) Breezy Hawk (GER) (Hawk Wing (USA))
3337[6] 5347[2] **5566**[2] ***5943***[3]
Budaiya Fort (IRE) *Phil McEntee* a46 54
3 b g Kodiac Knapton Hill (Zamindar (USA))
1141[11] *1430*[9] **2735**[4] 2870[11] *3319*[11] 3775[8] 5352[8] 5622[11]
Buddy Bob (IRE) *Wido Neuroth* 90
4 b g Big Bad Bob(IRE) Ahea (USA) (Giant's Causeway (USA))
6524a[2]
Buffer Zone *G M Lyons* a83 110
4 br g Bated Breath Buffering (Beat Hollow)
5205a[2] 5923a[5] **(7241a)** 7433[17]
Bug Boy (IRE) *Paul George* a63 73
3 b g Big Bad Bob(IRE) Velvetina (IRE) (Barathea (IRE))
1743 *1174*[5] 1825[8] *3440*[6] 3947[2]◆ 5085[2]◆ (5580) 6022[7] **(6805)** 7116[3] *7915*[7] *9067*[11]
Bugler Bob (IRE) *John Quinn* a77 53
3 ch g Dandy Man(IRE) Callanish (Inchinor)
(1488)◆ 1894[12] 2293[6] 3884[10] 4781[7] 7383[7] *8304*[3]◆ *8712*[8] *9218*[5] *9519*[5]
Buhturi (IRE) *Charles Hills* 86
2 ch g Raven's Pass(USA) Moon's Whisper (USA) (Storm Cat (USA))
3008[2]◆ (4550) **5415**[5] 6356[6] 7316[3]
Buhwarui Banseok (USA)
Bart Rice 82
6 b h Tizway(USA) Aim For The Moon (USA) (Deputy Minister (CAN))
284a[9] 730a[13]
Buildmeupbuttercup *W P Mullins* 103
5 ch m Sixties Icon Eastern Paramour (IRE) (Kris Kin (USA))
3952[2] **7216a**[2] 8114[11]
Bulldozer (IRE) *Michael Appleby* a28 24
2 b c Hallowed Crown(AUS) Phi Phi (IRE) (Fasliyev (USA))
8265[8] 8395[7] *9181*[11]
Bullfinch *Roger Charlton* a81 52
2 b c Kodiac Thistle Bird (Selkirk (USA))
8516[9] ***(8889)***
Bullington Boy (FR)
Jane Chapple-Hyam a70 75
3 b g Canford Cliffs(IRE) Borgia Gold (IRE) (Cape Cross (IRE))
2766[6]◆ 3675a[4] 4124[13] *4788*[5] *5270*[7] *7189*[4] 7681[3] 8207[5] *9217*[11] *9548*[9] *9657*[3]
Bullion Boss (IRE) *Michael Dods* 74
3 b g War Command(USA) Gold Bubbles (USA) (Street Cry (IRE))
2872[6] **3295**[4] **3882**[2] 5175[3] 5654[5] 6674[4]
Bullseye Bullet *Mark Usher* a38 34
4 ch g Kheleyf(USA) Satin Doll (Diktat)
2235[13] **3014**[9] *3325*[11]

Bumble Bay *Robert Stephens* a45 43
9 b g Trade Fair Amica (Averti (IRE))
5379[7]
Bumbledom *Michael Dods* a43 68
3 br g Epaulette(AUS) Miaplacidus (IRE) (Shamardal (USA))
1649[12] 3270[7] **(3932)** **4781**[3] 5619[4] 5847[6] *7632*[9]
Bumblekite *Steph Hollinshead* a43 51
3 ch f Nayef(USA) Harriet's Girl (Choisir (AUS))
1957[9] **3270**[2] 3684[13] 4794[7] *7909*[9] *9289*[8] *9446*[8]
Bungee Jump (IRE) *Grace Harris* a89 94
4 b m Canford Cliffs(IRE) Starchy (Cadeaux Genereux)
1143[9] *1388*[8] 1915[4] 2107[9] (2997) (3575)◆ 4353a[5] 5143[9] 5746[5] 5989[6] 6525[3] **(6803)**
Buniann (IRE) *Paul Midgley* a73 63
3 b g Tamayuz Darajaat (USA) (Elusive Quality (USA))
6206[3] *(6944)*◆ 7588[11] ***8429***[5]
Bunker Hill Lad *Michael Appleby* a16 63
4 b g Mount Nelson Enford Princess (Pivotal)
8270[13] *8670*[9] ***8870***[10]
Bunora De L'Alguer (IRE)
Gian Marco Pala 84
3 b f Battle Of Marengo(IRE) Rose Buck (Acclamation)
4171a[8]
Buonasera (IRE) *P L Giannotti* 100
4 b m Zebedee Rosina Bella (IRE) (Oratorio (IRE))
(2888a) 7254a[6] 8787a[7]
Burano Boy (IRE) *Ed Dunlop* 74
2 gr c Footstepsinthesand Ghost Of A Girl (IRE) (Verglas (IRE))
8460[6]◆
Burauq *Milton Bradley* a43 42
7 b g Kyllachy Riccoche (IRE) (Oasis Dream)
244[6] *8091*[0] *9201*[0] *1732*[7] 2287[7] 3036[5] 3527[16] 4182[8] 4494[10] 5081[12] 6329[9]
Burford Brown *Robert Cowell* a85 91
4 br g Swiss Spirit Sareb (FR) (Indian Ridge (IRE))
1929[5] **(2272)** 3375[4] 4301[3]
Burguillos *John Butler* a54 66
6 ch g Lope De Vega(IRE) Hazy Dancer (Oasis Dream)
255[7] 1829[9]◆ 2260[4] 3149[9] 3597[6] 6164[8] *6734*[7] 7545[5] 8434[12] *9132*[14] *9310*[16] *9503*[5]
Buridan (FR) *Richard Hannon* a100 96
4 b g Choisir(AUS) Lady McKell (IRE) (Raven's Pass (USA))
1459[7] 1829[5] 2117[7] 2837[4] 3164[2] (3597) 5664[17] ***(8425)***◆ *8851*[7]
Buriram (IRE) *Ralph Beckett* a79 87
3 b g Reliable Man Wild Step (GER) (Footstepsinthesand)
1696[2]◆ **(3295)** 4256[6] 5127[3] 5694[9] *7082*[5] **7683**[2] 8661[3]
Burj *Saeed bin Suroor* a65 60
3 b g Dansili Dysphonia (AUS) (Lonhro (AUS))
169a[7] 511a[11] 727a[5] 956a[8] **1857**[4] 3471[7] 4239[11]
Burmese Blazer (IRE) *Jim Goldie* a41 60
4 bb g Arakan(USA) Sr Pius (IRE) (Antonius Pius (USA))
1951[2] 2368[4] 2632[6] 2841[8] 4059[9] 4694[10] 4721[3] 4997[6] 5276[7] 5904[2] 6659[3] 6936[6] 7367[10] 7511[3] 7761[6] 8235[3] 8632[8]
Burmese Temple (FR) *V Devillars*
8 b g Sulamani(IRE) Goldarvor (FR) (Beat Hollow)
8737a[10]
Burnage Boy (IRE)
Micky Hammond 53
3 b g Footstepsinthesand Speedi Mouse (Alhaarth (IRE))
2152[7] 3219[6] **4443**[3]◆ 4990[12] 5814[4]
Burning (IRE) *Charlie Fellowes* a60 49
2 br c Gutaifan(IRE) Rayon Rouge (IRE) (Manduro (GER))
5774[8] 7981[5]◆ ***8546***[5]
Burning Lake (IRE) *J F Levins* a68 56
3 br g Le Havre(IRE) Baby Houseman (Oasis Dream)
4726[4]
Burning Topic (GER) *David Lanigan* a63 73
3 b f Maxios Burning Sunset (Caerleon (USA))
5062[2] 5969[6] *7278*[4] *7843*[7]
Burning Victory (FR) *S Wattel* a70 94
3 br f Nathaniel(IRE) M'Oubliez Pas (USA) (El Corredor (USA))
3391a[6]
Burniston Rocks *Ed Vaughan* a62 64
2 ch g Monsieur Bond(IRE) Miss Fridaythorpe (Pastoral Pursuits)
4798[5] 5381[7] **6807**[6] 8201[4] *9060*[4] *9307*[12]
Burn Some Dust (IRE) *Brian Ellison* a70 75
4 b g Shirocco(GER) Chilly Filly (IRE) (Montjeu (IRE))
3816[3] **(5241)**
Burnt Sugar (IRE) *Roger Fell* a107 109
7 b g Lope De Vega(IRE) Lady Livius (IRE) (Titus Livius (FR))
2100[6] **3588**[8] 4921[17] 5413[15]
Burren View Lady (IRE)
Denis Gerard Hogan a56 58
9 br m Dansili Westerly Gale (USA) (Gone West (USA))
2944[6]
Burrows Seaside (FR) *Philip Kirby* 41
2 b g Sidestep(AUS) See Your Dream (Siyouni (FR))
5234[8]
Burtonwood *Julie Camacho* a68 64
7 b g Acclamation Green Poppy (Green Desert (USA))
3474 3975[9] 4519[10] 5169[5] 5244[6] **5515**[2] 6099[3] 6503[2] 7050[8] *8429*[8] *8925*[2] *9223*[7] *9473*[5]
Busby (IRE) *Conrad Allen* a87 73
4 b g Kodiac Arabian Pearl (IRE) (Refuse To Bend (IRE))
(247) 3301[6] 5000[3] *5942*[7] *6319*[2] *7188*[5] *7789*[2] *(8063)* *8827*[2] ***(9176)***
Bushtucker Trial (IRE) *Michael Bell* 77
2 b g Bungle Inthejungle Universal Circus (Imperial Dancer)
2282[3] (2903) 4433[5] 5390[7] **(6158)** **(6498)** 7896[22]

Bustaan (USA) *Owen Burrows* a59
3 b f Distorted Humor(USA) Aryaamm (IRE) (Galileo (IRE))
9038[4] ***9400***[4]
Busy Street *Michael Appleby* a99 96
7 b g Champs Elysees Allegro Viva (USA) (Distant View (USA))
(349) *7043* *7992* ***(1172)*** ***1483***[3] 2801[5] 3081[6] *4381*[6] 4899[2] 6255[8] *9065*[2] *9222*[3] *9366*[2] *9588*[5]
Buthela (FR) *A Fabre* a61 97
5 b g Acclamation Tribune (FR) (Grand Slam (USA))
(1827a) **2429a**[3]
But I Like It (IRE) *Fergal Birrane* a46 56
3 b g Ruler Of The World(IRE) Cawett (IRE) (Danehill Dancer (IRE))
9552[10] ***9573***[6]
Buto *Eve Johnson Houghton* 62
2 ch g Nathaniel(IRE) Mea Parvitas (IRE) (Oasis Dream)
6106[5] 7124[5] 7562[7] 8244[8]
Butterfield (IRE) *Brian Forsey* a56 54
6 b g Fastnet Rock(AUS) Cozzene's Angel (USA) (Cozzene (USA))
8511 ***619***[4] ***810***[6] 1463[12] 2468[3] 2974[3] 4777[4] 5290[6] 5802[2] 7759[8] *8347*[3] *8828*[7] *9447*[4] *(9553)*
Butterfly Pose (IRE) *J S Moore* a46 55
2 gr f Hallowed Crown(AUS) She's A Minx (IRE) (Linamix (FR))
2282[5] **5469a**[8] 5794[4] *6584a*[8] 7056[10] *9009*[7] *9643*[7]
Buwardy *John Gosden* a77 60
2 gr c Invincible Spirit(IRE) Rumya (NZ) (Red Ransom (USA))
7661[6] ***7996***[2] ***8504***[2]
Buxlow Belle (FR) *David Menuisier* a34 49
4 gr m Authorized(IRE) Steel Woman (IRE) (Anabaa (USA))
2283[5] 2733[9] 3740[7]
Buyer Beware (IRE) *Liam Bailey* a63 68
7 br g Big Bad Bob(IRE) Adoring (IRE) (One Cool Cat (USA))
3481[5] 4056[5] **4404**[3] 4825[8] 5487[7] 6583[2] 7001[11]
Buy Me Back *Archie Watson* a70
3 b f Lethal Force(IRE) Delft (Dutch Art)
9211[2] *9514*[3]
Buy Nice Not Twice (IRE)
Richard Hannon a26 50
2 b f Teofilo(IRE) Petit Adagio (IRE) (Cape Cross (IRE))
4544[7] 5088[4] 5366[7] 6394[5] *6884*[7] 7111[4] *8603*[12]
Buzz (FR) *Hughie Morrison* a104 101
5 gr g Motivator Tiysha (IRE) (Araafa (IRE))
1927[7] **3864**[3] 5657[6] 7616[3]
Buzz Lightyere *Patrick Chamings* a52 57
6 b g Royal Applause Lady Gloria (Diktat)
4235[13] **4771**[4] 5680[6] *5946*[4] 6560[10] *7376*[7] 7984[9]
Buzztothemoon *Marco Botti* a50
2 ch c Dandy Man(IRE) Luna Mission (IRE) (Acclamation)
9174[13] *9326*[12]
Bye Bye Euro (IRE) *Keith Dalgleish* a31 61
2 ch f Dragon Pulse(IRE) Miss Frime (IRE) (Xaar)
4819[5] 5273[5] 6226[6] **7429**[4] *8303*[7]
Bye Bye Hong Kong (USA)
Andrew Balding a109 111
3 b g Street Sense(USA) Light And Variable (USA) (Tiznow (USA))
(1713) **(2688)** 3343[4] 4092[13]
Bye Bye Lady (FR) *Andrew Balding* a75
3 b f Sea The Stars(IRE) Peinture Rose (USA) (Storm Cat (USA))
8013[5]◆ ***(8671)***
Bygeorgemygeorge (FR) *P Adda* 62
3 b c George Vancouver(USA) Margot Mine (IRE) (Choisir (AUS))
3139a[5]
By Jove *Michael Bell* 53
2 b c Nathaniel(IRE) Calima Breeze (Oasis Dream)
6912[10] 7346[11] 7981[11]
Byline *Kevin Ryan* 85
2 b g Muhaarar Lauren Louise (Tagula (IRE))
4098[2] (5118)◆ **6422**[7] 7399[13]
By My Side (IRE) *Michael Bell* 41
2 ch f Siyouni(FR) Fill My Heart (IRE) (Peintre Celebre (USA))
8759[9]
By My Standards (USA)
W Bret Calhoun a112
3 b c Goldencents(USA) A Jealous Woman (USA) (Muqtarib (USA))
2425a[11]
By Rail *Nick Littmoden* a69
5 br g Rail Link Soldata (USA) (Maria's Mon (USA))
6733[7] ***7083***[2] *7790*[5]
Byronegetonefree *Stuart Coltherd* a35 35
8 b g Byron Lefty's Dollbaby (USA) (Brocco (USA))
3447[13] *5435*[11]
Byron Flyer *Ian Williams* a92 110
8 b g Byron Nursling (IRE) (Kahyasi (IRE))
2742[13] **3346**[2] 4053[8] 4646[16] 6452[4]
Byron Green (IRE)
Thomas Gallagher a53
7 b g Byron Exit Stage Left (IRE) (Exit To Nowhere (USA))
6887[6] *9091*[6] *9425*[10]
Byron's Choice *Michael Dods* a54 97
4 b g Poet's Voice Byrony (IRE) (Byron)
2844[10] 3563[2] **4127**[4] 5173[8] 7430[6]
Byzantia *John Gosden* 75
2 b f Golden Horn Hoyam (Royal Applause)
3049[5]
Byzantine Empire *John Gosden* a74 48
2 b c Golden Horn Mainstay (Elmaamul (USA))
6926[2]◆ 7338[9]
Caballetta *Roger Varian* 82
2 gr f Mastercraftsman(IRE) Allegretto (IRE) (Galileo (IRE))
(8432)◆

Caballero (IRE) *Keith Dalgleish* a83 90
3 ch c Camacho Dame D'Honneur (IRE) (Teofilo (IRE))
9472[6]
Caballero Chopper
Grizzetti Galoppo SRL 93
2 b c Mukhadram Vandergirl (IRE) (Dutch Art)
4172a[6]
Cabanac *Bent Olsen* a61
6 b h Falco(USA) Ibizane (USA) (Elusive Quality (USA))
7494a[8]
Cabarita *Ralph Beckett* a77 38
3 ch f Leroidesanimaux(BRZ) Catadupa (Selkirk (USA))
556[3] ***1166***[3]◆ 2612[P] *4022*[3] 5565[8]
Cabarita (GER) *H-J Groschel* a63 89
4 ch m Areion(GER) Caesarina (Hernando (FR))
4461a[10] **6270a**[6] 7250a[7]
Cable Speed (IRE) *Charles Hills* a75
2 b c Cable Bay(IRE) Hear My Cry (USA) (Giant's Causeway (USA))
9471[4]◆
Cabot Cliffs (IRE) *Charles Hills* a57 36
2 ch c Gleneagles(IRE) Hallouella (Halling (USA))
6424[14] ***6926***[8]
Cachaca *John Best* a25
3 b f Foxwedge(AUS) Elounta (Dubawi (IRE))
733[9]
Cacophonous *David Menuisier* a56 76
4 b g Cacique(IRE) Zee Zee Gee (Galileo (IRE))
2353[4] 3545[8] 4112[3] *4791*[7]
Cadeau D'Amour (IRE)
Richard Fahey a65 65
3 br g Camacho Perfect Pose (IRE) (Amadeus Wolf)
65[3] *524*[7]
Cadeau D'Or (FR) *Andrew Balding* 73
2 ch g Le Havre(IRE) Hill Of Grace (Desert Prince (IRE))
7162[5]
Cadeo *Marco Botti* a69
2 br g Raven's Pass(USA) Waldena (USA) (Storm Cat (USA))
7030[9] *7605*[3] ***7994***[4]
Cadre Du Noir (USA)
Martyn Meade a92 88
3 b c War Front(USA) Dynamic Feature (USA) (Rahy (USA))
(4120) 6836[3] ***7517***[3] *7815*[4]
Caen Na Coille (USA) *Ed Dunlop* a64 73
3 bb f Medaglia d'Oro(USA) Strathnaver (Oasis Dream)
7943 3860[5] 4326[11] 4870[3] **5429**[2] 5828[6]
Caesara *Jean-Pierre Carvalho* 90
4 b m Pivotal Chantra (GER) (Lando (GER))
4461a[7] **6270a**[4] 6769a[14]
Caesar's Comet (IRE)
Denis Gerard Hogan a68 68
5 b g Acclamation Star Now (Librettist (USA))
2328[2] *7086a*[4]
Caesonia *Charles Hills* a45 48
3 ch f Garswood Agrippina (Timeless Times (USA))
1852[11] **2506**[6] 3421[6] *6052*[P] *7282*[10] *8295*[4] *8547*[13] *9384*[9]
Cafe Americano (USA)
Chad C Brown 105
3 b f Medaglia d'Oro(USA) Roxy Gap (CAN) (Indian Charlie (USA))
8139a[4]
Cafe Espresso *Chelsea Banham* a62 63
3 b f Sir Percy Forest Express (AUS) (Kaaptive Edition (NZ))
(1494) *(1730)* 1885[2] **3012**[6] (3253) 4339[4] 6129[9] *7575*[9] *8298*[6] *8692*[10] *9134*[7] *9303*[13]
Cafe Milano *Simon Dow* a56
2 b c Al Kazeem Selka (FR) (Selkirk (USA))
6684[6] ***9634***[9]
Cafe Sydney (IRE) *Tony Carroll* a30 62
3 ch f Foxwedge(AUS) Carafe (Selkirk (USA))
4991[9] (5680) **(5880)**◆ 6759[3] **7343**[5] 7984[12]
Caffe Macchiato (IRE)
Mme Pia Brandt 89
4 b h Fast Company(IRE) Cappuccino (IRE) (Mujadil (USA))
1827a[9] **2429a**[7] (7062a)
Caged Lightning (IRE)
Steve Gollings a54 53
9 b g Haatef(USA) Rainbow Melody (IRE) (Rainbows For Life (CAN))
8945[8] ***9626***[11]
Caja Primera (GER) *H-A Pantall* a75 76
3 ch f Lord Of England(GER) Centinela (Caerleon (USA))
6063a[5] *9058a*[5]
Calaconta (FR) *S Dehez* a73 82
4 b m Muhtathir Triki Miki (FR) (Della Francesca (USA))
1491a[2]
Caladiyna (FR) *M Planard* 68
4 b m Poet's Voice Clarinda (FR) (Montjeu (IRE))
6031a[7]
Cala D'Or (IRE) *Samuel Farrell* 30
3 ch f Society Rock(IRE) Cala (FR) (Desert Prince (IRE))
1855[11] 3532[5]
Calaf (FR) *H Fortineau* a75 73
7 b g Elusive City(USA) Tianshan (FR) (Lahint (USA))
4747a[11] *5715a*[13]
Calamity May *Luke Dace* a50
2 ch f Helmet(AUS) Romantic Retreat (Rainbow Quest (USA))
9130[8] *9385*[10]
Cala Sveva (IRE) *Mark Usher* a47 33
3 b f Footstepsinthesand Sveva (IRE) (Danehill Dancer (IRE))
532[7] *3299*[8] *3996*[9] **4735**[6] *5648*[12]
Cala Tarida *F Rossi* 107
3 b f Garswood Capsicum (Holy Roman Emperor (IRE))
1795a[4] 3121a[4] **3905a**[5]

Calatrava (IRE) *Ralph Beckett* 54
2 b f Havana Gold(IRE) Intizara (Dansili)
8458[10]

Calbuco *Rod Millman* 54
2 b c Showcasing Empress Rock (IRE) (Fastnet Rock (AUS))
5794[6] **6330**[8] 6845[14] 7296[5] *9061*[12]

Calcite (FR) *G Mousnier* a48 63
8 gr m Sulamani(IRE) Jaillissante (FR) (Verglas (IRE))
8966a[2]

Calculation *Sir Michael Stoute* a97 89
3 br g Dubawi(IRE) Estimate (IRE) (Monsun (GER))
2208[9] *3446*[4] (4327) (5127) ***(6437)***◆ 6955[9]

Calder Prince (IRE) *Tom Dascombe* a96 85
6 gr g Dark Angel(IRE) Flame Of Ireland (IRE) (Fasliyev (USA))
2526[12] 3268[3]◆ 3846[8] 4108[7] 4607[8] 5130[3] 5820[6] (6700) 7145[2] 7678[4] ***8320***[2]

Caledonia Duchess *Jo Hughes* a68 63
6 b m Dutch Art Granuaile O'Malley (IRE) (Mark Of Esteem (IRE))
1543 *2567* **(479)** *724*[6]

Caledonia Laird *Gay Kelleway* a58 57
8 b g Firebreak Granuaile O'Malley (IRE) (Mark Of Esteem (IRE))
1597 ***(599)*** *925*[8] *2944*[8] 4567[10] *5003*[2] *5633*[5] *6117*[7] *7859*[4] *(8915)* *9090*[9]

Caledonian Crusade (IRE)
David Simcock a48 70
2 gr g Gleneagles(IRE) Convocate (USA) (Exchange Rate (USA))
6163[4] **6892**[4] *7834*[5]

Caledonian Gold *Lisa Williamson* a47 48
6 b m Acclamation Moonlight Rhapsody (IRE) (Danehill Dancer (IRE))
244[8] *383*[8] *531*[6] ***594***[3] *718*[4] *828*[5] *1060*[13] *1478*[5] *1883*[6] *2235*[3] *3007*[6] 3067[5] *3425*[7] 3476[4] 3772[5] 3843[8] *4455*[10] *4589*[10] 4880[12] 5768[4] 5918[4] *6462*[7] 6806[5] *7470*[8] *7912*[4] *8547*[11] *8689*[9]

Cale Lane *Julie Camacho* a57 83
4 ch m Mastercraftsman(IRE) Bruni Heinke (IRE) (Dutch Art)
2292[2] 2893[13] 3722[3] (4442)◆ 5143[5] 5419[2] **(5670)**

Calevade (IRE) *Ben Haslam* a52 45
3 gr g Gregorian(IRE) Avoidance (USA) (Cryptoclearance (USA))
2912[7] 5156[4] 5915[9] *7960*[6] ***9470***[2]◆

California Lad *Fergal Birrane* a74 63
6 b g Aussie Rules(USA) Medaille D'Or (With Approval (CAN))
3321[3] *9570*[9]

California Love *Richard Spencer* a101 99
3 ch f Power La Pantera (Captain Rio)
4052[6]◆ (4922) ***5944***[2] 7146[7] *8708*[5] *9603a*[2]

Calima Calling (IRE)
Michael Appleby a46 49
3 ch f Gale Force Ten Incoming Call (USA) (Red Ransom (USA))
6587[5] ***7190***[7] *8294*[10] *8924*[11] *9209*[9] *9548*[12]

Calin's Lad *Michael Appleby* a70 60
4 ch g Equiano(FR) Lalina (GER) (Trempolino (USA))
3430[2] 3657[11] *(9420)* ***9566***[3]◆

Calippo (IRE) *Archie Watson* a73 65
2 b f Cappella Sansevero Zelie Martin (IRE) (Invincible Spirit (IRE))
2907[3] (3257) 3652[3] 3812[6] (4652) 5196[2] 5968[2] *6584a*[7] ***7029***[2] 7329[4]

Caliste *H-A Pantall* a80 79
4 b g Intense Focus(USA) Russian Hill (Indian Ridge (IRE))
992a[3]

Called To The Bar (IRE)
Mme Pia Brandt 112
5 b g Henrythenavigator(USA) Perfect Hedge (Unfuwain (USA))
2169a[3] **(3123a)** 4015[8] (7008a) 9376a[5]

Calle Nevada (FR) *D Windrif* a54 75
2 b f Style Vendome(FR) Miss Annie (FR) (Dubawi (IRE))
8239a[6]

Callherwhatyoulike *Tim Pinfield* a17
2 b f Outstrip Aswaaq (IRE) (Peintre Celebre (USA))
8060[8]

Call Him Al (IRE) *Richard Fahey* a62 51
3 b g Alhebayeb(IRE) Exempt (Exceed And Excel (AUS))
1504[4] 2101[14] 3270[10] 3780[6] 4606[5] 4785[5] 5248[11]

Calling Out (FR) *David Simcock* a101 66
8 bb g Martaline Exit The Straight (IRE) (Exit To Nowhere (USA))
89[4] *368*[5] *800*[6] 1413[14] *2320*[5] *3322*[2]

Calling The Wind (IRE)
Richard Hughes a78
3 b g Authorized(IRE) Al Jasrah (IRE) (Shirocco (GER))
3358[9] ***9633***[7]

Calliope *Dianne Sayer* a58 66
6 b m Poet's Voice Costa Brava (IRE) (Sadler's Wells (USA))
4274[2] 5301[7] 5727[9]

Callipygian *James Given* a53 55
2 b f Magician(IRE) Soft Drink (USA) (Lemon Drop Kid (USA))
2052[4] 2579[5] *3578*[6] 4756[5] 5912[5] 6539[8] *7306*[7] *8085*[12]

Call Me Cheers *David Evans* a52 53
2 ch g Kyllachy Tweety Pie (IRE) (Rock Of Gibraltar (IRE))
2694[4] 2903[6] *5280*[10] ***6182***[2]◆ 6557[4] *7853*[6] *8118*[5] *8452*[10]

Call Me Ginger *Jim Goldie* a85 91
3 ch g Orientor Primo Heights (Primo Valentino (IRE))
211[5]◆ *806*[2]◆ (7313)◆ **7894**[6] 8512[8]

Call Me Grumpy (IRE)
Roger Varian a79 84
5 b g Holy Roman Emperor(IRE) Miss Rochester (IRE) (Montjeu (IRE))
840[2] ***1143***[3] *1329*[10]

Call Me Katie (IRE) *John Gosden* a74 75
2 b f Kodiac Carry On Katie (USA) (Fasliyev (USA))
5961[3] **6831**[3] 7393[5] *7832*[5] *8665*[9] *9137*[9]

Call Me Love *A Botti* 107
3 ch f Sea The Stars(IRE) Fresnay (Rainbow Quest (USA))
2887a[3] 4171a[3] (8153a) **(8790a)**

Call Me Madam *James Bethell* a52 47
4 b m Passing Glance Shazana (Key Of Luck (USA))
6499[5] 7048[7] *8072*[6] *8406*[8] ***9467***[2]

Call My Bluff (IRE)
Dominic Ffrench Davis a63 24
2 b c Make Believe Ocean Bluff (IRE) (Dalakhani (IRE))
8517[5] ***9363***[5]

Call Out Loud *Michael Appleby* a90 86
7 b g Aqlaam Winner's Call (Indian Ridge (IRE))
4[5] *104*[2]◆ *213*[4] ***(807)*** *1181*[4] *1356*[3] 2799[3] (3649) 4319[2] 5319[3] 5626[6] *8606*[12] *8918*[12]

Call The Wind *F Head* a112 114
5 ch g Frankel In Clover (Inchinor)
1441a[3] 3123a[3] 4962a[4] 6266a[2] **7928a**[2] 8589a[2]

Calonne (IRE) *J F Levins* a64 74
3 gr g Alhebayeb(IRE) Lady Pastrana (IRE) (Key Of Luck (USA))
9349[5]

Calvados Spirit *Richard Fahey* a83 83
6 b g Invincible Spirit(IRE) Putois Peace (Pivotal)
1308a[19] **1413**[6] **4079**[4] **4692**[3] 4723[6] 5155[2] 5693[12] **(6164)** 7212[9] 7906[10]

Calvinist *Kevin Frost* a63 56
6 b g Holy Roman Emperor(IRE) Sharp Relief (IRE) (Galileo (IRE))
2344[7] *9168*[6] *9275*[2]◆ ***9626***[2]

Calypso Rose (IRE) *H-F Devin* a71 69
2 b f Invincible Spirit(IRE) Calypso Beat (USA) (Speightstown (USA))
8447a[3]

Calyx *John Gosden* 118
3 b c Kingman Helleborine (Observatory (USA))
(2270) 3083[2]

Camachess (IRE) *Philip McBride* a69 80
3 b f Camacho Heeby Jeeby (Lawman (FR))
918[7] *(1081)* *(1167)* *(1170)* (2024) **(3742)** 4123[10] *8420*[8] *8921*[13] *9108*[9]

Camachita (IRE) *J P Murtagh* a83 93
2 ch f Camacho Where We Left Off (Dr Devious (IRE))
7215a[8] **8356a**[4]

Camacho Chief (IRE) *Michael Dods* 104
4 b g Camacho Passage To India (IRE) (Indian Ridge (IRE))
2557[5] 3589[3] **(3883)** 5454[6] 6351[10] 6960[4] 7894[4]

Camacho Man (IRE)
Jennie Candlish a53 52
2 ch c Camacho Ezilii (IRE) (Lawman (FR))
4302[8] 4734[7] 4992[8] 7111[9] *7767*[4] *8061*[8] ***8526***[2] ***9009***[4] *9164*[5] *9399*[5]

Camahawk *Tim Easterby* 73
2 b g Camelot Septembers Hawk (IRE) (Machiavellian (USA))
8511[3] 8858[8]

Camakasi (IRE) *Ali Stronge* a65 51
8 b g Camacho Innocence (Unfuwain (USA))
1653[13] 1934[7] 3700[RR] 4220[13] **6419**[8]

Camanche Grey (IRE)
Lucinda Egerton a56 48
8 gr g Camacho Sense Of Greeting (IRE) (Key Of Luck (USA))
25[8] *2631*[10] *2771*[2] 1505[9] ***2247***[4] 3504[10] *3592*[12] 3723[3] 4219[8] 4478[6] 4500[3] 4911[8] 5094[8] 5278[4] 5620[9]

Cambeleza (IRE) *Kevin Ryan* 56
3 b g Camacho Blessed Beauty (IRE) (Alhaarth (IRE))
3651[5] 4726[8] 5552[6]

Camber *Richard Fahey* a75 77
3 b g Garswood Topflightcoolracer (Lujain (USA))
(1720) **2333**[2] 3779[5]

Cambier Parc (USA) *Chad C Brown* 107
3 b f Medaglia d'Oro(USA) Sealy Hill (CAN) (Point Given (USA))
(8139a)

Cambria (USA) *Wesley A Ward* a90 92
2 ch f Speightstown(USA) Teen Pauline (USA) (Tapit (USA))
8745a[9]

Cambric *Roger Charlton* 84
3 ch f Australia Poplin (Medicean)
2795[7] (3888)◆ 4656[4] (5623)◆ **(6419)**◆ 7239[4]

Came From The Dark (IRE)
Ed Walker a44 100
3 gr c Dark Angel(IRE) Silver Shoon (IRE) (Fasliyev (USA))
1728[9] (3590) 3971[2] 5173[6] 5951[7] 6220[8] (6921)◆ **7894**[2]

Camelot Rakti (IRE) *James Tate* a80 43
3 b f Camelot Carioca (IRE) (Rakti)
3468[4] 4007[5] *5651*[10] *8548*[3]

Cameo Star (IRE) *Richard Fahey* a68 74
4 ch g Camacho Passionforfashion (IRE) (Fasliyev (USA))
1760[10] **2478**[2] 2898[6] 3930[6] 4630[5] 5237[5] *5852*[3] 6628[3] *7305*[8] 7779[6] 8234[8] *(8306)*

Camile (IRE) *Iain Jardine* a52 66
6 b m Captain Rio Heroic Performer (IRE) (Royal Applause)
7828 **(2631)**

Camino *Andi Brown* a42 40
6 b m Equiano(FR) Juncea (Elnadim (USA))
848[5] ***1383***[5] *1716*[10] 6126[4] *7690*[10]

Camorra (IRE) *G M Lyons* 85
2 b c Zoffany(IRE) Mauralakana (FR) (Muhtathir)
7744a[4]

Camouflaged (IRE) *Mark Johnston* a53 51
2 gr c Dark Angel(IRE) Inner Secret (USA) (Singspiel (IRE))
7902[9] ***8714***[10]

Campari *Roger Charlton* a74 78
2 b g Due Diligence(USA) Spritzeria (Bigstone (IRE))
6395[7] **7162**[4] *8604*[4]

Camphor (IRE) *Mrs John Harrington* 101
3 b f Camelot Paraphernalia (IRE) (Dalakhani (IRE))
6090a[5] **8368a**[3]

Camprond (FR) *Mme Pia Brandt* a72 97
3 b g Lope De Vega(IRE) Bernieres (IRE) (Montjeu (IRE))
421a[5] **5717a**[6]

Canadian George (FR)
Jennie Candlish a58 59
4 b g George Vancouver(USA) Connaissance (IRE) (Choisir (AUS))
9006[13] ***9626***[8]

Canagat *Archie Watson* a80
2 ch c Zoffany(IRE) Caskelena (IRE) (Galileo (IRE))
8288[3] ***(8810)***

Canal Rocks *Henry Candy* a85 87
3 br g Aussie Rules(USA) In Secret (Dalakhani (IRE))
1516[3] 3170[4]◆ 3647[5] (4562) 5292[4] **6155**[2] 7349[4] *8606*[3]

Canasta *James Fanshawe* a75 61
3 b f Charm Spirit(IRE) Morzine (Miswaki (USA))
787 *1142*[5] 3218[4] 4284[4]◆ *5284*[3] *6393*[3]◆ *(7858)*◆ ***8705***[4] *9443*[6]

Canavese *Eve Johnson Houghton* a36 52
3 ch f Mastercraftsman(IRE) Rivara (Red Ransom (USA))
2253[14] 2760[10] 4179[7] **4568**[9]

Can Can Nights *Olly Williams*
3 br f Sayif(IRE) Can Can Dancer (Fantastic Light (USA))
2301[8]

Can Can Sixty Two *R Mike Smith* a34 41
4 b m Sixties Icon Natalie Jay (Ballacashtal (CAN))
2962[5] 3250[8] **3718**[6] 4917[6] **5240**[5] 5937[8] 6343[10] 7489[10] 7513[9] 7783[8]

Candelisa (IRE) *David Loughnane* a83 86
6 br g Dream Ahead(USA) Vasilia (Dansili)
(1561) 2273[6] 3149[3] 3813[11] 4320[2] 4879[5] **5516**[2] 5948[12] 6700[6] 7142[11] *9658*[3]◆

Candesta (USA) *Julia Feilden* a59 50
9 b g First Defence(USA) Wandesta (Nashwan (USA))
6[11] *590*[8] ***1214***[10] *9225*[10] *9544*[10]

Candid (IRE) *Jonathan Portman* a46 50
2 b f Requinto(IRE) Afnoon (USA) (Street Cry (IRE))
2918[8] 3798[6] 4840[9] 7234[11] *8118*[4]◆ *8603*[7] *9322*[4]

Canessar (FR) *Arnaud Delacour* 108
6 rg g Kendargent(FR) Candara (FR) (Barathea (IRE))
3561a[4]

Canford Art (IRE) *Peter Fahey* a52 68
4 b m Canford Cliffs(IRE) Saldenart (GER) (Areion (GER))
2638[9] **7299**[4]

Canford Bay (IRE) *Antony Brittain* a85 88
5 b g Canford Cliffs(IRE) Maundays Bay (IRE) (Invincible Spirit (IRE))
970[2]◆ *1342*[7] *1403*[3] *1507*[3] (1899) 2079[5] **(2589)** 3097[10] 3509[3] 4100[4] **(4364)**◆ 4894[5] 5420[5] 5691[8] 7700[3] *8023*[5]◆ *8470*[3] *9030*[3] *9166*[6] *9286*[2] *9550*[4]

Canford Dancer *Richard Hughes* a68 71
3 b f Canford Cliffs(IRE) Petite Nymphe (Golan (IRE))
1171[3] **2125**[5] 2719[5] 3598[5] *4247*[10] 6505[5]

Canford Heights (IRE)
William Haggas a89 97
4 b g Canford Cliffs(IRE) Highindi (Montjeu (IRE))
3466[7] ***4381***[9]

Canford's Joy (IRE) *Alexandra Dunn* a58 72
4 b g Canford Cliffs(IRE) Joyful (IRE) (Green Desert (USA))
(3540) **5760a**[2] 7125[10]

Canford Thompson
Micky Hammond a71 56
6 b g Canford Cliffs(IRE) Sadie Thompson (IRE) (King's Best (USA))
1718[13] **3511**[4]

Can I Kick It (IRE) *Stuart Williams* a30 16
3 b f Acclamation Church Melody (Oasis Dream)
5650[11] *6594*[8] 7319[9]

Canimar *Shaun Keightley* a48 65
4 b m Havana Gold(IRE) Acquifer (Oasis Dream)
379[5] ***599***[2] *702*[4] *1093*[2] *1265*[4] *1477*[6] *1715*[3] *1969*[6] *9247*[8] *9439*[9] *9539*[7]

Canneyhill Bob *Kenny Johnson*
4 b g Arabian Gleam Politelysed (Courteous)
5555[11]

Canny Style *Joanne Foster*
6 b m Canford Cliffs(IRE) Stylish One (IRE) (Invincible Spirit (IRE))
8635[12]

Canoodling *Ian Williams* 69
3 b f Nathaniel(IRE) Tequila Sunrise (Dansili)
2770[11] **3482**[5] 3958[5] 4628[6] 5214[4] 6045[6]

Canouville (FR) *Mlle Y Vollmer* a74 79
4 b m Air Chief Marshal(IRE) Our Dream Queen (Oasis Dream)
2182a[2] **2956a**[2] 6267a[4]

Can't Beat It *Gavin Hernon* a18
2 b c Showcasing My Broken Drum (Slickly (FR))
8239a[10]

Can't Hold Us (FR) *D Allard* 56
2 b f Stormy River(FR) First Zita (GER) (Zieten (USA))
1240a[5] **1709a**[6] **3562a**[4] 5166a[8]

Cantiniere (USA) *Saeed bin Suroor* a94
4 b m War Front(USA) Up (IRE) (Galileo (IRE))
97a[10] *4640*[3] *5267*[5] *(6280)* ***(6981)*** *8701*[6]

Canton Queen (IRE)
Richard Hannon a82 96
3 b f Shamardal(USA) Hana Lina (Oasis Dream)
1939[6] 6451[3] **6951**[2]◆ 7901[5]◆ *9010*[4]

Can't Stop Now (IRE) *Clive Cox* a60 74
2 ch g Starspangledbanner(AUS) Sorry Woman (FR) (Ivan Denisovich (IRE))
2267[5] **5501**[4] **5980**[3] *9172*[6]

Canvassed (IRE) *Roger Varian* a63 56
4 b g Shamardal(USA) Painter's Pride (FR) (Dansili)
(1517)◆ 2271[5]

Capala (IRE) *Adam West*
3 b g Swiss Spirit Jezebel (Owington)
4378[15]

Cap D'antibes (IRE)
John Joseph Murphy a55 69
2 b c Society Rock(IRE) Miss Verdoyante (Montjeu (IRE))
5997a[5]

Cape Agulhas (IRE) *W J Martin* a52 44
5 gr g Famous Name Kat Act Two (Act One)
4498[9] ***8406***[2] *9042*[6]

Cape Byron *Roger Varian* 118
5 ch g Shamardal(USA) Reem Three (Mark Of Esteem (IRE))
(2609) **(4095)** 4923[11] 6472[3] (7892) 8331[12]

Cape Cavalli (IRE) *Simon Crisford* 89
3 b g Cape Cross(IRE) Matauri Pearl (IRE) (Hurricane Run (IRE))
1856[2] 2566[2] 3152[3] 4066[3] 6043[2] (6836) **7342**[2] 8092[9]

Cape Cova (IRE) *Marjorie Fife* a64 70
6 b g Cape Cross(IRE) Sina Cova (IRE) (Barathea (IRE))
6975[11] *7414*[4]

Cape Cyclone (IRE) *Stuart Williams* a51 57
4 b m Cape Cross(IRE) Dubai Cyclone (USA) (Bernardini (USA))
7810 *7532* 2740[8] **(4657)**◆ 5380[3] 6412[6]

Cape Greco (USA) *Jo Hughes* a68 64
4 b g Cape Blanco(IRE) High Walden (USA) (El Gran Senor (USA))
(180)◆ ***250***[3] *548*[5] 2026a[7] *2264a*[5] 4747a[9] ***6434a***[4]

Cape Hill Cotter (FR) *Ann Duffield* a54 43
4 b m Dabirsim(FR) Nelly Dean (Pivotal)
293[10]

Cape Islay (FR) *Mark Johnston* 87
3 b f Cape Cross(IRE) Eilean Ban (USA) (Silver Hawk (USA))
2110[3] 2618[6] 3548[6] **(4362)** 4864[6] 5253[7] 5706[6] 6576[6] 7332[3] 8341[10]

Capelli Rossi (IRE)
Miss Clare Louise Cannon 49
2 ch f Cappella Sansevero Lady Magdalena (IRE) (Invincible Spirit (IRE))
2957[7]

Cape Of Good Hope (IRE)
David A & B Hayes & Tom Dabern 112
3 b c Galileo(IRE) Hveger (AUS) (Danehill (USA))
(2031) **3390a**[4] 4013[10] **(8136a)** 8579a[10] 8952a[16]

Cape Palace *John Gosden* a91 91
2 b c Golden Horn Mia Diletta (Selkirk (USA))
(6664)◆ **7410**[3]

Cape Victory (IRE) *James Tate* a88 96
3 b c Dawn Approach(IRE) Cape Alex (Cape Cross (IRE))
1970[2] (2677) 4077[3] 4565[4] *6026*[2] *6686*[2] **(7213)** 8130[19]

Capezzano (USA) *S bin Ghadayer* a119 77
5 b g Bernardini(USA) Cableknit (USA) (Unbridled's Song (USA))
(282a)◆ *(513a)* ***(1114a)*** *1447a*[12]

Cap Francais *Ed Walker* 106
3 b g Frankel Miss Cap Ferrat (Darshaan)
2031[2] 2619[4] 4013[7] 5585[9] 6952[11] 7864[8]

Capla Berry *Rae Guest* a55 63
3 b f Roderic O'Connor(IRE) Salsa Brava (IRE) (Almutawakel)
6325[3] *7032*[5] *8472*[8]

Capla Crusader *Nick Littmoden* a70 34
3 b g Archipenko(USA) Desert Berry (Green Desert (USA))
(8451) *9178*[5]

Capla Cubiste *Sir Mark Prescott Bt* a66 60
2 b f Archipenko(USA) Eurolink Artemis (Common Grounds)
7981[3] ***8402***[2]◆ ***9063***[4]

Capla Demon *Antony Brittain* a54 59
4 b g Kodiac Namu (Mujahid (USA))
2147 *586*[10] *788*[9] 6273[12] *8123*[5] ***8502***[4] (Dead)

Capla Gilda *Andrea Marcialis* a76 75
3 b f Compton Place Respondez (Oasis Dream)
(1658a) 2090a[3] 3878a[2] *(5408a)*

Capla Huntress *Chris Wall* a69 52
3 gr f Sir Percy Great White Hope (IRE) (Noverre (USA))
5656[8] 6290[11] *6732*[6] *7280*[4] ***(7857)***◆

Capla Spirit *Gay Kelleway* 72
2 b g Cable Bay(IRE) Warden Rose (Compton Place)
6064[4] 6911[12] 7538[4]

Caplin *Mark Johnston* a87 66
3 b g Cape Cross(IRE) Party Line (Montjeu (IRE))
(1233) ***(1386)***

Capofaro *Jamie Osborne* a78 74
3 b g Kyllachy Pious (Bishop Of Cashel)
1331[0] *554*[6] *733*[8] *(1354)* *1726*[2] *(2007)* *(2350)* *(2597)* ***(2965)*** 3170[5] 4562[5]

Cappananty Con *Charlie Wallis* a81 75
5 gr g Zebedee Fairmont (IRE) (Kingmambo (USA))
433[2]◆ *849*[5] *1061*[3] *1357*[6] *(1767)* *2122*[4] ***(2515)*** *3303*[2]◆ *3443*[3] *4458*[4] *5000*[9] *9257*[11] *9584*[3]

Cappella Fella (IRE)
Sarah Hollinshead a48 29
2 b g Cappella Sansevero Almatlaie (USA) (Elusive Quality (USA))
4876[6] 6528[8] ***7030***[8] *9009*[6] *9399*[8]

Capp It All (IRE) *David Loughnane* 50
2 b f Cappella Sansevero Katy Daly (IRE) (Amadeus Wolf)
3194[6] 4323[4] 4819[7] 5313[8]

Capri (IRE) *A P O'Brien* 112
5 gr h Galileo(IRE) Dialafara (FR) (Anabaa (USA))
2158a[5] **4015**[6] 6191a[4] 7246a[10] 7717a[3] 8332[6]

Capricorn Prince *Gary Moore* a56 41
3 ch g Garswood Sakhee's Pearl (Sakhee (USA))
2795[17] 4452[13] 5592[10] 6367[6] 8553[5] 9312[7]

Capriolette (IRE) *Ed Walker* a82 74
4 b m Most Improved(IRE) Greta D'Argent (IRE) (Great Commotion (USA))
(370) 756[9] 1457[19] 1727[9] 4300[11] 4994[8] (5785) 6165[4] 7238[2] 7756[6] 8247[2] 8812[3] 9273[5] 9510[3]

Captain America (SWE) *Annike Bye Hansen* a91 100
9 b g Academy Award(IRE) Muja Maiy (IRE) (Mujadil (USA))
6523a[2] 7497a[4]

Captain Colby (USA) *Paul Midgley* a66 88
7 b g Bernstein(USA) Escape To Victory (Salse (USA))
1501[6] 1946[12] 2396[11] 2743[18] 3589[13] 4406[11] 5444[2]◆ 6162[9] 6676[15] 7467[9] 7700[8]

Captain Cook *Chris Waller* a90 101
6 b g Dubawi(IRE) Canda (USA) (Storm Cat (USA))
8803a[4]

Captain Corelli (IRE) *Julie Camacho* a59 56
2 ch g Anjaal Disprove (IRE) (Approve (IRE))
5845[7] 6943[7] 7619[5] 8085[6] 9009[3]

Captain Dan (IRE) *John James Feane* a72 59
5 b g Henrythenavigator(USA) Danielli (IRE) (Danehill (USA))
344[2] 4873[5]

Captain Dion *Ivan Furtado* a74 79
6 gr g Equiano(FR) Bandanna (Bandmaster (USA))
1177[8] 1366[3]◆ 1973[6] 3221[6] (3656)◆ (3989)◆ 4148[3] 7621[5] (8339) 9048[6] 9245[8]

Captain James (FR) *Mrs C Gilbert* a18 49
9 bb g Linngari(IRE) Chopassing (FR) (Indian Rocket)
2673a[2] 4686a[5] 6009a[7]

Captain Jameson (IRE) *John Quinn* a86 89
4 b g Camacho Cross Section (USA) (Cape Cross (IRE))
1459[10] 2061[7] 3770[3] 4369[7] 5951[3] 7402[8] 8101[3] 8342[2] 8636[3] 9308[5]

Captain Kissinger *Jo Hughes* a55 56
4 b g Captain Gerrard(IRE) Nigella (Band On The Run)
6[12] 257[7] 717[2] 887[8] 1390[10] 1717[4] 2170a[9] 2647a[15] 3711a[16]

Captain Lancelot (FR) *F Chappet* a74 51
3 b g Captain Marvelous(IRE) Rubies (Inchinor)
2090a[7] 3878a[7]

Captain Lars (SAF) *Archie Watson* a86 87
9 b g Captain Al(SAF) Polar Charge (Polar Falcon (USA))
35[3] 551[7] (787) 987[5] 1100[3] 1394[3] 1547[5] 1969[5]

Captain Marmalade (IRE) *Jimmy Fox* a44 53
7 gr g Duke Of Marmalade(IRE) Elisium (Proclamation (IRE))
599[7] 1836[3] 2513[3] 3592[3] 5310[8] 6049[5] 8416[10]

Captain Peaky *Liam Bailey* a50 45
6 b g Captain Gerrard(IRE) Multi-Sofft (Northern State (USA))
1060[2] 2012[7] 2963[11] 3730[7] 4512[5] 4914[10] 8405[6] 8694[8]

Captain Power (IRE) *Gordon Elliott* a52 56
7 b g Captain Rio Invincible Power (IRE) (Invincible Spirit (IRE))
307a[9] 9439[2] 9457[6]

Captain Pugwash (IRE) *Stef Keniry* a70 69
5 b g Sir Prancealot(IRE) Liscoa (IRE) (Foxhound (USA))
536[8] 803[9] 1169[3] 1343[6] 1648[4] 2106[13] (2512) 2785[7]

Captain Ryan *Geoffrey Deacon* a62 66
8 b g Captain Gerrard(IRE) Ryan's Quest (IRE) (Mukaddamah (USA))
(26) (118) 322[9] 986[4] 1266[3] 1820[14] 1987[5] 2728[10] 3425[8] 8697[4]

Captain Scott (IRE) *Heather Main* a62 62
4 b g Tamayuz Capriole (Noverre (USA))
968[4] 1517[5] 1989[6] 3547[12] 3941[7] 4633[6] 5001[5]

Captain Sedgwick (IRE) *John Spearing* a45 55
5 b m Approve(IRE) Alinda (IRE) (Revoque (IRE))
4378[5] 5081[3] 5675[2] (6529) 7236[9] 8123[6] 9298[6]

Captain St Lucifer *Ivan Furtado* a65
2 b g Casamento(IRE) Delaware Dancer (IRE) (Danehill Dancer (IRE))
9500[3]◆

Captain Tatman (FR) *M Krebs* 57
2 b g Olympic Glory(IRE) Florida (FR) (King's Best (USA))
1240a[7] 1709a[4] 2263a[8]

Captivated *John Gosden* a76 28
2 b c Bated Breath Capella's Song (IRE) (Oratorio (IRE))
7899[12] 8250[3]

Captivating Moon (USA) *Chris Block* a86 104
4 b h Malibu Moon(USA) Appealing Storm (USA) (Valid Appeal (USA))
6001a[7]

Capton *Michael Easterby* a46 78
6 b g Cape Cross(IRE) Flavian (Catrail (USA))
2563[11] 3338[7] 4875[8] 5820[7] 6456[2] 7003[5] 7510[6]

Caracas *Kevin Frost* a53 51
5 b g Cacique(IRE) Bourbonella (Rainbow Quest (USA))
160[5] 363[4] 721[3] 2196[7] 6046[7]

Caradoc (IRE) *Ed Walker* a93 104
4 b g Camelot Applause (IRE) (Danehill Dancer (IRE))
2803[5] (3605) 5440[4] (6021) 6420[3] (7457) 9003[4]

Carambole (GER) *Julien Morel* a60 58
3 b f Rock Of Gibraltar(IRE) Co Blue Splash (FR) (Anabaa Blue)
9280a[3]

Caramel Curves *Lisa Williamson* a48 49
3 b f Mayson Shannon Spree (Royal Applause)
1486[10] 2708[7] 2870[9] 4316[9] 5424[6]

Caravagio (FR) *Alain Couetil* a92 105
6 ch h American Post Semire (FR) (Mizoram (USA))
2428a[7] 6820a[5] 8580a[4]

Caravan Of Hope (IRE) *Hugo Palmer* a84 93
3 b g Nathaniel(IRE) Caravan Of Dreams (IRE) (Anabaa (USA))
3247[2]◆ 4066[4] 5634[2] 6211[3] 6641[2] (7867) (8513)

Carbon Dating (IRE) *Andrew Hughes* a76 77
7 b g The Carbon Unit(USA) Advertising Space (IRE) (Galileo (IRE))
2435[6] 2784[6] 4274[7] 4913[4]◆ 5122[2] 6658[2] 7510[3] 8524[6]

Carbutt's Ridge (IRE) *N Caullery* a46 54
6 br g Alfred Nobel(IRE) Tallassee (Indian Ridge (IRE))
3711a[11]

Cardano (USA) *Ian Williams* a64 93
3 b g Oasis Dream Astorgs Galaxy (Galileo (IRE))
472[4] 913[4] 1346[8] 2101[3] (2630) (3478) 3797[2] (4392) 5194[3] 5973[2]◆ (6454) 7396[4] 8092[5]

Cardaw Lily (IRE) *Ruth Carr* a46 52
4 b m Lawman(FR) Chervil (Dansili)
210[7] 533[6] 3771[3] 4651[7] 4824[7] 5237[4] 5486[2] 5767[8] 6058[2] 6680[3] 7591[11] 7780[4]

Card High (IRE) *Wilf Storey* a71 74
9 b g Red Clubs(IRE) Think (FR) (Marchand De Sable (USA))
4009[4] 5728[12]

Cardino (FR) *Carmen Bocskai* a65 67
3 gr c Rajsaman(FR) Facilita (IRE) (Fasliyev (USA))
9058a[8]

Cardsharp *Mark Johnston* a115 116
4 b g Lonhro(AUS) Pure Illusion (IRE) (Danehill (USA))
1103[3] (1181)◆ 1289[3] 1922[10] 2109[3] 2609[21] (3094) 3987[26] 4389[7]

Careful Thought *Mark Johnston* a51
2 b f Brazen Beau(AUS) Sharp Terms (Kris)
9631[6]

Carey Street (IRE) *John Quinn* a60 70
3 b g Bungle Inthejungle Undulant Way (Hurricane Run (IRE))
1662[10] 2635[17] 3805[3] 5593[3] 6341[7] 7363[4] 8434[2]◆ 8713[9]

Caribbean Spice (IRE) *Brian Meehan* 53
2 b g Gutaifan(IRE) Rumline (Royal Applause)
8722[10]

Caribbean Spring (IRE) *George Margarson* a64 64
6 b g Dark Angel(IRE) Bogini (IRE) (Holy Roman Emperor (IRE))
1208[3]◆ 1369[5] 1766[8] 7604[3] 8757[5] 8915[3]◆ 9185[8]

Caribeno *Sir Mark Prescott Bt* 45
2 ch c Archipenko(USA) Cubanita (Selkirk (USA))
4925[7]

Caribou Club (USA) *Thomas F Proctor* 113
5 ch g City Zip(USA) Broken Dreams (USA) (Broken Vow (USA))
1442a[13]

Carif (AUS) *Peter & Paul Snowden* 102
3 br c So You Think(NZ) Norzita (NZ) (Thorn Park (AUS))
8767a[2]

Carla Koala *Natalie Lloyd-Beavis* a44 40
3 b f Kuroshio(AUS) Bold Love (Bold Edge)
605[9] 1650[7] 2300[7] 8249[4] 8697[9]

Carleen *Chris Wall*
3 ch f Sepoy(AUS) Generous Lady (Generous (IRE))
2764[10]

Carlos Felix (IRE) *David Simcock* a74 73
2 ch g Lope De Vega(IRE) Quad's Melody (IRE) (Spinning World (USA))
7392[4]◆ 8424[4] 8823[3]

Carlovian *Mark Walford* a59 56
6 b g Acclamation Mimisel (Selkirk (USA))
2788[9] 3320[7] (3772) 4149[7] 4519[9] 4823[5] 5938[8] 6273[4] 6621[3] (7050) 7507[6] 7824[5] 8263[4] 8638[3] 8925[5] 9185[10]

Carlow Boy (IRE) *Christopher Kellett* a28 47
3 b g Elzaam(AUS) Whitershadeofpale (IRE) (Definite Article)
5100[7] 5866[5] 6361[4] 8863[8]

Carlton Bella *Michael Easterby* a19
2 b g Equiano(FR) The Clan Macdonald (Intikhab (USA))
9107[13] 9624[12]

Carlton Choice (IRE) *Laurent Loisel* a98 93
5 b g Bushranger(IRE) Choice House (USA) (Chester House (USA))
9210a[2]

Carmague (IRE) *J S Moore* 60
2 ch g Anjaal Dancing Lauren (IRE) (Oratorio (IRE))
2686[3] 3171a[4] 3714a[6] 4679a[6] 5600a[6] 6196a[10] 6384a[13]

Carmel *Archie Watson* a54 60
2 b f Cable Bay(IRE) Across The Galaxy (Cape Cross (IRE))
4221[5] 5514[4] 5887[4] 6799[3] 7234[8] 7767[11] (8180)

Carmena (IRE) *Charlie Fellowes* a63
2 b f No Nay Never(USA) Thewaytosanjose (IRE) (Fasliyev (USA))
5045[4] 6028[9]

Carnage *Nikki Evans* a56 49
4 b g Holy Roman Emperor(IRE) Sylvestris (IRE) (Arch (USA))
1102[10] 4868[3] 5378[9] 6400[13]

Carnageo (FR) *P Monfort* a63 69
6 b g Pivotal Sudarynya (IRE) (Sadler's Wells (USA))
6521a[16] 7536a[10] 7860a[5]

Carnival Rose *James Fanshawe* a77 72
3 b f Harbour Watch(IRE) Gypsy Carnival (Trade Fair)
2236[2] 3278[5] 5813[4] 7554[7] 8549[7] 9455[10]

Carnival Zain *E J O'Neill* a80 94
2 b c Youmzain(IRE) Lady Fashion (Oasis Dream)
7774a[6]

Carnwennan (IRE) *Charlie Fellowes* a99 99
4 b g Cacique(IRE) Slieve (Selkirk (USA))
2080[2] (2781) (3145) (4381) 5183[15] 6355[5] 9468[8]

Carolingien (FR) *F Vermeulen* a75 71
3 gr g Kendargent(FR) Calasetta (IRE) (Montjeu (IRE))
868a[6] 5165a[6]

Carouse (IRE) *Evan Williams*
4 b g Excelebration(IRE) Terre Du Vent (FR) (Kutub (IRE))
252[7]

Carpet Time (IRE) *Leanne Breen* a62 60
4 b g Intense Focus(USA) Beal Ban (IRE) (Daggers Drawn (USA))
28[2] 236[12] 1595[7] 1765[4] 7086a[7]

Carp Kid (IRE) *John Flint* a73 80
4 b g Lope De Vega(IRE) Homegrown (IRE) (Mujadil (USA))
346[7] (2353) 2793[5] 3545[5] 4561[2] 4841[4] 5571[5] 6331[2] 6812[3] 7233[2]

Carraigin Aonair (IRE) *Olly Murphy* a56 52
7 b m Fastnet Rock(AUS) Omanah (USA) (Kayrawan (USA))
5001[2] 6046[8]

Carrera *Mrs A Malzard* a22 22
9 b g Sixties Icon Aileen's Gift (IRE) (Rainbow Quest (USA))
2501a[3] 3642a[4]

Carriage Clock *Steph Hollinshead* 57
2 b f Coach House(IRE) Circadian Rhythm (Lujain (USA))
5170[9] 5895[6] 6458[5] 7234[7]

Carriageway *Jonathan Portman*
3 b f Coach House(IRE) Emma Peel (Emarati (USA))
615[9]

Carriesmatic *David Barron* 55
2 b f Passing Glance Concentrate (Zamindar (USA))
3968[9] 4623[6] 5387[8] 6497[6] 7585[4]◆

Carrington (FR) *A bin Harmash* a85 90
6 b g New Approach(IRE) Winning Family (IRE) (Fasliyev (USA))
(1748a)

Carry On Deryck *Ollie Pears* a63 70
7 b g Halling(USA) Mullein (Oasis Dream)
121[6] 2873[7] 4097[10] 4730[7] 5555[5] 6496[2]

Carry Out (FR) *D Allard* a53 71
7 bb g Air Chief Marshal(IRE) Respite (Pivotal)
2391a[3]

Carta Blanca (IRE) *David Thompson*
6 gr m Authorized(IRE) Alicante (Pivotal)
5728[16] 6545[9]

Cartiem (FR) *J-C Rouget* 106
3 bl f Cape Cross(IRE) Mintaka (FR) (Zamindar (USA))
(2312a) 3905a[13] 5470a[7] 6250a[3] 7942a[11]

Cartmell Cleave *Ruth Carr* a82 89
7 br g Pastoral Pursuits There's Two (IRE) (Ashkalani (IRE))
1895[3] 2416[6] 2893[7] 3868[9] (4369) 5191[5]

Carvelas (IRE) *J R Jenkins* a61 53
10 b g Cape Cross(IRE) Caraiyma (IRE) (Shahrastani (USA))
38[5] 262[7] 923[8] 1548[4] 1710[5] 3006[5] (3497) 4019[4] 4568[7] 4991[4] 5499[6] 6635[8] 7109[5] 7318[9] 7685[11] 8551[6] 8869[3]

Casablanca Kid (IRE) *Denis Quinn* a23
2 b c Worthadd(IRE) Coill Cri (IRE) (Shinko Forest (IRE))
6368[16] 6684[7] 7103[7]

Casa Comigo (IRE) *John Best* a75 61
4 b g Cape Cross(IRE) Belanoiva (IRE) (Motivator)
(369)◆ 619[5] 5974[7] (6601) (7558)◆ (7818) 8654[7] 9056[3] 9215[2]

Casado (IRE) *Linda Jewell*
5 b g Casamento(IRE) Sense Of Greeting (IRE) (Key Of Luck (USA))
2970[14]

Casa Loupi *Gary Moore* a51 69
2 ch g Casamento(IRE) Kameruka (Auction House (USA))
7981[4] 8722[4] 9174[7]

Casanova *John Gosden* a95 100
3 b g Frankel Karen's Caper (USA) (War Chant (USA))
2034[2] 2713[5] (6732) (7163)◆ 7891[5] 8320[8] 9200[6]

Casaruan *Michael Appleby* a47
2 b c Casamento(IRE) Aruan (Equiano (FR))
8912[7] 9043[9] 9195[11]

Casarubina (IRE) *Nick Littmoden* a61 60
3 br f Casamento(IRE) Mi Rubina (IRE) (Rock Of Gibraltar (IRE))
2123[2]◆ 2976[4] 3532[8] 6181[2] 7032[3] 7576[10]

Cascadian *James Cummings* 102
4 ch g New Approach(IRE) Falls Of Lora (IRE) (Street Cry (IRE))
8768a[3]

Case Key *Michael Appleby* a55 75
6 gr g Showcasing Fluttering Rose (Compton Place)
2508[8] 3056[8] 3550[9] 4303[12] 5107[5] 5352[2] 5799[3]◆ (6220) 6972[6] 7321[5] 8339[7] 8755[8]

Casement (IRE) *Michael Appleby* a53 86
5 b g Casamento(IRE) Kirk Wynd (Selkirk (USA))
(1660)◆ 1859[8] 2291[2] 2902[3] 4445[8] 5255[3] 5863[2] (7128) 7312[10] 8634[8]

Casey Banter *Julia Feilden* a57 51
4 bb m Holy Roman Emperor(IRE) Sinister Ruckus (USA) (Trippi (USA))
1214[8] 1353[3] 1717[3] 2240[4] (3142)◆

Cashel (IRE) *Michael Appleby* a70 66
4 b g Sepoy(AUS) Snow Dust (First Defence (USA))
138[2]◆ (250) (828) 942[8] 1271[5] 1479[4] 2106[14] 4787[4] 5807[5] 6317[5] 7609[4] 8223[4] 8756[8]

Cash In Mind (FR) *Des Donovan* a63 52
8 b g Creachadoir(IRE) Dynamic Dream (USA) (Dynaformer (USA))
3322[4] 3769[4]

Cash N Carrie (IRE) *Michael Appleby* a52
5 b m Casamento(IRE) Tales Of Erin (IRE) (Moss Vale (IRE))
67[9] 459[3] 616[9] 829[12] 1354[3] 1519[4] 1717[13] 2004a[4] 7375[3] 8001[5] (8753) 9090[7] 9362[2]◆ 9444[5]

Casi Casi *Charlie Wallis*
2 ch f Casamento(IRE) Violet (IRE) (Mukaddamah (USA))
2918[11] 5045[9] 5265[10]

Casima *Philip Kirby* a60 62
4 b m Dark Angel(IRE) Caskelena (IRE) (Galileo (IRE))
2374[6]

Casina Di Notte (IRE) *Marco Botti* a76 76
5 ch g Casamento(IRE) Nightswimmer (IRE) (Noverre (USA))
1355[8] 1566[2] 2124[6] (2978)

Caso Do Lago (IRE) *Robyn Brisland* a41 33
8 b g Balmont(USA) Dasha (Kyllachy)
6547[7] 7384[8]

Caspar The Cub (IRE) *Alan King* a97 75
4 ch g Casamento(IRE) Esposa (IRE) (Three Valleys (USA))
368[3] 758[2] 1422[7]

Caspian Prince (IRE) *Michael Appleby* a99 113
10 ch g Dylan Thomas(IRE) Crystal Gaze (IRE) (Rainbow Quest (USA))
3084[6] 3344[9] 4665[3] 4932[4] 5222a[5] 5927[7] 6149[6] 6351[16] 7243a[7]

Caspian Queen (IRE) *Mohamed Moubarak* a67 84
2 b f Sepoy(AUS) Rhythm Excel (Exceed And Excel (AUS))
3689[5]◆ (4993) 6019[4] (6833) 7696[4] 8724[14]

Cassard (FR) *P Monfort* a85 75
4 b g Air Chief Marshal(IRE) Corvette (Araafa (IRE))
6434a[2]

Cassata *R Rohne* a65 24
2 b f Casamento(IRE) Captain's Paradise (IRE) (Rock Of Gibraltar (IRE))
2890a[6]

Cassy O (IRE) *Tim Easterby* 73
2 b g Camacho Hawaajib (FR) (Elusive City (USA))
6336[5] 7398[6] 7677[9]

Castashadow *Alan Brown* a52 25
2 b g Harbour Watch(IRE) Dareesha (IRE) (Naaqoos)
2707[8] 3245[14] 7821[9] 9392[11] 9641[5]

Castel Angelo (IRE) *Henry Candy* a58 55
2 b c Anjaal La Chita Bonita (IRE) (Verglas (IRE))
5447[5] 5859[9] 6368[7] 6837[4] 7275[2] 8415[4]

Castelo (IRE) *Daniel Kubler* a50 59
3 b f Casamento(IRE) Fortress (Generous (IRE))
8847[10] 9133[10] 9450[4]

Castelvecchio (AUS) *Richard Litt* 116
2 b c Dundeel(NZ) St Therese (AUS) (Dehere (USA))
8579a[2]

Casterbridge *Eric Alston* a82 76
7 b g Pastoral Pursuits Damalis (IRE) (Mukaddamah (USA))
1194[5]

Caster Semenya *Steph Hollinshead* 26
3 gr f Albaasil(IRE) Goldeva (Makbul)
3050[10]

Casting (IRE) *Richard Hannon*
3 b c Society Rock(IRE) Suffer Her (IRE) (Whipper (USA))
319[12]

Casting Spells *Tom Dascombe* a59 68
3 ch f Lope De Vega(IRE) Ballymore Celebre (IRE) (Peintre Celebre (USA))
3050[6] 3974[5] 6890[4] 7643[5] 9273[9]

Castle Dream (FR) *Andrew Hollinshead* a76 61
5 b g Wootton Bassett Haut La Main (IRE) (Beat Hollow)
2956a[17] 7800a[10]

Castle Force *John O'Shea*
2 ch g Lethal Force(IRE) Breda Castle (Dutch Art)
2686[P]

Castle Hill Cassie (IRE) *Ben Haslam* a105 98
5 ch m Casamento(IRE) Angel Bright (IRE) (Dark Angel (IRE))
30[2] (460)◆ 1918[10]

Castlehill Retreat *Ben Haslam* a68 64
2 ch g Casamento(IRE) Ansina (USA) (Distant View (USA))
3220[3] 3702[9] 8195[6] (8815) 9110[3]◆ 9515[7]

Castle Lady (IRE) *H-A Pantall* a81 112
3 b f Shamardal(USA) Windsor County (USA) (Elusive Quality (USA))
(1795a) (2669a) 4051[5] 8139a[2] 8772a[10]

Castlelyons (IRE) *Robert Stephens* a96 72
7 br g Papal Bull Summercove (IRE) (Cape Cross (IRE))
82[2] 558[4] 1735[5]

Castle Of May (IRE) *F-H Graffard* 94
3 b f Raven's Pass(USA) Seschat (IRE) (Sinndar (IRE))
8376a[11]

Castle Quarter (IRE) *Seb Spencer* a74 58
3 b g Zoffany(IRE) Queen's Pudding (IRE) (Royal Applause)
2630[6] 4000[7] (5852) 6679[8] 7418[3] (8025) 8719[3]

Castlerea Tess *Sarah Hollinshead* a60 55
6 ch m Pastoral Pursuits Zartwyda (IRE) (Mozart (IRE))
116[10] (4481) 5083[5]

Castle Talbot (IRE) *Tom Clover* a45 65
7 b g Rock Of Gibraltar(IRE) Louve Sacree (USA) (Seeking The Gold (USA))
1546[7] 2233[5] 3473[12]

Castletownshend (IRE) *T M Walsh* 81
4 ch g Equiano(FR) Idonea (CAN) (Swain (IRE))
7241a[6]

Casual Reply *Roger Charlton* a78
3 b f Frankel Passing Parade (Cape Cross (IRE))
8013[2]◆ 8500[2] 9051[5]

Catalina Cruiser (USA)
John W Sadler a121
5 ch h Union Rags(USA) Sea Gull (USA) (Mineshaft (USA))
8773a[7]

Catalogue *Christine Dunnett* a55 26
3 b f Zoffany(IRE) Catopuma (USA) (Elusive Quality (USA))
3299[12] 3989[11]

Catapult *Shaun Keightley* a54 55
4 b g Equiano(FR) Alectrona (FR) (Invincible Spirit (IRE))
6[3] 365[3] (476) 830[2] 1021[4] 1192[4] 2741[3] 3208[3] 3738[7] 4501[10] 5264[6] 5678[5] 6051[7] 6441[4] 7389[2] 7632[3] (7838) 8249[5] 8547[7] (8840) 9161[4] 9335[5]

Catapult (USA) *John W Sadler* 116
6 bb h Kitten's Joy(USA) Gata Bella (USA) (Storm Cat (USA))
444a[4]

Catch My Breath *John Ryan* 69
3 ch g Bated Breath Likeable (Dalakhani (IRE))
1856[9] 2677[3]◆ 3278[3] 3741[6] 4801[3] 5866[2] 6164[3] (6610) 8186[4] 8434[8]

Catcho En Die (ARG)
Naipaul Chatterpaul 111
6 bb g Catcher In The Rye(IRE) Lola Grill (ARG) (Engrillado (ARG))
6001a[9]

Catch The Cuban *Colin Tizzard* a23 61
3 b g Havana Gold(IRE) Reyamour (Azamour (IRE))
2341[2] 3034[5] 3418[10]

Catechism *Richard Spencer* a65 50
2 b f Dutch Art Postulant (Kyllachy)
5772[8] 7546[3] 8218[4] 8841[5] 9196[10]

Catenda *R Rohne* a47 69
2 b f Hot Streak(IRE) Highland Jewel (IRE) (Azamour (IRE))
7724a[7]

Caterpillar (IRE) *Marco Gasparini* 83
4 b h Arakan(USA) Cenere (IRE) (Priolo (USA))
8585a[4]

Catheadans Fiyah *Martin Bosley* a54 34
3 b f Firebreak Dualagi (Royal Applause)
5890[3] 6598[10] 8018[10] 8450[10]

Catheadans Fury *Martin Bosley* a64 64
5 ch m Firebreak Dualagi (Royal Applause)
1265[P] 6329[2] 7230[10] 8217[6] 8896[2] 9507[6] 9670[7]

Cathedral Street (IRE)
Mark Johnston a56 67
3 b g Holy Roman Emperor(IRE) Raydaniya (IRE) (In The Wings)
7543[2]◆ 8645[4] 9038[8]

Catherine Bay *Henry Candy* a42
2 b f Hot Streak(IRE) Respondez (Oasis Dream)
9062[8]

Cath The Great (IRE) *Gary Moore* a34
2 b f War Command(USA) Lady Marl (Duke Of Marmalade (IRE))
9062[12] 9327[14]

Cat Royale (IRE) *John Butler* a55 58
6 b g Lilbourne Lad(IRE) Call This Cat (IRE) (One Cool Cat (USA))
1297[8] 1841[8] 2350[8] 2698[7] 3006[4] 3298[7] 4217[14] 6049[2] 6723[5] 8251[5] 9139[5] 9384[5] 9446[2]◆

Cats On Trees (FR) *L Gadbin* a62 79
4 ro m Myboycharlie(IRE) Cat Nova (FR) (Hurricane Cat (USA))
1245a[18]

Caustic Love (IRE) *Keith Dalgleish* a66 86
3 b f Fast Company(IRE) Moss Top (IRE) (Moss Vale (IRE))
21[2] (3921) (4243) 4822[4] 5333[2] (5790)◆ 6609[6] 7491[8]

Cauthen (IRE) *Milton Harris* a63 54
3 b g Dandy Man(IRE) Chellalla (Elnadim (USA))
855[9] 1141[5] 1515[2] 1726[5] 6024[2] 6329[7] (7282) 8223[2] 8698[3]◆ 8847[2]◆

Cava (IRE) *Joseph Patrick O'Brien* 99
3 b f Acclamation Royal Fizz (IRE) (Royal Academy (USA))
2156a[3] 2605a[8] 3359[4] 4242[2] 5325a[4]

Cavalry Park *Charlie Fellowes* a40 43
3 b g Epaulette(AUS) Sarah Park (IRE) (Redback)
2772[10] 4606[8]

Caviar Royale *Nikki Evans*
4 b g Royal Applause Precious Secret (IRE) (Fusaichi Pegasus (USA))
5379[10]

Cawthorne Lad *Tim Easterby* a56 60
3 ch g Coach House(IRE) Upton Seas (Josr Algarhoud (IRE))
3478[F] (8234) 8818[5] 9253[8]

Cayenne Pepper (IRE)
Mrs John Harrington 109
2 ch f Australia Muwakaba (USA) (Elusive Quality (USA))
(6689a) 8091[4]

Cayirli (FR) *Seamus Durack* a95 95
7 b g Medicean Clarinda (FR) (Montjeu (IRE))
82[6] (558) 1943[9] 4505[8]

Cazaline (FR) *M Delaplace* a75 92
4 b m Kentucky Dynamite(USA) Teatime (FR) (Loup Solitaire (USA))
2226a[13] 6651a[7]

Cece Ceylon *Ralph Beckett* a61 61
2 b f Iffraaj Scent Of Roses (IRE) (Invincible Spirit (IRE))
3259[4] 3968[8] 5772[14] 7079[4] 7767[6]

Cedar *Mohamed Moubarak* a54 52
3 ch f Sepoy(AUS) Lilli Marlane (Sri Pekan (USA))
1678[11] 1954[8] 2240[14] 3410[6] 4346[3] 4836[6] 5354[6] 7984[15]

Cedar Cage *Sir Mark Prescott Bt* a78
2 b g Golden Horn Faslen (USA) (Fasliyev (USA))
8503[5]◆ 8889[2] (9181)

Ceinture Noire (FR)
R Le Dren Doleuze 82
2 b f Wootton Bassett Meandra (IRE) (Dubawi (IRE))
7925a[2] 8482a[4]

Celebrity Dancer (IRE) *Kevin Ryan* 88
3 ch g Excelebration(IRE) Dance Hall Girl (IRE) (Dansili)
2570[3] 3357[5] 4099[3] 4895[9] 6207[10] 7781[10]

Celerity (IRE) *Lisa Williamson* a51 54
5 ch m Casamento(IRE) Shinko Dancer (IRE) (Shinko Forest (IRE))
118[8] 286[5] 503[9] 597[10] 811[7] 848[8] 2876[9] 3475[12] 3577[5] 3846[10] 3975[11] 4105[8] 4555[2] 4765[8] 4880[5] 5181[7] 5478[6] 5765[9] 5893[2] 6168[5] 6639[5] 8119[12] 8668[3] 9135[10] 9257[10] 9390[7] 9507[10]

Celestial *Michael Blanshard* a23
3 b f Motivator Celebrity (Pivotal)
6316[9]

Celestial Bliss *Kevin Ryan* 76
2 b c Oasis Dream La Pomme D'Amour (Peintre Celebre (USA))
7398[4]

Celestial Force (IRE)
Tom Dascombe a70 89
4 b g Sea The Stars(IRE) Aquarelle Bleue (Sadler's Wells (USA))
1761[7] 2374[5] (4208) 4899[3] 5849[2] 6340[2] 6716[3] 7181[2] 7830[2] 8513[6]

Celestial Object (IRE)
Mrs John Harrington 96
2 b f Galileo(IRE) Sea Siren (AUS) (Fastnet Rock (AUS))
8165a[5] 8763[4]

Celestial Spheres (IRE)
Charlie Appleby a102 101
5 b g Redoute's Choice(AUS) Copernica (IRE) (Galileo (IRE))
284a[10] 730a[9]

Celestial Wood (IRE)
Keith Dalgleish a63
2 b g Ivawood(IRE) Angelic Angie (IRE) (Approve (IRE))
9471[9]

Celestran *John Gosden* a75 75
2 b c Dansili Starscope (Selkirk (USA))
8721[3]◆ (9007)

Cellini (ITY) *G Botti* 52
2 b c Dandy Man(IRE) Folle Blanche (USA) (Elusive Quality (USA))
6776a[9]

Celsius (IRE) *Tom Clover* a32 89
3 ch g Dragon Pulse(IRE) Grecian Artisan (IRE) (Mastercraftsman (IRE))
(3508) 4183[2] (4604) (4829)◆ (5589) 7894[12]

Celtic (IRE) *A Fabre* a79 69
3 b f Speightstown(USA) Lady Of Shamrock (USA) (Scat Daddy (USA))
4204a[4]

Celtic Art (FR) *Paul Cole* 96
2 ch c Mastercraftsman(IRE) Irish Song (FR) (Singspiel (IRE))
4886[11] 5665[2]◆ 6424[2] (6832) 8483a[2]

Celtic Artisan (IRE)
Rebecca Menzies a68 69
8 ch g Dylan Thomas(IRE) Perfectly Clear (USA) (Woodman (USA))
784[6] 1399[7] 1659[3] (2692) 4194[3]◆ 4446[2] 5025[11] 7858[6]

Celtic Beauty (IRE) *K J Condon* 100
2 b f No Nay Never(USA) Keystone Gulch (USA) (Gulch (USA))
2881a[3] 4048[2] 4883[7] 6374[7]

Celtic Classic (IRE) *Paul Cole* a62 59
3 b g Cacique(IRE) Dabtiyra (IRE) (Dr Devious (IRE))
4498[12] (5425) 5648[4] 5987[3] 6531[2] (7280) 7759[4]

Celtic High King (IRE) *A P O'Brien* 86
2 b c Galileo(IRE) Homecoming Queen (IRE) (Holy Roman Emperor (IRE))
8582a[8]

Celtic Manor (IRE) *William Haggas* a76 82
3 b g Dandy Man(IRE) Celtic Lynn (IRE) (Celtic Swing)
(3167)◆ (3884)◆ 4638[5]

Celtic Mist (IRE) *Shaun Keightley* a58
2 ch f Camacho Celtic Heroine (IRE) (Hernando (FR))
8849[11] 9062[6] 9242[11] 9407[10]

Cemhaan *John Gosden* a56
2 b c Muhaarar Shalwa (Galileo (IRE))
8605[9]

Cenario *Richard Fahey* a42
2 b c Fountain Of Youth(IRE) Clodianna (IRE) (Clodovil (IRE))
2694[8]

Cenotaph (USA) *Simon Crisford* a82 81
7 b g War Front(USA) Sanserif (IRE) (Fasliyev (USA))
136[2] 563[6] 1891[9] 4095[20] 6706[15]

Cent Flying *William Muir* a71 78
4 b g Sepoy(AUS) Sea Of Leaves (USA) (Stormy Atlantic (USA))
2339[5] 3089[6] 3188[2] 3772[4] 4227[5] 4733[5] 5050[6] (5883)◆ 6132[3] (6162) 6756[3] 6916[4] (7130) 7467[3] 7564[8] 8063[6] 8550[12]

Central City (IRE) *Ian Williams* a81 88
4 b g Kodiac She Basic (IRE) (Desert Prince (IRE))
29[5] (292) 521[3]◆ (552) 825[4] 1291[5] (1418) 1664[3] 2095[10] 5195[7] 5858[6] 6291[4] 7185[7] 7680[4] 8412[8] 9642[7]

Centrifuge (IRE) *Michael Blanshard* a33
2 b f G Force(IRE) Of Course Darling (Dalakhani (IRE))
7787[10] 8651[13]

Centurion Song (IRE)
Brian Meehan 67
2 ch g Camacho New Music (IRE) (New Approach (IRE))
3943[4] 4839[3] 5845[6]

Century Dream (IRE)
Simon Crisford a95 108
5 b h Cape Cross(IRE) Salacia (IRE) (Echo Of Light)
846a[2] 1115a[4] 1445a[7] 8334[7] 8765[2] 9210a[5]

Cepheus *Brian Meehan* 84
2 ch c Sea The Stars(IRE) Crimson Cheer (USA) (Van Nistelrooy (USA))
(5908)

Cersei Lannister (IRE)
Adrian Nicholls a14 48
2 b f Acclamation Lafleur (IRE) (Grand Lodge (USA))
4206[7] 4819[8] 5295[6] 6435[6]

Certain Lad *Mick Channon* a98 106
3 b g Clodovil(IRE) Chelsey Jayne (IRE) (Galileo (IRE))
1713[5] 2414[6] 3082[4] 4016[14] (4607) 5711a[12] 6513[4] 7122[2] (7434)

Cesifire (IRE) *Adam West* a56 50
2 b f War Command(USA) Caterina Di Cesi (Cape Town (IRE))
6846[8] 8026[6] 9158[8] 9438[2] 9630[9]

C'Est No Mour (GER) *Peter Hedger* a82 85
6 b g Champs Elysees C'Est L'Amour (GER) (Whipper (USA))
2209[2] 2763[2] 3861[5] 4425[2]◆ 5305[3]◆ 5840[6] (6535) 7127[3] 8014[4] 8421[5]

Ceyhan *Barry Brennan* a10
7 ch g Rock Of Gibraltar(IRE) Alla Prima (IRE) (In The Wings)
3209[8] 8703[13]

Chablis (IRE) *A P O'Brien* a77 99
3 b f Galileo(IRE) Vadawina (IRE) (Unfuwain (USA))
2157a[10] 2642a[5] 2853a[4] 3820a[4] 5223a[4] 7242a[8] 8368a[9] 8734a[13]

Chacha Boy (FR) *Y Barberot* a68 43
3 b c Myboycharlie(IRE) Aquavenus (FR) (Elusive City (USA))
216a[3] 6328a[7]

Chachnak (FR) *F Vermeulen* 100
2 b c Kingman Tamazirte (IRE) (Danehill Dancer (IRE))
7940a[6]

Chai Chai (IRE) *Tom Dascombe* a71 58
4 b g Zoffany(IRE) Flamenco Red (Warning)
3072[7] 4249[13] 8197[6]

Chains Of Love (IRE) *K R Burke* 70
3 b f Society Rock(IRE) Sportsticketing (IRE) (Spectrum (IRE))
2200[5] 2689[9] 4080[10]

Chairlift Chat (IRE)
Eve Johnson Houghton 70
2 b g Delegator Letizia (IRE) (Tamayuz)
3694[4] 4544[4] 5775[3]

Chairmanic (IRE) *Brian Meehan* 50
2 b c G Force(IRE) Beauty Of The Sea (Elusive Quality (USA))
7661[7]

Chairmanoftheboard (IRE)
Mick Channon a93 84
3 b g Slade Power(IRE) Bound Copy (USA) (Street Cry (IRE))
1035[4] 1736[10] 1940[6] 2746[17] 7349[5] 8253[4] 8606[4]

Chairman Power *Sir Michael Stoute* a48
2 b c Galileo(IRE) Best Terms (Exceed And Excel (AUS))
7996[6]

Chakrii (IRE) *Henry Spiller* a57 40
3 b g Mukhadram Chalet Girl (Oasis Dream)
(593) 695[3] 802[2] 1066[5] 1332[7] 2213[5] 3593[8] 4485[6] 5054[2] 5653[2] 6153[2] 6983[4] 7375[6] 8001[7] 8553[6]

Chaleur *Ralph Beckett* a102 104
3 b f Dansili Lilyfire (USA) (First Defence (USA))
4922[4] 5525[3]◆ 6379[3] 7657[7] 8708[2]

Challet (IRE) *Michael Dods* a63 71
2 b g Clodovil(IRE) Eileenlilian (Authorized (IRE))
6457[3] 7285[2] 7870[4]

Chamade *Ralph Beckett* a23 79
2 b f Sepoy(AUS) Colima (IRE) (Authorized (IRE))
6718[10] (8458)

Chambonas (FR) *S Cerulis* a69 71
2 b c Wootton Bassett Elusive Queen (FR) (Elusive City (USA))
6262a[4]

Chamomile *Daniel Kubler* a60 59
3 b f Teofilo(IRE) Al Joza (Dubawi (IRE))
3546[6] 5808[8] 7190[9] (7909) 8870[9]

Champagne Angel (IRE)
Tim Easterby 48
2 gr f Dark Angel(IRE) On High (Exceed And Excel (AUS))
3968[12] 5590[4]◆ 5913[7]

Champagne Bob *Richard Price* a45 68
7 gr g Big Bad Bob(IRE) Exclusive Approval (USA) (With Approval (CAN))
2145[4] 2717[9] 3430[10] 3549[9]

Champagne Champ *Rod Millman* a84 84
7 b g Champs Elysees Maramba (Rainbow Quest (USA))
291[3]◆ 2254[6] 7464[4] (8726)

Champagne Clouds *Brian Ellison* a41 43
3 b g Equiano(FR) Procession (Zafonic (USA))
1081[9] 1380[5] 1982[9]

Champagne Cuddles (AUS)
Bjorn Baker 112
4 ch m Not A Single Doubt(AUS) Sky Cuddle (AUS) (Snippets (AUS))
1974a[4]

Champagne Highlife (GER)
Eve Johnson Houghton a39 64
2 b g Holy Roman Emperor(IRE) Casanga (IRE) (Rainbow Quest (USA))
2282[4] 3165[6] 3595[9] 5340[5] 5800[3] 7079[10]

Champagne Marengo (IRE)
Ian Williams a76 76
3 b g Battle Of Marengo(IRE) Sidney Girl (Azamour (IRE))
1360[9] 1656[11] 2125[10] 2511[6] 3197[2] (3931) (4594) (4862)◆ (5028) 5943[4] 7209[9] 8321[5]

Champagne Mondays *Scott Dixon* a54 52
3 ch g Milk It Mick La Capriosa (Kyllachy)
228[9] 505[2] 585[6] 834[8] (1043) 1430[2] 1863[10] 3319[8] 3775[6] 5147[3] 5299[7] 5738[4] 6277[14] 7869[3] 9539[11] 9643[8]

Champagne Pink (FR)
Vaclav Luka Jr a66 60
5 b m Teofilo(IRE) Carruba (IRE) (Marju (IRE))
1491a[10]

Champagne Rules *Sharon Watt* a73 74
8 gr g Aussie Rules(USA) Garabelle (IRE) (Galileo (IRE))
120[4] (241) 495[2]◆ 1398[3] 1648[2]◆ 1988[6] (3054) 3816[17] 4762[6] 5473[8] 9512[3]

Champagne Supanova (IRE)
Richard Spencer a73 62
2 b g Camacho Flawless Pink (More Than Ready (USA))
1651[3] 1953[5] 2257[5] 5146[6] 6113[4] (6387) 6705[4] 7369[4] 8219[5] 9205[8]

Champagne Terri (IRE)
Adrian Paul Keatley 74
3 b f Elzaam(AUS) Cresta Rise (Authorized (IRE))
(3246) (4400) 5599a[5]

Champagne Victory (IRE)
Brian Ellison 6
2 b f Bungle Inthejungle Golittlebadgirl (USA) (Giant's Causeway (USA))
2476[9] 2707[5] 3244[U] 5145[8] 6539[11]

Champarisi *Grant Tuer* a86 89
4 b m Champs Elysees Parisi (Rahy (USA))
101[2] 346[4] 803[5] (1159) (1503) (1971) 2781[4] 4146[3] 6256[2] (7033) (7439)◆

Champ Ayr *David Menuisier* a56 59
3 b g Champs Elysees Rose Ayr (Refuse To Bend (IRE))
3860[8] 4600[6] 5578[8] 6320[6] 7280[12]

Champers Elysees (IRE)
J P Murtagh 85
2 b f Elzaam(AUS) La Cuvee (Mark Of Esteem (IRE))
7247a[6]

Champion Brogie (IRE) *J S Moore* a72 73
3 b g Alhebayeb(IRE) Defensive Boast (USA) (El Gran Senor (USA))
142[5] 2274[3] 2567[7] 3420[5] 4236[11] 5408a[7] 5644a[4] 6267a[15] 7760[6] 8449a[4] (8698) 9217[5] (9329) 9669[7]

Championship (IRE) *A bin Harmash* a74 102
8 ch g Exceed And Excel(AUS) Aljafliyah (Halling (USA))
397a[6] 846a[8]

Champs De Reves *Michael Blake* a80 77
4 b g Champs Elysees Joyeaux (Mark Of Esteem (IRE))
2471[2]◆ 2732[4] 4220[7] (6331) 7816[4] (8692)◆

Champs Inblue *Chris Gordon* a40 54
4 ch g Champs Elysees Ellablue (Bahamian Bounty)
2593[7] (3252) 4111[5]

Chance *Simon Crisford* a61 94
3 ch c Lope De Vega(IRE) Harem Lady (FR) (Teofilo (IRE))
2192[2] (2995) (4662)◆ (5394) 6447[5] 7694[30]

Chance Of Glory (FR)
Mark Johnston a60 18
3 b c Olympic Glory(IRE) Miss Carmie (FR) (Excellent Art)
1970[4] 2517[11] 2930[7] 3938[9]

Changouro Basc (FR)
Gianluca Bietolini a75 75
4 b g Silver Frost(IRE) Olga Luck (Inchinor)
1245a[4]

Chankaya *Hugo Palmer* 39
2 ch c Dubawi(IRE) Splashdown (Falbrav (IRE))
8028[8]

Channel (IRE) *F-H Graffard* 109
3 b f Nathaniel(IRE) Love Magic (Dansili)
(3905a) 5586[7] 7252a[6]

Channel Cat (USA) *Todd Pletcher* 110
4 ch h English Channel(USA) Carnival Kitten (USA) (Kitten's Joy (USA))
8776a[7]

Channel Maker (CAN) *William Mott* a101 117
5 ch g English Channel(USA) In Return (USA) (Horse Chestnut (SAF))
444a[5] (2646a) 8776a[12]

Channel Packet *Michael Appleby* a73 69
5 b h Champs Elysees Etarre (IRE) (Giant's Causeway (USA))
154[5] 429[6] 801[3] 1065[3] 1647[10] 3053[8]

Chant (IRE) *Ann Duffield* a54 66
9 b g Oratorio(IRE) Akarita (IRE) (Akarad (FR))
4190[7] 5513[4]◆ 6939[8]

Chantresse (IRE) *Mark Usher* a69 46
4 b m Holy Roman Emperor(IRE) Woodland Chant (USA) (War Chant (USA))
616[5] 859[7] 1024[7] 1710[6] 2685[9] 2974[9] 3473[13] 4287[9]

Chaparral Dream (IRE)
Adrian McGuinness a82 65
4 b g High Chaparral(IRE) Dream Time (Rainbow Quest (USA))
479[4] 5599a[6]

Chapeau Bleu (IRE) *Mrs C Gilbert* a64 48
7 b m Haatef(USA) La Petite Bleue (GER) (Fantastic Light (USA))
3173a[4] (5232) 6553a[3]

Chapelli *Mark Johnston* a99 92
3 b f Poet's Voice Indian Petal (Singspiel (IRE))
1662[2] 1851[3] 2319[2] 2525[12] 3075[13] 4122[7] 4242[5] 4669[8] 4904[3] 5546[11]

Chaplin Bay (IRE) *Ruth Carr* a78 61
7 b g Fastnet Rock(AUS) Green Castle (IRE) (Indian Ridge (IRE))
1925[3] 2242[3] 2681[8] 3178[10] 3716[8] 4335[7] 4767[5] 5517[10] (5938) (6275) 7418[13] 7779[5]

Charabanc *Richard Hughes* 38
2 b f Coach House(IRE) Dolly Daydreamer (Equiano (FR))
2716[7]

Characteristic (IRE) *Tom Clover* a78
3 ch g Casamento(IRE) Stunned Silence (USA) (Officer (USA))
1677^2 5270^8 6186^6 7278^2

Charcor (IRE) *Mrs John Harrington* a99 94
5 b g Choisir(AUS) Sanadaat (Green Desert (USA))
1308a^{10}

Chares (GER) *C Ferland* 100
2 ch c Ivawood(IRE) Coco Demure (IRE) (Titus Livius (FR))
(7673a)

Charlemaine (IRE) *Paul Cole* 77
2 b c War Command(USA) Newyearresolution (USA) (Arch (USA))
1448a^3 (1931) 3988^{18} 5185^{17} (5562)

Charlene Du Champ (FR) *Tamara Richter* 24
3 bb f Myboycharlie(IRE) Screen Legend (IRE) (Invincible Spirit (IRE))
3066a^8 7642a^{12}

Charles Kingsley *Mark Johnston* a88 106
4 b h New Approach(IRE) Kailani (Monsun (GER))
1989^2 2435^2 2620^2 2786^4 (3222) (3408)◆ 4102^5 4646^{12} 5199^4 (5443)◆ 5662^5 6355^9 6958^4 7147^2 7464^5

Charles Molson *Patrick Chamings* a102 91
8 b g Monsieur Bond(IRE) Arculinge (Paris House)
2363^4 3040^4 3991^2 4902^2 5546^8 6706^3 7448^4 8707^{12} 9000^{10}

Charlesquint (IRE) *Y Barberot* a74 73
2 b c Showcasing Commute (Rail Link)
7675a^{10}

Charles Road (AUS) *Lance O'Sullivan & Andrew Scot* 106
5 b g Myboycharlie(IRE) Giant Mystique (AUS) (Giant's Causeway (USA))
1784a^{19}

Charles Street *George Scott* a66
2 ch g Helmet(AUS) Fleur De Lis (Nayef (USA))
5052^3

Charlie Alpha (IRE) *Roger Ingram* a51 37
5 b g Dandy Man(IRE) Maroussies Rock (Rock Of Gibraltar (IRE))
161^3 402^9 597^{11} 2318^{10}

Charlie Arthur (IRE) *Richard Hughes* a72 37
3 b g Slade Power(IRE) Musical Bar (IRE) (Barathea (IRE))
359^6 753^6 1570^5 4454^5 5284^5 6361^{11} (7685) 8293^2 8669^2 (8903)

Charlie D (USA) *Tom Dascombe* a88 89
4 b g Animal Kingdom(USA) Ocicat (USA) (Storm Cat (USA))
(3000) 3073^7 4363^4 5055^2 (5604) (6530) 7033^3 (7231) 8120^3 8321^2

Charlie's Boy (IRE) *Michael Dods* a50 60
3 b g Poet's Voice Royal Sister Two (IRE) (Teofilo (IRE))
4519^{11} 5215^8 5816^3 6678^7 7404^9 7956^8 8301^4

Charline Royale (IRE) *Silvia Amendola* 107
4 b m Zebedee Royal Majestic (Tobougg (IRE))
2888a^2 8648a^{15}

Charmed Spirit *Jonathan Portman* a63 59
3 b g Charm Spirit(IRE) Arch Of Colours (Monsun (GER))
1481^9

Charming Guest (IRE) *Mick Channon* a72 62
4 b m Kodiac Na Zdorovie (Cockney Rebel (IRE))
1061^6 2588^7 3014^8 3543^6

Charming Kid *Dean Ivory* a83 86
3 b g Charm Spirit(IRE) Child Bride (USA) (Coronado's Quest (USA))
57^3 (306a) 1920^6 2779^6 3865^{22} 9660^{10}

Charming Rose *John Gosden* a60
2 b f Kingman Sweet Rose (New Approach (IRE))
8913^{11} 9327^5

Charming Spirit (IRE) *Roger Varian* a69 73
2 b f Invincible Spirit(IRE) Willow View (USA) (Lemon Drop Kid (USA))
5772^5 6514^3 6928^6 7522^4 8303^4

Charmore *Ann Duffield* a8
2 b f Swiss Spirit Caramelita (Deportivo)
7958^{11} 8302^{13} 8919^{14}

Chartered *Ralph Beckett* 90
3 b f Frankel Time Saved (Green Desert (USA))
3013^4◆ (3800)◆ 8727^7

Chasanas De Bianca (FR) *M Cesandri* a60 53
3 bl f Saonois(FR) Chalouna (FR) (Marchand De Sable (USA))
6063a^{11}

Chasanda *David Evans* a68 74
2 ch f Footstepsinthesand Miss Chamanda (IRE) (Choisir (AUS))
(1651) 1923^4 2520^4 2805^{17} 3530^4 6800^2 6900^4 7785^9 9205^5

Chasedown (IRE) *A Botti* 105
5 gr h Nathaniel(IRE) Whipcla (IRE) (Whipper (USA))
8391a^2

Chasing Dreams *Charlie Appleby* a88 95
2 ch f Starspangledbanner(AUS) A Huge Dream (IRE) (Refuse To Bend (IRE))
(1833) (8316)

Chasing The Rain *K R Burke* a70 29
3 b f Toronado(IRE) Susi Wong (IRE) (Selkirk (USA))
1985^6

Chasselay (FR) *S Dehez* a92 94
5 b g Peer Gynt(JPN) La Minardiere (FR) (Verglas (IRE))
9210a^8

Chateau Conti (FR) *Joseph Patrick O'Brien* a34
7 b g Vendangeur(IRE) Regina Conti (FR) (Lavirco (GER))
1572a^7

Chateau Peapod *Lydia Pearce* a56 36
2 b f Coach House(IRE) Dash Of Lime (Bold Edge)
3441^5 4018^8 4999^8 5907^4 6884^2 7516^6 7767^5 8493^3 8824^2 9045^3

Chatez (IRE) *Alan King* 109
8 b g Dandy Man(IRE) Glory Days (GER) (Tiger Hill (IRE))
(1753) 2105^5

Chatham House *Richard Hannon* a82 92
3 gr g Dark Angel(IRE) Timely (Pivotal)
1423^2 2094^7 4338^3◆ 4909^4◆ 5270^3 (5773) 6220^2 6756^2 (7059) 7462^3

Chattanooga Boy (IRE) *Ahmed Kobeissi* a77 75
2 b g Acclamation Sign From Heaven (IRE) (Raven's Pass (USA))
1733^3 (2108) 3451^4 3812^7 9582a^8

Cheam Avenue (IRE) *Paul Midgley* 51
3 b f Garswood Gerash (FR) (Layman (USA))
2823^9 3499^7 3920^5 5771^7

Cheap Jack *Ronald Thompson* a65 43
3 b g Coach House(IRE) Ice Mayden (Major Cadeaux)
229^6 461^6 1084^3 1385^8 8669^{13}

Cheat (IRE) *Richard Hannon* a79 74
2 gr g Gutaifan(IRE) Beguiler (Refuse To Bend (IRE))
4826^9 5523^8 6078^2 6375^{19} (6963) 7409^7 8252^4 8505^8

Chebsey Beau *John Quinn* a68 78
9 b g Multiplex Chebsey Belle (IRE) (Karinga Bay)
5739^4 7053^5

Check In Check Out (IRE) *Richard Hannon* a44
3 gr f Zebedee Bruno Maris (IRE) (Bachelor Duke (USA))
141^P (Dead)

Cheeky Rascal (IRE) *Tom Ward* a69 70
4 b g Most Improved(IRE) Bessie Lou (IRE) (Montjeu (IRE))
1363^5 6830^8 7233^5 7756^3 8033^{10} 8813^3 9067^3 9303^{11} 9663^2

Cheerfilly (IRE) *Archie Watson* a68 71
5 br m Excelebration(IRE) Classic Remark (IRE) (Dr Fong (USA))
1216^5 1563^8

Cheerful *Michael Squance* a40 51
3 b f Toronado(IRE) Isla Azul (IRE) (Machiavellian (USA))
5627^{10} 6259^5 6701^5 7374^{11} 8009^4 8416^8 9090^{10}

Cheer The Title (IRE) *Tom Clover* a76 82
4 b g Acclamation Galistic (IRE) (Galileo (IRE))
3268^6 5320^2 5970^4 6730^3 8552^2

Cheese And Wine *Chris Wall* a52 53
2 b f Nathaniel(IRE) Meet Me Halfway (Exceed And Excel (AUS))
8458^{11} 9046^{12}

Chef D'Etat (FR) *J Bertran De Balanda* 55
3 b g Vision D'Etat(FR) Mademoiselle Adele (FR) (Le Havre (IRE))
6094a^5

Chef De Troupe (FR) *Dr Richard Newland* 61
6 b g Air Chief Marshal(IRE) Tazminya (Fantastic Light (USA))
6730^5

Chef Oui Chef (FR) *M Boutin* a71 71
9 b g Medecis Romantic Pearl (FR) (Kahyasi (IRE))
2182a^4 (4532a) 4960a^2

Cheikeljack (FR) *C Boutin* a90 83
6 b h Myboycharlie(IRE) Senderlea (IRE) (Giant's Causeway (USA))
9483a^8

Cheng Gong *Tom Clover* a59 56
3 b g Archipenko(USA) Kinetica (Stormy Atlantic (USA))
1690^{10} 3275^5 4568^3 5987^7 6982^2 (8204) 9201^3 9481^2

Cheongdam Dokki (USA) *Luigi Riccardi* a108
5 ch g To Honor And Serve(USA) Elusive Gold (USA) (Strike The Gold (USA))
7011a^2

Cherbourg (FR) *Dr Jon Scargill* a74 74
7 b g Dunkerque(FR) Seduisante (FR) (Anabaa (USA))
248^5 1183^6 3537^6

Cheries Amours (FR) *S Cerulis* a38 47
5 b m Air Chief Marshal(IRE) Cherie Bibie (FR) (Statue Of Liberty (USA))
2391a^9

Cherisy (FR) *Cedric Rossi* a92 95
4 bl m Le Havre(IRE) Cherish Destiny (USA) (Grand Slam (USA))
4432a^4 5168a^8

Cherokee Mist (CAN) *Charlie Appleby* a60
2 ch g City Zip(USA) Forest Gamble (USA) (Forest Wildcat (USA))
4030^8 4456^4

Cherokee Trail (USA) *John Gosden* 91
2 b c War Front(USA) Moth (IRE) (Galileo (IRE))
(6948) (7453) 8112^7

Cherries At Dawn (IRE) *Dominic Ffrench Davis* a73 28
4 ch m Dawn Approach(IRE) Cherry Orchard (IRE) (King's Best (USA))
1397^4 2017^2 3495^8 4869^7 7915^8 8200^6 9611^{11}

Cherry Cola *Sheena West* a51 73
3 ch f Sixties Icon Rose Cheval (USA) (Johannesburg (USA))
137^4 296^{10} 2566^5 3348^4 (3418) (3777) (4447) 4795^4 5778^5 6463^3

Cherry Lady (GER) *P Schiergen* 98
4 bb m Soldier Hollow Cherry Danon (IRE) (Rock Of Gibraltar (IRE))
2621^5 3907a^5 4706a^4

Cherry Oak (IRE) *Ben Haslam* a68 62
4 b m Society Rock(IRE) Blue Holly (IRE) (Blues Traveller (IRE))
129^6 411^{10}

Chesapeake Shores (IRE) *J A Stack* 86
3 b f Camelot Flamingo Sea (USA) (Woodman (USA))
5364a^5

Cheshire *James Bethell* a47
2 ch f Nathaniel(IRE) Hazy Dancer (Oasis Dream)
8717^8

Cheshmeh (FR) *Henk Grewe* 90
4 gr m Kendargent(FR) Cherriya (FR) (Montjeu (IRE))
1627a^7 5510a^{11}

Chess Grand Master *Joseph Patrick O'Brien* a91 88
6 b g Galileo(IRE) Rimth (Oasis Dream)
5508a^{19}

Chessman (IRE) *Richard John O'Brien* a99 104
5 b g Acclamation Dulcian (IRE) (Shamardal (USA))
1434a^2 2879a^2 3103a^5 5205a^{16} 6648a^7 7243a^9 7713a^3

Chess Master (IRE) *M Al Mheiri* a91 75
6 br g Shamardal(USA) Cassandra Go (IRE) (Indian Ridge (IRE))
1001^{11}

Chesterfield (IRE) *Seamus Mullins* 86
9 ch g Pivotal Antique (IRE) (Dubai Millennium)
7974^5

Chestnut Express (IRE) *D J Bunyan* 79
3 ch f Camacho Kermana (IRE) (Selkirk (USA))
2156a^9 2605a^7

Chestnut Honey (IRE) *A Botti* 109
3 b c No Nay Never(USA) Ardea Brave (IRE) (Chester House (USA))
(7504a) 8391a^5

Chetan *Tony Carroll* a71 66
7 b g Alfred Nobel(IRE) Island Music (IRE) (Mujahid (USA))
138^{11} 876^5 2797^7 3540^7 4615^5 5302^2 6121^5 6904^8 8711^4 9209^{11}

Chetwynd Abbey *James Fanshawe* a69 60
4 b m Nathaniel(IRE) Chetwynd (IRE) (Exit To Nowhere (USA))
(2528) 3205^{10}

Cheval Grand (JPN) *Yasuo Tomomichi* 120
7 ch h Heart's Cry(JPN) Halwa Sweet (JPN) (Machiavellian (USA))
1446a^2 5414^6 6354^8 9153a^9

Chevalier Cathare (FR) *S Wattel* 93
3 b c Sea The Moon(GER) Zain Al Boldan (Poliglote)
6005a^5

Chevallier *Michael Attwater* a97 72
7 b g Invincible Spirit(IRE) Magical Romance (IRE) (Barathea (IRE))
205^3 441^4 880^4 988^4 (1018) 3944^7 4300^9 4833^5 5351^9

Chez Vegas *Scott Dixon* a59 56
6 gr g Hellvelyn Lola Sapola (IRE) (Benny The Dip (USA))
467^8 3208^{10} 5107^3 6547^6

Chiarodiluna *Philip McBride* a60
2 b f Kyllachy Falling Angel (Kylian (USA))
6407^8 7031^5 8651^7

Chiavari (IRE) *Alexandra Dunn* a65 46
5 b m Born To Sea(IRE) Chiarezza (AUS) (Fantastic Light (USA))
1620a^9 4859a^{13} 5761a^7 6362^{10} 9256^6 9663^5

Chica Buena (IRE) *Keith Dalgleish* a25 59
4 b m Thewayyouare(USA) Easter Parade (Entrepreneur)
(7492)◆ 7732^3 8019^{13}

Chica Da Silva *Scott Dixon* a55 51
4 b m Kheleyf(USA) Cora Pearl (IRE) (Montjeu (IRE))
387^{11} 504^8

Chica De La Noche *Simon Dow* a79 81
5 b m Teofilo(IRE) Welsh Cake (Fantastic Light (USA))
256^3 366^2 (697)◆ 1382^5 1586^3 (2365) (3146) 3892^2 4113^5 5090^4 (5573) 6318^7 7165^7

Chicago Doll *Alan King* a87 81
3 ch f Cityscape Crooked Wood (USA) (Woodman (USA))
2942^3 3264^5 (4653) 5623^2◆ (6736) 8064^2

Chicago Guy *Alan King* a63 64
3 ch g Cityscape Hail Shower (IRE) (Red Clubs (IRE))
7559^5

Chicago May (IRE) *G M Lyons* a81 90
3 b f Charm Spirit(IRE) Urgele (FR) (Zafonic (USA))
2156a^6 2605a^{12}

Chicago School (IRE) *Nikki Evans* a47 45
6 ch g Approve(IRE) Ms Sasha Malia (IRE) (Verglas (IRE))
298^8 478^{10}

Chicago Socks *William de Best-Turner*
9 b g Catcher In The Rye(IRE) Sachiko (Celtic Swing)
6811^{10}

Chicas Amigas (IRE) *Mrs John Harrington* a75 91
3 b f Dragon Pulse(IRE) Veronica Falls (Medicean)
1306a^7 1601a^6 2156a^{10}

Chichester *Sir Michael Stoute* 61
2 b c Dansili Havant (Halling (USA))
8257^4

Chickenfortea (IRE) *Eric Alston* a39 62
5 gr g Clodovil(IRE) Kardyls Hope (IRE) (Fath (USA))
1565^9 2203^6 2847^7 3921^{14} 4785^{13} 5299^9 5767^5 6276^6 7590^2

Chief Ironside *David Menuisier* 109
4 b h Lawman(FR) Moment Of Time (Rainbow Quest (USA))
2573^6 3343^3 3987^{14} 4612^6 8138a^{13} (8578a) 8768a^{15}

Chief Mambo (FR) *H-F Devin* a71
3 b g Into Mischief(USA) Mama Lulu (USA) (Kingmambo (USA))
5407a^4

Chiefofchiefs *Charlie Fellowes* a103 95
6 b g Royal Applause Danvers (Cape Cross (IRE))
(56)◆ 565^4 879^5 1753^{23} 6915^4 8062^7 8336^9

Chief Sittingbull *Tony Carroll* a56
6 ch g Indian Haven Saharan Song (IRE) (Singspiel (IRE))
246^9 482^5 1146^5

Chikoko Trail *Gary Moore* a66 66
4 ch g Sixties Icon Search Party (Rainbow Quest (USA))
294^6 1175^2 1591^9 2617^{10} 3539^3 4115^4 (4797) 5351^5 5678^4 6602^4

Chil Chil *Andrew Balding* a81 89
3 b f Exceed And Excel(AUS) Tiana (Diktat)
2938^4 3532^2 4010^7 (6598) (6806) 6930^3 (7613)

Chilean *Martyn Meade* a71 96
4 b h Iffraaj Childa (IRE) (Duke Of Marmalade (IRE))
3987^{18} 8116^9

Chili Petin (USA) *Wesley A Ward* a85 75
2 b f City Zip(USA) Cat's Claw (USA) (Dynaformer (USA))
4048^{12}

Chill Chainnigh (FR) *Y Barberot* a84 96
2 b c Wootton Bassett Ella's Honour (Makfi)
6251a^4 7887a^5 8508a^6

Chillon Castle *David O'Meara* a42
3 br f Swiss Spirit Positivity (Monsieur Bond (IRE))
130^6

Chimney Rock (USA) *Michael J Maker* 109
2 b c Artie Schiller(USA) What's Your Point (USA) (Wheaton (USA))
8745a^2

Chinese Alphabet *Michael Appleby* a64 68
3 b g Leroidesanimaux(BRZ) Kesara (Sadler's Wells (USA))
1396^4 2096^5 3797^5 5580^3 6042^2 7116^5 7858^8 9168^{11} 9542^3 9646^5

Chinese Emperor *Lars Kelp* 65
2 b c Royal Applause Susi Wong (IRE) (Selkirk (USA))
7495a^{11}

Chinese Spirit (IRE) *Linda Perratt* a49 71
5 gr g Clodovil(IRE) In The Ribbons (In The Wings)
2439^6 2785^{12} 3177^3 (3720) 3922^5 4982^3◆ 5239^3 5490^2 5938^7 6341^{13} 6937^5 7364^3 7776^4 8818^{12} 9395^6

Chinese Whisperer (FR) *Alan King* a73 56
2 b c Poet's Voice Shanghai Noon (FR) (Turtle Bowl (IRE))
7162^9 7814^9 (8346)

Chingachgook *Tristan Davidson* a79 78
4 b g Al Kazeem Natty Bumppo (IRE) (Kheleyf (USA))
2104^2 2629^4 4241^6◆ 5305^4

Chipiron (FR) *Y Barberot* a86 86
3 ch g Rio De La Plata(USA) Chicago May (FR) (Numerous (USA))
3139a^3

Chisana *Chris Wall* 38
2 b f Bated Breath Sewards Folly (Rudimentary (USA))
5745^9 8409^8

Chitra *Daniel Kubler* a85 83
3 b f Sea The Moon(GER) Persian Star (Shamardal (USA))
(2772) (3596) 4008^5 5372^7 6835^2 7206^3 7914^3 8456^{11} 9203^7 (9390) (9584)

Chizzi *Rod Millman* 9
3 b f Coach House(IRE) Ziggy Zaggy (Diktat)
3090^{11}

Chloellie *J R Jenkins* a78 75
4 b m Delegator Caramelita (Deportivo)
(256) 697^2 1880^4 2971^3 4247^2 5386^3 5828^3 6408^4 6839^9 8254^3 8924^7

Chocco Star (IRE) *Chelsea Banham* a56 47
3 b f Lawman(FR) Sharplaw Star (Xaar)
520^5 1380^8 3775^8 8450^3 9272^3◆

Choco Box *Ed Vaughan* 85
4 b m Harbour Watch(IRE) Bible Box (IRE) (Bin Ajwaad (IRE))
2977^3

Chocoholic *Bryan Smart* a47 55
2 b g Due Diligence(USA) Unwrapit (USA) (Tapit (USA))
1843^{10} 4125^{10} 5017^2 5618^8 7208^9 8527^8 8815^5 9330^3 9643^4

Chocolaat Heer *John Quinn* a49
2 b g Heeraat(IRE) Calakanga (Dalakhani (IRE))
9099^{11} 9251^9 9607^8

Chocolate Box (IRE) *Mark Loughnane* a88 91
5 b g Zoffany(IRE) Chocolate Mauk (USA) (Cozzene (USA))
480^3

Chocolate Music (IRE) *Mrs John Harrington* 91
3 br f Dark Angel(IRE) Speedy Sonata (USA) (Stravinsky (USA))
6235a^3 7934a^{10} 8367a^9

Chocolat Noir (IRE) *Martin Todhunter* 41
6 b m Yeats(IRE) Valrhona (IRE) (Spectrum (IRE))
3686^{11}

Choice Encounter *Archie Watson* a79 47
4 ch g Choisir(AUS) Gimme Some Lovin (IRE) (Desert Style (IRE))
(139) (361) 755^4 1098^7 1290^5 1357^4 1487^4 2416^{11} 3462^{11}

Choice Of Mine (AUS) *Joseph Patrick O'Brien* a81
1 b c Redoute's Choice(AUS) Thislilsoulofmine (CAN) (Perfect Soul (IRE))
8889^4

Choise Of Raison *F Rossi* 99
2 b c Zoffany(IRE) Miss Plimsoll (USA) (Arch (USA))
7673a^2 8483a^3 9059a^3

Chookie Dunedin *Keith Dalgleish* a78 74
4 b g Epaulette(AUS) Lady Of Windsor (IRE) (Woods Of Windsor (USA))
230[4] ***786***[5] *1487*[10] 1950[6] 2368[9] 2788[4] 3221[9] 4721[4] 5123[2] 5770[8] *6631*[5] *8023*[10] *(8471)* *9140*[5] *(9365)*
Choosey (IRE) *Michael Easterby* a73 62
4 ch g Choisir(AUS) Petit Chou (IRE) (Captain Rio)
3309[9] 4625[8] 5027[4] 5595[4] ***(7855)***◆ *8712*[12]
Chop Chop (IRE) *Brian Barr* a45 59
3 b f Rip Van Winkle(IRE) Mince (Medicean)
554[3] *761*[6] 2798[10] 3354[3] 3839[3] 4328[8] 5582[6] *6737*[11] *8417*[10] *8864*[7] *8998*[9]
Choral Clan (IRE) *Brendan Powell* a75 73
8 b g Oratorio(IRE) Campbellite (Desert Prince (IRE))
248[4]◆
Choral Music *John E Long* a78 65
4 b m Equiano(FR) Gospel Music (Beat Hollow)
548 *1074*[3] *1392*[3] **3462**[2] 4424[9] 5677[6] *6317*[10] *7684*[8] *(8652)* *9453*[12]
Choral Work *William Haggas* 61
2 gr f Nathaniel(IRE) Chapel Choir (Dalakhani (IRE))
8758[7]
Choreograph *Roger Charlton* a50
2 b g Dansili Across The Floor (Oasis Dream)
9174[8]
Chorus of Lies *Alexandra Dunn* a34 33
7 b g Teofilo(IRE) Cherry Orchard (IRE) (King's Best (USA))
160[7]
Chosen Star *Michael Bell* a61 41
2 ch f Dubawi(IRE) Yodelling (USA) (Medaglia d'Oro (USA))
7054[10] ***8453***[8] *8913*[8]
Chosen World *Julie Camacho* a79 63
5 b g Intikhab(USA) Panoptic (Dubawi (IRE))
23[5] *609*[2] *(808)* *1273*[2] ***1925***[2] *2242*[6] *8197*[7] *8766*[11] *9047*[13] *9351*[3]
Chouain (FR) *M Rulec* 99
3 gr g Rajsaman(FR) Our Dream Queen (Oasis Dream)
3031a[2]
Christmas (IRE) *Flemming Velin* a37 95
3 b c Galileo(IRE) Christmas Kid (USA) (Lemon Drop Kid (USA))
3902a[3] *7494a*[10]
Christmas Diamond *Ollie Pears* 70
2 ch f Bated Breath Velma Kelly (Vettori (IRE))
4819[3]
Christmas Night *Ollie Pears* a66 64
4 ch g Compton Place Night Haven (Night Shift (USA))
808[7] *1426*[6] **2203**[3] 2681[5] 3215[6] *4195*[6] 5517[12] *(7443)* *8306*[12]
Chromium *Michael Attwater* a60 66
2 gr f Cable Bay(IRE) Ghedi (IRE) (Aussie Rules (USA))
2694[5] *3491*[12] **4222**[2] 5340[4] 5576[4] 6394[9] *7029*[6] *(7469)* *7994*[3] *9060*[10] *9307*[9] *9630*[8]
Chrysalism (IRE)
Joseph Patrick O'Brien a91 87
2 ch f Starspangledbanner(AUS) Song Of The Sea (Bering)
7879a[5] 9059a[6]
Chutzpah (IRE) *Mark Hoad* a48 40
3 b g Alhebayeb(IRE) Cheeky Weeky (Cadeaux Genereux)
442[7] *1174*[9] ***1332***[8] *2240*[8] 3348[11] *9216*[14]
Chynna *Mick Channon* a81 87
3 gr f Gregorian(IRE) Natalie Jay (Ballacashtal (CAN))
989[5] **2627**[4]◆ 3075[10] 3293[6] 4442[5] 4922[6] 5419[4]
Ciachope (FR) *L Rovisse* 46
2 b f Panis(USA) Cortina (FR) (Falco (USA))
5759a[9]
Ciao (IRE) *Gavin Cromwell* a82 83
4 ch m Lord Shanakill(USA) Selouma (FR) (Grape Tree Road)
1308a[9] **5597a**[5]
Cielo D'Irlanda (IRE) *D Grilli* 90
3 ch f Roderic O'Connor(IRE) Lady Conway (USA) (El Corredor (USA))
2161a[8]
Cigalera (FR) *M Delcher Sanchez* a90 92
3 b f Elusive City(USA) Macarella (IRE) (Shamardal (USA))
1200a[2] **2564a**[3] 6252a[6]
Cima Emergency (IRE)
Grizzetti Galoppo SRL 102
2 b c Canford Cliffs(IRE) Golden Song (Singspiel (IRE))
8390a[2]
Cima Fire (FR)
Grizzetti Galoppo SRL 88
3 b f Holy Roman Emperor(IRE) Gaudiana (GER) (Monsun (GER))
4171a[6] 7503a[8]
Cimeara (IRE)
Joseph Patrick O'Brien 102
4 b m Vocalised(USA) Gold Mirage (IRE) (Galileo (IRE))
(1620a) 2158a[7] 4351a[8] 4856a[3] 6191a[5]
Cindy Bear (IRE) *Roger Varian* a60 47
2 b f Kodiac My Twinkle (IRE) (Sea The Stars (IRE))
3461[7] 5737[6] *7813*[6]
Cindy Looper *Richard Whitaker* a58
2 gr f Coach House(IRE) Velvet Band (Verglas (IRE))
8084[8] 8395[9] *9097*[7]
Cinephile (FR) *Mlle Y Vollmer* a62 56
3 ch f Muhtathir Seance (GER) (Manduro (GER))
6063a[8]
Cinnabar *Roger Charlton* a57
2 b f Al Kazeem Moonlight Rhapsody (IRE) (Danehill Dancer (IRE))
9063[13] ***9500***[4]

Cinquain *Jo Hughes* 48
3 b f Poet's Voice Duo De Choc (IRE) (Manduro (GER))
1512a[10] **2265a**[10] 2759a[10] 3710a[9]
Cinzento (IRE) *Stuart Williams* a38 50
3 gr g Lawman(FR) Silver Samba (Dalakhani (IRE))
3648[9] 4452[8] 5193[6] 5784[7] *7192*[6] 8003[10]
Cipango *Marco Botti* a80 63
2 b c Dutch Art Poppets Sweetlove (Foxhound (USA))
4324[5] *5940*[3]◆ ***8605***[2]
Circe (FR) *J-M Beguigne* 73
2 gr f Kendargent(FR) Roche Ambeau (FR) (Chichicastenango (FR))
4533a[10] **9123a**[3]
Circle Dream (IRE) *S Seemar* a62 62
4 b g Oasis Dream Vezina (FR) (Bering)
49a[12]
Circle Of Stars (IRE)
Charlie Fellowes a68 67
3 b g Magician(IRE) Stars Above Me (Exceed And Excel (AUS))
359[7] *1676*[7] 2146[6] *2965*[9] 6304[2] 6760[7] ***7474***[3] ***8200***[3] *8696*[4]
Circuit *Wilf Storey* a45 43
5 br m Foxwedge(AUS) Lady Circe (USA) (Spinning World (USA))
1083[10] 2633[9] **2963**[7] 7732[6]
Circus Couture (IRE)
Jane Chapple-Hyam a97 100
7 ch g Intikhab(USA) Bois Joli (IRE) (Orpen (USA))
1414[6] 1753[13] 1890[8] 2271[7] **(3472)** 3987[21] 5192[9] 8336[16] *8892*[5] *9309*[7] *9588*[2]
Circus Maximus (IRE) *A P O'Brien* 119
3 b c Galileo(IRE) Duntle (IRE) (Danehill Dancer (IRE))
(2558) 3345[6] (3951) **5543**[2] 6354[7] **(7007a)** 8774a[4]
Cirque Royal *Charlie Appleby* a90 95
3 b g Cape Cross(IRE) Botanique (IRE) (Pivotal)
606[2]◆ *(723)* *(1221)* **6952**[9]
Citron Major *Nigel Tinkler* a81 95
4 ch g Major Cadeaux Citron (Reel Buddy (USA))
2378[7] 2743[9] **(3100)** 4127[12] 5217[3] **(5746)** 6229[3] 7152[4] 7431[6] 7701[6]
Citron Spirit (IRE) *P F Yiu* 113
7 b g Invincible Spirit(IRE) Citron Presse (USA) (Lemon Drop Kid (USA))
9379a[6]
Citta D'Oro *James Unett* a66 68
4 b g Cityscape Corsa All Oro (USA) (Medaglia d'Oro (USA))
(835) *(1231)* 2106[7] **3046**[3] *4194*[9] 4907[8] 5528[10]
City Escape (IRE) *Rae Guest* 61
2 b f Cityscape Lady Gabrielle (IRE) (Dansili)
4366[5] 6118[12]
City Light (FR) *S Wattel* a114 118
5 b h Siyouni(FR) Light Saber (FR) (Kendor (FR))
4094[9] (7255a) **7944a**[2]
Cityman *Andrew Slattery* a84 98
3 br g Slade Power(IRE) Ebrah (Singspiel (IRE))
306a[3] **(6986a)**
City Master *Ralph Beckett* a58 61
3 gr g Mastercraftsman(IRE) City Girl (IRE) (Elusive City (USA))
2798[9] ***3440***[4] 4284[7] *4642*[9]
City Of Light (USA)
Michael McCarthy a125
5 b h Quality Road(USA) Paris Notion (USA) (Dehere (USA))
(445a)
City Of Love *David Lanigan* a77 73
3 b f Exceed And Excel(AUS) Heart's Content (IRE) (Daylami (IRE))
6856[3] ***7608***[2] *7912*[3] *8548*[9] *9112*[4]
City Tour *Lydia Richards* a83 73
3 b g Dutch Art Privacy Order (Azamour (IRE))
(1504) 1846[5] 2897[4]◆ 5863[6] *6593*[2] 7413[3] *7816*[2] *8421*[7] ***9178***[2] ***(9418)***
City Walk (IRE) *Saeed bin Suroor* 81
2 b c Brazen Beau(AUS) My Lucky Liz (IRE) (Exceed And Excel (AUS))
1887[3]
City Wanderer (IRE) *Mick Channon* 82
3 b g Kodiac Viletta (GER) (Doyen (IRE))
1755[7] 2405[3] 2790[6]◆ 3638[5] (4225) (4909) 5574[4] **(6468)**◆
Claire Underwood (IRE)
Richard Fahey a92 92
4 b m Declaration Of War(USA) Sindjara (USA) (Include (USA))
1573◆ *(522)* *803*[2] 2119[3] (2370) 3070[3] 3655[6] 4407[5] ***5437***[2] **5902**[3] 6355[6] **6975**[2] 7403[7] 8245[9]
Clair Matin (FR) *T Lemer* 71
3 bb c Vertigineux(FR) Coriante (FR) (Indian Rocket)
1741a[10]
Clandestine Affair (IRE)
Jamie Osborne a38 60
2 b c Kodiac Sanaya (IRE) (Barathea (IRE))
5131[13] **5493**[4] 5956[7] 6394[7] *6884*[6]
Clan Royale *Roger Varian* 86
2 b g Siyouni(FR) Ascot Family (IRE) (Desert Style (IRE))
2610[2] 3008[3] 6167[4] (6997)◆ 8095[6]
Clap Your Hands *David Simcock* a94 60
3 b g Universal(IRE) Woop Woop (IRE) (Oratorio (IRE))
1182[5] *1344*[4]◆ 2925[4]◆ *9134*[2]◆ *(9442)* ***(9611)***
Clarabola (FR) *B De Montzey* a45 66
2 ch f Lucayan(FR) Astrobola (FR) (Astronomer Royal (USA))
6141a[6]
Clara Peeters *Gary Moore* a66 93
3 b f Epaulette(AUS) Musical Key (Key Of Luck (USA))
3041[2] *3468*[8] (4393) 5525[6] 6081[5] 6913[3] 7341[3] **7901**[2]

Clare Island (IRE) *Edward Lynam* a73 59
5 gr m Holy Roman Emperor(IRE) Les Alizes (IRE) (Cadeaux Genereux)
307a[12]
Clareyblue (IRE) *Martyn Meade* 83
2 gr c Zebedee Fancy Feathers (IRE) (Redback)
3601[3] **4401**[2]◆
Clarion *Sir Michael Stoute* 87
3 b f Dubawi(IRE) Caraboss (Cape Cross (IRE))
2762[4] 3546[2] 4474[4] **(5687)**◆ 6398[3]
Clary (IRE) *Alistair Whillans* a53 52
9 b m Clodovil(IRE) Kibarague (Barathea (IRE))
1717[9] *2241*[8] **2964**[3] *3448*[11] **5100**[3] 6628[7]
Clashaniska (IRE) *Tony Carroll* a51 59
3 b g Dark Angel(IRE) Spirit Watch (IRE) (Invincible Spirit (IRE))
9402[13]
Class Clown (IRE) *David Barron* a65 9
2 ch g Intense Focus(USA) Joli Elegant (IRE) (Dylan Thomas (IRE))
7285[12] *8069*[5] *8919*[10] ***(9330)***
Classic Charm *Dean Ivory* a69 77
4 b m Rip Van Winkle(IRE) Classic Lass (Dr Fong (USA))
33[2] *430*[7] *828*[3] *1231*[9] (2585) *4787*[11] *5309*[2] **(5593)** 6170[3] 8031[6] *9273*[11]
Classic Design (IRE)
Simon Crisford a82
3 b g Pivotal Fashion Line (IRE) (Cape Cross (IRE))
7630[8] *8351*[3] ***(9011)*** ***9628***[6]
Classic Joy (FR) *L Viel* a63 68
4 b h Cacique(IRE) Singapore Joy (FR) (Sagacity (FR))
(5115a) 7860a[P]
Classic Pursuit *Marjorie Fife* a50 64
8 b g Pastoral Pursuits Snake's Head (Golden Snake (USA))
163[5] *389*[7] ***797***[5] *1194*[9] *1487*[8] *1860*[8] 1946[13] 2589[6] 2841[16] 2893[14] 3928[11] 4586[5]◆ 5094[3] 5276[9] 5722[12] 7488[7] 8235[9] *8401*[8] *9335*[11] *9539*[10]
Classic Star *Dean Ivory* a60 64
3 b g Sea The Moon(GER) Classic Lass (Dr Fong (USA))
1347 3651[4] *4642*[5] 5561[2] **5957**[2]◆ *6389*[6] 8008[4] *8698*[5]
Classified (IRE) *Ed de Giles* a65 54
5 b m Lope De Vega(IRE) Crossbreeze (USA) (Red Ransom (USA))
3687[5] 4371[9] 4991[6] *6049*[11]
Classique Legend (AUS)
Les Bridge 114
3 gb g Not A Single Doubt(AUS) Pinocchio (AUS) (Encosta De Lago (AUS))
8362a[6] 8805a[10]
Classy Cailin (IRE) *Pam Sly* a56 55
4 b m Kodiac Waroonga (IRE) (Brief Truce (USA))
116[3] *484*[8] *530*[3] *1026*[6] ***1722***[4] 3352[9] 4376[9] (5063) *6284*[8] *6682*[3] *8018*[7]
Classy Lady *Ollie Pears* a47 57
2 b f Garswood Classic Vision (Classic Cliche (IRE))
2051[6] **2907**[4] 3812[16] 4075[2] 5196[4] 5295[5] ***8527***[3]◆ *9330*[5] *9515*[12]
Classy Moon (USA) *K R Burke* 95
2 b g Malibu Moon(USA) Contentious (USA) (Giant's Causeway (USA))
(3679)◆ 4846[6] **5228a**[6]
Claudia Jean (IRE) *Richard Hannon* 50
2 b f Camacho Quickstyx (Night Shift (USA))
3530[3] 4992[6] **5427**[5] 5958[9]
Claudine (IRE) *Alexandra Dunn* a43 67
4 b m Zoffany(IRE) Hamalka (IRE) (Alhaarth (IRE))
364[6] *760*[8] *923*[12] *1494*[5] *1769*[12]
Claudio Monteverdi (IRE)
Adam West
6 b g Galileo(IRE) Dance For Fun (Anabaa (USA))
1524[P]
Clay Motion (IRE) *David Barron*
2 b g Morpheus Click And Go (IRE) (Kodiac)
2907[9]
Clay Regazzoni *Keith Dalgleish* a80 78
2 b g Due Diligence(USA) Shifting Moon (Kheleyf (USA))
2957[2] 3703[2] 4091[10] 5185[12] 5485[5] 6653[9] 6969[2] 7429[10] 7778[2] 7904[9] ***(8505)*** 8760[3]
Clayton *Archie Watson* a55 78
10 b g Peintre Celebre(USA) Blossom (Warning)
(1949) **(2335)** 2901[6]
Clayton Hall (IRE) *John Wainwright* a45 50
6 b g Lilbourne Lad(IRE) Hawk Dance (IRE) (Hawk Wing (USA))
3447[6] **3705**[4] 4690[12] *9345*[6]
Clearance *Iain Jardine* a58 69
5 b g Authorized(IRE) Four Miracles (Vettori (IRE))
(482) *(695)* *1334*[7] (5939)◆ **(6583)** 6611[4]
Clear For Take Off *D Moser* a92 92
5 gr m Soldier Hollow Chantra (GER) (Lando (GER))
4534a[3] 6006a[7] **7250a**[4]
Clear Spring (IRE) *John Spearing* a75 74
11 b g Chineur(FR) Holly Springs (Efisio)
3164[4] **4835**[5] 5503[4] 6109[7]
Clegane *Ed Walker* a67 70
2 ch f Iffraaj Cradle Of Life (IRE) (Notnowcato)
4790[6]◆ **6019**[6] *7304*[5] 8026[3] *9137*[8]◆
Clem A *Alan Bailey* a79 69
3 b g Helmet(AUS) Mondovi (Kyllachy)
2689[4] 5031[10] 5531[5] (6121) 6529[4] *7609*[9] *9361*[5] ***(9573)***
Clematis (USA) *Charles Hills* a80 22
3 bb f First Defence(USA) Faraway Flower (USA) (Distant View (USA))
2445[7]
Clement (IRE) *Marjorie Fife* a58 50
9 b g Clodovil(IRE) Winnifred (Green Desert (USA))
243[7] *467*[11] *600*[5] *925*[11] *1478*[2] ***(1683)*** *1717*[6] ***1837***[3] 2145[8] ***2235***[2] 2513[6] *8301*[14] *8915*[10] *9111*[12]
Clemento (IRE) *John Quinn*
5 b g Canford Cliffs(IRE) Street Style (IRE) (Rock Of Gibraltar (IRE))
8696[P]

Cleonte (IRE) *Andrew Balding* 108
6 ch g Sir Percy Key Figure (Beat Hollow)
2269[3] 2575[6] (4096) **4670**[3] 6473[11] **7148**[2] 7928a[7] 8332[7]
Cleostorm (FR) *P Monfort* a70 74
3 ch f Stormy River(FR) Esquinade (FR) (Archange D'Or (IRE))
(216a)
Clerisy *Sir Michael Stoute* a65 81
3 b f Kingman Exemplify (Dansili)
(1855) **2806**[8] 7901[10]
Clevedon (IRE) *Ronald Harris* a44 51
3 br g Bungle Inthejungle Sandy Smile (IRE) (Footstepsinthesand)
137[10]
Clever Candy *Michael Bell* 67
2 b f Intello(GER) True Course (Dubawi (IRE))
4897[11] 5906[7] 6514[5]◆ **(7522)**
Clever Cookie *Peter Niven* a92 100
11 b g Primo Valentino(IRE) Mystic Memory (Ela-Mana-Mou (IRE))
6355[7] 6958[14]
Clever Trick *Kevin Ryan* a55 35
2 b g Pivotal Trick Or Treat (Lomitas)
5848[10] ***9095***[7]
Cliff (IRE) *Nigel Tinkler* a60 57
9 b g Bachelor Duke(USA) Silesian (IRE) (Singspiel (IRE))
1765[10] 2638[5] **3475**[5] 3738[4] 4519[15]
Cliff Bay (IRE) *Keith Dalgleish* a53 57
5 b g Elzaam(AUS) Lost Highway (IRE) (Danehill Dancer (IRE))
2298[3] 3681[7] (3924) 4513[2] **4978**[3] 6036[9] 6628[9] 7210[7] 7509[4] 7776[8] 8234[5]
Cliff's Edge (AUS)
Ciaron Maher & David Eustace 109
4 b h Canford Cliffs(IRE) Simulation (AUS) (Snaadee (USA))
8138a[6] **8578a**[2] 8768a[14]
Cliffs Of Capri *Jamie Osborne* a95 101
5 b g Canford Cliffs(IRE) Shannon Spree (Royal Applause)
173a[4] 640a[4] 847a[3] 961a[12] *4020*[3] 5188[3] 5546[4] **6445**[4] *6706*[14] 7865[3] *8320*[7]
Cliffs Of Dooneen (IRE)
Ralph Beckett a101 51
4 b g Galileo(IRE) Devoted To You (IRE) (Danehill Dancer (IRE))
1943[5] 2575[10]
Cliffs Of Freedom (IRE)
Kevin Thomas Coleman a54 79
2 b c Canford Cliffs(IRE) By Jupiter (Sea The Stars (IRE))
7386[7] ***8528***[8]
Clifftop Heaven *Mark Walford* 66
2 b g Canford Cliffs(IRE) Heaven's Sake (Cape Cross (IRE))
6065[9] 6368[6] **7285**[4] 8259[11]
Cliff Wind *Sir Mark Prescott Bt* a52
2 gr f Invincible Spirit(IRE) Fork Lightning (USA) (Storm Cat (USA))
9036[6] ***9393***[7] *9623*[9]
Clifton *Michael Easterby* a65
3 b g Sepoy(AUS) Humility (Polar Falcon (USA))
3324[5] *4196*[4] ***7303***[2]
Climax *Wilf Storey* a35 55
5 b m Acclamation Blue Rocket (IRE) (Rock Of Gibraltar (IRE))
1085[6] *1402*[11] *2189*[9]
Clinician *Sir Michael Stoute* a70
2 b f Kingman Clinical (Motivator)
9159[4]
Clipsham Tiger (IRE)
Michael Appleby a71 57
3 b g Bungle Inthejungle Texas Queen (Shamardal (USA))
4219[9] 4563[10] 5797[3] 6844[8] 7335[2] *8251*[10] *(8694)* *(8942)* ***(9028)*** *9331*[4] *9453*[10]
Clive Clifton (IRE) *Kevin Frost* a48 49
6 b g Wootton Bassett Dearest Daisy (Forzando)
62[5] *208*[7] *436*[9] *835*[7] *1015*[8] *1333*[3]◆ *3429*[6] **4475**[2] 5049[8] 6499[8]
Cloak And Dagger (IRE)
Ibrahim Al Malki 83
3 b c Lope De Vega(IRE) Redoutable (IRE) (Invincible Spirit (IRE))
893a[10]
Cloak Of Darkness (IRE)
Paul Nolan a49 43
4 b g Iffraaj Cape Of Night (IRE) (Cape Cross (IRE))
7087a[8]
Cloak Of Spirits (IRE)
Richard Hannon 108
2 ch f Invincible Spirit(IRE) Pivotique (Pivotal)
(5366) 7120[6] **7659**[3]
Clog Maker (IRE) *Mark Johnston* 71
2 b c Dark Angel(IRE) Utrecht (Rock Of Gibraltar (IRE))
3047[4]
Clon Coulis (IRE) *David Barron* a96 109
5 b m Vale Of York(IRE) Cloneden (IRE) (Definite Article)
(1063) *1918*[9] **3987**[2] 4758[5] 5610[18] 6379[8] 7657[10] 8336[12]
Clooney *Lydia Pearce* a60 69
4 b g Dansili Love Divine (Diesis)
8294[9] *8641*[7] *8828*[12]
Close Pass *S Seemar* a19
4 b g Shamardal(USA) Toolentidhaar (USA) (Swain (IRE))
1742a[15]
Closer Than Close
Jonathan Portman 65
3 b g Lope De Vega(IRE) Close At Hand (Exceed And Excel (AUS))
3696[5] **4423**[4] 5249[3] 6022[8] 6367[8] 8205[11] *8903*[9]
Close Your Eyes (ITY) *A Botti* 97
4 b m Mujahid(USA) Too In Love (IRE) (Galileo (IRE))
4170a[2]

Clotherholme (IRE) *Ann Duffield* a48 64
2 b c Sir Prancealot(IRE) Giorgi (IRE) (Kodiac)
7698[7] 8395[4] 8631[5] 9515[10]

Cloud Dancer (FR) *Mario Hofer* a80 81
4 gr g Kendargent(FR) Cavaliere (FR) (Traditionally (USA))
7136a[3] 7861a[9]

Cloud Drift *Michael Bell* 81
2 b g Toronado(IRE) Humdrum (Dr Fong (USA))
4480[4] 5512[2]◆ (6054) 7612[2]

Cloudea (IRE) *Richard Fahey* 76
2 gr f Clodovil(IRE) Maria Luisa (IRE) (King's Best (USA))
4142[4] (5197) 5788[4]

Cloud Eight (IRE) *P Monfort* a77 74
4 b g Dream Ahead(USA) Night Cam (IRE) (Night Shift (USA))
2956a[13] (7223a)

Cloudlam *William Haggas* a79 71
4 b m Arch(USA) Sharnberry (Shamardal (USA))
(18) (459)◆

Cloud Nine (FR) *Tony Carroll* a44 52
6 b m Sakhee(USA) Heaven (Reel Buddy (USA))
593[9] 1145[11] 1362[8] 2972[6] (Dead)

Cloud Thunder *Heather Main* a58 9
2 gr g Poet's Voice Cloud Illusions (USA) (Smarty Jones (USA))
7814[13] 8518[11]

Clovelly Bay (IRE)
Marcus Tregoning a65 72
8 b g Bushranger(IRE) Crystalline Stream (FR) (Polish Precedent (USA))
257[6] 859[4]

Clovenstone *Alistair Whillans* a49 63
3 b g Mazameer(IRE) Macqueen (Hawkeye (IRE))
2438[3] 3248[8] 4055[5] 4915[12] 7581[13] 8423[10] 8818[14] 9090[5] 9279[10] 9552[5]

Clubora (USA) *Richard Hannon* a41 37
3 b f Medaglia d'Oro(USA) Middle Club (Fantastic Light (USA))
1288[8] 2007[9] 2772[11] 3409[7]

Club Tropicana *Richard Spencer* a73 76
4 ch m Helmet(AUS) Twenty Seven (IRE) (Efisio)
1065[10] (3279) 4615[2] 5626[9] 6160[9] 7526[9]

Club Wexford (IRE) *Roger Fell* 98
8 b g Lawman(FR) Masnada (IRE) (Erins Isle (IRE))
2480[4] 3216[5] (3268) (4097) 4240[5] (4981) 5708[2] 5948[4] 6376[17] 7430[7]

C'Moi Cesar (FR) *Laurent Loisel* a51 76
2 ch c Power Cannes To Capri (IRE) (Galileo (IRE))
7925a[5] 8483a[5]

Cmon Cmon (IRE) *Nigel Tinkler* 59
2 b g Slade Power(IRE) Ramamara (IRE) (Trans Island)
1758[6] 2707[6] 3866[13]

Cnicht (FR) *D Henderson* a88 95
5 gr h Silver Frost(IRE) Gibraltar Bay (IRE) (Cape Cross (IRE))
682a[13] 6145a[2] (8375a)

Cnoc An Oir (IRE)
Joseph Patrick O'Brien a79 92
3 b f Born To Sea(IRE) Witch Of Fife (USA) (Lear Fan (USA))
5075a[6] 6090a[8] 7347[5] 8734a[11]

C Note (IRE) *Heather Main* a90 88
6 b g Iffraaj Alexander Queen (IRE) (King's Best (USA))
368[4] 521[4] 1757[8] 2800[5] 3663[3] 3806[6] 4425[3] 5667[14] 6217[6] 6967[11] 7829[11]

Coachella (IRE) *Ed de Giles* a58 56
5 gr g Kyllachy Indian Belle (IRE) (Indian Ridge (IRE))
2513[8] 3038[9] 3966[2] 4349[4] 4771[7] 5867[12] 7028[9]

Coal Front (USA) *Todd Pletcher* a117
5 bb r Stay Thirsty(USA) Miner's Secret (USA) (Mineshaft (USA))
(1440a) 3618a[7] 8771a[6]

Coase *Hugo Palmer* 89
2 b g Zoffany(IRE) Sharnberry (Shamardal (USA))
(3245)◆ 3949[17] 4876[2]

Coastal Cyclone *Harry Dunlop* a59 46
5 b g Canford Cliffs(IRE) Seasonal Cross (Cape Cross (IRE))
483[4] 759[6] 1210[4] 1952[4] 2145[6] 3476[5] 5147[14] 5302[14] 6174[10] 7172[15]

Coastal Drive *Paul Midgley* a66 54
4 gr g Harbour Watch(IRE) Added Attraction (FR) (Kendor (FR))
1161[7] 1976[5] 2638[13] 3413[5] 4149[12] 4434[6] 5147[12]

Coastal Mist (IRE) *John Quinn* 74
2 gr g Gutaifan(IRE) She's A Character (Invincible Spirit (IRE))
(3265)◆ 4032[2] 4486[3] 5390[3] 5612[9] 6053[7] 7247a[10] 8095[11]

Coastguard Watch (FR)
Natalie Lloyd-Beavis a56 45
3 b g Olympic Glory(IRE) Miss Hygrove (IRE) (Exceed And Excel (AUS))
1385[5] 1557[9] 2504a[3] 3174a[8] 4684a[6] 6531[11]

Coastline (IRE) *James Tate* a73 81
3 br f Cape Cross(IRE) Without Precedent (FR) (Polish Precedent (USA))
(1272) 2552[7] 3273[4] (4566) 5827[5]

Coast Ofalfujairah (IRE)
Kevin Ryan 61
2 b g Brazen Beau(AUS) Khameela (Equiano (FR))
1499[4] 3245[5] 5145[6]

Coast Of Dubai (IRE) *Kevin Ryan* a24 36
2 b g Elzaam(AUS) Instant Memories (IRE) (Ad Valorem (USA))
1416[11] 3954[8]

Cobber Kain *John Gosden* a82
2 ch g Sepoy(AUS) Doctor Serena (USA) (Cape Blanco (IRE))
(6858) (7605) 8252[5]

Cobnut (IRE) *James Fanshawe* a46
2 b g Kodiac Macadamia (IRE) (Classic Cliche (IRE))
8012[7]

Cobra Eye *John Quinn* 87
2 b c Kodiac Annie The Doc (Nayef (USA))
5125[2]◆ (5523) 8125[6] 9059a[9]

Cobweb Catcher *Rod Millman* a55 62
3 b g Swiss Spirit Sugar Beet (Beat Hollow)
1650[2] 1954[4] 2474[8] 3376[6] 5449[5]

Cochise *Roger Charlton* a64 75
3 b g Intello(GER) Ship's Biscuit (Tiger Hill (IRE))
4842[8] 5578[3] 6290[6] 7300[5] 7520[4] (8246)◆

Cock A Hoop (IRE) *Ben Haslam* a58
2 ch f Ivawood(IRE) Dancing With Stars (IRE) (Where Or When (IRE))
9514[5]

Cockalorum (IRE) *Roger Fell* a80 93
4 b g Cape Cross(IRE) Opinionated (IRE) (Dubai Destination (USA))
3515[7] 3867[4]◆ 4689[5] (5198) 5489[2] 5741[3] 6475[9] 7694[21] 8130[2] 8725[4]

Cockney Boy *Michael Appleby* a56 40
6 ch g Cockney Rebel(IRE) Menha (Dubawi (IRE))
180[5] 386[7]

Cockney Cracker (FR)
Niels Petersen 92
8 b g Cockney Rebel(IRE) Lady An Co (FR) (Lavirco (GER))
4419a[3] 6524a[7]

Cockney Hill *Joseph Tuite* a78
3 b g Bated Breath Espagnolette (Oasis Dream)
289[8] (753) 8894[3] 9441[9]

Cock Robin *Kevin Ryan* 58
2 b g Hot Streak(IRE) Rohesia (High Chaparral (IRE))
1843[5] 2869[8]

Cococabala (IRE) *Tareq Abdulla* a74 87
3 b g Sir Prancealot(IRE) Dream Applause (IRE) (Royal Applause)
893a[3]

Coco Chamelle (IRE) *Y Durepaire* a61
3 b f Alhebayeb(IRE) Antibes (IRE) (Grand Lodge (USA))
955a[5]

Coco City (FR) *M Delcher Sanchez* a75 103
5 b g Elusive City(USA) Coco (USA) (Storm Bird (CAN))
2667a[8] 5471a[4]

Coco Motion (IRE) *Michael Dods* 43
3 b g Es Que Love(IRE) Beguiler (Refuse To Bend (IRE))
2912[8] 3972[10] 6342[11]

Coconut Sugar (IRE) *Robert Cowell* a24
2 b f Gutaifan(IRE) Murrieta (Docksider (USA))
9668[13]

Code Of Conduct *Roger Charlton* a79 84
2 b c Siyouni(FR) Sequence (IRE) (Selkirk (USA))
7410[5]◆ 8810[2]

Code Of Honor (USA)
Claude McGaughey III a121
3 ch c Noble Mission Reunited (USA) (Dixie Union (USA))
2425a[2] 8777a[7]

Coeur Blimey (IRE) *Sue Gardner* 94
8 bb g Winged Love(IRE) Eastender (Opening Verse (USA))
(1735) 4096[10] 8114[23]

Coeur D'amour (IRE)
Madeleine Tylicki 83
4 b m Zoffany(IRE) Adoring (IRE) (One Cool Cat (USA))
2451a[5] 2961[3] 6090a[14]

Coeur De Lion *Alan King* a98 99
6 b g Pour Moi(IRE) Hora (Hernando (FR))
1735[2] (2578) 3952[5] 4381[3] 5183[3] 8114[24]

Coffeemeanscoffee (IRE)
W J Martin a37 53
4 b m Elzaam(AUS) Smart Starprincess (IRE) (Soviet Star (USA))
365[12] 4494[2] 8821[9]

Cogital *Amanda Perrett* a75 71
4 b g Invincible Spirit(IRE) Galaxy Highflyer (Galileo (IRE))
2472[3] 3022[8] 4426[4]◆ 4561[9] 5744[3] 6419[2] (6720)◆ 7845[5]

Cognac (IRE) *Mark Johnston* 86
2 b c Invincible Spirit(IRE) Rose De France (IRE) (Diktat)
5704[3] (6606) 7139[2]

Cohesion *David Bridgwater* a52 96
6 b g Champs Elysees Winter Bloom (USA) (Aptitude (USA))
2554[4] 3646[5] 4382[18] 5199[9] 5657[11] 6151[6] 6686[8]

Coiste Bodhar (IRE) *Scott Dixon* a45 59
8 b g Camacho Nortolixa (FR) (Linamix (FR))
167[5] 586[9] 830[11] 1554[7] 2532[9]

Colada Cove (IRE) *Tom Ward* a50
2 b c Harbour Watch(IRE) Sweet Coconut (Bahamian Bounty)
8346[9] 9085[9] 9156[9]

Cold Fire (IRE) *Robyn Brisland* a58
6 ch g Frozen Power(IRE) Eleanor Eloise (USA) (Minardi (USA))
451[10] 273[4]◆ 436[12] (940) 1176[7] 1546[P]

Cold Front *William Haggas* 84
2 b c Lope De Vega(IRE) Cloud Line (Danehill Dancer (IRE))
8516[2]◆

Cold Fusion (IRE) *Dai Williams* a44 55
6 b m Frozen Power(IRE) Tuscania (USA) (Woodman (USA))
8373a[6] 8737a[6]

Cold Harbour *Robyn Brisland* a68 65
4 b g North Light(IRE) Pilcomayo (IRE) (Rahy (USA))
(207) 923[6] 1297[6] 1680[3] (2345) 2819[3] (3209)◆ 4004[2] 4370[11] 7629[7] (7873) 8300[11] 8641[3] 8948[3] 9033[4] 9336[2] 9412[3] 9646[2]

Cold Light Of Day (FR)
Robert Collet a48 40
3 b f Anodin(IRE) Pepples Beach (GER) (Lomitas)
216a[14]

Cold Light Of Day *Michael Dods* 65
2 gr f Sea The Moon(GER) Frosty Welcome (USA) (With Approval (CAN))
5553[5]◆ 6175[6] 6970[6] 7585[3]◆

Cold Stare (IRE) *David O'Meara* 103
4 b g Intense Focus(USA) Ziria (IRE) (Danehill Dancer (IRE))
2100[9] 2572[10] (3589) 7433[15] 7701[4]◆ 7891[7] 8127[16] 8512[3]

Cold War Steve *Roger Fell* a56
2 ch g Lope De Vega(IRE) Balamana (FR) (Sinndar (IRE))
8528[11] 9029[6] 9181[3]◆

Colfer Me (IRE)
Joseph Patrick O'Brien a98 95
3 b g Canford Cliffs(IRE) Thistlestar (USA) (Lion Heart (USA))
1049a[5] 1306a[11]

Colibri Cael (FR) *P Leblanc* a63 35
7 b g Fuisse(FR) Dallia (FR) (Anabaa (USA))
115a[8]

Collate *Amy Murphy* a69 56
4 b m Oasis Dream Homepage (Dansili)
(399) 924[4]

Collect Call (IRE) *K R Burke* a59 64
3 b f Kodiac Payphone (Anabaa (USA))
1816[7] 3159[8]

Collegeville Girl (USA)
Richard Vega a26
3 b f Central Banker(USA) Lifelong (USA) (Vindication (USA))
7479a[11]

Collette (IRE) *Hugo Palmer* a50 68
2 ch f New Approach(IRE) Shallow Lake (USA) (Bernardini (USA))
5823[3]◆ 6146[4] 7023[4]

Collide *Hugo Palmer* a105 105
4 b h Frankel Scuffle (Daylami (IRE))
(1681)◆ 2742[4] 4053[5] 4884[15] 9302[4]

Collodi (GER) *Conor Dore* a42 56
10 b g Konigstiger(GER) Codera (GER) (Zilzal (USA))
1988[11]

Colomano *Markus Klug* 108
5 b h Cacique(IRE) Codera (GER) (Zilzal (USA))
2455a[5] 4427a[3] 5719a[4] 6771a[4] 7500a[4] 8391a[3]

Colonel Frank *Mick Quinn* a60 85
5 b g Dutch Art Loquacity (Diktat)
2739[8] 3649[5] 4300[12] (5628) 5911[4] 8766[8] (8860)

Colonelle (USA) *Ed Vaughan* a48 58
3 b f Lemon Drop Kid(USA) Sigurwana (USA) (Arch (USA))
2762[10] 3598[3] 4196[7] 4804[5] 5287[5]

Colonel Slade (IRE) *Phillip Makin* a73 64
3 b g Dandy Man(IRE) Sense Of A Woman (USA) (Street Sense (USA))
4120[8] 4452[5] 4774[2] 5031[9] 5304[2] (7581) (8345)◆ 8807[4] 9047[3]

Colonel Whitehead (IRE)
Heather Main a78 70
2 b c Showcasing Lady Brigid (IRE) (Holy Roman Emperor (IRE))
4839[8] 5500[3] 5859[3] 6219[3] (7186) 7754[10] 8650[7] (9099) 9205[10]

Colonize *John Gosden* a76
2 b c Empire Maker(USA) Nayarra (IRE) (Cape Cross (IRE))
8914[6] (9154)

Colony Queen *Steve Gollings* a63 77
3 b f Gregorian(IRE) Queen Margrethe (Grand Lodge (USA))
66[2] 403[2] (836) 1066[2] 1270[5] 2125[7] (3310) 4110[4] 5518[2] (7343) 7900[6] (8519)

Colour Contrast (IRE) *Iain Jardine* a18 66
6 b g Rock Of Gibraltar(IRE) Colour Coordinated (IRE) (Spectrum (IRE))
(2328) (2681) 2898[8] 3178[4] 4060[5] 4978[4] 5616[5] 6572[10] 8233[4]

Colourfield (IRE) *Charlie Fellowes* a61 70
4 b m Makfi Rainbow Desert (USA) (Dynaformer (USA))
1688[4] 2376[8]

Colourful Sky (FR) *J S Moore* a10 23
3 ch f Dalakhani(IRE) Sky Colours (IRE) (Galileo (IRE))
4452[12] 5641a[9]

Colour Image (IRE)
Saeed bin Suroor 84
2 b c Kodiac Chroussa (IRE) (Holy Roman Emperor (IRE))
7661[2]◆ 8128[6]

Colouring *Ed Walker* a76 57
2 b f Showcasing Blue Lyric (Refuse To Bend (IRE))
6919[10] 7786[2] 8418[2] 9205[2]◆ (9401)

Colwood *Robert Eddery* a76 72
5 ch g Champs Elysees La Colline (GER) (Ocean Of Wisdom (USA))
385[3] 700[3] 991[4] 2528[4]◆ (3444) 4825[7] 6720[3] 7631[3] 8523[2] 8726[3]

Combat Des Trente (FR) *C Lotoux* a76 76
6 gr g Kendargent(FR) Canalside (Nayef (USA))
4748a[6]

Combine (IRE) *Hugo Palmer* 76
2 b f Zoffany(IRE) Unity (IRE) (Sadler's Wells (USA))
8432[3]◆

Comeatchoo (IRE) *Phil McEntee* a54 57
2 b g Camacho La Estatua (Lope De Vega (IRE))
1844[10] 2415[6]◆ 2820[10] 4778[4] 5196[8] 5618[6] 6182[4] 7208[5] 7329[2] 7440[7] 7734[6] 8527[2] 9061[4] 9330[8] 9394[11]

Come Dancing (USA)
Carlos F Martin a113
5 bb m Malibu Moon(USA) Tizahit (USA) (Tiznow (USA))
8769a[6]

Comedia Eria (FR) *P Monfort* a101 100
7 b m Lope De Vega(IRE) Vola Vola (IRE) (Danehill Dancer (IRE))
2670a[2] 3994[4] 4948a[4] 6520a[5] 7254a[5] 8141a[11] 8648a[4]

Come On Bear (IRE) *Alan Bailey* a47 36
4 b m Dandy Man(IRE) Blusienka (IRE) (Blues Traveller (IRE))
2900[9] 3989[4] 4589[4]◆ 4753[6] 9659[4]

Come On Come On (IRE)
Clive Cox a87 83
5 br g Lord Shanakill(USA) Maridiyna (IRE) (Sinndar (IRE))
440[4]

Come On Dave (IRE) *John Butler* a67 61
10 b g Red Clubs(IRE) Desert Sprite (IRE) (Tagula (IRE))
431[10] 626[5] 1590[2] 2010[7] 2632[19] 3404[8] 4027[7] (5046) 6048[4] 6685[4]

Comeonfeeltheforce (IRE)
Lee Carter a72 55
3 b f Slade Power(IRE) Balladiene (IRE) (Noverre (USA))
183[4] 319[4] 537[5] 765[8] (1726) 2007[2] 3264[4] (4244) 4642[6] 5573[6] 6075[6] 7573[2] 9427[8]

Come On Girl *Tony Carroll* a62 62
2 gr f Outstrip Floating (Oasis Dream)
2205[10] 3573[5] 4191[6] 4652[4] 5010[5] 5576[3] 5958[2] (6313) 7522[2] 7827[8]

Come On Leicester (IRE)
Richard Hannon 88
3 b f Kodiac Graphic Guest (Dutch Art)
1832[8] 1913[8] 2627[5] 4242[6] 4904[6] 5459[8]

Come On Linda *Michael Easterby* a55
2 b f Alhebayeb(IRE) Friendship Is Love (Byron)
9623[8]

Come On My Son *Mark Loughnane* a76
2 b g Mayson Slinky McVelvet (Refuse To Bend (IRE))
(4766) 9029[5] 9500[6]

Come On Sal *Kevin Frost* a16
4 b m Sayif(IRE) Immortelle (Arazi (USA))
4196[11]

Come On Tier (FR) *Lee Carter* a68 55
4 b g Kendargent(FR) Milwaukee (FR) (Desert King (IRE))
19[3] 252[4] 552[6] 1025[6] 1294[7] 1544[4] (2006) 3944[10] 6050[7] 6839[11]

Come Say Hi (FR) *M Nigge* a76 72
3 b c Le Havre(IRE) Show Flower (Shamardal (USA))
7138a[2]

Come September (IRE)
Gavin Cromwell a79 90
3 b f Roderic O'Connor(IRE) Arakans Secret (IRE) (Arakan (USA))
7038a[4] 7635a[11] 8367a[5] 8572a[5] 8734a[10]

Comical (USA) *Doug O'Neill* a105
2 b f Into Mischief(USA) Kayce Ace (USA) (Tiznow (USA))
8747a[7]

Comicas (USA) *Charlie Appleby* a108 93
6 ch g Distorted Humor(USA) Abby's Angel (USA) (Touch Gold (USA))
1109a[4]◆

Cominginonmonday (IRE)
Robyn Brisland 45
4 ch m Dandy Man(IRE) Masakira (IRE) (Royal Academy (USA))
3339[5] 4129[9] 4367[8] 8901[12] 9220[12]

Comin' Through (AUS)
George Scott 96
5 b g Fastnet Rock(AUS) Mica's Pride (AUS) (Bite The Bullet (USA))
397a[7] 846a[7] 2609[23] 3315[11] 3987[22] 4805[6]

Commanche Falls *Michael Dods* 74
2 br g Lethal Force(IRE) Joyeaux (Mark Of Esteem (IRE))
(3703) 4516[7] 5934[4] 7896[6]

Commander (FR) *F Chappet* 85
2 b c War Command(USA) Dance Toupie (FR) (Dansili)
4961a[5]

Commander *Denis Gerard Hogan* 63
5 b g Frankel Model Queen (USA) (Kingmambo (USA))
5599a[16]

Commander Cole *Saeed bin Suroor* a110 100
5 b g Kyllachy Welsh Angel (Dubai Destination (USA))
7106[3]◆ 7686[2]◆ 8336[20]

Commander Han (FR)
Stuart Williams a83 77
4 ch g Siyouni(FR) Acentela (IRE) (Shirocco (GER))
1944[3] 2419[2]◆ 2778[13] 3160[7] 3581[6] 4403[14] 5434[8] 7090a[3] 7836[8] 8289[4] 9108[2]◆ 9348[5]◆

Commes (FR) *J-C Rouget* 113
3 b f Le Havre(IRE) Leaupartie (IRE) (Stormy River (FR))
2669a[2] 3905a[2] 6142a[3] 7942a[4]

Commit No Nuisance (IRE)
William Knight a73 70
2 ch c Ivawood(IRE) Free Lance (IRE) (Grand Lodge (USA))
4184[4] 4839[2] 5676[6] 7247a[9] 8850[3]

Communique (IRE) *Mark Johnston* a86 117
4 ch h Casamento(IRE) Midnight Line (USA) (Kris S (USA))
1750[7] (2410) 3314[4] 4093[8] (4848) 6007a[2] 6771a[9] 7500a[8]

Companion *Mark Johnston* a82 87
2 b f Dark Angel(IRE) Merry Jaunt (USA) (Street Sense (USA))
(2020) 2805[9] 3689[3] 4387[3] 5116a[8] 7156[2]

Company Minx (IRE) *Clive Cox* 80
2 gr f Fast Company(IRE) Ice Haven (IRE) (Verglas (IRE))
2918[9] (4798) 6019[2] 7117[6]

Compas Scoobie *Stuart Williams* a89 81
6 br g Kheleyf(USA) Fantastic Santanyi (Fantastic Light (USA))
247[6] 755[3] 1036[10] 1098[5] 1561[5]

Compassionate
Eve Johnson Houghton a45
3 b f Charm Spirit(IRE) Bathilde (IRE) (Generous (IRE))
4768[10]

Compass Point *Robyn Brisland* a69 63
4 b h Helmet(AUS) Takarna (IRE) (Mark Of Esteem (IRE))
6241 8295 (1214)◆ (1378) (1710) 70605 76098 86696 92246 936210

Compatriot (IRE) *Roger Fell* a75 61
5 b g Pour Moi(IRE) Wooded Glade (Oasis Dream)
52908 70539 75458 903310 91348

Compensate *Andrew Balding* a59 55
2 b g Sixties Icon Hala Madrid (Nayef (USA))
636811 71244 84025

Competitionofideas (USA)
Chad C Brown 112
4 b m Speightstown(USA) Devil By Design (USA) (Medaglia d'Oro (USA))
5978a3 7224a3

Completion (IRE) *Charlie Appleby* a87 102
4 b g Arch(USA) Minute Limit (IRE) (Pivotal)
847a16

Complexity (USA) *Chad C Brown* a102
3 b c Maclean's Music(USA) Goldfield (USA) (Yes It's True (USA))
9639a4

Comporta *Ismail Mohammed* a55 48
4 b g Iffraaj Hot Wired (Rock Of Gibraltar (IRE))
22567

Compton Abbey *Alexandra Dunn* a57 62
5 b m Compton Place Bolsena (USA) (Red Ransom (USA))
4783 13359

Compton Brave *J R Jenkins* a43 36
5 b g Compton Place Willmar (IRE) (Zafonic (USA))
15515 3799

Compton Mill *Hughie Morrison* a78 89
7 b g Compton Place Classic Millennium (Midyan (USA))
175712

Compton Poppy *Tony Carroll* a65 65
5 b m Compton Place Miss Poppy (Averti (IRE))
271712 44947 (5375) 63657 711211 81942

Compton Prince *Milton Bradley* a48 43
10 ch g Compton Place Malelane (IRE) (Prince Sabo)
2444 2939 80912 9254 303610

Compton River *Bryan Smart* a53 58
7 b g Compton Place Inagh River (Fasliyev (USA))
264

Compton's Finale
Adrian Paul Keatley a67 68
3 b g Compton Place Finalize (Firebreak)
2113 4083 (5236) 52764◆

Compulsive (IRE) *Gary Moore* a45 48
4 ch g Lope De Vega(IRE) Fand (USA) (Kingmambo (USA))
3911

Computable *Tim Easterby* a58 76
5 ch g Compton Place Kummel Excess (IRE) (Exceed And Excel (AUS))
305612 43648 46257 50423◆ 527610 65039

Comvida (IRE) *Hugo Palmer* a45 50
2 b g Camacho Savida (IRE) (King's Best (USA))
49929 52657 55017 72758 79804 839410 88973 917910 96407

Conaglen *James Bethell* a74 81
3 b c Toronado(IRE) Infamous Angel (Exceed And Excel (AUS))
7852 14588 (1723) 274613 33402

Concello (IRE) *Archie Watson* a89 90
3 b f Society Rock(IRE) Daneville (IRE) (Danetime (IRE))
2027a4 33596 405223 424210 58053

Concierge (IRE) *David Loughnane* a92 93
3 br g Society Rock(IRE) Warm Welcome (Motivator)
893a8 19205 241210 48665 55895 61483 64137 69543 71875 86079 96699

Concrete Rose (USA)
George R Arnold II 112
3 bb f Twirling Candy(USA) Solerina (USA) (Powerscourt)
(5645a)

Concur (IRE) *Rod Millman* a40 49
6 ch g Approve(IRE) Tradmagic (IRE) (Traditionally (USA))
1398 2636 5339

Confab (USA) *George Baker* a45 65
3 gr g Exchange Rate(USA) Callmenancy (USA) (Political Force (USA))
24054 30197 346412 478712 543110 656911 841712

Confederate *Hugo Palmer* a72
4 b g Teofilo(IRE) Merry Jaunt (USA) (Street Sense (USA))
849 2725

Confessional *Tim Easterby* a82 94
12 b g Dubawi(IRE) Golden Nun (Bishop Of Cashel)
25573 28439 35897 38834 43597 56919

Confetti (FR) *Yannick Fouin* a50 54
3 b g Myboycharlie(IRE) You Or No One (IRE) (Falbrav (IRE))
3878a11 5407a8

Confident Kid *Adrian McGuinness* a55 63
6 b g Dubawi(IRE) Longing To Dance (Danehill Dancer (IRE))
(7090a)

Confils (FR) *George Baker* a46 70
3 b f Olympic Glory(IRE) Mambo Mistress (USA) (Kingmambo (USA))
12176 234310 34075 (4232) 44982 (5349)

Confrerie (IRE) *George Baker* a59 65
4 b g Society Rock(IRE) Intellibet One (Compton Place)
11779 13286 1683P 22314◆ 29303 (3187) (3410) 44722 53023 58427 77587 798213 84362

Confrontational (IRE)
Jennie Candlish a84 84
5 b g Footstepsinthesand Chevanah (IRE) (Chevalier (IRE))
8567 10253 12736 19553 25842 33089 38454 41088 57094 61796 71453 (7678) 83424

Conga *Kevin Ryan* 85
3 ch f Footstepsinthesand Palais Glide (Proclamation (IRE))
21034 30505 38159 54193 64085 (7762)

Congratulate *Tim Easterby* a44 51
2 b f Fountain Of Youth(IRE) Bravo (Indian Charlie (USA))
17588 32456 44867 730611

Congress Place (IRE)
Michael Appleby a56 50
3 b f Compton Place Queen Of The Tarts (Royal Applause)
36518 51479 61309 63898 67942

Conker *Charlie Wallis* a28 44
2 b g Swiss Spirit Starlight Walk (Galileo (IRE))
40189 48028 53535

Conkering Hero (IRE) *Joseph Tuite* a80 63
5 ch g Arakan(USA) Brioney (IRE) (Barathea (IRE))
7008 40197 47914 63337 (7109) (7370) 78458 865410 92156

Connaught Ranger (IRE)
Denis Coakley a63 48
4 ch g Finsceal Fior(IRE) Mona Brown (IRE) (Dylan Thomas (IRE))
20058 27149 402811

Connect *A bin Harmash* a25 106
4 b g Roderic O'Connor(IRE) Robema (Cadeaux Genereux)
637a6 844a8 957a9

Connemera Queen *John Butler* a48 45
6 ch m Major Cadeaux Cashleen (USA) (Lemon Drop Kid (USA))
93059 956610

Conqueress (IRE) *Simon Pearce* a30 47
5 ch m Dandy Man(IRE) Sesmen (Inchinor)
15869 20198 29449 32766 374011 50605 58679 613111 940311

Conqueror (AUS)
David A & B Hayes & Tom Dabern 102
2 br c Fastnet Rock(AUS) Diademe (NZ) (Savabeel (AUS))
8137a6

Conquest Hardcandy (USA)
Michelle Nihei 100
5 b m Candy Ride(ARG) Dade Babe (USA) (Cimarron Secret (USA))
6491a5 7920a13

Consequences (IRE) *Ian Williams* a81 80
4 b g Dandy Man(IRE) Originate (Oasis Dream)
189211 33094 38835 440615 50404 66313 74703 76076 82205 85499

Consortium (IRE) *Alastair Ralph* a49 44
7 b g Teofilo(IRE) Wish List (IRE) (Mujadil (USA))
221711

Conspiritor *Charles Hills* a66 74
3 b g Charm Spirit(IRE) Royal Confidence (Royal Applause)
32613 36386 (4773) 52922 65583 71297 797512

Constancio (IRE) *Donald McCain*
6 b g Authorized(IRE) Senora Galilei (IRE) (Galileo (IRE))
257811

Constant *David O'Meara* a38 74
3 ch g Dutch Art West Of The Moon (Pivotal)
20783 34795 37195 386822 500210 57866 63429

Constantino (IRE) *F Vermeulen* a81 67
6 b g Danehill Dancer(IRE) Messias Da Silva (USA) (Tale Of The Cat (USA))
115a3 7136a4

Constantinople (IRE)
David A & B Hayes & Tom Dabern 115
3 b c Galileo(IRE) One Moment In Time (IRE) (Danehill (USA))
(3063a) 40172 55852 63532 8361a4◆ 8844a13

Constanzia *Jamie Osborne* a67 64
2 b f Dandy Man(IRE) Mara Grey (IRE) (Azamour (IRE))
22827 34916 (3579) 58852 62216 63723 67288 70796 75156 79945 91969

Constituent *Michael Appleby* a54 35
4 b g High Chaparral(IRE) Arum Lily (USA) (Woodman (USA))
403 18512 32054 34978 368615

Constitutional (IRE) *K R Burke* a63 46
2 b g Society Rock(IRE) Last Hooray (Royal Applause)
19683 26866 40326 60329 (7306) 75827 90609 93463 95412

Constraint *Andrew Balding* a57 67
3 b f Sinndar(IRE) Inhibition (Nayef (USA))
23016 27319 50483 55964 636611 85006

Consultant *Andrew Balding* a46 74
4 b g Kodiac Mary Goodnight (King's Best (USA))
14183 235310 279314

Contingency Fee *Phil McEntee* a72 64
4 b g Helmet(AUS) Hearsay (Dubai Destination (USA))
1606 2042 3694 5042 5893 16806 (1858) (1935) (2127) 23455 24715 37787 42156 4686a2 502510 53544 552812 (5679) 63036 65563 67963 731810 90336 (9221) 93334 95113

Continuum *Peter Hedger* a73 86
10 bb g Dansili Clepsydra (Sadler's Wells (USA))
2462 559P 47919 67202 75582 81968 92046 95114

Contract Kid (IRE) *Mark Loughnane* a39 44
2 b g G Force(IRE) Danamight (IRE) (Danetime (IRE))
19106 43026 57045

Contrapposto (IRE)
Mrs A M O'Shea 84
5 b g Cacique(IRE) Interim Payment (USA) (Red Ransom (USA))
7216a14

Contrast (IRE) *Michael Easterby* a80 65
5 ch g Dutch Art Israar (Machiavellian (USA))
2056 3518 7405 12329 141813 22917 394112 46583 (6324) (7560) 91777

Contrebasse *Tim Easterby* a60 76
4 b g Champs Elysees Viola Da Braccio (IRE) (Vettori (IRE))
28196 39739 43702 51792 (5897) 63403 70014 78304 81296 85132

Contrive (IRE) *Roger Varian* a95 99
4 gr m Mastercraftsman(IRE) Sixpenny Sweets (IRE) (Dalakhani (IRE))
194113 26082 33426 4706a6 59496 900211

Conundrum *Jedd O'Keeffe* 81
3 ch g Sir Percy Famusa (Medicean)
(1819) 23333 (3195) 43212 49883 65894 71415

Convene (IRE) *K R Burke* a54
2 b g Kodiac Altogether (IRE) (King's Best (USA))
76276

Converter (IRE) *John Butler* a84 62
3 b c Swiss Spirit Beylerbey (USA) (Street Cry (IRE))
17294 22554 34799 47938 842011

Convertible (IRE) *Hugo Palmer* a71
2 b g Helmet(AUS) Empress Ella (IRE) (Holy Roman Emperor (IRE))
87094

Convict *William Haggas* 95
2 ch c Australia Tweed (Sakhee (USA))
61546 70006◆ (7586)◆ 81242 (8462)

Cookie Ring (IRE) *Liam Bailey* a40 28
8 b g Moss Vale(IRE) Talah (Danehill (USA))
18013 46512 198310

Cookupastorm (IRE) *Martin Smith* a47 63
3 b f Camacho No Clubs (IRE) (Red Clubs (IRE))
14927 29049 37424 43433 45566 604810 702413 870410 92098

Coolagh Forest (IRE) *Paul D'Arcy* a83 107
3 b c Elzaam(AUS) Ekagra (Barathea (IRE))
903 3913 (1945) (2369) 44906 55839 64258 (6998)◆ (8126)◆ 833618 9125a7

Coolagh Magic *Seb Spencer* a83 79
3 b g Sepoy(AUS) Miliika (Green Desert (USA))
(21) (506) 8383◆ 13889 17624 21497 34796 38444 43683 53352 75408 80258 95128

Cool And Dry (ITY) *A Botti* 96
2 b c Sakhee's Secret Penfection (IRE) (Orpen (USA))
8789a4

Cool Echo *J R Jenkins* a58 73
5 b m Mount Nelson Ellcon (IRE) (Royal Applause)
(132) 36511 94113 14786 22356 31426

Cooler Mike (CAN)
Nicholas Nosowenko 47
4 ch g Giant Gizmo(USA) Executive Affair (CAN) (Bold Executive (CAN))
7226a6

Cool Exhibit *Simon Crisford* a86 81
3 b g Showcasing Frigid (Indian Ridge (IRE))
14583 20235 34653

Cool Kitty *Rebecca Menzies* a53 55
3 b f Kodiac Ligeia (Rail Link)
2748 3416 148614

Coolongolook *Gordon Elliott* a81 90
4 b g Invincible Spirit(IRE) Cascata (IRE) (Montjeu (IRE))
7216a16

Cool Possibility (IRE) *Charles Hills* 64
3 b g Dark Angel(IRE) Pink Diva (IRE) (Giant's Causeway (USA))
279012 31843 36486 42256 47376

Cool Reflection (IRE)
Sofie Lanslots a81 85
3 b g Showcasing Miss Lacey (IRE) (Diktat)
24129 29976 44952 50906 61084 8449a8

Cool Sphere (USA) *Robert Cowell* a83 83
2 ch c Orb(USA) Faringdon Circle (USA) (Speightstown (USA))
31902◆ 401212 43733 49932 554211 (6047) 61472 68992 7876a3

Cool Spirit *Olly Williams* a45 84
4 b g Swiss Spirit Marmot Bay (IRE) (Kodiac)
2306 (2788) 53957 56705 69218 826711

Cool Strutter (IRE) *John Spearing* a48 53
7 b g Kodiac Cassava (IRE) (Vettori (IRE))
22873 29249 42193 45004 50836 61073 79866 82799

Cool The Jets *F Vermeulen* a65 65
4 b g Swiss Spirit Small Fortune (Anabaa (USA))
992a10

Cool To Be A Cat (FR) *Ian Williams* a41
2 b g Style Vendome(FR) Forward Feline (IRE) (One Cool Cat (USA))
95679

Cool Vixen (IRE)
Mrs John Harrington 89
2 b f Dandy Man(IRE) Cool Tarifa (IRE) (One Cool Cat (USA))
6690a9

Cool Walk *Derek Shaw* a41
3 br f Poet's Voice Lady Elalmadol (IRE) (Shamardal (USA))
21510

Cooperess *Adrian Wintle* a50 52
6 b m Sixties Icon Vilnius (Imperial Dancer)
677 10159 121510 25137 48706 54983 60513 63633 65296 728613 80097

Coorg (IRE) *John Butler* a70 49
7 ch g Teofilo(IRE) Creese (Halling (USA))
129210 15887 22172◆

Copacabana Dancer (IRE)
Joseph Tuite a69 59
2 b g Zebedee Tipperary Boutique (IRE) (Danehill Dancer (IRE))
16515 (1879) 22285 30397

Copal *Ralph Beckett* a75 72
3 b g Dark Angel(IRE) Mirabilis (USA) (Lear Fan (USA))
27656 347110 44534

Copia Verborum (IRE) *J S Bolger* 85
3 b g Vocalised(USA) Gold Focus (IRE) (Intense Focus (USA))
13066 1600a6

Copleys Walk (IRE)
Mohammed Hussain a61 92
7 b g Excellent Art Silk Slippers (Oasis Dream)
869a7

Coply (FR) *R Chotard* 70
2 b c Reply(IRE) Coriante (FR) (Indian Rocket)
4228a9 5263a3 5713a2 6060a2 6384a12

Coppelia (GER) *Frau C Barsig* 93
4 b m Soldier Hollow C'Est L'Amour (GER) (Whipper (USA))
3907a4

Copper And Five *John Gosden* a21
3 ch g Paco Boy(IRE) Peachez (Observatory (USA))
9304

Copper Baked (FR) *L Rovisse* a61 53
5 bb m Never On Sunday(FR) Shakila (Cadeaux Genereux)
7136a13 7861a13 9014a10

Copper Knight (IRE) *Tim Easterby* a111 107
5 b g Sir Prancealot(IRE) Mystic Dream (Oasis Dream)
19464◆ 25572 (2775) 30973 334412◆ 43312 (4932) 56117 64235 66987 719321 80043 81822

Copperlight (IRE) *Ben Haslam* a65 37
2 b g Poet's Voice Delighted (IRE) (Danehill (USA))
70679 74166 830212 (9346)◆ 94492

Copper Rose (IRE) *Mark Johnston* a71 56
3 b f Lawman(FR) Rose Of Mooncoin (IRE) (Brief Truce (USA))
4428 7234 10642 15686 240610

Coral Beach (IRE) *A P O'Brien* a100 103
3 b f Zoffany(IRE) Abbasharjah (GER) (Tiger Hill (IRE))
2669a8 31158 40524 5223a5 5645a4 7220a6 87084

Coral Caye *Steph Hollinshead* a31 49
5 b m Pastoral Pursuits Vermilion Creek (Makbul)
53211

Corando *C Laffon-Parias* a87 98
3 b c Dark Angel(IRE) Norway Cross (Cape Cross (IRE))
3108a2

Corazonada (IRE)
Ismail Mohammed 64
2 ch f Camacho Giant Dancer (USA) (Giant's Causeway (USA))
74615

Corazon Espinado (IRE)
Simon Dow a91 89
4 b h Iffraaj Three Decades (IRE) (Invincible Spirit (IRE))
11435 13566 24874 (3318) 429911 82893 86062 92004 96692

Corelli (USA) *John Gosden* a103 107
4 b g Point Of Entry(USA) Vignette (USA) (Diesis)
24402 40967 59092 64202 695815

Corgi *Hughie Morrison* 105
4 b g So You Think(NZ) Ermyn Express (Selkirk (USA))
27423◆ 40534 566213

Corinthia Knight (IRE)
Archie Watson a111 106
4 ch g Society Rock(IRE) Victoria Lodge (IRE) (Grand Lodge (USA))
1365 5638 8773 9872 11058 12953 (1839) 409526 (5154) 59275 61498 66989 70582 (7497a) 8328a3 88514 90046 91662 94787 95716 96123

Corinthian *Derek Shaw* a70 93
6 b g Sea The Stars(IRE) Contradictive (USA) (Kingmambo (USA))
9156 129112

Corinthian Girl (IRE) *David Lanigan* a68 57
3 ch f Raven's Pass(USA) Elegant Beauty (Olden Times)
29093 34643 47685 57312 63934

Corinthian Star *George Scott*
3 b f Camelot Star Search (Zamindar (USA))
294311

Corked (IRE) *Alistair Whillans* a64 54
6 b m Mastercraftsman(IRE) Dama'A (IRE) (Green Desert (USA))
1256 4798 8142◆ 13993 17108 38436 45126 509910 54387 61023 73353 (7578) 79563 88184 (9391)

Cormier (IRE) *Stef Keniry* a69 72
3 b g Born To Sea(IRE) Scotch Bonnet (IRE) (Montjeu (IRE))
8043 20756 35852 51757 63407 76436 803315 84237 88378

Cormolain (FR) *Andrea Marcialis* a62 28
2 b c Rajsaman(FR) Coutances (Shamardal (USA))
6485a7

Cormorant (IRE) *A P O'Brien* a98 99
2 gr c Kingman Shemya (FR) (Dansili)
7217a5 87522

Cornborough *Mark Walford* 81
8 ch g Sir Percy Emirates First (IRE) (In The Wings)
26282◆ 43927 489210

Corncrake *Richard Hannon* a66 88
3 ro c Mastercraftsman(IRE) Harvest Queen (IRE) (Spinning World (USA))
14956 220811 27694 (4109)◆ (4663) (4830)◆

Corndavon Lad (IRE)
Richard Fahey 73
2 b g Camacho Wild Ways (Green Desert (USA))
22885 27068 33712 39984 46473 53908 637521

Cornerstone Lad *Micky Hammond* 77
5 b g Delegator Chapel Corner (IRE) (Alhaarth (IRE))
32942 (8635)

Cornwall Cottage *A Schaerer*
5 b g Lawman(FR) Bit By Bit (Rail Link)
592a7 694a5

Coronado Beach *Mlle A Wattel* a83
2 b c Toronado(IRE) Bay Laurel (IRE) (Baltic King)
(6584a) (8508a)

Coronation Cottage
Malcolm Saunders a69 73
5 b m Pastoral Pursuits Avrilo (Piccolo)
(2206) 24737 30322 35319 42308 52896 57936 723015 (8501) 90133 93905

Coronet *John Gosden* 117
5 gr m Dubawi(IRE) Approach (Darshaan)
24104 (4430a) (6265a) 83356

Corralejo (IRE) *John Wainwright* a4 18
3 b g Heeraat(IRE) Lady Caprice (Kyllachy)
1723[12] **2506[10]** 3157[9]
Correggio *Micky Hammond* 53
9 ch g Bertolini(USA) Arian Da (Superlative)
3054[7]◆ **3511[5]** 4446[10] 5473[6]
Corrida De Toros (IRE) *Ed de Giles* a68 67
3 b g Lope De Vega(IRE) The Shrew (Dansili)
2900[8] 3696[4] 4225[5] **4767[6]** 5797[11] 7681[7]
Corton Lad *Keith Dalgleish* a69 73
9 b g Refuse To Bend(IRE) Kelucia (IRE) (Grand Lodge (USA))
2436[10] **2962[2]** **3250[4]** 3925[5] 4274[5] 4491[4] 4724[5] 5301[4] **(5621)** 6658[3] 6933[7] 7368[9] 7510[4]
Corton Lass *Keith Dalgleish* a2 48
4 gr m Showcasing Elbow Beach (Choisir (AUS))
2324[5] 2678[11] 2789[8] 3723[7] 4493[10] 5491[6] **6574[2]** 6936[12] 7214[11] 7367[17] 7737[3] 8235[5]
Corvair (IRE) *Simon Crisford* a85
2 b c Toronado(IRE) Nagham (IRE) (Camacho)
9085[2] *9392[2]* ***(9631)***
Cosa Orga (IRE) *Brian Meehan* 54
2 b c Golden Horn New Morning (IRE) (Sadler's Wells (USA))
7162[10]
Cosmeapolitan *Alan King* a101 60
6 b g Mawatheeq(USA) Cosmea (Compton Place)
368[2]◆ **878[3]** 1422[10] 2105[10] 2832[14] *9055[5]*
Cosmelli (ITY) *Gay Kelleway* a101 47
6 b g Mr Vegas(IRE) Victorian Girl (GER) (Lomitas)
82[7] *349[5]* *1017[6]* ***1483[2]***◆ *1943[4]* *3466[3]* 3952[17] ***4382[5]*** *5437[6]* *8350[10]* *9419[9]*
Cosmic Chatter *Ruth Carr* a38 57
9 b g Paris House Paradise Eve (Bahamian Bounty)
2122[11] **2580[3]** 2847[8] 3221[12] 3657[3] 3921[8] 4440[11] 4978[9] 5767[4] 7761[2] *8266[9]* *8469[8]* 8637[7]
Cosmic City *J-P Gauvin* a85 85
7 gr g Elusive City(USA) Cosmic Fire (FR) (Dalakhani (IRE))
5410a[3]
Cosmic Horizon (IRE)
Joseph Patrick O'Brien 94
3 b c Excelebration(IRE) Flavia Tatiana (IRE) (Holy Roman Emperor (IRE))
6693a[13]
Cosmic Landscape *William Jarvis* a79 75
4 b g Lawman(FR) Dancingintheclouds (IRE) (Rainbow Quest (USA))
(239)◆ *945[6]* 1418[5] ***1566[3]*** *6888[4]*
Cosmic Law (IRE) *Richard Fahey* a100 99
3 b g No Nay Never(USA) Dhamma (USA) (Broad Brush (USA))
2525[2] 3865[4] ***4379[2]*** 5664[14]
Cosmic Power (IRE)
Eve Johnson Houghton 80
2 br g Power Dhamma (USA) (Broad Brush (USA))
5374[2] 6415[2]◆ **(6911)** 7409[9]
Cosmic Princess *Hughie Morrison* a65
2 b f Kingman Galaxy Highflyer (Galileo (IRE))
8602[6]
Cosmic Ray *Les Eyre* a58 62
7 b g Phoenix Reach(IRE) Beat Seven (Beat Hollow)
1251[3] *792[10]* *1339[7]* (1958) **2330[2]** 2738[10] 7060[4] 7545[7] 8033[4]
Cosmo Charlie (USA)
Doug Watson a111
5 br g Stay Thirsty(USA) Lake Como (USA) (Salt Lake (USA))
638a[3] *1114a[10]*
Cosmogyral (IRE)
Dominic Ffrench Davis a59 56
4 b m Camelot Fanditha (IRE) (Danehill Dancer (IRE))
(257)
Costello *Mike Murphy* a63 61
2 b g Makfi Samba Chryss (IRE) (Galileo (IRE))
5676[4] ***7605[4]*** *8288[8]* *8699[7]*
Cotai Again (IRE) *Charles Hills* 76
2 b g Kodiac Incessant (IRE) (Elusive Quality (USA))
4098[7] **5339[2]** 5879[2]◆ 6403[3] 6807[5]
Cote D'Azur *Les Eyre* a86 88
6 ch g Champs Elysees Florentia (Medicean)
1461[5] 1813[5] 2486[5] 6513[6] 6998[5]◆ 7185[8]◆ *8692[5]* *8918[2]* *9199[6]*
Coto Donana *Ed Vaughan* a60
2 b f Kingman Nyarhini (Fantastic Light (USA))
9130[4]◆
Cottingham *Kevin Frost* a58 44
4 b g Dalakhani(IRE) Echelon (Danehill (USA))
62[3] *1145[6]* *6663[4]* *7578[10]* *8008[2]* *8256[5]* *8417[11]*
Cotton Club (IRE) *George Boughey* a85 82
8 b g Amadeus Wolf Slow Jazz (USA) (Chief's Crown (USA))
5290[3] 6016[4] (6556) 6901[4] 7231[8] ***7819[2]*** *9215[5]*
Cottonopolis *Mark Johnston* a66 67
2 b c Ruler Of The World(IRE) Jamboree Girl (Bahamian Bounty)
5838[2] *9624[6]*
Cotton Socks (IRE) *Ann Duffield* a41 40
4 b g Dream Ahead(USA) Kartella (IRE) (Whipper (USA))
4078[12] 5038[11]
Cotubanama *Mick Channon* 71
3 b f Heeraat(IRE) Saona Island (Bahamian Bounty)
1894[10] 2144[10] **2356[2]** 3193[4] 3892[5] 4420[8] 4908[7] 5308[2] 6638[4] 7065[9] 7527[5] 8009[3]
Cougar Kid (IRE) *John O'Shea* a47 42
8 b g Yeats(IRE) Western Skylark (IRE) (Westerner)
2468[6] **2733[7]** 4868[7]
Could Be Gold (IRE) *John Butler* a15
5 b g Delegator Outshine (Exceed And Excel (AUS))
3142[12] 3533[11] *3996[12]*
Could Be King *John M Oxx* 102
3 b g Bated Breath Poyle Dee Dee (Oasis Dream)
1600a[3]
Couldn't Could She *Adam West* a42 70
4 b m Sixties Icon Emperatriz (Holy Roman Emperor (IRE))
2631[9] 2998[3] (3186)◆ 3276[8] **(4215)** 4499[5] 5316[8] 5795[4] 6568[3] 7229[5] 7984[14] *8641[6]*
Couleur Cafe (IRE) *Wido Neuroth* 70
2 b f Rock Of Gibraltar(IRE) Chiquette (Selkirk (USA))
7495a[6]
Coulonces (FR) *M Delzangles* a59 77
4 b m Le Havre(IRE) Talwin (IRE) (Alhaarth (IRE))
6521a[9]
Count Calabash (IRE)
Eve Johnson Houghton a109 98
5 b g Big Bad Bob(IRE) Tinaheely (IRE) (Intikhab (USA))
825 ***(758)*** *1422[6]* 2827[7]
Count D'orsay (IRE) *Tim Easterby* a63 100
3 b g Dandy Man(IRE) Deira (USA) (Green Desert (USA))
(5791)◆ 6476[15] 6976[2] (7700)◆ 8099[2]◆ **(8340)**
Counterfeit *Paul George* a11 24
4 b m Iffraaj Money Note (Librettist (USA))
4115[14] 6107[13] **7973[8]**
Counter Spirit (IRE)
Ismail Mohammed a82 71
5 b m Invincible Spirit(IRE) Counterclaim (Pivotal)
2977[9]
Counting Sheep (IRE)
Gordon Elliott a61 70
3 b g Morpheus Sheppard's Watch (Night Shift (USA))
486[3]
Count Montecristo (FR) *Roger Fell* a51 52
7 b g Siyouni(FR) Blackberry Pie (USA) (Gulch (USA))
63[5]
Count Of Amazonia (IRE)
Richard Hannon a80 71
2 b c Lope De Vega(IRE) Queen Myrine (IRE) (Oratorio (IRE))
6912[6] 7392[6] ***(8424)***
Count Otto (IRE) *Amanda Perrett* a85 96
4 b g Sir Prancealot(IRE) Dessert Flower (IRE) (Intikhab (USA))
1829[8] 2402[11] *3492[6]* 4186[8] (4545) 5524[11] 5661[6] 5911[2] 6565[2] **6953[5]** 7175[3] 7697[9] *8607[5]* *9660[7]*
Country *William Haggas* 101
3 b g Dubawi(IRE) Birjand (Green Desert (USA))
1458[6] (1975) (4989)◆ **(5973)**◆ 6725[4] 8092[8]
Country Blue (FR) *Mrs A Malzard* 56
10 bl g Country Reel(USA) Exica (FR) (Exit To Nowhere (USA))
2671a[2] **3173a[2]** 3641a[3] 4685a[8] 5232[4] 6553a[6]
Country House (USA) *William Mott* a117
3 ch c Lookin At Lucky(USA) Quake Lake (USA) (War Chant (USA))
(2425a)
Country'N'Western (FR)
Robert Eddery a79 71
7 b g Samum(GER) Cracking Melody (Shamardal (USA))
404[5] ***703[2]***◆ 1463[7] *1840[4]* *2351[4]* 5993[7] 7053[10] 8033[6] 8414[6] (8663) *9033[12]*
Country Rose (IRE) *Ronald Harris* a46 60
3 b f Bungle Inthejungle Fitrah (IRE) (Tamayuz)
3422[7] **4374[9]** 5014[5] 6851[4] *8194[9]*
Coup De Gold (IRE)
David Thompson a63 69
3 br g Maxios Astroglia (USA) (Montjeu (IRE))
1484[4] 4520[7] 5792[7] *6940[12]* *8814[5]* *9467[8]*
Courteva *Richard Price* a36
4 b m Multiplex Court Princess (Mtoto)
9011[7] *9368[8]*
Court House (IRE) *John Gosden* a111 110
4 b g Dawn Approach(IRE) Crossanza (IRE) (Cape Cross (IRE))
(143) *565[3]* ***879[2]*** *1921[6]* *9587[2]*
Courtney Rose *Ivan Furtado* 8
2 b f Heeraat(IRE) Dockside Strike (Docksider (USA))
5145[9] 5547[8] **7179[8]**
Court Of Appeal (IRE) *James Tate* a64 60
2 b c Golden Horn Gwael (USA) (A.P. Indy (USA))
7055[7] ***7821[4]***
Court Order *James Tate* a49 64
3 b c Lawman(FR) Polygon (USA) (Dynaformer (USA))
6169[3] *7035[7]*◆
Court Poet *Charlie Appleby* a78 96
3 b g Dubawi(IRE) Belenkaya (USA) (Giant's Causeway (USA))
3031a[6]
Courtside (FR) *David O'Meara* a76 82
4 ch g Siyouni(FR) Memoire (FR) (Sadler's Wells (USA))
1457[11] **1813[2]**
Cousin Khee *Hughie Morrison* a68 58
12 b g Sakhee(USA) Cugina (Distant Relative)
8414[8]
Coutts De Ville *Paul George* a40 29
3 ch f Dawn Approach(IRE) Samdaniya (Machiavellian (USA))
3839[8]
Covefe (FR) *Frau Hella Sauer* a76 71
3 b f Acclamation Mythical Border (USA) (Johannesburg (USA))
3028a[4]
Coverham (IRE) *James Eustace* a78 76
5 b g Bated Breath Mark Too (IRE) (Mark Of Esteem (IRE))
1561[8] *1880[2]* 2418[4] ***(2971)*** *3462[6]* 4336[3] 5144[3] 5870[4] *6350[5]* *7684[4]* 8206[7]
Covfefe (USA) *Brad H Cox* a114
3 b f Into Mischief(USA) Antics (USA) (Unbridled (USA))
(8769a)
Coviglia (IRE) *Jacqueline Coward* a72 68
5 gr g Invincible Spirit(IRE) Bright Snow (USA) (Gulch (USA))
2509[15] 3199[5] 4207[3] 4875[4] 6102[9] 7364[6]
(9453)◆
Cowboy Soldier (IRE)
Robert Cowell a98 93
4 b g Kodiac Urgele (FR) (Zafonic (USA))
(1938)◆ 2775[6] *3582[9]*
Cox Bazar (FR) *Ivan Furtado* a43 68
5 b g Nombre Premier Dame De Montlebeau (FR) (Dyhim Diamond (IRE))
2030[10] 3375[7] **4100[9]** 4654[10] 5180[9] 5972[9] 7800a[9] *8401[9]*
Cozone *Amanda Perrett* a50
2 b c Pour Moi(IRE) Bella Nouf (Dansili)
9052[11]
Cozy Sky (USA) *Gordon Elliott* a39 45
3 rg f Animal Kingdom(USA) Lets Get Cozzy (USA) (Cozzene (USA))
7488[9]
Crackaway (FR) *Harry Dunlop* a62 74
3 b g Whipper(USA) Ellary (FR) (Equerry (USA))
2141[10] **3538[4]** 4176[7]
Cracker Factory *Alan King* a63 63
4 b g Poet's Voice Pure Song (Singspiel (IRE))
8591[10]
Crackin Dream (IRE) *Clive Cox* a70 67
3 b g Oasis Dream Gothic Dance (IRE) (Dalakhani (IRE))
1516[7] 2098[10] 5050[2] 5358[3] *7447[8]* ***(7811)***
Cracking Name (IRE)
David Marnane a38 71
5 ch m Famous Name Christmas Cracker (FR) (Alhaarth (IRE))
3843[5]
Cracking Speed (IRE)
Richard Hannon a68 72
3 gr c Alhebayeb(IRE) Summer Glow (IRE) (Exceed And Excel (AUS))
2204[10] 2772[4] **(3406)**◆
Crafty Madam (IRE) *K J Condon* a85 98
5 gr m Mastercraftsman(IRE) Dani Ridge (IRE) (Indian Ridge (IRE))
(4353a) 6379[7] **7934a[3]**
Craigburn *Tom Clover* a37 66
2 b g Casamento(IRE) Craighall (Dubawi (IRE))
1879[9] 2282[6] **4114[4]** 4647[9] 5353[3] *5885[4]* (7284) 7896[19]
Crakadawn *Chelsea Banham* a24
3 ch f Excelebration(IRE) Atacama Sunrise (Desert Sun)
8689[8] *9439[14]*
Crakehall Lad (IRE) *Andrew Crook*
8 ch g Manduro(GER) My Uptown Girl (Dubai Destination (USA))
8072[12]
Cranberry *Richard Hughes* a80
2 ch f Toronado(IRE) Raymi Coya (CAN) (Van Nistelrooy (USA))
7547[2]◆ ***(8706)*** *9063[3]*
Craneur *Harry Dunlop* a68 72
3 ch g Showcasing Paris Winds (IRE) (Galileo (IRE))
2517[6] 3311[5] 3809[9] 4931[2] 5497[4] **6083[2]** 6671[2] 7413[11]
Crantock Bay *George Scott* 84
3 b g Havana Gold(IRE) Orton Park (IRE) (Moss Vale (IRE))
3661[2] **4367[2]** 4827[2]
Crash Helmet *Micky Hammond* a71 43
4 b g Helmet(AUS) Hot Secret (Sakhee's Secret)
6260[8] *7652[9]*
Craving (IRE) *Simon Crisford* a91 77
4 b h Equiano(FR) Pretty Bonnie (Kyllachy)
(197a) *573a[4]* *1001[10]* ***(1322a)*** 1748a[8]
Craylands *Michael Bell* 81
2 b f Golden Horn Madame Defarge (IRE) (Motivator)
4918[2] **5588[2]**◆ 7826[4]
Crazy Daisy *Jane Chapple-Hyam*
3 b f Gregorian(IRE) Darling Daisy (Komaite (USA))
547[5]
Crazy Love *Mick Channon* a44
2 b f Sixties Icon Follow The Faith (Piccolo)
9211[9] ***9631[11]***
Crazy Spin *Ivan Furtado* a56 46
3 b f Epaulette(AUS) George's Gift (Haafhd)
4001[0] *931[3]* *1593[3]* 1957[7] *2350[4]* *(2531)* *3204[2]* *4029[10]* *8270[9]* *9220[4]* *9410[2]*◆ ***(9544)***
Crazy Tornado (IRE)
Keith Dalgleish a59 56
6 b g Big Bad Bob(IRE) All Day (CHI) (Jaded Dancer (USA))
2328[3] 2681[11] 3177[7] 3721[11] 4003[8] 4915[10] 5100[9] 5766[12] 5899[2] 6655[8] 6937[9] 7508[7]
Creationist (USA) *Roger Charlton* a98 29
3 b g Noble Mission Bargain Blitz (USA) (Rahy (USA))
(133) *(523)* *1926[5]* 3341[9] 4342[9] *8222[5]* *8701[4]*◆ ***9055[2]***◆ *9454[4]*
Creative Talent (IRE) *Tony Carroll* a66 75
7 br g Mastercraftsman(IRE) Pitrizzia (Lando (GER))
2575 *792[2]* *(1015)*◆ *1362[2]* *2692[9]* 3572[4] 3766[6] (5803) 6507[7] 7270[7] *9256[10]* ***9609[2]***
Creativity (FR) *J E Hammond* a56 69
4 b m Motivator Kirkinola (Selkirk (USA))
6651a[5]
Creativity *Richard Fahey* a70 65
2 ch f Mayson Fantasize (Groom Dancer (USA))
5456[4] 6710[4] *7388[3]* ***7871[2]***◆ *8402[6]*
Credenza (IRE) *A P O'Brien* a75 104
3 b f Galileo(IRE) Bye Bye Birdie (IRE) (Oasis Dream)
2157a[6] 2451a[3] 2642a[7] 6239a[5] 6692a[2] **7242a[3]** 7635a[10]
Creedence (AUS)
David A & B Hayes & Tom Dabern 88
4 b g Helmet(AUS) Boracay (AUS) (Red Ransom (USA))
8803a[10]
Creek Harbour (IRE) *Milton Bradley* a68 56
4 b g Kodiac Allegheny Creek (IRE) (Teofilo (IRE))
31[8] ***154[2]*** *508[5]* *965[5]* *1355[4]* *1933[7]* *2774[3]* *(3688)* *4764[3]* *5281[7]* ***(5889)*** *6631[7]* *7078[4]* *7552[7]* *7855[5]* *9013[11]* *9386[9]* *9627[2]*
Creek Horizon *Saeed bin Suroor* a71
2 b g Invincible Spirit(IRE) Satin Kiss (USA) (Seeking The Gold (USA))
8455[5] *8912[3]*
Creek Island (IRE) *Mark Johnston* a65 74
3 ch c Iffraaj Jumeirah Palm Star (Invincible Spirit (IRE))
9433◆ *1195[5]* *1381[3]* *2200[7]* **(3226)** 3957[6] **4773[2]** 5124[5] 5557[3] 6164[4] 7512[4] 7906[7] *8548[8]*
Cressida *John Gosden* a82
2 b f Dansili Modern Look (Zamindar (USA))
(4502)◆
Crew Dragon (FR)
M Delcher Sanchez 82
2 b c Poet's Voice Vintage Red (FR) (Turtle Bowl (IRE))
1657a[2]
Crikeyitswhykie *Derek Shaw* a36 40
4 b g Piccolo Kitty Kitty Cancan (Warrshan (USA))
8341[3] *9731[2]*
Crimean Queen *Charlie Fellowes* a67 44
3 b f Iffraaj Victoria Cross (IRE) (Mark Of Esteem (IRE))
2322[3]◆ 3797[8]
Crime Of Passion (IRE)
Jamie Osborne a65 66
2 b f Acclamation Golden Shadow (IRE) (Selkirk (USA))
1821[7] 3259[5] 4373[7] **(6041)** *6436[3]* *7029[10]* *8750[4]* *8841[7]*
Crimewave (IRE) *Tom Clover* a78 77
3 b g Teofilo(IRE) Crossover (Cape Cross (IRE))
2766[7] *3584[5]* 4306[4] **4838[3]** 5445[4] 5959[5] *6840[5]* *7773[4]* *8652[2]* *9047[5]* *9273[3]*
Crimson King (IRE)
Michael Appleby a72 54
3 b g Kingman Toi Et Moi (IRE) (Galileo (IRE))
9028[3] ***9305[2]*** *9642[4]*
Crimson Kiss (IRE) *Pat Phelan* a57 49
3 ch f Sepoy(AUS) Crimson Year (USA) (Dubai Millennium)
556[9] 5092[6] 5561[9] 6569[13]
Crimson Princess *Nikki Evans* a44 45
4 ch m Sayif(IRE) Crimson Queen (Red Ransom (USA))
3352[12] 4376[10] **5678[6]** 6018[10] 6365[6]
Crimson Skies (IRE) *John Davies* a40 42
4 ch m Declaration Of War(USA) Emily Blake (IRE) (Lend A Hand)
5201[8] **5694[10]** 6341[14] *6945[10]* 7587[10]
Crindle Carr (IRE) *John Flint* a48 53
5 ch g Compton Place Arley Hall (Excellent Art)
619[7] 4868[9] 6366[7]
Crisaff's Queen *Agostino Affe'* 92
3 b f Zoffany(IRE) Monster Munchie (JPN) (Deep Impact (JPN))
2161a[12]
Criseyde *Sylvester Kirk* a53
2 b f Brazen Beau(AUS) Flemish School (Dutch Art)
9322[5] ***9506[8]***
Crispina *Ralph Beckett* a62
2 b f Kingman Dawn Of Empire (USA) (Empire Maker (USA))
8602[10]
Cristal Breeze (IRE)
William Haggas a84 88
3 b g Gale Force Ten Sapphire Spray (IRE) (Viking Ruler (AUS))
1676[4] (2334)◆ *(3324)* 3859[5] 4669[3] 5442[3]◆ **6451[2]**
Cristal Marvelous (FR) *M Boutin* 73
2 b f Captain Marvelous(IRE) Cristal Gem (Cadeaux Genereux)
4949a[4] **(6060a)** 8330a[6]
Cristal Pallas Cat (IRE)
Roger Ingram a52 54
4 b g Kodiac Flower Of Kent (USA) (Diesis)
250[7] *717[3]* *1060[8]* *1731[5]* *3007[3]* *3989[6]* **(5842)** 6758[5] 7028[6] *8255[10]* *9157[4]*
Cristal Spirit *George Baker* a77 78
4 b g Nathaniel(IRE) Celestial Girl (Dubai Destination (USA))
1463[2] 2400[4] *3467[3]* 3940[2] 5540[16] *6929[2]* **(8523)**
Cristofano Allori (IRE)
Abdulaziz Al-Kathiri 91
5 b h Shamardal(USA) Perfect Touch (USA) (Miswaki (USA))
892a[4]
Critical Thinking (IRE)
David Loughnane a81 71
5 b g Art Connoisseur(IRE) Cookie Cutter (IRE) (Fasliyev (USA))
917 ***260[3]*** *623[6]* *812[7]* *914[8]* 4108[5] 4320[6] *4767[7]* 5178[10] 5816[7] *6026[8]*
Critical Time *William Haggas* a81 77
3 b f Pivotal Winds Of Time (IRE) (Danehill (USA))
4298[5] 4806[2]◆ 5690[2] ***(7583)*** 8761[15]
Critical Voltage (IRE)
Richard Fahey a25 71
3 gr c Dark Angel(IRE) Elektra Marino (Mount Nelson)
6944[7] **7313[3]**
Critique (IRE) *Ed Walker* a62
2 b g Cacique(IRE) Noble Fantasy (GER) (Big Shuffle (USA))
8858[11] ***9326[7]*** *9509[10]*
Crochet (USA) *Hugo Palmer* 26
3 b f First Defence(USA) Magic Motif (USA) (Giant's Causeway (USA))
4377[6]
Crockford (IRE)
Joseph Patrick O'Brien a76 76
3 b g Camelot Meiosis (USA) (Danzig (USA))
1306a[3]
Croeso Cymraeg *James Evans* a69 30
5 b g Dick Turpin(IRE) Croeso Cusan (Diktat)
245[3] *(504)* *(721)*◆ *(2970)* *3497[3]* *4594[5]* *5271[3]* *6077[2]* ***6939[2]*** *7790[9]*
Cromwell *Alexandra Dunn* a43 58
3 bl g Swiss Spirit Brooksby (Diktat)
1067[3] 2141[6] 2407[5] 2914[7] **3256[5]** 3764[11] 4794[3] 5505[4] 5842[P] *6111[5]* *9629[13]*

Crop Over Queen (FR)
Andrea Marcialis a62 63
3 b f Planteur(IRE) Capannacce (IRE) (Lahib (USA))
3028a[3]

Croqueta (IRE) *Richard Hannon* a41
3 b f Camacho Oatcake (Selkirk (USA))
1359[9] 1726[10] 2007[8]

Cross Counter *Charlie Appleby* a96 119
4 b g Teofilo(IRE) Waitress (USA) (Kingmambo (USA))
(1441a) 4015[4] 5522[3] 7246a[4] 8844a[8]

Crossed Baton *John Gosden* a109 100
4 b g Dansili Sacred Shield (Beat Hollow)
2033[9] 6536[2] (9003)

Crosse Fire *Scott Dixon* a87 55
7 b g Monsieur Bond(IRE) Watersilk (IRE) (Fasliyev (USA))
43[3] 165[2] 230[2] 508[3] 832[2] (1160) 1366[4] (1426) (1552) 2065[7] 2348[2] 2638[6] 3206[4] 3656[10] 3928[10] 5300[6] 5768[6] (6549)◆ 7052[4] (7387)◆ 8267[7] 8900[3] 9030[4] 9334[5]

Crossing The Bar (IRE)
Sir Michael Stoute 45
2 b c Poet's Voice Ship's Biscuit (Tiger Hill (IRE))
8028[7]

Crossing The Line *Andrew Balding* a105 94
4 br m Cape Cross(IRE) Terentia (Diktat)
30[7] (1289) 1918[5] 3069[8] 3994[2]◆ 4921[13] 5944[3]◆ 6770a[5] 8708[7]

Cross Step (USA) *C Moore* a60 52
5 b g Kitten's Joy(USA) Maid Service (USA) (Arch (USA))
4209[8] 4634[9] 9275[11] 9310[12]

Cross Swords *Roger Fell* a60
4 b g Invincible Spirit(IRE) Alaia (IRE) (Sinndar (IRE))
100[12]

Crotchet *Joseph Patrick O'Brien* a98 99
4 gr m Lethal Force(IRE) Humouresque (Pivotal)
4353a[10] 7222a[7] 8734a[2] 9002[4] 9603a[3]

Croughavouke (IRE) *Jeff Mullins* 99
2 b f Dandy Man(IRE) Coin Case (IRE) (Frozen Power (IRE))
8748a[6]

Crowded Express *Stuart Kittow* a16
2 b g Fast Company(IRE) Dilys (Efisio)
7030[11]

Crowned Eagle *Marco Botti* a97 109
5 b g Oasis Dream Gull Wing (IRE) (In The Wings)
1113a[9] 1460[3] 2119[5] 4173a[2] 6466[4] 7498a[8]

Crown Leah *Peter Charalambous* a59 80
4 b m Swiss Spirit Starbotton (Kyllachy)
1598[6]

Crown Of Flowers *Richard Hannon* a63
3 ch f Garswood Ring Of Love (Magic Ring (IRE))
289[14]

Crownthorpe *Richard Fahey* a99 101
4 b g Monsieur Bond(IRE) Normandy Maid (American Post)
1308a[5] 2116[4] (2480) 2563[5] (3450)◆ 4292[U] 4934[3] 5398[6] 6376[F] (8096)

Crown Vallary (FR) *K R Burke* a48 41
4 b m Manduro(GER) Troiecat (FR) (One Cool Cat (USA))
1644[16]

Crown Walk *H-A Pantall* a79 104
4 ch m Dubawi(IRE) Dunnes River (USA) (Danzig (USA))
1451a[5] 7898[9]

Cruising *David Brown* 76
2 b g Helmet(AUS) Lanai (IRE) (Camacho)
3265[3] 4125[2] 4631[2] 5553[3] 6337[4] 8095[3]

Crushed (IRE) *Mark Walford* a62 73
5 b g Beat Hollow Sel (Salse (USA))
6939[7]

Cruyff *Richard Spencer* a70 51
2 b c Dutch Art Piano (Azamour (IRE))
6424[12] 8751[4]

Cry Baby (IRE) *Y Barberot* a94 93
5 b m Power Monteleone (IRE) (Montjeu (IRE))
1918[4] 5715a[3]

Cry Havoc (IRE) *Rae Guest* a80
2 b f War Command(USA) Na Zdorovie (Cockney Rebel (IRE))
8250[2] (9062)

Cryogenics (IRE) *Kenny Johnson* a44 34
5 b g Frozen Power(IRE) New Blossom (IRE) (Shirocco (GER))
1080[5] 1550[8] 3158[15] 3447[14]

Crystal Beach Road (FR) *J Parize* a53 60
7 gr m Silver Frost(IRE) Lily Bolero (King's Best (USA))
6031a[13]

Crystal Blanc (FR)
Guillaume Courbot a53 68
4 ch g Desert Blanc Cristal Gem (Cadeaux Genereux)
2170a[15]

Crystal Carole *John Quinn* 33
3 b f Canford Cliffs(IRE) Crystal Gale (IRE) (Verglas (IRE))
5771[11]

Crystal Casque *Rod Millman* a80 78
4 ch m Helmet(AUS) Crystal Moments (Haafhd)
1355[9] 2339[3] 2774[2] (4248) 5137[3] 6085[2] (7165) (7788) 8456[10]

Crystal Deauville (FR)
Gay Kelleway a73 81
4 b g Equiano(FR) Crystal Plum (IRE) (Rock Of Gibraltar (IRE))
1932[3] 2227[7] 3207[12] 3576[7] 3967[3] 4213[5] 4775[3]

Crystal King *Sir Michael Stoute* a94 98
4 ch g Frankel Crystal Star (Mark Of Esteem (IRE))
(2126) 2742[11] 4102[3] 5368[8] 6958[11] 7974[10]

Crystalle (USA) *John C Kimmel* 102
2 bb f Palace Malice(USA) Undo (USA) (Flatter (USA))
8748a[11]

Crystal Moonlight
Sir Michael Stoute a93 93
4 ch m New Approach(IRE) Crystal Capella (Cape Cross (IRE))
2401[5] 4145[7] 5682[7]

Crystal Ocean *Sir Michael Stoute* a127 129
5 b h Sea The Stars(IRE) Crystal Star (Mark Of Esteem (IRE))
(2083) (2827) (3985) 5414[2] 6354[2]

Crystal Pegasus *Sir Michael Stoute* a81 75
2 ch c Australia Crystal Etoile (Dansili)
6912[3]◆ 7579[2] 8346[6]

Crystal Tiara *Mick Channon* 60
3 gr f Gregorian(IRE) Petaluma (Teofilo (IRE))
3777[5] 4400[7] 4834[6] (5548) (5784)

Crystal Tribe (IRE) *William Haggas* a72 82
3 b c Dansili Crystal Music (USA) (Nureyev (USA))
1754[10] 2023[9] 2764[7] (3594) (4476)

Cry Wolf *Alexandra Dunn* a86 84
6 ch g Street Cry(IRE) Love Charm (Singspiel (IRE))
432[3] 735[3] (948) 1503[4] 1914[4] 2278[3] 6218[8] 9288[7] 9633[12]

Cuban *Christine Dunnett* a9
2 b g Havana Gold(IRE) Dignify (IRE) (Rainbow Quest (USA))
9156[11]

Cuban Affair *Richard Fahey* 18
2 b f Havana Gold(IRE) Cecily (Oasis Dream)
8337[8]

Cuban Spirit *Lee Carter* a54 38
4 b g Harbour Watch(IRE) Madam Mojito (USA) (Smart Strike (CAN))
483[7] 1179[10] 4025[8] 4733[10] 6117[4]◆ 6885[14] 8295[12] 9445[5]

Cuban Sun *James Given* a58 76
3 b f Havana Gold(IRE) Sunseek (Rail Link)
1697[2] (2253) 2935[6] 4034[5] 5175[9] 5785[2] 7682[8] 8300[8]

Cuba Ruba *Tim Easterby* a46 64
3 ch g Havana Gold(IRE) Diksie Dancer (Diktat)
3565[6] 3932[4] 4211[5] 5023[5] 5915[4]◆ 6232[4] (6612) 6938[4] 7493[5] 8238[14] 8641[5]

Cubswin (IRE) *Neil King* a78 84
5 b m Zamindar(USA) Moonlight Rhapsody (IRE) (Danehill Dancer (IRE))
1291[6] 6224[3]

Cuckoo's Calling *Keith Dalgleish* a29 14
5 b m So You Think(NZ) Sinndarina (FR) (Sinndar (IRE))
602[11]

Cue's Folly *Ed Dunlop* a57 58
4 b m Nathaniel(IRE) Island Odyssey (Dansili)
1548[11] 2974[6] 3272[10]

Cuillin (USA) *Noel Williams* a76 31
4 b m Arch(USA) Zahrah (USA) (Kitten's Joy (USA))
434[4] (9012) 9303[6]

Culmination *Jo Hughes* a80 93
7 b g Beat Hollow Apogee (Shirley Heights)
3879a[16] 4748a[5] 5035a[2] (5410a) 6521a[15] 7536a[14]

Culture (FR) *George Baker* 87
3 bb g Dream Ahead(USA) Talon Bleu (FR) (Anabaa Blue)
2354[5] 3011[8] 3710a[10] (6022) (6812) 7729[6]

Cupboard Love *Mark Johnston* a33 53
3 b f Iffraaj Sri Kandi (Pivotal)
9278[7] 9519[13]

Cupid's Arrow (IRE) *Ruth Carr* a57 50
5 b g Majestic Missile(IRE) Kiss And Don'Tell (USA) (Rahy (USA))
2013[4] 2958[5] 3413[7] 3771[2] (4037) 4912[8] 5235[8] 5768[5] 6058[4] 7286[11] 7590[5]

Cupid's Beau *David Loughnane* 58
2 b g Brazen Beau(AUS) Oilinda (Nayef (USA))
6911[11] 7333[7]

Cuppacoco *Ann Duffield* a67 61
4 b m Stimulation(IRE) Glen Molly (IRE) (Danetime (IRE))
279[2] 498[7] 1162[9] 1765[8] 2183[13] 2633[3] 3213[2] (4132) 4586[15] 5018[11] 5393[3] 6277[10] 6829[8] 7824[2] 8638[10]

Curfewed (IRE) *Tracy Waggott* a66 69
3 br g Most Improved(IRE) Evening Sunset (GER) (Dansili)
409[6] 804[4] 1645[5] 1819[3] 2711[6] 3513[5] 4210[10] 6342[5] 6582[4] 8713[8] 8818[3] 9391[4]

Curious Fox *Anthony Carson* a77 78
6 b m Bertolini(USA) Doric Lady (Kyllachy)
123[7]

Curren Bouquetd'or (JPN)
Sakae Kunieda 117
3 b f Deep Impact(JPN) Solaria (CHI) (Scat Daddy (USA))
9153a[2]

Current *Richard Hannon* 14
2 ch f Equiano(FR) Updated (FR) (New Approach (IRE))
8758[14]

Current (USA) *Todd Pletcher* a96 99
3 ch c Curlin(USA) Crosswinds (USA) (Storm Cat (USA))
6994a[6]

Current Option (IRE)
Adrian McGuinness a75 93
3 b g Camelot Coppertop (IRE) (Exceed And Excel (AUS))
2034[3] 3184[2] (3972)◆ 6693a[2] (7222a)

Curtiz *Hughie Morrison* a71
2 b c Stimulation(IRE) Supatov (USA) (Johannesburg (USA))
6718[9] 9029[2]◆

Custard The Dragon *John Mackie* a89 79
6 b g Kyllachy Autumn Pearl (Orpen (USA))
4[2] 213[5] (499) 805[6] 929[6] 1560[3] 2242[4] 3649[6] 3944[8] 8766[12] 9183[6] 9517[6]

Custodian (IRE) *Richard Fahey* 81
2 b c Muhaarar Zuhoor Baynoona (IRE) (Elnadim (USA))
5234[4] (5815)

Cuttin' Edge (IRE) *William Muir* a69 69
5 b g Rip Van Winkle(IRE) How's She Cuttin' (IRE) (Shinko Forest (IRE))
175[4] 944[8] 1392[5] 1655[10] 5498[4] (6123)◆ 6334[3] 7663[4] 8413[13] 8807[8]

Cutting Humor (USA)
Todd Pletcher a102
3 bb c First Samurai(USA) Pun (USA) (Pulpit (USA))
2425a[10]

Cutty Pie (IRE) *J Phelippon* a35 75
5 b m Cape Cross(IRE) Whisper To Dream (USA) (Gone West (USA))
6790a[5] 7676a[3] 7860a[4] (8966a) 9537a[11]

Cwynar *Andrew Balding* a62 63
4 b m Kodiac Modern Art (New Approach (IRE))
2998[2] 3572[5] 4499[8] 5344[9] (7859)

Cypress Creek (IRE) *A P O'Brien* 113
4 gr h Galileo(IRE) Dialafara (FR) (Anabaa (USA))
2560[5] 3314[9] 4015[11] 7246a[8] 7717a[2] 8114[14]

Daafr (IRE) *Antony Brittain* a75 82
3 b g Invincible Spirit(IRE) Kitty Love (USA) (Kitten's Joy (USA))
1035[8] 4099[6] 4895[7] 5422[4] 5984[5] 7310[5] 7856[10] 8712[6] 9106[8] 9351[11]

Daahyeh *Roger Varian* 110
2 ch f Bated Breath Affluent (Oasis Dream)
(2836)◆ (4048) 4883[2] 7244a[2] (7659) 8748a[2]

Daarik (IRE) *John Gosden* a103 38
3 b g Tamayuz Whip And Win (FR) (Whipper (USA))
(1423) 1926[2]

Daatis (GER) *Waldemar Hickst* 62
3 rg c Dabirsim(FR) Dramraire Mist (Darshaan)
6094a[3]

Daawy (IRE) *Roger Fell* a91 96
5 ch g Teofilo(IRE) Juno Marlowe (IRE) (Danehill (USA))
1927[12] 3726[9] 5199[8]

Dabbersgirl *Brian Baugh* a37
2 b f Heeraat(IRE) Shustraya (Dansili)
8865[12] 9008[9] 9324[9] 9623[11]

Dabouk (IRE) *David O'Meara* a64 70
3 b c Kyllachy Amanda Carter (Tobougg (IRE))
1570[4] 1975[4] 2507[9] 3570[12]

Daddies Diva *Rod Millman* 66
2 b f Coach House(IRE) Pixey Punk (Mount Nelson)
1821[11] 2248[2] (2579) 3055[3] 3835[3] 5185[24] 6053[8] 6637[7] 7827[9]

Daddies Girl (IRE) *Rod Millman* a88 94
4 b m Elzaam(AUS) La Cuvee (Mark Of Esteem (IRE))
(2252) 2608[6] 3374[7] (4113) 5187[7] 5944[8] 6721[8]

Daddy's Daughter (CAN)
Dean Ivory a81 89
4 b m Scat Daddy(USA) Golden Stripe (CAN) (El Corredor (USA))
1941[12] 2555[4] (3892) 5195[4] 6155[10] 8521[8] 9126[7] 9480[11]

Dadoozdart *Noel Meade* 99
3 br c Dawn Approach(IRE) Hairpin (USA) (Bernardini (USA))
(4136a)

Daffg (USA) *A bin Harmash* a78 77
4 ch g Discreet Cat(USA) Liza Too (USA) (Olmodavor (USA))
1001[3]

Daffy Jane *Nigel Tinkler* a61 84
4 b m Excelebration(IRE) Final Dynasty (Komaite (USA))
1895[9] 2809[12] 3309[10] 3815[2] 4442[3]◆ 4904[5] 5395[4] 5846[2]

Daghash *Stuart Kittow* a51 58
10 b g Tiger Hill(IRE) Zibet (Kris)
2718[3] 4251[7]

Dagian (IRE) *James Moffatt* 7
4 ch g Dawn Approach(IRE) Hen Night (IRE) (Danehill Dancer (IRE))
4241[17]

Dagueneau (IRE) *Emma Lavelle* a80 78
4 b g Champs Elysees Bright Enough (Fantastic Light (USA))
1559[6] 2080[12] 2936[4] 3377[2] 4112[8] 7830[12]

Dahawi *Hugo Palmer* a56 54
3 b g Heeraat(IRE) Piranha (IRE) (Exceed And Excel (AUS))
(384) (752) 1104[4] 1662[3] 2078[9] 3465[7]

Daheer (USA) *Owen Burrows* a60
2 ch c Speightstown(USA) Elraazy (USA) (Malibu Moon (USA))
5940[5]

Dahik (IRE) *Michael Easterby* a60 62
4 ch g Society Rock(IRE) Bishop's Lake (Lake Coniston (IRE))
3921[15] 4632[10] 6321[5] (6462) 7552[10] 8643[10] 9352[13]

Daily Times *John Gosden* a78 79
2 b f Gleneagles(IRE) Sunday Times (Holy Roman Emperor (IRE))
3601[4] 4245[2] 4849[2] 6793[2] (8067) 8659[3] 9099[10]

Daimyo *F Vermeulen* a63 72
4 b h Holy Roman Emperor(IRE) Hayaku (USA) (Arch (USA))
7136a[7]

Daisy Bere (FR)
Flurina Wullschleger a40 40
6 b m Peer Gynt(JPN) Jackette (USA) (Mr Greeley (USA))
592a[5] 780a[6]

Daiwa Cagney (JPN)
Takanori Kikuzawa 114
5 bb h King Kamehameha(JPN) Triplex (JPN) (Sunday Silence (USA))
9153a[6]

Dakharo (FR) *C E Cayeux* 57
3 ch g Dream Well(FR) Gallery's Native (FR) (Gallery Of Zurich (IRE))
7291a[7]

Dakota Gold *Michael Dods* a98 115
5 b g Equiano(FR) Joyeaux (Mark Of Esteem (IRE))
4331[5] (5454) (6229) (6351) (6999)◆ 7454[2] (7889)

Dalaalaat (IRE) *William Haggas* a93 92
3 b g Kingman Gile Na Greine (IRE) (Galileo (IRE))
2581[5]◆ 3471[3] (4639) 5583[8] 6258[2]

Dalacrown (IRE) *J-V Toux* a47 42
2 gr f Hallowed Crown(AUS) Dalaway (IRE) (Dalakhani (IRE))
8447a[7]

Dalakina (IRE) *David Weston* a61 61
3 ro f Mastercraftsman(IRE) White Cay (Dalakhani (IRE))
884[3] 9178[4] 9421[8]

Dalanijujo (IRE) *Mick Channon* 80
2 ch f Night Of Thunder(IRE) Kiss From A Rose (Compton Place)
(5170) 5964[6] 7412[5]

Dalasan (AUS)
Leon Macdonald & Andrew Gluyas 106
2 ch c Dalakhani(IRE) Khandallah (AUS) (Kitten's Joy (USA))
8137a[5]

Dalgarno (FR) *Jane Chapple-Hyam* a104 95
6 b g Sea The Stars(IRE) Jakonda (USA) (Kingmambo (USA))
1681[4] 2560[4] 8725[6] (9210a) 9587[3]

Dal Harraild
Ciaron Maher & David Eustace a108 109
6 ch g Champs Elysees Dalvina (Grand Lodge (USA))
8600a[10]

Dal Horrisgle *William Haggas* a79 104
3 b g Nathaniel(IRE) Dalvina (Grand Lodge (USA))
(3372)◆ (4553)◆ 5585[5] 6446[5]

Daligar (FR) *A De Royer-Dupre* 89
3 b c Invincible Spirit(IRE) Dalkala (USA) (Giant's Causeway (USA))
1450a[9]

Dalileo (IRE) *Mark Johnston* a88 85
4 b g Galileo(IRE) Snow Queen (IRE) (Danehill Dancer (IRE))
(291)

Dalkelef (FR) *M Boutin* 55
2 bl g Kheleyf(USA) Nanouk (IRE) (Nombre Premier)
1709a[7] 6060a[7] 7641a[9]

Dalness Express *Archie Watson* a45 46
6 b g Firebreak Under My Spell (Wizard King)
60[5] 357[2] 553[8] 1093[5] 1383[8] 2483[2] 2728[2] 3476[8] 4733[8] 4873[9] 6462[8] 6758[6] 6897[7] 7384[12] 8256[6] 8689[5]

Dalton *Julie Camacho* a70 91
5 b g Mayson Pious (Bishop Of Cashel)
2201[8] 2843[3] (3770) 4379[10] 5120[12] 5740[3] 6227[8] 8512[5]

Dalton Highway (IRE) *D K Weld* 87
6 b g Zoffany(IRE) Poinsettia (IRE) (Galileo (IRE))
5508a[2]

Daltrey *A R Al Rayhi* a62 28
4 b g Iffraaj Roger Sez (IRE) (Red Clubs (IRE))
1742a[14]

Dalvini (FR) *A De Royer-Dupre* 87
4 b h Lawman(FR) Daltama (IRE) (Indian Ridge (IRE))
8980a[8]

Damage Control *Andrew Balding* 78
2 ch g Zoffany(IRE) One So Marvellous (Nashwan (USA))
6905[7] 7755[4] 8028[2] 8461[5]

Damavand (GER) *Mario Hofer* a75 96
4 b g Teofilo(IRE) Diamantgottin (GER) (Fantastic Light (USA))
8240a[10]

Dame Denali *Anthony Carson* a49
2 b f Casamento(IRE) Doric Lady (Kyllachy)
8849[10] 9155[10] 9451[7]

Dame Freya Stark *Mark Johnston* a63 72
3 ch f Leroidesanimaux(BRZ) Lady Jane Digby (Oasis Dream)
1217[3] 1288[5] (5866)◆ 7629[4] 8033[14]

Dame Gladys *E Zahariev* a57 75
3 b f Mukhadram Nurse Gladys (Dr Fong (USA))
9280a[5]

Dame Malliot *Ed Vaughan* a82 111
3 b f Champs Elysees Stars In Your Eyes (Galileo (IRE))
3495[2] (5190) (6263a) 7118[6]

Damlaj *Owen Burrows* 47
3 b g Shamardal(USA) Mahaatheer (IRE) (Daylami (IRE))
1852[9]

Damon Runyon *John Gosden* a82 84
3 b g Charm Spirit(IRE) Tawaasul (Haafhd)
1592[2] 2524[6] 3860[2] 4474[2]

Dan *J-C Rouget* 102
3 b c Slade Power(IRE) Moonlit Garden (IRE) (Exceed And Excel (AUS))
5480a[2]

Dana Forever (IRE) *Tom Dascombe* a76 62
2 b f Requinto(IRE) Positive Step (IRE) (Footstepsinthesand)
4659[4] 5280[2] 6028[2]◆ 6637[3]

Danburite (JPN) *Hidetaka Otonashi* 114
5 b h Rulership(JPN) Tanzanite (JPN) (Sunday Silence (USA))
9153a[14]

Dance Diva *Richard Fahey* 91
4 b m Mayson Dance East (Shamardal (USA))
4758[10] 5525[9] 6379[11] 6974[4] 7735[4] 8101[4] 8521[2] 8766[6]

Dance Fever (IRE) *Clive Cox* a91 80
2 b c Sir Prancealot(IRE) Silk Fan (IRE) (Unfuwain (USA))
(6807) (7570) (8850)

Dance King *Tim Easterby* a57 80
9 ch g Danehill Dancer(IRE) One So Wonderful (Nashwan (USA))
2563[3] 3073[8] 4241[12] 4890[5] 5436[7] 5694[4] 6255[6] 6535[7] 6975[10] 7625[3] 7907[4]◆ 8515[16]

Dance Legend *Rae Guest* a91 100
4 b m Camelot Syvilla (Nayef (USA))
(2620)◆ 3586[5] 4145[2] 5190[8] 5510a[5] 6820a[6] 8245[3] 8710[9]

Dance Of Fire *N W Alexander* a43 46
7 b g Norse Dancer(IRE) Strictly Dancing (IRE) (Danehill Dancer (IRE))
7069[13] 8186[13]
Dance Teacher (IRE)
Shaun Keightley a79 88
5 ch m Lope De Vega(IRE) Fairnilee (Selkirk (USA))
2097[7] 2799[8]
Danceteria (FR) *David Menuisier* 116
4 b g Redoute's Choice(AUS) Bal De La Rose (IRE) (Cadeaux Genereux)
(1708a) 3025[3] (3678a) 4668[4] (5483a) 8579a[14]
Dance To Freedom *Stuart Williams* a51 39
3 b g Equiano(FR) Posy Fossil (USA) (Malibu Moon (USA))
32[5] 2735[8] 4244[10] 4794[9] 5797[8]
Dance To Paris *Lucy Wadham* a84 70
4 b m Champs Elysees Riabouchinska (Fantastic Light (USA))
3467[10] 4112[9] 4881[5] 9134[3]◆ 9288[3] (9570)
Dancin Boy *Michael Dods* a74 81
3 br g Gregorian(IRE) La Gifted (Fraam)
(2336)◆ 3358[7] 4077[7] 5970[3] 6961[8] 7782[9] 8237[10]
Dancing Approach *Roger Charlton* a66
2 b f Camelot Dream Approach (IRE) (New Approach (IRE))
8848[10] 9163[4] 9437[4]
Dancing Ballerina (IRE) *K R Burke* a58
3 b f Es Que Love(IRE) Vexatious (IRE) (Shamardal (USA))
141[4] 412[8]
Dancing Brave Bear (USA)
Ed Vaughan a94 91
4 b m Street Cry(IRE) Baghdaria (USA) (Royal Academy (USA))
1941[7] 4332[8] 5229a[10]
Dancing Doll (IRE) *M Flannery* a70 69
6 b m Invincible Spirit(IRE) Dancing Diva (FR) (Sadler's Wells (USA))
5599a[10]
Dancing Feet (IRE) *David O'Meara* 65
2 b f Footstepsinthesand Speronella (Raven's Pass (USA))
4366[4]
Dancing Girl (FR) *Harry Dunlop* a54
2 b f Style Vendome(FR) Aljafliyah (Halling (USA))
7515[9] 9243[5] 9501[4]
Dancing Harry (IRE)
Roger Charlton 77
2 b c Camelot Poisson D'Or (Cape Cross (IRE))
(8517)
Dancinginthesand (IRE)
Bryan Smart 62
2 b g Footstepsinthesand Omanome (IRE) (Acclamation)
2707[3] 3411[9] 4237[3] 4985[6] 7538[3]
Dancinginthewoods *Dean Ivory* 77
2 b c Garswood Pachanga (Inchinor)
(2761) 3312[4] 4324[2] 7409[11]
Dancing Jaquetta (IRE)
Mark Loughnane a50 20
3 b f Camacho Skehana (IRE) (Mukaddamah (USA))
437[12] 620[11] 4180[16] 4657[13]
Dancing Jo *Mick Channon* a62 74
3 b g Mazameer(IRE) Remix (IRE) (Oratorio (IRE))
(174) 1174[2] 1264[4] 1656[2] 2125[8] 2689[7] 2965[6] 6123[7] 6904[10] 7084[6] 7573[U] 7758[3] 8698[4] 9305[7] 9573[8]
Dancing Leopard (IRE) *K R Burke* a66 65
2 b f Fulbright Heavenly River (FR) (Stormy River (FR))
1821[4] 6096[5] 6570[4] 7386[3] 8085[3]◆ 8815[2] 9029[3] 9097[5] 9640[3]
Dancing Lilly *Debbie Hughes* a43 47
4 ch m Sir Percy Bhima (Polar Falcon (USA))
2354[11] 2731[11] 4177[5] 5378[6] 6400[4] 7558[5] 9204[9] 9336[8]
Dancing Master (FR) *J-V Toux* a61 61
4 b g George Vancouver(USA) Lindfield Dancer (Byron)
1391a[7]
Dancing Mountain (IRE) *P Monfort* a66 67
3 b f Kodiac Pearl Mountain (IRE) (Pearl Of Love (IRE))
972[5] 1894[11] 2683[2] 2908[6] 3417[4] 4033[3] 4493[11] 4720[14] 5393[2] 5559[7] (5765) 8449a[3] 9280a[7] 9504a[7]
Dancing On A Dream (IRE)
Joseph Patrick O'Brien a89 74
3 b f Dream Ahead(USA) Slip Dance (IRE) (Celtic Swing)
8734a[7]
Dancing Rave *David O'Meara* a73 79
3 b f Coach House(IRE) Right Rave (IRE) (Soviet Star (USA))
2098[13] 2635[9] 3292[4] (3709)◆ 4033[5] (5123) 5670[2] 6261[6] 7762[3] 7777[2] 8636[8] 9106[4]◆ 9349[2]◆ 9512[4]
Dancing Speed (IRE) *Marjorie Fife* a43 61
3 br g Dandy Man(IRE) Air Maze (Dansili)
2200[10] 2896[6] 3650[6] 3969[7] 4784[10] 8923[10]
Dancing Star *Andrew Balding* 107
6 b m Aqlaam Strictly Dancing (IRE) (Danehill Dancer (IRE))
2621[8] 3094[7]
Dancing Vega (IRE) *Ralph Beckett* 92
3 ch f Lope De Vega(IRE) We Can Say It Now (AUS) (Starcraft (NZ))
1751[12]
Dancing Warrior *William Knight* 87
3 b f War Command(USA) Corps De Ballet (IRE) (Fasliyev (USA))
2086[5] 5252[9] 5589[10] 6208[9]
Dancingwithwolves (IRE)
Ed Dunlop a74 74
3 b g Footstepsinthesand Clodovina (IRE) (Rock Of Gibraltar (IRE))
1495[4] 1975[2] 3195[10] 3885[5] 4479[2] 4874[2] 5202[6] 6518[6]

Dancin Inthestreet *William Haggas* a79 76
2 b f Muhaarar Souvenir Delondres (FR) (Siyouni (FR))
8758[2]◆ (9130)◆ 9364[5]
Dandhu *David Elsworth* a97 107
3 ch f Dandy Man(IRE) Poldhu (Cape Cross (IRE))
(1751) 2443[10] 7893[10] 9064[6]
Dandilion (IRE) *Alex Hales* a58 43
6 b m Dandy Man(IRE) Free Angel (USA) (Mystery Storm (USA))
286[2]◆ 823[4] 1818[7] 2153[10] 3320[8] 4376[RR] 5629[4] 5884[5] (6284) 7770[4]◆ 8018[4] 9246[2] 9551[3]
Dandizette (IRE) *Adrian Nicholls* a71 74
2 ch f Dandy Man(IRE) Interlacing (Oasis Dream)
2415[2] 2820[4] 3451[3] (3997) 4361[5] 4985[2] (5275)◆ 6436[5] 6900[2] 7440[6]
Dandy Belle (IRE) *Richenda Ford* a59 67
3 bb f Dandy Man(IRE) Jeunesse Doree (IRE) (Rock Of Gibraltar (IRE))
2995[8] 3418[12] 4931[9] 5431[8] 5878[4]
Dandy Dancer *Richard Hughes* a50 43
2 b g Dandy Man(IRE) Last Of The Dixies (Halling (USA))
4290[6] 4871[5] 5186[12] 7275[4] 7516[9]
Dandy Highwayman (IRE)
Ollie Pears a69 89
5 ch g Dandy Man(IRE) Paradise Blue (IRE) (Bluebird (USA))
(277) 788[5] 2633[2] 3214[4] 3704[10] 4523[3] 5020[3]◆ 6665[7] 7286[5] 7823[2]◆ 8839[4]
Dandy Lad (IRE)
Natalie Lloyd-Beavis a64 68
3 ch g Dandy Man(IRE) Lucky Pipit (Key Of Luck (USA))
854[6] 1079[2] 1296[6] 1557[5] 2995[12] 4765[7] 5264[9]
Dandy Lass (IRE) *Richard Phillips* 43
3 b f Dandy Man(IRE) El Mirage (IRE) (Elusive Quality (USA))
2919[12] 9416[8]
Dandyman Port (IRE) *Des Donovan* 77
5 b m Dandy Man(IRE) Fillthegobletagain (IRE) (Byron)
5181[2]
Dandy Pearl (IRE)
Denis Gerard Hogan a35 42
3 b f Dandy Man(IRE) Certainly Brave (Indian Ridge (IRE))
7468[6]
Dandy's Angel (IRE)
John Wainwright a53 71
2 b f Dandy Man(IRE) Party Pipit (IRE) (Desert Party (USA))
6336[3] 7063[3] 7958[5]◆
Dandy's Beano (IRE) *Kevin Ryan* a91 92
4 ch m Dandy Man(IRE) Hear My Cry (USA) (Giant's Causeway (USA))
1507[4] 2294[7] (2637) 3201[8] 3706[5] (4330) 4593[5] (5432) (5936) 7401[6]
Dandys Gold (IRE)
William J Fitzpatrick a62 80
5 b m Dandy Man(IRE) Proud Penny (IRE) (King Charlemagne (USA))
(307a)
Dandys Ocean (IRE)
Mrs John Harrington 74
3 b f Dandy Man(IRE) Ocean Myth (Acclamation)
1306a[16]
Danecase *David Dennis* a81 80
6 ch g Showcasing Yding (IRE) (Danehill (USA))
4226[10] 4844[8] 6898[3]◆ 7299[3] 8220[6] 8652[9]
Danehill Desert (IRE)
Richard Fahey a70 71
4 b g Clodovil(IRE) Misplace (IRE) (Green Desert (USA))
1403[5] 1765[17] 2638[3] 3550[6] 4037[6]
Danehill Kodiac (IRE)
Richard Hannon a112 114
6 b g Kodiac Meadow (Green Desert (USA))
2269[5] 2554[2] 3077[2]
Dangeroffizz (IRE) *Tim Easterby* 45
2 ch g Champs Elysees Tingleo (Galileo (IRE))
7000[5] 7586[10] 8857[9]
Dangerous Ends *Brett Johnson* a77 75
5 b g Monsieur Bond(IRE) Stolen Glance (Mujahid (USA))
1095[4] 1566[4] 4561[7] 6050[3] 6439[9] 8422[3] 9067[4]
Danglydontask *Mike Murphy* a51 53
8 b g Lucky Story(USA) Strat's Quest (Nicholas (USA))
4796[3] 5379[2] 6366[3] 6601[4] 7558[7] 8347[9]
Dani Blue (FR) *E Lyon* a63 65
6 gr m Slickly(FR) Angelic Girl (USA) (Swain (IRE))
6031a[8]
Daniel Dravot *Michael Attwater* a49 45
3 b g Nathaniel(IRE) Zubova (Dubawi (IRE))
2285[3] 3409[6] 4029[8] 4400[8] 4834[8] 7818[14] 8072[10] 8552[9] 9279[8]
Danielsflyer (IRE) *Michael Dods* a63 97
5 b g Dandy Man(IRE) Warm Welcome (Motivator)
1459[2]◆ 2396[12] 2844[2] 3863[6] 4127[9] 4981[3] 5692[10]
Danish Duke (IRE) *Ruth Carr* a50 56
8 ch g Duke Of Marmalade(IRE) Bridge Note (USA) (Stravinsky (USA))
1973[11] 2532[13]
Danking *Alan King* a57 49
2 b g Dansili Time Saved (Green Desert (USA))
4456[5] 5177[11] 8657[7]
Danny Ocean (IRE) *K R Burke* a73 77
2 b g Dandy Man(IRE) Loud Applause (Royal Applause)
1556[3] 1812[3] 2957[5] 5101[2]◆ 5777[6] 6653[5] 7064[3] 7419[2] (7827) 9137[6] 9347[5] 9414[4]
Danon Roman (JPN)
Anthony Freedman 84
5 bb h Deep Impact(JPN) Immaculate Cat (USA) (Storm Cat (USA))
9016a[6]
Danon Smash (JPN)
Takayuki Yasuda 114
4 b h Lord Kanaloa(JPN) Spinning Wildcat (USA) (Hard Spun (USA))
9377a[8]

Dan's Dream *Mick Channon* 106
4 br m Cityscape Royal Ffanci (Royal Applause)
2493a[2] 3557a[2] 3986[17] 5916[2] 6646a[7]
Danse A Rio (FR) *J Bossert* 52
5 b g Rio De La Plata(USA) Dance Idol (Groom Dancer (USA))
1073a[8]
Dansepo *Adam West* a48 61
3 ch g Sepoy(AUS) Danzanora (Groom Dancer (USA))
7114[9] 7572[8] (8006) 8408[8]
Danseur D'Argent (FR) *Jo Hughes* 67
3 gr f Le Havre(IRE) Sardinelle (FR) (Verglas (IRE))
1489a[5] 2091a[7] 2954a[6] 6062a[3] 7061a[8]
Dante's Peak *Gabor Maronka* 89
3 b c Harbour Watch(IRE) Disco Ball (Fantastic Light (USA))
6006a[10]
Dante's View (IRE)
Sir Michael Stoute a83 84
3 ch g Galileo(IRE) Daivika (USA) (Dynaformer (USA))
3584[3] 4143[3] 4636[3] 6589[2] 7057[2] 7577[4] 8398[3]
Danuska's My Girl (USA)
Dan Ward a107
5 b m Shackleford(USA) Amaday (USA) (Dayjur (USA))
8769a[5]
Danyah (IRE) *Owen Burrows* a78 84
2 b g Invincible Spirit(IRE) Cuis Ghaire (IRE) (Galileo (IRE))
(6167) 6891[7] 8418[3]
Danzan (IRE) *Andrew Balding* a103 99
4 b g Lawman(FR) Charanga (Cadeaux Genereux)
136[4] 389[6] 786[7] 2917[2] 3945[3] 6920[6] 8015[4]
Danzdanzdance (AUS)
Chris Gibbs & Michelle Bradley 102
4 gr m Mastercraftsman(IRE) Night Danza (AUS) (Danzero (AUS))
1783a[7]
Danzena *Michael Appleby* 35
4 b m Denounce Danzanora (Groom Dancer (USA))
5357[5] 7313[4]
Danzeno *Michael Appleby* a99 111
8 b g Denounce Danzanora (Groom Dancer (USA))
(3375) 4095[3] (4648) 5927[3] 6698[4] 6999[2] 7889[3] 8127[3]
Danzig Issue (FR)
Matthieu Palussiere 79
2 b c Orpen(USA) Angelic News (FR) (American Post)
2890a[5]
Daphinia *Dean Ivory* a56 68
3 b f Kuroshio(AUS) Phantom Spirit (Invincible Spirit (IRE))
2810[13] 5251[7] 5990[6]
Dapper Man (IRE) *Roger Fell* a93 93
5 b g Dandy Man(IRE) Gist (IRE) (Namid)
953[10] 1194[10] 1551[3]◆ 1899[6] 2368[8] 2876[4] (3056) (4279)◆ (4555) (4593)◆ 5154[5] 5371[13] 6208[6] 6607[4] 7700[5]
Dapper Power (IRE) *Edward Lynam* a70 78
5 ch g Dandy Man(IRE) Rumuz (IRE) (Marju (IRE))
7085a[4]
Dardenne (NOR) *Wido Neuroth* 89
5 b g Footstepsinthesand Distant Beat (NOR) (Muhtathir)
7497a[7]
Dargel (IRE) *Clive Cox* a84 83
3 b g Dark Angel(IRE) Lady Duxyana (Most Welcome)
1352[5] 2140[4] (5080) (5731)◆ 6075[2] 6671[3] 8498[3] 8809[3]
Daring Guest (IRE) *Tom Clover* a67 61
5 b g Fast Company(IRE) Balm (Oasis Dream)
159[3] 467[3] 920[8] 1179[3] 1335[2]◆ 2318[2] 3143[2] 4025[3] (5629) 5889[8] 9386[2]◆ 9622[4]
Daring Match (GER) *J Hirschberger* a43 73
8 ch h Call Me Big(GER) Daring Action (Arazi (USA))
2955a[16] 5643a[12]
Daring Venture (IRE) *Roger Varian* a75 70
3 b f Dabirsim(FR) Glorious Adventure (IRE) (Galileo (IRE))
(2550) 3603[4] 4288[5] 8702[4] 9048[7] 9203[6]
Dariyza (FR) *A De Royer-Dupre* a78 101
3 ch f Dawn Approach(IRE) Daryakana (FR) (Selkirk (USA))
3391a[7] 7477a[4] (8377a)
Dark Alliance (IRE)
Mark Loughnane a78 76
8 b g Dark Angel(IRE) Alinda (IRE) (Revoque (IRE))
31[2] (237) 466[4] 840[4] 962[4] 1392[2] 1511[8] 2005[7]
Dark American (FR) *V Sartori* a86 96
5 gr g Dark Angel(IRE) Tres Americanqueen (FR) (American Post)
4704a[2]
Darkange (FR) *J-P Sauvage* a73 37
3 b f Archange D'Or(IRE) Anse Crawen (FR) (Muhtathir)
7061a[10]
Darkanna (IRE)
Mohammed Hussain 74
4 br m Dark Angel(IRE) Jadanna (IRE) (Mujadil (USA))
892a[7]
Dark Confidant (IRE)
Donald McCain a49 55
6 b g Royal Applause Sleek Gold (Dansili)
599[4] 1192[9] 3413[13] 4455[9]
Dark Crocodile (IRE)
Seamus Durack a62 62
4 b g Dark Angel(IRE) Heaven's Vault (IRE) (Hernando (FR))
3462[14] 4194[12] 5003[9]
Dark Crystal *Linda Perratt* a24 43
8 b m Multiplex Glitz (IRE) (Hawk Wing (USA))
3721[13] 4512[10] 4726[12] 5100[10] 5237[5] 5933[5] 7780[11]

Dark Defender *Rebecca Bastiman* a69 91
6 b g Pastoral Pursuits Oh So Saucy (Imperial Ballet (IRE))
2201[5] (2588)◆ 3589[6] 4521[7] 5120[7] 5476[6] 7402[10] 8099[15] 8634[7]
Dark Devil (IRE) *Patrick Morris* a57 69
6 gr g Dark Angel(IRE) Ride For Roses (IRE) (Barathea (IRE))
1418[14] 1813[8] 2629[6] 3161[7] 3217[2] 3845[5] 4109[2] 4907[6] 5709[3] 6173[4] 6573[10] 7544[4] 7829[8] 9256[8] 9609[12]
Dark Discretion *Kevin Frost* a24
2 b f Fountain Of Youth(IRE) So Discreet (Tragic Role (USA))
8198[11] 9097[9]
Dark Dream (AUS) *F C Lor* 111
4 gb g All American(AUS) Buchanan Girl (AUS) (Lion Hunter (AUS))
9380a[7]
Dark Dream (FR) *Mlle M Henry* a79 57
8 ch g Maille Pistol(FR) Anse Crawen (FR) (Muhtathir)
8240a[11]
Dark Glory (IRE) *Brian Meehan* a48 67
3 b c Alhebayeb(IRE) Glyndebourne (USA) (Rahy (USA))
1656[8] 2517[10] 2995[3] 3204[8] 3697[7] 4180[10]
Dark Heart *Mark Johnston* a65
2 b c Nathaniel(IRE) Danehill Dreamer (USA) (Danehill (USA))
6185[3]
Dark Impulse (IRE) *John Bridger* 28
3 bz g Dark Angel(IRE) Invincible Me (IRE) (Invincible Spirit (IRE))
2140[8] 2773[5] 3045[10] 4183[12]
Dark Intention (IRE)
Lawrence Mullaney a80 89
6 b m High Chaparral(IRE) Ajiaal (Cape Cross (IRE))
2526[14] 3100[2] 3813[6] 4240[6] 4892[7]
Dark Jedi (IRE) *Charles Hills* a92 90
3 b g Kodiac Whitefall (USA) (Street Cry (IRE))
1926[7] 2558[5] 4016[23] 4934[6] 7617[5] 8253[8]
Dark Kris (IRE) *Richard Hughes* a70 72
2 b g Dark Angel(IRE) My Spirit (IRE) (Invincible Spirit (IRE))
2767[5] 3542[2] 4456[2] 7409[6]
Dark Lady *Richard Hannon* a87 105
2 b f Dark Angel(IRE) Ladyship (Oasis Dream)
4557[2]◆ (5045)◆ 5411[4] 5964[3]◆ 6444[2] (6907) 7692[7]
Dark Lochnagar (USA)
Keith Dalgleish a84 94
3 b c Australia Virginia Waters (USA) (Kingmambo (USA))
1926[9] 2811[4] 3358[5] 4689[6] 4913[2]◆ (5424) 5706[3] 6657[2] 7209[5] 7436[6] 8514[2]
Dark Magic *Dean Ivory* a60 44
5 b g Invincible Spirit(IRE) Dark Promise (Shamardal (USA))
138[8] 439[3]◆ 596[6] 857[2] 1037[5] 1328[4]
Dark Miracle (IRE) *Marco Botti* a83
3 b c Mukhadram Eolith (Pastoral Pursuits)
(1344) 2582[12] (2697)
Dark Moonlight (IRE) *Phil McEntee* a24
2 b g Kodiac On Location (USA) (Street Cry (IRE))
3890[5] 4282[7] 8067[8] 8118[9]
Dark Mystique *Dean Ivory* 37
3 b c Sea The Moon(GER) Apple Blossom (IRE) (Danehill Dancer (IRE))
6169[7] 8030[10] 8698[12]
Dark Of Night (IRE)
Saeed bin Suroor a72 57
2 gr g Dark Angel(IRE) Moonvoy (Cape Cross (IRE))
1937[4] 2594[5] 3274[7] 4878[6]
Dark Optimist (IRE) *David Evans* a34 80
2 b g Alhebayeb(IRE) Luvmedo (IRE) (One Cool Cat (USA))
1416[10] 1910[4] 2338[3] 2830[8] (3088) 4647[7] 6158[3] 6515[4] 7182[6] 9031[11]
Dark Phoenix (IRE) *Paul Cole* a62 51
2 gr c Camacho Alba Verde (Verglas (IRE))
8195[3] 8409[6] 9195[14] 9630[5]
Dark Poet *Ruth Carr* a61 56
3 b g Lethal Force(IRE) Poetic Dancer (Byron)
289[9] 2357[5] 2926[3] 3697[8] 4029[2] 6101[8] 7404[13]
Dark Pursuit *S Ibido* 79
3 b g Pastoral Pursuits Ogre (USA) (Tale Of The Cat (USA))
893a[12]
Dark Red (IRE) *Ed Dunlop* a96 99
7 gr g Dark Angel(IRE) Essexford (IRE) (Spinning World (USA))
284a[7] 514a[6] 847a[11] 1031[5] 3005[3] 3726[7] 4877[4] 5440[3]◆ 6447[4]
Dark Regard *Mark Johnston* a81 67
2 br f Dark Angel(IRE) Best Regards (IRE) (Tamayuz)
5118[2]◆ 5550[5] (8640) (9031)◆ (9162)
Dark Seraphim (IRE) *Charles Hills* 40
4 ro g Dark Angel(IRE) Win Cash (IRE) (Alhaarth (IRE))
4452[9] 7159[11]
Dark Shadow (IRE) *Clive Cox* 95
3 gr g Dark Angel(IRE) Djinni (IRE) (Invincible Spirit (IRE))
1691[12] (2274) (3422)◆ 4236[4] 4736[2] 5504[8] 6525[4] (7077)
Dark Shot *Scott Dixon* a87 94
6 b g Acclamation Dark Missile (Night Shift (USA))
2030[2] 2775[5] 3097[2] 3344[2] 4313a[3] 4932[2] 5524[12] 5661[14] 6549[3] 7073[6] 7541[2] 8099[20] 8267[5] 8340[4]
Dark Side Division *John Ryan* a18 60
2 b g Due Diligence(USA) Belle Of Honour (USA) (Honour And Glory (USA))
2257[4] 2973[8] 3739[6] 4802[7] 7315[6] 7910[11] 9045[12]
Dark Side Dream *Charlie Wallis* a72 66
7 b g Equiano(FR) Dream Day (Oasis Dream)
1880[10] 3462[13] 4455[7] 5889[9] (6321) 7320[5] 8501[2] 9013[4] 9365[5] 9627[10]

Darksideoftarnside (IRE)
Ian Williams a77 90
5 b g Intense Focus(USA) Beautiful Dancer (IRE) (Danehill Dancer (IRE))
4118[8] 5321[5] (6044) 7866[2] 8114[13]

Dark Side Prince *Charlie Wallis* a2
2 b g Equiano(FR) Dark Side Princess (Strategic Prince)
3739[8] 7316[8] 7546[9]

Dark Silver (IRE) *Ed Walker* a72 73
2 b g Dark Angel(IRE) Silver Shoon (IRE) (Fasliyev (USA))
3660[9] 4558[3] 5145[4] 5612[6] 6184[2] 7391[2] 7785[7] 8817[7]

Dark Templar (USA) *Kelsey Danner* a89 96
4 ch h Tapit(USA) Hurricane Flag (USA) (Storm Cat (USA))
5484a[4]

Dark Thunder (IRE) *Doug Watson* a70 83
3 gr g Alhebayeb(IRE) Call This Cat (IRE) (One Cool Cat (USA))
169a[11] 570a[3] 1742a[2]

Dark Vision (IRE) *Mark Johnston* a108 103
3 b c Dream Ahead(USA) Black Dahlia (Dansili)
1713[3] 2411[12] 3026[4] 4016[8] 4882[4] 5610[15] 6425[6] 6696[5] 7694[6] 8126[3] 8336[11]

Darwina *Alistair Whillans* a40 52
3 gr f Dark Angel(IRE) Anadolu (IRE) (Statue Of Liberty (USA))
4726[5] 5272[8] 5771[5] 6575[8] 7512[6] 7776[12] 8234[6] 8666[5] 9349[10] 9396[13] 9548[7]

Darwin Dream *Sophie Leech* a41 64
3 b g Australia Snoqualmie Girl (IRE) (Montjeu (IRE))
1754[6] 2289[6] 3311[10] 4400[12] 4998[12] (Dead)

Daryana *Eve Johnson Houghton* a47 75
3 b f Dutch Art Darysina (USA) (Smart Strike (CAN))
2762[9] 3463[10] 4341[4] 5349[7] 5777[10] 6362[4] (7298)

Daschas *Stuart Williams* a81 91
5 b g Oasis Dream Canada Water (Dansili)
2272[2] (2839) 3344[19] 4186[7] 4894[6] 4995[2] (5252) 5371[4] 6724[6] 7077[12] (7348)

Dash D'or (IRE) *Kieran P Cotter* a79 80
6 gr m Le Cadre Noir(IRE) Dash For Gold (Highest Honor (FR))
4313a[12] 6986a[10]

Dashed *Roger Varian* a58 76
3 b f Pivotal Shatter (IRE) (Mr Greeley (USA))
2102[6] 2760[3] 3258[2] 3892[3] 5105[3] 6025[8]

Dasheen *Karen Tutty* a56 53
6 b g Bahamian Bounty Caribbean Dancer (USA) (Theatrical (IRE))
2076[10] 2478[5] 2898[10] 3215[9] 3721[9] 4078[8] 5100[8]

Dashing Poet *Heather Main* a72 71
5 b m Poet's Voice Millisecond (Royal Applause)
202[2] 392[3] 507[3] 1216[2] 1563[4] 2617[2] 2714[2] 3691[2] 4426[5] 5373[10] 8902[11]

Dashing Roger *William Stone* a64 67
2 b g Fast Company(IRE) Croeso Cusan (Diktat)
7981[2] 9585[8] 9668[4]

Dashing Willoughby
Andrew Balding a81 113
3 b g Nathaniel(IRE) Miss Dashwood (Dylan Thomas (IRE))
1737[2] 2523[3] (3984) 4848[4] 5522[5] 7196[7] 7927a[9]

Das Kapital *John Berry* a45 52
4 b g Cityscape Narla (Nayef (USA))
3473[3]◆ 3834[8] 4868[2] 5378[12] 7553[5] 8204[3] 9470[8]

Das Rote (IRE) *Mario Giorgi* 94
2 ch f Dandy Man(IRE) Texas Queen (Shamardal (USA))
8791a[2]

Dassom (IRE) *Mlle A Wattel* a91 78
3 b g Frozen Power(IRE) Rosina Bella (IRE) (Oratorio (IRE))
2265a[5] 2953a[7]

Data Protection *William Muir* a71 87
4 b g Foxwedge(AUS) Midnight Sky (Desert Prince (IRE))
3027[5]◆ 3763[8] 4300[8] 4837[3] 5255[2] (5574) 6538[2] 7378[2] (7663) 8411[3] 9041[11]

Dathanna (IRE) *Charlie Appleby* a99 102
4 b m Dubawi(IRE) Colour (AUS) (More Than Ready (USA))
3288a[6] 4706a[8]

Dato *S Smrczek* 96
3 ch c Mount Nelson Dear Lavinia (USA) (Grand Slam (USA))
6487a[6]

Daubney's Dream (IRE)
Paddy Butler
4 b g Power Belle Of The Lodge (IRE) (Grand Lodge (USA))
4615[13] 6116[12]

Daughter In Law (IRE)
Roger Charlton a71 87
2 br f Requinto(IRE) Shizao (IRE) (Alzao (USA))
3983[24] 5544[5] 6474[7]

Dave (FR) *Mme Pia Brandt* a63 102
3 b c Wootton Bassett Dance Toupie (FR) (Dansili)
(1241a) 3029a[2] 5480a[3] 6249a[2] 7478a[8]

Dave Dexter *Ralph Beckett* a76 94
3 b g Stimulation(IRE) Blue Crest (FR) (Verglas (IRE))
2522[7] 3587[5] 3865[14] 6222[9]

David's Beauty (IRE) *Brian Baugh* a62 65
6 b m Kodiac Thaisy (USA) (Tabasco Cat (USA))
1507[6] 1767[4] 2473[3] 3577[2] 4230[9] 4632[3] 5181[10] 5986[9] 7112[8] 7488[3] 7757[7] 8117[10]

Davina *Bill Turner*
4 b m Delegator Devon Diva (Systematic)
7241[4] 4753[13] 5293[13]

Davydenko *Sir Michael Stoute* 108
3 ch c Intello(GER) Safina (Pivotal)
(2488) (3412) 4016[21] (5963)◆ (7122)

Dawaaleeb (USA) *Les Eyre* a82 96
5 b g Invincible Spirit(IRE) Plaza (USA) (Chester House (USA))
1413[4] 1694[5] 2419[7] 2803[2] 4079[3] 5776[7] 6580[6] 7312[7]

Dawaam (USA) *Owen Burrows* a100
3 b c Kitten's Joy(USA) Nereid (USA) (Rock Hard Ten (USA))
(8294)◆

Dawaaween (IRE) *Owen Burrows* a78 67
3 ch f Poet's Voice Ghandoorah (USA) (Forestry (USA))
2518[6] 3013[5] 3972[4] (8254) 8702[5]

Dawn Breaking *Richard Whitaker* a57 64
4 b g Firebreak Jubilee Dawn (Mark Of Esteem (IRE))
4148[8] 4584[9] 5593[7] (5817) (6036) 6628[4] 7875[10] 8306[6]

Dawn Commando *Daniel Kubler* a54 42
4 ch g Dawn Approach(IRE) Dynacam (USA) (Dynaformer (USA))
288[11] 553[7] 717[6] 1032[2] (1353) 1732[9]

Dawn Crusade (IRE)
Charlie Appleby a76
3 ch f Dawn Approach(IRE) Magical Crown (USA) (Distorted Humor (USA))
474[2] 794[2]

Dawn Delight *Hugo Palmer* a73
4 b m Dawn Approach(IRE) Al Mahmeyah (Teofilo (IRE))
27[6] (275) 464[3] 741[4]

Dawning (IRE) *Martyn Meade* a74
2 ch f Iffraaj Arabian Mirage (Oasis Dream)
8849[13] (9159)

Dawn Rising (IRE) *A P O'Brien* 88
2 b c Galileo(IRE) Devoted To You (IRE) (Danehill Dancer (IRE))
8574a[5]

Dawn The Destroyer (USA)
Kiaran McLaughlin a104
5 b m Speightstown(USA) Dashing Debby (USA) (Medaglia d'Oro (USA))
8769a[3]

Dawn Treader (IRE)
Richard Hannon a45 69
3 b g Siyouni(FR) Miss Elena (Invincible Spirit (IRE))
3261[8] 4322[11] 4874[6] 5747[6] 6860[2] 7270[3] (7973)

Dawn Trouper (IRE) *Nigel Hawke* a88 77
4 b g Dawn Approach(IRE) Dance Troupe (Rainbow Quest (USA))
3070[6] 4257[9]

Dawn View (IRE) *Stuart Williams* a61 11
2 b f Dawn Approach(IRE) Viletta (GER) (Doyen (IRE))
8458[19] 9155[4]

Dawry (IRE) *Heather Main* a74
3 b g Showcasing May Day Queen (IRE) (Danetime (IRE))
7841[6] 8552[4] 9011[2] 9350[2]◆

Daysaq (IRE) *Owen Burrows* a70
2 b c Invincible Spirit(IRE) Fawaayed (IRE) (Singspiel (IRE))
7911[4]◆ 8494[9]

Days Of Glory (CAN)
Richard Hannon a75 83
3 b c Scat Daddy(USA) Charming Thunder (USA) (Thunder Gulch (USA))
(1652) 2075[3]

Dayyan (FR) *U Schwinn* 81
2 b g Dabirsim(FR) Daraa (IRE) (Cape Cross (IRE))
(7043a)

Daze Out (IRE) *Richard Fahey* a59 27
4 b m Acclamation Maid To Order (IRE) (Zafonic (USA))
64[7] 410[9] 830[10] 1026[11]

Dazzling Dan (IRE) *Pam Sly* 107
3 b g Dandy Man(IRE) Scrumptious (Sakhee (USA))
2078[2]◆ (2835) 3865[6] 4847[3] (6222) 7193[12] 7868[4]

Dazzling Darren (IRE) *Adam West* a49 42
2 ch g Dragon Pulse(IRE) Top Of The Art (IRE) (Dark Angel (IRE))
5676[10] 6402[6] 7162[13] 8824[4] 9037[3] 9346[7]

Dazzling Des (IRE) *David O'Meara* a82 76
2 b g Brazen Beau(AUS) Secret Liaison (IRE) (Dandy Man (IRE))
1759[5] 2747[4] (4191) 4610[8] 5275[8] 6436[2] 7369[3] 8095[14] 8817[2] 9162[8] 9661[3]

Dazzling Rock (IRE) *Ralph Beckett* a83 74
4 ch g Rock Of Gibraltar(IRE) Dazzling Light (UAE) (Halling (USA))
(2239)

D'bai (IRE) *Charlie Appleby* 115
5 b g Dubawi(IRE) Savannah Belle (Green Desert (USA))
(397a)◆ 1974a[8] 9015a[4]

D B Pin (NZ) *J Size* a103 118
6 b g Darci Brahma(NZ) Pins 'N' Needles (NZ) (Pins (AUS))
9377a[7]

D Day (IRE) *Richard Hannon* a61 83
2 b g War Command(USA) Outshine (Exceed And Excel (AUS))
4925[12] (5775) 6344[5] 7119[19] 7896[28]

Deacon *F Head* a75 74
3 b c Dansili Latice (IRE) (Inchinor)
7291a[4]

Deadly Accurate *Roy Brotherton* a38 41
4 br g Lethal Force(IRE) Riccoche (IRE) (Oasis Dream)
4631[0] 1343[12] 2596[6] 5807[11]

Deal A Dollar *David Simcock* a100 87
3 b c Frankel Cape Dollar (IRE) (Cape Cross (IRE))
1824[2] 2375[2] 5614[7] (6349) 6981[2] (7302)◆ 8098[15] 9454[3]

Deansgate (IRE) *Julie Camacho* a85 73
6 b g Dandy Man(IRE) Romarca (IRE) (Raise A Grand (IRE))
499[4] 952[5] 3813[16] 4365[8] 6204[5] 6461[8] 7289[2]◆

Dean Street Doll (IRE)
Richard John O'Brien 98
3 b f Oasis Dream Soho Rose (IRE) (Hernando (FR))
2661a[2] 3115[5] 6692a[11] 7635a[7]

Dearly Beloved (IRE)
Keith Dalgleish 66
2 b f No Nay Never(USA) Forever More (IRE) (Galileo (IRE))
4583[5] 5185[11]

Dear Miriam (IRE) *Mick Channon* a59 65
3 b f Acclamation Phillippa (IRE) (Galileo (IRE))
1397[6] 2770[12] 3219[2] 3528[4] 3965[6] (4794) 5307[7]

Dear Power (IRE) *Roger Varian* a83 63
2 b f Acclamation Debuetantin (Big Shuffle (USA))
(5646) 6907[8]

Deauville (IRE) *Fawzi Abdulla Nass* 115
6 b h Galileo(IRE) Walklikeanegyptian (IRE) (Danehill (USA))
51a[11] 395a[6] 514a[14]

Debatable (IRE) *Gay Kelleway* a80 80
4 b m Cape Cross(IRE) Controversy (Elusive Quality (USA))
1578a[5] 1908a[3] 3140a[7]

Debawtry (IRE) *Phillip Makin* a64 75
4 b m Camacho Muluk (IRE) (Rainbow Quest (USA))
2846[2]◆ 3470[6] 3975[3]◆ 4632[6]◆ 4911[2]◆ 5169[3] 5515[8]

Debbie Dawn (IRE)
Cathrine Erichsen 64
2 ch f Dawn Approach(IRE) Barracade (IRE) (Barathea (IRE))
7495a[10]

Debbi's Dream *Ronald Thompson* 12
4 b m Foxwedge(AUS) Let's Dance (IRE) (Danehill Dancer (IRE))
2350[9]

Debbonair (IRE) *Hugo Palmer* a72 70
3 b g Slade Power(IRE) Bryanstown Girl (IRE) (Kalanisi (IRE))
258[3] 567[2] 917[5] 2096[8] 3092[6] 3947[5] (5334) 6022[6] 6940[3] 7756[2] 8300[3] 9303[5]

De Beau Tant *Dai Burchell* a25 22
4 b m Delegator Miss Beaudacious (IRE) (Antonius Pius (USA))
2733[10] 6043[6] 7081[8]

Debonair Don Juan (IRE)
Ed Vaughan a72 68
3 b c Lope De Vega(IRE) Dolled Up (IRE) (Whipper (USA))
3463[5] 4367[3]

De Bruyne Horse *Bernard Llewellyn* a62 100
4 b g Showcasing Right Rave (IRE) (Soviet Star (USA))
2714[14] 4281[12] 4797[7]

Deb's Delight *Richard Fahey* 87
2 b c Dark Angel(IRE) Royal Rascal (Lucky Story (USA))
(6336) 7179[7] 8026[9]

Debt Agent (NZ) *Jim Conlan* 106
6 b g Thorn Park(AUS) Prompt Payment (IRE) (In The Wings)
8578a[7] 8952a[15]

Debt Of Honour *Michael Bell* a51 51
2 b g Kyllachy Capacious (Nayef (USA))
5908[9] 6402[5] 7661[8] 8286[11]

Decanter *Sylvester Kirk* a64
2 ch f Slade Power(IRE) Buttercross (Zamindar (USA))
6629[5] 7031[3] 7515[8]

December Second (IRE)
Philip Kirby 97
5 b g Teofilo(IRE) Bulbul (IRE) (Shamardal (USA))
4066[2] 4600[2] 5098[2] (5849)

Decima (IRE) *Michael Easterby* a54 68
5 b m Dream Ahead(USA) Snowtime (IRE) (Galileo (IRE))
2345[6]

Decision Maker (IRE) *Roy Bowring* a63 57
5 b g Iffraaj Consensus (IRE) (Common Grounds)
43[8] (1085)◆ 1817[5] 2580[12] (3452) 4335[3] 5244[7] 5986[10] 8840[3] 9219[9] 9539[8]

Declamation (IRE) *John Butler* a46 49
9 ch g Shamardal(USA) Dignify (IRE) (Rainbow Quest (USA))
5807[8] 6547[10] 7080[8] 8404[6] 8822[9] 9133[8] 9659[9]

Declared Interest *Ralph Beckett* a73 73
2 b f Declaration Of War(USA) Wiener Valkyrie (Shamardal (USA))
7458[3] 8848[2]

Declaring Love *Charlie Appleby* 82
2 gb f Dubawi(IRE) Wedding March (IRE) (Dalakhani (IRE))
2836[3]

Deconso *Christopher Kellett* a61 54
3 b g Dandy Man(IRE) Tranquil Flight (Oasis Dream)
(235) 406[7] (620) 813[7] 1167[5] 1430[3] 1863[8] 2871[5] 3775[4] 4457[5] 4874[4] 5869[3] (6024)◆ 6389[7]

Decora (IRE) *Mick Channon* 62
2 ch f Conduit(IRE) Grevillea (IRE) (Admiralofthefleet (USA))
3257[4] 3798[3]

Decorated Invader (USA)
Christophe Clement 105
2 b c Declaration Of War(USA) Gamely Girl (USA) (Arch (USA))
8746a[4]

Decoration Of War (IRE)
Michael Appleby a75 57
4 b g Declaration Of War(USA) Sea Paint (IRE) (Peintre Celebre (USA))
22[6] 886[6] 1025[5] 1511[7] 9361[13]

Decrypt *P Twomey* 102
3 gr c Dark Angel(IRE) She's A Worldie (IRE) (Kodiac)
3104a[3]

Deebaj (IRE) *Gary Moore* a49 53
7 br g Authorized(IRE) Athreyaa (Singspiel (IRE))
4251[10]

Deebee *Declan Carroll* a26 72
3 ch g Dawn Approach(IRE) Tooraweenah (Notnowcato)
2250[2] 2507[6] 3373[8] 4068[6] 5124[7] 5947[5]

Dee Dee Dottie *Mark Loughnane* a37 1
3 b f Delegator Pantita (Polish Precedent (USA))
2967[7] 3574[7] 5748[9] 8251[8] 8553[10]

Deeds Not Words (IRE)
Tracy Waggott a42 59
8 b g Royal Applause Wars (IRE) (Green Desert (USA))
(144) (177) 407[7] 741[7] 1082[3] 1818[3] 2294[5] 2709[8] 3656[11] 4335[13] 5767[2] 6273[8] 6462[9] 7050[9] 7307[12] 7591[9] 7962[9] 8301[7] 8530[8]

Dee Ex Bee *Mark Johnston* 121
4 b h Farhh Dubai Sunrise (USA) (Seeking The Gold (USA))
(2269) (3024)◆ 4015[2] 5522[2] 6421[2] 7928a[3]

Deemster (IRE) *A Fabre* a97 102
4 b g Invincible Spirit(IRE) Tribune (FR) (Grand Slam (USA))
2782a[5] 9483a[4]

Deep Intrigue *Mark Johnston* a98 94
3 gr c Dark Angel(IRE) Abbakova (IRE) (Dandy Man (IRE))
57[6] (261) (806) 989[2] 1920[7] 2570[4] 3075[9]◆ 4379[7] 4654[6] 5195[2]

Deep Resolve (IRE) *Barry Leavy*
8 b g Intense Focus(USA) I'll Be Waiting (Vettori (IRE))
1971[9]

Deep Snow *Saeed bin Suroor* 78
2 b f Bated Breath Polar Circle (USA) (Royal Academy (USA))
5342[2]◆

Deep State (IRE) *H-A Pantall* a60 71
3 b c Archipenko(USA) Hayaku (USA) (Arch (USA))
2390a[4]

Deerfoot *Anthony Carson* 32
3 ch g Archipenko(USA) Danceatdusk (Desert Prince (IRE))
1690[11] 2366[7] 2926[9] 3275[8]

Deer Song *John Bridger* a52 50
6 b g Piccolo Turkish Delight (Prince Sabo)
(244) 357[10] 553[9] 919[9] 1093[7] 1210[5] 3014[10] 3688[4] 4026[4] 5750[6]

Deevious Beau *David Barron* 55
2 b g Brazen Beau(AUS) Vespasia (Medicean)
6822[8] 7333[8] 7538[5]

Defence Treaty (IRE)
Richard Fahey a83 84
3 b g Dandy Man(IRE) Just Like Ivy (CAN) (Street Cry (IRE))
2055[3] 3202[6] (3650) (4288) 5434[5] 5971[4] 6935[4] 7312[3] 7653[10] 8412[3]

Deference *Amanda Perrett* a75 59
3 ch g Showcasing Quiet (Observatory (USA))
2405[5] 5813[6] 6418[8] 7839[3]

Defoe (IRE) *Roger Varian* 122
5 gr g Dalakhani(IRE) Dulkashe (IRE) (Pivotal)
1750[4] 2410[2] (3314) (4093) 5414[9]

Degas (GER) *Markus Klug* 109
6 ch g Exceed And Excel(AUS) Diatribe (Tertullian (USA))
51a[10] 397a[12] 1793a[3] 3287a[9] 4157a[7] 5230a[7]

Degraves (IRE)
Joseph Patrick O'Brien 104
2 b c Camelot Daganya (IRE) (Danehill Dancer (IRE))
(8574a)

Degrisement (FR) *J Reynier* a95 83
5 b g Lawman(FR) Maria Gabriella (IRE) (Rock Of Gibraltar (IRE))
9483a[2]

Dehara (IRE) *Rinaldo Boccardelli* 95
3 b f Canford Cliffs(IRE) Marhaba (Nayef (USA))
2161a[3]

Deia Glory *Michael Dods* a90 90
3 b f Kyllachy Blue Lyric (Refuse To Bend (IRE))
2779[4] 4101[6] 4932[5] 5471a[6] 6648a[4] 7401[12] 8328a[10]

Deidra (IRE) *M D O'Callaghan* 78
2 gr f Dark Angel(IRE) Lethal Lena (IRE) (Thousand Words)
7742a[9]

Deinonychus *Michael Appleby* a60 76
8 b g Authorized(IRE) Sharp Dresser (USA) (Diesis)
2629[5] 3377[4] 3500[10] 3937[4] 5743[2] (6059) 6658[6] 6896[3] (7829) (8033) 8515[5] 8862[9] 9221[6]

Deira Surprise *Hugo Palmer* a73 78
3 ch f Slade Power(IRE) Beautiful Filly (Oasis Dream)
1360[8] 2144[8] 3323[8] 4338[4] 4626[2]

Deirdre (JPN) *Mitsuru Hashida* 118
5 b m Harbinger Reizend (JPN) (Special Week (JPN))
1445a[4] 3985[6] (5586) 7219a[4] 8335[3] 9376a[4]

Deja (FR) *Peter Chapple-Hyam* a106 96
4 b h Youmzain(IRE) Atarfe (IRE) (Anabaa (USA))
(4504)◆ 9094[5]

Delachance (FR) *P Monfort* a80 74
3 b g Linngari(IRE) Three French Hens (IRE) (Elnadim (USA))
2243[3]◆ 2976[2] 4489[4] 5492[2] (6013) 9281a[6]

Delagate The Lady *Michael Attwater* a50 29
3 b f Delegator Lady Phill (Avonbridge)
137[2] 296[4]◆ 402[5]

Delagate This Lord
Michael Attwater a57 83
5 b g Delegator Lady Filly (Atraf)
1915[5] 3164[5] 3856[10] 4230[10] (4495) 4926[2] 5318[4] 6203[2] 6668[3] (7230) 7564[5]

Delaire *N Dooly* a44 42
7 b g Sakhee's Secret Moody Margaret (Bahamian Bounty)
4777[6]

Delannoy *Neil Mulholland* a22 34
5 ch g Le Havre(IRE) Raving Monsun (Monsun (GER))
6055[9] 6843[14]

De Latour *Jason Ward* a56 60
3 b g Epaulette(AUS) Zerka (Invincible Spirit (IRE))
2327[5] 4823[9] 5038[10] 5738[5] 6275[11] 6978[6]

Delaware *A Fabre* a97 112
3 b c Frankel Zatsfine (Oasis Dream)
(5480a) (6249a) 7007a[9]

Delcia *Emma Lavelle* a41
3 b f Delegator Fiducia (Lawman (FR))
8808[7] 9157[11]

Delectable *Adrian Nicholls* a27 28
3 b f Cape Cross(IRE) Dulcet (IRE) (Halling (USA))
3270[13] 4000[9]

Delegating *Keith Henry Clarke* a64 49
5 b m Delegator Whispered Wish (Rainbow Quest (USA))
784[5]

Deleyll *John Butler* a59 61
5 ch g Sepoy(AUS) Strings (Unfuwain (USA))
5282[8] 6317[8] 7858[9] 9006[9] 9479[4]

Delicate Kiss *John Bridger* a82 78
5 b m Delegator Desert Kiss (Cape Cross (IRE))
175[2] (516) 4453[8] 5136[5] 5351[2] 6469[6] 6729[2] 7165[2] 7343[2] 7839[5] (8807) 9126[3]◆ 9304[5] 9658[2]

Delilah Park *Chris Wall* a86 65
5 b m Delegator Sarah Park (IRE) (Redback)
2484[9] 3549[6] (4247) 5283[8] 6076[2] (6968) 8017[2]

Delirium (IRE) *Ed de Giles* a51 62
5 b m Tamayuz Coeur De La Mer (IRE) (Caerleon (USA))
3267[7] 4232[5] 4499[4] 4869[5] 5795[6]

De Little Engine (IRE)
Alexandra Dunn a70 73
5 ch g Power Reveuse De Jour (IRE) (Sadler's Wells (USA))
9[11] 701[13] 1338[2] 1768[7] (1933) 2929[2] 3540[8] 4479[4] 5839[2] 6116[3] 6795[3] (7273) 9140[12] 9244[10]

Dell' Arca (IRE) *David Pipe* 85
10 b g Sholokhov(IRE) Daisy Belle (GER) (Acatenango (GER))
5496[4]

Del Mar May (USA) *Richard Baltas* a92
3 b f Jimmy Creed(USA) Big Lou (USA) (Malibu Moon (USA))
9638a[6]

Delph Crescent (IRE)
Richard Fahey a88 80
4 gr g Dark Angel(IRE) Zut Alors (IRE) (Pivotal)
1461[12] 1813[3] 2374[2] 2748[5] 3338[4] 3811[8] 4548[5] 5198[6] 5741[4] (6210) 6686[7] 7127[4] 7589[3] 7907[3] 8396[13]

Delphinia (IRE) *A P O'Brien* a93 114
3 b f Galileo(IRE) Again (IRE) (Danehill Dancer (IRE))
1307a[6] 2642a[3] 3316[5] 6239a[3] 7118[2] 7926a[2] 8333[2] (8710)◆

Del's Edge *Christopher Mason* a10 20
3 b f Harbour Watch(IRE) Elidore (Danetime (IRE))
5448[6] 6023[7] 6561[4] 8672[7]

Delta Bravo (IRE) *J S Moore* a55 50
3 b f Mastercraftsman(IRE) Rhiannon (IRE) (High Chaparral (IRE))
2341[9] 4447[6] 5641a[5] 6094a[10] 7474[5] 8869[10]

Delta Prince (USA) *James Jerkens* a78 114
6 bb h Street Cry(IRE) Delta Princess (USA) (A.P. Indy (USA))
444a[3]

Delta River *Jo Hughes* a77 85
4 b g Kodiac Waterways (IRE) (Alhaarth (IRE))
1346[2] 1827a[5]

Delta's Royalty (IRE) *Roger Varian* a76
2 b f Galileo(IRE) Royal Delta (USA) (Empire Maker (USA))
(9327)◆

Deluree (FR) *N Caullery* a46 43
3 b f Kheleyf(USA) Comedienne (FR) (Deportivo)
4229a[5] 5165a[10] 7642a[11]

Democracy (GER) *P Schiergen* 92
2 b f Areion(GER) Djidda (GER) (Lando (GER))
8586a[2]

Demons And Wizards (IRE)
Lydia Richards a54 44
4 b g Elnadim(USA) Crystal Theatre (IRE) (King's Theatre (IRE))
801[3] 717[9] 925[12]

Demophon *Steve Flook* a47 47
5 b g Oasis Dream Galatee (FR) (Galileo (IRE))
58[4] 257[8] 321[11] 482[6] 947[2] 1341[6] 2239[6] 3205[9] 4019[5] 4777[7] 5379[4] 5891[4] 6366[6] 6824[3] 7818[7] 8916[7] 9497[4]

Denis The Diva *Rae Guest* a45 55
3 b g Aussie Rules(USA) Lunarian (Bahamian Bounty)
3170[13] 3574[5] 5797[10] 6389[9]

Dennis' Moment (USA)
Dale Romans a109
2 b c Tiznow(USA) Transplendid (USA) (Elusive Quality (USA))
8749a[8]

Denzille Lane (IRE) *Doug Watson* a58 58
7 ch g Iffraaj Alexander Youth (IRE) (Exceed And Excel (AUS))
97a[5] 1322a[14]

Deolali *Stella Barclay* a44
5 b g Sleeping Indian Dulally (Dubawi (IRE))
210[12] 501[4] 1083[8]

Depardieu *M C Grassick* a54 59
2 ch g Leroidesanimaux(BRZ) Stellaire (Archipenko (USA))
7247a[25] 9501[7]

Department Of War (IRE)
Stuart Williams 79
4 ch g Declaration Of War(USA) Danetime Out (IRE) (Danetime (IRE))
3040[6]◆

Depeche Toi (IRE)
Jonathan Portman 40
2 ch f Camacho Dew (IRE) (Whipper (USA))
3165[9] 4062[5] 4840[10]

Dependable (GER) *Charles Hills* a42 58
4 ch m Reliable Man Dessau (GER) (Soldier Hollow)
3264[9] 5309[10] 6302[3] (7335)

Depose *Hugo Palmer* a75
2 b f Kingman Tested (Selkirk (USA))
5045[7] 8218[2] 8849[6] 9300[4]

Deposit (IRE) *David Simcock* a59
2 b g Sea The Stars(IRE) Interim Payment (USA) (Red Ransom (USA))
8823[12] 9052[8] 9326[9]

Deptford Mick (IRE) *Rae Guest* a46 69
3 br g Bated Breath Be Joyful (IRE) (Teofilo (IRE))
3167[4] 3839[10] 4328[11]

Deputise *William Haggas* a104 77
3 b g Kodiac Dolly Colman (IRE) (Diamond Green (FR))
1920[2] 2434[4] 3166[4] 7449[5]

Deputy Star *Ben Haslam* a48
3 b g Epaulette(AUS) Starkat (Diktat)
9350[5]

Dereham *John Berry* 53
3 b g Sir Percy Desiree (IRE) (Desert Story (IRE))
7159[9] 7730[6]

Derek Duval (USA) *Stuart Williams* a85 90
5 b g Lope De Vega(IRE) Lady Raj (USA) (El Prado (IRE))
184[6] 434[2]

Derek Le Grand *Grace Harris* 59
2 b g Mukhadram Duo De Choc (IRE) (Manduro (GER))
7235[8] 7755[9] 8244[9]

Derevo *Sir Michael Stoute* a100 101
3 b c Dansili Pavlosk (USA) (Arch (USA))
(1711) 2321[4] (4144) (5437) 8092[6]

Derma Louvre (JPN) *Hirofumi Toda* a102
3 br c Pyro(USA) Caribbean Romance (JPN) (Commands (AUS))
1443a[4]

Derry Boy *David Evans* a70 43
3 b g Havana Gold(IRE) Steppe By Steppe (Zamindar (USA))
367[2] 554[2] 761[4] 1094[2] 2114[12] 3302[5] 8496[7] 8852[9] 9256[5]

Dersu Uzala (IRE) *Marco Gasparini* 94
6 b g Windsor Knot(IRE) Ma Vai (IRE) (Be My Guest (USA))
4432a[7]

Desai *Noel Wilson* a60 64
5 br g Dansili Arabesque (Zafonic (USA))
500[RR] 608[5] 785[6] 2147[8] 3178[8] 3969[9] 4060[7] 4513[10]

Descendant *Miss Katy Brown* a65 59
4 b g Paco Boy(IRE) Eve (Rainbow Quest (USA))
5632[8]

Descouvrir Baileys (FR) *J-V Toux* a52 55
4 b g George Vancouver(USA) Frissonante (Sri Pekan (USA))
2170a[10]

Desert Ace (IRE) *Paul Midgley* a59 76
8 ch g Kheleyf(USA) Champion Place (Compton Place)
1194[13] 2079[7] 2421[12] 3658[3] 4230[15] (4514) 4880[13] 5244[10] 6099[11] 6699[2]◆ 6932[2] (7334) 7736[4] 8400[11]

Desert Caravan *William Haggas* a85
3 b g Oasis Dream Sequence (IRE) (Selkirk (USA))
(8718)◆ (9038)

Desert Doctor (IRE) *Ed Walker* a103 96
4 ch g Society Rock(IRE) Dorn Hill (Lujain (USA))
203[5] (382) 762[5] (1105) 1421[3]◆ 1829[7] 2743[17] 3480[5] 3863[13] 5942[4] 6920[8] (7372) 9478[2]◆

Desert Dream *Michael Easterby* a62 75
5 b g Oasis Dream Rosika (Sakhee (USA))
2899[11] 3704[9] 3957[9] 4322[12]

Desert Encounter (IRE)
David Simcock 119
7 b g Halling(USA) La Chicana (IRE) (Invincible Spirit (IRE))
1113a[3] 1446a[8] 3985[8] 4848[3] (5613) (6467) (7455) (8155a)

Desert Fire (IRE) *Saeed bin Suroor* a113 104
4 b h Cape Cross(IRE) Crystal House (CHI) (Golden Voyager (USA))
(285a)◆ 637a[2] 961a[3] 1927[4] 3992[2]◆ 5657[4] 6536[3] (6861)

Desert Flyer *John Gosden* a72
2 b f Shamardal(USA) White Moonstone (USA) (Dynaformer (USA))
(9471)◆

Desert Fox *Mike Murphy* a74 61
5 b g Foxwedge(AUS) Snow Moccasin (IRE) (Oasis Dream)
(2318) 3147[8] 5352[5] 5889[2] (6631) 7552[4] 7837[2] 8419[10] 9365[7]

Desert Friend (IRE) *David Simcock* a80 82
3 ch g Universal(IRE) Assabiyya (IRE) (Cape Cross (IRE))
5055[5] 5734[6]

Desert Frost (IRE)
Saeed bin Suroor a91 96
5 b g Dark Angel(IRE) Layla Jamil (IRE) (Exceed And Excel (AUS))
282a[10]

Desert Heights (IRE) *Mme V Deiss* a71 77
5 b g So You Think(NZ) Desert Fantasy (Oasis Dream)
115a[4]

Desert Icon (FR) *William Haggas* 101
3 b g Sea The Stars(IRE) Plume Rose (Marchand De Sable (USA))
1852[4]◆ (2289) 2802[3] (4256)◆ 5541[8] 5966[2] 6696[2]

Desert Land (IRE) *David Simcock* a63 76
3 b c Kodiac La Chicana (IRE) (Invincible Spirit (IRE))
2488[7] 3696[3] 4655[2] 5494[4] 7313[2] 7854[3]

Desert Lantern (USA)
Mark Johnston a78 53
3 b f More Than Ready(USA) Shuruq (USA) (Elusive Quality (USA))
1925[7] 2251[11] 3041[7] 3570[11] 4454[3] 4751[3]

Desert Lion *David Simcock* a81 73
3 b g Lope De Vega(IRE) Sorella Bella (IRE) (Clodovil (IRE))
1352[2] 2198[4] (4774) 5782[8] (8548)

Desert Lord (AUS)
Michael, Wayne & John Hawkes 98
4 b g High Chaparral(IRE) Nova Star (AUS) (Iglesia (AUS))
8360a[9]

Desert Mission (IRE)
Simon Crisford a70 63
3 b f Shamardal(USA) Jathabah (IRE) (Singspiel (IRE))
2128[8] 2731[3] 3495[5] 4187[6]

Desert Palms *Richard Hannon* 73
2 b c Oasis Dream Be My Gal (Galileo (IRE))
3542[7] 5131[4] 6464[6] 8465[12]

Desert Peace (USA)
Charlie Appleby a84
2 b c Curlin(USA) Stoweshoe (USA) (Flatter (USA))
(8011) 8751[3]

Desert Point (FR) *Keith Dalgleish* a62 88
7 b g Le Havre(IRE) Bonne Mere (FR) (Stepneyev (IRE))
2680[3] 3081[3] 3514[4] 4381[12] 5097[4] 6012[2]

Desert Ride (CAN) *Neil J Howard* a99 68
3 b f Candy Ride(ARG) Fun In The Desert (CAN) (Distorted Humor (USA))
6993a[8]

Desert Ruler *Jedd O'Keeffe* a90 84
6 b g Kheleyf(USA) Desert Royalty (IRE) (Alhaarth (IRE))
522[3] (803) 1559[5] 1761[3] 2748[8] 3073[9] 4241[9] 5201[7] 7003[12] 7577[6]

Desert Safari (IRE) *Mark Johnston* a95 93
2 b c Slade Power(IRE) Risen Sun (Shamardal (USA))
(7030) (7569) 7904[3] 8426[2]

Desert Secret *Saeed bin Suroor* a60
3 ch c Pivotal Secret Keeper (New Approach (IRE))
5634[5]

Desert Skyline (IRE) *David Elsworth* a105 113
5 ch g Tamayuz Diamond Tango (FR) (Acatenango (GER))
2807[5] 3864[5] 4382[11] 4884[3] 5662[7] 6473[3]

Desert Son *Sir Michael Stoute* a57
4 ch g Dubawi(IRE) Russelliana (Medicean)
2555[7] 3445[5]

Desert War (USA) *Hugo Palmer* a64
3 gr g Oasis Dream Gracie Square (USA) (Awesome Again (CAN))
2550[4]

Desert Warrior (IRE) *F Foresi* a50 68
6 ch g Peintre Celebre(USA) Danse Grecque (USA) (Hold That Tiger (USA))
5035a[5] 6521a[13]

Desert Wind (IRE) *Ed Vaughan* a104 94
4 b h Worthadd(IRE) Matula (IRE) (Halling (USA))
1422[3]◆ 2033[10] (3466) 4884[11] 7122[6]

Designated *Clive Cox* a65
3 ch f Dutch Art Entitled (Pivotal)
316[5] 1020[7]

Desire For Freedom (USA)
Roger Varian a67
3 b f Fed Biz(USA) Leinster Lady (USA) (E Dubai (USA))
1423[4]

Desirous *Ralph Beckett* a78 93
3 b f Kingman Emulous (Dansili)
(3041)◆ 4052[7] 4667[6] 5910[2] 6951[4] 7728[5]

Despoina (IRE) *Jedd O'Keeffe* a56
2 ch f New Approach(IRE) Dream Child (IRE) (Pivotal)
7579[4] 9095[10]

Destinata *Mme Pia Brandt* a62 72
4 b m Canford Cliffs(IRE) Hurricane Lady (IRE) (Hurricane Run (IRE))
1908a[5]

Destination *William Haggas* a82 94
3 b g Mukhadram Danehill Destiny (Danehill Dancer (IRE))
2094[5] (2506) 3463[2] 4347[2]

Destination Aim *Fred Watson* a24 51
12 b g Dubai Destination(USA) Tessa Reef (IRE) (Mark Of Esteem (IRE))
3924[7] 4584[12] 5517[15]

Destinys Rock *Mark Loughnane* a69 67
4 b m Zoffany(IRE) Special Destiny (Tobougg (IRE))
67[4] 536[9] 835[6] 1506[5] 2692[8] 3473[9] 4371[2]◆ (5025) 5850[5] 7060[12] 7858[10]

Destroyer *Tom Tate* a80 70
6 b g Royal Applause Good Girl (IRE) (College Chapel)
5398[9] 6460[12] 6729[8] 7074[7] 7378[3]◆ 8087[12] 8305[6] 9512[10]

Detachment *Shaun Harris* a45 79
6 b g Motivator Argumentative (Observatory (USA))
1413[13] 2710[14] 3867[15] 5245[3] 5516[3]◆ 6210[4] 7782[7] 7907[5] 8341[6] 9109[12]

Detective *Sir Michael Stoute* a50
3 b g Kingman Promising Lead (Danehill (USA))
7373[10]

Detonation *Shaun Harris* 62
3 gr c Sun Central(IRE) Tomintoul Star (Dansili)
5477[8] 6274[4] 6890[6]

Devant (FR) *H-A Pantall* 102
3 ch f Showcasing Davantage (FR) (Galileo (IRE))
1706a[4] 2621[3] 3621a[9] 4621a[5] 5608[16]

De Vegas Kid (IRE) *Tony Carroll* a78 89
5 ch g Lope De Vega(IRE) Fravolina (USA) (Lemon Drop Kid (USA))
(3185) (4061) 4322[4] (5804) 8253[7] 9198[9]

Deverell *John Gosden* a68 65
2 b c Kingman Lizzie Siddal (Dansili)
2973[6] 6708[7] 8319[6] 8890[9]

Deviant (CAN) *Danny Pish* a51 92
2 ch c Daredevil(USA) Alkmaar (CAN) (Monashee Mountain (USA))
8746a[13]

Devil (IRE) *F Head* 109
2 b c Siyouni(FR) Burma Sea (FR) (Lope De Vega (IRE))
(5468a) 6264a[8] (7292a) 8140a[2]

Devilla (FR) *J Bertran De Balanda*
2 b f American Devil(FR) Vila Flor (FR) (Sandwaki (USA))
5600a[10]

Devil Or Angel *Bill Turner* a63 58
4 ch m Assertive Level Pegging (IRE) (Common Grounds)
4396[4] 4749[6] 5084[7] (5884) 6602[5] (7557) 7844[6]

Devil's Angel *Jedd O'Keeffe* a69 51
3 gr g Dark Angel(IRE) Rocking The Boat (IRE) (Zebedee)
(500) 1720[8]

Devils Roc *Jonathan Portman* a73 75
3 gr f Lethal Force(IRE) Ring For Baileys (Kyllachy)
1687[4] (2276) 3045[3] 4185[12] 4556[3] 5289[3] 6286[9] (6857) 7157[5] 7230[12] 7843[3] 8254[4] 9218[6]

Devizes (IRE) *Pat Phelan* a59 41
3 b g Dubawi(IRE) Dalasyla (IRE) (Marju (IRE))
6290[12] 6836[7] 8828[2]

Devolution (FR) *F Vermeulen* 25
3 b f Makfi Dolce Cabana (Authorized (IRE))
5329a[7]

Dew Pond *Tim Easterby* a53 61
7 b g Motivator Rutland Water (IRE) (Hawk Wing (USA))
1861[5] 2373[3] 3272[8] (3705) 4004[4] 4208[3] 4435[2] 4990[6] 5743[5] 5905[2] 6180[2] 6827[4] 7368[12] 7441[13]

Dezba *M Nigge* a83 83
3 b f Kingman Vedela (FR) (Selkirk (USA))
683a[6]

Dhangadhi (FR) *L Gadbin* a46 83
7 bl m American Post Darmagi (IRE) (Desert King (IRE))
7860a[3]

Dharma Rain (IRE) *Clare Hobson* a50 59
4 b m High Chaparral(IRE) Crazy Volume (IRE) (Machiavellian (USA))
2196[5] 2528[6]

Dhevanafushi *H-A Pantall* a79 96
6 gr g Kendargent(FR) Tejaara (USA) (Kingmambo (USA))
3030a[6] 3879a[15]

Diaboleo (FR) *Ian Williams* a72 73
3 ch g Galileo(IRE) Beautifix (GER) (Bering)
1198a[3] 7143[6]

Diajaka (GER) *Markus Klug* 92
3 b f Kamsin(GER) Diacada (GER) (Cadeaux Genereux)
2137a[6] 3119a[8]

Diamanta (GER) *Markus Klug* 103
3 b f Maxios Diamantgottin (GER) (Fantastic Light (USA))
3877a[3] (5720a)

Diamond Avalanche (IRE)
Liam Bailey
6 b g Alfred Nobel(IRE) Queens Flight (King's Best (USA))
1506[12]

Diamond Cara *Stuart Williams* a10 41
3 ch f Equiano(FR) Tychy (Suave Dancer (USA))
4396[6] 5062[7] 5622[10] 5960[6] 6325[5] 7319[7] 8697[10]

Diamond Cottage
Malcolm Saunders a55
2 ch f Cappella Sansevero Avrilo (Piccolo)
7571[8] 9284[8] 9569[5]

Diamond Cruz (FR) *S Dehez* 50
2 b f Diamond Boy(FR) Alta Cruz (FR) (Poliglote)
9123a[7]

Diamond Dougal (IRE)
Mick Channon 95
4 b g Zebedee Blue Saphire (Acclamation)
(1654) 2117[2] 2568[5] 3589[4] 3945[7] 5476[7] 6396[5] 6714[5]◆ (7701)◆ 8512[11]

Diamond Falls (IRE)
Amanda Perrett a68
2 br g Alhebayeb(IRE) Saint Lucia (IRE) (Whipper (USA))
7787[3]◆ 8287[12]

Diamond Hill (IRE) *W P Mullins* 96
6 b m Beat Hollow Sixhills (FR) (Sabrehill (USA))
8245[7]

Diamond Jill (IRE)
Sarah Hollinshead a45
2 b f Footstepsinthesand Sindiyma (IRE) (Kalanisi (IRE))
9284[9]

Diamond Lady *William Stone* a70 83
8 b m Multiplex Ellen Mooney (Efisio)
1586[2] (1930) 2484[5] (3536) 3963[2] 4835[6]

Diamond Oasis *Hugo Palmer* a76 45
3 ch f Iffraaj Belonging (Raven's Pass (USA))
(1543)◆ 1985[2] 8809[11] 9424[6]

Diamond Oops (USA)
Patrick L Biancone a106 107
4 b g Lookin At Lucky(USA) Patriotic Viva (USA) (Whywhywhy (USA))
7922a[2] 8771a[8]

Diamond Pursuit *Ivan Furtado* a47 47
4 b m Pastoral Pursuits Broughtons Jewel (IRE) (Bahri (USA))
166[3] 484[7] 587[7] 887[4] 1026[9] 1192[6] 1553[12] 2298[4] 3410[4] 3996[6] 4582[10]

Diamond Reflection (IRE)
Alexandra Dunn a57 55
7 b g Oasis Dream Briolette (IRE) (Sadler's Wells (USA))
(62) 207[6] 399[2] 792[11] 1215[9] 1297[4] 1680[2] 2970[13] 4460[13] 6855[9]

Diamonds A Dancing
Laura Morgan a54 58
9 ch g Delta Dancer Zing (Zilzal (USA))
457[P]

Diamonds And Rust *Bill Turner* a63 28
2 b f Casamento(IRE) Constant Craving (Pastoral Pursuits)
6793[6] 7030[4] 7627[13] 9196[2]

Diamonds Forever (FR) *L Gadbin* a70 60
2 b f Footstepsinthesand Dalawala (IRE) (Hawk Wing (USA))
4533a[9] 9123a[12]

Diamond Shower (IRE) *John Flint* 62
3 b f Clodovil(IRE) Star Lodge (Grand Lodge (USA))
3157[3] 3920[2] 4367[4] 4912[9] 5893[4] (6526) 6856[4] 8247[9]

Diamond Sparkles (USA) *Mark Casse* 96
2 b f War Front(USA) Diamondsandrubies (IRE) (Fastnet Rock (AUS))
4819[4]◆ (5387)◆ 7267a[4]

Diamond Vendome (FR) *C Escuder* a97 108
4 b g Style Vendome(FR) Ordargent (FR) (Kendargent (FR))
(5079a) 6144a[7]

Diamonique *Keith Dalgleish* a74 76
3 b f Kyllachy Al Joudha (FR) (Green Desert (USA))
2149[9] 4604[2] 4986[3] 5617[3] 5854[3] 5901[2] 6070[2] 6607[10] 7402[14] 7511[8] 8419[3] 9402[6]

Dia Socks (USA) *Ji Yong Cheol* a104
5 ch h Langfuhr(CAN) Royal Strategy (USA) (Woodman (USA))
7010a[2]

Diavolaccia (ITY) *Nicolo Simondi* 64
2 b f Sakhee's Secret Doudounes (IRE) (Azamour (IRE))
8393a[9]

Dick Datchery (IRE) *David O'Meara* 78
2 b g Make Believe Bayja (IRE) (Giant's Causeway (USA))
4688[4] (5234)◆ 7437[5]

Dieulefit (IRE)
J C Cerqueira Germano a94 59
4 b m Oasis Dream Tereschenko (USA) (Giant's Causeway (USA))
9603a[6]

Di Fede (IRE) *Ralph Beckett* a91 106
4 b m Shamardal(USA) Dibiya (IRE) (Caerleon (USA))
3069[10] 3986[5] 4706a[3] 5475[2] 6508[4] 7146[9] (7893)

Digicode (FR) *P Monfort* a71 75
4 ch g Soul City(IRE) Solitudine (Inchinor)
992a[5] 3715a[6]

Digital Age (IRE) *Chad C Brown* 105
3 b c Invincible Spirit(IRE) Willow View (USA) (Lemon Drop Kid (USA))
6994a[8]

Digosville (FR) *F-H Graffard* 42
2 b f Siyouni(FR) Dasani (FR) (Dansili)
1448a[6]

Diligent Deb (IRE) *William Muir* a65 77
2 b f Due Diligence(USA) Kummel Excess (IRE) (Exceed And Excel (AUS))
(3660) 4048[9]◆ 5411[9] 6073[4] 6833[8]

Diligent Lass *Michael Blanshard* 22
2 b f Due Diligence(USA) Sunny York (IRE) (Vale Of York (IRE))
5314[13] 6527[4]

Dilithium (FR) *Kevin Ryan* 60
2 b g Dabirsim(FR) Lady Family (FR) (Sinndar (IRE))
6337[6] 7902[5]

Dilly Dilly (IRE) *John Wainwright* 42
3 b f Moohaajim(IRE) Scarlet Rosefinch (Cockney Rebel (IRE))
2909[9] 3339[6] 4629[3] 5914[15]

Dilmun Dynasty (IRE)
Sir Michael Stoute a80 76
3 b c Sea The Stars(IRE) Elegant Shadow (GER) (Shamardal (USA))
2764[3]◆ 3584[4] 4177[3] 4996[4]

Diluvien (FR) *Gianluca Bietolini* 102
4 b g Manduro(GER) Soldera (USA) (Polish Numbers (USA))
6095a[3] (6521a)

Dimanche A Bamako (FR)
C Boutin a31 35
4 b g Deportivo Route Des Indes (FR) (Dernier Empereur (USA))
1578a[9] 2647a[14]

Di Matteo *Marco Botti* a72 69
3 b f Bated Breath Pantile (Pivotal)
795[4] 1142[9] 1838[6] (2212) 3427[4] 4507[2] 5056[4] 5622[5] 6027[6] 8254[6]

Dimmesdale *John O'Shea* a62 54
4 b g Nathaniel(IRE) Diara Angel (IRE) (Hawk Wing (USA))
242[5] 696[6] 1331[7] 2468[5] 2998[8] 4498[3] 5378[11] 7790[11] 8854[13]

Dina (GER) *Markus Klug* 96
4 b m Nathaniel(IRE) Diatribe (Tertullian (USA))
3288a[10]

Dinah Washington (IRE)
Michael Bell a17 55
3 ch f Australia Gainful (USA) (Gone West (USA))
1834[6] 2102[8] 3275[7] 5028[6] 5648[11]

Dinard Rose (IRE) *Noel Meade* a58 82
3 b f Champs Elysees Rose Of Petra (IRE) (Golan (IRE))
5712a[5]

Diocles Of Rome (IRE)
Ralph Beckett a93 91
4 b g Holy Roman Emperor(IRE) Serisia (FR) (Exit To Nowhere (USA))
2363[5] (3308) 4385[6] 5413[14] 6318[2] 7188[8] 8016[7]

Diocletian (IRE) *Andrew Balding* a86 100
4 b g Camelot Saturday Girl (Peintre Celebre (USA))
291[4] 558[6] 2578[9] 3861[2] 5423[2] 6044[3] (7181)◆

Diodorus (IRE) *Karen McLintock* a71 75
5 b g Galileo(IRE) Divine Proportions (USA) (Kingmambo (USA))
2186[9] 3222[10] 3816[6] 4817[5] 5097[3] 6016[2] 6674[2] 9288[6]

Dioresse (IRE) *M Figge* a78 66
4 b m So You Think(NZ) Diora (IRE) (Dashing Blade)
682a[16]

Diplomat (GER) *Carina Fey* 99
8 b h Teofilo(IRE) Desidera (IRE) (Shaadi (USA))
869a[4]

Dirchill (IRE) *David Thompson* a62 67
5 b g Power Bawaakeer (USA) (Kingmambo (USA))
23[3] 355[6] 496[7] 808[3] 952[6] 1487[5] 1760[12] 2379[3] 2899[8] 3221[7] 3706[14] 3921[4] 4335[14] 6945[12] 8306[14] 9106[10]

Directory *James Eustace* a86 57
4 b g Oasis Dream Minority (Generous (IRE))
1727[10] (2297) 2966[10] 4249[2] 4506[3] 6964[10] 8658[5] 9199[4] (9561)

Dirk (IRE) *A Botti* 104
5 b h Mujahid(USA) Docksil (Docksider (USA))
2886a[4]

Dirty Dancer (FR) *Ralph Beckett* 76
2 b f No Nay Never(USA) Super Marmelade (IRE) (Duke Of Marmalade (IRE))
5132[4] 5684[2] 6710[5]

Dirty Rascal (IRE) *Tom Ward* a85 95
3 b c Acclamation Refusetolisten (IRE) (Clodovil (IRE))
1888[6] 2570[5] 2821[3] 3465[5] 4124[2] 4887[3] (5546) 7411[5]

Disarming (IRE) *Dr Jon Scargill* a59 52
2 b f War Command(USA) Gloved Hand (Royal Applause)
5250[6] 6161[9] 7104[6] 7516[3] 8061[11]

Discay *Philip Kirby* a22 37
10 b g Distant Music(USA) Caysue (Cayman Kai (IRE))
2351[7]

Disciple (IRE) *Amy Murphy*
5 b g Fastnet Rock(AUS) Gift From Heaven (IRE) (Excellent Art)
7518[11]

Disco Fever *John Gosden* a85
2 b f Oasis Dream Penelopa (Giant's Causeway (USA))
9324[4]◆ (9506)

Disco Flash (FR) *C Plisson* a66 65
5 b g Martillo(GER) Flash McQueen (SPA) (Dyhim Diamond (IRE))
1245a[8]

Discotheque (FR) *A Junk* 61
4 ch m Sinndar(IRE) Disco Dancing (Singspiel (IRE))
6790a[7]

Discovery Island *Charlie Appleby* 85
2 b g Dubawi(IRE) Sperry (IRE) (Shamardal (USA))
6163[2] 6669[5] 7611[2]

Discreet Hero (IRE) *Noel Wilson* a60 71
6 ch g Siyouni(FR) Alfaguara (USA) (Red Ransom (USA))
787[3]

Disey's Edge *Christopher Mason* a44 44
3 b f Harbour Watch(IRE) Edge Of Light (Xaar)
4421[7] 5448[4] 6198[5] 7032[9] 7298[5] 8249[6] 9276[10]

Di's Gift *Michael Appleby* a63 77
10 b g Generous(IRE) Di's Dilemma (Teenoso (USA))
387[6] 1196[4] 1334[6]

Displaying Amber *Ben Haslam* a52 44
4 ch m Showcasing Amber Lane (Compton Place)
973[4]

Disque Rouge (FR) *J-M Capitte*
3 b f Evasive Pink And Red (USA) (Red Ransom (USA))
4229a[11]

Disruptor (FR) *David Evans* a58 60
3 ch g Siyouni(FR) Ultradargent (FR) (Kendargent (FR))
5826[4] 6197[5] 6602[6] 8949[11] 9298[2] 9403[3] 9659[3]

Distant Applause (IRE)
Dominic Ffrench Davis a59
4 b g Acclamation Spacecraft (USA) (Distant View (USA))
53[2] 383[5] 9133[12]

Distant Chimes (GER)
Sir Mark Prescott Bt a97 93
4 b g Campanologist(USA) Dyveke (GER) (Lando (GER))
(5055) (5311) (5631) (6348) 6530[3]

Distant Image (IRE)
Saeed bin Suroor 39
3 b f Exceed And Excel(AUS) Sander Camillo (USA) (Dixie Union (USA))
2919[13]

Distant Mirage *James Tate* a64 40
3 b f Toronado(IRE) Oasis Jade (Oasis Dream)
(555) 1219[3] 1337[6] 1720[5]

Distingo (IRE) *Gary Moore* a67 69
6 b g Smart Strike(CAN) Distinctive Look (IRE) (Danehill (USA))
135[8]

Disturbing Beauty
Natalie Lloyd-Beavis a27
3 b f Mazameer(IRE) Deftera Fantutte (IRE) (Amadeus Wolf)
8653[7]

Diva D (IRE) *Mark Johnston* a72 48
3 b f Shamardal(USA) Say No Now (IRE) (Refuse To Bend (IRE))
798[4] 1476[5] 2212[7] 2904[10]

Diva Du Dancing (FR) *P Decouz* 72
2 gr f Silver Frost(IRE) Rava (IRE) (Nayef (USA))
1657a[7] (3714a) 4228a[7] 5166a[2]

Diva Kareem (IRE) *George Baker* a70 67
2 b f Al Kazeem Pennard (IRE) (High Chaparral (IRE))
3461[3] 3798[2] 4544[2]

Diva Morita (FR) *J Boisnard* 58
3 b f Pedro The Great(USA) Diba (GER) (Big Shuffle (USA))
7061a[7]

Diva Rock *George Baker* a67 72
2 b f Zoffany(IRE) Dashing (IRE) (Sadler's Wells (USA))
4233[5] 5045[3] 5588[8]◆ (6372)

Diva Star *Rae Guest* a63 69
4 ch m Siyouni(FR) Kissin Sign (Turtle Bowl (IRE))
2318[4] (2741) 2978[3] 3540[6]

Divergente (FR) *Jane Soubagne*
2 b f Vale Of York(IRE) L'Aventura (FR) (Librettist (USA))
1240a[10]

Divied (USA) *John Quinn* a61
3 b g Lope De Vega(IRE) Vied (USA) (Elusive Quality (USA))
500[3] 908[5] 1385[11]

Divina Gloria (FR) *Kevin Ryan* 77
2 b f Dabirsim(FR) Amouage (GER) (Tiger Hill (IRE))
(6675)◆

Divin Bere (FR) *Iain Jardine* a66 72
6 b g Della Francesca(USA) Mofa Bere (FR) (Saumarez)
1981[2] 2591[2] 3334[6] 6674[5]

Divine Call *Charlie Wallis* a55 52
12 b g Pivotal Pious (Bishop Of Cashel)
167[2] 503[7] 587[4] 919[5] 1192[10]

Divine Connection
Jonathan Portman a61 58
2 b f Cable Bay(IRE) Divine Power (Kyllachy)
4502[6] 5342[6] 6592[7] 7277[6] 8061[5] 8603[4] 8824[3] 9045[4] 9501[2]

Divine Covey *Richard Hannon* 67
2 gr f Dark Angel(IRE) Pack Together (Paco Boy (IRE))
3259[6] 3835[5] 4323[2] 5777[3]◆

Divine Gift (IRE) *Iain Jardine* a57 84
3 b g Nathaniel(IRE) Souter's Sister (IRE) (Desert Style (IRE))
2562[6] 3729[4] 4327[3] 9543[6]

Divine Image (USA)
Charlie Appleby a107 91
3 ch f Scat Daddy(USA) Sure Route (Ishiguru (USA))
510a[2]◆ (845a) (1110a) 1443a[13] 6250a[7]

Divine Messenger *Emma Owen* a88 28
5 b g Firebreak Resentful Angel (Danehill Dancer (IRE))
(248)◆ 557[6] 699[3] (1074) 1727[2] 2966[6]

Divine Queen *James Tate* a3
2 b f Kingman El Manati (IRE) (Iffraaj)
3461[12]

Diviner (IRE) *Mark Johnston* a58 56
3 b f Charm Spirit(IRE) Water Fountain (Mark Of Esteem (IRE))
1819[6] 2965[7] 3513[6] 4285[3] 4917[5] 5272[2]◆ 5561[8] 5619[6] 6582[8] 7270[4]

Divine Spirit *Charlie Appleby* 102
2 b f Kingman Shyrl (Acclamation)
(2918) 3983[14] 4883[5] 6791a[2] 7775a[2] 8724[13]

Divine Summer (USA) *Ed Walker* 57
2 rg f Summer Front(USA) Seattle Grey (USA) (Friends Lake (USA))
5170[8]

Divinity *K R Burke* 93
3 b f Dutch Art Elysian (Galileo (IRE))
(1897) 2806[11] 3728[4] 5187[6] 5790[2] 6379[15]

Divisidero (USA) *Kelly Rubley* 115
7 b h Kitten's Joy(USA) Madame Du Lac (USA) (Lemon Drop Kid (USA))
7922a[7]

Division (FR) *J-M Baudrelle* a64 64
3 b g Evasive Indian Princess (IRE) (Mujadil (USA))
216a[11] 2090a[12]

Diwan Senora (FR) *Y Barberot* a100 96
6 b h Youmzain(IRE) Kiss Senora (FR) (Chichicastenango (FR))
3879a[5] 4704a[6]

Dixieland (IRE) *Marjorie Fife* a46 49
3 b g Red Jazz(USA) Signora Lina (IRE) (High Chaparral (IRE))
4820[10] 5235[16] 5914[10] 7051[7] 7961[4] 8301[6] 9220[8] 9470[11]

Dixie Moon (CAN)
Catherine Day Phillips a100 96
4 ch m Curlin(USA) Dixie Chicken (USA) (Rahy (USA))
7224a[5]

Dixit Confucius (FR) *F Chappet* a66 73
4 b g Wootton Bassett Whitby (FR) (Gold Away (IRE))
992a[8] 4747a[12]

Diyani (FR) *M Delzangles* 97
3 ch g Rock Of Gibraltar(IRE) Dilafara (FR) (Singspiel (IRE))
3789a[3]

Diyari (IRE) *John Gosden* a72 72
2 b c Dubawi(IRE) Mutebah (IRE) (Marju (IRE))
6163[6] 7055[5] 9155[3]

Dizoard *Iain Jardine* a46 47
9 b m Desideratum Riviere (Meadowbrook)
99[5]◆ 1718[12] 3272[11] 5277[12] 5621[9] 6611[8]

Dizzy G (IRE) *K R Burke* a88 85
4 b m Red Jazz(USA) Altogether (IRE) (King's Best (USA))
2874[4] 3309[7] 4442[4] 5040[5] 5839[6] 5989[2] 6565[5] (7206) 7402[3] (8349)◆ 9010[5] 9214[11]

Django (ITY) *Riccardo Bandini* 90
4 b h Bold Fact(USA) Come O'Er The Sea (IRE) (Oratorio (IRE))
8787a[3]

Django Freeman (GER)
Henk Grewe 111
3 ch c Campanologist(USA) Donna Lavinia (GER) (Acatenango (GER))
(2310a) 3674a[2] 4707a[2]

Djukon *Andreas Suborics* 107
3 ch c Jukebox Jury(IRE) Djumama (IRE) (Aussie Rules (USA))
7249a[2]

Dltripleseven (IRE)
David W Drinkwater a18 14
6 gr g Dark Angel(IRE) Namu (Mujadid (USA))
947[10] 1235[11] 1361[11]

Dobbia (USA) *A bin Harmash* a16 67
3 b c Medaglia d'Oro(USA) Queen Of Denmark (USA) (Kingmambo (USA))
727a[4]

Dobrianka *Ralph Beckett* a77 67
3 ch f Sea The Stars(IRE) Topaze Blanche (IRE) (Zamindar (USA))
133[7] 761[3] 6290[4] 6931[2] 7915[5]

Doc Sportello (IRE) *Tony Carroll* a90 81
7 b g Majestic Missile(IRE) Queen Of Silk (IRE) (Brief Truce (USA))
(254) 1098[11] 1654[10] 2588[9] 3945[6] 4866[8] 5746[6] 6109[3] 6916[8] 7337[2] (8242) 9131[5] 9348[12]

Doctor Cross (IRE) *Richard Fahey* a78 81
5 b g Cape Cross(IRE) Doctrine (Barathea (IRE))
3514[6] 4407[2]◆ 4924[4] 5743[4] 6255[2] 7003[4] 7436[5] 8129[5] (8524) 8726[6]

Doctor Jazz (IRE) *Michael Appleby* a64 55
4 b g Most Improved(IRE) Daliyana (IRE) (Cadeaux Genereux)
4601[9] 7756[9] 8196[7] 8639[9] 8904[3] 9221[7] 9405[4] (9497) 9553[3]

Doctor Nuno *Mark Loughnane* a55 50
2 b g Due Diligence(USA) Aubrietia (Dutch Art)
6684[5] 7406[10] 9243[8]

Doctor Parkes *Natalie Lloyd-Beavis* a50 58
13 b g Diktat Lucky Parkes (Full Extent (USA))
2503a[2] 2671a[4] 3173a[7] 4685a[6]

Doctor Sardonicus *Tom Dascombe* a111 99
8 ch g Medicean Never A Doubt (Night Shift (USA))
837[8] 1295[6]

Doctor Wonderful *Kevin Frost* a63 60
4 ch g Medicean Wonderful Desert (Green Desert (USA))
536[6] 835[8] 3473[5] 4346[7] 5001[7] 5499[12]

Documenting *Kevin Frost* a110 54
6 b g Zamindar(USA) Namaskar (Dansili)
(623)◆ 1103[5] 1922[6] 5413[19] 6706[2] 7448[2] 8707[4] (9129)◆ 9612[2]

Dodgy Bob *Michael Mullineaux* a53 58
6 b g Royal Applause Rustam (Dansili)
60[3] 116[2] 483[2] 553[3] 887[3] 1026[2] 1335[12] 3716[15] 5723[9] 7468[9] 8007[3] 8117[6] 8295[5] 8469[7] 9445[8] (9516)

Dogged *David Elsworth* a59 85
2 b c Due Diligence(USA) Bling Bling (IRE) (Indian Ridge (IRE))
5125[9] 5809[9] 7162[2] (7612)

Do It In Rio (FR) *Tamara Richter* a72 86
5 b m Rio De La Plata(USA) Double Dollar (Agnes World (USA))
6769a[8]

Dolkong (USA) *Bae Dae Sun* a108
5 ch h Afleet Alex(USA) Swampoodle (USA) (Broken Vow (USA))
171a[6] 396a[3] (959a) 1114a[3] 1447a[11] 7011a[5]

Dolla Dolla Bill (IRE)
Richard Hannon a60
2 b c Epaulette(AUS) My Uptown Girl (Dubai Destination (USA))
9174[11] 9324[6] 9607[7]

Dollar Bid *Sir Michael Stoute* a70
2 b c Frankel Cape Dollar (IRE) (Cape Cross (IRE))
9136[4]◆

Dollar Value (USA) *Robert Cowell* a46 53
4 gr g Exchange Rate(USA) Makoma (USA) (Malibu Moon (USA))
2[2] 233[4] 463[5]◆

Dolly Dupree *Paul D'Arcy* a58 51
3 b f Poet's Voice Meddle (Diktat)
228[7] (585) (931) 1067[2] 1549[5] 4664[6] 5552[3] 6173[3] 6550[2] 7280[13] 7873[5] 8072[6] 8205[3] 8663[7]

Dolly McQueen *Anthony Carson* a63 50
3 b f Canford Cliffs(IRE) Caterina De Medici (FR) (Redoute's Choice (AUS))
2583[11] 3067[9] 3741[7] 6152[4] 7232[2] 8553[12] (8944) 9201[5] 9542[9]

Dollywaggon Pike *J R Jenkins* a32 32
5 b m Hellvelyn Once Removed (Distant Relative)
6199[3] 8898[14]

Dolphin Village (IRE) *Shaun Harris* a52 54
9 b g Cape Cross(IRE) Reform Act (USA) (Lemon Drop Kid (USA))
262[5] (602) 984[5] 1146[7] 1498[10] 1680[5] 9090[6] 9345[14]

Dolphin Vista (IRE) *Ralph Beckett* a100 106
6 b g Zoffany(IRE) Fiordiligi (Mozart (IRE))
1244a[8] 3953[16] 5182[4] (5926a) 8116[8]

Dolydaydream *Pat Phelan* a47 30
4 b m Equiano(FR) Ellie In The Pink (IRE) (Johannesburg (USA))
293[8] 402[11]

Dolynska (FR) *M Boutin* a56 42
3 bb f Dabirsim(FR) Veronique (GER) (Big Shuffle (USA))
1658a[5] 4959a[4]

Domagnano (IRE) *D Smaga* a78 78
4 b g Planteur(IRE) Daloisi (FR) (Marchand De Sable (USA))
3005[7] 4020[8] 4319[8] 7861a[2]

Dominannie (IRE) *Ron Barr* a42 51
6 b m Paco Boy(IRE) English Rose (USA) (Kafwain (USA))
1850[5] 2911[5] 3296[5] 4584[3] 5020[5] 5918[5] 6276[10]

Domino Darling *William Haggas* 85
2 b f Golden Horn Disco Volante (Sadler's Wells (USA))
(8510)

Dominus (IRE) *Brian Meehan* a94 93
3 ch c Zoffany(IRE) Gwen Lady Byron (IRE) (Dandy Man (IRE))
1562[2] 2060[2] (2405) 2835[2] 3479[U] 3945[8] 4420[2] (5126) 5442[7] 5983[4] 6413[5] 7868[6] (8289)

Dommersen (IRE) *Roger Fell* a87 75
6 ch g Dutch Art Kelowna (IRE) (Pivotal)
102[2]◆ 272[2] 390[2] (434) 950[2] 1106[3] 1422[9] 3004[5] 3514[7]

Donald Llewellyn *Gary Moore* 30
2 b c Pivotal Rose Law (New Approach (IRE))
8857[7]

Don Armado (IRE) *Robert Cowell* a91 87
3 b c Camacho Bella Ophelia (IRE) (Baltic King)
57[4] 806[3] 989[6] 1851[7] 2412[7] 2835[8] 4123[7] 4402[18]

Doncaster Rosa *Ivan Furtado* a63 67
2 b f Alhebayeb(IRE) Mosa Mine (Exceed And Excel (AUS))
2476[2]◆ 2820[11] 5547[4] 6097[4] 7029[5] 7438[6]

Doncaster Star *Ivan Furtado* 20
4 b m Doncaster Rover(USA) Pucker Up (Royal Applause)
2094[16] 2823[12] 4367[9] 6885[15]
Don Diego Vega *Daniel Kubler* 20
3 b g Toronado(IRE) Jules (IRE) (Danehill (USA))
2715[8] 5054[10]
Done Deal (IRE)
Sir Mark Prescott Bt a82 75
4 b g Azamour(IRE) Dundel's Spirit (IRE) (Invincible Spirit (IRE))
3222[5] 5012[4] 5625[7] 6634[5]
Donjah (GER) *Henk Grewe* 110
3 b f Teofilo(IRE) Dyanamore (USA) (Mt. Livermore (USA))
5720a[6] 6771a[2] 7500a[3] (8391a) 8792a[5]
Donjuan Triumphant (IRE)
Andrew Balding a107 120
6 b h Dream Ahead(USA) Mathuna (IRE) (Tagula (IRE))
2109[6] 3501[2] 5184[4] 5521[8] 6215[6] 7892[2] (8331)
Don Jupp (USA) *Marco Botti* a78
3 b c More Than Ready(USA) Dame Ellen (USA) (Elusive Quality (USA))
(615)◆ 1034[6]
Donnachies Girl (IRE)
Alistair Whillans a69 66
6 b m Manduro(GER) Russian Society (Darshaan)
2436[5] 3175[3] 4274[4] 4724[3] 4983[2] (5219) 5855[5] (6658) 7510[9] 8027[6]
Donnago (IRE) *Brian Ellison* 51
3 b f Power Redona (IRE) (Le Vie Dei Colori)
3570[4] 4487[8] 5213[10]
Donna Leon (FR) *Werner Glanz* 49
4 b m Masterstroke(USA) Denissa (GER) (Second Set (IRE))
4859a[11]
Donna Veloce (USA)
Simon Callaghan a112
2 b f Uncle Mo(USA) Coin Broker (IRE) (Montjeu (IRE))
8747a[2]◆
Donncha (IRE) *Seb Spencer* a90 93
8 br g Captain Marvelous(IRE) Seasonal Style (IRE) (Generous (IRE))
1097[5] 4079[8] 5726[2] 6231[2] 7517[6] 8096[9] 9517[10]
Donnelly's Rainbow (IRE)
Rebecca Bastiman a20 71
6 b g Lilbourne Lad(IRE) Donnelly's Hollow (IRE) (Docksider (USA))
1695[9] 2203[5] 2681[2] 3178[3] 3924[2] 4207[4] 4513[3] 4784[3] (4979) 5274[3]◆ (5616) 6628[10] 6935[6] (7363) 7738[3] 8237[5]
Donnybrook (IRE) *John Gosden* a75 75
2 b f Invincible Spirit(IRE) Mayhem (IRE) (Whipper (USA))
6928[3] (8202)
Dono Di Dio *Michael Madgwick* a85 86
4 b m Nathaniel(IRE) Sweet Cecily (IRE) (Kodiac)
292[2] 754[2] 1096[2] (1518) 2342[2] 3010[2]◆ 4257[2] 5321[8] 6842[4] 7566[4] 8064[6] 9215[3]
Don Ramiro (IRE) *Kevin Ryan* a81 62
2 b g Sir Prancealot(IRE) Centenerola (USA) (Century City (IRE))
2906[4] 4486[5] 4984[8] 7582[7] 8022[4]
Dontaskmeagain (USA)
Mark Johnston 89
2 ch c Karakontie(JPN) Al Beedaa (USA) (Swain (IRE))
(7023)◆ (7539)◆ 8112[8]
Don't Be Surprised *Seb Spencer* a59 59
4 ch g Monsieur Bond(IRE) Julie's Gift (Presidium)
125[4] 1083[4] 4300[2] 5248[13] 6036[12] 7960[8] 9516[13]
Don't Cry About It (IRE) *Ali Stronge* a38 44
4 ch g Casamento(IRE) Back At De Front (IRE) (Cape Cross (IRE))
288[4] 923[7] 1333[7] 2930[2] 3533[9] 5310[11] 5837[4] 6305[8]
Don't Do It (IRE) *Michael Appleby* a61 55
4 b g Casamento(IRE) Innclassic (IRE) (Stravinsky (USA))
62[2] 245[9] 436[2] 593[4] (724) 792[4] (984) 1231[7] 1333[4] 1482[4] 1710[3] 2111[5] 3774[6] 4287[6]
Don't Fence Me In (IRE)
Paul Webber a54
4 b m Fame And Glory Great Idea (IRE) (Lion Cavern (USA))
1102[7]
Don't Give Up *Tony Newcombe* a82 79
5 b h Dubawi(IRE) Avongrove (Tiger Hill (IRE))
6915[7]
Don't Joke *Mark Johnston* 69
2 ch g Slade Power(IRE) Lady Frances (Exceed And Excel (AUS))
1910[3] 2257[3] 2869[6] 5340[8] 7309[5]
Don't Jump George (IRE)
Shaun Lycett a70 74
4 b g Canford Cliffs(IRE) My Sweet Georgia (IRE) (Royal Applause)
2912[3] 6838[2] 7278[11] 8086[4] 8862[5] 9443[7]
Don't Stop Dancing (IRE)
Ronald Harris 85
2 ch c Anjaal Elayoon (USA) (Danzig (USA))
4480[6] (5082) 5584[11] 6364[2]◆ 6845[4] 7896[17]
Don'tstophimnow (IRE) *J S Moore* a4
2 b g Es Que Love(IRE) Off Stage (IRE) (Danehill Dancer (IRE))
7469[9] 7768[10]
Don't Tell Claire *Daniel Kubler* a41
2 ro f Gutaifan(IRE) Avenbury (Mount Nelson)
9062[11]
Don'tyouwantmebaby (IRE)
Richard Spencer a54 50
2 b f Kodiac Miss Corinne (Mark Of Esteem (IRE))
6159[6] 7786[6] 8431[7]
Doogan's Warren (IRE) *John Butler* a44 53
4 br g Canford Cliffs(IRE) Ochre (IRE) (Diktat)
8417[5] 8547[6] 9157[8]
Doon Star *Jim Goldie* a43 50
4 b m Sulamani(IRE) La Vecchia Scuola (IRE) (Mull Of Kintyre (USA))
2376[9] 3705[7] 4690[5] 4983[7] 5239[4] 5933[8] 7492[8] 7739[3] 8238[12]

Dorah *Archie Watson* 84
3 b f Camelot Rosie Probert (Dylan Thomas (IRE))
2148[4] (3153) 3729[6] 4599[3] 4881[6]
Doraonpogyeongseon (USA)
Min Jang Gi a102
6 ch h Kantharos(USA) Smartybegone (USA) (Smarty Jones (USA))
7010a[6]
Dorcha Knight (IRE)
David C Griffiths
2 gr c Make Believe Stella River (FR) (Stormy River (FR))
2780[12]
Dorchester *Marco Botti* a62
3 b f Lope De Vega(IRE) Cloud Line (Danehill Dancer (IRE))
78[4] 380[8] 547[3] 1385[9] 2007[12]
Dorchester Dom (IRE)
Nigel Twiston-Davies a48 69
2 ch g Starspangledbanner(AUS) Moriches (IRE) (Alhaarth (IRE))
1416[4] 4652[8] 5280[6] 9401[9]
Dories Delight (IRE) *Scott Dixon* a64 66
4 b g Dandy Man(IRE) She's My Rock (IRE) (Rock Of Gibraltar (IRE))
1070[3] 1274[9]
Doris Bleasedale (IRE)
Richard Fahey a45 61
3 b f Intikhab(USA) Sheba Five (USA) (Five Star Day (USA))
316[10]
Dormio *Stuart Kittow* a70 70
3 b g Equiano(FR) Diska (GER) (Kallisto (GER))
8242[5] 8806[9]
Dor's Diamond *Dean Ivory* a59
3 gr g Gregorian(IRE) Primavera (Anshan)
1587[5] 2236[6] 8894[4]
Dorset Blue (IRE) *Richard Hannon* 71
2 b g Canford Cliffs(IRE) Spinning Lucy (IRE) (Spinning World (USA))
3257[3] 3601[7] 4750[4] 5382[4] 5781[6]
Dor's Law *Dean Ivory* a58 65
6 b m Lawman(FR) Law Of Chance (Pennekamp (USA))
2740[12] 3006[2] (3774)
Dosc (IRE) *M Al Mheiri* a60 71
4 b h Dream Ahead(USA) Flanders (IRE) (Common Grounds)
997[11]
Dose *Richard Fahey* a54 49
6 b m Teofilo(IRE) Prescription (Pivotal)
5560[8] 6102[8] 7508[9]
Dosila *C Laffon-Parias* 65
3 b f Galileo(IRE) Stormina (USA) (Gulch (USA))
5329a[4]
Dothraki (IRE) *Ronald Thompson* a51 46
3 b g Bungle Inthejungle Ellistown Lady (IRE) (Red Sunset)
2281[4] 3271[9] 4434[10] 5559[17] 6578[6]
Doti *Rod Millman* a22
3 b f Charm Spirit(IRE) Garanciere (FR) (Anabaa (USA))
3591[2] 9431[1] 1236[13] 1554[11]
Dotted Swiss (IRE) *Archie Watson* a64 64
4 b m Swiss Spirit Luxuria (IRE) (Kheleyf (USA))
187[3] 314[5] 824[4] 1208[7] 1766[4] 2010[4] 2122[3]
Dotty Grand *Jamie Osborne* a36 50
3 b f Dream Ahead(USA) Dartrix (Dutch Art)
1379[4] 4021[2] 458[4] 5941[2]
Double Coffee *Peter Hiatt* a21 52
3 b f Mawatheeq(USA) Maimoona (IRE) (Pivotal)
2280[5] 2904[8]
Double D's *Michael Dods* a50 54
2 b g Archipenko(USA) Florentia (Medicean)
7398[10] 8424[9]
Double Esprit *Donald McCain* 53
3 b g Invincible Spirit(IRE) Nature Spirits (FR) (Beat Hollow)
5656[9] 6274[7]
Double Honour *James Bethell* a68 75
3 b c Garswood Snake's Head (Golden Snake (USA))
1458[4]◆ 3306[2] 4334[4] 5557[7] 6544[3] 7512[7]
Double Kodiac (IRE)
Simon Crisford a80 97
3 b g Kodiac Via Lattea (IRE) (Teofilo (IRE))
1888[2] 6207[6]
Double Legend (IRE)
Amanda Perrett a67 64
4 b g Finsceal Fior(IRE) Damask Rose (IRE) (Dr Devious (IRE))
85[2] (560) 1096[3] 2400[12] 2733[5] 4251[11] 5338[8]
Double Martini (IRE) *Roger Fell* a69 73
3 ch c Mastercraftsman(IRE) Dusty Moon (Dr Fong (USA))
6206[6] 6551[4] 7486[5] 8025[4] 8719[5] 9351[4]
Double Or Bubble (IRE) *Chris Wall* 70
2 b f Exceed And Excel(AUS) Mango Lady (Dalakhani (IRE))
5865[2]◆
Double Or Quits (GER) *M Nigge* a74 86
3 b f Tai Chi(GER) Dora Bella (GER) (Johan Cruyff)
(6789a)
Double Reflection *Michael Appleby* a63 77
4 b m Showcasing Green And Bleue (Green Tune (USA))
1719[7] 2230[2] 2612[8] 3255[4] 5458[7] 5841[4] 6512[7] 7366[9] 8027[3] 9050[12] 9333[6] 9570[10] 9611[9]
Double Up *Ian Williams* a96 70
8 b g Exceed And Excel(AUS) My Love Thomas (IRE) (Cadeaux Genereux)
639a[10] 843a[11] 2100[13] 2743[19] 3636[9] 4649[7] 5395[14] 9549[3]
Doubling Dice *Hugo Palmer* a47
2 br g Teofilo(IRE) Garanciere (FR) (Anabaa (USA))
8424[10]
Doubly Beautiful (IRE) *Ed de Giles* a46 73
3 ch g Born To Sea(IRE) Bella Bella (IRE) (Sri Pekan (USA))
6594[6] 7976[10] 8419[12] 9276[9]

Doughan Alb *Richard Hannon* a75 70
3 b c Havana Gold(IRE) Sandtime (IRE) (Green Desert (USA))
1495[2] 1856[8] 2715[5] 3373[5]
Douglas Fir (IRE) *Mark Johnston* a41
2 b g Australia Danehill Music (IRE) (Danehill Dancer (IRE))
7834[6]
Doukhan (IRE) *Kris Lees* 104
10 b g Dansili Luna Wells (IRE) (Sadler's Wells (USA))
1784a[5]
Doune Castle *Andrew Balding* a58 54
3 b g Camelot Ape Attack (Nayef (USA))
1756[7] 2142[7] 2999[5] 6104[10] 6864[4] 7390[5] 7818[2]
Dounyapour (FR)
Dr Richard Newland 77
6 ch g Lope De Vega(IRE) Diamond Tango (FR) (Acatenango (GER))
5540[15]
Dourado (IRE) *Patrick Chamings* a86 88
5 b h Dark Angel(IRE) Skehana (IRE) (Mukaddamah (USA))
2237[3] 3149[2] 6863[8] 7731[4] 8197[9] 8412[5] 9304[7]
Dove Divine (FR) *Hughie Morrison* a66 61
3 b f Le Havre(IRE) Numerieus (FR) (Numerous (USA))
3440[7] 8254[8] 9180[4]
Dove Mountain (IRE) *Olly Murphy* a53 63
8 b g Danehill Dancer(IRE) Virginia Waters (USA) (Kingmambo (USA))
207[5]◆ 910[7] 1333[8]
Dover Light *Dean Ivory* a51 39
2 ch g Sir Prancealot(IRE) Miss Mediator (USA) (Consolidator (USA))
1651[9] 2761[17] 3141[6]
Downdraft (IRE)
Joseph Patrick O'Brien a100 114
4 b h Camelot Cinnamon Rose (USA) (Trempolino (USA))
4053[6] (4745a) (5404a) 6191a[2] 8577a[3] (8767a) 8844a[22]
Downforce (IRE) *W McCreery* a58 107
7 b g Fast Company(IRE) Spinning Ruby (Pivotal)
1434a[8] 3062a[11] 7713a[2] 8166a[2]
Downtown Diva (IRE)
Adrian Paul Keatley a51 45
4 b m Approve(IRE) Sovereign Street (Compton Place)
2328[6]
Draco (USA) *N Bachalard* a102
4 b h Astrology(USA) Bring Me Luck (USA) (Pentelicus (USA))
282a[7]
Drafted (USA) *Doug Watson* a112 51
5 gr g Field Commission(CAN) Keep The Profit (USA) (Darn That Alarm (USA))
50a[2]◆ (512a) (1109a)◆ 1444a[5]◆
Dragon Beat (IRE) *Michael Appleby* a72 53
3 ch f Dragon Pulse(IRE) Dreamaway (IRE) (Oasis Dream)
182[2] 342[7] 4128[6] 4829[9] 5027[5]
Dragon Command *George Scott* a74 80
2 b g War Command(USA) Zari (Azamour (IRE))
2093[5] 2892[2] 3312[5] (4486) 4938[4] 5587[13] (7994) 8430[5]
Dragoness *F-H Graffard* 74
3 b f Frankel Dahama (Green Desert (USA))
(6486a)
Dragon Flight (IRE) *George Scott* 48
2 b f No Nay Never(USA) Real Charm (IRE) (Duke Of Marmalade (IRE))
3259[7]
Dragonfly (FR) *D Windrif* a47
3 b f Excelebration(IRE) Xcape To Victory (IRE) (Cape Cross (IRE))
509a[11]
Dragon Girl (IRE) *Roy Brotherton* 3
4 ch m Dragon Pulse(IRE) Raise Your Spirits (IRE) (Generous (IRE))
1021[13] 4657[14] 5499[13]
Dragon Kuza *Hugo Palmer* a37 31
3 b g Dragon Pulse(IRE) Mylaporyours (IRE) (Jeremy (USA))
1514[5] 1725[9] 2240[10] 3410[13]
Dragon Mall (USA)
Rebecca Menzies a96 97
6 b g Blame(USA) Petition The Lady (USA) (Petionville (USA))
121[4] 240[2] (625) 6475[14]
Dragon Mountain *Keith Dalgleish* a70 77
4 b g Sir Percy Rouge Dancer (Elusive City (USA))
1503[8] 2370[5] 2962[3] 3222[3] 4102[13] 4907[11] 5423[11] 6658[5]◆ 7301[7] 7513[11] 7872[7] 9367[3] 9570[6]
Dragons Call (IRE)
John James Feane a73 85
3 b f Dragon Pulse(IRE) Harriers Call (IRE) (Atraf)
7380[8]
Dragons Tail (IRE) *Tom Dascombe* a86 87
4 b g Dragon Pulse(IRE) Mastoora (IRE) (Acclamation)
2572[9] 3308[7] 3846[5] 4320[8] 5320[3] 5708[6] 6026[3] 6686[6] 7142[8] 7678[2] 8521[6]
Dragon Sun *Richard Hannon* a78 77
3 ch g Pivotal Moon Sister (IRE) (Cadeaux Genereux)
(1358)◆ (2055)◆ 3278[4] 3580[2]
Dragons Voice *David Menuisier* a86 92
5 b g Poet's Voice China (Royal Academy (USA))
1727[14] 2486[6] (3663) 3973[2] 5902[4] 6895[4] 7974[8]
Dragons Will Rise (IRE)
Micky Hammond 50
3 b g Dragon Pulse(IRE) Jaldini (IRE) (Darshaan)
2152[9] 3270[6] 5299[8] 6679[10]
Drakefell (IRE) *Antony Brittain* a85 57
4 b h Canford Cliffs(IRE) Cake (IRE) (Acclamation)
139[6] 517[3] 907[4] (1100) (1394) 1547[9] 1899[8]
Drakensberg (IRE) *A J Martin* a75 79
5 ch g Samum(GER) Djidda (GER) (Lando (GER))
2578[7]

Dramatica (IRE) *Stuart Williams* 42
2 ch f Lope De Vega(IRE) Miss Georgie (IRE) (Verglas (IRE))
8093[13] 8759[11]
Dramatic Device *Chris Wall* 96
4 b g Dansili Surprise Moment (IRE) (Authorized (IRE))
3192[4]◆ 4392[2]◆ (5103) (6411) (7616)
Dramatic Queen (USA)
William Haggas a103 111
4 ch m Kitten's Joy(USA) Midnight Music (IRE) (Dubawi (IRE))
2167a[8] (3096) 4645[2] 5663[7] 6473[P]
Dramatic Sands (IRE)
Archie Watson a84 82
2 b g Footstepsinthesand Melodrama (IRE) (Oratorio (IRE))
3274[2] 4091[14] (4480) 6020[2] (6965) 7840[5]
Dramatista (IRE) *Archie Watson* a66
2 ch f Lope De Vega(IRE) Aoife Alainn (IRE) (Dr Fong (USA))
4502[5]
Draw Lots (IRE) *Brian Meehan* a47 53
2 b g Zoffany(IRE) Foolish Act (IRE) (Sadler's Wells (USA))
6409[7] 7023[3] 7437[9] 8493[9]
Dr Doro (IRE) *Ian Williams* a58 78
6 b m Holy Roman Emperor(IRE) Stellarina (IRE) (Night Shift (USA))
2625[9] 2997[5] 4253[4] 4560[7] 4926[3] 5058[5] (5532) 7161[5]
Dreadnoughtus *Michael Appleby* a39
3 ch c Americain(USA) Sharp Dresser (USA) (Diesis)
9368[9]
Dream Academy (IRE) *Kevin Ryan* a63
2 b g Acclamation Modello (IRE) (Intikhab (USA))
8084[8]
Dream Ally (IRE) *John Weymes* a53 53
9 b g Oasis Dream Alexander Alliance (IRE) (Danetime (IRE))
28[10] 166[8] 702[3] 1192[7] 1368[2] 1553[10] 2189[6] 2532[10]
Dream And Do (IRE) *F Rossi* 101
2 b f Siyouni(FR) Venetias Dream (IRE) (Librettist (USA))
(8647a)
Dream Ascot *J A Stack* 90
4 b m Oasis Dream World Class (Galileo (IRE))
4745a[4]
Dreamboat Annie *Mark Usher* a47 49
4 b m Piccolo Bold Rose (Bold Edge)
430[6] 824[3] 1038[7] 7837[8] 8123[8] 8469[10] 8917[6] 9160[10] 9423[2] 9507[4]
Dreamboat Dave (IRE)
Sarah Humphrey a66 68
3 b g Morpheus Gatamalata (IRE) (Spartacus (IRE))
6393[9] 7685[3] (8001)◆ 8705[9] 9202[6] 9443[2] 9663[4]
Dreamboat Girl (IRE) *Rae Guest* a27
2 b f Dream Ahead(USA) Junia Tepzia (IRE) (Rock Of Gibraltar (IRE))
9251[11]
Dream Castle *Saeed bin Suroor* a30 116
5 b g Frankel Sand Vixen (Dubawi (IRE))
(51a)◆ (395a)◆ (1115a) 1445a[13] 3122a[5] 3948[14] 8136a[9] 8578a[11]
Dream Catching (IRE)
Andrew Balding a82 82
4 b g Dream Ahead(USA) Selfara (Oasis Dream)
1932[2] 2568[9] 3040[7] 3963[3] 4833[3] 5882[7] 6567[8] (7078) 7568[6] 8063[8]◆
Dream Chick (IRE) *Kevin Ryan* a64 46
3 br f Dream Ahead(USA) Dollar Chick (IRE) (Dansili)
354[3]◆ 1816[8] 2337[11] 2896[8] 3570[9] 4731[11]
Dreamfield *John Gosden* 113
5 b h Oasis Dream Izzi Top (Pivotal)
1853[8]
Dreamforce (AUS)
John P Thompson 110
6 b g Fastnet Rock(AUS) Eskimo Queen (NZ) (Shinko King (IRE))
8578a[5]
Dream Free *David Pipe* a56 55
6 b g Oasis Dream Freedonia (Selkirk (USA))
3834[5]
Dream Game *Ben Haslam* a49
2 bl f Brazen Beau(AUS) Dreamily (IRE) (New Approach (IRE))
9392[6]
Dream House *Tim Easterby* a68 65
3 b g Coach House(IRE) Kummel Excess (IRE) (Exceed And Excel (AUS))
1649[13] 2199[7] 2507[10] 3508[5] 3921[6] (4081) 4604[4] 5236[9] 5904[4] (6183) 7367[6] 7855[9]
Dreaming Away (IRE)
Simon Crisford a67 66
3 b f Shamardal(USA) Dreaming Beauty (Oasis Dream)
2823[2]
Dreaming Blue *Richard Fahey* a55 68
2 b g Showcasing Got To Dream (Duke Of Marmalade (IRE))
7361[12] 8424[7] 8858[4]
Dreamingofdiamonds (IRE)
David Lanigan a42 52
3 b f Alhebayeb(IRE) Jemima's Art (Fantastic Light (USA))
5062[4] 5428[3] 6152[11] 7549[9]
Dreaming Of Paris
Patrick Chamings a76 61
5 b m Oasis Dream Parisi (Rahy (USA))
2005[2] 2797[12] 3691[4] 4751[6] 7299[8] 7758[8]
Dream Isle (IRE) *Steph Hollinshead* a25 44
2 b g Tagula(IRE) Desert Location (Dubai Destination (USA))
3335[10] 3644[12] 4075[9] 9449[5]
Dream Kart (IRE) *Mark Johnston* a51 88
2 b f Dream Ahead(USA) Kartiste (IRE) (Kalanisi (IRE))
2968[4] 3244[3] 3803[3] (4448) 4799[2] 5243[3] (5703) 6713[4] 7400[8]

Dream Life (FR) *J-P Dubois* a75 83
3 b f Authorized(IRE) Tender Night (USA) (Elusive Quality (USA))
2091a[5] 6267a[8] 9504a[9]

Dream Machine (IRE) *Neil Mulholland* a53 89
5 ch g Dream Ahead(USA) Last Cry (FR) (Peintre Celebre (USA))
1757[13]

Dream Magic (IRE) *Mark Loughnane* a77 53
5 b g Lord Shanakill(USA) Pursuit of Passion (Pastoral Pursuits)
119[5] 481[2] 1024[4] (1498) 1988[5] 2696[6] 3150[3] 3428[3] 4190[11] 5570[7] 9012[5] (9367) 9611[4]

Dream Model (IRE) *Mark Loughnane* a53 25
3 b f Dream Ahead(USA) Twiggy's Girl (IRE) (Manduro (GER))
316[11] 4196[9] 6361[13] 6983[7] 7385[7] 7873[13]

Dream Mount (IRE) *Julie Camacho* a62 48
4 b g Dream Ahead(USA) Mistify (IRE) (Elusive Quality (USA))
355[9] 801[5] 8923[13] 9337[5]

Dream Night (FR) *H-A Pantall* a73 60
3 b f Olympic Glory(IRE) Claveria (FR) (Nayef (USA))
7505a[10]

Dreamofdiscovery (IRE) *Julie Camacho* a66 60
5 b g Henrythenavigator(USA) Dreamwriter (USA) (Tale Of The Cat (USA))
1399[13] 1647[12]

Dream Of Dreams (IRE) *Sir Michael Stoute* a110 121
5 ch g Dream Ahead(USA) Vasilia (Dansili)
(2062) (2916) 4094[2] 4923[10] 6959[8] 8331[16]

Dream Of Honour (IRE) *Tim Easterby* a38 72
3 b g Dream Ahead(USA) Pernica (Sir Percy)
2506[5] 3058[3] 4444[4] 4629[2] 6176[9] 6944[6]

Dream Of Words (IRE) *J C Cerqueira Germano* a94 63
4 ch m Dream Ahead(USA) Cleofila (IRE) (Teofilo (IRE))
9603a[5]

Dream On Dreamer (IRE) *Lucinda Egerton* a23 37
5 b m Dream Ahead(USA) Marula (IRE) (Sadler's Wells (USA))
608[8] 1478[10] 1850[10]

Dream Round (IRE) *Andrew Balding* 61
2 b f Gleneagles(IRE) Mythie (FR) (Octagonal (NZ))
7695[8]

Dreams And Visions (IRE) *Michael Easterby* a63 76
3 b g Archipenko(USA) Kibini (Galileo (IRE))
405[4] 5656[5] (7368)

Dreamseller (IRE) *Tim Easterby* a62 65
3 ch g Dream Ahead(USA) Picture Of Lily (Medicean)
4080[6] 4584[4]◆ 4725[2] 5517[3] 6101[10] 6679[2] (6983) 7404[3] 7875[11] 8234[2] 9361[8]

Dream Shot (IRE) *James Tate* a104 105
2 b c Dream Ahead(USA) Miss Buckshot (IRE) (Tamayuz)
(3039) 3566[3] 4610[2] 5584[7] (5887) 6474[8] 7149[2]◆ 8328a[2] 8745a[7]

Dream Today (IRE) *Jamie Osborne* a94 100
4 b g Dream Ahead(USA) Macheera (IRE) (Machiavellian (USA))
(170a) 639a[3] 843a[3] 960a[8] 6953[7] 7372[5]◆ 7913[5]

Dream Together (IRE) *Jedd O'Keeffe* 63
2 ch g Dream Ahead(USA) Shamsalmaidan (IRE) (Fantastic Light (USA))
6457[5]◆

Dream Walker (FR) *Brian Ellison* a71 71
10 gr g Gold Away(IRE) Minnie's Mystery (FR) (Highest Honor (FR))
3813[10] 4240[12] 5022[4] 5820[4] 6066[7] 7074[14]

Dreamweaver (IRE) *Ed Walker* a84 81
3 b g Mastercraftsman(IRE) Livia's Dream (IRE) (Teofilo (IRE))
(2406) 4671[2] (5124) 5861[4] 6722[2] (7301) 8092[7]

Dream With You (FR) *N Caullery* a23 81
3 b f George Vancouver(USA) Azucar (IRE) (Desert Prince (IRE))
168a[9] 845a[9] 1512a[2] 2091a[3] 5644a[7]

Dream World (IRE) *Michael Appleby* a61 78
4 b m Dream Ahead(USA) Tetard (IRE) (Lawman (FR))
1387[5] 1688[6] (2081) (2261) 2809[5] 3470[4] (5376) 5870[5] 6408[3] 7491[4] 8521[3] 9224[5] 9351[7] 9625[6]

Dreamy Rascal (IRE) *Richard Hannon* a66 60
2 b f Dream Ahead(USA) Emirates Challenge (IRE) (Cape Cross (IRE))
1821[6] 4802[6] 5288[4] 6415[6] (6837) 7234[6] 8506[7]

Dr. Edgar (USA) *Barclay Tagg* 104
6 ch g Lookin At Lucky(USA) Sennockian Storm (USA) (Storm Cat (USA))
5977a[7]

Dress Circle *James Tate* a47
2 b f Showcasing Minnaloushe (IRE) (Lawman (FR))
9474[5] 9623[10]

Drew Breeze (IRE) *Richard Spencer* a21 62
2 ch g Camacho Three Cheers (IRE) (Azamour (IRE))
3644[7]

Drifting Star (IRE) *Gary Moore* a32 41
4 b g Sea The Stars(IRE) Drifting (IRE) (Sadler's Wells (USA))
59[13] 245[12]

Dr Jekyll (IRE) *David Simcock* a62 71
3 b g Scat Daddy(USA) Similu (Danehill Dancer (IRE))
2023[6] 7373[6] 7999[6]

Dr Julius No *Murty McGrath* a38 40
5 b g Dick Turpin(IRE) Royal Assent (Royal Applause)
940[11] 8416[12]

Drogon (IRE) *Jackie Stephen* a55 68
3 b g Zoffany(IRE) Flames To Dust (GER) (Oasis Dream)
2559[11] 3082[14] 5947[7] 7435[10] 8304[11] 8719[12]

Droichead Atha (IRE) *Donal Kinsella* a34 34
4 ch m Tamayuz Indus Ridge (IRE) (Indian Ridge (IRE))
9400[7]

Dromara King *Richard Hughes* a72
2 ch c Mayson Spirit Na Heireann (IRE) (Dubawi (IRE))
8700[3]◆

Drombeg Dream (IRE) *Augustine Leahy* 101
4 b m Arcano(IRE) Drombeg Dawn (IRE) (Orpen (USA))
1307a[8] 2493a[7] 6235a[5] 7038a[12] 7794a[10]

Drop Kick Murphi (IRE) *Christine Dunnett* a52 72
5 b g Sir Prancealot(IRE) Rindiseyda (IRE) (Arakan (USA))
8435[4] 8697[2] 9160[4] 9298[3]◆ 9439[6]

Drosay (FR) *Georgios Alimpinisis* a71
3 b c Rajsaman(FR) Don't Worry Me (IRE) (Dancing Dissident (USA))
9058a[12] 9504a[6]

Dr Richard Kimble (IRE) *Marjorie Fife* a73 44
4 b g Lawman(FR) Aoife Alainn (IRE) (Dr Fong (USA))
2126[8] 2479[8] 3514[8] 3929[4] 4724[11] 6180[11] 8200[10]

Dr Simpson (FR) *Tom Dascombe* a102 97
2 b f Dandy Man(IRE) New Romantic (Singspiel (IRE))
1821[2] (4903) 5542[8] 6157[3] 6474[2] 6907[7] 7400[4] (8328a) 8745a[5]

Drummer *Denis Gerard Hogan* a29 54
4 b g Smart Strike(CAN) Sense Of Joy (Dansili)
7087a[7]

Drummer Jack (IRE) *K Kukk* a35 28
3 b g Toronado(IRE) Fligaz (FR) (Panis (USA))
79[8] 174[6] 400[4] 1140[13] 2004a[3] 2673a[10] 3174a[6] 4175a[4] 4684a[5] 6009a[8]

Drummond Warrior (IRE) *Pam Sly* a29 90
3 b g Zoffany(IRE) Ulanova (IRE) (Noverre (USA))
(3421) (4421) 6413[2] 7121[16] 8607[11]

Drumnadrochit *Charles Hills* a55 51
3 b g Coach House(IRE) Blissamore (Kyllachy)
2772[8] 4185[8]

Drumshanbo Destiny (FR) *Ronald Harris* a41 31
3 ch g Nathaniel(IRE) Lacy Sunday (USA) (King's Best (USA))
3299[7] 6049[10] 6505[8] 9139[8]

Drums Of War (IRE) *Chris Grant* a57
7 b g Youmzain(IRE) Min Asl Wafi (IRE) (Octagonal (NZ))
9350[4] 9469[7]

Dschingis First (GER) *Markus Klug* 105
3 b c Soldier Hollow Divya (GER) (Platini (GER))
2310a[3] 3674a[4] 4707a[6]

Dubai Acclaim (IRE) *Richard Fahey* a79 79
4 b g Acclamation Bahati (IRE) (Intikhab (USA))
19[5] 1925[9] 2509[5] 2842[4] 3199[11] 3880[2] 5117[6] 5782[2] 6370[2] (7074) (7540) 8305[13] 8658[2]

Dubai Avenue (IRE) *Clive Cox* a74 65
2 b c Bated Breath Starfly (IRE) (Invincible Spirit (IRE))
3644[6] 4295[5]

Dubai Beauty (IRE) *Saeed bin Suroor* a75 103
3 b f Frankel Minidress (Street Cry (IRE))
48a[14] 510a[4] 845a[11]

Dubai Blue (USA) *Saeed bin Suroor* a103 46
3 b f More Than Ready(USA) Speckled (USA) (Street Cry (IRE))
2745[10] (6721)

Dubai Canal *S Seemar* a57 36
3 b c Nayef(USA) It's The War (USA) (Consolidator (USA))
1742a[13]

Dubai Discovery (USA) *Saeed bin Suroor* a75 79
3 bb f Hard Spun(USA) Caramel Snap (USA) (Smart Strike (CAN))
5627[5] 6187[3] 6902[3] 7279[7]

Dubai Dominion *Ed Vaughan* 102
3 b c Pivotal Hoodna (IRE) (Invincible Spirit (IRE))
1830[6] 3621a[5] 4092[11] 6894[2] 7934a[12]

Dubai Elegance *Derek Shaw* a64 58
5 ch m Sepoy(AUS) Some Sunny Day (Where Or When (IRE))
31[9] 209[6] 356[13] 1716[8] 1883[9] 2632[8] 3001[4] 3425[5] 3738[6] 5147[2] 5558[4] (5659) 5828[5] 7345[4] 7590[8] 9477[5] (9551)

Dubai Empire (FR) *Mme G Rarick* a76 79
4 ch g Motivator Cable Beach (USA) (Langfuhr (CAN))
76a[2]

Dubai Eye *Hugo Palmer* a20
4 ch m Pivotal Jumeirah Palm Star (Invincible Spirit (IRE))
206[7]

Dubai Falcon (IRE) *Saeed bin Suroor* 93
3 b c Teofilo(IRE) Star Blossom (USA) (Good Reward (USA))
2581[2] (3152)

Dubai Future *Saeed bin Suroor* a99 85
3 b c Dubawi(IRE) Anjaz (USA) (Street Cry (IRE))
4608[2] (5254) (9051)◆

Dubai Horizon (IRE) *Saeed bin Suroor* a85 103
5 b g Poet's Voice Chibola (ARG) (Roy (USA))
7694[15]

Dubai Ice (USA) *Saeed bin Suroor* a67 60
3 ch f More Than Ready(USA) Cableknit (USA) (Unbridled's Song (USA))
2900[4]

Dubai Icon *Saeed bin Suroor* a97 99
3 b c New Approach(IRE) Arabian Beauty (IRE) (Shamardal (USA))
(7373) (8130)◆

Dubai Instinct *Brian Meehan* 92
3 b g Le Havre(IRE) Riotous Applause (Royal Applause)
1417[4] (1956)◆ 2828[14] (6730)

Dubai Legacy (USA) *Saeed bin Suroor* a101 104
3 b g Discreet Cat(USA) Afsana (USA) (Tiznow (USA))
(2378) 3075[3] 4016[20] 5963[3] 6915[3] (7697)

Dubai Life (USA) *Saeed bin Suroor* 72
2 bb f Dubawi(IRE) Carnival Court (USA) (Street Sense (USA))
6322[4]

Dubai Love *Saeed bin Suroor* a79 79
2 b f Night Of Thunder(IRE) Devotion (IRE) (Dylan Thomas (IRE))
(7826)◆ 8848[3]

Dubai Metro *George Scott* a36
3 ch g Shamardal(USA) Fragrancy (IRE) (Singspiel (IRE))
251[12] 979[11]

Dubai Mirage (IRE) *Saeed bin Suroor* 85
2 ch c Dubawi(IRE) Calipatria (Shamardal (USA))
5860[2] 6424[3]

Dubai Mission (IRE) *Adrian Wintle* a45 43
6 b g New Approach(IRE) Al Joza (Dubawi (IRE))
2692[12]

Dubai Opera *H-A Pantall* 47
3 b f Invincible Spirit(IRE) Emily Bronte (Machiavellian (USA))
3713a[9]

Dubai Paradise (IRE) *Charlie Appleby* 70
2 ch f Exceed And Excel(AUS) Good Place (USA) (Street Cry (IRE))
4849[4] 5366[8]

Dubai Philosopher (FR) *Michael Bell* a75 64
3 b g Tamayuz Elopa (GER) (Tiger Hill (IRE))
2128[3] 3254[4] 4291[5]

Dubai Quality (USA) *Saeed bin Suroor* a67
2 ch f Dubawi(IRE) Local Time (Invincible Spirit (IRE))
9284[2]

Dubai Romance (IRE) *Saeed bin Suroor* a64
2 ch f Dubawi(IRE) Gracefield (USA) (Storm Cat (USA))
2968[6] 7103[4]

Dubai Souq (IRE) *Saeed bin Suroor* a82 97
2 b c Dubawi(IRE) Balsamine (USA) (Street Cry (IRE))
4925[4] 5563[3] (6185) 6965[5] (8029)

Dubai Station *K R Burke* 97
2 b c Brazen Beau(AUS) Princess Guest (IRE) (Iffraaj)
2931[2] (3507) 4012[3] 5481a[3] 6422[11] 7904[10]

Dubai Tradition (USA) *Saeed bin Suroor* a97 93
3 b c Medaglia d'Oro(USA) Wavering (IRE) (Refuse To Bend (IRE))
2795[3] 3482[2] (4143) (4924) 5541[13] 8350[3]

Dubai Warrior *John Gosden* a113 93
3 b c Dansili Mahbooba (AUS) (Galileo (IRE))
(5808) 6861[2] 7478a[7] (8892) (9587)

Duba Plains *Kenny Johnson* a60 53
4 b g Sixties Icon Selinda (Piccolo)
2789[7] 3296[7] 3452[10] 3932[8] 4518[13]

Dubawi Fifty *Karen McLintock* a107 101
6 b g Dubawi(IRE) Plethora (Sadler's Wells (USA))
4382[2] 5540[11] 6355[12] 8114[9] 9468[4]◆

Dubawi Meeznah (IRE) *David Simcock* a67
4 b m Dubawi(IRE) Meeznah (USA) (Dynaformer (USA))
2017[7] 3495[9]

Dubby Dubbie (USA) *Robert B Hess Jr* 96
4 bb g Ice Box(USA) I'm Cozy (USA) (Grand Slam (USA))
444a[8]

Dubhe *Charlie Appleby* 103
4 b g Dubawi(IRE) Great Heavens (Galileo (IRE))
398a[6] (635a) 1784a[12]

Dubious Affair (IRE) *Sir Michael Stoute* a78 80
3 b f Frankel Dubian To (IRE) (Sea The Stars (IRE))
2361[5] 3553[7] 5421[3]◆ 6069[2] 6812[2] 8013[4] 8812[4] 9202[2] (9425)

Dublin Pharaoh (USA) *Roger Varian* a75
2 ch c American Pharoah(USA) Wile Cat (USA) (Storm Cat (USA))
9197[4] 9471[3]◆

Dublin Rocker (IRE) *Kevin Ryan* 50
2 b f No Nay Never(USA) Rocking (Oasis Dream)
3506[8] 4583[9]

Dubrava *Roger Varian* a82 62
3 gr f Dansili Rose Diamond (IRE) (Daylami (IRE))
3264[10] 4590[2]◆ (5813) 7788[6]

Dub Steps (FR) *F Guillossou*
5 b m Air Chief Marshal(IRE) Safe Steps (FR) (Footstepsinthesand)
7501a[9]

Duca Di Como (IRE) *Cathrine Erichsen* a103 100
4 br g Clodovil(IRE) Quality Love (USA) (Elusive Quality (USA))
3902a[5] (6523a) (7494a)

Duchess Of Avon *Gary Moore* a64 68
4 ch m Dutch Art Avon Lady (Avonbridge)
386[5] 835[10] 3187[9] (3966) 5151[3] 5380[2] 5804[7] 6844[2] 7982[7] 9427[3]

Duchess Of Danzig (GER) *H-F Devin* a65 95
4 ch m Sea The Stars(IRE) Djumama (IRE) (Aussie Rules (USA))
1627a[5] 5510a[7] 7062a[4]

Duck And Vanish *William Haggas* 73
2 b c Lope De Vega(IRE) Froglet (Shaamit (IRE))
7897[6]

Duck Egg Blue (IRE) *Liam Bailey* a8 40
5 b m Haatef(USA) Sapphire Spray (IRE) (Viking Ruler (AUS))
2509[13] 4109[RR] 6656[RR]

Duckett's Grove (USA) *Ed Walker* a94 105
3 b g Point Of Entry(USA) Xylonia (USA) (Horse Chestnut (SAF))
(2321) 3042[5] (4863)

Ducky Mallon (IRE) *Donal Kinsella* a72 79
8 gr g Jeremy(USA) Indus Ridge (IRE) (Indian Ridge (IRE))
7222a[6]

Dudley's Boy *Andrew Balding* 88
3 b g Passing Glance Lizzie Tudor (Tamayuz)
(2925) (3690)

Due A Diamond *Derek Shaw* a48
2 b f Due Diligence(USA) Shaws Diamond (USA) (Ecton Park (USA))
9641[4]

Due A Win *Bryan Smart* 38
2 b g Due Diligence(USA) Malelane (IRE) (Prince Sabo)
6891[10]

Due Care *Roger Charlton* a69
2 gr f Due Diligence(USA) Dolly Colman (IRE) (Diamond Green (FR))
8454[3] 9085[6]

Duende *Mlle L Kneip* a76 76
3 b f Lawman(FR) Venteuse (Beat Hollow)
9280a[10]

Duesenberg (IRE) *Richard Fahey* 82
2 b g Elzaam(AUS) Alabama Grace (IRE) (Teofilo (IRE))
(6891) 7398[5] 7902[3]

Duhail (IRE) *A Fabre* 100
3 ch g Lope De Vega(IRE) Single (FR) (Singspiel (IRE))
4703a[2]

Duhallow Noelie (IRE) *Adrian Paul Keatley* a70 73
3 ch g Dragon Pulse(IRE) Al Euro (FR) (Mujtahid (USA))
524[5] 855[3] 5238[7] 5272[9]

Duhr (IRE) *Ralph J Smith* a12 21
5 b g Mawatheeq(USA) Dijlah (Linamix (FR))
2283[RR] 3834[13] 4475[12] 5310[10]

Duke Bere (FR) *J Boisnard* a72 67
6 b g Peer Gynt(JPN) Realdad (ARG) (Victory Speech (USA))
1631a[8]

Duke Cosimo *Michael Herrington* a74 63
9 ch g Pivotal Nannina (Medicean)
214[2] 356[6] (788) 982[7] 1274[2] 1487[6] 1686[7] 2183[11] 4335[11] 4764[2] 5330[6] 6027[7] 6665[4] 7210[6]

Duke Debonair (IRE) *Jamie Osborne* a54
3 b g Dream Ahead(USA) Nurture (IRE) (Bachelor Duke (USA))
9276[5]

Duke Of Alba (IRE) *John Mackie* a64 71
4 b g Lope De Vega(IRE) Royal Alchemist (Kingsinger (IRE))
5[6] 241[3] 835[2] 1647[4]◆ 2202[2] 3054[4] 7643[2] 7873[12] 9093[12]

Duke Of Condicote *Alan King* a66 73
2 b g No Nay Never(USA) Duchess Of Gazeley (IRE) (Halling (USA))
5655[11] 6926[6] 7562[5] 8029[4]

Duke Of Dunabar *Roger Teal* a54 54
3 b g Dunaden(FR) Litewska (IRE) (Mujadil (USA))
2341[8] 6636[3] 7232[6] 7817[12] 8299[6]

Duke Of Dundee (FR) *A De Mieulle* 100
7 b g Duke Of Marmalade(IRE) Santa Louisia (Highest Honor (FR))
894a[7]

Duke Of Firenze *David C Griffiths* a80 96
10 ch g Pivotal Nannina (Medicean)
2030[5] 2368[5] 2576[2] (2841) (3097) 3344[7] 3883[2] 4313a[9] 5454[11] 5524[4] 5661[18] 6351[14] 6534[2] 7073[3] 7541[4] 8099[16] 8340[12]

Duke Of Hazzard (FR) *Paul Cole* 115
3 b c Lope De Vega(IRE) With Your Spirit (FR) (Invincible Spirit (IRE))
1794a[3] 2668a[5] 3082[7] 4092[5]◆ (4850) (5609) (6443)

Duke Of North (IRE) *Jim Boyle* a63 59
7 b g Danehill Dancer(IRE) Althea Rose (IRE) (Green Desert (USA))
1392[7] 1655[7] 1936[3] 2233[8] 3966[8] 5087[4] 5255[4] 5574[5] 6305[5] 6568[2] 7028[2] 7982[5] 8416[7] 8998[5] 9209[5] 9384[4] 9505[5]

Duke Of Yorkie (IRE) *Adam West* a46 45
3 b g Morpheus Fingal Nights (IRE) (Night Shift (USA))
4217[12] 4642[13] 5797[6] 6636[4] 7685[12] 8753[4] 9201[7]

Duke Of Yorkshire *Tim Easterby* a52 62
9 b g Duke Of Marmalade(IRE) Dame Edith (FR) (Top Ville (IRE))
1648[12] 3511[6] 4274[3] 4825[3] 5621[6] 6278[7] 7053[2] 8843[4]

Dukes Meadow *Roger Ingram* a45 27
8 b g Pastoral Pursuits Figura (Rudimentary (USA))
386[6] 595[9] 724[11] 1215[4]◆ 1378[5] 1717[8] 2972[5] 4473[9] 7374[10] 8417[9] 9157[5] 9456[5]

Dukessa (FR) *D Smaga* a54 58
3 gr f Makfi Dariena (FR) (Highest Honor (FR))
509a[5]

Dukhan *Hugo Palmer* a88 90
4 br g Teofilo(IRE) Vedela (FR) (Selkirk (USA))
1664[6] 2574[10] 3992[8]

Dulas (IRE) *Charles Hills* a83 73
2 b c Raven's Pass(USA) Petit Calva (FR) (Desert King (IRE))
4886[6] 7521[5] (9347)◆

Dulcina *S Donohoe* a41 34
5 b m Compton Place Alushta (Royal Applause)
7214^{10}

Dunbar Road (USA) *Chad C Brown* a113
3 b f Quality Road(USA) Gift List (USA) (Bernardini (USA))
8775a^{5}

Duneflower (IRE) *John Gosden* a76 107
3 b f Dubawi(IRE) Desert Blossom (IRE) (Shamardal (USA))
2507^{4} 2934^{3} (4828)◆ **(5369)** 6726^{2} 7477a^{2} 8116^{7}

Dunkerron *Joseph Tuite* a95 88
3 b g Kuroshio(AUS) Triple Cee (IRE) (Cape Cross (IRE))
2826^{7} 3075^{7} 4016^{25} 4648^{4} *8350*^{11} ***9214***^{2} *9660*^{6}

Dunkirk Harbour (USA)
Debbie Mountain a94 99
3 rg c Declaration Of War(USA) Goodness Gray (USA) (Pulpit (USA))
2660a^{4} 4016^{22} 5207a^{7} 9590a^{11}

Dunstall Dreamer *Denis Quinn* a29
4 b h Swiss Spirit Nordic Theatre (IRE) (King's Theatre (IRE))
178^{8} ***384***^{8} *1215*^{12}

Dupioni (IRE) *Rae Guest* a79 86
3 ch f Siyouni(FR) Kincob (USA) (Kingmambo (USA))
4072^{3} 4922^{3}◆ 5441^{3} **5827**^{2}◆

Duplication (IRE) *John Ryan* a78 73
5 b g Requinto(IRE) Primeshade Promise (Opening Verse (USA))
5965^{6} **6465**^{6}

Duplicitous (IRE) *James Tate* a48
3 b f Oasis Dream Eleanora Duse (IRE) (Azamour (IRE))
380^{9}

Duquesa Penguin *Sofie Lanslots* a72 64
7 ch g Winker Watson Quaker Parrot (Compton Place)
4532a^{4}

Durance (GER) *P Schiergen* 104
3 b f Champs Elysees Djidda (GER) (Lando (GER))
(3877a) (4683a) 5720a^{3} **6747a**^{2} **8154a**^{2}

Duration (IRE) *J R Jenkins* a51 46
4 b g Champs Elysees Fringe (In The Wings)
1601^{0} 5596^{13} 6601^{12} ***8081***^{6} 8523^{7} *8639*^{8}

Durrell *James Fanshawe* a89 93
3 b g Animal Kingdom(USA) Royal Order (USA) (Medaglia d'Oro (USA))
2210^{2} *(3584)* **5194**^{2} 5861^{3} 6917^{5} *7574*^{5}

Durston *David Simcock* 103
3 ch g Sea The Moon(GER) Caribana (Hernando (FR))
2208^{4} (3337) (3842)◆ 5541^{2} **6213**^{3}

Dusk Till Down (FR) *L Gadbin* a63 44
4 ch m Sri Putra Cormeilles (Dubawi (IRE))
1631a^{6}

Dusty Damsel *Mike Murphy* a60 45
3 ch f Toronado(IRE) Dusty Answer (Zafonic (USA))
556^{7} *979*^{8} ***1543***^{3} *2322*^{7} 3154^{9}

Dusty Dream *William Haggas* 70
2 b f Dubawi(IRE) Memory (IRE) (Danehill Dancer (IRE))
6918^{6} **8758**^{4}

Dutch Artist (IRE) *Nigel Tinkler* a59 47
7 ch g Dutch Art Baltic Princess (FR) (Peintre Celebre (USA))
3959^{7} *4460*^{4}◆ 4658^{11} 5024^{11} 5302^{7} 5560^{7} 6173^{5} **7545**^{6} *8000*^{7} *8299*^{8} *8694*^{7} *8942*^{5}

Dutch Chop (FR) *Jane Soubagne* a90 87
2 b g Amadeus Wolf Tulipe Rouge (FR) (Panis (USA))
5228a^{10}

Dutch Coed *Nigel Tinkler* a65 69
7 b g Dutch Art Discoed (Distinctly North (USA))
1648^{10} 2112^{10} 3225^{7} (3960) (4633) (5096)◆ 5850^{4} **(6068)** 6500^{4} 7513^{7} *8300*^{13}

Dutch Decoy *Richard Fahey* a69 78
2 ch g Dutch Art The Terrier (Foxhound (USA))
2184^{4} 3098^{4} 5553^{2} **(6653)**◆ 7399^{5}

Dutch Harbor *Sir Mark Todd* a67 47
2 b c Kodiac Complexion (Hurricane Run (IRE))
7030^{5} 7677^{8}

Dutch Masterpiece
Jaber Ramadhan a92 103
9 b g Dutch Art The Terrier (Foxhound (USA))
49a^{5} 393a^{6}

Dutch Melody *Lucinda Egerton* a41 47
5 b m Dutch Art Mystic Melody (IRE) (Montjeu (IRE))
1500^{7} 1663^{10} 1849^{7} *2244*^{9} **2911**^{6} 3296^{9} 4215^{8} 4475^{9} 4496^{4}

Dutch Monument *Richard Fahey* a47
2 ch f Dutch Art Lovina (ITY) (Love The Groom (USA))
8084^{12}

Dutch Painting *Michael Bell* 76
2 b f Dutch Art Lisiere (IRE) (Excellent Art)
5132^{10} 6019^{5} **(6831)** 7696^{13}

Dutch Pursuit (IRE)
Rebecca Menzies a74 69
3 b g Canford Cliffs(IRE) Dansili Dutch (IRE) (Dutch Art)
(20) 4980^{8} 6677^{9} *8428*^{8} *9329*^{7} *9512*^{13}

Dutch Story *Amanda Perrett* a59 68
3 ch g Dutch Art Shamandar (FR) (Exceed And Excel (AUS))
3003^{15} 3661^{10} 4116^{11} (5869)◆ *6389*^{2} *6840*^{8} 8207^{2} **(8436)**

Dutch Treat *Andrew Balding* a86 93
3 ch f Dutch Art Syann (IRE) (Daylami (IRE))
1751^{11} 6445^{12} 7123^{4} **(7901)** *9010*^{3} *9603a*^{14}

Dutch Uncle *Tom Clover* a52 78
7 b g Dutch Art Evasive Quality (FR) (Highest Honor (FR))
88^{2} *(204)* *552*^{4} *1291*^{10} 3541^{7} (3766) 4035^{3} 5198^{5} 5858^{4} *6736*^{7} 8033^{7} 8515^{15}

Dutiful Son (IRE) *Emma Owen* a33 6
9 b g Invincible Spirit(IRE) Grecian Dancer (Dansili)
2971^{11} *4501*^{11} *5051*^{12} *6284*^{11}

Dutugamunu (IRE) *Richard Spencer* a54
2 ch c Ivawood(IRE) Bunditten (IRE) (Soviet Star (USA))
7605^{5}

Dwyfran *David Loughnane* 41
2 b f Multiplex Buddug (Formidable I (USA))
3551^{6}

Dyagilev *Simon Pearce* a54 50
4 ch g Kheleyf(USA) Dancemetothemoon (Medicean)
4639^{11} 5245^{8} 5816^{9} *6731*^{10} *7281*^{12} *7685*^{7} *8001*^{3} 8204^{4} ***(8553)*** 8854^{11} ***9090***^{3} *9444*^{7}

Dyami (FR) *George Baker* 84
2 bb c Bated Breath Zaltana (USA) (Cherokee Run (USA))
4252^{5} 5665^{5} **6433a**^{2} 7410^{7}

Dylan Dancing (IRE) *C Le Veel* a55 80
6 b h Dylan Thomas(IRE) Raindancing (IRE) (Tirol (IRE))
2955a^{4} *5643a*^{9}

Dylan De Vega *Richard Fahey* 94
2 ch g Poet's Voice Colorada (Lope De Vega (IRE))
1953^{2} (2475)◆ 3988^{14} 4893^{2} 5612^{2} 6474^{10} **7400**^{6} 7904^{12}

Dynamic Kitty (USA)
Georgios Alimpinisis a65 66
3 b f Kitten's Joy(USA) Dyning Out (USA) (Dynaformer (USA))
2137a^{8} **4964a**^{7}

Dynamighty *Richard Spencer* a61 69
2 b f Due Diligence(USA) Weisse Socken (IRE) (Acclamation)
2918^{4} 3350^{3} 4802^{5} 5185^{20} *6029*^{3} *7556*^{4} *8195*^{8}

Dynamo Walt (IRE) *Derek Shaw* a81 63
8 b g Acclamation Cambara (Dancing Brave (USA))
1279 ***353***^{4} ***551***^{2}◆ *791*^{8} *1547*^{10} *1929*^{10} *2556*^{8} *3303*^{7} *9257*^{6} *9458*^{4} *(9550)*

Dyna Passer (USA)
Thomas Albertrani 104
3 ch f Lemon Drop Kid(USA) Dynaire (USA) (Dynaformer (USA))
6993a^{3}

Dyslexic (AUS)
Michael, Wayne & John Hawkes 99
4 b m Foxwedge(AUS) Easy To Read (AUS) (Encosta De Lago (AUS))
8138a^{18}

Eadbhard (IRE) *Peter Fahey* a51 74
4 b g Elzaam(AUS) Only Exception (IRE) (Jeremy (USA))
2331^{2} 5712a^{S} (Dead)

Eagle Court (IRE) *David O'Meara* 61
2 b g Free Eagle(IRE) Classic Remark (IRE) (Dr Fong (USA))
7586^{5}

Eagle Hunter *F-H Graffard* 99
3 b c Dansili Zeva (Zamindar (USA))
1241a^{2} **3029a**^{4} 3903a^{5}

Eagle Queen *Andrew Balding* a61 57
3 ch f Dubawi(IRE) Opera Gal (IRE) (Galileo (IRE))
2771^{9} 3889^{6} ***4641***^{8} 5744^{6} *6636*^{7} *7280*^{7}

Eagle Reel (IRE) *Luke Comer* a57 52
4 b h Zoffany(IRE) Ufallya (IRE) (Statue Of Liberty (USA))
419a^{5}

Eagles By Day (IRE) *Michael Bell* a76 111
3 bb c Sea The Stars(IRE) Missunited (IRE) (Golan (IRE))
1509^{2} (2142)◆ 2619^{6} **4049**^{3} 4845^{8}

Eagle Way (AUS) *John Moore* 116
6 ch g More Than Ready(USA) Wedgetail Eagle (AUS) (Lure (USA))
9376a^{10}

Eagleway (FR) *Andrea Marcialis* a93 102
3 b c Sakhee's Secret Tearsforjoy (USA) (Street Cry (IRE))
(3621a) 4703a^{5}

Eagre *Derek Shaw* a29
3 b g Dutch Art Tahlia Ree (IRE) (Acclamation)
2281^{3} ***595***^{13}

Eardley Road (IRE) *Clive Cox* a80 73
3 b c No Nay Never(USA) Corking (IRE) (Montjeu (IRE))
(943)◆ 1423^{5} 2147^{5} 3261^{5} 4188^{4}

Earl (GER) *Lennart Hammer-Hansen*
4 b g Tertullian(USA) Ericarrow (IRE) (Bollin Eric) 2002a^{7}

Earl Of Bunnacurry (IRE)
Kevin Frost a60 62
5 b g Approve(IRE) Bonkers (Efisio)
1159^{8} ***8348***^{6} ***9336***^{3} *9646*^{10}

Earl Of Harrow *Mick Channon* 79
3 b g Sixties Icon The Screamer (IRE) (Insan (USA))
2511^{5} (2914) (3505) 4187^{5} **(5954)** 8002^{6}

Early Edition (IRE) *Roger Fell* a28 48
3 b f Dawn Approach(IRE) Newsroom (IRE) (Manduro (GER))
1979^{5} 2482^{12} 2870^{10}

Early Enough (FR) *T Mercier* a68 68
6 b g Gold Away(IRE) Sayoko (IRE) (Rainbow Quest (USA))
(5761a)

Early Morning Mist (IRE)
Amy Murphy a44 15
2 bb f Pour Moi(IRE) Incense (Unfuwain (USA))
5052^{9} 6161^{13} ***6314***^{7}

Early Riser (IRE) *James Tate* a69
3 b f Dawn Approach(IRE) Cape Good Hope (Cape Cross (IRE))
7572^{5} ***8467***^{2}

Early Strike (FR) *Gavin Cromwell* a53 46
3 ch g Dawn Approach(IRE) Buille Cliste (IRE) (Smart Strike (CAN))
7240^{4}

Early Summer (IRE)
Hughie Morrison a79 82
4 b m Sea The Stars(IRE) Summer's Eve (Singspiel (IRE))
3635^{10} 4483^{6} **(5047)** 5540^{17} *6634*^{4}

Earnshaw (USA) *S Jadhav* a66 101
8 gr h Medaglia d'Oro(USA) Emily Bronte (Machiavellian (USA))
47a^{7} **284a**^{3} 514a^{4} 635a^{5} *959a*^{5}

Earth And Sky (USA) *George Scott* a83 70
3 b f Noble Mission Youre So Sweet (USA) (Storm Cat (USA))
2581^{7} 3553^{5} 4073^{4} 5060^{4} *5855*^{6} 8515^{14} *(8806)* *(9173)* ***9329***^{2} *9417*^{5}

Earthlight (IRE) *A Fabre* 119
2 ch c Shamardal(USA) Winters Moon (IRE) (New Approach (IRE))
(5481a) **(6264a)**◆ (7693)◆

Earthly (USA) *Bernard Llewellyn* a49 58
5 b g Spring At Last(USA) Geographic (USA) (Empire Maker (USA))
2344^{4} 2720^{6} 3017^{7} **3511**^{2} 4036^{7} *6681*^{4} *7553*^{6} *9312*^{5} *9553*^{6}

East *Kevin Ryan* 108
3 ch f Frankel Vital Statistics (Indian Ridge (IRE))
2669a^{3} 3115^{10} 5479a^{5}

East End Girl *Lucy Wadham* a44 58
2 b f Youmzain(IRE) Bermondsey Girl (Bertolini (USA))
6673^{5} *7515*^{10}

Eastern Racer (IRE)
Denis Gerard Hogan a63 77
7 b g Bushranger(IRE) Queen Cobra (IRE) (Indian Rocket)
748a^{11} **5537a**^{10}

Eastern Sheriff *Hugo Palmer* a81
2 b c Lawman(FR) Abunai (Pivotal)
(9063)

Eastern World (IRE)
Charlie Appleby a84
2 ch c Dubawi(IRE) Eastern Joy (Dubai Destination (USA))
9415^{2}

East Indies *Gary Moore* a75 59
6 b g Authorized(IRE) Elan (Dansili)
84^{3}

East Of Eden (IRE) *Hugo Palmer* a58 77
2 b f Exceed And Excel(AUS) Allegation (FR) (Lawman (FR))
4849^{3}◆ 5906^{4} *9251*^{3}

East Street Revue *Tim Easterby* a77 82
6 ch g Pastoral Pursuits Revue Princess (IRE) (Mull Of Kintyre (USA))
1899^{11} 2368^{11} **(2709)** 3375^{2} 3868^{17} 4406^{17} 4625^{3} 5217^{8} 6607^{2} **(6972)** *8921*^{14} *9519*^{4}

Easy Desire *Richard Fahey* a60 52
2 ch f Outstrip Dularame (IRE) (Pivotal)
8021^{5} 8458^{12}

Easy Money (IRE) *Roger Fell* a51
4 b g Iffraaj Ezalli (IRE) (Cape Cross (IRE))
384^{6} ***1236***^{8} *1427*^{6}

Easy Tiger *David Weston* a85 83
7 b g Refuse To Bend(IRE) Extremely Rare (IRE) (Mark Of Esteem (IRE))
8016^{12} ***8606***^{8} *9176*^{11} *9422*^{7}

Ebbisham (IRE) *John Mackie* a59 60
6 b g Holy Roman Emperor(IRE) Balting Lass (IRE) (Orpen (USA))
2203^{16} **2509**^{8} 3473^{7} *5003*^{8} *6977*^{4} *8667*^{6} *9040*^{7} *9168*^{9}

Eben Dubai (IRE) *John Flint* a13 27
7 b g New Approach(IRE) Eldalil (Singspiel (IRE))
4498^{11} 5993^{11}

Ebitda *Scott Dixon* a70 63
5 b m Compton Place Tipsy Girl (Haafhd)
4829^{7} *6549*^{8} **8263**^{3} 8861^{5} *8943*^{6} *9219*^{10} *9335*^{12}

Ebony (FR) *J-C Rouget* a93 102
3 b f Le Havre(IRE) Ennaya (FR) (Nayef (USA))
3905a^{9} 4964a^{2} 7978a^{4} *9170a*^{7}

Ebony Adams *Brian Meehan* 65
2 b f Fountain Of Youth(IRE) Mortitia (Dansili)
2915^{9} 3644^{5} 4394^{6} **(5146)** 5912^{6} 6372^{4} 7522^{6} 7896^{16}

Ebony Belle (IRE) *Patrick Martin* a37 47
3 b f Tough As Nails(IRE) Ebonywood (USA) (Montbrook (USA))
9035^{7}

Ebony Legend *John Quinn* 66
2 b f Camacho Cross Section (USA) (Cape Cross (IRE))
3652^{5} **4142**^{5} 4624^{7}

Ebqaa (IRE) *James Unett* a71 67
5 b m Cape Cross(IRE) Estedaama (IRE) (Marju (IRE))
(1341) ***1988***^{3}◆ *2214*^{5} ***3321***^{2} 3708^{7} 4363^{6} 5423^{8} *6681*^{6} 7682^{3} *8868*^{5} *9626*^{7}

Ebury *Martyn Meade* a89 100
3 ch c Iffraaj Alabelle (Galileo (IRE))
(1034)◆ *1594*^{2} *1926*^{10} **(6914)**◆ **8728**^{2}

Ecclesiastical *Martyn Meade* 62
2 ch c Pastoral Pursuits Bazzana (Zebedee)
3943^{6} 4734^{5}

Eccleston *Paul Midgley* a45 63
8 b g Acclamation Miss Meggy (Pivotal)
1895^{10} 2416^{12}

Echauffour (FR) *J-C Rouget* a71 79
6 b g Le Havre(IRE) Langrune (IRE) (Fasliyev (USA))
46a^{7}

Echelle Du Levant (IRE) *F Chappet* a61 65
3 b f Dabirsim(FR) Elnadwa (USA) (Daaher (CAN))
3028a^{13}

Echo (IRE) *Jedd O'Keeffe* a69 78
4 b g Zoffany(IRE) Aweebounce (IRE) (Dubawi (IRE))
(782) *(1398)* (1981) **3334**^{2} 3653^{7} 4491^{3} 6100^{3} 7001^{8} *8945*^{6}

Echo Brava *Suzi Best* a50 51
9 gr g Proclamation(IRE) Snake Skin (Golden Snake (USA))
33^{11}

Echo Cove (IRE)
Jane Chapple-Hyam a71 71
4 ch g Roderic O'Connor(IRE) Russian Rave (Danehill Dancer (IRE))
435^{5}

Echo Of Lightning *Roger Fell* a49 71
9 b g Echo Of Light Classic Lass (Dr Fong (USA))
3868^{15} 4207^{10} 4875^{9} 5021^{8} 5820^{8} **(6572)** 6937^{4} 7383^{8} *8199*^{12} *9028*^{13}

Echo Park (IRE)
Mrs John Harrington a93 92
4 br m Elusive Pimpernel(USA) Pershaan (IRE) (Darshaan)
1620a^{6}

Echo's Love (IRE) *John Gosden* 44
2 b f Invincible Spirit(IRE) Sound Reflection (USA) (Street Cry (IRE))
8093^{12} 8510^{12}

Eclipse Storm *J A Stack* 98
3 ch g Dream Ahead(USA) Gentle Breeze (IRE) (Dubawi (IRE))
2156a^{5} **2492a**^{2} 4016^{28} 5205a^{8} 7241a^{24}

Eclittica (IRE) *Marco Botti* a60
3 b f Pour Moi(IRE) Ekta (Danehill Dancer (IRE))
66^{4} *403*^{6}

Ecolo (FR) *C Laffon-Parias* a71 95
3 b c Invincible Spirit(IRE) Never Green (IRE) (Halling (USA))
8982a^{2}

Economic Crisis (IRE) *Alan Berry* a64 70
10 ch m Excellent Art Try The Air (IRE) (Foxhound (USA))
1505^{8} 1951^{7} 2433^{9} 2637^{4}◆ 3504^{6} (3933) 4555^{9} 4911^{7} 5276^{5} 5620^{4} (5904) **6607**^{3} 6829^{2} 7367^{9} 7736^{8} 8183^{7} 8339^{6} 8632^{7}

Ecrivain (FR) *C Laffon-Parias* 111
2 ch c Lope De Vega(IRE) Sapphire Pendant (IRE) (Danehill Dancer (IRE))
(7005a) **7940a**^{4}

Ecstasea (IRE) *Rae Guest* a57 57
3 b f Born To Sea(IRE) Rhapsodize (Halling (USA))
3019^{6} 4121^{8} **5269**^{5} 5869^{6} **6302**^{2} *8256*^{7} *8822*^{6} *9090*^{11}

Edaraat *Roger Varian* a97 91
3 b g Exceed And Excel(AUS) Deglet Noor (New Approach (IRE))
2023^{3}◆ 2802^{8} 4305^{5} *(4789)* (5557) 6425^{9} ***7517***^{2}

Ed Cuvee *Christine Dunnett*
3 ch g Mazameer(IRE) Flaming Telepath (Storming Home)
4590^{10}

Eddie Cochran (IRE)
Richard Hannon a63 74
3 bl g Society Rock(IRE) Crossreadh (USA) (Sahm (USA))
2216^{7} 2690^{5} **4178**^{3} *4788*^{7} *6886*^{5} *7560*^{13}

Eddie Haskell (USA) *Mark Glatt* 113
6 b g Square Eddie(CAN) Teresa Ann (USA) (Boston Harbor (USA))
8770a^{11}

Eddystone Rock (IRE) *John Best* a92 105
7 ch g Rock Of Gibraltar(IRE) Bayberry (UAE) (Bering)
82^{4} *349*^{6} *878*^{4} *1220*^{6} (1559) 2032^{2} 2606^{3} (3070) 3346^{3} 4646^{5} 4884^{7} (5928) **(6355)** 8114^{17}

Edebez (IRE) *Seamus Mullins* 47
2 b g Zebedee Silk City (IRE) (Barathea (IRE))
6845^{9} 7981^{7} **8858**^{5}

Eden Gardens (IRE) *Simon Crisford* a88 68
3 ch g Mukhadram Showerproof (Peintre Celebre (USA))
8606^{5} ***9050***^{4}

Eden Rose *Mick Channon* a96 94
4 b m Dansili Gallic Star (IRE) (Galileo (IRE))
(1330)◆ ***(1943)*** 3081^{2} (Dead)

Ede's Pat Phelan a56 59
3 b g Sir Percy My Amalie (IRE) (Galileo (IRE))
765^{7}

Edessann (IRE) *Michael Herrington* a57 73
3 ch g Lope De Vega(IRE) Edelmira (IRE) (Peintre Celebre (USA))
9351^{12} ***9519***^{12}

Edgar (GER) *David Bridgwater* a35
9 b g Big Shuffle(USA) Estella (GER) (Acatenango (GER))
40^{8}

Edgar Allan Poe (IRE)
Rebecca Bastiman a46 81
5 b g Zoffany(IRE) Swingsky (IRE) (Indian Ridge (IRE))
1271^{12} 2330^{5} 3177^{5} (3681) 3922^{2} (4446)◆ **(4762)** 5060^{6} 5725^{5} 7589^{9}

Edge (IRE) *Bernard Llewellyn* a65 58
8 b g Acclamation Chanter (Lomitas)
2145^{16} **2714**^{5} 2998^{4} 3541^{4} 4797^{5} 5337^{4} 5867^{5} 6334^{9} 6643^{7} *7549*^{4} *8466*^{11}

Edged Out *Christopher Mason* a56 60
9 b m Piccolo Edge Of Light (Xaar)
2729^{5} 3577^{6} **4230**^{2} 4556^{2} 4772^{2} 5582^{5} 5793^{3} 7112^{12} *7844*^{3} *8450*^{7} *9169*^{8} *9572*^{8}

Edge Of The Bay
Christopher Mason a38
2 b f Cable Bay(IRE) Sharpened Edge (Exceed And Excel (AUS))
6019^{11} ***7786***^{9}

Edgewood *Paul Midgley* a77 75
3 b g Garswood Heskin (IRE) (Acclamation)
972^{3}◆ 1662^{5} 2333^{4} *4288*^{7} 5786^{4}

Edification *Mark Fahey* a86 85
6 b g Dream Ahead(USA) Elegant Pride (Beat Hollow)
7216a^{4}

Edinburgh Castle (IRE)
Andrew Balding a82 81
3 b g Sea The Stars(IRE) Evensong (GER) (Waky Nao)
(7730) ***8552***^{3}

Edington (GER) *Frau S Steinberg* a80 101
7 b h Dansili Enrica (Niniski (USA))
46a^{5}

Edisa (USA) *A De Royer-Dupre* 110
3 ch f Kitten's Joy(USA) Ebiyza (IRE) (Rock Of Gibraltar (IRE))
(2759a) (3676a) 4429a^{2} 5470a^{2} (6993a) 8378a^{2} **9380a**^{5}

Edith (GER) *R Dzubasz* 99
5 ch m It's Gino(GER) Eliza Fong (GER) (Dr Fong (USA))
8587a[8]

Edmond Dantes (IRE) *David Menuisier* a72 74
3 gr g Alhebayeb(IRE) Abhasana (IRE) (Hawk Wing (USA))
3052[2] (3797) 4068[7] 5779[6] 6722[4] 8433[3]

Edraak (IRE) *Owen Burrows* 60
3 b g Elzaam(AUS) So Blissful (IRE) (Cape Cross (IRE))
6802[2]

Education *Ismail Mohammed* 20
3 ch c Mukhadram Pasithea (IRE) (Celtic Swing)
7177[2] 8398[9]

Eeh Bah Gum (IRE) *Tim Easterby* a92 93
4 b g Dandy Man(IRE) Moonline Dancer (FR) (Royal Academy (USA))
1946[14] 2775[4] 3097[8] 3344[4] 4331[4] 4896[12]

Eesha My Flower (USA) *Marco Botti* a72 75
3 b f English Channel(USA) Bella Bandita (USA) (Dynaformer (USA))
(2017) 3169[3]◆ 4599[4] 6595[6] 9273[4]◆

Eesha Says (IRE) *Tony Carroll* a59
4 b m Fast Company(IRE) Admire The View (IRE) (Dubawi (IRE))
(7628) 9335[3] 9539[2]

Eesha's Smile (IRE) *Ivan Furtado* a45 70
3 ch f Toronado(IRE) Lamentation (Singspiel (IRE))
2253[5] 4000[3] 4628[3] 5138[4] 6370[3] 8087[13] 9093[11] 9306[13] 9503[11]

Eevilynn Drew *Robert Eddery* a80
2 b c Epaulette(AUS) Halicardia (Halling (USA))
(8700) 9451[2] 9585[2]

Effernock Fizz (IRE) *Miss Katy Brown* a70 66
4 b m Lovelace Manx Fizz (Efisio)
273[11] (5214) 5633[10] 7216a[13]

Ego Dancer (FR) *M Delzangles* a75 90
4 b m Pour Moi(IRE) Sarabande (USA) (Woodman (USA))
2429a[5] 3136a[5]

Egotistic *David Simcock* a42 48
2 ch f Sepoy(AUS) Self Centred (Medicean)
5139[6] 5646[5] 6019[8]

Egypsyan Crackajak *Dominic Ffrench Davis* a37 43
2 b g Kutub(IRE) Three Scoops (Captain Rio)
8516[13]

Eight And Bob *W P Mullins* a53 76
6 b g Big Bad Bob(IRE) Mare Nostrum (Caerleon (USA))
5712a[2]

Eight Bells *Michael Bell* 17
2 b g Henrythenavigator(USA) Dawn Glory (Oasis Dream)
7981[14]

Eighteenhundred (IRE) *Paul Nicholls* 47
3 b g Battle Of Marengo(IRE) Kawaha (IRE) (Danehill Dancer (IRE))
3946[6] 5254[11]

Eight Rings (USA) *Bob Baffert* a116
2 bb c Empire Maker(USA) Purely Hot (USA) (Pure Prize (USA))
8749a[6]

Eightsome Reel *Michael Bell* a77 106
3 b g Iffraaj Set To Music (IRE) (Danehill Dancer (IRE))
1856[3] (2120) 2833[2] 4013[4]

Eileen's Magic *Lisa Williamson* 45
2 b f Zebedee Art Critic (USA) (Fusaichi Pegasus (USA))
3506[9] 3841[9] 4317[6] 4876[7]

Einar (IRE) *M Delcher Sanchez* a75 77
3 b g George Vancouver(USA) Pyramid Painter (IRE) (Peintre Celebre (USA))
(3878a)

Eirene *Dean Ivory* a101 103
4 b m Declaration Of War(USA) Za Za Zoom (IRE) (Le Vie Dei Colori)
1412[7] 2062[3] 2621[7]

Ejabah (IRE) *Charles Smith* a30 40
5 b m Iffraaj Relinquished (Royal Applause)
41[6] 1068[2] 2112[9] 2481[5] 2901[8]

Ejbaar *S Seemar* a78 93
7 b g Oasis Dream Habaayib (Royal Applause)
196a[6]

Ejtilaab (IRE) *Roger Varian* 85
3 b g Slade Power(IRE) Miranda Frost (IRE) (Cape Cross (IRE))
(4367)◆

Ekaitzana (FR) *Andrea Marcialis* 57
2 b f Dabirsim(FR) Urakana (IRE) (Teofilo (IRE))
3714a[3] 4228a[8]

Ekayburg (FR) *David Pipe* 65
5 b g Sageburg(IRE) Kayseri (FR) (Dress Parade)
2731[6] 3263[10] 3664[6] 4287[2] 7756[12]

Ekhtiyaar *Doug Watson* a70 116
5 b g Bated Breath Bayja (IRE) (Giant's Causeway (USA))
52a[3] (843a) 1111a[2] 1442a[9]

Elaire Noire (IRE) *R Biondi* 103
2 b c Footstepsinthesand Miss Brazil (IRE) (Exceed And Excel (AUS))
8390a[3]

Ela Katrina *Roger Varian* a78 43
3 gr f Kendargent(FR) Ela Athena (Ezzoud (IRE))
2771[6] 4641[7] 9051[2]

Elamirr (IRE) *Roger Varian* a84 74
3 b c Exceed And Excel(AUS) Ameerat (Mark Of Esteem (IRE))
4329[3] 4865[7] 7176[5]

Elara *S Wattel* a73 82
5 ch m Raven's Pass(USA) Moon Sister (IRE) (Cadeaux Genereux)
(4859a)

Elarqam *Mark Johnston* 122
4 b h Frankel Attraction (Efisio)
1890[4] (3074) 3953[3] (4612) (5455) 6354[3] 7219a[7]

El Astronaute (IRE) *John Quinn* a100 111
6 ch g Approve(IRE) Drumcliffe Dancer (IRE) (Footstepsinthesand)
1501[2]◆ 2409[6] 2744[6] 3097[9] (3818a) (4313a) 5222a[2] 5611[5] 6423[8] 7073[5] 7943a[3]

Elate (USA) *William Mott* a116
5 bb m Medaglia d'Oro(USA) Cheery (USA) (Distorted Humor (USA))
8777a[4]

El Borracho (IRE) *Simon Dow* a80 79
4 br g Society Rock(IRE) Flame Of Hibernia (IRE) (One Cool Cat (USA))
945[9] 1291[13] 3016[3] 3633[4]◆ 4112[5] (4425) 4929[5] 5091[5] 6291[7] (6634) 7370[4] 8014[7] 8468[8]

El Chapo *Fawzi Abdulla Nass* a80 74
4 b g Lethal Force(IRE) Never Lose (Diktat)
1001[8]

El Conquistador (USA) *Shaun Keightley* a59
2 ch c Kitten's Joy(USA) Bonita Donita (USA) (Fusaichi Pegasus (USA))
8494[11]

Eldelbar (SPA) *Geoffrey Harker* a52 59
5 ch g Footstepsinthesand Malinche (Hernando (FR))
1976[10] 2898[11] 4784[5]◆ 5213[9] 5770[5] 6276[8] 6666[7] 7050[2] 7443[5] 7962[3] 8469[3] 9111[8]

Elecktric Cafe (FR) *J Carayon* a50 43
8 b g Panis(USA) Dietrich (FR) (Anabaa (USA))
4748a[10]

Elector *Sir Michael Stoute* a97 101
4 b g Dansili Enticement (Montjeu (IRE))
(2408) 3315[8] 4613[6] 6513[5]

Electrical Storm *Saeed bin Suroor* 88
2 b g Dubawi(IRE) Mujarah (IRE) (Marju (IRE))
1887[2]◆ 2444[2] 4069[3] 6449[2] 7119[11]

Electric Ladyland (IRE) *Archie Watson* a92 87
2 b f Cable Bay(IRE) Conversational (IRE) (Thousand Words)
(1493) (1937) 2520[6] 3023[4] 3988[7] 5185[7] 5544[7] 6979[2] (7546)

Electric Landlady (IRE) *Denis Coakley* a74 87
4 b m Red Jazz(USA) Margie (IRE) (Marju (IRE))
1561[2] 2809[9]

Elegant Drama (IRE) *Jane M Foley* a65 75
4 b m Dandy Man(IRE) Speronella (Raven's Pass (USA))
5537a[7]

Elegant Erin (IRE) *Richard Hannon* 77
2 b f Dandy Man(IRE) Eriniya (IRE) (Acclamation)
4840[3] 5132[6] (6118) 7155[4] 7696[6] 8465[2]

Elegant Light *H-A Pantall* a71 93
3 bb f Teofilo(IRE) Ethereal Sky (IRE) (Invincible Spirit (IRE))
(8373a)

Elegant Love *David Evans* a68 72
3 b f Delegator Lovellian (Machiavellian (USA))
2355[7] 3665[4] 4562[6] 5253[4] 5580[4] 6039[4] 6505[2] 7081[4] (7295) 7973[2] 8519[2] 9201[4] 9542[8]

Elegiac *Mark Johnston* a109 108
4 b g Farhh Lamentation (Singspiel (IRE))
1062[2] (1693)

Elena *Charles Hills* a64 66
3 b f Toronado(IRE) Red Intrigue (IRE) (Selkirk (USA))
2762[7] 3598[2] 4211[3] 5549[4] 6362[9] 7526[3] 7858[5] 9279[4] 9426[5]

Elena Osorio (IRE) *Ed Walker* a57 53
3 ch f Lope De Vega(IRE) Artwork Genie (IRE) (Excellent Art)
3464[7] 5627[8] 6169[4] 6643[10] 9039[5] 9305[3] 9552[6]

Eleni (FR) *Waldemar Hickst* 103
4 ch m Kendargent(FR) Encore Merci (IRE) (Danehill Dancer (IRE))
7137a[6] 8587a[12]

Elenora Delight *Ron Barr* a76 65
4 b m Dansili Missy O' Gwaun (IRE) (King's Best (USA))
123[3] (364) 1511[6] 2261[6] 3930[9] 5436[11]

Elerfaan (IRE) *Rebecca Bastiman* a91 93
5 b g Shamardal(USA) Gorband (USA) (Woodman (USA))
2015[2] 2526[2] 3563[7]

Eleuthera *J F Levins* a60 63
7 ch g Bahamian Bounty Cha Cha Cha (Efisio)
(5238) 7777[4] 9352[4]

Elevate Her (IRE) *Richard Spencer* a61 6
2 b f Bungle Inthejungle Betty Fontaine (IRE) (Mujadil (USA))
2191[3]◆ 2469[6]

Eleven One (FR) *Gianluca Bietolini* a45 42
3 ch g Kheleyf(USA) Yellow Ground (USA) (Langfuhr (CAN))
2311a[7]

Elfin Queen (USA) *A P O'Brien* 76
2 ch f American Pharoah(USA) Pretty 'N Smart (USA) (Beau Genius (CAN))
8093[4]

Elfrida Beetle *Tim Easterby* a45 12
2 b f Fountain Of Youth(IRE) Parisianna (Champs Elysees)
7063[10] 7580[11]

El Ghazwani (IRE) *Hugo Palmer* a97 85
4 b h Cape Cross(IRE) Almansoora (USA) (Bahri (USA))
(1395) (1589) 2320[3] 4021[7] 4504[7] 7396[5] 7686[6] 8701[5] 9206[6] (9510)

El Guanche (FR) *M Delcher Sanchez* a74 94
3 ch c Power Miss Gran Canaria (Selkirk (USA))
1199a[10] 2564a[10] 3855[6]

El Gumryah (IRE) *Simon Crisford* a91 75
3 b f No Nay Never(USA) Dancing Shoes (IRE) (Danehill (USA))
(1939) 2806[10] 4052[20]

Elhafei (USA) *Michael Appleby* a67 78
4 br g Speightstown(USA) Albamara (Galileo (IRE))
4333[6] 4907[3] 5529[3] 6210[3] 6512[3] 7166[2] 7875[8] 8507[10] 8642[8]

Elham Valley (FR) *Andrew Balding* 60
2 gr c Tin Horse(IRE) Dame Du Floc (IRE) (Peintre Celebre (USA))
7972[9] 8517[4]

El Hombre *Keith Dalgleish* a97 81
5 ch g Camacho Nigella (Band On The Run)
127[8] 909[2] 1105[4] 1388[3] 4331[3] 5664[12] 8317[4] 9348[3]◆ 9571[3]

Eliade (FR) *F Rohaut* a76 101
3 b f Teofilo(IRE) Elodie (Dansili)
3391a[4] 6385a[2]

Eliaure (FR) *N Leenders* 69
2 b f Muhtathir Irrationnelle (IRE) (Astronomer Royal (USA))
9123a[4]

Elieden (IRE) *Mlle A-S Crombez* a64 63
3 b f Camacho Ohwhatalady (IRE) (Invincible Spirit (IRE))
401[2] 1658a[2] 2390a[7] 3066a[7] (4959a)

Eligible (IRE) *Clive Cox* a87 85
3 b g Dark Angel(IRE) Secrets Away (IRE) (Refuse To Bend (IRE))
2900[3]◆ 4226[4] 4788[2] (5350) 6282[3] 6729[3] 8024[4]

Elikapeka (FR) *Kevin Ryan* a63 63
3 b f War Command(USA) Regatta (FR) (Layman (USA))
405[3] 1400[2] 3414[4] 3650[8] 4284[10] 5247[15]

El Indio (FR) *H-A Pantall* a71 81
4 b h Meshaheer(USA) Belle Suisse (FR) (Hamas (IRE))
1449a[10] 2226a[9] 3136a[15] 4747a[6]

El Ingrato (FR) *M Delcher Sanchez* 102
3 b c Toronado(IRE) Narya (IRE) (Halling (USA))
(2311a)

Elisa Again *R Biondi* 102
3 ch f Champs Elysees Sunny Again (Shirocco (GER))
4171a[5] 8153a[2] 8790a[3]

Elisheba (IRE) *John Gosden* a80 83
3 b f Australia Laugh Out Loud (Clodovil (IRE))
556[5]◆ (794) 2618[4] 3099[5] 4068[5] 5687[4]◆ 6280[5]

Elite Icon *Jim Goldie* a41 53
5 b g Sixties Icon Sailing Days (Kris)
100[8] 607[5] 782[13] 1163[11] 1500[3] (2373) 2684[3] 3175[9] 3500[3] 3718[7] 4510[4] 5277[9] 5727[4] 5939[5] 6611[6] 7070[4] 8238[5] 8635[6]

Elixir Sky *Kevin Frost* a25
2 b f Fountain Of Youth(IRE) Millinsky (USA) (Stravinsky (USA))
9284[10] 9569[10]

Elixsoft (IRE) *Karen Tutty* a76 59
4 b m Elzaam(AUS) Grandegrandegrande (IRE) (High Chaparral (IRE))
355[4] 525[3] 784[2] (1271)◆ 1399[2] 1563[2] 1850[7] 2246[3] 2911[9] 3449[2]◆ 4333[10] 5178[9] 6940[9] 7288[7] 7526[5]◆ 7583[2] 8305[10] 8719[7] 9109[9] 9202[5] 9642[2]

Elizabeth Bennet (IRE) *Robert Cowell* a48 66
4 b m Acclamation Littlepromisedland (IRE) (Titus Livius (FR))
2687[6] 3427[8] 5251[6] 6668[8] 7022[7]

Eljaddaaf (IRE) *Dean Ivory* a96 78
8 b g Shamardal(USA) Almansoora (USA) (Bahri (USA))
255[6] 800[7] 6841[6] 7372[9] 8016[10] 9669[6]

El Jefe (IRE) *Brian Ellison* a41 53
2 b g Born To Sea(IRE) Ros Mountain (IRE) (Montjeu (IRE))
6943[14] 7388[10] 7870[6] 8394[3]

El Junco (FR) *M Boutin* a85 68
3 b c Style Vendome(FR) Oasis Valley (FR) (Naaqoos)
1340a[7] 5538a[6]

Elleanthus (IRE) *Joseph Patrick O'Brien* 88
3 b f War Command(USA) Holy Alliance (IRE) (Holy Roman Emperor (IRE))
1601a[7]

Ellenor Gray (IRE) *Richard Fahey* 68
2 gr f Gutaifan(IRE) Gender Dance (USA) (Miesque's Son (USA))
3265[8] 3968[7] 4433[2] 5472[5] 6585[3] 7399[16]

Ellerslie Lace (FR) *M Delzangles* 91
2 b f Siyouni(FR) Indiana Wells (FR) (Sadler's Wells (USA))
9059a[2]

Ellheidi (IRE) *K R Burke* 61
3 b f Invincible Spirit(IRE) Mythie (FR) (Octagonal (NZ))
2146[5] 2630[7] 3176[3] 3591[9]

Elliot The Dragon (IRE) *Derek Shaw* a51
4 b g Raven's Pass(USA) Somerset Falls (UAE) (Red Ransom (USA))
293[3]◆ (357) 919[10] 1368[10] 3143[3]

Ellthea (IRE) *J A Stack* 98
4 b m Kodiac Tropical Lady (IRE) (Sri Pekan (USA))
1307a[7] 1776a[9]

Elmetto *Hughie Morrison* a73
2 b f Helmet(AUS) Italian Connection (Cadeaux Genereux)
8849[2]

El Misk *John Gosden* a109 96
3 b c Dansili Igugu (AUS) (Galileo (IRE))
(1484)◆ 1856[7] 6290[2] (6842)◆ 7317[2] 8350[2]◆ (8655)◆

El Naseri (IRE) *Michael Dods* 80
2 b c Battle Of Marengo(IRE) Dubaya (Dubawi (IRE))
6971[2]◆ 7398[2] 8128[3]

Eloquent Style (IRE) *Ivan Furtado* a33 67
3 b c Dandy Man(IRE) Eloquent Rose (IRE) (Elnadim (USA))
5969[4] 6944[8] 7772[8]

Elpheba (IRE) *David Loughnane* a62 56
2 b f Anjaal Broadway Musical (IRE) (Exceed And Excel (AUS))
4238[7] 4903[3] 5280[3] 6387[2]

El Picador (IRE) *Sir Michael Stoute* a66 78
3 b g Dansili West Of Venus (USA) (Street Cry (IRE))
1594[4] 2582[5] (4176) 4663[2] 5594[9] 6331[5]

El Rey Brillante (CHI) *I Endaltsev* a47 87
4 rg h Dunkirk(USA) Golden Victory (CHI) (Winged Victory (USA))
8583a[6] 9014a[12]

Elsie Violet (IRE) *Robert Eddery* a61 67
3 ch f Gale Force Ten Kuaicoss (IRE) (Lujain (USA))
2114[14] 2760[8] 3256[8] 3593[2] (4346) 4568[4] 5337[6] 6173[2] 6810[5] 7526[6] 9427[6]

Eltham Palace *David Simcock* a66
2 b f Invincible Spirit(IRE) Moment In Time (IRE) (Tiger Hill (IRE))
5732[6]

El Tormenta (CAN) *Gail Cox* 115
4 bb g Stormy Atlantic(USA) Torreadora (USA) (El Prado (IRE))
(7225a) 8774a[6]

Elusif (IRE) *Shaun Keightley* a57 49
4 b g Elusive Quality(USA) Appealing (IRE) (Bertolini (USA))
33[12] 553[5] (701)◆ (924) (1177) 1338[4] 1973[10] 2483[6] 3701[7] 4195[5] 4501[5] 5051[8] 8123[11] 8666[7] 9410[6] 9505[2] 9659[8]

Elusive Exclusive (IRE) *P J Rothwell* a47 62
6 b g Elusive Pimpernel(USA) On Duty (IRE) (Night Shift (USA))
5712a[7]

Elusive Heights (IRE) *Roger Fell* a77 63
6 br g Elusive Pimpernel(USA) Berg Bahn (IRE) (Big Bad Bob (IRE))
6179[9] 7363[9] 8305[3]

Elwazir *Owen Burrows* a69 109
4 ch g Frankel Dash To The Front (Diktat)
3025[6] 7076[2] 7565[5] 8892[6]

Elysees (IRE) *Alan King* a76 76
4 ch g Champs Elysees Queen Of Tara (IRE) (Sadler's Wells (USA))
916[3] 3044[8] 3861[10]

Elysees Mumtaza (IRE) *A Peraino* 81
2 b f Champs Elysees Mumtaza (Nayef (USA))
8789a[11]

Elysees Palace *Sir Mark Prescott Bt* a88
5 b g Champs Elysees Ventura Highway (Machiavellian (USA))
(102)◆ 272[3] 735[2] 803[3] 1144[3] 1572a[5] (Dead)

Elysee Star *Mark Walford* a46 49
4 b m Champs Elysees Alushta (Royal Applause)
2911[4] 3657[7] 4130[6] 5392[5] 7336[2] 7544[3] 8423[6] 8949[2] 9035[3] 9220[6] 9544[5]

Elysian Flame *Michael Easterby* a44 95
3 ch g Champs Elysees Combustible (IRE) (Halling (USA))
5818[6] (6657)◆ 6955[3] 8098[2]

Elysian Lady *Michael Wigham* a29 40
3 b f Champs Elysees King's Guest (IRE) (King's Best (USA))
79[6] 400[2]

Elysian Star (FR) *B Moreno-Navarro* 83
5 b g Champs Elysees Karistar (IRE) (Montjeu (IRE))
6521a[12] 7536a[7]

Elysium Dream *Richard Hannon* a79 81
4 b m Champs Elysees Dream Of Wunders (Cape Cross (IRE))
2487[5] 3183[2] 3494[4] 4061[6] 4662[5] 7462[6] 8456[8] 8761[10]

Elzaa *Anthony McCann* a37 55
5 b m Elzaam(AUS) All Began (IRE) (Fasliyev (USA))
2963[8]

Elzaam's Dream (IRE) *Ronald Harris* a63 57
3 b f Elzaam(AUS) Alinda (IRE) (Revoque (IRE))
(3645) 4377[5] 5057[6] 5957[7] 6638[2] 8007[4] 9277[2]◆ 9548[3]

Emaraaty Ana *Kevin Ryan* 105
3 b c Shamardal(USA) Spirit Of Dubai (IRE) (Cape Cross (IRE))
2411[18] 3104a[12] 3891[5] (6847)

Emaraty Hero *K R Burke* a74 64
2 b c Lope De Vega(IRE) Valtina (IRE) (Teofilo (IRE))
7821[3]◆ 8459[7]

Embajadores (IRE) *M Maillard* a77 81
5 ch g Pivotal Freedom Flashing (USA) (Proud Citizen (USA))
2675a[6]

Embankment *Michael Attwater* a48 44
10 b g Zamindar(USA) Esplanade (Danehill (USA))
1145[10] 1519[8]

Ember's Glow *Mark Loughnane* a55 65
5 ch g Sepoy(AUS) Fading Light (King's Best (USA))
257[2] (363) 560[7] 910[6] 1334[5] 1718[9] 2127[3] 2698[4] 2975[12] 6843[9] 7857[6] 8869[4] (9289) 9481[5]

Emblazoned (IRE) *John Gosden* a88 110
4 b g Invincible Spirit(IRE) Sendmylovetorose (Bahamian Bounty)
2614[2] 4094[17] 4932[7]

Emblematique (FR) *F Rossi* 87
2 b f Siyouni(FR) Sage Melody (FR) (Sageburg (IRE))
5116a[6]

Embolden (IRE) *Richard Fahey* 90
2 b c Kodiac Sassy Gal (IRE) (King's Best (USA))
5172[3]◆ 5845[3] 6606[2] 7140[7] (7902) 8762[5]

Embour (IRE) *Richard Hannon* a95 101
4 b g Acclamation Carpet Lady (IRE) (Night Shift (USA))
1654[6] (1942) 2393[3] (2791) 3602[5] 3993[3] (4451) 4896[4] 5504[5] 5664[11] 6404[2] 6724[3] 7193[6] 7433[5]

Embrace The Moment (IRE) *Richard Hannon* a63 73
3 b f Le Havre(IRE) Kithonia (FR) (Sadler's Wells (USA))
1462[5] 2719[7]

Emenem *Simon Dow* a87 89
5 b g Sir Percy Kahalah (IRE) (Darshaan)
310[4] 758[5] 1395[3] 1588[2] 2032[4] 3044[9] 3663[2] 4614[4] (5321) (6156) 6437[3] 9633[5]

Emerald Fox *Patrick Chamings* a50 26
4 b m Foxwedge(AUS) Roshina (IRE) (Chevalier (IRE))
1849[6] *4022*[9] ***9416***[3]

Emerald Rocket (IRE) *Olly Murphy* a53 74
4 b g Society Rock(IRE) Lady From Limerick (IRE) (Rainbows For Life (CAN))
559[6]

Emeralds (AUS) *John Sargent* 96
2 ch f Sebring(AUS) Doulmera (USA) (Mr Greeley (USA))
8135a[6]

Emerald Swalk (IRE) *Tim Easterby* 41
2 gr g Zebedee Telegraphy (USA) (Giant's Causeway (USA))
8511[11]

Emerita (GER) *H-J Groschel* 101
4 b m Areion(GER) Edmee (GER) (Green Tune (USA))
3288a[4] 4461a[4] **(6270a)** 7750a[6]

Emigrated (IRE) *Derek Shaw* a53 63
6 b g Fastnet Rock(AUS) Ecoutila (USA) (Rahy (USA))
6249 ***717***[10]

Emilene *John Groucott* a42 7
5 b m Clodovil(IRE) Spark Up (Lahib (USA))
8694[11] ***9001***[5] *9165*[7]

Emily Goldfinch *Phil McEntee* a90 97
6 ch m Prime Defender Lakelands Lady (IRE) (Woodborough (USA))
1063[3] *1234*[6] *1382*[4] *1712*[3] 1932[6] (2804) 3536[6] **(4340)** **5143**[2] **5628**[2] *5944*[9] 6453[10] *9010*[2] *9129*[6] *9424*[7] *9645*[6]

Emily's Sea (IRE) *Nick Littmoden* a67 47
3 b f Born To Sea(IRE) See Emily Play (IRE) (Galileo (IRE))
4343[8]

Emin (IRE) *Enrique Leon Penate* 57
4 b h Camelot Chocolat Chaud (IRE) (Excellent Art)
8375a[10]

Eminence (IRE) *A P O'Brien* a100 101
3 b c Sea The Stars(IRE) Coolree Marj (IRE) (Marju (IRE))
4017[3] 5541[3] **6471**[8] 7216a[8]

Eminent (IRE) *Sir Mark Todd* 107
5 b h Frankel You'll Be Mine (USA) (Kingmambo (USA))
1783a[8]

Eminent Authority (IRE)
Joseph Patrick O'Brien 99
3 b g Frankel L'Ancresse (IRE) (Darshaan)
3984[5] 6191a[6] 7216a[11]

Emirates Currency *Clive Cox* a78
2 b c Muhaarar Loulwa (IRE) (Montjeu (IRE))
7911[5]◆ ***8751***[2] *9252*[3]

Emirates Empire (IRE) *Michael Bell* a84 83
3 b c Authorized(IRE) Ana Shababiya (IRE) (Teofilo (IRE))
1182[2]◆ (1771) ***(2317)*** 3337[4] *8754*[7]

Emirates Knight (IRE) *Roger Varian* a92 88
3 b c Dark Angel(IRE) Interim Payment (USA) (Red Ransom (USA))
2128[2] (2634)◆ 3262[6] 4325[3] 5973[4] ***(6596)*** *7574*[3] 8098[11] ***9055***[4]

Emirates Skycargo (IRE)
R Bouresly a40 47
7 b g Iffraaj Catchline (USA) (Bertolini (USA))
170a[12]

Emissary *Hugo Palmer* a86
2 b c Kingman Soviet Moon (IRE) (Sadler's Wells (USA))
(8121)◆

Emjayem *Patrick Chamings* a55 45
9 ch g Needwood Blade Distant Stars (IRE) (Distant Music (USA))
26[11]

Emma Cappelen *K R Burke* 49
2 b f Kingman Centime (Royal Applause)
7644[8]

Emma Point (USA)
Edouard Monfort a75 84
3 ch f Point Of Entry(USA) Emma Darling (USA) (Hennessy (USA))
134[6] *510a*[15] 727a[7] *(2125)* 3264[2] 4424[2] **6652a**[2]

Emmaus (IRE) *Conor Murphy* 108
5 b h Invincible Spirit(IRE) Prima Luce (IRE) (Galileo (IRE))
7225a[6]

Emojie *Jane Chapple-Hyam* a54 49
5 b g Captain Gerrard(IRE) Striking Pose (IRE) (Darshaan)
2321[8] 2690[13] 3277[8] 4349[14] *6885*[6] *7549*[2] *8694*[5] **9028**[2] ***9544***[2]

Emperor Sakhee *Karen McLintock* a35 50
9 ch g Sakhee(USA) Pochard (Inchinor)
100[7]

Emphatic (IRE) *J Larkin* a66 75
4 br g Epaulette(AUS) Wild Ocean (Pivotal)
5597a[2]

Empire Line (IRE) *J A Stack* a93 98
3 b c Holy Roman Emperor(IRE) Many Hearts (USA) (Distorted Humor (USA))
306a[2] **2882a**[7]

Employer (IRE) *Jim Goldie* a74 76
4 b g Camelot Close Regards (IRE) (Danehill (USA))
1461[2]◆ *1719*[4] *2186*[6] 2786[3] 3160[12] 4241[16] 4723[7] 5240[9] 6658[4] 6975[3] 7364[4] 7436[2] 7782[3] 8185[5] 8513[9]

Empress Ali (IRE) *Tom Tate* 90
8 b m Holy Roman Emperor(IRE) Almansa (IRE) (Dr Devious (IRE))
2563[10] 3811[12] 5458[4] **5741**[2]◆ 6172[2]

Empty Promises *Frank Bishop* a63
3 b g Mazameer(IRE) Rathlin Sound (Equiano (FR))
621[2]◆ *908*[3] *1236*[5] *2592*[9]

Emraan (IRE) *Ian Williams* a77
3 b g Invincible Spirit(IRE) Wissal (USA) (Woodman (USA))
(9635)

Emten (IRE) *Jamie Osborne* a72 90
2 b f Bungle Inthejungle Lucky Leigh (Piccolo)
(2205) 4012[5]◆ 5185[14] *6704*[3] **7149**[5] 7896[12]

Enable *John Gosden* a125 128
5 b m Nathaniel(IRE) Concentric (Sadler's Wells (USA))
(4668) (5414) **(6377)** 7941a[2]

Enbihaar (IRE) *John Gosden* a86 118
4 b m Redoute's Choice(AUS) Chanterelle (FR) (Trempolino (USA))
(2401) 3096[2] (4645) **(5663)**◆ (7118) 7926a[3]

Encapsulation (IRE)
Andrew Balding 105
3 b f Zoffany(IRE) Supercharged (IRE) (Iffraaj)
2157a[2] 4667[2]◆ 5397[6] **(7365)**

Encashment *Alan King* a46
2 b f Casamento(IRE) Burton Ash (Diktat)
8454[13] ***9311***[10] *9437*[10]

Enchanted Island (IRE) *Nick Kent* a7
4 b m Rip Van Winkle(IRE) Ekhraaj (USA) (El Prado (IRE))
9011[11]

Enchanted Linda
Michael Herrington a79 83
3 b f Charm Spirit(IRE) Enchanted Princess (Royal Applause)
1691[6] 2121[4] 2730[3] 2810[8] 3159[2] 3531[2] 4128[4] 4595[3] **(4783)** 5356[3] *6735*[5] 7380[9] *8470*[7] *9030*[7]

Enchantee (IRE) *Sir Mark Todd* a39
2 b f Gale Force Ten Love Valentine (IRE) (Fruits Of Love (USA))
7787[9] *8287*[8]

Enchanting Man *Charlie Appleby* a82 75
3 ch g Dawn Approach(IRE) Al Baidaa (Exceed And Excel (AUS))
133[2]

Enchanting Skies (IRE) *A Fabre* 99
4 b m Sea The Stars(IRE) Estefania (GER) (Acatenango (GER))
5510a[6]

Encipher *John Gosden* 87
2 b c Siyouni(FR) Ennaya (FR) (Nayef (USA))
4551[2] **(5131)**

Encoded (IRE) *Lynn Siddall* a52 39
6 ch m Sakhee's Secret Confidentiality (IRE) (Desert Style (IRE))
(25) ***129***[3] *411*[3] 3723[9] 4212[15] 4586[8] 5018[10] 5278[13] *7651*[12] *8720*[8] *9398*[13]

Encoder (USA) *John W Sadler* 100
2 b c English Channel(USA) Nono Rose (USA) (Hard Spun (USA))
8745a[6]

Encore D'Or *Robert Cowell* a109 108
7 b g Oasis Dream Entente Cordiale (IRE) (Ela-Mana-Mou (IRE))
(352)◆ *877*[6] *1919*[6] 2409[10] ***3582***[3] *4331*[11] 5142[2] 5371[11] 5927[9] *6149*[7] *7107*[5]

Encrypted *Hugo Palmer* a110 105
4 b g Showcasing Disclose (Dansili)
1919[11] ***4380***[4] *5942*[8]

Encryption (IRE) *David Simcock* a78 72
4 b g High Chaparral(IRE) Challow Hills (USA) (Woodman (USA))
2793[11] ***(4791)***

Endean *William Muir* a20 56
4 b g Doncaster Rover(USA) Tellmethings (Distant Music (USA))
5378[15] **6042**[8]

Endless Joy *Archie Watson* a77 97
2 b f Showcasing Funny Enough (Dansili)
2020[3] 2840[4] *6028*[3] (6637)◆ **7432**[3]

Endlessly (IRE) *Olly Murphy* a81 72
4 b g Nathaniel(IRE) What's Up Pussycat (IRE) (Danehill Dancer (IRE))
(562)◆ ***(1022)***

Endless Tangent (IRE) *John M Oxx* 72
4 b m Lawman(FR) Passion Planet (IRE) (Medicean)
1620a[10]

Endorphine (FR) *Hiroo Shimizu* a48 103
4 b m Muhtathir Polemique (IRE) (Poliglote)
8581a[2]

End Over End *Archie Watson* a60
3 b f Intello(GER) Overturned (Cape Cross (IRE))
7630[3] *7999*[4] ***8451***[3] *8868*[11]

Endowed *Richard Hannon* a93 87
2 gr g Dark Angel(IRE) Muqantara (USA) (First Samurai (USA))
2610[5] 3071[3] 4238[3] 4938[3]◆ (5501) ***(6073)***

Endowment *Clive Cox* a64
2 b f Garswood Inheritance (Oasis Dream)
8891[6] ***9623***[6]

End Zone *David Simcock* a77 79
2 b g Dark Angel(IRE) Brown Eyed Honey (Elusive City (USA))
5848[2] *7571*[3]

Enemy *John Gosden* 86
2 b c Muhaarar Prudenzia (IRE) (Dansili)
(6912)◆

Enemy Of The State (IRE)
R Mike Smith a40 39
5 b g Kodiac Bacchanalia (IRE) (Blues Traveller (IRE))
1500[8] 2373[9] 2819[8] *3447*[12] 4056[10] 4515[8] 6933[9]

Energia Flavio (BRZ) *Patrick Morris* a66 62
8 gr g Agnes Gold(JPN) Lira Da Guanabara (BRZ) (Pitu Da Guanabara (BRZ))
315[3] *465*[8] *912*[6] *1511*[2] *1769*[10] *1986*[5] *2693*[7]

Engage (USA) *Steven Asmussen* a114
4 b h Into Mischief(USA) Nefertiti (USA) (Speightstown (USA))
8773a[4]

Engaging Smile *W Delalande* a57 41
7 b m Exceed And Excel(AUS) Bronze Star (Mark Of Esteem (IRE))
5760a[6]

Engles Rock (IRE)
Mark Michael McNiff 83
3 b f Excelebration(IRE) Lisa Gherardini (IRE) (Barathea (IRE))
1306a[12]

English King (FR) *Ed Walker* a87 71
2 b c Camelot Platonic (Zafonic (USA))
8464[7] ***(9095)***◆

Englishman *Milton Bradley* a58 64
9 b g Royal Applause Tesary (Danehill (USA))
2107[10] 2484[10] 3079[5] **3543**[5] 4649[12] **5050**[3] 5495[6] 6018[5] 6401[7] *6889*[3] *7447*[7] *7770*[U] *8457*[6] *9169*[2] *9406*[4]

Engrave *Hugo Palmer* a68
3 gr f Dark Angel(IRE) Hot Wired (Rock Of Gibraltar (IRE))
8693[3] ***9091***[2]

Engrossed (IRE) *Martyn Meade* a82 45
3 ch f Tamayuz Last Cry (FR) (Peintre Celebre (USA))
289[7] *1567*[2] *5283*[4]◆ ***(6026)*** *9422*[9]

Enhanced *Hughie Morrison* 75
3 ch g New Approach(IRE) Complexion (Hurricane Run (IRE))
1755[10] **2113**[4] **3311**[3]◆ 4231[7]

Enigmatic (IRE) *Alan Bailey* a85 94
5 b g Elnadim(USA) Meanwhile (IRE) (Haafhd)
(2273) 2803[4] *4020*[5] 4851[5] **5155**[3] 6166[3] 6914[6] *8062*[12] 8725[12]

Enjazaat *Owen Burrows* a111 108
4 b g Acclamation Miliika (Green Desert (USA))
3043[5] 4648[2] 6453[7] (7152) ***(8015)***

Enjoy The Moment *Adrian Nicholls* 56
2 b f Captain Gerrard(IRE) Stella Rise (IRE) (Dutch Art)
4903[2] **5197**[2] 5547[5] 5968[3] 6271[2] 6792[3] *9164*[11] (Dead)

Enjoy The Moon (IRE) *P Schiergen* 106
3 b c Sea The Moon(GER) Enjoy The Life (Medicean)
2310a[7] **8171a**[4]

Enjoy The Silence (FR) *C Boutin* a57 76
6 b h Elusive City(USA) Cerita (IRE) (Wolfhound (USA))
2675a[5]

Enmeshing *Alexandra Dunn* a67 53
6 ch g Mastercraftsman(IRE) Yacht Club (USA) (Sea Hero (USA))
859[8] ***1022***[2] *1235*[4] 1500[9] *1988*[10] *2696*[2] 2998[13] *5631*[5] 6104[9] *6977*[7] 8248[12] *9168*[3] *(9481)* *9553*[7]

Ennjaaz (IRE) *Marjorie Fife* a61 48
5 b g Poet's Voice Hall Hee (IRE) (Invincible Spirit (IRE))
3502[14] 3973[10] **4689**[11] 5556[13]

Ennobled Friend (USA)
A bin Harmash a73 53
9 b g Malibu Moon(USA) Seek To Soar (USA) (Seeking The Gold (USA))
280a[7]

Enough Already *Kevin Ryan* 88
3 b g Coach House(IRE) Funny Enough (Dansili)
3510[2] **4635**[2] 5128[3]

Enough Said *Matthieu Palussiere* a80 79
3 b g Kyllachy Fenella Rose (Compton Place)
1028a[5] **1200a**[6] *1340a*[4] 2392a[9]

Entangling (IRE) *David Elsworth* a98 85
5 b g Fastnet Rock(AUS) Question Times (Shamardal (USA))
(9053)◆ *9309*[4] ***(9588)*** ***9667***[3]◆

Entertaining (IRE) *Richard Hannon* a65 78
3 b g Dandy Man(IRE) Letizia Sophia (IRE) (Shamardal (USA))
1886[5] **2470**[2]◆ 3307[9] 4188[5] *8122*[10] *8652*[11] *9047*[6]

Entertaining Ben *Amy Murphy* a75 73
6 b g Equiano(FR) Fatal Attraction (Oasis Dream)
179[2] *317*[9] *823*[6] *1507*[7]

Enthaar *Stuart Williams* a81 80
4 ch g Sepoy(AUS) Caledonia Princess (Kyllachy)
158[2] *618*[4] ***1061***[2] *1357*[2] 1822[4] 2107[7] 3021[2] 4301[6] 4374[6] (5843) 6301[6] 6756[4] (7337) *8601*[4] *9458*[5]

Entitle *John Gosden* a73 101
3 b f Dansili Concentric (Sadler's Wells (USA))
2745[2]◆ **3905a**[10]

Entrancing *Richard Fahey* 79
2 br f Mayson Hypnotize (Machiavellian (USA))
(5547)

Entrusting *James Fanshawe* a83 93
3 br g Nathaniel(IRE) Royal Empress (IRE) (Holy Roman Emperor (IRE))
1643[3] 2208[3] 3471[5] *6662*[2] **(7413)**

Envisaging (IRE) *James Fanshawe* a87 87
5 b g Zoffany(IRE) Star Of Stars (IRE) (Soviet Star (USA))
2977[2] 4365[6] **(5870)**◆ *6968*[5] ***8893***[3]

Envoy *James Eustace* a95 81
5 gr g Delegator La Gessa (Largesse)
82[9] *3466*[11]

Enyama (GER) *Michael Attwater* a53 50
3 b f Camelot Ella Ransom (GER) (Ransom O'War (USA))
2598 *858*[6] ***1221***[5] *1770*[11] *2530*[5] 3253[2] 3809[8] 5987[8]

Enzemble (IRE) *James Fanshawe* a69 71
4 b g Zoffany(IRE) Fifer (IRE) (Soviet Star (USA))
252[5] *557*[3] *922*[4] 2480[3] **(3255)**

Enzo (IRE) *John Butler* a67 55
4 b g Exceed And Excel(AUS) Zamhrear (Singspiel (IRE))
331[0] 1653[9] 2256[8] 4349[3] ***(5633)*** ***6977***[2] *8669*[5] ***9256***[3] ***9663***[3]

Enzo's Lad (AUS) *Michael Pitman* 109
6 b g Testa Rossa(AUS) Sheerama (AUS) (Catbird (AUS))
3950[11] 4094[15]

Eos Quercus (IRE) *N Leenders* a49 63
7 ch g Arcano(IRE) Khaizarana (Alhaarth (IRE))
7062a[9] **8737a**[2]

Epaulement (IRE) *Tom Dascombe* a101 113
4 b g Epaulette(AUS) Little Whisper (IRE) (Be My Guest (USA))
(1896) 2574[2] 3160[9] 4646[3] 6420[5] **(6895)**

Epaulini *Michael Dods* a11 59
3 b g Epaulette(AUS) Baylini (Bertolini (USA))
4288[11] **4823**[6] 5237[8] 5695[7] 5981[3] 6462[13]

Epeius (IRE) *Ben Haslam* a80 76
6 b g Arakan(USA) Gilda Lilly (USA) (War Chant (USA))
356[3] *(496)* *(741)* *970*[5] *1487*[11] 1976[2] ***(2379)*** 3221[10] 3999[2] 4280[2] *7656*[4] *8304*[2] *8921*[3] *9519*[6]

Ephemeral (IRE) *N Clement* a75 68
3 b f Footstepsinthesand Mycenae (Inchinor)
7061a[2]

Epic Adventure (FR) *Roger Teal* a68 59
4 ch g Shamalgan(FR) Larafale (FR) (Lion Heart (USA))
6350[8] 8761[9]

Epical (USA) *James M Cassidy* a82 107
4 b g Uncle Mo(USA) Klondike Hills (USA) (Deputy Minister (CAN))
2646a[5]

Epic Hero (FR) *A Fabre* a97 103
3 b g Siyouni(FR) Grace Lady (FR) (Muhtathir)
1794a[2] 4703a[6] 5714a[6]

Epistrophy (FR) *S Kobayashi* a94 104
3 b f Charm Spirit(IRE) Cheriearch (USA) (Arch (USA))
1795a[3]

Epitaph (IRE) *Michael Appleby* a66 69
5 b g Henrythenavigator(USA) Chartres (IRE) (Danehill (USA))
61[7] ***(481)*** *833*[3] *927*[2] *1159*[4] *1508*[8] 2202[12]

Epona *Keith Dalgleish* a50 71
3 b f Epaulette(AUS) Jackline (Diktat)
2098[3] 2787[4] 3685[6] 3923[4] *4330*[9] 5237[11] *8266*[6] *8646*[6] *9106*[9]

Epona (ITY) *Andrea Marcialis*
2 b f Kheleyf(USA) Pomone (IRE) (Orpen (USA))
6060a[8]

Eponina (IRE) *Michael Appleby* a62 71
5 b m Zoffany(IRE) Dame Rochelle (IRE) (Danehill Dancer (IRE))
232[6] *467*[12] *525*[4] (3843) 4438[2] 5030[8] 5419[6] *6025*[6] 6825[5] 7288[2] **(8031)** *8471*[8] *9223*[4]

Epouville (FR) *F Vermeulen* a89 79
4 b m Footstepsinthesand Vidiyna (FR) (Danehill Dancer (IRE))
1449a[13] **7250a**[8]

Epsom Faithfull *Pat Phelan* a75 72
2 b f Coach House(IRE) La Fortunata (Lucky Story (USA))
3595[5] 5745[2] (6442) ***(8219)***

Eqtidaar (IRE) *Sir Michael Stoute* a75 102
4 b h Invincible Spirit(IRE) Madany (IRE) (Acclamation)
2109[5]

Equally Fast *Roy Brotherton* a68 67
7 b g Equiano(FR) Fabulously Fast (USA) (Deputy Minister (CAN))
8501[9]

Equal Sum *Richard Hannon* a76
3 br f Paco Boy(IRE) Hypoteneuse (IRE) (Sadler's Wells (USA))
7373[5] ***7788***[4]

Equiano Perle *Michael Appleby* a9 49
3 b f Equiano(FR) Perle D'Or (IRE) (Entrepreneur)
1275[9] *1476*[6]

Equiano Springs *Tom Tate* a89 86
5 b g Equiano(FR) Spring Clean (FR) (Danehill (USA))
24[2] ***407***[2] ***(786)*** 2416[2]◆ (2824)◆ 4649[4] 5395[5] 6581[4] 6916[15] (7467) *8425*[14]

Equidae *Iain Jardine* a73 72
4 ch h Equiano(FR) Dularame (IRE) (Pivotal)
8085 ***(1369)*** 2509[3] 3503[5] 3970[4] 5117[5] 5490[3] 5933[3] 7069[2] 7364[12] 7776[6] *9397*[10]

Equilateral *Charles Hills* a104 112
4 b g Equiano(FR) Tarentaise (Oasis Dream)
1412[3] 1853[4] **2409**[2] 3950[7] 5222a[6] (7073) 7454[6]

Equimou *Robert Eddery* a85 93
5 ch m Equiano(FR) Culture Queen (King's Best (USA))
3[8] ***1547***[3] 1892[7] *2556*[5] 2839[9] *3303*[8]

Equinozio (IRE) *A Giorgi* a46 63
2 ch g Equiano(FR) Kasalla (IRE) (Footstepsinthesand)
3714a[7] ***6141a***[8]

Equipped *Mick Channon* a63 9
3 b f Equiano(FR) Marjong (Mount Nelson)
3661[12]

Equitant *Joseph Patrick O'Brien* a98 92
4 ch g Equiano(FR) Intrusion (Indesatchel (IRE))
173a[14] *513a*[13] **3062a**[12] 6693a[15]

Equitation *Stuart Williams* a85 98
5 b g Equiano(FR) Sakhee's Song (IRE) (Sakhee (USA))
127[3] *786*[6] *1098*[2] 1654[2] 2568[8] (2917) 3945[2] 4451[2] 5504[6] 6455[4] **(6916)** 7193[8]

Eraidah (IRE) *H-F Devin* 78
3 b f Toronado(IRE) Al Thakhira (Dubawi (IRE))
(1489a)

Erastus *Ruth Carr* a41 50
4 b g Swiss Spirit Blakeshall Rose (Tobougg (IRE))
2682[4]◆ *3304*[12] 4823[RR] 5247[6]

Eric The Eel (AUS) *Stuart Kendrick* 99
2 b g Olympic Glory(IRE) Modave (NZ) (Montjeu (IRE))
8137a[15]

Erika *Neil Mulholland* 19
2 ch f Hot Streak(IRE) Fame Is The Spur (Motivator)
6287[10] 6800[6] **7755**[13] 8243[7]

Erissimus Maximus (FR)
Robert Cowell a82 83
5 b g Holy Roman Emperor(IRE) Tegan (IRE) (Cape Cross (IRE))
163[6] *588*[6] *1098*[3] **(2484)** *3301*[8] 3883[7] 4369[10] 7467[7] 7894[9] 8262[8] *8900*[4] *9030*[10]

Ernest Aldrich *Ibrahim Al Malki* 90
3 b g Oasis Dream Wallis (King's Best (USA))
9590a[12]

Ernesto (GER) *Markus Klug* 101
4 ch h Reliable Man Enrica (Niniski (USA))
2666a[8] **7249a**[6]

Ernesto De La Cruz (FR) 91
Andrea Marcialis
2 b g Wootton Bassett Green Empire (IRE) (Second Empire (IRE))
8970a[3]

Ertidaad (IRE) *Emma Owen* a53 51
7 b g Kodiac Little Scotland (Acclamation)
155[9] 436[6] 719[5] 1214[11] 1520[12] 1717[12] 2298[10]

Escalade (IRE) *Sir Mark Prescott Bt* a75
2 b f Canford Cliffs(IRE) Sliding Scale (Sadler's Wells (USA))
7304[7] 7832[8] (8265)

Escalator *Charlie Fellowes* a72 111
4 br g Cape Cross(IRE) Sayyedati Symphony (USA) (Gone West (USA))
51a[7] (515a)

Escapability (IRE) *Alan King* a79 85
4 b g Excelebration(IRE) Brief Escapade (IRE) (Brief Truce (USA))
945[4] 1365[3] 2207[3] 7974[2] 9055[10]

Escape Clause (IRE) *Grant Tuer* a53 77
5 b g Lawman(FR) Discophilia (Teofilo (IRE))
22[8]

Escape Proof *Roger Charlton* a60 70
2 b f Cityscape Prove (Danehill (USA))
5052[5] (6368)

Escape The City *Hughie Morrison* a71 78
4 b m Cityscape Jasmeno (Catcher In The Rye (IRE))
2691[6] 3698[6] 4283[5] 4841[7] 5305[2] 5686[3] (7026) 7663[2] 7895[11] 8519[6]

Escape To Oz *Anthony Carson* 25
2 ch f Cityscape Munchkin (Tiger Hill (IRE))
2228[7]

Escobar (IRE) *David O'Meara* a98 115
5 b g Famous Name Saying Grace (IRE) (Brief Truce (USA))
1753[15] 2105[9] 2778[10] 4666[2] (4934) 5610[3] 6470[5] 6950[4] 7891[3] (8336)

Eshaasy *John Gosden* a79 88
2 b g Oasis Dream Galicuix (Galileo (IRE))
4886[7] (5809) 6727[5] 7897[11]

Es'hail (USA) *R Al Jehani* 104
4 bb h Giant's Causeway(USA) Much Obliged (USA) (Kingmambo (USA))
894a[5]

Eshtiraak (AUS) *David A Hayes* a46 81
4 br g Street Cry(IRE) Succeeding (AUS) (Flying Spur (AUS))
173a[6] 515a[5] 847a[7] 960a[7]

E Si Si Muove (IRE) *Andrew Crook* a45
7 b g Galileo(IRE) Queen Of France (USA) (Danehill (USA))
2301[7]

Esme Kate (IRE) *Ivan Furtado* a44 29
4 b m Arch(USA) Francisca (USA) (Mizzen Mast (USA))
589[7] 1163[5] 1365[5] 1680[12]

Espaldinha (FR)
Mme M Bollack-Badel a41 70
4 b m George Vancouver(USA) Bidart (FR) (Elusive City (USA))
2170a[11]

Esperitum (FR) *Carina Fey* a96 86
5 b g Siyouni(FR) Nona Allegrina (FR) (Scribe I (IRE))
4704a[14]

Espionne (FR) *H De Nicolay* a62 64
4 b m George Vancouver(USA) Ejina (FR) (Highest Honor (FR))
2170a[4] 7505a[6]

Espirit D'escalier (IRE) *J F Levins* a51 55
3 b f Dark Angel(IRE) Patience Alexander (IRE) (Kodiac)
9539[12]

Espoir Et Bonheur (IRE)
Gavin Cromwell 44
3 b f Dansili Adeste Fideles (USA) (Giant's Causeway (USA))
9337[12]

Espoir Parfait (FR) *C Theodorakis* a57 44
4 b g Le Havre(IRE) Eviane (FR) (American Post)
2647a[11]

Espresso Freddo (IRE)
Robert Stephens a76 73
5 b g Fast Company(IRE) Spring Bouquet (IRE) (King's Best (USA))
91[5] 364[4] 699[6] 886[3] 4235[10] 4479[6] 5497[5] 6103[3]◆ 6507[4] 7527[9] (7758) 8030[2] 8413[2] 8761[2] 9047[15]

Esprit De Corps *David Barron* a79 79
5 b g Sepoy(AUS) Corps De Ballet (IRE) (Fasliyev (USA))
4[4]◆ 508[2] 812[4] 952[2] 1457[16] 2348[3] 3649[2] 3813[17] 4693[2] 4980[2] 5303[3] 5692[5] 6261[5] 6461[5] 7289[4] 8070[2] 8719[6] (8946) 9334[6]

Esprit Rose (IRE) *Roger Varian* 75
2 b f Invincible Spirit(IRE) Intense Pink (Pivotal)
6919[3] 7393[2]

Es Que Magic (IRE) *Alex Hales* a60 49
3 b g Es Que Love(IRE) Itzakindamagic (IRE) (Indian Haven)
1141[4] 1385[3] 1678[4] 3996[5] 5799[7] 7281[11]

Es Que Pearl (IRE) *Rod Millman* 45
2 ch f Es Que Love(IRE) Pearl Power (Dutch Art)
1556[8] 2716[6] 3695[7] 5576[10] 8897[7]

Essaka (IRE) *Tony Carroll* a60 72
7 b g Equiano(FR) Dream Vision (USA) (Distant View (USA))
2206[2] (3404)◆ 3527[3] 3961[2] 4478[5] 5289[7] 5843[4] 6562[4] 7230[9]

Essenaitch (IRE) *David Evans* a47 64
6 b g Zoffany(IRE) Karlisse (IRE) (Celtic Swing)
1653[6] 3572[3] 5747[5] 6804[3]◆ 7116[9] 8414[3] 8663[5]

Essential *Olly Williams* a57 52
5 b g Pivotal Something Blue (Petong)
233[8] 410[10] 742[3] 1192[2] 1339[5] 1967[10] 2532[11] 3428[7] 4807[2] 6051[8] 6174[8] 6546[13]

Essenza (IRE) *Richard Fahey* a69 55
3 b f Alhebayeb(IRE) Eleganza (IRE) (Balmont (USA))
3935[5] 4822[6] 5392[7] 6070[5] 7384[5] 7869[4]

Essgee Nics (IRE) *Paul George* a37 49
6 b g Fairly Ransom(USA) Vannuccis Daughter (IRE) (Perugino (USA))
185[11] 3017[3] 4796[5] 6601[3]

Esspeegee *Alan Bailey* a55 68
6 b g Paco Boy(IRE) Goldrenched (IRE) (Montjeu (IRE))
88[7] 362[8] 754[12] 3511[15] 3941[5] 4547[3]◆ 5106[4] (6303) 6796[4] 8019[10]

Establish *Roger Varian* a77 87
2 ch c Australia Azenzar (Danehill Dancer (IRE))
6912[7] 7458[2] 8810[3]

Esta Bonita (IRE) *H-A Pantall* a72 51
2 b f Sepoy(AUS) Arabian Beauty (IRE) (Shamardal (USA))
9605a[9]

Estate House (FR)
James Fanshawe a54
2 b g Oasis Dream Alsace Lorraine (IRE) (Giant's Causeway (USA))
8455[10] 9155[11]

Estibdaad (IRE) *Paddy Butler* a34 25
9 b g Haatef(USA) Star Of Siligo (USA) (Saratoga Six (USA))
58[14] 1333[12] 1683[10] 1935[10]

Estibere (FR) *Edouard Thueux* a64 68
3 b g Alianthus(GER) Marthamia (FR) (Timboroa)
4357a[7]

Estihdaaf (USA) *Saeed bin Suroor* a108 87
3 br g Arch(USA) Enrichment (USA) (Ghostzapper (USA))
168a[8] 394a[2] (636a) 1110a[13]

Estranged (IRE) *Tom Clover* a47
3 b f Morpheus Compton Girl (Compton Place)
477[5]

Estrela Star (IRE) *Ali Stronge* a63 59
3 ch g Casamento(IRE) Reem Star (Green Tune (USA))
4931[3] 5680[4] 6531[5] 9042[2]◆ 9275[3]◆

Es Vedra (FR) *N Clement* a59 56
2 b f Dutch Art Faithful One (IRE) (Dubawi (IRE))
9605a[8]

Etalondes (FR) *F Vermeulen* a70 64
9 b g Royal Applause Fancy Dance (Rainbow Quest (USA))
5115a[6]

Etario (JPN) *Yasuo Tomomichi* 115
4 br h Stay Gold(JPN) Hot Cha Cha (USA) (Cactus Ridge (USA))
9153a[7]

Eternal Destiny *Ian Williams* a44 39
4 b m Poet's Voice Mrs Mogg (Green Desert (USA))
2740[14] 3142[14] 3774[9] 4358[9] 4915[11]

Eternal Summer (FR)
Jean-Pierre Carvalho 75
3 b f Sommerabend Evening Breeze (GER) (Surumu (GER))
1512a[4]

Eternal Sun *Ivan Furtado* a82 50
4 b m Mayson Golden Dirham (Kheleyf (USA))
163[3] 610[4] 1194[2] 1551[5] 2637[11] 3206[12] 8943[7]

Etheric *Marco Botti* a71
2 b f Brazen Beau(AUS) Wakeup Little Suzy (IRE) (Peintre Celebre (USA))
8250[8] 9158[2]

Ethic *William Haggas* 80
2 b g Dark Angel(IRE) Magique (IRE) (Jeremy (USA))
4558[2]◆ (5447)◆ 6352[9] 7072[6] 8110[9]

Ethics Boy (FR) *John Berry* a24
3 ch g Anodin(IRE) Ethics Girl (IRE) (Hernando (FR))
8753[7]

Etijaah (USA) *Doug Watson* a107 86
9 b g Daaher(CAN) Hasheema (IRE) (Darshaan)
171a[7] 638a[5] 959a[2]

Etikaal *Grant Tuer* a73 63
5 ch g Sepoy(AUS) Hezmah (Oasis Dream)
1925[12] 2418[8] 2846[6] 3199[12] 3657[9] 5247[2] (5526)◆ 5616[12] 6572[9] (8923) (9397)

Etisalat *A R Al Rayhi* a88 81
4 gr g Lethal Force(IRE) Chalet Girl (Oasis Dream)
1001[5] 1322a[6]

Et Moi Alors (FR) *Gary Moore* a67
5 b g Kap Rock(FR) Qui L'Eut Cru (FR) (Lavirco (GER))
921[3]

Etoile (FR) *J-C Rouget* 107
3 b f Siyouni(FR) Milena's Dream (IRE) (Authorized (IRE))
1626a[2] (3137a) 3905a[4] 6250a[6] 7942a[9]

Etoile (USA) *A P O'Brien* 100
2 b f War Front(USA) Gagnoa (IRE) (Sadler's Wells (USA))
(2881a) 7692[8]◆ 8748a[10]

Etoile Diamante (FR)
Andreas Suborics 63
3 b f Dabirsim(FR) Etoile Nocturne (FR) (Medicean)
4959a[9]

Eton College (IRE) *Mark Johnston* a87 87
2 b c Invincible Spirit(IRE) Windsor County (USA) (Elusive Quality (USA))
3419[7] 3660[3] (3962) (4861) 5612[14] 6228[2] 6705[3] 7438[2]

Etruria *A Fabre* a78 60
3 b f Invincible Spirit(IRE) Taranto (Machiavellian (USA))
2498a[7] 4621a[12]

Etymology (AUS) *James Cummings* 97
6 b g New Approach(IRE) Weaver Of Words (Danehill (USA))
8577a[8]

Eufemia *Amy Murphy* a63 31
3 ch f Dream Ahead(USA) Shyrl (Acclamation)
27[3] 211[4] 476[11] (918)

Eugenic *Tracey Barfoot-Saunt* a34 33
8 bb g Piccolo Craic Sa Ceili (IRE) (Danehill Dancer (IRE))
1841[12] 2277[11]

Euginio (IRE) *Fawzi Abdulla Nass* a81 105
5 b h Fastnet Rock(AUS) Starstone (Diktat)
395a[5]◆ 514a[7]

Eula Varner *Henry Candy* a70 82
5 gr m Showcasing Tremelo Pointe (IRE) (Trempolino (USA))
3575[4] 5105[2] 5688[3] 6170[7] 7519[5]

Eurato (FR) *Derek Shaw* a50 64
9 ch g Medicean Double Green (IRE) (Green Tune (USA))
1024[10] 1548[8] 2014[8]

Euro Implosion (IRE)
Keith Dalgleish 78
3 b g Battle Of Marengo(IRE) Mikes Baby (IRE) (Key Of Luck (USA))
2711[3] 3226[5] 3926[4] 4729[3] 4913[3] 5792[2]◆ (5905) (6232) (6589) 7209[10] 7441[7] 8098[16]

Euro No More (IRE) *Keith Dalgleish* a44 60
3 b f Kodiac Gerobies Girl (USA) (Deposit Ticket (USA))
2101[6] 2897[9] 3176[4] 3709[8] 4000[6]

European Blue (FR) *P Peltier* 33
4 b g Apsis Cadette Bleue (FR) (Cadoudal (FR))
5762a[6]

Euryale (IRE) *J-V Toux* a101 101
5 gr g Kendargent(FR) Russian Hill (Indian Ridge (IRE))
2648a[2] 8373a[5]

Evadala (FR) *Michael Blanshard*
4 b m Evasive Song Of India (Dalakhani (IRE))
242[12] 2999[8]

Eva Glitters (FR) *P Demercastel* a70 55
4 b m Evasive Loupy Glitters (FR) (Loup Solitaire (USA))
3715a[5] 4532a[7]

Eva Maria *Richard Fahey* a76 98
3 b f Sea The Stars(IRE) Whazzat (Daylami (IRE))
4520[3]◆ (5690) 6259[2] (7366) (7895) 9002[12]

Evangeline Samos *Kevin Ryan* a62 65
3 b f Foxwedge(AUS) Vive Les Rouges (Acclamation)
972[4] 1337[10] 2063[5] 2293[9]

Evaporust (IRE) *Mark Usher* a29 43
2 b g Gale Force Ten Bigalo's Laura B (IRE) (Needwood Blade)
6911[13] 8297[8] 8546[9]

Evasive Power (USA)
Denis Gerard Hogan a80 80
3 b g Elusive Quality(USA) Casting Director (USA) (Bernardini (USA))
4722[6] 7470[2]

Eve Harrington (USA)
Sir Mark Prescott Bt a68 66
3 b f Flatter(USA) Unbridled Empire (USA) (Empire Maker (USA))
(229) 500[2] 4804[4]

Evening Attire *William Stone* a78 71
8 b g Pastoral Pursuits Markova's Dance (Mark Of Esteem (IRE))
91[6] 381[5] 801[10] 1329[6] 1561[3] 2318[3]◆ 3781[3] 4281[4] (5107) 5551[4] 6373[5] 7446[9]

Evening Spirit *Ralph Beckett* a76 70
2 b f Invincible Spirit(IRE) Evita Peron (Pivotal)
7695[5]◆ 8453[2] 9158[3]

Evening Sun *Roger Charlton* 78
2 b c Muhaarar Fiery Sunset (Galileo (IRE))
7453[4] 8459[2]

Eventful *Hugo Palmer* a74 70
2 b f Oasis Dream Spectacle (Dalakhani (IRE))
6675[8] 7330[2] 8021[3] 8760[6] 9250[2]

Eventura *Tony Carroll* 46
3 ch f Lope De Vega(IRE) Demi Voix (Halling (USA))
4120[10] 4738[9] 5193[4] 5677[9]

Ever Amber (IRE)
Jonathan Portman a56
2 ch f Ivawood(IRE) Much Faster (IRE) (Fasliyev (USA))
8848[13] 9243[3] 9506[7]

Everfast (USA) *Dale Romans* a111
3 b c Take Charge Indy(USA) Awesome Surprise (USA) (Awesome Again (CAN))
2856a[2] 3620a[7]

Everkyllachy (IRE) *Karen McLintock* a67 68
5 br m Kyllachy Superfonic (FR) (Zafonic (USA))
(1402) (2122) 2379[4] (3227) 3504[4] 4330[5] 4911[6] 5432[4] 5972[6] 6659[9] 7307[10] 8925[9] 9272[2]◆

Everlasting Sea *Stuart Kittow* a47 46
5 b m Harbour Watch(IRE) Doliouchka (Saumarez)
1497[11] 2695[12] 5029[9] 6366[8] 6601[6] 6853[5]

Ever Love (FR) *C Boutin* a47 68
4 gr m Alianthus(GER) Evergrey (FR) (Verglas (IRE))
1073a[4] 1578a[11] 2264a[8]

Ever Rock (IRE) *J S Moore* a52 58
3 b f Society Rock(IRE) Alhaadh (USA) (Diesis)
60[2] 296[5] 402[2] 620[5] 1384[7] (1650) 2276[8] 3442[9] (3839) (4183) 4651[3] 4844[6] 5793[5] 6286[4] 6851[5]

Eversweet (FR) *J E Hammond* a76 86
2 b f Sommerabend Quatuor (IRE) (Kodiac)
5469a[6]

Everymananempror
James Fanshawe a35
3 br g Gregorian(IRE) Winterbourne (Cadeaux Genereux)
9416[6]

Everything For You (IRE)
Kevin Ryan a85 100
5 b g Pivotal Miss Delila (USA) (Malibu Moon (USA))
1896[3] 2370[2] 2742[9] 3655[5] 4646[8] (5199) 5657[2]

Evie May *Mick Channon* a31
3 b f Excelebration(IRE) Visanilla (FR) (Danehill (USA))
133[12] 370[10]

Evie Speed (IRE) *Jedd O'Keeffe* a50 62
3 br f Dawn Approach(IRE) French Bid (AUS) (Anabaa (USA))
2510[7] 2896[7] 4781[5] 7418[10]

Evolutionary (IRE) *Iain Jardine* a65 66
3 b f Morpheus Lilium (Nashwan (USA))
1985[5] 4507[9] 6176[6] 6609[4] 7069[9] 7405[11] 7779[10]

Evora Knights *Michael Easterby* a45 31
2 ch g Equiano(FR) Ewenny (Warrshan (USA))
7386[4] 8097[8] 8899[9]

Ewell Spring *Brett Johnson* a19 20
3 b f Captain Gerrard(IRE) Hey Mambo (Bertolini (USA))
3353[6] 6074[11] 6594[10] 7371[13]

Exalted Angel (FR) *K R Burke* a77 81
3 b g Dark Angel(IRE) Hurryupharriet (IRE) (Camacho)
1161[2]◆ 1924[3] (4204a) 4609[7] 5791[5] 6715[5]

Exasperate (AUS) *Matthew Brown* 89
4 b g Tough Speed(USA) I Gotcha Babe (AUS) (Mukddaam (USA))
9016a[3]

Excalibur (POL) *Micky Hammond* a45 43
6 gr g Youmzain(IRE) Electra Deelites (With Approval (CAN))
1718[7] 3500[7] 5727[7] 6343[7] 8343[7]

Exceedingly Diva *George Baker* a64 63
4 b m Exceed And Excel(AUS) Anqooda (USA) (Oasis Dream)
3020[6] 3404[6] 3961[3] 4027[2]

Exceeding Power *Martin Bosley* a96 84
8 b g Exceed And Excel(AUS) Extreme Beauty (USA) (Rahy (USA))
(878) 1267[4] 3466[10] 4381[13] 6437[4] 8701[7] 9177[2] 9667[4]

Excel And Succeed (IRE)
Michael Dods a51 69
2 b f Exceed And Excel(AUS) Kiyra Wells (IRE) (Sadler's Wells (USA))
6096[3]◆ 7580[8]

Excelcius (USA) *G M Lyons* a81 81
3 b g Exceed And Excel(AUS) Crying Shame (USA) (Street Cry (IRE))
4723[4]◆

Excelinthejungle (IRE)
Seamus Durack a44 53
3 b g Bungle Inthejungle Kannon (Kyllachy)
5960[4] 6198[4] 6838[5]

Excelled (IRE) *James Fanshawe* a78 69
3 b f Exceed And Excel(AUS) Elle Woods (IRE) (Lawman (FR))
2078[11] 3048[8] 4507[4] 5002[2] 6111[7] 7345[5]

Excellency (FR) *H-F Devin* 96
3 b f Sea The Stars(IRE) Twyla Tharp (IRE) (Sadler's Wells (USA))
8377a[5]

Excellent George *Stuart Williams* a83 85
7 b g Exceed And Excel(AUS) Princess Georgina (Royal Applause)
247[3] 551[5] 5503[9] 6809[2] 7321[2] 7607[2] 8826[5] 9286[7] 9550[6]

Excellently Poised *Mark Loughnane* a38 44
4 b g Sepoy(AUS) Excelette (IRE) (Exceed And Excel (AUS))
7959[13]

Excellent Magic *Roger Charlton* 58
3 ch f Exceed And Excel(AUS) Magic Nymph (IRE) (Galileo (IRE))
2790[7]

Excellent Times *Tim Easterby* 97
4 b m Excelebration(IRE) Al Janadeirya (Oasis Dream)
2097[5] 2874[3] 3815[7] (6379) (6974) 7893[8] 8184[9]

Excel Mate *Roy Bowring* a46 31
5 ch m Captain Gerrard(IRE) Exceedingly Good (IRE) (Exceed And Excel (AUS))
973[7] 1100[4] 2298[8]

Exceptional *Richard Fahey* 75
2 b f Dutch Art Expressive (Falbrav (IRE))
(3244)◆ 4048[19]

Excessable *Tim Easterby* a71 85
6 ch g Sakhee's Secret Kummel Excess (IRE) (Exceed And Excel (AUS))
2421[6] 2841[4] 4100[3] 4406[2] 4894[8] 5154[3] 5617[6] 6455[8] 6699[8] 6932[4] 7334[4] 8023[3]

Exchequer (FR) *Lucinda Russell* a8 23
3 gr g Equiano(FR) Cumbrian Princess (Mtoto)
7213[10] 8185[6]

Exchequer (IRE) *Richard Guest* a95 64
8 ch g Exceed And Excel(AUS) Tara's Force (IRE) (Acclamation)
255[3] 470[2] 805[8] 1097[3] 1916[6] 1942[3] 2418[15] 4149[11] 5144[7] 6680[14] 7210[3] 7443[7] 7591[3] 8016[8]

Exciting Days (USA) *Robert Cowell* a65 41
2 bb g Blame(USA) Whenthetimeisright (USA) (Devil His Due (USA))
4018[5]◆ 4564[9] 8709[7]

Exclusively *Archie Watson* 84
2 b f Showcasing Sweet Cecily (IRE) (Kodiac)
(1642)◆ 2138[2] 4048[17] 4659[2] 5275[4] 6272[4] 7333[6]

Exclusive Oro (FR) *Mme Pia Brandt* a53 55
3 b f Elusive City(USA) Negra Del Oro (GER) (Danehill Dancer (IRE))
216a[9]

Exclusive Waters (IRE)
Garvan Donnelly a63 54
9 b g Elusive City(USA) Pelican Waters (IRE) (Key Of Luck (USA))
4690[8]

Exec Chef (IRE) *Jim Boyle* a104 103
4 ch g Excelebration(IRE) Donnelly's Hollow (IRE) (Dockside (USA))
1413[2]◆ 1753[21] 2408[4] 3005[2] 3992[3] 4613[4] 4935[10] 5519[7] 7457[8] 7727[4] 8253[6]

Exclusive (IRE) *Archie Watson* a59 72
2 b f Kodiac Miss Mariduff (USA) (Hussonet (USA))
(2707) 3564[8] 4191[4] (5010) 5562[5] 6053[10] 6557[5] 7227[5]

Executive Force *Michael Wigham* a104 66
5 b g Sepoy(AUS) Mazuna (IRE) (Cape Cross (IRE))
(526) (611) (722) (825) 1031[2] (1232) (1294) 1545[3] 1681[3] 1921[7]

Exeter (AUS)
David A & B Hayes & Tom Dabern 86
2 b c Fastnet Rock(AUS) Vivacious Spirit (AUS) (Bel Esprit (AUS))
8137a[16]

Exhalation *Mark Johnston* a51
2 ch f Bated Breath Pamushana (IRE) (Teofilo (IRE))
8717[7]

Exhibit (IRE) *Richard Hannon* a77 61
2 b f Showcasing Timely (Pivotal)
8758[6] **(9158)**

Exhort *Richard Fahey* 102
4 ch m Dutch Art Entreat (Pivotal)
1889[7] 2961[2] 3374[4] (4758) **5475**[4] 6726[6] **7365**[4] 7657[5] 8094[6]

Existential (IRE) *Clive Cox* 92
4 br m Lethal Force(IRE) Fascination (IRE) (Galileo (IRE))
2252[7] 2608[7] **3192**[2] 4007[3]

Exmoor Beast *Peter Charalambous* a76
3 ch g Sepoy(AUS) Junket (Medicean)
6732[4] 7559[4] 7999[2] 8705[7] 9453[2] **(9662)**

Exning Queen (IRE) *Julia Feilden* a6 43
3 b f Camacho Seven Sing (USA) (Machiavellian (USA))
2976[8] 3603[9] **4298**[6] 5063[8] 5864[4] 6131[10] 7603[9]

Exoptable *William Haggas* a59
3 gr f Dark Angel(IRE) Executrix (Oasis Dream)
979[6] **1287**[5]◆

Exotic Escape *David Lanigan* a61 15
2 b f Muhaarar Zacheta (Polish Precedent (USA))
5684[9] **7304**[6] 7832[9]

Exousia *Henry Spiller* a26
3 b g Epaulette(AUS) Lady McGonagall (USA) (Malibu Moon (USA))
1066[13] **2240**[9] 5358[7]

Expensive Dirham *Mark Johnston* a71 81
2 ch f Dubawi(IRE) Hush Money (CHI) (Hussonet (USA))
5170[7] 5732[3] 6675[3] 6949[2] **7620**[2] 7874[4] 8505[9]

Explain *Ruth Carr* a49 66
7 ch g Kyllachy Descriptive (IRE) (Desert King (IRE))
1457[13] 1977[5] 2588[5] **2899**[5] 4523[13] 5021[5] 5616[7] 5770[12] 7780[9]

Expressionism (IRE)
Charlie Appleby a91 69
3 b f Galileo(IRE) Lady Springbank (IRE) (Choisir (AUS))
5148[5] (5810) **8710**[4]

Expressionist (IRE) *Charlie Appleby* 89
2 ch g Night Of Thunder(IRE) Permission Slip (IRE) (Authorized (IRE))
(2610) 4012[9] 4610[5]

Express Pass (AUS) *Nick Ryan* 99
2 b c Wandjina(AUS) Pass The Parcel (AUS) (More Than Ready (USA))
8137a[12]

Extra Elusive *Roger Charlton* a110 111
4 ch g Mastercraftsman(IRE) Nessina (USA) (Hennessy (USA))
1420[2]◆ 2083[3] 3074[5] **4612**[2]

Extra Large *M Al Mheiri* a74 60
4 b h Dubawi(IRE) Check The Label (USA) (Stormin Fever (USA))
997[8]

Extra Shot (IRE) *David Evans* a43
2 b f Cappella Sansevero Ja One (IRE) (Acclamation)
9252[8]

Extrasolar *Geoffrey Harker* a54 66
9 b g Exceed And Excel(AUS) Amicable Terms (Royal Applause)
2847[9] 3928[8] **4434**[2] 4630[4] 5038[3] 5300[9] 6590[8] 6826[7] 6945[7] 7420[3] 7961[11] 8821[5] 8925[4] 9398[10]

Extreme Appeal (IRE) *Kelly Morgan* a62 62
7 b g Excellent Art Silk Mascara (IRE) (Barathea (IRE))
1361[4] **(1463)** **(1718)** 1981[6] 8828[6] 9049[6] 9336[7]

Extreme Force (IRE) *Jonjo O'Neill* a72 66
3 ch g Exceed And Excel(AUS) Great Hope (IRE) (Halling (USA))
2406[9] 4838[11] 5779[12]

Extrodinair *Jane Chapple-Hyam* a82 47
4 b g Captain Gerrard(IRE) Mindfulness (Primo Dominie)
4189[7] 7373[2] 8086[7] (8693) 9199[5] **9455**[2]

Exultant (IRE) *A S Cruz* 123
5 b g Teofilo(IRE) Contrary (IRE) (Mark Of Esteem (IRE))
9376a[3]

Eyelool (IRE) *N Bachalard* a88 76
3 b g Dragon Pulse(IRE) Lady Heartbeat (Avonbridge)
636a[7]

Eye Of The Storm (IRE)
Conor Dore a71 79
9 ch g Galileo(IRE) Mohican Princess (Shirley Heights)
1947[8] 2118[6] 2435[7] (2901) 4019[6] 4386[6] 4792[9] 5311[10] (6055) 7830[13]

Eye Of The Water (IRE)
Ronald Harris a65 86
3 b g Lilbourne Lad(IRE) Desert Location (Dubai Destination (USA))
620[2] (813) 1296[3] 1678[2] 2357[9] 2939[2] 3354[4] (3697) 4227[3] 5056[6] (5985) **(6286)** 6913[9] **8522**[3] 9549[12]

Eyes That Dazzle
Matthieu Palussiere a59 67
3 b f Showcasing Golden Secret (Sakhee's Secret)
683a[10]

Eynhallow *Charlie Appleby* 100
5 b g Nathaniel(IRE) Ronaldsay (Kirkwall)
5966[4] 6420[6] **7394**[3]

Eyreborn (IRE) *Keith Dalgleish* a14 48
5 b m Born To Sea(IRE) Eyrecourt (IRE) (Efisio)
2373[4] 2684[8] 2964[10] 4690[10]

Ey Up Its Mick *Tony Coyle* a48 65
3 b g Milk It Mick Silky Silence (High Chaparral (IRE))
1982[8] 2197[2] 2870[5] 3709[4] 4080[5] 5771[6] (6176) 6546[10] **7764**[2]

Ezanak (IRE) *John Wainwright* a43 61
6 b g Sea The Stars(IRE) Ebaza (IRE) (Sinndar (IRE))
231[3] 432[4] 469[6] 2400[11] 2819[11] 4216[5] 4446[6] 5029[10] 5571[10] (6098) 6545[4] 7001[7] 7492[9] 8019[12] 9447[7] 9560[7]

Ezzrah *Charlie Fellowes* a60 57
3 b g Garswood Tessie (Tiger Hill (IRE))
3724[7] 4636[5] 5656[13] 7070[10] **9201**[2] **9467**[5]

Faakhirah (IRE) *Saeed bin Suroor* a78 78
2 b f Dawn Approach(IRE) Rawaaq (Invincible Spirit (IRE))
6514[2]◆ 7304[3] **(8453)**

Faatinah (AUS) *David A Hayes* 112
6 b g Nicconi(AUS) Alqwah (IRE) (Danehill (USA))
(49a) 393a[3] 725a[2] 1111a[10]

Fabled (FR) *Matthieu Palussiere* a51 45
3 b g George Vancouver(USA) Fabiola (GER) (Medicean)
3066a[10] **3878a**[9]

Fabricate *Michael Bell* a100 115
7 b g Makfi Flight Of Fancy (Sadler's Wells (USA))
1420[4] **2083**[4] 3074[6]

Fabulist *John Gosden* a77 88
3 b f Dubawi(IRE) Melodramatic (IRE) (Sadler's Wells (USA))
1739[3] **(4341)** 4898[5] **5441**[2]◆ 6081[6] 6968[6] 7901[12]

Fabulous Las Vegas (FR)
Krzysztof Ziemianski 95
4 b h Air Chief Marshal(IRE) Coleene (King's Best (USA))
8980a[5]

Fabulous View (FR) *Ruth Carr* 14
3 b f Intello(GER) I'm So Glad (Clodovil (IRE))
1723[13] 2018[13] 3218[6] **3651**[14]

Faccio Io *Grizzetti Galoppo SRL* 93
2 ch f Bated Breath Fularmada (Manduro (GER))
8393a[5]

Face Like Thunder *John Butler* a48 58
4 b g Passing Glance Violet's Walk (Dr Fong (USA))
248[6] 507[11] 1653[11] 2349[10] 7758[10] 7973[9] 8207[7] 8942[4] 9225[3]◆ **9544**[3]

Facethepuckout (IRE) *John Ryan* a76 86
3 b g Excelebration(IRE) Taarkod (IRE) (Singspiel (IRE))
320[5] **1178**[2] 1285[8] 1685[3] 3018[4] 3273[6] 3805[2] 4124[10] 4591[3]

Fact Or Fable (IRE) *J S Moore* a56 60
2 gr g Alhebayeb(IRE) Unreal (Dansili)
1651[7] 1910[5] **2315a**[3] **2890a**[4] 3634[5] 4394[7] 4679a[5] 5713a[12] 6196a[8] 6384a[11] 8824[8] 9009[5] 9307[6] 9449[4] 9630[10]

Fading Icon *Philip Kirby* a14 22
4 b m Sixties Icon Fading Away (Fraam)
5814[5]

Fahad *Roger Varian* 69
2 b c Farhh Radhaadh (IRE) (Nayef (USA))
4611[4]

Fahan Mura (USA) *Vladimir Cerin* 105
5 ch m English Channel(USA) Celtic Cross (USA) (Giant's Causeway (USA))
444a[10]

Fair Alibi *Tom Tate* a71 68
3 b g Paco Boy(IRE) Alybgood (CAN) (Alydeed (CAN))
(831) **1193**[2] 1662[9] 2149[4] 2635[5] 3202[10] 3884[3] 5551[7] 5951[6] 7418[8] 9185[6]

Fair Cop *Andrew Balding* a74 83
5 b m Exceed And Excel(AUS) Speed Cop (Cadeaux Genereux)
1082[4]◆ 1822[11] **(2358)** 3201[10]

Fair Maiden (USA) *Eoin Harty* 104
2 ch f Street Boss(USA) Shieldmaiden (USA) (Smart Strike (CAN))
7267a[3] 8748a[12]

Fairmet *Marco Botti* a67
2 b f Helmet(AUS) Fairdal (Shamardal (USA))
8602[12] **9327**[3]

Fairmont (FR) *C Ferland* a99 96
3 gr g Orpen(USA) Figurelibre (IRE) (Verglas (IRE))
(421a) **3108a**[3]

Fair Pass (IRE) *Marco Botti* a71 63
2 b f Raven's Pass(USA) Fair Nashwan (Nashwan (USA))
3461[2] 4557[5] 6028[4] 7029[4]◆ 8318[6]

Fair Power (IRE) *John Butler* a69 62
5 b g Power Pitrizzia (Lando (GER))
1675[11] 2256[6] 3186[2] 3537[3] 4346[5] 5803[3] 6152[2] (6860) (7376) 7685[4] 8422[11] **(9479)** 9663[7]

Fair Sabra *David Elsworth* a56 54
2 b f Swiss Spirit Silver Sail (Daylami (IRE))
5961[5] 6281[6] 7276[9] **7785**[6] 8452[6] 8825[5]

Fair Warning *Henry Spiller* a57 56
2 b g Helmet(AUS) Critical Path (IRE) (Noverre (USA))
2761[13] 3491[14] **6161**[8] 7626[7] 8815[6] 9346[2]◆

Fairway To Heaven (IRE)
Paul George a51 56
10 b g Jeremy(USA) Luggala (IRE) (Kahyasi (IRE))
132[4] **(809)**

Fairy Falcon *Bryan Smart* 100
4 ch m Sepoy(AUS) Easy To Imagine (USA) (Cozzene (USA))
3360[4] 3956[3] 4891[8] 6056[4] **6698**[3] 7401[11] 8166a[4]

Fairy Fast (IRE) *George Boughey* a68 68
3 b f Requinto(IRE) Fairy Trader (IRE) (Hawk Wing (USA))
2123[3] 2683[4] (2871) 3148[2] 3376[2] 3417[2] 4731[13] 5738[2] **6048**[2] 6183[5] 6685[2] 7022[6] **7286**[2] 7869[10]

Fairyland (IRE) *A P O'Brien* 112
3 b f Kodiac Queenofthefairies (Pivotal)
2443[5] 3115[6] 3950[5]◆ 4923[3] 6423[10] 6959[6] **(7243a)** 7943a[10]

Fairy Stories *Richard Fahey* a62 87
3 b f Mayson Fairy Shoes (Kyllachy)
2635[3]◆ (3376) 3596[2] 4335[4] 5123[4] 5660[3] (6715)◆ (7511) **(7908)**

Fairy Tale (IRE) *Gay Kelleway* a92 88
4 b g Kheleyf(USA) Singapore Fairy (FR) (Sagacity (FR))
1449a[5] 2226a[16] 3136a[17] **4250**[2] 4899[8] 5686[2] 6535[6] 8421[11]

Fairy Tango (IRE) *Sarah Lynam* a58 55
4 b m Elnadim(USA) Suntory (IRE) (Royal Applause)
419a[6]

Faith And Fortune (ARG)
M F De Kock a27
3 b g Cityscape Fortune In Faith (USA) (Grand Slam (USA))
169a[10] 511a[15]

Faithful Mount *Ian Williams* a68 87
10 b g Shirocco(GER) Lady Lindsay (IRE) (Danehill Dancer (IRE))
2578[5] 3145[7]

Fajjaj (IRE) *Hugo Palmer* 67
4 ch g Dawn Approach(IRE) Pleasantry (Johannesburg (USA))
1890[10] **7694**[29]

Fake News *David Barron* a66 68
4 b g Paco Boy(IRE) Day Creek (Daylami (IRE))
1413[15] **2628**[6] 3199[6] 3704[7] 3922[11] 5020[8] 5239[8]

Fakir Bere (FR) *P Adda* a68 52
4 b g Pedro The Great(USA) Triple Witching (USA) (Pulpit (USA))
2264a[7]

Falacho (IRE) *David Loughnane* a56 17
2 b f Requinto(IRE) Picabo (IRE) (Elusive City (USA))
6899[7] 7546[6] **7995**[3] 8750[8] 8841[6]

Falathaat (USA) *Saeed bin Suroor* a75 23
3 ch f Union Rags(USA) Mezah (USA) (Tapit (USA))
2909[12] **4329**[11]

Falcao (IRE) *John Butler* a62 75
7 b g Majestic Missile(IRE) Cafe Lassere (USA) (Giant's Causeway (USA))
1179[5] 1265[7] 1553[7] **(1969)** 2194[6] 2532[4] 9182[4] 9670[6]

Falcao Negro *P Vidotto* a48 74
6 b h Canford Cliffs(IRE) Really Lovely (IRE) (Galileo (IRE))
6145a[11]

Falcata *Jo Hughes* 70
2 b c Sayif(IRE) Timeless Elegance (IRE) (Invincible Spirit (IRE))
6776a[6] 7675a[14]

Falco Delavilliere (FR)
R Avial Lopez a84 85
4 b g Air Chief Marshal(IRE) Betty Bowl (FR) (Turtle Bowl (IRE))
2226a[15] **3136a**[10]

Falcon Claws (USA) *Marco Botti* a65
2 ch c Union Rags(USA) Brown Eyed Mary (USA) (Pulpit (USA))
5940[4] 7473[5] 7834[4]

Falcon Cliffs (IRE) *Tony Carroll* a68 72
5 b m Canford Cliffs(IRE) Circle (IRE) (Galileo (IRE))
119[2] 318[2] 535[3] 991[5]◆ 7344[9] 7845[6] 8347[2] 8703[3] (8916) (9447)◆

Falcon Eight (IRE) *D K Weld* 114
4 b h Galileo(IRE) Polished Gem (IRE) (Danehill (USA))
(4670) 6421[4] 7928a[5]

Falconidae (IRE) *Richard Hannon* a63 65
2 b f Kodiac Dhuma (Falco (USA))
2338[4] 2836[6] **4849**[5] 5683[11] 6330[6] 7296[4] 7785[5]

Falcon Run (FR) *F Head* 83
3 b c Hurricane Run(IRE) Germance (USA) (Silver Hawk (USA))
1347a[10]

Faldetta *Eve Johnson Houghton* 74
2 b f Helmet(AUS) Perfect Cover (IRE) (Royal Applause)
2996[3] (3405)◆ **4214**[2] 4861[3]

Falls Creek (USA) *Andrew Balding* a52 8
4 bb m Street Cry(IRE) Trickski (USA) (Peteski (CAN))
245[5] **482**[2] 721[7] 6077[4] 8000[5] 8551[4] 9275[4] 9412[P]

Falmouth Light (FR) *Iain Jardine* 84
4 b g Cape Cross(IRE) Wonderous Light (IRE) (Montjeu (IRE))
1461[10] **3502**[4] 3726[4] 8237[9]

Falsehood (IRE) *John Gosden* 60
3 gr c Kingman Half Truth (IRE) (Verglas (IRE))
2794[6]

False Id *Fred Watson* a60 61
6 b g Aqlaam Miss Dutee (Dubawi (IRE))
120[2] 241[5] 410[6] 910[8] 1176[3] 1390[6] 1506[2] 1722[5] (1983) **(2112)**◆ 2231[6] 3046[7] 3547[9] 3959[8] 4657[7] 7418[12] 7956[6] 9391[13]

Fame N Fortune *Joseph Tuite* a64 41
3 b g Thewayyouare(USA) Acapella Star (IRE) (Oratorio (IRE))
3594[5] 4038[4] 5987[9] 6279[2] (6723) **7375**[2] 7817[9]

Famiglia (FR) *Charley Rossi* 85
2 b f George Vancouver(USA) Renascent Rahy (Rahy (USA))
5469a[7]

Family Fortunes *Michael Madgwick* a95 93
5 ch g Paco Boy(IRE) Barawin (IRE) (Hawk Wing (USA))
56[2] 310[2] **(557)** **988**[2] 1294[9] 3423[3] 4255[8] 5991[5] 6347[8] 6964[5] 7567[4] 9177[5] 9510[4]

Famous Dynasty (IRE)
Michael Blanshard a65 62
5 b g Famous Name Daffodil Walk (IRE) (Captain Rio)
85[6] **859**[4] **1363**[3] 1826[4] 3545[9] 4231[11] 4795[5] 6077[11] 7240[8] 7759[3] 8204[6] 8854[12] 9310[3]

Famous Wolf (FR) *A Fabre* a102 99
3 b g Kendargent(FR) More Than Famous (FR) (More Than Ready (USA))
1347a[5] **2499a**[4]

Fanaar (IRE) *William Haggas* a99 106
3 b g Dark Angel(IRE) Inca Trail (USA) (Royal Academy (USA))
(989) 1713[7] 3075[4] 4016[3] 5413[17] **6425**[3] 6950[16]

Fan Club Rules (IRE)
Matthieu Palussiere 101
2 b c Gutaifan(IRE) Mia Divina (Exceed And Excel (AUS))
3333a[9] 4417a[4] **5228a**[4] 5542[4]

Fancy Blue (IRE) *A P O'Brien* 100
2 b f Deep Impact(JPN) Chenchikova (IRE) (Sadler's Wells (USA))
(8165a)

Fancy Dress (IRE) *Ralph Beckett* a20 44
3 ro f Mastercraftsman(IRE) What Style (IRE) (Teofilo (IRE))
2034[6] 2518[11] 3888[11]

Fancy Flyer *Dean Ivory* a72 72
3 b g Archipenko(USA) Lucky Flyer (Lucky Story (USA))
3440[9] 4183[9] 5092[3] **(6052)** **7204**[2] 7514[8] 9306[10]

Fancy Footings (IRE)
Tom Dascombe a85 77
3 b g Dandy Man(IRE) Mystical Past (IRE) (Majestic Missile (IRE))
(8902) 9183[3] 9480[9]

Fanfaronade (USA) *John Gosden* a66
3 gr f Exchange Rate(USA) Fanzine (USA) (Cozzene (USA))
524[6] **1066**[3] 1270[4] **1481**[3]

Fannie By Gaslight *Mick Channon* 80
4 b m Sixties Icon Inffiraaj (IRE) (Iffraaj)
5174[5] 5571[7] 5982[3] 6509[4] 7366[3] **(7682)** 7782[4] 7974[7] 8519[3]

Fanny Chenal *Jim Boyle* a41 49
3 b f Kodiac Maakrah (Dubai Destination (USA))
2623[8] 3421[7] 4244[9] **5049**[5] 5987[13] 8406[9]

Fanny Logan (IRE) *John Gosden* 112
3 b f Sea The Stars(IRE) Linda Radlett (IRE) (Manduro (GER))
(2148)◆ 2521[3] 4014[9] (5397) **(6082)**◆ (7347) (8094) 8772a[4]

Fansurper (IRE) *Roger Fell* a65 54
2 b g Gutaifan(IRE) Twiggy's Girl (IRE) (Manduro (GER))
7285[7] 7698[4] **7911**[6] 8815[12]

Fantail *Simon Crisford* a80
2 b f Zoffany(IRE) Red Fantasy (IRE) (High Chaparral (IRE))
(9046)

Fantastic Bere (FR) *E Leenders* a61 58
4 gr g Pedro The Great(USA) Kanonette (FR) (Kaldoun (FR))
5760a[3]

Fantastic Blue *Ismail Mohammed* 88
3 ch c Iffraaj Blue Beacon (Fantastic Light (USA))
3373[6] 5779[2]◆ **(6463)** (7057) 7459[5] 8002[7]

Fantastic Diamond (FR)
H-A Pantall 91
2 b f Sommerabend Fine Emotion (GER) (Big Shuffle (USA))
5228a[8]

Fantastic Flyer *Dean Ivory* a80 49
4 br m Harbour Watch(IRE) Lucky Flyer (Lucky Story (USA))
(1731) (2235) 3146[4] 4247[4] (5282) (5632) 6025[9] **(7552)** 8063[5] 8550[7]

Fantastic Glory (FR)
A De Watrigant a58 68
3 b f Olympic Glory(IRE) Mud Hilah (FR) (Kingsalsa (USA))
9280a[6]

Fantastic Ms Fox *Richard Fahey* a60 67
3 b f Foxwedge(AUS) Cracking Lass (IRE) (Whipper (USA))
1697[5] 2096[6] 2712[2] (3197) 3886[3] **5028**[4] 5566[4] **6068**[3] **6589**[3] **6938**[2] **7441**[3]

Fantasy (IRE) *A P O'Brien* a74 90
3 b f Invincible Spirit(IRE) Cassandra Go (IRE) (Indian Ridge (IRE))
1434a[15] 2605a[9] **2880a**[4] 3818a[8] 5222a[7] 5325a[17]

Fantasy Believer (IRE)
Charles Hills a83 73
2 b c Make Believe Avizare (IRE) (Lawman (FR))
5186[6] 5774[3] 6528[4] 7612[7] 8665[7] **(9172)**

Fantasy In March (FR) *S Renaud*
3 b f Manduro(GER) Sideville (IRE) (Acclamation)
7476a[11]

Fantasy Justifier (IRE)
Ronald Harris a60 63
8 b g Arakan(USA) Grandel (Owington)
28[4] 483[8] 882[4] 920[2] 1820[7] 3143[9] 3527[4] 4181[13] 4481[6] (6107) **6363**[2]◆ 7084[12] 7299[10] 8408[9]

Fantasy Keeper *Michael Appleby* a87 90
5 b g Mayson Expressive (Falbrav (IRE))
2611[7] 3636[2] (3856) 5951[2] 6549[2] **(7828)** 8099[8] 8262[12] 9030[5] 9183[8]

Fantasy Lover (IRE)
Michael Appleby a46
2 b f Due Diligence(USA) Jollification (IRE) (Acclamation)
9409[7]

Fantom Force (IRE)
Richard Hannon a65 76
2 gr c Gutaifan(IRE) Aja (IRE) (Excellent Art)
3660[4] 3962[3] 4254[4] 5101[3] **(5340)** 5896[5] 6416[7] 7391[9] 8219[7]

Fan Zone (FR) *B De Montzey* 89
3 ch f Zizany(IRE) Queen's Garden (USA) (Kingmambo (USA))
1626a[7]

Fanzone (IRE) *Archie Watson* a70 80
2 b c Gutaifan(IRE) Dame Alicia (IRE) (Sadler's Wells (USA))
4889[2] 5288[2] 5780[4] 9242[3]

Faraasah (IRE) *Jamie Osborne* a76 78
4 br g Arcano(IRE) Falsafa (Dansili)
7085a[8] 7552[11]

Far Above (IRE) *James Tate* 100
3 b c Farhh Dorraar (IRE) (Shamardal (USA))
(1886) 2834[4] (3661) **(4703a)**

Farah Di Belle (FR) *Alain Couetil* 39
4 b m Doctor Dino(FR) Saone Et Loire (FR) (Always Fair (USA))
5762a[5]

Faramman *John Gosden* a32
2 b c Fastnet Rock(AUS) Nessina (USA) (Hennessy (USA))
9325[12]

Faraway Fields (USA) *Peter Hiatt* a49 70
4 b g First Defence(USA) Faraway Flower (USA) (Distant View (USA))
562[7] **962**[10] 2112[11] 2698[11]

Far Cry *Hughie Morrison* a54 41
6 b m Sakhee's Secret Yonder (And Beyond (IRE))
59[6] 245[7] 1679[7] 2901[4] 3497[7] 6049[12]

Fard *Roger Fell* a66 72
4 b g Dutch Art Rose Blossom (Pastoral Pursuits)
2847[6] 3215[8] 3721[5] 4131[4] 4523[7] 4785[4] 4820[2] 5247[7] 5299[6] 5918[6] 6066[5] 6275[6] 6666[4] (7286) **(7420)** 7654[9] 7959[5]

Fareeq *Charlie Wallis* a63 65
5 gr g Dark Angel(IRE) Spate (IRE) (Danehill Dancer (IRE))
298[7] 596[4] 1021[2] **(1266)** 1590[3] 2010[3] 2473[9] 6048[5] 6685[3] 7446[7] 9092[10] 9386[6] 9583[7] 9664[4]

Fares Alpha (USA) *Marco Botti* a66 42
3 gr g Exchange Rate(USA) Relampago Azul (USA) (Forestry (USA))
1568[4] 2336[9] 4031[6] 5731[6]

Fares Kodiac (IRE) *Marco Botti* a53 71
3 b c Kodiac Artemis (IRE) (Marju (IRE))
838[6] **1388**[4] 1920[8] 4420[7] 5335[6] 5647[8]

Fares Poet (IRE) *Marco Botti* a81 62
3 b c Poet's Voice Moon Over Water (IRE) (Galileo (IRE))
1696[6] 2942[2] 4789[2] 6026[7] 6593[4] **7554**[2] 8197[5] 9273[6]

Farewell Kiss (IRE) *Michael Bell* a7 57
2 ch f Exceed And Excel(AUS) Kiss Me Goodbye (Raven's Pass (USA))
4849[8] 5772[10] 6514[9] 7275[12]

Farhh Away *Michael Dods* a73 65
4 ch g Farhh Bukhoor (IRE) (Danehill (USA))
1659[12] **2246**[2]◆ 4130[4] 5213[5] 6180[10]

Farhhmorecredit *Michael Attwater* 35
2 b c Farhh Espresso Romano (Pastoral Pursuits)
3943[12] **4750**[6]

Farhhmoreexciting *David Elsworth* a60 22
4 ch g Farhh Something Exciting (Halling (USA))
1423[8] 2009[7] 2192[9] 2738[13] 6116[9]

Farl (IRE) *Ed Walker* a53
4 b m Cape Cross(IRE) Oatcake (Selkirk (USA))
178[6] 399[11] 718[7]

Farnham *Roger Varian* a83 72
3 b f Farhh Purple Tiger (IRE) (Rainbow Quest (USA))
1740[5] **(8497)**◆

Farol *James Given* a54 51
3 br f Kuroshio(AUS) Spate Rise (Speightstown (USA))
550[4]◆ 5264[10] 5969[11] 6587[6]

Farout (IRE) *F-H Graffard* 62
2 b c Dark Angel(IRE) Transhumance (IRE) (Galileo (IRE))
7675a[7]

Farrdhana *Phillip Makin* a44
3 ch f Farhh Dhan Dhana (IRE) (Dubawi (IRE))
739[2] 1272[8] 2677[6] 8667[11]

Far Rockaway *William Haggas* a70
2 b f Frankel Darinza (FR) (Dalakhani (IRE))
8913[5]◆ **9154**[2] 9624[2]

Farump *Robert Eddery* a50 46
3 b f Zebedee Grey Again (Unfuwain (USA))
341[4] 476[9]

Farzeen *Roger Varian* a91 93
3 ch f Farhh Zee Zee Gee (Galileo (IRE))
251[7] (5554) (6074)◆ **7146**[6] 8115[10]

Fas (IRE) *Mme Pia Brandt* a100 95
5 b h Fastnet Rock(AUS) Sotka (Dutch Art)
640a[11] 843a[13] **3289a**[9] 7255a[11]

Fascinating Spirit (IRE)
Marjorie Fife a51 54
4 b m Fastnet Rock(AUS) Maryellen's Spirit (IRE) (Invincible Spirit (IRE))
6572[7] 9446[12] 9544[12]

Fashion Advice *Keith Dalgleish* 78
2 ch f Dandy Man(IRE) Secret Advice (Sakhee's Secret)
3196[3] **(3927)**

Fashionesque (IRE) *Rae Guest* a59 71
3 b f Fast Company(IRE) Featherlight (Fantastic Light (USA))
2976[3] (4129)◆ **5357**[2] 6225[4] 7189[9]

Fashion Free *Archie Watson* a69 71
2 b f Muhaarar Ighraa (IRE) (Tamayuz)
2915[7] 3441[3] 4245[4] 4756[3] 5313[5] **(5576)** 6113[3] 6792[4]

Fashion Royalty *Roger Charlton* a76 69
2 b f War Front(USA) Royal Decree (USA) (Street Cry (IRE))
6407[7] 7235[3] **(8319)**

Fashion's Star (IRE) *Roger Charlton* 88
3 ch f Sea The Stars(IRE) Ninas Terz (GER) (Tertullian (USA))
2268[8]

Fashion Stakes (IRE)
Jeremy Noseda 66
3 b f Dark Angel(IRE) Warshah (IRE) (Shamardal (USA))
2397[3]

Fasika (AUS) *Joseph Pride* 99
3 bb f So You Think(NZ) Jarada (AUS) (Redoute's Choice (AUS))
8805a[9]

Fast And Free *William Haggas* 72
2 b f Iffraaj Dame Helen (Royal Applause)
4849[7] **5342**[4] 6675[5]

Fast And Friendly (IRE)
Barry Murtagh 20
5 b g September Storm(GER) Merewood Lodge (IRE) (Grand Lodge (USA))
5555[10] 6824[6]

Fast And Furious (IRE)
James Bethell a53 54
6 b g Rock Of Gibraltar(IRE) Ocean Talent (USA) (Aptitude (USA))
7656[7] 8719[13]

Fastar (IRE) *Gerard O'Leary* a85 87
5 ch g Fast Company(IRE) Asterism (Motivator)
1308a[8] **(9404)**◆

Fast Boy (IRE) *David Simcock* a66
3 b g Fast Company(IRE) Celtic Heroine (IRE) (Hernando (FR))
90[5] 518[P] (Dead)

Fast Deal *Tim Easterby* 71
2 ch g Fast Company(IRE) Maven (Doyen (IRE))
5512[5] 5764[2]◆ 6175[10]◆ **6579**[2]◆ 6969[7]

Fast Endeavour *Ian Williams* a53 54
3 b f Pastoral Pursuits Scented Garden (Zamindar (USA))
813[6] **918**[4] 1141[6] 1514[6]

Fasterkhani *Philip Kirby* 49
3 b g Fast Company(IRE) Musikhani (Dalakhani (IRE))
2912[9] 3200[8] 3680[8] **8343**[3]

Fastman (IRE) *David O'Meara* 95
3 br g Elzaam(AUS) Manalisa (IRE) (Manduro (GER))
2078[8] 2510[4] 2746[3] 4099[2] 4895[4] **5685**[2] 6425[14]

Fast'n Furious (GER)
Adrian Nicholls a23
3 bb c Kendargent(FR) Fantanella (IRE) (Montjeu (IRE))
949[8] 1195[13]

Fast Pass (USA) *Peter R Walder* a99
6 b g Successful Appeal(USA) Passionate Dancer (USA) (Cat Thief (USA))
7010a[14]

Fast Track *Marjorie Fife* a37 38
8 b g Rail Link Silca Boo (Efisio)
31[6]◆ 237[3] 468[4] 883[4] 4694[14]

Fast Track Flyer (IRE) *Brian Ellison* a42 52
2 b f Free Eagle(IRE) Chanter (Lomitas)
5764[12] **6065**[7] 6664[6] 7306[13]

Fata Morgana *Christine Dunnett* a13 14
4 b m Society Rock(IRE) Life's A Whirl (Machiavellian (USA))
3279[10] 3688[RR]

Father McKenzie *James Eustace* a48 47
5 b g Sixties Icon Queen Of Narnia (Hunting Lion (IRE))
132[P] (Dead)

Faunus D'Emra (FR) *T Poche* a39 29
4 b g Naaqoos Talka (FR) (Vettori (IRE))
2170a[18]

Faux Pas *F Head* 41
3 b f Anodin(IRE) Rarement (IRE) (Monsun (GER))
7561a[6]

Favori Royal (FR) *E Lyon* a60 56
4 b g Wootton Bassett Matin De Tempete (FR) (Cardoun (FR))
178[5] **384**[4] 1349a[10] 2955a[13]

Favorite Moon (GER)
William Haggas a73 75
2 b c Sea The Moon(GER) Favorite (GER) (Montjeu (IRE))
8028[6] **8518**[4] 9007[3]

Favre (USA) *Robert Cowell* a56 32
3 ch c Munnings(USA) Ice Crystal (USA) (Henny Hughes (USA))
2550[6] 3277[10]

Fawaareq (IRE) *Doug Watson* a75 77
6 b g Invincible Spirit(IRE) Ghandoorah (USA) (Forestry (USA))
573a[13]

Fayetta *David Loughnane* a70 72
3 b f Champs Elysees Starfan (USA) (Lear Fan (USA))
409[4]◆ 598[3] 794[4] 917[3] 3708[4] 3955[4] 4443[2] 4769[6] **5599a**[2] 5712a[9] 5954[5] 6405[4] 6901[6] 9367[2] 9542[7] 9611[10]

Fayez (IRE) *David O'Meara* a98 106
5 b g Zoffany(IRE) Gems (Haafhd)
276[2] 521[5] 807[4] (1106) 1413[9] 2116[3] (2873) (3515) 4021[6] 4692[4] 4935[11] 5199[3] **(5519)** 6543[3]

Faylaq *William Haggas* a110 103
3 b c Dubawi(IRE) Danedream (GER) (Lomitas)
2524[4] (4034)◆ (4296)◆ 4901[2] **(7574)**◆ 7890[4]

Fear And Fire (FR) *Mme G Rarick* 4
3 b f Elusive City(USA) Fanurio's Angel (FR) (Sanglamore (USA))
4204a[6]

Fearaun (IRE) *Stella Barclay* a41 71
4 b g Arakan(USA) Brosna Time (IRE) (Danetime (IRE))
101[9] 3461[0] 5354 **789**[7] 1032[12]

Fearless King *Frau S Steinberg* 86
2 b c Kingman Astrelle (IRE) (Makfi)
6746a[6]

Fearlessly (IRE) *Roger Varian* a69 84
3 gr f Dalakhani(IRE) Mid Mon Lady (IRE) (Danetime (IRE))
4372[3] **(4804)**◆ 5138[5]

Fearless Warrior (FR)
Eve Johnson Houghton a84 81
3 ch g Sea The Stars(IRE) Mambo Light (USA) (Kingmambo (USA))
1911[3]◆ 2905[3] 3842[6] 4739[3] 6454[3] 8421[2] **(9066)** 9418[7]

Fear Naught *George Baker* a70 48
2 gr g Brazen Beau(AUS) Tanda Tula (IRE) (Alhaarth (IRE))
7338[8] 7983[6] **8265**[4]◆

Fearsome *Nick Littmoden* a102 99
5 b g Makfi Lixian (Linamix (FR))
(345)◆ (440)◆ 878[5] 1017[3] 1220[4] **1917**[5] 3024[5] 4382[12]

Federico *Enrique Leon Penate* a76 89
6 b g Acclamation Frangy (Sadler's Wells (USA))
6145a[10] **8375a**[4]

Fedora Fits *Mark Loughnane* a22 55
2 ch f Helmet(AUS) Lee Miller (IRE) (Danehill Dancer (IRE))
5780[5] 6368[8] 7030[10]

Feebi *Chris Fairhurst* a49 53
3 b f Pour Moi(IRE) Scorn (USA) (Seeking The Gold (USA))
1643[10] 2148[10] 3197[8] 3931[7] 5242[7] 6030[6] **(7290)** 8269[4]

Fee Historique (FR) *Hiroo Shimizu* 86
2 ch f Lucayan(FR) Xachusa (FR) (Xaar)
7939a[6]

Feel Good Factor *Richard Fahey* a58 56
2 ch f Dutch Art Meeting Waters (Aqlaam)
4275[4] 5093[3] **5635**[3] 6369[8]

Feeling Easy (IRE) *R K Watson* a11 43
7 b m Bushranger(IRE) Easy Feeling (IRE) (Night Shift (USA))
5933[7]

Feelinlikeasomeone
Jack W Davison a61 75
2 b f Requinto(IRE) Mocca (IRE) (Sri Pekan (USA))
4550[2] 4876[4] 5737[2] 6442[7] 7547[6] 9499[8]

Feel The Thunder *Scott Dixon* a37
3 b c Milk It Mick Totally Trusted (Oasis Dream)
9032[6] 9644[7]

Feel The Vibes *Michael Blanshard* a57 50
5 b g Medicean Apple Dumpling (Haafhd)
207[13]

Feheriq (FR) *E Rocton* a44
4 bb g Air Chief Marshal(IRE) Hickory Hill (FR) (Gold Away (IRE))
76a[10]

Feisty Katerina (IRE)
Gerard O'Leary a49 63
4 b m Vocalised(USA) Miss Ekaterina (IRE) (Teofilo (IRE))
9403[5]

Feleena's Spell *Peter Charalambous* a23
3 b f Epaulette(AUS) Bella's Charm (Hernando (FR))
8497[6] 8753[8]

Felicia Blue *Richard Fahey* a52 72
2 ch f Mayson Diamond Blue (Namid)
4006[2] **(8337)** 9099[7]

Feliciana De Vega *Ralph Beckett* a101 111
3 b f Lope De Vega(IRE) Along Came Casey (IRE) (Oratorio (IRE))
5949[3] 7886a[5] **(8116)**◆

Felix *Marco Botti* a97 93
3 ch g Lope De Vega(IRE) Luminance (IRE) (Danehill Dancer (IRE))
2075[4] 3548[8] 4830[4] (7618) **(9610)**

Felix The Poet *Archie Watson* a92 67
3 ch g Lope De Vega(IRE) Ensemble (FR) (Iron Mask (USA))
3086[4] 3548[5] **4639**[2] 5422[7] **6347**[4] 6964[9] 7836[9]

Femina (IRE) *C Laffon-Parias* a80 92
2 b f Siyouni(FR) Legerete (USA) (Rahy (USA))
6777a[5]

Feminista (IRE) *J S Bolger* 80
2 ch f Dawn Approach(IRE) My Fere Lady (USA) (Mr Greeley (USA))
2881a[8]

Fen Breeze *Rae Guest* a82 73
3 b f Bated Breath Ruffled (Harlan's Holiday (USA))
(796)◆ 1475[2] **2319**[7] 4122[6] 4595[7]

Fendale *Bryan Smart* a92 87
7 b g Exceed And Excel(AUS) Adorn (Kyllachy)
(353) **953**[2] 2775[8] 4406[5] 5154[4] 9098[7] 9348[2]◆

Fenjal (IRE) *Gay Kelleway* a73 50
3 gr g Kodiac Spinamix (Spinning World (USA))
1223[3] **(461)**◆ 2711[10] 3538[6] 4215[7] 6186[8]

Fennaan (IRE) *Phillip Makin* a92 91
4 br g Footstepsinthesand Sanadaat (Green Desert (USA))
1502[5] 2419[5] 2873[2] 3160[6] 4021[8] 5693[7] 6231[5] 6580[2] 6998[12] **(8024)** 8606[9]

Fennann *Frank Bishop* a30
8 b g Dutch Art Embraced (Pursuit Of Love)
9626[13]

Ferblue (FR) *J-C Rouget* 100
3 ch c Motivator Blue Fern (USA) (Woodman (USA))
5718a[6]

Fergus D'Ana (FR) *F-X Belvisi* a44
4 b g Khalkevi(IRE) Island Doree (IRE) (King's Best (USA))
76a[14]

Ferid *M Delzangles* 78
3 b c Oasis Dream Flotilla (FR) (Mizzen Mast (USA))
3675a[3]

Fern Owl *John Butler* a63 51
7 ch g Nayef(USA) Snow Goose (Polar Falcon (USA))
1429[9] 1861[7] 2695[9] 3428[4] 4190[2] **(5285)**◆ 5631[8] 6681[5]

Fersen (FR) *F Chappet* a62 74
3 b g Rajsaman(FR) Mahiladipa (FR) (Librettist (USA))
421a[13]

Festina *Sir Mark Prescott Bt* a56 28
3 gr f Lethal Force(IRE) Quite A Thing (Dutch Art)
7032[4] 7303[4] 7976[7]

Festina Plente *J P Murtagh* a92 88
3 b f Toronado(IRE) Hasty (IRE) (Invincible Spirit (IRE))
8734a[3]

Festival Day *Mark Johnston* 86
2 b f Dubawi(IRE) Ama (USA) (Storm Cat (USA))
6831[2] **(7297)** 7659[8]

Festival Of Ages (USA)
Charlie Appleby a61 44
5 b g Medaglia d'Oro(USA) November (USA) (A.P. Indy (USA))
238[2]◆ 1735[7]

Festive Star *Simon Crisford* 104
2 b f Golden Horn Festoso (IRE) (Diesis)
5684[4] (6322) **(7724a)** 8482a[6]

Fethiye Boy *Ronald Harris* a59 70
5 br g Pastoral Pursuits Ocean Blaze (Polar Prince (IRE))
43[6] **626**[7] 1023[5] 2473[10] 3577[8]

Fflur *K R Burke* a53 53
3 b f Lethal Force(IRE) Exceedingly (Exceed And Excel (AUS))
319[6] 612[6]

Fiannoglaigh (IRE)
Rebecca Menzies 48
2 b f Kodiac Garra Molly (IRE) (Nayef (USA))
7285[10] 8100[10] 9095[12]

Fibonacci *Alan King* a84 74
5 ch g Galileo(IRE) Tereschenko (USA) (Giant's Causeway (USA))
1943[3] 2613[3]

Ficelle Du Houley (FR) *Y Barberot* a97 97
4 b m Air Chief Marshal(IRE) Facilita (IRE) (Fasliyev (USA))
1244a[7] 1627a[4] 5926a[6] **6992a**[5] 9210a[9]

Fiction Writer (USA) *Mark Johnston* a70 69
3 b g Super Saver(USA) Peggy Jane (USA) (Kafwain (USA))
208 289[5] **1178**[4] 2299[4] 2933[3] 4000[8] 5731[8] 6439[4] 7609[6] 8270[6]

Field Gun (USA) *Stuart Williams* a82 40
4 b g More Than Ready(USA) D'Wild Beach (USA) (D'Wildcat (USA))
(548) **1496**[2] 2237[5] 3032[5] 3492[7] 4660[6]

Field Of Vision (IRE) *John Flint* a43 64
6 b g Pastoral Pursuits Grand Design (Danzero (AUS))
2339[7] 2717[13] 3543[7] 4227[11] 4994[10] 6045[5] 6529[7] 7273[5] 8009[2] 8408[4] 8666[6]

Fieldsman (USA) *Tony Carroll* a71 74
7 b g Hard Spun(USA) R Charlie's Angel (USA) (Indian Charlie (USA))
(2145) 2774[4] **(4281)** 5416[3] 5560[5] 6414[6] 6795[4] 8902[2] 9559[5]

Fields Of Athenry (USA)
James Tate a94 68
3 b c Candy Ride(ARG) Purple (IRE) (Galileo (IRE))
1293[2]◆ 1823[6] (2942)◆ **3493**[2] **4639**[4] 6150[8] **8320**[5]

Fields Of Dreams *Roger Charlton* a83
3 b g Champs Elysees Dylanesque (Royal Applause)
836[7] 1984[3] 8294[4] 8656[7] 9202[8] **(9422)**

Fields Of Fire *Alistair Whillans* a42
5 b g Aqlaam Blazing Field (Halling (USA))
18[6] **208**[8] 5891[2]

Fields Of Fortune *Joseph Tuite* a53 73
5 b g Champs Elysees Widescreen (USA) (Distant View (USA))
2936[3] 3778[4] **4661**[3] 5840[7] 6419[5] 8696[7] 9367[9]

Fierce Impact (JPN)
Matthew A Smith a100 108
5 b h Deep Impact(JPN) Keiai Gerbera (JPN) (Smarty Jones (USA))
1974a[7] **(8138a)** **(8768a)**

Fierement (JPN) *Takahisa Tezuka* 123
4 b h Deep Impact(JPN) Lune D'Or (FR) (Green Tune (USA))
7941a[12]

Fierte D'Amour (FR) *L Gadbin* 92
4 b m Siyouni(FR) Alexandrina (GER) (Monsun (GER))
5229a[9]

Fiery Breath *Robert Eddery* a71 61
4 br g Bated Breath Sunset Kitty (USA) (Gone West (USA))
144[12] 1265[2]◆ 1766[2] 4115[9] 4472[7] 5063[3]◆ 6018[3] (7052) 8199[4] 8711[3] **(9185)** 9245[6]

Fiery Mission (USA)
Sir Michael Stoute a64 74
3 b g Noble Mission Quickfire (Dubai Millennium)
4423[3] 5268[4] 6034[4] 7305[9]

Fiesole *Olly Murphy* a85 83
7 b g Montjeu(IRE) Forgotten Dreams (IRE) (Olden Times)
6452[7] **8608**[4] 9167[5]

Fiesta (SWI) *P Schaerer* a63
5 b m Jukebox Jury(IRE) Fujairah (SWI) (Sri Pekan (USA))
592a[2] 694a[2] 780a[7]

Fifth Position (IRE) *Roger Varian* 106
3 b g Dark Angel(IRE) Ballet Move (Oasis Dream)
1754[4] (2249) 3042[3] **4612**[5] 5609[5] 7694[8]

Fifty Days Fire (FR) *D Allard* a50 49
3 bb g Kheleyf(USA) Ghada Amer (FR) (Anabaa (USA))
216a[12]

Fifty Five (USA) *Chad C Brown* 101
5 b m Get Stormy(USA) Soave (USA) (Brahms (USA))
6491a[4]

Fiftyshadesfreed (IRE)
Lennart Jarven a94 89
8 gr g Verglas(IRE) Vasilia (Dansili)
6523a[6]

Fifty Stars (IRE)
David A & B Hayes & Tom Dabern 110
4 b h Sea The Stars(IRE) Swizzle Stick (IRE) (Sadler's Wells (USA))
8768a[2] 8952a[5]

Fight Hero *Y S Tsui* a107 65
8 b g Footstepsinthesand Jarhes (IRE) (Green Desert (USA))
1444a[6]

Fighting Don (FR) *Harry Dunlop* a73 68
2 ch g Anodin(IRE) Mazayyen (American Post)
5131[14] 6449[5]◆ 7043a[4] **8508a**[7] 9363[4]

Fighting Irish (IRE) *Harry Dunlop* a77 89
4 b h Camelot Quixotic (Pivotal)
2791[6] **3501**[5] 4095[18] 5188[8] **8982a**[4] 9483a[7]

Fighting Temeraire (IRE)
Dean Ivory a83 81
6 b g Invincible Spirit(IRE) Hot Ticket (IRE) (Selkirk (USA))
1036[8] 1355[10] 1695[5] 2076[5] (4115) (5144) 5626[3] 6898[6] 7205[2] 8221[7] 9048[U] **(9455)**

Fightwithme (IRE) *John Gosden* a89 77
3 b c Shamardal(USA) Music Show (IRE) (Noverre (USA))
2569[P]

Filament Of Gold (USA)
Roy Brotherton a57 57
8 b g Street Cry(IRE) Raw Silk (USA) (Malibu Moon (USA))
504[4] 2127[12] 2733[3]◆ 4498[5] 4777[2] 5290[2] 6333[5] **(6853)** 7231[9] 8196[11]

Filbert Street *Roy Brotherton* a55 42
4 ch g Poet's Voice Tinnarinka (Observatory (USA))
236[11] 503[4] 1335[10] **1521**[4] **2295**[2] 3527[7] 6546[7] 7384[11] 7606[5] 8268[4] **(8643)** 8898[6] 9551[11]

Fille De Reve *Ed Walker* a66 91
4 b m Iffraaj Danehill Dreamer (USA) (Danehill (USA))
2791[8] 4891[14] **6453**[6]◆ 6953[13] 7411[8]

Filles De Fleur *George Scott* a76 59
3 rg f Gregorian(IRE) Big Moza (Pastoral Pursuits)
(2238) 2597[3] 4226[17] 4789[7] 5651[2] 8549[6] 8902[6] 9202[16]

Fillydelphia (IRE) *Liam Bailey* a46 49
8 b m Strategic Prince Lady Fonic (Zafonic (USA))
1500[5] 2373[8] 3708[11] 3929[3] 4515[10] 5301[3] 5766[7] 6012[4] 7048[14]

Filo's Flyer (IRE) *Archie Watson* a50
2 b f Teofilo(IRE) Floating Along (IRE) (Oasis Dream)
7555[9]

Filou (SWI) *P Schaerer* 92
8 b h Lord Of England(GER) Fujairah (SWI) (Sri Pekan (USA))
780a[5]

Final *Mark Johnston* a91 85
7 b g Arabian Gleam Caysue (Cayman Kai (IRE))
4437[4] 4988[4] 5437[4] 5739[3] 6255[3]

Final Attack (IRE) *Sarah Hollinshead* a52 55
8 b g Cape Cross(IRE) Northern Melody (IRE) (Singspiel (IRE))
120[7] 912[2] 1015[3] 1339[4] 1390[7] 1841[10] 6733[8] 7857[3] 8299[12] 8466[7] 9362[9] 9481[4]

Final Choice *Adam West* a77 56
6 b g Makfi Anasazi (IRE) (Sadler's Wells (USA))
291[6] 991[7] 1524[4] 2239[7] 5596[8]

Final Deal *Mark Usher* 53
2 b f Due Diligence(USA) Investiture (Invincible Spirit (IRE))
4557[8]

Final Energy (KOR) *Kim Jae Sub* a96
4 br g Testa Matta(USA) Pureun Energy (KOR) (Menifee (USA))
7010a[5]

Final Frontier (IRE) *Ruth Carr* a76 74
6 b g Dream Ahead(USA) Polly Perkins (IRE) (Pivotal)
2151[8] 3053[4] 4207[5] 4693[6] (6373) 6826[5] 8221[3] 8495[4]

Final Frontier (USA)
Thomas Albertrani 110
4 b h Ghostzapper(USA) Sahara Gold (USA) (Seeking The Gold (USA))
8770a[9]

Final Go *Grant Tuer* a75 74
4 b g Equiano(FR) Ipsa Loquitur (Unfuwain (USA))
2588[2] 2893[12] 3722[5] 6972[7] 7656[2] 8304[13]

Finalize (FR) *Rosine Bouckhuyt* a67 65
5 b m Vertigineux(FR) Fligane (FR) (Bering)
7800a[5]

Final Legacy *Derek Shaw* a51 33
3 b f Coach House(IRE) Tartatartufata (Tagula (IRE))
3836[6] 4129[12] 5917[4] 6277[15] 8643[4]◆ 8840[8]

Final Option *William Muir* 92
2 bl f Lethal Force(IRE) If So (Iffraaj)
(5737) 6907[4] 7432[5] 8724[10]

Final Orders *Simon Crisford* a69 79
3 b g Camelot Trapeze (Pivotal)
5103[2]◆ 5742[4] 7559[3] 8020[5]

Final Rock *Sir Mark Prescott Bt* a67 84
4 b g Rock Of Gibraltar(IRE) Up At Last (Cape Cross (IRE))
3349[3] 4890[4] 5391[4] 5840[9] 8014[10]

Final Song (IRE) *Saeed bin Suroor* a97 103
2 b f Dark Angel(IRE) Rahiyah (USA) (Rahy (USA))
(2565)◆ 3983[3] 4883[3] 8089[6]

Final Venture *Paul Midgley* a104 109
7 b g Equiano(FR) Sharplaw Venture (Polar Falcon (USA))
1946[2] 2880a[2] 3956[2] 5927[2] 6351[22]

Finche *Chris Waller* 111
5 ch g Frankel Binche (USA) (Woodman (USA))
8361a[5]◆ 8844a[7]

Finch Hatton *Robert Cowell* a44 44
3 b g Showcasing Fifty (IRE) (Fasliyev (USA))
2123[4] 2489[10]

Findhorn *Kevin Ryan* 35
2 br c Kyllachy Palais Glide (Proclamation (IRE))
7698[6]

Finely Tuned (IRE) *Simon Crisford* a72 72
2 b g Gleneagles(IRE) Turning Top (IRE) (Pivotal)
7821[5] 8657[3]◆ 9007[5]

Finery *K R Burke* a73
2 b f Al Kazeem Elysian (Galileo (IRE))
7304[2]◆ (8402)◆

Finespun (IRE) *John Gosden* a74
3 b f Sea The Stars(IRE) Gossamer (Sadler's Wells (USA))
8467[5] 9011[3] 9469[2]◆

Finest Sound (IRE) *Simon Crisford* 77
2 b c Exceed And Excel(AUS) Amplifier (Dubawi (IRE))
6669[3] 7338[3] 7899[3]

Fingal's Cave (IRE) *Philip Kirby* a75 73
7 ch g Fast Company(IRE) Indiannie Moon (Fraam)
23[7] 1367[9] 2418[7] 3305[8] 3682[4] 3922[13] 4785[11]

Finisher (USA) *Mark Gillard* a50 42
4 br g Street Cry(IRE) Morena (PER) (Privately Held (USA))
7560[14] 8224[10] 8904[8] 9312[3]

Fink Hill (USA) *Richard Spencer* a65 65
4 b g The Factor(USA) Matroshka (IRE) (Red Ransom (USA))
43[9] 131[9] 383[10]

Finniston Farm *Tom Dascombe* a61 85
4 b g Helmet(AUS) Logic (Slip Anchor)
2095[6] 2574[7]◆ (3087) 4342[8] 5437[7] 6923[8] 7903[4]

Finoah (IRE) *Tom Dascombe* a93 96
3 b g Kodiac Burstingdalak (IRE) (Dalakhani (IRE))
2525[9] 3048[4] 3479[7] (3591) 4016[12] 4669[5] (5953) 6207[4] 8572a[8] 9254[5] 9472[7]

Finsbury Square (IRE)
M Delcher Sanchez a89 101
7 b g Siyouni(FR) Diamond Square (FR) (Dyhim Diamond (IRE))
7943a[7] 8648a[9]

Finsceal Rose (IRE)
Gavin Cromwell a24 46
3 ch f Finsceal Fior(IRE) North Light Rose (USA) (North Light (IRE))
5099[6]

Fintas *David O'Meara* a84 88
3 b c Lope De Vega(IRE) Free Rein (Dansili)
636a[5] 1110a[11] 3493[6] 4669[7] 5666[6] 6225[3] 6410[3]

Fintech (IRE) *Colin Heard*
5 b g Dark Angel(IRE) Final Legacy (USA) (Boston Harbor (USA))
4687a[9]

Fira (FR) *S Dehez* a77 100
4 b m Siyouni(FR) Nakamti (FR) (Lahint (USA))
5229a[4] 6263a[6] 6992a[10]

Firby (IRE) *Michael Dods* a53 69
4 b g Rock Of Gibraltar(IRE) Huffoof (IRE) (Dalakhani (IRE))
3511[8] 4054[3]◆ 5560[11] 5728[11]◆ 6456[3] 8515[11] 8862[4]

Fire At Midnight (FR) *N Caullery* a59 64
3 ch g Siyouni(FR) Almogia (USA) (Gone West (USA))
1241a[9] 2091a[8] 3878a[4]

Fire Away (USA) *M F De Kock* 67
7 b h War Front(USA) Salute (USA) (Unbridled (USA))
285a[11]

Firebird Song (IRE) *H-A Pantall* a86 102
3 b f Invincible Spirit(IRE) Policoro (IRE) (Pivotal)
(7250a) 7886a[3] 8376a[10]

Fire Brigade *Michael Bell* a97 103
5 b g Firebreak Island Rhapsody (Bahamian Bounty)
1753[22]

Fire Diamond *Tom Dascombe* a82 64
6 b g Firebreak Diapason (IRE) (Mull Of Kintyre (USA))
812[10] 1164[5] 1511[3] (2193) 2596[2] 2998[5] 3305[12]

Fire Fighting (IRE) *Mark Johnston* a102 99
8 b g Soldier Of Fortune(IRE) Savoie (FR) (Anabaa (USA))
1220[3] 1267[2]◆ 1422[13] 1664[5] 2032[9] 2440[4] 2786[2] 3346[6] 4102[12] 9055[14] 9366[4] 9588[9]

Fire Fly (IRE) *A P O'Brien* 94
3 ch f Galileo(IRE) Massarra (Danehill (USA))
1601a[10] 2661a[5] 3786a[4] 4092[16] 4954a[6] 6646a[12]

Fire Island *Tom Ward* a55
3 b f Iffraaj Pink Flames (IRE) (Redback)
7841[7] 8467[6] 8718[6] 9207[7]

Fire Jet (IRE) *John Mackie* a89 93
6 ch m Ask Lightning Jet (Dutch Art)
1947[12] 2801[3] 3600[12]

Firelight (FR) *Andrew Balding* a85 92
3 b f Oasis Dream Freedom's Light (Galileo (IRE))
3166[3] 3865[12] 4340[4] 8607[3] 9129[7]

Firenze Fire (USA) *Jason Servis* a118
4 b h Poseidon's Warrior(USA) My Every Wish (USA) (Langfuhr (CAN))
3618a[5] 8773a[5]

Firenze Rosa (IRE) *John Bridger* a51 62
4 b m Zebedee Our Nana Rose (IRE) (Viking Ruler (AUS))
1820[10] 2206[7] 3596[7] 3961[4] 4556[4] 5046[7] 5750[5] 6510[3] 7568[3] 7757[2] (7986) 8242[2] 8279[3]

Fire Of Beauty (FR)
Andrea Marcialis a67 66
3 b g Siyouni(FR) Clariyn (FR) (Acclamation)
2390a[5] 6328a[5]

Firepower (FR) *Clive Cox* 89
2 b g Starspangledbanner(AUS) Torentosa (FR) (Oasis Dream)
(2338) 2830[6] 4012[10] 7456[6]

Firewater *Richard Fahey* a64 72
3 ch g Monsieur Bond(IRE) Spirit Na Heireann (IRE) (Dubawi (IRE))
2125[4] 2711[8] 3513[8] (3938) 5474[2] 5898[2] 6341[3] 7368[7] 7829[5] 8515[3]

Firlinfeu *Jim Goldie* a63 74
4 b g New Approach(IRE) Antara (GER) (Platini (GER))
7489[2] 8186[9]

Firmament *David O'Meara* a103 104
7 b g Cape Cross(IRE) Heaven Sent (Pivotal)
2419[11] 2778[2] 3313[12] (3863) 5413[6] 6376[4] 6706[5] 7188[4] 7697[6] 8096[2] 9440[5]

Firmdecisions (IRE) *Nigel Tinkler* a86 90
9 b g Captain Rio Luna Crescente (IRE) (Danehill (USA))
1273[7] 1561[11] 2107[2] (2893) (4492) 4902[8] 5626[7] 7059[2] 7467[6] 8425[9] 8921[6]

Firnas *S bin Ghadayer* a97 84
6 b g Dubawi(IRE) Crystal Music (USA) (Nureyev (USA))
1748a[5]

First Breath *Ben Haslam* a43 46
4 b g Bated Breath Miss Rimex (IRE) (Ezzoud (IRE))
613[7]

First Call (FR) *Patrick Morris* a54 55
4 ch g Shamardal(USA) Reponds Moi (USA) (More Than Ready (USA))
467[10] 983[2] 1146[2] 1398[5] 1841[3]

First Contact (IRE) *Charlie Appleby* a90 107
4 gr g Dark Angel(IRE) Vanishing Grey (IRE) (Verglas (IRE))
395a[7] 846a[3] 1115a[3] 1890[6] 2271[6] 7905[2]

First Dance (IRE) *Tom Tate* a73 71
5 b m Cape Cross(IRE) Happy Wedding (IRE) (Green Tune (USA))
2822[5] 3267[4] 4371[4]◆ 4892[6] 5213[3] 5474[4] 6661[2] 7301[5] 7650[6] (8669) 9273[7]

Firsteen *Alistair Whillans* a63 62
3 b f Requinto(IRE) Teide Mistress (USA) (Medaglia d'Oro (USA))
211[6] 406[3]◆ 1081[3]◆ 1486[2]◆ 2337[10] 2958[2]◆ 3921[12] 4725[4] (5215) 5852[2] 6609[5] 6945[2]◆ 7583[8]

First Eleven *John Gosden* 116
4 b h Frankel Zenda (Zamindar (USA))
(2742) 4646[11]

First Excel *Roy Bowring* a73 47
7 ch g First Trump Exceedingly Good (IRE) (Exceed And Excel (AUS))
42[2] 131[2] 278[3] 586[5] 3476[7] 5107[7] 8066[8] 8839[2] 9223[3]

First Flight (IRE) *Tony Newcombe* a78 78
8 b g Invincible Spirit(IRE) First Of Many (Darshaan)
3356[7] 3567[RR] 4333[3] 5216[2] (5555) 5948[3] (6012) 7465[6] 7663[3] 8633[3] 9138[2]◆ 9443[14]

First Impression (IRE) *John Quinn* a67 77
2 b g Make Believe Charmgoer (USA) (Nureyev (USA))
6497[5] 7416[3] (7778)◆

First In Line *John Gosden* a115 110
3 ch c New Approach(IRE) Hidden Hope (Daylami (IRE))
1956[2]◆ (3445) (5656)◆ 6471[2] 6955[10] 8092[2] (8754)

First Kingdom (IRE)
William Haggas 53
2 b f Frankel Simple Magic (IRE) (Invincible Spirit (IRE))
8759[7]

First Link (USA) *Jean-Rene Auvray* a81 65
4 b m First Defence(USA) Magic Motif (USA) (Giant's Causeway (USA))
144[5] (366)◆ (760) 1063[4] (1329)◆ 1586[4] 2273[14] 2927[6] 3892[7] 4838[8] 5565[6] 6898[2] 7236[12] 8419[9] 9126[5]◆ 9424[5]

Firstman (FR) *J-C Rouget* a64 75
2 b c Zoffany(IRE) Tortsanlottie (IRE) (Teofilo (IRE))
6433a[4] 7675a[2]

First Nation *Charlie Appleby* a79 110
5 b g Dubawi(IRE) Moyesii (USA) (Diesis)
(284a)◆ 844a[3] 1890[5] 3953[13] 4612[3] 5182[3] 5718a[3]

First Premio (USA) *Mark Casse* a87 107
5 ch h Pure Prize(USA) Perils Of Pauline (USA) (Stravinsky (USA))
7922a[4]

First Quest (USA) *Jim Boyle* a55 76
5 b g First Defence(USA) Dixie Quest (USA) (Coronado's Quest (USA))
1269[10] (1653) 2360[6]

First Receiver *Sir Michael Stoute* a77 84
2 b c New Approach(IRE) Touchline (Exceed And Excel (AUS))
4886[3]◆ 8823[2]

First Response *Linda Stubbs* a82 79
4 b g First Defence(USA) Promising Lead (Danehill (USA))
1457[14] 1925[10] 3199[2] 5136[2] 6129[6] 6500[2] 7069[6] 7378[5] (8427) 8918[7] 9050[7] 9628[2]

First Sitting *Chris Wall* 106
8 b g Dansili Aspiring Diva (USA) (Distant View (USA))
2408[9] 3160[14] 4342[4] 5519[14] 7122[5] 8130[12]

First Star (USA) *Ronald W Ellis* a98
3 ch f First Dude(USA) Via Regina (USA) (English Channel (USA))
9638a[4]

First View (IRE) *Saeed bin Suroor* a86
2 b c Exceed And Excel(AUS) Love Charm (Singspiel (IRE))
(7814) (8823)◆

First Voyage (IRE) *Michael Appleby* a63 87
6 ch g Dubawi(IRE) Concordia (Pivotal)
3300[6] 8032[5] 9086[5]

First Winter (IRE) *Charlie Appleby* a77
2 b g Dubawi(IRE) Abhisheka (IRE) (Sadler's Wells (USA))
9634[2]

Fitzgerald (USA) *S Jadhav* a79
7 b g Elusive Quality(USA) Filarmonia (ARG) (Slew Gin Fizz (USA))
282a[11] 425a[6]

Fitzrovia *Ed de Giles* a66 71
4 br g Poet's Voice Pompey Girl (Rainbow Quest (USA))
3430[12] (3781) (3939) 4552[10] 5373[9] 5782[6] 7305[7] 7652[8] 8031[7]

Fitzwilly *Mick Channon* a72 71
9 b g Sixties Icon Canadian Capers (Ballacashtal (CAN))
1497[7] 2217[10] 2359[3] 3444[5] 4251[5] (4796) 5047[4] 5891[9]

Fitzy *Paddy Butler* a37 59
3 b g Epaulette(AUS) Zagarock (Rock Of Gibraltar (IRE))
1084[8] 1979[2] 2262[7] (3270) 3721[3] 4487[9] 5247[4] 5556[15] 6502[4] 8998[11] 9423[7]

Fiveandtwenty *Mark Johnston* a61
2 br f Farhh Fen Guest (Woodborough (USA))
8848[6] 9154[4] 9325[11]

Five Diamonds *William Haggas* 74
3 b f Mukhadram Felwah (Aqlaam)
4211[2]◆ (5062)◆ 5955[5]

Five Helmets (IRE) *Iain Jardine* a44 81
3 b g Helmet(AUS) Sweet Home Alabama (IRE) (Desert Prince (IRE))
1485[5] 2054[4] 2635[14] 2897[6] (4000)◆ (4689) 6232[5] (6500)◆ 6998[11] 7332[2]

Five Ice Cubes (FR) *D Smaga* a76 79
4 ch h Rip Van Winkle(IRE) Victoria College (FR) (Rock Of Gibraltar (IRE))
(5009a)

Fivetwoeight *Peter Chapple-Hyam* a84 69
5 b h Kyllachy Super Midge (Royal Applause)
247[4]

Fizzy Feet (IRE) *David Loughnane* a90 72
3 b f Footstepsinthesand Champagne Mistress (Kyllachy)
1219[4] 1337[8] (1492) 4128[5] 4458[3] 4904[7] 5819[8] 8349[7] 8470[2] 9131[2] 9286[3] (9387) 9660[4]

Flag Festival *S Seemar* a82 72
4 gr g New Approach(IRE) Blue Bunting (USA) (Dynaformer (USA))
1748a[11]

Flag Of Honour (IRE) *A P O'Brien* 116
4 b h Galileo(IRE) Hawala (IRE) (Warning)
1777a[2] 2494a[2] 3114[2] 4015[5]

Flag Of St George (FR) *G Botti* a57 57
3 gr c Tin Horse(IRE) Bon Escient (Montjeu (IRE))
5641a[7]

Flambeur (USA) *C Laffon-Parias* a99 101
3 rg g Mizzen Mast(USA) Flamenba (USA) (Kingmambo (USA))
(868a) 4431a[4] 6005a[2] 7923a[6]

Flames Of York *K R Burke* a70
2 b g Rock Of Gibraltar(IRE) Special Miss (Authorized (IRE))
5433[3]

Flaming Heart (FR) *H-A Pantall* a72 73
3 b f Sommerabend Fine Emotion (GER) (Big Shuffle (USA))
509a[6]

Flaming Marvel (IRE)
James Fanshawe a95 93
5 b g Redoute's Choice(AUS) Flame Of Hestia (IRE) (Giant's Causeway (USA))
(184)◆ (916) 1596[5] 6981[3] 7394[6] 8350[4]

Flamingo Girl (GER) *Henk Grewe* a73 93
2 b f Soldier Hollow Flamingo Sky (USA) (Silver Hawk (USA))
7749a[3] 8371a[7]

Flaming Princess (IRE)
Richard Fahey 99
2 b f Hot Streak(IRE) Qatar Princess (IRE) (Marju (IRE))
(3469) 3983[7] 5411[8] (5976a) 6791a[3] 7149[4] 8088[6]

Flaming Red *Kevin Bishop*
3 ch f Phenomena Just Puddie (Piccolo)
1739[10] 2142[12]

Flaming Spear (IRE) *Dean Ivory* a106 111
7 ch g Lope De Vega(IRE) Elshamms (Zafonic (USA))
5521[5] 6215[7] 8336[17] 9064[12]

Flaming Star (FR) *H-A Pantall* a68 98
3 gr f Captain Marvelous(IRE) Fantasia (GER) (Monsun (GER))
3621a[2] 4621a[10] 8141a[4]

Flarepath *William Haggas* a78 85
3 b f Exceed And Excel(AUS) Fiery Sunset (Galileo (IRE))
3603[2]◆ 4922[9]

Flashcard (IRE) *Andrew Balding* 110
3 ch g Fast Company(IRE) Portico (Pivotal)
3075[6] 3599[5] 4919[2] (5412) 6122[3]

Flash Gordon (IRE)
Mrs John Harrington 97
3 b c Kodiac Oasis Sunset (IRE) (Oasis Dream)
2492a[3] 2882a[3]

Flash Henry
Mohammed Jassim Ghazali 86
2 b c Cable Bay(IRE) Angels Wings (IRE) (Dark Angel (IRE))
3039[5] 3644[2] 4062[3] 4295[2] 9582a[4]

Flashing Approach (IRE)
Mark Johnston 69
2 b c New Approach(IRE) Flashing Green (Green Desert (USA))
5088[5] 5848[4]

Flash Point (IRE) *Tracy Waggott* a72 66
3 ch g Iffraaj Permission Slip (IRE) (Authorized (IRE))
4989[3] 5742[5] 6034[5] 6940[5]◆ 7209[7] 8524[5] 9093[8]

Flash To Bang *Ivan Furtado* a52 66
2 b c Telescope(IRE) Fangfoss Girls (Monsieur Bond (IRE))
2610[6] 9408[8]

Flashy Flyer *Dean Ivory* a39 45
2 ch f Helmet(AUS) Lucky Flyer (Lucky Story (USA))
2248[10] 2579[8] 3350[4] 7896[21] 8603[9]

Flat Stone *Daniele Camuffo* a64
3 ch g Champs Elysees Something Exciting (Halling (USA))
1268[4] 2142[10]

Flat To The Max (FR) *Tim Fitzgerald* a81 77
4 b g Maxios Another Name (USA) (Giant's Causeway (USA))
3384a[5] 9570[3]

Flaunt It (IRE) *Jane Chapple-Hyam* a41 31
3 b f Mukhadram Labisa (IRE) (High Chaparral (IRE))
8206[11] 9047[14]

Flavius Titus *Roger Varian* a94 104
4 ch g Lethal Force(IRE) Furbelow (Pivotal)
(1829)◆ 2442[3] (3602) 5664[27] 7152[8]

Fleeting (IRE) *A P O'Brien* 115
3 b f Zoffany(IRE) Azafata (SPA) (Motivator)
2443[15] 3316[3] 4014[2] 5208a[2] 5978a[4] 7252a[5] 7942a[2] 8333[4]◆

Fleeting Freedom *Alan Bailey* a76 80
4 b m Equiano(FR) Fleeting Image (Sir Percy)
3185[4] 3743[7]

Fleeting Prince (IRE) *Charles Hills* 86
2 b c No Nay Never(USA) My Sweet Georgia (IRE) (Royal Applause)
4482[2] (4992) 5584[13] 6375[15]

Fleeting Princess *Charles Hills* 73
2 b f Dandy Man(IRE) Queen Of The Tarts (Royal Applause)
(2257) 2805[13] 4048[16] 4802[4]

Fleet Street *John Gosden* a67 66
2 b f Pivotal Archive (Dansili)
7054[7] 8913[9] 9159[5] 9328[4]

Fleur Irlandaise (FR) *Yannick Fouin* 68
4 b m No Risk At All(FR) Orlandaise (FR) (Goldneyev (USA))
6095a[7]

Flight Command (FR)
Mme M Bollack-Badel 40
3 ch g Norse Dancer(IRE) Angel Wing (Barathea (IRE))
1450a[11]

Flight Officer *Michael Easterby* a20 44
8 b g New Approach(IRE) Danuta (USA) (Sunday Silence (USA))
8260[9] 8396[14] 8862[10]

Flight Of Thunder (IRE) *Kevin Ryan* 64
2 b f Night Of Thunder(IRE) Thames Pageant (Dansili)
1642[8] 2052[7] 3644[9] 4778[2] 5618[3] 6822[2] 7308[7]

Flight Risk (IRE) *J S Bolger* a78 112
8 ch g Teofilo(IRE) Raghida (IRE) (Nordico (USA))
3062a[2] (3786a) 5207a[5] (6235a) 8166a[5]

Flight To Dubai (IRE) *C Escuder* 73
5 ch h Dubai Destination(USA) Cahirleske (IRE) (Saffron Walden (FR))
1349a[2]

Flight To Nowhere *Richard Price* a16
7 ch m Aeroplane River Beauty (Exit To Nowhere (USA))
239[9]

Flighty Almighty *Tom Dascombe* a80 85
3 b f Elusive Quality(USA) Wall Of Sound (Singspiel (IRE))
(1594) 2806[6] 4052[25] 5253[5] 5861[7]

Flighty Lady (IRE) *Gavin Hernon* 105
2 b f Sir Percy Airfield (Dansili)
7006a[3] 7939a[3]

Flint Hill *Michael Dods* a56 78
3 ch g Excelebration(IRE) Modify (New Approach (IRE))
1645[4] 2096[9] 4077[6] 5898[5] 7782[5]

Flintrock (GER) *Andrew Balding* a85 84
4 br g Sinndar(IRE) Four Roses (IRE) (Darshaan)
1425[4] 2143[6] 2571[3] 3044[10] 4936[5]

Flint Said No *Bryan Smart* a38 69
3 gr g Harbour Watch(IRE) Rock Ace (IRE) (Verglas (IRE))
2897[8] 5847[3] 7066[9]

Flippa The Strippa (IRE)
Charles Hills 95
2 gr f Outstrip Celsius Degre (IRE) (Verglas (IRE))
2248[3]◆ (2716) (3023) 3983[8] 5544[3] 6374[9] 8088[9]

Flirtare (IRE) *Amy Murphy* a65 61
4 b m Oasis Dream Federation (Motivator)
144[7] 439[5] 1177[3] 2286[4]

Flit (AUS) *James Cummings* 102
2 b f Medaglia d'Oro(USA) Glissade (AUS) (Redoute's Choice (AUS))
(8135a)

Float (IRE) *David Simcock* 62
2 b f Nathaniel(IRE) Honorine (IRE) (Mark Of Esteem (IRE))
8432[5]

Floating Artist *Richard Hannon* 108
3 b c Nathaniel(IRE) Miss Kenton (IRE) (Pivotal)
1737[5] (4901) 5585[4]

Flo Jo's Girl *Tim Easterby* 49
3 b f Mastercraftsman(IRE) Portraitofmylove (IRE) (Azamour (IRE))
2712[5] 3197[6] 3931[9]

Flood Defence (IRE) *Iain Jardine* a67 69
5 b m Harbour Watch(IRE) Krynica (USA) (Danzig (USA))
346[3] 607[6] 1024[5] 4914[2]◆ 5905[3] (6038) 6658[7] 7366[7] 8515[18]

Flop Shot (IRE) *A Fabre* a81 109
3 b c New Approach(IRE) Dancequest (IRE) (Dansili)
(2499a) 4431a[3] 6143a[3]

Flora Tristan *Ivan Furtado* a59 54
4 ch m Zoffany(IRE) Red Roxanne (Rock Of Gibraltar (IRE))
2297[8] 4028[8] 5030[11] 8896[7] 9128[5]◆ 9248[3] 9287[6]

Floravise (FR) *E Caroux* a64 83
4 ch m Evasive Mariposa (IRE) (Oasis Dream)
2675a[12]

Flor De Seda (FR) *Jo Hughes* a63 63
4 b m George Vancouver(USA) Toile De Soie (FR) (Peintre Celebre (USA))
1245a[17] 1491a[13] 2391a[7] 2955a[10] 6031a[6] 6651a[4] 7062a[2] 7505a[8]

Florence Rose *Jonathan Portman* a53 45
3 b f Medicean Masque Rose (Oasis Dream)
1593[9] 3256[14]

Florencio *Jamie Osborne* a89 82
6 b g Equiano(FR) Mary Pekan (IRE) (Sri Pekan (USA))
(260) 441[10] 618[5] 734[2] 1213[7] 7089a[10] 7551[8] 8062[8] 8496[3]◆

Florenza *Chris Fairhurst* a63 89
6 b m Haafhd Danzatrice (Tamure (IRE))
1763[5] (2097) 2809[13] 3450[9] 4058[4] 4828[7] 6179[4] 6677[7] 6974[5] 7288[4] 8024[10]

Florissante (FR)
J Bertran De Balanda a47 46
3 gr f Tin Horse(IRE) Vila Flor (FR) (Sandwaki (USA))
1658a[9]

Flourishable *Tony Carroll* a46
3 ch f Equiano(FR) Choral Rhythm (IRE) (Oratorio (IRE))
365[14]

Flowering Peach (IRE) *A P O'Brien* 104
3 b f Galileo(IRE) Naples Bay (USA) (Giant's Causeway (USA))
4856a[6] 5364a[4] 5663[4]

Flower Of Thunder (IRE)
Richard Hannon a66
2 b f Night Of Thunder(IRE) Flower Fairy (USA) (Dynaformer (USA))
8602[5] 9046[9]

Flower Power *Tony Coyle* 67
8 br m Bollin Eric Floral Rhapsody (Alflora (IRE))
1848[2] 2254[9] 3054[9] 3269[5] 3955[6] 4370[6] 4601[3] 5019[3] 5974[8] (6828) 7048[3] 7070[9] 7441[9]

Flowing Clarets *Roger Ingram* a51 54
6 ch m Pastoral Pursuits Flying Clarets (IRE) (Titus Livius (FR))
3543[12] 3961[9] 4374[7] 4556[9] 5884[7] 6048[7] 6285[3] 6510[4] 7557[5] 7784[8] 7986[7] 8279[7] 8410[2] 8649[6] 9246[9]

Flowing Magic (IRE) *George Scott* a28 65
2 b c Iffraaj Brimful (IRE) (Invincible Spirit (IRE))
3739[4] 4384[7] 5280[9]

Fluttershy *John Ryan* 46
2 ch f Roderic O'Connor(IRE) Twilight Sparkle (IRE) (Rock Of Gibraltar (IRE))
5961[7] 6606[8]

Fly At Dawn (USA) *Charlie Appleby* a73 73
5 ch g Discreet Cat(USA) Emirates Girl (USA) (Unbridled's Song (USA))
285a[5]◆ 513a[12]

Fly Falcon (IRE) *Richard Hannon* a78 71
2 b c Free Eagle(IRE) Regalline (IRE) (Green Desert (USA))
7897[8] (8504)

Flying Dandy (IRE) *M Bouckaert* a50 53
3 b c Dandy Man(IRE) Double Vie (IRE) (Tagula (IRE))
4229a[9] 4959a[11]

Flying Dragon (FR) *Richard Hannon* 76
3 b g War Command(USA) Histoire De Jouer (FR) (Kaldounevees (FR))
1462[8] 2569[5] 3011[7] 4585[4] 5085[5] 5350[4] 5561[3] 6045[2] 6540[5] 6904[2] 7074[3] 7404[2] 8413[5]

Flying Foxy *George Scott* a63 66
5 b m Foxwedge(AUS) Fauran (IRE) (Shamardal (USA))
1521[5] 1952[9] 2527[4] 3001[5]

Flying Moon (GER)
Jonathan Portman a52 50
3 b g Sea The Moon(GER) Finity (USA) (Diesis)
2284[3] 2715[6] 4787[10] 6030[8] 6860[8] 7240[5]

Flying Pursuit *Tim Easterby* a65 91
6 ch g Pastoral Pursuits Choisette (Choisir (AUS))
1763[6] 2117[8] 2743[12] 3602[13] 3863[4]◆ 4402[8] 5454[5] 5692[15] 6227[12] 6676[8] 7431[5]◆ 7701[3] 8101[2]◆ 8766[4]

Flying Raconteur *Nigel Tinkler* a69 73
5 b g Bated Breath Abunai (Pivotal)
4131[3]◆ 4728[4] 5156[8] 5556[7] 6204[8] (6582)

Flying Sakhee *John Bridger* a49 51
6 b m Sakhee's Secret Sister Moonshine (Averti (IRE))
2365[6] 3352[13] 4378[3] 5430[4] 6120[5] 6605[2] 6897[4] 7281[2] 7812[8] 8417[14] 9249[6] 9298[10]

Flying Standard (IRE) *Chris Wall* 38
2 ch g Starspangledbanner(AUS) Snow Scene (IRE) (Singspiel (IRE))
7346[10] 8203[9]

Flying Tiger (IRE) *Nick Williams* 74
6 bl g Soldier Of Fortune(IRE) Ma Preference (FR) (American Post)
2354[4]◆ 3263[9]

Fly Lightly *Robert Cowell* a76 56
3 b c Dawn Approach(IRE) Step Lightly (IRE) (Danehill Dancer (IRE))
251[6] 967[2]◆ 2582[11] 3445[4] 4663[6] 6662[4]

Flylikeaneagle (IRE) *Mark Johnston* a74 86
2 b g Free Eagle(IRE) Dulcian (IRE) (Shamardal (USA))
5433[2] (6065) 6654[2] (7331) 8029[9] 8462[6]

Fly The Flag *John Gosden* a80 77
3 gr f Australia Approach (Darshaan)
4641[3]◆ 5254[4] (6633) 8727[4]

Fly The Nest (IRE) *Tony Carroll* a78 52
3 b g Kodiac Queen Wasp (IRE) (Shamardal (USA))
1424[7] 2567[9] 3422[6] 5343[7] 5750[8] 6598[6] 9420[8]

Fly True *Ivan Furtado* a66 47
6 b m Raven's Pass(USA) Have Faith (IRE) (Machiavellian (USA))
586[7] 926[5]◆ (1158) (1967) 3939[8] 5632[2] 6546[4] 7384[9] 8068[4] 8404[4] 8949[7]

Foad *Ed Dunlop* a60 65
2 b c Kodiac Slatey Hen (IRE) (Acclamation)
1556[5] 1953[6] 5125[8] (5958) 6387[3] 7315[3]

Focus Group (USA) *Chad C Brown* 108
5 bb h Kitten's Joy(USA) Cocktail Hour (USA) (Dynaformer (USA))
2646a[6] 7226a[3]

Foggy Flight (USA) *S Jadhav* a81
3 gr f Rattlesnake Bridge(USA) Successful Verdict (USA) (Successful Appeal (USA))
48a[11] 510a[12]

Folamour *A Fabre* a98 109
4 b h Intello(GER) Zagzig (Selkirk (USA))
2428a[2] 3389a[4] 9210a[3]

Folie D'Amour
Eve Johnson Houghton a39 54
2 b f Nathaniel(IRE) Rock Follies (Rock Of Gibraltar (IRE))
7695[10] 8454[11]

Folie De Louise (FR)
Carmen Bocskai a100 100
5 gr m Tin Horse(IRE) Folie Folie (GER) (Observatory (USA))
3288a[5] 4157a[5] 7477a[7] 9124a[3]

Folie Douze *Henry Spiller* a52
4 b g Foxwedge(AUS) Chicklade (Firebreak)
1356[9] 1880[13] 3002[11]

Folies Bergeres *Grace Harris* a62 56
4 ch m Champs Elysees May Fox (Zilzal (USA))
1024[11] 1341[4] 1569[6] 2344[11] 2998[14]

Foligno (FR) *E Libaud* 70
3 b c Orpen(USA) Feerie Stellaire (FR) (Take Risks (FR))
(7476a)

Folk Dance *David Simcock* a73 69
2 b f Golden Horn Folk Opera (IRE) (Singspiel (IRE))
7695[6] 8913[3]◆

Follia *Marco Botti* 70
2 b f Toronado(IRE) Filona (IRE) (Motivator)
5381[3] 6603[2]◆

Follow A Dream (USA)
John Gosden a62
3 rg f Giant's Causeway(USA) Dream Of Summer (USA) (Siberian Summer (USA))
1165[3] 1397[7]

Following Breeze (IRE) *Jim Boyle* a14 15
4 b m Kodiac Xaloc (IRE) (Shirocco (GER))
1037[9] 1383[12] 2231[11] 2930[9]

Follow Intello (IRE) *Chris Wall* a77 81
4 b g Intello(GER) Sauvage (FR) (Sri Pekan (USA))
2207[5] (2793)◆ 3973[6] (5179) 6924[6] 7830[11]

Followme Followyou (IRE)
Mark Johnston a44 60
3 b f Holy Roman Emperor(IRE) Capall An Ibre (IRE) (Traditionally (USA))
2199[9] 2506[4] 2909[13] 3409[4] 4003[5] 4690[3]

Followthesteps (IRE) *Ivan Furtado* a82 80
4 b g Footstepsinthesand Excellent Mariner (IRE) (Henrythenavigator (USA))
117[2] 499[5] 790[4] 1597[2] 2611[5] 3504[3] 9108[8] 9519[9]

Fonthill Abbey (IRE) *A Fabre* a89 78
3 b f Dubawi(IRE) Fair Hill (New Approach (IRE))
2954a[4]

Foolaad *Roy Bowring* a105 103
8 ch g Exceed And Excel(AUS) Zayn Zen (Singspiel (IRE))
127[2] 389[2] 588[4] 1105[10] (1459) 1814[3] 2396[7] 2775[2] 4331[7] 5927[8] 6351[18] 6960[5] 8099[21] 9562[5]

Fool For You (IRE) *Richard Fahey* a97 88
4 b m Lawman(FR) Bosphorus Queen (IRE) (Sri Pekan (USA))
2557[6] 3344[18] 3883[3] (4331) 4896[9] 6351[15] 7401[13]

Foolish Humor (USA)
Wesley A Ward 80
2 ch f Distorted Humor(USA) Foolish Cause (USA) (Giant's Causeway (USA))
3988[20]

Fool To Cry (IRE) *Johnny Farrelly* a26 28
6 ch m Fast Company(IRE) Islandagore (IRE) (Indian Ridge (IRE))
2695[13] 9553[8]

Fooraat (IRE) *Roger Varian* a84
2 b f Dubawi(IRE) Nahrain (Selkirk (USA))
(8525)◆

Football Friend *Antony Brittain* a40
3 ch g Monsieur Bond(IRE) Mozayada (USA) (Street Cry (IRE))
408[8]

Foot Of King (IRE) *Endo Botti* 100
3 br c Footstepsinthesand Icebreaking (IRE) (Elusive City (USA))
2162a[8] 2888a[3]

Footstepsanpie (IRE) *A Botti* a79 55
3 b c Most Improved(IRE) Good Chocolate (IRE) (Fayruz)
1028a[2]

Footsteps At Dawn (IRE)
Shane Nolan a60 47
4 b m Footstepsinthesand Miss Gorica (IRE) (Mull Of Kintyre (USA))
(8502)◆ (Dead)

Footstepsintherain (IRE)
J R Jenkins a51 45
9 b g Footstepsinthesand Champagne Toni (IRE) (Second Empire (IRE))
701[12] 925[6] 1042[4] 3007[12] 3304[9]

Forban Du Large (FR)
Xavier Hondier a56 53
4 b g George Vancouver(USA) Gulf Stream Lady (IRE) (Cadeaux Genereux)
2264a[12]

Forbidden City (FR) *S Cerulis* a72 56
4 b h Style Vendome(FR) Funny Crazy (FR) (Chichicastenango (FR))
2264a[10]

Forbidden Dance *Hughie Morrison* a73 73
3 ch f Dutch Art Strictly Lambada (Red Ransom (USA))
2488[8] 2919[8] 3761[3] 4788[6] 5549[3] 6069[3] 7474[2] (8200) 9012[3]

Forbidden Land (IRE)
Richard Hannon a68 82
2 b g Acclamation Week End (Selkirk (USA))
2780[2]◆ 3890[3] 5577[3] 6728[2] 7197[4] 7840[8] 8252[8]

Forbidden Planet *Roger Charlton* a101 56
4 b h Pivotal Aiming (Highest Honor (FR))
(86) (310)◆ 825[2]◆ (1422)◆ 1927[2]

Forced *Richard Hughes* a41 62
2 br f Lethal Force(IRE) Danehill Revival (Pivotal)
1493[4] 2469[2] 2996[6] 5279[5]

Force Of Cashen (IRE)
Tom Gretton a39 52
3 b g Gale Force Ten Elegant Girl (IRE) (Amadeus Wolf)
6885[10] 7236[7]

Force Of Impact (IRE) *Paul George* a59 38
2 gr c Lethal Force(IRE) Corncockle (Invincible Spirit (IRE))
4999[7] 5729[2] 6330[9] 7556[9]

Foreign Legion (IRE)
Luke McJannet a49 68
4 ch g Declaration Of War(USA) Solar Event (Galileo (IRE))
37[2]◆ (155) (293) (467) (596)◆ 982[10] 3188[5] 3543[4] 3781[4] 4123[6] 4378[2] 4657[6]

Foresee (GER) *Tony Carroll* a62 55
6 b g Sea The Stars(IRE) Four Roses (IRE) (Darshaan)
85[4] 560[6] 3209[3] 4547[5] 6104[7] 7390[6] 7759[5] (8854) (9042) 9207[2]

Foreshore *K R Burke* a64
2 b g Footstepsinthesand Skinny Love (Holy Roman Emperor (IRE))
8424[6] 9181[6] 9252[5] 9513[5]

Forest Of Dean *John Gosden* a81 116
3 b g Iffraaj Forest Crown (Royal Applause)
(949)◆ 1645[2]◆ (2075) 2828[4] (5583) (6475)◆ 7457[11]

Forest Ranger (IRE) *Richard Fahey* a105 114
5 b g Lawman(FR) Alava (IRE) (Anabaa (USA))
1115a[7] 1890[2] (2573) 5455[6] 6470[6] 7365[6] 8126[4]

Forever A Lady (IRE)
Keith Dalgleish a49 66
6 b m Dark Angel(IRE) Unicamp (Royal Academy (USA))
2203[15] 2785[10] 3223[2] 3685[5] 4060[3] 4512[2] 4979[3] 5238[5] (5486) 5935[3] 6033[4] 6572[8] 7207[8] 7507[3] 7780[2] (8233)

Forever Coco (FR) *Andrea Marcialis* a68 70
2 ch f Rio De La Plata(USA) Asiana (FR) (Westerner)
5759a[8]

For Ever Fun (FR) *L Gadbin* a65 72
4 b m Linngari(IRE) Superstition (FR) (Kutub (IRE))
1449a[4] 3136a[11] 7062a[7]

Forever In Dreams (IRE)
Aidan F Fogarty 113
3 gr f Dream Ahead(USA) Dora De Green (IRE) (Green Tune (USA))
2605a[5] (3085) 4050[2] 6959[10] 7944a[7] 8331[3]

Forever Mine *Eve Johnson Houghton* 10
3 ch f Iffraaj Best Regards (IRE) (Tamayuz)
1740[18] 2077[9]

Forever Yours (FR) *S Wattel* a84 95
4 ch m Motivator Everlast (FR) (Anabaa (USA))
6095a[2] 8980a[3]

Forewarning *Julia Brooke* a62 77
5 b g Cacique(IRE) Buffering (Beat Hollow)
4146[2] 5487[6] (6256) 7001[2]◆ 7381[2] 8129[9]

Forgetful Agent
Eve Johnson Houghton a54 63
2 ch g Anjaal Bronze Star (Mark Of Esteem (IRE))
3660[7] 4191[5]

Forge Valley Lad *Ed Vaughan* a56 57
2 b c Cityscape Tamara (Marju (IRE))
8722[8] 9130[6]◆

Forgotten Girl *Christine Dunnett* a31 21
3 b f Sir Prancealot(IRE) College Doll (Piccolo)
6325[6] 7278[9] 8290[11] 9439[10]

Forjatt (IRE) *N Bachalard* a98 104
11 b g Iffraaj Graceful Air (IRE) (Danzero (AUS))
425a[4] 847a[6]

Forked Lightning
Dominic Ffrench Davis a30
2 b g Night Of Thunder(IRE) Darrfonah (IRE) (Singspiel (IRE))
9585[11]

Formality *Michael Bell* 76
2 b c Frankel Silver Mirage (Oasis Dream)
8460[5]

Formally *Tony Carroll* a41 13
3 ch c Showcasing Adaptability (Mastercraftsman (IRE))
943[8] 6283[9] 7024[10]

Formal Order *J P Murtagh* a75 74
3 b g Iffraaj Full Mandate (IRE) (Acclamation)
523[2]

Formi (IRE) *L Gadbin* a66 64
4 b g High Chaparral(IRE) Derivatives (IRE) (Dansili)
2647a[4] 3711a[7]

Formiga (IRE) *Seamus Durack* a51
4 b m Worthadd(IRE) Hymn Of Love (IRE) (Barathea (IRE))
1021[7] 1328[12] 1837[12]

Foronceinmylife (IRE)
Jamie Osborne a63
2 ch f Zoffany(IRE) Kirinda (IRE) (Tiger Hill (IRE))
9437[5]

Forrest Gump (FR) *J-M Lefebvre* a52 68
4 b h George Vancouver(USA) Marcela Howard (IRE) (Fasliyev (USA))
5009a[2]

For Richard *John Best* a55
3 b g Muhtathir Retainage (USA) (Polish Numbers (USA))
1677[10] 2550[8] 2967[6]

Forseti *Michael Appleby* a70 42
3 b g Charm Spirit(IRE) Ravensburg (Raven's Pass (USA))
(312) 2559[9] 4360[8] (5102) 5804[12] 7839[10] 8420[10] 9048[12] 9349[6] 9642[3]

Fortamour (IRE) *Ben Haslam* a80 54
3 b g Es Que Love(IRE) Kathy Sun (IRE) (Intikhab (USA))
3157[7] (7303)◆ 8718[3]◆ 9517[4]

Fort Benton (IRE) *David Barron* a59 41
3 b g Big Bad Bob(IRE) Pira Palace (IRE) (Acclamation)
27[5] 477[6] 1720[6] 2016[10] 7286[12]

For The Trees (IRE)
Mrs John Harrington a56 88
2 bb f Ivawood(IRE) Siesta Time (Oasis Dream)
8724[9]

Forthwith *Tony Carroll* a36 41
3 b f Footstepsinthesand Admirable Spirit (Invincible Spirit (IRE))
4116[8] 5062[5] 5797[4] 6361[5]◆ 7027[9]

Fortinbrass (IRE) *John Balding* a47 55
9 b g Baltic King Greta D'Argent (IRE) (Great Commotion (USA))
1192[3] 1368[4] 2532[6]

Fortissimo (GER) *Nicolo Simondi* 75
5 b g Lord Of England(GER) Francfurter (Legend Of France (USA))
3643a[7]

Fortissimo (IRE) *Mark Johnston* a69
3 b g Dream Ahead(USA) Double Diamond (FR) (Muhtathir)
8427[4] 9109[10] 9573[7]

Fort Myers (USA) *A P O'Brien* a105 108
2 b c War Front(USA) Marvellous (IRE) (Galileo (IRE))
2830[2] 3949[4] 4413a[3] 6690a[3] 7195[4] (7879a) 8746a[7]

Fort Templier (FR) *Vaclav Luka Jr* a78 79
3 ch c Champs Elysees Askania Nova (IRE) (New Approach (IRE))
2758a[7]

Fortunate Move *Richard Fahey* a46
3 b f Heeraat(IRE) Fortunately (Forzando)
408[7] 795[6] 1180[3] 2190[8]

Fortune And Glory (USA)
Joseph Tuite a79 79
6 b g War Front(USA) Spain (USA) (Thunder Gulch (USA))
2714[8] 3462[7] 4226[7] (4787)◆ (5136) 5667[15] 6925[2] 7975[4] 8702[9] 9173[4]

Forty Bere (FR) *Robert Collet* a32 60
4 b g Pedro The Great(USA) Kunoichi (USA) (Vindication (USA))
7601a[7]

Forty Four Sunsets (FR)
Richard Hannon a58 54
3 gr f Showcasing Scarlet Empire (IRE) (Red Ransom (USA))
1828[7] 2341[6] 3348[5] 4754[9] 5552[8] 6279[3]

Forus *Jamie Osborne* a67 64
2 b g Mukhadram Anbella (FR) (Common Grounds)
4114[7] 4766[4] 5676[8] 7874[6] 8286[10] (8546)

Forwardly (FR) *Charley Rossi* 60
2 ch f Zoffany(IRE) Ardingly (IRE) (Danehill Dancer (IRE))
6384a[5]

Forza Capitano (FR) *H-A Pantall* a109 109
4 bl h Captain Marvelous(IRE) Fantasia (GER) (Monsun (GER))
1919[7] 2667a[5] 4205a[2] 7254a[8] 8648a[7]

Foulognes (IRE) *F Vermeulen* a77 75
5 gr m Lope De Vega(IRE) Desisterna (GER) (Sternkoenig (IRE))
6031a[10]

Fount *A Fabre* 109
3 b f Frankel Ventura (USA) (Chester House (USA))
3121a[6] 5227a[2] (6142a)

Fountain Of Life *Philip McBride* a57 57
3 b g Garswood Suerte Loca (IRE) (Peintre Celebre (USA))
2550[10] 3277[9] 4121[10] 5031[5] 5653[6] 7450[2] 8292[5]

Four Feet (IRE) *Henry Candy* a46 43
3 b g Harbour Watch(IRE) Royal Connection (Bahamian Bounty)
2790[10] 3464[9] 6119[U] 6802[4] 7374[12]

Four Kingdoms (IRE) *R Mike Smith* a65 79
5 b g Lord Shanakill(USA) Four Poorer (IRE) (Oasis Dream)
1503[5] 2326[6] 2785[2] 3046[6] 4001[2] 4689[4] 4983[3] 5423[5] (5850) 6576[2] 7212[11] 7436[13]

Four Mile Beach *Michael Chapman* a23 27
6 gr g Dalakhani(IRE) Rappel (Royal Applause)
1369[12] 1858[P]

Four Mile Bridge (IRE) *Mark Usher* a57 60
3 b g Acclamation Agent Allison (Dutch Art)
134[3] 1516[13] 2355[5] 2689[5] 3195[8] 4476[3] 5085[4] 6279[7] 6805[4] 7375[4] 7817[5] 8299[3] 8667[3] 8822[5]

Fourni (IRE) *Mrs A Malzard* 29
10 ch m Rakti Eckbeag (USA) (Trempolino (USA))
2003a[4] 4687a[4]

Four Wheel Drive *David Brown* a67 94
3 b g Doncaster Rover(USA) Lawless Bridget (Alnasr Alwasheek)
5244[2] (5738) (6070) 6339[3] (6699) (6976) 7524[6] 8340[2]

Four Wheel Drive (USA)
Wesley A Ward 112
2 b c American Pharoah(USA) Funfair (USA) (More Than Ready (USA))
(8745a)

Four White Socks *Joseph Tuite* a97 106
4 ch m Lope De Vega(IRE) Peppermint Green (Green Desert (USA))
3820a[5] 5190[12] (7635a)

Foxboro (GER) *P Schiergen* a63 71
4 b g Maxios Fair Breeze (GER) (Silvano (GER))
4748a[4] 5410a[5]

Fox Chairman (IRE)
Andrew Balding 113
3 b c Kingman Starfish (IRE) (Galileo (IRE))
(1754) 2558[3] 4013[2] (5182)

Fox Champion (IRE)
Richard Hannon a81 111
3 b c Kodiac Folegandros Island (FR) (Red Rocks (IRE))
(1458)◆ (1888) (2889a) 3951[7] 4705a[3] 5716a[9] 6508[7] 8765[7]

Fox Duty Free (IRE)
Andrew Balding 81
2 b c Kingman Bugie D'Amore (Rail Link)
5186[3]◆ 6424[10] 8128[2]

Foxes Flyer (IRE) *Luke McJannet* a68 63
3 b g Foxwedge(AUS) Midnight Fling (Groom Dancer (USA))
1677[5]◆ 2967[5] 3517[4] 4225[8] 7452[10] 7610[9]

Fox Fearless *K R Burke* a67 75
3 b g Camelot Silent Music (IRE) (Peintre Celebre (USA))
1558[3] 1928[5] 3474[7] 5127[6] 8398[2]

Fox Happy (IRE) *Richard Hannon* a63 52
3 b c Showcasing Roo (Rudimentary (USA))
359[5] 554[4] 1296[5] 1678[12] 3182[4]

Fox Hill *Eric Alston* a53 65
3 b f Foxwedge(AUS) Siryena (Oasis Dream)
1894[13] 3685[8] 4823[2] 5392[2] (5559) 6033[5] (7047) 7486[3]

Fox Kasper (IRE) *Tim Easterby* a70 68
3 ch g Society Rock(IRE) Easy Times (Nayef (USA))
133[5] 698[6] 1178[3] 1568[7] 6678[9] 7049[5] 7540[9]

Fox Leicester (IRE) *Andrew Balding* a79 93
3 gr g Dark Angel(IRE) Pop Art (IRE) (Excellent Art)
(1379) 2082[4] 2414[3] (3261) 4325[6] 5666[12] 7863[10]

Fox Mafia (IRE) *Andrew Balding* a53 27
4 b h Dawn Approach(IRE) Zibilene (Rainbow Quest (USA))
2347[4]

Fox Morgan *Andrew Balding* a32 27
3 b g Paco Boy(IRE) Alovera (IRE) (King's Best (USA))
2624[8]

Fox Power (IRE) *Richard Hannon* a106 98
3 gr c Dark Angel(IRE) Zenella (Kyllachy)
(1926) 9440[4]

Fox Premier (IRE) *Andrew Balding* a88 102
3 b g Frankel Fann (USA) (Diesis)
(2553) (3262) 4017[9] 5583[2]

Foxrush Take Time (FR)
Richard Guest a48 49
4 b g Showcasing Stranded (Montjeu (IRE))
155[3] 273[8] 533[2] 829[3] 984[2] 1078[4] 1431[3] 1679[4] 2234[7] 2595[4] 3006[8] 3298[2] 3705[3] 5435[10] 5653[10] 6499[6] 7375[7] 7732[8] 7873[8] 8072[9]

Fox Shinji *Andrew Balding* a22 60
3 b c Iffraaj Keene Dancer (Danehill Dancer (IRE))
8407[6]

Fox Tal *Andrew Balding* 117
3 b c Sea The Stars(IRE) Maskunah (IRE) (Sadler's Wells (USA))
(7076) 8335[4]◆

Foxtrot Knight *Ruth Carr* a67 65
7 b g Kyllachy Rustam (Dansili)
1507[2]◆ 1818[4] 2294[3] 2709[5]

Foxtrot Lady *Andrew Balding* a94 106
4 ch m Foxwedge(AUS) Strictly Dancing (IRE) (Danehill Dancer (IRE))
2062[6] 2916[4] 4095[16] 4891[7] 5608[6] 6847[3] 7146[5] 7657[6]

Foxtrot Liv *P Twomey* 102
3 ch f Foxwedge(AUS) Bestfootforward (Motivator)
2493a[5] 3115[3]

Fox Vardy (USA) *Martyn Meade* 90
3 b g Frankel Dance With Another (IRE) (Danehill Dancer (IRE))
3699[3] (4187) 5614[6] 6411[2] 8098[9]

Foxy Boy *Rebecca Bastiman* a55 55
5 ch g Foxwedge(AUS) Suzy Wong (Auction House (USA))
60[9] (322) 597[4] 809[11] 1505[7] 2324[11] 2678[8] 3213[13] 3518[11]

Foxy Eloise *Robyn Brisland* 34
4 b m Foxwedge(AUS) Eleanor Eloise (USA) (Minardi (USA))
3707[10]

Foxy Femme *John Gallagher* 73
3 ch f Foxwedge(AUS) Pusey Street Vale (Moss Vale (IRE))
3090[7] 3839[2] (4651)◆ 6286[3] 7022[3] 7299[2] 8521[4]

Foxy Forever (IRE)
Michael Wigham a85 87
9 b g Kodiac Northern Tara (IRE) (Fayruz)
353[7] 551[4] 837[6] 1098[9] 1938[4] 2368[2] 2839[5] 3056[9] (3531) 4253[5] 5606[3]◆ 6455[5] 6809[7] 7321[3] 7771[2] 8023[2] 8601[6] 9057[8] 9550[2]

Foxy Lady *Kevin Ryan* a58 58
4 b m Foxwedge(AUS) Catherine Palace (Grand Lodge (USA))
(462) 814[6] 2330[9]

Foxy Power (FR) *R Le Gal* a49 64
3 b f Power Foxxy Cleopatra (FR) (Slickly (FR))
955a[3] 6094a[4]

Foxy Rebel *Ruth Carr* a22 47
5 ch g Cockney Rebel(IRE) Foxholes Lodge (Nasheyt)
2963[4] 3682[5] 3939[5] 4512[3] 5151[6] 7336[5]

Foxy's Spirit *Clare Hobson* a49 54
4 b m Foxwedge(AUS) Jessie's Spirit (IRE) (Clodovil (IRE))
1710[4] 1935[8] 2234[12] 2595[11]

Fragrant Belle *Ralph Beckett* a84 74
3 ch f Sir Percy Palace Princess (FR) (Dubawi (IRE))
1495[5] 3324[7] 3955[3] 4656[3] 5307[5] 5898[8] (7192) 7845[7] (8696)

Fragrant Dawn *Charles Hills* a64 77
3 b f Iffraaj Festivale (IRE) (Invincible Spirit (IRE))
1975[3] 3195[4] 4663[3] 5355[3] 5734[5] (6540)

Frame (FR) *C Lotoux* a37 73
3 b f Maxios Free Flying (FR) (Authorized (IRE))
6652a[3]

Frame Rate *Iain Jardine* a63 61
4 b g Arcano(IRE) Miss Quality (USA) (Elusive Quality (USA))
2373[2] 2684[5] 3705[9] 5277[11]

Framley Garth (IRE) *Liam Bailey* a81 76
7 b g Clodovil(IRE) Two Marks (USA) (Woodman (USA))
1518[5] 2435[4] 2748[7] 3095[5] 3816[8] 4437[5] 7003[13]

Francisco Bay *Ed de Giles* a73 70
3 b g Paco Boy(IRE) Lucky Breeze (IRE) (Key Of Luck (USA))
3548[2] 3808[6] 4788[3]

Francisco Pizarro (IRE)
Adam West a10
2 b g Bungle Inthejungle Gemini Diamond (IRE) (Desert King (IRE))
9631[12]

Francis Xavier (IRE) *Kevin Frost* a106 105
5 b g High Chaparral(IRE) Missionary Hymn (USA) (Giant's Causeway (USA))
3074[7] 4935[16] 5657[5] (6917) 7622[2] (9094) 9366[7]

Franconia *John Gosden* a76
2 b f Frankel Winter Sunrise (Pivotal)
8913[2]◆

Francophilia *Mark Johnston* a80 78
4 b m Frankel Lady Jane Digby (Oasis Dream)
41[3] 536[4] 1065[14] 2279[2] 2732[5] (3015)◆ 3415[2] 4009[6] (4383) 4752[4] 5623[6]

Frankadore (IRE) *Tom Dascombe* a71 72
3 ch g Frankel Adoration (USA) (Honor Grades (USA))
2101[9] 3052[3]◆ 4291[2] 4549[6] 5385[3]

Frank Bridge *Alexandra Dunn* a24 40
6 b g Avonbridge First Among Equals (Primo Valentino (IRE))
9304[10]

Frankelio (FR) *Micky Hammond* a54 75
4 b g Frankel Restiadargent (FR) (Kendargent (FR))
2526[8] 3268[4] 3867[8] 4445[7] 5416[4] 7678[5] 8396[11]

Frankellina *William Haggas* 105
3 ch f Frankel Our Obsession (IRE) (Shamardal (USA))
2745[2]◆ 3316[6] 4014[6] 5397[3] 6378[8]

Frankel's Storm *Mark Johnston* 90
2 b f Frankel Gale Force (Shirocco (GER))
4918[7] 5387[2] (6035)◆ 6212[5] 7004a[2] 8482a[5]

Frankenstella (IRE) *John Quinn* 49
2 b f Frankel L'Ancresse (IRE) (Darshaan)
8855[6]

Franklin Street (IRE)
Joseph Patrick O'Brien 94
2 b c No Nay Never(USA) Queen Bodicea (IRE) (Revoque (IRE))
8574a[4]

Frankly Darling *John Gosden* 80
2 b f Frankel Hidden Hope (Daylami (IRE))
8432[2]◆

Frankly Mr Shankly (GER)
Michael Bell 72
2 b g Maxios Four Roses (IRE) (Darshaan)
7346[5] 8203[7] 8722[5]

Frank's Law *Keith Dalgleish* 21
3 b g Orientor Berberana (IRE) (Acclamation)
2327[7] 2708[10]

Frank's Legacy *Nikki Evans*
5 ch g Aqlaam Quite A Thing (Dutch Art)
1339[11] 6844[10]

Frankster (FR) *Micky Hammond* a3 63
6 b g Equiano(FR) Milwaukee (FR) (Desert King (IRE))
2290[4] 3053[5] 3704[5] 5474[7] 5816[4] 8663[6]

Frankuus (IRE) *David O'Meara* a92 105
5 gr g Frankel Dookus (IRE) (Linamix (FR))
2119[2] 2574[6]

Frantical *Tony Carroll* a58 59
7 b g Observatory(USA) Quest For Freedom (Falbrav (IRE))
4232[2] 5378[14] 6059[7] 6560[2] 6855[4]

Franz Kafka (IRE) *John Gosden* a85 100
3 ch g Dubawi(IRE) Kailani (Monsun (GER))
1458[2] 1886[2] 2506[3] (3184)◆ 6076[6]

Frasard *Bryan Smart* 84
2 ch c Casamento(IRE) Katabatik Katie (Sir Percy)
3245[4]◆ 4206[2] 4623[2]

Fraser Island (IRE) *Mark Johnston* a74 82
3 ch g Australia Ponty Acclaim (IRE) (Acclamation)
(1845)◆ 2446[2] 2811[7] 3086[3] 4549[5] 4996[2] 5347[5] 5840[4] 6323[5] 7379[5]

Fraternity (IRE) *Richard Fahey* 80
2 ch f Zoffany(IRE) Aurora Borealis (IRE) (Montjeu (IRE))
4605[2] 5170[5] 6697[4]

Frea *Harry Dunlop* a47 46
3 b f Sea The Moon(GER) Patronella (IRE) (High Chaparral (IRE))
78[14] 289[10] 1236[7] 2357[6] 2926[7] 7606[4] 7838[7]

Freckles *Marcus Tregoning* a69 78
4 ch m Arakan(USA) Tarneem (USA) (Zilzal (USA))
(2277) 4235[12] 5373[7] 6160[2] (6804) 7026[2] 8812[7]

Fred *Mark Johnston* 85
2 ch g Frankel Deirdre (Dubawi (IRE))
2957[8] (4282) (5177) 5587[6]

Freddy With A Y (IRE) *J R Jenkins* a50 64
9 b g Amadeus Wolf Mataji (IRE) (Desert Prince (IRE))
1209[9] 1732[3] 3142[15]

Freebe Rocks (IRE) *Ian Williams* a65 59
4 ch g Camacho Shamardyh (IRE) (Shamardal (USA))
309[4] 985[6]

Free Bounty *Clare Ellam*
6 b g Dick Turpin(IRE) Native Ring (FR) (Bering)
1429[12] (Dead)

Free Cash (IRE) *Nigel Tinkler* a28 32
2 b g Cable Bay(IRE) Mill Point (Champs Elysees)
8511[13] 8919[12]

Free Cover (USA) *Andrew Lerner* a80
3 rg f Congrats(USA) Candybedandy (USA) (Holy Bull (USA))
9638a[9]

Freedom And Wheat (IRE)
Michael Blake a63 42
3 b g Fast Company(IRE) Rustam (Dansili)
65[5] 1685[7] 2204[13] 2939[3] 3440[8] 4193[3] 4454[7] 8266[3] 8711[14] 8839[3] 9503[2]

Freedom Rising (GER)
Yasmin Almenrader a93 93
3 b f Reliable Man Focal (Pivotal)
5720a[11] 7499a[4] 7978a[11] 9170a[8]

Freedom's Breath *Michael Appleby* a39 46
3 b f Bated Breath Quest For Freedom (Falbrav (IRE))
598[5] 931[8] 1270[9] 3741[12]

Freedreams *Tony Carroll* a47
3 b f Born To Sea(IRE) Sinaadi (IRE) (Kyllachy)
1034[10] 1358[12]

Free Gift *Tony Carroll* a59 62
3 b g Makfi Aldeburgh Music (IRE) (In The Wings)
1141[9]

Free Love *Michael Appleby* a89 92
3 b f Equiano(FR) Peace And Love (IRE) (Fantastic Light (USA))
(1691) (2255)◆ 2810[9] 3844[6] (4736) 5504[11] 6476[8] 7058[3] 7524[4] 8099[11] 8340[11] 8900[2] 9030[12]

Freerolling *Charlie Fellowes* a88 90
4 ch g Exceed And Excel(AUS) Overturned (Cape Cross (IRE))
(2555) 3680[3] 4305[3] 5174[3] 6347[5] 6964[4] 7457[12] 8130[15] 8498[10]

Freescape *David Marnane* a99 101
4 ch g Cityscape Careless Freedom (Bertolini (USA))
49a[11] 640a[3] 847a[4] 960a[9] 3062a[8] 5205a[15] 6396[8]

Freesia Gold (IRE) *Daniel Kubler* a53 52
3 ch f Havana Gold(IRE) Secret Happiness (Cape Cross (IRE))
319[9] 941[6] 1725[7] 2240[6]

Freestyler (SWE) *Jessica Long* 100
5 bb g Areion(GER) Swedish Girl (SWE) (Swedish Shave (FR))
7498a[2]

Free Talkin *Michael Attwater* a38 35
4 b m Equiano(FR) Where's Broughton (Cadeaux Genereux)
293[RR] 4219[7] 5430[7] 8279[11]

Freiheit (IRE) *N Clement* a69 67
4 b m Acclamation Freedom (GER) (Second Empire (IRE))
1073a[2] 7505a[7]

Frelene (FR) *C Lerner* a72 46
3 b f Dream Ahead(USA) Love Liu (FR) (Librettist (USA))
2090a[6]

French *Antony Brittain* a64 67
6 ch m Monsieur Bond(IRE) Guadaloup (Loup Sauvage (USA))
587[6]

French Asset (IRE)
Sir Michael Stoute a72 32
2 b c Siyouni(FR) Blue Chip (Galileo (IRE))
8504[4] 8858[6]

French Flyer (IRE)
Rebecca Bastiman a44 52
4 b g Pour Moi(IRE) Leavingonajetplane (IRE) (Danehill (USA))
1647[8] 2111[11] 4518[11] 5099[2] 5787[14] 6036[7] 7509[5] 8406[11]

French Heroine *Declan Carroll* a65 63
4 b m Redoute's Choice(AUS) Hasaiyda (IRE) (Hector Protector (USA))
101[6]

French King *H-A Pantall* 118
4 ch h French Fifteen(FR) Marina Piccola (IRE) (Halling (USA))
(894a) (2455a) (4427a) (6007a) 7941a[9]

Frenchmans Creek (IRE)
Seamus Durack a49 25
3 b g Most Improved(IRE) Reveuse De Jour (IRE) (Sadler's Wells (USA))
1344[6] 1725[10] 2216[4] 2941[8] 3407[9] 4485[11]

French Mix (USA) *Alexandra Dunn* a81 82
5 b m Dalakhani(IRE) Alharmina (Linamix (FR))
(404) (457) 3541[3] 3862[8] 4543[2] 5858[5] 6511[5] 7053[8] 8829[6] 9496[11]

French Pegasus (FR) *Y Barberot* a94 77
4 b g French Fifteen(FR) Etrangere (USA) (Fusaichi Pegasus (USA))
2782a[9] 4704a[9]

French Polish *William Haggas* a60
2 ch f New Approach(IRE) French Dressing (Sea The Stars (IRE))
8848[7]

French Rain (IRE) *G M Lyons* 85
2 ch f Siyouni(FR) Evening Rain (USA) (Raven's Pass (USA))
6429a[9] 8164a[5]

French Riviera (FR) *Ralph Beckett* a77 74
4 b m Intello(GER) Ecume Du Jour (FR) (Hawk Wing (USA))
1569[2] 3545[10] 4296[7]

French Twist *David Loughnane* a65 57
3 ch f Animal Kingdom(USA) Braided (USA) (Elusive Quality (USA))
360[4] 1385[4] 6039[8] 6317[6] (6731) 7875[3] 8070[5] 8499[13] 9006[12] 9361[11] 9548[2] 9629[12]

Frequency Code (FR)
Jedd O'Keeffe a66 66
3 ch g Le Havre(IRE) Stylish (Anshan)
1417[11] 2245[2] 2581[8] 4914[3]◆ 5175[6]

Freshfield Ferris *Brian Rothwell* a23 34
3 b f Kuroshio(AUS) Artistic Dawn (IRE) (Excellent Art)
2334[6] 2912[11] 3200[12] 8645[6] 8837[10] 9276[11]

Freshwater Cliffs *Richard Hughes* a70 30
2 b c Canford Cliffs(IRE) Morant Bay (IRE) (Montjeu (IRE))
6755[3] 7186[5] 7605[2] 8201[9] 8546[8]

Fresnel *Jack W Davison* a98 98
3 b f Sea The Stars(IRE) Candle Lit (IRE) (Duke Of Marmalade (IRE))
1307a[5] 2157a[4] 2745[4] 4014[7] 6090a[6] 6692a[4] 7668a[4] 8710[11]

Freyja (IRE) *Mark Johnston* 84
2 ch f Gleneagles(IRE) Crystal Valkyrie (IRE) (Danehill (USA))
6118[2]◆ (6697) (7330) 8397[6]

Frida Kahlo (IRE) *Archie Watson* a42 55
2 br f Society Rock(IRE) Wild Affaire (IRE) (High Chaparral (IRE))
1879[8] 2331[3] 3212[5]

Friday Fizz (IRE) *Mark Loughnane* a53 54
3 b f Kodiac Sugarhoneybaby (IRE) (Docksider (USA))
4367[6] 5057[5] 6587[3] 7472[8] 9547[3]

Friendly Advice (IRE)
Keith Dalgleish a67 81
3 ch g Orientor Secret Advice (Sakhee's Secret)
1337[5] (2477) 2960[3] 3999[3] (4280)◆ 4908[2]◆ 5422[5] 7049[3] 7402[9]

Frightened Rabbit (USA)
Dianne Sayer a49 54
7 b g Hard Spun(USA) Champagne Ending (USA) (Precise End (USA))
3686[7] 6343[2] 7070[11] 7492[2] 7783[2]

Frisella *John Gosden* a77 79
3 b f Frankel Panzanella (Dansili)
(1064) 2768[5]

Frivola *A Botti* 80
2 b f Dawn Approach(IRE) Finidaprest (IRE) (Dylan Thomas (IRE))
7724a[5]

Frivolous Prince (IRE)
Mrs C Gilbert a43 39
6 b g Baltic King Sweet Reflection (IRE) (Victory Note (USA))
2673a[4] 3640a[7] 4175a[5] 4687a[3]

From Me To Me (IRE) *Endo Botti* 95
5 ch g Lope De Vega(IRE) Love In The City (IRE) (Dr Devious (IRE))
8787a[2]

Fromnowon (IRE) *Richard Hannon* 74
2 b f Showcasing Jeanie Johnston (IRE) (One Cool Cat (USA))
4840[2] 5189[3]

Fronsac *Daniel Kubler* a70 66
4 ch g Frankel Riberac (Efisio)
4249[11] 6083[8] 6839[5] 7204[4] 7812[4]

Frontispiece *Amanda Perrett* a40 92
5 b g Shamardal(USA) Free Verse (Danehill Dancer (IRE))
1757[5] 3806[4] (4224) 5811[8] (6156) 8727[6]

Frontman *John Gosden* 79
3 b g Kingman Winter Sunrise (Pivotal)
4121[4] 4452[2]

Front Of Line *Chris Wall* a50
2 b f Cable Bay(IRE) Pivotal Drive (IRE) (Pivotal)
9085[7]

Frost At Midnight (USA)
Mark Johnston 69
2 ch f City Zip(USA) Midnight Watch (USA) (Stormy Atlantic (USA))
5294[4] 5801[2]◆

Frosted Lass *David Barron* a31 42
3 gr f Zebedee Jofranka (Paris House)
1982[3] (2908) 3417[5] 4328[12] 5236[4] 5660[6] 7047[8] 7286[10]
Frosty (IRE) *A P O'Brien* a77 98
3 gr f Galileo(IRE) Laddies Poker Two (IRE) (Choisir (AUS))
6090a[4] 6378[10] 7635a[8] 8367a[6] 8734a[12]
Frosty Tern *Geoffrey Deacon*
3 gr f Aussie Rules(USA) Frosty Welcome (USA) (With Approval (CAN))
2690[14]
Frow (IRE) *Des Donovan* a42 50
3 b g Swiss Spirit Royal Arruhan (Royal Applause)
6737[6]
Frozen Juke (IRE) *Fabio Marchi* 101
3 br c Frozen Power(IRE) Labba (Tiger Hill (IRE))
2887a[4] 8788a[5]
Frozen Lake (USA) *John O'Shea* a69 77
7 b g Elusive Quality(USA) Creative Design (USA) (Stravinsky (USA))
64[10] 599[9]
Frozen Ocean (FR)
Saeed bin Suroor a73
2 b c Dabirsim(FR) Sailor Moon (IRE) (Tiger Hill (IRE))
9107[3]◆
Fruition *William Haggas* a75 65
2 b g Oasis Dream Ananas (Nayef (USA))
6669[9] 8455[3] (8999)
Fruit Salad *K Kukk* a59 59
6 ch m Monsieur Bond(IRE) Miss Apricot (Indian Ridge (IRE))
2671a[3] 3173a[3] (3641a) 4174a[6] 4685a[3] 5232[3] 6553a[5]
Frutireu (IRE) *A Botti* 97
4 ch h Casamento(IRE) Farthing (IRE) (Mujadil (USA))
4432a[6]
Fryerns *George Scott* a56
2 b f Helmet(AUS) Beyond Fashion (Motivator)
8093[16]
Fuchsia *James Fanshawe* a56
2 b f Bated Breath Esteemable (Nayef (USA))
9413[5]
Fuel Injection *Ruth Carr* a49 44
8 gr g Pastoral Pursuits Smart Hostess (Most Welcome)
25[9] 129[10] 322[2] 411[9] 1987[9]
Fuente *Keith Dalgleish* a85 81
3 ch g Havana Gold(IRE) Bounty Box (Bahamian Bounty)
3865[20] 4379[12] 5692[12] 6015[2]◆ 6588[4] 7068[4] 7781[7] 9404[2]
Fugacious (IRE) *John James Feane* 71
3 b g Fast Company(IRE) Dazzling Day (Hernando (FR))
7486[8]
Fujaira King (USA) *Stuart Williams* a73 69
3 b g Kitten's Joy(USA) Cat On A Tin Roof (USA) (Catienus (USA))
2023[4] 9171[6] 9540[2]
Fujaira Prince (IRE) *Roger Varian* 106
5 rg g Pivotal Zam Zoom (IRE) (Dalakhani (IRE))
(2095)◆ 2742[2] 4053[3]
Fujimoto Flyer (JPN)
Emmet Mullins a69 78
3 b f Admire Moon(JPN) Picture Princess (Sadler's Wells (USA))
4136a[8]
Fulbeck Rose *Nigel Tinkler* 38
2 b f Free Eagle(IRE) Penny Rose (Danehill Dancer (IRE))
3196[10] 4075[7] 5196[7] 5789[14] 6271[3] 6539[9]
Full Authority (IRE) *David O'Meara* 94
2 b c Kingman Ashley Hall (USA) (Maria's Mon (USA))
(2561)◆ 3023[5]
Full Court Press (IRE) *P Leblanc* a61 65
6 b g Frozen Power(IRE) Share The Feeling (IRE) (Desert King (IRE))
5761a[5]
Full Flat (USA) *Hideyuki Mori* a96 86
2 b c Speightstown(USA) Golden Flair (USA) (Medaglia d'Oro (USA))
8749a[5]
Full House *John Davies* a58 41
2 b g Lethal Force(IRE) Tamalain (USA) (Royal Academy (USA))
6943[6] 7506[7] 8084[11]
Full Intention *Simon Pearce* a74 74
5 b g Showcasing My Delirium (Haafhd)
253[9] 944[4] 1329[7] (1880) 2611[15] 3462[5] 4028[10] 4643[6] 5144[2] 5821[5] 7684[7] 8495[7] (8827) 9176[3] 9455[4]◆
Fullness Of Life (IRE) *A Botti* 99
3 b f Holy Roman Emperor(IRE) La Badia (IRE) (Stravinsky (USA))
(2161a)
Full Of Beauty (AUS) *J Size* 119
4 b g Darci Brahma(NZ) Pennacchio (NZ) (Align (AUS))
9377a[5]
Full Secret (IRE) *Richard Fahey* a56
2 b f Footstepsinthesand Meadow (Green Desert (USA))
9284[4]◆
Full Spectrum (IRE) *Paul George* a58 52
2 b f Fulbright With Colour (Rainbow Quest (USA))
3257[6] 6029[5] 6287[8] 6799[4] 9330[12]
Full Speight (USA)
Sir Mark Prescott Bt a57
2 ch g Speightstown(USA) Athenian (IRE) (Acclamation)
9392[9] 9607[4]
Full Spirit (FR) *J-M Lefebvre* a60 71
4 b g Youmzain(IRE) Lorie De Ples (FR) (Satri (IRE))
2026a[8]
Full Strength *Ivan Furtado* a35 24
2 ch g Helmet(AUS) Cafe Express (IRE) (Bertolini (USA))
4289[8] 5655[12] 6054[7]
Full Suit *Ralph J Smith* a53 47
5 gr m Dalakhani(IRE) Perfect Hand (Barathea (IRE))
4447[8] 5310[13]
Full Verse (IRE) *Charlie Appleby* 87
2 b g Kodiac Anthem Alexander (IRE) (Starspangledbanner (AUS))
1887[6] 2267[3] (3335) 5587[8] 6727[6]
Fulminato (GER) *Dr A Bolte* a77 87
5 b g Excelebration(IRE) Fulminante (GER) (Dashing Blade)
1827a[4] 2429a[6]
Fulminix (ITY) *Endo Botti* 104
4 ch h Blu Air Force(IRE) Miss Manouche (IRE) (Peintre Celebre (USA))
3643a[3] 4432a[5] 8786a[3]
Fumbleintheforest *Robyn Brisland* a56 40
2 b f Bungle Inthejungle Blacke Forest (Manduro (GER))
3141[4] 3803[2] 5547[7]
Fumbo Jumbo (IRE)
Rebecca Bastiman a41 70
6 b m Zebedee Baraloti (IRE) (Barathea (IRE))
1973[12] 2433[8] 3658[10] 4519[4]◆ (5392) 5659[5] 7507[10]
Fume (IRE) *James Bethell* a48 72
3 b g Frankel Puff (IRE) (Camacho)
289[3] 1894[3] 2293[7] 3202[11] 4728[3] 5215[11] 7915[10]
Fun Fact (AUS) *Bjorn Baker* 93
3 bg g The Factor(USA) Fill The Page (AUS) (Dane Shadow (AUS))
8805a[15]
Funkadelic *Ben Haslam* a46 51
4 ch g Dandy Man(IRE) Cape Elizabeth (IRE) (Invincible Spirit (IRE))
25[10] 2789[3]◆ 3518[13] 4493[4] 6829[9]
Funky Dunky (IRE) *Keith Dalgleish* 50
2 b g Requinto(IRE) Red Blanche (IRE) (Red Clubs (IRE))
7506[6] 7765[4] 8232[6]
Fun Legend *P Bary* a78 90
3 b c Frankel Body And Soul (IRE) (Captain Rio)
1198a[4] 2953a[2]
Fun Mac (GER) *Hughie Morrison* a70 94
8 ch g Shirocco(GER) Favorite (GER) (Montjeu (IRE))
2575[5] 3952[4] 5540[12] 7181[7] (8399) 8726[4]
Funny Kid (USA) *C Ferland* a110 109
6 b h Lemon Drop Kid(USA) Pitamakan (USA) (Danzig (USA))
3123a[8] 7928a[10] 9468[2]◆
Funny Man *David O'Meara* 86
3 b g Distorted Humor(USA) Midnight Thoughts (USA) (Henrythenavigator (USA))
2875[6] 3517[10] 3965[2] (4345) (5175) (5426) 6232[3] 6459[2] 7001[3] 7493[2] 7864[6] 8513[8]
Fureur De Vivre (FR) *B De Montzey* 93
3 ch c Gemix(FR) Martiniquaise (FR) (Anabaa (USA))
3108a[6]
Furia Cruzada (CHI) *E Charpy* a99 96
7 b m Newfoundland(USA) Nuestra Machi (CHI) (Hussonet (USA))
51a[8] 283a[3] 728a[5] 1114a[8]
Furious *David Simcock* a103 94
3 b f Oasis Dream Noyelles (IRE) (Docksider (USA))
(3427) 4023[2] 5143[4] (6148) (6859) 7449[4]
Furiously Fast (IRE) *Dai Burchell* a36 39
7 b g Fast Company(IRE) Agouti (Pennekamp (USA))
85[13]
Furni Factors *Ronald Thompson* a60 56
4 b g Captain Gerrard(IRE) Calgary (Pivotal)
167[6] (973) 1364[7] 2527[9] 3213[15] 3933[7] 4765[9] 5765[11] 7628[9] 8638[8]
Furore (NZ) *F C Lor* 115
4 b g Pierro(AUS) Stormy Choice (AUS) (Redoute's Choice (AUS))
9380a[4]
Furqaan (IRE) *Owen Burrows* a63
3 b f Dark Angel(IRE) Surrey Storm (Montjeu (IRE))
8290[4]
Furyan *Nigel Tinkler* 49
3 b g Coach House(IRE) Lily Lily (Efisio)
1982[11] 2098[8] 2482[8] 4328[5]◆ 4731[8] 5031[8] 5215[6] 5695[11] 6499[7]
Fury And Fire *William Jarvis* a61
3 b c Equiano(FR) Luanshya (First Trump)
367[4] 752[5]
Furzig *Richard Fahey* a98 90
4 b g Monsieur Bond(IRE) Princess Cocoa (IRE) (Desert Sun)
2348[4] (2842)◆ 3356[3] 3867[2]◆ 4403[7] 4892[2] (5436)◆ 6475[6] 8130[13] 9041[2]◆ 9309[6] (9667)
Future Investment *Ralph Beckett* 93
3 b g Mount Nelson Shenir (Mark Of Esteem (IRE))
1824[3] (2524) (3482) 4136a[3] 5541[10] 8098[4]
Futuristic (IRE) *James Tate* a90 77
3 b g Shamardal(USA) Aqlaam Vision (Aqlaam)
6206[5] (7319) 7655[2] (8304) 8495[3]
Fuwairt (IRE) *Lee Carter* a73 70
7 b g Arcano(IRE) Safiya Song (IRE) (Intikhab (USA))
104[5] (618) 856[6] 1143[4] 1644[11] 7789[8] 8690[6] 9054[6]◆ 9176[8] 9283[4] 9453[7]
Fuwayrit (IRE) *Mark Johnston* a87 84
2 gr c Gutaifan(IRE) Can Dance (Manduro (GER))
5523[2] (5934) (6704)◆ 7679[7] 9175[4] 9582a[11]
Fyodor *Seamus Mullins* 17
3 b c Dunaden(FR) Sir Kyffin's Folly (Dansili)
1824[14] 2142[11]
Gabrial (IRE) *Richard Fahey* a97 105
10 b g Dark Angel(IRE) Guajira (FR) (Mtoto)
1414[3] 2105[8] 2573[5] 3069[3] 3863[12] 4319[5]
Gabrials Boy *Richard Fahey* a87 88
3 b g Paco Boy(IRE) Statua (IRE) (Statoblest (IRE))
5656[4] 6274[3] (6544) 6955[12] 9274[4] 9628[5]
Gabrials Centurion (IRE)
Richard Fahey a73 75
4 b g Society Rock(IRE) Flamanda (Niniski (USA))
1271[9] 2785[11]
Gabrial's Kaka (IRE) *Patrick Morris* a64 78
9 b g Jeremy(USA) Love In May (IRE) (City On A Hill (USA))
276[5] 463[7] 1025[8] 1399[6] 1769[4] 1836[9] 2106[10] 2692[11]
Gabrial The Devil (IRE)
Richard Fahey a75 92
4 b g Epaulette(AUS) Grasshoppergreen (IRE) (Barathea (IRE))
1459[9] 2844[8] 3318[9] 3846[6] 4369[2] (4649) 5420[3] 5661[19] 5951[4] 7183[2] 7678[7] 8522[5] (8636)
Gabrial The Giant (IRE)
Patrick Morris a60 67
3 b g Battle Of Marengo(IRE) Compassion (Tiger Hill (IRE))
614[9] 966[7] 1166[4] 1770[4] 2213[6] 2697[10]
Gabrial The One (IRE)
Richard Fahey 83
3 b g Zoffany(IRE) Guilia (Galileo (IRE))
1845[3] 2562[5] (3073) 3842[4] 4321[3] 4362[5] 4906[2] 5424[2] 5706[5] 6716[4] 7144[2] 7683[4]
Gabrial The Saint (IRE)
Richard Fahey a97 97
4 ch g Society Rock(IRE) Green Briar (Compton Place)
1654[9] 1946[9] 2572[2] 3069[4] (4359) 4896[11] 5205a[17] 5420[2] 5661[20] 6714[8] 7142[2] 7431[2] 8317[3] 8512[4]
Gabrial The Tiger (IRE)
Richard Fahey a74 80
7 b g Kodiac Invincible (Slip Anchor)
31[5] 463[4] (840) 1164[4] 1366[6] 1768[9] 2679[4] (3214) 3846[3]◆ 4320[3] (4879) 5274[8] 5708[9] (7183)◆ 7678[11]
Gabrial The Wire *Richard Fahey* 97
3 b g Garswood Nightunderthestars (Observatory (USA))
2525[8] 2825[2] (3307) 3599[4]◆ (4360)◆ 4847[10] 6222[8] 6711[9] (7184)
Gabriela Laura *Alexandra Dunn* a66 48
3 b f Swiss Spirit Tintac (Intikhab (USA))
556[12] 1142[2] 1359[3] 2689[11] 5429[5] 5677[10] 7472[12]
Gabriel Oak *Donald McCain* a55 69
3 b g Sir Percy Maleficent (Azamour (IRE))
4104[4] 6890[5] 9469[8]
Gabriel's Oboe (IRE) *Mark Walford* a49 50
4 b g Rip Van Winkle(IRE) Tinaar (USA) (Giant's Causeway (USA))
1648[11] 2202[14] 3447[9] 3769[6]
Gabster (IRE) *K Kukk* a51 46
6 ch m Iffraaj Mozie Cat (IRE) (Mozart (IRE))
(2003a) 2500a[2] 4687a[5] 6554a[5]
Gaelic Kingdom (IRE) *Charles Hills* a34
2 b g Gleneagles(IRE) Impressionist Art (USA) (Giant's Causeway (USA))
7842[9]
Gailo Chop (FR) *Matthew Williams* a107 111
8 ch g Deportivo Grenoble (FR) (Marignan (USA))
8136a[7] 8578a[9] 8952a[11]
Gaining *Brad H Cox* 105
5 b m American Post Acquisition (Dansili)
8154a[7]
Gainsay *Jonathan Portman* a73 73
4 b m Sayif(IRE) Pesse (IRE) (Eagle Eyed (USA))
(1216) 1655[3] 1850[11] 5087[6] 6717[6]
Galactic Glow (IRE) *William Jarvis* 77
2 b c No Nay Never(USA) Shine Like A Star (Fantastic Light (USA))
2093[3]◆ 4889[5]
Galactic Spirit *James Evans* a72 75
4 ch g Dutch Art Gino's Spirits (Perugino (USA))
617[5] 1095[5] 1291[7] 3467[12] 4224[8] 5625[3] 6278[8] 6830[2] 7816[5] 8248[4]
Galadine (FR) *F Head* a50 66
2 b f Anodin(IRE) Galanaa (IRE) (Naaqoos)
6873a[3]
Galadriel *Kevin Ryan* 82
2 b f Dutch Art Handbell (IRE) (Acclamation)
2805[4]◆ 4048[14] 5387[4] (6096) 7117[5]
Gala N Dandy (IRE) *S M Duffy* a46 41
4 b m Dandy Man(IRE) Luggala (IRE) (Kahyasi (IRE))
8840[11] 8898[9]
Galata Bridge *Sir Michael Stoute* a69
2 b c Golden Horn Infallible (Pivotal)
8604[6]
Galaxy Road (USA) *M Al Mheiri* a70
3 br c Elusive Quality(USA) Nana Anna (USA) (Henny Hughes (USA))
169a[12]
Gale Force Maya *Michael Dods* a64 92
3 ch f Gale Force Ten Parabola (Galileo (IRE))
(2293) 2897[3] 3719[3] 4288[9] (4822) (5724) (6623) 7380[2] 7613[2]
Galileo Jade (IRE) *Richard Hannon*
3 b f Australia Dusty In Memphis (USA) (Broken Vow (USA))
3761[7] 4641[10]
Galileo Silver (IRE) *Alan King* a89 76
4 gr g Galileo(IRE) Famous (IRE) (Danehill Dancer (IRE))
2769[8] 3860[4] (4792)
Galileo's Spear (FR)
Sir Mark Prescott Bt a73 74
6 b h Galileo(IRE) Lady Shakespeare (USA) (Theatrical (IRE))
99[3]◆ 700[6] 1196[3] 1429[5] 1815[3]
Galio Chop (FR) *A Chopard* 58
2 b c Kheleyf(USA) Gooseley Lane (Pyramus (USA))
3333a[8]
Galispeed (FR) *Archie Watson* a63 54
2 b g Galiway Becquaspeed (FR) (Country Reel (USA))
3990[7] 7154[8] 8717[6] 9137[5]◆
Galitello *Mark Johnston* a67 68
4 b g Intello(GER) Coventina (IRE) (Daylami (IRE))
262[8] (566) 1144[10] 1330[8] 1663[6] 2373[10] 3017[8] 3481[5] (Dead)
Galiva (FR) *Mlle Y Vollmer* a50
3 b f Evasive Lady Anouchka (IRE) (Vettori (IRE))
9058a[15]
Gallaside (FR) *Archie Watson* a87 87
2 b c Lucayan(FR) Gallaecia (SPA) (Choisir (AUS))
2761[3] 3245[3] (4289) (5781) (6942)◆ 8029[7]
Gallatin *Andrew Balding* a75 72
3 b f Kingman Fantasia (Sadler's Wells (USA))
3584[6] 4641[4] 5748[3] 6331[6] 7083[5] 7835[2] 9050[9]
Gallia D'Emra (IRE)
Remy Nerbonne 60
3 ch f Tin Horse(IRE) Belua (GER) (Lomitas)
2390a[6]
Gallic *Ed Walker* a92 89
3 b f Kodiac Gallipot (Galileo (IRE))
1857[3]◆ 2821[4] 4393[2] 5253[2] (6709) 7347[12] 7895[6] 8809[10]
Gallic Chieftain (FR)
Archie Alexander a90 108
6 ch h Tamayuz Katerini (FR) (Cacique (IRE))
1784a[6]
Gallipoli (IRE) *Richard Fahey* a97 84
6 b g Compton Place Altadena Lady (IRE) (Imperial Ballet (IRE))
351[7] 805[2] 1181[2] 1916[4] 2378[5] 2609[12] 3100[6] 4385[7] 5200[7] 5546[14]
Galloon (FR) *Y Barberot* a62 67
2 b c Dandy Man(IRE) Haute Couture (FR) (Invincible Spirit (IRE))
1448a[4] 5713a[3]
Galloway Hills *Phillip Makin* a74 87
4 b g Kyllachy Bonnie Brae (Mujahid (USA))
(1976) 2416[4] 2824[7] 3503[3] (3868) 4369[5] 5217[6] 5821[9] 7183[13] 7621[11] 8428[7] 8921[12]
Galope Americano (BRZ)
Mme Pia Brandt a74 88
4 b h Silent Times(IRE) Sul Americana (BRZ) (Baronius (BRZ))
6095a[4] 8240a[8]
Galouska (FR) *D Smaga* a53 79
4 b m Kentucky Dynamite(USA) Calia (FR) (Orpen (USA))
2391a[4]
Galsworthy *John Gosden* a79 80
2 b c Dansili Gallipot (Galileo (IRE))
8460[2] 9095[3]
Galvanize (USA) *Doug Watson* a103 89
6 b h Medaglia d'Oro(USA) Enthused (USA) (Seeking The Gold (USA))
282a[3]◆ 513a[6] 959a[3]
Galzoche (FR)
Mme C Barande-Barbe a44
3 b f Tigron(USA) Genereuse Thocleva (FR) (Gold Away (IRE))
977a[10]
Gamba (IRE) *Richard Hannon* a58 69
3 b f Cape Cross(IRE) Gravitation (Galileo (IRE))
183[13]
Gambon (GER)
Eve Johnson Houghton 82
3 b g Dutch Art Guajara (GER) (Montjeu (IRE))
2139[8] 3421[3]◆ 4116[12] (4655)◆ 5343[5] (6108) 6525[5] 7205[6] 8521[11]
Game And Set *Andrew Balding* 86
2 b f Zoffany(IRE) Grace And Favour (Montjeu (IRE))
4337[2] 5366[3] (6159) 6746a[8]
Game Over (IRE) *Richard Hannon* a28 64
2 gr c Toronado(IRE) Match Point (FR) (Verglas (IRE))
4117[6] 5131[9] 5809[11]
Game Player (IRE) *Roger Varian* a80 104
4 gr g Dark Angel(IRE) Lucky Clio (IRE) (Key Of Luck (USA))
1891[4] (2363) 3009[2] 4097[3] 5610[9]
Gamesome (FR) *Paul Midgley* a73 75
8 b g Rock Of Gibraltar(IRE) Hot Coal (USA) (Red Ransom (USA))
278[8] 610[6] 907[10] 1505[2] 1952[2] 2709[14] (3975) (4632) 5244[8] 6057[4] 7367[3] 8400[5]
Gamesters Icon *Oliver Greenall* a55 83
4 b m Sixties Icon Gamesters Lady (Almushtarak (IRE))
2106[3] 2685[5] 3267[9] 4914[7] 7508[2] (7776) (8247)◆ (8515) (8862)
Game Winner (USA) *Bob Baffert* a118
3 b c Candy Ride(ARG) Indyan Giving (USA) (A.P. Indy (USA))
2425a[5]
Ganbaru (IRE) *A Fabre* a79 71
2 gr c Dark Angel(IRE) Rachelle (IRE) (Mark Of Esteem (IRE))
5468a[4]
Gangster Of Love (FR)
Carmen Bocskai a60 69
3 b c Dream Ahead(USA) Trombe (FR) (Bering)
6062a[5]
Gang Warfare *Alexandra Dunn* a82 57
8 b g Medicean Light Impact (IRE) (Fantastic Light (USA))
1144[9] 1524[3] 1971[6] 2571[8] 3481[6] 4483[9]
Gannicus *Brendan Powell* a47 49
8 b g Phoenix Reach(IRE) Rasmani (Medicean)
436[15]
Gantier *John Gosden* a78 83
3 b g Frankel Kid Gloves (In The Wings)
299[2] (598) 839[2] 1386[3] (1928) 2796[3] 4256[7]
Ganton Eagle *Michael Easterby* 37
3 b g Poet's Voice Our Faye (College Chapel)
3565[8] 4629[4] 4732[7]
Gaon Champ (KOR) *An Byung Ki* a104
4 b h Ecton Park(USA) Ruby Queen (KOR) (Badge Of Silver (USA))
7010a[3]
Garbanzo (IRE) *Ed Walker* a94 92
5 gr g Mastercraftsman(IRE) Noble Fantasy (GER) (Big Shuffle (USA))
(5811) 6958[5] 8114[29]
Garden Oasis *Tim Easterby* a71 79
4 b g Excelebration(IRE) Queen Arabella (Medicean)
2116[5] 3515[10] 4907[9] 5398[5] 6231[3] 6580[3]◆ 7185[5]

Garden Of Eden (ITY) *F Saggiomo* 88
3 b c War Command(USA) Tina Donizetti (IRE) (Monsun (GER))
2887a[9]

Gardol Man (IRE) *G Botti* a74 65
3 b g Dandy Man(IRE) Tullyorior Glory (IRE) (Desert Style (IRE))
217a[4]

Garigliano (FR) *N Caullery* a63
2 bb c Gutaifan(IRE) Green Ridge (FR) (Green Tune (USA))
6141a[5]

Garlizain (FR) *Alexandros Giatras* a79
4 b g Youmzain(IRE) Garlinote (FR) (Poliglote)
8240a[5]

Garnock Valley *R Mike Smith* 52
2 b f Orientor Midnight Bahia (IRE) (Refuse To Bend (IRE))
5485[6] 6606[10] 7211[5] 7506[4] 8180[2]◆

Garrel Glen *James Eustace* 91
3 ch f Mount Nelson Azure Mist (Bahamian Bounty)
2443[12] 3012[5] 4052[27] 7466[3]◆ 7900[11]

Garrick *Tim Easterby* a69 80
5 b g Galileo(IRE) Rimth (Oasis Dream)
1944[U] 2419[9]

Garrison Commander (IRE)
Eve Johnson Houghton a60 75
3 b g Garswood Malea (IRE) (Oratorio (IRE))
1897[9] 2697[8] 3195[5] 3538[5] 4476[2] 4761[4]

Garrison Law *David Simcock* a49 62
3 b g Garswood Cushat Law (IRE) (Montjeu (IRE))
3696[7] 5085[3] 5784[9] 7280[10] 7685[10] 7998[6] 8551[11]

Garrus (IRE) *Charles Hills* a93 108
3 gr c Acclamation Queen Of Power (IRE) (Medicean)
(1692) (2779) 4665[2] 5222a[3] 6423[11]

Garth Rockett *Mike Murphy* a64 57
5 b g Delegator Leelu (Largesse)
430[3] 1684[8] 2971[9] 5144[9] 5526[7] 6131[2] 7527[7] 7811[2] 8018[3] 8255[6] (8757) (9128) 9420[3] 9629[6]

Gaslight *James Fanshawe* a72 61
3 br f Aussie Rules(USA) Isis (USA) (Royal Academy (USA))
2967[2] 4247[6]

Gas Monkey *Julia Feilden* a69 88
4 b g Cityscape Bavarica (Dansili)
250[2] 722[2] 1065[8] 1482[2] (2259) (4220) (4601) 5436[6] (6218) 7729[7]

Gate City (USA) *Adrian Nicholls* a39
3 br g Animal Kingdom(USA) Fu Cat (USA) (Fusaichi Pegasus (USA))
103[7] 4051[3] 5371[0] 1555[8]

Gates Of Horn (IRE) *P Riccioni* 89
3 b c Morpheus Lovegood (IRE) (Desert Style (IRE))
2162a[4]

Gates Pass *Brian Barr* a69 65
4 bb g Showcasing Molly Mello (GER) (Big Shuffle (USA))
464[4] 732[4] 1065[6] 2998[9] 4235[4] 5284[10] 6334[12]

Gatesy (IRE) *John Davies*
3 gr g Swiss Spirit Firoza (FR) (King's Best (USA))
2111[0] 3499[10]

Gatting (AUS) *Darren McAuliffe* 115
5 b g Hard Spun(USA) Stubborn (AUS) (Lonhro (AUS))
8136a[10]

Gaur D'Emra (FR) *Brian Beaunez* a75 75
3 ch c Tin Horse(IRE) Talka (FR) (Vettori (IRE))
2953a[8]

Gavi Di Gavi (IRE) *Alan King* a67 59
4 b g Camacho Blossom Deary (IRE) (Duke Of Marmalade (IRE))
3648[7] 4305[9] 5003[4] 5282[3] 6204[17] (7080) 7812[3] 8923[2] 9361[9]

Gavlar *William Knight* a79 69
8 b g Gentlewave(IRE) Shawhill (Dr Fong (USA))
1291[8] 1943[7] 2571[5] 3377[3] 4791[3] 5812[5] 6720[5] 7845[11] 8654[6]

Gawdawpalin (IRE) *Sylvester Kirk* a73 68
6 b g Holy Roman Emperor(IRE) Dirtybirdie (Diktat)
345[5] 617[9] 1291[11] 2793[13] 3766[3] 4220[3] 9421[7]

Gazelle *Roger Charlton* a67
2 b f Al Kazeem Perfect Practice (Medicean)
8651[4]◆ 9062[5]

Gazton *Ivan Furtado* a61 70
3 b g Equiano(FR) Duchess Of Seville (Duke Of Marmalade (IRE))
4760[2] 5477[5] 6259[6] 7126[5] 8472[3]

Gear Jockey (USA)
George R Arnold II a18 106
2 b c Twirling Candy(USA) Switching Gears (USA) (Tapit (USA))
8746a[3]

Geepower (IRE) *Brian Ellison* 56
2 b g Power Geesala (IRE) (Barathea (IRE))
2475[8] 2706[4] 3098[7] 5146[7] 5800[4] 6563[5] 7284[4]

Gee Rex (IRE) *J C Hayden* 82
3 b g Requinto(IRE) Valentine Hill (IRE) (Mujadil (USA))
2882a[5]

Geetanjali (IRE) *Michael Bell* a89 89
4 b m Roderic O'Connor(IRE) Scylla Cadeaux (IRE) (Cadeaux Genereux)
2230[5] (2902) 3336[3] 4318[5] 4997[5] 6280[3] (6512) (6672) 6854[2] 7895[14] 8701[3]

Geizy Teizy (IRE) *Marco Botti* a82 77
3 b f Lawman(FR) For Joy (Singspiel (IRE))
(2690) 3495[4] 5253[6] 6170[8] 8427[2] 9199[3] 9417[6] (9625)

Gelsmoor Bay *Derek Shaw* a30
2 b f Cable Bay(IRE) Mutheera (Oasis Dream)
5243[10] 5646[8] 6029[8] 6837[10] 7582[12]

Gembari *David Brown* a63 55
4 b g Denounce Zagarock (Rock Of Gibraltar (IRE))
6[10] 9847[7]

Gemini *John Quinn* a49 68
4 b m Makfi Gaze (Galileo (IRE))
1666[5] 2214[6] 5604[3] 6256[6] (6824) 7231[12]

Gemologist (IRE) *Lucinda Russell* a42 56
4 b m Sir Percy Tiffany Diamond (IRE) (Sadler's Wells (USA))
721[5] 6611[5] 6933[3] 7732[4] 8238[8]

Gem Song (AUS) *Kris Lees* 104
3 b c Your Song(AUS) Beautiful Gem (AUS) (Peintre Celebre (USA))
8805a[16]

Gendarme (IRE) *Alexandra Dunn* a71 80
4 b g Lawman(FR) Gravitation (Galileo (IRE))
135[7] 362[5] 859[2] 1292[7] 1848[9] 2279[3] (2468) 2733[2] 2928[2] 3408[3] (3572) 4209[7] 5009a[4] 5012[5] (5570) 5881[3] 6331[8] 6804[4] 7127[7]

General Allenby *Shaun Keightley* a45 51
5 b g Medicean Cat Hunter (One Cool Cat (USA))
3272[2] 3653[10] 5379[5] 5993[9] 8551[5] 8843[DSQ] 9087[5] 9312[4] 9560[5]

General Brook (IRE) *John O'Shea* a55 62
9 b g Westerner Danse Grecque (IRE) (Sadler's Wells (USA))
2468[7] 2720[4] 3000[3] 3571[9] 5378[8] 6104[5] 6599[4] 6843[5] 7116[2] 7492[3] 7985[4]

General Joe (IRE) *Clive Cox* a53 70
2 ch g Siyouni(FR) Shapoura (FR) (Sinndar (IRE))
5809[12] 7113[2] 7842[8]

General Mischief (IRE)
Michael Dods 51
3 b g Dream Ahead(USA) Dorothy Parker (IRE) (Mujadil (USA))
3247[8] 3972[8]

General Patton *Lydia Pearce* a43 14
5 b g Intense Focus(USA) Blandish (USA) (Wild Again (USA))
5867[11] 6327[14] 6733[10]

General Zoff *William Muir* a74 74
4 b g Zoffany(IRE) Aunt Julia (In The Wings)
3091[2] 3693[2] 4257[3] 6044[4] 6348[2] 7239[5] 7845[9]

Genesius (IRE) *Julie Camacho* a70 15
2 ch g Teofilo(IRE) Craic Agus Spraoi (IRE) (Intense Focus (USA))
5512[7] 7579[3] 8717[3]

Genetics (FR) *Andrew Balding* a80 98
5 b g Manduro(GER) Garmerita (FR) (Poliglote)
2574[5] 3346[9] 4418a[4] 5929[2] 6420[12] 7147[6]

Geneva Spur (USA) *Roger Varian* a47 62
3 b f Distorted Humor(USA) My Dark Rosaleen (Sadler's Wells (USA))
5357[4]◆ 6569[12] 7157[6] 7472[11] 8822[7] 9032[7] 9298[5] 9439[7]

Geneva Trumpet *Seb Spencer* a25 36
8 b g Virtual Quotation (Medicean)
1171[0] 3162[10]

Genever Dragon (IRE)
Tom Dascombe a72 71
2 b g Dragon Pulse(IRE) Glen Ginnie (IRE) (Red Clubs (IRE))
2594[7] 5177[7] 5655[3] 8394[9] 9110[2]◆ 9250[6] 9513[6]

Geniale (JPN) *S Kobayashi* 92
5 b h Deep Impact(JPN) Sarafina (FR) (Refuse To Bend (IRE))
3906a[5]

Gennaro (IRE) *Ivan Furtado* a42 68
3 b g Harbour Watch(IRE) Buzkashi (IRE) (Nayef (USA))
1819[2] 2299[7] 4602[8] 5975[7] 7129[8] 8291[10] 8499[10]

Gentle Look *Saeed bin Suroor* a85 94
3 ch g Dubawi(IRE) Rosewater (IRE) (Pivotal)
1823[4] (2333) (2825) 3493[5] 5434[7] 8016[11] 9053[12]

Gentlemen *Phil McEntee* a84 59
8 ch g Ad Valorem(USA) Stoney Cove (IRE) (Needwood Blade)
43 255[4] 381[4] 508[6] (609) (797) 981[3] 1160[3] 1552[5] 1881[F] (Dead)

Gentlewoman (IRE) *John Gosden* a76 82
3 b f Shamardal(USA) Satin Kiss (USA) (Seeking The Gold (USA))
1855[2] 2762[8] 3431[3] 4124[5] 4592[3] (5105)

Gently Spoken (IRE) *Martyn Meade* a48 50
2 b f Gutaifan(IRE) Always Gentle (IRE) (Redback)
5132[9] 7995[5]

Genuine Approval (IRE)
John Butler a66 81
6 ch m Approve(IRE) Genuinely (IRE) (Entrepreneur)
2595[10] 4287[14] (5001) 5285[2] 7474[8] 8703[12] 9168[10]

Geography Teacher (IRE)
R Mike Smith a60 61
3 b g Bungle Inthejungle Magical Bupers (IRE) (Intikhab (USA))
21[7] 341[5] (505) 834[6] 1081[5] 1430[4] 2337[7] 2943[6] (3204)◆ 6610[3] 6937[13] 8646[2] 8903[2] 9337[8]

Geological (IRE)
Damian Joseph English a98 87
7 b g Rock Of Gibraltar(IRE) Bean Uasal (IRE) (Oasis Dream)
748a[5] 7089a[7]

Geomatrician (FR) *Andrew Balding* a57 71
3 b c Mastercraftsman(IRE) Madonna Dell'Orto (Montjeu (IRE))
1852[10] 2795[4] 3724[4] 4929[4] 5954[6] 6681[8] 8065[8]

Geometrical (IRE) *J S Bolger* a64 105
2 ch c Dawn Approach(IRE) Symmetrical (USA) (Unbridled's Song (USA))
6430a[3] 7245a[6] 8356a[5] 8716[10]

Geonpi (IRE) *N Bellanger* a76 76
8 b g Footstepsinthesand Maria Gabriella (IRE) (Rock Of Gibraltar (IRE))
4747a[2]

Geordielad *Oliver Sherwood* a56 49
5 ch g Geordieland(FR) Adees Dancer (Danehill Dancer (IRE))
(38) 810[2] 1341[5] 3272[6]

Georgearthurhenry *Amy Murphy* a47
3 b g Iffraaj Mea Parvitas (IRE) (Oasis Dream)
229[8] 723[9] 827[7] 1732[12]

George Bowen (IRE) *Richard Fahey* a111 97
7 gr g Dark Angel(IRE) Midnight Oasis (Oasis Dream)
1105[3] 1295[8] (1421) 1919[2] 2744[8] 3891[6] 4402[7] 5120[9] 5664[21] 6229[11] 7433[19] 8127[22]

George Cornelius (IRE)
Kieran P Cotter a96
2 b c Bungle Inthejungle Havinaconniption (Aqlaam)
7876a[4]

George Dryden (IRE) *Denis Quinn* a40 78
7 gr g Zebedee Key To Fortune (GER) (Big Shuffle (USA))
791[7] 1394[4] 2272[11] 2611[14] 2940[4] 5289[2] 5532[7] 6335[8] 7078[5] 7690[9] 9089[10] 9219[12] 9386[11]

George Formby *Hugo Palmer* a56 44
3 ch g Mayson Supa Sal (King's Best (USA))
1423[7] 1649[11] 1676[10] 3938[10] 4568[8]

George Hastings *K R Burke* a50 47
3 gr g Gregorian(IRE) Pachanga (Inchinor)
122[8] 765[11] 1270[11]

George Junior *Ed Walker* a46 52
3 b g Paco Boy(IRE) Basque Beauty (Nayef (USA))
7772[6] 9090[12] 9282[5] 9446[13]

George Mallory *Kevin Ryan* a59 71
3 b g Kingman Rose Et Noire (IRE) (Dansili)
1819[4] 2200[6] 3052[6] 3926[6] 5023[7] (5898) 7493[3] 8641[4]

George Of Hearts (FR)
George Baker a71 84
4 gr g Kendargent(FR) Bugie D'Amore (Rail Link)
1753[10] 2609[13] 3009[8] 4255[9] 7413[5] 7975[3] 8412[6] (8761)

George Ridsdale *Michael Easterby* 57
3 ch g Ruler Of The World(IRE) Cape Rising (IRE) (Cape Cross (IRE))
1764[4] 2152[8] 7405[6] 7783[9]

George's Law *Tim Easterby* 39
3 b g Lawman(FR) Despatch (Nayef (USA))
3270[11] 4210[13] 4582[6] 5389[9]

George The Prince (FR) *G Doleuze* a88 91
5 b h My Risk(FR) Sea Starling (FR) (Slickly (FR))
4704a[16] (6267a) 9483a[5]

George Thomas *Robert Eddery* a64 63
3 b g Heeraat(IRE) Lexington Rose (Captain Gerrard (IRE))
2976[7] 3836[4] 4827[6] 7319[6] 8263[16] (9583)

Georgeville *D K Weld* 104
3 b c Dawn Approach(IRE) Big Break (Dansili)
4411a[3]

George Villiers (IRE) *S Seemar* a96 68
4 b h Dubawi(IRE) Comic (IRE) (Be My Chief (USA))
(1001)

George William *Ed Walker* a92 97
6 b g Paco Boy(IRE) Basque Beauty (Nayef (USA))
4299[5]◆ 5188[2] 6214[6] 8062[9]

Georgia Du Rabutin (FR)
N Bellanger 22
3 ch f George Vancouver(USA) Meniska (FR) (Invincible Spirit (IRE))
5165a[11]

Georgian Bay (IRE) *Thomas Coyle* a71 68
9 b g Oratorio(IRE) Jazzie (FR) (Zilzal (USA))
(1572a) (Dead)

Geranium *Hughie Morrison* a77 82
4 ch m Sakhee's Secret Kasumi (Inchinor)
2714[12] 3700[7] (5316)◆ (6412) 6672[2] 7465[2] 8014[5] 8812[11]

Gerardino Jet (IRE) *Mario Marcialis* 98
2 b c Henrythenavigator(USA) Ardena (IRE) (Dalakhani (IRE))
4172a[8] 8390a[5]

Gerry The Glover (IRE) *Lee Carter* a63 61
7 b g Approve(IRE) Umlani (IRE) (Great Commotion (USA))
4226[8] 4615[3] 5087[9] 5675[4] 6723[6] 8416[2] (9207)

Gert Lush (IRE) *Roger Teal* a60 68
2 b f Bated Breath Agent Allison (Dutch Art)
3033[3] 4222[6] (6527) 7297[3] 8699[6]

Gervais (USA) *A R Al Rayhi* a83 42
5 br g Distorted Humor(USA) Ruth E (USA) (A.P. Indy (USA))
196a[5] 997[2]

Get Back Get Back (IRE) *Clive Cox* a89 90
4 b g Lord Shanakill(USA) Bawaakeer (USA) (Kingmambo (USA))
(2092)◆ 2748[4] 3663[8] 4224[6] 4792[3]

Get Boosting *Keith Dalgleish* a88 75
2 b g Swiss Spirit Inagh River (Fasliyev (USA))
6336[9] 6606[5] 6934[2] 7398[9] 7765[7] (8315) 8817[3] 9162[5]◆ 9364[2] 9607[2]

Getchagetchagetcha *Clive Cox* a105 105
3 b g Champs Elysees Paella (IRE) (Oasis Dream)
1035[2] 1625a[6] (3646)◆ 4013[8] 7565[4] 8005[3] (9366)◆

Get Even *Jo Hughes* a77 75
4 b m Multiplex Retaliator (Rudimentary (USA))
1391a[6] 2182a[3] 2956a[16] 3715a[4] 4532a[6] 7223a[3]

Get Knotted (IRE) *Michael Dods* a96 101
7 ch g Windsor Knot(IRE) Genuinely (IRE) (Entrepreneur)
2396[5] 2843[12] 3863[11] 5453[3] 6922[6] 7431[3] (7781) 8127[19]

Getonsam *Tristan Davidson*
7 ch g Black Sam Bellamy(IRE) Pennepoint (Pennekamp (USA))
7665[7]

Get Set (IRE) *Matthieu Palussiere* 90
2 b c French Navy Almarada (FR) (Le Havre (IRE))
5286a[5] (5600a) 6002a[4] 6746a[5]

Get The Look (IRE) *J S Moore* a43 54
2 b f Brazen Beau(AUS) Confidente (IRE) (Awesome Again (CAN))
3441[8] 4048[21] 5759a[6] 6196a[11] 6584a[6]

Get The Rhythm *Richard Fahey* 84
3 b c Garswood Star Kodiak (IRE) (Kodiac)
(4128) 5589[16] 5661[12] 6676[13] 7402[16]

Geyser *Barry Murtagh* a21 45
3 b g Gale Force Ten Popocatepetl (FR) (Nashwan (USA))
2438[6] 3198[5] 4039[4] 5915[13]

G For Gabrial (IRE) *Richard Fahey* 69
2 gr g Gutaifan(IRE) Cockney Rhyme (Cockney Rebel (IRE))
2561[9] 3071[6] 3841[5] 4317[3] 4878[5] 5781[2] (6097) 6579[3] 6969[6] 7585[5]

Ghaamer (USA) *R Bouresly* a59 74
9 b g Hard Spun(USA) Teeba (USA) (Seeking The Gold (USA))
52a[14] 170a[9]

Ghadbbaan *Sir Michael Stoute* a63
3 ch c Intello(GER) Rock Choir (Pivotal)
6316[6]

Ghaith *David Loughnane* a87 79
4 b g Invincible Spirit(IRE) Wild Mimosa (IRE) (Dynaformer (USA))
1286[3] 1728[4] 5057[3] 5579[2] 8290[3] (9606)

Ghaiyyath (IRE) *Charlie Appleby* 128
4 b h Dubawi(IRE) Nightime (IRE) (Galileo (IRE))
(1628a) 2168a[3] (6771a) 7941a[10]

Ghalib (IRE) *Rebecca Bastiman* a60 80
7 ch g Lope De Vega(IRE) Gorband (USA) (Woodman (USA))
2015[9] 2480[8] (3502) 3811[9] 4445[5] 5095[3] 5594[7] 7829[7] 8237[7]

Ghaly *Saeed bin Suroor* a82 79
3 ch c Dubawi(IRE) Hanky Panky (IRE) (Galileo (IRE))
3003[12] 3648[5] 5268[2] (6169)

Ghalyoon *Marcus Tregoning* a54 93
4 b g Invincible Spirit(IRE) Swiss Lake (USA) (Indian Ridge (IRE))
4298[2]◆ (4927)

Ghanim (IRE) *H-A Pantall* 61
3 b c Shamardal(USA) Dulkashe (IRE) (Pivotal)
4120[6] 4732[4] 6062a[4]

Gharabeel (FR) *F Rohaut* a90 91
3 b f Toronado(IRE) Mi Dica (Green Desert (USA))
9170a[10]

Ghathanfar (IRE) *Tracy Waggott* a66 59
3 br g Invincible Spirit(IRE) Cuis Ghaire (IRE) (Galileo (IRE))
1764[7] 1975[6] 2895[6] 3970[2] 5215[7] 5695[12] 6276[3]◆ (6945)◆ 8025[3]

Ghayadh *George Boughey* a71 71
4 b g Kyllachy Safe House (IRE) (Exceed And Excel (AUS))
1031[6] 1912[12] 2837[6] 3313[14] 4300[10] 6469[7] 7305[10] 8221[10]

Ghayyar (IRE) *Tim Easterby* a73 76
5 b g Power Al Ihtithar (IRE) (Barathea (IRE))
1813[6] 2369[6] 2894[3]◆ 3216[2] 3547[10] 3957[5] 4634[2] 5022[3] 5725[4] 6341[6] 6573[4] 7069[11]

Ghazan (IRE) *Ivan Furtado* a60 66
4 ch g Iffraaj Sweet Firebird (IRE) (Sadler's Wells (USA))
344[6] 1343[7] 1563[6] 1983[2] 2692[3] 3429[9] 4194[2] 4657[5] 5282[10] 6102[7] 7812[7] 8806[5] 9006[8] 9277[6]

Ghaziyah *William Haggas* a85 96
3 gr f Galileo(IRE) Fork Lightning (USA) (Storm Cat (USA))
(4520)◆ (5269)◆ 6406[4] 7895[2]

Ghepardo *Patrick Chamings* a60 67
4 b m Havana Gold(IRE) Clincher (Royal Applause)
2010[5] 2729[2] 3404[2] 4230[12] 5449[2] 6299[4] 7274[7] 8217[9]

Ghislaine *A Wohler* 99
3 b f Soldier Hollow Good Donna (GER) (Doyen (IRE))
6769a[4] 8376a[7]

Ghost Buy (FR) *Ivan Furtado* a57 58
3 b g Orpen(USA) Nantha (IRE) (King's Best (USA))
408[4] 1236[9] 1598[7] 2296[5] 2908[5] 3884[5] 4328[3] 8264[7] 9001[2] 9276[6] 9287[4] 9538a[7]

Ghost Of Alcatraz (IRE)
Richard Fahey 50
2 gr f Society Rock(IRE) Best Steps (IRE) (Acclamation)
4727[6]

Ghost Queen *William Jarvis* a67 73
3 gr f Mukhadram Deire Na Sli (IRE) (Aussie Rules (USA))
48a[13] 997[12] 9203[10]

Giacomo Casanova (IRE)
Kevin Ryan a67 56
3 b c Es Que Love(IRE) Off Stage (IRE) (Danehill Dancer (IRE))
(215) (783) 1193[4]

Giant Expectations (USA)
Peter Eurton a118
6 ch h Frost Giant(USA) Sarahisittrue (USA) (Is It True (USA))
8771a[10]

Giant Hero (USA) *N Bachalard*
3 b g Giant's Causeway(USA) Hollywood Heroine (USA) (Medaglia d'Oro (USA))
169a[8]

Giant Steps (IRE) *Jo Hughes* 44
2 b g Footstepsinthesand Saysim West (IRE) (Kheleyf (USA))
6776a[11] 7674a[7]

Gibbs Hill (GER) *Roger Varian* a108 113
6 gr g Mastercraftsman(IRE) Gold Charm (GER) (Key Of Luck (USA))
4382[P] 6420[4] 6962[8] 7457[3]

Gibraltar (IRE) *Michael Bell* a70 58
2 b g Tamayuz Red Halo (IRE) (Galileo (IRE))
8257[6] 8605[7] 8889[3] 9250[4]

Gibraltarian (IRE) *Jim Boyle* a54 52
3 b f War Command(USA) Star Of Gibraltar (Rock Of Gibraltar (IRE))
5748[5] 6290[7] 6811[7] 9005[11] 9216[12] 9481[6]

Gidu (IRE) *Todd Pletcher* a66 101
4 rg h Frankel Manerbe (USA) (Unbridled's Song (USA))
5977a[9]

Gift Account *Mick Channon* 17
2 b g Captain Gerrard(IRE) Outside Art (Excellent Art)
1240a[9]

Gifted Dreamer (IRE) *Mark Usher* a33 34
2 b g Morpheus Bronntanas (IRE) (Spectrum (IRE))
4114[12] 4766[9] 5907[5] 7910[8] 8415[13]

Gifted Master (IRE) *Hugo Palmer* a110 96
6 b g Kodiac Shobobb (Shamardal (USA))
1111a[6] 1853[6] 2442[8] 4095[25] 8707[2] 9004[8]

Gifted Ruler *Tom Dascombe* 93
2 b c Muhaarar Dubai Bounty (Dubai Destination (USA))
5845[4]◆ (7645) **8446a**[4]

Gifted Zebedee (IRE)
Anthony Carson a44 49
3 b g Zebedee Zakyah (Exceed And Excel (AUS))
2123[5] 2940[10] 4301[9] **5064**[5] 5532[6] 6048[9] 6321[7]

Gift From God *Hugo Froud* a50 67
6 b g Teofilo(IRE) Piffling (Pivotal)
58[10] 369[14]

Gift In Time (IRE) *Paul Collins* a58 60
4 b g Society Rock(IRE) Gift Of Time (Cadeaux Genereux)
907[8] 2379[8] 2633[4] 3504[9] 3657[8] **6017**[3]◆ 6277[11]

Gift Of Kings *Kevin Ryan* 67
2 b c Kingman Indian Love Bird (Efisio)
6424[6] 7398[8]

Gift Of Raaj (IRE) *Ivan Furtado* a68 70
4 br g Iffraaj Gift Of Spring (USA) (Gilded Time (USA))
8300[5] 9012[7]

Gift Of Youth *Amanda Perrett* a64 54
2 b g Fountain Of Youth(IRE) Margrets Gift (Major Cadeaux)
6287[9] 6807[8] **7570**[4]

Gifts Of Gold (IRE)
Saeed bin Suroor 110
4 b g Invincible Spirit(IRE) Sanna Bay (IRE) (Refuse To Bend (IRE))
(4258) (5667)◆ **6513**[2]

Giga White (IRE) *G M Lyons* 90
3 gr g Dark Angel(IRE) Lightwood Lady (IRE) (Anabaa (USA))
7435[7]

Gigi's Beach *Hugo Palmer* 56
2 b g Oasis Dream Clenor (IRE) (Oratorio (IRE))
7346[9] 7899[7] 8128[7]

Gilded Heaven *Roger Varian* a76 64
4 ch m Medicean Heavenly (Pivotal)
67[6]

Gilgamesh *George Scott* a100 104
5 b g Foxwedge(AUS) Flaming Cliffs (USA) (Kingmambo (USA))
1421[7] **1891**[7]

Gilmer (IRE) *Stef Keniry* a35 40
8 b g Exceed And Excel(AUS) Cherokee Rose (IRE) (Dancing Brave (USA))
2638[12] 3413[6] 4725[6] **4912**[6] 5237[10] 6655[6] 7507[11] 7761[5] 8233[11]

Gilt Edge *Christopher Mason* a60 72
3 b f Havana Gold(IRE) Bright Edge (Danehill Dancer (IRE))
5083[7] 5377[3] (5799)◆ (6397) **(6638)**◆ 7115[5] 7760[5] 8349[8] 8702[7] 9218[7]

Gimme Joy (FR) *Y Barberot* a60
3 b f Rio De La Plata(USA) Milwaukee (FR) (Desert King (IRE))
(5641a)

Gina Bere (FR) *D Guillemin* 82
3 b f Hurricane Cat(USA) Shadow Of The Day (FR) (Until Sundown (USA))
1242a[6]

Gina D'Cleaner *Keith Dalgleish* a21 60
2 ch f Equiano(FR) Sally Can Wait (Sakhee (USA))
1499[7] 7211[6] **8338**[6] 8640[10]

Gin Gembre (FR) *K R Burke* a71 62
2 ch g Dandy Man(IRE) Repechage (FR) (Gold Away (IRE))
1651[4] **1844**[2] 2586[5] 4657[10] 5196[5] 5968[5] 6196a[3]

Ginge N Tonic *Adam West* a50 47
3 ch g Sixties Icon Romantic Retreat (Rainbow Quest (USA))
(765) 1270[8] 1555[7] 2011[6] 3275[9] 3593[6] 3809[P]

Ginger Box *Karen George* a32 28
2 rg f Mastercraftsman(IRE) Ellbeedee (IRE) (Dalakhani (IRE))
7972[12] **8604**[12]

Ginger Fox *David Loughnane* a86 81
3 ch g Iffraaj Rimth (Oasis Dream)
1424[4] 2078[12] 2766[2] 3340[4] 3885[2] 4325[2] 4607[2] 4865[5] 5947[4] 6729[4] 7213[2] 7465[4] 8017[9] (9057) **9476**[2]

Ginger Jam *Nigel Tinkler* a61 87
4 ch g Major Cadeaux Day By Day (Kyllachy)
(502)◆ 742[4] 1765[3] 2153[4] (2638) 2846[3] (4212) (4586)◆ (5244) **(5515)**◆

Ginger Lacey *Harry Dunlop* a34 24
4 b g Showcasing Flying Hi (Kyllachy)
2555[8] 3017[12] **6601**[11]

Ginger Max *Richard Fahey* a60 50
3 b c Garswood Miss Bunter (Bahamian Bounty)
1336[5]◆ 2397[9] 8268[5] 8949[8]

Gin In The Inn (IRE) *Richard Fahey* a67 86
6 b g Alfred Nobel(IRE) Nose One's Way (IRE) (Revoque (IRE))
2117[5] 2526[11] **3971**[3] 4406[10] 4987[6] 5740[6] 6826[3] 7621[12] 8339[8]

Ginistrelli (IRE) *Ed Walker* 84
3 b g Frankel Guaranda (Acatenango (GER))
1824[5] 4063[6] 6411[6] **(6924)** 8513[14]

Ginmann (IRE) *Bolette Rosenlund* 93
5 b g Fast Company(IRE) Auspicious (Shirley Heights)
3902a[6] 4419a[6]

Gino Wotimean (USA)
Noel Williams a66 37
3 bb g Gio Ponti(USA) Promulgation (USA) (Street Cry (IRE))
66[5] 343[3] **2697**[6] 3765[5]

Gin Palace *Eve Johnson Houghton* a75 89
3 b g Swiss Spirit Regal Curtsy (Royal Applause)
2035[6] (2927) 3471[8] 4994[4] (5505) **(6155)** 6670[3] 7617[6]

Ginvincible *James Given* a60 68
3 gr f Zebedee Gone Sailing (Mizzen Mast (USA))
412[4] 3339[2] **(4033)** 4783[5] **5791**[3] 6715[4] 8263[17] 8861[8]

Giogiobbo *Nick Littmoden* a94 80
6 b h Bahamian Bounty Legnani (Fasliyev (USA))
297[5] **762**[8] 909[9] 1289[4] 1916[3] 2442[6] 3301[5] 3492[4] 4379[4]

Giorgio (FR) *C Scandella*
2 ch c George Vancouver(USA) Berceuse (Mtoto)
5763a[10]

Giovanna Blues (USA)
Francine A Villeneuve a94 91
6 b m Gio Ponti(USA) Blues Legend (USA) (Mr Greeley (USA))
7224a[6]

Giovanni Tiepolo *Henry Candy* a63
2 b c Lawman(FR) Leopard Creek (Weldnaas (USA))
9008[7] 9385[6]

Gipsy Song (FR) *M Delzangles* 87
4 b m Makfi Singing Machine (USA) (Rossini (USA))
(1245a) 5410a[9] (9537a)

Girl From Mars (IRE)
Tom Dascombe 56
2 b f Make Believe Miss Lucy Jane (Aqlaam)
7677[7] **8258**[4] 8855[7]

Girl Of Dreams *Nikki Evans* a22
2 b f Heeraat(IRE) Princess Of Rock (Rock Of Gibraltar (IRE))
8999[12] 9323[9] **9641**[7]

Giuseppe Cassioli *Charles Hills* 51
2 b c Bated Breath Olympic Medal (Nayef (USA))
5186[10]

Giuseppe Garibaldi (IRE)
John M Oxx 96
4 b h Galileo(IRE) Queenscliff (IRE) (Danehill Dancer (IRE))
894a[11] 5404a[3] 5874a[6]

Giuseppe Piazzi (IRE)
Flemming Velin 85
7 b h Galileo(IRE) Belesta (Xaar)
7498a[10]

Give Battle (IRE) *C Byrnes* a57 54
7 b g Intikhab(USA) Hugs 'n Kisses (IRE) (Noverre (USA))
3500[5] 7300[8]

Give Em A Clump (IRE)
Victor Dartnall a43 54
4 br g Camacho Pixie's Blue (IRE) (Hawk Wing (USA))
920[11] **3475**[11]

Give Him Time *Nick Gifford* a76 76
8 b g Kalanisi(IRE) Delayed (FR) (Fijar Tango (FR))
2400[9] **2793**[4] 3633[12] 7083[11]

Give It Some Teddy *Tim Easterby* a45 90
5 b g Bahamian Bounty Croeso Cariad (Most Welcome)
(1644) 2584[6] 2873[8] 3867[12] 4079[7] 4403[10] 5693[11] 5970[2] 6460[3] 6998[4]◆ (7312) **(7906)**

Give Me Breath *Sir Michael Stoute* a64 37
3 b f Bated Breath Watchoverme (Haafhd)
4110[10] **5138**[7]

Given (IRE) *Debbie Hughes* 24
2 b f Ivawood(IRE) Annacurra (IRE) (Verglas (IRE))
6640[10]

Given Choice (IRE) *Simon Crisford* a86 62
4 b m Teofilo(IRE) Eldalil (Singspiel (IRE))
(119) 291[5]

Givepeaceachance *Denis Coakley* a62 58
4 b m Declaration Of War(USA) Mount Crystal (IRE) (Montjeu (IRE))
1334[2] **2595**[2]◆ 3015[6] 3834[2] 5285[3] 6077[5] 7759[2] 8347[5] 8696[3]

Giving Back *Alan King* a72 68
5 bg m Midnight Legend Giving (Generous (IRE))
3495[13] 4503[6] 5048[5] 5891[7] (6849) (7300) 7558[4] **(9204)**

Giving Glances *Alan King* a86 89
4 b m Passing Glance Giving (Generous (IRE))
7900[4]

Giving Wings (FR)
Matthieu Palussiere 47
3 b g Elusive City(USA) Dovima (IRE) (Dream Well (FR))
2265a[12] 3139a[11]

Givinitsum (SAF)
Eve Johnson Houghton a63 91
3 b g Lateral Fine Hope (SAF) (Fine Edge I)
1414[9] 2260[3] **4348**[4] 5173[10] 5862[4] 6319[7]

Giza Goddess (USA) *John Shirreffs* 102
3 rg f Cairo Prince(USA) Comfort And Joy (USA) (Harlan's Holiday (USA))
9637a[4]

Glaceon (IRE) *Tina Jackson* a56 58
4 b m Zoffany(IRE) Ihtiraam (IRE) (Teofilo (IRE))
2580[4] 3297[7] 3970[7] **(4131)** 4728[8] **5096**[2] 5556[10]

Glaciate *P Bary* a77 80
3 b f Kingman Winter Silence (Dansili)
9058a[3]

Glacier Fox *Mark Loughnane* a38 57
4 ch g Foxwedge(AUS) Beat Seven (Beat Hollow)
1080[3] **(2056)** 2628[5] 3217[5] 3959[9] 4658[8] 8422[13] 8862[13] 9310[15]

Gladden (IRE) *Lee Carter* a52 44
4 ch m Teofilo(IRE) Ballantrae (IRE) (Diktat)
474[6] 5430[11] 7200[4] 8553[4] **9289**[2] 9589[16]

Gladice *Marco Botti* a68 71
2 b f Intello(GER) Amurra (Oasis Dream)
3990[5] 4766[3] 6629[3]◆ (7031) **7724a**[6]

Glad Memory (GER) *F Head* a63 69
3 b f Medicean Glady Romana (GER) (Doyen (IRE))
993a[9]

Glaer *John Gosden* a65
2 b c Siyouni(FR) Glorious Sight (IRE) (Singspiel (IRE))
8714[6]

Glamorous Anna
Christopher Mason a82 84
2 b f Cable Bay(IRE) Go Glamorous (IRE) (Elnadim (USA))
3419[11] 3835[6] (4871) 5544[6] 6157[5] **6713**[3]◆ 7156[3] 7813[3] 8219[3]

Glamorous Crescent *Grace Harris* a63 60
3 ch f Stimulation(IRE) Go Glamorous (IRE) (Elnadim (USA))
2474[3] 2995[2] 3697[3] (4180) 4874[3] 5377[4] 6856[2] 7236[14] 8255[2] **8698**[2]

Glamorous Force *Ronald Harris* a51 37
2 b g Lethal Force(IRE) Glamorous Spirit (IRE) (Invincible Spirit (IRE))
4373[6] 4871[6] **6979**[3] 7853[4]

Glamorous Rocket (IRE)
Christopher Mason a50 75
4 gr m Dark Angel(IRE) Glamorous Spirit (IRE) (Invincible Spirit (IRE))
2272[13] 3037[4] 3576[9] 5375[5] **5990**[2] 6299[2] 7178[4] 9135[9] 9390[8]

Glance *Ralph Beckett* a98 103
3 b f Dansili Look So (Efisio)
2806[3] 3387a[3] 4332[5] **5397**[2] 6775a[7] (9170a)

Glan Y Gors (IRE) *David Thompson* a83 81
7 bb g High Chaparral(IRE) Trading Places (Dansili)
(101)◆ (272) 522[5] (737) 948[2] **1220**[2] 1425[6] 1596[3] 2092[5] 2636[2] 2748[6] 3653[9] 4381[8] 4913[11] 6736[4] 7003[10] 7301[8]

Glasgon *Ray Craggs* a54 46
9 gr g Verglas(IRE) Miss St Tropez (Danehill Dancer (IRE))
208[14]

Glasses Up (USA) *R Mike Smith* 84
4 ch g English Channel(USA) Hurricane Hallie (USA) (Hurricane Run (IRE))
4057[3] 4692[5] 5240[4] 5489[4] 5849[3] 6475[10] 7212[7]◆ 7379[3] 7782[2] 8237[3]◆ 8396[10]

Glass Slippers *Kevin Ryan* 117
3 b f Dream Ahead(USA) Night Gypsy (Mind Games)
1751[14] 3085[5] 4101[2] 4891[4] (5714a) (7254a) **(7943a)**

Glassy Waters (USA)
Saeed bin Suroor a98 45
5 ch h Distorted Humor(USA) Captivating Lass (USA) (A.P. Indy (USA))
172a[11] (Dead)

Glasvegas (IRE) *Keith Dalgleish* 98
2 b g Zebedee Rejuvenation (IRE) (Singspiel (IRE))
2367[2] (2783) **3988**[3] 7119[8] (7506) 7904[11]

Gleaming Arch *Fred Watson* a63 42
5 b g Arabian Gleam Mrs Quince (Mark Of Esteem (IRE))
4586[10] 5094[9] (7307) 7959[4] **8925**[3]

Gleeds Girl *Mick Channon* 71
2 ch f Equiano(FR) Linda (FR) (Tamayuz)
5772[11] 6300[3]◆ 7407[3] **(7754)**

Gleeful *David O'Meara* a71 72
3 b f Pivotal Merletta (Raven's Pass (USA))
1985[4] 2630[4] 3146[3] **3801**[2] 4335[6] 7298[3] (9032) 9559[6]

Glenamoy Lad *Michael Wigham* a81 97
5 b g Royal Applause Suzy Alexander (Red Ransom (USA))
170a[6] 639a[8] 729a[8] 843a[7] 6404[6] 6953[6] 7431[20] 9348[9]

Glencoe Boy (IRE) *David Flood* a58
2 b g Gleneagles(IRE) Eastern Appeal (IRE) (Shinko Forest (IRE))
6344[7] **7842**[7] 8919[5]

Glendevon (USA) *Richard Hughes* a108 85
4 ch g Scat Daddy(USA) Flip Flop (FR) (Zieten (USA))
1289[2] **1922**[3] 3074[8] 3987[28] 4292[10] 5188[7] 5546[18] 6150[9] 6861[6] 9053[3]◆ 9418[8]

Glen Esk *Chris Wall* a66 62
2 b g Kyllachy Ski Slope (Three Valleys (USA))
5655[6] 6161[7] 6673[6] **7277**[2]◆

Glen Force (IRE)
Sir Mark Prescott Bt a76
2 b c Gleneagles(IRE) Lethal Quality (USA) (Elusive Quality (USA))
9107[2]◆ 9347[3]◆

Glengarry *Keith Dalgleish* a90 87
6 b g Monsieur Bond(IRE) Lady McBeth (IRE) (Avonbridge)
2242[2] 3179[5] 4292[6] 4511[5] 4980[6] 5434[4] 5903[6] (6935) 7212[4] 7362[9] 8024[12] 8498[8]

Glenglade *Ismail Mohammed* a100 82
4 b h Shamardal(USA) Nantyglo (Mark Of Esteem (IRE))
97a[7]

Glengowan (IRE) *Paul Cole* 80
2 b f Kingman Pink Damsel (IRE) (Galileo (IRE))
(6774a) 8482a[7]

Gleniffer *Jim Goldie* 69
3 b g Orientor Glenlini (Bertolini (USA))
4827[5] 5554[6] 6206[4] 6608[5] **6932**[3]

Glenn Coco *Stuart Williams* a93 91
5 gr g Aussie Rules(USA) Las Hilanderas (USA) (El Prado (IRE))
34[3] (381) (1143)◆ **(1881)** (2799) 4654[4] 5195[3] 6220[9] 7164[5] 7462[4] 9053[7] 9254[4]

Glenorchy (IRE) *Mme Pia Brandt* a75 81
3 b g Makfi Celestina Agostino (USA) (Street Cry (IRE))
9504a[5]

Glen Shiel *Archie Watson* a98 105
5 ch g Pivotal Gonfilia (GER) (Big Shuffle (USA))
6861[5] **7563**[2] 8336[4] 9014a[9] 9309[8]

Glenties (USA) *Mark Johnston* a82
2 b c Karakontie(JPN) Candy Kitty (USA) (Lemon Drop Kid (USA))
7821[2]◆ **8121**[2]◆ 8717[4]

Global Academy (IRE)
Gay Kelleway a89 66
4 b g Zebedee Lady Meagan (IRE) (Val Royal (FR))
1098[4] 1290[3] 1938[3] 2556[9] 4236[7] 4593[6]

Global Acclamation *Ed Dunlop* a61 59
3 b g Acclamation High Luminosity (USA) (Elusive Quality (USA))
437[7] (550) **1167**[2] 2016[6] 2357[11] 3442[8] 3964[3] 4567[4] 5526[3] 6131[7] 6983[9] 8256[3]

Global Agreement *Milton Harris* 64
2 ch g Mayson Amicable Terms (Royal Applause)
5879[3] **6300**[5] 6528[7] **7754**[4] 7980[5] 8430[4] 8856[3]

Global Art *Ed Dunlop* a86 83
4 b g Dutch Art Constant Dream (Kheleyf (USA))
157[2] 434[5] 552[5] **(2124)** **3004**[2] 4209[5] 5436[5] 6289[4] 7465[3] 8197[8] 8692[9] 9199[2] 9480[5]

Global Captain (USA) *Jung Ho Ik* a84
3 ch c Munnings(USA) Queen Mercury (USA) (Langfuhr (CAN))
7010a[7]

Global Challenger (IRE)
Gay Kelleway a44
3 gr g Dark Angel(IRE) Silca Boo (Efisio)
6283[8] **7655**[5]

Global Cloud (GER) *R Dzubasz* 83
3 b f Soldier Hollow Global Beauty (Tiger Hill (IRE))
3639a[7] **7250a**[5]

Global Command (IRE) *Ed Dunlop* a59
3 b g War Command(USA) Parsley (IRE) (Zebedee)
3003[10]

Global Destination (IRE)
Ed Dunlop a63 73
3 b g Slade Power(IRE) Silk Trail (Dubai Destination (USA))
954[4] 1346[7] 3354[6] (3764) **(4218)** 5002[8] 5847[5] 7731[3] 8691[5]

Global Esteem (IRE) *Gay Kelleway* a56 73
2 b c Kodiac Baltic Belle (IRE) (Redback)
7055[3] 9567[5]

Global Exceed *Karen Tutty* a65 67
4 b g Exceed And Excel(AUS) Blue Maiden (Medicean)
928[3]◆ 1160[4] **1684**[3] 1932[7] 2318[7] 2847[11] 3704[3] 5021[6]◆ 7652[3]◆ 8405[11] 8713[12] 8923[12]

Global Express *Ed Dunlop* a66 76
3 ch g New Approach(IRE) All For Laura (Cadeaux Genereux)
1898[4] **2289**[3] 5124[4] 6083[9] 7773[7] 8413[11]

Global Falcon *Charles Hills* a74 85
3 ch c Siyouni(FR) Maggi Fong (Dr Fong (USA))
1034[4]◆ 1652[5] 2354[6] (4656) **(4929)** 5943[6] 8082[8]

Global Freedom *Ed Dunlop* a53 57
3 b g Maxios Modesty's Way (USA) (Giant's Causeway (USA))
1754[12] 2128[7] 2941[5] **3275**[4]

Global Giant *Ed Dunlop* a113 100
4 b h Shamardal(USA) Aniseed (IRE) (Dalakhani (IRE))
3953[15] **4411a**[5]

Global Gift (FR) *Ed Dunlop* a64 94
3 b g Invincible Spirit(IRE) Special Gift (IRE) (New Approach (IRE))
1381[4] 1886[8] 2147[2]◆ (3249) (3728) (4325) 5192[8] 6258[3] 7068[3] **7680**[3] 8260[6]

Global Goddess (IRE)
Gay Kelleway a60 44
3 b f Morpheus Church Mice (IRE) (Petardia)
1831[1] **476**[2] 2926[14] 5377[8] 5866[7]

Global Heat (IRE) *Saeed bin Suroor* a80 94
3 b g Toronado(IRE) Raskutani (Dansili)
2208[2] **(2872)**

Global Hope (IRE) *Gay Kelleway* a75 70
4 b g Oasis Dream Classic Remark (IRE) (Dr Fong (USA))
2002a[11] 2782a[11] 3351[3] 4081[7] 4303[5] 4733[3] 5526[2] (5864) 6518[3] (7320) 7402[19] **8419**[2] 9306[7]

Global Humor (USA) *Jim Goldie* a67 57
4 b g Distorted Humor(USA) In Bloom (USA) (Discreet Cat (USA))
463[6] 5852[8] 6978[3] 8712[4] **(9106)**◆ 9223[6] 9397[6]

Global Hunter (IRE)
Saeed bin Suroor 90
3 b c Kodiac Romie's Kastett (GER) (Halling (USA))
(4738) **(5451)** 6258[6]

Global Melody *Phil McEntee* a71 72
4 b g Hellvelyn Dash Of Lime (Bold Edge)
2[4]◆ 1522[4] 1973[3] 2296[4] **2580**[2] 3207[6] 3701[4] 3771[4] 3936[4] 9089[8] 9185[3] 9337[4] 9545[2] 9622[8]

Global Myth (USA) *Robert Cowell* a42 48
3 b c Scat Daddy(USA) Excelente (IRE) (Exceed And Excel (AUS))
215[9]

Global Orchid (IRE)
Tom Dascombe a46
2 b f Showcasing Law Keeper (IRE) (Lawman (FR))
7580[10] 8510[15]

Global Prospector (USA) *Clive Cox* a85 62
3 bb c Scat Daddy(USA) Alegendinmyownmind (Cape Cross (IRE))
(1236) 1909[3]

Global Quality *Charles Hills* 69
3 ch g No Nay Never(USA) Dynacam (USA) (Dynaformer (USA))
1886[14]

Global Rock (FR) *Ed Dunlop* a48 66
3 b g Siyouni(FR) Baino Rock (FR) (Rock Of Gibraltar (IRE))
1755[8] 3247[11] **4806**[4]◆ 7858[11] 8434[13]

Global Rose (IRE) *Gay Kelleway* a51 67
4 b m Dark Angel(IRE) Classic Falcon (IRE) (Dubawi (IRE))
4074[7] **4751**[2]

Global Spirit *Roger Fell* a68 83
4 b g Invincible Spirit(IRE) Centime (Royal Applause)
2788[2] (3221) 3706[6] 3722[4] 4552[2] (4693) 5303[4] **6677**[2] 8342[6]

Global Storm (IRE) *Charlie Appleby* a76 86
2 ch g Night Of Thunder(IRE) Travel (USA) (Street Cry (IRE))
5331[2] 5940[2] 7162[3] **(8760)**

Global Style (IRE) *Tony Carroll* a70 67
4 b g Nathaniel(IRE) Danaskaya (IRE) (Danehill (USA))
135[11] **364**[3] **836**[3] 1025[7] 1653[5]

Global Tango (IRE) *Luke McJannet* a93 90
4 gr g Zebedee Beautiful Dancer (IRE) (Danehill Dancer (IRE))
24[5] 361[5] 1036[4] (1357) **(1496)** 1942[6] 2791[4] 5649[5] 6220[10] 6440[4] 7205[5] 7372[7]

Global Warning *Ed Dunlop* a87 43
3 b g Poet's Voice Persario (Bishop Of Cashel)
1423^3 ***(1925)*** 2414^{10} *3465^4 4793^7*

Global Wonder (IRE) *Suzi Best* a65 59
4 b g Kodiac Traveller's Tales (Cape Cross (IRE))
145^2 ***(309)*** 473^8 1065^9 9047^{10} 9306^8 9426^8 *9663^{10}*

Globe Theatre (USA) *A P O'Brien* a76 77
3 b c War Front(USA) Was (IRE) (Galileo (IRE))
3104a^{13}

Gloria *Mme M Bollack-Badel* a90 90
4 gr m Showcasing Go East (GER) (Highest Honor (FR))
(1391a) 3136a^8 4704a^4

Gloria Bere (FR) *J Boisnard* a73 67
3 gr f Peer Gynt(JPN) Miss Fine (FR) (Kaldoun (FR))
7061a^3

Gloriano (IRE) *Paul Webber*
2 b c Authorized(IRE) Gloriana (FR) (Footstepsinthesand)
9052^{14}

Glorious Artist (IRE) *F C Lor* a101 92
5 b g Zoffany(IRE) Queenie Keen (IRE) (Refuse To Bend (IRE))
7011a^4

Glorious Caesar *Ed Walker* a69 54
2 b g Holy Roman Emperor(IRE) Electric Feel (Firebreak)
6905^9 **9208**^{5} *9509^7*

Glorious Charmer
Michael Herrington a71 64
3 b g Charm Spirit(IRE) Fantacise (Pivotal)
3048^5 3659^4 *9348^{10} 9517^9*

Glorious Dane *Mark Walford* a67 70
3 b g Olympic Glory(IRE) Kaminari (IRE) (Sea The Stars (IRE))
1494^2 (2417) **3415**^{3} 4602^{11} 5975^6 *8019^3 9093^2*

Glorious Emaraty (FR)
Mme G Rarick a69 72
3 b g George Vancouver(USA) Ascot Glory (IRE) (Kheleyf (USA))
217a^2 1598^5 **3590**^{2} 4103^6 *9058a^9*

Glorious Forever *F C Lor* 116
5 ch g Archipenko(USA) Here To Eternity (USA) (Stormy Atlantic (USA))
9380a^6

Glorious Jem *David Lanigan* a68 72
4 b g Helmet(AUS) Polar Jem (Polar Falcon (USA))
4283^7 **5373**^{3} *6050^5*

Glorious Journey *Charlie Appleby* 114
4 b g Dubawi(IRE) Fallen For You (Dansili)
2609^8 2916^2 4389^2 4923^8 **(6215)** 7944a^9

Glorious Lover (IRE) *Ed Walker* a101 96
3 b g Tamayuz Love Match (Danehill Dancer (IRE))
2378^2 2834^5 4016^9

Glorious Poet *S bin Ghadayer* a76 80
6 ch g Poet's Voice Sky Wonder (Observatory (USA))
1322a^{13}

Glorious Return (IRE)
Jonathan Portman a59 27
2 ch c Camacho Coming Back (Fantastic Light (USA))
3760^6

Glorious Rio (IRE) *Charles Hills* 23
2 b g Gutaifan(IRE) Renaissance Rio (IRE) (Captain Rio)
5172^9

Glorious Rocket *John Hodge* a44 38
5 b g Bated Breath Up And About (Barathea (IRE))
210^{13}

Glorious Warrior (IRE)
Caroline Fuchs 39
4 ch g Shamardal(USA) Guangzhou (GER) (Konigstiger (GER))
9537a^{12}

Glorious Zoff (IRE) *Charles Hills* 72
2 b g Zoffany(IRE) Ardbrae Lady (Overbury (IRE))
5125^7 **5572**^{4}

Glory *Richard Hannon* a70 61
3 b g Olympic Glory(IRE) Updated (FR) (New Approach (IRE))
1352^4 **2114**^{4} 2630^5 4926^5 *5731^3* 6083^7 6810^8 *7083^7*

Gloryana *Archie Watson* a71 58
2 b f Invincible Spirit(IRE) Tymora (USA) (Giant's Causeway (USA))
4605^6 ***5732***^{4} *6185^6*

Glory Awaits (IRE) *David Simcock* a81 81
9 ch g Choisir(AUS) Sandbox Two (IRE) (Foxhound (USA))
34^8 **429**^{3} *548^6 1213^4 1479^2 1859^{10}* 2739^2 2977^7 3743^4 4566^7 *5267^6 5651^3 6391^2 7191^4 (8549)*

Glory Days (NZ) *Bill Thurlow* 103
6 b m Red Giant(USA) Bilancia (NZ) (Montjeu (IRE))
1784a^3 8134a^9

Gloryella *Brian Rothwell* a36 27
3 b f Yorgunnabelucky(USA) Ceiriog Valley (In The Wings)
1764^{12} ***2375***^{5} 3200^{10} 3721^{12} 4210^{12} 5028^8 *6612^6 8944^7*

Glory Fighter *Charles Hills* a76 71
3 b g Kyllachy Isola Verde (Oasis Dream)
5014^4 5589^{15} 6332^7 ***7771***^{5}

Glory Maker (FR) *K R Burke* 79
2 ch c The Wow Signal(IRE) Storia Dell'Isola (FR) (Vespone (IRE))
3498^3 4551^5 **(5286a)**

Glory Of Paris (IRE)
Michael Appleby a79 51
5 b g Sir Prancealot(IRE) Paris Glory (USA) (Honour And Glory (USA))
34^4 209^3 (276) 526^3 **812**^{2} *1099^5* 1694^{12} *6863^{11} 7191^6 7551^6 8428^{10} 8496^8 8827^4 9048^2 9304^6 9422^4 9561^5*

Glory Street *Paddy Butler* a28
3 ch g Resplendent Glory(IRE) Quality Street (Fraam)
1587^6 4116^{16}

Glory Vase (JPN) *Tomohito Ozeki* 122
4 bb h Deep Impact(JPN) Mejiro Tsubone (JPN) (Swept Overboard (USA))
(9376a)

Gloves Lynch *Gordon Elliott* 92
3 b g Mukhadram Suelita (Dutch Art)
2492a^8

Gloweth *Stuart Kittow* a53 68
4 b m Pastoral Pursuits Dancing Storm (Trans Island)
1586^8 2277^7 **(3541)** 5178^7 7756^5

Glutnforpunishment *Nick Littmoden* a74 75
3 b g Dawn Approach(IRE) Oxsana (Dubawi (IRE))
(1039) 1555^3 2213^4 (2530) (3446) **(4339)** 4906^3 *5778^7 9421^4*

Glyder *John Holt* a43 48
5 b m Camacho Blades Princess (Needwood Blade)
1987^8 **2924**^{3} 3213^5 3577^3 4132^{14} 5765^8 *7628^{12} 8263^{10}*

Gmasha *Robert Cowell* a27 51
2 ch f Intrinsic She's So Pretty (IRE) (Grand Lodge (USA))
8202^4 *8640^8*

Gm Hopkins *Jaber Ramadhan* a74 105
8 b g Dubawi(IRE) Varsity (Lomitas)
51a^9 173a^{13} 961a^4◆ *1112a^9*

Gms Princess *Sarah Hollinshead* a46
3 b f Albaasil(IRE) Zartwyda (IRE) (Mozart (IRE))
6732^{10} 8294^{11} 9011^6 ***9481***^{8}

Gnaad (IRE) *Alan Bailey* a74 82
5 b g Invincible Spirit(IRE) Areyaam (USA) (Elusive Quality (USA))
2781^0 **2272**^{3} 2625^8 5595^2◆ 6080^3 **6668**^{2} 6954^7 7337^5 7828^{12} *8946^{RR} 9203^5 9632^4*

Go Annie Go *Mandy Rowland*
3 b f Es Que Love(IRE) Make It Snappy (Mujadil (USA))
9403^{13}

Go Bananas *Ron Barr* a14 24
4 b m Bahamian Bounty Ribbon Royale (Royal Applause)
5558^{16}

Gobi Desert *P Twomey* 82
4 b h Oasis Dream Household Name (Zamindar (USA))
3103a^8

Gobi Sunset *Mark Johnston* a76 83
3 b c Oasis Dream Dark Promise (Shamardal (USA))
2108^5◆ *2594^4* 3542^5 (4098) **(7391)**◆

Go Bob Go (IRE)
Eve Johnson Houghton a48
2 b g Big Bad Bob(IRE) Fire Up (Motivator)
6344^8

Go Canada (IRE) *A Giorgi* a37 52
2 gr c Alhebayeb(IRE) Zain Joy (CAN) (Survivalist (USA))
5763a^5 **7641a**^{5}

Gocrazyprince (FR)
Mlle L Payet-Burin
6 b g Chichi Creasy(FR) Queenofnerverland (IRE) (Kheleyf (USA))
7223a^8

Goddess (USA) *A P O'Brien* 105
3 b f Camelot Cherry Hinton (Green Desert (USA))
5223a^2 (6090a) (6692a) **7242a**^{2} 7942a^P (Dead)

Goddess Of Fire *John Ryan* a72 51
2 b f Toronado(IRE) Burnt Fingers (IRE) (Kheleyf (USA))
2761^9 *6629^7 6883^7* 7315^7 *(8493)* 8859^3 *9250^3 (9399)*◆ ***(9449)***◆ *9546^4*

Goddess Of Rome (IRE)
Simon Crisford a37
2 b f Holy Roman Emperor(IRE) Gariepa (GER) (Black Sam Bellamy (IRE))
6858^9 ***7515***^{11} *8069^7*

Godfather (IRE) *Tom Dascombe* 46
2 ch c Night Of Thunder(IRE) Aqlaam Vision (Aqlaam)
3866^7◆

God Has Given *Ivan Furtado* a60 68
3 b g Nathaniel(IRE) Langs Lash (IRE) (Noverre (USA))
1857^9 2114^9 **2933**^{5} 3805^5 4994^7 5104^6 6304^7 *8223^5 8903^5 9005^9 9275^7*

Godhead *John Gosden* a86
3 b c Charm Spirit(IRE) Hello Glory (Zamindar (USA))
(9213)◆ ***9502***^{2}

God Of Dreams *Iain Jardine* 53
3 b g Morpheus Bella Chica (IRE) (Bigstone (IRE))
2438^4 3226^6 **4488**^{3} 4820^6 5272^6 6575^3 7207^{10} 7404^5 7780^8

God Willing *Declan Carroll* a67 48
8 b g Arch(USA) Bourbon Ball (USA) (Peintre Celebre (USA))
1026^6 ***722***^{5} 1418^{11} 1647^7 2335^5 4322^9 4582^5

Go Fast (IRE) *N Caulley* a61 88
3 b h Born To Sea(IRE) Juno Blackie (JPN) (Sunday Silence (USA))
5035a^{15}

Go Fox *Tom Clover* a73 72
4 ch g Foxwedge(AUS) Bling Bling (IRE) (Indian Ridge (IRE))
2259^6 4220^{10} **(5354)** *6439^6* 7026^8

Go Guarantor *R Mike Smith* a38 43
5 b g Medicean Furbelow (Pivotal)
2436^7 3175^{10} 4004^7

Going Native *Olly Williams* a56 52
4 ch m Speightstown(USA) Latin Love (IRE) (Danehill Dancer (IRE))
62^7 208^{12} 462^{11} 590^2 829^6 ***(1163)*** *1426^4 1858^3 2196^4 2345^3 2737^8 7873^9 8406^7 8639^7 8904^2 9333^8 9646^3*

Going Places *Roger Varian* 77
3 ch c Frankel Khor Sheed (Dubawi (IRE))
4120^4

Golconda Prince (IRE)
Mark Pattinson a49 56
5 b g Arcano(IRE) Mujarah (IRE) (Marju (IRE))
391^2 941^{14} 1297^7 ***1679***^{6} 2111^{14} 3740^{13} 4615^{12} 5430^5 5675^{10}

Gold (GER) *Markus Klug* 89
3 b f Sea The Moon(GER) Gold Charm (GER) (Key Of Luck (USA))
3119a^9

Gold Arch *David Lanigan* a74 69
3 b g Archipenko(USA) Goldrenched (IRE) (Montjeu (IRE))
(2213)◆ 3418^4 4038^2 *(4769)*◆ 5792^5 *6320^7* ***(7474)***

Gold Arrow *Ralph Beckett* a57 81
3 b f Havana Gold(IRE) Pearl Spirit (IRE) (Invincible Spirit (IRE))
3293^3 4072^6 4635^5

Gold At Midnight *William Muir* a84 82
3 b f Havana Gold(IRE) Midnight Ransom (Red Ransom (USA))
1104^6 1516^6 1857^{14} 2204^{14} (4286) 4651^2 (5191) 5882^5 6162^6 ***6930***^{2} 7351^2◆ *9054^{10} 9387^6*

Gold Bere (FR) *M Rolland* a67 63
3 bb g Hurricane Cat(USA) Sanisa (FR) (Panis (USA))
(442) **698**^{5} *1568^5* 2311a^2 *5407a^5*

Gold Brocade (IRE)
Michael Appleby a69 71
2 ch f Dragon Pulse(IRE) Primal Snow (USA) (Langfuhr (CAN))
9515^3

Gold Club *Lee Carter* a56 55
8 b g Multiplex Oceana Blue (Reel Buddy (USA))
365^8 595^8 2693^{11} **4376**^{2} 5050^9 *6284^6 7784^6*

Gold Desert *Richard Hannon* 74
2 ch c Mastercraftsman(IRE) Tendency (IRE) (Galileo (IRE))
7338^5 **8128**^{5} 8721^5

Golden Air Force (ITY)
F Boccardelli 91
2 ch c Blu Air Force(IRE) Black County (ITY) (Black Minnaloushe (USA))
4172a^3

Golden Apollo *Tim Easterby* a89 97
5 ch g Pivotal Elan (Dansili)
2100^7 2743^{10} 3480^7 3863^5 4402^3◆ 5120^8 5454^4 5971^8◆ 6676^3 6953^4 7152^6 **(7431)**

Golden Box (USA)
A De Royer-Dupre a73 100
3 ch f Kitten's Joy(USA) Gold Round (IRE) (Caerleon (USA))
3676a^2 **6003a**^{4} **7137a**^{2} 7927a^6

Golden Boy (FR) *S Wattel* 83
2 b c Siyouni(FR) Straight Lass (IRE) (Machiavellian (USA))
5468a^3 **(6262a)** **7292a**^{3}

Golden Circle (IRE) *Patrick Owens* a24 77
3 gr f Kingman Wrong Answer (Verglas (IRE))
3654^9 ***8470***^{11}

Golden Cygnet *Ralph Beckett* a61 37
2 b f Cable Bay(IRE) Dark Swan (IRE) (Zamindar (USA))
5132^{11} ***6072***^{4} *9063^6*

Golden Deal (IRE) *Richard Phillips* a51 51
4 b m Havana Gold(IRE) Lady Rockfield (IRE) (Rock Of Gibraltar (IRE))
3352^6 *3687^8* 4232^{14} ***6723***^{2} *8000^4 9139^9 9481^{11}*

Golden Dragon (IRE)
Stuart Williams 101
2 b c Starspangledbanner(AUS) Emerald Cutter (USA) (Henrythenavigator (USA))
4564^6 (5500) (6464) **8088**^{5}

Golden Etoile (FR) *Colin Tizzard* a31
5 b m Muhtathir Golden Firebird (IRE) (Old Vic)
242^{13}

Golden Footsteps (IRE)
Mark Gillard a35 34
4 b m Footstepsinthesand Contemplate (Compton Place)
1820^{13} 2145^{18}

Golden Force *Clive Cox* a82 83
3 b g Lethal Force(IRE) Malilla (IRE) (Red Clubs (IRE))
3048^6 4420^5 (5303) 5862^6 **6913**^{4} 7351^6 *7789^4*◆

Golden Fountain (IRE)
Mark Johnston a58
2 br c Fountain Of Youth(IRE) Art Of Gold (Excellent Art)
9323^6 *9668^{12}*

Golden Grenade (FR) *Ian Williams* a45
3 b g Zanzibari(USA) King's Parody (IRE) (King's Best (USA))
534^6 *967^4 1165^{12} 2530^7* 4039^6

Golden Guest *Les Eyre* a76 65
5 ch g Bated Breath Si Belle (IRE) (Dalakhani (IRE))
1271^4 ***1392***^{4} 5020^9 6627^3 *6839^8*

Golden Guide *K R Burke* a55 58
4 b m Havana Gold(IRE) Blonde (IRE) (Pivotal)
6^6 2101^0 387^7

Golden Hind *David O'Meara* 70
2 b f Golden Horn Messias Da Silva (USA) (Tale Of The Cat (USA))
8338^2

Golden Horde (IRE) *Clive Cox* 117
2 ch c Lethal Force(IRE) Entreat (Pivotal)
2792^4 (3419)◆ 3949^5 (5584) 6264a^3 **7693**^{2}

Golden Jaguar (USA)
A bin Harmash a76 98
3 ch c Animal Kingdom(USA) Golden Sunray (USA) (Crafty Prospector (USA))
(511a) **956a**^{2} *1443a^{14}*

Golden Jeffrey (SWI) *Iain Jardine* 76
6 b g Soldier Hollow Ange Doree (FR) (Sinyar (IRE))
2326^7 3511^{14} 4056^9 5241^5

Golden Legend (FR) *H-F Devin* a77 109
5 b m Doctor Dino(FR) Gold Harvest (FR) (Kaldounevees (FR))
3138a^4 5079a^7

Golden Lips (IRE) *Harry Dunlop* 76
2 b f Golden Horn Lady Penko (FR) (Archipenko (USA))
3049^6 4223^4 6675^2 (7203) **8393a**^{6}

Golden Nectar *Laura Mongan* a73 74
5 ch m Sakhee's Secret Mildoura (FR) (Sendawar (IRE))
944^3 *1216^8 1880^{15}* 3967^{10} *4787^6*

Golden Parade *Tim Easterby* a74 79
3 ch g Pivotal Fondled (Selkirk (USA))
3051^5 3478^7 3885^8 4606^2 *(5056)*◆ (5335) 5972^2 6533^3 **7311**^{2} 7828^{11}

Golden Pass *Hugo Palmer* 77
2 b f Golden Horn Lovely Pass (IRE) (Raven's Pass (USA))
7461^3◆

Golden Rajsa (FR) *Pauline Menges* a90 93
5 b m Rajsaman(FR) Golden Clou (FR) (Kendor (FR))
7885a^6 *9603a^{12}*

Golden Salute (IRE)
Andrew Balding a71 80
4 b m Acclamation Golden Shadow (IRE) (Selkirk (USA))
365^5 ***317***^{4}

Golden Sandbanks *Iain Jardine* a45
2 b c Havana Gold(IRE) Serrenia (IRE) (High Chaparral (IRE))
9107^{10}

Golden Slumbers *Bill Turner* a27
2 ch f Equiano(FR) Halfwaytoparadise (Observatory (USA))
3689^{10} **9506**^{14}

Golden Spectrum *Gay Kelleway* a83 98
3 b g Dutch Art Lady Darshaan (IRE) (High Chaparral (IRE))
(554) (893a) 1854^7 **2889a**^{5} 4013^9

Golden Times (SWI) *Mark Johnston* a47 45
2 ch f Lord Of England(GER) Ange Doree (FR) (Sinyar (IRE))
3881^5 *9243^{10}* ***9448***^{6}

Golden Warrior (FR) *G Botti* 51
2 ch c George Vancouver(USA) Elusive Jewel (FR) (Elusive City (USA))
3171a^5

Golden Wolf (IRE) *Tony Carroll* a72 73
5 bb g Big Bad Bob(IRE) Jeunesse Doree (IRE) (Rock Of Gibraltar (IRE))
238^6 522^7 7815^8 8253^{13} ***9053***^{10} *9611^8*

Gold Filigree (IRE) *Richard Hughes* a101 102
4 gr m Dark Angel(IRE) Gold Lace (IRE) (Invincible Spirit (IRE))
(1295)◆ 1913^2 **(2874)** 3085^9 4101^8 5325a^3 5705^4 6648a^5 7401^3 8115^9

Gold Flash *Rod Millman* a63 57
7 b g Kheleyf(USA) My Golly (Mozart (IRE))
3430^4 *4195^8* 4873^8 5498^5 *5633^4 6117^8*

Gold Fleece *Hugo Palmer* a76 74
3 b f Nathaniel(IRE) Conquete (FR) (Kyllachy)
370^5 615^2 2914^3 3708^2 3955^2 ***4769***^{2}◆

Goldfox Girl *Robyn Brisland* a53 43
4 b m Phenomena Baileys Honour (Mark Of Esteem (IRE))
1163^{12}

Goldfox Grey *Robyn Brisland* a42 40
3 gr g Equiano(FR) Beautifull Mind (IRE) (Zebedee)
5193^9 5592^8 5969^{10} ***8944***^{5} *9225^{14}*

Gold Hunter (IRE) *Steve Flook* a58 77
9 b g Invincible Spirit(IRE) Goldthroat (IRE) (Zafonic (USA))
1215 ***254***^{3} *564^7 914^7 1208^R 1357^{11}* 2107^{14} 3089^7 4181^2 4479^U **(4873)** 5373^4 5839^9 *6978^4 7299^7 8199^8 8690^8 9006^{10} 9423^3 9629^8*

Goldie Hawk *Chris Wall* a49
2 b f Golden Horn Always Remembered (IRE) (Galileo (IRE))
9284^6

Goldino Bello (FR) *Harry Dunlop* a77 64
3 b g Anodin(IRE) Valse Legere (FR) (Falco (USA))
1424^{11} 2635^{10}

Gold Lake (FR) *Frau Hella Sauer* a85 80
4 b g Reckless Abandon Guiana (GER) (Tiger Hill (IRE))
3136a^{12}

Gold Maze *Mrs John Harrington* 99
2 b c Golden Horn Astonishing (IRE) (Galileo (IRE))
7744a^3

Goldmembers (FR) *M Boutin* a58 74
2 b g Kheleyf(USA) Ana Style (FR) (Anabaa Blue)
1448a^5 **3171a**^{2} 7674a^8 *8239a^5*

Gold Moonlight (FR) *F Head* 74
2 ch c Anodin(IRE) Memoire (FR) (Sadler's Wells (USA))
7925a^6

Gold Mount *Ian Williams* a74 117
6 b g Excellent Art Dolcetto (IRE) (Danehill Dancer (IRE))
1441a^4 **(3864)** 4933^2 8361a^{12}◆

Goldslinger (FR) *Gary Moore* a61 50
7 b g Gold Away(IRE) Singaporette (FR) (Sagacity (FR))
38^4◆ *1679^5*◆ 2283^4

Gold Souk (IRE) *Mark Johnston* 90
2 b c Casamento(IRE) Dubai Sunrise (USA) (Seeking The Gold (USA))
3760^7 4388^3 5665^{10} (6564) 7699^2 **8509**^{2}

Gold Step (FR) *F Rossi* 92
2 bb f Sidestep(AUS) Fedora (FR) (Kendor (FR))
8446a^3 8970a^6

Gold Stick (IRE) *John Gosden* 94
3 b c Dubawi(IRE) Gamilati (Bernardini (USA))
1755^5◆ (2505) 3263^4 **5502**^{3}

Gold Stone *Kevin Ryan* a77 73
4 b m Havana Gold(IRE) Slatey Hen (IRE) (Acclamation)
5647 ***953***^{4} 1950^3 2416^7 2637^3 3056^{11}

Gold Tail (IRE) *Paola Maria Gaetano* 81
4 b h Dream Ahead(USA) Reign (IRE) (Elusive City (USA))
2888a^{12}

Gold Town *Charlie Appleby* a112 101
4 b g Street Cry(IRE) Pimpernel (IRE) (Invincible Spirit (IRE))
171a^4 513a^4 ***842a***^{7}

Gold Tyranny (DEN) *Lennart Reuterskiold Jr* 98
5 b g Zoffany(IRE) Thara (USA) (Hennessy (USA))
7498a[12]
Gold Venture (IRE) *Philip Kirby* a49 68
2 ch f Dandy Man(IRE) Monroe (Tomba)
(2331) 2716[5] (3694) 5295[4] 5683[13] 6272[7] 7064[11] 7767[9] 8815[13] 9009[9] 9330[7]
Gold Vibe (IRE) *P Bary* a95 113
6 ch g Dream Ahead(USA) Whisper Dance (USA) (Stravinsky (USA))
2667a[4] 3388a[4] 4948a[3] 5471a[3] 7254a[3] 7943a[6]
Gold Wand (IRE) *Roger Varian* 84
2 b f Golden Horn Los Ojitos (USA) (Mr Greeley (USA))
8510[2]
Goldy Baby (FR) *N Paysan* 57
9 ch m Gold Away(IRE) Nobly Baby (FR) (Volochine (IRE))
5761a[3] 8737a[3]
Golega (FR) *P Van De Poele* a70 71
4 ch m Masterstroke(USA) Bealli (IRE) (Bering)
76a[7]
Gometra Ginty (IRE) *Keith Dalgleish* a61 81
3 b f Morpheus Silver Cache (USA) (Silver Hawk (USA))
(3920) 4334[5] 5274[4]◆ (5619) 5903[7] 6609[3] 7213[6] 7491[6] (7735) 8237[4]
Gonbutnotforgotten (FR) *Philip McBride* a54
3 b f Showcasing Porcini (Azamour (IRE))
1570[7] 1838[11] 2762[P] 3277[12] 4244[7] 5054[7]
Gone Solo (IRE) *Robert Collet* a77 75
4 ch g Shamardal(USA) Go Lovely Rose (IRE) (Pivotal)
992a[6] 6267a[2]
Gone With The Wind (GER) *Rebecca Bastiman* a48 57
8 b g Dutch Art Gallivant (Danehill (USA))
155[4] 532[6] 595[4] 1354[5] 1836[11]
Gonna Dancealot (IRE) *Jane Chapple-Hyam* a68 62
2 b f Sir Prancealot(IRE) Lilium (Nashwan (USA))
5189[5] 8287[4]◆ 8651[3]
Gonzaga *James Bennett* a65 51
4 b g Oasis Dream Symposia (Galileo (IRE))
1570[8] 2009[2] 2624[5] 3543[9] 4194[13] 5051[10]
Gonzalo *N Bellanger* a77 69
6 b g Zoffany(IRE) Singapore Belle (FR) (Sagacity (FR))
5035a[10] 7536a[16]
Goobinator (USA) *Donald McCain* a78 72
3 ch g Noble Mission Lilac Lilly (USA) (Bluegrass Cat (USA))
6034[3] 8020[2] (8838)
Good Answer *Robert Cowell* a70 68
3 b g Iffraaj Cool Question (Polar Falcon (USA))
3351[5] (3836) 5660[5] 6806[8] 8755[7] 9218[2] 9498[12]
Good Birthday (IRE) *Andrew Balding* 103
3 b g Dabirsim(FR) Chica Loca (FR) (American Post)
(1462)◆ 2828[3] 4017[10] 4882[5] (6696) 7694[3]
Good Business (IRE) *Henry Spiller* a46 52
5 ch m Dutch Art Parakopi (IRE) (Green Desert (USA))
1883[10] 3001[10] 3738[3] 6126[5] 6889[13] 7838[9]
Goodbye To Jane (FR) *Jo Hughes* 18
2 b f Slade Power(IRE) Bashasha (USA) (Kingmambo (USA))
4533a[12]
Good Curry (TUR) *Bayram Kocakaya* a106
7 b h Sharp Humor(USA) Laud (USA) (Honour And Glory (USA))
729a[4]◆ 1112a[2] 1440a[12]
Good Earth (IRE) *Jamie Osborne* a66 76
2 b g Acclamation Madhatten (IRE) (Dream Ahead (USA))
3542[3] 4394[3] 4734[2] 5186[5] 5635[4] 7619[2] 9031[5]
Good Effort (IRE) *Ismail Mohammed* a107 102
4 b h Shamardal(USA) Magical Crown (USA) (Distorted Humor (USA))
173a[16] 640a[7] 842a[10]◆ 4921[9] 5413[16] (5911) 6453[8] 7433[13] 7892[5] 9098[2] (9483a)
Good Fortune *Charlie Appleby* 100
3 b g New Approach(IRE) Mazuna (IRE) (Cape Cross (IRE))
(168a) 956a[6] 5963[2]
Good Impression *Dai Burchell* a57 60
4 b g Showcasing Daintily Done (Cacique (IRE))
5378[13] 6042[3] 6830[6] (7240) 7759[8] 9168[4] 9481[12]
Good Job Power (IRE) *Richard Hannon* a77 76
2 b c Acclamation Thousandfold (USA) (Giant's Causeway (USA))
5125[5] 5523[6] 6078[5] (6563) 8665[3]
Good Looker (IRE) *Tony Coyle* 46
3 ch g Zoffany(IRE) Looker (Barathea (IRE))
2482[11] 2871[8] 6678[12]
Good Luck Charm *Gary Moore* a64 65
10 b g Doyen(IRE) Lucky Dice (Perugino (USA))
2365[8] 2774[8] 3540[9] 4589[8] (6117) 6305[3] 6758[8] 7982[4] 8711[2]
Good Luck Fox (IRE) *Richard Hannon* a37 84
3 b g Society Rock(IRE) Violet Ballerina (IRE) (Namid)
2086[10] 2810[6] 3151[5] 3531[11] 4008[2] 4872[5] 5589[12] 7178[5] 8550[13]
Good Man (IRE) *Karen McLintock* a54 38
6 ch g New Approach(IRE) Garden City (FR) (Majorien)
2081[1] 607[2] 782[6] 1718[6]
Goodman Square *Mark Usher* a34 30
2 b f Kyllachy Freedom Rock (Rock Of Gibraltar (IRE))
4840[13] 5907[6] 6719[12] 7110[6] 7833[12] 8118[8]
Goodnight Girl (IRE) *Jonathan Portman* a97 97
4 gr m Clodovil(IRE) Leenavesta (USA) (Arch (USA))
1712[2] 2917[3] 3492[2] 3994[11] 5143[6] 5746[3] 5846[6] 6908[2] 7613[7] 8522[12]
Good Night Mr Tom (IRE) *Mark Johnston* 85
2 b g Tagula(IRE) Babylonian (Shamardal (USA))
1893[7] 3679[3]◆ 4401[4] (5668) 6272[3] 7763[3]
Good Of Saints *C Lerner* a61 68
2 b f War Command(USA) Goona Chope (FR) (Namid)
7044a[8]
Good Ole Winnie *Ali Stronge*
3 b f Gale Force Ten Dalliefour (IRE) (Cape Cross (IRE))
6074[14]
Good Question (FR) *C Escuder* a71 106
4 b g Manduro(GER) Question Of Time (FR) (Olden Times)
6820a[2] 8980a[2]
Good Reason *Saeed bin Suroor* a79 62
2 gr f Dark Angel(IRE) Sander Camillo (USA) (Dixie Union (USA))
5588[11] 6205[3] 6675[6] (8286)◆ 9044[4]
Good Smash (FR) *F Pardon* a71 75
7 b g Orpen(USA) Salon Musique (GER) (Black Sam Bellamy (IRE))
2226a[6]
Good Tidings (FR) *John Gosden* a94 74
3 bb g Teofilo(IRE) Nouvelle Bonne (FR) (Desert Style (IRE))
7159[3] (7559) (8020) 8701[2] 9055[3] 9454[9]
Good Time Charlie *Clive Cox* a57
2 b c Due Diligence(USA) Our Faye (College Chapel)
8418[7] 9668[7]
Good Times Too *Mick Channon* 53
2 b g Captain Gerrard(IRE) Mistic Magic (IRE) (Orpen (USA))
1651[8] 1931[5] 3088[5] 5340[10] 6799[9]
Good Try *Michael Bell* a52
2 b f Iffraaj Good Hope (Cape Cross (IRE))
8914[11] 9158[7] 9324[8]
Good Tyne Girl (IRE) *Heather Main* a64 77
3 gr f Requinto(IRE) Hardy Pink (IRE) (Clodovil (IRE))
813[5]
Good Vibes *David Evans* 105
2 b f Due Diligence(USA) Satsuma (Compton Place)
1833[2]◆ (2138) (2805) 5411[5] 6157[7] 6374[3] 6907[6] (8088)
Goodwood Rebel (IRE) *Ralph Beckett* 75
2 b g Dandy Man(IRE) Our Valkyrie (IRE) (High Chaparral (IRE))
2338[5] 3088[4] 3694[2] 5088[3] 7155[10] 7754[9]
Goodwood Sonnet (IRE) *William Knight* a47 53
3 b g Lope De Vega(IRE) Surface Of Earth (USA) (Empire Maker (USA))
2341[11] 3593[12] 3965[4] 5249[2] 6202[5] 6982[8] 8003[7]
Gordalan *Philip Kirby* a47 63
3 b g Foxwedge(AUS) Mad Annie (USA) (Anabaa (USA))
2912[10] 3200[9] 5425[5] 6660[6] (8344)
Gordon Lord Byron (IRE) *T Hogan* a107 107
11 b g Byron Boa Estrela (IRE) (Intikhab (USA))
1434a[12] 3103a[3] 3786a[3] 5207a[4] 5923a[3] 6472[6] 6894[5] 7241a[4] 7713a[6]
Gorgeous General *Lawrence Mullaney* a62 63
4 ch g Captain Gerrard(IRE) Gorgeous Goblin (IRE) (Lujain (USA))
(167) (411)◆ 503[2] (702)◆ (834) 926[4] 1368[5] 1973[4] 2183[3] 4586[4] 5722[2] 6178[7] 6547[3] 7307[3] 7651[3] 8306[9]
Gorgeous Gobolina *Susan Corbett* a55 59
3 b f Captain Gerrard(IRE) Gorgeous Goblin (IRE) (Lujain (USA))
4010[6] 4367[5] 4827[9] 5854[5] 6277[12]
Gorgeous Noora (IRE) *Archie Watson* a103 83
5 b m Raven's Pass(USA) Aneedah (IRE) (Invincible Spirit (IRE))
203[4]◆ (297) 563[2] (877) 1412[6] 1918[8]
Gorham's Cave *Ali Stronge*
5 b g Rock Of Gibraltar(IRE) Moiava (FR) (Bering)
59[2]◆ 245[8] 1145[4]
Goring (GER) *Eve Johnson Houghton* a106 85
7 b g Areion(GER) Globuli (GER) (Surako (GER))
121[2] 880[5] 1101[8] (1916) 2402[5] 3581[9] 9000[3] 9309[10] 9666[2]
Go Sandy *Lisa Williamson* a3 1
4 ch m Captain Gerrard(IRE) Lily Jicaro (IRE) (Choisir (AUS))
811[8] 1076[5]
Goscote *Henry Candy* a69 79
4 ch m Pivotal Gosbeck (Dubawi (IRE))
2017[3] 2999[2] (4661)◆ 5452[7] 6044[5] 7239[6] 8661[7]
Goshen (FR) *Gary Moore* a31 97
3 b g Authorized(IRE) Hyde (FR) (Poliglote)
(3538) (3809)◆ (8661)◆
Gospel *Mick Channon* a83 77
3 b f Holy Roman Emperor(IRE) Heavenly Sound (Street Cry (IRE))
1242a[5] 1939[5] 3591[8]
Gossamer Wings (USA) *A P O'Brien* 98
3 b f Scat Daddy(USA) Lavender Baby (USA) (Rubiano (USA))
2605a[6] 2880a[6] 3388a[5] 4954a[7] 5325a[7]
Gossip *Martyn Meade* a65 62
2 b f Exceed And Excel(AUS) Al Sharood (Shamardal (USA))
6846[3] 8865[5]
Gossip Column (IRE) *Ian Williams* a63 96
4 b g Arcano(IRE) Monicalew (Refuse To Bend (IRE))
2095[14] 2563[6] 3338[6] 3605[6] 3847[3] (4407)◆ 4877[7] 5370[4] 5706[2] (6067) 7144[3] (7680)
Gossipe (FR) *J-L Pelletan* a25 56
4 bb m Deportivo Suricat Girl (IRE) (Antonius Pius (USA))
2170a[6]
Gossiping *Gary Moore* a85 100
7 b g Dubawi(IRE) Gossamer (Sadler's Wells (USA))
557[11] (1355) (2526) (3313) 5610[7] 6445[10] 6964[8] 7697[11] 8016[4]◆ 8728[12]
Got Charm (FR) *Edouard Monfort* a26
2 b f Rajsaman(FR) Bon Escient (Montjeu (IRE))
8448a[9]
Go To Hollywood (FR) *Y Barberot* 100
3 b c Penny's Picnic(IRE) Agence Belge (FR) (Librettist (USA))
1243a[3] 3287a[3] 5480a[5] 6249a[4]
Got Stormy (USA) *Mark Casse* 116
4 ch m Get Stormy(USA) Super Phoebe (USA) (Malabar Gold (USA))
(5977a) 7225a[2] 8774a[2]
Gottardo (IRE) *Ed Dunlop* a71 66
4 b g Choisir(AUS) Chantarella (IRE) (Royal Academy (USA))
(1209)◆ 1766[3] 3838[6] 4281[10] 5723[5] 6631[9] 7447[3] 7837[3] 8199[2] 8713[2] 9006[3] 9427[4]
Got The T Shirt *Keith Dalgleish* a63 69
2 ch g Casamento(IRE) Lolamotion (Equiano (FR))
7398[7] 7902[4] 8302[5] 9250[8] 9515[9]
Gotti (USA) *A R Al Rayhi* a65 52
4 b h More Than Ready(USA) Soot Z (USA) (Empire Maker (USA))
97a[11]
Got Will (FR) *Y Barberot* a74 74
3 ch f Mayson Miranda Frost (FR) (Vespone (IRE))
3028a[8]
Got Wind *C Ferland* a77 87
3 b f Olympic Glory(IRE) Sarvana (FR) (Dubai Destination (USA))
2027a[3] 3137a[6]
Gourel (FR) *Mme M Bollack-Badel* a85 73
5 b g Le Havre(IRE) Racemate (Hurricane Run (IRE))
7136a[11]
Governor Of Punjab (IRE) *Mark Johnston* a74 92
2 ch g Footstepsinthesand Simla Bibi (Indian Ridge (IRE))
3702[5] (3990)◆ (4750) (5587) 6417[6]
Gowanbuster *Susan Corbett* a80 70
4 b g Bahri(USA) Aahgowangowan (IRE) (Tagula (IRE))
496[3] 743[4] 788[3] (1403) 1951[3] (2247)◆ 2379[2] 2893[9] 9108[10]
Gowanlad *Philip Kirby* a75
2 b c Mayson Aahgowangowan (IRE) (Tagula (IRE))
8337[9] 9099[5] 9393[2]
Go Well Spicy (IRE) *Tim Fitzgerald* a69 74
2 gr f Gutaifan(IRE) Best New Show (IRE) (Clodovil (IRE))
2579[2] 3573[2] (3934) (4323) 4647[6] 5683[5] 6221[5] 6833[5] 7522[5] 8261[5] 8465[7] 9031[7] (9307)
Go With Grace *J S Moore* a15
2 gr f Gutaifan(IRE) Love Action (IRE) (Motivator)
3461[11]
Goya Senora (FR) *Y Barberot* a77 105
3 b c Anodin(IRE) Nina Senora (FR) (My Risk (FR))
2314a[4] 6005a[4] 7478a[3]
Grab And Run (IRE) *Richard Fahey* a69 71
3 b g Kodiac Private Alexander (IRE) (Footstepsinthesand)
2713[6] 3932[2] 4334[3] 5561[4] 5938[2]◆
Grace And Danger (IRE) *Andrew Balding* 104
3 b f Teofilo(IRE) Opinionated (IRE) (Dubai Destination (USA))
2521[4] 3012[8] 6466[2] 7180[3]◆ 8245[4]
Grace And Virtue (IRE) *Richard Fahey* a62
2 b f Iffraaj Spiralling (Pivotal)
7580[4] 8316[3] 8913[6]
Grace Bere (FR) *S Cerulis* a72
3 b f Pedro The Great(USA) Help From Heaven (IRE) (Titus Livius (FR))
509a[2]
Graceful (IRE) *Richard Hannon* a40 47
3 b f Zoffany(IRE) Tahara (IRE) (Caerleon (USA))
186[8]
Graceful Act *Ron Barr* a50 52
11 b m Royal Applause Minnina (IRE) (In The Wings)
3163[14] 4036[8] 4633[3] 5024[5] 5214[5] (5518) 6103[7] 6545[2] 7956[12]
Graceful James (IRE) *Jimmy Fox* a82 61
6 ch g Rock Of Gibraltar(IRE) Little Miss Gracie (Efisio)
86[2] 294[2]
Graceful Kitten (USA) *Amador Merei Sanchez* 95
2 b c Kitten's Joy(USA) Alexandra's Grace (USA) (Hard Spun (USA))
8746a[12]
Graceful Lady *Robert Eddery* a63 85
6 b m Sixties Icon Leitzu (IRE) (Barathea (IRE))
2571[4] 3145[6] 4404[6] 5047[3] (5967)◆ 6530[2] 7464[7] 8114[16] 8726[5]
Graceful Magic *Eve Johnson Houghton* a78 99
2 gr f Gutaifan(IRE) Magic Escapade (IRE) (Azamour (IRE))
(3259) 4048[22] 4790[4] (5683) 6221[8] 6833[2] (7117) 7432[2]
Grace Note *Archie Watson* a42 57
2 b f Swiss Spirit Darling Grace (Nayef (USA))
4766[7] 5527[5] 7269[2] 8022[8]
Grace Of Cliffs (FR) *A De Watrigant* a16 59
3 b f Canford Cliffs(IRE) Grace Of Dubai (FR) (Dubai Destination (USA))
9281a[15]
Grace Plunkett *Richard Spencer* a53 51
2 b f Brazen Beau(AUS) Goodnightsuzy (IRE) (Azamour (IRE))
1642[11] 2108[7] 3055[4] 5958[4] 6313[4] 6837[9] 7275[3] 7516[2] 7910[2] 8415[12]
Grace Spirit *A De Royer-Dupre* a68 99
3 b f Invincible Spirit(IRE) Gracefully (IRE) (Orpen (USA))
6142a[7] 7360a[3] 8376a[8] 8983a[2]
Graciarose *Tracy Waggott*
3 ch f Piccolo Ex Gracia (Efisio)
3707[11] 5554[12] 6578[9]
Gracie *James Fanshawe*
3 b f Champs Elysees Fallen From Grace (Singspiel (IRE))
3200[11]
Gracie's Girl *Michael Appleby* a54 45
2 b f Heeraat(IRE) Queens Revenge (Multiplex)
1879[3] 2052[6] 9029[7] 9643[3]
Gracie Stansfield *Tony Carroll* a57 52
5 ch m Peintre Celebre(USA) Ex Gracia (Efisio)
80[6] 363[12] 1032[8]
Gracious George (IRE) *Jimmy Fox* a55 57
9 b g Oratorio(IRE) Little Miss Gracie (Efisio)
207[11]
Gracious John (IRE) *Ian Williams* a95 86
6 b g Baltic King Dorn Hill (Lujain (USA))
35[6] 877[4] 987[3] 1295[4] 1734[8] 1839[7] 4521[9] 6339[5] 6724[8] 7183[9] 9088[2] 9389[7]
Graignes (FR) *Y Barberot* 113
3 b c Zoffany(IRE) Grey Anatomy (Slickly (FR))
1707a[2] 2668a[4] 4705a[8] 6004a[5]◆ 7255a[2] 7944a[5]
Grain Of Sense (IRE) *Ralph Beckett* 80
2 ch g Teofilo(IRE) Grain Of Truth (Gulch (USA))
7897[3]◆ 8461[4]
Grandads Best Girl *Linda Perratt* a58 56
2 b f Intrinsic Mitchelland (Namaqualand (USA))
7733[5] 8232[7] 8816[3]
Grandad's Legacy *Ali Stronge* a58 48
3 b g Harbour Watch(IRE) Vodka Shot (USA) (Holy Bull (USA))
2341[13] 3354[7] 4244[12]
Grand Argentier (FR) *Doug Watson* a97 69
7 b g Palace Episode(USA) Ashkadima (IRE) (Ashkalani (IRE))
573a[8]
Grand Bazaar *John Gosden* a74 73
2 b c Golden Horn Damaniyat Girl (USA) (Elusive Quality (USA))
6892[3] 8424[3] 8823[5]
Grand Canal (IRE) *Tom Clover* a48
2 b c Australia Loreto (IRE) (Holy Roman Emperor (IRE))
8823[13] 9156[7]
Grandee (IRE) *Roger Fell* a95 94
5 b g Lope De Vega(IRE) Caravan Of Dreams (IRE) (Anabaa (USA))
1461[4] (1719) 2808[4] 3346[5] 4102[7] 4884[5] 5457[3] 5928[4] 6981[6] 7414[3] 7819[5]
Grandee Daisy *Michael Appleby* a46 44
3 ch f Sepoy(AUS) Chili Dip (Alhaarth (IRE))
79[9] 550[7] 918[2] 1170[6] 1678[5] 1842a[4] 2390a[9] 3028a[7] 4357a[6] 4959a[10] 6598[8] 9505[9]
Grandfather Tom *Robert Cowell* a75 86
4 b g Kheleyf(USA) Kassuta (Kyllachy)
(2025) 3021[5] 4301[8] (5027) (5990) 6954[8]
Grand Glory *Gianluca Bietolini* a76 108
3 b f Olympic Glory(IRE) Madonna Lily (IRE) (Daylami (IRE))
3905a[3]
Grand Inquisitor *Conor Dore* a79 90
7 b g Dansili Dusty Answer (Zafonic (USA))
1949[5] (3300) (3929) 4437[2] 4522[2] 5055[4] 5436[9] 6842[6] 7610[6] 8014[13] 8692[6] 9012[10] 9202[15]
Grandmaster Flash (IRE) *Joseph Patrick O'Brien* a100 82
3 ch c Australia Kittens (Marju (IRE))
8655[2] 9454[2]
Grandma Tilly *Steph Hollinshead*
4 b m Hellvelyn Sleep Dance (Sleeping Indian)
8242[11] 8638[11]
Grand Pianola *Tim Easterby* 47
2 b g Firebreak Grand Liaison (Sir Percy)
4238[9] 5331[7]
Grand Rock (IRE) *William Haggas* 93
2 b c Acclamation Miss Gibraltar (Rock Of Gibraltar (IRE))
4550[4] (6654) (7726) 8397[3]
Grandscape *Ed Dunlop* a68 74
4 b g Lemon Drop Kid(USA) Unnatural (USA) (Proud Citizen (USA))
1463[4] 2059[4] 3541[5] 4446[8] 5337[5] 5728[8] 6343[4] 8843[2]◆ (9542)
Grand Secret (FR) *M Boutin* a64 64
3 b g Orpen(USA) Scarley Secret (IRE) (Royal Applause)
4229a[4] 7642a[7]
Grand Shang (IRE) *Gianluca Bietolini* 55
2 b c Shanghai Bobby(USA) Starship Scarlett (USA) (Dixie Union (USA))
6776a[8]
Grandstand (IRE) *Richard Price* a34 47
3 b g Kodiac Lady Shanghai (IRE) (Alhaarth (IRE))
140[6] 401[3] 4286[10] 5147[11] 6329[12] 6638[5]
Grange Walk (IRE) *Pat Phelan* a69 69
4 ch g Thewayyouare(USA) A Woman In Love (Muhtarram (USA))
242[6] 562[6] 1182[4] 1653[4] 2617[9] 3015[5] 4737[2] 5316[3] 6568[4]
Granite City Doc *Lucy Normile* a70 71
6 b g Arabian Gleam Hansomis (IRE) (Titus Livius (FR))
2436[3] 2785[5] (3448) 4333[4] 5725[2] 7301[4] 7513[2] 8300[4]
Granny Grey (IRE) *David Barron* 28
2 ch f Tagula(IRE) Ever Evolving (FR) (Elusive Quality (USA))
7063[9]

Granny Roz *Ray Craggs* a75 78
5 b m Bahamian Bounty Hulcote Rose (IRE) (Rock Of Gibraltar (IRE))
928[2] 1194[12] 1760[18] 3207[11] 8066[12] 8429[12] 8924[9] 9397[9]

Gran Pierino (ITY) *Andrea Marcialis* a77 84
5 b g Montalegre(IRE) Universal Shade (ITY) (Pursuit Of Love)
7861a[10]

Gran Risa (IRE) *A Giorgi* 47
2 ch f Dream Ahead(USA) So Katie (IRE) (Iffraaj)
1657a[11]

Grape Shot *Richard Hannon* a59 55
3 b f Nathaniel(IRE) Angara (Alzao (USA))
1543[4] 2210[8] 3310[7]

Grapevine (IRE) *Charles Hills* a78 85
6 b g Lilbourne Lad(IRE) High Vintage (IRE) (High Chaparral (IRE))
1934[2]◆ 2486[3] 2797[14] 3424[2] (3944) 4450[3]

Graphite (FR) *A Fabre* a109 113
5 gr g Shamardal(USA) Fairly Grey (FR) (Linamix (FR))
1451a[2] 2313a[5]

Graphite (IRE) *Geoffrey Harker* a61 67
5 ro g Galileo(IRE) Simply Perfect (Danehill (USA))
784[13] 2335[4] 4078[P]

Graphite Storm *Clive Cox* a85 92
5 gr g Delegator Ice Haven (IRE) (Verglas (IRE))
2363[3] 2832[9] 3632[5] 4654[2] (5386) 6214[4] 6803[3] 7462[5] 8253[3]

Grasmere (IRE) *Alan Bailey* a56 52
4 b m Society Rock(IRE) Silk Point (IRE) (Barathea (IRE))
1841[11] 2738[6] 3298[8] 6049[3] 7376[10] 8204[8]

Gravistas *Mark Johnston* a82 87
3 b c Dansili Gaze (Galileo (IRE))
2697[2]◆ 3358[2]◆ (3604)

Gravity Force *K R Burke* a73 91
2 b c Fountain Of Youth(IRE) Itsinthestars (Zoffany (IRE))
6943[2]◆ (7398)◆ 7902[2] 8762[4]

Gravity Wave (IRE) *John Flint* a68 71
5 br g Rip Van Winkle(IRE) Phrase (Royal Anthem (USA))
246[8] 481[3] 1463[8] 2217[3] 3175[6] 4543[4] 5338[2] (6173) 6343[3]

Grayboy *David Brown* a29 64
3 gr g Aussie Rules(USA) Grace Hull (Piccolo)
1195[8]

Gray Magician (USA) *Peter Miller* a99
3 rg c Graydar(USA) Burg Berg (USA) (Johannesburg (USA))
1443a[2] 2425a[19]

Grazano (FR) *Alain Couetil* 63
3 gr c Mastercraftsman(IRE) Madonje (GER) (Monsun (GER))
7476a[2]

Grazeon Roy *John Quinn* a92 86
3 ch g Archipenko(USA) Graze On And On (Elmaamul (USA))
2192[5] 2507[5] 5969[3] 7405[4] 8515[2]◆ (8641) (8948) (Dead)

Greach (IRE) *Diego Dettori* 87
3 br f Gregorian(IRE) Ach Alannah (IRE) (Marju (IRE))
2161a[9] 7503a[7]

Great Aim (IRE) *James Tate* a64 21
2 b c Shooting To Win(AUS) Jillanar (IRE) (Lawman (FR))
6719[4] 7269[5]

Great Ambassador *Ralph Beckett* a85 85
2 ch g Exceed And Excel(AUS) Snoqualmie Girl (IRE) (Montjeu (IRE))
4246[2] 4925[2] 5665[3] 7119[14] (9197)

Great America (IRE) *F Bossert* a64 64
4 gr m Lethal Force(IRE) Miss Legal Eagle (IRE) (Authorized (IRE))
2002a[10]

Great Aspirations *Mark Johnston* a47 31
2 b f Fast Company(IRE) Asinara (GER) (Big Shuffle (USA))
2906[7] 3491[10]

Great Aventura (IRE)
Cristiano Davide Fais 87
5 b m Clodovil(IRE) Gold Blended (IRE) (Goldmark (USA))
4170a[5] 8153a[6] 8585a[2]

Great Bear *Roger Charlton* a86 84
3 b g Dansili Great Heavens (Galileo (IRE))
2099[4] (2731) 3604[3] 4327[6] 6411[4] 7082[2] 8120[7]

Great Colaci *Gillian Boanas* a58 57
6 b g Sulamani(IRE) Fairlie (Halling (USA))
410[12] 738[2]

Great Dame (IRE) *David O'Meara* a36 87
2 ch f Dandy Man(IRE) Dame Hester (IRE) (Diktat)
1642[7] (1893) (2520) 2805[14] 3333a[5] 4417a[5] 5185[19] 5976a[5] 6498[5] 9162[13]

Greater Love *Jonathan Portman* 32
2 br f Brazen Beau(AUS) Lovellian (Machiavellian (USA))
5132[13]

Great Esteem (IRE) *Charlie Appleby* a83 81
3 b g Dubawi(IRE) Woven Lace (Hard Spun (USA))
6732[2] 7525[2]

Great Example *Saeed bin Suroor* a82 105
3 b c Cape Cross(IRE) Gower Song (Singspiel (IRE))
1764[6] 2321[3] (2875) 4256[4] (5149)◆ 6506[2] 7457[2]

Great Fengshui (IRE)
Richard Hannon a64 39
2 ch g Anjaal Vexatious (IRE) (Shamardal (USA))
5439[7] 6402[RR] 9326[6]

Great Gunnar *Vaclav Luka Jr* 60
3 b c Aussie Rules(USA) Blaise Chorus (IRE) (Singspiel (IRE))
7561a[4]

Great Hall *Mick Quinn* a69 79
9 b g Halling(USA) L'Affaire Monique (Machiavellian (USA))
231[5] 3600[13] 4118[9] 6224[7] 7394[8] 8433[9]

Great Image (IRE) *Saeed bin Suroor* a76 73
2 b g Exceed And Excel(AUS) Beautiful Forest (Nayef (USA))
6409[8] 7437[2] 8059[2] 8890[4]

Great Midge *Henry Candy* a75 78
4 b g Kyllachy Super Midge (Royal Applause)
2997[2] 3661[5] 4303[9]

Great Order (USA)
Saeed bin Suroor a56 84
6 bb g Distorted Humor(USA) Michita (USA) (Dynaformer (USA))
5440[8] (Dead)

Great Prospector (IRE)
Richard Fahey a96 102
4 b g Elzaam(AUS) Guana (IRE) (Dark Angel (IRE))
1415[13] 2100[3] 3863[3] 4402[10] 6229[14]

Great Scot *Tom Dascombe* 115
3 b g Requinto(IRE) La Rosiere (USA) (Mr Greeley (USA))
1752[2] 2411[9] 2889a[3] 4013[11] 6122[4] (6956)

Great Shout (IRE) *Amy Murphy* a74 75
3 b f Kodiac By Jupiter (Sea The Stars (IRE))
251[8] 4207[9] 5056[2] 5985[7] (6132) 6533[4] 7345[2] 8304[8] 8866[4] 9140[6]

Great Suspense *David O'Meara* a70 63
3 b g Bated Breath Gimasha (Cadeaux Genereux)
3661[6] 4396[2] 5057[8] 7651[4] 8268[3] (8672)

Great Tonio (FR) *N Leenders* a69 69
5 bb g Great Journey(JPN) Starmaria (FR) (Starborough)
1245a[7]

Great Trango (IRE)
David Harry Kelly 84
6 b g Canford Cliffs(IRE) Tarascon (IRE) (Tirol (IRE))
5508a[8] 8114[6]

Great White Shark (FR)
W P Mullins 90
5 gr m Le Havre(IRE) Trip To Fame (FR) (Lordmare (FR))
(5508a) 8114[10]

Grecko (ARG) *Kenneth McPeek* a73
3 gr c Not For Sale(ARG) Grecian (ARG) (Equalize (USA))
394a[4] 1110a[12]

Greek Hero *Declan Carroll* 87
3 ch g Champs Elysees Za Za Zoom (IRE) (Le Vie Dei Colori)
2845[7] 3248[4] (3707) 4403[9] 4895[6] 5984[2]◆ 6961[5] (8237)

Greek Kodiac (IRE) *Mick Quinn* a63 78
3 b g Kodiac Greek Easter (IRE) (Namid)
1886[6] 2569[4] 3278[2] 3779[8] 4338[5] 5445[6] 6132[5] 7462[7] 9662[5]

Greek Oasis *Chris Wall* 60
2 b f Oasis Dream Greek Goddess (IRE) (Galileo (IRE))
7393[11] 8093[8]

Greeley (IRE) *Rod Millman* 79
3 b g Sir Prancealot(IRE) Hannah Greeley (USA) (Mr Greeley (USA))
1823[7] 2470[3] 3647[6] 4176[6] 4773[3] (5446) (6045) 6331[3]

Green Backspin (IRE)
Gavin Hernon 54
2 b c Exceed And Excel(AUS) Mireille (IRE) (Dalakhani (IRE))
8447a[6]

Green Book (FR) *Brian Ellison* 74
2 b g Authorized(IRE) Mantissa (Oratorio (IRE))
4324[8] 6054[2] 7623[3] 8029[3] 8462[3]

Green Door (IRE) *Robert Cowell* a84 68
8 b g Camacho Inourhearts (IRE) (Pips Pride)
551[6] 1211[8] 2940[2] 3443[2] (4026) 5649[3] 5888[8] 8262[9] 9131[6] 9390[3] 9550[8]

Green Etoile *Alan King* a62 71
3 ch g Nathaniel(IRE) Myriades D'Etoiles (IRE) (Green Tune (USA))
(2343) 4339[5]

Greengage (IRE) *Tristan Davidson* a68 59
4 b m Choisir(AUS) Empowermentofwomen (IRE) (Manduro (GER))
3251[9] 4690[2]◆ 5214[2] 5851[7] 7544[7] (8466) (9040) 9256[2]◆

Green Power *John Gallagher* 102
4 b g Kheleyf(USA) Hakuraa (IRE) (Elnadim (USA))
1459[4]◆ 1829[3] 2609[22] 3043[7] 4186[5] (5524) (6404) 7193[18] 7892[9]

Greenside *Henry Candy* a96 104
8 b g Dubawi(IRE) Katrina (IRE) (Ela-Mana-Mou (IRE))
1753[4] (2487) 3313[3] 3857[4] 4666[5] 7891[2]

Green Siren (FR)
Mme M Bollack-Badel a74 78
3 ch f Siyouni(FR) Green Speed (FR) (Green Tune (USA))
8983a[9]

Green Spirit (FR)
Mme M Bollack-Badel 75
2 b g Charm Spirit(IRE) Green Speed (FR) (Green Tune (USA))
(8481a)

Greenview Paradise (IRE)
Jeremy Scott a55 45
5 gr m Exchange Rate(USA) Senza Rete (IRE) (Barathea (IRE))
1145[5] 1361[5] (1861) (2014) 4251[9] 5285[4] 6599[6] 7202[8]

Gregarious Girl *Stuart Williams* a56 57
3 b f Gregorian(IRE) Wiki Tiki (Dixie Union (USA))
296[7] 412[2] 497[4]

Gregorian Girl *Dean Ivory* a72 68
3 b f Gregorian(IRE) Jackie's Opera (FR) (Indian Ridge (IRE))
(1515) 2238[4] 2904[11] 3764[4]◆ 4248[2] 5622[2] 5786[2] 6703[3] (7573) 8807[6]

Gregory The Great
Steph Hollinshead
3 b g Heeraat(IRE) Word Perfect (Diktat)
2932[11] 3499[11]

Greg Pass (IRE) *Nicolo Simondi* 87
7 b g Raven's Pass(USA) Baranja (USA) (St Jovite (USA))
7502a[6] 8392a[7]

Gremoboy *Tim Easterby* a60 46
3 ch g Mayson Largo (IRE) (Selkirk (USA))
1646[7] 2510[9] 3516[8] 4000[5] 4761[8] 7732[9] 8070[4]◆ 8233[3] 8642[5]

Grenadier Guard (IRE)
Mark Johnston a71 88
3 ch g Australia Another Storm (USA) (Gone West (USA))
3482[4] (3724) 4143[2] 4862[3] 5967[7] 6340[4] 9543[4]

Grenadine (IRE) *A P O'Brien* 63
2 b f Galileo(IRE) Words (IRE) (Dansili)
8758[6]

Grey Berry (IRE) *Tim Easterby* a38 60
3 gr f Alhebayeb(IRE) Ur Secret Is Safe (IRE) (Dylan Thomas (IRE))
1816[5] 2147[4] 2590[8] 3414[11] 4278[7] 5031[7] 5389[4] 6024[7] 6502[11] 7336[4]

Grey Britain *John Ryan* a110 106
5 gr g Arcano(IRE) Reaching Ahead (USA) (Mizzen Mast (USA))
(519) 757[3] 1062[5] (Dead)

Greybychoice (IRE) *Nick Littmoden* a65 57
3 b g Dark Angel(IRE) Khalice (Bahamian Bounty)
(881) 1035[7] 1285[12] 2204[8] 2939[6] 3440[5] 4454[RR] 7105[4] 7811[11]

Greycoat *James Fanshawe* a74
2 gr c Lethal Force(IRE) Scarlet Royal (Red Ransom (USA))
8494[3]◆

Grey D'Ars (FR) *Nick Littmoden* a84 80
3 gr g Rajsaman(FR) Prisenflag (FR) (Pyrus (USA))
5614[8] 6349[2] 6454[4] 7279[3] 8014[9]

Grey Destiny *Antony Brittain* a69 54
9 gr g Desideratum Mother Corrigan (IRE) (Paris House)
(64) (233) 463[2] 609[6] 705[3] 830[8] (1338) 1684[5] 2183[7] 2692[4] 4194[8] 4455[6] 4767[3] 5282[11]

Grey Eminence *James Given* a67 53
2 gr g Outstrip Laurena (GER) (Acatenango (GER))
8511[7] 8810[4] 9181[12]

Grey Flash (USA) *Bent Olsen* 68
2 rg c The Factor(USA) Wildcat Lily (USA) (D'Wildcat (USA))
7495a[9]

Grey Fox (IRE) *Emma Lavelle* a68 60
2 gr c Gutaifan(IRE) Boucheron (Galileo (IRE))
8516[5] 9208[6]

Grey Galleon (USA) *Clive Cox* a79 79
5 gr g Mizzen Mast(USA) Floresta (USA) (Forest Camp (USA))
91[10] 2484[4] 3462[4] 3838[8] 4501[2] 4786[3] 5677[4] 6084[5] 6401[5] 9245[7] 9453[9]

Grey Gem (IRE) *K Kukk*
8 gr g Danehill Dancer(IRE) Tiffany Diamond (IRE) (Sadler's Wells (USA))
4687a[8]

Grey Hare *Tony Carroll* a39 47
3 gr g Captain Gerrard(IRE) Ya Halla (IRE) (Dark Angel (IRE))
3319[10] 3887[8] 4180[5] 4754[8] 5377[7] 6361[10]

Grey Lion (IRE) *Matthew A Smith* a75 102
7 gr g Galileo(IRE) Grey Lilas (IRE) (Danehill (USA))
8600a[8]

Grey Mist *Karen McLintock* a70 75
5 gr g Mastercraftsman(IRE) Kekova (Montjeu (IRE))
(99)◆ (2217) (2591) 9405[9]

Grey Mystere *J-C Rouget* 97
2 gr f Lethal Force(IRE) Creamcake (USA) (Mr Greeley (USA))
(6384a)

Grey Panel (FR) *T Le Brocq* 43
11 gr g Largesse Minnie's Mystery (FR) (Highest Honor (FR))
2003a[5] 3642a[6]

Grey Rasko (FR) *Edouard Thueux* a14 64
3 b g Rajsaman(FR) Barossa (FR) (Hannouma (IRE))
9280a[14]

Grey Spirit (IRE)
Sir Mark Prescott Bt a86 88
4 gr g Dark Angel(IRE) Buttonhole (Montjeu (IRE))
3300[5] (4837)◆ 5130[5] 7212[3] 7816[3]

Greyzee (IRE) *Rod Millman* a62 62
3 gr g Zebedee Curl (IRE) (Duke Of Marmalade (IRE))
183[6]◆ 537[2] 829[2] (1173) 1481[6] 2734[3] 5337[8] 5580[7] 6123[8]

Griffin Street *Alistair Whillans* a37 50
6 gr g Zebedee Twilight Belle (IRE) (Fasliyev (USA))
6936[11] 7214[8] 7488[8] 7737[10] 8233[12]

Griffone (FR) *J D Hillis* a81 70
4 b h Vision D'Etat(FR) Infini (GER) (Sinndar (IRE))
2002a[6]

Griggy (IRE) *Sean Curran* a61 63
3 b g Dandy Man(IRE) Joint Destiny (IRE) (Desert Prince (IRE))
906[4] 1337[4] 2063[11] 2939[12] 3442[12] 4192[6] 8119[7] 8821[4] 9161[3] 9272[4] (9457) (9508)

Grimbold *K R Burke* a29 54
2 b g Kyllachy Breve (Observatory (USA))
4275[6] 5212[7] 5655[9] 6271[4] 6884[8]

Grimsdyke *Tim Easterby* a36 61
3 b g Firebreak Katie Boo (IRE) (Namid)
4584[13] 4823[7] (5558) 5914[2]◆ 6462[6] 7389[7] (7590) 7764[6]

Grimsthorpe Castle *Ed Walker* a45 50
2 b c Dawn Approach(IRE) Willoughby (IRE) (Oasis Dream)
5774[9] 6395[8] 6858[8] 7516[11] 8061[10]

Grinling (IRE) *Richard Hannon* a64 59
2 b c Mastercraftsman(IRE) Gravitation (Galileo (IRE))
6912[8] 7755[10] 9007[7]

Grinty (IRE) *Michael Dods* a59 68
5 b g Elnadim(USA) Fire Line (Firebreak)
45[9] 231[11] 830[7]

Gripper *Lucinda Russell* a68 63
4 b g Thewayyouare(USA) Hold On Tight (IRE) (Hernando (FR))
8236[6] 9093[13]

Grise Lightning (FR) *Richard Fahey* a73 81
4 gr m Wootton Bassett Tenepia (FR) (Keltos (FR))
42[9] 279[9]

Grise Magicienne (FR)
Gerard Aidant a28 7
4 gr m Gris De Gris(IRE) Aurore Fleurie (FR) (Cadoudal (FR))
2002a[12] 2264a[13]

Grisons (FR) *Robert Cowell* a78 74
3 b c Iffraaj Fig Roll (Bahamian Bounty)
4421[2] 4827[7] 6023[3] (6198) (7157) 7552[2] 9458[3] 9632[5]

Gritti (FR) *C Ferland* a75 91
3 ch c Le Havre(IRE) Grenadia (USA) (Thunder Gulch (USA))
1347a[6]

Gronkowski (USA) *S bin Ghadayer* a119 79
4 b h Lonhro(AUS) Four Sugars (USA) (Lookin At Lucky (USA))
1114a[5] 1447a[2]

Groundswell (AUS)
Anthony Freedman 106
2 b c Fastnet Rock(AUS) The Broken Shore (AUS) (Hussonet (USA))
8137a[3]

Groundworker (IRE) *Paul Midgley* a52 62
8 b g Tagula(IRE) Notepad (King's Best (USA))
1554[9] 2189[3] 2678[5] 3213[3] (3723) 4132[7] 5018[12] 5276[11] (6659) 7307[7] 7766[2]

Groupie *Tom Tate* a54 66
5 b m Requinto(IRE) Amour Fou (IRE) (Piccolo)
3414[5] 3969[8] 4523[8] 6025[4] 6590[7] 7051[5] 7420[9] 7654[5] 8469[2] 8901[2] 9160[8]

Group Stage (GER) *Alan King* 76
3 b g Maxios Good Hope (GER) (Seattle Dancer (USA))
2582[3] 3765[2] 4739[6] 8002[5]

Grouseman *Pam Sly* a48 56
2 b g Kyllachy Speciosa (IRE) (Danehill Dancer (IRE))
4324[7] 8504[10]

Grove Ferry (IRE) *Andrew Balding* 88
2 b g Excelebration(IRE) Rebelline (IRE) (Robellino (USA))
2761[8] (3695) (4832)

Grove Hill (IRE) *Michael Mulvany* a59 57
6 b m Millenary Knocka Beauty (IRE) (Allegoric (USA))
5712a[13] 7088a[6]

Groveman *Jedd O'Keeffe* a81 84
4 b g Holy Roman Emperor(IRE) Raving Monsun (Monsun (GER))
2080[5] 4241[2]

Growl *Richard Fahey* a67 103
7 b g Oasis Dream Desert Tigress (USA) (Storm Cat (USA))
2100[10] 2557[8] 3480[4] 3589[5] 4402[2]◆ 4896[17] 5454[7] 5664[9] (6227) 6714[6] 7433[2] 8127[12]

Guandi (USA) *Tom Dascombe* a77 71
3 ch g Declaration Of War(USA) Hoh Buzzard (IRE) (Alhaarth (IRE))
1754[5] 3067[2] 3510[5] 4188[6] 9012[2] 9138[5]

Guaracha *Alexandra Dunn* a49 51
8 ch g Halling(USA) Pachanga (Inchinor)
1341[10] 1679[9] 2014[9] 2695[5] 3497[5] 5053[2] 6046[3] 7390[10] 7818[10] 8196[10] 8916[6] 9087[7] 9312[9]

Guarana (USA) *Chad C Brown* a113
3 b f Ghostzapper(USA) Magical World (USA) (Distorted Humor (USA))
7479a[2]

Guaranteed (IRE) *J S Bolger* 109
3 b c Teofilo(IRE) Gearanai (USA) (Toccet (USA))
1603a[6] 2662a[6] 3104a[10] 4414a[5] 5874a[2] 6192a[3] 7218a[6]

Guarded Secret *Michael Dods* 40
3 ch f Bated Breath Hill Welcome (Most Welcome)
2823[11] 3565[5] 3920[8] 5554[8]

Guardian Fay (IRE)
Jean-Pierre Carvalho 86
3 b f Soldier Hollow Guardia (GER) (Monsun (GER))
3639a[8] 7291a[2] 8792a[11]

Guardian Witch (IRE)
Jean-Pierre Carvalho
4 b m Lawman(FR) Guadalupe (GER) (Monsun (GER))
8804a[P]

Guardia Svizzera (IRE) *Roger Fell* a59 64
5 b g Holy Roman Emperor(IRE) Winged Harriet (IRE) (Hawk Wing (USA))
165[7] 237[7] 1521[7] 5042[10] 5330[9] 5722[3] 6099[8] 6659[11] 7286[3] 7487[2] 7507[4] 8071[6] 8263[8] 8720[7] 8840[9] 8925[7] (9161) 9272[5] 9477[12] 9518[9]

Guardiola (USA) *Bernard Llewellyn* a49 50
4 b g Lonhro(AUS) Badalona (Cape Cross (IRE))
2998[10] 4111[9] 4232[9] (5293) 5867[7] 6507[8]

Gueraty (FR) *Angel Imaz-Beloqui* 85
3 b c Captain Chop(FR) Guerendiain (SPA) (Dyhim Diamond (IRE))
6145a[9]

Guernsey (USA) *Doug Watson* a78
5 gr g Tapit(USA) Channel (USA) (Storm Cat (USA))
196a[3] 997[4]

Guiding Spirit (IRE) *Clive Cox* a62 49
3 bz g Zebedee Miss Smilla (Red Ransom (USA))
384[7] 752[4] 1458[9] 4606[9]

Guiding Star *Patrick J McKenna* a44 52
5 b m Iffraaj Still I'm A Star (IRE) (Lawman (FR))
1085[4]

Guildhall *Ralph Beckett* 78
3 b g Cityscape Ecstasy (Pursuit Of Love)
1462[3] 2141[4] 2796[10] 4321[7] 5124[3] 6165[6] 7126[6] 7907[10]

Guildsman (FR) *Archie Watson* 106
2 b g Wootton Bassett Dardiza (IRE) (Street Cry (IRE))
(3542)◆ 3949[3] 4846[4] 5584[12] 6690a[2] 7602a[5]

Guipure *K R Burke* a68 74
2 ch f Dutch Art Interlace (Pivotal)
3506[6] 4142[6] 4605[8] 8022[2] (8394)

Gulf Of Poets *Michael Easterby* a79 99
7 b g Oasis Dream Sandglass (Zafonic (USA))
1413[5]◆ 1753[20] 4035[2] 7430[8] 8096[11]

Gulfstream Tiger (USA)
Francisco Castro 59
2 ch c Elusive Quality(USA) Chulula (USA) (Leroidesanimaux (BRZ))
7495a[15]

Gulland Rock *Anthony Carson* a51 47
8 b g Exceed And Excel(AUS) Sacre Coeur (Compton Place)
3142[10] 3781[5] 4067[9] 5081[6] 5302[6] 6131[6] 7603[4] 8547[8] 8949[5] 9249[9]

Gullane One (IRE) *Tim Easterby* a60 72
4 ch g Dream Ahead(USA) Shamsalmaidan (IRE) (Fantastic Light (USA))
1760[17] (3706)◆ 4103[8] 4440[7] 4829[8] 5395[11] 5723[3] (6581) 7311[8] 7703[4] 8403[4]

Gulliver *David O'Meara* a106 108
5 b g Sayif(IRE) Sweet Coincidence (Mujahid (USA))
136[3] 470[4] 762[3] 909[7] 2743[11] 3480[3] 3945[4] (4402)◆ 5454[15] 5664[6] 6229[12] 6706[12] 7241a[3] 7433[3] (8127)

Gumball (FR) *Philip Hobbs* a86 93
5 gr g No Risk At All(FR) Good Time Girl (FR) (Slickly (FR))
(921) (1331) (2143) 2801[4]

Gun Case *Alistair Whillans* a69 47
7 b g Showcasing Bassinet (USA) (Stravinsky (USA))
355[7] 738[8] 3922[14] 4979[4] 6174[11] 7654[11] 7961[9] 8530[7]

Gunmaker (IRE) *Ruth Carr* a72 55
5 b g Canford Cliffs(IRE) Can Dance (Manduro (GER))
1329[3] 1880[3] 2247[2] 3207[10] 3656[5] 4148[10] 4784[8] 5282[9] 5852[6] 6373[9] 6945[6]

Gunmetal (IRE) *David Barron* 104
6 gr g Clodovil(IRE) March Star (IRE) (Mac's Imp (USA))
2442[5] 3097[4] 4095[6] 5664[15] 6351[13] 7193[17] 7433[9] 7701[2] 8127[14] 8512[9]

Gunmetal Jack (IRE)
M D O'Callaghan a69 69
2 gr g Outstrip Polly Adler (Fantastic Light (USA))
5710a[4]

Gunnabedun (IRE) *Iain Jardine* a59 40
3 gr g Gregorian(IRE) Green Vision (IRE) (Green Desert (USA))
21[5] 215[4] 406[5] 1167[9] (1554)◆ 1863[4] (2300) 2683[8] 3417[7] 4276[7] 4493[8] 5278[12]

Gunner Moyne *Emma Owen* a11
7 b g Excellent Art Maramkova (IRE) (Danehill Dancer (IRE))
9446[11]

Gunnery (FR) *Nicky Henderson* 54
6 ch g Le Havre(IRE) Loup The Loup (FR) (Loup Solitaire (USA))
3952[16]

Gunnevera (USA) *Antonio Sano* a121
5 ch h Dialed In(USA) Unbridled Rage (USA) (Unbridled (USA))
445a[6] 1447a[3]

Gunnison *Richard Fahey* a56 57
3 b g Mayson Kinkajou (Distinctly North (USA))
2243[5] 2590[5] 3339[4] 3771[6] 4286[6] 4726[3] 5215[12] 6101[9] (6678) 6983[3] 7385[4] 7960[4] 8301[8]

Guns Of Leros (USA) *Gary Moore* a66 87
6 bb g Cape Blanco(IRE) Zappeuse (USA) (Kingmambo (USA))
2032[8] 2781[6] 3635[8] 5321[6] 5540[18]

Gupta *David Brown* a63
3 b g Equiano(FR) Lanai (IRE) (Camacho)
831[3] 1161[4] 1336[6] 7959[11] 8839[8] 9092[11] 9219[8]

Gurkha Friend *Karen McLintock* a95 101
7 b g Showcasing Parabola (Galileo (IRE))
929[9] 1232[3] 2187[7] 2873[RR]

Guroor *Marco Botti* a79 62
3 ch f Lope De Vega(IRE) Shalwa (Galileo (IRE))
2253[13] 4110[8] 5355[5] 6030[5] 7344[5] 7817[3] 8200[2] (8293) (9067)◆ 9511[2]

Gustave Aitch (FR) *Sophie Leech* a54 42
3 b g Maxios Alyssandre (IRE) (Oasis Dream)
1824[12] 7035[5] 7999[7] 8644[7]

Gustavo Fring (IRE)
Richard Spencer a58 31
5 b g Kodiac Maleha (IRE) (Cape Cross (IRE))
3147[10] 4501[9] 6373[12]

Gustavus Weston (IRE)
Joseph G Murphy 111
3 br g Equiano(FR) Chrissycross (IRE) (Cape Cross (IRE))
2156a[8] 2882a[2] 5205a[10] (5923a) 7713a[4]

Guvenor's Choice (IRE)
Marjorie Fife a52 62
4 ro g Intikhab(USA) Exempt (Exceed And Excel (AUS))
874 625[3] 2335[3] 2962[4] 3541[6] 4067[7] 4602[4] 6341[16] 7060[9] 8186[14] 8753[2]

Gwafa (IRE) *Paul Webber* a88 91
8 gr g Tamayuz Atalina (FR) (Linamix (FR))
4614[5] 5967[2] (6848)

Gweedore *Katie Scott* a59 65
2 b g Epaulette(AUS) Ares Choix (Choisir (AUS))
6314[5] 6684[4] 7361[6] 9640[5]

Gwendola *C Laffon-Parias* a96 96
3 b f Oasis Dream Gwenseb (FR) (Green Tune (USA))
9170a[2]

Gworn *R Mike Smith* a51 62
9 b g Aussie Rules(USA) Crochet (IRE) (Mark Of Esteem (IRE))
3180[4] 3867[7] 4057[4] 4982[8] 5239[6] 5937[7] 6341[8] 6937[8] 7492[10] 7739[2] 8238[4] 8423[5] 8904[7] 9345[13] 9470[6]

Gyllen (USA) *A Fabre* a71 104
4 bb g Medaglia d'Oro(USA) Miss Halory (USA) (Mr Prospector (USA))
2428a[6] 3389a[5] 5718a[5] 6522a[8]

Gylo (IRE) *David O'Meara* a44 77
3 b g Tamayuz She's A Character (Invincible Spirit (IRE))
1723[8] 2094[9] 2635[7] 2933[6] 3478[6] 5215[4] 5695[5] 5814[2] (6702)◆ (6827) (7048) 7441[11] 8341[4]

Gymkhana *P De Chevigny* a78 88
6 ch g Equiano(FR) Village Fete (Singspiel (IRE))
3589[15] 4079[9] 4319[4] 5692[3] 5951[5] 9483a[6]

Gypsy Moth (USA) *A bin Harmash* 53
5 b g Medaglia d'Oro(USA) Gentle Gale (USA) (Storm Cat (USA))
1742a[7]

Gypsy Rocker (IRE) *Brian Meehan* 43
2 ch g Slade Power(IRE) Delira (IRE) (Namid)
2792[11] 3419[10] 5780[10]

Gypsy Rosaleen *David Evans*
2 b f Sayif(IRE) Buredyma (Dutch Art)
4480[11]

Gypsy Spirit *Tom Clover* a78 97
3 b f Gregorian(IRE) Romany Gypsy (Indesatchel (IRE))
1751[7] 2498a[3] 4052[17] 4621a[2] 5608[15] 6270a[2] 7496a[4] 8115[4] 8983a[5]

Gypsy Traveller *Kevin Frost* a55
2 b g Alhebayeb(IRE) Romany Gypsy (Indesatchel (IRE))
8503[8] 8865[9] 9251[6]

Gypsy Whisper *David Menuisier* 77
2 b f Helmet(AUS) Secret Insider (USA) (Elusive Quality (USA))
4798[4] 5772[6] (6603) 7409[4]

Haabis (USA) *Patrick Chamings* a48 1
6 b g Super Saver(USA) Raise Fee (USA) (Menifee (USA))
80[10] 2240[11] 6051[12]

Haadef *Brian Meehan* 50
3 b g Delegator Peace Concluded (Bertolini (USA))
2280[6] 2900[7]

Haader (FR) *Derek Shaw* a59 54
4 ch g Sepoy(AUS) Idle Tears (Selkirk (USA))
316[6] 431[6] 706[3] 914[10] 1403[7] 1595[3] 2532[8] 2741[6]◆ 3304[10] 3738[9]

Haafel (IRE) *Charles Hills* 22
2 gr c Dark Angel(IRE) Enfijaar (IRE) (Invincible Spirit (IRE))
3194[12]

Haats Off *Brian Barr* a63 73
3 ch f Haatef(USA) Lahqa (IRE) (Tamayuz)
555[7] 1043[2] 2503a[3] 3191[4] 3836[7]

Habah (USA) *Doug Watson* a78
3 b f Twirling Candy(USA) Dear Mama (ARG) (Mutakddim (USA))
510a[6] 845a[4]

Habub (USA) *Owen Burrows* a109 75
4 b h War Front(USA) Sweet Lulu (USA) (Mr Greeley (USA))
(2009) 2791[7] (5945)◆ 6706[7] 7188[2] (7997)

Hackbridge *Pat Phelan* a77 79
4 br g Archipenko(USA) Famcred (Inchinor)
876[2] 1095[2] 1655[2] 4548[7] 5311[12] 9303[12]

Hackle Setter (USA) *Sylvester Kirk* a75 71
3 b g Noble Mission Zaharias (USA) (Grand Slam (USA))
1736[9] 3465[11] 4793[5] 5505[5] 6538[4] 7542[7] 8806[4]

Hackney Road
Fernando Perez-Gonzalez a86 93
6 b m Aqlaam West Lorne (USA) (Gone West (USA))
4948a[5] 7254a[10]

Haddaf (IRE) *Stuart Williams* a83 84
4 b g Dawn Approach(IRE) Deveron (USA) (Cozzene (USA))
1421[11] 1892[5] 2442[10] 2910[9] 5195[6] 5626[5] 6517[2] 7164[7] 7467[8] 9054[3] 9176[4] 9455[3] 9519[7]

Hadeer (IRE) *R Al Jehani* a64 57
3 b c Rock Of Gibraltar(IRE) Elhareer (IRE) (Selkirk (USA))
893a[11]

Hadfield (IRE) *Neil Mulholland* a72 80
7 b g Sea The Stars(IRE) Rezyana (AUS) (Redoute's Choice (AUS))
1330[4]

Hafeet Alain (IRE) *Adrian Nicholls* 100
3 b g Elzaam(AUS) Batuta (New Approach (IRE))
2078[3] 2787[2] 3479[2] 3654[5] (8101) (8728)◆

Haggswood Boy *Ronald Thompson* a32 20
3 ch g Coach House(IRE) Bustling Darcey (Assertive)
458[7]

Haida Gwaii (IRE) *Charles Hills* a47
2 b f Zoffany(IRE) Briolette (IRE) (Sadler's Wells (USA))
9509[9]

Haighfield *Paul Midgley* a49 53
3 b f Garswood Crawford Avenue (Equiano (FR))
4508[8]

Haitian Spirit *Gary Moore* a60 49
3 b f Swiss Spirit Haiti Dancer (Josr Algarhoud (IRE))
438[5] 4477[7]

Hajey *Mark Johnston* a45
2 ch c Raven's Pass(USA) Almashooqa (USA) (Dubawi (IRE))
7958[9]

Hajjam *David O'Meara* a98 95
5 b g Paco Boy(IRE) Amanda Carter (Tobougg (IRE))
1891[5] 2378[4] 2609[9] 4127[6] 4385[4] 4921[12] 5312[3] 5692[9] 5971[7]

Haky (IRE) *J E Hammond* a79 106
5 ch g Muhtathir Marah Dubai (FR) (Dubawi (IRE))
6266a[3] 7008a[2] 8134a[11] 8600a[3] 8767a[8]

Haldane (IRE) *Phillip Makin* 62
2 b g Gleneagles(IRE) One Chance (IRE) (Invincible Spirit (IRE))
3998[5]◆

Halfacrown (IRE) *Jamie Osborne* a48 49
2 b c Hallowed Crown(AUS) Ava's World (IRE) (Desert Prince (IRE))
4114[9] 5602[5] 5887[6] 6435[5] 6604[7] 8526[3] 8824[6] 9045[2] 9399[3]

Half Bolly *Mark Walford* a51 61
3 ch g Haafhd Zefooha (FR) (Lomitas)
405[9] 971[7] 1195[9] 5898[9] 6180[3] 6400[7] 7290[3]

Half Full *Stuart Coltherd* a43 49
3 ch g Monsieur Bond(IRE) Choral Singer (Daylami (IRE))
20[9] 612[8] 2213[7] 2587[4] 3299[10] 5096[7] 5766[14]

Half Nutz (IRE) *Ms Sheila Lavery* 66
2 ch g Sir Prancealot(IRE) Segoria (IRE) (Shinko Forest (IRE))
7247a[17]

Half Of Seven *Jonjo O'Neill*
2 b f Harbour Watch(IRE) Neila (GER) (Diktat)
6019[10]

Halfwaytothemoon (IRE)
John Gosden a41
2 b f Sea The Stars(IRE) Reflective (USA) (Seeking The Gold (USA))
9415[9]

Halimi (IRE) *J S Bolger* 99
3 bb c Teofilo(IRE) Vincennes (King's Best (USA))
4136a[4]

Hallalulu *S Cerulis* a83 88
3 br f Kyllachy Cat O' Nine Tails (Motivator)
3264[3] 4110[2] 4549[3] 6902[5] 7702[9] (9281a)

Halle's Harbour *Paul George* a62 57
3 ch f Harbour Watch(IRE) Clifton Dancer (Fraam)
(137) 813[4] 1170[5] 2357[3] 6286[13] 7770[7] 8018[2] 8896[3] 9246[5]

Hallings Comet *Shaun Lycett* a32 53
10 ch g Halling(USA) Landinium (ITY) (Lando (GER))
560[11]

Hamariyna (IRE) *M Halford* 99
3 b f Sea The Moon(GER) Hanakiyya (IRE) (Danehill Dancer (IRE))
(2661a)

Hameem *John Gosden* a106 99
4 br m Teofilo(IRE) Tres Ravi (GER) (Monsun (GER))
(2763) 4145[8] 4864[4] (5735)◆ 6378[4] 8710[2] 9302[3]

Hamish *William Haggas* 114
3 b g Motivator Tweed (Sakhee (USA))
2198[2]◆ (3946) 4842[3] (6471) (8098)◆ 8520[2]

Hamish Macbeth *Hugo Palmer* a79 93
2 b g Due Diligence(USA) Brick Tops (Danehill Dancer (IRE))
2761[5] (5381) (6415) 7247a[3] 8426[5] 9582a[5]

Hamley (FR) *Peter Fahey* a90 98
6 b m Fastnet Rock(AUS) Mary Arnold (IRE) (Hernando (FR))
5535a[13]

Hamlul (FR) *Sir Michael Stoute* a83 93
4 gr h Frankel Alix Road (FR) (Linamix (FR))
2022[4] (Dead)

Hammer Gun (USA) *Derek Shaw* a85 78
6 b g Smart Strike(CAN) Caraboss (Cape Cross (IRE))
44[4] 255[2] 381[8] 557[9] 812[6]◆ 1036[6] (1197) (1367) 1428[5] 2015[8] (2076) (3305) 3880[3] 4322[6] 5741[8] 6841[7] 7074[2] (7378) 8642[2] 8761[13]

Hammerindown (USA)
Mohamed Al Farsi a57 47
8 bb g Put It Back(USA) Baba's Mandate (USA) (Full Mandate (USA))
869a[14]

Hammy End (IRE) *William Muir* a62 65
3 b g Mount Nelson Northern Affair (IRE) (Giant's Causeway (USA))
156[9] 403[5] 765[10] (4485) 5601[3] 6128[3] 6702[2] 7290[2] 7984[2] 8248[5] 9005[6]

Hamper (FR) *P Adda* a51 48
3 b g Penny's Picnic(IRE) Barbieri (IRE) (Encosta De Lago (AUS))
1842a[6] 3066a[12] 7642a[10]

Hanabaal Tun (FR)
R Le Dren Doleuze a74 69
5 b h Elusive City(USA) Annatto (USA) (Mister Baileys)
5715a[6] 7861a[8]

Hanakotoba (USA) *Stuart Williams* a68 68
3 b f Can The Man(USA) Dalis On Stage (USA) (Yankee Gentleman (USA))
215[2] 287[3] (605) 1275[7] 1492[5] 1954[2] 2281[5] 3045[5] 3742[3] 4343[6]

Hanalei Moon (USA) *Mark Casse* a87 100
4 ch m Malibu Moon(USA) Authenticity (USA) (Quiet American (USA))
7920a[5]

Hanati (IRE) *Brian Ellison* a55 34
3 ch f Camacho Royal Visit (IRE) (King's Best (USA))
1[2] (186)◆ 388[2] 1275[5] 4330[8] 6057[5] 6575[10] 6685[5] 7307[13] 8119[10]

Hanbury Dreams *Tom Clover* a62 43
3 b f Heeraat(IRE) Lady O Malley (IRE) (Oratorio (IRE))
380[3] 798[9] 2251[9] 3258[6] 4029[7]

Handful Of Gold (IRE)
Kevin Bishop a36 17
2 ch f No Nay Never(USA) Golden Passion (IRE) (Arakan (USA))
6330[10] 6800[7] 9363[10]

Handiwork *Steve Gollings* a88 90
9 ch g Motivator Spinning Top (Alzao (USA))
(2080) 2781[10] 4146[6] 4782[6] 7819[3] 8661[4]

Handlebars (IRE) *Keith Dalgleish* 65
2 br f Footstepsinthesand Amodio (IRE) (Cape Cross (IRE))
6570[3] 6934[3] 7361[9] 7874[7]

Handmaiden *H-A Pantall* a80 78
3 b f Invincible Spirit(IRE) Zabeel Park (USA) (Medicean)
1855[6] 3712a[5]

Hand On Heart (IRE) *J A Stack* 98
4 ch m Mastercraftsman(IRE) Insight (FR) (Sadler's Wells (USA))
1307a[2]◆ 2493a[4] 3986[15]

Hand On My Heart *Clive Cox* 92
2 ch f Iffraaj Place In My Heart (Compton Place)
(4398) 5542[9] 6791a[7]

Hands Down (IRE) *Nigel Tinkler* a24 53
2 b f Mukhadram Flurry Of Hands (IRE) (Acclamation)
4517[11] 6064[10] 6457[12] 6919[11] 8022[10]

Handsome Bob (IRE) *Neil King* a17 14
4 b g Most Improved(IRE) Beautiful Dreamer (Red Ransom (USA))
387[12] 927[5] 1235[10] 9497[7]

Handsome Yank (USA)
Ivan Furtado 62
2 bb g Kitten's Joy(USA) Upper East Sider (USA) (Forest Wildcat (USA))
3194[10] 7361[8] 7870[11]

Handytalk (IRE) *Rod Millman* a74 84
6 b g Lilbourne Lad(IRE) Dancing With Stars (IRE) (Where Or When (IRE))
1654[3] 2107[11] 2472[2] 3040[3] (3701) 3838[5] 4545[7] (5495) 5882[8] 7115[2]

Hang Man (IRE) *Michael Moroney* 94
5 ch g Windsor Knot(IRE) Halliard (Halling (USA))
8134a[5] 8803a[3]

Han Solo Berger (IRE) *Chris Wall* a68 82
4 b g Lord Shanakill(USA) Dreamaway (IRE) (Oasis Dream)
1822[8] 3206[7] 4829[2] 5318[2] 5532[2]◆ 6162[8] (6455) 7077[13]◆ (7321) 7894[16]

Ha'penny Bridge (IRE)
Mrs John Harrington 89
2 ch f Tamayuz Diminish (IRE) (Raven's Pass (USA))
7215a[4]

Happen (USA) *A P O'Brien* a52 102
3 b f War Front(USA) Alexandrova (IRE) (Sadler's Wells (USA))
1601a[2] (2493a) 4051[6] 5645a[2] 7221a[6]

Happy Bean (USA) *C Laffon-Parias* a65 35
3 bl f Medaglia d'Oro(USA) Happy Week (USA) (Distorted Humor (USA))
993a[10]

Happy Bere (FR) *A De Watrigant* 105
2 bl c Pedro The Great(USA) Miss Fine (FR) (Kaldoun (FR))
(6002a) 7005a[4] 7887a[4] 9582a[3]

Happy Chrisnat (FR) *C Plisson* a61 79
2 b c Red Dubawi(IRE) Impedimanta (IRE) (Aussie Rules (USA))
6485a[6] 7043a[5] 8448a[7]

Happy Clapper (AUS)
Patrick Webster 121
8 b g Teofilo(IRE) Busking (AUS) (Encosta De Lago (AUS))
1783a[4]

Happy Company (IRE) *P J Hassett* a50 70
5 ch g Fast Company(IRE) Miss Mauna Kea (IRE) (Observatory (USA))
5599a[13]

Happy Ending (IRE)
Seamus Mullins a48 60
4 b m Big Bad Bob(IRE) Heroic Performer (IRE) (Royal Applause)
85[12] 482[11] 7891[10] 2234[13] 3834[3] 4216[7]

Happy Escape *Tony Carroll* a87 81
5 b m Delegator Saharan Song (IRE) (Singspiel (IRE))
(81) (255)◆ 475[3] 756[10] 1234[5]

Happy Face (IRE) *Joseph Tuite* a67 71
3 b f Kingman Intense Pink (Pivotal)
5141[4] 5690[3] 6315[5] 9644[4]

Happy Hannah (IRE) *John Davies* 51
3 ch f Gale Force Ten Sli Na Fiarana (Dr Fong (USA))
1764[5] 2337[13] 4002[9] 4584[11] 5214[10]

Happy Hiker (IRE) *Michael Bell* 83
3 b f Dalakhani(IRE) Travelling Light (USA) (Gone West (USA))
1738[4] 2148[3] (2838) 5190[7] 6124[6]

Happy Odyssey (IRE) *N Clement* 98
3 b f Camacho Casual Remark (IRE) (Trans Island)
1200a[3] 1780a[2] 2564a[6] 4703a[8]

Happy Pepite (FR) *C Plisson* 35
2 b f Soul City(IRE) Armelle D'Haguenet (FR) (Sleeping Car (FR))
1240a[12]

Happy Power (IRE) *Andrew Balding* 116
3 gr c Dark Angel(IRE) Tamarisk (GER) (Selkirk (USA))
(1736) 2615[3] (3814) 4092[7] 5543[4] 6443[3] 7660[5] 8334[6]

Happy Star (FR) *C Escuder* a57 46
2 gr f Milanais(FR) Cousine (FR) (Slickly (FR))
6196a[12]

Hapt (FR) *M Nigge* a49 67
3 b f Masterstroke(USA) Honey Gem (FR) (Gold Away (IRE))
3139a[2]

Haqeeqy (IRE) *John Gosden* 71
2 b c Lope De Vega(IRE) Legal Lyric (IRE) (Lawman (FR))
7458[4]

Haraz (IRE) *Paddy Butler* a50 56
6 b g Acclamation Hanakiyya (IRE) (Danehill Dancer (IRE))
263[5] 365[5] 760[7] 1731[8] 1935[9] 2006[3] 3592[11] 6051[11] (6414) 6844[4] 7603[7] 8417[8] 9249[7] 9384[3]

Harbour Bay *Jedd O'Keeffe* a61 51
4 b h Harbour Watch(IRE) Three Secrets (IRE) (Danehill (USA))
608[7] 968[5]

Harbour Breeze (IRE)
Lucy Wadham a92 85
4 b g Le Havre(IRE) Retiens La Nuit (USA) (Grand Slam (USA))
1102[3]◆ 1757[17] (2186) (2969) 4035[8] 4613[7] 5174[6]

Harbour City (USA) *James Tate* a59
3 b f Australia Who Is Camille (USA) (Dixie Union (USA))
5269[4] 6074[5] 6862[3] 7376[12] 8405[7]

Harbour Force (FR) *Neil Mulholland* a53 55
5 b g Harbour Watch(IRE) Dam Beautiful (Sleeping Indian)
59[9] 288[10] 724[8] 1679[8]
Harbour Front *Robyn Brisland* a70
3 b g Iffraaj Wosaita (Generous (IRE))
8500[3] 9469[4]
Harbour Mist (IRE) *Tim Easterby*
2 b g Harbour Watch(IRE) Ittasal (Any Given Saturday (USA))
9471[13]
Harbour Patrol (IRE)
Rebecca Bastiman a48 51
7 b g Acclamation Traou Mad (IRE) (Barathea (IRE))
116[6] 273[3] 501[9]
Harbour Point *Michael Appleby* a40 68
2 ch f Harbour Watch(IRE) Stunning Icon (Dr Fong (USA))
8202[5] 8431[4] 9181[7]
Harbour Quay *Patrick Chamings* a6 2
5 b g Foxwedge(AUS) Whatcameoverme (USA) (Aldebaran (USA))
242[7] 435[3] 833[2] 927[3] 1292[5] 1861[6] 3150[4] 9542[11]
Harbour Spirit (FR) *Richard Hughes* a87 72
3 b g Charm Spirit(IRE) Save Me The Waltz (FR) (Halling (USA))
1360[4] 1857[11] 3526a[4] (4506) 5667[10] 6347[6] 7191[3] 8320[6]
Harbour Sunrise *Shaun Harris* a16 38
4 b m Harbour Watch(IRE) Nairobi (FR) (Anabaa (USA))
969[10] 5293[9]
Harbour Times (IRE)
Patrick Chamings a41 48
3 br f Harbour Watch(IRE) Elegant Times (IRE) (Dansili)
2734[9] 4217[8] 5377[2] 6052[4] 6569[10] 7523[7]
Harbour Vision *Derek Shaw* a77 76
4 gr g Harbour Watch(IRE) Holy Nola (USA) (Silver Deputy (CAN))
(430) 5484 (801) 1099[2] 1479[5] (2065) 2739[4] 3147[5] 3813[12] 4249[7] 5178[6] 5688[2] 6220[11] 6863[4] 8549[3] 8692[8] 9054[8] 9224[7] 9453[6]
Hard Knock Life *Tim Easterby* 40
3 b g Dream Ahead(USA) Little Annie (Compton Place)
2713[9] 3157[8] 4210[11]
Hard Not To Love (CAN)
John Shirreffs a113
3 b f Hard Spun(USA) Loving Vindication (USA) (Vindication (USA))
(9638a)
Hard Nut (IRE) *Richard Hannon* a85 85
2 b c Gutaifan(IRE) With A Twist (Excellent Art)
3660[5] (4018) (4839) 5612[5]◆ 6356[5] 6705[2]
Hard Rock (FR) *Louis Baudron* a59 39
2 b g Slickly(FR) Halesia (One Cool Cat (USA))
9605a[7]
Hard Solution *David O'Meara* a72 73
3 ch g Showcasing Copy-Cat (Lion Cavern (USA))
1894[6] 2293[5] 2939[5] 3516[6] 3645[7] 4081[2] (4276) (4434) 4911[3]◆ 5236[3] 5620[8] (7588) 8296[7] 8429[4] 8715[11] 9135[11]
Hard Times (IRE) *Philip Kirby* a32 37
8 b g Moss Vale(IRE) Graze On Too (IRE) (Rainbow Quest (USA))
3181[6] 4914[8]
Hard Toffee (IRE) *Louise Allan* a64 63
8 b g Teofilo(IRE) Speciale (USA) (War Chant (USA))
39[2] 724[12] 2738[2] 3276[7] 6636[5] 7376[11]
Hard To Handel *Mrs A Malzard* a59 60
7 b g Stimulation(IRE) Melody Maker (Diktat)
2501a[2] 4686a[6] 5233[3] 6010a[2] 6554a[4]
Hareem Queen (IRE) *K R Burke* a100 77
3 gr f Dark Angel(IRE) Dulcian (IRE) (Shamardal (USA))
1272[4] 2077[4] (8268) (8900) 9562[2]
Hareeq *Richard Hughes* a87 93
4 b h New Approach(IRE) Fallen Star (Brief Truce (USA))
(1914)◆ 2801[6] 4102[4] 4924[5] 5811[9]
Hares Rocket (IRE) *Joseph Tuite* 37
2 ch g Zebedee Ichiuma (USA) (Mizzen Mast (USA))
3943[14] 4394[10] 4734[10]
Hariboux *Hugo Palmer* a81 97
2 b g Havana Gold(IRE) Royal Warranty (Sir Percy)
(5052) 5527[3] (5801) (6450) 7072[2]
Hark *P Van De Poele* a56 56
5 b m Bated Breath Ancestral Way (Mtoto)
3711a[6]
Harlan Strong (ARG)
Kenneth McPeek 100
4 br h Harlan's Holiday(USA) Muequita Fitz (ARG) (Fitzcarraldo (ARG))
284a[6] 398a[8] 961a[14]
Harlem
David A & B Hayes & Tom Dabern 109
7 b g Champs Elysees Casual (Nayef (USA))
1783a[9] 8136a[3] 8579a[8] 8952a[12]
Harlem Shake (IRE)
Marco Gasparini 95
8 b g Moss Vale(IRE) Ladylishandra (IRE) (Mujadil (USA))
2888a[14]
Harlequin *William Knight* a70 67
2 b g Swiss Spirit Falcon In Flight (Shamardal (USA))
4030[2] 6079[3] 7407[6] 8890[7]
Harlequin Dancer (IRE)
Lawrence Mullaney a59 19
4 b m Zoffany(IRE) April Green (FR) (Green Tune (USA))
504[9]
Harlequin Rose (IRE)
Patrick Chamings a47 57
5 ch m Dutch Art Miss Chaussini (IRE) (Rossini (USA))
2286[8] 3410[3]◆ 4472[4] (4753) 5806[12] 6305[4] (6758) 7028[4] 7549[11] 8416[6]

Harlow *Ian Williams* a77 45
5 b g Harlan's Holiday(USA) Glowing (IRE) (Dansili)
536[5] 754[5] 5337[7]
Harmless (FR) *C Ferland* a86 71
3 ch g Anodin(IRE) Snowbright (Pivotal)
1707a[7]
Harmonie Royale (FR) *P Monfort* a54 40
2 b f Elusive City(USA) Beijaline (FR) (Naaqoos)
6386a[7]
Harmonise *Sheena West* a67 75
5 b m Sakhee's Secret Composing (IRE) (Noverre (USA))
2400[6] 2793[3] 5344[7] (5744) 6104[2] (6371)◆ 8433[4] 8696[9]
Harome (IRE) *Roger Fell* a83 97
5 ch g Bahamian Bounty Clytha (Mark Of Esteem (IRE))
1946[10] 2775[10] 3097[6] 3344[6] 4100[6] (4691) 4722[2] 4896[3] 5317[8] 6351[21] 6534[6] 6920[11] 8099[22]
Harperelle *Alistair Whillans* a42 50
3 ch f Burwaaz She's So Pretty (IRE) (Grand Lodge (USA))
787[3] 1023[10] 1488[7] 2197[14] 3249[10] 3720[B] 4487[6] 4917[7] 5851[11] 6524[5] 7336[7] 7780[10]
Harpocrates (IRE) *A P O'Brien* 108
2 b c Invincible Spirit(IRE) Ideal (Galileo (IRE))
4091[5] 5997a[2] 6352[2] 7119[7]
Harpo Marx (IRE) *A P O'Brien* 98
3 b c Galileo(IRE) Nechita (AUS) (Fastnet Rock (AUS))
3984[6] 5522[7]
Harriet's Force (IRE)
Keith Henry Clarke a95 95
3 b f Lethal Force(IRE) Its On The Air (IRE) (King's Theatre (IRE))
1601a[9] 2157a[9] 6692a[6] 7668a[6] 8734a[9]
Harrison Point (FR) *Archie Watson* a80
2 ch c Speightstown(USA) Summer Surprice (FR) (Le Havre (IRE))
5809[2] (9385)
Harrogate (IRE) *Jim Boyle* a73 83
4 br g Society Rock(IRE) Invincible Me (IRE) (Invincible Spirit (IRE))
1394[8] 2484[11] (3021) 3347[12] 3443[6] 4545[5] (4835) 5606[6] 6534[3] 7268[5] 8285[6] 8895[7]
Harrovian *John Gosden* a79 102
3 b g Leroidesanimaux(BRZ) Alma Mater (Sadler's Wells (USA))
2764[2]◆ 3445[2] (4760)◆ 5614[3] 6506[3] (7396) 8126[7]
Harry Beau *David Evans* a78 65
5 ch g Kheleyf(USA) Lovellian (Machiavellian (USA))
1822[12] 2339[9] 3089[5] 4733[4] 5579[5] 6027[2] 6329[3] 6602[3] 8291[7] 8847[6]
Harry Callahan (IRE) *Mick Channon* a59 58
4 b g Dutch Art Sovana (IRE) (Desert King (IRE))
59[7] 245[2] 363[3] (549) (1145) 1361[3] (1519) 2014[2] 2127[10]
Harry Hurricane *George Baker* a87 88
7 b g Kodiac Eolith (Pastoral Pursuits)
987[4] 2030[6]◆ 2227[2] 2403[3] 2839[2] 3662[5] 4253[2] 4495[6] 5524[13] (6288) (6809) 8267[4] 9131[9]
Harry Love (IRE) *Ollie Pears* 82
2 b g Lawman(FR) Gimmick (IRE) (Siyouni (FR))
3702[2]◆ (4516) (5514) 6498[4]
Harry's Bar *James Fanshawe* a102 68
4 ch g Exceed And Excel(AUS) Firenze (Efisio)
1286[2]◆ 1728[3] 2484[8] 2823[5] (3443) (4458)◆ (5888)◆ 7107[3] 7687[2] 9098[3] (9301)
Harry's Dancer (IRE)
Osama Omer E Al-Dafea 94
7 b m Kodiac Dance On (Caerleon (USA))
892a[5]
Harry's Ridge (IRE) *Eric Alston* a55 54
4 b g Acclamation Dani Ridge (IRE) (Indian Ridge (IRE))
2094[14] 2506[9] 3416[5] 9169[3]◆ 9572[3]
Harry The Norseman *Jonjo O'Neill* a41 60
3 ch g Norse Dancer(IRE) Titled Lady (Sir Percy)
9010 2518[10] 3418[6] 3888[3] 5596[9] 6550[7]
Harswell (IRE) *Liam Bailey* 72
2 b g Kodiac Golden Flower (Royal Applause)
2115[7] (2367) 2747[8] 4893[5] 5275[3]◆
Harswell Approach (IRE)
Liam Bailey 66
2 b g Camacho Maiden Approach (New Approach (IRE))
4623[7] 5273[3]◆ 5615[4] 6226[3] 6969[10]
Hart Fell *Kevin Frost*
3 b g Nayef(USA) Dumfriesshire (Oasis Dream)
8398[10]
Hartnell *James Cummings* 116
8 b g Authorized(IRE) Debonnaire (Anabaa (USA))
1783a[3] 8361a[7] 8952a[3]
Hart's Dream *Kevin Ryan* 11
2 b g Poet's Voice Angel Song (Dansili)
5894[6]
Hartside (GER) *Peter Winks* 22
10 b g Montjeu(IRE) Helvellyn (USA) (Gone West (USA))
8399[6]
Hart Stopper *Stuart Williams* a89 89
5 b g Compton Place Angel Song (Dansili)
2442[7] 3164[6] 4123[9] 4805[2] (5058) 5868[4] 6162[2] 7121[3] 9057[2]◆
Hartswood *Richard Fahey* 80
2 b g Garswood Nihal (IRE) (Singspiel (IRE))
6337[5] 6891[2] (7285)◆ 7904[6]
Harvest Day *Michael Easterby* a78 78
4 b m Harbour Watch(IRE) Miss Wells (IRE) (Sadler's Wells (USA))
23[2] (355)◆ 3567[3] 4243[3] 4626[3] 4831[6] 6609[2] (7288) 7820[2] 8719[9]
Harvestfortheworld (IRE)
J A Stack a80 97
4 bb m So You Think(NZ) Israar (Machiavellian (USA))
1531a[9]

Harvest Ranger *Michael Appleby* a44 45
5 b g Bushranger(IRE) Time Of Gold (USA) (Banker's Gold (USA))
2256[9] 2972[14]
Harvey Dent *Archie Watson* a82 94
3 ch g Mayson Accede (Acclamation)
90[4] (403) 826[2] 1645[9] 2616[4] 3011[4] 3683[2] 4001[5] 4316[2] (4634) 4909[2] (5095) 7068[2]
Harvey Wallbanger (USA)
Kenneth McPeek a106
3 b c Congrats(USA) Adorabell (USA) (Distorted Humor (USA))
7011a[6]
Hasanabad (IRE) *Ian Williams* 97
4 b g Nathaniel(IRE) Hasanka (IRE) (Kalanisi (IRE))
7615[5]
Has D'Emra (FR) *F Rossi* a47 96
2 b c Kheleyf(USA) Royalrique (FR) (Enrique)
1240a[4] (3171a) 5116a[3] 5976a[3] 7775a[3]
Hashtagmetoo (USA)
Jamie Osborne a71 72
2 b f Declaration Of War(USA) Caribbean Princess (USA) (Henrythenavigator (USA))
3578[4] 4221[4] 4840[5] 5777[4] 6161[2] 6504[2] (6629) 7696[7] 8465[3]
Hasili Filly *Lawrence Mullaney* a45 5
3 b f Zoffany(IRE) Miss Marvellous (USA) (Diesis)
2420[7] 3482[11] 7655[6] 7962[7] 8819[4] 9220[11]
Hassaad *Archie Watson* a79 74
3 b f Kodiac Samaah (IRE) (Cape Cross (IRE))
2623[3] (6797) 7854[2] 8285[5] 8715[5] 9106[2]◆ 9218[11] 9519[2]
Hasturies (FR) *Mme Pia Brandt* a67 60
3 ch f Le Havre(IRE) Hasturianita (IRE) (Dubawi (IRE))
(3139a)
Hateya (IRE) *Jim Boyle* a97 100
4 b m Footstepsinthesand Selfsame (USA) (Dansili)
1294[3] 2252[2] 3318[2] 3857[7] 5525[5] 6406[3] 6721[2] 7496a[3]
Hathal (USA) *Jamie Osborne* a111 111
7 ch h Speightstown(USA) Sleepytime (IRE) (Royal Academy (USA))
(121) (601) 879[7]
Hathiq (IRE) *Denis Gerard Hogan* a75 104
5 b g Exceed And Excel(AUS) Madany (IRE) (Acclamation)
3344[17] 4313a[16]◆ 6648a[12] 6986a[8]
Hatsaway (IRE) *Pat Phelan* a47 68
8 b g Dubawi(IRE) Scotch Bonnet (IRE) (Montjeu (IRE))
2400[7] 2928[4] 3778[5] 5089[7] 5679[6] 6566[5] 7202[2] 7759[7]
Hats Off To Larry *Mick Channon* a61 90
5 b g Sixties Icon Highland Jig (Norse Dancer (IRE))
(3072) 3250[2] 4144[2] 4613[5] 4997[2] (5594)
Hattaab *Graeme McPherson* a33 48
6 b g Intikhab(USA) Sundus (USA) (Sadler's Wells (USA))
7818[12]
Hat Yai (IRE) *Andrew Balding* 58
3 b c Garswood Takizada (IRE) (Sendawar (IRE))
1562[10] 2250[4]
Hautot (FR) *Gerald Geisler* a72 76
4 b g Zoffany(IRE) Super Hantem (IRE) (Royal Anthem (USA))
1449a[7] 7861a[6]
Havana Bere (FR) *J Boisnard* 72
2 b f Hurricane Cat(USA) Ajab Bere (FR) (Peer Gynt (JPN))
(2315a)
Havana Dawn *Phillip Makin* a67 73
2 gr f Havana Gold(IRE) Rock Ace (IRE) (Verglas (IRE))
3156[5] 3703[4] (3968) 4647[4] 6369[3] 6653[4] 7029[11] 9031[2] 9401[4] 9515[6]
Havana Go *Keith Dalgleish* a50 66
4 ch g Havana Gold(IRE) Stagecoach Jade (IRE) (Peintre Celebre (USA))
1951[8] 2433[11] 2958[3] 3227[7] 3716[5]◆
Havana Jane *Andrew Balding* a64
4 b m Havana Gold(IRE) Le Badie (IRE) (Spectrum (IRE))
6074[4] (7032) 7788[7]
Havana Ooh Na Na *K R Burke* a71 67
3 ch g Havana Gold(IRE) Blanc De Chine (IRE) (Dark Angel (IRE))
1141[7] (1385) 1721[6] (2016) 2942[7] 3273[2] 3884[7] 4635[4]
Havana Princess *Dr Jon Scargill* a19 20
2 b f Havana Gold(IRE) Yat Ding Yau (FR) (Air Chief Marshal (IRE))
4790[10] 6314[8] 8432[9]
Havana Rocket (IRE)
Andrew Balding a84 80
3 b g Havana Gold(IRE) Mawaakeb (USA) (Diesis)
(354)◆ 1345[3] 1888[5]
Havana Sunset *Mike Murphy* a58
3 b g Havana Gold(IRE) Sunset Kitty (USA) (Gone West (USA))
7573[8] 8223[6] 8756[10]
Have A Nice Day *T G McCourt* a65 74
9 b g Oratorio(IRE) Centrepiece (Pivotal)
5537a[12] 5597a[12]
Havelock (IRE) *Peter Fahey*
5 ch g Helmet(AUS) Pearl Grey (Gone West (USA))
232[2] 507[7]
Haveoneyerself (IRE) *John Butler* a52 67
4 b g Requinto(IRE) Charismas Birthday (IRE) (Choisir (AUS))
1266[10] 2876[10] 4563[5] (5822)◆ 6562[5] 6798[4] 7274[2]
Hawaam (IRE) *Roger Fell* a82 86
4 b g Swiss Spirit Anne Bonney (Jade Robbery (USA))
2079[10] 2625[3]◆ 3360[3] 3936[2] 4301[5] 5298[7] 5420[11] (5691) 6178[6] 7624[2] 7908[4] 8262[5] 8340[14] 8400[2]

Hawafez (IRE) *Saeed bin Suroor* 53
3 ch f Shamardal(USA) Devotee (USA) (Elusive Quality (USA))
3013[9]
Hawaiian Freeze *J Moon* a45 45
10 b m Avonbridge Autumn Affair (Lugana Beach)
2672a[5]
Hawkamah (IRE) *A Fabre* 76
3 ch f New Approach(IRE) Board Meeting (IRE) (Anabaa (USA))
2759a[2]
Hawk Cliff (FR) *Jo Hughes* 51
3 b g Panis(USA) Valse Mystique (IRE) (Grand Lodge (USA))
1450a[12] 1741a[9] 2758a[10]
Hawk In The Sky *Richard Whitaker* a24 71
3 ch g Coach House(IRE) Cocabana (Captain Rio)
1665[8] 4129[5] (4629) 5791[7] 7065[7] 7624[4] 8083[11] (8632)
Hawridge Storm (IRE) *Rod Millman* a65 82
3 b g Intello(GER) Aneedah (IRE) (Invincible Spirit (IRE))
3465[12] 4065[2] 5947[8] 6399[2] 7159[5] 7865[2] 8761[12]
Hayadh *Rebecca Bastiman* a98 97
6 gr g Oasis Dream Warling (IRE) (Montjeu (IRE))
1502[3]◆ 1944[2] (2419)◆ 2778[3] 3863[7] 4403[13] 5693[15] 6231[6] 7312[6] 7906[8]
Haya Of Fortune (FR) *N Leenders* a88 84
5 b m Soldier Of Fortune(IRE) Haya Samma (IRE) (Pivotal)
6651a[11]
Haymarket *R Mike Smith* a40 47
10 b g Singspiel(IRE) Quickstyx (Night Shift (USA))
2330[8] 2682[7] 3181[5] 4054[8] 4690[7] 5100[11] 6628[11] 7738[5] 8234[9]
Hayuplass *Tim Easterby* a48 3
2 b f Showcasing Music In Exile (USA) (Diesis)
8510[13] 8919[11] 9347[6]
Hayward Field (IRE) *Noel Wilson* a41 49
6 b g Cape Blanco(IRE) Keepers Hill (IRE) (Danehill (USA))
1949[4] 3163[5] 4190[3] 4515[5] 5555[4] 7048[10]
Hazapour (IRE) *D K Weld* 111
4 ch h Shamardal(USA) Hazarafa (IRE) (Daylami (IRE))
1777a[5] (2660a) 3948[12]
Hazaranda *Sir Michael Stoute* a60 72
3 b f Dansili Hazariya (IRE) (Xaar)
2770[5] 5148[6] 6438[5]
Haze *Sir Mark Todd* a57
3 b f Oasis Dream Dorelia (IRE) (Efisio)
4383 4763[7] 6598[9]
Hazel Bay (IRE) *D K Weld* a71 94
4 b m Iffraaj Sadima (IRE) (Sadler's Wells (USA))
1309a[2] 1620a[4]
Hazienda (IRE) *T Castanheira* a62 67
3 b f Thewayyouare(USA) Hauville (FR) (Hurricane Run (IRE))
6063a[10] 6789a[3]
Hazm (IRE) *Tim Vaughan* 77
4 br g Shamardal(USA) Hikari (IRE) (Galileo (IRE))
3664[8] 4600[4] 5451[2] 6211[8] 7159[8]
Headhunter (FR) *Andrea Marcialis* a63 63
2 gr c Style Vendome(FR) Home And Away (USA) (Skip Away (USA))
7799a[7]
Headland *Martyn Meade* 62
3 b g Harbour Watch(IRE) Bazzana (Zebedee)
4546[6]
Headman *Roger Charlton* a91 117
3 b c Kingman Deliberate (King's Best (USA))
1737[6] (2828) (4431a) (6143a) 7219a[5]
Heads Together *S Kobayashi* a64 71
4 b m Kodiac Sand Grouse (Mr Greeley (USA))
7505a[2]
Healing Power *Ivan Furtado* a76
3 b g Kodiac Loch Ma Naire (IRE) (Galileo (IRE))
(8290) 8645[3]
Heart Ahead (IRE) *J D Hillis* a56 35
5 b g Dream Ahead(USA) Hungry Heart (IRE) (Hawk Wing (USA))
2026a[9]
Heartbreak Hotel (IRE)
Michael Bell 46
3 gr f Le Havre(IRE) Daliana (Verglas (IRE))
3648[8] 4121[11]
Heart In Havana *Michael Easterby* a6 54
3 bb g Havana Gold(IRE) Fine Lady (Selkirk (USA))
2250[8] 3412[4] 4211[6] 5552[5] 6666[13] 7048[15]
Heart Of Soul (IRE) *Ian Williams* a78 83
4 b g Makfi Hadrian's Waltz (IRE) (Holy Roman Emperor (IRE))
1182[3] 1365[2] 1989[3] (2577) 3073[5] 3847[6] 4362[7] 4907[7] 5423[7] 5709[2] 6716[9] 7683[12]
Heart Reef (FR) *Ralph Beckett* 87
2 b f Australia Ignis Away (FR) (Gold Away (IRE))
(6918) 8763[5]
Heartstar *John Mackie* a49
2 b f Heeraat(IRE) Available (IRE) (Moss Vale (IRE))
6028[7] 7769[9] 8067[4]
Heartstring *Ann Duffield* a46 63
3 br f Slade Power(IRE) The Terrier (Foxhound (USA))
2380[6]
Heartwarming *Clive Cox* 90
3 b f Showcasing Place In My Heart (Compton Place)
1913[3] 4101[P] 6724[10] 7348[6]
Heartwood (USA)
James K Chapman a102
5 rg h Tapit(USA) Maple Forest (USA) (Forestry (USA))
7010a[8]
Heath Charnock *Michael Dods* a92 89
3 b c Showcasing Bayleaf (Efisio)
2397[10] (3302) 4638[2] 5658[3] 6339[4] 7187[2] 9088[3]◆ 9348[4]◆
Heatherdown (IRE) *Ian Williams* a58 61
3 b g Morpheus Hapipi (Bertolini (USA))
79[2] (341) 1173[10] 1957[3] 4400[10] 4931[5] 5287[7] 6117[2] 6723[8] 7376[5] 8001[6] 8405[8]

Heaven Forfend *Sir Michael Stoute* 92
2 b c Frankel Heaven Sent (Pivotal)
2792[2] 4091[6] 7338[4]
Heavenhasmynikki (USA)
Robert B Hess Jr a100
4 ch m Majestic Warrior(USA) Floral Park (USA) (Forest Wildcat (USA))
8769a[9]
Heavenly Bliss *Sir Michael Stoute* a52 67
3 ch f Intello(GER) Heaven Sent (Pivotal)
3306[5] 4285[4] 5030[10]
Heavenly Holly (IRE) *Hugo Palmer* a98 98
4 b m Shamardal(USA) Happy Holly (IRE) (Holy Roman Emperor (IRE))
(1918) 3085[3] 3994[8] 4954a[5] 5325a[6] 6769a[5] 7401[7] 9603a[9]
Heavenly Rainbow (IRE)
Michael Herrington a61 70
3 b g Havana Gold(IRE) China Pink (Oasis Dream)
7855[6] 8429[10] 8698[9] 9106[7] 9477[9]
Heavenly Secret (IRE) *Tony Coyle* 36
4 b g Sea The Stars(IRE) Prime Run (Dansili)
1849[5] 2146[7] 2506[11]
Heavenly Tale (IRE) *Ralph Beckett* a64 55
3 b f Shamardal(USA) Angels Story (IRE) (Galileo (IRE))
518[2] 1221[6] 6811[6]
Heaven On Earth (IRE) *A P O'Brien* 90
3 b f Galileo(IRE) Lillie Langtry (IRE) (Danehill Dancer (IRE))
4351a[10]
Heavens Open *Richard Fahey* 76
2 b f Pivotal Celeste (Green Desert (USA))
3679[4] 4142[2] 5737[3]
Heavy Metal *S bin Ghadayer* a115 106
9 b g Exceed And Excel(AUS) Rock Opera (SAF) (Lecture (USA))
171a[9] 726a[3] 1112a[4] 1440a[2]
Hector Loza *Simon Dow* a82 92
2 b c Kodiac Queen Sarra (Shamardal (USA))
4246[3] (5265) (6112)◆ 6727[4] 7602a[7] 9582a[6]
Hector's Here *Ivan Furtado* a58 73
3 b g Cityscape L'Addition (Exceed And Excel (AUS))
1721[4] 2152[2] 3270[4] (4002) 4585[2]◆
Hedging (IRE)
Eve Johnson Houghton a42 70
5 rg g Mastercraftsman(IRE) Privet (IRE) (Cape Cross (IRE))
2145[9] 2774[6] 3540[2] 3966[3] (4472) 4753[4] 5498[8] 5804[11] 6305[6] 6414[5] (7982)
Hediddodinthe (IRE) *Peter Winks* a64 51
5 gr g Kendargent(FR) Damoiselle (USA) (Sky Classic (CAN))
535[2] 1196[7] 1341[9] 1660[12]
Hedidit *C Lerner* a68 48
3 b c Cape Cross(IRE) Tossoff (FR) (Slickly (FR))
4357a[11]
Hee Haw (IRE) *Adrian McGuinness* a74 72
5 b g Sleeping Indian My American Beauty (Wolfhound (USA))
307a[5] 7088a[2]
Heer I Am *Paul George* a37
2 b c Heeraat(IRE) Lexington Rose (Captain Gerrard (IRE))
8011[11] 8865[10] 9242[14]
Heer We Go Again *David Evans* a76 75
2 b c Heeraat(IRE) Madam Mojito (USA) (Smart Strike (CAN))
1416[7] 1493[3] 1758[2] 2108[2] (2469) 7679[11] 8890[8] 9205[3] 9401[7] (9499)
Heezararity *David Weston*
11 b g Librettist(USA) Extremely Rare (IRE) (Mark Of Esteem (IRE))
7759[13]
Heidiava *Chris Grant*
3 b f Captain Gerrard(IRE) Endless Night (GER) (Tiger Hill (IRE))
4276[10]
Heiress *John Gosden* 84
2 b f Kingman Love Divine (Diesis)
(8758)◆
Helcia (IRE) *C Ferland* a76
3 gr f Olympic Glory(IRE) Mizdirection (USA) (Mizzen Mast (USA))
683a[7]
Heldtoransom *Joseph Tuite* 33
3 b f Dick Turpin(IRE) Wassendale (Erhaab (USA))
2488[13] 2773[4] 3463[13] 4005[9]
Helen Sherbet *K R Burke* a74 45
4 br m Makfi Clifton Dancer (Fraam)
91[9] 2331[0]
Heleta *Peter Hedger* a51
2 b f Helmet(AUS) Juno Moneta (IRE) (Holy Roman Emperor (IRE))
6719[11] 7276[8] 7786[7]◆ 9438[7]
Helf (IRE) *Oliver Greenall* a57 73
5 b g Helmet(AUS) Causeway Song (USA) (Giant's Causeway (USA))
185[3] 8347[12]
Helfire *Martin Bosley* a64 52
6 b m Archipenko(USA) Relkida (Bertolini (USA))
1075[6] 1216[3] 1586[6] 1683[2] 2692[5] 3540[5] 3967[8]
Heliaebel *Charlie Fellowes* a68 54
2 b f Camelot Zamzama (IRE) (Shamardal (USA))
6928[7] 7826[6] 8504[3]
Helian (IRE) *Ed Dunlop* a71 71
3 b c Shamardal(USA) Amathia (IRE) (Darshaan)
3003[11] 3768[3] 4178[6] 5898[4] 7116[7] (9132)◆
Helioblu Bareliere (FR)
Mme G Rarick a59 75
6 b g Heliostatic(IRE) Lonia Blue (FR) (Anabaa Blue)
46a[14]
Hellavashock *Alistair Whillans* a30 35
6 gr g Hellvelyn Surprise Statement (Proclamation (IRE))
100[9]
Hello Baileys *Mark Johnston* a72 76
2 b c Supplicant Jane Jubilee (IRE) (Mister Baileys)
4937[4] 5186[4] 5624[2]◆ 6971[3] 8714[3] 9242[7] 9414[6]

Hello Bangkok (IRE)
Andrew Balding a64 79
3 b f Tamayuz Ziria (IRE) (Danehill Dancer (IRE))
2285[5] 2937[7]
Hellofagame *Richard Price* a48 24
4 b g Hellvelyn Gracie's Games (Mind Games)
2391[0] 3577[7] 4182[14] 4733[11] 6107[10] 7527[13] 8263[15] 8408[13] 8901[3] 9332[4]
Hell Of A Joker *Bill Turner* a5 21
2 br c Hellvelyn Oceanico Dot Com (IRE) (Hernando (FR))
1416[14] 1843[9] 7186[6]
Hell Of A Lady *Johnny Farrelly* a51 45
5 gr m Hellvelyn Lady Killer (IRE) (Daggers Drawn (USA))
1914[8]
Hello Girl *Nigel Tinkler* a56 59
4 ch m Bated Breath Elysee (IRE) (Fantastic Light (USA))
253[11] 849[6] 1023[6] 1820[8] 2206[5] 3143[4] 3738[5] (4376) 4720[6] 5018[5] 5393[5]
Hello Is You (FR) *Mme J Hendriks* a52 49
3 b g Anodin(IRE) Young Majesty (USA) (Maria's Mon (USA))
421a[10] 3066a[11] 3878a[8] 9538a[3]
Hellovaqueen *Richard Hughes* a71 62
4 gr m Hellvelyn Regal Quest (IRE) (Marju (IRE))
3645[6] 4181[6] 5837[5] 6018[4] 6526[2] 7274[6]
Hellovasinger *Richard Hughes* a58 45
3 b g Hellvelyn Sing Alana Sing (Singspiel (IRE))
6838[4] 7319[8] 7976[5] 8711[12] 9161[14]
Hello Youmzain (FR) *Kevin Ryan* 121
3 b c Kodiac Spasha (Shamardal (USA))
1752[4] (3083) 4050[3] (6959) 8331[8]
Hells Babe *Michael Appleby* a96 101
6 gr m Hellvelyn Blues In Cee (IRE) (Sinndar (IRE))
1414[5] 3815[5] 4442[2]◆ 4905[5] (6014) 6646a[3]
Helluvasunset *Mark Usher* 13
2 ch f Helmet(AUS) Arabian Sunset (IRE) (Dubawi (IRE))
3942[8] 4798[13] 5630[8]
Helmoona *Karen Tutty* a8 56
2 ch g Helmet(AUS) Maimoona (IRE) (Pivotal)
6970[8] 7579[7]
Helovaplan (IRE) *Bryan Smart* a87 91
5 b g Helmet(AUS) Watsdaplan (IRE) (Verglas (IRE))
213[3] (740) 1644[15] 5246[2] 6543[5] 8024[13]
Helter Skelter (FR) *J-C Rouget* 110
2 b c Wootton Bassett Winna Chope (FR) (Soave (GER))
4961a[2] (6251a) 7940a[5]
Helvetian *Kevin Frost* a89 83
4 b g Swiss Spirit Lucky Dip (Tirol (IRE))
2403[9] 2917[5] 3347[6] 4236[8] 4835[4] (8470) 9057[5] 9458[9]
Helvic Dream (IRE) *Noel Meade* 92
2 b g Power Rachevie (IRE) (Danehill Dancer (IRE))
5710a[3]
Hembree (USA) *Michael J Maker* 107
5 bb h Proud Citizen(USA) Knockatrina (USA) (Langfuhr (CAN))
5977a[6]
Hemera (FR) *T Lemer* a13
3 b f Palace Episode(USA) Tengeline (FR) (Cardoun (FR))
1658a[11]
Hen (IRE) *Jamie Osborne* a63 45
3 b f Camelot Lily Of Kenmare (IRE) (Exceed And Excel (AUS))
358[5] 794[7] 967[5] 1217[9] 2213[3] 2697[3] 3418[9] 6505[7]
Hendrix (IRE) *Hughie Morrison* a62
3 b g War Command(USA) Monzza (Montjeu (IRE))
518[3] 1711[4]
Henley *Tracy Waggott* a82 72
7 b g Royal Applause Making Waves (IRE) (Danehill (USA))
1929[8] 2421[10] 2589[4] 2775[21] 3971[7] 4821[6] 5691[10] 5819[6] 7624[6] 7700[4] 8023[13] 8715[9]
Henley's Joy (USA)
Michael J Maker a87 109
3 ch c Kitten's Joy(USA) Blue Grass Music (USA) (Bluegrass Cat (USA))
6994a[5]
Henrietta's Dream *Robyn Brisland* a45 47
5 b m Henrythenavigator(USA) Timeless Dream (Oasis Dream)
159[11] 613[9] 954[5] 1192[11] 2633[12] 2912[6] 4130[11] 4358[6] 4720[16] 5918[3] 6066[8] 7335[6] 8407[4] 8942[8]
Henry Croft *Tony Carroll* a66 79
6 b g Dubawi(IRE) Karen's Caper (USA) (War Chant (USA))
9168[2]
Henry Mouth (IRE) *A Botti*
4 b h Henrythenavigator(USA) Cottonmouth (IRE) (Noverre (USA))
2885a[5]
Henrytheaeroplane (USA) *Z Koplik* 44
7 b g Henrythenavigator(USA) April Pride (Falbrav (IRE))
8982a[9]
Henry The Sixth *Scott Dixon* a10
3 b c Milk It Mick Six Wives (Kingsalsa (USA))
8407[8] 8947[3] 9332[9]
Heptathlete (IRE) *Mme B Jacques* a70 65
4 gr m Mount Nelson Jessica Ennis (USA) (English Channel (USA))
1391a[10] 4960a[4]
Heraldic (USA) *S Seemar* a77 67
6 br g Discreet Cat(USA) Chilukki's Song (USA) (Elusive Quality (USA))
1322a[15]
Herbert Pocket *Tim Easterby* 57
2 b g Helmet(AUS) Marysienka (Primo Dominie)
2780[9] 6336[6] 6622[11]
Herculean *Roger Charlton* a78 96
4 ch g Frankel African Rose (Observatory (USA))
3806[5] 5440[2]◆ 6151[5] 7863[8]

Hereby (IRE) *Ralph Beckett* a68 102
3 b f Pivotal Look Here (Hernando (FR))
2770[6]◆ (3802) 4503[3] (5706) (6255) (7144) (7864)
Here Comes When (IRE)
Andrew Balding a102 116
9 br g Danehill Dancer(IRE) Quad's Melody (IRE) (Spinning World (USA))
3025[4] 6956[5]
Here's Rocco (IRE) *John Quinn* 44
3 b g Charm Spirit(IRE) Aqraan (In The Wings)
1646[8] 2630[12] 3292[5] 3709[7] 4979[7] 7444[7]
Here's Two *Ron Hodges* a74 79
6 b m Hellvelyn There's Two (IRE) (Ashkalani (IRE))
(2005) 2622[3] 3468[9] 3892[6] 6201[8] 7554[5] 8413[12]
Her Indoors (IRE) *Alan King* a68 48
2 b f Raven's Pass(USA) Superfonic (FR) (Zafonic (USA))
6281[2] 7154[9]
Heritage *Clive Cox* a87 94
3 b f Garswood Inheritance (Oasis Dream)
2144[3] 2687[2] 3151[4] 4072[5] (4496)◆ (5015) 5291[2] 6332[3] 6954[5] 7449[3]
Herm (IRE) *David Evans* a61 43
5 b g Bushranger(IRE) School Holidays (USA) (Harlan's Holiday (USA))
39[9] 399[3] 760[6] 1390[4] 1841[5] (2500a) 3186[8] (8869) (9275)◆ 9626[12]
Herman Hesse *John Gosden* 75
2 b c Frankel Dream Peace (IRE) (Dansili)
3274[6] 5860[3] 7562[4] 8244[3] 8461[8]
Hermano Bello (FR)
Richard Hannon a62 54
2 b c Youmzain(IRE) Pasaquina (GER) (Acatenango (GER))
4897[8] 5439[6] 6368[10] (7516) 7910[9] 8415[5]
Hermaphrodite (FR) *F-H Graffard* 103
4 b m Le Havre(IRE) Decency (IRE) (Celtic Swing)
1627a[8] 5510a[2] 6263a[5]
Hermiona (USA) *F Chappet* a84 93
3 ch f Kitten's Joy(USA) Darajah (CAN) (Hard Spun (USA))
2954a[2] 3677a[6] 5227a[5] 9170a[16]
Hermocrates (FR) *Richard Hannon* a70 74
3 b g Farhh Little Shambles (Shamardal (USA))
(122)◆ 2125[6] 2485[3] 4231[2] 4547[6] 5012[3] 5426[3] 5778[6] 7625[4] (7984) 8507[6]
Hermosa (IRE) *A P O'Brien* 115
3 b f Galileo(IRE) Beauty Is Truth (IRE) (Pivotal)
(2443) (3115) 4051[2] 5588[9] 7221a[2] 7898[8]
Hermosa Vaquera (IRE)
Gary Moore a15 21
9 b m High Chaparral(IRE) Sundown (Polish Precedent (USA))
7985[10] 8551[15]
Hermoso Mundo (SAF)
Hughie Morrison 98
6 b g Ideal World(USA) Escoleta Fitz (ARG) (Fitzcarraldo (ARG))
961a[10] 4670[4] 5183[10] 5662[6] 6420[10] 7394[5] 8114[18]
Hermosura *Ralph Beckett* a81 67
3 b f Shamardal(USA) Honorlina (FR) (Linamix (FR))
4768[8] 5254[5] 5656[7] 6367[4]◆ (6595) 7279[6] (8064) 9302[8]
Hernan *Andrea Marcialis* a85 84
2 b c Bated Breath La Cuesta (IRE) (Showcasing)
7043a[3] 8239a[2] 9605a[2]
Herodotus (IRE) *Andrew Balding* 62
2 b g Iffraaj Merry Me (IRE) (Invincible Spirit (IRE))
6757[2] 7983[5]
Hero Hero (IRE) *Andrew Balding* a80 95
3 b c No Nay Never(USA) Fancy (IRE) (Galileo (IRE))
2060[3] (3067) 4016[10] 5932[8] 6711[8]
Heroic *Charles Hills* 75
3 b c Heeraat(IRE) Aquasulis (IRE) (Titus Livius (FR))
(3353) 4124[12]
Heroine (FR) *J-C Rouget* a77 90
4 b m Camelot Elusive Galaxy (IRE) (Elusive City (USA))
(1578a)
Heron (USA) *Brett Johnson* a70 63
5 b g Quality Road(USA) Dreamt (Oasis Dream)
160[2] 560[8] 731[7] (1548) 2593[2] (3205)◆ 3940[6] 5891[3] 8065[11] 9049[8] 9336[6]
Herre Dittery *Pat Phelan* 45
2 bb g Cable Bay(IRE) Young Dottie (Desert Sun)
5314[11] 5992[9] 6532[6]
Herring Bay *John Holt*
2 b f Heeraat(IRE) Hikkaduwa (Sakhee (USA))
7644[10]
Herringswell (FR) *Henry Spiller* a73 56
4 b m Pour Moi(IRE) Sovereign's Honour (USA) (Kingmambo (USA))
377[7] 2631[1] 5957 940[5] 1353[12] 2234[9] 3298[12] 5081[13] 6131[4] 7374[7] (8435) (8821) (9352)◆
He's A Keeper (IRE)
Tom Dascombe 92
2 b g Brazen Beau(AUS) Silver Grey (IRE) (Chineur (FR))
5177[2] (5894)◆ 6957[6] 8397[4]
He's A Laddie (IRE) *Archie Watson* a85 80
2 ch g Fast Company(IRE) Crimson Lass (IRE) (Dubawi (IRE))
(5635) (6029)◆ 6474[9] 7369[2] 8817[5]
He's Amazing (IRE) *Ed Walker* a83 78
4 b g Fastnet Rock(AUS) Kahyasi Moll (IRE) (Brief Truce (USA))
(2207) 3168[P] 3806[7] 4863[6] 5776[5] 6347[7] 7413[4] 8608[2]
Heshem (IRE) *A De Mieulle* a92 100
6 b h Footstepsinthesand Doohulla (USA) (Stravinsky (USA))
894a[13]
He's Our Star (IRE) *Ali Stronge* a67 73
4 b g Lord Shanakill(USA) Afilla (Dansili)
(2232) 2927[5] 5373[11] 6050[8] 8507[7] 9067[9] 9361[3] 9663[9]

Hesslewood (IRE) *James Bethell* a87 87
3 b g Slade Power(IRE) Rochitta (USA) (Arch (USA))
(1485)◆ 1897[3] 2821[5] 4107[2] 8101[13] 8809[4]
Hesssa *K R Burke* 69
2 b f Zoffany(IRE) Ana Shababiya (IRE) (Teofilo (IRE))
7054[6]
Hexagon (IRE) *Roger Charlton* a86 79
2 b g Acclamation Somerset Falls (UAE) (Red Ransom (USA))
3419[6] 4252[2] 4925[3] (6040) 6965[2] 7840[3]
Hexis (IRE) *Guillaume Courbot* a55 68
5 b h Henrythenavigator(USA) Hunza Dancer (IRE) (Danehill Dancer (IRE))
(3711a) 9537a[7]
Heyday *Richard Fahey* 21
2 b f Showcasing Bimbo (Iffraaj)
6971[10]
Hey Doc (AUS)
Tony McEvoy & Calvin McEvoy 118
5 b g Duporth(AUS) Heyington Honey (AUS) (General Nediym (AUS))
9015a[3]
Hey Gaman *James Tate* 116
4 b h New Approach(IRE) Arsaadi (IRE) (Dubawi (IRE))
(2109)◆ (3289a) 5207a[2] 5521[2] 6215[5] 7944a[6] 8774a[7]
Hey Gracie *Mark Usher* a37
3 b f Delegator Capestar (IRE) (Cape Cross (IRE))
8451[8]
Hey Ho Let's Go *Mark Hoad* a64 67
3 b c Dream Ahead(USA) Lookslikeanangel (Holy Roman Emperor (IRE))
1180[2] 1728[5] 3090[6] 3651[3]◆ 4181[15] 5431[2] 6418[5] 8007[6] 8419[7] 8840[2]◆ 9539[4]◆
Hey Jazzy Lady (IRE)
Andrew Crook a23 54
3 b f Red Jazz(USA) First Bunting (IRE) (Hawkeye (IRE))
5914[13] 6462[12] 7303[6] 9395[12]
Hey Jonesy (IRE) *Kevin Ryan* a106 112
4 b g Excelebration(IRE) Fikrah (Medicean)
2062[2] 2744[5] 4095[9] 5129[2] 5413[12] 7433[16] 8127[15]
He'Zanarab (IRE) *Jim Goldie* 80
3 b g Footstepsinthesand Ziggy's Secret (Sakhee's Secret)
1752[8] 2412[8] 2835[13] 4236[12] 5936[3] 6607[5] 7002[9] 7362[12] 7402[15]
Hibernian Warrior (USA)
Roger Varian a75 75
2 bb c War Front(USA) Quarter Moon (IRE) (Sadler's Wells (USA))
7661[3] 8999[2]
Hic Bibi *David Loughnane* a67 70
4 b m Cityscape Real Me (Mark Of Esteem (IRE))
138[3] 366[4] 701[3] 1158[7] (1715) (2153) 3014[7] 7066[4] 7383[5] 8199[8] 8755[9] 9498[7]
Hiconic *Alex Hales* a58 52
2 b f Sixties Icon Hi Note (Acclamation)
5342[7] 5630[2] 6281[3] 7079[7] 8061[8] 8603[5]
Hidden Depths (IRE)
Neil Mulholland a65 58
4 b g Dark Angel(IRE) Liber Nauticus (IRE) (Azamour (IRE))
562[2] 703[3] 876[10] 6010a[3] 6830[10] 7790[4] 9367[8] 9497[2]
Hidden Dream (FR) *John Butler* a53
4 b m Oasis Dream Hideaway Heroine (IRE) (Hernando (FR))
3661[13] 4116[14] 5051[6] 5633[9] 6051[10]
Hidden Dream (IRE)
Christine Dunnett a51 51
4 b m Casamento(IRE) Anything (IRE) (Rock Of Gibraltar (IRE))
399[5] 593[6] 984[6] 1297[5] 1546[4] 2112[3] 2738[3] 3298[13] 4346[13] 4568[2] 5354[2] 5653[5] (8000) 8434[7]
Hidden Message (USA)
William Haggas 106
3 bb f Scat Daddy(USA) Secret Charm (IRE) (Green Desert (USA))
2268[4] 3387a[4] (4667)
Hidden Pearl *John Berry* a55 67
3 ch f Dunaden(FR) Volkovkha (Holy Roman Emperor (IRE))
4372[6] 4803[8] 5880[5] 9442[2] 9626[10]
Hidden Spell (IRE) *K R Burke* a66 72
2 b f Dandy Man(IRE) Dara's Image (IRE) (Moss Vale (IRE))
3652[2]◆ 3997[4] 6919[6] 7377[3] 7995[2] (8395)
Hidden Stash *William Stone* a46 58
5 b g Sakhee's Secret Marajuana (Robellino (USA))
2234[8] 3187[11] 3966[4] 4217[10] 4753[10] 5802[9]
Hide Your Heart (IRE)
David Loughnane a48 39
3 b f Bungle Inthejungle Cookie Cutter (IRE) (Fasliyev (USA))
4358[7] 5083[11]
Hieronymus *George Baker* a57 75
3 b g Dutch Art Sleek (Oasis Dream)
5505[7] 5773[6] 8242[4] 8660[2]◆ 8860[8] 9171[5] 9632[9]
High Above *Charlie Fellowes* 77
3 b f Australia Gertrude Gray (IRE) (Hurricane Run (IRE))
2838[2] 3553[10]
High Acclaim (USA) *Roger Teal* a80 78
5 b g Elusive Quality(USA) La Reine Lionne (USA) (Leroidesanimaux (BRZ))
29[4] 294[4] 962[7] 1025[2] 1655[6] 2207[4] 2797[4] 4283[4] 4561[5] 5086[7] (5747) 6289[3]
High Accolade (IRE) *James Tate* a78
2 gr c Outstrip Honeymead (IRE) (Pivotal)
(7958)◆
High Anxiety *Andrew Crook* a43 3
5 ch m Bated Breath Odense (USA) (Medaglia d'Oro (USA))
2771[0] 503[6] 742[6] 1402[8] 1811[1]
High As A Kite (FR) *Jan Bjordal* 98
5 b m Manduro(GER) Troiecat (FR) (One Cool Cat (USA))
4419a[8] 7496a[6]

High Ball (FR) *F Vermeulen* a75 93
3 b f Doctor Dino(FR) Heavenly Music (IRE) (Oratorio (IRE))
1626a[6] 4429a[7]

Highbrow *David Simcock* a97 103
4 b g Intello(GER) Wild Gardenia (Alhaarth (IRE))
3005[4] 3992[7] 4504[4] 6021[6] 7686[3]

Highcastle (IRE) *Lisa Williamson* a57 53
4 b g High Chaparral(IRE) Green Castle (IRE) (Indian Ridge (IRE))
2014[11] 4358[3] 4818[4] 6758[P]

High Charm (FR) *S Wattel* a71
2 gr c Kendargent(FR) High Story (FR) (Zanzibari (USA))
8448a[4]

High Cliff (FR) *F Vermeulen* a74 78
3 ch f French Fifteen(FR) Billette (FR) (Thunder Gulch (USA))
683a[8]

High Command (IRE) *Brian Barr* a70 52
6 b g High Chaparral(IRE) Plaza (USA) (Chester House (USA))
390[7] 927[6] 1159[6] 1429[6] 1861[4] 1971[2] 2351[2] 2528[5] 4791[13]

High Commissioner (IRE) *Paul Cole* 88
3 ch g Australia Winesong (IRE) (Giant's Causeway (USA))
2795[2] 3152[5] 4842[3] 5614[5] 6216[3] 6903[2]

High Contrast *K R Burke* a62 51
3 b g Kingman Parisi (Rahy (USA))
1819[5] 2510[11] 3208[11]

Higher Kingdom *Archie Watson* a83
2 b c Kingman Noozhah (Singspiel (IRE))
(8012)◆

Higher Power *James Fanshawe* a107 95
7 b g Rip Van Winkle(IRE) Lady Stardust (Spinning World (USA))
757[4] 1062[3] 1917[4] 2554[3]

Higher Power (USA) *John W Sadler* a120 107
4 b h Medaglia d'Oro(USA) Alternate (USA) (Seattle Slew (USA))
8777a[3]

Highest Ground (IRE) *Sir Michael Stoute* 86
2 b c Frankel Celestial Lagoon (JPN) (Sunday Silence (USA))
(7521)◆

Highest Mountain (FR) *Joseph Tuite* a63 69
3 b g Siyouni(FR) Chanson Celeste (Oratorio (IRE))
868a[5] 1381[5] 1909[4] (6874a)

Highfaluting (IRE) *James Eustace* a84 72
5 b g High Chaparral(IRE) Walk On Water (Exceed And Excel (AUS))
1653[3] 2629[2]◆ 3700[9] (6317) 6839[2] 7519[2] (8220)

Highfield Haven *John Quinn*
2 b c Le Havre(IRE) Alla Breve (Dansili)
8857[10]

High Flying Bird (FR) *Tom Dascombe* 78
2 b f Reliable Man Supernova Heights (IRE) (Oasis Dream)
5895[4] 6697[5] 7054[2] 7620[3] (8465)

High Fort (IRE) *Karen McLintock* a57 55
4 b g Acclamation Barracade (IRE) (Barathea (IRE))
3412[6] 3932[6] 5477[10] 7960[3] 8530[9] 8818[2] 9282[9] (9395)

Highgarden *John Gosden* a108 109
4 b m Nathaniel(IRE) Regalline (IRE) (Green Desert (USA))
3995[3] 4645[6]

High Glory (FR) *J F Levins* a43 57
3 b g Olympic Glory(IRE) High Princess (FR) (High Chaparral (IRE))
9345[10] 9544[6]

High Gloss *James Fanshawe* a58 29
3 b f Invincible Spirit(IRE) So Silk (Rainbow Quest (USA))
5554[9] 6316[7] 8013[7]◆ 8669[12]

Highjacked *John Davies* a40 53
3 b g Dick Turpin(IRE) Vera Richardson (IRE) (Dutch Art)
2337[14] 2870[3] 3292[7] 5914[8]

Highland Acclaim (IRE) *David O'Meara* a61 81
8 b g Acclamation Emma's Star (ITY) (Darshaan)
91[2] (260) (564) 734[4] 964[5] 3309[6] 3846[11] 4545[4] 4835[3] 5040[3] 5476[8] 6567[3] 6826[8] 7130[4] 7837[9] 8496[11] 8690[5] 9140[10] 9283[8] 9423[4]

Highland Bobby *David O'Meara* a61 60
4 b g Big Bad Bob(IRE) Eolith (Pastoral Pursuits)
1836[5] 2202[4]

Highland Chief (IRE) *Paul Cole* 99
2 b c Gleneagles(IRE) Pink Symphony (Montjeu (IRE))
(1733) 4091[3] 7691[6]

Highland Dreamer (IRE) *Charlie Fellowes* 37
2 b f Gleneagles(IRE) Seolan (IRE) (Alhaarth (IRE))
7203[9]

Highland Sky (IRE) *David Simcock* a60 73
4 b g Camelot Healing Music (FR) (Bering)
2928[8] (4843) 5825[3] 6348[5]

Highland Sky (USA) *Barclay Tagg* a75 104
6 bb g Sky Mesa(USA) Kristi With A K (USA) (Petionville (USA))
3561a[3]

Highland Sun (IRE) *Richard Phillips* a39
3 ch f Helmet(AUS) Cintsa Sun (IRE) (Medicean)
7912[7] 8842[7] 9038[6] 9368[10]

High Language (IRE) *Philip McBride* a32 90
5 b m Lawman(FR) Benedicte (IRE) (Galileo (IRE))
1017[8] 1218[5]

Highlight Reel (IRE) *Rebecca Bastiman* a75 79
4 b g Big Bad Bob(IRE) Dance Hall Girl (IRE) (Dansili)
1457[15] 2116[6] 2584[3] 3179[4] 3567[10] 4322[8] 7289[13] 8181[4] 8761[11] 9109[14]

Highly Approved (IRE) *Adrian McGuinness* a78 77
4 b m Approve(IRE) High Society Girl (IRE) (Key Of Luck (USA))
5537a[9]

Highly Focussed (IRE) *Ann Duffield* a66 70
5 b g Intense Focus(USA) Mood Indigo (IRE) (Indian Ridge (IRE))
(2789)◆ 3999[7] 4632[11] 5478[9]

Highly Sprung (IRE) *Les Eyre* a67 86
6 b g Zebedee Miss Donovan (Royal Applause)
24[9] 381[10] 840[5] 1164[12] 1817[3] (2292) 2893[10] 3868[13] 4148[2] (5476) 5821[6] 6677[6] 7402[2] (7621) 8101[9]

High Maintenance *Mark Loughnane* a52
2 b f Due Diligence(USA) Random (Shamardal (USA))
8546[6] 9062[7] 9448[5]

High Moor Flyer *Jedd O'Keeffe* a18 39
2 b f Pour Moi(IRE) A Media Luz (FR) (Johann Quatz (FR))
8021[10] 8855[9]

High On Life *S bin Ghadayer* a107 85
8 b g Invincible Spirit(IRE) Lovely Thought (Dubai Destination (USA))
50a[5] 639a[2] 1111a[8]

High River (FR) *N Paysan* a77 49
3 gr g Stormy River(FR) High Perfection (IRE) (High Chaparral (IRE))
7476a[5]

High Shine *Michael Bell* 60
2 b f Paco Boy(IRE) Hypoteneuse (IRE) (Sadler's Wells (USA))
6603[4] 7755[11] 8458[15]

Highway Bess *Patrick Chamings* a48 48
4 br m Dick Turpin(IRE) Bob's Princess (Bob's Return (IRE))
2732[8] 6077[6] 7759[11]

Highwaygrey *Tim Easterby* 72
3 b g Dick Turpin(IRE) Maybeagrey (Shamardal (USA))
1819[8] 2200[2] 2711[2] (3052) 3505[3] 4077[2] 5394[3] 5898[6] 6540[4] 7213[5] 7829[6]

Highwayman *David Thompson* a57 51
6 b g Dick Turpin(IRE) Right Rave (IRE) (Soviet Star (USA))
210[5] 436[4] 969[9] 1431[9] 1648[8] 2335[6] 2631[8] 3224[5] 3297[2] 4002[8] 4633[14] 5216[5]

Highway One (USA) *George Baker* a67 62
5 b m Quality Road(USA) Kinda Wonderful (USA) (Silver Train (USA))
85[8] 145[3] 295[8] 616[3] 965[3] 1497[10] 7756[4]◆ 8422[5] 8813[6] 9310[5]

Highway Robber *Wilf Storey* a56 49
6 b g Dick Turpin(IRE) Lawyers Choice (Namid)
99[4] 208[6] 782[14] 1981[3] 2591[8] 3929[2] 5277[10]

Highway Robbery *Julia Feilden* a51 52
3 gr g Dick Turpin(IRE) Minty Fox (Dalakhani (IRE))
1593[7] 2011[4] 2941[3] (3593) 3965[5] 4834[3]◆ 5648[6] 6681[3] 7202[5] 8414[9] 9201[6]

Highway To Heaven (IRE) *T G McCourt* a23 62
4 b m Pour Moi(IRE) Lillebonne (FR) (Danehill Dancer (IRE))
7776[2]

Hi Harry (IRE) *Declan Carroll* 37
2 b g Epaulette(AUS) Emerald Fire (Pivotal)
4125[9] 4984[10]

Hi Ho Silver *Chris Wall* a62 61
5 gr g Camacho Silver Spell (Aragon)
2019[5] 2740[2] 3279[4] 4349[13] 5051[7] 6327[3] (6897) 7527[10] 8436[11]

Hijran (IRE) *Henry Oliver* a42 48
6 ch m Mastercraftsman(IRE) Sunny Slope (Mujtahid (USA))
8247[11]

Hikayah *David O'Meara* a61
3 b f Bated Breath Aubrietia (Dutch Art)
971[6] 1400[4] 2018[9] 3057[8]

Hilborough *Les Eyre* a54 71
4 b g Makfi Ambrix (IRE) (Xaar)
1163[P]

Hilbre Lake (USA) *Lisa Williamson* a44 12
3 bb g Revolutionary(USA) Countess Clare (USA) (Sun King (USA))
66[8] 621[7] 4358[10] 4909[8] 6024[12] 6505[9] 7141[8] 7681[12]

Hilight *Martin Bosley* a42 49
4 b m Archipenko(USA) Relkida (Bertolini (USA))
2693[8]

Hillgrove Angel (IRE) *Jim Goldie* a47 67
7 gr g Dark Angel(IRE) Theben (GER) (Monsun (GER))
2244[8] (3181)◆ (3718)◆

Hill Hollow (IRE) *David Simcock* a71
3 ch g Helmet(AUS) Bint Doyen (Doyen (IRE))
8086[3] 8718[4]

Hills And Dales (IRE) *Hans-Inge Larsen* a40 89
7 b g Acclamation Soul Mountain (IRE) (Rock Of Gibraltar (IRE))
7494a[9]

Hillwalker *Thomas Cleary* 84
3 b g Foxwedge(AUS) Dance A Daydream (Daylami (IRE))
3104a[14]

Himola (FR) *C Laffon-Parias* 97
3 b c Dalakhani(IRE) Campanillas (IRE) (Montjeu (IRE))
3031a[5]

Hindaam (USA) *Owen Burrows* a74 64
3 b f Arch(USA) Saraama (USA) (Bahri (USA))
3495[10] 4258[4] 6836[5] (7609) (8705)

Hinemoa (FR) *N Clement* a65
3 ch f Tamayuz Leah Claire (IRE) (Tomba)
217a[5] 993a[7] 1658a[8]

Hiorne Tower (FR) *John Best* a56 55
8 b g Poliglote Hierarchie (FR) (Sillery (USA))
6601[8]

Hipodamo De Mileto (FR) *J Calderon* 100
5 ch g Falco(USA) La Atalaya (Montjeu (IRE))
(4418a) 8375a[3]

Hippeia (IRE) *Lawrence Mullaney* a54 43
4 b m Lilbourne Lad(IRE) Majestic Oasis (Oasis Dream)
525[5] 886[12] 1399[12] 1973[9] 2329[8] 2682[9] 6066[2]◆ 6276[12] 7335[7] 7587[8] 7654[12]

Hiroshima *John Ryan* a76 98
3 b g Nathaniel(IRE) Lisiere (IRE) (Excellent Art)
(2301)◆ 2619[8] 3345[11] 4136a[10] 8520[3]

Historic (IRE) *Saeed bin Suroor* 74
2 bb c Shamardal(USA) Galician (Redoute's Choice (AUS))
2973[4] 3866[4]

Historic Event (IRE) *Alexandros Giatras* a67 72
5 gr m Invincible Spirit(IRE) Scenica (ARG) (Interprete (ARG))
8240a[9]

History Dream (FR) *B Audouin* a36 72
8 gr g Sagacity(FR) Manixa (FR) (Manninamix)
7501a[2]

History Wotton (FR) *R Martens* 60
3 b f Wootton Bassett Histoire (IRE) (Whipper (USA))
5329a[5] 6062a[2]

History Writer (IRE) *David Menuisier* 103
4 b g Canford Cliffs(IRE) Abhasana (IRE) (Hawk Wing (USA))
1753[7] 3027[3] 3313[13] (3857) 4666[7] 5610[14] 6376[15] 7694[16] 8379a[3] (9124a)

Hi There Silver (IRE) *Michael Madgwick* a38 42
5 gr g Clodovil(IRE) Elaborate (Sadler's Wells (USA))
(1520) 2283[3] 5310[5] 5499[7]

Hitman *Rebecca Bastiman* a51 57
6 b g Canford Cliffs(IRE) Ballymore Celebre (IRE) (Peintre Celebre (USA))
1660[11] 2418[13] 4523[12] 5214[7] 5593[6] 6275[5] 7581[6] 8031[5]

Hit The Beat *Clive Cox* a64 35
4 br m Fast Company(IRE) Dance Express (IRE) (Rail Link)
256[6] 759[10] 9128[2]◆ 9420[6] 9629[3]

Hit The Bid *D J Bunyan* a111 112
5 b h Exceed And Excel(AUS) Selinka (Selkirk (USA))
49a[2] 393a[2] 1111a[7] 6648a[6] 7243a[8] 7454[3] 8328a[4]

Hit The Road (USA) *Dan Blacker* 104
2 b c More Than Ready(USA) Highway Mary (USA) (US Ranger (USA))
8746a[DSQ]

Hit The Silk (IRE) *P J F Murphy* a80 83
6 br g Majestic Missile(IRE) Queen Of Silk (IRE) (Brief Truce (USA))
5711a[7]

Hit The Track Jack *D De Waele* 66
3 b g Swiss Spirit Athenia (IRE) (Fath (USA))
2090a[9] 2392a[7] 3066a[2] (4229a) 5165a[2] 6061a[7] 9538a[5]

Hiva'Oa (FR) *T Poche* 19
4 b m George Vancouver(USA) Melodya (FR) (Great Palm (USA))
2170a[17]

Hlaitan *Hugo Palmer* a72 77
2 b g Iffraaj The Madding Crowd (Dansili)
6948[4]◆ 7392[2]◆ 7814[5]

HMS President (IRE) *Eve Johnson Houghton* a81 52
2 b c Excelebration(IRE) Dance Hall Girl (IRE) (Dansili)
6528[6] 8012[4] (8717)◆

Hochfeld (IRE) *Mark Johnston* a79 108
5 b g Cape Cross(IRE) What A Charm (IRE) (Key Of Luck (USA))
1947[10] 2440[7]

Hodeng (IRE) *J-C Rouget* a78 77
3 br c Cape Cross(IRE) Seasons (Dubai Destination (USA))
5407a[2]

Hoffa *Michael Dods* a62 67
3 b g Iffraaj Minoan Dancer (IRE) (Galileo (IRE))
1845[5] 3226[12]

Hogans Holiday (USA) *Robert N Falcone Jr* 98
4 rg m The Factor(USA) Hogan Beach (USA) (Harlan's Holiday (USA))
6491a[6]

Hog Creek Hustle (USA) *Vickie L Foley* a111
3 bb c Overanalyze(USA) Candy Fortune (USA) (Candy Ride (ARG))
8773a[6]

Ho Ho Khan (NZ) *D J Hall* 110
4 b h Makfi China Choice (AUS) (Encosta De Lago (AUS))
9376a[6]

Holbox (FR) *F Vermeulen* a57 68
3 bb c Alhebayeb(IRE) Normale Sup (IRE) (Authorized (IRE))
5641a[3] 6094a[2]

Holdenhurst *Bill Turner* a69 69
4 gr g Hellvelyn Michelle Shift (Night Shift (USA))
(53) 383[2] 857[8] 1179[6] 1266[5] 2287[2] 2847[2] 3527[12] (4776) 5289[4] (7470) 8217[4] 9089[4]

Hold Fast (IRE) *Andrew Balding* 67
2 b f Fastnet Rock(AUS) Rohain (IRE) (Singspiel (IRE))
5588[7] 6402[2]

Hold Still (IRE) *William Muir* a73 83
3 b g Bated Breath Effervesce (IRE) (Galileo (IRE))
3261[2] 4497[4] 5104[3]◆ 5749[2] 6425[12] 7176[6] 7836[6]

Hold Sway (IRE) *Doug Watson* a60 91
5 b g Dubawi(IRE) Annabelle's Charm (IRE) (Indian Ridge (IRE))
573a[9]

Holdthasigreen (FR) *B Audouin* a90 115
7 ch g Hold That Tiger(USA) Greentathir (FR) (Muhtathir)
(2169a) 3123a[5] 4962a[5] (7928a) 8589a[3]

Hold True *D Smaga* a81 97
3 ch f Bated Breath Honest Quality (USA) (Elusive Quality (USA))
1242a[3] 2954a[5] 5644a[8]

Hold Your Breath *Tony Carroll* a35 48
4 b m Bated Breath Chittenden (USA) (Raven's Pass (USA))
4733[12] 5083[10] 5675[12] 5981[2] 6529[12]

Holiday Magic (IRE) *Lee Carter* a72 67
8 gr g Dark Angel(IRE) Win Cash (IRE) (Alhaarth (IRE))
8471[4] (9217)

Hollaback Girl *Richard Spencer* a58 56
2 ch f Camacho Jimmy's Girl (IRE) (Equiano (FR))
1513[8] 1968[2] 2248[7] 3441[6] 5279[4] 5800[5] 6436[6] 7853[7] 8067[2] 8640[5]

Hollander *Alexandra Dunn* a57 50
5 ch g Dutch Art Thrill (Pivotal)
187[5]◆ 430[9] 849[7] 1038[2] 1208[9] 1768[8] 2286[7] 4501[4] 6058[12] 6546[12] 7811[7] (8697) 9246[8] 9298[4] 9420[13]

Holloa *Tim Easterby* a66 63
2 b f Acclamation Blue Echo (Kyllachy)
2115[5] 2747[9] 3220[7] 7284[2]◆ 7584[10] (8085)◆ 8817[10]

Hollywood Dream *Neil Mulholland* a60 51
4 b m Delegator Royal Obsession (IRE) (Val Royal (FR))
1431[8]

Hollywood Road (IRE) *Gary Moore* a86 91
6 b g Kodiac Rinneen (IRE) (Bien Bien (USA))
1395[2] 1914[3] 2620[5] 3016[5] 4752[3]

Hollywood Waltz *Mick Channon* a47 47
2 b f Free Eagle(IRE) Pesse (IRE) (Eagle Eyed (USA))
3652[6] 4221[6] 5602[4] 6182[7]

Holmeswood *Julie Camacho* a77 93
5 b g Mayson Angelzarke (IRE) (Acclamation)
2743[14] 3097[13] 4894[4] 5119[4] (6607) 7348[2] 8099[17] 8867[8]

Holmgarth (FR) *Philip Kirby* 8
2 b g Youmzain(IRE) Dispol Diva (Deportivo)
6035[3] 7067[14]

Holy Bere (FR) *Edouard Monfort* a44
2 b f Peer Gynt(JPN) Valibi Bere (FR) (Russian Blue (IRE))
6386a[6]

Holy Eleanor (IRE) *Archie Watson* a68 55
2 b f Holy Roman Emperor(IRE) Tennessee Moon (Darshaan)
9137[4] 9307[2] 9448[2] 9568[5]

Holy Heart (IRE) *John Gosden* a79 74
4 b g Holy Roman Emperor(IRE) Heart Of Ice (IRE) (Montjeu (IRE))
34[2] (252)

Holy Helena (CAN) *James Jerkens* a75 106
5 bb m Ghostzapper(USA) Holy Grace (USA) (Holy Bull (USA))
7224a[4] 8154a[5]

Holy Hymn (IRE) *Kevin Frost* a51 55
3 b g Holy Roman Emperor(IRE) Missionary Hymn (USA) (Giant's Causeway (USA))
2249[8] 3938[7] 7290[8] 7857[7] 8644[6]

Holy Kingdom (IRE) *Tom Clover* a93 85
3 gr c Australia Cable (USA) (Dynaformer (USA))
156[6] 442[2] 2765[2] 3604[2]◆ 6224[5] 6952[7] (7689) 8098[3]◆ 8754[2]

Holy Legal (BRZ) *Ignacio Correas IV* a60 61
5 b m Holy Roman Emperor(IRE) Hora Legal (BRZ) (Minstrel Glory (USA))
7010a[10]

Holy Tiber (IRE) *Chelsea Banham* a55 56
4 b m Holy Roman Emperor(IRE) Quiet Waters (USA) (Quiet American (USA))
467[7] 596[2] 1075[7] 1179[11] 1553[9] 1715[2] 2741[2] 3143[7] 4807[5] 5144[10] 6441[9] 7281[9] 7684[9] 9161[2]

Home Before Dusk *Keith Dalgleish* a93 70
4 b g Medicean Flylowflylong (IRE) (Danetime (IRE))
495[4] 1022[6] 1500[6] 2436[4] 3181[3] 3705[6] 4054[6] (4293) 4633[5] 5239[11] 6341[2] (6663) 6940[6] 7305[2] 7653[2] (8087) (8305) 9096[5] (9480)

Home For Half Past (IRE) *David O'Meara* a48
2 b g Elusive Pimpernel(USA) Spiritville (IRE) (Invincible Spirit (IRE))
8528[9] 8919[6]

Home Of The Brave (IRE) *James Cummings* a98 115
7 ch g Starspangledbanner(AUS) Blissful Beat (Beat Hollow)
9015a[2]

Homer (IRE) *A Fabre* 96
3 b g Sea The Stars(IRE) Synchronic (IRE) (Dansili)
6773a[3]

Homerique (USA) *Chad C Brown* 109
4 gr m Exchange Rate(USA) Chiquita Picosa (USA) (Congaree (USA))
4950a[3]

Homesick Boy (IRE) *Ed Dunlop* a66 64
3 b g Data Link(USA) Don't Cry For Me (USA) (Street Cry (IRE))
2021[5] 2712[3] 3092[10] 3538[7] 4346[4] 5354[5] 6128[6] 7280[3] 7857[5] 8204[9] (8551) 9049[2] 9275[6]◆

Homesman (USA) *Liam Howley* a77 112
5 bb g War Front(USA) My Annette (USA) (Red Ransom (USA))
8136a[6] 8579a[11]

Homespin (USA) *Mark Johnston* a77 91
2 ch c Speightstown(USA) Vaguely Familiar (USA) (A.P. Indy (USA))
2931[4] 3426[2] (4394) (5612) 6356[17]

Honcho (IRE) *Mrs A Malzard* a46 54
7 gr g Dark Angel(IRE) Disco Lights (Spectrum (IRE))
(2004a) 2671a[5] (3174a) 4685a[9] 5233[4] 6555a[3]

Honest Albert *John Gosden* a95 93
3 ch g Sepoy(AUS) Mini Mosa (Indian Ridge (IRE))
(4305)◆ 5434[2]

Honey Bear (IRE) *Mark Johnston* a47 56
3 ch f Animal Kingdom(USA) Ishitaki (ARG) (Interprete (ARG))
795[11] 1400[8] 4774[3]

Honey Gg *Declan Carroll* a72 72
4 b m Mayson Local Fancy (Bahamian Bounty)
(1364) 1521[2] 2296[2] 2637[2]◆ 3206[8] 4074[5] 4911[10] 7387[3]◆ 7831[5] 8263[14] 8643[U] 9219[2] 9335[7]

Honey Lane (IRE) *William Jarvis* a55 15
3 gr f Nathaniel(IRE) All Hallows (IRE) (Dalakhani (IRE))
5656[12] 6887[5]◆

Honeysuckle Moon *Tim Easterby*
2 b f Make Believe Zerka (Invincible Spirit (IRE))
5780[P]

Honfleur (IRE) *Sir Michael Stoute* a73 74
3 ch f Le Havre(IRE) Galistic (IRE) (Galileo (IRE))
4641[6] 6114[3] 7395[3] 8064[10] 8468[6]

Hong Kong (USA) *A P O'Brien* 86
2 rg c American Pharoah(USA) Mekko Hokte (USA) (Holy Bull (USA))
8762[7]

Hong Kong Dragon *George Scott* a54
2 ch g Harbour Watch(IRE) Blue Maiden (Medicean)
9174[10] 9242[9] 9413[12] 9607[6]

Hong Kong Star (FR) *O Trigodet* 69
2 ch f Helmet(AUS) Cheg (FR) (Kheleyf (USA))
8330a[11]

Honnold *Donald McCain* 52
2 br g Sea The Moon(GER) Aloha (With Approval (CAN))
4238[6] 5152[6] 6336[8]

Honorable (FR) *Gary Moore*
4 b g Lawman(FR) Petite Noblesse (FR) (Galileo (IRE))
9633[14]

Honorable Treasure (USA)
Kenneth McPeek a98
4 b h To Honor And Serve(USA) Tempest Treasure (USA) (Dixie Union (USA))
280a[2] 513a[8] 842a[9]

Honore Daumier (IRE)
Henry Candy a77 73
2 b c Lawman(FR) Feis Ceoil (IRE) (Key Of Luck (USA))
5439[9] 6154[5] 6912[4] 9300[2]◆

Honor Oak (IRE) *T Hogan* a86 91
7 gr m Zebedee Ishimagic (Ishiguru (USA))
1308a[7] 5597a[8]

Hooflepuff (IRE) *Brian Ellison* a71
3 b g Gale Force Ten Hflah (IRE) (Dubawi (IRE))
278 1173[3] 1725[4] 5054[3] 6077[3] (7034) 7415[4] 8293[4] (9168) 9345[4]

Hook (FR) *A Giorgi* 43
2 b c Frozen Power(IRE) Super Super (IRE) (Medicean)
7043a[8]

Hoorayforthegrey *Robyn Brisland* a47
2 gr g Henrythenavigator(USA) Jillolini (Bertolini (USA))
9408[9]

Hooray Henry *Henry Candy* 44
2 gr c Brazen Beau(AUS) All That Jas (IRE) (Jeremy (USA))
6899[6] 7160[8]

Hooriya *Marco Botti* a54
3 b f Dark Angel(IRE) Jellwa (IRE) (Iffraaj)
1142[11] 1288[7] 3431[8] 3989[9] 5652[8]

Hooroo (IRE) *K R Burke* a60 66
2 b g Hallowed Crown(AUS) Hflah (IRE) (Dubawi (IRE))
5152[5] 5433[8] 6065[6] 6625[6] 7874[3] 8394[5] (8856)

Hootenanny (IRE) *Adam West* a40 58
2 b g Shooting To Win(AUS) Marju Lass (IRE) (Marju (IRE))
5780[9] 6300[6] 7569[10] 7980[13] 8897[8] 9127[8]

Hopalong Cassidy (FR)
D & P Prod'Homme a55 65
4 ch g Air Chief Marshal(IRE) Dear Maria (FR) (Kendor (FR))
2170a[8]

Hopeful (FR) *C Laffon-Parias* 107
2 b g Motivator Monst (IRE) (Monsun (GER))
7005a[2] (7774a)

Hope Is High *John Berry* a75 72
6 b m Sir Percy Altitude (Green Desert (USA))
5316[5] 6333[3] (6854) 7231[7] 7688[9] 8468[7]

Hopeless (FR)
Mme C Barande-Barbe a82 96
6 ch g Tigron(USA) Phalaee (FR) (Ski Chief (USA))
5168a[9]

Hop Maddocks (IRE) *Fred Watson* a44 65
4 b g Roderic O'Connor(IRE) Yurituni (Bahamian Bounty)
2638[15] 3921[17] 4824[9]

Hoquilebo (FR) *T Castanheira* a59 69
4 b g Falco(USA) Honey Gem (FR) (Gold Away (IRE))
(2170a)

Horatio Star *Brian Meehan* 81
4 b g Mount Nelson Star Entry (In The Wings)
2208[8] 3545[4] 4283[6] 4841[6] (5290) 5604[2] 6848[2] 7866[8]

Hornby *Michael Attwater* a56 31
4 b g Equiano(FR) Kindia (IRE) (Cape Cross (IRE))
478[9] 986[9] 2924[8] 3404[7] 4219[10] 6023[6]

Hornsby *S Jadhav* a91 78
6 b g Dubawi(IRE) Moonlife (IRE) (Invincible Spirit (IRE))
51a[13] 282a[8] 515a[6]

Horologist (USA) *John Mazza* a100
3 b f Gemologist(USA) Cinderella Time (USA) (Stephen Got Even (USA))
7479a[3]

Hors De Combat *Denis Coakley* a78 103
8 ch g Mount Nelson Maid For Winning (USA) (Gone West (USA))
173a[11] 515a[9] 847a[10] 2832[5]◆ 3313[11]◆ 4255[3]

Hortzadar *David O'Meara* 100
4 b g Sepoy(AUS) Clouds Of Magellan (USA) (Dynaformer (USA))
(1813) (1977) 2778[6] 3313[5]◆ 4097[7] 4863[5] 5489[3] (6231) 6693a[12] 8096[7] 8728[6]

Hostelry *Michael Dods* 68
2 ch f Coach House(IRE) Queens Jubilee (Cayman Kai (IRE))
4826[5]◆ 5388[3]◆ 7063[2]

Hot Affair *Tom Dascombe* 86
2 b f Ivawood(IRE) Romp (Pivotal)
5317[6] 5788[2]◆ (6577) 8791a[10]

Hot Beat (IRE) *T M Walsh* a86 83
7 b g Dylan Thomas(IRE) Hungry Heart (IRE) (Hawk Wing (USA))
3384a[3]

Hot Date *George Margarson* a14 40
2 b f Hot Streak(IRE) Speed Date (Sakhee's Secret)
2761[12] 5527[7] 5745[6] 6313[8] 7896[24]

Hot Heels *Tom Dascombe* a70 77
2 ch g Hot Streak(IRE) Poulaine Bleue (Bertolini (USA))
5280[4] 5418[2] 6029[4]◆ 7182[3]◆ 8315[3] 9031[12]

Hot Heir (IRE) *Adrian Nicholls* 27
2 ch f Hot Streak(IRE) Maid In Heaven (IRE) (Clodovil (IRE))
2367[5] 4516[12]

Hot Hot Hot *Tony Carroll* a50 24
2 ch f Hot Streak(IRE) Just Emma (Bertolini (USA))
6019[9] 6846[13] 7407[11] 8315[9] 9407[11]

Hot King Prawn (AUS) *J Size* 122
4 gr g Denman(AUS) De Chorus (AUS) (Unbridled's Song (USA))
9377a[2]

Hot News (IRE) *Sylvester Kirk* 27
2 b f Camelot Media Room (USA) (Street Cry (IRE))
5342[9] 6592[12]

Hot Poppy *John Gallagher* a16 35
2 ch f Hot Streak(IRE) Columella (Kyllachy)
3689[9] 4233[7] 5011[4] 6019[12]

Hot Summer (FR) *C Lerner* a56 75
3 b c Sommerabend American Nizzy (FR) (American Post)
3710a[14]

Hot Summer *Richard Hannon* a75 82
2 b c Hot Streak(IRE) Lahqa (IRE) (Tamayuz)
6409[2] 6927[4] 7235[2]

Hotsy Totsy (IRE) *Ed Walker* a89 95
3 b f Casamento(IRE) Siphon Melody (USA) (Siphon (BRZ))
1740[3] (2340)◆ (2967) 4052[3]

Hot Team (IRE) *Hugo Palmer* a87 94
3 b g Zoffany(IRE) Ahd (USA) (Elusive Quality (USA))
2163a[9] 3581[8] 4016[27] 6923[4] 7728[3] 8320[9]

Hot Touch *Hugo Palmer* a81 89
2 ch f Hot Streak(IRE) Stroll Patrol (Mount Nelson)
3968[2] (4790)◆ 7659[5] 8724[16]

Houesville (FR) *C Lerner* a79 77
3 b f Rajsaman(FR) Keira (FR) (Turtle Bowl (IRE))
2498a[8] 7978a[12]

Houlton *Marco Botti* a87 65
4 ch g Declaration Of War(USA) Greek Goddess (IRE) (Galileo (IRE))
559[2] 700[2] 1144[4] (2059) 2398[7] 4383[3] 5631[2] 6634[2] 7033[2] 8120[4]

Hour Of The Dawn (IRE)
Ed Vaughan a70 67
3 b c Bated Breath Burning Dawn (USA) (Bernstein (USA))
3661[3] 4334[2]

House Call (IRE) *Gordon Elliott* a44 57
4 b m Clodovil(IRE) Zalanga (IRE) (Azamour (IRE))
7087a[5] (7509) 7783[10]

House Deposit *Roger Fell* 58
3 ch g Sepoy(AUS) Rosaceous (Duke Of Marmalade (IRE))
2098[9] 2635[8] 3570[3] 4070[8] 5335[5] 5486[5] 5914[7] 6176[8] 6679[4] 7523[6]

House Of Kings (IRE) *Clive Cox* 91
3 b g Camelot Celestial Bow (IRE) (Raven's Pass (USA))
2616[6] 4325[4] 5140[3] 5749[3] 5947[2] 7163[6] 7728[4]

Hout Bay (FR) *Mario Hofer* a81 92
6 bb g Whipper(USA) Iocaste (GER) (Acatenango (GER))
9014a[3]

Houtzen (AUS) *Martyn Meade* 113
4 b m I Am Invincible(AUS) Set To Unleash (AUS) (Reset (AUS))
3950[8] 5611[2] 7243a[10]

Hovingham (IRE) *Nigel Tinkler* 36
2 b g Captain Gerrard(IRE) Taro Tywod (IRE) (Footstepsinthesand)
1843[8] 7000[7] 7539[8] 8128[9]

Howardian Hills (IRE)
Victor Dartnall a60 49
6 b g Vale Of York(IRE) Handsome Anna (IRE) (Bigstone (IRE))
2595[6] 3640a[4] 4232[10]

Howbaar (USA) *James Bethell* a60 53
4 b g Lonhro(AUS) Going Day (USA) (Daylami (IRE))
3247[12] 4076[5] 5156[9]

How Bizarre *Liam Bailey* a63 78
4 ch g Society Rock(IRE) Amanda Carter (Tobougg (IRE))
1768[11] 2372[3] 2679[5] 3199[14] 4511[4] 4728[5] (5022) 5274[2] 5516[5] 5903[3] 6573[2] 6935[8] 7212[10] (7738) 8181[2] 8237[6]

How Far (IRE) *Simon Crisford* a96 92
4 b g Kodiac Akuna Magic (IRE) (Whipper (USA))
382[5] 1459[15]

Ho Whole Dream (IRE)
Michael Easterby a38 64
3 ch g Pivotal Dream Play (IRE) (In The Wings)
1417[15] 6732[7] 7143[5] 8635[11]

Howizeegeezer *Charlie Wallis*
2 b g Mukhadram Tadpole (Sir Percy)
8494[14]

Howling Wolf (IRE) *Anthony Mullins* 92
2 gr c Footstepsinthesand Aussie Opera (IRE) (Aussie Rules (USA))
7217a[7]

Howman (IRE) *Roger Varian* a87 80
4 b g Sea The Stars(IRE) Hoity Toity (Darshaan)
4386[2] 5966[6]

Howzer Black (IRE) *Keith Dalgleish* a81 84
3 b g Requinto(IRE) Mattinata (Tiger Hill (IRE))
1104[2]◆ 1360[3] 1945[6] 2371[3] (2896) 4099[5] 4492[4] 4980[5] 6015[3] 6935[7] 7402[21] 7435[4] 7781[2] 8766[5] 9348[8] 9476[6]

Htilominlo *Sylvester Kirk* a83 86
3 b c Zoffany(IRE) Haven's Wave (IRE) (Whipper (USA))
486[4] 1034[3] 2141[2] 2407[2] 2828[11] 3373[2] 3808[8] 4901[6] 5840[2]◆ 9167[4] 9633[P]

Hua Hin (IRE) *E Lyon* a55 55
3 ch g Dandy Man(IRE) Midnight Oasis (Oasis Dream)
360[5] 620[9] 1549[9] 6061a[5]

Hua Mulan (IRE) *Keith Dalgleish* a63 65
2 gr f Harbour Watch(IRE) Ultimate Best (King's Best (USA))
7733[3] 8232[2] 8528[5]

Hubert (IRE) *Sylvester Kirk* a69 78
2 b g Kodiac Qalahari (IRE) (Bahri (USA))
3942[3] 4394[2] 4992[3] (5577) 6073[3] 7725[3] 8318[4]

Huboor (IRE) *Mark Johnston* 87
2 b f More Than Ready(USA) Glorification (Champs Elysees)
3776[3] (4482)◆ 7179[3]◆ (7696)

Huddle *William Knight* a66 61
3 gr f Aussie Rules(USA) Purest (Shamardal (USA))
1359[5] 1676[5] 2598[4] 3041[8] 4248[5] 4870[4] 5730[5] 6844[7] (9209) 9427[10] 9657[6]

Hudson Hornet (FR) *Jiri Chaloupka* 33
2 ch c Outstrip Love And War (GER) (War Blade (GER))
5763a[6] 8330a[12]

Hugoigo *Jim Goldie* a48 60
5 b g Sulamani(IRE) Gargoyle Girl (Be My Chief (USA))
100[3] 208[2] 607[3] 782[9] 1398[10] 1718[5]◆ 4056[3] 4510[8] 4825[4] 5241[2] 5487[2] 5939[6] (6343) 6611[7]

Hukum (IRE) *Owen Burrows* a83 69
2 b c Sea The Stars(IRE) Aghareed (USA) (Kingmambo (USA))
7453[3] (9052)

Hula Girl *Charles Hills* a65 52
4 gr m Oasis Dream Tropical Paradise (IRE) (Verglas (IRE))
298[3] 411[7]

Hulcote *Clive Cox* a99 95
4 b m Frankel Polly's Mark (IRE) (Mark Of Esteem (IRE))
1461[3]◆ 3010[7] (3726) 4145[5] 8245[2] 9002[8] 9302[5] 9588[7]

Humanitarian (USA) *John Gosden* a88 106
3 b g Noble Mission Sharbat (USA) (Dynaformer (USA))
(2769) 3345[7] 4049[7]

Human Nature (IRE)
Stuart Williams a91 69
6 b g Kodiac Sundown (Polish Precedent (USA))
139[5] 382[2] 981[5] 1356[4] 1560[7] 2272[8] 2804[5] 3701[5] 5050[8] 8063[4] (8496) 9476[8]

Humbert (IRE) *David O'Meara* a94 93
5 b g Kodiac Fee Eria (FR) (Always Fair (USA))
1415[17] 1753[P] 8096[8] 8728[11] 9053[11] 9388[3]◆

Humble Gratitude *Ian Williams* a79 92
4 ch g Foxwedge(AUS) Gilt Linked (Compton Place)
2015[5] 2526[6] 3072[2] 3845[6] 4403[8] 4875[5] (5708) (6166) 6711[5] 7184[2]

Humidor (NZ)
Ciaron Maher & David Eustace 109
6 b g Teofilo(IRE) Zalika (NZ) (Zabeel (NZ))
8136a[5] 8577a[4] 8952a[9]

Hummdinger (FR) *Alan King* a43 68
3 ch g Planteur(IRE) Interior (USA) (Fusaichi Pegasus (USA))
1957[2] 2485[4] 3092[2] 3809[6] 4656[5] 5954[4] 8224[9]

Hummingbird (IRE)
David Loughnane a40 59
3 b f Fast Company(IRE) Rocking (Oasis Dream)
8306[13] (8637) 8864[9]

Hungarian Rhapsody
Jamie Osborne a61 54
5 b g Exceed And Excel(AUS) Sharp Terms (Kris)
(484) 9241[0]

Hunni *Tom Clover* a65 81
4 b m Captain Gerrard(IRE) Lady O Malley (IRE) (Oratorio (IRE))
3336[6] 3743[3] 4393[3] 4828[6] 5573[4] 6408[2] 7165[5] 7901[4] 8691[4]

Hunters Step *Nigel Tinkler* a41 47
3 b g Mukhadram Step Softly (Golan (IRE))
4636[7] 5690[10] 6177[5] 6575[9] 8820[3] 9516[7]

Hunter Valley (FR) *Cedric Rossi* 58
2 bb f Power Meulles (FR) (Scat Daddy (USA))
5600a[2]

Hunterwali *Michael Dods* a77 79
3 ch f Kyllachy Samasana (IRE) (Redback)
2420[4]◆ (3570) 4585[5] 5844[6] (7189)

Hunting Horn (IRE) *A P O'Brien* 115
4 b h Camelot Mora Bai (IRE) (Indian Ridge (IRE))
894a[3] 1446a[4] 2646a[4] 3985[4] 4668[6] 5414[5] 6001a[8] 7219a[8] (8577a) 8844a[15]

Huraa *Bryan Smart* 69
2 b f Brazen Beau(AUS) Hakuraa (IRE) (Elnadim (USA))
2907[2]

Huraiz (IRE) *Mark Johnston* a97 93
2 ch c Sepoy(AUS) Samaah (IRE) (Cape Cross (IRE))
(5856)◆ (6449) 6966[3] 8125[4]

Hurcle (IRE) *Archie Watson* a79
2 b c Exceed And Excel(AUS) Switcher (IRE) (Whipper (USA))
(4384)

Hurricane Alert *Mark Hoad* a53 43
7 b g Showcasing Raggle Taggle (IRE) (Tagula (IRE))
478[5] 823[3] (986)◆ 1210[8] 1716[2] 2010[2] 3404[4] 4027[6] 5046[3] 5884[9]

Hurricane Alex *Richard Hannon* a76 6
2 b c Canford Cliffs(IRE) Azharia (Oasis Dream)
8516[20] 8700[2] 9063[2] 9328[3]

Hurricane Ali (IRE) *John Mackie* a65 60
3 b g Alhebayeb(IRE) Hurricane Irene (IRE) (Green Desert (USA))
3510[7] 3972[7] 7772[4]◆

Hurricane Gold (FR)
Matthieu Palussiere a66 58
3 b g Hurricane Cat(USA) Midas Medusa (FR) (Elusive City (USA))
216a[15] 5408a[3]

Hurricane Heidi *Derek Shaw* a29
3 gr f Kyllachy The Manx Touch (IRE) (Petardia)
795[12] 3003[16] 3598[8] 9410[8]

Hurricane Hero (FR) *K R Burke* a77 49
3 b g George Vancouver(USA) Memoire (FR) (Sadler's Wells (USA))
1386[5] 1972[2] 2323[3] 3139a[10] 3253[3]

Hurricane Ivor (IRE) *F Chappet* 90
2 b c Ivawood(IRE) Quickstep Queen (Royal Applause)
4417a[7]

Hurricane Speed (IRE) *Kevin Ryan* a32 30
3 ch g Gale Force Ten Ma Nikitia (IRE) (Camacho)
4371[1] 612[10]

Hurry Kane *Paul George* a47 63
3 ch g Dunaden(FR) Flotation (USA) (Chapel Royal (USA))
4459[P] 6043[5] 6641[6] 7035[10] 8696[8]

Hurstwood *Tim Easterby* 90
2 bg c Dark Angel(IRE) Haigh Hall (Kyllachy)
1893[3] 3290[2] (3810) (4441)◆ 4846[7] 5707[5] 6356[13] 7072[7] 7399[12]

Hush Writer (JPN)
Gai Waterhouse & Adrian Bott 105
4 b g Rulership(JPN) Star Of Sapphire (USA) (Tapit (USA))
8767a[6]

Hussar Ballad (USA)
Antony Brittain a61 63
10 b g Hard Spun(USA) Country Melody (USA) (Gone West (USA))
481[4] 782[7] 1334[3] 1341[3] 1548[7] 2014[10] 2593[5] (2695) 3769[8] 4190[8]

Huwaiteb *Owen Burrows* a63 74
2 b g Oasis Dream Zahoo (IRE) (Nayef (USA))
5809[10] 8459[5] 8889[5]

Hyanna *Eve Johnson Houghton* a89 100
4 b m Champs Elysees Highly Spiced (Cadeaux Genereux)
1681[6] (2342)◆ 3010[3] 3800[2] 4613[3] 5370[3] 5929[6] (6725) 7457[6] 7895[4] 8710[7]

Hyba *Robert Cowell* 55
2 b f Muhaarar Jellwa (IRE) (Iffraaj)
4659[5]

Hydroplane (IRE)
Sir Mark Prescott Bt a84 83
3 b g Pour Moi(IRE) Walk On Water (Exceed And Excel (AUS))
3226[10] (4931) (5054)◆ (5385)◆ 6842[2] 7209[8] 7729[2]

Hygrove Dan (FR) *L Gadbin* a57 68
4 ch h Planteur(IRE) Hygrove Welshlady (IRE) (Langfuhr (CAN))
1908a[9]

Hyperfocus (IRE) *Tim Easterby* a83 101
5 bb g Intense Focus(USA) Jouel (FR) (Machiavellian (USA))
2378[6] 2843[2] (3480) 3863[17] 4402[15] 5454[9] 5664[24] 6227[2] 6920[3]◆ 7431[12] 8127[2] 8340[6]

Hypnos (IRE) *David Simcock* a71 66
3 b g Morpheus Winter Song (IRE) (Pivotal)
140[2] 561[2] 885[3] 1066[6] (1481) 2021[9]

Hypochondriac *Claes Bjorling* a36 57
2 br f Pastoral Pursuits Mondovi (Kyllachy)
1493[6] 1931[3] 2331[2] 7495a[14]

Hypothetical (IRE) *John Gosden* a82
2 ch c Lope De Vega(IRE) Peut Etre (IRE) (Whipper (USA))
(9452)

Hystery Bere (FR) *J Boisnard* 56
2 b c Pedro The Great(USA) Mysteryonthebounty (USA) (Mystery Storm (USA))
2315a[5]

I Am A Dreamer *Mark Johnston* a68 88
3 b g Dream Ahead(USA) Alexander Ballet (Mind Games)
2054[7] 2746[4] 3357[6] 4338[2] (4635) 4887[13] 5246[4] 5459[9] 5862[3] (6015) 6440[7] 6803[7] 7205[7]

I Am Charlie (FR) *J-P Gauvin* a94 94
6 bb m Great Journey(JPN) Freedom Sweet (FR) (Sicyos (USA))
8240a[6]

I Am Dandy (IRE) *James Ewart* a56 55
4 b g Dandy Man(IRE) Acushladear (IRE) (Tagula (IRE))
210[4] 738[6] 1967[3]◆ 2329[7] 3225[3] 4002[7] 9516[14]

I Am Eloquent (AUS)
Trent Busuttin & Natalie Young 88
2 b f I Am Invincible(AUS) Choice Words (AUS) (Choisir (AUS))
8135a[8]

I Am Magical *Charlie Fellowes* a74 85
3 b f Declaration Of War(USA) Lady Wingshot (IRE) (Lawman (FR))
2103[2] (2760) 2934[5] 3807[3] 4922[10]

I Am Superman (IRE)
M D O'Callaghan 107
3 b c Footstepsinthesand Fastnet Lady (IRE) (Fastnet Rock (AUS))
2492a[5] 3104a[6] 4092[12] 6137a[3] 8805a[13]

Iballisticvin *Gary Moore* a44 59
6 b g Rail Link Guntakal (IRE) (Night Shift (USA))
1936[8] 2617[11] 2928[7] 4111[2] 5049[4] 6843[8] 7985[7]

Iberia (IRE) *A P O'Brien* 108
2 b c Galileo(IRE) Beauty Bright (IRE) (Danehill (USA))
6430a[7] 7245a[5] 7691[3]◆ 8356a[2]
Iberica Road (USA) *Grant Tuer* a60 60
6 bb g Quality Road(USA) Field Of Clover (CAN) (Bluegrass Cat (USA))
410[8] 593[8] 829[11]
Ibn Malik (IRE) *M Al Mheiri* a110 93
6 ch g Raven's Pass(USA) Moon's Whisper (USA) (Storm Cat (USA))
49a[3] 512a[3] 639a[5] 957a[3] 1112a[7] 1440a[8]
Ibn Medecis (FR) *P-J Fertillet*
4 b g Medecis Soft Gold (USA) (Gulch (USA))
8737a[11]
Ibraz *Roger Varian* a102 101
4 b g Farhh Wadaa (USA) (Dynaformer (USA))
1753[11] 2408[6] 3450[4] 5965[2] (6543) 7106[4] (Dead)
I Can (IRE) *Sir Mark Todd* a73 54
4 b g So You Think(NZ) Walk On Water (Exceed And Excel (AUS))
1517[3] 2488[9] 7684[5] 8221[5]◆ 8652[8]
I Can Dream (FR) *Yannick Fouin* 58
3 gr f Montmartre(FR) Inaya (FR) (Majorien)
6094a[7]
I Can Fly *A P O'Brien* a101 115
4 b m Fastnet Rock(AUS) Madonna Dell'Orto (Montjeu (IRE))
1445a[11] 2829[6] 3105a[2] 3986[3] 4885[3] 5543[3]
6265a[4] 7221a[5] 7898[5] 8335[7]
Ice Age (IRE)
Eve Johnson Houghton a88 101
6 b g Frozen Power(IRE) Incendio (Siberian Express (USA))
1734[5] 2117[6] 2791[9] 3480[2] 3662[6] 4451[3] 5504[16]
6229[7] 6847[2] 7397[5] 8127[8] 8522[13]
Icebee (IRE) *Vaclav Luka Jr* a70 64
3 b f Xtension(IRE) Voom Voom (IRE) (Bahamian Bounty)
509a[10]
Ice Canyon *Kevin Frost* a68 66
5 b g Raven's Pass(USA) Picture Hat (USA) (El Prado (IRE))
(61) 346[2] 945[8] 1095[7] 2696[12] 3321[8] 5706[4]
6736[8] 7790[12] (8703)
Ice Cave (IRE) *Saeed bin Suroor* a84
3 ch c Shamardal(USA) La Collina (IRE) (Strategic Prince)
2060[6] 2938[9] (8653)◆ 9057[6]◆
Ice Cold In Alex (IRE) *K J Condon* a87 88
5 b g Olden Times Telesina (ITY) (Marju (IRE))
5205a[3] 6693a[4] 7222a[3]
Ice Cool Cullis (IRE)
Mark Loughnane a41 23
4 ch g Frozen Power(IRE) Kathoe (IRE) (Fayruz)
239[7] 1362[9] 4346[11] 4868[8]
Icefinger (IRE) *Gavin Hernon* a94 95
3 gr c Kodiac Miss Spinamix (IRE) (Verglas (IRE))
6249a[6]
Ice Gala *William Haggas* 98
3 b f Invincible Spirit(IRE) Ice Palace (Polar Falcon (USA))
(2144) 3359[7] 4052[16] 4922[5]
Ice Galley (IRE) *Philip Kirby* a62 67
6 br g Galileo(IRE) Ice Queen (IRE) (Danehill Dancer (IRE))
2398[9]
Ice Lord (IRE) *Chris Wall* a59 100
7 gr g Verglas(IRE) Special Lady (FR) (Kaldoun (FR))
1829[4]◆ 5911[6] 6404[7] 6920[9] 8522[2]
Ice Pyramid (IRE) *Philip Kirby* a69 81
4 ch g New Approach(IRE) Coolnagree (IRE) (Dark Angel (IRE))
18[3]◆ 9469[3]◆
Ice Royal (IRE) *Mrs A Malzard* a65 61
6 b g Frozen Power(IRE) Salford Princess (IRE) (Titus Livius (FR))
4686a[3] 5233[5] 6010a[5] 6555a[6]
Ice Skate *Tim Easterby* a33 51
2 gr f Due Diligence(USA) Skiing (Sakhee's Secret)
2115[10] 2892[7] 3411[7] 4006[6] 4985[3]◆ 5789[7] 6032[6]
6683[8] 7208[11]
Ice Sprite *William Haggas* 66
2 ch f Zoffany(IRE) Queen Of Ice (Selkirk (USA))
8759[5]◆
Ickworth (IRE) *W McCreery* a88 98
2 b f Shamardal(USA) Ishitaki (ARG) (Interprete (ARG))
(2491a) 3983[RR] 4352a[8] 7400[3] 8088[11] 8328a[8]
Iconic Belle *Philip Kirby* a82 80
5 ch m Sixties Icon Five Bells (IRE) (Rock Of Gibraltar (IRE))
803[7] 3269[2] 4363[3] 7301[9] 9570[2]
Iconic Boy *Alexandra Dunn* a8
4 b g Cape Cross(IRE) Snoqualmie Girl (IRE) (Montjeu (IRE))
185[10]
Iconic Choice *Tom Dascombe* 106
3 ch f Sixties Icon Adorable Choice (IRE) (Choisir (AUS))
1751[2]◆ 2443[7] 3119a[7] 4416a[7] 7365[5] 8367a[13]
8765[5]
Iconic Code *Keith Dalgleish* a62 70
4 ch m Sixties Icon Silca Key (Inchinor)
3502[9] 3925[7] 4917[2] 5117[4] 5844[2] 6341[5] 7491[3]◆
(7783)
Iconic Girl *Andrew Balding* a68 72
4 b m Cape Cross(IRE) Snoqualmie Star (Galileo (IRE))
732[3] 963[4] 1343[5] 1848[5] 2720[2]
Iconic Knight (IRE) *Ed Walker* a75 83
4 b g Sir Prancealot(IRE) Teutonic (IRE) (Revoque (IRE))
2272[7] 2824[10] 3636[3]◆ 4236[6] 4995[7] 5395[2] 6465[2]
6916[2] 8420[7] 8766[13]
I Could Do Better (IRE)
Ian Williams 96
3 b g Canford Cliffs(IRE) Shebelia (GER) (Black Sam Bellamy (IRE))
(2895)◆ (4439) 5609[6] 6453[9] 7411[4]
Ideal Candy (IRE) *Karen Tutty* a69 80
4 b m Canford Cliffs(IRE) Forever More (IRE) (Galileo (IRE))
1850[2] 2290[2] 3095[9] 3568[4] 4371[7] 5245[2] 5725[9]
6500[3] 7288[10] 8305[7] 8719[11] 9109[6] 9351[10]
Ideal Destiny *Karen Tutty* a62
3 b f Dawn Approach(IRE) Early Morning Rain (IRE) (Rock Of Gibraltar (IRE))
6941[3] 7630[7] 8718[5]
Ideal Grace *Brian Barr* a38 57
3 ch f Poet's Voice Sunday Bess (JPN) (Deep Impact (JPN))
1677[11] 2690[6] 3263[12] 3888[4] 4547[8] 5601[4] 5987[5]
8837[6] 9139[11]
Ideal Option (IRE) *Tim Easterby* 37
3 ch g Camacho Practicallyperfect (IRE) (King Charlemagne (USA))
2590[9]
Ideological (IRE) *Mark Johnston* a83 84
3 b f Dawn Approach(IRE) Micaela's Moon (USA) (Malibu Moon (USA))
1897[8] 2768[4] 3468[10] 4729[2] 5201[5] 5741[10]
Idiosa (GER) *Mlle L Kneip* 88
3 b f Soldier Hollow Indikova (IRE) (Bushranger (IRE))
3121a[11] 6005a[7] 6385a[7]
Idle Wheel (FR) *F-X Belvisi* a61 58
7 b g Youmzain(IRE) Island Doree (IRE) (King's Best (USA))
2266a[9]
Idoapologise *James Bethell* a72 67
2 b g Havana Gold(IRE) Shiba (FR) (Rail Link)
3866[11] 5396[5] 6175[9] (7283) (8022)◆
Idol Deputy (FR) *James Bennett* a61 33
13 gr g Silver Deputy(CAN) Runaway Venus (USA) (Runaway Groom (CAN))
62[11] 485[11]
If At Sea *Amanda Perrett* 35
3 b f Pour Moi(IRE) Ebble (Oasis Dream)
3013[11] 4189[8] 4800[5]
Iffraaz (IRE) *Mark Johnston* 92
2 b c Iffraaj Zofzig (USA) (Danzig (USA))
(3290) 3988[16] (4564) 6422[10] 7072[3] 8113[9]
Ifreet (QA) *Richard Hannon* a69 37
3 ch c Toronado(IRE) Bella Varenna (IRE) (Lawman (FR))
251[3] 1165[2] 1550[4] 3093[4]
Iftiraaq (IRE) *David Loughnane* a72 72
8 b g Muhtathir Alzaroof (USA) (Kingmambo (USA))
61[6] 318[P]
Iftitah (IRE) *S Seemar* a88 47
5 b g Harbour Watch(IRE) Solstice (Dubawi (IRE))
(997)
Ifton *Ruth Carr* a62 66
3 b g Iffraaj Flambeau (Oasis Dream)
2896[4] 3650[10] 4606[3]◆ 4820[7] 5575[3] 6130[2]◆
6840[4] 7460[6] 8291[9]
If We Can Can *Olly Williams*
4 ch g Sepoy(AUS) Kirk (Selkirk (USA))
8664[9] 9033[11] 9470[13]
Ignacius Reilly *Vaclav Luka Jr* a52 98
3 gr c Worthadd(IRE) In The Pink (IRE) (Indian Ridge (IRE))
1198a[6]
Ignatius (IRE) *John Best* a56 61
3 b g Casamento(IRE) Free Lance (IRE) (Grand Lodge (USA))
400[5] 1332[6] (1957) 2406[5] 3275[6] 4547[4] 4834[5]
5648[5] 7202[3] 7520[3] 8551[3] 9049[5] 9310[9]
I Had A Dream *Tom Clover* a63 68
2 b f Dream Ahead(USA) Grandmas Dream (Kyllachy)
3644[10] 4222[3] 5895[2] 7787[4]
I Hear Thunder (FR) *James Tate* a56
2 ch f Night Of Thunder(IRE) Keeping Quiet (GER) (Samum (GER))
9311[9] 9585[7]
Iiex Excelsa (IRE) *J A Stack* a65 93
4 ch m Excelebration(IRE) Holly Blue (Bluebird (USA))
1307a[4] 2627[3] 3786a[7] 6646a[10]
Ikebana *Roger Varian* 70
2 b f Pivotal Sea The Bloom (Sea The Stars (IRE))
6846[7] 7644[5] 8431[3]
Ikigai *Mrs Ilka Gansera-Leveque* 95
2 b f Sayif(IRE) Usem (Bahamian Bounty)
(5527) 7602a[3] 8647a[8]
I Kirk (SWE) *Susanne Berneklint* a110
5 ch g Eishin Dunkirk(USA) I Could (USA) (Johannesburg (USA))
(280a) 1109a[6]
I Know How (IRE) *Julie Camacho* a68 69
4 b g Epaulette(AUS) Blue Crystal (IRE) (Lure (USA))
1760[7] 2247[6] 3970[3] 4523[14] 6058[8] (7066) 8083[8]
8923[4] 9352[2]◆ (9518)
Ilanga (FR) *D Guillemin* 104
3 b f Penny's Picnic(IRE) Molly Mara (GER) (Big Shuffle (USA))
1780a[5] (2564a) 6520a[9] 8648a[3]
Il Capitano (FR) *Roger Charlton* a72
3 ch c Dawn Approach(IRE) Manyara (Manduro (GER))
258[4]
Il Decamerone (FR)
Elias Mikhalides a74 50
3 b g Born To Sea(IRE) Letizia Relco (IRE) (Lucky Story (USA))
1241a[8]
Iley Boy *John Gallagher* a60 56
5 b g Delegator Menha (Dubawi (IRE))
321[6] 560[3] 923[3] (1679) 1935[6] 3015[4]
Ilhabela Fact *Tony Carroll* a87 75
5 b h High Chaparral(IRE) Ilhabela (IRE) (Azamour (IRE))
84[7] 362[2] (559) (945) 1425[5] 2209[7] 2969[9] 9066[7]
9303[3]◆
Ilikehim (IRE) *William Durkan* 63
5 b g Lawman(FR) Slip Dance (IRE) (Celtic Swing)
5712a[11]
I'll Be Brief *Julie Camacho* a59 53
3 b f Epaulette(AUS) Shesastar (Bahamian Bounty)
9397[5]
I'll Be Good *Alan Berry* a53 55
10 b g Red Clubs(IRE) Willisa (Polar Falcon (USA))
2576[5] 3723[4]◆ 4132[3] 4493[9] 5278[7] 5892[5] (6174)
6277[4] 6659[7] 7052[11] 7488[6] 7766[3] 8638[2] 8901[7]
Illegitimate Gains *Adam West* a13 40
3 b f Zebedee Jillolini (Bertolini (USA))
5044[8] 5575[6] 6754[6] 7172[14]
I'lletyougonow *Mick Channon* a76 79
3 b f Bated Breath Upskittled (Diktat)
2251[3]◆ 4424[5] 5255[6] (5749) 6362[8] 6973[3] 7341[5]
7975[2] 8606[7] 9126[3] 9417[4]
I'll Have Another (IRE)
Mark Johnston a98 102
3 b f Dragon Pulse(IRE) Jessie Jane (IRE) (Dylan Thomas (IRE))
1831[6] 2445[3] 2745[6] 5133[6] 5735[3] (6223) 6952[5]
7566[2] 7864[4] 8754[5]
Illumina *Gavin Hernon* 34
2 ch f Helmet(AUS) Cheerio Sweetie (IRE) (Captain Rio)
2263a[9]
Illumined (IRE) *John Gosden* a92 103
3 br f Sea The Moon(GER) Nenuphar (IRE) (Night Shift (USA))
2481[2] (4503)◆ 5810[2] (6893) 7565[3]
Illusionist (GER) *Archie Watson* 94
2 b g Hot Streak(IRE) Irishstone (IRE) (Danehill Dancer (IRE))
2362[2] 2686[2] (3530) 3988[5] 4580a[7] 6899[4]
Illustrious Lad (AUS)
Peter Gelagotis 92
7 b g I Am Invincible(AUS) Industrious (AUS) (Zeditave (AUS))
1442a[12]
Illustrious Spirit *Ali Stronge* a49 34
4 b g Swiss Spirit Darling Daisy (Komaite (USA))
3352[11] 8697[5] 9445[9] 9508[2]
Illustrissime (USA) *Mark Walford* a87 58
6 b g Mizzen Mast(USA) Ghost Friendly (USA) (Ghostzapper (USA))
29[2] 184[5] (793)◆ 1232[6] 1719[2] 3502[12] 8396[8]
Illywhacker (IRE) *Gary Moore* a57 60
3 b c Oasis Dream Rebecca Rolfe (Pivotal)
2210[7] 2794[9] 3665[13] 5377[12] 5957[10]
Il Maestro (IRE) *John Quinn* a55 65
2 b g Camacho Dance On (Caerleon (USA))
1758[4] 2288[4] 2783[7] 5275[7] 5789[12] 7833[7] 8750[3]
9061[10]
I Love Thisgame (IRE)
Annalisa Umbre 82
2 ch c Es Que Love(IRE) Fitrah (IRE) (Tamayuz)
4172a[4]
I Love You Baby *Michael Appleby* a70
3 b f Cityscape Ashtaroth (Royal Applause)
(9547) 9644[3]
Il Paradiso (USA) *A P O'Brien* 118
3 ch c Galileo(IRE) Famous (IRE) (Danehill Dancer (IRE))
4414a[7] 6421[3] 7196[5] 8844a[3]◆
Il Pittore (FR) *C Escuder* a82 81
8 b g Mr Greeley(USA) Spira (IRE) (Sadler's Wells (USA))
5643a[13]
Ilsereno *Scott Dixon* a60
2 gr f Lethal Force(IRE) She's A Worldie (IRE) (Kodiac)
8899[7] 9393[4]
Il Sicario (IRE) *Bill Turner* a69 69
5 b g Zebedee Starring (FR) (Ashkalani (IRE))
2732[3] 3150[2] 3537[2] 4547[9] 5086[4] 5747[4]
Image Of The Moon
Shaun Keightley a81 74
3 b f Mukhadram Hamsat Elqamar (Nayef (USA))
1173[2] 1358[2]◆ 2125[3] 4225[2] 5561[6] (6075) (6593)
7471[4] 8024[8]
Imaging *D K Weld* 107
4 b h Oasis Dream Mirror Lake (Dubai Destination (USA))
(1531a) (1776a) 3287a[2] 7934a[2] 8334[15]
Imago Jasius (FR) *F Monnier* 80
6 ch g Spanish Moon(USA) Issoria (FR) (Saint Cyrien (FR))
1245a[3] (8737a)
Imajorblush *Philip Kirby* a59 59
3 ch g Mukhadram Winter Dress (Haafhd)
4608[4] 5004[2]
I'm Available (IRE) *Andrew Balding* a82 91
3 b f Nathaniel(IRE) Night Carnation (Sleeping Indian)
359[4] 761[2] (1033) 1480[5] (2251) 2569[2] 4052[14]
7728[2] 8519[5] 9041[9]
I'm Billy Murphy (IRE) *Nigel Tinkler* a31 60
3 b g Bated Breath Tonle Sap (IRE) (Manduro (GER))
2016[11]
I'm Brian *Julia Feilden* a43 42
3 b g Sepoy(AUS) Emily Carr (IRE) (Teofilo (IRE))
1171[12] 2023[10] 2925[7] 4400[15] 4568[11]
I'm British *Don Cantillon* a61 40
6 b g Aqlaam Libritish (Librettist (USA))
979[5] 1212[5] 1381[7] 2376[11] 2740[13]
Imbucato *Tony Carroll* a48 56
5 b g Paco Boy(IRE) L'Invitata (Dr Fong (USA))
484[6] 2145[13] 3187[3] 3966[6] 5806[4] (5837) 6758[4]
7982[15]
Im Dapper Too *John Davies* a69 64
8 b g Dapper Lonely One (Perryston View)
1660[7] 2203[7] 3296[4] 3922[8] 4293[4] 5213[7] 5438[2]
6666[2]
I'm Digby (IRE) *Richard Hughes* 73
2 b g Gutaifan(IRE) Lathaat (Dubai Destination (USA))
2205[5] 3165[4] 3644[3]◆
I'm Easy *Michael Easterby* 43
2 b g Archipenko(USA) Eminencia (Sadler's Wells (USA))
7902[10] 8858[7]
I'm Freezing (IRE) *P Monfort* a65 47
3 b f Iffraaj Morning Frost (IRE) (Duke Of Marmalade (IRE))
5538a[5]
Imhotep *Roger Charlton* a69 67
3 b g Kingman African Rose (Observatory (USA))
6838[3]◆ 7319[3] 7841[4]
I'm Improving (IRE) *Keith Dalgleish* a51 87
4 b g Most Improved(IRE) Shebelia (GER) (Black Sam Bellamy (IRE))
611[6]
Imminent Approach
Tony Newcombe a67 43
4 b m New Approach(IRE) Nashmiah (IRE) (Elusive City (USA))
1176[9] 3834[10] 4475[13] 5338[6]
Immoral (IRE) *Ed Walker* 69
3 b g Helmet(AUS) Loose Julie (IRE) (Cape Cross (IRE))
2139[7] 2794[12] 3565[7] 4180[2] (4801)
Imotep (FR) *M Boutin* 68
3 b f Captain Marvelous(IRE) Melivea (FR) (Green Tune (USA))
1842a[7] 2090a[10] 3066a[3] (6061a) 9538a[10]
Impart *Laura Mongan* a69 65
5 b g Oasis Dream Disclose (Dansili)
179[4] 439[11]
Impatient *Ralph Beckett* a81 73
2 b g More Than Ready(USA) Regardez (Champs Elysees)
5809[5] 6528[3] 7162[8] 7840[7] (8252)
Imperative (USA)
Anthony T Quartarolo a88 70
9 b g Bernardini(USA) Call Her (USA) (Caller I.D. (USA))
445a[8]
Imperial Act *Andrew Balding* a71 68
4 b m Frankel Victrix Ludorum (IRE) (Invincible Spirit (IRE))
436[13] 532[5] 717[7] 1717[2]◆ (2240) 2930[4] (3325)
3533[6] (5016) 6414[2] 6717[2] 6904[6] 7812[9]
Imperial Charm *Simon Crisford* 107
3 b f Dubawi(IRE) Reem Three (Mark Of Esteem (IRE))
1795a[2] 2669a[4] 3121a[3] 4416a[3] 6910a[3] 8154a[4]
Imperial Command (IRE)
Jonjo O'Neill 71
2 b g War Command(USA) Acts Out Loud (USA) (Mr Greeley (USA))
2205[4] 8511[9]
Imperial Court (IRE) *David Simcock* a73 76
4 b g Zoffany(IRE) La Vita Bella (Mtoto)
(3778) 4308[7] 5443[4]◆
Imperial Eagle (IRE)
Lawrence Mullaney a46 53
2 br f Free Eagle(IRE) Wild Step (GER) (Footstepsinthesand)
4517[5] 5243[7] 6064[9] 7306[10] 7768[8] 8526[8]
Imperial Empire *Charlie Appleby* a74 78
2 ch g Dubawi(IRE) Falls Of Lora (IRE) (Street Cry (IRE))
4324[6] 5059[4] 6127[2] (6728) 7840[6]
Imperial Focus (IRE) *Simon Waugh* a61 76
6 b g Intense Focus(USA) Mrs Cee (IRE) (Orpen (USA))
8186[12] 8423[4] 8713[11] 9345[7] 9542[6]
Imperial Gloriana (IRE)
David O'Meara 80
2 b f Kingman Songbird (IRE) (Danehill Dancer (IRE))
3968[4]◆ 4596[2] 5387[3] 6221[2] 6606[3]
Imperial Hint (USA) *Luis Carvajal Jr* a126
6 bb h Imperialism(USA) Royal Hint (USA) (Lahint (USA))
1444a[3]
Imperial Square (IRE)
Mark Johnston a77
2 b c Sea The Stars(IRE) Miss Cambridge (Dubawi (IRE))
7579[5] 7996[3] 8504[7]
Imperial State *Michael Easterby* a60 85
6 b g Holy Roman Emperor(IRE) Seldemosa (Selkirk (USA))
2526[4] 3503[10] 4078[2] 4319[6] 6978[5] 7145[5] 8031[10]
8181[3]
Imperial Tango (FR) *A Schutz* a80 84
5 b m Sageburg(IRE) Driving Miswaki (USA) (Miswaki (USA))
5715a[11] 7800a[6] 8648a[10]
Imperium (IRE) *Roger Charlton* a82 75
3 ch g Frankel Ramruma (USA) (Diesis)
2566[4] 4234[3] 4842[6] (7279) 7845[2]◆
Impertinente (IRE) *A Fabre* 105
4 b m Redoute's Choice(AUS) Incroyable (USA) (Singspiel (IRE))
3123a[11]
Imphal *Gary Moore* a87 89
5 b g Nathaniel(IRE) Navajo Rainbow (Rainbow Quest (USA))
3635[6] 4614[3]
Important Mission (USA) *S Jadhav* a95 94
5 br g More Than Ready(USA) Laura's Pleasure (USA) (Cactus Ridge (USA))
197a[12]
Impression *Amy Murphy* a52 53
2 b f Dutch Art Past Forgetting (IRE) (Pivotal)
4206[4] 5387[9] 6592[9] 7516[4]
Impressionable *William Muir* a61 42
3 b f Exceed And Excel(AUS) Appealing (IRE) (Bertolini (USA))
1740[15] 2332[8] 3431[7] 4763[8] 5869[4] 7281[4] 7909[2]
8299[2] 9279[5]◆ 9573[10]
Impressor (IRE) *Marcus Tregoning* 99
2 b c Footstepsinthesand Little Empress (IRE) (Holy Roman Emperor (IRE))
5523[4] (6079) 7456[8] 8762[3]
Imprimis (USA) *Joseph Orseno* 117
5 bb g Broken Vow(USA) Shoppers Return (USA) (Put It Back (USA))
3950[6] 8770a[6]

Improbable (USA) *Bob Baffert* a116
3 ch c City Zip(USA) Rare Event (USA) (A.P. Indy (USA))
2425a[4] 2856a[6] 7480a[4] 8771a[5]

Improvising (IRE) *P Monfort* a72 69
3 ch f Showcasing Magic Art (IRE) (Nayef (USA))
3526a[5]

Impulsif *A Fabre* a89 112
4 ch g New Approach(IRE) Violante (USA) (Kingmambo (USA))
(3879a) 7924a[4]

Impulsion (IRE) *Roger Varian* a91 94
3 b f Footstepsinthesand Danidh Dubai (IRE) (Noverre (USA))
2144[7] 2806[7] 3583[2] 4242[4] 4891[12] 5441[4]

Impulsive Force (IRE) *Ruth Carr* a25 27
4 gr g Lethal Force(IRE) A Mind Of Her Own (IRE) (Danehill Dancer (IRE))
6665[11]

Imrahor *Hugo Palmer* 82
2 b c Kingman She's Mine (IRE) (Sea The Stars (IRE))
7453[2]

I'm Watching You *Ronald Harris* a65 5
2 ch g Harbour Watch(IRE) Victrix Ludorum (IRE) (Invincible Spirit (IRE))
7113[10] 8297[3]◆ 8865[8]

Inaam (IRE) *John Butler* a79 77
6 b g Camacho Duckmore Bay (IRE) (Titus Livius (FR))
(31) 564[2] 1487[14] 1880[9] 2966[13] 5283[12] 6547[8] 7080[10] (9140)◆

In A Bubble (IRE) *A Oliver* 63
2 ch f Anjaal Dirtybirdie (Diktat)
7247a[24]

Inattendu (FR) *F Chappet* a82 84
3 b g Anodin(IRE) Suama (FR) (Monsun (GER))
868a[4]

Inaugural (GER) *P Schiergen* 70
2 b c Soldier Hollow Independant (Medicean)
8964a[5]

Inca Man (FR) *Paul Cole* a70 75
2 b c Rajsaman(FR) Aztec Queen (Holy Roman Emperor (IRE))
5572[3]◆ 6433a[5] 7555[2] 7983[3] 8481a[6]

Incampo (FR) *J-P Gauvin* a76 80
5 b h Campanologist(USA) Indian Cat (IRE) (One Cool Cat (USA))
5035a[3]

Incentive *Stuart Kittow* a54 68
5 b m Stimulation(IRE) Folly Drove (Bahri (USA))
(1820) 2339[11] 3470[3] 4281[7] (5498) 6567[11] 7758[5] 8247[6] 8711[9]

Inceyquincyspider (IRE)
Julia Feilden
3 b g Requinto(IRE) Grand Isla (Selkirk (USA))
8003[U]

Incinerator *Hugo Palmer* a85 81
2 b c Oasis Dream Bella Nostalgia (IRE) (Raven's Pass (USA))
3962[4] 4564[2] (5294) 5962[3] 6416[4] (6808) 7197[5] 7840[4] 8252[2]

Inclyne *Andrew Balding* a84 84
3 ch f Intello(GER) Lady Brora (Dashing Blade)
1828[5] 2612[2] 2935[3] 3699[5] 5421[2] (6345) 6967[2] 7682[4]

Incognito (IRE) *Mick Channon* a70 77
2 gr f Elusive City(USA) Gallice (IRE) (Fuisse (FR))
4223[6] 4918[4] 5189[2] 5588[5] 6118[4] 6629[2] 7117[10] 7547[4]

Incredible Dream (IRE)
Conrad Allen a52 57
6 b g Vale Of York(IRE) Finnmark (Halling (USA))
246[4] 4589[10] 2593[6] 3834[7] 4287[8] 5285[8] 5528[4] 5824[5] 7318[6] 8251[11]

Incredulous *William Haggas* a77 85
3 b f Intello(GER) Fantasize (Groom Dancer (USA))
3517[5] 3974[2] (4768) 5341[2] 5682[8]

Incus *Ed de Giles* a22 39
6 b g Bertolini(USA) Cloudchaser (IRE) (Red Ransom (USA))
1235[9] 1429[10] 8828[13]

Indeed *Dominic Ffrench Davis* a105 112
4 b g Showcasing Argumentative (Observatory (USA))
1753[2] (3992) (5192) 5610[19] 8116[2] 8764[3]

In Demand (IRE) *Roger Charlton* a67 70
4 b g Dalakhani(IRE) Fleur De Cactus (IRE) (Montjeu (IRE))
3686[4] 9405[3]

Independence Day (IRE)
Chelsea Banham a54 53
6 b h Dansili Damson (IRE) (Entrepreneur)
144[3] 468[7] 790[10] 982[9] 1177[7] 1364[10] 1883[12] 2527[11] 6126[3] 7282[5] 7824[4] 8457[2] 8821[6]

Independent Missy (IRE)
Tracey Collins 78
3 br f Dandy Man(IRE) Springfort (IRE) (Captain Rio)
8166a[6]

India *Michael Bell* a83 89
4 b m Poet's Voice Miss Brown To You (IRE) (Fasliyev (USA))
311[6]

Indian Affair *Milton Bradley* a61 49
9 br g Sleeping Indian Rare Fling (USA) (Kris S (USA))
28[6] 144[8] (483) 882[7] 1021[5] 1335[6] 1837[6] 2215[7] 3144[8] 4481[10] 4873[U] 5081[10] 6018[8] 6363[9] 7282[7]

Indianapolis (IRE) *James Given* a100 105
4 b h Galileo(IRE) Adoration (USA) (Honor Grades (USA))
1460[2]◆ 2742[6] 4102[8] 4646[4] (5929) 6420[8] (8005)

Indian Blessing *Ed Walker* a104 104
5 ch m Sepoy(AUS) Alpen Glen (Halling (USA))
2493a[8] (3359) 3986[10] 4954a[3] 5230a[2] 6491a[2] 7920a[11]

Indian Creak (IRE) *Mick Channon* a71 87
2 b c Camacho Ushindi (IRE) (Montjeu (IRE))
2792[8] 3419[2] 4030[3] (4544) 5587[5] 6020[4] (6403) 7119[15] 7409[2] 7896[4]

Indian Harbour *Sue Gardner*
6 b g Indian Haven Hawait Al Barr (Green Desert (USA))
2354[16]

Indian Pacific (FR) *Louis Baudron* a75 73
3 b g Exceed And Excel(AUS) Acatama (USA) (Efisio)
3675a[5] 6486a[3]

Indian Pursuit (IRE) *John Quinn* a78 59
6 b g Compton Place Church Melody (Oasis Dream)
187[8] 1895[11] 2379[9] (2632) 2876[11] 3928[4] 4519[2] 4586[3] 5042[5] 5892[4] 6591[8] 6826[4] 7051[6] 7286[15]

Indian Raj *Stuart Williams* a56 82
5 b g Iffraaj Princess Georgina (Royal Applause)
2272[4]◆ 3375[5] 4805[3] (5318) 6288[3] 6668[6] 7161[6] 9257[9]

Indian Road (IRE) *Mark Johnston* a61
2 b c Invincible Spirit(IRE) Anna Salai (USA) (Dubawi (IRE))
9107[9]◆ 9392[12]

Indian Sea *Dr Jon Scargill* a34
3 b f Born To Sea(IRE) Indian Dumaani (Indian Ridge (IRE))
7190[10] 8000[12] 8553[13]

Indian Sounds (IRE)
Mark Johnston a72 72
3 b g Exceed And Excel(AUS) Sarinda (Dubawi (IRE))
2364[9] 2997[8] 4001[6] 4723[8] 5270[5] 5651[7] 6111[2] 6840[12] 7310[4] 7811[4]

Indian Tinker *Robert Cowell* a66 58
10 b g Sleeping Indian Breakfast Creek (Hallgate)
1521[8]

Indian Tygress *James Fanshawe* a90 84
4 b m Sepoy(AUS) Persario (Bishop Of Cashel)
1382[3]◆ 1942[4] 2627[8]◆ 4023[8] 5143[10]

Indian Viceroy *Hughie Morrison* a84 70
3 b g Kodiac Broadlands (Kheleyf (USA))
3075[8] 3591[7] 4300[13] 5813[2] (6350) 7128[5] 8017[6]

Indian Vision (IRE)
Micky Hammond 68
5 ch g Iffraaj Sweet Fairnando (Hernando (FR))
3481[3]

Indiaro *Linda Perratt* 57
3 b g Sleeping Indian Cafe Express (IRE) (Bertolini (USA))
3499[9] 4055[9] 4489[4] 4979[8] 5235[7] 5486[12] 5935[8]

Indie Angel (IRE) *John Gosden* a74
2 gr f Dark Angel(IRE) Indigo Lady (Sir Percy)
8454[5] 9158[4] (9437)

Indie Groove (IRE) *Linda Perratt* 43
4 b g Intikhab(USA) Cristal Groove (IRE) (Marju (IRE))
3225[11] 4054[12] 5933[10]

Indignation (FR) *Sir Michael Stoute* a57 57
3 b g Frankel This Time (FR) (Zafeen (FR))
3263[11]

Indigo Lake *John Gosden* a68
2 b c Frankel Responsible (Oasis Dream)
9326[5] 9634[5]

Indigo Times (IRE) *David Simcock* a59
2 gr g Alhebayeb(IRE) Easy Times (Nayef (USA))
7555[6] 9408[7] 9668[8]

Indiscretion (IRE)
Jonathan Portman a75 78
4 b m Big Bad Bob(IRE) Fleeting Affair (USA) (Gone West (USA))
516[3] 1387[4] 2797[13]

Indisposed
Mrs Ilka Gansera-Leveque a36 8
3 b g Born To Sea(IRE) Disposition (Selkirk (USA))
6687[7] 8662[5]

Indomeneo *Richard Fahey* a79 74
4 b g Piccolo Cherrycombe-Row (Classic Cliche (IRE))
1461[6] 2095[13] 2577[5] 3072[8] 3568[5] 4627[4] 5130[4] (5178) 5725[6] 6165[3] 7185[9] 7489[5] 7903[2] 9138[3]◆ 9273[2]◆

Indomitable (IRE) *Andrew Balding* a71 73
3 b g Invincible Spirit(IRE) Mousse Au Chocolat (USA) (Hennessy (USA))
2570[6] 3591[6] 4669[9] 6801[5] 8017[7]

Indra Dawn (FR) *Archie Watson* a49 50
2 b g Panis(USA) Andolorise (IRE) (Footstepsinthesand)
3245[11] 3990[12] 6029[7] 6604[2] 7306[5]◆ 7626[6] 8526[6]

Inductive *Michael Dods* a55 53
2 b g Canford Cliffs(IRE) Princess Rose (Royal Applause)
3245[12] 4517[7] 5553[10] 7306[9] 7582[5] 8022[9] 8526[9]

Indy (IRE) *John Quinn*
8 b g Indian Haven Maddie's Pearl (IRE) (Clodovil (IRE))
3726[11]

Indy Champ (JPN)
Hidetaka Otonashi 121
4 b h Stay Gold(JPN) Will Power (JPN) (King Kamehameha (JPN))
9379a[7]

Indyco (FR) *H-A Pantall* a113 99
4 ch h Rio De La Plata(USA) Indyca (GER) (Panis (USA))
1922[2] 3030a[7] 3879a[9]

Indyzeb (IRE) *Seamus Mullins* a58 59
2 b f Zebedee Indy Gal (IRE) (Intikhab (USA))
6364[4] 6793[3] 7813[7]

Inevitable Outcome (IRE)
David Simcock a44 54
2 b f Ivawood(IRE) Foreplay (IRE) (Lujain (USA))
5988[5] 6846[6] 7569[7]

Inexes *Ivan Furtado* a70 80
7 gr g Exceed And Excel(AUS) Likeable (Dalakhani (IRE))
1969[2] 2348[7] 3207[7] 3722[2] 4149[2] 4912[5]◆ (5551) (6260) 7402[12] 8827[7]

Infanta Isabella *George Baker* 99
5 b m Lope De Vega(IRE) Shemissa (IRE) (Fairy King (USA))
1757[2] 2612[3] (3763) 4113[3] 5525[4] 6406[2] 9124a[9]

In Favour *A Fabre* 103
3 ch c Frankel Popular (Oasis Dream)
4963a[6] 5717a[3] 6773a[5]

Inference *John Gosden* a90 84
3 b f Intello(GER) Dublino (USA) (Lear Fan (USA))
2148[2]◆ 2770[4] 4022[2] 4641[5] (6438) 7347[11]

Infinite Grace *David O'Meara* 79
2 ch f Sepoy(AUS) Pepper Lane (Exceed And Excel (AUS))
1893[2] (2476) 2805[16] 3927[8] 4756[2] (4985) 5683[7] 6272[5] 6713[5]

Infiniti (IRE) *Barry Leavy* a3 2
6 b m Arcano(IRE) Seraphina (IRE) (Pips Pride)
2593[12]

Infirmier (USA) *Mlle A Wattel* a97 98
4 b h Distorted Humor(USA) Etincelle (USA) (Dynaformer (USA))
(3136a)

Inflamed *Ed Walker* a68 51
2 ch g New Approach(IRE) Indignant (Gold Away (IRE))
4925[9] 5493[6] 5980[7] 6435[2] 6884[5] (7277) (7910)◆

Inflexiball *John Mackie* a44 49
7 b m Refuse To Bend(IRE) Sphere (IRE) (Daylami (IRE))
2244[13] 3547[7] 3959[5] 4371[8] 5248[12] 6059[4] 8072[13] 8664[10]

Influencer *A Fabre* a66 98
3 ch c New Approach(IRE) Avongrove (Tiger Hill (IRE))
5480a[4]

Informed Front (USA) *John Gosden* a82 83
3 gr g War Front(USA) Informed Decision (USA) (Monarchos (USA))
3277[3]◆ 7572[2] 8294[3]

Infox (FR) *Guillaume Courbot* a67
3 b g Reliable Man Seltitude (IRE) (Fairy King (USA))
9280a[2]

Infrastructure *Martyn Meade* a100 99
4 ch g Raven's Pass(USA) Foundation Filly (Lando (GER))
3605[4]◆ (4877) 5443[3]◆ 6355[3] 9065[4] 9468[6]

Infuse (IRE) *Roger Charlton* a63 82
3 b f Lope De Vega(IRE) Fusion (IRE) (Cape Cross (IRE))
2103[3] 3050[2] 4304[4] 5529[2] 6438[4]

Ingelara (IRE)
Joseph Patrick O'Brien a54 52
4 ch m Zoffany(IRE) Playamongthestars (AUS) (Galileo (IRE))
419a[9]

Ingenium (IRE) *David O'Meara* a54 29
3 ch f Exceed And Excel(AUS) Lady Docker (IRE) (Docksider (USA))
2123[7] 3416[7]

Ingleby Angel (IRE) *Fred Watson* a31 37
10 br g Dark Angel(IRE) Mistress Twister (Pivotal)
2241[10]

Ingleby George *Jason Ward* 6
5 b g Rail Link Ingleby Princess (Bold Edge)
4636[8] 9011[12]

Ingleby Hollow *David O'Meara* a65 82
7 ch g Beat Hollow Mistress Twister (Pivotal)
2092[5] 2591[6] 3095[6] (3415) 3973[3] 4437[3]◆ 5743[3]◆ 7441[12]

Ingleby Mackenzie *Eoin Doyle* a56 58
5 b g Sixties Icon Natalie Jay (Ballacashtal (CAN))
9042[5]

Ingleby Molly (IRE) *Jason Ward* a55 48
4 ch m Choisir(AUS) Mistress Twister (Pivotal)
2013[8] 2633[8] 3476[14] 5299[4] 5629[7] (5857) 6276[7] 7420[11] 7591[2]

Inglorious *E Lyon* a73 73
5 gr g Kheleyf(USA) Impulsive Decision (IRE) (Nomination)
115a[5]

Inhalation *Ed Vaughan* a71
2 b g Bated Breath Al Joudha (FR) (Green Desert (USA))
8709[3]◆ 9085[4]◆ 9569[6]

Inhale *Amanda Perrett* a77 87
3 b f Bated Breath Innocent Air (Galileo (IRE))
4341[7]◆ (5333)

In Her Time (AUS) *Kris Lees* 119
6 bb m Time Thief(AUS) Hell It's Hot (AUS) (Zeditave (AUS))
8362a[9]

Initial Approach (IRE) *Alan Brown* a40
3 b f Dawn Approach(IRE) Coquette Noire (IRE) (Holy Roman Emperor (IRE))
128[7] 795[10] 1165[9] 4628[9] 9470[12]

Initiative (IRE) *Richard Price* 39
4 b g Excelebration(IRE) Viking Fair (Zamindar (USA))
6630[5] 7299[12]

In Memory (IRE) *S Richter* 95
3 ch f Reliable Man Iojo (USA) (Giant's Causeway (USA))
6747a[10] 8587a[13]

Innamorare (IRE) *Gavin Cromwell* a86 88
4 b m Intense Focus(USA) Duchess Dee (IRE) (Bachelor Duke (USA))
4353a[6] 5535a[2] 6693a[20] 7222a[16] 9278[4]◆

Innenminister (GER) *Dr A Bolte* a77 63
4 b h Masterstroke(USA) Intschu Tschuna (GER) (Lando (GER))
46a[6]

Inner Charm *Kevin Ryan* a47 67
3 b f Charm Spirit(IRE) Elusive Pearl (USA) (Medaglia d'Oro (USA))
1489a[6] 2091a[10] 6259[9] 7486[7] 7959[8] 8840[4]◆ 9185[P] (Dead)

Inner Circle (IRE) *Mark Loughnane* a64 79
5 b g Choisir(AUS) Eternity Ring (Alzao (USA))
3969[6] 4239[4] (4523) 4980[4] 5903[4]◆ (6066) 6734[8] 8030[6] 8702[8] 9331[6]

Innervisions (IRE) *W McCreery* 75
2 b f Dubawi(IRE) Fiesolana (IRE) (Aussie Rules (USA))
5362a[4]

Innings *Richard Fahey* a61
2 b c Intello(GER) Red Bloom (Selkirk (USA))
8084[10]

Innisfree (IRE) *A P O'Brien* a110 108
2 b c Galileo(IRE) Palace (IRE) (Fastnet Rock (AUS))
(7744a) 8716[2]

Innocent (IRE) *Ralph Beckett* a70 70
3 b f Cape Cross(IRE) Pirans Rock (IRE) (Rock Of Gibraltar (IRE))
1594[3] 4110[6] 5349[6]

Innovation *John Gosden* a61
2 b f Dubawi(IRE) Free Verse (Danehill Dancer (IRE))
9471[7]

Inns Of Court (IRE) *A Fabre* a77 121
5 b h Invincible Spirit(IRE) Learned Friend (GER) (Seeking The Gold (USA))
(3388a) 4948a[2]

Innstigator *Sue Gardner* a38 23
5 b g Delegator Page (Elmaamul (USA))
2998[12] 4498[8] 5081[11]

Inn The Bull (GER) *Alan King* a86 74
6 ch g Lope De Vega(IRE) Ile Rousse (Danehill (USA))
1559[7] 2126[3] 3467[11]

Inn With The Gin *Scott Dixon* a35
3 b f Coach House(IRE) Tipsy Girl (Haafhd)
8407[5] 9032[5] 9332[6]

Inosanto *Robyn Brisland*
3 b g Charm Spirit(IRE) Astromagick (Rainbow Quest (USA))
1332[13]

Insania *K R Burke* 84
2 gr f Gregorian(IRE) Mysterious Girl (IRE) (Teofilo (IRE))
2051[5] (2415)◆ 2906[2] 3196[2] 5171[4] 5587[11] (6369) 7117[8]

Inseo (FR) *M Boutin* a74 72
8 b g King's Best(USA) Insan Mala (IRE) (Bahhare (USA))
7136a[10] 7861a[5]

Insider (FR) *Alex Fracas* a79 53
7 ch g Saddex Integration (GER) (Lando (GER))
4748a[9]

Insignia Of Rank (IRE)
Joseph G Murphy a80 103
4 b g Epaulette(AUS) Let Me Shine (USA) (Dixie Union (USA))
1308a[15] 5535a[14] 5711a[13] 7038a[8]

Inspirational (IRE) *Ed Dunlop* 49
3 b f Slade Power(IRE) Refuse To Give Up (IRE) (Refuse To Bend (IRE))
1852[12] 2583[12] 3080[8] 4217[11] 5680[8]

Inspired Thought (IRE)
Archie Watson a83 94
3 br f Dandy Man(IRE) Alice Liddel (IRE) (Dark Angel (IRE))
(1523)◆ (1862) 2380[2] (3202) (3719) 4375[4] 5058[2] (5581) 6006a[4] 7401[15] 8141a[10]

Instantly *Robert Cowell* a61 69
2 b c Intrinsic One Moment (Notnowcato)
4993[7]◆ 5427[2] 5689[2] 6147[4]

Insurgence *James Fanshawe* a94 94
4 ch g Sepoy(AUS) Isis (USA) (Royal Academy (USA))
441[2] 988[3] 1294[6] (4598)

Insurplus (IRE) *Jim Goldie* a77 64
6 b g Bushranger(IRE) Emily Express (IRE) (High Estate)
609[5] 808[6] (1083) 1271[2] (1399) 1925[8] 2246[8] 3178[7] 3305[13] 4060[8] 4725[8] (5560) 6461[13] (6665) 7305[5] (7652) 8087[11] 9109[4] 9349[3] 9512[5]

Intaglio (POR) *Andre Vale* 50
6 ch h Bugatti(GER) Debony (POR) (Sorcerous)
4418a[13]

Inteldream *Marco Botti* a75 13
3 b g Intello(GER) Libys Dream (IRE) (Invincible Spirit (IRE))
5592[11] 6732[8] (7035) (9134)◆

Intellogent (IRE) *F Chappet* 113
4 ch h Intello(GER) Nuit Polaire (IRE) (Kheleyf (USA))
1628a[3] 2168a[5] 3122a[4] 6001a[6] 7293a[2] 8378a[7] 9125a[5]

Intense Battle (IRE)
Marco Gasparini 96
3 b f Intense Focus(USA) Tofa (IRE) (Alhaarth (IRE))
2161a[2] 7503a[9]

Intense Pleasure (IRE) *Ruth Carr* a48 46
4 b g Sepoy(AUS) Promesse De L'Aube (FR) (Galileo (IRE))
1644[8] 2246[10] 2842[9] 3177[13] 3704[8] 4148[11] 4785[10] 5213[6] 5556[14] 6499[10]

Intense Romance (IRE)
Michael Dods a81 107
5 b m Intense Focus(USA) Hedera (USA) (Woodman (USA))
2221a[6] 3587[6] 6698[10] 6960[6] 7889[11]

Intense Starlet (IRE) *Brian Ellison* a44 38
8 ch m Intense Focus(USA) Glady Starlet (GER) (Big Shuffle (USA))
834[3]◆ 973[11] 1553[5] 2324[13]

Intense Style (IRE) *Denis Quinn* a71 54
7 ch g Intense Focus(USA) Style Queen (IRE) (Galileo (IRE))
740[2] 922[12] 1213[9] 2246[9] 2710[6] 3880[4] 4207[13] 5274[10] 5816[8] 7145[12] 7587[2] 8070[9] 8861[3]

Intercessor *John Gallagher* 2
2 b g Due Diligence(USA) Miss Meticulous (Bahamian Bounty)
4254[6]

Interchoice Star *Ray Peacock* a37 27
14 b g Josr Algarhoud(IRE) Blakeshall Girl (Piccolo)
586[12]

Intermodal *Julia Brooke* a62 59
5 b g Rail Link Rule Of Nature (Oasis Dream)
1858[13]

Internationalangel (IRE)
Richard Fahey 63
2 gr f Dark Angel(IRE) Wrong Answer (Verglas (IRE))
2248[6] 3506[7]

International Guy (IRE)
Richard Fahey 72
3 b g Alhebayeb(IRE) America Alone (Dalakhani (IRE))
1649[7] 2058[2]◆ 4520[6] 6067[9]

International Law *Antony Brittain* a77 70
5 gr g Exceed And Excel(AUS) Cruel Sea (USA) (Mizzen Mast (USA))
(1025) 1271[10] (1511) 2596[5] 3053[6] 3567[11] 6026[6] 7378[4] 8507[3] (9285)

International Lion *Richard Fahey* 68
2 ch c Kyllachy Redskin Dancer (IRE) (Namid)
3098[5] 3866[8] 4401[5] 5101[5] 5781[3] (6969) 7429[5] 8124[3] 8859[4]

International Man *Richard Fahey* 84
4 b g Epaulette(AUS) Right Answer (Lujain (USA))
1644[3] 2057[7] 2710[13] 4403[5] 4982[4] 5398[7] (5770) (6626) 7142[9]

Internationaltiger *Richard Fahey* 65
2 b c Garswood Elusive Sue (USA) (Elusive Quality (USA))
5456[5] 6368[5] 6970[9]

Interrogation (FR) *Alan Bailey* a27 31
4 b g Redback Amalea (IRE) (Dylan Thomas (IRE))
239[8] 435[7] 3740[14] 4475[11] 4868[6] 5596[11] 6152[7]

Interrogator (IRE) *Alan Bailey* a37 42
3 b g Tamayuz Arbeel (Royal Applause)
2932[8] 4590[7] 5193[7] 6860[11] 7271[10] 7685[14]

Interrupted Dream *Gay Kelleway* a66 56
2 b g Oasis Dream Interception (IRE) (Raven's Pass (USA))
3739[5] 4290[5] 5197[6] 5562[7] 6313[6] 6571[7] 6884[4] 7111[5] (7275) 7626[2] 8259[10] 9568[8]

Interstellaire (FR) *Mme B Jacques* a40 44
4 ch m Tin Horse(IRE) Billette (FR) (Thunder Gulch (USA))
2170a[13]

In The Cove (IRE) *Richard Hannon* a78 66
3 b c Footstepsinthesand Vatrouchka (USA) (Kingmambo (USA))
2238[3] 2597[2] (3440) 4789[5] 5343[3] 5651[11] 6204[6] (6840) 7189[6] 8220[2] 8427[3] 9173[9]

In The Lope (IRE) *Mme Pia Brandt* a94 94
5 b g Lope De Vega(IRE) Biswa (USA) (Kafwain (USA))
565[6]

In The Night (IRE) *Charlie Appleby* a76
2 b g Shamardal(USA) Surprise Moment (IRE) (Authorized (IRE))
8319[4]◆ 9452[3]

In The Present (USA)
Mrs John Harrington a88 88
2 b f Karakontie(JPN) Dreams Of Fire (USA) (Dynaformer (USA))
2491a[3] 2881a[6]

In The Red (IRE) *Martin Smith* a84 83
6 b g Elusive Pimpernel(USA) Roses From Ridey (IRE) (Petorius (IRE))
(249) 962[2] 1036[3] (1392) 5667[17] 6347[11] 6916[16] 7268[7] 8289[12] 8755[11] 9422[10]

Intimate Moment *Philip McBride* 79
2 b f Mustajeeb Firebelly (Nicolotte)
4222[9] (4802) 7896[14]◆

Intisaab *David O'Meara* a101 104
8 b g Elnadim(USA) Katoom (IRE) (Soviet Star (USA))
170a[3] 397a[13] 639a[12] 843a[14] 2117[4] 2743[5] 4095[11] 4402[4]◆ 5205a[4] 5413[20] 6706[9] 7152[3] 7433[12]◆ 7913[3] 8127[9] 8425[6] 8851[9] 9308[2] 9472[4]◆ 9660[8]

Into Debt *Camilla Poulton* a54
3 b g Paco Boy(IRE) Katherine Parr (Haafhd)
9213[12] 9635[8]

Into Faith (FR) *David Menuisier* 81
2 b c Intello(GER) Have Faith (IRE) (Machiavellian (USA))
5331[6] 6669[4] (7925a)

Into The Sound (IRE) *G Botti* a72 70
3 gr g Mastercraftsman(IRE) Donoma (IRE) (Beat Hollow)
421a[8]

Into The Zone *Simon Crisford* a70 48
3 b g New Approach(IRE) Lady Zonda (Lion Cavern (USA))
5254[9] 7872[8]

Intransigent *Andrew Balding* a87 91
10 b g Trans Island Mara River (Efisio)
176[4]◆ 3009[7] 4320[11]

Intrepid Heart (USA) *Todd Pletcher* a109
3 rg c Tapit(USA) Flaming Heart (USA) (Touch Gold (USA))
3620a[8]

Intrepid Italian *Richard Hannon* 65
2 b c Havana Gold(IRE) Pizzarra (Shamardal (USA))
6528[5]

Intrepidly (USA) *Charlie Fellowes* a93 80
5 b g Medaglia d'Oro(USA) Trepidation (USA) (Seeking The Gold (USA))
557[2] 922[9] 1544[2] 2419[10]

Intricate *Clive Cox* a39 41
3 b f Showcasing Last Slipper (Tobougg (IRE))
4285[11] 6286[11] 7080[13]

Intrinsic Bond *Tracy Waggott* 75
2 b g Intrinsic Misu Billy (Misu Bond (IRE))
5968[12] 7698[2] 8631[3]

In Trutina *Archie Watson* a67 68
3 ch f Firebreak Yearbook (Byron)
2199[2]◆ 2590[6] (3157) 3801[6] 4454[2] 4767[12]

Intuitive (IRE) *James Tate* a106 80
3 b g Haatef(USA) Majraa (FR) (Invincible Spirit (IRE))
(1728) 2412[6] 3151[3] 4638[3] 5266[2] (7187) (8016)◆

Invasion Day (IRE) *David O'Meara* a91 82
3 b g Footstepsinthesand Van De Cappelle (IRE) (Pivotal)
6067[8] 6501[3] 6913[8] 7653[4]◆ (8017)

Inverarity *Frank Bishop* a51
3 b c Mazameer(IRE) Tripti (IRE) (Sesaro (USA))
186[7] 388[6] 1168[7]

Inverleigh (IRE) *G M Lyons* a42 87
3 br c Excelebration(IRE) Sommorell (IRE) (Fast Company (IRE))
(2156a) 2882a[8] 3786a[2]

Inver Silver *Ollie Pears* 13
2 ch f Fast Company(IRE) My Best Bet (Best Of The Bests (IRE))
5968[13] 6822[9]

Investor (FR) *Carmen Bocskai* 82
4 b g Champs Elysees I'm Right (USA) (Rahy (USA))
6521a[8]

Invictus Spirit *Sir Michael Stoute* a74 93
3 b c Frankel Daring Aim (Daylami (IRE))
5254[3]◆ 5634[4] (7143) (Dead)

Invincible Army (IRE) *James Tate* a118 118
4 b h Invincible Spirit(IRE) Rajeem (Diktat)
(1412) (2744) 4094[7] (4380) 5716a[13] 6959[5] 7243a[3] 7943a[4]

Invincible Bertie (IRE) *Nigel Tinkler* a52 53
2 gr g Zebedee Miss Moody (IRE) (Frozen Power (IRE))
3507[7] 3810[8] 4984[6] 5618[5] 6182[5] 7208[7]

Invincible Diva (IRE)
Mrs John Harrington 75
2 br f Invincible Spirit(IRE) Lulawin (Kyllachy)
4580a[6]

Invincible Larne (IRE) *Mick Quinn* a70 70
3 b g Invincible Spirit(IRE) Caphene (Sakhee (USA))
2060[5] 2489[6] 4343[4] 5064[3] (5826) 7105[2] 7320[3]

Invincible One (IRE) *Sylvester Kirk* a37 44
3 b g Invincible Spirit(IRE) Photophore (IRE) (Clodovil (IRE))
943[4] 1337[11] 3354[9] 4286[8] 4794[10] 5552[4] 5957[5] 6284[9] 9157[10] 9450[12]

Invincible Sea (IRE) *Linda Jewell* a57 8
3 b f Born To Sea(IRE) Melaaya (USA) (Aljabr (USA))
943[7] 1296[11] 1725[11] 3348[13]

Invincible Strike (IRE) *S Seemar* a83 89
8 gr g Invincible Spirit(IRE) Lazaretta (IRE) (Dalakhani (IRE))
197a[5] 1322a[8]

Invisible (IRE) *Keith Henry Clarke* a37 51
4 b g Zebedee Cafe Creme (IRE) (Catrail (USA))
600[7]

Inviolable Spirit (IRE)
Richard Fahey a79 82
4 b g Zebedee Mediska (Medicean)
1487[13] 2372[8]

Invisible Shadow *Alex Hales* a41
4 b g Oasis Dream Tavy (Pivotal)
155[11] 1145[9]

Invisible Storm *William Stone* a57 47
4 gr m Multiplex Dawn Lightning (Dark Angel (IRE))
383[3] 597[7] 4074[8] 9161[10] 9411[7] 9508[8]

Invitation (IRE) *A P O'Brien* a86 83
3 ch f Galileo(IRE) Night Lagoon (GER) (Lagunas)
6239a[6] 8368a[12] 8710[8] 8784a[7]

Invitational *Roger Varian* a102 98
3 ch f Poet's Voice Platinum Pearl (Shamardal (USA))
(78) (1838)◆ 4052[21] 5944[7] 6721[6] 8115[2] (8983a)

Involved *Daniel Kubler* a79 83
4 b g Havana Gold(IRE) Trick Or Treat (Lomitas)
434[3] 1096[8] (7185)◆ 7680[6]

Inyamazane (IRE) *Mick Channon* 75
2 b f Requinto(IRE) Yasmeena (USA) (Mr Greeley (USA))
2565[4] 3033[2] 3534[2] 4142[3] 4398[4] 5171[5]

Iolani (GER) *Dianne Sayer* 69
7 b g Sholokhov(IRE) Imogen (GER) (Tiger Hill (IRE))
2080[10] 3511[3] 4036[4] 5277[5] 5728[4] 6343[11] 6828[6]

Iona Island *Jean-Rene Auvray* a43 49
6 b m Dutch Art Still Small Voice (Polish Precedent (USA))
257[12] 482[10]

Ipcress File *Scott Dixon* a49 52
4 ch g Sixties Icon Solmorin (Fraam)
1070[2] 1163[6] 2196[14]

I Remember You (IRE) *A P O'Brien* 97
3 b f Australia Remember You (IRE) (Invincible Spirit (IRE))
1601a[13] 2493a[9] 3786a[6] 4353a[7] 4954a[4] 6137a[7] 6646a[4] 7635a[9]

Irene May (IRE) *Sylvester Kirk* a84 84
3 b f Moohaajim(IRE) Poker Hospital (Rock Of Gibraltar (IRE))
5736[7] 6668[5] (6851) 7613[6] 8349[4]◆ 8852[7]

Iridessa (IRE)
Joseph Patrick O'Brien 114
3 b f Ruler Of The World(IRE) Senta's Dream (Danehill (USA))
1601a[3] 2443[8] 3115[4] (4354a) 5208a[7] (7221a)◆ 7898[3] (8772a)

Irish Acclaim (IRE) *Clive Cox* a76 71
2 b c Acclamation Irish Cliff (IRE) (Marju (IRE))
4184[3]◆ 4734[4] 9043[2]

Irish Art (IRE) *David Lanigan* a65 63
3 b g Dutch Art Slieve Mish (IRE) (Cape Cross (IRE))
3034[4] 3594[9] 4215[9]

Irish Charm (FR) *Ivan Furtado* a51
5 b g Siyouni(FR) Danclare (USA) (Stravinsky (USA))
913[9] 4334[7]

Irish Diana *P Monfort* 47
2 ch f Coach House(IRE) Bossy Kitty (Avonbridge)
7641a[6]

Irish Eileen *Michael Easterby* 74
2 b f Coach House(IRE) El Molino Blanco (Royal Applause)
2093[6] 2747[10] 3506[3] 3881[4] 7620[6]

Irish Emperor (IRE)
Mme Pia Brandt a73 90
4 b g Holy Roman Emperor(IRE) Irish Queen (FR) (Speedmaster (GER))
1449a[6] 5643a[8]

Irish Freedom (USA) *S Seemar* a50
5 b h Pioneerof The Nile(USA) Island Striker (USA) (Smart Strike (CAN))
282a[9] 959a[7]

Irish Girl *Georgi Zhekov*
3 b f Burwaaz Vale Of Belvoir (IRE) (Mull Of Kintyre (USA))
2887a[12]

Irish Minister (USA)
David Thompson a56 62
4 b g Americain(USA) Spanked (USA) (Deputy Minister (CAN))
1273[12] 3922[6] 4239[9] 4634[6] 5560[9] 6663[8] 7903[5] 8301[10] 8639[3] 9560[2]

Irish Times *Henry Spiller* a58 43
4 b g Swiss Spirit Amouage Royale (IRE) (Mr Greeley (USA))
273[2] (717) (1060) 1214[4] 2740[9] 3774[11] 4460[8] 5652[9] 7374[14]

Irish Trilogy (IRE) *Nina Lensvik* 91
3 gr g Gregorian(IRE) Maya De La Luz (Selkirk (USA))
168a[4] 511a[2] 956a[3] 5609[9]

Irish Tweed *Andrew Balding* 20
2 b f Roderic O'Connor(IRE) Lady Brora (Dashing Blade)
6603[6]

Iris's Spirit *Tony Carroll* a42 38
3 b f Sayif(IRE) Dubawi's Spirit (IRE) (Dubawi (IRE))
79[7] 614[6] 1358[8] 4476[6] 5287[6] 5842[9] 8256[12] 8915[12]

Ironclad *Hugo Palmer* a91 92
3 br g Dubawi(IRE) Heat Haze (Green Desert (USA))
1033[3]◆ 1417[5] 3584[2]◆ (3958) (5194) 5734[4]

Iron Duke (GER) *P Schiergen* 96
3 rg c Dark Angel(IRE) Invisible Flash (Invincible Spirit (IRE))
3369a[4] 4534a[4] 6006a[5] 6519a[6]

Iron Heart *Andrew Balding* a70 50
2 b c Muhaarar Kiyoshi (Dubawi (IRE))
8516[10] 9323[3]◆

Iron Mike *Keith Dalgleish* a76 75
3 gr g Gregorian(IRE) Regal Velvet (Halling (USA))
1504[9] 2336[6] 4820[9] 6342[4] (6938)◆ 7368[2] 7782[6] 8298[3] 8705[3] 9012[8]

Iron Ryan (FR) *Lee Smyth* a55 67
7 ch g Namid Forces Sweetheart (Allied Forces (USA))
7823[4] 9277[7]

Iron Spirit (FR) *J Phelippon* a60 70
9 b g Turtle Bowl(IRE) Irish Vintage (FR) (Loup Solitaire (USA))
2391a[10]

Irregardless (IRE) *Donal Kinsella* a53 43
3 b g Requinto(IRE) Bonkers (Efisio)
7544[11]

Irreverent *Richard Fahey* 94
3 b g Iffraaj Royal Rascal (Lucky Story (USA))
(2146) 3340[5] (4099) 4895[3] 5693[8] 6543[6] (6973) 7430[4]

Irv (IRE) *Micky Hammond* 87
3 ch g Zoffany(IRE) Marion Antoinette (IRE) (Antonius Pius (USA))
1897[5] 2746[9] 3412[2] (4403)◆ (5398)◆ 6425[16] 7312[9] 8101[14]

Irving's Girl *Brett Johnson* a51
4 b m Rip Van Winkle(IRE) High Cross (IRE) (Cape Cross (IRE))
242[U] (Dead)

Isaac Murphy (USA)
Mark H Tompkins
3 b g Medaglia d'Oro(USA) Marietta (USA) (Machiavellian (USA))
3584[13] 4121[12]

Isaan Queen (IRE) *Archie Watson* a100 99
3 b f War Command(USA) Dundel's Spirit (IRE) (Invincible Spirit (IRE))
261[3] (2319) 2874[2] 4023[3]◆ 4891[16] 5846[4]

Isabeau (IRE) *M D O'Callaghan* 98
2 b f Cable Bay(IRE) Semblance (Pivotal)
3983[18] 4580a[3] 5361a[7] 6190a[2] 7400[5]

Isabella Brant (FR) *Ralph Beckett* a81 78
3 rg f Mastercraftsman(IRE) Walk In Beauty (IRE) (Shamardal (USA))
2771[10] 3699[2] 4913[13] 5735[2] 6597[3] (7704)

Isabella Red (IRE) *Lisa Williamson* a48 25
3 b f Dark Angel(IRE) Littlepromisedland (IRE) (Titus Livius (FR))
341[8] 400[9] 887[9] 1353[9] 2238[11] 2871[10] 3067[10]

Isabella Ruby *Lisa Williamson* a54 50
4 b m Power Scarlet Rocks (IRE) (Chineur (FR))
293[7] 483[10] 809[9] 4358[2] 5130[6] 5918[9] 6013[2] 6590[4] 7444[10] 7681[6] 8119[3] 8637[8] 9276[4] (9445)

Isalys (FR) *D Guillemin* a89 84
3 b f Panis(USA) Ipshanda (FR) (Siyouni (FR))
683a[5] 3029a[7]

Isango *Charlie Fellowes* a76 74
3 b f Dansili Incheni (IRE) (Nashwan (USA))
(1567) 2251[8] 3193[6]

Isayalittleprayer *Gary Moore* 60
2 b f Nathaniel(IRE) I Say (IRE) (Oratorio (IRE))
5588[10] 7972[7] 8458[9]

Iseebreeze (IRE)
Anthony Mulholland a56 30
4 b m Frozen Power(IRE) Brizana (USA) (Diesis)
419a[7]

Ise Lodge Babe *Ronald Thompson* a37 33
4 b m Librano Scented Garden (Zamindar (USA))
1085[5] 2295[10]

Iserman (FR) *Vaclav Luka Jr* a61 73
4 b h Scalo Indian Cat (IRE) (One Cool Cat (USA))
3136a[13]

Ishallak *Mark Usher* 31
4 b g Cityscape Shallika (IRE) (Alhaarth (IRE))
2617[13] 2901[7] 3774[7] 4336[6]

Isharah (USA) *Noel C Kelly* a75 60
6 b g Kitten's Joy(USA) Menekineko (USA) (Kingmambo (USA))
99[7] 589[5]

Ishebayorgrey (IRE) *Iain Jardine* a62 71
7 gr g Clodovil(IRE) Superjet (IRE) (Soviet Star (USA))
2241[6] 3181[2]◆ 3448[3] 3922[3] 4916[3]◆ 6663[7] 7443[12] 7823[8] 8306[4] (8864) 9253[4] 9518[4]

Ishvara *Robert Cowell* 80
2 b f Dutch Art Cloud's End (Dubawi (IRE))
(5590) 6157[10] 6997[9]

Isidor Bonheur Yes (FR)
David O'Meara 68
5 b g Sageburg(IRE) Isarnixe (GER) (Banyumanik (IRE))
3655[8]

Isidro (FR) *H-F Devin* a82 92
3 b g Lope De Vega(IRE) Ondoyante (IRE) (Slickly (FR))
2953a[4]

Is It Off (IRE) *Sean Curran* a56 61
4 b g Clodovil(IRE) French Doll (IRE) (Titus Livius (FR))
3429[7] 5284[4] 7084[10] 8068[8] 8863[5] 9403[7]

Iskandarani (USA) *R Bouresly* a48 70
3 ch c Eskendereya(USA) Pick And Choose (USA) (Street Cry (IRE))
168a[10] 394a[14]

Iskanderhon (USA) *I Endaltsev* a74 105
3 b g Exchange Rate(USA) Beiramar (IRE) (Monsun (GER))
421a[4] 7927a[3] 8589a[6]

Island Brave (IRE) *Heather Main* a104 104
5 b h Zebedee Tip the Scale (USA) (Valiant Nature (USA))
1422[4] 1927[9] (4102) 4646[6] 4933[6] 5662[11] 6452[5] 8853[3] 9055[9] 9366[5]

Island Flame (IRE) *Jennie Candlish* a51 47
6 b m Kodiac Noble Flame (IRE) (Doyoun)
120[12] 2244[6] 3006[10] 5285[10]

Island Glen (USA) *Heather Main* a52 64
3 ch g More Than Ready(USA) Miss Lavinia (USA) (Speightstown (USA))
2794[5] 3663[9] 8025[11] 8652[13]

Island Hideaway *David Lanigan* a77 54
2 b f Mukhadram Interstella (Sea The Stars (IRE))
7695[9] 8454[4] 9046[2] (9383) 9665[2]

Island Jungle (IRE) *Mark Usher* a70 43
3 b g Teofilo(IRE) Loreto (IRE) (Holy Roman Emperor (IRE))
1419[5] 2035[11] 5311[4] 6030[4] 6320[5] 7192[5]

Island Nation (IRE) *Heather Main* a64 63
2 ch g Ruler Of The World(IRE) Rethink (Raven's Pass (USA))
7453[8] 8058[5] 8464[8]

Island Of Life (USA)
William Haggas a105 93
5 b m Dubawi(IRE) Pimpernel (IRE) (Invincible Spirit (IRE))
(30) 1103[2] 1918[2]◆ 3085[6] 3994[5] 4380[3]◆ 4891[10] 5608[14] 5944[6]

Island Reel (IRE) *Heather Main* a46 43
3 b f Ruler Of The World(IRE) Bridge Note (USA) (Stravinsky (USA))
1739[9] 2719[8] 8348[10]

Island Song (IRE) *Mrs A Malzard* a71 64
5 b m Equiano(FR) Fortuna Limit (Linamix (FR))
2026a[3] (2672a) 3640a[2] 6008a[3] 6554a[2]

Island Sound *H Al Alawi* a67 74
4 gr g Havana Gold(IRE) Cloud Illusions (USA) (Smarty Jones (USA))
1322a[4]

Island Storm (IRE) *Heather Main* a78 52
2 b c Anjaal She's Neat (IRE) (Frozen Power (IRE))
5992[7] 6314[3] (7416) 8029[8] (9110)◆ 9546[6]

Island Warrior (IRE) *Heather Main* 54
2 ch g Power Light Sea (IRE) (King's Best (USA))
5339[5] 6287[11]

Isla Skye (IRE) *Barry Brennan* 3
3 b f Zebedee Sky Ranger (IRE) (Bushranger (IRE))
3598[6] 4496[5] 9423[9]

Islay Mist *Lee Carter* a51 49
3 ch f Coach House(IRE) Amary (IRE) (Acclamation)
458[5] 1167[7] 1340a[8] 1557[7] 3442[7] 4029[4] 4244[11] 6052[2] 6605[3] 7371[8] 7604[2] 8547[10] 9423[8]

Isle Of Avalon (IRE)
Sir Mark Prescott Bt a74 66
4 b m Camelot Adeste (Dansili)
101[7] 469[2] 566[5]

Isle Of Innisfree (USA) *Paul D'Arcy* a72 87
3 b c Scat Daddy(USA) Dream The Blues (IRE) (Oasis Dream)
5649[6] 6225[6] 9030[11] 9455[13] 9632[11]

Isle Of Wolves *Jim Boyle* a59 75
3 b g Nathaniel(IRE) L'Ile Aux Loups (IRE) (Rock Of Gibraltar (IRE))
1264[9] 1696[7] 2035[7] 2406[3] 3947[6] 4836[2] 6022[2] (6568) 7126[4]

Ismene (GER) *Jean-Pierre Carvalho* 98
3 b f Tertullian(USA) Imagery (GER) (Monsun (GER))
5720a[U] 6487a[8] 7862a[4] 8587a[5]

Isobar Wind (IRE) *David Evans* a65 69
2 b g Baltic King Zeeoneandonly (IRE) (Zebedee)
1733[5] 1953[3] 2205[6] 3634[6] (5196) 5789[6] 6041[3] 6637[4] 7056[5] (7768) 8856[8] 9127[7] (9501)

Isocrates (USA) *Simon Crisford* 39
3 b c Dansili I Am Beautiful (IRE) (Rip Van Winkle (IRE))
7382[5]

Isola Bella May (IRE) *Jedd O'Keeffe* 66
2 b f Free Eagle(IRE) Heart Of Hearts (Oasis Dream)
8258[3]◆

Isolate (FR) *Martyn Meade* a67 80
3 b g Maxios Unaided (Dansili)
1509[3] 2142[3] 3699[6] 4296[3] 5779[11]

Isolde (IRE) *Amy Murphy* a5 53
2 b f Camelot Zanzibar Girl (USA) (Johannesburg (USA))
5956[5] 7473[8]

Isole Canarie (IRE) *Gavin Hernon* 101
4 b m Rip Van Winkle(IRE) Hairicin (IRE) (Hurricane Run (IRE))
1708a[8] 2670a[9] 4397[7]

Isomer (USA) *Andrew Balding* a93 85
5 ch g Cape Blanco(IRE) Nimue (USA) (Speightstown (USA))
2054[4] 441[7] 521[2] 764[6] 1413[7]◆ 2273[5] 4997[7] 5858[3] 6925[5] 7618[4]
I Spied *Mark Johnston* a65
2 ch c Australia Super Sleuth (IRE) (Selkirk (USA))
9154[5]
Ispolini *Charlie Appleby* a79 117
4 b g Dubawi(IRE) Giants Play (USA) (Giant's Causeway (USA))
47a[2] (281a) (958a) 1441a[2] 2807[4] (7249a)
Is She The One *Denis Quinn* a16 12
2 b f Equiano(FR) Lady Vermeer (Dutch Art)
1493[7] 1879[5] 2331[4] 7469[11] 8527[14]
Istanbul (IRE) *Richard Fahey* 100
2 gr c Gutaifan(IRE) Anadolu (IRE) (Statue Of Liberty (USA))
3512[3] (4624) 5228a[5]
Is That Love (IRE) *Kevin Ryan* a64
2 b c Es Que Love(IRE) Winnifred (Green Desert (USA))
7769[3]◆
Istoria (IRE) *Joseph G Murphy* 71
3 b f Camelot Brooklyn's Storm (USA) (Storm Cat (USA))
8784a[9]
Istorius (FR) *H-A Pantall* 49
3 b c Pastorius(GER) Indianapolis (GER) (Tiger Hill (IRE))
2519a[8]
Itchingham Lofte (IRE)
David Barron a44 75
3 gr g Worthadd(IRE) Lady Georgina (Linamix (FR))
1643[4] 2301[5] 2875[3] 3513[4] 4077[5] (4779)
It Had To Be You *William Haggas* a72
3 b c Frankel Fallen For You (Dansili)
7373[3] 8693[2]
I Think So (IRE) *David Loughnane* a58 42
4 b m So You Think(NZ) Nawaashi (Green Desert (USA))
4600[8] 5148[7] 5549[6] 6059[10] 6731[2] 6977[5] 7859[6] 8466[5] 8863[2] 9450[7]
Itizzit *Hughie Morrison* a81 83
3 ch f Mukhadram Whatizzit (Galileo (IRE))
2715[3] 3266[2] (4424) 4838[9] 5545[10] 7128[7] 8456[4] 9126[6]
Itkaann (IRE) *Owen Burrows* a81 69
3 b c Gutaifan(IRE) Mimisel (Selkirk (USA))
4282[4] 5493[2] (9325)◆
Itlaaq *Michael Easterby* a66 75
13 b g Alhaarth(IRE) Hathrah (IRE) (Linamix (FR))
3816[14] 5728[15]
Itmakesyouthink *Mark Loughnane* a60 59
5 b g So You Think(NZ) Anbella (FR) (Common Grounds)
5057[7] 6177[3] 6594[5] 7299[11] 8123[9] 8417[2] 8666[4] 9305[11]
It Must Be Faith *Michael Appleby* a64 61
9 b g Mount Nelson Purple Rain (IRE) (Celtic Swing)
381[9] 548[2] 849[4] 1100[2] 1329[4] 1426[8] 1686[4] 1880[12] (2503a) 6857[3] 7178[6] 7855[7] 8296[2] 9106[5] 9219[6]◆ 9335[10] 9406[8] (9477)
Itmusthavebeenlove (IRE)
Michael Bell a58 63
2 b f Galileo(IRE) Nijoom Dubai (Noverre (USA))
5139[4] 6322[5] 6906[11] 8699[5]
Itobo (GER) *H-J Groschel* 114
7 ch g Areion(GER) Iowa (GER) (Lomitas)
(3386a) 4622a[4] 6487a[4] (7862a) 8372a[4]
Itojeh *Michael Easterby* 39
2 ch g Cityscape Croeso Cariad (Most Welcome)
7902[14] 8657[10]
Itoldyoutobackit (IRE) *Jonjo O'Neill* 40
2 ch c Ivawood(IRE) Jawlaat (IRE) (Shamardal (USA))
4373[8] 6078[11] 7055[9]
Its A Given *Roger Charlton* a71
2 ch f Bated Breath Emergency (Dr Fong (USA))
(9195)◆
It's A Heartache (IRE) *H-F Devin* 77
2 b f Holy Roman Emperor(IRE) Fate (FR) (Teofilo (IRE))
2757a[P]
Itsakindamagic *Geoffrey Deacon* a58 63
5 b g Mount Nelson Carsulae (IRE) (Marju (IRE))
(2064) 2739[7] 8412[13]
Itsallaboutluck (IRE)
Richard Hughes a66
2 b g Kodiac Lucky (IRE) (Sadler's Wells (USA))
8605[8] 9181[2] 9634[7]
It's All A Dream (FR)
Matthieu Palussiere 86
3 b c Elusive City(USA) Kataragama (Hawk Wing (USA))
1243a[6]
It's All A Joke (IRE)
Adrian McGuinness a56 71
4 ch g Dandy Man(IRE) Jesting (Muhtarram (USA))
36[8] 317[3] 433[4] (763) 907[6] 1394[9] 2053[6] 7085a[6]
Its All Class (FR) *J Reynier* a66 77
9 b g Hurricane Cat(USA) She's All Class (USA) (Rahy (USA))
6434a[5]
Itsalonglongroad *John C McConnell* a76 71
5 b g Lawman(FR) Alabelle (Galileo (IRE))
5712a[8]
It's Been Noted *Tom Dascombe* 72
2 b c Heeraat(IRE) Trixie Malone (Ishiguru (USA))
2115[4] 2561[2] 3071[5]
It's Good To Laugh (IRE) *Clive Cox* 85
2 b g Tamayuz London Plane (IRE) (Danehill Dancer (IRE))
5345[2] (6640) 7410[8] 8760[2]
It's How We Roll (IRE)
John Spearing a59 58
5 b g Fastnet Rock(AUS) Clodora (FR) (Linamix (FR))
3298[3] 4991[2] (5499) 6042[5] 6599[2] 6843[2] 7271[2]
It'Smabirthday (IRE) *Archie Watson* a80
2 ch g Society Rock(IRE) Birthday (IRE) (Singspiel (IRE))
(9607)
It's Never Enough *James Ewart* a45 74
5 b g Equiano(FR) Swynford Pleasure (Reprimand)
5486[11] 8269[6] 8922[12]
Its Nice Tobe Nice *William Muir* a61 57
3 b f Dalakhani(IRE) Bright Halo (IRE) (Bigstone (IRE))
1359[4] 7159[4] 7867[5]
It's Not My Fault (IRE) *Paul Midgley* 55
2 b f Lawman(FR) Paddy Again (IRE) (Moss Vale (IRE))
3725[3] 4366[6] 4876[5] 5295[2] 6097[5] 7283[5] 7584[11]
Its Toytown *R Mike Smith* a28
3 ch g Orientor Sleeper Class (Sleeping Indian)
5669[6] 6941[6] 7303[9]
Itsupforgrabsnow (IRE)
Susan Corbett a43 37
4 b m Footstepsinthesand Rye Rhythm (IRE) (Fasliyev (USA))
2376[12] 3158[8] 4078[10] 5041[6] 5300[11]
Itwouldberudenotto *Richard Fahey* a64 47
2 b g Fountain Of Youth(IRE) Jive (Major Cadeaux)
2415[8] 7958[4] 8302[6] 9307[8] 9513[3]
Ivadream *Roger Charlton* a61 60
2 b g Ivawood(IRE) Midnight Fling (Groom Dancer (USA))
6078[8] 6807[9] 7406[9] 9061[3] 9196[4]
Iva Go (IRE) *Tim Easterby* 76
2 b f Ivawood(IRE) Enliven (Dansili)
1642[2]◆ (2051) 2805[7] 3156[4] 3927[3] 4893[4]
Ivamonet (IRE) *Michael Wigham*
2 b f Ivawood(IRE) Picture Of Lily (Medicean)
4448[10]
Ivanka (GER) *A Wohler* 96
3 bb f Dabirsim(FR) Irresistable (GER) (Monsun (GER))
2137a[7] 3119a[11]
Iva Reflection (IRE) *Tom Dascombe* a72 81
2 b g Ivawood(IRE) Mirror Image (Acclamation)
(2093) 2520[2] 3988[17] 4647[8] 4938[5] 7140[9] 7871[4]
Ivatheengine (IRE) *Paul Cole* a85 79
2 br g Ivawood(IRE) Sharp Applause (IRE) (Royal Applause)
2716[2]◆ (3165) (9413)
I'vegotthepower (IRE)
Brian Meehan 88
5 b g Power Waterways (IRE) (Alhaarth (IRE))
2487[7] 3027[4] 3423[6]
Ivictory (AUS) *J Size* 115
5 b g Mossman(AUS) Inca Lagoon (AUS) (Hussonet (USA))
9377a[11]
Ivor *Richard Hannon* a59 77
2 b g Iffraaj Ligeia (Rail Link)
1931[6] 3190[3] 3534[3] 8605[6]
Ivory Charm *Richard Fahey* a64 69
3 b f Charm Spirit(IRE) Ivory Gala (FR) (Galileo (IRE))
229[4]◆ 798[6] 1166[6] 2337[2] (3223) 4000[2] 4321[4] 4628[4]
Izvestia (IRE) *Archie Watson* a51 56
3 b f Battle Of Marengo(IRE) Westcote (USA) (Gone West (USA))
2029a[11] (2587) (3150) 4522[5] 4735[2] 5304[5] 5548[4]
Izzer (IRE) *Osama Omer E Al-Dafea* a65 71
3 gr g Clodovil(IRE) Broadway Musical (IRE) (Exceed And Excel (AUS))
893a[13]
Izzthatright (IRE)
Jassim Mohammed Ghazali 111
7 b g Moss Vale(IRE) Miss Adelaide (IRE) (Alzao (USA))
892a[3]
Jaaneh *William Haggas* 60
2 b f Dubawi(IRE) Ethaara (Green Desert (USA))
6514[6] 6919[9]
Jaaref (IRE) *A R Al Rayhi* a45 103
6 ch g Sea The Stars(IRE) Tabassum (IRE) (Nayef (USA))
47a[9] 284a[4] 515a[15] 847a[8]
Jaarim (USA) *Fawzi Abdulla Nass* a59 67
3 b c Distorted Humor(USA) Cherokee Jewel (USA) (Cherokee Run (USA))
(1742a)
Jaariyah (USA) *Roger Varian* a75
2 bb f Shamardal(USA) Jiwen (CAN) (Singspiel (IRE))
(8602)
Jaayiz (IRE) *P Monfort* a67 71
3 b g Zoffany(IRE) So Devoted (IRE) (Holy Roman Emperor (IRE))
7561a[3]
Jabalaly (IRE) *Ed Dunlop* a89 79
3 b g Moohaajim(IRE) Bahati (IRE) (Intikhab (USA))
2094[4] 2713[2] 3307[7] 5267[9] 6840[3] (7519) 8101[5] (8498)
Jabbaar *Iain Jardine* a91 93
6 ch g Medicean Echelon (Danehill (USA))
558[5] 2435[3] 3070[5] 3655[2] 5097[2]◆ 5199[6] 5902[2] 6255[7] 6657[3] 7181[6] 8633[2] 9222[2]
Jabbarockie *Eric Alston* a85 101
6 b g Showcasing Canina (Foxhound (USA))
1860[2] 2421[3] 2841[3] (3509) 4100[2] 4894[2] (5617) 6351[12]
Jacbequick *David Pipe* a78 83
8 b g Calcutta Toking N' Joken (IRE) (Mukaddamah (USA))
1914[5]
Jackamundo (FR) *Declan Carroll* 86
3 b g Fast Company(IRE) Luxie (IRE) (Acclamation)
1504[6]◆ 1846[7] (2582) (3548) 5489[5] 6955[8] 8098[5]
Jackate *Ollie Pears* a59 59
2 b g Sleeping Indian Anushka Noo Noo (Makfi)
5815[4] 8714[8] 9136[10]
Jack Bear *Roger Teal* a78 56
8 b g Joe Bear(IRE) Colins Lady (FR) (Colonel Collins (USA))
119[6]
Jack Berry House *George Boughey* a69 63
3 b g Harbour Watch(IRE) Dularame (IRE) (Pivotal)
1212[4] 1677[4] 2630[10] 4288[6] 5847[4] 7080[4] 7609[10] 9244[4]
Jackblack *Nikki Evans* a25 30
7 b g Crosspeace(IRE) Saharan Royal (Val Royal (FR))
2003a[6] 2502a[3] 7474[12]
Jack D'Or *Ed Walker* a79 77
3 b g Raven's Pass(USA) Inchberry (Barathea (IRE))
3353[3]◆ 4189[2] 4789[3]◆ 5779[5] 6469[3] (7278) 8122[5]
Jackfinbar (FR) *Harry Dunlop* a78 110
4 b h Whipper(USA) Anna Simona (GER) (Slip Anchor)
4670[5]
Jackhammer (IRE) *Dianne Sayer* a49 74
5 b g Thewayyouare(USA) Ask Annie (IRE) (Danehill (USA))
2330[3] (2963) 3177[3] (3297) (3682)◆ 4054[2] (4239)◆
Jack Is Back *Lawrence Mullaney*
2 b g Due Diligence(USA) Rosa Luxemburg (Needwood Blade)
8395[10]
Jack Louie *Dean Ivory* a42 35
3 ch g Mazameer(IRE) Fleetwood Nix (Acclamation)
594[7] 941[7] 1354[7] 1732[4]
Jackman *Lee James* a22 45
5 gr g Aussie Rules(USA) Fit To Burst (Pastoral Pursuits)
2335[7] 5043[8] 8637[9] 8901[10]
Jacko (IRE)
Jassim Mohammed Ghazali a74 74
3 gr c Dark Angel(IRE) Tartessian (IRE) (Lawman (FR))
893a[7]
Jack Of Diamonds (IRE)
Roger Teal a49 40
10 b g Red Clubs(IRE) Sakkara Star (IRE) (Mozart (IRE))
886[11] 1343[10] 1958[10] 2698[8]
Jackpot Royale *Michael Appleby* a57 88
4 b g Sixties Icon Sofia Royale (Royal Applause)
2821[10] 3763[9] 4061[3] 4867[10] 5150[3] 6155[9] 6217[7] 7350[6] 8342[7] 8521[7]
Jack Randall *Tim Easterby* a59 60
3 gr g Cityscape Skiing (Sakhee's Secret)
1649[9] 2152[4] 3246[10] 4286[7] (5847) 6575[2] 8306[3]
Jack Ruby (IRE) *Richard Hannon* a56 58
2 b g Havana Gold(IRE) Make Me Blush (IRE) (Makfi)
5345[6] 6040[4] 6926[10] 8061[6]
Jack Ryan (IRE) *John Ryan* 62
2 b g Harbour Watch(IRE) Anything (IRE) (Rock Of Gibraltar (IRE))
5273[6] 6161[6] 8459[9]
Jacksonfire *Michael Mullineaux* a36 50
7 ch g Firebreak Fitolini (Bertolini (USA))
60[10] 180[12] 2717[14] 3475[4] 4481[7] 5486[7] 5551[3] 6107[4] 7065[11] 7590[10]
Jackson Hole (FR) *M Rulec* 75
3 b f Elusive City(USA) Snake River (IRE) (Bachelor Duke (USA))
8584a[5]
Jacksonian *Ralph Beckett* 82
2 ch c Frankel Kalima (Kahyasi (IRE))
5439[2]
Jack's Point *William Muir* a96 98
3 b g Slade Power(IRE) Electra Star (Shamardal (USA))
1851[10] 3075[2] 3599[6] 4360[7] 4847[13] 5666[2] 5932[5] 6847[5] 7448[3] 8016[13] 9198[8]
Jackstar (IRE) *Tom Dascombe* a89 83
3 gr g Dark Angel(IRE) Starbright (IRE) (Duke Of Marmalade (IRE))
(1346) 1854[8] 2412[12] 6922[9] 7362[6] 8522[8] 8852[5] (9476) 9669[4]
Jacksun (FR) *M Figge* a74 95
5 b g Zambezi Sun Jackanory (FR) (Marchand De Sable (USA))
780a[4] 8980a[4]
Jack Taylor (IRE) *Richard Hughes* a74 76
4 b g Invincible Spirit(IRE) Glory Power (IRE) (Medicean)
2227[4]◆ 3021[4] 3536[5] 4495[9]
Jack The Truth (IRE) *George Scott* a80 85
5 ch g Dandy Man(IRE) Friendly Heart (CAN) (Lion Heart (USA))
2[3] 165[6] 610[3] 741[5] 849[3] 1061[5] 1551[4] (4301) (4556)◆ 4821[4]◆ 5444[3] 6455[7] 7387[4]
Jack Yeats (IRE) *A P O'Brien* 85
3 b c Galileo(IRE) Fire Lily (IRE) (Dansili)
4049[8]
Jacob Black *Keith Dalgleish* a41 77
8 b g Amadeus Wolf First Eclipse (IRE) (Fayruz)
1948[3]◆ 2372[6] (2679) 2898[3] 4001[4] 4058[6] 4239[3] 4511[7] 4982[10] 5616[11] 6573[7]
Jacob Cats *William Knight* a82 84
10 b g Dutch Art Ballet (Sharrood (USA))
1330[3] 2400[8] 3044[RR] 3467[8] 4483[2] (6105)
Jacob's Pillow *Rebecca Bastiman* a57 60
8 b g Oasis Dream Enticing (IRE) (Pivotal)
163[7] 498[6] 707[4] 1023[11] 1368[7] 2053[10] 2632[7] 3221[13] 3413[3] 3656[3] 3921[13] 5094[4] 5235[2] 5491[3] 5935[5] 6174[15]
Jadeer (IRE) *Mick Channon* 39
2 b c Roderic O'Connor(IRE) Gush (USA) (Empire Maker (USA))
7458[9] 7899[8] 8460[11]
Jadeerah *John Gosden* a93 95
3 b f Frankel Maqaasid (Green Desert (USA))
4124[4] (4592)◆ 5369[6] 5944[4] 7893[12]
Jadella Willfin (FR) *Richard Hannon* a64
3 gr f Tin Horse(IRE) Sienna May (USA) (Dixie Union (USA))
1677[3]
Jaega (IRE) *D K Weld* 97
4 b m Fastnet Rock(AUS) Farranjordan (Galileo (IRE))
1620a[5] 3820a[7]
Jafetica *Mark Johnston* a73 61
5 ch m New Approach(IRE) Fann (USA) (Diesis)
(145)
Jaganory (IRE) *Christopher Mason* a44 60
7 b g Dylan Thomas(IRE) Jacquelin Jag (IRE) (Fayruz)
2206[15] (2728) 3036[7] 3577[4] 4181[5] 4494[4] 4776[3] 5083[2] 5498[7] 5607[2] 6110[5] 6329[10] 6857[5] 7172[5] 7784[3] 8249[3] 8697[7] 9034[4]
Jagerbond *Andrew Crook* a44 46
3 ch g Monsieur Bond(IRE) Velvet Jaguar (Hurricane Run (IRE))
1486[12] 1721[8] 2350[6] 2531[6] 3246[3] 4587[8] 4914[13] 5477[7] 6036[11] 6502[10] 7024[8] 8942[2] 9028[4] 9337[9] 9391[8]
Jaggy Nettle (IRE) *Andrew Hughes* a20
2 b f The Carbon Unit(USA) Storminateacup (IRE) (Galileo (IRE))
8525[8]
Jahaafel (FR) *M Al Mheiri* a40 40
4 gr g Style Vendome(FR) Irisijana (GER) (Diktat)
197a[8]
Jahbath *William Haggas* a106 79
3 b g Mukhadram Oulianovsk (IRE) (Peintre Celebre (USA))
(391) (1035) 1443a[11]
Jahrawi (USA) *Kevin Ryan* a69
2 b c Fed Biz(USA) Honimiere (IRE) (Fasliyev (USA))
8528[4]
Jaidaa *P Monfort* a67 53
3 b f Dark Angel(IRE) Angelic Air (Oasis Dream)
2018[7] 2838[4] 3584[9] 4284[12] 9281a[7]
Jai Hanuman (IRE)
Michael Wigham a74 56
5 b g Requinto(IRE) Almost Blue (USA) (Mr Greeley (USA))
760[2] (969) (1032) (1175) (1591) 4426[10]
Jailbreak (IRE) *Conrad Allen* a42 40
3 b g Lawman(FR) Luminata (IRE) (Indian Ridge (IRE))
1728[10] 2238[5] 2943[7] 3697[4] 4217[9] 4485[10] 6885[12] 8915[7] 9216[13] 9442[4]
Jakodobro *Bryan Smart* 24
2 b g Fountain Of Youth(IRE) Equinox (Medicean)
1844[8] 2331[9] 4517[10] 5295[9] 5968[15]
Jalaad (IRE) *Saeed bin Suroor* a90 92
4 b g Kodiac Surrey Storm (Montjeu (IRE))
(2094)◆ 2598[2] 3496[4] 4598[2] 5626[8] (7653) 8809[6]
Jaleel *Roger Varian* a87 87
3 b g Iffraaj Precariously Good (Oasis Dream)
2366[3] 3051[2] (4124) 4887[9] 5685[3] (6076) 6913[7] 7551[4] 8016[9]
Jalingo (IRE) *Ali Stronge*
8 b g Cape Cross(IRE) Just Special (Cadeaux Genereux)
6077[13]
Jaliska (FR) *S Cerulis* a77 64
3 b f Elusive City(USA) Adamantina (FR) (Muhtathir)
977a[4]
Jalmoud *Charlie Appleby* a83 110
3 ch g New Approach(IRE) Dancing Rain (IRE) (Danehill Dancer (IRE))
(1856) (2426a) 3984[13] 4431a[2] 4963a[3] 5585[7] 6353[4]
Jalwan (USA) *John Butler* a74
2 b c Wicked Strong(USA) City Run (USA) (Cherokee Run (USA))
6344[3] 9174[4] 9448[4]
Jamaal Danehill *Kevin Ryan* a38
2 ch f Casamento(IRE) Danega (Galileo (IRE))
5856[11] 7304[8]
Jamacho *Charlie Longsdon* a70 72
5 ch g Camacho Obsessive Secret (IRE) (Grand Lodge (USA))
9303[7] 9626[3]
Jamaheery (IRE) *Richard Hannon* 87
2 b f Kodiac Ambiguous (Kheleyf (USA))
(7393)◆ 8088[10]
Jamaican Jill *William Muir* a80
4 b m Teofilo(IRE) Kahlua Kiss (Mister Baileys)
818[6] 459[7] 1065[2] 1688[3] 8812[10]
Jamais Assez (USA) *K R Burke* 79
2 b g Invincible Spirit(IRE) Ana Luna (Dream Well (FR))
4098[5] 6891[3] 7645[2] 8125[7]
Jamal (FR) *R Le Dren Doleuze* 16
3 b g Dabirsim(FR) Ante Portas (GER) (American Post)
1741a[11]
James Park Woods (IRE)
Ralph Beckett a66 79
3 b g Australia Happy Holly (IRE) (Holy Roman Emperor (IRE))
2088[7] 3247[3] 4362[6] 5140[2] 5688[4] 6418[3] (7681)
James Street (IRE) *Hugo Palmer* a89 79
3 b c Gale Force Ten Paris Glory (USA) (Honour And Glory (USA))
57[2] 261[2] 470[5] 1920[3] 2746[19]
James Watt (IRE) *Michael Bell* 90
3 b g Morpheus Tomintoul Singer (IRE) (Johannesburg (USA))
2054[3] 2412[3] 2835[7] 3659[2] 3935[2] 5058[3] 5442[9] 5791[2]◆ 6476[18] 7431[22] 8101[18]
James' Will *David Marnane* a47
3 b g Heeraat(IRE) Obsessive Secret (IRE) (Grand Lodge (USA))
306a[8]
Jamih *Tina Jackson* a50 72
4 ch g Intello(GER) Hannda (IRE) (Dr Devious (IRE))
3811[14] 7185[12] 7589[8] 7907[11] 8300[12]
Jamil (IRE) *Tina Jackson* 51
4 b g Dansili Havant (Halling (USA))
7622[5] 8260[10]
Jampower *Natalie Lloyd-Beavis* a48 3
4 b g Equiano(FR) Wiki Tiki (Dixie Union (USA))
379[12]

Janajka (FR) *J-L Guillochon* a47 45
4 b m Monitor Closely(IRE) Shaimix (FR) (Pinmix (FR))
5762a[3]

Janaya (FR) *Mme J Hendriks* a55 45
8 b m Deportivo Relire (FR) (Fabulous Dancer (USA))
4960a[9]

Jan De Heem *Tina Jackson* a55 63
9 ch g Dutch Art Shasta (Shareef Dancer (USA))
3054[11] 3447[4] 4126[4] 4435[3] 4990[5]◆ 5219[2] 5766[5] 5975[3] 6278[2] 6827[2] (7053) 7314[3] 7441[5]◆ 8343[5] 8423[11]

Jane Camille *Peter Hedger* a35 28
3 b f Harbour Watch(IRE) Emulate (Alhaarth (IRE))
6594[9] 7278[10] 7976[6] 8547[9] 8942[11]

Jane Victoria *Luke McJannet* a23 53
2 ch f Helmet(AUS) Winter Hey Lane (USA) (Speightstown (USA))
4221[10] 5011[3] 5427[3] 5958[11] 6799[8] 9438[8]

Jangkhe (FR) *K Borgel* 78
2 ch c Kheleyf(USA) Kadjang (FR) (Panis (USA))
7674a[3]

Janoobi (SAF) *M F De Kock* a23 99
5 b h Silvano(GER) Shasta Daisy (SAF) (Rakeen (USA))
52a[13] 397a[11] 726a[6] 846a[6] 1115a[8]

Jan Van Hoof (IRE)
Michael Herrington a77 56
8 b g Dutch Art Cosenza (Bahri (USA))
131[4] 353[8] (743) 970[3] 1403[2] 1929[7] 2379[6] 2709[11] 4149[10] 9473[7]

Japan *A P O'Brien* 125
3 b c Galileo(IRE) Shastye (IRE) (Danehill (USA))
2777[4] 3345[3] (4049) (4963a) (6354) 7941a[4]

Jardin Fleuri (FR) *B Legros* a56 59
6 b m Myboycharlie(IRE) Bashful (IRE) (Brief Truce (USA))
3711a[13]

Jarrocho (IRE) *David Marnane* a45 61
3 b g Requinto(IRE) Wing Diva (IRE) (Hawk Wing (USA))
5492[3]

Jash (IRE) *Simon Crisford* 107
3 b c Kodiac Miss Azeza (Dutch Art)
(2834) 4050[6]

Jashma (IRE) *Richard Hughes* a88 86
5 b g Power Daganya (IRE) (Danehill Dancer (IRE))
3[4] 3043[8] 3443[5] 4213[6]

Jasmine A La Plage (FR)
Ludo Van Beylen a57 57
4 b m Palace Episode(USA) Diner En Ville (FR) (Barathea (IRE))
6031a[16]

Jasmine B (IRE) *John Ryan* a36 38
3 ch f Exceed And Excel(AUS) Fashionable (Nashwan (USA))
155[13] 437[10] 802[7] 1066[10] 1358[10]

Jasnin (FR) *Waldemar Hickst* a96 81
7 gr g Palace Episode(USA) Jaillissante (FR) (Verglas (IRE))
3879a[11]

Jassaar *D K Weld* 101
4 b g Dansili Rasmeyaa (IRE) (New Approach (IRE))
(3062a) 5535a[11] (6693a) 7222a[10]

Jaunty *Conrad Allen* a47 47
2 b f Acclamation Merletta (Raven's Pass (USA))
2840[8] 8454[8]

Javea Magic (IRE) *Tom Dascombe* a47 60
2 br g Society Rock(IRE) Cape Karli (IRE) (Cape Cross (IRE))
3194[7] 3477[3] 4550[5] 4985[7] 6683[5] 7469[7]

Javelin *William Muir* a78 69
4 ch m Lethal Force(IRE) Amitola (IRE) (Choisir (AUS))
(1684) 2097[4] (2237) 3020[3] 3147[7] 4243[4] 4994[9] 7843[5] 8456[2] 9140[11] 9455[12]

Jawshan (USA) *Ian Williams* a71 69
4 b g Denman(AUS) Diamond Baby (USA) (Southern Image (USA))
2819[10] 4308[6] 5091[2] 5571[6] 6224[4] 6566[6]

Jawwaal *Michael Dods* a87 95
4 ch g Bahamian Bounty Avenbury (Mount Nelson)
1459[3]◆ 2393[2] 2843[14] 4402[9] 5454[3] 6676[10] 7431[13] 8099[9]

Jayadeeva (FR) *Guillaume Courbot* a35 56
2 b g Kheleyf(USA) Dame Caprice (IRE) (Bering)
2263a[2] 5263a[2] 5713a[7] 6485a[5] 6873a[6] 7641a[8]

Jaycols Star *Tim Vaughan* a52 53
4 ch g Medicean A Lulu Ofa Menifee (USA) (Menifee (USA))
2127[7]

Jay Me Lo (IRE) *Lawrence Mullaney* a60 31
2 b f Equiano(FR) Arabian Spell (IRE) (Desert Prince (IRE))
4516[10] 8640[12] 9471[8]

Jaywalk (USA) *John C Servis* a108
3 rg f Cross Traffic(USA) Lady Pewitt (USA) (Orientate (USA))
7479a[7]

Jazeel (IRE) *Jedd O'Keeffe* a87 103
4 b g Roderic O'Connor(IRE) Simla Bibi (Indian Ridge (IRE))
2408[2] 3315[2] (4613) 4935[9] 5519[2] 6420[9] 7694[7]

Jazirat (IRE) *S Al Shamsi* a76 51
4 b g Dark Angel(IRE) Layla Jamil (IRE) (Exceed And Excel (AUS))
97a[9] 197a[7]

Jazzameer *Debbie Hughes* a21 34
4 ch m Mazameer(IRE) Jinks And Co (Ishiguru (USA))
1475[7] 2280[9] 5494[7] 8295[11] 9544[13]

Jazz Hands (IRE) *Richard Fahey* a69 56
3 b g Red Jazz(USA) Ishimagic (Ishiguru (USA))
1957[10] (2325) 2712[8] 3348[10] 4487[3] 5031[2] 5552[7] 6130[6] 6610[2] 7581[5] 7956[5] (8405) 8818[7] (9331)

Jazz Legend (USA) *Mandy Rowland* a59 62
6 b g Scat Daddy(USA) Champion Ride (USA) (Candy Ride (ARG))
166[2] (1071) (1553) 2532[7] 8071[11] 8666[11]

Jazz Magic (IRE) *Lynn Siddall* a41 43
4 ch g Red Jazz(USA) Caerella (IRE) (Alzao (USA))
3224[11] 3682[8] 6627[7] 8086[8]

Jazz Melodie (FR) *P De Chevigny* a97 101
5 b m Soul City(IRE) Quatz Melody (FR) (Johann Quatz (FR))
1127a[3] 1708a[6] 9603a[4]

Jazz Party *Paul Cole* a70
2 b c New Approach(IRE) Harlem Dancer (Dr Devious (IRE))
9208[4]

Jazz Style (IRE) *David Brown* a42 53
2 b g Red Jazz(USA) Gypsy Style (Desert Style (IRE))
3371[6] 4238[8] 5294[10] 7079[9] 8527[10] 8897[6] 9037[5] 9110[6]

Jazz Warrior (FR) *G Verheye* a40 38
5 gr g Ransom O'War(USA) Jaragua (FR) (Medaaly)
3711a[8]

Jazzy Card (IRE) *Linda Jewell* a51 43
3 ch f Red Jazz(USA) Gilda Lilly (USA) (War Chant (USA))
547[4] 1359[6] 2210[11] 3256[13]

Jazzy J (IRE) *Anthony McCann* a58
4 b g Red Jazz(USA) Lady Elsie (Singspiel (IRE))
2127[9]

Jean Baptiste (IRE)
Sir Michael Stoute a82 68
2 b c Invincible Spirit(IRE) Pioneer Bride (USA) (Gone West (USA))
5860[4] 6927[2] 7571[2]

Jeanette May *William Stone* a44 40
3 b f Dick Turpin(IRE) Clock Opera (IRE) (Excellent Art)
978[4] 1562[9] 2236[9] 3182[5] 4244[3]

Jean Excels *Roy Bowring* a25 26
4 b m Captain Gerrard(IRE) Exceedingly Good (IRE) (Exceed And Excel (AUS))
1402[14] 1554[8]

Jeanie B *Mick Channon* a81 81
2 ch f Bated Breath Effie B (Sixties Icon)
6846[4] (7377) 7765[2] 8243[3] 8723[2] (8913)

Jean Mary *Stef Keniry* a17
2 ch f Cityscape Ananda Kanda (USA) (Hero's Tribute (USA))
8631[11] 8816[8] 9347[13]

Jean Merci (FR) *Keith Dalgleish* a44 50
3 b g Panis(USA) Fabulatrice (FR) (Turtle Bowl (IRE))
2530[8] 2712[10] 3246[13]

Jean Racine (FR) *H-A Pantall* 73
2 bb c Rajsaman(FR) Paola Lisa (FR) (Pomellato (GER))
7675a[3]

Jeans Maite *Roy Bowring* a38
3 b f Burwaaz Misu's Maite (Misu Bond (IRE))
4367[10] 8947[2] 9540[5]

Jean Valjean *Richard Spencer* a51 64
3 b g Bated Breath Waitingonacloud (In The Wings)
2078[7] 5202[8] 6085[3] 7523[2] 8009[8]

Jedhi *Hughie Morrison* a84 90
4 b m Big Bad Bob(IRE) Capriolla (In The Wings)
(2613) 3586[6] 3995[5] (5133) 6223[3]

Jeffrey Harris *Jim Goldie* a63 56
4 b g Orientor Theatrical Dancer (Theatrical Charmer)
1403[9] 1950[4] 2433[6] 4059[6] 4694[3] 5276[8] 5491[4] 5620[6] 6574[8] 7488[5] 7737[2] (7962)◆ (8925) 9352[5]

Jellmood *Chris Gordon* a89 87
4 b g Acclamation Emotif (ARG) (Giant's Causeway (USA))
56[5] 1727[7] 2487[6] 3040[5] 3763[6] 4249[10] 5343[6] 8017[13]

Jellystone (IRE) *Ralph Beckett* a73 71
2 b g Kodiac Scholarly (Authorized (IRE))
5908[7] 7235[5] 7814[4] 8518[6]

Jeltrin (USA) *Alexis Delgado* a100
3 b f Tapizar(USA) Song To The Moon (USA) (Successful Appeal (USA))
7479a[9]

Je M'En Fiche *Patrick Chamings* a37 43
3 b f Rock Of Gibraltar(IRE) Katya Kabanova (Sadler's Wells (USA))
1676[9] 2925[6] 3965[8] 9544[8]

Jems Bond *Alan Brown* a62 53
2 ch g Monsieur Bond(IRE) Saphire (College Chapel)
6337[11] 6943[8] 7645[4] 8085[2] (8452)

Jem Scuttle (USA) *Declan Carroll* a69 68
3 ch g City Zip(USA) Elegantly Wild (IRE) (Galileo (IRE))
1857[8]◆ 2101[10] 2510[5] 3307[6] 4288[4] 4606[4] 4767[9] 6678[4] 7404[10] 8025[10] 9180[5] 9455[7]

Je Ne Regretterien *A Fabre* 99
3 b f Galileo(IRE) Prudenzia (IRE) (Dansili)
3391a[3]

Jenilat Pearl (FR) *J Phelippon*
4 b m Tin Horse(IRE) Perchance (Oasis Dream)
8966a[6]

Jennies Gem *Ollie Pears* a50 48
6 b g Mount Nelson Kaspirit (IRE) (Invincible Spirit (IRE))
501[12] 2241[7] 3199[9] 3959[3] 5024[8] 5513[7]

Jen's Lad (IRE) *Richard Hannon* 48
2 b g Dandy Man(IRE) Strawberry Queen (Dr Fong (USA))
7162[12] 7562[10] 8517[11]

Jenufa (FR) *H-A Pantall* a30 69
2 ch f Hunter's Light(IRE) Jezlay (FR) (Layman (USA))
8447a[2]

Jeopardy John *Michael Attwater* a61 62
4 b g Delegator Daysiwaay (IRE) (Daylami (IRE))
4449[4] 4797[9]

Jerbourg *Tim Easterby* 69
2 b g Mayson Tabrina (IRE) (Fasliyev (USA))
6337[7] 6891[6] 7645[3]

Jered Maddox *David Marnane* a77 77
3 b g Lawman(FR) Al Janadeirya (Oasis Dream)
(5494)

Jeremiade (FR) *Mme J Hendriks* a62
4 b m Tin Horse(IRE) Mowaajaha (USA) (Invincible Spirit (IRE))
6434a[8]

Jeremy's Jet (IRE) *Tony Carroll* a54 43
8 b g Jeremy(USA) Double Vie (IRE) (Tagula (IRE))
62[12] 485[5] 624[6] 941[4] 1032[6] 1527[11] 2012[8] 4991[5]

Jersey Grey (FR) *Jamie Osborne* a52
2 gr g Rajsaman(FR) Akoyama (Peintre Celebre (USA))
8604[10] 9154[10] 9363[9]

Jersey Jack (JER) *K Kukk*
3 b g Saddler's Rock(IRE) La Verte Rue (USA) (Johannesburg (USA))
6555a[8]

Jersey Wonder (IRE)
Jamie Osborne a92 92
3 ch g Zoffany(IRE) Magena (USA) (Kingmambo (USA))
3262[4] 4256[8] (4739) 5614[13] 8350[8] 8853[5] 9056[2] 9215[7]

Jervaulx *James Bethell* 16
2 gr g Champs Elysees Perfect Haven (Singspiel (IRE))
6673[8]

Jesse Jude (IRE) *Simon West* 48
6 ch g Doyen(IRE) La Belle Bleu (IRE) (Lahib (USA))
2505[9] 4600[7]

Jessely (FR) *Andrea Marcialis* 97
2 b f Charm Spirit(IRE) Lapland (FR) (Linamix (FR))
7602a[2] 8140a[8]

Jessie Allan (IRE) *Jim Goldie* a44 51
8 b m Bushranger(IRE) Ishimagic (Ishiguru (USA))
1021[11] 1505[3] 1765[11] 2958[12] 4059[8] 4720[10] 5235[4]◆ 5278[8] 5486[3] 5722[7] 5935[4] 6462[11] 7214[5] 7367[12] 7780[6]

Jessinamillion *James Bethell* a62 56
5 b g Mine(IRE) Miss Apricot (Indian Ridge (IRE))
4293[8] 5787[9] 6462[14]

Jetcologne (GER) *Miss V Haigh* a59 31
3 rg f Sehrezad(IRE) Jasmin Blanche (GER) (Tannenkonig (IRE))
9281a[11]

Jet Set Go *Seb Spencer* 61
4 ch m Equiano(FR) Golden Valley (Three Valleys (USA))
1649[5] 2397[8] 2823[6]

Jet Setteuse (FR) *F Rohaut* a72 103
3 ch f Makfi Pretty Panther (FR) (Hurricane Run (IRE))
1242a[2] 1706a[3] 4621a[11] 8376a[3] 9603a[11]

Jetstream (IRE) *D J Jeffreys* a59 63
4 b g Galileo(IRE) Bewitched (IRE) (Dansili)
1399[8] 4370[5] 5106[6] 5803[10]

Jet Streaming (IRE) *Samuel Farrell* 79
5 ch m Born To Sea(IRE) Sateen (Barathea (IRE))
2404[6] 3096[RR] 3586[RR]

Jeu De Mots (FR) *Dianne Sayer* 10
6 b g Saint Des Saints(FR) Nanouska (GER) (Dashing Blade)
6034[7]

Jeweller *Sir Michael Stoute* a81 62
3 ch g Mastercraftsman(IRE) Allegretto (IRE) (Galileo (IRE))
2289[5] 6290[9] 7192[3] (7998) (8292)

Jewel Maker (IRE) *Tim Easterby* 78
4 b g Invincible Spirit(IRE) Sapphire (IRE) (Medicean)
6677[8] 7310[7] 7908[2] 8183[3] 8636[2]

J Gaye (IRE) *Richard Phillips* a74 69
3 b f Canford Cliffs(IRE) Ice Pie (Mount Nelson)
1419[4] 2361[3] 4326[4] 5344[4]◆ 8644[2] 9033[2]

Jighen (IRE) *A Botti* 96
3 ch c Teofilo(IRE) Pocket A Pound (IRE) (Azamour (IRE))
2887a[7]

Jilbaab *Brian Meehan* a77 68
3 b g Havana Gold(IRE) Sand Dancer (IRE) (Footstepsinthesand)
2140[3] (2598) 3580[4] 4124[11]

Jill Rose *Richard Whitaker* a66 67
3 ch f Coach House(IRE) Wotatomboy (Captain Rio)
1894[14] 2939[4] 3516[9] 4192[4] 4586[16] 4783[4] 5629[8] (5914) 7047[6] 7632[4] 8071[5] 8839[5]

Jimmy Greenhough (IRE)
Richard Fahey 60
3 gr g Dream Ahead(USA) Expedience (USA) (With Approval (CAN))
1975[7] 3195[7] 4284[2] 4761[7]

Jimmy Krankyar (USA)
Phillip Makin a33 52
3 rg g Exchange Rate(USA) Lastroseofsummer (IRE) (Haafhd)
4916[9] 5248[5] 5766[10] 6499[9]

Jim 'N' Tomic (IRE)
Dominic Ffrench Davis a28 76
2 b g War Command(USA) Anna David (Sleeping Indian)
2205[7] 2792[3]◆ 4839[6] 6911[15] 7971[8] 8890[12] 9127[9]

Jinambo (JPN) *Noriyuki Hori* 105
4 b h Deep Impact(JPN) Apapane (JPN) (King Kamehameha (JPN))
9153a[13]

Jizellita (FR) *A De Royer-Dupre* a82 91
4 b m Muhtathir Jacira (FR) (Sillery (USA))
8980a[7]

JJ's Journey (IRE) *Andrew Hughes* 14
4 b h The Carbon Unit(USA) Advertising Space (IRE) (Galileo (IRE))
4274[8]

Jm Barrie *David Marnane* a61 68
2 ch g Sir Percy Maleficent (Azamour (IRE))
5710a[12]

Jm Jackson (IRE) *Mark Johnston* a76 91
2 bb f No Nay Never(USA) Kawn (Cadeaux Genereux)
1759[2] 3023[2] 4048[23] 5125[3] 5646[2]

Joa De Gibraltar (IRE) *J Reynier* 78
2 b f Rock Of Gibraltar(IRE) Fetan Joa (FR) (Enrique)
(5166a)

Joanie Stubbs *Richard Spencer* 59
2 b f Garswood Cherry Malotte (Pivotal)
8458[8]

Joan Jet (FR) *N Milliere* a7 19
4 b m Equiano(FR) Amarinda (GER) (Tiger Hill (IRE))
7223a[7]

Joanna Vassa *Roger Ingram* a36 42
2 b f Equiano(FR) Quotation (Medicean)
5250[10] 8700[14] 8912[8]

Jochi Khan (USA)
Mohamed Moubarak a55 44
2 bb g Daredevil(USA) Awesome Mama (USA) (Awesome Again (CAN))
3371[7] 4734[11] 5265[9] 7833[5]◆ 9060[6] 9179[3] 9330[2]

Jock Talk (IRE) *Patrick Morris* a36 34
5 b g Famous Name Katdogawn (Bahhare (USA))
1506[10] 3251[8] 3718[9]

Jodies Jem *Stuart Edmunds* a81 83
9 br g Kheleyf(USA) First Approval (Royal Applause)
617[4]

Joe Blining (FR) *C Lerner* a60 67
3 ch g Kentucky Dynamite(USA) Pomposa (IRE) (Barathea (IRE))
5641a[4]

Joe Francais (FR) *J-C Rouget* 98
3 b c George Vancouver(USA) Gibraltar Bay (IRE) (Cape Cross (IRE))
1243a[5] 1797a[4] 3390a[11]

Joegogo (IRE) *David Evans* a85 74
4 b g Approve(IRE) Joyfullness (USA) (Dixieland Band (USA))
36[3] (433) 471[2] 763[3] 4872[8] 5252[8] 5959[3] 6080[6] 7337[3] 8470[9] 8895[3] 9131[4]◆ 9203[8] 9257[4]

Joe's Way *Tim Easterby* 34
2 b g Equiano(FR) Nos Da (Cape Cross (IRE))
4238[10]

Joe The Beau *Michael Easterby* 76
3 ch g Mukhadram Divine Power (Kyllachy)
(2200) 2942[12]

Joevia (USA) *Gregory D Sacco* a114
3 bb c Shanghai Bobby(USA) Peace Process (USA) (War Front (USA))
3620a[3]

Joey Boy (IRE) *Kevin Ryan* a61 56
3 b g Zebedee Lady Day (Selkirk (USA))
524[8] 783[2] 918[5] 1982[15] 2958[3] 4731[4] 5558[11]

Johan *William Haggas* 87
2 b c Zoffany(IRE) Sandreamer (IRE) (Oasis Dream)
5439[4]◆ (5956) (7733)◆ 8112[6]

Johann Strauss *R Bouresly* 16
8 br g High Chaparral(IRE) Inchmina (Cape Cross (IRE))
725a[6] 960a[14]

John Betjeman *Mark Gillard* a65 76
3 b g Poet's Voice A Great Beauty (Acclamation)
1516[10] 1587[3] 2204[4] 2339[8] 3764[2] 4562[9] 5813[9] 6084[2] 8521[9]

John Caesar (IRE)
Rebecca Bastiman a42 51
8 b g Bushranger(IRE) Polish Belle (Polish Precedent (USA))
912[10] 1519[6] 2112[8] 3224[9] 3959[4] 4633[7] 5024[7] 5248[2] 5518[5] 6103[6] 6499[4]

John Clare (IRE) *Pam Sly* a74 77
3 b g Poet's Voice Specialty (IRE) (Oasis Dream)
2114[2] 3273[3] 3930[7] 4440[13] 7542[4] 8549[2] 9047[11]

Johni Boxit *Brian Barr* a40 63
4 ch g Sakhee's Secret Pink Supreme (Night Shift (USA))
2277[3] 2975[6] 5016[7] 6121[9] 8863[11] 9207[10]

John Joiner *Shaun Keightley* a58 57
7 b g Captain Gerrard(IRE) Nigella (Band On The Run)
1987[10] 3001[11] 3320[10] 3772[3] 4182[6]

John Kirkup *Michael Dods* a85 86
4 ch g Assertive Bikini (Trans Island)
1978[5] 2416[9] 2899[4] (3550) 3868[7] 4879[3] 5395[8] 5692[4] 6677[14] 7289[5] (7777) 8428[3] 8921[9] 9334[10]

John Leo's Son (IRE) *David Evans* 26
2 b g Elzaam(AUS) Mountain Glow (Araafa (IRE))
6106[7] 6395[11] 6640[12]

Johnny Cavagin *Paul Midgley* a66 79
10 b g Superior Premium Beyond The Rainbow (Mind Games)
214[5] 356[9] (1818) 2053[2] 2709[4]◆ 3504[11] 3868[8] 4307[2] (5478) 5819[4] 7624[5]

Johnny Drama (IRE)
Andrew Balding 106
4 b g Lilbourne Lad(IRE) Quelle Histoire (IRE) (Whipper (USA))
4053[13] 5519[6] 6475[2] 7457[10] 8126[2]

Johnny Kidd *Andrew Balding* a82 77
3 ch g Australia Sabreon (Caerleon (USA))
2142[5] 2731[4]◆ 3802[2] 4739[5] 5452[3] 6597[2]

Johnny Reb *Charlie Fellowes* a79 72
3 b g Showcasing Specific Dream (Danehill Dancer (IRE))
2823[3] 3302[2]◆ 3661[9] 6968[10] 7607[5]

Johnny Utah (IRE) *Richard Spencer*
2 b g Dandy Man(IRE) Caramel Sundae (Oratorio (IRE))
8721[10]

Johnyfortycoats (IRE)
Michael Mulvany 11
3 b g Tough As Nails(IRE) Miss Ailbhe (Polish Precedent (USA))
2853a[5]

Joie De Vivre (IRE)
Martin Todhunter a65 74
4 gr m Mastercraftsman(IRE) Fragonard (Teofilo (IRE))
(3708)◆ 5039[3] 5728[9]

Jojo (IRE) *Jo Hughes* a67 69
3 b f Battle Of Marengo(IRE) Swingsky (IRE) (Indian Ridge (IRE))
2598[3] 3712a[3] 4621a[13] 6063a[9] 7138a[6]

Joker On Jack (USA) *Wesley A Ward* a88 87
2 ch c Declaration Of War(USA) Aventure Love (FR) (Orpen (USA))
2830[7]

Jolie (FR) *Andrea Marcialis* 100
2 b f Power Elettra (FR) (Literato (FR))
1709a[3] (2263a) 3333a[2] 4417a[2] 5228a[3] 5481a[4] 6791a[4] 7292a[4] 7943a[12]

Jolyon *Michael Scudamore* a45
3 ch g Raven's Pass(USA) Fleurissimo (Dr Fong (USA))
9662[7]

Jomrok *Owen Burrows* a81 74
3 b f Mukhadram Shadow Dancing (Unfuwain (USA))
3889[2] 4641[2] 5656[3] 6501[4]

Jonah Jones (IRE) *Tom Dascombe* 89
3 b c No Nay Never(USA) Conniption (IRE) (Danehill Dancer (IRE))
5953[6] 6425[11] 7002[8]

Jonboy *David Brown* a76 79
4 b g Delegator Cavallo Da Corsa (Galileo (IRE))
8712[2] 9108[5] 9334[7] 9519[10]

Jonker (AUS) *David Atkins* 109
3 b c Spirit Of Boom(AUS) Hearts And Arrows (AUS) (Kempinsky (AUS))
8805a[8]

Jonnysimpson (IRE) *Lee Carter* a39 29
4 gr m Zebedee Applauding (IRE) (Royal Applause)
1682[10] 4501[6] 5046[8] 9508[7]

Joplin (GER) *D Fechner* a75 105
5 b m Soldier Hollow Jane (GER) (Samum (GER))
2182a[10] (4706a) 5479a[4]

Jordan Electrics *Linda Perratt* 72
3 b g Dandy Man(IRE) Ruby Slippers (Sir Percy)
2683[5] 2960[4] 3719[2]◆ (3999) 4492[2] 4721[6] 5670[6] 5901[5] 6608[4] 6932[6]

Jordan's Chris (IRE) *Linda Perratt* 14
3 ch f Society Rock(IRE) Crimson Sunrise (IRE) (Holy Roman Emperor (IRE))
4489[8] 5094[11]

Jorgie (FR) *Iain Jardine* a51
2 ch c George Vancouver(USA) Capannacce (IRE) (Lahib (USA))
9347[7]

Jorvik Prince *Julia Brooke* a55 35
5 br g Kheleyf(USA) Wotatomboy (Captain Rio)
179[6] 970[7] 3452[9] 3933[9] 4763[12] 9169[7] 9272[11]

Josephine Bettany *Hughie Morrison* a32
2 b f Dansili Household Name (Zamindar (USA))
8848[12]

Jo's Girl (IRE) *Micky Hammond* a40 69
4 b m Zebedee Diamond Finesse (IRE) (Red Clubs (IRE))
1660[6] 2290[8] 2509[11] 3199[13] 5117[7] 7583[9] 8664[5]

Joshua R (IRE) *David Barron* 66
2 b g Canford Cliffs(IRE) Khobaraa (Invincible Spirit (IRE))
6457[9] 7377[4]

Josiebond *Rebecca Bastiman* a56 57
3 ch f Monsieur Bond(IRE) Smiddy Hill (Factual (USA))
2197[5] 2871[7] 3319[3] 3775[2] 4731[3] 5063[7] 5914[9] 7486[6] 7962[6]

Journey Of Life *Gary Moore* a75 71
3 ch g Exceed And Excel(AUS) Maria Bella (IRE) (Raven's Pass (USA))
2567[10] 2938[2] 3167[3] 4193[2] 4507[7]

Jouska *Henry Candy* 101
2 b f Cable Bay(IRE) Quiet Protest (USA) (Kingmambo (USA))
4557[6] (5317)◆ 6157[4] 6907[5]◆ 8088[3]

J'Ouvert (IRE) *David Evans* a70 63
3 b f Dawn Approach(IRE) Areyaam (USA) (Elusive Quality (USA))
380[5] 547[2] 795[9] 6801[6] 7237[3] 7682[11] 8499[2] (8756) 9202[9] 9453[15]

Jovial *Sir Michael Stoute* a76 82
2 b f Dubawi(IRE) Joyeuse (Oasis Dream)
5646[3] (6514) (7580)

Joycetick (FR) *Nick Littmoden* a70 47
5 b g Myboycharlie(IRE) Joyce (GER) (Chato (USA))
2696[3] 3444[4] 5271[9] 7033[8] 8868[7]

Joyful Dream (IRE) *John Butler* a50 62
5 ch m Dream Ahead(USA) Tearsforjoy (USA) (Street Cry (IRE))
155[10] 462[4] 941[3] 1158[2] 1431[7] 1731[3] 1967[12] 3410[2] 4217[2] 4753[5] 5284[9] (5806) 6758[3] (7024) 7273[2] 7982[6]

Joyful Mission (USA) *Sir Michael Stoute* 92
3 b g Noble Mission Hint Of Joy (USA) (Empire Maker (USA))
1886[4] 4608[3] (5477) 6506[4]

Joyful Star *Fred Watson* a52 55
9 b g Teofilo(IRE) Extreme Beauty (USA) (Rahy (USA))
1722[10] 2329[5] 3177[11] 4293[10] 7207[6] 7961[2] 9111[13]

Joza (IRE) *Adrian Paul Keatley* a59 58
3 b g Morpheus Dubai Princess (IRE) (Dubai Destination (USA))
409[5]

Juals Spirit (IRE) *Brian Ellison* a39 40
3 b f Raven's Pass(USA) Bahama Spirit (IRE) (Invincible Spirit (IRE))
1721[13] 2190[6] 2530[4] 2941[7] 3246[11] 3684[9] 6036[10]

Juan De Valdes *Shaun Keightley* a57 13
3 bg c Exceed And Excel(AUS) Vayasa (FR) (Zamindar (USA))
1940[7] 2900[11]

Juan Elcano *Kevin Ryan* 109
2 ch c Frankel Whatami (Daylami (IRE))
(3551)◆ 4920[2] 7195[3]

Juan Horsepower *Denis Quinn* a42 47
5 b g Foxwedge(AUS) Elysee (IRE) (Fantastic Light (USA))
166[9] 7770[12] 9034[12] 9161[11] 9384[10] 9505[6]

Juanito Chico (IRE) *Michael Attwater* a78 77
5 br g Pour Moi(IRE) Miss Kittyhawk (IRE) (Hawk Wing (USA))
56[8] 252[2] 557[8] 722[3] 915[3] 1367[8] 1479[7] 1882[2] (1955) 2273[19] 2739[6] 2927[4] 4403[4] 4662[4] 5155[6] 5863[3] 6261[3] 6567[2] 7272[3] 7839[6]

Juan Les Pins *Ed Walker* a72 54
2 b g Invincible Spirit(IRE) Miss Cap Ferrat (Darshaan)
7458[7] 8059[3] 9174[2]◆

Jubilance (IRE) *Bent Olsen* a76 87
10 b g Oratorio(IRE) Literacy (USA) (Diesis)
6524a[9]

Jubiloso *Sir Michael Stoute* a87 111
3 b f Shamardal(USA) Joyeuse (Oasis Dream)
(2060) (2794)◆ 4051[3] 5608[3]◆ 6726[7]

Judicial (IRE) *Julie Camacho* a114 108
7 b g Iffraaj Marlinka (Marju (IRE))
2409[7] 3950[12] (5142) 5611[6] (6698) 7454[5] (9004)◆

Judith Gardenier *R Mike Smith* a28 31
7 b m Rip Van Winkle(IRE) Millagros (IRE) (Pennekamp (USA))
607[7] 1398[13] 4004[9] 4054[11] 4914[14]

Jukebox Blues (FR) *Mark Johnston* a46 23
3 b c Jukebox Jury(IRE) Attima (Zafonic (USA))
4459[7] 4779[7] 5153[3] 5803[13]

Jukebox Jive (FR) *Jamie Osborne* a79 92
5 b g Jukebox Jury(IRE) Sweetheart (Sinndar (IRE))
281a[7] 635a[3] 3952[15] 4096[6] 5183[12] 5496[3] 6100[2] 6888[5]

Jukov (FR) *Y Barberot* a73 54
3 b g American Devil(FR) Grinta Noire (FR) (Redback)
5407a[3] 7561a[10]

Julia's Magic (IRE) *Mrs Denise Foster* a83 95
4 b m Dandy Man(IRE) Fly By Magic (IRE) (Indian Rocket)
2880a[3] 3557a[4] 6648a[10] 8328a[13]

Juliet Foxtrot *Brad H Cox* a91 107
4 b m Dansili Kilo Alpha (King's Best (USA))
7920a[2]

Julio (GER) *Henk Grewe* 89
4 b h Exceed And Excel(AUS) Julissima (Beat Hollow)
892a[6] 3369a[6] 6006a[6]

Juliusjuliusson (USA) *P Bary* 77
2 b c War Front(USA) Hoop Of Colour (USA) (Distorted Humor (USA))
5468a[2]

Julius Limbani (IRE) *Jassim Mohammed Ghazali* 89
3 b c Anodin(IRE) Kshanti (USA) (Diesis)
893a[9]

Jumaira Bay (FR) *Roger Varian* a55 74
2 b c Siyouni(FR) Desert Sunrise (Green Desert (USA))
7571[5] 8203[2] 8657[5]

Jumeirah (IRE) *Eve Johnson Houghton* a36 59
3 b f Acclamation Scarlet Plum (Pivotal)
1838[8] 2340[11] 2938[8]

Jumellea (IRE) *Joseph Patrick O'Brien* a88 92
3 b f Zoffany(IRE) In My Dreams (IRE) (Sadler's Wells (USA))
8367a[3] 8734a[14] 8784a[6]

Jumira Bridge *Robert Cowell* a92 98
5 b g Invincible Spirit(IRE) Zykina (Pivotal)
354[4] 389[5] (4609) 4995[4] 5371[14] 5888[4] 6149[5] 6724[5]◆ 7175[6] 8607[4] 9098[9]

Jumping Cats *Chris Wall* a83 77
4 ch g Champs Elysees Pivotal Drive (IRE) (Pivotal)
2059[6] 3334[5] (4019) 4782[3] 5812[6] 7033[6] 7464[6]

Jumping Jack (IRE) *Chris Gordon* a77 74
5 b g Sir Prancealot(IRE) She's A Character (Invincible Spirit (IRE))
3022[7] 3766[4] 4426[9] 5091[4] 6507[3] 7984[7] 8705[12]

Jumpin' Jack Flash (FR) *T Lemer* a81 87
5 b g Sunday Break(JPN) Slap Shade (IRE) (Invincible Spirit (IRE))
4704a[7]

Jump The Gun (IRE) *Jamie Osborne* a79 78
2 b g Make Believe Sound Of Guns (Acclamation)
3098[3] 3451[5] 5591[3]◆ 6637[2]◆ 6980[3] (7386) 7870[3] 8337[3]

Junderstand *Alan King* a70 81
4 ch m Champs Elysees Sienna Sunset (IRE) (Spectrum (IRE))
2207[6] 4283[2] 5594[3]◆ 6967[9]

Juneau (IRE) *Mark Johnston* a73 92
4 b m Dubawi(IRE) Snow Rose (USA) (Elusive Quality (USA))
1589[5] 1882[7] 3161[4]

Jungle Boogaloo (IRE) *Andi Brown* a51 58
2 b f Bungle Inthejungle Newton Bomb (IRE) (Fast Company (IRE))
2918[6] 3835[9] 5500[9] 7833[6]

Jungleboogie (GER) *Carina Fey* a79 82
5 b g Nicaron(GER) Jive (GER) (Montjeu (IRE))
780a[2]

Jungle Book (GER) *Jonathan Portman* a64 64
2 ch c Sea The Moon(GER) Josefine (GER) (Kallisto (GER))
2761[10] 3990[8] 4766[5] 6394[2] 7277[3] 7767[8] 8259[3]

Jungle Capers (IRE) *Mick Channon* a50 29
2 b g Bungle Inthejungle Kidmeforever (Piccolo)
7406[13] 7899[11] 8418[10] 9407[2]◆

Jungle Cove (IRE) *Mrs John Harrington* 94
2 gr c Mastercraftsman(IRE) Purple Glow (IRE) (Orientate (USA))
6430a[6]

Jungle Inthebungle (IRE) *Mick Channon* a79 79
3 ch g Bungle Inthejungle Princess Banu (Oasis Dream)
1424[6] 2008[6] 2773[2] 3191[3] 4736[6]

Jungle Jane (IRE) *W McCreery* a85 63
3 b f Bungle Inthejungle Funcheon Vale (IRE) (Acclamation)
6648a[11]

Jungle Juice (IRE) *Mick Channon* a68 76
3 b f Bungle Inthejungle Riymaisa (IRE) (Traditionally (USA))
1656[9] 2212[4] 2995[4] 3440[3] (3887) 4181[7] (4479) (4874)◆ 5137[5] 5450[5] 5573[5] 6418[6] 6801[3] 7345[3] 7514[6] 7901[7] 8247[10]

Jungle Rock (IRE) *Iain Jardine* 56
2 ch g Bungle Inthejungle Green Vision (IRE) (Green Desert (USA))
6622[12] 7046[7] 7506[3]

Jungle Room (USA) *Denis Quinn* a35 26
4 b g Violence(USA) Raised Right (USA) (Giant's Causeway (USA))
3158[11]

Jungle Secret (IRE) *Richard Fahey* a56 57
3 ch f Bungle Inthejungle Secret Circle (Magic Ring (IRE))
1[3] 4129[10] 4508[2] 5202[P]

Jungle Speed (FR) *F Chappet* 76
3 b c Bungle Inthejungle Velvet Revolver (IRE) (Mujahid (USA))
5589[9]

Jungle Warfare (IRE) *Richard Hannon* a55
3 ch g Bungle Inthejungle Fanditha (IRE) (Danehill Dancer (IRE))
316[9] 1549[12]

Junior Rip (IRE) *Roger Charlton* a79 70
3 b g Rip Van Winkle(IRE) Sarawati (IRE) (Haafhd)
2101[7] 2941[2] 3418[2] 3777[8] 5249[7] (5946) 6393[2] (7452) 7816[6]

Juniors Dream (IRE) *Ivan Furtado* a31 22
3 gr g Holy Roman Emperor(IRE) Lagoa (FR) (Dark Angel (IRE))
3860[9] 4608[6] 5477[11] 8469[12]

Juniors Fantasy (IRE) *Tim Easterby* a56 60
3 b g War Command(USA) Natural Choice (Teofilo (IRE))
1979[6] 2943[2] 3684[2] 4488[4] 4915[2]◆ 5272[3]◆ 5817[8] 6342[8]

Junius Brutus (FR) *Ralph Beckett* a96 101
3 ch g Cockney Rebel(IRE) Tricked (Beat Hollow)
2826[8] 4422[2]◆ 5932[9] 6476[19] 7187[8] 7913[7] 8851[2] 9571[5]

Junkanoo *Gary Moore* 72
2 b c Epaulette(AUS) Bahamian Music (IRE) (Bahamian Bounty)
5665[9] 7339[4] 8657[2]

Junoesque *John Gallagher* a58 73
5 b m Virtual Snake Skin (Golden Snake (USA))
(1936) 3038[4] (3691) (4426) 5138[3] (5881) 6566[3] 7200[5] 8519[4]

Junooh (IRE) *Sir Michael Stoute* a69 89
3 b g Le Havre(IRE) Mumayeza (Indian Ridge (IRE))
1852[5]◆ 6887[2] (7543) 8260[2]◆

Junvieve (FR) *Richard Hannon* a67 68
2 b f Orpen(USA) Tengeline (FR) (Cardoun (FR))
5189[11] 5733[6]◆ 6106[2] 6504[4]

Jupiter *Alexandra Dunn* a55 60
4 b g Finjaan Medicea Sidera (Medicean)
86[7] 1328[8] 2513[10] 2930[6] 4481[3] 5083[8] 5430[3] (5675) 6529[3] 7236[4] 7812[6] 8223[8] 8757[6] 9629[10]

Jupiter Custos (FR) *Michael Scudamore* a49 49
7 b g Le Havre(IRE) Angel Rose (IRE) (Definite Article)
5271[13] 6115[7]

Jupiter Road *Nigel Tinkler* a80 88
3 b g Charm Spirit(IRE) Thankful (Diesis)
5557[8] 6209[5] 6541[5] 6973[4] 8515[13]

Jus Pires (USA) *Declan Carroll* a89 90
5 b g Scat Daddy(USA) Liza Lu (USA) (Menifee (USA))
7872[2]◆ 8727[10] 9066[5]

Just A Formality (FR) *C Escuder* a76 86
5 bb h Spirit One(FR) Formalite (FR) (Equerry (USA))
5035a[12]

Just A Minute *Steph Hollinshead* a42 43
4 b m Poet's Voice Inaminute (IRE) (Spectrum (IRE))
1397[9] 2361[8] 9011[9]

Just An Idea (IRE) *Roger Ingram* a57 54
5 b g Lilbourne Lad(IRE) Emreliya (IRE) (Danehill Dancer (IRE))
144[11] 383[11] 1682[5] 2235[7] 2693[2]◆ 5302[8] 6174[12] 6682[7] 7603[5] 7977[3] 8408[2] 9185[7] (9439)

Justanotherbottle (IRE) *Declan Carroll* 102
5 ch g Intense Focus(USA) Duchess K (IRE) (Bachelor Duke (USA))
2775[13] 4402[12]◆ 5664[5] 6351[9] (6724) 7193[10] 7433[23]

Just Another Idea (IRE) *Mandy Rowland* a9 29
4 ch g Casamento(IRE) Emreliya (IRE) (Danehill Dancer (IRE))
2698[12] 5053[11]

Just A Penny (IRE) *Doug Watson* a98 67
7 b g Kodiac Privet (IRE) (Cape Cross (IRE))
425a[7]

Just A Rumour (IRE) *Noel Wilson* a46 41
3 gr f Bungle Inthejungle Rectify (IRE) (Mujadil (USA))
2871[9] 4439[4] 5099[12] 5558[10] 5904[6] 6174[16]

Just A Touch (IRE) *Jane Chapple-Hyam* a51
3 gr f Alhebayeb(IRE) Mary Pekan (IRE) (Sri Pekan (USA))
8894[5] 9032[8] 9425[6]

Just Because *M Bouckaert* a51 46
7 b g Mawatheeq(USA) Muwakaba (USA) (Elusive Quality (USA))
9537a[13]

Just Benjamin *William Haggas* a63 92
3 b g Epaulette(AUS) Desert Royalty (IRE) (Alhaarth (IRE))
1171[8] 1344[2] (2284) (3358)◆ 4063[2]

Just Brilliant (IRE) *Peter Chapple-Hyam* a81 80
4 b h Lope De Vega(IRE) Mauresmo (IRE) (Marju (IRE))
1517[2] 2207[7] 4249[9]

Just Call Me Ella *Rebecca Menzies* a37 44
2 ch f Iffraaj Daughter Dawn (IRE) (New Approach (IRE))
6971[7] 7304[9] 8021[9]

Just Champion *John Flint* 3
3 b g Dunaden(FR) Koliakhova (FR) (Literato (FR))
4774[7]

Justfirstlady (IRE) *J-C Rouget* a80 87
3 b f Siyouni(FR) Just Little (FR) (Grand Slam (USA))
7360a[12]

Just For The Craic (IRE) *Neil Mulholland* a59 45
4 b g Most Improved(IRE) Beziers (IRE) (Fasliyev (USA))
1038[4]◆ 1426[5] 2206[11] 3936[7] 5629[11] 6273[10] 8249[10]

Just Glamorous (IRE) *Grace Harris* a57 85
6 ch g Arcano(IRE) Glamorous Air (IRE) (Air Express (IRE))
2403[2] 3344[11] 3662[2] 4313a[15] 4995[6] 5606[5] 6080[4] 6809[8] 7831[7]

Just Heather (IRE) *John Wainwright* a49 39
5 gr m Zebedee Miss Sundance (IRE) (Desert Sun)
241[13] 607[8] 951[6] 1506[7] 1983[12] 3067[8] 3296[6] 3681[6] 4690[14] 5421[7] 6069[5] 6098[10] 6499[13] 7491[9] 7681[10]

Just Hiss *Tim Easterby* 94
6 b g Lawman(FR) Feather Boa (IRE) (Sri Pekan (USA))
2105[3] 2873[6] 3515[2] 4097[8] 5398[3]

Just Hubert (IRE) *William Muir* a89 95
3 b g Dunaden(FR) La Tulipe (FR) (Authorized (IRE))
1911[6] 2562[4] 4559[3] (4729) (5347) 6471[5] (7209) 7864[5] 8754[6]

Justice Lady (IRE) *Robert Cowell* a82 81
6 br m Dream Ahead(USA) Celestial Dream (IRE) (Oasis Dream)
953[6] 2358[6] 2637[6] 3596[6]

Justice Shallow (FR) *Alan Berry*
3 ch g Shakespearean(IRE) Try The Air (IRE) (Foxhound (USA))
2197[18] 2870[12]

Justified *Mark Johnston* 59
2 br g Authorized(IRE) Caribbean Dancer (USA) (Theatrical (IRE))
8244[7] 8857[3] 9063[14]

Justifier (IRE) *G M Lyons* a105 103
2 ch c Free Eagle(IRE) Pale Orchid (IRE) (Invincible Spirit (IRE))
(5997a) 6430a[5] 7879a[2] 8574a[3]

Just Jean (IRE) *Micky Hammond* 61
2 b f Society Rock(IRE) Yashila (IRE) (Indian Haven)
3512[2] 4032[5] 4517[9] 6458[7]

Just Later *Amy Murphy* a62 68
3 b g Equiano(FR) Lucky Legs (IRE) (Danehill Dancer (IRE))
4218[4] 4874[5] 5531[9] 7189[8] 7685[5] 8068[14]

Justlookatmenow *Karen George*
3 b f Pastoral Pursuits Cassie's Choice (IRE) (Fath (USA))
8013[11]

Just Magic *Tim Easterby* a60
3 ch g Sepoy(AUS) Magic Music (IRE) (Magic Ring (IRE))
9038[5] 9276[3]◆ 9475[7]

Just Martha *John Flint* a56 18
4 b m Sepoy(AUS) Porthcawl (Singspiel (IRE))
3090[10]

Just May *Clive Cox* a44 60
2 br f Lethal Force(IRE) Milly's Gift (Trade Fair)
5794[3]◆ 6800[5] 7569[8]

Just My Type *Roger Varian* 82
3 ch f Iffraaj Sweet Cecily (IRE) (Kodiac)
3080[3] 4554[2] 6418[7]

Just Norman *Paul D'Arcy* 60
2 b g Sepoy(AUS) Nurai (Danehill Dancer (IRE))
4564[10] 5145[5] 5624[10] 6372[10]

Just Once *Mrs Ilka Gansera-Leveque* a60 64
3 b f Holy Roman Emperor(IRE) Nur Jahan (IRE) (Selkirk (USA))
20[5] 977a[6] 1979[8] 3208[8] 3777[2] 6039[3]◆ 7240[3] 7643[8] 9216[4] 9609[4]

Just Proud (FR) *S Wattel* a25 54
3 b g Rajsaman(FR) Haut La Main (IRE) (Beat Hollow)
4357a[5]

Just Right *John Flint* a40 48
4 ch m Medicean Rightside (High Chaparral (IRE))
2733[6] 2998[6] 4232[6] 4498[6] 7271[7] 9312[13]

Just Sherry (IRE) *Edouard Monfort* a87 100
4 b m Intense Focus(USA) Crafty Notion (IRE) (Viking Ruler (AUS))
(6820a)

Just That Lord *Michael Attwater* a92 90
6 ch g Avonbridge Lady Filly (Atraf)
(791) 1394[6] 1839[5] (2030) 3344[16] 3993[5] 4458[2] 8867[6] 9131[3]◆ 9389[4] 9458[8]

Just The Man (FR) *Clive Cox* a97 94
3 bz g Rajsaman(FR) Yachtclubgenoa (IRE) (Teofilo (IRE))
1754[3] 2569[3] 3647[3] (5341)◆ 5861[2] 7342[5] (8701)◆ 9055[13] (9388) 9667[5]

Just Wait (IRE) *Mark Johnston* a63 84
4 b m Teofilo(IRE) Winesong (IRE) (Giant's Causeway (USA))
1525[4] 1848[8] (2819) 3054[5] 3861[12]

Just Wonderful (USA) *A P O'Brien* 112
3 b f Dansili Wading (IRE) (Montjeu (IRE))
2443[6] 3115[7] 4051[8] 5586[5] **7221a**[3] *7920a*[7] 8772a[5]

Just You Wait *Charlie Appleby* 79
3 b g Dubawi(IRE) Speirbhean (IRE) (Danehill (USA))
1417[6] **2113**[3] 2845[4]

Juthoor (IRE) *E Charpy* a61 88
4 ch g Shamardal(USA) Dehbanu (IRE) (King's Best (USA))
1748a[15]

Kaafy (IRE) *Grant Tuer* a66 65
3 b g Alhebayeb(IRE) Serene Dream (Oasis Dream)
2794[8] 3964[5] 5236[2] **5620**[2] 5985[8] 6608[6]◆ 7047[2] 7486[4] 7703[7] *8083*[3] *8712*[11]

Kachumba *Rae Guest* a49 82
4 b m Mayson Native Nickel (IRE) (Be My Native (USA))
1932[4] 2365[3] 3185[3] 4473[8] (4751) 5380[7] (5805) 6567[9] **(7205)**

Kachy *Tom Dascombe* a119 113
6 b h Kyllachy Dubai Bounty (Dubai Destination (USA))
(563)◆ ***(1919)*** 3084[5] 4094[3]

Kadar (USA) *Michael J Maker* 98
3 bb c Scat Daddy(USA) Kaloura (IRE) (Sinndar (IRE))
1831[4] **6994a**[7]

Kadiz (IRE) *Paul George* a43 49
3 b f Lope De Vega(IRE) Looby Loo (Kyllachy)
186[2] *388*[3] *831*[4] 2276[6] 3665[10] *4642*[11] *6737*[9] *7784*[7]

Kadrizzi (FR) *Dean Ivory* a80 73
6 ch g Hurricane Cat(USA) Kadiania (FR) (Indian Rocket)
158[4] ***381***[2] *1164*[7] 1561[9] *2124*[4] 2628[3] 3255[3]

Kaeso *Nigel Tinkler* 106
5 b g Excelebration(IRE) Bahia Breeze (Mister Baileys)
1694[9] 2116[2] 2609[3]◆ (3069) 3863[9] 4403[12] **(5173)** **5413**[2]

Kafee (IRE) *Andrew Balding* 47
2 b c Make Believe Dream Date (IRE) (Oasis Dream)
8516[11]

Kafeel (USA) *Alexandra Dunn* a47 55
8 b g First Samurai(USA) Ishraak (USA) (Sahm (USA))
248[8] *760*[10] ***1328***[5]◆ 4797[4] 5081[14] *6317*[8] *8257*[6]

Kafoo *Michael Appleby* a58 47
6 b g Dansili Nidhaal (IRE) (Observatory (USA))
1880[5] *3989*[5] *4195*[4] *4589*[9] 5100[5] *5633*[6] *7282*[12]

Kaftan *G M Lyons* a93 91
3 b f Dansili Sense Of Pride (Sadler's Wells (USA))
8734a[8]

Kahala Queen (IRE) *Roger Varian* a63
3 b f Shamardal(USA) Whazzis (Desert Prince (IRE))
(7912)

Kahina (IRE) *Hugo Palmer* a58 58
3 b f Camelot Close Regards (IRE) (Danehill (USA))
2262[5] **(2930)** 4071[9]

Kahpehlo *John Bridger* a33 58
2 b f Helmet(AUS) Anosti (Act One)
3076[5] 3695[6] 4114[8] 6118[9] *6837*[7] **7203**[5]

Kailyn (GER) *M Krebs* a76 76
6 bb m Manduro(GER) Kaziyma (FR) (Daylami (IRE))
4859a[4]

Kairos (ITY) *Andrea Marcialis* 64
2 gr f Kingston Hill Siendra (IRE) (Refuse To Bend (IRE))
7799a[9]

Kaiser Soze (FR) *G Botti* 71
3 b c Camelot Rugosa (Oasis Dream)
1450a[4]

Kaizer *Alistair Whillans* a57 66
4 ch g Nathaniel(IRE) Perse (Rock Of Gibraltar (IRE))
968[7] 3247[7] 3680[7] 4515[9] 5277[3]◆ 6933[5] 7492[4] **(7739)** *9093*[6]

Kajaki (IRE) *Kevin Ryan* a61 81
6 gr g Mastercraftsman(IRE) No Quest (IRE) (Rainbow Quest (USA))
1666[4] 2326[5] 4983[6]

Kalagia (IRE) *Mark Johnston* a82 85
4 b m Kodiac Esuvia (IRE) (Whipper (USA))
5095[4]◆

Kalani Rose *Mrs A Corson* 19
5 b m Sixties Icon Dance To The Blues (IRE) (Danehill Dancer (IRE))
2004a[5] 2673a[6] 3174a[4] **4175a**[3] 4684a[7] 6009a[3] 6555a[7]

Kalaya (IRE) *Archie Watson* a37 60
3 b f Thewayyouare(USA) Kalabaya (IRE) (Sinndar (IRE))
2195[4] 2690[10] 3254[3] **3886**[4] *4998*[7] *5648*[8] 6098[4]

Kalfu *Clive Cox* a42
2 b f Pivotal Synergy (FR) (Victory Note (USA))
5733[10]

Kalimotxo *William Knight* a48
2 b f Equiano(FR) Royal Ivy (Mujtahid (USA))
9385[7] ***9668***[9]

Kalk Bay (IRE) *Michael Easterby* a61 59
12 b g Hawk Wing(USA) Politesse (USA) (Barathea (IRE))
4078[14] **4319**[7]

Kall To Alms *Stef Keniry* 7
3 b g Dick Turpin(IRE) Lady Amakhala (Val Royal (FR))
7704[7]

Kaloor *Brian Meehan* 98
3 b g Nathaniel(IRE) Blinking (Marju (IRE))
1737[3] 2523[7] 3042[6] 4256[5] 6917[3] 7459[6]

Kalsara *Andrew Balding* a75 75
2 b f Muhaarar Kalsa (IRE) (Whipper (USA))
5342[5] ***(6072)*** **7412**[2]

Kameko (USA) *Andrew Balding* a117 111
2 bb c Kitten's Joy(USA) Sweeter Still (IRE) (Rock Of Gibraltar (IRE))
(5345) 6727[2]◆ 7691[2] ***(8716)***◆

Kamikaze Lord (USA) *John Butler* a76 62
3 ch c First Samurai(USA) Le Sang Royale (USA) (Henrythenavigator (USA))
1857[12] 2835[10] *5000*[5] *5647*[6] ***6350***[4] *7519*[4] *8221*[6] *8496*[9]

Kamra (USA) *Michael Appleby* a83 78
5 b g Stay Thirsty(USA) Milliondollarbill (USA) (Speightstown (USA))
361[3] *832*[5] ***9387***[2]◆ *9549*[8]

Kamran (GER) *Henk Grewe* a49 44
2 rg c Outstrip Konigin Shuttle (GER) (Big Shuffle (USA))
6196a[7]

Kanderas *H-A Pantall* a95 93
3 b g Rip Van Winkle(IRE) Kheshvar (IRE) (Shamardal (USA))
2027a[7]

Kannapolis (IRE) *Michael Easterby* a76 77
4 b g Makfi Alta Definizione (IRE) (Hawk Wing (USA))
1418[8] 2057[3] 3305[5] **4728**[2] 5725[3] 6370[5] 7074[6] *(8300)*

Kanuka (FR) *J Reynier* 97
3 b f Footstepsinthesand Spirit Of Pearl (IRE) (Invincible Spirit (IRE))
8377a[8]

Kapono *Roger Fell* a82 82
3 b g Kuroshio(AUS) Fair Maiden (JPN) (Carnegie (IRE))
342[8] *1219*[6] *1360*[6] 2635[18] 3508[3] ***(4335)*** 4436[7] 4603[3] **5459**[2] 5953[4] 7781[3]

Karaginsky *S Seemar* a86 60
4 ch g Dubawi(IRE) Belenkaya (USA) (Giant's Causeway (USA))
634a[3]

Karak (USA) *Wesley A Ward* 87
2 b f Karakontie(JPN) Down The Well (IRE) (Mujadil (USA))
3988[15]

Karam Albaari (IRE) *J R Jenkins* a62 78
11 b h King's Best(USA) Lilakiya (IRE) (Dr Fong (USA))
1078[6]

Karankawa (USA) *H-F Devin* 75
2 b f Karakontie(JPN) Southbound (USA) (Southern Image (USA))
8483a[4]

Karasheni (IRE) *Iain Jardine* 69
3 ch g Poet's Voice Karasiyra (IRE) (Alhaarth (IRE))
7493[8]

Karawaan (IRE) *G M Lyons* a91 98
5 b g Sea The Stars(IRE) Magic Sister (Cadeaux Genereux)
(1308a)

Karbayane (FR) *W Walton* a49 73
6 b m Air Chief Marshal(IRE) Karbayouna (FR) (Kouroun (FR))
7223a[2]

Kareena Kapoor (USA)
Simon Crisford a75 71
3 ch f More Than Ready(USA) Tabreed (Sakhee (USA))
(211) 2874[6]

Karibana (IRE) *Richard Hughes* a78 76
2 b c Hallowed Crown(AUS) Queen Wasp (IRE) (Shamardal (USA))
6927[3] 7611[3] *8494*[2]

Karisoke *Simon Crisford* a69 71
3 b g Lope De Vega(IRE) In The Mist (Pivotal)
6701[3] *7373*[4] 8006[4] *9165*[3]

Karlarina (FR) *M Nigge* 79
2 b f Le Havre(IRE) Karsabruni (FR) (Speedmaster (GER))
9123a[2]

Karlsburg (FR)
Carlos Fernandez-Balcones 85
5 bl h Sageburg(IRE) Yes My Love (FR) (Anabaa (USA))
4418a[8]

Karlstad (FR) *Mme Pia Brandt* a63 86
4 b g Stormy River(FR) Kill The Crab (IRE) (Petorius (IRE))
6521a[2] 7536a[4]

Karnavaal (IRE) *Sir Michael Stoute* a85 81
3 b g Dubawi(IRE) Qareenah (USA) (Arch (USA))
1857[6] 2746[5] 3858[7] ***5945***[2]

Karsador *M Rolland* a60 70
4 gr g Kendargent(FR) Karsabruni (FR) (Speedmaster (GER))
992a[4] 3140a[6]

Karynia (FR) *J Parize* a63 63
6 ch m Footstepsinthesand Keisha (FR) (Green Tune (USA))
6031a[9]

Kasaman (FR) *M Delzangles* 103
3 b c Charm Spirit(IRE) Kasatana (IRE) (Hernando (FR))
3904a[4] **4963a**[7] 6385a[10]

Kasbaan *Michael Appleby* a105 82
4 br g Dansili Aghareed (USA) (Kingmambo (USA))
2563[12] *(6841)*◆ *(6964)* 8062[4] ***8892***[2] ***9309***[3] *9587*[5]

Kasbah (IRE) *Adrian McGuinness* a75 67
7 b g Acclamation Dance Hall Girl (IRE) (Dansili)
307a[4]

Kaser (IRE) *David Loughnane* a90 73
4 b g Invincible Spirit(IRE) Lethal Quality (USA) (Elusive Quality (USA))
345[4] *617*[7] *5055*[7] 6210[5] *(6686)* 7185[6] *7610*[7] *(8197)*◆ *9041*[8] *9255*[3] ***(9628)***

Kashagan *Archie Watson* a88 82
3 b g New Approach(IRE) Card Shop (USA) (Chester House (USA))
(2375) 2845[5] 4136a[11] 5694[2] 6044[6] ***(7773)***

Kashgar (SWE) *Roy Arne Kvisla* a76
5 b h Eishin Dunkirk(USA) Angels' Share (SWE) (Most Welcome)
7494a[6]

Kashid (USA) *J J Lambe* a35 44
4 b g Elusive Quality(USA) Fiesta Lady (ARG) (Southern Halo (USA))
7087a[6]

Kashmirella (IRE)
Eve Johnson Houghton 63
2 ch f Camacho Pashmina (IRE) (Barathea (IRE))
6118[7] 7203[7]

Kasperenko *Clive Cox* a67 56
5 b g Archipenko(USA) Jardin (Sinndar (IRE))
4053[17]

Kassab *Peter Chapple-Hyam* 71
2 ch c Exceed And Excel(AUS) Homily (Singspiel (IRE))
4564[5] 5059[5] **6807**[4] 7391[3]

Kastasa (IRE) *D K Weld* 113
3 b f Rock Of Gibraltar(IRE) Kasanka (IRE) (Galileo (IRE))
(7216a) **(7717a)**

Kasuku *Ralph Beckett* a30 54
3 b f Delegator Hobby (Robellino (USA))
2210[9] 3574[6] *5808*[11] **(6531)** 7240[7]

Katara (FR) *Sir Michael Stoute* 54
2 b f Deep Impact(JPN) Asyad (IRE) (New Approach (IRE))
8093[10]

Katelli (IRE) *Richard Fahey* a57
2 br g Dragon Pulse(IRE) Kateeva (IRE) (Statue Of Liberty (USA))
9393[9] ***9514***[8]

Kates Star *Christine Dunnett* a19 24
2 b f Casamento(IRE) Naady (Mawatheeq (USA))
6858[11] **7346**[12] *9159*[12]

Katheefa (USA) *Ruth Carr* a97 57
5 gr g Street Cry(IRE) Wid (USA) (Elusive Quality (USA))
24[6] *214*[8] *317*[8] *498*[3] *610*[8] *970*[6] *1366*[2] *(1522)* 1976[7] *(2194)*◆ *2515*[6] *(3301)*◆ 3706[12] *4379*[3] *5266*[4] *5942*[2] *6319*[8] ***(9549)***

Katherine Place *Bill Turner* a61 42
4 b m Showcasing Folly Drove (Bahri (USA))
6285[2] 6797[2] *7468*[5] *7628*[6] *(7784)* *8450*[2] ***(9169)*** ***9583***[2]

Kath's Boy (IRE) *Tony Carroll* a54 59
5 b g Bushranger(IRE) Elayoon (USA) (Danzig (USA))
476[6] ***(926)*** *1162*[3] *1364*[6] *2527*[6]

Kath's Lustre *Richard Hughes* a64 67
4 b m Dick Turpin(IRE) It's Dubai Dolly (Dubai Destination (USA))
2729[4] 4556[5] 5107[6] 6605[7] *7690*[7] *8501*[8] *(8896)* *9386*[3]

Kathy *Scott Dixon* a17 23
4 b m Bated Breath Lolita Lebron (IRE) (Royal Applause)
1527[9] *2196*[11]

Katiba (IRE) *D K Weld* 98
2 b f Footstepsinthesand Katiola (IRE) (Oratorio (IRE))
8356a[3]

Katie Gale *Robyn Brisland* a69 68
9 b m Shirocco(GER) Karla June (Unfuwain (USA))
(40) *947*[8] *1196*[5] *1429*[4] *2351*[6] *2528*[3]

Katie Lee (IRE) *Henry Candy* a83 66
4 b m Camacho Katherine Lee (IRE) (Azamour (IRE))
(54)

Katie O'Hara (IRE) *Samuel Farrell* a23 19
3 ch f Born To Sea(IRE) Cochin (USA) (Swain (IRE))
1984[5] ***2550***[11] 3182[9] 4244[13]

Katie Or (FR) *F Vermeulen* a64
4 b m Orpen(USA) Katika (FR) (High Yield (USA))
2264a[2]

Katiesheidinlisa *Tom Dascombe* 86
3 b f Camelot Spritza (IRE) (Spectrum (IRE))
(1739) **(2399)** 2562[10] 3800[5] 5332[2] 6124[7] 6893[4] 7682[10]

Katinka (FR) *Archie Watson* 71
4 b m Siyouni(FR) Gribatune (FR) (Green Tune (USA))
(1849)

Katiymann (IRE) *M Halford* a93 92
7 b g Shamardal(USA) Katiyra (IRE) (Peintre Celebre (USA))
5711a[5] 6693a[14]

Katniss Everdeen (IRE)
Richard Spencer 65
2 b f Camacho Luanas Pearl (IRE) (Bahri (USA))
6078[3]◆ 6458[4]

Katoki Karwin *Mlle A Wattel* a53 54
3 ch g Compton Place Odense (USA) (Medaglia d'Oro (USA))
4959a[3] ***5408a***[6]

Kattani (IRE) *D K Weld* a84 87
3 b g Tamayuz Katiola (IRE) (Oratorio (IRE))
6693a[17]

Katzoff (IRE) *Richard Hannon* a73
2 b c Mastercraftsman(IRE) Loved (IRE) (Galileo (IRE))
8999[4] *9323*[2]

Kavadi *Hughie Morrison* a60 57
2 b f Siyouni(FR) Ensemble (FR) (Iron Mask (USA))
6949[6] 7826[7] ***8602***[11]

Kavakney (BEL) *Gerard Aidant* a68 35
3 b c Cockney Rebel(IRE) Kavasole (FR) (Kavafi (IRE))
868a[8]

Kavora *Micky Hammond* a54 45
4 b m Havana Gold(IRE) Anadiya (FR) (Bahri (USA))
210[9] ***809***[2] 2298[13]

Kawkabba (USA) *P Monfort* a64 64
3 gr f Oasis Dream Wid (USA) (Elusive Quality (USA))
993a[8]

Kayat *David Simcock* a65 49
2 b g Intrinsic Red Kyte (Hawk Wing (USA))
5381[8] ***5856***[5] *6704*[7]

Kayenne (FR) *C Escuder* a93 97
7 ch m Air Chief Marshal(IRE) Victorian Dancer (IRE) (Groom Dancer (USA))
5168a[4]

Kayewhykelly (IRE) *Julie Camacho* a65 67
2 ch f Dragon Pulse(IRE) Meduse Bleu (Medicean)
3702[3] 4516[3] *5856*[4] **6653**[2]◆ *7419*[4]

Ka Ying Star *A S Cruz* 114
4 b g Cityscape Casual Glance (Sinndar (IRE))
9379a[9]

Kaylen's Mischief *D J Jeffreys* a43 57
6 ch g Doyen(IRE) Pusey Street Girl (Gildoran (IRE))
3205[7] (3740) 3941[3]◆ **(5378)** *6077*[8]

Kay Sera *Tony Newcombe* a57 45
11 b g Kayf Tara Inflation (Primo Dominie)
2698[10] **4498**[4]◆ 5290[7]

K Club (IRE) *J Hirschberger* a85 92
3 b f Kodiac Big Boned (USA) (Street Sense (USA))
57[5] *261*[5] *1340a*[6] **2137a**[3] **6270a**[3] 6519a[7] **8376a**[4] 8983a[13]

Keats (IRE) *A P O'Brien* 73
2 b c Galileo(IRE) Airwave (Air Express (IRE))
8721[4]

Keep Busy (IRE) *John Quinn* a63 96
2 b f Night Of Thunder(IRE) Look Busy (IRE) (Danetime (IRE))
2184[3] 3927[2] (4238) (4647) 6542[6] 7117[7] 7399[4] 7679[2] 7896[5] 8724[4] **(8970a)**

Keeper's Choice (IRE)
Denis Coakley a43 69
5 ch m Intikhab(USA) Crossing (Cape Cross (IRE))
2797[3] 4226[13] 4902[10] 6084[6] 6469[10] *8652*[12]

Keep It Country Tv *Pat Phelan* a47 51
3 ch g Archipenko(USA) Monda (USA) (Cozzene (USA))
400[6] 3410[9] *4029*[9] 6049[8] **7027**[4] *9384*[7] *9659*[11]

Keep Me Company (IRE)
James Fanshawe 93
3 b g Fast Company(IRE) Chirkova (USA) (Sadler's Wells (USA))
(3648)◆

Keep On Fly (IRE) *A Botti* 107
3 ch g Rip Van Winkle(IRE) So Many Shots (IRE) (Duke Of Marmalade (IRE))
(2887a) **4173a**[3]

Keep On Laughing (IRE)
John Butler a38
4 b m Henrythenavigator(USA) Outshine (Exceed And Excel (AUS))
5004[11] *6074*[12] ***6316***[8] *6885*[13] *7371*[7]

Keepup Kevin *Pam Sly* a64 80
5 b g Haafhd Black Salix (USA) (More Than Ready (USA))
(3215) **(4207)** 5303[5] 6326[7] 7540[4] *8495*[8]

Keith *Rod Millman* a51 51
3 b g Rip Van Winkle(IRE) Serenity Spa (Excellent Art)
2140[6] 2932[6] *3593*[13] 3888[5] 6805[8] **8003**[3] ***8406***[3] *8644*[3] *8843*[3]

Kelinda Dice *Mick Quinn* a55 25
2 b f Hot Streak(IRE) Dora's Sister (IRE) (Dark Angel (IRE))
2020[6] 5906[8] ***9195***[8] *9407*[6]

Kelis (IRE) *Heather Main* a38
3 ch f No Nay Never(USA) Apple Spirit (USA) (Lemon Drop Kid (USA))
8467[10] ***9038***[7] ***9368***[6]

Kellington Kitty (USA)
Mike Murphy a53 53
4 bb m Kitten's Joy(USA) Keeping Watch (IRE) (Danehill (USA))
116[4] *485*[7] *717*[5] *1477*[3] *2066*[6] 2728[7] 3410[10] 5806[3] **(6199)** *6889*[6] *7420*[8] *8123*[10] 8638[4]

Kelly's Dino (FR) *K R Burke* a101 112
6 b g Doctor Dino(FR) Sabolienne (FR) (Marchand De Sable (USA))
1017[2] *1428*[2] 1947[6] 4102[2] (4646) 4933[5] **(5909)**◆ 6473[19] 7218a[8]

Kelsey's Cross (USA)
Patrick L Biancone 102
3 b f Anthony's Cross(USA) Amy's Allie (USA) (Trippi (USA))
5645a[3] 8139a[7]

Kelydor (FR) *F Foresi* 59
2 gr f Kendargent(FR) Liberty Island (FR) (Statue Of Liberty (USA))
5166a[5]

Kemble (IRE) *Richard Hannon* 98
2 b f Kodiac Cherrington (IRE) (Lope De Vega (IRE))
1833[3]◆ (2686) 4048[18] 4861[5] 5976a[2] 6474[6] 6907[9] **8088**[4]

Kemmeridge Bay *Grant Tuer* a26 28
3 b f Coach House(IRE) Bookiesindexdotnet (Piccolo)
26[7] *341*[10] 7737[9] ***8920***[3] *9034*[9]

Kenava (FR) *J-P Gauvin* a71 67
3 ch f Kendargent(FR) Lana (GER) (Montjeu (IRE))
7505a[9]

Kenbaio (FR) *P Bary* a92 100
3 gr c Kendargent(FR) Baia Chope (FR) (Deportivo)
1780a[3] 2564a[8] **5714a**[3] 8141a[9]

Ken Colt (IRE) *F Chappet* 108
4 b g Kendargent(FR) Velvet Revolver (IRE) (Mujahid (USA))
2667a[3] 4205a[3] **(5471a)** 7943a[16]

Kendergarten Kop (IRE)
David Flood a75 65
4 ch g Kendargent(FR) Elsa T (IRE) (Duke Of Marmalade (IRE))
(4378) 4873[2] ***(5309)*** *6317*[4] ***7560***[2] *7839*[7] *8070*[10] 8413[9] *8702*[3]

Kendred Soul (IRE) *Jedd O'Keeffe* 71
2 ch f Kendargent(FR) Champion Place (Compton Place)
4125[7] 4727[3] 5294[2] **(6064)** 7046[2] 7679[8]

Kenfaro (FR) *Yannick Fouin* 51
3 gr c Kendargent(FR) Zamfara (Azamour (IRE))
2311a[6]

Kenica (IRE) *K R Burke* 57
3 b f Camelot Za'hara (IRE) (Raven's Pass (USA))
2505[5] 2875[7] 3553[6]

Kenlova (FR) *P Bary* 97
2 bb f Kendargent(FR) Ice Love (FR) (Three Valleys (USA))
4417a[3] 5469a[3] 7006a[6] 7939a[8]

Kenmare River *Tim Vaughan* a28 60
4 gr g Kendargent(FR) Isabella Glyn (IRE) (Sadler's Wells (USA))
2127[8] 2720[13]

Kennerton Green (IRE) *Lydia Pearce* a36 26
4 b g Rip Van Winkle(IRE) Parvenue (FR) (Ezzoud (IRE))
4475[10] 5106[11]

Kennocha (IRE) *Amy Murphy* a64 62
3 b f Kodiac Of Course Darling (Dalakhani (IRE))
(3442) 4763[2] 5526[9] 6441[6] (7027) 7472[4] 7982[14] 9128[10]

Kenny (GER) *Waldemar Hickst* a64 62
4 b g Santiago(GER) Kinetio (GER) (Three Coins Up (USA))
5115a[4]

Kenny The Captain (IRE) *Tim Easterby* a71 71
8 ch g Captain Rio Kelso Magic (USA) (Distant View (USA))
1760[13] 2201[14] 2824[11] 3221[3] 3503[4] 5723[8] 6373[7] 6680[6] 7065[3] 7511[4] (7591) 7828[16] 8339[4] 9113[2]

Kenoughty (FR) *J Moon* a34 48
3 b g Kendargent(FR) Meandra (IRE) (Dubawi (IRE))
8551[0] 1935[7] 2240[7] 3642a[2] (4687a) 6010a[4] 6554a[6]

Kensai (FR) *Laurent Loisel* a65 65
5 gr h Jukebox Jury(IRE) Olive Danon (IRE) (Dylan Thomas (IRE))
7136a[6]

Kensington Art *Richard Fahey* a72 77
3 b g Dutch Art Lady Luachmhar (IRE) (Galileo (IRE))
1979[3] 2482[4] 3052[5] 3505[4] 4038[6] 4587[2] 5242[2] (6586) (6864) 6924[4] 7830[6] 8635[4]

Ken's Sam's (IRE) *Adrian McGuinness* a68 67
6 b m Intense Focus(USA) Hannah's Smile (IRE) (Cape Cross (IRE))
277[2] 7089a[3]

Kenstone (FR) *Adrian Wintle* a79 87
6 gr g Kendargent(FR) Little Stone (FR) (One Cool Cat (USA))
1955[4] 2691[7] 3575[6] 7125[7]

Kentuckyconnection (USA) *Bryan Smart* a74 68
6 b g Include(USA) Youcanringmybell (USA) (Street Cry (IRE))
214[4] 356[7] (2183) 2898[7] 4148[5] 4523[6] 5517[5] 6665[6]◆ 7305[13] (7820) 9351[6]

Kentucky Hardboot (IRE) *Mick Channon* 58
2 ch g Starspangledbanner(AUS) Fanditha (IRE) (Danehill Dancer (IRE))
4897[7] 5345[7] 5801[5] 6394[11] 6808[2] 7277[12] 7585[13]

Kentucky Kingdom (IRE) *James Evans* a63 40
3 b g Camacho Venetian Rhapsody (IRE) (Galileo (IRE))
20[3] 290[4] 7772[5] 8606[13] 9276[2] 9545[7]

Kenway (FR) *F Rossi* 107
2 ch c Galiway Kendam (FR) (Kendargent (FR))
1448a[2] (6777a) 7940a[7]

Kenwina (FR) *P Bary* 58
3 ch f Kendargent(FR) Ponte Bawi (IRE) (Dubawi (IRE))
7061a[4]

Kenzai Warrior (USA) *Roger Teal* 102
2 bb c Karakontie(JPN) Lemon Sakhee (CAN) (Lemon Drop Kid (USA))
(6905) (8762)◆

Kenzohope (FR) *C Boutin* a53 55
3 gr c Kendargent(FR) Bedford Hope (GER) (Chato (USA))
1741a[8] 6874a[7]

Kenzydancer (FR) *P Sogorb* 44
2 bl c Kendargent(FR) Dime Dancer (IRE) (Azamour (IRE))
7775a[6]

Kepala *Eve Johnson Houghton* a72
2 gr f Mastercraftsman(IRE) Kebaya (Montjeu (IRE))
7832[6] 9163[2]

Kepou (FR) *C Escuder* 52
2 b f Kheleyf(USA) Peaceful Deia (FR) (King's Best (USA))
5166a[7]

Kerascouet (FR) *J-V Toux* a37 66
5 gr g Siyouni(FR) Delvita (FR) (Pinmix (FR))
7800a[4]

Keravnos (FR) *Y Barberot* a80 82
9 b g Elusive City(USA) Kypriano's Angel (FR) (Kendor (FR))
4747a[3]

Kerka (FR) *J-C Rouget* a86 76
3 b f Dansili Kerasona (FR) (Oasis Dream)
5644a[3]

Kermouster *Grant Tuer* a61 76
3 b f Garswood Rise (Polar Falcon (USA))
2635[13] (2870) 3414[6] 3685[3] (5552) (5984)◆ (6624)◆ 7213[7] 7491[7]

Kerosin (GER) *Denis Gerard Hogan* a94 94
8 b g Tertullian(USA) Karavel (GER) (Monsun (GER))
3952[11]

Kerrera *Dean Ivory* a54 53
6 ch m Champs Elysees Questa Nova (Rainbow Quest (USA))
2014[7] 2593[13] 3252[8] (9157) 9456[6]

Kesia (IRE) *John Gosden* a78 87
3 ch f Australia Caserta (Dansili)
(2566)◆ 5190[9] 8671[3]

Keska *Richard Fahey* a45 35
3 b f Iffraaj Imperialistic (IRE) (Imperial Ballet (IRE))
2420[6] 3246[8] 3777[6] 4488[5]

Kestrel Dot Com *Charlie Wallis* a22 29
7 br g Oasis Dream Tanfidh (Marju (IRE))
2977[10] 4226[P]

Keswick *Heather Main* a87 81
5 b g Dansili Marywell (Selkirk (USA))
7567[5] 8024[14] 8658[6] 9050[5] 9285[3] 9480[4]

Ketchup (FR) *Ali Stronge*
3 b f Nathaniel(IRE) Chutney (IRE) (Exceed And Excel (AUS))
8698[13]

Ketil (USA) *P Bary* a82 86
2 b c Karakontie(JPN) Matroshka (IRE) (Red Ransom (USA))
8483a[6]

Ketts Hill *Mohamed Moubarak* 38
3 b g Mayson Grapes Hill (Kingsalsa (USA))
4298[7]

Kew Gardens (IRE) *A P O'Brien* 122
4 b h Galileo(IRE) Chelsea Rose (IRE) (Desert King (IRE))
2560[2] 3314[2] 7246a[2] (8332)◆

Key Bid *A R Al Rayhi* a44 78
5 ch g Dubawi(IRE) Silca Chiave (Pivotal)
172a[3] 396a[4] 959a[4]

Key Choice *Eric Alston* a53 58
3 ch g Iffraaj Strictly Silca (Danehill Dancer (IRE))
3510[11] 4010[11] 4818[2] 6983[5] 7960[12]

Keyhaven *James Fanshawe* a71 69
3 b f Raven's Pass(USA) New Fforest (Oasis Dream)
1492[6]

Key Master (IRE) *R Biondi* 83
4 b m Mastercraftsman(IRE) Maggie Lou (IRE) (Red Ransom (USA))
4170a[6]

Key Player *Eve Johnson Houghton* a87 90
4 ch g Kheleyf(USA) My Pretty Girl (Arakan (USA))
4418 915[2] 1213[8] 1727[4] 2273[12] (3183) 3536[2] 4598[4] 5090[3] 5804[6] (6567) 6968[7] 7563[9]

Keyser Soze (IRE) *Richard Spencer* a109 101
5 ch g Arcano(IRE) Causeway Queen (IRE) (Giant's Causeway (USA))
(176)◆ (805) 1922[5] 3588[6] 4921[14] 6706[11] 7891[10] 9198[4]

Keystroke *Stuart Williams* a109 112
7 b h Pivotal Fondled (Selkirk (USA))
(136) 1103[6] (1853) 4094[12] 5184[3] 6520a[6] 7454[4] 7892[3] 8331[10]

Key To Power *Mark Johnston* a80 81
3 b f Slade Power(IRE) Key To Peace (IRE) (Kheleyf (USA))
(520) 796[2] 1193[3] 1929[4] 2121[3] 2255[3] 2730[4] 3068[8] (3535) 3742[5] 4128[8] (4374) 4759[5]

Key Victory (IRE) *Charlie Appleby* a73 109
4 b g Teofilo(IRE) Patroness (Dubawi (IRE))
51a[12] 285a[4] 514a[8] 961a[11] 3987[15] 4666[4] 5610[13] 6150[10]

Khaadem (IRE) *Charles Hills* 119
3 br c Dark Angel(IRE) White Daffodil (IRE) (Footstepsinthesand)
(2826)◆ 4050[7] 5184[2] (5664) 6959[11] 8331[11]

Khaan *Michael Appleby* a57 52
4 ch h Kheleyf(USA) Sharp Dresser (USA) (Diesis)
2094[13] 2972[3] (3208) 3744[6] 5373[6] 6560[4] 7385[2]

Khabeerah *Roger Varian* a69
3 gr f Dubawi(IRE) Hadaatha (IRE) (Sea The Stars (IRE))
5808[3] 6594[4]

Khafooq *Robert Cowell* a73 73
3 b g Kodiac Al Manaal (Echo Of Light)
1691[2] 2255[5] 3045[9] 3836[2] (4396)

Khafoo Shememi (IRE) *Sir Michael Stoute* a104 106
5 b g Dark Angel(IRE) Appleblossom Pearl (IRE) (Peintre Celebre (USA))
4397[3]◆ 5475[3]

Khagan (IRE) *A Fabre* 105
3 b c Le Havre(IRE) Knyazhna (IRE) (Montjeu (IRE))
2426a[3] 3120a[2] 3904a[3]

Khalaty *James Given* 10
2 b f Poet's Voice Tia Mia (Dr Fong (USA))
4826[15] 5780[12] 6368[17]

Khalhinkha (FR) *Simone Brogi* 42
2 bb f American Post Midnight Miracle (IRE) (Danehill Dancer (IRE))
6060a[6]

Khalifa Sat (IRE) *Andrew Balding* 80
2 b c Free Eagle(IRE) Thermopylae (Tenby)
6905[6] (7562)

Khaloosy (IRE) *Roger Varian* a86
2 gr c Dubawi(IRE) Elshaadin (Dalakhani (IRE))
8424[2] (9136)◆

Khan (GER) *Henk Grewe* 95
5 b h Santiago(GER) Kapitol (GER) (Winged Love (IRE))
2455a[7] 6266a[6] 8391a[4] 8804a[2]

Khanchaym (FR) *M Delcher Sanchez* 70
3 ch f Siyouni(FR) Breath Of Love (USA) (Mutakddim (USA))
1489a[7]

Kharbetation (IRE) *David O'Meara* a63 75
6 b g Dream Ahead(USA) Anna's Rock (IRE) (Rock Of Gibraltar (IRE))
1955[5] 2479[5] 2710[12] 4035[5] 4689[7]

Khatm *Saeed bin Suroor* a44
2 b c Dubawi(IRE) Hawaafez (Nayef (USA))
9415[10]

Khawaatem (USA) *Keith Henry Clarke* a36
4 ch g Smart Strike(CAN) Charmed Gift (USA) (A.P. Indy (USA))
1572a[8]

Khazaf *Ruth Carr* 52
4 b g Dawn Approach(IRE) Winds Of Time (IRE) (Danehill (USA))
1643[8]

Khazix (IRE) *J F Levins* a53 61
4 b g Al Kazeem Burlesque Star (IRE) (Thousand Words)
145[9] 1936[2] 2231[5] 3187[6] 4349[12] 7779[9]

Kheleyf's Girl *Clare Ellam* a25 22
4 br m Kheleyf(USA) Handsome Molly (Halling (USA))
532[10]

Kheros *Archie Watson* a91 86
3 b g Harbour Watch(IRE) Almunia (IRE) (Mujadil (USA))
103[5] 3341[6] 4445[4] 5089[5] 5516[7] (6160)◆ (6925)

Khismet *John Flint* a70 56
6 b m Kheleyf(USA) Bisaat (USA) (Bahri (USA))
1333[13] 3571[5] 6545[7] 6853[2] 7231[10]

Khitaamy (IRE) *Tina Jackson* a25 33
5 b g Approve(IRE) Halliwell House (Selkirk (USA))
2509[14] 3203[12] 3969[10] 4293[9] 4784[9] 5558[14] 7048[13]

Khochenko (FR) *M Nigge* a83 75
4 ch g Pastoral Pursuits Flam (Singspiel (IRE))
1349a[5]

Khuzaam (USA) *Roger Varian* a112 93
3 ch c Kitten's Joy(USA) Afraah (USA) (Hard Spun (USA))
2833[5] 7349[2] (8253) 9064[2]

Kiastep (FR) *Mme E Vibert* a4
2 b f Sidestep(AUS) Kialoskar (IRE) (Refuse To Bend (IRE))
1240a[11] 6386a[9]

Kibaar *Ruth Carr* a47 64
7 b g Pastoral Pursuits Ashes (IRE) (General Monash (USA))
1817[2] 2153[7] 2632[12] 6829[7] 7307[11] 7824[8] 8450[5] 8720[10] 8925[6] 9398[4] 9572[6]

Kickham Street *John Quinn* a64 50
3 ch g Olympic Glory(IRE) Alzanti (USA) (Arch (USA))
813[9] 1275[3] 1954[6] 2708[5]

Kick On *John Gosden* 111
3 b c Charm Spirit(IRE) Marika (Marju (IRE))
(1831) 2411[7] 3390a[9] 4013[13] (6122)◆ 8336[19]

Kick On Kick On *Ian Williams* a91 91
4 b g Swiss Spirit Catmint (Piccolo)
1734[3] 2403[11] 5371[10] 6208[5] 9166[5]

Kidda *Richard Fahey* 78
2 gr g Gutaifan(IRE) Lily Again (American Post)
1758[5] (2288) 2747[6]

Kidd Malibu (USA) *M Al Mheiri* a79 79
6 ch g Malibu Moon(USA) Kiddari (USA) (Smarty Jones (USA))
196a[2]

Kiefer *Eve Johnson Houghton* 94
3 gr g Pour Moi(IRE) Dali's Grey (Linamix (FR))
1756[6] 2142[2] (2796)◆ 4256[2]◆ 5417[3] 6471[7] 8092[14]

Kiev (FR) *Mme Pia Brandt* a84 74
3 ch g Olympic Glory(IRE) Lunashkaya (Muhtathir)
3710a[5]

Kikana (FR) *L Rovisse* a32 61
2 b c Elusive City(USA) Kensita (FR) (Soviet Star (USA))
3562a[6] 5600a[7]

Kilbaha Lady (IRE) *Nigel Tinkler* a71 72
5 b m Elnadim(USA) Sidney Girl (Azamour (IRE))
724[5] 835[3] 1015[2]◆ 1231[3] 1378[4] (1647) 3057[4] (3217) 3957[4]◆ 4371[3] 4627[6] 6663[2] 7074[4] 7835[3] 8300[2]

Kilbarchan (GER) *Mark Johnston* a11 10
3 gr f Jukebox Jury(IRE) Kellemoi De Pepita (Hawk Wing (USA))
7782[11]

Kilconquhar *David O'Meara* a72
2 b c Hallowed Crown(AUS) Passing Stranger (IRE) (Dixie Union (USA))
9008[3] 9195[12] 9514[7]

Kilcoran *Philip Kirby* a43 49
4 ch m Champs Elysees India Spirit (Dr Fong (USA))
100[5]

Kilham *Declan Carroll* 71
2 ch g Pivotal Russian Heroine (Invincible Spirit (IRE))
3290[3] 3810[4] 5485[2] 5913[6] 6653[7] 7904[14]

Kilig *Tim Easterby* a61 61
2 b g Fountain Of Youth(IRE) Today's The Day (Alhaarth (IRE))
2707[2] 3507[5] 4032[7] 5896[6] 7309[2]◆ 7582[4] 7871[6]

Killer Queen *David C Griffiths* a34
4 b m Havana Gold(IRE) Radio Gaga (Multiplex)
621[6] 831[7] 1195[11] 5857[14] 6013[5]

Killing Joke (FR) *R Roels* a50 56
5 bl g Sageburg(IRE) Zanyeva (IRE) (Oasis Dream)
4960a[6]

Killing Zoe (FR) *D Guillemin* a66 78
2 b f Wootton Bassett Pin Up Girl (IRE) (New Approach (IRE))
9605a[3]

Kiloecho (FR) *J-V Toux* a86 88
3 b g Whipper(USA) Ammia (IRE) (Medicean)
2953a[3]

Kilowatt *Tim Easterby* 78
5 ch g Power Bogside Theatre (IRE) (Fruits Of Love (USA))
3250[5] 3816[13]

Kimari (USA) *Wesley A Ward* a101 105
2 b f Munnings(USA) Cozze Up Lady (USA) (Cozzene (USA))
3983[2] 8745a[4]

Kimbear (USA) *Doug Watson* a103
5 b h Temple City(USA) Sky Dreamer (USA) (Sky Mesa (USA))
171a[2] 726a[4] 1440a[4]

Kimberley Girl *Michael Easterby* a59 43
3 b f Heeraat(IRE) Black Baccara (Superior Premium)
1195[10] 1504[10] 2197[8] 3208[6] 4488[8] 4725[11]

Kimblewick (IRE) *John Gosden* a77 85
3 b f Iffraaj Kiyra Wells (IRE) (Sadler's Wells (USA))
1711[2] 2831[8] 4052[15] 5030[6] 6170[6]

Kimbriki *Ed Walker*
3 b g Dansili Cascata (IRE) (Montjeu (IRE))
3445[13]

Kimifive (IRE) *Joseph Tuite* a100 101
4 ch g Born To Sea(IRE) Appletreemagic (IRE) (Indian Danehill (IRE))
1829[12] (2402) 2609[7] 3062a[7] 4299[6] 4650[2] 5413[10] 5664[10] 6445[6] 6950[7] 8016[2]

Kinch (IRE) *J F Levins* a62 65
3 b g Dark Angel(IRE) Lapis Blue (IRE) (Invincible Spirit (IRE))
(4720) 7776[9]

Kindly *Michael Easterby* a80 82
6 b m Kyllachy Touching (IRE) (Kheleyf (USA))
4822[3] 6825[3]◆ 6972[4] 7380[4] 8428[5] 9183[9]

Kind Review *Tracy Waggott* 66
3 b g Kodiac Melodique (FR) (Falco (USA))
3158[2] 3517[6] 3972[6] 4635[3] 5215[5]

Kinetic Cross *Werner Glanz* a65 60
5 b g Cape Cross(IRE) Kinetica (Stormy Atlantic (USA))
4860a[7]

King (GER) *C J M Wolters* a84 105
3 ch c Lord Of England(GER) Kaiserwiese (GER) (Sholokhov (IRE))
2163a[3] 3385a[6]

King Ademar (USA) *Martyn Meade* a74 99
3 bb c Scat Daddy(USA) Parisian Affair (USA) (Mr Greeley (USA))
1690[2] 3471[2]◆ 4016[17] 4738[2] 5193[3]

King And Queen (FR) *Mark Johnston* 72
3 b c Le Havre(IRE) Queen's Logic (IRE) (Grand Lodge (USA))
2519a[9] (4914)◆ (5122)◆ 5473[4]

King Athelstan (IRE) *Gary Moore* a63 67
4 b g Mayson Ashtaroute (USA) (Holy Bull (USA))
2617[6] 3186[3] 3941[10] 4991[7] 6303[5] (7271) 8414[4] 9310[7] (9589)

Kingbrook *Mark Johnston* 90
2 bg c Kingman Warling (IRE) (Montjeu (IRE))
4551[3] (4897)◆ 6352[8] 7197[3]

King Carney *Charlie Fellowes* a70 96
2 ch c Australia Petit Trianon (Dansili)
5848[5] 6664[2] (8028) (8397)

King Christophe (IRE) *Peter Fahey* a61 64
7 b g Duke Of Marmalade(IRE) Mini Brush (USA) (Broad Brush (USA))
2321[0] 2593[4] 3209[2] 5712a[4] 7300[4]

King Cole (USA) *Doug Watson* a65 54
6 ch g Scat Daddy(USA) Volver (IRE) (Danehill Dancer (IRE))
1001[6]

King Crimson *John Butler* a63 76
7 ch g Captain Gerrard(IRE) Elegant Lady (Selkirk (USA))
1817[9] 2515[7] (3188) 3531[12] (3961) 4660[4] 5532[4] 5843[2] 6335[7] 7831[6] 8285[8]

King David (DEN) *Marc Stott* 107
4 b h Elusive City(USA) Jeunesse Lulu (IRE) (Montjeu (IRE))
3902a[2] (4622a) 6144a[6] 7498a[6]

Kingdom Brunel *David O'Meara* a57 74
4 gr g Mastercraftsman(IRE) Messias Da Silva (USA) (Tale Of The Cat (USA))
2246[5] 2785[8] 3216[7] 3704[2] 4131[5]◆ 4762[7]

Kingdom Of Dubai (FR) *Roger Varian* a70 64
3 b g Iffraaj Caprarola (USA) (Rahy (USA))
133[4] 289[4] 785[3] 2021[6] 2597[4] 2965[2] 4071[5] 6439[5] 7083[4]

King Fan *Mark Johnston* 68
2 b c Kingman Forever Times (So Factual (USA))
6622[5]

Kingfast (IRE) *David Dennis* a56 66
4 b g Fast Company(IRE) Monarchy (IRE) (Common Grounds)
(1390) 1680[11] 2111[3] 2970[5] (3571) (4111) 4287[4] 5425[3] 6104[8]

King Gold (FR) *N Caullery* 27
2 gr c Anodin(IRE) Miss Gandelia (FR) (Kingsalsa (USA))
7675a[12]

Kingi Compton *Marian Falk Weissmeier* a65 47
3 b g Compton Place Missprint (Ishiguru (USA))
(287)◆ 854[4] 906[8] 4959a[8]

Kinglami *John O'Shea* a61 67
10 b g Kingsalsa(USA) Red Japonica (Daylami (IRE))
2483[7] 3576[5] 4181[3] 4733[6] 4872[4] 6084[8] (6682) 7115[4] 7576[7] 9247[7]

King Lenox *Nigel Tinkler* 62
2 b g Heeraat(IRE) Tidal (Bin Ajwaad (IRE))
1759[6] 2475[4] 2869[4] 4125[11] 6337[10] 7284[6]

King Leonidas *John Gosden* 85
2 b c Kingman Reem (AUS) (Galileo (IRE))
(8459)◆

King Lothbrok (FR) *A bin Harmash* a74 65
3 b g Elusive City(USA) Madawaska (USA) (Leroidesanimaux (BRZ))
168a[14] 570a[11]

King Malpic (FR) *T Lemer* a101 115
6 gr g King's Best(USA) Sablonniere (FR) (Verglas (IRE))
3289a[2] (4948a) 5716a[12]

Kingmans Spirit (IRE) *David Loughnane* a60
2 b f Kingman Kaabari (USA) (Seeking The Gold (USA))
7769[6] 8865[7] 9409[6]

King Neptune (USA) *A P O'Brien* a86 110
2 bb c War Front(USA) Agreeable Miss (USA) (Speightstown (USA))
2491a[2] 4012[6] 4846[5] 5584[10] 6190a[5] 7119[5] 7693[4] 8745a[11]

King Nonantais (FR) *Andreas Suborics* a76 85
7 ch g Air Chief Marshal(IRE) Castries (IRE) (Captain Rio)
7536a[9] 9537a[3]

King Of Ace (USA) *Peter Wolsley*
5 b h Malibu Moon(USA) Cintarosa (USA) (Grand Slam (USA))
7011a[11]

King Of Arms *John Gosden* a72
2 b c Kingman Marika (Marju (IRE))
8346[2]◆ 9136[6] 9509[3]

King Of Athens (USA) *A P O'Brien* a91 89
2 b c War Front(USA) Together Forever (IRE) (Galileo (IRE))
3949[13] 5665[8] (8709)

King Of Change *Richard Hannon* a79 122
3 b c Farhh Salacia (IRE) (Echo Of Light)
(1690) 2411[2] (7340) (8334)◆

King Of Comedy (IRE)
John Gosden 121
3 b c Kingman Stage Presence (IRE) (Selkirk (USA))
(2023)◆ (3026) 3951[2] 6354[4] 7660[2] 8334[13]

King Of Glory (USA) *Peter Wolsley* a73
4 b g Ghostzapper(USA) Goldfield (USA) (Yes It's True (USA))
7011a[8]

Kingofmerrows (IRE) *Karen Tutty* a66 60
5 br g Kodiac Tamara Gervasoni (IRE) (Namid)
125[10]

King Of Naples *Ruth Carr* a53 65
6 b g Excellent Art Avon Lady (Avonbridge)
63[6] 344[3]◆ 536[3] 793[11] (911) 3162[5] 3568[10] 4054[5] 4513[8] 5003[6] 5851[13] 6502[6] 6860[5]

King Of Rooks *Henry Spiller* a60 83
6 b g Acclamation Slap Shot (IRE) (Lycius (USA))
33[8] 295[6] 701[4]◆ 919[7] 2013[11] 2235[11] 8821[12]

King Of The North (IRE)
Jonathan Portman a64
2 b g Kodiac Scotch Bonnet (IRE) (Montjeu (IRE))
8823[9] 9154[6] 9325[4]

King Of The Ring *Paul Nicholls* 14
3 b g Sepoy(AUS) Anosti (Act One)
3696[10] 4794[12]

King Of The Sand (IRE)
Gary Moore a78 84
4 ch g Footstepsinthesand Lough Mewin (IRE) (Woodman (USA))
86[3] 2360[5] (2928) 3321[4] 4543[9] 6291[3] 7026[4] (7729)

King Of The Throne (USA)
Emmet Mullins a93 70
2 ch c Hard Spun(USA) You Make Luvin Fun (USA) (A.P. Indy (USA))
8716[6]

King Of Tonga (IRE) *David O'Meara* 93
3 gr g Dark Angel(IRE) Bronze Queen (IRE) (Invincible Spirit (IRE))
2054[2]◆ 2559[4] 3357[2] 4403[11] 6425[10] 6922[8] 7362[5] 8101[7] (8766)

King Oswald (USA) *James Unett* a66 61
6 b g Street Cry(IRE) Northern Melody (IRE) (Singspiel (IRE))
125[3] 479[6] 784[3] 1065[11] (1506) 2972[2] 4349[6] 5016[8] 5531[4] 7858[7] 8863[6] 9609[10]

King Ottokar (FR) *Charlie Fellowes* 108
3 b c Motivator Treasure (FR) (Anabaa (USA))
(1737) 2523[4] 4013[3] 6122[5]

King Platin (FR)
Mme C Barande-Barbe a84 99
7 ch h Konig Shuffle(GER) Couture Platine (FR) (Top Waltz (FR))
1244a[6] 9124a[11]

King Power *Andrew Balding* a78 84
3 ch f Frankel Prowess (IRE) (Peintre Celebre (USA))
2087[2] 2618[3] 4171a[10] 6633[3] 7867[4] 8398[4] 9051[4]

King Ragnar *Roger Varian* a77 77
2 b c Hot Streak(IRE) Park Law (IRE) (Fasliyev (USA))
7406[2]◆ 8912[2] (9107)◆

King Robert *Charlie Wallis* a92 82
6 b g Royal Applause Generously Gifted (Sakhee (USA))
254[6] 382[3] 797[2] (1211)◆ 1822[5] 2061[6] 3856[2] 4364[4] 5661[16] 5990[4] 7161[7] 7771[9]

Kings Academy *John Mackie* a36 35
5 ch g Mayson Intrusion (Indesatchel (IRE))
3939[12] 4767[10] 5151[8] 6275[15]

King's Advice *Mark Johnston* a105 118
5 ch h Frankel Queen's Logic (IRE) (Grand Lodge (USA))
(985) (1291)◆ (1596) (1761) (2119) (3078) 4382[6] (4884) (5662) 6473[18] 7158[2]

King's Caper *Mark Johnston* a95 95
2 br c New Approach(IRE) Karen's Caper (USA) (War Chant (USA))
3804[4] 4317[2] (4623) (6226) (6707)◆ 7726[3] 8462[2]

King's Castle (IRE) *William Haggas* 62
2 b c Camelot Kikonga (Danehill Dancer (IRE))
8464[9] 8857[4]

King's Charisma (IRE)
David O'Meara 67
2 b g Teofilo(IRE) Bawaakeer (USA) (Kingmambo (USA))
4623[5] 5512[4] 7285[3] 8259[5]

King's Command *Charlie Appleby* 116
2 b g Dubawi(IRE) O'Giselle (AUS) (Octagonal (NZ))
(4069) 4920[8] 6002a[3] (7887a)

King's Counsel *Daniel Kubler* a67
3 b g Camelot Love Everlasting (Pursuit Of Love)
1419[6] 7689[3] 8500[5]

Kings Creek (IRE) *Alan King* a67 49
2 b g Elusive Quality(USA) Nunavik (IRE) (Indian Ridge (IRE))
5493[7] 7571[9] 8346[5]

King's Field (IRE)
Joseph Patrick O'Brien a106 102
4 b h Kodiac Mimiteh (USA) (Maria's Mon (USA))
173a[9] 2879a[3] 3987[25]

King's Girl *Sir Michael Stoute* a56 76
3 b f Kingman Damaniyat Girl (USA) (Elusive Quality (USA))
2251[2] (3258)

King Shamardal *Mark Johnston* a66 61
3 b c Shamardal(USA) Model Queen (USA) (Kingmambo (USA))
1379[2] 2147[7] 2900[6] 3478[9]

Kings Highway (IRE) *Ivan Furtado* a84
4 b g Shamardal(USA) Bimini (Sadler's Wells (USA))
(4249)

Kingsholm (IRE) *Archie Watson* 67
2 b c Tagula(IRE) Fixed Gaze (USA) (Speightstown (USA))
4394[5]

Kings Inn (IRE) *Paul Nicholls* a59 70
5 b g Mawatheeq(USA) Afnoon (USA) (Street Cry (IRE))
1363[10] 2279[7]

Kingslady *Eve Johnson Houghton*
3 b f Kingman Kazeem (Darshaan)
3761[6]

Kingsley Klarion (IRE) *John Butler* a69 54
6 b g Arcano(IRE) May Day Queen (IRE) (Danetime (IRE))
1715[11] 4025[9] 5629[3] 7552[8] (7837) 9089[7] 9386[5]

King's Lynn *Andrew Balding* 92
2 b c Cable Bay(IRE) Kinematic (Kyllachy)
6464[2]◆ (7119)◆

Kingson (IRE) *Richard Fahey* 76
3 b g Kingman Gaditana (Rainbow Quest (USA))
2058[3] 3957[10] 4663[4] 5245[7] 6209[3] (7512) 8413[8]

King's Pavilion (IRE) *Jason Ward* a81 94
6 b g King's Best(USA) Embassy (Cadeaux Genereux)
1414[8] 1896[10] 2419[8] 3515[4] 4403[3]◆ 4730[6] 5246[5] (5516) 5948[8] 7184[5] (7865) 8096[4]

Kings Royal Hussar (FR) *Alan King* a70 72
3 b g Zebedee Ile Rouge (Red Ransom (USA))
2933[2] 3580[9] 4664[3] 5350[3] 6075[4] 8652[6]

King's Slipper *Clive Cox* a98 92
4 b g Leroidesanimaux(BRZ) Last Slipper (Tobougg (IRE))
(1727) 2419[15] 4255[5] 6964[11] 7686[5] 9041[7]

Kingstar (FR) *Mme Pia Brandt* 101
4 ch h Evasive King's Parody (IRE) (King's Best (USA))
9124a[10]

Kingston Kurrajong *William Knight* a81 84
6 b g Authorized(IRE) Kingston Acacia (King Of Roses (AUS))
2273[4] 2797[9] 3185[2]◆ 4249[2] 4994[3] 5667[6] (6469) (7125) 8197[13] 8253[5]

King's View (IRE) *Richard Hannon* a59 67
2 b g Dark Angel(IRE) Encore View (Oasis Dream)
3760[9] 4388[5] 4992[4] 5781[7] 6792[2] 7155[9] 7754[11] 8650[6]

King's Vow (FR)
Joseph Patrick O'Brien a95 97
3 b g Frankel Seven Magicians (USA) (Silver Hawk (USA))
4136a[2] 6471[12]

Kings Will Dream (IRE)
Chris Waller 111
5 ch g Casamento(IRE) Road Harbour (USA) (Rodrigo De Triano (USA))
8579a[6] 8952a[6]

King Torus (IRE) *Lee Carter* a37 44
11 b g Oratorio(IRE) Dipterous (IRE) (Mujadil (USA))
295[11]

Kinks *Mick Channon* a78 96
3 b g Sixties Icon Crazee Diamond (Rock Of Gibraltar (IRE))
1662[7] 2078[4] 2525[6] 2835[3] 3654[8] 4422[3]◆ 4847[11] (5442)◆ 5932[4] 6222[7] 7002[3]◆ 7397[3]

Kinloch Pride *Noel Wilson* a68 70
7 ch m Kyllachy Pride Of Kinloch (Dr Devious (IRE))
1950[5] 2324[4] 2632[5]

Kinross *Ralph Beckett* a104 101
2 b c Kingman Ceilidh House (Selkirk (USA))
(7899)◆ 8716[5]◆

Kinsman *William Haggas* a77 73
2 ch c Exceed And Excel(AUS) Peeress (Pivotal)
7346[3]◆ (8503)

Kinver Edge (USA) *Charlie Appleby* a87
3 b g Speightstown(USA) Peace Preserver (USA) (War Front (USA))
156[4]◆ 343[2] (827) 1485[4]

Kion (IRE) *Jaber Ramadhan* a79 72
4 ch g Dragon Pulse(IRE) Diamond Duchess (IRE) (Dubawi (IRE))
196a[15]

Kiowa *Philip McBride* a31 35
3 b g Foxwedge(AUS) Colombia (IRE) (Art Connoisseur (IRE))
606[4] 1019[8] 2550[12] 4219[13] 4755[5] 5084[9]

Kipling (IRE) *A P O'Brien* 82
2 b c Galileo(IRE) La Traviata (USA) (Johannesburg (USA))
4886[5]

Kipps (IRE) *Hughie Morrison* a78
2 gr c War Command(USA) Sixpenny Sweets (IRE) (Dalakhani (IRE))
9007[2] (9634)

Kiraleah *Ivan Furtado* a50
3 b f Pastoral Pursuits Jocasta Dawn (Kyllachy)
7822[5] 8467[8] 9416[4]

Kira's Star *Richenda Ford* a31 14
3 b f Denounce Choisirez (IRE) (Choisir (AUS))
7228[5] 7841[9] 8467[12]

Kirkland Forever
Eve Johnson Houghton a57 73
5 ch m Sakhee(USA) Maystock (Magic Ring (IRE))
(1826) 2353[2] 3545[2]

Kirstenbosch *James Fanshawe* a99 92
3 b f Mount Nelson Kassiyra (IRE) (Kendor (FR))
(2912) (4022)◆ 5397[5]

Kirtling *Andi Brown* a62 62
8 gr g Araafa(IRE) Cape Maya (Cape Cross (IRE))
(1334)◆ 2111[12] 5528[9] 6303[3] (6796) 7318[7] 8019[6]

Kiruna Peak (IRE) *Fergal O'Brien* 54
5 ch m Arcano(IRE) Kirunavaara (IRE) (Galileo (IRE))
5795[7] 6853[10]

Kiseki (JPN) *Katsuhiko Sumii* 120
5 bb h Rulership(JPN) Blitz Finale (JPN) (Deep Impact (JPN))
7251a[3] 7941a[7]

Kismat *Alan King* a48 70
4 b m Sepoy(AUS) Magic Destiny (Dubai Destination (USA))
2737[4]◆ 3267[8] 4220[12] 4615[11] 5338[7] 5993[4]

Kissesforeveryone *Andrew Crook* a35 37
4 b m Havana Gold(IRE) Kisses For Me (IRE) (Sadler's Wells (USA))
3162[8] 4004[6] 4915[13]

Kiss For A Jewel (IRE) *D K Weld* 95
3 b f Kingman Sapphire (IRE) (Medicean)
8368a[10]

Kiss Me Forever (FR) *K Borgel* 44
2 b f Soul City(IRE) Voie Des Tsars (FR) (Early March)
5166a[10]

Kitaabaat *David Simcock* a96 93
4 b g Dansili Ausus (USA) (Invasor (ARG))
3027[7] 6596[3] (7199) 7688[3] (8853) 9055[8]

Kitcarina (FR) *Andrew Balding* a81 77
4 b m Shamardal(USA) Kitcat (GER) (Monsun (GER))
(3468) 5419[5] 6050[6] 7165[4]

Kitos *Sir Mark Prescott Bt* a41 47
2 b f Showcasing Cool Question (Polar Falcon (USA))
5733[11] 6028[8] 6548[10] 7234[2] 7582[RR] 8201[8]

Kitten's Dream *Richard Fahey* a65
2 b c Kitten's Joy(USA) Strathnaver (Oasis Dream)
8346[7]

Kitty's Cove *Tim Easterby* a48 57
4 b m High Chaparral(IRE) Juniper Girl (IRE) (Revoque (IRE))
3251[5] 4510[6] 5053[6] 5277[2]◆ 5596[3] 5975[2] (6611) 7070[5] 7381[4]

Kiunguja (FR) *C Plisson* a43 72
4 ch m Linda's Lad Nera Divine (FR) (Divine Light (JPN))
1245a[6]

Klara Spirit (IRE) *R Mike Smith* 4
2 b f Sir Prancealot(IRE) Mokama (Motivator)
6606[11] 7211[8] 7506[9] 7778[10]

Klass Action (IRE)
Sir Mark Prescott Bt a76 71
3 b f Iffraaj Alutiq (IRE) (Kodiac)
182[3] 838[7] 1219[2] 2024[4]

Klassique *William Haggas* a91 108
4 b m Galileo(IRE) Chachamaidee (IRE) (Footstepsinthesand)
2401[2] (3586) 4645[3] 6263a[3] 8333[5]

Klipperty Klopp *Antony Brittain* a62 52
3 ch g Monsieur Bond(IRE) First Harmony (First Trump)
524[2] 931[10] 1084[5] 1486[5] 2016[5] 3271[10] 5304[3] 7335[4] 8301[11] 9139[2] 9289[5] 9470[9]

Klopp *Antony Brittain* a71 60
3 b f Monsieur Bond(IRE) Caranbola (Lucky Story (USA))
215[6] (412) 972[2]◆ 1081[2] 1337[2] 1488[5] 2380[3] 2635[16] (2939) 3508[6] 4330[6] 5056[8] 8924[4] 9113[5]◆ 9397[3]

Klopp Of The Kop (IRE) *Clive Cox* 80
2 ch g Excelebration(IRE) Avomcic (IRE) (Avonbridge)
1733[4] 6375[3] 6911[3] 8459[6]

Kluger (JPN) *Tomokazu Takano* a99 115
7 bb h King Kamehameha(JPN) Addicted (GER) (Diktat)
1783a[2] 8579a[13] 8952a[8]

Klungel (GER) *Markus Klug* 96
4 b h Jukebox Jury(IRE) Konigstochter (GER) (Dai Jin)
2666a[10]

Klute (IRE) *Mrs John Harrington* a89 92
3 br g Kodiac Fonda (USA) (Quiet American (USA))
7222a[17]

Knapsack (IRE) *Clive Cox* a51
2 b f Nathaniel(IRE) Packed House (Azamour (IRE))
9284[5]

Knightcap *Tim Easterby* 73
2 b f Sir Percy Mookhlesa (Marju (IRE))
1759[3] 2052[5] 2906[5] 4727[4] 5296[5] 5789[5] 6064[6] (6272) 6369[2]

Knight Commander *Steve Flook* a65 56
6 br g Sir Percy Jardin (Sinndar (IRE))
566[4] 810[3] 1497[4]◆ 1840[2]◆ 2936[6] 4483[4] 5053[7] 5604[5] 6042[7]

Knight Crusader *John O'Shea* a87 89
7 b g Sir Percy Lac Marmot (FR) (Marju (IRE))
242[3] 562[4] 696[3] (1144)◆ 2254[2] 3044[2] 3467[7] (4614) 5368[6] 8129[7] 8654[3]

Knighted (IRE) *Kevin Ryan* 95
4 b g Sir Prancealot(IRE) Olympia Theatre (Galileo (IRE))
1694[6] 2105[4] 2873[9]

Knightfall *David Lanigan* a62 47
3 b g Nathaniel(IRE) Enchanted (Magic Ring (IRE))
5193[8] 5650[8] 6119[5] 6731[4]

Knightly Spirit *Iain Jardine* a46 63
4 br g Dalakhani(IRE) Elysian (Galileo (IRE))
5156[7] 6343[6] (6578) 7513[8] 7903[3] 8185[3]

Knightshayes *Paul George* 74
3 ch f Mukhadram Today's The Day (Alhaarth (IRE))
2356[7] 3193[3] 4226[15]

Knight Shield (IRE) *William Haggas* 87
2 b c Starspangledbanner(AUS) Three Decades (IRE) (Invincible Spirit (IRE))
(4184) (5339)◆

Knight To Behold (IRE)
Harry Dunlop 117
4 b h Sea The Stars(IRE) Angel Of The Gwaun (IRE) (Sadler's Wells (USA))
2083[2] 3122a[7] 5455[3]

Knockabout Queen *Tony Carroll* a67 72
3 b f Sixties Icon Rough Courte (IRE) (Clodovil (IRE))
1656[12] 2114[10] 2730[6] 3839[14] 4651[9] 5607[4] 5884[RR] 6285[7] 6737[4] (6794) 7022[2] (7172) 7523[4] 8296[4] 9218[9] 9402[10]

Knockacullion (USA)
Richard Hughes a92 77
3 b c Bernardini(USA) Vole Vole Monamour (USA) (Woodman (USA))
5269[3] 6316[3] 6811[2] (7630)◆

Knockacurra (IRE) *Mark Loughnane* a38 26
2 b c Anjaal Ohh Lala (IRE) (Clodovil (IRE))
3595[8] 8297[7] 9036[9]

Knock Annie (IRE) *K R Burke* 59
2 b f Dandy Man(IRE) Knock Twice (USA) (Two Punch (USA))
3469[8] 3968[11]

Knock Knock (IRE) *Sylvester Kirk* a49
2 br g Slade Power(IRE) Knock Stars (IRE) (Soviet Star (USA))
6979[4] 7538[9] 8195[9]

Knockout Blow *John E Long* a64 60
4 b g Lethal Force(IRE) Elidore (Danetime (IRE))
177[3] 286[4] 483[3] 596[7] 920[6] 1179[4] 1328[10] 4219[6] (4749) 5883[4] 6605[10] 7274[8] 8450[4] 8917[7] (9247) (9507) 9670[4]

Knowing *James Fanshawe* a68 83
3 b g Pour Moi(IRE) Wedding Speech (IRE) (Acclamation)
2023[7]◆ 2582[3] 3946[2] (5529)◆ 6323[2] (7126)

Knowing Glance (IRE)
Richard Fahey a73 78
4 b g Kodiac Shauna's Princess (IRE) (Soviet Star (USA))
2418[2] 2899[7] 3649[8] 4365[4] 5488[4] (6037) 9048[4] 9140[3]◆ 9351[9]

Know It All *J P Murtagh* 103
2 b f Lord Kanaloa(JPN) Common Knowledge (Rainbow Quest (USA))
6429a[7] 7742a[3]

Know It's Possible (FR) *H-A Pantall* a61 50
3 b c George Vancouver(USA) Connaissance (IRE) (Choisir (AUS))
421a[14]

Know No Limits (IRE)
Tom Dascombe 87
2 b f Outstrip Singing Field (IRE) (Singspiel (IRE))
2579[3] 3469[4] (3841) 4233[3] (4878) 5683[9] 6713[2]◆ 7140[2] 7904[8]

Kocasandra (IRE) *Archie Watson* a69 76
2 b f Kodiac Sudood (USA) (Shamardal (USA))
2491a[6] 6980[6]◆ 7419[6] 7754[8] 8118[2]

Kodiac Dancer (IRE)
Julie Camacho a51 52
3 b f Kodiac Kaiulani (IRE) (Danehill Dancer (IRE))
2377[4] 3416[4] 4731[10] 5181[5]

Kodiac Express (IRE) *Mike Murphy* a77 71
4 b m Kodiac Excel Yourself (IRE) (Exceed And Excel (AUS))
1814[9] 3303[3] 3856[9] 5843[5] 6288[4] 8895[4] 9135[8] 9257[7]

Kodiac Harbour (IRE) *Paul George* a89 93
4 b g Kodiac Operissimo (Singspiel (IRE))
316[2]◆ (732)◆ 2555[2] (3149) 4399[4]

Kodiac Lass (IRE) *Katie Scott* a68 68
3 b f Kodiac Awwal Malika (USA) (Kingmambo (USA))
(1570) 2340[18] 3323[7] 4248[6] 4831[5] 5941[5] 7084[5] 7573[9] 8436[3] 9396[12]

Kodiac Pride *Sir Mark Prescott Bt* a74 74
3 b g Kodiac Queen Of Mean (Pivotal)
(3218) 4065[3] 9404[7] 9669[10]

Kodiak Attack (IRE) *Sylvester Kirk* a68 79
3 b g Kodiac Good Clodora (IRE) (Red Clubs (IRE))
3302[4] 4116[4] 4396[3] (5960) (6197) 7112[2] 7568[2] 7760[3]◆

Kodicat (IRE) *Kevin Ryan* a66 64
5 b m Kodiac Mimiteh (USA) (Maria's Mon (USA))
2203[10] 2847[4] 3656[4] 4335[5] 4720[2]◆ 5235[3] 5767[3] 7050[7] 7507[2] 8839[12]

Kodi Dream *Roger Fell* a62 70
3 b g Coach House(IRE) Gumhrear (IRE) (Kodiac)
235[8] (524) 585[4] 1084[4] 1486[4] 1720[10] 1980[2] (2337)

Kodiellen (IRE) *Richard Hannon* 65
2 b f Kodiac Newellen (IRE) (Montjeu (IRE))
5906[3] 6159[5] 7297[5]

Kodi King (IRE) *K R Burke* a55 68
3 b g Kodiac Throne (Royal Applause)
1458[5]◆ 1924[6] 2624[4]◆ 3590[10]

Kodi Koh (IRE) *Simon West* a53 52
4 b m Kodiac Laywaan (USA) (Fantastic Light (USA))
120[6] 295[5] 590[9] 1506[9] 2112[4] (2376) 3447[2]◆ 4287[5] 4515[7] 5851[14] 6499[2]◆ 6663[5] 7335[5] 7578[5] 9391[3]

Kodiline (IRE) *David Evans* a61 68
5 b g Kodiac Kris Spring (Kris S (USA))
(91) 260[5] 734[5] 922[7] 1098[10] 1290[7] 1496[8] 1880[11] 2201[7] 2824[8] 3215[7] 5021[2] 5282[5] 6045[4] 7028[8] 8755[10] 8949[9] 9209[6]◆ (9423) 9505[12] 9657[9]

Kodimoor (IRE) *Mark Walford* a43 59
6 b g Kodiac Victoria Lodge (IRE) (Grand Lodge (USA))
2324[9] 2789[4] 3518[5] (4584) (4978) (5430) 6276[2] 6655[5] 7444[9] 7961[12]

Koditime (IRE) *Clive Cox* 96
4 b h Kodiac Eponastone (IRE) (Footstepsinthesand)
3097[5] 4896[15] 5371[7] 5524[8] 6534[8] 6954[13]

Koduro (IRE) *K R Burke* 68
3 b f Kodiac Affability (IRE) (Dalakhani (IRE))
7366[12] 7900[10]

Kodyanna (IRE) *S Wattel* a85 87
3 b f Kodiac Jadanna (IRE) (Mujadil (USA))
1199a[7]

Koeman *Mick Channon* a100 100
5 b g Dutch Art Angelic Note (USA) (The Minstrel (CAN))
2440[3] 2969[2] 4646[7] 5199[7] 5929[4] 6917[6] 7201[2] (7459)

Kohoof *William Haggas* a67
2 b f Tamayuz Nozhar (IRE) (Iffraaj)
6704[4] 8891[4]◆ 9085[3] 9414[8]

Kolding (NZ) *Chris Waller* 114
3 b g Ocean Park(NZ) Magic Star (AUS) (Danzero (AUS))
(8805a)

Kolossus *Michael Dods* a64 73
3 ch g Assertive Bikini (Trans Island)
2510[6] 2896[9] 4977[2] 5215[3] 5724[3] 6338[8] 7311[9]

Kolsche Jung (GER) *Dr A Bolte* a71 70
3 b c Wiener Walzer(GER) Kaiserblumchen (GER) (Platini (GER))
2758a[4]

Kommander Kirkup
Michael Herrington a64 74
8 ch g Assertive Bikini (Trans Island)
2[6] 214[9] 586[13] 705[4] 9113[11] 9352[6] 9518[5]

Komodo (FR) *R Chotard* a83 81
6 b g Le Havre(IRE) Kinlochrannoch (Kyllachy)
5715a[4]

Konchek *Clive Cox* a84 100
3 bl g Lethal Force(IRE) Soar (Danzero (AUS))
2270[3] 2826[11] 4050[8] 5442[4]◆ 7193[19]

Kondratiev Wave (IRE) *Tony Carroll* a88 86
2 ch c Dragon Pulse(IRE) Right Reason (IRE) (Manduro (GER))
8164a[4] 9364[6] 9661[2]◆

Kongastet (FR) *S Wattel* a71 73
2 b c American Devil(FR) Sikkim (FR) (Linamix (FR))
4679a[2] 5713a[8] 6141a[3] 7674a[5]

Konigin *John Berry* a68 65
4 b m Shamardal(USA) Kitty Wells (Sadler's Wells (USA))
38[3] 5824[3]◆ 6371[5] 7318[11] 8347[10] 9049[9] 9336[9]

Konig Platon (GER) *J Hirschberger* 93
3 b c Soldier Hollow Konigin Platina (GER) (Platini (GER))
3385a[8]

Kool And The Gang (IRE)
J Albrecht a79 84
9 b g Elusive City(USA) Knightsbridge (BRZ) (Yagli (USA))
2429a[12]

Koosto (FR) *A Junk* a60 66
4 b g Zanzibari(USA) Kriska (FR) (Kaldou Star)
2647a[12]

Koovers (IRE) *Gay Kelleway* a57 38
2 b g Requinto(IRE) Silk Feather (USA) (Silver Hawk (USA))
5527[6] 5838[6] 6719[6] 7275[10] 7853[10] 8118[11]

Korcho *Hughie Morrison* a76 97
3 b c Toronado(IRE) Locharia (Wolfhound (USA))
(1823) 2828[8] 3548[3] (4188) 4882[2] 5583[6] 7694[20]

Koroneki (IRE) *M Delcher Sanchez* a68 34
3 b g War Command(USA) Alland (IRE) (Teofilo (IRE))
421a[11]

Kosciuszko (IRE) *John Gosden* 94
3 b c Australia Nobilis (Rock Of Gibraltar (IRE))
4842[5] 5541[12] 6917[4] 7459[2] 8098[10]

Koshi *K Kukk* 21
4 b m Kyllachy Espagnolette (Oasis Dream)
2004a[F] 2673a[9] 3174a[2] 3642a[7] 6008a[6]

Kostantina *Olly Williams* a15 48
3 b f Oasis Dream Missy O' Gwaun (IRE) (King's Best (USA))
2148[8] 2802[12] 3882[3] 4628[8] 4990[15] 5648[9] 5915[14]

Koubalibre (FR) *F Head* a57 79
3 ch f Galileo(IRE) Kheleyf's Silver (IRE) (Kheleyf (USA))
2759a[7]

Koukiboy (FR) *F Foucher* a61 67
5 ch g Siyouni(FR) Flaminga Tremp (FR) (Trempolino (USA))
1631a[3]

Kourkan (FR) *J-M Beguigne* 113
6 bb g American Post Kourka (FR) (Keos (USA))
8583a[2] 9124a[8]

Koutsounakos *Mario Hofer* a69 69
4 b g Captain Gerrard(IRE) Saorocain (IRE) (Kheleyf (USA))
2956a[6] 7800a[3]

Koybig (IRE) *David Marnane* a77 83
7 b g Kodiac Amber Nectar (IRE) (Barathea (IRE))
5597a[4] 7089a[5]

K P Dreamin (USA) *Jeff Mullins* a99
2 ch f Union Rags(USA) Litigating (USA) (Point Given (USA))
8747a[8]

K P Slickem (USA) *Jeff Mullins* a67 92
3 b f Include(USA) Queens Plaza (USA) (Forestry (USA))
9637a[7]

Krabi *Tim Easterby*
2 b f Gutaifan(IRE) Miskin Diamond (IRE) (Diamond Green (FR))
2840[14]

Kraka (IRE) *Christine Dunnett* a75 62
4 b g Dark Angel(IRE) Manuelita Rose (ITY) (Desert Style (IRE))
430[4] 759[3] 982[2] 1037[2] (1393) 1565[2] 2107[12] 3207[3] 3868[18] 4307[7] 5352[6] 6132[6] 6631[4] 7552[5] 7986[3] 8435[8] 9337[3] 9498[4] 9622[7]

Krampus (USA) *William Mott* 104
5 b g Shakespeare(USA) Midtown Girl (USA) (Rahy (USA))
5977a[8]

Kranachberg (FR) *J D Hillis*
4 b h Vision D'Etat(FR) Semina (GER) (Mamool (IRE))
2002a[13]

Kraquante *F Chappet* 84
2 b f Bated Breath Desert Image (Beat Hollow)
9059a[4]

Krazy Paving *Olly Murphy* a59 72
7 b g Kyllachy Critical Path (IRE) (Noverre (USA))
161[4] (920) (1335) 2013[7] 9133[11] 9287[12] 9551[10]

Kripke (IRE) *David Barron* a79 88
4 b g Fast Company(IRE) Tranquil Sky (Intikhab (USA))
1644[4]◆ (2291) 2873[5] 4108[2] 5149[5] 5693[9] 6460[7] 6998[8] 7906[2]

Kris Black (IRE) *Kieran P Cotter* a52
6 b g Le Cadre Noir(IRE) Folk Kris (IRE) (Kris Kin (USA))
419a[11] 1553[4]

Krishmaya (IRE) *Adam West* a6 44
2 b f Dandy Man(IRE) Tomintoul Magic (IRE) (Holy Roman Emperor (IRE))
3798[4] 4798[11] 5317[9] 6563[3] 7079[13]

Kronprinz (GER) *Pavel Tuma* a88 105
4 ch h Lord Of England(GER) Kaiserwiese (GER) (Sholokhov (IRE))
173a[5] 515a[13] 637a[5] 847a[9] 3287a[6] 4157a[3] 5230a[9] (7750a) 8786a[4]

Kroy *Ollie Pears* a60 45
5 b g Sleeping Indian Valley Of The Moon (IRE) (Monashee Mountain (USA))
410[4] 1765[7] 2183[9] 3214[9] 8819[11]

Krunch *X Thomas-Demeaulte* a70
3 b f Sea The Stars(IRE) Spinacre (IRE) (Verglas (IRE))
509a[3] 977a[2]

Krystal Crown (IRE)
Andrew Hughes a27 41
2 b f Famous Name Dancing Cosmos (IRE) (Holy Roman Emperor (IRE))
6606[7] 7506[5] 7765[6] 8527[13]

Krystallite *Scott Dixon* a69 52
6 ch m Kheleyf(USA) Chrystal Venture (IRE) (Barathea (IRE))
1023[8] 1507[10]

Kubrick (AUS) *Chris Waller* 106
2 ch c Shooting To Win(AUS) Alcatraz (AUS) (Fastnet Rock (AUS))
8137a[14]

Kudbegood (IRE)
John C McConnell a60 66
4 b g Most Improved(IRE) Orpens Peach (IRE) (Orpen (USA))
8345[4]

Kukulkan (MEX) *Fausto Gutierrez* a106
4 bb h Point Determined(USA) The Real Mayo (USA) (Bernardini (USA))
445a[11]

Kulin Rock (USA) *Michael J Maker* 105
5 bb g Lonhro(AUS) Miracle Moment (USA) (Chester House (USA))
2646a[9]

Kumasi *David O'Meara* a75 50
2 ch c New Approach(IRE) Ghanaian (FR) (Shamardal (USA))
6424[13] 8714[2]◆ 9197[5]

Kunani (USA) *M Al Mheiri* a84 59
5 br g Arch(USA) Sweet Sonnet (USA) (Seeking The Gold (USA))
1322a[5]

Kung Fu *Simon Crisford* 66
3 b g Kingman Cubanita (Selkirk (USA))
1852[6] 2634[8] 4178[P] (Dead)

Kupa River (IRE) *Roger Fell* a82 84
5 b g Big Bad Bob(IRE) Lamanka Lass (USA) (Woodman (USA))
187[2] 347[2] (1016) (1560) 1895[7] 2151[3] (2372) 2679[3] 3179[3] 3813[15] 8921[5] 9348[7] 9476[7]

Kuramata (IRE) *John Gosden* a84
2 b c Australia Blue Kimono (IRE) (Invincible Spirit (IRE))
9415[3]

Kuredu *Julie Camacho* a28
3 b g Intello(GER) Wait It Out (USA) (Swain (IRE))
6941[5]

Kurious *Henry Candy* 105
3 b f Kuroshio(AUS) Easy To Imagine (USA) (Cozzene (USA))
2086[2] 2826[12] (3855) (4665)

Kuwait Currency (USA)
Richard Hannon a106 90
3 ch g Kitten's Joy(USA) Thebignbadestbunny (USA) (Smart Strike (CAN))
1830[7] 2084[6] 4017[16] 5192[4] 5412[5] 5948[5] (6347) 6964[2] (7815) 8222[2] 9003[2] 9309[5] 9666[3]

Kuwait Direction (IRE)
Richard Hannon a74 95
2 b c Kodiac Open Verse (USA) (Black Minnaloushe (USA))
2205[8] 3335[2] 3949[10] 8723[4] 9043[4]

Kuwait Shield *Richard Fahey* a77 73
2 ch g Kyllachy Varnish (Choisir (AUS))
4098[6] 5172[6] 5764[5] (7438)◆ 7874[2]

Kuwait Station (IRE) *David O'Meara* a71 83
3 br g Swiss Spirit Summer Spice (IRE) (Key Of Luck (USA))
2054[6] 2510[8] 3051[3] 3930[5] 4107[4] 4565[3] 5095[5] 5557[4] 6186[7]

Kuwaity *Mohamed Moubarak* a59 58
2 b g Cable Bay(IRE) Broughtons Flight (IRE) (Hawk Wing (USA))
6532[4]◆ 7285[5] 7981[12] 8603[2]

Kvetuschka *Peter Chapple-Hyam* a78 81
3 rg f Mastercraftsman(IRE) Signella (Selkirk (USA))
(1397) 2618[5] 3800[3] 5982[4] 6672[4] 7682[9] 8705[2]

Kwanza *Mark Johnston* a64 69
4 b m Exchange Rate(USA) Kiswahili (Selkirk (USA))
1269[8] 2244[2] 2911[8] 4371[6] (5156) 5899[3] 6500[6]

Kwela *Eve Johnson Houghton* a85 80
3 b f Kodiac Funday (Daylami (IRE))
1687[2]◆ 2204[5] (2904) 4909[6] 5450[7] 6111[3]◆ 6801[4] 7078[3] (7514) (8456) 9054[2] 9424[4]

Kybosh (IRE) *Michael Appleby* a57 9
3 b g Dansili Super Sleuth (IRE) (Selkirk (USA))
2943[3] 3275[11] 8863[3]◆ 9446[3] 9479[5]

Kylie Rules *Ruth Carr* a67 91
4 bl m Aussie Rules(USA) Africa's Star (IRE) (Johannesburg (USA))
(1850) (2057) (2710) (3216) 3552[3] 4626[4] 5246[7] (5693) 6379[16] 6974[7] 7430[3] 7735[5]

Kyllachy Castle *Lynn Siddall* a41 46
3 ch g Kyllachy Amicable Terms (Royal Applause)
3972[11] 4367[7] 5914[11] 6338[5] 8295[6] 8666[10]

Kyllachy Dragon (IRE) *Mark Rimell* a67 65
4 b g Dragon Pulse(IRE) Lafayette (GER) (Artan (IRE))
446 618[6] 1018[6] 8220[8] 8806[7] 9054[11] 9361[2]

Kyllachy Gala *Marco Botti* a93 88
6 b g Kyllachy Tenuta Di Gala (IRE) (Nashwan (USA))
368[7] 1031[7] 2808[11] 3346[11] 3663[7] 8014[3] (8608) 9055[7] 9418[5]

Kyllachy Princess *David Loughnane* a44 44
3 ch f Kyllachy Inagh River (Fasliyev (USA))
1346[11] 1816[10] 2420[5] 2940[8] 3319[5] 4481[12]

Kyllachys Tale (IRE) *Roger Teal* a46 71
5 b m Kyllachy Betray (King's Best (USA))
5071[10] 2714[10] 4067[5] (4870) 5677[7] 6362[5] (7237) 7982[2]◆ 8806[11]

Kyllachy Warrior (IRE)
Lawrence Mullaney a72 73
3 gr g Kyllachy Silver Act (IRE) (Aqlaam)
130[2] 408[5] 2477[2]◆ 3159[11] 4128[7] 6944[3] 8066[3] 8715[4] 9182[3]

Kyllang Rock (IRE) *James Tate* a91 96
5 b g Kyllachy Megec Blis (IRE) (Soviet Star (USA))
1839[6] (6056) 7541[3] 8182[4]

Kyllukey *Charlie Wallis* a52 47
6 b g Kyllachy Money Note (Librettist (USA))
357[5] 834[4] 920[4] 1384[6] (1716) 1987[7] 2066[2] 3001[7] 3143[8] 8901[11] 9411[6] 9457[4]

Kyllwind *Martyn Meade* a72 65
2 b c Kyllachy Trust The Wind (Dansili)
4184[8] 4826[7] 5185[22] (7582) 7980[9]

Kynren (IRE) *David Barron* a76 112
5 b g Clodovil(IRE) Art Of Gold (Excellent Art)
1415[2] 2609[2] 3987[5] 6376[3] 7430[2] (7891) 8336[6]

Kyoto Star (FR) *Tim Easterby* a74 54
5 b g Oasis Dream Hanami (Hernando (FR))
272[6]◆ 754[9] 7053[13] 7439[8] 8515[4]

Kyroc (IRE) *Susan Corbett* a32 64
3 br f Society Rock(IRE) Dispol Kylie (IRE) (Kheleyf (USA))
412[6] 783[6] 1081[6] 2197[17] 7737[12] 7959[14]

Kyvon Des Aigles (FR)
Mme C Barande-Barbe a67 60
4 gr g Style Vendome(FR) Kiva Des Aigles (FR) (Enrique)
1391a[8]

Laafy (USA) *Sir Michael Stoute* a92 96
3 b g Noble Mission Miner's Secret (USA) (Mineshaft (USA))
(2113) 2811[2] 4063[4] 5734[2] (6171) 6955[6] 7866[6]

La Base (IRE) *A Botti* 93
4 ch m Arcano(IRE) Secret Fashion (King's Best (USA))
4170a[4]

La Belle De Mai (FR) *I Endaltsev* 39
3 b f Penny's Picnic(IRE) Rada Angel (IRE) (Le Vie Dei Colori)
4621a[14] 7642a[8]

Labelleepoque (IRE) *V Fazio* 56
2 b f Gale Force Ten Dabousiya (IRE) (Barathea (IRE))
7724a[9]

La Belle Mayson *P Monfort* a56 45
4 ch m Mayson Excellent Show (Exceed And Excel (AUS))
4532a[3]

Labrega *Hugo Palmer* a90 62
4 b m Cacique(IRE) Postale (Zamindar (USA))
2064[3] 2608[9] 4108[11]

Lacan (IRE) *Michael Bell* a42 57
8 b g New Approach(IRE) Invincible Isle (IRE) (Invincible Spirit (IRE))
34[9] 962[5] 1269[5] 2006[2] 2797[8] 4067[11] 4566[8] 6058[11] 6605[9] 8207[6] 9456[8]

La Canche (FR) *Carina Fey* 98
4 bb m Le Havre(IRE) L'Authie (FR) (Linamix (FR))
1827a[7] 2782a[8]

Laccario (GER) *A Wohler* 115
3 b c Scalo Laccata (Lomitas)
(3674a) (4707a) 6771a[3] 7862a[2]

Lacento (IRE) *A Wohler* 83
3 b c Harbour Watch(IRE) Night Party (IRE) (Dansili)
2163a[10]

La Chica Lobo *Lisa Williamson* a43 57
2 b f Captain Gerrard(IRE) Senora Lobo (IRE) (Amadeus Wolf)
5280[7] 5635[5] 6029[6] 6585[5]◆ 7853[8]

La Cumparsita (IRE)
Tristan Davidson a57 56
5 b m Papal Bull Silk Slippers (Oasis Dream)
1083[3]◆ (1478) 1967[2] 3716[12] 4725[9] 5051[5] 5852[12] 7286[17]

Ladies First *Michael Easterby* a61 89
5 b m Monsieur Bond(IRE) Forever Bond (Danetime (IRE))
2809[7] 3867[5] 4278[5] 5030[4] (5458) 6998[13] 7366[2] 8130[3]

La Dragontea *Michael Bell* 61
2 b f Lope De Vega(IRE) La Concorde (FR) (Sadler's Wells (USA))
8758[9]

Lads Order (IRE) *Michael Appleby* a71 53
3 b g Lilbourne Lad(IRE) Maid To Order (IRE) (Zafonic (USA))
21[4]

Ladweb *John Gallagher* a45 70
9 ch g Bertolini(USA) Adweb (Muhtarram (USA))
2206[10] 2709[7] 3576[2]◆ 3961[7] 4307[6] 5986[8]

Lady Adelaide (IRE) *Roger Charlton* a83 71
3 b f Australia Confusion (FR) (Anabaa (USA))
2445[4] 8519[7] 9050[6] 9418[4]

Lady Alavesa *Michael Herrington* a76 70
4 b m Westlake Matilda Peace (Namaqualand (USA))
(202)◆ 460[3] 1063[5] 1387[3] 1688[2] 2612[4] 3276[5] 4007[2] 6025[5] 6230[2] 7491[5] 7682[2] 8247[8] 9109[8]

Lady Aria *Michael Bell* a93 79
3 b f Kodiac Dot Hill (Refuse To Bend (IRE))
2319[5]◆ 8115[8] 8983a[15]

Lady Athena (FR) *Y Durepaire* 106
4 b m Redoute's Choice(AUS) Monblue (Monsun (GER))
1627a[12]

Lady Bergamot (FR)
James Fanshawe a92 91
5 gr m Mastercraftsman(IRE) Mahima (FR) (Linamix (FR))
1927[8] 2822[3] 3995[2] 7688[7] 8710[5]

Lady Bowthorpe *William Jarvis* a77 86
3 b f Nathaniel(IRE) Maglietta Fina (IRE) (Verglas (IRE))
5650[5] (6283) 7341[2] 8463[2]

Lady Calcaria *Tim Easterby* a71 80
3 b f Mayson Ride The Wind (Cozzene (USA))
(1894) 2293[3] (3293) 3719[7] 3935[3] 4330[3] 4822[5] 5399[2] 7613[11] 8025[9]

Lady Camelot (IRE) *Philip Kirby* 61
4 b m Camelot Queen Jock (USA) (Repent (USA))
5849[8] 6924[7]

Lady Carduros (IRE)
Michael Appleby a45 15
5 b m Byron Saranjo (IRE) (Carrowkeel (IRE))
4589[12] 5528[15] 6059[13] 6529[10] 8915[5] 9220[5]◆ 9403[4]

Lady Celia *Richard Fahey* a49 60
2 b f Mayson Fairy Shoes (Kyllachy)
4509[4] 5294[9] 5788[5] 7029[8] 7734[8]

Lady Codee *Michael Attwater* a62
2 b f Coach House(IRE) Lady Prodee (Proclamation (IRE))
6852[6] 7547[10] 8453[7] 9568[6]

Lady Cosette (FR) *Harry Dunlop* a79 63
3 b f Wootton Bassett Faviva (USA) (Storm Cat (USA))
320[3] 884[2] 2618[7] 3012[9] 4653[5] 6111[8]

Lady Dancealot (IRE)
David Elsworth a101 90
4 b m Sir Prancealot(IRE) Mayorstone (IRE) (Exceed And Excel (AUS))
2442[9] 2809[8] 3164[3]◆ 3815[3] 4560[3] 5143[7] 5628[3] 6319[3] 6908[3] 7467[2] 8851[3] (9088) 9301[6] (9660)

Lady Dandy (IRE) *Ivan Furtado* a32
2 b f Dandy Man(IRE) Rupa (IRE) (Acclamation)
8198[10] 8865[11] 9097[10]

Lady Dauphin (IRE)
Charlie Fellowes a73 77
3 b f Bungle Inthejungle Chateau Dauphin (USA) (First Defence (USA))
(5969) 6559[3] 7350[3] 8692[7]

Lady Eleanor *James Fanshawe* a72
2 ch f Iffraaj Firenze (Efisio)
8454[10] 9159[3]

Lady Elysia *Harry Dunlop* a33 54
3 ch f Champs Elysees Lost In Lucca (Inchinor)
2771[13] 3035[3] 3889[7] 4998[8] 5987[6] 7202[6] 8916[14]

Lady Erimus *Kevin Ryan* a22 62
2 b f Due Diligence(USA) Orapids (Oratorio (IRE))
1642[12] 2476[8] 3954[4] 5296[11] (5912) 6969[12] 7626[8]

Lady Fanditha (IRE) *Clive Cox* 74
2 b f Kodiac Lady Ro (Showcasing)
(2248) 2805[11]

Lady Florence (IRE)
Malcolm Saunders a14
2 b f Zebedee Lady Caprice (Kyllachy)
6078[10] 6330[11] 7569[9]

Lady G (IRE) *William Haggas* 73
2 b f Golden Horn Hikari (IRE) (Galileo (IRE))
8510[4]

Lady Galore (IRE) *C Ferland* 96
2 b f Raven's Pass(USA) Green Diamond Lady (USA) (Johannesburg (USA))
(5116a) 6791a[5] 8140a[7]

Lady Georgie (IRE)
John C McConnell 86
2 b f Lawman(FR) Jeritza (Rainbow Quest (USA))
8165a[6]

Lady Greta (IRE)
Adrian McGuinness a58 26
3 b f Morpheus Greta D'Argent (IRE) (Great Commotion (USA))
341[9]

Lady Gwhinnyvere (IRE)
John Spearing 19
5 b m Sir Prancealot(IRE) Johar Jamal (IRE) (Chevalier (IRE))
3304[13]

Lady In France *K R Burke* a70 104
3 b f Showcasing Sacre Coeur (Compton Place)
(2377) 3587[2] 4205a[4] (7401) 8648a[8]

Lady Isabel (IRE) *Alan Bailey* 72
2 b f Hallowed Crown(AUS) Meanwhile (IRE) (Haafhd)
8202[3] 8758[11]

Lady Jane Wilde (IRE) *John M Oxx* 87
2 ch f Dragon Pulse(IRE) Lastdanceforme (IRE) (Danehill Dancer (IRE))
7215a[6] 8164a[6]

Lady Joanna Vassa (IRE)
Richard Guest a33 35
6 ch m Equiano(FR) Lady Natilda (First Trump)
2678[12] 3933[11] 4493[7] 4685a[5] 5491[9] 6574[9] 7651[11] 7737[7]

Lady Kaya (IRE) *Ms Sheila Lavery* 111
3 b f Dandy Man(IRE) Kayak (Singspiel (IRE))
(1601a) 2443[2] (Dead)

Lady Kermit (IRE) *Archie Watson* a90 91
2 b f Starspangledbanner(AUS) Empress Theodora (Dansili)
(1513)◆ (1923) 2805[3] 3333a[4] 4398[3]

Ladykiller (GER) *A Wohler* 106
3 ch c Kamsin(GER) Lady Jacamira (GER) (Lord Of England (GER))
(8171a) 8792a[9]

Lady Kinsale *Eric Alston* 12
3 gr f Farhh Night Haven (Night Shift (USA))
2897[10] 3417[10] 4508[7]

Lady Kyria (FR) *Philip Kirby* a63 61
5 b m Holy Roman Emperor(IRE) Segesta (IRE) (Vettori (IRE))
6038[5] 7048[8] 7441[8] **8343**[2]

Lady Latte (IRE) *K R Burke* 51
2 b f Anjaal Cappuccino (IRE) (Mujadil (USA))
5988[7] **7067**[7]

Lady Lavender (ITY)
Sebastiano Guerrieri a79 53
2 ch f Le Vie Infinite(IRE) Pietracamela (ITY) (Blu Air Force (IRE))
8791a[9]

Lady Lavinia *Michael Easterby* a48 50
3 b f Burwaaz El Molino Blanco (Royal Applause)
1980[5] **2904**[3] **3191**[2] 3414[9] 4554[4] 4785[9] 5389[6] *6024*[3] 7443[13] *8469*[5]

Lady Lawyer (USA) *John Gosden* a99 91
3 b f Blame(USA) Profess (USA) (War Front (USA))
4597[2] *(5268)* ***(5944)*** 7657[9]

Ladyleys Beluga *K R Burke* a74
2 b f Showcasing Terse (Dansili)
9607[3]

Lady Light *Michael Bell* 92
2 ch f Showcasing Bird Key (Cadeaux Genereux)
(8431)◆ **8724**[3]◆

Lady Lizzy *K R Burke* a65 73
3 ch f Rio De La Plata(USA) Elzebieta (IRE) (Monsun (GER))
2935[5] 5030[5] 5844[5] **6624**[3] 7288[5]

Lady Lynetta (IRE) *Richard Hughes* 80
2 b f Tamayuz Cristal Fashion (IRE) (Jeremy (USA))
5772[3] 6831[4] **(7695)**

Lady Madison (IRE)
Richard Hughes a89 89
3 b f No Nay Never(USA) Sparkling Rock (IRE) (Rock Of Gibraltar (IRE))
(2210) 4052[22] 4865[8] ***6721***[3] 7657[13]

Lady Magda *Jonathan Portman* a66
2 b f Sir Percy Alice's Dancer (IRE) (Clodovil (IRE))
8651[5] *9052*[7]

Lady Makfi (IRE) *Johnny Farrelly* a61 52
7 b m Makfi Dulcet Tones (IRE) (Singspiel (IRE))
(185) *1022*[7] *1196*[6] *1429*[3] *2196*[13] *3205*[6]

Lady Marigold (IRE)
Eve Johnson Houghton a67 68
4 b m Intense Focus(USA) Peace Lily (Dansili)
138[5] *366*[9]

Lady Mascara *James Fanshawe* a66 79
3 b f Cacique(IRE) Avon Lady (Avonbridge)
1336 *1288*[4] *2018*[5]◆ 2933[4] 4664[2] 5349[3] **(6304)** 6902[2] 7682[6]

Lady Maura (IRE) *J P Murtagh* a67 58
2 b f Muhaarar Mathuna (IRE) (Tagula (IRE))
7876a[5]

Lady Mayhem (IRE) *Roger Fell* a49 42
3 b f Zebedee Novelina (IRE) (Fusaichi Pegasus (USA))
4488[10]

Lady Mazie (IRE)
Dominic Ffrench Davis a52 58
3 ch f Excelebration(IRE) Blessing Box (Bahamian Bounty)
3409[3] 4235[5]

Lady Melody (IRE) *David O'Meara* a51 59
2 b f Kodiac Hope And Faith (IRE) (Zebedee)
3927[5] *9251*[5] *9607*[5]

Lady Minx *Edouard Monfort* a60 57
2 b f Planteur(IRE) Nouf (FR) (Invincible Spirit (IRE))
6386a[2]

Lady Monica *John Holt* a18 66
3 b f Bated Breath Sina (GER) (Trans Island)
(2624)◆ 3189[9] 3884[8] 5622[4] **6120**[4] 6569[7]

Lady Morpheus *Gary Moore* a52 56
3 b f Morpheus Tatora (Selkirk (USA))
2926[12] *4244*[2] **(5092)** 5806[2] 6897[16] *8822*[12] *9439*[3]

Lady Muk *Steph Hollinshead* a21 52
3 b f Mukhadram Green Poppy (Green Desert (USA))
2524[9] **3680**[4] *4768*[12] 6624[7] 8003[9]

Lady Natasha (IRE)
James Grassick a31 49
6 b m Alfred Nobel(IRE) Hot To Rock (IRE) (Kalanisi (IRE))
3847[9] 5012[6] 6200[6] 6556[4] **6853**[3] 7231[11] *9204*[11]

Lady Navarra (IRE) *Gay Kelleway* a59 58
3 ch f Iffraaj Natural Flair (USA) (Giant's Causeway (USA))
4189[5] ***4592***[7] 6371[4] *7280*[8]

Lady Nectar (IRE) *Ann Duffield* a58 65
2 b f Zebedee Mitchelton (FR) (High Chaparral (IRE))
6254[3] 6822[3] 6997[6] ***8841***[4]◆

Lady Ninja (USA) *Richard Baltas* a104
5 bb m Majesticperfection(USA) Dressed To Kill (USA) (Formal Gold (CAN))
8769a[8]

Lady Of Aran (IRE) *Charlie Fellowes* a87 87
4 b m Sir Prancealot(IRE) Tipperary Boutique (IRE) (Danehill Dancer (IRE))
1955[7] *4023*[9] 4552[3] *5651*[4] *6350*[2] 6916[10] **(7380)** 7613[10] ***8456***[3] *9424*[2]

Lady Of Authority *Richard Phillips* a59 33
4 b m Kheleyf(USA) Miss Authority (Authorized (IRE))
2071[2] *7923* *1390*[8] *2127*[2] ***(2698)*** *2970*[8] 6599[10]

Lady Of Mercia *John Flint* 49
3 b f Dunaden(FR) Ambella (IRE) (Dark Angel (IRE))
4774[4] **5578**[7] 6043[7] 7985[11]

Lady Of Shalott *David Simcock* 96
4 b m Camelot Silent Act (USA) (Theatrical (IRE))
2822[2]◆ 3336[5] **(4391)** 6223[4] 7201[3]

Lady Of York *Chelsea Banham* a55 47
5 b m Sir Percy Parsonagehotelyork (IRE) (Danehill (USA))
587 *363*[14] *1334*[10] 6599[5] ***6843***[4] *7685*[8] *8406*[6] *8916*[8]

Lady Olenna (IRE) *R P Cody* 85
3 ch f Lope De Vega(IRE) Luce (IRE) (Sadler's Wells (USA))
6090a[13]

Lady Parma (USA) *S Seemar* a94 35
3 br f Exchange Rate(USA) Angle (USA) (Dynaformer (USA))
510a[3]◆ 956a[10]

Lady Pauline (USA) *Wesley A Ward* a85 86
2 ch f Munnings(USA) D'Wildcat Speed (USA) (Forest Wildcat (USA))
2267[2]

Lady Pendragon *Martin Smith* 59
2 b f Camelot Arthur's Girl (Hernando (FR))
5588[9]

Lady Penelope (IRE)
Joseph Patrick O'Brien 101
2 ch f Night Of Thunder(IRE) Step Sequence (Nayef (USA))
7400[2] **8140a**[4] 8970a[5]

Lady Phyllis *Michael Attwater* a58 43
2 b f Coach House(IRE) Lady Phill (Avonbridge)
6047[3] 6852[5] ***7546***[4]◆ *8452*[12] *9407*[8]

Lady Prancealot (IRE)
Richard Baltas a69 104
3 b f Sir Prancealot(IRE) Naqrah (IRE) (Haatef (USA))
6993a[6] **(9637a)**

Lady Quickstep (IRE) *Gay Kelleway* 81
2 b f Sir Prancealot(IRE) Quick Sketch (IRE) (Excellent Art)
(2282) 2805[15] **3156**[2] 3564[4]

Lady Red Moon *Marco Botti* a74 74
2 b f Havana Gold(IRE) Sparkling Montjeu (IRE) (Montjeu (IRE))
3776[4] 4366[3] *5052*[4] *(5885)* **(6221)** ***7548***[3] *9608*[6]

Lady Reset *David Evans* a51 79
3 ch f Yorgunnabelucky(USA) Reset City (Reset (AUS))
(2355) **(2719)** 3153[4]

Lady Rouda (IRE) *Philip Kirby* a45 46
3 b f Swiss Spirit Jida (IRE) (Refuse To Bend (IRE))
4487[7] 5389[11]

Ladysane (FR) *J Boisnard* a83 74
2 b f Dabirsim(FR) Lady Anouchka (IRE) (Vettori (IRE))
7925a[4]

Lady Sarah *Tony Carroll* 17
2 ch f Mukhadram Atyaab (Green Desert (USA))
7406[14] **7981**[13]

Lady Scathach (IRE) *T G McCourt* a48 61
4 b m Zoffany(IRE) Lady Aoy (IRE) (Indian Haven)
4851[3]

Lady Scatterley (FR) *Tim Easterby* a64 74
3 ch f No Nay Never(USA) Camdara (FR) (Hawk Wing (USA))
4285[10] 4628[2] 5156[2] 5334[2] 5785[5] 6500[5] 7704[3] *8020*[4] **(8398)**

Lady Schannell (IRE) *Marco Botti* a63 59
3 b f Teofilo(IRE) Royal Guinevere (Invincible Spirit (IRE))
1142[3]◆ *1838*[9] *2598*[6] 3258[5] *4247*[11]

Lady Sebastian *Jason Ward* 8
3 b f Morpheus Starburst (Fantastic Light (USA))
3218[7] **4520**[8] 5336[7]

Lady Shanawell (IRE) *Ben Haslam* a55 32
3 ch f Lord Shanakill(USA) Lukes Well (IRE) (Shirocco (GER))
5855[3]◆ ***6982***[3]

Lady Sidney (FR)
R Le Dren Doleuze a93 98
5 b m Mr. Sidney(USA) Marechale (FR) (Anabaa (USA))
682a[5] **1627a**[3] 2167a[7]

Lady's Maid (USA) *A Fabre* a80 48
3 b f More Than Ready(USA) Lady Samuri (USA) (First Samurai (USA))
1512a[7]

Lady Snazz (USA) *S Seemar* a40 41
3 ch f Curlin(USA) Redaspen (USA) (Bianconi (USA))
1742a[10]

Lady Steps *Jim Goldie* a61
3 ch f Equiano(FR) Millsini (Rossini (USA))
2377[6] 3176[6]

Lady Stormborn (IRE)
Andrew Slattery 96
3 b f Camelot Chiming (IRE) (Danehill (USA))
8784a[8]

Lady Tati (IRE) *David Simcock* a51 37
2 b f Charm Spirit(IRE) Melodique (FR) (Falco (USA))
6047[4] 8431[8]

Lady Te (GER) *Carina Fey* a86 94
3 b f Tertullian(USA) Lady Luck (GER) (Monsun (GER))
1626a[3] 2889a[11] 3676a[7]

Lady Walli (FR) *Gianluca Bietolini* a52 70
3 ch f Anodin(IRE) Lady Sadowa (Nayef (USA))
7138a[10]

Lady Wannabe (IRE) *J A Stack* 104
3 b f Camelot Wannabe Better (IRE) (Duke Of Marmalade (IRE))
2661a[8] **4411a**[4] 5075a[2] 7242a[7]

Lady Wedad (USA) *Doug Watson* a67
3 b f Elusive Quality(USA) Up The Street (USA) (Street Cry (IRE))
48a[9]

Lady Wolf *Rod Millman* a53 57
3 b f Kuroshio(AUS) Angry Bark (USA) (Woodman (USA))
695[5]◆ ***(802)*** *1066*[7] *1332*[4] *1770*[7]

Lady York (IRE) *Charlie Wallis* a46 51
4 b m Vale Of York(IRE) Brave Truth (IRE) (Brief Truce (USA))
1383[10]

Lafilia (GER) *Giuseppe Fierro* a57 64
4 b m Teofilo(IRE) Labrice (Dubawi (IRE))
1369[10] *1617*[5] *2217*[9] 2720[5] 4036[6] 4777[3] 4869[2]◆ *5001*[3] **5301**[2] 5513[3] *9134*[5] *9275*[10]

La Foglietta *Ralph Beckett* a74 68
2 ch f Lope De Vega(IRE) Mamma Morton (IRE) (Elnadim (USA))
8100[7] *9163*[6]

Lafontaine (FR) *Sylvester Kirk* a50 46
2 b f Canford Cliffs(IRE) Moma Lee (Duke Of Marmalade (IRE))
3257[12] 3694[7] 4222[7] *7516*[5] *7910*[U] *8061*[4] *(8824)* ***9037***[2]

La Force (GER) *Patrick Gallagher* a109 95
5 bb m Power La Miraculeuse (GER) (Samum (GER))
8775a[10]

La Fortuna *Charlie Wallis* a76 71
6 b m Zamindar(USA) Hyperspace (Dansili)
1712[5] *3303*[6] 3596[5] 4253[6] **5013**[2] 6335[3] *7447*[6]

La Fripouille (FR) *K Borgel* 64
2 b f Evasive's First(FR) Paroledefripouille (FR) (Marchand De Sable (USA))
5166a[3]

L'Age D'Or *Robert Cowell* a44 49
4 b m Iffraaj Goleta (IRE) (Royal Applause)
4027[8]

Lagenda *Liam Bailey* a58 65
6 b g Dick Turpin(IRE) Whirly Dancer (Danehill Dancer (IRE))
2106[11] 2964[9] 3730[6] *4195*[10] (6937) **(7207)** 7738[6] 8186[11] *9047*[12] *9361*[7] *9503*[7]

Laguna Spirit *Pat Phelan* a43 21
3 ro f Swiss Spirit Laguna Belle (Dutch Art)
141[7] *855*[8] *1515*[9]

Lahessar *George Scott* a49 70
3 b c Exceed And Excel(AUS) Burlesque Star (IRE) (Thousand Words)
65[6]

Lahore (USA) *Phillip Makin* a87 102
5 br g Elusive Quality(USA) Nayarra (IRE) (Cape Cross (IRE))
2061[8] 3501[6] 5217[5]◆ (5740) 6229[6] **6676**[2] 7431[11] 8127[5]◆ 8512[6]

Lah Ti Dar *John Gosden* 116
4 b m Dubawi(IRE) Dar Re Mi (Singspiel (IRE))
(2776) 3314[6] 4430a[3] 6377[3] 7926a[4] 8589a[4]

Laieth *Saeed bin Suroor* a95 101
4 b g Dubawi(IRE) First City (Diktat)
280a[3] *513a*[14] ***(2803)***◆ 3308[4] *3991*[8]

Laikaparty (IRE) *Archie Watson* 81
2 ch g Havana Gold(IRE) Raggiante (IRE) (Rock Of Gibraltar (IRE))
4798[2] **5381**[2] 6300[2] (6852) 7904[16]

Lairig Ghru *Micky Hammond* a70 70
2 b g Canford Cliffs(IRE) Word Perfect (Diktat)
7619[3] ***8084***[3] *9107*[6]

Laith Alareen *Ivan Furtado* a53 79
4 b g Invincible Spirit(IRE) Bewitchment (Pivotal)
5444[5] 6332[8] *8267*[10] *9203*[12]

La Java Bleue (FR) *C Escuder* 51
2 bb f Tin Horse(IRE) Dark Beauty (Singspiel (IRE))
6060a[5]

Lake Alexandrina (IRE) *A Fabre* a59 74
3 ch f Australia Fountain Of Peace (USA) (Kris S (USA))
2759a[9]

Lakeland Magic (IRE) *Grant Tuer*
2 b g Magician(IRE) Thewandaofu (IRE) (Clodovil (IRE))
8395[11]

Lake Lucerne (USA) *John Gosden* a45
2 b f Dubawi(IRE) Round Pond (USA) (Awesome Again (CAN))
9437[7]

Lakeside (FR) *T Mercier* 18
4 b m Harbour Watch(IRE) Parcimonie (Nombre Premier)
5762a[8]

Lakeview (IRE) *David Loughnane* a71 48
2 b g Tagula(IRE) Eye Catching (Exceed And Excel (AUS))
1493[9] 1893[6] ***9569***[2] *9661*[6]

Lake Volta (IRE) *Mark Johnston* a92 107
4 b g Raven's Pass(USA) Ghanaian (FR) (Shamardal (USA))
1944[4] (2260) 2609[10] 2844[3] **(3043)** 3347[2] 4095[8] 4402[14] 4921[5] 5120[2] 5413[9] 5664[7] 6229[8] 6445[8] 6711[11] *7188*[10] 7891[11]

Lalacelle (FR) *S Cerulis* a69 63
2 gr f Rajsaman(FR) La Rouge (FR) (Le Havre (IRE))
2263a[6] 3714a[2] 4228a[3] 5600a[4] ***(6141a)*** ***6584a***[2] *9605a*[10]

Lala Dance (FR) *C Lerner* a56 74
3 ch f Motivator Goritie (FR) (Anabaa (USA))
977a[7]

La La Land (GER) *Henk Grewe* 85
2 ch f Outstrip La Caldera (Hernando (FR))
7004a[3]

Lalania *William Stone* a73 71
4 br m Kheleyf(USA) George's Gift (Haafhd)
314[3] ***824***[2] *1209*[6] 5532[3] 6132[2] 6857[4] 7345[6] 7977[7] *8755*[3] ***(9092)***◆ *9584*[2]

La Lune *Henry Candy* 87
3 ch f Champs Elysees Moonlight Mystery (Pivotal)
2087[6] **(2771)**

Lamaire (IRE) *Riccardo Santini* 101
3 b f Casamento(IRE) Lilanga (IRE) (Kalanisi (IRE))
2161a[6] **(4171a)** 7503a[6]

La Maquina *George Baker* a87 89
4 b g Dutch Art Miss Meltemi (IRE) (Miswaki Tern (USA))
(1036) *1727*[11] (3040) *4506*[9] **4887**[2] 5546[12] 6468[6]

La Mariniere (FR) *D De Watrigant* 64
3 b f Boby Di Job(BRZ) Infinitely (Fantastic Light (USA))
2954a[8]

La Maruca (IRE) *F Rossi* 52
2 ch f Ivawood(IRE) Duchess Diva (IRE) (Duke Of Marmalade (IRE))
6873a[8]

Lambeth Walk *Archie Watson* a82 96
2 ch f Charm Spirit(IRE) Cockney Dancer (Cockney Rebel (IRE))
(1821) *(2316)* 3983[10] **4883**[4] 6542[2] 7432[6] 7896[7]

Lambrini Lullaby *Lisa Williamson* a47 34
4 b m Captain Gerrard(IRE) Lambrini Lace (IRE) (Namid)
117[9] ***621***[5] *1020*[8] *2318*[11] 3067[7] 3846[12] 4555[10] 5181[11] 6590[10]

Lambristo (IRE) *J S Moore* a40 6
3 b c Bungle Inthejungle Amodio (IRE) (Cape Cross (IRE))
3463[14] *4774*[6] ***9644***[6]

Lamh Ar Lamh (IRE) *Nigel Hawke* a36 40
5 ch m Teofilo(IRE) Tintreach (CAN) (Vindication (USA))
731[13]

L'Ami De Baileys (FR) *J-V Toux* 4
2 bl c Supplicant Maggi Fong (Dr Fong (USA))
1709a[10]

L'Ami Pierrot *Matthieu Palussiere* a53 63
4 bb g Invincible Spirit(IRE) Green Swallow (FR) (Green Tune (USA))
7536a[15]

La Mirada (FR) *Mlle V Dissaux* a33 63
3 b f Dobby Road(FR) Surtsey (FR) (Anabaa Blue)
1512a[11] 2091a[9] **7138a**[9]

La Miura (FR) *T Castanheira* a62
3 ch f Evasive Top Wave (FR) (Medaaly)
217a[12] ***509a***[7] *1658a*[10]

Lamloom (IRE) *David O'Meara* a84 92
5 b g Cape Cross(IRE) Lulua (USA) (Bahri (USA))
2015[6] 2622[6] 2894[4] **(4058)** 4240[16] **5246**[3] 6588[5]

Lampang (IRE) *Tim Easterby* 95
2 b c Dandy Man(IRE) Black Mascara (IRE) (Authorized (IRE))
(6622)◆ **(7698)** 8125[8]

Lanana (FR) *Robert Collet* a76 101
4 b m Sepoy(AUS) Anandara (IRE) (Dylan Thomas (IRE))
(6651a) 6992a[2] **(7885a)** 8584a[4] 8790a[5]

Lancaster House (IRE) *A P O'Brien* 107
3 b c Galileo(IRE) Quiet Oasis (IRE) (Oasis Dream)
(7038a) 7220a[7]

Lancelot Du Lac (ITY) *Dean Ivory* a108 90
9 b g Shamardal(USA) Dodie Mae (USA) (Capote (USA))
563[9] ***837***[4] 5927[6] 6229[10] *7687*[3] 8127[13] *8851*[6] *9088*[6] *9478*[6]

Lanciato (NZ) *Mark Newnham* 108
6 br g Per Incanto(USA) Surreptitious (NZ) (O'Reilly (NZ))
1974a[13]

Landa Beach (IRE) *Andrew Balding* a81 90
3 b g Teofilo(IRE) Jameela's Dream (Nayef (USA))
1558[5] *2321*[6] 3295[5] 6218[2] 6924[2] **(7866)**

Landing Night (IRE)
Rebecca Menzies a78 71
7 b g Kodiac Night Delight (IRE) (Night Shift (USA))
3[6] *278*[6] *610*[5] *1929*[2] 2421[7] 2508[3] 2841[11] 3360[5] 5042[4] 5298[4] (6829) 7367[11] *7855*[4] *8296*[5] *8715*[3] *9108*[3] *9365*[4] *9473*[4] *9622*[3]

Land Of Legends (IRE)
Saeed bin Suroor a85 107
3 b c Iffraaj Homily (Singspiel (IRE))
2023[2]◆ 2802[5] *(3464)* (4299) **(5666)** 6453[5]

Land Of Mind *M Delcher Sanchez* a81 81
4 b g Myboycharlie(IRE) Coco (USA) (Storm Bird (CAN))
1449a[3] 2226a[10]

Land Of Oz *Sir Mark Prescott Bt* a93 99
3 ch c Australia Madame Defarge (IRE) (Motivator)
3197[4] (4803)◆ (5487)◆ *(5812)* (6125)◆ 6471[3] *(6929)*◆ **(7464)** 8114[27]

Land Of Plenty (AUS)
Peter & Paul Snowden 112
5 bb h Stratum(AUS) Dancing (Spectrum (IRE))
8360a[5] 8768a[13]

Land Of Winter (FR) *Rae Guest* a71 70
3 b g Camelot Gaselee (USA) (Toccet (USA))
2712[6] *3593*[9] 3777[3] 5915[5] *(7390)* 7629[2] 8246[2] ***9087***[2]◆

Land's End (DEN) *Francisco Castro* a96 96
7 b h Academy Award(IRE) Lois (SWE) (Fraam)
6523a[4]

Landue *Marcus Tregoning* a95 70
4 b g Champs Elysees Time Of Gold (USA) (Banker's Gold (USA))
2969[6] ***3466***[5]

Langholm (IRE) *Declan Carroll* 69
3 b g Dark Angel(IRE) Pindrop (Exceed And Excel (AUS))
2337[12] 2913[8] 4039[2] (4210) (5023) 5654[4] **6068**[2] 7213[3]

Langley Vale *Roger Teal* a54 54
10 b g Piccolo Running Glimpse (IRE) (Runnett)
2693[5] **3533**[4] 4873[7] 6107[8] 6529[9] *9157*[12]

Lansky (IRE) *S bin Ghadayer* a89 91
4 b g Dark Angel(IRE) Goldthroat (IRE) (Zafonic (USA))
397a[3] 640a[5] 960a[5] *1109a*[8]

Laoise (USA) *Linda Perratt* a34 38
3 b f Noble Mission Lilbourne Eliza (IRE) (Elusive City (USA))
6608[9] **6936**[8] 7214[13] 7737[14]

La Pentola (FR) *F Belmont* 80
2 b f Planteur(IRE) Lady Oriande (Makbul)
4533a[3]

La Pergola (FR) *S Cerulis* a74 65
3 b f Penny's Picnic(IRE) Elusive Queen (FR) (Elusive City (USA))
4959a[5] ***5408a***[4]

La Petite Sauvage (USA)
A bin Harmash a16
3 br f Colonel John(USA) La Defense (USA) (Wild Again (USA))
570a[14]

Lapidary *Heather Main* a83 77
3 b f Kodiac Carved Emerald (Pivotal)
3463[3] (4116) ***(5736)*** *6346*[4] *7914*[5] *8456*[9]

La Poutanesca (IRE) *D Smaga* a51 85
5 ch m Falco(USA) Victoria College (FR) (Rock Of Gibraltar (IRE))
6651a[F]

Lappet (IRE) *Gavin Cromwell* a56 63
4 b m Epaulette(AUS) Aqraan (In The Wings)
(4513) 4784^{6} 7089a^{6} 9503^{3}

La Pradera *Henk Grewe* 84
3 b f Wiesenpfad(FR) La Dane (IRE) (Danehill (USA))
3877a^{7}

Lapses Linguae (FR)
Emmet Mullins a78 77
2 ch f Dandy Man(IRE) Idle Tears (Selkirk (USA))
9062^{2} 9393^{3}

Lapulced'acqua (IRE)
Grizzetti Galoppo SRL 97
4 b m Epaulette(AUS) Rosa Del Ponte (Authorized (IRE))
4170a^{3} (4432a)

Laqab (IRE) *Derek Shaw* a69 53
6 b g Teofilo(IRE) Ghaidaa (IRE) (Cape Cross (IRE))
812^{11} 886^{4} 1065^{12} 1675^{4}◆ 1859^{6} 2692^{10} 3567^{12} 4567^{8} 5003^{7} 5248^{7} 5817^{5} 7578^{13}

Laraaib (IRE) *Owen Burrows* 116
5 b h Pivotal Sahool (Unfuwain (USA))
1750^{3} 2827^{2} (Dead)

Lara Silvia *Iain Jardine* 67
2 ch f Casamento(IRE) Idyllic Star (IRE) (Choisir (AUS))
1642^{5} 2367^{3} 2840^{6} 5618^{4} 6032^{7} (7110) (7734)

La Rav (IRE) *Michael Easterby* a81 66
5 b g Footstepsinthesand Swift Acclaim (IRE) (Acclamation)
6677^{12} 7362^{14} 8305^{2}◆ 8918^{4} 9351^{2}◆

Larchmont Lad (IRE) *Joseph Tuite* 112
5 b h Footstepsinthesand Fotini (IRE) (King's Best (USA))
2109^{2} 2615^{7} 4389^{4} 5413^{7} 6508^{3} 7255a^{3}

La Reconquista *C Laffon-Parias* 72
2 gr f Dark Angel(IRE) Foreign Legionary (IRE) (Galileo (IRE))
4947a^{3}

Laredo Chop (FR) *J-M Capitte* 42
3 b c Amadeus Wolf Lavistahermosa (FR) (Deportivo)
955a^{9}

La Regle Du Jeu (FR) *Y Barberot* a65 65
3 b f Pedro The Great(USA) Darwin's Rhea (FR) (Della Francesca (USA))
3028a^{6} 4357a^{3} 9280a^{4}

Lariat *Andrew Balding* 95
3 ch c Poet's Voice Lasso (Indian Ridge (IRE))
2088^{2} 2562^{2} 3086^{2} 3842^{2} 5417^{4} 6657^{6} 7459^{4}

Larno (FR) *M Boutin* a79 98
5 gr g Milanais(FR) Honorable Sister (FR) (Highest Honor (FR))
2226a^{4} 4704a^{3} 8379a^{5} 9124a^{7}

Laser Show (IRE) *Saeed bin Suroor* a88 87
2 ch c New Approach(IRE) Entertains (AUS) (Street Cry (IRE))
(4611) 9052^{2}

La Sioux (IRE) *Richard Fahey* a57 72
5 ch m Casamento(IRE) Dakota Sioux (IRE) (College Chapel)
120^{5} 348^{7} 814^{4} 1339^{3} (2330) (2911) 4828^{3} 7125^{8} 7738^{8} 9040^{8}

Last Chance Paddy (USA)
Sarah-Jayne Davies a42 45
5 gr g Paddy O'Prado(USA) Mizzcan'tbewrong (USA) (Mizzen Mast (USA))
810^{9} 8868^{10}

Last Date *Ivan Furtado* a64
2 br g Music Master Tanning (Atraf)
4246^{10} 5280^{5} 6254^{7} (7833) 8825^{4} (9196)

Last Days Of May *Christine Dunnett* a10
2 rg f Outstrip Fenella Rose (Compton Place)
8287^{13} 9158^{10}

Last Edition (FR) *A Fabre* a86 59
3 gr f Kendargent(FR) Apperella (Rainbow Quest (USA))
(993a) 3878a^{5}

Last Empire *Kevin Ryan* 97
3 b f Pivotal Final Dynasty (Komaite (USA))
(3499) (4489) (5951) 7401^{4} 8115^{12}

Last Enchantment (IRE)
Neil Mulholland a62 74
4 b m Camelot Illandrane (IRE) (Cape Cross (IRE))
1934^{4} 2685^{7} 4371^{12} 4869^{4} 6511^{6} 6854^{5} 7233^{4} 7790^{14} 9132^{6} 9367^{4}

Last Glance (IRE) *Tracy Waggott* a19 49
4 b g Shamardal(USA) Linda Radlett (IRE) (Manduro (GER))
18^{7} 5297^{8}

Lasting Legacy *Chris Fairhurst* a80 61
2 gr f Lethal Force(IRE) Araminte (One Cool Cat (USA))
5553^{7} 6336^{4} (7304)◆

Last Look (IRE) *Saeed bin Suroor* a91 103
3 b f Pivotal Gonbarda (GER) (Lando (GER))
(4641)◆ (5783) (6398)

Lastochka *Roger Varian* a72 88
3 ch f Australia Lashyn (USA) (Mr Greeley (USA))
2831^{7} 3762^{4}

Last Opportunity (IRE) *G M Lyons* 91
2 b c Dandy Man(IRE) Opportuna (Rock Hard Ten (USA))
7247a^{11}

Last Page *Tony Carroll* a89 71
4 b g Pastoral Pursuits No Page (IRE) (Statue Of Liberty (USA))
361^{2} 734^{3} 1356^{5} (2107) 4649^{9} 8317^{8} (8826) 9214^{10}

Last Surprise (IRE) *Simon Crisford* a88 87
2 ch f No Nay Never(USA) Beta Tauri (USA) (Oasis Dream)
(3441) 4048^{25} 4398^{5} (7103) 7696^{3} 8318^{2}

Last Winter (SAF)
Sir Michael Stoute a100 97
5 b h Western Winter(USA) Field Flower (SAF) (Silvano (GER))
7340^{6} 8811^{4}

La Taniere (FR) *S Gouyette* 31
5 b m Myboycharlie(IRE) La Teranga (FR) (Beat Hollow)
7009a^{3} 7501a^{8}

Late For The Sky *Stella Barclay* a8 30
5 b m Shirocco(GER) China Lily (USA) (Street Cry (IRE))
532^{9} 1146^{9} 3960^{7} 5043^{5} 8344^{8}

Latent Heat (IRE) *Tony Carroll* a64 60
3 b g Papal Bull Taziria (SWI) (Zilzal Zamaan (USA))
9548^{4}

Late Romance *Charlie Appleby* a50
2 b f Dubawi(IRE) Voleuse De Coeurs (IRE) (Teofilo (IRE))
9311^{8}

Late Shipment *Nikki Evans* a48 58
8 b g Authorized(IRE) Time Over (Mark Of Esteem (IRE))
2359^{7} 7300^{10}

Lathom *Paul Midgley* a71 84
6 b g Compton Place Wigan Lane (Kheleyf (USA))
1951^{6} 2433^{2} 2841^{2} (3658) (4100) 4894^{7} 6607^{9} 6921^{3} 7700^{7} 7908^{5}

Latin Five (IRE)
Joseph Patrick O'Brien 90
2 b c Camacho Penolva (IRE) (Galileo (IRE))
6375^{12}

Latinius (FR) *J-M Beguigne* a67 77
4 b g Kouroun(FR) Latinia (FR) (Barathea (IRE))
1449a^{11} 4747a^{10}

Latoyah Of North (IRE)
Michael Mulvany 91
6 b m Mustameet(USA) Mariah Mooney (IRE) (Moonax (IRE))
7635a^{13}

La Trinidad *Roger Fell* a60 54
2 b g Bated Breath High Drama (IRE) (High Chaparral (IRE))
7067^{8} 7539^{5} 7958^{6}

Latrobe (IRE) *Joseph Patrick O'Brien* 114
4 br h Camelot Question Times (Shamardal (USA))
1777a^{3} 2494a^{4} 3953^{4} 4351a^{2} (5874a) 7246a^{6} 8844a^{18}

Laubali *David O'Meara* a80 51
4 ch g Kyllachy Different (Bahamian Bounty)
131^{7} 347^{5} 5281^{3} 5972^{8} 7470^{7} 8470^{8} 8866^{6} 9365^{12} 9622^{9}

Lauberhorn Rocket (GER)
Tim Vaughan a60 45
4 b g Maxios La Hermana (Hernando (FR))
1236^{12} 1346^{10} 2127^{4} 2970^{3} 3769^{3} (6077) 6550^{3}

Laucitu (FR) *Mlle M-L Mortier*
6 b m Kingsalsa(USA) Voitudon (Lujain (USA))
2955a^{15}

Lauderdale (FR) *Charley Rossi* a60
3 ch g Desert Guest(IRE) Ladoga (Exceed And Excel (AUS))
6328a^{8}

Lauenen (FR) *J-C Rouget* a86 84
2 b c Canford Cliffs(IRE) Peppy Miller (FR) (Iffraaj)
6776a^{7} 8508a^{3}

Laugh A Minute *Roger Varian* a106 108
4 b g Mayson Funny Enough (Dansili)
2109^{4} 2614^{3} 4380^{2}◆ 5120^{11} 7433^{24}

Laughifuwant (IRE) *Gerard Keane* 102
4 b g Roderic O'Connor(IRE) Red Fanfare (First Trump)
(5711a) 7794a^{3} 8572a^{3}

Laughing Crusader *David O'Meara* a13
2 b c Outstrip Sitting Pretty (IRE) (Compton Place)
2783^{8} 3451^{8}

Laughing Fox (USA)
Steven Asmussen a108
3 ch c Union Rags(USA) Saskawea (CAN) (Stormy Atlantic (USA))
2856a^{5}

Laughter Lounge (IRE)
David Evans 57
2 b f Ivawood(IRE) Mafaaza (USA) (Jazil (USA))
3049^{5} (5295)

Laulloir (IRE) *Kevin Ryan* a44 44
3 ch f More Than Ready(USA) Legs Lawlor (USA) (Unbridled (USA))
913^{5} 5690^{9}

Laura Game (FR) *M Brasme* a55 62
3 b f Zambezi Sun Les Tourelles (IRE) (Sadler's Wells (USA))
977a^{8}

Laura Louise (IRE) *Nigel Tinkler* a21 42
3 b f Farhh Autumn Sun (IRE) (Invincible Spirit (IRE))
2262^{8} 2943^{8} 3271^{13} 6678^{11} 7290^{10}

Laura's Legacy *Andrew Balding* a39 24
3 b f Passing Glance Rebecca Romero (Exceed And Excel (AUS))
1523^{6} 1909^{5} 2300^{4} 3148^{6}

Laurens (FR) *K R Burke* 117
4 b m Siyouni(FR) Recambe (IRE) (Cape Cross (IRE))
2829^{2} 3948^{6} (5479a) 6472^{2} 7221a^{4} 7898^{7}

Laurentia (IRE) *Dean Ivory* a49
3 b f Iffraaj Brynica (FR) (Desert Style (IRE))
9171^{9} 9425^{8} 9635^{9}

Laurier (USA) *Kevin Ryan* a66 53
3 bb f Scat Daddy(USA) Abundantly Blessed (USA) (Phone Trick (USA))
3463^{6} 4608^{5}

Lavaspin *S Seemar* a101
5 b g Hard Spun(USA) Belenkaya (USA) (Giant's Causeway (USA))
(729a) 1109a^{10}

Lavender's Blue (IRE)
Amanda Perrett 109
3 b f Sea The Stars(IRE) Beatrice Aurore (IRE) (Danehill Dancer (IRE))
(1834) 2831^{2} 3316^{14} (6726)◆ 7898^{4}

Lavengro Lad (IRE) *Andrew Slattery* a60 14
3 ch g Showcasing Jolie Etoile (USA) (Diesis)
306a^{6}

La Venus Espagnola (IRE)
C Laffon-Parias 77
2 ch f Siyouni(FR) Sureyya (GER) (Monsun (GER))
7925a^{7}

La Voix Magique *Steph Hollinshead* 82
3 ch f Poet's Voice Inaminute (IRE) (Spectrum (IRE))
1740^{6} (2103) 2521^{6} 2934^{6} 5947^{9} 7366^{10}

Lawaa (FR) *Richard Fahey* 72
2 b g Bated Breath Smaisma (IRE) (Galileo (IRE))
4544^{3}◆ 5665^{11} 6654^{5} 7699^{4} 8394^{8}

Lawanda (IRE) *T Lemer* a68 75
4 gr m Lawman(FR) Cheyrac (FR) (Smadoun (FR))
6651a^{12}

Law Equity (FR) *Rebecca Menzies* a47 46
8 bb g Lawman(FR) Basse Besogne (IRE) (Pursuit Of Love)
3251^{3}

Lawmaking *Michael Scudamore* a90 87
6 b g Zamindar(USA) Canada Water (Dansili)
1401^{5} 1757^{4} 2800^{2} 3315^{10} 4108^{3} 4386^{3} 5267^{3}◆ (6863) 7517^{5} 8253^{2}

Lawn Ranger *Michael Attwater* a95 98
4 b g Cityscape Baylini (Bertolini (USA))
945^{3}◆ 1291^{3} 1518^{2} (2486) 3016^{2} (3424)◆ 4504^{6} 6021^{5} (6447) 8701^{8} 9055^{6} 9206^{7}

Law Of One (IRE)
Sir Michael Stoute a78
2 ch c Galileo(IRE) Strawberry Fledge (USA) (Kingmambo (USA))
8288^{2}

Law Of Peace *Charlie Appleby* 85
2 b c Shamardal(USA) Certify (USA) (Elusive Quality (USA))
4282^{2}◆ 6912^{2}◆ 7521^{4}

Lawyersgunsn'money *Roger Teal* a60 60
4 gr g Indian Haven Non Disclosure (IRE) (Clodovil (IRE))
921^{6} 1331^{5} 1989^{7} 4220^{4} 5425^{9} 6855^{6} 9403^{2} 9657^{5}

Laxmi (IRE) *Brian Meehan* a69 63
3 b f War Command(USA) Princess Patsky (USA) (Mr Greeley (USA))
966^{4} 1567^{7} 1985^{3} 2355^{8} 5575^{7}

Laxxia (GER) *M Nigge* 69
4 b m Maxios Laccata (Lomitas)
1578a^{10}

Layaleena (IRE) *Sir Michael Stoute* a79 93
3 b f Sea The Stars(IRE) Nectar De Rose (FR) (Shamardal (USA))
2088^{8} (2934) 4052^{26} 5525^{10}

Layla (FR) *Mme Pia Brandt* 76
2 b f Lope De Vega(IRE) She Loves You (Lawman (FR))
6774a^{5}

Layla's Dream *Tony Carroll* 41
3 b f Assertive Layla's Oasis (Oasis Dream)
4116^{15} 4772^{6} 5492^{4} 5793^{7}

Lazarus (IRE) *Amy Murphy* a52 53
5 b g Zoffany(IRE) Knysna (IRE) (Rock Of Gibraltar (IRE))
38^{9} 560^{9} 789^{6} 1548^{10} 5029^{4} 5891^{5} 6601^{2} 6982^{5} 7558^{9} 9087^{4}

Lazuli (IRE) *Charlie Appleby* 97
2 b c Dubawi(IRE) Floristry (Fasliyev (USA))
(5624)◆ (7071) 8088^{8}

Lazy Daisy (USA) *Doug O'Neill* a102
2 b f Paynter(USA) Romantic Intention (USA) (Suave (USA))
8747a^{6}

Leader Writer (FR) *David Elsworth* a76 83
7 b g Pivotal Miss Emma May (IRE) (Hawk Wing (USA))
2710^{3} 3763^{5} 4851^{10} 6347^{9} 6925^{4} 7618^{6} (7975) 8412^{RR}

Leafhopper (IRE) *John Gosden* 83
2 gr f Dark Angel(IRE) Layla Jamil (IRE) (Exceed And Excel (AUS))
(5961)◆

Leagan Gaeilge (IRE) *J S Bolger* 82
3 b f Vocalised(USA) Feile Bride (IRE) (Dylan Thomas (IRE))
1306a^{15}

Leannes Lady (IRE) *Alan Berry* 31
7 b m Ask Wizzy (IRE) (Presenting)
5421^{8}

Lean On Pete (IRE) *Ollie Pears* a68 50
10 b g Oasis Dream Superfonic (FR) (Zafonic (USA))
387^{5} 1163^{4} 2196^{6}

Leapers Wood *Michael Dods* 83
2 b c Garswood Skipton (IRE) (Dark Angel (IRE))
2892^{3}◆ 3411^{5} 5234^{3} 6053^{2} 6336^{2} 6997^{7} 7904^{13}

Learn By Heart *Bent Olsen* 100
4 b h Frankel Memory (IRE) (Danehill Dancer (IRE))
(3902a) 6524a^{5} 7498a^{4}

Leave Em Alone (IRE) *David Evans* a40 61
2 b f War Command(USA) Tides (Bahamian Bounty)
1642^{4} 1843^{4} 2907^{8} 5313^{6} 5630^{6} 7079^{8} 7275^{7}

Le Baol (FR) *Hughie Morrison* a83 101
3 b g Orpen(USA) La Teranga (FR) (Beat Hollow)
8092^{15}

Le Bayou (FR) *Christopher Head* a74 74
2 b c Dabirsim(FR) Kastiya (FR) (Desert Style (IRE))
5642a^{3}

Le Brivido (FR) *A P O'Brien* a75 113
5 b h Siyouni(FR) La Bugatty (IRE) (Dr Fong (USA))
1776a^{3} 2829^{5}◆ 3948^{5} 4094^{5} 5716a^{11} 6472^{7}

Le Chiffre *David O'Meara* 72
2 b c Zoffany(IRE) Bondesire (Misu Bond (IRE))
6606^{4} 6970^{2}◆ 8232^{4}

Led Astray *Michael Bell* 64
2 b f Oasis Dream Oshiponga (Barathea (IRE))
4849^{6} 5737^{5} 6577^{5}

Ledbury (IRE) *J R Jenkins* a45 7
7 b g Lawman(FR) Truly Magnificent (USA) (Elusive Quality (USA))
1044^{2} 1519^{7}

Ledham (IRE) *Sir Michael Stoute* a94 94
4 b h Shamardal(USA) Pioneer Bride (USA) (Gone West (USA))
2105^{2}

Le Don De Vie *Hughie Morrison* a67 106
3 b g Leroidesanimaux(BRZ) Leaderene (Selkirk (USA))
(2034) (3341) 5541^{4} (6506) 7694^{17}

Leebellinsummerbee (IRE)
Donald McCain a48 23
3 b f Footstepsinthesand Paint The Town (IRE) (Sadler's Wells (USA))
2531^{10} 5548^{6}

Lee Roy *Michael Attwater* a71 15
3 ch c Leroidesanimaux(BRZ) Steppin Out (First Trump)
79^{3} 698^{2}◆ (1174) 2101^{12}

Leeshaan (IRE) *Rebecca Bastiman* a57 51
4 b g Bated Breath La Grande Elisa (IRE) (Ad Valorem (USA))
277^{5} 502^{8} 834^{11} 2433^{3} 3227^{9} 3291^{4} 3723^{6} 4720^{7} 4823^{3} 5238^{4} 6276^{P} 7207^{9} 7779^{3} 8234^{7}

Lefortovo (FR) *Jo Hughes* a84 64
6 b g Arcano(IRE) Lorientaise (IRE) (Xaar)
347 2558 1164^{2} 1631a^{4} 2675a^{8} 5715a^{9} 7136a^{8} 7601a^{8}

Legalized *Dianne Sayer* a18 19
5 br m Authorized(IRE) Laurena (GER) (Acatenango (GER))
8344^{6}

Legal Mind *Emma Owen* a55
6 ch h Firebreak La Sorrela (IRE) (Cadeaux Genereux)
53^{7} 244^{5} 531^{3} 1093^{6} 1384^{4} 1732^{8}

Legal Spin (IRE) *W P Mullins* 88
4 b g Lawman(FR) Spinning Well (IRE) (Pivotal)
5508a^{15}

Legal Tender (IRE) *Bryan Smart* 29
3 b g Camacho A Childs Dream (IRE) (Intense Focus (USA))
1954^{10} 4436^{8} 5393^{10}

Legendary Lunch (IRE)
Fawzi Abdulla Nass a76 102
5 ch g Dragon Pulse(IRE) Taalluf (USA) (Hansel (USA))
843a^{4}

Legend Island (FR) *Ed Walker* a54 58
3 b g Dabirsim(FR) Carolla Bay (IRE) (Duke Of Marmalade (IRE))
2238^{7} 2734^{7} 3938^{8} 4584^{14}

Legends Of War (USA)
Doug O'Neill 112
3 b c Scat Daddy(USA) Madera Dancer (USA) (Rahy (USA))
8770a^{12}

Le Gitan (FR) *C Boutin* a72 66
4 ch h Dunkerque(FR) Voyageuse (FR) (Kentucky Dynamite (USA))
7601a^{10}

Leg It Lenny (IRE) *Robert Cowell* a61 62
2 b g Baltic King El Morocco (USA) (El Prado (IRE))
3644^{8} 4282^{5} 5381^{9} 5885^{3} 6387^{5} 9438^{3}

Lehoogg *Roger Varian* a79 81
3 ch c Bated Breath Button Moon (IRE) (Compton Place)
(1352)◆ 1764^{2} 2395^{4}

Leinster (USA) *George R Arnold II* 116
4 b h Majestic Warrior(USA) Vassar (USA) (Royal Academy (USA))
8770a^{7}

Le Maharajah (FR) *Tom Clover* a69 71
4 b g Cacique(IRE) Sign Of Life (Haafhd)
3276^{2} 4426^{11} 6160^{10} 7060^{8}

Le Maitre Chat (USA)
Micky Hammond a83 87
8 b g Tale Of The Cat(USA) Bedside Story (Mtoto)
5457^{P} (Dead)

Le Manege Enchante (IRE)
Derek Shaw a51 50
6 gr g Zebedee Beth (Deportivo)
26^{6} 161^{2}◆ 293^{5} 483^{6} 1383^{3} 2066^{7} 2527^{3}◆ 3001^{3} 3425^{3} 3975^{13} 4212^{5} 4765^{3} 5264^{5} 5892^{6} 6220^{12} 8643^{9} 8898^{5} 9398^{5}

Le Mont (FR) *P Bary* 80
3 b c Le Havre(IRE) Miss Bio (FR) (River Mist (USA))
1450a^{3}

Le Moqueur (FR) *K Borgel* a58 31
3 bb c Penny's Picnic(IRE) Melinee (FR) (Blackdoun (FR))
955a^{6}

Le Musee (FR) *Nigel Hawke* a58 69
6 b g Galileo(IRE) Delicieuse Lady (Trempolino (USA))
1989^{5} 2518^{8} 3017^{6} 3686^{2}

Lennybe *David Brown* a64
3 b g Epaulette(AUS) Destiny Of A Diva (Denounce)
(1070) 2192^{6}

Lenny The Lion *Lydia Pearce* a41
2 ch g Lethal Force(IRE) Agony And Ecstasy (Captain Rio)
6858^{10} 7787^{12} 8287^{10}

Lenya *John Gosden* a74 57
3 gr f Dark Angel(IRE) Lixirova (FR) (Slickly (FR))
5141^{5} (7451)

Leoch *Kevin Ryan* a51 71
2 ch g Hot Streak(IRE) Acquiesced (IRE) (Refuse To Bend (IRE))
7506^{2} 8337^{5} 9099^{8}

Leo Davinci (USA) *George Scott* a63 82
3 b g Artie Schiller(USA) Sweet Temper (USA) (Stormy Atlantic (USA))
2236^{5} 2802^{9} 3665^{3} (4080) 4281^{2} 4566^{3} 5255^{5} 8017^{11}

Leo De Fury (IRE)
Mrs John Harrington 112
3 ch c Australia Attire (IRE) (Danehill Dancer (IRE))
5585^{8} 6192a^{2} 7218a^{5} 7923a^{4}

Leodis (IRE) *Micky Hammond* a41 43
7 ch g Shirocco(GER) Leonica (Lion Cavern (USA))
1663^{9} 2591^{13} 3272^{14}

Leodis Dream (IRE) *David O'Meara* a109 104
3 b g Dandy Man(IRE) Paddy Again (IRE) (Moss Vale (IRE))
(1762) (2086) (2522) 3097[19] 3855[8] **(7449)** 8328a[7] 9004[7] 9166[7]

Leo Minor (USA) *Robert Cowell* a71 69
5 b g War Front(USA) Kissed (IRE) (Galileo (IRE))
1814[8] 2272[12] 2839[7] 3536[7] **4301**[4]◆ 4609[3] 5252[5] 5647[7] 6455[6] 6857[2] 7337[7] 7690[3]◆ 8063[9] 8429[3]

Leonio (FR) *Andrea Marcialis* a95 97
4 b h Myboycharlie(IRE) Katelyns Kiss (USA) (Rahy (USA))
2782a[7]

Leopardina (IRE) *David Simcock* a63 63
3 b f Lawman(FR) Leopard Creek (Weldnaas (USA))
2332[2]◆ 3535[3] 4454[6]

Leo's Luckyman *David Flood* a15 20
2 b g Cable Bay(IRE) Atalis (Holy Roman Emperor (IRE))
4652[7] 7113[11] 7842[12]

Lep *Michael Attwater* a65
3 b g Nathaniel(IRE) Liel (Pivotal)
9425[4]◆ **9662**[3]

Le Pin (FR) *B Legros* a86 74
6 gr g Holy Roman Emperor(IRE) Night Dhu (Montjeu (IRE))
4748a[7] 5035a[13] 5410a[8]

Le Rafale (FR) *J C Rosell* 93
4 ch h Le Havre(IRE) Elzebieta (IRE) (Monsun (GER))
4418a[6]

Le Romain (AUS) *Kris Lees* 115
6 b g Hard Spun(USA) Mignard (AUS) (Strategic (AUS))
1974a[6]

Leroy Leroy *Richard Hannon* a92 90
3 b g Compton Place Small Fortune (Anabaa (USA))
1940[4] 2414[5] **3160**[2] 4342[5] 4935[17] 5121[4] 6652a[4] 7122[7] 7622[4] 8412[7]

Lesanti *Ed de Giles* a48 55
5 b g Royal Applause Kammaan (Diktat)
595[5] 941[10] 1214[9] 1477[9] (Dead)

L'Es Fremantle (FR)
Michael Chapman a17 39
8 b g Orpen(USA) Grand Design (Danzero (AUS))
5302[13]

Les Gar Gan (IRE) *Ray Peacock* a48 58
8 b m Iffraaj Story (Observatory (USA))
465[10] 590[10]

Leshlaa (USA) *Saeed bin Suroor* a107 114
5 ch h Street Cry(IRE) Vine Street (IRE) (Singspiel (IRE))
395a[2] (Dead)

Les Hogues (IRE) *J-C Rouget* 100
2 b f Bated Breath Hatsepsut Queen (FR) (Peintre Celebre (USA))
6777a[4] **8647a**[2]

Le Solaire *P Bary* a83 68
2 b c Siyouni(FR) Apsara (FR) (Darshaan)
8508a[2]

Less Of That (IRE) *Debbie Hughes* a42 60
5 b m Canford Cliffs(IRE) Night Glimmer (IRE) (Night Shift (USA))
1355[11] **2353**[5] 2714[7] 7756[11]

Lestrade *David O'Meara* a75
3 b g Lawman(FR) Ninas Rainbow (Rainbow Quest (USA))
733[4]◆ (1212)◆ **1587**[2] 2082[10] 7856[9] 8220[11] 8495[9]

Lethal Angel *Stuart Williams* a76 75
4 gr m Lethal Force(IRE) Heliograph (Ishiguru (USA))
2081[3] 2804[2] 4074[2] 4560[2] 5191[3] 5750[2] 6220[4] 6401[3] (7022) 7613[5] 7837[4] 8349[5] **(9013)**

Lethal Blast *Karen George* a42 43
2 b f Lethal Force(IRE) Having A Blast (USA) (Exchange Rate (USA))
5250[9] 6028[6] 8912[9]

Lethal Guest *Ollie Pears* a66 41
3 gr g Lethal Force(IRE) Holberg Suite (Azamour (IRE))
122[6] 2325[9] 3271[11] 4518[9] 5023[10]

Lethal Laura *Kevin Frost* a55 41
3 ch f Lethal Force(IRE) Laurena (GER) (Acatenango (GER))
406[10] 2197[11] 2531[3] 3299[6] 3938[5] **(4642)** 5031[4] 5389[7] 6575[5] 7404[11] 8819[3] 9282[7] 9410[10]

Lethal Look *Sarah Hollinshead* a21
3 gr g Lethal Force(IRE) Look Here's Dee (Dansili)
6732[12] **9502**[5]

Lethal Lover *Clive Cox* a67 55
3 b f Lethal Force(IRE) Sadaharu (FR) (Dansili)
442[5] **1142**[4] 2356[6] 3154[5] 4225[10] 5284[11]

Lethal Lunch *Clive Cox* a104 83
4 gr g Lethal Force(IRE) Pin Cushion (Pivotal)
1097[4] (6318) 6953[9] (7188) 8707[10] **9301**[2]

Lethal Missile (IRE) *Clive Cox* a83 82
3 b g Lethal Force(IRE) Lostintheclouds (Firebreak)
1285[2] (1656) (3170) 4662[2] **9304**[4]◆

Lethal Power (IRE)
Joseph G Murphy 91
4 b h Acclamation Land Army (IRE) (Desert Style (IRE))
6693a[10]

Lethal Promise (IRE) *W McCreery* a87 102
3 b f Invincible Spirit(IRE) Lethal Quality (USA) (Elusive Quality (USA))
(2605a) 3557a[5] 5222a[8] 5325a[15] 8328a[12]

Lethal Sensation *Paul Webber* 46
2 b f Lethal Force(IRE) Exceed Sensazione (Exceed And Excel (AUS))
3835[8] 4302[9] 5988[13] 6799[10]

Lethal Shadow *Marco Botti* a68
2 b g Lethal Force(IRE) Danehill Shadow (IRE) (Danehill Dancer (IRE))
9252[9] **9567**[6]

Lethal Steps *Gordon Elliott* a90 96
4 gr g Lethal Force(IRE) Tanda Tula (IRE) (Alhaarth (IRE))
4053[11]

Lethal Talent *Jonathan Portman* a78 61
2 gr f Lethal Force(IRE) Talent Spotter (Exceed And Excel (AUS))
2915[10] 3491[5] 4222[4] (6071) 6808[4] 7155[8] **(8198)** **9175**[3]

Let Her Loose (IRE) *Richard Fahey* 65
2 ch f Mukhadram Passionable (New Approach (IRE))
7000[3]◆ 7778[3] 8338[5]

Letmestopyouthere (IRE)
Archie Watson a63 61
5 ro g Sir Prancealot(IRE) Romanylei (IRE) (Blues Traveller (IRE))
187[7] 468[11] 759[7] 926[8] 1179[12] 2145[2] 3203[7] 3716[7] 4115[12] 4481[7] 4807[3] 6844[6] 7603[2] **8757**[2] 9185[4]

Le Torrent *Emma Lavelle* a80 67
7 ch g Sir Percy Cinnas Ransom (Red Ransom (USA))
(700)◆ 991[8] 1330[7] 4791[2] **5812**[2]

Let Right Be Done *Linda Perratt* a50 50
7 gr g Lawman(FR) Cheerfully (Sadler's Wells (USA))
501[8] 2329[11] 2963[12] 4054[10] 4513[4] **4726**[2] 4979[5] 6572[5] 7738[9]

Let Rip (IRE) *Henry Candy* a84 78
5 b g Rip Van Winkle(IRE) Al Ihsas (IRE) (Danehill (USA))
4249[5] 5320[4] 6331[4] **6390**[4]

Letsbe Avenue (IRE) *Bill Turner* a77 78
4 b g Lawman(FR) Aguilas Perla (IRE) (Indian Ridge (IRE))
2064[4] 2273[13] 3423[5] 3944[6] 4506[5]◆ 4838[10] 6164[7] 6469[9] 6717[4] 7084[3]◆ 8291[8] 9185[11]

Let's Be Happy (IRE)
Mandy Rowland a63 58
5 gr m Mastercraftsman(IRE) Corrozal (GER) (Cape Cross (IRE))
61[8] 1163[10] 1858[12] 5285[11]

Letscrackon (IRE) *Gary Moore* a73 79
2 b f Camacho Laetoli (ITY) (Footstepsinthesand)
5988[4] **(8409)** 8891[3]

Lets Go Flo (IRE) *Brian Ellison* a41 46
3 b f Finsceal Fior(IRE) Lost Icon (IRE) (Intikhab (USA))
5169[6] **5278**[3]◆ 5768[9]

Lets Go Lucky *David Evans* a74 63
2 ch f Yorgunnabelucky(USA) Reset City (Reset (AUS))
4480[10] 5577[5] 6028[5] (6604) **(7767)**◆ 8318[9] 9300[12]

Levanter (FR) *Harry Dunlop* a66 48
3 b f Rock Of Gibraltar(IRE) Seasonal Cross (Cape Cross (IRE))
2790[8] **7772**[3]◆ 8808[5] 9361[4] 9573[5]

Levendi (AUS) *Peter Gelagotis* 99
4 b h Pierro(AUS) Lipari (AUS) (Redoute's Choice (AUS))
9015a[8]

Lever Du Soleil (FR)
Gavin Cromwell a87 81
4 b g Le Havre(IRE) Morning Dust (IRE) (Invincible Spirit (IRE))
(4510) (4724) **(4782)**◆ (5097)◆

Lewandowski (IRE) *Edward Lynam* a66 46
5 gr g Zebedee Chelsy (IRE) (Statue Of Liberty (USA))
419a[3]

Lewis Slack *Richard J Bandey* a33 50
3 b g Coach House(IRE) Pelican Key (IRE) (Mujadil (USA))
1723[11] **4477**[5] 5430[8]

Lexikon *Ollie Pears* a51 56
3 b f Mayson Fairy Steps (Rainbow Quest (USA))
612[2] 931[9] 1721[2] (1979) **2482**[3] 3292[10] 3569[9] 4518[7] 5389[12]

Lexington Dash (FR)
Richard Hannon a80
2 b c Siyouni(FR) Mythical Border (USA) (Johannesburg (USA))
9130[2]◆ 9392[4]

Lexington Empire *David Lanigan* a96 56
4 ch g Intello(GER) Emperice (USA) (Empire Maker (USA))
(1882) 2969[7] **4021**[2] 5437[3] 6151[2] 6981[4]

Lexington Flair (FR) *Hugo Palmer*
4 b g Dabirsim(FR) Kyleam (King's Best (USA))
8944[8]

Lexington Law (IRE) *Alan King* a97 87
6 b g Lawman(FR) Tus Nua (IRE) (Galileo (IRE))
87[3] 758[6] 1017[5] 1422[12] 2126[6] 3428[2] (4522) 5135[5]

Lexington Palm (IRE)
Keith Dalgleish a57 51
3 b f Elzaam(AUS) Easter Girl (Efisio)
1567[6] 2212[8] 3414[10] 4059[7] 4720[15] 5300[5] 5768[8]

Lexington Place *Ruth Carr* a65 69
9 ch g Compton Place Elidore (Danetime (IRE))
1364[5] **1767**[2] 2324[10] 2632[9]

Lexington Quest (IRE)
Richard Hannon a58 71
2 b g Ivawood(IRE) Serenata (IRE) (Oratorio (IRE))
1651[6] 1887[7] **3767**[5] 4756[4]◆ 5146[8] 5313[4] **5907**[2] 6394[4] 7277[5] 7910[4] 8493[6]

Lexington Rebel (FR)
Richard Hannon a85 84
2 b c Dabirsim(FR) Silent Sunday (IRE) (Testa Rossa (AUS))
5577[4] (6364) **6966**[6] **7445**[2] 8709[2] 9364[8] 9608[7]

Lexington Warfare (IRE)
Richard Fahey a66 66
2 b c Acclamation Soul Mountain (IRE) (Rock Of Gibraltar (IRE))
2869[3] 5118[4] 5764[8] 7247a[14] **9608**[3]

Lexington Warlord *Richard Hannon* 33
3 b g War Command(USA) Archina (IRE) (Arch (USA))
1652[12] 1956[8] 2581[13] 3197[10]

Lexi The One (IRE) *Richard Fahey* a52 65
2 b f Dandy Man(IRE) Garter Star (Mark Of Esteem (IRE))
1879[6] 2520[7] 3595[3] 3841[4] **4647**[2] 5703[5] **6458**[2] 7140[5] 7677[3]

Lezardrieux *Grant Tuer* a62 48
2 b g Due Diligence(USA) M'selle (IRE) (Elnadim (USA))
6822[10] 7046[9] 7308[5] (8527) 9061[5] **(9394)**

Liamba *David O'Meara* a77 61
4 b m Equiano(FR) Hisaronu (IRE) (Stravinsky (USA))
42[3] 279[5] 702[2] 1368[3]◆ 1986[2] 2349[2] **(3207)**◆ 3470[7] 8070[7] 8403[3] 8946[3] 9224[4] (9545)

Liam's Lass (IRE) *Pam Sly* a61 60
3 b f Dandy Man(IRE) Rupa (IRE) (Acclamation)
2016[4] 2735[3] (3352) 3780[7] 7051[4] **7472**[3]

Liam The Charmer (USA)
Michael McCarthy 110
6 bb g Smart Strike(CAN) Charm The Giant (IRE) (Giant's Causeway (USA))
894a[14]

Libbretta *John E Long* 68
4 ch m Libranno Dispol Katie (Komaite (USA))
2361[4] **2770**[7]

Libello (IRE) *C Boutin* 100
6 ch h Archipenko(USA) Scarlett's Pride (FR) (Singspiel (IRE))
2169a[6]

Liberata Bella *George Scott* a58 49
3 b f Iffraaj Namaadhej (USA) (Swain (IRE))
183[12]

Liberation Day *Philip Kirby* a80 54
3 b g Iffraaj Welsh Cake (Fantastic Light (USA))
(316) **(838)** 1424[9] 2522[9] 3048[9] 4552[12] 5002[9] 7213[11] 7773[11]

Liberation Point (IRE)
Richard Fahey a68
2 b c Iffraaj Botanique (IRE) (Pivotal)
9471[6]◆

Liberri (IRE) *G Arizkorreta Elosegui* 86
3 b c Camelot Kirinda (IRE) (Tiger Hill (IRE))
6145a[7]

Liberte Absolue (FR) *C Lerner* a58 55
2 b f Olympic Glory(IRE) Fenella's Link (Linamix (FR))
9123a[6]

Liberty Beach *John Quinn* 108
2 b f Cable Bay(IRE) Flirtinaskirt (Avonbridge)
(3156) (3564) 3983[4]◆ (4610) (5542)◆ **6374**[2]◆

Liberty Diva (IRE) *Alan Berry* a2 26
3 b f Palavicini(USA) Alpine Mysteries (IRE) (Elusive City (USA))
2327[8] 4606[10] 4909[9] **5297**[7] 7764[8]

Liberty Filly *Roger Charlton* a62 58
2 ch f Iffraaj Safe House (IRE) (Exceed And Excel (AUS))
5733[9] 7331[3] **7787**[5] 8415[7] 8824[7]

Liberty London (GER)
H-J Groschel 95
3 b f Maxios Ledicea (Medicean)
4683a[4] 5720a[12] 7499a[9]

Libline (FR) *H-F Devin* a59
3 gr f Martaline Libaute (FR) (High Yield (USA))
977a[5]

Librisa Breeze *Dean Ivory* a105 113
7 gr g Mount Nelson Bruxcalina (FR) (Linamix (FR))
6215[2]◆ 8331[15] 9064[7] 9440[8]

Licankabur (FR) *H-A Pantall* a71 73
2 b c Rajsaman(FR) Adamantina (FR) (Muhtathir)
7674a[2]

Licit (IRE) *Mohamed Moubarak* a68
2 b f Poet's Voice Deserted (Oasis Dream)
8058[7] **8651**[2]

Licorice *Archie Watson* a57
2 b g Lawman(FR) Tutti Frutti (Teofilo (IRE))
6718[7] 7605[9]

Lidena (FR) *J-C Rouget* 93
3 b f Iffraaj Ludiana (FR) (Dalakhani (IRE))
2029a[4]

Lieutenant Conde *Hughie Morrison* a68 58
3 b g Havana Gold(IRE) Jasmeno (Catcher In The Rye (IRE))
186[3]◆ 561[4] 614[4] **(2517)** 4176[5] 4769[8] 6810[8] 8003[6]

Lifeboat (IRE) *Kevin Frost* a40 53
4 b g Born To Sea(IRE) Mrs Seek (Unfuwain (USA))
120[8] 288[12]

Life Knowledge (IRE) *Liam Bailey* a52 57
7 ch g Thewayyouare(USA) Rosa Bellini (IRE) (Rossini (USA))
3155[4] 3447[7] 4004[3] 4274[6] 7739[6] 8423[9] 9470[5]

Life Less Ordinary (IRE)
Chris Waller a89 109
7 b g Thewayyouare(USA) Dont Cross Tina (IRE) (Cape Cross (IRE))
8768a[7] **8952a**[4]

Life Matters (USA) *Richard Hughes* a60
2 ch c Candy Ride(ARG) Moon Catcher (USA) (Malibu Moon (USA))
9415[6] 9631[10]

Life's A Breeze (IRE) *R Le Gal* a71 96
3 b g Gale Force Ten Aubusson (IRE) (Montjeu (IRE))
1797a[6] 7561a[8]

Light And Dark *Saeed bin Suroor* 94
3 b c Shamardal(USA) Colour (AUS) (More Than Ready (USA))
4121[3] **(4887)**◆ 5546[16] 6517[4]

Light Angel *John Gosden* a87 93
2 gr c Dark Angel(IRE) Light The Stars (IRE) (Sea The Stars (IRE))
2394[2] (2792) 3949[15] **5382**[2] 5962[5] 6632[2] 6957[7] 7612[4] 7983[2]

Light Bay *Henry Candy* a52
2 b f Cable Bay(IRE) Key Light (IRE) (Acclamation)
8700[8]

Light Blush (IRE) *Charlie Appleby* 98
2 b f Kodiac Marsh Daisy (Pivotal)
(4918) **5346**[2] 5964[7]

Lightening Dance *Amanda Perrett* a78 82
5 b m Nathaniel(IRE) Dance Lively (USA) (Kingmambo (USA))
2685[3] 3010[5] 4447[3] (5344) **6511**[2] 7395[4] 7900[7]

Light Lily *Paul D'Arcy* a46
2 ch f Iffraaj Night Lily (IRE) (Night Shift (USA))
5590[5] 8891[12] **9195**[10] 9438[5]

Lightly Squeeze *Harry Fry* a74 82
5 b g Poet's Voice Zuleika Dobson (Cadeaux Genereux)
(6896) 7974[4]

Light My Fire (FR) *Karoly Kerekes* a70 87
4 b m Camelot Dixie Dance (IRE) (Orpen (USA))
4170a[7] **8153a**[5]

Lightness (IRE) *John Gosden* a69
2 b f Shamardal(USA) Serene Beauty (USA) (Street Cry (IRE))
9163[3]

Lightning Attack *Richard Fahey* a77 72
3 b g Lethal Force(IRE) Afrodita (IRE) (Montjeu (IRE))
1504[2] 1846[10] **2630**[3] **3249**[2] **3885**[3] 4316[4] 6258[5] 6940[4]◆ 7213[8] 7363[8] (7903)

Lightning Blue *Mick Channon* 41
2 b f Harbour Watch(IRE) Blue Beacon (Fantastic Light (USA))
7826[9] 8258[7] **8458**[14]

Lightning Bug (IRE) *Suzy Smith* a31 43
2 b f Starspangledbanner(AUS) Redinha (Dansili)
3578[8] **4221**[7] 5314[10] 5886[7] 7111[11] 7910[10]

Lightning Charlie *Iain Jardine* a81 75
7 b g Myboycharlie(IRE) Lighted Way (Kris)
1290[4] 1654[8] **2568**[6] 3536[4] 3963[6] 4866[4] 5661[9] 6301[4] 6916[14] 8063[10] 9113[9] 9397[4] 9545[3]

Light Of Air (FR) *Gary Moore* a65 70
6 b g Youmzain(IRE) Height Of Vanity (IRE) (Erhaab (USA))
1333[2] **2233**[2] 4215[5] 4838[5] 5337[2] 5570[4] 6173[6] (6760) 7984[5]

Lightoller (IRE) *P Monfort* a78 71
5 ch g Harbour Watch(IRE) April (IRE) (Rock Of Gibraltar (IRE))
2956a[11] **5715a**[7]

Light The Fuse (IRE) *K R Burke* a61 72
2 b c Dandy Man(IRE) Mandhooma (Oasis Dream)
4688[6] 4984[11] 5294[5]◆ 6175[4] **6563**[2] 7309[4] 7725[4] 7827[13] **8201**[2] 8465[6]

Light The Lights (SAF)
M F De Kock a90 112
7 b g Western Winter(USA) First Arrival (SAF) (Northern Guest (USA))
51a[6]◆ 172a[6] 514a[12]

Light Up Our Stars (IRE)
Richard Hughes a85 87
3 b c Rip Van Winkle(IRE) Shine Like A Star (Fantastic Light (USA))
1755[6] (2715) **4671**[3] **6909**[3] 7153[5] 8498[6]

Ligne D'Or *A Fabre* 109
4 b m Dansili Louve Nationale (IRE) (Galileo (IRE))
3678a[7] 4962a[3] 6263a[4] 7252a[3] **7942a**[7]

Lihou *David Evans* a84 85
3 ch g Mayson Kodiac Island (Kodiac)
1736[7] **(2525)** 6222[5] 7868[5] 8420[5] 9214[9]

Lijian (GER) *J Hirschberger* a75 107
5 b g Soldier Hollow Larena (GER) (Big Shuffle (USA))
9014a[7]

Likala (FR) *J-C Rouget* 103
3 gr f Exceed And Excel(AUS) Lidiyana (FR) (Motivator)
2027a[5] 8969a[7]

Li Kui *Paul Cole* a71 76
3 br g Poet's Voice Lily Again (American Post)
4071[4] **(4761)**

Lilbourne Star (IRE) *Clive Cox* a59 73
4 b g Lilbourne Lad(IRE) Make Amends (IRE) (Indian Ridge (IRE))
3464[6] 4227[12] **5107**[2] 5352[7] 6401[4]

Lil Grey (IRE) *Ms Sheila Lavery* 97
2 gr f Starspangledbanner(AUS) Vera Lilley (IRE) (Verglas (IRE))
4048[6] **5206a**[2] 6190a[3] 7692[9] 8164a[7]

Liliofthelamplight (IRE)
Mark Johnston a81 76
3 ch f Helmet(AUS) Lilakiya (IRE) (Dr Fong (USA))
1034[5] (1984) 2925[3] 3807[4] **(4329)** 4626[5] 5688[5] 6026[11] 6630[4] 7452[9]

Lili Wen Fach (IRE) *David Evans* a41 59
2 gr f Gregorian(IRE) Zuzinia (IRE) (Mujadil (USA))
1642[6] 1844[3] 2191[7] 2716[4] 2996[2] **(3573)** 3812[2] 4647[5] 5777[8] 6637[6] 7296[3] 8841[8]

Lilkian *Shaun Keightley* a69 55
2 ch g Sepoy(AUS) Janie Runaway (IRE) (Antonius Pius (USA))
4999[2]◆ 5527[4] 6167[7] 7179[5] 7556[5]◆ 8195[2] 8650[3]◆ **(8841)** 9031[6]

Lille *Kevin Ryan* a75 65
3 b f Equiano(FR) Interlace (Pivotal)
(1161) 1492[4] 3659[8] 4128[9]

Lillian Russell (IRE) *H-A Pantall* 104
4 b m Dubawi(IRE) Be Fabulous (GER) (Samum (GER))
2169a[8] 6266a[7] **8171a**[3]

Lilligram *Roger Varian* a64 61
3 ch f Leroidesanimaux(BRZ) Millistar (Galileo (IRE))
128[6] **3050**[8]

Lilly Kafeine (FR) *A Schutz* a77 101
5 b m Myboycharlie(IRE) Hamida (USA) (Johannesburg (USA))
7255a[7] 8583a[4]

Lilly's Legacy *Nikki Evans* a8 16
3 b f Piccolo Lilly Blue (IRE) (Hawk Wing (USA))
7228[4] 7772[10] 8451[10]

Lil Rockerfeller (USA) *Neil King* a63 101
8 ch g Hard Spun(USA) Layounne (USA) (Mt. Livermore (USA))
5540[6]

Lily Ash (IRE) *Mike Murphy* a47 60
6 b m Lilbourne Lad(IRE) Ashdali (IRE) (Grand Lodge (USA))
5679[2] 6324[8] 7318[12] 8068[7] 8664[3]

Lily Bonnette *Julia Feilden* a21 24
2 ch f Helmet(AUS) Wish You Luck (Dubai Destination (USA))
2761[19] 4502[8] **6322**[6] 8824[12]

Lily Jean *Stuart Kittow* 30
4 ch m Makfi Eastern Lily (USA) (Eastern Echo (USA))
2280[8] 3533[10]
Lily Like *Andrew Balding* a55
2 gr f Kodiac Lixirova (FR) (Slickly (FR))
9413[6]
Lily Of Year (FR) *Denis Coakley* a57 57
4 b m Siyouni(FR) Arpagone (FR) (Victory Note (USA))
1820[5] 2728[6] 4115[15] 6018[7] 6107[7] 8008[5] 8689[6]
Lilypad (IRE) *Amy Murphy* a46 58
4 b m New Approach(IRE) Vow (Motivator)
2737[6] 3708[6] 8904[6]
Lily's Candle (FR) *F Head* 108
3 gr f Style Vendome(FR) Golden Lily (FR) (Dolphin Street (FR))
1795a[9]
Lily's Prince (IRE) *Garvan Donnelly* a75 57
9 b g Strategic Prince Miss Sabre (Sabrehill (USA))
307a[5] 748a[8]
Limalima (IRE) *Stuart Williams* a51
3 ch f Sea The Stars(IRE) Katla (IRE) (Majestic Missile (IRE))
7190[8] 8552[7]
Limaro Prospect (IRE) *Sir Mark Prescott Bt* a57
2 b c Camacho Ibecke (Exceed And Excel (AUS))
9130[7] 9413[10] 9569[7]
Limato (IRE) *Henry Candy* a93 119
7 b g Tagula(IRE) Come April (Singspiel (IRE))
2744[4] (4389) 4923[12] 6508[6] 8090[2]
Limelighter *Sheena West* 61
3 b g Harbour Watch(IRE) Steal The Curtain (Royal Applause)
2407[4] 4836[7] 6505[4]
Limelite (IRE) *K Kukk* 44
5 b m Dark Angel(IRE) Light It Up (IRE) (Elusive City (USA))
2671a[6] 3173a[6] 3641a[5] 4174a[5] 4685a[7] 5232[5]
Limerick Lord (IRE) *Julia Feilden* a58 52
7 b g Lord Shanakill(USA) Hollow Green (IRE) (Beat Hollow)
6[13] (485) 760[3] 912[3] 1075[3] (1431) 1527[10] 3592[9] 4460[7] 5302[5] 5806[7] 6758[2] 7028[5] 8942[9] 9225[13]
Limited Reserve (IRE) *Christian Williams* 38
7 b g Court Cave(IRE) Lady Blackie (IRE) (Definite Article)
1365[7] 3946[9] 4177[9]
Limit Long *D J Bunyan* a62 89
3 ch g Lope De Vega(IRE) Framed (Elnadim (USA))
2492a[6] 7189[10]
L'Improviste (FR) *Alain Couetil* a65 66
4 bl h Vision D'Etat(FR) Mojo Moon (IRE) (Slickly (FR))
1908a[8]
Lim's Cruiser (AUS) *Stephen Gray* 109
6 b g Casino Prince(AUS) Hope Downs (AUS) (Good Journey (USA))
4094[8] 4923[6]
Linaria (GER) *J Hirschberger* 88
3 b f Soldier Hollow Lavela (GER) (Nayef (USA))
3119a[10]
Lin Chong *Paul Cole* 82
2 b c Muhaarar Reroute (IRE) (Acclamation)
4839[7] 5374[3] 6262a[3] 7160[5] (8447a)
Lincoln (IRE) *Denis Gerard Hogan* a47 83
8 b g Clodovil(IRE) Gilt Linked (Compton Place)
5537a[8]
Lincoln Blue *Jane Chapple-Hyam* a79 79
2 b c Bated Breath Garden Row (IRE) (Invincible Spirit (IRE))
3190[7] 3739[2] (4361) 5624[8] 9043[7] 9364[7]
Lincoln Gamble *Richard Fahey* a51 57
2 gr g Zebedee Lincolnrose (IRE) (Verglas (IRE))
7308[4] 8395[5] 8816[6]
Lincoln Park *Michael Appleby* 96
3 b c Kyllachy Twilight Pearl (Pastoral Pursuits)
1736[13] 1945[4] (2559) 3632[6] 4650[3] 5422[2] 5983[5] 6922[7] 7431[23] 7868[9]
Lincoln Red *Olly Williams* a51 60
3 ch g Monsieur Bond(IRE) Roxy Hart (Halling (USA))
1549[7] 1982[2] (2735) (3775) 4328[6] 4807[6] 5914[4] 6174[9] 6737[7] 7654[10]
Lincoln Spirit *David O'Meara* a58 43
3 gr f Piccolo Lincolnrose (IRE) (Verglas (IRE))
(296) 437[2] 620[7] 813[3]◆ 940[6] 1140[11] 1296[9]
Lincoln Tale (IRE) *David O'Meara* 67
3 b f Intello(GER) Pine Chip (USA) (Nureyev (USA))
2152[3]◆ (2712) 3311[9] 3708[3] 3955[7] 5028[5] 5974[4] 6371[3] 7314[8] 7732[2] 8238[10]
L'Indomptable (FR) *C Escuder* a78 80
4 b m Rajsaman(FR) Kitty D'Argos (FR) (Ecossais I (FR))
6651a[3]
Line Des Ongrais (FR) *P Chemin & C Herpin* a70 101
8 b m Voix Du Nord(FR) Kitzmaid (GER) (Midyan (USA))
2169a[5] 7008a[5] 7928a[9]
Line Drummer (FR) *J Reynier* 82
9 b g Galileo(IRE) Miss Bio (FR) (River Mist (USA))
2675a[2]
Line of Duty (IRE) *Charlie Appleby* 117
3 ch c Galileo(IRE) Jacqueline Quest (IRE) (Rock Of Gibraltar (IRE))
2777[7] 3345[9] 6004a[3] 7007a[3] 7923a[3] (Dead)
Line Of Enquiry *James Tate* a73
2 b c New Approach(IRE) Cadenza (FR) (Dansili)
9208[3]
Line Of Reason (IRE) *Paul Midgley* a88 94
9 br g Kheleyf(USA) Miss Party Line (USA) (Phone Trick (USA))
1847[2] 1946[5] 2775[17] 3344[13] 4331[6] 4406[3]◆ 4896[13] 5524[7] 6332[6] 6809[3] 7077[2] 7348[7]

L'Inganno Felice (FR) *Iain Jardine* a65 56
9 br g Librettist(USA) Final Overture (FR) (Rossini (USA))
9221[4]
Linger (IRE) *Joseph Patrick O'Brien* a62 83
6 b g Cape Cross(IRE) Await So (Sadler's Wells (USA))
(5712a)
Linguine (FR) *Dai Williams* a24 38
9 ch g Linngari(IRE) Amerissage (USA) (Rahy (USA))
5744[8]
Linked (IRE) *E J O'Neill* a14 61
2 b c Cable Bay(IRE) L'Amour Toujours (IRE) (Montjeu (IRE))
6386a[8]
Linngaria (FR) *F Foucher* a64 61
4 b m Linngari(IRE) Syllable (Halling (USA))
6031a[5]
Lionel (FR) *C Lerner* a58 76
2 b c Toronado(IRE) Chega De Saudade (FR) (Fastnet Rock (AUS))
5642a[4] 6433a[3]
Lion Hearted (IRE) *Michael Appleby* a89 59
5 b g Lope De Vega(IRE) Ros The Boss (IRE) (Danehill (USA))
(379) (501) (738) (784) (1164) 1197[9] (1544)◆ (1714) 1916[10]
Lion's Vigil (USA) *Richard Fahey* 53
2 ch g Kitten's Joy(USA) Keeping Watch (IRE) (Danehill (USA))
4623[4]
Lippy Lady (IRE) *Paul George* a57 50
3 b f Bungle Inthejungle Sayrah (Sakhee (USA))
855[5] 1140[4] 2007[3] 2734[2]◆ 3256[10] 4797[3] (5304) 6117[5] 6643[12] 7295[4] 7909[4] 8822[10]
Lips Eagle (GER) *Andreas Suborics* 86
3 b f Gleneagles(IRE) Lips Arrow (GER) (Big Shuffle (USA))
7749a[4] 8586a[3]
Lipslikecherries *Jamie Osborne* a56
2 b f Dark Angel(IRE) Manaaber (USA) (Medicean)
7813[6] 8602[13]
Lips Queen (GER) *Eva Fabianova* 101
3 bb f Kamsin(GER) Lady Lips (GER) (Zinaad)
(8587a)
Liquid Mercury (SAF) *R Bouresly* 76
7 gr g Trippi(USA) Skip Poker (USA) (Skip Away (USA))
960a[12]
Lisbet *John Gosden* a60
2 ch f Frankel Angel Terrace (USA) (Ghostzapper (USA))
9046[7] 9327[8]
Lisbeth Salander (IRE) *Richard Spencer* a44 33
2 b f Camacho Laheen (IRE) (Bluebird (USA))
6079[10] 6719[9] 7104[8] 7833[11]
Liscahann *Seamus Mullins* 65
2 ch f Coach House(IRE) Athwaab (Cadeaux Genereux)
5317[4]◆ 5859[7] 6800[4] 7754[13]
Lismore (IRE) *Sir Mark Prescott Bt* a55 38
2 b f Zoffany(IRE) Tecla (IRE) (Whipper (USA))
7473[7] 7814[11] 8258[6]
Lisnamoyle Lady (IRE) *Martin Smith* a45 45
4 ch m Roderic O'Connor(IRE) Allegheny Dawn (IRE) (Teofilo (IRE))
243[9] 920[9] 1384[10] 3476[10] 5430[6] 7336[3]
Lissitzky (IRE) *Andrew Balding* a87 91
4 b g Declaration Of War(USA) Tarfshi (Mtoto)
2342[4] (2801) 3600[14] 4381[10] 4884[17]
Listen In (IRE) *F Head* 109
5 ch m Sea The Stars(IRE) Es Que (Inchinor)
3138a[2] 3389a[6] 5510a[3] 6263a[7]
Listen To The Wind (IRE) *William Haggas* a84 90
3 b f Toronado(IRE) Henties Bay (IRE) (Cape Cross (IRE))
2103[6] (3278) 4497[2] 8222[8]
Litigation *Jaber Ramadhan* a78 62
3 b m Foxwedge(AUS) Torcross (Vettori (IRE))
573a[11]
Litigator (IRE) *Henry Spiller* 63
2 b c Elzaam(AUS) Lady Elsie (Singspiel (IRE))
4947a[5]
Litigious *John Gosden* 96
3 b f Lawman(FR) Field Of Miracles (IRE) (Galileo (IRE))
(3637)◆ (5421) 6124[3] 7075[2] 7566[6]
Litterale Ci (FR) *Harry Fry* 94
6 b m Soldier Of Fortune(IRE) Cigalia (Red Ransom (USA))
5183[9] 5508a[3] 6171[6]
Little Anxious *Grace Harris* 34
3 ch f Coach House(IRE) Allmost Inti (Intikhab (USA))
1557[11] 2276[9] 2995[5] 4180[15] 5083[12]
Little Becky *Ed Vaughan* a78
2 b f Sir Percy Amelia May (Dansili)
(8454)
Little Bird (IRE) *Richard Hannon* a74 77
2 b f Free Eagle(IRE) Burma Star (Shamardal (USA))
2761[6] (4366) 5314[2] (6281)
Littlebitofmagic *Michael Dods* a50 48
3 b g Phoenix Reach(IRE) Magic Echo (Wizard King)
1643[9] 5969[7] 7903[6]
Little Boy Blue *Bill Turner* a87 96
4 gr g Hellvelyn Dusty Dazzler (IRE) (Titus Livius (FR))
981[2] 1098[6] 1915[3] 2227[3] 3037[3] 3531[4] (3963) 4236[5] 4545[2] 5746[4] 6565[3] 7175[5] 8522[4]
Little Brown Trout *William Stone* a82 80
2 b g Casamento(IRE) Clock Opera (IRE) (Excellent Art)
3601[6] 4564[7] 5145[3]◆ 6515[3] 7391[4] (8430) 8723[5] 9162[9] (9661)

Little Choosey *Roy Bowring* a54 48
9 ch m Cadeaux Genereux Little Nymph (Emperor Fountain)
2731[2] 485[8] 969[5] 3473[10] 4657[4] 5106[8] 8068[12] 8942[P] (Dead)
Little Devil *Bill Turner* a37 45
2 ch f Hot Streak(IRE) Sunburnt (Haafhd)
1513[7] 1821[10] 2694[9]
Littledidyouknow (IRE) *Archie Watson* a79 77
2 b f Due Diligence(USA) Solfilia (Teofilo (IRE))
(1968) (2191) 3333a[7] 9322[2]
Little Downs *Richard Hannon* 49
2 b f Siyouni(FR) Asaawir (Royal Applause)
8759[8]
Little Floozie *Brett Johnson* a40
2 b f Brazen Beau(AUS) Sweet Wind Music (Zamindar (USA))
7813[9] 9062[10]
Little Fortune *Henry Candy* a33
2 b f Swiss Spirit Chevise (IRE) (Holy Roman Emperor (IRE))
8891[13]
Little India (FR) *K R Burke* a76 77
3 ch f Manduro(GER) Jolie Laide (IRE) (Sakhee (USA))
1730[4] 2229[3] 3310[3] 4602[2] 6186[4] 9138[4] 9480[7] 9496[5]
Little Jo (FR) *P Monfort* a64
3 b g Planteur(IRE) Fanny Des Hardys (IRE) (Fasliyev (USA))
217a[9]
Little Jo *Brian Ellison* a89 47
5 b g Major Cadeaux Discoed (Distinctly North (USA))
7694[28] 8918[3] 9517[8]
Little Kim *K R Burke* 87
3 b f Garswood Primo Lady (Lucky Story (USA))
4101[4] 4891[13] 5471a[9]
Little Lady Luck *Mark Usher*
3 ch f Yorgunnabelucky(USA) Dockside Strike (Docksider (USA))
1142[13] 5595[9] 6559[5] 7278[12]
Little Legs *Brian Ellison* a74 87
3 b f Captain Gerrard(IRE) Livia Drusilla (IRE) (Holy Roman Emperor (IRE))
1762[9] 1929[11] 3293[8] 4294[6] (5042)◆ 5399[6] 6332[5] 6476[12] 7387[8] 8023[9]
Little Lotte (IRE) *Mrs A Corson*
6 b m Kodiac Dancing Steps (Zafonic (USA))
2003a[8] 2500a[3] 3642a[8] 6008a[7]
Little Lulu (IRE) *Archie Watson* a44
2 b f Muhaarar Queen Of Tara (IRE) (Sadler's Wells (USA))
3689[8] 4245[6] 6072[7] 6884[10]
Littlemissattitude *Derek Shaw* a57
2 b f Due Diligence(USA) Lady Elalmadol (IRE) (Shamardal (USA))
7995[9] 9036[11] 9393[6]
Little Miss Daisy *William Muir* a65 59
5 b m Arabian Gleam Desert Liaison (Dansili)
179[8] 433[7] 920[3] 1179[7] 1266[6] 1477[8] 1837[11] (2215) (2944) 3352[5]
Little Miss Kodi (IRE) *Mark Loughnane* a56 57
6 b m Kodiac Sensasse (IRE) (Imperial Ballet (IRE))
243[5] 553[2] 594[4] 719[2] 887[7] 2693[6] 3007[10] 5081[2] 6131[8] 6897[13] 7420[12]
Little Miss Lilly *Clive Cox* a61 62
4 b m Lethal Force(IRE) Malilla (IRE) (Red Clubs (IRE))
9507[3] 9670[2]
Little Miss Lola *Lynn Siddall* a51 57
5 ch m Dandy Man(IRE) Purepleasureseeker (IRE) (Grand Lodge (USA))
3975[14] 4493[12] 6936[7] 7737[5] 8720[13]
Little Miss Muffin *Sam England* a30 50
3 b f Doncaster Rover(USA) Guava (Kyllachy)
3707[8] 4439[3] 5128[5] 5771[8] 6273[9] 9185[12] 9398[12] 9539[13]
Little Palaver *Clive Cox* a80 67
7 b g Showcasing Little Nymph (Emperor Fountain)
(253) 564[4]◆ 755[6] 1329[5] 2339[6] 2971[2] 3701[8] 6335[4] 7080[2]◆ (8221) 9329[6]
Little Rock (IRE) *Richard Hughes* a76 79
3 gr g Zebedee Lakatoi (Saddlers' Hall (IRE))
403[9] (930) 1264[2]◆ 1823[3] 2406[6]
Little Ted *Tim Easterby* a60 62
2 ch c Cityscape Speedy Utmost Meg (Medicean)
3335[9] 3954[5] 4623[8] 5789[3] 6053[3] 6372[9] 6625[3] 7140[4] 7438[4] 8201[6] 9031[10] 9164[3] 9568[4]
Little Thornton *Stella Barclay* a34 6
3 b f Swiss Spirit Lee Miller (IRE) (Danehill Dancer (IRE))
4193[9] 4629[5] 5236[10] 5559[20]
Little Tipple *John Ryan* a40 39
3 b f Gregorian(IRE) Back On Baileys (Kyllachy)
2238[13] 3148[9] 3442[11] 3775[7] 4749[7] 5102[6] 5304[4] 5548[3] 5803[11] 5880[4] 8003[8]
Little Tipsy *Adam West* 25
2 b f Harbour Watch(IRE) B Berry Brandy (USA) (Event Of The Year (USA))
4223[9]
Littleton Hall (IRE) *Mick Channon* a73 41
2 br g Camacho When Not Iff (IRE) (Iffraaj)
1733[9] 1937[2] 2316[3] 2476[7] 7754[12] 8430[9]
Liva (IRE) *Stef Keniry* a58 52
4 ch g Champs Elysees Resistance Heroine (Dr Fong (USA))
4404[10] 5423[12] 9167[6] 9626[9]
Live Dangerously *John Bridger* a44 44
9 b g Zamindar(USA) Desert Lynx (IRE) (Green Desert (USA))
1675[12]
Live In The Moment (IRE) *Adam West* a72 74
2 ch g Zebedee Approaching Autumn (New Approach (IRE))
5591[6] 6845[8] 7407[4] 7754[2] 8069[2] 8890[5]

Lively Lydia *Eve Johnson Houghton* a44 51
3 b f Charm Spirit(IRE) Coventina (IRE) (Daylami (IRE))
2937[6] 4507[10]
Live Your Dream (IRE) *Saeed bin Suroor* a77 76
2 b c Iffraaj Dream Book (Sea The Stars (IRE))
6708[2] 7392[3] (7957)
Living In The Past (IRE) *K R Burke* 110
2 b f Bungle Inthejungle Ayr Missile (Cadeaux Genereux)
4006[3]◆ (4583)◆ 5411[3] (6374) 7692[5] 8748a[14]
Living Legend (IRE) *Mark Johnston* a89 99
3 b g Camelot Jazz Girl (IRE) (Johar (USA))
(1419) (1911) 2558[4]
Livvys Dream (IRE) *Charles Hills* a84 82
4 b m Declaration Of War(USA) Briolette (IRE) (Sadler's Wells (USA))
(2516)◆ 3300[2] 5741[6] 6331[7]
Lizzie Loch *Alistair Whillans* a51 60
3 br f Maxios Quenched (Dansili)
103[8] 739[4] 971[10] 3721[10] 4690[11] (4983) 6938[7] 7493[6] 8238[7]
Lleyton (IRE) *J R Finn* a53 62
7 b g Kalanisi(IRE) Bonnie Parker (IRE) (Un Desperado (FR))
5599a[11]
Lloyd (IRE) *Mlle J Soudan* a92 93
2 b c Zebedee Liesl (IRE) (Iffraaj)
(4949a) 7602a[6]
Local Affair *Simon Crisford* a64
3 ch f Teofilo(IRE) Local Spirit (USA) (Lion Cavern (USA))
2017[4]
Local History *James Tate* a72 72
3 b f Sepoy(AUS) Local Fancy (Bahamian Bounty)
(2976) 4248[3] 5392[4] 6132[4]
Loch Lady *Ralph Beckett* a57 48
3 b f Camelot Highland Shot (Selkirk (USA))
370[7] 2343[12] 3418[7]
Loch Laggan (IRE) *David Menuisier* 8
3 b g Sea The Stars(IRE) Magic Sister (Cadeaux Genereux)
1755[11] 2505[11]
Loch Ness Monster (IRE) *Michael Appleby* a87 93
3 b g War Command(USA) Celestial Dream (IRE) (Oasis Dream)
1485[3]◆ 2082[3] 2616[2] 3082[11] 3857[5] 4792[7] 5095[2] 5973[5] 6730[6]
Locked N' Loaded *Tim Fitzgerald* a80 48
2 b c Morpheus La Roumegue (USA) (Henrythenavigator (USA))
5980[8] 6402[7] 6858[4] 7548[7] (9250) 9546[2] (9608)
Lock Seventeen (USA) *Charlie Fellowes* a52 59
3 b g Kitten's Joy(USA) Spirit Line (USA) (Indian Charlie (USA))
1165[7] 1417[9] 2343[11] 2941[4] (3528) 4345[6]
Loco Dempsey (FR) *Richard Hannon* a38 51
2 b f Cityscape L'Addition (Exceed And Excel (AUS))
5988[12] 6205[6] 7461[7] 8452[9] 9045[10]
Locommotion *Matthew Salaman* a61 56
7 gr g Proclamation(IRE) Miss Madame (IRE) (Cape Cross (IRE))
365[4] 2235[5]
Lodi (FR) *L Rovisse* a71 74
5 b h Whipper(USA) Grise Bomb (USA) (Mr Greeley (USA))
1073a[5] 2026a[2]
Lofty *David Barron* a71 77
3 b g Harbour Watch(IRE) Curly Come Home (Notnowcato)
1195[2] 1523[2]◆ 2334[3] 4286[2] 7976[3] 8268[6]
Logan Roy *Andrew Balding* a53
2 ch c Bated Breath Masandra (IRE) (Desert Prince (IRE))
9155[7] 9415[7]
Logan's Choice *Roger Charlton* a54
4 b g Redoute's Choice(AUS) Bright Morning (USA) (Storm Cat (USA))
3445[11] 5269[9] 7240[15]
Logi (IRE) *Rebecca Bastiman* a75 72
5 b g Kodiac Feet Of Flame (USA) (Theatrical (IRE))
812[9] 1273[11] 1760[6] 2437[3] 2679[6] 3221[5] 3657[4] 4058[2] 4879[4] 5488[7] 5903[2] 6204[11]
Logician *John Gosden* 119
3 ro c Frankel Scuffle (Daylami (IRE))
(2795)◆ (4073) (4559) (6353) (7196)
Log Out Island (IRE) *S Seemar* a60 85
6 b g Dark Angel(IRE) White Daffodil (IRE) (Footstepsinthesand)
843a[10] 1111a[11]
Logrado (ARG) *E Charpy* a94 101
4 b h Manipulator(USA) Lincay (ARG) (Interprete (ARG))
1114a[7] 1440a[7]
Lola Paige (IRE) *David O'Meara* a48 76
2 b f Galileo(IRE) Timbuktu (IRE) (Fastnet Rock (AUS))
3881[2]◆ 4605[5] 7203[2] 8699[8]
Lola's Theme *Tom Dascombe* a55 75
3 gr f Iffraaj Lady's Art (FR) (Verglas (IRE))
2559[5]◆ 3548[4] 3842[7] 4553[5] 5124[2] 5424[5] 6230[6]
Lolita Pulido (IRE) *Eve Johnson Houghton* a43 64
3 b f Toronado(IRE) Myth And Magic (IRE) (Namid)
5350[6] 6075[8] 6558[5] 7027[12]
Lollipop Lady *Mme M-C Chaalon* a50 43
3 gb f Garswood Nolas Lolly (IRE) (Lomitas)
1739[8] 2113[7] 2361[12] 9281a[14]
Lomu (IRE) *Iain Jardine* a97 89
5 ch g Dandy Man(IRE) Miss Me (Marju (IRE))
3501[4]◆ 4406[18] 5120[10] 6549[5] 7736[7] (9286)◆ (9571)◆

London (GER)
Mrs Ilka Gansera-Leveque 40
2 b f Lord Of England(GER) La Reine Noir (GER) (Rainbow Quest (USA))
8203[8] 8759[12]

London Arch *Charlie Fellowes* a71
2 b c Fastnet Rock(AUS) Mount Crystal (IRE) (Montjeu (IRE))
9452[2]

London Calling (IRE)
Richard Spencer a71 69
2 b g Requinto(IRE) Bellechance (Acclamation)
2761[7] 3257[5] 4480[3] 5777[5] 6372[8] 7548[2] 8402[3]◆ 8699[4]

London Eye (USA)
Sir Michael Stoute a74 75
3 ch c Australia Circle Of Life (USA) (Belong To Me (USA))
1652[6] 2406[2] 3295[3] 4291[4]

London Grammar (IRE)
Ralph J Smith a42 44
5 b m Sir Prancealot(IRE) Emmas Princess (IRE) (Bahhare (USA))
204[4] 369[13] 736[10]

London Memories (FR) *A Spanu* a64 54
2 b c Hurricane Cat(USA) Elusive Lily (Elusive City (USA))
7675a[11]

London Pride *Jonathan Portman* a54 38
3 ch f Cityscape Heartsease (Pursuit Of Love)
2965[10] 3947[8] 4794[11] 5652[5] 6117[3] 7374[13]

London Protocol (FR) *John Mackie* a48 68
6 ch g Muhtathir Troiecat (FR) (One Cool Cat (USA))
2480[9] 3450[11] 3880[6] 6961[12] 8070[8] 8766[14]

London Rock (IRE) *Richard Hannon* a72 73
3 b c Society Rock(IRE) Scottish Exile (IRE) (Ashkalani (IRE))
142[4] 458[5]

Lone Peak (FR) *F Head* a69 74
3 b c Lope De Vega(IRE) Oh Beautiful (Galileo (IRE))
1797a[8]

Lone Sailor (USA) *Thomas Amoss* a111
4 b h Majestic Warrior(USA) Ambitious (USA) (Mr Greeley (USA))
7011a[10]

Lone Voice (IRE) *Tony Carroll* a47 65
4 b g Poet's Voice Zain Joy (CAN) (Survivalist (USA))
940[14] 1527[8] 2587[8]

Long Call *Tony Carroll* a80 82
6 b g Authorized(IRE) Gacequita (URU) (Ride The Rails (USA))
2926◆ (5841) 7026[3] (7465) 8829[4]

Long Game (FR) *P Decouz* a55
3 b c Toronado(IRE) Bea Remembered (Doyen (IRE))
421a[9]

Long Haired Lover (IRE)
James Fanshawe a75
2 b f Night Of Thunder(IRE) Love And Laughter (IRE) (Theatrical (IRE))
8453[3]

Long Range Toddy (USA)
Steven Asmussen a108
3 bb c Take Charge Indy(USA) Pleasant Song (USA) (Unbridled's Song (USA))
2425a[16]

Longroom *Noel Wilson* a63 70
7 b g Oasis Dream Phantom Wind (USA) (Storm Cat (USA))
1501[8] 2841[10] 4100[7] 4514[2] 5042[9] 5901[4] 6829[4] 7959[7] 8296[3] 8715[6] 9013[6]

Longsider (IRE) *David Lanigan* a69
2 b c Ruler Of The World(IRE) Lady Dettoria (FR) (Vettori (IRE))
9509[4]

Long Socks *Alan King* a68 66
5 ch g Notnowcato Sienna Sunset (IRE) (Spectrum (IRE))
(232) 1526[5]

Longville Lilly *Trevor Wall* a43 39
4 b m Mawatheeq(USA) Curtains (Dubawi (IRE))
2731[12] 4554[5] 5081[8] 6059[8] 6628[12] 6977[8] 8646[7] 9028[10] 9609[8]

Lonicera *Henry Candy* a63 65
3 gr f Lethal Force(IRE) Puya (Kris)
2355[2] 3182[2]◆ 3651[10] 4642[3] 5284[8] 6643[8] 7236[6] 8008[8]

Look Around *Andrew Balding* a78 105
3 b f Kingman Magic America (USA) (High Yield (USA))
1832[4] 2443[9] 5369[2] 6726[3]

Look At Him *Jo Hughes* 29
2 ch c Anjaal Vaughn Got Style (Champs Elysees)
1657a[14] 2263a[10]

Look Back (FR) *H-A Pantall* a82 77
4 gr g Rajsaman(FR) Like It Is (FR) (Kendor (FR))
4747a[8]

Look Closely *Roger Varian* 91
3 b g Sea The Stars(IRE) Lady Heidi (High Chaparral (IRE))
4073[5] 5103[3] 6836[2] (7525)

Looking For Carl *Mark Loughnane* a73 65
4 b g Lope De Vega(IRE) Dam Beautiful (Sleeping Indian)
1497[5] 2626[8] 3686[6] 4251[12]

Look Out Louis *Tim Easterby* 75
3 b g Harbour Watch(IRE) Perfect Act (Act One)
1662[6] 2149[3] (2635) (3048) 3479[3] 4008[6] 4847[20] 5724[7] 6623[4] 7005[2] 7402[23]

Looks Good (IRE) *Richard Hughes* a54
2 b f Morpheus Unfortunate (Komaite (USA))
6146[3] 7031[7] 8287[9] 8651[11] 9212[8] 9449[6]

Look Surprised *Roger Teal* a72 75
6 ch m Kier Park(IRE) Cloridja (Indian Ridge (IRE))
317[7] 763[P] 2206[8] 3838[3] 4230[7] 4494[9] (5750) 6288[2] 6809[P] 9135[5]◆ 9402[7]

Looktothelight (USA)
Jamie Osborne a69 32
2 bb c Mineshaft(USA) Julie Napp (USA) (Curlin (USA))
3601[10] 6926[5] 8121[5]

Look Twice (JPN) *Hideaki Fujiwara* 113
6 b h Stay Gold(JPN) Esyoueffcee (IRE) (Alzao (USA))
9153a[10]

Look Who It Isnae (IRE) *Alan Berry* 34
3 b f Thewayyouare(USA) Forest Delight (IRE) (Shinko Forest (IRE))
5669[5] 6013[4]

Loolabelle *Tim Easterby* 38
2 b f Harbour Watch(IRE) Hamloola (Red Ransom (USA))
2475[7]

Loolwah (IRE) *Sir Michael Stoute* a71 87
3 gr f Pivotal Yanabeeaa (USA) (Street Cry (IRE))
3372[2] (3974) 4898[4] 6406[5]

Loose Chippings (IRE)
Ivan Furtado a61 56
5 b g Rock Of Gibraltar(IRE) Karjera (IRE) (Key Of Luck (USA))
1861[2] 2196[2]◆ 2345[2] 2738[7] 4518[2] 5080[3] 5593[10] 6098[2] (7087a) 7873[2] 8072[3] 8269[3]

Lope Athena *Stuart Williams* a54 54
3 b f Lope De Vega(IRE) Elas Diamond (Danehill Dancer (IRE))
2366[5] 3603[10] 5268[6] 6635[6]

Lope De Loop (IRE) *Aytach Sadik* a40 52
4 b m Lope De Vega(IRE) Patroller (USA) (Grand Slam (USA))
464[5] 1020[10] 2128[12] 4764[6] 8668[5] 9182[8]

Lope Scholar (IRE) *Ralph Beckett* a70 33
3 b f Lope De Vega(IRE) Varsity (Lomitas)
4592[5] 5193[5] 6187[P]

Lopes Dancer (IRE) *Brian Ellison* a82 66
7 b g Lope De Vega(IRE) Ballet Dancer (IRE) (Refuse To Bend (IRE))
124[4] (495) 803[4] 1840[5] 2185[2] 2636[6] (7577) 8082[3] 8396[6] 8948[4]

Lope Y Fernandez (IRE)
A P O'Brien 108
2 b c Lope De Vega(IRE) Black Dahlia (Dansili)
4091[2] 5520[3] (6690a) 7693[6]

L'Optimiste (FR) *J Parize* a70 75
6 b g Makfi Shapoura (FR) (Sinndar (IRE))
2182a[9] 2675a[3]

Loquen (IRE) *Andrea Marcialis* 60
3 b g Lawman(FR) Emouna Queen (IRE) (Indian Ridge (IRE))
1842a[5] 2392a[3]

Lord Campari (IRE) *Roger Varian* 70
2 b c Kingman Blanche Dubawi (IRE) (Dubawi (IRE))
6669[6]

Lord Chapelfield *Amy Murphy* a49
2 b g Delegator Diamond Vanessa (IRE) (Distinctly North (USA))
8605[11] 9155[12] 9242[10]

Lord Cooper *Marjorie Fife* a53 53
5 b g Sir Percy Zooming (IRE) (Indian Ridge (IRE))
439[6] 599[3] 742[9] 912[7]

Lord Del Boy *Michael Attwater* a30
4 b g Delegator Lady Prodee (Proclamation (IRE))
159[9]

Lord Digby *Adam West* a31
4 b g Dick Turpin(IRE) Chrissycross (IRE) (Cape Cross (IRE))
435[9] 732[6] 1070[4] 2006[5]

Lordelio (IRE) *G Botti* a84 85
2 ch c Dandy Man(IRE) Nurama (Daylami (IRE))
6141a[4]

Lord George (IRE)
James Fanshawe a108 85
6 gr g Sir Percy Mahima (FR) (Linamix (FR))
82[10] 311[3] 519[4] 1917[7] 6848[7]

Lord Glitters (FR) *David O'Meara* a96 120
6 gr g Whipper(USA) Lady Glitters (FR) (Homme De Loi (IRE))
1445a[3] 2829[13] (3948) 5543[5] 6354[6] 8334[8] 8774a[9]

Lord Halifax (IRE) *Charlie Fellowes* a84 70
3 b g Famous Name Neutral (Beat Hollow)
2690[9] 3664[4] 4459[2] 8433[8] (9303)◆ 9421[3]

Lord Howard (IRE) *Mick Channon* a57 54
3 b g Havana Gold(IRE) Lady Gabrielle (IRE) (Dansili)
6119[6] 6505[6] 7295[6] (8003) 8205[6] (9216) 9481[10]

Lord Lamington *Mark Johnston* a84 85
3 b g Australia Lady Eclair (IRE) (Danehill Dancer (IRE))
917[4]◆ (1270)◆ 1396[2] (1884) 2317[5] (3260) 4024[5] 4782[2] 5487[8] 6716[5] 6888[2] 7209[6]

Lord Murphy (IRE) *Mark Loughnane* a57 41
6 b g Holy Roman Emperor(IRE) Tralanza (IRE) (Traditionally (USA))
180[11] 462[2] 624[8] 3592[5] 5675[7] 6731[9]

Lord Neidin *Alan King* a73
2 br c Outstrip Cosmea (Compton Place)
7814[3] 8455[4] 9052[3]

Lord North (IRE) *John Gosden* a92 114
3 b g Dubawi(IRE) Najoum (USA) (Giant's Causeway (USA))
(2188) 3026[8] 6915[2]◆ (7694) 8336[2] (8764)◆

Lord Oberon *K R Burke* a84 100
4 b g Mayson Fairy Shoes (Kyllachy)
2100[8] 3589[2] 3863[18]

Lord Of The Alps (IRE)
Mark Johnston a73 73
2 ch g Lord Of England(GER) Adalawa (IRE) (Barathea (IRE))
3954[3]◆ 5052[2] 5512[3] 6097[2] 7309[6]

Lord Of The Glen *Jim Goldie* a68 55
4 b g Orientor Glenlini (Bertolini (USA))
131[8] 278[7] 498[5] 743[5] 1505[5] 1950[7] 2324[7] 2678[9] 3452[8] 6462[10] 6574[6] 7214[6] 7737[8] 7959[6] 8720[4]◆ 9398[2] 9518[3]

Lord Of The Lodge (IRE)
K R Burke 108
2 b c Dandy Man(IRE) Archetypal (IRE) (Cape Cross (IRE))
(2957) 3949[12] 5134[6] (5845) 6422[2]

Lord Of The Rock (IRE)
Lawrence Mullaney a75 90
7 b g Rock Of Gibraltar(IRE) La Sylphide (Rudimentary (USA))
(2104) 5693[2] 8130[18]

Lord Of The Sky *James Tate* a66
2 b c Dansili Cloud Castle (In The Wings)
8823[8] 9156[4]

Lord P *Richard Hannon* a52
2 b c Brazen Beau(AUS) Netta (IRE) (Barathea (IRE))
9156[6] 9415[8]

Lord Riddiford (IRE) *John Quinn* a97 94
4 gr g Zebedee Beacon Of Hope (IRE) (Barathea (IRE))
2557[7] 3097[11] (3582) 3993[4] 4313a[5] 4888[6] 5524[5] 6351[11] 7107[2] 7524[7] 8099[18]

Lord Rob *David Thompson* a46 47
8 b g Rob Roy(USA) First Grey (Environment Friend)
969[8] 1083[9] 1647[9] 2241[9] 3163[13] 4078[9] 4131[8] 5213[8] 5555[9] 5766[11] 7444[8] 7587[5] 7961[5] 8530[12]

Lordsbridge Boy *Dean Ivory* a69 67
3 b g Equiano(FR) Fontaine House (Pyramus (USA))
3764[8] (5622) 6598[2] 6930[5] (8217) 9089[11] 9218[4]

Lord Spirit (FR) *T Castanheira* 67
3 b g Spirit One(FR) Lady Verde (FR) (Meshaheer (USA))
1450a[10]

Lord Torranaga (FR) *Alain Couetil* a73 73
4 b h Planteur(IRE) Marie Cuddy (IRE) (Galileo (IRE))
1631a[5]

Lord Warburton (IRE) *Michael Bell* 43
2 ch g Zoffany(IRE) Portrait Of A Lady (IRE) (Peintre Celebre (USA))
8459[11] 8721[6]

Lorelei Rock (IRE) *G Botti* 94
2 b f Camacho Laureldean Lady (IRE) (Statue Of Liberty (USA))
4048[7] 4352a[4] 7775a[5] 8446a[5] (8791a) 8970a[10]

Lorelina *Andrew Balding* a53 97
6 b m Passing Glance Diktalina (Diktat)
2401[4] 3315[5] 3726[8] 5133[4] 5928[7] 7566[3] 8245[6]

Loretta (IRE) *Julie Camacho* a60 44
3 b f Iffraaj Marlinka (Marju (IRE))
3920[7] 6206[7] 9112[3]◆ 9547[4]

Loretta Lass *Adam West* a50 7
2 b f Elzaam(AUS) Irina Princess (Selkirk (USA))
4106[8] 5732[9] 6281[5] 8603[11] 9045[11]

Lorna Cole (IRE) *William Muir* a74 72
3 gr f Lethal Force(IRE) Suedehead (Cape Cross (IRE))
(130) 342[6] 4595[4] 5372[5] 5736[4] 6183[4] 6397[2] 6851[3] 7514[9]

Lorraynio (FR) *C Lerner* a64 63
4 b h Elusive City(USA) Suvretta Queen (IRE) (Polish Precedent (USA))
1449a[16]

Lorton *Julie Camacho* a82 89
3 b f Sepoy(AUS) Oilinda (Nayef (USA))
1662[8] 2510[2] 3293[2] 3583[5] 4987[5]◆ 5442[8]

Los Camachos (IRE)
John Gallagher a71 79
4 b g Camacho Illuminise (IRE) (Grand Lodge (USA))
381[7] (466) (517) 1018[2] 6155[7] 7567[3] 7975[7] 8412[10] 9496[4]

Los Campanos (GER) *Dr A Bolte*
5 b g Campanologist(USA) La Salvita (GER) (Big Shuffle (USA))
1793a[9]

Los Cerritos (SWI) *Milton Harris*
7 ch g Dr Fong(USA) La Coruna (SWI) (Arazi (USA))
4216[12] 4771[9]

Los Ojos (FR) *S Jeddari* 3
6 b g Satri(IRE) La Gioconda (SWI) (King Of Kings (IRE))
1349a[11]

Lost Empire (IRE) *Harry Dunlop* 75
2 b g Footstepsinthesand Ballerina Rose (Duke Of Marmalade (IRE))
5775[2] 6845[6] 8517[6]

Lost History (IRE) *John Spearing* a78 65
6 b g Strategic Prince Prelude (Danzero (AUS))
1988[2] 2696[8] (3321) 3545[7] 5502[5] 5817[6] 6736[6]

Lost In Alaska (USA)
Jeremy Noseda 70
3 b g Discreet Cat(USA) Truly Blushed (USA) (Yes It's True (USA))
1886[9] 2736[5] 3157[2]

Lost In France (IRE) *R Le Gal* a67 67
2 b f Epaulette(AUS) Lostinparadise (Exceed And Excel (AUS))
1657a[12] 2263a[5] (4228a) 5263a[6]

Lost In Time *Saeed bin Suroor* a68 86
2 b c Dubawi(IRE) Reunite (IRE) (Kingmambo (USA))
4588[2] 5523[3] 6287[2] (6845) 7725[2]

Lost Treasure (IRE) *A P O'Brien* a110 111
4 b h War Front(USA) Wading (IRE) (Montjeu (IRE))
1442a[10]

Lothario *Dean Ivory* a79 74
5 gr g Dark Angel(IRE) Kisses For Me (IRE) (Sadler's Wells (USA))
942[5] (1176) 1355[3] 2596[3] (3002) 3944[5] 4322[10] 5267[8] (6050) 6630[3]

Lots Ov (IRE) *John Wainwright* a54 39
5 b m Rock Of Gibraltar(IRE) Bright Enough (Fantastic Light (USA))
607[10] 984[9] 1663[8] 3057[10] 3272[13] 3929[5] 3955[8] 5421[9]

Lottie Deno *D J Jeffreys* a47 36
3 b f Havana Gold(IRE) Rapid Revalation (USA) (Bianconi (USA))
6131[13] 8469[4] 8819[9]

Lottie Marie *Robert Cowell* a67
2 ch f Intello(GER) Heavenly Dawn (Pivotal)
8453[5] 9324[2]◆

Loud And Clear *Jim Goldie* a85 79
8 b g Dalakhani(IRE) Whispering Blues (IRE) (Sadler's Wells (USA))
(124) 349[3] 522[2] 948[3] 1483[5] 2435[5] 2781[8] 3361[4]

Loudest Whisper (IRE) *E D Delany* a43 51
4 b m Maxios Legal Lyric (IRE) (Lawman (FR))
8406[13]

Louganini *Roger Charlton* 84
2 ch g Zoffany(IRE) Princess Loulou (IRE) (Pivotal)
(8721)◆

Lougher (IRE) *Richard John O'Brien* 78
2 ch f Teofilo(IRE) Lightstream (IRE) (Shamardal (USA))
5997a[4] 6689a[6]

Lough Salt (IRE) *Richard Guest* 61
8 b g Brian Boru Castlehill Lady (IRE) (Supreme Leader)
7704[4]

Louie De Palma *Clive Cox* a69 101
7 b g Pastoral Pursuits Tahirah (Green Desert (USA))
1459[5] (2568) 3602[2] 4186[3] 4866[3] 7433[6] 8127[4]

Louis D'Or (IRE) *Laurent Loisel* a50 97
4 ch h Intello(GER) Soudanaise (IRE) (Peintre Celebre (USA))
3906a[4]

Louisiana Beat (IRE) *Mike Murphy* a48 38
3 ch f Helmet(AUS) Union City Blues (IRE) (Encosta De Lago (AUS))
8870[7] 9216[6] 9481[9]

Louis Treize (IRE) *Richard Spencer* a82 83
3 ch g Slade Power(IRE) Black Rodded (Bahamian Bounty)
2412[11] 5180[3]

Loulin *Ruth Carr* a58 59
4 ch g Exceed And Excel(AUS) Wimple (USA) (Kingmambo (USA))
1403[4] 2013[9] 2532[3] 2958[16] 7962[5] 8401[7] (8898) 9219[4] 9335[2] (9411)◆

Loupedra (FR) *J Boisnard* 43
2 b f Pedro The Great(USA) Loupana (FR) (Loup Solitaire (USA))
7641a[7]

Louve Dream (IRE) *Carina Fey* a92 88
3 b g Oasis Dream Louve Nationale (IRE) (Galileo (IRE))
3713a[3]

Love (IRE) *A P O'Brien* 111
2 ch f Galileo(IRE) Pikaboo (Pivotal)
(5361a) 6429a[5] (7244a) 8091[3]

Love And Be Loved *John Flint* a54 71
5 b m Lawman(FR) Rightside (High Chaparral (IRE))
2685[4] 3572[2] 4220[9] 8248[8]

Loveatfirstlight (IRE) *James Unett* a42
3 b f Es Que Love(IRE) Spark Up (Lahib (USA))
1838[10] 7681[9] 8472[6] 9445[10]

Love Bracelet (USA) *A P O'Brien* 74
2 b f War Front(USA) Bracelet (IRE) (Montjeu (IRE))
3983[20] 7695[7]

Love Destiny *Mark Johnston* a81 77
2 b c Lethal Force(IRE) Danehill Destiny (Danehill Dancer (IRE))
(6106)◆ 6375[16] (7104) 7612[6] 8124[8]

Love Dreams (IRE) *Jamie Osborne* a90 99
5 b g Dream Ahead(USA) Kimola (IRE) (King's Theatre (IRE))
515a[16] 843a[9] 1097[2] 2402[2] 2778[4] 3009[4] 3318[3] (3563) 3863[10] 4299[10] 4650[5] 5453[8] 5708[5] 6214[3] 6391[8] 6517[3] (6978) 7563[7] 8062[5]◆ 8690[3]

Lovee Dovee *Joseph Patrick O'Brien* a67 82
3 b f Galileo(IRE) Celestial Lagoon (JPN) (Sunday Silence (USA))
8367a[14]

Love Explodes *Ed Vaughan* a67 76
3 b f Champs Elysees Acquainted (Shamardal (USA))
827[5] 3012[7] 4326[6] 6559[4] 7288[6] 7772[2] 9400[2]

Loveheart *Michael Bell* a61 51
3 b f Dubawi(IRE) Love Divine (Diesis)
6316[5] 6587[4] 6862[4] 7609[12] 8205[10]

Loveisthehigherlaw *P Twomey* 99
3 b f Kodiac Sweet Stream (ITY) (Shantou (USA))
8368a[4]

Love Kisses (IRE) *Mark Johnston* a66 70
3 b c Dream Ahead(USA) Coconut Kisses (Bahamian Bounty)
134[8] 461[9]

Lovelett (IRE) *M Figge* a76 90
5 b m Arcano(IRE) Lucky Pipit (Key Of Luck (USA))
3288a[8] 4170a[9]

Love Locket (IRE) *A P O'Brien* 87
2 b f No Nay Never(USA) Starlet (IRE) (Sea The Stars (IRE))
7742a[7]

Love Love *Richard Hannon* a76 74
2 b f Kodiac Perfect Blessings (IRE) (Kheleyf (USA))
2138[5] 2915[3] 3689[2] 4233[4]

Lovely Acclamation (IRE)
Debbie Hughes a37 44
5 b m Acclamation Titova (Halling (USA))
1478[9] 3687[10] 5293[4] 6643[9] 9544[11]

Lovely Approach *Hugo Palmer* a84
4 ch g New Approach(IRE) Lovely Pass (IRE) (Raven's Pass (USA))
827[3] 1169[5] (1525)◆

Lovely Jubbly *Pat Phelan* a23
4 ch m Harbour Watch(IRE) Ruthie (Pursuit Of Love)
1351[9]

Lovely Lou Lou *John Ryan* a65 64
3 b f Sir Percy Silver Linnet (IRE) (Acclamation)
(8662) 9368[3] 9662[8]

Lovely Melody (FR) *R Rohne* a57 57
2 b f Penny's Picnic(IRE) Sensible Song (FR) (Kingsalsa (USA))
5600a[9]

Lovely Miss (FR) *H De Nicolay* a55 64
3 ch f Excelebration(IRE) I Should Care (FR) (Loup Solitaire (USA))
2265a[9] 4357a[4]
Lovely Smile (ITY) *A Botti* 95
2 b c Mujahid(USA) Caractere (IRE) (Indian Ridge (IRE))
4172a[7] 8791a[3]
Love My Life (IRE) *Jamie Osborne* a54 37
2 ch f Ivawood(IRE) Cradle Brief (IRE) (Brief Truce (USA))
3165[11] 3461[9] 3943[11] 4448[8]
Love Not Money *John Bridger* a51
2 b f Dawn Approach(IRE) Maggie Lou (IRE) (Red Ransom (USA))
7605[7] 7896[27] 8195[5] 8640[7] 9061[11] 9212[9] 9323[8]
Love Powerful (IRE)
Richard Hannon 76
2 b f Gutaifan(IRE) Montefino (IRE) (Shamardal (USA))
4245[P] 5170[6] 5500[2] (6019) 7156[4]
Love Rat *Scott Dixon* a68
4 b g Mawatheeq(USA) Watersilk (IRE) (Fasliyev (USA))
162[2] 833[5] (1040) 2345[4] 3054[12] 3205[8] 3769[7] 7415[9]
Lovers' Gait (IRE) *Ed Dunlop* 52
2 b f Gleneagles(IRE) Liberally (IRE) (Statue Of Liberty (USA))
5684[8] 7203[6] 8093[14]
Lover's Knot *H-A Pantall* a69 75
3 b f Invincible Spirit(IRE) Patroness (Dubawi (IRE))
510a[13] 3677a[10]
Love So Deep (JPN)
Jane Chapple-Hyam a64 109
3 b f Deep Impact(JPN) Soinlovewithyou (USA) (Sadler's Wells (USA))
(1696) (2021) 2521[7] 3012[3] 4014[5] 5190[4] (5682) 6263a[2] 6993a[5]
Love To Breeze *Jonathan Portman* a71 70
4 b m Azamour(IRE) Burn The Breeze (IRE) (Beat Hollow)
1497[3] 2400[10] 2718[5]
Love To Excel (IRE) *F Foresi* a45 53
3 ch c Es Que Love(IRE) Sakal (Exceed And Excel (AUS))
5165a[4] 6061a[9]
Love Your Work (IRE) *Adam West* a73 67
3 ch g Helmet(AUS) Little Italy (USA) (Proud Citizen (USA))
(1067) 1285[11] (2299)◆ 3278[8] 4306[7] 4506[10] 5270[6] 5651[8] 6393[7] 7083[9] 7875[2] 8642[4] 9180[7] 9349[4]
Lovin (USA) *David O'Meara* a72 65
3 ch f Orb(USA) Innocent Love (USA) (Grand Slam (USA))
838[8] 2121[9] 5335[7] 5854[4] 7105[8]
Loving Glance *Martyn Meade* a80 85
3 b f Invincible Spirit(IRE) Kissable (IRE) (Danehill Dancer (IRE))
5141[2]◆ 5627[2]◆ 6315[2] 7341[6] 9011[4] (9165) 9404[5]
Loving Life (IRE) *Martin Bosley* a19 24
2 b f Society Rock(IRE) Edelfa (IRE) (Fasliyev (USA))
3964[9] 4376[12]
Loving Pearl *John Berry* a24 49
3 b f Dunaden(FR) Forever Loved (Deploy)
2760[11] 3741[8] 4834[7] 5648[10]
Loving Your Work
Ken Cunningham-Brown a41 59
8 b g Royal Applause Time Crystal (IRE) (Sadler's Wells (USA))
58[13] 288[9] 1520[7] (3700) 4111[7] (Dead)
Low Profile *Rebecca Bastiman* a61 72
4 ch g Galileo(IRE) Dynaforce (USA) (Dynaformer (USA))
1666[8] 2479[6] 3054[2] 4208[6] 5473[5] 6576[4]
Low Sun *W P Mullins* a84 108
6 b g Champs Elysees Winter Solstice (Unfuwain (USA))
2575[4]
Loxley (IRE) *Charlie Appleby* a112 113
4 b g New Approach(IRE) Lady Marian (GER) (Nayef (USA))
1115a[5] 7076[6] 7662[2] 8811[2] 9302[2]
Loyalty *Derek Shaw* a90 44
12 b g Medicean Ecoutila (USA) (Rahy (USA))
517[2] (734) 1218[3] 2514[5]
Lualiwa *Kevin Ryan* a46 67
5 b g Foxwedge(AUS) Sunpearl (Compton Place)
1502[9] 2116[9] 2894[8] 3813[18]
Luath *Suzzanne France* a53 53
6 ch g Archipenko(USA) Delaware Dancer (IRE) (Danehill Dancer (IRE))
6[7] 590[6] 1527[5] 2350[2] 3142[9]
Lucander (IRE) *Ralph Beckett* a74 88
2 b g Footstepsinthesand Lady Sefton (Oratorio (IRE))
5314[5] (5992) 6718[3] (7197) (8124)
Luce Des Aigles (FR)
Mme C Barande-Barbe a66 68
3 b f Zanzibari(USA) Folie Des Aigles (FR) (Ocean Of Wisdom (USA))
7138a[7]
Luceita (IRE) *J S Bolger* 68
4 ch m Dawn Approach(IRE) Lura (USA) (Street Cry (IRE))
2493a[10]
Luchador
Jassim Mohammed Ghazali a65 87
3 b f Holy Roman Emperor(IRE) Bride Unbridled (IRE) (Hurricane Run (IRE))
893a[2]
Lucie Manette *A Fabre* a77 102
4 b m Shamardal(USA) Padmini (Tiger Hill (IRE))
2670a[6]
Lucifers Shadow (IRE)
Mrs C Gilbert
10 gr g Dark Angel(IRE) Marianne's Dancer (IRE) (Bold Fact (USA))
4175a[6]
Lucipherus (IRE) *Marco Botti* a69 72
3 b g Dark Angel(IRE) Nitya (FR) (Indian Ridge (IRE))
2021[3] 2485[5] 3947[10]
Lucius Tiberius (IRE)
Charlie Appleby 110
4 b g Camelot Keegsquaw (IRE) (Street Cry (IRE))
1628a[4] 2033[5] 2808[2] 4053[10] 4646[2] 6466[3]
Lucknow *Alexandros Giatras* a73 79
5 b g Sepoy(AUS) Meetyouthere (IRE) (Sadler's Wells (USA))
8240a[7]
Luck Of Clover *Andrew Balding* a66 69
3 b f Phoenix Reach(IRE) Diktalina (Diktat)
1351[4] 1771[4] 2343[3] 3153[2] 3809[2] 4459[3] 4862[2] 6125[5] 8248[3]
Lucky Beggar (IRE)
David C Griffiths a74 71
9 gr g Verglas(IRE) Lucky Clio (IRE) (Key Of Luck (USA))
(1765) 2824[5] 3706[3] 3928[3] 5330[3] 5972[7] 6220[6] 6373[2] 6591[6] 6972[13] 7121[11] 7507[5]
Lucky Bird (FR) *Louis Baudron* a61 69
3 b g Orpen(USA) Blessed Catch (USA) (Storm Cat (USA))
1340a[5] 3713a[6]
Lucky Charm *Chris Wall* a71 73
3 b f Charm Spirit(IRE) Drift And Dream (Exceed And Excel (AUS))
6388[3] (7417)
Lucky Circle *David Evans* a42 40
3 b f Yorgunnabelucky(USA) Circle Of Angels (Royal Applause)
2341[10] 2913[9] 3593[10] 4485[12]
Lucky Clover *Malcolm Saunders* a25 29
8 ch m Lucky Story(USA) Willisa (Polar Falcon (USA))
2940[9]
Lucky Deal *Mark Johnston* a101 108
4 ch g Mastercraftsman(IRE) Barter (Daylami (IRE))
558[2] (799)◆ 1483[4] 1947[4] 2118[2]◆ 2575[12] (3081) 4096[4] 5183[13]
Lucky Draw *Ed de Giles* a57
2 b f Roderic O'Connor(IRE) Lucky Breeze (IRE) (Key Of Luck (USA))
8849[9] 9211[8]
Luckyforsome (IRE) *Eric Alston*
2 b f Henrythenavigator(USA) Samadilla (IRE) (Mujadil (USA))
4006[7]
Lucky Icon (IRE) *Philip Kirby* a32 34
5 b g Sixties Icon Sauterelle (IRE) (Key Of Luck (USA))
6343[9]
Lucky Jolie (USA) *A Fabre* a50 99
3 b f More Than Ready(USA) Lucky Copy (USA) (Unbridled's Song (USA))
1706a[6]
Lucky Lilac (JPN) *Mikio Matsunaga* 112
4 ch m Orfevre(JPN) Lilacs And Lace (USA) (Flower Alley (USA))
9376a[2]
Lucky Lips (GER) *Mario Hofer* a88 64
5 ch g Mamool(IRE) Lips Arrow (GER) (Big Shuffle (USA))
7861a[12]
Lucky Lodge *Antony Brittain* a76 52
9 b g Lucky Story(USA) Melandre (Lujain (USA))
214[6] 496[3] 741[2] 914[2] 1274[4] 1487[2]◆ 1686[6] 1768[5] 2122[2] 2247[3] 2638[7] 3549[7] 4335[2] 4764[5] 5281[4] 6027[3] 7418[9] 7820[3] 8471[2] (8712) 9106[3] 9402[4]
Lucky Lou (IRE) *Patrick Chamings* a48 61
3 b f Most Improved(IRE) Bessie Lou (IRE) (Montjeu (IRE))
78[5] 1094[5] 1825[6] 2341[4] 3418[13] 6531[10] 7280[14]
Lucky Louie *Roger Teal* a67 83
6 ch g Dutch Art Ardessie (Bahamian Bounty)
3305[2] 4365[2] 5136[3] (5579) 7121[6] 8101[12]
Lucky Lover Boy (IRE)
Oliver Greenall a42 43
4 b g Teofilo(IRE) Mayonga (IRE) (Dr Fong (USA))
7683[9]
Lucky Lucky Man (IRE)
Richard Fahey a79 83
4 gr g Clodovil(IRE) Regrette Rien (IRE) (Chevalier (IRE))
2117[13] 2393[7] 3309[3] 3971[6] 4369[8] 5670[3]◆ 6227[5] 6972[2] 7402[17] 8425[8]
Lucky Lycra (IRE) *F Rohaut* 100
3 ch f Olympic Glory(IRE) Pearl Banks (Pivotal)
2029a[8] 7927a[10]
Lucky Number *William Haggas* a52 79
3 gr g Dark Angel(IRE) Keep Dancing (IRE) (Distant Music (USA))
2507[8] 3510[8] 3932[5] 5334[3] (5797)◆ 6558[2] 8305[8]
Lucky's Dream *Ian Williams* a75 73
4 ch g Yorgunnabelucky(USA) Dream Esteem (Mark Of Esteem (IRE))
2111[8] (3276) (3473) 4283[3] 5338[4] 9443[4]
Lucky Turn (IRE) *Michael Bell* a84 64
3 b f Zoffany(IRE) Lucky Spin (Pivotal)
3050[9] (7835)◆ 8064[7] (9202)
Lucky Violet (IRE) *Linda Perratt* a62 68
7 b m Dandy Man(IRE) Rashida (King's Best (USA))
22[7] 525[6] 2963[3] 3178[2] 4058[7] 4278[3] 4693[4] 4723[5] 5274[5]◆ 5616[8] 5899[5] 6573[9] 8922[6] 9111[2]◆ 9396[10]
Lucky You (FR) *C Lerner* a72 72
3 b f Poet's Voice Lucky Look (FR) (Teofilo (IRE))
9058a[6]
Lucullan (USA) *Kiaran McLaughlin* 109
5 b h Hard Spun(USA) Golden Velvet (USA) (Seeking The Gold (USA))
7225a[4] 8774a[11]
Lucy Lou (IRE) *Charles Hills* 64
3 b f Galileo(IRE) Baraka (IRE) (Danehill (USA))
1738[8] 2731[7] 6043[3] 6720[8]
Lucymai *Dean Ivory* a106 70
6 b m Multiplex Miss Lesley (Needwood Blade)
30[4] 351[6] 8708[12] 9198[6] 9586[2]
Lucy's Law (IRE) *Tom Tate* a56 67
5 b m Lawman(FR) Lucy Limelites (Medicean)
784[7] 2512[3] 3449[6] 4036[10] 5178[5] 6059[11] 6663[10] 7578[12] 8466[12]
Luduamf (IRE) *Michael Chapman*
5 ch g Tamayuz Aphorism (Halling (USA))
1661[0] 1369[13]
Lufricia *Roger Varian* a86 93
3 br f Kodiac Lucrece (Pivotal)
(1924) 2319[13] 3544[4] 4595[2]◆ 5589[3] 6476[10]
Luigi Pirandello (USA)
Agostino Affe' 99
2 b c The Factor(USA) Regalo Mia (USA) (Sligo Bay (IRE))
8789a[2]
Luigi Vampa (FR) *David Menuisier* 80
2 b c Elvstroem(AUS) Sunday Rose (Red Ransom (USA))
5775[7] (6504) 7154[2] 7925a[3]
Luis Vaz De Torres (IRE)
Richard Fahey a80 85
7 b g Tagula(IRE) Tekhania (IRE) (Dalakhani (IRE))
213[2] 508[7] 952[8] 1768[4] 2242[5] 2893[5] 3813[3] 4546[3] (5246) 6014[3] 6588[3] 7128[3] (9245) 9669[5]
Lukoutoldmakezebak
David Thompson a57 53
6 b g Arabian Gleam Angelofthenorth (Tomba)
969[3]◆ 1083[2]◆ 1431[4] 1836[4] 2631[6] 2682[3] 3225[2] 3720[4] 4512[9] 4633[4] 5214[8] (5787) 7207[3] 7443[9] (7654) 8922[9]
Lulu Star (IRE) *Julia Feilden* a62 45
4 b m Oasis Dream Jeanie Johnston (IRE) (One Cool Cat (USA))
459[4] 616[7] 983[7] 1546[8] 2737[5] 3298[6] 3740[8]
Lumen *Roger Charlton* a53
4 ch g Rip Van Winkle(IRE) Luminance (IRE) (Danehill Dancer (IRE))
160[8]
Lumination *Martyn Meade* a60 79
3 b g Toronado(IRE) Sparkling Eyes (Lujain (USA))
1033[5] 1652[3] 6811[4]
Luminosa (FR) *D Smaga* 70
4 b m Makfi Katchagua (FR) (Anabaa (USA))
4859a[12] 6521a[11]
Luna Magic *Archie Watson* a78 78
5 b m Mayson Dayia (IRE) (Act One)
736[5] 1363[8] 1591[6] 2112[2]◆ 2259[3] (4460) 4658[2] 4838[2] (6102) 6507[2] 6760[2] (8186) 8515[9] 8862[8] 9496[2]
Luna Princess *Michael Appleby* a51 54
3 b f Equiano(FR) Enford Princess (Pivotal)
1665[6] 1862[6] 2550[7] 3204[7] 3684[3] 4029[6] 5102[2]
Lunar Deity *Stuart Williams* a80 66
10 b g Medicean Luminda (IRE) (Danehill (USA))
(154) 429[7] (1269) 1936[4] 2233[6] 3279[2] 4615[7] 5087[3] 5316[7] 5824[6] 6327[2] 6844[3] 9050[13] 9496[10]
Lunar Jet *John Mackie* a80 99
5 ch g Ask Lightning Jet (Dutch Art)
(1757) 2095[5] (2800) 3160[11] 3605[7] 3726[3] 4877[2] 5519[13] 5950[6] 6923[6] 9094[7] 9366[8] 9610[6]
Luna Wish *George Margarson* a63 56
2 b f Sea The Moon(GER) Crystal Wish (Exceed And Excel (AUS))
2020[5] 2836[9] 4337[8] 5886[2] 6071[2] (6435) (6884) 7315[4] 7548[9] 8699[3] 9044[3] 9212[10]
Lunch Lady *F Head* a98 107
4 gr m Shamardal(USA) High Maintenance (FR) (Highest Honor (FR))
1451a[3] 2167a[4] 3906a[3]
L'Un Deux Trois (IRE) *Michael Bell* a69 74
3 gr g Mastercraftsman(IRE) Moment Juste (Pivotal)
1510[4] 2150[2] 3358[8] 4803[4]◆ 5778[8] 7439[6] 8414[12]
Luscifer *Richard Hughes* a38 49
2 b c Heeraat(IRE) Nut (IRE) (Fasliyev (USA))
3595[7] 4214[3] 4766[8] 5576[8] 6071[9]
Lush Life (IRE) *Jamie Osborne* a94 99
4 gr m Mastercraftsman(IRE) Break Of Day (USA) (Favorite Trick (USA))
2487[3]◆ (3027)◆ 3450[6] 4666[13] 5610[20] 6151[3] 6951[5] 7863[9] 9064[8] 9200[9]
Lusis Naturea *Paul Traynor* a80 77
8 b g Multiplex Kenny's Dream (Karinga Bay)
5599a[3]
Lustrous Light (IRE) *J Motherway* a27 70
6 ch g Galileo(IRE) Glinting Desert (IRE) (Desert Prince (IRE))
5508a[20]
Luv U Whatever *Marjorie Fife* a73 73
9 b g Needwood Blade Lady Suesanne (IRE) (Cape Cross (IRE))
703[5] 1463[16] 1666[9] 1861[12]
Luxford *Gary Moore* a55 45
5 b m Mullionmileanhour(IRE) Dolly Parton (IRE) (Tagula (IRE))
80[7] 3006[3] 4217[5] 4753[12] 5652[7] 6049[13] 6723[9] 7376[6]
Luxor *William Haggas* a83 91
3 b g Oasis Dream Eminently (Exceed And Excel (AUS))
2835[14] 3865[15] 4638[6]
Luxor Temple (USA) *A R Al Rayhi* a59 59
3 br c Cairo Prince(USA) May Fine (CAN) (In Excess I (IRE))
570a[7] 727a[11]
Luxuriant *D K Weld* 84
3 b f Kingman Sense Of Joy (Dansili)
6090a[12]
Luzum (IRE) *Michael Easterby* a67 74
4 b g Epaulette(AUS) Empress Ella (IRE) (Holy Roman Emperor (IRE))
2709[6] 3207[2]◆ (3969) 4320[4] 5488[9] 5821[12] 7065[10] 7632[10]
Lydiate Lady *Eric Alston* a60 67
7 b m Piccolo Hiraeth (Petong)
2296[7] 2637[9] 3518[4] 4105[4] 5181[9] 7488[2]◆ 7588[2] 8066[10] 8660[5] (8861)
Lyford (IRE) *Alistair Whillans* a58 49
4 ch g Intense Focus(USA) Nurture (IRE) (Bachelor Duke (USA))
5905[4] 6939[4]◆ 7415[10] 8423[12] 8670[2] 9087[8] 9275[8] 9553[4]
Lynchpin (IRE) *Lydia Pearce* a46 56
3 b c Camacho River Bounty (Bahamian Bounty)
3665[11] 4070[7] 4787[8] 5866[6] 6279[11] 6636[11] 6860[12] 7817[11] 8205[4] 8434[4] 8869[5]
Lyndon B (IRE) *George Scott* 99
3 b g Charm Spirit(IRE) Kelsey Rose (Most Welcome)
2094[2] 3727[2] 4298[3] (5104)◆ 5546[3] (6670)
Lyn's Secret (IRE) *Seamus Mullins* 38
4 ch m Sakhee's Secret Blase Chevalier (IRE) (Chevalier (IRE))
1934[6] 2345[9] 4771[8]
Lyons Lane *Michael Dods* a54 37
3 ch f Showcasing Bruni Heinke (IRE) (Dutch Art)
1816[9] 5669[4] 6551[2] 7628[7] 7962[12]
Lyre (AUS) *Anthony Freedman* 106
2 br f Lonhro(AUS) Erato (AUS) (Street Cry (IRE))
8135a[4]
Lyrical *Ed Dunlop* 72
2 gr f Poet's Voice Reaching Ahead (USA) (Mizzen Mast (USA))
7054[9] 8458[5] 8759[3]
Lyrical Ballad (IRE) *Neil Mulholland* a52 45
3 gr f Dark Angel(IRE) Iffraaj Pink (IRE) (Iffraaj)
2713[7] 3306[6] 6009a[4] 6555a[5] 9420[11]
Lyrical Waters
Eve Johnson Houghton 59
3 b g Poet's Voice Golden Waters (Dubai Destination (USA))
2208[14] 3802[5] 4066[6] 4834[10]
Lyrica's Lion (IRE) *Sheena West* a44 56
5 b g Dragon Pulse(IRE) Shishangaan (IRE) (Mujadil (USA))
3022[14] 3633[11] 5425[8] 6830[7]
Lyric Gold *Richard Hannon* a66
2 b c Dubawi(IRE) The Sound Of Music (IRE) (Galileo (IRE))
8494[8]
Lyricist Voice *Marco Botti* a71
2 b c Poet's Voice Lyricist (Librettist (USA))
5433[5] 6344[2] 7787[2] 8546[7] 9172[4]
Lyronada *M Figge* a51
3 b f Toronado(IRE) Lyra's Daemon (Singspiel (IRE))
683a[11]
Lysander Belle (IRE) *Sophie Leech* a64 57
3 b f Exceed And Excel(AUS) Switcher (IRE) (Whipper (USA))
437[8] 555[8] 1167[4] 1557[10] 2300[2] 3148[7] (3319) 3839[7] 4763[5] 4772[7] 6024[5] (6181) 6685[6]
Lys Gracieux (JPN) *Yoshito Yahagi* 124
5 bb m Heart's Cry(JPN) Liliside (FR) (American Post)
(8579a)
Lyzbeth (FR) *Martyn Meade* 94
3 b f Zoffany(IRE) Arcangela (Galileo (IRE))
(4597)◆ 5608[10] 6379[9] 7893[11]
Lzaaz (IRE) *Alan King* a30 54
4 gr g Clodovil(IRE) Solandia (IRE) (Teofilo (IRE))
2720[8] 3209[6]
Maamora (IRE) *Simon Crisford* a102 101
3 b f Dubawi(IRE) Zoowraa (Azamour (IRE))
1834[2] 2321[2] 3013[2] (3517) 4052[13] (5564) (7106)◆ 7496a[2]
Maared (IRE) *Luke McJannet* a62 62
3 ch g Born To Sea(IRE) Hollow Quaill (IRE) (Entrepreneur)
614[7] 802[10] 1140[10]
Maarek *Miss Evanna McCutcheon* a22 79
12 b g Pivotal Ruby Rocket (IRE) (Indian Rocket)
3846[7] 3945[5] 4313a[6] 7241a[19]
Maaward (IRE) *Richard Hannon* a101
4 b g Kodiac Caterina Di Cesi (Cape Town (IRE))
3991[11]
Maazel (IRE) *Lee Carter* a62 61
5 b g Elzaam(AUS) Laylati (IRE) (Green Desert (USA))
365[9] 924[6] 1069[2] (1075) 1328[2] 1477[5] 1933[5] 2286[2] 3187[4] 4025[10] 8874[4]◆ 9249[2] 9298[8]◆ 9505[7]
Mable Lee (IRE) *Bryan Smart* a44 47
4 ch m Zoffany(IRE) Mexican Milly (IRE) (Noverre (USA))
3503[11] 8925[12] 9352[9] 9539[9]
Mabo *Grace Harris* a61 58
4 gr g Aussie Rules(USA) Crochet (IRE) (Mark Of Esteem (IRE))
2717[10] 3430[8] 4181[14] 5498[2] 6045[3] 6334[6] 6643[4] 6977[6] (7236) 7758[2] 8256[4] (8416) 8667[4] 9305[8]
Ma Boy Harris (IRE) *P Monfort* a59 58
2 b c Dandy Man(IRE) Stones Peak (IRE) (Rock Of Gibraltar (IRE))
4631[3] 5093[4] 5472[4] 6182[3] 6683[10] 7283[3] 8330a[8]
Mabre (IRE) *David Evans* a63 46
2 gr c Make Believe Slope (Acclamation)
8516[12] 9187[8]
Mabs Cross *Michael Dods* a74 117
5 b m Dutch Art Miss Meggy (Pivotal)
(2409) 3084[3] 3950[4] 6423[4] 7243a[6] 7943a[5] 8331[9]
Mac Ailey *Tim Easterby* a50 61
3 ch g Firebreak Rosabee (IRE) (No Excuse Needed)
3570[2] 4284[3] 4728[6] 5215[9] 5816[6] 6036[5] 6678[8] 7405[5] 7859[9] (8205) 8434[5]
Machiavelian Storm (IRE)
Richard Mitchell
7 gr m Dark Angel(IRE) Terri's Charmer (USA) (Silver Charm (USA))
2145[17] 3038[12] 4215[10]
Machiavelli *Denis Gerard Hogan* a59 67
4 b g Leroidesanimaux(BRZ) Kleio (Sadler's Wells (USA))
3163[3] 4724[9]
Machine Head (USA)
Geoffrey Harker a19 29
5 ch g Paddy O'Prado(USA) Dixie Song (USA) (Fusaichi Pegasus (USA))
5766[13]
Machine Learner *Joseph Tuite* a90 92
6 b g Sir Percy My First Romance (Danehill (USA))
2278[4] 3070[7] 4614[2] 5321[3] 7216a[6] 7688[6]

Machios *Andrew Balding* 63
2 br g Maxios Astragal (Shamardal (USA))
5774[7] 7154[4]◆

Macho Boy (IRE) *Brian Meehan* 76
2 b g Camacho Tartiflette (Dr Fong (USA))
6948[6] 7521[2]◆

Macho Lady (IRE) *David O'Meara* a58 56
3 br f Camacho Jouel (FR) (Machiavellian (USA))
235[10]

Macho Time (IRE) *K R Burke* a84 83
2 b g Camacho Galeaza (Galileo (IRE))
(4688) (5553) 7409[8] 8426[4]

Macho Touch (IRE) *K R Burke* a53 76
2 b f Camacho Hint Of Red (IRE) (Fast Company (IRE))
1923[6] 2805[5]

Macho Wind (IRE) *M M Peraino* 69
3 b c Camacho Cry Of Liberty (IRE) (Statue Of Liberty (USA))
2888a[13]

Machree (IRE) *Declan Carroll* a84 88
4 b m Lord Shanakill(USA) Faleena (IRE) (Verglas (IRE))
1899[9] (3201) 4896[18] 5617[5] 6714[7] 7183[8] 8349[10] 8900[6] 9458[6]

Mac Jetes *David Loughnane* a70 57
3 b f Archipenko(USA) Real Me (Mark Of Esteem (IRE))
7298[2] (7772) 8122[9]

Mackaar (IRE) *Roger Varian* a92 101
3 b g Cape Cross(IRE) Albemarle (King's Best (USA))
(1592)◆ 2031[4] 2828[10] 4224[2] 5121[6] 6712[4]

Mackelly (IRE) *Richard Hughes* a54
2 b g Ivawood(IRE) Last Gold (FR) (Gold Away (IRE))
7571[6] 8418[9] 9043[10]

Mack The Knife (IRE)
Jamie Osborne a39
2 b g Australia Kitty Matcham (IRE) (Rock Of Gibraltar (IRE))
8605[13] 9154[13] 9363[11]

Mac McCarthy (IRE)
Richard Hughes a71 73
2 ch g Anjaal Kitty Softpaws (IRE) (Royal Applause)
3165[12] 3491[8] 3990[10] (5886) (6394) 6728[6] 7173[4] 7994[2] 8259[7]

Mac O'Polo (IRE) *Donald McCain* a57 42
5 b g Henrythenavigator(USA) Topka (FR) (Kahyasi (IRE))
241[8] 482[12] 1334[4] 6098[7] 7060[7]

Macquarie (IRE) *A P O'Brien* 71
3 ch c Australia Beyond Brilliance (IRE) (Holy Roman Emperor (IRE))
5712a[14]

Macs Blessings (IRE) *Stef Keniry* a58 63
3 b g Society Rock(IRE) Lear's Crown (USA) (Lear Fan (USA))
341[2] 537[3] (612) 1084[2] 1721[5] 2337[3] 3270[5] 4720[5] (4784) 5238[2] 5300[3] 5771[2] 5935[2] 6276[13] 6338[10]

Madame Bounty (IRE) *P Monfort* a77 63
5 b m Bahamian Bounty Madame Boulangere (Royal Applause)
4960a[3]

Madame Jo Jo *Sarah Hollinshead* a53 56
4 ch m Havana Gold(IRE) Paradise Place (Compton Place)
180[7] 531[7] 600[2] 1032[11]

Madame Peltier (IRE)
Charlie Fellowes a63 62
2 b f Exceed And Excel(AUS) Airline Hostess (IRE) (Sadler's Wells (USA))
6906[8] 7832[7] 8602[9]

Madame Ritz (IRE) *Richard Phillips* a45
4 b m Canford Cliffs(IRE) Sky Red (Night Shift (USA))
5629[12] 7770[10] 8457[8] 8898[12] 9160[11] 9457[3]

Madame Tantzy
Eve Johnson Houghton a77 73
3 b f Champs Elysees Roodle (Xaar)
(1288) 1751[15] 5341[5] 5749[6] 6840[6]

Madame Vitesse (FR) *P Monfort* a65 54
3 b f Vertigineux(FR) Do I Worry (FR) (Charge D'Affaires)
215[3] 620[6] 813[8] 2871[12] 6874a[4] 7642a[6]

Madame Winner *Stuart Williams* 26
2 ch f Sir Percy Lady Guinevere (Pivotal)
8458[18] 8758[13]

Madam Seamstress (IRE)
J S Bolger 95
3 b f Vocalised(USA) Stitch Night (IRE) (Whipper (USA))
2661a[6] 5325a[5] 5711a[14] 6693a[16]

Maddfourmaggy (IRE)
Steph Hollinshead a37 40
3 b f Heeraat(IRE) Matron (Bahamian Bounty)
585[9]

Madeeh *Philip Kirby* a78 81
3 b c Oasis Dream Ashaaqah (IRE) (Dansili)
3003[5]◆ 3958[2] 4671[6] 6541[4]◆ 7141[6] 7680[7] 9096[7]

Made For All (FR) *K R Burke* 74
2 bb f Dabirsim(FR) Rainbows For All (IRE) (Rainbows For Life (CAN))
7644[3]◆ 8431[5]

Made For You *Olly Murphy* a64 65
4 b g Cape Cross(IRE) Edallora (IRE) (Refuse To Bend (IRE))
1331[4]

Made Guy (USA) *J S Moore* a47 15
2 b g Street Boss(USA) But She's Ours (USA) (Lawyer Ron (USA))
3419[12] 3760[8] 6141a[7] 7768[5]

Made In Italy (IRE) *Marco Botti* a68
2 b f Mukhadram Delicatezza (Danehill Dancer (IRE))
9585[4]◆

Made In Lewisham (IRE)
David Evans a38 61
3 b g Morpheus River Beau (IRE) (Galileo (IRE))
537[8] 829[14]

Madeleine Bond *Henry Candy* a65 80
5 ch m Monsieur Bond(IRE) Spin A Wish (Captain Rio)
2252[8] 2966[11] 3698[3] 4450[7] 5782[5] 6362[2] 7237[4] (8413) 8761[3]

Madeleine Must (FR) *H-A Pantall* 103
3 b f Motivator Danny's Choice (Compton Place)
3677a[2] 4621a[6] (6910a) 7898[6]

Mad Endeavour *Stuart Kittow* a44 56
8 b g Muhtathir Capefly (Cape Cross (IRE))
1595[5] 3543[3] 5083[4] 6107[2] 8018[5]

Made Of Honour (IRE)
David Loughnane a86 77
5 ch m Casamento(IRE) Bonne (Namid)
(104)◆ (475) 756[5] 7471[5] 7856[11] 8197[12]

Made To Lead (FR) *Laurent Loisel* a95 98
4 b m Linngari(IRE) Magic Artiste (FR) (Art Sebal (USA))
8377a[3] 8969a[4]

Made To Order (FR) *E J O'Neill* 59
3 ch f Rio De La Plata(USA) Dakhla Oasis (IRE) (Night Shift (USA))
3712a[6] 6874a[5]

Made You Look (USA)
Chad C Brown a26 105
5 bb h More Than Ready(USA) Night And Day (USA) (Unbridled's Song (USA))
5977a[5] 7225a[8]

Madhmoon (IRE) *Kevin Prendergast* 117
3 b c Dawn Approach(IRE) Aaraas (Haafhd)
1600a[2] 2411[4] 3345[2] 4414a[4] (6137a) 7219a[6]

Madison County (NZ)
Murray Baker & Andrew Forsman 106
3 b g Pins(AUS) Red Delicious (NZ) (No Excuse Needed)
8138a[7] 8578a[8]

Madison Vanzales (FR) *M Boutin* a57 60
3 b f George Vancouver(USA) Eva Gonzales (IRE) (Peintre Celebre (USA))
7642a[3] 9538a[2]

Madita (GER) *S Smrczek* 106
4 rg m Soldier Hollow Manita (IRE) (Peintre Celebre (USA))
1793a[2] 3288a[2] 4461a[3]

Madiva (FR) *Vaclav Luka Jr* a69 70
7 gr m Aussie Rules(USA) Mahradeva (GER) (Medicean)
1491a[6]

Madkhal (USA) *Saeed bin Suroor* a93 74
3 ch g Distorted Humor(USA) Almurra (USA) (Street Cry (IRE))
7551[7] 8289[2]

Madrinho (IRE) *Tony Carroll* a83 78
6 ch g Frozen Power(IRE) Perfectly Clear (USA) (Woodman (USA))
139[4] 253[7] 790[2] 1357[3] 2107[8] 2804[6] 3549[3] 4649[6] 4880[8] 5723[2] 6203[7] 7337[9] 7828[13]

Madulain (FR) *H-A Pantall* a79 75
4 b m Paolini(GER) Mandel Island (IRE) (Turtle Island (IRE))
76a[5]

Maerchengarten *Ed de Giles* a41 44
3 b f Bated Breath Kammaan (Diktat)
7114[5] 7854[5] 8249[9] 9034[5] 9225[12] 9397[8]

Mafia Power *Richard Hannon* 74
2 b c Gleneagles(IRE) Rivara (Red Ransom (USA))
8459[4]

Magadan (GER) *J M Snackers* 68
3 b c Soldier Hollow Meransa (USA) (Fusaichi Pegasus (USA))
4707a[15]

Magari (FR) *Charley Rossi* a99 100
6 b h Denon(USA) Shakila (Cadeaux Genereux)
682a[12]

Magellan *Philip Kirby* a82 76
5 b g Sea The Stars(IRE) Hector's Girl (Hector Protector (USA))
3081[9]

Mageva *F Chappet* 90
2 b f Wootton Bassett Melilot (FR) (Elusive City (USA))
(4533a) 8647a[5]

Maggies Angel (IRE) *Richard Fahey* 81
4 b m Dark Angel(IRE) Last Bid (Vital Equine (IRE))
2809[14] 3815[6] 4320[9] 5453[5] 5971[3] (6609) 7362[10]

Maggi Rockstar (IRE) *Paul D'Arcy* 74
3 b f Slade Power(IRE) Maggi Rocks (IRE) (Fastnet Rock (AUS))
1740[4] 2102[7]

Maghaweer (IRE) *H Al Alawi* a23 41
4 ch h Dubawi(IRE) Indian Ink (IRE) (Indian Ridge (IRE))
197a[11] 997[13]

Maghfoor *Eric Alston* a62 72
5 b g Cape Cross(IRE) Thaahira (USA) (Dynaformer (USA))
1648[3] 2092[8] 3046[15] 4602[6] 4907[10] 5025[5] 5556[5] 6586[4]

Magic Act (IRE) *Mark Johnston* 50
3 b g New Approach(IRE) Pure Illusion (IRE) (Danehill (USA))
5103[5] 5742[9] 6274[6] 6805[6]

Magical (IRE) *A P O'Brien* 123
4 b m Galileo(IRE) Halfway To Heaven (IRE) (Pivotal)
(1777a) (2494a) (3114) 3985[2] 4668[2] 6377[2] (7219a) 7941a[5] (8335)

Magical Dreamer (IRE) *E J O'Neill* a77 97
5 b m Acclamation Double Fantasy (GER) (Indian Ridge (IRE))
5479a[8] 7293a[5]

Magical Duchess *Michael Dods* a10 38
3 b f Morpheus Idyllic Star (IRE) (Choisir (AUS))
3416[6]

Magical Effect (IRE) *Ruth Carr* a72 83
7 ch g New Approach(IRE) Purple Glow (IRE) (Orientate (USA))
1714[7] 1978[4] 2588[4] 3179[2] 3813[8] (4440)◆ 5476[3] 5821[3] 6260[3] 6677[11] 7311[4] 7621[7] 8339[2] 8634[5]

Magical Force *Rod Millman* a61 57
2 b f Lethal Force(IRE) Mythical City (IRE) (Rock Of Gibraltar (IRE))
2767[7] 4993[5] 6846[10] 8452[2] 9060[7] 9414[5]

Magical Forest (IRE) *H Blume* a85 83
5 b m Casamento(IRE) Hurry Home Hydee (USA) (Came Home (USA))
6521a[6] 7536a[8] (8240a)

Magical Journey (IRE) *James Tate* 94
2 ch f Night Of Thunder(IRE) Aljaazya (USA) (Speightstown (USA))
(7333) 8724[2]◆

Magical Max *Mark Walford* 82
2 gr g Coach House(IRE) Vellena (Lucky Story (USA))
(3866) (4517)

Magical Molly Joe *David Barron* a60 45
5 b m Arabian Gleam Magical Music (Fraam)
410[3]◆ 484[9] 1722[7] (1837) (2693) 3430[7] 3716[11] 7444[11]

Magical Moment (FR) *Kevin Ryan* a26 70
2 b f Dubawi(IRE) Maka (FR) (Slickly (FR))
6919[5]◆ 7546[8]

Magical Morning *John Gosden* a70
2 b c Muhaarar The Lark (Pivotal)
8455[6]

Magical Rhythms (USA)
John Gosden a81 89
3 b f Pioneerof The Nile(USA) Nayarra (IRE) (Cape Cross (IRE))
2919[6] 4341[3] 5627[3] (6316) (7341)

Magical Ride *Richard Spencer* a62 98
4 ch g Paco Boy(IRE) Decorative (IRE) (Danehill Dancer (IRE))
1286[5] 1728[7] 2060[7] 2774[5] 3208[9] 4115[2] (4349) (4567) 4801[4] (5677) (5959) 6953[U]

Magical Spirit (IRE) *Kevin Ryan* a88 82
3 ch g Zebedee La Dame De Fer (IRE) (Mr Greeley (USA))
1488[2]◆ 3202[2] (3516) 4603[6] 5399[5] (7656) 8921[2]

Magical Touch *H-A Pantall* 100
4 b m Dubawi(IRE) Criticism (Machiavellian (USA))
3123a[9] 7249a[11] 8581a[3]

Magical Wish (IRE) *Richard Hannon* a95 101
3 b g Heeraat(IRE) Tomintoul Magic (IRE) (Holy Roman Emperor (IRE))
1424[2] (1685) 2746[6] 3865[3]◆ 4669[2] 4847[12] 5711a[10] 5932[7] 7431[18]

Magic Attitude *F Chappet* 91
2 b f Galileo(IRE) Margot Did (IRE) (Exceed And Excel (AUS))
7673a[3]

Magic Circle (IRE) *Ian Williams* a92 108
7 b g Makfi Minkova (IRE) (Sadler's Wells (USA))
2560[3] 4015[9]

Magic City (IRE) *Michael Easterby* a76 76
10 b g Elusive City(USA) Annmarie's Magic (IRE) (Flying Spur (AUS))
1457[10] 2710[7] 3100[3] 3567[7] 3867[11] 5770[7] 6628[8]

Magic Dust *Marco Botti* a38 73
2 b f Casamento(IRE) Lady Artemisia (IRE) (Montjeu (IRE))
8258[2]◆ 9046[13]

Magicienmake Myday *H De Nicolay* a60 53
8 b h Whipper(USA) Whisper To Dream (USA) (Gone West (USA))
115a[11] 2391a[11]

Magic Image *H-A Pantall* a61 80
3 ch f Dubawi(IRE) White Rose (GER) (Platini (GER))
168a[13] 511a[14] 6270a[7]

Magicinthemaking (USA)
John E Long a69 51
5 br m Wildcat Heir(USA) Love In Bloom (USA) (More Than Ready (USA))
53[U] (161) 718[2] 919[2] 3304[3] (3996) 6441[2] (7576) (7812)

Magic J (USA) *Ed Vaughan* a91 86
3 ch c Scat Daddy(USA) Miss Lamour (USA) (Mr Greeley (USA))
1926[8] 7655[3] 8267[3]

Magic Lily *Charlie Appleby* a94 100
4 ch m New Approach(IRE) Dancing Rain (IRE) (Danehill Dancer (IRE))
7885a[2] 9002[6]

Magic Mirror *Mark Rimell* a79 51
6 b m Dutch Art Balatoma (IRE) (Mr Greeley (USA))
135[5] 364[2] 616[2] (942) 1269[6] 1518[3] 2106[9] 2797[6] 4249[8] 8807[11] 9067[5] 9173[2]

Magic Sea (IRE) *Sarah Dawson* a69 55
4 b g Born To Sea(IRE) Annmarie's Magic (IRE) (Flying Spur (AUS))
1861[9]

Magic Ship (IRE) *John Norton* a33 43
4 b g Kodiac Baltic Belle (IRE) (Redback)
2146[9] 3730[5] 4728[14] 5787[16] 8008[9]

Magic Shuffle (IRE) *Barry Brennan* a62 71
3 b g Ruler Of The World(IRE) Himiko (IRE) (Aussie Rules (USA))
(4235) 4737[3] 5338[3] 5880[3] 7116[10] 7573[4] 8756[7]

Magic Song (FR) *S Kobayashi* a71 70
5 bb m Kendargent(FR) Magic Potion (FR) (Divine Light (JPN))
4747a[14] 6031a[2] 7505a[4]

Magic Timing *Tim Fitzgerald* a77 73
2 b g Hot Streak(IRE) Enchanted Princess (Royal Applause)
5118[3] 5615[3] 6622[7] 7064[2] 8239a[3]

Magic Twist (USA) *Mark Johnston* a14 69
2 b f Elusive Quality(USA) Tourner (USA) (Hard Spun (USA))
4688[3] 5572[2] 7113[7] 9172[11] 9515[13]

Magic Wand (IRE) *A P O'Brien* 115
4 b m Galileo(IRE) Prudenzia (IRE) (Dansili)
444a[2] 1446a[5] 2646a[3] 3953[2] 4354a[2] 5414[11] 6001a[2] 7219a[2] 8579a[4] 8844a[10] (8952a) 9380a[2]

Magna Grecia (IRE) *A P O'Brien* 121
3 b c Invincible Spirit(IRE) Cabaret (IRE) (Galileo (IRE))
(2411) 3104a[5] 8334[14]

Magna Moralia (IRE) *John Quinn* 73
2 gr g Gregorian(IRE) Trentini (IRE) (Singspiel (IRE))
5273[4]◆ 5764[7] (6497)◆ 6969[8] 8029[2] 8394[2]

Magnet (FR) *L Gadbin* a84
4 ch g Exceed And Excel(AUS) Molly Malone (FR) (Lomitas)
1578a[12]

Magnetic (IRE) *J S Moore* a45 20
3 b g Alhebayeb(IRE) Telltime (IRE) (Danetime (IRE))
141[9] 437[13] 2357[12] 2734[11]

Magnetic Charm *William Haggas* 112
3 b f Exceed And Excel(AUS) Monday Show (USA) (Maria's Mon (USA))
(2806) 4052[2] 5369[3] 7224a[2] 8139a[8]

Magnetic North (IRE)
Ms Sheila Lavery a83 91
4 ch g Born To Sea(IRE) No Trimmings (IRE) (Medecis)
5535a[7] 5711a[3]

Magnetique (IRE) *J Parize* 40
4 b h Leroidesanimaux(BRZ) Magique (IRE) (Jeremy (USA))
1578a[8]

Magnetised *Roger Varian* 77
2 b c Shamardal(USA) Princess Nada (Barathea (IRE))
(8511)◆

Magnificat (IRE) *Alan King* a32
2 b c Dandy Man(IRE) Retrato (USA) (Fusaichi Pegasus (USA))
9385[9]

Magnificia (IRE) *Ed Dunlop* a39 72
2 b f Sir Prancealot(IRE) Star Bonita (IRE) (Invincible Spirit (IRE))
5189[10] 5527[2] 9409[8]

Magnolia Springs (IRE)
Eve Johnson Houghton a91 98
4 b m Shamardal(USA) Rainbow City (IRE) (Rainbow Quest (USA))
1627a[6] 2642a[6] 3586[4] 5190[6] 6082[4]

Magny Cours (USA) *A Fabre* a89 111
4 b g Medaglia d'Oro(USA) Indy Five Hundred (USA) (A.P. Indy (USA))
1244a[2] 8379a[2]

Magojiro (USA) *W J Martin* a34 32
4 b g Hat Trick(JPN) Rebuke (USA) (Carson City (USA))
369[12] 7240[16]

Magrevio (IRE) *Liam Bailey* 60
3 b g Helmet(AUS) Queen Althea (IRE) (Bach (IRE))
2150[8] 3226[11] 4990[2] 6612[3] 6938[5]

Magwadiri (IRE) *Mark Loughnane* a57 66
5 b g Casamento(IRE) Hankering (IRE) (Missed Flight)
1659[8] 2256[13] (3158) 7811[9] 9566[6] 9657[7]

Mahamedeis (AUS) *Nick Ryan* 106
4 ch g Magnus(AUS) Elusive Magic (AUS) (Elusive Quality (USA))
8138a[10] 8768a[11]

Mahari (IRE) *Kerry Lee*
6 b g Duke Of Marmalade(IRE) Mission Secrete (IRE) (Galileo (IRE))
2486[7]

Mahna Mahna (IRE)
David W Drinkwater a44 43
5 b g Kodiac Namu (Mujahid (USA))
243[12] 2929[8] 3186[6] 4216[8] 5081[5]

Mahoe (FR) *A Junk* a78 105
4 b h Doctor Dino(FR) Marabounta (FR) (Zieten (USA))
2169a[4]

Mahuika *John Gallagher* a41
3 b f Firebreak Adweb (Muhtarram (USA))
8808[6]

Maiden Castle *Henry Candy* a67 86
3 b g Nayef(USA) Danae (Dansili)
2354[2]◆ 3263[5]

Maiden Navigator *David Simcock* a53 52
3 b f Sea The Moon(GER) Captain's Paradise (IRE) (Rock Of Gibraltar (IRE))
259[4] 836[8] 4447[7] 5001[9] 5548[5]

Maiden Voyage (FR) *Archie Watson* 85
4 b m Motivator Atlantic Light (Linamix (FR))
7026[5] 7294[7] 7625[5]

Maid For Life *Charlie Fellowes* a101 95
3 b f Nathaniel(IRE) Dream To Be Maid (Oasis Dream)
1400[10] 2060[4] (3323) 4793[3]◆ (5525) 5949[4] 6709[2] 7347[8] 9002[14]

Maid From The Mist *John Gallagher* 56
3 gr f Hellvelyn Ball Burst (IRE) (Imperial Ballet (IRE))
1219[9] 1650[8] (2708) 3801[3] 5084[4] 5607[6] 6120[2] 7824[14] 8263[12]

Maid In India (IRE) *Eric Alston* 110
5 br m Bated Breath Indian Maiden (IRE) (Indian Ridge (IRE))
(3587) 4101[15] (7454)

Maid In Manhattan (IRE)
Rebecca Menzies a56 87
5 b m Fame And Glory Silly Goose (IRE) (Sadler's Wells (USA))
(3272) (3769) 3886[2] 4661[2] (6016) (6674) 6924[5] (7830)◆ (8027)

Maid Millie *Jane Chapple-Hyam* a57 48
3 b f Dream Ahead(USA) Maid A Million (Kyllachy)
27[11] 1170[4] 1385[7] 2007[4] 3651[7] 5890[2] 6181[4] 6737[3] 7105[3]◆ 8847[4] 9039[4] 9133[3] 9572[4]

Maid Of Spirit (IRE) *Clive Cox* a67 81
4 br m Invincible Spirit(IRE) Indian Maiden (IRE) (Indian Ridge (IRE))
2009[3] 3021[3] 3470[5] 5659[3] (6080) 6809[6] 8115[11]

Maid Up *Andrew Balding* a80 107
4 gr m Mastercraftsman(IRE) Complexion (Hurricane Run (IRE))
2410[7] 3096[5] 3995[6] 4933[8]

Maifalki (FR) *Jason Ward* a78 95
6 b g Falco(USA) Makila (IRE) (Entrepreneur)
47a[6] 398a[9] 730a[11] 4102[14] 4890[3] 5440[7]

Mailshot (USA) *S bin Ghadayer* a91 92
5 ch g Hard Spun(USA) Newsreel (IRE) (A.P. Indy (USA))
173a[12] 425a[8] 1748a[6]

Main Edition (IRE) *Mark Johnston* 111
3 b f Zoffany(IRE) Maine Lobster (USA) (Woodman (USA))
1832[7] (3119a) 4051[9] 5369[7] (7905) 8765[6]

Main Reef *David Simcock* 50
2 ch c Pivotal Coral Mist (Bahamian Bounty)
2367[4] 8202[8]

Mainsail Atlantic (USA)
James Fanshawe a85 82
4 b h Speightstown(USA) Minakshi (FR) (Footstepsinthesand)
2022[3]◆ 4250[9] 5348[5] 6026[5] 7350[2] 8240a[3]

Main Stage (NZ)
Trent Busuttin & Natalie Young 93
4 b g Reliable Man Kiri (NZ) (Prized (USA))
9016a[8]

Main Street *David Elsworth* a100 99
4 b g Street Cry(IRE) My Special J'S (USA) (Harlan's Holiday (USA))
565[7] 880[3] 1181[6] 1545[7]

Maisie Ellie (IRE) *Paul George* a33 59
2 ch f Starspangledbanner(AUS) Pina Colada (Sabrehill (USA))
2248[5] 2996[9] 3660[8] 6979[5] 7522[9] 7853[11] 8825[8]

Maisie Moo *Shaun Keightley* a57 45
3 b f Swiss Spirit Al Hawa (USA) (Gulch (USA))
556[10] 913[3] 1170[2] 1285[9] 1863[6] 2939[10] 3697[5] 5730[4] (8256) 8667[12] 8864[5] 9305[12]

Majaalis (FR) *William Haggas* 99
3 b g Invincible Spirit(IRE) High Surf (USA) (Storm Cat (USA))
2790[5] 4120[7] (4827)◆ 5530[2]◆ 6413[6] (7351)

Majarra (IRE) *Adrian Nicholls* 37
2 b f Swiss Spirit Berry Baby (IRE) (Rainbow Quest (USA))
3335[8] 4206[6]

Majdool (IRE) *Noel Wilson* a59 56
6 b g Acclamation Maany (USA) (Mr Greeley (USA))
3177[12] 5038[6] 5282[7] 6441[5] 8306[8] 8666[9]

Majeski Man (IRE)
Mrs Denise Foster 64
2 ch c Dandy Man(IRE) Fly By Magic (IRE) (Indian Rocket)
5710a[6]

Majeste *Rebecca Bastiman* a53 71
5 b g Acclamation Winged Valkyrie (IRE) (Hawk Wing (USA))
2012[6] 2439[3] (3225) (3296) 3718[3]◆ 3960[3] 5285[5] 5728[2]◆ 6180[7] 6343[8] 7783[7] 8238[6] 8515[10]

Majestic Ace *Richard Hannon*
2 ch c Paco Boy(IRE) Dark Quest (Rainbow Quest (USA))
4254[7]

Majestic Dawn (IRE) *Paul Cole* a75 101
3 ch c Dawn Approach(IRE) Jolie Chanson (FR) (Mount Nelson)
32[2]◆ 1034[2] (1756) 2828[7] 4017[7] 4882[3] 7694[5] (8260) 8725[3]

Majestic Endeavour *Mark Johnston* a45
2 b f Shamardal(USA) Majestic Manner (Dubawi (IRE))
8849[12]

Majestic Mac *Hughie Morrison* a71 82
3 b g Cape Cross(IRE) Talent Spotter (Exceed And Excel (AUS))
2035[4] 2927[2] 4124[3] 4546[4] 5343[2] 5804[10] 7460[4] 8017[8]

Majestic Mambo (SAF)
M F De Kock 110
4 b g Mambo In Seattle(USA) Regal Classic (SAF) (Al Mufti (USA))
1115a[6] 1445a[8]

Majestic Man (IRE)
Ronald Thompson a43 38
6 b g Majestic Missile(IRE) Windomen (IRE) (Forest Wind (USA))
462[8] 2346[6]

Majestic Moon (IRE) *Julia Feilden* a76 79
9 b g Majestic Missile(IRE) Gala Style (IRE) (Elnadim (USA))
237[5] 392[4] 1074[2] 1367[3] 1526[2] 1859[2] 2193[5] 2297[5] 2739[3] 3541[9]

Majestic Noor *John Gosden* a77
2 b f Frankel Nouriya (Danehill Dancer (IRE))
8848[5] 9156[2]

Majestic Sands (IRE)
Richard Fahey 88
2 b c Kodiac La Grande Zoa (IRE) (Fantastic Light (USA))
(3190)◆ 3949[14]

Majestic Stone (IRE)
Julie Camacho a54 55
5 b g Casamento(IRE) Pretty Majestic (IRE) (Invincible Spirit (IRE))
2244[3] (3251) 3925[4] 4601[4] 5248[9] 6059[5] 6939[3]◆ 7415[5] 8423[2] 9289[3] 9470[7]

Majestyk Fire (IRE) *David Flood* a25 11
2 ch g Ivawood(IRE) Dream Impossible (IRE) (Iffraaj)
6718[11] 7972[13] 8605[12]

Major Assault *Debbie Hughes* a38 42
6 b g Kyllachy Night Premiere (IRE) (Night Shift (USA))
9670[11]

Major Blue *James Eustace* a71 76
3 b g Delegator Bahama Blue (Bahamian Bounty)
313[6] (621) 1336[3] 2098[6] 2730[2] 4236[9] (4757) 5356[5] 7337[10] 7837[10] 8117[4] 8296[9]

Major Crispies *Ronald Thompson* a58 65
8 b g Pastoral Pursuits Nellie Melba (Hurricane Sky (AUS))
232[9] 586[6] 788[6] 882[5] 1158[5] 1553[8] 1722[11] 1967[8] 2298[7] 3476[3] 5767[10]

Majorette *Brian Barr* a67 58
5 ch m Major Cadeaux So Discreet (Tragic Role (USA))
144[4] 439[4] 759[8] 1076[2]◆ (2010) 6120[6] 7078[6] 8861[7] 9386[12]

Major Jumbo *Kevin Ryan* a91 113
5 gr g Zebedee Gone Sailing (Mizzen Mast (USA))
1412[2] 2409[3] 2744[2] 3388a[3] 4923[9] (5705) 6959[7] 7433[14]

Major Muscari (IRE) *Shaun Harris* a34 33
11 ch g Exceed And Excel(AUS) Muscari (Indian Ridge (IRE))
973[9] 1192[13] 1384[11] 1967[11] 2287[9]

Major Partnership (IRE)
Saeed bin Suroor a97 106
4 gr h Iffraaj Roystonea (Polish Precedent (USA))
170a[8] 515a[10] (847a) 1440a[11] 6953[12] 8707[11]

Major Pusey *John Gallagher* a51 75
7 ch g Major Cadeaux Pusey Street Lady (Averti (IRE))
1654[5] 2625[7] 3509[6] 6921[7] 7568[8] 7986[2]◆ 8285[7]

Major Reward (IRE)
Adrian Paul Keatley a90 85
3 b g Dawn Approach(IRE) Zanzibar Girl (USA) (Johannesburg (USA))
2492a[9]

Major Snugfit *Michael Easterby* a65 66
3 ch g Ruler Of The World(IRE) Bridle Belle (Dansili)
2096[11] 6940[7] 7545[4] 8200[7] 9467[6]

Major Valentine *John O'Shea* a72 93
7 b g Major Cadeaux Under My Spell (Wizard King)
(1952) 2358[3] (2717) 2804[8] 3701[3] (4872) (6109) (6525) 7431[13] 8607[10]

Makaarim *Seamus Durack* a51 39
5 b g Tamayuz Dubawi Cheetah (IRE) (Dubawi (IRE))
158[8] 507[9] 944[7] 1338[8] 1986[9]

Makahiki (JPN) *Yasuo Tomomichi* 117
6 b h Deep Impact(JPN) Wikiwiki (JPN) (French Deputy (USA))
9153a[4]

Makambe (IRE) *Chelsea Banham* a79 64
4 gr g Dark Angel(IRE) Pink Diva (IRE) (Giant's Causeway (USA))
54[7] 473[4] 876[6] 985[4] 1363[6] 1463[3] 2928[5] 3633[7] 4296[6] 5824[4] 6317[3] (6839) (7875) 8902[4] 9180[2] 9561[3]

Makanah *Julie Camacho* a84 101
4 b g Mayson Diane's Choice (Komaite (USA))
(2421)◆ 2910[2] (3360)◆ 4331[10] 6351[4] 7193[7] 8340[7]

Makawee (IRE) *David O'Meara* 99
4 b m Farhh Storming Sioux (Storming Home)
2436[2] (3095) (3269)◆ 3862[5] 4145[6] 4936[2] 5457[2] 6355[13] 7075[3]

Makda (FR) *J Boisnard* a69 77
3 b f Makfi Dajariyda (FR) (Cape Cross (IRE))
9281a[3]

Make A Challenge (IRE)
Denis Gerard Hogan a69 115
4 b g Invincible Spirit(IRE) Crinoline (USA) (Street Cry (IRE))
(5537a) 7241a[2] (8166a) 8331[5]

Make A Wish (IRE) *Simon Crisford* 91
3 ch f No Nay Never(USA) Saturn Girl (IRE) (Danehill Dancer (IRE))
(2909) 4124[6] (4669)

Make Good (IRE) *David Dennis* a59 70
4 b g Fast Company(IRE) Rectify (IRE) (Mujadil (USA))
85[7] 559[3] 1024[2] 1363[2] 1498[6] 2279[6] (5029) 6105[5]

Make It Rain (IRE) *Simon Crisford* a76 69
2 b f Night Of Thunder(IRE) Badalona (Cape Cross (IRE))
8093[9] 8510[5] (9326)

Make Me *Tim Easterby* 72
4 ch g Makfi Magic Music (IRE) (Magic Ring (IRE))
2842[3] 3268[5] 3922[9] 4108[9] 5616[10] 6037[3] 6461[6] 7363[5] 8031[2]

Make Me Laugh (IRE)
Richard Fahey 65
2 ch c Iffraaj Tickle Me (GER) (Halling (USA))
5848[8] 6892[5] 7539[7]

Make My Day (IRE) *John Gosden* 89
3 b c Galileo(IRE) Posset (Oasis Dream)
2099[2] 3699[4] (4066)

Makeno (FR) *D Guillemin* a70 62
2 gr c Kendargent(FR) Marelle (GER) (Raven's Pass (USA))
6196a[4]

Make On Madam (IRE) *Les Eyre* a54 51
7 b m Captain Rio Rye (IRE) (Charnwood Forest (IRE))
2256[11] 3214[5] 4584[8] 5517[11] 6102[10]

Making History (IRE)
Saeed bin Suroor a60 86
2 b g Dubawi(IRE) Important Time (IRE) (Oasis Dream)
1953[4] 2686[5] 3419[3] (5101)◆ 5382[3] 6020[3] 6705[6] 7827[4]

Making Miracles *Mark Johnston* a112 113
4 b g Pivotal Field Of Miracles (IRE) (Galileo (IRE))
1947[5] (2118) (2575) 3024[4] 3864[6] 4382[7] 5183[14] 6473[P]

Makito *C Laffon-Parias* a77
2 b g Makfi Pale Pearl (IRE) (King's Best (USA))
(8448a)

Makmour (FR) *J-C Rouget* a80 99
3 b c Rock Of Gibraltar(IRE) Makana (FR) (Dalakhani (IRE))
2499a[7]

Makofitwhatyouwill *Ruth Carr* a44 32
4 b g Makfi Frequent (Three Valleys (USA))
132[6] 501[5] 738[11]

Maksab (IRE) *Mick Channon* a88 84
4 b g Makfi Azeema (IRE) (Averti (IRE))
(856) 1097[7] 1881[7] 2363[6] 4887[4] 5386[4] 5945[4] 6567[5] 7205[4] 8017[5]

Maktabba *William Haggas* 74
3 b f Dansili Mudaaraah (Cape Cross (IRE))
2481[3] (5048)◆ 5982[6] 6854[3]

Maktay *David Bridgwater* a49 46
3 b g Makfi Cinta (Monsun (GER))
2357[7] 2943[12] 3645[10]

Makyon (IRE) *Mark Johnston* 94
2 b c Make Believe Mise (IRE) (Indian Ridge (IRE))
3098[2]◆ (3498) 3949[11] 4610[10] (5485) 5900[2] 7763[4]

Makzeem *Roger Charlton* a90 108
6 b g Makfi Kazeem (Darshaan)
3009[5]◆ 4299[8] (5188) 5413[22] 7905[4] 9064[10]

Malaguerra (AUS) *Peter Gelagotis* 92
7 b g Magnus(AUS) Tennessee Morn (AUS) (Bletchingly (AUS))
1974a[11]

Malaspina (ITY) *Ivan Furtado* a73 65
7 b m Pounced(USA) Modern Goddess (USA) (Gulch (USA))
276[4] 499[7] 840[6] 4371[11]

Malaysian Boleh *Phil McEntee* a49 39
9 ch g Compton Place Orlena (USA) (Gone West (USA))
116[9] 159[4] 379[6] 478[6] 613[4] 719[4] 925[9] 1215[5] 1383[4] 1478[4] 1732[5] 1933[8] 3007[11] 3475[10] 3996[8] 4336[7] 4797[8] 5806[5] 5837[7] 6152[6]

Maldonado (FR) *Michael Easterby* a60 63
5 ch g Rio De La Plata(USA) Spanish Winner (IRE) (Choisir (AUS))
3939[11] 4633[8] 5518[3] (6305) 7544[6] 8669[8]

Malevra (FR) *G Botti* a73 101
3 b f Le Havre(IRE) Marania (IRE) (Marju (IRE))
3391a[2] 4171a[7]

Malibu Roan (USA) *Agostino Affe'* 78
3 rg c Malibu Moon(USA) Maria's Dane (USA) (Maria's Mon (USA))
2162a[6]

Malika I Jahan (FR) *David Lanigan* a71 68
3 b f Australia Have Faith (IRE) (Machiavellian (USA))
7451[2] 7999[5]

Malizia *Amy Murphy* a20
2 b f Epaulette(AUS) Sleepy Dust (IRE) (Rip Van Winkle (IRE))
8919[13]

Malkoboy (FR) *Claudia Erni* a80 105
5 gr h Rajsaman(FR) Goldy Honor (FR) (Highest Honor (FR))
3123a[4]

Mallet Head *Philip McBride*
3 b c Rajsaman(FR) Attachee De Presse (IRE) (Danehill (USA))
518[5]

Mallons Spirit (IRE)
Michael Appleby 41
3 b f Rip Van Winkle(IRE) Que Sera Sera (Dansili)
2932[10] 3421[8] 5358[6] 5869[8]

Malmesbury Abbey (FR) *Ed Walker* 48
2 b g Wootton Bassett Darice (IRE) (Cape Cross (IRE))
6079[8] 6845[11] 7406[11]

Malotru *Marco Botti* a81 100
2 b c Casamento(IRE) Magika (Dubawi (IRE))
(3141) (4172a) 6422[4] 7456[5]

Malt Teaser (FR) *John Best* a18 15
5 ch g Muhtathir Abondante (USA) (Thunder Gulch (USA))
6077[10]

Malvern *Richard Hannon* 79
2 ch c Outstrip Perfect Muse (Oasis Dream)
(5374) (5879) 6356[20] 7399[17]

Mama Africa (IRE) *John Flint* a43 50
5 br m Big Bad Bob(IRE) Colourpoint (USA) (Forest Wildcat (USA))
164[3] 392[2] 951[7] 1367[2] 1526[7] 1859[5] (2346) 3541[12] 4872[6] 5560[13] 7977[6] 8946[7] 9185[9]

Mambila (FR) *Geoffrey Harker* 71
5 b g Rio De La Plata(USA) Maka (FR) (Slickly (FR))
5330[8] 6099[12] 7051[8]

Mambo Nights (IRE)
Richard Hannon 86
2 b c Havana Gold(IRE) Inez (Dai Jin)
5177[8] 5665[6] 6154[2] 6905[3]

Mamdood (IRE) *Stef Keniry* a53 48
5 gr g Clodovil(IRE) Fact (American Post)
7581[9] 8238[3]◆ (8423) 8670[3] 8843[6] 9168[8] 9345[9] 9552[7]

Mametz Wood (IRE) *K R Burke* a78 76
4 b g Elzaam(AUS) Shaanbar (IRE) (Darshaan)
102[9] 392[5]

Mamillius *George Baker* a84 86
6 b g Exceed And Excel(AUS) Laika Lane (USA) (Street Cry (IRE))
1143[6] 1496[3] (1932) 3183[3] 3963[8] 5090[2] 5839[5] 6567[7] 7128[8] 7268[3]

Mamnoon (IRE) *Roy Brotherton* a37 37
6 b g Cape Cross(IRE) Masaafat (Act One)
2998[11] 4498[7] 4771[6] 6855[8] 7232[10]

Manahir (FR) *S Jadhav* a72 94
5 ch h Naaqoos Lerina (FR) (Priolo (USA))
52a[11] 639a[9]

Manana Chica (IRE) *Clive Cox* 72
3 b f Kodiac Bayalika (IRE) (Selkirk (USA))
2340[6] (2762) 3307[11] 4603[7]

Manap *Archie Watson* a53 64
2 b g Sepoy(AUS) Monshak (IRE) (Monsun (GER))
4114[6] 9500[9]

Mancini *Jonathan Portman* a82 99
5 ch g Nathaniel(IRE) Muscovado (USA) (Mr Greeley (USA))
2143[4] 2781[2] 3952[7] (4936) 5540[7] 6355[11] 7181[3]

Mandalayan (IRE)
Jonathan Portman a59 92
4 b g Arakan(USA) Danza Nera (IRE) (Dansili)
1559[2] 2342[3] 4505[10] 5321[9] 6156[3] 7127[5] 7729[5]

Mandarin (GER) *Ian Williams* a85 98
5 ch g Lope De Vega(IRE) Margarita (GER) (Lomitas)
2273[17] 2739[5] 3338[2] 3806[2] (4997) (5625)◆ 5929[3] 6420[13]

Mandarin Princess *Kenny Johnson* a37 39
4 b m Vale Of York(IRE) Little China (Kyllachy)
2587[5] 3448[12] 3929[6] 5297[6] 5555[7]

Mandocello (FR) *Rod Millman* a53 76
3 b g Motivator Serenada (FR) (Anabaa (USA))
1352[8] 1690[6] 2250[3]◆ (2689) 5779[9] 6414[4] (7756)

Mandolin Wind (FR) *E J O'Neill* a48 76
5 bb m Equiano(FR) Dhurwah (IRE) (Green Desert (USA))
6267a[6]

Manfadh (IRE) *Kevin Frost* a69 68
4 b g Iffraaj Asiya (USA) (Daaher (CAN))
(344) 793[7] 1169[8] 3046[5] 3429[5] 4109[3] 5709[10] 7083[6] 7858[3] 8664[8]

Mangaia (FR) *Vaclav Luka Jr* a84 70
5 b m Orpen(USA) Mapiya (Green Tune (USA))
4532a[8]

Mangkhut (FR) *Andrea Marcialis* 86
2 b c Sommerabend Fantastic Fire (GER) (Platini (GER))
6746a[7] 9059a[8]

Mango Chutney *John Davies* a47 70
6 b g Sleeping Indian Crimson Topaz (Hernando (FR))
4239[7] 5020[11] 5770[10] 9512[14]

Mango Tango (FR) *Archie Watson* a102 106
6 b m Siyouni(FR) Alexandrina (GER) (Monsun (GER))
682a[10]

Manguzi (FR) *A R Al Rayhi* a108 63
3 b c Planteur(IRE) My Girl Charlie (IRE) (Kodiac)
169a[2] (394a) 1110a[3] 1443a[3]

Manigordo (USA) *Richard Hannon* 94
2 bb c Kitten's Joy(USA) Cutting Edge (USA) (Silver Deputy (CAN))
4388[4] 4897[2] 7119[4]◆ 7614[5]

Manipur (GER) *Markus Klug*
5 b h Lord Of England(GER) Manipura (GER) (Dansili)
780a[9]

Manjaam (IRE) *Ian Williams* a85 89
6 ch g Tamayuz Priory Rock (IRE) (Rock Of Gibraltar (IRE))
1422[11] 2032[6] 2781[11] 4102[6] 4884[8] 5443[6] 7181[4]◆ 7688[5] 8350[9] 9288[5] 9419[7] 9570[5]

Manjeer (IRE) *John M Oxx* a92 95
3 b c Footstepsinthesand Navajo Moon (IRE) (Danehill (USA))
1049a[6] 6235a[6] 7038a[13]

Mankayan (IRE) *Charlie Fellowes* 85
3 b g Intello(GER) Angelic Note (IRE) (Excellent Art)
(3699) 5153[2] 7525[4] 8513[11]

Mankib *William Haggas* a102 116
5 ch h Tamayuz Natagora (FR) (Divine Light (JPN))
2615[2] 3588[9]

Mannaal (IRE) *Simon Crisford* 99
3 b f Dubawi(IRE) Soraaya (IRE) (Elnadim (USA))
(2481) 3169[2] 3762[6] (4996) (5545) 6124[4] 7137a[7]

Manny Wah (USA) *Bob Baffert* a101
3 ch c Will Take Charge(USA) Battlefield Angel (USA) (Proud Citizen (USA))
9639a[3]

Man Of Letters (FR) *R Chotard* a60 62
5 gr g Literato(FR) Snake River (IRE) (Bachelor Duke (USA))
1073a[7]

Man Of Promise (USA)
Charlie Appleby 80
2 b c Into Mischief(USA) Involved (USA) (Speightstown (USA))
5367[3]◆

Man Of The Night (FR)
Richard Hannon 93
2 b c Night Of Thunder(IRE) Mandheera (USA) (Bernardini (USA))
(4558)◆ 6417[4] 7410[2] 7897[12]

Man Of The Sea (IRE)
Neil Mulholland a63 62
3 ch g Born To Sea(IRE) Hurricane Lily (IRE) (Ali-Royal (IRE))
2276[3] (2671a) (3173a) 3641a[2] (4685a) 5232[6] (6553a) 9664[3]

Man Of Verve (IRE) *Philip Kirby* a64 46
5 b g Dandy Man(IRE) She's Our Rock (IRE) (Rock Of Gibraltar (IRE))
22[4] 348[6] 910[11]

Manolith *David O'Meara* 72
2 b g Dandy Man(IRE) Eolith (Pastoral Pursuits)
1812[7] (2115) 2415[3]◆ 2903[7] 4893[3] 5185[16] 6032[8] (6900)

Manolo Blahniq (NZ) *Tony Noonan* 104
5 b g Jimmy Choux(NZ) Floramour (AUS) (More Than Ready (USA))
8360a[4]

Manomine *R K Watson* a52 55
10 b g Manduro(GER) Fascinating Hill (FR) (Danehill (USA))
208[3] 1083[6]

Man On The Moon (GER)
Jean-Pierre Carvalho a47 90
3 ch c Sea The Moon(GER) Maricel (GER) (Silvano (GER))
2163a[7] 3674a[8]

Manorah (IRE) *Roger Varian* a83 89
3 b f The Factor(USA) Fifth Avenue Doll (USA) (Marquetry (USA))
2354[13] (2935) 4391[2] 5687[3] 6280[4] 7137a[8] 8064[4]

Manor Park *Alan King* a79 78
4 b g Medicean Jadeel (Green Desert (USA))
2626[5]

Mansfield *Stella Barclay* a62 62
6 b g Exceed And Excel(AUS) Jane Austen (IRE) (Galileo (IRE))
496[8] 907[8] 1565[3] 1986[3] 2122[5] (3203) 3475[9] 4630[7] 5558[3] 6680[4] 7051[3] 7443[3] 7823[7] 9133[2] 9287[3] 9551[6]

Manshood (IRE) *Paul Midgley* a84 85
6 b g Iffraaj Thawrah (IRE) (Green Desert (USA))
1487[9] 2079[6] (2508) 3347[9] 3868[6] 4313a[2] 5205a[14] 5619[6] 7077[3] 7908[6] 8601[8]

Mans Not Trot (IRE) *Brian Barr* a60 57
4 b g Kodiac Turuqaat (Fantastic Light (USA))
39[6] 462[3] 940[3] 1060[14] 1214[3] (2012) 3006[7] 4787[7] 5003[11] 5633[8]

Mantega (FR) *H-A Pantall* a64 65
3 b f Manduro(GER) Tegan (IRE) (Cape Cross (IRE))
9280a[8] 9504a[8]

Manthoor (IRE) *H Al Alawi* a62 75
4 gr h Swiss Spirit Enchanting Way (Linamix (FR))
97a[8] 573a[12]

Manton Grange *George Baker* a90 89
6 b g Siyouni(FR) Emulate (Alhaarth (IRE))
2402[7] 2966[2]

Manton Warrior (IRE)
Charlie Fellowes a82 72
3 b g War Command(USA) Kotdiji (Mtoto)
2021[8] 3311[7] (4024) 4729[4] 5825[2] (6392) 7082[4] 7370[3] 7845[3] 8468[2]

Mantovani (FR) *Harry Fry* a54 81
4 b g High Chaparral(IRE) Ripley (GER) (Platini (GER))
7518[6]

Manucci (IRE) *Amanda Perrett* 79
3 b g Nathaniel(IRE) American Spirit (IRE) (Rock Of Gibraltar (IRE))
2566[6] 7159[7] 7730[2] (8248)◆

Manuel (AUS) *Tony McEvoy* 112
5 b g Commands(AUS) Girl Hussler (AUS) (Hussonet (USA))
1974a[5]

Manuela De Vega (IRE)
Ralph Beckett 108
3 b f Lope De Vega(IRE) Roscoff (IRE) (Daylami (IRE))
2521[2]◆ 3316[4] 5208a[5] 5663[2] 6446[3] 7180[2] 8792a[2]

Many A Star (IRE) *James Given* a75 71
2 ch c Starspangledbanner(AUS) Many Hearts (USA) (Distorted Humor (USA))
5908[8] 6449[3] 7160[4] 8890[2] 9162[10]

Manzil (IRE) *Michael Easterby* a53 65
4 ch g Bated Breath Pointed Arch (IRE) (Rock Of Gibraltar (IRE))
7436[11] 8129[11]

Manzo Duro (IRE) *David O'Meara* 73
2 bb g Slade Power(IRE) Miss Cape (IRE) (Cape Cross (IRE))
6226[2]◆ 6971[4] 7778[7]

Manzoni *Mohamed Moubarak* a45 47
3 b g Equiano(FR) Gauchita (Invincible Spirit (IRE))
1523[5] 2199[11] 2976[9] 6889[10] 7838[6] 8295[7]

Maori Knight (IRE) *Richard Hughes* 80
2 b c Camelot Chatham Islands (USA) (Elusive Quality (USA))
5131[3] 7151[4]

Mapocho (FR)
Frederic Lamotte D'Argy a24 16
4 gr g Style Vendome(FR) Miss Santiago (FR) (Smadoun (FR))
2264a[14] 2955a[14]

Mapped (USA) *Iain Jardine* a65 70
4 b g Mizzen Mast(USA) Geographic (USA) (Empire Maker (USA))
1461[9] 2116[11] 3095[7] 3467[6] 4009[5] 4724[10] 5240[6]

Maqaadeer *Ed Dunlop* a74 77
3 b g Mukhadram Burnt Fingers (IRE) (Kheleyf (USA))
1217[2] 1480[4] 2336[4] 4070[3] (4664) 5245[9] 6165[7]

Maqboola (USA) *Richard Hughes* a71 55
3 b f Tamayuz Asiya (USA) (Daaher (CAN))
5650[10] 7976[4] 8672[4] 9450[2]◆ (9629)

Maqsad (FR) *William Haggas* 111
3 b f Siyouni(FR) Amerique (IRE) (Galileo (IRE))
(1828) (2445) 3316[8] 5586[8] 7657[12]

Maqtal (USA) *Roger Varian* a74 75
2 b g Distorted Humor(USA) Almoutezah (USA) (Storm Cat (USA))
5331[3] (7346) 8319[5]

Maquisard (FR) *Michael Madgwick* a84 81
7 ch g Creachadoir(IRE) Gioiosa Marea (IRE) (Highest Honor (FR))
3635[9] 4505[9] 6596[7] 7729[8] 8421[3] 9056[7]

Maratha (IRE) *Stuart Williams* a89 77
5 gr g Cape Cross(IRE) Middle Persia (Dalakhani (IRE))
3423[7] 4450[8] 4566[4]

Maratino (FR) *C Lotoux* a71 86
4 gr g Tin Horse(IRE) Maracena (FR) (Marju (IRE))
1245a[2]

Marble Bar *Iain Jardine* a76 42
4 b g Makfi Presbyterian Nun (IRE) (Daylami (IRE))
241[9] 484[11] 809[4] 882[6] (1192) (1366)◆ 1522[3] 1552[3]

Marble Bay (IRE) *David Evans* a62
2 gr f Toronado(IRE) Indian Dumaani (Indian Ridge (IRE))
8455[7] 9211[5] 9506[6]

Marcela De Vega *Ralph Beckett* a62
2 b f Lope De Vega(IRE) Lunar Phase (IRE) (Galileo (IRE))
9046[8] 9452[5]

Marcella *Ruth Carr* a43 43
4 b m Showcasing Cool In The Shade (Pastoral Pursuits)
3320[9]

Marcelle (FR) *M Seror* a71 72
4 b m French Fifteen(FR) Polychrome (FR) (Bering)
1073a[3] 1578a[3]

March To The Arch (USA)
Mark Casse 109
4 b g Arch(USA) Daveron (GER) (Black Sam Bellamy (IRE))
5977a[4] 7922a[5]

Mardle *K R Burke* a61 66
3 ch g Mukhadram Hoh Chi Min (Efisio)
126[2] 3858[8] 6037[5] 7404[8] 8024[7] 8690[7]

Marengo *Bernard Llewellyn* a51 75
8 gr g Verglas(IRE) Cloudchaser (IRE) (Red Ransom (USA))
2577[8] 3545[6] 3847[2] 5423[9] 6104[3] 6642[4] 7239[3] 7683[7]

Marengo Sally (IRE) *Ben Haslam* a38 22
2 b f Battle Of Marengo(IRE) Saldenaera (GER) (Areion (GER))
3652[7] 8919[9]

Margaretha (IRE) *Amy Murphy* 43
2 b f Dawn Approach(IRE) Hollow Green (IRE) (Beat Hollow)
5676[7] 6832[3] 8244[11]

Margaret J *Phil McEntee* a50 41
3 gr f Bated Breath Louverissa (IRE) (Verglas (IRE))
122[4] 259[6] 533[4] 802[11] 1726[4] 2517[3] 3256[6] 3741[11] 4071[6] 4801[7] 5380[5] 5946[7] 6153[7] 9157[3] 9279[11] 9395[13]

Margie's Choice (GER)
Michael Madgwick a77 60
4 b m Redoute's Choice(AUS) Margie's World (GER) (Spinning World (USA))
81[6] 516[4] 699[2] 1099[3] 1688[8] 2365[7] 2797[16] 3264[8] 4249[14] 7982[16] 8422[4] 8812[9] 9067[2]

Margub *Marcus Tregoning* a102 79
4 ch g Bated Breath Bahamian Babe (Bahamian Bounty)
(2015) 2551[5] 4866[9]

Marhaba Milliar (IRE) *John Gosden* a91 97
3 b c Kodiac Lady Of The Desert (USA) (Rahy (USA))
(4348) 5666[4]

Marhaban (IRE) *Charlie Appleby* a90 96
3 b g New Approach(IRE) Arsaadi (IRE) (Dubawi (IRE))
(299) (606) 1835[4] 6670[2]

Maria Magdalena (IRE) *Alex Hales* a43 68
3 b f Battle Of Marengo(IRE) Few Words (Fraam)
606[3] 884[5] 1351[7] (7200)

Marianafoot (FR) *J Reynier* a109 111
4 ch h Footstepsinthesand Marianabaa (FR) (Anabaa (USA))
(869a) 3289a[5] 4581a[2] 7255a[4] 7944a[11]

Maria Rosa (USA) *John Gosden* a84
2 b f War Front(USA) Seeking Gabrielle (USA) (Forestry (USA))
8525[2]◆

Marie's Diamond (IRE)
Mark Johnston a99 107
3 b c Footstepsinthesand Sindiyma (IRE) (Kalanisi (IRE))
1707a[5] 1926[4] 2889a[4] 3317[3] 4092[8] 4905[4] (5129) (5475) 6122[P]

Marie's Gem (IRE) *Mark Johnston* a50 62
2 b g Showcasing Les Alizes (IRE) (Cadeaux Genereux)
7733[4] 8494[13] 9136[9]

Marie's Picnic (FR) *J Reynier* a86 88
3 b f Penny's Picnic(IRE) Marie D'o (FR) (Librettist (USA))
683a[9]

Marieta (FR) *M Delcher Sanchez* 107
2 b f Siyouni(FR) Macarella (IRE) (Shamardal (USA))
(4947a) 6248a[2] 7939a[2]

Marietta Robusti (IRE)
Stella Barclay a62 70
4 b m Equiano(FR) La Tintoretta (IRE) (Desert Prince (IRE))
1929[9] 2296[6] 5181[6] 5432[3] (5892) 6921[5] 7511[5] 7766[6]

Marilyn *Shaun Keightley* a61 65
5 ch m Sixties Icon Donatia (Shamardal (USA))
2977[8] 4393[6] 4643[9] 5144[8]

Marina Grove (IRE) *Tim Easterby* a42 34
2 b f Kodiac Charlie Em (Kheleyf (USA))
8631[6] 9036[4]◆ 9251[7]

Marina Marshall (FR)
Frau Doris Ursula Smith
5 bl m Air Chief Marshal(IRE) Dubai Marina (Polish Precedent (USA))
9537a[14]

Marinaresco (SAF) *M F De Kock* 106
6 b g Silvano(GER) Gay Fortuna (SAF) (Fort Wood (USA))
397a[8] 846a[5] 1113a[6] 1441a[5]

Marina's Legacy (USA)
Aaron M West 74
5 ch m Divine Park(USA) Marina (USA) (Theatrical (IRE))
7920a[12]

Marine One *Denis Gerard Hogan* a76 66
5 b g Frankel Marine Bleue (IRE) (Desert Prince (IRE))
5599a[8]

Marion's Boy (IRE) *Roger Teal* 59
2 ch c Mastercraftsman(IRE) Freddie's Girl (USA) (More Than Ready (USA))
6154[8] 7339[7]

Marju's Quest (IRE) *Adrian Wintle* a24 44
9 b g Marju(IRE) Queen's Quest (Rainbow Quest (USA))
9042[12]

Markazi (FR) *David O'Meara* a86 95
5 gr g Dark Angel(IRE) Marasima (IRE) (Barathea (IRE))
1694[10] 2116[8] 2784[2] 3268[2] 3867[3] 4403[2]◆ 4867[7] 5516[6] 5948[10] (7362) 8016[6]

Market King (USA) *D Wayne Lukas* a94
3 b c Into Mischief(USA) Divine Presence (USA) (A.P. Indy (USA))
2856a[12]

Markhan (USA) *Gordon Elliott* a87 78
6 b g Birdstone(USA) Royal Flush (USA) (Smart Strike (CAN))
480[2]

Markhor (IRE) *S Ibido* 98
3 ch c Frankel Vorda (FR) (Orpen (USA))
9590a[7]

Mark Of Excellence (IRE) *L Gadbin* a69 60
5 ch g Sepoy(AUS) Cheyenne Star (IRE) (Mujahid (USA))
7223a[6]

Mark's Choice (IRE) *Ruth Carr* 86
3 b g Bungle Inthejungle Ramamara (IRE) (Trans Island)
1894[9] (2121) 2635[11] (2960) (3479) 4008[4] 4368[4] 5126[3] 5335[3] 6227[3] 6676[9] 7077[5] 7621[4]

Marlborough Sounds
John Joseph Murphy 84
4 b g Camelot Wind Surf (USA) (Lil's Lad (USA))
7216a[12]

Marlyn (IRE) *Martyn Meade* 72
3 b f Exceed And Excel(AUS) Myrine (IRE) (Sadler's Wells (USA))
1740[10] 2340[4]

Marmalade Day *Gary Moore* a64
3 ch f Mukhadram Pink Stone (FR) (Bigstone (IRE))
8693[5] 9425[9] 9635[2]

Marmarr *William Haggas* 34
3 b f Dubawi(IRE) Anaamil (IRE) (Darshaan)
2583[13] 3482[9] 3664[11]

Marmelo *Hughie Morrison* a85 117
6 b h Duke Of Marmalade(IRE) Capriolla (In The Wings)
(1750) 3314[5] 4430a[5] 4962a[2] (6266a)

Marnie James *Jedd O'Keeffe* a99 106
4 b g Camacho Privy Garden (IRE) (Oasis Dream)
49a[6] 393a[6] 1946[11] 2775[3] 3097[14] 4095[21] 4896[16] 6351[2] 6999[3] 7193[20] 8015[3]

Marobob *R Le Dren Doleuze* a72 72
5 b m Big Bad Bob(IRE) Maroochydore (IRE) (Danehill (USA))
1491a[5] 6651a[14]

Maroc *Nikki Evans* a46 73
6 b g Rock Of Gibraltar(IRE) Zietory (Zieten (USA))
3547[6] 5993[3] 6568[6] 8248[11] 9132[11]

Maroon Bells (IRE) *David Menuisier* a64 70
4 ch m Mount Nelson Chelsea Morning (USA) (Giant's Causeway (USA))
2975[3] 3705[2]◆ 4287[7] 5528[5]◆ (6599) 7200[3] 8064[9]

Marouche (FR) *A De Royer-Dupre* a72 96
4 ch m Dalakhani(IRE) Mansera (FR) (Manduro (GER))
7137a[3]

Marquisette *Marcus Tregoning* a42
4 b m Archipenko(USA) Maria Di Scozia (Selkirk (USA))
2555[6]

Marrakech Express (FR)
Laurent Loisel a82 84
3 b c Rio De La Plata(USA) Chagrin D'Amour (IRE) (Sir Percy)
1347a[7] 6652a[6]

Marronnier (IRE) *Stuart Williams* 97
3 ch g Lope De Vega(IRE) Beach Bunny (IRE) (High Chaparral (IRE))
3779[3] (4671) 5348[2] 5861[5] 7342[4] (7728)

Marselha Prince (FR) *Cedric Rossi* 78
2 b c Prince Gibraltar(FR) Moune (IRE) (Whipper (USA))
6384a[3]

Marshal Dan (IRE) *Heather Main* a76 86
4 b g Lawman(FR) Aunt Nicola (Reel Buddy (USA))
1329[2] 1768[3] (2774) 4067[2] 4634[7] (5343) 6155[4] 6468[3] 7865[4]

Marshall Aid (IRE) *Mark Usher* a63 58
6 b g Lawman(FR) Dievotchkina (IRE) (Bluebird (USA))
318[6] 724[10] 810[8]

Marshall Jennings (IRE)
Mrs John Harrington a94 106
7 b g Lawman(FR) Zuniga's Date (USA) (Diesis)
1308a[14] 1531a[6] 5535a[5] 6235a[8] 7222a[11]

Marsh Harbour (FR)
Mme Pia Brandt 51
4 b g Zafeen(FR) Moon Romance (FR) (Nayef (USA))
1631a[7]

Mars Landing (IRE)
Sir Michael Stoute a53 77
2 b g Dark Angel(IRE) Psychometry (FR) (Danehill Dancer (IRE))
6669[8] 7339[2] 8011[9]◆

Martalouna (FR) *N Paysan* a66 71
6 gr m Martaline Dalva (FR) (Johann Quatz (FR))
5761a[6]

Martha McEwan (IRE) *David Barron* a13 45
3 b f Lilbourne Lad(IRE) Ever Evolving (FR) (Elusive Quality (USA))
1523[7] 2146[8] 2713[8]

Martineo *John Butler* a87 86
4 b g Declaration Of War(USA) Woodland Scene (IRE) (Act One)
54[10] (347)◆ (914) (1487)◆ 2611[3] 3043[3] 4123[3] 4851[9] 5862[5] 6162[4] 6968[4] 8893[2] 9441[7] 9669[11]

Martin King *John Butler* a56
3 b c Oasis Dream I'm A Dreamer (IRE) (Noverre (USA))
1034[8] 7373[8] 9420[9]

Martin's Brig (IRE) *Iain Jardine* a70
2 b c Equiano(FR) Weeza (IRE) (Sakhee (USA))
8919[3] 9408[2]

Marvel *Julie Camacho* a74 71
3 b g Poet's Voice Baralinka (IRE) (Barathea (IRE))
954[8] 5917[2] 6206[2] 6944[2]◆ 7417[2] 8407[2]

Marvellous Night (FR)
H De Nicolay a76 82
4 b m Captain Marvelous(IRE) Makaye (FR) (Kendor (FR))
2956a[10] 6267a[14]

Mary Elise (IRE) *Michael Blake* a70 54
4 b m Mastercraftsman(IRE) Je T'Adore (IRE) (Montjeu (IRE))
135[3]◆ 2342[5] 3444[9] 4447[9]

Maryellen *Alan Bailey* a54
3 b f Mayson Granny McPhee (Bahri (USA))
4590[9] 5193[11] 7032[6] 8998[7] 9403[9]

Marylebone *Joseph Patrick O'Brien* a71 50
6 b g Shamardal(USA) Mary Boleyn (IRE) (King's Best (USA))
7088a[7]

Mary Le Bow *Paul George* a56 45
8 b m Sir Percy Bermondsey Girl (Bertolini (USA))
8466[4] 9362[8]

Marylin (FR) *S Cerulis* a85 88
3 b f Motivator Rocaille (FR) (Anabaa (USA))
9281a[10]

Mary Salome (IRE)
Madeleine Tylicki 85
3 gr f Zebedee Christa Maria (Alhaarth (IRE))
7241a[10]

Mary Somerville *John Gosden* a74 76
3 ch f Galileo(IRE) Maureen (IRE) (Holy Roman Emperor (IRE))
2251[7] 2765[5] 7608[3] 8290[10]

Marzipan *Jonathan Portman* 36
2 gr f Zebedee Ficelle (IRE) (Chineur (FR))
5988[9] 7160[9]

Masaakin *Richard Hannon* a77 71
2 b f Kodiac Ebtisama (USA) (Kingmambo (USA))
3506[5] 5646[4] 6407[3] 7155[5] (7813)

Masaarr (USA) *N Bachalard* a80 102
4 ch h Distorted Humor(USA) Aryaamm (IRE) (Galileo (IRE))
171a[8]

Masaff (IRE) *D K Weld* 105
3 ch c Raven's Pass(USA) Masiyma (IRE) (Dalakhani (IRE))
2853a[3] 4351a[6] 4745a[3] 5364a[3]

Masai Spirit *Philip McBride* a60 43
3 b f Charm Spirit(IRE) Eastern Lily (USA) (Eastern Echo (USA))
2018[6] 2762[13] 4336[10] 5080[8] 7282[3] (7549)◆ 8001[2]

Masar (IRE) *Charlie Appleby* a13 113
4 ch h New Approach(IRE) Khawlah (IRE) (Cape Cross (IRE))
4093[5] 4848[6]

Masaru *Richard Hannon* a89 100
3 b c Lethal Force(IRE) Spontaneity (IRE) (Holy Roman Emperor (IRE))
(1676) (2082) 3082[12] 4092[10]

Mascalino (GER) *H Blume* a75 89
5 b h Jukebox Jury(IRE) Marny (GER) (Dashing Blade)
(2675a) 4747a[13]

Mascat *Ralph Beckett* 86
2 ch c Zoffany(IRE) Critical Acclaim (Peintre Celebre (USA))
6669[2]◆ (7611)

Mascha (FR) *Chad C Brown* 89
4 b m Le Havre(IRE) Calima Mon Amour (FR) (Shirocco (GER))
6491a[9]

Masetto (FR) *M Nigge* a79 71
3 b g Mayson Acacalia (GER) (Ransom O'War (USA))
9058a[4]

Mashael (FR) *A Fabre* 105
3 b f Dubawi(IRE) Al Jassasiyah (IRE) (Galileo (IRE))
(7978a) 8584a[2]

Masham Moor *Chris Fairhurst*
2 b g Music Master Jane's Payoff (IRE) (Danetime (IRE))
7698[9]

Masham Star (IRE) *Mark Johnston* a103 99
5 b g Lawman(FR) Croisiere (USA) (Capote (USA))
1101[6] 1415[15] 1753[19] 2100[12] 2487[2] 2551[6] 2832[3] 3069[2] 3313[4] 3472[3] 3857[8] 4020[2] 4934[4] 5155[10] 8062[14] 8521[15] 9285[6]

Masked Identity *Shaun Keightley* a69 86
4 b g Intello(GER) Red Bloom (Selkirk (USA))
(841) 1102[2] (2347)◆ 3027[6] 3867[17] 4867[2] 5320[5] 6326[2] 6841[8] 9053[13]

Mask Of Time (IRE)
Ciaron Maher & David Eustace a73 98
5 b h Holy Roman Emperor(IRE) Mission Secrete (IRE) (Galileo (IRE))
1783a[6]

Masquerade Bling (IRE)
Neil Mulholland a65 60
5 b m Approve(IRE) Mataji (IRE) (Desert Prince (IRE))
2145[7] 3430[3]◆ 4124[2] 4479[3] 6529[8]

Massam *David Simcock* a74 59
3 ch g Dubawi(IRE) Shumoos (USA) (Distorted Humor (USA))
2031[6] 2821[6] 4559[5]

Massif Central (IRE) *M Halford* a108 101
5 b g Arcano(IRE) Melaaya (USA) (Aljabr (USA))
4745a[2] 5874a[5] 7668a[4]

Mass Media *John Gosden* a74 80
2 ch c Exceed And Excel(AUS) Entertainment (Halling (USA))
3274[5] 4117[2] 4886[9] 5572[6] 6185[2]

Master Archer (IRE)
James Fanshawe a92 91
5 gr g Mastercraftsman(IRE) Kinigi (IRE) (Verglas (IRE))
2801[8] 3635[4] 4505[3] 4899[5]

Master Bloom (SWE)
Cathrine Erichsen 99
4 b g Pastorius(GER) Milibloom (SWE) (Miesque's Son (USA))
7498a[3]

Master Burbidge *Neil Mulholland* a66
8 b g Pasternak Silver Sequel (Silver Patriarch (IRE))
9447[2]◆

Master Dancer *Tim Vaughan* a47 68
8 gr g Mastercraftsman(IRE) Isabella Glyn (IRE) (Sadler's Wells (USA))
3940[5]

Master Diver *Sir Mark Prescott Bt* a84
4 gr g Mastercraftsman(IRE) Lottie Dod (IRE) (Invincible Spirit (IRE))
117[5]◆ 275[2] (419a) 807[3]◆ 1036[5] 1367[5] 2348[6]

Master Fencer (JPN)
Koichi Tsunoda a112 74
3 ch c Just A Way(JPN) Sexy Zamurai (USA) (Deputy Minister (CAN))
2425a[6] 3620a[5]

Master Grey (IRE) *Rod Millman* a51 78
4 gr g Mastercraftsman(IRE) Market Day (Tobougg (IRE))
1463[13] 2344[5] (2718) 2936[5] 3700[4] (4257) 4928[2] 5452[6] 6105[9] 8246[6]

Master Matt *Matthew J Smith* a74 85
3 b g Slade Power(IRE) Ahaaly (Exceed And Excel (AUS))
2098[15] 7241a[16]

Master McGrath (IRE) *Kevin Ryan* 99
2 br c No Nay Never(USA) Dacio (USA) (Harlan's Holiday (USA))
5234[2]◆ (5859) 6791a[6]
Master Milliner (IRE) *Emma Lavelle* a63 38
3 ch g Helmet(AUS) Aqualina (IRE) (King's Theatre (IRE))
2795[16] 6836[6] 7278[7] 8224[2]
Master Of Irony (IRE) *John Quinn*
7 b g Makfi Mother Of Pearl (IRE) (Sadler's Wells (USA))
8513[10]
Master Of Reality (IRE)
Joseph Patrick O'Brien 119
4 b g Frankel L'Ancresse (IRE) (Darshaan)
(2158a) 4015[3] 6191a[3] 7246a[5] 8844a[4]
Master Of The Moon
Ismail Mohammed a69 67
4 b g Sea The Stars(IRE) Crystal Mountain (USA) (Monashee Mountain (USA))
7518[5]
Master Poet *Gary Moore* a53 56
4 b g Poet's Voice Lilli Marlane (Sri Pekan (USA))
2513[5] 3298[14] 5430[2] 6363[14] 7282[9] 7982[11]
Master Rocco (IRE)
Jane Chapple-Hyam a60 37
2 ch c Dawn Approach(IRE) Mama Rocco (Shirocco (GER))
5439[8] 5940[6] 6704[6] 8493[8] 9154[9] 9399[4]
Masters Apprentice (IRE)
Mark Walford a62 55
4 ch g Mastercraftsman(IRE) Maghzaa (IRE) (Aqlaam)
385[4] 619[10] 1024[9] 1235[5] 1548[3] 1718[11] 6827[8] 7314[6] 8344[2]
Master Speaker (IRE)
Adrian McGuinness a72 88
9 b g Danehill Dancer(IRE) First Breeze (USA) (Woodman (USA))
748a[9] 1308a[3] 5597a[14] 5711a[11]
Master Spy (IRE) *Paul Cole* a67 65
2 gr g Mastercraftsman(IRE) Stealth Bolt (USA) (Stormy Atlantic (USA))
4839[5] 8028[10] 8302[3]
Master's Spirit (IRE) *J Reynier* a92 107
8 gr h Mastercraftsman(IRE) Lavayssiere (FR) (Sicyos (USA))
5718a[4] 6522a[5]
Master The Stars (GER) *Ed Dunlop* 63
2 b c Sea The Stars(IRE) Magma (GER) (Dubai Destination (USA))
8203[5]
Master The World (IRE)
David Elsworth a110 107
8 gr g Mastercraftsman(IRE) Zadalla (Zaha (CAN))
879[6] 1420[3] 1921[8] 3953[12] 5519[16]
Matador (FR) *Matthieu Palussiere* 80
4 b g Style Vendome(FR) Tina Bull (USA) (Holy Bull (USA))
1073a[10]
Match Maker (IRE) *Simon Crisford* 89
4 b g Declaration Of War(USA) I'm In Love (USA) (Zafonic (USA))
(4055) (4841) 5348[3]
Matchmaking (GER)
Sir Mark Prescott Bt a86 86
4 ch g Mastercraftsman(IRE) Monami (GER) (Sholokhov (IRE))
5967[4] 6437[2]
Matchwinner (GER) *J M Snackers* 95
8 ch h Sternkoenig(IRE) Mahamuni (IRE) (Sadler's Wells (USA))
3386a[8]
Matello (FR) *C Laffon-Parias* 76
2 b c Intello(GER) Mama Lulu (USA) (Kingmambo (USA))
6262a[2]
Matematica (GER) *C Laffon-Parias* 103
3 b f Rock Of Gibraltar(IRE) Mathematicienne (IRE) (Galileo (IRE))
2669a[5] 3387a[5] 4416a[4] 6142a[5] 6910a[4] (7886a) 8376a[6] 8583a[7]
Matera *Kevin Ryan* a63 72
2 ch g Showcasing Navajo Charm (Authorized (IRE))
3507[4] 3998[3]
Matera Sky (USA) *Hideyuki Mori* a116 97
5 ch h Speightstown(USA) Mostaqeleh (USA) (Rahy (USA))
1444a[2] 8773a[8]
Material Girl *Richard Spencer* a71 80
3 b f Pivotal Apace (IRE) (Oasis Dream)
126[4] (2420)◆ 2760[6] 3552[2] 3892[4] 5573[3] 6170[4] 6974[9] 7901[3] 8766[2]
Matewan (IRE) *Ian Williams* a84 82
4 b g Epaulette(AUS) Cochin (USA) (Swain (IRE))
3022[13] 3925[2] 4913[6] (5743) 9274[2]◆ 9421[2]
Math Wizard (USA)
Saffie A Joseph Jr a109
3 ch c Algorithms(USA) Minister's Baby (USA) (Deputy Minister (CAN))
(7480a) 8777a[5]
Matilda Bay (IRE) *Jamie Osborne* a45 32
3 b f Australia Teddy Bears Picnic (Oasis Dream)
884[6] 1509[6] 1824[15] 3299[9] 4372[9] 4998[10]
Matista (IRE) *H-A Pantall* 77
3 b c Acclamation Rajastani (IRE) (Zamindar (USA))
6267a[11] 8449a[9]
Matravers *Martin Keighley* a63 50
8 b g Oasis Dream Maakrah (Dubai Destination (USA))
85[14] 2111[15]
Matricienne (FR) *M Delaplace* 41
3 b f Motivator Theoricienne (FR) (Kendor (FR))
6652a[7]
Matterhorn (IRE) *Mark Johnston* a121 115
4 b h Raven's Pass(USA) Tanaghum (Darshaan)
(87) (800)◆ (1031) 1420[7] (1921) 2573[2]◆ 3025[2] 3948[10] (4397)◆ 4900[5] 5483a[7] 6467[2] 6956[2] 7220a[2] 8116[4]

Maulesden May (IRE)
Keith Dalgleish a77 77
6 b m Dark Angel(IRE) Jemima's Art (Fantastic Light (USA))
1503[6] 2326[4] (2962) 3267[6] 5937[6] 6576[5] 7366[6] 7510[8] 8236[7]
Maureb (IRE) *Tony Coyle* a53 63
7 br m Excellent Art Almost Blue (USA) (Mr Greeley (USA))
502[9] 1967[4] 2295[9]
Maurice Dancer *Julie Camacho* a65 61
2 b g Kodiac Kind Of Hush (IRE) (Marju (IRE))
5172[8] 5689[5] 6254[6] 7284[5] 8085[9] (9164)
Mauricio (IRE) *Stella Barclay* a71 73
5 ch g Helmet(AUS) Essexford (IRE) (Spinning World (USA))
(5824) 6278[5] 6896[2] 9570[4]
Maurimo *Roger Charlton* 41
2 b f Kingman Lynnwood Chase (USA) (Horse Chestnut (SAF))
7458[8]
Ma Valentine (FR)
Mme Anne-Marie Gareau a52 58
7 b m Kingsalsa(USA) Commana (FR) (Octagonal (NZ))
3711a[4]
Maven (USA) *Wesley A Ward* a90 106
2 ch c American Pharoah(USA) Richies Party Girl (USA) (Any Given Saturday (USA))
(4417a) 5542[10]
Mawakib *Roger Varian* a92 86
3 b c Havana Gold(IRE) Keladora (USA) (Crafty Prospector (USA))
(1389)◆ 1729[4]◆ 2412[2] (3465)◆ 4360[3] 6841[10]
Mawde (IRE) *Rod Millman* 73
3 ch f Sir Prancealot(IRE) Rise Up Lotus (IRE) (Zebedee)
1692[5] 2086[7] 2810[11] 3420[6] 3893[6] 4556[7]
Mawsool (IRE) *Ed Dunlop* a70 74
3 b g Kodiac Habaayib (Royal Applause)
(1587) 2114[8]
Max Dynamite (FR) *W P Mullins* a73 114
9 b g Great Journey(JPN) Mascara (GER) (Monsun (GER))
4096[3] 6473[12] 7148[3] 8332[8]
Max Guevara (IRE) *William Muir* a41 53
3 b g Alhebayeb(IRE) Assumption (IRE) (Beckett (IRE))
3170[12] 4225[9] 4789[9] 5092[4] 5304[6] 6202[6] 6600[5] 7375[11] 8003[2] 8753[6] 8822[13]
Maxi Boy *Michael Bell* 99
2 b c Oasis Dream Lavender And Lace (Barathea (IRE))
(2973) 3949[8] 4920[3]◆ 5584[9]
Maximilius (GER) *Ralph Beckett* 59
2 bg g Soldier Hollow Macuna (Acatenango (GER))
6106[6] 7113[5] 7899[9] 8394[6]
Maximize *Peter Chapple-Hyam* a41
2 b f Garswood Dazzling View (USA) (Distant View (USA))
9437[8]
Maximum Aurelius (FR)
F-H Graffard 78
6 b g Showcasing Feld Marechale (FR) (Deputy Minister (CAN))
9014a[6]
Maximum Effect *John Gosden* a87
3 ch f Iffraaj Dubai Bounty (Dubai Destination (USA))
5269[2] 6187[2] 6886[3] (8013) 8812[2] 9050[14]
Maximum Power (FR) *Tim Pinfield* a66 66
4 b g Power Keisha (FR) (Green Tune (USA))
313[5] 759[2] 1038[6] 4453[9]
Maximum Security (USA)
Jason Servis a121
3 b c New Year's Day(USA) Lil Indy (USA) (Anasheed (USA))
2425a[17]
Max L (IRE) *Alistair Whillans* a22 22
2 ch g Ivawood(IRE) Silcasue (Selkirk (USA))
6585[7] 6943[12]
Max's Thunder (IRE)
David Simcock a71 59
2 b g Night Of Thunder(IRE) Alaia (IRE) (Sinndar (IRE))
3694[8] 4839[4] 4999[10] 5907[3] 6808[3]
Max's Voice (IRE) *David Loughnane* 55
2 b g Poet's Voice Duljanah (IRE) (Dream Ahead (USA))
5294[7] 5956[6] 6654[6] 7111[6]
Max Vega (IRE) *Ralph Beckett* 105
2 ch c Lope De Vega(IRE) Paraphernalia (IRE) (Dalakhani (IRE))
6905[2] (7623) (8111)
Max Zorin (IRE) *Andrew Balding* 93
5 b g Cape Cross(IRE) My (King's Best (USA))
2408[10] 2832[11] 3472[5] 5155[8] 5708[7]
Mayaadeen (IRE) *Doug Watson* a88 82
4 b h Invincible Spirit(IRE) Rose De France (IRE) (Diktat)
997[5]
Mayana Chope (FR) *A Chopard*
2 b f Vale Of York(IRE) Moon Serenade (Key Of Luck (USA))
2757a[7]
Maybellene (IRE) *Alan Berry* a50 63
2 b f Camacho Chute Hall Lady (IRE) (Dark Angel (IRE))
1821[3] 2052[3] 5185[21] 5602[3] 5968[6] 6539[4] 7208[3] 7440[2] 7734[4] 8180[4] 9541[6]
Maybe Today *Simon Crisford* a93 97
4 b m Cacique(IRE) Quiza Quiza Quiza (Golden Snake (USA))
310[6] (1267) 2032[3] 2680[4] (7075) 7900[3]
Maydanny (IRE) *Mark Johnston* 85
3 b g Dubawi(IRE) Attraction (Efisio)
3218[2] 3768[2]
Mayfair Madame *Stuart Kittow* a36 56
3 ch f Mayson Talqaa (Exceed And Excel (AUS))
2489[5] 3801[7] 4183[4] 5181[8] 6397[3] 7757[5] 8018[9] 8457[10]

Mayfair Pompette (FR)
Charlie Fellowes 70
3 ch f Toronado(IRE) Tipsy Me (Selkirk (USA))
1740[7] 2340[7]
Mayfair Rock (IRE) *K R Burke* a60
4 ch m Society Rock(IRE) Tara Too (IRE) (Danetime (IRE))
388[7]
Mayfair Spirit (IRE)
Charlie Fellowes a88 84
3 b g Charm Spirit(IRE) Sassy Gal (IRE) (King's Best (USA))
1174[3] (1697) (2141) 3373[3] (4107) (5176) 5948[6] 6964[7] (7610)◆
Mayflower Lady (IRE)
Ronald Harris a44 23
2 b f Bungle Inthejungle Disc Play (Showcasing)
3573[7] 5011[5] 6106[8] 7110[7] 8198[6]
Maygold *Ed Walker* a88 103
4 b m Mayson Spanish Gold (Vettori (IRE))
2625[2]◆ 3303[4] (3893) 5524[3] 6257[5] (6960) 7889[6] 8141a[5] 9004[9]
May Happen *Jamie Osborne* a40
2 b f Mayson Jasmine Royale (Royal Applause)
8250[9] 9062[9] 9242[13] 9407[7]
Maykir *J R Jenkins* a45 44
3 b g Mayson Kiruna (Northern Park (USA))
4476[8] 4735[4] 7280[9] 7520[6] 9442[3]
Mayleaf Shine (IRE)
Mme Doris Schoenherr a52 75
5 b m Mayson Let Me Shine (USA) (Dixie Union (USA))
2648a[6]
Mayne (IRE) *Andrew Balding* a84 83
3 b g Dansili Pink Damsel (IRE) (Galileo (IRE))
5650[6] 6316[2]◆ 7143[2]
Maysong *Ed Dunlop* a82 73
2 ch g Mayson Aldeburgh Music (IRE) (In The Wings)
3601[8] 3767[2] 5234[5] (9414)
May Sonic *Charles Hills* a79 80
3 b g Mayson Aromatherapy (Oasis Dream)
1171[7] (1677)◆ 2397[7] 3858[4]
Mayson Mount *Shaun Keightley* a34
2 b c Mayson Epernay (Tiger Hill (IRE))
8751[5]
Maystar (IRE) *Archie Watson* a91 97
2 b g Mayson Oakley Star (Multiplex)
(5427)◆ 6011[2] (6548) 7247a[2] 8446a[6] (9364) (9582a)
Mazeed (USA) *S Seemar* a83 52
5 ch g Street Cry(IRE) Speed Succeeds (USA) (Gone West (USA))
97a[2] (573a) 1001[4]
Mazekine *Roger Ingram* a45
2 b f Mukhadram Dea Caelestis (FR) (Dream Well (FR))
8605[10] 9156[10]
Mazeltof (FR) *J Phelippon* a76 70
3 ch g Kheleyf(USA) Acroleine (FR) (Indian Rocket)
7138a[8]
Mazikeen *Richard Hughes* a71
2 b f Dunkerque(FR) Salome (FR) (Fuisse (FR))
8706[4] (9408)◆
Mazmerize *Christine Dunnett* a20 17
3 b g Mazameer(IRE) Patience (Kyllachy)
1381[12] 2023[14] 5650[12] 6128[9] 8251[13] 9456[10]
Mazyoun *Hugo Palmer* a93 87
5 br g Mayson Hypnotize (Machiavellian (USA))
2572[6] 3268[7] 4506[4]
Mazzini *Fawzi Abdulla Nass* a111 115
6 ch g Exceed And Excel(AUS) Firenze (Efisio)
(393a)◆ (639a)◆ 1111a[3] 1442a[11]
Mazzuri (IRE) *Amanda Perrett* a91 95
4 ch m Raven's Pass(USA) Essexford (IRE) (Spinning World (USA))
2033[8] 2401[3] 3346[7] 4391[4] 6509[3]
McKinzie (USA) *Bob Baffert* a123
4 b h Street Sense(USA) Runway Model (USA) (Petionville (USA))
3618a[2] 8777a[2]
McQueen (FR) *Yasmin Almenrader* a83 96
7 gr g Silver Frost(IRE) Misdirect (Darshaan)
3369a[3] 4534a[6] 6006a[8] 8982a[7]
Mea Culpa (IRE) *Julie Camacho* a44 58
3 b g Dandy Man(IRE) La Dama Boba (IRE) (Lope De Vega (IRE))
954[7] 2199[5] 3157[6]
Meagher's Flag (IRE) *Paul Nicholls* a46 72
4 b g Teofilo(IRE) Gearanai (USA) (Toccet (USA))
1914[6] 2902[4] 4190[4]
Mearing *Iain Jardine* a65 80
4 b g Aussie Rules(USA) Director's Dream (IRE) (Act One)
833[4] 1169[9] (2439)
Mecca's Gift (IRE) *Michael Dods* 76
3 b f Dark Angel(IRE) Frizzante (Efisio)
2200[9] 2482[6] 3478[5] (4488) 4761[10] 6342[3] (6679) 7512[5]
Mecca's Hot Steps *Michael Dods* 70
2 ch f Hot Streak(IRE) Vintage Steps (IRE) (Bahamian Bounty)
2051[4]◆ 2820[2] 3156[3] 5197[4] 6032[2] 7377[5]
Medahim (IRE) *Ivan Furtado* a93 103
5 b g Kodiac Novel Fun (IRE) (Noverre (USA))
2832[8]◆ 4299[4] 5453[2] 6014[7] 7152[2]
Medalla De Oro *Tom Clover* a79 85
5 b g Teofilo(IRE) Nyarhini (Fantastic Light (USA))
2032[5] 2763[6] 3816[12] (4907) 5849[6] 6289[5] 7185[4] 8396[12]
Medal Winner (FR) *Archie Watson* 89
3 gr g Olympic Glory(IRE) Pax Mina (FR) (Keltos (FR))
2581[14] 4076[2] (4474)◆
Medburn Cutler *Peter Hedger* a39 65
9 ch g Zafeen(FR) Tiegs (IRE) (Desert Prince (IRE))
1735[6] 2571[7] 3044[12] 4614[10]

Medici Moon *Richard Price* a62 49
5 ch g Medicean Cockney Fire (Cockney Rebel (IRE))
1369[8] (1769) 2111[13] 2631[7] 6334[11] 6643[13] 8223[3] 8863[9] 9040[11] 9503[6]
Medicine Jack *G M Lyons* 95
5 ch g Equiano(FR) Agony Aunt (Formidable I (USA))
1434a[13] 2221a[8] 5205a[9]
Medieval (IRE) *Paul Cole* a89 84
5 b g Kodiac Quickstyx (Night Shift (USA))
1727[5] 2273[3] 2803[3] 4300[4] 4887[6] 5804[2] 6155[3] 6468[4] 7975[11]
Medika (IRE) *Andrew Balding* a47
2 b f Australia Weeping Wind (Oratorio (IRE))
8604[9]
Medoras Childe *Heather Main* a58 54
3 b f Nayef(USA) Byroness (Byron)
1081[8] 1515[3] (1725) 2597[6]
Meetings Man (IRE) *Ali Stronge* a1 4
12 gr g Footstepsinthesand Missella (IRE) (Danehill (USA))
58[12]
Meet The Parents *John Best*
2 b g Casamento(IRE) Elounta (Dubawi (IRE))
3943[15]
Meghan Sparkle (IRE) *Clive Cox* a56 57
3 b f Showcasing Poppet's Lovein (Lomitas)
3421[5]
Mehanydream (FR) *C Boutin* a49 68
2 b c Silver Frost(IRE) Mehany (FR) (Danehill (USA))
1657a[5] 5713a[14] 6584a[9] 8239a[8] 8330a[4]
Mehdaayih *John Gosden* a97 116
3 b f Frankel Sayyedati Symphony (USA) (Gone West (USA))
(1885)◆ (2521) 3316[7] (4429a) 5586[2] 7942a[10] 8335[5]
Mekong *Sir Michael Stoute* a97 113
4 b g Frankel Ship's Biscuit (Tiger Hill (IRE))
3024[2]◆ 3864[7] 4670[2] 6473[10] 8332[4]
Melabi (IRE) *Stella Barclay* a51 54
6 b g Oasis Dream Briolette (IRE) (Sadler's Wells (USA))
3447[5] 4515[2] 5106[9] (6502) 6982[7] 7578[7] 8466[6] 9289[4] 9446[4]
Melanna (IRE) *Stella Barclay* a36 31
8 b m Camacho Colour's Red (IRE) (Red Ransom (USA))
1861[13]
Melba Rose *H-A Pantall* 58
3 ch f Toronado(IRE) Maid To Dream (Oasis Dream)
7061a[5] (Dead)
Melburnian (FR) *A J Martin* 85
4 ch m Zambezi Sun Moscow Nights (FR) (Peintre Celebre (USA))
7900[2]
Melburnian *Jane Chapple-Hyam* a64
3 b g Hallucinate(USA) Bedouin Bride (USA) (Chester House (USA))
5808[10] 6345[7] 9213[6] 9469[5]
Melgate Magic *Michael Easterby* a69 55
3 ch g Harbour Watch(IRE) Corn Rigs (Exceed And Excel (AUS))
505[3]
Melgate Majeure *Michael Easterby* a67 58
3 br g Lethal Force(IRE) Ambrix (IRE) (Xaar)
3271[4]◆ 5023[4]◆ (5851) 6068[5] 7452[6] 8713[6] 9180[8]
Melicertes *A Fabre* 103
3 b c Poet's Voice Neptune's Bride (USA) (Bering)
(2953a) 3903a[4]
Melissa (FR) *Ivan Furtado* a63 44
3 ch f Evasive Snow Jasmine (IRE) (Exceed And Excel (AUS))
183[9] 6789a[4] 7561a[9] 9058a[7] 9504a[11]
Mellad *Peter Chapple-Hyam* 76
2 b c Oasis Dream Clarentine (Dalakhani (IRE))
2957[4] 3551[4] 5624[4] 7155[2]
Melnikova *Sir Michael Stoute* a81 78
2 ch f Frankel Safina (Pivotal)
(5733)◆ 7412[3]
Melodic Charm (IRE) *James Tate* a90
2 ch f Exceed And Excel(AUS) Folk Melody (IRE) (Street Cry (IRE))
(6028) 6966[4]
Melodies *Ed Dunlop* a73 92
4 ch m Iffraaj Singersongwriter (Raven's Pass (USA))
5441[5]
Melodino (GER) *K Demme* 98
4 b h Dabirsim(FR) Melody Fair (IRE) (Montjeu (IRE))
3287a[8] 4157a[6]
Melody Belle (NZ) *Jamie Richards* 109
4 b m Commands(AUS) Meleka Belle (NZ) (Iffraaj)
8952a[2]
Melody D'Amour (FR) *E Kurdu* 8
3 ch f Tertullian(USA) City Of Light (FR) (Kingsalsa (USA))
4229a[10]
Melody King (IRE) *John Quinn* 83
2 b c Kodiac Mekong Melody (IRE) (Cape Cross (IRE))
(6970) 7398[3]
Melo Pearl *Mrs Ilka Gansera-Leveque* a42 47
3 ch f Paco Boy(IRE) Jewelled (Fantastic Light (USA))
594[6] 941[12] 1383[7] 2926[4] 4477[2]◆ 5287[3] 5842[5] 7273[6]
Melrose (IRE) *E Lyon* a57 59
2 b f Zoffany(IRE) Mary's Daughter (Royal Applause)
7044a[9] 7641a[3] 8330a[7]
Melrose Way *Paul Midgley* 72
3 ch f Mayson Winter's Night (IRE) (Night Shift (USA))
(1816) 2334[5] 4129[4] (5660) 6976[7] 7762[6]
Melting Dew *Sir Michael Stoute* a92 100
5 b g Cacique(IRE) Winter Sunrise (Pivotal)
2440[9] 3600[9] 4646[9] 5929[9] 6355[4] 6958[P]

Melwood *Antony Brittain* a11
3 b g Monsieur Bond(IRE) Melandre (Lujain (USA))
1984[6] 3200[13] 4078[15]

Memory Hill (IRE) *David Evans* a68
3 gr g Zebedee Munaasaba (IRE) (Elnadim (USA))
8472[5] 8842[3]◆ 9032[4] 9475[8]

Memphis Bleek *Ivan Furtado* a71 80
3 ch g Olympic Glory(IRE) Party (IRE) (Cadeaux Genereux)
1956[6] 4055[3] 5594[4]◆ 5937[5] 7129[3] 7730[5] 8507[5]

Memyselfandmoi (IRE) *W McCreery* 88
3 b f Pour Moi(IRE) Sar Oiche (IRE) (Teofilo (IRE))
7038a[10]

Menardais (FR) *N Caullery* a59 74
10 b g Canyon Creek(IRE) Madeleine's Blush (USA) (Rahy (USA))
1349a[7]

Mendacious Harpy (IRE) *Mrs A Malzard* a26 33
8 b m Dark Angel(IRE) Idesia (IRE) (Green Desert (USA))
2504a[2] 2673a[11] 3174a[7] 3642a[3] 4175a[2] 4684a[2] 6009a[2]

Mendamay *Tim Easterby* a20 70
3 b f Mayson Sand And Deliver (Royal Applause)
2332[3]◆ (3416) 5057[9]

Mendeleev *James Given* a47 31
3 b g Hellvelyn Wightgold (Golden Snake (USA))
802[6] 1270[12]

Mendoza (IRE) *James Eustace* a82 78
3 ch g Zebedee Strange Magic (IRE) (Diamond Green (FR))
3302[7] (4507) 5000[10] 6111[6] 6930[10] 8221[2] (8702) 9054[7]

Mengli Khan (IRE) *Gordon Elliott* a87 83
6 b g Lope De Vega(IRE) Danielli (IRE) (Danehill (USA))
3952[12]

Menina Atrevida *Ivan Furtado* a48 54
3 ch f Nayef(USA) Delaware Dancer (IRE) (Danehill Dancer (IRE))
971[5] 1458[7] 2094[11]

Menin Gate (IRE) *Richard Fahey* a65 65
3 gr g Farhh Telegraphy (USA) (Giant's Causeway (USA))
971[6] 2634[7] 3226[9] 3926[5] 4443[4] 5175[2] 5792[3] 6531[7] 7048[9] (7956)

Mensen Ernst (IRE) *Richard Hannon* 79
2 ch c Intello(GER) Vivacity (Trempolino (USA))
3767[3]◆ 4750[2] 5710a[14]

Menthe Pastille (FR) *N Clement* a60 79
3 bb f Style Vendome(FR) Age Of Refinement (IRE) (Pivotal)
6063a[2]

Menuetto *H-A Pantall* a58 84
4 b m Dubawi(IRE) Measured Tempo (Sadler's Wells (USA))
2002a[4] 5035a[9] 7536a[2]

Men United (FR) *Roy Bowring* a35 32
6 b g Acclamation Moore's Melody (IRE) (Marju (IRE))
322[7] 1402[10] 1554[10]

Mephisto (IRE) *Ralph Beckett* 60
2 gr g Kendargent(FR) Save Me The Waltz (FR) (Halling (USA))
5345[4] 6154[10]

Meqdam (IRE) *Saeed bin Suroor* 70
3 ch g Dubawi(IRE) Scatter Dice (IRE) (Manduro (GER))
2802[4]◆ 3372[6] 4474[3]

Mequinenza (IRE) *Vaclav Luka Jr* a55 61
2 ch f Starspangledbanner(AUS) Sifter (USA) (Henrythenavigator (USA))
8239a[7]

Mera Di Breme *R Biondi* 65
2 b f Holy Roman Emperor(IRE) Disposition (Selkirk (USA))
7724a[8]

Meraki *Tim Pinfield* a47 49
3 b g Heeraat(IRE) Sound Of Life (IRE) (Cape Cross (IRE))
4244[5] 5102[3] 6284[10]

Mercenary Rose (IRE) *Paul Cole* a87 84
3 b f Sepoy(AUS) Hulcote Rose (IRE) (Rock Of Gibraltar (IRE))
1832[10] 3167[2] 4330[2] 4783[3] 5589[2] 6148[4] 7894[14] (8601) 8826[7] 9131[8]

Mercers *Paddy Butler* a57 57
5 b m Piccolo Ivory's Joy (Tina's Pet)
53[3] 179[F] 1590[8] 1930[7] 4025[7] 5046[9] 6284[4] 7977[9] 8279[10] (8457) 9507[8] 9670[5]

Mercer's Troop (IRE) *Alistair Whillans* a74 60
4 b g Canford Cliffs(IRE) Meek Appeal (USA) (Woodman (USA))
4404[13] 5122[6] 5728[14] 9467[13]

Merchant Of Venice *James Fanshawe* a90 66
4 b g Bated Breath Isola Verde (Oasis Dream)
(608) (1099) 1727[3] 2273[10] 2966[3] 4639[7] 9517[5]

Merchants Breath *Shaun Keightley* a48 10
2 b c Bated Breath Wiki Tiki (Dixie Union (USA))
6047[5] 6548[6] 6911[16]

Merci Capucine *S Wattel* a76 74
4 b m Falco(USA) Tocopilla (FR) (Medaaly)
4859a[8]

Mercurist *Rod Millman* a50
2 b c Muhaarar Xceedingly Xcited (IRE) (Exceed And Excel (AUS))
9174[14] 9413[11]

Mercury *Stephen Michael Hanlon* a58 58
7 ch g Showcasing Miss Rimex (IRE) (Ezzoud (IRE))
1335[11] 8864[4] 9450[11]

Mercury Dime (IRE) *Ed Dunlop* a66
3 ch f Teofilo(IRE) Margravine (USA) (King's Best (USA))
8467[7] 9011[5] 9425[2] 9662[4]

Mer De Glace (JPN) *Hisashi Shimizu* 115
4 b h Rulership(JPN) Glacier Blue (JPN) (Sunday Silence (USA))
(8361a) 8844a[6]

Merdon Castle (IRE) *Michael Blake* a49 49
7 b g Acclamation Siren's Gift (Cadeaux Genereux)
924[5] 1177[6] 1477[4] 2234[3] 3142[13] 4346[8] 4753[9] 6855[3] 7550[5] 8694[9]

Mere Anarchy (IRE) *Robert Stephens* a68 66
8 b g Yeats(IRE) Maracana (IRE) (Glacial Storm (USA))
700[7] 3693[5] 4483[8]

Mereside Blue *David Barron* a33
2 b f Sepoy(AUS) Blue Oyster (Medicean)
7063[12] 8714[11]

Mer Et Nuages (FR) *A Fabre* a78 112
4 b g Lope De Vega(IRE) Mahnaz (Dansili)
1708a[2] 2313a[3] 3879a[3]

Merhoob (IRE) *John Ryan* a109 107
7 b g Cape Cross(IRE) Lady Slippers (IRE) (Royal Academy (USA))
203[2] 352[6] 762[2] (909)◆ 1105[2] 1295[2] 1501[7] 1919[3] (2557) 3602[12] 4331[12] 4905[6] 5705[9] 7433[11] 8182[3] 9088[12] 9198[3] 9478[5] 9612[5] 9660[3]

Merimbula (USA) *F Head* 103
3 b f Dalakhani(IRE) Urban Ball (IRE) (Galileo (IRE))
3121a[5] 4429a[3]

Meri Senshi (FR) *S Wattel* a81 81
3 b f Elusive City(USA) Folle Biche (FR) (Take Risks (FR))
993a[6]

Merlin *Michael Bell* a85 77
5 b g Oasis Dream Momentary (Nayef (USA))
56[7]

Mericourt (IRE) *Iain Jardine* a79 69
3 gr g Mizzen Mast(USA) Elite (Invincible Spirit (IRE))
9476[10]

Merry Banter *Paul Midgley* a82 88
5 b m Bated Breath Merry Diva (Bahamian Bounty)
1501[5] 2030[3] 2910[6] 4101[5] 4722[4] 4986[2] 5298[6] 6178[10] (6534) 7321[4] 7771[8] 8099[19]

Merry Vale *John Gosden* a65 79
3 b f Intello(GER) Monturani (IRE) (Indian Ridge (IRE))
3637[2]◆ 4326[3] 9425[3]

Merryweather *Michael Appleby* a80 69
2 b f Dunaden(FR) Pearl Princess (FR) (Astronomer Royal (USA))
6054[3] 7562[8] (9311)

Merweb (IRE) *Heather Main* a79 71
4 gr g Shamardal(USA) Ashley Hall (USA) (Maria's Mon (USA))
2186[8] 2966[9] 3944[9] 6050[2] 6201[5]◆ 6961[11] 7554[9] 9109[3] 9304[2]

Meryems Way (IRE) *Patrick Martin* a45 64
3 b f Tough As Nails(IRE) Anne-Lise (Inchinor)
9028[6]

Meshardal (GER) *Ruth Carr* a52 48
9 b g Shamardal(USA) Melody Fair (IRE) (Montjeu (IRE))
1368[8] 1765[12] 2183[6] 2741[8] 3475[6] 3921[5] 4037[3] 8901[8] 9457[2] 9518[7]

Message *Mark Johnston* a66 72
3 b c Dansili Melikah (IRE) (Lammtarra (USA))
1221[7] 1509[4] 1771[5] 3311[2] 3538[2] 4024[4] 4484[2] 4656[2] 4803[5]

Metal Exchange *Marjorie Fife* a67 66
3 b f Helmet(AUS) Bochafina (FR) (High Chaparral (IRE))
(408)◆ 1020[9] 4129[3] 4977[5] 7286[19]

Metallic Black *Richard Fahey* a70 82
3 br g Bated Breath Silken Express (IRE) (Speightstown (USA))
8712[7]

Metatron (IRE) *Tom Dascombe* a80 72
3 gr g Dark Angel(IRE) Orikawa (FR) (Gold Away (IRE))
1293[4] 1897[7] 2559[10] 4329[9]

Met By Moonlight *Ron Hodges* a75 70
5 b m Sakhee's Secret Starlight Walk (Galileo (IRE))
1216[4] (1586) 2339[15] 3462[3] 4247[7] 6025[10] 6203[5] 7230[14] 7760[8]

Methag (FR) *Alex Hales* a69 72
6 b m Pour Moi(IRE) Kyria (Grand Lodge (USA))
1330[11] 8027[2]

Metier (IRE) *Andrew Slattery* 94
3 b g Mastercraftsman(IRE) We'll Go Walking (IRE) (Authorized (IRE))
4136a[7]

Me Too Nagasaki (IRE) *Stuart Williams* a83 71
5 b g Iffraaj Distinguish (IRE) (Refuse To Bend (IRE))
4[6] 699[5] 922[6] 1695[6] 2193[3] 2584[5] 2710[10] 3633[5] 3766[5] 4067[12]

Metronomic (IRE) *Peter Niven* a46 50
5 b g Roderic O'Connor(IRE) Meon Mix (Kayf Tara)
2290[7] 3297[3] 3959[6] 4990[9] (5301) 5766[3] 6499[11]

Mews House *David Brown* a63 22
2 ch c Coach House(IRE) Beauty Pageant (IRE) (Bahamian Bounty)
4937[8] 8899[5] 9036[7] 9394[4] 9541[5]

Mezidon (FR) *D & P Prod'Homme* a70 75
6 gr g Le Havre(IRE) Belliflore (FR) (Verglas (IRE))
3879a[13]

Mezmaar *Mark Usher* a67 78
10 b g Teofilo(IRE) Bay Tree (IRE) (Daylami (IRE))
138[9] 925[5] 1715[5] 2972[9] 3687[2] 3989[7]

Mia Diva *John Quinn* a67 75
2 ch f Exceed And Excel(AUS) Imperialistic Diva (IRE) (Haafhd)
1923[5] (4433) 5093[2]◆ 5683[12] 6375[11] 7227[3] 7785[8]

Miaella *Chelsea Banham* a53 42
4 b m Captain Gerrard(IRE) Sweet Applause (IRE) (Acclamation)
380[2] 1336[11] 2976[8] 3781[6] 6441[7] 7576[8] 7844[4] 8401[10] 9298[9] 9508[3]

Mia Maria (IRE) *D K Weld* 91
3 gr f Dansili Majestic Silver (IRE) (Linamix (FR))
6692a[9] 8367a[10]

Mia Mento (IRE) *Thomas Mullins* 88
3 b f Casamento(IRE) Mia Divina (Exceed And Excel (AUS))
2661a[7]◆ 2882a[6] 4353a[4]

Miarka (FR) *Harry Dunlop* a71 43
2 b f Siyouni(FR) Bearlita (GER) (Lomitas)
4790[8] 5879[4]

Mia Tesoro (IRE) *Charlie Fellowes* a94 100
6 b m Danehill Dancer(IRE) Souter's Sister (IRE) (Desert Style (IRE))
283a[7] 728a[2] 961a[9]

Mia Vittoria *Amy Murphy* a27
3 b f Nathaniel(IRE) Frequently (Dansili)
7375[13] 8837[9]

Mi Capricho (IRE) *Keith Dalgleish* a44 64
4 b g Elzaam(AUS) Mavemacullen (IRE) (Ad Valorem (USA))
1511[9] (2329) (2682) 8923[11] 9352[14]

Michaels Choice *William Jarvis* a72 74
3 b g War Command(USA) Todber (Cape Cross (IRE))
2086[12] 4603[5] 5647[5] 5882[6] 6197[4] 6756[5] 7337[4] (8285) 8860[7]

Michael's Mount *Ian Williams* a75 89
6 ch g Mount Nelson Dumnoni (Titus Livius (FR))
1559[8] 2578[4] (3653) 4381[11] 4936[4]

Michele Strogoff *Michael Appleby* a90 89
6 b g Aqlaam Maschera D'Oro (Mtoto)
29[6] 121[3] (240) 601[4] 800[3] 915[4] 1232[7] 1589[4] 1882[3] 3992[4] 4662[3] 4997[6] 5564[3] 5796[5] 6390[2] 6886[2] 7551[2] 7836[5] 9041[3] 9206[5] 9285[4] 9388[4] 9510[5] 9666[4]

Michigan Blue (IRE) *Richard Hannon* a43 51
3 b f War Command(USA) Regency Girl (IRE) (Pivotal)
1754[8] 2340[13]

Mickey (IRE) *Tom Dascombe* a92 86
6 b g Zoffany(IRE) Enchantment (Compton Place)
176[6] 623[4] 1395[5] 1694[11] 3072[6] 4322[3] (4552) 7184[4] 7856[6] 9255[2] 9658[9]

Mickey Drippin (IRE) *Noel Williams* a60
2 b g Mustajeeb Ghaidaa (IRE) (Cape Cross (IRE))
9585[9]

Microclimate *Mark H Tompkins*
2 b g Casamento(IRE) Lady Bellatrix (Singspiel (IRE))
3812[18]

Micronize (IRE) *Richard Fahey* a62 56
3 b g Dream Ahead(USA) Marmaria (SPA) (Limpid)
341[2] 4080[11] (4457) 4764[4]

Microscopic (IRE) *David Simcock* a59 64
2 br f Intense Focus(USA) Royal Esteem (Mark Of Esteem (IRE))
2579[4] 3196[5] 3595[2] 4448[4] 5026[2] 6011[3] 6900[3] 7369[5]

Midas Girl (FR) *Ed Walker* a69 63
3 bb f Dabirsim(FR) Takara Girl (FR) (Kodiac)
4592[6] 5494[2] 6074[3] 7519[9] 8254[9] 8499[11]

Midas Maggie *Philip Kirby* a49 61
4 b m Archipenko(USA) Algarade (Green Desert (USA))
1341[8] 1398[12]

Midas Spirit *Ed Walker* a59
3 b c Charm Spirit(IRE) Pearlofthequarter (Rock Of Gibraltar (IRE))
4178[8] 4590[6]

Mid Atlantic Storm (IRE) *Tom Ward* a60 65
3 b g Gale Force Ten Altogether (IRE) (King's Best (USA))
5041[3]◆ 8220[4] 8419[8]

Middlescence (IRE) *Lucinda Egerton* a69 52
5 ch g Lope De Vega(IRE) Silesian (IRE) (Singspiel (IRE))
101[8] 262[9] 309[7] 1042[2] 1212[3] 1328[7] 1715[10] 2242[7] 3716[9] 4217[4] 4472[5]

Midgrey (IRE) *F-X Belvisi* a78 74
4 gr m Camelot Tasharowa (FR) (Linamix (FR))
3140a[2] 4859a[14] 6031a[3] 7505a[3]

Midnight Bisou (USA) *Steven Asmussen* a120
4 bb m Midnight Lute(USA) Diva Delite (USA) (Repent (USA))
8775a[2]

Midnight Drift *Clive Cox* a47
2 b f Lethal Force(IRE) Malilla (IRE) (Red Clubs (IRE))
9211[7]

Midnight Guest (IRE) *David Evans* a41 51
4 b m Acclamation Midnight Martini (Night Shift (USA))
439[8] 626[10] 2206[9] 2473[6] 4772[4] 5051[11] 5629[13] 8668[4]

Midnight In Havana *Bryan Smart* a61 50
3 b g Havana Gold(IRE) Eleventh Hour (IRE) (Invincible Spirit (IRE))
1720[3] 2337[4] 6945[3]◆ 7444[5] 8233[10] 9516[4]

Midnightly *Rae Guest* a78 71
5 b m Acclamation Midnight Shift (IRE) (Night Shift (USA))
36[9] 317[5] 626[6]

Midnight Malibu (IRE) *Tim Easterby* a93 94
6 b m Poet's Voice Midnight Martini (Night Shift (USA))
163[4] (389) 588[8] (1860) 2030[9] 3201[6] 4101[13] 4986[5]

Midnight Mimosa (IRE) *Tim Easterby* a29 47
2 ch f Anjaal Miss Prim (Case Law)
4237[5] 5788[6] 6096[7] 7029[12]

Midnight Mood *Dominic Ffrench Davis* a53 52
6 b m Aqlaam Inflammable (Montjeu (IRE))
4426[7] 4991[8] 5344[6] 6153[5] 6860[3] 7857[9] 8299[13]

Midnight Sands (USA) *Doug Watson* a103 83
3 ch c Speightstown(USA) It's Midnight (USA) (Shamardal (USA))
634a[2]◆

Midnights' Gift *Alan King* a78 81
3 gr f Midnight Legend Giving (Generous (IRE))
5148[3] 6114[2] (6903) 7574[4]

Midnight Shine (FR) *A Fabre* 98
3 b g Siyouni(FR) Zaneton (FR) (Mtoto)
1489a[2] (2091a) 3621a[7]

Midnights Legacy *Alan King* 79
2 b c Midnight Legend Giving (Generous (IRE))
7755[5]◆ (8244)◆

Midnight Vixen *Ben Haslam* a61 59
5 b m Foxwedge(AUS) Midnight Ransom (Red Ransom (USA))
120[9] 1399[4] (1722) 2241[12] 2911[3] 3223[5] 5438[11] 7509[7] 8819[8]

Midnight Warrior *Ron Barr* a53 59
9 b g Teofilo(IRE) Mauri Moon (Green Desert (USA))
3162[11] 4126[10] 4435[7] 4990[7] 5301[8] 6586[5] 7314[10]

Midnight Welcome *Patrick Chamings* a45 3
2 b f Fast Company(IRE) Eleventh Hour (IRE) (Invincible Spirit (IRE))
7407[10] 9327[13]

Midnight Wilde *John Ryan* a67 72
4 gr g Poet's Voice Si Belle (IRE) (Dalakhani (IRE))
2254[7] 2577[9] 4392[8]

Midnitemudcrabs (IRE) *John James Feane* a63 67
6 ch m Arcano(IRE) Ma Nikitia (IRE) (Camacho)
4979[2] 7236[2]

Midnite Rendezvous *Derek Shaw* a35
3 b f Coach House(IRE) Midnite Motivation (Motivator)
90[11] 343[4] 537[9] 1173[9] 1270[7] 1726[6] 2213[9]

Midoura *Laura Mongan*
3 b f Delegator Mildoura (FR) (Sendawar (IRE))
2967[8] 3697[13] 5249[12] 6860[14]

Midport (IRE) *Roger Charlton* a44 55
3 b g Dabirsim(FR) Monspa (Monsun (GER))
3092[7] 8551[10]

Midterm *Liam Howley* a85 97
6 b g Galileo(IRE) Midday (Oasis Dream)
1784a[9]

Mid Winster *Andrew Slattery* a60 92
3 b f Burwaaz Cayman Fox (Cayman Kai (IRE))
5325a[8] 6476[14]

Mienvee Flyer *F-H Graffard* 75
2 b f Pivotal Blue Aegean (Invincible Spirit (IRE))
7044a[7]

Mightaswellsmile *Ron Barr* a46 51
5 b m Elnadim(USA) Intishaar (IRE) (Dubai Millennium)
3933[13] 4132[10] 4586[12] 5038[4] 5300[2] 5559[8] 5768[2] 6275[12] 6590[5] 7052[9] 7591[12] 8632[6] 8720[6] 9398[8]

Mightily *Doug Watson* a82 64
5 b g Dubawi(IRE) Mandellicht (IRE) (Be My Guest (USA))
97a[13]

Mighty Mac (IRE) *Karen McLintock* a74 64
4 b g Dragon Pulse(IRE) Invincible Fire (IRE) (Invincible Spirit (IRE))
784[12] 1560[4] 3221[8]

Mighty Matilda *Simon Earle*
3 ch f Execute(FR) Try And See (TUR) (Wolf (CHI))
7159[10]

Mighty Rock *Sebastiano Guerrieri* 83
2 b f Cable Bay(IRE) Marigay's Magic (Rock Of Gibraltar (IRE))
7724a[4]

Mighty Spirit (IRE) *Richard Fahey* a81 93
2 b f Acclamation Majestic Alexander (IRE) (Bushranger (IRE))
1923[2]◆ 2805[2] 3983[6] 4583[2] 5185[3] 5544[2] 6474[5] 7211[2] (8631)

Migration (IRE) *David Menuisier* 103
3 b g Alhebayeb(IRE) Caribbean Ace (IRE) (Red Clubs (IRE))
1754[2]◆ 2082[2] (2766) 4016[7] 4882[7] (5861) 6725[2] 7457[5]

Mikmak *Tim Easterby* a85 91
6 b g Makfi Rakata (USA) (Quiet American (USA))
2710[8] 3072[4]◆ 3811[5] 4240[8]◆ 4490[5] 4730[2] 5693[5] (5948) 6543[4] 7068[6] 8096[14]

Milabella *R Mike Smith* 38
3 b f Bated Breath Miss Noble (Exceed And Excel (AUS))
2683[6] 3176[5] 4726[10] 5486[8] 7487[8]

Mi Laddo (IRE) *Oliver Greenall* a54 53
3 b g Lilbourne Lad(IRE) Fritta Mista (IRE) (Linamix (FR))
1486[8] 2016[8] 2531[8] 4003[3] 4485[5] 5054[6] 5248[3] 5851[9]

Milagre Da Vida (IRE) *K R Burke* a61
3 b f Bated Breath Eucharist (IRE) (Acclamation)
8920[4] 9332[2] 9644[2]

Milan Reef (IRE) *David Loughnane* a9 64
4 br m Famous Name Jagapaw (IRE) (Manduro (GER))
2106[6] 3225[4] 3296[3] 3547[2] 3682[3] 3720[6] (8009) 8247[7] 8414[13]

Mildenberger *Mark Johnston* a111 111
4 b h Teofilo(IRE) Belle Josephine (Dubawi (IRE))
2033[7]◆ 2410[3] 2807[3] 9302[6] 9468[3]◆

Mild Illusion (IRE) *Jonathan Portman* 96
2 br f Requinto(IRE) Mirror Effect (IRE) (Shamardal (USA))
4221[2] 5250[2] (5745) 6221[3] (7156)◆ 7696[8] 7896[2] (8724)

Milestone (FR) *A Fabre* a76 99
3 b c Mastercraftsman(IRE) Mission Secrete (IRE) (Galileo (IRE))
3031a[3]

Milistorm *Michael Blanshard* a53
3 b f Sepoy(AUS) Oasis Breeze (Oasis Dream)
1726[11] 2531[9] 3593[14] 5054[8] 6636[10]

Military Hill (IRE) *Paul Stafford* a55 63
6 b g Majestic Missile(IRE) Grateful Thanks (FR) (Bering)
5712a[15]

Military Law *John Gosden* a108 87
4 b g Dubawi(IRE) Marine Bleue (IRE) (Desert Prince (IRE))
(29) 1757[10] (4292)◆

Military Madame (IRE) *John Quinn* a62 66
4 b m Epaulette(AUS) Sweet Kristeen (USA) (Candy Stripes (USA))
125[11] 462[5]◆

Military March *Saeed bin Suroor* 113
2 b c New Approach(IRE) Punctilious (Danehill (USA))
(5439)◆ (8112)◆

Military Move *Roger Varian* 61
3 ch c Dubawi(IRE) Rainbow Dancing (Rainbow Quest (USA))
2795[6]

Military Tactic (IRE)
Saeed bin Suroor a65 76
3 b c Iffraaj Lunar Spirit (Invincible Spirit (IRE))
2023[8] 2634[2] 4196[3] 5176[4]

Military Zone (AUS)
Peter & Paul Snowden 106
3 b g Epaulette(AUS) Loading Zone (AUS) (Street Sense (USA))
8805a[7]

Militia *Richard Fahey* a68 79
4 b g Equiano(FR) Sweet As Honey (Duke Of Marmalade (IRE))
4303[10] 4894[9] 5330[7] 5819[5] 6261[4] 6339[9] (7367) (8183) 8400[3]

Militry Decoration (IRE)
Dr Jon Scargill a69 66
4 b g Epaulette(AUS) Funcheon Vale (IRE) (Acclamation)
91[8] 1355[6] 1675[3] 3002[4] 4028[5] 4787[5] 6059[2] 7083[12] 8033[8] 8434[10]

Milldean Felix (IRE) *Suzi Best* a51 56
3 br g Red Jazz(USA) Plausabelle (Royal Applause)
5679[5] 6279[12] 6723[13] 7232[5] 8406[4]

Milldean Panther *Suzi Best* a55 48
3 b g Mayson Silver Halo (Paris House)
296[9] 1380[7] 1863[7] 2240[13] 2924[7] 3182[10]

Mille Et Mille *C Lerner* a77 105
9 b g Muhtathir Quezon Sun (GER) (Monsun (GER))
6266a[4] 7928a[8] (8580a)

Mille Fois Merci (IRE) *A Fabre* 80
2 b f Galileo(IRE) High Celebrity (FR) (Invincible Spirit (IRE))
6774a[2]

Millesime (IRE) *J-C Rouget* a68 64
3 ch f Dawn Approach(IRE) Ermine And Velvet (Nayef (USA))
2390a[10]

Millfield (FR) *D Smaga* a93 97
6 b h Whipper(USA) Victoria College (FR) (Rock Of Gibraltar (IRE))
4704a[12]

Millicent Fawcett *John Gosden* a80 77
3 b f Kingman Mainstay (Elmaamul (USA))
1740[2] 8529[2] 8842[4] (9400)

Millie Lily (IRE) *R Le Gal* a60 72
3 b f Makfi Holly Polly (GER) (Dylan Thomas (IRE))
(7138a)

Millie May *Jimmy Fox* a48 48
5 b m Sixties Icon Maydream (Sea Freedom)
257[11] 1498[4] 2468[4] 2733[8] 4796[7] 6046[10] 7271[3] 7985[5] 8916[3]

Millie The Minx (IRE) *Dianne Sayer* a14 54
5 b m Medicean Popocatepetl (FR) (Nashwan (USA))
3681[3] 4633[10] 5099[4]◆ 5766[4] 7048[6]

Millionaire Waltz *Paul Cole* a79 78
2 b c Heeraat(IRE) Radio Gaga (Multiplex)
1887[5] 7453[6] 9195[5] (9448)◆

Million Dreams (FR) *Laurent Loisel* a57 54
3 b f Dabirsim(FR) Oliandra (FR) (Lando (GER))
1658a[3] 3028a[10] 9280a[9]

Millions Memories *Laura Mongan* a74 79
3 b g Zoffany(IRE) Millestan (IRE) (Invincible Spirit (IRE))
2875[2] 3471[6] 5267[7] 8692[11] 9173[12]

Millisle (IRE) *Mrs John Harrington* 116
2 ch f Starspangledbanner(AUS) Green Castle (IRE) (Indian Ridge (IRE))
(6190a) 6907[2] (7692)

Millswyn (IRE)
Joseph Patrick O'Brien 92
3 b g Camelot Condition (Deploy)
4136a[5]

Milltown Star *Mick Channon* a85 96
2 b c Roderic O'Connor(IRE) Hail Shower (IRE) (Red Clubs (IRE))
3245[9] 3990[2] (4254) (4999)◆ 5520[7] 6002a[U] 7247a[5] 7612[3] 8110[2] (9059a)

Milord's Song (FR) *S Wattel* 105
3 b c Siyouni(FR) Secret Melody (FR) (Inchinor)
1200a[4] 2564a[2] 3621a[4] 4703a[4] 6252a[2] 7886a[2]

Milos (FR) *H-A Pantall* a61 32
2 b f Planteur(IRE) Little Hippo (Halling (USA))
1448a[8]

Milton Road *Rebecca Bastiman* a61 60
4 b g Mazameer(IRE) Blakeshall Girl (Piccolo)
742[8] 1021[3] 1765[5] 2329[2] 2638[8] 3475[7] 3924[4] 4725[7]

Mi Manchi (IRE) *Marco Botti* a58 52
3 b f Sea The Moon(GER) Carraigoona (IRE) (Rock Of Gibraltar (IRE))
836[5] 1077[3] 1397[8] 2011[8] 3777[4] 4400[9]

Mime Dance *John Butler* a56 76
8 b g Notnowcato Encore My Love (Royal Applause)
1369[11] 1527[7] 1679[11] (3592) 4460[12] 7604[7] 8663[9]

Mimic's Memory *T G McCourt* a51 50
5 b m Sayif(IRE) Blue Crest (FR) (Verglas (IRE))
7086a[9]

Mina Vagante *Hugo Palmer* a80 79
3 b f Exceed And Excel(AUS) Unity (IRE) (Sadler's Wells (USA))
3889[4] 4341[8] 5213[2] 5556[2] 6412[2] (7344) 8064[3] 8811[6]

Mina Velour *Bryan Smart* 75
3 ch f Garswood Ardessie (Bahamian Bounty)
1649[3] (2332) 3499[5] 4822[2] (6338)

Mind Mapping (USA) *A Fabre* a100 105
4 b g Medaglia d'Oro(USA) Visual Mind (USA) (Kingmambo (USA))
1708a[3]

Mind The Crack (IRE)
Mark Johnston a79 97
3 b g Jukebox Jury(IRE) Mountain Melody (GER) (Refuse To Bend (IRE))
(3254)◆ (3585) 4644[2] 4901[5] 5541[5]

Mineche (FR) *N Milliere*
3 ch f Alexandros Minnaloushe (FR) (Black Minnaloushe (USA))
2390a[12]

Minhaaj (IRE) *William Haggas* a74 80
2 b f Invincible Spirit(IRE) Sharqeyih (Shamardal (USA))
8097[2]◆ 8724[8] 9036[3] (9393)

Mini Milk *Jonathan Portman* 57
3 b f Archipenko(USA) Milkie Way (Cape Cross (IRE))
3889[8] 4842[9] 5451[8] 6367[7] 6849[7]

Mininggold *Michael Dods* a79 73
6 b m Piccolo Rosein (Komaite (USA))
(43) 230[3] 743[6] 1194[3] (1551) 1860[3] 2053[8] 2637[5] 3206[6] 5181[4] 7387[2] 8066[2] 8267[9]

Minnehaha (FR) *A Schouteet* a63 65
4 b m Poet's Voice Sosquaw (FR) (Numerous (USA))
2170a[2] 2647a[7]

Minnelli *Philip McBride* a62 67
3 ch f Showcasing Clear Voice (USA) (Cryptoclearance (USA))
2765[7] 4804[3] 5307[8] 6128[4] 6702[4] (7318) 8868[6] 9093[9]

Minoria *Rae Guest* a76
4 ch m Harbour Watch(IRE) Mina (Selkirk (USA))
(141) 464[2]

Minty Jones *Michael Mullineaux* a27 42
10 b g Primo Valentino(IRE) Reveur (Rossini (USA))
118[11] 3291[8] 3723[11] 5491[10] 5551[6] 5986[4] 6277[13] 7761[4]

Minuty (FR) *F Head* 93
2 b f Charm Spirit(IRE) Galaxidi (High Chaparral (IRE))
(7044a) 7602a[4]

Minuty *Rae Guest* a61
4 b m Acclamation Million Faces (Exceed And Excel (AUS))
27[4] 178[4] 476[10] 811[6]

Miqyaas *R Bouresly* 59
4 b g Oasis Dream Fawaayed (IRE) (Singspiel (IRE))
1742a[5]

Mirabelle (FR) *C Laffon-Parias* a76 68
3 b f Anodin(IRE) Minted (USA) (Mineshaft (USA))
2265a[3]

Mirabelle Plum (IRE)
Robyn Brisland a41 43
3 b f Casamento(IRE) Spirit Of Alsace (IRE) (Invincible Spirit (IRE))
2932[7] 4277[3] 5004[7] 8944[4] 9646[8]

Miracle Des Aigles (FR)
Mme C Barande-Barbe a100 80
6 b g Siyouni(FR) Folie Des Aigles (FR) (Ocean Of Wisdom (USA))
2429a[10] 8240a[2]

Miracle Garden *Roy Brotherton* a57 57
7 ch g Exceed And Excel(AUS) Sharp Terms (Kris)
187[4] 463[8] 801[7] (1038) 1208[6] 1765[16] 2971[4] 3476[6] (3838) 4303[8] 4879[7] 5289[5] 5503[8] 8866[7] 9217[12] 9477[4]

Miracle Of Medinah *Mark Usher* a87 95
8 ch g Milk It Mick Smart Ass (IRE) (Shinko Forest (IRE))
2791[2] 4609[4] 5628[5] 6318[5] 6916[5]

Miracle Works *Robert Cowell* a85 83
4 gr g Kyllachy Eastern Destiny (Dubai Destination (USA))
131[3] 253[8] (849) (1342) 1822[10] 2556[7] 3021[6] 5606[2] 5888[2]

Mirage Dancer
Trent Busuttin & Natalie Young 118
5 b h Frankel Heat Haze (Green Desert (USA))
(3077) 4093[3] 4848[2] 5613[2] 8361a[3] 8844a[14]

Mirage Vert (FR) *S Wattel* a65
3 gr g Kheleyf(USA) Cocopalm (FR) (Linamix (FR))
9058a[10]

Mirasch (FR) *Waldemar Hickst* a65 64
3 b g Vespone(IRE) Manon I (Alzao (USA))
6328a[6]

Mira Star (IRE) *Ed Vaughan* 69
2 b f Sea The Stars(IRE) Spinaminnie (IRE) (Moss Vale (IRE))
5684[6] 6640[6] 7799a[6]

Miraz (IRE) *Richard Hannon* a65
2 b c Kodiac Summer Blues (USA) (Summer Bird (USA))
8121[3] 9634[8]

Miro (GER) *M Le Forestier* 40
4 ch g Peintre Celebre(USA) Montezuma (GER) (Monsun (GER))
7676a[9]

Mirrii Yanan (IRE) *Carla O'Halloran* 62
4 b m Society Rock(IRE) Miss Chaumiere (Selkirk (USA))
2170a[3]

Mirsaale *Keith Dalgleish* a75 93
9 ch g Sir Percy String Quartet (IRE) (Sadler's Wells (USA))
1947[9] 2118[5] 2575[11] 3929[7] 4522[3]

Mirth (USA) *Philip D'Amato* 106
4 bb m Colonel John(USA) Di's Delight (USA) (French Deputy (USA))
8772a[6]

Mischief Managed (IRE)
Tim Easterby a71 75
5 ch g Tagula(IRE) Cape Clear (Slip Anchor)
7364[11]

Mischief Star *David O'Meara* a79 74
2 b g Due Diligence(USA) Red Mischief (IRE) (Red Clubs (IRE))
3703[3]◆ 4401[7] (5764) 6625[10] 7140[3] (8318) 8665[5]◆

Mishriff (IRE) *John Gosden* 88
2 b c Make Believe Contradict (Raven's Pass (USA))
8203[4] 8518[3] (8857)◆

Misread *Geoffrey Deacon* 40
3 ch f Nayef(USA) Widescreen (USA) (Distant View (USA))
4842[11] 5428[7] 6315[9] 8406[12]

Miss Alpha (FR) *F Vermeulen* 35
4 b m Cape Cross(IRE) Motivation (FR) (Muhtathir)
2647a[9]

Miss Australia (FR)
Guillaume Courbot a39 7
7 gr m Mr. Sidney(USA) Dedicace (USA) (El Prado (IRE))
9014a[13]

Miss Bar Beach (IRE)
Keith Dalgleish a86 96
4 b m Choisir(AUS) Whitegate Way (Greensmith)
30[6] 756[7] 4891[15]

Miss Bassett (FR) *T Lemer* 57
2 b f Wootton Bassett Sunday Surprise (FR) (Orpen (USA))
1657a[6]

Miss Bates *Ann Duffield* a58 72
5 b m Holy Roman Emperor(IRE) Jane Austen (IRE) (Galileo (IRE))
(273) 624[7] 9039[10]

Miss Blondell *Marcus Tregoning* a72 70
6 ch m Compton Place Where's Broughton (Cadeaux Genereux)
4841[3] 5565[3] 6083[5] 6830[5] 7229[2] 8422[8] 8813[5] 9132[13]

Miss Carla (IRE) *Jamie Osborne* a64 36
2 b f Kodiac Sindjara (USA) (Include (USA))
6846[9] 8891[5]

Misscarlett (IRE) *Philip Kirby* a51 60
5 b m Red Rocks(IRE) Coimbra (USA) (Trempolino (USA))
1718[3] 3272[5] 3686[8] 5435[4]

Miss Celestial (IRE)
Sir Mark Prescott Bt a69 103
3 b f Exceed And Excel(AUS) Liber Nauticus (IRE) (Azamour (IRE))
3317[7] (5291) 5705[3] 6257[3] 6769a[2] 7893[2]

Miss Chilli *Michael Easterby* a45 35
2 rg f Monsieur Bond(IRE) Poetic Verse (Byron)
1759[11] 2594[8] 5295[8] 6675[7]

Miss Communicate *Lydia Pearce* a53 59
3 b f Gregorian(IRE) Love Quest (Pursuit Of Love)
855[6] 1381[11] 1678[10] 4179[4] 5526[10] 6885[9]

Miss Crick *Alan King* a78
8 b m Midnight Legend Kwaheri (Efisio)
41[2] 696[2] (884)

Miss Ditsy (IRE) *Michael Attwater* a44 3
3 b f Most Improved(IRE) Maramkova (IRE) (Danehill Dancer (IRE))
6119[7] 7278[8] 8808[4]

Miss Elsa *Eve Johnson Houghton* a68 75
3 b f Frozen Power(IRE) Support Fund (IRE) (Intikhab (USA))
2114[13] 3189[4] 3532[3] 4218[5] 4651[5] 5315[5] 6904[11] 7295[2] 7817[4] (8348) 9367[6]◆ (9426) 9663[8]

Miss Enigma (IRE) *Richard Hughes* a65 60
3 b f Kodiac Mysteriousness (FR) (Beat Hollow)
1142[8] 1293[8] 1514[3] (2211) 2592[2] 3045[7] 3839[9] 4192[3] 4457[7]

Miss Firecracker (IRE)
Dr Jon Scargill a17
3 ch f Dragon Pulse(IRE) Miss Otis (Danetime (IRE))
4592[8] 6345[8]

Miss Fizz (FR) *P De Chevigny* 23
3 b f Sri Putra Kalimba De Luna (FR) (Green Tune (USA))
6094a[9]

Miss Gargar *Harry Dunlop* a60 53
3 b f Garswood Verge (IRE) (Acclamation)
1687[6] 2276[5] 2995[7] 3887[6] 4457[3] 5890[5] 6181[3] (6737) 7557[7] 8194[3] 8704[6] 9135[7] 9287[11]

Miss Gradenko *Robert Cowell* a55 46
3 b f Foxwedge(AUS) Instructress (Diktat)
7854[4] 8249[7] (8450) 8840[7] 9272[6] 9572[9]

Miss Green Dream *Julia Feilden* a50 51
3 b f Oasis Dream Miss Corniche (Hernando (FR))
79[4] 400[3] 765[3] 1332[12] 1770[5] 3275[2] 4400[3] 6128[7] 7025[5] 7450[6] 8916[12] 9279[12]

Miss Harriett *Stuart Kittow* a42 50
3 b f Arvico(FR) Ivorsagoodun (Piccolo)
2354[14] 2999[6] 3889[9] 5378[10] 6400[12] 8869[6]

Miss Havana *Eve Johnson Houghton* a53 54
3 b f Havana Gold(IRE) Tamalain (USA) (Royal Academy (USA))
183[8] 1935[3] 3092[9] 3407[8]

Miss Icon *Patrick Chamings* a64 66
5 b m Sixties Icon Pretty Miss (Averti (IRE))
4378[9] (5081) 6116[2] 6529[2] 7024[2] 7527[4] 8499[9]

Missile Mantra (AUS)
Peter & Paul Snowden 101
2 b f Smart Missile(AUS) Wecansay Mak (AUS) (Starcraft (NZ))
8135a[2]

Mission Boy *A Botti* 108
3 b c Paco Boy(IRE) Miss Mission (IRE) (Second Empire (IRE))
2162a[2] 2887a[2] 3903a[6] 7502a[2] 8392a[8] 8786a[5]

Mississippi Miss *Dr Jon Scargill* a55 56
5 ch m Equiano(FR) Junket (Medicean)
1216[6] 1769[11] 2740[11]

Miss Jabeam (IRE)
Aidan Anthony Howard a78 83
3 ch f Bungle Inthejungle Semper Fi (Royal Applause)
6986a[5] 7241a[23]

Miss Lara (IRE) *A Fabre* 63
2 b f Galileo(IRE) Miss France (IRE) (Dansili)
4533a[8]

Miss Latin (IRE) *David Simcock* a88 81
4 b m Galileo(IRE) Breeze Hill (IRE) (Danehill (USA))
2399[6] 3269[3] 4881[3] 5540[14] (6200) 7395[2] 8710[6]

Miss Liberty Belle (AUS)
William Jarvis a62 59
2 ch f Starspangledbanner(AUS) Alpine Belle (NZ) (Rock Of Gibraltar (IRE))
2340[15] 2939[7] 3964[4] 4755[2] 5526[4] 6389[5] (7446) 8007[RR]

Miss Lucy (IRE) *K R Burke* 81
2 b f Kodiac Fifth Avenue Doll (USA) (Marquetry (USA))
3244[4] 3927[6] (4849)

Miss M (IRE) *William Muir* a67 68
5 b m Mastercraftsman(IRE) Tintern (Diktat)
3015[3] (3834) 4447[5] 5089[4] 5344[3] 6291[6] 6830[9] 6854[4] 7790[2] 8065[2] 8812[6]

Miss Maben *Iain Jardine*
3 ch f Compton Place Miss Trish (IRE) (Danetime (IRE))
6575[11]

Miss Mae (GER) *Henk Grewe* 88
3 b f Mamool(IRE) Matchday (Acclamation)
2137a[5]

Miss Matterhorn
Eve Johnson Houghton a63 71
2 b f Swiss Spirit Support Fund (IRE) (Intikhab (USA))
2228[4]◆ 2694[3] 3257[2] (4114) 5101[7] 5777[9]

Miss Me (GER) *N Clement* 25
3 b f Footstepsinthesand Miss Lady (GER) (Lawman (FR))
3712a[8]

Miss Moon (FR) *A Botti* 99
3 b f Elusive City(USA) Miss Bikini (IRE) (Titus Livius (FR))
2161a[5]

Miss Morocco *John Gosden* a71
3 b f Nathaniel(IRE) Morocco Moon (Rock Of Gibraltar (IRE))
103[4]◆

Miss Mumtaz (IRE) *Ian Williams* a79 79
4 ch m Lope De Vega(IRE) Ispanka (Invincible Spirit (IRE))
3169[4] 4391[3] 4627[7]

Miss O Connor (IRE)
William Haggas 108
4 b m Roderic O'Connor(IRE) Magadar (USA) (Lujain (USA))
(5592)◆ (5949) (8583a)

Miss Paxman *Martyn Meade* a30 71
2 b f Exceed And Excel(AUS) Half Truth (IRE) (Verglas (IRE))
4557[4] 5447[4] 7786[10]

Miss Pollyanna (IRE) *Roger Ingram* a49 36
3 ch f Helmet(AUS) Ivy Batty (IRE) (King's Best (USA))
141[6] 4306[8] 5092[8] 5803[12] 7081[5] 7817[13] 9216[5] 9589[15]

Miss President *Robert Cowell* a52 58
3 b f Oasis Dream Madam President (Royal Applause)
2908[10] 5063[11] 5960[8]

Miss Ranger (IRE) *Roger Fell* a43 59
7 gr m Bushranger(IRE) Remiss (IRE) (Indian Ridge (IRE))
1418[6] 2244[12] 2628[7] 3251[7] 3886[9] 4126[7] 4510[9] 4661[12] 4881[2] 5423[10] 5727[11] 5975[5] 6550[6] 7314[4] (8343) 8635[5]

Miss Rebero *Gary Sanderson*
9 b m Cockney Rebel(IRE) One Zero (USA) (Theatrical (IRE))
277[13]

Miss Recycled *Michael Madgwick* a36 53
4 b m Royal Applause Steel Free (IRE) (Danehill Dancer (IRE))
(4217) 4753[7] 6897[12] 7343[9] 8251[7]

Miss Roazhon *P Monfort* a46 72
2 ch f Outstrip Roxy Hart (Halling (USA))
7799a[4]

Miss Rouge (IRE)
Sebastiano Guerrieri 89
2 ch f Dream Ahead(USA) Playful (Piccolo)
8791a[5]

Miss Sabina *Ann Duffield* a48 51
3 ch f Mayson Some Diva (Dr Fong (USA))
2788[10]

Miss Sheridan (IRE)
Michael Easterby a68 77
5 br m Lilbourne Lad(IRE) Sues Surprise (IRE) (Montjeu (IRE))
2418[14] (3053) 5245[4] 5844[7] 7378[8]

Miss Siska (AUS) *Grahame Begg* 101
5 bb m So You Think(NZ) Sing Hallelujah (AUS) (Is It True (USA))
8138a[8]

Miss Sixtina (FR) *J Parize*
4 b m Sinndar(IRE) Miss Sixty (IRE) (Barathea (IRE))
2002a[8]

Miss Spotsy (FR) *H-A Pantall* a82 65
3 ch f Vespone(IRE) Miss Sissy (FR) (Sicyos (USA))
993a[4]

Miss Swift *Marcus Tregoning* a48 8
3 b f Sir Percy Lady Hestia (USA) (Belong To Me (USA))
3324[11] 6531[8] 7450[5] 8292[3] 8916[5] 9087[6]

Miss Thoughtful *Jamie Osborne* a66 61
2 gr f Gutaifan(IRE) Lovely Thought (Dubai Destination (USA))
6442[6] (6719)◆ 7104[5] 8650[2] 9300[9]

Misstic (FR) *Edouard Monfort* a51 57
3 b f Wootton Bassett Misdirect (Darshaan)
7642a[2]

Miss Tiche (IRE) *S Wattel* 73
2 ch f Ivawood(IRE) Miss Wicklow (IRE) (New Approach (IRE))
1240a[8] 1709a[2] 2757a[5] 5286a[2]

Miss Villanelle *Charles Hills* a60 76
2 b f Ivawood(IRE) Parabola (Galileo (IRE))
3076[2] 3426[4] 4897[6] (5777) 6221[4] 6833[7] 8303[6]

Miss Wow (IRE) *Stef Keniry* a8 48
3 b f Elusive Pimpernel(USA) Hannah's Magic (IRE) (Lomitas)
585[7]

Miss Yoda (GER) *John Gosden* a78 97
2 ch f Sea The Stars(IRE) Monami (GER) (Sholokhov (IRE))
(5732)◆ (7162) 8111[2]

Mister Charlie (FR) *A Le Duff* a80 72
3 b c Myboycharlie(IRE) Alianza (Halling (USA))
7138a[3]

Mister Chiang *Mark Johnston* a86 82
3 b g Archipenko(USA) Robe Chinoise (Robellino (USA))
1462[4] 2562[7] 3474[5] 4034[3] (4443)◆ (5012) 5840[5] 6232[6] 6634[3] 7439[2] (7631)◆ 8098[17]

Mister Fawkes *Richard Hughes* a35 45
3 b g Phoenix Reach(IRE) Sister Moonshine (Averti (IRE))
3299[13] 6153[10] 7240[12]

Mister Freeze (IRE)
Patrick Chamings a57 55
5 ch g Frozen Power(IRE) Beacon Of Hope (IRE) (Barathea (IRE))
1820[15] 2349[7] 4115[10] 5003[13] 6546[2] 7384[2] 8279[2] 8847[8] 8949[3] 9225[5]

Mister Gabriel (FR) *J Piednoel* 33
3 gr g Silver Frost(IRE) Pierre Bleue (FR) (Poliglote)
6094a[8]

Mister Jingle (FR) *K Borgel* 76
2 gr c Never On Sunday(FR) Tell Me Why (FR) (Distant Relative)
7674a[4]

Mister Magic (IRE)
Gianluca Bietolini a94 74
4 b g Red Jazz(USA) Luvmedo (IRE) (One Cool Cat (USA))
7136a[2]

Mister Manduro (FR) *Brian Ellison* a40 44
5 ch g Manduro(GER) Semenova (FR) (Green Tune (USA))
3862[12]

Mister Music *Tony Carroll* a89 75
10 b g Singspiel(IRE) Sierra (Dr Fong (USA))
(63) 466[2] 929[3] 1428[3] 2346[2] (4455) 4867[8] 5416[8] 6370[8] 7145[10] 8642[6] 9183[5]

Mister Musicmaster *Ron Hodges* a55 66
10 b g Amadeus Wolf Misty Eyed (IRE) (Paris House)
2277[9] 2472[5] 3038[3] 4235[6] 4873[3] 5373[5] 6334[8] 6731[5] 7232[3] 8417[3] 8822[4] 8998[4] 9207[11]

Mister Nino (FR) *J-M Beguigne* 100
3 b c Magician(IRE) Desideria (USA) (Desert Party (USA))
5717a[5] 6385a[4]

Mister Vancouver (FR) *Y Barberot* a78 68
3 ch c George Vancouver(USA) Mowaajaha (USA) (Invincible Spirit (IRE))
9504a[2]

Mist In The Valley *David Brown* a37 36
2 b f Hellvelyn Katie Elder (FR) (High Chaparral (IRE))
2191[9] 3196[8] 8338[11]

Mistiroc *John Quinn* a93 97
8 br g Rocamadour Mistinguett (IRE) (Doyoun)
2095[2] 2808[7] 4021[5] 4877[5] 6535[3] 7436[7] 8082[5]

Mistral Song (FR)
Michael Blanshard 56
5 b m Hurricane Cat(USA) Song Of India (Dalakhani (IRE))
3889[5]

Mistress Nellie *William Stone* a55 54
4 ch m Mount Nelson Watchoverme (Haafhd)
58[3] 2571[0] 2975[2] 3252[2] 3740[2] 4111[3] 5106[2] 6599[7] 7318[8] 7985[2] 8204[5] 8854[2] 9139[6] 9310[2] 9589[3]

Mistress Of Love (USA) *K R Burke* a80 88
3 b f Scat Daddy(USA) Beloveda (USA) (Ghostzapper (USA))
1832[9] 3677a[9] 4347[5]

Mistress Of Venice *K J Condon* a71 82
4 b m Bated Breath Rohlindi (Red Ransom (USA))
6648a[9]

Mistress Viz (IRE)
Sarah Hollinshead a54 51
5 gr m Mastercraftsman(IRE) Vizean (IRE) (Medicean)
185[9]

Mistry Girl *John Holt* a38
2 b f Cable Bay(IRE) Goodie Twosues (Fraam)
9506[12]

Misty *Ralph Beckett* a14 60
3 b f Oasis Dream Ceilidh House (Selkirk (USA))
1740[12] 2488[10] 3546[5] 4285[9]

Misty Birnam (SAF) *Ian Williams* a77 80
5 gr g Toreador(IRE) In The Mist (SAF) (Verglas (IRE))
237[6]

Misty Breese (IRE)
Sarah Hollinshead a44 40
4 b m Zebedee Geordie Iris (IRE) (Elusive City (USA))
2975[4] 3740[4] 4658[6] 5421[6] 5981[8] 6049[6] 6733[9] 7034[5] 7390[9]

Misty Grey (IRE) *Mark Johnston* 100
2 ch c Dark Angel(IRE) Chinese White (IRE) (Dalakhani (IRE))
2362[3] (2869) 3312[3] 4012[7] 5134[2] 5584[6] 6422[9] 7071[2] 8125[10]

Misu Pete *Mark Usher* a67 68
7 b g Misu Bond(IRE) Smart Ass (IRE) (Shinko Forest (IRE))
159[8] (595) 941[2] 1418[9] 2797[10] 3325[6] 4460[6]◆ (5137) 5633[2] 6085[4] 7527[11] 9132[9] 9427[7]

Mitchell Road (USA) *William Mott* 107
4 b m English Channel(USA) Quake Lake (USA) (War Chant (USA))
4950a[5] 7920a[8]

Mitchum *Ron Barr* a41 39
10 b g Elnadim(USA) Maid To Matter (Pivotal)
2632[15] 3203[9] 3518[6] 3933[12] 5767[9] 6174[7] 6680[8] 7389[9] 8638[7] 9395[14]

Mitchum Swagger *Ralph Beckett* a104 109
7 b g Paco Boy(IRE) Dont Dili Dali (Dansili)
2085[5] 2688[4] 3588[5] 3987[17] 7905[3] 8336[3] 8765[4] 9124a[2]

Mithayel Style (FR)
David Thompson a30 56
3 b f Style Vendome(FR) Tis Mighty (IRE) (Fruits Of Love (USA))
2123[6] 5041[8] 5558[15] 7303[8]

Mithmaar (IRE) *Mark Johnston* 59
3 b g Sea The Stars(IRE) Nufoos (Zafonic (USA))
2113[5]

Mitigator *Lydia Pearce* a71 69
3 b g Delegator Snake Skin (Golden Snake (USA))
966[8] 1264[10] 2238[8] 3580[10] 3780[4] (4029) (5531) 5632[5] 6164[10] 7084[2] 7405[3] 8207[10]

Mitole (USA) *Steven Asmussen* a127
4 b h Eskendereya(USA) Indian Miss (USA) (Indian Charlie (USA))
(3618a) (8773a)

Mitty's Smile (IRE) *Archie Watson* a72 72
2 b f No Nay Never(USA) Lace (IRE) (Sadler's Wells (USA))
4840[4] (5250) 5934[5] 6369[4] 7104[3] 7495a[13] (8650) 9300[11] 9401[10]

Mixboy (FR) *Keith Dalgleish* a98 97
9 gr g Fragrant Mix(IRE) Leston Girl (FR) (Lesotho (USA))
231[4] (1524) 3952[P] 5457[6]

Mixed Up Miss (IRE) *Bryan Smart* a23 47
3 b f Kodiac Kerfuffle (IRE) (Kheleyf (USA))
3932[10] 7651[8] 7962[14]

Mixologist (FR) *Y Barberot* a60
2 b c Gemix(FR) Ideal Step (FR) (Footstepsinthesand)
8448a[5]

Mizaah (IRE) *Owen Burrows* a104 100
6 b g Invincible Spirit(IRE) Miss Beabea (IRE) (Catrail (USA))
6894[4] 7448[6]

Mizuki (IRE) *Andrew Balding* 68
4 b m Sea The Stars(IRE) Bright Snow (USA) (Gulch (USA))
3263[7] 3946[3]

Mizzy (AUS) *Anthony Cummings* 105
3 bk f Zoustar(AUS) Missy Cummings (AUS) (Magnus (AUS))
8805a[3]

Mkfancy (FR) *Mme Pia Brandt* 109
2 b c Makfi Fancy Green (FR) (Muhtathir)
6776a[3] (7675a) (8582a)

Mm Sixsevei (IRE) *John M Oxx* 19
4 ch m Dragon Pulse(IRE) Lara Celeb (IRE) (Peintre Celebre (USA))
3557a[8]

Mneef (USA) *S Jadhav* a41 10
3 ch g Overanalyze(USA) Wickie's Flame (USA) (Kafwain (USA))
168a[16] 570a[12]

Moans Cross (USA)
David Bridgwater a54 46
5 ch g Spring At Last(USA) Playful Wink (USA) (Orientate (USA))
7857[8]

Moayadd (USA) *Neil Mulholland* a80 79
7 b g Street Cry(IRE) Aryaamm (IRE) (Galileo (IRE))
2672a[2] 3091[4] 4928[4] 5452[10] 6931[7]

Mobham (IRE) *J R Jenkins* a69 70
4 b g Teofilo(IRE) Elegant Beauty (Olden Times)
242[9] 562[3] 1022[8] 1826[3] 2353[7] 3700[5] 4601[2] 5528[13] 5744[7] 8703[4] 9005[2] 9589[2]

Mocead Cappall *John Holt* a37 50
4 b m Captain Gerrard(IRE) All Fur Coat (Multiplex)
7468[10] 8668[6] 8898[11]

Mochalov *Jane Chapple-Hyam* a66 40
4 b g Denounce Awesome Asset (USA) (Awesome Again (CAN))
33[7] 175[6] 595[2] (718) 982[5] 1177[12] 2019[7] 2741[12] 4807[9] 5309[3] 5807[2] (6116) 7080[3] 7839[8] 8083[12] 8756[3] 9086[3] 9629[9]◆

Modakhar (IRE) *K R Burke* a85 83
3 b g Battle Of Marengo(IRE) Lost Highway (IRE) (Danehill Dancer (IRE))
3510[4] 6823[2] (7490) 8514[8] 8918[5]

Model Guest *George Margarson* a91 92
3 ch f Showcasing Looks All Right (IRE) (Danehill Dancer (IRE))
2268[5] 2608[4] 4052[5] 4806[3] 7697[12] 7863[3] 8222[4]

Modern British Art (IRE)
Michael Bell a65 80
2 b c Cable Bay(IRE) Let Me Shine (USA) (Dixie Union (USA))
4246[9] 4992[2] (5794) 7072[5] 7391[8] 8494[12]

Modern Millie *Mick Channon* 94
3 b f Sixties Icon Hairspray (Bahamian Bounty)
1751[6] 2268[3] 2806[5] 4052[12] 4667[5] 4898[8]

Modmin (IRE) *Marcus Tregoning* 73
2 b c Tamayuz Arsheef (USA) (Hard Spun (USA))
6640[4]◆

Modular Magic *David Barron* 71
2 b g Swiss Spirit Lucy Parsons (IRE) (Thousand Words)
(7308)

Mo Emmad Ali (IRE) *Kevin Ryan* 66
3 b g No Nay Never(USA) Special Assignment (USA) (Lemon Drop Kid (USA))
1764[10] 3569[10]

Mofaaji *Simon Crisford* 59
3 ch g Animal Kingdom(USA) My Dubai (IRE) (Dubai Millennium)
4421[3] 6198[3]

Moftris *William Haggas* a58 76
3 b g Iffraaj Baheeja (Dubawi (IRE))
978[3] 1293[5] 4452[3]◆ 5394[10] 5985[3]◆

Moghram (IRE) *Marcus Tregoning* 69
3 b g Sir Percy Red Blossom (USA) (Silver Hawk (USA))
2142[8] 2731[2] 3699[8] 4231[10]

Mo Green (FR) *W Gulcher* a56 55
9 b g Marchand De Sable(USA) Ma Belle Tef (FR) (Medaaly)
5410a[7]

Mogsy (IRE) *Tom Dascombe* a58 83
3 br g Dandy Man(IRE) Dictatrice (FR) (Anabaa (USA))
3067[6] 4196[6] 5128[2] 6177[2] (7442) 8101[10]

Mogul *A P O'Brien* a109 110
2 b c Galileo(IRE) Shastye (IRE) (Danehill (USA))
(7217a) 8716[4]◆

Mohaather *Marcus Tregoning* 114
3 b c Showcasing Roodeye (Inchinor)
(1752) 8334[5]

Mohareb *Michael Appleby* a96 73
3 b g Delegator Irrational (Kyllachy)
1886[13] 2634[4] 8472[2] (8695) (9203) 9404[3] 9517[2] (9669)

Mohawk (IRE) *A P O'Brien* 114
3 b c Galileo(IRE) Empowering (IRE) (Encosta De Lago (AUS))
2558[2] 3104a[8] 3390a[7] (5112a) 7253a[3] (Dead)

Mohican Heights (IRE)
David Simcock 100
2 ch c Australia Mohican Princess (Shirley Heights)
(6417)◆

Mohogany *Tom Clover* a34 53
3 b g Foxwedge(AUS) Jadeamie (Raven's Pass (USA))
2238[9] 2798[13]

Mohtarrif (IRE) *Marcus Tregoning* a78 41
3 b g Cape Cross(IRE) Sharedah (IRE) (Pivotal)
979[4] (1293)◆ 4304[8]

Mojambo (IRE)
Stephen Michael Hanlon a56 50
4 ch m Zoffany(IRE) Mojita (IRE) (Montjeu (IRE))
8404[7] (9446) 9479[2]

Mojano (FR) *S Richter* 85
3 ch c Denon(USA) Metaline (FR) (Dr Fong (USA))
2758a[8] 4707a[13]

Mojave *Roger Charlton* a78 78
3 b g Dream Ahead(USA) Desert Image (Beat Hollow)
2690[2] 6345[2] 6687[2] (7177) 8298[10]

Mojito (IRE) *William Haggas* a80 113
5 b g Requinto(IRE) Narva (USA) (Grand Slam (USA))
(4666) 5610[6]

Mojo Boy (FR) *Gerald Geisler* a44 75
4 b g Pedro The Great(USA) Reine Amandine (FR) (Marignan (USA))
2182a[7]

Mokaatil *Ian Williams* a90 92
4 br g Lethal Force(IRE) Moonlit Garden (IRE) (Exceed And Excel (AUS))
470[6] 837[5] (1814) 1946[3] 2557[4] 3344[14] 4379[9] 5530[3] 5661[13] 5746[2] (6565) 6953[11] 9088[4] 9478[8] 9549[4]

Mokammal *Sir Michael Stoute* a68 91
3 b g Mukhadram My Inspiration (IRE) (Invincible Spirit (IRE))
2216[3] (3266) (4321) 5861[6]

Mokarris (USA) *Simon Crisford* a100 45
5 b h More Than Ready(USA) Limonar (IRE) (Street Cry (IRE))
563[4]◆ 1412[8]

Mokhalad *Damian Joseph English* a68 88
6 ch g Dubawi(IRE) Model Queen (USA) (Kingmambo (USA))
6693a[22] 7222a[13]

Mokuba (IRE) *Brian Meehan* a58 42
3 b c Helmet(AUS) Rocking Horse (Rock Of Gibraltar (IRE))
32[4]

Molaaheth *Alexandra Dunn* a63 74
3 b g Heeraat(IRE) All Fur Coat (Multiplex)
1337[7]◆ 2098[2] 4010[5] 4507[8] 5622[8] (6801)

Molatham *Roger Varian* 104
2 ch c Night Of Thunder(IRE) Cantal (Pivotal)
5367[2] (6424) (7150) 8112[4]

Molinari (IRE) *William Muir* 61
2 gr c Mastercraftsman(IRE) Moon Empress (FR) (Rainbow Quest (USA))
7235[6]◆ 7755[12] 8028[5]

Molino (FR) *C Ferland* a65
2 b c Makfi Parma (FR) (Intikhab (USA))
6386a[3]

Molivaliente (USA) *John Best* a82
3 ro c The Factor(USA) Bee Brave (Rail Link)
2550[2]◆ (4793) 8017[10]

Moll Davis (IRE) *George Scott* a74 97
3 b f Kingman Stupendous Miss (USA) (Dynaformer (USA))
2102[5] 2713[4] 3495[3] 4110[3] (4913)◆ 5545[5] (6209)◆ 7347[10] 8580a[3]

Molliana *Neil Mulholland* a46 49
4 b m Olden Times The Screamer (IRE) (Insan (USA))
(2673a) 3174a[S] (3642a) (4175a) (5233) (6008a) (6554a)

Molls Memory *Ed Walker* a76 94
4 ch m Helmet(AUS) Bright Moll (Mind Games)
1760[2] (2611) (3945) 5504[9] 6396[4] 6922[2] 7613[12] (8521)

Molly Blake *Clive Cox* a59 50
3 b f Bated Breath Park Melody (IRE) (Refuse To Bend (IRE))
2204[12] 5044[4] 6181[7] 7172[4] 7557[3] 7757[14] 8119[5]

Molly King (GER) *V B Buda* a53 53
6 rg h Lando(GER) Molly Maxima (GER) (Big Shuffle (USA))
8375a[11]

Molly Mai *Philip McBride* a64 68
3 b f Mayson Handsome Molly (Halling (USA))
798[8] 1140[8] 1567[3] (2482)◆ 2760[7] 3779[4] 4454[4] 5272[4] 6101[6] 7452[8] 8713[7]

Mollys Best (FR) *Katerina Berthier* 41
5 b g Elusive City(USA) Bubbly Molly (FR) (Wagon Master (FR))
6006a[13]

Molly's Game *David Elsworth* a47 68
3 b f Heeraat(IRE) Molly Marie (IRE) (Fasliyev (USA))
2762[5] 3273[7] 4286[3] 5315[4] 7157[7] 8653[5]

Molly Shaw *Chris Wall*
2 b f Helmet(AUS) Paradise Isle (Bahamian Bounty)
8431[9]

Molotov (IRE) *Jamie Osborne* 59
3 ch g No Nay Never(USA) Brigids Cross (IRE) (Sadler's Wells (USA))
2210[10] 3768[4] 4189[4] 4931[8] 5784[10]

Molten Lava (IRE) *Steve Gollings* a58 49
7 b g Rock Of Gibraltar(IRE) Skehana (IRE) (Mukaddamah (USA))
80[2] 210[6] 829[10] 1339[2] 1527[3] 2112[6] 2972[8] 7960[7] 8405[9] 8942[7] 9282[6] 9456[4]

Momentarily *Mick Channon* a62 58
4 b m Cityscape Firebelly (Nicolotte)
3572[7] 4028[7] 4473[3] 4751[4]

Moment Of Hope (IRE)
David Simcock a78 81
3 b f Casamento(IRE) Hikayati (IRE) (Iffraaj)
(1351) 2838[5] (4459) 5545[4] 6223[6]

Moment Of Peace *Christine Dunnett* a52 16
2 b g Gregorian(IRE) Penny's Pearl (IRE) (Royal Applause)
8203[10] 8455[12]

Moment Of Silence (IRE)
Saeed bin Suroor a93
3 b f Slade Power(IRE) Sleeping Beauty (IRE) (Oasis Dream)
7655[4] 8497[2]◆ (9010)

Moments Linger (IRE) *J S Bolger* a80 81
2 b f Dawn Approach(IRE) Vocal Nation (IRE) (Vocalised (USA))
2491a[5]

Momentum *Antony Brittain* a58
2 b f Swiss Spirit Valiantly (Anabaa (USA))
7580[5] 8084[7] 8816[9]

Momentum Swing *Robert Cowell* a40
2 br g Dark Angel(IRE) Winning Express (IRE) (Camacho)
6047[6]

Momkin (IRE) *Roger Charlton* 110
3 b c Bated Breath Contradict (Raven's Pass (USA))
1854[2] 2411[10] 4092[6] 4850[2] 5609[3] 6508[2] 7255a[5]

Momtalik (USA) *Derek Shaw* a71 76
4 b g Point Of Entry(USA) Sacred Feather (USA) (Carson City (USA))
1331[3] 2185[5] 8842[2] 9180[9] 9443[13] 9559[10]

Monaadhil (IRE) *Marcus Tregoning* a86 89
5 b g Dark Angel(IRE) Urban Daydream (IRE) (Oasis Dream)
3496[5] 4300[5] 5267[4]

Monaafasah (IRE)
Marcus Tregoning 83
3 bb f Cape Cross(IRE) Salhooda (IRE) (Nayef (USA))
2771[4] (4234) 7525[3]

Monadante *John Butler* a48 40
3 b g Kyllachy Roslea Lady (IRE) (Alhaarth (IRE))
1332[14]

Mona Lisa's Smile (USA)
A P O'Brien a56 71
3 b f War Front(USA) Imagine (IRE) (Sadler's Wells (USA))
2445[5] 2661a[10] 5075a[11] 5325a[13]

Monarch Maid *Peter Hiatt* a50 53
8 b m Captain Gerrard(IRE) Orange Lily (Royal Applause)
244[3] 293[2] 402[4] 919[6] 1038[3] (5393) 5884[2] 6126[2] 6321[4] 6794[4] 7022[5]

Monarch Of Egypt (USA)
A P O'Brien 114
2 b c American Pharoah(USA) Up (IRE) (Galileo (IRE))
4413a[2] 5922a[2] 7693[8] 8113[5]

Mon Choix *Andrew Balding* 68
2 b g Pivotal Privacy Order (Azamour (IRE))
4252[7] 6669[10] 7661[5]

Mondain *Mark Johnston* a89 92
3 ch g Dubawi(IRE) Mondalay (Monsun (GER))
1510[3] 1972[3] (4031) (4491) 4928[3] 5127[2] (5391)◆ 5566[5] 5943[5] 6955[5] 8098[8]

Monde Chat Luna (JPN)
Hiroo Shimizu a73 103
8 b h Neo Universe(JPN) Wind In Her Hair (IRE) (Alzao (USA))
46a[12] 7293a[4]

Moneta *Ronald Harris* a56 58
3 b f Kodiac Money Note (Librettist (USA))
1287[2] 1838[7] 2356[4] 2904[4] 3189[8] 3964[10] 5044[3] 6018[11] 7573[12] 8119[9] 8469[6] 8697[3] (9034) 9169[5] 9335[8]

Money Back (FR) *F Vermeulen* a68 66
3 b f Never On Sunday(FR) Relais D'Aumale (Rainbow Quest (USA))
5329a[6] 6789a[6]

Moneyball *Keith Dalgleish* a34 5
2 b f Swiss Spirit Lady Estella (IRE) (Equiano (FR))
1923[8] 3245[15] 3717[7]

Mon Frere (IRE)
Sir Mark Prescott Bt a80 58
3 b g Pour Moi(IRE) Sistine (Dubai Destination (USA))
3446[5] 5053[4] (5648) (6115) 6392[2]

Mongolia *Michael Appleby* a63 59
3 b f Maxios Bianca De Medici (Medicean)
1287[8] 1725[3] 1935[2] 2719[3] 3348[3] 3888[8] 6531[6] 7270[6] 7873[3]◆ (8269) 8551[2]

Mongolian Groom (USA)
Enebish Ganbat a119 72
4 bb g Hightail(USA) Bourbonesque (USA) (Dynaformer (USA))
8777a[P] (Dead)

Moni (FR) *S Culin* a74 95
3 ch g Confuchias(IRE) Nimohe (FR) (Excellent Art)
7886a[6]

Monica Sheriff *William Haggas* a89 107
3 b f Lawman(FR) Require (Montjeu (IRE))
2770[9] (3553) (6043)◆ (6661)◆ (7566) (8581a)

Monks Stand (USA) *John Mackie* a86 74
5 b g More Than Ready(USA) Return The Jewel (USA) (Broken Vow (USA))
2[9]

Monogamy *Martyn Meade* a26 47
3 bg f Poet's Voice White Wedding (IRE) (Green Desert (USA))
2087[10] 7772[9]

Monoski (USA) *Mark Johnston* 98
2 b c Street Boss(USA) Wipe Out (USA) (Hard Spun (USA))
2747[2]◆ (3055)◆ 3949[16] 4441[3] 5707[3] 6356[4] 7245a[4] 7614[4]

Monoxide *Martyn Meade* a88 75
4 b g Galileo(IRE) Breathe (FR) (Ocean Of Wisdom (USA))
2022[5] 6211[9]

Mon Paris (FR) *Edouard Thueux* a77 56
4 b g Elusive City(USA) Queen Lyric (FR) (King's Best (USA))
992a[2]

Monsaraz *James Given* a55
2 b c Cityscape Rattleyourjewellery (Royal Applause)
8424[11] 8889[7] 9181[13]

Monsieur Croco (FR)
Mlle Y Vollmer 113
4 b g Croco Rouge(IRE) Nana Desir (FR) (Dananeyev (FR))
8378a[5]

Monsieur Fox *Lydia Richards* a60 59
4 b g Foxwedge(AUS) Demoiselle Bond (Monsieur Bond (IRE))
288[3] 923[9] 1215[2]◆ 4453[11] 5309[11] 6152[10] 8224[13]

Monsieur Jimmy *Brian Ellison* a78 61
7 ch g Monsieur Bond(IRE) Artistic License (IRE) (Chevalier (IRE))
4329[8] 5434[11] 5787[13] 7088a[10]

Monsieur Lambrays *Tom Clover* a83 79
3 b g Champs Elysees Windermere Island (Cadeaux Genereux)
1690[7] 2406[7] 2914[2] 4339[3] 5355[4] 5778[3] (6687) (7915) 8655[3]

Monsieur Mel *Andre Hermans* a20
5 b g Monsieur Bond(IRE) Melandre (Lujain (USA))
9483a[14]

Monsieur Noir *Roger Varian* 85
3 b g Shamardal(USA) Night Frolic (Night Shift (USA))
3090[4] 4654[5] (5448) 6413[4] 7362[4]

Monsieur Piquer (FR) *K R Burke* a56 53
3 ch g French Fifteen(FR) Madeenh (FR) (Pivotal)
1140[6] 1720[11] 1825[4] 2152[6] 3204[4] 3721[6] 4488[2]

Monsieur Vic (FR) *Jessica Long* 64
2 gr c Lawman(FR) Jeune Et Jolie (IRE) (Verglas (IRE))
7495a[12]

Mons Star (IRE) *Saeed bin Suroor* a89 84
3 b c Sea The Stars(IRE) Something Mon (USA) (Maria's Mon (USA))
1856[4]◆ 2524[5] (9091) (Dead)

Montalvan (IRE) *Roger Fell* a37 63
3 ch g Lope De Vega(IRE) Shermeen (IRE) (Desert Style (IRE))
2197[15] 2477[9] 3159[7] 4033[4] 4328[2] 4731[2] (5202) 5308[4] 6070[7] 6608[7] 7050[4] 7703[6] 8264[6]

Montaly *Andrew Balding* a82 103
8 b g Yeats(IRE) Le Badie (IRE) (Spectrum (IRE))
2575[13]

Montanari *Andrew Balding* 80
2 ch c Sea The Moon(GER) Pax Aeterna (USA) (War Front (USA))
4091[12] 6832[2]

Montatham *William Haggas* a93 93
3 gr g Showcasing Eastern Destiny (Dubai Destination (USA))
(6177)◆ (6701)◆ 7349[3] 8184[2]◆ 9053[4]

Montather (IRE) *Roger Varian* a84
2 ch c Dubawi(IRE) Lanansaak (IRE) (Zamindar (USA))
(9156)

Monte Cinto (IRE) *Louis Baudron* a74 74
2 b c Make Believe Bailonguera (ARG) (Southern Halo (USA))
5642a[8]

Montelimar *Andrew Crook* 42
4 b m Raven's Pass(USA) Mascarene (USA) (Empire Maker (USA))
7543[4] 8398[7] 8662[3] 9336[11]

Monteverdi (FR) *G Botti* a87 92
6 b g Kyllachy West Of Saturn (USA) (Gone West (USA))
2955a[11]

Montfiquet (FR) *N Caullery* a62 63
3 b g Le Havre(IRE) Kilava (FR) (Invincible Spirit (IRE))
5538a[8] 7138a[12]

Montgaroult (FR) *B De Montzey* a81 66
4 b g Air Chief Marshal(IRE) Foresta (FR) (Forestier (FR))
2264a[4]

Montilien (FR) *X Thomas-Demeaulte* 55
3 b g Shamalgan(FR) Miss Louise (FR) (Country Reel (USA))
3139a[7]

Montina (FR) *Werner Glanz* 75
5 b m Soldier Of Fortune(IRE) Montanarella (GER) (Zieten (USA))
6031a[4] 6651a[8]

Mont Kiara (FR) *Simon Dow* a76 64
6 b g Kendargent(FR) Xaarienne (Xaar)
(253) 564[9] 763[5] 1061[7] 1357[8] 2611[10] 3188[4] 5050[7] 5503[11] 8704[9] (9248) 9420[10] 9629[2]

Mont Kinabalu (IRE) *Kevin Ryan* a77 79
4 b g Society Rock(IRE) Startori (Vettori (IRE))
209[5] 350[4] 812[8] 1099[7] (1659) 1948[2] 2480[6] 2842[10] 3356[4] 3957[7] 4445[2]◆

Mont Plaza (FR) *J Reynier* a77 80
4 ch h Mount Nelson Plaza Mayor (FR) (Kyllachy)
1391a[9]

Mont Royal (FR) *Ollie Pears* a54 64
5 gr g Naaqoos Take Blood (FR) (Take Risks (FR))
1398[7] 2056[9] 3162[12] 3960[6]

Montsarrat (IRE) *S bin Ghadayer* a102 96
6 br g Poet's Voice Flying Flag (IRE) (Entrepreneur)
172a[7] 396a[2]◆ 1114a[9]

Montviette (FR) *J-C Rouget* 102
3 bb f Le Havre(IRE) Lady Meydan (FR) (American Post)
1795a[7] 3121a[7] 4431a[6]

Monty (FR) *A De Royer-Dupre* 98
4 b g Motivator Antebellum (FR) (Anabaa (USA))
(9014a)

Monty Saga (FR) *D Chenu* 73
3 b g Toni Blue(FR) Dolce Bambina (FR) (Sagacity (FR))
2519a[3]

Montys Angel (IRE) *John Bridger* a37 48
9 b m Definite Article Montys Bank (IRE) (Montelimar (USA))
7202[9] 7558[10] 8246[4] 8523[3]

Montys Inn (IRE) *Richard Hannon* a68
3 b g Kodiac Bailonguera (ARG) (Southern Halo (USA))
8653[4] 9171[4] 9475[6]

Monumental Man *Jamie Osborne* a70 73
10 b g Vital Equine(IRE) Spark Up (Lahib (USA))
347[3] 790[3] 883[3] 1016[4] 1209[7] 5959[6] 7086a[5]

Monya (IRE) *Charles Hills* a67
3 gr f Dark Angel(IRE) Bridal Dance (IRE) (Danehill Dancer (IRE))
9475[3]◆

Monza (IRE) *Bent Olsen* 96
4 bb m Footstepsinthesand Carini (Vettori (IRE))
283a[6] 728a[6] 7497a[13]

Monzino (USA) *Michael Chapman* a21 1
11 bb g More Than Ready(USA) Tasso's Magic Roo (USA) (Tasso (USA))
5043[7] 6173[9] 7545[11]

Mood For Mischief *James Bennett* a65 52
4 b g Nathaniel(IRE) Tina's Spirit (IRE) (Invincible Spirit (IRE))
135[6] 385[2] 731[4] 1024[3] 1497[6] 1826[8] 2695[11] 3015[7] 4251[6] 4796[6] 5053[8] 6853[7]

Moolhim (FR) *Simon Crisford* a77 78
2 b c Siyouni(FR) Melbourne Shuffle (USA) (Street Cry (IRE))
4117[3] 4611[3] (5940) 6728[7]

Mooltazem (IRE) *Michael Dods* a51 69
5 b g Elzaam(AUS) Whisper Dance (USA) (Stravinsky (USA))
1896[8] 2370[RR] 3180[RR]

Moomba (IRE) *Amanda Perrett* a65
2 ch c Australia Beatrice Aurore (IRE) (Danehill Dancer (IRE))
9208[8]

Moon Artist (FR) *Michael Blanshard* a43 43
3 b f Archipenko(USA) Moonavvara (IRE) (Sadler's Wells (USA))
765[6] 2011[5] 2343[13] 4400[5] 4931[10] 5842[4] 6569[8] 7027[7] 7376[9] 8416[9] 9456[9]

Moonbi Creek (IRE) *Stella Barclay* a50 46
12 b g Fasliyev(USA) Moonbi Range (IRE) (Nordico (USA))
180[10] 273[5] 530[6] 613[5]

Moondance *Gary Moore* a65 59
2 b f Mayson Amontillado (IRE) (Pastoral Pursuits)
5588[15] 7124[2] 7570[7] 7980[6] 9060[11] (9212)

Moongazer *Charles Hills* a76 32
3 br f Kuroshio(AUS) Sonnellino (Singspiel (IRE))
(438) 1033[2] 1495[3] 5030[9] 8305[14]

Moonhak Chief (USA)
Kim Soon Keun a113
4 bb h Pioneerof The Nile(USA) Talullah Lula (USA) (Old Trieste (USA))
(7011a)

Moon King (FR) *Ralph Beckett* a61 96
3 br g Sea The Moon(GER) Maraba (IRE) (Danehill Dancer (IRE))
(2150) (2511) (3474) (3729) (4906) 6955[4] 8098[6]

Moonlight Escapade *John Quinn* a38 47
3 ch g Cityscape Marmalade Moon (Shamardal (USA))
4785[14]

Moonlighting *Kevin Ryan* 58
2 gr f Hot Streak(IRE) Blue Moon (Trade Fair)
3196[11] 3919[2] 4516[4]

Moonlight In Japan (FR)
Andrea Marcialis a46 47
3 gr g Rajsaman(FR) Moonlight Kiss (IRE) (Verglas (IRE))
2090a[4]

Moonlight In Paris (IRE)
John Gosden 78
2 b f Camelot Malayan Mist (IRE) (Dansili)
(8855)

Moonlight Man (GER) *Markus Klug* 105
3 rg c Reliable Man Moonlight Symphony (GER) (Pentire)
2163a[2] 3385a[5] 4707a[7]

Moonlightnavigator (USA)
John Quinn a52 70
7 br g Henrythenavigator(USA) Victorica (USA) (Exbourne (USA))
2187[8]

Moonlight Shadow *N Caullery* a58 50
2 gr c Fountain Of Youth(IRE) Lone Angel (IRE) (Dark Angel (IRE))
9605a[11]

Moonlight Spirit (IRE)
Charlie Appleby a81 109
3 b c Dubawi(IRE) Moonsail (Monsun (GER))
(967) (2110)◆ 3120a[3] 3984[4] (6773a) 7927a[2]

Moonlit Sands (IRE) *Brian Ellison* a44 61
4 b m Footstepsinthesand Dusty Moon (Dr Fong (USA))
5018[7]◆ 5244[9] (5722) 6099[6] 6699[11] 7210[5] 7590[6] 8637[3] 8925[13]

Moonlit Sea *Pat Phelan* a67 48
3 b g Sea The Moon(GER) Angeleno (IRE) (Belong To Me (USA))
358[7] 615[4] 1173[8] 1825[12] 4834[11]

Moon Of Baroda *Charles Hills* a81 78
4 gr g Dubawi(IRE) Millennium Star (IRE) (High Chaparral (IRE))
84[4] (480) 700[4] 1022[4] 2080[6] 4483[10]

Moon Of Love (IRE) *Richard Fahey* a83 83
2 b f Kodiac Moon Club (IRE) (Red Clubs (IRE))
3564[3]◆ 4048[24] 6374[10] (6979) 7692[10] 9162[3]

Moonoon (FR) *C Ferland* 104
3 ch f Sea The Moon(GER) Cloon (USA) (Lure (USA))
4429a[5] 8790a[2]

Moon Power *K R Burke* 47
2 b f Exceed And Excel(AUS) Shepherdia (IRE) (Pivotal)
6254[4]◆

Moonracer (FR) *S Smrczek* a90 93
4 b h Linngari(IRE) Auto Rouge (IRE) (Testa Rossa (AUS))
2002a[2]

Moonraker *Michael Appleby* a92 87
7 ch g Starspangledbanner(AUS) Licence To Thrill (Wolfhound (USA))
(3) 389[3] (588) 786[8] 4331[13] 4995[3] 5252[4] 5504[13] 6954[12] 7321[6] 7913[10] 8317[6] 8867[9] 9030[9] 9562[4] (9645)

Moonshine Mo *Kevin Frost* 56
2 b g Pastoral Pursuits Topflight Princess (Cockney Rebel (IRE))
3335[7] 5780[11]

Moonshiner (GER)
Jean-Pierre Carvalho 105
6 ch h Adlerflug(GER) Montezuma (GER) (Monsun (GER))
2666a[3] 7249a[3] 8171a[5]

Moon Song *Clive Cox* a77 81
4 gr m Lethal Force(IRE) West Of The Moon (Pivotal)
36[6]

Moontide (IRE) *J S Moore* a42 64
2 ch g Society Rock(IRE) Independent Girl (IRE) (Bachelor Duke (USA))
3405[4] 4114[10] 4679a[3] 5286a[7] 5759a[7] 7768[6] 8824[11]

Moon Trouble (IRE)
Michael Appleby a96 84
6 ch g Lope De Vega(IRE) Shake The Moon (GER) (Loup Solitaire (USA))
1421[6] 1734[6] 2402[8] 3301[4] (3492) 4521[6] 8607[6] 9088[11] 9389[6] 9562[6]

Moorland Spirit (IRE)
Archie Watson a66 64
2 ch f Kyllachy Dutch Courage (Dutch Art)
5838[3] 6118[10] 6532[3] 7277[4] 8286[3]

Mooroverthebridge *Grace Harris* a65 44
5 b m Avonbridge Spennymoor (IRE) (Exceed And Excel (AUS))
(315) 467[4] 701[9] 1820[6] 2206[3] 2483[5] 2729[U] 3089[4] 4494[6] 4870[8] 6526[3] 7236[13] 8123[4] 8469[11]

Moor Top *Jennie Candlish* 42
3 b g Garswood Light Hearted (Green Desert (USA))
2099[9] 2941[10]

Moosmee (IRE) *William Haggas* a78 82
2 br c Society Rock(IRE) Tara Too (IRE) (Danetime (IRE))
6891[5] (8026) 8865[4] 9195[7]

Mootasadir *Hugo Palmer* a116 102
4 b h Dansili Mahbooba (AUS) (Galileo (IRE))
(1017) (1420)◆ 2807[6] 3561a[7] 4382[16] 6962[2] 7668a[7]

Mooteram (IRE) *Mick Channon* 22
3 br f Moohaajim(IRE) Easee On (IRE) (Hawk Wing (USA))
1740[16] 2103[9]

Moqarrab (USA) *M Al Mheiri* a104 58
4 b g Speightstown(USA) Grosse Pointe Anne (USA) (Silver Deputy (CAN))
842a[2]◆ 1112a[11]

Moqarrar (USA) *E Charpy* a94 83
4 gr g Exchange Rate(USA) Time To Enjoy (USA) (Distorted Humor (USA))
513a[7] 957a[7]

Moqtarreb *Roger Varian* 94
3 b g Kingman Elshaadin (Dalakhani (IRE))
2802[2] 3340[3] (4121) 4851[4]

Moraawed *Roger Varian* a76 92
3 b g Swiss Spirit Hot Secret (Sakhee's Secret)
1728[2] (2078)◆ 2835[4] 3865[10] (5319) 6451[6] 7142[7]

Morando (FR) *Andrew Balding* 119
6 gr g Kendargent(FR) Moranda (FR) (Indian Rocket)
(2560) 3314[8] 4093[4] 5414[8] 6213[2] (7890)◆

Mordin (IRE) *Simon Crisford* a94 111
5 b g Invincible Spirit(IRE) Bryanstown (IRE) (Galileo (IRE))
(2105) 3343[5] 3987[10] 4935[13] 5657[3] 6725[5] 7694[4]

Mordred (IRE) *Richard Hannon* a79 91
3 b c Camelot Endure (IRE) (Green Desert (USA))
1835[5] 2414[9] 4016[13] 4851[6] 5614[4] 6021[2] 7436[8] 7727[5] 8725[9] 9050[11]

More Buck's (IRE) *Peter Bowen* 62
9 ch g Presenting Buck's Blue (FR) (Epervier Bleu)
4234[4]

More Harry *Clare Ellam*
4 b g Aussie Rules(USA) Native Ring (FR) (Bering)
160[9] 504[13] 1146[10] 3298[P] 5631[11]

Moremi (FR) *D Guillemin* 71
2 ch c Kheleyf(USA) Mephala (FR) (Muhaymin (USA))
(7641a)

More No Never (GER)
Jean-Pierre Carvalho 68
2 b c No Nay Never(USA) Magali (GER) (Monsun (GER))
7937a[5]

More Salutes (IRE)
Michael Attwater a58 30
4 b g Acclamation Champion Place (Compton Place)
243[8] 701[5]◆ 925[7] 1353[5] 1933[9] 4378[12] 5960[5] 6838[6]

More Than A Prince
Richard Hannon a71 79
2 b c Oasis Dream La Petite Reine (Galileo (IRE))
6219[4] 6708[5] 7162[7] 7548[5] (7980)◆

More Than Likely *Richard Hughes* a64 77
3 b f Coach House(IRE) Moss Likely (IRE) (Clodovil (IRE))
2997[7] 3427[2]◆ 4422[4] 5015[2] 5251[4] (6602) 7178[3] 7568[7] 8668[2]

More Than Love *Tim Easterby* a62 26
2 b g Kitten's Joy(USA) He Loves Me More (USA) (More Than Ready (USA))
7000[8]◆ 7586[11] 8503[6]

More Than More (USA)
James Fanshawe a68 40
4 b m More Than Ready(USA) Donamour (USA) (Langfuhr (CAN))
1586[10]

Moretti (IRE) *Les Eyre* a52 60
4 b m Requinto(IRE) Hassaya (IRE) (King's Best (USA))
969[6] 3057[7] 3414[3] (6131) (6518)

Morgan Le Faye *A Fabre* 111
5 b m Shamardal(USA) Molly Malone (FR) (Lomitas)
(1627a) (2167a) (3138a) 4430a[6]

Morgenstern (FR) *D Windrif* a53 59
2 b c Sommerabend Pink And Red (USA) (Red Ransom (USA))
3171a[6] 5763a[3] 6384a[10]

Morisco (IRE) *Tom Dascombe* a77 94
2 b g Requinto(IRE) Mattinata (Tiger Hill (IRE))
4611[5] (5433) 6352[5] (7361)

Morlaix *David Simcock* a69
2 b g Mayson Estemaala (IRE) (Cape Cross (IRE))
8058[8] 8700[4]◆ 9063[5]

Morley Gunner (IRE) *S Donohoe* a43 47
4 b g Elzaam(AUS) Lovingit (IRE) (Fasliyev (USA))
2681[7] 2963[14] 3718[10] 4690[9] 5939[7]

Morning Basma (FR) *E J O'Neill* 76
3 ch f Born To Sea(IRE) La Ville Lumiere (USA) (Rahy (USA))
1512a[3] 3713a[2] 4204a[2]

Morning Dew (FR) *N Caullery* 95
3 b f Dabirsim(FR) Fancy Diamond (GER) (Ransom O'War (USA))
3121a[9] 3905a[16]

Morning Duel (IRE) *David O'Meara* 79
3 ch g Dawn Approach(IRE) Days Of Summer (IRE) (Bachelor Duke (USA))
3517[3] 3932[3] 4732[2] 5690[7] 6582[3] (6823)

Morning Shadow *Mark Johnston* a71
2 ch f New Approach(IRE) Elle Shade (Shamardal (USA))
9197[2] 9327[9]

Morning Wonder (IRE) *Kevin Ryan* a98 99
4 ch g Dawn Approach(IRE) Mount Elbrus (Barathea (IRE))
2786[7] 3726[10]

Morpho Blue (IRE)
Mrs John Harrington a85 91
3 b f Mastercraftsman(IRE) Butterfly Blue (IRE) (Sadler's Wells (USA))
5075a[8] 5369[8] 6646a[11] 7222a[12]

Morro Castle *Jamie Osborne* a37
3 b g Havana Gold(IRE) Cultured Pride (IRE) (King's Best (USA))
401[7]

Morticia *Keith Dalgleish* 79
4 b m Dandy Man(IRE) Diksie Dancer (Diktat)
4001[7] 4278[8]

Mortirolo (FR) *Andrea Marcialis* a65 75
3 b g Dream Ahead(USA) Diena (FR) (Librettist (USA))
217a[8] 4959a[2] 6061a[2]

Mosakhar *Ollie Pears* a80
3 b g Dawn Approach(IRE) Min Banat Alreeh (IRE) (Oasis Dream)
8529[3] (8842)

Moseeb (IRE) *A bin Harmash*
4 b g Invincible Spirit(IRE) Boastful (IRE) (Clodovil (IRE))
997[14]

Mo See Cal (USA) *Peter Miller* a101
4 rg m Uncle Mo(USA) Do Dat Blues (USA) (Lydgate (USA))
8775a[6]

Moses (FR) *Mario Hofer* a85 80
4 b g Dabirsim(FR) Mon Zamin (IRE) (Zamindar (USA))
1449a[14]

Moshaher (USA) *Doug Watson* a84
3 b g Goldencents(USA) Miss Valiant (USA) (Valiant Nature (USA))
636a[6] 1110a[10]

Mosseyb (IRE) *Paul Midgley* a52 52
4 b g Epaulette(AUS) Allegrissimo (IRE) (Redback)
1722[12] 3656[2] 4148[6]

Moss Gill (IRE) *James Bethell* a73 105
3 b g No Nay Never(USA) Sharaarah (IRE) (Oasis Dream)
1236[2] 2377[2] 2810[2]◆ (3339) (4008)◆ 4847[2] 6476[2] (8099) 8340[9]

Moss 'N' Dale (NZ) *Peter Gelagotis* 104
6 b g Castledale(IRE) Hot 'N' Moss (NZ) (Strategic Image (AUS))
8360a[6] 9016a[10]

Mossy's Lodge *Rebecca Menzies* a63 50
6 b m Royal Applause Tee Cee (Lion Cavern (USA))
348[5] 462[7] 911[2] 912[9] 1399[11] 1769[9]
Mostahel *Paul Midgley* a70 72
5 b g Acclamation Entente Cordiale (IRE) (Ela-Mana-Mou (IRE))
1654[11] 2201[10] 2824[12] 4660[3] 6461[3] 6972[8] 7418[5] 8181[8]
Mostaqel (IRE) *Richard Hannon* 43
2 b g Society Rock(IRE) Sunny Days (IRE) (Areion (GER))
7521[11]
Mostawaa *Heather Main* a87 85
3 ch g Poet's Voice Mumtaza (Nayef (USA))
6315[4] 7191[5] 7863[7] 8411[5] 9096[10]
Most Celebrated (IRE)
Neil Mulholland a38 89
6 b g New Approach(IRE) Pietra Santa (FR) (Acclamation)
7185[13]
Most Empowered (IRE)
Enrique Leon Penate a60 85
5 ch m Soldier Of Fortune(IRE) Sirenita (IRE) (Mull Of Kintyre (USA))
8375a[5]
Mostly *John Gosden* 78
2 b f Makfi Montare (IRE) (Montjeu (IRE))
8458[2]
Motafaawit (IRE) *Richard Hannon* a89 108
3 bb g Intikhab(USA) Rayaheen (Nayef (USA))
(2054) (2570) 4016[16] 4850[5] 6207[8]
Motagally *Charles Hills* a96 86
3 b g Swiss Spirit Gilt Linked (Compton Place)
2008[3] 2567[5] 4123[5] 5685[4] 6108[3] 6930[4] (7268) (7913)◆
Motahassen (IRE) *Declan Carroll* a66 64
5 br g Lonhro(AUS) Journalist (IRE) (Night Shift (USA))
1858[7] 2202[6] 2819[4] 3163[11] (3547) 3681[4] 4109[5] 4914[11] 6055[4] 7070[6] 7830[10] (9225)◆ 9331[3]
Motajaasid (IRE) *P Monfort* a74 81
4 b g Harbour Watch(IRE) Cape Joy (IRE) (Cape Cross (IRE))
856[2] 962[8] 1526[3]◆ 2273[7] (3018) 3701[6] 4455[4] 5643a[11]
Motakhayyel *Richard Hannon* a80 101
3 b c Heeraat(IRE) Virtuality (USA) (Elusive Quality (USA))
(3306)◆ 4348[2] (4919) 5412[6]
Motamarris (IRE) *F Head* a88 113
3 b c Le Havre(IRE) Thamarat (Anabaa (USA))
3390a[3]◆
Motamayiz *Roger Varian* a59 56
2 b g Charm Spirit(IRE) Chanterelle (FR) (Trempolino (USA))
8516[7] 9043[6] 9195[9]
Motaraabet *Owen Burrows* a70 75
4 b g Dansili Hawaafez (Nayef (USA))
1989[4] 2999[3] 4661[4]◆
Motarajel *F Rohaut* a71 78
2 b c Camacho Vereri Senes (Nayef (USA))
8508a[8]
Motawaafeq (FR) *Michael Appleby* a74 78
3 b c Wootton Bassett Crossed Fingers (IRE) (Cape Cross (IRE))
(9475) 9628[11]
Motawaazy *Roger Fell*
3 b g Kingman Shimah (USA) (Storm Cat (USA))
9644[8]
Motawaj *Roger Varian* a102 96
3 b g Dubawi(IRE) Tantshi (IRE) (Invincible Spirit (IRE))
4306[3]◆ (4788)◆ (5320)◆ 5963[6] 6964[3]
Moteo (IRE) *John M Oxx* a84 98
4 gr m Teofilo(IRE) Modeeroch (IRE) (Mozart (IRE))
2451a[2] 3820a[3] 4856a[2] 6239a[4] 7717a[4] 8710[10]
Motfael (IRE) *Owen Burrows* a85 87
3 b c Invincible Spirit(IRE) Fidelite (IRE) (In The Wings)
3463[4] 5650[3] (6399) 7191[7]
Mother Brown *Bill Turner* 10
3 ch f Coach House(IRE) Lisa Jane (Compton Place)
3532[6] 4927[5] 5960[7]
Mother Mother (USA) *Bob Baffert* a104
3 bb f Pioneerof The Nile(USA) Mother (USA) (Lion Hearted (USA))
9638a[3]
Mother Of Dragons (IRE)
Phil McEntee a65 67
4 ch m Society Rock(IRE) Queen O'The Desert (IRE) (Green Desert (USA))
236[4] 596[9] 1037[7] 1565[5] 1682[9] 2025[5] 2287[6] 3144[5] 3476[12] 3738[11]
Mother's Approach (IRE)
Gavin Cromwell a66 46
3 b f Dawn Approach(IRE) Rice Mother (IRE) (Indian Ridge (IRE))
8020[3]
Motion Emotion (USA)
Richard Baltas a100
3 b f Take Charge Indy(USA) Golden Motion (USA) (Smart Strike (CAN))
9638a[8]
Motivate Me (FR) *Roger Varian* 84
3 b f Motivator Jomana (IRE) (Darshaan)
2087[7] (2770) 3553[2] 5133[5]
Mot Juste (USA) *Roger Varian* 104
3 b f Distorted Humor(USA) Time On (Sadler's Wells (USA))
1832[2] 2443[13] 4885[6] 5608[8]◆ 6508[8] 7146[3]
Mottaham (FR) *Christian Williams* 33
4 b g Siyouni(FR) Moune (IRE) (Whipper (USA))
3421[10] 3946[12] 4178[7]
Mottrib (IRE) *Roger Varian* 85
2 b c Invincible Spirit(IRE) Freezy (IRE) (Dalakhani (IRE))
(3760) 4282[3]
Motym (FR) *Mme V Seignoux* a45 45
4 b g Motivator Ymlaen (IRE) (Desert Prince (IRE))
9537a[10]
Mouchee (IRE) *Michael Blake* a75 50
4 b g Zebedee Nashaat (Redoute's Choice (AUS))
404[9] 985[7] 1159[11] 3000[6] 3571[12] 4231[12] 5802[6]
Moudallal *Robert Cowell* a32 36
3 b f Poet's Voice Elhaam (IRE) (Shamardal (USA))
6013[3] 7417[5] 7976[9] 8469[13]
Moulmein *Sylvester Kirk* 20
2 ch c Australia Natty Bumppo (IRE) (Kheleyf (USA))
6564[7]
Mountain Angel (IRE) *Roger Varian* a74 111
5 b g Dark Angel(IRE) Fanciful Dancer (Groom Dancer (USA))
(2033) (3315) 3953[5] 4935[7] 6144a[2] 7923a[2] 9125a[13]
Mountain Brave *Mark Johnston* a70
2 b f Sepoy(AUS) Plucky (Kyllachy)
9623[2]
Mountain Hunter (USA)
Saeed bin Suroor a110 111
5 b g Lonhro(AUS) Tamarillo (Daylami (IRE))
284a[5] (730a) (961a) 1445a[12] 3953[7] 5519[8] 6962[5] (7662)
Mountain Of Stars *Suzzanne France* a46 22
4 b g Equiano(FR) Ivory Silk (Diktat)
166[5] 1192[12] 2189[10] 3144[10] 3970[10] 8269[7] 9220[9]
Mountain Peak *Ed Walker* a91 94
4 b g Swiss Spirit Nolas Lolly (IRE) (Lomitas)
2403[8] 3347[13] 4186[9] (4888) 5371[5] 6724[11] 6954[9] 7175[2]◆
Mountain Rescue (IRE)
Michael Attwater a81 89
7 b g High Chaparral(IRE) Amber Queen (IRE) (Cadeaux Genereux)
1881[6] 2273[18] (4067) 4867[6] 5862[2] 6729[7] 7563[3] 8521[13]
Mountain Rock (IRE)
Johnny Farrelly a29 58
7 b g Mountain High(IRE) Ajo Green (IRE) (Moscow Society (USA))
2718[6] 6849[8]
Mount Ararat (IRE) *K R Burke* a64 79
4 b g Sea The Stars(IRE) Divine Authority (IRE) (Holy Roman Emperor (IRE))
239[4] 696[4] 1849[3] 2291[3] (3680) 5948[13] 7363[10]
Mount Barina *John Davies* a15
4 b m Mount Nelson Sambarina (IRE) (Victory Note (USA))
9469[10]
Mount Cleshar *John Butler* a37 39
5 b g Mount Nelson Resal (IRE) (Montjeu (IRE))
6046[11] 6552[8]
Mount Everest (IRE) *A P O'Brien* 112
3 b c Galileo(IRE) Six Perfections (FR) (Celtic Swing)
7218a[4] 7662[4] 8776a[6] 9376a[14]
Mount Fuji (IRE) *Debbie Mountain* 97
2 gr g Dark Angel(IRE) Shermeen (IRE) (Desert Style (IRE))
4012[11] 5206a[5] 5922a[4] 6690a[8] 9582a[10]
Mount Mogan *Ed Walker* a62
2 b g Helmet(AUS) Super Midge (Royal Applause)
9299[5]
Mount Pelion (IRE) *A Fabre* a78 104
4 ch g Raven's Pass(USA) Sundrop (JPN) (Sunday Silence (USA))
8379a[4] 9014a[2]
Mount Tahan (IRE) *Kevin Ryan* a106 85
7 b g Lope De Vega(IRE) Sorpresa (USA) (Pleasant Tap (USA))
1664[7] 2032[11] 3005[8] 4988[5] 5594[10]
Mount Wellington (IRE)
Stuart Williams a68 76
4 b g Invincible Spirit(IRE) Marvada (IRE) (Elusive City (USA))
249[4] 468[2] 982[3] 1682[8] 2580[14] 9113[10] (9277)◆
Mouriyani (USA) *Tom Ward* a71 73
3 b g City Zip(USA) Mouraniya (IRE) (Azamour (IRE))
9418[10]
Mousebird (IRE) *Hughie Morrison* a68 66
3 b f Zoffany(IRE) Firecrest (IRE) (Darshaan)
2361[9] 2770[8] 3637[7] 5473[7] 9542[4]
Mousquetaire (FR) *David Menuisier* a50 33
3 b g Anodin(IRE) Cavaliere (FR) (Traditionally (USA))
1562[13] 3353[5] 5004[4] 6723[10] 8205[13]
Move In Faster *Michael Dods* a46 63
4 ch g Monsieur Bond(IRE) Tibesti (Machiavellian (USA))
2512[6] 3415[8] 4002[3] 4915[3]◆ 5239[5] 6036[3] 8405[5]
Move In Time *Paul Midgley* a87 91
11 ch g Monsieur Bond(IRE) Tibesti (Machiavellian (USA))
1892[9] 2839[6] 3509[5] 4279[4] 5027[2] (5819)
Moveonup (IRE) *Gay Kelleway* a68 69
3 gr g Zebedee Emma Dora (IRE) (Medaglia d'Oro (USA))
1385[2] 2529[3] 3574[2] 3884[9] 4218[3] 5002[7] 5730[7] 6325[4] 9218[8] 9386[10] 9548[8]
Move Swiftly *William Haggas* a101 115
4 b m Farhh Hurricane Harriet (Bertolini (USA))
(3986) 5479a[6] 8334[12]
Movie Set (USA) *Richard Spencer*
7 bb g Dubawi(IRE) Short Skirt (Diktat)
1518[11]
Movie Star (GER) *C J M Wolters* a62 63
4 b m Soldier Hollow Mouette (GER) (Tertullian (USA))
1343[2] 1988[12] 3276[3] 3941[2] 4601[5] 6059[6] 6324[7] 7318[5]◆ 8224[7] 9537a[9]
Moving Forward (IRE) *Tony Coyle* a79 75
4 b g Street Cry(IRE) Floristry (Fasliyev (USA))
2748[17] 5201[4] 5849[9] 6586[8]
Mowaeva (FR) *G Botti* a91 91
2 b c Evasive Mowaajaha (USA) (Invincible Spirit (IRE))
4961a[4] 5481a[5]
Moxy Mares *Mark Loughnane* a54 82
4 ch g Motivator Privalova (IRE) (Alhaarth (IRE))
1757[11] 2691[5] 2894[6] 4209[4] 5130[2] 5537a[3] 6164[9] 7069[8] 8031[3] 8521[5] 8902[8]
Moyassar *Richard Hannon* a89 110
3 ch g Tamayuz Catwalk (IRE) (Pivotal)
1851[8] (2412) 2826[10] 4896[19]
Mozzarella (FR) *Mlle L Kneip* a62 55
2 gr f Power Melting Ice (IRE) (Verglas (IRE))
7799a[10]
Mr Adjudicator *W P Mullins* 89
5 b g Camacho Attlongglast (Groom Dancer (USA))
5508a[4]
Mr Andros *Brendan Powell* a29 31
6 b g Phoenix Reach(IRE) Chocolada (Namid)
116[7] (365)
Mr Bold (FR) *O Trigodet* a53 65
3 b g Charm Spirit(IRE) Supergirl (USA) (Woodman (USA))
7138a[11]
Mr Bowjangles *Gay Kelleway* a12 15
2 b g Acclamation Fiftyshadesofpink (IRE) (Pour Moi (IRE))
3739[7] 4517[12] 9127[10]
Mr Buttons (IRE) *Linda Stubbs* a74 76
3 b g Elzaam(AUS) Clann Force (Kyllachy)
1557[3] 1969[3] 3420[2] 3884[6] 4343[2] 4604[3] 5356[4] 5826[3] 6070[3] 6806[3] 7514[2] 8712[9]
Mr Carbonator *Philip Kirby* a74 67
4 b g Bated Breath Diamond Lass (IRE) (Rock Of Gibraltar (IRE))
102[3] 390[6] 1367[7] 1660[2] 1859[7] 2629[3] 3162[4] 3681[2] 4036[2] 4627[2] 5301[6] 9093[7] 9333[5]
Mr Carpenter (IRE) *David Lanigan* a79 66
3 rg g Mastercraftsman(IRE) Satwa Pearl (Rock Of Gibraltar (IRE))
2764[5] 5254[10] 6315[3] 6941[2] 8290[13]
Mr Clarify (NZ) *Wayne Walters* 90
6 br g Savabeel(AUS) Clareta (AUS) (Pauillac (AUS))
9016a[9]
Mr Coco Bean (USA) *David Barron* a71 86
5 b g Gio Ponti(USA) Ing Ing (FR) (Bering)
(507) (1648)◆ 2512[7] 3046[2] (3162)◆ (4602) 4892[9] (5556) 6998[15] 7589[4]
Mr Cool Cash *John Davies* a51 53
7 b g Firebreak Cashleen (USA) (Lemon Drop Kid (USA))
3297[5] 4584[6] 5099[3] 6036[6] 6627[2] 7508[6] 7960[5] 8530[2]
Mr Diamond (IRE) *Richard Fahey* a69 87
3 b g Bated Breath Diamond Lass (IRE) (Rock Of Gibraltar (IRE))
(2510) 3075[5] 3599[3]
Mr Dib Dab (FR) *Mark Loughnane* a63
2 b c Dabirsim(FR) Naan (IRE) (Indian Charlie (USA))
9624[9]
Mr Duepearl *Robyn Brisland* a73 71
2 b c Due Diligence(USA) Midnight Pearl (USA) (Woodman (USA))
(5026) 7186[2]
Mr Everest (IRE) *A J Martin* 90
6 b g Cape Cross(IRE) Incitatus Girl (IRE) (Galileo (IRE))
5508a[13] 8114[5]
Mr Fox *Michael Attwater* a66 61
3 b g Foxwedge(AUS) Shared Moment (IRE) (Tagula (IRE))
403[4] (1066) 1593[2] 2322[5] 3407[7] 4400[6] 5679[4] 9589[7]
Mr Frankie *Alan Phillips*
8 b g Sleeping Indian Shes Minnie (Bertolini (USA))
62[6] 485[3] 792[7] 1146[8] 9552[11]
Mr Fudge *Richard Fahey* a51 54
2 ch g Anjaal Clann Force (Kyllachy)
1556[2] 2476[3] 3220[4] 5668[7] 5968[8] 7469[6]
Mr Gallivanter (IRE) *Mlle B Renk* a72 69
8 ch g Heliostatic(IRE) Purepleasureseeker (IRE) (Grand Lodge (USA))
46a[9]
Mr Gent (IRE) *Ed Dunlop* a68 69
4 br g Society Rock(IRE) Furnival (USA) (Street Cry (IRE))
249[7] 811[2] 1037[8] 1266[9] 1715[6]
Mr Greenlight *Tim Easterby* a50 64
4 b g Bahamian Bounty Nos Da (Cape Cross (IRE))
1760[9] 4132[13] 4586[2]◆ 4694[5] 5018[4] (5300) 5768[11] 6174[2] 6273[5] 6621[4] 7051[9] 7367[2] 7831[4] 8235[2] 8429[11]
Mr Gus (IRE) *Richard Fahey* 53
2 b g Slade Power(IRE) Perfect Venture (Bahamian Bounty)
2820[9] 3245[13] 3679[8] 5146[4] 5789[8] 7284[7]
Mr Jack Daniels *Peter Hiatt* 12
2 b g Paco Boy(IRE) Day Creek (Daylami (IRE))
4184[12] 6640[11] 7981[16]
Mr Jones And Me *Tom Dascombe* 78
2 b g Brazen Beau(AUS) Posy Fossil (USA) (Malibu Moon (USA))
4826[2]◆ 5456[3] 5707[4] 6356[19]
Mr Kiki (IRE) *Michael Bell* 88
2 b g No Nay Never(USA) Jacquelin Jag (IRE) (Fayruz)
5367[4] (5865)◆ 7456[7]
Mr Kodi (IRE) *David Evans* a51 59
2 b g Kodiac Khaimah (Nayef (USA))
2108[4] 3047[6] 4925[13] 5958[5] 6604[5] 8061[12] 8603[6] 8897[4] 9164[7] 9330[6]
Mr Lupton (IRE) *Richard Fahey* a101 115
6 ch g Elnadim(USA) Chiloe Wigeon (IRE) (Dockslder (USA))
(3103a) 4380[6] 5207a[6] 5716a[10] 6472[9] 7433[20]
Mr Mac *Peter Hedger* a75 71
5 b g Makfi Veronica Franco (Darshaan)
(175)◆ 295[2] 962[9] 1655[5] 7554[10] 8807[7] 9453[14] 9663[11]
Mr Millarcky *Rae Guest* a56
3 b g Equiano(FR) Fatal Attraction (Oasis Dream)
9332[7] 9475[9]
Mr Minerals *Alexandra Dunn* a77 46
5 ch g Poet's Voice River Song (USA) (Siphon (BRZ))
840[3] 952[4] 1106[7] 1329[9] 4281[11] 6026[10] 6931[8] 8549[10] 9256[11]
Mr. Money (USA) *W Bret Calhoun* a112
3 b c Goldencents(USA) Plenty O'Toole (USA) (Tiznow (USA))
7480a[2] 8771a[7]
Mr Money Bags (AUS)
Robbie Griffiths 106
4 ch g Written Tycoon(AUS) Biggietupac (AUS) (Dubai Destination (USA))
9016a[5]
Mr Nice Guy (IRE) *Clare Hobson* a51 60
3 b g Nathaniel(IRE) Three Choirs (IRE) (Rock Of Gibraltar (IRE))
2795[15] 4234[5] 5254[7] 5778[9] 6202[4] 6805[2] 7202[10] 7998[5]
Mr Nutherputt (IRE) *William Knight* 12
2 b g Camacho Right After Moyne (IRE) (Imperial Ballet (IRE))
4897[12]
Mr Orange (IRE) *Paul Midgley* a62 84
6 b g Paco Boy(IRE) Shirley Blake (IRE) (Acclamation)
1895[6] 2292[3] 2893[6] 3706[7] 4440[10] (5157) (5821) 6916[11] 7621[6] 8101[6] 8342[10]
Mr Pommeroy (FR) *M Ramadan* a24 34
8 ch g Linngari(IRE) Amerissage (USA) (Rahy (USA))
1748a[13]
Mr Potter *Richard Guest* a59 49
6 ch g Assertive Enclave (USA) (Woodman (USA))
371[0] 357[9] 1032[10] (1093) (1477) 2153[6] 2681[3] 3007[5] 3996[7] 4684a[8]
Mr Poy *Hughie Morrison* 80
2 ch c Sepoy(AUS) Quiz Mistress (Doyen (IRE))
5774[2]◆
Mr Quickie (AUS) *Phillip Stokes* 110
3 bb g Shamus Award(AUS) Special Favour (AUS) (General Nediym (AUS))
8361a[11] 8577a[2]
Mr Red Clubs (IRE) *Henry Tett* a72 62
10 b g Red Clubs(IRE) Queen Cobra (IRE) (Indian Rocket)
181[5]
Mr Rusty (IRE) *Richard Hannon* 62
2 b c Zebedee Imtidaad (USA) (Lemon Drop Kid (USA))
7972[8] 8518[7]
Mrs Benson (IRE)
Michael Blanshard a71 52
4 ch m Rip Van Winkle(IRE) Ebble (Oasis Dream)
202[3] 364[7] 1216[7] 2617[12] 4115[11] 5309[12] 6123[3] 6904[7]
Mrs Bouquet *Mark Johnston* a76 97
2 b f Toronado(IRE) Riva Royale (Royal Applause)
(3451)◆ 3841[6] 4384[2] (4780) (4893) (5544)
Mrs Burbidge *Neil Mulholland* a55 45
9 b m Pasternak Twin Time (Syrtos)
602[8] 3640a[3]
Mr Scaramanga *Simon Dow* a95 90
5 b h Sir Percy Lulla (Oasis Dream)
176[7] (441) 856[4] 880[6] 1294[5] 1916[11] 2486[2] 3315[3] 3806[8] (4548) 5667[7] 6537[3] 9003[5] 9206[3] 9666[5]
Mr Scarlet *Ms Sheila Lavery* a79 70
5 b g Dandy Man(IRE) Scarlet Buttons (IRE) (Marju (IRE))
5205a[18]
Mrs Discombe *Mick Quinn* 72
3 b f Garswood Dora's Sister (IRE) (Dark Angel (IRE))
2077[5] 3532[4] 4297[2] (5357)
Mrs Dukesbury (FR) *Archie Watson* a70 75
2 ch f Ruler Of The World(IRE) Sunshinesonleith (IRE) (Danehill Dancer (IRE))
4114[2]◆ 4544[6] 5189[7] 5912[3] (6386a)
Mrs Flanders (IRE) *Charles Hills* 75
2 gr f Dark Angel(IRE) Havin' A Good Time (IRE) (Jeremy (USA))
2565[2]◆
Mr Shady (IRE) *J S Moore* a71 70
2 gr g Elzaam(AUS) Whitershadeofpale (IRE) (Definite Article)
5468a[6] 5642a[11] 6141a[2] 6433a[6] 8448a[6] 9243[2]
Mr Shelby (IRE) *S Donohoe* a61 61
5 b g Casamento(IRE) Notepad (King's Best (USA))
2324[3] 2678[3] 2958[10] 4694[11] (5935) 6574[7]
Mrs Hoo (IRE) *Richard Fahey* a66 58
3 b f Lawman(FR) Wingspan (USA) (Silver Hawk (USA))
1462[9] 7069[10] 7829[14] 8669[7] 9256[4] 9479[7]
Mrs Ivy *Ralph Beckett* a59 51
3 ch f Champs Elysees Just Wood (FR) (Highest Honor (FR))
1738[5] 7035[8] 8000[10] (8670) 9310[14]
Mr Slicker (FR) *Andrew Hollinshead* a78 50
5 b g Exceed And Excel(AUS) Glory Power (IRE) (Medicean)
2955a[9]
Mrs Meader *Seamus Mullins* a62 65
3 b f Cityscape Bavarica (Dansili)
370[4] 1064[4] 1730[5] 2343[6] 3947[3] 5565[4]
Mrs Merton *William Knight* 66
2 b f Iffraaj Merton Matriarch (Cadeaux Genereux)
6442[5] 6911[9] 7644[6] (Dead)
Mr Smith *C Byrnes* a26 60
8 gr g Galileo(IRE) Intrigued (Darshaan)
(3686) 8523[5]
Mr Spirit (IRE) *Marco Botti* a47 67
3 b g Invincible Spirit(IRE) Sharapova (IRE) (Elusive Quality (USA))
2238[12] 4787[9] 5946[8] 6731[6] 7909[8]
Mrs Sippy (USA) *H Graham Motion* a74 108
4 b m Blame(USA) Qushchi (Encosta De Lago (AUS))
2776[6] 3586[7] 8772a[9]
Mrs Tiffen *Lisa Williamson* 14
2 b f Finjaan Fancy Rose (USA) (Joyeux Danseur (USA))
5704[6] 6205[7]
Mrs Todd *Tony Carroll* a51 29
5 b m Foxwedge(AUS) Orange Pip (Bold Edge)
27[13] 811[3] 3527[14]

Mr Strutter (IRE) *Ronald Thompson* a63 77
5 ch g Sir Prancealot(IRE) Khajool (IRE) (Haafhd)
42[4] 1522[7] 1760[15] 2349[9] 3656[6] 4519[5] (4785) 5151[2] 5593[5] 5852[10] 6461[11] 7632[6] 8068[3] 8270[5] 9395[2]

Mr Stunning (AUS) *F C Lor* 125
6 b g Exceed And Excel(AUS) With Fervour (USA) (Dayjur (USA))
9377a[4]

Mr Sundowner (USA)
Michael Herrington a50 55
7 bb g Scat Daddy(USA) Bold Answer (USA) (Dynaformer (USA))
5214[6] 6275[14] 6827[6] 7048[11] 7441[10] 7859[8] 8530[10]

Mrs Upjohn (FR) *Archie Watson* a75
2 b f Dabirsim(FR) Zamiria (FR) (Zanzibari (USA))
8717[2]◆ 9311[2]

Mrs Worthington (IRE)
Jonathan Portman a41 64
3 gr f Dark Angel(IRE) Mirror Effect (IRE) (Shamardal (USA))
2340[14] 3258[3] 3801[5] 4183[5] 5315[3] 7157[4] 7812[10] 7976[2] 8242[7]

Mr Terry (IRE) *Jamie Osborne* a48
2 gr c Gutaifan(IRE) Carallia (IRE) (Common Grounds)
9130[10]

Mr Top Hat *David Evans* a94 94
4 b g Helmet(AUS) Tut (IRE) (Intikhab (USA))
164[4] 623[3] 764[2] 915[5] 1912[5] (2563) 3515[3] 5776[3] 6166[4] 6725[6] 6895[5] 7863[5] 8260[5] 8411[9] 9041[6] 9255[6]

Mr Tyrrell (IRE) *Richard Hannon* a80 92
5 b g Helmet(AUS) Rocking (Oasis Dream)
(1655) 1955[6] (2472) 2799[5] 3423[2] 4902[4] 5104[5] 5546[9] 5991[3] 6155[6] 6729[10]

Mr Wagyu (IRE) *John Quinn* a63 73
4 ch g Choisir(AUS) Lake Louise (IRE) (Haatef (USA))
1895[13] 2201[13] 2788[6] 3999[4] 4280[6] 5972[3]◆ 6261[7] 6898[4] 7311[3] 8083[4]

Mr Wilton (IRE) *Charles Hills* 43
2 b c Raven's Pass(USA) Full Moon Fever (IRE) (Azamour (IRE))
5523[10]

Mr Wing (IRE) *John Wainwright* a18 14
4 b g Dandy Man(IRE) Siesta Time (Oasis Dream)
237[8] 465[11] 587[8] 2350[11] 3067[11] 3158[13] 4319[9] 4358[11]

Mr Zoom Zoom *Luke McJannet* a69 73
3 b g Toronado(IRE) Gay Mirage (GER) (Highest Honor (FR))
1711[3] 2034[5] 2485[2] 2914[5] 3604[5] 4024[3]

Msaikah (IRE) *H-F Devin* a48 95
4 b m Galileo(IRE) Light Quest (USA) (Quest For Fame)
5229a[8]

Ms Bad Behavior (CAN)
Richard Baltas a92 105
4 bb m Blame(USA) Cumulonimble (USA) (Stormy Atlantic (USA))
7920a[10]

Muatadel *John Wainwright* a65 69
6 b g Exceed And Excel(AUS) Rose Blossom (Pastoral Pursuits)
315[4] 586[2] (788) 1768[6] 1976[3] 2478[4] (4582) 5517[6] 6066[3] 6496[4] 6628[2] 6937[3] 7587[4]

Mubaalegh *J E Hammond* 98
5 b g Dark Angel(IRE) Poppet's Passion (Clodovil (IRE))
6006a[2] 7254a[11] 8141a[7]

Mubakker (USA) *Sir Michael Stoute* a101 84
3 gr c Speightstown(USA) Ready To Act (USA) (More Than Ready (USA))
(6838)◆ 7868[7]

Mubariz *Roger Charlton* 94
3 br g Dansili Could It Be (IRE) (Galileo (IRE))
3859[3] 4553[3] 5796[7]

Mubarmaj (FR) *E J O'Neill* a55 76
3 b g Oasis Dream Gooseley Chope (FR) (Indian Rocket)
1489a[3] 3713a[10] 9058a[16]

Mubhij (IRE) *Roger Varian* a102 96
4 b g Dark Angel(IRE) Diva (GER) (Oasis Dream)
(2977) 3632[2] (4385) 5413[23] 6150[5]

Mubtasim (IRE) *Charlie Appleby* a105 114
5 b g Arcano(IRE) Start The Music (IRE) (King's Best (USA))
(640a)◆ 960a[2] (1891)

Mubtasimah *William Haggas* 99
3 b f Dark Angel(IRE) Midnight Hush (FR) (Anabaa (USA))
(4405)◆ (5128) (5910) 6379[6] 6951[6] 8463[3]

Much Better (USA) *Bob Baffert* a101 91
3 bb r Pioneerof The Nile(USA) Dust And Diamonds (USA) (Vindication (USA))
9639a[5]

Muchly *John Gosden* a95 102
3 b f Iffraaj Ego (Green Desert (USA))
1751[8] (2268) 3012[4]◆ 4667[3] 5949[5] 7893[3] 8708[9]

Mucho Macho (FR) *Simone Brogi* a43 82
2 b c Machucambo(FR) Khanbaligh (FR) (Panis (USA))
7674a[6]

Mucho Unusual (USA) *Tim Yakteen* 103
3 b f Mucho Macho Man(USA) Not Unusual (USA) (Unusual Heat (USA))
9637a[2]

Mudawwan (IRE) *James Bethell* a72 71
5 b g Invincible Spirit(IRE) Louve Sacree (USA) (Seeking The Gold (USA))
355[3] 609[4] 1273[8] 3215[11] 3969[3] 4523[11] 6204[14] 6665[9]

Mudeer (IRE) *G Botti* a67 59
3 b g Kendargent(FR) Makisarde (FR) (Xaar)
2392a[6] 5408a[2]

Muette *A Fabre* 99
3 b f Deep Impact(JPN) Blarney Stone (IRE) (Peintre Celebre (USA))
(7137a) 7927a[4]

Muftakker *John Norton* a51 62
5 gr g Tamayuz Qertaas (IRE) (Linamix (FR))
2695[4]◆ 4126[3]

Mugatoo (IRE) *David Simcock* a82 95
4 b g Henrythenavigator(USA) Elopa (GER) (Tiger Hill (IRE))
(2398) 3799[5] 4877[6]

Muhaarar's Nephew *Owen Burrows* a88 73
3 b g Mukhadram Rufoof (Zamindar (USA))
3324[3] (4211) 5808[2] (6886)

Muhallab (IRE) *Adrian Nicholls* a57 59
3 b g War Command(USA) Andrea Bellevica (IRE) (Aussie Rules (USA))
785[5] 954[3] 1427[4] 2197[16] 3202[5] 4033[6] 4276[5] 4586[7] 5215[2] 6024[6] 6389[3] (6575) 6897[2] 7210[10]

Muhtaram *M Al Mheiri* a82 81
9 b g Shamardal(USA) Neshla (Singspiel (IRE))
97a[6]

Muito Obrigado (JPN)
Koichi Tsunoda 112
5 b h Rulership(JPN) Pisa No Graf (JPN) (Sunday Silence (USA))
9153a[8]

Mujaafy (AUS) *M F De Kock* 79
4 b g Star Witness(AUS) Pearl Of The Sea (AUS) (Fastnet Rock (AUS))
725a[4]

Mujassam *Sophie Leech* a80 81
7 ch g Kyllachy Naizak (Medicean)
1552[4]◆ 1859[4] 2297[6] 2788[7] 3214[6] (3928) (4060) 4280[3] 4440[3] 4833[2] 5274[6] 5770[2] (6027) 6567[10] 7121[9] 7601a[2] 8031[8] 8649[4]

Mujeeb *E Charpy* a75 88
5 b g Dubawi(IRE) Naahedh (Medicean)
1748a[4]

Mukha Magic *Gay Kelleway* a60 73
3 b g Mukhadram Sweet Lemon (IRE) (Oratorio (IRE))
1593[5] 2712[7] 3256[3] 3938[2] (5249) 5502[4] 6463[4]

Mukhayyam *Tim Easterby* a83 95
7 b g Dark Angel(IRE) Caster Sugar (USA) (Cozzene (USA))
1664[4] 2119[4]

Mulan (IRE) *Sir Michael Stoute* a68 79
3 b f Kingman Platonic (Zafonic (USA))
(3193)◆ 4119[5] 6672[6]

Mulfit (USA) *S Jadhav* a78
3 gr c Exchange Rate(USA) Sita (USA) (Giant's Causeway (USA))
636a[8]

Mulhima (IRE) *A bin Harmash* a76
3 ch f Mukhadram Excellerator (IRE) (Exceed And Excel (AUS))
48a[4] 510a[8] 845a[10]

Mullarkey *John Best* a65 65
5 b g Mullionmileanhour(IRE) Hannah's Dream (IRE) (King's Best (USA))
39[4] (288) 724[9] 1546[3] 2111[2] 2617[5] 3473[2] 4426[6] 5309[5] 6320[4] 6566[2] (7790) 8422[7]

Mulligatawny (IRE) *Roger Fell* a88 92
6 b g Lope De Vega(IRE) Wild Whim (IRE) (Whipper (USA))
1948[5] 2563[4] (3180) (3356) 4035[9] 5657[9] 6580[7] 7694[25]

Mullion Dreams *James Ewart* 26
5 b g Mullionmileanhour(IRE) High Meadow Rose (Emperor Fountain)
2505[10] 3248[11] 4004[8]

Mulsanne Chase *Conor Dore* a52 48
5 b g Sixties Icon Hot Pursuits (Pastoral Pursuits)
59[11] 436[7] 549[8]

Multamis (IRE) *Owen Burrows* a51 90
3 gr g Charm Spirit(IRE) Dabista (IRE) (Highest Honor (FR))
1345[6] (2035) 3859[6] (5089) 5841[5]

Multellie *Tim Easterby* a59 82
7 b g Multiplex Bollin Nellie (Rock Hopper)
1761[8] 3222[9] 3862[7] 4241[14] 5201[6] 5694[7] 6255[5] 6657[5] (7510) 7702[5]

Multicurrency (USA) *H Al Alawi*
4 gr g Exchange Rate(USA) Istamara (Teofilo (IRE))
634a[7]

Multigifted *Michael Madgwick* a71 69
6 b m Multiplex Attlongglast (Groom Dancer (USA))
560[10] 731[9]

Multiply By Eight (FR)
Tom Dascombe a61 83
2 b f Muhaarar Baldovina (Tale Of The Cat (USA))
3259[3]◆ 3983[12] 5045[5] 5772[9]

Multitask *Gary Moore* a64 52
9 b g Multiplex Attlongglast (Groom Dancer (USA))
399[6] 941[8] 1383[6]

Multiviz *S M Duffy* a43 42
6 b m Multiplex Vizean (IRE) (Medicean)
1572a[6]

Mulzim *Mike Murphy* a68 64
5 b g Exceed And Excel(AUS) Samaah (IRE) (Cape Cross (IRE))
2065[8]

Mumsbirthdaygirl (IRE)
Mark Loughnane a41 40
2 ch f Dandy Man(IRE) Dutch Party (Dutch Art)
1968[5] 2415[10] 2694[6] 7110[5] 7584[5] 8825[10] 9330[9]

Mums Hope *Hughie Morrison* a80 80
3 gr f Lethal Force(IRE) Jadwiga (Pivotal)
3323[5] 3552[5] 4898[2] 5505[3] 6593[3] 7788[3] 8221[8]

Mums The Law *Jane Chapple-Hyam* a62 57
2 b f Lawman(FR) Tell Mum (Marju (IRE))
6449[8] 7547[5] 9437[12]

Mums Tipple (IRE) *Richard Hannon* 119
2 ch c Footstepsinthesand Colomone Cross (IRE) (Xaar)
(5367) (6375) 7693[7]

Munaazil (IRE) *Roger Varian* 69
3 b g Dubawi(IRE) Aljaaziah (Medaglia d'Oro (USA))
1956[5]

Mundersfield *David Simcock* a65
5 b m Nathaniel(IRE) Captain's Paradise (IRE) (Rock Of Gibraltar (IRE))
385[5] 566[2] 991[6] 1858[9]

Mungo's Quest (IRE) *Simon Dow* a54 11
2 ch g Sir Prancealot(IRE) Sheila Blige (Zamindar (USA))
2767[10] 3579[6] 4030[6] 6313[9] 7605[6] 8058[3] 8415[9]

Munhamek *Ivan Furtado* a78 92
3 b g Dark Angel(IRE) Cadenza (FR) (Dansili)
(1171) 1723[2] (2198) 3082[2]◆

Munitions (USA) *A Fabre* 113
3 b c War Front(USA) War Echo (USA) (Tapit (USA))
(1707a) 2668a[9] 4705a[4] 5716a[14]

Munstead Moonshine
Andrew Balding a46 38
3 ch f Sir Percy Royal Patron (Royal Academy (USA))
299[6] 723[8] 1555[5] 1770[8] 3197[7]

Muntadab (IRE) *Roger Fell* a89 102
7 b g Invincible Spirit(IRE) Chibola (ARG) (Roy (USA))
1763[2] 7701[9] 7905[6] 8184[8] 9198[7] 9472[9]

Muntahaa (IRE)
David A & B Hayes & Tom Dabern a74 95
6 gr g Dansili Qertaas (IRE) (Linamix (FR))
8600a[11]

Muntazah *Doug Watson* a119 111
6 b g Dubawi(IRE) Rumoush (USA) (Rahy (USA))
171a[3]◆ (726a)◆ (1112a)◆ 1440a[3]

Muqarred (USA) *Karen Tutty* a71 49
7 bb g Speightstown(USA) Bawaara (FR) (Quiet American (USA))
5[8] 209[7] 392[7] 1197[6] (1526) 1859[3] 2193[3] 2297[4] 2346[3] 3163[9] 3297[4] 5099[13] 5247[11] 5852[11] 6276[5] (7385) 7875[5] 8266[2] 8902[10] 9180[10]

Muraabit *Tim Easterby* a25 55
7 ch g Makfi Ho Hi The Moon (IRE) (Be My Guest (USA))
5657[10]

Muraad (IRE) *Owen Burrows* a91 95
3 gr g Dark Angel(IRE) Hidden Girl (IRE) (Tamayuz)
(2128) 3003[3] 4865[2] 5564[8]

Muraadef *Ruth Carr* a56 53
4 b g Kodiac Dominatrix (Whipper (USA))
1837[4] 2215[8] 2693[10] 3924[3] 4584[7] 5284[13] 6036[2] 6627[11] 7783[11]

Muraahib (IRE) *R Bouresly* 51
5 b h Shamardal(USA) Amathia (IRE) (Darshaan)
1742a[8]

Muraahin *Jamie Osborne* a31 36
4 ch g Teofilo(IRE) Fatanah (IRE) (Green Desert (USA))
3100[8]

Muraaqeb (AUS) *David A Hayes* 78
4 b h Snitzel(AUS) Tafseel (AUS) (Starcraft (NZ))
285a[10] 960a[11]

Muraaqeb *Milton Bradley* a59 42
5 b g Nathaniel(IRE) Tesary (Danehill (USA))
241[7] (533) 1015[7] 1145[3] 1520[11] (1680) 2127[11] (2234) 2698[3] (3006) 3298[4] 4547[10] 5285[9] 5378[7] (5653) 5946[2] (6153) 9362[3] 9444[2] 9552[8]

Muraikh (FR) *H-F Devin* a80 84
3 b c Toronado(IRE) Plumba (Anabaa (USA))
3029a[8]

Murdanova (IRE) *Rebecca Menzies* a79 79
6 gr g Zebedee Agnista (IRE) (Iffraaj)
260[6] 496[6] 812[3] 1329[11] 1768[2] 2151[5] 2514[3] 3147[4] (3930)

Murhib (IRE) *Lydia Richards* a60 62
7 b g Sea The Stars(IRE) Mood Swings (IRE) (Shirley Heights)
58[8] 257[4] 549[4] 736[11] (1146) 1520[6] 1679[3] (3298)◆ 3444[3] 3700[3]◆ 5271[5] 6320[3] 8065[4]

Muritz *John Quinn* a65
2 ch f Free Eagle(IRE) Super Saturday (IRE) (Pivotal)
9107[5]◆ 9409[4]

Murqaab *John Balding* a50 52
3 b g Showcasing Ahwahnee (Compton Place)
1954[7] 2380[4] (2633) 3202[8] 3516[7] 6373[11] 7472[10] 7869[9] 8264[5] 8840[10] 9643[5]

Murraymint (FR) *Ralph Beckett* a27 62
2 b c Wootton Bassett Diamond Nizzy (IRE) (Sadler's Wells (USA))
5980[5] 6504[6] 7677[5] 8699[9]

Murray River (USA) *John Gosden* a86 82
3 b g Australia Waterway Run (USA) (Arch (USA))
(567) 6211[4]

Musaddas *R Bouresly* a70 83
9 b g Exceed And Excel(AUS) Zuleika Dobson (Cadeaux Genereux)
51a[15] 425a[9] 960a[10]

Musa D'Oriente *M Gonnelli* 99
8 b m Nayef(USA) Musa Golosa (Mujahid (USA))
7503a[3]

Musawaat *Fawzi Abdulla Nass* a107 98
5 b h Equiano(FR) Starry Sky (Oasis Dream)
1112a[3] 1440a[6]

Musbaq (USA) *Ben Haslam* a66 60
4 b g Union Rags(USA) Eraada (Medicean)
116[12] 501[13]

Muscika *David O'Meara* a94 98
5 b g Kyllachy Miss Villefranche (Danehill Dancer (IRE))
1978[6] 2393[6] (2843) 3097[12] 4521[2] 4805[4] 5217[2] 5454[2] 5740[2] 6229[4] 6676[6] 7193[11] 7431[8] 7701[5] 8425[4]

Musetta *H-F Devin* a39 74
2 gr f Dark Angel(IRE) Miss Quality (USA) (Elusive Quality (USA))
2890a[2]

Mushaageb (IRE) *Roger Varian* a71 66
3 b g War Command(USA) Divisme (USA) (Elusive Quality (USA))
405[6] 1195[4] 1285[10] 1656[5] 1979[9]

Musharrif *Declan Carroll* a71 85
7 b g Arcano(IRE) Cefira (USA) (Distant View (USA))
1760[4] 2053[4] 2294[4] 2508[6] (2876) 3056[4] 3706[13] 4406[9] 4555[4] (4759) 5157[3] 5476[2] 5911[5] 6972[9]

Mushtaq (IRE) *Richard Hannon* a89 94
4 b g Zoffany(IRE) Iamfine (IRE) (Whipper (USA))
1757[16] 4639[9]

Musical Mast (USA) *P Bary* 70
2 gr c Mizzen Mast(USA) Flute (USA) (Seattle Slew (USA))
6776a[5]

Musical Sky *Michael Dods* 53
3 ch f Mayson Sky Wonder (Observatory (USA))
2635[20] 4129[7] 4820[5] 5695[13]

Music Major *Michael Attwater* a62 39
6 br g Bertolini(USA) Music Maid (IRE) (Inzar (USA))
321[4] 736[4] (859) 1292[4] 1498[7] 8065[13] 8703[10] 9005[3] 9310[6] 9426[2]

Music Man (IRE) *Hughie Morrison* a74 69
9 b g Oratorio(IRE) Chanter (Lomitas)
1095[6] 1330[6]

Music Seeker (IRE) *Declan Carroll* 88
5 b g Henrythenavigator(USA) Danehill Music (IRE) (Danehill Dancer (IRE))
1418[7] 1695[7] 2104[3] (2629)◆ 3161[6] (3811) 4892[3] 5594[6] 6998[6] 7694[27] 7829[3] 8260[4] 8661[6]

Music Society (IRE) *Tim Easterby* a97 90
4 gr g Society Rock(IRE) Absolutely Cool (IRE) (Indian Ridge (IRE))
1895[12] 2588[3] 3221[4] (3504) 3868[2] 4406[19] 6178[2] (6339) (7402) 8099[12]

Music Therapist (IRE)
George Scott a78 73
2 gr g Zebedee Provence (Averti (IRE))
5913[5] 6300[4] 6704[2] (7296) 7785[2] 8095[7]

Musikaline (FR) *Y Barberot* 99
4 b m Martaline Natt Musik (FR) (Kendor (FR))
3138a[5]

Musis Amica (IRE) *A Fabre* 110
4 b m Dawn Approach(IRE) White Star (IRE) (Darshaan)
5229a[2] 6265a[7] 7252a[2] 7926a[8]

Mustaaqeem (USA)
Bernard Llewellyn a70 68
7 b g Dynaformer(USA) Wasseema (USA) (Danzig (USA))
2359[5] 2718[8] 6105[11] 6366[9]

Mustadun *Mark Johnston* a82 63
3 b g Lethal Force(IRE) Tiger Stone (Tiger Hill (IRE))
354[4] (785) 978[2] 1480[3] 1897[6] 2369[2] 3011[9] 3885[9] 4634[8] 6101[11] 6600[3] 7295[7]

Mustajeer *Kris Lees* a101 114
6 b g Medicean Qelaan (USA) (Dynaformer (USA))
1777a[7] 2158a[2] 3114[3] 4351a[5] (6473) 8361a[6]◆ 8844a[23]

Mustaqbal (IRE) *Michael Dods* a56 82
7 b g Invincible Spirit(IRE) Alshamatry (USA) (Seeking The Gold (USA))
3567[6] 4322[5] 5490[8] 5726[9] 7363[7]

Mustarrid (IRE) *Ian Williams* a93 95
5 b g Elzaam(AUS) Symbol Of Peace (IRE) (Desert Sun)
3991[4]◆ 4650[4] 5948[11] 7212[2] (8658)◆ 9309[9]

Mustashry *Sir Michael Stoute* a113 122
6 bb g Tamayuz Safwa (IRE) (Green Desert (USA))
1890[3] (2829) 3948[7] 4668[5] (8090)

Must Be An Angel (IRE)
Sylvester Kirk a72
2 gr f Dark Angel(IRE) Lapis Blue (IRE) (Invincible Spirit (IRE))
8849[3] 9159[6] 9506[3]

Must Be Late (IRE) *A Botti* 100
3 b f Champs Elysees Delphica (IRE) (Acclamation)
2161a[4] 4171a[2] 8153a[7]

Must Be Magic (IRE)
Andrew Balding a44 78
4 b m Camelot Saturn Girl (IRE) (Danehill Dancer (IRE))
696[8]

Must Dream *Seb Spencer* a5 49
2 ch g Mustajeeb Golden Valley (Three Valleys (USA))
1759[8] 2780[10] 4106[7] 6097[7] 6884[9]

Must See The Doc *Iain Jardine* 80
3 b g Sea The Moon(GER) Kong Moon (FR) (Hernando (FR))
1645[7]

Mutaabeq (IRE) *Marcus Tregoning* a82 93
4 ch g Teofilo(IRE) Khulood (USA) (Storm Cat (USA))
4613[9] 5796[2] 6725[7] 7563[6]

Mutabaahy (IRE) *Antony Brittain* a70 75
4 b g Oasis Dream Habaayib (Royal Applause)
790[9] 1016[6] 1164[8] 1487[12] 1952[7] 3550[2] 3706[4] 4037[2] 4335[9] 5330[4] 6373[6] 7311[5] 7703[5] 8083[9] 8896[8] 9352[12] (9406)◆ 9473[3] (9572)

Mutadaawel (IRE) *Anthony McCann* a83 79
4 b g Invincible Spirit(IRE) Elshabakiya (IRE) (Diktat)
2128[5] 6164[2]

Mutafani *Simon Crisford* a95 95
4 b g Exceed And Excel(AUS) Hokkaido (Street Cry (IRE))
2778[11] 3472[4]◆ 5173[11] 8707[7] 9200[2]

Mutafarrid (IRE) *Paul Midgley* a69 73
4 gr g Dark Angel(IRE) Margarita (IRE) (Marju (IRE))
1457[18] 2841[15] 3549[5] 4103[10] 4440[8] 6204[7] 6461[9]

Mutafawwig *Saeed bin Suroor* 85
3 b c Oasis Dream Reunite (IRE) (Kingmambo (USA))
(6206)◆

Mutahaddith *A R Al Rayhi* a82
9 b g Shamardal(USA) Castaway Queen (IRE) (Selkirk (USA))
196a[12]

Mutalahef (IRE) *Marcus Tregoning* a74
2 b c Kingman Raasekha (Pivotal)
9631[2]

Mutamaasik *Roger Varian* a94 107
3 ch g Dubawi(IRE) Muhawalah (IRE) (Nayef (USA))
3464[2] (4196) (5650)◆ (6225)◆ (7123)◆

Mutamaded (IRE) *Ruth Carr* a70 91
6 b g Arcano(IRE) Sahaayeb (IRE) (Indian Haven)
1545[8] 1896[6] 2119[6] 2563[9] 3180[3] 3862[2] 4035[4] 4241[4] 4988[2] 5199[5] 5417[7] 5818[5] (6576) 7436[10] 7702[6] 8130[16] 8633[4]

Mutamakina *C Laffon-Parias* 111
3 b f Nathaniel(IRE) Joshua's Princess (Danehill (USA))
6250a[2] **7253a[2]** 7926a[9]

Mutaraffa (IRE) *Charles Hills* 96
3 b g Acclamation Excellent View (Shamardal (USA))
1852[3] (2366) (3019) 4650[7] **(5312)** 5971[6]

Mutarakez (IRE) *Ruth Carr* a55 66
7 ch g Fast Company(IRE) Nightswimmer (IRE) (Noverre (USA))
1955[2] 2291[5] 2842[6] 3215[4] 3704[6] 4078[5] 4582[2]

Mutasaamy (IRE) *Roger Varian* a84 73
3 b g Oasis Dream Eswarah (Unfuwain (USA))
3003[7]◆ 3306[7] 5176[2]◆ ***(5730)***

Mutawaffer (IRE) *Phillip Makin* a37 80
3 b g Kodiac Golden Flower (Royal Applause)
1762[8] **2086[6]** 3531[8] 4495[4] *8023[14]* *8403[9]*

Mutawakked (IRE) *M Al Mheiri* a75 75
5 b g Kodiac Your Opinion (IRE) (Xaar)
196a[7]

Mutawathea *Simon Crisford* a101 86
8 b g Exceed And Excel(AUS) Esteemed Lady (IRE) (Mark Of Esteem (IRE))
515a[11] **847a[12]**

Muthhila (IRE) *S Jadhav* a79 75
3 b f Kodiac Rose Lilas (Cape Cross (IRE))
48a[3] *510a[9]* 956a[13]

Muthmir (IRE) *William Haggas* a101 110
9 b g Invincible Spirit(IRE) Fairy Of The Night (IRE) (Danehill (USA))
3344[5] 4665[8] 4896[10] *6149[4]* 7193[14]

Muzaawel *Ralph J Smith* a49 47
4 ch g New Approach(IRE) Jilnaar (IRE) (Dansili)
1102[9] **1331[8]** *9450[8]*

Muzdawaj *M Al Mheiri* a85 99
6 b g Dansili Shabiba (USA) (Seeking The Gold (USA))
844a[6] 1115a[9]

Muzy (FR) *Andrea Marcialis* 81
2 b c Penny's Picnic(IRE) Madeenh (FR) (Pivotal)
6002a[5] **6873a[5]**

Mya George (FR) *G Doleuze* 52
3 b f George Vancouver(USA) Mya (FR) (Dr Fong (USA))
3713a[8] 8449a[7]

My Amigo *Marjorie Fife* a68 75
6 gr g Stimulation(IRE) Blue Crest (FR) (Verglas (IRE))
2526[9] 3503[7] 3813[14] 4240[15] 4875[11] 5490[11] 7363[11] *7609[2]*◆ *7875[4]* *8291[3]* *8499[3]* *8753[3]*

My Boy Lewis (IRE) *Roger Fell* a66 69
3 b g Dandy Man(IRE) Flamelet (USA) (Theatrical (IRE))
2635[19] **3249[3]** 4070[9] 4761[5] 5176[9] 6101[5] 6342[6] 6678[10]

My Boy Monty *Gary Sanderson*
3 b g Passing Glance Sudden Impulse (Silver Patriarch (IRE))
5552[10] 6036[15]

My Boy Sepoy *Stuart Williams* a88 86
4 ch g Sepoy(AUS) Emily Carr (IRE) (Teofilo (IRE))
2360[4] (3022)◆ 4407[6] 5149[6] (5858) 6725[9] 7166[3] 7413[8] *8421[4]* *8829[2]* ***9418[2]***

My Brother Mike (IRE) *Kevin Frost* a70 44
5 b g Bated Breath Coming Back (Fantastic Light (USA))
(135) ***362[6]*** *754[8]* 2112[12] 4232[7]

My Bubba *Malcolm Saunders* a21 24
7 b g Dutch Art Moyoko (IRE) (Mozart (IRE))
6051[13] 6363[13] 6855[11]

My Buddy (FR) *E Libaud* a60 81
4 b h Orpen(USA) Lungwa (IRE) (One Cool Cat (USA))
5643a[6]

My Catch (IRE) *Doug Watson* a104 96
8 b g Camacho Catch The Sea (IRE) (Barathea (IRE))
50a[3] ***512a[5]*** *1109a[9]*

My Dandy Doc (IRE) *John Quinn* a54 60
2 b f Dandy Man(IRE) Atishoo (IRE) (Revoque (IRE))
5118[5] **5553[4]** 6697[7] *8085[8]*

My Dear Friend *Ralph Beckett* a78 57
3 b g Kodiac Time Honoured (Sadler's Wells (USA))
290[2] ***(698)*** 4841[9] 5445[8] *6186[5]* *6886[4]*

My Dream Of You (IRE) *Tony Coyle*
2 ch f Equiano(FR) A Childs Dream (IRE) (Intense Focus (USA))
2051[9]

My Excelsa (IRE) *J F Levins* a70 59
3 b f Exceed And Excel(AUS) Emirates Joy (USA) (Street Cry (IRE))
(9540)

My Footsteps *Paul D'Arcy* a33 37
4 b g Footstepsinthesand Luminous Gold (Fantastic Light (USA))
4189[9] *5004[8]* 5254[12] **5842[8]** 6131[12]

My Frankel *Sir Michael Stoute* 67
2 b c Frankel My Special J'S (USA) (Harlan's Holiday (USA))
6669[7]

My Girl Maisie (IRE) *Richard Guest* a50 57
5 b m Fast Company(IRE) Queen Al Andalous (IRE) (King's Best (USA))
5531[10] *613[6]* *973[10]* ***1383[2]*** *1478[3]* *1731[6]* *3304[11]* 7286[18] 7590[13]

My Good Brother (IRE)
T G McCourt a66 65
10 b g Elusive City(USA) Final Favour (IRE) (Unblest)
307a[8] ***7086a[2]***

My Havana *Nigel Tinkler* a54 52
2 gr g Havana Gold(IRE) Si Belle (IRE) (Dalakhani (IRE))
3411[10] 3703[7] 5396[7] 5815[7] 6625[7] ***7306[6]*** *7582[6]* *8286[6]*

My Kinda Day (IRE) *Richard Fahey* 71
2 b g Exceed And Excel(AUS) Sound The Alarm (Compton Place)
2780[7] **3355[2]** 3810[3] 4938[6]

Mykindofsunshine (IRE) *Clive Cox* a65 73
3 gr g Zebedee Silk Fan (IRE) (Unfuwain (USA))
2024[3] 2730[5] 4185[4] 6373[4] *7189[7]*

Myklachi (FR) *David O'Meara* a69 67
3 b g Style Vendome(FR) Perle Noire (FR) (King's Best (USA))
1980[7] 3246[6] (4005) 4690[4] 4990[3]◆ 5425[2] 5915[8] ***(6660)*** 7368[14] *8019[8]*

My Lady Claire *Patrick Chamings* a52 54
3 ch f Cityscape Lady Sylvia (Haafhd)
1142[12] *1677[8]* **2340[8]** 3170[10] 3797[6] 4473[2] 4931[7] 6123[6] 7982[8] *9160[6]* *9439[4]*

My Law *Jim Boyle* a59 57
3 b f Mayson Lawyers Choice (Namid)
1687[8] 2204[3] ***3442[6]*** 3887[4] 8009[6] *8666[8]* *8998[2]* *9209[10]* *9659[5]*

My Little Orphan *Keith Dalgleish* 48
3 b g Heeraat(IRE) Costa Brava (IRE) (Sadler's Wells (USA))
4487[12]

My Lord *Paddy Butler* a38 35
11 br g Ishiguru(USA) Lady Smith (Greensmith)
1519[12]

My Lord And Master (IRE)
William Haggas a88 107
4 ch g Mastercraftsman(IRE) Affability (IRE) (Dalakhani (IRE))
4935[20] **6790a[3]** 7676a[10]

My Lovely One (FR) *E Libaud* a66 63
4 b m Muhtathir Nadrashaan (FR) (Darshaan)
1491a[7]

My Love's Passion (FR) *Y Barberot* 106
2 b f Elvstroem(AUS) Amber Two (Cadeaux Genereux)
(1657a) 3333a[3] **5228a[2]**

My Mate (IRE)
L W J Van Der Meulen a73 68
7 ch g Approve(IRE) Date Mate (USA) (Thorn Dance (USA))
5643a[5]

My Mo (FR) *Tristan Davidson* a55 43
7 b g Silver Frost(IRE) Anna Ivanovna (FR) (Fasliyev (USA))
3447[3] ***5435[2]***

My Motivate Girl (IRE)
Archie Watson a69 69
2 b f Requinto(IRE) Albaraaha (IRE) (Iffraaj)
2903[8]◆ **3405[2]** 3644[4] *4018[2]* 4344[3] 4727[5] *(5630)* *6113[5]* ***(7029)***

My Name Is Rio (IRE) *John Davies* a68 43
9 ch g Captain Rio Walk In My Shadow (IRE) (Orpen (USA))
43[7] *356[12]* 1765[14] 2638[14]

My Poem *Sir Michael Stoute* a75 67
2 ch f Poet's Voice Watchoverme (Haafhd)
7203[4] ***7832[4]*** 8432[4]

My Premier County (FR)
Matthieu Palussiere a59 67
2 b c Elusive City(USA) Premier Acclaim (IRE) (Acclamation)
2263a[3] 4949a[6] 5713a[9] 6384a[7] 7641a[2]

My Renaissance *Sam England* a58 50
9 bb g Medicean Lebenstanz (Singspiel (IRE))
4990[11] ***5851[3]*** *7578[9]*

My Reward *Tim Easterby* a87 94
7 b g Rail Link Tarot Card (Fasliyev (USA))
1947[13] 2742[16] 3081[8] 3655[3] 4102[11] **5199[2]** 5818[7] 6355[14] 6657[12] 6958[10] 7181[5]

Myrmidons (IRE) *Michael Dods* 73
3 ch g Casamento(IRE) Allegrissimo (IRE) (Redback)
2334[4] 3707[5]

My Sharona
Jassim Mohammed Ghazali a58 60
10 gr m Dark Angel(IRE) Tanda Tula (IRE) (Alhaarth (IRE))
892a[8]

My Snowdrop (IRE) *Claudia Erni* 82
4 b m Lilbourne Lad(IRE) Khatela (IRE) (Shernazar)
6769a[11]

My Society (IRE) *David Dennis* a63 59
4 b g Society Rock(IRE) Greek Easter (IRE) (Namid)
1565[10] **2741[10]** 3476[11] 4657[10]

Mysterious Look *Sarah Hollinshead* a7 12
6 ch m Sakhee's Secret Look Here's Carol (IRE) (Safawan)
6168[8] *7389[11]*

Mystery Power (IRE)
Richard Hannon 111
2 b c No Nay Never(USA) Gems (Haafhd)
(4106) **(4920)** 5520[6] 7456[2] 8113[7]

Mystical Jadeite *Grace Harris* a44 62
3 b g Finjaan Striking Pose (IRE) (Darshaan)
1652[9] **2690[7]** 3354[5] 4179[6] 5497[8] *6075[7]* 7025[8] *7573[11]*

Mystical Mac (IRE) *Iain Jardine* a33 42
4 b g Clodovil(IRE) Long Lost Love (Langfuhr (CAN))
3682[6] 4130[10]

Mystical Moon (IRE)
David C Griffiths a56 39
4 ch m Excelebration(IRE) Boast (Most Welcome)
117[6] *379[7]* *476[13]* *1020[6]* *1286[6]* *(1383)* ***(1565)*** **1837[5]** 2081[10] *2318[5]*◆ 4440[12] *5889[6]* *6682[10]* *6889[12]* *7281[14]* *7371[5]* *7606[7]*

Mystic Dragon
Mrs Ilka Gansera-Leveque a58 44
3 ch f Intello(GER) Portrait (Peintre Celebre (USA))
7704[5] ***8013[6]*** *8467[4]* *9573[4]*

Mystic Journey (AUS)
Adam Trinder 108
3 bk f Needs Further(AUS) White Gold (NZ) (Colombia (NZ))
8579a[5]

Mystic Knight (IRE) *Tim Easterby* a20 48
2 b c Sir Prancealot(IRE) Mystic Dream (Oasis Dream)
1499[5] *1968[6]* 2869[7] 4756[7]

Mystic Meg *Hughie Morrison* a77 88
4 b m Camelot Hypnology (USA) (Gone West (USA))
3010[8] **3698[2]** 7413[7]

Mystic Monarch (FR)
Andrea Marcialis 80
2 b f Holy Roman Emperor(IRE) Western Mystic (GER) (Doyen (IRE))
5976a[6]

Mystic River (IRE) *James Ferguson* a67
2 b c Animal Kingdom(USA) Harriet Tubman (USA) (Medaglia d'Oro (USA))
9452[4]◆ *9624[8]*

Mystique Moon *Doug Watson* a108
5 ch g Shamardal(USA) Celestial Girl (Dubai Destination (USA))
396a[5]◆ ***957a[5]***

Mystiquestar (IRE) *Roger Charlton* a58 68
3 b f Sea The Stars(IRE) Magique (IRE) (Jeremy (USA))
1543[5]◆ 2087[5] **2719[2]** 3310[5]

My Style (IRE)
Eve Johnson Houghton a62 77
3 gr g Holy Roman Emperor(IRE) That's My Style (Dalakhani (IRE))
2249[4] 3372[5] *4196[5]* 5494[3] 6220[3]◆

Mysusy (IRE) *Robert Cowell* a37 32
3 b f Dawn Approach(IRE) Gold Lace (IRE) (Invincible Spirit (IRE))
3425[9] 5822[6] *7468[8]* *8898[13]*

My Swashbuckler (IRE)
Alain Couetil 105
4 b h Pour Moi(IRE) Avventura (USA) (Johannesburg (USA))
3123a[10]

My Target (IRE) *Michael Wigham* a85 67
8 b g Cape Cross(IRE) Chercheuse (USA) (Seeking The Gold (USA))
19[2] *205[5]* *441[9]* *807[7]* *1018[5]* *8197[10]* *(8918)* *9255[5]* *9422[3]* *9510[2]*

Myth Creation (USA)
Joseph Patrick O'Brien a47 90
4 b m More Than Ready(USA) Mabadi (USA) (Sahm (USA))
7087a[4] 7794a[8] **8572a[4]**

Mythic (FR) *A De Royer-Dupre* 101
3 b f Camelot Gyrella (IRE) (Oasis Dream)
2498a[5] **7477a[5]** 7978a[8]

Mythica (IRE) *Jean-Pierre Carvalho* 94
3 b f Adlerflug(GER) Madhyana (GER) (Monsun (GER))
3877a[2] **5720a[9]** **7499a[2]** 7978a[13] 8587a[7]

Mythical (FR) *A P O'Brien* 103
2 b c Camelot Inchmina (Cape Cross (IRE))
8111[4] **8582a[3]**

Mythical Madness *Simon Dow* a88 87
8 b g Dubawi(IRE) Miss Delila (USA) (Malibu Moon (USA))
87[2]◆ *240[4]* *764[5]* *988[5]* *1232[5]* *1589[2]* 2033[4] ***(2320)*** 2808[5] *9309[11]* *9588[8]*

Mythical Magic (IRE)
Charlie Appleby 115
4 b g Iffraaj Mythie (FR) (Octagonal (NZ))
397a[2] **(846a)** 2829[12] 3948[13]

Mythical Spirit (IRE) *Julie Camacho* a72 77
5 b m Dragon Pulse(IRE) Call This Cat (IRE) (One Cool Cat (USA))
2637[7]◆

Mythmaker *Bryan Smart* a100 94
7 b g Major Cadeaux Mythicism (Oasis Dream)
2614[5] 6351[20] *7372[8]* *8607[7]*

Mythological (IRE) *Louise Allan* a12 11
4 gr g Galileo(IRE) Pembina (IRE) (Dalakhani (IRE))
3700[12] 4287[15] ***4594[12]*** *5285[12]*

My Thought (IRE) *John Gosden* 47
2 b g Kodiac Aricia (IRE) (Nashwan (USA))
5367[7]

My Town Chicago (USA)
Kevin Frost a68 52
4 b g Medaglia d'Oro(USA) Say You Will (IRE) (A.P. Indy (USA))
117[4] *239[6]* *1176[4]* *1378[10]* *(1986)* 2349[8] 2971[6] 4494[3] *6685[8]* *7576[2]* *8083[7]* ***(8704)*** *9365[9]* *9622[6]*

My Ukulele (IRE) *John Quinn* a60 78
3 ch f Power Island Music (IRE) (Mujahid (USA))
4725[5] (5272)◆ (5695) 6679[6] (7404) **7735[2]** 8031[4]

My Valentino (IRE) *Dianne Sayer* a31 59
6 ch g Duke Of Marmalade(IRE) Nadwah (USA) (Shadeed (USA))
1158[10] 2329[3] 2964[7] 3716[6] 4513[7] (5100) 6628[6] (7210) **(7508)** 8637[5]

My Vision *Saeed bin Suroor* a70
2 b g Showcasing Shembara (FR) (Dylan Thomas (IRE))
8346[3]◆ *9007[10]*

Mywayistheonlyway (IRE)
Grant Tuer a66 79
6 b g Tamayuz Soul Custody (CAN) (Perfect Soul (IRE))
2203[8] 2964[2] 3214[7] ***5852[4]***◆

Naadirr (IRE) *Kevin Ryan* a89 80
8 b g Oasis Dream Beach Bunny (IRE) (High Chaparral (IRE))
1459[8] *1942[7]* 2393[9] 3770[8] 5038[5] 6109[4] 6335[2] 6591[9] 7777[7]

Naaeebb (USA) *A bin Harmash* a70 64
5 b g Lonhro(AUS) My Dubai (IRE) (Dubai Millennium)
997[3]

Naantali (NZ)
Ciaron Maher & David Eustace 102
4 b m Rip Van Winkle(IRE) Zaloot (NZ) (Zabeel (NZ))
1974a[9]

Nabbeyl (IRE) *Roger Varian* a74 79
3 b c New Approach(IRE) Sajjhaa (King's Best (USA))
1697[3] 2229[2] *2697[7]*

Nabeyla *Roger Varian* a82
3 bb f New Approach(IRE) Feedyah (USA) (Street Cry (IRE))
(795) ***8294[2]***

Nabhan *Bernard Llewellyn* 76
7 b g Youmzain(IRE) Danidh Dubai (IRE) (Noverre (USA))
1463[6] 2901[2] 4112[4] **(4543)** 6218[4] 6642[5] 7294[4]

Nablawyh (IRE) *Ismail Mohammed* a49
2 b f Acclamation Simkana (IRE) (Kalanisi (IRE))
9163[10]

Nabunga (FR) *J Phelippon* a66 91
7 b g Aussie Rules(USA) Grantsville (GER) (Trempolino (USA))
6790a[4] **7860a[2]**

Nabvutika (IRE) *John Butler* a35 55
3 b f Poet's Voice Elope (GER) (Tiger Hill (IRE))
1957[12] 2262[3] **4485[2]** 4794[5] *6723[14]* *7375[12]* *8001[8]* *9282[11]*

Nacida (GER) *Yasmin Almenrader* a58 99
5 b m Wiener Walzer(GER) Nacella (GER) (Banyumanik (IRE))
7249a[5] **8171a[2]** 8804a[3]

Nafaas *Roger Charlton* a56
2 gr c Mastercraftsman(IRE) Woodland Scene (IRE) (Act One)
8999[9]

Nafaayes (IRE) *Jean-Rene Auvray* a67 69
5 ch m Sea The Stars(IRE) Shamtari (IRE) (Alhaarth (IRE))
84[8] *369[2]* *731[6]* *946[5]* *3444[2]*◆ *4251[3]* **(4881)** 5897[4] 6716[7] *8654[11]* *9204[3]*

Nagano Gold *Vaclav Luka Jr* a90 120
5 b h Sixties Icon Never Enough (GER) (Monsun (GER))
2428a[3] **4093[2]** 6522a[3] 7941a[8]

Nahaarr (IRE) *William Haggas* a101 100
3 b c Dark Angel(IRE) Charlotte Rua (IRE) (Redback)
(2397) (3351)◆ (4338) ***(4591)*** 5965[3]

Nahham (IRE) *Alexandra Dunn* a76 73
4 b g Dawn Approach(IRE) Anna's Rock (IRE) (Rock Of Gibraltar (IRE))
(1094) **(2280)** 2966[7] 3529[4] *4643[P]* *9054[P]*

Naida (GER) *Yasmin Almenrader* 100
3 rg f Reliable Man Nacella (GER) (Banyumanik (IRE))
5720a[2]

Naif (FR) *Y Durepaire* a93 94
4 b h French Fifteen(FR) Safia (FR) (Diktat)
2782a[4]

Naizagai *Roger Varian* a77 77
2 b c Dark Angel(IRE) Nazym (IRE) (Galileo (IRE))
8203[3] **8721[2]** ***9208[2]***◆

Najashee (IRE) *Roger Fell* a75 70
5 gr g Invincible Spirit(IRE) Tonnara (IRE) (Linamix (FR))
2959[4] 3867[6] ***4329[3]*** 4892[12] 5490[7] 6341[9] *6940[10]* *8713[13]*

Najib (IRE) *Roger Fell* a42 61
3 b g Invincible Spirit(IRE) Angel's Tears (Seeking The Gold (USA))
2208[6] 2795[10] 8181[5] *9109[13]*

Najm *F Rossi* a77 25
2 b c Intrinsic Paint The Star (IRE) (Acclamation)
5082[8] *5265[4]* *5856[3]*◆ *6980[10]* *(7419)* *7871[3]* *(8239a)* ***(9605a)***

Nakakande (IRE) *Karl Thornton* a56 64
3 b f Bungle Inthejungle Tallawalla (IRE) (Oratorio (IRE))
5938[6]

Nakeeta *Linda Jewell* a76 92
8 b g Sixties Icon Easy Red (IRE) (Hunting Lion (IRE))
2158[8] **3081[7]** 4899[10] 6834[6] 7866[10] *8654[9]*

Namasjar (FR) *F Vermeulen* a49 59
5 gr m Rajsaman(FR) Dame Phanie (FR) (Kaldoun (FR))
2675a[7]

Name The Wind *James Tate* a100 87
3 b c Toronado(IRE) Trust The Wind (Dansili)
(1940) 2411[19] *3581[5]* *4385[5]* 5150[4] *6841[3]*◆ *7448[7]* *8253[11]*

Namos (GER) *D Moser* 107
3 b c Medicean Namera (GER) (Areion (GER))
(3369a) **4705a[5]** 5716a[15] 6519a[4]

Nampara *Paul D'Arcy* a71 69
4 b m Kyllachy Nurai (Danehill Dancer (IRE))
8895[2] *9092[6]* *9498[5]*

Nananita (IRE) *Mark Loughnane* a52 55
3 b f War Command(USA) Causeway Queen (IRE) (Giant's Causeway (USA))
137[3] *437[6]* *1141[8]* *8502[11]* *9161[12]* *9445[12]*

Nancho (GER) *Gabor Maronka* 110
4 b g Tai Chi(GER) Nantana (GER) (Paolini (GER))
(8372a) **(8792a)**

Nanjoe *Jim Goldie* a53
4 b m Helmet(AUS) Hanella (IRE) (Galileo (IRE))
1400[7] *2241[13]*

Nanning City (IRE) *B A Murphy* a63 18
4 b g Vocalised(USA) Carina Ari (IRE) (Imperial Ballet (IRE))
1195[12]

Nantucket (IRE) *Sir Michael Stoute* a60 74
3 b f Sea The Stars(IRE) Lucy Cavendish (USA) (Elusive Quality (USA))
2087[9] 4738[3] **7526[2]**◆

Naples Bay *Katie Scott* a39 59
5 b g Kodiac Trombe (FR) (Bering)
2203[9] 2788[11] 4060[11] 4726[7] 4978[6] 6276[11] **(6621)** 7065[4] 7507[9] 7766[7] 8234[4] 8637[11]

Napping *Amy Murphy* a68 66
6 b m Sleeping Indian Vax Rapide (Sharpo)
159[5] (3738) *4025[5]* 4567[12] 5883[3] (6605) ***7446[4]*** *8199[6]* *8711[11]* *9386[8]* *9545[6]*

Naqaawa (IRE) *William Haggas* a98 98
4 b m Shamardal(USA) Hammiya (IRE) (Darshaan)
(4640) **5545[3]** 6378[9] 7347[4] 7658[8]

Narak *George Scott* 76
3 ch f Dubawi(IRE) Chachamaidee (IRE) (Footstepsinthesand)
3761[8] 5554[3] 6587[2] **(7204)**

Naralsaif (IRE) *Derek Shaw* a60 42
5 b m Arcano(IRE) Mejala (IRE) (Red Ransom (USA))
2508 (553) (719) (887) 10604 11755 18372 19867 424712

Nardo (FR) *F Foucher* a61 92
9 b g Aussie Rules(USA) Nannetta (IRE) (Mark Of Esteem (IRE))
7536a13

Nareia (GER) *Frau Erika Mader* 80
5 b m Areion(GER) Navicella (FR) (Beat Hollow)
7499a7

Narina (IRE) *William Haggas* a32 73
3 b f Rip Van Winkle(IRE) Savanna Days (IRE) (Danehill Dancer (IRE))
25835 30352 40227 (4484) 54264

Narjes *Laura Mongan* a75 75
5 b m Sepoy(AUS) Dubai Sea (USA) (Street Sense (USA))
3092 (473) 8763 23602 26918 31855 35394 45486 50875 55743 62807 65387 73448 756011 870513 91324 931010

Narrate *Hugo Palmer* a55
2 b f Dansili Indication (Sadler's Wells (USA))
84546

Narynkol *Roger Varian* a64 89
4 ch g Declaration Of War(USA) Nazym (IRE) (Galileo (IRE))
57832 65442

Nasaiym (USA) *James Tate* 91
2 b f More Than Ready(USA) Beyond Our Reach (IRE) (Danehill Dancer (IRE))
28402◆ (5132) 63748 74124

Nasee *John Joseph Hanlon* a60 72
4 b g Intello(GER) Mischief Making (USA) (Lemon Drop Kid (USA))
22592 (2975) 37783 5599a12

Naseeb (IRE) *Richard Fahey* a40 62
2 b g Elzaam(AUS) Las Encinas (Pastoral Pursuits)
45166 49996

Nashirah *H-A Pantall* a71 99
3 b f Dubawi(IRE) Perfect Light (IRE) (Galileo (IRE))
48a2 511a5 18325 231911 6252a3

Nashy (IRE) *Sir Michael Stoute* a64
2 b c Camelot Venus De Milo (IRE) (Duke Of Marmalade (IRE))
86054

Nataleena (IRE) *Ben Haslam* a66 53
3 b f Nathaniel(IRE) Hayyona (Multiplex)
28758 40764 56906 66602 74157 (8081) 85243 94674◆

Natalie Express (FR) *Henry Spiller* a74 69
5 b m Excelebration(IRE) Miss Emma May (IRE) (Hawk Wing (USA))
2568 6977

Natalie's Joy *Mark Johnston* 73
3 b f Lope De Vega(IRE) Semaphore (Zamindar (USA))
28069

Natch *Michael Attwater* a45 52
4 b g Nathaniel(IRE) Angara (Alzao (USA))
619 3093 7244 11837 47377 53104

Nate The Great *Archie Watson* 101
3 b c Nathaniel(IRE) Theladyinquestion (Dubawi (IRE))
26193 398410 48453 5364a6 5717a8

Nathanielhawthorne *Marco Botti* a68 61
3 ch g Nathaniel(IRE) Gino's Spirits (Perugino (USA))
11658 15095 17713 33118

Nathaniella *Mme M-C Chaalon* a60
3 b f Nathaniel(IRE) Cherry Malotte (Pivotal)
9058a11 9281a13

National Glory (IRE) *Archie Watson* a73 68
4 b g Invincible Spirit(IRE) Ponty Acclaim (IRE) (Acclamation)
1393 3616 56410 7555 9286 12098 19305 24833 28047 30143 31883 35763 39363 46945

National League (IRE)
Richard Fahey 86
2 gr g Gutaifan(IRE) Margarita (IRE) (Marju (IRE))
40324◆ 44862 (4876) 63755 (7763)

National Treasure (IRE)
Charlie Appleby a70 83
2 b f Camelot Flawless Beauty (Excellent Art)
51393◆ 65924

Native Appeal (IRE) *Doug Watson* a71 81
4 b g Exceed And Excel(AUS) Picture Hat (USA) (El Prado (IRE))
573a7

Native Fighter (IRE) *Jedd O'Keeffe* a76 77
5 b g Lawman(FR) Night Of Magic (IRE) (Peintre Celebre (USA))
5224 7375 20927 23984 2636F 56213

Native Silver *Robert Eddery* a75 58
3 gr g Olympic Glory(IRE) Kendorova (IRE) (Kendor (FR))
(1195) 21924 366410 422612

Native Tribe *Charlie Appleby* 85
2 b c Farhh Anything Goes (IRE) (Nayef (USA))
51312 (5860)

Nat Love (IRE) *Mick Channon* a69 72
2 b g Gregorian(IRE) Chaguaramas (IRE) (Mujadil (USA))
31412◆ 34912 39437 57772 61064◆ (6532) 70646 71556 77255

Natsovia *Jamie Osborne* a74
3 ch f Nathaniel(IRE) So Belle (Singspiel (IRE))
3582 (917) 12335 40312

Natty Dresser (IRE) *Debbie Hughes* a23 26
4 b g Dandy Man(IRE) Parlour (Dansili)
93315

Natty Night *William Muir* a82 82
3 b g Nathaniel(IRE) Danehill Dreamer (USA) (Danehill (USA))
22995 29146 (3692) 45592 73022 809212 86085 91672

Natural Power (IRE) *Mrs D A Love* 81
2 bb c Slade Power(IRE) Miss Intimate (USA) (War Chant (USA))
5710a2

Nature Strip (AUS) *Chris Waller* 128
4 ch g Nicconi(AUS) Strikeline (AUS) (Desert Sun)
8362a4

Naughty Rascal (IRE)
Richard Hannon a89 92
3 ch g Kyllachy Gerika (FR) (Galileo (IRE))
18514 28356 34222 41866

Nausha *Roger Varian* a83 102
3 b f Kingman Nazym (IRE) (Galileo (IRE))
19394 (2745) 3905a14 7242a6 833310

Nautical Haven *Suzi Best* a68 58
5 b g Harbour Watch(IRE) Mania (IRE) (Danehill (USA))
231812 59907 90924

Navadir (JPN) *Marco Botti* a70
3 b f Deep Impact(JPN) Zumoorooda (AUS) (Encosta De Lago (AUS))
1222◆ 5673 14815 17306

Navajo Dawn (IRE) *Robyn Brisland* a62 64
2 b f Dawn Approach(IRE) Patience Alexander (IRE) (Kodiac)
284011 34695 42752 51465 56189 88994 93947

Navajo Pass *Donald McCain* 92
3 b g Nathaniel(IRE) Navajo Charm (Authorized (IRE))
37242 57422 (6340) 809812

Navajo Star (IRE) *Robyn Brisland* a79 81
5 b m Mastercraftsman(IRE) Champagne Aerial (IRE) (Night Shift (USA))
2912 (385) 9164 (991) 11728 133010 15032 19714 23985 29367

Navajo War Dance *Ali Stronge* a65 72
6 br g Makfi Navajo Rainbow (Rainbow Quest (USA))
27937 411210

Navalmoral *M Boutin* a67 60
3 b g Charm Spirit(IRE) Rose Memory (IRE) (Elusive City (USA))
3710a12

Navarra Princess (IRE)
Don Cantillon a47 49
4 b m Intense Focus(USA) Navarra Queen (Singspiel (IRE))
20668 27403 31423 35927 916012 94509

Navigate By Stars (IRE)
Gordon Elliott 71
3 br f Sea The Stars(IRE) Bitooh (Diktat)
18244◆ 22536 (3057)◆ 33104 46719 56238 77828

Nawar *Martin Bosley* a79 62
4 b g Henrythenavigator(USA) Nouriya (Danehill Dancer (IRE))
11026 20053 302211 (4028) 85485 91738 96586

Nayala *A Wohler* 91
3 b f Maxios Ninfea (GER) (Selkirk (USA))
5227a6 7250a3

Nayef Road (IRE) *Mark Johnston* 113
3 ch c Galileo(IRE) Rose Bonheur (Danehill Dancer (IRE))
(2446) 27776 33415 39843 48452 (5585) 63535 71963 7927a7

Nayel (IRE) *Richard Hannon* a34 80
7 b g Acclamation Soliza (IRE) (Intikhab (USA))
142214 20957 28006 741310

Nayibeth (USA) *Wesley A Ward* a95 74
2 b f Carpe Diem(USA) Le Relais (USA) (Coronado's Quest (USA))
404813

Nayslayer (IRE) *Ali Jan* a44 58
3 b g No Nay Never(USA) Elaflaak (USA) (Gulch (USA))
511a7 956a5

Nazeef *John Gosden* a91 106
3 b f Invincible Spirit(IRE) Handassa (Dubawi (IRE))
36033◆ (4298) (6862) (7463)◆

Near Kettering *Sam England* a70 68
5 ch g Medicean Where's Broughton (Cadeaux Genereux)
309512 35688 (6180) 74397 84226

Nearly Perfection (IRE) *Alan King* a58
3 b f Camacho Leenavesta (USA) (Arch (USA))
96357

Nearly There *Wilf Storey* a60 60
6 b g Virtual Nicoise (IRE) (Lear Spear (USA))
13989 17188 34478 (4126)◆ 52193 59745 68275 70485 823813 93458

Nearooz *Roger Varian* a85 94
3 b f New Approach(IRE) Modeyra (Shamardal (USA))
(2018) 29342 43182◆ 55459 (6902) 78958

Near Poet (GER) *Markus Klug* 82
2 b c Poet's Voice Near Galante (GER) (Galileo (IRE))
8964a3

Nebo (IRE) *T Hogan* a72 100
4 b g Kodiac Kindling (Dr Fong (USA))
1776a8

Necoleta *Sylvester Kirk* a63 47
3 b f Intello(GER) Ellbeedee (IRE) (Dalakhani (IRE))
10196 135211 57486 62799 67023◆ 76852 (8251) 85537 90904 94465 (9552) 96095

Ned Mackay *Roger Charlton* a67 64
3 b g Kodiac Marywell (Selkirk (USA))
4617◆

Ned Pepper (IRE) *Alan King* a77 74
3 b g Intello(GER) Storyland (USA) (Menifee (USA))
358411 42583 48427 57782 82985◆ 86563

Needs To Be Seen (FR) *Jim Goldie* a68 72
4 b g Motivator Morning Line (FR) (Anabaa (USA))
27633 33618 59025 70038 736811 94677

Neelakurinji (FR) *F Foresi* a68 65
3 b f Rio De La Plata(USA) Ballerina Girl (FR) (Moscow Ballet (USA))
6063a3

Neesaan *Simon Crisford* a55
3 b f New Approach(IRE) Red Dune (IRE) (Red Ransom (USA))
21882

Nefarious (IRE) *Henry Candy* a92 84
3 ro c Zebedee Tellelle (IRE) (Trans Island)
(320)◆ 20545 27467 34652 38583 44203 47932 57734

Neff (GER) *Gary Moore* a57 68
4 b g Pastorius(GER) Nouvelle Fortune (IRE) (Alzao (USA))
11838 (2617) 342910 53164 71166

Nefyn Beach (IRE) *Jo Hughes* a66 56
3 b f Big Bad Bob(IRE) Lucky Date (IRE) (Halling (USA))
2896 10948 15155 2759a6 5329a2 6486a5

Nehaall *Roger Varian* a77
2 ch f Pivotal Khatiba (IRE) (Kheleyf (USA))
93472◆

Neige Eternelle (FR) *H-A Pantall* a69 58
4 ch m Makfi Still I'm A Star (IRE) (Lawman (FR))
1578a6 2264a3

Neigh Dramas *Bryan Smart* 13
3 ch g Equiano(FR) Silvee (Avonbridge)
263311 407813

Neileta *Tim Easterby* 64
3 b g Epaulette(AUS) Neila (GER) (Diktat)
24825◆ 32713◆ 35132 40032 (4690) 555611 57924 67026 72909

Nelkan (IRE) *H-A Pantall* a39
4 ch m Dubawi(IRE) Brom Felinity (AUS) (Encosta De Lago (AUS))
9483a12

Nelly (FR) *S Smrczek* a59 76
4 bl m Manduro(GER) Nebraska I (FR) (Octagonal (NZ))
1491a12

Nelson River *Tony Carroll* a58 64
4 b g Mount Nelson I Say (IRE) (Oratorio (IRE))
75758

Nelson Road (IRE) *Tristan Davidson* a35 75
6 b g Mount Nelson Merciful (IRE) (Cape Cross (IRE))
19717

Nelson's Hill *William de Best-Turner* a38
9 b g Mount Nelson Regal Step (Royal Applause)
4399 9904 126511

Nemean Lion (GER) *A Fabre* 75
2 b c Golden Horn Ninfea (GER) (Selkirk (USA))
8481a2

Neon Sea (FR) *Sir Michael Stoute* a92 88
3 b f Siyouni(FR) Carnoustie (FR) (Acclamation)
23405 (3080) (3583) 42429

Neroli *Derek Shaw*
2 gr f Tamayuz Ming Meng (IRE) (Intikhab (USA))
799510

Nervous Nerys (IRE) *Alex Hales* a45 53
3 b f Kodiac Sassy (FR) (Sinndar (IRE))
9186 11409 314810 36455 (4219) (5878) 67945

Nespola *Roger Varian* 36
3 b f New Approach(IRE) Nargys (IRE) (Lawman (FR))
21038 27718

Ness Of Brodgar *Mark H Tompkins* a56 25
4 b m Harbour Watch(IRE) Missouri (Charnwood Forest (IRE))
273812 34972 425113 45943 52717

Nessun Dorma (IRE) *W P Mullins* 97
6 b g Canford Cliffs(IRE) Idle Chatter (IRE) (Galileo (IRE))
7216a5

Nessy (USA) *Ian R Wilkes* 104
6 bb g Flower Alley(USA) Flower Forest (USA) (Kris S (USA))
7226a2 8155a6

Netley Abbey *Paul George* a43 35
5 b g Myboycharlie(IRE) Ana Style (FR) (Anabaa Blue)
36911 73110

Nette Rousse (GER) *Ralph Beckett* 91
3 ch f Mastercraftsman(IRE) Nina Celebre (IRE) (Peintre Celebre (USA))
25816 32633◆ (3860) 54588 (5982) 75665

Nettie Honeyball *Nigel Tinkler* a30 19
3 ch f Coach House(IRE) Concentration (IRE) (Mind Games)
12758

Neufbosc (FR)
David A & B Hayes & Tom Dabern a76 103
4 gr g Mastercraftsman(IRE) Nonsuch Way (IRE) (Verglas (IRE))
8600a9 8844a21

Nevada *Steve Gollings* a69 76
6 gr g Proclamation(IRE) La Columbina (Carnival Dancer)
1002◆ 7822 13982◆ 22023 (4036)

Nevendon *Michael Bell* 43
2 b c Nathaniel(IRE) Unex Mona Lisa (Shamardal (USA))
846412

Never Alone *Charlie Appleby* 84
2 b g Dubawi(IRE) Yummy Mummy (Montjeu (IRE))
64093 73382 78979

Never A Word (USA)
Alexandra Dunn a59 46
5 br g Lonhro(AUS) Janetstickettocats (USA) (Storm Cat (USA))
83476 86395 94975 95604

Never Back Down (IRE)
Adrian McGuinness a87 74
4 b g Kodiac Steer By The Stars (IRE) (Pivotal)
52a10 640a12 843a12 39917 46485 6986a11

Never Be Enough *Keith Dalgleish* a88 89
4 ch m Sir Percy Camp Fire (IRE) (Lahib (USA))
20568 (2785)◆ 30572◆ 34497 40572 (4278) 44903 47587 52182 66564 94173

Never Come Back (FR) *M Nigge* a78 64
3 bl g Manduro(GER) Nijenrode (GER) (Tertullian (USA))
1241a6 1741a4

Never Dark *Andrew Balding* a72
2 b c No Nay Never(USA) Dark Missile (Night Shift (USA))
92993◆

Never Do Nothing (IRE)
Andrew Balding a71 97
3 b g Casamento(IRE) Purple Tigress (Dubai Destination (USA))
18353 24463 30732 (4063) 49013 59312 69523

Nevereversaynever (IRE)
J A Stack a78 79
3 b f No Nay Never(USA) Dowager (Groom Dancer (USA))
5325a10

Never In Paris (IRE) *K R Burke* a71 83
2 b f No Nay Never(USA) Meeting In Paris (IRE) (Dutch Art)
(4659)◆ 51858 96235

Never In Red (IRE) *Robyn Brisland* a65 67
2 b c Anjaal Bank On Black (IRE) (Big Bad Bob (IRE))
49103◆ 55147 68833 (7269) 83028 85463

Never No More (IRE) *A P O'Brien* a93 109
3 ch c No Nay Never(USA) Law Of The Jungle (IRE) (Catcher In The Rye (IRE))
(1306a) (1600a) 71942 8805a14

Never Said Nothing (IRE)
Jonathan Portman a61 61
2 b g Hallowed Crown(AUS) Semiquaver (IRE) (Mark Of Esteem (IRE))
15569 21916 32457 52968 65712 84158 88592 91792 939911

Never Say Never (FR) *S Jesus* a52 56
6 gr m Never On Sunday(FR) Teatime (FR) (Loup Solitaire (USA))
3711a12

Never Surrender (IRE)
Charles Hills a71 83
5 b g High Chaparral(IRE) Meiosis (USA) (Danzig (USA))
194311 257810 37996 488414 60442◆ 64486 72948

Never To Forget *John Butler* a59
4 b g Medicean Fontaine House (Pyramus (USA))
72785 77727 86455 920712

Neverushacon (IRE)
Mrs John Harrington 81
8 b g Echo Of Light Lily Beth (IRE) (Desert King (IRE))
5508a5

Never Without You (FR) *P Capelle* a47 48
5 bl g Slickly Royal(FR) Isula Di Isula (IRE) (Anabaa (USA))
6267a13 7800a11

New Agenda *Paul Webber* a78 72
7 b g New Approach(IRE) Prove (Danehill (USA))
2928 (592a) 780a10 22078 36339 93039

New Angel *John Gosden* a75
3 ch f New Approach(IRE) Angel Terrace (USA) (Ghostzapper (USA))
60742◆ 71902 (7822)

New Arrangement *James Tate* a96 95
3 b g New Approach(IRE) Sooraah (Dubawi (IRE))
35172◆ (5098) (7228)◆ 83203

New Arrival (IRE) *James Tate* a59
2 gr f Gutaifan(IRE) Doula (USA) (Gone West (USA))
90624 96683

Newbolt (IRE) *Ralph Beckett* a78 42
2 gr c Bated Breath Nirva (IRE) (Verglas (IRE))
86579 (9155)

New Cracker's (IRE) *N Caullery* a60
2 b c Toronado(IRE) Pastiches (Street Cry (IRE))
8508a9

Newcross (IRE) *A J Martin* 90
6 b g Cape Cross(IRE) Miss Polaris (Polar Falcon (USA))
(3384a) 5508a16

New Day Dawn (IRE)
Tom Dascombe a83 97
4 ch m Dawn Approach(IRE) Roo (Rudimentary (USA))
28094◆ 33595 47584 59497 637917

New Expo (IRE) *Julia Feilden* a42 49
3 ch g New Approach(IRE) Anayid (A.P. Indy (USA))
21509 32753 43457 49986 58802 70254 75205

Newgate Angel *Tony Coyle* a42 49
3 b f Heeraat(IRE) Rio's Girl (Captain Rio)
19826 23005 29084 421212 45085 903411

Newgate Duchess *Tony Coyle*
5 b m Haafhd Arctic Queen (Linamix (FR))
79037

Newgirlintown (IRE) *Gerard O'Leary* a53 52
3 b f Clodovil(IRE) La Chassotte (FR) (Until Sundown (USA))
92484 94036

New Graduate (IRE) *James Tate* 112
4 ch h New Approach(IRE) Srda (USA) (Kingmambo (USA))
(2116) 398719 43972 5168aP

New Jack Swing (IRE)
Richard Hannon a51 57
2 b g Dandy Man(IRE) Boca Dancer (IRE) (Indian Ridge (IRE))
34198 47986 50826 55765 59583 84525

New Jazz (USA) *John Gosden* a78 84
3 ch f Scat Daddy(USA) Seanchai (USA) (English Channel (USA))
20182 27605 35803 (4806) 55652

New King *John Gosden* a86 105
3 b c Frankel Marine Bleue (IRE) (Desert Prince (IRE))
1563 20884 (3859)

New Legend (KOR)
Kim Young Kwan a73
4 b h Menifee(USA) Smarty Kota (USA) (Smarty Jones (USA))
7011a9

New Look (FR) *Tim Easterby* a56 71
4 gr g Style Vendome(FR) Tara's Force (IRE) (Acclamation)
210511 33086 38139 424011 572610 65829 73787 790713

New Man *Tim Easterby*
2 b g Equiano(FR) Magic Myth (IRE) (Revoque (IRE))
6175[14] 6970[11]

Newmarket Warrior (IRE) a73 73
Iain Jardine
8 b g Dalakhani(IRE) Heavens Peak (Pivotal)
22[3] 209[4] 355[2]◆ 2246[4] 4108[4] 4329[6] 5817[2] 6626[7] 7305[6] 8087[1] 8173[3] 9256[9]

New Queen *L Bietolini* a74 89
3 b f Charm Spirit(IRE) Air Biscuit (IRE) (Galileo (IRE))
2161a[11]

New Rhythm *Alistair Whillans* a40 41
4 b m Monsieur Bond(IRE) Social Rhythm (Beat All (USA))
5554[11] 6663[12] 7489[7] 8663[8]

New Rich *Eve Johnson Houghton* a58 49
9 b g Bahamian Bounty Bling Bling (IRE) (Indian Ridge (IRE))
(60) 244[2] 484[10] 1210[7] 2728[12] 3592[8]

Newsflash *Amy Murphy* a35
3 ch f Showcasing Pivotal Bride (Dubawi (IRE))
442[10] 723[10]

New Show (IRE) *Michael Bell* 92
4 ch g New Approach(IRE) Music Show (IRE) (Noverre (USA))
1757[14] (2209) 2440[8] 3087[4] 3663[4] (4437)

Newsical *Mark Walford* a47 61
2 b g Music Master Front Page News (Assertive)
3702[10] 4516[8] 4903[4] 5703[7] 7064[7] 7584[8] 8085[10] 9394[9] 9499[6]

Newspeak (IRE) *Fred Watson* a11 40
7 b g New Approach(IRE) Horatia (IRE) (Machiavellian (USA))
3224[12] 4513[9] 5098[4]

Newstead Abbey *Rebecca Bastiman* a69 41
9 b g Byron Oatcake (Selkirk (USA))
315[7] (586) 830[4] 1016[7] 1522[6] 6204[15] 7066[8] 7507[8] 7869[6] 8233[9] 8646[9] 9039[7] 9283[10]

New Street (IRE) *Suzi Best* a64 61
8 gr g Acclamation New Deal (Rainbow Quest (USA))
39[10] 145[5] 309[9]

Newton Jack *Stuart Kittow* a61 26
2 b g Fast Company(IRE) Jackline (Diktat)
2767[9] 8418[4] 9008[6]

Newton Kyme (IRE) *David Simcock* a49
3 b g Vale Of York(IRE) My Lucky Liz (IRE) (Exceed And Excel (AUS))
442[6] 554[10]

New Trails (USA) *A bin Harmash* a112 87
5 b g Medaglia d'Oro(USA) Issaqueena (USA) (Mr Prospector (USA))
(172a) 638a[2] 1114a[4] 1447a[10]

New Tune *Ralph Beckett* 31
2 b f Fastnet Rock(AUS) Pure Song (Singspiel (IRE))
5342[8] 9163[11]

New World Tapestry (USA) a87 86
A P O'Brien
2 b c War Front(USA) Tapestry (IRE) (Galileo (IRE))
(7661) 8716[8]

New York Girl (IRE)
Joseph Patrick O'Brien 105
2 ch f New Approach(IRE) Annee Lumiere (IRE) (Giant's Causeway (USA))
(7742a)

Newyorkstateofmind *William Muir* a74 68
2 b g Brazen Beau(AUS) Albany Rose (IRE) (Noverre (USA))
3595[6] 3942[2] 6755[2] 7227[6] 7556[2] (7785)

Next Shares (USA) *Richard Baltas* a1 111
6 bb g Archarcharch(USA) Two Dot Slew (USA) (Evansville Slew (USA))
444a[7] 7922a[6] 8774a[13]

Nezar (IRE) *Dean Ivory* a81 75
8 ch g Mastercraftsman(IRE) Teddy Bears Picnic (Oasis Dream)
361[7] 914[4] 1329[8] 1655[8] (2596)◆ 3649[7] 4226[6] 5283[9] 6026[9] 6717[5] 9498[8]

Nguni *Paul Cole* a62 62
3 ch f Mount Nelson Flashbang (Dubawi (IRE))
235[7] 437[3]

Niamh's Starlight (IRE)
Bryan Smart a39 41
2 b f Baltic King Brillano (FR) (Desert King (IRE))
7063[7] 8084[13]

Nibras Again *Paul Midgley* a77 86
5 b g Kyllachy Regina (Green Desert (USA))
953[5] 1342[5] 1899[2] 2294[8] 2910[3] 4301[2] (4406)◆ 4691[2] 6178[9] 6455[9] 7077[7] 7771[6] 8304[7]

Nibras Shadow (IRE)
Ismail Mohammed a68 68
2 gr f Dark Angel(IRE) Althea Rose (IRE) (Green Desert (USA))
6831[5] 7695[12] 8525[5]

Nibras Time (USA)
Ismail Mohammed a38
4 gr h Exchange Rate(USA) Clever Timing (USA) (Elusive Quality (USA))
634a[6]

Nibras Wish (IRE)
Ismail Mohammed a51 71
2 ch c Tamayuz Viking Rose (IRE) (Norse Dancer (IRE))
6704[8] 7346[6] 8257[3]

Nica (GER) *Dr A Bolte* 106
4 rg m Kamsin(GER) Narrika (GER) (Santiago (GER))
(3288a) 5230a[3] 6770a[2] 7750a[4] 8392a[4]

Nicco (FR) *S Smrczek* a69 59
3 bb c Orpen(USA) Nightdance Sun (GER) (Monsun (GER))
421a[15]

Nice One Too *David C Griffiths*
2 b f Swiss Spirit Bondi Beach Babe (Misu Bond (IRE))
4433[11] 4903[7] 6011[6] 6577[6]

Nice To Sea (IRE) *Olly Murphy* a56 61
5 b m Born To Sea(IRE) Campessa (IRE) (Intikhab (USA))
67[11] 602[3] 910[2] 1334[11] 2014[5]

Nice To See You (FR) *Robert Collet* a103 108
6 b h Siyouni(FR) Around Me (IRE) (Johannesburg (USA))
682a[4]

Nicholas T *Jim Goldie* a87 103
7 b g Rail Link Thorntoun Piccolo (Groom Dancer (USA))
2187[5] 2419[3]◆ 2609[20] 3160[4] 4097[6] 4490[2]◆ (4692)◆ 4981[2] (5240)◆ (5489) 5930[4] 7122[3] 7434[2] 7694[12]

Nickajack Cave (IRE) *G M Lyons* 96
3 gr g Kendargent(FR) Could You Be Loved (IRE) (Montjeu (IRE))
6192a[5]

Nicki's Angel (IRE) *Richard Fahey* 85
3 gr f Dark Angel(IRE) Titova (Halling (USA))
3359[8] 3865[17] 4368[5] 4894[12] 5399[4] 5972[5] 6607[7]

Nicklaus *William Haggas* a99 99
4 ch g Exceed And Excel(AUS) Nianga (GER) (Lomitas)
3313[8] 3581[3] 4255[2] 5519[15] 6150[2] 7617[3]

Nickorette (FR) *A Kahn*
3 bl f Nicaron(GER) Banderille Royale (FR) (Kapgarde (FR))
7476a[10]

Nickos (GER) *S Smrczek* a64 63
3 b g Pomellato(GER) Navicella (FR) (Beat Hollow)
9504a[4]

Nicks Not Wonder *Jamie Osborne* a74
2 b c Siyouni(FR) Singuliere (IRE) (Singspiel (IRE))
7555[8] 8528[2]

Nick Vedder *Robyn Brisland* a75 72
5 b g Rip Van Winkle(IRE) Devotion (IRE) (Dylan Thomas (IRE))
(24) 748a[6] 964[4] 4649[10] 5395[12] 5868[3] 6326[5] 7121[14] 7607[3] 8016[5] 8267[8] 8642[7] 9030[6] 9476[12] 9645[4]

Nicky Baby (IRE) *Dean Ivory* a51 51
5 gr g Dark Angel(IRE) Moon Club (IRE) (Red Clubs (IRE))
155[6] 436[8] 593[7] 1362[6] (1717) 2240[2] 3142[5] 3687[9] 6049[9] 6723[7] 6885[8]

Nicky Nook *Stella Barclay* a33
6 b m Captain Gerrard(IRE) Rose Bounty (Polar Falcon (USA))
608[9] 1080[7]

Nicky Style (FR) *G Botti* a57 49
3 gr f Style Vendome(FR) Green Shadow (FR) (Green Tune (USA))
5329a[3]

Nicolina (GER) *Jo Hughes* 29
4 b m Tertullian(USA) Navalde (GER) (Alkalde (GER))
8737a[7]

Nietzsche *Brian Ellison* a72 78
6 ch g Poet's Voice Ganga (IRE) (Generous (IRE))
948[5] 1159[9] 2092[3]

Nifty Niece (IRE) *Ann Duffield* a21 52
5 gr m Zebedee Hasty Harriet (IRE) (Choisir (AUS))
3413[15] 4257[8] 5558[5] 6462[4] 6590[2] 9034[14]

Nigel Nott *David Simcock* a66
3 ch g Dutch Art Baileys Jubilee (Bahamian Bounty)
8695[3]

Nigg Bay (IRE) *J F Levins* a79 78
5 b g Exceed And Excel(AUS) Muaamara (Bahamian Bounty)
(4721) 5495[2] 6203[8] 7085a[5]

Night Bear *Ed Vaughan* a64
2 ch c Dragon Pulse(IRE) Contenance (IRE) (Dansant)
9095[5] 9634[6]

Night Closure *John Butler* a20 38
3 b g Royal Applause Easter Diva (IRE) (Dansili)
1594[5]

Night Colours (IRE) *Simon Crisford* a62 103
2 b f Night Of Thunder(IRE) Many Colours (Green Desert (USA))
6592[5] (7235)◆ 7726[2] (8393a)

Night Fury *Lucinda Egerton* a22 41
3 b g Sir Percy Hell Hath No Fury (Oratorio (IRE))
1898[6] 2195[6] 3372[9] 5235[17]

Nightingale Valley *Stuart Kittow* a68 82
6 ch m Compton Place Dancing Storm (Trans Island)
(2584) 3468[7] 4283[8] 5709[6] 6362[6] 7975[13]

Night Law *Katie Scott* a28 58
5 b m Lawman(FR) Night Carnation (Sleeping Indian)
4720[13] 5235[13] (5767) (6273) 7066[10] 8235[8] 8638[9]

Night Of Fashion (IRE)
Ralph Beckett a45
2 b f Camelot Shirley A Star (USA) (Cozzene (USA))
9634[13]

Night Of The Opera (IRE)
Matthieu Palussiere 62
2 ch c Rio De La Plata(USA) She's Got The Beat (FR) (Slickly (FR))
2263a[7]

Night Secret (IRE) *William Haggas* a73 78
3 b f Dark Angel(IRE) Providencia (Oasis Dream)
(3420)

Night's Watch (NZ) *Chris Waller* 107
5 br g Redwood Glory Run (AUS) (Exceed And Excel (AUS))
8138a[2] 8768a[6] 8952a[13]

Night Time Girl *Ismail Mohammed* a53
2 ch f Night Of Thunder(IRE) Assabiyya (IRE) (Cape Cross (IRE))
9383[5] 9634[10]

Nikisophia (IRE) *Maurizio Grassi* 95
3 b f No Nay Never(USA) Apache Dream (IRE) (Indian Ridge (IRE))
(8787a)

Nikkei (GER) *P Schiergen* 108
4 ch h Pivotal Nicella (GER) (Lando (GER))
2666a[5] 3678a[6] 4622a[2] 5719a[6] 7249a[10] 8792a[10]

Nikolayeva *Sir Mark Prescott Bt* a52
2 b f Archipenko(USA) Nezhenka (With Approval (CAN))
8454[12] 8913[14] 9242[6] 9501[3]

Nimocis (FR) *C Boutin* a60 40
4 ch h Medecis Nimohe (FR) (Excellent Art)
1391a[11] 2182a[8]

Nimr *J Phelippon* a78 77
6 b g Shamardal(USA) Riberac (Efisio)
1349a[4]

Nimrod (IRE) *M Weiss* a90 92
6 b h High Chaparral(IRE) Night Of Magic (IRE) (Peintre Celebre (USA))
592a[4] 780a[3]

Nina Bailarina *Ed Walker* 101
2 b f Lope De Vega(IRE) Vesnina (Sea The Stars (IRE))
5132[2]◆ (5906) 7292a[2] 7692[11] 8970a[8]

Ninario (GER) *Waldemar Hickst* a93 102
4 ch h Areion(GER) Ninigretta (GER) (Dashing Blade)
3879a[8] 6770a[4] 7750a[2] 8392a[5]

Nine Below Zero
Fawzi Abdulla Nass a111 93
4 b g Showcasing Finesse (Shamardal (USA))
512a[4] 729a[3] 842a[4] 1109a[2] 1444a[7]

Nine Elms (USA) *Roy Bowring* a59
4 ch g Street Cry(IRE) Nawaiet (USA) (Zilzal (USA))
971[4] 1080[6] 1550[6]

Ninepin Bowler *Ann Duffield* a64 64
5 b g Rip Van Winkle(IRE) Smooth As Silk (IRE) (Danehill Dancer (IRE))
3163[6] 3718[5] (4004)◆ 4587[5] 6180[8] 6586[7]

Nineteenrbo'Malley *Robyn Brisland* 49
7 b g Beat All(USA) My Nora (IRE) (Rossini (USA))
2417[4] 3882[5] 4760[6] 5891[10]

Ningaloo (GER) *Rebecca Bastiman* a52 59
5 b g Siyouni(FR) Notre Dame (GER) (Acatenango (GER))
4732[5] 5656[11] 6259[3] 6666[6]◆ 7513[5] 7956[10]

Ninjago *Paul Midgley* a64 71
9 b g Mount Nelson Fidelio's Miracle (USA) (Mountain Cat (USA))
883[5] 1976[8] 2203[13] 2958[8] (3413) 4276[2] (4823) 5330[2] 6058[3] 6621[2] 7066[5]

Nipozzano (IRE) *Marc Stott* 85
3 b c War Command(USA) Amor Fatal (IRE) (Kheleyf (USA))
7497a[10]

Nirodha (IRE) *Amy Murphy* a74 74
2 ch f Camacho Ekagra (Barathea (IRE))
4766[2] (5353) (6458) 7117[11] 7620[5] 8665[4] 9137[11]

Nitro (USA) *Doug Watson* a28
3 b c Candy Ride(ARG) Secret Jewel (USA) (Bernardini (USA))
169a[13]

Nitro Boost (IRE) *W McCreery* a72 101
3 b f Dandy Man(IRE) Esuvia (IRE) (Whipper (USA))
2221a[7] 2605a[3] 4313a[14] 5325a[11] (6648a)

Nitro Express *Roger Charlton* 58
2 b c Dubawi(IRE) Flotilla (FR) (Mizzen Mast (USA))
8722[6]

Nkosikazi *William Haggas* a91 96
4 gr m Cape Cross(IRE) Whatami (Daylami (IRE))
4113[2]◆ 4851[2] 6721[4] 7895[3] 8710[3] 9210a[12]

Noafence (IRE) *Adam West*
2 gr f Outstrip Strasbourg Place (Compton Place)
6564[8]

No Approval (IRE) *David Bridgwater* a41 47
6 b g Approve(IRE) Night Cam (IRE) (Night Shift (USA))
399[8] 533[8] 719[8]

Nobel Joshua (AUT)
Denis Gerard Hogan a35 70
3 br g Joshua Tree(IRE) Namat (IRE) (Daylami (IRE))
2511[3]

No Bills *Michael Easterby* a56 57
3 ch f Mayson Brave Mave (Daylami (IRE))
3508[11]

Noble Account *Julia Feilden* 68
3 b g Dansili Illustrious Miss (USA) (Kingmambo (USA))
2764[6] 3277[4] 4073[6] 4838[4] 5394[7] 5841[3] 6760[4]

Noble Ancestry
Jassim Mohammed Ghazali a47 47
3 b g Dubawi(IRE) Joys Of Spring (IRE) (Invincible Spirit (IRE))
9590a[16]

Noble Behest *Ian Williams* a83 77
5 b g Sir Percy Lady Hestia (USA) (Belong To Me (USA))
4363[5] 5135[4] 5502[6] 6105[12] 6967[8] 8196[2]◆ (9087)◆ (9405)

Noble Bertie (USA) *Tim Easterby* 51
2 ch g Noble Mission Oxbow Lake (USA) (Dynaformer (USA))
5512[6] 6065[8] 7067[11]

Noble Dawn (GER) *Ivan Furtado* a73 68
2 ch f Dawn Approach(IRE) Neuquen (IRE) (Rock Of Gibraltar (IRE))
6943[5] 7644[4] (9284)

Noble Deed *Michael Attwater* a49 50
9 ch g Kyllachy Noble One (Primo Dominie)
1093[11] 1265[10] 1682[4] 2287[5] 3406[U] 5883[6]

Noble Expression *R K Watson* a81 87
4 b g Sir Percy Disposition (Selkirk (USA))
204[3] (469) 622[4] 2032[10] (3428) 5404a[4]

Noble Fox *Clive Cox* a75 73
3 b g Foxwedge(AUS) Woolfall Rose (Generous (IRE))
2210[3] 2715[4] 3463[9] 4306[6] 5505[2] 6469[8] 7560[6] 8413[10] 9132[2] 9443[3]

Noble Gift *William Knight* a93 88
9 ch g Cadeaux Genereux Noble Penny (Pennekamp (USA))
1681[5] 2620[4] 3806[9] 4792[4] 5811[4] 6967[3] 8608[6] 8656[4]

Noble Lineage (IRE) *James Tate* a90 75
3 ch c Iffraaj Regal Hawk (Singspiel (IRE))
(1568) 2088[9] 4639[5]◆

Nobleman's Nest *Simon Crisford* a79 97
4 br g Poet's Voice Tamzin (Hernando (FR))
3318[12]

Noble Moon (GER) *P Schiergen* 105
3 b c Sea The Moon(GER) Nouvelle Noblesse (GER) (Singspiel (IRE))
2163a[5] 2889a[10]

Noble Music (GER) *Ralph Beckett* a71 75
3 b f Sea The Moon(GER) Noble Lady (GER) (Sholokhov (IRE))
1417[3]◆ 6034[2] 6890[3] 7518[2] 8245[10]

Noble Peace *Simon Pearce* a72 71
6 b g Kyllachy Peace Concluded (Bertolini (USA))
252[6] 1367[6] 1588[6] 2584[9] 5061[4] 5820[5] 6717[3] 7560[7] 8206[8] 8756[12] (9427)

Noble Prospector (IRE)
Richard Fahey a85 92
3 b g Elzaam(AUS) Seraphina (IRE) (Pips Pride)
1562[4] 2198[3] 3218[3] 4055[4] 4989[2] 5973[3] (6734) (7141)

Noble Sky (FR) *H Blume* 31
3 bl f Never On Sunday(FR) Nachita (FR) (Sagamix (FR))
3710a[8] 6061a[8]

Noble Thought (USA)
Michael J Maker 104
6 bb g Harlan's Holiday(USA) No Use Denying (USA) (Maria's Mon (USA))
3561a[8]

No Can Do *Jamie Osborne* a57 40
2 b c Toronado(IRE) Frigid (Indian Ridge (IRE))
5991[2] 6314[4] 6532[7] 9037[7] 9127[6]

No Comment (DEN) *Bent Olsen* a72 86
6 b h Naaqoos Vytinna (FR) (Victory Note (USA))
6523a[8]

Nocturnal Fox (IRE) *A Fabre* 104
4 b h Farhh Nabati (USA) (Rahy (USA))
1628a[6] 2169a[7]

Noddy Shuffle *Michael Easterby* 53
2 b g Heeraat(IRE) Sophie'Jo (Agnes World (USA))
1844[4] 3810[7] 5294[11] 9640[8]

No Dress Rehearsal
Michael Easterby a72 69
3 b f Cityscape Sailing Days (Kris)
3200[2] 3729[7] 5156[3] 6810[4] 7287[3]

Noel (IRE) *Daniel Kubler* a51
4 b g Requinto(IRE) Santacus (IRE) (Spartacus (IRE))
827[8] 1212[8] 1517[6] 1958[12]

No Faith (FR) *C Ferland* a71 69
4 b m Le Havre(IRE) Macina (IRE) (Platini (GER))
8373a[4]

No Limit Credit (GER)
Andreas Suborics 67
2 ch f Night Of Thunder(IRE) Nasrine (IRE) (Barathea (IRE))
8964a[6]

No Mercy *K R Burke* 77
2 b c Sepoy(AUS) Isola Verde (Oasis Dream)
2783[3] 3411[4] 4937[3] 5390[2] 6167[5] 6997[4] 7896[11]

No More Regrets (IRE)
Patrick Morris a60 65
3 b f Kodiac Shifting (IRE) (Oratorio (IRE))
2522[10] 3068[7] 3479[8] 3844[5] 4908[6] 5419[7] 6181[5] 6945[11] 9477[11]

Nona (GER) *Mario Hofer* 82
2 b f Pastorius(GER) Niyama (GER) (Tertullian (USA))
6746a[9] 8371a[5] 8964a[7]

Nonayneverornore (IRE)
A Le Duff a65 45
3 ch g No Nay Never(USA) Choose Me Please (IRE) (Choisir (AUS))
2090a[14] 3878a[10]

Nonchalance *John Gosden* a63 92
3 b f Dubawi(IRE) Tearless (Street Cry (IRE))
2518[4]◆ (3050) (3603) 4052[24]

No Needs Never (IRE)
Joseph Patrick O'Brien a101 100
3 br c No Nay Never(USA) Opera Fan (FR) (Cape Cross (IRE))
1776a[2]

Noneedtotellme (IRE) *James Unett* a51 45
6 gr m Fast Company(IRE) Gemma's Delight (IRE) (Clodovil (IRE))
911[8]

Nonios (IRE) *David Simcock* a101 88
7 b g Oasis Dream Young And Daring (USA) (Woodman (USA))
240[3] (521) 764[3] 1031[3] 1294[4]◆ (1545) 2022[2] 2320[4] 3005[6] 4021[3] 4490[7] 4997[3] 5796[3] 9610[4]

Nonkono Yume (JPN) *Yukihiro Kato* a110
7 ch g Twining(USA) Nonko (JPN) (Agnes Tachyon (JPN))
1440a[10]

No Nonsense *David Elsworth* a98 102
3 b c Acclamation Gift Of Music (IRE) (Cadeaux Genereux)
(57) 1752[6] 2270[2] 2779[5] 4092[14]

Noor Al Hawa (FR) *G E Mikhalides* 101
6 ch h Makfi Majestic Roi (USA) (Street Cry (IRE))
894a[8]

Nooramunga (FR) *M Delzangles* 97
3 b f Siyouni(FR) Turtle Bow (FR) (Turtle Island (IRE))
4621a[3] 6142a[9]

Noordhout (FR) *R Martens* a63 82
4 b m Elusive City(USA) Anatolie (IRE) (Peintre Celebre (USA))
(7601a)

Noor Sahara (IRE) *F Chappet* a69 102
3 b f Lope De Vega(IRE) By Invitation (USA) (Van Nistelrooy (USA))
(3029a) 3905a[11] 6142a[6] 7360a[10]

Nooshin *Amy Murphy* a75 78
3 b f Declaration Of War(USA) Queen Sarra (Shamardal (USA))
1288[2] 1838[4] 2420[2] **3807**[2] 4828[4] 5565[5] 7583[4] 8305[12]

Nope (IRE) *Mrs John Harrington* 99
2 b f No Nay Never(USA) Bright Sapphire (IRE) (Galileo (IRE))
7742a[5] **8089**[4]

Norab (GER) *Bernard Llewellyn* a64 66
8 b g Galileo(IRE) Night Woman (GER) (Monsun (GER))
2359[6] 2718[7] **4146**[4] 4483[7] 6105[2] **6366**[2] 7033[5] **7300**[3]

Norathir (FR) *D De Watrigant* 95
3 b f Muhtathir Loonora (FR) (Valanour (IRE))
2029a[9]

Nordano (GER) *Neil King* a70 70
3 ch g Jukebox Jury(IRE) Navajo Queen (GER) (Monsun (GER))
1661[3] 2099[7] 2511[2] 2712[11] **3931**[6] *7520*[2]

Nordenfelt (IRE) *Sue Gardner* a35 51
6 b g Lilbourne Lad(IRE) There With Me (USA) (Distant View (USA))
6105[8] 6366[10]

Nordic (GER) *Wido Neuroth* 75
2 ch g Gleneagles(IRE) Norwegian Pride (FR) (Diktat)
7495a[4]

Nordic Dream (IRE)
Jassim Mohammed Ghazali a70 86
6 b h Dream Ahead(USA) Nyramba (Night Shift (USA))
869a[8]

Nordic Fire *David O'Meara* a82 87
3 b g Dream Ahead(USA) Nordic Spruce (USA) (Dynaformer (USA))
6207[9] **7435**[11] 8101[19]

Nordic Flight *James Eustace* a45 66
4 b g Norse Dancer(IRE) Winged Diva (IRE) (Hawk Wing (USA))
2690[12] 4067[4] **4561**[8]◆ 5316[9] 6324[6] *6931*[6]

Nordic Lights *Charlie Appleby* a81 107
4 ch g Intello(GER) Marika (Marju (IRE))
284a[2] **(637a)**◆ *1114a*[6]◆

Noriac (ITY) *Roberto Di Paolo* 79
6 b h St Paul House Purple Paradise (IRE) (Fasliyev (USA))
2888a[9]

Norma *James Fanshawe* a83 92
3 ch f New Approach(IRE) Deirdre (Dubawi (IRE))
2208[5]◆ 2770[2] 3637[5] (5565) **6398**[2] 7347[9] *8064*[8]

Normal Equilibrium *Ivan Furtado* a70 68
9 b g Elnadim(USA) Acicula (IRE) (Night Shift (USA))
2824[3] 3404[5] 4369[4] 5169[7] 6017[4] 7077[18] *8264*[8] *9272*[10]

Normal Norman *John Ryan* a83 81
5 ch g Shamardal(USA) Ambria (GER) (Monsun (GER))
6594[2]◆ 7212[5] 8236[2] ***(9304)***◆

Normandel (FR) *J S Bolger* 102
5 b m Le Havre(IRE) Lidana (IRE) (King's Best (USA))
(1307a) **3105a**[5]

Normandy Barriere (IRE)
Nigel Tinkler a70 91
7 b g Rock Of Gibraltar(IRE) Ma Paloma (FR) (Highest Honor (FR))
1829[13]◆ 2117[12] 2791[5] 3094[5] 3945[9] 4649[3] **4866**[2] 5416[7] 6162[7] 6916[6] 7121[10] 7621[8] *8289*[10]

Normandy Blue *Luke McJannet* a43 53
4 ch g Le Havre(IRE) Ballerina Blue (IRE) (High Chaparral (IRE))
185[4] *549*[3] *946*[9] *1548*[5] 2359[8] *3497*[4] 4287[3] 5029[13] 7759[6] *8347*[11] *9412*[6]

Normcore (JPN) *Kiyoshi Hagiwara* 112
4 gr m Harbinger Chronologist (JPN) (Kurofune (USA))
9379a[4]

Norohna (FR) *Nicolo Simondi* 95
2 ch f Spirit One(FR) Norina (Linamix (FR))
5759a[3] 7724a[3] **8789a**[3]

North America *S Seemar* a118 84
7 b g Dubawi(IRE) Northern Mischief (USA) (Yankee Victor (USA))
(171a)◆ *(638a)* *1447a*[7]

North End (FR) *F Rossi* a57 60
6 gr g Elusive City(USA) Fruta Bomba (FR) (Nombre Premier)
7601a[9]

Northern Celt (IRE) *Tim Easterby* a36 38
2 b g Gutaifan(IRE) Scent Of Summer (USA) (Rock Hard Ten (USA))
4624[8] **6997**[10] 7619[10] *8527*[6]

Northern Daggers (ITY)
Andrea Marcialis a65 79
4 b g Mujahid(USA) Daggers Girl (IRE) (Daggers Drawn (USA))
(76a)

Northern Footsteps *Ollie Pears* 17
3 b f Footstepsinthesand Raktina (Polish Precedent (USA))
1980[6] *2530*[6] 3270[9] 3570[10]

Northern Grace *Brian Ellison* a23 47
2 ch f Helmet(AUS) Amelia Grace (IRE) (Starspangledbanner (AUS))
1923[10] *5280*[8] **5689**[8] 6053[6] **6625**[9]

Northern Hope *David O'Meara* a65 74
2 b g Equiano(FR) Heading North (Teofilo (IRE))
3954[2]◆ *4289*[5] 5273[2] 6097[8]

Northern Lyte *Nigel Tinkler* a67 75
3 b f Sir Percy Phoenix Clubs (IRE) (Red Clubs (IRE))
2200[11] 2711[U] 3226[7] 3947[4] 4210[3] (4628) 5023[3] 5307[2] 6101[3] **(6501)** 7213[4]

Northernpowerhouse *Bryan Smart* a88 79
3 b c Harbour Watch(IRE) Mortitia (Dansili)
2635[2] 3202[3] 4444[2] (5274)◆ 5903[5] 6700[5] *8025*[2] ***(9517)***◆

Northern Queen (IRE) *Brian Ellison* a48 66
4 gr m Dark Angel(IRE) Queen Bodicea (IRE) (Revoque (IRE))
1389[6] **1816**[4]

Northern Society (IRE)
Keith Dalgleish a52 65
3 b f Camacho La Estatua (Lope De Vega (IRE))
(2683)◆ 3159[4] 3516[4] 4059[5] 4632[7] 4911[9] 5236[6] 5620[5] 5904[5] (6608) 6936[4] 7588[5] *7959*[9] 8235[10]

North Face (IRE) *Marco Botti* a103 75
4 b g Declaration Of War(USA) Queen Titi (IRE) (Sadler's Wells (USA))
398a[7] 514a[13] ***2320***[6] *2969*[10]

North Korea (IRE) *Brian Baugh* a51 45
3 b f Bungle Inthejungle Betty Fontaine (IRE) (Mujadil (USA))
605[6] *813*[10] *2211*[9] 2474[6] 2908[8] 3417[3] 5084[8] 6017[5] 7172[7] *8119*[4] *8839*[11] *9283*[9]

North Point *David Elsworth* a68 72
2 b g Norse Dancer(IRE) Cascades (IRE) (Montjeu (IRE))
6079[4]◆ *6718*[2]◆ 7154[3] **8465**[5]

Northwest Frontier (IRE)
Micky Hammond a75 90
5 b g Galileo(IRE) Francesca D'Gorgio (USA) (Proud Citizen (USA))
2118[4] 2781[14]

North Wind (IRE)
Damian Joseph English a83 83
3 b g No Nay Never(USA) Kawn (Cadeaux Genereux)
5207a[9] 7241a[22]

Norton Lad *Tim Easterby* a29 46
2 b c Helmet(AUS) Oasis Breeze (Oasis Dream)
5689[10] 6175[13] 6585[6] **7308**[6] *8527*[12]

Norway (IRE) *A P O'Brien* 109
3 ch c Galileo(IRE) Love Me True (USA) (Kingmambo (USA))
2523[2] 3345[8] 3984[9] 4414a[3] 5414[7] 6353[3] **(7218a)**

Nosdargent (FR)
D & P Prod'Homme a76 81
4 b g Kendargent(FR) Nostaltir (FR) (Muhtahir)
1449a[9] 3136a[7] **4747a**[4]

No Show (IRE) *Richard Hannon* 75
2 ch c Showcasing Innocent Air (Galileo (IRE))
5345[3] 5845[5] **6710**[3]

Nostalbowl (FR) *D & P Prod'Homme* a52 65
6 ch g Turtle Bowl(IRE) Nostaltir (FR) (Muhtathir)
1245a[11]

Nostalgic Air *Ruth Carr* 13
2 b f Hot Streak(IRE) Steal The Curtain (Royal Applause)
1844[9] **2586**[6]

Nostrovia (IRE) *Richard Spencer* 63
3 gr f Alhebayeb(IRE) Na Zdorovie (Cockney Rebel (IRE))
2251[10] **3598**[4] 4651[6]

Not Another Word *Nigel Tinkler* 49
2 ch f Monsieur Bond(IRE) Venus Rising (Observatory (USA))
2415[11] 3212[4] 4075[8] 5017[3] **5514**[5] 5968[14]

Notation (IRE) *Mark Johnston* 70
2 b f Poet's Voice Party Line (Montjeu (IRE))
7067[4]◆ **7826**[3]

Note Bleu *Gary Moore* a64
2 b c Camelot Silent Music (IRE) (Peintre Celebre (USA))
9385[8]

Notforalongtime *Clive Cox* a77
2 b c Paco Boy(IRE) Punchy Lady (Invincible Spirit (IRE))
9195[4] ***(9451)***

No Thanks *William Jarvis* a61 66
3 b g Pour Moi(IRE) Miss Fifty (IRE) (Whipper (USA))
2529[5] 3273[5] 3741[10] 4345[3] *4998*[2] (5601) 6128[5] **7318**[3] *8065*[6]

No Tinc Por *N Clement* 92
3 b f Authorized(IRE) Tierceville (IRE) (Oratorio (IRE))
6385a[8]

Not Never *Gary Moore* 92
7 ch g Notnowcato Watchoverme (Haafhd)
3952[10]

Notnowcedric (FR) *B Le Regent* 31
8 ch g Notnowcato Miss Loulou (FR) (Gold Away (IRE))
7501a[5]

Not On Your Nellie (IRE)
Nigel Tinkler 64
2 b f Zebedee Piccadilly Filly (IRE) (Exceed And Excel (AUS))
4984[9] 5388[6] **5689**[3] 7734[3]◆ 8180[6]

Notre Same (GER)
Stephanie Gachelin 61
8 b g Samum(GER) Nordtanzerin (GER) (Danehill Dancer (IRE))
6790a[8]

No Trouble (IRE) *Stuart Williams* a58 49
3 b g No Nay Never(USA) Lady Babooshka (Cape Cross (IRE))
3170[11] 3741[9] 4485[13]

Not So Shy *Lisa Williamson* a36 39
3 b f Heeraat(IRE) Littlemisstutti (IRE) (Noverre (USA))
296[2] *505*[6] *605*[5] *620*[3] *918*[9] *1167*[10] *4192*[8] *4457*[12] 4555[11] 4908[9] 5582[7] 5847[8] *6024*[11] 6754[7]

Not So Sleepy *Hughie Morrison* a84 105
7 ch g Beat Hollow Papillon De Bronze (IRE) (Marju (IRE))
2032[7] 3655[4] 4884[4] **6171**[2] 6958[7] 8114[4]

Notwhatiam (IRE) *Alan Berry* 30
9 b g Morozov(USA) Riverfort (IRE) (Over The River (FR))
7681[11] **8399**[5]

Nouvelli Solo (FR) *Lucinda Egerton*
3 ch f Coach House(IRE) Cheap N Chic (Primo Valentino (IRE))
3218[9]

Novabridge *Karen Tutty* a53 48
11 ch g Avonbridge Petrovna (IRE) (Petardia)
25[2] *129*[4] *411*[5] *834*[5] *973*[3] ***1402***[2]

Nova Roma *John Gosden* a67
2 b c Golden Horn Ragsah (IRE) (Shamardal (USA))
8604[7]

Novelty Seeker (USA)
Michael Easterby a40 47
10 b g Street Sense(USA) Nawaiet (USA) (Zilzal (USA))
8260[7] 8862[14]

N Over J *William Knight* a55 52
4 b g Kodiac Risk A Look (Observatory (USA))
1933[3] 2774[9] *3304*[5] *3687*[4] 4753[3] 6121[4] 6507[6] *8416*[5]

Noverre Dancer (IRE)
Nick Littmoden a39
3 ch g Le Havre(IRE) Irish Cliff (IRE) (Marju (IRE))
1217[10] *6283*[7] *6594*[12] ***8869***[8]

No War (USA) *F Rohaut* a72
3 b f War Front(USA) Peace Burg (FR) (Sageburg (IRE))
1199a[12]

No Way Jose (IRE) *Brian Meehan* a81 92
3 b f No Nay Never(USA) Crystal Valkyrie (IRE) (Danehill (USA))
2144[9] **3193**[2] 4052[11]

Now Children (IRE) *Clive Cox* a96 104
5 ch g Dragon Pulse(IRE) Toberanthawn (IRE) (Danehill Dancer (IRE))
2606[6]

Now I'm A Believer *Mick Channon* a34 49
2 b f Gregorian(IRE) Alpha Spirit (Sixties Icon)
4750[7] 5196[6] 5577[6] *6071*[11] 6604[4] **(7111)** *7516*[8]

Noxareno (GER) *F Chappet* a78 74
3 b c Maxios Nobilissima (GER) (Bluebird (USA))
3710a[2]

Nsnas (IRE) *Saeed bin Suroor* a85
3 b c Bated Breath Burn The Breeze (IRE) (Beat Hollow)
7559[2] ***(8351)***◆

Nuala (FR) *A Fabre* a95 98
3 gr f Soldier Hollow Blowaway (FR) (Linamix (FR))
7360a[4] 8376a[5] *9170a*[4] *9603a*[15]

Nubbel (GER) *Markus Klug* 91
3 ch c Wiener Walzer(GER) Norderney (GER) (Dai Jin)
2163a[8]

Nubius (IRE) *P Schiergen* 91
3 b c Dylan Thomas(IRE) Nicolaia (GER) (Alkalde (GER))
3674a[7]

Nubough (IRE) *Iain Jardine* a83 87
3 b g Kodiac Qawaasem (IRE) (Shamardal (USA))
(431) *1104*[3] **2364**[3] 2997[3] 5724[4] **6225**[2] 6451[4] 7068[8] 7781[9]

Nugget *Richard Hannon* a80 73
2 b c Siyouni(FR) Gemstone (IRE) (Galileo (IRE))
7406[4] ***8011***[2]◆

Nuits St Georges (IRE)
David Menuisier a71 86
4 ch g Mount Nelson Twelfth Night (IRE) (Namid)
2092[9] (2626)◆ (3635)◆ **5897**[2] 7239[2] 8114[12]

Numerian (IRE)
Joseph Patrick O'Brien a103 107
3 b g Holy Roman Emperor(IRE) Delicate Charm (IRE) (High Chaparral (IRE))
1049a[3] 4016[5]◆ 5535a[6] 6693a[3] ***7668a***[2]

Numero Uno *Tim Vaughan*
3 b g Dubawi(IRE) Casual Look (USA) (Red Ransom (USA))
134[9] *8298*[12]

Numinous (IRE) *Henry Candy* a37 42
2 ch g Anjaal Emma Dora (IRE) (Medaglia d'Oro (USA))
4482[5] 4798[12] **6807**[10] 7174[4] *9307*[11]

Nunzia (FR) *F Vermeulen* 98
2 b f Epaulette(AUS) Netsuke (IRE) (Aragorn (IRE))
7006a[5] 7939a[9]

Nurse Barbara (IRE) *G M Lyons* 101
2 b f Kodiac Finagle (IRE) (Azamour (IRE))
7215a[2] **7692**[6]

Nurse Finch (FR) *Andrew Balding* a18
2 b f Camelot Nyanza (GER) (Dai Jin)
6592[10]

Nutopia *Antony Brittain* a49 41
4 b m Monsieur Bond(IRE) Carambola (Lucky Story (USA))
277[6] *502*[6] *738*[10] 5041[5] *7032*[8] ***8472***[4] *8819*[7] *9111*[11]

Nuzha *Tony Newcombe* a48 53
5 ch m Mayson Always On My Mind (Distant Relative)
293[6]

Nyaleti (IRE) *Mark Johnston* a109 109
4 ro m Arch(USA) America Nova (FR) (Verglas (IRE))
2441[2] 2776[4] 3342[8] 3986[7] ***4332***[2] 4645[4] 5586[6] 6443[6] 7565[6]

Nyanga (IRE) *David Menuisier* a45 41
3 b f Born To Sea(IRE) Mujadil Shadow (IRE) (Mujadil (USA))
1359[7] *1726*[8]

Nylon Speed (IRE) *Alan King* a84 70
5 b g Campanologist(USA) Neuquen (IRE) (Rock Of Gibraltar (IRE))
(88) *292*[4] *754*[3] *(1096)* **1425**[2] 2092[13]

Oakenshield (IRE) *Kevin Ryan* 74
2 b c Invincible Spirit(IRE) War Effort (USA) (War Front (USA))
6891[4] 7765[5]

Oasis Charm *Charlie Appleby* a100 109
5 b g Oasis Dream Albaraka (Selkirk (USA))
(514a) 844a[5] 3953[9] 4612[7]

Oasis Fantasy (IRE) *David Simcock* a91 93
8 br g Oasis Dream Cara Fantasy (IRE) (Sadler's Wells (USA))
1031[4] *1267*[5] **(3016)** **4395**[2] 4890[6] 5686[4]

Oasis Prince *Mark Johnston* a60 99
3 b g Oasis Dream Demisemiquaver (Singspiel (IRE))
1346[5]◆ (1562) (2058) (2616) 3082[10] 3728[3] **(4347)** 4882[6] 5150[2] 5790[3] 6513[3] 7457[7] 7727[3] 8514[7]

Oasis Song *Hughie Morrison* a52
2 b f Oasis Dream Wahylah (IRE) (Shamardal (USA))
6719[7] *7104*[7] *8316*[8] *8825*[2] *9330*[11]

Obee Jo (IRE) *Tim Easterby* 75
3 b g Kodiac Maleha (IRE) (Cape Cross (IRE))
1665[5] (2199) **2624**[2]◆ 3654[6] 4099[8] 5191[6] 5983[6]

Oberyn Martell
Eve Johnson Houghton a66 59
3 b g Charm Spirit(IRE) Nickels And Dimes (IRE) (Teofilo (IRE))
838[4] 1851[11] 2086[11] 3166[5] 4420[9] 5335[8] *9203*[9] *9632*[10]

Obeyaan (USA) *Fawzi Abdulla Nass* a58
3 b c Tiznow(USA) Street Girl (USA) (Street Hero (USA))
394a[7]

Oblate *Robyn Brisland* a68 53
3 b f Epaulette(AUS) Lady Benedicte (IRE) (Shamardal (USA))
930[6] 4211[4] 5041[4] 6101[13] *8270*[2]◆ ***8645***[2] *9028*[9]

Obligate *P Bary* 111
3 b f Frankel Responsible (Oasis Dream)
(2498a) (3387a) **5479a**[3] 7007a[8]

Oborne Lady (IRE) *Seamus Mullins* a52 57
6 b m Watar(IRE) Lady Shackleton (IRE) (Zaffaran (USA))
2428 *562*[5] *921*[6] *1297*[9] **(2344)** *2593*[9] 5301[10]

Obsession For Gold (IRE)
Mrs Ilka Gansera-Leveque a53 1
3 b g Acclamation Campfire Glow (IRE) (Invincible Spirit (IRE))
1198a[8] ***1379***[3] 1665[7] *5890*[6] *6441*[8] *7374*[4] *7838*[3] *8119*[2] *8469*[9] *9439*[12]

Ocala *Andrew Balding* a89 90
4 ch m Nathaniel(IRE) Night Carnation (Sleeping Indian)
1517[4] 2509[6] (2994) 3502[3] (4318) 5545[6] 6217[3] **6923**[3] 7729[3] *9177*[4]

Ocamonte (IRE)
X Thomas-Demeaulte a61 64
5 gr g Kendargent(FR) Pestagua (IRE) (Lawman (FR))
7601a[6]

Ocasio Cortez (IRE)
Richard Hannon a70 81
2 rg f Gutaifan(IRE) Novel Fun (IRE) (Noverre (USA))
2093[4] *2594*[6] 2918[3] (3595) 4221[3] 5185[5] **(5418)** 6157[8] 6833[6] 7247a[16] *9162*[6] *9608*[8]

Ocean Air (FR) *John C McConnell* a47 54
5 b g Rio De La Plata(USA) Silver Miss (FR) (Numerous (USA))
(4916)◆

Ocean Crystal *Mrs A Malzard* a32 37
7 b m Stimulation(IRE) Crystal Gale (IRE) (Verglas (IRE))
2673a[7]

Ocean Fantasy (FR)
Jean-Pierre Carvalho 100
2 b f Make Believe Oceanie (FR) (Dansili)
(8371a)

Ocean Paradise *William Knight* a68 82
3 gr f New Approach(IRE) Tropical Paradise (IRE) (Verglas (IRE))
1755[2] 2919[3] **(3768)** 4393[7] 8463[5] *9176*[10] *9422*[8]

Ocean Reach *Richard Price* a51 47
3 b f Phoenix Reach(IRE) Ocean Transit (IRE) (Trans Island)
3204[12] **4177**[4] 5249[5] 5784[6] 6367[3] 6805[5]

Ocean Rouge *Tony Carroll* a24 17
3 b g Kuroshio(AUS) Madame Rouge (Major Cadeaux)
4029[11] 4931[11]

Ocean Spray *Eugene Stanford* a12 4
4 ch m Showcasing Gibraltar Lass (USA) (Concerto (USA))
1546[10] **3279**[8] 4568[12] *8404*[8]

Ocean Temptress *Louise Allan* a33 44
5 b m Equiano(FR) Ipsa Loquitur (Unfuwain (USA))
3470[8] 3967[11] 5144[6] 6058[10] 7977[5] 8279[6] 8436[5] *8915*[13]

Oceanus (IRE) *Julia Feilden* a52 67
5 b g Born To Sea(IRE) Alkhawarah (USA) (Intidab (USA))
3871[10] **2738**[8] 3276[9]

Ocelot *Robert Cowell* a78 96
5 b m Poet's Voice Desert Lynx (IRE) (Green Desert (USA))
1913[7] **3085**[4] 4101[14] 4891[11]

Och Aye *Mark Johnston* a44
4 b g Declaration Of War(USA) Di Moi Oui (Warning)
1989[8]

Ocho Grande (IRE)
Eve Johnson Houghton 66
2 b g Tamayuz Soul Custody (CAN) (Perfect Soul (IRE))
5563[6] 6415[5] **7113**[4] 7980[12]

Ochre Riu (IRE) *Ivan Furtado* a15
2 ch g Tagula(IRE) Raseel (Aqlaam)
6943[13] *7870*[10] ***9029***[8]

Octave (IRE) *Mark Johnston* a79 79
3 ch f Dawn Approach(IRE) Calando (USA) (Storm Cat (USA))
2835[9] 3082[13] ***3494***[5] **4072**[4] *8456*[7]

Octeville (IRE) *C Lotoux* a46 70
4 b m Le Havre(IRE) My Memoir (IRE) (King's Best (USA))
6651a[13] **7062a**[3]

October Storm *Mick Channon* a77 82
6 br g Shirocco(GER) Cyber Star (King's Best (USA))
2080[3] 3044[6] 3635[5] 4404[5] 5368[5] 5967[5] 6901[2]

Odds On Oli *Richard Fahey* a63 62
4 b g Camelot Red Blooded Woman (USA) (Red Ransom (USA))
2241[11] 3162[6] **3720**[2]◆ 9225[9] 9503[8] (9609)
O Dee *Patrick Dejaeger* a62 74
7 ch g Iffraaj Queen's Grace (Bahamian Bounty)
2956a[5]
Odeon (NZ)
Mathew Ellerton & Simon Zahra 110
5 bb g Zacinto Theatre Buff (USA) (Theatrical (IRE))
9015a[5]
Odina *Mario Hofer* 44
2 b f Outstrip Oulianovsk (IRE) (Peintre Celebre (USA))
8586a[7]
Odyssey Girl (IRE) *Richard Spencer* a77 77
2 gr f Gutaifan(IRE) Lady Marita (IRE) (Dandy Man (IRE))
(4840) 5185[9] **6442**[3] 7247a[7] **8297**[2] (9242)
Oeil De Tigre (FR) *Tony Carroll* a67 86
8 b g Footstepsinthesand Suerte (Halling (USA))
2917[6] 3531[10] 4186[4] 4872[3] (5503) 5839[3] 6465[4] 7175[7]
Oenophile (GER) *Tom Gretton* a8 33
4 b m Mamool(IRE) Ormita (GER) (Acatenango (GER))
482[13]
Officer Drivel (IRE) *Paddy Butler*
8 b g Captain Rio Spiritville (IRE) (Invincible Spirit (IRE))
1591[8] 2005[10] 2513[9] 2970[12] 3298[10]
Off Piste *Tim Easterby* 60
3 gr g Reliable Man Hamloola (Red Ransom (USA))
1897[10] 2872[7] 5973[7]
O Fortuna (FR) *Mme Pia Brandt* a60 74
4 b m Myboycharlie(IRE) Karmina Burana (FR) (Highest Honor (FR))
1578a[7]
O'Goshi (FR) *J Boisnard* a70 70
5 b g Kentucky Dynamite(USA) Hier Deja (FR) (Neverneyev (USA))
7136a[5]
Oh It's Saucepot *Chris Wall* a83 91
5 b m Sir Percy Oh So Saucy (Imperial Ballet (IRE))
2064[7] 3004[4] 4250[3] 5502[2] (6224) (7395)◆ 7900[5]
Oh Mary Oh Mary *Michael Easterby* a12 62
2 b f Mukhadram How Fortunate (Haafhd)
5764[3]◆ 6654[4] 7388[9]
Oh My Oh My (IRE)
Matthieu Palussiere a44 73
3 b g Slade Power(IRE) Sylvan Mist (IRE) (Footstepsinthesand)
1028a[9]
Ohnotanotherone *Stuart Kittow* 41
2 b f Camacho Saint Lucy (Selkirk (USA))
3573[8] 4233[6] **5374**[7] 6604[3] 7111[7]
Oh Purple Reign (IRE)
Richard Hannon a98 96
2 b c Sir Prancealot(IRE) Warda (Pivotal)
(2931) 3312[2] 3566[2] 4637[2] (4937) 5415[4] (5707) 6542[3] **6966**[2] 7614[6]
Oh Say Can You See (FR)
Matthieu Palussiere 51
3 b c Starspangledbanner(AUS) Doubleyou One (AUS) (Danehill Dancer (IRE))
2392a[8] 3066a[16]
Oh So Nice *Tony Carroll* a54 50
3 b f Kyllachy Femme De Fer (Hamas (IRE))
5306[3] 6023[4] 8672[2] 9169[6] 9272[7] **9664**[5]
Oh So Terrible (USA)
Bradley S Ross a61 97
5 b m Cape Blanco(IRE) Miss Terrible (ARG) (Numerous (USA))
5978a[7]
Oh This Is Us (IRE) *Richard Hannon* a117 114
6 b h Acclamation Shamwari Lodge (IRE) (Hawk Wing (USA))
601[2] (880) 1103[7] (1922) 2085[6] 2688[2] 3343[2] 3814[3] 4397[6] 4905[2] 5475[5] 6445[9] (6711)◆ 8090[3] 9064[9]
Oh Yes Please *Michael Dods* 58
3 b f Lethal Force(IRE) Valentina Guest (IRE) (Be My Guest (USA))
3684[14]
Oi The Clubb Oi's *Ian Williams* a57 73
4 gr g Champs Elysees Red Boots (IRE) (Verglas (IRE))
2620[3] (3377) 3861[11] 5219[4]
Ojooba *Owen Burrows* a98 100
3 b f Dubawi(IRE) Rumoush (USA) (Rahy (USA))
1855[3] 4341[5]◆ (5148) (6172) 7662[5] 9002[3]
O'Juke (FR) *Nicolo Simondi* 101
4 ch g Jukebox Jury(IRE) O'Keefe (FR) (Peintre Celebre (USA))
2885a[3]
Okarina Dream (FR) *H De Nicolay* a89 71
3 ch f George Vancouver(USA) Osceola (IRE) (Layman (USA))
9170a[12] 9504a[3]
Okiam Des Mottes (FR) *P Lenogue* a67 63
4 b g Diamond Green(FR) Oktodez (GER) (Java Gold (USA))
2170a[7]
Oklahoma Dancer (USA)
A Selvaratnam 59
3 b c Beggarthyneighbor(USA) She'satroublemaker (USA) (Volponi (USA))
9590a[15]
Oksana Astankova *Mick Channon* 53
2 b f Cable Bay(IRE) Royal Ffanci (Royal Applause)
8516[6]
Olaf *George Boughey* a47 56
3 b g Frozen Power(IRE) Khafayif (USA) (Swain (IRE))
6290[16] (6600) **7228**[2] 7909[6] 9049[10]
Olaudah *Henry Candy* a67 53
5 b g Equiano(FR) Bookiesindexdotnet (Piccolo)
(2013) 3144[2] 3527[6] 4219[12] (4763) 6048[8] 6605[4] 7447[4] 8217[10]
Olcan *David O'Meara* a76 60
2 b g Showcasing Pickle (Piccolo)
3451[2]◆ 3810[5] 4384[5] 4938[8]
Old Fashioned (CHI)
A bin Harmash a77 87
6 ch g Neko Bay(USA) Hebrides (CHI) (Schossberg (CAN))
97a[3] **573a**[6]
Old Friend (FR) *Ed Walker* a56 56
2 b g Fast Company(IRE) Alpen Glen (Halling (USA))
6912[9] **8012**[6]
Old Glory (IRE) *H Al Ramzani* a96 103
3 b c Frankel Belesta (Xaar)
3104a[9] 4013[12] **5609**[4] 9590a[14]
Old News *Richard Hughes* a83 86
2 b c Dutch Art Queen's Charter (Oasis Dream)
(4734) **5134**[5] **6464**[3] 6963[5] (7495a) 8110[6] 8850[7]
Old Persian *Charlie Appleby* a90 122
4 b h Dubawi(IRE) Indian Petal (Singspiel (IRE))
(1113a) (1446a) 3314[7] 6007a[3] (7226a) 8776a[11]
Old Red Eyes (USA) *Joseph Tuite* a51 58
3 ch g Speightstown(USA) Grand Mere (USA) (Bob And John (USA))
2798[5] **3650**[7] 4180[9]
Oleksander *Archie Watson* 82
2 b c Teofilo(IRE) Ollie Olga (USA) (Stormy Atlantic (USA))
(7154) (7983)◆
Olendon (FR) *Chad C Brown* 107
3 ch f Le Havre(IRE) Talema (FR) (Sunday Break (JPN))
3121a[2] 5645a[5]
Oliver Hardy *Paul Cole* a68 76
3 b g Foxwedge(AUS) Astrantia (Dansili)
836[4] 1033[10] 1770[6] 3092[4] (3407)◆ (3965) **5954**[2] 6722[5]
Olivers Pursuit *Gay Kelleway* 64
2 br g Pastoral Pursuits Deep Blue Sea (Rip Van Winkle (IRE))
2561[10] 5992[5] **6532**[2]
Olivia On Green *Ronald Thompson*
3 b f Assertive Dimashq (Mtoto)
1417[17] 3218[8] 4439[6] 6982[9]
Olivia R (IRE) *David Barron* a51 68
3 ch f Excelebration(IRE) Rozene (IRE) (Sleeping Indian)
3202[9] **3650**[4] **4080**[3] 4820[4] 5238[9] 5659[10] 7032[10] 8068[6]
Ollie's Candy (USA) *John W Sadler* a112 99
4 bb m Candy Ride(ARG) Afternoon Stroll (USA) (Stroll (USA))
8775a[4]
Ollivander (IRE) *David O'Meara* a76 79
3 b g Heeraat(IRE) Coy (IRE) (Danehill (USA))
1523[4] 1970[3] 2299[2]◆ (2529) 3249[6] (3569) 4193[5] 4585[3] (5021) (5297) 6015[4] 6700[4] **7540**[2] 8181[12] 8642[3] 8902[3] 9642[5]
Olmedo (FR) *J-C Rouget* 115
4 b h Declaration Of War(USA) Super Pie (USA) (Pivotal)
1451a[4] 2313a[2] 3948[15] (6144a) **7007a**[4] 7924a[2]◆
Oloroso (IRE) *Andrew Balding* a77 78
3 ch g Fast Company(IRE) Convidada (IRE) (Trans Island)
(1285)◆ **1846**[4] 2364[7] 3465[10] 4316[5] 5351[4] **6081**[2] 6468[5] 7460[7] 7975[10]
Olwen's Dream (IRE) *Jimmy Frost* a23 45
3 b f Requinto(IRE) High Chart (Robellino (USA))
7295[9]
Olympe (FR) *J-C Rouget* a98 95
3 b f Charm Spirit(IRE) Naissance Royale (IRE) (Giant's Causeway (USA))
2498a[6] **3387a**[6]
Olympic Conqueror (IRE)
James Fanshawe a75 80
3 b g Olympic Glory(IRE) Queen's Conquer (King's Best (USA))
4305[6] 5477[4] 6169[2] 6624[2]◆ 7452[3] (7907) 8514[5] 9273[8]
Olympic Light (FR) *F Chappet* a73 73
3 b f Olympic Glory(IRE) Atlantic Light (Linamix (FR))
2759a[4]
Olympic Odyssey *Harry Fry* 69
4 b g Camelot Field Of Hope (IRE) (Selkirk (USA))
6055[6]
Olympic Spirit *David Barron* a71
3 ch g Olympic Glory(IRE) Magic Florence (IRE) (Zebedee)
130[3] **408**[2] 1161[5] 1924[10]
Om (USA) *Peter Miller* a99 114
7 ch h Munnings(USA) Rare Cat (USA) (Tabasco Cat (USA))
8770a[2]
Omaha Beach (USA)
Richard E Mandella a121
3 bb c War Front(USA) Charming (USA) (Seeking The Gold (USA))
8771a[2] (9639a)
Omnivega (FR) *David Simcock* a75 67
3 b g Siyouni(FR) Vermentina (IRE) (Darshaan)
5783[3] **7518**[3]
Omotesando *Oliver Greenall* a55 64
9 b g Street Cry(IRE) Punctilious (Danehill (USA))
916[5] 1330[P] 1508[9] **2359**[4] 2819[9] 3940[8] 5053[10]
Omran *Michael Wigham* a69 66
5 ch g Choisir(AUS) Ruff Shod (USA) (Storm Boot (USA))
8893[8] 9057[10] 9441[8]
On A Session (USA)
Aidan F Fogarty 100
3 b c Noble Mission Destiny Calls (USA) (With Approval (CAN))
2882a[10] 4092[15] 5205a[13] **5711a**[2] 6693a[19] 7934a[11]
Onassis (IRE) *Charlie Fellowes* a81 73
2 b f Dubawi(IRE) Jacqueline Quest (IRE) (Rock Of Gibraltar (IRE))
4223[5] 5045[2] 6019[7] 6963[2] 7696[5] (8303)
Onda District (IRE) *Stella Barclay* a55 52
7 b g Oasis Dream Leocorno (IRE) (Pivotal)
100[4]◆ 321[12] 1145[8] **3251**[2] 3500[9]
Ondin (IRE) *C Ferland* 58
3 gr c Oasis Dream Mia Capri (IRE) (Dalakhani (IRE))
3139a[8]
On Display *Nigel Tinkler* a40
2 b g Showcasing Miss Giler (High Chaparral (IRE))
9107[12] **9347**[8]
One Alc (FR) *Dean Ivory*
2 b g Wootton Bassett Caspian Breeze (USA) (Henrythenavigator (USA))
5956[9] 7104[9]
Onebaba (IRE) *Tony Carroll* a74 72
3 ch g No Nay Never(USA) Enharmonic (USA) (E Dubai (USA))
1381[6] **1570**[3] 3170[6] 3580[6] 7656[6] 8496[6] 8690[2] **9140**[2] 9349[9]
One Bite (IRE) *Keith Dalgleish* a66 74
2 b g Kodiac Rose Lilas (Cape Cross (IRE))
3245[8] 4238[4] (5093)◆ 5668[5] 6548[5] 7399[6] 8318[5]
One Boy (IRE) *Paul Midgley* a48 58
8 ch g Captain Gerrard(IRE) Paris Song (IRE) (Peintre Celebre (USA))
1817[4] 2294[10] 2632[17] 3213[6] 3723[12] 4132[11] 5018[8] 5491[2]◆ 5986[2] (6168) 6659[5] 7487[5] 7737[6] 7824[12]
One Cool Daddy (USA) *Dean Ivory* a80 29
4 b g Scat Daddy(USA) Coup (USA) (Empire Maker (USA))
2128[6] 2966[12] 3944[11] **8702**[2] 9054[5] 9304[8]
One Cool Poet (IRE)
Matthew J Smith a61 99
7 b g Urban Poet(USA) Oasis Star (IRE) (Desert King (IRE))
(5599a) **7216a**[10]
Onedin (IRE) *Kevin Ryan* a39 28
2 gr g Lethal Force(IRE) Dutch Heiress (Dutch Art)
6971[9] **9471**[12]
Onedownunder *Jonathan Portman* 45
3 b g Aussie Rules(USA) Saffron Fox (Safawan)
1652[11]
One Flew Over (IRE) *Ian Williams* 47
4 b g Jeremy(USA) Coill Cri (IRE) (Shinko Forest (IRE))
6131[14]
One For Brad (IRE) *Alan Berry* 42
4 b m Watar(IRE) Our Jaffa (IRE) (Bin Ajwaad (IRE))
3932[9] **4917**[8]
One Hart (IRE) *Mark Johnston* a86 84
2 b c Gutaifan(IRE) Crystal Morning (IRE) (Cape Cross (IRE))
3998[2]◆ (4275)◆ 5172[4] **6073**[2] 7399[11] 7763[5] 8665[2] 8850[5]
One Idea *Simon Crisford* a70
2 ch c Dubawi(IRE) Rose Diamond (IRE) (Daylami (IRE))
9174[3]◆
One Last Hug *Jim Goldie* a43 38
4 b g Orientor Gargoyle Girl (Be My Chief (USA))
954[6] 1212[7] 1722[9] 7420[7] 7779[4] 8819[5] 9220[10] 9391[9]
One Last Look (IRE) *G M Lyons* 91
2 b f Fastnet Rock(AUS) Celestial Bow (IRE) (Raven's Pass (USA))
5361a[5]
One Last Night (IRE) *Robert Cowell* a89 86
4 ch m Elusive Quality(USA) Danuta (USA) (Sunday Silence (USA))
1913[9] **2627**[6] 3587[8] 4101[11]
One Liner *John O'Shea* a46 40
5 b g Delegator Quip (Green Desert (USA))
462[6] 532[2] 1354[9] 2012[11] 2471[6]
One Master *William Haggas* 117
5 b m Fastnet Rock(AUS) Enticing (IRE) (Pivotal)
3105a[4] 3948[3] 4885[2] 5716a[5] (7944a) 8331[2]
One More Chance (IRE)
Michael Appleby a64 57
4 b m Epaulette(AUS) Hi Katriona (IRE) (Second Empire (IRE))
123[RR] 315[8] **814**[3] 1158[12]
One Night Stand *William Jarvis* 78
2 b g Swiss Spirit Tipsy Girl (Haafhd)
6449[4] **7316**[2] 7896[10]
One One Seven (IRE)
Antony Brittain a59 55
3 b g Arcano(IRE) Maany (USA) (Mr Greeley (USA))
497[5] 783[5] 1954[3] 2477[7] 2870[8] 3159[5] 4212[7] 4436[5] 5308[3] 5985[6] (7468) 7770[2] 7824[11] 8720[11] 9133[7] (9287)
Oneovdem *Tim Pinfield* a81 69
5 ch g Yorgunnabelucky(USA) Noor El Houdah (IRE) (Fayruz)
206[2] (886) 1099[4] 1395[4] 2472[4] 4320[12] 7554[4] 8122[8]
Onesarnieshort (FR) *F Bertrand* a54 56
4 b g Penny's Picnic(IRE) La Atomica (FR) (Silent Times (IRE))
2647a[8]
One Step Beyond (IRE)
Richard Spencer 70
2 b c Exceed And Excel(AUS) Yours Truly (IRE) (Dark Angel (IRE))
4394[4]◆ 4826[8]
One To Go *Tim Easterby* a72 74
3 gr g Champs Elysees Tina's Spirit (IRE) (Invincible Spirit (IRE))
1645[8] 2150[5] 2712[4] 3226[4] 4210[2] 4761[2] 5214[3] 5557[2] 5695[4] (6101) **6501**[2] 7074[8] 7512[3] 7906[4] 8186[8]
One Vision (IRE) *Charlie Appleby* a1
3 ch g Shamardal(USA) Music Chart (USA) (Exchange Rate (USA))
(103)◆ 1856[5]
On Guard *John Gosden* 76
2 b c Invincible Spirit(IRE) Palitana (USA) (Giant's Causeway (USA))
5894[2]◆
Only Alone (IRE) *Jedd O'Keeffe* a43 42
2 b f Starspangledbanner(AUS) Only Together (IRE) (Montjeu (IRE))
7333[9] **9099**[9]
Onlyhuman (IRE)
Mrs John Harrington 105
6 b g Invincible Spirit(IRE) Liscune (IRE) (King's Best (USA))
5535a[8] 6693a[25]
Only Orsenfoolsies
Micky Hammond 67
10 b g Trade Fair Desert Gold (IRE) (Desert Prince (IRE))
2591[12] (3294) 8344[5]
Only Spoofing (IRE) *Jedd O'Keeffe* a89 94
5 b g Approve(IRE) Golden Anthem (USA) (Lion Cavern (USA))
1860[6] 3658[4] 4279[3] (4625) (4821) (5371) 5888[3] 6724[9]◆ **6986a**[2] 8099[6]
Only Ten Per Cent (IRE)
J R Jenkins a46 42
11 b g Kheleyf(USA) Cory Everson (IRE) (Brief Truce (USA))
719[9] **1731**[2] 2298[11]
Onomatopoeia *Camilla Poulton* a47 59
5 b m Raven's Pass(USA) Manoeuvre (IRE) (Galileo (IRE))
3690[3] 4547[11] 7560[12] 8414[14] 9207[13]
On Route *Sir Mark Prescott Bt* a63 56
3 b f Pivotal Expect (Invincible Spirit (IRE))
6930[7] 7307[6] **7576**[4] 7844[7]
On The Bob *Paddy Butler* a7 34
3 b g Big Bad Bob(IRE) Favourite Girl (IRE) (Refuse To Bend (IRE))
2926[13] **3253**[4] 8249[11]
On The Edge (FR) *Mme A Rosa* a61 67
3 b f George Vancouver(USA) Life Of Risks (FR) (Take Risks (FR))
9504a[12]
On The Go Again (IRE)
Michael Mulvany 96
6 b g Arakan(USA) Lady Bolino (IRE) (King's Theatre (IRE))
7038a[14]
On The Line (IRE) *Hugo Palmer* a83 95
3 gr c Dark Angel(IRE) Crimson Cheer (USA) (Van Nistelrooy (USA))
720[4] 966[2] (1264) 1646[2] 1945[5] (4079)
On The Nod *E J O'Neill* 10
2 b g Slade Power(IRE) Marmaria (SPA) (Limpid)
3171a[7]
Ontheradar (IRE) *Ronald Thompson* a34 46
2 b g Morpheus Tap The Dot (IRE) (Sharp Humor (USA))
4516[9] **5331**[8] 5764[11] 7626[3]
On The Rhine (IRE) *Andrew Hughes* a49 46
2 b c War Command(USA) Janna's Jewel (IRE) (Traditionally (USA))
7235[10] 7778[9]
On The Right Track *Mark Usher* a64 52
2 gr g Mukhadram Jessica Ennis (USA) (English Channel (USA))
7453[5] 8517[10] **8810**[6] 9212[12]
On The Sea *N Caullery* a87 78
5 b g Oasis Dream Quenched (Dansili)
9483a[10]
On The Stage *K R Burke* a64 74
3 b f Swiss Spirit Spotlight (Dr Fong (USA))
2121[8] **2960**[5]
On The Warpath *Charlie Appleby* a92 115
4 ch g Declaration Of War(USA) Elusive Pearl (USA) (Medaglia d'Oro (USA))
173a[2] 515a[3] (960a) 1891[2] (2442)
On Tick (IRE) *Miss Katy Brown* a73 67
2 b c Epaulette(AUS) Vale Of Paris (IRE) (Vale Of York (IRE))
5635[2] 6899[3] 7876a[7] 8195[4]
On Your Marks *Andrea Marcialis* a54 66
2 b g Showcasing White House (Pursuit Of Love)
5468a[7]
Ooby Douby (FR) *N Leenders* a48 53
4 gr g Soul City(IRE) Yasmara (FR) (Kendor (FR))
5009a[6]
Oofy Prosser (IRE) *Harry Dunlop* a55 63
3 br g Tough As Nails(IRE) Choir Lady (IRE) (Ad Valorem (USA))
2190[7] (2773) 3018[7] 3150[5]
Opening Verse (IRE)
John Joseph Murphy 79
3 b g Dark Angel(IRE) Silk Slippers (Oasis Dream)
6235a[7]
Open Wide (USA) *Amanda Perrett* a88 104
5 bb g Invincible Spirit(IRE) Nunavik (IRE) (Indian Ridge (IRE))
1892[3] 2403[5] 2775[7] 3344[10] (4186) 4896[2] 5504[2] 5664[2] 6404[4] **6953**[3] 7193[8]
Opera Kiss (IRE) *Ivan Furtado* a45 34
3 ch f Slade Power(IRE) Shamardal Phantom (IRE) (Shamardal (USA))
954[9] 1427[5] 1816[12] 3270[12] 5063[6] 5857[13] **6885**[4] 7336[6] 8547[12] 9138[9] 9283[11]
Operatic Export (IRE) *J S Bolger* 80
3 b f Vocalised(USA) Teofolina (IRE) (Teofilo (IRE))
1601a[14]
Ophelia's Dream *H-A Pantall* a57 78
3 ch f Dubawi(IRE) Hibaayeb (Singspiel (IRE))
7505a[11]
Opine (IRE) *Michael Bell* a56
2 b g Authorized(IRE) Tocqueville (FR) (Numerous (USA))
6314[6] **6927**[7] 7787[7] 8287[11]
Opportunist *Martyn Meade* a58
3 b c Cape Cross(IRE) Argent Du Bois (USA) (Silver Hawk (USA))
9425[5]
Optima Petamus *Liam Bailey* a53 49
7 gr g Mastercraftsman(IRE) In A Silent Way (IRE) (Desert Prince (IRE))
1390[2] 1520[5] 1958[6] 3225[6] 3448[2] 4003[6] 4293[11] 5025[4] 5518[6] 5851[4] 6545[6] 8694[6] 9362[4] (9470)
Optimickstickhill *Scott Dixon* a43 43
4 gr m Milk It Mick Stylistickhill (IRE) (Desert Style (IRE))
2295[5] 2527[7] 3213[4]◆ (3518) 3975[7] 4212[8] 5765[6] 6547[11] 7286[6] 7590[11]
Optio *Brian Meehan* a69 62
2 b c Equiano(FR) Aarti (IRE) (Oasis Dream)
5186[9] 5775[5] **6708**[6] 7438[5]
Optionality *D J Bunyan* a32 82
5 b m Bated Breath Celebrity (Pivotal)
3818a[9]

Orange Blossom *Richard Fahey* a55 78
3 ch f Showcasing Satsuma (Compton Place)
752[2] (1139) 5659[4] 6533[2] 7367[5] 7828[2] 8403[7]
Orangefield (FR) *M Boutin* a69 86
8 b g Soave(GER) Moon Serenade (Key Of Luck (USA))
2648a[5]
Orange Justice *David Loughnane* a45 29
2 ch f Harbour Watch(IRE) Jord (IRE) (Trans Island)
6979[6] 7377[9] 8067[5] 8527[11] 8825[9]
Orange Suit (IRE) *Ed de Giles* a74 73
4 b g Declaration Of War(USA) Guantanamera (IRE) (Sadler's Wells (USA))
2628[8] 2966[8] 4250[8] 4817[6] 7060[2] (7229) 7829[10] 8806[2] 9273[12] 9510[6] 9642[6]
Orbaan *A Fabre* 105
4 b g Invincible Spirit(IRE) Contradict (Raven's Pass (USA))
3030a[4]
Orchidees (FR) *N Leenders* a39 38
3 b f Spider Flight(FR) Orchidee Divine (FR) (Divine Light (JPN))
7476a[6]
Orchidia (IRE) *Roger Charlton* a76 72
3 ch f Bated Breath New Orchid (USA) (Quest For Fame)
2102[4] 4768[2] (8467)
Orchid Star *Charlie Appleby* a80 100
3 b f Dubawi(IRE) Pleione (FR) (Sadler's Wells (USA))
(547) (739) 1832[6] 8376a[2] 8983a[3]
Orczy (IRE) *Richard Hannon* a72
2 b c Sir Percy Maria Kristina (FR) (Footstepsinthesand)
9325[5]◆ 9509[2]
Ordalie Jem (FR) *S Jesus* 65
2 ro f Tin Horse(IRE) Beauty Jem (FR) (Red Ransom (USA))
4533a[7]
Order Again (NZ) *Brian Smith* 100
5 b g Iffraaj Glass Half Full (NZ) (Van Nistelrooy (USA))
8138a[16]
Order Of Command (AUS)
Danny O'Brien 108
4 b g Squamosa(AUS) Commanding Angel (AUS) (Commands (AUS))
9015a[7]
Order Of Merritt (IRE)
Sir Mark Prescott Bt a20 38
2 b g Kyllachy Merritt Island (Exceed And Excel (AUS))
5865[7] 6147[6] 6548[11] 7111[12] 7584[9]
Order Of St John *John Ryan* 71
2 b g Coach House(IRE) Gospel Music (Beat Hollow)
3274[8] 4564[4] 5780[2] 7391[7] 8430[2]
Ord River *Henry Candy* 1
4 b m Intello(GER) Free Offer (Generous (IRE))
2770[14]
Oribi *William Haggas* a51 52
2 b f Muhaarar Shamandar (FR) (Exceed And Excel (AUS))
4337[7] 4790[9] 5427[4] 6182[8] 6837[5]
Oriental Eagle (GER)
J Hirschberger 107
5 bb h Campanologist(USA) Oriental Pearl (GER) (Big Shuffle (USA))
3386a[6] 4427a[4] 5719a[3] 7249a[4]
Oriental Lilly *Jim Goldie* a76 77
5 ch m Orientor Eternal Instinct (Exceed And Excel (AUS))
786[9] 1502[7] (1929) 2161[6] 3309[5] 4103[5] 4330[4] 4722[5] 5432[2] 5903[8] 6609[7] 6972[5] (7310) 7402[20] 7583[6] 8304[9] 8719[10] 8924[2] 9113[6] 9519[3]
Oriental Mystique *David Simcock* a76 71
2 b f Kingman Madame Chiang (Archipenko (USA))
8464[4]◆ (8848)◆
Oriental Queen (FR) *M Nigge* a69 78
4 b m Declaration Of War(USA) Orion Girl (GER) (Law Society (USA))
6521a[7]
Oriental Relation (IRE)
John Balding a65 55
8 gr g Tagula(IRE) Rofan (USA) (Cozzene (USA))
236[9] 1364[9] 2153[8] 2632[18]
Oriental Splendour (IRE) *Ruth Carr* a47 55
7 br g Strategic Prince Asian Lady (Kyllachy)
2189[5] 2789[6] (3213) 4212[9] 4694[7] (5018) 5722[6] 6503[7] 7051[10] 7591[7]
Orient Class *Paul Midgley* a53 76
8 ch g Orientor Killer Class (Kyllachy)
610[10] 953[9] 1403[8] 1950[9]
Orient Express *Richard Fahey* a65 23
4 b g Orientor Midnight Dynamo (Lujain (USA))
117[3] 500[5] 2847[10]
Originaire (IRE) *William Haggas* a80 104
3 b c Zoffany(IRE) Polly Perkins (IRE) (Pivotal)
(32) 312[2]
Original Choice (IRE)
Nick Littmoden a100 100
5 ch g Dragon Pulse(IRE) Belle Watling (IRE) (Street Cry (IRE))
173a[15] 637a[8] 961a[5] 4342[6] 4935[19] 5610[8] 5930[8] 6861[4] (7201) 7616[6] 9041[10] 9667[2]
Orin Swift (IRE) *Jonathan Portman* a83 89
5 b g Dragon Pulse(IRE) Hollow Green (IRE) (Beat Hollow)
(2254) 2571[2] 3635[2] 4118[5] 5457[4] 6448[7] 8129[2]
Orion's Bow *Tim Easterby* a77 80
8 ch g Pivotal Heavenly Ray (USA) (Rahy (USA))
2201[4] 2843[13] 3509[10] (5119) 5395[16] 5901[3] 6227[14] 6826[9]
Orion's Shore (IRE) *Jamie Osborne* a60
3 ch c Sea The Stars(IRE) Bright Snow (USA) (Gulch (USA))
8351[9] 9213[8]
Orlaith (IRE) *Iain Jardine* 97
2 b f Fastnet Rock(AUS) Cmonbabylitemyfire (IRE) (Piccolo)
3244[8] 4006[5] 4433[4] (4984) 5544[4] (6157) 7432[4] 8125[3] 8724[6]
Orliko (IRE) *Richard Hannon* a54 64
3 b g Kodiac Lisieux Orchid (IRE) (Sadler's Wells (USA))
2798[6] (3409) 3697[6] 4179[2] 4453[5] 4642[12] 5031[6] 5431[9] 6052[5] 6361[14]
Ormesher *Donald McCain* a50 66
4 b g Sir Percy Marakabei (Hernando (FR))
7643[3] 8944[3]
Ormskirk *Johnny Farrelly* a19 41
6 gr g Hellvelyn River Song (USA) (Siphon (BRZ))
6601[7]
Ormuz (GER) *Henk Grewe* 89
3 b f Mamool(IRE) Ormita (GER) (Acatenango (GER))
3877a[4] 4707a[10] 8585a[5]
Ornate *David C Griffiths* a101 109
6 b g Bahamian Bounty Adorn (Kyllachy)
3[3] (163) (230) 352[2] 588[2] 877[5] (1892)◆ 2409[5] 2744[9] (3344) (3956) 5371[6] 5611[3] 5664[18] 6423[7] 6698[6] 7454[8]
Orobas (IRE) *Lucinda Egerton* a65 69
7 b g Dark Angel(IRE) Miss Mujadil (IRE) (Mujadil (USA))
1040[2]◆ 1183[11] 1297[11] (1333) 1482[7] 2959[5] 3038[6] 3217[7] 3297[6] 4216[2] (4473) 4915[7] 5043[3] 5239[7] 5274[7] 5782[7]
Oromo (IRE) *Karl Thornton* a47 52
6 b g High Chaparral(IRE) Miss Beatrix (IRE) (Danehill Dancer (IRE))
482[7] 5939[2] 8081[3]
Orsino (IRE) *Seb Spencer* a72 76
5 b g Galileo(IRE) Birmanie (USA) (Aldebaran (USA))
4383[10] 5739[5] 6674[3]
Orvar (IRE) *Paul Midgley* a94 98
6 b g Dandy Man(IRE) Roskeen (IRE) (Grand Lodge (USA))
49a[4] 393a[4] 837[7] 1734[7] 2775[15] 3097[7] 4313a[4] 4888[5] 5420[6] (6208) 6351[7] 7193[13] 8099[3] 8867[5]
Osborne Bulls (AUS)
James Cummings 119
5 b g Street Cry(IRE) Jerezana (AUS) (Lonhro (AUS))
1974a[2]
Osho *Richard Hannon* a62 66
3 b c Oasis Dream Maid Of Killeen (IRE) (Darshaan)
1217[5] 1423[6] 2140[5] 4070[2]◆ 4476[5]
Oslo *Sir Michael Stoute* a78 70
2 b g Gleneagles(IRE) Intercontinental (Danehill (USA))
5131[6] 5809[6] 6402[3] (7548)◆
Osmosis *Jason Ward* a65 65
3 gr f Tamayuz Spectacle (Dalakhani (IRE))
2058[3] 2711[4] 3099[4] 3708[6] 4628[5] 5334[4] 5556[8] 6101[3] 6610[4] 7542[2] 8205[9] 8903[7]
Oso Rapido (IRE) *David O'Meara* 75
2 b g Kodiac Burke's Rock (Cape Cross (IRE))
2869[2] 3411[3] 3866[5] 4938[7] 6653[6] (7309)
Ossco *Mohamed Moubarak* a67 11
2 b g Sepoy(AUS) Forbidden Love (Dubawi (IRE))
2903[8] 3579[3] 4018[3] 4637[5] 6113[2] 6719[3]
Ostilio *Simon Crisford* a86 116
4 ch h New Approach(IRE) Reem Three (Mark Of Esteem (IRE))
2313a[7] 2829[8] 5977a[10]
Ostrich *Roger Charlton* a51
3 b c Phoenix Reach(IRE) Tamso (USA) (Seeking The Gold (USA))
66[7]
Otago *Michael Bell* 77
2 b g Cable Bay(IRE) Spinning Top (Alzao (USA))
3194[5] 3739[3] (4344) 6356[18]
Oti Ma Boati *William Haggas* a78 82
2 b f Iffraaj Mania (IRE) (Danehill (USA))
(3652)◆ (4290)◆ (5171) 6356[7] 7696[11]
Ottoman Court *Charlie Appleby* a91 88
2 b g Shamardal(USA) Tulips (IRE) (Pivotal)
2931[5] 3601[2] 6154[3] (8912)◆
Oudini (FR) *Simone Brogi* 50
2 b c Due Diligence(USA) Kointreau (IRE) (Desert King (IRE))
4949a[8]
Oud Metha Bridge (IRE)
Julia Feilden a77 78
5 ch g Helmet(AUS) Central Force (Pivotal)
1563[5] (2256) 2978[2] (3743) 4566[6] 5726[8] 8658[4] 9173[10] 9512[9]
Oui Madame (IRE)
Hue & Lamotte D'Argy 43
3 b f No Nay Never(USA) Mitchelton (FR) (High Chaparral (IRE))
3066a[9]
Oulmes Dream (FR)
Mme E Siavy-Julien a2 40
4 ch g Alexandros Belle Dream (IRE) (Indian Haven)
4748a[11]
Our Boy Zeus (IRE)
Micky Hammond
3 b g Morpheus Alexander Duchess (IRE) (Desert Prince (IRE))
2150[11] 2587[7]
Our Charlie Brown *David C Griffiths* a68 72
5 b g American Post Cordoba (Oasis Dream)
1925[11] 2372[5] 2898[9] 3771[5] 3969[4] 4523[10] 4784[4] (6276) 6572[4] 8199[3] 8471[5] 9545[5]
Our Cilla *Andrew Crook* a48 63
5 gr m Sixties Icon Kinetix (Linamix (FR))
8081[4]
Our Country (USA) *George Weaver* 102
2 b c Constitution(USA) Light And Variable (USA) (Tiznow (USA))
8746a[8]
Our Dave *John Quinn* a50 65
2 b g Due Diligence(USA) Lady Sledmere (IRE) (Barathea (IRE))
3703[8] 4075[3] 4623[9] 5295[7] (6271) 6673[4] 7306[12] 8022[7]
Our Girl Sheila (IRE) *K R Burke* 62
2 b f Nathaniel(IRE) Amazon Beauty (IRE) (Wolfhound (USA))
8855[4]
Our Kylie (IRE) *Donald McCain* a48 56
7 b m Jeremy(USA) Prakara (IRE) (Indian Ridge (IRE))
5728[10]
Our Last Summer (IRE)
Niels Petersen 104
6 br g Zamindar(USA) Hoh My Darling (Dansili)
3902a[8] 4419a[10]
Our Little Pony *Lawrence Mullaney* 86
4 b m Bated Breath Cracking Lass (IRE) (Whipper (USA))
2637[8] 2874[5] 3868[3]◆ 5395[6] 5691[2] (6178)◆ 6379[13] 6972[11] (8400)
Our Lord *Michael Attwater* a87 73
7 gr g Proclamation(IRE) Lady Filly (Atraf)
3893[7] 4495[8] 5281[10]
Our Manekineko
Stephen Michael Hanlon a50 32
9 b g Kyllachy Gallivant (Danehill (USA))
273[7] (912) 1769[7] 4190[12]
Our Man In Havana *Tony Carroll* a54 49
4 b g Havana Gold(IRE) Auntie Kathryn (IRE) (Acclamation)
187[10] 236[10] 468[9] 1682[11] 1986[10] 9287[13] 9551[5]
Ourmullion *David Pipe* a75 64
5 b g Mullionmileanhour(IRE) Queen Ranavola (USA) (Medaglia d'Oro (USA))
4231[8]
Our Oystercatcher *Mark Pattinson* a72 78
5 br g Pastoral Pursuits The Dark Eider (Superlative)
2272[6] 2556[4] 3856[3] 4230[4] 5252[6] 5889[5] (6668) 7161[2] 8242[6]
Our Patron Saint (IRE)
Sarah Dawson 33
2 b g Epaulette(AUS) Ocean Talent (USA) (Aptitude (USA))
7247a[22]
Our Place In Loule *Noel Wilson* a52 73
6 ch g Compton Place Show Off (Efisio)
(1505) 1951[4] 2368[10] 4059[13] 4691[4] 4911[11] 7367[15] 7511[10] 8183[5]
Our Rodney (IRE) *Donald McCain* a39 69
3 b g Canford Cliffs(IRE) Sea Swell (USA) (Elusive Quality (USA))
2101[11] 4109[6]
Our Secret (IRE) *Liam Bailey* a44 44
3 ch f Dandy Man(IRE) Classic Style (IRE) (Desert Style (IRE))
1486[11] 2197[6] 4078[7] 5297[4] 5771[9]
Ours Puissant (IRE) *Hugo Palmer* a93 83
3 b g Kodiac Lady Emily (IRE) (Jeremy (USA))
893a[5] 2082[9]
Outback Traveller (IRE)
Nikki Evans a57 54
8 b g Bushranger(IRE) Blue Holly (IRE) (Blues Traveller (IRE))
3838[10]
Out Bound (IRE) *J-V Toux* 40
2 ch c Dragon Pulse(IRE) Gan Locht (USA) (Whywhywhy (USA))
1709a[9]
Outbox *Simon Crisford* 111
4 b g Frankel Emirates Queen (Street Cry (IRE))
4884[6] 5662[2] 5909[3] 6712[3]
Outcrop (IRE) *Jennie Candlish* a47 56
5 b g Rock Of Gibraltar(IRE) Desert Sage (Selkirk (USA))
8414[5]
Outer Space *John Flint* a65 61
8 b g Acclamation Venoge (IRE) (Green Desert (USA))
2994[4] 4235[8] 6334[10] 7236[11]
Out For A Duck *Michael Appleby* a43
2 b f Due Diligence(USA) Three Ducks (Diktat)
8640[4] 9046[14] 9383[7]
Outlaw Torn (IRE) *Richard Guest* a46 42
10 ch g Iffraaj Touch And Love (IRE) (Green Desert (USA))
436[11] 532[8] 593[3] 983[3] 1078[3] 1546[6] 1680[9] 2234[10] 5652[6] 5946[6] 6153[6] 6502[7]
Out Of Breath *Grant Tuer* 73
2 b g Bated Breath Parisi (Rahy (USA))
1651[2] 1931[4] 2275[5] 3812[8] 4652[2] 5896[3] (6571) 6969[5] 7585[2] 8394[11]
Out Of Here (IRE) *Kevin Ryan* a56 54
2 ch g G Force(IRE) Wee Jean (Captain Gerrard (IRE))
2706[5] 3265[6] 4125[5] 6071[6]
Out Of The Ashes
Mohamed Moubarak a38 30
6 ch g Phoenix Reach(IRE) Shrewd Decision (Motivator)
1715[12] 2235[12] 3738[10] 4589[7] 5653[8]
Outofthegloom *Brian Rothwell* a39
2 b f Heeraat(IRE) Srimenanti (Diktat)
9107[11] 9393[8]
Outofthequestion *Alan King* a69 76
5 b g Delegator Why Dubai (USA) (Kris S (USA))
754[7] 1292[8] 2254[10] 2793[8]
Out Of Time (ITY) *A Botti* 112
3 ch c Sakhee's Secret Calma Apparente (Rainbow Quest (USA))
(2162a) 3643a[2] 4432a[3] (8392a) (8786a)
Outrage *Daniel Kubler* a99 85
7 ch g Exceed And Excel(AUS) Ludynosa (USA) (Cadeaux Genereux)
(127)◆ 352[4] 786[4] 1938[9] 2775[19]
Outragusandangerus (USA)
Roy Arne Kvisla 75
2 bb c Summer Front(USA) Everdeen (USA) (Lemon Drop Kid (USA))
7495a[5]
Outrath (IRE) *Suzi Best* a54 45
9 b g Captain Rio Silver Grouse (IRE) (Zagreb (USA))
2234[14]
Outside Inside (IRE)
Mark Johnston a82 80
4 b m Holy Roman Emperor(IRE) Humble And Proud (IRE) (Pivotal)
1273[5]◆ 2959[3] 3743[5] 3843[4] 4278[2] 4643[8] 4982[5]
Outtake *Richard Hannon* 69
2 br g Outstrip Cambridge Duchess (Singspiel (IRE))
4558[5] 4871[3] 5456[6] 6372[11] 7391[6]
Ouzo *Richard Hannon* a93 95
3 b c Charm Spirit(IRE) Miss Meltemi (IRE) (Miswaki Tern (USA))
2101[2] (3471)◆ (3805) (4300) 8728[4] 9053[5]
Over Attracted (USA) *F Chappet* 47
2 bb f Atreides(USA) Appearance (USA) (Harlington (USA))
8447a[8]
Overbeck (IRE) *Dean Ivory* a61
4 b g Camelot Brigid (USA) (Irish River (FR))
6887[3] 7559[6]
Overdose D'Oroux (FR)
Carmen Bocskai 60
4 b h Overdose Illiana (GER) (Tertullian (USA))
7136a[9]
Overhaugh Street *Ed de Giles* a67 77
6 b g Bahri(USA) Bom Chicka Wah Wah (USA) (Dynaformer (USA))
3222[6] 4362[2] (5423) 5840[8] (6716) 7683[5] 8513[4]
Overpriced Mixer *Jamie Osborne* a79 76
2 b c Harbour Watch(IRE) Chincoteague (IRE) (Daylami (IRE))
3257[7] 4480[2] 6314[2] (6673) (7787)
Over The Guns (IRE) *K R Burke* a63 63
3 b g Garswood Princess Rose (Royal Applause)
2333[6] 3548[7]
Over The Moon (IRE) *P Sogorb* a62 77
3 b f Invincible Spirit(IRE) Hit The Sky (IRE) (Cozzene (USA))
8377a[7]
Over The River *Alexandra Dunn*
3 b f Avonbridge First Among Equals (Primo Valentino (IRE))
5057[12]
Overtrumped *Mike Murphy* a54 65
4 b m Champs Elysees Perfect Hand (Barathea (IRE))
1482[10] 2617[14] 3547[5] 3937[2] 5785[6] 5982[5] 7643[10] 7973[7]
Overwrite (IRE) *Mark Johnston* a25 83
2 ro c Zebedee Negotiate (Red Ransom (USA))
7388[7] 7677[2] (7981)◆
Owendale (USA) *Brad H Cox* a111
3 b c Into Mischief(USA) Aspen Light (USA) (Bernardini (USA))
2856a[3] 8777a[10]
Ower Bush Mills *Richard Hannon* a43
2 br c Dick Turpin(IRE) Mary's Pet (Where Or When (IRE))
8999[10] 9325[9]
Ower Fly *Ruth Carr* a62 81
6 b g Pastoral Pursuits Contrary Mary (Mujadil (USA))
1459[12] 1944[7] 4759[6] 5416[5] 5821[10] 6588[8] 7820[7] 8304[10] 8712[5] 8946[6] 9253[11]
Owhatanight *Ed Dunlop* 50
2 gr c Night Of Thunder(IRE) White Wedding (IRE) (Green Desert (USA))
5501[6]
Owney Madden *Martyn Meade* 88
2 b c Oasis Dream Terre Du Vent (FR) (Kutub (IRE))
3542[4] 4252[3] (5186) 5612[11] (6356) 7072[4] 7399[7]
Oxalis (IRE) *F Head* 81
2 b c Invincible Spirit(IRE) Lady Of Shamrock (USA) (Scat Daddy (USA))
7887a[6]
Oxford Blu *Olly Murphy* a65 68
5 b g Aqlaam Blue Zealot (IRE) (Galileo (IRE))
385[7]
Oxted *Roger Teal* 115
3 b g Mayson Charlotte Rosina (Choisir (AUS))
(2139) 2826[2] 5184[6] 5658[4] 6222[2] (7193)
Oxygenic *David O'Meara* a53 56
3 b f Showcasing Viola D'Amour (IRE) (Teofilo (IRE))
215[11] 605[3] 1167[8] 2211[6]
Oya (IRE) *S Seemar* a42
3 b f Farhh Zumurudah (FR) (Dubawi (IRE))
48a[10]◆
Oydis *Ralph Beckett* 96
3 b f Nathaniel(IRE) Opera Dancer (Norse Dancer (IRE))
2770[10] 3152[4] (3947) (5452)◆ 6223[2] 7118[7]
Oyster Card *Michael Appleby* a44 40
6 b g Rail Link Perle D'Or (IRE) (Entrepreneur)
1548[12] 4594[13] 6853[9] 7271[9]
Ozark *Jennie Candlish* a29 40
3 b f Archipenko(USA) Shimoni (Mark Of Esteem (IRE))
2099[8] 2845[6] 4143[4] 7035[9] 8081[10]
Pablo Escobarr (IRE)
William Haggas a113 112
3 b c Galileo(IRE) Bewitched (IRE) (Dansili)
1911[2] 2619[2] 4049[5] 8764[2] (9302)
Pablo Hernandez *David O'Meara* a52
2 b c Zoffany(IRE) Miss Delila (USA) (Malibu Moon (USA))
9363[8]
Pablow *Alan Bailey* a54 20
4 b g Delegator Limonia (GER) (Perugino (USA))
602[5] 695[8]
Pachadargent (FR) *J-P Gauvin* a84 99
8 b g Kendargent(FR) Sabasha (FR) (Xaar)
7676a[5]
Pacificadora (USA) *Simon Dow* a67 43
3 bb f Declaration Of War(USA) Rau Breck (USA) (Mr Greeley (USA))
78[3] (380) 2731[10] 4788[8]
Pacific Coast *Antony Brittain* a40 38
2 b g Monsieur Bond(IRE) Sea Crest (Xaar)
3265[9] 4191[7] 4433[8] 9394[12]
Pacific Salt (IRE) *Pam Sly* a66 60
6 gr g Zebedee Villa Nova (IRE) (Petardia)
33[9]

Pacino *Richard Fahey* a76 76
3 b g Heeraat(IRE) Ringtail (USA) (Street Cry (IRE))
1360[2]◆ (1846) 2559[7] 3357[9] 4316[3] 4360[4] 4909[5] 5422[6] 5708[8] 7145[11]

Packet Racket *Ann Duffield*
2 b c Fast Company(IRE) Saralea (FR) (Sillery (USA))
4433[10] 4719[5]

Packington Lane *Tim Easterby* a51 55
3 b g Heeraat(IRE) Blades Princess (Needwood Blade)
4128[10] 4757[3] 6685[7] 7286[9] 7651[10]

Pacodali (IRE) *Lindsey Smith* 109
6 br g Paco Boy(IRE) Dont Dili Dali (Dansili)
8578a[4] (9016a)

Paco Dawn *Tony Carroll* a43 42
5 ch m Paco Boy(IRE) First Dawn (Dr Fong (USA))
476[7] 3410[12] 5498[9] 7028[10] 7237[7] 8255[13]

Paco Escostar *Julie Camacho* a48 65
4 ch m Paco Boy(IRE) Shesastar (Bahamian Bounty)
1952[6] 2632[13] 4132[6] 4824[5] 5478[8] 6277[8] 7052[2] 7824[9]

Paco's Prince *Nick Littmoden* a78 63
4 b g Paco Boy(IRE) Equitissa (IRE) (Chevalier (IRE))
2124[2] 2516[3] 3004[3] 3816[9] 4250[11] 6439[7] 7083[10]

Pact Of Steel *Ivan Furtado* a56 49
4 ch g Declaration Of War(USA) She's My Dandy (IRE) (Holy Roman Emperor (IRE))
3325[5] (6977) 7374[8] 7859[7] 8466[8] 8998[12]

Pactolus (IRE) *Stuart Williams* a108 84
8 b g Footstepsinthesand Gold Marie (IRE) (Green Desert (USA))
(368) 879[3] 1101[13] 1921[3] 4255[7] 4613[8] 5320[6] 6537[4] 7396[2] 8062[3] 9003[3] 9309[2] 9610[2]

Paddy A (IRE) *Ian Williams* a84 84
5 b g Holy Roman Emperor(IRE) Lilting (IRE) (Montjeu (IRE))
2578[2] 3467[5] 4019[8] 4791[11]

Paddy Elliott (IRE) *Brian Ellison* a71 68
2 b g French Navy Siphon Melody (USA) (Siphon (BRZ))
1416[8] 1758[3] 4384[4] 4999[4] 6457[2] 7064[4] 7827[5]

Paddyplex *Tristan Davidson* a76 68
6 b g Multiplex Turtle Bay (Dr Fong (USA))
1220[5] 8082[7] 9096[6] 9628[9]

Paddy Power (IRE) *Richard Fahey* a85 86
6 ch g Pivotal Rag Top (IRE) (Barathea (IRE))
1487[7] 1895[5] (2416)◆ 2843[4]◆ (3079) 3893[3] 4402[16] 4492[3] 5454[8] 5661[5] 6227[19] 6972[3] 7402[6] 8425[11] (8921)

Paddys Motorbike (IRE)
Nigel Twiston-Davies a95 95
7 ch g Fast Company(IRE) Saffa Garden (IRE) (King's Best (USA))
(3799) 4096[5] 5540[10]

Paddy's Pursuit (IRE)
David Loughnane a65 57
3 b g Pastoral Pursuits Anaya (Tobougg (IRE))
316[4] 841[7] 1178[5] 3354[10] 6037[6] 6569[5] 7024[5] 7549[8] 8822[11]

Paddy's Rock (IRE) *Lynn Siddall* a36 41
8 b g Whipper(USA) Hedera (USA) (Woodman (USA))
2695[8] 3511[9] 5518[8]

Paddys Runner *Graeme McPherson* a64 67
7 gr g Sir Percy Frosty Welcome (USA) (With Approval (CAN))
946[6]

Paddy The Chef (IRE) *Ian Williams* a79 77
4 b g Dandy Man(IRE) The Reek (Tiger Hill (IRE))
3192[8] 4296[4] 5086[6] 5528[3]◆ 6303[8] (7116)◆

Padmavati *Ed Walker* a58 30
3 b f New Approach(IRE) Padmini (Tiger Hill (IRE))
1730[7] 2341[14] 3593[11] 4753[11]

Padura Brave *Mark Usher* a62 57
3 b f Havana Gold(IRE) Audaz (Oasis Dream)
2965[5] 3665[9] 4284[6] 4789[4] 5731[4] 6279[10] 7573[5] 8254[12] 8667[8] 9042[8] 9446[6]

Pageant Master (IRE)
Michael Appleby a24 11
3 ch g Casamento(IRE) Skiphall (Halling (USA))
1486[9] 2735[7] 3780[10] 9516[12]

Paintball Wizard (IRE) *Julia Feilden* 51
3 ch g Mastercraftsman(IRE) Dance Avenue (IRE) (Sadler's Wells (USA))
5783[5] 6216[4] 8662[2]

Painted Dream *George Margarson* a67 51
3 b f Showcasing Speed Date (Sakhee's Secret)
1475[3] 2204[11] 5281[6] 5622[9] 6286[12] 7105[6] 8071[4] 9249[5] 9420[12]

Paint It Black *Sylvester Kirk* a57
2 b g Iffraaj Sister Ship (Sulamani (IRE))
8700[11] 9448[7]

Paisley's Promise (IRE)
Mike Murphy
2 ch f Dandy Man(IRE) Relinquished (Royal Applause)
5527[8] 6368[18]

Palace Pier *John Gosden* 96
2 b c Kingman Beach Frolic (Nayef (USA))
(6669)◆ (7339)

Palace Prince (GER)
Jean-Pierre Carvalho a97 103
7 bb h Areion(GER) Palace Princess (GER) (Tiger Hill (IRE))
682a[7] 1793a[4] 3287a[5] 4157a[2] 5230a[8] 6770a[6]

Palao (GER) *Markus Klug* 85
2 ch c Champs Elysees Plissetskaia (FR) (Caerleon (USA))
7937a[3]

Palavas (FR) *Cedric Rossi* a91 104
4 b g Redoute's Choice(AUS) Peinted Song (USA) (Unbridled's Song (USA))
5168a[3]

Palavicini Run (IRE) *Linda Perratt* a42 43
6 ch m Palavicini(USA) Dawn's Sharp Shot (IRE) (Son Of Sharp Shot (IRE))
2328[11] 4720[11] 4979[6] 5237[7] 5486[10] 5935[7]

Palawan *Katy Price* a5 18
6 b g Mount Nelson Apple Sauce (Prince Sabo)
1231[13]

Palazzo *Bryan Smart* a43 45
3 b g Morpheus Sweet Power (Pivotal)
3513[11] 5099[11] 9220[7] 9544[4]

Palermo (IRE) *Michael Wigham* a56 44
5 b g Intikhab(USA) La Spezia (IRE) (Danehill Dancer (IRE))
810[10] 2373[6] 2684[6]

Palimero (GER) *Mario Hofer* 81
2 b c Amaron Pearl Of Love (GER) (Sholokhov (IRE))
7937a[4]

Palladium *Martyn Meade* a72 78
3 ch g Champs Elysees Galicuix (Galileo (IRE))
1771[2] 2096[4] 3474[2] 4803[3]

Pallasator *Gordon Elliott* a87 107
10 b g Motivator Ela Athena (Ezzoud (IRE))
4096[2] 6266a[8]

Palmerino (FR) *E Leenders* a80 88
8 b g Doctor Dino(FR) Palmeriade (FR) (Kouroun (FR))
5035a[4]

Palmina (FR) *D Zarroli* a60 69
3 b f Rock Of Gibraltar(IRE) Gal O Gal (USA) (Manlove (USA))
216a[13]

Palmyre (FR) *H-F Devin* 98
4 b m Dansili Purely Priceless (IRE) (Galileo (IRE))
1708a[5] 5229a[5] 6992a[7] 7885a[4] 8969a[8]

Paloma Ohe *Jan Korpas* 93
2 ch f Rio De La Plata(USA) Pom Pom Pom (Big Shuffle (USA))
(8586a)

Palomba (IRE) *C Laffon-Parias* 108
3 b f Lope De Vega(IRE) Australienne (IRE) (Monsun (GER))
4964a[3] 6003a[3] (8445a)

Pal O'Mine (IRE) *Tina Smith* 89
9 b g Dylan Thomas(IRE) Xaara (SWE) (Xaar)
6523a[7]

Palpitator (FR) *C Bresson* 105
5 b h Motivator Feerie Stellaire (FR) (Take Risks (FR))
6266a[5] 7008a[6]

Paminah *Hughie Morrison* a43
4 b m Bated Breath Starry Sky (Oasis Dream)
178[7]

Pammi *Jim Goldie* a62 54
4 b m Poet's Voice Bright Girl (IRE) (Invincible Spirit (IRE))
1015 1500[2] 2436[6] 3175[8] 3500[4] 4004[5] 4056[6] 4515[6] 4724[4] 5122[5] 5435[6] 5939[3] 6611[3] 6933[6] 7070[7] 7492[6] 7783[6] 8238[11]

Pamper *James Fanshawe* a51 72
3 b f Lethal Force(IRE) Cosseted (Pivotal)
2713[3] 3707[6] 5592[3] 6204[13] 7278[6] 8206[10]

Panatos (FR) *Alexandra Dunn* a58 66
4 b g Denon(USA) Prairie Scilla (GER) (Dashing Blade)
1429[7] 1858[4] (2359) 2718[2] 3686[5] 5115a[3] 5379[3] 6200[4] 6642[6] 7860a[7] 8639[6] 9333[7] 9497[6] 9560[3]

Panda Seven (FR) *Gavin Hernon* 82
2 b c Wootton Bassett Hermanville (IRE) (Hurricane Run (IRE))
6262a[5]

Pandora's Minder *Lucinda Egerton* 23
3 b f Bungle Inthejungle Dream Day (FR) (Spectrum (IRE))
2147[11] 2243[6] 2912[12] 3035[4]

Pandora Star *John Quinn* a58 47
3 b f Epaulette(AUS) Gracefilly (Invincible Spirit (IRE))
585[2] 931[2] 1140[12]

Panic Room (IRE) *Tom Dascombe* 81
2 br c Cappella Sansevero Varnay (Machiavellian (USA))
6167[3]◆ 6622[2] (6892)

Panist (IRE) *Mark Johnston* a64 64
2 b c Starspangledbanner(AUS) Caribbean Ace (IRE) (Red Clubs (IRE))
5234[7] 6943[9] 7437[4] 8085[4]

Panko (IRE) *Alex Hales* a76 88
6 b g Iffraaj Engraving (Sadler's Wells (USA))
1425[8]

Panthera Tigris *Jo Hughes* 57
2 b f Heeraat(IRE) Tiger Cub (Dr Fong (USA))
1240a[6] 1709a[5] 2263a[4] 2757a[6] 3714a[8] 4228a[5] 6060a[4] 6485a[3] 6873a[4] 7641a[4]

Pantomime (IRE) *Mme G Rarick* a67 62
7 gr m Mastercraftsman(IRE) Dama'A (IRE) (Green Desert (USA))
46a[10]

Pao Enki (FR) *Mme A Rosa* a83 60
5 b g Muhtathir Lady Needles (IRE) (Sri Pekan (USA))
46a[2]

Papa Delta *Tony Carroll* a65 60
5 b g Makfi Step Softly (Golan (IRE))
2580[8] 3352[2] (4025) 5081[9] 5889[4] 6329[4]◆ 6363[7] 8217[5] 9128[7] 9246[4]

Paparazzi *Tracy Waggott* a83 71
4 b g Iffraaj Columella (Kyllachy)
(22) 125[2] (209) 2842[7] 3305[7] 4239[8] 4329[2] 5436[8]

Papa Stour (USA) *Stuart Williams* a79 64
4 b g Scat Daddy(USA) Illaunglass (IRE) (Red Clubs (IRE))
3147[3]◆ 3991[6] 4867[9] 5945[6] 9512[2]◆

Papa Winner (FR) *S Jesus* a44 48
5 b g Salut Thomas(FR) Palea (GER) (Red Ransom (USA))
3711a[9]

Paper Star *George Baker* 69
2 b f Make Believe Roxy Star (IRE) (Fastnet Rock (AUS))
2282[2] 2586[3]◆ 3220[2] 3634[3] 3988[19] 4799[3] (5263a)

Pappalino (FR) *J Reynier* 105
3 bb c Makfi Bartira (Cape Cross (IRE))
1347a[4] 2314a[2]

Parabellum (IRE)
Denis Gerard Hogan 70
5 b g Dubawi(IRE) Pacifique (IRE) (Montjeu (IRE))
5597a[16]

Paradise Boy (FR) *Andrew Balding* a60 78
3 ch c Mamool(IRE) Palace Secret (GER) (Big Shuffle (USA))
(259) 836[2] 1233[2] 1386[2] 3585[4] 4362[3] 4906[4] 5424[4]

Paradise Papers *David Barron* a66 38
3 b f Lethal Force(IRE) Day Creek (Daylami (IRE))
1272[3]◆ 1649[8] 2148[9] 6176[12] 6945[13]

Paradise Woods (USA)
John Shirreffs a115
5 b m Union Rags(USA) Wild Forest (USA) (Forest Wildcat (USA))
8775a[11]

Paradoxal (FR) *H-A Pantall* a55 66
3 gr c Kendargent(FR) Nanty (IRE) (Nashwan (USA))
(4357a)

Parafection (IRE) *C Ferland* a78 92
3 b c Mastercraftsman(IRE) Your Game (FR) (Montjeu (IRE))
9281a[4]

Parallel World (IRE) *K R Burke* a82 38
3 b g Morpheus Miss Glitters (IRE) (Chevalier (IRE))
1649[10] (1970) (9644)

Para Mio (IRE) *Seamus Durack* a72 72
4 b g Pour Moi(IRE) Malaspina (IRE) (Whipper (USA))
61[2] 1988[9] 9306[4]

Paramount (FR) *C Ferland* 101
3 b f Siyouni(FR) Pagua (IRE) (Zamindar (USA))
2029a[2] 3137a[4] 3905a[12] 5470a[6] 6249a[3] 7360a[9]

Paraponera Jem (FR) *S Jesus* a63 54
3 b c Palace Episode(USA) Beauty Jem (FR) (Red Ransom (USA))
421a[6]

Para Queen (IRE) *Heather Main* a60 63
3 b f Slade Power(IRE) Dancer's Leap (Pivotal)
3445[8] 4177[6] (5987) 7873[6] (8414) 8663[3] 9093[4] 9467[11]

Paravent *F Rohaut* 90
3 b f Oasis Dream Paratonnerre (Montjeu (IRE))
2029a[10]

Pardon My French (IRE)
Vaclav Luka Jr a66 83
3 b c Kodiac Redstone Dancer (IRE) (Namid)
1200a[5] 1340a[2] 1842a[3] 5644a[2]

Parikarma (IRE) *Ed Dunlop* a67 72
2 b f Canford Cliffs(IRE) Pushkar (Danehill Dancer (IRE))
5684[7] 6407[5] 7304[4] (8201) 8856[6]

Parinacota (FR) *Stephanie Gachelin* a41 30
5 b m Dobby Road(FR) Surtsey (FR) (Anabaa Blue)
7136a[14]

Parion *Richard Fahey* a39 51
3 b f Mayson Delft (Dutch Art)
1862[5] 2332[9] 2708[8] 3413[10] 4080[7] 4584[5] 5021[3] 5389[8] 7210[4]

Pari Passu (IRE) *Peter Fahey* a69 61
6 ch g New Approach(IRE) Tiz The Whiz (USA) (Tiznow (USA))
7088a[5]

Parisean Artiste (IRE)
Eve Johnson Houghton a55 55
3 ch f Zoffany(IRE) Meeting In Paris (IRE) (Dutch Art)
1894[8] 2689[6] 3154[10] 4567[7] 4931[4]

Parish Poet (IRE) *Paul Cole* a70 70
3 ch f Lope De Vega(IRE) Tinaheely (IRE) (Intikhab (USA))
3080[4] 3495[6] 4110[11]

Parisian Affair *Neil King* a55 57
4 b m Champs Elysees Trinkila (USA) (Cat Thief (USA))
6114[5] 6345[5] 6903[3] 7300[7]

Paris Protocol *Mark Walford* a67 45
6 b g Champs Elysees Island Vista (Montjeu (IRE))
272[9] 6586[6]

Park Bloom (IRE) *H-F Devin* a71 93
4 b m Galileo(IRE) Alluring Park (IRE) (Green Desert (USA))
1827a[8] 2266a[5] 6992a[8] 7499a[5]

Parker's Boy *Brian Barr* a42 54
2 b g Hot Streak(IRE) Shannon Spree (Royal Applause)
4254[5] 4999[5] 6079[7] 7275[11] 9009[8] 9330[10] 9607[9]

Parkers Hill (IRE) *J P Murtagh* a72 78
3 ch c No Nay Never(USA) Chiarezza (AUS) (Fantastic Light (USA))
1306a[10]

Parker's Pride *Brian Rothwell* a40
3 b g Burwaaz Lady Norlela (Reset (AUS))
354[5] 785[8] 1665[9] 3219[7] 3684[15]

Park Lane Dancer (IRE)
John Quinn a40 57
2 br g Elzaam(AUS) Greatest Dancer (IRE) (Iffraaj)
8026[5] 9008[10] 9347[11]

Parknacilla (IRE) *Henry Spiller* a68 53
3 br f Mukhadram Patuca (Teofilo (IRE))
1332[5]◆ 2262[4] 3275[10] 4485[9] 5293[3] 5797[2] 6131[3] (6885) (7374)◆ 8291[2] 8756[2]

Park Tower (FR) *H-A Pantall* a50 83
4 ch h Manduro(GER) Adeje Park (IRE) (Night Shift (USA))
1449a[15] 2226a[12]

Parole (IRE) *Tim Easterby* a46 58
7 ch g Mastercraftsman(IRE) Leniency (IRE) (Cape Cross (IRE))
5709[7] 6179[5] 6341[15] 7513[10]

Parousia *H-A Pantall* 74
3 ch f Shamardal(USA) National Day (IRE) (Barathea (IRE))
8983a[14]

Parsifal (SPA) *G Arizkorreta Elosegui* 93
6 ch h Rip Van Winkle(IRE) Shemanikha (FR) (Sendawar (IRE))
398a[5] 730a[10] 959a[8] 4418a[7] 6145a[5]

Partridge (IRE) *Richard Hannon* 78
2 b f Zoffany(IRE) Lasilia (IRE) (Acclamation)
3088[2] 3507[2] 3983[19] 5427[6]

Party Goer (IRE) *Endo Botti* 96
4 ch m Intense Focus(USA) Savana Pearl (IRE) (Byron)
7503a[4]

Party Island (IRE) *Denis Coakley* a28 50
2 ch g Tagula(IRE) Pretty Demanding (IRE) (Night Shift (USA))
6845[13] 7407[7] 8751[6]

Party Playboy (GER)
Anthony Mullins a72 90
5 ch g Samum(GER) La Parabol (FR) (Trempolino (USA))
5540[5] 8114[2]◆

Party Popper *David Simcock* 41
2 ch c Outstrip Pink Flames (IRE) (Redback)
7023[5]

Party Potential (USA) *Alan King* a40 56
2 b g Congrats(USA) Lil Miss Richie (USA) (Half Ours (USA))
4480[9] 5052[11] 5775[6] 7079[12] 7971[6]

Party Royal *Nick Gifford* a63 54
9 b g Royal Applause Voliere (Zafonic (USA))
457[2] 2217[8]

Parys Mountain (IRE) *Tim Easterby* a67 85
5 gr g Dark Angel(IRE) Muzdaan (IRE) (Exceed And Excel (AUS))
1944[8] 2419[16] 3450[8] 4127[8] 4511[6] 5453[6] 5692[14] 6588[2]◆ 6922[9] (7145) 7362[13] 7865[6] 8342[9] 8634[4]

Pascasha D'Or (FR) *S Wattel* a83 82
5 ch g Mr. Sidney(USA) Reine Annicka (FR) (Lord Of Men)
(46a) (7676a)

Pas De Secrets (IRE) *Wido Neuroth* a96 91
6 b g High Chaparral(IRE) Quiet Waters (USA) (Quiet American (USA))
4419a[7]

Paseo *Amanda Perrett* 18
3 b g Champs Elysees Posteritas (USA) (Lear Fan (USA))
2769[7]

Passing Clouds *Michael Attwater* a57 51
4 b g Kheleyf(USA) Steppin Out (First Trump)
245[10] 695[4] 1146[6] 1520[2] 3186[4] 5425[10] 5744[5] 6836[4] 7518[4] 8224[3] 8854[8] 9589[6] 9662[6]

Passing Fashion (IRE)
Ralph Beckett 87
2 b g Raven's Pass(USA) Fashion Statement (Rainbow Quest (USA))
5374[4]◆ (5676) 6417[5] 7755[7]

Passing Nod *William Haggas* a40 51
2 b g Zoffany(IRE) Superstar Leo (IRE) (College Chapel)
3942[6] 8026[7] 8202[7]

Passion (IRE) *A P O'Brien* 95
2 b f Galileo(IRE) Dialafara (FR) (Anabaa (USA))
7120[7]

Passion And Glory (IRE)
Saeed bin Suroor 100
3 b c Cape Cross(IRE) Potent Embrace (USA) (Street Cry (IRE))
4842[2] 5384[3] (6290) 6998[7] (8514)

Passionate Love (IRE)
Mark Walford a52 53
4 b m Bated Breath Magic Nymph (IRE) (Galileo (IRE))
784[9] 984[8]

Passion Return (IRE)
Gianluca Verricelli 91
3 ch c Casamento(IRE) Fillthegobletagain (IRE) (Byron)
2887a[8]

Passive (IRE) *David Elsworth* a17
3 rg g Alhebayeb(IRE) Peacemaker (IRE) (High Chaparral (IRE))
2891[2] 752[8]

Pass The Cristal (IRE) *William Muir* a43 41
5 b g Raven's Pass(USA) Crystal Melody (Nureyev (USA))
155[8] 717[12]

Pass The Gin *Andrew Balding* a63 86
3 br f Passing Glance Oasis Spirit (Oasis Dream)
2086[3] 2525[4]◆ 3068[3] 3544[3] 3815[4] 4736[5] (4904) 5589[11] 6108[5] 7183[12]

Pass The Vino (IRE) *Paul D'Arcy* a86 101
3 b g Power Excellent Mariner (IRE) (Henrythenavigator (USA))
306a[7] (1168) (4847) 5442[2]◆ 5932[2] 6476[5] 7010a[16] 8127[20] 8851[8]

Pastfact *Malcolm Saunders* a56 50
5 br g Pastoral Pursuits Matterofact (IRE) (Bold Fact (USA))
1682[7] 2339[14] 3527[U] 4181[9]

Pastichop (FR) *C Gourdain* a86 82
5 b g Bertolini(USA) Perle De Star (FR) (Indian Rocket)
2226a[8]

Pastime *Kevin Frost* a80 80
5 b g Pastoral Pursuits Piddies Pride (IRE) (Indian Lodge (IRE))
1694[7] 9255[4]◆ 9422[5]

Past Master *Henry Candy* a87 88
6 gr g Mastercraftsman(IRE) Millestan (IRE) (Invincible Spirit (IRE))
2748[11] 3663[5] 5135[3] 5625[2] (6448) 7394[4] 9056[8]

Patchewollock (IRE) *G Nicot* a74 74
5 b g Fastnet Rock(AUS) Place De L'Etoile (IRE) (Sadler's Wells (USA))
6434a[3]

Patchouli *Mick Channon* a61 77
3 b f Sixties Icon Inffiraaj (IRE) (Iffraaj)
1386[6] 2253[3]◆ 2582[6] 2935[4] (3513) 3762[5] 4110[5]

Path Of Thunder (IRE)
Charlie Appleby 92
2 ch g Night Of Thunder(IRE) Sunset Avenue (USA) (Street Cry (IRE))
2444[3] 2973[2] (4551) (5382)

Paths Of Glory *Hugo Palmer* a103 91
4 gr g Mastercraftsman(IRE) Pacific Rim (IRE) (Singspiel (IRE))
3664[3] 4104[2] (5578) 6657[10] (7294) (8082)◆ (8350)◆ 9094[2] 9366[3]

Path To The Stars (GER)
James Tate a35
3 b g Sea The Stars(IRE) Path Wind (FR) (Anabaa (USA))
156[11] 486[5]

Patienceisavirtue *Christine Dunnett* a31 34
4 b m Libranno Patience (Kyllachy)
4589[14]

Patrick (IRE) *Paul Midgley* a60 53
7 b g Acclamation Red Liason (IRE) (Selkirk (USA))
1342[8] 1817[6] 2847[5] 5235[9] 5857[2]◆ 6174[5] 7065[6] 8457[4] 8720[5]

Patrick Erin (NZ) *Chris Waller* 105
7 b g Gallant Guru(AUS) Mega Babe (NZ) (Personal Escort (USA))
1784a[7] 8767a[10]

Patronus *Brian Meehan*
3 b g Zoffany(IRE) Miss Complex (Compton Place)
174[4]

Patternrecognition (USA)
Chad C Brown a114
6 b h Adios Charlie(USA) Almost A Valentine (USA) (High Cotton (USA))
445a[12]

Pattie *Mick Channon* a101 95
5 ch m Sixties Icon Excellent Day (IRE) (Invincible Spirit (IRE))
30[3] 756[3] 1063[2] 1753[8] 1918[6] 3857[10] 3994[7] 4758[9] 5187[3] 5525[8] 5944[5] (6214) 6445[7] 6974[2] 7435[8]

Patzefredo (FR) *F Rossi* 95
2 b c Penny's Picnic(IRE) Lili St Cyr (IRE) (Rock Of Gibraltar (IRE))
6251a[5] 6777a[8]

Paved With Gold (IRE)
Tristan Davidson a60 62
6 b g Champs Elysees Luminous Gold (Fantastic Light (USA))
4293[13]

Pavel (USA) *Doug O'Neill* a114
5 rg h Creative Cause(USA) Mons Venus (CAN) (Maria's Mon (USA))
1447a[4] 3618a[6]

Pavers Pride *Noel Wilson* a57 71
5 ch g Bahamian Bounty Pride Of Kinloch (Dr Devious (IRE))
2876[6] 3291[7] 6829[5] 7367[8] 7736[6] 8235[7]

Pavlichenko (IRE)
John James Feane a47 45
4 b g Captain Gerrard(IRE) Hawk Eyed Lady (IRE) (Hawk Wing (USA))
2324[8] (Dead)

Pawpaw *Clive Cox* a63
2 b g Showcasing Papaya (IRE) (Teofilo (IRE))
8605[5] 9136[8] 9509[8]

Pax Britannica (IRE)
David Simcock a61 56
2 b f Zoffany(IRE) Athreyaa (Singspiel (IRE))
6928[8] 7695[11] 8432[7]

Paycheck *David Simcock* a73 61
2 ch f Raven's Pass(USA) Fibou (USA) (Seeking The Gold (USA))
6911[8] 7547[3] 8706[2]

Pazeer (FR) *Ibrahim Al Malki* 97
5 b h Siyouni(FR) Parandeh (FR) (Kahyasi (IRE))
894a[9]

Peace Achieved (USA) *Mark Casse* 109
2 b c Declaration Of War(USA) Sense Of Class (USA) (Fusaichi Pegasus (USA))
8746a[11]

Peace Charter *G M Lyons* 101
2 b f War Front(USA) Emollient (USA) (Empire Maker (USA))
2881a[2] 4352a[3]

Peace Dreamer (IRE)
Robert Cowell a67 80
5 b m Sir Prancealot(IRE) See Nuala (IRE) (Kyllachy)
3037[2] 4105[7] 4495[3] 5015[3] 5959[4]

Peaceful (IRE) *A P O'Brien* 101
2 bb f Galileo(IRE) Missvinski (USA) (Stravinsky (USA))
8763[2]

Peaceful City (FR) *M Boutin* a67 71
4 b m Elusive City(USA) Peaceful Paradise (Turtle Island (IRE))
(2647a) 6790a[9] 7505a[5]

Peace Of Paris (GER) *Markus Klug* 92
3 ch f Helmet(AUS) Peace Of Glory (GER) (Sholokhov (IRE))
4461a[6] 6270a[5] 6769a[6]

Peace Prevails *Jim Boyle* a63 70
4 ch m Declaration Of War(USA) Miss Mediator (USA) (Consolidator (USA))
202[5] 3276[4] 4111[4] (4547)◆ 5091[3]◆ (5571) (6566) 8813[9]

Peace Treaty (IRE) *Mark Johnston* a38
2 b f War Command(USA) Naomh Geileis (USA) (Grand Slam (USA))
9383[6]

Peachey Carnehan
Michael Mullineaux a63 61
5 ch g Foxwedge(AUS) Zubova (Dubawi (IRE))
28[3] 64[8] 790[8] (1021) 1338[3] 1597[9] 2478[6] 3550[5] 3924[6] 4281[8] 4763[10] 5051[4] 6174[14] 6682[5] 7145[8] 7183[10] (7527) 7770[6] 8083[2] 8306[7] 9253[7] 9277[5] 9477[6] 9566[7]

Peach Pavlova (IRE) *Ann Duffield* 25
5 b m Elzaam(AUS) Zvezda (USA) (Nureyev (USA))
3414[13] 5100[12] 5559[10]

Peach Tree (IRE) *A P O'Brien* 100
3 ch f Galileo(IRE) Pikaboo (Pivotal)
2642a[4] 3316[10] 3820a[2] 4014[10] (4856a) 5208a[6] 5663[6] 6263a[9] 7118[8]

Peak Princess (IRE) *Archie Watson* a94 82
5 b m Foxwedge(AUS) Foot Of Pride (IRE) (Footstepsinthesand)
30[5] 460[6] 756[6]

Pearl Acclaim (IRE)
David C Griffiths a81 68
9 b g Acclamation With Colour (Rainbow Quest (USA))
43[5] (166) 433[8] 586[8]

Pearl Beach *William Knight* a43 47
2 b f Footstepsinthesand Western Pearl (High Chaparral (IRE))
4223[7] 5088[6] 6205[5] 7516[7]

Pearl Fly (FR) *J Jouin* 15
4 gr m Dragon Dancer Miss De La Noe (FR) (Visionary (FR))
1908a[12]

Pearl Jam *James Fanshawe* a64 40
3 br f Showcasing Dance Pearl (Danehill Dancer (IRE))
2909[11] 4305[7] 6074[8] 6885[3] 8251[2] 8822[2]

Pearl Noir *Scott Dixon* a38 59
9 b g Milk It Mick Cora Pearl (IRE) (Montjeu (IRE))
503[8] 1071[4] 1952[3] 2632[2] 3213[7] 3518[2] 3933[5] 4212[2]◆ 4586[14] 5018[13] 7052[5] 7389[8] 9335[6] 9539[6]

Pearl Of Freedom *H-A Pantall* a75
3 ch f Pivotal La Pelegrina (USA) (Redoute's Choice (AUS))
6486a[2]

Pearl Of India *Robyn Brisland* a40 42
2 b f Sleeping Indian Misty Pearl (Royal Applause)
6548[8] 7063[6] 7627[8]

Pearl Of Qatar *Tristan Davidson* a68 59
3 gr f Footstepsinthesand Musical Molly (IRE) (Mastercraftsman (IRE))
1846[8] 2098[11] 2477[8] 2708[2] 2940[7] 5629[2] 6033[2] 6365[4] 7764[4] (7823)◆

Pearl Of The West (IRE)
John C McConnell a88 88
5 b m Teofilo(IRE) Creese (Halling (USA))
3384a[2]

Pearl's Calling (IRE) *Ron Barr* a43 51
4 ch m Dandy Man(IRE) Celtic Heroine (IRE) (Hernando (FR))
3203[4] 3932[7] 4519[18]

Pearl Spectre (USA) *Phil McEntee* a58 63
8 ch g Street Cry(IRE) Dark Sky (USA) (Storm Cat (USA))
5[3] (158) 249[6] 392[6] 611[3] 944[6] 1366[7] 1479[6] 1880[6] 2065[6] 2237[2] 3002[3] 3147[9] 3744[4] 4219[2] 4472[6] 5144[5] 5677[5] 6441[10] 6703[4] 7527[6] 8917[4] 8998[3] 9028[5] 9157[2] 9249[4] 9427[9]

Pearl Stream *Michael Dods* a51 58
2 b f Fountain Of Youth(IRE) Seaperle (Firebreak)
2892[8] 3679[6] 5485[4] 6313[7] 7584[6] 8022[6] 9346[4]◆

Pearlwood (IRE) *Richard Fahey* 54
2 b f Ivawood(IRE) Rio's Pearl (Captain Rio)
2906[6] 3717[4] 4237[8] 4756[8] 5296[13]

Pea Shooter *Brian Ellison* a82 55
10 b g Piccolo Sparkling Eyes (Lujain (USA))
(131) 610[2] 907[11] 1082[5] 4406[16] 5038[8] 6335[6] 7077[16]

Pecheurs De Perles (IRE)
John Butler
5 b g Pour Moi(IRE) Annacloy Pearl (IRE) (Mull Of Kintyre (USA))
348[10] 590[4] 8207[11] 8949[13]

Peckinpah (IRE) *Alan King* a72 48
3 ch g Excelebration(IRE) Melodrama (IRE) (Oratorio (IRE))
1568[3] 2407[8] 9067[12]

Pecorino *Richard Hughes* a51 60
3 ch g Intello(GER) Puff Pastry (Pivotal)
2690[8] 3463[11] 3946[7] 6367[5] 7240[13] 7985[3] 8551[12]

Pedal Power *Andrew Balding* a8
2 b g Nayef(USA) Rebecca Romero (Exceed And Excel (AUS))
9156[12]

Pedro Cara (FR) *M Delcher Sanchez* 108
3 b g Pedro The Great(USA) Magic Cara (FR) (Akarad (FR))
2426a[5] 6994a[2] (9590a)

Pedro The First (FR) *F Rossi* a91 94
4 b g Pedro The Great(USA) Pink Candie (FR) (Fath (USA))
2782a[6] 5643a[3]

Pedrozzo (FR) *E Leenders* a66 55
3 b g Pedro The Great(USA) Helguera (FR) (Hamas (IRE))
7476a[4]

Peerless Percy (IRE) *Michael Dods* a45 47
2 b g Sir Percy Victoria Montoya (High Chaparral (IRE))
6892[7] 7586[8] 8302[10]

Pegasus *A Kleinkorres* a76 77
4 b g Sageburg(IRE) Pyramid Lake (USA) (Broad Brush (USA))
6434a[7]

Pegasus Bridge
Eve Johnson Houghton a63 43
3 b g Camacho Fire Line (Firebreak)
2995[9] 3697[14] 4193[3] 4477[6]

Peggie Sue *Adam West* a82 90
4 b m Captain Gerrard(IRE) Aunt Minnie (Night Shift (USA))
1394[10] 1822[6] (2294) (2625)◆ 4105[5] (4375) 5372[6] 5736[5] 6056[2] 6714[11] 7687[6] 7828[7] 8262[4] 8900[7]

Peggotty *Tony Carroll* 30
3 ch f Assertive Level Pegging (IRE) (Common Grounds)
4421[5] 5494[6] 6023[5]

Peggy McKay *Andrew Balding* 64
4 b m Iffraaj Miss Lacey (IRE) (Diktat)
3603[11] 4737[5] 5528[16] 6039[7]

Peggy's Angel *Stef Keniry* a50 56
4 b m Captain Gerrard(IRE) Dora's Sister (IRE) (Dark Angel (IRE))
139[2] 254[5] 1382[8] 1760[14] 2081[2] 2637[10] 9334[13]

Pelligrina (IRE) *A Fabre* 105
3 b f Soldier Hollow Pearls Or Passion (FR) (Monsun (GER))
(3391a) 8378a[8]

Pempie (IRE) *Andrew Balding* a70 78
3 ch f Lope De Vega(IRE) Penelope Star (GER) (Acatenango (GER))
1855[8] 2689[2] (3093) 3698[4] 4671[8] 8806[10] 9067[7] 9421[6]

Penarth Pier (IRE)
Christine Dunnett a64 56
3 b f Dark Angel(IRE) Waveband (Exceed And Excel (AUS))
1219[8] 2772[9] 3688[3] 4567[6] 5526[6] 6389[4] 7024[4] 7549[3] 7982[12] (8255) 8457[3] 9217[8] 9548[6]

Pendleton *Michael Dods* a81 98
3 b g Garswood Anglezarke (IRE) (Acclamation)
(2243)◆ 3590[5] 4603[2] 5126[2] 6623[3] 7002[2]◆ 7402[5] (7894) 8512[2]

Pendo *John Best* a74 70
8 b g Denounce Abundant (Zafonic (USA))
942[7] 1269[3] 1591[2] 2259[5] 2617[3] 4028[4]

Penelope Queen *Agostino Affe'* 92
2 b f Dream Ahead(USA) Belvoir Diva (Exceed And Excel (AUS))
8791a[7]

Penmellyn (IRE) *Phillip Makin* a67 58
2 b f Dark Angel(IRE) Red Avis (Exceed And Excel (AUS))
1923[7] 2783[5] 8084[6] 8815[4] 9060[2] 9513[2]

Penniesfromheaven (IRE)
Ken Wingrove
3 gr f Lethal Force(IRE) Dittander (Exceed And Excel (AUS))
6027[9]

Penn Kalet (FR) *B Legros* a50 53
3 b c The French(FR) Libre Amour (FR) (Lost World (IRE))
421a[12]

Pennsylvania Dutch *Kevin Ryan* a101 96
5 b g Dutch Art Map Of Heaven (Pivotal)
(1760) (1951) (2201)◆ 2843[10] (3636) 3971[8] (4521)

Penny Diamond *Amanda Perrett* a40 45
2 b f War Command(USA) Penny Sixpence (FR) (Kheleyf (USA))
3076[4] 5045[8] 5501[8] 8825[7] 9212[7]

Penny Green *C Moore* a5
5 b m Halling(USA) Penelewey (Groom Dancer (USA))
1841[13]

Penny Pot Lane *Richard Whitaker* a60 75
6 b m Misu Bond(IRE) Velvet Band (Verglas (IRE))
1895[8] 2081[5] 2580[9] 3470[2] 3657[6] (4149) 4440[6] 5333[4] 5821[4] 6260[2] 7066[7] 7383[4] (7703) 8400[12] 8712[10] 8924[6] 9108[11]

Pennywhistle (IRE) *John Gosden* a86 93
3 b f Iffraaj Folk Melody (IRE) (Street Cry (IRE))
2552[2]◆ 3041[3] 4147[2] 5910[3]

Penpal (IRE) *James Fanshawe* a73
2 b f Invincible Spirit(IRE) French Friend (IRE) (Teofilo (IRE))
6072[3] (8849)

Penrhos *Charles Hills* a50 73
3 b c Kodiac Bereka (Firebreak)
2794[3] 3464[8] 4306[5] 6399[3] 8495[10]

Pensee *Roger Charlton* a58 57
3 b f Dansili Fleur De Cactus (IRE) (Montjeu (IRE))
4503[5] 5421[5] 6641[5]

Pensee Spirituelle *A Fabre* a69 61
3 b f Invincible Spirit(IRE) Penne (FR) (Sevres Rose (IRE))
3710a[7]

Pensierieparole
Grizzetti Galoppo SRL a59 85
7 ch g Exceed And Excel(AUS) Pursuit Of Charge (Pursuit Of Love)
2888a[8] 8787a[8]

Pensiero D'Amore (IRE) *A Botti* 101
3 b c Zoffany(IRE) Ira Brevis Furor (IRE) (King's Best (USA))
2162a[3] 8786a[6]

Pentewan *Phillip Makin* a73 76
2 b f Havana Gold(IRE) Serena's Pride (Danbird (AUS))
3702[6] 4290[3] 4583[3] 5171[3] 5668[2] 6625[4] 7072[8] 7419[3] 7871[7]

Pentimento *John Best* a78
3 b g Garswood M'selle (IRE) (Elnadim (USA))
5808[6] 8290[2] 8653[2] 9173[3]

Pentland Lad (IRE) *Charlie Fellowes* a69 53
3 b g Camacho First Lady (IRE) (Indian Ridge (IRE))
848[3]◆ 1140[3]◆ (1514) (1678) 2063[2] 2204[7] 3440[12] 8221[9]

Penwood (FR) *Joseph Tuite* a46 49
4 b m Orpen(USA) In The Woods (You And I (USA))
6302[4] 7024[9] 7557[6] 7784[4] 8119[6] 8697[8]

Penwortham (IRE) *Richard Fahey* a65 88
6 b g Dandy Man(IRE) Portofino Bay (IRE) (Montjeu (IRE))
1459[17] 1881[9] 2526[5] 3179[6] 3846[4] (4320)◆ 5453[10] 5708[4] 6711[6] 7142[5] 7678[6]

Pepito (IRE)
Tania Filipa Vieira Teixeira a37
4 b g Lilbourne Lad(IRE) Sustain (Zamindar (USA))
2264a[15]

Pepper Bay *Michael Bell* a76
2 b f Cable Bay(IRE) Selinka (Selkirk (USA))
7570[2] (8250) 8891[11] 9099[2]

Pepper Street (IRE) *Amy Murphy* a48 62
4 b m Born To Sea(IRE) Mindy (IRE) (Zamindar (USA))
4112[6] 5053[9] 6115[6]

Peppone (GER) *A Wohler* 94
3 bb c Pastorius(GER) Pivoline (FR) (Pivotal)
3385a[7]

Pepys *Bryan Smart* a63 85
5 b g Aqlaam Generously Gifted (Sakhee (USA))
4511[8]

Perceived *Antony Brittain* a57 58
7 ch m Sir Percy New Light (Generous (IRE))
671[0] 792[8] 1958[4] (2244) 2513[4] 3267[3] 3774[4] 5285[7]

Percy (IRE) *Frank Bishop* a57 72
5 gr g Kodiac Bysshe (Linamix (FR))
4407[7] 4988[6] 5706[9] 7631[6] 8635[10]

Percy Alexander *James Tate* a63
3 ch g Sir Percy Rosy Alexander (Spartacus (IRE))
251[9] 615[5] 913[6] 1174[6] (1593) 2322[2]

Percy Green (IRE) *K R Burke* a53 63
2 b g Sir Percy All In Green (IRE) (Diamond Green (FR))
1887[8] 2594[10] 3190[6] 5296[2] 5886[5] 6571[6] 7056[4] 7315[2]

Percy Prosecco *Archie Watson* a72 70
4 b g Sir Percy Grapes Hill (Kingsalsa (USA))
946[3] 2344[3] (4569) 4825[5] 5277[8] 5528[2] (6278) (6681) 8829[9]

Percy's Prince *Amanda Perrett* a60 26
3 b g Sir Percy Attainable (Kalanisi (IRE))
3299[4] 4769[4] 4998[11] 7280[5] (7520) 7818[4] 8854[3] 9204[8]

Percy Street *David Pipe* 91
6 br g Sir Percy Star Of Gibraltar (Rock Of Gibraltar (IRE))
3952[14]

Percy Toplis *Christine Dunnett* a50 52
5 b g Kheleyf(USA) West Lorne (USA) (Gone West (USA))
594[2] 924[9] 1478[7] 1715[9] 2019[4] 2256[10] 2972[4] 3142[2] 4801[5] 5354[3] 5652[3] 5867[2] 6324[3] 7318[4] 8001[9] 8204[10] 8434[11]

Perfecimperfection (IRE)
Marco Botti a75 73
3 b f Camelot Sunbird (Echo Of Light)
1656[3] 2200[4] 3310[2] 3773[4] (6439) 7835[9] 8807[5]

Perfect Alibi (USA) *Mark Casse* a106
2 bb f Sky Mesa(USA) No Use Denying (USA) (Maria's Mon (USA))
8747a[4]

Perfect Arch (IRE)
Saeed bin Suroor a80
2 b g Dawn Approach(IRE) Willow Beck (Shamardal (USA))
8121[8] 8752[3]

Perfect Beauty *J P Murtagh* a52 65
4 gr m Mount Nelson Bruxcalina (FR) (Linamix (FR))
7087a[2]

Perfect Charm *Archie Watson* 72
3 b f Charm Spirit(IRE) Indignant (Gold Away (IRE))
3351[6] 3920[4] 4489[6] (5492) (5582) 5822[7] 6562[7] 7112[6] 7568[9]

Perfect City (IRE) *Jonjo O'Neill* a94 84
4 b g Elusive City(USA) Tall Perfection (USA) (Distorted Humor (USA))
2742[14] 5667[16]

Perfect Cracker *Patrick Chamings* a56 52
11 ch g Dubai Destination(USA) Perfect Story (IRE) (Desert Story (IRE))
2207[9]

Perfected *Roger Varian* a63
2 ch c Night Of Thunder(IRE) Semayyel (IRE) (Green Desert (USA))
5809[8]

Perfect Empire *Mark Johnston* a66 60
2 b c Holy Roman Emperor(IRE) Pink Tequila (Teofilo (IRE))
7778[4]◆ 8069[4] 8494[7]

Perfect Focus (IRE) *Simon Crisford* a75
2 b c Acclamation Tonle Sap (IRE) (Manduro (GER))
8084[2]

Perfect Grace *Archie Watson* a66 75
3 b f Bated Breath Bassinet (USA) (Stravinsky (USA))
370[6] 761[7] 4499[2] (4771) 5307[4] 5795[2] 6104[12] 7233[6] 7756[7] 8705[6] 9006[5] 9427[2]

Perfect Hustler (USA)
Jeremy Noseda a86 89
4 ch g Jimmy Creed(USA) Jacqui's Promise (USA) (Loup Sauvage (USA))
1714[8] 2837[5]

Perfect Illusion *Andrew Balding* a82 88
4 b g Nathaniel(IRE) Chicita Banana (Danehill Dancer (IRE))
2209[4] 2800[7] 3095[3] 3408[2]◆ 4224[5] (4752)

Perfect Inch *Charlie Fellowes* 56
2 b f Dark Angel(IRE) Inchina (Montjeu (IRE))
4337[6]

Perfection *David O'Meara* a87 106
4 ch m Dutch Art Cantal (Pivotal)
2621[2]◆ 3085[10] 4095[7] 4954a[2] 5608[2] (6257) 6999[4] 7713a[5]

Perfect Number *Saeed bin Suroor* a74
3 b f Cape Cross(IRE) Wizara (IRE) (Teofilo (IRE))
(7190) 7822[3] 8294[5] 8812[8]

Perfect Outing *Clive Cox* a56 59
2 gr f Outstrip Makara (Lion Cavern (USA))
5775[4] 9506[5]

Perfect Pitch (GER) *S Smrczek* a71 82
5 b m Campanologist(USA) Prima Directa (GER) (Big Shuffle (USA))
2266a[7] 3879a[10]

Perfect Refuge *Clive Cox* a78 73
4 gr m Champs Elysees Perfect Haven (Singspiel (IRE))
(67) 459[2] 793[10] 4426[8] 5316[6] 5747[2] 6289[6] 7083[8] 7756[10]

Perfect Rose *Mark Johnston* a55 78
2 b f Oasis Dream Maid To Perfection (Sadler's Wells (USA))
1513[3] 3049[2]

Perfect Showdance *Clive Cox* a78 56
3 ch f Showcasing Perfect Star (Act One)
2583[9] 3264[11] 7237[6] 7773[9]

Perfect Soldier (IRE)
Shaun Keightley a44 49
5 b g Kodiac Independent Girl (IRE) (Bachelor Duke (USA))
138[10] 386[9] 1983[6] 3325[4] 3592[10] 5633[11] 6860[13]

Perfect Summer (IRE) *Ian Williams* a67 75
9 b m High Chaparral(IRE) Power Of Future (GER) (Definite Article)
1172[7] 3886[6] 4881[7] 5379[8]

Perfect Sunset *Andrew Balding* a8 68
2 b f Iffraaj Perfect Star (Act One)
7813[10] **8758**[5]

Perfect Swiss *Tim Easterby* a69 60
3 b g Swiss Spirit Perfect Practice (Medicean)
2871[4]◆ 3319[2] 3651[12] 4720[3] 5202[2] 5558[2] 6275[7] 7207[4] (7960)◆ **(8301)** 9109[7]

Perfect Symphony (IRE)
Mark Pattinson a68 66
5 b g Dandy Man(IRE) Fields Of Joy (GER) (Waky Nao)
1329[13] 1933[4] 2145[5] 2929[5] **(3143)** 4501[3] 4833[6] 5351[3] 5799[5] 7130[6] 7576[3] 8408[7] 8704[5] 9420[14] 9507[7] 9670[3]

Perfect Tapatino (FR)
Joseph Patrick O'Brien a93 96
5 ch h Perfect Soul(IRE) Tapatina (USA) (Seeking The Gold (USA))
8784a[4]

Perfect Winter (IRE)
Saeed bin Suroor a76
3 b f Invincible Spirit(IRE) Heartily (IRE) (Dubawi (IRE))
8808[2]

Peri Lina (TUR) *Hasan Boyraz* 97
4 gr m Falco(USA) Efisia (FR) (Efisio)
283a[5] **728a**[3] 961a[13]

Peripherique *James Eustace* a50 51
3 ch f Champs Elysees Somersault (Pivotal)
1344[7] **2690**[11] 3445[6] 4594[6]

Perique *Peter Hiatt* a59 21
3 b g Cacique(IRE) Meetyouthere (IRE) (Sadler's Wells (USA))
259[7] **518**[4] 723[7] 4484[8] 4803[9] 7985[9]

Peristera (IRE) *Gavin Hernon* 17
2 ch f New Approach(IRE) Prem Ramya (GER) (Big Shuffle (USA))
9123a[13]

Perla Blanca (USA) *Ed Dunlop* a48 75
5 gr m Dalakhani(IRE) Trend Line (IRE) (Holy Roman Emperor (IRE))
(3175) **(4825)** 5727[10]

Perpetrator (IRE) *Roger Charlton* a72 69
4 b g Shamardal(USA) Palmeraie (USA) (Lear Fan (USA))
157[6]

Perregrin *Mark Johnston* a62 55
2 b g Fountain Of Youth(IRE) New Falcon (IRE) (New Approach (IRE))
2469[3] 2783[6] 3265[4] **(9640)**

Persepone *Hugo Palmer* a60 52
3 b f Dubawi(IRE) Filia Regina (Galileo (IRE))
2361[10] **4503**[4] 5384[4] 6642[7]

Persia (IRE) *A P O'Brien* a104 103
2 bb c Galileo(IRE) Just Pretending (USA) (Giant's Causeway (USA))
8112[5] 8574a[2] **(8752)**◆

Persian Beauty (IRE)
Simon Crisford a48
3 b f Dubawi(IRE) Zeeba (IRE) (Barathea (IRE))
2245[4]

Persian King (IRE) *A Fabre* 117
3 b c Kingman Pretty Please (IRE) (Dylan Thomas (IRE))
(1794a) (2668a) **3390a**[2]

Persian Knight (JPN)
Yasutoshi Ikee 117
5 bb h Harbinger Orient Charm (JPN) (Sunday Silence (USA))
9379a[5]

Persian Moon (IRE) *Mark Johnston* 106
3 b c Makfi Lune Rose (High Chaparral (IRE))
2084[3] 2413[3] 3042[4] 4017[4] 4901[7] 5121[2] 5541[6] 6420[7] 6712[2] **6952**[2]

Persian Sun *Stuart Williams* a76 74
4 b g Dansili Khor Sheed (Dubawi (IRE))
2209[5] 7616[4] 8727[8] 9066[4] 9405[5]

Persona (FR) *J-C Rouget* a70
3 ch f Kendargent(FR) Pioneer Girl (IRE) (Anabaa (USA))
993a[5]

Persuading (IRE) *Charlie Appleby* a74 82
3 b g Oasis Dream Short Skirt (Diktat)
723[3] **4073**[3]

Persuasion (IRE) *Charles Hills* 99
2 b c Acclamation Effervesce (IRE) (Galileo (IRE))
(5665) 6352[6] **7614**[2]

Persuer *David Simcock* a68 59
3 ch f Intello(GER) Chase The Lady (USA) (Atticus (USA))
7081[2] **7451**[3] 8500[4]

Peruvian Lily (FR) *Michael Appleby* a69 79
3 ch f Mayson Rosa Mundi (Alhaarth (IRE))
9199[11] 9278[5]

Peruvian Summer (IRE)
Kevin Frost a67
3 ch g Lope De Vega(IRE) Need You Now (IRE) (Kheleyf (USA))
316[8] 1173[6] 1549[3]◆ 2016[7] **(2190)** 3204[6]

Peshkova (IRE) *W McCreery* a66 74
4 gr m Shamardal(USA) Walkamia (FR) (Linamix (FR))
3818a[11]

Pesto *Richard Hannon* a95 95
3 br g New Approach(IRE) Pickle (Piccolo)
(3858)◆ 4865[6] 5564[5] 6347[2] **7517**[4]

Peters Pudding (IRE)
Lisa Williamson a49 48
3 ch g Fast Company(IRE) Whats For Pudding (IRE) (Kheleyf (USA))
122[7] 228[8] 401[4] **1557**[4] 2016[12] 8472[7] 8864[11] 9276[7] 9473[10] 9508[10]

Pete So High (GER) *Julia Brooke* a68 76
5 b g High Chaparral(IRE) Paulaya (GER) (Peintre Celebre (USA))
4689[9] 5474[8]

Petit Bay *Sir Mark Todd* a43
3 b f Dick Turpin(IRE) Sky High Diver (IRE) (Celtic Swing)
6074[6] 7912[5] 8497[5]

Petite Jack *Neil King* a103 93
6 ch g Champs Elysees Pilcomayo (IRE) (Rahy (USA))
878[2] **(1220)** 1267[6] 1917[8] 3992[9] 9003[6] **9588**[3]

Petite Magician (IRE) *David Barron* a42 28
3 b f Requinto(IRE) Personal Design (IRE) (Traditionally (USA))
211[8]

Petite Malle (USA)
James Fanshawe a66 55
3 b f Super Saver(USA) Vuitton (USA) (Smart Strike (CAN))
3003[9] 4452[6] 5269[7] 6130[8] **(6636)** 7344[7] 7835[6]

Petite Mustique (IRE) *A P O'Brien* 107
2 b f Galileo(IRE) Inca Princess (IRE) (Holy Roman Emperor (IRE))
6429a[2]

Petite Steps (IRE) *Miss Katy Brown* a44 30
2 ch f Dragon Pulse(IRE) Angel Stevens (IRE) (Hawk Wing (USA))
5197[7] 5630[5] 7308[9]

Petit Fils (FR) *J-P Gauvin* a93 110
4 b g Makfi Mamie Zane (FR) (Orpen (USA))
(2428a) 3389a[7] 7008a[4]

Petitioner (IRE) *John Davies* a57 73
5 b g Dansili Reflective (USA) (Seeking The Gold (USA))
522[6] **7001**[6]

Petit Palais *Tom George* a51 29
4 ch g Champs Elysees Galicuix (Galileo (IRE))
9633[13]

Petits Fours *Charlie Fellowes* a59 63
3 b f Lawman(FR) Praline (IRE) (Pivotal)
1656[6] 2253[7] 3594[8] 4372[7]

Petra's Pony (IRE) *Brian Meehan* a50 36
4 b g Big Bad Bob(IRE) Gabriellina Klon (IRE) (Ashkalani (IRE))
362[9] 876[9] **1018**[4] 1431[11] 9310[11] 9553[10]

Petrastar *Clive Cox* a85 85
4 b g Passing Glance Petrarchick (USA) (Arch (USA))
1559[9] 1914[7] **2691**[2] 3424[3] 4250[7] 5321[4] 5812[3] 6929[3]

Petrify *Bernard Llewellyn* a49 42
9 b g Rock Of Gibraltar(IRE) Frigid (Indian Ridge (IRE))
1520[13]

Petrus (IRE) *Brian Meehan* 106
4 b g Zoffany(IRE) Ambrosine (Nashwan (USA))
(1413) (1912) 2832[4]◆ 3987[24] **4666**[3] 6376[14] 7694[19]

Pettifogger (IRE) *Marco Botti* a90 93
4 b g Lope De Vega(IRE) Desert Version (Green Desert (USA))
1714[6] 2363[2] **(2837)** 3308[8] 4299[7]

Pettinger *Charles Hills* a62 66
2 b f Hot Streak(IRE) Joshua's Princess (Danehill (USA))
5547[6] **6442**[4] 6883[4] 7419[7] 8287[7]

Pettochside *John Bridger* a76 77
10 b g Refuse To Bend(IRE) Clear Impression (IRE) (Danehill (USA))
1822[13] 2403[10] 2568[10] 3443[4] 3856[4]◆ 3893[4] **4253**[3] 4844[5] 5252[7] 6288[5] 7112[4] (7568) 7757[3] **7894**[10] 8285[4] 8410[3] 8649[2]

Phaidra Jasmin (FR) *Mlle L Kneip* a3 69
3 b f Dabirsim(FR) Parijan (GER) (Dashing Blade)
1658a[12]

Phalasteen (USA) *R Bouresly* 62
3 ch c Kitten's Joy(USA) Mambo With G (USA) (Old Trieste (USA))
570a[5] 727a[8]

Phantasmal *Stuart Coltherd* a68 53
5 b g Pivotal Asaawir (Royal Applause)
3452[6]◆ 4916[8] 5852[14]

Phantom Bride (IRE) *K R Burke* 64
2 b f Fastnet Rock(AUS) Absolute Music (USA) (Consolidator (USA))
5588[12] **6226**[5] 6697[8]

Pharoa (FR) *J-P Dubois* a83 77
3 b g Bated Breath Pyramid Street (USA) (Street Sense (USA))
3710a[6]

Pharoah King (USA) *John Gosden* a74
2 b c American Pharoah(USA) Dancing Trieste (USA) (Old Trieste (USA))
8823[10] **9154**[3]

Pharoh Jake *John Bridger* a44 44
11 ch g Piccolo Rose Amber (Double Trigger (IRE))
(179) 298[2] **478**[2] 857[7] 986[3] 1210[6] 1590[5] 2010[6] 4027[9] 4376[3] 5449[4] 5884[6] 6048[6] 7986[5] 8279[5] 9423[6] 9583[6] 9664[7]

Phase After Phase (IRE)
Joseph Patrick O'Brien a84 89
2 b c Siyouni(FR) Pollyana (IRE) (Whipper (USA))
7876a[2]

Phebes Dream (IRE)
John C McConnell a50 50
6 b m Roderic O'Connor(IRE) Alexander Family (IRE) (Danetime (IRE))
3209[4] **4914**[6]

Pheidippides *Tom Clover* a83 72
4 ch g Sepoy(AUS) Bounty Box (Bahamian Bounty)
206[3] 732[2] **(962)** 1213[6] 1882[6] 6050[4] 6863[10] 7554[8]

Phenakite *Ollie Pears* 51
3 b g Dream Ahead(USA) Cats Eyes (Echo Of Light)
5969[9] **6578**[5] 7335[9]

Philamundo (IRE) *Richard Spencer* a85 61
4 b g Sir Prancealot(IRE) Rublevka Star (USA) (Elusive Quality (USA))
(33) 175[9] **(429)** 548[3] 807[6] 1213[3]◆ 1757[18] 3004[6] 4653[5] 5267[2] 5651[5] 6151[4] 7191[2] 8289[5] 8549[4] 9199[12]

Philipine Cobra *Phil McEntee* 86
3 b f Showcasing Lavender And Lace (Barathea (IRE))
2736[2]◆ (3532) **(3815)** 4122[3] 4847[7] 5251[5]

Philippine Cobra (FR) *G Botti* a71 64
3 b f Siyouni(FR) Bermondsey Girl (Bertolini (USA))
1658a[4] 2090a[2] 2954a[9] 4229a[6]

Philip's Wish *Keith Dalgleish* 65
3 b g Maxios Queen's Dream (GER) (Oasis Dream)
3248[10] **3707**[3] 4277[2]

Philonikia *Ralph Beckett* a74 68
3 b f Kingman Colima (IRE) (Authorized (IRE))
156[8] 3482[6] 5175[4] 6232[7] **(8065)**◆ 8656[5]

Philosophical *Jedd O'Keeffe* a60 60
2 ch g Mukhadram Incarnation (IRE) (Samum (GER))
5655[4] **6664**[4] 7586[7]

Philosophy (FR) *N Leenders* a55 64
4 b g Kentucky Dynamite(USA) Hucking Hope (IRE) (Desert Style (IRE))
1908a[7]

Philyaboots *Donald McCain* a41 48
3 b g Oasis Dream Miracle Maid (Selkirk (USA))
3248[9] **4055**[6] 4488[9] 8819[6] 9287[8]

Phobos *Michael Blanshard* a52 58
4 b m Intello(GER) Jolie Etoile (USA) (Diesis)
250[10] **1362**[10] 2231[7] 3252[9] 4498[13]

Phoceene (FR) *F Rossi* 102
3 ch f Olympic Glory(IRE) Atlantic Slew (FR) (Helissio (FR))
2312a[2] 3121a[8] 6250a[8]

Phoebe Agnes *Shaun Harris* a20
3 b f Phoenix Reach(IRE) Medam (Medicean)
5062[6] **6187**[8]

Phoenix Approach (IRE)
Tim Easterby 59
2 b g Dawn Approach(IRE) Purple Warrior (USA) (Quality Road (USA))
4106[6] **4937**[5] 5396[6]

Phoenix Aquilus (IRE)
Seamus Durack 71
2 b c Slade Power(IRE) Permsiri (IRE) (Ad Valorem (USA))
8257[2]◆ 8858[3]

Phoenix Dawn *Louise Allan* a45 72
5 b g Phoenix Reach(IRE) Comtesse Noire (CAN) (Woodman (USA))
9204[12]

Phoenix Lightning (IRE)
Kevin Bishop a27 33
4 b g Lawman(FR) Royal Fizz (IRE) (Royal Academy (USA))
5099[9] 9283[12]

Phoenix Of Spain (IRE)
Charles Hills a87 120
3 gr c Lope De Vega(IRE) Lucky Clio (IRE) (Key Of Luck (USA))
(3104a) 3951[6] 5543[6] 7007a[5] 8334[10]

Phoenix Queen *Gay Kelleway*
3 b f Phoenix Reach(IRE) Chocolada (Namid)
403[8] 930[7]

Phoenix Star (IRE) *Stuart Williams* a65 62
3 b g Alhebayeb(IRE) Volcanic Lady (IRE) (Invincible Spirit (IRE))
621[3] 1691[5] 2421[11] 4185[7] 5064[4] 5826[2] 6183[7] 7320[4] 7837[7] 8435[3] 8704[4] 8896[4] (9218) 9477[3]

Phoenix Strike *Ben Haslam* a41
2 b c Casamento(IRE) Promise You (Teofilo (IRE))
8424[13] **8717**[10]

Phosphor (IRE) *Martyn Meade* a70 58
3 b c Havana Gold(IRE) Luminous Gold (Fantastic Light (USA))
1236[3] 3590[8] 5450[6]

Photograph (IRE) *Richard Hannon* 76
2 b c Kodiac Supreme Occasion (IRE) (Teofilo (IRE))
8722[2]◆

Phuket Power (IRE)
Tom Dascombe a73 78
2 b g Kodiac Brazilian Bride (IRE) (Pivotal)
5859[4] **6464**[4] 6807[3] 7419[10] (9324)

Physics (IRE) *Paul Cole* a63
3 b g Acclamation Precipitous (IRE) (Indian Ridge (IRE))
943[5]◆ **1139**[6] 2009[4]

Pianissimo *Anthony Carson* a94 83
3 b g Teofilo(IRE) Perfect Note (Shamardal (USA))
1756[2] 6662[3] 7382[2] 7867[2] (8500) (9056) **(9454)**

Piano Solo (FR) *K J Condon* 95
3 b g Planteur(IRE) Pianiste (FR) (Anabaa (USA))
2492a[4]

Piazon *Julia Brooke* a65 64
8 br g Striking Ambition Colonel's Daughter (Colonel Collins (USA))
43[2] 167[4] 503[3] 926[2] 1521[6] 3518[RR] 3975[4] 4132[2] 5276[3] (5491) 6659[6] 7052[10] 7588[3] 8401[3] 8643[2] 8840[6] 9219[7] 9473[6]

Picc And Go *Debbie Hughes* 29
6 b m Piccolo Just Down The Road (IRE) (Night Shift (USA))
4182[10] 4481[15] 7172[10] 7757[15]

Piccata (FR) *T Van Den Troost* 54
2 b f Sommerabend Waldeslust (IRE) (Medicean)
7044a[6]

Pic Cel (FR) *J-C Rouget* a64 64
2 b c Penny's Picnic(IRE) Celesteen (IRE) (Azamour (IRE))
4679a[9] **5286a**[6] 5759a[5] 6196a[6]

Piccolita *Hughie Morrison* a44 29
3 b f Piccolo Violet's Walk (Dr Fong (USA))
604[2] 795[8] **1332**[10] 2531[7] 3271[7] 4642[10]

Piccolo Ramoscello
Lisa Williamson
6 b m Malinas(GER) Dusky Dancer (Ziggy's Dancer (USA))
3067[12] 3553[12] 4104[5] 4358[12] 7682[12] 8553[16]

Piccolo Ristretto (FR)
Louisa Carberry 47
4 ch g Vision D'Etat(FR) Infusion (Efisio)
1908a[11]

Piccothepack *Richard Fahey* a55 43
3 b f Piccolo Cards (Tobougg (IRE))
235[9] 505[8] 887[11]

Piccupaprosecco *Derek Shaw*
3 b f Piccolo Saktoon (USA) (El Prado (IRE))
1924[11] 2624[12] 2736[9]

Picket Line *Geoffrey Deacon* a67 51
7 b g Multiplex Dockside Strike (Docksider (USA))
144[10] **3089**[9] 6018[12] 7281[13]

Pickett's Charge *Brian Ellison* a82 76
6 b g Clodovil(IRE) Chelsea Morning (USA) (Giant's Causeway (USA))
3549[11] 3861[9] 4329[7] 5020[4] 5517[2] 5726[3] (5839) 6201[3] **6700**[3] 7212[8] 7305[10]

Picks Pinta *John David Riches* a53 52
8 b g Piccolo Past 'N' Present (Cadeaux Genereux)
502[5] **(613)** 809[4]◆ 973[6] 1335[5] 2329[10] 4493[2] 4823[4] 5276[6] 5559[9] 7962[10] 8295[10] 8638[6]

Picnic Boreal (FR) *D Allard* a57 45
2 b g Penny's Picnic(IRE) Dyhim Boreale (FR) (Dyhim Diamond (IRE))
1448a[9]

Picture Frame *Saeed bin Suroor* a81 82
2 b f Showcasing Hello Glory (Zamindar (USA))
2836[4]◆ 3469[6] **(4223)** 5587[7] 7696[9] 8850[2]

Picture Painter (IRE) *David Pipe* a58 45
6 gr g Zoffany(IRE) Sisceal (Dalakhani (IRE))
482[3] 789[8] 1361[10]

Picture Poet (IRE) *Henry Spiller* a61 57
3 b g Camacho Cockney Rhyme (Cockney Rebel (IRE))
274[4] **614**[2] 1173[5] 2322[4] 3299[2] 4038[7] 5284[5] 7376[4] 7909[5] 8854[5] 9087[9]

Picture Your Dream *Seb Spencer* a61 57
4 ch m Kheleyf(USA) Another Sunset (Doyen (IRE))
785[4] **1272**[7] 1723[10] 2638[4] 3414[12] 3921[16] 9516[11]

Piece Of History (IRE)
Saeed bin Suroor a99 91
4 b g Iffraaj Moonlife (IRE) (Invincible Spirit (IRE))
5173[7] 6214[5] 7188[7] **(8606)**

Piece Of Paradise (IRE) *J A Stack* 98
2 b f Holy Roman Emperor(IRE) Double Fantasy (GER) (Indian Ridge (IRE))
6375[4] **(7400)** 7432[7]

Piedita (IRE) *Sir Mark Prescott Bt* a82 89
5 b m Authorized(IRE) Archina (IRE) (Arch (USA))
5368[7] **5769**[2]

Pierata (AUS) *Gregory Hickman* 118
4 b h Pierro(AUS) November Flight (AUS) (Flying Spur (AUS))
(1974a) **8362a**[5]

Pierre Lapin (IRE) *Roger Varian* 111
2 b c Cappella Sansevero Beatrix Potter (IRE) (Cadeaux Genereux)
(3047)◆ **(7456)**

Pietra Della Luna (IRE) *M Figge* a11 88
3 ch f Lope De Vega(IRE) Pietra Dura (Cadeaux Genereux)
4416a[8] 5227a[7]

Pike Corner Cross (IRE)
David Evans a57 47
7 b g Cape Cross(IRE) Smart Coco (USA) (Smarty Jones (USA))
241[6] 481[5] 603[3] 912[5] **1231**[4] 1506[4] 2111[6] 2698[6] 3322[3] 4460[3]◆ 5081[4] 5363[3] 6153[3] 7240[11] 7859[3] (8299) 8417[4] 8870[2] 9207[5] 9362[6] 9456[7] 9552[2]

Pilansberg *Mark Gillard* a49 77
7 b g Rail Link Posteritas (USA) (Lear Fan (USA))
1750[U] 2607[4] **4096**[9]

Pilaster *Roger Varian* a101 109
4 b m Nathaniel(IRE) Portal (Hernando (FR))
1693[3] 3096[4] 3586[3] 5663[5] **7926a**[5]

Pilgrim Soul *Kerry Lee* a5 15
4 b m Yeats(IRE) Sabah (Nashwan (USA))
3698[7]

Pillar *Adrian McGuinness* a65 55
6 b g Rock Of Gibraltar(IRE) Ceilidh House (Selkirk (USA))
7086a[3]

Pillar Of Society (IRE)
Doug Watson a95 91
5 b g Roderic O'Connor(IRE) Specific (IRE) (Dubawi (IRE))
513a[9] **1001**[2]

Pillars Of Earth *James Eustace* 51
2 b g Nathaniel(IRE) Aliena (IRE) (Grand Lodge (USA))
8464[11]

Pilot Wings (IRE) *David Dennis* a69 41
4 b g Epaulette(AUS) Intaglia (GER) (Lomitas)
1653[12] 3547[11] 7083[13] 7858[4] **8348**[5] 8813[8] 9040[10]

Pilsdon Pen *Joseph Tuite* a55 51
2 b g Helmet(AUS) Bisou (Tiger Hill (IRE))
2792[12] **3990**[9] 4394[8] **5886**[4] 6394[12]

Pimpinehorse (FR) *M Drean*
4 gr g Tin Horse(IRE) Pimpinella (FR) (Highest Honor (FR))
7062a[8]

Pinaclouddown (IRE) *J-Y Artu* a51 63
3 b g Battle Of Marengo(IRE) Saffa Garden (IRE) (King's Best (USA))
1741a[5] 5407a[7] 6328a[12]

Pinarella (FR) *Ben Haslam* a60 69
3 ch f Kendargent(FR) Ponte Di Legno (FR) (Sinndar (IRE))
1275[2] 2199[3] 3292[8] **(4731)** 5854[6] 7050[5] 8083[6] 8924[8] 9396[9]

Pinatar (IRE) *John Best* a64
2 b c Holy Roman Emperor(IRE) Burn The Breeze (IRE) (Beat Hollow)
7445[5] 7571[4] **7814**[8] 8415[6]

Pinatubo (IRE) *Charlie Appleby* a87 128
2 b c Shamardal(USA) Lava Flow (IRE) (Dalakhani (IRE))
(2594)◆ (3312) (4091) (5520) **(7245a)** (8113)

Pincheck (IRE) *Mrs John Harrington* 109
5 b g Invincible Spirit(IRE) Arty Crafty (USA) (Arch (USA))
5112a[5] 6137a[5] **7220a**[3] 7794a[2] 8116[5] 8572a[7]

Pinchpoint (IRE) *John Butler* a52 68
4 ch g Excelebration(IRE) Al Amlah (USA) (Riverman (USA))
2512[8] 3251[6] 3966[10] **4568**[5] 6327[13]

Pinctada *John Bridger* a46 24
3 b f Finjaan Oyster (IRE) (Diamond Green (FR))
615[8] 855[11]

Pindaric *Declan Carroll* a38 41
5 ch g Poet's Voice Hunter's Fortune (USA) (Charismatic (USA))
430[2] 718[5]

Pink Clover (FR) *M Brasme* a58 57
2 b f Mawatheeq(USA) Adobe Pink (Motivator)
7799a[8]

Pink Dogwood (IRE) *A P O'Brien* 112
3 br f Camelot Question Times (Shamardal (USA))
(2157a) **3316**[2] 4354a[3] 5208a[3] 7252a[8] 7942a[8] 8333[8]

Pink Flamingo *Michael Attwater* a86 90
3 b f Dream Ahead(USA) Naivasha (Captain Gerrard (IRE))
215[5] 412[3] 605[2] (854) 1023[7] (1687) (2281) 3535[2]◆ 4185[5] (4478) 5372[2] 6301[3] 6859[3] 7178[2] **7524**[2]

Pink Iceburg (IRE) *Peter Crate* a57 66
3 b f Kodiac Twinkling Ice (USA) (Elusive Quality (USA))
1691[8] 2687[5] 3659[5] **4736**[4] 5318[6] **6299**[3] 6754[4] 7337[11] 8704[8] 9583[5]

Pinkie Pie (IRE) *Andrew Crook* 44
3 b f Tagula(IRE) Bidable (Auction House (USA))
3938[4] 4210[9] 5784[8] 7027[10] 7780[7] 8270[12]

Pink Princess *P Monfort* a73 77
2 b f Hallowed Crown(AUS) Hikayati (IRE) (Iffraaj)
3171a[3] 5713a[11] **6384a**[2]

Pink Sands (IRE) *William Haggas* 82
2 b f No Nay Never(USA) First Breeze (USA) (Woodman (USA))
2918[2] **(4006)**

Pink Tulip *David Simcock* a56
2 ch f Dutch Art Tahirah (Green Desert (USA))
3578[5] 4840[12] **6072**[6] 7079[14]

Pinnata (IRE) *Stuart Williams* a100 87
5 b g Shamardal(USA) Lavande Violet (GER) (Hurricane Run (IRE))
(351)◆ 805[3] 1101[9] 5445[2]◆ 6166[2] (6370) 7163[2] 7350[7] 8062[2] 9053[8] 9472[10]

Pinter *E Charpy* a88 88
7 b g Exceed And Excel(AUS) Pickle (Piccolo)
(196a)

Pinzolo *Ismail Mohammed*
8 b g Monsun(GER) Pongee (Barathea (IRE))
958a[6]

Pioneering (IRE) *Roger Fell* a66 77
5 b g Shamardal(USA) Oregon Trail (USA) (Gone West (USA))
3547[3] 3811[6] 4602[5] **(5899)** 7513[12] 8237[8] 8300[9] 9033[5] 9337[7]

Piper Arrow *Andrew Balding* a86 80
3 b g War Command(USA) Zeyran (IRE) (Galileo (IRE))
1690[5] 2192[3] **(3003)**

Piper Bomb (IRE)
Adrian McGuinness a52 59
4 bb m Dandy Man(IRE) Distant Piper (IRE) (Distant Music (USA))
60[4] 116[8]

Pipers Note *Ruth Carr* a75 88
9 ch g Piccolo Madam Valentine (Primo Valentino (IRE))
1421[9] **1814**[2]◆ 2117[10] 2843[11] 3480[11] 4521[5] 4987[4] 5217[7] 5740[5] 6581[7] 7077[15] 7624[7]

Pipes Of Peace (IRE)
Seamus Durack a97 95
5 b g Galileo(IRE) Coachella (Danehill (USA))
758[4] **1422**[2] 1947[3] 2781[12]

Pipoca *James Given*
3 ch f Archipenko(USA) Trick Or Treat (Lomitas)
2581[12]

Pirandello *A Fabre* a97 97
5 b h Invincible Spirit(IRE) Taranto (Machiavellian (USA))
4205a[7]

Pirate King *Charlie Fellowes* a89 86
4 br g Farhh Generous Diana (Generous (IRE))
2398[3] 3081[4] 4407[3] 8421[6] 9056[6] 9215[4] **(9633)**

Pirate's Cove (IRE) *S Jadhav* a84 78
6 b g Dubawi(IRE) Dunnes River (USA) (Danzig (USA))
573a[5]

Pistoletto (USA) *A P O'Brien* 106
2 b c War Front(USA) Lerici (USA) (Woodman (USA))
5206a[6] 6422[6] 7119[6] 7532a[4] **8088**[2]

Pitchcombe *Clive Cox* a74 68
2 b g Lethal Force(IRE) Emmuska (Sir Percy)
2761[11] 3165[7] 3694[5] (7079) 7409[3] **7840**[2]

Pitcher *Richard Hannon* a58 67
2 ch c Sepoy(AUS) Samdaniya (Machiavellian (USA))
3274[9] **3890**[4] **4558**[6] 5587[9] 6416[6] 6808[6] 8493[5]

Pivello *Tom Clover* a38 56
4 ch g Intello(GER) Pivotting (Pivotal)
2112[7] 5310[6]

Pivoine (IRE) *Andrew Balding* a105 114
5 b g Redoute's Choice(AUS) Fleur De Cactus (IRE) (Montjeu (IRE))
1545[6] 2083[6] 2827[4] 4053[18] **(4935)** 6001a[5] 6962[9] 7455[2] 8155a[4] 9125a[6]

Pivotal Flame (IRE) *Pat Phelan* a71 61
6 b m Pivotal Saadiah (IRE) (Dubai Destination (USA))
(262) 309[5] **404**[3]

Pizzo Carbonara (IRE)
Valentina Oglialoro 66
6 ch m Dandy Man(IRE) Gibilmanna (IRE) (Croco Rouge (IRE))
4170a[10]

Placebo Effect (IRE) *Ollie Pears* a74 75
4 b g Lilbourne Lad(IRE) Hawaiian Dream (IRE) (Catcher In The Rye (IRE))
2057[2] 2710[9] **3199**[4] 3568[6] 4627[3] 5556[3] 6068[6] (6627) 7074[13] 7542[5] 8087[5]

Place Des Vosges (IRE)
David Menuisier a54 61
4 b m Rip Van Winkle(IRE) Red Blossom (USA) (Silver Hawk (USA))
1463[9] 1858[11]

Plain Beau *Mme Conny Whitfield* a79 84
4 b g Thewayyouare(USA) Preveza (FR) (Dalakhani (IRE))
(2002a)

Plait *Michael Bell* a90 88
4 ch m Bated Breath Quiff (Sadler's Wells (USA))
(435) 682a[14] 2401[6] 2961[5] 5735[5] 6709[5] 7567[2] 7973[4]

Planetoid (IRE) *Suzi Best* a52 58
11 b g Galileo(IRE) Palmeraie (USA) (Lear Fan (USA))
369[10] 1361[6]

Plansina *Tom Symonds* a66 70
4 b m Planteur(IRE) Sina (GER) (Trans Island)
1387[6]

Plantadream *John Best* 70
4 b g Planteur(IRE) Phantom Ridge (IRE) (Indian Ridge (IRE))
7143[3]

Plantlove (FR) *M Nigge* a68 83
4 b m Planteur(IRE) Pennylove (FR) (Pennekamp (USA))
4747a[5] 6651a[2]

Platane *C Laffon-Parias* a83 104
3 ch f Le Havre(IRE) Modestie (FR) (Nayef (USA))
(1626a) 3121a[10] 3905a[8] 6250a[5] **8154a**[3]

Plata O Plomo (USA)
Susanne Berneklint a98
5 rg g Paddy O'Prado(USA) Profitability (USA) (Cherokee Run (USA))
282a[5] 513a[5] 957a[6] 7494a[5]

Platform Nineteen (IRE)
Michael Bell 90
3 ch g Australia Susan Stroman (Monsun (GER))
2120[4] 2769[6] 3931[2] (5242) (5596)◆ (6100)◆ **(7001)**◆ 7866[7]

Plath *Sir Michael Stoute* a67
2 b f Poet's Voice Ebble (Oasis Dream)
8602[4] 9085[10]

Platinum Coast (USA) *James Tate* a33
3 ch f Speightstown(USA) Aerocat (USA) (Tale Of The Cat (USA))
78[13] 431[5] 1081[7] **1725**[8]

Platinum Prince *Gary Moore* a63 3
2 gr g Harbour Watch(IRE) Sakhee's Pearl (Sakhee (USA))
8518[13] 9243[4] **9585**[6]

Platinum Star (IRE)
Saeed bin Suroor a77 108
2 b c Lope De Vega(IRE) Toquette (IRE) (Acclamation)
2594[2]◆ (3194)◆ 3988[2] 4846[2] 5520[5] **(6542)** 8088[7]

Platinum Warrior (IRE)
John W Sadler a85 106
4 gr h Galileo(IRE) Laugh Out Loud (Clodovil (IRE))
1441a[6]

Platitude *Amanda Perrett* a93 101
6 b g Dansili Modesta (IRE) (Sadler's Wells (USA))
3078[6] 4884[9] **6834**[2] 7158[RR] **7615**[3] 7866[3] 9065[5] 9419[8]

Playa Del Puente (IRE) *M Halford* a86 99
3 b g Elzaam(AUS) Playamongthestars (AUS) (Galileo (IRE))
(1049a)

Playfull Spirit *John Gosden* a73 69
4 b m Invincible Spirit(IRE) Annabelle's Charm (IRE) (Indian Ridge (IRE))
366[3] 525[2] (706)

Play It By Ear (IRE) *David O'Meara* 63
3 ch g Dragon Pulse(IRE) Seriously (FR) (Sinndar (IRE))
2200[12] **3198**[7] 4039[3]

Play With Me *Ken Wingrove* a31 31
5 ch m Captain Gerrard(IRE) Plead (FR) (Bering)
599[10]

Playwriter (IRE) *M Ibrahim*
5 b g New Approach(IRE) The Shrew (Dansili)
1742a[16]

Pleasant Gesture (IRE) *J S Moore* a46 48
3 ch f Dandy Man(IRE) Validate (Alhaarth (IRE))
217a[11] 401[U] 620[8]

Pleasure Garden (USA)
Sir Mark Prescott Bt a39
2 b c Union Rags(USA) Garden of Eden (USA) (Curlin (USA))
9208[9] **9325**[10] 9509[11]

Pledge Of Honour *Dean Ivory* a75
3 b g Shamardal(USA) Lura (USA) (Street Cry (IRE))
9213[3]◆ 9502[3]

Plegastell (FR) *Edouard Monfort* 100
2 ch f Planteur(IRE) Pariolina (FR) (Muhtathir)
7939a[5]

Plein Ciel (GER) *Anthony Freedman* 106
6 bb g Mamool(IRE) Picobella (GER) (Big Shuffle (USA))
9016a[7]

Plissken *Richard Price* 35
3 b f Bated Breath Blast Furnace (IRE) (Sadler's Wells (USA))
1834[5] 2583[7] 3372[8] 4372[10] 5380[8] 7526[11] 8009[9] 8247[13]

Plough Boy (IRE) *Garvan Donnelly* a85 83
8 b g Dandy Man(IRE) Ribald (Alhaarth (IRE))
748a[7] 6986a[12] **(7085a)**

Plucky Dip *John Ryan* a47 57
8 b g Nayef(USA) Plucky (Kyllachy)
161[10] 263[8] **485**[6] 1060[10] 1208[8] 1378[9] 1717[10] 2235[10] 2298[6] 4589[11] 5302[15]

Plumatic *A Fabre* 115
5 b h Dubawi(IRE) Plumania (Anabaa (USA))
(2313a) **8583a**[3]

Plum Duff *Michael Blanshard* a36 39
3 b f Showcasing Lady Macduff (IRE) (Iffraaj)
554[8] **6802**[3] 7298[7] 8249[8] 9457[P]

Plumette *David Loughnane* a58 71
3 b f Compton Place Belatorio (IRE) (Oratorio (IRE))
211[2] 841[2] 1168[5] (1557) **(2356)** 2897[5] 3552[4] 4316[8] 5176[5] 5985[5] **6801**[2]◆ 7299[6] 7843[8]

Plunger *John Butler* a80 82
4 ch g Helmet(AUS) Percolator (Kheleyf (USA))
2584[10] 3149[7] **3944**[4] 4506[7] 4994[5] (5643a) 6538[6] 7164[6] 7839[4] 8305[4] 9455[9] 9642[8]

Plunkett *Ed Dunlop* 52
2 b c Gleneagles(IRE) Araqella (IRE) (Oasis Dream)
6409[6]

Plus Que Parfait (USA)
Brendan P Walsh a110 98
3 ch r Point Of Entry(USA) Belvedera (USA) (Awesome Again (CAN))
(1443a) 2425a[8]

Plutonian (IRE) *Charles Hills* a84 105
5 b g Raven's Pass(USA) Ripalong (IRE) (Revoque (IRE))
1753[5] 2778[14] 3992[10] 5519[11] 6150[11]

Plymouth Rock (IRE) *John Quinn* 78
2 b g Starspangledbanner(AUS) Welcome Spring (IRE) (Lawman (FR))
4401[6] 5591[2] **(6971)** 7429[7]

Pocket Dynamo (USA)
Robert Cowell a70 99
3 br c Dialed In(USA) Little Bit Tiny (USA) (Cuvee (USA))
1692[2] 2270[4] 3084[4] 4665[9] 5471a[2]

Pocket Square *Roger Charlton* 107
2 ch f Night Of Thunder(IRE) Shared Account (Dansili)
6322[3] (6949)◆ **(8482a)**

Pocket Warrior *Paul D'Arcy* a47 57
8 b g Tobougg(IRE) Navene (IRE) (Desert Style (IRE))
1215[11] 1477[10] (2924) **(3036)** 3320[6] 3527[8] 7986[11] 8502[9]

Poco Contante *David Thompson* a8 43
2 b f Fast Company(IRE) Littlemoor Lass (Motivator)
6970[10] 8021[11]

Poeta Brasileiro (IRE) *Henry Spiller* a73 54
4 b g Poet's Voice Top Act (FR) (Fantastic Light (USA))
1023[4] 1208[4] 1767[5] 2122[9] 3207[5] 5281[5] 5889[3] 6503[5] 7446[3] 7690[2] 8071[3] (8264) 8755[4] **8946**[2] 9224[3]

Poetic Charm *Charlie Appleby* a88 109
4 b m Dubawi(IRE) Speirbhean (IRE) (Danehill (USA))
(283a)◆ **(728a)**

Poetic Choice *Keith Henry Clarke* a59 58
8 b m Byron Ennobling (Mark Of Esteem (IRE))
7960[11]

Poetic Diva (FR) *N Clement* a60 61
3 b f Poet's Voice Academic Angel (USA) (Royal Academy (USA))
509a[8]

Poetic Era *David Simcock* a59 70
3 b f Poet's Voice Secret Era (Cape Cross (IRE))
2216[6] **3266**[3] 4804[6]◆ 5419[9]

Poetic Force (IRE) *Tony Carroll* a93 84
5 ch g Lope De Vega(IRE) Obligada (IRE) (Beat Hollow)
557[10] 922[2] **(1356)** 1916[5] 2273[9] (3529) 4545[6] 4867[4] 5804[3] 6729[11] 7128[6] 8606[10]

Poetic Legacy (IRE) *Mark Johnston* a62 51
3 b f Lope De Vega(IRE) Cottonmouth (IRE) (Noverre (USA))
6259[8]◆ 6703[5] 7027[3]◆ (7375)◆ **7578**[2] **7859**[2] 8001[11]

Poetic Light *Adrian McGuinness* a44 51
4 b g Poet's Voice Point Perfect (Dansili)
7088a[8]

Poetic Lilly *David Menuisier* a45 49
2 b f Poet's Voice Lilly Junior (Cape Cross (IRE))
4302[5] 5082[7] 7203[8] 8603[8]

Poetic Motion *Jim Boyle* a54 53
3 b f Toronado(IRE) Sonnetation (IRE) (Dylan Thomas (IRE))
1731[4] (2734) 3256[11] 4029[3] **4642**[2] 5957[4] 6885[7]

Poetic Principle (IRE) *J S Moore* a69 74
5 b g Royal Applause Lady Links (Bahamian Bounty)
1565[8]

Poet Pete (IRE) *Mark Usher*
3 ch g Poet's Voice My Body Is A Cage (IRE) (Strategic Prince)
251[14] 1824[16] 6361[15] 6860[15] 7973[10]

Poetry *Michael Bell* 98
3 b f Kingman Swiss Diva (Pivotal)
2564a[9] **4665**[4] 4932[3] **6520a**[4] 7254a[9] 7889[7]

Poets Dance *Rae Guest* 81
2 b f Poet's Voice Whirly Dancer (Danehill Dancer (IRE))
3469[3] 5317[2] 5590[2] 6577[2] (6899) **8088**[12]

Poet's Dawn *Tim Easterby* a80 89
4 ch g Poet's Voice Dudley Queen (IRE) (Excellent Art)
2480[5] 3216[3] 3563[5] **(3867)** 4403[6] 6475[11] 6998[2] 7434[7] 8130[14] 8918[8]

Poet's Lady *David Barron* 73
2 gr f Farhh La Gessa (Largesse)
6175[3] **6919**[4]

Poet's Magic *Jonathan Portman* a42 68
3 b f Poet's Voice Magic Destiny (Dubai Destination (USA))
1825[3] 2355[9] 3665[8] 4227[13] 5092[2] 5575[4] **6569**[2] 7731[5]

Poet's Mind (USA) *Charlie Appleby* a81
2 bb g Dubawi(IRE) Arethusa (USA) (A.P. Indy (USA))
8319[2] 9007[8]

Poet's Pride *David Barron* a72 72
4 b g Arcano(IRE) Amber Heights (Kyllachy)
586[4] 706[2] (811) 2580[10] 2846[4] **(4195)**◆ 4767[4]◆ 5123[3] **6204**[3] 6461[7] 7074[11]

Poet's Prince *Mark Johnston* a84 98
4 b g Poet's Voice Palace Affair (Pursuit Of Love)
1896[2] 2320[8] 5667[4]

Poet's Quest (FR) *S Wattel* 75
3 b c Poet's Voice Alta Lilea (IRE) (Galileo (IRE))
2519a[5]

Poet's Society *A bin Harmash* a101 106
5 ch g Poet's Voice Rahiyah (USA) (Rahy (USA))
285a[7] **640a**[2]

Pogo (IRE) *Charles Hills* a96 108
3 b c Zebedee Cute (Diktat)
1926[6] (2414) 2889a[7] 4016[19] 5666[9] **(6425)** 6950[10] 8336[8]

Point In Time (IRE) *Mark Usher* a84 84
4 b m Champs Elysees Creme Anglaise (Motivator)
(2214) 3861[9] 4504[5] 5133[2] 5735[6] 7466[2] 8064[5] **(8727)** **9056**[4]

Point Of Honour (IRE) *Phillip Makin* a51 49
4 b g Lope De Vega(IRE) Shamayel (Pivotal)
2202[9] **3705**[5] 4126[9] 4435[4] 4990[8] 6098[3] 6828[2] **7578**[3] 8072[7]

Point Of Order *Archie Watson* a70 77
2 ch c Showcasing Cross My Heart (Sakhee's Secret)
4624[3] 5093[5] **5577**[2] 6158[6] 6436[4] 7440[3] 8067[7]

Point Of Woods *Tina Jackson* a62 64
6 b g Showcasing Romantic Myth (Mind Games)
2632[3] 3213[9] 3518[9] 4037[5] **(5169)** 5393[8] 6099[9] 6273[7] 7051[11] 8263[13] 8429[14]

Point Taken (IRE) *Micky Hammond* a74 76
5 b g Papal Bull Grand Isla (Selkirk (USA))
4304[5] 4989[4] 5849[4] 6674[9]

Point Zero (IRE) *Michael Appleby* a75 62
4 b g Dandy Man(IRE) Alchimie (IRE) (Sri Pekan (USA))
1[4] 42[7] (388) (587) 707[3] 823[5] **(928)** 1194[11] 1366[5] 1551[6] 2025[6] 2296[3]

Poitin *Keith Henry Clarke* a65 59
9 b m Kheleyf(USA) Port Providence (Red Ransom (USA))
3175[4]

Polar Cloud *Heather Main* a56
3 gr g Mount Nelson Cloud Illusions (USA) (Smarty Jones (USA))
9425[7]

Polaris Angel *Mark Walford* a49
3 rg f Lethal Force(IRE) Grand Slam Maria (FR) (Anabaa (USA))
1168[6]

Polish *John Gallagher* a76 84
4 b g Teofilo(IRE) Polygon (USA) (Dynaformer (USA))
1943[10] 3861[4] 4543[7] **5179**[3] 5540[9] 7819[4] 8661[8]

Polished Article *Lawrence Mullaney* a49
4 b m Intense Focus(USA) File And Paint (IRE) (Chevalier (IRE))
275[5] 706[4] 1192[8]

Politicise (IRE) *William Haggas* a80 89
3 b g Camelot Politesse (USA) (Barathea (IRE))
1945[3] **2616**[3] 3341[7] 4068[4]

Politicum (FR) *Arslangirej Savujev* 63
3 gr c Lethal Force(IRE) Patanegra (IRE) (Barathea (IRE))
6006a[11]

Pollyissimo *Henry Spiller* a58 56
4 ch m Nathaniel(IRE) Fleurissimo (Dr Fong (USA))
1546[9] 2234[15]

Polly's Gold (IRE) *Paul George* a54 67
4 ch m Havana Gold(IRE) Keyta Bonita (IRE) (Denon (USA))
180[8] 1354[8]

Polybius *David Simcock* a98 92
8 b g Oasis Dream Freedonia (Selkirk (USA))
3094[6] 4451[6] 4866[6] 5530[5] 5942[5] 7397[6] 8425[7]◆ 8607[8] 9088[10] **(9214)** 9301[5]

Polydream (IRE) *F Head* 119
4 b m Oasis Dream Polygreen (FR) (Green Tune (USA))
2313a[6] **3289a**[3] (4581a) 5716a[7]

Polyphony (IRE) *John Mackie* a45 81
4 b m Power Start The Music (IRE) (King's Best (USA))
(3178) 3685[2] 4243[2]◆ **5030**[2] 6170[5] 6961[4] 7526[4]

Pondus *James Fanshawe* 111
3 b c Sea The Moon(GER) Diablerette (Green Desert (USA))
1690[4] (2581) (3263) 4049[6] **5182**[2] **5950**[2] 7455[3] 8335[9]

Pontecarlo Boy *Richard Whitaker* a46 60
5 ch g Piccolo Dahshah (Mujtahid (USA))
1723[9] 1849[8] 2901[9]

Pontille (FR) *Elias Mikhalides* 107
4 b m Whipper(USA) Ponte Brolla (FR) (Highest Honor (FR))
(8980a)

Pont Neuilly (FR) *H De Nicolay* a24 24
9 ch h Medecis Panzella (FR) (Kahyasi (IRE))
115a[13]

Poor Auld Paddy *David Elsworth* a57 22
3 b g Swiss Spirit Moment In The Sun (Dubai Destination (USA))
615[7] **1033**[7] **1217**[4] 1696[9] 2007[10]

Poor Duke (IRE) *Michael Mullineaux* a5 12
9 b g Bachelor Duke(USA) Graze On Too (IRE) (Rainbow Quest (USA))
62[13]

Pop Dancer (IRE) *Richard Fahey* 90
2 b g Kodiac Pop Art (IRE) (Excellent Art)
5152[2] **(5472) (5900)** 6356[15] 7679[5] 8095[12]

Popping Corks (IRE) *Linda Perratt* a58 56
3 b f Camacho Shamardyh (IRE) (Shamardal (USA))
21[6] **497**[3] 1504[12] 2327[3] 2683[3] 3292[U] 4493[5] 4720[8] 5094[2] 5236[5] 5491[5] 6338[4] 6659[2] 6936[9] (7487) 7766[4] 8235[4]

Poppy In The Wind *Alan Brown* a59 56
7 b m Piccolo Vintage Steps (IRE) (Bahamian Bounty)
25[3] 129[8] 411[4] 9398[6] 9518[10]

Poppy Jag (IRE) *Kevin Frost* a47 46
4 b m Kodiac Jacquelin Jag (IRE) (Fayruz)
1554[3] 2295[8] 2924[6] 3475[8] 4481[13] 7737[11]

Poppy May (IRE) *James Given* a57 51
5 b m Zoffany(IRE) Lara Amelia (IRE) (Ishiguru (USA))
161[9] 379[8] 1192[5] **(1384) 2013**[2] 3143[6] 3738[8] 8821[7] 9161[8] 9445[3]

Pop Song *H-A Pantall* a72 87
4 b m New Approach(IRE) Lyric Of Light (Street Cry (IRE))
6651a[9]

Pop The Cork *Jonjo O'Neill* a68 41
3 b g Harbour Watch(IRE) Gospel Music (Beat Hollow)
2485[6]

Pop The Hood (USA) *Doug Watson* a87
7 br g Street Cry(IRE) Prophetically (CAN) (Pulpit (USA))
280a[4] 729a[6] 957a[11]

Populaire (FR) *Amanda Perrett* a40 67
2 gr f Zebedee Monspa (Monsun (GER))
5772[4] 7406[8] 8250[6]

Porcelain Girl (IRE) *Michael Bell* a79 74
3 ch f Exceed And Excel(AUS) Dresden Doll (USA) (Elusive Quality (USA))
2144[11] 3583[3] 4023[6] 5105[5] 5989[5] 6930[6] 8924[5]

Porrima (IRE) *Ben Haslam* a70 66
4 gr m Kodiac El Morocco (USA) (El Prado (IRE))
(410)◆ (525) 808[2] 1271[6] 2097[3]

Portamento (IRE) *A R Al Rayhi* a92 97
7 gr h Shamardal(USA) Octave (USA) (Unbridled's Song (USA))
52a[9] 397a[10] 725a[3] 1111a[9]

Porthos (FR) *Mme G Rarick* a58
3 b g Sommerabend Pepperrose (GER) (Big Shuffle (USA))
217a[10]

Porth Swtan (IRE) *Garry Moss* a78 97
4 b g Invincible Spirit(IRE) Propaganda (IRE) (Sadler's Wells (USA))
(1502) 1944[F] (Dead)

Port Lairge *Michael Chapman*
9 b g Pastoral Pursuits Stylish Clare (IRE) (Desert Style (IRE))
508[8] 8639[11]

Portledge (IRE) *James Bethell* a91 82
5 b g Acclamation Off Chance (Olden Times)
104[3] (213) 499[2] (952) 1143[8] 1457[12] 4887[10] 5434[3]◆

Port Noir *Grace Harris* a53 52
2 bl f Harbour Watch(IRE) Cocabana (Captain Rio)
1821[13] 3194[9] 4480[8] 5576[7] 6071[4] 6683[2] 7234[3]

Porto Ferro (IRE) *John Bridger* a73 60
5 b m Arcano(IRE) Sassari (IRE) (Darshaan)
2206[6] 2483[9] 3020[7] 4227[14] 5050[5] 6806[2] 7337[8] 8242[10] 9247[2] 9507[9] 9670[8]

Portofino (IRE) *David O'Meara* 9
3 ch g Australia Song Of My Heart (IRE) (Footstepsinthesand)
5742[7]

Port Of Leith (IRE) *Mark Johnston* a73 68
3 b g Dark Angel(IRE) Tender Is Thenight (IRE) (Barathea (IRE))
561[3] 2055[5] 2896[5]

Port Soif *Scott Dixon* a57 45
5 b m Foxwedge(AUS) Positivity (Monsieur Bond (IRE))
1158[4] 1369[2] 1527[4] 2350[3] 4349[5] 7385[10] 8405[10] 8942[13]

Portugueseprincess (IRE)
Archie Watson a62
2 b f Camacho Royal Visit (IRE) (King's Best (USA))
4999[3]

Port Winston (IRE) *Alan King* a68 74
2 b g Harbour Watch(IRE) Volkovkha (Holy Roman Emperor (IRE))
2205[3] 2931[5] 5052[8] 6073[5] (6667) 7391[10] 8219[6] 8506[3]

Positive *Clive Cox* 109
2 b c Dutch Art Osipova (Makfi)
(4252)◆ 5520[2] (6727)◆ 8113[6]

Positive Light (IRE)
Sir Mark Prescott Bt a48 57
2 b f No Nay Never(USA) Sharplaw Star (Xaar)
5265[6] 5646[6] 5838[4] 6313[3] 6683[7] 7980[10]

Posted *Richard Hannon* 99
3 b f Kingman Time Away (IRE) (Darshaan)
2790[4] 4597[3] 4927[2] (5450) (6451) 7146[4] 7657[4]

Postie *James Eustace* a52 43
3 b f Medicean Postage Stampe (Singspiel (IRE))
2581[9] 3263[14] 4022[5] 7390[2] 8072[5]

Potala Palace
Joseph Patrick O'Brien 81
2 b c Dansili Sanjida (IRE) (Polish Precedent (USA))
5710a[7]

Potemkin (GER) *A Wohler* 109
8 bb g New Approach(IRE) Praia (GER) (Big Shuffle (USA))
(4157a) 5079a[6]

Potencia (IRE) *Declan Carroll* a34
2 b f Free Eagle(IRE) Appetina (Perugino (USA))
9181[10] 9471[11]

Potenza (IRE) *James Eustace* a46 77
3 b g Born To Sea(IRE) Cranky Spanky (IRE) (Spectrum (IRE))
813[11] 2355[4] 3246[7] (4070) (4284) 5394[5] 5898[3] 6232[2] 8433[2]

Pot Luck *Sharon Watt* a44 45
3 b f Phoenix Reach(IRE) Marajuana (Robellino (USA))
79[12] 400[7] 537[4] 931[12] 6117[9] 8670[5] 8869[9]

Pot Of Paint *Tom Dascombe* a65 71
2 b c New Approach(IRE) Regency (JPN) (Tanino Gimlet (JPN))
6424[4]◆ 8121[4]◆

Potters Lady Jane *Lucy Wadham* a74 78
7 b m Sir Percy Arabescato (UAE) (Gone West (USA))
3269[6] 4118[2] 4569[3] 5623[4] (6323) 7395[6] 8696[6]

Potters Question *Amy Murphy* a60 32
3 ch g Cardinal Scipmylo (Doyen (IRE))
1587[4] 2192[7] 3184[5] 9128[13] 9444[9]

Poucor *Mick Channon* a45 54
4 b g Pour Moi(IRE) Corinium (IRE) (Turtle Island (IRE))
7240[6] 7985[8] 8204[2]

Pounamu (AUS) *Michael Kent* 80
7 gr g Authorized(IRE) Tangiwai (AUS) (Street Cry (IRE))
8578a[10]

Pound Off You *Gillian Boanas* 27
3 ch f Haafhd Let It Be (Entrepreneur)
5742[6] 6274[U] 6544[5]

Pour Joie *Ian Williams* a37 26
4 b g Pour Moi(IRE) Lupa Montana (USA) (Giant's Causeway (USA))
2208[16] 9017[10] 9416[5]

Pour La Victoire (IRE) *Tony Carroll* a75 78
9 b g Antonius Pius(USA) Lady Lucia (IRE) (Royal Applause)
2273[20] 3040[8] 3536[3] 3963[5] 4867[11] 5804[9] 5882[3] 6301[7] (6795) 7268[2] 8649[5] 8827[5]

Pour Me A Drink *Clive Cox* a81 88
3 ch g Nathaniel(IRE) Euroceleb (IRE) (Peintre Celebre (USA))
1755[4] (2101) 3262[5] 3859[2] 6217[5]◆ 6967[6] 7413[2] 8002[4]

Pourmorechampagne *Paul Webber* 36
3 b g Pour Moi(IRE) Aqua Aura (USA) (Distorted Humor (USA))
2932[9] 3372[10] 4176[8]

Pour Sioux (IRE) *Gordon Elliott* 52
3 b f Pour Moi(IRE) Sweet Sioux (Halling (USA))
7493[7]

Powerage (IRE) *Malcolm Saunders* a48 44
3 b f Slade Power(IRE) Ice On Fire (Iceman)
3697[9] 5085[6] 5373[8] 6052[3] 6361[6] 8255[7]

Powerallied (IRE) *Richard Fahey* 91
6 b g Camacho Kaplinsky (IRE) (Fath (USA))
1814[5] 2775[20] 3846[9] 4364[2] (4880) 5420[8] 5661[10] 5951[8] (6714)◆ 6960[7]

Power Best (IRE) *G Botti* a98 64
3 b c Power Kathy Best (IRE) (King's Best (USA))
1199a[4] 5538a[3]

Power Euro (IRE) *Henk Grewe* 98
7 ch g Peintre Celebre(USA) Power Penny (GER) (Galileo (IRE))
(2026a) 7249a[8]

Powerful Breeze *Hugo Palmer* 114
2 b f Iffraaj Power Of Light (IRE) (Echo Of Light)
(6407) (7120) 8091[2]

Powerful Dream (IRE)
Ronald Harris a76 70
6 b m Frozen Power(IRE) Noble View (USA) (Distant View (USA))
1915[6]◆ 2358[5] 2473[2] 2729[3] 3531[7] 4230[3] 4495[7] 5013[4] 5449[6] 7230[7] (7757) (8194) 8470[6] 9257[5]

Powerful Society (IRE) *Mark Gillard* a41 47
4 b m Power Society Gal (IRE) (Galileo (IRE))
2720[9]

Powerful Sole *Andrea Marcialis* a78 78
3 b c Sir Percy Piper's Ash (USA) (Royal Academy (USA))
(1842a)

Powerful Star (IRE) *David Lanigan* a66 70
3 ch f Slade Power(IRE) Star Studded (Cadeaux Genereux)
2762[3] 3431[6] 4341[10] 6350[6] 6840[9]

Power Home (IRE) *Denis Coakley* a68 65
5 ch m Power Ascendancy (Sadler's Wells (USA))
85[5] 616[4] (910) (1363) 1988[4] 7790[10] 8414[10] 9367[7] (9626)

Power Link (USA) *James Tate* a104 68
3 rg g Data Link(USA) Greyciousness (USA) (Miswaki (USA))
169a[5]◆ 5266[7] (6319)◆ 7913[2] (8317) (9254)

Power Of Darkness
Marcus Tregoning 105
4 b g Power Summer's Lease (Pivotal)
1889[2] 2408[7] (4255) (5930)

Power Of Life (USA) *Michael Bell* a52 45
3 bb g Hat Trick(JPN) Asuncion (USA) (Powerscourt)
319[11] 612[9] 1725[2] 2262[6] 2943[5]

Power Of Love *George Baker* a8
2 b g Paco Boy(IRE) A Legacy Of Love (IRE) (Sea The Stars (IRE))
3419[13] 4030[9] 7571[11] 9172[10]

Power Of States (IRE)
Hugo Palmer a83 83
3 b c Lope De Vega(IRE) Allegation (FR) (Lawman (FR))
1737[9] 4304[3]◆ 4924[3] 5694[3] 6217[8] 7452[2] 8092[17]

Power Of Time (IRE)
Charlie Appleby a74
2 b c Galileo(IRE) Terror (IRE) (Kodiac)
8810[5] 9156[3]

Power Of You (IRE) *William Knight* a57
3 ch g Dragon Pulse(IRE) Add Up (IRE) (Ad Valorem (USA))
1293[6] 1677[7] 2236[8]

Power Packed *Henry Candy* 38
2 b f Slade Power(IRE) Piping Dream (IRE) (Approve (IRE))
5250[11] 7297[6]

Power Player *K R Burke* 75
3 b g Slade Power(IRE) Varnish (Choisir (AUS))
2147[9] 2634[10] 3727[3] 4732[3] 5176[3] 5898[7] 6342[2] (7405) 8396[9]

Power Point *John Wainwright* 37
2 br g Cable Bay(IRE) Frabjous (Pivotal)
8128[8]

Power Seeker (IRE) *Rod Millman* a13 46
3 b g Power Eclat Royale (Royal Applause)
2066[10] 2734[13] 4180[11]

Power Surge (IRE) *Robert Stephens*
5 ch g Power Silver Skates (IRE) (Slip Anchor)
242[10]

Powertrain (IRE) *Hugo Palmer* 88
2 ch g Zoffany(IRE) Emerald Ring (IRE) (Johannesburg (USA))
4826[6] 5501[3] (6219) (7140) 8110[5]

Power Zone (IRE) *A Wohler* 87
3 ch f Lope De Vega(IRE) Up In Time (Noverre (USA))
4534a[7] 6769a[13]

Poyle George Two *John Hodge* a46 51
4 b g Sepoy(AUS) Poyle Dee Dee (Oasis Dream)
45[8] 2183[8] 2682[8] 3177[9] 3721[2] 5100[4] 7508[8] 7956[9]

Poyle Vinnie *Ruth Carr* a94 97
9 b g Piccolo Poyle Dee Dee (Oasis Dream)
791[6] (1547) 1814[7] (2556) 2775[9] 3582[6] 4406[12] 5119[3] 5524[2] (5661) 6229[9] 6565[6] 7121[12]

Praetorius (GER) *A Wohler* 68
2 rg c Novellist(IRE) Ponte Tresa (FR) (Sicyos (USA))
7004a[6]

Prairie Moppins (USA)
Sylvester Kirk a47 2
2 rg f Creative Cause(USA) Saratta (USA) (Flower Alley (USA))
6118[13] 8198[9] 8546[4] 8824[10] 9045[6] 9127[5] 9399[10]

Prairie Spy (IRE) *Mark Johnston* a83 72
3 b f Sepoy(AUS) Vista Bella (Diktat)
2008[4]◆ 2552[3] 2927[7] 3923[5] 5030[7] 5565[7] 6186[2] 6540[6] 7272[6] 7773[12]

Prairie Town (IRE) *Tony Carroll* a59 54
8 b g High Chaparral(IRE) Lake Baino (Highest Honor (FR))
2591[7] 3205[5]

Praise You (IRE) *Tom Ward* a61 65
2 b c Acclamation Kanshe (IRE) (Dalakhani (IRE))
9605a[5]

Praleen (FR) *P Nador* a66 70
4 b m Tin Horse(IRE) Perpetual Glory (Dansili)
1491a[14]

Pranceabootthetoon (IRE)
Milton Bradley a44 41
4 ch h Sir Prancealot(IRE) Cabopino (IRE) (Captain Rio)
179[3] 322[4] 919[8] 3036[11]

Prancing Oscar (IRE) *Ben Haslam* a55 50
5 b g Sir Prancealot(IRE) Beguiler (Refuse To Bend (IRE))
125[12] 462[12] 2376[7] 3224[7] 9447[6]

Praxedis *Robert Cowell* a24 41
4 b m Dutch Art Angel Song (Dansili)
2081[4] 2580[13] 3738[12] 5063[4] 5864[5] 6199[2] 7838[13]

Praxeology (IRE) *Mark Johnston* a81 92
2 b g Dark Angel(IRE) Hartstown House (IRE) (Primo Dominie)
2316[2] 2610[3] (3512) (3890) 5612[4] 6356[11] (7182)◆ 7904[17] 8659[4]

Praxidice *K R Burke* a60 75
3 b f Toronado(IRE) Cross My Heart (Sakhee's Secret)
3293[4] 3923[3] 5459[3] 5953[7] 7471[6] 7901[9] 8403[8]

Pray (GER) *Andreas Suborics* a66 88
3 b f Maxios Paraisa (Red Ransom (USA))
9281a[9]

Preciosa (GER) *R Dzubasz* 94
3 ch f Sea The Moon(GER) Prakasa (FR) (Areion (GER))
5470a[8] 7862a[5]

Precious Moments (IRE)
A P O'Brien 106
2 b f Gleneagles(IRE) Tarbela (IRE) (Grand Lodge (USA))
4048[5] 4352a[2] 5361a[4] 6374[6] 7244a[8] 8724[12]

Precious Plum *Charlie Wallis* a67 59
5 b m Equiano(FR) Miss Polly Plum (Doyen (IRE))
286[7] 483[9] (1210)◆ 1883[5] (3001) 4074[4] 4563[4] (6685) 7690[5] 8194[6] 9627[8]

Precision Prince (IRE)
Mark Loughnane a65 61
3 b g Dragon Pulse(IRE) Little Live Wire (IRE) (Dubawi (IRE))
319[2] (537) 802[3] 1593[8] 1957[5] 2517[8] 3246[5] 3684[6] 4473[7]

Precision Storm *Mark Loughnane* a70 61
2 gr g Dragon Pulse(IRE) Way To The Stars (Dansili)
4317[4] 5052[7] 5848[6] 6394[10] 7677[6] (8415) 8699[2]

Precocity (IRE) *Richard Fahey* 62
2 b f Kodiac Days Of Summer (IRE) (Bachelor Duke (USA))
3477[4] 4984[3]

Predetermined (IRE) *J-V Toux* a43 42
6 b g Lope De Vega(IRE) Queen Bodicea (IRE) (Revoque (IRE))
7800a[8]

Predictable Tully (IRE) *Clive Cox* a79 80
2 b f Kodiac Alerted (USA) (First Defence (USA))
4790[4] 5772[2] 7832[3]

Preening *James Fanshawe* a104 102
4 b m Dutch Art Striving (IRE) (Danehill Dancer (IRE))
1941[2] 3986[14] 5369[4] 7146[2]◆ 8708[6] 9064[4] (9603a)

Prefontaine (IRE) *Roger Varian* 92
3 gr g Mastercraftsman(IRE) Cochabamba (IRE) (Hurricane Run (IRE))
3260[2] 3842[3] 4644[3]

Prejudice *David Simcock* 91
3 ch g Dubawi(IRE) Ever Rigg (Dubai Destination (USA))
2796[4]◆ 4342[3]◆ 5135[2]

Premier Lion (FR) *Vaclav Luka Jr* a79 84
4 b h Zanzibari(USA) Fammi Sognare (IRE) (Bertolini (USA))
6522a[6]

Premier Power *Roger Varian* a100 87
2 ch c Siyouni(FR) Pelerin (IRE) (Shamardal (USA))
6219[2]◆ (8060)◆

Premium Bond *Richard Hannon* a36 45
2 b g Outstrip Gennie Bond (Pivotal)
4114[11] 4925[8] 5314[9] 6071[10]

Premium Pink (IRE) *Luke McJannet* a29 22
4 b m Camacho Ride For Roses (IRE) (Barathea (IRE))
161[13] 379[11] 5310[9] 5675[13]

Prerogative (IRE) *Tony Carroll* a40 45
5 b g Rock Of Gibraltar(IRE) Tedarshana (Darshaan)
207[3] (436) 602[6] 983[8] 1163[7] 2111[7] 3186[5] 4232[3] 4771[3] 5310[3] 5802[5] 6560[9] 7270[8]

Presence Process *Pat Phelan* a66 66
5 b g Dansili Loulwa (IRE) (Montjeu (IRE))
292[9] 859[6] 985[5] 1269[9] 1498[8] 6077[9] 7375[5] 8756[4] 9207[6]

Preservation *Jedd O'Keeffe* a44 50
3 b f Kyllachy Protectress (Hector Protector (USA))
1458[10] 2531[5] 3226[8] 4038[8]

Presidential (IRE) *Roger Fell* a63 92
5 b g Invincible Spirit(IRE) Poetical (IRE) (Croco Rouge (IRE))
1891[3] 2609[17] 4127[7] 4299[9] 5173[5] 5488[2]◆ 5971[9] 6207[2] 6445[11] 6922[5] 8766[7]

Presidential Sweet (ITY)
Marco Botti a55
2 b f Golden Horn Biz Bar (Tobougg (IRE))
8021[7]◆ 8848[8]

Presley (ITY) *A Botti* 105
6 b h Gladiatorus(USA) Pasionaria (IRE) (Celtic Swing)
2885a[4] 4173a[5] 7502a[4] 8788a[2]

Press Gang *Harry Fry* a72 70
6 b g Mount Nelson Rutba (Act One)
2059[5]

Prestbury Park (USA)
Sofie Lanslots a80 81
4 bb g Shamardal(USA) Sutra (USA) (Meadowlake (USA))
1760[8] 2053[3]◆ 2824[2] 3706[7]◆ 4059[11] 4630[6] 6058[7] 6099[4] 7511[6] (7624) 7855[2] 8262[11] 8400[9] 9483a[13]

Prestigious (IRE) *Archie Watson* a61 55
2 ch f Camacho Western Sky (Barathea (IRE))
3049[8] 5732[7] 6592[8] 8286[4] 8493[4] 9250[7]

Pretending (ITY) *A Botti* 104
6 b h Librettist(USA) Brumeux (IRE) (Machiavellian (USA))
(8585a)

Pretorio (IRE) *M Nigge* a102 62
7 b g Aussie Rules(USA) England's Legend (FR) (Lure (USA))
682a[2]

Pretreville (FR) *J-C Rouget* a84 101
4 b h Acclamation Pegase Hurry (USA) (Fusaichi Pegasus (USA))
2782a[2]

Pretty Baby (IRE) *William Haggas* a82 105
4 b m Orpen(USA) Premiere Danseuse (Gold Away (IRE))
(2621) 3986[13] 5608[11] 7146[13]

Pretty Boy (IRE) *Mme Pia Brandt* 105
3 b c Siyouni(FR) Fast And Pretty (IRE) (Zamindar (USA))
1707a[6] 3621a[3] 4705a[7] 5714a[7] 7886a[4]

Pretty Fantasy (IRE)
Gavin Cromwell a29 51
3 b f Casamento(IRE) Pixie Belle (IRE) (Echo Of Light)
8837[7]

Pretty In Grey *Marco Botti* a72 66
2 gr f Brazen Beau(AUS) Maglietta Fina (IRE) (Verglas (IRE))
5988[3] 6919[8] 7393[6] (8699)◆

Pretty Lady (IRE) *Mark Johnston* a61 60
2 b f Es Que Love(IRE) Quality Love (USA) (Elusive Quality (USA))
7046[5] 7769[5] 8084[5] 9196[5]

Pretty Passe *Martin Todhunter* a57 41
5 b m Exceed And Excel(AUS) Passe Passe (USA) (Lear Fan (USA))
410[5] 2183[12] 4130[9]

Pretty Pickle (IRE) *William Haggas* 67
2 b f Born To Sea(IRE) Onomatomania (USA) (Mr Greeley (USA))
4222[5]

Pretty Point (USA) *Patrick Gallagher* 100
3 b f Point Of Entry(USA) Pretty Syrie (USA) (Street Boss (USA))
9637a[3]

Pretty Pollyanna *Michael Bell* 109
3 b f Oasis Dream Unex Mona Lisa (Shamardal (USA))
3115[2] 4051[7] 4923[4] 5716a[6] 6453[2]

Prevent *Ian Williams* a67 81
4 br g Poet's Voice Emergency (Dr Fong (USA))
1457[17] 2151[10] 3149[5] 3305[11] (4561) 5178[8] 6289[9] 7003[3]◆ 7294[6]

Price Range (USA) *P Bary* a101 98
3 b c First Defence(USA) Price Tag (Dansili)
1794a[4] 3029a[5]

Pride Of America (FR)
Harry Dunlop a84
2 b c American Post Atarfe (IRE) (Anabaa (USA))
9007[4] (9624)◆

Pride Of Angels *Gary Moore* a68 71
6 gr m Dark Angel(IRE) Openness (Grand Lodge (USA))
9308[9]

Pride's Gold (USA) *Simon Crisford* a96 92
4 b m Animal Kingdom(USA) Royal Order (USA) (Medaglia d'Oro (USA))
460[2] (1213)◆

Priest (IRE) *Martyn Meade*
2 b c Hallowed Crown(AUS) Chica Whopa (IRE) (Oasis Dream)
7407[12]

Prigioniera (IRE) *Marco Gasparini* 81
4 ch m Duke Of Marmalade(IRE) Peaceful Light (Doyen (IRE))
4170a[8]

Prime Approach (IRE)
Brett Johnson a34 7
3 ch g Dawn Approach(IRE) Remarkable Story (Mark Of Esteem (IRE))
2488[12] 2795[19] 4066[8] 7518[9]

Primeiro Boy (IRE) *Richard Fahey* a68 67
3 gr g Zebedee House Of Roses (New Approach (IRE))
1488[6] 2293[8] 2960[7] 3508[10] 4148[9] (4454) 5020[6] 5632[4] 6176[3] 7652[7] 8070[3]

Primeravez (IRE) *Michael Dods* a55 69
3 b f Dark Angel(IRE) Evening Frost (IRE) (Invincible Spirit (IRE))
3844[7]

Prime Red (DEN) *Birgitte Nielsen* 85
6 ch g Victorious Soul(USA) On Line (SWE) (Songline (SWE))
7497a[11]

Primero (FR) *David O'Meara* a105 104
6 b g Cape Cross(IRE) Flamenba (USA) (Kingmambo (USA))
311[2] 799[4] 1017[7]
Primogeniture (IRE)
Martin Keighley a75 44
8 b g Glory Of Dancer Jacqueline (IND) (King Charlemagne (USA))
703[4] 1815[5] (Dead)
Primo's Comet *Jim Goldie* a86 81
4 b g Orientor Primo Heights (Primo Valentino (IRE))
127[5] 353[3]◆ 791[4]◆ (953) 1211[4] 1946[6] 2421[4] 2843[6] 3360[2] 4100[5] 4691[3] 5661[4] 9098[8] 9348[11]
Primo Uomo (IRE) *Gerard O'Leary* a93 103
7 b g Strategic Prince Mooching Along (IRE) (Mujahid (USA))
1434a[9] 2221a[3] 3818a[6] 6986a[4] 7241a[12] 8328a[9]
Prince Ahwahnee *Phillip Makin* a75 76
4 b g Harbour Watch(IRE) Ahwahnee (Compton Place)
4691[5] 5217[P] (Dead)
Prince Caspian *Richard Hannon* a78
2 b c Muhaarar Riskit Fora Biskit (IRE) (Kodiac)
9008[2] 9631[5]
Prince Charmin' (IRE) *Tim Vaughan* a62 58
6 b g High Chaparral(IRE) Dream Club (Dansili)
2344[6]
Prince Consort (IRE)
John Wainwright a50 54
4 b g Most Improved(IRE) Fame And Fortune (IRE) (In The Wings)
154[6] 495[6] 782[11] 983[6] 1981[8] 2587[3] 3163[12] 3682[9] 4131[10] 4582[3] 5517[13] 6102[6] 6502[5] 6578[8] 7681[2] 8295[8] 8942[10] 9282[4] 9450[6]
Prince Eiji *Roger Varian* 108
3 ch c Dubawi(IRE) Izzi Top (Pivotal)
7340[4] 8116[3]◆
Prince Elzaam (IRE)
Jaber Ramadhan 86
3 b c Elzaam(AUS) Emmas Princess (IRE) (Bahhare (USA))
168a[6] 511a[4] 956a[7]
Prince Hamlet (FR)
M Delcher Sanchez 97
3 b c Sommerabend Calle A Venise (IRE) (Invincible Spirit (IRE))
1243a[4] 1794a[5]
Prince Imperial (USA)
Sir Michael Stoute a80 34
2 b c Frankel Proportional (Beat Hollow)
6409[9] (7996)
Prince Llyr (IRE) *Heather Main* a69 71
3 b g Zoffany(IRE) Zadalla (Zaha (CAN))
1264[3]
Prince Lucky (USA) *Todd Pletcher* a112
4 b g Corinthian(USA) Lucky Notion (USA) (Great Notion (USA))
3618a[9]
Princely *Tony Newcombe* a71 70
4 b h Compton Place Royal Award (Cadeaux Genereux)
253[6] 433[6] 741[6] 982[8] 1522[5] 3701[2] 4181[4] 4872[2] 6203[3] 6562[3] 7230[2] 7757[10] 8242[9] 9013[8]
Prince Mamillius *Derek Shaw* a2
3 ch c Coach House(IRE) Queen Hermione (IRE) (Camacho)
9012 316[12] 604[6]
Prince Of Arran *Charlie Fellowes* a111 113
6 b g Shirocco(GER) Storming Sioux (Storming Home)
1113a[4] 1441a[9] 5613[5] 6473[8] 6962[3] 8134a[2] (8600a) 8844a[2] 9376a[11]
Prince of Eagles (IRE)
David Lanigan a72
2 b c Free Eagle(IRE) Sleeping Beauty (IRE) (Oasis Dream)
9415[4]
Prince Of Harts *Rod Millman* a75 96
3 br g Dalakhani(IRE) Reaf (In The Wings)
(1345)◆ 2088[6] 2630[2] 3580[5] (4306)◆ 4865[3] 5412[2] (8412)
Prince Of Naples (IRE)
Ms Sheila Lavery a87 93
2 b c Holy Roman Emperor(IRE) Armoise (Sadler's Wells (USA))
6690a[7] 7247a[4]
Prince Of Rome (IRE)
Richard Hughes a94 66
3 gr c Lethal Force(IRE) Garraun (IRE) (Tamayuz)
2086[9] 3075[14] 4294[3] 5649[2] 6735[3] 7187[4] 9214[3] 9389[2] 9660[2]
Prince Of Time *Stella Barclay* a49 53
7 ch g Bahamian Bounty Touching (IRE) (Kheleyf (USA))
1837[8] 2298[9] 4824[2] 5237[9] 5629[5] 5857[5] 6621[5] 7282[8] 7761[3] 8233[8] 9035[10]
Prince Oliver (FR) *M Figge* 64
2 b c Penny's Picnic(IRE) Comnena (Tiger Hill (IRE))
8964a[8]
Prince Percy *Gary Moore* a61 40
2 b g Sir Percy Crystal High (High Chaparral (IRE))
8721[7] 9242[5]
Prince Rock (IRE) *Simon Dow* a58 53
4 ch g Society Rock(IRE) She's A Queen (IRE) (Peintre Celebre (USA))
3144[7] 3989[2] 4589[3] 5264[2] 6199[4] 6284[3] 6889[2] 7281[5] 7371[2] 7606[3] 8547[4] 9160[2] (9249) 9505[3] (9659)
Princesa Carolina (USA)
Kenneth McPeek 101
3 rg f Tapit(USA) Pure Clan (USA) (Pure Prize (USA))
8139a[3]
Princes Des Sables *Kevin Ryan* a68 101
3 ch f Monsieur Bond(IRE) Hopes N Dreams (IRE) (Elusive City (USA))
3654[7] 4442[6] (5846) 6257[4] 6999[8] 9098[11]
Princess Apollo *Donald Whillans* a30 32
5 b m Mullionmileanhour(IRE) Speedy Senorita (IRE) (Fayruz)
2678[13] 3933[10] 4726[11] 5558[9] 5857[10]
Princess Bride *Saeed bin Suroor* 76
2 b f Shamardal(USA) Peacoat (Doyen (IRE))
7054[3] 7695[4] 8461[2]
Princess Carly *Ali Stronge* 27
2 b f Swiss Spirit Amary (IRE) (Acclamation)
5988[11]
Princesse Animale *Pat Phelan* a65
2 b f Leroidesanimaux(BRZ) Isabella Beeton (Archipenko (USA))
7555[2]
Princesse Bassett (FR)
George Baker a58 24
3 b f Wootton Bassett Mariposa (IRE) (Oasis Dream)
1142[6] 2340[16]
Princesse Mathilde
Charlie Fellowes a68 92
3 gr f Dalakhani(IRE) Halle Bop (Dubai Millennium)
4964a[6] 8514[4] 9066[6]
Princess Florence (IRE) *John Ryan* a47 55
3 b f Zebedee Villa Nova (IRE) (Petardia)
1650[13] 2190[9] 3182[7] 3409[2] 3964[6] 4217[3] (4477) 4754[7] 5107[8] 5377[13] 5806[10] 6130[7] 6610[5] 7738[2] 8205[8] 8436[10]
Princess Gold (FR) *F Rohaut* a74 89
4 gr m Style Vendome(FR) Princess Love (FR) (Verglas (IRE))
6031a[12]
Princess Harley (IRE) *Mick Quinn* a64 68
4 gr m Dark Angel(IRE) Tonle Sap (IRE) (Manduro (GER))
162[4] 616[10] 1482[6] 2974[4] 3778[2] 5271[12] 6371[7] 7998[7] 9033[3] 9333[3] (9646)
Princess Isla *J-C Rouget* a72 79
3 b f Frankel Peinture Abstraite (Holy Roman Emperor (IRE))
(977a)
Princess Jenni (NZ)
David Brideoake 105
3 b f High Chaparral(IRE) Glitzabeel (NZ) (Zabeel (NZ))
8138a[12]
Princess Juliana (IRE)
Brian Meehan
3 b f Rip Van Winkle(IRE) Conveyor Belt (IRE) (Pivotal)
1834[9]
Princess Keira (IRE) *Mick Quinn* a65 67
4 b m Acclamation La Reine De Pearls (IRE) (Dubawi (IRE))
2025[3] 3020[2] (4074) 4733[7] 5352[4] 7345[7]
Princess Nearco (IRE) *Liam Bailey* 44
5 b m Elzaam(AUS) Royal Jubilee (IRE) (King's Theatre (IRE))
4370[9] 5277[7] 7492[7]
Princess Palliser (IRE) *John Quinn* a58 57
3 b f Slade Power(IRE) Piccola Sissi (IRE) (Footstepsinthesand)
1272[6] 2098[4] 3719[6] 4440[9] 5092[10] 5767[7] 5914[3] 6338[9]
Princess Power (IRE) *Nigel Tinkler* 91
3 b f Slade Power(IRE) Flurry Of Hands (IRE) (Acclamation)
1762[2] 2078[10] 2525[3] 3068[5] 3479[4] (4368)◆ 4847[4] 5442[6] 5983[3] 6476[4] 7002[7]
Princess Siyouni (IRE) *Mick Quinn* a21 47
2 b f Siyouni(FR) Librettista (AUS) (Elusive Quality (USA))
5961[6] 7695[15] 9159[11]
Princess T *Neil Mulholland* a55
4 gr m Aussie Rules(USA) Fairy Slipper (Singspiel (IRE))
9368[4]
Princess Way (IRE) *Paul George* a57 72
5 gr m Zebedee Stef's Girl (IRE) (Petardia)
2277[2] (3533) 4657[2] (5795) 7229[4]
Principia *Adam West* a40 61
4 b m High Chaparral(IRE) Zero Gravity (Dansili)
2626[10] 4220[8] 4653[3] 5106[RR] 5425[6] 5803[8] 6153[8] 6843[10]
Printemps D'Avril (FR)
J-P Perruchot
3 b f Panis(USA) Avril (GER) (Samum (GER))
4204a[7]
Prisma (IRE) *Ivan Furtado*
2 ch f Starspangledbanner(AUS) Doubleyou One (AUS) (Danehill Dancer (IRE))
5590[6] 6096[10]
Prissy Missy (IRE)
David Loughnane a30 63
2 b f Gutaifan(IRE) Maracuja (Medicean)
3190[8] 3679[5] 4373[5] 5010[2] 5279[7] 6041[2] 6557[2] (6799) 7284[3] 7522[8]
Pritty Livvy *Noel Wilson* a28 26
3 b f Gregorian(IRE) Sitting Pritty (IRE) (Compton Place)
2197[19] 3975[17] 4358[13] 5236[7] 5738[6]
Private Matter *Amy Murphy* a78 81
5 b g Mayson Privacy Order (Azamour (IRE))
1654[4] 2484[7] 3636[8] 4365[3] 5821[7] 6319[4] 7183[4]◆ 7564[6] 8943[5] 9223[2] (9559)
Private Romance (IRE) *N Clement* 85
2 ch f Siyouni(FR) Private Eye (FR) (American Post)
9059a[5]
Private Ryan (USA) *H Al Alawi* a14
3 b c Declaration Of War(USA) Grace Anatomy (USA) (Aldebaran (USA))
570a[10]
Private Secretary *John Gosden* 107
3 b c Kingman Intrigued (Darshaan)
(1643) (2088) (3042) 4049[4]
Probability (IRE) *Archie Watson* a92 91
3 b f Moohaajim(IRE) Fine Prospect (IRE) (Namid)
27[2] (313) 555[3] (720) (1424)◆ (1729) 2008[5] (3068) 4023[4] 5325a[9] 6148[2] 6735[7] 7401[16]
Probable Cause *Archie Watson* a71 80
2 ch f Lethal Force(IRE) Wink (Salse (USA))
(2694) 3350[2] 3997[7] (4799)
Proceed (IRE) *Archie Watson* a73 59
4 ch m Mastercrafstman(IRE) Roanne (USA) (Lemon Drop Kid (USA))
67[2] 404[8]
Proceeding *Tracy Waggott* a61 46
4 b g Acclamation Map Of Heaven (Pivotal)
275[3] 2203[11] 2899[9] 3924[8] 4207[11] 5438[6] 6666[7] 7587[6] 8530[3] (8818) (8922) 9395[3]
Proclaimer *Julie Camacho* a67 63
2 b c Free Eagle(IRE) Pious (Bishop Of Cashel)
5172[7] 5553[6] 6337[8] (9515)
Prodigious *Sir Michael Stoute* a32 16
3 ch f Intello(GER) Spacious (Nayef (USA))
4022[6]
Production *Alan King* a65 83
3 b g Oasis Dream Pure Excellence (Exceed And Excel (AUS))
2395[8] 2766[5] 3307[5] (4077) 4671[4] 5417[5] 9274[5]
Professor *William Knight* a60 83
9 ch g Byron Jubilee (Selkirk (USA))
6317[12] 7084[4]
Profile Prince *Micky Hammond*
3 b g Harbour Watch(IRE) Princess Luna (GER) (Grand Lodge (USA))
5742[10] 6544[U] (Dead)
Profit (IRE) *Henk Grewe* 56
3 b f Nayef(USA) Polite Reply (IRE) (Be My Guest (USA))
3028a[11]
Profound (IRE) *Mark Usher* a73 70
4 b g Intello(GER) Bahama Spirit (IRE) (Invincible Spirit (IRE))
8294[8] 8809[9] 9012[9] 9138[6] 9361[10]
Progressive Rating *William Knight* a88 67
2 br c Bated Breath Foxtrot Alpha (IRE) (Desert Prince (IRE))
3274[10] 6415[3] (7276)◆ (8297)
Project Bluebook (FR) *John Quinn* a68 83
6 bl g Sinndar(IRE) Apperella (Rainbow Quest (USA))
7403[6]
Projection *Roger Charlton* 110
6 b g Acclamation Spotlight (Dr Fong (USA))
2744[10] 4094[10] 5184[8]
Prominna *Tony Carroll* a58 60
9 ch g Proclamation(IRE) Minnina (IRE) (In The Wings)
402[6]◆ 597[6] 986[2] 1266[2] 1590[4] 3425[4] (3936) 4307[8]
Promise Of Peace (JPN)
Donald McCain a45 58
5 ch g King Kamehameha(JPN) Peace Of World (JPN) (Sunday Silence (USA))
3862[11]
Promise Of Success
Saeed bin Suroor a75 76
3 b f Dansili Summer School (IRE) (Street Cry (IRE))
727a[12] 2770[3] 3261[9]
Promises Fulfilled (USA)
Dale Romans a117
4 ch h Shackleford(USA) Marquee Delivery (USA) (Marquetry (USA))
1444a[4] 3618a[4]
Promissory (IRE) *John Gosden* 104
3 b f Dubawi(IRE) Seal Of Approval (Authorized (IRE))
3013[3]◆ (4600)◆ 6446[2] 7658[3]
Promote (IRE) *James Tate* a68 83
3 b f Dandy Man(IRE) Park Haven (IRE) (Marju (IRE))
5057[2] 5868[2] 8550[9]
Prompting *Olly Murphy* a73
3 br g Bated Breath Enticing (IRE) (Pivotal)
8653[3] 9165[2]
Pronghorn *Michael Easterby* 3
2 ch g Casamento(IRE) Be Lucky (Kyllachy)
3477[7] 3812[14] 8631[10]
Pronouncement (USA) *J P Murtagh* 95
2 ch f Declaration Of War(USA) Terrific Tiffany (USA) (Strong Hope (USA))
7215a[3]
Proper Beau *Bryan Smart* a52 83
2 b g Brazen Beau(AUS) Olivia Grace (Pivotal)
(1499)◆ 3023[6] 5900[3] 6498[3]◆ 8817[9]
Proposed *Jaber Ramadhan* a87 95
7 b h Invincible Spirit(IRE) On A Soapbox (USA) (Mi Cielo (USA))
9125a[10]
Proschema (IRE) *Tom Dascombe* a109 111
4 ch g Declaration Of War(USA) Notable (Zafonic (USA))
1750[6] 2742[8] 3600[3] 4382[3] 5183[6] 5662[9]
Prosecute (FR) *Sean Regan* a12 44
6 b g Lawman(FR) Dissitation (IRE) (Spectrum (IRE))
3681[5] 4513[5] 4658[9] 6036[14] 6663[13]
Prosecution *J P Murtagh* a72 79
5 b g Lawman(FR) Convention (Encosta De Lago (AUS))
526[4]
Prosecutor (IRE) *Mark H Tompkins* a37 19
2 b f Mayson Arrowood (IRE) (Motivator)
1416[13] 2191[8] 5265[8]
Prospectus *Gavin Cromwell* a63 84
6 b g Sakhee(USA) Some Sunny Day (Where Or When (IRE))
5508a[12]
Protagonist (FR) *Jamie Osborne* a76 73
2 b g Wootton Bassett Sagariya (FR) (Shamardal (USA))
5131[10] 5809[3]◆ 6395[4] 7235[4]
Protected Guest *George Margarson* a74 104
4 b g Helmet(AUS) Reem Star (Green Tune (USA))
1889[8] 5370[5] (6513) 6917[2] 7394[2]
Proton (IRE) *Jedd O'Keeffe* a75 86
3 b g Slade Power(IRE) Singing Bird (IRE) (Excellent Art)
(3248) 4076[3] 6209[2] 7302[4] 8002[3]
Proud And Elated (FR)
Joseph Patrick O'Brien a65 65
4 b m Makfi Danceabout (Shareef Dancer (USA))
419a[8]
Proud Archi (IRE) *Michael Dods* a52 88
5 b g Archipenko(USA) Baharah (USA) (Elusive Quality (USA))
1457[6] 2057[5] 2893[2]◆ 3813[2]◆ 4879[10] 5246[9] 5692[11]
Proun (FR) *Andrea Marcialis* 47
2 b f Sidestep(AUS) Celestia (Anabaa (USA))
1709a[8] 3562a[9]
Proven Strategies (USA)
Mark Casse 104
2 bb c Sky Mesa(USA) Stormbeforethecalm (CAN) (Quiet American (USA))
8746a[6]
Provocation (IRE) *Mark Johnston* a72 63
2 b g Lawman(FR) Kalandara (IRE) (Rainbow Quest (USA))
7623[4] 8528[10] 8914[3] 9155[6]
Psara *H-F Devin* 96
3 b f Invincible Spirit(IRE) Pacifique (IRE) (Montjeu (IRE))
2426a[4] 3391a[5] 4964a[5]
Psychedelic Funk *G M Lyons* 103
5 ch g Choisir(AUS) Parabola (Galileo (IRE))
1776a[7] 2660a[6] 6693a[21] 7794a[6] 7934a[4] (8572a)
Ptarmigan Ridge *Richard Hughes* a83 96
5 b g Kyllachy Joshua's Princess (Danehill (USA))
2100[2] 2572[8] 3632[8] 6920[2] 9000[8]
Published (IRE) *E J O'Neill* 56
2 b c Exceed And Excel(AUS) Alsalwa (IRE) (Nayef (USA))
7043a[6]
Puchita (IRE) *Antony Brittain* a58 53
4 b m Acclamation Violet Ballerina (IRE) (Namid)
62[9] 208[10] 1018[3] 1431[5] 1683[5] 2241[3] 5517[4] 7527[3] 7961[8] 8502[2] 8666[3] 8922[8] 9039[3] 9551[2]
Puckle *Tim Easterby* 48
2 b f Poet's Voice Pasithea (IRE) (Celtic Swing)
7586[6] 8100[9]
Pudding Chare (IRE) *R Mike Smith* a68 71
5 b g Arcano(IRE) Rosy Dudley (IRE) (Grand Lodge (USA))
2439[5] 2963[6] (3177) 4060[4] 4693[3]◆ (4725) 4982[7] 5490[9] 5933[9] 7364[13] 7776[13]
Puds *Richard Hughes* a95 96
4 br m Bated Breath Missy Wassie Gal (USA) (High Chaparral (IRE))
(1382) 1822[3] 1938[2] (2403) 3043[2]◆ 3544[2] 5661[11] 6149[2] 6908[7] 7497a[3] 8867[3]
Puelo (FR) *Carina Fey* 74
5 b h Sinndar(IRE) Premiere Danseuse (Gold Away (IRE))
1245a[14]
Puerto Banus *Ian Williams* a75 74
3 b g Bated Breath Three Ducks (Diktat)
2794[4] 3499[2] 4358[5] 7069[3] 7816[7] 9140[8] 9244[2]
Puerto Sol (IRE) *Brian Ellison* a55 53
2 b g Camacho Reina De Luz (IRE) (Echo Of Light)
1844[5]◆ 2184[5] 2957[3] 7208[10] 7584[3] 8022[11]
Puffthemagicdragon *George Scott* 56
2 b g Brazen Beau(AUS) Marmot Bay (IRE) (Kodiac)
2820[8]
Pukka Tique *Ivan Furtado* a45 24
3 b g Sepoy(AUS) Flylowflylong (IRE) (Danetime (IRE))
8351[8] 8869[12]
Pull Harder Con *Robyn Brisland* a44 51
2 b c Mayson Cut The Cackle (IRE) (Danetime (IRE))
5125[10] 5780[8] 6167[6] 7046[11] 7627[9] 9640[6]
Pullman Brown (USA) *Philip Kirby* a49 48
7 b g Big Brown(USA) Touch Too Much (USA) (Holy Bull (USA))
789[4] 1163[13] 1431[10]
Pumaflor (IRE) *Philip Kirby* a42 54
7 b g Aussie Rules(USA) Krasotka (IRE) (Soviet Star (USA))
1659[11] 2335[9] 2978[6] 4633[11] 5024[9] 6327[5] 6937[12] 7960[13]
Pumblechook *Iain Jardine* a74 71
6 b g Dalakhani(IRE) Chiang Mai (IRE) (Sadler's Wells (USA))
2626[7] 7631[4] 8523[4] 8945[4] 9184[5] 9570[8]
Pumpkin Rumble (USA)
Kevin Attard a103 105
8 ch g English Channel(USA) Clarins (USA) (Storm Cat (USA))
5484a[3] 8155a[5]
Pump Pump Palace (FR)
J-P Gauvin a103 103
6 b h King's Best(USA) Pump Pump Girl (FR) (Kendor (FR))
(682a) 9210a[6]
Punchbowl Flyer (IRE)
Eve Johnson Houghton a70 77
2 b g Dream Ahead(USA) All On Red (IRE) (Red Clubs (IRE))
4480[5] 5774[5] (6300)◆ 6963[6] 7391[5]
Punctuate (FR) *Richard Hannon* a19 63
2 b c Clodovil(IRE) Apostrophe (IRE) (Barathea (IRE))
8011[10] 8460[8]
Punita Arora (IRE)
Mrs John Harrington a97 97
2 ch f Sepoy(AUS) Wojha (IRE) (Pivotal)
7215a[5] 7879a[3]
Punjab Mail *Tim Fitzgerald* a73 76
3 b g Charm Spirit(IRE) Harryana (Efisio)
1388[5] 1662[11] 3307[3] 4552[7] 4895[5] 6085[5] 6518[4] 7189[3] 7652[5] 8495[5] 8548[4] 9453[11]
Punkawallah *Alexandra Dunn* a70 52
5 b g Sepoy(AUS) Max One Two Three (IRE) (Princely Heir (IRE))
457[3] 1463[15] 2696[7] 3511[10] 4216[11] 6681[9] 7474[10] 9312[11]
Punkie (FR) *Laura Lemiere* 51
3 gr f Makfi Peace Mine (CAN) (Mineshaft (USA))
6789a[5]
Punting (IRE) *Richard Hughes* a69
2 ch f Power Lakatoi (Saddlers' Hall (IRE))
9211[4]◆ (9500)◆

Purbeck Gem *Robyn Brisland* a45 49
5 ch m Sakhee's Secret Porcelana (IRE) (Highest Honor (FR))
117[7] 275[4] 599[8] 1731[12]

Purbeck Hills (IRE) *Richard Hannon* a58 64
3 b g Oasis Dream Albisola (IRE) (Montjeu (IRE))
1857[13] 2141[9] 3092[11] 3594[6] 3888[9] 4931[6]

Purdey's Gift *Andrew Balding* a86 74
3 b c Camelot Saphira's Fire (IRE) (Cape Cross (IRE))
1484[3] 7816[9] (8298) 9066[3]

Pure Country *Noel Williams* a79
4 b g Frankel Plante Rare (IRE) (Giant's Causeway (USA))
46a[15] 469[4]

Purely Prosecco *Derek Shaw* a39
3 b f Poet's Voice Nabat Sultan (Invincible Spirit (IRE))
604[4] 753[7] 908[7] 2300[3] 7628[13] 8643[11] 8840[12]

Pure Purfection (IRE) *Jim Boyle* a28 51
2 b f Dream Ahead(USA) Rose Of Africa (IRE) (Cape Cross (IRE))
5500[10] 6532[5] 7124[3] 7980[8] 8415[11]

Pure Sensation (USA)
Christophe Clement a90 114
8 rg g Zensational(USA) Pure Disco (USA) (Disco Rico (USA))
8770a[5]

Pure Shores *Ian Williams* a83 88
5 b m Dubawi(IRE) Polly's Mark (IRE) (Mark Of Esteem (IRE))
81[2] 4393[4] 4706a[9] 5187[2] 5475[6]

Pure Zen (FR) *Gianluca Bietolini* 103
3 b f Zoffany(IRE) Dolce Attesa (Dr Fong (USA))
1706a[7] 2498a[2] 3387a[2] 4705a[9]

Purgatory *Chris Wall* a71 82
3 b g Dark Angel(IRE) Meet Me Halfway (Exceed And Excel (AUS))
2238[6] 3780[2] 4284[8] 5784[5] (6130) 6678[3] (7084) (8206)

Purple Empress *Ivan Furtado* 37
2 ch f Mayson Purple Silk (Holy Roman Emperor (IRE))
2093[7]

Purple Jazz (IRE) *Jeremy Scott* a56 57
4 b g Red Jazz(USA) Breakmeheart (IRE) (Galileo (IRE))
3834[12] 4868[5] 5378[3] 6400[6] 7240[9]

Purple Paddy *Jimmy Fox* a63 46
4 b g Swiss Spirit Stunning In Purple (IRE) (Kheleyf (USA))
175[7] (941)◆ 1032[3] 1675[2] 2145[12] 4235[7] 6051[9] (8417) (8822) 9305[6]

Purple Power *Mick Quinn* 65
2 bb f Slade Power(IRE) Peace Summit (Cape Cross (IRE))
7393[7]

Purple Rock (IRE) *Gay Kelleway* a84 79
7 b g Fastnet Rock(AUS) Amethyst (IRE) (Sadler's Wells (USA))
390[5] (703) (927)◆ 1073a[9]

Purple Sandpiper *Robyn Brisland* a6 58
2 b c Mayson The Lady Lapwing (Mark Of Esteem (IRE))
8012[10] 8257[7] 8402[7]

Purple Tommy *Jimmy Fox* a31
3 ch g Assertive Stunning In Purple (IRE) (Kheleyf (USA))
2140[9] 9171[8] 9416[7]

Purple Victory (FR) *F Head* 95
3 b g War Command(USA) Lana Girl (USA) (Arch (USA))
(6094a)

Pushaq (IRE) *Anthony McCann* a60 62
6 b g Roderic O'Connor(IRE) Et Dona Ferentes (Green Desert (USA))
2513[2] 5003[3] 8345[6]

Push Back *George Scott* a43
3 b g Kyllachy Cara Gina (Bahamian Bounty)
27[12] 1353[7]

Pushkin Museum (IRE) *John Butler* a20 15
8 gr g Soviet Star(USA) Chaste (Groom Dancer (USA))
439[2] 2194[8] 4767[11] 5632[10] 9518[11]

Pushmi Pullyu (IRE)
Jane Chapple-Hyam 71
3 b f Roderic O'Connor(IRE) Russian Rave (Danehill Dancer (IRE))
(3780) 4071[7] 5730[8] 6412[8] 8030[9]

Pushover *Steph Hollinshead* a48 61
2 gr f Hellvelyn Soft Touch (IRE) (Petorius (IRE))
6919[7] 7644[9] 8816[5]

Put The Law On You (IRE)
Alistair Whillans a45 53
4 b g Declaration Of War(USA) Spirit Of Tara (IRE) (Sadler's Wells (USA))
968[8] 1643[14] 2245[7] 3686[9] 6611[2] 7070[2] 8081[5] 8635[7]

Putting Green *Neil Mulholland* a45 61
7 ch g Selkirk(USA) Ryella (USA) (Cozzene (USA))
6958[13]

Putumayo (FR) *J-M Osorio* a83 95
4 b h Myboycharlie(IRE) Djebel Amour (USA) (Mt. Livermore (USA))
4418a[3] 8375a[8]

Puzzle *Richard Hughes* a60 72
3 b g Paco Boy(IRE) Appleton Drove (USA) (Street Cry (IRE))
943[6] 1168[3] 2334[2] 2912[4] 4288[12]

Puzzlebook *David Evans* 29
2 b f Fountain Of Youth(IRE) Find The Answer (Vital Equine (IRE))
5493[8] 6185[8]

Puzzle Cache *Rod Millman* a48 44
5 b m Phoenix Reach(IRE) Secret Queen (Zafeen (FR))
370[12] 921[9] 1351[6] 1680[4] 1958[5] 6104[13] 6560[7] 6855[7]

Pyledriver *William Muir* 103
2 b c Harbour Watch(IRE) La Pyle (FR) (Le Havre (IRE))
(4925) 6212[4] (6957) 7691[7]

Pyramid Place (IRE) *John Gosden* a60
2 b g Authorized(IRE) Attima (Zafonic (USA))
9052[4] 9325[6]

Pythion (FR) *G M Lyons* 100
3 b g Olympic Glory(IRE) Paragua (GER) (Nayef (USA))
1603a[3] 2662a[7] 2853a[2] 3984[11] 7216a[15]

Pytilia (USA) *Richard Hughes* a84 70
3 rg f Mizzen Mast(USA) Infanta (IRE) (Cape Cross (IRE))
(1359) 2141[8] 2942[6] 3468[2] 4424[6] (7554) 8197[11]

Qaabil (IRE) *William Haggas* a75 68
3 b g Charm Spirit(IRE) Kartica (Rainbow Quest (USA))
421a[7] 8894[2] 9213[4]

Qaaddim (IRE) *Roger Varian* a80 75
2 ch g Hot Streak(IRE) Never In (IRE) (Elusive City (USA))
4246[4] 5172[5] 5624[7] 6403[2]◆ 7155[3] (7840) 8509[3]

Qaaraat *Antony Brittain* a71 67
4 b g Acclamation Ladyship (Oasis Dream)
1023[2] 1393[8] 2515[4] 2709[2] 2876[2] 3206[5] 3658[8] 4364[6] 4458[6] 5042[7] 5395[13] 5515[6] 5986[6] 7334[5] 7823[6] 8643[3] (8715) 9135[2] 9406[7] 9473[8]

Qabala (USA) *Roger Varian* 110
3 b f Scat Daddy(USA) Entwine (USA) (Empire Maker (USA))
(1832) 2443[3] 3115[9] 4885[4] 5479a[7]

Qaffaal (USA) *Michael Easterby* a99 81
8 b g Street Cry(IRE) Wasseema (USA) (Danzig (USA))
212[4] 1101[4]

Qafila (AUS)
David A & B Hayes & Tom Dabern 102
3 b f Not A Single Doubt(AUS) Zighy Bay (USA) (Tapit (USA))
8134a[8] 8361a[17]

Qallaab (IRE) *Michael Appleby* a65 40
4 ch g Dawn Approach(IRE) Gazebo (Cadeaux Genereux)
702[5] 919[4] 1177[11]

Qamka *Roger Varian* a94 80
3 br f Mastercraftsman(IRE) First (Highest Honor (FR))
2583[3] (3761) (8529) 9170a[6]

Qarasu (IRE) *Roger Charlton* 109
3 br g Le Havre(IRE) Bella Qatara (IRE) (Dansili)
2581[3] (3664)◆ 5194[5] (6211)◆ 6923[2] 7565[2] 8445a[5]

Qaroun *Sir Michael Stoute* a98 93
4 b h Dark Angel(IRE) Exotic Isle (Exceed And Excel (AUS))
1881[2] 2402[3] 3581[2] 4292[2] 4666[12] 6150[6] 7106[6]

Qasbaz (IRE) *Jamie Osborne* a74 74
2 b g Make Believe Esuvia (IRE) (Whipper (USA))
6911[4]◆ 7569[2] 8250[4]

Qaseeda *William Haggas* a67 69
2 b f Poet's Voice Diala (IRE) (Iffraaj)
7160[2]◆ 7813[5] 8706[3]

Qasr *Keith Dalgleish* a43 71
5 b g Excelebration(IRE) Blur (Oasis Dream)
3500[8] 7368[3]

Qatar Bolt *H-A Pantall* a75 86
4 ch h French Fifteen(FR) Yellow And Green (Monsun (GER))
1449a[2] 2226a[2] 3136a[9]

Qatar Queen (IRE)
James Fanshawe a75
3 b f Kodiac Alina (IRE) (Galileo (IRE))
5808[4] 6862[2] 9213[5] 9547[2]

Qatar River (FR) *Leyla Ennouni* a73 79
4 b h French Fifteen(FR) Mud Hilah (FR) (Kingsalsa (USA))
4418a[10]

Qawamees (IRE) *Michael Easterby* a83 82
4 b g Exceed And Excel(AUS) Jabhaat (USA) (Hard Spun (USA))
2748[16] 3515[6] 3845[3] 4208[2] 4491[2] (5818) 7003[9] 7403[5] 8341[5]

Qayed (CAN) *Kevin Frost* a56 9
4 b g Blame(USA) Endless Journey (USA) (A.P. Indy (USA))
61[10] 321[5] 810[7] 1334[9] 2014[4] 2698[2] 2970[10] 3321[6] 4287[13] 6843[13]

Qayes *P Ventena Alves* 71
4 b g Exceed And Excel(AUS) Time Control (Sadler's Wells (USA))
5471a[8]

Qaysar (FR) *Richard Hannon* a86 110
4 b g Choisir(AUS) Coco Demure (IRE) (Titus Livius (FR))
1694[8] 2609[11] 3563[3] 4020[4] 5319[2] (5776) (5965) 6376[6] (6894) (7198) 7891[8]

Q Cee *Eugene Stanford* a17 17
6 b g Denounce Gibraltar Lass (USA) (Concerto (USA))
1732[10]

Qinwan *Andrew Balding* a58 66
2 b c Paco Boy(IRE) Figment (Acclamation)
5859[6] 6852[4] 7386[2] 8650[9] 9196[11]

Q Twenty Boy (IRE) *Mark Usher* a55 65
4 ch g Dandy Man(IRE) Judies Child (IRE) (Majestic Missile (IRE))
4227[6] 4555[8]

Quadrilateral *Roger Charlton* 115
2 ch f Frankel Nimble Thimble (USA) (Mizzen Mast (USA))
(6154)◆ (7412)◆ (8091)

Quaint (IRE) *Hughie Morrison* a63 56
2 b f Dandy Man(IRE) Destiny's Kitten (IRE) (Naaqoos)
4448[5] 8067[3] 8640[2] 9300[7]

Qualisaga (FR) *Carina Fey* 107
5 b m Sageburg(IRE) Qualita (GER) (Konigstiger (GER))
1127a[2] 1708a[9] 2167a[6] 2670a[3] (8379a) 9124a[5]

Quanah (IRE) *Liam Bailey* a36 66
3 ch g Dandy Man(IRE) Boucheron (Galileo (IRE))
1488[9] 2055[4] 4286[11] 4563[8] 7488[4] 7590[4] (7764) (8235)

Quantum Dot (IRE) *Ed de Giles* a72 76
8 ch g Exceed And Excel(AUS) Jeed (IRE) (Mujtahid (USA))
2358[8] 4364[10] 4880[11] 5375[7]

Quantum Joy (GER)
Lennart Hammer-Hansen 88
3 b f Maxios Qelle Amie (CAN) (Beau Genius (CAN))
3877a[6] 6747a[7]

Quantum Love (GER) *Frau J Mayer*
4 b m Maxios Qelle Amie (CAN) (Beau Genius (CAN))
2002a[3]

Quare Lucky (IRE) *Mark Loughnane* a67 46
3 b g Excelebration(IRE) Dama'A (IRE) (Green Desert (USA))
7295[5] 8293[9]

Quarry Bay (IRE) *William Knight* a41
2 b g Ivawood(IRE) Sandbox Two (IRE) (Foxhound (USA))
9415[13]

Quarry Beach *Henry Candy* a74 75
3 b f Dutch Art Free Offer (Generous (IRE))
4562[2] 5350[2] 5863[5] 6418[2] 7165[3] 7460[2] 8030[7] 8807[3]

Quarrystreetmagic (IRE)
Brian Meehan 35
2 b c Zebedee Another World (GER) (Night Shift (USA))
4394[11] 4993[9] 5501[9] 6053[9] 6313[12]

Quarterback (GER) *Yvonne Durant* a83 86
7 b h American Post Quebra (GER) (Surumu (GER))
6524a[10] 7498a[9]

Quartier Francais (USA)
A R Al Rayhi a85 74
5 br h Street Cry(IRE) Divine Dixie (USA) (Dixieland Band (USA))
573a[2]

Quarto Cavallo *Adam West* a46 48
5 b m Epaulette(AUS) Oriental Romance (IRE) (Elusive City (USA))
137[8] 437[9] 2190[12] 2734[12] 3410[5] 4180[4] 4657[12] 5092[U] 5431[7] 5806[13] 6181[12]

Quayside *S Seemar* a96 93
4 ch g Harbour Watch(IRE) Fantacise (Pivotal)
843a[8]

Quduraat *Michael Appleby* a59 45
3 ch f Teofilo(IRE) Ejadah (IRE) (Clodovil (IRE))
134[5] 409[7] 3213[11] 4567[13] 5247[12] 5864[2] 7371[9]

Que Amoro (IRE) *Michael Dods* a75 102
3 b f Es Que Love(IRE) Onomatomania (USA) (Mr Greeley (USA))
1762[10] 4128[3]◆ 4294[4] (5399) (6476) 7401[2]

Queen (FR) *Mme Pia Brandt* 106
3 b f Kingman Pride (FR) (Peintre Celebre (USA))
6775a[2] 7478a[2] 8094[2]

Queen Aya *Ed Walker* a55 64
2 ch f Helmet(AUS) Show Aya (IRE) (Showcasing)
3689[6] 4448[6] 4993[3] 6158[4] 6667[4] 7556[7]

Queen Constantine (GER)
William Jarvis a83 81
3 b f Holy Roman Emperor(IRE) Quilita (GER) (Lomitas)
2253[2]◆ 3260[6] 4739[2] 5982[2] 7452[4] (9177) 9418[9]

Queen Daenerys (IRE)
Roger Varian 103
2 b f Frankel Song To Remember (USA) (Storm Cat (USA))
5366[2] (7461) 8091[6]

Queendara (FR) *D Guillemin* a70 93
3 b f Kendargent(FR) Dance In The Park (FR) (Walk In The Park (IRE))
2029a[3] 3676a[6]

Queen Emily *Conor Dore* 15
3 b f Toronado(IRE) Daysiwaay (IRE) (Daylami (IRE))
2417[6] 2901[10]

Queen Flawless (FR) *J-P Dubois* 69
3 gr f Makfi Flawless (FR) (Invincible Spirit (IRE))
6486a[6]

Queen Gamrah *Mark Johnston* a87 62
2 b f Toronado(IRE) Rainbow's Edge (Rainbow Quest (USA))
8458[6] (8651) (9097)◆ 9608[2]

Queen Jo Jo *Kevin Ryan* 102
3 br f Gregorian(IRE) River Song (USA) (Siphon (BRZ))
1751[5] (2627)◆ 3557a[3]

Queen Josephine (GER) *M Figge* a76 92
3 b f Soldier Hollow Quintessa (GER) (Shirocco (GER))
8153a[4]

Queen Kahlua *H-F Devin* 74
2 b f Kingman Kahlua Kiss (Mister Baileys)
4947a[2]

Queen Mia (IRE) *Declan Carroll* a52 47
3 ch f Famous Name Agnetha (GER) (Big Shuffle (USA))
8819[2]◆ 9111[5]◆ 9282[3] 9544[7]

Queen Monaco (IRE) *H Al Alawi* a67 32
3 b f Bungle Inthejungle My Uptown Girl (Dubai Destination (USA))
48a[7]

Queen Morny (FR) *H-A Pantall* a75 61
3 gr f Kendargent(FR) Tres Americanqueen (FR) (American Post)
2390a[8] 3028a[5]

Queen Moya (IRE) *Nigel Tinkler* a34 37
2 b f Cappella Sansevero Midnight Muscida (IRE) (Kodiac)
3411[8] 3812[11] 4778[7] 9515[11]

Queen Of All *Richard Hughes* a75
2 b f Mukhadram Dhuyoof (IRE) (Sinndar (IRE))
(9211)

Queen Of Bradgate *Ivan Furtado* a13 24
3 b f Compton Place Russian Ruby (FR) (Vettori (IRE))
3256[9] 5031[11] 5890[7]

Queen Of Burgundy
Christine Dunnett a77 81
3 b f Lethal Force(IRE) Empress Adelaide (Pivotal)
1855[7] (3189) 3516[2] 4297[7] 4660[2] 5191[4] 5647[3] (6326) 7351[4] 7828[17]

Queen Of Clubs *Roger Charlton* a56 22
2 b f Gleneagles(IRE) Fondly (IRE) (Dansili)
5772[15] 8913[7] 9159[8] 9630[11]

Queen Of Desire (IRE)
Roger Varian a68 96
4 b m Dubawi(IRE) Beyond Desire (Invincible Spirit (IRE))
(1913)◆ 2409[11] 4101[3] 4891[6] 6351[17] 6534[4]

Queen Of Kalahari *Les Eyre* a72 53
4 b m Lethal Force(IRE) Aromatherapy (Oasis Dream)
25[4] 742[7] 1093[8] 2532[2] 3007[2] 3475[2] (3716) 5147[4] 5517[8] 6546[5] (7389) (7632) (8071) 8924[3] (9223)◆

Queen Of Mayfair *John Gosden* a65 54
3 b f Dubawi(IRE) Wonder Why (GER) (Tiger Hill (IRE))
2249[7]

Queen Of Paris *William Knight* a69 41
4 b m Champs Elysees Beldarian (IRE) (Last Tycoon)
262[4] 619[6] 946[4] 1497[8] 2359[10]

Queen Of Rock (IRE) *Philip Kirby* a35 17
2 b f Ruler Of The World(IRE) Lady Gibraltar (Rock Of Gibraltar (IRE))
7046[10] 7627[12] 8525[9] 9330[4]

Queen Of Silca *Mick Channon* a61 63
2 b f Kingman Silca Chiave (Pivotal)
6911[7] 7393[9] 7832[10] 9665[3]

Queen Of Style (IRE) *Rod Collet* a51 56
4 gr m Style Vendome(FR) Emouna Queen (IRE) (Indian Ridge (IRE))
2170a[12]

Queenoftheclyde (IRE) *K R Burke* a56 58
2 ch f Dandy Man(IRE) Coconut Kisses (Bahamian Bounty)
2579[6] 3689[7] 4992[7] (6182) 6667[2] 7208[6] 7853[5] 8452[7]

Queen Of The Sea (IRE)
Saeed bin Suroor a70
2 b f Sea The Stars(IRE) Knyazhna (IRE) (Montjeu (IRE))
4245[3]

Queen Of Time *Henry Candy* a97 100
5 b m Harbour Watch(IRE) Black Belt Shopper (IRE) (Desert Prince (IRE))
1941[9] 2404[5] 2776[5] 3374[3] 4332[6] (4930) 6082[6] 6992a[3] 7694[24]

Queen Penn *Richard Fahey* a77 80
4 gr m Dark Angel(IRE) The Manx Touch (IRE) (Petardia)
1457[4] 2252[5] 3323[3] 3843[2] 4278[4] 5218[4] 6170[2]

Queen Power (IRE)
Sir Michael Stoute 103
3 ch f Shamardal(USA) Princess Serena (USA) (Unbridled's Song (USA))
2268[2] (2831) 4014[4] 6467[4]

Queen Salamah (IRE)
Richard Spencer 60
2 b f No Nay Never(USA) Cape Jasmine (IRE) (Danehill (USA))
5250[4] 5745[10] 6793[P] (Dead)

Queens Blade *Tim Easterby* a59 57
2 b f Heeraat(IRE) Blades Princess (Needwood Blade)
2586[4] 2820[5] 3469[9] 4985[5] 5279[6] 5618[7] (5968) (6539) (7329) 8430[10] 8506[4]

Queens Care (IRE) *Julie Camacho* a41 56
4 b m Born To Sea(IRE) Athlumney Dancer (Shareef Dancer (USA))
123[8]

Queen's Course (IRE)
William Haggas a63
2 b f Gleneagles(IRE) Dingle View (IRE) (Mujadil (USA))
9008[5] 9347[4]

Queen's Favour *Sir Michael Stoute* a63 46
2 b f Muhaarar Queen's Best (King's Best (USA))
7695[13] 8453[6]

Queens Gift (IRE) *Michael Dods* a81 101
4 b m Canford Cliffs(IRE) Jawaaneb (USA) (Kingmambo (USA))
2588[8] 3201[2] 3815[10] (4595) (4986) 6698[2] 7073[2]

Queen's Order *Kevin Ryan* 88
2 b f Delegator Kirunavaara (IRE) (Galileo (IRE))
5472[2]◆ (6254) 6791a[8] 7400[12]

Queens Road (IRE) *Bill Turner* a54 50
2 b f Make Believe Okba (USA) (Diesis)
1556[4] 7308[8] 7786[8] 8750[2]

Queens Royale *Michael Appleby* a65 72
5 b m Stimulation(IRE) Sofia Royale (Royal Applause)
45[3] 233[9] 2585[10] 3146[9]

Queen's Sargent (FR) *Kevin Ryan* a56 86
4 gr g Kendargent(FR) Queen's Conquer (King's Best (USA))
1457[3] 2526[10] 3632[4] 4320[7] 5173[9] 5692[2] (6677) 7362[8] 8101[17] 8918[11]

Queen's Soldier (GER)
Andrew Balding a51 70
3 b g Soldier Hollow Queen Mum (GER) (Manduro (GER))
1510[5] 2407[3] 3418[3] 3797[3] 4547[2] 5497[3] 6202[2] (6505)

Queen's Way (FR) *J-L Guillochon*
3 gr f Stormy River(FR) Marie Du Lys (FR) (Polish Summer)
993a[11]

Queen Tomyris *William Jarvis* a54
4 b m Declaration Of War(USA) Caphene (Sakhee (USA))
6[9]

Quel Destin (FR) *Paul Nicholls* a50 73
4 ch g Muhtathir High Destiny (FR) (High Yield (USA))
8246[3]

Quemonda *Ken Cunningham-Brown* a61 53
3 ch f Mount Nelson Quesada (IRE) (Peintre Celebre (USA))
1142[10] 1495[7] 2340[12] *(6279)* ***6723[4]***

Quench Dolly *John Gallagher* a58 82
5 gr m Hellvelyn Hollybell (Beveled (USA))
1892[10] 2403[7] 3636[10] **4105[3]** 5180[7] 7564[4] 7894[17] 8262[10] 8660[3]

Que Quieres (USA) *Simon Dow* a58
3 b g Bernardini(USA) Christine Daae (USA) (Giant's Causeway (USA))
7518[8] 8292[2] 9049[3] ***(9201)*** *9412[4]*

Quercus (IRE) *Ann Duffield* 63
2 b g Nayef(USA) Dufoof (IRE) (Shamardal (USA))
6970[7] 7285[6] 7698[5]

Questionare *John Gosden* a76 98
3 b g Galileo(IRE) Dream Peace (IRE) (Dansili)
(1019) 2258[2] **3152[2]** 4017[14]

Question Of Faith *Martin Todhunter* a51 74
8 b m Yeats(IRE) Anastasia Storm (Mozart (IRE))
2185[9] 3294[8] **4056[4]** 4491[5] 4983[8] 5241[4] 5487[5] 5727[5] 6827[7] 7053[4]

Quest The Moon (GER)
Frau S Steinberg 110
3 b c Sea The Moon(GER) Questabella (GER) (Rock Of Gibraltar (IRE))
2310a[2] **(3120a)** 4707a[4] **5483a[3] 7253a[5]**

Quevillon (FR) *S Cerulis* a76 71
5 ch g Siyouni(FR) Princess Roseburg (USA) (Johannesburg (USA))
7676a[4]

Quian (GER) *P Schiergen* 85
3 rg c Mastercraftsman(IRE) Quiana (GER) (Monsun (GER))
2310a[8] 3674a[10]

Quick *Richard Hannon* 89
3 b f Olympic Glory(IRE) The Giving Tree (IRE) (Rock Of Gibraltar (IRE))
(1740) 2268[9] 3696[2] 4898[7] 6081[7] (6759) **7618[2]**

Quick Breath *Jonathan Portman* a89 89
4 b g Bated Breath Shy Appeal (IRE) (Barathea (IRE))
1714[2] 2065[3] 2611[11] *3147[6] (3462)* 4061[2] ***4786[2]*** 5319[5] **5626[2]** *6318[4] 6968[3] 7517[7] 8289[6]*

Quick Look *Michael Easterby* a70 93
6 b g Kheleyf(USA) Weqaar (USA) (Red Ransom (USA))
1459[13] 2201[11] 2775[11] 3480[6] **(3846)** 8636[9]

Quickly Does It *Brian Ellison* a21 17
3 b f Havana Gold(IRE) Mylington Maid (Dubai Destination (USA))
6551[5] 7065[12]

Quick Monet (IRE) *Shaun Harris* a52 42
6 b g Excellent Art Clinging Vine (USA) (Fusaichi Pegasus (USA))
(3304) *3996[3]* 5247[8] *6546[8] 7550[6]* ***(8547)*** *8757[3] 9160[9]*

Quick Recap (IRE) *Tom Dascombe* a73 77
2 ch f No Nay Never(USA) Princess Patsky (USA) (Mr Greeley (USA))
7063[4]◆ **7644[2]** *8316[2]*

Quick Recovery *Jim Boyle* a58 56
4 gr m Lethal Force(IRE) Lisiere (IRE) (Excellent Art)
1265[5] 1820[9] 3020[5] 4115[8] 4776[4] *5264[3] 6284[5] 6888[8] 7606[10] 8689[4] 8915[2] 8998[10]*

Quicksand (IRE) *Hughie Morrison* a81 86
4 ch m Footstepsinthesand Miss Bellbird (IRE) (Danehill (USA))
2399[3] 3269[4] 5305[6] 6509[2] 7395[7]

Quicksilver *Ed Walker* a58 60
3 b f Coach House(IRE) Poulaine Bleue (Bertolini (USA))
137[5] 406[4]

Quickstep Lady *Andrew Balding* 69
2 b f Australia Strictly Dancing (IRE) (Danehill Dancer (IRE))
6154[7] **6906[5]**

Quickthorn *Hughie Morrison* 77
2 b c Nathaniel(IRE) Daffydowndilly (Oasis Dream)
8028[9] **8461[6]**

Quiet Endeavour (IRE)
George Baker a84 86
3 b g Society Rock(IRE) My Eurydice (Exceed And Excel (AUS))
806[5] 989[4] ***1199a[6]*** 1920[10] 2525[7] 3865[19] *7187[6]* 7564[7] *8289[9] 8691[6]*

Quiet Moment (IRE)
Maurice Barnes a32 45
5 b m Dandy Man(IRE) Easee On (IRE) (Hawk Wing (USA))
2012[12] 2328[7] 2963[9] **3158[4]** 3681[8] 3720[8]

Quiet Night (IRE) *Charles Hills* a33
2 b f Dark Angel(IRE) Pindrop (Exceed And Excel (AUS))
9347[10]

Quiet Note *Saeed bin Suroor* 71
3 b f Invincible Spirit(IRE) Lady Marian (GER) (Nayef (USA))
2919[7] 3517[9]

Quiet Place (IRE) *Saeed bin Suroor* a76 75
2 b f Kodiac Need You Now (IRE) (Kheleyf (USA))
2020[2]◆ 2706[2] ***3441[2]*** *4191[3]*

Quiet Shy (FR) *Michael Scudamore* a36 40
4 b m Youmzain(IRE) Quiet Queen (Sulamani (IRE))
2771[7] 3553[11] 4326[8] 5499[11]

Quiet Word (FR) *Archie Watson* a48 37
2 b f Dandy Man(IRE) Angel Spirit (IRE) (Invincible Spirit (IRE))
2579[7] ***8250[5]*** *8899[8] 9394[10]*

Quila Saeda (GER) *Michael Appleby* a58
5 b m Campanologist(USA) Quirigua (Intikhab (USA))
7395 ***1525[3]*** *1858[6]*

Quimerico *John Best* a70 39
2 b g Due Diligence(USA) Peyto Princess (Bold Arrangement)
4798[9] *8012[9]* ***8494[5]***

Quindio (FR) *X Thomas-Demeaulte* a88 102
3 b g Evasive Desilusion (FR) (Dyhim Diamond (IRE))
2027a[2] 3029a[6]

Quintada *Mark Johnston* a79 84
3 b f Leroidesanimaux(BRZ) Quiza Quiza Quiza (Golden Snake (USA))
2768[3] 3099[3] **(5039)**◆ 5614[11] 6230[5] *6736[3]* **(7466)** *8608[8]*

Quintarelli (GER) *Dr A Bolte* 75
4 b h Campanologist(USA) Quiaba (GER) (Big Shuffle (USA))
2666a[11]

Quirky Gertie (IRE) *Mick Channon* 80
3 b f Fast Company(IRE) Acushladear (IRE) (Tagula (IRE))
2623[5] 3574[3] 4129[2] (5428) 5575[2] 6286[5] **7762[2]** 8007[7]

Quita *Waldemar Hickst* 82
3 b f Footstepsinthesand Quiania (IRE) (Dansili)
8804a[5]

Quite Subunctious (IRE)
Keith Henry Clarke a55 54
4 b m Rip Van Winkle(IRE) Beyond The Sea (IRE) (Fasliyev (USA))
602[2] *782[10]*

Quixote (GER) *James Unett* a52 57
9 b h Pivotal Quebrada (IRE) (Devil's Bag (USA))
2015[10] **3149[8]** 3649[11] 7145[6] 7527[8]

Quizical (IRE) *Ms Sheila Lavery* 98
4 b g Roderic O'Connor(IRE) Twenty Questions (Kyllachy)
1308a[11] 1531a[7] **5535a[3]** 5711a[6] 6693a[8] 7934a[7]

Quloob *Gary Moore* a65 95
5 b g New Approach(IRE) Jadhwah (Nayef (USA))
2143[5] **5368[4] 6848[3]** 7866[4]

Quote *A P O'Brien* a93 100
3 b f Galileo(IRE) Sasuela (GER) (Dashing Blade)
8368a[5] **8784a[2]** *9002[7]*

Quoteline Direct *Micky Hammond* a62 68
6 ch g Sir Percy Queen's Pudding (IRE) (Royal Applause)
1659[9] **2291[4]** 3053[3]◆ 3547[8] 4446[7] 4762[4] 5024[4] 5817[4] 6456[6] 7545[3] *8870[3] 9391[10]*

Qutob (IRE) *Charles Hills* a88 90
3 b g Acclamation When Not Iff (IRE) (Iffraaj)
1886[3] 2405[2] 3058[2] *(4590)* **(5195)**

Raa Atoll *Luke Comer* 110
4 b h Sea The Stars(IRE) Meetyouthere (IRE) (Sadler's Wells (USA))
(2666a) 3561a[6] 4351a[3]

Raabeh *Brian Meehan* 48
2 b g Showcasing Twinkle Twinkle (Exceed And Excel (AUS))
4558[9]

Raadea *Marcus Tregoning* 30
2 ch g Showcasing Dream Melody (Selkirk (USA))
4252[8]

Raaeb (IRE) *Saeed bin Suroor* a89 87
2 ch c Raven's Pass(USA) Kalaatah (USA) (Dynaformer (USA))
(7151)◆ 7899[2] ***(8418)*** *9364[4]*

Raaeq (IRE) *Brian Meehan* 88
2 b c Kingman Jamaayel (Shamardal (USA))
6845[2] **(7458)**

Raafid *A R Al Rayhi* a87 96
6 b g Shamardal(USA) Time Away (IRE) (Darshaan)
170a[11]

Raahy *George Scott* a81 94
2 b g Brazen Beau(AUS) Moonlight Mystery (Pivotal)
3335[3] 3943[2] (4373)◆ **5542[6]** 6375[6] 7182[5] *7546[2]*

Raajin *Charles Hills* a69
2 b g Raven's Pass(USA) Atab (IRE) (New Approach (IRE))
8011[4]

Raakib Alhawa (IRE)
David Simcock 109
3 b c Kingman Starlet (IRE) (Sea The Stars (IRE))
3026[7] 3814[5] **(6466)** 7890[5]

Raasel *Marcus Tregoning* 82
2 ch c Showcasing Dubai Affair (Dubawi (IRE))
(8243)◆ 8723[3]

Raashdy (IRE) *Sam England* a48 46
6 b g Intikhab(USA) Maghya (IRE) (Mujahid (USA))
481[6] **910[4]** 1666[6] *1988[7] 2595[7] 5001[4] 7415[6]*

Raatea *Marcus Tregoning* a76 84
2 b c Invincible Spirit(IRE) Darajaat (USA) (Elusive Quality (USA))
6640[3]◆ **7410[6]** *8455[2]*

Raayan (USA) *A R Al Rayhi* a65 59
3 ch c Animal Kingdom(USA) Tale Of The Fox (CAN) (Tale Of The Cat (USA))
394a[8] **570a[6]**

Race Day (IRE) *Saeed bin Suroor* a101 100
6 ch g Dubawi(IRE) Nadia (Nashwan (USA))
49a[10] **285a[2]** 640a[8]

Race For Fame (IRE) *S Smrczek* a46 51
8 b g Meshaheer(USA) Rocky Mixa (FR) (Rock Of Gibraltar (IRE))
4960a[7]

Rachel Wall (IRE) *Henry Candy* 64
2 b f Kodiac Anne Bonney (Jade Robbery (USA))
4337[4]

Rachel Zane (IRE) *Hugo Palmer* a57 67
3 b f Sea The Moon(GER) Mark Of An Angel (IRE) (Mark Of Esteem (IRE))
2210[4] 2919[10] **3665[5]**

Rachmaninov (USA) *Hugo Palmer* a58
2 b c Mizzen Mast(USA) Solo Piano (USA) (Empire Maker (USA))
6718[6]

Racing History (IRE)
Saeed bin Suroor 112
7 b h Pivotal Gonbarda (GER) (Lando (GER))
51a[2] 395a[3] 844a[2] **1113a[2]** 1446a[7]

Racquet *Ruth Carr* a48 45
6 br g Pastoral Pursuits Billie Jean (Bertolini (USA))
1883[7] 2189[7] 2527[5] 2958[14] **3518[3]** 3723[8] 3933[8] 5393[4] 5765[10] 6174[13] 7286[4]◆ 7590[7]

Radio Source (IRE) *Tim Easterby* a56 63
4 ch g Raven's Pass(USA) Roshanak (IRE) (Spinning World (USA))
2116[12]

Radja (FR) *V Sartori* a77 71
4 bb h Rajsaman(FR) Gone South (IRE) (Zamindar (USA))
3715a[2]

Radjash *Declan Carroll* a59 59
5 b g Shamardal(USA) White Moonstone (USA) (Dynaformer (USA))
3158[5] **5559[2] 5918[2]** 6275[3] 6628[5]

Raffle King (IRE) *Julia Brooke* a53 48
5 b g Kodiac Tap The Dot (IRE) (Sharp Humor (USA))
1987[4] 2958[7] 3518[8] 3975[8] 4586[13] *7468[4] 7628[3] 7962[11]*

Raffle Prize (IRE) *Mark Johnston* 114
2 ch f Slade Power(IRE) Summer Fete (IRE) (Pivotal)
2836[2]◆ (3071)◆ (3983) (4883) **6264a[2]** 7692[2]

Raflot (USA) *Gary Moore* a81 80
3 b g Elusive Quality(USA) Viva Rafaela (BRZ) (Know Heights (IRE))
7865[U]

Raging Bull (FR) *Chad C Brown* 113
4 b h Dark Angel(IRE) Rosa Bonheur (USA) (Mr Greeley (USA))
5977a[2] 7225a[3]

Ragnar *Roger Charlton* a77 87
3 b g Toronado(IRE) Inner Sea (USA) (Henrythenavigator (USA))
723[2]◆ (1165)◆ 1824[8] 2470[4] **(3808)**

Ragstone Cowboy (IRE)
Gary Moore a44 64
3 b g Slade Power(IRE) Three Decades (IRE) (Invincible Spirit (IRE))
2204[15] 3354[8] 4794[4] 5784[3] (6202) *7817[10]* **8205[2]**

Ragstone View (IRE) *Rod Millman* a68 80
4 b g Requinto(IRE) Highland Miss (USA) (Theatrical (IRE))
1561[10] 2365[2] 2994[2] *4249[6]* **(4838)** 5343[4] 5776[8] 6803[4]

Ragtime Sally *Harry Dunlop* a48 63
2 b f Iffraaj Honky Tonk Sally (Dansili)
8093[7] 8759[10] *9156[5]*

Raha *Julia Feilden* 65
3 b f Mukhadram Cefira (USA) (Distant View (USA))
2023[12] **2762[6]** 3603[8] 4070[5] 5062[3] 5724[5]

Raheeb (IRE) *Owen Burrows* a80 67
3 b f Kodiac Dream Date (IRE) (Oasis Dream)
2319[12] 4595[8]

Raheen House (IRE)
William Haggas 114
5 b g Sea The Stars(IRE) Jumooh (Monsun (GER))
3864[2] **4933[3]** 6473[9] 8134a[6] 8803a[13]

Raheeq *Roger Varian* 89
2 b f Muhaarar Shimah (USA) (Storm Cat (USA))
(4233)◆

Rahmah (IRE) *Geoffrey Deacon* a63 64
7 b g Vale Of York(IRE) Sweet Home Alabama (IRE) (Desert Prince (IRE))
2720[12] *6077[12]* ***6843[12]***

Raihaan (IRE) *Ed Dunlop* a50
3 ch g Intello(GER) Masaafat (Act One)
9012[11]

Rail Dancer *Shaun Keightley* a75 71
7 b g Rail Link Mara Dancer (Shareef Dancer (USA))
3213 560[5] 923[2] 1235[8] ***(2595)*** (2738) 4220[6] *4792[10] 5631[7] 8656[6] 9067[10] 9303[14]*

Railport Dolly *David Barron* a73 80
4 b m Rail Link Polly Adler (Fantastic Light (USA))
2822[6] (3267) 4653[2] 5474[3] 6230[3] 7379[7]◆ **7907[2]** 8515[6] *9096[8] 9278[3] 9496[6]*

Rainbow Charlie *Mrs A Corson* 17
8 b g Rainbow High Natacha Rostow (Pursuit Of Love)
2003a[7] **2502a[4]** 4687a[6] 6010a[7]

Rainbow Dreamer *Alan King* a104 92
6 b g Aqlaam Zamhrear (Singspiel (IRE))
(704) 6958[8] 8114[21] 8726[2] ***(9419)***

Rainbow Girl (IRE) *Richard Hannon* a60 72
3 b f Kodiac Toppled (IRE) (Pivotal)
1336[4] *2212[6]*

Rainbow Heart (IRE)
William Haggas a92 96
3 bb f Born To Sea(IRE) Sea Of Heartbreak (IRE) (Rock Of Gibraltar (IRE))
1939[3] *4332[7]*

Rainbow Jazz (IRE) *Adam West* a68 54
4 b g Red Jazz(USA) Let's Pretend (Rainbow Quest (USA))
135[9] *1183[14] 1525[6]* 3941[11] 4475[4] 4547[7] 5049[10] 5570[8] *5653[4] 6152[3]*

Rainbow Jet (IRE) *John Mackie* 76
2 b f Dream Ahead(USA) Star Jet (IRE) (Teofilo (IRE))
5170[10] 5895[5] 6918[2] **7826[2]**

Rainbow Lad (IRE) *Michael Appleby* a54 50
6 b g Lilbourne Lad(IRE) Carmona (Rainbow Quest (USA))
100[10]◆ 457[6] ***789[3]*** 2003a[2] (2502a)

Rainbow Moonstone (IRE)
Joseph Patrick O'Brien 94
3 b f Holy Roman Emperor(IRE) Moonstone Magic (Trade Fair)
1601a[8] **2156a[4]** 2605a[4]

Rainbow Spirit *Ed Dunlop* a44 48
3 b f Charm Spirit(IRE) Navajo Rainbow (Rainbow Quest (USA))
2253[11] 3528[9] *6723[12]*

Raincall *Henry Candy* a65 83
4 b m Pivotal Lone Rock (AUS) (Fastnet Rock (AUS))
2623[4]◆ (3089) 4227[4] (6120)◆ **7401[10] 8115[6]**

Rain Cap *Mick Channon* a49 55
2 b g Fountain Of Youth(IRE) Rough Courte (IRE) (Clodovil (IRE))
3008[7] 3257[8] 3812[13] **(4075)** 5296[9] 5781[5] *5886[6]*

Raining Fire (IRE) *James Fanshawe* a78 58
3 ch g Kitten's Joy(USA) Flame Of Hestia (IRE) (Giant's Causeway (USA))
2795[9] *8351[6]* ***8671[2]***

Rain Prancer (IRE) *Richard Spencer* 63
2 b g Sir Prancealot(IRE) Singingintherain (IRE) (Kyllachy)
8280[3]

Rains Of Castamere *Mick Channon* a61 41
2 ch g Harbour Watch(IRE) Shrimpton (Cadeaux Genereux)
7981[9] *8912[6]* ***(9127)***

Raise A Billion *Alan Berry* 28
8 b g Major Cadeaux Romantic Destiny (Dubai Destination (USA))
4514[4] 4694[13] 5491[8] 6574[12] 7487[9] 7761[8] 8632[12]

Raise A Little Joy *J R Jenkins* a40 44
4 b m Pastoral Pursuits Ray Of Joy (Tobougg (IRE))
3475[14] ***4026[5]*** 4378[16] **5822[5]** 6199[5]

Raise You (IRE) *Andrew Balding* 108
3 ch c Lope De Vega(IRE) Hikari (IRE) (Galileo (IRE))
(1755) **(2833)** 3390a[10] **5950[3]**

Raising Sand *Jamie Osborne* a94 114
7 b g Oasis Dream Balalaika (Sadler's Wells (USA))
2609[4] 3987[3] **(5413)** 6956[3] 7891[16] 8334[9]

Rajan *Tom Clover* a23 45
2 b c Fountain Of Youth(IRE) Dayville (USA) (Dayjur (USA))
3165[10] *7605[8]*

Rajapur *David Thompson* a34 47
6 rg g Dalakhani(IRE) A Beautiful Mind (GER) (Winged Love (IRE))
208[13] ***(1068)*** *1718[10] 2196[9]* 4435[12]

Rajguru *Tom Clover* a71
2 ch c Dutch Art Gakalina (IRE) (Galileo (IRE))
5314[14] ***5887[2]*** *6344[4] 8850[9] 9414[2]*

Rajinsky (IRE) *Tom Dascombe* a94 87
3 b g Zoffany(IRE) Pink Moon (IRE) (Namid)
(8411)◆ *9096[4]*◆ ***(9288)***

Rajman *Tom Clover* a65 40
3 ch c Zoffany(IRE) Mutheera (Oasis Dream)
79[5] (437) ***1141[3]*** *1358[11]* 5092[9] *7576[6] 8698[8] (9298) 9629[5]*

Rakan *D K Weld* 101
3 b c Sea The Stars(IRE) Tarfasha (IRE) (Teofilo (IRE))
2662a[4] 4414a[8]

Rakassah (IRE) *Richard Hughes* a74 62
2 ch f Night Of Thunder(IRE) Elegant Peace (IRE) (Intense Focus (USA))
6928[5] 7539[4] ***8218[3]***

Rakastava (IRE) *Mick Channon* a64 54
3 b g Clodovil(IRE) Shemissa (IRE) (Fairy King (USA))
621[4] **908[2]** *1139[5]* 2101[7] *2965[8]* 3478[8] 3839[11] 4180[13]

Rakematiz *Brett Johnson* a77 73
5 ch g Pivotal Regal Velvet (Halling (USA))
473[3] ***(876)*** *1292[6]* 4453[7] 5747[7] 7125[9] *9202[14]*

Rake's Progress *Heather Main* a82 84
5 b g Sir Percy Cartoon (Danehill Dancer (IRE))
2104[11] 2793[6] (3633) 4241[10] 6218[5] **(8032)** 8396[5] 8725[10]

Raksha (IRE) *David O'Meara* 58
3 b f Dandy Man(IRE) Violet Lashes (USA) (Badge Of Silver (USA))
3157[4] **3416[3]** 4129[8] 4508[6] 5041[7] 5559[18]

Rally Driver *Mick Channon* 47
2 b g Gregorian(IRE) Exentricity (Paco Boy (IRE))
7623[7] **7983[4]** 8244[10]

Ralphy Boy Two (IRE)
Alistair Whillans 72
2 b g Gutaifan(IRE) St Athan (Authorized (IRE))
4237[6] 4688[7] 5934[2] **(6625)** 7064[8] **7827[2]**◆

Ramatuelle *Laura Mongan* a52 58
3 ch f Champs Elysees Florentia (Medicean)
3204[10] 4771[5] 5795[3]◆ *6279[6]* 7025[3] **(7270)** *8854[9] 9207[8]*

Rambaldi (IRE) *Marco Botti* a70 73
3 b g Rip Van Winkle(IRE) Shorana (IRE) (Holy Roman Emperor (IRE))
1285[4] 1720[4] **(2933) 4562[3]** *6075[5] 7773[8] 8549[8]*

Ramblow *Alexandra Dunn* a45 46
6 b m Notnowcato Nsx (Roi Danzig (USA))
80[8] 1354[6] 1683[8] 1967[14] 3038[7] **5016[6]** 5803[6] **5842[3]** 6305[7] *8416[11] 8756[9] 8915[6] 9403[10]*

Ramesses *Richard Fahey* 79
3 b g Invincible Spirit(IRE) Songbird (IRE) (Danehill Dancer (IRE))
(2114) 2896[3] 3683[5] 4552[4] **(4980)** 5459[5] 6015[5] 6700[9] 8181[7]

Rampant Lion (IRE) *William Jarvis* a90 83
4 ch g Bahamian Bounty Mamma Morton (IRE) (Elnadim (USA))
(922) 1413[8] 1912[8] 2480[7] *2966[5]* 4300[6] 4887[8] 5574[2] 5863[4] *6841[9]* 7364[5] *(8320)*

Ramsbury *Charlie Fellowes* a90
4 b g Dansili Disco Volante (Sadler's Wells (USA))
242[2] *2321[5]*

Ramsha (IRE) *Mark Johnston* a38 60
2 ch f Raven's Pass(USA) Bishara (USA) (Dubawi (IRE))
7832[11] **8338[7]**

Ranch Hand *Andrew Balding* a89 104
3 b g Dunaden(FR) Victoria Montoya (High Chaparral (IRE))
(1365)◆ (2195)◆ 2619[5] 4845[5] **(6955)** 8114[15]

Rangali Island (IRE) *David Simcock* a85 73
3 b c Camacho Tender Surprise (Doyen (IRE))
2395[5] *8122[4]*◆ ***(8809)***◆ *9304[9]*

Rangefield Express (IRE)
Geoffrey Harker a54 52
3 b g Born To Sea(IRE) Bogini (IRE) (Holy Roman Emperor (IRE))
4010[4] 4731[7] 5215[10] 5771[10] 5914[12] *6944[4] 7417[4] 7824[7]* ***(8720)***◆ *9335[9] 9572[5]*

Rannan (FR) *R Martens* a69 81
4 b h Style Vendome(FR) Footsteppy (IRE) (Footstepsinthesand)
5035a[7] 6521a[10]

Ransomed Dreams (USA)
Ed Walker a53 63
3 bb g Arch(USA) Dark Sky (USA) (Storm Cat (USA))
1979[7] **3052[7]**

Rantan (IRE) *Paul Midgley* a49 61
6 b g Kodiac Peace Talks (Pivotal)
1162[7]◆ 1403[6] 2183[14]

Rapid Applause *Michael Easterby* a91 83
7 b g Royal Applause Madam Ninette (Mark Of Esteem (IRE))
6676[14] 7431[9] 7541[5] 8900[8]

Rapidash *Richard Hannon* a56 66
2 b f Dark Angel(IRE) Lottie Dod (IRE) (Invincible Spirit (IRE))
6415[7] 6911[6] 7160[7] 9401[6]

Rapid Reaction (IRE) *J F Grogan* a88 97
4 ch m Shamardal(USA) Bratislava (Dr Fong (USA))
2880a[5] 3557a[6] 3818a[5] 4313a[3] 5222a[9] 5325a[12] 6648a[2] 8328a[11]

Rapid Rise (IRE) *Milton Bradley* a51 40
5 b g Fast Company(IRE) French Doll (IRE) (Titus Livius (FR))
243[2] (530) 887[6] 1026[5] 1215[7] 1731[10] 2286[6] 3352[10]

Rapid Russo *Michael Dods* 79
2 b g Coach House(IRE) Rapid Recruit (IRE) (Fast Company (IRE))
4624[4] 5388[7] (6011) 7399[15] 8631[7]

Rapsody (FR) *E Libaud* 19
3 b f Charm Spirit(IRE) Commute (Rail Link)
3028a[12]

Rapture (FR) *Archie Watson* a80 70
3 ch f Pivotal Rosa Bonheur (USA) (Mr Greeley (USA))
4597[5] 5268[3] 5808[5] 7237[8] (7843) 8496[10]

Raquelle (IRE) *Tim Easterby* a25 47
3 b f Requinto(IRE) Zuccini Wind (IRE) (Revoque (IRE))
1982[13] 2300[6] 2908[3] 3417[9] 4212[4] 4493[6]

Rare (IRE) *Archie Watson* a71 76
4 b m Galileo(IRE) Miarixa (FR) (Linamix (FR))
262[2]◆ 457[4] 619[12]

Rare Groove (IRE) *Jedd O'Keeffe* a101 105
4 ch h Lope De Vega(IRE) Ascot Lady (IRE) (Spinning World (USA))
1559[3] (2435) 2742[10] 4381[2] 5183[5] 6355[2]◆

Rare Kylla (IRE) *Peter Fahey* 55
2 b f Kyllachy Rare Ransom (Oasis Dream)
7247a[19]

Rasaasy (IRE) *Anthony Carson* a81
3 b g Cape Cross(IRE) Drops (IRE) (Kingmambo (USA))
(9543)◆

Raselasad (IRE) *Tracy Waggott* 94
5 b g Acclamation Wajaha (IRE) (Haafhd)
1502[2] 1944[5] 2419[13] 3308[3] 4511[2] 6014[2]

Rashdan (FR) *Iain Jardine* a83 77
4 b g Big Bad Bob(IRE) On Fair Stage (IRE) (Sadler's Wells (USA))
1518[7] 1971[3] 3973[8] 4383[5] 5489[6]◆ 6460[9] 6940[11] 7489[9]

Rasheeq (IRE) *Mohamed Moubarak* a71 82
6 b g Vale Of York(IRE) Limber Up (IRE) (Dansili)
1521[3] 1973[5] 2194[4] (2580) 2846[9] 3549[4] (4227) 5395[10]

Rasima *Roger Varian* a107 95
4 gr m Iffraaj Raushan (IRE) (Dalakhani (IRE))
1918[12] 2441[5] 3374[6] 4332[4] 5397[4] 6962[6] 7658[6] 8710[12]

Raspberry *Olly Williams* a69 70
3 b f Avonbridge Spennymoor (IRE) (Exceed And Excel (AUS))
2332[4]◆ 2736[6] (3176) 4444[5] 5392[9] 5854[2] 7656[9] 8194[7] 8715[13]

Raspoutin (FR) *P Journiac* a63 30
5 ch g Soul City(IRE) Omarie (FR) (Johann Quatz (FR))
8737a[9]

Raster (FR) *M Boutin* a50 62
4 b g Mastercraftsman(IRE) Marania (IRE) (Marju (IRE))
2647a[2]

Rathagan *Richard Hughes* a63 69
2 b c Kyllachy Ardessie (Bahamian Bounty)
7546[5] 7825[2] 8899[6] 9205[7] 9541[4]

Rathbone *Kevin Ryan* 96
3 b g Foxwedge(AUS) Frequent (Three Valleys (USA))
(1665) (3151) 3865[8] 4847[19] 6476[11] 7431[15]

Ratnaraj (ITY) *Ottavio Di Paolo* 79
4 b h St Paul House Ruby Dancer (IRE) (King's Best (USA))
8787a[6]

Rattan (NZ) *Richard Gibson* 120
5 br g Savabeel(AUS) Grand Princess (AUS) (Last Tycoon (IRE))
9377a[10]

Rattling Jewel *J J Lambe* a62 70
7 b g Royal Applause Mutoon (IRE) (Erhaab (USA))
7777[5]

Raucous *Robert Cowell* a104 110
6 b g Dream Ahead(USA) Shyrl (Acclamation)
762[4] 909[3]◆ 1105[6] 1421[2] 1916[2] 2551[2] 3009[6] 4095[4] (4805) 5664[3] (6453) 7892[4]

Ravenhoe (IRE) *Mark Johnston* a61 64
6 ch g Bahamian Bounty Breathless Kiss (USA) (Roman Ruler (USA))
2513[12]

Ravenous *Luke Dace* a75 80
8 b g Raven's Pass(USA) Supereva (IRE) (Sadler's Wells (USA))
735[5] 1693[4] 3070[2] 4257[4] 5417[6] 5840[10] 6848[6] 7683[3] 8829[7] 9012[6] 9303[10]

Ravenscar (IRE) *Grant Tuer* a68 69
3 b f Helmet(AUS) Cry Pearl (USA) (Street Cry (IRE))
5969[2] 7303[5] 8086[2]

Raven's Corner (IRE) *S Seemar* a111 87
6 ch g Raven's Pass(USA) Beautiful Filly (Oasis Dream)
(50a)◆

Raven's Cry (IRE) *P Twomey* 89
2 b f Raven's Pass(USA) Sagami (USA) (Street Cry (IRE))
(5710a) 7215a[7]

Raven's Raft (IRE) *David Loughnane* a66 60
4 gr m Raven's Pass(USA) Sea Drift (FR) (Warning)
(1988) 4220[P] 4362[4] 5631[6] 5706[7] 6371[6] 6736[9] 7300[9] 8348[9] 8670[7] 8870[5] 9042[10]

Rawdaa *Sir Michael Stoute* a102 115
4 b m Teofilo(IRE) Lady Lahar (Fraam)
1941[3]◆ 2776[2] 3986[2] 5586[3]

Raydiance *K R Burke* a103 98
4 b g Mayson Iridescence (Dutch Art)
1415[12] 1753[18] (4127)◆ 4385[3]◆ 5188[4] 5916[3] 5971[5] 7435[3] 7865[5] 7891[9] 9472[3]◆

Rayig *A R Al Rayhi* a71 69
3 ch c Exceed And Excel(AUS) Kaabari (USA) (Seeking The Gold (USA))
169a[9] 1742a[3]

Raymond Tusk (IRE)
Richard Hannon a108 114
4 b h High Chaparral(IRE) Dancing Shoes (IRE) (Danehill (USA))
894a[6] 2269[2]◆ 2827[3] 4015[7] 6473[4] 8844a[16] (9468)◆

Rayna's World (IRE) *Philip Kirby* 76
4 b m Poet's Voice Salmon Rose (IRE) (Iffraaj)
1757[7] 2822[7] 3816[16] 6278[10] 7683[8] 8635[2]

Rayong *K R Burke* 95
2 b c Mayson Lydiate (IRE) (Acclamation)
(2892)◆ 3988[10] 4610[3] 5228a[7] 6375[2] 7119[12]

Rayon Vert (FR) *Laurent Loisel* a102 102
5 b h Harbour Watch(IRE) Mansoura (IRE) (Kalanisi (IRE))
3030a[5] 4704a[15] 5715a[2]

Raypeteafterme *Declan Carroll* a43 49
3 ch g Harbour Watch(IRE) Trump Street (First Trump)
1691[9] 2380[5] 2477[12] 3159[10] 3569[8] 4328[17] 4586[11] 7651[9]

Razeena (CAN) *Doug Watson* a82
3 b f Malibu Moon(USA) Pink Palace (USA) (Empire Maker (USA))
510a[11] 845a[3] 1443a[10]

Razin' Hell *John Balding* a61 45
8 b g Byron Loose Caboose (IRE) (Tagula (IRE))
43[F] (Dead)

Reaction (GER) *Eva Fabianova* 83
3 b f Tertullian(USA) Red Pearl (FR) (Zieten (USA))
7250a[6]

Reaction Time *Saeed bin Suroor* a80 80
4 b g Dubawi(IRE) Cloudspin (USA) (Storm Cat (USA))
6259[10] 6732[5] 8827[3]

Real Appeal (GER) *J S Bolger* 99
2 b g Sidestep(AUS) Runaway Sparkle (Green Desert (USA))
(3333a) 4012[14] 5206a[7] 6190a[4] 7532a[5]

Real Estate (IRE) *Michael Attwater* a78 75
4 b g Dansili Maskunah (IRE) (Sadler's Wells (USA))
91[3] 314[2] 790[6] (982) 1393[6] 1930[2] (2483) 3014[5] 3963[4] 4835[7] 7552[6]◆ 7837[6] 9306[5] (9498) (9632)◆

Real Force *Gerard O'Leary* 99
2 gr c Lethal Force(IRE) Real Me (Mark Of Esteem (IRE))
4413a[4]

Realityhacking (FR) *F Chappet* a75 54
3 b g Bungle Inthejungle You Got The Love (Hawk Wing (USA))
217a[6] 1028a[4] 9538a[4]

Really Super *Amy Murphy* 77
5 b m Cacique(IRE) Sensationally (Montjeu (IRE))
2254[3]

Real Poet (IRE) *Sir Michael Stoute* 44
2 b g Poet's Voice Milady Eileen (IRE) (Footstepsinthesand)
7521[10]

Real Smooth (IRE) *Richard Hannon* 81
3 b g Teofilo(IRE) Amber Silk (IRE) (Lawman (FR))
2139[5] 2802[7] 3090[2] 4116[2] 5303[6]

Real Story (USA) *Ignacio Correas IV* 104
4 rg g Fast Bullet(USA) My Own Story (USA) (Lasting Approval (USA))
7922a[14]

Realtin Fantasy (IRE) *W P Browne* a39 53
3 b f Power Perfect Fantasy (IRE) (Oratorio (IRE))
7487[6]

Reasoned (IRE) *James Eustace* a73 62
3 ch f Intello(GER) Do The Honours (IRE) (Highest Honor (FR))
1816[6] 2199[4] 2965[3] 4080[4] 4642[4] 7835[8] 8207[4] 8436[4] 9039[2] 9253[2] (9548)

Reassurance *Tim Easterby* a56 68
4 b m Champs Elysees Timely Words (Galileo (IRE))
3267[5] 3708[9] 4724[8] 6069[4] 7314[2] 8196[5]

Reassure *William Haggas* a85 76
2 b f Oasis Dream Blhadawa (IRE) (Iffraaj)
5317[8] (6147) 7333[2]◆ 8095[9] (8817) 9162[11]

Reaver (IRE) *John Hodge* a56 58
6 b g Sabiango(GER) Mattinata (Tiger Hill (IRE))
9512[11]

Rebecamille (FR) *H De Nicolay* a61 70
6 b m Anabaa Blue Burgaudine (FR) (Marchand De Sable (USA))
4859a[5] 6031a[11]

Rebecca Rocks *Henry Candy* 96
5 b m Exceed And Excel(AUS) Rebecca Rolfe (Pivotal)
(4101) 5611[9]

Rebecke (IRE) *Lee Carter* a38 42
3 b f Camacho Ibecke (Exceed And Excel (AUS))
3080[6] 3696[9] 5306[5] 6107[9] 9450[10]

Rebel Cause (IRE) *John Holt* a57 45
6 b g Cockney Rebel(IRE) Happy Go Lily (In The Wings)
2512[9] 3046[11] 3720[9] 4475[7] 5025[12] 5560[10]

Rebel Lightning (IRE) *P Monfort* a83 80
6 gr g Zebedee Bellechance (Acclamation)
2226a[5]

Rebel Queen (FR) *P Monfort* a61 66
4 b m Cockney Rebel(IRE) Sunmoon Royale (GER) (Royal Dragon (USA))
1908a[6] 5762a[2]

Rebel Redemption *John Quinn* a65 61
2 gr g Lethal Force(IRE) Tempting (Pivotal)
3702[7] 4826[10] 5388[9] 7283[2] 7584[4] 9061[6] 9307[5] (9407)

Rebel Soldier Boy *David O'Meara* 71
2 b g Sepoy(AUS) Intrusion (Indesatchel (IRE))
7308[2] 7538[2] 8337[4]

Rebel State (IRE) *Jedd O'Keeffe* a61 60
6 b g Zoffany(IRE) Stately Princess (Robellino (USA))
2076[7] 2241[4] 2963[2] 3704[11] 3720[5] 4293[3] 4512[7] 5099[7] 5247[9] 5787[5] 7444[6] 7654[8] 7960[2] 8301[3] (8530) 8922[7]

Rebel Streak *Ali Jan* a47 80
4 b g Dark Angel(IRE) Siren's Gift (Cadeaux Genereux)
393a[5] 639a[6] 725a[5]

Rebel Tale (USA) *Andrew Slattery* 108
2 ch c Tale Of The Cat(USA) Purr And Prowl (USA) (Purim (USA))
5997a[3] 6430a[2] 7217a[4]

Rebel Woods (FR) *Joseph Tuite* a18 33
6 br g Cockney Rebel(IRE) In The Woods (You And I (USA))
695[11]

Recall It All *Ivan Furtado* a46
2 b g Toronado(IRE) Rotunda (Pivotal)
8121[9] 8503[7]

Reckless Endeavour (IRE)
David Barron a85 71
6 b g Kodiac Red Fanfare (First Trump)
176[5] 499[3] 909[4]◆ 1290[6] 1502[6] 1727[6] 2015[7] 8428[2] 8921[4]◆ 9476[3]◆

Reclaim Victory (IRE) *Brian Ellison* a70 72
2 b f Helmet(AUS) Doctor's Note (Pursuit Of Love)
4289[2] 5433[4] (5895) 6675[4] 7072[9]

Recondite (IRE) *Ralph Beckett* a78 76
3 b g Acclamation Aquarius Star (IRE) (Danehill Dancer (IRE))
2139[6] 2802[6] 4178[4] 5782[4] 6469[2]◆ 7839[2]

Recon Mission (IRE) *Tony Carroll* 108
3 b c Kodiac Ermine Ruby (Cape Cross (IRE))
2086[4] 2522[2] 3344[15] (3865) 5184[10] 5927[4] 6476[13] 7943a[13]

Reconnaissance *Tom Clover* a52 63
3 b g Lope De Vega(IRE) Victrix Ludorum (IRE) (Invincible Spirit (IRE))
2114[6]◆ 4225[7] 5002[6] 5531[2] 6130[5] 7027[6] 8207[8]

Recover Me (FR) *J-C Rouget* 89
4 gr m Fastnet Rock(AUS) Marie Rossa (Testa Rossa (AUS))
9124a[4]

Recovery Road (IRE) *I Endaltsev* a59 52
3 br c No Nay Never(USA) Hannahs Turn (Dubai Destination (USA))
7642a[9]

Rectory Road *Ronald Harris* a87 90
3 b g Paco Boy(IRE) Caerlonore (IRE) (Traditionally (USA))
90[6] (289)◆ 5412[3] 6076[7] 6841[4] 7815[6] 8222[3] 9255[7]

Recuerdame (USA) *Simon Dow* a70 40
3 b g The Factor(USA) B R's Girl (USA) (Pulpit (USA))
1285[6] 2035[10] 4787[2] 5731[7] 6569[14] 8698[10] 9128[8] 9305[10]

Red Alert *Tony Carroll* a85 88
5 b g Sleeping Indian Red Sovereign (Danzig Connection (USA))
361[4] 797[3] 1496[9] 2611[13] (3032) 3164[7] 4236[3] 5058[6] 5882[2] 6525[6] (6756) 9057[7] 9441[5]

Red Allure *Michael Mullineaux* a50 54
4 ch m Mayson Lark In The Park (IRE) (Grand Lodge (USA))
2081[9] 3476[U] 3921[11] 4182[11] 5181[3] 5893[3] 7591[4] 7962[2] 8720[9] 9398[3] 9518[8]

Red Archangel (IRE)
Richard Spencer a44 59
3 b f Dark Angel(IRE) Illuminating Dream (IRE) (High Chaparral (IRE))
174[7] 1957[6] 2341[3] 3407[3] 3741[4] 4346[2] 5049[3] 5653[9] 6130[4]

Red Armada (IRE) *Clive Cox* 93
3 b c Invincible Spirit(IRE) Alumni (Selkirk (USA))
2790[2] (4178) (4865)

Red Armour *Luke McJannet* a55 60
3 b f Nayef(USA) Ansina (USA) (Distant View (USA))
4922[11] 9244[9]

Redarna *Dianne Sayer* a56 96
5 ch g Aqlaam Curtains (Dubawi (IRE))
2076[8] 2509[7] (2898) (3922) 4239[5] 4875[2] (5416) (5726) 7068[7] 7435[2]

Red Balloons *Richard Fahey* 96
3 b f Kyllachy Cecily (Oasis Dream)
4891[3] 6257[8] 6999[9] 7431[24]

Red Bond (IRE) *Keith Dalgleish* a84 81
3 b c Red Jazz(USA) Faithfulbond (IRE) (Elbio)
(472) (826) 1462[2] 9628[3]◆

Red Bravo (IRE) *Charles Hills* a71 75
3 b g Acclamation Vision Of Peace (IRE) (Invincible Spirit (IRE))
2082[8] 3591[5] 4793[6] 6111[4] 7731[6] 8220[7] 8496[4]

Red Cactus (USA) *Bent Olsen* a90
3 ch c Hard Spun(USA) Strut The Canary (USA) (Mineshaft (USA))
169a[6] 636a[3] 1110a[6]

Red Cardinal (IRE) *Kris Lees* a74 107
7 b g Montjeu(IRE) Notable (Zafonic (USA))
1784a[17] 8600a[4]

Red Chois (IRE) *William Jarvis* a80
5 b m Choisir(AUS) Red Blossom (Green Desert (USA))
81[4]

Red Cinderella *David Evans* a21 44
2 b f Heeraat(IRE) Littlemisstutti (IRE) (Noverre (USA))
2918[10] 3165[8] 3573[6] 5576[9] 6799[7] 7110[8] 8750[9]

Red Cossack (CAN) *Dean Ivory* a51 51
8 ch g Rebellion Locata (USA) (Stravinsky (USA))
39[5] 245[6] 532[3] 717[4] 983[4] 1353[2] 1717[7] 2740[7] 3304[2]◆ 7549[5] 8416[4] 9160[7]

Red Curry (FR) *H-A Pantall* a54 59
3 ch f Denon(USA) Red Shot (FR) (Gentlewave (IRE))
2954a[7]

Red Cymbal *Anthony McCann* a74 63
4 b g Pivotal Red Baton (Exceed And Excel (AUS))
260[8] 381[11] 2122[6] 2958[15]

Red Derek *Lisa Williamson* 64
3 b g Steele Tango(USA) Maydream (Sea Freedom)
4358[4] 5128[6] 5656[6] 7773[10]

Red Desert (IRE) *Roger Varian* a62
3 b g Australia Arbaah (USA) (Invasor (ARG))
32[7]

Reddiac (IRE) *Ed Dunlop* a61 61
3 b g Kodiac Margarita (IRE) (Marju (IRE))
3440[13] 5358[4] 5866[4] 6635[2] 7376[3] 7685[9] 8205[5]

Red Douglas *Scott Dixon* a27
5 ch g Sakhee(USA) Chrystal Venture (IRE) (Barathea (IRE))
7390[11]

Redemptive *Phil McEntee* a68 67
3 b f Royal Applause Hope And Fortune (IRE) (High Chaparral (IRE))
55[2] 474[5] 1264[4] 1825[2] 2798[2] 3154[6] 4071[8] 5431[4] (7472) 8254[5] 9048[11] 9244[8]

Redemptorist (IRE) *Olly Murphy* a78 67
4 b g Frozen Power(IRE) Fly With Me (IRE) (Montjeu (IRE))
598[2] 1508[4]

Redemptress (IRE) *John O'Shea* a30
3 b f Zebedee Sina Cova (IRE) (Barathea (IRE))
472[7] 1352[12] 6531[9] 8251[14]

Red Epaulette (IRE)
M D O'Callaghan 90
2 b c Epaulette(AUS) Shall We Tell (Intikhab (USA))
3988[9]

Redesdale Rebel *Susan Corbett* a65
3 ch g Mayson Jubilee (Selkirk (USA))
9112[2]◆ 9332[5]

Red Fedora *Clive Cox* a58
3 b f Lethal Force(IRE) Red Turban (Kyllachy)
370[3]◆ 761[5]

Red For All *Ed Dunlop* 62
2 b c Muhaarar All For Laura (Cadeaux Genereux)
5956[4] 6564[5]

Red Force One *Paul Nicholls* a95 95
4 ro g Lethal Force(IRE) Dusty Red (Teofilo (IRE))
617[2] 3087[2]

Red Forever *Helen Cuthbert* a37 49
8 ch g Major Cadeaux Spindara (IRE) (Spinning World (USA))
4694[9] 5722[10]

Red Galileo *Saeed bin Suroor* a113 114
8 b g Dubawi(IRE) Ivory Gala (FR) (Galileo (IRE))
281a[3] 635a[2] 730a[2] 958a[2] 1441a[8] 2742[7] (3600)◆ 4382[8] 6473[2] 8600a[5]

Redgrave (IRE) *Joseph Tuite* a83 74
5 b g Lope De Vega(IRE) Olympic Medal (Nayef (USA))
2516[2] 2797[15] 3944[3] 4108[6] 4907[5] 5594[5] 5709[9] 7489[3] 8507[4]

Red Gunner *Mark Loughnane* a66 58
5 b g Oasis Dream Blue Maiden (Medicean)
181[3] 250[12] 364[5] 595[10] 941[5] 3533[2] 4349[7] 5016[2] 6123[9] 6334[7] 6855[2] 7232[7] 8000[3] 8224[4] 8466[3] (8870) (9090)◆ 9207[4]

Red Hot (FR) *Richard Fahey* a73 93
3 b f Siyouni(FR) Green China (FR) (Green Tune (USA))
2521[5] 3341[8] 4318[4] 5458[2] 6172[3]

Red Hot Chili (SWE) *Patrick Wahl* a90 90
6 ch g Eishin Dunkirk(USA) Delta Downs (Deputy Minister (CAN))
3902a[9] 7494a[3]

Red Hot Fusion (IRE) *Alan Berry* 16
5 b g Kodiac Unfortunate (Komaite (USA))
3416[8] 6174[17] 7052[12] 7761[9]

Red Hot Streak *Tim Easterby* 64
2 b g Hot Streak(IRE) Perfect Act (Act One)
3512[4] 3841[8] 4631[4]

Red Hottie *Michael Appleby* a29 30
2 ch f Hot Streak(IRE) Descriptive (IRE) (Desert King (IRE))
4302[7] 5317[10] 6514[8] 7833[10] 8824[9]

Redicean *Alan King* a106 85
5 b g Medicean Red Halo (IRE) (Galileo (IRE))
311[4] 757[5]

Red Impression *Roger Charlton* a97 87
3 gr f Dark Angel(IRE) Purissima (USA) (Fusaichi Pegasus (USA))
2319[3]◆ 2826[5] 7401[9] 9098[6]

Red Invader (IRE) *John Butler* a69 73
9 b g Red Clubs(IRE) Tifariti (USA) (Elusive Quality (USA))
236[7] 1265[8] 1507[9] (1987) (2295) 2527[8] 6685[RR] 7632[11] 8066[9] 8501[7] 9545[8]

Red Jasper *Michael Appleby* a65 62
2 ch g Showcasing Spate (IRE) (Danehill Dancer (IRE))
3512[6] 4588[4] 5865[5] 6313[2] 6683[3] 7283[4] 7827[6] 8201[5] 8415[2] 9172[8] 9328[5]

Red Kitten (FR) *D De Waele* a82 69
6 b g Kitten's Joy(USA) Red Diadem (Pivotal)
2955a[6]

Red Knight (USA) *William Mott* 107
5 ch g Pure Prize(USA) Isabel Away (USA) (Skip Away (USA))
3561a[5]

Red Lark (IRE) *J P Murtagh* a75 72
2 b f Epaulette(AUS) Firecrest (IRE) (Darshaan)
7247a[8]

Red Line Alexander (IRE)
Simon Crisford a63 74
2 b f Sea The Stars(IRE) Tayma (IRE) (Exceed And Excel (AUS))
6949[3]◆ 8021[4]

Red Maharani *James Given* a57
2 ch f Sepoy(AUS) Vintage Gardenia (Selkirk (USA))
1879[4]◆ 2761[18] 3579[4] 6387[4] 7306[4] 8022[12] 8897[2] 9179[6] 9407[9]

Red Missile (IRE) *William Haggas* a71 76
2 b c Battle Of Marengo(IRE) Plym (Notnowcato)
5908[4] 7154[6] 9136[3]◆

Red Mist *Simon Crisford* a94 107
4 b h Frankel Red Dune (IRE) (Red Ransom (USA))
2873[3]

Red Moon Lady *Dean Ivory* 9
3 b f Epaulette(AUS) Maisie's Moon (USA) (Curlin (USA))
2550[13] 3421[9] 4738[10] 5431[11]

Red October (IRE) *Hugo Palmer* a81 84
3 ch g Dawn Approach(IRE) Mamonta (Fantastic Light (USA))
1645[3]

Red Onion *Gaspar Vaz* a59 86
5 b h Fast Company(IRE) Capsicum (Holy Roman Emperor (IRE))
6145a[6] 7062a[5]

Red Phoenix (IRE) *Mark Johnston* a47 47
3 ch g Pivotal Huma Bird (Invincible Spirit (IRE))
(855) (1141) 1516[8] 2689[12]

Red Pike (IRE) *Bryan Smart* a82 79
8 ch g Kheleyf(USA) Fancy Feathers (IRE) (Redback)
36[2] 278[9] 3706[15] 4821[3] 5244[4] (5901) 6178[8] 6699[6] 8066[5] 8660[6] 8860[3]

Red Poppy *William Haggas* a58
2 ch f Declaration Of War(USA) Valiant Girl (Lemon Drop Kid (USA))
9163[5]

Red Reflection (IRE) *Richard Fahey* 29
2 b g Zebedee Hazarayna (Polish Precedent (USA))
2093[8]

Red Romance *Clive Cox* a70 75
3 ch f Dutch Art Semblance (Pivotal)
2762[2] 3603[7] 5002[5] (5429) 6362[11]

Redrosezorro *Eric Alston* 76
5 b g Foxwedge(AUS) Garter Star (Mark Of Esteem (IRE))
1895[4] 2418[12] 2893[3] 3549[8] 4880[6] (5723)◆ 6591[2] 7183[5]◆ 7828[14]

Red Royalist *Stuart Edmunds* a81 81
5 b g Royal Applause Scarlet Royal (Red Ransom (USA))
84[2] 480[4] 4363[2]◆

Red Saree (IRE) *Michael Wigham* a12 53
3 b f Moohaajim(IRE) Red Japonica (Daylami (IRE))
2255[6] 4185[10]

Red's Comet *Laura Mongan* a24
3 b f King Raedwald(AUS) Emperor's Hope (IRE) (Holy Roman Emperor (IRE))
401[8]

Red Secret (CAN) *Ed Dunlop* a68 60
3 b c Lemon Drop Kid(USA) Parley (USA) (Street Cry (IRE))
3584[7] 5103[4] 5656[10] 7817[6] (8196) 8696[2]

Red Seeker *Tim Easterby* a56 76
4 ch g Red Jazz(USA) Purepleasureseeker (IRE) (Grand Lodge (USA))
3162[2] 3473[6] 4130[2] 4633[9] (5247) (5517) (6204) 6700[8] 7289[9]

Red Skye Delight (IRE)
Luke McJannet a56
3 gr f Clodovil(IRE) Sole Bay (Compton Place)
156[10] 1167[6] 1514[8] 5264[4] 6441[3] 6885[2] 7550[2] 9248[6] 9439[5]

Red Snapper *William Stone* a46 46
4 b m Kheleyf(USA) Amistress (Kalanisi (IRE))
402[7] 596[3] 2287[4] 4749[2] 5264[7] 6794[7]

Red's Rocket *Laura Mongan* a25
2 b f King Raedwald(AUS) Arrival Time (Rail Link)
7103[6] 7995[8]

Red Star Dancer (IRE)
David Thompson
5 b g Tamayuz Red Planet (Pivotal)
7903[8]

Red Starlight *Richard Hannon* a104 105
4 br m Pivotal Star Chart (IRE) (Dubawi (IRE))
1414[2] 1753[6] 2608[3] 3359[3] 3987[8] 5187[5] 5949[2] 6726[8] 7411[7] 7893[7]

Red Striker (IRE) *G M Lyons* a68 77
4 b g Sea The Stars(IRE) Coolree Marj (IRE) (Marju (IRE))
5537a[11]

Red Stripes (USA) *Lisa Williamson* a65 62
7 b g Leroidesanimaux(BRZ) Kaleidoscopic (USA) (Fortunate Prospect (USA))
118[4] 471[8] (597) 823[7] 1076[3] 1210[2] 1364[2] (1521) 1716[6] 2433[5] (2527) 2876[8] 3452[3] 3846[14] 4493[3] 4555[3] 4829[6] 4880[3] 5180[5] 5819[3] 5952[2] (6510) 6829[3] 7112[3] (7690) 8066[7] 8296[6] 9013[9] 9092[8] 9219[5] 9286[5] 9406[9] 9627[5]◆

Red Sun (IRE) *Charles Hills* a65 70
2 b g Gutaifan(IRE) Island Sunset (IRE) (Trans Island)
3530[2] 4246[7] 4558[4] 5340[7] 5612[13]

Red Tea *Joseph Patrick O'Brien* a86 110
6 ch m Sakhee(USA) Maimoona (IRE) (Pivotal)
3105a[3] 3986[8] (5223a) 6265a[3] 8154a[8]

Red Torch (FR) *H-A Pantall* a91 99
4 b h Air Chief Marshal(IRE) Red Kiss (IRE) (Fasliyev (USA))
5471a[5] (6006a) 7255a[9] 8648a[5] (8982a)

Red Tornado (FR) *Chris Fairhurst* a85 73
7 ch g Dr Fong(USA) Encircle (USA) (Spinning World (USA))
349[7] 737[4] 2781[13] 4404[12]

Red Touch (USA) *Michael Appleby* a76 63
7 bb g Bluegrass Cat(USA) Touchnow (CAN) (Pleasant Tap (USA))
5[4] 603[4] 965[6] 1369[7] 1526[8] 1858[8]

Red Treble *Rebecca Menzies* a54 75
2 b f Iffraaj Threetimesalady (Royal Applause)
4550[3] 6175[5] (6570) 7117[9] 7438[3] 8303[5]

Red Tycoon (IRE) *Patrick Chamings* a63 63
7 b g Acclamation Rugged Up (IRE) (Marju (IRE))
1682[3]◆ 2339[10] 3014[11] 3527[5] 4025[2] 4749[5] 5147[7] (5607) 6329[5] 6794[3] 7446[5]

Red Verdon (USA) *Ed Dunlop* a109 115
6 ch g Lemon Drop Kid(USA) Porto Marmay (IRE) (Choisir (AUS))
(1460) 2410[5] 2827[6] (4933) 6473[14] 8361a[8]

Redzel (AUS) *Peter & Paul Snowden* 119
6 b g Snitzel(AUS) Millrich (AUS) (Rubiton (AUS))
8362a[8]

Redzone *Bryan Smart* a58 55
2 b g Sepoy(AUS) Mythicism (Oasis Dream)
4826[11] 5553[9] 6175[11] 8816[4] 9196[7] 9515[5]

Reedway (IRE) *Robyn Brisland* a8 39
6 ch g Intikhab(USA) Mistress Bailey (IRE) (Mister Baileys)
2192[10] 3482[10]

Reehaam *John Gosden* a56 69
2 b f Kingman Umneeyatee (AUS) (Encosta De Lago (AUS))
5366[4] 8889[9] 9046[11]

Reeth (IRE) *John Gosden* a83 72
3 b g Kodiac Tanouma (USA) (Mr Greeley (USA))
(55) 6670[5]

Reeves *Robert Cowell* a99 91
3 b g Tamayuz Mania (IRE) (Danehill (USA))
1736[2] 2082[5] 2746[2] 3357[3]◆ 4065[4] 5685[5] 5953[5] 7049[7] (8691) (9198) (9478)◆

Reflektor (IRE) *Tom Dascombe* a97 88
6 ch g Bahamian Bounty Baby Bunting (Wolfhound (USA))
203[4] 909[8] (1388) 1839[4] 2557[9] 3589[10] 4759[3] 5705[10] 7913[8] 8317[7] 9404[8]

Reformed Character (IRE)
Lydia Pearce a43 40
3 b c Zoffany(IRE) Sallysaysso (IRE) (Danehill Dancer (IRE))
1389[7] 1690[12] 2550[9] 3352[7] 3996[10] 5531[7] 6152[9] 6635[5] 6860[9] 8434[9]

Refuge *Michael Easterby* 53
2 b g Harbour Watch(IRE) Beldale Memory (IRE) (Camacho)
3411[6] 3866[10]

Refulgence Star (IRE) *S Seemar* a62 56
3 b g Fast Company(IRE) Zalanga (IRE) (Azamour (IRE))
570a[8] 1742a[11]

Regal Ambition *Clive Cox* a59
3 ch f Pivotal Regal Salute (Medicean)
78[9] 698[7] 931[6]

Regal Banner *Roger Varian* a74 76
3 ch f Lope De Vega(IRE) Regal Riband (Fantastic Light (USA))
2583[4] 3685[4] 4248[4]◆ 5941[6] 6362[3]◆ 7583[3] 8519[8]

Regal Director (IRE) *Archie Watson* a91 85
4 b g New Approach(IRE) Dubai Queen (USA) (Kingmambo (USA))
2374[3] 3861[6] (6456) 6734[4] 7465[7] (8014)

Regal Gait (IRE) *Simon Dow* a59 7
6 b g Tagula(IRE) Babylonian (Shamardal (USA))
38[6] 619[8] 947[6]

Regal Glory (USA) *Chad C Brown* 103
3 ch f Animal Kingdom(USA) Mary's Follies (USA) (More Than Ready (USA))
8139a[6]

Regal Lilly (IRE) *David Simcock* a59 69
3 b f Iffraaj Sweet Lilly (Tobougg (IRE))
3050[4]◆ 3680[2]◆ 9400[3]

Regal Mirage (IRE) *Tim Easterby* a76 79
5 ch g Aqlaam Alzaroof (USA) (Kingmambo (USA))
1666[7] 2636[9] 3250[7] 3816[11] 4209[2] 4446[5]◆ 4689[3] 4913[8] 5178[4] (5474) 6067[7] (7332) 7872[4] 8396[7]

Regal Miss *Patrick Chamings* a17 16
7 b m Royal Applause Pretty Miss (Averti (IRE))
4500[6] 6794[8]

Regal Reality *Sir Michael Stoute* 121
4 b g Intello(GER) Regal Realm (Medicean)
2085[3] (3025) 4668[3] 5455[4] 6354[5] 8335[8]

Regency Legend (NZ) *C S Shum* 106
3 b g Pins(AUS) Sparkling (NZ) (O'Reilly (NZ))
9377a[12]

Reggae Runner (FR)
Mark Johnston a85 88
3 b c Lethal Force(IRE) Caribbean Dancer (USA) (Theatrical (IRE))
313[4] 534[2]◆ (761) 1945[2] 2082[6] 3082[9] 3683[3] 4079[10] (4497) 5104[4] 5667[13] 6231[7] 7191[8]

Reggino (FR) *Jedd O'Keeffe* a62 59
2 b g Farhh Musikhani (Dalakhani (IRE))
6497[4]◆ 7416[5] 7958[8]

Regimented (IRE) *Richard Hannon* a78 85
4 b h Epaulette(AUS) Colour Coordinated (IRE) (Spectrum (IRE))
2065[5] 2622[4] 2797[2] 3255[2] 3763[3] 4300[3] 4786[7] 6201[7]

Rego Park Lady (IRE)
Adrian Murray a28 62
4 b m Requinto(IRE) Henrietta Mews (Compton Place)
(4493) 7052[8] 7487[4]

Regular *Michael Bell* a77 80
3 ch g Exceed And Excel(AUS) Humdrum (Dr Fong (USA))
1516[2] 2146[2] (2900) 3599[9] 4099[10]

Regular Income (IRE) *Adam West* a74 86
4 b g Fast Company(IRE) Max Almabrouka (USA) (Hennessy (USA))
4294 (536) 754[11] 1065[7] (2290) (2628)◆ 3315[6] 3424[4] (3845) 4241[11] 7413[9] 7829[4] 8411[2] 8725[5]

Regulator (IRE) *Alexandra Dunn* a78 57
4 b g Acclamation Rasana (Royal Academy (USA))
139[7] 699[7] 922[11] 1496[5] 1880[8] 6588[7] 8420[9] 8755[5] 9132[5]◆

Reigning Ice *Clive Cox* 39
3 br f Xtension(IRE) Ice Haven (IRE) (Verglas (IRE))
5428[8] 6594[11]

Reignite *Emma Owen* a67
4 b g Firebreak Resentful Angel (Danehill Dancer (IRE))
141[8] 476[5] 924[7] 1177[13]

Reims *William Haggas* a68
3 b f Invincible Spirit(IRE) Riberac (Efisio)
8497[3]◆ 8695[4] 9165[5]

Reine De Lune (FR) *S Morineau* a61 33
3 gr f Kingsalsa(USA) Louna De Vati (FR) (Sinndar (IRE))
7061a[11]

Reine De Vitesse (FR)
Jane Chapple-Hyam a79
3 b f Wootton Bassett Vitesse Superieure (Statue Of Liberty (USA))
5650[4]◆ (7841) 8498[12] 9422[6]

Reine Magnifique (FR)
James Fanshawe a46 24
3 ch f Excelebration(IRE) Mahima (FR) (Linamix (FR))
3324[9] 4211[7]

Related *Paul Midgley* a81 88
9 b g Kheleyf(USA) Balladonia (Primo Dominie)
832[8] 1160[5] 3657[10] (4519)

Relative Ease *J S Moore* a52 45
3 b f Sayif(IRE) Shohrah (IRE) (Giant's Causeway (USA))
1739[7] 2249[9] 9139[3]◆

Relativity (FR) *Harry Dunlop* 25
2 ch c Rio De La Plata(USA) Relation (USA) (Distant View (USA))
8518[8]

Relaxed Boy (FR) *Mrs A Malzard* a66 69
6 b h Le Havre(IRE) Joyce (GER) (Chato (USA))
(4174a) 4685a[2] 5232[2] 6553a[4]

Reliable Son (FR) *N Clement* a90 90
3 gr g Reliable Man Hot Fudge (SWE) (Lomitas)
2758a[2]

Relight My Fire *Tim Easterby* a56 55
9 ch g Firebreak Making Music (Makbul)
2478[7] 3215[10] 4207[7] 4512[8] 5021[4] 5247[13] 5560[4] 6102[4] 7654[13] 9111[6]

Reloaded (IRE) *George Scott* a90 89
3 b g Excelebration(IRE) Wooded Glade (Oasis Dream)
1646[3] 7205[3] 7617[4] 7856[2]◆ 8606[6]

Remarkable *David O'Meara* a68 102
6 b g Pivotal Irresistible (Cadeaux Genereux)
1414[4] 2609P 5129[4] 5916[4] 6207[7] 7891[15]

Remember Daisy (USA)
Gary Scherer a67 99
4 ch m Misremembered(USA) Very Speightstown (USA) (Speightstown (USA))
5978a[6]

Remembering You (IRE) *Clive Cox* a62 69
3 b f Es Que Love(IRE) Tallassee (Indian Ridge (IRE))
313[7] 841[4] 1140[5] (2152) 3665[2] 4285[2]

Remember Nerja (IRE) *Barry Leavy* a31 31
5 ch m Lord Shanakill(USA) Tequise (IRE) (Victory Note (USA))
2593[11] 3155[6]

Remember Rocky *Lucy Normile* a62 67
10 ch g Haafhd Flower Market (Cadeaux Genereux)
2330[7] 3181[4] (4054) 5096[3] 6341[4] 6827[3] 7048[2] 7368[5] 8019[5]

Remember The Days (IRE)
Jedd O'Keeffe a73 78
5 b g Kyllachy Pointed Arch (IRE) (Rock Of Gibraltar (IRE))
2636[4] 3415[6] 4009[2] 4817[3] 5391[2] 6256[7] 6933[2]

Remember The Man (IRE)
Neil King a75 64
6 b g Dalakhani(IRE) Perfect Hedge (Unfuwain (USA))
2254[8] 2626[6] 4019[2] 7631[9]

Remission *Derek Shaw* a48 38
3 b g Epaulette(AUS) Fenella Fudge (Rock Hard Ten (USA))
2300[8] 5864[3] 5985[9] 8839[7]

Remmy D (IRE) *Jim Goldie* a73 62
4 b g Lawman(FR) Evening Time (IRE) (Keltos (FR))
102[5] 740[4] 950[3] 1418[12] 1647[11] 2244[7] 2962[6] 3448[10] 4054[4] 4690[6] 5178[3] 5556[12] 5937[4] (6655) 7513[3] 7776[14]

Renardeau *Ali Stronge* a83 73
3 b g Foxwedge(AUS) La Cucina (IRE) (Last Tycoon)
2689[8] 3665[5] 4176[4] (5497) 6022[5] 8641[9] (9421) (9511) 9611[2]

Renegade Master *George Baker* a83 61
3 b g Paco Boy(IRE) Candle (Dansili)
(90) (258) 3261[10] 4188[7] 6593[6] 7295[8]

Rent's Dew (IRE) *Tim Easterby* 52
3 b g Shirocco(GER) Rutland Water (IRE) (Hawk Wing (USA))
5690[8] 6177[6] 6701[7] 7048[12] 8204[13]

Repartee (IRE) *Kevin Ryan* 100
2 br c Invincible Spirit(IRE) Pleasantry (Johannesburg (USA))
(2780) 5134[4] 6422[3] 7119[2]◆

Repentir *Mme M Bollack-Badel* a45 19
2 b f Roderic O'Connor(IRE) Miaplacidus (IRE) (Shamardal (USA))
9123a[11]

Repercussion *Gavin Hernon* a106 106
6 b g Manduro(GER) Summertime Legacy (Darshaan)
4581a[6]

Replenish (FR) *S Cerulis* a98 95
6 ch g Le Havre(IRE) Brambleberry (Cape Cross (IRE))
1708a[12] 2266a[3] 5718a[7] 9210a[14]

Reponse Exacte (FR) *Amy Murphy* a80 82
3 gr f Rajsaman(FR) Barmaid (FR) (Cape Cross (IRE))
8456[6]◆ 8852[3] 9199[8] 9510[7]

Repulse Bay (IRE) *Ralph Beckett* a62 51
3 b f Dark Angel(IRE) Soxy Doxy (IRE) (Hawk Wing (USA))
258[6]

Reputation (IRE) *Ruth Carr* a87 102
6 b g Royal Applause Semaphore (Zamindar (USA))
(2117) 2743[8] 3347[4] 3602[4]◆ 4299[2]◆ 4607[4] 5413[21] 6229[13] 6706[13] 7152[7]

Requiems Dream (IRE)
Mark Johnston a67 75
2 ch f Dream Ahead(USA) Kerrys Requiem (IRE) (King's Best (USA))
3919[5] 4727[2] (5011) (5037)◆ 9401[5]

Requinto Dawn (IRE)
Richard Fahey a88 85
4 br g Requinto(IRE) Till Dawn (IRE) (Kheleyf (USA))
2079[8] 2416[10] 2910[7] 3360[6] 3999[6] 4625[9] 5157[2]

Requited (IRE) *Hughie Morrison* a75 55
3 b g Requinto(IRE) Joyfullness (USA) (Dixieland Band (USA))
3590[11] 4185[11] 5056[7] 5595[3] (6048) 7387[7] 7632[2] (7869) 8242[8] 8943[3] 9365[8]

Reshaan (IRE) *Alexandra Dunn* a50 46
4 b g Dark Angel(IRE) Bluebell (IRE) (Mastercraftsman (IRE))
835[11] 2193[7] 2971[8] 3687[12] 3939[6] 4479[7] 6059[12] 6363[6] 6897[8] 7389[5] 7632[7] 8256[8] 8435[5] 8901[5] 9035[6] 9220[2] 9410[4] 9439[13]

Reshoun (FR) *Ian Williams* a100 100
5 b g Shamardal(USA) Radiyya (IRE) (Sinndar (IRE))
2143[3] 2801[9] 5183[8] 5929[8] 6958[3] (9065)

Resounding Silence (USA)
James Tate a43
3 ch f Lemon Drop Kid(USA) Night Song (Oasis Dream)
299[5]

Resplendent Rose
Michael Madgwick a13 35
2 b f Heeraat(IRE) Attlongglast (Groom Dancer (USA))
2915[12] 3798[5] 5956[8] 6313[10]

Restive (IRE) *Michael Appleby* a76 64
6 b g Rip Van Winkle(IRE) I Hearyou Knocking (IRE) (Danehill Dancer (IRE))
737[6] 950[6] 1159[3] 1398[4] 1648[5] 2330[6] 2785[4]◆ 3177[8] 3448[9] 3721[7] (4003) 4689[10] 5095[7] 5555[6] 6218[3] 7053[7] (8843) 9033[7] 9221[2] 9496[7]

Restive Spirit *Charlie Wallis* a50 54
4 b g Intello(GER) Hooray (Invincible Spirit (IRE))
7372[10] 7913[11]

Restless Endeavour (IRE)
Jamie Osborne a70 68
2 b f Dandy Man(IRE) Belgique (IRE) (Compton Place)
6146[2] (6344) 6603[3] 7585[9]

Restless Rose *Stuart Williams* a85 87
4 ch m Power Albany Rose (IRE) (Noverre (USA))
2687[4] 4023[5] 4340[3] 5015[4] 5515[5]◆ 5990[3] 6631[2] 7130[2] (7345) 7613[3] 8115[14] 8550[5] 9057[4] 9549[6]

Restorer *Ian Williams* a104 103
7 gr g Mastercraftsman(IRE) Moon Empress (FR) (Rainbow Quest (USA))
2574[4] 3600[10] 4646[14] 4935[14] 5929[5] 6420[15] 6958[12] 7680[2]

Resurrected (IRE) *Philip McBride* a53 30
3 b f Clodovil(IRE) Puca (IRE) (Arcano (IRE))
2581[10] 4022[8] 4582[7] (7371)

Reticent Angel (IRE) *Clive Cox* a83 85
3 ro f Dark Angel(IRE) Sioduil (IRE) (Oasis Dream)
1729[3] 2086[8] 2274[4] 3427[3] 3855[3] 4703a[9] 7401[8] 7889[10]

Retirement Beckons *Linda Perratt* 57
4 b g Epaulette(AUS) Mystical Ayr (IRE) (Namid)
2329[9] 2964[4] 4725[3] 4978[2] (5099) 5238[3] (5933) 6655[3] 6937[10] 7509[2] 7779[2]

Return To Senders (IRE)
Jassim Mohammed Ghazali a79 79
2 b c Sir Prancealot(IRE) Bougainvilia (IRE) (Bahamian Bounty)
2594[9] 3194[3]◆ 3512[5] 3812[5] 4861[2] 5265[2] 5562[4] 9582a[7]

Reux *F Head* 59
2 b c Dansili Neartica (FR) (Sadler's Wells (USA))
6433a[7]

Revamp (USA) *David Simcock* a65
3 bb g Tapizar(USA) Lady Siphonica (USA) (Siphon (BRZ))
1165[4]◆ 1689[3] 2192[12]

Revelstoke *A Wohler* a90 96
3 ch c Toronado(IRE) Crown (IRE) (Royal Applause)
2889a[9] 3907a[8]

Reverberation *J J Lambe* a54 69
4 ch g Excelebration(IRE) Echo Ridge (IRE) (Oratorio (IRE))
7090a[4]

Reverend Jacobs *Alan King* a87 50
5 b g Nathaniel(IRE) Light Impact (IRE) (Fantastic Light (USA))
1220[7] 1559[11]

Revestar (IRE) *Simon Crisford* a78 51
2 b c Sea The Stars(IRE) Danseuse De Reve (IRE) (Invincible Spirit (IRE))
7000[4] (7555)

Revich (IRE) *Richard Spencer* a88 92
3 b g Requinto(IRE) Kathleen Rafferty (IRE) (Marju (IRE))
2525[5]◆ 3048[2] 4123[4] (4546) 5546[15] 7142[3] 7868[3] 8707[8] 9088[7] 9308[3]

Reviette *Kevin Ryan* 70
2 b f Kyllachy Readyandaway (USA) (More Than Ready (USA))
5243[4] 6064[3] 7644[7]

Revolutionary Man (IRE)
Mark Loughnane a55 75
4 b g Exceed And Excel(AUS) Bint Almukhtar (IRE) (Halling (USA))
6898[5] 8006[6] 9402[11]

Revolutionise (IRE) *Stuart Williams* a88 83
3 gr g Lope De Vega(IRE) Modeeroch (IRE) (Mozart (IRE))
7964 3440[2] (4185) 4793[4] 5442[10] 6220[15] (6930) 7789[3] 8420[3]◆ 9441[3]

Revolver (IRE) *Sir Mark Prescott Bt* a36 48
2 b g Slade Power(IRE) Swizzle Stick (IRE) (Sadler's Wells (USA))
7388[6] 7842[10] 8203[6]

Rewaayat *Charles Hills* a70 80
4 br g Pivotal Rufoof (Zamindar (USA))
1684[2] 2183[4] (5050) 5551[5] 6080[5] 7161[3]

Rewrite The Stars (IRE)
James Tate a70 54
3 ch f Sea The Stars(IRE) Table Bay (IRE) (Nayef (USA))
2919[11] 4503[2] 5810[10] 8552[5]

Rex Place (IRE) *H Al Ramzani* a50 70
3 b c Battle Of Marengo(IRE) Green Chorus (IRE) (Oratorio (IRE))
893a[U]

Rey De Oro (JPN) *Kazuo Fujisawa* 122
5 b h King Kamehameha(JPN) La Dorada (JPN) (Symboli Kris S (USA))
1446a[6] 9153a[11]

Rey Loopy (IRE) *Ben Haslam* a92 79
5 b g Lope De Vega(IRE) Al Basar (USA) (Sahm (USA))
(23) 209[2] (350) 611[2] 807[2] (1401) 1644[2] 2242[8] 4292[P] 7312[8] 8024[11] 8918[P]

Reynolds *Eve Johnson Houghton* 84
3 ch g Exceed And Excel(AUS) L'Affaire Monique (Machiavellian (USA))
2790[3]◆ 4121[2]

Rey Pelayo (FR) *F Chappet* a82 67
3 b c Wootton Bassett Darkova (USA) (Maria's Mon (USA))
(9058a)

Rgeebee *David O'Meara* a29
3 b f Showcasing Milford Sound (Barathea (IRE))
9400[8]

Rhea *Kevin Ryan* 97
2 ch f Siyouni(FR) Titian's Pride (USA) (Giant's Causeway (USA))
(3049) 5346[3]

Rhossili Down *Charles Hills* a70 77
3 b f Kingman Exceptionelle (Exceed And Excel (AUS))
1570[2] 3080[2]◆ 3920[3] 4655[3] 7901[8] 8695[2] (9112)

Rhubarb Bikini (IRE)
Archie Watson a76
2 b c Zoffany(IRE) Pearlitas Passion (IRE) (High Chaparral (IRE))
8287[2] (9585)

Rhydwyn (IRE) *T Hogan* 89
3 b g Kodiac Pilates (IRE) (Shamardal (USA))
6235a[4] 7241a[18] 8166a[7]

Rhyme Scheme (IRE)
Mick Channon 75
2 b f Poet's Voice Tidal Moon (Sea The Stars (IRE))
4605[7] 7203[3] 8093[3]

Rhythmic Intent (IRE)
Stuart Williams 92
3 ch c Lope De Vega(IRE) Kerry Gal (IRE) (Galileo (IRE))
2249[3] 3808[2] 4841[10] 5341[3] (6216) 6952[6]◆ 8092[3]

Rhythmic Motion *Jim Boyle* a37
2 ch f Toronado(IRE) Sonnetation (IRE) (Dylan Thomas (IRE))
8849[14] 9085[12]

Rich And Famous (USA) *S Jadhav* a74 93
5 b g Bernardini(USA) Enrichment (USA) (Ghostzapper (USA))
196a[10]

Rich Approach (IRE) *James Bethell* a70 62
3 b g Dawn Approach(IRE) Kiss Me Goodbye (Raven's Pass (USA))
(274)◆ 698[4] 1720[9] 2418[5] 3569[7] 4606[6] 5852[9]

Richard Of Cambria *Adrian Nicholls* 8
2 b g Cityscape Porthgain (Bertolini (USA))
3954[10] 4206[8]

Richard R H B (IRE)
David Loughnane a69 70
2 b g Fulbright Royal Interlude (IRE) (King's Theatre (IRE))
1416[15] 2108[3] 2706[7] 5101[4] 6372[6] 8259[4] 8665[6]◆ (9137)◆ 9568[3]

Richard Strauss (IRE) *Philip Kirby* a63 63
5 bb g Kheleyf(USA) Symfony (IRE) (Monsun (GER))
2202[15] 2684[7] 3511[13] 4435[8] 5766[8] 8344[4]

Rich Belief *James Bethell* a86 86
2 b g Make Believe Realt Eile (IRE) (Dark Angel (IRE))
2869[5] 3702[4] (4456) 5896[2] 6184[3] 6942[3]◆ 8124[4]

Rich Cummins *Mark Johnston* a65 65
3 ro g Dalakhani(IRE) Claxon (Caerleon (USA))
1270[2] 1770[2] 2011[2] 2150[7] 3198[2] 4039[7]

Richenza (FR) *Ralph Beckett* a92 104
4 b m Holy Roman Emperor(IRE) Nantha (IRE) (King's Best (USA))
2627[9] (3544) 3891[3] 6229[15] 7892[7] (8115)

Rich Girl (IRE) *Sylvester Kirk* a26
2 b f Gutaifan(IRE) Queenofthenorth (IRE) (Halling (USA))
9448[8] 9585[12]

Richmond Avenue (IRE) *A Fabre* 101
4 b m Invincible Spirit(IRE) Ragsah (IRE) (Shamardal (USA))
4706a[7] 6910a[2] 7657[3]

Rickyroadboy *Mark Walford* a44 70
4 b g Mazameer(IRE) Black Baccara (Superior Premium)
1760[11] 2294[2] 2625[6] 3936[5] 5157[6] 6680[9] 7065[8] 7511[9]

Ricochet (IRE) *C Boutin* a63 65
3 b g Lope De Vega(IRE) Sound Of Guns (Acclamation)
3421[4] 4116[6] 4655[6] 5306[2] 6598[7] 7157[3] 7447[9] 8408[3] 8712[3] 9106[11] (9280a) 9538a[8]

Ridaa (IRE) *J E Hammond* a94 96
3 ch f New Approach(IRE) Halaqa (IRE) (Pivotal)
(5329a) 9170a[5]

Ride And Prejudice *Julia Feilden* a58 8
2 b f Casamento(IRE) Emma's Gift (IRE) (Aussie Rules (USA))
1937[5] 2469[5] 4502[7]

Rideson *Roger Varian* a79
2 b f Golden Horn Rekdhat (IRE) (Shamardal (USA))
7832[2]◆ 9046[3]

Ride The Monkey (IRE)
Michael Dods 54
3 b g Bungle Inthejungle Eileenlilian (Authorized (IRE))
2895[7] 4077[4] 5124[8] 6578[3] 7405[12]

Ridgy (FR) *Gerard Aidant* a56
3 gr f Electric Beat Rowina (GER) (Hamond (GER))
9058a[13]

Rifft (IRE) *Lydia Richards* a52 63
4 b g Iffraaj Toquette (IRE) (Acclamation)
1094[11] 5268[7] 6119[3] 6839[10] 8223[9] 8822[8] 9305[14]

Riflescope (IRE) *S Seemar* a95 104
6 b g Raven's Pass(USA) Red Intrigue (IRE) (Selkirk (USA))
843a[2] 1111a[4]

Right About Now (IRE)
Charlie Wallis a48 51
5 b g Famous Name Right Reason (IRE) (Manduro (GER))
2259[7] 3744[8] 5354[8] 6324[10] 6860[7] 7318[13] 8466[10]

Right Action *Richard Fahey* a81 88
5 b g Dandy Man(IRE) Rockaby Baby (IRE) (Beckett (IRE))
(1457) 2679[2] 3100[5] 3813[4] 5195[5] 5692[7] 6922[11] 7362[7] 8342[13]

Right Flank (USA) *Doug Watson* a86 64
5 b h War Front(USA) Principal Role (USA) (Empire Maker (USA))
997[10]

Rimmal (USA) *Jeremy Noseda* 16
3 b f Bellamy Road(USA) Shooting Party (USA) (Sky Classic (CAN))
1834[8] 2332[12]

Rince Deireanach (IRE) *J J Lambe* a49 65
4 b m Teofilo(IRE) National Swagger (IRE) (Giant's Causeway (USA))
7779[7]

Ring Cycle *Sylvester Kirk* a69 43
3 ch g Norse Dancer(IRE) Opera Glass (Barathea (IRE))
156[7] 2914[8]

Ringerdingding (AUS)
Anthony Freedman 110
3 bl c Sebring(AUS) Maybe I (AUS) (Red Ransom (USA))
9015a[6]

Ringo Kid *Mrs Olivia Byrne* a57 54
6 b g Bushranger(IRE) Clincher (Royal Applause)
8406[10] 9042[7]

Ring Out The Bells (IRE)
Charles Hills a45 55
3 br f Kodiac Newlywed (IRE) (Authorized (IRE))
400[8]

Rio Glamorous *Roy Bowring*
6 b g Aussie Rules(USA) Glamorous Spirit (IRE) (Invincible Spirit (IRE))
2296[8] 3475[15]

Rioja Day (IRE) *Jim Goldie* a55 69
9 b g Red Clubs(IRE) Dai E Dai (USA) (Seattle Dancer (USA))
350[7] 611[5] 1083[5] 2436[11] 2964[8] 3224[8]

Rionach *M D O'Callaghan* a76 101
4 b m Sea The Stars(IRE) Forest Crown (Royal Applause)
1307a[9] 2493a[3] 2879a[7] 3786a[5] 6646a[6] 7794a[9]

Rio Ronaldo (IRE) *Mike Murphy* a50 93
7 b g Footstepsinthesand Flanders (IRE) (Common Grounds)
2272[10] 2839[3] 3301[9]

Riot (IRE) *John Gosden* a81 90
2 b c Kingman Alexander Queen (IRE) (King's Best (USA))
3804[2]◆ 4611[2] 5563[2] (6927)

Rio Tigre (IRE) *S Jadhav* a96 99
8 b h Teofilo(IRE) Braziliz (USA) (Kingmambo (USA))
281a[5] 730a[6]

Rioviejo (FR) *X Thomas-Demeaulte* 32
2 gr c Kendargent(FR) Precious Promise (FR) (Kandahar Run)
1657a[13]

Ripley (IRE) *Charles Hills* a64 46
4 b m Declaration Of War(USA) La Conquerante (Hurricane Run (IRE))
473[5] 782[3] 1024[8] 4869[6]

Ripon Spa *Jedd O'Keeffe* 62
3 b g Rock Of Gibraltar(IRE) Lady Lahar (Fraam)
2506[7] 3510[6] 3972[9] 5695[8]

Ripplet *Hughie Morrison* a65 22
4 b m Rip Van Winkle(IRE) Seradim (Elnadim (USA))
435[4] 1064[5] 1287[6] 1861[11] 2344[12]

Rippling Waters (FR)
Jamie Osborne a66 78
5 b m Areion(GER) Pepples Beach (GER) (Lomitas)
33[3] (386) 697[5] 828[6] 1216[9] 7088a[9]

Ripp Orf (IRE) *David Elsworth* a87 101
5 b g Rip Van Winkle(IRE) Barzah (IRE) (Darshaan)
1415[5]◆ 1753[16] 2609[5] 3318[10] 4921[6] 5413[4] 6214[2] 6950[2] 7891[13]

Risaala (IRE) *Charles Hills* a66
3 bb f Mukhadram Maayaat (USA) (Jazil (USA))
2216[2]

Rise Hall *Martyn Meade* 105
4 b g Frankel Forever Bond (Danetime (IRE))
(1694) 4342[2]◆ 4934[2] (5440)◆ 6475[4]◆ 7457[13]

Rise High (FR) *C Fownes* 120
5 b g Myboycharlie(IRE) Lana Girl (USA) (Arch (USA))
9380a[3]

Rising Sunshine (IRE)
Milton Bradley a49 43
6 b g Dark Angel(IRE) Little Audio (IRE) (Shamardal (USA))
243[10] 263[9] 531[4] 924[2] 1214[6]

Risk Mitigation (USA) *David Evans* a54 52
3 bb g Hat Trick(JPN) Island Escape (USA) (Petionville (USA))
913[11] 1094[9] 1344[5] 4794[8] 5548[2] 6042[4] 6361[3] 7025[7] 8003[4] 8269[2] (8406) 8843[F] (Dead)

Risk Taker (IRE) *Clive Cox* a63 67
2 ch g Lope De Vega(IRE) What A Treasure (IRE) (Cadeaux Genereux)
8516[4] 9130[5]

Rita's Folly *Anthony Carson* a49 60
3 b f Harbour Watch(IRE) Doric Lady (Kyllachy)
3780[11] (5358) 5869[7] 6389[11] 7472[7] 8847[12]

Ritas Legacy *Roy Brotherton* a7 31
5 b g Passing Glance Rita's Rock Ape (Mon Tresor)
926[9]

Ritchie Star (IRE) *Ben Haslam* a59 59
3 b g Lilbourne Lad(IRE) Array Of Stars (IRE) (Barathea (IRE))
1764[9] 2711[7] 3246[2] 4039[5] 5915[6] 7578[6] 8922[2] 9225[8] 9516[5]

Ritchie Valens (IRE)
Richard Hannon a86 86
3 ch g Helmet(AUS) Miss Cape (IRE) (Cape Cross (IRE))
1293[3]◆ 2075[2] 2553[3] 2828[6] 3808[4] 5451[3] (5779) 6217[2] 6967[4] 7702[7]

Rivas Rob Roy *John Gallagher* a61 52
4 ch g Archipenko(USA) Rivas Rhapsody (IRE) (Hawk Wing (USA))
37[3] 250[4] 484[2] 925[3] 1075[4] 1933[6] 2286[5] 2741[4] 3187[10] 7024[14] 8818[6] (9111)◆ 9277[8] 9629[7]

Riven Light (IRE) *W P Mullins* 107
7 b g Raven's Pass(USA) Vivacity (Trempolino (USA))
3953[6] 7038a[5] 8784a[5]

River Cafe (IRE) *John Bridger* a32 35
4 b m High Chaparral(IRE) Dingle View (IRE) (Mujadil (USA))
257[13] 9248[9] 9426[12]

River Cam *James Tate* a69 75
2 b f Fountain Of Youth(IRE) Cadeaux Power (Major Cadeaux)
5353[2] 5856[2] 6883[2] 7308[3] 8302[4] 9300[3] 9515[4]

River Cannes (FR) *T Castanheira* a61 69
4 b m Orpen(USA) Cannes To Capri (IRE) (Galileo (IRE))
2670a[5]

River Dart (IRE) *Tony Carroll* a67 48
7 ch g Dutch Art Sky Galaxy (USA) (Sky Classic (CAN))
124[5] 947[9] 1363[9] 2353[9] 4543[8] 6303[11] 8224[12]

River Dawn *Paul Cole* a74 69
3 ch g Dawn Approach(IRE) Echo River (USA) (Irish River (FR))
1346[P] 2794[7] 3184[4] 3661[4] 4185[6] (4754) 8807[2] 9306[6]

Riverfront (FR) *Andrew Balding* 78
3 gr g Reliable Man Why Worry (FR) (Cadeaux Genereux)
5592[6] 5955[6] (6811)

River Glades *Tom Tate* a76 74
4 b g Cape Cross(IRE) Everglades (Teofilo (IRE))
124[3] 2781[7]

River Icon *Iain Jardine* 85
7 b m Sixties Icon River Alder (Alderbrook)
7510[2] 8129[3] 8513[3]

Riverina *Harry Dunlop* a54 52
3 ch f Australia Peace Palace (Archipenko (USA))
1730[8] 2343[8] 3593[4] 5049[9] 6046[6] 7520[8] 8293[8]

River Nymph *Clive Cox* a80 82
2 b c Cable Bay(IRE) Little Nymph (Emperor Fountain)
6845[3] 7407[2] (9008)

River Of Kings (IRE)
Keith Dalgleish a59 58
2 b g Kodiac Esedra (IRE) (Hurricane Run (IRE))
2288[3] 2780[8] 3498[6] 5185[23] 5789[11] 6625[8] 7306[3] 7582[9] 7904[15] 8815[7] 9037[6]

River On The Hills (FR)
Mme Pia Brandt 99
5 b m Sinndar(IRE) Ronda (Bluebird (USA))
5510a[4] 7137a[4]

River Rule *Adrian Wintle* a42 47
4 b m Bated Breath Ocean Countess (IRE) (Storming Home)
58[11] 1519[5] 4190[9]

River Song (IRE) *Archie Watson* a69
2 b f Battle Of Marengo(IRE) Yurituni (Bahamian Bounty)
9097[4]

River Sprite *Daniel Kubler* a62
2 b f Swiss Spirit Camp Riverside (USA) (Forest Camp (USA))
7276[2] 8198[5]

Riviera Claire *Jamie Osborne* a63 53
3 b f Showcasing Seldemosa (Selkirk (USA))
319[7]

Riviera Nights *Richard Hannon* a96 98
3 b c Kingman Turama (Pivotal)
1940[3] 2828[13] 3599[11] (6913) 7697[3]

Rizzichop (FR) *O Trigodet* a85 79
7 b g Deportivo Yamouna (FR) (Danehill Dancer (IRE))
2226a[7]

Rizzle Dizzle *Rebecca Menzies* a60 43
4 b m Foxwedge(AUS) Greensand (Green Desert (USA))
123[6] 356[10] 1368[12]

Road Rage (IRE) *Michael Dods* 74
2 b g Requinto(IRE) Grid Lock (IRE) (Van Nistelrooy (USA))
1758[10] 4206[5] 4976[3] (5896) 6450[4]

Roadster (USA) *Bob Baffert* a115
3 rg c Quality Road(USA) Ghost Dancing (USA) (Silver Ghost (USA))
2425a[15] 9639a[2]

Road To Paris (IRE)
Sir Mark Prescott Bt a80 75
3 b g Champs Elysees Alchemilla (Dubai Destination (USA))
3195[11] 5028[3] 5378[2] (5825)◆ 6055[2] (6333) (7845)

Roar (IRE) *Ed de Giles* a72 81
5 b g Pour Moi(IRE) Evening Rushour (IRE) (Mull Of Kintyre (USA))
246[6] 1291[4] 2092[2] (3250) 3816[18] 6038[6]

Roaring Forties (IRE)
Rebecca Bastiman a50 67
6 b g Invincible Spirit(IRE) Growling (IRE) (Celtic Swing)
1338[9] 2203[14] 2372[2] 2898[12] 3215[2] 3781[8] 4060[9] 4584[10] 4978[7] (5237) 5938[4] 7364[14] 7540[10] 8233[5]

Roaring Rory *Ollie Pears* a59 59
6 ch g Sakhee's Secret Barbieri (IRE) (Encosta De Lago (AUS))
277[7] 502[4] 738[4] 1765[6] 2153[3] 2678[10] 4823[8] 5559[4] 5857[6] 7286[7] 7770[3]◆ 8457[5] 9133[9] 9551[9]

Robben Rainbow *Katie Scott* a41 55
5 b g Delegator Sally Can Wait (Sakhee (USA))
1158[9] 1765[13] 2328[4] (2682) 3178[9] 4060[10] 4513[6] 4784[7] 5852[13] 6572[2] 7210[11] 7443[8] 7738[7] 8123[7]

Robbian *Charles Smith* a42 53
8 b g Bertolini(USA) Crathes (Zilzal (USA))
1554[5] 4212[13] 8071[9] 8263[6] 8632[11] 8861[2] 9182[7]

Robeam (IRE) *Richard Fahey* a58 59
3 b g Helmet(AUS) Secret Flame (Machiavellian (USA))
228[5] 612[5] 1721[7] 2125[2] 2517[7] 3198[3] 3593[5] 3931[4] (4435) 4998[3] 5915[2] 7192[4]

Robero *Gay Kelleway* a82 79
7 b g Piccolo Ceilidh Band (Celtic Swing)
44[5] 260[4] 929[5] 2015[4] 2526[13] 3018[2] 4078[4] 6164[5] 6734[2] 7653[9] 8122[2]◆ 8761[14] 9606[3] (9642)

Robert Bruce (CHI) *Chad C Brown* 115
4 bb h Fast Company(IRE) Lady Pelusa (ARG) (Orpen (USA))
6001a[4]

Robert Fitzroy (IRE) *Michael Bell* a67 69
3 b g Big Bad Bob(IRE) Semiquaver (IRE) (Mark Of Esteem (IRE))
1697[7] 2697[4] 3311[4] 3888[6] 4484[9] (6128) 6586[2]

Robert Frost (USA)
Jane Chapple-Hyam a62 64
2 ch g Munnings(USA) Sorenstam (USA) (Tiznow (USA))
5353[4] 5887[3] 6344[6]

Robert Guiscard (IRE)
Mark Johnston a67 71
2 b g Exceed And Excel(AUS) Beneventa (Most Welcome)
5865[4]◆ 6219[6] 6970[3] 7419[5] 8201[3]

Robert L'Echelle (IRE)
Hughie Morrison a78 70
3 b g Big Bad Bob(IRE) Damhsa Le Cheile (IRE) (Teofilo (IRE))
(66) 1911[7] 4068[8] 5055[3] 7279[5] 7915[12]

Robert Walpole *George Scott* 71
2 b c Golden Horn Whazzat (Daylami (IRE))
6409[5] 7392[5]

Robiano (IRE) *Ottavio Di Paolo* a10 30
6 b h Dubawi(IRE) Reggane (Red Ransom (USA))
2888a[15]

Robin Du Bois (FR)
Carmen Bocskai 78
3 b g Kandahar Run Ballymaloe (GER) (Big Shuffle (USA))
7291a[8]

Robin Of Navan (FR) *Harry Dunlop* a90 110
6 ch h American Post Cloghran (FR) (Muhtathir)
1420[8] 1890[7] 2271[3] 2832[7]◆ 3987[20] (5230a) 7007a[7] 7922a[13] 8392a[3]

Robin Weathers (USA)
Fawzi Abdulla Nass a80 75
5 ch g Elusive Quality(USA) Sharnberry (Shamardal (USA))
97a[4]

Robot Boy (IRE) *Marjorie Fife* a74 74
9 ch g Shamardal(USA) Pivotal's Princess (IRE) (Pivotal)
2079[12] 2421[9] 3360[7] 3658[12] 3928[9] 4514[3] (4694) 4911[5] 5169[RR] 5723[6] 5892[3]

Robotique Danseur (FR) *K R Burke* a74 32
3 b f Siyouni(FR) Dawn To Dance (IRE) (Selkirk (USA))
(1400) 2102[10] 7822[2] 8427[5] 9109[11]

Robranov (ITY) *Roberto Di Paolo* 89
6 b h St Paul House Jasmine Joli (IRE) (Cape Cross (IRE))
2888a[11]

Robsdelight (IRE) *Gay Kelleway* a47 70
4 br g Harbour Watch(IRE) Silca Boo (Efisio)
1413[16] 3183[4] 4061[5] 8206[9] 9182[6]

Roca Magica *Ed Dunlop* a51 40
3 b f Garswood Marigay's Magic (Rock Of Gibraltar (IRE))
4642[P] 6666[11] 7282[4] 7961[7] 8408[5] 9160[5] 9410[9] 9659[2]

Roc Angel (FR) *F Chappet* a105 106
5 ch g Rock Of Gibraltar(IRE) Forewarned (IRE) (Grand Lodge (USA))
682a[3] 1921[4] 3987[6] 9210a[10]

Roc Astrale (IRE) *Phil McEntee* a73 50
5 ch g Teofilo(IRE) Lumiere Astrale (FR) (Trempolino (USA))
1482[5] 2059[8] 2301[4] 2468[8] 2975[10] 3428[5] 3740[6]

Roccabascerana (AUS) *David Jolly* 100
2 ch g Fighting Sun(AUS) Checklist (AUS) (Reset (AUS))
8137a[11]

Rochenka (FR) *M Brasme* a64 68
6 bl m Rock Of Gibraltar(IRE) Lunashkaya (Muhtathir)
6031a[15]

Rochester House (IRE)
Mark Johnston a85 100
3 ch g Galileo(IRE) Kalla (Monsun (GER))
1484[2]◆ (1661)◆ 2258[3] 2811[3] 3358[4] 3729[3] 4327[2] (5019) (5769)◆ 6171[3] 6471[11] 8114[19] 8754[9] 9065[7]

Rochford (IRE) *Henry Spiller* a61 36
2 b c Ivawood(IRE) Lady Berta (Bertolini (USA))
4069[7] 4588[3] 5265[5] 6884[3]◆ 7306[2] 8061[3] 8760[9] 9045[8]

Rock (AUS)
Michael, Wayne & John Hawkes 98
3 b g Pierro(AUS) Subtitle (AUS) (Fastnet Rock (AUS))
8768a[12]

Rockafilly (FR) *J A Nash* a31 34
4 b m Dabirsim(FR) Barzas River (IRE) (Dalakhani (IRE))
504[11]

Rock At The Park (FR) *H-A Pantall* 60
3 ch g Denon(USA) Adeje Park (IRE) (Night Shift (USA))
1450a[7]

Rock Blanc (FR) *R Le Dren Doleuze* 63
2 b c Youmzain(IRE) Rock Harmonie (FR) (Rock Of Gibraltar (IRE))
7675a[13]

Rock Bottom *Richard Hughes* a73
3 ch c Coach House(IRE) La Tinta Bay (Compton Place)
(182) 287[2]

Rock Boy Grey (IRE)
Mark Loughnane a78 42
4 gr g Dark Angel(IRE) Encore View (Oasis Dream)
3768[5] 5137[4] 6116[5]◆ 6665[2] 7418[4]◆ 8199[7]◆ 8471[3]◆ 8923[5] 9217[2] **(9622)**◆

Rock Eagle *Ralph Beckett* 111
4 ch g Teofilo(IRE) Highland Shot (Selkirk (USA))
3077[4]

Rockemperor (IRE) *Simone Brogi* a88 110
3 b c Holy Roman Emperor(IRE) Motivation (FR) (Muhtathir)
1625a[2] 3390a[6]

Rockesbury *David Loughnane* a62 57
4 b g Foxwedge(AUS) Nellie Ellis (IRE) (Compton Place)
1986[6] **2215**[2] 2944[4] 3430[5] 4195[3] 4875[6] 9128[9] 9253[3] 9566[4]

Rocket Action *Robert Cowell* a109 88
3 gr g Toronado(IRE) Winning Express (IRE) (Camacho)
1924[2] 2434[3] 2835[11] 5530[4] (6735) 7449[2] (8867) **(9166)**

Rocket Dancer *Sylvester Kirk* a60 71
2 b g Toronado(IRE) Opera Dancer (Norse Dancer (IRE))
3760[5]◆ **6368**[2] 6858[6] 7971[7] 8124[9]

Rocket Power *A bin Harmash* a90 94
6 ch g Kyllachy Rhal (IRE) (Rahy (USA))
425a[5] 847a[13]

Rocket Ronnie (IRE) *Adrian Wintle* a49 60
9 b g Antonius Pius(USA) Ctesiphon (USA) (Arch (USA))
59[12] 436[5] **721**[6]

Rock Force (IRE) *Alan King* a71 89
4 b g Fastnet Rock(AUS) Sweepstake (IRE) (Acclamation)
2969[8] 3663[9] 4224[7]

Rock Hill (IRE) *Paul Midgley* a50 67
4 br g Rock Of Gibraltar(IRE) Pascali (Compton Place)
1402[4] 2633[10]

Rock Icon *Ali Stronge* a57 63
6 b g Sixties Icon Monashee Rock (IRE) (Monashee Mountain (USA))
922[10] **1356**[7] 1727[13] 2064[8] 3529[5] 6289[10]

Rockies Spirit *Denis Quinn* a79 83
4 br h Swiss Spirit Red Mischief (IRE) (Red Clubs (IRE))
158[7] 317[11] **1767**[9] 2804[11]

Rockingham Jill *Jo Hughes* 66
2 b f Cable Bay(IRE) Bubbly Ballerina (Footstepsinthesand)
2275[2]◆

Rocking My Boat (IRE)
Nick Littmoden a52
2 ch g Gale Force Ten Lady Pitrizza (IRE) (Night Shift (USA))
8455[11] **9085**[8]

Rocking Reg (IRE) *Roger Teal* a68 54
2 gr c Gutaifan(IRE) Princess Of Troy (IRE) (Tiger Hill (IRE))
8409[5] **9036**[2] 9474[2]

Rockin' N Raven *Sylvester Kirk* a50
2 b g Raven's Pass(USA) Solva (Singspiel (IRE))
7276[7]

Rock In Society (IRE) *John Butler* a60 56
4 ch g Society Rock(IRE) Arabela (IRE) (Medicean)
1383[9] 1554[4] 1732[2] 2066[3] (3007) 3304[8] 4217[7] 5302[11] 5806[15] 5837[2] 6546[6] 7281[3] 8018[11] **8256**[2]

Rock Island Line *Mark Walford* a38 39
5 b g Haafhd Diablo Dancer (Zafeen (FR))
784[11] **1231**[12] 2290[9] 3162[P] 4633[15]

Rockley Point *Katie Scott* a55 47
6 b g Canford Cliffs(IRE) Statua (IRE) (Statoblest (IRE))
(742) 1162[11] 1766[10] 2183[5] 3227[10] 3452[4] 3933[6] 4335[12] 5765[5] 6659[10] 7420[4] 7824[3] 7962[4] 8632[5] 8821[2] (9398) 9473[12]

Rockliffe *Micky Hammond* a33 44
6 b g Notnowcato Hope Island (IRE) (Titus Livius (FR))
4435[9] 5043[6] 5766[6] **6583**[3]

Rock N Roll Queen *John Mackie* a58 50
3 gr f Coach House(IRE) Misty's Choice (Hellvelyn)
2016[9] 2871[11] 4193[7] 5293[12]

Rock N'Stones (IRE) *Gillian Boanas* a49 53
8 b g Stowaway Rock Abbey (IRE) (College Chapel)
40[4] 589[11] 1718[4] **(2684)** 4510[10] 5435[8] 5727[12]

Rock Of Estonia (IRE)
Michael Squance a72 54
4 ch g Society Rock(IRE) Estonia (Exceed And Excel (AUS))
253[5]◆ 755[7] 1522[2] **(2348)**◆ **2799**[2]◆ 3575[2] 4365[7] 6968[11] 7789[9] 8220[10] 8946[4] 9223[5] 9559[9] 9627[3]

Rock Of Fame *Roger Varian* a64
2 b f Fastnet Rock(AUS) Familliarity (Nayef (USA))
7580[6] **8218**[5] 8891[9]

Rock Of Glenstal *S Gouyette* a62 9
9 b g Mount Nelson Amandian (IRE) (Indian Ridge (IRE))
7501a[7]

Rock Of Pensax (IRE)
Mark Loughnane a26
2 br g Society Rock(IRE) China Pink (Oasis Dream)
9567[10]

Rock Of Redmond (IRE)
Dean Ivory a55
2 b f Rock Of Gibraltar(IRE) Classic Lass (Dr Fong (USA))
8058[6] **8700**[7] 9631[9]

Rock On Baileys *Amy Murphy* a94 101
4 ch m Rock Of Gibraltar(IRE) Ring For Baileys (Kyllachy)
2062[7] 2627[10] 3994[10] 4904[2] 5705[2] **6453**[3] 6999[5]◆ 7892[8] 8708[11] 9088[8] 9301[10] (9586)

Rock On Bertie (IRE) *Derek Shaw* a55 55
4 b g Rock Of Gibraltar(IRE) Princess Banu (Oasis Dream)
1983[8] 2112[13] 2741[11]

Rocksette *Adam West* a58 53
5 b m Mount Nelson Native Nickel (IRE) (Be My Native (USA))
1935[5] 2277[8] 3348[7] 3941[8] 4475[6] 5049[6] **(5310)** 5993[10] 6560[8] 7232[8] 7375[8] 8000[13]

Rock Sound (IRE) *Declan Carroll* a85 76
4 ch g Lope De Vega(IRE) Thoughtless Moment (IRE) (Pivotal)
(8839)◆ 9334[2]

Rockstar Max (GER) *Denis Coakley* a46
3 b g Maxios Remote Romance (USA) (Irish River (FR))
7841[8] 8653[6] 9165[8]

Rock Steady (IRE) *Alan King* a105 95
6 ch g Intikhab(USA) Mannsara (IRE) (Royal Academy (USA))
6848[5]

Rock The Cradle (IRE) *Ed Vaughan* 93
3 ch g Ruler Of The World(IRE) Independent Girl (IRE) (Bachelor Duke (USA))
3170[2]◆ 4071[3] 5060[2]◆ (5863) 6468[2] **(7350)**

Rock Up In Style *Clare Ellam* a73 60
3 b g Showcasing Flora Trevelyan (Cape Cross (IRE))
(1166) 1481[8] 2336[8] 2942[8] 3665[14] 4070[10] 5054[9]

Rock Warbler (IRE)
Michael Mullineaux a53 44
6 ch g Raven's Pass(USA) Rare Tern (IRE) (Pivotal)
356[8] 468[8] 914[6] 1231[10] 3046[13] 3705[10] 4460[10] 4875[10] 5024[6] 5302[9] 5723[11] 9395[10] 9445[7] 9643[6]

Rockwood *Karen McLintock* a68 77
8 b g Rock Of Gibraltar(IRE) Hannah Frank (IRE) (High Chaparral (IRE))
102[4] 950[4] 1169[11]

Rocquemont (FR) *F Rohaut* a87 104
3 b c Anodin(IRE) Rebecca's Filly (FR) (Elusive City (USA))
(5538a)

Rocques (FR) *F Chappet* 103
3 b f Lawman(FR) Regina Mundi (IRE) (Montjeu (IRE))
1795a[5] **2669a**[7] 3387a[7] 5608[4]

Rodaini (USA) *A bin Harmash* a108 90
5 ch g Exchange Rate(USA) Blessings Count (USA) (Pulpit (USA))
282a[6] **(842a)** 1112a[5]

Roddy Ransom *Ben Haslam* a20
2 b g Roderic O'Connor(IRE) Midnight Ransom (Red Ransom (USA))
7821[10]

Rodin *Andrew Balding* a68 46
2 b c Mayson Moon Goddess (Rainbow Quest (USA))
8409[7]◆ **9008**[4]

Rodnee Tee *David O'Meara* a83 80
2 b g Roderic O'Connor(IRE) Sugar Free (IRE) (Oasis Dream)
(1844) 2115[2] **2694**[2] 3566[5] 4361[4]

Rodney After Dave (IRE)
Marjorie Fife 47
3 b g Intense Focus(USA) Ceol Cois Tine (IRE) (Teofilo (IRE))
3218[5] 3684[10] 4210[6] 5915[10]

Rodney Le Roc *John Best* a51 40
2 b g Garswood French Accent (Elnadim (USA))
3257[9] **9631**[8]

Rodrico (AUS) *Bjorn Baker* 99
6 b g High Chaparral(IRE) Truly A Beauty (USA) (Seeking The Gold (USA))
1784a[13]

Rodrigo Diaz *David Simcock* a44
2 b g Golden Horn Kitty Wells (Sadler's Wells (USA))
9052[13] **9415**[11]

Rogue *Alexandra Dunn* a93 84
4 b g Epaulette(AUS) Miskin Diamond (IRE) (Diamond Green (FR))
1881[3] 3496[6] 4860a[3] 5564[7] 6201[4] 6863[6] (7861a)

Rogue Runner (GER) *Carina Fey* a60 79
7 b g King's Best(USA) Rosa Di Brema (ITY) (Lomitas)
(1073a)

Rolando (IRE) *A Wohler* a109 105
5 b h Campanologist(USA) Rosa Di Brema (ITY) (Lomitas)
5926a[3] 8372a[5] 9210a[4]

Rolladice *Michael Easterby* a24 76
4 ch g Bated Breath Selkirk Sky (Selkirk (USA))
2709[13] 3221[14] 6972[10] **(8342)** 8400[10]

Roller *Mark Loughnane* a72 82
6 b g Rail Link Buffering (Beat Hollow)
2151[6] 4078[3] **4319**[3] 5351[6] 5804[5] 6582[10] 7305[12] 7587[11] (9006) 9453[5] 9606[6]

Rollicking (IRE) *Richard Hannon* a61 59
3 b f Holy Roman Emperor(IRE) Maghzaa (IRE) (Aqlaam)
7166[5] **7839**[11] 8247[12]

Roma Bangkok *Marco Botti* a67
3 b g Mount Nelson Magika (Dubawi (IRE))
1033[6] **1570**[6]

Roman Candle *A Fabre* 110
3 b c Le Havre(IRE) Holy Dazzle (Sunday Break (JPN))
1625a[3] (2314a) 3390a[5] 4963a[4] **6143a**[2]

Romance d'Amour (IRE)
Ottavio Di Paolo 87
4 bl m Kendargent(FR) Regina Mundi (IRE) (Montjeu (IRE))
8790a[8]

Romanciere (IRE) *A Fabre* 106
3 b f Dansili Balladeuse (FR) (Singspiel (IRE))
2312a[3] **4416a**[2] 5470a[3] 6775a[4]

Roman De Brut (IRE)
Rebecca Menzies a67 76
7 ch g Rock Of Gibraltar(IRE) Nesmeh (USA) (More Than Ready (USA))
181[2] **886**[5] 1025[4] 1399[5] 2124[3] 4293[7]

Romanised (IRE) *K J Condon* 119
4 b h Holy Roman Emperor(IRE) Romantic Venture (IRE) (Indian Ridge (IRE))
1776a[5] 2829[4] 3948[4] **(5207a)** (6004a) **7007a**[2]

Roman Legend (IRE)
Jassim Mohammed Ghazali a52 92
8 b h Holy Roman Emperor(IRE) Taking Liberties (IRE) (Royal Academy (USA))
869a[6]

Roman Melody *David Elsworth* a65 76
2 b g Holy Roman Emperor(IRE) Gift Of Music (IRE) (Cadeaux Genereux)
6078[6] 6845[5] **7406**[3] 8059[4] 8430[6]

Roman River *Martin Smith* a87 96
4 b h Holy Roman Emperor(IRE) Inagh River (Fasliyev (USA))
563[7] 1098[8] **1892**[2] 4406[8]

Roman's Empress (IRE)
David Loughnane a33 57
2 b f Holy Roman Emperor(IRE) Dabtiyra (IRE) (Dr Devious (IRE))
3049[7] 3954[6] 7067[10] 7585[7] 8603[10]

Roman Spinner *Rae Guest* a80 76
4 ch m Intikhab(USA) Pompeia (Singspiel (IRE))
81[3] **618**[2] 756[4] 1143[7] 4113[6] 4786[4] 5376[2] 5828[2] 6326[6] 7080[6]◆ 8254[7] 8652[5]◆ (9244) (9417) 9658[5]

Roman Stone (USA) *Keith Dalgleish* a48 81
3 b g Noble Mission Winendynme (USA) (Dynaformer (USA))
4636[2] (6034)◆ **7490**[2] 8082[9]

Romantic (IRE) *Noel C Kelly* a61 57
10 b g Holy Roman Emperor(IRE) Welsh Love (Ela-Mana-Mou (IRE))
100[11]

Romantic Pur (FR) *Mlle B Renk* a55 64
7 bb g Soldier Of Fortune(IRE) Romantic Notion (IRE) (Mujadil (USA))
2391a[6]

Romantic Pursuit (USA)
Kiaran McLaughlin 104
3 b f Medaglia d'Oro(USA) Questing (Hard Spun (USA))
6993a[4]

Romantic Vision (IRE) *Kevin Ryan* 83
2 b c Dandy Man(IRE) Lily White Socks (IRE) (Arakan (USA))
5689[7] (6585)◆ **(7437)**◆ 8095[4]

Roman Turbo (IRE) *M Halford* 104
2 b c Holy Roman Emperor(IRE) Swish (GER) (Monsun (GER))
(5206a) **6430a**[4] 7245a[7]

Roman Warrior *Fergal Birrane* a64 67
4 b g Holy Roman Emperor(IRE) Meet Marhaba (IRE) (Marju (IRE))
9566[9]

Romany Rose (IRE) *Conor Dore*
3 b f Requinto(IRE) Five Star Maria (IRE) (Carrowkeel (IRE))
258[8]

Romero (IRE) *Kevin Ryan* 83
2 b g Brazen Beau(AUS) Out Of Thanks (IRE) (Sadler's Wells (USA))
(2820)◆ 4413a[5]

Romínintheglomin (IRE)
Andrew Hughes a3 54
2 br f Society Rock(IRE) The Real Thing (IRE) (Traditionally (USA))
4275[5] 5118[6] 6606[6] (7234) **7763**[6] 8526[11]

Rominou (FR) *C Lerner* a99 99
6 ch g Excellent Art La Romana (Bijou D'Inde)
3879a[7]

Romola *Sir Michael Stoute* a99 95
3 b f Pivotal Dianora (New Approach (IRE))
2395[6] 3494[3] 4318[6] 5827[3] (6170) (6410) **7815**[2]

Romsey *Hughie Morrison* a81 99
2 b f Mukhadram Broadlands (Kheleyf (USA))
3165[3]◆ (3578) 5346[4] 5964[4] 6444[5] (7749a) **8393a**[3]

Ronaldo (GER) *Andreas Suborics* a96 42
5 b h Scalo Reine Galante (IRE) (Danehill (USA))
8372a[6]

Roncey (FR) *Edouard Monfort* a89 102
5 b h Pivotal Mixed Intention (IRE) (Elusive City (USA))
8373a[2]

Rondinella (NZ)
Roger James & Robert Wellwood 104
4 b m Ocean Park(NZ) Valpolicella (NZ) (Red Ransom (USA))
1784a[4]

Rondo (USA) *Charles Hills* 66
2 b c Twirling Candy(USA) Short Dance (USA) (Hennessy (USA))
6219[5]

Ronnie The Rooster *Les Eyre* a61 43
5 b g Captain Gerrard(IRE) Piranha (IRE) (Exceed And Excel (AUS))
2012[5] 2290[6]

Ronni Layne *Louise Allan* a51 40
5 b m Native Ruler Cindy Incidentally (Shinko Forest (IRE))
829[13] 1145[7] 1520[9] **2234**[2] 3006[11] 3298[11] 3774[5] 5025[6] 5302[4]

Roodeparis *Mark Usher* a58 51
4 ch g Champs Elysees Roodeye (Inchinor)
4287[16]

Roof Garden *Mike Murphy* a68 41
4 ch g Cityscape Celebrity (Pivotal)
1479[8] 3002[6] **3429**[2] 4370[10] 4801[6] 6839[13]

Room To Roam (IRE) *Peter Fahey* a64 69
5 b g Fast Company(IRE) Lady's Locket (IRE) (Fasliyev (USA))
7085a[10]

Roong Roong (IRE)
Richard Hannon 55
3 gr f Dark Angel(IRE) Cut No Ice (IRE) (Verglas (IRE))
1740[8]

Rope A Dope (IRE) *P Schiergen* 71
3 b f Bungle Inthejungle Ronja (USA) (El Corredor (USA))
6006a[9]

Ropey Guest *George Margarson* 101
2 b c Cable Bay(IRE) Hadeeya (Oratorio (IRE))
2931[7] 3274[4] **3949**[6] 4920[4] 5415[3] **6352**[3] 6948[5] 7614[3] 8112[3] **8762**[2]

Rory And Me (FR) *Micky Hammond* 76
4 b g Shamardal(USA) Rosawa (FR) (Linamix (FR))
7382[3] **7704**[2] 8398[8]

Rosa (IRE) *Richard Fahey* a76 43
2 b f Camacho Topiary (IRE) (Selkirk (USA))
(7786)◆ 8097[7] 9251[4]

Rosadora (IRE) *Ralph Beckett* a77 88
2 ch f Camacho Adoring (IRE) (One Cool Cat (USA))
2915[4] (3689) 4387[4]◆ 5171[2] 5683[4] **7117**[3] 7696[10]

Rosa Gold *Rae Guest* a53
2 b f Havana Gold(IRE) Rosa Grace (Lomitas)
9211[10] **9408**[6]

Rosamour (IRE) *Richard Hughes* a48 70
3 b f Paco Boy(IRE) Goldamour (IRE) (Fasliyev (USA))
2798[7] **3764**[3] 4562[7] 5105[6] 5575[5] 6363[8] 7027[2] 7573[7]

Rosamunde (FR) *Mme N Verheyen* a62 64
5 b m Nayef(USA) Rosie Thomas (IRE) (Dylan Thomas (IRE))
4859a[9]

Rosa P *Steph Hollinshead* 41
2 br f Pastoral Pursuits Fortunately (Forzando)
6457[11] 7063[11] 8118[10]

Rosardo Senorita *Rae Guest* a77 66
2 b f Requinto(IRE) Poudretteite (Royal Applause)
6118[3]◆ 6570[2] **(7515)** 8651[6]

Rosarno (IRE) *Chelsea Banham* a54 57
5 b g Fastnet Rock(AUS) Jouet (Reprimand)
812[12] 1143[10] 1367[12] 1768[10] **2019**[6] 2596[9] 3007[13] 7508[4] 8251[3] 8694[2] 8915[4]

Rose Bandit (IRE) *Stef Keniry* 71
2 b f Requinto(IRE) Poppy's Rose (Diktat)
3997[3] **(4910)**◆ 5037[2]◆ 5668[6] 7064[9]

Rose Berry *Charlie Wallis* a89 88
5 b m Archipenko(USA) Desert Berry (Green Desert (USA))
755[2] 1382[6] **(1712)** 1913[6] 3427[7] 4101[12] 4904[4] 5291[3] 5736[3] 8349[8] 8691[3]

Rose Crown *Mick Channon* a20 67
5 b m New Approach(IRE) Silver Touch (IRE) (Dansili)
4216[4] **4762**[2] 4869[3] 5301[9] 6303[10]

Rose Diamant (FR) *E J O'Neill* 45
2 gr f Rajsaman(FR) Touch Me Now (IRE) (King's Best (USA))
4533a[11]

Rose Flower (GER) *G Botti* 101
3 b f Dabirsim(FR) Representera (Lomitas)
2954a[3] **(4621a)**

Rose Hip *Tony Carroll* 85
4 b m Acclamation Poppy Seed (Bold Edge)
2623[7]◆ (3470) 4227[2] (4775) (5606) **(6835)**

Roseina's Voice *David Loughnane* 80
2 b f Poet's Voice Signorina Roseina (Captain Gerrard (IRE))
3244[6] **(7179)**◆ 7677[4]

Roselane (FR) *M Delcher Sanchez* a38
2 b f Dabirsim(FR) Marie Dar (FR) (Sinndar (IRE))
8239a[9]

Roseman (IRE) *Roger Varian* 117
3 b c Kingman Go Lovely Rose (IRE) (Pivotal)
1755[3] (2250) 3026[2]◆ 4013[5] **(8765)**◆

Rose Marmara *Brian Rothwell* a60 72
6 ch m Exceed And Excel(AUS) Show Rainbow (Haafhd)
2151[11] 2809[10] 3928[7] 4438[6] 4595[6] 5040[2]◆ 6591[5] **6825**[2] 7051[2] 8643[7] 8946[5]

Rosemay (FR) *R Mike Smith* a56 56
5 b m Mayson Maine Rose (Red Ransom (USA))
2964[6] 3224[6] (4917) **(5239)**

Rose Of Kildare (IRE)
Mark Johnston 104
2 b f Make Believe Cruck Realta (Sixties Icon)
2228[2]◆ 2561[4]◆ (2907) (3220) 3564[2] 4091[8] 5390[5] (5683) 6356[3] 6833[4] (7432) **(8089)**

Roser Moter (IRE) *Michael Appleby* a35 27
4 b m Motivator Rosia Bay (Rock Of Gibraltar (IRE))
2737[9] 3740[12] 4287[12] 5029[15] 5499[8] 6098[9] 6860[10] 7034[7] **7549**[7] 8270[8] 8694[12]

Rose Secret (ITY) *A Botti* 103
2 b f Sakhee's Secret Rose Celtic (ITY) (Celtic Swing)
8393a[2]

Rose Tinted Spirit *Karen McLintock* a84 81
4 b g Swiss Spirit Woolfall Rose (Generous (IRE))
3356[6] 4386[8]

Roseya (FR) *A De Royer-Dupre* 71
3 b f Invincible Spirit(IRE) Rosanara (FR) (Sinndar (IRE))
4204a[3]

Rosie Royale (IRE) *Roger Teal* a64 65
7 gr m Verglas(IRE) Fearn Royal (IRE) (Ali-Royal (IRE))
3571[6] 4231[4]◆ (4869) 5290[4] 6105[7] **6333**[2] 7231[5] 9570[7] 9626[5]

Rosina *Ann Duffield* a85 72
6 b m Showcasing Mondovi (Kyllachy)
4406[14] 4821[7] 5515[9]

Rosin Box (IRE) *Tristan Davidson* a58 58
6 b m New Approach(IRE) Burn The Floor (IRE) (Indian Haven)
3177[6] 3448[6] 3924[10] 4460[9] 5560[12] 7783[5] 8301[12] 9028[12]

Rosny (FR) *M Planard* a52 49
8 b g Soldier Of Fortune(IRE) Frissonante (Sri Pekan (USA))
5035a[14]

Rossetti *Natalie Lloyd-Beavis* a8 7
11 gr g Dansili Snowdrops (Gulch (USA))
1914[9]

Rossita (GER) *Andreas Suborics* a78
5 b m It's Gino(GER) Royal Fong (GER) (Dr Fong (USA))
46a[3]

Ross Raith Rover *Lee Carter* a65 67
6 b g Oasis Dream Baqah (IRE) (Bahhare (USA))
560[12] 910[12]

Rostropovich (IRE)
David A & B Hayes & Tom Dabern 108
4 b g Frankel Tyranny (Machiavellian (USA))
8361a[16] 8844a[24]

Rosy Ryan (IRE) *Tina Jackson* a42 55
9 b m Tagula(IRE) Khaydariya (IRE) (Akarad (FR))
2585[8] 2911[7] 3414[7] 4584[2] 5099[8] 5247[3] 5787[6] (6103) 7545[10]

Rotherhithe *Henry Spiller* a57 50
4 b m Finjaan Reeling N' Rocking (IRE) (Mr Greeley (USA))
1061[11] 2261[5] 4336[9]

Rotherwick (IRE) *Paul Cole* a82 91
7 ch g Starspangledbanner(AUS) Pivotalia (IRE) (Pivotal)
2800[9] 3806[3] 4450[5] 4997[4] 5667[3]◆ 6021[4] 6447[3] 6909[4] 7294[3] 7729[4] 8727[5] 9050[10]

Roudrapour (FR) *Tony Carroll* a72 63
4 gr g Redoute's Choice(AUS) Rosanara (FR) (Sinndar (IRE))
8862[7]

Roue De Charrette *Amy Murphy* a47 33
4 ch m Champs Elysees Somersault (Pivotal)
1850[9] 3740[9] 4594[10]

Roulston Scar (IRE) *Kevin Ryan* 107
3 b g Lope De Vega(IRE) Pussycat Lips (IRE) (Holy Roman Emperor (IRE))
(2149) 2810[3] (3654)◆ 6476[3] (7002)◆ 7868[10]

Roundabout Magic (IRE)
Simon Dow a67 65
5 ch h Zebedee Cayo Largo (IRE) (Captain Rio)
3443[8] 4027[5] 4374[4]◆ 6048[3] 6605[5] 7690[8] 7986[9] 9092[2]◆ 9583[3] (9664)

Roundhay Park *Nigel Tinkler* 90
4 ch g Mayson Brave Mave (Daylami (IRE))
2117[11] 2396[8] 2743[6] 3480[10] 4369[3] 4649[2] 4987[3] 5691[4] 6208[7] 6676[7] 7077[4] 8400[6]

Roundhead *Richard Phillips* 59
4 ch g Helmet(AUS) Blue Mistral (IRE) (Spinning World (USA))
6812[6]

Round The Island *Richard Whitaker* a56 64
6 b g Royal Applause Luanshya (First Trump)
1818[5] 2292[4] 2709[9] 3214[8] 3656[8] 4440[5] 5157[5] 7066[3] (7383) 7590[3] 8264[4] 8923[8] 9128[6] 9277[9]

Rousayan (IRE) *Roger Fell* a88 95
8 b g Invincible Spirit(IRE) Rose Quartz (Lammtarra (USA))
2710[4] 3563[6] (4240) (4445)◆ 6014[5] 6496[3] 6543[8] 7068[5] 7815[5]

Roussel (IRE) *Charlie Appleby* a102 104
4 b g Kodiac Sodashy (IRE) (Noverre (USA))
170a[5]

Rovaniemi (IRE) *David Simcock* a78 73
2 b c Oasis Dream Landmark (USA) (Arch (USA))
5956[2] (7842)◆

Rovetta (FR) *Mrs John Harrington* 84
5 b m So You Think(NZ) Rosa Brett (ITY) (Green Tune (USA))
5508a[14]

Roving Mission (USA)
Ralph Beckett a77 70
3 ch f Noble Mission Preferential (Dansili)
4641[9] 6043[4] 7159[2] 7730[3] 8507[2] 9202[12]

Rowland Ward *Ralph Beckett* 92
3 b g Sea The Stars(IRE) Honor Bound (Authorized (IRE))
1661[2] (2096)◆ 3260[4] 5201[2] 6975[7]

Roxy Art (IRE) *Ed Dunlop* a78 87
3 ch f Dutch Art Chicago Girl (IRE) (Azamour (IRE))
1751[10] 2319[10] 4638[7]

Royal Admiral (IRE)
Adrian McGuinness a76 71
5 b g Royal Applause Royal Visit (IRE) (King's Best (USA))
5599a[15] (7089a)

Royal Affair (IRE)
Joseph Patrick O'Brien 77
2 b f Kingman Gimasha (Cadeaux Genereux)
4580a[5]

Royal Ambition (IRE) *Clive Cox* a71 76
2 ch c Anjaal Petite Georgia (IRE) (Camacho)
2275[4] 2903[4] 5500[5] (6113) (7155)

Royal Astronomer *Hughie Morrison* a67
2 b c Telescope(IRE) Regal Fairy (IRE) (Desert King (IRE))
9063[11] 9325[7] 9500[2]

Royal Bassett (FR) *Robin Dickin* 19
2 b g Wootton Bassett Donna Roberta (GER) (Dashing Blade)
5374[8]

Royal Big Night (USA)
Mark Johnston a50 72
3 ch g Distorted Humor(USA) Tamboz (USA) (Tapit (USA))
8032[3] 8411[4]

Royal Birth *Stuart Williams* a107 93
8 b g Exceed And Excel(AUS) Princess Georgina (Royal Applause)
35[2]◆ 877[2] (987) 1295[5] 1919[8] 1938[5] 2775[16] 3582[5] 3993[2] 4896[14] (4995) 5504[14] 5942[9] 6954[11] (7107)◆ (7687)◆ 8015[2] 9004[5] 9088[5] 9166[3] 9301[4] 9571[2] 9612[6]

Royal Born (IRE) *Richard Price* a42
3 b g Born To Sea(IRE) Albarouche (Sadler's Wells (USA))
1182[7] 9368[7]

Royal Bowl (FR) *F Seguin* a53 56
6 b g Turtle Bowl(IRE) Monarquia (IRE) (Danehill Dancer (IRE))
8737a[4]

Royal Brave (IRE)
Rebecca Bastiman a81 95
8 b g Acclamation Daqtora (Dr Devious (IRE))
1501[4] 1946[8] 2843[8] 3480[9] 5617[4] 6227[6] 6607[8] 7736[3] 8023[4] 8470[4] 8921[8]

Royal Charmer *Mark Usher* a56
2 b g Hallowed Crown(AUS) Yaqootah (USA) (Gone West (USA))
7276[3]

Royal Commando (IRE)
Charles Hills 102
2 b c No Nay Never(USA) Online Alexander (IRE) (Acclamation)
4069[4] (4596)◆ 5584[8] 7456[4] 8113[8]

Royal Connoisseur (IRE)
Richard Fahey a64 71
8 b g Art Connoisseur(IRE) Valferno (IRE) (Val Royal (FR))
1366[8] 1766[12] 2076[11] 2846[10] 3203[6] 3716[13] 6682[9] 7761[7]

Royal Context (IRE) *Michael Dods* a75
2 b g Acclamation Out Of Context (IRE) (Intikhab (USA))
6548[4] (7627)◆ 8899[3]

Royal Cosmic *Richard Fahey* a77 78
5 b m Wootton Bassett Cosmic Case (Casteddu)
101[4] (387) (607) 737[3] 1525[2] 2185[4] 3222[2] (3361) 3816[7] 3973[4] 4913[10] 7577[5] 7872[5] 8129[10]

Royal Council (IRE)
Michael Appleby a65 68
2 b g Clodovil(IRE) Queen Zain (IRE) (Lawman (FR))
2394[3] 3426[5] 3954[7] 5562[2] 6041[4] 7556[3] 9300[10]

Royal Countess *Lucy Normile* 48
3 b f Coach House(IRE) Dont Tell Nan (Major Cadeaux)
2325[6] 3226[3] 3684[5] 4488[7] 5096[5] 6938[3] 7732[5]

Royal County Down (IRE)
A P O'Brien a59 97
2 ch c Gleneagles(IRE) Pearl Grey (Gone West (USA))
7217a[6] 8716[11]

Royal Crusade *Charlie Appleby* 111
2 b c Shamardal(USA) Zibelina (IRE) (Dansili)
(6409) 7195[2] (8114)

Royal Dancer *Sylvester Kirk* a57 60
3 b g Norse Dancer(IRE) King's Siren (IRE) (King's Best (USA))
79[10] 5987[12] 6511[3] 7025[2] 7553[2] (7985)◆ 8224[5] 8644[4] 8916[2] 9042[3] 9216[7]

Royal Diplomat (IRE) *P Monfort* a77 67
4 b g Zebedee Pretty Priceless (IRE) (Pearl Of Love (IRE))
1391a[2] 2956a[9]

Royal Dornoch (IRE) *A P O'Brien* 112
2 b c Gleneagles(IRE) Bridal Dance (IRE) (Danehill Dancer (IRE))
5584[3] 6264a[7] 7195[5] (7691)

Royal Duchess *Lucy Normile* 70
9 b m Dutch Art Royal Citadel (IRE) (City On A Hill (USA))
3178[6] 4060[6] (4726) 5237[2] 5938[5]

Royal Dynasty *Mohamed Moubarak* a68 67
3 b f Charm Spirit(IRE) Millisecond (Royal Applause)
8419[6] 8920[2] 9217[7] (9670)

Royale Theyss (FR) *C Boutin* a60 58
3 bb f Penny's Picnic(IRE) Royale Demeure (FR) (Gentlewave (IRE))
3028a[9]

Royal Family (FR) *Amy Murphy* a79 89
3 b f Frankel Crafty (AUS) (Manhattan Rain (AUS))
474[3] 5810[6] 6633[2] 7081[3] (8433) 8980a[6]

Royal Flag *Brian Ellison* a65 70
9 b g New Approach(IRE) Gonbarda (GER) (Lando (GER))
1429[11] 2080[8] 2613[2] 3294[5] 3940[7] 4522[4] 5391[3] 5513[2] 5727[2] 6200[5] 6340[6] 7301[3] 7830[9] 8019[9]

Royal Gift (FR) *Matthieu Palussiere* a80 71
4 b m Palace Episode(USA) Laureldean Desert (Green Desert (USA))
(992a)

Royal Goldie (IRE) *Lydia Richards* a62 65
4 b m Havana Gold(IRE) Dream Maker (IRE) (Bahamian Bounty)
135[10] 473[7] 1183[10]

Royal Guild (IRE)
Sir Mark Prescott Bt a57
3 b g Mastercraftsman(IRE) Be My Queen (IRE) (Sadler's Wells (USA))
258[7] 461[8]

Royal Gunner (ITY) *G Botti* a56 56
3 b g Le Vie Infinite(IRE) Raganella (IRE) (Fasliyev (USA))
6874a[3]

Royal Hall (FR) *Gary Moore* a59 51
7 b g Halling(USA) Royal Fantasy (IRE) (King's Best (USA))
3252[6] 4796[2] 5379[6]

Royal Illusion (IRE) *W P Mullins* 96
7 b m King's Theatre(IRE) Spirit Run (IRE) (Luso)
5508a[7]

Royal Intervention (IRE) *Ed Walker* a94 109
3 ch f Exceed And Excel(AUS) Exciting Times (FR) (Jeune Homme (USA))
2319[4] 3083[3] 4050[5] (4891) 5608[5] (6519a)

Royal Julius (IRE) *J Reynier* a98 107
6 b h Royal Applause Hflah (IRE) (Dubawi (IRE))
894a[2] 2428a[4] 3678a[4] 5079a[3] 6144a[5] 7504a[2] (9125a)

Royal Liberty *Geoffrey Harker* a28 41
4 b g Acclamation Anadolu (IRE) (Statue Of Liberty (USA))
3163[8] 4518[15] 4990[13] 5216[3] 5555[8] 6098[8] 6824[5]

Royal Lightning *James Given* 58
2 b f Hot Streak(IRE) Royal Obsession (IRE) (Val Royal (FR))
2415[4]◆ 2903[5] 3652[4] 6683[11] 7283[10]

Royal Line *John Gosden* a114 115
5 ch h Dubawi(IRE) Melikah (IRE) (Lammtarra (USA))
4612[4] (6962) 8332[3]◆ 8811[5]

Royal Lytham (FR) *A P O'Brien* 113
2 b c Gleneagles(IRE) Gotlandia (FR) (Anabaa (USA))
3949[7] (4846) 5922a[3]

Royal Marine (IRE)
Saeed bin Suroor a75 113
3 b g Raven's Pass(USA) Inner Secret (USA) (Singspiel (IRE))
169a[4] 1854[4] 2411[13] 3951[9] 4705a[12]

Royal Meeting (IRE)
Saeed bin Suroor 112
3 b c Invincible Spirit(IRE) Rock Opera (SAF) (Lecture (USA))
8360a[3] 8768a[16]

Royal Mezyan (IRE) *Henry Spiller* a62 43
8 b g Royal Applause Rice Mother (IRE) (Indian Ridge (IRE))
279[4] 626[4] 1179[9] 1883[4] 3001[9] 6126[6] 7371[3]◆ 7838[11]

Royal Nation *Archie Watson* a80 63
2 b f Nathaniel(IRE) Royal Empress (IRE) (Holy Roman Emperor (IRE))
6592[6] 7297[4] 8849[4]◆ 9172[2] (9513)

Royal Optimist (IRE) *David Evans* 30
2 b g Acclamation Chances Are (IRE) (Dandy Man (IRE))
3088[7]

Royal Prize *Mme M Bollack-Badel* a69 64
9 ch g Nayef(USA) Spot Prize (USA) (Seattle Dancer (USA))
3715a[8]

Royal Prospect (IRE)
Julie Camacho a89 93
4 b g Thewayyouare(USA) Jillian (USA) (Royal Academy (USA))
24[4] 353[6] (3971) 4521[8] (5217) 6227[17]

Royal Rattle *John Norton* a49 23
4 b g Delegator Rattleyurjewellery (Royal Applause)
501[10] 2147[10] 3158[14] 4455[11]

Royal Regent *Lucy Normile* a37 73
7 b g Urgent Request(IRE) Royal Citadel (IRE) (City On A Hill (USA))
2369[4] 3180[5] 4057[6] 5240[3] 5937[3]

Royal Reserve *Lucinda Russell* a66 66
6 b g Duke Of Marmalade(IRE) Lady Hawkfield (IRE) (Hawk Wing (USA))
7436[14]

Royal Residence *James Tate* a75 98
4 b g Epaulette(AUS) Jubilant Queen (Kyllachy)
2396[6] 2568[3] 3597[2] 3770[U] (5530) 6396[3] 6920[4] 7431[19]

Royal Sands (FR) *James Given* a77 49
3 bb g Dabirsim(FR) Agent Mimi (FR) (Medecis)
1643[7] 2094[12] 3464[4] 7189[13] (8407)◆ 8943[4] 9334[9]

Royal Shaheen (FR)
Alistair Whillans a60 76
6 b g Myboycharlie(IRE) Viola Royale (IRE) (Royal Academy (USA))
1644[14] 2291[6] 2894[7] 3502[11] 3922[12] 5490[5] 5726[4] (6341) 6626[3] 7069[5] 7829[12]

Royal Star *Roger Charlton* a73 77
3 b f Sea The Stars(IRE) Altesse Imperiale (IRE) (Rock Of Gibraltar (IRE))
1738[3] 2142[6] 9303[8] 9502[4]

Royal Sunday (FR) *Alex Hales*
5 gr g Never On Sunday(FR) Royale Malaisie (FR) (Villez (USA))
1525[P]

Royal Town (FR) *Z Koplik* 91
4 b h Wootton Bassett Tehamana (IRE) (Pleasantly Perfect (USA))
2429a[9]

Royal Welcome *James Tate* a71 78
3 b f Kingman Deveron (USA) (Cozzene (USA))
2332[6] 2909[2] 3431[4] 4520[5] 5554[5] 6518[7] 9199[9]

Royal Youmzain (FR) *A Wohler* 113
4 b h Youmzain(IRE) Spasha (Shamardal (USA))
3386a[2] 4427a[2] 6007a[4] 6487a[3] 7500a[6]

Roy Rocket (FR) *John Berry* a38 61
9 gr g Layman(USA) Minnie's Mystery (FR) (Highest Honor (FR))
1355[12] 1934[5] 2233[4] 2928[6] 3537[5] 4216[3]◆ 4796[8] 5528[6] 5993[2] 6303[7] 6796[5]

Roys Dream *Paul Collins* a58 75
5 b m Monsieur Bond(IRE) Velvet Jaguar (Hurricane Run (IRE))
(2729) 4280[7] 4822[8]

Roy's Legacy *Shaun Harris* a54 46
10 b h Phoenix Reach(IRE) Chocolada (Namid)
26[10] 787[5] 848[2] 986[5] 1383[11] 1716[9]

Rubaiyat (FR) *Henk Grewe* 114
2 b c Areion(GER) Representera (Lomitas)
(7004a) (7937a) (8390a)

Rubenesque (IRE) *Tristan Davidson* a81 82
7 b m Getaway(GER) Shouette (IRE) (Sadler's Wells (USA))
(1815) (7381) (7819) 8129[8] 8399[3] 9405[7]

Rubensian *David Dennis* a67 45
6 ch g Medicean Hymnsheet (Pivotal)
559[4] 1169[6] 1566[5] 2233[7] 7474[11]

Rubia Bella *David Simcock* a73
2 ch f Bated Breath Sky Crystal (GER) (Galileo (IRE))
2968[2]

Rubiglia (FR) *G Botti* a70
2 b f Charm Spirit(IRE) Marania (IRE) (Marju (IRE))
8448a[3]

Ruby Gates (IRE) *John Butler* a75 63
6 b m Avonbridge Wild Academy (IRE) (Royal Academy (USA))
459[6] 793[6] 3022[12] 3468[3] 4028[9] (6733) 7560[8] 8507[8] 9278[6]

Ruby Power (IRE) *Richard Hannon* a67 63
2 b f Kodiac Coquette Rouge (IRE) (Croco Rouge (IRE))
5588[13] 6079[5] 6948[7] 7522[10] 9307[3] 9414[9]

Ruby Shield (USA) *Richard Fahey* 56
2 b f War Front(USA) Ruby Tuesday (IRE) (Galileo (IRE))
6205[4]

Ruby Wine *Jeremy Scott* 60
3 b f Phenomena Para Siempre (Mujahid (USA))
5748[4] 6641[4] 7518[10]

Ruby Wonder *David O'Meara* 69
2 b f Swiss Spirit Nurse Gladys (Dr Fong (USA))
2052[2] 2475[2] 2805[18] 5788[3]

Rudaina *Amy Murphy* a61
2 b f Dark Angel(IRE) Bouyrin (IRE) (Invincible Spirit (IRE))
9506[4]

Rudimental (FR) *C Lerner* 99
3 ch c Mastercraftsman(IRE) Russiana (IRE) (Red Ransom (USA))
(1450a) 6385a[9]

Rudy Lewis (IRE) *Charlie Fellowes* a62 78
3 b g Excelebration(IRE) Bless You (Bahamian Bounty)
3324[6] 3972[5] 5269[6]◆ 6081[3]◆ 6678[2]◆ 7452[7] 8030[8]

Rue Dauphine (FR)
Artus Adeline De Boisbrunet a46 59
3 b f Sommerabend Idria (GER) (Kings Lake (USA))
2311a[4] 3139a[4]

Rue De Paradis (FR) *Mlle C Neveux* a45 65
4 ch m Satri(IRE) Duchesse Valentine (FR) (Bachelor Duke (USA))
2782a[13]

Rufus King *Mark Johnston* a105 96
4 ch g Iffraaj Mosqueras Romance (Rock Of Gibraltar (IRE))
1891[10] 2100[14] 2402[9] 2837[3] 3313[9] 4021[4] 4607[3] 4730[3] 5535a[4] 5711a[9]

Ruled By The Moon *Ivan Furtado* a49 61
5 b g Mawatheeq(USA) Hallingdal (UAE) (Halling (USA))
969[11]

Rule Of Honour *Ismail Mohammed* a40 50
4 ch h New Approach(IRE) Our Queen Of Kings (Arazi (USA))
1742a[9]

Ruler Of Natives *Robyn Brisland*
3 b g Native Ruler Misty Pearl (Royal Applause)
9368[11]

Ruler Of The Nile *Marjorie Fife* a74 45
7 b g Exceed And Excel(AUS) Dinka Raja (USA) (Woodman (USA))
40[7] 589[8] 8072[11] 8343[4] 8551[13]

Rulers Kingdom (IRE)
Mark Johnston a64 39
2 b c Shamardal(USA) Illustrious Miss (USA) (Kingmambo (USA))
7586[9] 8069[6] 8424[5] 8815[8] 9060[5] 9307[6] 9513[7]

Rum Baba *Charlie Fellowes* a77 80
3 ch g New Approach(IRE) Soft Centre (Zafonic (USA))
1886[12] 3445[3] (4452)

Rumble Inthejungle (IRE)
Richard Spencer 102
3 ch c Bungle Inthejungle Guana (IRE) (Dark Angel (IRE))
4050[9] 4665[7] 5611[4] 6423[9]

Rumbo Norte (IRE)
Gianluca Bietolini a76 80
4 ch h Declaration Of War(USA) Sushi Tuna (Halling (USA))
76a[4]

Rum Lad *Jo Hughes* a52 54
3 b g Heeraat(IRE) Madame Mojito (USA) (Smart Strike (CAN))
1379[4] 2098[12] 2926[6] 3878a[6] 4357a[10] 4959a[6] 7223a[5] 7642a[4]

Rum Runner *Richard Hannon* a80 93
4 b h Havana Gold(IRE) Thermopylae (Tenby)
3009[9] 3632[3] 4666[10] 4887[12] (5626)◆ 6207[3] 6950[12] 7678[10]

Rumshak (IRE) *Michael Dods* a83 76
4 ch g Arcano(IRE) Scarlet Rosefinch (Cockney Rebel (IRE))
953[11] 1760[19] 1950[8]

Run After Genesis (IRE)
Brett Johnson a68 70
3 gr g Archipenko(USA) She Is Great (IRE) (Dalakhani (IRE))
(1140) 1825[9] (3651) 3964[7] 4737[4] 7189[12] 8806[3] 9663[6]

Runaiocht (IRE) *Brian Forsey* a49 41
9 ch g Teofilo(IRE) Julie Girl (USA) (Jules (USA))
80[5] 288[8] 1032[9] 9248[10]

Run Ashore (FR) *M Nigge* a73 73
3 b g Le Havre(IRE) Banville (FR) (Lando (GER))
216a[10] (1741a) 9281a[12]

Run Like Hell (FR) *Jane Soubagne* 68
2 b f Holy Roman Emperor(IRE) Final Call (Rail Link)
1657a[4]

Running Cloud (IRE)
Mark Loughnane a83 82
4 b g Cacique(IRE) Nimbus Star (Nayef (USA))
1425[3] 2209[3] 2781[5] 4257[5] 5811[5] 7575[6] 9496[9]

Runnymede *Frau S Steinberg* a72 97
3 b c Dansili Indication (Sadler's Wells (USA))
3385a[4] 5483a[8]

Runway Dreamer (USA)
Josie Carroll 85
2 rg f Tonalist(USA) Runway Rosie (USA) (Include (USA))
7267a^7

Run Wild (GER) *John Gosden* a91 104
2 ch f Amaron Rondinay (FR) (Cadeaux Genereux)
5132^3 *5733*^{4} *(6592)*◆ 7120^4 **8482a**^{2} 8763^3

Rupture (AUS) *Paul Preusker* 92
5 ch g Street Boss(USA) Dara Seans (AUS) (Giant's Causeway (USA))
8803a^6

Rusalka (IRE) *Tim Easterby* 57
2 b f Ivawood(IRE) Song To The Moon (IRE) (Oratorio (IRE))
2707^7 **3196**^{4} 3703^6 **4780**^{3}◆ 5296^6 6571^3 7309^3 7522^3

Rushcutters Bay *Hugo Palmer* a59 51
2 b c Cable Bay(IRE) Kicker Rock (Fastnet Rock (AUS))
4798^{10} *5856*^{9} ***7186***^{4} *7754*^{7} *8195*^{7}

Rush Hour (IRE) *N Clement* a65 57
3 b f Zoffany(IRE) Place De L'Etoile (IRE) (Sadler's Wells (USA))
6062a^6

Rushing Fall (USA) *Chad C Brown* 115
4 b m More Than Ready(USA) Autumnal (USA) (Forestry (USA))
4950a^2 7920a^4

Rusper Dreams (IRE)
Jamie Osborne a61 51
3 b g Dream Ahead(USA) Daganya (IRE) (Danehill Dancer (IRE))
228^3◆ *437*^{4} *931*^{11}

Rusper's Gift (IRE) *Jamie Osborne* a63
3 b g Requinto(IRE) Cadescia (IRE) (Cadeaux Genereux)
6317^{13} *7034*^{6} ***8348***^{3}

Rusper's Lad *Tom Clover* 75
2 b c Brazen Beau(AUS) Camelopardalis (Tobougg (IRE))
2973^3

Russian Realm *Paul Midgley* a84 82
9 b g Dansili Russian Rhythm (USA) (Kingmambo (USA))
407^4◆ *832*^{10} *2247*^{8} 3971^5 5395^9

Russian Royale *Micky Hammond* a53 59
9 b m Royal Applause Russian Ruby (FR) (Vettori (IRE))
1981^5

Russian Rum *James Given* a15 43
3 b g Archipenko(USA) Bebe De Cham (Tragic Role (USA))
585^{10} ***1270***^{10}

Russian Rumour (IRE)
Jonathan Portman a55 56
2 b f Make Believe Russian Rave (Danehill Dancer (IRE))
6118^8 *7515*^{7} *8651*^{9}

Rustang (FR) *Allan Smith* a92 105
4 b g Holy Roman Emperor(IRE) Oppamattox (FR) (Munir)
9125a^3

Rux Power *Andrew Balding* a93 79
3 b f Kingman Cut Short (USA) (Diesis)
(1381) ***1939***^{2}◆

Rux Ruxx (IRE) *Tim Easterby* a72 87
4 b m Dark Angel(IRE) Lady Duxyana (Most Welcome)
2893^8◆ *3323*^{6} (3685) (4438)◆ 4902^6 5333^3 (5903) 6379^{10} **(6825)** 7735^7

Rydan (IRE) *Gary Moore* a89 83
8 ch g Intense Focus(USA) Lough Mewin (IRE) (Woodman (USA))
(2400) **3044**^{4} 3799^4 6448^4 7127^2 *9056*^{10}

Rye House (IRE) *Patrick Dejaeger* a61 51
10 b g Dansili Threefold (USA) (Gulch (USA))
5115a^7

Sa'ada (USA) *A bin Harmash* a74 68
4 b m Bellamy Road(USA) Hey Seattle (USA) (Seattle Slew (USA))
1322a^{12}

Saaheq *Michael Appleby* a96 94
5 b g Invincible Spirit(IRE) Brevity (USA) (Street Cry (IRE))
353^5 *(551)* *981*^{4} *1552*^{2} (1946) 2775^{12} *3582*^{7} 4888^4 5524^{10} 6208^2 6724^4 7348^4 7894^5 ***(8267)***

Saam (FR)
Mme P Butel & J-L Beaunez a60 80
3 gr c Kendargent(FR) Super Hantem (IRE) (Royal Anthem (USA))
6486a^7

Sabaaya (IRE) *Charles Hills* 59
2 b f Oasis Dream Rufoof (Zamindar (USA))
3835^4 4323^3 (Dead)

Sabai Sabai (IRE) *K R Burke*
3 b f Shamardal(USA) Semayyel (IRE) (Green Desert (USA))
5126^6

Sablet *Eve Johnson Houghton* 44
2 b f Fulbright Garabelle (IRE) (Galileo (IRE))
7695^{14}

Sacred Dance *Charlie Appleby* 81
2 b f Sea The Stars(IRE) Janey Muddles (IRE) (Lawman (FR))
3049^3◆ **(3881)**◆

Sacred Legacy (IRE) *Ronald Harris* a52 59
2 ch g Zebedee Sacred Love (IRE) (Barathea (IRE))
6911^{10} *8059*^{8} *9299*^{7}

Sacred Life (FR) *S Wattel* 109
4 b h Siyouni(FR) Knyazhna (IRE) (Montjeu (IRE))
1244a^4

Sacred Sprite *John Berry* a64 58
4 b m Nathaniel(IRE) Lively Sprite (Dansili)
921^8 *1331*^{6} ***(2593)*** 3272^7 *5271*^{6} ***5891***^{2} 6556^2 6853^{11} *8347*^{7}

Sacred Warner (IRE) *Clive Cox* a52 47
3 b g Holy Roman Emperor(IRE) Alerted (USA) (First Defence (USA))
554^9 ***1094***^{6} 1562^8 *2007*^{6} 2734^{10}

Sadlers Beach (IRE)
Marcus Tregoning a53 67
3 b f Pour Moi(IRE) Dusty Boots (IRE) (Footstepsinthesand)
2517^4 (3034) (4499) **5601**^{2} 6463^5

Sadler's Soul (USA) *Archie Watson* a63 14
3 b f Revolutionary(USA) Sadler's Secretary (IRE) (Sadler's Wells (USA))
1397^2 *2018*^{12} 2361^{13}

Saeer (IRE) *Sir Michael Stoute* a49 63
2 ch g Australia Pivotalia (IRE) (Pivotal)
7055^6 *7814*^{14}

Safe Voyage (IRE) *John Quinn* a90 117
6 b g Fast Company(IRE) Shishangaan (IRE) (Mujadil (USA))
(2100) (2615) **(3588)** 5207a^3 6215^3 7944a^4 **8334**^{3}

Saffo (IRE) *D Zarroli* a63 69
4 b m Henrythenavigator(USA) My Meltemi (IRE) (Hawk Wing (USA))
1245a^{13}

Saffran (IRE) *Simon Crisford* 79
3 b g Teofilo(IRE) Oriental Step (IRE) (Tamayuz)
3337^3 **(4177)**

Saffron Lane *Harry Dunlop* a56
2 b f Mukhadram Sabreon (Caerleon (USA))
8012^8 *9130*^{9} ***9299***^{6}

Safira Menina *Mrs A Malzard* a49 50
7 b m Paco Boy(IRE) Isla Azul (IRE) (Machiavellian (USA))
2003a^3 3640a^6 **4687a**^{2} **6008a**^{2}

Saga Bee (FR) *C Boutin* 57
2 b f Dragon Dancer Circus Bee (IRE) (Cape Cross (IRE))
3562a^8

Sagama *M Delzangles* 70
3 gr f Sinndar(IRE) Saghaniya (FR) (Rock Of Gibraltar (IRE))
3391a^8

Saga Sprint (IRE) *J R Jenkins* a48 47
6 b m Excellent Art Queen Of Malta (IRE) (Exceed And Excel (AUS))
1333^9 **6324**^{4} *9312*^{8}

Saga Timgad (FR)
Francesco Santella a73 80
3 bb c Excelebration(IRE) Manaaqeb (Cape Cross (IRE))
2162a^7

Sagauteur (FR) *D Guillemin* 104
3 b g Literato(FR) Saga D'Ouilly (FR) (Linamix (FR))
1243a^2 (2027a) 3108a^5

Sagittarian Wind *Archie Watson* a53 47
3 b f Iffraaj Bahia Breeze (Mister Baileys)
7298^4 *8123*^{3} *8255*^{9} *9161*^{13} ***9445***^{2} *9508*^{5}

Sagittarius Rising (IRE)
John C McConnell 79
4 ch g Camacho Ophelia's Song (Halling (USA))
5537a^{13} **7781**^{4}

Saglyacat (FR) *Noam Chevalier* a62 64
4 b m Hurricane Cat(USA) Saglyana (FR) (Sagamix (FR))
5009a^3

Sahaafy (USA) *M Al Mheiri* a86 87
7 br g Kitten's Joy(USA) Queen's Causeway (USA) (Giant's Causeway (USA))
196a^8

Saharan Shimmer *David Menuisier* 18
2 b c Oasis Dream Come Touch The Sun (IRE) (Fusaichi Pegasus (USA))
8516^{17}

Sahhab (USA) *Geoffrey Deacon* 24
2 b f Declaration Of War(USA) Princess Consort (USA) (Dixieland Band (USA))
5745^8

Sahreej (IRE) *Paul W Flynn* a53 53
6 gr g Zebedee Petite Boulangere (IRE) (Namid)
3206^{11}

Saikung (IRE) *Charles Hills* a88 88
3 b f Acclamation Glitter Baby (IRE) (Danehill Dancer (IRE))
1562^3 2356^3 2798^3 3923^2 (4554) 5140^5 (5782) 6160^5 7463^3 **8412**^{2} *9126*^{10} ***9417***^{2} *9658*^{7}

Sailing (GER) *Roger Charlton* a56
3 b f Lope De Vega(IRE) Sail (IRE) (Sadler's Wells (USA))
7822^4◆

Sailing South (IRE) *J S Bolger* 75
2 ch f Teofilo(IRE) Twin Sails (USA) (Boston Harbor (USA))
7215a^9

Saint Andrews (FR) *H Blume* 61
3 b c Makfi Step With Joy (CAN) (Kitten's Joy (USA))
3710a^4

Saint Equiano *Keith Dalgleish* a97 92
5 b g Equiano(FR) St Athan (Authorized (IRE))
(4) *929*^{8} 1502^8 2116^{10}

Saint Mac *Michael Appleby* a69 57
4 b g Nathaniel(IRE) Noahs Ark (IRE) (Charnwood Forest (IRE))
162^3 ***390***^{3}◆

Saint Of Katowice (IRE)
Richard Fahey a77 77
2 b c Elzaam(AUS) Silesian (IRE) (Singspiel (IRE))
4125^3◆ 4719^2 **5212**^{2} **5615**^{2} 6450^3 ***7958***^{2}

Saint Pois (FR) *J-P Sauvage* a74 73
8 b g Le Havre(IRE) Our Dream Queen (Oasis Dream)
115a^6

Saint Romain (FR) *C Boutin* a72 74
2 b g Rajsaman(FR) Sandouville (Lope De Vega (IRE))
7799a^3

Saisons D'Or (IRE) *Jedd O'Keeffe* a83 86
4 ro g Havana Gold(IRE) Deux Saisons (Chineur (FR))
740^3 *1164*^{3} (1695) (2151) 2842^2 4240^4 **5200**^{2} 5246^8 6588^6 7310^8 *8024*^{3} *8918*^{10}

Sajanji *Simon Crisford* a71 61
4 ch m Iffraaj Soraaya (IRE) (Elnadim (USA))
18^2 ***344***^{6} *608*^{4}

Sakura (FR) *Ms Sheila Lavery* 62
3 br f Dabirsim(FR) Salcita (GER) (Zieten (USA))
3557a^7

Sakura Zensen (FR) *Hiroo Shimizu* a77 94
3 ch f Planteur(IRE) Sheema (Teofilo (IRE))
4429a^6 7978a^{10} *9170a*^{15}

Salaasel *Georgios Alimpinisis* a51 55
4 b g Teofilo(IRE) Pearl Spirit (IRE) (Invincible Spirit (IRE))
3140a^9

Salamanca School (FR)
Mark Johnston 76
2 b c Rock Of Gibraltar(IRE) Princess Sofia (UAE) (Pennekamp (USA))
7361^3◆ 8244^2 **(8858)**

Salam Zayed *Richard Fahey* 78
3 b g Exceed And Excel(AUS) Long Face (USA) (Whywhywhy (USA))
3373^4 3926^9 4446^{11} (4875) (5151) 5422^3 5557^6 **6582**^{2} 6961^{16} 7145^7 7542^8

Salar Island (ITY) *Andrea Marcialis* 91
2 ch c Sakhee's Secret Salar Violet (IRE) (Orpen (USA))
(3562a) **5228a**^{9} (7674a)

Salateen *David O'Meara* a108 107
7 ch g Dutch Art Amanda Carter (Tobougg (IRE))
(89)◆ 869a^{12} *1181*^{5} *1922*^{4} 3094^4 4389^8 4905^3 5129^3 5965^4 *6391*^{9}

Salayel *Roger Varian* a76 96
3 b f Bated Breath Hurry Home Hillary (USA) (Deputed Testamony (USA))
4922^2◆ **6379**^{4} **6951**^{3} 7463^2

Salerne *D Guillemin* 85
2 b f Charm Spirit(IRE) Salicorne (USA) (Aragorn (IRE))
4417a^8

Salina (FR) *J-C Rouget* a68 68
3 b f Pedro The Great(USA) Valibi Bere (FR) (Russian Blue (IRE))
6328a^2

Sally Hope *John Gallagher* 51
3 ch f Coach House(IRE) First Term (Acclamation)
5592^4 **6169**^{5} 7114^4 8008^7 8408^{12}

Salmana (FR) *Laura Lemiere* 92
3 ch f Nathaniel(IRE) Saraluna (USA) (Unbridled's Song (USA))
6773a^4

Salmon Fishing (IRE)
Mohamed Moubarak a53 54
3 b g Dragon Pulse(IRE) Lake Wanaka (IRE) (Fasliyev (USA))
2798^4 3651^9 **4567**^{5} *5807*^{6} 6130^{10} *6737*^{8} *7420*^{5} *7654*^{7} *8000*^{11} *8547*^{5}

Salouen (IRE) *Sylvester Kirk* 118
5 b h Canford Cliffs(IRE) Gali Gal (IRE) (Galileo (IRE))
(2607) 3314^3 4093^7 **5414**^{4} 7246a^9

Salsa (IRE) *A P O'Brien* 68
2 b f Galileo(IRE) Beauty Is Truth (IRE) (Pivotal)
5588^6◆

Salsabeel (IRE) *Charlie Appleby* 110
5 b g Exceed And Excel(AUS) Tokyo Rose (UAE) (Jade Robbery (USA))
51a^3◆ (Dead)

Salsada (IRE) *Jedd O'Keeffe* a67
2 ch f Mukhadram Mokaraba (Unfuwain (USA))
9471^5◆

Salsa Verde (IRE) *Ed de Giles*
4 b g Canford Cliffs(IRE) Bridal Dance (IRE) (Danehill Dancer (IRE))
4131^{11}

Saltarin Dubai (ARG) *S Seemar* a109 78
6 ch g E Dubai(USA) Saltarina Fitz (ARG) (Fitzcarraldo (ARG))
172a^4 ***(396a)*** *959a*^{6}

Saltie Girl *David Barron* a15 58
3 b f Intikhab(USA) Marine Girl (Shamardal (USA))
2332^{10} **2590**^{4} 3516^5 3921^7◆ 4725^{10} 5202^5 5914^6

Salt Lake City (FR) *B Audouin* a96 97
4 b h Holy Roman Emperor(IRE) Fleur De Sel (Linamix (FR))
(2782a) **3879a**^{4}

Saltonstall *Adrian McGuinness* 99
5 ch g Pivotal Macleya (GER) (Winged Love (IRE))
1415^{18} 3062a^{10} **(5535a)** 5711a^8 6693a^6 7934a^8 8336^{13}

Salt Whistle Bay (IRE) *Rae Guest* a73 78
5 b g Royal Applause Quantum (IRE) (Alhaarth (IRE))
1881^4 *2237*^{4} **2622**^{2} 3529^2 4061^4 5776^{10} 8030^5

Salty Kiss (FR) *F Foresi* a39 52
3 b f Evasive Silver Forest (IRE) (Mujadil (USA))
6063a^7

Salute The Soldier (GER)
Clive Cox a100 109
4 br g Sepoy(AUS) Street Fire (IRE) (Street Cry (IRE))
1232^2 1912^2 2832^{13} 4666^8 5546^2 (6445) **(6950)**◆ 7411^3

Saluti (IRE) *Paul Midgley* a83 86
5 b g Acclamation Greek Easter (IRE) (Namid)
1457^2◆ 1978^2 3100^7 3813^{13} 4303^6 4649^5 6261^2 6677^3 **(7121)** 7621^3 *8425*^{5}

Salvadori (IRE) *R Bouresly* a83 75
8 b g Teofilo(IRE) Rachelle (IRE) (Mark Of Esteem (IRE))
196a^9

Salve Etoiles (IRE) *Henry Candy* 26
3 b f Sea The Stars(IRE) Salve Diana (GER) (Dalakhani (IRE))
2838^6

Salve Helena (IRE) *T Le Brocq* a30 39
4 b m Soldier Hollow Salve Diana (GER) (Dalakhani (IRE))
4174a^4 4687a^7

Samagace Du Vivien (FR)
S Gouvaze a71 64
5 b g Air Chief Marshal(IRE) Queen Du Vivien (FR) (Kingsalsa (USA))
115a^9

Samasthiti (IRE) *Carina Fey* a71 72
4 b m Camelot Navajo Moon (IRE) (Danehill (USA))
3879a^{14}

Samba Pa Ti (IRE) *Mlle E Schmitt* a66 62
5 b m Hat Trick(JPN) Amourette (FR) (Halling (USA))
1491a^8

Samba Saravah (USA)
Charlie Fellowes a71 62
3 bb g Union Rags(USA) Caragh Queen (USA) (Hard Spun (USA))
1852^7 2208^{13} 2802^{13} ***(4291)*** *6392*^{4}

Sambucca Spirit *Paul Midgley* a52 52
3 b g Charm Spirit(IRE) Hokkaido (Street Cry (IRE))
2477^{11} 5765^3 *7651*^{6} ***8268***^{2}◆ ***8632***^{2} ***8898***^{3}

Sam Cooke (IRE) *Ralph Beckett* a83 95
3 b g Pour Moi(IRE) Saturday Girl (Peintre Celebre (USA))
(2562)

Sameem (IRE) *James Tate* a98 102
3 b c New Approach(IRE) Ahla Wasahl (Dubai Destination (USA))
(1645)◆ 2031^7 2872^3 3262^2 4016^{24} (4730) **(5121)**◆ 6213^5 *8853*^{4}

Sameer (FR) *Ian Williams* a78 73
3 b g Nathaniel(IRE) Sanabyra (FR) (Kahyasi (IRE))
7291a^9

Samharry *H Al Alawi* a65 61
5 b g Exceed And Excel(AUS) Ballymore Celebre (IRE) (Peintre Celebre (USA))
97a^{14} ***997***^{9}

Samille (IRE) *Amy Murphy* a73 68
2 b f Kodiac Monicalew (Refuse To Bend (IRE))
7330^3 8338^4 ***9327***^{2}

Sam Missile (IRE)
Patrick J McKenna a74 89
6 b g Smart Strike(CAN) Kitty Matcham (IRE) (Rock Of Gibraltar (IRE))
1531a^8

Sa Mola (GER) *N Clement* a49 74
4 bb m Dabirsim(FR) Salona (GER) (Lord Of England (GER))
7861a^7

Samothrace (FR) *F-H Graffard* 93
3 b f Iffraaj Hunza Dancer (IRE) (Danehill Dancer (IRE))
2029a^6 **7978a**^{3}

Samovar *Scott Dixon* a87 79
4 b g Finjaan Chrystal Venture (IRE) (Barathea (IRE))
163^0 *230*^{7} *389*^{4} *471*^{4} *588*^{7} *832*^{4}◆ *1072*^{2} *1194*^{4} *1860*^{7} *(2296)* 2841^6◆ ***3206***^{3} 3504^2 *6549*^{8} 7077^{14} *7387*^{11} *(8066)* *8267*^{2} *8403*^{5} *8660*^{8} *8943*^{2} *9030*^{2} *(9334)* ***9562***^{3} *9645*^{5}

Sampers Seven (IRE) *M Halford* a69
2 b f Anjaal Sampers (IRE) (Exceed And Excel (AUS))
7876a^8

Samphire Coast *Derek Shaw* a86 57
6 b g Fastnet Rock(AUS) Faslen (USA) (Fasliyev (USA))
34^6 *157*^{5} *(699)* *922*^{5} ***1213***^{2}◆ *1401*^{4} *1544*^{5} *1714*^{4} *2064*^{6} 2509^{10} *8809*^{2} *9053*^{6} *(9199)* *9440*^{6} *9561*^{4}

Samsar (IRE) *Adrian Nicholls* a11 38
2 br g Dandy Man(IRE) Lady Mandeville (IRE) (Strategic Prince)
3156^7 **4433**^{7} *4999*^{9} 6011^5 **6539**^{7} 7056^7

Sam's Call *Michael Easterby* 70
2 b c Finjaan Winner's Call (Indian Ridge (IRE))
5388^4 6997^5◆ 7619^7 8097^9

Samskara (IRE) *C Laffon-Parias* a75 85
3 gr f Kodiac Chiara Wells (IRE) (Refuse To Bend (IRE))
(3713a) 7254a^{12}

Samson's Reach *Richard Price* a32 10
6 b g Phoenix Reach(IRE) Court Wing (IRE) (Hawk Wing (USA))
1989^{10} **8246**^{8}

Samstar *Mark Johnston* a62 60
3 ch f Nathaniel(IRE) Gossamer Seed (IRE) (Choisir (AUS))
1397^3◆ 1738^{10} *2017*^{5} 3057^3 3407^6

Samurai (IRE) *M Weiss* a72 92
6 b g Shamardal(USA) Sevenna (FR) (Galileo (IRE))
694a^4

Sanaadh *Michael Wigham* a100 97
6 ch g Exceed And Excel(AUS) Queen's Logic (IRE) (Grand Lodge (USA))
470^3◆ *805*^{4} ***(1097)***◆ 2609^{15} 3062a^{14} 4921^8 6445^5 6950^{11} 8096^{15} *9666*^{P}

San Andreas (IRE) *A P O'Brien* a88 79
3 b g Dark Angel(IRE) Last Bid (Vital Equine (IRE))
1306a^9 1600a^7 **2156a**^{7} 5207a^{10} 5923a^9

San Bernardo *Shaun Keightley*
2 ch g Raven's Pass(USA) Ayun (USA) (Swain (IRE))
7571^{12}

San Carlos *Shaun Keightley* a88
3 b c Havana Gold(IRE) Ittasal (Any Given Saturday (USA))
(2236) ***3493***^{3} ***4638***^{4} ***5945***^{3}

Sancho (FR) *M Delcher Sanchez* a71 72
5 b h Motivator Donna Roberta (GER) (Dashing Blade)
7536a^6

Sand Diego (IRE) *Peter Crate* 77
2 ch g Starspangledbanner(AUS) Supreme Quest (Exceed And Excel (AUS))
4993^4◆ 5859^2 6330^2 **(7160)**

Sandfrankskipsgo *Peter Crate* a64 65
10 ch g Piccolo Alhufoof (USA) (Dayjur (USA))
(298) *1266*^{8} *1590*^{9} *2010*^{8} *5046*^{5} *6285*^{4} *7557*^{9} *(7844)*

San Diaco (IRE) *Ed Dunlop* a64 5
3 gr g Kodiac Cland Di San Jore (IRE) (Lando (GER))
979^{12} ***1165***^{5} 1754^{11} *2965*^{12}

Sandkissed (IRE) *Amy Murphy* a43 53
4 b m Sir Prancealot(IRE) Hapipi (Bertolini (USA))
3475[13] 4376[7] 5063[10]

San Donato (IRE) *Roger Varian* a95 112
3 b c Lope De Vega(IRE) Boston Rocker (IRE) (Acclamation)
2668a[3]

Sandoside (FR) *C Boutin* a65 65
8 b g Palace Episode(USA) Sandside (FR) (Marchand De Sable (USA))
2391a[5]

Sandra's Secret (IRE) *Les Eyre* a77 94
6 gr m Zebedee Good For Her (Rock Of Gibraltar (IRE))
1814[4] 2117[15] 2743[21] 4759[8]

Sandret (IRE) *Ben Haslam* a94 96
3 b g Zebedee Sava Sunset (IRE) (Manduro (GER))
(954)◆ (1649) 2787[3] 4895[2] 5790[4] 6410[2] (7153)◆ 9041[4]◆

Sandridge Lad (IRE) *John Ryan* a76 68
3 b g Equiano(FR) Quixada (GER) (Konigstiger (GER))
342[4] 506[4] (1193) 1388[6] 1691[11] 1920[11] 2810[12] 3659[7] 4343[5] 5064[6] 6455[10] 7387[6] 8066[4] 8267[6]◆ 8550[2] 9245[11] 9441[2] 9498[2]

Sands Chorus *Scott Dixon* a68 80
7 b g Footstepsinthesand Wood Chorus (Singspiel (IRE))
1413[10] 1757[3] 2104[4] 2479[2] 3072[3] 3160[13] 3502[5] 3867[14] 5741[5] 6580[4] 7074[12]

Sand Share *Ralph Beckett* a74 98
3 br f Oasis Dream Shared Account (Dansili)
2745[8] 3676a[3] 6082[2] 6775a[6] 7978a[9]

Sands Of Mali (FR) *Richard Fahey* 121
4 b h Panis(USA) Kadiania (FR) (Indian Rocket)
1442a[6] 3501[3] 4094[16] 8331[14]

Sandtastic (FR) *Bettina Andersen* 86
5 ch g Footstepsinthesand Persian Sea (UAE) (Dubai Destination (USA))
7497a[9]

Sandy Dream (FR)
Mme R Philippon a67 69
3 b f Anodin(IRE) Sandy Winner (FR) (Priolo (USA))
1658a[6] (3028a)

Sandyman *Paul Cole* a82 77
3 ch g Footstepsinthesand Quiz Mistress (Doyen (IRE))
5451[5] (5955) 6967[5] 7974[9]

Sandyssime (FR) *G Botti* a94 86
4 bl g Camelot Sandy Light (IRE) (Footstepsinthesand)
3136a[4] (4704a)

Sandy Steve *Stuart Williams* a70 62
3 b g Aussie Rules(USA) Lady Guinevere (Pivotal)
1562[11] 1886[10] 2366[6] 4070[4] 5803[2]◆ (6152) 7025[6] (7817) 9202[13]

Sandy Street *Donald McCain* a30
3 b g Nayef(USA) Apsara (Groom Dancer (USA))
6544[6] 8944[6]

Sandytown (IRE) *David C Griffiths* a2 1
4 b g Tamayuz Wild Ways (Green Desert (USA))
1016[9] 4367[11] 6462[15]

Sangarius *Sir Michael Stoute* 114
3 b c Kingman Trojan Queen (USA) (Empire Maker (USA))
3026[3] (4013)

San Huberto (IRE) *F Chappet* a75 102
3 b c Speightstown(USA) Sediciosa (IRE) (Rail Link)
(2519a) (3031a) 3904a[5] (5717a) 6994a[3] 7927a[8]

San Juan (IRE) *Shaun Keightley* a59
2 b c Tagula(IRE) Bigasiwannabe (IRE) (King Charlemagne (USA))
7103[5] 7570[5]

San Pablo (FR) *H-A Pantall* 69
3 b c Joshua Tree(IRE) Aroma Bella (FR) (King's Best (USA))
2758a[9]

San Paolo (FR) *C Lerner* a72
3 ch g Kendargent(FR) Serandine (IRE) (Hernando (FR))
6328a[11]

San Pedro (IRE) *A P O'Brien* 88
2 b c Gleneagles(IRE) Elle Woods (IRE) (Lawman (FR))
8762[10]

San Rafael (IRE) *Mark Johnston* a77
2 b g Tamayuz Babberina (IRE) (Danehill Dancer (IRE))
(7911) 8503[4] 8889[11]

San Sebastian (IRE) *Ed Dunlop* 76
3 b g Iffraaj Invincible Cara (IRE) (Invincible Spirit (IRE))
1562[5] 3372[4] 4120[5] 5529[6]

Sans Regret (FR) *S Wattel* a64 76
4 b m Manduro(GER) Blue Lullaby (IRE) (Fasliyev (USA))
4859a[6]

Santa Ana Lane (AUS)
Anthony Freedman 127
6 b g Lope De Vega(IRE) Fast Fleet (AUS) (Fastnet Rock (AUS))
8362a[2]

Santafiora *Julie Camacho* a62 50
5 b m Poet's Voice Acquifer (Oasis Dream)
(28) (236) 468[6] 2153[5] 3291[2] 4330[7] 4763[3] 5392[6] 5659[6] 6273[6] 6682[6] 7591[8] (8469) 9133[6] 9551[8]

Santana Slew *James Given* a37 48
3 gr f Gregorian(IRE) Saratoga Slew (IRE) (Footstepsinthesand)
7912[6] 8530[11]

Sant Angelo (GER) *S Smrczek* a58 64
5 b g Areion(GER) St Aye (USA) (Nureyev (USA))
3715a[7] 7800a[2]

Santi Del Mare (FR) *J-C Rouget* 81
3 b c Lope De Vega(IRE) Salicorne (USA) (Aragorn (IRE))
2953a[6]

Santorini Sal *John Bridger* a46 57
2 b f Gregorian(IRE) Aegean Mystery (Dr Fong (USA))
2915[5] 3595[4] 5250[5] 5745[3] 6071[8] 7110[2] 8280[4] 8452[11]

Santurin (FR) *Henk Grewe* a75 85
2 b c Sommerabend Semina (GER) (Mamool (IRE))
7673a[6]

Saoirse's Gift (IRE) *Tim Easterby* 48
2 ch g Tagula(IRE) Fritta Mista (IRE) (Linamix (FR))
3551[5] 4317[7] 5655[13]

Sapa Inca (IRE) *Mark Johnston* a77 99
3 b f Galileo(IRE) Inca Princess (IRE) (Holy Roman Emperor (IRE))
1730[2]◆ 2096[3] 2685[2] 2905[2] (3765) 4064[3] 5614[2] (5931) 6657[4] 7864[2] (8245)◆

Sa Paradura *Grizzetti Galoppo SRL* 64
2 b f Poet's Voice Ring For Baileys (Kyllachy)
8393a[8]

Sapphire Jubilee *Ollie Pears* a62 35
3 b f Lethal Force(IRE) Queens Jubilee (Cayman Kai (IRE))
1862[3] 2377[3] 3291[5] 5392[8] (5854)

Saqqara King (USA)
Charlie Appleby a84 95
2 gr c American Pharoah(USA) Joyful Victory (CAN) (Tapit (USA))
3335[4] (4117) 4961a[3] 6251a[2] 6707[3]

Saracen Spirit *Mick Channon* 48
2 b c Poet's Voice Precariously Good (Oasis Dream)
6971[8] 7619[8] 8026[10]

Saracen Star *J S Moore* a59 31
2 b f Make Believe Singing Sky (Oasis Dream)
8516[15] 9127[2] 9311[7] 9665[7]

Sarah Jessica (IRE)
Gavin Cromwell 70
3 b f Makfi Zamid (FR) (Namid)
(7238)

Saras Hope *John Gallagher* 66
2 b g Swiss Spirit Rivas Rhapsody (IRE) (Hawk Wing (USA))
3507[6] 4302[3] 5500[8]

Sarasota (IRE) *Paul George* a62 61
4 b m Zoffany(IRE) Saldenaera (GER) (Areion (GER))
913[2] 1102[4] 1286[4] 1586[7] 4455[2] 4749[3] 5297[3] 5747[3] 6304[6] 9566[5]

Sarasota Bay *John Quinn* a52 71
3 ch f Coach House(IRE) Bird Key (Cadeaux Genereux)
1389[4] 3292[2] 3801[4] 4651[8] 5893[5] 6338[7]

Sarasota Star (IRE) *Martin Keighley* a70
3 rg g Zebedee Riviera Rose (IRE) (Dalakhani (IRE))
229[7] 1396[5] 2299[3]

Sarati (FR) *M Maillard* a61 60
3 ch f Anodin(IRE) Quillaja (GER) (Tiger Hill (IRE))
7561a[5]

Saratoga Vision (USA)
Alexander P Patykewich 87
2 bb f Court Vision(USA) Unchecked (USA) (Unbridled (USA))
7267a[6]

Sarayaat (IRE) *James Fanshawe* 32
2 b f Exceed And Excel(AUS) Stravina (GER) (Platini (GER))
6514[7]

Sargento *Simon Dow* a42 51
4 b g Dick Turpin(IRE) Vezere (USA) (Point Given (USA))
363[13]

Sarim (IRE) *Warren Greatrex* a80 77
4 b g Declaration Of War(USA) Silver Star (Zafonic (USA))
(8829)◆ 9177[9]

Sari Mareis *Denis Coakley* a49 52
3 b f Toronado(IRE) Fanny May (Nayef (USA))
2280[7] 2734[8] 4485[3] 5049[RR] 5287[RR]

Sark (IRE) *David Evans* a57 68
6 b g Zoffany(IRE) Breezeway (IRE) (Grand Lodge (USA))
58[6] 736[P] 1235[7]

Saroog *Simon Crisford* a88 103
5 b g Nathaniel(IRE) Bahama Bay (GER) (Dansili)
4224[4] (4899)◆ (6452) 7147[5]

Sarookh (USA) *Jessica Long* a85 93
4 b h Speightstown(USA) Yaqeen (Green Desert (USA))
6523a[10] 7497a[5]

Sarsaparilla Kit *Stuart Williams* a54 45
3 b f Footstepsinthesand Cincinnati Kit (Cape Cross (IRE))
1139[7] 1381[13] 3148[4] 4183[7] 4396[5] (9001) 9161[5] 9411[2] 9508[4]

Sarvi *Jim Goldie* a67 76
4 br m Intello(GER) Crystal Swan (IRE) (Dalakhani (IRE))
1503[7] 4724[6] 5179[5] 5621[7] 5937[2] (6656) 7366[5] 7491[2] 7735[6]

Saryshagann (FR) *David O'Meara* a85 86
6 gr g Iffraaj Serasana (Red Ransom (USA))
1588[3] 2104[5] 2577[2]◆

Sash *Amanda Perrett* a76 95
3 b c Oasis Dream Surcingle (USA) (Empire Maker (USA))
(1495) 2141[5] 2796[6] (4994) 5412[4] 5991[4] (7176) 7617[2]

Sashenka (GER) *Sylvester Kirk* a86 80
3 b f Maxios Sarabia (GER) (One Cool Cat (USA))
1359[2] 1738[2] 2284[2] (3598) 5779[8] 6211[6] 7279[4] (7650) (8812) 9178[3] 9418[3]

Sassie (IRE) *Michael Easterby* a85 88
4 b m Rip Van Winkle(IRE) Star Of Gibraltar (Rock Of Gibraltar (IRE))
2400[5] 2626[3]◆ (3467) 3653[3] 4505[4] 7001[5] 7403[3] 7830[5] (8129)◆

Sassoon *Paul Cole* a47 74
3 ch g Poet's Voice Seradim (Elnadim (USA))
1886[7] 2280[3] 3170[3] 3638[8] 5350[7] 8761[4] 9244[11]

Sassy Lassy (IRE)
David Loughnane a41 35
2 b f Cappella Sansevero Dissonance (IRE) (Rossini (USA))
1843[7] 2694[7] 7377[8] 7833[13] 8526[13]

Satchville Flyer *Milton Bradley* a52 61
8 ch g Compton Place Palinisa (FR) (Night Shift (USA))
155[2]◆ 553[6] 717[8] 4797[6] 6363[10] 7236[8] 8502[7] 8864[6] 9249[8] 9298[7] 9439[8]

Satisfy (IRE) *B A Murphy* a10 79
5 b m New Approach(IRE) Venturi (Danehill Dancer (IRE))
1197[10] 1309a[5] 7635a[14]

Satis House *Susan Corbett* a35 17
5 b m Bahri(USA) Ex Mill Lady (Bishop Of Cashel)
7739[8]

Satomi (GER) *Markus Klug* 106
3 b f Teofilo(IRE) Swordhalf (Haafhd)
3119a[6] 3639a[2] 5720a[4] 6747a[5] 7926a[6] 8587a[11]

Satono Japan (JPN)
Sir Michael Stoute a80
2 b c Deep Impact(JPN) Dubawi Heights (Dubawi (IRE))
(8455)◆

Sauchiehall Street (IRE)
Noel Williams a76 59
4 b g Mastercraftsman(IRE) Top Trail (USA) (Exchange Rate (USA))
1096[5] 1292[3] 1826[9] 4796[4] 5106[5] 7109[3] 8468[3] 8696[5]

Sauron's Eye *Ivan Furtado* a65 57
3 b g Delegator Stylish Dream (USA) (Elusive Quality (USA))
5594[11] 6101[14]

Savaanah (IRE) *Roger Charlton* a97 98
4 b m Olden Times Tanouma (USA) (Mr Greeley (USA))
1941[6] 3374[5] 5525[11] 6910a[6]

Savage Beauty (IRE) *Richard Fahey* a34 68
2 b f Starspangledbanner(AUS) Sister Sylvia (Fantastic Light (USA))
8338[3] 9347[9]

Savaheat (NZ)
Mick Price & Michael Kent Jnr 89
4 br g Savabeel(AUS) Heat Storm (AUS) (Green Desert (USA))
9016a[4]

Savalas (IRE) *Robert Cowell* a94 94
4 gr g Zebedee Tap The Dot (IRE) (Sharp Humor (USA))
1946[16] 2743[4] 3589[12] 4402[17] 4888[2] 5454[13] 7121[5] 7431[17] 8099[5] 9098[5] 9458[2] 9571[8]

Savanna Gold (IRE) *Hugo Palmer* a65
2 b g Havana Gold(IRE) Prospera (IRE) (Cape Cross (IRE))
7814[12] 8346[8] 9007[9]

Savannah Beau *Scott Dixon* a31 41
7 b m Major Cadeaux Mancunian Way (Green Desert (USA))
5018[14] 7628[11] 9445[11]

Savarin (JPN) *A Fabre* 100
2 b f Deep Impact(JPN) Sarafina (FR) (Refuse To Bend (IRE))
(7006a) 7939a[7]

Save You (FR) *J-Y Artu* a51 51
3 ch f Montmartre(FR) Our Beautiful (FR) (Sinndar (IRE))
2265a[11]

Savile Row (FR) *Carina Fey* a89 73
5 b g Ransom O'War(USA) Shikoku (Green Desert (USA))
(5760a)

Savitar (IRE) *Lee Carter* a68 67
4 b g Shamardal(USA) Foofaraw (USA) (Cherokee Run (USA))
1393[7] 2365[5] 3543[2]◆ 5309[6] 6121[3] (6717) 7125[6] 7811[3] 8270[4] 9132[3]◆ 9426[10]

Savlad *Shaun Harris* a49
4 b g Delegator Dubai Legend (Cadeaux Genereux)
275[7] 500[6] 785[12]

Savoir Aimer (FR) *T Castanheira* 83
3 b c Authorized(IRE) Magic Date (FR) (Sagamix (FR))
2519a[4]

Savoyard (IRE) *J Boisnard* 52
6 b g Canford Cliffs(IRE) World's Heroine (IRE) (Spinning World (USA))
7501a[3]

Savoy Brown *Michael Attwater* a42 53
3 b g Epaulette(AUS) Kindia (IRE) (Cape Cross (IRE))
1678[7] 2926[11] 5431[5] 5957[8] 6279[8] 7280[11] 9216[11]

Savvy Nine (FR) *William Haggas* a72 88
3 bl g Anodin(IRE) Insan Mala (IRE) (Bahhare (USA))
2499a[3] 3029a[3]

Sawasdee (IRE) *Andrew Balding* a70 68
3 br g Shamardal(USA) Beneventa (Most Welcome)
1419[3] 2769[5] 4031[4] 4795[2] 5311[7]

Sawwaah *Owen Burrows* a88 98
4 b g New Approach(IRE) Mudaaraah (Cape Cross (IRE))
1889[3] 3857[11] 6923[9] (7863) 8728[7]

Saxo Jack (FR) *Sophie Leech* a48 60
9 b g King's Best(USA) Gamma (FR) (Sadler's Wells (USA))
5086[8] 9273[13] 9542[12]

Sayesse *Lisa Williamson* a71 66
5 b g Sayif(IRE) Pesse (IRE) (Eagle Eyed (USA))
3002[8] 3781[9] 4281[9] 4552[11] 5130[7]

Say Good Buy (GER) *Henk Grewe* 99
3 b c Showcasing Strela (GER) (Lomitas)
8372a[2] 9590a[13]

Sayidah Kodiac *E J O'Neill* 74
2 b f Kodiac Samira Gold (FR) (Gold Away (IRE))
2757a[4]

Say It Simple *Richard Fahey* a68 72
2 ch f Iffraaj Nashama (IRE) (Pivotal)
6096[2]◆ 7030[2]

Say Nothing *Hughie Morrison* a74 76
3 b f Nathaniel(IRE) I Say (IRE) (Oratorio (IRE))
2253[12] 3505[2] 3886[8] 5421[4] 6030[2] 6371[8] 8641[2]

Say The Word *Simon Crisford* a72
3 b g Authorized(IRE) Soryah (IRE) (Shamardal (USA))
2195[2]

Sbraase *Noel C Kelly* a76 75
8 ch g Sir Percy Hermanita (Hernando (FR))
4724[2] 5712a[3] 7368[8]

Scabbard (USA) *Eddie Kenneally* a105
2 ch c More Than Ready(USA) Cowgirl Mally (USA) (Gone West (USA))
8749a[4]

Scale Force *Gay Kelleway* a78 71
3 gr g Lethal Force(IRE) Alectrona (FR) (Invincible Spirit (IRE))
506[2] 2708[4] 3508[2] 4008[7] 4192[2] 4343[7] 5660[4] 6183[3] 6735[2]

Scallywagtail (IRE) *Gary Moore* a41 47
2 br c Gutaifan(IRE) Eminence Gift (Cadeaux Genereux)
6300[8] 7124[6] 7981[8] 9061[7]

Scandinavian Lady (IRE)
Ivan Furtado a60 57
3 b f Swiss Spirit Azzurra Du Caprio (IRE) (Captain Rio)
(406) 6945[5]◆ 7443[4] 8083[5] 8264[3] 8502[3]

Scaramanga (IRE) *Paul Nicholls* a75 90
4 b g Mastercraftsman(IRE) Herboriste (Hernando (FR))
2143[2]

Scarlet Dragon *Alan King* a108 105
6 b g Sir Percy Welsh Angel (Dubai Destination (USA))
143[2] 4935[21] 5662[4] 6420[11] 7408[3] 9588[4]

Scarlet Red *Malcolm Saunders* a34 50
4 b m Equiano(FR) Crimson Fern (IRE) (Titus Livius (FR))
1676[11] 3090[12] 3532[7] 3836[5] 7468[7] 7784[9]

Scarlet Ruby *Roger Charlton* a47
2 b f Al Kazeem Monisha (FR) (Sinndar (IRE))
9063[8] 9327[10]

Scarlet Skis *Stef Keniry* a41 40
3 b f Kodiac Red Lady (IRE) (Dutch Art)
1863[9] 4487[13]

Scarlett Of Tara (GER)
Karoly Kerekes a69 69
3 bb f Tai Chi(GER) Staraya (FR) (King's Best (USA))
(6063a)

Scarlett Sun *George Margarson*
3 b g Sun Central(IRE) Red To Violet (Spectrum (IRE))
6811[9] 8645[9]

Scarlet Tufty (FR) *C Ferland* 95
3 b c Siyouni(FR) Marie Dar (FR) (Sinndar (IRE))
6385a[5] 8445a[4]

Scat King (IRE) *Richard Hughes* a84 56
3 b g Scat Daddy(USA) Come To Heel (IRE) (Elnadim (USA))
(1550)◆ 3465[13] 4643[4]

Scenery *Marjorie Fife* a64 45
4 ch g Elnadim(USA) Widescreen (USA) (Distant View (USA))
277[9] 410[2]◆ 738[9] 1765[9] 1836[8] 2235[9] 3158[10]

Scenesetter (IRE) *Marco Botti* a65 70
3 gr f Shamardal(USA) Freezy (IRE) (Dalakhani (IRE))
1288[3]◆ 1739[5] 3495[7] 4447[2] 5855[4] 6412[4] 7343[3]

Scenic Lady *Michael Attwater* a35 26
3 b f Frozen Power(IRE) Dazzling View (USA) (Distant View (USA))
296[11] 400[12]

Scentasia *John Gosden* a107 101
3 b f Cape Cross(IRE) Sweet Rose (New Approach (IRE))
2087[3] 4258[2] (5827)◆ 6721[5] (7349) 7895[13] (8708) (9002)◆

Schang (GER) *P Vovcenko* 97
6 b h Contat(GER) Shaheen (GER) (Tertullian (USA))
1451a[6]

Scheme *Sir Mark Prescott Bt* a80
3 b f Pivotal Between Us (Galileo (IRE))
4768[9] 5855[2]◆ 6280[2] 6686[3]◆ 7554[6] 8427[7]

Schhili (IRE) *H-A Pantall* a79 73
3 b f Kodiac Galaxie Sud (USA) (El Prado (IRE))
(509a)

Schindlers Ark (USA)
Jane Chapple-Hyam a54 46
5 gr g Exchange Rate(USA) Sweet Science (USA) (Diesis)
369[9] 589[4] 1145[2] 1361[8] 1519[2] 1858[5]

Schmoozie (IRE) *Jonathan Portman* a70
2 b f Zoffany(IRE) Steal The Show (NZ) (High Chaparral (IRE))
9163[9] 9383[3] 9624[3]

Schnapps *Jedd O'Keeffe* a54 56
3 b f Swiss Spirit Where's Broughton (Cadeaux Genereux)
1385[6] 3154[8] 6678[6] 7581[10]

School Of Thought *James Tate* a75
2 ch c Sir Percy Lady Sylvia (Haafhd)
8287[6] 9155[2]

Schroders Mistake (IRE)
K J Condon 85
2 b f Cable Bay(IRE) Spectacular Show (IRE) (Spectrum (IRE))
5361a[6] 8164a[2]

Schumli *David O'Meara* a52 59
2 b f Swiss Spirit Noble Cause (Showcasing)
4142[7] 4517[6] 5294[3] 5789[13] 6271[5] 7283[8] 7768[4] 8526[4] 8815[11] (9009) 9164[8] 9346[6] 9501[5] 9643[9]

Schwesterherz (FR) *Henk Grewe* 100
2 b f Areion(GER) Nouvelle Noblesse (GER) (Singspiel (IRE))
6248a[4] 8371a[6] 8964a[2]

Scintilating *Ralph Beckett* 77
3 b f Siyouni(FR) Photo Flash (IRE) (Bahamian Bounty)
2687[8]

Scofflaw *David Evans* a85 86
5 b g Foxwedge(AUS) Belle Des Airs (IRE) (Dr Fong (USA))
(34) 381[3] 557[4] 625[5] 922[3] 1099[6] 1560[5] 1925[6] 2472[6] 3018[3] (3322) (5130) (5709) 5948[9] 6686[4] 7185[2] 7680[5] 7975[5] 8412[4] 9041[5] (9138)◆ 9304[3] 9628[8]

Scoffsman *Kevin Frost* a64 68
4 b g Dansili Purissima (USA) (Fusaichi Pegasus (USA))
(2740) 4336[2]◆ 7758[9] 8199[11] 9006[4] 9256[RR]

Scorched Breath *Charlie Fellowes* a70 39
3 b g Bated Breath Danvers (Cape Cross (IRE))
477[3] 1171[2] 1516[5] 8220[9] 8521[10] 9244[12] 9329[4] 9559[13]

Scorching Heat *Adrian McGuinness* a80 84
5 b g Acclamation Pink Flames (IRE) (Redback)
7241a[11]

Scorpio's Dream *Charlie Wallis* a18
2 b g Due Diligence(USA) Small Fortune (Anabaa (USA))
7570[9] 8058[11] 8546[11]

Scotch Corner (IRE)
David C Griffiths 9
2 b g Elzaam(AUS) Campbellite (Desert Prince (IRE))
2475[10] 2707[9]

Scots Sonnet *Jim Goldie* a71 55
5 b g Poet's Voice Jabbara (IRE) (Kingmambo (USA))
608[6] 971[2] 1723[3] 2247[7] 2784[4] 3704[13] 5239[10] 8923[9]

Scottish Blade (IRE) *Charles Hills* a59 18
3 b c Exceed And Excel(AUS) Hecuba (Hector Protector (USA))
2139[10] 4457[10]

Scottish Jig (USA) *William Mott* a83 96
4 ch m Speightstown(USA) Light Jig (Danehill (USA))
6491a[7]

Scottish Summit (IRE)
Geoffrey Harker a69 89
6 b g Shamardal(USA) Scottish Stage (IRE) (Selkirk (USA))
2808[9] 3087[3] 5741[7] 6460[4] 7142[10] (7589) 8130[9]

Scottsdale *Peter Winks* a16 64
6 b g Cape Cross(IRE) High Praise (USA) (Quest For Fame)
1334[12] 1463[17] 9312[10]

Scrafton *Tony Carroll* a41 40
8 b g Leporello(IRE) Some Diva (Dr Fong (USA))
162[7] 8862[15] 9033[9] 9367[11] 9560[6]

Screaming Gemini (IRE)
Tony Carroll a70 62
5 b g Shamardal(USA) Littlefeather (IRE) (Indian Ridge (IRE))
175[3] 705[5] 1675[10] 2256[4] 3038[5]

Screeching Dragon (IRE)
Kevin Frost 39
2 b g Tagula(IRE) Array Of Stars (IRE) (Barathea (IRE))
6368[14] 8857[5]

Scribner Creek (IRE) *R Le Gal* a81 79
6 b g Roderic O'Connor(IRE) Nebraska Lady (IRE) (Lujain (USA))
(2391a)

Scripturale (FR) *M Delcher Sanchez* 97
2 b f Makfi Skysweeper (FR) (Hurricane Run (IRE))
8482a[3]

Scrutiny *Kevin Ryan* a65 68
8 b g Aqlaam Aunty Mary (Common Grounds)
295[7]

Scuzeme *Phillip Makin* a83 76
5 ch g Kheleyf(USA) Barbieri (IRE) (Encosta De Lago (AUS))
1364[4]◆ 1765[2] 2183[2] (2847) 3706[2] 3999[5] 4440[4] 5670[8] 6373[8] (6547)◆

SDH Dream Team *Tim Easterby* 60
3 b g Epaulette(AUS) Donatia (Shamardal (USA))
1819[9]

Sea Art *William Knight* a56 68
3 b g Born To Sea(IRE) Kekova (Montjeu (IRE))
1510[7] 2343[4] 3197[5] 3888[2] 4484[6] 5249[6] 6405[3] 7280[6] (7759)

Sea Battle (FR) *Jane Chapple-Hyam* a69 51
3 ch g Lope De Vega(IRE) Francisca (USA) (Mizzen Mast (USA))
3741[5] (6722) 7450[8] 7973[6] 8291[5]

Seaborn (IRE) *Patrick Chamings* a85 80
5 b g Born To Sea(IRE) Next To The Top (Hurricane Run (IRE))
(2233) 3015[2] (3941) 4215[2] (5086) (6830) 7575[4] (8120)◆

Seaborough (IRE) *David Thompson* a53 66
4 b g Born To Sea(IRE) Nobilissima (IRE) (Orpen (USA))
86[5] 950[7] 1271[8] 1647[3]◆ 2290[5] 2512[4] 3046[8] 3163[2] 3718[8] 4333[11] 5029[11] 5219[5] 5556[6] 6180[5] 7314[9]

Sea Bright *Michael Attwater* a47
2 b g Fulbright Mary Sea (FR) (Selkirk (USA))
8604[11] 9085[11]

Sea Countess (IRE) *J-V Toux* a54
3 b f Born To Sea(IRE) Alltherightmoves (IRE) (Namid)
977a[9]

Seadance *Richard Hannon* a62
2 b c Harbour Watch(IRE) Sand Dancer (IRE) (Footstepsinthesand)
9326[8] 9624[11]

Sea Ewe *Alistair Whillans* a46 50
2 b f Proclamation(IRE) Dispol Katie (Komaite (USA))
7580[8] 8232[5] 9347[12]

Seafarer (IRE) *Marcus Tregoning* a99 95
5 br g Henrythenavigator(USA) Rose Of Petra (IRE) (Golan (IRE))
311[5] 980[5] 2278[2] 2786[6] 3466[6] 4224[P] 9094[8] 9588[6] 9633[6]

Seafaring Girl (IRE)
Mark Loughnane a42 54
3 ch f Born To Sea(IRE) Elayoon (USA) (Danzig (USA))
1549[6] 2350[10] 3271[8] 4244[6] 4518[4] (5377) 5806[9] 6600[2] 7443[10] 8256[10]

Seaforth (IRE) *Adrian Wintle* a57 73
7 b g Acclamation Hendrina (IRE) (Daylami (IRE))
484[5] (1026) 1339[6] 1837[9] 2013[5] 2693[4] 4481[11] 4873[12] 5837[6] (9282) 9450[5] 9609[6]

Sea Fox (IRE) *David Evans* a91 73
5 b g Kodiac City Maiden (USA) (Carson City (USA))
441[6] 856[5] 988[6] 1912[10] 2273[11] 2799[6] (8122)◆ (9255) 9480[8] 9658[10]

Sea It My Way (IRE)
James Fanshawe a61 26
3 b g Sea The Stars(IRE) Take The Ribbon (USA) (Chester House (USA))
6290[15] 6887[4] 7518[7] 9091[3]

Sea Me Win (IRE) *Brian Ellison* a47
6 b g Sea The Stars(IRE) Silk Trail (Dubai Destination (USA))
9350[6]

Seamour (IRE) *Brian Ellison* a97 99
8 b g Azamour(IRE) Chifney Rush (IRE) (Grand Lodge (USA))
1927[13] 4381[4]

Seamster *David Loughnane* a60 61
12 ch g Pivotal Needles And Pins (IRE) (Fasliyev (USA))
2053[5] 2358[4] 3227[5] 3291[3] 3658[9] 4307[9] 5018[3] 5084[5] (6017) 6590[9] 7052[6]

Seanie (IRE) *Karl Thornton* a52 56
10 b g Kodiac Cakestown Lady (IRE) (Petorius (IRE))
484[4] 1021[9]

Seanjohnsilver (IRE) *Declan Carroll* a55 64
3 ch g Power Fulminata (IRE) (Holy Roman Emperor (IRE))
1336[10] 2197[3] 2871[2] 3202[12] 3709[6] 6024[9]

Sea Of Class (IRE) *William Haggas* 121
4 ch m Sea The Stars(IRE) Holy Moon (IRE) (Hernando (FR))
3985[5] (Dead)

Sea Of Cool (IRE) *John Ryan* a50 37
2 b g Sea The Stars(IRE) Magh Meall (Monsieur Bond (IRE))
2362[4] 7611[5] 8461[10] 8856[5] 9045[5] 9179[DSQ]

Sea Of Faith (IRE) *William Haggas* 107
3 b f Sea The Stars(IRE) Jumooh (Monsun (GER))
2087[4]◆ 2831[5] (3882)◆ 5133[3] (6124)◆

Sea Of Flames *Richard Spencer* a37 26
6 ch g Aqlaam Hidden Fire (Alhaarth (IRE))
3496[8]

Sea Of Love (GER) *Markus Klug* 76
2 b f Sea The Moon(GER) Soprana (GER) (Cadeaux Genereux)
7749a[5]

Sea Of Marengo (IRE) *Grace Harris* a68 59
3 b g Battle Of Marengo(IRE) Margie (IRE) (Marju (IRE))
(1041)◆ 2517[5] 5497[9] 5797[5] 6123[4] 6810[12]

Sea Of Marmoon *Mark Johnston* 59
2 b f Golden Horn Sibling Honour (Bernardini (USA))
5139[5] 7755[6]

Sea Of Mystery (IRE)
Michael Appleby a68 68
6 b g Sea The Stars(IRE) Sassenach (IRE) (Night Shift (USA))
4241[15] 4791[10] 5891[8] 6796[2]◆ (7060) 7318[2] 7629[3] 8065[7] 8341[7] 9049[7] 9336[5] (9560)

Sea Of Reality (IRE)
William Haggas a70
3 b f Born To Sea(IRE) Girouette (IRE) (Pivotal)
313[2] 384[2]

Sea Of Shadows *Michael Easterby* 29
2 gr f Sea The Stars(IRE) Pink Opaque (Nayef (USA))
8510[11] 8855[10]

Seaport *Seamus Durack* a58 66
8 ch g Champs Elysees Cochin (USA) (Swain (IRE))
4224[10] 5321[10]

Sea Prose (FR) *F Head* a91 106
4 b m Lope De Vega(IRE) Calasetta (IRE) (Montjeu (IRE))
1827a[2]

Seaquinn *John Best* a49 46
4 b m Equiano(FR) Marine Girl (Shamardal (USA))
365[6] 594[8] 830[12] 1214[2]◆ 1717[5] 3142[4] 3966[5] 6327[8] 7374[2] 7609[7] 8000[2] 9444[6]

Sea Race (IRE) *Paul Fitzsimons* 94
3 b f Charm Spirit(IRE) Sea Chorus (Singspiel (IRE))
7496a[5]

Searanger (USA) *Rebecca Menzies* a50 56
6 b g US Ranger(USA) Baby Lets Cruise (USA) (Tale Of The Cat (USA))
1274[7] 1766[9] 2638[10] 3413[12] 3924[5] 5558[6] 6036[4] 6275[10] 6666[10] 7384[4] 8068[5] 8295[2] 8819[12]

Search For A Song (IRE) *D K Weld* 118
3 ch f Galileo(IRE) Polished Gem (IRE) (Danehill (USA))
5208a[4] (6378) (7246a)

Search For Light (IRE)
Saeed bin Suroor a81 81
3 gr f New Approach(IRE) Fire Blaze (IRE) (Dubawi (IRE))
(2102) 3003[4]

Searching (IRE) *Grace Harris* a52 73
7 ro g Mastercraftsman(IRE) Miracolia (IRE) (Montjeu (IRE))
2185[8] 2591[4] 2819[5] 3361[3] 3940[4] 7116[11]

Sea's Aria (IRE) *Mark Hoad* a51 51
8 b g Sea The Stars(IRE) Speed Song (Fasliyev (USA))
59[8] 369[8] 721[4] (1044) 1361[7] 3017[2] 3252[7] 4777[5] 6601[10] 9310[13]

Seascape (IRE) *Henry Candy* a29 74
3 b f Sea The Moon(GER) Feis Ceoil (IRE) (Key Of Luck (USA))
(2341) 5549[2]◆ 6672[3] 7343[10]

Sea Sculpture *Andrew Balding* a79 77
3 b g Archipenko(USA) Seaflower Reef (IRE) (Robellino (USA))
(2216)◆ 3324[4] 3808[5]

Seasearch *Andrew Balding* a70 44
4 b g Passing Glance Seaflower Reef (IRE) (Robellino (USA))
99[6] 387[3] (589) 731[12] 927[4] 1861[3] 2351[3] 2718[10]

Sea Shack *Julia Feilden* a49 56
5 b g Equiano(FR) Folly Bridge (Avonbridge)
241[4] 479[2] 624[2] 792[9] 1060[3] 1215[3] 1390[3] 2012[4] 2631[4] 3006[12] 6117[6] 6731[3] 7281[6] 8667[7] 8942[3] 9220[3] 9516[9]

Seaside Song *Cathrine Erichsen* a88 93
5 b m Harbour Watch(IRE) Sea Chorus (Singspiel (IRE))
4461a[9] 7496a[7]

Sea Sister (IRE) *Olly Murphy* a50 24
3 b f Born To Sea(IRE) Campessa (IRE) (Intikhab (USA))
4452[11]

Seas Of Elzaam (IRE)
David O'Meara 73
2 b g Elzaam(AUS) Ocean Sands (IRE) (Desert Prince (IRE))
7046[3] 7377[6] 8337[2]

Seasons Bloom (AUS) *C S Shum* 116
6 br g Captain Sonador(AUS) Pyramisa's Lass (AUS) (Not A Single Doubt (AUS))
9377a[9]

Seasony (IRE) *Mark Johnston* a80
2 b c Siyouni(FR) Rosie Cotton (IRE) (King's Best (USA))
(7445)◆

Sea Sovereign (IRE) *Ian Williams* a59 51
6 b g Sea The Stars(IRE) Lidakiya (IRE) (Kahyasi (IRE))
5320[7] 6218[7] 8065[9] 8868[3] 9204[10]

Sea Storm *Martyn Meade* a62
3 ch f Monsieur Bond(IRE) Chez Cherie (Wolfhound (USA))
1168[4] 1346[3]

Sea Tea Dea *Adrian Wintle* a42 50
5 b m Archipenko(USA) Half Sister (IRE) (Oratorio (IRE))
204[5] 482[6] 2234[11] 2930[5] 3352[4] 5016[3] 5293[2] 6643[5] 6897[6] 7374[5] 9446[7]

Sea The Lion (IRE) *Jarlath P Fahey* 110
8 b g Sea The Stars(IRE) Ramona (Desert King (IRE))
4933[7]

Sea The Spirit *Mike Murphy* a18
2 b g Sea The Stars(IRE) My Country (IRE) (Invincible Spirit (IRE))
2594[11]

Sea Tide *Laura Mongan* a69 75
5 b m Champs Elysees Change Course (Sadler's Wells (USA))
1882[5] 2353[6] 3022[9]

Sea Trout Reach (IRE)
William Haggas 76
2 ch c Mukhadram Caelica (IRE) (Sea The Stars (IRE))
5655[2] 6905[5]

Sea Voice *Richard Hannon* 81
2 b c Poet's Voice Always Like This (IRE) (Cape Cross (IRE))
6905[10] (7113) 8517[2]

Sea Weed (FR) *G Doleuze* a35
4 b m Alianthus(GER) Sea Starling (FR) (Slickly (FR))
2264a[11]

Sea Willow *Henry Spiller* a49 55
2 ch f Dream Ahead(USA) Showbird (Showcasing)
4849[9] 6146[5] 7393[12] 9438[4]

Sea Wings *William Haggas* a75 68
3 ch g Sea The Stars(IRE) Infallible (Pivotal)
4121[5] 5268[5] 5808[9] 7773[5]

Sebastiano Ricci (IRE)
Mark Loughnane a61 81
4 b g Lope De Vega(IRE) Dear Dream (IRE) (Montjeu (IRE))
250[6] 2349[11] 3225[9]

Sebastian's Wish (IRE)
Keith Dalgleish a62 74
6 b g Aqlaam Swish (GER) (Monsun (GER))
2326[2] 3361[5]

Second Collection *Tony Carroll* a87 88
3 b f Delegator Quelle Affaire (Bahamian Bounty)
235[2]◆ 477[2] (1020) (1337)◆ 2212[2] (2687) 3544[5] (4420) 5504[4] 9214[6]

Second Love (IRE) *K R Burke* a82 67
2 ch c Es Que Love(IRE) In Seconds (USA) (Giant's Causeway (USA))
3491[3] 4302[2] 6064[5] (6883) 8297[5]

Secondo (FR) *Robert Stephens* a70 66
9 b g Sakhee's Secret Royal Jade (Last Tycoon)
31[3] 237[4] 600[3] 883[2] 1682[6] 1930[3] 2717[3] 4455[8] 4873[6] (5083) 5495[4] 6363[4] 7977[10] (8199) 9048[9]

Second Page *Richard Hannon* a80 66
5 b g Harbour Watch(IRE) Almunia (IRE) (Mujadil (USA))
390[4] 704[2]◆ 1159[5]

Second Sight *Charlie Fellowes* a65
3 b c Showcasing Dream Vision (USA) (Distant View (USA))
2375[4] 3003[13] 3584[10] 4769[11] 5695[14]

Second Summer (USA)
A R Al Rayhi a84 101
7 ch g Summer Bird(USA) Greenstreet (USA) (Street Cry (IRE))
638a[6] 1113a[10]

Secret Ace *Archie Watson* a71
3 ch f Compton Place Secret Romance (Sakhee's Secret)
141[2] 458[3]

Secret Acquisition *Daniel Kubler* a67
2 b f Sea The Moon(GER) Maria Letizia (Galileo (IRE))
7031[2] 7515[2] 8700[9]

Secret Advisor (FR)
Charlie Appleby 96
5 b g Dubawi(IRE) Sub Rose (IRE) (Galileo (IRE))
4053[12] 4884[12]

Secret Ambition *S Seemar* a107 71
6 b h Exceed And Excel(AUS) Inner Secret (USA) (Singspiel (IRE))
282a[4] (425a) 726a[2] 1112a[6] 1440a[5]

Secretarial (IRE) *Tim Easterby* 78
3 b f Kingman Wadaat (Diktat)
2094[8] 2634[5]◆ (3247)

Secret Art (IRE) *Gary Moore* a93 72
9 ch g Excellent Art Ivy Queen (IRE) (Green Desert (USA))
1545[5] 2320[7] 2800[8] 3300[3] 3806[12] 6211[7] (6390) 7166[4] 8253[14]

Secret Asset (IRE) *Lisa Williamson* a49 58
14 gr g Clodovil(IRE) Skerray (Soviet Star (USA))
161[12]

Secret Cecil (FR) *Joseph Tuite* 50
2 b g Holy Roman Emperor(IRE) Cruise Dancer (IRE) (Ishiguru (USA))
2338[6] 3039[8] 4394[13] 4778[8]

Secret Diary *Declan Carroll* a60 29
2 b f Mukhadram Yearbook (Byron)
7538[8] 7958[3] 8640[11] 9060[3] 9346[5]

Secret Escape (IRE)
Donald McCain 3
7 ch m Getaway(GER) Portorosa (USA) (Irish River (FR))
7704[6]

Secretfact *Malcolm Saunders* a81 81
6 br g Sakhee's Secret Matterofact (IRE) (Bold Fact (USA))
1915[9] 3531[5] 3856[5] 4374[2] 6110[3] 6332[2] 6668[4] (7178) 7771[3] 8470[5] 8601[7] 9131[7] 9286[6]

Secret Footsteps (IRE) *K R Burke*
3 br g Footstepsinthesand Secret Friend (IRE) (Royal Applause)
1970[6]

Secret Glance *Adrian Wintle* a48 57
7 b g Sakhee's Secret Look Here's Dee (Dansili)
263[3] 530[5] 4115[7] 6363[12] 7384[10] 7811[8]

Secret Identity *Michael Mullineaux* a26 65
2 b f Equiano(FR) Onlyyouknowme (IRE) (Martino Alonso (IRE))
3196[5] 3968[6] 4583[6] 5789[9] 7283[6] 9164[10]

Secretinthepark *Michael Mullineaux* a84 83
9 ch g Sakhee's Secret Lark In The Park (IRE) (Grand Lodge (USA))
1760[16] (2053) 2416[5] 2841[5] 4100[10] 4406[4] (4894) 5661[7] 6455[3] 6954[15] 7077[11] (8023) 8428[9] 9098[10]

Secret Lightning (FR)
Michael Appleby a56 60
7 ch m Sakhee's Secret Dimelight (Fantastic Light (USA))
599[5] 719[7] 1477[7]

Secret Magic (IRE)
Mark Loughnane a47 24
3 b f Alhebayeb(IRE) No Secrets (USA) (El Corredor (USA))
1515[8] 3270[8] 4518[8] 6024[8] 7523[8]

Secret Message (USA)
H Graham Motion 110
4 bb m Hat Trick(JPN) Westside Singer (USA) (Gone West (USA))
4950a[4] 6491a[8] 8154a[10]

Secret Passion *Archie Watson* a55 59
2 b f Havana Gold(IRE) Hamsat Elqamar (Nayef (USA))
4819[6] 5387[6] 5733[8] 7277[8]

Secret Pearl (FR) *P Monfort* a48 64
5 b m Palace Episode(USA) L'Ecuyere (GER) (Black Sam Bellamy (IRE))
5761a[2]

Secret Picnic (FR) *John Quinn* a52 52
3 b g Penny's Picnic(IRE) Secret Marks (FR) (Echo Of Light)
783[3]◆ 918[8] 1380[2] 1982[10] 2300[9]

Secret Player (FR) *G Botti* a70
2 b c Rio De La Plata(USA) Sertolina (USA) (Bertolini (USA))
8448a[8]

Secret Potion *Ronald Harris* a74 72
5 b g Stimulation(IRE) Fiancee (IRE) (Pivotal)
626[2] 907[5] 1037[3] (1682) 2122[8] 2717[5] 4230[5] 5281[9] 5607[5] (5986) 6203[6] (6365) 7112[5] 7831[3] 8063[2] 8242[3]

Secret Potion (GER) *Henk Grewe* 95
3 bb g Dabirsim(FR) Sola Gratia (IRE) (Monsun (GER))
6385a[6] 7249a[13]

Secret Return (IRE) *Karen George* a76 83
6 ch m Roderic O'Connor(IRE) Quick Return (Polish Precedent (USA))
2584[4] 3763[2] 4639[8] (6201)◆ 7975[8] 8412[9] 8809[8] 9126[8]

Secret Smile (IRE) *Mark Johnston* a72
2 ch f Exceed And Excel(AUS) Zam Zoom (IRE) (Dalakhani (IRE))
8338[10] 8700[6] 8913[4] 9159[7] 9448[3] 9665[6]

Secret Spice (USA) *Richard Baltas* a114
4 b m Discreet Cat(USA) Chimayo (USA) (A.P. Indy (USA))
8775a[9]

Secret Stash (IRE) *Mark Casse* 96
2 b f Mukhadram Poppet's Lovein (Lomitas)
7267a[5]

Secret Thoughts (USA) *A P O'Brien* 98
3 b f War Front(USA) Chicquita (IRE) (Montjeu (IRE))
1601a[5] 2521[10] 5075a[5]

Secret Time (GER) *F Chappet* 98
2 b f Camacho Song Of Time (IRE) (Kheleyf (USA))
7006a[2] 7925a[10]

Secret Treaties *Christine Dunnett* a46 55
3 b f Heeraat(IRE) Honky Tonk Queen (USA) (Mizzen Mast (USA))
1855[9] 2623[10]◆ 4328[13] 5358[2] 6130[13] 7281[8] 8207[3]

Secret Venture *Kevin Ryan* 93
3 b g Kyllachy Resort (Oasis Dream)
2434[2] 3865[21]

Secret Victory *Charlie Appleby* a70 79
2 ch c Dubawi(IRE) Hidden Gold (IRE) (Shamardal (USA))
7996[4] 8464[2]

Secret Wedding *P Monfort* a42 32
2 ch f Casamento(IRE) Sacred Bond (Exceed And Excel (AUS))
5600a[8]

Sedrina (IRE) *S Wattel* a73 77
3 b f Dream Ahead(USA) Spring Wave (IRE) (Dr Fong (USA))
3710a[13]

Seduction (FR) *C Escuder* 85
3 b f Evasive Absent Minded (Medicean)
3031a[7]

Seductive Moment (GER) *Mark Johnston* a79 96
3 ch g Shamardal(USA) Sexy Lady (GER) (Danehill Dancer (IRE))
126[5] (5255) (5445)◆ 6425[4]

Seed Of Love (FR) *Simone Brogi* 61
3 b c Planteur(IRE) Tauranga (FR) (Gold Away (IRE))
1741a[7]

Seeing Red (IRE) *Amanda Perrett* a49 61
3 b f Sea The Stars(IRE) Red Fantasy (IRE) (High Chaparral (IRE))
2087[8] 3013[10] 5730[9] 9305[13]

Seeking Revenge (FR) *Mme E Siavy-Julien* a58 59
4 b g Spirit One(FR) European Style (FR) (Ezzoud (IRE))
2647a[3]

Seeking The Soul (USA) *Dallas Stewart* a114
6 b h Perfect Soul(IRE) Seeking The Title (USA) (Seeking The Gold (USA))
445a[2] 1447a[8] 8777a[6]

Seek The Moon (USA) *Lawrence Mullaney* a56 60
4 b m Giant's Causeway(USA) Crescent Moon (USA) (Seeking The Gold (USA))
1169[12] 1399[10] 3414[8] 4130[3] 4371[5] 4990[4] 5438[5]

See My Baby Jive *Donald Whillans* a44 47
5 ch f Coach House(IRE) Lady Fiona (Royal Applause)
4489[5]

Seenit Doneit Next (IRE) *Andrew Hughes* 44
3 b f The Carbon Unit(USA) Janna's Jewel (IRE) (Traditionally (USA))
2438[5] 4915[14]

Seen The Lyte (IRE) *Nigel Tinkler* a66 87
4 b m Kodiac Highest Praise (Acclamation)
1978[3] 2292[5] 2589[3] 3201[3] 3868[4] (4105) 4625[6] 4986[4] 5372[4] 5846[3] 6714[4] 7183[7]

Seeusoon (IRE) *Andrew Balding* a67 74
3 b g Sea The Moon(GER) Village Fete (Singspiel (IRE))
358[4] (1080)◆ 1884[4] 2562[3] 3260[5] 3729[5] 7683[10] 8433[11]

Seeyoubyme (FR) *Debbie Mountain* 99
3 gr g Siyouni(FR) Peinted Song (USA) (Unbridled's Song (USA))
9590a[6]

Sefton Warrior *Richard Spencer* a69 61
2 b g Frankel Maid To Master (IRE) (Danehill Dancer (IRE))
7346[8] 8346[4] 9208[7]

Segarelli (IRE) *A Fabre* 73
3 ch g Sea The Stars(IRE) Samba Brazil (GER) (Teofilo (IRE))
2758a[3]

Se Green *Tim Easterby* 44
3 b f Sepoy(AUS) Nos Da (Cape Cross (IRE))
1982[14] 3417[8] 3684[7] 5297[5]

Seinesational *William Knight* a86 89
4 b g Champs Elysees Kibara (Sadler's Wells (USA))
(1840) 2398[6] 3044[3] (3861) 4505[6] 5540[2] 6834[3] 7403[4] 8114[22] 8654[4]

Seize The Time (IRE) *K R Burke* a69 75
2 ch f Siyouni(FR) Teeba (USA) (Seeking The Gold (USA))
(5243) 6157[9] 7149[7]

Selcourt (USA) *John W Sadler* a110
5 ch m Tiz Wonderful(USA) Azure Spring (USA) (Open Forum (USA))
8769a[7]

Selectif *O Briand* a33 39
7 b g Elusive City(USA) Born Again (FR) (Cape Cross (IRE))
7009a[9] 7501a[10]

Selecto *Roger Charlton* a62 72
2 b c Paco Boy(IRE) Telescopic (Galileo (IRE))
4925[6] 5774[4] 6858[5] 8760[5]

Self Assessment (IRE) *K R Burke* a84 77
3 b g Elzaam(AUS) Little Miss Diva (IRE) (Diktat)
1345[4] 1857[10] 2825[5] 5002[3] 5270[4] 5947[6] 7049[2] 8342[12] (8495) 9054[9] 9476[9]

Selflessly (USA) *Chad C Brown* 100
2 bb f More Than Ready(USA) Uniformly Yours (CAN) (Grand Slam (USA))
8748a[5]

Self Sense (AUS) *David Brideoake* 105
8 br g Street Sense(USA) Be My Person (AUS) (Personal Flag (USA))
8134a[13]

Selini Mou (IRE) *Georgios Alimpinisis* a70 50
4 ch m Thewayyouare(USA) Moonboat (Starcraft (NZ))
1491a[3]

Selino *James Fanshawe* a103 87
3 b g Champs Elysees Air Kiss (Red Ransom (USA))
2289[2] 2845[2]◆ 3802[3]◆ 5734[3] (6459) (8321)

Sellingallthetime (IRE) *Mark Usher* a53 45
8 ch g Tamayuz Anthyllis (GER) (Lycius (USA))
38[8] 346[9] 622[5] 1498[9] 2344[10] 2698[5]◆ 2970[7] 3834[4] 4498[10] 5379[9] 5802[4] 6681[10]

Selsey Sizzler *William Knight* a60 65
2 b g Nathaniel(IRE) Heho (Dansili)
3274[11] 4117[5] 6402[4] 7562[9] 8286[5]

Semari (NZ) *Trent Busuttin & Natalie Young* 100
4 b m Sebring(AUS) Kumari (NZ) (Zabeel (NZ))
1784a[15]

Semoum (USA) *Roger Varian* 99
3 b c Bernardini(USA) No Curfew (USA) (Curlin (USA))
(2434) 4122[5]

Sempre Presto (IRE) *Richard Fahey* 72
4 b m Nathaniel(IRE) Flandre (USA) (Elusive Quality (USA))
1666[2] 2399[7] 3054[8] 3816[5] 4817[4] 5473[3] 6371[2] 7057[3] 7368[6]

Sena *William Haggas* a51
2 b f Dutch Art Vallado (IRE) (Clodovil (IRE))
9299[10] 9413[9] 9569[8]

Sendacard *Richard Fahey* a71 71
2 br f Showcasing Valentine Glory (Kyllachy)
5913[2]◆ 7063[5] 8891[2]

Sendeed (IRE) *Saeed bin Suroor* a88 93
3 b c Shamardal(USA) Petrushka (IRE) (Unfuwain (USA))
2023[11] 3510[3] (4277) 4996[3] 5984[2] (6967) 7829[2]◆

Senior Investment (USA) *Kenneth McPeek* a99 79
5 ch h Discreetly Mine(USA) Plaid (USA) (Deputy Commander (USA))
396a[6] 638a[4]

Seniority *William Haggas* a107 107
5 ch g Dubawi(IRE) Anna Palariva (IRE) (Caerleon (USA))
52a[4] 515a[8] 3313[2] 4292[4] 5610[4] 6391[3] 6915[5] 8062[11]

Senorita Grande (IRE) *John Quinn* a66 57
3 b f Garswood Spring Green (Bahamian Bounty)
2243[4] 2624[3]◆ 3499[8] 4328[4] 5659[8] 6737[2] (6889) 7446[2] 7869[8] 8755[6]

Sensazione Poy *G Botti* a85 77
4 b g Sepoy(AUS) Queen Sensazione (IRE) (King Charlemagne (USA))
(1908a) (2264a) (6790a)

Sense Of Belonging (FR) *Kevin Ryan* a76 76
3 ch g Dutch Art Bertie's Best (King's Best (USA))
1862[4] 3638[4] 4288[2]

Sense Of Direction *K R Burke* a65
3 b f Kodiac One Giant Leap (IRE) (Pivotal)
229[3]◆ 1195[6]

Senza Limiti (IRE) *William Haggas* a99 102
3 ch c Lope De Vega(IRE) Senza Rete (IRE) (Barathea (IRE))
1940[2] 2668a[8] (Dead)

Sepahi *Henry Spiller* a65 65
3 ch f Sepoy(AUS) Katevan (IRE) (Heliostatic (IRE))
720[5] 1170[7] (1380) 3189[6] 3709[3]◆ 4457[9] 5377[10] 5869[2] 7105[5] 8083[10] 8896[10] (9253) 9548[5]

Separable *Tim Easterby* 54
3 ch g Sepoy(AUS) Poyle Meg (Dansili)
1980[8] 2870[6] 3570[5] 4519[17]

Separate *Richard Hannon* 100
2 b f Cable Bay(IRE) Miss Moses (USA) (Gulch (USA))
1733[2] 2805[6] (3350) 4048[15] 4398[2] 5185[6] 5612[8] 6356[8] (7409) 7696[2] 8089[3] 8763[7]

Sephira Park *Chris Wall* a31 39
4 b m Sepoy(AUS) Sparkle Park (Kyllachy)
5336[5] 6594[7]

Sephton *Alan King* a40 56
3 b g Shamardal(USA) Honour (Dansili)
2965[11] 4664[4] 5249[8]

Sepia Belle *Amy Murphy*
2 b f
9668[5]

Seprani *Amy Murphy* a75 76
5 b m Sepoy(AUS) King's Guest (IRE) (King's Best (USA))
2804[3] 3543[11] 3967[2] 4833[4] 5870[2] 5959[2] 6401[2] 6795[6] 7684[2] 7843[2] 8471[7]

September Power (IRE) *Roger Varian* a56
2 b f Mastercraftsman(IRE) Lisanor (Raven's Pass (USA))
9159[10] 9323[7] 9567[4]

Septems (FR) *Mme J Hendriks* a80 72
3 ch c Vespone(IRE) Rosen Opera (FR) (Rosen Kavalier (JPN))
868a[2] 9058a[2]

Seqania *Mario Hofer* a70 66
4 b m Equiano(FR) Singuna (GER) (Black Sam Bellamy (IRE))
2391a[2]

Seraphim *Marco Botti* a66 45
3 gr f Dark Angel(IRE) Moma Lee (Duke Of Marmalade (IRE))
1272[5]◆ 2018[6] 2550[3] 3146[2] 4247[3] 4807[7] 5807[4] 8499[4] 8698[7] 9089[3] 9277[4] (9477) 9627[4]

Seraphinite (IRE) *Jamie Osborne* a74 76
2 gr f Gutaifan(IRE) Ellasha (Shamardal (USA))
2579[9] (2968) 4048[20] 4637[4] 5340[2] 5683[6] 5988[2] 6667[3] 7896[15] 8315[6] 9205[9]

Serena (GER) *H-J Groschel* 99
4 b m Soldier Hollow Salonshuffle (GER) (Big Shuffle (USA))
4622a[6]

Serenading *James Fanshawe* a66 67
3 br f Iffraaj Constant Dream (Kheleyf (USA))
6074[7] 6701[2] 7190[5] 8254[13]

Serendipite (FR) *F Head* a63 64
3 b f Le Havre(IRE) Instant (USA) (Gone West (USA))
3139a[6]

Serengeti Empress (USA) *Thomas Amoss* a111
3 bb f Alternation(USA) Havisham (USA) (Bernardini (USA))
7479a[6] 8775a[3]

Serengeti Song (IRE) *K R Burke* a71 76
3 b g Poet's Voice African Plains (Oasis Dream)
1389[3] 1649[6] 2098[5] 2635[6] 3565[4] 4288[10]

Serenu (FR) *A Sagot* a47 59
9 gr g Walk In The Park(IRE) Doraflor (FR) (Kendor (FR))
2026a[10]

Sergei Prokofiev (CAN) *A P O'Brien* a88 107
3 b c Scat Daddy(USA) Orchard Beach (CAN) (Tapit (USA))
(1434a) 2409[4] 3950[10] 4665[6]

Serienschock (GER) *Mme A Rosa* a76 71
11 bb g Sholokhov(IRE) Saldenehre (GER) (Highest Honor (FR))
6095a[8]

Serious Jockin *Mick Channon* a53 30
2 b g Footstepsinthesand Crazee Diamond (Rock Of Gibraltar (IRE))
5775[9] 6254[5] 6464[9] 7768[2] 7994[6] 8452[8] 8750[4]

Sermandakfi (FR) *F Monnier* 77
3 ch f Makfi Josephjuliusjodie (IRE) (Galileo (IRE))
7291a[3]

Sermon (IRE) *Tom Dascombe* a80 79
2 gr g Dark Angel(IRE) Kermana (IRE) (Selkirk (USA))
3507[3] 4191[2] 4361[2] 5703[2] 6375[7] 7437[3] 8261[2]

Servalan (IRE) *Mrs John Harrington* a75 100
3 b f No Nay Never(USA) Catch The Eye (IRE) (Oratorio (IRE))
2605a[2] (5325a) 5923a[6] 6472[8] 7146[12]

Servo (IRE) *Lynn Siddall* a73 60
5 b g Power Parade Scene (USA) (Parade Ground (USA))
(125)

Sesame (IRE) *Michael Appleby* a34 42
3 b f Slade Power(IRE) Tiger Spice (Royal Applause)
2933[9] 3683[7] 6342[10] 7550[9]

Sesame Birah (IRE) *Richard Hannon* 94
2 b f Gregorian(IRE) Limousine (Beat Hollow)
3934[2] (4317) 5469a[4] (5774) 6212[2] 6957[5]

Sestilio Jet (FR) *Andrea Marcialis* a103 112
4 b h French Fifteen(FR) Hideaway Girl (Fasliyev (USA))
(2667a) 3388a[2] 7254a[4] 7943a[8]

Set In Stone (IRE) *Andrew Hughes* 74
5 b m Famous Name Storminateacup (IRE) (Galileo (IRE))
1308a[16] 2369[5] 2784[5] 3502[10] 4278[6] 4917[3]◆ (5117) 6656[2] (7489)

Set Piece *Hugo Palmer* a112 107
3 b g Dansili Portodora (USA) (Kingmambo (USA))
(128) 1854[3] 2411[14] 5480a[7] (9064)

Set Point Charlie (IRE) *Seamus Durack* a52 63
3 b g Holy Roman Emperor(IRE) Love Thirty (Mister Baileys)
3464[13] 4196[10] 4738[7] 5867[8] (6361) 6643[6] 9479[10]

Setting Sail *Charlie Appleby* a100 112
4 b g Dansili West Wind (Machiavellian (USA))
(1989) 2606[4] 3315[4] (4342)◆ 4935[2] 5519[3] (6536) 9016a[2]

Settle For Bay (FR) *David Marnane* a84 98
5 b g Rio De La Plata(USA) Dissitation (IRE) (Spectrum (IRE))
51a[14] 285a[8] 2879a[8] 3987[27]

Settle Petal *Pat Phelan* a71 64
5 b m Peintre Celebre(USA) Shall We Dance (Rambo Dancer (CAN))
5087[8] 5570[6] 6160[6] 7083[3] 7560[9] 9426[4] 9663[13]

Seven Clans (IRE) *Karen Tutty* a83 54
7 b g Cape Cross(IRE) Cherokee Rose (IRE) (Dancing Brave (USA))
4249[12] 6733[4] 7185[11] 8014[12] 8692[3] 9096[9] 9543[2]◆ 9611[6]

Seven Emirates (IRE) *K R Burke* a45 70
2 b c Dark Angel(IRE) Blockade (IRE) (Kheleyf (USA))
6175[7] 7179[4] 7870[5] 8430[7]

Seven For A Pound (USA) *Richard Fahey* a59 45
3 b g Scat Daddy(USA) Gimlet Witha Twist (USA) (Tale Of The Cat (USA))
1819[7] 3594[7] 4210[8] 5023[8] 5905[5] 8068[9]

Sevenleft (IRE) *Ms Sheila Lavery* a64 76
6 br g Manduro(GER) Fleeting Affair (USA) (Gone West (USA))
7085a[9]

Sevenna Star (IRE) *John Ryan* a61 100
4 b h Redoute's Choice(AUS) Sevenna (FR) (Galileo (IRE))
2807[7] 4053[19] 7615[4] 9222[4]

Seventeen O Four (IRE) *Michael Bell* a57
2 ro g Gutaifan(IRE) Bali Breeze (IRE) (Common Grounds)
9197[6] 9451[6]

Seventeenpointfour *Amy Murphy* 34
3 b g Le Havre(IRE) Laguna Salada (IRE) (Invincible Spirit (IRE))
5384[5]

Seventii *Robert Eddery* a51 49
5 b m Medicean Lowndes (Rail Link)
245[13] 549[6] 1341[7] 1519[11] 2111[10] 2975[5] 3252[3] 3740[3] 3941[6] 4216[5] 5029[8] 5513[5] 6601[5] 7202[7] 8072[2] 8551[14] 8843[5] 9444[10]

Severance *Mick Channon* a95 96
3 b g Nathaniel(IRE) Decorative (IRE) (Danehill Dancer (IRE))
1756[3] (2099) 2619[7] 4017[6] 4845[9] 5541[9] 6349[3] 8725[7]

Severnaya (IRE) *John Gosden* a74 94
3 b f Dubawi(IRE) Zibelina (IRE) (Dansili)
(971)◆ (7114)◆ 8728[3]

Sextant *Sir Michael Stoute* 111
4 b g Sea The Stars(IRE) Hypoteneuse (IRE) (Sadler's Wells (USA))
(2606) 3346[4] (4395) (5370) 6213[4] (7180)◆ 7890[2]

Sexy Metro (FR) *D Guillemin* 99
3 b g Diamond Green(FR) Mindset (IRE) (Vettori (IRE))
2564a[4] 4205a[6]

Sexy Secret *Simon Pearce* a43 37
8 b g Sakhee's Secret Orange Walk (IRE) (Alzao (USA))
4346[12] 5528[14] 7318[15] 9481[7]

Sezim *Mohamed Moubarak* a84 84
3 b g Dansili Serres (IRE) (Daylami (IRE))
2765[3] 3779[2] (4316) 6081[4] 6700[7] 7653[5] 8809[5] 9199[7] 9388[5] 9480[6]

Sfumato *Adrian Nicholls* a69 70
5 br g Bated Breath Modern Look (Zamindar (USA))
2203[4] 2846[5] 3656[9] 4519[7] 4785[2]◆ (5051) 5632[3]◆ 6680[7] (7051) 7289[6]

Shabaaby *Owen Burrows* 112
4 br g Kyllachy On The Brink (Mind Games)
(2614)

Shabeeb (USA) *Ian Williams* a92 64
6 b g Smart Strike(CAN) Sortita (GER) (Monsun (GER))
2575[P] 4382[13] 4899[9] 5443[7] 5657[P]

Shabrice (GER) *H Blume* a53
4 b m Shirocco(GER) Schwarzach (GER) (Grand Lodge (USA))
76a[9]

Shackled N Drawn (USA) *Peter Hedger* a57 57
7 b g Candy Ride(ARG) Cajun Flash (USA) (Bertrando (USA))
298[5] 857[9] 986[5] 1716[11] 4500[8]

Shades Of Blue (IRE) *Clive Cox* 112
3 br f Kodiac Enjoyable (IRE) (Verglas (IRE))
2077[3] 2779[2] (4205a) 4891[2] 6257[2] 7254a[2] 7943a[11]

Shades Of Silver *Alexandra Dunn* a47 47
9 b g Dansili Silver Pivotal (IRE) (Pivotal)
833[6] 1144[8] 1330[9]

Shadn (IRE) *Andrew Balding* a81 107
2 b f No Nay Never(USA) Amethyst (IRE) (Sadler's Wells (USA))
(3461)◆ 3983[13] (5134)◆ 6444[3] 7456[3] (8140a) 8748a[9]

Shadow Glen *Eve Johnson Houghton* 68
2 b g Gleneagles(IRE) Milady (Shamardal (USA))
4184[6] 7407[9] 8517[7]

Shadow Leader *Michael Dods* 63
2 b g Equiano(FR) Midnight M (Green Desert (USA))
5234[6] 5689[4]

Shadow's Girl *Bernard Llewellyn* a39 17
7 gr m Fair Mix(IRE) Special Beat (Bustino)
1519[10]

Shady McCoy (USA) *Ian Williams* a85 95
9 b g English Channel(USA) Raw Gold (USA) (Rahy (USA))
2100[11] 2572[7] 3318[6] 4127[10] 4887[11]◆ 5319[4] 5416[2] 6950[15] 7563[4] 8062[10] 8690[4] 9086[4] 9283[7]

Shaffire *Harry Whittington* a58 68
3 b f Clodovil(IRE) Wigan Lane (Kheleyf (USA))
2356[8] 3442[10] 7976[8] 8279[8] 8457[9] 9384[2]◆ 9657[4]

Shafia (FR) *J-C Rouget* 96
3 b f Le Havre(IRE) Shalaiyma (FR) (New Approach (IRE))
3676a[5]

Shafran Mnm (IRE) *Andrea Marcialis* 91
3 b f Shamardal(USA) Powdermill (Oasis Dream)
4703a[7]

Shagalla *Roger Varian* a74 69
3 b f Lawman(FR) Shabyt (Sadler's Wells (USA))
2445[6] 2685[6] 5039[4]

Shahnaza (FR) *A De Royer-Dupre* 107
4 b m Azamour(IRE) Shanndiyra (IRE) (King's Best (USA))
1627a[2] 2167a[3] 3138a[3] 4962a[6] 7885a[5]

Shailene (IRE) *Andrew Balding* a98 105
4 ch m Rip Van Winkle(IRE) Snow Key (USA) (Cozzene (USA))
1927[6] 2440[6] 3374[2] (4170a) 4645[5] 5662[3] 6747a[3] (7408) 7658[4]

Shaji *David Bridgwater* a61 45
4 b g Exceed And Excel(AUS) Eclaircie (IRE) (Thunder Gulch (USA))
731[11] 910[10] 1680[7]

Shake Me Handy *Roger Teal* a75 62
4 gr g Eastern Anthem(IRE) Cloridja (Indian Ridge (IRE))
438[2] 963[2] 5292[5] 6806[4] 9632[3]

Shakespear'sgalley (IRE) *Joseph Patrick O'Brien* 87
4 b h Galileo(IRE) Lady Shakespeare (USA) (Theatrical (IRE))
5508a[10]

Shakiah (IRE) *Sharon Watt* a46 55
4 b m Farhh Dubai Sea (USA) (Street Sense (USA))
1431[6] 1967[7] 2376[6] 3162[9] 5156[6] 6827[9]

Sha La La La Lee *Tom Dascombe* a94 99
4 b g Helmet(AUS) Shamara (IRE) (Spectrum (IRE))
623[2] (988) 1294[2] 1916[8] (2572) 3069[5] 4097[5] 5708[10] 7184[6]

Shaleela's Dream *Jane Chapple-Hyam* a69 60
3 b g Oasis Dream Shaleela (IRE) (Galileo (IRE))
472[6] 723[5] 1019[3] 1481[7] 2125[9] 4070[6] 4567[3] 5092[7] 5526[5] 7050[11]

Shallow Hal *K R Burke* a85 85
3 b g Mayson Bazelle (Ashkalani (IRE))
1736[6] 2746[11] 3654[4] 3865[7]◆ 7402[18] 8921[7] 9348[6]

Shall We Begin (IRE) *Michael Easterby* a47 49
3 ch f Bungle Inthejungle Shone Island (IRE) (Desert Sun)
1924[8] 2823[8] 4212[11] 4436[4] 5393[7] 6608[8] 7047[7]

Shalona (FR) *Henk Grewe* 101
3 b f Soldier Hollow Salona (GER) (Lord Of England (GER))
(2137a) 3119a[3] 4461a[2] 5230a[6]

Shamaal Nibras (USA) *Doug Watson* a107 105
10 b g First Samurai(USA) Sashay Away (USA) (Farma Way (USA))
425a[2]

Shamad (IRE) *Peter Fahey* a77 84
5 b g Shamardal(USA) Maryellen's Spirit (IRE) (Invincible Spirit (IRE))
5599a[4] (7003)◆ (7436)

Shamaheart (IRE) *Geoffrey Harker* a44 50
9 b g Shamardal(USA) Encouragement (Royal Applause)
3199[7] 4523[5] 5247[10] 6627[8] 7587[3] 7960[9] 8818[10]

Shamalov (IRE) *Denis Gerard Hogan* a42 56
3 gr g Alhebayeb(IRE) Over Rating (Desert King (IRE))
4726[9]

Shaman (IRE) *C Laffon-Parias* a98 115
3 ch c Shamardal(USA) Only Green (IRE) (Green Desert (USA))
(1243a) (1625a) 2668a[2] 3951[5] 6004a[2] 7007a[6] 7924a[3]

Shamarouski (IRE) *Louise Allan* a61 47
3 b g Bungle Inthejungle Masela (IRE) (Medicean)
(8666)

Shambolic (IRE) *John Gosden* 101
3 b f Shamardal(USA) Comic (IRE) (Be My Chief (USA))
2445[2] 3012[2] 4014[8] 5682[3] 6378[7]

Shambra (IRE) *Lucy Wadham* a55 66
5 b m Clodovil(IRE) Shambodia (IRE) (Petardia)
2400[3] 3708[5]

Shamdor *A De Royer-Dupre* a69 79
4 b g Kendargent(FR) Shamiyra (FR) (Medicean)
2956a[15] 7861a[4]

Shamitsar *Ray Craggs* a41 45
5 b g Shami Tsarina Louise (Red Ransom (USA))
2245[6] 2634[11] 4076[6] 4435[10] 6550[8]

Shamiyla (FR) *A De Royer-Dupre* 97
3 b f Kingman Shamakiya (IRE) (Intikhab (USA))
3137a[5]

Shamkha (IRE) *Richard Hannon* a53 64
3 b f Teofilo(IRE) Shivaree (Rahy (USA))
1346[6] 2103[5] 2689[10] 3310[6] 3594[11]

Shamlahar *Simon Crisford* a73 68
4 b m Shamardal(USA) Miss Lahar (Clodovil (IRE))
(206)

Shamlan (IRE) *Marjorie Fife* a63 55
7 br g Shamardal(USA) Atamana (IRE) (Lahib (USA))
64[4] 243[3] 467[2] 1177[5] 1328[3] 1986[11] 2215[11] 2681[10] 2972[13]

Shammah (IRE) *Richard Hannon* a67 81
2 b f Frankel Biscaya Bay (Dansili)
2767[3] 3461[8] (3942) 4387[6] 4893[6] 5703[3] 6158[2]◆ 9393[5]

Shamrad (FR) *Ian Williams* a44
3 b g Casamento(IRE) Shamsa (FR) (Selkirk (USA))
606[6] 1019[7] 9644[5]

Shamrock Emma (IRE) *Gary Moore* a24 5
4 ch m Mizzen Mast(USA) Lisselan Diva (IRE) (Barathea (IRE))
37[8]

Shams Brazilero (IRE) *Andrea Marcialis* a75 51
5 b h Shamardal(USA) Lumiere Du Soir (FR) (Anabaa (USA))
6434a[9]

Shamshon (IRE) *Stuart Williams* a93 89
8 b g Invincible Spirit(IRE) Greenisland (IRE) (Fasliyev (USA))
(36) 297[2] (470) 837[2] 1105[7] 1211[5] 1892[6] 2030[4] (2227) 3079[3] 3963[7] 4213[3] 4888[3] 5252[3] (5444)◆ 5504[10] 6534[7] 7175[4] (7524) 9088[13] 9301[9]

Shamsoun (FR) *G Guillermo* a39 26
5 b g Medicean Shamsa (FR) (Selkirk (USA))
7009a[7]

Shamtee (IRE) *X Thomas-Demeaulte* 106
4 b m Shamardal(USA) Truth Beauty (IRE) (Dubai Destination (USA))
1127a[6]

Shanaghai City (USA) *R Bouresly* a66 36
3 b c Shanghai Bobby(USA) Anysaturdayinmay (USA) (Any Given Saturday (USA))
511a[13]

Shanakill Star (IRE) *Dean Ivory* a23 29
5 b m Lord Shanakill(USA) Lola Rosa (IRE) (Peintre Celebre (USA))
309[10]

Shancelot (USA) *Jorge Navarro* a121
3 bb c Shanghai Bobby(USA) True Kiss (USA) (Is It True (USA))
8773a[2]

Shandon (IRE) *Lucinda Egerton*
4 b g Big Bad Bob(IRE) Rum Raisin (Invincible Spirit (IRE))
273[13]

Shandoz *Roger Varian* a80 84
2 b c Golden Horn Shabyt (Sadler's Wells (USA))
6163[3] 6905[4] (7473)

Shanghai Grace *Charles Hills* a85 85
3 b c Kyllachy Lavinia's Grace (USA) (Green Desert (USA))
20[2] 289[2]◆ 733[3] (978) (1178) (1360) 1685[5] 4099[4] 4497[3]

Shanghai Superfly (USA) *Marcos Zulueta* a49
3 b c Shanghai Bobby(USA) Wicked Wish (USA) (Gold Case (USA))
7480a[6]

Shanghaizhengchang *M Delzangles* a51 64
3 b f Mawatheeq(USA) Shanghai Noon (FR) (Turtle Bowl (IRE))
5165a[8]

Shani *John Bridger* a60 58
2 b f Heeraat(IRE) Limegrove (Captain Gerrard (IRE))
2561[8] 2915[8] (3634) 4373[4] 5045[6] 6563[7] 7296[6] 7556[8] 7754[3] 8243[5] 8409[4]

Shanty Star (USA) *R Bouresly* a65 90
3 gr c Hard Spun(USA) Little Nellie (USA) (Mizzen Mast (USA))
394a[10] 570a[2] 956a[4] 1110a[8]

Shaqwar *Kevin Ryan* 71
3 ch f Sea The Moon(GER) Majestic Roi (USA) (Street Cry (IRE))
2420[3]◆ 3974[3] 5554[2]

Sharamm (IRE) *N Bachalard* a45 68
4 b g Shamardal(USA) Oojooba (Monsun (GER))
197a[9]

Shared Belief (IRE) *Archie Watson* 95
2 b g Dandy Man(IRE) Hidden Belief (IRE) (Holy Roman Emperor (IRE))
(3804) 4920[5] 6251a[3] 6957[8] 7673a[4]

Shareef Star *Sir Michael Stoute* a91 92
4 b g Sea The Stars(IRE) Gotlandia (FR) (Anabaa (USA))
1461[7] (2374) 3168[2] 4021[9]

Share The Honour *A J Martin* a75 81
6 ch g Shamardal(USA) Hometime (Dubai Destination (USA))
7216a[9]

Shargiah (IRE) *Michael Appleby* a78 88
6 ch g New Approach(IRE) Zacheta (Polish Precedent (USA))
87[5] 4144[6] 4892[5] 5440[6]

Sharing (USA) *H Graham Motion* a88 110
2 ch f Speightstown(USA) Shared Account (USA) (Pleasantly Perfect (USA))
(8748a)

Sharja Bridge *Roger Varian* 115
5 b g Oasis Dream Quetena (GER) (Acatenango (GER))
(1414) 2085[2] 2829[10] 3948[9] 6956[6]

Sharja Silk *Roger Varian* a91 75
4 b g Dubawi(IRE) So Silk (Rainbow Quest (USA))
1943[2] 2613[4]

Shark (FR) *James Fanshawe* a62
3 b g Siyouni(FR) Sea Life (FR) (Anabaa (USA))
4334[6] 6315[7]

Sharney *Archie Watson* a48
2 b f Mastercraftsman(IRE) Champagne Ceri (Montjeu (IRE))
9634[12]

Sharoka (IRE) *Markus Klug* 94
3 b f Rock Of Gibraltar(IRE) Sharin (GER) (Areion (GER))
2137a[2] 3119a[5] 4683a[6]

Sharpalo (FR) *A bin Harmash* a102 106
7 b g Shamardal(USA) Pony Girl (IRE) (Darshaan)
47a[3] 398a[2] 730a[4] 1113a[5] 1441a[7]

Sharp Breath *Richard Fahey* 55
3 b f Bated Breath First Approval (Royal Applause)
2199[6] 2909[10]

Sharp Defence (USA) *Richard John O'Brien* a81 82
5 b g First Defence(USA) Jazz Drummer (USA) (Dixieland Band (USA))
2437[4]

Sharp Operator *Charlie Wallis* a58 62
6 ch g Medicean Helen Sharp (Pivotal)
39[3] 207[2] 288[6] (465) 595[6] 912[4] 1015[5] 1231[8] 1546[2] 2231[2] 3006[13] 3187[5] 3966[7] 4753[2] 5003[5] 5310[2] 5531[6] 6152[5] 6860[4] 7028[3] (7550) 8000[6]

Sharp Rock (GER) *Frau S Steinberg* 62
3 ch c Tertullian(USA) So Royal (GER) (Royal Solo (IRE))
2758a[5]

Sharp Suited *Brian Ellison* a73
4 b g Dansili Appearance (Galileo (IRE))
8814[3] 9368[2] (9469)◆

Sharp Talk (IRE) *Shaun Keightley* a67 37
3 b g Vocalised(USA) Invincible Wings (IRE) (Invincible Spirit (IRE))
4196[8] 4800[4] 5592[9] (6389) 6840[10] 7472[2]◆ 8025[12]

Sharqeyya (IRE) *Owen Burrows* a51 59
3 b f Oasis Dream Daymooma (Pivotal)
3603[6] 4180[8]

Sharqi (IRE) *Jean-Rene Auvray* a68 64
3 ch f Kitten's Joy(USA) Rosby Waves (USA) (Distorted Humor (USA))
3889[10] 4768[11] 5048[6]

Sharrabang *Stella Barclay* a59 58
3 b g Coach House(IRE) Dulally (Dubawi (IRE))
841[6] 1168[8] 1336[7] 1863[2] 2211[4] 2592[3] 2939[11] 3839[6] 4328[7] (4820) 5852[5] 6575[4] 7444[4] (8119)◆ 8502[6] 9548[11]

Shatharaat (IRE) *A Oliver* 91
4 b g Kodiac Party Whip (IRE) (Whipper (USA))
1308a[13]

Shattering (IRE) *Paul Cole* a52 66
3 b g Zoffany(IRE) Lexy May (USA) (Lear Fan (USA))
6836[8] 7373[9] 7730[4] 8761[6] 9138[P] (Dead)

Shaun's Delight (IRE) *Ronald Harris* a38 51
2 ch g Camacho Leopard Hunt (USA) (Diesis)
3088[6] 3695[8] 4373[9] 5010[4] 5958[7] 6837[6] 7110[4]

Shauyra (IRE) *William Haggas* a78 76
3 ch f Sea The Moon(GER) Donnelly's Hollow (IRE) (Dockside (USA))
6290[3]◆ (6941)◆ 8351[4]

Shawaaheq (IRE) *Ed Dunlop* a84 77
3 b g Tamayuz Jabhaat (USA) (Hard Spun (USA))
2900[2] (3565) 5270[2] (6282) 6913[6] 7653[6]

Shawaamekh *Declan Carroll* a72 94
5 b g Born To Sea(IRE) Frances Stuart (IRE) (King's Best (USA))
2151[2] 2509[2] (3813) (5692) 7222a[8] 8184[6]

Shawaf *F Head* a55 46
3 gr g Mukhadram Dijlah (Linamix (FR))
4204a[5]

Shawwaslucky *Derek Shaw* a19 23
3 ch f Coach House(IRE) Shaws Diamond (USA) (Ecton Park (USA))
2550[14] 2938[11] 4592[9] 6181[11] 6389[12] 6680[15]

Shazzab (IRE) *Richard Fahey* a65 65
4 b m Elzaam(AUS) Ceylon Round (FR) (Royal Applause)
1850[3] 2106[5] 2585[4] 3939[9] 4915[8] 5438[8]

Sh Boom *Peter Chapple-Hyam* a87 99
3 b f War Command(USA) Nouvelle Lune (Fantastic Light (USA))
2831[6] 3316[13] 6726[5] 7347[13] 7657[8] 9002[10]

Shearian *Declan Carroll* a73 55
9 b g Royal Applause Regal Asset (USA) (Regal Classic (CAN))
507[8] 830[9]

She Believes (IRE) *Sylvester Kirk* a81 81
4 ch m Arcano(IRE) African Moonlight (UAE) (Halling (USA))
2005[4] (2360) (2612) 3336[4] 3698[5]

Shebberghan (IRE) *Ed Dunlop* a80 80
4 bb g Sea The Stars(IRE) Shebella (IRE) (Dubai Destination (USA))
310[3]◆ 625[4] 1644[10] 7379[6] 8014[11] 8433[10]

She Can Boogie (IRE) *Tom Dascombe* a85 94
3 b f Dandy Man(IRE) Disko (IRE) (Kodiac)
2522[3] (2576) 3844[2] 4101[9] 4359[4] 6476[9] 6960[3] 8340[13]

She Can Dance *Kevin Ryan* a84 74
2 b f Acclamation Corazon Canarias (FR) (Caradak (IRE))
2840[5] 3810[6] 4889[3]◆ (6436) 7400[11]

Sheepscar Lad (IRE) *Nigel Tinkler* a50 75
5 b g Arcano(IRE) Piccadilly Filly (IRE) (Exceed And Excel (AUS))
1899[5] 2201[3] 2588[6] 3056[7] 3658[6] 3971[4] 4406[7] 5027[3] 6099[2] 6699[3] 7334[3] 7624[3] 7908[3] 8400[4]

Shehreen (IRE) *D K Weld* 98
2 b f Iffraaj Shareen (IRE) (Bahri (USA))
7742a[4] 8165a[4]

Sheila (IRE) *Hugo Palmer* a65
2 ch f Australia Donnelly's Hollow (IRE) (Dockside (USA))
9509[5]

Sheila's Empire (IRE) *Gavin Cromwell* a62 52
4 b m Holy Roman Emperor(IRE) Silk Mascara (IRE) (Barathea (IRE))
58[5] 160[11] 5043[2]

Sheila's Showcase *Denis Coakley* a77 79
3 b g Showcasing Loreto Rose (Lahib (USA))
1851[6] 2364[10] 3858[5] 4669[4] 5450[4] 7663[6] 8122[3]◆ 8806[8]

Sheila's Treat (IRE) *Ivan Furtado* a81 67
6 b g Frozen Power(IRE) Bonny Rose (Zaha (CAN))
276[3]

Shekhem (IRE) *D K Weld* 107
2 ch c Zoffany(IRE) Shelina (IRE) (Dalakhani (IRE))
7744a[2]

Shekiba (IRE) *Joseph G Murphy* a81 100
4 ch m Arcano(IRE) Catbells (IRE) (Rakti)
2451a[4] 3105a[7] 4353a[11] 7794a[12]

Shekky Shebaz (USA) *Jason Servis* 114
4 b g Cape Blanco(IRE) Rose Ransom (USA) (Red Ransom (USA))
8770a[3]

Sheldon Cooper (IRE) *David Dennis* a47 46
6 b g Excellent Art Lapis Lazuli (Rainbow Quest (USA))
695[6]

Shelir (IRE) *D K Weld* 101
3 gb g Dark Angel(IRE) Shelina (IRE) (Dalakhani (IRE))
(2492a) 3104a[11] 6192a[6] 7038a[7]

Shellebeau (IRE) *Alexandra Dunn* a62 61
3 b f War Command(USA) Attracted To You (IRE) (Hurricane Run (IRE))
2356[5] 4247[8] 4870[10] 8217[7] 8839[6] 9035[11]

She Looks Like Fun *K R Burke* a55 69
2 ch f Kyllachy My Propeller (IRE) (Holy Roman Emperor (IRE))
2820[3]◆ 3355[3] 4624[2] 5026[3] 7029[9] 7329[3] 8506[10]

Shelter (IRE) *A J McNamara* a58 50
3 b f Le Havre(IRE) Peut Etre (IRE) (Whipper (USA))
9646[9]

She Makes Me Smile (USA) *Trevor Gallimore* a41
3 ch f Include(USA) Verona Dale (USA) (Siphon (BRZ))
7479a[10]

Shenanigans (IRE) *Roger Varian* a102 103
5 b m Arcano(IRE) Ladylishandra (IRE) (Mujadil (USA))
1941[4] (2961) 3986[9] 4332[3] 7635a[12]

Shendail (FR) *Mlle Emmanuelle Barrier* a2 29
5 b g Elusive City(USA) Shendama (FR) (Dr Fong (USA))
7009a[6]

Shendam (FR) *M Delzangles* 99
3 b c Charm Spirit(IRE) Shemima (Dalakhani (IRE))
6249a[5] 7886a[7]

Shenouni (GER) *Jean-Pierre Carvalho* 84
2 b f Siyouni(FR) She Bang (FR) (Monsun (GER))
8371a[4]

Shepherd Market (IRE) *Clive Cox* a87 102
4 b m Reckless Abandon Shepherdia (IRE) (Pivotal)
1941[11] 2621[4] 3588[4] 4706a[10] 7657[11] 7893[4] 8367a[4]

Shepherd's Purse *Ruth Carr* a67 66
7 b g Pastoral Pursuits Neyraan (Lujain (USA))
1164[9] 1686[5] 2194[5] 2514[2] 3203[5] 3658[2]◆ 3975[10] (4059) 4625[4] 4911[4]◆ 5478[7] 5972[4] 6227[15] 6699[9] 7066[8]◆ 7576[5] 7959[3] (8296) 8501[3] 9013[5] 9108[7]

Shepherds Way (IRE) *Michael Dods* 69
2 gr f Dark Angel(IRE) Strait Power (IRE) (Rock Of Gibraltar (IRE))
2840[12] 4984[5] 5388[5] 5789[10] (7208) 7734[2]

Shepton Joa (FR) *N Paysan* a52 68
6 b m Kentucky Dynamite(USA) Sherakat (IRE) (Inchinor)
7536a[11] 8580a[5]

Shere Calm (FR) *G Doleuze* a97 71
6 gr g Peer Gynt(JPN) Blowaway (FR) (Linamix (FR))
(5715a)

Sherella *J R Jenkins* a50 46
3 b f Delegator Mediterranean Sea (IRE) (Medecis)
1825[11] 2238[10] 2943[10] 5552[11] 8255[4] 9410[3]

Sheriffmuir (USA) *John Gosden* a79 74
3 bb c War Front(USA) Lerici (USA) (Woodman (USA))
7841[2] 9213[2] 9416[2]

Sherpa Trail (USA) *Ed Walker* a65
3 rg g Gio Ponti(USA) Vapour Musing (Manduro (GER))
(9276)◆

Sherwood Forrester *Paul George* a3 58
3 b g Nayef(USA) Panoptic (Dubawi (IRE))
2354[8] 3946[4] 5577[8] 8248[10] 8870[11]

Sherzy Boy *Michael Easterby* a59 40
4 b g Champs Elysees Sherzam (Exceed And Excel (AUS))
2846[8] 4195[2]◆ 4293[5] 5024[10]

She's A Babe (IRE) *Aidan F Fogarty* a86 82
3 b f Kodiac Surf's Up (IRE) (Encosta De Lago (AUS))
8734a[6]

Shesadabber *Brian Baugh* a39 46
3 b f Heeraat(IRE) Saorocain (IRE) (Kheleyf (USA))
604[3] 908[4] 1567[8] 2357[4] 4481[9] 5083[9]

She's A Diamond *Mick Channon* 41
2 b f Captain Gerrard(IRE) Symboline (Royal Applause)
2138[6] 2331[8]

She's A Novelty (IRE) *Dai Williams* a39 68
4 b m Approve(IRE) Novel Fun (IRE) (Noverre (USA))
8862[3]◆

She's Apples (IRE) *Roger Charlton* a69 51
3 b f Redoute's Choice(AUS) Steal The Show (NZ) (High Chaparral (IRE))
1287[3] 1696[8] 3052[8]

She's A Stunner (IRE) *Matthieu Palussiere* a60
3 b f Morpheus Indian Navy (IRE) (Elusive City (USA))
216a[6]

She's A Unicorn *Tom Dascombe* a77 79
2 b f Garswood Shatter (IRE) (Mr Greeley (USA))
5895[7] 7031[6] 7623[2] (8259) (8509) 8856[2] 9044[2]

She's Awake *Michael Easterby* a50 50
3 b f Iffraaj Porthcawl (Singspiel (IRE))
2896[10] 3684[11]

She's Easyontheeye (IRE) *John Quinn* a53 61
2 b f Kodiac Bonnie Lesley (IRE) (Iffraaj)
1759[10] 2051[8] 5037[3]◆ 5514[8] 6272[8] 7208[8] 7440[4] 7853[3] 8527[5]

She's Gina (GER) *Seamus Mullins* 59
6 b m It's Gino(GER) Song Of Night (GER) (Tiger Hill (IRE))
4257[8]

She's Got You *John Gosden* a101 101
3 b f Kingman Without You Babe (USA) (Lemon Drop Kid (USA))
2340[3] (4119) (6951)◆ 7657[2] 8708[3]

She's On The Edge (IRE) *Anthony Carson* a53
2 b f Canford Cliffs(IRE) Tea Cup (Danehill Dancer (IRE))
8891[8]

She's Royal *Bryan Smart* a65 55
4 b m Delegator Sukuma (IRE) (Highest Honor (FR))
(2241)

She's Still Mine *Matthieu Palussiere* a74 67
3 b f Kodiac Night Lily (IRE) (Night Shift (USA))
5538a[4] 6061a[4]

Shesthedream (IRE) *Lisa Williamson* a41 59
6 b m Dream Ahead(USA) Tatiana Romanova (USA) (Mr Greeley (USA))
26[9] 118[6] 322[8] 503[10]

She Strides On *Mick Channon* 52
2 ch f Paco Boy(IRE) Pose (IRE) (Acclamation)
3942[7] 8758[10]

Sheung Wan *Richard Fahey* a37 52
2 b c Swiss Spirit Russian Dance (USA) (Nureyev (USA))
7179[6] 7627[10] 8069[8] 8526[7]

Shevchenko Park (IRE) *Tom Dascombe* 73
2 b g Epaulette(AUS) Compton Girl (Compton Place)
2561[7] 5331[4] 5848[9]

She'Zanarab *Iain Jardine* a59 53
3 ch f Orientor Rafta (IRE) (Atraf)
1486[6]◆ 1720[7] 1982[5] 2327[6] 2708[3]

Shielding (USA) *S Labate* 84
5 b g First Defence(USA) Kithira (Danehill (USA))
2226a[3]

Shifted Strategy (IRE) *J A Stack* a56 81
4 b g Choisir(AUS) Pure Greed (IRE) (Galileo (IRE))
5537a[14] 5597a[18]

Shifting Gold (IRE) *William Knight* a71 66
3 b f Fast Company(IRE) Elusive Gold (IRE) (Elusive City (USA))
1825[5] 2355[6] 3594[10] 4453[6] (5031) 5680[2] 6635[3] 7343[4] 7984[4] (9005) 9132[7]

Shifting Star (IRE) *John Bridger* a42 64
14 ch g Night Shift(USA) Ahshado (Bin Ajwaad (IRE))
132[8]

Shillelagh (NZ) *Chris Waller* 105
7 b m Savabeel(AUS) Trocair (AUS) (Flying Spur (AUS))
1783a[5]

Shimmering (IRE) *John Gosden* a71
2 b f Lope De Vega(IRE) Crysdal (Dalakhani (IRE))
8602[3] (9509)

Shimmering Dawn (IRE)
James Tate a96 86
3 b f Morpheus Subtle Shimmer (Danehill Dancer (IRE))
(1476) (2787) (4023)◆ 5325a[14] 7372[2] 7687[4]

Shine Baby Shine *Philip Kirby* a69 70
5 b m Aqlaam Rosewood Belle (USA) (Woodman (USA))
99[2] 1429[2]◆ 3175[2] 3886[7] 4404[4] 4983[4] 7001[9] 7631[5]◆ 8639[2] 8945[2] 9467[3]◆

Shine On Brendan (IRE) *Clive Cox* a77
2 b g Society Rock(IRE) Something Magic (Proud Citizen (USA))
8865[2] 9413[2]

Shine So Bright *Andrew Balding* 114
3 gr c Oasis Dream Alla Speranza (Sir Percy)
(1830) 2411[6] (6472) 7194[4] 8090[5]

Shinghari (IRE) *Alexandra Dunn* a29 83
7 br g Cape Cross(IRE) Sindiyma (IRE) (Kalanisi (IRE))
88[8] 390[9]

Shining *Jim Boyle* a76 79
3 b f Lethal Force(IRE) Spring Clean (FR) (Danehill (USA))
1492[3] (2730) 3422[5] 4375[3] 7789[10] 8601[2] 8895[9] 9131[10] 9245[9]

Shining Armor *John Ryan* a81 74
3 b g Morpheus Kenyan Cat (One Cool Cat (USA))
168a[5] 511a[12] 1295[10] 1388[7] 1692[4] 1920[9] 5617[7] 7049[8] 8181[10] 8495[11]

Shining Emerald *A Wohler* 99
8 b g Clodovil(IRE) Janayen (USA) (Zafonic (USA))
3369a[7] 6006a[12] 8982a[8]

Shining Pass (GER) *A Wohler* 95
3 b f Raven's Pass(USA) Serienhoehe (IRE) (High Chaparral (IRE))
3639a[6] 4683a[3] 5720a[8]

Shining Sea (IRE)
Sir Mark Prescott Bt a63
3 b f Sea The Stars(IRE) Shamwari Lodge (IRE) (Hawk Wing (USA))
4768[7] 5268[P]

Shining Valley (IRE) *Brett Johnson* a29
5 b g Clodovil(IRE) Shining Vale (USA) (Twilight Agenda (USA))
940[13]

Ship Of The Fen *Ian Williams* a73 93
4 b g Champs Elysees Ruffled (Harlan's Holiday (USA))
(3091) 3799[2] 4614[8] 4899[4] 5967[3]

Shir Khan *Paul Cole* a84 84
3 ch g Leroidesanimaux(BRZ) Sterling Sound (USA) (Street Cry (IRE))
1713[8] 2446[4] 2942[5] 4392[3]

Shiso (IRE) *R Rohne* a32 69
2 b f Sir Prancealot(IRE) Maria Montez (Piccolo)
4228a[2] 6060a[3] 7724a[10]

Shoal Of Time (FR) *A Fabre* 79
2 b c Lope De Vega(IRE) Hawaiian Heat (IRE) (Galileo (IRE))
7675a[9]

Shoot For Gold *Saeed bin Suroor* 85
3 b g Sea The Stars(IRE) Lamazonia (IRE) (Elusive City (USA))
5489[9]

Shoot The Moon (IRE)
William Jarvis a68 64
2 b g Lawman(FR) Luna Moon (Equiano (FR))
7346[7] 9385[5]

Shoot To Kill (IRE) *George Scott* a77 74
2 b g Dandy Man(IRE) Nancy Astor (Shamardal (USA))
4826[4] 5367[6] 7103[2] 8110[10] 8890[6]

Shoplifted (USA) *Steven Asmussen* a95
2 b c Into Mischief(USA) Shopit (USA) (Yes It's True (USA))
8749a[7]

Shore Step (IRE) *J P Murtagh* a80 77
9 br g Footstepsinthesand Chatham Islands (USA) (Elusive Quality (USA))
7085a[2]

Shortbackandsides (IRE)
Tim Easterby a57 72
4 b g Fast Company(IRE) Whatagoodcatch (IRE) (Bachelor Duke (USA))
2416[13] 2846[7] 3549[2] 4037[7] 5282[6] 6066[4] 6680[12] (7507)

Shorter Skirt *Eve Johnson Houghton* a74 83
3 ch f Showcasing Heading North (Teofilo (IRE))
(1475) 2567[6] 3427[6] (4560) 5143[8] 5773[3] 6346[5] 6916[7] 7206[5] 7789[6]

Shoshone Warrior (IRE)
A P O'Brien 75
2 b c Galileo(IRE) Runway Dancer (Dansili)
7897[5]

Shot In The Dark (FR) *C Boutin* a42 45
6 b g Dark Angel(IRE) Velvet Revolver (IRE) (Mujahid (USA))
4532a[10]

Shouranour (IRE) *Peter Niven* a40 55
9 b g Lawman(FR) Sharesha (IRE) (Ashkalani (IRE))
6582[6] 7385[5] 7960[10]

Shovel It On (IRE) *Steve Flook* a53 71
4 br g Elusive Pimpernel(USA) Fitrah (IRE) (Tamayuz)
116[5] 485[10] 912[8] 941[9] 1215[8] 1494[3] 1679[2] 2111[9] 2593[10] 3017[11] (4190) 4594[7] 5499[10] 5802[7] 6733[5] 7034[3] 7857[4] 8196[13]

Showboating (IRE) *John Balding* a85 74
11 b g Shamardal(USA) Sadinga (IRE) (Sadler's Wells (USA))
(5) 164[2] 1428[6] 2509[9] 3922[7] 5434[10] 5593[4] 6068[4] 6967[10] 7542[6]

Showdance Kid *Kevin Frost* a59 55
5 b g Showcasing Maid To Dance (Pyramus (USA))
840[7] 1177[10] 2215[4] 2741[7] 3430[11] 4460[5] 4749[4]

Showing *Michael Blanshard* a23
2 ch f Showcasing Blaugrana (IRE) (Exceed And Excel (AUS))
5733[12]

Show Kena (FR) *P Sogorb* 78
2 b f Kendargent(FR) Show Gorb (SPA) (Caradak (IRE))
3333a[6]

Show Me A Sunset *Richard Fahey* a55
3 b c Showcasing Sunrise Star (Shamardal (USA))
1924[7]

Show Me Heaven *Bill Turner* 68
2 b f Stimulation(IRE) Hot Pursuits (Pastoral Pursuits)
1733[8] 2469[4] 2996[8] (3798) 4282[6] 5010[6]

Show Me Show Me *Richard Fahey* 100
5 b g Showcasing Springing Baroness (Bertolini (USA))
(1416) 2520[5] 3055[2] 5185[2] 5542[3] 6375[17] 7400[10]

Show Me The Bubbly *John O'Shea* a79 74
3 b f Showcasing Folly Bridge (Avonbridge)
1139[2]◆ 1475[5] (2474) 3045[4] 4368[6] 4783[2] 5375[3] 7855[3] 8117[2]◆ 8470[10] 8895[8]

Showmethedough *Richard Fahey* a66 81
4 ch g Showcasing Silver Purse (Interrex (CAN))
45[6]

Showmethemoon *J-C Rouget*
3 b f Le Havre(IRE) Pacific Queen (FR) (Sunday Break (JPN))
6486a[4]

Showmolina *David Lanigan* a61
2 b c Showcasing Crossmolina (IRE) (Halling (USA))
9451[5]

Show Must Go On (FR)
Aidan F Fogarty 49
3 b g Reply(IRE) Luna Negra (GER) (Big Shuffle (USA))
2880a[9]

Show Palace *Jennie Candlish* a76 82
6 ch g Showcasing Palais Polaire (Polar Falcon (USA))
1860[4] 2508[9] 2709[3]◆ 3206[10] 3509[7] (4307) 5180[8] (5595) 6178[3] 6921[9] 8183[2] 8660[4] 8860[4]

Showroom (FR) *Mark Johnston* a32 91
4 b g Motivator Lemon Twist (IRE) (Marju (IRE))
1559[4] 1927[14] 2563[8] 4997[8]

Showshutai *Christopher Kellett* a44 38
3 b g Showcasing Sleeper (Rail Link)
405[12] 913[7] 1430[7] 2190[11] 2582[10] 3219[5]

Show Stealer *Rae Guest* a102 99
6 ch m Showcasing Winifred Jo (Bahamian Bounty)
2917[4] 4451[4] 4805[5] (5504) (5989) 6404[3] 6908[5] 7193[3] 7431[4]◆ (8851) 9004[11]

Show The Money *Ivan Furtado* a41 63
4 ch g Showcasing Rio Belle (IRE) (Captain Rio)
759[11] 2740[4] 4131[2] 6731[8]

Show The Way (IRE) *F Foresi* 72
5 b g Whipper(USA) Calasetta (IRE) (Montjeu (IRE))
5035a[8] 6521a[14]

Show The World *Lucinda Egerton* a40 46
3 ch g Showcasing Moving Sea (IRE) (Rock Of Gibraltar (IRE))
1034[9] 2908[9] 5098[5] 5238[11]

Showu *Tony Carroll* a64 69
3 b f Showcasing Travelling (Dubai Destination (USA))
83[5] 3189[7]

Shoyd *Richard Hannon* a40 41
4 ch m Showcasing Yding (IRE) (Danehill (USA))
6116[10] 7273[7] 7843[9] 8255[12]

Shraaoh (IRE) *Chris Waller* a97 102
6 b g Sea The Stars(IRE) Jumooh (Monsun (GER))
(1784a) 8577a[6]

Shrewd *Iain Jardine* a64 80
9 b g Street Sense(USA) Cala (FR) (Desert Prince (IRE))
2435[8] 3450[10] 4057[5] 5240[8] 5849[7] 6658[11] 7368[13] 8236[8]

Shrewdness *William Haggas* a85 77
3 br f Lawman(FR) Shama (IRE) (Danehill Dancer (IRE))
2361[2] 3637[3] 4234[2] (6186) 6709[3] 7895[9]

Shufoog *Mark Usher* a69 73
6 b m Mawatheeq(USA) Hamloola (Red Ransom (USA))
1183[3] 4561[11] 5344[2] 7343[6]

Shug *Ed Walker* a63 47
3 b g Slade Power(IRE) Midnight Fantasy (Oasis Dream)
130[5] 367[5] 855[2]◆ 1174[4] 1358[6] 1982[12] 2926[8] 3697[11]

Shumba (USA) *David Simcock* a67
2 ch c Kitten's Joy(USA) Jalal (USA) (Johar (USA))
9136[7] 9325[2]

Shumookhi (IRE) *Archie Watson* a65 87
3 ch f Society Rock(IRE) Three Knots (IRE) (Chineur (FR))
1200a[9] 1913[5] 2605a[13]

Shuraffa (IRE) *Charles Hills* 74
2 b f Shamardal(USA) Shamtari (IRE) (Alhaarth (IRE))
6906[4]◆

Shut Down (FR) *Mario Hofer* a69 73
2 b c Siyouni(FR) Drifting (IRE) (Sadler's Wells (USA))
6776a[4] 7925a[8]

Shutterbug (FR) *W Mongil* a83 76
7 ch h Soldier Of Fortune(IRE) Nazlia (FR) (Polish Precedent (USA))
4860a[4]

Shyarch *Christine Dunnett* a56 54
5 b g Archipenko(USA) Coconut Shy (Bahamian Bounty)
159[10] 553[4]◆ 887[5] 1032[4] 4589[5]

Shymay *George Margarson* a60 54
2 b f Mayson Coconut Shy (Bahamian Bounty)
8431[6] 9211[6]◆ 9641[3]

Shyron *Lee Carter* a72 59
8 b g Byron Coconut Shy (Bahamian Bounty)
(294)◆ 557[5] 764[4] 1040[3] 1269[7] 2006[4] 6925[3]

Sibelius (GER) *Markus Klug* 101
3 b c Pastorius(GER) Shiramiyna (IRE) (Invincible Spirit (IRE))
2163a[4] 2889a[8] 3674a[5] 4707a[11] 6487a[7]

Siberian Night (IRE) *Ed Walker* a69 53
2 b g Siyouni(FR) Sweet Dream (Oasis Dream)
6891[9] 8011[7] 8709[5] 9212[2] (9328)◆

Siberius (ITY) *Cristiano Davide Fais* 92
3 b c Moohaajim(IRE) Rosa Del Ponte (Authorized (IRE))
7502a[5]

Sible Hedingham *James Eustace* a55 55
3 ch f Rip Van Winkle(IRE) Emily Blake (IRE) (Lend A Hand)
4760[4] 6345[6] 6903[5] 8644[5]

Sibylline *David Simcock* a56 56
3 ch f Leroidesanimaux(BRZ) Selenography (Selkirk (USA))
2102[9] 3013[8] 3690[5] 4476[7] 5287[4] 6595[3] 7450[3] 8292[4] (9412)

Sicilia *C Laffon-Parias* a99 98
3 b f Kingman Palitana (USA) (Giant's Causeway (USA))
1199a[2] 1795a[8] 2564a[7]

Sicilian Focus (IRE)
Sebastiano Guerrieri a64 91
2 b g Anjaal Magical Bupers (IRE) (Intikhab (USA))
8791a[6]

Sicomoro (ITY) *Nicolo Simondi* 102
2 ch c Sakhee's Secret Saluggia (IRE) (Galileo (IRE))
4172a[2] 8390a[4]

Side Effect *Michael Appleby* a77 67
4 br m Harbour Watch(IRE) Fame Is The Spur (Motivator)
(392) 475[4]

Siege Of Boston (IRE) *John Butler* a71 58
6 ch g Starspangledbanner(AUS) Milton Of Campsie (Medicean)
5283[5]

Siege Of Quebec (AUS)
Gai Waterhouse & Adrian Bott 112
4 b h Fastnet Rock(AUS) Rose Of Cimmaron (AUS) (Bite The Bullet (USA))
1974a[3]

Siempre Rapido *Stuart Kittow*
2 b c Outstrip Cape Mystery (Cape Cross (IRE))
8517[12]

Siena Bay *Tim Easterby* a18 18
2 b f Cable Bay(IRE) Siena Gold (Key Of Luck (USA))
1923[9] 2051[7]

Siena Mia *Philip Kirby* a61 50
4 b m Bated Breath Serenata Mia (Mark Of Esteem (IRE))
5969[5] 7032[2] 8529[4] 8818[8] 9113[4] 9396[8]

Sienna Dream *Alistair Whillans* a59 57
4 b m Swiss Spirit Angry Bark (USA) (Woodman (USA))
5486[9] 5938[3] (7779)

Siglo Six *Hugo Palmer* a86 92
3 ch g Havana Gold(IRE) Yensi (Doyen (IRE))
1723[7] 3972[2] 4520[2] (5336) 6166[5] (6729) 7163[3] 8222[7] 9041[12]

Signalman (USA) *Kenneth McPeek* a110
3 b c General Quarters(USA) Trip South (USA) (Trippi (USA))
2856a[9]

Signal Twenty Nine *William Knight* a42
2 gr g Gregorian(IRE) Beacon Lady (Haafhd)
9415[12]

Significant Form (USA)
Chad C Brown 106
4 rg m Creative Cause(USA) Church By The Sea (USA) (Harlan's Holiday (USA))
(6491a)

Signora Cabello (IRE) *John Quinn* 97
3 b f Camacho Journalist (IRE) (Night Shift (USA))
2270[4] 3085[7] 3950[9] 7401[14]

Signore Piccolo *David Loughnane* a57 81
8 b g Piccolo Piccolo Cativo (Komaite (USA))
2079[3] 2893[11] 3309[8] 3509[4]

Sign O'The Time (FR) *J Parize* a41 73
3 b f Wootton Bassett Slap Shade (IRE) (Invincible Spirit (IRE))
3066a[13]

Signsealdelivered *Clifford Lines* a23
5 b g Mawatheeq(USA) Confluence (Milk It Mick)
242[11]

Signs Of Success (IRE)
Mme J Hendriks a46 44
6 b g Elusive City(USA) Quartz (FR) (Muhtathir)
6434a[11]

Sigrid Nansen *Alexandra Dunn* a59 69
4 b m Cityscape Hail Shower (IRE) (Red Clubs (IRE))
789[9] 1146[3] 1520[3] 2283[2] 3252[5] 3571[4] (4216) (4498) (4868)◆ 5138[2] 5571[3] 5762a[7]

Sigurd (GER) *Joanne Foster* a19 54
7 ch g Sholokhov(IRE) Sky News (GER) (Highest Honor (FR))
99[8] 7053[14]

Sikandarabad (IRE)
David A & B Hayes & Tom Dabern 107
6 b g Dr Fong(USA) Sindiyma (IRE) (Kalanisi (IRE))
8138a[4] 8578a[6] 8768a[10]

Silca Mistress *Clive Cox* a87 83
4 ch m Dutch Art Strictly Silca (Danehill Dancer (IRE))
2097[6] 2809[6] 5105[4] 6465[5] 6835[4] 7519[8] 8866[5]

Silencious (FR) *M Boutin* a58 65
2 b f Dabirsim(FR) Bruyante (USA) (Awesome Again (CAN))
4949a[2] (6196a) 6584a[4]

Silent Agenda *Archie Watson* a70 48
2 b f Kyllachy Kerry's Dream (Tobougg (IRE))
3461[4] 3962[5] 4790[11]

Silent Attack *Tony Carroll* a103 100
6 b g Dream Ahead(USA) Chanterelle (FR) (Trempolino (USA))
173a[3] 514a[10] 726a[7] 961a[7] 8062[6] 8707[13] 9198[2] 9440[3]

Silent Bullet (IRE) *R Bouresly* a29 48
8 b g Exceed And Excel(AUS) Veil Of Silence (IRE) (Elusive Quality (USA))
196a[16]

Silent Echo *Peter Hedger* a101 107
5 b g Oasis Dream Quiet (Observatory (USA))
8707[9] 9129[3]◆ 9301[3]◆

Silent Night (SWE) *Patrick Wahl* a53 82
2 b f Night Of Thunder(IRE) Raihaana (USA) (Dynaformer (USA))
7495a[2]

Silent Poet (CAN)
Nicholas Gonzalez 110
4 bb g Silent Name(JPN) Cara Bella (USA) (Ghostzapper (USA))
7225a[9]

Silent Wave *Charlie Appleby* 84
2 b f War Front(USA) Secret Gesture (Galileo (IRE))
(3076) 4048[8]

Silk Forest (IRE) *P Twomey* 104
3 b f Kodiac Rosa Parks (Sadler's Wells (USA))
(8367a)

Silk Island (IRE) *Michael Wigham* a45 41
3 b f Tagula(IRE) Silk Affair (IRE) (Barathea (IRE))
802[8] 1270[6]

Silk Mill Blue *Richard Whitaker* a52 56
5 b g Piccolo Marysienka (Primo Dominie)
2012[9] 3215[5] 4518[5] 4728[12] 5555[2] 7578[11] 8301[5] 8530[6] 8666[2] 9111[7] 9282[8]

Silkstone (IRE) *Pam Sly* 83
3 b g Alhebayeb(IRE) Fine Silk (USA) (Rahy (USA))
1697[4] 2582[7] 3195[2] (3885) 4392[4] 5104[2] 5984[4] 6729[6]

Sils Maria *Ann Duffield* a53 38
3 gr f Swiss Spirit Snow Cover (Verglas (IRE))
128[4] 6701[6] 7578[14]

Silva (IRE) *Mme Pia Brandt* a100 110
3 b f Kodiac Sotka (Dutch Art)
(510a) 845a[8] 2669a[10] 6142a[4] (7477a)

Silver Amerhican (FR)
Matthieu Palussiere a42 73
3 b c American Post Silver Diane (FR) (Silver Rainbow)
8449a[6]

Silverbook *Charlie Appleby* a47
4 b g New Approach(IRE) Sahraah (USA) (Kingmambo (USA))
9368[5]

Silver Character (IRE)
Donald McCain a36 17
4 gr g Camelot Convocate (USA) (Exchange Rate (USA))
6556[5]

Silver Cristal (USA) *F-H Graffard* a59 74
2 gr f The Factor(USA) Sayedah (IRE) (Darshaan)
6774a[6]

Silver Dust (IRE) *Richard Fahey* a73 68
3 gr g Clodovil(IRE) Silesian (IRE) (Singspiel (IRE))
1504[7] 7364[9] 8719[4]◆ 9559[8]

Silver Falcon (IRE)
Cathrine Erichsen 70
5 gr g Mastercraftsman(IRE) Dacca (Deploy)
4419a[11]

Silverkode (IRE) *Joseph G Murphy* 98
5 b g Kodiac Silver Tide (USA) (Silver Hawk (USA))
7222a[14]

Silver Line (IRE) *Saeed bin Suroor* 107
5 gr g Dark Angel(IRE) Admire The View (IRE) (Dubawi (IRE))
(5150) 6376[5]◆ 7340[3] 7891[12]

Silver Machine *Archie Watson* a80
2 gr f Brazen Beau(AUS) Blue Crest (FR) (Verglas (IRE))
(8891)

Silver Mission (IRE) *Richard Fahey* a65 76
2 gr g Dark Angel(IRE) Miss Indigo (Indian Ridge (IRE))
2892[5] (4032) 5550[3] 6728[4] 8318[7]

Silver Quartz *Archie Watson* a85 96
4 gr g Frankel Rosamixa (FR) (Linamix (FR))
601[3] 1101[11] 1415[11] 1922[11]

Silverrica (IRE) *Malcolm Saunders* 66
9 gr m Ad Valorem(USA) Allegorica (IRE) (Alzao (USA))
2358[7] 4230[11] 4374[5] 5013[5] 5375[6] 5607[7] 7112[10]

Silver Samurai *Marco Botti* a78 77
2 gr c Cable Bay(IRE) High Tan (High Chaparral (IRE))
6684[3] 7104[2] (8280) 8850[4]

Silver Service (IRE)
Michael Mulvany 87
3 gr f Tough As Nails(IRE) Love Is The Key (IRE) (Azamour (IRE))
4353a[8]

Silver Spear (IRE) *Andrew Slattery* 84
2 gr f Clodovil(IRE) Sophie Germain (IRE) (Indian Ridge (IRE))
8164a[3]

Silver Start *Charles Hills* a71 74
2 gr f Cable Bay(IRE) Silver Rainbow (IRE) (Starspangledbanner (AUS))
(2275)◆ 2805[10] 3573[3] 7896[25] 8506[8] 9205[4] 9499[9]

Silverstrand (IRE) *H-F Devin* a73 41
3 gr g Mastercraftsman(IRE) Sunday Nectar (IRE) (Footstepsinthesand)
7291a[10]

Silvertown (IRE) *A Oliver* 60
2 b c Make Believe Levanto (IRE) (Lawman (FR))
7744a[5]

Silverturnstogold *Tony Carroll* a72 65
4 ch g Equiano(FR) Saharan Song (IRE) (Singspiel (IRE))
125[7] 1176[5] 1355[2] 3533[5] 6305[2] 7024[3]◆ 7982[3] 8847[3] (9035) (9180) (9224)

Silverwave (FR) *F Vermeulen* a77 112
7 b h Silver Frost(IRE) Miss Bio (FR) (River Mist (USA))
3389a[3] 7251a[4] 8378a[3] 8980a[11]

Silvery Mist (FR) *F Chappet* a98 101
4 gr m Stormy River(FR) Misty Heights (Fasliyev (USA))
1918[3] 2670a[7] 4706a[2]

Silvington *Mark Loughnane* a41 51
4 b g Firebreak Millinsky (USA) (Stravinsky (USA))
185[6] 535[5] 3774[8] 4873[10] 5302[10] 6327[12] (6844) 7527[12] 8299[9]

Simba Samba *Philip McBride* a58 60
3 b g Leroidesanimaux(BRZ) Rouge Dancer (Elusive City (USA))
606[5] (1084)◆ 1141[2]◆ 1721[9] 3775[3] 3989[13] 5064[2] (6126) 6321[6]

Simbirsk *John O'Shea* a48 75
4 ch g Al Kazeem Oulianovsk (IRE) (Peintre Celebre (USA))
1653[2] (2471) 2732[7] 3700[8] 5086[2] 5850[3] 7233[7] 8422[12]

Similaire (FR) *Gianluca Bietolini* a82 76
3 b c Linda's Lad Similitudine (FR) (Brief Truce (USA))
6874a[2]

Simona (FR) *F-H Graffard* a91 96
3 b f Siyouni(FR) Monava (FR) (El Prado (IRE))
(2954a) 8983a[7] 9603a[8]

Simon's Smile (FR) *Mme G Rarick* a38 39
3 b g Anodin(IRE) Nebraska I (FR) (Octagonal (NZ))
1972[6] 2336[2]◆ 2677[5] 3513[9] 4005[7] 6874a[6]

Simoon (IRE) *Andrew Balding* a85 91
5 b g Sixties Icon Astragal (Shamardal (USA))
(1479) (2691) 3072[5] 3992[6] 4837[4] 6730[2] (7567)

Simple Thought (IRE)
Simon Crisford a79 79
4 b m Teofilo(IRE) Punita (USA) (Distorted Humor (USA))
239[2] 474[4]

Simplicity (FR) *F Chappet* a78 96
3 b f Casamento(IRE) Sleek Gold (Dansili)
(1512a) 2498a[4] 3677a[4] 4621a[8] 5227a[3] 7360a[8]

Simply Beautiful (IRE) *A P O'Brien* a95 105
3 gr f Galileo(IRE) Simply Perfect (Danehill (USA))
4856a[5] 5075a[3] 5364a[2] 6239a[2] 6692a[5] 7658[2] 8094[3] 8368a[8] 9002[5]

Simply Brilliant *F C Lor* 113
5 ch g Frankel Red Bloom (Selkirk (USA))
9379a[10]

Simply Silca (IRE) *Richard Hughes* a68 54
2 b f Showcasing Just Silca (Teofilo (IRE))
5729[3] 6719[2] 8395[6]

Simply Sin (IRE) *Neil Mulholland* a52 36
4 b g Footstepsinthesand Miss Sally (IRE) (Danetime (IRE))
3946[10] 8018[5]

Simply Striking (FR)
M Delcher Sanchez a94 103
3 ch c Kheleyf(USA) Reech Band (Choisir (AUS))
2668a[10]

Simply Susan (IRE)
Eve Johnson Houghton a58 57
2 ch f Canford Cliffs(IRE) Garraun (IRE) (Tamayuz)
5011[2] 5602[2] 7269[4] 7833[9] 8452[4]

Simply True (IRE) *A Oliver* 76
2 ch c Camacho Faussement Simple (IRE) (Beat Hollow)
7247a[21]

Simul Amicis *Dianne Sayer* a40 36
3 b f Hurricane Run(IRE) Xaphania (Sakhee (USA))
405[11] 785[11] 4818[3] 6583[5]

Sinawann (IRE) *M Halford* 107
2 b c Kingman Simawa (IRE) (Anabaa (USA))
7217a[2]

Sincerely Resdev *Philip Kirby* a54 55
4 br g Rock Of Gibraltar(IRE) Sincerely (Singspiel (IRE))
7390[8] 8639[4]

Sincerity *James Fanshawe* 75
3 b f Iffraaj Affinity (Sadler's Wells (USA))
2249[5] 3248[3] 3958[4] (6039) 7238[4]

Sinfonietta (FR) *Sophie Leech* a40 49
7 b g Sinndar(IRE) Final Whistle (IRE) (Rossini (USA))
5283[11] 6050[10] 6734[10] 7811[10]

Sing Bertie (IRE) *Derek Shaw* a47 22
3 b g Zebedee Emirates Challenge (IRE) (Cape Cross (IRE))
215[8] 412[7] 906[2]◆ 1380[3] 2211[3]◆ 2592[4] 5765[12] 6183[6] 7628[10] 9411[4]

Singe Anglais (IRE) *Nigel Tinkler* 71
2 ch g Footstepsinthesand Callanish (Inchinor)
3866[9] 4516[5] (5017)◆ (5789)◆ 6653[8] (7064) 8095[5]

Singe Du Nord *Nigel Tinkler* a55 45
3 b f Mayson Siena Gold (Key Of Luck (USA))
79[11] 931[7] 1549[4]

Singer In The Sand (IRE)
Pat Phelan a41
4 b m Footstepsinthesand Village Singer (USA) (Rahy (USA))
141[10] 736[12] 2283[9]

Singing Sheriff *Ed Walker* a86 73
4 b g Lawman(FR) La Felicita (Shareef Dancer (USA))
54[11] 362[3]◆ 793[2] (1095) 1508[2] 2092[10] 3022[4] 3567[14] 8014[2] 9274[3]

Singing The Blues (IRE)
Rod Millman a75 79
4 b g Sir Prancealot(IRE) Atishoo (IRE) (Revoque (IRE))
257[3] 363[6] (789) (923) (1235)◆ 1497[2] 2059[2] (2279) 2626[2]◆ 3700[2] 4231[3] 4929[2] 5571[8] 6200[2] 6848[4] 7231[3] 7830[8]

Singing Tower (FR) *N Clement* a78 78
3 ch f Siyouni(FR) La Tour Rouge (Monsun (GER))
1199a[9] 3526a[6]

Single (IRE) *Mick Channon* a66 63
2 ch f Nathaniel(IRE) Solita (USA) (Thunder Gulch (USA))
6118[5]◆ 6504[3]◆ 7515[3] 7778[5]

Single Handed (AUS) *Nick Smart* 95
4 br g Ambidexter(AUS) Miss Eclipse (AUS) (El Moxie (USA))
8803a[12]

Sing Out Loud (IRE)
Michael Madgwick a70 73
4 b g Vocalised(USA) Tus Maith (IRE) (Entrepreneur)
3806[10] 4506[8] 6289[8] 7125[5] 9173[7]

Sing Something *Mrs C Gilbert* a55 55
6 gr h Paco Boy(IRE) Rock Ace (IRE) (Verglas (IRE))
3173a[5] 3641a[4] 4174a[3] 4685a[4] 6553a[2]

Singstreet (FR)
Mme M Bollack-Badel a78 104
3 b g Evasive Sinnderelle (FR) (Sinndar (IRE))
(1198a)

Sinjaari (IRE) *William Haggas* 102
3 b g Camelot Heavenly Song (IRE) (Oratorio (IRE))
1643[2]◆ (2208) 2828[2] 4017[8] 5583[3] 6895[2] 8092[13]

Sinndarella (IRE) *Sarah Hollinshead* a52 52
3 b f Fast Company(IRE) Alafzara (IRE) (Nayef (USA))
2150[6] 3528[2] 4484[3] 5798[2] 6531[4] 7818[5] 8293[3] 8828[3] 9275[5]

Sin Sin (IRE) *Nigel Hawke* a40 41
5 b m Intense Focus(USA) Saor Sinn (IRE) (Galileo (IRE))
9231[3] 2359[9]

Sin To Win (NZ)
David A & B Hayes & Tom Dabern 97
6 b g Sir Percy Ledahead (NZ) (Jugalug (NZ))
8803a[9]

Sionnach Rua *Jimmy Fox*
4 ch m Foxwedge(AUS) My Jeanie (IRE) (King Charlemagne (USA))
359[13]

Sioux Frontier (IRE) *Iain Jardine* a58 77
4 b g Excelebration(IRE) Sioux Rising (IRE) (Danetime (IRE))
886[9] (1500) (2436) 3073[4] 3250[3] 3925[3] 4208[4] 4913[7] 7368[10]

Si Que Es Buena (ARG)
H Graham Motion 99
5 b m Equal Stripes(ARG) Epoca Buena (ARG) (Mutakddim (USA))
8154a[6]

Sir Arthur Dayne (IRE)
Mick Channon 83
2 b c Sir Prancealot(IRE) Shoshoni Wind (Sleeping Indian)
4184[9] 4480[7] 4832[3] (5313) 5576[2] 5962[4] 6375[8] 6728[5] 7429[3] (7971) 8397[5]

Sir Bibi (FR)
Lennart Hammer-Hansen a79 79
7 b g Touch Down(GER) Elli (Polar Falcon (USA))
2675a[10]

Sir Boris (IRE) *Tom Dascombe* 108
2 b c Due Diligence(USA) Queens Park (FR) (King's Best (USA))
5082[3] (5591)◆ (5780) 6542[4] (7532a) 8140a[3]

Sir Busker (IRE) *William Knight* a98 93
3 b g Sir Prancealot(IRE) Street Kitty (IRE) (Tiger Hill (IRE))
2364[5] 2567[4] (3638) 4546[2] 5090[5] 5953[2]◆ 6711[4] (7517) 8222[6]

Sir Canford (IRE) *Ali Stronge* a58 63
3 b g Canford Cliffs(IRE) Alexander Divine (Halling (USA))
761[8] 1034[7] 1562[7] (3348) 5679[3] 6279[5] 8828[8] 9168[7]

Sir Chancealot (IRE)
Amanda Perrett 26
2 b g Sir Prancealot(IRE) Hypocrisy (Bertolini (USA))
2767[11] 3257[10] 3694[9] 5313[9] 5907[7]

Sir Charles Punch *James Given* a66 81
2 b g Sir Percy Russian Punch (Archipenko (USA))
6065[5] 6664[5] 7151[3] 7539[3] 8505[6]

Sir Charles Road (AUS)
Lance O'Sullivan & Andrew Scot 103
5 b g Myboycharlie(IRE) Giant Mystique (AUS) (Giant's Causeway (USA))
8767a[4]

Sir Chauvelin *Jim Goldie* a106 104
7 b g Authorized(IRE) Jabbara (IRE) (Kingmambo (USA))
1460[6] 1947[7] 2742[18] 9094[3] 9468[4]

Sir Dancealot (IRE) *David Elsworth* a97 119
5 b g Sir Prancealot(IRE) Majesty's Dancer (IRE) (Danehill Dancer (IRE))
2829[7] 3814[4] (5521) 6215[4] 6472[5]◆ (7194) 7944a[10]

Sir Dandy *Lucy Wadham* a20
2 b g Sir Percy Cartoon (Danehill Dancer (IRE))
8823[14] 9208[12]

Sir Dotti (IRE) *John C McConnell* 61
2 b c Dandy Man(IRE) Midas Haze (Pivotal)
7247a[13]

Sir Dragonet (IRE) *A P O'Brien* 117
3 b c Camelot Sparrow (IRE) (Oasis Dream)
(2523)◆ 3345[5] 6192a[4] 7196[4]

Sir Dylan *Polly Gundry* a43 36
10 b g Dylan Thomas(IRE) Monteleone (IRE) (Montjeu (IRE))
1146[4]

Siren's Fury (AUS) *Jason Coyle* 102
5 bb m Myboycharlie(IRE) De Chorus (AUS) (Unbridled's Song (USA))
1974a[10]

Sir Fred (IRE) *Julia Feilden* a54 50
4 gr g Born To Sea(IRE) Diamond Line (FR) (Linamix (FR))
2974[7] 3740[5] 5029[5] 5528[8] 6853[6] 7558[6]

Sir Geoffrey (IRE) *Scott Dixon* a40 44
13 b g Captain Rio Disarm (IRE) (Bahamian Bounty)
586[11] 702[7]

Sir George (FR) *E Libaud* a79 78
3 b c George Vancouver(USA) Yours Ever (Dansili)
1243a[8]

Sir George Somers (USA)
Nigel Twiston-Davies a60 76
6 ch g Cape Blanco(IRE) Sense Of Class (USA) (Fusaichi Pegasus (USA))
292[10] 473[9] 911[9] 1175[6] 1841[9]

Sir Gnet (IRE) *Ed Dunlop* a66 52
5 b g Galileo(IRE) Ecoutila (USA) (Rahy (USA))
386[4] 1183[5] (1362) 1591[5] 1983[4] 2696[5] 5528[7] 7109[4] 7956[7] 8703[7] 8916[9] 9207[3] 9479[9]

Sir Gordon *Ralph J Smith* a45 64
2 br g Sixties Icon Potternello (IRE) (Captain Marvelous (IRE))
1556[6] 3634[2] 3812[10] 4652[3] 8650[11] 8890[11]

Sir Hamilton (IRE) *Alan Bailey* a52 71
4 b g Canford Cliffs(IRE) Cawett (IRE) (Danehill Dancer (IRE))
1213[11] 2516[8] 8206[2] 8413[4] 9176[12] 9496[12]

Sir Havelock (IRE) *Richard Fahey* a59 57
2 br g Hallowed Crown(AUS) Gemma's Pearl (IRE) (Marju (IRE))
3919[4] 4486[6] 4826[13] 6097[3]◆ 6625[5]◆ 7582[2] 8259[9]

Sir Hector (IRE) *Charlie Wallis* a60 43
4 ch g Sir Prancealot(IRE) Awwal Malika (USA) (Kingmambo (USA))
1342[6] 2025[7] 2206[13] 4026[2] 5889[P] 6631[8] 7447[2] 7837[5] 8839[9] (9272)◆ 9406[2] 9572[2]

Sirinapha (IRE) *Richard Hannon* a57 62
3 b g Alhebayeb(IRE) Sassari (IRE) (Darshaan)
3440[11]

Sirius Slew *Alan Bailey* a66 74
3 b g Epaulette(AUS) Slewtoo (Three Valleys (USA))
2024[2]◆ 2976[5] 3420[3] 4655[7] 5622[6] 6204[10] (6569) 7189[11] 8702[6]

Sirjack Thomas (IRE)
Adrian McGuinness a89 94
4 gr g Fast Company(IRE) Veliyka (IRE) (Linamix (FR))
5597a[11] 6693a[9] 7241a[13]

Sir Jamie *Tony Carroll* a55 57
6 ch g Monsieur Bond(IRE) First Dawn (Dr Fong (USA))
80[9] 399[7] 595[11] 1354[2] 1683[7] 2631[12] (2972) 4349[2] 5136[4]

Sir Lancelott *Adrian Nicholls* a49 44
7 b g Piccolo Selkirk Rose (IRE) (Pips Pride)
180[4] 379[4] 479[5] 533[3] 1015[10] 1060[6] 1353[6]

Sir Magnum *Tony Carroll* a50 56
4 ch g Sakhee(USA) Queen Of Heaven (USA) (Mr Greeley (USA))
3966[13] 4453[2] 5633[7] 6327[11] 8251[4] 8694[10] 9282[2]◆ 9552[9]

Sir Maximilian (IRE) *Ian Williams* a96 101
10 b g Royal Applause Nebraska Lady (IRE) (Lujain (USA))
(2396) 4095[17] 4402[6] 5664[20] 6404[5] (7142)

Sir Oliver (IRE) *Richard Hughes* a72 65
2 b g Dark Angel(IRE) Folga (Atraf)
2792[6] 5186[8] 7030[3]◆ 8465[9] 8890[3]

Sir Ottoman (FR) *Ivan Furtado* a62 71
6 b g Excellent Art Hali Layali (Green Desert (USA))
31[4] 187[6] 701[2] (1037) 1682[2] 2194[3] 2929[10] 3549[10] 4060[2] 4103[7] 5678[8] (7088a)

Sir Ox (USA) *Robert Cowell* a70 59
3 b g Oxbow(USA) Lady Melesi (USA) (Colonial Affair (USA))
134[4] (400) (614) 698[3] 1656[7] 5730[3]

Sir Plato (IRE) *Rod Millman* a66 71
5 b g Sir Prancealot(IRE) Dessert Flower (IRE) (Intikhab (USA))
1727[12] 2273[16] 2691[9] 3529[3] 4615[8] 4994[6] 6334[2] 6904[9] 8031[9] 8413[DSQ]

Sir Prize *Dean Ivory* a84
4 b g Sir Percy Three Sugars (AUS) (Starcraft (NZ))
(85)◆ (362) 7544◆ (6320) 6931[3] 7575[2] 8321[3] 9066[2] 9633[8]

Sir Roderic (IRE) *Rod Millman* a58 80
6 b g Roderic O'Connor(IRE) Begin The Beguine (IRE) (Peintre Celebre (USA))
1563[3] 2339[4] (2714) 3100[4] 3575[3] 3944[2] 4226[2] 5579[4] 6201[6] 6803[2] 7164[10] 7975[9]

Sir Rodneyredblood *J R Jenkins* a61 54
2 ch g Roderic O'Connor(IRE) Red Blooded Woman (USA) (Red Ransom (USA))
3644[14] 3943[10] 4344[5] 6313[5] 6837[3] 7110[9] 7833[9] (8825)◆ 9061[9] 9407[3]

Sir Ron Priestley *Mark Johnston* 114
3 ch c Australia Reckoning (IRE) (Danehill Dancer (IRE))
(1898) (3086) 4017[13] (4644) (5541) (6446) 7196[2]

Sir Sahib (USA) *Kevin Attard* 100
4 b g Fort Larned(USA) Xs Belle (USA) (Dynaformer (USA))
5484a[2] 7226a[5]

Sir Thomas Gresham (IRE)
Tim Pinfield a104 104
4 b h Dutch Art Loquacity (Diktat)
563[5] 909[5] 1853[5]◆ 2409[9] 6453[4] 7411[2]

Sir Titan *Tony Carroll* a85 88
5 b g Aqlaam Femme De Fer (Hamas (IRE))
2622[7] 3636[7] 4902[7] 5626[4]◆ 6326[3] (7462) 9308[4]

Sir Victor (IRE) *Tom Dascombe* a73 71
3 b g Sir Prancealot(IRE) Victoria Lodge (IRE) (Grand Lodge (USA))
1685[6] 2035[5] 2872[4] 3471[9] 4107[5] 4552[9] 5080[6] 5817[7] 6342[7]

Sir Walter (IRE) *Eric Alston* a47 40
4 b g Camacho Damalis (IRE) (Mukaddamah (USA))
129[11] 167[3] 286[8] 411[6] 503[5] 2633[6] 5278[6]

Sir Winston (USA) *Mark Casse* a117
3 ch c Awesome Again(CAN) La Gran Bailadora (USA) (Afleet Alex (USA))
(3620a)

Siskin (USA) *G M Lyons* 116
2 bb c First Defence(USA) Bird Flown (Oasis Dream)
(4413a) (5922a)

Sissi Doloise (FR) *A Bonin* a70 70
5 b m Motivator Sirene Doloise (FR) (Marchand De Sable (USA))
1491a[11] 4859a[3]

Sistercharlie (IRE) *Chad C Brown* a75 118
5 b m Myboycharlie(IRE) Starlet's Sister (IRE) (Galileo (IRE))
(4950a) (5978a) 8772a[3]

Sister Midnight (IRE) *P Bary* 76
3 b f Dark Angel(IRE) Yoga (IRE) (Monsun (GER))
7291a[5]

Sister Of The Sign (IRE)
James Given a64 43
3 b f Kodiac Summer Magic (IRE) (Desert Sun)
235[6] (497) 783[4] (1079) 1275[6] 2211[10] 2592[10] 4183[11]

Sittin Handy (IRE) *Dean Ivory* a47 34
3 ch g Helmet(AUS) Three Times (Bahamian Bounty)
406[8] 1514[7] 3246[12] 5431[6] 5867[10] 6389[10] 7550[4] 8001[12]

Six Gun *Jassim Mohammed Ghazali* 62
2 b g Sepoy(AUS) Three By Three (IRE) (Invincible Spirit (IRE))
1556[7] 2331[5] 4075[4] 9582a[14]

Six Strings *Michael Appleby* a80 87
5 b g Requinto(IRE) Island Music (IRE) (Mujahid (USA))
54[9] 249[2] (6591)◆ 6935[2] 7059[4] 7607[4] 8636[6] 8921[10] 9176[5]

Sixth Of June *Simon Earle* a33 48
5 b m Crosspeace(IRE) Eccentricity (Emarati (USA))
7603[3] 8256[9] 9629[11]

Sixties Coed *Nigel Tinkler* a16
4 b g Sixties Icon Discoed (Distinctly North (USA))
9112[5] 9350[7]

Sixties Idol *Sheena West* a35 43
6 b m Sixties Icon Fading Away (Fraam)
731[14]

Six Til Twelve (IRE) *Robyn Brisland* a58
3 b g Bungle Inthejungle Cuiseach (IRE) (Bachelor Duke (USA))
7630[4] 8290[9] 9032[3] 9332[3]

Siyahamba (IRE) *Bryan Smart* a49 52
5 ch g Helmet(AUS) Kalabunga (IRE) (Val Royal (FR))
504[3] 1163[2] 2196[3] 2684[2] 3205[3] 4510[3] (5513) 6098[5]

Siyarafina (FR) *A De Royer-Dupre* 110
3 b f Pivotal Siyenica (FR) (Azamour (IRE))
(3121a) 3905a[6]

Size Matters *Mike Sowersby* a52 46
5 b g Captain Gerrard(IRE) Icky Woo (Mark Of Esteem (IRE))
1722[6] 2349[6] 3960[5] 4587[7] 6103[8]

Skalleti (FR) *J Reynier* a100 113
4 gr g Kendargent(FR) Skallet (FR) (Muhaymin (USA))
682a[8] (2429a) (5168a) (7923a)◆ (8788a)

Skalleto (FR) *J-P Gauvin* a83 77
5 b g Kendargent(FR) Skallet (FR) (Muhaymin (USA))
7601a[4]

Skardu *William Haggas* 114
3 ch c Shamardal(USA) Diala (IRE) (Iffraaj)
(1854) 2411[3] 3104a[4] 3951[4] 6443[4]

Ska Ridge *Rebecca Menzies* a55
7 b g Distant Peak(IRE) Tandawizi (Relief Pitcher)
8814[4] 9469[9]

Skating Away (IRE) *Joseph Tuite* a36 54
3 b f Bungle Inthejungle She Runs (FR) (Sheyrann (IRE))
7236[10] 8553[8]

Skazino (FR) *Cedric Rossi* a66 99
3 ch g Kendargent(FR) Skallet (FR) (Muhaymin (USA))
4431a[5]

Skeetah *John Quinn* a61 64
3 b f Heeraat(IRE) Skylla (Kyllachy)
1924[5] 2477[6] 3508[7] 4081[5] 5738[3] 6397[4] (8263) 8643[5] 9219[3]◆

Skerryvore *James Fanshawe* a82 77
3 ch g Toronado(IRE) Succinct (Hector Protector (USA))
2250[5] 2690[4] 4304[2] 5654[3] (6940)◆ 8692[4]◆ 9096[3]

Skiddaw (AUS) *Danny O'Brien* 98
2 b c Hinchinbrook(AUS) Hidden Message (NZ) (Pentire)
8137a[9]

Skill Set (IRE) *Henry Candy* a85 91
4 b m Mastercraftsman(IRE) Rakiza (IRE) (Elnadim (USA))
2961[4] 5190[11] 6082[3] 7885a[7]

Skip The Queue (IRE) *H Al Jehani* 68
2 b c Acclamation Red Perdita (IRE) (Approve (IRE))
5263a[5] 5763a[4] 6485a[2] 6873a[2] 9582a[12]

Skip To My Lou *Peter Crate* a59
4 b m Foxwedge(AUS) Alhufoof (USA) (Dayjur (USA))
(478) 597[2]◆

Skirrid Mountain (IRE) *David Evans* a23
2 b f Elzaam(AUS) Shadow Mountain (Selkirk (USA))
9252[10]

Skito Soldier *Ruth Carr* a41 48
4 b g Sepoy(AUS) Kotsi (IRE) (Nayef (USA))
2964[11] 3781[11]

Skitter Scatter (USA) *John M Oxx* a77 102
3 b f Scat Daddy(USA) Dane Street (USA) (Street Cry (IRE))
2443[14] **6646a**[2] 7221a[7]

Skontonovski *Richard Spencer* 77
2 b c Harbour Watch(IRE) An Ghalanta (IRE) (Holy Roman Emperor (IRE))
5624[5] **6395**[2] 7119[17]

Skrei (IRE) *Dr A Bolte* 63
4 gr m Approve(IRE) Midsomer Mist (IRE) (Lawman (FR))
6270a[8]

Sky Bolt (FR) *Pauline Menges* a69 69
6 ch h Denon(USA) Suvretta Queen (IRE) (Polish Precedent (USA))
5115a[5]

Sky Commander (IRE) *James Tate* a90 49
2 b c War Command(USA) Queen Of Skies (IRE) (Shamardal (USA))
3194[8] ***(9323)***◆

Sky Cross (IRE) *Mark Johnston* 59
3 b c Cape Cross(IRE) Lil's Jessy (IRE) (Kris)
2120[5] 2914[10]

Sky Defender *Mark Johnston* a95 87
3 b c Farhh Al Mahmeyah (Teofilo (IRE))
(2470)◆ 2828[15] *9206*[4] *9388*[7]

Skydiving *Mlle S Houben* a62 61
4 b g Al Kazeem How High The Sky (IRE) (Danehill Dancer (IRE))
63[2] *364*[8] *600*[6] **2955a**[5] 4960a[8]

Sky Flyer *Ralph Beckett* a54 67
2 b g Zoffany(IRE) Highland Shot (Selkirk (USA))
5131[12] *6185*[5] **6564**[4]◆ 8029[5]

Skyful Sea (FR) *P Schiergen* 101
3 b f Sea The Stars(IRE) Saldentigerin (GER) (Tiger Hill (IRE))
3385a[2] **4427a**[5] 5720a[7]

Sky Lake (GER) *Marco Botti* a79
2 b f Dabirsim(FR) Salona (GER) (Lord Of England (GER))
7547[8] ***(8528)***

Skylark Lady (IRE) *Nikki Evans* a37 37
6 ch m Tamayuz Allegrissimo (IRE) (Redback)
4870[9] **5680**[5] 6599[8]

Skyllachy *Mark Usher* a58
2 b c Kyllachy Sweetest Revenge (IRE) (Daggers Drawn (USA))
9036[10] ***9413***[8]

Skyman *Roger Charlton* a72 83
3 b g Mukhadram Skyrider (IRE) (Dalakhani (IRE))
3247[5] 4306[2] *4789*[6] **6160**[3] **(6671)** **8260**[3]

Skymax (GER) *Ralph Beckett* 96
3 br g Maxios Set Dreams (FR) (Galileo (IRE))
2811[5] 3337[5] 4327[4] (5135) **6471**[4] 8092[11]

Sky Moon (IRE) *Peter Fahey* a69 77
4 b h Swiss Spirit Carte D'Oro (IRE) (Medaglia d'Oro (USA))
5537a[16]

Sky Orchid (FR) *F Head* a56 59
3 b f Wootton Bassett Acampe (Sky Mesa (USA))
977a[3]

Sky Patrol (IRE) *Lucy Wadham* a51 71
3 b g Camacho Patroller (USA) (Grand Slam (USA))
6325[2]

Sky Power (FR) *G Barbedette* a83 77
2 b c Stormy River(FR) Feltzer (FR) (Indian Rocket)
8508a[5]

Sky Power (IRE) *Richard Hannon* 73
2 b c Fastnet Rock(AUS) Dame Blanche (IRE) (Be My Guest (USA))
8722[3]◆

Sky Storm *Hughie Morrison* 67
2 ch f Night Of Thunder(IRE) Dinvar Diva (Dalakhani (IRE))
8516[3]

Skyva *Brian Ellison* a63 56
4 b g Dick Turpin(IRE) Skylla (Kyllachy)
277[4] 1818[8] *2189*[8] *2527*[2] *2944*[3]

Sky Vega (IRE) *Tom Ward* a65 74
2 b c Lope De Vega(IRE) Danaskaya (IRE) (Danehill (USA))
5331[5] **5801**[3] 7113[3] 7754[5] *9110*[5] *9414*[7] *9605a*[4]

Slade King (IRE) *Gary Moore* a71 76
3 ch g Slade Power(IRE) Lough Mewin (IRE) (Woodman (USA))
2406[8] 4836[5] 6304[3] 6810[2] **7342**[3] *9067*[6]

Slaidburn *Tim Easterby* 25
2 b g Mayson Medina (IRE) (Pennekamp (USA))
5472[7] 6175[12]

Slainte (IRE) *Sarah Dawson* a48 45
3 b g Elusive Pimpernel(USA) Rangooned (Bahamian Bounty)
1863[3]

Slaithwaite (IRE) *Roger Fell* a55 54
3 br g Society Rock(IRE) Wild Whim (IRE) (Whipper (USA))
1549[14] *1721*[14] **3513**[3] **4005**[3] 5023[9] 5216[4]

Slalom (FR) *A Fabre* a85 111
3 b c Intello(GER) Zagzig (Selkirk (USA))
(1797a) 3390a[12] **4963a**[2]◆

Slavonic Dance (IRE)
Ralph Beckett a42 60
2 b f Muhaarar Najam (Singspiel (IRE))
5131[8] 5801[4] 6395[6] 6808[5] 7277[8]

Sleepdancer (IRE) *John Ryan* 30
3 b g Rip Van Winkle(IRE) Dancing Eclipse (IRE) (Danehill Dancer (IRE))
2932[5] 5103[7] 5193[10] *6046*[12] 6612[5] *7192*[10] *9412*[7] *9560*[8]

Sleeping Giant (GER) *P Schaerer* a69 79
9 gr g Dalakhani(IRE) Special Delivery (IRE) (Danehill (USA))
694a[3]

Sleeping Lion (USA)
James Fanshawe a96 99
4 ch g Teofilo(IRE) Flame Of Hestia (IRE) (Giant's Causeway (USA))
2126[2] *2969*[3] 4102[10] 5368[2] 6355[8] **(7147)**

Sleepy Haven (IRE)
Jennie Candlish a51 62
9 b g Indian Haven High Society Girl (IRE) (Key Of Luck (USA))
162[5] *504*[12]

Slickteg (FR) *H-A Pantall* a34 79
4 bl h Slickly(FR) Tegan (IRE) (Cape Cross (IRE))
(2956a)

Slieve Donard *Noel Wilson* 36
3 b g Hellvelyn Bladewood Girl (Needwood Blade)
2197[9] **2327**[4] 2633[7] 3158[12] 4010[9] 4434[9]

Slingshot *Bryan Smart* a64 50
2 b f Due Diligence(USA) Nizhoni (USA) (Mineshaft (USA))
6622[8] ***8084***[4]◆ *9107*[7] *9541*[3]

Slipalongtrevaskis *Paul Howling* a49 49
6 b g Kheleyf(USA) Tilly's Dream (Arkadian Hero (USA))
357[6] *594*[5] ***1477***[2] *2066*[4] *3007*[9] 3352[8]

Slipper Satin (IRE) *Simon West* a40 46
9 b m Excellent Art In The Ribbons (In The Wings)
4510[13]

Slivio (FR) *F Rossi* a43
3 gr g Slickly(FR) Izaline (FR) (Orpen (USA))
955a[8]

Sloane Garden *James Tate* a71 76
3 ch f Iffraaj Sloane Square (Teofilo (IRE))
5357[3] *6283*[2] 6823[3] **7288**[3]

Slowfoot (GER) *Suzi Best* a59 96
11 b h Hernando(FR) Simply Red (GER) (Dashing Blade)
363[8] ***549***[5]

Slowmo (IRE) *Tom Dascombe* a70 70
3 b g Kodiac Motion Lass (Motivator)
(458)◆

Sly Minx *Mick Channon* 72
2 b f Sixties Icon Tanojin (IRE) (Thousand Words)
7897[7] **8464**[3]

Smart Champion *David Simcock* a89 91
4 b g Teofilo(IRE) Soryah (IRE) (Shamardal (USA))
6834[4] ***7464***[2]◆ *9419*[6]

Smarter (IRE) *William Haggas* a84 85
3 gr g Dark Angel(IRE) Coquette Rouge (IRE) (Croco Rouge (IRE))
1166[7] *(1555)*◆ *1928*[2] *2317*[3] **4339**[2] *6597*[5] **7830**[3]

Smart Lady (FR) *M Delzangles* 72
3 b f Makfi Rosa Linda (FR) (Teofilo (IRE))
3710a[3]

Smart Lass (IRE) *Iain Jardine* a54 61
4 b m Casamento(IRE) Smart Ass (IRE) (Shinko Forest (IRE))
4914[12] *6939*[5]◆ *7415*[2] (7732) **(8238)**

Smart Move (FR)
D & P Prod'Homme a53 79
4 b g Style Vendome(FR) Ideechic (FR) (Chichicastenango (FR))
2956a[8] **4747a**[7] 7601a[5]

Smart Project (IRE) *Adrian Nicholls* a50 46
2 b g Gutaifan(IRE) Heeby Jeeby (Lawman (FR))
9394[6]

Smart Rag (IRE) *A Botti* 96
2 b c Gleneagles(IRE) Paint In Green (IRE) (Invincible Spirit (IRE))
8390a[6]

Smart Samba (IRE) *Chris Wall* a39 10
3 b g Intello(GER) Brazilian Bride (IRE) (Pivotal)
7525[6] 7999[8] ***8451***[9]

Smart Stinger (USA)
Andrew Slattery a40 20
5 ch m Dominus(USA) Float And Sting (USA) (Two Punch (USA))
307a[11]

Smart Whip (FR) *C Lotoux* a87 100
8 b g Dylan Thomas(IRE) Green Girl (FR) (Lord Of Men)
7536a[3] **8580a**[2]

Smashing Lass (IRE) *Ollie Pears* a43 49
3 ch f Sir Prancealot(IRE) Gilded Truffle (IRE) (Peintre Celebre (USA))
1486[13] *2190*[10] 3158[7] 3569[5] 4518[10] **5389**[2] 6578[4] 7290[5]

Smash Williams (IRE) *J S Bolger* 106
6 ch g Fracas(IRE) Take Flight (IRE) (Pivotal)
1434a[3] 1776a[4] 3103a[6] 3818a[2] 4313a[7] 5205a[11]

Smeaton (IRE) *Roger Fell* a52 65
3 b g Sir Prancealot(IRE) Sunny Harbor (IRE) (Indian Haven)
1643[5] *2245*[5] 2677[4] **3226**[2] 3505[6] 4664[5] 5023[6] 5552[2] 5695[9] 6540[3] 7405[7]

Smile A Mile (IRE) *Mark Johnston* a92 97
3 ch g Slade Power(IRE) Bergamask (USA) (Kingmambo (USA))
(2371)◆ 2766[4] (3051) 4445[6] 4692[2] (5061) 5200[4] 5564[6] **(6258)** 6516[5] **6973**[2] **7184**[3] 7430[10] 7694[22] *9200*[5] *9610*[5]

Smiley Bagel (IRE)
Mark Loughnane a40 49
6 b g Kyllachy Epistoliere (IRE) (Alzao (USA))
88[4] *346*[6] *754*[10] *985*[2] *1363*[4] 3155[5] *7915*[11] *8507*[12]

Smith (IRE) *Lydia Richards* a44 57
3 ch g Dawn Approach(IRE) Alazeya (IRE) (Shirocco (GER))
1652[10] 2734[6] 3409[5] *4029*[5] 4400[4] **(4735)** *6636*[9]

Smoke On The Water
Charlie Fellowes a67 57
3 ch g Iffraaj Fullaah (IRE) (Shamardal (USA))
2802[10] ***9635***[4]

Smokey Bear (IRE) *Roger Charlton* a85 85
2 b c Kodiac Shamankiyna (FR) (Azamour (IRE))
4734[3]◆ 5501[2] **(7407)** ***(8059)***

Smokey Lane (IRE) *David Evans* a79 81
5 ch g Zebedee Masela (IRE) (Medicean)
260[7] ***618***[3]◆ *797*[4] *1357*[9] 1822[7] 2107[3] 2841[14] *3462*[9] 4926[4] 5495[3] 6109[2] 7115[3] 7299[9] (7977) (8007) 8522[10] 8860[5] *9334*[3] *9606*[4]

Smoki Smoka (IRE) *Donald McCain* a73 59
3 ch g Dragon Pulse(IRE) Creating Speed (IRE) (Lord Shanakill (USA))
316[7]◆ ***461***[2]◆ *839*[4] 1696[5] 2562[9] 4602[10] *5632*[6] *6024*[10]

Smuggler *Marcus Tregoning* 77
2 b g Sir Percy Patronella (IRE) (High Chaparral (IRE))
4062[2]◆ 5665[7] 7458[6]

Smugglers Creek (IRE)
Iain Jardine a71 74
5 b g Medicean Crystany (IRE) (Green Desert (USA))
234 *356*[5] 2372[7] (2899) 4239[13] 4693[7] **5616**[2] *6665*[10] 7289[8] *7820*[6] *9283*[6]

Snapper Sinclair (USA)
Steven Asmussen a103 101
4 b h City Zip(USA) True Addiction (USA) (Yes It's True (USA))
8771a[4]

Snapraeceps (IRE)
Joseph Patrick O'Brien a89 100
3 b f Canford Cliffs(IRE) Snap Alam (IRE) (Alamshar (IRE))
5075a[4] 6090a[7] 6692a[10] 7347[14] **7635a**[2] 8368a[6] *8734a*[5] *9002*[9]

Snazzy Jazzy (IRE) *Clive Cox* 113
4 b h Red Jazz(USA) Bulrushes (Byron)
3588[3] **(3891)** 5184[9]

Sneaky *T Van Den Troost* a57 62
2 b f Charm Spirit(IRE) Crafty (AUS) (Manhattan Rain (AUS))
2968[5] **3259**[2] 3927[P] 4448[2] 4985[8] 5562[3] 6041[5] *9605a*[6]

Sneaky Getaway (IRE)
Emmet Mullins 96
6 b g Getaway(GER) Aguida (FR) (Kahyasi (IRE))
7148[5] **8114**[8]

Sneaky Peek *Andrew Balding* 86
3 b f Nayef(USA) Casual Glance (Sinndar (IRE))
1739[2] 2524[7] (3200) 4064[2] **4864**[3]◆

Snejinska (FR) *Mrs C Gilbert* a13 15
5 gr m Sageburg(IRE) Pearlescence (USA) (Pleasantly Perfect (USA))
2673a[8] 4684a[9] **5233**[2] 6008a[4] **6555a**[4]

Snookered (IRE) *Brian Ellison* a75 76
5 b g Born To Sea(IRE) Secret Quest (Pivotal)
2628[4] ***4383***[4] **5019**[2] 5712a[6] 6278[4]

Snooker Jim *Steph Hollinshead* a58 57
4 b g Holy Roman Emperor(IRE) Lucia De Medici (Medicean)
180[6] ***1769***[6] **2631**[2] *3325*[3] 3730[2] 3939[4] *4460*[11] 5787[7] 6059[9] 6627[4] 7509[3] 7776[5] 8008[3] *9111*[3] *9384*[6]

Snooze Button (IRE)
Jamie Osborne a52
4 b g Zoffany(IRE) Myrtle Beach (IRE) (Kenmare (FR))
431[4] *706*[5] ***753***[4] *882*[9]

Snoozy Sioux (IRE)
T Van Den Troost a63 68
5 b m Sleeping Indian Castalian Spring (IRE) (Oasis Dream)
(7800a)

Snowball Jackson *Richard Hannon* a69
2 br c No Nay Never(USA) Emeralds Spirit (IRE) (Rock Of Gibraltar (IRE))
9413[3]

Snowdon *Michael Dods* a80 79
4 b m Iffraaj Solva (Singspiel (IRE))
3449[3] 5198[8] *6280*[6] *6940*[8] *7650*[7]

Snow Falcon (IRE) *Noel Meade* 80
9 b g Presenting Flocon De Neige (IRE) (Kahyasi (IRE))
3952[13]

Snow Hope *A Oliver* a59 41
3 gr f Exceed And Excel(AUS) Riva Snows (IRE) (Dalakhani (IRE))
306a[5]

Snow In Spring *Ralph Beckett* a55
3 b g Oasis Dream Khione (Dalakhani (IRE))
259[5] 3528[11] 3965[9]

Snow Leopard (IRE) *Tony Carroll* a47 47
3 gr g Mount Nelson La Gandilie (FR) (Highest Honor (FR))
8854[10] ***9289***[6]

Snow Ocean (IRE) *David Evans* a84 70
3 b g Exceed And Excel(AUS) Callistan (IRE) (Galileo (IRE))
7114[2] *7875*[7] *(8645)* ***(9273)***◆ ***9628***[4]

Snow Patch (IRE) *D J Bunyan* a69 71
4 b m Epaulette(AUS) Radha (Bishop Of Cashel)
307a[13] ***7690***[4]

Snow Shower *Sir Michael Stoute* 80
2 b f Lope De Vega(IRE) Solar Pursuit (Galileo (IRE))
(6906)

Snow Storm (IRE) *Saeed bin Suroor* a73 75
3 b c Slade Power(IRE) Snowdrops (Gulch (USA))
2101[5] *2942*[4] 3779[7]

Snowy Sunday (FR) *Frank Sheridan* a64 63
5 ch g Medecis Many Dreams (FR) (Lando (GER))
3711a[3]

Soala (IRE) *J E Hammond* a52 67
4 ch m Al Kazeem Shada (IRE) (Galileo (IRE))
4859a[10]

Soar Above *John Butler* a82 43
4 rg g Lethal Force(IRE) Soar (Danzero (AUS))
253[4] *944*[2] *2971*[7] *(4501)* ***(4786)*** *5283*[7] *8702*[10] *8827*[8] *9606*[2]

Soaring Spirits (IRE) *Dean Ivory* a62 63
9 ch g Tamayuz Follow My Lead (Night Shift (USA))
760[9] *1328*[9] 2483[10] **3406**[2] 3540[4] 3966[12] 5675[9] 6058[6] 7024[7] 7273[8] 8436[6] *9384*[12] *9505*[11]

Soaring Star (IRE) *Kevin Ryan* 75
2 b c Starspangledbanner(AUS) Peig (IRE) (Refuse To Bend (IRE))
4826[3]◆ **6175**[2] 7119[18]

So Beloved *David O'Meara* a102 108
9 b g Dansili Valencia (Kenmare (FR))
1763[3] **2100**[4] **3094**[2] 3987[9] 4921[7] 5610[16] 6376[7] 7164[3] 7891[14] 8336[7] *9000*[2] *9129*[4]

So Brave *Eve Johnson Houghton* a74 83
3 b f Kyllachy Valiantly (Anabaa (USA))
9214[12] ***9549***[7]

Sobriquet (IRE) *Ed de Giles* 68
2 ch f Night Of Thunder(IRE) Broadway Duchess (IRE) (New Approach (IRE))
3469[7] **3835**[2]◆

So Chivalry (GER)
Jean-Pierre Carvalho 101
3 b c Camelot So Smart (GER) (Selkirk (USA))
3674a[6] **4707a**[9]

Social Butterfly (IRE)
Mick Channon a70 57
4 gr m Clodovil(IRE) Bank On Black (IRE) (Big Bad Bob (IRE))
279[10]

Social Calendar *James Tate* a48
3 b c Gregorian(IRE) Beautiful Lady (IRE) (Peintre Celebre (USA))
3324[10] (Dead)

Social City *Tony Carroll* a60 30
3 b g Cityscape Society Rose (Saddlers' Hall (IRE))
7525[5] *8451*[6] *8944*[2] ***9216***[3]

Socialites Red *Scott Dixon* a66 74
6 ch m Sakhee's Secret Tipsy Girl (Haafhd)
1162[4] *(1368)* *1553*[2] (1817) *1973*[2] *2194*[2] 2292[6] 2824[9] **3056**[2] *3207*[4] 3658[7] 3928[6]

Socially Shady *K R Burke* a70
2 ch g Zoffany(IRE) Executrix (Oasis Dream)
9363[3] *9624*[5]

Social Network (IRE) *James Tate* a64 62
3 ch f Australia Mona Lisa (Giant's Causeway (USA))
128[3] 5627[7] *6393*[6]

Society Guest (IRE) *Mick Channon* a64 73
3 b f Society Rock(IRE) Bronze Baby (USA) (Silver Charm (USA))
2919[5] 3546[3] **4120**[3] 4405[2] 4655[5] 5445[5] 5785[3] 6083[10] 6810[6] 7237[2] 7460[3] 7681[4] *7912*[2] *8290*[6] *(8920)* *9089*[5]

Society Lion *Sir Michael Stoute* 80
2 b c Invincible Spirit(IRE) Pavlosk (USA) (Arch (USA))
7661[4] **(8203)**

Society Prince (IRE)
James Fanshawe a68 72
4 br g Society Rock(IRE) Princess Atoosa (USA) (Gone West (USA))
(6325) 6972[16]

Society Queen (IRE) *Richard Fahey* 81
3 b f Society Rock(IRE) Passion Fruit (Pursuit Of Love)
2522[4] 3068[4] 3815[8] 4595[5] 5476[5]

Society Red *Richard Fahey* a72 97
5 ch g Arcano(IRE) Idonea (CAN) (Swain (IRE))
1308a[12] **1664**[2] 1896[5] **2808**[2] 3160[8] 4646[10] 5440[5] 6475[7] 7434[4]◆ 8130[6]

Society Star *Robert Cowell* a55 65
3 b f Society Rock(IRE) Clapperboard (Royal Applause)
3596[4] *4192*[7] 5603[3] (5917) **6197**[2] 7047[5] *8194*[8]

Society Sweetheart (IRE)
J S Moore 33
3 br f Society Rock(IRE) Breakmeheart (IRE) (Galileo (IRE))
1740[11] 2250[6] 3664[12] 4485[8] 5293[8] 5797[9] 7523[9]

Sociologist (FR) *Scott Dixon* a67 67
4 ch g Society Rock(IRE) Fabiola (GER) (Medicean)
390[8] 1418[10] *7629*[5] 8033[5] 8434[6] **8664**[2] *9221*[3] *9333*[2] ***9542***[2] *9646*[4]

Socks And Shares (IRE)
Derek Shaw a36 10
6 b g Elnadim(USA) Al Andalyya (USA) (Kingmambo (USA))
1176[8]

So Claire *William Muir* a50 58
3 br f Kyllachy If So (Iffraaj)
3019[3]◆ 3697[12] 4218[6] 4754[4] 5429[4] *6052*[7] 6361[9] *(8295)* *8547*[2]◆ *8915*[8]

Socru (IRE) *Michael Easterby* a62 73
3 b g Kodiac Hemaris (IRE) (Sri Pekan (USA))
(2098) 2937[4] **3884**[4] 4781[6] 5459[7] 5692[6] 6176[13] 6626[4] 7828[5] *9113*[7] *9351*[5] *9559*[12]

Sod's Law *Hughie Morrison* a74 88
4 b g Mayson Lawyers Choice (Namid)
1511[11] 3149[4] 3763[4] 5149[3] 5474[6] 8032[2] **8396**[2]

Soffia *Edward Lynam* 118
4 br m Kyllachy Rime A Rien (Amadeus Wolf)
1434a[6] 2221a[2] (2880a) (3557a) **(5222a)** 7243a[5]

Soffika (IRE) *Sir Michael Stoute* 99
2 b f Zoffany(IRE) Rosika (Sakhee (USA))
(4142) **5964**[2]◆

Soft Cover *William Haggas* a64 67
3 bb f Shamardal(USA) Sentaril (Danehill Dancer (IRE))
2909[4] **4178**[5] *4590*[5]

Soft Icing *Niels Lantsoght* a23 14
3 b f Swiss Spirit Chantilly Beauty (FR) (Josr Algarhoud (IRE))
9538a[9]

Soft Light (FR) *J-C Rouget* 114
3 b c Authorized(IRE) Light Saber (FR) (Kendor (FR))
1797a[5] 2426a[2] 3904a[2] 4963a[5] **6522a**[2] 7941a[6]

Soft Summer Rain *Michael Easterby* a50 50
3 ch f Champs Elysees Modern Art (New Approach (IRE))
1417[13] **2099**[6] ***2301***[3]

Soghan (IRE) *Richard Hughes* a95 92
5 br g Cape Cross(IRE) Quiet Dream (USA) (Seattle Slew (USA))
(311)

So Hi Cardi (FR) *Roger Fell* a54 62
3 b f So You Think(NZ) Zongoraora (FR) (Bering)
1019[5] 1690[8] **3802**[4] *4769*[7] 5974[6] *6552*[7] 7739[4] *8200*[8]

So High *John Gosden* a86 92
3 ch c Nathaniel(IRE) Fugitive Angel (USA) (Alphabet Soup (USA))
(1689) **2110**[2]

So Hi Speed (USA) *Robert Cowell* a49 39
3 b g Central Banker(USA) Quietly Elegant (USA) (Quiet American (USA))
831[2] 1161[3] 1427[2]
So Hi Storm (IRE) *K R Burke* a68 65
3 b g Holy Roman Emperor(IRE) Great Joy I (IRE) (Grand Lodge (USA))
140[5] 409[2]
Soho Starlight *H-A Pantall* a92 91
6 ch h Pivotal Soho Star (Smarty Jones (USA))
8373a[3]
Soho Vicky (IRE) *H-A Pantall* a50 67
3 b f Motivator Soho Star (Smarty Jones (USA))
7138a[4]
Soie D'Leau *Linda Stubbs* a72 86
7 b g Monsieur Bond(IRE) Silky Silence (High Chaparral (IRE))
1892[8] 2910[8] 3589[14] 4301[7]
So I'm Told (IRE) *Gary Moore* a42 36
3 b g Lope De Vega(IRE) Satopanth (Medicean)
229[9] 695[7] 1770[9] 3528[7] 3965[7]
So I Told You (IRE) *Richard Hughes* 78
2 b f Gleneagles(IRE) Nocturne (GER) (Rock Of Gibraltar (IRE))
7755[2]◆ (8258)
Sokudo (IRE) *Madeleine Tylicki* a31 45
3 ch g Bungle Inthejungle Sapporo (IRE) (Distorted Humor (USA))
613[10]
Solage *J S Bolger* 98
3 b f Galileo(IRE) Secrete (FR) (Cape Cross (IRE))
6692a[7] 7635a[6] (8368a) 8784a[3]
Solar Gold (IRE) *William Haggas* a102 103
4 b m Sea The Stars(IRE) Jessica's Dream (IRE) (Desert Style (IRE))
3085[2]◆ 3994[3]◆ 4921[2] 5608[13] 6726[4] 7146[10] 8090[4] 8708[8]
Solar Heights (IRE) *James Tate* a98 72
3 b f Cape Cross(IRE) Solar Moon (Pivotal)
78[6] 534[3] (979) 2333[5] (3580) 4639[3]◆ (6630) 7106[8] 9625[5]
Solar Park (IRE) *Michael Attwater* a77 71
3 ch c Kendargent(FR) Solandia (IRE) (Teofilo (IRE))
20[4]◆ 354[2] (604) (972) 1424[8] 2024[5] 4507[5] 5990[5] 6288[6] 6930[9]
Solar Screen (IRE) *Roger Varian* 72
2 gr c Golden Horn Screen Star (IRE) (Tobougg (IRE))
8464[6]
Solar Wave (IRE) *J S Bolger* 95
4 b m Vocalised(USA) Solar Outburst (IRE) (Galileo (IRE))
4353a[12] 6693a[23]
Soldier Blue (FR) *Brian Ellison* a48 51
5 ch g Sepoy(AUS) Kocooning (IRE) (King's Best (USA))
356[4] 8098[8]◆ 1384[5] 1595[6] 3325[9] 4434[7]
Soldier Of War (USA) *Ben Pauling* 39
4 b g War Front(USA) Praise (USA) (Mr Prospector (USA))
4258[5] 4452[10] 5103[6] 5803[9]
Soldier On Parade *Amy Murphy* a69
2 b g Dunaden(FR) Litewska (IRE) (Mujadil (USA))
9500[8] 9634[11]
Soldier's Call *Archie Watson* 116
3 b c Showcasing Dijarvo (Iceman)
2779[3] 3950[3]◆ 5222a[4] 6423[2] 7243a[4] 7943a[15]
Soldier's Minute *Keith Dalgleish* a106 105
4 b g Raven's Pass(USA) Hadba (IRE) (Cape Cross (IRE))
(1290) 1421[5] 1946[15] (2743) 4095[19] 4402[11] 5664[16] 7433[7] 8127[7] (8607) 9004[3]◆ 9478[3]
Soldier's Son *Henry Candy* a64 69
3 b g Epaulette(AUS) Elsie's Orphan (Pastoral Pursuits)
2794[10] 3463[7] 4927[4] 5786[3] 6638[3] 6930[8] 7157[2]
Soleil Marin (IRE) *A Fabre* a102 114
5 b g Kendargent(FR) Sousmarine (IRE) (Montjeu (IRE))
(1244a) 1628a[2] 2168a[4] 3678a[2] 5079a[2] 6144a[9]
Solemn Pledge *K R Burke* 69
2 b f Showcasing Lovers' Vows (Dubawi (IRE))
5485[3] 6622[10] 7211[3] (7584) 7896[20]
Solesmes *Tony Newcombe* a32 39
3 b f Gregorian(IRE) Bridie ffrench (Bahamian Bounty)
1557[12] 2276[7] 3319[12] 4376[11] 6397[5] 6754[8]
Solfeggio (IRE) *Chris Wall* a63 64
3 br f Bated Breath Superfonic (FR) (Zafonic (USA))
2114[7] 3154[3] 4285[8] 4788[4]◆ 5284[12] 8847[9] 9040[4] 9391[5]
Solid Stone (IRE)
Sir Michael Stoute a82 100
3 br g Shamardal(USA) Landmark (USA) (Arch (USA))
(1835)◆ 2828[9] 4882[11] 5564[2] 6516[2] 6725[3]
Soliers (FR) *G Botti* 71
2 b c Rajsaman(FR) Shaheen Zain (IRE) (Oasis Dream)
(4679a) 5286a[4]
Solitary Sister (IRE) *John Berry* a43 57
5 br m Cockney Rebel(IRE) Sweet Afton (IRE) (Mujadil (USA))
245[11] 436[10] 721[8]
Solmina (FR) *J-L Dubord* 93
7 b m Solon(GER) Ominneha (FR) (Exit To Nowhere (USA))
6820a[8] 8375a[2]
Soloist (IRE) *Alexandra Dunn* a76 75
3 b f Camelot Ayshea (Mr Greeley (USA))
1738[11] 2148[7] 3050[7] 3513[7] 3926[2] 4803[7] (5855) 7493[4] 7650[3] 9611[12]
Solstalla *David Weston* a60 66
7 b m Halling(USA) Solstice (Dubawi (IRE))
9405[6]
Solsticia (IRE) *A Fabre* 79
2 b f Le Havre(IRE) Solilea (IRE) (Galileo (IRE))
6774a[4]

Soltanaa (FR) *F Vermeulen* 28
3 b f Makfi Epatha (IRE) (Highest Honor (FR))
5329a[8]
Solveig's Song *Steve Woodman* a58 46
7 b m Norse Dancer(IRE) Ivory Lace (Atraf)
250[9] 940[4]◆ 2231[8] 4753[8] 5049[7] 5803[7] 7028[7] 8417[6] 8822[14]
So Macho (IRE) *Grant Tuer* a68 68
4 ch g Camacho Turban Heights (IRE) (Golan (IRE))
2895[3] 5283[10] 5817[6] (6302) 7310[6] 8087[10]
Sombra De Mollys *Brian Ellison* a11 53
2 gr f Mayson Musical Molly (IRE) (Mastercraftsman (IRE))
4624[5] 5243[9] 5689[6] 6683[9]
Somekindasuperstar *Paul Collins* a59 34
2 b f Fast Company(IRE) Passkey (Medicean)
6336[10] 6943[10] 7580[3] 8085[7]
Someone Exciting *David Thompson* a52 60
6 b m Notnowcato Quite Something (Footstepsinthesand)
2189[2] 2638[2] 2678[6] 3413[11] 3723[5] 4132[8] 4434[8] (5299) 5559[13] 5768[3] (6590) 7307[5] 7591[10] 7962[8] 8637[4] 9111[9] 9398[7]
Some Picture (IRE) *Mick Channon* 67
2 b f Kodiac Windy Lane (Dubai Destination (USA))
8093[15] 8759[4]
Somethingaboutjack (IRE)
Eve Johnson Houghton a63 71
3 br c No Nay Never(USA) City Dazzler (IRE) (Elusive City (USA))
1728[6] 2397[4] 3090[3]
Something Awesome (CAN)
Jose Corrales a94 79
8 b g Awesome Again(CAN) Somethinaboutlaura (USA) (Dance Floor (USA))
445a[10]
Something Blond (IRE)
Marco Botti a57
3 ch f Olympic Glory(IRE) Broadway Duchess (IRE) (New Approach (IRE))
556[8]
Something Brewing (FR)
Iain Jardine a62 40
5 gr g Clodovil(IRE) Talwin (IRE) (Alhaarth (IRE))
100[6] 7070[8] 8238[9]
Something Lucky (IRE)
Michael Attwater a76 69
7 gr g Clodovil(IRE) Lucky Leigh (Piccolo)
3[5] 230[5] 382[7] 471[5] 763[2] 791[2] 964[2] 1194[8] 1211[2]◆ 1394[7] 2272[5] 2556[2] 2940[6] 3303[5] 3443[7] 3936[6] 4593[3] 5042[2] 5298[5] 5647[4] 8755[2] 9245[4] 9390[2]
Somewhat Sisyphean *Wilf Storey* a47 50
3 b g Mount Nelson Nine Red (Royal Applause)
201[0] 971[11] 1721[12] 4487[5]◆ 5915[3] 9391[7]
Somewhere Secret
Michael Mullineaux a67 74
5 ch g Sakhee's Secret Lark In The Park (IRE) (Grand Lodge (USA))
125[9] 2076[4] 2418[9] 3215[3] (3549) 3706[9]◆ 3921[3] (4181) 5180[2] 5661[23] (5952) 6110[2] 6921[11] 7766[5] 8304[12] 8660[9]
Sommer Katze (FR) *Declan Carroll* a80 57
3 b g Sommerabend Forward Feline (IRE) (One Cool Cat (USA))
8006[2] (8947) (9332)◆
So Much Happy (USA)
George Papaprodromou 93
3 bb f Twirling Candy(USA) Black Valentine (USA) (Cindago (USA))
9637a[8]
Sonaiyla (IRE) *M Halford* 87
3 gr f Dark Angel(IRE) Sinaniya (USA) (More Than Ready (USA))
4353a[3]
Son Cesio (FR) *F Chappet* 77
8 b h Zafeen(FR) Slitana (FR) (Dansili)
4205a[5]
So Near So Farhh *Mick Channon* a55 76
4 ch m Farhh Protectress (Hector Protector (USA))
1663[2] 2591[3] 3294[6] 3693[4] (4483) 4881[4] (5379) 6105[3] 6716[2] 7403[9]
Songkran (IRE) *David Elsworth* a73 78
3 b g Slade Power(IRE) Choose Me (IRE) (Choisir (AUS))
(359) 733[5] 2140[2] 2746[8] 3051[7] 4124[9] 4789[8]
Song Of Life *Andrea Marcialis* a86 85
5 b m Poet's Voice Sign Of Life (Haafhd)
(4860a)
Song Of Summer *Phil McEntee* a29 36
4 ch m Choisir(AUS) Height Of Summer (IRE) (Alhaarth (IRE))
273[6] 501[7] 2930[8] 3143[10] 3279[7] 3781[2] 4217[13] 5981[7] 9086[6] 9160[14]
Song Of The Isles (IRE)
Heather Main a68 78
3 ch f Tagula(IRE) Musicology (USA) (Singspiel (IRE))
2772[7] (3354) 4378[7] 4870[2] 5380[4] (6418) 7460[8] 9126[9] 9351[13]
Song Without End (IRE)
Sir Michael Stoute a62
3 b g Pour Moi(IRE) Amathusia (Selkirk (USA))
1984[4] 2690[15]
Sonja Henie (IRE) *David Loughnane* a80 85
3 b f Exceed And Excel(AUS) Cold Cold Woman (Machiavellian (USA))
1838[5] 2552[5] 3278[7] 4591[2] (6025) 6286[2] (6533) 7188[12] 7380[7] 8023[6] 9203[4]
Sonnetina *Denis Coakley* a43 61
3 b f Poet's Voice Tebee's Oasis (Oasis Dream)
1726[7] (2926) 3697[2] 4477[4]
Sonnetist *Johnny Farrelly* a46 49
5 b g Poet's Voice Society Rose (Saddlers' Hall (IRE))
135[12] 1159[12]
Sonnet Rose (IRE) *Conrad Allen* a71 67
5 ch m Poet's Voice Arabian Pearl (IRE) (Refuse To Bend (IRE))
366[8] 697[3] 1234[7] 1382[7] 1586[5] 1880[14] 2261[2] 3744[5] 4248[7] 4567[2] (4807) 5282[2] 5828[4] 6703[2] (7684) 8254[2] 8711[6] 9048[10] 9217[6] 9455[6] 9586[4]

Son Of Beauty (IRE) *Shaun Harris* a25 69
3 b g Vocalised(USA) Sunset Beauty (IRE) (Whipper (USA))
6066[6] 7630[6]
Son Of Normandy *F Head* a51 77
3 ch g Galileo(IRE) Sansiwa (IRE) (Dansili)
2519a[2]
Son Of Prancealot (IRE)
David Evans a36 59
2 b g Sir Prancealot(IRE) Startori (Vettori (IRE))
3165[13] 5493[5] 5775[8] 6394[8] 7277[10]
Son Of Red (IRE) *Alan King* a59 54
2 b c French Navy Tarziyma (IRE) (Kalanisi (IRE))
6927[6] 7521[9] 8709[6] 9172[5]
Son Of Rest *J A Stack* 113
5 b h Pivotal Hightime Heroine (IRE) (Danetime (IRE))
1434a[7]
Sonoma (FR) *W Gulcher* 31
3 b f Siyouni(FR) Paper Profits (Kendor (FR))
6063a[12]
Sooqaan *Antony Brittain* a51 37
8 bl g Naaqoos Dream Day (FR) (Spectrum (IRE))
5[7] 45[2]◆ 232[5] 508[4] (705) 830[6] 1158[6] 1426[2] 2193[6] 2349[3] 2944[5] 4195[9] 5051[9] 7385[6] 7859[10] 8646[4] 9035[4] 9225[4] 9544[9]
Sootability (IRE) *Richard Fahey* 75
3 br f Camelot Balaagha (USA) (Mr Greeley (USA))
2872[5] 3862[10] 4626[6] 5394[8] 5844[3] (6342) 7126[2] 7404[4] 8413[3]
Sooty's Return (IRE) *J S Moore* a29 23
2 b g Anjaal Apasiona (IRE) (Invincible Spirit (IRE))
3634[7] 4652[6] 7056[8] 7516[13] 9045[9]
So Perfect (USA) *A P O'Brien* 112
3 b f Scat Daddy(USA) Hopeoverexperience (USA) (Songandaprayer (USA))
1751[3] (2882a) 4092[9] 4923[5] 5716a[8] 6423[3] 6959[9] 7243a[2] 7943a[2] 8331[17]
Sophar Sogood (IRE) *Paul D'Arcy* a61 45
2 b g French Navy Cloud Break (Dansili)
5052[10] 6054[5] 6368[9] (7626) 8286[2] 8493[2]
Sophia Maria *James Bethell* a61 63
3 b f Swiss Spirit Malelane (IRE) (Prince Sabo)
1816[3] 2418[11] 3146[10] 4080[12] 5202[9] 5767[5] 6275[2] (6666) 7444[2] 7823[9] 8306[11]
Sophia's Princess *Ivan Furtado*
3 ch f Coach House(IRE) Rosa Luxemburg (Needwood Blade)
1272[9] 2146[11]
Sophisticated Heir (IRE)
Kevin Frost a46 47
9 b g New Approach(IRE) My Girl Sophie (USA) (Danzig (USA))
60[8]
Sophosc (IRE) *Joseph Tuite* a88 88
3 ch g Society Rock(IRE) Ichiuma (USA) (Mizzen Mast (USA))
3011[5] (4065) 4830[2] 5341[4] 5931[9] 6390[3] 7342[6] 8421[10]
Sopran Ival (IRE)
Grizzetti Galoppo SRL 103
2 br f Ivawood(IRE) Reign (IRE) (Elusive City (USA))
8647a[7]
Soramond (GER) *Ed Dunlop* a52 58
2 b f Sea The Moon(GER) St Aye (USA) (Nureyev (USA))
8855[5] 9243[6] 9437[9]
Sorbet *Lucy Wadham* a47
4 b m Passing Glance Fireburst (Spectrum (IRE))
696[7] 1771[11]
Sorbonne *David Barron* 67
3 ch g Cityscape Sorcellerie (Sir Percy)
5041[2]◆ 5554[4] 6259[7]
Sorrel (IRE) *Sir Michael Stoute* a74
2 b f Dansili Anice Stellato (IRE) (Dalakhani (IRE))
6928[4] 8454[2]
Sors (IRE) *Andrew Slattery* a59 84
7 b g Acclamation Maid Of Ailsa (USA) (Pivotal)
5537a[15]
Sorteo (IRE) *Andrew Balding* 63
2 b f Invincible Spirit(IRE) Sweepstake (IRE) (Acclamation)
5132[7] 5772[7]
So Sharp *Archie Watson* a81 92
2 b f Bated Breath Theladyinquestion (Dubawi (IRE))
(4557) 5411[7] 6907[10] 7813[2]
Sosian *Richard Fahey* a55 63
4 b m Showcasing Leonica (Lion Cavern (USA))
67[5] 321[7] 533[5] 984[3] 1500[4] 2376[10] (3163)◆ 3718[2] 4515[4] 5277[4]
So Si Bon (AUS)
David A & B Hayes & Tom Dabern 110
5 bk g So You Think(NZ) Black Minx (NZ) (Lonhro (AUS))
8138a[14] 8768a[4] 8952a[14]
Sosoft (FR) *C Laffon-Parias* 76
3 b c Pivotal Soft Lips (Rahy (USA))
3712a[7]
So Special *William Muir* a55 54
2 gr f Lethal Force(IRE) Secret Era (Cape Cross (IRE))
6949[7] 8651[8]
So Strictly *Paul Cole* 59
3 b c So You Think(NZ) Salsa Steps (USA) (Giant's Causeway (USA))
4258[6] 4738[5] 5808[13] 6810[10]
Sosume (FR) *Gavin Hernon* a73 84
3 b g Siyouni(FR) Louve Rouge (FR) (Gold Away (IRE))
2667a[9] 5644a[6]
Sotomayor *Jane Chapple-Hyam* a74 72
4 b g Havana Gold(IRE) No Frills (IRE) (Darshaan)
985[3]◆ (1292) (1588)
Soto Sizzler *William Knight* a99 101
4 b g Mastercraftsman(IRE) Jalousie (IRE) (Barathea (IRE))
1422[5]◆ (2032) (3346) 4504[2] 5519[9] 7408[2]
Sottsass (FR) *J-C Rouget* 123
3 ch c Siyouni(FR) Starlet's Sister (IRE) (Galileo (IRE))
1625a[5] (3390a) (7253a) 7941a[3]

Soudania *F Head* a86 110
3 b f Sea The Stars(IRE) Sahel (GER) (Monsun (GER))
(6775a) (7478a) 8378a[4]
Soul Patch (AUS) *Ken Keys* 108
2 b c Shamus Award(AUS) God Bless Us (AUS) (Flying Spur (AUS))
8137a[8]
Soul Search (IRE) *G M Lyons* 106
2 b f Zoffany(IRE) Ecoutila (USA) (Rahy (USA))
5206a[3] 6429a[3] 7244a[4] 7532a[2]
Soul Searching *Pat Phelan* a53 29
3 ch f Iffraaj Remember (Selkirk (USA))
795[2] 1346[9] 2630[11] 8698[11] 9128[12]
Sound (GER) *Michael Moroney* 107
6 bb h Lando(GER) Sky Dancing (IRE) (Exit To Nowhere (USA))
1784a[8] 8361a[10] 8844a[12]
Sound Machine (GER) *Mario Hofer* 95
2 b f Pastorius(GER) Sing Hallelujah (GER) (Big Shuffle (USA))
4417a[6] 7749a[2] 9582a[9]
Sound Mixer *William Haggas* a61 37
2 b f Cable Bay(IRE) Medley (Danehill Dancer (IRE))
8458[16] 9099[4]◆ 9299[4]
Sound Of Cannons *Brian Meehan* 100
2 b c Nathaniel(IRE) Rock Choir (Pivotal)
(6163) 6957[2] 7691[5] 8582a[4]
Sound Of Iona *Jim Goldie* a70 70
3 ch f Orientor Eternal Instinct (Exceed And Excel (AUS))
1336[2]◆ 1924[9] 3176[2] 4081[4] 4722[7]
Sound Of Victory (IRE) *P Bary* a67 92
3 b g Sea The Stars(IRE) Sakarya (IRE) (Duke Of Marmalade (IRE))
2314a[5]
Soundproof (FR)
Mme M Bollack-Badel 47
2 b f Norse Dancer(IRE) Speed Of Sound (Zafonic (USA))
9123a[8]
So Unique (FR) *N Clement* a79 92
3 ch f Siyouni(FR) Trully Blessed (FR) (Street Sense (USA))
3677a[7] 5227a[4]
Souter Johnnie (IRE)
Richard Hughes a67 61
2 b g Elzaam(AUS) Too Close (IRE) (Danehill Dancer (IRE))
3694[6] 4798[7] 5314[8] 5886[3]◆ 7079[3] (8061) 8286[12]
South Africa (GER)
Waldemar Hickst 83
2 b c Maxios Salontasche (GER) (Dashing Blade)
7004a[4]
Southbank (AUS)
Anthony Freedman 101
2 b f Fastnet Rock(AUS) Rezoned (NZ) (Zabeel (NZ))
8135a[3]
South Coast (USA)
Saeed bin Suroor a72 72
2 b f War Front(USA) Moyne Abbey (USA) (Charismatic (USA))
5732[5] 6564[2] 7834[2]
Southern Dancer *Brian Meehan* 63
2 b g Cable Bay(IRE) Mambo Halo (USA) (Southern Halo (USA))
7339[3]
Southern France (IRE)
Ciaron Maher & David Eustace 115
4 b h Galileo(IRE) Alta Anna (FR) (Anabaa (USA))
2158a[3] 2807[2] 4093[6] 4351a[4] 5522[4] (6191a) 7246a[3] 8844a[19]
Southern Hills (IRE) *A P O'Brien* 101
2 ch c Gleneagles(IRE) Remember You (IRE) (Invincible Spirit (IRE))
(3988)
Southern Horse (ARG) *J S Bolger* 103
3 b c Roman Ruler(USA) Southern Beauty (ARG) (Southern Halo (USA))
4095[14] 5923a[7]
Southern Legend (AUS) *C Fownes* 119
6 b g Not A Single Doubt(AUS) Donna's Appeal (AUS) (Carnegie (IRE))
1445a[6] 9376a[8]
Southern Rock (IRE)
David O'Meara 95
3 b g New Approach(IRE) Country Music (Street Cry (IRE))
(2438) (4001)◆ 4553[2] 5121[5] (5741) (6541)
South Light (IRE) *Antony Brittain* a35 44
2 b f Elzaam(AUS) Rien Ne Vas Plus (IRE) (Oasis Dream)
2475[6] 3196[9] 4778[6] 5968[10] 7329[5] 8527[7]
South Pacific *A P O'Brien* 110
3 b c Galileo(IRE) Tonnara (IRE) (Linamix (FR))
(4017) 5522[6]
South Sea Pearl (IRE) *A P O'Brien* 105
3 b f Galileo(IRE) Cassydora (Darshaan)
4856a[4] (5364a) 5663[3] 6263a[8] 6377[4] 7118[4] 7926a[7] 8333[7]
South Seas (IRE) *Philip Kirby* a89 106
5 ch g Lope De Vega(IRE) Let It Be Me (USA) (Mizzen Mast (USA))
1415[19]
Souvigne (FR) *J-P Gauvin* a69 47
5 b h Zanzibari(USA) Senanques (FR) (Apeldoorn (FR))
5035a[16]
Sovereign (IRE) *A P O'Brien* 117
3 ch c Galileo(IRE) Devoted To You (IRE) (Danehill Dancer (IRE))
1603a[2] 2662a[3] 3345[10] (4414a)
Sovereign Beauty (IRE) *Clive Cox* a58 72
2 b f Free Eagle(IRE) Indian Maiden (IRE) (Indian Ridge (IRE))
(4062) 4840[8] 7458[5] 8650[8]

Sovereign Duke (GER)
Henry Candy a75 95
4 b g Jukebox Jury(IRE) Shadow Queen (GER) (Lando (GER))
3078[4]◆ **5443[2]**◆ 8114[26]

Sovereigns Bright (IRE)
Ms Sheila Lavery a83 83
3 gr f No Nay Never(USA) Gleaming Silver (IRE) (Dalakhani (IRE))
2157a[8]

Sovereign State *Tony Newcombe* a47 58
4 b g Compton Place One Night In May (IRE) (Choisir (AUS))
1616[6] **(3577)** *4763[9]* 5768[7] 7977[8]

So When (FR) *P Sogorb* 75
3 b f Never On Sunday(FR) Etty's Diary (IRE) (Enrique)
3526a[2]

So Wonderful (USA) *A P O'Brien* 107
2 b f War Front(USA) Wonder Of Wonders (USA) (Kingmambo (USA))
2881a[5] 4048[11] 5361a[3] 6429a[4] 6689a[2] **7244a[3]**

Soyounique (IRE) *Sir Mark Todd* a70
2 ch g Siyouni(FR) Adventure Seeker (FR) (Bering)
8288[5]◆

So You Thought (USA)
Simon West a14 63
5 b g So You Think(NZ) Lady Of Akita (USA) (Fantastic Light (USA))
3209[7] **3718[4]** 4109[7] 8664[6]

Space Ace (FR) *Archie Watson* a72 77
2 ch f The Wow Signal(IRE) Imperial Topaz (FR) (Dutch Art)
3579[2] 3919[3] **(5314)** 5777[7] 6106[3] 6527[2] *6629[4]* 7174[3]

Space Bandit *Michael Appleby* a84 50
4 ch g Shamardal(USA) Hometime (Dubai Destination (USA))
19[4] 436[6] (508) 929[2]◆ ***(1428)***◆ 1813[7]

Space Blues (IRE) *Charlie Appleby* 116
3 ch c Dubawi(IRE) Miss Lucifer (FR) (Noverre (USA))
1737[4] 2249[2] (2746) (3317) 4092[2] **4705a[2]** **5716a[3]**◆

Space Traveller *Richard Fahey* 114
3 b c Bated Breath Sky Crystal (GER) (Galileo (IRE))
1830[2] 2826[3] 3621a[7] **(4092)** 5521[6] 6470[3] **(7220a)** 8774a[8]

Space Walk *William Haggas* a87 87
3 b g Galileo(IRE) Memory (IRE) (Danehill Dancer (IRE))
1756[4] 2142[4] **(4104)** 5347[3] ***5943[2]*** 8098[7]

Space War *Michael Easterby* a59 62
12 b g Elusive City(USA) Princess Luna (GER) (Grand Lodge (USA))
1553[3] 1967[5] (2532) 2741[5] **(3475)** 3716[3] 4207[8] 6174[4] 6680[5] *7389[4]*

Spaliburg Rosetgri (FR) *F Fouquet*
8 b g Sageburg(IRE) Spalitas (FR) (Medaaly)
7501a[11]

Spandavia (IRE) *Ed Dunlop* a59
2 ch f Showcasing Bronte Sister (IRE) (Acclamation)
8453[10] 8913[12] ***9158[5]***

Spanish Angel (IRE)
Andrew Balding 78
2 br g Gutaifan(IRE) City Dazzler (IRE) (Elusive City (USA))
2444[4] 3039[2] 5418[4] **(6755)**

Spanish Archer (FR)
James Fanshawe a103 103
4 b g Lope De Vega(IRE) Parcelle Perdue (FR) (Coroner (IRE))
4021[10] **(5657)** 6895[3] **8005[2]** ***9094[4]***

Spanish Aria *John Gosden* a78 86
3 b f Lope De Vega(IRE) Woodland Aria (Singspiel (IRE))
3468[6] 4052[10] **5253[2]** 5785[4] 6509[5]

Spanish Bounty *Mrs A Malzard* 8
14 b g Bahamian Bounty Spanish Gold (Vettori (IRE))
3173a[8] 4684a[10]

Spanish City *Roger Varian* a92 104
6 ch g Exceed And Excel(AUS) Annabelle's Charm (IRE) (Indian Ridge (IRE))
2837[2] 3347[5] 3602[3] 4921[4] 5664[19] (6517) 6950[5] **7697[2]**

Spanish Kiss *William Knight* a72
2 b c Lope De Vega(IRE) Kissable (IRE) (Danehill Dancer (IRE))
7814[10] ***8914[4]***

Spanish Mane (IRE) *Julia Feilden* a52 60
4 b m Havana Gold(IRE) Kiva (Indian Ridge (IRE))
2019[3] 2261[F] 2972[12] 4349[9] 5144[11] (5828) 6131[5]

Spanish Miss (IRE) *Mlle A Wattel* a71 63
3 b f Lilbourne Lad(IRE) Hundredsnthousands (IRE) (Thousand Words)
2091a[4] **(3066a)** 8449a[5]

Spanish Mission (USA)
David Simcock a92 113
3 b c Noble Mission Limonar (IRE) (Street Cry (IRE))
1035[5] 3042[2] **(4845)** **5585[3]** (6994a)

Spanish Persuader (FR)
Mark Johnston a55 65
2 b g Motivator Alava (IRE) (Anabaa (USA))
8528[7] **8857[2]** *9095[9]*

Spanish Star (IRE)
Patrick Chamings a61 82
4 b g Requinto(IRE) Rancho Star (IRE) (Soviet Star (USA))
(2473) 3014[2] **(3543)** 4374[3] 4844[4] 6301[5] 6668[7] 7130[8] (7760) 8285[3] *8826[8]*

Spanish Time *Keith Dalgleish* a60 61
2 b g Kendargent(FR) Really Lovely (IRE) (Galileo (IRE))
2707[4] 3290[5] **4688[5]** 6571[4]

Spantik *Roger Fell* a73
2 b c Canford Cliffs(IRE) Syrdarya (Galileo (IRE))
5856[7] ***(6718)*** *9154[12] 9500[7]*

Spare Parts (IRE) *Phil McEntee* a96 51
5 b g Choisir(AUS) Grandel (Owington)
260[P]

Spargrove *Hughie Morrison* a70 57
3 b c Cacique(IRE) Capriolla (In The Wings)
2530[2] 3809[3] *4594[2]* ***(4998)***

Sparkalot *Simon Dow* a89 78
5 br g Bated Breath Three Wrens (IRE) (Second Empire (IRE))
6319[5] ***7107[4]***◆ *8420[6] 9214[4]*

Sparklealot (IRE) *Ivan Furtado* a72 92
3 b g Sir Prancealot(IRE) Monsusu (IRE) (Montjeu (IRE))
1736[5] 2559[6] 3591[4] 4320[5] 4909[3] 5459[4] **(6588)** 7362[2] 8101[11] 8634[3] *8893[7]*

Sparkle In His Eye *Mme Pia Brandt* a82 84
3 ch c Sea The Stars(IRE) Nyarhini (Fantastic Light (USA))
128[2]◆ *(405)*◆ **2488[3]** 3261[4] 4321[6] *(5407a)* 6652a[5]

Sparkle Roll (FR) *John Gosden* 104
3 gr f Kingman Ysoldina (FR) (Kendor (FR))
(2087) 2745[7] **4014[3]** 5190[3] 8333[12]

Sparkling Breeze *Michael Dods* a55 53
2 ch g Coach House(IRE) African Breeze (Atraf)
1759[9] 2115[6] 2907[5] **3812[4]** 5296[10] 5968[7] 6539[3] 7056[6] *7469[4]*

Sparkling Diamond *Philip McBride* a61 42
2 b f Cable Bay(IRE) Read Federica (Fusaichi Pegasus (USA))
2761[6] *3491[7] 3990[6]* 5101[6] ***6837[2]***◆ *7079[2]* 7767[3]

Sparkling Olly (IRE) *Michael Bell* 69
2 b f Gleneagles(IRE) Sogno Verde (IRE) (Green Desert (USA))
8093[5]

Sparkling Or Still (IRE)
David Lanigan a63
2 b f Kendargent(FR) West Of Venus (USA) (Street Cry (IRE))
8706[11] 9197[9] ***9408[4]***◆

Spark Of War (IRE) *Keith Dalgleish* a56 62
4 b g Declaration Of War(USA) Acts Of Grace (USA) (Bahri (USA))
2330[4] 3054[10] 3568[11] 4056[8] 4515[3] 4983[5] 5277[6] 5766[2] 6828[4] 7509[6] *8922[4] 9207[9] 9345[3]*◆

Spark Plug (IRE) *Brian Meehan* a103 85
8 b g Dylan Thomas(IRE) Kournikova (SAF) (Sportsworld (USA))
757[2] ***1917[3]*** 4053[15]

Sparrow Hawk *J S Moore* a21
2 b f Free Eagle(IRE) Calico Moon (USA) (Seeking The Gold (USA))
9208[10]

Spartan Fighter *Declan Carroll* 99
2 b c Dutch Art Survived (Kyllachy)
2892[4] (3477) (4889) 6422[8] **8140a[6]** 8970a[7]

Speak In Colours
Joseph Patrick O'Brien 113
4 gr h Excelebration(IRE) Maglietta Fina (IRE) (Verglas (IRE))
3103a[2] 4094[4] **5521[4]** 6472[4] (7713a) 7944a[3] 8331[6]

Speak Softly (FR) *T Poche* a51 45
10 b m Layman(USA) Libera (Turtle Island (IRE))
5761a[8]

Specialise *Roger Varian* a93 95
3 gr f Mastercraftsman(IRE) My Special J'S (USA) (Harlan's Holiday (USA))
1828[6] 2488[4] 2919[4] (4110) *4640[2]* 6893[2] **(7900)**

Special Secret
Eve Johnson Houghton 84
2 b f Kodiac Love's Secret (Pivotal)
(4221) 4840[7] 6019[3] **7117[4]** 7696[12]

Spectaculis *Denis Quinn*
4 b g Champs Elysees Merry Diva (Bahamian Bounty)
6687[8]

Spectrum Of Light (IRE)
Charlie Appleby a75
2 br g Golden Horn Elegant Shadow (GER) (Shamardal (USA))
9471[2]◆

Speed Company (IRE) *Ian Williams* a72 94
6 b g Fast Company(IRE) Trentini (IRE) (Singspiel (IRE))
368[8] 2095[11] (3514) 3816[2] **4395[3]** 4890[2] **5818[2]**

Speed Dating (FR) *Derek Shaw* a60 50
2 gr g Outstrip Sign Your Name (GER) (Areion (GER))
2475[5] **3812[3]** 5655[5] *6073[6]* 6563[6] 7056[9] 7584[7] *7767[10] 8286[8] 9037[8] (9179) 9346[8] 9640[2]*

Speed Lady (FR) *C Lecrivain* 48
3 b f Planteur(IRE) Speed Run (FR) (Soldier Of Fortune (IRE))
7476a[8]

Speed Merchant (IRE)
Michael Appleby a75 62
2 ro g Zebedee Tanyeli (IRE) (Mastercraftsman (IRE))
4558[8] 4897[9] 5381[5] 6394[3] *7079[11] 7626[4] (8118)*◆ *(9060) 9196[6]* ***(9541)***◆ *9665[5]*

Speedo Boy (FR) *Ian Williams* a70 103
5 ch g Vision D'Etat(FR) Shamardanse (IRE) (Shamardal (USA))
281a[6] 635a[6] 2575[7] **3600[2]** *4382[17]*

Speed Skater *Amanda Perrett* a54
3 b f Olympic Glory(IRE) My Love Thomas (IRE) (Cadeaux Genereux)
186[5] *476[12] 918[11] 1384[9]*

Speedymining (IRE) *Bryan Smart* 16
2 b g Moohaajim(IRE) Spacecraft (USA) (Distant View (USA))
4624[10]

Speedy Move (IRE) *S Seemar* a83 83
7 b g Iffraaj Beautiful Filly (Oasis Dream)
997[7]

Spencer *J Phelippon* a11 74
2 b g Finjaan Star Kodiak (IRE) (Kodiac)
3562a[2] 8330a[10]

Spencers Son (IRE)
Richard Spencer a66 68
3 b g Arcano(IRE) Zalama (FR) (Red Ransom (USA))
2075[10] **3278[6]** 3805[4] *5813[10] 6925[6]* 8033[12] 8206[4] 8436[8]

Spenny's Lass *John Ryan* a59 44
4 br m Bated Breath Midnight Hush (FR) (Anabaa (USA))
144[9] 383[6] 1061[8] ***1209[2]***◆ *1883[3] 2318[8] 3144[4]* 4074[6] *4763[6] 5629[9] 6051[4]* 6572[11] 7214[12] 8235[6] 8435[7] *9411[8] 9457[8]*

Spiced *Ron Hodges* a64
4 b m Dansili Superstar Leo (IRE) (College Chapel)
202[6] ***467[6]***

Spiced Perfection (USA)
Peter Miller a109
4 b m Smiling Tiger(USA) Perfect Feat (USA) (Pleasantly Perfect (USA))
8769a[4]

Spice Of Life *Ralph Beckett* a59 59
3 b f Sea The Stars(IRE) So In Love (Smart Strike (CAN))
1397[5] 2505[7] **4447[4]** 5249[11]

Spice War *Oliver Sherwood* a66 66
4 b g Declaration Of War(USA) Blast Furnace (IRE) (Sadler's Wells (USA))
(6843) ***(7553)***◆ *7998[4]*

Spietata *Nicolo Simondi* 87
3 b f Epaulette(AUS) Spunger (Fraam)
4171a[9]

Spinacia (IRE)
Eve Johnson Houghton a70
2 b f Charm Spirit(IRE) Spinola (FR) (Spinning World (USA))
7813[4]◆ *8218[10]* ***8849[5]***

Spinart *Pam Sly* a71 73
6 ch g Dutch Art Spinneret (Pivotal)
2349[4]◆ **3279[5]**

Spinning Memories (IRE) *P Bary* a88 115
4 b m Arcano(IRE) Hanalei Memories (USA) (Hard Spun (USA))
(2670a) 3289a[4] 4581a[3] 5716a[4] **(6520a)** 7943a[9]

Spinning Mist *J Phelippon* 69
2 b f Toronado(IRE) Rhagori (Exceed And Excel (AUS))
6196a[5] (6485a) **(6873a)** 8330a[9]

Spinoff (USA) *Todd Pletcher* a111 81
3 ch c Hard Spun(USA) Zaftig (USA) (Gone West (USA))
2425a[18] ***3620a[6]***

Spiorad (IRE) *David O'Meara* 97
4 b g Invincible Spirit(IRE) Gift From Heaven (IRE) (Excellent Art)
1849[4]◆ (4130)◆ 4445[3]◆ (5970)◆ **(6179)** 6998[10]

Spiorad Saoirse *Andrew Slattery* a89 81
4 b g Iffraaj Alsalwa (IRE) (Nayef (USA))
1308a[17] **5597a[10]**

Spirit Dancer *Richard Fahey* a80
2 b c Frankel Queen's Dream (GER) (Oasis Dream)
8319[3]◆

Spirited Guest *George Margarson* a83 71
3 b g Swiss Spirit Choisette (Choisir (AUS))
1139[3]◆ *7319[2]*◆ *(7854)*◆ *8117[3]*◆ ***(8895)***◆ *9203[3]*

Spirit Kingdom (USA)
Mark Johnston a69 68
3 ch f Animal Kingdom(USA) Infinite Spirit (USA) (Maria's Mon (USA))
290[3] 409[3] ***524[4]*** *1358[5]*

Spirit Noir (IRE)
Sebastiano Guerrieri 94
2 br c Dragon Pulse(IRE) Appletreemagic (IRE) (Indian Danehill (IRE))
8789a[10]

Spirit Of Angel (IRE)
Marcus Tregoning a72 63
3 b g Dark Angel(IRE) Spirit Of Cuba (IRE) (Invincible Spirit (IRE))
359[8] 1396[3] (2322) 3204[9] 6393[5] 6931[4] 7984[6] 8414[2] ***(9093)***◆

Spirit Of Appin *Brian Meehan* a109 108
4 b m Champs Elysees Oshiponga (Barathea (IRE))
(3010) 4145[4] 5190[2] 5682[4] 6378[3] (7658) ***8811[3]***

Spirit Of Epsom *Brett Johnson* a27
5 b g Captain Gerrard(IRE) Bettina Blue (IRE) (Paris House)
359[10]

Spirit Of Ishy *Stuart Kittow* a24 46
4 b m Hellvelyn Our Piccadilly (IRE) (Piccolo)
1732[11] **3036[2]** 3527[15] 4481[16] 4776[5] 5081[7] 5806[11]

Spirit Of Light (IRE)
Charlie Appleby a67
2 gr g Dark Angel(IRE) Inspiriter (Invincible Spirit (IRE))
5809[7]

Spirit Of Lucerne (IRE)
Phil McEntee a59 49
3 br f Swiss Spirit Fascination Street (IRE) (Mujadil (USA))
141[3] *384[5]* ***550[5]*** *1167[11]* 2281[6] 2735[11] 3182[3] 3780[8] 4754[3] 5293[5] 5867[6] 6128[8] 6302[5]

Spirit Of Lund (IRE) *Iain Jardine* a74 75
3 b g Fast Company(IRE) Kyrielle (Medicean)
1504[5]◆ 2101[15] **2677[2]** 3565[2] 5274[9] 6068[7] 6612[4] 7404[6]

Spirit Of May *Roger Teal* a94 82
3 ch g Coach House(IRE) Bengers Lass (USA) (Orientate (USA))
(2063) 2772[2] 3638[7] 4185[3] (4908) 5581[3] 7467[5] *(8550)* ***(9441)***

Spirit Of Nelson (IRE) *J Reynier* a98 110
4 b m Mount Nelson Spirit Of Pearl (IRE) (Invincible Spirit (IRE))
(5229a) 6265a[5] 7477a[3] **(8584a)** 8969a[6]

Spirit Of Nicobar *Andrew Balding* a55 44
3 b f Dunaden(FR) Sweet Mandolin (Soviet Star (USA))
1824[13] ***2195[3]*** 4066[7] *4594[8] 5648[7]* 6400[9]

Spirit Of Sarwan (IRE) *Stef Keniry* a56 71
5 b g Elzaam(AUS) Hidden Heart (USA) (Kingmambo (USA))
1399[9] 2106[4] 2439[7] 3224[2] 3681[9] (3721) 4658[10] (4915)◆ **5933[4]** 6341[10] 6658[10] **(7513)** 8186[5] *8507[11]* 8862[12]

Spirit Of Scotland (USA)
R Bouresly a75 54
5 b h Girolamo(USA) Forty Greeta (ARG) (Roar (USA))
1322a[3]

Spiritofthenorth (FR) *Kevin Ryan* a51 69
2 br g Bated Breath Danlepordamsterdam (IRE) (War Front (USA))
5152[3] 5591[4] *7276[5]*

Spirit Of The Sky *Richard Fahey* 73
2 b f Swiss Spirit Clouds Rest (Showcasing)
7377[2]◆ **(7825)** 8097[5]

Spirit Of Wedza (IRE)
Julie Camacho a70 80
7 b g Footstepsinthesand Sampers (IRE) (Exceed And Excel (AUS))
1597[8] **(2433)** 4279[2] 4821[5] 5040[7] 5444[4] 6591[7] *8023[11] 8866[3] 9365[6] 9622[2]*

Spirit Of Zebedee (IRE)
John Quinn a67 54
6 gr g Zebedee Sampers (IRE) (Exceed And Excel (AUS))
(857) 1179[2] ***(1265) 1393[2]*** 1930[4] 2638[11] 3213[14] 3933[4] 4519[6] 4720[4] 5299[3] 5558[7] 6273[3] 6590[6] 7590[12]

Spirit Power *Eric Alston* a70 69
4 b g Swiss Spirit Verasina (USA) (Woodman (USA))
28[5] 236[8] (286) 411[2] ***(707)***◆ *1162[6]* 1817[7] 2632[14] 3413[9] (5180) 5952[8] *7959[10] 9498[10]*

Spirit Ridge *Amanda Perrett* 99
4 b g Nathaniel(IRE) Tates Creek (USA) (Rahy (USA))
2440[5] 3600[11] **7616[2]** 8005[4]

Spirit's Revench (FR)
P Demercastel a76 83
9 ch g Spirit One(FR) European Style (FR) (Ezzoud (IRE))
6521a[3]

Spiritual Boy (IRE) *David O'Meara* a55 46
3 b g Paco Boy(IRE) Spiritual Air (Royal Applause)
1979[4] *2517[9]* 2913[10] 3271[5] 4518[6] *5001[10]*

Spiritual Command (IRE)
Michael Dods 52
3 b g War Command(USA) Emeralds Spirit (IRE) (Rock Of Gibraltar (IRE))
3707[7]

Spiritually *Chris Wall* a58
3 b f Charm Spirit(IRE) Lalectra (King Charlemagne (USA))
384[3] *1139[9] 2592[8]*

Spiritual Man (IRE) *Jonjo O'Neill* a72 67
7 b g Lawman(FR) Vee Gita (IRE) (Vettori (IRE))
84[5] 622[2] ***1022[3]*** *1508[5]*

Spiritual Son (IRE) *Jarlath P Fahey* 72
2 b c Pour Moi(IRE) Million Spirits (IRE) (Invincible Spirit (IRE))
5710a[10]

Spiritual Star (IRE) *Paul George* a64 73
10 b g Soviet Star(USA) Million Spirits (IRE) (Invincible Spirit (IRE))
295[4] 701[6]◆ *942[10]* **1769[3]** 2215[5] 4479[9] *5003[12]*

Spiritulist *David Evans* 47
2 b c Fountain Of Youth(IRE) Spirit Glance (Invincible Spirit (IRE))
1931[7] **2275[6]** 3212[7]

Spirit Warning *Andrew Balding* a90 94
3 b g Charm Spirit(IRE) Averami (Averti (IRE))
134[2] (290)◆ *(561)*◆ *885[4]* 2035[2] 2559[2] *(3493)* 4399[3] **5312[2]** **(5991)** 6425[15] 7184[7]

Splash Around *Bernard Llewellyn* a42 56
5 ch g Nathaniel(IRE) Splashdown (Falbrav (IRE))
4190[6] ***5001[6]***

Splash Of Verve (IRE)
David Thompson a56 55
7 b g Fast Company(IRE) Ellistown Lady (IRE) (Red Sunset)
(208) 602[4] 782[5] 983[5] 1398[8] 1841[2] 2376[2] 3162[3] 3224[3] 4003[7] 4633[13] *5851[10]* 6502[3]

Splendidly *K R Burke* a87
2 ch g Garswood Regal Riband (Fantastic Light (USA))
(9392) ***(9514)***

Splinter *Richard Fahey* 79
2 b c Garswood Cracking Lass (IRE) (Whipper (USA))
8128[4]◆

Split Down South *Phil McEntee* a72 62
3 gr g Dark Angel(IRE) Brown Eyed Honey (Elusive City (USA))
7447[5] (8917) 9035[2] (9089)◆ ***9217[3]***◆ *9455[5]*◆

Spoken Words *John David Riches* a42 44
10 b m Fruits Of Love(USA) Jerre Jo Glanville (USA) (Skywalker (USA))
63[7] ***279[11]*** *1085[7] 4764[7]*

Spokesman (IRE)
Andrew Hollinshead a62 52
3 b g Alhebayeb(IRE) Xema (Danehill (USA))
3710a[11]

Spoof *Charles Hills* a86 95
4 b g Poet's Voice Filona (IRE) (Motivator)
1734[4] 2743[7] 3375[3] *3993[7]* 6724[7] 7524[3] 7894[8] *9214[7] 9549[5] 9660[9]*

Sporting Bill (IRE) *James Fanshawe* a49 61
4 br g Society Rock(IRE) Pandoras Secret (IRE) (Monashee Mountain (USA))
275[6] ***463[9]***

Sporting Chance *Simon Crisford* a85 102
3 b c Kodiac Elpida (USA) (Giant's Causeway (USA))
168a[12] 511a[3] *636a[4]* **(956a)** 2411[17] 3075[11]

Sporting Times *Ed Dunlop* a83 84
5 ch g Sir Percy Queen Of Iceni (Erhaab (USA))
6596[5] 7688[8]

Sports Reporter *Richard Fahey* a63 55
2 b c Dark Angel(IRE) By Invitation (USA) (Van Nistelrooy (USA))
7902[7] 8714[7] 9195[6]

Sporty Yankee (USA) *Aytach Sadik* a47 76
6 gr g Paddy O'Prado(USA) I Insist (USA) (Green Dancer (USA))
184[8] 345[8] 469[7]

Spotify (FR) *Charlie Appleby* a104 110
5 b g Redoute's Choice(AUS) Gwenseb (FR) (Green Tune (USA))
(398a) (844a) 1113a[7] 3678a[3]

Spot Lite *Rod Millman* a61 60
4 b g Compton Place High Class Girl (Royal Applause)
2483[13] 3036[6] 3527[10] 4772[3] 5084[2] 5393[9] 5582[2] 6365[3] 6639[2] 7230[13] 8450[8]

Spotton (IRE) *Rebecca Bastiman* a38 45
3 b g Tamayuz Farbenspiel (IRE) (Desert Prince (IRE))
133[11] 5477[9] 6177[4] 6575[6] 7486[9] 8025[14]

Spreadsheet (IRE) *Jim Boyle* a79 86
2 b g Exceed And Excel(AUS) Mundana (IRE) (King's Best (USA))
4290[2] 5059[2] 7160[3] 9569[4]

Spring Ability (IRE) *Laura Mongan* a52
4 b g Oasis Dream Because (IRE) (Sadler's Wells (USA))
145[6]

Spring Back (USA) *An Byung Ki* a97
3 b g Gemologist(USA) Frangible (USA) (Broken Vow (USA))
7010a[4]

Spring Bloom *K R Burke* 72
2 ch g Power Almond Branches (Dutch Art)
2903[2]◆ 3717[2] 4517[3]

Springbourne *Bill Turner* 76
5 b g Hellvelyn Musical Key (Key Of Luck (USA))
4116[3] 5959[7]

Spring Campaign (IRE)
Michael Bell 59
2 ch f Dandy Man(IRE) Doctrine (Barathea (IRE))
5243[6]

Spring Dixie (IRE)
Natalie Lloyd-Beavis a37 54
7 gr m Zebedee Dixie Jazz (Mtoto)
145[7] 385[8] 481[7] 859[13]

Spring Holly (IRE) *Milton Bradley* a20 21
3 b f Zebedee Blue Holly (IRE) (Blues Traveller (IRE))
848[11] 906[11] 2211[11] 5044[9] 5582[8] 6329[13]

Spring Loaded (IRE) *Paul D'Arcy* a110 111
7 gr g Zebedee Nisriyna (IRE) (Intikhab (USA))
2916[5] 4095[15]

Spring Of Love *Charlie Appleby* 82
2 b f Invincible Spirit(IRE) Desert Blossom (IRE) (Shamardal (USA))
(8093)

Spring Romance (IRE) *Dean Ivory* a80 81
4 bb g Zebedee Love And Devotion (Shamardal (USA))
763[4] 1061[9] 2339[12] (4303)◆ 5395[15] 9203[11] 9632[6]

Spring Run *Jonathan Portman* a41 63
3 ch f Nathaniel(IRE) May Fox (Zilzal (USA))
1739[6] 2361[7] 3092[5] 3809[4] 4345[4] 5242[4] 6400[2] (7202) 7818[13]

Spring Street (FR) *S Wattel* a74 74
2 gr f Penny's Picnic(IRE) Loshad (Lomitas)
7044a[5]

Spring To Freedom (IRE)
Mark Walford a51 16
3 b g Zebedee Liberty Grace (IRE) (Statue Of Liberty (USA))
612[12]

Spring To Mind *Ralph Beckett* a13 35
2 b f Archipenko(USA) Soft Morning (Pivotal)
7972[11] 8914[13]

Springvale Lad *Mark Loughnane* a51 39
2 b c Archipenko(USA) Combustible (IRE) (Halling (USA))
8516[14] 9500[10]

Springwood Drive *Tim Easterby* a55 78
3 b f Mayson Ocean Boulevard (Danehill Dancer (IRE))
4010[3]◆ 4439[2]◆ 5057[4] 5659[2] (5893) (6261)◆

Spun To Run (USA)
Juan Carlos Guerrero a118
3 b c Hard Spun(USA) Yawkey Way (USA) (Grand Slam (USA))
7480a[5] (8771a)

Spurofthemoment *Charles Hills* 55
2 b f Brazen Beau(AUS) Royal Blush (Royal Applause)
5132[8] 5859[8] 6159[7]

Sputnik Planum (USA)
Michael Appleby a78 91
5 b g Quality Road(USA) Shiva (JPN) (Hector Protector (USA))
2574[8] 3502[2] 3811[10] 5174[4] 6211[2] 7872[6] 8260[8] 8411[6]

Spy Fi *John Norton* a15
5 b m Dick Turpin(IRE) Sindarbella (Sinndar (IRE))
6662[5] 8020[7]

Spygate *Richard Fahey* 77
2 b c Brazen Beau(AUS) Virginia Hall (Medicean)
3703[5] 4516[2] 4910[4] 6375[20] 6822[4] 7763[2] 8395[2]

Square De Luynes (FR)
Niels Petersen 111
4 b g Manduro(GER) Power Girl (GER) (Dashing Blade)
(4419a) (6524a) (7498a)

Squats (IRE) *Ian Williams* a84 87
7 b g Dandy Man(IRE) Light Sea (IRE) (King's Best (USA))
2568[7] 3347[3]

Squelch *Rae Guest* a77 73
3 b f Dark Angel(IRE) Blancmange (Montjeu (IRE))
4189[10] 4341[6] 7572[3] 8206[5] 9047[2]

Squire *Marjorie Fife* a54 50
8 b g Teofilo(IRE) Most Charming (FR) (Darshaan)
125[8] 386[3] 552[2] 724[13] 1378[3] 1482[9] 1660[9] 2145[11] 5239[9] 5653[11] 6456[7] 6860[6] 7374[3] 7550[8] 8068[11] 8694[4] 8915[9]

Squizzy Boy (IRE) *Laura Mongan*
3 b g Sepoy(AUS) Run Of The Day (Three Valleys (USA))
4800[6]

Sri Prada (FR) *G Doleuze* a80 78
5 gr m Air Chief Marshal(IRE) Fenella's Link (Linamix (FR))
(7505a)

Sri Sene Power (IRE)
Richard Hannon a14 52
2 b f Dark Angel(IRE) Fanciful Dancer (Groom Dancer (USA))
2968[7] 5906[5]

Stade Velodrome (FR) *J Bourgeais* a71 60
3 bb g Evasive Stunning (USA) (Nureyev (USA))
1028a[8] 6789a[10] 9504a[10]

Staffa (IRE) *Denis Coakley* a63 61
6 b m Rock Of Gibraltar(IRE) Gabriellina Klon (IRE) (Ashkalani (IRE))
4026[6] 4556[8] 7557[10] 7757[13]

Stagehand *Charles Hills* a86 82
3 b f Kodiac Silent Entrance (Beat Hollow)
1828[9] (4732) 5198[3] 6736[2] 7466[4] 8608[9]

Stage Magic (IRE) *Charlie Appleby* 97
4 b g Dark Angel(IRE) Witnessed (Authorized (IRE))
514a[5] 730a[7]

Stage Play (IRE) *Michael Bell* 98
3 gr f Oasis Dream Boastful (IRE) (Clodovil (IRE))
5608[17] 6257[10]

Stag Horn *Archie Watson* 76
2 b c Golden Horn Starfala (Galileo (IRE))
7067[3] 7562[3] 8244[4]

Stagiaire *Ralph Beckett* a71
2 b f Sea The Moon(GER) So In Love (Smart Strike (CAN))
9052[12] 9327[7]

Stainforth Swagger
Ronald Thompson
3 b g Havana Gold(IRE) Ferayha (IRE) (Cape Cross (IRE))
4328[15] 5389[13] 6502[12] 8942[12]

Stake Acclaim (IRE) *Dean Ivory* a102 111
7 b g Acclamation Golden Legacy (IRE) (Rossini (USA))
(1734) 3587[4] 6056[3] 6520a[2] 7254a[7] 7889[5] 9004[4] 9389[3]

Stallone (IRE) *Richard Spencer* a68 75
3 b g Dandy Man(IRE) Titian Queen (Tobougg (IRE))
1488[4]◆ 2482[9] (3771) 3887[3] 4507[3] 5056[5] 5622[7] 5985[2] 6598[5] 7828[3] (8008) (8207) 8413[6]

Stamford Raffles
Jane Chapple-Hyam a96 90
6 b g Champs Elysees Romantic Retreat (Rainbow Quest (USA))
432[2] (757) 980[3] 1917[10] 2801[7] 4381[14] (5686) 6411[5] 7616[5] 9206[8]

Stamp Duty (IRE) *Suzzanne France* a49 56
11 b g Ad Valorem(USA) Lothian Lass (IRE) (Daylami (IRE))
63[4]

Stamp Of Authority (IRE)
T G McCourt a52 62
7 b g Invincible Spirit(IRE) Silver Bracelet (Machiavellian (USA))
(7780)

Stanarley Pic *Susan Corbett* a42 67
8 b g Piccolo Harlestone Lady (Shaamit (IRE))
272[10]

Stand Firm (IRE) *Robert Cowell* a51 46
4 b g Kodiac Refuse To Give Up (IRE) (Refuse To Bend (IRE))
2235[8] 2741[9] 3007[7] 3687[3] 4378[11]

Stand Free *Suzzanne France* a54
2 b f Helmet(AUS) Ivory Silk (Diktat)
9163[8]

Stand N Deliver *Clive Cox* a65
5 b g Dick Turpin(IRE) Drifting Gold (Bold Edge)
138[7] 348[4] 925[2] 1176[6] 1836[10]

St Andrews (IRE) *Gillian Boanas* a64 61
6 ch g Rip Van Winkle(IRE) Stellavera (FR) (Anabaa (USA))
2217[7] 2684[4] 3272[9] 3653[4] 4510[11] 4825[2] 5435[7] 5727[6] 6256[4] 7053[3] 8344[3] 8635[3]

Stand To Attention (AUS)
Leon & Troy Corstens 98
2 b c Starspangledbanner(AUS) Baltics (AUS) (Fusaichi Pegasus (USA))
8137a[10]

Stanford (IRE) *Andrew Balding* a79
2 ch c Zoffany(IRE) Almost Always (IRE) (Galileo (IRE))
6926[3] 7814[2]

Staplegrove (IRE) *Stella Barclay* a20 53
4 b g Camelot Teddy Bears Picnic (Oasis Dream)
1232[10] 1418[17] 1813[4] 2106[8] 3046[10] 4365[10] 7820[8] 8345[9] 9220[13]

Star Alexander *Clive Cox* 90
2 ch f Starspangledbanner(AUS) Triggers Broom (IRE) (Arcano (IRE))
2565[3] (3835)◆ 4387[5] 8724[11]

Star Approach (IRE)
Ismail Mohammed a66
2 ch c New Approach(IRE) Starletina (IRE) (Sea The Stars (IRE))
9624[10]

Star Archer *Michael Easterby* a79 91
5 b g Champs Elysees Postale (Zamindar (USA))
6475[13] 6975[5] 7434[10] 8130[17] 8701[9] 9199[10]

Star Ascending (IRE)
Jennie Candlish a77 62
7 ch g Thousand Words Sakaka (Tobougg (IRE))
61[3]◆ (346) 803[8] 1159[7] 1508[6] 2202[5] (2696) 3321[5] 4208[7] 4601[8] 5122[7] 5728[6] 6499[3] 7544[5] 8186[3] 8664[4] 9496[3]

Star At Midnight *Jo Hughes* a31 53
3 b f Heeraat(IRE) Intense Feeling (IRE) (Intense Focus (USA))
7061a[6] 7476a[7]

Star Attraction (FR) *Tony Carroll* a40 46
4 b m Orpen(USA) Heaven (Reel Buddy (USA))
132[3] 553[11] 924[8] 3410[7] 5675[6] 6324[9]

Starbo (IRE) *John Quinn* 53
2 ch g Starspangledbanner(AUS) Jamesbo's Girl (Refuse To Bend (IRE))
7285[9] 7902[12] 8395[8]

Starcaster *Jedd O'Keeffe* a77 96
4 b g Dansili Shirocco Star (Shirocco (GER))
1761[2] (2748)

Starcat *Hughie Morrison* a86
2 ch c Lope De Vega(IRE) Purr Along (Mount Nelson)
(9415)◆

Star Catcher *John Gosden* a59 115
3 b f Sea The Stars(IRE) Lynnwood Chase (USA) (Horse Chestnut (SAF))
(1738) 2831[3] (4014) (5208a) (7252a) (8333)◆

Starchant *John Bridger* a48 56
3 b f Gregorian(IRE) Aegean Mystery (Dr Fong (USA))
520[4] 854[5] 1170[9] 1650[9] 2281[4] 3045[8] 4183[10] 5046[4] 5960[2] 6023[2] 6754[5] 7557[8] 7784[5] 9508[9] 9583[8] 9664[10]

Star Citizen *Fred Watson* a30 45
7 b g New Approach(IRE) Faslen (USA) (Fasliyev (USA))
8339[5] 9113[14]

Star Command (IRE) *Denis Coakley* a22
3 b f War Command(USA) Megaspiel (Singspiel (IRE))
7114[8] 7841[10]

Star Cracker (IRE) *Jim Goldie* a52 46
7 ch g Starspangledbanner(AUS) Champagne Cracker (Up And At 'Em)
25[7] 129[9] 613[2] 742[5] 973[2] 1085[3] 1402[9] (2189) 2958[6] 3227[8] 3723[10] 4720[9] 5235[5] 5486[4] 5722[5] 6574[5] 7214[7] 7367[7] 7487[7] 7651[5] 8233[7] 8720[2]◆ 9398[9]

Starczewski (USA) *David Simcock* a86 84
3 b g Magician(IRE) Lucifer's Stone (USA) (Horse Chestnut (SAF))
2518[5] 3093[2] 4176[2] 4549[2] (5355) (5943) 6471[9]

Starfield Song (IRE) *Iain Jardine* 28
2 b f Cappella Sansevero Feabhas (IRE) (Spectrum (IRE))
3679[9] 4778[5]

Starfighter *Ed Walker* 85
3 b g Sea The Stars(IRE) Starlit Sands (Oasis Dream)
2082[7] 3195[3]◆ 4392[5] 4841[2] 5355[2] 6463[2] (6909) 7413[6] 8092[16]

Stargazer (IRE) *Philip Kirby* a109 100
6 b g Canford Cliffs(IRE) Star Ruby (IRE) (Rock Of Gibraltar (IRE))
349[2] 519[3] (1483)◆

Star Guide (GER) *David Menuisier* a44 55
3 b g Maxios Summarily (IRE) (Shamardal (USA))
1417[10] 6290[10] 6887[7] 7240[10]

Star In The Making *Clive Cox* 86
2 b f Muhaarar Lonely Ahead (USA) (Rahy (USA))
2915[2] 6159[2] (6846) 7696[14]

Starkers *Tom Clover* a37
3 ch f Mukhadram Undress (IRE) (Dalakhani (IRE))
5004[6]

Starlight *Michael Bell* 40
3 b f Iffraaj Ighraa (IRE) (Tamayuz)
1855[10] 2250[7] 4120[9] 4485[7]

Starlight Red (IRE) *Charles Hills* a70 68
3 gr f Sea The Stars(IRE) Turning Point (Dalakhani (IRE))
1592[3] 2521[11] 3311[11] (4179) 4761[9]

Starlight Romance (IRE)
Richard Fahey a81 80
5 b m Excelebration(IRE) Takizada (IRE) (Sendawar (IRE))
351[5]◆ 805[7] 1234[3]◆ 1916[12] 2809[2] 3308[10] 4072[7] 5453[9] 6379[14] 6974[6] 7362[11]

Starmaniac *C Laffon-Parias* 100
3 b c Sea The Stars(IRE) Plumania (Anabaa (USA))
2314a[3] 3390a[15]

Star Of Athena *Ali Stronge* a66 62
4 b m Champs Elysees Aswaaq (IRE) (Peintre Celebre (USA))
2928[3] 3834[6] 6303[2] (8868) 9005[5] 9412[5] 9626[4]◆

Star Of Bengal *John Gosden* a110 105
4 b h Oasis Dream Stage Presence (IRE) (Selkirk (USA))
(3005) 3953[8] 6467[5] 7686[9]

Star Of Namibia (IRE)
Michael Mullineaux
9 b g Cape Cross(IRE) Sparkle Of Stones (FR) (Sadler's Wells (USA))
5897[6]

Star Of Southwold (FR)
Michael Appleby a100 98
4 bl g Le Havre(IRE) Into The Wild (FR) (Great Journey (JPN))
(157)◆ 625[2] 737[2] 1422[16] 2800[4] (4021) 4240[2] (5155) 6150[4] (6391) 7686[8] 9200[7] 9610[3]

Star Of St James (GER)
Richard Fahey 73
2 b g Equiano(FR) Slight Advantage (IRE) (Peintre Celebre (USA))
2892[6] 3265[2] 4302[4] 5390[6] 7064[5]

Star Of St Louis (FR) *Denis Quinn* a45 44
2 b c Style Vendome(FR) Momix (Selkirk (USA))
3990[11] 4564[8] 5059[6] 7275[6] 7833[4] 8526[5] 8825[6] 9438[6]

Star Of The Seas (NZ) *Chris Waller* 98
4 ch g Ocean Park(NZ) Stella Livia (Titus Livius (FR))
8768a[9]

Star Of Valour (IRE) *Lynn Siddall* a71 61
4 b g Invincible Spirit(IRE) Birthstone (Machiavellian (USA))
971[9] 1381[10] 1659[5] 2056[6] 2738[5] 3163[7] 5817[3] 6655[2] 7513[4] 8186[6] (8667) 9006[2] (9361)

Star Of War (USA) *Richard Hannon* a81 84
3 b f Declaration Of War(USA) Sunshine For Life (USA) (Giant's Causeway (USA))
(1287) 2144[2] 2552[4] 4052[18] 4841[5] 5687[5]

Star Of Wells (IRE) *William Haggas* a69 58
2 b c Sea The Stars(IRE) Seas Of Wells (IRE) (Dansili)
5345[5] 6185[4] 8012[2]

Starplex *Keith Dalgleish* a32 60
9 b g Multiplex Turtle Bay (Dr Fong (USA))
272[11] 1719[8] 1977[8] 2092[16] 2509[12] 2842[11] 8238[2]

Star Prize (IRE) *Noel Wilson* a54
2 b f Power In My Dreams (IRE) (Sadler's Wells (USA))
8297[6] 8714[9]

Star Quality *Mrs John Harrington* a77 79
5 b m Champs Elysees Starfan (USA) (Lear Fan (USA))
5597a[9]

Starry Eyes (USA) *Simon Crisford* a85 72
3 ch f Animal Kingdom(USA) Starship Elusive (USA) (Elusive Quality (USA))
510a[5] 845a[7]

Star Safari *Charlie Appleby* 93
3 b g Sea The Stars(IRE) Intimhir (IRE) (Muhtathir)
6005a[6]

Star's Daughter *Lucinda Egerton* 16
2 b f Fast Company(IRE) Michelle Shift (Night Shift (USA))
2316[4] 3033[5] 4910[5]

Star Shield *David O'Meara* a89 90
4 ch g Helmet(AUS) Perfect Star (Act One)
1561[7] 2372[4]◆ 2898[5] 3649[3] (4322) 4566[2] (4867)◆ 5693[5] 6460[2] 7312[2] 7906[3] 8918[6]

Starship Jubilee (USA)
Kevin Attard 112
6 b m Indy Wind(USA) Perfectly Wild (USA) (Forest Wildcat (USA))
6491a[3] (7224a) (8154a)

Stars In The Night (IRE)
Kevin Ryan a76 67
2 b f Starspangledbanner(AUS) On The Dark Side (IRE) (Kheleyf (USA))
1923[3] 2561[3] 3244[5] 5243[5] 6053[4]

Stars In The Sky *William Haggas* a41 74
2 b f Galileo(IRE) Maureen (IRE) (Holy Roman Emperor (IRE))
5366[5] 6205[2] 6926[9] 8760[8]

Star Talent (IRE) *Gay Kelleway* a69 69
3 b g Lilbourne Lad(IRE) High Vintage (IRE) (High Chaparral (IRE))
2519a[6] 3584[8] 4459[4] 4779[3] 5654[6] 6030[7] 7035[3] 8200[4] 9279[9]◆ 9646[7]

Startego *Archie Watson* a60 71
3 b g New Approach(IRE) Tafiya (Bahri (USA))
1697[6] 3170[9] 3580[8] 4000[4] 4473[6]

Star Terms *Richard Hannon* 102
3 ch f Sea The Stars(IRE) Best Terms (Exceed And Excel (AUS))
1751[4]◆ 2443[11] 2831[4] 3762[2] (4964a) 6003a[2] 7118[5] 7658[7]

Start Time (IRE) *Paul Midgley* a48 79
6 b g Invincible Spirit(IRE) Silca's Sister (Inchinor)
1457[8] 3318[8] 3868[11] 4879[9] (5488) 6179[7] 6677[4] 7289[15] 7621[9] 8342[8]

State Crown (IRE) *Charlie Appleby* a76
2 ch c New Approach(IRE) Patroness (Dubawi (IRE))
6632[3]◆

State Of Affair (USA) *Ed Walker* a84 81
3 ch g Giant's Causeway(USA) Circumstances (IRE) (Galileo (IRE))
1756[8] 2336[5] (4549) 5347[4] 6736[5] (7816)

Station To Station *Clive Cox* a62 66
2 b g Cacique(IRE) Jubilant Queen (Kyllachy)
5186[7] 6424[8] 8494[10]

Statuario *Richard Spencer* a75 84
4 b g Helmet(AUS) Cat Hunter (One Cool Cat (USA))
3973[5] 4548[4] 5178[2] 6289[7]

Staxton *Tim Easterby* a105 103
4 b g Equiano(FR) Snake's Head (Golden Snake (USA))
2117[3]◆ 2743[13] 3602[8] 3863[8] (4379) 5120[3] 5454[14] 6229[5] 7433[10] 8127[18] 8425[13]

Staxton Hill *Richard Fahey* a40 41
2 gr g Outstrip Snake's Head (Golden Snake (USA))
4937[7] 5856[10] 8631[8]

Staycation (IRE) *Rebecca Bastiman* a75 76
3 b g Acclamation Staceymac (IRE) (Elnadim (USA))
1504[3] 1894[2] 2293[2] 2937[2]

Staycee *Rod Millman* 45
2 ch f Bated Breath Under Milk Wood (Montjeu (IRE))
4223[8] 4992[10] 6640[7]

Stay Classy (IRE) *Richard Spencer* a94 90
3 ch f Camacho Hollow Green (IRE) (Beat Hollow)
1751[9] 4052[19] 4891[5] 5705[7] 6379[18] 6999[6] 7613[9] 8766[9] (9126) 9278[2]◆ (9424)◆ 9625[3]◆

Stay Forever (FR) *Andrew Balding* a65 68
3 br f Harbour Watch(IRE) Stybba (Medicean)
66[6] 360[6] 930[2] 1171[9] 3887[2] 4378[6] 5137[2] (5561) 6084[4] 7977[12]

Stay In The Light *Roger Ingram* a52 51
4 b m Showcasing Starlight Walk (Galileo (IRE))
207[8] 479[11] 1353[10] 3279[6] 3691[5] 4346[14] 9426[11]

St Brelades Bay (IRE)
Mrs John Harrington a94 92
7 b g Camacho Tides (Bahamian Bounty)
3062a[6]

Stealth Command *Murty McGrath* a63
2 b g War Command(USA) Akhila (IRE) (Dalakhani (IRE))
7787[6] 9243[9]

Steal The Scene (IRE) *Kevin Frost* a69 58
7 b g Lord Shanakill(USA) Namoos (USA) (Sahm (USA))
33[6] 315[5] 944[5] 1660[10] 5526[8] 6327[4] 6731[7] 7859[5] 8299[5] 8667[9]◆ (9039) (9503) (9566)

Stealth Fighter (IRE)
Saeed bin Suroor a86 96
4 b g Kodiac Green Chorus (IRE) (Oratorio (IRE))
1561[4] (2022) 2742[12] 3515[8] (4450) 6537[2]

Steaming (IRE) *Ralph Beckett* a66 71
5 b g Rail Link Dazzling Day (Hernando (FR))
2254[5] 3145[5] 5179[7]

Steccando (IRE) *Rebecca Menzies*
6 b g Lawman(FR) Second Act (Sadler's Wells (USA))
5001[11]

St Edward's Crown (AUS)
Shane Fliedner 94
2 bb f Epaulette(AUS) Patina (AUS) (Anabaa (USA))
8135a[10]

Steel Helmet (IRE) *William Bethell* a56 49
5 ch g Helmet(AUS) Marine City (JPN) (Carnegie (IRE))
39[8] 593[5] (3447) 4914[4] 5271[2] (5435) (6046) 6552[5]

Steel Prince (IRE)
Anthony Freedman 107
5 b g Nathaniel(IRE) Steel Princess (IRE) (Danehill (USA))
8600a[7] 8844a[9]

Steelriver (IRE) *Michael Herrington* a83 64
9 b g Iffraaj Numerus Clausus (FR) (Numerous (USA))
129[2] 279[3] 742[2] (882) 1016[3] 1357[5] 1597[3] (1686) (1766) 2153[2] (2940) 3203[3] 3492[5] 5000[4] 5299[2] 5559[14] 6027[5] 8649[3] 8866[2] 9257[2] 9402[5]

Steel Train (FR) *David O'Meara* a84 82
8 b g Zafeen(FR) Silent Sunday (IRE) (Testa Rossa (AUS))
212[5] 381[6] 466[5]

Steeve *Rod Millman* 77
3 ch g Lethal Force(IRE) Club Tahiti (Hernando (FR))
3261[7] 3885[7] 5450[3] 5858[2] 6083[3] 6671[6] 7465[8] 7973[5]

Stela Star (IRE) *Thomas Mullins* a75 102
2 b f Epaulette(AUS) Compostela (Sea The Stars (IRE))
(8356a)

Stellar Mass (IRE) *Carina Fey* a93 93
6 b h Sea The Stars(IRE) Juno Marlowe (IRE) (Danehill (USA))
1309a[6] 1777a[6] 9210a[7]

Stellina (GER) *P Schiergen* 58
2 ch f Neatico(GER) Startsissima (Green Tune (USA))
8371a[9]

Stelvio (FR) *A Giorgi* 83
2 b g Style Vendome(FR) Sabi Sabi (FR) (Orpen (USA))
2315a[2] 4679a[7]

Stepaside Boy *David Evans* 37
3 b g Dick Turpin(IRE) Mookhlesa (Marju (IRE))
2900[10] 3353[4] 4927[6]

Stepney Causeway *Michael Bell* a75 51
2 b c New Approach(IRE) Wake Up Call (Noverre (USA))
4886[12] (8914)

Step To The Beat *Clive Cox* a56
2 b c Fast Company(IRE) Dance Express (IRE) (Rail Link)
8060[6] 9130[11]

Sterling Price *James Eustace* a55
3 b g War Command(USA) Chantry (Galileo (IRE))
2938[7] 4590[8]

Sterling Stamp (IRE) *Paul Cole* a73 51
2 b c Teofilo(IRE) Aneedah (IRE) (Invincible Spirit (IRE))
4184[11] 7569[3] 8058[2] 8297[9] 8856[4]

Stevie Smith *Amy Murphy* 24
3 b f Roderic O'Connor(IRE) Poem (IRE) (Dylan Thomas (IRE))
4779[6] 5955[8]

Stewardess (IRE) *Richard Fahey* a70 76
4 gr m Dandy Man(IRE) Smart Hostess (Most Welcome)
3201[5] 3658[5] 4149[4] (4660) 5392[10] 6220[16] 6972[14] 7656[8]

Stex (IRE) *R Dzubasz* 100
3 b f Lord Of England(GER) Sun Society (GER) (Law Society (USA))
3639a[3] 4622a[5] 6747a[4] 8587a[6]

Still In Deauville (IRE)
Miss V Haigh a48 43
3 ch f Camacho Mastoora (IRE) (Acclamation)
216a[8]

Still Standing (IRE)
Mrs John Harrington 101
4 ch g Mastercraftsman(IRE) Il Palazzo (USA) (Giant's Causeway (USA))
(1309a) 1777a[4] 7038a[9]

Stirred (USA) *Michael McCarthy* a95
3 b f Shakin It Up(USA) Fay Na Na (USA) (Majestic Warrior (USA))
9638a[7]

Stittenham *Michael Easterby* 7
2 b f Helmet(AUS) Kibenga (Oasis Dream)
1642[13] 2780[11] 3212[8]

Stittenham Wood *Michael Easterby* a53 60
2 br g Garswood Handsome Molly (Halling (USA))
7388[4] 7765[3]◆

Stivers (ARG) *D K Weld* 88
5 gr h Lasting Approval(USA) Salapaia (ARG) (Hidden Prize (USA))
6712[5] 7218a[9] 8784a[10]

St Ives *William Haggas* a79 77
2 b c Cable Bay(IRE) Galaktea (IRE) (Statue Of Liberty (USA))
2973[5] 3866[3]◆ (4826)◆ 5853[2]◆ 6375[9] 7409[5] 7679[4] 8219[8]

St Just *William Haggas* a73 34
2 b c Golden Horn Alfajer (Mount Nelson)
8464[13] 8810[7] 9323[5] (9665)

Stockbridge Tap *James Bethell* 68
2 ch c Nayef(USA) Last Supper (Echo Of Light)
5894[3]

Stonebridge (FR) *C Alonso Pena* 78
4 gr h Silver Frost(IRE) Vingt Six (FR) (Octagonal (NZ))
5035a[6]

Stone Circle (IRE) *Michael Bell* 94
2 ch c No Nay Never(USA) Candlehill Girl (IRE) (Shamardal (USA))
3419[4] 4482[4] (5172) 5587[4] (7247a) 8125[9]

Stone Cougar (USA)
Mark Johnston 69
3 ch f Kitten's Joy(USA) Fitful Skies (IRE) (Dubawi (IRE))
1975[5] 2289[4] 2731[8] 3219[3] 3965[3] (4038) 4372[4]

Stone Mason (IRE) *Roger Charlton* 71
3 b c Pivotal Victoria Star (IRE) (Danehill (USA))
2505[3] 3248[6] 3860[6] 5779[7]◆

Stone Of Destiny *Andrew Balding* a106 103
4 b g Acclamation Irishstone (IRE) (Danehill Dancer (IRE))
352[3]◆ 563[3]◆ 892a[2] 1295[7] 1919[10] 3347[8] 4095[13] 4896[6] 5664[8] (5927) 6351[19] 6953[8] 7433[18]

Stone Princess (IRE) *Brian Ellison* 55
2 gr f Camacho Stone Roses (IRE) (Zebedee)
1893[5] 2415[5] 4433[9]

Stone Soldier *James Given* a81 85
2 ch c Mayson La Adelita (IRE) (Anabaa (USA))
3290[4] 4984[4] 5780[3] (6980) (7679) 8095[13] 9364[9]

Stone The Crows *Iain Jardine* a87 87
5 b g Cape Cross(IRE) Stars In Your Eyes (Galileo (IRE))
2080[9] 2680[5]

Stone Tornado *C Ferland* 99
3 b f Toronado(IRE) Irishstone (IRE) (Danehill Dancer (IRE))
2161a[13] 6142a[10] 7503a[2]

Stoneyford Lane (IRE)
Steph Hollinshead a68 68
5 b g Bushranger(IRE) Peace Talks (Pivotal)
187[9] 1973[8] 2632[11] 3199[10] 3550[7] 4182[12] 5633[12] 6051[5] 7024[6] 7236[5] 7779[8]

Stoney Lane *Richard Whitaker* a76 79
4 b g Mayson Spin A Wish (Captain Rio)
2146[3]◆ (2507) 2823[4] 3813[7] 4303[4] 5692[13] 6339[2] 6699[12] 7621[10] 8087[3]

Stonific (IRE) *David O'Meara* a55 71
6 b g Sea The Stars(IRE) Sapphire Pendant (IRE) (Danehill Dancer (IRE))
(1461) 1761[5] 6067[5] 6975[4] 7510[5] 7907[6] 8185[4]

Stony Look (IRE) *Andrew Balding* a61
2 b f Passing Glance Chesil Beach (Phoenix Reach (IRE))
7515[4] 8058[4] 8700[13]

Stopdworldnletmeof *David Flood* a52 53
5 b g Piccolo Dilli Dancer (Dansili)
177[6] 357[8] 597[8]

Stop Going On (IRE) *David Evans*
2 b f Gutaifan(IRE) Classic Style (IRE) (Desert Style (IRE))
6040[5]

Stopnsearch *Brett Johnson* a45 25
2 b g War Command(USA) Secret Suspect (Invincible Spirit (IRE))
5314[12] 6719[10]

Storm Ahead (IRE) *Tim Easterby* a85 81
6 b g Iffraaj Loose Julie (IRE) (Cape Cross (IRE))
2480[2] 2710[11] 3567[8] (3880) 4239[10]◆ 5200[5] 5516[4] 5820[2] 6231[8] 6370[4] 6961[10] 7363[3] 8197[3] 8761[8] (9041)◆ 9285[2] 9480[3] 9628[7]

Storm Approaching
James Fanshawe a58 36
3 b f Dawn Approach(IRE) Dubai Cyclone (USA) (Bernardini (USA))
2488[11] 3247[9] 8467[3]

Storm At Dawn (IRE)
Ismail Mohammed a43
2 b f Dawn Approach(IRE) Portland River (FR) (Stormy River (FR))
9158[9]

Storm Blitz (IRE) *Robert Cowell* a52 37
3 b g Dandy Man(IRE) Stormy View (USA) (Cozzene (USA))
186[6]

Stormbomber (CAN) *Ed Walker* a82 60
3 ch g Stormy Atlantic(USA) Swanky Bubbles (CAN) (Ascot Knight (CAN))
2094[6]◆ 3302[6] 3764[10] 5284[2] 5730[2] 6350[3] 6840[2] 7560[3] 8087[2]◆ (8507)

Storm Boy *Michael Attwater* a55
4 b h Paco Boy(IRE) Evenstorm (USA) (Stephen Got Even (USA))
359[11] 919[3]◆

Stormbringer *Gavin Hernon* a87 95
4 b g Dutch Art Riva Royale (Royal Applause)
2648a[3] 4948a[6]

Storm Eleanor *Hughie Morrison* a65 46
3 b f Mukhadram Alkhana (IRE) (Dalakhani (IRE))
2354[10] 5592[5] 6187[4] 6595[5] 7629[6] 8345[3] 9279[7]

Storm Girl *Sarah-Jayne Davies*
3 b f Paco Boy(IRE) Evenstorm (USA) (Stephen Got Even (USA))
78[12] 1094[7] 1676[6] 3764[9] 9139[10]

Stormingin (IRE) *Gary Moore* a79 82
6 gr g Clodovil(IRE) Magadar (USA) (Lujain (USA))
1269[2] 1934[3] 3633[3] (4283) 5089[6] 6160[4] 7452[5] 8862[6]

Stormin Norman *Micky Hammond* 69
4 b g Sir Percy Roses (Muhtarram (USA))
2505[8] 3200[7] 3482[8] (4990) (5727)◆ 6256[3] 7381[3]

Stormin Tom (IRE) *Tim Easterby* a62 73
7 b g Dylan Thomas(IRE) She Storm (IRE) (Rainbow Quest (USA))
2080[11] 2591[11] 3481[4] 4400[8] 4782[4] (5739) 6586[3] 6933[8] 7439[4]

Storm Katy (FR) *M Boutin* a72 67
3 b f Sommerabend Anasy (USA) (Gone West (USA))
2090a[11] 3028a[2] 5408a[8]

Storm Lightning *Kevin Frost* a45 44
10 b g Exceed And Excel(AUS) All For Laura (Cadeaux Genereux)
26[5] 322[5] 357[3] 809[6] 1093[3] 2728[11] 2924[11] 5084[3] 6503[4] 7838[4] 9411[5]

Storm Melody *Ali Stronge* a68 81
6 b g Royal Applause Plume (Pastoral Pursuits)
249[3] 701[8] 924[3] 1037[6] 1820[4] 2929[4] (3527) 4230[13] (4494) (4926) 5291[5] 6335[5]

Storm Over (IRE) *Phillip Makin* a89 93
5 b g Elnadim(USA) Stormy View (USA) (Cozzene (USA))
1839[2] 2061[4] 2917[7] 3301[3] 3662[3] 3883[6] 8099[13] 8400[8] 9549[2]

Storm Steps (IRE) *Timothy Doyle* a72 62
4 br g Footstepsinthesand Travel Treat (IRE) (Kalanisi (IRE))
5599a[7]

Storm The Court (USA)
Peter Eurton a115
2 b c Court Vision(USA) My Tejana Storm (USA) (Tejano Run (USA))
(8749a)

Storm The Hill (USA)
Philip D'Amato 106
5 b m Get Stormy(USA) Thornhill (USA) (Good And Tough (USA))
7920a[9]

Storm Trooper (IRE) *Charlie Wallis* a53 78
8 b g Acclamation Maid To Order (IRE) (Zafonic (USA))
26[2] 118[3] 478[7] 597[9] 848[4]

Storm Wave (FR) *J-V Toux* 9
2 b c Charm Spirit(IRE) Enfant Modele (Peintre Celebre (USA))
5763a[9]

Stormwave (IRE) *Ralph Beckett* 61
3 b g Dalakhani(IRE) Celtic Slipper (IRE) (Anabaa (USA))
1737[8] 2833[6] 3604[7] 5311[11]

Storm Wings (IRE) *Jo Hughes* 25
2 b f Battle Of Marengo(IRE) Goodie Goodie (Shirocco (GER))
2275[8] 5166a[11]

Stormy Antarctic *Ed Walker* a109 116
6 ch g Stormy Atlantic(USA) Bea Remembered (Doyen (IRE))
(1793a) (2886a) 3948[11] 5483a[6]

Stormy Bay *Keith Dalgleish* 49
2 b g Cable Bay(IRE) Tarando (Equiano (FR))
2892[10] 3220[5] 3498[5] 4756[6] 5296[14]

Stormy Belle (IRE) *P A Fahy* a68 88
5 ch m Dandy Man(IRE) Herrera (IRE) (High Chaparral (IRE))
5597a[6] 8367a[8]

Stormy Blues *Nigel Hawke* a77 81
5 b g Sepoy(AUS) Miss Brown To You (IRE) (Fasliyev (USA))
88[6] 346[5] 473[2] 1169[4] 1329[12] 5311[13]

Stormy Girl (IRE) *David Loughnane* 86
2 ch f Night Of Thunder(IRE) Refusetolisten (IRE) (Clodovil (IRE))
4993[6] (7063)◆ 8125[5] 8724[5]

Stormy Liberal (USA) *Peter Miller* 120
7 b g Stormy Atlantic(USA) Vassar (USA) (Royal Academy (USA))
1442a[3] 8770a[8]

Storting *Mick Channon* 93
3 b g Iffraaj Stella Point (IRE) (Pivotal)
1756[5] 2120[2] 2769[3] 3248[2] 3885[4] 5667[5] (6259) 7153[2] 8514[6]

Story Begins (FR) *A Spanu* a56 64
4 ch m Never On Sunday(FR) Groovin High (USA) (Elusive Quality (USA))
3140a[5]

Story Of Light (IRE)
Charlie Appleby a85 76
2 b g Dark Angel(IRE) Beautiful Ending (Exceed And Excel (AUS))
2780[5] (9043) 9385[2]

Stosur (IRE) *Gay Kelleway* a62 67
8 b m Mount Nelson Jules (IRE) (Danehill (USA))
39[7] 399[9]

St Ouen (IRE) *K Kukk* a45 45
3 b c Alhebayeb(IRE) Heat (King's Best (USA))
4686a[9] 6010a[6]

Stoweman *Clive Cox* 79
2 gr g Lethal Force(IRE) Poetic Dancer (Byron)
5447[2]◆ 6079[2] (6528) 7725[6]

St Patrick's Day (USA) *A P O'Brien* a106 106
4 b h Pioneerof The Nile(USA) Littleprincessemma (USA) (Yankee Gentleman (USA))
3103a[9] 3818a[10]

St Peters Basilica (IRE)
John Gosden a74 78
3 b c Galileo(IRE) Crystal Gaze (IRE) (Rainbow Quest (USA))
(367)

Stradivarius (IRE) *John Gosden* a80 123
5 ch h Sea The Stars(IRE) Private Life (FR) (Bering)
(2807) (4015) (5522) (6421) (7148) 8332[2]

Straight Ash (IRE) *Ollie Pears* a61 70
4 gr g Zebedee Blackangelheart (IRE) (Danehill Dancer (IRE))
1659[7] 2478[3] 3053[2] 3305[3] 3567[5] 4657[3] 5214[9] 6103[2] 6573[6] 7542[3] 8087[9]

Straight Right (FR) *Andrew Balding* a113 83
5 b g Siyouni(FR) Sailor Moon (IRE) (Tiger Hill (IRE))
89[2] 351[2] 1922[7] 2609[18] 4095[23] 9472[5]

Strait Of Hormuz (IRE)
Andrew Balding a79 77
2 b g Sir Percy Sliabh Luachra (IRE) (High Chaparral (IRE))
3601[9] 6858[2] (7677)

Straitouttacompton *Ivan Furtado* a66 67
3 b g Compton Place Red Mischief (IRE) (Red Clubs (IRE))
1819[10] 2529[7] 7048[4]◆ 7441[6] 8019[4] 9367[5]

Strait Run (IRE) *Micky Hammond* 37
8 ch g Rock Of Gibraltar(IRE) Gentlemen's Guest (USA) (Gentlemen (ARG))
1663[5]

Strange Brew *Michael Attwater* a43
2 b f Helmet(AUS) Baylini (Bertolini (USA))
9585[10]

Strategic (IRE) *Eric Alston* a39 52
4 b g Kodiac Run To Jane (IRE) (Doyoun)
2681[9] 3682[7] (4515) 4990[14] 6180[12] 6828[8] 7739[7]

Strategic Heights (IRE)
Richard Spencer a52 47
10 b g Strategic Prince Shot Of Redemption (Shirley Heights)
1061[12]

Strathspey Stretto (IRE)
Marcus Tregoning 31
4 ch m Kyllachy Rhythm And Rhyme (IRE) (Elnadim (USA))
4421[6] 5448[5]

Stratification (USA) *John Gosden* a78 76
3 ch f Australia Rags To Riches (USA) (A.P. Indy (USA))
2771[3] 6438[3]

Stratton Street (USA) *S Seemar* a83 90
5 br g Street Cry(IRE) Ihtifal (Dansili)
285a[6]

Stratum *W P Mullins* a102 110
6 b g Dansili Lunar Phase (IRE) (Galileo (IRE))
4382[10] (8114)

Strawberryandcream
James Bethell a62 68
4 ch m Cityscape Miss Apricot (Indian Ridge (IRE))
117[8] 784[14] (5041)◆ 5816[5] 6461[2] 6825[6] 7762[5] 8924[10] 9396[4]

Strawberry Hind (IRE)
Mick Channon 74
2 b f Kodiac Fonseca (IRE) (Red Clubs (IRE))
2996[7] 5906[2] 6442[2] 6919[12]

Strawberry Jack *George Scott* a90 81
3 b g Foxwedge(AUS) Strawberry Leaf (Unfuwain (USA))
1140[2] 1720[2] 2055[2] 2200[3] 2927[3] (3273) 3569[4] 4300[7] 4872[7] 5839[7] (9048) 9176[2]

Strawberry Morn (IRE)
W McCreery 47
2 ch f Dream Ahead(USA) Morning Jewel (IRE) (Dalakhani (IRE))
7247a[20]

Strawman (IRE) *Adrian Nicholls* 80
2 b c Starspangledbanner(AUS) Youve Got A Friend (IRE) (Alhaarth (IRE))
6065[4] 6673[2] (7067) 7699[3]

Streaker *Kevin Ryan* 71
2 b c Showcasing La Napoule (Piccolo)
2957[6] 4688[2] 5815[6] 6356[10] 7827[11]

Streamline *Clive Cox* a101 97
2 b c Due Diligence(USA) Ahwahnee (Compton Place)
(5288) (5729) 6474[3] (6966)

Street Band (USA) *J Larry Jones* a113
3 ch f Istan(USA) Street Minstrel (USA) (Street Cry (IRE))
(7479a) 8775a[8]

Street Jester *Robert Stephens* a47 53
5 b g Avonbridge Street Diva (USA) (Street Cry (IRE))
3571[11] (4777) 5290[5] 7231[13]

Street Life *Richard Fahey* a56 54
2 ch g Hot Streak(IRE) Atheera (IRE) (Shamardal (USA))
3451[7] 4238[5] 5388[8] 6032[3] 6683[4] 7309[8] 8085[5] 8315[4]

Street Of Dreams *Doug Watson* a97 69
6 b h Shamardal(USA) Express Way (ARG) (Ahmad (ARG))
172a[8]

Streeton (IRE) *Ralph Beckett* a61
2 b g Siyouni(FR) Graphic Guest (Dutch Art)
7769[4]◆ 8418[5] 8912[5]

Street Parade *Stuart Williams* a100 104
3 b g Swiss Spirit Jollification (IRE) (Acclamation)
(3166)◆ 3855[7] 4122[2] 4847[17] 5504[15] 5927[10] 6476[17] 6859[2]

Street Poet (IRE)
Michael Herrington a79 82
6 b g Poet's Voice Street Star (USA) (Street Cry (IRE))
603[5] 784[10] 1271[3]◆ 1983[3] 2596[11] 2692[2] 2944[2]◆ (3429) (4194) (4767) (5283) 6026[4] 6961[17] 7856[4] 8122[7] 9480[10] 9628[10]

Streets Of Avalon (AUS)
Shane Nichols 112
4 b g Magnus(AUS) Kamuniak (NZ) (Black Minnaloushe (USA))
8138a[11] (8360a) 8768a[8]

Strelka *Ralph Beckett* a83 80
3 b f Kingman Soviet Moon (IRE) (Sadler's Wells (USA))
5748[2] 6438[2] (7081) 7900[9]

Strict (IRE) *Michael Appleby* a59 66
3 b g Slade Power(IRE) Thawrah (IRE) (Green Desert (USA))
2790[9] 3277[5] 3696[6] 4225[3] 8646[8] 8949[10] 9279[6]

Strictly Art (IRE) *Alan Bailey* a64 66
6 b g Excellent Art Sadinga (IRE) (Sadler's Wells (USA))
404[6] 946[7] 1235[6] 1815[6] 2974[2] 3175[7] 4216[9] 6278[9] 6853[8] 8551[8]

Strictly Legal (IRE) *David O'Meara* a37 25
3 b f Lawman(FR) Sensational Samba (IRE) (Exceed And Excel (AUS))
6587[7] 7287[5] 8467[9] 9139[12]

Strict Tempo *Andrew Balding* a87 88
3 ch f Norse Dancer(IRE) Strictly Dancing (IRE) (Danehill Dancer (IRE))
2144[5] 3293[5] 4922[7] 5450[2] 5773[2] 6346[2] 7176[3] 7836[2]◆

Striding Edge (IRE) *Mark Johnston* a66 66
2 b c Canford Cliffs(IRE) Assault On Rome (IRE) (Holy Roman Emperor (IRE))
4246[6] 5339[3] 6757[4] 7315[5] 8665[10]

Strike Bomber (FR)
Andrea Marcialis a73 75
3 ch g Le Havre(IRE) Now Again (GER) (Lomitas)
1450a[6] 3675a[7] 5407a[6]

Striking Approach *Roger Charlton* a63 65
2 b c New Approach(IRE) Nazli (IRE) (Invincible Spirit (IRE))
6409[4] 9252[6]

Strindberg *Marcus Tregoning* a57 52
3 b c Sea The Moon(GER) Summer Night (Nashwan (USA))
3664[7] 4443[5] 6392[5]

Strings Of Life *H-A Pantall* a88 87
3 b f Slade Power(IRE) Nashama (IRE) (Pivotal)
1199a[11]

Stringybark Creek
David Loughnane a80 85
5 b g Bushranger(IRE) Money Note (Librettist (USA))
1695[2] 2057[8] 2898[2] (3957) 4283[9] 5597a[7] 6370[6] 6734[6] 7145[4] 7540[7] 8515[19] (9054) 9173[5] 9329[3] 9658[8]

Strive For Glory (USA)
Robert Cowell a72 101
2 b c Dialed In(USA) Chu And You (USA) (You And I (USA))
(2184) 3023[3]◆ 4012[4] (4580a)

Strong And Stable (FR)
Mme Pia Brandt a91 92
4 b m Motivator Adjudicate (Dansili)
5229a[7]

Strong Power (IRE) *George Scott* a75 84
2 b g Kodiac Soft Power (IRE) (Balmont (USA))
1416[2] 1887[4] (2362) 6548[3] 8097[4] 8817[8]

Strong Steps *Jim Goldie* a78 75
7 br g Aqlaam Wunders Dream (IRE) (Averti (IRE))
1644[6] 2439[4] 2959[2] 3502[15] 3922[10] 4058[3] 4693[8]◆ 4982[2] 5117[2] (5490) 6204[12] 6460[10]

Stronsay (IRE) *Bryan Smart* 74
3 b g Gale Force Ten Perfect Blossom (One Cool Cat (USA))
1846[6] 2371[2] 3249[7] 3930[3] 4781[4] 5335[4] 6176[11] 8070[11]

Stroxx (IRE) *Tim Easterby* a65 74
2 b g Camacho Labisa (IRE) (High Chaparral (IRE))
5396[4] 6622[3] 7179[2]◆ 8297[4]

Structor (USA) *Chad C Brown* 109
2 b c Palace Malice(USA) Miss Always Ready (USA) (More Than Ready (USA))
(8746a)

Stubbins (USA) *Doug O'Neill* a100 117
3 b c Morning Line(USA) Sierra Vista (Atraf)
1443a[6] 8770a[4]◆

Stuckinthemoment (IRE) *D Chenu* 12
3 b g Society Rock(IRE) Gift Of Time (Cadeaux Genereux)
6061a[10]

Study Of Man (IRE) *P Bary* 118
4 b h Deep Impact(JPN) Second Happiness (USA) (Storm Cat (USA))
2168a[2] 3122a[2] 6004a[6]

Stunning Spirit *F Head* a105 110
5 b h Invincible Spirit(IRE) Stunning View (USA) (Dynaformer (USA))
3030a[3] 3879a[2] 5926a[2] 7255a[6]

Styledargent (FR) *J-P Gauvin* 97
3 b c Style Vendome(FR) Feriadargent (FR) (Kendargent (FR))
6385a[3]

Stylehunter *John Gosden* a93 105
4 ch g Raven's Pass(USA) Sunday Bess (JPN) (Deep Impact (JPN))
3605[3] 3987[4] 4935[18]

Style Major (FR) *Mlle V Dissaux* a22 28
2 b c Style Vendome(FR) Major's Love (FR) (Majorien)
8447a[10]

Style Presa (FR) *Rod Collet* a68 106
4 gr m Style Vendome(FR) Sorpresa (USA) (Pleasant Tap (USA))
2670a[4] (7503a)

Stylistique *Roger Varian* a80 109
2 b f Dansili Sleek (Oasis Dream)
5342[3]◆ 5733[2] 6444[4] 7117[2] 7659[2] 8089[7]

Suakin (IRE) *John Gosden* a50 62
3 b f Motivator Adeste (Dansili)
1824[6] 2017[6] 3153[5] 9201[9]

Suave Richard (JPN)
Yasushi Shono 121
5 ch h Heart's Cry(JPN) Pirramimma (USA) (Unbridled's Song (USA))
1446a[3] (9153a)

Subaana (IRE) *Roger Varian* 88
3 b f Cape Cross(IRE) Suba (USA) (Seeking The Gold (USA))
(5627)

Subedar (AUS) *James Cummings* 104
2 cg g Sepoy(AUS) Virage De Fortune (AUS) (Anabaa (USA))
8137a[4]

Subjectivist *Mark Johnston* a87 95
2 b c Teofilo(IRE) Reckoning (IRE) (Danehill Dancer (IRE))
3551[2] 4106[2] (4588)◆ 5415[6] 6417[2] 6957[4] 8111[7]

Subliminal *Simon Dow* a70 50
4 b g Arcano(IRE) Rare Virtue (USA) (Empire Maker (USA))
246[3] 559[5] 923[5] (1183) 1297[2] 1591[3] 2202[11] 3429[4] 4028[2] 4194[7] 5570[9] 6317[14] 6717[7] 8499[8] 9209[3]◆ 9426[3] 9657[10]

Subutai (IRE) *Clive Cox* 58
2 b g Camacho The Hermitage (IRE) (Kheleyf (USA))
3008[5] 4394[9]

Subway Dancer (IRE) *Z Koplik* a101 116
7 b g Shamardal(USA) Sub Rose (IRE) (Galileo (IRE))
3122a[9] 5079a[5] 6144a[4] (8378a)

Success Days (IRE) *K J Condon* 108
7 gr h Jeremy(USA) Malaica (FR) (Roi Gironde (IRE))
1777a[8] 2573[3] 3678a[5] 6004a[7] 7007a[10]

Sucellus *John Gosden* a89 96
3 b c Dansili Primevere (IRE) (Singspiel (IRE))
1419[2] 2113[2] 3011[3] (7342)

Such Promise *Mike Murphy* a56 56
3 b g Dansili Much Promise (Invincible Spirit (IRE))
1516[11] 2735[10] 3442[5] 5430[9] 6284[7] 7105[7] 7838[10] 8417[13]

Sudfaa (FR) *M Le Forestier* a64 75
4 ch m Sri Putra Montagne Lointaine (IRE) (Numerous (USA))
7676a[6]

Sudona *Hugo Palmer* a66 79
4 b m Zoffany(IRE) Vickers Vimy (Montjeu (IRE))
2360[3] 3022[5] 4561[4] 5529[4]◆ 6512[2]

Suedois (FR) *David O'Meara* a100 113
8 b g Le Havre(IRE) Cup Cake (IRE) (Singspiel (IRE))
2085[4] 2615[4] 3588[2] 4389[3] 4900[3] 5521[3] (6508) 7220a[4] 7922a[3]

Suegioo (FR) *Ian Williams* a75 90
10 ch g Manduro(GER) Mantesera (IRE) (In The Wings)
2578[2] 3635[7] 3847[4] 4146[5] 4381[P]

Suestar *David Simcock* 52
2 gr f Dark Angel(IRE) Momentus (IRE) (Montjeu (IRE))
8510[7]

Sufficient *Rod Millman* 89
3 gr f Showcasing Good Enough (FR) (Mukaddamah (USA))
2144[4] 2768[6] (3807) 4828[2] (5187) 8463[6]

Sufi *Milton Harris* a78 80
5 ch g Pivotal Basanti (USA) (Galileo (IRE))
2793[2] 3633[6] (4231) 5452[8] 6419[3] 7231[2] 7575[3] 8120[5]

Sugar Daddy (GER)
Lennart Hammer-Hansen a59 87
5 b h Areion(GER) Sugar Baby Love (GER) (Second Empire (IRE))
9124a[6]

Sugar Plum Fairy *Tony Carroll* a49 43
4 ch m Halling(USA) Atyaab (Green Desert (USA))
60[7] 293[4] 596[8] 2728[9] 3527[9] 4776[2] 5806[14] 6897[14] 7172[12] 9411[3]

Suitcase 'N' Taxi *Tim Easterby* a83 61
5 br g Major Cadeaux Finalize (Firebreak)
1817[8] 3056[10] 3658[11] 4519[8] 4630[3] 5393[6] 5722[4] 6099[10] 7066[2] 7443[2] (8404) (8646) (9183)

Sujet Libre (FR) *J-C Rouget* 105
2 b c Hurricane Cat(USA) Tiziana (USA) (Dixie Union (USA))
6777a[3]

Sukalia *John Bridger* a48 53
3 b f Swiss Spirit Perception (IRE) (Hawk Wing (USA))
1825[7] 2253[9] 3154[4] 4284[5] 4794[6] 5957[P] (Dead)

Sulafaat (IRE) *Rebecca Menzies* a65 55
4 ch m Haatef(USA) Elraabeya (CAN) (Seeking The Gold (USA))
1399[14] 2376[4] 3162[7] 3448[5] 4518[12] 5851[2] (6545) 7415[3] 7650[2] 8423[8] (9345)◆ 9391[2]

Sula Island *Alan King* a75 75
5 ch m Sulamani(IRE) Cosmea (Compton Place)
1569[4] 2214[2]

Sulal Nair (FR) *X-L Le Stang* a49 38
6 b g Naaqoos Sol Schwarz (Hernando (FR))
7501a[4]

Sully (FR) *Rod Collet* 81
4 gr m Siyouni(FR) Shaama Rose (FR) (Verglas (IRE))
2167a[10]

Sully (NZ)
Trent Busuttin & Natalie Young 105
4 gr g Reliable Man Lady Winifred (NZ) (Casual Lies (USA))
8134a[3] 8803a[7]

Sulochana (IRE) *Hughie Morrison* a57
2 br f Lope De Vega(IRE) Yakshini (IRE) (Monsun (GER))
8999[8] 9383[8]

Suman (FR) *Rod Collet* 60
3 b g Rajsaman(FR) Sorpresa (USA) (Pleasant Tap (USA))
1450a[8]

Summa Force (IRE)
Richard Hannon a53 40
3 b g Gale Force Ten Queen Myrine (IRE) (Oratorio (IRE))
1825[13] 3777[9] 4232[13]

Summer Angel (IRE)
Michael Appleby a48 46
4 gr m Mastercraftsman(IRE) City Image (IRE) (Elusive City (USA))
37[11] 4657[11] 4751[5] 5531[8]

Summer Bride (IRE) *Tim Easterby* 66
3 b f Mayson Spring Fashion (IRE) (Galileo (IRE))
2909[6] 3412[3] 3565[3] 4147[4] 4820[7]

Summerbridge (IRE) *James Bethell* a35
2 ch f Ruler Of The World(IRE) Huffoof (IRE) (Dalakhani (IRE))
9097[6]

Summer Daydream (IRE)
Keith Dalgleish a82 82
3 b f Footstepsinthesand Summer Dream (IRE) (Oasis Dream)
4242[8] 4692[7] 4987[7] 5846[5] 6656[3] 7366[11] 7735[8] 8342[15] (8924) 9351[14]

Summer Flair (IRE) *Charlie Appleby* 72
3 gr f Dubawi(IRE) Summer Fete (IRE) (Pivotal)
2361[6]

Summerghand (IRE) *David O'Meara* a98 107
5 b g Lope De Vega(IRE) Kate The Great (Xaar)
1829[2] 2442[2] 4095[5] 4648[3] 5664[4] 6229[2] 7433[4] 7891[4]◆ 8127[10] (9612)

Summer Glamour (IRE)
Adrian Paul Keatley 45
3 b f Holy Roman Emperor(IRE) Sheer Glamour (IRE) (Peintre Celebre (USA))
5915[7]

Summer Heights *Jim Goldie* 56
2 b f Orientor Primo Heights (Primo Valentino (IRE))
5485[7] 5900[4] 6606[9] 7208[2] 7734[7] 8180[5]

Summer Lake *Roger Charlton* 42
2 b f Poet's Voice Random Success (IRE) (Shamardal (USA))
3695[9] 4222[8] 4840[11]

Summer Moon *Mark Johnston* a69 103
3 ch g Sea The Moon(GER) Songerie (Hernando (FR))
(2485) (2811) 3337[3] 4017[12] 4644[4] 5347[6] (7394)◆ 8114[3]◆ 8520[4]

Summeronsevenhills (USA)
Richard Hughes a92 70
2 bb c Summer Front(USA) Iboughtheranyway (USA) (Dixie Union (USA))
6905[8] 7339[6] 8069[3] (9044) (9546)

Summer Palace (USA) *Alan King* a68
2 b c Giant's Causeway(USA) Luvly Rita (USA) (Danehill Dancer (IRE))
7555[5]

Summer Romance (IRE)
Charlie Appleby 107
2 gr f Kingman Serena's Storm (IRE) (Statue Of Liberty (USA))
(3776)◆ (4387)◆ 5411[6] 6907[3]

Summer Sands *Richard Fahey* 112
2 b c Coach House(IRE) Koharu (Ishiguru (USA))
2747[3] (3566) 3988[6] 6422[5] 7693[3] (7904)

Summer Skies *Marcus Tregoning* a57 49
3 b f Leroidesanimaux(BRZ) Sunset Shore (Oasis Dream)
7228[3] 8013[8]

Summers Way *Bill Turner* 22
2 gr f Coach House(IRE) Starlight June (Hellvelyn)
2767[8] 3835[10]

Summer Valley *Gary Moore* a64 52
2 b f Mukhadram Pink Stone (FR) (Bigstone (IRE))
6603[5] 8093[11] 8706[6]

Summit Reach *Ralph Beckett* a86
2 b c Dansili Casual (Nayef (USA))
9136[2]◆ 9415[5]

Sumner Beach *Brian Ellison* a48 59
5 ch g Aqlaam Cosmic Song (Cosmonaut)
3957[8] 4916[4]◆ 5438[9] (5816) 6102[5] 6655[7] 7385[8] 8299[11] 8667[5] 8922[10]

Sun And Polo (FR) *P Le Gal* a58 40
8 b g Zambezi Sun Rugianna (FR) (Kahyasi (IRE))
7009a[4]

Sun At Work (GER) *W Haustein* a88 103
7 ch g Areion(GER) So Royal (GER) (Royal Solo (IRE))
3879a[6] 7750a[5] 8583a[5]

Sun Bear *John Gosden* 78
2 b f Dubawi(IRE) Great Heavens (Galileo (IRE))
8855[2]◆

Sunblazer (IRE) *Kim Bailey* a81 76
9 gr g Dark Angel(IRE) Damask Rose (IRE) (Dr Devious (IRE))
291[7] 3091[6] 4118[7] 5812[7]

Sunbreak (IRE) *Mark Johnston* a69 60
4 b g Dawn Approach(IRE) Carry On Katie (USA) (Fasliyev (USA))
86[6] 784[8] 1183[12] 1362[4]

Sunbright (IRE) *Michael Appleby* a38 39
4 b m Dawn Approach(IRE) Crossover (Cape Cross (IRE))
1550[9] 2350[7] 3304[6] 4131[9]

Sun Crystal (IRE) *Richard Fahey* 68
2 ch f Exceed And Excel(AUS) Takizada (IRE) (Sendawar (IRE))
3866[6] 5387[5] 6918[5] 7585[10]

Sun Cuisine (USA) *Charlie Appleby* a76 70
2 b c Medaglia d'Oro(USA) Moulin De Mougin (USA) (Curlin (USA))
5823[4] 6708[3] 9095[4]

Sunday Sovereign *P Twomey* 103
2 b c Equiano(FR) Red Sovereign (Danzig Connection (USA))
4012[8]

Sunday Star *Ed Walker* 105
3 b f Kodiac Northern Star (IRE) (Montjeu (IRE))
1832[11] 2806[4] 3317[6] 4242[7] (5143)◆ 5714a[4] 6257[9] 7146[8]

Sun Devil (ITY) *Diego Dettori* 85
5 b h Desert Prince(IRE) Dondup (IRE) (Hurricane Run (IRE))
7502a[7]

Sundiata *Charles Hills* a74 63
3 b f Showcasing Dawn Of Empire (USA) (Empire Maker (USA))
380[4] 1020[2] (1296) 1476[2] 1894[5] 4926[6] 7914[2]

Sun Hat (IRE) *Simon Crisford* a85
4 ch m Helmet(AUS) Bright Water (Refuse To Bend (IRE))
252[3]

Sunhill Lad (IRE) *Julia Brooke* a53 50
4 gr g Lilbourne Lad(IRE) Gris Ladera (IRE) (Verglas (IRE))
3225[10] 8869[2] 9345[11]

Sunlight (AUS)
Tony McEvoy & Calvin McEvoy 114
3 b f Zoustar(AUS) Solar Charged (AUS) (Charge Forward (AUS))
8362a[10] 8805a[2]

Sun Maiden *Sir Michael Stoute* a111 112
4 b m Frankel Midsummer (Kingmambo (USA))
2776[3] (3374) (4332) 5586[4] 6962[4] 8333[3]

Sunnyside Lady *Michael Easterby* a49 51
4 ch m Kheleyf(USA) Skiddaw Wolf (Wolfhound (USA))
1026[10]

Sun Power (FR) *Richard Hannon* a86 102
2 b g Night Of Thunder(IRE) Sparkling Smile (IRE) (Cape Cross (IRE))
2747[5] (3426)◆ 4091[4] 5415[2] 6212[3] 6966[5]

Sunset Breeze *Sir Mark Prescott Bt* a71 64
2 b g Pivotal Sunrise Star (Shamardal (USA))
7627[4] 7911[2] 8280[2]

Sunset Flash (IRE) *David Lanigan* a86
3 b f Mayson Sunset Avenue (USA) (Street Cry (IRE))
1984[2] 2552[6]

Sunset Kiss *Michael Bell* 78
2 b f Kingman Because (IRE) (Sadler's Wells (USA))
7054[5] 7695[3]

Sunset Nova (IRE) *Andrew Slattery* a70 77
3 ch g Zebedee Melodize (Iceman)
7241a[14]

Sunshineandbubbles *David Evans* a60 50
6 b m Multiplex Dockside Strike (Dockside (USA))
67[3] 344[10] 876[11] 1591[7] 2345[7] 2595[3]◆ 3834[11] 4658[12] (9362) 9479[3] 9609[7]

Sunshine Coast *Jamie Osborne* a44
4 b g Kyllachy Sunseek (Rail Link)
7375[10] 8001[10] 8553[9] 8694[13]

Sunshine Fantasy (IRE)
Archie Watson a42 55
2 b f Make Believe Elshamms (Zafonic (USA))
5433[11] 6054[4]

Sunshine Fun (USA)
Jamie Osborne a63
2 b f Bernardini(USA) Claire Soleil (USA) (Syncline (USA))
8602[8]

Sunsprite (IRE) *Richard Hughes* 102
3 b c Kodiac Dutch Rose (IRE) (Dutch Art)
2826[6]◆ 3599[7] 4186[2] 4866[DSQ] 5504[12] 6396[2]

Sunstorm *Stef Keniry* a42 50
4 ch g Medicean Crimson Cloud (Kyllachy)
3203[8] 4131[7] 5458[13]

Sunvisor (IRE) *William Muir* a55 49
3 ch g Helmet(AUS) Island Sunset (IRE) (Trans Island)
3170[14] 6840[11] 7460[9] 8291[11]

Supaulette (IRE) *Tim Easterby* a67 74
4 b m Epaulette(AUS) Supreme Spirit (IRE) (Invincible Spirit (IRE))
2081[8] (2418)◆ 2899[3] 3203[2] 3414[2] 4243[5] 4822[7] 5392[3] 6033[3] 6260[4] 7418[14]

Superb Story (IRE) *Harry Fry* a83 76
8 b g Duke Of Marmalade(IRE) Yes My Love (FR) (Anabaa (USA))
3467[2] 4505[5]◆

Super Florence (IRE)
Adrian Nicholls a47 60
4 gr m Zebedee Top Of The Ridge (IRE) (Celtic Swing)
1951[9] 2433[4] 2789[5] 3930[8] 4785[8] 5094[7] 5300[8] 6273[11] 6574[4] 6936[2] (7214) 7651[7] 9397[11]

Super Girl (AUS) *Joshua Julius* 89
4 b m So You Think(NZ) Hailbella (AUS) (Giant's Causeway (USA))
8803a[8]

Superior (USA) *A bin Harmash* a96
3 b c Majesticperfection(USA) Tiz Fate (USA) (Tiznow (USA))
394a[5] 1110a[2] 1443a[8]

Superior Badolat (IRE)
Andrea Marcialis a62 65
2 gr c Dark Angel(IRE) Royal Fortune (IRE) (Invincible Spirit (IRE))
5468a[8]

Superiority (IRE) *K R Burke* a62 50
2 b f Exceed And Excel(AUS) Janina (Namid)
7619[6] 8316[4] 8640[6]

Superior Moment (IRE) *Tom Clover* a66
2 b c Pivotal Superior Charm (USA) (Elusive Quality (USA))
9136[5] 9509[U]

Super Julius *S Donohoe* a53 77
5 ch g Bated Breath Paradise Isle (Bahamian Bounty)
1818[2] (1950) 2368[7] 4059[10] (5094)◆ 5478[2] 5936[2] 6932[5]

Super Kid *Tim Easterby* a90 82
7 b g Exceed And Excel(AUS) Crimson Year (USA) (Dubai Millennium)
1761[6] 2186[7] 2636[3] 3070[4] (3847) 5055[6] 5391[5] 5706[8] 6981[5] 7144[4] 7702[8] 8341[9]

Supernova
Michael, Wayne & John Hawkes a77 102
4 b h Intello(GER) Carding (USA) (Street Cry (IRE))
8600a[6]

Superseded (IRE) *John Butler* a57 70
3 gr g Exceed And Excel(AUS) Satwa Ruby (FR) (Verglas (IRE))
27[7] 412[5] 1296[8] 1488[8] 2211[5] (2592) 3045[2] 3376[4] (4192) 4894[10] 6183[8] 7588[8] 8117[11] 8715[10] 9092[9] 9406[10] 9664[6]

Super Seth (AUS)
Anthony Freedman 111
2 b c Dundeel(NZ) Salutations (AUS) (Redoute's Choice (AUS))
(8137a)

Superstition *Eve Johnson Houghton* a7 48
3 b f Swiss Spirit School Fees (Royal Applause)
1863[11] 2357[8] 2773[3]

Super Titus
David A & B Hayes & Tom Dabern 97
5 b g Dansili Mirror Lake (Dubai Destination (USA))
8134a[10]

Suphala (FR) *A Fabre* 107
3 ch f Frankel Sefroua (USA) (Kingmambo (USA))
1706a[2] 2669a[9] (3677a) (4416a) 6250a[4]

Supreme Chance
Michael Blanshard a36
3 b g Delegator Avon Supreme (Avonbridge)
400[11] 2007[11] 3299[11] 5648[13]

Supreme Dream *Shaun Harris* a49 43
3 b f Captain Gerrard(IRE) Sweet Lily Pea (USA) (Hard Spun (USA))
2482[10] 3271[6] 3570[6] 4731[5] 5300[12] 5558[8] 6181[8] 7032[7] 7335[8] 9439[11]

Supreme Power (IRE)
Tracy Waggott a65 70
5 b g Power Supreme Spirit (IRE) (Invincible Spirit (IRE))
104[4] 410[14]

Suprimo (GER) *P Schiergen* 85
3 b c Maxios Survey (GER) (Big Shuffle (USA))
4534a[5]

Suquitho (FR) *H-A Pantall* 90
3 b f Authorized(IRE) Suvretta Queen (IRE) (Polish Precedent (USA))
1626a[5] 2029a[7] 2759a[8]

Sura (IRE) *Waldemar Hickst* a79 35
4 gr m Mastercraftsman(IRE) Seatone (USA) (Mizzen Mast (USA))
46a[4]

Sure I'm Your Man (IRE)
Roger Charlton a62 22
2 b g Sea The Moon(GER) All Hallows (IRE) (Dalakhani (IRE))
8518[9] 8914[5] 9155[9]

Surewecan *Andrew Hollinshead* a59 57
7 b g Royal Applause Edge Of Light (Xaar)
3715a[3] 4960a[5]

Sureyoutoldme (IRE) *Ruth Carr* a83 64
5 ch g Tamayuz Place De Moscou (IRE) (Rock Of Gibraltar (IRE))
1273[3] (1768) 2015[3] 2679[7] 3268[9] 3867[16]

Surf Dancer (IRE) *William Haggas* a88 87
2 b c Lope De Vega(IRE) Beach Belle (Invincible Spirit (IRE))
5367[5] (5980)◆ (6632) 8762[8]

Surfman *Roger Varian* a101 108
3 b c Kingman Shimmering Surf (IRE) (Danehill Dancer (IRE))
(2245)◆ 2777[3] 3390a[8]

Surprise Baby (NZ) *Paul Preusker* 112
4 bb g Shocking(AUS) Bula Baby (NZ) (Kaapstad (NZ))
8844a[5]◆

Surprise Encounter *David Simcock* a61
2 b f Iffraaj Counterclaim (Pivotal)
9046[10] 9437[6]

Surrajah (IRE) *Tom Clover* a53 39
2 b c Camelot Sharaarah (IRE) (Oasis Dream)
4295[7] 5859[10] 6147[5] (9438) 9630[7]

Surrey Blaze (IRE) *Joseph Tuite* a59 54
4 b g Thewayyouare(USA) Catadalya (IRE) (One Cool Cat (USA))
292[6] 754[6] 1095[3] 1518[6] 6511[7] 8702[11] 9054[12] 9443[12]

Surrey Breeze (IRE) *Archie Watson* a57 34
3 b g Footstepsinthesand Breezeway (IRE) (Grand Lodge (USA))
858[5] 1221[7] 2913[11]

Surrey Flame (FR) *Joseph Tuite* a49
2 ch g Teofilo(IRE) Ryedale Mist (Equiano (FR))
8709[8] 9299[9]

Surrey Hope (USA)
Hughie Morrison a80 89
5 b g Lemon Drop Kid(USA) She Be Classy (USA) (Toccet (USA))
4639[10] 5776[9] (6538) 7517[8]

Surrey Pride (IRE) *Joseph Tuite* 78
2 b c Lope De Vega(IRE) La Conquerante (Hurricane Run (IRE))
7162[6]◆ (7755)

Surrey Thunder (FR) *Joseph Tuite* 106
3 b c Le Havre(IRE) Zakania (IRE) (Indian Ridge (IRE))
1347a[2] 1797a[3] 3385a[3] 4707a[5] 5950[5] (6385a) 7890[6]

Surrey Warrior (USA)
Archie Watson a74 73
3 b g Data Link(USA) Spring Heather (IRE) (Montjeu (IRE))
1884[3] 3474[8] 4231[5] 4779[4]

Surrounding (IRE) *M Halford* a106 106
6 b m Lilbourne Lad(IRE) Roundabout Girl (IRE) (Doubletour (USA))
1531a[3] (2879a) 4353a[2] (4954a) 7220a[5] (8734a)

Survoltee (GER) *F Chappet* 85
3 b f Helmet(AUS) Silver Face (FR) (Iron Mask (USA))
1200a[7]

Sushi Power (IRE) *Tim Easterby* 51
2 b f No Nay Never(USA) Bright And Clear (Danehill (USA))
4323[5] 5553[8]

Susie Javea *Ollie Pears* 51
2 b f Coach House(IRE) Charlevoix (IRE) (King Charlemagne (USA))
2475[9] 4075[6] 5295[3] 5912[2] 7585[11]

Suspicious Mind (DEN)
Nina Lensvik a96 96
6 b g Appel Au Maitre(FR) Fleur En Fleur (FR) (Hernando (FR))
281a[2] 958a[4] 7498a[5]

Sussex Girl *John Berry* a35 52
5 ch m Compton Place Palinisa (FR) (Night Shift (USA))
2019[2]◆ 2585[9] 3186[7] 4475[5] 5802[3] 6560[5]

Sussex Solo *Luke Dace* a51 56
3 gr g Compton Place Grezie (Mark Of Esteem (IRE))
1173[11] 1264[7] 1726[9] 3354[11] (5431) 5957[6] 6117[10]

Sussex Spirit *Luke Dace* a28 39
3 b f Swiss Spirit Hip Hip Hooray (Monsieur Bond (IRE))
3352[14]

Sussudio *Richard Spencer* a65 53
3 b f Compton Place Glen Molly (IRE) (Danetime (IRE))
477[4] 1020[4] 1296[2] 1687[7] 2199[8] 2735[6] 3442[4] 4193[6] 4563[6]

Suttonwood Sally *Geoffrey Deacon* a18
5 b m Delegator Hip Hip Hooray (Monsieur Bond (IRE))
117[11] 516[5] 965[8]

Suwaan (IRE) *Ruth Carr* a81 74
5 ch g Exceed And Excel(AUS) Janina (Namid)
1950[2] 2841[7] 3206[9] 4059[3] 4632[4] 5244[3] 5819[2] 6099[5]

Suyoof (AUS) *M F De Kock* 99
6 ch g Magic Albert(AUS) Magic Harmony (AUS) (Danehill Dancer (IRE))
52a[5]◆ 285a[9]

Suzi's Connoisseur
Jane Chapple-Hyam a93 81
8 b g Art Connoisseur(IRE) Suzi Spends (IRE) (Royal Applause)
352[5] 588[3] 964[3] 1916[9] 2611[4] 2804[10] 3550[4] (4123) 5191[2] 5628[4] 6162[5] 7467[4] 7828[9] 9214[8] 9441[4] 9660[5]

Suzuka Devious (JPN)
Mitsuru Hashida 107
8 bb h King Kamehameha(JPN) Suzuka Laurent (JPN) (Sunday Silence (USA))
8136a[8] 8952a[7]

Swansdown *William Haggas* a73 72
3 ch f Dubawi(IRE) Pongee (Barathea (IRE))
3052[4] 3741[3] 4769[3]◆ 5623[3] 6595[4] 7835[7] (8713)◆ 8923[3] 9453[4]

Swansway *Michael Easterby* a67 71
6 ch g Showcasing Spring Stroll (USA) (Skywalker (USA))
1848[7]

Swanton Blue (IRE) *Ed de Giles* a61 74
6 b g Kodiac Cabopino (IRE) (Captain Rio)
2717[4] 3221[11] 3576[8] 4181[10] 4733[2] 5799[4] 7130[5] 7576[9]

Swapan (FR) *Mlle L Kneip* 27
2 b c Whipper(USA) Sainte Baume (FR) (Enrique)
2890a[DSQ]

Swedish Dream (FR)
Annike Bye Hansen 96
5 ch g Helmet(AUS) Demeanour (USA) (Giant's Causeway (USA))
3902a[4] 6524a[6]

Sweet And Dandy (IRE)
Luke McJannet a75 22
4 b m Dandy Man(IRE) Translator (IRE) (Choisir (AUS))
177[5] 1382[2]◆ 1712[4] 2065[2] 3146[7] 9455[11]

Sweet Cassie (IRE)
Leonard Paul Flynn 53
4 b m Casamento(IRE) Diyla (IRE) (Bahhare (USA))
3384a[DSQ]

Sweet Celebration (IRE)
Marco Botti a87 73
3 b f Excelebration(IRE) Snow Dust (First Defence (USA))
1171[5] 2216[5]◆ 2932[2] 4804[2] 6687[3]◆ 7650[5] 8298[2] (8656)◆ (9178) 9454[6]

Sweet Charity *Denis Coakley* a79 78
4 b m Mount Nelson Fanny May (Nayef (USA))
1589[3] 2230[4] 3264[7] 4392[10] 4898[3] 6538[5] 7560[5] 8422[10]

Sweet Dreamer *K R Burke* 60
3 br f Harbour Watch(IRE) Unasuming (IRE) (Orpen (USA))
3266[4] 3724[6] 4326[9]

Sweet Embrace (IRE)
John Wainwright a41 51
2 b f Kodiac Zarkalia (IRE) (Red Ransom (USA))
5037[4] 5514[9] 6096[8] 7208[4] 7584[12] 7833[8] 8527[9]

Sweetest Smile (IRE) *Ed de Giles* a52 43
4 b m Champs Elysees Scorn (USA) (Seeking The Gold (USA))
208[5] (535) 946[10] 1361[9] 1861[10] 3272[12] 3686[12] 5435[3] 5596[6] 7300[11] 8081[12] 8347[8]

Sweet Fong (FR) *P Le Gal* 23
7 b g Dr Fong(USA) Sweetner (FR) (Stravinsky (USA))
7009a[8]

Sweet Forgetme Not (IRE)
Phil McEntee a45 53
3 bb f Dream Ahead(USA) Amazon Beauty (IRE) (Wolfhound (USA))
2063[7] 2735[5]◆ 3650[12] 4183[3] 4500[2] 5063[2] (5352) 8757[4] 8864[8] 9161[9] 9398[14]

Sweet Jemima (USA) *William Muir* a42 61
3 ch f More Than Ready(USA) Sweet Nothings (USA) (Street Cry (IRE))
2340[9] 2762[11] 3650[9] 9209[12]

Sweet Joanna (IRE) *Richard Fahey* 72
2 gr f Gutaifan(IRE) Rugged Up (IRE) (Marju (IRE))
4517[2]◆

Sweet Man *J Hirschberger* 94
4 gr h Reliable Man Sworn Pro (GER) (Protektor (GER))
7249a[9]

Sweet Marmalade (IRE)
Brian Ellison a52 65
4 b m Duke Of Marmalade(IRE) Lady Chaparral (High Chaparral (IRE))
2417[2] 3200[3] 4370[8] 4779[5] 5728[13] 9362[11]

Sweet Melania (USA) *Todd Pletcher* 106
2 ch f American Pharoah(USA) Sweet N Discreet (USA) (Discreet Cat (USA))
8748a[3]

Sweet Nature (IRE) *Laura Mongan* a62 49
4 b m Canford Cliffs(IRE) High Figurine (IRE) (High Chaparral (IRE))
154[4] 366[5] 1042[3] 1653[14] 2232[4] 3187[8] 4217[6] 4787[3] 5807[12] 6568[5] 7271[4] 7790[7] 8224[14] 8854[7] 9204[2]

Sweet Poem *Clive Cox* a69 62
3 b f Poet's Voice Three Sugars (AUS) (Starcraft (NZ))
556[11] 2018[3] 3041[6] 3665[12] 4284[9]

Sweet Promise *James Fanshawe* a92 101
3 b f Intello(GER) Penny Rose (Danehill Dancer (IRE))
(4326) 5148[2] (6187) 6775a[3] 8094[8]

Sweet Pursuit *Rod Millman* a70 80
5 b m Pastoral Pursuits Sugar Beet (Beat Hollow)
4560[6] 5251[3] 5736[6] (6203) 6835[3] 7564[2] 8522[11]

Sweet Reward (IRE)
Jonathan Portman a57 66
2 b c Acclamation Dangle (IRE) (Desert Style (IRE))
6504[5] 8100[8] 8889[6]◆

Sweet Sami D (USA)
Patrick B McBurney a82
3 bb f First Samurai(USA) Treaty Of Kadesh (USA) (Victory Gallop (CAN))
7479a[5]

Sweet Serenade *James Tate* a62 59
2 b f Zoffany(IRE) Caster Sugar (USA) (Cozzene (USA))
5387[7] 6072[5] 8454[7] 9196[8]◆ 9407[5]

Sweet Sixteen (GER) *Amy Murphy* a51 65
2 b f Maxios Sugar Baby Love (GER) (Second Empire (IRE))
4114[3]◆ 5314[4] 6629[6] 8259[8] 8603[13]

Sweet Smoothie (FR) *H Blume* 17
3 b f Reliable Man Sternenkonigin (IRE) (Samum (GER))
3712a[9]

Sweet Thomas (GER)
Matthew A Smith a62 91
7 b g Dylan Thomas(IRE) Sworn Pro (GER) (Protektor (GER))
8134a[12]

Swell Song *Robert Cowell* a52 54
3 ch f Kyllachy Racina (Bluebird (USA))
3376[5] 4563[7] 5822[3] 6321[3] 6889[11] 7468[2] 7784[10]

Swendab (IRE) *John O'Shea* a30 51
11 b g Trans Island Lavish Spirit (USA) (Southern Halo (USA))
626[9] 920[7] 1384[3] 1595[10] 1952[10] 4182[13] 4500[7] 5084[6] 6107[14] 7112[13] 8649[7]

Swerved (IRE) *Ollie Pears* a55 52
3 b f Excelebration(IRE) Manoeuvre (IRE) (Galileo (IRE))
1972[4] 2913[7] 3708[10] 8293[7] 8819[10]

Swift Approval (IRE)
Stuart Williams a90 86
7 ch g Approve(IRE) Tiltili (IRE) (Spectrum (IRE))
176[3] 382[6] 856[8] 1097[6] 2622[5] 2977[4] 3649[9] (4226) 5386[5] (5862) 6567[6] 7059[3] 7731[2] 8766[3] 9214[5]

Swift Arion (IRE) *John Quinn* 9
2 b g Outstrip Wings Of Fame (IRE) (Namid)
3919[6] 6226[9]

Swift Blade (IRE) *Gary Moore* a53 40
11 ch g Exceed And Excel(AUS) Gold Strike (IRE) (Rainbow Quest (USA))
5802[8] 6046[9] 6599[9]

Swift Emperor (IRE) *David Barron* a74 85
7 b g Holy Roman Emperor(IRE) Big Swifty (IRE) (Intikhab (USA))
2584[7] 2710[2]◆ 3356[3] 3811[11] 4079[5] 4907[2] (Dead)

Swift Justice *Mark Loughnane* a47 48
3 b g Sixties Icon Wansdyke Lass (Josr Algarhoud (IRE))
1166[9] 2277[10]

Swift Rose (IRE) *Saeed bin Suroor* a89 99
3 b f Invincible Spirit(IRE) Tulips (IRE) (Pivotal)
48a[5] 510a[14] 845a[2] 1443a[5] 2745[9] 4255[4]

Swift Wing *John Gosden* a76 86
3 ch g Pivotal Gull Wing (IRE) (In The Wings)
2566[3]◆ 3724[3] 4104[3] 6890[2] 7689[2] 8398[5]

Swilly Sunset *Anthony Carson* a47 75
6 b g Kyllachy Spanish Springs (IRE) (Xaar)
6165[5] 6512[5] 7166[6] 7610[8]

Swindler *Ed Walker* 104
3 b g Invincible Spirit(IRE) Priceless Jewel (Selkirk (USA))
(4866)◆ 5442[5]◆ (6953)◆

Swinging Eddie *Kevin Ryan* a48 69
3 b g Swiss Spirit Bling Bling (IRE) (Indian Ridge (IRE))
3884[2]◆ 4286[9] 5236[8] 5669[3]

Swingy (FR) *D Smaga* a57
3 b c Anodin(IRE) La Fee De Breizh (FR) (Verglas (IRE))
5641a[6] 6328a[9]

Swinley (IRE) *Richard Hughes* a78 75
2 br g Dragon Pulse(IRE) Invincibile Stella (IRE) (Invincible Spirit (IRE))
3008[4] 3660[2] 3943[5] 5500[4] 6158[5] 6667[5] 7785[3] 8315[2] (8506)

Swinley Forest (IRE) *Brian Meehan* a68 77
2 b g Ivawood(IRE) Spring Bouquet (IRE) (King's Best (USA))
3760[3] 4482[3] 5082[5] 6161[4] 6728[3] 7119[20] 7871[5] 8318[8]

Swiper (IRE) *John O'Shea* a52 51
3 b g Clodovil(IRE) Hawk Dance (IRE) (Hawk Wing (USA))
4874[7] 5377[11] 6085[6] 6361[7] 6983[10] 9001[4] 9248[7]

Swiss Air *William Haggas* a71 74
3 b f Oasis Dream Swiss Lake (USA) (Indian Ridge (IRE))
4422[5]

Swissal (IRE) *David Dennis* a65 68
4 b g Swiss Spirit Al Gharrafa (Dutch Art)
1393[5] 1930[6] 2145[10] (2929) 3967[5] 5080[5] 6116[4] 9217[10] 9420[7] 9629[4]

Swiss Bond *J S Moore* a37 60
2 b f Swiss Spirit Verge (IRE) (Acclamation)
1513[6] 2792[5] 2996[5] 3562a[7] 5101[8] 5340[9] 7516[10]

Swiss Cheer (FR)
Jonathan Portman a84 49
3 b g Swiss Spirit Happy Clapper (Royal Applause)
1033[4]◆ 1352[3]◆ 8206[12] 8495[6] (9047)

Swiss Chill *Clive Cox* 64
4 b g Swiss Spirit Littlemisssunshine (IRE) (Oasis Dream)
(5306) 5793[4]

Swiss Chime *Alan Berry* a57 62
3 b f Swiss Spirit Dolly Daydreamer (Equiano (FR))
(1) 287[6] 854[3] 1193[5] 1380[4] 1650[10] 3508[13] 4508[9] 4604[7] 5738[7] 5893[6]

Swiss Connection *Bryan Smart* a68 60
3 b g Swiss Spirit Sofonisba (Rock Of Gibraltar (IRE))
2477[10] 4335[10] 6070[4] 6659[4]◆ 7307[2]◆ (7959) 8429[9] 9473[11]

Swiss Cottage *Karl Thornton* a57 80
4 b g Swiss Spirit Cheeky Girl (College Chapel)
1572a[4]

Swiss Cross *Phil McEntee* a54 60
12 b g Cape Cross(IRE) Swiss Lake (USA) (Indian Ridge (IRE))
53[6] 263[2] 365[7] 402[3] 531[5] 848[7] 920[5] 1384[8] 1478[8] 1731[9] 2286[3] 3187[7] 3410[11] 4378[8] (4684a)

Swiss Knight *Stuart Williams* a86 82
4 b g Oasis Dream Swiss Diva (Pivotal)
3602[7]◆ 4609[5] 4995[9] 5911[3] 6465[8] 7397[2] 7789[5] 8495[2] 8550[11]

Swiss Miss *John Gallagher* a21 45
3 b f Swiss Spirit Miss Meticulous (Bahamian Bounty)
2077[8] 2597[9] 3697[10] 3975[12] 4182[4] 4824[8]

Swiss Peak *Michael Bell* a60 62
3 b g Swiss Spirit Easy To Love (USA) (Diesis)
2021[4]◆ 2597[5] 3256[4]◆ 4346[6] 4568[6]

Swiss Pride (IRE) *Richard Hughes* a78 77
3 b g Swiss Spirit Encore Encore (FR) (Royal Applause)
(990) 1492[2] 2730[7] 3535[4] (4193) 5581[2] 5647[2] 6533[5] 7078[2] 7514[3] 7789[7] (8649) 9387[3]

Swiss Storm *Michael Bell* a94 95
5 b g Frankel Swiss Lake (USA) (Indian Ridge (IRE))
(915)◆ 1545[4] 2116[13]

Swissterious *Damian Joseph English* a63 82
3 b c Swiss Spirit Mysterious Girl (IRE) (Teofilo (IRE))
1306a[8] 1434a[11] 2525[13]

Swiss Vinnare *Phil McEntee* a49
5 b g Arabian Gleam Matilda Peace (Namaqualand (USA))
9453[13] 9642[9]

Switzerland (USA)
Steven Asmussen a108
5 br h Speightstown(USA) Czechers (USA) (Indian Charlie (USA))
512a[6] 729a[2] 1109a[5] 1444a[8]

Swooping Eagle (IRE)
Roger Varian a65
2 b g Free Eagle(IRE) Weekend Lady (IRE) (Bahamian Bounty)
8823[11] 9325[3]◆ 9509[6]

Sword Beach (IRE)
Eve Johnson Houghton a79 85
2 ch g Ivawood(IRE) Sleeping Princess (IRE) (Dalakhani (IRE))
3695[2] 4254[2] 5152[4] 5587[2] 6375[14] 7473[3] (8100)

Swordbill *Ian Williams* a78 74
4 ch g Champs Elysees Dream Wild (Oasis Dream)
2092[12] 2626[11] (3334) 4118[6] 4661[9] 6333[8] 7845[13] 8524[7]

Sword Exceed (GER) *Ivan Furtado* a83 69
5 b g Exceed And Excel(AUS) Sword Roche (GER) (Laroche (GER))
548[7] 2348[5] (3147)◆ 3991[10] 4643[7] 5770[13] 6440[6] 9402[9]

Sword Peinture (GER)
Andreas Suborics 101
4 ch m Peintre Celebre(USA) Swordhalf (Haafhd)
5483a[5] 6747a[8] 7504a[3] 8790a[9] 9125a[11]

Sybil Grand *Katy Price* a49 53
3 b f Canford Cliffs(IRE) Life Is Golden (USA) (Giant's Causeway (USA))
161[5] 458[2] 887[2]◆ 1141[12] 2066[9]

Sydney Express *Ismail Mohammed*
3 b g Australia Blanche Dubawi (IRE) (Dubawi (IRE))
6890[7]

Sydney Opera House *A P O'Brien* 112
3 ch c Australia Sitara (Salse (USA))
1603a[4]

Sylviacliffs (FR) *K R Burke* a60 44
3 b f George Vancouver(USA) Sienna Bella (Anabaa (USA))
(228) 585[3] 931[5] (1549) 1722[3] 2299[6] 2529[2] 2904[6] 3685[7] 8902[9] 9337[6] 9423[5] 9559[14]

Sylvia's Mother *Joseph Tuite* a75 75
3 b f Foxwedge(AUS) Majestic Song (Royal Applause)
2149[8] 3068[9] 3508[9] 4026[7]

Symbolic Star (IRE) *Barry Murtagh* a51 55
7 b g New Approach(IRE) Epitome (IRE) (Nashwan (USA))
3296[8] 4293[12] 5633[13]

Symbolization (IRE)
Charlie Appleby a85 102
4 b g Cape Cross(IRE) Yorkshire Lass (IRE) (Pivotal)
637a[4]◆ 847a[14]

Symbolize (IRE) *Andrew Balding* 98
2 ch c Starspangledbanner(AUS) French Flirt (Peintre Celebre (USA))
(2767)◆ 3988[4] 5584[5]

Symbol Of Love *Charlie Appleby* a76
2 b f Shamardal(USA) Policoro (IRE) (Pivotal)
9437[3]

Symphony (IRE) *James Unett* a46 50
3 gr f Gregorian(IRE) Anazah (USA) (Diesis)
228[12] 537[6] 1567[4] 2943[4] (4358) 6130[12]

Synchrone (FR) *J-P Gauvin* a71 72
3 b f Rajsaman(FR) Shinabaa (FR) (Anabaa (USA))
1028a[10] (7561a)

Synchrony (USA) *Michael Stidham* a94 111
6 ch h Tapit(USA) Brownie Points (USA) (Forest Wildcat (USA))
7225a[5]

Syphax (USA) *S Jadhav* a92 100
5 b h Arch(USA) Much Obliged (USA) (Kingmambo (USA))
172a[9]

Syrtis *A Fabre* 103
3 b c Frankel Sabratah (Oasis Dream)
1797a[2] 2499a[2]

Szoff (GER) *Yasmin Almenrader* a87 88
9 b h Shirocco(GER) Slawomira (GER) (Dashing Blade)
8240a[4]

Taaldara (IRE) *Ben Haslam* a45 43
3 b f Mukhadram Taaluf (IRE) (Nayef (USA))
2018[10] 3412[7]

Taamer *Charles Hills* a59
2 ch f Tamayuz Abhajat (IRE) (Lope De Vega (IRE))
7547[7]

Taamol (IRE) *A R Al Rayhi* a98 101
5 b g Helmet(AUS) Supreme Seductress (IRE) (Montjeu (IRE))
173a[7] 729a[7]

Tabaahy *David O'Meara* a73 74
4 b g Kyllachy Pious (Bishop Of Cashel)
(1598) 1951[5] 2508[5] 2841[9] 3706[10] 9498[6]

Tabarak (USA) *R Bouresly* a70 61
3 b c Quality Road(USA) Miss Drake (USA) (Afleet Alex (USA))
511a[8] (634a) 1110a[7]

Tabarrak (IRE) *Richard Hannon* a115 117
6 b g Acclamation Bahati (IRE) (Intikhab (USA))
2271[4] 4389[6] 6445[2] 6950[2] (7411)

Tabassor (IRE) *Charles Hills* 83
3 ch f Raven's Pass(USA) Thaahira (USA) (Dynaformer (USA))
2102[3]◆ (2932) 4377[3] 5687[2] 6209[4] 7238[6]

Tabdeed *Owen Burrows* 110
4 ch g Havana Gold(IRE) Puzzled (IRE) (Peintre Celebre (USA))
(5658)◆ 7892[6]

Tabera *M G Mintchev* 88
2 b f Gleneagles(IRE) Temida (IRE) (Oratorio (IRE))
8371a[3]

Tabla *Lee Carter* a2
7 b m Rail Link Questa Nova (Rainbow Quest (USA))
207[14] 717[11] 1078[7]

Table Mountain *Andrew Balding* a47
2 b f Phoenix Reach(IRE) Cape Victoria (Mount Nelson)
9154[11]

Tabou Beach Boy *Oliver Greenall* a55 56
3 b g Mukhadram Illandrane (IRE) (Cape Cross (IRE))
183[2] 1270[3] 2150[4] 2913[6] 3198[6] 4587[4] 5987[4] 6660[4]

Tabularasa (FR) *N Caulley* a94 84
4 b g Sea The Stars(IRE) Recreation (Dansili)
682a[8]

Taceec (IRE) *Adrian McGuinness* a55 62
4 b g Most Improved(IRE) Laemeen (IRE) (Danehill Dancer (IRE))
62[4] (116) 273[10]

Tacio *C Laffon-Parias* 56
2 b c Swiss Spirit Triple Dip (IRE) (Three Valleys (USA))
7043a[6]

Tacitly *Roger Charlton* a68
2 b f Dubawi(IRE) Timepiece (Zamindar (USA))
8848[4]◆ 9311[4]

Tacitus (USA) *William Mott* a115
3 rg c Tapit(USA) Close Hatches (USA) (First Defence (USA))
2425a[3] 3620a[2]

Tactical Approach (IRE)
Gavin Cromwell a62 37
3 b g Teofilo(IRE) Mathuna (IRE) (Tagula (IRE))
8351[7]

Tactile (FR) *M Nigge* a83 76
3 b c Wootton Bassett Zapiya (FR) (Panis (USA))
3675a[8]

Tadaany (IRE) *Ruth Carr* a56 58
7 b g Acclamation Park Haven (IRE) (Marju (IRE))
2183[10] 2958[4] 3476[2] 3772[2] 4037[4] 4519[16] 4912[4] 5235[11] 5765[4] 6057[3] 6659[12] 7420[6] 7628[5] 8401[4] 8901[6] 9034[10]

Tadaawol *Roger Fell* a76 88
6 b g Kyllachy Bright Edge (Danehill Dancer (IRE))
1644[5] 1977[3] 2526[3] 2842[8] (2894) 4240[14] 4634[3] 4723[2] 5155[4] 5398[8] 5970[6] 6014[4] 6677[10] 7310[3] 7820[4]

Tadasana *Archie Watson* a24 65
3 b f Battle Of Marengo(IRE) Letters (FR) (Raven's Pass (USA))
2195[5] 2690[3] 3200[4]

Tadleel *Ed Dunlop* a89 81
4 b g Dark Angel(IRE) Quelle Affaire (Bahamian Bounty)
6318[3] 6863[9] 7350[5] 7856[3]

Tadreej *Saeed bin Suroor* a80 80
2 ch f Mukhadram Wahgah (USA) (Distorted Humor (USA))
5170[2] 6906[6] (7832)◆ 8525[6]

Taekwondo (FR) *Mme Pia Brandt* a77 79
4 b h Excelebration(IRE) Tarawa (FR) (Green Tune (USA))
1578a[2]

Taexali (IRE) *Andrew Hughes* a61 80
6 ch g Raven's Pass(USA) Enchanted Evening (IRE) (High Chaparral (IRE))
2788[12]

Tafaakhor (IRE) *A R Al Rayhi* a75 92
5 bl g Dark Angel(IRE) Tellelle (IRE) (Trans Island)
1748a[7]

Tafish (IRE) *Richard Hughes* a81 74
2 b g War Command(USA) Zigarra (Halling (USA))
6395[5] 6926[7] (7870)◆ 8760[7]

Tag (FR) *F Rossi* a84 62
2 b c George Vancouver(USA) Tamada (Lucky Story (USA))
7925a[11]

Tagda *Mlle M Henry* a36 41
3 b f Tamayuz Ragda (Invincible Spirit (IRE))
9280a[12] 9504a[13]

Tagle (IRE) *Ivan Furtado* a64 48
4 b g Requinto(IRE) Beginners Luck (IRE) (Key Of Luck (USA))
344[8]

Tagur (IRE) *Kevin Ryan* a78 47
5 ch g Tagula(IRE) Westcote (USA) (Gone West (USA))
5[2] 1197[4] 1367[4] 1859[9] 4728[13] 5817[9] 7363[12] 8923[6] 9035[5] 9331[2]

Tahitian Prince (FR)
Richard Hannon a77 49
2 b c Siyouni(FR) Tehamana (IRE) (Pleasantly Perfect (USA))
7453[7] 8604[2]

Tahreek *Sir Michael Stoute* a78 81
4 b g Dansili Rifqah (USA) (Elusive Quality (USA))
3496[3] 4020[7] 5150[5]

Tailor Made *Mohamed Moubarak* 61
3 ch g Archipenko(USA) Malhadinha (IRE) (New Approach (IRE))
1752[7]

Tails I Win (CAN) *Roger Fell* a57 56
3 b f Shanghai Bobby(USA) Beshairt (USA) (Thunder Gulch (USA))
122[5] 319[3]◆ 1593[12] 1770[10] 3246[4] 3938[3]◆ 4210[4] 4653[4] 5389[5] 6578[7] 6983[2] 7578[8] 7909[3] 8299[4]

Taima *Sir Mark Prescott Bt* a54 33
2 b f Make Believe Highest (Dynaformer (USA))
7547[9] 8458[17]

Taisei Trail (JPN) *Yoshito Yahagi* 108
4 bb h Heart's Cry(JPN) Motherwell (JPN) (Symboli Kris S (USA))
9153a[15]

Tai Sing Yeh (IRE) *J F Levins* a54 70
5 b g Exceed And Excel(AUS) Cherry Orchard (IRE) (King's Best (USA))
(2958)◆ (5235) 7777[6]

Tajawoz (USA) *Owen Burrows*
3 b g War Front(USA) Stanwyck (USA) (Empire Maker (USA))
8500[7]

Tajdeed (IRE) *Michael Appleby* 62
4 br g Teofilo(IRE) Nufoos (Zafonic (USA))
2417[5] 3248[5] 4615[6] 5025[7] 5355[6]

Takatul (USA) *M Al Mheiri* a92 90
6 b g Smart Strike(CAN) Torrestrella (IRE) (Orpen (USA))
1748a[P]

Takbeer (IRE) *Nikki Evans* a24 20
7 b g Aqlaam Precious Secret (IRE) (Fusaichi Pegasus (USA))
6566[7]

Take A Guess (FR) *Claudia Erni*
7 b g Palace Episode(USA) Somewhere (FR) (Noverre (USA))
780a[8]

Take Fright *Hugo Palmer* a69 61
3 br f Bated Breath Tipping Over (IRE) (Aussie Rules (USA))
2366[4] 2909[5] 3970[5] 4767[2] 5281[8] 6025[7]

Take It Down Under *Amy Murphy* a60 75
4 b g Oasis Dream Roz (Teofilo (IRE))
1387[8] 1562[6] (2019) 2256[3] 8548[10]

Take Me To The Sky *Ed Dunlop* a76 74
2 b c Tamayuz Nassaakh (Cape Cross (IRE))
6161[3] 6684[2] 9585[3]

Takeonefortheteam
Mark Loughnane a71 69
4 b g Bahamian Bounty Miss Bond (IRE) (Danehill Dancer (IRE))
315[9] 1338[6] (1675) 2106[12] 2714[4] 2978[4] 4235[2] 4657[8] 5309[4] 6334[5] 6839[4] (8223) 8652[3] 9244[3] 9361[12]

Take That *Richard Fahey* a66 40
2 b g Iffraaj Letterfromamerica (USA) (Ghostzapper (USA))
6497[7] 7416[4]◆ 7821[8]

Take The Helm *Brian Meehan* a100 89
6 ch g Monsieur Bond(IRE) Oasis Breeze (Oasis Dream)
89[3] 176[8] 1181[7]

Take Two *Alex Hales* a76 57
10 b g Act One Lac Marmot (FR) (Marju (IRE))
404[4] 1144[5] 1463[10]

Takiah *Peter Hiatt* a52 51
4 b m Arcano(IRE) Elmaam (Nayef (USA))
120[10] 695[12] 940[7] 4475[8] 5307[3] 5549[5] 5867[3] 6327[9] 7060[6] 7526[8]

Takuendo (IRE) *F Head* a91 100
3 b c Deep Impact(JPN) Desertiste (Green Desert (USA))
5644a[9]

Takumi (IRE) *Roger Varian* a62 91
3 b g Mastercraftsman(IRE) Nebraas (Green Desert (USA))
(2407) 2872[2] 4068[2] 4450[2] 6411[3] 7589[6]

Talap *Roger Varian* a81 78
2 b g Kingman Tamarind (IRE) (Sadler's Wells (USA))
6912[5] 7151[5] 7586[3] 7971[2] 8505[2]

Talent To Amuse (IRE)
Emma Lavelle a75 81
6 b m Manduro(GER) Burn Baby Burn (IRE) (King's Theatre (IRE))
4505[7]

Tale Of Silence (USA) *Barclay Tagg* a113
5 bb h Tale Of The Cat(USA) Silence Beauty (JPN) (Sunday Silence (USA))
3618a[8]

Talking About You *Mick Channon* a57
2 b f Sixties Icon Ificaniwill (IRE) (Mastercraftsman (IRE))
9197[10] 9506[10]

Talk Like This (USA) *Tim Pinfield* a46
3 ch c More Than Ready(USA) Will Prevail (USA) (Storm Cat (USA))
753[5] 906[10]

Talk Or Listen (IRE) *F Rossi* a82 106
3 gr c Alhebayeb(IRE) Sodashy (IRE) (Noverre (USA))
(1347a) 3120a[4] 5079a[3] 6143a[4]

Tallinski (IRE) *Sofie Lanslots* a75 81
5 ch g Mayson Estonia (Exceed And Excel (AUS))
115a[12] 2956a[3] 6267a[3]

Tallulah's Quest (IRE) *Julia Feilden* a52 58
5 b m Tagula(IRE) Sarin Dubhe (IRE) (Catcher In The Rye (IRE))
5675[11] 6327[10]

Tally's Son *Grace Harris* a40 53
5 b g Assertive Talamahana (Kyllachy)
2714[6] 2994[6] 4453[3] 5080[7] 5497[6] 6045[8] 6904[12]

Tally's Song *Grace Harris* a38 38
6 b m Piccolo Talamahana (Kyllachy)
379[10] 834[10] 2473[4] 2729[7] 3036[8] 3527[13] 4182[9] 4873[11] 6199[6]

Tamachan *Roger Charlton* a48 73
3 b f Camelot Marmalade Cat (Duke Of Marmalade (IRE))
1739[4] 2771[5] 3538[3]◆ 4843[2] (Dead)

Tamao *Andrew Balding* a47
2 b f Tamayuz Starflower (Champs Elysees)
9284[7] 9409[9]

Tamar (IRE) *Alan King*
2 b g Tamayuz Tumooh (IRE) (Authorized (IRE))
5956[10]

Tambourine Girl *Roger Charlton* a75 70
2 b f Cable Bay(IRE) Triton Dance (IRE) (Hector Protector (USA))
4184[2] 4790[3] (8218)

Tamerlane (IRE) *Clive Cox* a76 74
4 b g Dark Angel(IRE) Coy (IRE) (Danehill (USA))
248[2] 942[3] 2774[7] 3305[4] 4028[3] 4506[2] 4994[2]

Tamkeen *Ruth Carr* 50
4 ch g Kyllachy Regatta (USA) (Giant's Causeway (USA))
6677[13]

Tamleek (USA) *David O'Meara* 72
5 bb g Hard Spun(USA) Tafaneen (USA) (Dynaformer (USA))
1460[5] 5657[7] 8185[2] 8633[5] 9138[P] (Dead)

Tammam Boss (IRE) *S Seemar* a34 40
3 b c Raven's Pass(USA) Hermia (IRE) (Cape Cross (IRE))
570a[9]

Tammani *William Haggas* a86 105
2 b c Make Believe Gentle On My Mind (IRE) (Sadler's Wells (USA))
4886[8] (5563) 6957[3] 7774a[4] (8483a) 8716[9]

Tammooz *Roger Varian* a97 96
3 b g Lawman(FR) La Concorde (FR) (Sadler's Wells (USA))
2488[5] 3446[2]◆ 4291[3] 5779[3]◆ (6291) (7702)◆ 8754[3]◆

Tammy Wynette (IRE) *W McCreery* a76 83
4 b m Tamayuz Cmonbabylitemyfire (IRE) (Piccolo)
2221a[5]

Tamniah (FR) *A Fabre* 102
3 b f Nathaniel(IRE) Ezdehar (IRE) (Rock Of Gibraltar (IRE))
(6003a) 7252a[9] 8094[7]

Tamok (IRE) *Michael Bell* a51 53
3 b f Australia Anklet (IRE) (Acclamation)
2583[10] 3277[7] 6202[3] 6531[3] 6982[4] 8204[7]

Tampere (IRE) *David Simcock* a55
2 b f Sea The Moon(GER) Brigitta (IRE) (Sadler's Wells (USA))
8706[8]

Tamreer *Roger Fell* a90 97
4 ch m New Approach(IRE) Reyaadah (Tamayuz)
968[3] 2104[9] 2186[5] 3095[2] (3449) 4145[3] 4599[2] (6420) 6962[12] 7658[5]

Tan *Lisa Williamson* a56 69
5 b g Aqlaam Sunburnt (Haafhd)
165[5] 297[4] 471[6] 953[8] 1496[10] 1899[7] 2227[5] 2709[10] 6058[9] 6547[2] 6798[2] 7334[6] 8066[6] (8668) 9013[10] 9092[3] 9219[11] 9402[12] 9550[10] 9627[9]

Tanaawol *Mark Johnston* 49
3 b c Dansili Eshaadeh (USA) (Storm Cat (USA))
2120[6] 3248[12] 4055[8]

Tanasoq (IRE) *Paul Midgley* a76 102
6 b g Acclamation Alexander Youth (IRE) (Exceed And Excel (AUS))
(1501) 9166[8]

Tangled (IRE) *Karen Tutty* a86 87
4 b g Society Rock(IRE) Open Verse (USA) (Black Minnaloushe (USA))
6460[6] 7121[13] 7678[8] 8024[2]◆ 8918[9]

Tango (IRE) *A P O'Brien* 105
2 b f No Nay Never(USA) Idle Chatter (IRE) (Galileo (IRE))
3983[9] 4352a[6] 6429a[6] 7244a[7] 7692[4] (8164a) 8748a[8]

Tangramm *Dean Ivory* a72 75
7 bb g Sakhee's Secret Tripti (IRE) (Sesaro (USA))
292[11] 536[7] 793[9] 1343[9] 3022[2] (3937) 4392[6] 5311[5] 5782[3] 6439[8] 7560[4] 8033[11] 8705[11] 9256[12]

Tanita *Sir Michael Stoute* a79
2 b f Frankel Shoal (Oasis Dream)
5733[3] 6592[2]

Tankerville (USA) *D K Weld* 92
3 b c Kitten's Joy(USA) Starformer (USA) (Dynaformer (USA))
1603a[5]

Tanqeeb *Ian Williams* a46 62
3 b g Garswood Oasis Mirage (Oasis Dream)
2285[4] 7204[7] 7975[6] 9217[13]

Tantivy *Richard Hannon* a56 77
2 b c Roderic O'Connor(IRE) Tamso (USA) (Seeking The Gold (USA))
6112[5] 7154[5] 7562[2] 8244[5] 8760[4] 9044[5]

Tantpispoureux (IRE) *F-H Graffard* a77 104
3 b g Showcasing T'As D'Beaux Yeux (Red Ransom (USA))
4428a[2] 5480a[6]

Tanzerin (IRE) *Charlie Fellowes* a57
3 b f Dansili Seolan (IRE) (Alhaarth (IRE))
370[11] 556[6] 979[10] 1549[13] 2152[11]

Taopix *Karen McLintock* a62 45
7 b g Rip Van Winkle(IRE) Sinister Ruckus (USA) (Trippi (USA))
9093[5]

Taos (FR) *J-C Rouget* 101
3 b c Toronado(IRE) Just With You (IRE) (Sunday Break (JPN))
(3108a) 6143a[5]

Tapis Libre *Jacqueline Coward* a59 75
11 b g Librettist(USA) Stella Manuela (FR) (Galileo (IRE))
2398[8] 2748[13] 3415[4] 3862[6] 4543[6] 5621[4] 5727[8] 6278[6] 7053[11]

Tapisserie *William Haggas* 102
3 ch f Le Havre(IRE) Miss Work Of Art (Dutch Art)
2077[2]◆ 2623[2]◆ (3696) (4242)◆ 6257[7] 7893[9]

Tappity Tap *Daniel Kubler* a72
4 b m Leroidesanimaux(BRZ) Dance Of Light (USA) (Sadler's Wells (USA))
239[3] 1064[3] 1569[5]

Taraayef (IRE) *Adrian Nicholls* a68
4 b m Teofilo(IRE) Shuhra (IRE) (Marju (IRE))
41[4] 794[6] 1065[13]

Taranta (IRE) *Mlle J Soudan* 83
2 b f Gleneagles(IRE) Kiss Of Spring (IRE) (Dansili)
7673a[5]

Tarbeyah (IRE) *Kevin Frost* a58 69
4 ch m Teofilo(IRE) Shamtari (IRE) (Alhaarth (IRE))
2148[6] 3247[4] 4285[5] 4870[5] 5593[9] 6187[5] 7474[9]

Tarboosh *Paul Midgley* a93 109
6 b g Bahamian Bounty Mullein (Oasis Dream)
1501[3] 2409[8] 3587[3] 4331[8] 6056[5] 6351[8] 6698[8] (7541) 8004[2] (8182)

Target Zone *David Elsworth* a94 88
3 ch c Champs Elysees Sailors Path (New Approach (IRE))
90[2] (251) 1035[3] 1940[5] 2833[4] 5194[4] 7863[6] 8728[9]

Tarnawa (IRE) *D K Weld* 111
3 ch f Shamardal(USA) Tarana (IRE) (Cape Cross (IRE))
2157a[3] (2642a) 3316[11] (6239a) (7242a) 8333[9]

Tarnhelm *Wilf Storey* a56 57
4 b m Helmet(AUS) Anosti (Act One)
952[7] 1271[11] 1648[7] 2244[10] 2376[5] 2911[11] 3163[10] 4131[6] (4630) (4824) 5235[15] 5723[4] 5857[9] 6275[4] 6627[6] 7210[8] 7443[11] 8233[2] 8530[5] 8821[10] 8922[5] 9396[2] 9516[6]

Tarrzan (IRE) *John Gallagher* a41 54
3 bb g Bungle Inthejungle Susiescot (IRE) (Verglas (IRE))
1296[7] 1557[6] 2281[3] 2926[2] 3182[8] 3645[4] 4218[2] 4754[2] 5837[3] 7027[11] 7273[3] 8502[8] 8821[13]

Tarseekh *Charlie Wallis* a59 54
6 b g Kyllachy Constitute (USA) (Gone West (USA))
60[6] 402[10]◆ (594) 1026[3] 3007[4] 3304[4] 3996[2] 4589[2] (5264) 6284[2] 6889[4]

Tartlette *Hughie Morrison* a81 66
3 b f Champs Elysees Tottie (Fantastic Light (USA))
2251[5] 2719[6] 3407[2] 4215[4]

Tasaaboq *Phil McEntee* a47 46
8 b g Aqlaam Seldemosa (Selkirk (USA))
64[9] 161[7] 530[4] 587[3] 594[9] 702[6] 925[10]

Tasalka (IRE) *D K Weld* 84
2 ch f Lope De Vega(IRE) Tarakala (IRE) (Dr Fong (USA))
7742a[8]

Tashman (IRE) *Gavin Cromwell* 37
4 b g Excelebration(IRE) Tanoura (IRE) (Dalakhani (IRE))
5599a[14]

Tasman Sea *Eve Johnson Houghton* a66 59
3 ch f Champs Elysees Makara (Lion Cavern (USA))
2253[10] 2697[9] 3310[8] 5377[9]

Taste The Nectar (USA)
Robert Cowell a76 70
2 ch f More Than Ready(USA) Alb (USA) (Pulpit (USA))
2257[2] 2805[12] 3461[10] 6515[2] 6705[5] 7117[12] (7995) (8890) 9175[5] 9401[2]

Tathmeen (IRE) *Antony Brittain* a76 73
4 b g Exceed And Excel(AUS) Deyaar (USA) (Storm Cat (USA))
2[8] (498) 743[3] (907)◆ 1194[7] 1394[5] 1929[6] 2079[4] 6260[5] 7470[4] 8023[8] (8429) 8895[6] 9108[6] 9257[3]◆ 9550[3]

Tato Key (ARG) *David Marnane* a110
4 b h Key Deputy(USA) Tatiana Cat (ARG) (Easing Along (USA))
512a[2]◆ 1109a[3] 1444a[9]

Tattenhams *Adam West* a44 51
3 b f Epaulette(AUS) Tattling (Warning)
1182[8] 3277[11] 3996[11] 4794[2] 5784[4] 6304[5] 7027[5]

Tattletime (USA) *David Loughnane* a56
2 b f Orb(USA) Miss Tattle Tale (USA) (Tale Of The Cat (USA))
9036[5] 9251[8] 9392[8] (9643)

Tatweej *Owen Burrows* 73
3 b f Invincible Spirit(IRE) Beach Frolic (Nayef (USA))
1834[4] 3889[3] (4304)

Tauran Shaman (IRE)
Mrs John Harrington 97
3 b c Shamardal(USA) Danelissima (IRE) (Danehill (USA))
7924a[5]

Taurean Dancer (IRE) *Roger Teal* a68 62
4 b g Intello(GER) Traou Mad (IRE) (Barathea (IRE))
246[7] 2696[4] 3700[10] 4843[5] 5631[9] 6560[3] 6853[4] 9005[14]

Taurean Star (IRE) *Luke Dace* a82 67
6 b g Elnadim(USA) Marhaba (Nayef (USA))
1097[9] 2609[19] 3632[7] 4299[12] 7563[8]

Tauteke *Roger Varian* a81 93
3 b f Sea The Stars(IRE) Tamarind (IRE) (Sadler's Wells (USA))
2618[2] 3316[12] 6378[6] 7347[7]

Tavener *David C Griffiths* a40 46
7 b g Exceed And Excel(AUS) Sea Chorus (Singspiel (IRE))
31[10] 439[7] 626[8] 857[5] 1021[6] 1061[4] 1075[2] (1179) 1265[3] 1393[3] 1496[7] 1684[6] 1715[7] 3430[9] 4025[6] 4833[7] 5038[9] 6462[5] 6897[10] 7282[2] 7604[5] 7770[11] 7961[13] 8689[7] 9508[11]

Tavus (IRE) *Roger Charlton* a74 83
3 b g Pour Moi(IRE) La Persiana (Daylami (IRE))
615[6] 1352[9] 3780[3]◆ 4991[3] (5778) (6642)◆ 7370[2] (8002)

Tawaafoq *Adrian Wintle* a49 62
5 b g Showcasing Gilt Linked (Compton Place)
5083[3] 5883[2] (6329) 6639[3] 7230[8] 7757[9] 9477[7] 9670[9]

Tawny Port *Stuart Williams* a105 91
5 ch g Arcano(IRE) Tawaasul (Haafhd)
2568[11] 3636[6]◆ (3662) 5628[6] 6227[16] 6920[7] 7894[11] (9030)◆ 9301[7] (9562)

Tawseef (IRE) *Donald McCain* a60 70
11 b g Monsun(GER) Sahool (Unfuwain (USA))
3686[3] (4308) 5241[3] 5727[3]

Tax (USA) *Danny Gargan* a115
3 bb g Arch(USA) Toll (USA) (Giant's Causeway (USA))
2425a[14] 3620a[4]

Taxiwala (IRE) *Archie Watson* 84
2 b g Holy Roman Emperor(IRE) It's True (IRE) (Kheleyf (USA))
2093[2] 2783[2] (3534) 3988[8] 5185[15]

Taxmeifyoucan (IRE)
Keith Dalgleish a72 92
5 b g Beat Hollow Accounting (Sillery (USA))
8399[4]
Taylor Velvet (IRE) *Fergal Birrane* a55 53
4 b m Intense Focus(USA) Rose Story (FR) (Observatory (USA))
3322[5]
Tazaman *Kevin Frost* a30 51
2 ch g Mukhadram Farletti (Royal Applause)
8058[10] 8657[6]
Tchapalo (FR) *N Leenders* 48
4 b g Whipper(USA) Tchastaya (FR) (Marju (IRE))
1908a[10]
Te Akau Caliburn (IRE)
Andrew Balding 105
4 b h Camelot Enchanted Evening (IRE) (High Chaparral (IRE))
2742[5] (3655)◆ 4884[2]
Te Akau Shark (NZ) *Jamie Richards* 117
4 ch g Rip Van Winkle(IRE) Bak Da Chief (NZ) (Chief Bearhart (CAN))
8579a[3]
Te Amo Te Amo *Simon Dow* a51 58
3 b g Kyllachy Caption (Motivator)
1139[8] 2063[6] 2489[4] 2939[9] 3440[10] 8457[11] 9161[7] 9246[6] 9384[8]
Team Talk *Saeed bin Suroor* a111 111
6 b g Teofilo(IRE) Native Blue (Seeking The Gold (USA))
51a[4] 514a[2] 844a[4] 1113a[8] 1441a[10]
Teasel's Rock (IRE) *Tim Easterby* 36
2 b f Society Rock(IRE) Laywaan (USA) (Fantastic Light (USA))
3245[10] 4623[10] 5553[13] 6097[9] 6539[6] 7329[6]
Tease Maid *John Quinn* a64 46
3 b f Heeraat(IRE) Flirtinaskirt (Avonbridge)
1523[3] 2063[4] 3709[9] 4457[4] 4763[4] 5620[7] 7389[3] 7823[12] 8071[2] 8407[3] 8949[12] 9185[5]
Tea Time Desert (ITY)
Simone Brogi 55
2 b f Desert Prince(IRE) Mugnaga (IRE) (Catrail (USA))
5166a[4]
Tebay (IRE) *John Best* a45 56
4 b g Elzaam(AUS) Maid Of Ale (IRE) (Barathea (IRE))
801[8] 1183[13] 2617[7] 2975[9] 3481[7] 4115[13] 8822[3] 9090[8]
Technician (IRE) *Martyn Meade* 115
3 gr c Mastercraftsman(IRE) Arosa (IRE) (Sadler's Wells (USA))
(1558)◆ 2084[2] 2523[5] (3789a) 5585[6] (6213) 7196[6] (7927a) (8589a)◆
Technological *George Margarson* a94 56
4 gr g Universal(IRE) Qeethaara (USA) (Aljabr (USA))
345[2] (617) 878[6] 980[2] 1172[4] 1596[4] 2748[14] 3145[4]
Teemlucky *Ian Williams* a40 55
3 ch f Yorgunnabelucky(USA) Dream Esteem (Mark Of Esteem (IRE))
4189[6] 4738[6] 5336[4] 5987[10] 7200[2] 8200[9] 8551[16]
Teenage Gal (IRE) *Gavin Hernon* a78 73
4 b m Acclamation Bobbie Soxer (IRE) (Pivotal)
2266a[4]
Teenar *Richard Fahey* a72 76
2 b g Mayson Bailadeira (Intikhab (USA))
3498[7] 3997[2] 4384[3] 4938[2] 5612[10]
Teepee Time *Michael Mullineaux* a46 52
6 b m Compton Place Deora De (Night Shift (USA))
322[6] 1952[8] 2632[10] 3291[6] 4694[2] 5181[12] 5722[9] 5892[2] 6277[2] 8117[7] 9627[6]
Tel Aviv (FR) *Andrea Marcialis* 90
3 b c Nathaniel(IRE) Grenade (FR) (Bering)
2499a[6] 4428a[4]
Telecaster *Hughie Morrison* 117
3 b c New Approach(IRE) Shirocco Star (Shirocco (GER))
1417[2] (1824) (2777) 3345[13] 4668[7]
Telekinetic *Tony Carroll* a52 51
4 b m Champs Elysees Kinetix (Linamix (FR))
257[9] 1958[3] 2738[4] 2975[7] 4346[9] 5025[8] 5824[2] 6855[5] 8663[2] 9289[7]
Telemaque (USA) *A Fabre*
2 b c War Front(USA) Treasure Trail (USA) (Pulpit (USA))
4947a[6]
Teleplay (AUS)
Mick Price & Michael Kent Jnr 109
4 b m Written Tycoon(AUS) Special Episode (AUS) (Redoute's Choice (AUS))
(9015a)
Tell Me All *Sir Mark Prescott Bt* a79 88
2 b c Lope De Vega(IRE) Confidential Lady (Singspiel (IRE))
5177[5] (5512) 6112[2] (7429) 8111[8]
Tellovoi (IRE) *Richard Guest* a50 60
11 b g Indian Haven Kloonlara (IRE) (Green Desert (USA))
159[6] 379[3] 613[3] 969[2] 1071[3] 1732[6] 1967[9] (2066) 2235[4] 2298[5] 2681[6] 3142[8] 6572[6] 6885[5] 7374[15] 7550[3] 7603[6] 8068[10]
Tell William *Marcus Tregoning* 79
3 b g Invincible Spirit(IRE) Swiss Kiss (Dansili)
5448[3] 6084[9] (6558) 7176[2]
Temper Trap *Tim Easterby* 39
2 br g Slade Power(IRE) Sloane Square (Teofilo (IRE))
5845[8] 6892[8]
Temple Boy (FR) *J Phelippon* a64 68
7 gr g Linda's Lad Temple Queen (GER) (Local Suitor (USA))
2026a[6]
Temple Church (IRE)
Hughie Morrison 106
5 b g Lawman(FR) All Hallows (IRE) (Dalakhani (IRE))
4053[16] 5183[11] 6657[13]
Temple Of Heaven *Richard Hannon* a104 98
2 b g Iffraaj Royal Whisper (Royal Applause)
(1953) (2830) 3988[13] (8426)◆

Temple Of Wonder (IRE)
Liam Bailey a53 62
3 b g Clodovil(IRE) Noble Fantasy (GER) (Big Shuffle (USA))
140[7] 506[3] 854[2] 2063[9] 2474[7] 2592[5] 3924[9] 4487[2]◆ 4915[9] 5272[7] 6036[8]◆ 7210[9] 7654[6] 7962[13]
Temple Road (IRE) *Milton Bradley* a65 51
11 b g Street Cry(IRE) Sugarhoneybaby (IRE) (Docksider (USA))
179[U] 9247[5]
Templier (IRE) *Gary Moore* a53 58
6 b g Mastercraftsman(IRE) Tigertail (FR) (Priolo (USA))
185[5] 3252[4] 5047[6] 5802[11]
Tempus *Roger Charlton* a95 83
3 b c Kingman Passage Of Time (Dansili)
(2518)◆ (3727) 8320[4]
Temujin (IRE) *Ali Stronge* a64 63
3 b g Moohaajim(IRE) Alhena (IRE) (Alhaarth (IRE))
2007[5] 3256[2] 3594[2] 6304[8]
Temur Khan *Tony Carroll* a84 62
4 br g Dansili Slink (Selkirk (USA))
(41) (390) 980[4] 1425[9] 2620[7] 3377[5] 9543[8]
Tenax (IRE) *Nigel Tinkler* 90
3 b g Slade Power(IRE) Stravina (GER) (Platini (GER))
1762[3] 2255[2] 2810[5] 3654[3] 4008[3] (4603) 5126[5] 5399[3] 5724[2]◆ 6451[5] 6623[2] 6976[5]
Tenbobmillionaire *Tim Easterby* 51
2 b c Heeraat(IRE) Otroolha (IRE) (Oasis Dream)
4624[9] 5689[9] 6064[12] 6539[10]
Tenbury Wells (USA) *John Gosden* a70
2 b c Medaglia d'Oro(USA) Dayatthespa (USA) (City Zip (USA))
9624[7]
Tencaratrubieslace (FR)
M Delcher Sanchez a71 64
3 b f Siyouni(FR) Diamond Square (FR) (Dyhim Diamond (IRE))
1512a[9] 8983a[12]
Ten Chants *Ed Dunlop* a64 57
2 gr g Gregorian(IRE) Tenbridge (Avonbridge)
5052[6] 5433[6] 5780[7] 6394[6]
Tenedos *Ed de Giles* a72 60
4 b g High Chaparral(IRE) Garanciere (FR) (Anabaa (USA))
345[6] 803[10] 1096[7] 1525[5] 1971[8]
Tenfold (IRE) *Martyn Meade* 71
2 b g Born To Sea(IRE) Dear Dream (IRE) (Montjeu (IRE))
8100[5]
Tenley (AUS) *James Cummings* 101
2 gr f Medaglia d'Oro(USA) Fratianne (AUS) (Lonhro (AUS))
8135a[7]
Tenorio (FR) *Mlle V Dissaux* a58 75
6 b h Dobby Road(FR) Surtsey (FR) (Anabaa Blue)
6267a[9]
Ten Sovereigns (IRE) *A P O'Brien* 125
3 b c No Nay Never(USA) Seeking Solace (Exceed And Excel (AUS))
2411[5] 4050[4] (4923) 6423[6] 8362a[12]
Ten Thousand Stars
Adrian Nicholls a54 70
2 ch f Toronado(IRE) Myriades D'Etoiles (IRE) (Green Tune (USA))
5433[10] (6161) 6654[3] 7309[7]
Teodora De Vega (IRE)
Ralph Beckett a82 82
3 b f Lope De Vega(IRE) Applauded (IRE) (Royal Applause)
7945 1165[6] 1652[4] 3773[2]◆ (4836) 5436[2] (5549) 6172[5] 7702[2]◆ 8513[7]
Teodula (IRE) *Henry Spiller* a64 58
3 ch f Tagula(IRE) Lady Kildare (IRE) (Bachelor Duke (USA))
274[7] 1954[9]
Tequila Boom Boom (FR)
Mlle M-L Mortier a25 57
3 b f Palace Episode(USA) Optica (FR) (Hernando (FR))
2311a[5]
Terbium (AUS) *Phillip Stokes* 104
3 gb g Terango(AUS) Serene Lass (AUS) (Not A Single Doubt (AUS))
8360a[8]
Terebellum (IRE) *John Gosden* 113
3 br f Sea The Stars(IRE) Marvada (IRE) (Elusive City (USA))
(3013)◆ 3762[3] (6250a) 7942a[5]
Tereshkova *Michael Bell* 60
3 b f Sea The Moon(GER) Fanny Squeers (New Approach (IRE))
1828[10] 2340[10] 2583[8]
Teresita Alvarez (USA)
Jeremy Noseda a68 61
3 b f Arch(USA) Stroll By (USA) (Stroll (USA))
55[F] 461[10]
Termonator *Grant Tuer* a68 67
3 ch g Monsieur Bond(IRE) Easy Terms (Trade Fair)
831[5] 1161[6] 1336[9] (1863) 2482[2] 3204[3]◆ 8025[7] 8713[4]
Terra Dina (FR) *H-F Devin* a79 95
3 b f Doctor Dino(FR) Terra Alta (FR) (Kaldounevees (FR))
7978a[7] 9170a[13]
Terre De France (FR) *F Rossi* a75 82
2 b c Intello(GER) Narya (IRE) (Halling (USA))
6386a[4] (7799a)
Terrestre (FR) *F Head* a46
3 ch f Motivator Gout De Terroir (USA) (Lemon Drop Kid (USA))
509a[12]
Terri Rules (IRE) *Lee Carter* a61 69
4 b m Camacho Hawaiian Storm (Jeremy (USA))
1076[4] 1595[8] 1766[6] 2025[4] 2473[8] 4772[5] 5046[2] 5315[2] 6285[5] 6602[2] 6889[5] (8018) 8896[9] 9246[3] 9583[4] 9664[2]

Tertius (FR) *M Nigge* a92 108
3 ch c Siyouni(FR) Rhenania (IRE) (Shamardal (USA))
(1200a) 5714a[5] 6520a[3] 8141a[6] 8648a[13]
Teruntum Star (FR)
David C Griffiths a90 101
7 ch g Dutch Art Seralia (Royal Academy (USA))
357 297[6] (1847) 2117[14] 3602[11] 5120[13] 5740[7] 7193[22] 7894[3] 8340[5] (8522)
Terzetto (IRE) *M Halford* a85 96
4 ch m Iffraaj Calando (USA) (Storm Cat (USA))
7635a[5] 8368a[11]
Tesorina (IRE) *William Knight* a61 57
4 b m Lilbourne Lad(IRE) Insieme (IRE) (Barathea (IRE))
207[9] 288[2] (736) 1297[3] 1362[3] 1498[5] 2595[12]
Testa (IRE) *S Wattel* a96 90
3 b f Acclamation Tecla (IRE) (Whipper (USA))
3712a[2] 7360a[5] 9603a[7]
Testa Rossa (IRE) *Jim Goldie* a73 76
9 b g Oratorio(IRE) Red Rita (IRE) (Kefaah (USA))
350[6] 611[4] 807[5] 1273[9] 1401[3] 1925[5] 2246[6] 2963[10] 4054[9] 4329[10]
Testiange (FR) *P Monfort* 53
3 ch g Archange D'Or(IRE) Testisun (FR) (Until Sundown (USA))
7476a[3]
Teston (FR) *P Bary* a90 93
4 ch g Rio De La Plata(USA) Tianshan (FR) (Lahint (USA))
3136a[6] 4704a[5]
Test Valley (IRE)
Tracey Barfoot-Saunt a34 63
4 b g Footstepsinthesand Rockabout (IRE) (Rock Of Gibraltar (IRE))
2128[11] 2280[4] 2731[5]◆ 3533[7] 6363[11] 7112[9]
Tete Raide (FR) *B Deniel* 48
4 b g Agent Secret(IRE) Tetaclak (FR) (Ballingarry (IRE))
8737a[5]
Tetradrachm *Shaun Harris* a68 51
6 b g Holy Roman Emperor(IRE) Dahlia's Krissy (USA) (Kris S (USA))
(321)◆ 607[4] 782[4] 1024[6] 2696[11]
Texas Radio (IRE)
John James Feane a53 47
6 b g Kyllachy Miss Rochester (IRE) (Montjeu (IRE))
7086a[10] (Dead)
Texas Rock (IRE) *M C Grassick* a77 100
8 b g Rock Of Gibraltar(IRE) Vestavia (IRE) (Alhaarth (IRE))
1434a[10] 1776a[6] 2879a[4] 3062a[3] 5205a[5]
Texting *Mohamed Moubarak* a64 87
3 b f Charm Spirit(IRE) Dreamily (IRE) (New Approach (IRE))
1816[2] 3058[4] 3742[2] (4343) (5372) 6080[2] (6954) 7894[15]
Thaayer *Michael Herrington* a74 55
4 b g Helmet(AUS) Sakhya (IRE) (Barathea (IRE))
1401[6] 4386[7] 4907[12] 9512[7]
Thahab Ifraj (IRE) *Alexandra Dunn* a65 63
6 ch g Frozen Power(IRE) Penny Rouge (IRE) (Pennekamp (USA))
160[3] (2196) 3205[2] (6552) 6864[5] (8639) 9336[10]
Thai Power (IRE) *Andrew Balding* 60
2 b c Kingman Roscoff (IRE) (Daylami (IRE))
7611[4] 8257[5]
Tha'ir (IRE) *Philip McBride* a57 57
9 b g New Approach(IRE) Flashing Green (Green Desert (USA))
241[11] 481[9] 1717[11] (1841) 2012[2] 2693[3] 3325[2]
Thais (FR) *Chad C Brown* 101
5 bb m Rio De La Plata(USA) Tianshan (FR) (Lahint (USA))
4950a[6] 5978a[5]
Thai Terrier (USA) *Mark Johnston* a75
3 b g Kitten's Joy(USA) Perfect Agility (USA) (Perfect Soul (IRE))
9662[2]◆
Thakaa (USA) *Charles Hills* a56 71
3 b f Lemon Drop Kid(USA) Yaqeen (Green Desert (USA))
1855[5] 3637[4] 4628[7]
Thammin *M Al Mheiri* a106 89
5 gr g Dark Angel(IRE) Gimme Some Lovin (IRE) (Desert Style (IRE))
1109a[7]
Thaniella (FR) *P Bary* a61 69
2 ch f Nathaniel(IRE) Matorio (FR) (Oratorio (IRE))
8239a[4]
Thanielle (FR) *Richard Hannon* 75
2 b f Nathaniel(IRE) Tingling (USA) (Storm Cat (USA))
5961[4] 6906[3]
Thanks Be *Charlie Fellowes* a68 92
3 ch f Mukhadram Out Of Thanks (IRE) (Sadler's Wells (USA))
2102[2] 2935[2] (4052)
Thank The Irish (IRE)
Jamie Osborne a59 56
2 b c Camacho Deira Dubai (Green Desert (USA))
6718[8] 6858[7] 7154[7] 7548[10] 8061[13]
Thaqaffa (IRE) *Amy Murphy* a85 81
6 b g Kodiac Incense (Unfuwain (USA))
345[3] 617[8] 945[10] 1291[2] 2092[6] 3091[3] 5625[6] 6888[6]
That Is The Spirit *Michael Appleby* a84 92
8 b g Invincible Spirit(IRE) Fraulein (Acatenango (GER))
(3496) 3991[3] 5386[2]◆ 6207[5]
That's Not Me (IRE)
Anthony McCann a52 76
3 ch f Dandy Man(IRE) Whimsical (IRE) (Strategic Prince)
306a[4] 6162[3] 6591[10] 7241a[15]
Thavors (ITY) *Andrea Marcialis* 67
2 b c Sakhee's Secret Dolce Nera (Dansili)
4949a[3] 5759a[4]

Thawry *Antony Brittain* a63 59
4 b g Iffraaj Salacia (IRE) (Echo Of Light)
272[4]◆ 495[5] 793[4] (950) 1106[6] 1395[7] 1508[3] 2185[6] 2696[9] 3161[5] 3816[10] 4333[8] 6663[6] 7034[4] 7415[8] 7956[4] 8348[4] 8669[9] 9345[5]
The Accountant *Amy Murphy* a51 59
4 ch g Dylan Thomas(IRE) Glorybe (GER) (Monsun (GER))
7382[4]
The Armed Man *Chris Fairhurst* a75 89
6 b g Misu Bond(IRE) Accamelia (Shinko Forest (IRE))
(1978) 2843[7] 3770[4] 4521[4] 5217[4] 5691[3] 6676[4] 7121[15]
Theatre Of War (IRE)
Keith Dalgleish a82 79
3 b g War Command(USA) Final Opinion (IRE) (King's Theatre (IRE))
3357[8] 3930[4] 4099[7] 4693[9]
Theatro (IRE) *Jedd O'Keeffe* a60 84
3 b f Camelot Bogside Theatre (IRE) (Fruits Of Love (USA))
1764[11] 2245[3] 2875[4] (4039) 4291[6] (5792)◆ 6924[3] 8661[2]
Theban Air *Lucy Wadham* a58 36
3 b f Bated Breath Temple Of Thebes (IRE) (Bahri (USA))
733[7] 1142[P] 7298[6]
The Bearfighter (IRE)
Charlie Fellowes a58
4 b g Society Rock(IRE) Absolute Fun (IRE) (Lawman (FR))
145[8]
The Bell Conductor (IRE)
Phillip Makin a74 79
2 b g Dandy Man(IRE) Saffian (Dubawi (IRE))
3411[2] 8097[3] 8631[2]◆ (8899)
Thebian *John Gosden* a34
2 b c Kingman Amarillo Starlight (IRE) (Dalakhani (IRE))
8889[10]
The Big House (IRE)
Adrian Nicholls a45 64
3 b g Coach House(IRE) Tekhania (IRE) (Dalakhani (IRE))
1430[8] 2197[10] 3271[2] 3650[2]◆ 4244[8] 4488[U] 4915[4] (5389) 5695[2] 5771[3] 6679[3] 6937[6] (7444)◆ 7780[5]
The Blue Bower (IRE) *Suzy Smith* a62 65
2 b f Morpheus Blue Holly (IRE) (Blues Traveller (IRE))
3491[4]◆ 4222[10] 5250[3] 5838[5] 6415[4] 7276[6] 8750[6] 9061[2] 9196[3]
The Blue Eye
Jassim Mohammed Ghazali 104
7 b h Dubawi(IRE) Soneva (USA) (Cherokee Run (USA))
894a[4]
The Blues Master (IRE) *Alan King* a72 74
5 gr g Mastercraftsman(IRE) Catch The Blues (IRE) (Bluebird (USA))
4383[2] 5631[4]
The British Lion (IRE)
Alexandra Dunn a68 65
4 b g Power Mala Mala (IRE) (Brief Truce (USA))
355[5] (463) 801[6] 1036[9] 1164[6] 1684[7] 1880[7] 2232[3] 3188[7] 3967[7] 5016[9] 8711[13] 9128[11] 9248[5] 9450[3]
The Broghie Man
Adrian Paul Keatley 95
4 ch g Cityscape Suelita (Dutch Art)
2667a[6] 3818a[7] 5916[5]
The Brora Pobbles *Alistair Whillans* a48 49
4 b m Helmet(AUS) Snow Blossom (Beat Hollow)
3224[10] 4916[5] 5560[14] 7508[5] 7783[4] 8664[7] 9395[7] 9470[3]
The Bull (IRE) *Ben Haslam* a55 57
4 ch g Camacho Zarara (USA) (Manila (USA))
1402[6] 2013[6] 3227[3] 3723[2] 4824[4] 5857[4] 6666[5] 6945[4] 7654[3] 8821[3]
The Cashel Man (IRE)
Nicky Henderson a89 94
7 b g High Chaparral(IRE) Hadarama (IRE) (Sinndar (IRE))
1735[4] 2781[9] 5540[4]
The Celtic Machine *Pat Phelan* a47
4 b g Rip Van Winkle(IRE) Lyra's Daemon (Singspiel (IRE))
206[5] 695[10] 1362[7] 1680[8]
The Cherokee Kid (IRE)
David Evans a22
2 ch g Anjaal Hazardous (Night Shift (USA))
9451[8] 9567[11]
Thechildren'strust (IRE)
Gary Moore a83 80
4 br g Society Rock(IRE) Estemaala (IRE) (Cape Cross (IRE))
5[5] 294[7] 5667[9] 6083[4] (6904) 7125[4] 8827[6] 9173[6] 9422[2] 9658[4]
The Chosen One (NZ)
Murray Baker & Andrew Forsman 108
3 b c Savabeel(AUS) The Glitzy One (AUS) (Flying Spur (AUS))
(8134a) 8361a[9] 8767a[5] 8844a[17]
The City's Phantom
Richard Spencer 75
2 b c Free Eagle(IRE) Meet Marhaba (IRE) (Marju (IRE))
4069[5] 5314[3]
The Conqueror (IRE) *A Botti* 102
4 ch h Excelebration(IRE) March Madness (Noverre (USA))
2888a[5] 8787a[5]
Thecornishbarron (IRE)
Aytach Sadik a52 52
7 b g Bushranger(IRE) Tripudium (IRE) (Night Shift (USA))
210[2] 1527[2] 1858[2] 2196[8] 2963[13] 7873[14] 8670[10]
The Corporal (IRE) *Chris Wall* 86
3 b g Dansili Ideal (Galileo (IRE))
1857[7]◆ 2766[10] 4296[5] (5060) (6129) 6671[5] 7396[3]

The Cruising Lord *Michael Attwater* 100
3 b g Coach House(IRE) Lady Filly (Atraf)
(1909) 2270[6] 2826[9] 3855[2] 4665[5] 5371[9] 5932[10] 7889[9]

The Cruix (IRE) *Dean Ivory* 60
4 ch g Galileo(IRE) Walklikeanegyptian (IRE) (Danehill (USA))
3263[13] 4304[6] 4600[3]

The Daley Express (IRE)
Ronald Harris a93 91
5 b g Elzaam(AUS) Seraphina (IRE) (Pips Pride)
1822[2] (1915)◆ 2403[6] 3531[13] 4236[10] 5252[2] 6208[4] 6332[4] (7771)◆ 8099[4] 8867[7] 9571[7]

The Dancing Poet *Ed Vaughan* a75 75
3 ch g Poet's Voice Caldy Dancer (IRE) (Soviet Star (USA))
1171[6] 5561[7] (6393) 7126[3] 7773[3] 8641[8]

The Defiant *Paul Midgley* a57 72
3 b g Morpheus Killer Class (Kyllachy)
(906) 1650[6] (2327) (3417) 4436[2]◆ 5042[8] 6715[8] 6976[6] 7367[4] 8117[9]

The Detainee *Neil Mulholland* a65 71
6 b g Aqlaam Jakarta Jade (IRE) (Royal Abjar (USA))
619[3] 947[7] 3000[2] 3511[7] 4661[10] 6200[3] 7231[6]

Thedevilinneville *Adam West* a52 39
3 b g Paco Boy(IRE) Ribbon Royale (Royal Applause)
438[4] 534[5] 753[8] 1071[2]◆ 1549[11] 3182[6] 3651[13] 4078[6] 4376[6] 4477[8] 5107[9]

The Eagle's Nest (IRE)
Alexandra Dunn a65 59
5 ch g Lope De Vega(IRE) Follow My Lead (Night Shift (USA))
942[9] 1169[7] 1343[11] 1675[7] 2471[4] 8813[7] 9362[7] 9479[6]

The Emperor Within (FR)
Martin Smith a97 97
4 b g Holy Roman Emperor(IRE) Watchful (IRE) (Galileo (IRE))
1694[2] 2429a[8] 2808[6] 4342[7] 7163[5] 8253[12]

The Establishment *John Butler* a67 44
4 b g Exceed And Excel(AUS) Sweet Coincidence (Mujahid (USA))
36[7] 564[5] (790) 1164[10] 1342[9] 1597[10] 1767[10] 2717[2] 4479[8] 6350[9] 6968[9] 7519[10] 9498[11]

The Fiddler *Chris Wall* a58 62
4 b g Big Bad Bob(IRE) Strings (Unfuwain (USA))
2202[7] 3272[3] 4251[8] 5029[2] (5974) (7314)

The First King (IRE) *Paul Cole* a80
2 b g War Command(USA) Rochitta (USA) (Arch (USA))
8448a[2]

The Fitzpiers Lion (IRE)
Ronald Harris a43 49
2 gr g Gutaifan(IRE) Miss Mary (Multiplex)
7113[8] 8058[9]

The Galla Girl (IRE) *Denis Quinn* a60 19
3 b f Footstepsinthesand Headborough Lass (IRE) (Invincible Spirit (IRE))
174[9]

The Game Is On
Sir Mark Prescott Bt a76 68
3 b g Garswood Paquerettza (FR) (Dr Fong (USA))
3208[4]◆ 5016[4] (5287) 5580[5] 8705[5] (9256)

The Game Of Life
Michael Herrington a85 64
4 b g Oasis Dream Velvet Star (IRE) (Galileo (IRE))
9255[10] 9476[11] 9606[8]

The Gates Of Dawn (FR)
George Baker a72 49
4 ch g Iffraaj Cheap Thrills (Bertolini (USA))
1356[8] 2107[13] 4786[5]

The Gill Brothers *Stuart Williams* a94 41
3 gr g Mukhadram Si Belle (IRE) (Dalakhani (IRE))
(7572) (8894)◆ 9200[3] 9440[2]

The Gingerbreadman
Chris Fairhurst a39 40
4 b g Misu Bond(IRE) Accamelia (Shinko Forest (IRE))
2532[5]◆ 3058[5] 3772[7] 4602[9] 5558[13] 7869[7] 8266[4] 8903[8]

The Ginger Bullet *Richard Fahey* a44 56
2 ch c Camacho Queen's Pudding (IRE) (Royal Applause)
1843[6] 2415[7] 2820[6] 4756[9] 5896[4] 6539[5] 7056[2] 7582[11]

Theglasgowwarrior *Jim Goldie* a93 97
5 b g Sir Percy Sweet Cando (IRE) (Royal Applause)
2370[3] 2680[2] (2786)◆ 3600[8] 4102[9] 4381[5] 5928[2] 6657[11] 7147[3] 7403[2]

The Golden Cue *Steph Hollinshead* a69 52
4 ch g Zebedee Khafayif (USA) (Swain (IRE))
(42) 586[3] 1973[7] 2194[7] 2580[6] 3504[12] 5952[7] 6168[4] 7757[11] 8263[7] 8646[11]

The Grand Visir *Ian Williams* a54 109
5 b g Frankel Piping (IRE) (Montjeu (IRE))
3600[7] (3952) 5183[7] 6473[16]

Thegreatcollection (USA)
Doug Watson a108
5 b g Saint Anddan(USA) Cactus Cadillac (USA) (Cactus Ridge (USA))
282a[2] 513a[2] 957a[4]

Thegreatestshowman *Amy Murphy* a93 89
3 ch g Equiano(FR) Conversational (IRE) (Thousand Words)
1729[6] 2149[2]◆ 3422[3] 4368[8] (5356) (5647) 6565[4] 6954[4] 7348[3] 8420[2] (9131)◆ 9166[4] 9389[5]

The Great Heir (FR) *Kevin Ryan* 95
3 b g Pedro The Great(USA) Lady McKell (IRE) (Raven's Pass (USA))
2746[16] 3599[12] 5953[3] 7123[2]◆

The Great Phoenix *Gay Kelleway* a28 66
3 ch g Phoenix Reach(IRE) Comtesse Noire (CAN) (Woodman (USA))
5622[12] 7573[10]

The Great Wall (USA)
Michael Appleby a86 91
5 b g Bernardini(USA) Music Room (USA) (Unbridled's Song (USA))
4[8] 499[6] 832[3] 1160[2] 1367[11] 1969[4] 2346[5]

The Grey Bay (IRE) *Julie Camacho* a52 39
2 gr g Gutaifan(IRE) Coursing (Kyllachy)
5913[8] 7769[7] 8067[6] 9394[5]

The Grey Dancer (IRE)
Joseph Tuite a41 49
3 gr g Alhebayeb(IRE) Key Girl (IRE) (Key Of Luck (USA))
79[13]

The Grey Goat (IRE)
Peter Charalambous a65 55
3 gr g Zebedee Empress Charlotte (Holy Roman Emperor (IRE))
7523[5] 7841[5] 8290[7] 8669[11]

Thegreyvtrain *Ronald Harris* a68 70
3 gr f Coach House(IRE) Debutante Blues (USA) (Dubawi (IRE))
298[4] 605[7] 906[9] 2474[2] (3148) (4772) 5013[3] 5449[7] 5603[2] 6183[2] 6397[6] 6562[2] 6754[2] 8117[5]

The Grey Zebedee *Tim Easterby* a64 63
3 gr g Zebedee Nippy (FR) (Anabaa (USA))
2197[7] 2908[7] 5620[3] 5765[2] (6277) 6608[3] 7047[3] 7307[8] 7959[2] 8632[4] 8925[10] 9352[11] (9539)

The Groove *David Evans* a68 75
6 b g Azamour(IRE) Dance East (Shamardal (USA))
181[6] 466[3] (600) (883) 1208[2] 1597[5] 1686[3] 1766[7] 2339[2] 2717[7] 2997[4] 3543[10] 4455[5] (4764) 6027[4] (6898) 7299[5] 8220[3] 8471[10] 9365[3]◆ 9427[5] 9622[5]

Theheartneverlies
Sir Mark Prescott Bt a48 34
2 b g Oasis Dream Albamara (Galileo (IRE))
7316[6] 7769[8] 8059[9]

The Inevitable (AUS) *Scott Brunton* 105
3 b g Dundeel(NZ) Gift Bouquet (AUS) (King's High (AUS))
8805a[12]

The Irish Rover (IRE) *A P O'Brien* a78 100
3 b c No Nay Never(USA) Shelley Beach (IRE) (Danehill Dancer (IRE))
1600a[5] 2156a[2] 2882a[9] 3951[11]

The Jean Genie *William Stone* a87 86
5 bb m Lawman(FR) Miracle Seeker (Rainbow Quest (USA))
884[4] 1065[5] 1292[2] (1688) (1934) 6289[2] 6759[2] 7153[3] 7610[3] 8725[13] 9388[2] 9510[10]

The King (IRE) *Mrs John Harrington* 107
4 ch h Mastercraftsman(IRE) Catch The Moon (IRE) (Peintre Celebre (USA))
2494a[3] 4351a[9] 5404a[2]

The King's Steed *Shaun Lycett* a58 42
6 b g Equiano(FR) King's Siren (IRE) (King's Best (USA))
463[3] 828[4] 1177[14] 1715[4] 2692[7] 4195[7] 4733[9] 8295[3] (8689) 8915[11] 9039[8] (9456) 9566[8]

The Kyllachy Touch *Derek Shaw* a37
2 gr c Kyllachy The Manx Touch (IRE) (Petardia)
9474[6] 9607[10]

The Lacemaker *Milton Harris* a66 43
5 b m Dutch Art Sospel (Kendor (FR))
2339[13] 3838[9] 4281[14] 5892[7] 6299[5] 7576[11] 8217[3] 8704[3] 8896[6] 9128[4] (9246) (9386) 9622[10]

The Lamplighter (FR)
George Baker a82 78
4 b g Elusive City(USA) Plume Rouge (Pivotal)
1036[2] 1560[6] 2514[4] 3014[4] 3462[10] 3645[2] 3967[6] 4281[13] 6109[5] (6401) 7130[7] 7760[2] 8285[2]

The Last Bow *Michael Easterby* 10
2 b f Casamento(IRE) Bow Bridge (Bertolini (USA))
7698[8] 8631[9]

The Last Emperor *Emmet Mullins* a79 58
4 b g Azamour(IRE) Raskutani (Dansili)
7489[4]

The Last Party *James Given* a40 41
3 b f Hellvelyn Third Party (Terimon)
2635[15] 4651[10] 5064[7]

The Lazy Monkey (IRE)
Mark Johnston a64 25
2 b f Rock Of Gibraltar(IRE) Idle Rich (USA) (Sky Classic (CAN))
1879[7] 2052[8] 3578[3] 4289[4] 4756[12]

The Lock Master (IRE)
Michael Appleby a45 37
12 b g Key Of Luck(USA) Pitrizza (IRE) (Machiavellian (USA))
504[7] 721[9] 1163[8]

Thelonious *Michael Bell* a66 61
3 b g Sea The Moon(GER) Miss Chaussini (IRE) (Rossini (USA))
967[3] 1268[3] 2208[10]

The Lords Walk *Bill Turner* a64 72
6 b g Dick Turpin(IRE) Mi Anna (GER) (Lake Coniston (IRE))
1591[4] 1710[7] (2111) 2617[4] 2998[7] 3571[7] 4561[6] (5087) 5570[2] 6121[2] 6904[3]

The Man Of Mode (IRE)
Michael Attwater a32 39
3 b g Society Rock(IRE) Prime Time Girl (Primo Dominie)
367[7] 597[12]

Thematic (USA)
Dominic Ffrench Davis a79 89
3 b g Noble Mission Gateway (USA) (A.P. Indy (USA))
5717a[7] 9667[7]

Themaxwecan (IRE) *Mark Johnston* a89 106
3 b c Maxios Psychometry (FR) (Danehill Dancer (IRE))
(156) 1558[2] 2619[9] 3337[2] 3984[8] 4644[5] (5368) 6452[2] (6834) 8114[20]

The Mcgregornator (IRE)
Adrian Paul Keatley a38 81
5 bz g Bushranger(IRE) Bridal Path (Groom Dancer (USA))
410[11]

The Mekon *Noel Wilson* 56
4 ch g Red Jazz(USA) Date Mate (USA) (Thorn Dance (USA))
2146[10] 2634[9] 3970[6] 6502[9] 7509[8]

The Met *David Loughnane* a85 68
3 b g Gregorian(IRE) Kasalla (IRE) (Footstepsinthesand)
(8472) (9502)◆

The Meter *Mohamed Moubarak* a69 49
3 b f Helsinki(USA) Lulea (Authorized (IRE))
32[6] 1819[11] 3146[8] 4110[9] 4642[8]

The Mystery Wizard *Tim Easterby* a35 39
2 b c Finjaan Samerous (FR) (Generous (IRE))
1812[6] 5052[12] 5553[12] 5968[11]

The Navigator *Dianne Sayer* 82
4 gr g Mastercraftsman(IRE) Blessing (USA) (Pulpit (USA))
2894[2]◆ 3250[6] 4240[13] 4817[2] 5725[10] 6626[5] (7069)

The New Marwan *Richard Fahey* 82
2 b c Dark Angel(IRE) Tiger Mist (IRE) (Galileo (IRE))
2561[6] 3071[2] (3998) 4878[3] 5704[2] 7139[3] 8124[5]

The Night King *Mick Quinn* a78 75
4 b g Arcano(IRE) Semplicita (IRE) (In The Wings)
(1065) 1418[4] 1882[4] 2259[4] 2763[5] 3937[3] 5060[3] 8761[16] 9202[11] 9443[9]

The Night Watch *William Haggas* a83 85
3 b g Dutch Art Scarlet Runner (Night Shift (USA))
2139[2] 2746[14] 3590[6] (4297) 5126[4] 7002[10]

The Nile Song (FR) *Y Barberot* 61
2 gr f Stormy River(FR) Italica (FR) (Slickly (FR))
1240a[2] 4679a[4] 5286a[8] 5759a[10]

The Numismatist (IRE)
Jamie Osborne a47
3 b c Sir Prancealot(IRE) Friendly Heart (CAN) (Lion Heart (USA))
908[6] 943[9] 1725[6] 2240[3]

Theobald (IRE) *J S Bolger* a100 101
4 ch g Teofilo(IRE) Sanaara (USA) (Anabaa (USA))
1308a[20]

Theodorico (IRE) *Lucinda Egerton* a27 80
6 b g Teofilo(IRE) Yes Oh Yes (USA) (Gone West (USA))
1457[9] 2151[7] 3649[12] 5490[4]◆ 5616[9]

The One Maybe (FR)
Stephanie Gachelin
4 bl m Henrythenavigator(USA) Kandalek (Hawk Wing (USA))
8240a[12]

Theory Of Time (IRE)
Charlie Appleby 86
2 b f Dubawi(IRE) Betimes (New Approach (IRE))
(2915) 3983[11]

Theotherside (IRE) *Richard Hannon* 77
2 br f Dandy Man(IRE) New Magic (IRE) (Statue Of Liberty (USA))
(7406)

The Pastoral Bear *Mark Pattinson*
3 ch f Pastoral Pursuits Torrecilla (General Monash (USA))
4423[6] 6074[13]

The Peckhampouncer (IRE)
D Broad 83
2 b c Cappella Sansevero Monivea (IRE) (Fasliyev (USA))
4098[4]

The Perch (IRE) *Patrick J McKenna* a52 44
4 b m Camacho Schull Harbour (IRE) (Greenwood Lake (USA))
1080[4]

The Perfect Crown (IRE)
Archie Watson a92
2 b c Hallowed Crown(AUS) Perfect Fun (Marju (IRE))
(9085)◆

The Pink'n *Seamus Mullins* 79
3 gr g Dunaden(FR) Lady Friend (Environment Friend)
1823[5] 2141[3] 2796[7] 3808[3] 4187[4]

The Pinto Kid (FR)
James Fanshawe a95 40
4 b g High Chaparral(IRE) Lake Palace (Nayef (USA))
2059[3] 2763[7] (4250)◆ 5811[2] 6596[6] (7688) 9055[11]

The Red Witch *Steph Hollinshead* 55
2 b f Cable Bay(IRE) Lady Macduff (IRE) (Iffraaj)
4221[8] 4557[9] 8243[4]

The Resdev Way *Philip Kirby* a77 76
6 b g Multiplex Lady Duxyana (Most Welcome)
1524[6] 1663[4] 1981[4] (2974) 4056[2] 4308[8] 4936[3]◆ 5769[4] 7001[12] 7631[7] 8524[4] 8945[3]◆ 9184[4]

The Retriever (IRE)
Micky Hammond a50 48
4 ch g Shamardal(USA) Silent Secret (IRE) (Dubai Destination (USA))
2505[12] 2895[5] 3517[7] 5300[7] 5768[10] 7207[7] 7961[3] 8530[4] 9225[2] 9396[11]

The Revenant *F-H Graffard* 120
4 ch g Dubawi(IRE) Hazel Lavery (IRE) (Excellent Art)
(1127a) (1451a) (3287a) (7924a)◆ 8334[2]◆

The Right Choice (IRE)
James Ferguson a69 54
4 ch g Choisir(AUS) Expedience (USA) (With Approval (CAN))
44[3] (165) 307a[7] 2611[9] 3503[8] 4148[7] 5677[11] 7085a[7] 8410[5] 9182[2] 9559[3]

The Right Man *D Guillemin* 110
7 br g Lope De Vega(IRE) Three Owls (IRE) (Warning)
1442a[5] 3369a[2] 8141a[2] 8648a[12]

Thermal (IRE) *Ian Williams* a53 33
3 b f Lawman(FR) Rising Wind (IRE) (Shirocco (GER))
1166[8] 7145[13]

The Rocket Park (IRE) *John Berry* a34 61
6 b g Rock Of Gibraltar(IRE) Snowpalm (Halling (USA))
7159[6] 9091[4]

The Rutland Rebel (IRE)
Micky Hammond 67
3 b g Delegator Do Disturb (IRE) (Sinndar (IRE))
2147[6] 2912[5] 3513[10] 4761[6] (5814) 7544[12]

The Saddle Rock (IRE)
John Wainwright 13
2 b f Bated Breath Dream Role (Acclamation)
5815[8]

The Secrets Out *Luke Dace* a61 68
5 bl g Sakhee's Secret Brooksby (Diktat)
1826[12] 2793[10]

The Simple Truth (FR) *John Berry*
2 gr g Rajsaman(FR) Minnie's Mystery (FR) (Highest Honor (FR))
6504[7] 7899[15] 8751[8]

The Song Of John (USA)
S Seemar a60
3 b c Colonel John(USA) Golden Silk (USA) (Songandaprayer (USA))
1110a[9]

The Special One (IRE)
Phil McEntee a61 44
6 br m Cape Cross(IRE) Capote West (USA) (Capote (USA))
256[4] 366[6] 430[5] 595[3] 801[2] 924[11] 1060[9] 1214[7] 1477[11] 1936[6] 3989[10] 4074[3] 4376[4] 4749[8] 5837[8]

Thespinningwheel (IRE)
Adam West a12 35
4 b g Arakan(USA) Dancing Jest (IRE) (Averti (IRE))
3584[12] 3946[11] 4305[8] 7869[11]

The Stalking Moon (IRE)
Adrian Nicholls a53 71
5 b m Arcano(IRE) Cornakill (USA) (Stormin Fever (USA))
2076[9] 2418[3] 3704[4] 3969[5] 5770[9] 6276[4] (7526) 7776[3]

The Summit (FR) *H-A Pantall* a71 106
2 b c Wootton Bassett Acola (FR) (Acatenango (GER))
7774a[3] 8582a[5]

The Taj Mahal (IRE) *Liam Howley* a85 109
5 b h Galileo(IRE) You'resothrilling (USA) (Storm Cat (USA))
1784a[18]

The Third Man *Henry Spiller* a58 67
8 gr g Dalakhani(IRE) Spinning Queen (Spinning World (USA))
1060[11] 3325[8]

The Thorny Rose *Michael Dods* a45 57
3 b f Delegator Muara (Wolfhound (USA))
1816[13] 2332[5] 2823[10] 3292[9] 4328[16] 5914[5] 7384[6] 8270[14]

The Throstles *Kevin Frost* a84 79
4 b g Poet's Voice Stylish Dream (USA) (Elusive Quality (USA))
2516[6] 4067[6] 4602[3] (5337) 6129[5] 6686[5] 7663[7] 9167[3] 9285[5] (9496)◆

The Tiger (GER)
Frau Anna Schleusner-Fruhriep 97
6 gr g Ogatonango(GER) Tiger Flame (FR) (Kendor (FR))
(8804a)

The Tin Man *James Fanshawe* 119
7 b g Equiano(FR) Persario (Bishop Of Cashel)
2916[3] 4094[6] 5184[7] 6959[2] 8331[13]

The Trader (IRE) *Mark Johnston* a96 97
3 gr g Mastercraftsman(IRE) Chinese White (IRE) (Dalakhani (IRE))
2553[2] 2828[5] 3341[2] 4882[10] 5583[11] 6541[2] 6861[3] 7199[2] 7434[8] 8092[4] 8655[4]

The Trendy Man (IRE)
David O'Meara a44 40
2 b g Dandy Man(IRE) Nutshell (Dubai Destination (USA))
2907[6] 3812[12] 4075[5] 5296[12] 6097[6] 7306[8] 7585[6]

The Tripple T (IRE) *Andrew Hughes* 53
2 b c War Command(USA) Devine Countenance (IRE) (Danehill Dancer (IRE))
7506[8] 7778[6]

The Truant (IRE)
Mrs John Harrington 73
2 b g Mastercraftsman(IRE) Invincible Cara (IRE) (Invincible Spirit (IRE))
5710a[5]

The Turpinator (IRE)
David Elsworth a79
2 b c Canford Cliffs(IRE) Bessichka (Exceed And Excel (AUS))
8011[6]◆ (8604)

The Very Moon *Sir Michael Stoute* a71 86
3 ch f Teofilo(IRE) Carisolo (Dubai Millennium)
2771[2] 4326[2] 5048[2] 6114[4]

The Warrior (IRE) *Lee Carter* a71 74
7 b g Exceed And Excel(AUS) Aymara (Darshaan)
54[3] 294[5] 722[6] 1392[5] 1655[4] 2005[6] 3002[7] 4028[12] 4837[5] 5309[9] 8223[7] 8422[9] 9209[2] 9305[5]

The Way You Dance (IRE)
Michael Attwater a46 67
7 b g Thewayyouare(USA) Beautiful Dancer (IRE) (Danehill Dancer (IRE))
318[5] 1144[7] 1363[7] 2400[13] 6901[3] 7300[6] 7845[14] 8246[9]

The Weed Machine (IRE)
Mark Johnston a76
2 b c Kodiac Noahs Ark (IRE) (Charnwood Forest (IRE))
9008[8] 9252[7] 9385[3]

The Wine Cellar (IRE)
Keith Dalgleish 64
2 ch c Dragon Pulse(IRE) Veronica Falls (Medicean)
4976[4]

The Wire Flyer *John Flint* a46 43
4 b g Champs Elysees Good Morning Star (IRE) (Shirocco (GER))
1212[6] 1520[8] 1958[11] 2593[3] 4868[4] 6115[8]

The Works (IRE) *Declan Carroll* a32 45
2 ch f No Nay Never(USA) Seinellanima (IRE) (Oratorio (IRE))
3968[10] 4516[11] 5017[5] 6969[11] 7275[9] 7582[10] 8897[5] 9179[7] 9438[9]

Theydon Bagel *Peter Charalambous* a12
2 b f Toronado(IRE) Kalon Brama (IRE) (Kodiac)
7461[9] 7899[13] 8751[7]

Theydon Boxer *Peter Charalambous* a52
4 b g Piccolo Angel Of Fashion (IRE) (Invincible Spirit (IRE))
9455[14]

Theydon Louboutin
Peter Charalambous 10
2 b f Toronado(IRE) Angel Of Fashion (IRE) (Invincible Spirit (IRE))
7461[8] 7899[14] **8458**[20]

Theydon Spirit *Peter Charalambous* a46
4 ch g Piccolo Ela Gorrie Mou (Mujahid (USA))
383[7] *1214*[5] *2234*[6] *9157*[6] *9410*[5]

The Young Master *Neil Mulholland* a37
10 b g Echo Of Light Fine Frenzy (IRE) (Great Commotion (USA))
7818[11]

Thibaan (USA) *Sir Michael Stoute* a72
2 b c War Front(USA) Lahudood (Singspiel (IRE))
8823[4]

Thimbleweed *Ralph Beckett* a83 86
4 b m Teofilo(IRE) Prairie Flower (IRE) (Zieten (USA))
5545[8] 6124[5] *6842*[5] 7618[5]

Think Big (IRE) *G E Mikhalides* 95
2 b c Night Of Thunder(IRE) Avenue Montaigne (IRE) (Showcasing)
5922a[5] **6474**[4] **9582a**[2]

Thinking Cutely *Antony Brittain*
3 ch f Monsieur Bond(IRE) Guadaloup (Loup Sauvage (USA))
3200[14]

Think Love (IRE) *J Parize* a59 41
3 b f So You Think(NZ) Meulles (FR) (Scat Daddy (USA))
7561a[7]

Think Of Me (GER) *F-H Graffard* 100
3 b f So You Think(NZ) Tosia (GER) (Big Shuffle (USA))
6773a[2]

Thinque Tank *Charlie Longsdon* a61 65
3 b g So You Think(NZ) Azharia (Oasis Dream)
1268[5] *1495*[8] **1824**[7] **2582**[4] 3195[9]

Third Time Lucky (IRE)
Richard Fahey a99 103
7 gr g Clodovil(IRE) Speckled Hen (IRE) (Titus Livius (FR))
1101[3] 1415[8] 1753[9]

Third World (IRE) *D K Weld* 87
3 b g Dansili Sense Of Purpose (IRE) (Galileo (IRE))
1306a[5]

Thirlmere *Julie Camacho* a66 71
4 b m Mayson Anglezarke (IRE) (Acclamation)
4827[3]◆ 6178[11]

This Girl *Tom Dascombe* a83 82
4 b m Nathaniel(IRE) Fibou (USA) (Seeking The Gold (USA))
29[3] *460*[5] *1106*[2] 2104[8] 2577[10] 4554[3] (5844) 6961[6]

Thistimenextyear *Richard Spencer* a74 95
5 gr g New Approach(IRE) Scarlet Empire (IRE) (Red Ransom (USA))
3726[2]

Thiswaycadeaux (IRE)
W McCreery 96
5 b m Thewayyouare(USA) Shuruk (Cadeaux Genereux)
4353a[9] 5075a[9] **8572a**[2]

Thomas Cranmer (USA)
Tina Jackson a57 78
5 b g Hard Spun(USA) House Of Grace (USA) (Limehouse (USA))
2748[9] 3160[5] 4035[7] 4407[4] **4892**[4] 6067[4] 6456[4] 8515[17]

Thomas Crown (FR)
Caroline Auvray a47 47
8 b g Hurricane Cat(USA) Quellaffaire (FR) (Charge D'Affaires)
3711a[10]

Thomas Cubitt (FR) *Michael Bell* 65
3 b g Youmzain(IRE) Helsinka (FR) (Pennekamp (USA))
1417[8] 1690[9] 2249[6] **2913**[2] 3219[4] 4345[5]

Thomas Hawk *Alan Brown* a37 26
2 b g Gregorian(IRE) Miss Mohawk (IRE) (Hawk Wing (USA))
4289[7] 5704[4] 6368[12] *7626*[10] 7957[4]

Thomas Hobson *W P Mullins* a68 116
9 b g Halling(USA) La Spezia (IRE) (Danehill Dancer (IRE))
2666a[2] 4015[10]

Thomas Lanfiere (FR)
David Simcock a60 45
2 b g No Nay Never(USA) Lexi The Princess (IRE) (Holy Roman Emperor (IRE))
4018[7] 4295[6] 4564[11] 5958[8]

Thora (IRE) *Simon Dow* a54
3 b f Iffraaj Authora (IRE) (Authorized (IRE))
1287[7] *1592*[4]

Thorkhill Star (IRE) *Allan Smith* a63 100
7 b g Equiano(FR) Reine De Romance (IRE) (Vettori (IRE))
9125a[9]

Thorn *Peter Hiatt* a32 72
3 b g Dansili Thistle Bird (Selkirk (USA))
3647[8] 5984[6] 6730[4] 7129[2] **8030**[3] *9180*[11]

Thornaby Nash *Jason Ward* a48 76
8 br g Kheleyf(USA) Mistress Twister (Pivotal)
1659[6] (2203) 2785[6] 3178[5] (3704) 4523[2] 5021[7] **5560**[2] 7587[9] *7875*[13] *9006*[11] *9395*[11]

Thornaby Princess *Jason Ward* a47 51
8 b m Camacho Ingleby Princess (Bold Edge)
2324[6] 2678[7] 5278[10] *5857*[11] 6277[9] **(6574) 6936**[3] **7214**[2] *7468*[3] *7737*[4] *8898*[10] *9185*[13]

Thornaby Spirit (IRE) *Jason Ward* 60
4 b g Swiss Spirit Ingleby Princess (Bold Edge)
5336[6] **7442**[2] *9032*[9]

Thornton Katie *Brian Rothwell*
3 b f Kuroshio(AUS) Byton (Byron)
5917[5]

Thornton Le Clay *Michael Easterby* a53 43
3 b g Nathaniel(IRE) Dance East (Shamardal (USA))
3247[10] 3482[7] 3882[4] 5248[14] ***6552***[2] *7390*[3]

Thorntoun Care *Karen Tutty* a58 75
8 b g Rail Link Thorntoun Piccolo (Groom Dancer (USA))
2056[5] 2512[5] 3175[5] (3511) 4036[5] 4446[4]◆ (5024) **5621**[2] 5728[3] 6456[5] 7053[6] (7544) 8515[7]

Thorntoun Lady (USA) *Jim Goldie* a58 41
9 b m Henrythenavigator(USA) Valery Lady (ARG) (Roy (USA))
123[5] *236*[5] ***502***[3] *738*[5] *788*[8] *1026*[4] *1335*[7] 2329[6] 2682[10] 2958[13] 3716[10] 4276[4] 4726[6] 5235[10]

Thounder (FR) *Gary Moore* 72
5 ch g Hurricane Cat(USA) Meldown (FR) (Until Sundown (USA))
2208[7]

Thrave *Henry Candy* 101
4 b g Sir Percy Feis Ceoil (IRE) (Key Of Luck (USA))
1889[4] 2832[2] 3857[9] **5192**[2] 6376[9]

Threading (IRE) *Mark Johnston* 110
4 b m Exceed And Excel(AUS) Chaquiras (USA) (Seeking The Gold (USA))
3986[12] **4758**[8]

Thread Of Silver *Charlie Appleby* 82
2 b f Shamardal(USA) Woven Lace (Hard Spun (USA))
5961[2] 6407[6] 7393[3]

Threat (IRE) *Richard Hannon* 115
2 ch c Footstepsinthesand Flare Of Firelight (USA) (Birdstone (USA))
(2444) 3949[2] 5584[2] (6422) **(7195)** 7693[5]

Three Card Trick *Kevin Ryan* a75 72
3 ch g Piccolo Card Games (First Trump)
1762[6] 2810[10] 4297[6] 4757[2] 6715[7] *7552*[3] ***8304***[4]

Three Castles *Keith Dalgleish* a54 70
3 b g Zoffany(IRE) Fountain Of Honour (IRE) (Sadler's Wells (USA))
405[8] *523*[3] *949*[6] 2325[4]◆ (3684)◆ 4002[5] 4914[9] (5937)◆ **6612**[2] 6938[6] 7404[7] 7783[3]

Three Coins *Richard Fahey* 78
2 b f Fountain Of Youth(IRE) Bereka (Firebreak)
(2586) 3564[7] 5243[2] 5683[10] **(6175)**◆

Three Comets (GER) *Roger Varian* 97
3 b g Sea The Moon(GER) Tickle Me Pink (Groom Dancer (USA))
2619[10] 5541[11] **6696**[3] 7317[3]

Three C's (IRE) *George Boughey* a54 54
5 b g Kodiac Ms Mary C (IRE) (Dolphin Street (FR))
3994 ***719***[3] *1683*[9] 3352[3] 4376[5] 5293[7] *(6051)* *6666*[9] *7281*[7] *7549*[6] *8255*[2]

Threediamondrings *Mark Usher* a63 52
6 ch g Geordieland(FR) Five Gold Rings (IRE) (Captain Rio)
3444[8] 5106[7] *6046*[RR] 6419[6] **6849**[4]

Three Dragons *Ben Haslam* a60 58
2 ch g Sakhee(USA) Three Heart's (Three Valleys (USA))
7067[6] ***7957***[3] *9095*[6] *9513*[8]

Three Fans (FR) *Tom Dascombe* a71 75
2 b g Dabirsim(FR) Shining Glory (GER) (Konigstiger (GER))
5125[4] 5815[3] 6287[4] 7971[5] *8505*[3]◆ *9137*[7]

Threefeetfromgold (IRE)
Martin Smith a49 70
3 ch g Helmet(AUS) Lady Pitrizza (IRE) (Night Shift (USA))
4298[4] 4800[3] 5678[3] **6569**[3] 7274[4]

Three Little Birds *Sylvester Kirk* a80 76
4 b m Dandy Man(IRE) Oilinda (Nayef (USA))
3032[4] 3596[3] 4230[6] 4844[3] 5372[3] (5793) 6798[3] 7230[5] *8895*[5] *9013*[2]◆ ***(9135)***◆ *9286*[9] *9390*[4]

Three Saints Bay (IRE)
David O'Meara a83 105
4 b g Kodiac Fiuise (IRE) (Montjeu (IRE))
1502[4] **(1944)** 2402[10] 2844[4] 3863[20] 4650[6] 4921[16] (5916) 6894[6] 8184[3]

Three Star General *David Pipe* a36 65
6 b g Montjeu(IRE) Honorlina (FR) (Linamix (FR))
2359[2]

Three Weeks (USA) *David O'Meara* a96 82
4 gr g Tapit(USA) Midnight Thoughts (USA) (Henrythenavigator (USA))
(164) ***440***[2] *929*[4] *1420*[6] *6151*[7]

Thresholdofadream (IRE)
Amanda Perrett a62 54
4 b m Camelot Signella (Selkirk (USA))
1851[3] *5663*◆ *(731)* 2344[8] 3017[5] ***(4251)*** *5271*[8] *8828*[10] *9204*[5]

Thrilla In Manila *Richard Spencer* a75 84
3 b g Iffraaj Tesary (Danehill (USA))
7892[10] ***9171***[2]

Thriller's Moon *Richard Whitaker* a12
2 ch g Mayson Rio's Rosanna (IRE) (Captain Rio)
8717[13] *9181*[14]

Thrill Seeker (IRE) *William Haggas* 65
2 b c Invincible Spirit(IRE) Galvaun (IRE) (Galileo (IRE))
6948[8]

Throckley *Katy Price* a76 76
8 b g Passing Glance Porcelain (IRE) (Peintre Celebre (USA))
2126[5] *5055*[9]

Throne Hall *Kevin Ryan* 77
2 b c Kingman Appearance (Galileo (IRE))
5848[3]

Thrones Game (FR) *Yannick Fouin* a49 71
6 b m Soldier Of Fortune(IRE) Sirenita (IRE) (Mull Of Kintyre (USA))
9537a[5]

Throttle Control (IRE) *J-V Toux*
2 gr f Zebedee Trisara (Exceed And Excel (AUS))
(1240a)

Thumur (USA) *Owen Burrows* a76
2 bb c Golden Horn Time Being (Zamindar (USA))
8605[3]

Thunder And Light *Marco Botti* a71
3 b c Australia Que Puntual (ARG) (Contested Bid (USA))
1352[7] ***3003***[6] *3445*[9]

Thunderbell *Scott Dixon* a52 53
5 ch m Haafhd Trustthunder (Selkirk (USA))
3781[10]

Thunder Buddy *K R Burke* a67 41
4 b g Mayson Inchcoonan (Emperor Jones (USA))
(45) *232*[4] *738*[3] ***(830)*** *1426*[3] *1859*[11] *2349*[5] 3970[8] 4582[8]

Thundercloud *Scott Dixon* a44 65
4 gr m Aussie Rules(USA) Trustthunder (Selkirk (USA))
465[9]

Thunderdome (FR) *Gay Kelleway* a56 77
2 b g Orpen(USA) The Lucky Go Girl (GER) (Dr Devious (IRE))
7276[4] **8330a**[2]

Thunder Flash *Ed Walker* 48
2 b g Night Of Thunder(IRE) Sultanah Heyam (Manduro (GER))
6464[8] 7338[12]

Thunderhooves *John Ryan* a44 40
4 ro g Raven's Pass(USA) Regrette Rien (USA) (Unbridled's Song (USA))
3744[7] 3966[14] 4216[10] 4838[12]

Thundering Blue (USA)
David Menuisier a103 115
6 rg g Exchange Rate(USA) Relampago Azul (USA) (Forestry (USA))
2083[7] **3074**[3] **4430a**[7] 6354[9] *6962*[10]

Thunder King (FR) *Amy Murphy* 59
2 b g Hunter's Light(IRE) Lady McKell (IRE) (Raven's Pass (USA))
4106[5] 5655[10] 8657[8]

Thunderman (ITY) *A Botti* 102
3 gr c Blu Air Force(IRE) Yaldas Girl (USA) (Unbridled's Song (USA))
8788a[3]

Thunderoad *Tony Carroll* a66 52
3 b g Street Sense(USA) Royal Crystal (USA) (Tapit (USA))
299[4] ***917***[2] *1233*[4] 2096[12] *3446*[6] *4789*[10] 5505[6] 6022[9] *6636*[2] 7027[8] *7685*[6]◆ *8348*[7] *8837*[2] *9005*[4]

Thunderous (IRE) *Mark Johnston* 100
2 b c Night Of Thunder(IRE) Souviens Toi (Dalakhani (IRE))
(4324) (5212) **(6212)**

Thunder Snow (IRE)
Saeed bin Suroor a121 100
5 b h Helmet(AUS) Eastern Joy (Dubai Destination (USA))
1114a[2]◆ *(1447a)* ***3618a***[3]

Thunderspeed (FR) *C Ferland* 89
2 b c Night Of Thunder(IRE) Marmoom Flower (IRE) (Cape Cross (IRE))
8582a[7]

Thurstan (FR) *J Parize* 50
2 ch c Vatori(FR) Zhuhai (IRE) (Indian Lodge (IRE))
5763a[8]

Thyme White (FR) *B De Montzey* 73
3 b g Anodin(IRE) Jane (GER) (Samum (GER))
1797a[7]

Tiar Na Nog (IRE) *Denis Coakley* a76 77
7 b m Ask Carmencita (Rock Of Gibraltar (IRE))
1588[4] 2209[8] **(2685)** 4425[5] 6812[5] 8248[7] *8705*[10] *9421*[5]

Tiberian (FR) *Mlle L Kneip* 99
7 b h Tiberius Caesar(FR) Toamasina (FR) (Marju (IRE))
2428a[8] 6522a[7]

Tickle Me Green (GER)
Markus Klug 100
2 b f Sea The Moon(GER) Tickle Me Pink (Groom Dancer (USA))
8371a[2] 8964a[4]

Ticklish (FR) *Mark Johnston* a67 67
3 b f Dalakhani(IRE) Cosquillas (IRE) (Selkirk (USA))
3295[6] 3773[5] 5055[8] ***6328a***[3]

Ticks The Boxes (IRE) *Brian Ellison* a63 63
7 ch g Fast Company(IRE) Swan Sea (USA) (Sea Hero (USA))
45[5] *244*[7] *587*[2] *(1973)* 2298[2] (2349) 2876[3] 3475[3] **3657**[2] 3921[9] 4912[10] *5857*[3] **6546**[3] *7088a*[4]

Tick Tock Croc (IRE) *Bryan Smart* 53
3 b g Requinto(IRE) Quinine (Dark Angel (IRE))
5018[6] 5559[16] 6503[3]

Ticolet (IRE) *M Delcher Sanchez* a63 15
3 b f Garswood Up At Last (Cape Cross (IRE))
1512a[12] **2390a**[11]

Tidal Point (IRE) *Steph Hollinshead* 77
3 br g Sea The Moon(GER) Centred (IRE) (Dalakhani (IRE))
1558[6] 1898[5] 2099[3] 3260[3] **3729**[2] 4644[7] 5127[4]

Tidal Racer *Clive Cox* a54
2 b g Heeraat(IRE) Making Waves (IRE) (Danehill (USA))
8059[7] *9242*[12]

Tidal's Baby *John O'Neill* a24 34
10 b g Dutch Art Tidal (Bin Ajwaad (IRE))
4684a[3]

Tidal Surge (IRE) *Les Eyre* a40 63
4 ch m Showcasing Oke Bay (Tobougg (IRE))
116[11] *250*[11]

Tidal Watch (IRE) *Jonjo O'Neill* a79 70
5 b g Harbour Watch(IRE) Najmati (Green Desert (USA))
119[3] 4231[6]

Tie A Yellowribbon *James Bethell* a69 68
3 gr f Poet's Voice Silver Games (IRE) (Verglas (IRE))
1488[3]◆ 1894[7] *2212*[5] 2904[5] 3189[2] 4081[3] 4436[3]

Tiempo Vuela *John Gosden* a83
2 b f Lope De Vega(IRE) Tempest Fugit (IRE) (High Chaparral (IRE))
(8021)◆

Tiercel *Rebecca Bastiman* a73 82
6 b g Olden Times Sharp Mode (USA) (Diesis)
526[5] ***(1273)*** *1925*[13] 3214[10]

Tiffindell (IRE) *Robert Eddery* a39
3 ch f Raven's Pass(USA) Nadia (Nashwan (USA))
8753[5] *9138*[8] *9213*[10]

Tifosa (IRE) *Mme Pia Brandt* a82 108
3 b f Kodiac Toquette (IRE) (Acclamation)
(1242a) 1795a[6] 6142a[8] 8583a[9]

Tiger Balm *George Boughey* a52
2 b f Universal(IRE) Limber Up (IRE) (Dansili)
7546[7] *7995*[6] ***8891***[10]

Tiger Crusade (FR) *David Simcock* 79
2 b c No Nay Never(USA) Folle Allure (FR) (Poliglote)
6127[3] **(7316)**◆

Tiger Eye (IRE) *James Fanshawe* a99 97
4 b m Frankel Crystal Gaze (IRE) (Rainbow Quest (USA))
(464)◆ *(963)* *(1234)* *1941*[5] 2404[4] ***3994***[6]

Tigerfish (IRE) *William Stone* a56 69
5 b m Lilbourne Lad(IRE) Nisriyna (IRE) (Intikhab (USA))
(59) *736*[8] *910*[5] (2283) *2595*[5] **(3537)** 4215[3] **5025**[3] **(5528)**

Tigerinmytank *John Holt* a41 44
3 b f Heeraat(IRE) Tiger Cub (Dr Fong (USA))
1557[8] 2197[12] *3208*[7] 3645[9] **5102**[4] 5559[6] 5884[3] 5960[3] *6889*[9]

Tiger Lyon (USA) *John Butler* a59 63
4 b g Kitten's Joy(USA) Hold It (USA) (Discreet Cat (USA))
882[10] *2013*[10] *3001*[6] ***3320***[2] *8457*[12] *9169*[9]

Tigerskin *Ralph Beckett* a57 78
3 ch g Nathaniel(IRE) Jamboretta (IRE) (Danehill (USA))
1754[9] 2485[7] 5175[10] (6042) **(6400)** 7239[P] 8002[8]

Tigerten *Joseph Tuite* a51 51
2 b g Born To Sea(IRE) Morning Bride (IRE) (Danehill Dancer (IRE))
5339[7] **5992**[8] ***6927***[8]

Tiger Voice (FR)
Henry De Bromhead a57 91
4 b g Poet's Voice Tarsia (GER) (Tiger Hill (IRE))
1309a[4]

Tiger Zone (IRE) *Clive Cox* a56 57
2 b g Society Rock(IRE) Shalabina (Nayef (USA))
5860[5] 7521[8] *8011*[8]

Tigray (USA) *Michael Appleby* a78 68
3 gr g Tapit(USA) Daisy Devine (USA) (Kafwain (USA))
1884[2] *(1972)* **2317**[2] 2905[4] 3474[4] *7370*[5] ***7631***[2] *8321*[4] *8945*[7] *9184*[3]

Tigresse Tianjin *C Plisson* a46 62
4 b m Nathaniel(IRE) Turtle Point (USA) (Giant's Causeway (USA))
2647a[6]

Tilda (IRE) *A Fabre* 88
3 b f Motivator Rock My Soul (IRE) (Clodovil (IRE))
7978a[5]

Tilett *F Rohaut* a74 89
3 b f Rock Of Gibraltar(IRE) Cloghran (FR) (Muhtathir)
2027a[6]

Tilghman (IRE) *David O'Meara* a46 50
4 b g Lawman(FR) Poppet's Lovein (Lomitas)
2736[7] **7442**[3]

Tilly Devine *Scott Dixon* a29 3
5 gr m Aussie Rules(USA) Cora Pearl (IRE) (Montjeu (IRE))
387[9] ***504***[5]

Tilly Tamworth *Rod Millman* 56
2 br f Lethal Force(IRE) Bonnie Grey (Hellvelyn)
2686[4] **4871**[4] 5250[8] 6799[5] 7227[4]

Tilsworth Diamond *Mike Murphy* a34 49
4 b m Delegator Lady Bonanova (IRE) (Haatef (USA))
2967[9] **5428**[6] *6074*[9] 6897[15] **8006**[3] *8251*[12] 8637[10]

Tilsworth Lukey *J R Jenkins* a59 58
6 b g Sixties Icon Chara (Deploy)
2196[12] *2720*[10] *3298*[5] **3774**[2]◆ 4111[6] *5653*[7] 6059[3]

Tilsworth Prisca *J R Jenkins* a35 33
4 ch m Equiano(FR) Ashwell Rose (Anabaa (USA))
2624[9] *3304*[14] 5107[4] 5526[11] 6131[15] ***9001***[6] *9475*[10]

Tilsworth Rose *J R Jenkins* a47 51
5 b m Pastoral Pursuits Pallas (Statue Of Liberty (USA))
2451[4] *718*[6] *848*[6] *2295*[7] 3476[9] 3933[3] **(4563)** 5063[5] 5532[5] 6126[8] 7172[6] *7371*[12] *8901*[4] *9034*[2] *9247*[3] *9457*[4]

Tilsworth Sammy *J R Jenkins* a56 48
4 b g Mount Nelson Chara (Deploy)
369[5]◆ *7318* ***1361***[2] 2344[9] 2718[9] *3444*[7] *4594*[9] 5596[10] *6046*[5] *6552*[4]

Tiltilys Rock (IRE) *Andrew Crook* a45 45
2 ch g Society Rock(IRE) Tiltili (IRE) (Spectrum (IRE))
3702[8] 4125[12] 4433[6] *5279*[8] **5764**[9] **6228**[5] 7284[8] *8815*[10] ***9394***[2]

Time Change *Ralph Beckett* a95 92
4 ch m Dutch Art Time Honoured (Sadler's Wells (USA))
1757[9] 2822[4] *4386*[5] 4930[2] (5796) 6082[5] 6992a[11] 7347[6] ***9206***[2]

Time For A Toot (IRE) *Charles Hills* a69 93
4 b m Oasis Dream Market Forces (Lomitas)
1127a[5] 1757[6] 2252[4] 3763[10] **(6961)**

Time For Bed (IRE) *Richard Hannon*
3 b f Zebedee Violet Flame (IRE) (Kalanisi (IRE))
2077[6] 2937[5] 3764[7] 4449[3]

Time Force (IRE) *K R Burke* 63
2 ch g Gale Force Ten Groupetime (USA) (Gilded Time (USA))
4344[4] 4509[5] 5273[8]

Time Immemorial (IRE)
Roger Varian a64
3 b g Mastercraftsman(IRE) Await So (Sadler's Wells (USA))
486[2] *1066*[8] *1233*[6]

Timeless Flight *A R Al Rayhi* a77 71
5 b h Helmet(AUS) Kathy's Rocket (USA) (Gold Legend (USA))
197a[6] *573a*[10]

Time's Arrow (IRE) *David O'Meara* a78 80
5 b h Redoute's Choice(AUS) Gilt Edge Girl (Monsieur Bond (IRE))
1853[7] 2396[13]

Times Past (IRE) *Archie Watson* a15
3 b c Dandy Man(IRE) Cant Hurry Love (Desert Prince (IRE))
320[2]

Time Stands Still *W J Martin* a58 83
5 b m Dandy Man(IRE) Adele Blanc Sec (FR) (Marchand De Sable (USA))
366[7]

Time To Choose *A Botti* 103
6 b h Manduro(GER) Penfection (IRE) (Orpen (USA))
3643a[4] 4432a[2] 7502a[3] 8788a[4]

Timetodock *Tim Easterby* a57 73
3 b g Harbour Watch(IRE) Unwrapit (USA) (Tapit (USA))
2098[7] 2477[3] 2871[3] (3292) 3709[5] 4033[2] (4436) 5298[3] 5660[7] 6070[8] 7387[9] 7588[7]

Time To Fly (FR) *M Seror* a79 90
4 b h Wootton Bassett Alpinette (FR) (Pyramus (USA))
9483a[9]

Time To Reason (IRE)
Charlie Wallis a71 82
6 b g Kyllachy Danehurst (Danehill (USA))
236[6] 626[3] (823) 1209[3] 2318[13] 4027[4] 5352[9] 8895[10] 9092[5] 9477[10]

Time To Rock *John Bridger* a29
4 b g Olden Times Five Bells (IRE) (Rock Of Gibraltar (IRE))
1094[12] 1517[7] 3018[8]

Time To Strike (IRE)
David Simcock 73
2 b f Muhaarar Up In Time (Noverre (USA))
5132[5] 5906[6]

Time To Study (FR) *Ian Williams* a88 105
5 ch g Motivator Dissertation (FR) (Sillery (USA))
565[8] 2575[8] 3952[3] 4382[15] 4884[16] (6095a) (6958) 8114[25]

Time Trialist *Pat Phelan* a4 51
3 b g Footstepsinthesand Les Verguettes (IRE) (Iffraaj)
4738[8] 6117[11] 7973[P]

Time Voyage (IRE) *John Quinn* a76
2 b f Raven's Pass(USA) Katherine Lee (IRE) (Azamour (IRE))
8525[4]◆ 9097[2] 9585[5]

Time Warp *A S Cruz* a79 115
6 ch g Archipenko(USA) Here To Eternity (USA) (Stormy Atlantic (USA))
9380a[8]

Time Zone *Louise Allan* a74 55
5 b g Kheleyf(USA) Be Joyful (IRE) (Teofilo (IRE))
876[4]

Timon (IRE) *Mick Channon* a52 50
2 ch g Anjaal Malekat Jamal (IRE) (Dutch Art)
4734[9] 5186[11] 5447[6] 6071[5] 6435[4] 6563[4] 7056[3] 7234[10]

Timoshenko *Sir Mark Prescott Bt* a22 89
4 ch g Archipenko(USA) Nezhenka (With Approval (CAN))
(5540) 8114[28]

Tinalixa (FR) *C Plisson* 17
2 ro f Tin Horse(IRE) Lixariva (FR) (Slickly (FR))
1448a[10]

Tinandali (IRE) *D K Weld* 106
3 b g Oasis Dream Timarwa (IRE) (Daylami (IRE))
3063a[7] 5112a[6] 7794a[11]

Tina Teaspoon *Derek Shaw* a45 43
5 b m Kheleyf(USA) Button Moon (IRE) (Compton Place)
834[9] 986[8] 1402[13] 2295[11] 2924[4] 3404[3] 4563[3] 4776[8] 5822[8] 9034[13] 9411[9]

Tindrum *Heather Main*
2 ch g Mukhadram Tinshu (IRE) (Fantastic Light (USA))
8857[U]

Tin Fandango *Mark Usher* a71 62
4 b g Steele Tango(USA) Littlemoor Lass (Motivator)
619[2] 946[2] (1497) 2239[5] 6720[7] 7845[12] 8654[8]

Tingo In The Tale (IRE)
Tony Forbes a43 46
10 b g Oratorio(IRE) Sunlit Skies (Selkirk (USA))
387[8] 2901[5] 8868[9]

Tin Hat (IRE) *Eve Johnson Houghton* a70 88
3 ch g Helmet(AUS) Precautionary (Green Desert (USA))
1736[12] 2274[6] 2997[10] 4297[3] 4908[8] 5503[3] (5882) 6301[2] 6465[7] 7351[3] 8852[8]

Tinkerbird *Eugene Stanford* a35
3 br c Gregorian(IRE) Swan Queen (In The Wings)
8451[11] 9051[6]

Tinnahalla (IRE) *Jamie Osborne* a70 70
2 b g Starspangledbanner(AUS) Bright Bank (IRE) (Sadler's Wells (USA))
5563[5] 7388[2] 7972[2] 8657[4]

Tintern Spirit (IRE) *Milton Bradley* a45 34
3 b f Swiss Spirit Tintern (Diktat)
296[6] 550[8] 1141[10] 1515[6] 1678[6] 2276[10] 6107[12] 6361[8] 6703[8] 7024[12] 7812[11] 9248[8]

Tinto *Amanda Perrett* a105 106
3 b g Compton Place Amirah (IRE) (Holy Roman Emperor (IRE))
1729[2]◆ 2274[2] 2567[3] 2835[5] 4420[4]◆ 4609[2] (5014) 5589[4] 5661[22] 6222[6] 6413[3] 6724[2] (7397)◆ (7868)◆ 8648a[6] 9004[2]

Tintoretto (IRE)
John Joseph Murphy a75 84
4 b g Lilbourne Lad(IRE) Fanacanta (IRE) (Olden Times)
5537a[6] 5597a[17]

Tiny Titan *Richard Fahey* 29
2 gr f Zebedee Katora (Kodiac)
2331[7]

Tio Esteban (FR) *W J Martin* a56 51
4 b g Captain Marvelous(IRE) Angel Voices (IRE) (Tagula (IRE))
(8863)

Tipitena *W McCreery* 99
4 b m Camelot Flora Trevelyan (Cape Cross (IRE))
1620a[7] 3820a[6] 6090a[2] 7038a[11] 7635a[3] 8094[5]

Tipperary Jack (USA) *John Best* a88 74
3 b c Violence(USA) Indian Miss (USA) (Indian Charlie (USA))
2397[5] (3463) 4827[4] 6076[8] 6593[5] (8852)◆ 9669[8]

Tippler *Sir Mark Todd* a60
2 gr g Iffraaj Present Day (Cadeaux Genereux)
8455[8]

Tiptop (FR) *Hue & Lamotte D'Argy* a65 77
3 bb f Zanzibari(USA) Tinera (FR) (Kendor (FR))
1028a[6]

Tip Two Win *Roger Teal* 94
4 gr h Dark Angel(IRE) Freddie's Girl (USA) (More Than Ready (USA))
4094[11] 4900[8]

Tiramisu (GER) *Andreas Suborics* 83
2 b f Amaron Tiger Lilly (GER) (Tiger Hill (IRE))
8586a[4]

Tiritomba (IRE) *Richard Hannon* a77 68
2 b f Exceed And Excel(AUS) Starry Messenger (Galileo (IRE))
4184[7] 4918[8] 8602[2] 9172[3]

Tis Marvellous *Clive Cox* a101 114
5 b g Harbour Watch(IRE) Mythicism (Oasis Dream)
1412[4] 1942[8] 3043[4] 4095[2] (4896)◆ 6698[5] 7073[4] 7889[4]

Tisona *Matthieu Palussiere* a61 68
3 b f Bated Breath Kheleyf Magic (Kheleyf (USA))
1200a[8]

Titan Goddess *Mike Murphy* a89 86
7 b m Equiano(FR) Phoebe Woodstock (IRE) (Grand Lodge (USA))
158[3]◆ 429[10] 697[6] 942[6]

Titanium Grey *Jedd O'Keeffe* 14
2 b c Outstrip Cheerfully (Sadler's Wells (USA))
7067[13] 8402[8]

Titanium Sky (IRE) *D K Weld* a85 95
3 gr f Dark Angel(IRE) She's Our Mark (Ishiguru (USA))
2493a[6] 2661a[4] 6646a[8] 8367a[11] 8734a[4]

Titus Secret *Malcolm Saunders* a59 64
7 ch g Sakhee's Secret Crimson Fern (IRE) (Titus Livius (FR))
6203[9]

Tiz A Slam (CAN) *Roger L Attfield* a103 111
5 b h Tiznow(USA) Flaming Rose (CAN) (Grand Slam (USA))
(5484a) 7226a[4]

Tizwotitiz *Steph Hollinshead* a47 56
3 b g Finjaan Girl Of The Rain (IRE) (Refuse To Bend (IRE))
1430[5] 2357[2] 2870[4] 3158[3] 4328[9] 4763[11] 6168[3] 6462[2] 7590[9] 7824[6] 8821[8]

Tobacco Road (IRE)
Mark Pattinson a64 67
9 b g Westerner Virginias Best (King's Best (USA))
145[4] 724[3] 876[7] 1333[10] 2112[5] 3006[9] 4615[9] 5499[4] 7060[11] 7553[7]

Tobaco (ARG) *Doug Watson* a55
6 b g Roman Ruler(USA) Tacanuya (ARG) (Southern Halo (USA))
997[6]

Tobeeornottobee *Declan Carroll* a63 63
3 ch c Coach House(IRE) Lady Le Quesne (IRE) (Alhaarth (IRE))
505[4] 720[3] 5478[3] 5985[4] 6699[13] 7047[4] 7527[2] 7591[6] 8008[6] 8306[10] 9106[6]◆ 9287[7]

To Be Wild (IRE)
Jane Chapple-Hyam a97 106
6 br g Big Bad Bob(IRE) Fire Up (Motivator)
1062[6] 8853[6] 9065[3] 9468[7]

Toboggan's Fire *Donald McCain* a63 64
6 b m Firebreak Toboggan Lady (Tobougg (IRE))
162[6]

Tobouggaloo *Stuart Kittow* a41 63
8 ch m Tobougg(IRE) Let Alone (Warning)
4112[7] 5344[5]◆ 6104[11]

Toda Joya (IRE) *Giuseppe Renzi* 24
5 b m Lilbourne Lad(IRE) Vermilliann (IRE) (Mujadil (USA))
8787a[9]

Today (KOR) *Kim Young Kwan* a90
5 ch g Drosselmeyer(USA) Gone Goodbye (USA) (Gone For Real (USA))
7010a[11]

Today Power (IRE) *Richard Hannon* a63 63
2 b g Dark Angel(IRE) Todegica (Giant's Causeway (USA))
4252[9] 6163[7] 6564[6] 7111[2]◆ 9665[4]

To Dibba *N Bachalard* a80 100
5 gr g Dubawi(IRE) Rose Diamond (IRE) (Daylami (IRE))
1001[9]

Tofan *Marco Botti* a75
4 ch h Helmet(AUS) Countermarch (Selkirk (USA))
239[5] 8351[5] 9173[14]

Toffee Galore *Archie Watson* a45 71
3 b f Lope De Vega(IRE) Poppets Sweetlove (Foxhound (USA))
360[7] 917[6]

Togoville (IRE) *Anthony McCann* a93 79
9 gr g Verglas(IRE) Road Harbour (USA) (Rodrigo De Triano (USA))
307a[10] (748a)

Toijk (FR) *M Nigge* a89 108
3 ch c Siyouni(FR) Eire (Medicean)
1707a[4] 2499a[5]

Tolmount *Charlie Appleby* a71
2 b c Dubawi(IRE) Fintry (IRE) (Shamardal (USA))
9624[4]

Tolosa (FR) *D Guillemin* a56 72
3 gr f Elusive City(USA) Kiritsou (FR) (Great Palm (USA))
5538a[7]

Tomahawk Ridge (IRE)
John Gallagher a55 66
3 gr g Alhebayeb(IRE) Low Cut Affair (IRE) (Fast Company (IRE))
1275[4] 1982[4] (2489) 2908[2] 3508[12] 4586[9] 5603[4] 7588[10] 8925[14]

Tombolo (FR) *Michael Dods* 73
2 b c Le Havre(IRE) Sandbar (Oasis Dream)
6892[2]

Tom Collins *David Elsworth* a82 84
2 br c Dubawi(IRE) Cocktail Queen (IRE) (Motivator)
6891[8] 8060[2]◆ (8460) 8762[11]

Tom Dooley (IRE) *Philip Kirby* a31 38
8 b g Dylan Thomas(IRE) Shizao (IRE) (Alzao (USA))
3279[9] 4567[11] 4916[7]

Tomfre *Ralph Beckett* 96
2 b c Cable Bay(IRE) Kurtanella (Pastoral Pursuits)
3943[3] (4295) (5152) (5962)◆ 7150[5] (8110) 8762[6]

Tomily (IRE) *David O'Meara* a86 89
5 b g Canford Cliffs(IRE) Cake (IRE) (Acclamation)
1938[7] 2272[9] 2940[3] 3301[7] 3597[5] (4449) (4977) (5298)◆ 5454[10] 5888[6] 6227[10] 6921[2] 7121[8] 7700[6] 7908[7] 8428[4] (8690)

Tom Melbourne (IRE) *Chris Waller* a73 103
8 b g Dylan Thomas(IRE) Roshanak (IRE) (Spinning World (USA))
8360a[7]

Tommycole *Olly Williams* a56 50
4 b g Native Ruler Tancred Miss (Presidium)
1274[5] 1862[7] 2347[3] 2740[5] 3473[11] 4518[14] 6050[11] 6666[12]

Tommy Cooper (IRE) *Michael Bell* 67
2 ch c Dandy Man(IRE) Imelda Mayhem (Byron)
3660[6]

Tommy De Vito *Charles Hills* a67
2 b c Dandy Man(IRE) Rohlindi (Red Ransom (USA))
8816[2]

Tommy Docc (IRE) *Keith Dalgleish* a81 89
7 b g Thewayyouare(USA) Liturgy (IRE) (Catcher In The Rye (IRE))
469[3] (622)

Tommy G *Jim Goldie* a86 82
6 ch g Makfi Primo Heights (Primo Valentino (IRE))
24[7] 407[8] 741[3] 953[7] 1082[2] 2437[2] 2788[5] (3179) 4058[5] 4511[3] 4980[7] 5661[3] 6208[8] 7121[7] 7402[13] 7781[5] 8425[12]

Tommy Hallinan (IRE) *Brian Ellison* a55 64
5 b g Intense Focus(USA) Bowstring (IRE) (Sadler's Wells (USA))
948[6] 1106[8] 1271[13] 6210[2] 6828[3] 7441[4]

Tommy Rock (IRE) *Clive Cox* a65 66
2 gr c Society Rock(IRE) Chiara Wells (IRE) (Refuse To Bend (IRE))
6330[3]◆ 7406[12] 8060[4]

Tommys Geal *Michael Madgwick* a55 58
7 b m Halling(USA) Steel Free (IRE) (Danehill Dancer (IRE))
736[6]

Tommy Taylor (USA) *Kevin Ryan* a85 87
5 b g Mizzen Mast(USA) Sharp Apple (USA) (Diesis)
1459[6] 1829[15] 2396[3] 2775[18] 3308[2] 4759[4] 4887[5] 5453[4] 6676[5] 7362[3] 8101[8] 8550[4]

Tomorrow's Angel *Iain Jardine* a68 68
4 ch m Teofilo(IRE) Funday (Daylami (IRE))
2326[3] 3046[14] 3686[13] 4056[7] 4510[5] 4869[8]

Tomorrow's Dream (FR)
William Haggas a75
2 b f Oasis Dream Midnight Thoughts (USA) (Henrythenavigator (USA))
9392[5] (9623a)◆

Tomouh (IRE) *Saeed bin Suroor* 63
2 b f Dubawi(IRE) Sundrop (JPN) (Sunday Silence (USA))
6407[4]

Tom's Anna (IRE) *Sean Regan* a21 48
9 b m Antonius Pius(USA) Vanilla Delight (IRE) (Orpen (USA))
2328[10] 3296[2] 3939[2] 4785[12] 5213[4] 5787[4] 6627[9] 7776[11]

Tom's D'Etat (USA) *Albert M Stall Jr* a120
6 b h Smart Strike(CAN) Julia Tuttle (USA) (Giant's Causeway (USA))
445a[9]

Tomshalfbrother *Robert Cowell* a58 69
3 b g Sir Percy Kassuta (Kyllachy)
8672[3] 9540[3]

Tom Tulliver *Declan Carroll* 79
2 b g Hot Streak(IRE) Belle Isle (Pastoral Pursuits)
3371[3] (3739) 4433[3] 5275[5] 6498[2] 7399[8] 8261[4]

To Nathaniel *John Gosden* a57
2 ch c Nathaniel(IRE) Too The Stars (IRE) (Sea The Stars (IRE))
9326[10]

Tone Broke (CAN)
Steven Asmussen a95 81
3 bb c Broken Vow(USA) Mendocino Beano (CAN) (Smart Strike (CAN))
394a[6] 1110a[14] 6994a[9]

Tone The Barone *Stuart Williams* 72
3 ch g Lope De Vega(IRE) A Huge Dream (IRE) (Refuse To Bend (IRE))
(2204) 3508[8] 4297[5] (5064)◆ 5356[2] 6286[8]

Toni's A Star *Tony Carroll* a65 64
7 b m Avonbridge Canina (Foxhound (USA))
28[9] 286[3] (626) 926[6] 1507[8] 4555[5] 5750[3] 5986[3] (7274) 7651[2] 7986[8] 9135[3]◆

Tonquin Valley *Brian Ellison* 42
2 b g Camacho Vita Mia (Central Park (IRE))
1843[U] 2288[6] 2892[U]

Tonto's Spirit *Dianne Sayer* a51 70
7 b g Authorized(IRE) Desert Royalty (IRE) (Alhaarth (IRE))
6016[3]

Tony The Gent (IRE) *G M Lyons* a88 92
6 b g Kodiac Becuille (IRE) (Redback)
1308a[6]

Tonyx *Ed Walker* a67 86
3 b f Nathaniel(IRE) Kadoma (Danehill Dancer (IRE))
(7159) (8814)◆

Too Big To Fail (IRE)
Mark Johnston 69
2 b f Teofilo(IRE) Pretty Diamond (IRE) (Hurricane Run (IRE))
8028[4] 8432[6]

Too Darn Hot *John Gosden* 125
3 b c Dubawi(IRE) Dar Re Mi (Singspiel (IRE))
2777[2] 3104a[2] 3951[3] (4705a) (5543)

Toofi (FR) *John Butler* a75 85
8 b g Henrythenavigator(USA) Silver Bark (Royal Applause)
3079[4] 3657[5]

Too Hard To Hold (IRE)
Mark Johnston a73 73
2 b g Camacho Bilderberg (IRE) (Big Bad Bob (IRE))
4062[4] 4486[4] 4903[6] 5288[3] (5618) 6147[3] 6883[5] 7186[3] 7785[4] 8315[8]

Tookiedoo (IRE) *Kieran P Cotter* a50 73
5 b m Art Connoisseur(IRE) Eur Elusive (IRE) (Elusive City (USA))
1554[2]◆

Toolatetodelegate *Brian Barr* a58 55
5 b m Delegator Little Caroline (IRE) (Great Commotion (USA))
53[4] 244[10] 809[7] 1093[9] 2503a[4] 2728[5] 3527[2] 4219[4] (4500) 4776[6] 5582[4] 5884[8] 6329[11]

Toolmaker *David Flood* a35
2 b g Harbour Watch(IRE) Calypso Dream (IRE) (Danehill Dancer (IRE))
7269[6] 8069[9] 8604[13]

Too Shy Shy (IRE) *Richard Spencer* a66 79
2 gr f Kodiac Satwa Ruby (FR) (Verglas (IRE))
2836[7] 3461[6] 3983[15] 4583[8] 6375[18] 8465[8]

Top Attraction *Chris Fairhurst* 16
2 b g Fountain Of Youth(IRE) Symphonic Dancer (USA) (Smart Strike (CAN))
5856[12] 6673[7]

Top Boy *Tony Carroll* a73 73
9 b g Exceed And Excel(AUS) Injaaz (Sheikh Albadou)
433[5] 832[7] 1357[7] 2107[6] 2515[5] 3147[14] (4733) (5013) 7230[4] 8063[3]

Top Breeze (IRE) *Richard Hughes* a87 94
3 b g Gale Force Ten Shamarlane (Shamardal (USA))
(1336)◆ (1851) 2522[5] 3166[2] 4847[9] 5589[6]

Top Buck (IRE) *Brian Meehan* a73 79
2 ch g Dandy Man(IRE) Tip It On The Top (IRE) (War Chant (USA))
2205[2] 2520[3] 3047[5] 3695[3] 6375[10] 6963[4] (7173) 7429[9] 8252[7] 8505[5]

Top By Cocooning (FR) *J-P Gauvin* 76
6 ch g American Post Cocooning (FR) (Galetto (FR))
5035a[11] 6790a[2]

Top Class Angel (IRE)
Richard Hannon a59 71
2 b f Dark Angel(IRE) Expensive Date (Monsieur Bond (IRE))
4030[4]◆ 4605[4]

Top Face (USA) *H Al Ramzani* a86 99
6 bb h Tiznow(USA) Toppisme (USA) (Saint Ballado (CAN))
869a[3]

Top Flight Cool *Tim Easterby* a58 70
2 b g Monsieur Bond(IRE) Topflightcoolracer (Lujain (USA))
6971[6] 7285[8] 8302[9]

Topflighttoafrica *David O'Meara* 39
2 b f Sir Percy Hispalis (IRE) (Barathea (IRE))
5764[10]

Topical *Richard Hannon* a76 82
3 b g Toronado(IRE) Star Value (IRE) (Danehill Dancer (IRE))
1736[4] 2078[6]

Topkapi Star *Roger Varian* a61 75
2 b f Golden Horn Burlesque Star (IRE) (Thousand Words)
3881[3] 4245[5] 5170[3] 6969[4] 7620[4]

Top Max (FR) *H-A Pantall* 98
3 b g Joshua Tree(IRE) Risky Nizzy (Cape Cross (IRE))
1241a[4] (6652a)

Topmeup *Gay Kelleway* a55 59
5 ch m Mayson Ambrix (IRE) (Xaar)
1349a[8]

Top Mission *Marco Botti* a89 85
5 b g Dubawi(IRE) Ever Love (BRZ) (Nedawi)
2064[2]◆ 2487[8] 3496[7] 4867[5] 5688[6]

Top Notch Tonto (IRE)
Brian Ellison a69 77
9 ch g Thousand Words Elite Hope (USA) (Moment Of Hope (USA))
3811[7] 4241[7]◆ 4383[8] 4913[12] 5694[5] 6067[6] 7003[11] 7185[3] 7589[7]

Top Offer *Patrick Morris* a59 52
10 b g Dansili Zante (Zafonic (USA))
210[3] 792[6] 5003[10] 5438[4] 5851[6] (6327) 7581[11] 8818[11]

Top Of The Range (NZ)
Michael Moroney 100
5 bb g Savabeel(AUS) Spiriting (NZ) (Montjeu (IRE))
1784a[11] (8803a)

Topology *Joseph Tuite* a69 54
6 br g Passing Glance Bold Byzantium (Bold Arrangement)
1675[9] 1983[5] 2692[6] 3429[3] 6507[5] (7083) 7790[8] 8422[2] 8813[2] 9067[8]

Top Power (FR) *Andrew Balding* a57 84
3 ch g Le Havre(IRE) Altamira (Peintre Celebre (USA))
103[2]◆ 858[4] 5614[12] 7141[4] 7974[3] 8727[3]

Top Rank (IRE) *James Tate* a74 92
3 gr c Dark Angel(IRE) Countess Ferrama (Authorized (IRE))
(1764) (7617)

Top Rock Talula (IRE)
Warren Greatrex a65 65
4 b m Lord Shanakill(USA) Spirit Watch (IRE) (Invincible Spirit (IRE))
59[4] (245) 369[6] 736[2] 1341[2] 1548[2] (2733) 2974[5] 5344[8]

Top Score *Saeed bin Suroor* a100 113
5 br g Hard Spun(USA) Windsor County (USA) (Elusive Quality (USA))
52a[2]◆ 397a[5] 639a[11] 846a[9] (Dead)

Top Secret *Clive Cox* a69
2 ch g Anjaal Just Devine (IRE) (Montjeu (IRE))
9385[4] 9631[3]

Tops No *William Muir* a25 49
4 b m Mount Nelson China Beads (Medicean)
6043[8] *7081[6]* **7973**[3] *8553[11]* *8869[11]*

Top Space (USA) *C Laffon-Parias* a42
3 b c Speightstown(USA) Top Order (USA) (Dayjur (USA))
***1198a**[9]*

Topsy Turvy (IRE) *Ibrahim Al Malki* 95
7 b g Pivotal Helter Skelter (USA) (Seeking The Gold (USA))
869a[13]

Top Top (IRE) *Sir Michael Stoute* a44 46
3 b c Frankel Jira (Medicean)
1956[7] 3604[6] ***7560**[10]*

Top Tug (IRE) *Alan King* a99 106
8 ch g Halling(USA) Top Romance (IRE) (Entrepreneur)
2827[5] 4053[14] 5662[12]

Tor *Marjorie Fife* a51 76
5 ch g Orientor Dance In The Sun (Halling (USA))
61[4] **1947**[11] 2118[7] 2786[8] 3222[4]◆ 3847[5] 4913[5] 5423[4] 5743[6] 6933[4] 8236[4] 8635[8] *9467[12]*

Torbellino *John Best* a65 71
3 b f Maxios Tiny Smile (IRE) (Celtic Swing)
6290[8] **6811**[3] *8451[2]* *9633[11]*

Torcello (IRE) *Shaun Lycett* a67 94
5 ch g Born To Sea(IRE) Islandagore (IRE) (Indian Ridge (IRE))
3466[12] 4224[9] *4792[12]* *5811[7]* (6217) **(7727)** (7974)

Torch *Laura Morgan* a42 46
6 b g Paco Boy(IRE) Singed (Zamindar (USA))
789[5] **2373**[5] 2626[9] *4190[5]*

Toriano (FR) *Waldemar Hickst* 61
4 b g Dutch Art Tu Eres Mi Amore (IRE) (Sadler's Wells (USA))
1631a[2] **2182a**[6]

Toriano *Nick Littmoden* a70 60
6 ch g Equiano(FR) Ticki Tori (IRE) (Vettori (IRE))
(1042)◆ *2596[7]* 3018[6]

Torna A Surriento (ITY)
Gianluca Bietolini a72 72
6 b h Blu Air Force(IRE) Black County (ITY) (Black Minnaloushe (USA))
2955a[7]

Tornibush (IRE) *P Decouz* a94 109
5 b h Dream Ahead(USA) Celenza (FR) (Dansili)
2313a[4] 3289a[7] 4581a[4]

Torochica *John Best* a86 85
3 ch f Toronado(IRE) Biased (Haafhd)
2236[7] 3067[3] (5193) 7141[2] 7895[12] ***9050**[2]* *9177[3]* *9510[8]*

Toro Dorado *Ed Dunlop* a77 61
3 b g Toronado(IRE) Rawoof (IRE) (Nayef (USA))
1481[4] 1980[4] 2798[11] 3256[7] *4293[2]* 4836[3] *(5284)* 5797[12] *6317[2]* *7305[3]* 7982[9] *9202[3]* ***9453**[3]*

Torolight *Nicky Henderson* a73 52
3 b g Toronado(IRE) Tuscan Light (Medicean)
826[4] *1173[4]* ***(2011)*** *3446[7]* *4769[9]* *9303[2]*

Toronado Queen (IRE)
Richard Fahey a74 76
3 b f Toronado(IRE) Queenofthenorth (IRE) (Halling (USA))
(6587)◆ *7190[3]* 7681[5] 8463[7]

Toronto (IRE) *A P O'Brien* 94
2 b c Galileo(IRE) Mrs Marsh (Marju (IRE))
5362a[2] 6430a[8] 7245a[8]

Toro Strike (USA) *Richard Fahey* 91
2 b c Toronado(IRE) Scarlet Strike (USA) (Smart Strike (CAN))
2830[5] (3411) 4441[2]◆ **5587**[3] **7119**[3]

Torpen (FR) *P Monfort* a93 79
2 b c Orpen(USA) That's The Spirit (FR) (Country Reel (USA))
7925a[9]

Torquato (ITY) *A Botti* 94
2 b c Ruler Of The World(IRE) Torrechiara (FR) (Halling (USA))
8789a[5]

Torque Of The Town (IRE)
Noel Wilson a35 55
3 gr g Zebedee Elaysa (Shamardal (USA))
2199[10] 2590[7] **3157**[5] 5202[4] 6176[10] *8502[10]*

Torrealta (FR) *H-F Devin* a68
3 b f Toronado(IRE) Santa Agata (FR) (Anabaa (USA))
***993a**[3]*

Tosen Ciara (IRE) *J-C Bertin* a48 57
3 ch f Dandy Man(IRE) Eliza Snow (IRE) (Majestic Missile (IRE))
2390a[3] 4229a[8]

Tosen Gift (IRE) *S Kobayashi* 106
4 b m Lope De Vega(IRE) Miracolia (IRE) (Montjeu (IRE))
1244a[9] **2167a**[2] 3138a[6] (6992a) 7885a[3] 8584a[3] 8969a[3]

Tosen Shauna (IRE) *M Rulec* a81 94
3 b f Alhebayeb(IRE) Naked Poser (IRE) (Night Shift (USA))
(2390a) *5538a[2]* 8449a[2] **8983a**[4]

Toshima (IRE) *Robert Stephens* a84 86
4 b g Sea The Stars(IRE) Sabreon (Caerleon (USA))
4614[9] **(5496)** 5967[6] *6348[3]* *8321[7]*

Total Commitment (IRE)
Peter Hedger a98 83
3 b g Exceed And Excel(AUS) Crysdal (Dalakhani (IRE))
(6413) 6916[12] *(7789)*◆ ***(8420)*** 9478[4]

Total Distraction *K R Burke* 31
2 b g Fountain Of Youth(IRE) Mad Annie (USA) (Anabaa (USA))
7619[9]

Totally Boss (USA)
George R Arnold II 118
4 b g Street Boss(USA) Totally Tucker (USA) (Elusive Quality (USA))
8770a[10]

Totally Magic (IRE)
Richard Whitaker a59 61
7 b m Captain Rio Hypocrisy (Bertolini (USA))
210[8] ***501**[2]*

Total Perfection (IRE)
Richard Hannon a56
2 br c Fountain Of Youth(IRE) Day By Day (Kyllachy)
***7555**[7]* *8059[10]*

To The Moon *John Gosden* a80 68
3 b f Sea The Stars(IRE) Ladys First (Dutch Art)
2488[6] 3761[4] ***6346**[3]* *(7999)*

Touchthesoul (ITY) *Gary Moore* a79 71
4 b g Red Rocks(IRE) Easy Hawk (Hawk Wing (USA))
7567[7]

Tough Remedy (IRE)
Keith Dalgleish a94 91
4 b g Tough As Nails(IRE) Remediate (USA) (Miswaki (USA))
(212) ***800**[2]*◆ ***1232**[4]* 1753[17] ***2187**[2]* 2808[8] *3450[5]* 4240[7] 5095[6] 5709[8] *6630[2]*

Tour De Magie (IRE) *Mlle J Soudan* a24 20
3 b f Olympic Glory(IRE) Magie Noire (IRE) (Marju (IRE))
2311a[8]

Tour De Paris (IRE) *Alan King* a70 42
4 b g Champs Elysees Disco Lights (Spectrum (IRE))
85[10] *(810)* ***1235**[2]* 2239[4] *6681[11]* *7845[10]*

Touriga (BRZ) *H Graham Motion* 98
3 b f Put It Back(USA) Just Perfect (BRZ) (Nugget Point (IRE))
7224a[7]

Tour To Paris (FR) *Mme Pia Brandt* a108 108
4 b h Fuisse(FR) Theoricienne (FR) (Kendor (FR))
3289a[8] 7255a[10] **(8141a)**

Town Bee (USA) *Doug Watson*
3 b c Jersey Town(USA) Bees (USA) (Rahy (USA))
634a[9]

Toybox *Jonathan Portman* a62 67
3 ch f Paco Boy(IRE) Play Street (Tobougg (IRE))
1264[8] 2407[9] **3170**[7] 3665[7] 4424[4] 5561[5] 6810[3] 7343[8] *8291[6]* *9216[2]* *9589[5]*

Toy Theatre *Michael Appleby* a93 74
5 b m Lonhro(AUS) Puppet Queen (USA) (Kingmambo (USA))
(756) ***(951)*** *1234[4]* *1918[11]* 2252[10] 6214[7]

Tracker Saga (IRE) *J S Bolger* 73
3 b c Vocalised(USA) Gold Mirage (IRE) (Galileo (IRE))
5712a[12]

Tractive Effort *Michael Attwater* a40 26
6 b g Rail Link Anastasia Venture (Lion Cavern (USA))
***363**[9]*

Trade Talks *Chris Wall* a77 50
4 b g Cacique(IRE) Esteemed Lady (IRE) (Mark Of Esteem (IRE))
4283[10]

Trading Point (FR)
Damian Joseph English a96 98
5 b g Siyouni(FR) Zita Blues (IRE) (Zieten (USA))
1308a[2] 5535a[9] 7222a[15]

Traditional Dancer (IRE)
Iain Jardine a47 48
7 b g Danehill Dancer(IRE) Cote Quest (USA) (Green Desert (USA))
***208**[4]* *9470[4]*

Trailboss (IRE) *Ed Vaughan* a80 76
4 b g High Chaparral(IRE) Seeking Solace (Exceed And Excel (AUS))
2301[2] *2555[3]* 3263[8] (4370) 5825[4] 7026[7] *7915[4]* ***(8422)***

Train To Georgia (USA)
Joseph Tuite a74 74
3 bb g Scat Daddy(USA) Ghost Galaxy (USA) (Ghostzapper (USA))
(1217)◆ **4177**[2]

Trais Fluors *K J Condon* a107 113
5 b h Dansili Trois Lunes (FR) (Manduro (GER))
2083[5] **3122a**[3] **3906a**[2] 6144a[3] 7293a[3] 8774a[11]

Tralee Hills *Peter Hedger* a81 85
5 b g Mount Nelson Distant Waters (Lomitas)
88[3] ***(735)*** 3806[11] *4250[10]* 5417[8] *7915[9]* *8608[3]* *8829[5]*

Trancoso (FR) *E Leenders* a71
6 b g Rock Of Gibraltar(IRE) Tropa De Elite (USA) (Street Cry (IRE))
***46a**[11]*

Tranquil Storm (IRE) *Kevin Ryan* a62 72
4 b m Oasis Dream Sparkle Plenty (IRE) (Galileo (IRE))
1908a[2] 5009a[5] **7287**[2] *8838[2]*

Transcendent (ITY) *F Chappet* a105 105
3 b g Dabirsim(FR) Resaca (GER) (Touch Down (GER))
683a[2] *(1199a)* ***(1920)*** **3903a**[2]

Transcript *James Tate* a69 54
2 b f Night Of Thunder(IRE) Storyland (USA) (Menifee (USA))
8759[6] ***9311**[3]*

Transition *Amanda Perrett* a78
2 b c Oasis Dream Nancy O (IRE) (Pivotal)
6112[3]◆ *7842[4]* ***(9208)***◆

Transpennine Gold *Michael Dods* a51 51
3 gr g Gregorian(IRE) Perfect Cover (IRE) (Royal Applause)
2198[6] **3680**[6] 5915[12] ***6983**[6]* *7909[7]* *8863[10]*

Trapani *John Gosden* a61
3 gr f Shamardal(USA) Claba Di San Jore (IRE) (Barathea (IRE))
***103**[6]* *358[6]*

Tras Os Montes (FR) *Mlle L Kneip* a61 65
2 b c Sommerabend Sottovoce (Oratorio (IRE))
4949a[7]

Trautmann (IRE) *Rebecca Menzies* a74 75
5 ch g Casamento(IRE) Klang (IRE) (Night Shift (USA))
101[3] *495[3]* *803[6]* **(4056)** 4404[11] 7001[10] 7368[15]

Traveller (FR) *Antony Brittain* a62 59
5 b g Henrythenavigator(USA) Nantes (GER) (Night Shift (USA))
125[5] ***479**[3]* ***911**[3]* *1015[4]* *1506[3]* ***1769**[2]* *1983[9]* *3448[8]* *5438[3]* *7581[2]* *8087[4]* *8345[2]* *8713[5]* *9040[3]* *9395[9]*

Travel On *John Gosden* a98 98
3 b g Lope De Vega(IRE) Teeky (Daylami (IRE))
(1268)◆ **2084**[4] *2553[5]* ***6349**[4]*◆ 6952[4] 7616[7]

Trawangane (FR) *N Clement* a85 96
5 ch m Dutch Art On The Line (FR) (Green Tune (USA))
***46a**[8]*

Treacherous *Ed de Giles* a88 72
5 b g Paco Boy(IRE) Black Baroness (Ishiguru (USA))
253[3] ***(407)*** *(755)* *(1098)* *1290[2]* *1942[9]* 2611[12]

Treasured Company (IRE)
Richard Guest a46 41
3 b g Fast Company(IRE) Lady's Locket (IRE) (Fasliyev (USA))
1515[7] ***2190**[3]* *2531[4]* 4487[10] 6610[7] *7549[10]*

Treasured Times (IRE) *R Bouresly* a60 79
5 ch h Teofilo(IRE) Last Resort (Lahib (USA))
***1322a**[9]*

Treasure Me *Charlie Fellowes* a90 98
4 b m Poet's Voice Treasured Dream (Oasis Dream)
475[2] *756[2]* *951[3]* *1234[2]* *1918[7]* ***2627**[2]*◆ 3587[7] 4340[6] 8115[13]

Treasure Quest *Brian Meehan* a65 73
3 b c Sepoy(AUS) Collectable (Excellent Art)
657[7]

Treaty Of Dingle *Hughie Morrison* a66 57
2 b f Roderic O'Connor(IRE) Josefa Goya (Sakhee's Secret)
3039[6]◆ 5500[6] *5729[5]* *6683[6]* *7275[5]* *7910[3]* *8415[3]* ***(9037)*** *9250[5]*

Treble Clef *Lee Carter* a63
4 b g Helmet(AUS) Musical Key (Key Of Luck (USA))
1352[10] *2555[5]* ***9171**[3]*

Treble Treble (IRE) *Kevin Ryan* 88
2 b c Brazen Beau(AUS) Sugar Blossom (IRE) (Marju (IRE))
4401[3]◆ **(5125)** 6474[11] 8125[11]

Trecco Bay *David Elsworth* a54
2 b f New Approach(IRE) Porthcawl (Singspiel (IRE))
***7786**[5]*◆ ***8218**[11]* *9631[7]*

Trefoil *Ralph Beckett* 77
2 b f Teofilo(IRE) Prairie Flower (IRE) (Zieten (USA))
(8464)

Trekking (AUS) *James Cummings* 118
4 b g Street Cry(IRE) Outdoor (AUS) (Redoute's Choice (AUS))
8362a[3]

Trelinney (IRE) *Marcus Tregoning* a56 67
3 b f Dandy Man(IRE) Silvertine (IRE) (Alzao (USA))
2965[4]◆ 3797[4] 4562[4]◆ **(5085)** 5795[5]

Tremont (FR) *D De Waele* a75 65
4 b h Most Improved(IRE) Sheema (Teofilo (IRE))
***2264a**[6]*

Tremor (IRE) *Alan King* 73
2 ch g Intello(GER) Shake The Moon (GER) (Loup Solitaire (USA))
7339[8] **(8657)**

Tremwedge *Miss Ellmarie Holden* 53
3 b g Foxwedge(AUS) Tremelo Pointe (IRE) (Trempolino (USA))
7984[10]

Trenchard (USA) *Doug Watson* a88
5 b g Elusive Quality(USA) Temporada (USA) (Summer Squall (USA))
***197a**[10]*

Trent (HUN) *Z Hegedus* a47 63
3 b f George Vancouver(USA) Temple Mount (IRE) (Montjeu (IRE))
2265a[7]

Trentatre (FR) *Andrea Marcialis* 61
2 b f Orpen(USA) Pen Du (FR) (Astronomer Royal (USA))
2315a[4] **8330a**[3]

Trentino (FR) *M Nigge* a79 73
3 ch g Harbour Watch(IRE) Added Attraction (FR) (Kendor (FR))
1241a[3]

Tresorerie (FR) *C Ferland* 102
4 b m Intello(GER) Treasure (FR) (Anabaa (USA))
6144a[8] **8969a**[5]

Tresorier *John James Feane* 80
5 b g Dunkerque(FR) Treasure (FR) (Anabaa (USA))
***7241a**[17]*

Tres Rush (IRE) *Mme Pia Brandt* 77
5 b g Rip Van Winkle(IRE) Tres Ravi (GER) (Monsun (GER))
4748a[2]

Tres Solid (FR) *M Boutin* a67 67
8 b g Honours List(IRE) Tres Passing (FR) (Medaaly)
5115a[2] *5410a[6]* 8966a[3]

Trethias *Mrs John Harrington* 105
3 b f Invincible Spirit(IRE) Evita (Selkirk (USA))
2157a[7] 2661a[3] 5208a[8] 6692a[3] 7242a[5] **8094**[4] 8367a[2]

Trevie Fountain *Richard Fahey* a60 68
2 b g Fountain Of Youth(IRE) Fantacise (Pivotal)
4826[12] *5433[9]* **5934**[3] 6653[10] *7419[8]* 7896[13]

Trevithick *Bryan Smart* a96 43
4 b g Champs Elysees New Choice (IRE) (Barathea (IRE))
(19) *350[2]* ***1401**[2]* *2187[3]* *2959[6]* *4292[8]* *9200[8]*

Tribal Commander *Ian Williams* 70
3 gr g Intikhab(USA) Jessica Ennis (USA) (English Channel (USA))
3373[P] 4392[9] **4671**[5] 5175[8] 6291[5] 7300[2]

Tribal Craft *Andrew Balding* 97
3 ch f Mastercraftsman(IRE) Snoqualmie Star (Galileo (IRE))
3263[6]◆ (3889) (5153) 5541[7] **6124**[2] 6712[6] 7864[7]

Tribal Warrior *James Tate* a83 95
4 b h New Approach(IRE) Lunda (IRE) (Soviet Star (USA))
(4511)◆ 8184[4]

Tribhuvan (FR) *H-A Pantall* a77 82
3 b c Toronado(IRE) Mahendra (GER) (Next Desert (IRE))
***868a**[3]*

Tribune *Sylvester Kirk* a55 35
3 ch g Medicean Giusina Mia (USA) (Diesis)
1344[3] *1676[8]* ***2322**[6]* 3528[10] 3965[10] 4400[14]

Trickbag (USA) *Susanne Berneklint* a85 75
5 br g Brilliant Speed(USA) Shining Appeal (USA) (Powerscourt)
50a[6] 640a[10] ***842a**[8]*

Tricky Dicky *Roger Fell* a80 89
6 b g Holy Roman Emperor(IRE) Tricky Situation (Mark Of Esteem (IRE))
407[6] *914[3]* *(1072)* 2580[11] (2846) *3206[2]* 3550[3] (3657) 3928[2] (4148) 4440[2]◆ **(5395)**

Trickydickysimpson *Richard Fahey* a50 20
2 b c Poet's Voice Ershaadaat (IRE) (Cape Cross (IRE))
3954[9] ***4289**[6]*

Tricorn (IRE) *Ruth Carr* a93 92
5 b g Helmet(AUS) Special Dancer (Shareef Dancer (USA))
1912[11] 2778[12] 3160[10] **4079**[6]◆

Tried And True (USA)
Doug Watson a97 96
7 b g Medaglia d'Oro(USA) Dearly (Rahy (USA))
***172a**[2]* *396a[8]*

Triggered (IRE) *Ed Walker* 93
3 b g Dandy Man(IRE) Triggers Broom (IRE) (Arcano (IRE))
1762[7] 2396[4] 3865[18] **6976**[3] 8512[12]

Trigger Happy (IRE)
Richard Spencer a65
2 b g Gutaifan(IRE) Boom And Bloom (IRE) (Lawman (FR))
***8546**[2]*

Trinity Girl *Mark Johnston* a67
2 b f Teofilo(IRE) Micaela's Moon (USA) (Malibu Moon (USA))
8198[2] ***8528**[3]* *8919[4]*

Trinity Lake *Declan Carroll* 84
3 b g Dansili Mirror Lake (Dubai Destination (USA))
(2147) 2634[6] 5690[4] **7141**[3] 7907[12]

Trinity Star (IRE) *Karen McLintock* a73 77
8 gr g Kheleyf(USA) Zamiyla (IRE) (Daylami (IRE))
1401[8] 3053[7] 3502[6] *4333[2]* 4762[5] 5122[4] **(5694)** 6038[4] 6975[7] 7643[9] *8300[7]*

Trio Gagnant (FR) *F Foucher* 49
4 bl g Silver Frost(IRE) Like Afleet (USA) (Afleet Alex (USA))
5762a[4]

Triple Distilled *Nigel Tinkler* 92
3 b g Tamayuz So Refined (IRE) (Cape Cross (IRE))
2395[7] 2825[3] 3307[4] 3654[2] 4297[3]◆ (4895) **(5459)**

Triple First *Seamus Mullins* a30 65
5 b m Dick Turpin(IRE) Orphina (IRE) (Orpen (USA))
1935[11] ***2240**[12]*

Triple Genius (IRE) *Ed Dunlop* a39 49
3 b g Mastercraftsman(IRE) Three Moons (IRE) (Montjeu (IRE))
2505[6] *3445[10]* 3860[7] 5596[12] 6400[11]

Triple Nickle (IRE)
Bernard Llewellyn a63 65
3 b f So You Think(NZ) Secret Shine (IRE) (Raven's Pass (USA))
7238[3] 7682[7] 8247[4] *9040[6]* *(9279)*◆ ***9573**[9]*

Triple Spear *Michael Appleby* a69 63
2 br g Showcasing Secret Romance (Sakhee's Secret)
6548[9] 7333[5]◆ 8026[4] *9137[3]*◆ ***9401**[3]*◆ ***(9474)***

Trita Sass (IRE) *A Botti* 98
3 b c Pounced(USA) Torrechiara (FR) (Halling (USA))
2887a[6] 7504a[4]

Tritonic *Alan King* 93
2 ch c Sea The Moon(GER) Selenography (Selkirk (USA))
5177[4] (6395) **(7410)** 8111[5]

Tritonix *Gavin Cromwell* a75 81
4 b m Nathaniel(IRE) Triton Dance (IRE) (Hector Protector (USA))
5404a[5]

Troilus (FR) *S Wattel* a85 101
2 b c Siyouni(FR) Resistance (FR) (King's Best (USA))
(5642a) **7005a**[5] 7925a[14]

Trois Bon Amis (IRE)
Mark Campion a24 41
5 gr g Lilbourne Lad(IRE) Vanozza (FR) (Dylan Thomas (IRE))
***6153**[11]*

Trois Mille (FR) *S Cerulis* a71 114
3 b g Evasive Indian Beauty (IRE) (Mujadil (USA))
(2090a) 4581a[5] (6252a) 8141a[3] **(8648a)**

Troisouni (FR) *Conrad Allen*
3 b f Siyouni(FR) Gamma (FR) (Sadler's Wells (USA))
4341[11] *8645[8]* *9165[9]*

Trois Roses (FR) *J-M Lefebvre* 47
5 gr m Vatori(FR) Spinohn (FR) (Take Risks (FR))
3711a[14]

Trolius (IRE) *Simon Crisford* a76 91
3 b g Cape Cross(IRE) Trikala (IRE) (High Chaparral (IRE))
168a[3] 511a[6] 727a[3] 956a[9] 6914[3]◆ 7863[4] *8253[10]*

Tronada *Alan King* a71 77
3 b f Toronado(IRE) Manbaa (USA) (Jazil (USA))
3041[5] 3773[3] 4663[8] 5349[5] *6282[4]* 6961[14]

Tronador (IRE) *David Lanigan* a61 50
3 ch g Lope De Vega(IRE) Autumn Leaves (FR) (Muhtathir)
2518[9] 3277[6] 3946[8] ***5946**[3]* *6635[4]*

Troop *Ann Duffield* a60 54
4 gr g Lethal Force(IRE) Bendis (GER) (Danehill (USA))
5438[12] *5787[3]* *7581[3]* *7956[2]* *8301[2]* ***8667**[2]* *8922[3]*

Troop Commander (IRE)
Kevin Prendergast 81
2 b c War Command(USA) Tempura (GER) (Cape Cross (IRE))
5710a^{11}

Tropbeau *A Fabre* 111
2 b f Showcasing Frangipanni (IRE) (Dansili)
(5469a) (6248a) 7692^{3}

Tropezienne (FR)
R Le Dren Doleuze a56 45
4 b m Whipper(USA) Alinade (FR) (Poliglote)
76a^{12} 3711a^{15}

Tropics (USA) *Dean Ivory* a112 86
11 ch g Speightstown(USA) Taj Aire (USA) (Taj Alriyadh (USA))
(35) 352^{7} 837^{3} 1839^{3} 2062^{4} 2917^{8} 3582^{2} (3993) 6149^{3}◆ 7687^{5} 8015^{5}

Trossachs *J S Bolger* 105
3 ch c New Approach(IRE) Falls Of Lora (IRE) (Street Cry (IRE))
7216a^{3}

Trotter *Stuart Kittow* a56 63
5 b g Piccolo Vintage Steps (IRE) (Bahamian Bounty)
1820^{2} 2717^{11} 3645^{3} 4181^{11}

Trou Aux Biches (FR) *Y Barberot* 47
2 b f Rajsaman(FR) Starsic (FR) (Sageburg (IRE))
4949a^{9} 5600a^{5} 6485a^{4}

Troubador (IRE) *Michael Dods* 100
2 gr g Poet's Voice Eastern Destiny (Dubai Destination (USA))
1844^{7} (2906) 3498^{2} (3919) (4938) (5390)◆ 6356^{2} 7904^{2}

Trouble And Strife (IRE)
Sir Mark Prescott Bt a83 88
4 br m Declaration Of War(USA) Rare Tern (IRE) (Pivotal)
3408^{4} 4782^{5} 5321^{7} 7033^{3} 7439^{3} 7819^{6}

Trouble Of Course (FR)
Mme Pia Brandt a95 92
5 gr g Rajsaman(FR) Sister Trouble (FR) (Spectrum (IRE))
4419a^{5} 6524a^{4} 9014a^{5}

Trouble Shooter (IRE)
Shaun Keightley a74 64
3 b g Delegator Khibraat (Alhaarth (IRE))
585^{5} 829^{7}◆ 1066^{4}◆ 2007^{7} 2597^{7} 3299^{3} (3741) 4998^{5} 5648^{2} (5915) (6367)◆ (7082) (8019) 8468^{4}

Trouser The Cash (IRE)
Amy Murphy 54
2 b f Starspangledbanner(AUS) Bint Malyana (IRE) (Bahamian Bounty)
1821^{9} 6793^{5} 8751^{9}

Trouville (FR) *C Ferland* a89 65
3 b g Le Havre(IRE) Dont Teutch (FR) (Country Reel (USA))
683a^{4} 1243a^{7}

Truckingby *Mark Johnston* a61 61
3 b g Raven's Pass(USA) Off Chance (Olden Times)
836^{6} 949^{5} 1358^{4} 1555^{6} 1957^{4} 2325^{3} 2734^{5}

True Belief (IRE) *Brett Johnson* a71 70
3 b g Excelebration(IRE) It's True (IRE) (Kheleyf (USA))
1728^{11} 2009^{5} 2489^{7} 3961^{8} 5044^{2} 6052^{9} (7976) 8217^{2} 9218^{3} 9498^{3}

True Believer (IRE) *Mark Johnston* a70
2 b f Make Believe Laviniad (IRE) (Lawman (FR))
9284^{3} 9409^{2} 9623^{7}

True Blue Moon (IRE)
Joseph Patrick O'Brien a78 94
4 gr g Holy Roman Emperor(IRE) Fancy Intense (Peintre Celebre (USA))
4313a^{10} 5205a^{12} 6986a^{9}

True Colors *Mark Pattinson* a29 24
5 b g Sir Percy Shesells Seashells (Tiger Hill (IRE))
7282^{11} 7859^{13}

True Destiny *Roger Charlton* a74 89
4 ch g Mastercraftsman(IRE) Holy Dazzle (Sunday Break (JPN))
622^{3} (947) 2239^{2} (2936) 3653^{2}◆ (4404)◆ 5540^{3}

True Hero *Nigel Tinkler* a83 78
3 b g Charm Spirit(IRE) Beldale Memory (IRE) (Camacho)
1691^{3} 2121^{7} 4128^{2} 4294^{2} 4604^{5} 5356^{6} 5791^{4} 6148^{6} 6715^{6} 6976^{4}

True Mason *K R Burke* 98
3 b g Mayson Marysienka (Primo Dominie)
1780a^{4} 3083^{4} 5664^{25} 6252a^{4} 7243a^{11} 7889^{8}

True Motion (IRE) *Aidan F Fogarty* a67 78
2 b c Kodiac Savana Pearl (IRE) (Byron)
7876a^{6}

True North (IRE)
Sir Mark Prescott Bt a74 64
4 b g Henrythenavigator(USA) Cosmic Fire (FR) (Dalakhani (IRE))
4791^{8} 5436^{10}

True Romance (IRE) *Julia Brooke* a55 71
5 gr g Mastercraftsman(IRE) Full Of Love (IRE) (Hawk Wing (USA))
(5277)◆ (5766)◆ 6180^{4} 7368^{4}

True Scarlet (IRE) *Ed Walker* a73 40
2 b f Make Believe Lady Pimpernel (Sir Percy)
8510^{9} 9437^{2}

True Self (IRE) *W P Mullins* 112
6 b m Oscar(IRE) Good Thought (IRE) (Mukaddamah (USA))
3586^{2} 4856a^{7} 6473^{6} 8600a^{2} 9376a^{7}

Trueshan (FR) *Alan King* a85 112
3 b g Planteur(IRE) Shao Line (FR) (General Holme (USA))
(5634) (6641) 6955^{2} (8092) (8520)

True Thoughts (IRE) *Laura Young* a52 38
4 b g So You Think(NZ) True Joy (IRE) (Zilzal (USA))
3000^{5} 8246^{7}

True Timber (USA)
Kiaran McLaughlin a110
5 b h Mineshaft(USA) Queen's Wood (USA) (Tiznow (USA))
445a^{7} 1440a^{9}

True Valour (IRE) *Simon Callaghan* 108
5 b h Kodiac Sutton Veny (IRE) (Acclamation)
8774a^{10}

Truffle Mac *Hughie Morrison* a42 5
2 b f Kendargent(FR) Chutney (IRE) (Exceed And Excel (AUS))
8516^{19} 8913^{13} 9159^{9}

Tru Grit (IRE) *Tom Clover* a43 73
3 b g Acclamation Qalahari (IRE) (Bahri (USA))
6286^{14}

Trulee Scrumptious
Peter Charalambous a50 64
10 b m Strategic Prince Morning Rise (GER) (Acatenango (GER))
2799^{7} 3185^{6} 4067^{3} 4336^{5} 5138^{6} (5380) 5870^{3} 6164^{6} 6412^{3}

Trulove *John David Riches* a41 54
6 b m Piccolo Snow Dancer (IRE) (Desert Style (IRE))
277^{8} 411^{8} 2481^{6} 4489^{7} 5094^{6} 6277^{3} 7052^{7} (7488) 8632^{9}

Trumpet Man *Mark Johnston* a80 75
2 b c Golden Horn Concordia (Pivotal)
6708^{4}◆ 7473^{2} 8464^{5}

Trumpets Call (IRE)
David Loughnane 69
2 ch g Anjaal Yellow Trumpet (Petong)
5894^{4} 6368^{4} 6892^{6} 7521^{6}

Trust Me (IRE) *Dean Ivory* a50 63
3 b g Shamardal(USA) Punita (USA) (Distorted Humor (USA))
2210^{6} 2736^{8} 3464^{10} 4185^{13} 5629^{6} 6058^{13}

Trust You *Endo Botti* 101
7 ch g Kheleyf(USA) Evening Guest (FR) (Be My Guest (USA))
2888a^{4} 8787a^{4}

Tsar *John Gosden* a78 82
2 b c Kingman Kilo Alpha (King's Best (USA))
4886^{4}◆ (7821)

Tsarmina (IRE) *David Evans* a55 16
3 b f Ruler Of The World(IRE) Caelis (Avonbridge)
1019^{4}◆ 1165^{11} 1293^{7} 1593^{11} 2943^{9} 5293^{10}

Tsundoku (IRE) *Alexandra Dunn* a44 60
8 ch m Medicean Toberanthawn (IRE) (Danehill Dancer (IRE))
619^{13} 1429^{8} 6366^{5}

Tucson *James Bethell* a47 73
3 b g Lawman(FR) Bruxcalina (FR) (Linamix (FR))
1646^{4} 2336^{3} 2811^{6} 3505^{5} 5242^{5} 8196^{12}

Tudo Bem (FR) *M Boutin* a81 89
3 b c Sommerabend Boulba D'Alben (FR) (Dark Angel (IRE))
1842a^{2} (2392a) 8982a^{6}

Tudor City (IRE) *A J Martin* a76 88
7 b g Yeats(IRE) She's Our Mare (IRE) (Commanche Run)
6475^{8}

Tukhoom (IRE) *David O'Meara* a87 88
6 b g Acclamation Carioca (IRE) (Rakti)
2076^{2} 3199^{3} 3957^{3} (4078) 4552^{5} 5173^{4} 5303^{2} 5616^{4} (5820) 6201^{2} (6496) 6978^{2} (7164) 7563^{5} 8634^{6} 9283^{3} 9404^{6} 9561^{2}

Tuk Power *Andrew Balding* a56
3 b f Dubawi(IRE) Soon (IRE) (Galileo (IRE))
3463^{8}

Tulane (IRE) *Richard Phillips* a63 63
4 br g Arcano(IRE) Jeunesse Doree (IRE) (Rock Of Gibraltar (IRE))
3022^{6} 3941^{9} 8224^{6} 8703^{2} 9168^{5} 9553^{2}

Tulfarris *Charlie Fellowes* 97
3 b c Zoffany(IRE) Eurolink Raindance (IRE) (Alzao (USA))
1736^{3} 2395^{2} 4016^{11} 4882^{9} 5693^{13} 6914^{2} 7863^{2}

Tulipe Angelique (FR) *Paul Webber* a25
3 b f Planteur(IRE) Belle Chasse (Kyllachy)
4768^{13}

Tulip Fields *Mark Johnston* a76 77
2 b f Golden Horn Vituisa (Bering)
4819^{2} 5588^{3} 6918^{3} 8021^{2} 8525^{3}

Tulloona *Tom Clover* a68 63
3 b g Coach House(IRE) Minnola (Royal Applause)
359^{3}◆ 796^{3} 1171^{4} 3764^{6} 4286^{5} 5352^{3} 7080^{11} 8435^{2}

Tum Tum *Michael Herrington* a81 44
4 ch g Dawn Approach(IRE) Lalectra (King Charlemagne (USA))
608^{3} 886^{7} 1197^{2}◆ 1526^{6} (2246) 3462^{12} 5178^{11} 5970^{10} (7305)

Tundra *Anthony Carson* a75 73
5 b m Bated Breath Tanouma (USA) (Mr Greeley (USA))
801^{9} 2081^{6} 2729^{6} (3020)

Tunky *James Given* a62 40
3 gr f Gregorian(IRE) Alushta (Royal Applause)
27^{10} 319^{8} 612^{4} 2262^{9} 3299^{5} 3777^{7} 4038^{5}

Turaath *Charles Hills* 50
2 b f Oasis Dream Fadhayyil (IRE) (Tamayuz)
7054^{8}

Turanga Leela *John Mackie* a78 75
5 ch m Paco Boy(IRE) Sunday Bess (JPN) (Deep Impact (JPN))
(468) 2081^{11} 2508^{2} 3323^{2} 3846^{2} 4320^{10} 4879^{8} 6025^{2} 7471^{2} 7914^{4} 8866^{9}

Turbine (IRE) *Denis Gerard Hogan* a88 90
6 b g Cape Cross(IRE) Chiquita Linda (IRE) (Mujadil (USA))
3062a^{13}

Turbiondo (ITY) *Fabio Marchi* 86
2 b c Turati Biondina (ITY) (Nil (IRE))
8789a^{9}

Turea *L Gadbin* a92 94
3 b f Dubawi(IRE) Dream Clover (Oasis Dream)
(3710a) 7360a^{7} 9170a^{14}

Turgenev *John Gosden* a94 113
3 b c Dubawi(IRE) Tasaday (USA) (Nayef (USA))
1737^{7} 2031^{3} 2777^{5} 4016^{2} 4850^{4} 6443^{2} 7340^{2} 9125a^{2}

Turjomaan (USA) *Roger Varian* a84 112
3 bb c War Front(USA) Almoutezah (USA) (Storm Cat (USA))
(4334)◆ 5609^{2}

Turkistan Express (FR)
Laurent Loisel 69
2 ch c Makfi Orsovia (Shamardal (USA))
8481a^{3}

Turnberry Isle (IRE) *A P O'Brien* 100
3 b c Galileo(IRE) Rosdhu Queen (IRE) (Invincible Spirit (IRE))
5535a^{18} 5711a^{4} 6137a^{4} 6693a^{5} 7220a^{8}

Turnbury *Nikki Evans* a45 44
8 b g Azamour(IRE) Scottish Heights (IRE) (Selkirk (USA))
2234^{5} 3473^{14} 5499^{5}

Turning Gold *Nigel Twiston-Davies* a52 73
5 ch g Pivotal Illusion (Anabaa (USA))
8661^{5}◆

Turn 'n Twirl (USA) *Simon Crisford* a92 60
3 b f Twirling Candy(USA) Kind Turn (USA) (Street Cry (IRE))
48a^{8} 3431^{2} 4639^{6} 5386^{6} (6346) 7188^{9} 8016^{3} 9129^{2}◆

Turn Of Luck (IRE) *I Endaltsev* a75 79
4 b h Pivotal Side Of Paradise (IRE) (Sadler's Wells (USA))
85^{3} 309^{6} 2266a^{8}

Turn On The Charm (FR)
James Fanshawe a75
2 b g Charm Spirit(IRE) Shendaya (FR) (Danehill Dancer (IRE))
6927^{5} 7996^{5}

Turn On The Tears (USA)
John James Feane a58 62
6 ch m Cape Blanco(IRE) Down The Well (IRE) (Mujadil (USA))
348^{12}

Turntable *Simon Crisford* a68 71
3 b g Pivotal Masarah (IRE) (Cape Cross (IRE))
2034^{4} 7272^{2}

Turn To Rock (IRE) *Ed Walker* a77
3 ch g Slade Power(IRE) Pivotal's Princess (IRE) (Pivotal)
367^{6} 752^{7} 943^{2} 7080^{7} 7514^{4} 7812^{2} 8221^{4} (8419)

Turquoise Friendly
Michael Easterby a49 47
3 b g Holy Roman Emperor(IRE) Cry Freedom (IRE) (Acclamation)
520^{2} 2009^{6} 2489^{9} 3650^{11} 3964^{8} 6176^{7} 9395^{4}◆

Tuscan Gaze (IRE) *John Gosden* 80
2 ch c Galileo(IRE) Crystal Gaze (IRE) (Rainbow Quest (USA))
(8722)◆

Tuscan Pearl *William Knight* a1 30
4 b m Medicean Western Pearl (High Chaparral (IRE))
1826^{13} 2626^{12}

Tuscany (IRE) *Grace Harris* a49 44
5 ch g Poet's Voice Avril Rose (IRE) (Xaar)
315^{10} 911^{10} 2145^{15}

Tutti (FR) *D De Waele* a57 54
4 bl m Slickly(FR) Chicaya (FR) (Kaldounevees (FR))
2264a^{9}

Tuvalu *J-M Osorio* 90
7 b g Shirocco(GER) Light Impact (IRE) (Fantastic Light (USA))
4418a^{11} 6145a^{4} 8375a^{7}

Twelve Bros (IRE) *Mme Pia Brandt* a64 68
2 b f Anjaal Hundredsnthousands (IRE) (Thousand Words)
6774a^{9}

Twelve Diamonds (IRE)
Charles Hills a61
2 ch f Raven's Pass(USA) Wardat Dubai (Mawatheeq (USA))
7569^{6} 8218^{6}

Twenty Minutes
Damian Joseph English a73 86
4 b g Rip Van Winkle(IRE) Wink (Salse (USA))
419a^{2} 7090a^{2} 7241a^{9}

Twentyonered *Grace Harris* 28
2 br g Due Diligence(USA) Eve (Rainbow Quest (USA))
2338^{8} 2716^{8} 3943^{13}

Twentysixthstreet (IRE)
Andrew Hughes 79
3 ch c Zoffany(IRE) Enchanted Evening (IRE) (High Chaparral (IRE))
3499^{6} 4277^{4} (4912)◆ 5123^{5} 6610^{9} (7486) 7511^{2} 7764^{7}

Twentysvnthlancers *Paul Midgley* a63 54
6 b g Hellvelyn Subtle Move (USA) (Known Fact (USA))
834^{2}◆ (1162) 1364^{3} 1818^{6} 2324^{12} 3518^{7} 3975^{15} 4586^{6} 5018^{9}

Twenty Years On *Richard Hughes* a69 70
3 b g Rip Van Winkle(IRE) Distinctive (Tobougg (IRE))
2407^{7} (3092) 3809^{7} 4031^{5} 4843^{4} 5798^{4} 6805^{3}

Twice As Likely *Richard Hughes* a64 72
2 b f Tamayuz Xaphania (Sakhee (USA))
1821^{14} 3039^{3}◆ 3573^{4} (4222) 4861^{4} 6637^{5} 7029^{3} 7276^{10} 8650^{4}

Twiggy *Karen McLintock* a50 48
5 b m Sixties Icon Queen's Pudding (IRE) (Royal Applause)
501^{3} 1400^{5} 2241^{5} 2681^{4} 3225^{5} 3720^{F} (Dead)

Twilighting *Henry Candy* a55 47
3 b f Kyllachy Night Affair (Bold Edge)
2623^{9}◆ 3090^{8} 3661^{7} 5890^{4} 6107^{6} 6737^{10} 7784^{2} (8249) 9169^{4}

Twilight Payment (IRE)
Joseph Patrick O'Brien 111
6 b g Teofilo(IRE) Dream On Buddy (IRE) (Oasis Dream)
2158a^{4} (4351a) 7246a^{7} 8844a^{11}

Twin Appeal (IRE) *Karen Tutty* a86 84
8 b g Oratorio(IRE) Velvet Appeal (IRE) (Petorius (IRE))
1925^{4} 2151^{4} 2899^{10} 3567^{4} 4728^{7} (5020) 5770^{3} 6461^{4} 6700^{2} (7289) 7540^{5} 7856^{7} 8101^{15}

Twin Paradox *John Quinn* 58
2 bb g Slade Power(IRE) Malyana (Mtoto)
6654^{7} 7361^{10} 7902^{11}

Twin Star (IRE) *Noel Williams* a96 96
5 ch g Tagula(IRE) Chronicle (Observatory (USA))
2742^{17} 3799^{3} 6171^{4}

Twist (FR) *C Laffon-Parias* 80
2 ch c Pivotal Distortion (Distorted Humor (USA))
6776a^{2}

Twist (IRE) *Nicky Henderson* a77
4 b g Invincible Spirit(IRE) Kahira (IRE) (King's Best (USA))
921^{5} 1269^{4}

Twist 'N' Shake *John Gosden* 109
3 b f Kingman Hippy Hippy Shake (Danehill Dancer (IRE))
1828^{2} (2583) 2806^{2} 4051^{4} (5227a) 6142a^{2}

Twist Of Hay *Michael Dods* 59
2 b f Showcasing Spinatrix (Diktat)
6175^{8} 8395^{3}◆

Twistsandturns (IRE) *Adrian Wintle* a23 12
8 b g Acclamation Shesthebiscuit (Diktat)
263^{12} 531^{8} 1353^{11} 3187^{12}

Twittering (IRE) *Oliver Signy* a56 66
2 b c Kodiac Swallow Falls (IRE) (Lake Coniston (IRE))
4897^{10} 5374^{5} 5635^{6} 6387^{6} (7056) 7767^{7} 8118^{6} 9212^{6} 9438^{10}

Two Bids *William Haggas* a62 84
3 b g Dalakhani(IRE) Echelon (Danehill (USA))
3860^{3}◆ 5254^{2} 5742^{3} 7143^{4} 7867^{3} 8814^{2}

Two Blondes (IRE) *Mick Channon* 86
3 ch g Dragon Pulse(IRE) Itaya (IRE) (Namid)
1897^{4} 2510^{10} 3011^{10}

Two Faced *Lydia Pearce* a40 38
3 b f Coach House(IRE) Blushing (IRE) (Fasliyev (USA))
1380^{6} 2063^{8} 2924^{10} 4472^{9} 5004^{10}

Two For Three (IRE) *Roger Fell* 35
3 ch g Dawn Approach(IRE) Antique (IRE) (Dubai Millennium)
1643^{12} 1898^{7} 2289^{8} 3271^{14}

Two Hearts *P Monfort* a61 63
2 b g Havana Gold(IRE) Miss Mullberry (Kodiac)
2115^{8} 3717^{6} 4778^{3} 5279^{3} 5618^{2} 6539^{2} (6683) 7584^{2} 7833^{2} 9605a^{13}

Two Penny'S (FR) *J-V Toux* a17 18
2 gr c Penny's Picnic(IRE) Kianga (Cadeaux Genereux)
5763a^{7}

Two Sixty (USA) *Mark Casse* a98
2 b f Uncaptured(CAN) Jim's Lonesa (USA) (Put It Back (USA))
8747a^{9}

Two Sox *Tim Easterby* 55
2 b g Nathaniel(IRE) Anna Sophia (USA) (Oasis Dream)
5177^{9} 5655^{7} 6226^{8}

Twpsyn (IRE) *David Evans* a74 65
3 b g Es Que Love(IRE) Gold Blended (IRE) (Goldmark (USA))
90^{9} 229^{5} 431^{3} 841^{3} 1173^{7} 1516^{12} 1957^{8} (2501a) 3594^{4} 5249^{U} 5497^{2} 5601^{6} (8837) 9033^{8}

Tyger Bay *Shaun Keightley* a60
2 b c Cable Bay(IRE) Ribbon Royale (Royal Applause)
8250^{10} 8912^{4} 9085^{5}

Tyler Durden (IRE) *Richard Spencer* 73
2 b g Bungle Inthejungle Starfleet (Inchinor)
5865^{3} 6457^{8} 7247a^{23} 8430^{8}

Tynamite (IRE) *David Marnane* a54 51
5 ch g Elnadim(USA) Madam Macie (IRE) (Bertolini (USA))
5498^{6}

Tynecastle Park *Robert Eddery* a73 69
6 b g Sea The Stars(IRE) So Silk (Rainbow Quest (USA))
40^{2} 369^{7} 589^{2} (1196) (1429) 1815^{2} 9184^{2} (9336)◆

Typhoon Lily (IRE) *Richard Hughes*
2 ch f G Force(IRE) Rise Up Lotus (IRE) (Zebedee)
7104^{P}

Typhoon Ten (IRE) *Richard Hannon* a95 90
3 b g Slade Power(IRE) Cake (IRE) (Acclamation)
1691^{4} 5503^{2} 5983^{2}◆ 6319^{9} 8766^{10} (9308) 9404^{9}

Typsy Toad *Richard Fahey* 52
2 b c Casamento(IRE) Coveted (Sinndar (IRE))
3498^{4} 4623^{3} 5273^{9} 5789^{15}

Tyrconnell (IRE) *Sarah Lynam* a70 63
5 ch g Bated Breath Miss Honorine (IRE) (Highest Honor (FR))
(7086a)

Ty Rock Brandy (IRE)
Miss Natalia Lupini a67 68
4 b m Dandy Man(IRE) Britain's Pride (Royal Applause)
468^{12} (8117)◆

Tyrsal (IRE) *Shaun Keightley* a45 47
8 b g Jeremy(USA) Blanchelande (IRE) (Subotica (FR))
363^{10} 2738^{14} 3740^{10} 5271^{11} 5946^{5} 6550^{4} 7873^{4} 8904^{5} 9310^{8} 9444^{4} 9646^{6}

UAE Jewel *Roger Varian* 112
3 b c Dubawi(IRE) Gemstone (IRE) (Galileo (IRE))
(1852)◆ (2413) 7660^{4}

UAE Prince (IRE) *Roger Varian* 109
6 b g Sea The Stars(IRE) By Request (Giant's Causeway (USA))
(2808)

UAE Soldier (USA) *Paddy Butler* a37 42
4 b g Dansili Time On (Sadler's Wells (USA))
419a^{10} 6903^{6} 7604^{6} 9312^{12}

Ubla (IRE) *Gay Kelleway* a64 44
6 ch g Arcano(IRE) Manuelita Rose (ITY) (Desert Style (IRE))
295^{9} 430^{10} 760^{4} 1060^{5} (1339) 1390^{9} 1769^{5} 2740^{10} 4115^{5} 6897^{9} (7281) 7654^{4} 8199^{5} 9277^{3}◆ 9420^{2}

Ucel (IRE) *F Hassine* a62 56
5 b g Kyllachy Umthoulah (IRE) (Unfuwain (USA))
7223a^{4}

Udontdodou *Richard Guest* a99 97
6 b g Fastnet Rock(AUS) Forever Times (So Factual (USA))
470^{7} 1421^{10} 1938^{6} 2061^{3} 3582^{4} 4995^{8}◆

Ugly Warrior (NZ) *Y S Tsui* a102 96
4 ch g Swiss Ace(AUS) Ugly Betty (AUS) (High Yield (USA))
7010a[13]

Ugo Gregory *Tim Easterby* 73
3 br g Gregorian(IRE) Raajis (IRE) (Dark Angel (IRE))
4080[9] 5176[6] (5786) (6058) 6338[6] 7828[4] 8181[6]

Uh Oh Chongo *Michael Easterby* a63 44
3 ch g Monsieur Bond(IRE) Champagne Katie (Medicean)
228[10] 524[3] 5814[6] 7404[12] 7776[10] 8348[11]

Ulshaw Bridge (IRE) *James Bethell* a90 94
4 b g High Chaparral(IRE) Sharaarah (IRE) (Oasis Dream)
2778[8] 3450[3] 4127[2] 4851[3] 5971[10] 6543[7]

Ulster (IRE) *Archie Watson* a98 97
4 rg g Intello(GER) Ronaldsay (Kirkwall)
(242) (696) 916[2] 1172[2] 1947[2] 3952[P] 4899[7] 5902[6] 7688[2]

Ultimate Avenue (IRE)
David Simcock a96 87
5 b g Excelebration(IRE) Dance Avenue (IRE) (Sadler's Wells (USA))
382[4] 762[7] 1097[8] 1714[3] 3301[2]◆ 4348[5] 5061[2] 9669[3]

Ultimate Fight (FR) *Z Koplik* a71 90
5 ch g Muhaymin(USA) Fantastica (GER) (Big Shuffle (USA))
5715a[12]

Ultimat Power (IRE) *Frank Bishop* a51 14
5 ch g Power Trumbaka (IRE) (In The Wings)
8255[8] 8547[3] 8689[10] 9160[3]

Ultim'Reve (FR) *F Foresi* a70 66
4 b g Evasive Oa Chereve (FR) (Kaldounevees (FR))
2182a[5]

Ultra Petita *K Borgel* a80 81
4 b h Aussie Rules(USA) Shuttle Mission (Sadler's Wells (USA))
3140a[3]

Ultra Violet *Ed Vaughan* 95
2 b f Gleneagles(IRE) Rive Gauche (Fastnet Rock (AUS))
(4337) 5964[8] 6577[3] 7117[13]

Uluru Park (IRE) *Brendan W Duke* 71
4 b m So You Think(NZ) I'm Sheikra (IRE) (Captain Rio)
5599a[17]

Um Aljadeela (IRE) *Kevin Ryan* a60 60
2 b f Iffraaj Ajaadat (Shamardal (USA))
6457[6] 7031[4]

Um Elnadim (FR) *Mark Johnston* a60 59
2 b f Elvstroem(AUS) Three French Hens (IRE) (Elnadim (USA))
5615[5] 6281[4] 6934[4] 7277[11]

Ummalnar *William Haggas* a93 104
4 ch m Shamardal(USA) Royal Secrets (IRE) (Highest Honor (FR))
4035[6] (4898)◆

Um Shama (IRE) *David Loughnane* a64 41
3 ch f Helmet(AUS) Night Club (Mozart (IRE))
174[5] (319) 461[11] 614[3] 4284[11] 4735[5] 5389[10]

Unabated (IRE) *Jane Chapple-Hyam* a92 63
5 b g Bated Breath Elhareer (IRE) (Selkirk (USA))
3993[6] 4805[7] 5266[6] (5942) 6920[10] 7372[4] 8015[6] 8893[4] (Dead)

Unauthorised Act (IRE) *Alan Berry* 9
2 b f Elzaam(AUS) Forest Delight (IRE) (Shinko Forest (IRE))
5418[5] 6713[6] 7211[7] 7734[9]

Unblinking *Nigel Twiston-Davies* a64 60
6 b g Cacique(IRE) Deliberate (King's Best (USA))
947[3]

Unbridled Light (FR)
Anthony Honeyball 21
2 ch f Hunter's Light(IRE) Polysheba (FR) (Poliglote)
6118[11] 6527[5] 7174[5]

Uncertain Smile (IRE) *Clive Cox* a62 65
3 b f Bungle Inthejungle Witnessed (Authorized (IRE))
3013[7] 3546[4] 4423[5] 5287[2] 5784[2] 6202[7] 7344[4] 7817[7] 8870[4] 9040[9]

Uncle Bernie (IRE)
Sarah Hollinshead a59 45
9 gr g Aussie Rules(USA) Alwiyda (USA) (Trempolino (USA))
457[5] 1840[6] 2217[12] 4190[10] 5053[5] 6681[7] 8868[8] (9312)

Uncle Charlie (IRE) *Ann Duffield* a63 67
5 b g Vale Of York(IRE) Velvet Kiss (IRE) (Danehill Dancer (IRE))
2418[6] 2893[4]◆ 3656[7] 4148[4] 4785[7] 7289[12] 7444[3] 8306[2] 8818[13] 9352[10]

Uncle Colum (FR) *Gavin Hernon*
3 b c Dabirsim(FR) Romina (FR) (Slickly (FR))
3675a[P]

Uncle Jerry *Mohamed Moubarak* a86 81
3 b g Kyllachy News Desk (Cape Cross (IRE))
83[2] 142[3] 342[3] 588[5] 838[2] 1424[3] 1729[8] 2525[11] 3422[4] 3659[3] 4103[9] 6440[3] 6913[5] 7519[3]◆ 8550[3]

Uncle Norman (FR) *Tim Easterby* a40 57
3 ch g Havana Gold(IRE) Holy Moly (USA) (Rock Of Gibraltar (IRE))
1504[8] 2152[10] 3650[5] 4149[9] 4731[9] 5771[4] 6176[4] 6679[5] 7581[8]

Uncle Sid *William Jarvis* 56
2 b g Free Eagle(IRE) Paisley (Pivotal)
7316[7] 7896[3] 8722[9]

Uncle Swayze *Ralph Beckett* a64
2 b g Dandy Man(IRE) Hold On Tight (IRE) (Hernando (FR))
8700[5]◆ 9500[5]

Undercolours (IRE) *Marco Botti* a70
3 b g Excelebration(IRE) Puddles (FR) (Holy Roman Emperor (IRE))
2967[4] 3324[8] 4590[4] 5730[6] 6733[2] 9047[7] 9349[8] 9573[3]

Undercover Brother *John Balding* a61 66
4 ch g Captain Gerrard(IRE) Socceroo (Choisir (AUS))
4307[10]

Under Curfew *Tony Carroll* a64 64
3 ch g Stimulation(IRE) Thicket (Wolfhound (USA))
555[5] 1729[7] 2114[5] 2772[3] 3406[3] 4457[6] 6018[2] 6286[6]

Understory (USA) *Tim McCarthy* a33 33
12 b g Forestry(USA) Sha Tha (USA) (Mr Prospector (USA))
436[16]

Under The Stars (IRE) *James Tate* 108
2 b f Night Of Thunder(IRE) Jumeirah Palm Star (Invincible Spirit (IRE))
(4727)◆ (5411)◆ 6374[4] 7244a[5] 7659[4] (7896)

Under The Storm *James Tate* a68
3 ch f Toronado(IRE) Under The Rainbow (Fantastic Light (USA))
1400[6] 2018[4]

Under Your Spell (IRE)
Jamie Osborne a60 36
2 gr c Dark Angel(IRE) Masaya (Dansili)
3767[6] 4018[6]

Undiscovered Angel (FR)
Mlle K Hoste a51 55
5 b m Wootton Bassett Angel Voices (IRE) (Tagula (IRE))
7861a[11]

Unforgetable (IRE)
Joseph Patrick O'Brien a96 97
2 b f Muhaarar Annabelle Ja (FR) (Singspiel (IRE))
5361a[2] 7119[10] 7879a[4] 8748a[13]

Unforgiving Minute *Sean Curran* a81 55
8 b g Cape Cross(IRE) Ada River (Dansili)
56[4] (1218) 1356[2] 1714[5] 2514[6] (9086) (9283)

Unguja (FR) *E Lyon* a80 66
4 b m Zanzibari(USA) That's The Spirit (FR) (Country Reel (USA))
1449a[18] 4860a[6]

Uni *Chad C Brown* a93 119
5 ch m More Than Ready(USA) Unaided (Dansili)
5977a[3] (7920a) (8774a)

Unifier *Michael Dods* 81
2 b g Showcasing Miss Chicane (Refuse To Bend (IRE))
3290[6] 6997[2]◆

Union (IRE) *Roger Varian* a67
2 b c New Approach(IRE) Shahnila (FR) (Elusive City (USA))
9174[5]

Union Rose *Ronald Harris* a79 85
7 b g Stimulation(IRE) Dot Hill (Refuse To Bend (IRE))
(317) 471[7] 1342[3] 1915[7] 2358[2] 3032[3] 3576[4] 5375[4] 5607[3] 5799[2] 6110[4] (6335) (7161) 7337[6] 9286[10] 9550[5]

Union Spirit *Peter Chapple-Hyam* a63 50
2 bb g Outstrip Nouvelle Lune (Fantastic Light (USA))
4886[13] 5774[10] 9451[3]

Unique Company (IRE)
David Thompson a36 31
4 ch g Fast Company(IRE) Unique Blanche (Mirio (FR))
1068[3] 1981[9] 2335[8]

United (USA) *Richard E Mandella* 114
4 ch g Giant's Causeway(USA) Indy Punch (USA) (Pulling Punches (USA))
8776a[2]

United Front (USA) *A P O'Brien* 88
2 b c War Front(USA) Shell House (IRE) (Galileo (IRE))
2830[4] 4091[9]

Unite The Clans (IRE)
Sandy Thomson
5 b g Danehill Dancer(IRE) Janna's Jewel (IRE) (Traditionally (USA))
5905[7]

Unit Of Assessment (IRE)
William Knight a82 85
5 b g Dragon Pulse(IRE) Before The Storm (Sadler's Wells (USA))
135[2]◆ (246) 362[7] (754) 1291[9] 1518[10] 2092[4] 2691[4] (3545) 4614[7] 5625[5] 7575[5] 8341[3]

Universal Command *Jack R Barber* a87 72
4 b g Delegator Telescopic (Galileo (IRE))
1757[15] 4257[6] 5452[9]

Universal Effect *Mark Loughnane* a79 70
3 b f Universal(IRE) Saaboog (Teofilo (IRE))
2103[7] 2912[2] 3324[2] 4109[4] 5380[6] (5941)◆ 6075[3] 8122[6] 8549[5] 9173[11] 9625[4]

Universal Gleam *Keith Dalgleish* a97 95
4 b g Sir Percy Mookhlesa (Marju (IRE))
(2784)◆ (2959) 3515[9] 4097[4] 5398[4] 5693[10] (6460) 7106[5] 7434[6] 7906[9] 9000[7] (9206)◆

Universal Order *David Simcock* a85 103
3 ch g Universal(IRE) My Order (Raven's Pass (USA))
(3035)◆ 4068[3] (5605)◆ 6471[10] (7317)

Universal Song *Seamus Mullins* a21 44
3 ch f Universal(IRE) Song Of The Desert (Desert Sun)
1738[9] 2142[9] 3092[8] 3888[10]

Unknown Pleasures (IRE)
Mrs John Harrington 86
2 b f Zoffany(IRE) Three Mysteries (IRE) (Linamix (FR))
7742a[6]

Unonothinjonsnow *Frank Bishop* a36 51
5 b g Arakan(USA) Kleio (Sadler's Wells (USA))
589[6] 1861[14]

Unplugged (IRE) *Andrew Balding* a66 72
3 b g Alhebayeb(IRE) Crown Light (Zamindar (USA))
2192[8] 3003[8] 3664[5] 4176[3]

Unresolved *Mark Johnston* 49
2 b c Frankel Lamar (IRE) (Cape Cross (IRE))
5345[8] 5894[5]

Unsuspected Girl (IRE)
Milton Bradley a25 8
6 b m Rip Van Winkle(IRE) Sweet Sioux (Halling (USA))
462[10] 549[7] 1519[13] 9553[11]

Until Midnight (IRE)
Eugene Stanford a60 52
9 b g Moss Vale(IRE) Emma's Star (ITY) (Darshaan)
734[6] 1036[11] 5526[P]

Untold Secret *S bin Ghadayer* a69 83
7 b g Shamardal(USA) Confidential Lady (Singspiel (IRE))
197a[2] 1322a[11]

Untouchable Beauty *Hugo Palmer* a60
2 ch f Raven's Pass(USA) Extreme Beauty (USA) (Rahy (USA))
7515[5] 8198[3] 8528[6]

Unwanted Beauty (IRE)
Annike Bye Hansen a70 89
3 b f Iffraaj Extreme Beauty (USA) (Rahy (USA))
7496a[8]

Upavon *Tony Carroll* a66 66
9 b g Avonbridge Blaina (Compton Place)
247[2] 1218[2] 1930[8] 3079[6] 3688[2] 4449[2] 5289[8] 5882[9]

Upgraded (IRE) *A J Martin* a69 73
5 b m Acclamation Dream Club (Dansili)
5712a[10]

Up Helly Aa (IRE) *W McCreery* 106
3 b c Galileo(IRE) Fiesolana (IRE) (Aussie Rules (USA))
5112a[2] (7794a)

Uponastar (IRE) *Ben Haslam* a28
3 b f Zebedee Eponastone (IRE) (Footstepsinthesand)
174[8] 614[8] 5430[10] 5890[8] 8086[6] 8924[12]

Upstage (IRE) *David Simcock* a54 61
2 b f Cable Bay(IRE) Spotlight (Dr Fong (USA))
6846[12] 7393[8] 7570[8]

Upstaging *Noel Wilson* a70 82
7 b g Mount Nelson Corndavon (USA) (Sheikh Albadou)
1459[14] 2201[12] 3868[12] 4103[2] 4364[9] 4879[11] 5740[4] 6581[6] 6972[12] 7402[4] 8304[6] 8866[8]

Upstate New York (IRE)
Richard Fahey 78
2 gr c No Nay Never(USA) Mizayin (IRE) (Clodovil (IRE))
3767[4] 4361[3]◆ 4903[5] 6167[2] 7247a[26]

Up Ten Down Two (IRE)
Michael Easterby a69 67
10 b g Hurricane Run(IRE) Darabela (IRE) (Desert King (IRE))
1398[6] 2217[4] 4126[5]◆ 4825[P]

Up To Speed *James Tate* a53 42
2 b f Invincible Spirit(IRE) Fann (USA) (Diesis)
5317[7] 9413[7]

Uptown Funk (IRE) *Keith Dalgleish* a46 47
5 b g Galileo(IRE) All's Forgotten (USA) (Darshaan)
6583[4]

Urban Beat (IRE) *J P Murtagh* a103 102
4 b g Red Jazz(USA) Closetocrazy (IRE) (Blues Traveller (IRE))
1434a[4] (2221a) 3103a[7] 3818a[4] 6648a[3] 8166a[3]

Urban Hero (IRE) *Archie Watson* a75 68
2 b g Elzaam(AUS) Anner Queen (IRE) (Invincible Spirit (IRE))
6673[3]◆ 7416[2] (9243) 9546[5]

Urban Highway (IRE) *Tony Carroll* a64 69
3 ch g Kodiac Viking Fair (Zamindar (USA))
360[3] 555[6] 1650[5] 2204[2] 3764[5] 4755[3] 5678[2] 5878[2] (6754) 8419[4]

Urban Icon *Richard Hannon* 109
3 b c Cityscape Fauran (IRE) (Shamardal (USA))
1752[3] 2411[8] 3317[2] 4092[4] 4850[3]

Urban Scene *Linda Jewell* a46 28
3 b f Cityscape Fashionable Gal (IRE) (Galileo (IRE))
5748[7] 6283[6] 8290[8]

Urban Spirit (IRE) *Karen McLintock* a40 59
5 b g Born To Sea(IRE) Rose Of Mooncoin (IRE) (Brief Truce (USA))
504[10] 1718[2] 2695[6] 4510[2]◆ 8081[7] 8635[9]

Urlucc (IRE) *R Le Gal* a67 69
3 b c Lord Shanakill(USA) Scala Romana (IRE) (Holy Roman Emperor (IRE))
1741a[2]

Ursa Minor (IRE) *John Gosden* 80
2 b c Sea The Stars(IRE) Kincob (USA) (Kingmambo (USA))
4388[2] 5439[3]◆ (7392)◆

Ursulina (IRE) *Tom Dascombe* 93
2 b f Kodiac Esterlina (IRE) (Highest Honor (FR))
(3725) 4387[2] 5346[6] 6918[4]

Ursus Arctos (IRE) *N Clement* a63 70
3 b c Kodiac Bikini Babe (IRE) (Montjeu (IRE))
216a[5]

Ursus Belle (IRE)
John James Feane a27 29
4 b m Kodiac Switcher (IRE) (Whipper (USA))
1506[8]

Urtzi (IRE) *Michael Attwater* a60
2 b f Due Diligence(USA) Yankee Belle (USA) (Yankee Gentleman (USA))
7786[4] 8218[8] 8891[7] 9407[4] 9630[2]

Urus *Grizzetti Galoppo SRL* 78
2 b c Sepoy(AUS) Fersah (USA) (Dynaformer (USA))
8390a[7] 8789a[6]

Urwald *A Fabre* 109
3 ch c Le Havre(IRE) Waldjagd (Observatory (USA))
1625a[7] 3289a[6] 4705a[10] 6249a[7] 7886a[8]

Usain Best (FR) *B Legros* a59 71
7 b g Whipper(USA) Take Grace (FR) (Take Risks (FR))
5761a[4]

Usain Boat (IRE) *Noel C Kelly* a54 60
3 b g Casamento(IRE) Emerald Peace (IRE) (Green Desert (USA))
1360[5] 2529[6] 3420[7] 3645[8] 4693[10]

Usanecolt (IRE) *Jamie Osborne* a56 52
3 b g Olympic Glory(IRE) Never Busy (USA) (Gone West (USA))
183[9] 9279[3]◆ 9552[4]

U S S Michigan (USA) *A P O'Brien* a103 98
3 gr g War Front(USA) Photograph (USA) (Unbridled's Song (USA))
1713[4] 2492a[7] 3063a[3]

Ustath *Owen Burrows* a81 79
3 ch g Exceed And Excel(AUS) Adorn (Kyllachy)
1389[2] (2123) 2810[14]

Utah (IRE) *J J Lambe* 85
5 b g Galileo(IRE) Healing Music (FR) (Bering)
5404a[7]

Uther Pendragon (IRE) *J S Moore* a75 83
4 b g Dragon Pulse(IRE) Unreal (Dansili)
1655[9] 1912[9] 2516[4] (2732) 3022[3] 4450[6] 4704a[11] 5796[6] 6211[5] 6447[6] 7756[8] 9611[3]

Utility (GER) *David Bridgwater* a71
8 b g Yeats(IRE) Ungarin (GER) (Goofalik (USA))
41[5]

Utopian Lad (IRE) *Tom Dascombe* a70 59
2 b g Society Rock(IRE) Perfect Pose (IRE) (Amadeus Wolf)
2561[5] 5501[5] 5980[6] 8061[2]◆ 9060[12]

Uzincso *John Butler* a65 65
3 b g Mayson Capacious (Nayef (USA))
5004[5] 6315[6] 7278[3] 8206[3]

Vadavar (FR) *A De Royer-Dupre* a90 94
4 b h Redoute's Choice(AUS) Vadapolina (FR) (Trempolino (USA))
1708a[7]

Vadivina (IRE) *F Vermeulen* 66
3 ch f New Approach(IRE) Celebre Vadala (FR) (Peintre Celebre (USA))
7499a[12]

Vadlana (FR) *Mlle B Renk* a63 73
4 b m Approve(IRE) Vanozza (FR) (Dylan Thomas (IRE))
2170a[14]

Vadrouilleur (FR) *J Phelippon* a59 50
3 gr g Dream Ahead(USA) Vita (FR) (Elusive City (USA))
6789a[9]

Vaerya *Frau C Barsig* 54
3 b f Poet's Voice Bravia (Shamardal (USA))
(9538a)

Vakilita (IRE) *Andrew Balding* 26
3 ch f Iffraaj Vakiyla (FR) (Galileo (IRE))
2354[15] 2770[13] 8553[15]

Valac (IRE)
David A & B Hayes & Tom Dabern 94
7 gr g Dark Angel(IRE) Polished Gem (IRE) (Danehill (USA))
8767a[9]

Valcartier (IRE) *Fawzi Abdulla Nass* a97 92
5 b g Redoute's Choice(AUS) Vadawina (IRE) (Unfuwain (USA))
1748a[3]

Valdermoro (USA) *Richard Fahey* 108
2 b g Declaration Of War(USA) Snooki (USA) (Empire Maker (USA))
4106[3] (5331) (6352)

Vale Do Sol (IRE)
Hesham Al Haddad a87 94
7 b g Vale Of York(IRE) Condilessa (IRE) (Key Of Luck (USA))
9125a[12]

Valence *Ed Dunlop* a67 75
3 b g Oasis Dream Independence (Selkirk (USA))
1696[4] 2096[10] (2711) 3808[7] 7915[6] 8411[8]

Valentine Mist (IRE)
James Grassick a51 51
7 b m Vale Of York(IRE) Silvertine (IRE) (Alzao (USA))
359[9] 697[8] 942[12] 1218[4] 1731[13] 3843[7] 5680[7] 5795[9] (6560) 6855[10] 7232[11] 9282[12] 9481[3] 9609[3]

Valentino (FR) *Alex Fracas* a59 74
3 b g Rajsaman(FR) Welcome Valentine (Johannesburg (USA))
1741a[3] 7061a[9]

Valentino Dancer *Olly Murphy* a87 81
4 ch g Mastercraftsman(IRE) Bertie's Best (King's Best (USA))
945[2]◆ 1518[4]◆

Valentino Sunrise *Mick Channon* a51 66
3 b g Sixties Icon Leleyf (IRE) (Kheleyf (USA))
1650[3] 2204[6] 2489[3] 3045[6] 3508[4] 4183[6] 5169[2] 6168[2] 6365[5] 7568[4] 7986[4] 8263[9]

Vale Of Kent (IRE) *Mark Johnston* a107 113
4 b g Kodiac Red Vale (IRE) (Halling (USA))
3987[7] 4385[8] (4921) 5413[13] 5610[2] 6376[2] 6706[4]

Valeria Messalina (IRE)
Mrs John Harrington 100
2 b f Holy Roman Emperor(IRE) Arty Crafty (USA) (Arch (USA))
8089[2]

Valid Point (USA) *Chad C Brown* 108
3 b c Scat Daddy(USA) Goldbud (USA) (Buddha (USA))
7922a[10]

Valkenburg *William Bethell* a61 68
4 b g Dutch Art Balamana (FR) (Sinndar (IRE))
(1663) 2254[4] 3653[8] 4661[6] 5391[6] 6256[5] 6824[2]

Vallachy *William Muir* a48 17
4 b g Kyllachy Valentina Guest (IRE) (Be My Guest (USA))
1286[7] 3661[11] 4116[13] 4589[13]

Vallarta (IRE) *Ruth Carr* a63 55
9 b g Footstepsinthesand Mexican Miss (IRE) (Tagula (IRE))
928[4] 1208[5]◆ 1505[6] 2328[8] 2788[8] 3413[4] 4149[5] 4720[12] 5300[4] 5559[12] 6590[3] 7443[6] (7761) 8264[2] 8638[5] 8925[11] 9185[2]

Vallee Des Fleurs (GER)
J Hirschberger 59
2 b f Soldier Hollow Vallanda (GER) (Lomitas)
6746a[10]

Valletta Sunset *Julia Feilden*
2 b g Casamento(IRE) Sunset Kitty (USA) (Gone West (USA))
7392[7]

Valley Belle (IRE) *Phil McEntee* a54 58
3 b f Slade Power(IRE) Al Sharood (Shamardal (USA))
235[5] 505[5] 550[3] 798[3] 918[3] 1170[8] 1476[4] 1650[12] 2238[2] 2735[2] 3148[5] 3442[2] 4244[4] 4457[8] 7447[10] 9161[6] 9398[11] 9445[6]

Valley Of Fire *Les Eyre* a85 72
7 b g Firebreak Charlie Girl (Puissance)
24[8] 1457[7] 2076[14] 2804[4]◆ 4149[6] 4552[6]◆ 5238[6] 6204[2] (6461) 7074[10] 7540[3] 8305[4] (8719)◆ (9351)◆

Valrose (FR) *Claudia Erni* 66
3 b f Kodiac Vadirima (FR) (Selkirk (USA))
6769a[12] 8377a[9]

Valse Au Taillons (FR)
Johnny Farrelly a69
6 b m Montmartre(FR) Eyaelle (FR) (Green Tune (USA))
2059[7]

Valtice Du Berlais (FR)
Robert Collet 34
2 b f Balko(FR) Crystal Du Berlais (FR) (Great Pretender (IRE))
9123a[9]

Vampish *Philip McBride* a78 79
4 b m Sir Percy Falling Angel (Kylian (USA))
292[12] 814[5] 1351[2] (1569) 2214[4] 3145[2] 4118[3] 5682[6] 6223[5] 7034[2] 8321[6]

Van Beethoven (CAN) *A P O'Brien* a104 105
3 bb c Scat Daddy(USA) My Sister Sandy (USA) (Montbrook (USA))
1049a[4] 1443a[9] 2668a[6] 3104a[7] 3951[8] 7922a[8]

Vanbrugh (USA) *Charles Hills* a91 105
4 b h First Defence(USA) Hachita (USA) (Gone West (USA))
(1763) 2615[5] 4095[10] 4905[7] 5664[23] 6894[3] 7411[6]

Vandad (IRE) *Mohamed Moubarak* a73 63
2 b c Dandy Man(IRE) Ruby Girl (IRE) (Fast Company (IRE))
7406[7] 8288[6] 9195[3]

Vandella (IRE) *David Evans* a45 59
3 b f Invincible Spirit(IRE) Lady Livius (IRE) (Titus Livius (FR))
78[2]◆ 370[2] 4496[2]◆ 8672[5]

Van Dijk *Antony Brittain* 60
2 b g Cable Bay(IRE) Stresa (Pivotal)
2476[6] 3098[6] 4098[8] 4756[10] 6372[13]

Van Gerwen *Paul Midgley* a62 65
6 ch g Bahamian Bounty Disco Ball (Fantastic Light (USA))
468[5] 790[12] 970[4] 1342[11] 2294[6] 2508[4] 3056[3] 3504[7] 6260[6]◆ 6699[10] 7286[8] 8263[2]◆ 8339[9]

Vanilla Gold (IRE) *N Clement* a95 100
3 b f No Nay Never(USA) Miss Childrey (IRE) (Dr Fong (USA))
1199a[3] 1706a[5]

Vanity Vanity (USA) *Denis Coakley* a65 54
4 ch m Kitten's Joy(USA) Blue Grass Music (USA) (Bluegrass Cat (USA))
262[6] 859[3] 1826[7] 4287[11] 4499[7] 8703[11] 9005[7]

Van Mayor (FR) *J Reynier* a75 39
3 b c Rip Van Winkle(IRE) Plaza Mayor (FR) (Kyllachy)
5165a[9]

Vape *Ralph Beckett* a42
2 gr c Dark Angel(IRE) Puff (IRE) (Camacho)
9569[9]

Vardon Flyer *Michael Easterby* 81
2 b g Fountain Of Youth(IRE) Harryana To (Compton Place)
1812[5] 2780[6] 3245[2] 3866[2] 4878[7] 6356[12] 8095[2]◆

Varenka (USA) *H Graham Motion* 100
3 b f Ghostzapper(USA) Dynamic Cat (USA) (Dynaformer (USA))
8139a[5]

Variation (USA) *Stephen Miller* 106
5 b g War Chant(USA) Fleeting Angel (AUS) (Don't Say Halo (USA))
8360a[2]

Various (IRE)
Eve Johnson Houghton a52
2 b g Fulbright Miss Frangipane (IRE) (Acclamation)
8250[7] 8700[12] 9668[10]

Varsha *Ismail Mohammed* 56
2 b f No Nay Never(USA) More Is To Come (USA) (War Front (USA))
6514[4]

Vasari (USA) *Sir Michael Stoute* a73 67
2 b g Muhaarar Honest Quality (USA) (Elusive Quality (USA))
5265[3] 5859[5] 7769[2]

Vasiliev *Clive Cox* a79 88
3 ch g Dutch Art Barynya (Pivotal)
1690[3] 3648[2] (4423)

Vasilika (USA) *Dan Ward* 113
5 ch m Skipshot(USA) La Belle Marquet (USA) (Marquetry (USA))
7920a[3] 8772a[2]

Vasy Sakhee (FR) *Y Barberot* a56 82
6 b m Sakhee(USA) Vasy Fleur De Roy (FR) (Balleroy (USA))
6521a[5]

Vatican City (IRE) *A P O'Brien* a87 72
2 ch c Galileo(IRE) You'resothrilling (USA) (Storm Cat (USA))
7899[5]

Vaudou Des Ongrais (FR)
P Chemin & C Herpin a64 71
10 gr g Della Francesca(USA) Kitzmaid (GER) (Midyan (USA))
4748a[3] 5410a[4]

Vedeux (IRE) *C Lerner* a87 90
8 b h Elusive City(USA) Qahatika (FR) (Polish Precedent (USA))
5715a[8]

Vee Man Ten *Ivan Furtado* a62 77
3 b g Mayson Sadiigah (Medicean)
2810[7] 3590[4] 4059[2] 4604[6] 5660[2] 5952[4] 6715[3] 8550[8]

Vega Magic (IRE) *Kevin Ryan* 83
2 b c Lope De Vega(IRE) Oriental Magic (GER) (Doyen (IRE))
7000[2]◆ 7902[8]

Vegas Boy (IRE) *Jamie Osborne* a86 91
4 ch g Society Rock(IRE) Consensus (IRE) (Common Grounds)
2061[5] 2568[2] 2917[9] 3597[4] 4123[6] 4866[7] 5503[6]

Vegas Knight (AUS) *Colin Little* 101
2 bb g Declaration Of War(USA) Lycra Lass (AUS) (Shamardal (USA))
8137a[7]

Vegatina *John Gosden* a71
3 b f Lope De Vega(IRE) Valtina (IRE) (Teofilo (IRE))
556[2] 1142[7]

Vekoma (USA) *George Weaver* a113
3 ch c Candy Ride(ARG) Mona De Momma (USA) (Speightstown (USA))
2425a[12]

Veleta *Clive Cox* a69 60
2 ch f Dutch Art Barynya (Pivotal)
5366[9] 6831[6] 7786[3] (8750)

Velma *Chris Fairhurst* a69
2 b f Fast Company(IRE) Valoria (Hernando (FR))
8714[4] 9097[3]

Velma Valento (FR) *C Ferland* a99 80
4 b m Dabirsim(FR) Bunny Lebowski (FR) (Echo Of Light)
9002[2]

Velorum (IRE) *Charlie Appleby* 98
3 b g Sea The Stars(IRE) Lily's Angel (IRE) (Dark Angel (IRE))
(2802)◆ (3277) 4016[26]

Velvet Morn (IRE) *William Knight* a69
4 b m Epaulette(AUS) El Soprano (IRE) (Noverre (USA))
732[5] 1094[4] (1286) 1687[10]◆ 8826[6] 9176[7] 9386[7]◆

Velvet Vision
Mrs Ilka Gansera-Leveque a65 74
4 b m Nathaniel(IRE) Battery Power (Royal Applause)
1482[3] 2056[3]◆ 2737[3] 3010[6] 3778[6] 4371[10] 5271[10] 8669[4] 9093[10]

Velvet Vista *Mark H Tompkins* a53 57
3 b f Sea The Moon(GER) Battery Power (Royal Applause)
598[4] 2150[10] 3777[10]

Velvet Vixen (IRE) *Jo Hughes* a45 59
3 b f Requinto(IRE) Theebah (Bahamian Bounty)
26[8] 287[4] 597[3] 1842a[10] 2090a[5] 2392a[4] 3066a[4] 3713a[7] 4229a[2] 5165a[3] 6061a[6]

Velvet Voice *Mark H Tompkins* a52 45
5 b m Azamour(IRE) Battery Power (Royal Applause)
436[14]

Vena D'Amore (IRE) *Dean Ivory* a46 71
3 b f Exceed And Excel(AUS) Sues Surprise (IRE) (Montjeu (IRE))
1650[11] 2063[10] 2943[13]

Venantimi (FR) *B De Montzey* a62 88
2 ch g Milanais(FR) Medievale (FR) (Lost World (IRE))
6777a[6]

Venedegar (IRE) *H Al Ramzani* 99
3 b g Dubawi(IRE) Cara Fantasy (IRE) (Sadler's Wells (USA))
1462[6] 2075[9] 2766[9] 9590a[4]

Vengeur Masque (IRE)
Michael Moroney 108
7 b g Monsun(GER) Venetian Beauty (USA) (Lear Fan (USA))
1784a[2]

Ventaron (FR) *C Boutin* a85 64
8 ch g Le Havre(IRE) Piemontaise (FR) (Ultimately Lucky (IRE))
7676a[8]

Vent Charlie (FR) *P Fleurie* a66 73
4 b g Myboycharlie(IRE) Vent Celeste (Peintre Celebre (USA))
1391a[4]

Vento Di Fronda (IRE) *G Botti* a48
3 b f Holy Roman Emperor(IRE) Catch Wind (USA) (Mr Greeley (USA))
509a[9]

Ventriloquist *Simon Dow* a68 58
7 ch g New Approach(IRE) Illusion (Anabaa (USA))
138[6] 295[10] 517[4] 3430[6] 3996[4] 4589[6]

Ventura Bay (IRE) *Richard Fahey* 68
3 b g Dragon Pulse(IRE) Meduse Bleu (Medicean)
1656[4] 2101[4] 3478[4] 4005[2] 5102[5] 6341[11]

Ventura Blues (IRE)
Alexandra Dunn a78 69
5 bb m Bated Breath Salmon Rose (IRE) (Iffraaj)
81[9] 177[4] 460[4]◆ 699[4] 951[2] 1234[8] 4248[9]

Ventura Bounty (FR)
Richard Hannon 74
2 b c Dabirsim(FR) Amazing Bounty (FR) (Tertullian (USA))
5145[2]◆ 6040[3]

Ventura Destiny (FR)
Keith Dalgleish a64 38
2 gr f Outstrip Medalha Milagrosa (USA) (Miner's Mark (USA))
6226[7] 7733[6] 8021[8] (8526) (8897) 9009[10]

Ventura Express *Richard Fahey* 51
2 ch c Mayson Mail Express (IRE) (Cape Cross (IRE))
6457[10]

Ventura Flame (IRE) *Keith Dalgleish* 83
2 b f Dandy Man(IRE) Kramer Drive (IRE) (Medicean)
3679[2]◆ 3983[17] 4509[2] 5418[3] 5737[4] (6032)◆ 6356[16] 7211[4] 7400[7] (7765) 8261[3]

Ventura Glory *Richard Hannon* a70 70
3 b f Olympic Glory(IRE) Fringe Success (IRE) (Selkirk (USA))
1285[5] 2101[13] 2760[4] 2933[7] 3570[7] 8407[7]

Ventura Gold (IRE) *Steve Gollings* a71 79
4 b g Red Jazz(USA) Desert Shine (IRE) (Green Desert (USA))
(1563) (1948) 2479[3] 3568[3] 4239[6] 6456[8] 7540[11]

Ventura Island (FR)
Richard Hannon a50 50
3 b f Le Havre(IRE) Sun Seeker (IRE) (Galileo (IRE))
1332[9] 2213[8] 3198[8]

Ventura Knight (IRE)
Mark Johnston a102 101
4 b g Casamento(IRE) Alltherightmoves (IRE) (Namid)
514a[9] 637a[12] 1101[7] 1415[14] 3160[3] 3605[2] 3992[5] 4292[3] 4981[4] 5519[4] 5667[11] 5966[5] 6475[3] 6725[8]

Ventura Lightning (FR)
Richard Fahey 101
2 gr c No Nay Never(USA) From This Day On (USA) (El Prado (IRE))
(5388)◆ (6228) 6690a[5] 7602a[8] 8125[2]

Ventura Ocean (IRE) *Richard Fahey* a75 99
3 b g Raven's Pass(USA) Tranquil Spirit (IRE) (Invincible Spirit (IRE))
(1662) 3865[16] 4402[13] 4759[2] 5173[2] (5685) 6950[14] 7435[6]

Ventura Rascal *Kevin Ryan* a61
2 b g Fountain Of Youth(IRE) Choisette (Choisir (AUS))
9514[6]

Ventura Rebel *Richard Fahey* 106
2 b c Pastoral Pursuits Finalize (Firebreak)
(1759) (2267) 4012[2] 5185[4]

Ventura Royal (IRE) *David O'Meara* a39 81
4 ch m Teofilo(IRE) Ermine And Velvet (Nayef (USA))
3960[2] 4728[9] 4917[4] (6573) 7364[8] (7542) 7835[11]

Ventura Secret (IRE) *Michael Dods* a52 61
5 ch g Roderic O'Connor(IRE) Bajan Belle (IRE) (Efisio)
1976[6] 2418[10] 3177[10] 3716[2] 3921[2] 4630[2] 5235[14] 5723[7] 6680[13]

Ventura Star (IRE) *David Lanigan* a60 44
2 b c Gutaifan(IRE) Galileo's Star (IRE) (Galileo (IRE))
6161[12] 7104[4] 7555[10]

Ventura Storm (IRE)
David A & B Hayes & Tom Dabern 105
6 b g Zoffany(IRE) Sarawati (IRE) (Haafhd)
8134a[7] 8577a[5]

Venture (IRE) *Tom Ward* a78 60
3 b g Showcasing Starfly (IRE) (Invincible Spirit (IRE))
(9171)◆

Venturous (IRE) *David Barron* a85 96
6 ch g Raven's Pass(USA) Bold Desire (Cadeaux Genereux)
1342[2] (1597) (2910) 3582[8] 4313a[8] 4722[3] 5420[9] 5661[2] 7241a[7] 7431[10]

Venusta (IRE) *Mick Channon* a64 74
3 b f Medicean Grevillea (IRE) (Admiralofthefleet (USA))
1828[4] 2583[6] 2967[3] (3665) 4147[3] 6370[7] 6902[4] 7344[3] 7643[4]

Veracious *Sir Michael Stoute* 116
4 b m Frankel Infallible (Pivotal)
2441[4] 3342[3] 3986[4] (4885) 7898[2] 8334[4]

Veranda (FR) *S Ibido* 93
5 bb h Canford Cliffs(IRE) Visinada (IRE) (Sinndar (IRE))
894a[12]

Verbal Dexterity (IRE) *J S Bolger* 111
4 b h Vocalised(USA) Lonrach (IRE) (Holy Roman Emperor (IRE))
1531a[5] 2660a[2] 3114[5]

Verboten (IRE) *John Gosden* a92 88
2 b c No Nay Never(USA) Far Away Eyes (IRE) (High Chaparral (IRE))
(5059)◆ 8716[7]

Verdana Blue (IRE)
Nicky Henderson a93 103
7 b m Getaway(GER) Blue Gallery (IRE) (Bluebird (USA))
921[2] 2269[4]

Verde E Rosa (IRE) *Nicolo Simondi* 98
3 b f Zoffany(IRE) Giant Dream (Giant's Causeway (USA))
2161a[10] 7503a[10]

Verdigris (IRE) *Ruth Carr* a62 71
4 b m Intense Focus(USA) Nimboo (USA) (Lemon Drop Kid (USA))
2290[10] 2911[2] (3199) 3743[6] 4322[7] 5218[3] 6204[9] 6461[10] 7583[5]

Vereny Ka (FR) *C Lerner* 60
2 b f Penny's Picnic(IRE) Dayaniguas (FR) (Commands (AUS))
3714a[4] 4228a[4] 5263a[4] 5713a[5] 6384a[8]

Vereta (IRE) *Emma Owen*
3 b f Dick Turpin(IRE) Vera Lou (IRE) (Manduro (GER))
2623[11]

Verhoyen *M C Grassick* a70 95
4 b g Piccolo Memory Lane (With Approval (CAN))
748a[10] 3062a[4] (5205a)

Verify *Ed Walker* a77 76
3 b g Dansili Victoire Finale (Peintre Celebre (USA))
1755[12] 2795[8] 3372[7] 5580[2] 6128[2] (6810) 8298[4]

Verimli (FR) *A De Royer-Dupre* 100
3 b g Born To Sea(IRE) Verriya (FR) (Zamindar (USA))
5717a[2]

Veritas (IRE) *A Fabre* 70
2 b c Camelot Dancequest (IRE) (Dansili)
5642a[10]

Verne Castle *Michael Wigham* a95 40
6 ch g Sakhee's Secret Lochangel (Night Shift (USA))
35[5] 987[7] 1211[3]◆ 1295[9] 3021[9] 9088[9] 9458[7]

Veronesi (FR) *J-C Rouget* 113
3 b c Kendargent(FR) Verone (USA) (Dixie Union (USA))
1625a[4] 3789a[4] 7253a[4]

Veronica's Napkin (IRE) *J Moon* 15
7 b m Yeats(IRE) Adjisa (IRE) (Doyoun)
6008a[5]

Verry Elleegant (NZ) *Chris Waller* 109
3 b f Zed(NZ) Opulence (NZ) (Danroad (AUS))
8579a[12]

Vertice (IRE) *Marco Botti* a46
2 ch f Toronado(IRE) Asima (IRE) (Halling (USA))
9063[10] 9500[11]

Verti Chop (FR) *C Boutin* a76 80
6 bb g Namid Very Astair (FR) (Astair (FR))
5715a[5]

Very Honest (IRE) *Brett Johnson* a71 71
6 b m Poet's Voice Cercle D'Amour (USA) (Storm Cat (USA))
144[2] 236[3]

Very Talented (IRE)
Saeed bin Suroor a109 83
6 b g Invincible Spirit(IRE) Crystal House (CHI) (Golden Voyager (USA))
730a[8] 959a[9] (Dead)

Vespera (IRE) *F-H Graffard* a77 100
4 ch m Teofilo(IRE) Plain Vanilla (FR) (Kendor (FR))
6651a[10] 8969a[2]

Vexed *David Simcock* 74
3 b g Charm Spirit(IRE) Kite Mark (Mark Of Esteem (IRE))
2258[4] 2914[4] 4663[5]

Via Con Me (FR) *M Pimbonnet* 41
2 b f Big Bad Bob(IRE) Tantivy (USA) (Giant's Causeway (USA))
5166a[9]

Viadera *G M Lyons* 102
3 b f Bated Breath Sacred Shield (Beat Hollow)
1601a[11] 4242[3] (5075a) 6692a[8] 7222a[9]

Via De Vega (FR) *Andrew Balding* 84
2 ch c Lope De Vega(IRE) Via Milano (FR) (Singspiel (IRE))
(7338) 8582a[6]

Viaduct *Martyn Meade* a72
2 b c Showcasing Folly Bridge (Avonbridge)
9008[P] 9130[3] 9324[3]

Via Pellegrina (FR) *J-P Gauvin* a60 43
3 gr f Palace Episode(USA) Veri Star (FR) (Verglas (IRE))
955a[4]

Via Serendipity *Stuart Williams* a112 101
5 b g Invincible Spirit(IRE) Mambo Light (USA) (Kingmambo (USA))
2609[25] 3094[8] (4020)◆ 4666[6] 5192[6] 5930[6] 6376[16] (8062) 9064[5]

Via Veritas (USA) *Michael Bell* a59
2 bb f Street Sense(USA) Win McCool (USA) (Giant's Causeway (USA))
6928[9]

Vibrance *James Fanshawe* a82 65
3 b f Nathaniel(IRE) Park Crystal (IRE) (Danehill (USA))
4326[5] 5254[6] 5810[4] 6595[2] 7287[4] 8019[2] 8398[6] (8828) (9215)

Vibrance (USA) *Michael McCarthy* a100 95
3 b f Violence(USA) Block (USA) (Dynaformer (USA))
9637a[6]

Vibrant Chords *Henry Candy* a73 84
6 b g Poet's Voice Lovely Thought (Dubai Destination (USA))
1942[2] 2743[20] 3602[10] 5371[12] 5746[7]

Viceregent *Richard Fahey* 73
2 b g Nathaniel(IRE) Simply Shining (IRE) (Rock Of Gibraltar (IRE))
5396[3] 6035[2] 6971[5] 7429[8] 8124[6]

Vicky Cristina (IRE) *John Holt* a32 37
4 b m Arcano(IRE) And Again (USA) (In The Wings)
3721[8] 4657[9] 5147[6] 6275[13] 8009[5] 8404[5] 9157[9]

Vicopisano (FR) *B Legros* a55 85
4 b g Elusive City(USA) Suama (FR) (Monsun (GER))
1449a[17]

Victochop (FR) *George Baker* a36 60
2 b g Captain Chop(FR) Ma Victoryan (FR) (Kheleyf (USA))
1416[12] 1493[8] 3943[9] 5313[2] (5763a)

Victoria Drummond (IRE)
Mark Johnston a96 94
4 b m Sea The Stars(IRE) Rezyana (AUS) (Redoute's Choice (AUS))
(4118)

Victoriano (IRE) *Archie Watson* a50 77
3 b g Teofilo(IRE) Victorian Beauty (USA) (Rahy (USA))
1555[4]◆ 2913[4] (3198) 3528[3]◆ 3931[3] 4345[2] 5012[2] 5596[5] (5798) 6125[3] 6419[4] 6642[2] 7231[4] 7631[8]

Victor Kalejs (USA) *Roy Arne Kvisla* a87 92
5 ch g Spring At Last(USA) Make A Promise (USA) (Mr Greeley (USA))
3902a[7] 6524a[8] 7494a[4]

Victor Ludorum *A Fabre* 113
2 b c Shamardal(USA) Antiquities (Kaldounevees (FR))
(6776a) (7940a)

Victors Lady (IRE) *Robert Cowell* a69 62
4 b m Society Rock(IRE) Novat (IRE) (Tagula (IRE))
1162[8]

Victory Ahead (IRE) *David Simcock* 66
3 b g Dream Ahead(USA) Rush (Compton Place)
3499[4]

Victory Angel (IRE) *Robert Cowell* 90
5 b g Acclamation Golden Shadow (IRE) (Selkirk (USA))
2442[4]◆ 2917[10] 4451[7] 5530[6] 6455[11]

Victory Bond *William Haggas* a108 106
6 b g Medicean Antebellum (FR) (Anabaa (USA))
1101[12] 1420[5]◆ 1921[5] 8892[3] (9309) 9587[4]

Victory Chime (IRE) *Ralph Beckett* a82 95
4 b g Campanologist(USA) Patuca (Teofilo (IRE))
2209[6] (3192) 4144[3] 4792[5] (5348) 5966[3] (6537)

Victory Command (IRE)
Mark Johnston a103 104
3 b c War Command(USA) Aguinaga (IRE) (Machiavellian (USA))
394a[3] 727a[9] 956a[12] 1830[4] 2414[8] 3082[3] 3341[4] 4016[6] (4490) 4919[4] 5192[5] 5583[4] (6151) 6475[5] 6696[4] 7457[9] 8126[6]

Victory Day (IRE) *William Haggas* 106
3 b g Bated Breath Night Sphere (IRE) (Night Shift (USA))
(2590) 3865[2]◆ (5932)

Victory Rose *Michael Squance* a66 70
3 b f Bated Breath Albany Rose (IRE) (Noverre (USA))
1236[6] 2623[6] 2938[3] (4328) 6598[4] 7320[2]

Victory Wave (USA)
Saeed bin Suroor a109 101
5 ch m Distorted Humor(USA) Angel Craft (USA) (A.P. Indy (USA))
52a[6] 283a[4] 640a[6] 729a[9] 960a[13] 1942[5] (2551) (3494)◆ 3994[13]

Vida Pura (FR) *A Fabre* 65
3 bl f Dabirsim(FR) Mi Vida Loca (IRE) (Sakhee (USA))
7561a[2]

Viddora (AUS) *Lloyd Kennewell* 113
6 b m I Am Invincible(AUS) Snow Flight (NZ) (Colombia (NZ))
1442a[4]

Video Diva (IRE) *James Fanshawe* 54
3 b f Camelot Caught On Camera (Red Ransom (USA))
1824[9] 2361[11] 3553[9] 4400[13]

Vienna Woods (FR) *Y Barberot* a73 72
5 bb m Cacique(IRE) Vienna View (Dalakhani (IRE))
1073a[11] 2026a[5] (4748a) 5410a[2]

Vienne (IRE) *J-C Rouget* 79
2 b f Showcasing Wadjet (IRE) (Shamardal (USA))
4533a[2]

Viento De Condor (IRE)
Tom Clover a56 46
4 b g Dragon Pulse(IRE) Polska (USA) (Danzig (USA))
309[8] 2975[8] 3774[10] 4349[11]

View The Bay (IRE) *Andrew Slattery* a84 72
4 b m Casamento(IRE) Princess Kyka (IRE) (Namid)
307a[2] 748a[2]

Vigo (FR) *L Gadbin* 65
2 b g Diamond Green(FR) Vivement Dimanche (Royal Applause)
8481a[5]

Vigorito *David Barron* a45 63
3 b f Arcano(IRE) Lucy Parsons (IRE) (Thousand Words)
2624[10] 3292[3]

Viking Honour (IRE) *Joseph Tuite* 6
2 b g Rock Of Gibraltar(IRE) Little Miss Gracie (Efisio)
7113[9] 7407[13] 7981[15]

Viking Prince (IRE) *Patrick Morris* a25 54
3 gr g Morpheus Sharp And Smart (IRE) (Dark Angel (IRE))
5783[4] 6290[13] 6732[9] 7141[7] 9168[12]

Viking Way (IRE) *Olly Williams* a54 55
4 ch g Society Rock(IRE) Patrimony (Cadeaux Genereux)
1335[4] 2295[3] (3476) 3738[2] 4212[6] 4519[14] 5767[11] 7420[13]

Vikivaki (USA) *David Loughnane* a51 63
3 ch f Congrats(USA) Smart Dancer (USA) (Smart Strike (CAN))
1427[3] 2332[11] 3535[5] 7472[9] 8071[12] 8417[7]

Vilaro (FR) *D Smaga* a83 91
6 b g Whipper(USA) Envoutement (FR) (Vettori (IRE))
1827a[6] 9014a[4]

Villa Anabaa (FR) *Charley Rossi* 56
2 b f Anabaa Blue Villa Tamaris (FR) (Gold Away (IRE))
5166a[6]

Villabate (IRE) *Nicolo Simondi* 101
4 b g Holy Roman Emperor(IRE) Alta Fedelta (Oasis Dream)
8786a[2]

Villa D'Amore (IRE) *A Fabre* a69 99
3 b f Mastercraftsman(IRE) Highest Ever (IRE) (Galileo (IRE))
3137a[2] 4429a[4] 6003a[5] 8581a[4]

Village King (ARG) *Todd Pletcher* a115 106
4 b h Campanologist(USA) Villard (USA) (Pleasant Tap (USA))
2646a[8]

Village Rock (IRE) *Richard Hughes* a53 50
2 ch c Society Rock(IRE) Village Singer (USA) (Rahy (USA))
2228[8] 3491[13] 6719[8] 7234[4] 7626[5] 7768[3] 8118[3]

Villain's Voice *Roger Varian* 71
2 ch c Poet's Voice Balayage (IRE) (Invincible Spirit (IRE))
4564[3]

Villalar (FR) *C Laffon-Parias* a68 87
3 b f Whipper(USA) Highphar (FR) (Highest Honor (FR))
8983a[8]

Villa Maria *S Donohoe* a51 61
4 b m Makfi An Ghalanta (IRE) (Holy Roman Emperor (IRE))
7207[2]

Villa Marina *C Laffon-Parias* 115
3 b f Le Havre(IRE) Briviesca (Peintre Celebre (USA))
2759a[3] (5470a) 7252a[4] (7942a) 8772a[7]

Villanelle *Jonathan Portman* a42
2 b f Muhaarar Station House (IRE) (Galileo (IRE))
8848[11] 9327[12]

Villa Paloma (IRE) *Mark Johnston* a50
2 ch f Rock Of Gibraltar(IRE) Ma Paloma (FR) (Highest Honor (FR))
7958[7] 8302[11] 8706[12] 9449[7]

Villa Rosa (FR) *H-F Devin* 108
4 b m Doctor Dino(FR) Villa Joyeuse (FR) (Kahyasi (IRE))
6522a[4] (7293a) 7923a[5]

Villette (IRE) *Dean Ivory* a91 85
5 b m Sixties Icon Spinning Lucy (IRE) (Spinning World (USA))
617[3] 945[7] 2252[9] 2612[6] 3300[4] 8032[4] 8761[5]

Villiersdorp *John Hodge* 53
4 b m Lucarno(USA) Ballinargh Girl (IRE) (Footstepsinthesand)
3248[7] 3680[5]

Vimy Ridge *Alan Bailey* a57 75
7 ch g American Post Fairy Shoes (Kyllachy)
790[11] 1023[9] 2206[12] 3975[16]

Vinaccia (IRE) *C Lerner* a58 68
4 b m Poet's Voice Chicane (Motivator)
2170a[5]

Vincent's Forever *Sophie Leech* a47 45
6 b g Pour Moi(IRE) Glen Rosie (IRE) (Mujtahid (USA))
835[9]

Vincenzo Coccotti (USA)
Patrick Chamings a62 42
7 rg g Speightstown(USA) Ocean Colors (USA) (Orientate (USA))
1820[12] 2483[8] 3089[8] 4227[10] 4797[2] 5151[5] 6051[2] (6441) 7684[3] 8711[5] 9209[7] 9505[4] 9659[6]

Vin D'Honneur (IRE)
Stuart Williams a62 62
3 ch f Le Havre(IRE) Happy Wedding (IRE) (Green Tune (USA))
122[9] 183[6] 765[2] 917[7] (1332) 3034[2] 3777[11] 4372[5] 5623[7] 6405[5] 8551[7] 8916[10]

Vindicate *Sir Michael Stoute* a78 71
2 ch c Lope De Vega(IRE) Aurore (IRE) (Fasliyev (USA))
5908[6] (6708)◆

Vindolanda *Charles Hills* a72 87
3 ch f Nathaniel(IRE) Cartimandua (Medicean)
1856[6] 2524[3] 3446[3] 3955[5] 5778[4] (6069) (7643) 8245[8]

Vingtcoeurs (FR) *C Plisson* 65
4 b g Air Chief Marshal(IRE) Ana Zghorta (Anabaa (USA))
1245a[15] 2647a[10] 3711a[2]

Vinnie's Wish (IRE)
John C McConnell a18 65
4 b g Most Improved(IRE) Sarella Loren (USA) (Theatrical (IRE))
3207[8]

Vino Rosso (IRE) *Michael Blanshard* a58 48
3 b f Zebedee Fonseca (IRE) (Red Clubs (IRE))
1687[11] 2204[9] 3442[3] 3839[13] 4328[14] 5731[5] 6052[8] 6361[12] 7172[13] 8697[6]

Vino Rosso (USA) *Todd Pletcher* a128
4 ch h Curlin(USA) Mythical Bride (USA) (Street Cry (IRE))
(8777a)

Vintage Brut *Tim Easterby* 109
3 b g Dick Turpin(IRE) Traditionelle (Indesatchel (IRE))
1780a[7] 2614[4] 3317[5] 3621a[11] 5705[5] 6229[17]

Vintage Polly (IRE) *Hugo Palmer* a56 71
2 br f Gutaifan(IRE) Payphone (Anabaa (USA))
6704[5] 7393[4] 7995[4] 8431[2] 9031[13]

Vintage Port (IRE) *Tony Carroll* 38
2 b g Canford Cliffs(IRE) Chittenden (USA) (Raven's Pass (USA))
7406[15] 7981[10]

Vintager *Charlie Appleby* 116
4 ro g Mastercraftsman(IRE) White And Red (IRE) (Orpen (USA))
844a[7]◆ 1890[9] 2408[3] 3074[4] (3906a) (6770a) 7922a[12]

Vintage Rascal (FR) *Tom Ward* 80
2 b c Nathaniel(IRE) Irish Vintage (FR) (Loup Solitaire (USA))
(7972)

Vintage Rose *Mark Walford* 68
3 ch f Cityscape Jozafeen (Zafeen (FR))
3200[5] 3553[8] 3724[5] 5473[2] 5974[3]

Vintage Times *Tim Easterby* 73
2 b f Firebreak Traditionelle (Indesatchel (IRE))
2840[7] 5514[2] (5788)◆ 6822[7] 7182[4] 7904[7] 8095[10]

Vinyl Track (IRE) *G Botti* a55 87
2 ch c Tamayuz Vittoria Vetra (Danehill Dancer (IRE))
5116a[9] 6262a[7]

Viola (IRE) *James Fanshawe* 47
2 ch f Lope De Vega(IRE) Sistine (Dubai Destination (USA))
8510[8]

Viola Park *Ronald Harris* a66 68
5 b g Aqlaam Violette (Observatory (USA))
64[2] 138[4] 243[6] 484[3] (925) 1177[2] 1715[8] 1986[8] 2944[7] 4767[8] 5051[3] 7080[12] (7770) (8123) 8704[2] 9253[9] 9420[5] 9566[2]

Violet's Lads (IRE) *Brett Johnson* a68 64
5 b m Myboycharlie(IRE) Cape Violet (IRE) (Cape Cross (IRE))
256[2] 476[8] 1075[5] (8847) 9217[4]

Violette Szabo (IRE) *Nigel Tinkler* 69
2 b f Excelebration(IRE) Forthefirstime (Dr Fong (USA))
5514[10] 6064[14] 6697[3] 8100[6]

Viomenil (FR) *J-P Gauvin* a70 63
3 ch g Saonois(FR) Villa Joyeuse (FR) (Kahyasi (IRE))
(955a)

Vipin (FR) *William Muir* a57 62
4 b g Approve(IRE) Heaven's Heart (IRE) (Captain Rio)
979[7] 5428[5] 6119[4] 6977[3] 7236[3] 7758[4] 8348[2] 8870[6] 9040[5] 9305[4] 9403[8]

Virginia Joy (GER) *J Hirschberger* 93
2 b f Soldier Hollow Virginia Sun (GER) (Doyen (IRE))
6746a[4]

Virgin Snow *Ed Dunlop* a73 72
2 b f Gleneagles(IRE) Snow Fairy (IRE) (Intikhab (USA))
5170[4] 6592[3]

Viridorix *J-C Rouget* a79 98
4 rg h Dawn Approach(IRE) Chill (FR) (Verglas (IRE))
6820a[7]

Visage (IRE) *J-C Rouget* 94
3 ch f Galileo(IRE) Just Pretending (USA) (Giant's Causeway (USA))
8445a[3]

Vischio (IRE) *Jonathan Portman* a55
2 b f Holy Roman Emperor(IRE) Drifting Mist (Muhtathir)
9363[7]

Viscount Barfield *Mme Pia Brandt* a103 106
6 gr g Raven's Pass(USA) Madonna Dell'Orto (Montjeu (IRE))
6520a[8] 8982a[3]

Viscount Wilson *S M Duffy* a50 55
4 b g Lethal Force(IRE) Highland Starlight (USA) (Dixieland Band (USA))
7492[5] 8843[7]

Visibility (IRE) *Martyn Meade* a64 56
2 b g Raven's Pass(USA) Cry Pearl (USA) (Street Cry (IRE))
5439[5]◆ 6911[14] 8504[5]

Visible Charm (IRE)
Charlie Appleby 87
2 b g Invincible Spirit(IRE) Mare Nostrum (Caerleon (USA))
3047[2] 3804[3] (5145) 5962[2] 6450[2] 8110[3]

Visinari (FR) *Mark Johnston* 106
2 gr c Dark Angel(IRE) Visinada (IRE) (Sinndar (IRE))
(3601)◆ 4846[3] 5520[4] 7150[4]

Visionara *Simon Crisford* a84 65
3 b f Kingman State Treasure (USA) (Mineshaft (USA))
3603[5] 4341[9] 5650[2] (6111)◆ 6721[7] 7471[3] 8456[5] 9054[4] 9424[3] 9586[3]

Visionary (IRE) *Robert Cowell* a102 89
5 b g Dream Ahead(USA) Avodale (IRE) (Lawman (FR))
786[3]

Visionary Dreamer (FR)
Matthieu Palussiere a62 68
3 ch g Anodin(IRE) Galilee (FR) (Mr. Sidney (USA))
4357a[9]

Vision Clear (GER) *Gary Moore* a59 77
4 b g Soldier Hollow Vive Madame (GER) (Big Shuffle (USA))
3349[4]

Vision Rebelle (FR)
Adrien Fouassier a50 62
5 b m Monitor Closely(IRE) Opportunity Girl (FR) (Ballingarry (IRE))
(7009a)

Visions (IRE) *Grizzetti Galoppo SRL* 38
2 b f Worthadd(IRE) Charming Woman (IRE) (Invincible Spirit (IRE))
8393a[10]

Visiteur Royal (FR) *J-P Dubois* 72
3 gr g Zanzibari(USA) Visite Royale (FR) (Muhtathir)
3675a[6]

Visor *James Fanshawe* a66 69
4 b g Helmet(AUS) Entitlement (Authorized (IRE))
4370[4] 5824[7] 7240[2] 8662[4] 9093[3] 9542[10]

Vitally Important (IRE)
H Al Ramzani a69 95
9 ch h Pivotal Kirkinola (Selkirk (USA))
869a[5]

Vitalogy *Joseph Patrick O'Brien* 106
2 b c No Nay Never(USA) Sylvestris (IRE) (Arch (USA))
6352[4]

Vitare (IRE) *Mick Channon* 33
2 b g Sidestep(AUS) Question (USA) (Coronado's Quest (USA))
8409[10]

Vita Vivet *Dianne Sayer* a35 52
3 ch f Bated Breath Cresta Gold (Halling (USA))
785[7] 3510[9] 3920[6]

Vitellius *Stuart Williams* 48
2 b g Lope De Vega(IRE) Lunar Spirit (Invincible Spirit (IRE))
5655[8]

Vitor (FR) *O De Montzey* a49 56
7 ch g Vatori(FR) Red Vixen (IRE) (Agnes World (USA))
115a[10]

Vitralite (IRE) *K R Burke* 103
3 br c Moohaajim(IRE) Nellie Forbush (Phoenix Reach (IRE))
(3510) (4608) 5128[4] 6425[2] 7697[5]

Vivacious Spirit *Phillip Makin* a75 65
3 b g Charm Spirit(IRE) Buredyma (Dutch Art)
4585[6] 5176[7] 7207[5] 7405[8]

Viva Gloria (GER) *J Hirschberger* 94
4 rg m Reliable Man Vive La Reine (GER) (Big Shuffle (USA))
3288a[7] 7499a[6]

Viva Voce (IRE) *David Barron* a56
2 b g Intense Focus(USA) Moonbi Haven (IRE) (Definite Article)
9474[4]◆

Vivax (IRE) *Ruth Carr* a52 52
3 b g Dandy Man(IRE) Princess Mood (GER) (Muhtarram (USA))
8642[9] 9093[14]

Vive En Liberte (GER)
Yasmin Almenrader 94
2 bb f Soldier Hollow Vive Madame (GER) (Big Shuffle (USA))
8371a[11]

Vive La Difference (IRE)
Tim Easterby a79 77
5 b g Holy Roman Emperor(IRE) Galaxie Sud (USA) (El Prado (IRE))
1644[12] 2509[4] 3502[13] 3867[9] 5200[3] 5490[6] 5726[8] 6961[13] 7364[7] 7738[4] 8030[4] 8206[8] 8719[2]◆ (9349)◆ (9512)

Vive L'Ami (GER) *Christina Bucher* a69 71
7 b g Soldier Hollow Vive La Reine (GER) (Big Shuffle (USA))
(2182a)

Vivernus (USA) *Adrian Nicholls* a89 40
6 b h Street Cry(IRE) Lady Pegasus (USA) (Fusaichi Pegasus (USA))
231[2]

Vivianite (IRE) *Archie Watson* a90 99
4 b m Teofilo(IRE) Crystany (IRE) (Green Desert (USA))
1941[10] 2404[3] 2961[6] 3342[5] 3994[9] 4758[11] 6910a[7]

Vivid Diamond (IRE) *Mark Johnston* 106
3 b f Cape Cross(IRE) Pretty Diamond (IRE) (Hurricane Run (IRE))
2521[8] 3099[2] 3877a[5] 4877[2] 5417[2] 5931[7] (6712) 7118[3] 7890[3] 8581a[6]

Vividly *Charles Hills* 81
2 b f Charm Spirit(IRE) Zero Gravity (Dansili)
4557[3]◆ (5588)◆ 8089[9]

Vivionn *Sir Michael Stoute* a96 105
3 ch f Dubawi(IRE) Giants Play (USA) (Giant's Causeway (USA))
1838[3] (2552) (3336) 4640[4] 5545[2] 6378[2]

Vivlos (JPN) *Yasuo Tomomichi* 114
6 bl m Deep Impact(JPN) Halwa Sweet (JPN) (Machiavellian (USA))
1445a[2]

Vixen (IRE) *Emma Lavelle* a61 78
5 b m Kodiac Radio Wave (Dalakhani (IRE))
2585[2] 3763[7] 4226[11] 5593[11] 6317[11] 7084[11] 8247[3]

Vlannon *Michael Madgwick* a46 57
4 b g Captain Gerrard(IRE) Attlongglast (Groom Dancer (USA))
2344[2] 8224[8] 8828[9]

Vocal Heir (IRE) *Olly Murphy* a41 56
7 b m Vocalised(USA) Heir Today (IRE) (Princely Heir (IRE))
602[9] 1333[11]

Vocal Music (IRE) *P Bary* 83
4 b h Vocalised(USA) Christinas Letter (IRE) (Galileo (IRE))
6004a[8]

Vodka Dawn (IRE) *Phillip Makin* 30
2 gr f Gutaifan(IRE) Bella Ophelia (IRE) (Baltic King)
1844[6] 2331[6] 3212[6]

Voi *Conrad Allen* a77 79
5 b m Holy Roman Emperor(IRE) Bride Unbridled (IRE) (Hurricane Run (IRE))
310[5] (616) 945[5] 1518[8] 2399[2] (2737) 3096[7] 3449[4] 5332[4] 5529[5] 8812[5] 9177[6] 9418[6]

Voice Of A Leader (IRE)
Chelsea Banham a50 79
8 b g Danehill Dancer(IRE) Thewaytosanjose (IRE) (Fasliyev (USA))
80[4] 399[10] 465[6] 1078[2] 1431[2] 1841[7] 2240[5] 2972[10] 3592[2] (6049) 6723[3] 7550[7] 8756[5] 9157[7] 9444[8]

Voice Of Calm *Harry Dunlop* a68 68
3 b f Poet's Voice Marliana (IRE) (Mtoto)
4768[4] 5955[3] 6345[3] 7618[3]

Voice Of Dubai *Hugo Palmer* a47
4 b g Poet's Voice Pencarrow (Green Desert (USA))
207[10]

Voice Of Dubawi *Paul Webber* a7 44
2 b f Poet's Voice Fame Game (IRE) (Fasliyev (USA))
7981[6] 9284[11]

Voice Of Salsabil *David Evans* 53
3 ch f Poet's Voice Mokaraba (Unfuwain (USA))
2999[7] 3637[6] 5578[4] 6367[9]

Voiceoftheemirates *Kevin Ryan* 49
3 b g Showcasing Makaaseb (USA) (Pulpit (USA))
1764[8] 2289[7] 3412[5]

Voices From War (IRE) *A Botti* 86
2 ch c Poet's Voice Raaya (USA) (Giant's Causeway (USA))
8789a[7]

Volatile Analyst (USA)
Keith Dalgleish 99
2 b c Distorted Humor(USA) Gentle Caroline (USA) (Street Sense (USA))
(4719)◆ 5584[4]

Volcanic Sky *Saeed bin Suroor* a87 93
4 b g Street Cry(IRE) Short Skirt (Diktat)
3466[4] 4241[3]◆ (5305) 5818[3]

Volcanique (IRE)
Sir Mark Prescott Bt a51 54
3 b f Galileo(IRE) Pink Symphony (Montjeu (IRE))
5242[6] 5601[5] 5975[4] 6366[4] 6864[2] 7390[4] 7998[2] 8828[5]

Volcano Bay *Ismail Mohammed* 32
2 b f Universal(IRE) Ras Shaikh (USA) (Sheikh Albadou)
7826[10] 8510[10] 8855[11]

Volfango (IRE) *F Vermeulen* a103 103
5 b h Dutch Art Celebre Vadala (FR) (Peintre Celebre (USA))
1628a[5] 3287a[4] 4157a[4] 5168a[5]

Volkan Star (IRE) *Charlie Appleby* 88
2 b g Sea The Stars(IRE) Chicago Dancer (IRE) (Azamour (IRE))
5908[2]◆ (6402)◆ 8111[6]

Volkstok'n'barrell (NZ)
Danny O'Brien 95
7 b g Tavistock(NZ) Volkster (NZ) (Volksraad)
8803a[14]

Volksha (FR) *Simone Brogi* 99
3 b f Le Havre(IRE) Balashkova (FR) (Montjeu (IRE))
(2029a) 3137a[3] 4416a[6] 6005a[3]

Voltaic *Paul Cole* a70 76
3 ch g Power Seramindar (Zamindar (USA))
2139[4] 2925[2] 3353[2] 4377[2] 4800[2] 5428[2] 7460[5] (8410)

Voltereta (IRE) *M Delcher Sanchez* a60 44
3 b f Kodiac Violet's Gift (IRE) (Cadeaux Genereux)
5165a[5]

Von Blucher (IRE) *Rebecca Menzies* a81 96
6 ch g Zoffany(IRE) Tropical Lady (IRE) (Sri Pekan (USA))
1459[11] 1829[10] 2396[10] **4127**[11] *4379*[6]◆ 4759[7] 5692[8] 7121[4]◆

Vormir (IRE) *Fergal Birrane* a70 78
2 bb g Elzaam(AUS) Gangster Squad (FR) (Astronomer Royal (USA))
9569[3]

Vow And Declare (AUS) *Danny O'Brien* 112
3 ch g Declaration Of War(USA) Geblitzt (AUS) (Testa Rossa (AUS))
8361a[2] **(8844a)**

Vrai (IRE) *Kevin Ryan* a69 61
3 b f Dark Angel(IRE) Sogno Verde (IRE) (Green Desert (USA))
21[3] *274*[5] *431*[2]

Vulcan (IRE) *Harry Dunlop* a70 75
2 b g Free Eagle(IRE) Quixotic (Pivotal)
3804[5] 4252[4] *6926*[4] **7755**[3]

Vysotsky (FR) *L Gadbin* 76
3 ch c Bated Breath Vologda (IRE) (Red Ransom (USA))
1241a[7]

Wa'ad *H Al Ramzani* a54 57
2 b f Cable Bay(IRE) Tamara Moon (IRE) (Acclamation)
6719[5]◆ 9582a[13]

Waady (IRE) *Doug Watson* a102 91
7 b g Approve(IRE) Anne Bonney (Jade Robbery (USA))
49a[8] 170a[10]

Waarif (IRE) *David O'Meara* a85 103
6 b g Arcano(IRE) Indian Belle (IRE) (Indian Ridge (IRE))
1415[10] 1912[7] 2419[6] 2778[9] (3168) 3515[5] 4097[2] **(4399)** 4935[15] 5155[9] 5930[10] 6376[8] 7122[4] **(7430)** 8096[5] 8336[5] 8728[5]

Wadacre Galoubet *Mark Johnston* a72 35
3 b g Born To Sea(IRE) Glenreef (Three Valleys (USA))
6274[5] *6687*[4] *7035*[2] *7450*[4] *8019*[11] ***(8644)*** *8945*[5]

Wadacre Gigi *Mark Johnston* a50 51
4 gr m Martaline Glenreef (Three Valleys (USA))
1981[7]

Wadah *J R Jenkins* 29
4 ch m Stimulation(IRE) Chase The Fox (Foxhound (USA))
1475[6] **2077**[7] 2624[11]

Waddat (IRE) *Richard Hughes* a79 60
2 b c Kodiac Luminous Gold (Fantastic Light (USA))
3942[4] 8516[8] *(8865)* ***(9300)***◆

Wade's Magic *Tim Easterby* 65
2 bg g Lethal Force(IRE) Miliika (Green Desert (USA))
5514[6]◆ 6064[11] **6457**[4] 7064[12] 7827[7] 8180[3]

Wadi Al Sail (IRE) *Gay Kelleway* 60
2 b c Holy Roman Emperor(IRE) Fruit O'The Forest (IRE) (Shinko Forest (IRE))
5523[7] 8721[9]

Wadi Al Salaam (IRE) *Tim Easterby* a74 59
2 b c Outstrip Candy Banter (USA) (Distorted Humor (USA))
7046[6] 7437[6] ***(8302)*** *8919*[7]

Wadigor *N Bachalard*
6 b g Champs Elysees Haven's Wave (IRE) (Whipper (USA))
398a[10]

Wadilsafa *Owen Burrows* 116
4 b h Frankel Rumoush (USA) (Rahy (USA))
2271[8] **3814**[2] 4900[6] 5950[4] 7455[5]

Waffleton *Derek Shaw*
3 gr f Epaulette(AUS) Ming Meng (IRE) (Intikhab (USA))
6388[5]

Wafrah *David O'Meara* 62
2 b f Dark Angel(IRE) Magic Florence (IRE) (Zebedee)
2565[5] 3679[7] 4583[7]

Wafy (IRE) *Charles Hills* 97
4 br g Dubawi(IRE) Ghanaati (USA) (Giant's Causeway (USA))
1753[25] 4863[2]◆ **5776**[2] 6376[13] 6914[4]

Waging War (AUS) *Leon Macdonald & Andrew Gluyas* 100
5 b g Rebel Raider(AUS) Fartoo Flashy (AUS) (Galileo (IRE))
8138a[5]

Wagnerian (JPN) *Yasuo Tomomichi* 118
4 b h Deep Impact(JPN) Miss Encore (JPN) (King Kamehameha (JPN))
9153a[3]

Wagram (FR) *Z Koplik* a76 100
4 b g Orpen(USA) Hopa Hopa (FR) (Muhtathir)
1349a[3] **5168a**[2]

Wahash (IRE) *Richard Hannon* a92 102
5 gr g Dark Angel(IRE) Delira (IRE) (Namid)
1101[10] 1415[9] **1912**[3] 2100[5] 2832[6] 3313[6] 4255[6] 4654[7]

Waheebah (IRE) *Rod Collet* 99
4 b m Camelot Wanna (IRE) (Danehill Dancer (IRE))
5510a[8]

Wahoo *Michael Dods* a71 95
4 b g Stimulation(IRE) Shohrah (IRE) (Giant's Causeway (USA))
2393[5]◆ 4127[5] **(5971)** 7435[9] 8096[10] *9183*[7]

Wai Key Star (GER) *Frau S Steinberg* 113
6 b h Soldier Hollow Wakytara (GER) (Danehill (USA))
3386a[7] **5483a**[2] 6487a[5] 8792a[7]

Waikuku (IRE) *J Size* 118
4 b g Harbour Watch(IRE) London Plane (IRE) (Danehill Dancer (IRE))
9379a[2]

Wailea Nights (IRE) *Marco Botti* a67 61
2 br f Lawman(FR) Jersey Brown (IRE) (Marju (IRE))
5676[3] *6858*[3] *7569*[5] *9137*[10] ***(9568)***

Waitaki (IRE) *James Given* a61 54
6 b m Invincible Spirit(IRE) Bluebell Park (USA) (Gulch (USA))
9516[2]

Wait Forever (IRE) *Marco Botti* a105 95
4 b h Camelot Mount McLeod (IRE) (Holy Roman Emperor (IRE))
2886a[3] 3643a[6] ***9000***[4]◆ *9440*[7]

Waiting For Richie *Tom Tate* a50 53
6 b g Rail Link Heart Of Hearts (Oasis Dream)
2781[15] 3653[12] **4404**[9]

Waitingfortheday (IRE) *Joseph Patrick O'Brien* a86 104
4 b m Elzaam(AUS) Wiolante (GER) (Lagunas)
(5597a) 6090a[9] **(6646a)** 7242a[4] 8790a[6]

Wakily (FR) *H Fortineau* a52 8
3 b f Literato(FR) Wakiglote (FR) (Sandwaki (USA))
3066a[14]

Waldblumchen (GER) *G Botti* a67 97
3 ch f Sea The Moon(GER) Waldblume (GER) (Halling (USA))
1242a[4] **3677a**[3] 8376a[9] 8983a[11]

Waldgeist *A Fabre* 128
5 ch h Galileo(IRE) Waldlerche (Monsun (GER))
(2168a) 3985[3] 5414[3] (7251a) **(7941a)**

Waldkonig *John Gosden* a94
2 b c Kingman Waldlerche (Monsun (GER))
(9363)

Waldpfad (GER) *D Moser* 116
5 b h Shamardal(USA) Waldbeere (Mark Of Esteem (IRE))
3907a[2] (4534a) **(5184)**◆ 6519a[2] 6959[3] 7944a[12]

Waldstern *John Gosden* 109
3 ch g Sea The Stars(IRE) Waldlerche (Monsun (GER))
3842[5] 4845[6] **(5966)** **7455**[4]

Walec *N Caulley* a85 88
7 b g Shamardal(USA) Sail (IRE) (Sadler's Wells (USA))
1827a[3] 2429a[4] 4704a[7]

Waleed (FR) *M Delcher Sanchez* a93 78
5 ch g Muhtathir Peachmelba (USA) (Theatrical (IRE))
4860a[5]

Waleydd *Roger Varian* a83 81
2 b c Nathaniel(IRE) Ta Ammol (Halling (USA))
8518[2] ***9095***[2]

Walhaan (IRE) *J-C Rouget* a96 83
3 gr g Dark Angel(IRE) Back In The Frame (Dutch Art)
683a[3]

Waliyak (FR) *Roger Varian* a81 81
2 br f Le Havre(IRE) Vadariya (Sea The Stars (IRE))
8093[2] **8759**[2] ***(9163)***

Walking Thunder (USA) *A bin Harmash* a106
3 b c Violence(USA) Street Show (USA) (Street Boss (USA))
(169a)◆ *636a*[2] *1443a*[7]

Walk In Marrakesh (IRE) *Mark Johnston* 101
2 ch f Siyouni(FR) Walk In Beauty (IRE) (Shamardal (USA))
3506[2] (4206) (4976) (5346) **6248a**[3] 7267a[2]

Walkinthesand (IRE) *Richard Hannon* 114
3 b c Footstepsinthesand Masseera (IRE) (Alzao (USA))
1831[2] 2413[2] 3026[5] **(4882)** 5583[7] 6956[4] 7076[3]

Walk In The Sun (USA) *S bin Ghadayer* a92 95
4 b h Street Sense(USA) Mystic Melody (USA) (Seattle Slew (USA))
637a[10] *957a*[8] **1748a**[9]

Walk It Talk It *Chris Wall* a25 64
3 b f Nathaniel(IRE) Windy Britain (Mark Of Esteem (IRE))
2505[4] 4326[7] *5810*[8]

Walkman (IRE) *Tim Pinfield* a70 63
3 b c War Command(USA) Mooching Along (IRE) (Mujahid (USA))
806[7] *1424*[10] 3838[7] 4297[8] *7080*[5] *8652*[7]

Walkonby *Mick Channon* a52 75
2 ch f Sixties Icon Shadows Ofthenight (IRE) (Fastnet Rock (AUS))
5366[6] *5732*[8] (5907) (6416) 6969[3] **(7620)** 8029[6] 8462[4]

Walk On Walter (IRE) *Jonathan Portman* a100 99
4 b g Footstepsinthesand Hajmah (IRE) (Singspiel (IRE))
(981) ***(2061)*** 2791[3] *3991*[9] 4451[5] *5266*[5] 6953[10] (7175) *7913*[4]

Wallaby (IRE) *Jonathan Portman* a54 61
2 ch f Australia Sky Boat (IRE) (Dansili)
4114[5]◆ **5189**[4] 5992[10] *7910*[5] *8286*[9]

Wallflower (IRE) *Rae Guest* a59 47
4 b m Thewayyouare(USA) Gaselee (USA) (Toccet (USA))
76a[11] *321*[10]

Wall Of Fire (IRE) *Ciaron Maher & David Eustace* a75 102
6 b g Canford Cliffs(IRE) Bright Sapphire (IRE) (Galileo (IRE))
8134a[4] 8767a[7]

Wall Of Sapphire (IRE) *Mark Loughnane* a70 68
3 b f Lawman(FR) Bright Sapphire (IRE) (Galileo (IRE))
174[2]◆ *461*[4] *826*[5] *1358*[7] (1825) 2200[8] 3223[4] 3797[9] *5807*[10] 6810[11]

Walls Have Ears (IRE) *Ivan Furtado* a47
2 b f War Command(USA) Shegotloose (USA) (Dynaformer (USA))
7870[7] ***8121***[7] *9623*[12]

Wally (IRE) *J-C Rouget* 99
2 gr c Siyouni(FR) Full Of Beauty (Motivator)
5642a[5] (6433a) **7774a**[5]

Wally's Wisdom *Mark Loughnane* a57 52
7 b g Dutch Art Faldal (Falbrav (IRE))
59[5] ***482***[4] *2695*[10]

Walsingham (GER) *P Schiergen* 108
5 b h Campanologist(USA) Winterkonigin (GER) (Sternkoenig (IRE))
2455a[6] **3386a**[5]

Walter White (FR) *Alan King* a74 71
4 b g Maxios Antique Rose (GER) (Desert King (IRE))
4792[6] 6156[5]

Walton Street *Charlie Appleby* 109
5 b g Cape Cross(IRE) Brom Felinity (AUS) (Encosta De Lago (AUS))
730a[3] 4390[2] 5718a[2]

Walton Thorns (IRE) *Charles Hills* a32 55
2 b g Zebedee Bishop's Lake (Lake Coniston (IRE))
1416[16] **2792**[9] **3371**[5] 5146[9] *6182*[10] 6557[6]

Wanaasah *David Loughnane* a80 61
3 b f Cape Cross(IRE) Eldalil (Singspiel (IRE))
316[3] *1019*[2] *1345*[5] *1730*[3] 2110[4] 2521[9] 4663[7] ***(6030)*** ***6320***[2] *6392*[3] *6888*[3] *8948*[6] *9288*[4]

Wanaway (FR) *P Bary* 90
2 b f Galiway Matwan (FR) (Indian Rocket)
7044a[4] **8647a**[4] 8970a[4]

Wan Chai (USA) *Ralph Beckett* a59 60
3 b f Speightstown(USA) Dansette (Dansili)
2511[10] ***615***[3]

Wand *Lucy Wadham* a62
2 b f Camelot Ape Attack (Nayef (USA))
8848[9] ***9311***[6]

Wanderwell *A Fabre* a69 82
3 b f New Approach(IRE) Ama (USA) (Storm Cat (USA))
7978a[6]

Waneen (IRE) *John Butler* a48 39
6 b g Approve(IRE) Million All Day (IRE) (Daylami (IRE))
298[9] *1266*[7] *1716*[7] **2728**[4] 2924[2] *3425*[6] 6126[9] 6794[6] *7606*[8] *7838*[8] *9664*[8]

Wannabe Betsy (IRE) *William Jarvis* a62
2 b f Siyouni(FR) Wannabe Special (Galileo (IRE))
9046[5]

Wannie Mae (IRE) *William Haggas* 74
3 ch f Australia Wurfklinge (GER) (Acatenango (GER))
2771[12] 3553[4]◆ (4064)◆ **5566**[3]

Wapping (USA) *Barry Brennan* a88 91
6 b g Smart Strike(CAN) Exciting Times (FR) (Jeune Homme (USA))
735[4]

Waqaas *Mark Usher* a44 50
5 b g Showcasing Red Mischief (IRE) (Red Clubs (IRE))
1357[10] ***9606***[9]

Waqt (IRE) *Alexandra Dunn* a65 70
5 b g Acclamation Needles And Pins (IRE) (Fasliyev (USA))
1177[4] *(1328)*◆ *1675*[6] *1986*[4] (2231) 2714[3] 3038[2] (3539) **4207**[2] 4566[5] 5760a[4] 6414[7] 6803[5] 7272[5]

War Advocate (IRE) *Adrian Paul Keatley* a63 57
4 ch g Declaration Of War(USA) Verbose (USA) (Storm Bird (CAN))
2963[5] 4378[10]

War and Glory (IRE) *James Tate* a68
3 b f War Command(USA) Foreplay (IRE) (Lujain (USA))
(65) *228*[4] *461*[5]

War Asset (ITY) *Gianluca Bietolini* a67 78
6 b g Blu Air Force(IRE) Tell Me (ITY) (Machiavellian (USA))
5760a[5]

War Beast (USA) *Doug O'Neill* 99
2 b c Declaration Of War(USA) Special One (USA) (Point Given (USA))
8746a[10]

War Brigade (FR) *Ian Williams* a69 75
5 b g Manduro(GER) Adjudicate (Dansili)
2819[7] **3633**[2]◆ **3940**[3] 5452[5] **5739**[2] 6156[4] 6896[4]

Wardachan (FR) *Laurent Loisel* a63 47
2 b f Milanais(FR) Sonia (GER) (Robellino (USA))
6196a[9]

War Defender *Tim Easterby* 50
2 b g War Command(USA) Never Lose (Diktat)
7285[11] **7623**[6]

War Drums *Alexandra Dunn* a22 56
5 b g Authorized(IRE) Crystal Swan (IRE) (Dalakhani (IRE))
6105[10] **6601**[9] 8246[10] *8670*[8]

War Eagle (IRE) *Ian Williams* a40 72
3 b g Australia Dorothy B (IRE) (Fastnet Rock (AUS))
2075[8] 2796[8] 5594[8] **6104**[4] 6849[3] *8468*[9]

Wareeda (IRE) *Richard Hannon* a44
3 b f War Command(USA) Areeda (IRE) (Refuse To Bend (IRE))
1543[6] 2581[11]

War Empress (IRE) *Julia Feilden* a68 58
3 b f War Command(USA) Alice Rose (IRE) (Manduro (GER))
1417[12] 2148[5] *8013*[9] ***8828***[4]◆ *9467*[9]

War Ensign (IRE) *Tim Easterby* 56
4 b g War Front(USA) Ventura (IRE) (Spectrum (IRE))
3225[8] 4132[5] 5202[3] **5278**[2]◆ 5559[5] 5917[3] 6503[6] 6574[11]

War Glory (IRE) *Richard Hannon* a114 99
6 b g Canford Cliffs(IRE) Attracted To You (IRE) (Hurricane Run (IRE))
1097[11] 1694[4] 1912[6] 2105[6] (2622)◆ 3027[2] 3318[5]◆ *(3581)*◆ 3987[11] 4399[5] 5188[6] 5610[10] 5930[5] *(6706)* *7188*[3] *(7448)*◆ ***(8707)*** *9064*[11]

Wargrave (IRE) *J A Stack* 102
3 b c Galileo(IRE) Scream Blue Murder (IRE) (Oratorio (IRE))
1600a[4] **2889a**[6] 5583[10] 7038a[2] 7794a[7]

War Hero (IRE) *Adrian McGuinness* a84 78
4 b g Declaration Of War(USA) Sugar Mint (IRE) (High Chaparral (IRE))
5537a[4] ***7089a***[2]

Warily *Richard Fahey* 41
2 b c Invincible Spirit(IRE) Slink (Selkirk (USA))
1893[8]

Warnaq (IRE) *Matthew J Smith* 100
5 b m Arcano(IRE) Ihtiraam (IRE) (Teofilo (IRE))
1308a[4] 1620a[3] 2560[6] 7038a[6] 8368a[2] **(8784a)**

Warne's Army *Mark Johnston* a14 75
2 b f Fast Company(IRE) Euro Empire (USA) (Bartok I (IRE))
7870[8] *8232*[3]◆ **8855**[3]

Warning Fire *Mark Johnston* a93 93
3 b f Shamardal(USA) Bright Beacon (Manduro (GER))
(1219) 2149[6] 2772[6] 3967[4] (4606) 4721[2] (4831)◆ (5218) **5525**[2] 5666[3] 5805[2] 6379[19] 6914[5] ***(7471)*** **7735**[3] 7901[11]

Warning Light *Shaun Keightley* a60 60
4 b m Lethal Force(IRE) Cefira (USA) (Distant View (USA))
1550[5] *2215*[9] 2737[7] *5284*[7] *(5652)* *(6635)* 6843[3] *7474*[4] **8466**[2] *9090*[F] (Dead)

Warning Shot (IRE) *Saeed bin Suroor* 58
2 ch c Exceed And Excel(AUS) Margravine (USA) (King's Best (USA))
7055[8]

War No More (USA) *Roger Varian* a64
4 br m War Front(USA) Moth (IRE) (Galileo (IRE))
78[8] *824*[6]

War Of Clans (IRE) *K R Burke* a52 67
2 b g Ivawood(IRE) Precautionary (Green Desert (USA))
1499[3] 1758[7] 2706[6] 4985[4] 5789[2] 6053[5] **(6792)** *8650*[12] *9401*[8]

Warofindependence (USA) *John O'Shea* a63 57
7 bb g War Front(USA) My Dear Annie (USA) (Smart Strike (CAN))
321[9] ***602***[10] *789*[11]

War Of Succession *Tony Newcombe* a43 63
5 b g Casamento(IRE) Rohlindi (Red Ransom (USA))
830[13] *1527*[6] 2233[3] **4771**[2] 5858[7] 6560[6] *8065*[10]

War Of Will (USA) *Mark Casse* a114 106
3 b c War Front(USA) Visions Of Clarity (IRE) (Sadler's Wells (USA))
2425a[7] ***(2856a)*** *3620a*[9] *7480a*[3] *8777a*[9]

War Princess (IRE) *Alan King* a59 61
3 b f War Command(USA) Starlight Princess (IRE) (Mastercraftsman (IRE))
4189[3] *9400*[6] *9635*[6]

Warranty (FR) *Mark Johnston* a67
2 b g Authorized(IRE) Ballymena Lassie (Giant's Causeway (USA))
7957[2] *8752*[4]

Warren (FR) *Y Barberot* 74
4 b g Elusive City(USA) Danlepordamsterdam (IRE) (War Front (USA))
2782a[12]

Warring States (JPN) *Mohammed Jassim Ghazali* 57
5 ch h Victoire Pisa(JPN) Ciliege (JPN) (Sakura Bakushin O (JPN))
869a[11]

Warrior Display (IRE) *Bernard Llewellyn* a59 57
3 b g Dandy Man(IRE) Clare Glen (IRE) (Sakhee (USA))
(183) *567*[4] *765*[5] 2341[5] 5548[8] 6643[14]

Warrior Goddess *John Butler* a60 62
4 b m Henrythenavigator(USA) Azenzar (Danehill Dancer (IRE))
7823[11]

Warrior's Charge (USA) *Brad H Cox* a108
3 bb c Munnings(USA) Battling Brook (USA) (Broken Vow (USA))
2856a[4]

Warrior's Valley *David C Griffiths* a72 51
4 b g Mayson Sand And Deliver (Royal Applause)
43[4] *278*[5] *(503)* *849*[2] *907*[7] *(1076)* *1162*[2] *(1194)* ***1394***[2] *1551*[2] 1860[5] 4593[7] 6099[13] *6549*[4] *7387*[10] *9390*[9] *9584*[4]

Warsaw Road (IRE) *Robert Cowell* a96 90
5 ch g Zebedee Warda (Pivotal)
8425[2]

War Storm *Archie Watson* a77 86
2 b g Due Diligence(USA) Primo Lady (Lucky Story (USA))
2594[3]◆ (3098) (4125) 4878[4] **(6515)** 7119[13]

War Tiger (USA) *Richard Fahey* a88 93
3 b g War Front(USA) Quarter Moon (IRE) (Sadler's Wells (USA))
103[3]◆ *(343)*◆ *(839)* **1835**[2] 2828[12]

War Whisper (IRE) *Paul Midgley* a70 88
6 b g Royal Applause Featherweight (IRE) (Fantastic Light (USA))
1814[6] 2368[6] 4406[6] 4625[2] 5617[2] **6455**[2] 7077[10] 8091[14] 8400[7]

Warzuzu (IRE) *C Ferland* 76
2 b f War Front(USA) Lady Zuzu (USA) (Dynaformer (USA))
7006a[7]

Wasaayef (IRE) *John Gosden* a82 91
2 b f Kingman Seagull (IRE) (Sea The Stars (IRE))
4502[2]◆ (5139) **7461**[2]

Wasachop (FR) *Jane Soubagne* a56 80
2 ch c Kheleyf(USA) Wa Zine (FR) (Iron Mask (USA))
9605a[12]

Waseem Faris (IRE) *Milton Harris* a56 87
10 b g Exceed And Excel(AUS) Kissing Time (Lugana Beach)
1915[8] (3037) **3531**[3] 4253[7] 5318[5] 6080[7] 6809[5] *8601*[9] *9057*[9]

Wasim (IRE) *Ismail Mohammed* a82 102
4 b h Acclamation Quiet Protest (USA) (Kingmambo (USA))
280a[5] **960a**[3]

Wasm *Ruth Carr* a54 67
5 ch g Exceed And Excel(AUS) Finchley (Machiavellian (USA))
1506[11] *2241*[14]

Wasmya (FR) *F-H Graffard* 106
3 ch f Toronado(IRE) Lamorlaye (IRE) (Danehill Dancer (IRE))
(6769a) 7944a[8]
Wasntexpectingthat *Richard Fahey* a84 73
3 b g Foxwedge(AUS) Carsulae (IRE) (Marju (IRE))
1306a[4] 1736[11] 5821[11] 7002[4]◆ 7402[24] 7781[8] 8342[14] (9113) (9519)◆
Watan *Richard Hannon* 106
3 ch c Toronado(IRE) Shotgun Gulch (USA) (Thunder Gulch (USA))
1854[6] 2834[3] 4705a[6]
Wat Arun (FR) *C Lotoux* a33
3 b g Alianthus(GER) Blue Sally (FR) (Della Francesca (USA))
5641a[8]
Watayouna (FR) *F-H Graffard* 99
4 b m Siyouni(FR) Pavie (USA) (Lomitas)
1708a[10] 2167a[5] 5229a[3]
Watchable *David O'Meara* a103 104
9 ch g Pivotal Irresistible (Cadeaux Genereux)
3[2] 127[4] 297[3] (964) 1847[4] (2393) (3347) 4095[12] 4896[8] 5266[3] 5942[3] 6351[5] 7193[16] 7913[6] 8317[5] 8867[2] (9098) (9389)
Watch And Learn *Donald McCain* a55 57
3 b f Havana Gold(IRE) Charlecote (IRE) (Caerleon (USA))
442[9] 761[9] 1288[6] 2941[6] 3528[8] 4400[2] 4834[4] 5766[9] 6505[3]
Watch Me (FR) *F-H Graffard* 117
3 b f Olympic Glory(IRE) Watchful (IRE) (Galileo (IRE))
(1706a) 2669a[6] (4051) 6004a[4] 7942a[3]
Watchmyeverymove (IRE)
Stuart Williams 64
3 b g War Command(USA) Glympse (IRE) (Spectrum (IRE))
2746[18] 3471[11] 3885[6] 4479[10] 4565[6]
Water Diviner (IRE) *Richard Hannon* a79 79
3 b c Bungle Inthejungle Khayrat (IRE) (Polar Falcon (USA))
4065[5] 4643[3] 5804[8] 6469[4] 8221[12]
Waterfall *Lucy Wadham* a45 61
3 b f Mukhadram Jump Ship (Night Shift (USA))
5004[3] 5810[9] 6811[5] 7520[9]
Waterfront (IRE) *Simon Crisford* a79 68
3 b g Cape Cross(IRE) Bright Water (Refuse To Bend (IRE))
4738[4] 6022[3] 6439[3] (7450) (8468)
Waterproof *Shaun Keightley* a54 43
3 b g Pour Moi(IRE) Laughing Water (FR) (Duke Of Marmalade (IRE))
4484[7] 6030[9] 6702[5] 7280[2] 8000[9] 8293[5] 8553[2]
Water's Edge (IRE) *George Baker* a77 79
3 b g Footstepsinthesand Sommer Queen (IRE) (Thousand Words)
258[2]◆ (518) 839[3] 1386[4] 5348[4] 6165[2] 6931[5] 7728[6]
Watersmeet *Mark Johnston* a109 98
8 gr g Dansili Under The Rainbow (Fantastic Light (USA))
238[3] 519[2] (1917) 2575[P] 3081[5]
Watheer *Roger Fell* a57 62
4 ch g Leroidesanimaux(BRZ) Sunset Shore (Oasis Dream)
3161[8] 3880[7] 4728[10] 5770[11] 7875[12] 8070[6] 8270[10] 9133[4]◆ 9516[10]
Wave Walker *Sylvester Kirk* a47 39
3 ch g Footstepsinthesand Winged Diva (IRE) (Hawk Wing (USA))
2942[11] 3947[9]
Way To Paris *Andrea Marcialis* 114
6 gr h Champs Elysees Grey Way (USA) (Cozzene (USA))
1244a[5] 2169a[2] 3123a[2] (4962a) 7251a[2] 7928a[6] 8589a[5]
Wazin *Simon Crisford* a78
4 b m Dutch Art Azameera (IRE) (Azamour (IRE))
196a[14]
Weardiditallgorong *Des Donovan* a23 27
7 b m Fast Company(IRE) Little Oz (IRE) (Red Ransom (USA))
3774[3]
We Are All Dottie *Pat Phelan* a47 27
3 b f Mayson Young Dottie (Desert Sun)
940[9] 1514[9] 2926[10] 4991[10]
Wearraah *Alan Brown* a29 39
3 b g Heeraat(IRE) Hoof's So Lucky (Compton Place)
4129[11] 4488[11] 4978[10] 5554[7] 5914[14]
Webuyanyhorse *Jamie Osborne* a67 75
2 gr g Gutaifan(IRE) Hairicin (IRE) (Hurricane Run (IRE))
5676[5] 6161[5] 6718[4] 7548[6] 8286[7]
Wedding Blue *Andrew Balding* 92
3 b g Kingman Wedding Morn (IRE) (Sadler's Wells (USA))
2354[3] (3011)◆
Wedding Breakfast (IRE)
Stella Barclay a47 28
5 ch m Casamento(IRE) Fair Countenance (IRE) (Almutawakel)
1983[7] 3959[10] 5025[13]
Wedding Date *Richard Hannon* a84 93
3 b f Dandy Man(IRE) Fiancee (IRE) (Pivotal)
83[4] 342[2] 2121[5] (2810) 3068[8] 3865[11] (4122) 4736[3] 5014[3] 5371[3] 6476[6] 6954[10]
Wedding Photo (USA) *Peter Fahey* a41 40
5 b m Lonhro(AUS) Well At The Top (IRE) (Sadler's Wells (USA))
9553[9]
Wedding Proposal (FR)
D & P Prod'Homme 66
2 ch c Casamento(IRE) Artistic Light (Fantastic Light (USA))
1240a[3] 6384a[9]
Wee Jim (IRE) *Luke Comer* a60 85
3 b c Canford Cliffs(IRE) Marydale (Aqlaam)
3063a[5] 5535a[16] 6693a[24]
Weekender *John Gosden* a115 117
5 b g Frankel Very Good News (USA) (Empire Maker (USA))
2269[6] (2554) 4933[4] 6473[20] (7158) 7662[3] 9302[7]
We Go (FR) *H-A Pantall* a98 100
3 b c No Nay Never(USA) Encore Merci (IRE) (Danehill Dancer (IRE))
1200a[10] 2564a[5] 3621a[6] 4703a[3] 5714a[8]
Wejdan (FR) *William Haggas* 103
2 b f Dabirsim(FR) War Bride (GER) (War Blade (GER))
(5772)◆ 6374[5] 8089[8]
Welcome Surprise (IRE)
Saeed bin Suroor a77 46
2 b g Exceed And Excel(AUS) New Style (USA) (Street Cry (IRE))
2767[6] 3426[3] 4290[4] 5896[7]
Welcoming (FR) *Mark Johnston* a44 83
3 b f No Nay Never(USA) Love Over Gold (FR) (Peintre Celebre (USA))
1424[5] 2567[8] 3935[4] 4693[5] 5022[2] 5292[3] 5970[7] 7129[6] (7491)
Weld Al Emarat *Michael Easterby* a95 86
7 b g Dubawi(IRE) Spirit Of Dubai (IRE) (Cape Cross (IRE))
(44)◆ (929)◆ 1428[2]◆ 2095[8] 2710[5] 3502[7] 4079[2]
Welford *S Seemar* a55 87
6 b g Dubawi(IRE) Avongrove (Tiger Hill (IRE))
573a[3]
Well Done Fox *Richard Hannon* 107
3 b c Acclamation Excelette (IRE) (Exceed And Excel (AUS))
2270[7] 3855[5]
Well Fleeced *F Vermeulen* a76 74
7 b g Excellent Art Diksie Dancer (Diktat)
1349a[6]
Well Funded (IRE) *James Bethell* a54 80
3 b f Camelot Malikayah (IRE) (Fasliyev (USA))
1484[5] 2150[3] 2913[3] (3886) 5028[2] 5596[2]◆ 6459[5] (7070)◆ (7683) 8027[5]
Welliesinthewater (IRE)
Derek Shaw a91 84
9 b g Footstepsinthesand Shadow Ash (IRE) (Ashkalani (IRE))
3649[10]
Well Of Wisdom *Charlie Appleby* 102
2 b c Oasis Dream Alessandria (Sunday Silence (USA))
(1887)◆ 2830[3] 3949[9] (4961a) 5481a[2] 6746a[2]
Well Prepared *Richard Hannon* a73 76
2 b c Due Diligence(USA) Amazed (Clantime)
7521[3] 8060[3] 8503[2]
Wells Farhh Go (IRE) *Tim Easterby* 113
4 b h Farhh Mowazana (IRE) (Galileo (IRE))
(4390)◆ 5522[8] 6473[15] 7890[7]
Weloof (FR) *John Butler* a64 48
5 b g Redoute's Choice(AUS) Peinted Song (USA) (Unbridled's Song (USA))
(295) 2005[9] 3002[10] 5282[12] 5632[9] 6317[7] 6839[7] 9006[7] 9361[6] 9657[2]◆
Welsh Back *Michael Bell* a32
2 bb f Harbour Watch(IRE) Clifton Dancer (Fraam)
9097[8] 9211[11] 9408[10]
Welsh Lord *Saeed bin Suroor* a96
4 gr g Dark Angel(IRE) Welsh Angel (Dubai Destination (USA))
172a[5] 396a[7] 573a[14]
Welsh Rarebit *Lucinda Egerton* 50
6 b g Dylan Thomas(IRE) Chelsey Jayne (IRE) (Galileo (IRE))
5783[6]
Welsh Warrior *Nikki Evans* 23
3 b g Harbour Watch(IRE) Crimson Queen (Red Ransom (USA))
6023[8] 6561[5]
Weltstar (GER) *Markus Klug* 100
4 bb h Soldier Hollow Wellenspiel (GER) (Sternkoenig (IRE))
7500a[7]
Wemyss Point *Philip Kirby* a63 69
7 b g Champs Elysees Wemyss Bay (Sadler's Wells (USA))
9405[8]
Wemyss Ware (IRE)
Sir Michael Stoute a78
3 b g Dubawi(IRE) White Moonstone (USA) (Dynaformer (USA))
8294[6] (8552)
Wendreda *Mrs Ilka Gansera-Leveque* 49
2 b f Casamento(IRE) Zagarock (Rock Of Gibraltar (IRE))
7826[8] 8432[8]
Wensley *Rebecca Bastiman* a49 52
4 b g Poet's Voice Keladora (USA) (Crafty Prospector (USA))
1565[7] 2053[7] 3716[14] 4726[13] 4785[6] 5247[5] 5517[9]
Wentwood *D K Weld* 87
4 b g Pour Moi(IRE) Desert Liaison (Dansili)
5597a[13]
Wentworth Amigo (IRE)
Jamie Osborne a45 77
2 gr c Gutaifan(IRE) Burning Dawn (USA) (Bernstein (USA))
3190[5] (3803) 4610[9] 5612[12] 9031[9]
Wentworth Falls *Geoffrey Harker* a99 101
7 gr g Dansili Strawberry Morn (CAN) (Travelling Victor (CAN))
1847[5] 2396[2] 2743[2] 3602[6] 4402[5]◆ 4521[3] 6676[11] 7193[5]◆
We Owen A Dragon
Tom Dascombe a66 66
2 ch g Dragon Pulse(IRE) Raktina (Polish Precedent (USA))
3071[4] 3841[7] 4106[4] 5177[10] 5781[4] 6372[2]◆ 6625[2] 7140[8] 7582[3]
We're Reunited (IRE) *Ronald Harris* a67 74
2 b g Kodiac Caelis (Avonbridge)
5447[3] 5980[2] 6395[3] 6807[2] 7679[9] 9031[4] 9300[6] 9541[7]
Werewolf *Archie Watson* a31 43
2 b c Siyouni(FR) Ysper (FR) (Orpen (USA))
6395[9] 6708[8]
We Ride The World (IRE)
Amandine Baudron a70 75
4 b g Orpen(USA) Meulles (FR) (Scat Daddy (USA))
6434a[6]
Westbrook Bertie *Mick Channon* 77
4 b g Sixties Icon Evanesce (Lujain (USA))
8033[3] 8433[7]
West Coast Flyer *David Simcock* a92 81
6 b g Cape Cross(IRE) La Felicita (Shareef Dancer (USA))
(432) 558[3] 758[3] 980[6]
West Drive (IRE) *Gary Moore* 90
6 ch g Sea The Stars(IRE) Fair Sailing (IRE) (Docksider (USA))
2032[12]
West End Charmer (IRE)
Mark Johnston 106
3 b c Nathaniel(IRE) Solar Midnight (USA) (Lemon Drop Kid (USA))
1911[4] 2562[8] (3338)
West End Girl *Mark Johnston* 103
2 b f Golden Horn Free Rein (Dansili)
(4605)◆ 5346[5] (5964)◆ 7120[8] 8091[9]
Western Australia (IRE)
A P O'Brien a103 105
3 ch c Australia What A Treasure (IRE) (Cadeaux Genereux)
1049a[2] 1831[5] (2853a) 3984[12] 4351a[7] 4963a[8] 7196[8] 8754[8]
Western Dawn (IRE) *Phillip Makin* a60 78
3 b g Dawn Approach(IRE) Yes Oh Yes (USA) (Gone West (USA))
7653[12] 8181[11] 8862[16]
Western Dixie (IRE)
Jennie Candlish a47
5 b m Westerner Flame Of Dixie (IRE) (Beneficial)
1771[9] 2017[P]
Western Duke (IRE) *Ian Williams* a89 93
5 b g High Chaparral(IRE) Witch Of Fife (USA) (Lear Fan (USA))
2969[5] 4224[3] 4425[4] (5417) 6420[16] 9056[5] 9419[4]
Western Dynamisme (FR)
Simon Dow a11
4 b m Manduro(GER) Western Hope (IRE) (High Chaparral (IRE))
752[9]
Western Frontier (USA)
A P O'Brien 95
3 b c Scat Daddy(USA) Missamerica Bertie (USA) (Quiet American (USA))
2882a[4] 4092[18]
Western Hero (IRE) *Kevin Ryan* 67
2 b g Excelebration(IRE) Kayak (Singspiel (IRE))
6424[9] 7247a[12]
Westfield Wonder
Ronald Thompson a33 33
4 b g Captain Gerrard(IRE) Flying Highest (Spectrum (IRE))
166[7] 587[5] 1969[7] 2298[12]
West Newton *Roger Charlton* a68 71
3 b c Kitten's Joy(USA) Queen's Prize (Dansili)
979[9] 1217[8] 2511[4] (3311) 4296[2]
Wetrov (FR) *R Rohne* a86 86
4 ch g Evasive Whoosh (FR) (Muhtathir)
1793a[7] 4704a[10]
We've Got The Love (IRE)
Clive Cox
3 b f Charm Spirit(IRE) Olympic Medal (Nayef (USA))
4326[10]
W G Grace (IRE) *Tim McCarthy* a11 12
4 b g Exceed And Excel(AUS) Ownwan (USA) (Kingmambo (USA))
6897[17]
Whatabird (IRE) *Richard Fahey* 77
2 b f Gleneagles(IRE) Inkling (USA) (Seeking The Gold (USA))
6919[2] (7644)◆
What About Carlo (FR)
Eve Johnson Houghton a59 103
8 b g Creachadoir(IRE) Boccatenera (GER) (Artan (IRE))
2607[2] 3315[9] 3646[4] 5182[5]
What A Business (IRE) *Roger Fell* a64 75
2 b g Gregorian(IRE) Lady Bee (IRE) (Lawman (FR))
1879[2] 2761[14] 3212[3] 4032[3] 4517[4] 5296[7] 5789[4]◆ (6053) 6653[3] 7399[2] 7827[3] 8095[8]
What A Dazzler *Bill Turner* a42 30
3 ch f Coach House(IRE) Dusty Dazzler (IRE) (Titus Livius (FR))
313[8] 943[12] 6107[11] 6526[5]
Whataguy *Paul Nicholls* 82
3 ch g Mayson La Fortunata (Lucky Story (USA))
2274[5] 3531[6] 3838[4] (4213) 5318[7] 5589[8] 6227[7] 7268[6]
What An Angel *Richard Hannon* 79
2 bg c Dark Angel(IRE) Mary Boleyn (IRE) (King's Best (USA))
4611[6] 5131[7] 6948[2] 7338[6] 7612[8]◆ 8110[12]
What A Queen (FR)
Matthieu Palussiere 57
3 ch f Siyouni(FR) Hieroglyph (Green Desert (USA))
1512a[5]
What A Turnup (IRE) *Mark Walford* a36
4 b m Frozen Power(IRE) Go Maggie Go (IRE) (Kheleyf (USA))
8086[9]
What A Welcome *Patrick Chamings* a94 104
5 ch g Nathaniel(IRE) Hometime (Dubai Destination (USA))
1943[8] 3078[2] 3600[4] 4884[10] 5662[8] 5928[3] 6834[5] 7459[3]
Whatdoesnotkillyou *John Mackie* a48 2
5 b g Camacho Verus Decorus (IRE) (Titus Livius (FR))
132[7] 485[12]
What Is Life (IRE) *Richard Fahey* 72
2 b f Iffraaj Media Luna (Oasis Dream)
4659[3]
What Secret (IRE) *C Boutin* a40 34
3 b g Exceed And Excel(AUS) So Secret (IRE) (Barathea (IRE))
216a[7] 9280a[11] 9538a[6]
What's The Story *Keith Dalgleish* a103 112
5 b g Harbour Watch(IRE) Spring Fashion (IRE) (Galileo (IRE))
2378[3]◆ (2778) 3987[12] 4935[3] 5610[11] (6376) 7365[2]
What Will Be (IRE) *Olly Murphy* a63 59
3 b g Thewayyouare(USA) Gali Gal (IRE) (Galileo (IRE))
855[4] 1358[3] 1721[3] 3311[6] 8200[5]
Whatwouldyouknow (IRE)
Richard Guest a68 72
4 b g Lope De Vega(IRE) Holamo (IRE) (Montjeu (IRE))
2056[4] 3217[6] 3960[4] 4194[10] (5213) 6102[2] 6573[3] 7074[9] 8122[12]
Wheels On Fire (FR)
Aidan F Fogarty 105
2 bb c Sidestep(AUS) Winds Up (USA) (Street Sense (USA))
3988[11] 5116a[2] 5542[5] 7149[3]
Whelans Way (IRE) *Roger Teal* a70 84
3 b g Requinto(IRE) Lupine (IRE) (Lake Coniston (IRE))
(2567) 3307[2] 3590[3] 4368[2] 6916[3] 8522[6]
Whenapoet *Michael Appleby* a72 52
3 b c Poet's Voice If Or When (IRE) (Dylan Thomas (IRE))
391[2] 826[6] 1480[2] 2075[7] 2582[13] 4306[9]
When Comes Here (IRE)
David Loughnane a54 78
2 br g Lawman(FR) Quads (IRE) (Shamardal (USA))
2338[2] 2780[4] 3962[2] 5587[12] 6364[3] 7119[16] 8665[11]
Where Next Jo *David Evans* a42 50
2 gr f Lethal Force(IRE) Almunia (IRE) (Mujadil (USA))
2915[6] 5745[5] 9567[7]
Where's Jeff *Michael Easterby* a68 88
4 b g Haafhd Piece Of Magic (Alflora (IRE))
1695[4] (2479)◆ 3862[3] (4241) 5694[8] (6975) 8633[6]
Where's Mick (IRE) *Jedd O'Keeffe* a72 64
2 b g Equiano(FR) She Storm (IRE) (Rainbow Quest (USA))
8337[6] 8631[4] 8919[2] 9392[3]
Where's Perle *Michael Wigham* a57 28
3 b f Kyllachy Highland Jewel (IRE) (Azamour (IRE))
406[6]
Wherewithal *Ralph Beckett* a65 25
3 b c Lope De Vega(IRE) Banks Hill (Danehill (USA))
7114[6] 7572[6]
Whigwham *Gary Sanderson* a32 41
5 ch m Sleeping Indian Normandy Maid (American Post)
281[1] 4132[9] 5147[13] 5559[11]
Whimbrel (IRE) *John Gosden* a81 81
3 gr f Dark Angel(IRE) Seagull (IRE) (Sea The Stars (IRE))
3050[3] (3495)◆ 4052[8]
Whimsical Dream *Michael Bell* a47 52
3 b f Oasis Dream Dream Whim (Nayef (USA))
1837◆ 532[4] 4499[3] (5049) 5680[3]
Whims Of Desire
Sir Mark Prescott Bt a44
3 b f Nathaniel(IRE) Clarietta (Shamardal (USA))
795[7] 979[13] 1217[7] 5242[8] 6046[U] 6367[10]
Whinging Willie (IRE) *Gary Moore* a70 81
10 b g Cape Cross(IRE) Pacific Grove (Persian Bold (IRE))
385[6] 1497[9]
Whinmoor *Nigel Tinkler* 91
4 gr g Havana Gold(IRE) Makhsusah (IRE) (Darshaan)
2260[2] 2743[15] 3308[5] 4598[3] 5453[7] 5971[2] 6460[13]
Whirling Dervish
Mrs John Harrington 97
4 b g Camelot Synergy (FR) (Victory Note (USA))
2158a[9]
Whirl Me Round *Robyn Brisland* a39 53
5 ch g Piccolo Give Her A Whirl (Pursuit Of Love)
448 982[11] 1969[8] 4449[5]
Whiskey And Water *Brian Ellison* a73 76
3 b g Harbour Watch(IRE) Bahamamia (Vettori (IRE))
1845[2] 2323[2] 4779[2] 7209[4]
Whiskey Sour (IRE) *W P Mullins* a82 105
6 b g Jeremy(USA) Swizzle Stick (IRE) (Sadler's Wells (USA))
2575[3]
Whisper Aloud *Archie Watson* a86 84
3 b f Swiss Spirit Lulla (Oasis Dream)
(1142)◆ 6388[2] (6561)◆ 7206[2] 7613[4]◆ 8115[15] 8349[3] 8852[5] 9387[4] 9549[9]
Whisper A Word (IRE)
Lucinda Egerton a31 45
5 ch m Bated Breath Affability (IRE) (Dalakhani (IRE))
971[12] 1083[7] 1368[13]
Whispering Angel (GER)
Markus Klug 100
3 b f Soldier Hollow Wamika (GER) (Shirocco (GER))
3639a[5] 4683a[5]
Whispering Beauty (USA)
William Haggas 89
3 bb f Arch(USA) She's A Beauty (USA) (Storm Cat (USA))
4341[2] (5141) (5748)
Whispering Leaves (IRE) *Clive Cox* 53
2 b f Acclamation Djinni (IRE) (Invincible Spirit (IRE))
1821[12] 3695[4] 4221[9]
Whispering Soul (IRE) *Brian Baugh* a48 51
6 b m Majestic Missile(IRE) Belle Of The Blues (IRE) (Blues Traveller (IRE))
28[8] 118[9] 3518[12] 5722[13]

Whisper Not *Richard Hannon* a66 3
2 b c Poet's Voice Poyle Meg (Dansili)
8287[5] 8517[8]

Whistler Bowl *Gary Moore* a53 72
3 b f Mukhadram Sablonne (USA) (Silver Hawk (USA))
(4372) 5249[4] 6125[2] **6405**[2]

White Chocolate (IRE)
David Simcock a89 88
5 gr m Mastercraftsman(IRE) Coco Demure (IRE) (Titus Livius (FR))
3010[4] 3800[4] ***3995***[4] 4864[5] *5735*[4]

White Coat *John Gosden* a82 74
3 ch c Dansili Clinical (Motivator)
133[3] *827*[2] *979*[2] *1381*[2] 1646[5] 2146[4] *3302*[3]

White Elusive (FR) *F Rossi* a68 71
2 b f Elusive City(USA) Kataragama (Hawk Wing (USA))
6584a[3]

White Feather *Jo Hughes* a47 55
4 ch g Bated Breath Just Wood (FR) (Highest Honor (FR))
2648a[7] 4960a[10]

Whitefountainfairy (IRE)
Andrew Balding a90 90
4 ch m Casamento(IRE) Groupetime (USA) (Gilded Time (USA))
1421[4]◆ *1881*[5] 2402[6] **5546**[6] 6379[12] 6922[3] 7142[6] 7678[9]

Whitehall *Geoffrey Harker* a27 42
4 b g Dansili Majestic Roi (USA) (Street Cry (IRE))
1813[9]

Whitehaven (FR) *Hughie Morrison* a40
2 bl g Le Havre(IRE) Passion Blanche (Dutch Art)
9181[9] *9448*[9]

White Iverson (IRE)
Richard Spencer a71 73
3 ch g Tale Of The Cat(USA) Illaunglass (IRE) (Red Clubs (IRE))
130[4]

White Moonlight (USA)
Saeed bin Suroor a76 93
2 b f Medaglia d'Oro(USA) Fitful Skies (IRE) (Dubawi (IRE))
(6928) **(7897)**◆

White Mountain *Saeed bin Suroor* a72
3 b f Raven's Pass(USA) Mujarah (IRE) (Marju (IRE))
9038[2]

White Shaheen *William Muir* a83 87
6 b g Makfi Likeable (Dalakhani (IRE))
184[4]◆ *735*[P]

White Turf (IRE) *Alastair Ralph* a64 45
4 gr g Clodovil(IRE) Holda (IRE) (Docksider (USA))
435[2] 2353[8]

White Valiant (FR) *T Le Brocq* 74
6 gr g Youmzain(IRE) Minnie's Mystery (FR) (Highest Honor (FR))
2672a[3] **(3640a)**

Whitmore (USA) *Ronald Moquett* a119
6 ch g Pleasantly Perfect(USA) Melody's Spirit (USA) (Scat Daddy (USA))
8773a[3]

Who Dares Wins (IRE) *Alan King* a108 108
7 b g Jeremy(USA) Savignano (Polish Precedent (USA))
1735[3] 2575[2] ***(4382)*** 5183[4] **7928a**[4] 8114[7]

Whosegottheshekles (IRE)
Nigel Tinkler 44
2 b g Footstepsinthesand Super Supreme I (IND) (Zafonic (USA))
8511[8]

Who's Steph (IRE) *G M Lyons* 109
4 gr m Zoffany(IRE) Llew Law (Verglas (IRE))
1620a[2] **(2451a)** 2642a[2] (3820a) 6090a[3] 7635a[4]

Who Told Jo Jo (IRE) *Joseph Tuite* a47 63
5 b g Bushranger(IRE) Shenkara (IRE) (Night Shift (USA))
2145[14] **(2287)** 2717[6] **3089**[2] 3203[10] 3527[11] 4181[12] 4824[6] 7757[12] 7977[11]

Wichita (IRE) *A P O'Brien* 117
2 b c No Nay Never(USA) Lumiere Noire (FR) (Dashing Blade)
7150[2]◆ **(7614)** 8113[3]

Wicked Whisper (USA)
Steven Asmussen a107
2 b f Liam's Map(USA) Zayanna (USA) (Bernardini (USA))
8747a[5]

Wicklow Warrior *Peter Niven* a48 22
4 b g Sleeping Indian Vale Of Clara (IRE) (Iffraaj)
241[12] *8270*[11]

Widaad *Owen Burrows* a58
2 b f Muhaarar Mudaaraah (Cape Cross (IRE))
8849[8]

Wide Acclaim (IRE)
Rebecca Menzies a64 45
4 b m Acclamation Riynaaz (IRE) (Cape Cross (IRE))
62[10] *273*[9]

Widgee Turf (AUS) *Patrick Payne* 110
5 ch g Turffontein(AUS) Greyhound (AUS) (Kala Dancer I)
8138a[9]

Widnes *Alan Bailey* a57 67
5 b g Showcasing Largo (IRE) (Selkirk (USA))
1297[10] 2975[11] 4111[10]

Wiff Waff *Chris Gordon* a72 65
4 b g Poet's Voice Eraadaat (IRE) (Intikhab (USA))
131[5] *278*[4] ***433***[3] *982*[4] *1507*[5] *1686*[2] 2025[2] 3021[8] 3856[6] 4227[8] 4844[7] 6401[8] 6510[6] 7172[11] *8018*[8]

Wightman (IRE) *Mick Channon* 76
2 b g Anjaal Defensive Boast (USA) (El Gran Senor (USA))
3890[2]◆ 4252[6] 5314[7]

Wikita (FR) *Charley Rossi* a78 77
8 b m Desert Style(IRE) Vagabonde (FR) (Valanour (IRE))
5715a[14]

Wild Abandon *Ralph Beckett* a48 65
3 b f Kingman Sant Elena (Efisio)
3892[8]

Wild Animal *Murty McGrath* a22 74
3 b g Kingman Epic Similie (Lomitas)
1852[8] **3664**[2] 4304[7] *9173*[13] *9453*[16]

Wildbeere (GER) *Waldemar Hickst* 85
3 bb f Maxios Wurfkette (GER) (Black Sam Bellamy (IRE))
4683a[7]

Wild Cat *Roger Charlton* 63
3 ch f Nathaniel(IRE) Desert Tigress (USA) (Storm Cat (USA))
3013[6] 3761[5] 4452[7]

Wild Dancer *Patrick Chamings* a63 60
6 b m Mawatheeq(USA) Pretty Miss (Averti (IRE))
4247[5] 5351[8] 6529[5] 7172[2] ***7812***[5] *8704*[7]

Wild Eagle (FR) *Vaclav Luka Jr* a15
3 b c Sommerabend Waajida (Dubawi (IRE))
1198a[10]

Wild Edric *Tom Dascombe* a88 90
3 ch g Equiano(FR) Lady Red Oak (Medicean)
1662[4] 2525[10] 3590[9] 4359[6] 4908[5] *(5000)* *5281*[2] **6715**[2]◆ 6921[10]

Wild Emotion (GER)
Andreas Suborics a73 75
3 b f Lord Of England(GER) Wildlife Lodge (GER) (Konigstiger (GER))
4229a[7]

Wild Flower (IRE) *Luke McJannet* a52 58
7 b m Approve(IRE) Midsummernitedream (GER) (Thatching)
1335[3] *1595*[9] 4182[3] 4481[5] *5264*[11] 5883[5] *6889*[7] *(7604)* **(8279)** *8839*[10] *8917*[3] *9247*[4] *9410*[7]

Wild Hero (IRE) *Andrew Balding* 70
2 b g Zoffany(IRE) Thought Is Free (Cadeaux Genereux)
4886[10] **5572**[5] **7139**[4] 7971[4]

Wild Hope *Kevin Ryan* a86 86
3 b g Kingman Wild Mimosa (IRE) (Dynaformer (USA))
2114[3] (2897)◆ 3249[9] 4001[3]◆ **(4723)** 5749[4] 6370[10] ***7653***[3]

Wild Illusion *Charlie Appleby* 108
4 b m Dubawi(IRE) Rumh (GER) (Monsun (GER))
3122a[6] 4354a[4] 6265a[6]

Wildmountainthyme *Stella Barclay*
3 b f Doncaster Rover(USA) Awaywithefairies (Courteous)
9547[5]

Wild Shot *Noel C Kelly* a77 69
5 br g So You Think(NZ) Highland Shot (Selkirk (USA))
4689[2]

Wild Thunder (IRE) *Richard Hannon* a89 92
2 b c Night Of Thunder(IRE) Shama's Song (IRE) (Teofilo (IRE))
(3008)◆ 4920[6] 6163[5] *6707*[2] **7197**[2] *8121*[6]

Wiley Post *Tony Carroll* a83 83
6 b g Kyllachy Orange Pip (Bold Edge)
2484[3] 3856[7] 4995[5] 5843[3] **(6798)** 7130[3] *8601*[5] ***9203***[2]

Wilfy *Sylvester Kirk* a68 71
2 br g Kyllachy Close To The Edge (IRE) (Iffraaj)
6287[6] *7030*[6] **7406**[5] 7980[11] *9205*[6] *9300*[5] *9499*[2]

Willa *Richard Hannon* a67 71
2 b f Dutch Art Holberg Suite (Azamour (IRE))
2836[8] **4223**[2] *4502*[4] 5587[10] 7173[3] 8465[4]

Willa's Wish (IRE) *Tony Carroll* a15 32
3 b f Zoffany(IRE) Supreme Spirit (IRE) (Invincible Spirit (IRE))
3839[12] 4755[6] 5084[10] **5981**[4] 6794[9]

Willett *Sarah Hollinshead* a26 50
3 br g Avonbridge Madame Elizabeth (Multiplex)
4193[8] 5981[5] **6361**[2] *7385*[11]

William Alexander *Les Eyre* 52
2 b g Zoffany(IRE) Xaloc (IRE) (Shirocco (GER))
4032[8] 5145[7] **5553**[11]

William Booth (IRE) *Mrs C Gilbert* a27 33
5 b g Born To Sea(IRE) Chaguaramas (IRE) (Mujadil (USA))
2004a[2] 2673a[3] 3174a[3] **3642a**[5] 4686a[7] 6009a[5]

William Hunter *Nigel Twiston-Davies* a74 79
7 b g Mawatheeq(USA) Cosmea (Compton Place)
2104[6] 3663[6] 4838[6] 5338[5] 5993[DSQ]

William McKinley *Ali Stronge* a54 41
3 b g Exceed And Excel(AUS) Pure Song (Singspiel (IRE))
472[3] 2210[13] 2795[18] *6052*[6] *8345*[10]

William Thomas (IRE)
Robert Eddery a53 38
2 b g Sepoy(AUS) Dream Day (Oasis Dream)
5887[5] 6449[9] *6883*[6] *8526*[10] *8897*[9]

Willie John *Roger Varian* 111
4 b h Dansili Izzi Top (Pivotal)
1460[4] **3074**[2]◆ 3953[14] 7076[5]

Willing To Please *David Barron* 46
2 b f Iffraaj Tebee's Oasis (Oasis Dream)
6997[8]

Willkommen *Marco Botti* a71
3 b c Epaulette(AUS) Weeza (IRE) (Sakhee (USA))
183[3]◆ *802*[9] *1770*[3] *2213*[2] ***(2941)***◆ *8868*[4] *9626*[6]

Will Ness (IRE) *D Allard* a51 50
3 b g Footstepsinthesand Keyta Bonita (IRE) (Denon (USA))
3066a[5] 4357a[8] **7642a**[5]

Will Of Iron *John Gosden* a56 79
3 b g Invincible Spirit(IRE) Astronomy Domine (Galileo (IRE))
128[5] **1652**[2] 2208[12]

Willow Brook *Julie Camacho* a38 35
3 ch f Sepoy(AUS) Portland River (FR) (Stormy River (FR))
215[6] ***497***[2] 2197[13] *5854*[7] *7959*[12]

Willow Grace *George Baker* a49 57
4 ch m Harbour Watch(IRE) Sparkling Montjeu (IRE) (Montjeu (IRE))
736[9] *965*[7]

Willow Tree (FR) *E Libaud* a66 68
4 b m Orpen(USA) Zilly Fish (FR) (Generous (IRE))
1491a[9]

Will Sommers *Kevin Ryan* 66
2 b c Teofilo(IRE) Dubai Queen (USA) (Kingmambo (USA))
7361[5]

Willsy *Frank Bishop* a42 47
6 b g Sakhee's Secret Blakeshall Rose (Tobougg (IRE))
37[9] ***180***[9] *533*[7]

Will To Win (GER) *Simon Crisford* a86 53
2 ch g Showcasing Win For Life (GER) (Dubawi (IRE))
3601[5] ***(4030)***

Willyegolassiego *Neil Mulholland*
6 br m Kheleyf(USA) Kryena (Kris)
5631[10]

Willy Nilly (IRE) *Clive Cox* 53
2 b g Morpheus Subtle Shimmer (Danehill Dancer (IRE))
6669[11] 7338[7] 8517[9]

Willy Sewell *Michael Appleby* a79
6 b g Multiplex Cherished Love (IRE) (Tomba)
41[7] *979*[3] ***(1102)*** *8918*[13] *9167*[7] *9418*[11]

Wilpena (IRE) *D Smaga* a55 54
3 ch f Makfi Loutka (FR) (Trempolino (USA))
3710a[15]

Wilson (IRE) *Julia Feilden* a73 69
4 b g Born To Sea(IRE) Alkhawarah (USA) (Intidab (USA))
249[5] *1684*[9] 2232[5] 2929[6] 3540[3] **(3967)** 5839[8] 7272[7] 7982[10]

Wimpole Hall *William Jarvis* a84 75
6 b g Canford Cliffs(IRE) Sparkling Eyes (Lujain (USA))
184[3] *617*[6] *825*[3] *2969*[4] *4250*[5] 5348[6] 6512[6] *6967*[7] *8656*[2] *(9050)* *9388*[6]

Winalotwithalittle (IRE) *J R Jenkins* a47
3 ch f Frozen Power(IRE) Easy Going (Hamas (IRE))
5592[12] 5748[8] *6315*[10] ***9171***[7]

Winander *Stuart Kittow* 8
2 b g Ruler Of The World(IRE) Rydal Mount (IRE) (Cape Cross (IRE))
8518[12]

Win Bright (JPN)
Yoshihiro Hatakeyama 120
5 gr h Stay Gold(JPN) Summer Eternity (JPN) (Admire Cozzene (JPN))
(9380a)

Windforpower (IRE) *Tracy Waggott* a51 57
9 b g Red Clubs(IRE) Dubai Princess (IRE) (Dubai Destination (USA))
25[6] ***129***[5] *279*[8] *613*[8] *973*[6] *1085*[2] *1402*[7] *3452*[7] 4434[11]

Windham Belle (IRE) *W McCreery* a75 84
2 b f Anjaal Belle Of The Blues (IRE) (Blues Traveller (IRE))
4352a[9] 7247a[18]

Wind In My Sails *Ed de Giles* a78 87
7 b g Footstepsinthesand Dylanesque (Royal Applause)
(2797) 3423[4] 4365[5] 5155[7] **(5292)** 5667[12] 7312[5]

Wind Place And Sho
James Eustace a66 81
7 b g Shirocco(GER) Coh Sho No (Old Vic)
3653[5] 4661[8] 5047[RR]

Windracer (IRE)
Mrs John Harrington 90
2 ch f Showcasing Fair Sailing (IRE) (Docksider (USA))
5361a[8] **6429a**[8]

Windsor Cross (IRE) *Richard Fahey* a83 84
4 gr g Camacho Lizzy's Township (USA) (Delaware Township (USA))
1273[4]◆ 1644[7] 2057[6] 2784[3] *4386*[4] 5240[7] 6129[3] 7074[15] 7489[8] *9202*[4]

Windsorlot (IRE) *Tony Carroll* a56 47
6 ch g Windsor Knot(IRE) Majestic Jenny (IRE) (Zamindar (USA))
2720[11] ***3325***[7] 4232[11] 4658[4] 5499[9] 6324[5] 6760[5] 7271[8]

Wind Storm *K R Burke* a64 63
4 b m Holy Roman Emperor(IRE) Imperialistic (IRE) (Imperial Ballet (IRE))
123[4] ***476***[3]

Windstoss (GER) *Markus Klug* 112
5 b h Shirocco(GER) Wellenspiel (GER) (Sternkoenig (IRE))
2455a[3] **3386a**[3]

Wind Test *Andrea Marcialis* a93 96
3 gr g Epaulette(AUS) Elbow Beach (Choisir (AUS))
1199a[5] 6252a[7]

Windy Writer (IRE) *Sam England* 18
9 br g Rudimentary(USA) Hardabout (IRE) (Alderbrook)
3929[8]

Winfola (FR) *X Thomas-Demeaulte* 84
5 gr m Motivator Romance Bere (FR) (Verglas (IRE))
4859a[7]

Wingate *J Cloerec* a34 51
9 b g Zamindar(USA) Sirene Doloise (FR) (Marchand De Sable (USA))
7009a[2]

Wing Dancer (FR)
Mme M Bollack-Badel 20
2 b f Norse Dancer(IRE) Angel Wing (Barathea (IRE))
9123a[10]

Winged Spur (IRE) *Mark Johnston* a84 86
4 ch m Motivator Mark Of An Angel (IRE) (Mark Of Esteem (IRE))
950[5] *1106*[5] *1395*[6] 2230[6] 2748[3] 3000[4] **(3349)** 4209[6] 4913[9] 5305[5] 6224[6] 7294[9] 8341[11]

Wingingit (IRE) *Andrew Balding* a67 99
5 ch m Helmet(AUS) Chirkova (USA) (Sadler's Wells (USA))
2033[6] 2401[7]

Wing Power (IRE) *S Dehez* 73
2 b c Power Wing Diva (IRE) (Hawk Wing (USA))
7799a[2]

Wingreen (IRE) *Martin Smith* a72 76
3 ch f Lope De Vega(IRE) Relation Alexander (IRE) (Dandy Man (IRE))
4506[6] *8552*[6] *8806*[6]

Wings Of Dubai (IRE)
Ismail Mohammed a43 44
3 b f Dark Angel(IRE) Aertex (IRE) (Exceed And Excel (AUS))
6399[4] **7319**[5] *8820*[2] *9160*[13]

Wings Of Time *Charlie Appleby* a74 100
3 b g Invincible Spirit(IRE) Marie De Medici (USA) (Medicean)
(534) 4120[2] **(4851)** 5412[7]

Winiata (IRE) *J P Murtagh* a64 92
3 bb f Society Rock(IRE) Bellacoola (GER) (Lomitas)
7038a[3] **8368a**[7]

Winklemann (IRE) *John Flint* a74 68
7 br g Rip Van Winkle(IRE) Kykuit (IRE) (Green Desert (USA))
1209[4] *1369*[6] 2145[3] 2580[7] 4281[6] (5302) 6680[11] ***(7603)***

Winklevi (FR) *Mrs A Malzard* 47
4 b g Maxios Wild Star (IRE) (Sternkoenig (IRE))
3640a[5]

Winman In Grey (FR) *Y Barberot* a69 72
3 b g Rajsaman(FR) Cinder's Post (FR) (American Post)
2265a[6]

Winnetka (IRE) *Richard Hannon* a64 69
2 ch g Camacho Little Audio (IRE) (Shamardal (USA))
3943[8] *4246*[8] **4544**[5] **5146**[2]

Winning Streak *Stuart Williams* a81 82
2 ch c Hot Streak(IRE) Positivity (Monsieur Bond (IRE))
4394[12] 5624[6] **(6287)** 7679[6] 8110[8] *9162*[4] *9661*[7]

Win O'Clock *Roger Charlton* a76
2 ch c Australia Gee Kel (IRE) (Danehill Dancer (IRE))
9326[4]

Win Tenderness (JPN)
Haruki Sugiyama 109
6 ch h Company(JPN) Moere Merci (JPN) (Magic Miles (USA))
9153a[12]

Winterfuchs (GER) *Carmen Bocskai* 106
3 ch c Campanologist(USA) Wunderblume (GER) (Lomitas)
(2163a) **3674a**[3] 7478a[4] 8378a[6]

Winter Gleam (IRE) *William Knight* a38 44
3 b f Kodiac Boo Boo Bear (IRE) (Almutawakel)
2035[12] **2798**[8] *8807*[10]

Winterkoenigin *David Lanigan* a60 69
3 b f Kingman Wittgenstein (IRE) (Shamardal (USA))
2904[7] 4285[6]◆ **4801**[2] 5354[7] 5797[7] *5941*[7] *7084*[8]

Winter Light *Richard Hughes* a89 89
3 ch f Bated Breath Moonglow (Nayef (USA))
1685[8] ***3323***[4]

Winter Lion (IRE) *John O'Shea* a62 56
9 ch g Galileo(IRE) Hill Of Snow (Reference Point)
2793[12] ***3467***[9]

Winterlude (IRE) *Jennie Candlish* a94 84
9 b g Street Cry(IRE) New Morning (IRE) (Sadler's Wells (USA))
82[11] ***345***[7]

Winter Snowdrop (IRE)
Julia Feilden a39 46
3 gr f War Command(USA) Morning Jewel (IRE) (Dalakhani (IRE))
251[11] *1077*[4] *1689*[4] 3407[4] 4476[4] 4836[4] **5866**[3] 6412[5] 7271[5]

Winter Spice (IRE) *Johnny Farrelly* a4 2
8 gr g Verglas(IRE) Summer Spice (IRE) (Key Of Luck (USA))
4019[9]

Win Vic (FR) *S Kobayashi* a60 61
4 b g Alex The Winner(USA) Matsot (FR) (Maresca Sorrento (FR))
76a[6]

Win Win Win (USA)
Michael Trombetta a106 104
3 bb c Hat Trick(JPN) Miss Smarty Pants (USA) (Smarty Jones (USA))
2425a[9] *2856a*[7]

Winx (AUS) *Chris Waller* 126
7 b m Street Cry(IRE) Vegas Showgirl (NZ) (Al Akbar (AUS))
(1783a)

Wireless (FR) *Vaclav Luka Jr* a78 108
8 ch h Kentucky Dynamite(USA) Sachet (USA) (Royal Academy (USA))
5168a[6]

Wiretap (FR) *David Simcock* a78 85
3 b g Charm Spirit(IRE) Ysper (FR) (Orpen (USA))
2364[8] **(3779)** 4347[3]

Wirral Girl (IRE) *Denis Quinn* a82 76
4 b m Kodiac Ursula (IRE) (Namid)
123[9]

Wisdom Mind (IRE)
Joseph Patrick O'Brien a86 95
4 b m Dark Angel(IRE) Alina (IRE) (Galileo (IRE))
2879a[5] **3359**[2] 4758[6] 5075a[10] 6090a[10] 6646a[5] 7794a[5] 7934a[5] 8367a[7]

Wise Coco *Alistair Whillans* a53 43
6 b m Shirocco(GER) Sensible (Almutawakel)
2373[7] **3500**[6] 3686[14]

Wise Counsel *Clive Cox* 99
3 b g Invincible Spirit(IRE) Noozhah (Singspiel (IRE))
3591[3] (3858) 5953[8] **(7435)**

Wise Glory (IRE) *Simon Crisford* 71
2 b g Muhaarar Bint Almukhtar (IRE) (Halling (USA))
6065[3]

Wiseiten (FR) *Frank Sheridan* a66 66
4 gr g Slickly(FR) Pilgrim Of Grace (FR) (Bering)
76a[8]

Wise Ruler *Simon Crisford* a92 78
3 ch g Dawn Approach(IRE) Bint Almukhtar (IRE) (Halling (USA))
5656[2] *(6662)*◆ ***7302***[3]

Wise Words *James Tate* a94 99
3 b f Sepoy(AUS) Akhmatova (Cape Cross (IRE))
954[2] *1236*[4] *1598*[3]◆ *(2380)* (3159) 3855[4] **5014**[2] *6735*[4] (7058)

Wishbone (IRE) *J S Moore* 22
3 b c Footstepsinthesand Royale Life (FR) (Anabaa (USA))
5538a9

Wishfully (IRE) *H-A Pantall* a93 98
3 b f Invincible Spirit(IRE) Tajriba (IRE) (Teofilo (IRE))
6769a3 7499a3 8377a2

Wishful Thinker (AUS)
Richard Gibson 119
5 b g I Am Invincible(AUS) Zebithea (AUS) (Barathea (IRE))
1442a7 9377a6

Wishing Well *Micky Hammond* a69 70
7 b m Bahri(USA) Amourallis (IRE) (Dushyantor (USA))
25915 368610

Wish You Well (GER)
Jean-Pierre Carvalho 97
3 bb f Soldier Hollow Walburga (GER) (One Cool Cat (USA))
4683a8 (7499a)

Wisperwind (GER) *Henk Grewe* a84 93
7 bl g It's Gino(GER) Wayumi (GER) (Samum (GER))
2666a12 7860a6

Wissahickon (USA) *John Gosden* a119 121
4 ch h Tapit(USA) No Matter What (USA) (Nureyev (USA))
(565)◆ (879) 19212 64704

Witch Hunt (IRE) *David Menuisier*
2 b c Lawman(FR) Witches Brew (IRE) (Duke Of Marmalade (IRE))
885810

With Approval (IRE) *Karen Tutty* a57 56
7 b g Approve(IRE) Kelsey Rose (Most Welcome)
(80) 2507 19365 22313 368711 39669 44753 504911 58035 66663 785911 830113 (8819) 903912 93963 95168

With A Start (IRE)
Denis Gerard Hogan a73 74
4 b g Sea The Stars(IRE) Sudden Blaze (IRE) (Soviet Star (USA))
1572a2

With Caution (IRE) *James Eustace* a91 79
3 ch f Dandy Man(IRE) Kitty Softpaws (IRE) (Royal Applause)
(477) (908)◆ 11682 30483 35834 45604 50002 550310 (7607) 83492 954910

With Good Grace (IRE)
Charles Hills a73
4 ch m Galileo(IRE) Withorwithoutyou (IRE) (Danehill (USA))
10966

Withhold *Roger Charlton* a111 116
6 b g Champs Elysees Coming Back (Fantastic Light (USA))
(5183)◆ 647313 (7615) 83325

Within Reach *Ralph Beckett* a41
2 b f Oasis Dream Grasped (Zamindar (USA))
91749

Withoutdestination *Marco Botti* a81 74
3 b g Epaulette(AUS) Where I Be (Dubawi (IRE))
3435 7236 10802◆ (1510) 23174 40242 56542 71083

Without Parole *Chad C Brown* a90 116
4 b h Frankel Without You Babe (USA) (Lemon Drop Kid (USA))
1445a5 2829a14 8774a3

With Pleasure *John Flint* a76 74
6 b g Poet's Voice With Fascination (USA) (Dayjur (USA))
68496 85236

With Pride *Clare Ellam* a37 40
3 b c Pour Moi(IRE) Aliena (IRE) (Grand Lodge (USA))
28913 6067 94010 159310 33486

With Promise *David Lanigan* 76
2 b c Shamardal(USA) Magical Crown (USA) (Distorted Humor (USA))
(5823)◆

With Respect (IRE)
Hughie Morrison 85
2 gr c Gutaifan(IRE) More Respect (IRE) (Spectrum (IRE))
(8516)

With Thanks (IRE) *William Haggas* 83
2 b f Camacho Thanks (IRE) (Kheleyf (USA))
(8759)◆

With Virtue *James Tate* 59
2 b f Iffraaj Lalectra (King Charlemagne (USA))
346910 43375 51973

With You *F Head* 115
4 b m Dansili In Clover (Inchinor)
3122a8 5479a2 6265a2 7942a6

Wizardry (FR) *George Scott* 42
2 b g Zoffany(IRE) March (Dutch Art)
42958 562411 62197

Wodanaz (FR) *D Chenu* 39
3 ch g Diogenes(IRE) Fleur Mongiron (FR) (Fasliyev (USA))
6062a7

Woggle (IRE) *Geoffrey Deacon* a53 35
4 ch m Camacho Radio Wave (Dalakhani (IRE))
803 4859 10327 13544 15193◆ 19588 32989 357110 55659 61168 61997

Wojood *Hugo Palmer* a49 67
3 b g Dansili Endless (Sadler's Wells (USA))
53116 60831

Woke (IRE) *K R Burke* 64
2 bb f Showcasing Analysis (Dubai Destination (USA))
37252 49765 538710

Wolfcatcherjack (IRE) *Nick Gifford* a77 78
5 b g Lawman(FR) Alleluia (Caerleon (USA))
93034

Wolf Chop (FR) *C Boutin* a8
3 b c Amadeus Wolf Via Appia I (FR) (Exit To Nowhere (USA))
1198a11

Wolfe (JPN)
Gai Waterhouse & Adrian Bott 101
4 ch g Novellist(IRE) Peace Of World (JPN) (Sunday Silence (USA))
8361a13

Wolf Hunter (IRE) *J Moon* a76 86
3 ch g Sir Prancealot(IRE) Sunny Hollow (Beat Hollow)
3641a6 (4686a)

Wolf Prince (IRE) *Amy Murphy* 82
3 b g Pour Moi(IRE) Preach (IRE) (Danehill Dancer (IRE))
62742 76836◆ 83412

Wonder Bolt (USA) *Ji Yong Cheol* a89
9 rg h Desert Warrior(USA) Little Champ (CAN) (Great Gladiator (USA))
7010a9

Wonderful Effort (IRE) *Ed Vaughan* a48
2 b f Acclamation Up At Last (Cape Cross (IRE))
56467 95069

Wonderful Moon (GER)
Henk Grewe 115
2 ch c Sea The Moon(GER) Wonderful Filly (GER) (Lomitas)
7937a2 (8964a)

Wonderful Tonight (FR)
David Menuisier 79
2 b f Le Havre(IRE) Salvation (Montjeu (IRE))
85103 (9123a)

Wonderment (IRE) *N Clement* 106
3 b f Camelot Wiwilia (Konigstiger (GER))
3905a7 6003a6 6993a2

Wonder Of Lips (GER) *H-F Devin* 86
4 b m Champs Elysees Wunderblume (GER) (Lomitas)
1627a10

Wonderwork (IRE) *K R Burke* 85
2 b g Night Of Thunder(IRE) First Party (Royal Applause)
(5689) 647412 733310

Wondrous Scene (IRE) *K J Condon* a47 62
3 b f Acclamation Rock Exhibition (Rock Of Gibraltar (IRE))
95404

Wonnemond (GER) *S Smrczek* a91 102
6 b g Areion(GER) Windaja (GER) (Surako (GER))
1793a5 5230a4 6770a3 7494a2 8583a8 9210a11

Wontgetfooledagen (IRE)
Rebecca Menzies a46 41
3 b g Zebedee No Way (IRE) (Rainbows For Life (CAN))
50111 8025 106612 40557

Wooded (IRE) *F-H Graffard* 107
2 b c Wootton Bassett Frida La Blonde (FR) (Elusive City (USA))
6777a2 7887a3

Wooden (FR) *M Nigge* a72 91
4 ch h French Fifteen(FR) La Boisserie (FR) (Dansili)
2266a6 7062a6

Woodhouse *Sir Michael Stoute* 73
2 b f Kingman Danvina (IRE) (Dansili)
61593◆ 70544

Woodland Opera (IRE)
Mrs John Harrington 48
9 br g Robin Des Champs(FR) Opera Hat (IRE) (Strong Gale (IRE))
3384a6

Woodlands (FR) *F Fouquet*
8 ch h Green Tune(USA) Someries (FR) (Kendor (FR))
7009a10

Woods (IRE) *William Haggas* a77 58
3 b g Garswood Flare Of Firelight (USA) (Birdstone (USA))
2514 7336 46554

Woodside Wonder *Keith Dalgleish* a80 83
3 br g Camacho Cambridge Duchess (Singspiel (IRE))
1263 25598 40999 43606 47812 56193 65914 (7049) 736410 75122 87617 92546 95177

Woodsmokehill *Rod Millman* 46
2 b f Brazen Beau(AUS) Zeyran (IRE) (Galileo (IRE))
525012 60787 716010

Woody Creek *J A Stack* 107
3 b f Zoffany(IRE) Belle Isle (Pastoral Pursuits)
5325a2 5923a2 74015◆

Woofie (IRE) *Laura Mongan* a37 42
7 b g Duke Of Marmalade(IRE) Violet Ballerina (IRE) (Namid)
22836 565312

Wookie (FR) *J-C Rouget* a92 96
3 b c Wootton Bassett Medical Kiss (FR) (Medicean)
3108a4

Wooldix (FR) *Mlle Stephanie Penot* a75 55
4 ch h Evasive In Love Kelty (FR) (Green Tune (USA))
4532a2

Woossett (FR) *H-A Pantall* a53 70
3 b c Wootton Bassett Starshine (Danehill Dancer (IRE))
1198a5

Wootton (FR) *Charlie Appleby* 113
4 b g Wootton Bassett American Nizzy (FR) (American Post)
846a4◆ 1115a2 1445a9 73405 8379a6

Wordismybond *Amanda Perrett* a47 56
10 b g Monsieur Bond(IRE) La Gessa (Largesse)
871110

World Title (IRE) *Archie Watson* 89
2 b c Dandy Man(IRE) Piccola Sissi (IRE) (Footstepsinthesand)
35513 (3954) 47503 (6579) (7699)

World War (IRE) *Martin Keighley* a12 89
5 ch g Galileo(IRE) Jacqueline Quest (IRE) (Rock Of Gibraltar (IRE))
7046

Worthamonkey *Denis Quinn* a10
2 b c Cable Bay(IRE) Zambujeiro (Dutch Art)
746910 77689 80679

Worth Waiting *David Lanigan* a101 111
4 b m Bated Breath Salutare (IRE) (Sadler's Wells (USA))
(2441) 4354a5 6265a8 696211

Wotadoll *Mike Murphy* a68 68
5 b m Harbour Watch(IRE) Rhapsilian (Dansili)
56787 (6018) 63296 68355 71618

Wotamadam *Dean Ivory* a55 51
4 gr m Lethal Force(IRE) Rhapsilian (Dansili)
538 4026 7188 109310

Wots The Wifi Code *Tony Coyle* 64
2 b g Fast Company(IRE) Velvet Jaguar (Hurricane Run (IRE))
32655 412513 49376 62283 728311

Woven *David Simcock* a95 95
3 ch g Dutch Art Regal Silk (Pivotal)
168a2 511a10 34934 43856 484714 59323 62223 71873 74485

Woven Quality (IRE)
Donald McCain 74
2 b g Epaulette(AUS) Amoreshari (Paco Boy (IRE))
42374 48763 57646 62726 706410

Wow (GER) *Andreas Suborics* a86 78
5 bb g Areion(GER) Wonderful Filly (GER) (Lomitas)
115a2 2675a9

Wow Cat (CHI) *Chad C Brown* a113
4 bb m Lookin At Lucky(USA) Winter Cat (CHI) (Cat Thief (USA))
8775a7

Wrath Of Hector *Tony Newcombe* 39
2 b c Mayson Dutch Mistress (Dutch Art)
53396 60789 82436

Wrecking Crew (USA) *Peter Miller* a107
2 bb r Sky Kingdom(USA) Truelladeville (CAN) (Yes It's True (USA))
8749a3

Wren *Roger Charlton* a79 80
2 b f Raven's Pass(USA) Magical Romance (IRE) (Barathea (IRE))
(4245) 56762 84534

Wrenthorpe *Bryan Smart* a75 87
4 b g Hellvelyn Milly-M (Cadeaux Genereux)
18993 22012 282415 35045 42795 489411 60572 73875 (7831) (8262) 83408

Written Broadcast (IRE)
Richard Hannon a74 83
2 gr g Gutaifan(IRE) Teeline (IRE) (Exceed And Excel (AUS))
45963 51862 55239 62873 69637 740910

Wrongroadtomayo *Fred Watson*
2 b f Paco Boy(IRE) Female Spring (Mujahid (USA))
47277

Wufud *Charles Hills* a77 87
4 b h Dubawi(IRE) Tahrir (IRE) (Linamix (FR))
30402 38805 61555 714212

Wutzelmann (GER)
Frau Anna Schleusner-Fruhriep 3
9 bb g Desert Prince(IRE) Walerie (GER) (Law Society (USA))
8804a7

Wyclif *Ralph Beckett* 94
2 b c Archipenko(USA) Altruiste (Montjeu (IRE))
(5655) 63683 (7000)◆ 83972

Wye Bother (IRE) *Milton Bradley* a47 57
3 b f Born To Sea(IRE) Enchantment (Compton Place)
1377 2354 6204 8489 22112 25926 31488 33199 71579 76066 811911

Wyndspelle (NZ) *Johno Benner* 111
5 b h Iffraaj Western Star (NZ) (High Chaparral (IRE))
8138a17

Wynfaul The Wizard (USA)
Laura Morgan a57 43
4 b g Bodemeister(USA) Red Dot (USA) (Diesis)
85912 300614 50434 54463 57878 61528

Wynford (IRE) *Lucinda Egerton* a67 72
6 ch g Dylan Thomas(IRE) Wishing Chair (USA) (Giant's Causeway (USA))
32947 54873 56218

Wyomia Jasmin (FR)
Waldemar Hickst a40 67
3 b f Dabirsim(FR) Wafiyah (GER) (Lord Of England (GER))
6789a2

Xaaros (FR) *P Sogorb* 89
2 gr c Kendargent(FR) Xaarina (FR) (Aussie Rules (USA))
5116a7

Xcelente *Mark Johnston* a81 83
2 b g Exceed And Excel(AUS) Vanity Rules (New Approach (IRE))
(1758) 22882 35664 46373 558714 69638 782710

Xenophanes (IRE) *M Boutin* a69 71
9 b g Shamardal(USA) Nipping (IRE) (Night Shift (USA))
2956a12 6267a5

X Force (IRE) *Archie Watson* a83 75
2 b g Bungle Inthejungle Nafa (IRE) (Shamardal (USA))
43732 48712 (5280) (6705)◆ 82194

Xian Express (IRE) *Michael Appleby* a69 82
2 ch g Dragon Pulse(IRE) Wind Inher Sleeves (USA) (Speightstown (USA))
95149 96412

Ximena *William Jarvis* a31 41
3 b f Poet's Voice Amanjena (Beat Hollow)
18347 276214 55927 61539

Xquisite (IRE) *J S Moore* a44 35
2 b f Xtension(IRE) Make Amends (IRE) (Indian Ridge (IRE))
291511 5286a9 91273 95016

X Rated (IRE) *Mark Johnston* a58 60
5 gr g Exceed And Excel(AUS) Screen Star (IRE) (Tobougg (IRE))
29627 34298 40058

Xtara (IRE) *Dina Danekilde* a80 87
3 b c Xtension(IRE) Brave Madam (IRE) (Invincible Spirit (IRE))
(83) 5552 7497a8

X Y Jet (USA) *Jorge Navarro* a121
7 rg g Kantharos(USA) Soldiersingsblues (USA) (Lost Soldier (USA))
(1444a)

Yaazaain *J E Hammond* a60 58
3 b g Iffraaj Tamazirte (IRE) (Danehill Dancer (IRE))
2758a6

Yabass (IRE) *Archie Watson* a95 97
4 ch g Lope De Vega(IRE) Fresh Mint (IRE) (Sadler's Wells (USA))
21183 3384a4 39529 54575 57693

Ya Boy Sir (IRE) *Alistair Whillans*
12 ch g Alhaarth(IRE) Champs Elysees (USA) (Distant Relative)
42769 469415 509412

Yabrave *N Bachalard*
5 b g Bahamian Bounty Dare To Dream (Exceed And Excel (AUS))
196a13

Yafta *Richard Hannon* a104 111
4 gr h Dark Angel(IRE) Swiss Dream (Oasis Dream)
18532 27443 409414

Ya Hala (IRE) *Charlie Appleby* 88
3 b f Shamardal(USA) Mount Elbrus (Barathea (IRE))
7360a6

Ya Hayati (USA) *Charlie Appleby* a80
2 b c Dubawi(IRE) Wedding Toast (USA) (Street Sense (USA))
78146◆ (8605)

Yalata *Charlie Appleby* a5
2 ro g Fast Company(IRE) Blanc De Chine (IRE) (Dark Angel (IRE))
34266

Yamato (IRE) *John C McConnell* a60 52
6 b g Big Bad Bob(IRE) Himiko (IRE) (Aussie Rules (USA))
(8347)◆ 946710

Yamuna River *Chris Gordon* a75 72
4 b m Foxwedge(AUS) Harryana To (Compton Place)
16538 22798 49296

Yanling (FR) *Matthieu Palussiere* a74 97
5 ch m Rio De La Plata(USA) Hijaziyah (Testa Rossa (AUS))
5168a7 6769a9

Yard Line (USA) *R Bouresly* a85 76
8 b g Discreet Cat(USA) Perceive (USA) (A.P. Indy (USA))
49a7

Yarrow Gate *Michael Dods* 72
2 b f Garswood Winter's Night (IRE) (Night Shift (USA))
24764◆ 32442 35646 56683 637215

Yasir (USA) *Sophie Leech* a57 48
11 b g Dynaformer(USA) Khazayin (USA) (Bahri (USA))
1194 4579 8104 13348◆ 20143◆ 26953 50533 52856 60466 66812 74747 78183 83474 90424 93122 94475

Yasmin From York *Brian Rothwell* 22
3 b f Sixties Icon Bonnie Burnett (IRE) (Hawk Wing (USA))
164313 214811 28458 31989 40389

Yattwee (USA) *Saeed bin Suroor* a106 92
6 bb g Hard Spun(USA) Alzerra (UAE) (Pivotal)
51885 (6150)◆

Ydra *Archie Watson* a68 64
3 b g Mayson Camelopardalis (Tobougg (IRE))
2592 8583 13654 25117 32542 37654

Year Of The Tiger (IRE) *A P O'Brien* a109 105
2 b c Galileo(IRE) Tiggy Wiggy (IRE) (Kodiac)
40917 49207 76914 81134 87163

Yellow Label (USA) *Andrew Balding* a46 66
3 br g Hat Trick(JPN) Kazam (USA) (Dynaformer (USA))
13448 16527 21136 30923 38887 50287

Yellow Storm (FR)
Stephane Chevalier 73
5 b m Tiberius Caesar(FR) Yellow Queen (FR) (Slickly (FR))
5510a10

Yellow Tiger (FR) *Ian Williams* a85 87
3 b g Wootton Bassett Comnena (Tiger Hill (IRE))
(4636) 56149 59314 83505 96334

Yer Tekkin Mick *Michael Appleby* a45
4 b g Native Ruler Lord Conyers (IRE) (Inzar (USA))
86714

Yes Always (IRE) *K R Burke* a76
2 b f No Nay Never(USA) Flavia Tatiana (IRE) (Holy Roman Emperor (IRE))
(8084)◆

Yes Can Do (USA) *Ed Dunlop* a18 37
3 b f No Nay Never(USA) Sheba's Humor (USA) (Distorted Humor (USA))
23569 27359 402912

Yestaahel *Kevin Frost* 2
3 b g Footstepsinthesand Azenzar (Danehill Dancer (IRE))
51287

Yesterdayoncemore (IRE)
J A Stack a77 89
2 bb f No Nay Never(USA) Danehill's Dream (IRE) (Danehill (USA))
2881a7 4352a5

Yes Yes Yes (AUS) *Chris Waller* 118
2 b c Rubick(AUS) Sin Sin Sin (AUS) (Fantastic Light (USA))
(8362a)

Yes You (IRE) *Bryan Smart* a47 78
5 ch m Choisir(AUS) Mexican Milly (IRE) (Noverre (USA))
37226 44925 49774 53953 56703 646112 77624 951911

Yet Another (IRE) *Grace Harris* a30 38
4 b g High Chaparral(IRE) Elaflaak (USA) (Gulch (USA))
309013 369611 4178DSQ 47745 529311 60189 65264 68576 825511

Yfenni (IRE) *Milton Bradley* a48 41
3 ch f Dutch Art Paisley (Pivotal)
296[3] 550[6] 906[6] 1296[10] 2211[7] 2357[13] 3839[4] 5044[7] 5377[5] 5957[3] 7024[11] 9659[12]
Y Fyn Duw A Fydd *Alan King* a39 7
4 b m Nathaniel(IRE) Dignify (IRE) (Rainbow Quest (USA))
9589[13]
Yimkin (IRE) *Marco Botti* a60 46
3 b f Kingman Orpha (New Approach (IRE))
(556) 1543[2] 2760[9] 9625[7]
Yimou (IRE) *Dean Ivory* a90 91
4 b g Kodiac Heroine Chic (IRE) (Big Bad Bob (IRE))
206[4] 3462[8] 4227[7] (4844) (5868)◆ (6465) 7397[4] 8420[4] 8867[4]
Yogi (NZ)
Ciaron Maher & David Eustace 103
6 b g Raise The Flag Malozza (AUS) (Grand Lodge (USA))
1784a[16]
Yoker (FR) *Mme Pia Brandt* a86 78
2 b c Manduro(GER) Nova Luz (Divine Light (JPN))
8508a[4]
Yolo Again (IRE) *Roger Fell* a91 93
3 b f Toronado(IRE) Suite (IRE) (Invincible Spirit (IRE))
182[4] (342) 1762[5] 1920[4] 2319[8] 2522[6] 2960[2] 3293[9] 4101[7] (4294) 4932[6] 5705[6] 6257[6] 6999[7] 8115[5]
Yomogi (FR) *Hiroo Shimizu* 92
2 b f Zoffany(IRE) Desert Red (IRE) (Green Desert (USA))
1657a[10] 2757a[3] 8647a[3]
Yorbelucky *Ian Williams* 60
4 b g Yorgunnabelucky(USA) Circle Of Angels (Royal Applause)
2151[9] 2628[9] 3572[6]
Yorkshire Gold *Kevin Ryan* 87
2 b c Muhaarar Swift Campaign (IRE) (Intikhab (USA))
(5550)◆ 6352[7] 8125[12]
Yorkshire Grey (IRE) *Ann Duffield* a28 55
2 gr g Lawman(FR) Magnifica (USA) (Mizzen Mast (USA))
4486[8] 5212[4] 5815[5] 6313[11] 7284[9] 8526[12]
Yoshida (JPN) *William Mott* a119 105
5 b h Heart's Cry(JPN) Hilda's Passion (USA) (Canadian Frontier (USA))
444a[6] 1447a[6] 8777a[8]
Yoshimi (IRE) *Richard Fahey* 84
2 gr g Dream Ahead(USA) Dawn Dew (GER) (Montjeu (IRE))
5396[2]◆ 6065[2] (6934)◆ 7429[2] 8100[3]
Yo Tambien *John C McConnell* a48 63
4 ch m Sir Percy Moi Aussi (USA) (Mt. Livermore (USA))
3205[RR]
Youarefullofchat *Robyn Brisland* 36
2 gr f Lethal Force(IRE) Chatalong (IRE) (Invincible Spirit (IRE))
4302[10] 5895[9] 7046[8]
Youarestar *William Haggas* 58
3 b g Sea The Stars(IRE) Alumna (USA) (Mr Greeley (USA))
2764[9]
You Can Smile (JPN)
Yasuo Tomomichi 119
4 b h King Kamehameha(JPN) Mood Indigo (JPN) (Dance In The Dark (JPN))
9153a[5]
You Don't Own Me (IRE)
Joseph Tuite a67 56
2 b f Evasive Hypatia (IRE) (Holy Roman Emperor (IRE))
5250[7] 5745[4] 5988[8] 7079[5] 8452[3] 8825[3] 9009[2] (9061) 9164[4]
Youkan (IRE) *Stuart Kittow* a78 88
4 b g Choisir(AUS) Ellikan (IRE) (Exceed And Excel (AUS))
2568[4]◆ 3509[9] 3636[5] 3893[2] 6920[5] 7564[9] 8262[7] 8601[10] 8826[3]
You Little Beauty *Ann Duffield* a46 44
3 b f Stimulation(IRE) Ziefhd (Haafhd)
501[6] 1982[7] 2197[4] 2633[5] 3158[6] 3684[4] 4003[4] 8942[6]
You Little Ripper (IRE)
Peter Chapple-Hyam a81 82
3 b c Rip Van Winkle(IRE) Sahara Sky (IRE) (Danehill (USA))
405[2] 1676[2] 2243[2] 2736[3] 4565[2]
Youmna (FR) *H-A Pantall* a74 88
3 b c French Fifteen(FR) Enfant Modele (Peintre Celebre (USA))
(7291a)
Younevercall (IRE) *Kim Bailey* 92
8 b g Yeats(IRE) Afarka (IRE) (Kahyasi (IRE))
4096[11]
You Never Can Tell (IRE)
Richard Spencer a92 63
3 b g Elzaam(AUS) Zanida (IRE) (Mujadil (USA))
57[7] 806[6] 989[3] 1920[P] 5312[5] 6440[8]
Youneverletmedown (IRE)
Keith Dalgleish a51
2 br f Footstepsinthesand Calorie (Sea The Stars (IRE))
8651[12]
Young Bernie *Andrew Balding* a71 66
4 b g Sixties Icon Hot Pursuits (Pastoral Pursuits)
3464[5] 4377[4] 7731[7]
Young Fire (FR) *David O'Meara* a94 95
4 b g Fuisse(FR) Young Majesty (USA) (Maria's Mon (USA))
2429a[2] 5948[7] 6460[8] (6922) 7781[6] 8096[5] 9053[9] 9254[2]
Young General (IRE)
Richard Hannon a56 58
3 gr c Dark Angel(IRE) Dust Flicker (Suave Dancer (USA))
5494[5] 5808[7] 6283[5]

Young John (IRE) *Mike Murphy* a90 85
6 b g Acclamation Carpet Lady (IRE) (Night Shift (USA))
1560[2] 2237[6] 2799[4] 3649[4] 5503[5] 6326[4] (7115)◆ 7621[2] (8403) 8522[14] 9183[2] 9441[6]
Young Merlin (IRE) *Roger Charlton* a75 79
3 b g Camelot Zelloof (IRE) (Kheleyf (USA))
2407[6] 4031[3] 4803[6] (5566) 6125[4] 7082[3]
Young Rascal (FR) *William Haggas* a117 111
4 b g Intello(GER) Rock My Soul (IRE) (Clodovil (IRE))
1750[5] 2410[6] (8811) 9376a[9]
Youngstar (AUS) *Chris Waller* 102
4 b m High Chaparral(IRE) Starspangled (IRE) (Danehill (USA))
1974a[12] 8844a[20]
Young Tiger *Tom Tate* a70 56
6 b g Captain Gerrard(IRE) Blades Princess (Needwood Blade)
3213[8] 4829[4] 5478[5] 6099[7] 7052[3] (7824) (8401) 8840[5] (9219) 9473[2]◆ 9645[3]
Youonlyliveonce (FR) *Lars Kelp* 72
2 b c Sidestep(AUS) Feelin Foxy (Foxhound (USA))
7495a[7]
You Owe Me *Mark Johnston* a67
2 ch g Champs Elysees Elpida (USA) (Giant's Causeway (USA))
8914[8] 9095[8] 9326[3]
Your Band *Jamie Osborne* a77 24
4 b g Helmet(AUS) Kampai (Sakhee (USA))
38[2]◆ (160)◆ 318[3] 481[10] 1022[5]
Your Choice *Laura Mongan* a69 52
4 ch m Foxwedge(AUS) Mildoura (FR) (Sendawar (IRE))
963[3] 5309[13] 6120[7] 8007[5] 8254[11] 8896[11] 9249[3] 9505[10]
Yourdeel (NZ)
David A & B Hayes & Tom Dabern 103
2 b g Dundeel(NZ) Miss Zapper (AUS) (Red Ransom (USA))
8137a[13]
You're Cool *John Balding* a86 53
7 b g Exceed And Excel(AUS) Ja One (IRE) (Acclamation)
3[7] 791[5] 1211[6] 1547[2] 1952[5] (3303) 4458[5] 5888[7] 7771[7] 8550[10]
You're Hired *Amanda Perrett* a86 92
6 b g Dalakhani(IRE) Heaven Sent (Pivotal)
2800[3] 4250[6] 4752[2] 5667[2] 6447[2] 6909[2] 7457[4] 7694[11]
You're My Rock *Richard Fahey* a75 69
2 ch c Rock Of Gibraltar(IRE) You're My Cracker (Captain Gerrard (IRE))
4289[3] 5177[6] 5780[6] 6980[8]
Your Just Desserts (IRE)
Paul Collins 41
4 b m Requinto(IRE) Whats For Pudding (IRE) (Kheleyf (USA))
5278[5] 5559[19]
Your Mothers' Eyes *Alan Bailey* a59 67
3 b c Aussie Rules(USA) Sanctum (Medicean)
476[4] 1296[4] 1549[8] 2016[2] (3182)◆ 3650[3] 3964[2] 4378[4] 5092[5] 5869[5] 7603[8] 9503[4] 9657[8]
Your Pal Tal *J F Levins* a61 61
9 b g Dark Angel(IRE) Good Health (Magic Ring (IRE))
502[2] (5278)◆
Your Thoughts (FR) *Paul Webber* a57 57
3 b f So You Think(NZ) Moraga (IRE) (Acclamation)
4121[7] 5141[7] 6187[6] 6810[7] 7344[6]
Yourtimeisnow *Roger Varian* 102
3 b f Charm Spirit(IRE) Maid For Winning (USA) (Gone West (USA))
1751[13] 2627[7] 3085[11]
Yousini *Kevin Ryan* a86 92
3 b g Siyouni(FR) War Effort (USA) (War Front (USA))
1851[2] 2835[12] 3865[5] 5120[5] 6227[18] 7002[6] 7431[21] 8900[5]
Youthfilly *Ollie Pears* 17
2 b f Fountain Of Youth(IRE) Quiet Elegance (Fantastic Light (USA))
2706[9]
Youthful *Michael Bell* a72
3 b g Shamardal(USA) Good Hope (Cape Cross (IRE))
2598[P]
Yu Change (JPN) *Hideyuki Mori* a81 85
6 bb h Swift Current(JPN) Yu Carat (JPN) (Winning Ticket (JPN))
869a[9]
Yuften *Denis Gerard Hogan* a95 94
8 b g Invincible Spirit(IRE) Majestic Sakeena (IRE) (King's Best (USA))
5597a[3] 6693a[7]
Yukon Mission (IRE) *John Quinn* a69
2 b f Kodiac Refuse To Give Up (IRE) (Refuse To Bend (IRE))
9043[5] 9623[3]
Yukon Thunder *Steph Hollinshead* a24
2 ch g Night Of Thunder(IRE) Yukon Girl (IRE) (Manduro (GER))
8999[11]
Yulong Gold Fairy *J S Bolger* 102
4 b m Mount Nelson Quite A Thing (Dutch Art)
1307a[3] 3105a[6] (7934a)
Yulong Prince (SAF) *M F De Kock* 105
4 b h Gimmethegreenlight(AUS) Congestion Charge (Diktat)
1445a[10]
Yuman (FR) *M Rulec* a89 91
5 gr g Literato(FR) Dianaba (FR) (Diktat)
2955a[3] 3369a[5] 3907a[6]
Yuri Gagarin *John Gosden* a72
3 ch g Sea The Moon(GER) Soviet Terms (Soviet Star (USA))
(9350)◆
Yusra *Marco Botti* a83 72
4 b m Invincible Spirit(IRE) Munyatee (ARG) (Dylan Thomas (IRE))
81[5] 516[2] 1387[2] 2252[6] 3994[14] 7788[2] 8498[11]

Yvette *Sir Mark Prescott Bt* a64
3 b f Le Havre(IRE) Macleya (GER) (Winged Love (IRE))
133[8] 370[8] 5269[8] 5851[5] 6720[6] 7817[2] 8423[2]
Zaaki *Sir Michael Stoute* a104 117
4 b g Leroidesanimaux(BRZ) Kesara (Sadler's Wells (USA))
(2271) (3343) 4900[2]◆ 5521[7] (6470) 7660[3] 9379a[8]
Zabarqan (IRE) *J-C Rouget* 66
2 b c Invincible Spirit(IRE) Tahaany (IRE) (Raven's Pass (USA))
5468a[5] 6262a[6]
Zabeel Champion *Mark Johnston* a81 74
2 b c Poet's Voice Stars In Your Eyes (Galileo (IRE))
(7174)◆ 8302[2]
Zabeel Prince (IRE) *Roger Varian* 120
6 ch g Lope De Vega(IRE) Princess Serena (USA) (Unbridled's Song (USA))
(1890) (3122a) 3985[7] 4668[8] 5543[7]
Zabeel Star (IRE) *Karen McLintock* a85 71
7 ch g Arcano(IRE) Deep Winter (Pivotal)
1719[5] 2186[3] 3811[13] 4383[6] 5436[3] 5970[5] 6658[8] 7653[7] 9496[8]
Zabriskie (IRE) *Luke Comer* 91
4 b h Frankel Moonlight's Box (USA) (Nureyev (USA))
2666a[9] 3343[6] 4411a[7] 5112a[7] 5535a[12] 6192a[P] (Dead)
Zacada (NZ)
Murray Baker & Andrew Forsman 103
6 b g Zabeel(NZ) Lacada (AUS) (Giant's Causeway (USA))
1784a[14]
Zac Brown (IRE) *Charlie Wallis* a86 77
8 b g Kodiac Mildmay (USA) (Elusive Quality (USA))
203[6] 964[6] 1496[4] 1547[6] 2556[3] 3301[U] 3492[3] (4253) 4593[4] 4880[7] (5649) 5888[5] 6510[2] 7130[9]
Zaccapa (FR) *F Chappet* 77
2 b f Muhaarar Soudanaise (IRE) (Peintre Celebre (USA))
7044a[2]
Zack Mayo *Philip McBride* a75 95
5 b g Air Chief Marshal(IRE) White Wedding (IRE) (Green Desert (USA))
8727[11] 9177[8] 9611[5]
Zaeem *Ivan Furtado* a56 48
10 b g Echo Of Light Across (ARG) (Roy (USA))
44[7] 386[8] 1197[7] 1369[9]
Zafaranah (USA) *Pam Sly* a85 72
5 ch m Raven's Pass(USA) Jiwen (CAN) (Singspiel (IRE))
(123) 564[6] 812[5] 4281[5] 4831[4] 6025[3] 6582[5] (7608) 8197[2] 8691[2] 9126[2]◆ 9476[5]
Zafeer (JPN) *Marco Botti* a73 74
2 b c Deep Impact(JPN) Zumoorooda (AUS) (Encosta De Lago (AUS))
5823[2] 7346[2] 8604[5]
Zafiro (FR) *D De Waele* a70 75
7 b g Sageburg(IRE) La Romagne (FR) (Art Francais (USA))
7676a[2] 9537a[15]
Zagitova (IRE) *A P O'Brien* 103
3 ch f Galileo(IRE) Penchant (Kyllachy)
1601a[4]
Zagrah *Owen Burrows* a72
2 b f Dansili Rewaaya (IRE) (Authorized (IRE))
5732[2]
Zahee (IRE) *Saeed bin Suroor* a80 74
4 b g Iffraaj Havin' A Good Time (IRE) (Jeremy (USA))
4927[3] 5650[7] 6594[3] 7470[5]
Zahirah *J R Jenkins* a64 54
5 b m Mullionmileanhour(IRE) Numanthia (IRE) (Barathea (IRE))
465[7]
Zahraani *J R Jenkins* a50 50
4 b g Mount Nelson Mediterranean Sea (IRE) (Medecis)
435[6] 562[8] 1858[10] 2417[3] 3017[9] 3705[8] 6843[11] 7873[11]
Zain Hana *John Butler* a88 89
4 b m Shamardal(USA) Lavender And Lace (Barathea (IRE))
1829[14] 3085[8] 4340[5] 5251[2]
Zainhom (USA) *M Al Mheiri* a95 100
5 ch g Street Cry(IRE) Kaseema (USA) (Storm Cat (USA))
173a[8]
Zain Storm (FR) *John Butler* a66 13
2 b c Lethal Force(IRE) Nickels And Dimes (IRE) (Teofilo (IRE))
1953[7] 3141[3] 4018[4] 6113[6] 6883[8] 8085[11]
Zakher Alain *Adrian Nicholls* 51
2 b c Sepoy(AUS) Madame Mere (IRE) (Dalakhani (IRE))
4631[5] 5017[4] 5472[6]
Zakouski *Charlie Appleby* a90 102
3 b g Shamardal(USA) O'Giselle (AUS) (Octagonal (NZ))
1854[5]
Zalkaya (FR) *N Milliere* a46 49
7 b m Chichi Creasy(FR) Zalka (FR) (Indian Rocket)
7800a[7]
Zalmi Angel *Adrian Nicholls* a52 53
3 b f Swiss Spirit Break Of Dawn (USA) (Mt. Livermore (USA))
1549[10] 2337[5] 2482[7] 2871[6] 3651[2] 4487[11]
Zalpa (USA) *David Evans* 64
3 bb f More Than Ready(USA) Sis City (USA) (Slew City Slew (USA))
1512a[6] 7237[9]
Zamaam *E Charpy* a80 94
9 br h Muhtathir Nasheed (USA) (Riverman (USA))
398a[4] 635a[4] 958a[5]
Zaman *Charlie Appleby* 111
4 b g Dutch Art Wake Up Call (Noverre (USA))
514a[3] 730a[5]

Zamani (GER) *David Bridgwater* a63 65
3 ch g Mamool(IRE) Zuccarella (GER) (Banyumanik (IRE))
7984[3] 8293[6] 8703[5]
Zambezi Magic *Clive Cox* a69 60
2 b g Zoffany(IRE) Millestan (IRE) (Invincible Spirit (IRE))
7521[7] 8012[3] 8823[7]
Zamharer
Mohammed Jassim Ghazali 91
3 b c Olympic Glory(IRE) Strawberrydaiquiri (Dansili)
9590a[10]
Zamjar *Robert Cowell* a86 88
5 b g Exceed And Excel(AUS) Cloud's End (Dubawi (IRE))
2079[2] 2556[6] 2839[8] 3597[3] 6954[6] 7348[8] (8428)
Zamoyski *Steve Gollings* a59 62
9 ch g Dutch Art Speech (Red Ransom (USA))
6055[8] 6674[7] 7998[3] 8828[11]
Zampano (FR) *A Kleinkorres*
4 gr g Ordenstreuer(IRE) Zappatera (FR) (Marchand De Sable (USA))
2002a[9]
Zampa Road (IRE) *David Evans* a49
2 ch f Camacho Nurture (IRE) (Bachelor Duke (USA))
1513[5] 1879[10]
Zamperini (IRE) *Gary Moore* a62 54
7 ch g Fast Company(IRE) Lucky Date (IRE) (Halling (USA))
560[2] 923[4] 1498[2] 5679[7]
Zander *G M Lyons* 91
3 b g Oasis Dream Zaminast (Zamindar (USA))
1306a[14] 4136a[9]
Zane Daddy (USA) *Mark Johnston* a55 69
3 bb c Scat Daddy(USA) Obsequious (USA) (Fusaichi Pegasus (USA))
7543[3] 8300[10]
Zan O'Bowney (ITY) *Nicolo Simondi* 98
7 b h Blu Air Force(IRE) Blu Ransom (IRE) (Fasliyev (USA))
2888a[10]
Zanzibar (FR) *Cedric Rossi* a78 77
5 b g Zanzibari(USA) First Legend (FR) (Montjeu (IRE))
5643a[4]
Zap *Richard Fahey* a80 96
4 b g Mayson Moonglow (Nayef (USA))
1891[8] 2609[14] 3094[3] 3563[4] 3857[6] 4921[10] 5546[5] 6693a[11] 7188[13] 8096[12] 8893[5]
Zapateado *Paul George* a55 61
4 b m Zoffany(IRE) Ziggy Zaggy (Diktat)
1074[4] 2714[13]
Zapel *A Botti* 96
6 b h Kyllachy Viadeigiardini (Dubai Destination (USA))
2888a[7]
Zapper Cass (FR) *Michael Appleby* a89 77
6 b g Elusive City(USA) Moonlight Cass (IRE) (Danehill Dancer (IRE))
2[7] 158[6] 237[2] 468[10] 600[4] 787[2] (970) (1208)◆ 1274[3] (1507) 1597[4] 1767[6] 2294[9] 2625[4] 3147[2] 3770[7] 4364[3]◆ 5000[6] 5889[7] 6027[8] 7828[6] 8007[2] 8263[5] (8943) 9013[7] 9286[8] 9390[6] 9550[9]
Zappiness (USA)
Peter Chapple-Hyam a62 44
3 ch f Stay Thirsty(USA) Zappeuse (USA) (Kingmambo (USA))
1740[14] 2925[5] 4022[4] 5652[2] 6279[14] 7318[14] 8299[7]
Zargun (GER) *Henk Grewe* 99
4 b g Rock Of Gibraltar(IRE) Zenaat (Galileo (IRE))
1793a[8] 3369a[8] 3907a[7] 6519a[5] 6770a[7] 8392a[6] 8787a[10]
Zarkallani (FR) *A De Royer-Dupre* 91
3 b c Invincible Spirit(IRE) Zarkava (IRE) (Zamindar (USA))
3390a[13]◆ 6005a[8]
Zarkavon *John Wainwright* a51 41
5 b m Avonbridge Zarkavean (Medicean)
465[2] 835[5] 1390[5] 1836[7] 2376[3] 3448[4] 3960[8] 8863[7] 9391[12]
Zarrar (IRE) *Rae Guest* a62 50
4 b g Thewayyouare(USA) Featherlight (Fantastic Light (USA))
6320[8] 7083[14] 7790[13] 7998[8] 9412[2]◆
Zarzyni (IRE) *M Halford* 102
2 b g Siyouni(FR) Zunera (IRE) (Invincible Spirit (IRE))
5362a[3] 6690a[4] 7532a[3]
Zascandil (FR) *C Delcher-Sanchez* 96
5 b h Motivator Magic Date (FR) (Sagamix (FR))
4418a[2] 6145a[8]
Zatorius (GER) *S Cerulis* a48 62
4 b g Pastorius(GER) Zarah Top (GER) (Big Shuffle (USA))
2026a[4]
Zaula *Mick Channon* a59 49
3 rg f Dark Angel(IRE) Zimira (IRE) (Invincible Spirit (IRE))
211[7] 555[4] 943[10] 1170[3] 1385[10] 1678[8] 3780[9] 4180[14] 4755[4] 5306[4] 5878[3] 6561[2] 6754[3] 7371[10]
Zaverna (IRE) *F Monnier* a71 71
5 b m Excelebration(IRE) Zalonia (Cape Cross (IRE))
(6031a)
Zavrinka (FR) *V Sartori* a87 95
4 b m Rajsaman(FR) Salvation (Montjeu (IRE))
2782a[3] 4706a[5] 9603a[10]
Zawadi (GER) *Frau V Henkenjohann* a59 68
6 b m Kallisto(GER) Zandra (GER) (Lagunas)
4859a[2]
Zaydanides (FR) *Tim Pinfield* 56
7 bl g American Post Ouarzazate (IRE) (Enrique)
2208[15] 4177[8] 5578[5] 6400[8] 7759[12]
Zayriyan (IRE) *Ali Stronge* a57 62
4 ch g Shamardal(USA) Zariyna (IRE) (Marju (IRE))
9362[5] 9659[10]
Zazen *A Fabre* 79
3 b f Oasis Dream Zantenda (Zamindar (USA))
(5644a) 7886a[9]

Zealandia (FR) *M Nigge* 66
2 b c Sea The Moon(GER) Belle Ambre (Teofilo (IRE))
7675a^{4}

Zealous (IRE) *Alistair Whillans* a69 68
6 br g Intense Focus(USA) Velvet Kiss (IRE) (Danehill Dancer (IRE))
1648^{9} *2244*^{11} 3297^{8} 4914^{5} **(5725)** 6545^{5} 7513^{6} 8186^{2} 8515^{8}

Zeb City (IRE) *Mark L Fagan* a48 47
4 b g Zebedee Mad About The Girl (IRE) (Excellent Art)
6574^{3} 7214^{9}

Zebulon (IRE) *Ruth Carr* a66 75
5 gr g Zebedee Novelina (IRE) (Fusaichi Pegasus (USA))
1565^{4} 1976^{9} *2379*^{5} *8839*^{13} ***9397***^{2} ***9518***^{2}

Zebzardee (IRE) *Richard Fahey* 68
3 ro g Zebedee Zarkalia (IRE) (Red Ransom (USA))
3719^{4}◆ 4280^{5} 4523^{9}

Zeebad (IRE) *Paul D'Arcy* a45
3 gr g Zebedee Love Intrigue (IRE) (Marju (IRE))
137^{6} *887*^{10}

Zefferino *Martin Bosley* a74 64
5 ch g Frankel Turama (Pivotal)
1209^{5}◆ *1684*^{4} *2318*^{6} 4115^{3} (6334) *7609*^{3} *(8291)* ***(8499)*** *9047*^{9} *9244*^{7}

Zegalo (IRE) *Roger Varian* 77
2 b c Zoffany(IRE) Mzyoon (IRE) (Galileo (IRE))
6948^{3} 7539^{2} (8257)

Zeimaam (IRE) *Owen Burrows* a74
2 ch c Slade Power(IRE) Jathaabeh (Nashwan (USA))
8288^{4} ***8999***^{3}◆ *9363*^{6}

Zelote (FR) *Mme M Bollack-Badel* 66
2 b g Literato(FR) Zython (FR) (Kabool)
8447a^{5}

Zenafire *Sarah Hollinshead* a48 66
10 b g Firebreak Zen Garden (Alzao (USA))
3511^{11} 4126^{11}

Zenagh (USA) *A Fabre* 81
3 b f Mizzen Mast(USA) Stormica (USA) (Storm Cat (USA))
4621a^{9}

Zenaida (IRE) *Ed Dunlop* a72
2 b f Kodiac Constellation (Cape Cross (IRE))
8454^{9} ***9506***^{2}

Zenith One (IRE) *Seamus Durack* a67 47
4 br g Footstepsinthesand Gemini Diamond (IRE) (Desert King (IRE))
246^{5} 1826^{10} *2595*^{8}

Zephyrina (IRE) *Daniel Kubler* 69
3 b f Big Bad Bob(IRE) Western Sky (Barathea (IRE))
2715^{2} (3574) 5451^{7}

Zephyros (GER) *David Bridgwater* a66 60
8 br g Areion(GER) Zandra (GER) (Lagunas)
344^{5} *911*^{6} 1936^{7} 2471^{3} 2732^{6} 3473^{8} 3834^{9}

Zerano (FR) *H-A Pantall* a59 59
3 ch g Denon(USA) Zariyana (IRE) (Desert Prince (IRE))
2265a^{8}

Zere *Archie Watson* a57
2 b f Iffraaj Zimira (IRE) (Invincible Spirit (IRE))
8021^{6}

Zero Limits *Marco Botti* a6 31
2 gr g Outstrip Mpumalanga (Observatory (USA))
8857^{6} *9500*^{12}

Zero To Hero (IRE) *Archie Watson* a56 13
4 ch m Arakan(USA) Blue Daze (Danzero (AUS))
6687^{6} *7035*^{6} 7177^{3} *7859*^{12}

Zeshov (IRE) *Rebecca Bastiman* a70 72
8 b g Acclamation Fathoming (USA) (Gulch (USA))
1271^{7} 1695^{8} **1948**^{4} 2369^{3} 2894^{5} 3957^{11} 5899^{4} 6573^{5} 6937^{2} 7212^{6} 8186^{7}

Zest Of Zambia (USA) *Dai Burchell* a49 55
3 bb f Lemon Drop Kid(USA) Lusaka (USA) (Distorted Humor (USA))
5254^{8} 5578^{6} **6290**^{5} 7238^{5} *8348*^{8}

Zeyzoun (FR) *Alexandra Dunn* a83 86
5 b g Excelebration(IRE) Zayanida (IRE) (King's Best (USA))
2824^{6} 4303^{3} 4879^{2} 5626^{10} *6440*^{2}◆ *6863*^{7} **(7731)** 8521^{12} 9537a^{8}

Zezenia (IRE) *Roger Varian* a66
2 b f Oasis Dream Lahaleeb (IRE) (Redback)
7580^{2}

Zhui Feng (IRE) *Amanda Perrett* a100 105
6 b g Invincible Spirit(IRE) Es Que (Inchinor)
3009^{3} 3987^{23} 4397^{5} 4666^{9} 5610^{17} 5930^{2} 6445^{3} 6915^{6} 7694^{23}

Zhukovsky (IRE) *Ismail Mohammed* a70
3 b g Zoffany(IRE) Sea Paint (IRE) (Peintre Celebre (USA))
9475^{5}◆

Ziggle Pops *Richard Hannon* 85
2 ch c Zoffany(IRE) Loch Ma Naire (IRE) (Galileo (IRE))
2792^{10} 5624^{3} 6154^{4} (6757) **7119**^{9}

Zighidi *Frank Sheridan* a73 75
3 b f Holy Roman Emperor(IRE) Mambo Gold (USA) (Medaglia d'Oro (USA))
1626a^{8}

Zig Zag (IRE) *Philip Kirby* a44 44
6 b g Zoffany(IRE) Le Montrachet (Nashwan (USA))
2202^{10}

Zig Zag Zyggy (IRE)
Andrew Hughes a60 87
4 b h The Carbon Unit(USA) Dancing Cosmos (IRE) (Holy Roman Emperor (IRE))
(2437) 3503^{9} 4279^{7} **5119**^{2} 6607^{6}

Zihaam *Roger Fell* a63 69
5 ch g Dutch Art Hymnsheet (Pivotal)
1848^{4} 2436^{8} 3054^{6} (3959) 4208^{5} **(4817)** **5245**^{5} 5728^{7} **6100**^{4} 7332^{4} *8019*^{7}

Zihba (IRE) *J A Stack* a89 104
4 b h Choisir(AUS) Fancy Vivid (IRE) (Galileo (IRE))
1531a^{2} **2660a**^{3} 3114^{4} 3953^{11} 4411a^{6} 5112a^{4}

Zillion (IRE) *Sue Gardner* a61 75
5 b g Zebedee Redelusion (IRE) (Hernando (FR))
6104^{6}◆

Zillione Sun (FR)
Mme P Butel & J-L Beaunez a69 98
4 ch m Zambezi Sun Zillione Beauty (FR) (Ocean Of Wisdom (USA))
6992a^{4} 8790a^{7}

Zim Baby *Paul George* a69 72
2 b f Roderic O'Connor(IRE) Kenyan Cat (One Cool Cat (USA))
3194^{2}◆ (3644) *9364*^{10} *9661*^{4}

Zingaro Boy (IRE) *Hugo Palmer* a73 59
2 b g Zoffany(IRE) Awohaam (IRE) (Iffraaj)
4246^{5} 4925^{11} *5809*^{4}◆ 6372^{7} ***6980***^{2}◆ *7419*^{9} 8465^{11}

Zip *Richard Fahey* a77 79
3 ro g Kyllachy Flycatcher (IRE) (Medicean)
(126) 2746^{10} 3591^{2} 3728^{2} 5200^{6} 5557^{5} 6179^{3} 6961^{9} 7906^{5} 8342^{3} **(8634)**

Zip Along (IRE) *Richard Fahey* a53 81
4 b m Iffraaj Wizz Up (IRE) (Whipper (USA))
6974^{8} 7380^{6}

Zipedeedodah (IRE) *Joseph Tuite* a55 45
7 gr g Zebedee Beverley Macca (Piccolo)
118^{7} *179*^{5} ***1716***^{4} *1987*^{6}

Ziveri (FR) *F Rossi* a77 81
4 b h Mayson Alma Thomas (IRE) (Orpen (USA))
(1349a) **3136a**^{2} 4704a^{13} *5643a*^{2}

Ziyad *C Laffon-Parias* 117
4 bb g Rock Of Gibraltar(IRE) Arme Ancienne (Sillery (USA))
3389a^{2} **4430a**^{2} (6522a) 8155a^{3}

Zizum *Alan Berry* 28
4 ch g Showcasing Proud Duchess (IRE) (Duke Of Marmalade (IRE))
2633^{13} 4319^{10} 4694^{12} 5491^{11} **5670**^{9}

Zlatan (IRE) *Ed de Giles* a85 90
6 b g Dark Angel(IRE) Guard Hill (USA) (Rahy (USA))
8658^{7}

Zmhar (IRE) *James Tate* a89 63
3 ch c Shamardal(USA) Guarantia (Selkirk (USA))
(798) ***(966)***

Zmile *Michael Bell* 76
2 b f Medaglia d'Oro(USA) Cay Dancer (Danehill Dancer (IRE))
3049^{4} 4091^{11}

Zock (FR) *F Rossi* a90 79
5 ch g Rock Of Gibraltar(IRE) Zanet (FR) (Enrique)
5643a^{7} **(7136a)**

Zodiacus (IRE) *T G McCourt* 79
3 b f Zoffany(IRE) Naval Affair (IRE) (Last Tycoon (IRE))
2605a^{14} **8166a**^{8}

Zodiakos (IRE) *Roger Fell* a75 77
6 b g Kodiac Zonic (Zafonic (USA))
22^{2} *429*^{2} *507*^{5} 1660^{3} 2439^{2} (2509) *3002*^{2} 3199^{8} **(3730)** 4067^{8} 5490^{10} 6496^{5} 7069^{12}

Zoelola (FR)
Mme P Butel & J-L Beaunez a76 76
5 b m Rajsaman(FR) Zillione Beauty (FR) (Ocean Of Wisdom (USA))
(1491a)

Zofar Zogood (IRE)
Joseph Patrick O'Brien 84
2 b f Zoffany(IRE) Inca Wood (UAE) (Timber Country (USA))
8165a^{7}

Zofelle (IRE) *Hugo Palmer* a75 82
3 b f Zoffany(IRE) Height Of Elegance (IRE) (Galileo (IRE))
1272^{2}◆ 2144^{6} 2809^{11} **4119**^{3} 4654^{9}

Zoffany Bay (IRE) *Ali Stronge* a58 63
5 b g Zoffany(IRE) Trois Graces (USA) (Alysheba (USA))
6200^{7} ***9443***^{11} *9611*^{7}

Zoffee *Tom Dascombe* a77 91
3 b g Zoffany(IRE) Mount Crystal (IRE) (Montjeu (IRE))
3051^{6} 4187^{2} (5502) **6291**^{2} 6955^{7}

Zo Lane (FR) *F Rossi* 64
2 b f Vale Of York(IRE) Park Lane (FR) (Orpen (USA))
4679a^{10} 5713a^{13}

Zolushka (IRE) *Marco Gasparini* 53
3 b f Lord Chaparral(IRE) Zolletta (IRE) (Brief Truce (USA))
4171a^{11}

Zoman (ITY) *Grizzetti Galoppo SRL* 92
3 b c Rajsaman(FR) Zobenigo (IRE) (Orpen (USA))
2162a^{5} **2887a**^{10}

Zoom Out *Nigel Tinkler* a54 33
3 ch g Haafhd Bigger Picture (IRE) (Raven's Pass (USA))
405^{10} *930*^{5} *1195*^{7} ***1486***^{7} *1721*^{10} 2337^{9} 2587^{6}

Zoran *Hugo Palmer* a71
2 b c Invincible Spirit(IRE) Filia Regina (Galileo (IRE))
8999^{7}◆ ***9363***^{2}

Zoravan (USA) *Keith Dalgleish* a72 72
6 ch g More Than Ready(USA) Zaralanta (IRE) (Danehill Dancer (IRE))
2899^{2} **4239**^{2} 4634^{4}◆ 4879^{6} **5117**^{3} 5726^{7} 6037^{4} **6626**^{2} 7069^{4} **7363**^{2} ***7652***^{2} *8305*^{9} *9113*^{8}

Zorawar (FR) *David O'Meara* a74 68
5 b g Shamardal(USA) Zerkeriya (IRE) (Soviet Star (USA))
37^{5} *(532)* *(624)*◆ *724*^{2} *801*^{4} ***965***^{2} *1343*^{4} 1647^{6} 2056^{7} *2596*^{8}

Zoraya (FR) *Pam Sly* a82 77
4 b m Zoffany(IRE) Aztec Queen (Holy Roman Emperor (IRE))
123^{2} *756*^{8} *992a*^{9} 4113^{4} 4424^{7} 5376^{3} 5573^{2}◆ (5981) 6898^{7} *7843*^{10}

Zorion *Charlie Appleby* 104
5 b g Smart Strike(CAN) Zofzig (USA) (Danzig (USA))
637a^{7} **961a**^{2} 3953^{10}

Zorro Cass (FR) *Matthieu Palussiere* 74
3 bl c Elusive City(USA) Moonlight Cass (IRE) (Danehill Dancer (IRE))
(7642a)

Zorro's Girl *Archie Watson* a58
3 b f Toronado(IRE) Broughtons Charm (IRE) (Invincible Spirit (IRE))
990^{3} *1171*^{10} *1514*^{2} *1678*^{3} ***2190***^{2} *2350*^{5}

Zouy's Comet (AUS)
Richard Laming 75
3 b g Zoustar(AUS) Queen's Elect (AUS) (Holy Roman Emperor (IRE))
9016a^{11}

Zuba *Amanda Perrett* a85 85
3 b g Dubawi(IRE) Purr Along (Mount Nelson)
2088^{3} 3765^{6} *5311*^{3} ***(5734)*** **5931**^{5} *6349*^{5} 6952^{10}

Zubayr (IRE) *Ian Williams* a89 78
7 b g Authorized(IRE) Zaziyra (IRE) (Dalakhani (IRE))
82^{3} ***349***^{4} 5540^{13}

Zucesso (FR) *S Smrczek* a66 59
2 b c Dabirsim(FR) Zaphira (GER) (Big Shuffle (USA))
7675a^{8}

Zuckerberg (IRE) *Ivan Furtado* a59 69
2 ch g Camacho Queenie Keen (IRE) (Refuse To Bend (IRE))
3190^{4} **4125**^{4} 5764^{4} 6424^{7} *6980*^{7}

Zuenoon (IRE) *D K Weld* 105
3 gr g Havana Gold(IRE) Zindana (IRE) (Dalakhani (IRE))
2660a^{5} **6137a**^{2}

Zulu Alpha (USA) *Michael J Maker* a33 113
6 bb g Street Cry(IRE) Zori (USA) (A.P. Indy (USA))
2646a^{7} **8776a**^{4}

Zulu Girl *Eve Johnson Houghton* a67 66
2 b f Lethal Force(IRE) Upskittled (Diktat)
3461^{5} 4223^{3} 4897^{3} 6118^{6}

Zulu Zander (IRE) *David Evans* a72 81
2 b g Bungle Inthejungle Fig Digliani (IRE) (Fasliyev (USA))
1416^{3} **(1556)** **(1910)** 2267^{4} *4637*^{6} 5542^{12} 8659^{2} *9162*^{7} *9499*^{4}

Zumurud (IRE) *Rebecca Bastiman* 88
4 gr g Zebedee Thaisy (USA) (Tabasco Cat (USA))
1895^{2} 2416^{8} 3503^{2} 3868^{5}◆ 4303^{2} **(5040)**◆ 6220^{7} 6676^{12} 8636^{5}

Zwayyan *Andrew Balding* a104 104
6 ch g Pivotal Mail The Desert (IRE) (Desert Prince (IRE))
(1101)◆ 1415^{7} **1912**^{4} 2085^{7} 3987^{16} **5930**^{3} *6391*^{4} 7164^{4}

Zylan (IRE) *Roger Fell* a98 78
7 ch g Kyllachy Belgique (IRE) (Compton Place)
(832)◆ *1105*^{9} *1274*^{8} *1428*^{4} 2201^{6} 2898^{4} 3930^{2} 5488^{6} *6549*^{7} 6826^{6} 7289^{3} 7540^{6} *9517*^{11}

Zyrjann (IRE) *Meret Kaderli*
7 ch g Rock Of Gibraltar(IRE) Zariziyna (IRE) (Dalakhani (IRE))
592a^{6}

Zyzzyva (FR) *Gavin Hernon* a73 94
4 b h Siyouni(FR) Zanatiya (FR) (Sinndar (IRE))
1127a^{4}

Zzoro (IRE) *Amanda Perrett* a84 86
6 br g Manduro(GER) Krynica (USA) (Danzig (USA))
2486^{4} 3726^{6} *4792*^{2} 5594^{2} 6217^{4} *6596*^{4} **(7166)** 7727^{2} 8725^{11} *9055*^{12}

Season Statistics Trainers - GB Flat 2019 (Jan 1-Dec 31)

	NAME	WINS–RUNS	%	2ND	3RD	WNR-RNRS	WIN PRIZE	TOTAL PRIZE	£1 STAKE
1	**John Gosden**	192-714	27%	141	100	126-223	£6,282,134	£8,000,228	-96.35
2	**A P O'Brien**	24-220	11%	31	20	21-101	£4,391,270	£7,680,548	-63.48
3	**Mark Johnston**	249-1459	17%	204	193	131-273	£3,174,443	£5,399,661	-346.92
4	**Richard Hannon**	153-1286	12%	159	150	96-273	£2,732,963	£4,012,259	-300.75
5	**Andrew Balding**	126-852	15%	117	102	91-191	£2,343,511	£3,601,158	-158.58
6	**Sir Michael Stoute**	84-395	21%	63	56	55-119	£1,815,793	£3,480,587	-36.05
7	**William Haggas**	142-646	22%	106	78	97-183	£1,635,918	£3,125,481	-116.59
8	**Roger Varian**	116-602	19%	104	89	86-170	£1,796,114	£2,662,806	-121.08
9	**Richard Fahey**	178-1514	12%	173	188	121-276	£1,391,189	£2,545,525	-200.33
10	**David O'Meara**	130-952	14%	123	117	72-144	£1,555,135	£2,421,589	-90.28
11	**Charlie Appleby**	71-275	26%	55	36	50-110	£1,688,273	£2,191,332	-80.84
12	**Charles Hills**	68-480	14%	53	59	48-114	£1,223,116	£1,623,004	-92.47
13	**Tim Easterby**	126-1244	10%	117	124	79-178	£856,773	£1,392,890	-155.17
14	**Clive Cox**	71-567	13%	74	81	50-130	£733,573	£1,271,686	-163.77
15	**Archie Watson**	133-776	17%	117	100	76-157	£668,302	£1,270,046	-208.49
16	**Ralph Beckett**	82-517	16%	58	53	52-133	£763,307	£1,242,801	-26.65
17	**Saeed bin Suroor**	81-346	23%	58	52	57-116	£725,045	£1,193,630	-20.57
18	**Kevin Ryan**	65-531	12%	56	56	43-130	£654,228	£1,166,192	-117.39
19	**Tom Dascombe**	67-457	15%	66	50	45-81	£712,086	£1,145,875	-57.88
20	**K R Burke**	68-583	12%	71	82	50-134	£565,303	£1,105,044	-107.58
21	**Michael Appleby**	99-922	11%	90	94	55-147	£652,842	£1,102,798	-295.85
22	**Roger Charlton**	54-324	17%	40	40	36-99	£734,555	£1,017,588	-21.57
23	**Stuart Williams**	74-577	13%	83	67	43-80	£577,463	£979,366	-18.65
24	**David Simcock**	52-423	12%	48	64	37-110	£615,986	£931,730	-131.30
25	**James Tate**	72-306	24%	44	36	42-75	£659,928	£926,098	-12.88
26	**Keith Dalgleish**	80-691	12%	74	82	46-105	£523,042	£889,457	-173.77
27	**Michael Dods**	44-462	10%	46	53	27-91	£455,710	£807,315	-101.75
28	**Ian Williams**	53-528	10%	52	42	34-94	£452,979	£791,108	-118.31
29	**Hugo Palmer**	53-383	14%	49	53	33-99	£445,491	£785,092	-105.83
30	**Ed Walker**	56-416	13%	61	36	37-87	£497,678	£728,509	-65.67
31	**Martyn Meade**	17-126	13%	19	18	13-40	£448,408	£718,623	+26.13
32	**Mick Channon**	65-636	10%	77	77	43-108	£351,644	£705,711	-267.58
33	**John Quinn**	36-370	10%	33	42	25-72	£333,597	£663,650	-109.76
34	**Simon Crisford**	52-263	20%	45	47	38-86	£450,826	£653,583	-2.23
35	**Alan King**	33-276	12%	29	36	23-75	£408,913	£648,767	+40.73
36	**James Fanshawe**	53-327	16%	46	51	34-77	£324,349	£621,966	-73.00
37	**Roger Fell**	58-558	10%	53	56	36-69	£354,864	£621,132	-128.22
38	**G M Lyons**	2-10	20%	0	1	2-10	£602,782	£611,414	+17.00
39	**Eve J'son Houghton**	44-382	12%	40	43	29-78	£331,195	£609,005	-50.24
40	**Tony Carroll**	74-669	11%	72	68	44-110	£385,656	£607,721	-100.10
41	**David Elsworth**	14-156	9%	12	18	11-32	£363,020	£593,858	-6.00
42	**David Evans**	67-599	11%	54	64	35-85	£326,038	£547,017	-87.23
43	**F-H Graffard**	1-3	33%	1	0	1-3	£283,550	£520,050	+18.00
44	**Richard Hughes**	55-450	12%	55	58	44-95	£284,256	£519,020	-44.96
45	**Hughie Morrison**	29-304	10%	34	35	23-68	£299,755	£518,380	-151.91
46	**Mitsuru Hashida**	1-3	33%	0	1	1-1	£340,260	£496,587	+18.00
47	**Michael Bell**	47-355	13%	30	33	33-93	£273,552	£493,468	-25.47
48	**Charlie Fellowes**	34-259	13%	35	30	23-61	£324,362	£490,650	-5.13
49	**Robert Cowell**	34-354	10%	43	42	24-76	£248,707	£488,222	-117.19

Season Statistics Jockeys - GB Flat 2019 (Jan 1-Dec 31)

	NAME	WINS–RUNS	%	2ND	3RD	4TH	WIN PRIZE	TOTAL PRIZE	£1 STAKE
1	**Oisin Murphy**	220-1106	20%	197	150	125	£2,801,466	£4,377,361	-77.77
2	**Daniel Tudhope**	159-792	20%	121	100	82	£1,802,923	£2,891,446	-7.75
3	**Ben Curtis**	137-916	15%	105	112	98	£1,011,096	£1,559,342	-30.45
4	**Tom Marquand**	136-1054	13%	127	132	109	£1,063,097	£1,764,905	+14.08
5	**Joe Fanning**	135-810	17%	109	92	94	£1,454,306	£1,983,622	-57.55
6	**P J McDonald**	132-901	15%	132	106	106	£1,094,210	£1,917,924	-100.34
7	**Jim Crowley**	126-575	22%	57	69	56	£2,312,090	£3,251,864	-15.46
8	**Adam Kirby**	126-795	16%	118	115	84	£1,211,609	£2,051,017	-101.85
9	**Hollie Doyle**	116-819	14%	113	87	109	£693,462	£1,201,634	-48.67
10	**David Probert**	112-1209	9%	133	138	155	£631,187	£1,194,353	-273.75
11	**Richard Kingscote**	106-738	14%	101	106	81	£987,074	£1,662,424	-130.67
12	**James Doyle**	105-561	19%	82	74	69	£2,300,898	£4,223,501	-84.32
13	**Luke Morris**	105-1265	8%	125	140	148	£549,753	£1,111,972	-612.06
14	**Silvestre De Sousa**	103-620	17%	67	60	70	£1,927,733	£3,144,444	-100.42
15	**Jason Watson**	97-744	13%	99	72	100	£1,237,908	£1,781,477	-31.98
16	**Robert Havlin**	91-640	14%	86	82	76	£733,556	£1,274,131	-287.68
17	**Franny Norton**	91-700	13%	101	95	88	£882,000	£1,612,722	-250.96
18	**Jack Mitchell**	89-521	17%	83	56	58	£470,303	£724,055	-98.52
19	**Jason Hart**	88-701	13%	72	78	68	£577,583	£951,436	-94.70
20	**Harry Bentley**	81-612	13%	71	70	75	£865,404	£1,484,957	-129.10
21	**David Egan**	77-688	11%	100	81	82	£634,806	£1,206,252	-190.33
22	**Andrea Atzeni**	76-480	16%	64	63	52	£1,490,329	£2,388,730	-16.64
23	**David Allan**	76-618	12%	84	71	67	£585,388	£927,787	-174.85
24	**Ryan Moore**	71-443	16%	81	56	56	£2,689,904	£5,179,345	-157.19
25	**Paul Hanagan**	71-567	13%	72	70	71	£576,460	£1,009,028	-78.58
26	**Kieran O'Neill**	71-764	9%	67	72	68	£388,748	£656,896	-167.63
27	**Frankie Dettori**	66-255	26%	45	33	21	£5,951,232	£7,365,868	-26.20
28	**Sean Levey**	66-485	14%	83	53	52	£1,369,950	£1,860,693	-27.51
29	**Graham Lee**	65-620	10%	65	72	49	£359,758	£620,700	-233.90
30	**Rossa Ryan**	65-621	10%	64	68	67	£396,155	£665,935	-179.36
31	**Hector Crouch**	63-509	12%	44	60	60	£338,587	£537,120	-128.64
32	**Cieren Fallon**	62-479	13%	60	61	49	£430,510	£892,795	-97.78
33	**Shane Kelly**	58-704	8%	73	75	75	£308,922	£577,460	-239.50
34	**Paul Mulrennan**	57-668	9%	72	79	62	£357,170	£765,590	-245.04
35	**Sean Davis**	56-640	9%	55	68	62	£301,069	£556,321	-214.91
36	**Rob Hornby**	55-619	9%	53	76	60	£456,292	£752,519	-78.99
37	**Clifford Lee**	53-387	14%	35	53	39	£297,911	£453,264	+22.93
38	**Dane O'Neill**	52-287	18%	48	31	39	£439,300	£648,442	-50.47
39	**Callum Shepherd**	52-577	9%	61	59	68	£298,508	£530,529	-209.51
40	**Jamie Spencer**	48-348	14%	40	43	36	£651,428	£1,387,430	-112.00
41	**Barry McHugh**	48-359	13%	31	36	33	£354,261	£546,003	+44.00
42	**Nicola Currie**	48-578	8%	47	48	43	£325,891	£550,638	-223.94
43	**Liam Keniry**	48-601	8%	58	49	46	£301,206	£508,419	-176.49
44	**Phil Dennis**	47-575	8%	56	45	60	£350,913	£573,663	-24.38
45	**Pat Cosgrave**	45-309	15%	39	34	41	£246,323	£407,765	-69.45
46	**Charles Bishop**	45-542	8%	52	55	57	£275,607	£613,822	-171.54
47	**Andrew Mullen**	45-655	7%	60	67	58	£190,419	£411,367	-266.21
48	**Alistair Rawlinson**	44-406	11%	42	44	47	£320,470	£536,566	-109.18
49	**Martin Dwyer**	44-438	10%	36	42	52	£312,392	£515,611	-55.55

Season Statistics Owners - GB Flat 2019 (Jan 1-Dec 31)

	NAME	WINS–RUNS	%	2ND	3RD	4TH	WIN PRIZE	TOTAL PRIZE
1	Hamdan Al Maktoum	151-638	24%	87	79	73	£2,551,693	£3,764,790
2	Smith/Magnier/Tabor	7-78	9%	15	13	9	£2,123,813	£3,688,569
3	K Abdullah	71-291	24%	41	39	35	£2,924,230	£3,407,944
4	Godolphin	157-654	24%	117	94	66	£2,385,395	£3,369,818
5	King Power Racing Co Ltd	59-375	16%	39	40	44	£1,536,543	£2,362,352
6	Magnier/Tabor/Smith	8-47	17%	4	2	5	£1,203,169	£1,798,586
7	Shk H bin M Al Maktoum	58-359	16%	57	47	42	£852,905	£1,610,654
8	Shk M Obaid Al Maktoum	41-212	19%	32	40	26	£1,012,840	£1,471,301
9	Cheveley Park Stud	50-328	15%	51	45	50	£663,632	£1,358,525
10	Sir Evelyn De Rothschild	5-21	24%	4	2	0	£533,506	£1,049,628
11	B E Nielsen	10-33	30%	3	3	1	£911,168	£1,022,877
12	Tabor/Smith/Magnier	4-60	7%	8	4	9	£408,862	£1,006,354
13	Clipper Logistics	50-247	20%	30	40	25	£509,669	£883,724
14	Lord Lloyd-Webber	5-15	33%	1	3	0	£673,595	£819,354
15	Ali Abdulla Saeed	3-7	43%	2	1	0	£650,375	£764,579
16	Sheikh Ahmed Al Maktoum	36-162	22%	37	32	22	£280,154	£753,370
17	A E Oppenheimer	13-49	27%	12	7	3	£526,810	£633,145
18	Saeed Manana	51-229	22%	37	26	29	£464,773	£629,929
19	David Spratt	2-3	67%	0	0	0	£603,429	£603,429
20	Flaxman/Magnier/Tabor/Smith	2-6	33%	1	0	1	£348,058	£598,077
21	Shk J Dalmook Al Maktoum	38-151	25%	22	23	15	£409,627	£561,035
22	Geoff & Sandra Turnbull	16-136	12%	19	17	12	£418,315	£559,347
23	The Queen	29-147	20%	24	19	24	£393,261	£542,543
24	Toji Morita	1-3	33%	0	1	0	£340,260	£496,587
25	Qatar Racing Limited	27-117	23%	24	13	9	£356,891	£486,688
26	HRH Princess Haya Of Jordan	12-69	17%	17	9	6	£225,899	£455,618
27	Dr Marwan Koukash	31-309	10%	35	31	28	£218,210	£449,939
28	Paul & Clare Rooney	24-163	15%	19	24	22	£240,277	£433,379
29	Mrs Fitri Hay	21-161	13%	20	16	23	£292,780	£407,111
30	BenhamWhitfordQuinnQuinn	2-39	5%	2	3	5	£238,267	£396,593
31	John Dance	17-135	13%	29	12	14	£114,571	£395,712
32	Phoenix T'bred Limited 1	1-6	17%	2	0	0	£283,550	£394,778
33	Helena Springfield Ltd	7-38	18%	5	2	4	£340,918	£388,165
34	George Strawbridge	17-94	18%	20	16	11	£203,481	£378,041
35	Weldspec Glasgow Limited	20-135	15%	17	21	10	£238,617	£370,108
36	Jaber Abdullah	15-64	23%	7	8	7	£281,774	£363,289
37	Tony Bloom	6-23	26%	2	2	0	£315,456	£359,850
38	HH Sheikha Al Jalila Racing	16-45	36%	7	8	3	£263,835	£358,642
39	Withernsea T'bred Limited	5-49	10%	3	9	6	£267,991	£357,680
40	Smith/Magnier/Tabor/Flaxman	2-9	22%	0	1	1	£300,447	£350,576
41	Saeed Suhail	9-65	14%	12	8	8	£129,382	£342,595
42	Paul Dean	5-7	71%	1	0	0	£180,111	£330,611
43	Lady Bamford	8-57	14%	11	10	6	£61,206	£318,645
44	David W Armstrong	22-131	17%	22	17	18	£174,573	£308,615
45	T W Morley	18-141	13%	22	13	10	£168,463	£305,846
46	Abdulla Al Mansoori	16-118	14%	13	13	20	£231,687	£292,648
47	Alexander Tamagni	1-1	100%	0	0	0	£283,550	£283,550
48	Mohamed Obaida	5-24	21%	5	4	3	£124,892	£277,993
49	The Cool Silk Partnership	16-101	16%	10	14	12	£186,105	£270,215

Season Statistics Sires - GB & Ire 2019 (Jan 1-Dec 31)

	HORSE	WNRS-RNRS	WINS-RUNS	STAKES	WNRS-RNRS	EARNINGS
1	**Galileo**	82-191	122-755	31	31-75	£11,945,529
2	**Sea The Stars**	68-143	99-587	7	7-34	£4,164,792
3	**Shamardal**	67-148	102-706	11	11-29	£3,512,973
4	**Frankel**	52-110	86-440	9	9-36	£3,495,105
5	**Dubawi**	80-177	127-650	12	12-43	£3,493,868
6	**Dark Angel**	109-270	167-1493	7	7-46	£3,164,568
7	**Kodiac**	135-334	188-1919	4	4-50	£2,736,385
8	**Invincible Spirit**	82-173	137-962	7	7-31	£2,384,010
9	**Nathaniel**	49-128	73-608	2	2-18	£2,298,583
10	**Lope De Vega**	69-186	105-852	10	10-24	£1,984,672
11	**Camelot**	59-132	81-607	7	7-20	£1,862,563
12	**Zoffany**	73-194	110-966	4	4-23	£1,828,010
13	**Dandy Man**	90-220	155-1404	4	4-18	£1,779,634
14	**No Nay Never**	43-101	57-439	8	8-31	£1,705,356
15	**Bated Breath**	65-164	90-805	6	6-18	£1,699,041
16	**Pivotal**	42-87	70-488	3	3-16	£1,594,592
17	**Australia**	36-107	65-439	8	8-21	£1,592,407
18	**Oasis Dream**	56-149	82-758	3	3-21	£1,517,426
19	**Kingman**	64-122	80-414	11	11-33	£1,514,655
20	**Acclamation**	61-160	93-1056	2	2-19	£1,485,312
21	**Showcasing**	48-163	65-779	3	3-16	£1,481,652
22	**Farhh**	21-36	32-154	5	5-10	£1,471,698
23	**Dansili**	42-115	69-523	4	4-16	£1,443,004
24	**Teofilo**	35-137	55-614	3	3-18	£1,436,829
25	**Dream Ahead**	35-99	58-513	5	5-11	£1,351,702
26	**Footstepsinthesand**	49-123	74-681	2	2-17	£1,318,225
27	**Iffraaj**	51-169	80-851	3	3-20	£1,299,831
28	**Champs Elysees**	49-110	74-623	4	4-12	£1,290,748
29	**Exceed And Excel**	64-161	97-973	3	3-11	£1,215,584
30	**Mastercraftsman**	49-140	80-691	3	3-21	£1,205,689
31	**Dawn Approach**	33-112	47-467	2	2-12	£1,089,757
32	**New Approach**	42-120	68-493	5	5-16	£1,076,294
33	**Dutch Art**	59-107	88-667	4	4-19	£1,026,603
34	**Kyllachy**	43-120	67-799	2	2-4	£980,459
35	**Equiano**	37-122	64-730	3	3-7	£902,703
36	**Zebedee**	50-152	73-986	1	1-7	£897,773
37	**Medicean**	16-46	27-276	0	0-3	£880,323
38	**Mayson**	43-110	71-658	0	0-8	£855,419
39	**Raven's Pass**	26-80	44-400	2	2-11	£842,160
40	**Canford Cliffs**	36-104	59-600	1	1-7	£819,467
41	**Cape Cross**	42-94	65-536	2	2-10	£818,653
42	**War Front**	27-66	40-296	3	3-20	£809,185
43	**Camacho**	44-165	64-940	0	0-10	£803,014
44	**Holy Roman Emperor**	31-94	48-556	4	4-12	£793,873
45	**Sir Prancealot**	24-74	41-505	2	2-6	£777,634
46	**Lethal Force**	36-100	58-553	1	1-7	£756,725
47	**Tamayuz**	22-71	30-334	1	1-8	£755,929
48	**Arcano**	36-78	59-563	2	2-8	£753,547
49	**Fast Company**	37-98	51-562	1	1-5	£744,294

Raceform Ratings - Flat 2019

Two-Year-Olds

122	**Pinatubo**	Charlie Appleby
119	**Mums Tipple**	Richard Hannon
118	**Earthlight**	A Fabre
117	**Arizona**	A P O'Brien
117	**Golden Horde**	Clive Cox
117	**Wichita**	A P O'Brien
116	**Millisle**	Mrs John Harrington
115	**Quadrilateral**	Roger Charlton
115	**Threat**	Richard Hannon
114	**Powerful Breeze**	Hugo Palmer
113	**Military March**	Saeed bin Suroor
113	**Raffle Prize**	Mark Johnston
112	**A'Ali**	Simon Crisford
112	**Al Suhail**	Charlie Appleby
112	**Royal Dornoch**	A P O'Brien
112	**Summer Sands**	Richard Fahey

All-Weather

121	**Matterhorn**	Mark Johnston
119	**Kachy**	Tom Dascombe
119	**Wissahickon**	John Gosden
118	**Invincible Army**	James Tate
117	**Kameko**	Andrew Balding
117	**Oh This Is Us**	Richard Hannon
117	**Young Rascal**	William Haggas
116	**Mootasadir**	Hugo Palmer
115	**Cardsharp**	Mark Johnston
115	**First In Line**	John Gosden
115	**Weekender**	John Gosden
114	**Bin Battuta**	Saeed bin Suroor
114	**Judicial**	Julie Camacho
114	**Royal Line**	John Gosden
114	**War Glory**	Richard Hannon
113	**Alrajaa**	John Gosden
113	**Desert Fire**	Saeed bin Suroor
113	**Dubai Warrior**	John Gosden
113	**Indyco**	H-A Pantall
113	**Pablo Escobarr**	William Haggas
113	**Red Galileo**	Saeed bin Suroor
113	**Straight Right**	Andrew Balding

Three-Year-Olds

125	**Japan**	A P O'Brien
125	**Ten Sovereigns**	A P O'Brien
122	**King Of Change**	Richard Hannon
121	**Advertise**	Martyn Meade
121	**Hello Youmzain**	Kevin Ryan
121	**King Of Comedy**	John Gosden
121	**Magna Grecia**	A P O'Brien
121	**Too Darn Hot**	John Gosden
119	**Anthony Van Dyck**	A P O'Brien
119	**Circus Maximus**	A P O'Brien
119	**Khaadem**	Charles Hills
119	**Logician**	John Gosden
118	**Calyx**	John Gosden
117	**Fox Tal**	Andrew Balding
117	**Madhmoon**	Kevin Prendergast
117	**Roseman**	Roger Varian
117	**Sir Dragonet**	A P O'Brien
117	**Telecaster**	Hughie Morrison
117	**Watch Me**	F-H Graffard

Older Horses

123	**Magical**	A P O'Brien
122	**Elarqam**	Mark Johnston
122	**Kew Gardens**	A P O'Brien
121	**Dee Ex Bee**	Mark Johnston
121	**Regal Reality**	Sir Michael Stoute
120	**The Revenant**	F-H Graffard
119	**Cross Counter**	Charlie Appleby
119	**Master Of Reality**	J P O'Brien
118	**Enbihaar**	John Gosden
118	**Invincible Army**	James Tate
117	**Aspetar**	Roger Charlton
117	**Communique**	Mark Johnston
117	**Knight To Behold**	Harry Dunlop
117	**Laurens**	K R Burke
117	**Zaaki**	Sir Michael Stoute
116	**Billesdon Brook**	Richard Hannon
116	**Cardsharp**	Mark Johnston
116	**Danceteria**	Davuid Menuisier
116	**First Eleven**	John Gosden
116	**Hey Gaman**	James Tate
116	**Lah Ti Dar**	John Gosden
116	**Romanised**	K J Condon

Raceform Flat Median Times 2019

Some distances have been omitted where insufficient data exists to establish a reliable median time

ASCOT

- **5f** 1m 0.7s
- **6f** 1m 13.7s
- **7f** 1m 27.5s
- **7f 213y (Rnd)** 1m 40.6s
- **1m (Str)** 1m 41.4s
- **1m 1f 212y** 2m 7.7s
- **1m 3f 211y** 2m 32.6s
- **1m 6f 34y** 3m 4.3s
- **1m 7f 209y** 3m 33.3s
- **2m 3f 210y** 4m 22.0s
- **2m 5f 143y** 4m 43.6s

AYR

- **5f** 1m
- **5f 110y** 1m 6.5s
- **6f** 1m 13.1s
- **7f 50y** 1m 32.5s
- **1m** 1m 42.8s
- **1m 1f 20y** 2m 0.2s
- **1m 2f** 2m 12.4s
- **1m 5f 26y** 2m 54.4s
- **1m 7f** 3m 27.0s
- **2m 1f 105y** 4m 1.5s

BATH

- **5f 10y** 1m 2.0s
- **5f 160y** 1m 11.1s
- **1m** 1m 41.7s
- **1m 2f 37y** 2m 11.1s
- **1m 3f 137y** 2m 30.8s
- **1m 5f 11y** 2m 52.8s
- **1m 6f** 3m 6.1s
- **2m 1f 24y** 3m 51.4s

BEVERLEY

- **5f** 1m 2.9s
- **7f 96y** 1m 32.6s
- **1m 100y** 1m 46.4s
- **1m 1f 207y** 2m 5.7s
- **1m 4f 23y** 2m 38.8s
- **2m 32y** 3m 37.9s

BRIGHTON

- **5f 60y** 1m 3.0s
- **5f 215y** 1m 11.1s
- **6f 210y** 1m 23.8s
- **7f 211y** 1m 36.9s
- **1m 1f 207y** 2m 5.0s
- **1m 3f 198y** 2m 36.0s

CARLISLE

- **5f** 1m 2.1s
- **5f 193y** 1m 14.6s
- **6f 195y** 1m 28.0s
- **7f 173y** 1m 40.0s
- **1m 1f** 1m 59.0s
- **1m 3f 39y** 2m 29.7s
- **1m 6f 32y** 3m 11.6s
- **2m 1f 47y** 3m 54.3s

CATTERICK

- **5f** 1m 0.5s
- **5f 212y** 1m 13.6s
- **7f 6y** 1m 27.4s
- **1m 4f 13y** 2m 40.6s
- **1m 5f 192y** 3m 7.6s
- **1m 7f 189y** 3m 36.0s

CHELMSFORD (AW)

- **5f** 1m 0.2s
- **6f** 1m 13.7s
- **7f** 1m 27.2s
- **1m** 1m 39.9s
- **1m 2f** 2m 8.6s
- **1m 5f 66y** 2m 53.6s
- **1m 6f** 3m 3.2s
- **2m** 3m 30.0s

CHEPSTOW

- **5f 16y** 59.4s
- **6f 16y** 1m 11.5s
- **7f 16y** 1m 23.9s
- **1m 14y** 1m 36.0s
- **1m 2f** 2m 12.8s
- **1m 4f** 2m 40.3s
- **2m** 3m 42.1s
- **2m 2f** 4m 9.9s

CHESTER

- **5f 15y** 1m 2.1s
- **5f 110y** 1m 9.0s
- **6f 17y** 1m 15.5s
- **7f 1y** 1m 27.5s
- **7f 127y** 1m 35.7s
- **1m 2f 70y** 2m 14.3s
- **1m 3f 75y** 2m 27.4s
- **1m 4f 63y** 2m 42.2s
- **1m 5f 84y** 2m 56.6s
- **1m 6f 87y** 3m 9.8s
- **1m 7f 196y** 3m 31.9s
- **2m 2f 140y** 4m 4.6s

DONCASTER

- **5f 3y** 59.6s
- **5f 143y** 1m 8.1s
- **6f 2y** 1m 12.7s
- **6f 111y** 1m 19.6s
- **7f 6y** 1m 26.4s
- **7f 213y (Rnd)** 1m 40.8s
- **1m (Str)** 1m 40.2s
- **1m 2f 43y** 2m 12.3s
- **1m 3f 197y** 2m 36.6s
- **1m 6f 115y** 3m 11.6s
- **2m 109y** 3m 40.4s
- **2m 1f 197y** 3m 55.0s

EPSOM

- **5f** 55.3s
- **6f 3y** 1m 9.9s
- **7f 3y** 1m 23.4s
- **1m 113y** 1m 46.4s
- **1m 2f 17y** 2m 10.0s
- **1m 4f 6y** 2m 40.8s

FFOS LAS

- **5f** 59.0s
- **6f** 1m 10.9s
- **7f 80y** 1m 33.1s
- **1m** 1m 42.9s
- **1m 2f** 2m 12.7s
- **1m 3f 209y** 2m 40.2s
- **1m 6f** 3m 8.6s
- **2m** 3m 36.7s

GOODWOOD

- **5f** 58.1s
- **6f** 1m 12.1s
- **7f** 1m 26.7s
- **1m** 1m 39.2s
- **1m 1f 11y** 1m 57.4s
- **1m 1f 197y** 2m 8.9s
- **1m 3f 44y** 2m 28.3s
- **1m 3f 218y** 2m 39.6s
- **1m 6f** 3m 3.7s
- **2m** 3m 30.9s
- **2m 4f 134y** 4m 31.8s

HAMILTON

- **5f 7y** 1m 0.4s
- **6f 6y** 1m 12.7s
- **1m 68y** 1m 48.4s
- **1m 1f 35y** 1m 59.0s
- **1m 3f 15y** 2m 25.5s
- **1m 4f 15y** 2m 38.6s
- **1m 5f 16y** 2m 54.7s

HAYDOCK

- **5f** 1m 0.4s
- **5f (Inner)** 1m 0.4s
- **6f** 1m 13.9s
- **6f (Inner)** 1m 13.9s
- **6f 212y (Inner)** 1m 29.3s
- **7f 37y** 1m 31.4s
- **7f 212y (Inner)** 1m 42.7s
- **1m 37y** 1m 44.9s
- **1m 2f 42y (Inner)** 2m 10.8s
- **1m 2f 100y** 2m 16.6s
- **1m 3f 140y (Inner)** 2m 33.3s
- **1m 3f 175y** 2m 33.3s
- **1m 6f** 3m 4.6s
- **1m 6f (Inner)** 3m 4.6s
- **2m 45y** 3m 36.7s
- **2m 45y (Inner)** 3m 36.7s

KEMPTON (AW)

- **5f** 1m 0.5s
- **6f** 1m 13.1s
- **7f** 1m 26.0s
- **1m** 1m 39.8s
- **1m 1f 219y** 2m 8.0s
- **1m 2f 219y** 2m 21.0s
- **1m 3f 219y** 2m 34.5s
- **1m 7f 218y** 3m 30.1s

LEICESTER

- **5f** 1m 1.8s
- **6f** 1m 12.1s
- **7f** 1m 25.7s
- **1m 53y** 1m 46.3s
- **1m 2f** 2m 9.2s
- **1m 3f 179y** 2m 35.0s

LINGFIELD

- **4f 217y** 58.7s
- **6f** 1m 11.5s
- **7f** 1m 24.3s
- **7f 135y** 1m 31.7s
- **1m 1f** 1m 56.9s
- **1m 2f** 2m 12.2s
- **1m 3f 133y** 2m 34.0s
- **1m 6f** 3m 11.2s
- **2m 68y** 3m 36.0s

LINGFIELD (AW)

- **5f 6y** 58.8s
- **6f 1y** 1m 11.9s
- **7f 1y** 1m 24.8s
- **1m 1y** 1m 38.2s
- **1m 2f** 2m 6.6s
- **1m 4f** 2m 33.0s
- **1m 5f** 2m 46.0s
- **1m 7f 169y** 3m 25.7s

MUSSELBURGH

- **5f 1y** 59.7s
- **7f 33y** 1m 29.0s
- **1m 2y** 1m 40.0s
- **1m 208y** 1m 53.1s
- **1m 4f 104y** 2m 44.5s
- **1m 5f** 2m 51.7s
- **1m 5f 216y** 3m 3.9s
- **1m 7f 217y** 3m 31.5s

NEWBURY

- **5f 34y** 1m 1.5s
- **6f** 1m 13.2s
- **6f 110y** 1m 20.1s
- **7f (Str)** 1m 27.0s
- **1m (Str)** 1m 39.9s
- **1m (Rnd)** 1m 40.5s
- **1m 1f** 1m 55.7s
- **1m 2f** 2m 9.7s
- **1m 3f** 2m 23.2s
- **1m 4f** 2m 38.0s
- **1m 5f 61y** 2m 54.4s
- **2m** 3m 39.4s
- **2m 110y** 3m 46.3s
- **2m 2f** 4m 6.8s

NEWCASTLE (AW)

- **5f** 59.5s
- **6f** 1m 12.5s
- **7f 14y** 1m 26.2s
- **1m 5y** 1m 38.6s
- **1m 2f 42y** 2m 10.4s
- **1m 4f 98y** 2m 41.1s
- **2m 56y** 3m 35.0s

NEWMARKET

- **5f (Row)** 59.1s
- **6f (Row)** 1m 11.9s
- **7f (Row)** 1m 25.4s
- **1m (Row)** 1m 38.4s
- **1m 1f (Row)** 1m 51.1s
- **1m 2f (Row)** 2m 5.4s
- **1m 4f (Row)** 2m 32.5s
- **1m 6f (Row)** 2m 57.1s
- **2m (Row)** 3m 29.3s
- **2m 2f (Row)** 3m 55.5s

NEWMARKET (JULY)

- **5f (July)** 58.7s
- **6f (July)** 1m 12.1s
- **7f (July)** 1m 25.7s
- **1m (July)** 1m 40.0s
- **1m 2f (July)** 2m 7.1s
- **1m 4f (July)** 2m 33.9s
- **1m 5f (July)** 2m 45.9s
- **1m 6f (July)** 2m 59.9s
- **2m (July)** 3m 28.4s

NOTTINGHAM

- **5f 8y** 1m 0.2s
- **5f 8y (Inner)** 1m 0.2s
- **6f 18y** 1m 13.8s
- **1m 75y** 1m 46.7s
- **1m 75y (Inner)** 1m 46.7s
- **1m 2f 50y** 2m 13.4s
- **1m 2f 50y (Inner)** 2m 13.4s
- **1m 6f** 3m 6.4s
- **1m 6f (Inner)** 3m 6.4s
- **2m** 3m 34.5s
- **2m** 3m 34.5s

PONTEFRACT

- **5f 3y** 1m 3.9s
- **6f** 1m 17.1s
- **1m 6y** 1m 45.9s
- **1m 2f 5y** 2m 15.0s
- **1m 4f 5y** 2m 41.1s
- **2m 1f 27y** 3m 49.2s
- **2m 2f 2y** 4m 7.7s
- **2m 5f 139y** 4m 58.0s

REDCAR

- **5f** 58.5s
- **5f 217y** 1m 11.8s
- **7f** 1m 25.4s
- **7f 219y** 1m 36.6s
- **1m 1f** 1m 54.5s
- **1m 2f 1y** 2m 6.9s
- **1m 5f 218y** 3m 7.0s
- **1m 7f 217y** 3m 33.7s

RIPON

- **5f** 59.4s
- **6f** 1m 12.5s
- **1m** 1m 41.0s
- **1m 1f** 1m 54.7s
- **1m 1f 170y** 2m 4.6s
- **1m 2f 190y** 2m 19.0s
- **1m 4f 10y** 2m 36.3s
- **1m 6f** 3m 2.4s
- **2m** 3m 32.4s

SALISBURY

- **5f** 1m 0.5s
- **6f** 1m 14.5s
- **6f 213y** 1m 28.7s
- **1m** 1m 43.5s
- **1m 1f 201y** 2m 10.5s
- **1m 4f 5y** 2m 37.6s
- **1m 6f 44y** 3m 6.6s

SANDOWN

- **5f 10y** 1m 1.3s
- **7f** 1m 29.3s
- **1m** 1m 43.3s
- **1m 1f** 1m 56.3s
- **1m 1f 209y** 2m 10.2s
- **1m 6f** 3m 6.0s
- **2m 50y** 3m 37.9s

SOUTHWELL (AW)

- **4f 214y** 59.7s
- **6f 16y** 1m 16.5s
- **7f 14y** 1m 30.3s
- **1m 13y** 1m 43.7s
- **1m 3f 23y** 2m 28.0s
- **1m 4f 14y** 2m 41.0s
- **1m 6f 21y** 3m 8.3s
- **2m 102y** 3m 45.5s
- **2m 2f 98y** 4m 11.5s

THIRSK

- **5f** 59.4s
- **6f** 1m 12.8s
- **7f** 1m 27.6s
- **7f 218y** 1m 41.7s
- **1m 4f 8y** 2m 40.0s
- **2m 13y** 3m 33.6s

WETHERBY

- **5f 110y** 1m 5.8s
- **7f** 1m 27.2s
- **1m** 1m 41.6s
- **1m 2f** 2m 9.3s
- **1m 6f** 3m 7.0s
- **2m** 3m 33.7s

WINDSOR

- **5f 21y** 1m 0.1s
- **6f 12y** 1m 12.1s
- **1m 31y** 1m 44.5s
- **1m 2f** 2m 9.0s
- **1m 3f 99y** 2m 29.7s

WOLVERHAMPTON (AW)

- **5f 21y** 1m 1.9s
- **6f 20y** 1m 14.5s
- **7f 36y** 1m 28.8s
- **1m 142y** 1m 50.1s
- **1m 1f 104y** 2m 0.8s
- **1m 4f 51y** 2m 40.8s
- **1m 5f 219y** 3m 1.0s
- **2m 120y** 3m 39.3s

YARMOUTH

- **5f 42y** 1m 1.9s
- **6f 3y** 1m 12.6s
- **7f 3y** 1m 25.1s
- **1m 3y** 1m 38.2s
- **1m 1f 21y** 1m 54.5s
- **1m 2f 23y** 2m 8.8s
- **1m 3f 104y** 2m 27.8s
- **1m 6f 17y** 3m 4.7s

YORK

- **5f** 58.2s
- **5f 89y** 1m 3.6s
- **6f** 1m 11.6s
- **7f** 1m 24.6s
- **7f 192y** 1m 37.5s
- **1m 177y** 1m 50.4s
- **1m 2f 56y** 2m 10.3s
- **1m 3f 188y** 2m 33.2s
- **1m 5f 188y** 3m 0.2s
- **2m 56y** 3m 33.9s

Raceform Flat Record Times

ASCOT

Distance	Time	Age	Weight	Going	Horse	Date
5f	58.80	2	9-1	Good To Firm	No Nay Never	Jun 20 2013
5f	57.44	6	9-1	Good To Firm	Miss Andretti	Jun 19 2007
6f	1m 12.39	2	9-1	Good To Firm	Rajasinghe	Jun 20 2017
6f	1m 11.05	3	9-1	Good To Firm	Blue Point	May 3 2017
7f	1m 25.73	2	9-3	Good	Pinatubo	Jun 22 2019
7f	1m 24.28	4	8-11	Good To Firm	Galician	Jly 27 2013
7f 213y	1m 39.55	2	8-12	Good	Joshua Tree	Sep 26 2009
7f 213y	1m 35.89	3	9-0	Good To Firm	Alpha Centauri	Jun 22 2018
1m	1m 36.60	4	9-0	Good To Firm	Ribchester	Jun 20 2017
1m 1f 212y	2m 1.90	5	8-11	Good To Firm	The Fugue	Jun 18 2014
1m 3f 211y	2m 24.60	4	9-7	Good To Firm	Novellist	Jly 27 2013
1m 7f 209y	3m 24.12	4	8-12	Good To Firm	Mizzou	Apr 29 2015
2m 3f 210y	4m 16.92	6	9-2	Good To Firm	Rite of Passage	Jun 17 2010
2m 5f 143y	4m 45.24	9	9-2	Good To Firm	Pallasator	Jun 23 2018

AYR

Distance	Time	Age	Weight	Going	Horse	Date
5f	56.98	2	8-11	Good	Boogie Street	Sep 18 2003
5f	55.68	3	8-11	Good To Firm	Look Busy	Jun 21 2008
6f	1m 9.73	2	7-10	Firm	Sir Bert	Sep 17 1969
6f	1m 8.37	5	8-6	Good To Firm	Maison Dieu	Jun 21 2008
7f 50y	1m 28.99	2	9-0	Good	Tafaahum	Sep 19 2003
7f 50y	1m 26.43	4	9-4	Good To Firm	Hajjam	May 22 2018
1m	1m 39.18	2	9-7	Good	Moonlightnavigator	Sep 18 2014
1m	1m 36.00	4	7-13	Firm	Sufi I	Sep 16 1959
1m 1f 20y	1m 50.30	4	9-3	Good	Retirement	Sep 19 2003
1m 2f	2m 4.02	4	9-9	Good To Firm	Endless Hall	Jly 17 2000
1m 5f 26y	2m 45.81	4	9-7	Good To Firm	Eden's Close	Sep 18 1993
1m 7f	3m 13.16	3	9-4	Good	Romany Rye	Sep 19 1991
2m 1f 105y	3m 45.20	4	6-13	Firm	Curry	Sep 16 1955

BATH

Distance	Time	Age	Weight	Going	Horse	Date
5f 10y	59.50	2	9-2	Firm	Amour Propre	Jly 24 2008
5f 10y	58.75	3	8-12	Firm	Enticing	May 1 2007
5f 160y	1m 8.70	2	8-12	Firm	Qalahari	Jly 24 2008
5f 160y	1m 8.10	6	9-0	Firm	Madraco	May 22 1989
1m	1m 37.41	3	9-5	Firm	I'vegotthepower	Jly 5 2017
1m 2f 37y	2m 5.80	3	9-0	Good To Firm	Connoisseur Bay	May 29 1998
1m 3f 137y	2m 25.74	3	9-0	Hard	Top The Charts	Sep 8 2005
1m 5f 11y	2m 47.20	4	10-0	Firm	Flown	Aug 13 1991
1m 6f	2m 58.97	4	9-10	Firm	Charlie D	Sep 15 2019
2m 1f 24y	3m 43.41	6	7-9	Firm	Yaheska	Jun 14 2003

BEVERLEY

Distance	Time	Age	Weight	Going	Horse	Date
5f	1m 0.89	2	8-12	Good To Firm	Langavat	Jun 8 2013
5f	59.77	5	9-3	Good To Firm	Judicial	Jun 20 2017
7f 96y	1m 31.10	2	9-7	Good To Firm	Champagne Prince	Aug 10 1995
7f 96y	1m 31.10	2	9-0	Firm	Majal	Jly 30 1991
7f 96y	1m 29.50	3	7-8	Firm	Who's Tef	Jly 30 1991
1m 100y	1m 43.30	2	9-0	Firm	Arden	Sep 24 1986
1m 100y	1m 42.20	3	8-4	Firm	Legal Case	Jun 14 1989
1m 1f 207y	2m 1.00	3	9-7	Good To Firm	Eastern Aria	Aug 29 2009
1m 4f 23y	2m 33.35	5	9-2	Good To Firm	Two Jabs	Apr 23 2015
2m 32y	3m 28.62	4	9-11	Good To Firm	Corpus Chorister	Jly 18 2017

BRIGHTON

Distance	Time	Age	Weight	Going	Horse	Date
5f 60y	1m 0.10	2	9-0	Firm	Bid for Blue	May 6 1993
5f 60y	59.30	3	8-9	Firm	Play Hever Golf	May 26 1993
5f 215y	1m 8.10	2	8-9	Firm	Song Mist	Jly 16 1996
5f 215y	1m 7.12	8	9-6	Good To Firm	Diamond Lady	Apr 20 2019
6f 210y	1m 19.90	2	8-11	Hard	Rain Burst	Sep 15 1988
6f 210y	1m 20.10	4	9-3	Good To Firm	Sawaki	Sep 3 1991
7f 211y	1m 32.80	2	9-7	Firm	Asian Pete	Oct 3 1989
7f 211y	1m 30.50	5	8-11	Firm	Mystic Ridge	May 27 1999
1m 1f 207y	2m 4.70	2	9-0	Good To Soft	Esteemed Master	Nov 2 2001
1m 1f 207y	1m 57.20	3	9-0	Firm	Get The Message	Apr 30 1984
1m 3f 198y	2m 25.80	4	8-2	Firm	New Zealand	Jly 4 1985

CARLISLE

Distance	Time	Age	Weight	Going	Horse	Date
5f	1m 0.10	2	8-5	Firm	La Tortuga	Aug 2 1999
5f	58.80	3	9-8	Good To Firm	Esatto	Aug 21 2002
5f 193y	1m 12.30	2	9-2	Good To Firm	Burrishoole Abbey	Jun 22 2016
5f 193y	1m 10.83	4	9-0	Good To Firm	Bo McGinty	Sep 11 2005
6f 195y	1m 26.39	2	8-11	Good To Firm	Kahlua Kliss	Sep 11 2005
6f 195y	1m 24.30	3	8-9	Good To Firm	Marjurita	Aug 21 2002
7f 173y	1m 40.67	2	9-0	Good To Firm	Jaad	Sep 19 2005
7f 173y	1m 35.84	5	8-12	Good To Firm	Waarif	Jun 27 2018
1m 1f	1m 53.84	3	9-0	Firm	Little Jimbob	Jun 14 2004
1m 3f 39y	2m 20.46	5	10-0	Good To Firm	Aasheq	Jun 27 2018
1m 6f 32y	3m 2.20	6	8-10	Firm	Explosive Speed	May 26 1994
2m 1f 47y	3m 46.20	3	7-10	Good To Firm	Warring Kingdom	Aug 25 1999

CATTERICK

Distance	Time	Age	Weight	Going	Horse	Date
5f	57.60	2	9-0	Firm	H Harrison	Oct 8 2002
5f	57.10	4	8-7	Firm	Kabcast	Jly 6 1989
5f 212y	1m 11.40	2	9-4	Firm	Captain Nick	Jly 11 1978
5f 212y	1m 9.86	9	8-13	Good To Firm	Sharp Hat	May 30 2003
7f 6y	1m 24.10	2	8-11	Firm	Linda's Fantasy	Sep 18 1982
7f 6y	1m 22.56	6	8-7	Firm	Differential	May 31 2003
1m 4f 13y	2m 30.50	3	8-8	Good To Firm	Rahaf	May 30 2003
1m 5f 192y	2m 54.80	3	8-5	Firm	Geryon	May 31 1984
1m 7f 189y	3m 20.80	4	7-11	Firm	Bean Boy I	Jly 8 1982

CHELMSFORD (A.W)

Distance	Time	Age	Weight	Going	Horse	Date
5f	58.52	2	9-6	Standard	Prince Of Rome	Sep 20 2018
5f	57.30	7	8-13	Standard	Brother Tiger	Feb 7 2016
6f	1m 11.14	2	8-10	Standard	Second Love	Sep 5 2019
6f	1m 10.00	4	9-2	Standard	Raucous	Apr 27 2017
7f	1m 23.62	2	9-2	Standard	Fintas	Sep 22 2018
7f	1m 22.59	7	8-0	Standard	Boy In The Bar	Sep 22 2018
1m	1m 37.15	2	9-3	Standard	Dragon Mall	Sep 26 2015
1m	1m 35.46	4	9-7	Standard	Mindurownbusiness	Nov 23 2015
1m 2f	2m 1.81	5	9-7	Standard	Bin Battuta	Sep 28 2019
1m 5f 66y	2m 47.00	4	8-7	Standard	Coorg	Jan 6 2016
1m 6f	2m 55.61	3	9-0	Standard	Brasca	Sep 5 2019
2m	3m 22.37	5	9-3	Standard	Notarised	Mar 3 2016

CHEPSTOW

Distance	Time	Age	Weight	Going	Horse	Date
5f 16y	57.60	2	8-11	Firm	Micro Love	Jly 8 1986
5f 16y	56.80	3	8-4	Firm	Torbay Express	Sep 15 1979
6f 16y	1m 8.50	2	9-2	Firm	Ninjago	Jly 27 2012
6f 16y	1m 8.10	3	9-7	Firm	America Calling	Sep 18 2001
7f 16y	1m 20.48	2	9-0	Good	Festival Day	Sep 17 2019
7f 16y	1m 19.30	3	9-0	Firm	Taranaki	Sep 18 2001
1m 14y	1m 33.10	2	8-11	Good To Firm	Ski Academy	Aug 28 1995
1m 14y	1m 31.60	3	8-13	Firm	Stoli	Sep 18 2001
1m 2f	2m 4.58	3	8-13	Good To Firm	Show Of Force	Jly 19 2018
1m 4f	2m 31.89	5	8-13	Good To Firm	Volpene Jelois	May 22 2018
2m	3m 27.28	4	8-12	Good	Hawkerland	Jly 4 2017
2m 2f	3m 56.40	5	8-7	Good To Firm	Laffah	Jly 8 2000

CHESTER

Distance	Time	Age	Weight	Going	Horse	Date
5f 15y	59.94	2	9-2	Good To Firm	Leiba Leiba	Jun 26 2010
5f 15y	58.88	3	8-7	Good To Firm	Peterkin	Jly 11 2014
5f 110y	1m 6.39	2	8-7	Good To Soft	Kinematic	Sep 27 2014
5f 110y	1m 4.54	5	8-5	Good	Bossipop	Sep 1 2018
6f 17y	1m 12.54	2	8-12	Good	Glass Slippers	Sep 1 2018
6f 17y	1m 12.02	5	9-5	Good To Firm	Deauville Prince	Jun 13 2015
7f 1y	1m 25.29	2	9-0	Good To Firm	Due Respect	Sep 25 2002
7f 1y	1m 23.75	5	8-13	Good To Firm	Three Graces (GER)	Jly 9 2005
7f 127y	1m 32.29	2	9-0	Good To Firm	Big Bad Bob	Sep 25 2002
7f 127y	1m 30.62	5	9-10	Good	Oh This Is Us	Sep 1 2018
1m 2f 70y	2m 7.15	3	8-8	Good To Firm	Stotsfold	Sep 23 2006
1m 3f 75y	2m 22.17	3	8-12	Good To Firm	Perfect Truth	May 6 2009
1m 4f 63y	2m 33.70	3	8-10	Good To Firm	Fight Your Corner	May 7 2002
1m 5f 84y	2m 45.43	5	8-11	Firm	Rakaposhi King	May 7 1987
1m 7f 196y	3m 20.33	4	9-0	Good To Firm	Grand Fromage	Jly 13 2002
2m 2f 140y	3m 58.89	7	9-2	Good To Firm	Greenwich Meantime	May 9 2007

DONCASTER

Distance	Time	Age	Weight	Going	Horse	Date
5f 3y	58.04	2	9-1	Good	Gutaifan	Sep 11 2015
5f 3y	57.31	7	9-10	Good	Tabaret	Aug 14 2010
5f 143y	1m 7.26	2	9-0	Good To Firm	Cartography	Jun 29 2003
5f 143y	1m 5.38	4	9-7	Good	Muthmir	Sep 13 2014
6f 2y	1m 10.33	2	9-4	Good To Firm	Comedy	Jun 29 2018
6f 2y	1m 9.56	3	8-10	Good To Firm	Proclaim	May 30 2009
6f 111y	1m 17.19	2	8-9	Good	Mr Lupton	Sep 10 2015
6f 111y	1m 16.62	4	8-10	Good	Badr Al Badoor	Sep 12 2014
7f 6y	1m 22.78	2	9-5	Good	Basateen	Jly 24 2014
7f 6y	1m 21.81	6	8-7	Good To Firm	Signor Peltro	May 30 2009
7f 213y	1m 38.37	2	8-6	Good To Soft	Antoniola	Oct 23 2009
7f 213y	1m 34.46	4	8-12	Good To Firm	Staying On	Apr 18 2009
1m	1m 36.72	2	8-12	Good	Dance Of Fire	Sep 13 2014
1m	1m 34.95	6	8-9	Firm	Quick Wit	Jly 18 2013
1m 2f 43y	2m 4.81	4	8-13	Good To Firm	Red Gala	Sep 12 2007
1m 3f 197y	2m 27.48	3	8-4	Good To Firm	Swift Alhaarth	Sep 10 2011
1m 6f 115y	3m 0.27	3	9-1	Good To Firm	Logician	Sep 14 2019
2m 109y	3m 34.52	7	9-0	Good To Firm	Inchnadamph	Nov 10 2007
2m 1f 197y	3m 48.41	4	9-4	Good To Firm	Septimus	Sep 14 2007

EPSOM

Distance	Time	Age	Weight	Going	Horse	Date
5f	54.00	6	8-13	Good To Firm	Ornate	Jun 1 2019
6f 3y	1m 7.85	2	8-11	Good To Firm	Showbrook	Jun 5 1991
6f 3y	1m 6.20	9	8-11	Good To Firm	Watchable	Jun 1 2019
7f 3y	1m 21.30	2	8-9	Good To Firm	Red Peony	Jly 29 2004
7f 3y	1m 20.15	4	8-7	Firm	Capistrano I	Jun 7 1972
1m 113y	1m 42.80	2	8-5	Good To Firm	Nightstalker	Aug 30 1988
1m 113y	1m 40.46	4	9-6	Good To Firm	Zaaki	Jun 1 2019
1m 2f 17y	2m 3.50	5	7-11	Firm	Crossbow I	Jun 7 1967
1m 4f 6y	2m 31.33	3	9-0	Good To Firm	Workforce	Jun 5 2010

FFOS LAS

Distance	Time	Age	Weight	Going	Horse	Date
5f	57.06	2	9-3	Good To Firm	Mr Majeika	May 5 2011
5f	56.35	5	8-8	Good	Haajes	Sep 12 2009
6f	1m 9.00	2	9-5	Good To Firm	Wonder Of Qatar	Sep 14 2014
6f	1m 7.46	6	10-2	Good To Firm	Handytalk	Jly 29 2019
7f 80y	1m 30.15	2	9-2	Good To Firm	Fox Tal	Jly 24 2018
7f 80y	1m 29.72	3	8-7	Good To Firm	Hellovaqueen	Jly 24 2018
1m	1m 39.36	2	9-2	Good To Firm	Hala Hala	Sep 2 2013
1m	1m 37.12	5	9-0	Good To Firm	Zebrano	May 5 2011
1m 2f	2m 4.85	8	8-12	Good To Firm	Pelham Crescent	May 5 2011
1m 3f 209y	2m 31.18	3	9-9	Good	Trueshan	Aug 29 2019
1m 6f	2m 58.61	4	9-7	Good To Firm	Lady Eclair	Jly 12 2010
2m	3m 25.42	4	9-3	Good To Firm	Long John Silver	Jly 24 2018

GOODWOOD

Distance	Time	Age	Weight	Going	Horse	Date
5f	58.22	2	9-1	Good	Rumble Inthejungle	Aug 1 2018
5f	56.20	5	9-5	Good To Firm	Battaash	Aug 2 2019
6f	1m 9.81	2	8-11	Good To Firm	Bachir	Jly 28 1999
6f	1m 9.10	6	9-0	Good To Firm	Tamagin	Sep 12 2009
7f	1m 24.99	2	8-11	Good To Firm	Ekraar	Jly 29 1999
7f	1m 23.75	4	9-3	Good	Billesdon Brook	Aug 2 2019
1m	1m 37.21	2	9-0	Good	Caldra	Sep 9 2006
1m	1m 35.28	3	8-13	Good To Firm	Beat Le Bon	Aug 2 2019
1m 1f 11y	1m 56.27	2	9-3	Good To Firm	Dordogne	Sep 22 2010
1m 1f 11y	1m 52.81	3	9-6	Good	Vena	Jly 27 1995
1m 1f 197y	2m 2.81	3	9-3	Good To Firm	Road To Love	Aug 3 2006
1m 3f 44y	2m 22.77	3	9-3	Good	Khalidi	May 26 2017
1m 3f 218y	2m 31.39	3	9-1	Good To Firm	Cross Counter	Aug 4 2018
1m 6f	2m 58.34	6	9-2	Good To Firm	Sir Chauvelin	Aug 4 2018
2m	3m 24.86	5	9-4	Good	Soldier In Action	Sep 4 2018
2m 4f 134y	4m 25.85	7	8-6	Good To Firm	Teak	Jly 30 2014

HAMILTON

Distance	Time	Age	Weight	Going	Horse	Date
5f 7y	57.95	2	8-8	Good To Firm	Rose Blossom	May 29 2009
5f 7y	57.20	5	9-4	Good To Firm	Dapper Man	Jun 27 2019
6f 6y	1m 10.00	2	8-12	Good To Firm	Break The Code	Aug 24 1999
6f 6y	1m 9.03	6	9-5	Good To Firm	George Bowen	Jly 20 2018
1m 68y	1m 45.46	2	9-5	Good To Firm	Laafiraaq	Sep 20 2015
1m 68y	1m 42.70	6	7-7	Firm	Cranley	Sep 25 1972
1m 1f 35y	1m 53.60	5	9-6	Good To Firm	Regent's Secret	Aug 10 2005
1m 3f 15y	2m 18.66	3	9-3	Good To Firm	Postponed	Jly 18 2014
1m 4f 15y	2m 30.52	5	9-10	Good To Firm	Record Breaker	Jun 10 2009
1m 5f 16y	2m 45.10	6	9-6	Firm	Mentalasanythin	Jun 14 1995

HAYDOCK

Distance	Time	Age	Weight	Going	Horse	Date
5f	58.51	2	9-1	Good	Four Dragons	Oct 14 2016
5f	58.56	2	8-2	Good To Firm	Barracuda Boy	Aug 11 2012
5f Inner	56.39	5	9-4	Firm	Bated Breath	May 26 2012
5f Inner	57.38	7	9-12	Good To Firm	Foxy Forever	Jly 21 2017
6f	1m 10.98	4	9-9	Good To Firm	Wolfhound	Sep 4 1993
6f Inner	1m 10.58	2	9-2	Good To Firm	Prestbury Park	Jly 21 2017
6f	1m 8.56	3	9-0	Firm	Harry Angel	May 27 2017
6f Inner	1m 9.04	3	8-11	Good To Firm	Princes Des Sables	Aug 8 2019
6f 212y	1m 27.20	2	9-6	Good	Brogan	Oct 14 2016
6f 212y	1m 25.28	3	9-8	Good To Firm	Mystic Flight	Jun 7 2018
7f 37y	1m 27.57	2	9-2	Good To Firm	Contrast	Aug 5 2016
7f 37y	1m 25.50	3	8-11	Good	Forge	Sep 1 2016
7f 212y	1m 39.41	2	9-0	Good	Star Archer	Sep 1 2016
7f 212y	1m 37.80	3	9-4	Good To Firm	Sidewinder	May 26 2017
1m 37y	1m 41.99	2	9-0	Good	Top Of The Glas	Aug 8 2013
1m 37y	1m 38.50	4	8-11	Good To Firm	Express Himself	Jun 10 2015
1m 2f 42y	2m 7.25	3	8-9	Good To Firm	Laraaib	May 26 2017
1m 2f 100y	2m 7.53	4	9-5	Good To Firm	Teodoro	Aug 11 2018
1m 3f 140y	2m 25.52	5	9-9	Good To Firm	December Second	Aug 8 2019
1m 3f 175y	2m 25.53	4	8-12	Good To Firm	Number Theory	May 24 2012
1m 6f	2m 55.20	5	9-9	Good To Firm	Huff And Puff	Sep 7 2012
2m 45y	3m 26.98	5	8-13	Good To Firm	De Rigueur	Jun 8 2013

KEMPTON (A.W)

Distance	Time	Age	Weight	Going	Horse	Date
5f	58.96	2	8-6	Standard	Glamorous Spirit	Nov 28 2008
5f	58.07	5	8-12	Standard	A Momentofmadness	Apr 7 2018
6f	1m 11.02	2	9-1	Standard To Slow	Invincible Army	Sep 9 2017
6f	1m 9.79	4	8-11	Standard	Trinityelitedotcom	Mar 29 2014
7f	1m 23.79	2	8-0	Standard	Elsaakb	Nov 8 2017
7f	1m 23.10	6	9-9	Standard	Sirius Prospect	Nov 20 2014
1m	1m 37.26	2	9-0	Standard	Cecchini	Nov 8 2017
1m	1m 35.73	3	8-9	Standard	Western Aristocrat	Sep 15 2011
1m 1f 219y	2m 2.93	3	8-11	Standard To Slow	Ply	Sep 25 2017
1m 2f 219y	2m 15.65	4	8-8	Standard To Slow	Forbidden Planet	Mar 30 2019
1m 3f 219y	2m 28.99	6	9-3	Standard	Spring Of Fame	Nov 7 2012
1m 7f 218y	3m 21.50	4	8-12	Standard	Colour Vision	May 2 2012

LEICESTER

Distance	Time	Age	Weight	Going	Horse	Date
5f	59.01	2	9-1	Good To Firm	Sayesse	Aug 16 2016
5f	58.00	6	9-7	Good	Encore d'Or	Oct 9 2018
6f	1m 11.14	2	8-6	Good To Firm	Clever Candy	Sep 23 2019
6f	1m 9.60	5	9-4	Good	Danecase	Oct 9 2018
7f	1m 23.33	2	9-5	Good To Firm	Highest Ground	Sep 23 2019
7f	1m 22.24	5	9-2	Good To Firm	Home Of The Brave	Apr 29 2017
1m 53y	1m 44.05	2	8-11	Good To Firm	Congressional	Sep 6 2005
1m 53y	1m 41.89	5	9-7	Good To Firm	Vainglory	Jun 18 2009
1m 2f	2m 5.25	3	9-7	Good To Firm	Desert Fire	Jly 19 2018
1m 3f 179y	2m 27.10	5	8-12	Good To Firm	Murghem	Jun 18 2000

LINGFIELD

Distance	Time	Age	Weight	Going	Horse	Date
4f 217y	56.76	2	9-2	Good	Glory Fighter	May 11 2018
4f 217y	56.09	3	9-4	Good To Firm	Whitecrest	Sep 16 2011
6f	1m 9.41	2	9-0	Good To Firm	Company Minx	Jly 10 2019
6f	1m 8.48	4	9-6	Good To Firm	Rewaayat	Jly 17 2019
7f	1m 21.22	2	9-9	Good To Firm	Sir Arthur Dayne	Jly 24 2019
7f	1m 20.46	4	9-4	Good To Firm	Magical Ride	Aug 3 2019
7f 135y	1m 29.32	2	9-3	Good To Firm	Dundonnell	Aug 4 2012
7f 135y	1m 26.73	3	8-6	Good To Firm	Hiaam	Jly 11 1987
1m 1f	1m 50.45	4	9-3	Good To Firm	Enzemble	May 30 2019
1m 2f	2m 4.83	5	9-8	Good To Firm	Hairdryer	Jly 21 2018
1m 3f 133y	2m 23.95	3	8-5	Firm	Night-Shirt	Jly 14 1990
1m 6f	2m 58.88	3	8-13	Good To Firm	Timoshenko	Jly 21 2018
2m 68y	3m 23.71	3	9-5	Good To Firm	Lauries Crusador	Aug 13 1988

LINGFIELD (A.W)

Distance	Time	Age	Weight	Going	Horse	Date
5f 6y	57.59	2	9-7	Standard	Augustus Caesar	Sep 24 2019
5f 6y	56.67	5	8-12	Standard	Ladies Are Forever	Mar 16 2013
6f 1y	1m 9.76	2	9-4	Standard	Red Impression	Nov 24 2018
6f 1y	1m 8.32	6	9-0	Standard	Kachy	Feb 2 2019
7f 1y	1m 22.67	2	9-3	Standard	Complicit	Nov 23 2013
7f 1y	1m 21.90	4	9-9	Standard	Cardsharp	Mar 13 2019
1m 1y	1m 35.70	2	8-13	Standard	Qaaddim	Oct 3 2019
1m 1y	1m 33.90	6	9-5	Standard	Lucky Team	Mar 30 2018
1m 2f	2m 0.99	4	9-0	Standard	Farraaj	Mar 16 2013
1m 4f	2m 26.99	6	9-11	Standard	Pinzolo	Jan 21 2017
1m 5f	2m 39.70	3	8-10	Standard	Hidden Gold	Oct 30 2014
1m 7f 169y	3m 15.18	4	9-1	Standard	Winning Story	Apr 14 2017

MUSSELBURGH

Distance	Time	Age	Weight	Going	Horse	Date
5f 1y	57.66	2	9-2	Good To Firm	It Dont Come Easy	Jun 3 2017
5f 1y	56.77	9	9-10	Good To Firm	Caspian Prince	Jun 9 2018
7f 33y	1m 27.46	2	8-8	Good	Durham Reflection	Sep 14 2009
7f 33y	1m 25.00	9	8-8	Good To Firm	Kalk Bay	Jun 4 2016
1m 2y	1m 40.34	2	8-12	Good To Firm	Succession	Sep 26 2004
1m 2y	1m 36.83	3	9-5	Good To Firm	Ginger Jack	Jly 13 2010
1m 208y	1m 50.42	8	8-11	Good To Firm	Dhaular Dhar	Sep 3 2010
1m 4f 104y	2m 36.80	3	8-3	Good To Firm	Harris Tweed	Jun 5 2010
1m 5f	2m 46.41	3	9-5	Good To Firm	Alcaeus	Sep 29 2013
1m 5f 216y	2m 57.98	7	8-5	Good To Firm	Jonny Delta	Apr 18 2014
1m 7f 217y	3m 25.62	4	8-3	Good To Firm	Aldreth	Jun 13 2015

NEWBURY

Distance	Time	Age	Weight	Going	Horse	Date
5f 34y	1m 1.64	2	8-5	Good To Firm	Ginger Nut	Jly 21 2018
5f 34y	58.79	10	9-1	Good	Take Cover	Sep 23 2017
6f	1m 10.64	2	8-11	Good	James Garfield	Sep 23 2017
6f	1m 10.27	3	9-0	Good To Firm	Never Back Down	May 19 2018
6f 110y	1m 18.06	2	9-5	Good To Firm	Twin Sails	Jun 11 2015
7f	1m 23.04	2	8-11	Good To Firm	Haafhd	Aug 15 2003
7f	1m 20.80	3	9-0	Good To Firm	Muhaarar	Apr 18 2015
1m	1m 38.45	2	8-12	Good	Tritonic	Sep 20 2019
1m	1m 35.07	4	8-11	Good To Firm	Rhododendron	May 19 2018
1m Rnd	1m 36.98	3	9-1	Good To Firm	He's Our Star	Jun 26 2018
1m 1f	1m 49.65	3	8-0	Good To Firm	Holtye	May 21 1995
1m 2f	2m 1.29	3	8-7	Good To Firm	Wall Street II	Jly 20 1996
1m 3f	2m 17.91	5	9-3	Good	Desert Encounter	Sep 23 2017
1m 4f	2m 28.61	4	9-4	Good To Firm	Teodoro	Jun 26 2018
1m 5f 61y	2m 49.34	3	8-1	Good To Firm	Galmarley	Jly 20 2018
1m 5f 61y	2m 44.90	5	10-0	Good To Firm	Mystic Hill	Jly 20 1996
2m	3m 25.42	8	9-12	Good To Firm	Moonlight Quest	Jly 19 1996

NEWCASTLE (A.W)

Distance	Time	Age	Weight	Going	Horse	Date
5f	58.05	2	8-6	Standard	Spin Doctor	Oct 25 2016
5f	57.78	3	8-9	Standard	Astraea	Dec 15 2018
6f	1m 9.95	2	9-2	Standard	Mazyoun	Oct 25 2016
6f	1m 9.86	3	9-2	Standard	Unabated	Mar 22 2017
7f 14y	1m 25.50	2	9-5	Standard	Commander Cole	Oct 18 2016
7f 14y	1m 24.10	3	9-0	Standard	Northernpowerhouse	Dec 18 2019
1m 5y	1m 36.26	2	9-1	Standard	Kameko	Nov 1 2019
1m 5y	1m 36.10	4	9-8	Standard	Alfred Richardson	Nov 9 2018
1m 2f 42y	2m 4.88	3	8-6	Standard	Palisade	Oct 16 2016
1m 4f 98y	2m 36.76	3	8-7	Standard	Ajman Prince	Oct 14 2016
2m 56y	3m 29.87	4	9-8	Standard	Dannyday	Jun 25 2016

NEWMARKET

Distance	Time	Age	Weight	Going	Horse	Date
5f	58.69	2	8-12	Good To Firm	Mrs Danvers	Oct 7 2016
5f	56.81	6	9-2	Good To Firm	Lochsong	Apr 30 1994
6f	1m 9.31	2	9-0	Good	Earthlight	Sep 28 2019
6f	1m 9.55	3	9-1	Good To Firm	Captain Colby	May 16 2015
7f	1m 22.37	2	9-1	Good	U S Navy Flag	Oct 14 2017
7f	1m 21.98	3	9-0	Good To Firm	Tupi	May 16 2015
1m	1m 35.13	2	9-0	Good	Royal Dornoch	Sep 28 2019
1m	1m 34.07	4	9-0	Good To Firm	Eagle Mountain	Oct 3 2008
1m 1f	1m 46.99	3	8-10	Good	Lord North	Sep 28 2019
1m 2f	2m 2.76	2	9-2	Good	Kew Gardens	Oct 14 2017
1m 2f	2m 0.13	3	8-12	Good	New Approach	Oct 18 2008
1m 4f	2m 29.13	3	9-0	Good	First Nation	Oct 13 2017
1m 6f	2m 51.59	3	8-7	Good	Art Eyes	Sep 29 2005
2m	3m 18.64	5	9-6	Good To Firm	Times Up	Sep 22 2011
2m 2f	3m 45.59	4	8-8	Good	Withhold	Oct 14 2017

NEWMARKET (JULY)

Distance	Time	Age	Weight	Going	Horse	Date
5f	56.09	6	9-11	Good	Borderlescott	Aug 22 2008
5f	57.31	4	9-2	Good To Firm	Mountain Peak	Jly 12 2019
6f	1m 10.35	2	8-11	Good	Elnawin	Aug 22 2008
6f	1m 9.09	2	9-3	Good To Firm	Raffle Prize	Jly 12 2019
6f	1m 9.09	2	9-3	Good To Firm	Raffle Prize	Jly 12 2019
6f	1m 9.11	4	9-5	Good To Firm	Lethal Force	Jly 13 2013
7f	1m 23.33	2	9-1	Good To Firm	Birchwood	Jly 11 2015
7f	1m 21.78	3	8-13	Good To Firm	Light And Dark	Jly 12 2019
1m	1m 37.47	2	8-13	Good	Whippers Love	Aug 28 2009
1m	1m 34.42	3	8-12	Good To Firm	Alice Springs	Jly 8 2016
1m	1m 35.89	4	9-7	Good To Firm	Veracious	Jly 12 2019
1m 2f	2m 0.61	3	9-7	Good To Firm	Walkinthesand	Jly 12 2019
1m 4f	2m 27.52	3	8-5	Good	Dame Malliot	Jly 20 2019
1m 5f	2m 39.96	3	9-1	Good To Firm	Spanish Mission	Jly 11 2019
1m 5f	2m 40.75	5	9-10	Good	Wadi Al Hattawi	Aug 29 2015
1m 6f	2m 53.53	5	9-4	Good To Firm	King's Advice	Jly 12 2019

NOTTINGHAM

Distance	Time	Age	Weight	Going	Horse	Date
5f 8y	59.05	2	9-0	Good To Firm	Main Desire	May 2 2017
5f 8y	57.90	2	8-9	Firm	Hoh Magic	May 13 1994
5f 8y	57.01	3	8-12	Good To Firm	Garrus	Apr 10 2019
5f 8y	57.58	5	7-11	Good To Firm	Penny Dreadful	Jun 19 2017
6f 18y	1m 11.40	2	8-11	Firm	Jameelapi	Aug 8 1983
6f 18y	1m 10.00	4	9-2	Firm	Ajanac	Aug 8 1988
1m 75y	1m 44.75	2	9-0	Good	Vivid Diamond	Oct 3 2018
1m 75y	1m 42.02	3	9-0	Good To Firm	Ganayem	May 11 2018
1m 75y	1m 41.60	4	8-13	Good To Firm	Rise Hall	Apr 10 2019
1m 2f 50y	2m 7.13	5	9-8	Good To Firm	Vasily	Jly 19 2013
1m 6f	2m 57.80	3	8-10	Firm	Buster Jo	Oct 1 1985
2m	3m 25.25	3	9-5	Good	Bulwark	Sep 27 2005

PONTEFRACT

Distance	Time	Age	Weight	Going	Horse	Date
5f 3y	1m 1.10	2	9-0	Firm	Golden Bounty	Sep 20 2001
5f 3y	1m 0.49	5	9-5	Good To Firm	Judicial	Apr 24 2017
6f	1m 14.00	2	9-3	Firm	Fawzi	Sep 6 1983
6f	1m 12.60	3	7-13	Firm	Merry One	Aug 29 1970
1m 6y	1m 42.80	2	9-13	Firm	Star Spray	Sep 6 1983
1m 6y	1m 42.80	2	9-0	Firm	Alasil	Sep 26 2002
1m 6y	1m 40.60	4	9-10	Good To Firm	Island Light	Apr 13 2002
1m 2f 5y	2m 10.10	2	9-0	Firm	Shanty Star	Oct 7 2002
1m 2f 5y	2m 8.20	4	7-8	Hard	Happy Hector	Jly 9 1979
1m 2f 5y	2m 8.20	3	7-13	Hard	Tom Noddy	Aug 21 1972
1m 4f 5y	2m 33.72	3	8-7	Firm	Ajaan	Aug 8 2007
2m 1f 27y	3m 40.67	4	8-7	Good To Firm	Paradise Flight	Jun 6 2005
2m 2f 2y	3m 51.10	3	8-8	Good To Firm	Kudz	Sep 9 1986
2m 5f 139y	4m 47.80	4	8-4	Firm	Physical	May 14 1984

REDCAR

Distance	Time	Age	Weight	Going	Horse	Date
5f	56.88	2	9-7	Good To Soft	Wolfofwallstreet	Oct 27 2014
5f	56.01	10	9-3	Firm	Henry Hall	Sep 20 2006
5f 217y	1m 8.84	2	8-3	Good To Firm	Obe Gold	Oct 2 2004
5f 217y	1m 8.60	3	9-2	Good To Firm	Sizzling Saga	Jun 21 1991
7f	1m 21.28	2	9-3	Firm	Karoo Blue	Sep 20 2006
7f	1m 21.00	3	9-1	Firm	Empty Quarter I	Oct 3 1995
7f 219y	1m 34.37	2	9-0	Firm	Mastership	Sep 20 2006
7f 219y	1m 32.42	4	10-0	Firm	Nanton	Sep 20 2006
1m 1f	1m 52.44	2	9-0	Firm	Spear	Sep 13 2004
1m 1f	1m 48.50	5	8-12	Firm	Mellottie	Jly 25 1990
1m 2f 1y	2m 10.10	2	8-11	Good	Adding	Nov 10 1989
1m 2f 1y	2m 1.40	5	9-2	Firm	Eradicate	May 28 1990
1m 5f 218y	2m 59.54	6	8-5	Good To Firm	Leodis	Jun 23 2018
1m 7f 217y	3m 24.90	3	9-3	Good To Firm	Subsonic	Oct 8 1991

RIPON

Distance	Time	Age	Weight	Going	Horse	Date
5f	57.80	2	8-8	Firm	Super Rocky	Aug 5 1991
5f	57.80	2	9-5	Good	Ornate	Jly 18 2015
5f	57.28	5	8-12	Good	Desert Ace	Sep 24 2016
6f	1m 10.40	2	9-2	Good	Cumbrian Venture	Aug 17 2002
6f	1m 9.09	5	8-13	Good To Firm	Sandra's Secret	May 20 2018
1m	1m 38.77	2	9-4	Good	Greed Is Good	Sep 28 2013
1m	1m 36.62	4	8-11	Good To Firm	Granston	Aug 29 2005
1m 1f	1m 49.97	6	9-3	Good To Firm	Ginger Jack	Jun 20 2013
1m 1f 170y	1m 59.12	5	8-9	Good To Firm	Wahoo Sam	Aug 30 2005
1m 4f 10y	2m 31.40	4	8-8	Good To Firm	Dandino	Apr 16 2011
2m	3m 23.90	4	9-10	Firm	Panama Jack I	Jun 23 1988

SALISBURY

Distance	Time	Age	Weight	Going	Horse	Date
5f	59.30	2	9-0	Good To Firm	Ajigolo	May 12 2005
5f	59.18	7	8-10	Good To Firm	Edged Out	Jun 18 2017
6f	1m 12.10	2	8-0	Good To Firm	Parisian Lady	Jun 10 1997
6f	1m 11.09	3	9-0	Firm	L'Ami Louis	May 1 2011
6f 213y	1m 25.97	2	9-0	Firm	More Royal	Jun 29 1995
6f 213y	1m 24.91	3	9-4	Firm	Chilworth Lad	May 1 2011
1m	1m 40.48	2	8-13	Firm	Choir Master	Sep 17 2002
1m	1m 38.29	3	8-7	Good To Firm	Layman	Aug 11 2005
1m 1f 201y	2m 4.72	6	8-9	Good To Firm	Alqirm	Jun 22 1988
1m 4f 5y	2m 31.69	3	9-5	Good To Firm	Arrive	Jun 27 2001
1m 6f 44y	3m 0.48	7	9-2	Good To Firm	Highland Castle	May 23 2015

SANDOWN

Distance	Time	Age	Weight	Going	Horse	Date
5f 10y	59.48	2	9-3	Firm	Times Time	Jly 22 1982
5f 10y	58.57	3	8-12	Good To Firm	Battaash	Jly 8 2017
7f	1m 26.56	2	9-0	Good To Firm	Raven's Pass	Sep 1 2007
7f	1m 26.36	3	9-0	Firm	Mawsuff	Jun 14 1986
1m	1m 43.90	2	9-5	Good	Via De Vega	Sep 18 2019
1m	1m 39.21	4	8-12	Good To Firm	El Hayem	Jly 8 2017
1m 1f	1m 54.63	2	8-8	Good To Firm	French Pretender	Sep 20 1988
1m 1f	1m 56.77	3	9-4	Good	Titi Makfi	Jun 8 2017
1m 1f	1m 52.40	7	9-3	Good To Firm	Bourgainville	Aug 11 2005
1m 1f 209y	2m 2.14	4	8-11	Good	Kalaglow	May 31 1982
1m 6f	3m 1.08	3	8-9	Good	Just Hubert	Jly 25 2019
1m 6f	2m 56.90	4	8-7	Good To Firm	Lady Rosanna	Jly 19 1989
2m 50y	3m 29.38	6	9-0	Good To Firm	Caucus	Jly 6 2013

SOUTHWELL (A.W)

Distance	Time	Age	Weight	Going	Horse	Date
4f 214y	57.61	2	9-2	Standard	The Bell Conductor	Nov 7 2019
4f 214y	56.80	5	9-7	Standard	Ghostwing	Jan 3 2012
6f 16y	1m 14.00	2	8-5	Standard	Panalo	Nov 8 1989
6f 16y	1m 13.49	4	9-7	Standard	Rock Sound	Nov 5 2019
7f 14y	1m 26.82	2	8-12	Standard	Winged Icarus	Aug 28 2012
7f 14y	1m 26.29	7	8-9	Standard To Slow	Weld Al Emarat	Feb 27 2019
1m 13y	1m 38.00	2	8-10	Standard	Andrew's First	Dec 30 1989
1m 13y	1m 38.00	2	8-9	Standard	Alpha Rascal	Nov 13 1990
1m 13y	1m 37.25	3	8-6	Standard	Valira	Nov 3 1990
1m 3f 23y	2m 21.50	4	9-7	Standard	Tempering	Dec 5 1990
1m 4f 14y	2m 33.90	4	9-12	Standard	Fast Chick	Nov 8 1989
1m 6f 21y	3m 1.60	3	7-8	Standard	Erevnon	Dec 29 1990
2m 102y	3m 37.60	9	8-12	Standard	Old Hubert	Dec 5 1990

THIRSK

Distance	Time	Age	Weight	Going	Horse	Date
5f	57.20	2	9-7	Good To Firm	Proud Boast	Aug 5 2000
5f	56.92	5	9-6	Firm	Charlie Parkes	Apr 11 2003
6f	1m 9.20	2	9-6	Good To Firm	Westcourt Magic	Aug 25 1995
6f	1m 8.80	6	9-4	Firm	Johayro	Jly 23 1999
7f	1m 23.70	2	8-9	Firm	Courting	Jly 23 1999
7f	1m 22.80	4	8-5	Firm	Silver Haze I	May 21 1988
7f 218y	1m 37.97	2	9-0	Firm	Sunday Symphony	Sep 4 2004
7f 218y	1m 34.80	4	8-13	Firm	Yearsley I	May 5 1990
1m 4f 8y	2m 29.90	5	9-12	Firm	Gallery God	Jun 4 2001
2m 13y	3m 22.30	3	9-0	Firm	Tomaschek	Jly 17 1981

WETHERBY

Distance	Time	Age	Weight	Going	Horse	Date
5f 110y	1m 6.14	2	9-5	Good To Firm	Coastal Mist	May 30 2019
5f 110y	1m 4.25	3	9-1	Good To Firm	Dapper Man	Jun 19 2017
7f	1m 26.23	2	8-9	Good	Rayaa	Jly 21 2015
7f	1m 24.72	4	9-2	Good	Slemy	Jly 21 2015
1m	1m 38.47	3	9-1	Good To Firm	Savaanah	Jun 22 2018
1m 2f	2m 5.13	5	9-5	Good	First Sargeant	Jly 21 2015
1m 6f	3m 0.41	3	9-7	Good To Firm	Davy's Dilemma	Jun 19 2017

WINDSOR

Distance	Time	Age	Weight	Going	Horse	Date
5f 21y	58.69	2	9-0	Good To Firm	Charles The Great	May 23 2011
5f 21y	58.08	5	8-13	Good To Firm	Taurus Twins	Apr 4 2011
6f 12y	1m 10.50	2	9-5	Good To Firm	Cubism I	Aug 17 1998
6f 12y	1m 9.58	7	9-0	Good To Firm	Tropics	Jun 1 2015
1m 31y	1m 41.73	2	9-5	Good To Firm	Salouen	Aug 7 2016
1m 31y	1m 39.47	4	9-6	Good To Firm	Matterhorn	Jun 29 2019
1m 2f	2m 4.24	7	9-8	Good To Firm	Desert Encounter	Aug 24 2019
1m 3f 99y	2m 21.50	3	9-2	Firm	Double Florin	May 19 1980

WOLVERHAMPTON (A.W)

Distance	Time	Age	Weight	Going	Horse	Date
5f 21y	59.75	2	9-6	Standard	Quatrieme Ami	Nov 13 2015
5f 21y	59.33	5	9-6	Standard	Lomu	Dec 3 2019
6f 20y	1m 12.16	2	9-2	Standard	Mubakker	Nov 1 2018
6f 20y	1m 11.44	5	9-6	Standard	Kachy	Dec 26 2018
7f 36y	1m 26.77	2	8-11	Standard	Richard R H B	Nov 23 2019
7f 36y	1m 25.35	4	9-3	Standard	Mister Universe	Mar 12 2016
1m 142y	1m 47.38	2	9-5	Standard	Jack Hobbs	Dec 27 2014
1m 142y	1m 45.43	4	9-4	Standard	Keystroke	Nov 26 2016
1m 1f 104y	1m 55.91	6	8-8	Standard	Storm Ahead	Nov 18 2019
1m 4f 51y	2m 33.44	4	9-5	Standard	Paths Of Glory	Oct 19 2019
2m 120y	3m 31.18	4	9-0	Standard	Aircraft Carrier	Jan 14 2019

YARMOUTH

Distance	Time	Age	Weight	Going	Horse	Date
5f 42y	1m 0.37	2	8-11	Good To Firm	Pink Iceburg	Jly 11 2018
5f 42y	59.16	5	8-8	Good To Firm	Daschas	Sep 18 2019
6f 3y	1m 10.40	2	9-0	Firm	Lanchester	Sep 15 1988
6f 3y	1m 9.14	3	9-0	Good To Firm	Cartographer	May 24 2017
7f 3y	1m 22.20	2	9-0	Good To Firm	Warrshan	Sep 14 1988
7f 3y	1m 22.12	4	9-4	Good To Firm	Glenbuck	Apr 26 2007
1m 3y	1m 36.30	2	8-2	Firm	Out Run	Sep 15 1988
1m 3y	1m 33.49	7	9-0	Firm	Bint Dandy	May 16 2018
1m 1f 21y	1m 52.00	3	9-5	Good To Firm	Touch Gold	Jly 5 2012
1m 2f 23y	2m 2.83	3	8-8	Firm	Reunite	Jly 18 2006
1m 3f 104y	2m 23.10	3	8-9	Firm	Rahil I	Jly 1 1993
1m 6f 17y	2m 57.80	3	8-2	Good To Firm	Barakat	Jly 24 1990

YORK

Distance	Time	Age	Weight	Going	Horse	Date
5f	57.11	2	9-0	Good	Big Time Baby	Aug 20 2016
5f	55.90	5	9-11	Good To Firm	Battaash	Aug 23 2019
5f 89y	1m 3.20	2	9-3	Good To Firm	The Art Of Racing	Sep 9 2012
5f 89y	1m 1.72	4	9-7	Good To Firm	Bogart	Aug 21 2013
6f	1m 8.90	2	9-0	Good	Tiggy Wiggy	Aug 21 2014
6f	1m 8.23	3	8-11	Good To Firm	Mince	Sep 9 2012
7f	1m 22.32	2	9-1	Good To Firm	Dutch Connection	Aug 20 2014
7f	1m 21.00	3	9-1	Good To Firm	Shine So Bright	Aug 24 2019
7f 192y	1m 36.92	2	9-5	Good	Awesometank	Oct 14 2017
7f 192y	1m 34.95	3	9-3	Good To Firm	Pogo	Aug 23 2019
1m 177y	1m 46.76	5	9-8	Good To Firm	Echo Of Light	Sep 5 2007
1m 2f 56y	2m 5.29	3	8-11	Good To Firm	Sea The Stars	Aug 18 2009
1m 3f 188y	2m 25.40	4	8-8	Good To Firm	Tamreer	Aug 23 2019
1m 5f 188y	2m 52.97	6	9-5	Good To Firm	Mustajeer	Aug 24 2019
2m 56y	3m 27.06	5	9-6	Good To Firm	Stradivarius	Aug 23 2019

SPLIT SECOND SPEED RATINGS

The following lists the fastest performances of 3yo+ and 2yo horses which have recorded a speed figure of 103 or over during the 2019 season.
Additional information in the parentheses following the speed figure shows the distance of the race in furlongs, course, state of going and the date on which the figure was achieved.

THREE-YEAR-OLDS AND UPWARDS -Turf

A Momentofmadness 110 *(5½f,Yor,G,Aug 21)*
A Sure Welcome 104 *(5f,Bri,GS,Jun 25)*
Aasheq 106 *(10½f,Chs,S,May 10)*
Abanica 103 *(6f,Cur,S,Sep 28)*
Abate 104 *(5f,Not,HY,Oct 16)*
Abel Handy 112 *(5f,Chs,GF,Jun 29)*
About Glory 108 *(10f,Bat,F,Sep 4)*
Above N Beyond 117 *(7f,Mey,G,Feb 28)*
Above Normal 114 *(7f,Mey,G,Jan 19)*
Absolute Dream 103 *(7f,Cat,GF,Sep 10)*
Absolutio 110 *(8f,Don,G,May 4)*
Abushamah 106 *(7½f,Bev,GS,May 29)*
Acari 103 *(8f,Cur,S,Aug 16)*
Accidental Agent 115 *(8f,Nby,G,May 18)*
Acclaim The Nation 107 *(5f,Don,S,Aug 17)*
Accomplice 106 *(8f,Ffo,G,Aug 29)*
Ace Combat 103 *(11½f,Wdr,G,Apr 15)*
Aces 110 *(7½f,Chs,G,Jun 28)*
Across The Sea 106 *(6f,Nby,GF,Jly 11)*
Act Of God 106 *(15f,Leo,G,Jun 13)*
Act Of Magic 106 *(10f,Lin,GF,Jun 1)*
Addeybb 121 *(10½f,Hay,HY,Aug 10)*
Addis Ababa 109 *(10f,Yor,S,Jun 14)*
Admirality 114 *(7f,Leo,G,Sep 14)*
Admirals Bay 103 *(11½f,Yar,GF,May 30)*
Advertise 116 *(6½f,Dea,G,Aug 4)*
Aegeus 106 *(10f,Lin,G,Aug 10)*
Aera 103 *(12f,Cur,GY,Aug 23)*
Afaak 114 *(8f,Asc,S,Jun 19)*
Afandem 108 *(5f,Not,HY,Nov 6)*
Affluence 106 *(11f,Goo,GF,Sep 3)*
After John 105 *(6f,Goo,HY,Sep 25)*
Agent Basterfield 110 *(12f,Bri,GF,Aug 8)*
Agent Gibbs 109 *(16f,Chp,GF,May 14)*
Agent Zigzag 109 *(10f,Cur,G,Jun 28)*
Agincourt 112 *(7f,Yor,G,Aug 22)*
Agrapart 106 *(16f,Asc,S,May 10)*
Agravain 108 *(14f,Red,GF,May 20)*
Ahlan Emarati 110 *(8f,Mey,G,Mar 2)*
Ahorsewithnoname 108 *(12f,Cat,S,Aug 19)*
Aim Power 103 *(8f,Asc,G,Jun 21)*
Air Dance 109 *(8f,Lon,GS,Jly 14)*
Air Force Amy 108 *(10f,Ffo,GS,Aug 13)*
Air Pilot 111 *(10f,Goo,HY,Sep 25)*
Air Raid 113 *(6f,Ham,S,Jly 19)*
Aircraft Carrier 107 *(16f,Asc,G,Aug 10)*
Airgead 110 *(8f,Leo,GF,Aug 8)*
Airshow 107 *(5f,Bev,GF,Apr 17)*
Aiya 110 *(10f,Pon,GF,Sep 19)*
Ajwad 122 *(8f,Mey,G,Mar 2)*
Aktau 111 *(11f,Goo,GF,Aug 2)*
Akvavera 103 *(7½f,Chs,GS,Aug 4)*
Akwaan 105 *(10f,Sal,GF,May 25)*
Al Erayg 106 *(7f,Lei,GF,Jly 6)*
Al Hilalee 103 *(10f,Nmk,G,May 18)*
Al Jellaby 105 *(8f,Don,G,Mar 30)*
Al Kout 107 *(16f,Asc,G,Aug 10)*
Al Messila 106 *(8½f,Not,G,Jly 16)*
Al Muffrih 112 *(10f,Red,GF,May 27)*
Al Mureib 104 *(8½f,Not,S,Oct 30)*
Alaadel 108 *(6f,Hay,S,Sep 6)*
Alandalos 103 *(8f,Bat,GF,Aug 27)*
Albanita 106 *(10f,Bat,F,Sep 15)*
Albert Finney 109 *(10½f,Hay,GF,Jly 4)*
Aleef 108 *(6f,Cur,G,Jun 29)*
Alemagna 110 *(12f,Goo,G,Aug 25)*
Alemaratalyoum 111 *(7f,Hay,S,Sep 6)*
Alexana 110 *(14f,Yor,GF,May 25)*
Alexander James 104 *(8f,Thi,GS,May 11)*
Alfa McGuire 105 *(8f,Ayr,G,Jly 15)*
Alfaatik 105 *(10f,San,GF,Apr 26)*
Alfie Solomons 104 *(6f,Nmk,GF,Jly 11)*
Alfolk 106 *(7f,Mey,G,Feb 7)*
Alfred Boucher 103 *(8f,Sal,S,Aug 14)*
Alfred Richardson 107 *(8f,Rip,G,Aug 26)*
Algaffaal 103 *(7f,Asc,GF,Jly 13)*
Alhaazm 103 *(11f,Nby,G,May 17)*
Alice Milligan 106 *(10f,Leo,G,Aug 15)*
Alicia Darcy 104 *(6f,Wdr,G,Aug 11)*
Alignak 108 *(12f,Ffo,G,Aug 29)*
Aljady 107 *(6f,Yor,GF,May 15)*
Alkaamel 109 *(8f,Nmk,G,May 4)*
Alkaraama 112 *(6f,Asc,GF,Sep 7)*
All Right 106 *(8f,Ffo,G,Aug 29)*
All The King's Men 104 *(7f,Leo,G,Jun 6)*
All Yours 106 *(12f,Ffo,GF,Aug 1)*
Allegiant 107 *(12f,Eps,G,Aug 1)*
Allmankind 110 *(10½f,Chs,GS,May 9)*
Almania 111 *(10f,Goo,G,Aug 1)*
Almashriq 108 *(10f,Nmk,GF,Jly 12)*
Almond Eye 116 *(9f,Mey,G,Mar 30)*
Almost Midnight 104 *(14f,Asc,S,Jun 19)*
Alnadir 105 *(10f,Bri,GF,Aug 8)*
Alnaseem 105 *(8f,Nmk,GF,Aug 3)*
Aloe Vera 114 *(10f,Chp,G,May 3)*
Alonso Cano 106 *(7f,Lon,G,May 16)*
Alotabottle 105 *(8f,Crl,GS,Sep 11)*
Alpha Delphini 115 *(5f,Hay,GF,May 25)*
Alrajaa 103 *(7f,Sal,GS,Aug 15)*
Alright Sunshine 112 *(17½f,Ayr,G,Sep 20)*
Alsvinder 104 *(5½f,Chs,G,Jly 12)*
Alternative Fact 107 *(8f,San,G,Jly 31)*
Altra Vita 110 *(16f,Asc,S,Oct 4)*
Aluqair 104 *(7f,Sal,GS,Aug 15)*
Always Resolute 104 *(16f,Rip,GS,Jun 5)*
Amadeus Grey 104 *(8½f,Not,G,Jun 5)*
Amanaat 105 *(6f,Cur,GF,May 25)*
Amanto 103 *(12f,Eps,G,Aug 1)*
Amaretto 103 *(10f,Bat,F,May 15)*
Amazing 117 *(7f,Sha,GF,Apr 22)*
Amazing Chocolate 116 *(7f,Sha,GF,Apr 22)*
Amazing Luck 118 *(7f,Sha,GF,Apr 22)*
Amazing Red 107 *(16f,Asc,GF,May 1)*
Amazing Satchmo 108 *(8f,Sha,G,Jan 1)*
Ambassadorial 106 *(7f,Nmk,GF,Jly 13)*
Ambient 107 *(8f,Hay,GF,Jly 5)*
Amedeo Modigliani 108 *(8f,Leo,GY,Apr 3)*
Amelia R 104 *(6f,Not,G,Jly 19)*
Amjaady 107 *(10f,Lei,GS,Jun 10)*
Amorously 107 *(8f,Wdr,GF,Jun 30)*
Amplify 107 *(6f,Sal,GF,May 25)*
Anapurna 112 *(12f,Lon,G,Sep 15)*
Anchises 105 *(8f,Ham,GF,May 17)*
Ancient Spirit 108 *(10f,Leo,SH,Oct 19)*
Angel Alexander 111 *(6f,Ayr,G,Sep 21)*
Angel Eyes 104 *(5f,Mus,GF,May 2)*
Angel Gabrial 108 *(14f,Red,G,Jun 22)*
Angel Islington 104 *(7f,Lon,VS,Oct 6)*
Angel's Hideaway 114 *(7f,Asc,G,Jun 22)*
Angel's Whisper 109 *(8½f,Eps,G,Aug 26)*
Anna Bunina 109 *(10f,Pon,GF,Sep 19)*
Anna Nerium 111 *(8½f,Eps,GF,Jun 1)*
Annie Fior 106 *(8f,Leo,G,Jun 6)*
Another Batt 112 *(7f,Mey,G,Jan 24)*
Another Lincolnday 106 *(14f,Red,G,Jun 22)*
Another Touch 105 *(10f,Yor,GF,Jly 13)*
Anthony Van Dyck 116 *(10f,Leo,G,Sep 14)*
Antico Lady 103 *(8f,Wet,GF,May 30)*
Antilles 104 *(10f,Cur,GF,Sep 15)*
Antonia De Vega 110 *(10f,Nby,S,Jun 13)*
Anyonecanhaveitall 108 *(16f,Mus,GF,Sep 14)*
Anythingtoday 109 *(8f,Thi,G,May 4)*
Apache Blaze 103 *(10f,Don,G,Mar 30)*
Aperitif 104 *(5f,Wwl... *

Aperitif 104 *(5f,Hay,GS,Jly 20)*
Apex King 109 *(7f,Nmk,G,Jun 27)*
Aplomb 115 *(6f,Asc,S,Oct 4)*
Apparate 108 *(12f,Sal,GF,Jun 26)*
Appeared 104 *(12f,Mey,G,Feb 14)*
Applause 106 *(7f,Sha,G,Apr 22)*
Appointed 108 *(11f,Crl,GF,Jun 26)*
Apterix 106 *(12f,Thi,GS,May 11)*
Aquarium 107 *(12f,Goo,GF,Aug 2)*
Arabeska 105 *(7f,Leo,G,Jly 18)*
Arabian Jazz 105 *(7f,Cat,GF,Jly 1)*
Arabist 105 *(12f,Nby,S,Aug 17)*
Arbalet 113 *(8f,Wdr,GF,Jun 29)*
Arcanada 108 *(8f,Hay,GS,Jun 22)*
Arcanears 108 *(6f,Cur,GF,May 25)*
Archaeology 112 *(8f,Don,G,May 4)*
Archer's Dream 111 *(6f,Sal,S,Jun 16)*
Archi's Affaire 109 *(12f,Rip,GS,Sep 28)*
Archie Perkins 107 *(10f,Yor,S,Jun 14)*
Archimedes 105 *(5f,Bev,GF,Aug 25)*
Archimento 105 *(14f,San,G,Jly 24)*
Arctic Fox 104 *(10f,Yor,GF,May 25)*
Arctic Ocean 107 *(12f,Bev,G,Jun 18)*
Arctic Sea 103 *(10f,Chp,G,Sep 2)*
Arctic Spirit 104 *(8f,Wdr,G,May 13)*
Ardhoomey 111 *(6f,Cur,GF,May 25)*
Arecibo 113 *(5f,Asc,S,Oct 5)*
Areen Heart 105 *(6f,Goo,GF,May 24)*
Arigato 104 *(8f,Nmk,GF,Jly 26)*
Arletta Star 106 *(7½f,Chs,GS,Jly 27)*
Armandihan 107 *(11f,Crl,GF,Jun 26)*
Armed 104 *(12f,Yor,GF,May 25)*
Army Of Angels 107 *(8f,Lon,GS,Jly 14)*
Arnold 104 *(5f,Bev,G,Jly 30)*
Arrowtown 107 *(17½f,Ayr,G,Sep 20)*
Art Song 104 *(8f,Nmk,GF,Aug 2)*
Arthur Kitt 107 *(12f,Chs,GS,May 8)*
Arthur Pendragon 108 *(14f,Lin,S,Jly 27)*
Arthurian Fame 107 *(12f,Gal,G,Aug 2)*
Artic Nel 103 *(14f,Cat,GF,Jly 1)*
Artistic Language 109 *(11f,Crl,HY,May 31)*
Artistic Rifles 109 *(8f,Don,GF,May 18)*
Arty Campbell 109 *(16f,Chp,GS,Aug 15)*
Asanda 107 *(8f,Leo,G,Jly 25)*
Ascot Day 110 *(12f,Chp,GS,Aug 15)*
Ascot Week 105 *(8f,Don,GF,Sep 11)*
Ashazuri 106 *(10f,Eps,G,Jly 4)*
Ashpan Sam 105 *(6f,Eps,G,Jly 4)*
Ashrun 111 *(15f,Lon,VS,Oct 5)*
Asian Angel 107 *(12f,Asc,G,Aug 10)*
Asoof 117 *(8f,Mey,G,Jan 17)*
Aspire Tower 109 *(12½f,Mus,GS,Jun 1)*
Assimilate 120 *(7f,Sha,G,Mar 31)*
Astrologer 105 *(7f,Thi,G,Sep 7)*
Atalanta's Boy 110 *(6f,Goo,HY,Sep 25)*
Athlumney Hall 104 *(8f,Cur,S,Sep 28)*
Athollblair Boy 108 *(7f,Don,GF,Jun 29)*
Atlas 113 *(8f,Cur,GF,May 26)*
Atletico 106 *(7½f,Bev,GS,May 29)*
Atomic Jack 110 *(16f,Chp,GS,Aug 15)*
Aubretia 106 *(8f,Nmk,G,Jun 22)*
Aurora Eclipse 106 *(6f,Cur,S,Aug 16)*
Aussie Breeze 105 *(12f,Chp,G,Aug 22)*
Aussie Valentine 117 *(8f,Cur,GF,May 26)*
Aussie View 103 *(8f,Wdr,GF,Aug 5)*
Australien 108 *(11f,Lon,GS,Apr 22)*
Australis 106 *(10f,Wet,G,May 7)*
Austrian School 114 *(14f,Mus,G,Apr 20)*
Autretot 104 *(10f,Ayr,GF,Jly 7)*
Autumn Flight 105 *(6f,Ham,S,Sep 22)*
Autumn War 108 *(10f,Don,G,Jly 20)*
Auxerre 112 *(8f,Don,G,Mar 30)*
Auxiliary 108 *(12f,Yor,S,Jun 14)*
Avalanche 107 *(8f,Leo,GF,Jly 11)*
Awaamir 105 *(7f,Lon,GS,Apr 22)*
Awake My Soul 106 *(10½f,Hay,HY,Jun 12)*
Away He Goes 105 *(10f,Nby,GF,Jly 11)*
Awe 113 *(8f,Hay,GF,May 25)*
Aweedram 114 *(8f,Hay,GF,May 25)*
Awesometank 109 *(8½f,Eps,GF,Jun 1)*
Ay Ay 103 *(12f,Mey,G,Jan 19)*
Ayutthaya 107 *(10f,Pon,G,Jun 23)*
Azano 110 *(7f,Nmk,G,May 18)*
Azraff 117 *(7f,Mey,G,Jan 19)*
Aztec Eagle 104 *(10f,Leo,G,Jun 13)*

B Fifty Two 105 *(6f,Thi,G,Aug 30)*
Baasem 109 *(12f,Don,S,Aug 3)*
Baashiq 105 *(8f,Bri,GF,Sep 16)*
Baba Ghanouj 103 *(8f,Nmk,GF,Jly 26)*
Baba Mama 118 *(7f,Sha,G,Jan 1)*
Babbo's Boy 104 *(12f,Lei,GF,May 20)*
Baby Power 114 *(6f,Cur,GF,May 26)*
Baby Steps 104 *(6f,Pon,G,Aug 7)*
Badenscoth 109 *(10f,San,S,Jun 14)*
Baghdad 108 *(12f,Asc,G,Jun 21)*
Bahamian Sunrise 107 *(5f,San,G,Sep 13)*
Bahkit 105 *(10f,Red,G,Apr 8)*
Bahlwan 107 *(5f,Mus,GF,May 2)*
Bailarico 106 *(18f,Pon,GF,Apr 9)*
Balefire 109 *(8f,Leo,GF,Jly 11)*
Balgair 106 *(8f,Nmk,G,Jun 27)*
Balladeer 105 *(8f,Nmk,GF,May 16)*
Ballet Red 109 *(10f,Chp,GF,May 14)*
Ballyquin 103 *(6f,Asc,GS,May 11)*
Balmoral Castle 104 *(10f,Wdr,G,May 13)*
Baltic Baron 109 *(8f,Goo,GF,Aug 2)*
Baltic Song 108 *(12f,Lei,HY,Oct 8)*
Bambino Lola 108 *(7f,Red,G,Jun 22)*
Bambys Boy 104 *(14f,Ffo,G,Aug 23)*
Band Of Brothers 119 *(7f,Sha,G,Apr 22)*
Banditry 109 *(11½f,Wdr,GF,Jun 29)*
Bangkok 110 *(12f,Asc,GS,Jun 21)*
Banksea 103 *(8f,Ayr,G,Jun 22)*
Banksy's Art 116 *(10f,Chp,GF,May 23)*
Banta Bay 109 *(14f,Lin,GF,Sep 14)*
Bar Room Bore 107 *(12f,Gal,G,Aug 1)*
Baraweez 107 *(7½f,Chs,S,May 10)*
Barbados 107 *(14f,Asc,S,Jun 19)*
Barbill 106 *(6f,Nmk,GF,Jly 11)*
Barend Boy 103 *(6f,Cur,GF,May 25)*
Barney Roy 112 *(8f,Asc,G,Jun 18)*
Baron Bolt 110 *(6f,Sal,GF,Sep 3)*
Baroot 117 *(8f,Mey,G,Jan 10)*
Barossa Red 108 *(8f,Hay,HY,Aug 10)*
Barristan The Bold 115 *(8f,Hay,GF,May 25)*
Barsanti 113 *(14f,Yor,GF,Aug 24)*
Bartholomeu Dias 106 *(14½f,Don,GF,Sep 13)*
Bashiyr 103 *(8f,Cur,S,Sep 28)*
Basilisk 107 *(8f,Ffo,G,Aug 29)*
Battaash 119 *(5f,Hay,GF,May 25)*
Battered 105 *(6½f,Don,GF,Sep 13)*
Battle Of Marathon 108 *(14f,Mus,GF,Sep 6)*
Battle Of Pembroke 103 *(14f,Red,GF,May 28)*
Battle Of Waterloo 104 *(7f,Mus,G,Aug 2)*
Battle Of Wills 106 *(12f,Hay,GF,Jly 4)*
Bay Hill 105 *(12f,Cur,G,Jly 20)*
Bay Of Poets 107 *(9f,Mey,G,Jan 24)*
Bayshore Freeway 116 *(14f,Yor,GF,May 25)*
Be Bold 103 *(8f,Pon,G,Aug 7)*
Be More 104 *(8f,Asc,GF,Jly 13)*
Be Perfect 104 *(14f,Cat,GF,Sep 21)*
Be Thankful 106 *(10f,Lin,S,Jun 11)*
Bear Force One 111 *(7f,Nby,GF,Sep 21)*
Beat Le Bon 113 *(8f,Goo,GF,Aug 2)*
Beat The Bank 117 *(8f,Asc,G,Jun 18)*
Beatboxer 119 *(8f,Hay,GF,May 25)*
Beaufort 103 *(11f,Crl,GS,Jun 17)*
Beautiful Gesture 103 *(8f,Thi,G,Apr 29)*
Beauty Filly 107 *(7f,Chs,G,Jly 13)*
Beauty Only 111 *(7f,Sha,G,Jan 1)*
Beckford 112 *(6f,Cur,G,Jun 29)*
Beckwith Place 106 *(8f,Leo,G,Jun 6)*
Bedouin's Story 117 *(7f,Yor,S,Jly 27)*
Bedtime Bella 105 *(6f,Crl,HY,Aug 13)*
Beechwood Jude 106 *(11f,Crl,GS,Jun 17)*
Beer With The Boys 106 *(17f,Bat,F,Aug 2)*
Belated Breath 106 *(6f,Wdr,GF,May 27)*
Bell Heather 105 *(7½f,Chs,G,Jly 12)*
Bell Rock 107 *(8f,San,GF,May 23)*
Bella Ragazza 106 *(8½f,Eps,GF,Jun 1)*
Bella Vita 112 *(10f,Sal,S,Jun 11)*
Bellakris 109 *(8f,Cur,G,Jly 20)*
Bellevarde 113 *(5f,Not,S,Oct 30)*
Belvoir Bay 108 *(6f,Mey,G,Mar 30)*
Ben Vrackie 112 *(14f,Yor,GF,Aug 24)*
Benadalid 109 *(10f,Don,G,Jly 20)*
Benbatl 117 *(8f,Nmk,G,Sep 27)*
Bengali Boys 104 *(5f,Not,S,May 11)*
Benny And The Jets 104 *(5f,Lei,GF,Sep 23)*
Bercasa 109 *(10f,Leo,GY,May 12)*
Beringer 109 *(8f,Don,G,Mar 30)*
Berrahri 105 *(14f,Goo,G,Aug 24)*
Beryl The Petal 103 *(6f,Pon,GF,Jly 1)*
Beshaayir 115 *(8f,Cur,GF,May 25)*
Best Effort 108 *(8f,Sha,G,Mar 31)*
Betancourt 103 *(14f,Cat,GF,Jly 1)*
Betsey Trotter 108 *(6f,Red,G,Aug 10)*
Better Choice 122 *(7f,Sha,G,Mar 31)*
Betty F 104 *(7f,Nmk,GF,Jly 12)*
Betty Grable 106 *(12f,Cat,GF,Sep 21)*
Beverley Bullet 107 *(10f,Yor,S,Jun 14)*
Beyond Equal 108 *(6f,Bat,G,Jun 26)*
Beyond Reason 105 *(7f,Goo,G,Aug 2)*
Beyond The Clouds 106 *(12f,Rip,GS,Aug 5)*
Bhodi 103 *(10f,Lei,GF,Sep 10)*
Bibbidibobbidiboo 105 *(7f,Cat,GF,Jly 1)*
Bielsa 115 *(6f,Thi,G,Aug 30)*
Big Challenge 110 *(10f,Mey,G,Jan 17)*
Big Country 104 *(10f,Don,GF,Sep 11)*
Big Kitten 105 *(11½f,Wdr,GF,Jun 29)*
Big Lachie 106 *(5f,Bat,G,Jun 26)*
Big Time Dancer 106 *(14f,Red,G,Jun 22)*
Big Time Maybe 103 *(5f,Bri,GF,Aug 20)*
Bighearted 103 *(10f,Yar,GF,Sep 18)*
Billesdon Brook 115 *(8f,Nmk,GS,Oct 5)*
Billingsgate 116 *(7f,Mey,G,Jan 19)*
Billy Dylan 105 *(5f,Bev,G,Jly 30)*
Billy No Mates 108 *(12f,Rip,GS,Sep 28)*
Billy Ray 112 *(16½f,Nby,GS,Jly 20)*
Billy Roberts 108 *(10f,Pon,GF,Sep 19)*
Bin Battuta 114 *(12f,Mey,G,Jan 24)*
Bint Soghaan 109 *(10f,Nmk,GF,Aug 24)*
Biometric 111 *(8f,Asc,GS,Jun 20)*
Birch Grove 105 *(12f,Nmk,GF,Jun 29)*
Bird To Love 107 *(10f,Ffo,GS,Aug 13)*
Bit Of A Quirke 104 *(10½f,Chs,G,Jly 13)*
Black Friday 104 *(7f,Mus,G,Aug 2)*
Black Kalanisi 110 *(12f,Bri,GF,Aug 8)*
Black Lotus 109 *(10f,Don,GF,Jun 1)*
Black Magic Woman 115 *(7f,Leo,G,Sep 14)*
Black Medick 103 *(7f,Eps,GF,Aug 27)*
Blackheath 112 *(7f,Lei,GF,Jly 6)*
Blacklooks 103 *(6f,Cur,Y,Aug 23)*
Blaine 107 *(6f,Goo,GS,Jun 9)*
Blair House 113 *(9f,Mey,G,Jan 24)*
Blairmayne 112 *(6f,Cur,G,Sep 15)*
Blakeney Point 106 *(12f,Nmk,G,Aug 9)*
Blame It On Sally 105 *(16f,Goo,G,Aug 23)*
Blame Roberta 103 *(5f,Bat,GF,Apr 19)*
Blankiedoodie 105 *(8f,Leo,GF,Aug 8)*
Blazing Saddles 108 *(11½f,Lin,GF,Jun 1)*
Blenheim Palace 116 *(10f,Leo,GY,May 12)*
Bless Him 110 *(8f,Asc,GF,Sep 6)*
Blistering Bob 104 *(10f,Sal,S,Aug 14)*
Blizzard 106 *(7f,Goo,G,Aug 2)*
Blizzing Away 112 *(7f,Sha,G,Jan 1)*
Blonde Warrior 103 *(7f,Yar,GF,Jun 28)*
Blooming Spirit 112 *(7f,Sha,G,Mar 31)*
Blowing Dixie 103 *(14f,Red,GF,May 20)*
Blown By Wind 110 *(7f,Mus,S,Oct 14)*
Blue De Vega 111 *(5f,Asc,GF,Sep 7)*
Blue Gardenia 107 *(12f,Nmk,G,Jly 20)*
Blue Laureate 105 *(18f,Nmk,GF,Sep 21)*
Blue Medici 107 *(10f,Wdr,GF,Jun 30)*
Blue Mist 112 *(7f,Asc,GS,May 11)*
Blue Point 121 *(5f,Mey,G,Feb 14)*
Blyton 105 *(6f,Cur,S,Aug 16)*
Bo Samraan 109 *(12f,Cat,HY,Oct 29)*
Bobby Shaft 104 *(7f,Red,G,Apr 8)*
Boerhan 104 *(13f,Nmk,GF,Jly 11)*
Bogardus 103 *(16f,Mus,GF,Jly 3)*
Boitron 111 *(7f,Nby,GS,Apr 13)*
Bold Approach 106 *(10f,Cur,GF,Sep 15)*
Bold Rex 117 *(8f,Mey,G,Mar 2)*
Bollihope 109 *(8f,Pon,G,Aug 7)*
Bollin Joan 107 *(12f,Cat,GF,Sep 21)*
Bollin Ted 104 *(10f,Bev,GF,Jly 22)*

Bombero 107 *(11f,Crl,GS,Jun 17)*
Bombyx 108 *(10f,San,GF,May 23)*
Bopedro 114 *(7f,Leo,G,Sep 14)*
Born In China 114 *(7f,Sha,G,Jan 1)*
Born Leader 104 *(12f,Don,G,Jly 20)*
Born To Reason 103 *(12f,Bri,GF,Aug 20)*
Borodin 115 *(8f,Thi,G,May 4)*
Bossipop 111 *(5½f,Chs,G,Aug 31)*
Boston Bruin 107 *(10f,Cur,G,Jun 28)*
Boston George 107 *(7f,Wet,GS,May 7)*
Boudica Bay 104 *(5f,Not,GS,Jun 27)*
Boundary Lane 111 *(5f,Chs,GF,Jun 29)*
Bounty Pursuit 104 *(7f,Chp,G,Sep 17)*
Bowerman 103 *(8½f,Not,GF,Apr 10)*
Bowson Fred 103 *(5½f,Chs,G,Jly 12)*
Boy In The Bar 103 *(6f,Ayr,G,Jun 22)*
Brando 115 *(6½f,Dea,G,Aug 4)*
Brasca 105 *(12f,Chp,GF,May 23)*
Brave Hero 106 *(7f,Mey,G,Jan 19)*
Bravo Sierra 114 *(6f,Dea,G,Aug 4)*
Bravo Zolo 116 *(7f,Mey,G,Jan 24)*
Breanski 108 *(7f,Don,S,Aug 17)*
Breathable 104 *(11f,Crl,GS,Aug 5)*
Breathtaking Look 115 *(7f,Don,GF,Sep 13)*
Breden 109 *(8f,Don,G,Mar 30)*
Breton Rock 111 *(7f,Don,GF,Sep 14)*
Brian Epstein 108 *(8f,Don,GF,May 18)*
Brian The Snail 109 *(5f,Asc,GF,Jly 13)*
Briardale 104 *(10f,Pon,GF,Sep 19)*
Bring It On 108 *(9f,Sha,G,Mar 31)*
Bring Us Paradise 107 *(8½f,Eps,G,Sep 12)*
Brittanic 103 *(10f,Yar,F,Aug 25)*
Broad Appeal 107 *(11f,Goo,GF,Sep 3)*
Broad Street 111 *(12f,Leo,GF,Aug 8)*
Brockagh Cailin 106 *(8f,Bat,F,May 24)*
Brockey Rise 104 *(6f,Thi,GF,Jun 3)*
Broken Spear 111 *(5f,Cat,S,Oct 19)*
Broome 118 *(10f,Leo,GY,May 12)*
Brother McGonagall 105 *(8½f,Bev,G,Jun 8)*
Broughtons Flare 106 *(7f,Nmk,GF,May 17)*
Brutalab 106 *(10f,Bev,GF,Jly 16)*
Bruyere 106 *(10f,Not,S,Oct 9)*
Bubble And Squeak 109 *(8f,Asc,GS,May 11)*
Buccaneers Vault 106 *(6f,Thi,G,Aug 30)*
Buckhurst 115 *(12f,Leo,G,Sep 14)*
Buckland Boy 109 *(12f,Thi,GS,Jun 18)*
Buckman Tavern 110 *(14f,San,G,Jly 25)*
Buddies 118 *(7f,Sha,G,Mar 31)*
Buffer Zone 117 *(6f,Cur,G,Sep 15)*
Bug Boy 107 *(10f,Ffo,GF,Aug 1)*
Buhwarui Banseok 109 *(10f,Mey,G,Jan 17)*
Building Bridges 107 *(10f,Leo,GY,Apr 3)*
Buildmeupbuttercup 104 *(18f,Nmk,S,Oct 12)*
Bullington Boy 104 *(8f,Nmk,GF,May 16)*
Bullion Boss 108 *(11f,Crl,HY,May 31)*
Bungee Jump 105 *(7f,Chp,G,Sep 2)*
Burford Brown 103 *(5f,Asc,GF,May 1)*
Buridan 105 *(6f,Don,GF,Mar 31)*
Buriram 112 *(11f,Crl,HY,May 31)*
Burmese Blazer 105 *(5f,Ham,S,Sep 23)*
Burn Some Dust 110 *(17½f,Ayr,GS,Jly 22)*
Burren View Lady 108 *(6f,Cur,GF,May 26)*
Burtonwood 105 *(5f,Bev,G,Jly 30)*
Buyer Beware 111 *(15f,Ayr,G,Jun 21)*
Buzz 108 *(14f,Yor,GS,Jun 15)*
Bye Bye Hong Kong 110 *(8½f,Eps,GF,Jun 1)*
Byron Flyer 106 *(12f,Eps,GF,Jun 1)*
Byron's Choice 111 *(7½f,Bev,GF,Jun 8)*

C Note 105 *(10f,Nby,S,Aug 17)*
C'Est No Mour 107 *(12f,Bri,GF,Aug 8)*
Cadre Du Noir 103 *(10f,Goo,GF,Sep 3)*
Caesar's Comet 109 *(6f,Cur,GF,May 26)*
Cafe Sydney 106 *(10f,Cur,GF,Aug 3)*
Calder Prince 104 *(8f,Hay,GF,Jly 5)*
Cale Lane 105 *(6f,Pon,GF,Jly 1)*
California Gungho 108 *(5f,Sha,G,Apr 22)*
California Love 111 *(7f,Nmk,GF,Jly 13)*
California Turbo 120 *(7f,Sha,G,Mar 31)*
California Whip 112 *(7f,Sha,G,Jan 1)*
Call Me Ginger 106 *(5f,Asc,S,Oct 5)*
Call Out Loud 109 *(7½f,Chs,G,Jun 28)*
Call The Wind 116 *(8f,Mey,G,Mar 30)*
Calvados Spirit 107 *(8f,Pon,GS,Jly 19)*
Calyx 109 *(6f,Asc,GF,May 1)*
Camacho Chief 111 *(5f,Chs,GS,May 9)*
Came From The Dark 108 *(6f,Hay,HY,Jun 8)*
Camphor 110 *(12f,Gal,G,Aug 2)*
Canal Rocks 108 *(8f,Nby,GS,Aug 16)*
Candelisa 107 *(7f,Lei,G,Apr 5)*
Canford Bay 108 *(5f,Rip,GS,May 10)*
Canford Dancer 108 *(10f,Chp,GF,May 14)*
Canning 105 *(8½f,Gal,G,Aug 5)*
Canton Queen 106 *(7f,Nmk,GF,Aug 24)*
Cap Francais 108 *(11½f,Lin,S,May 11)*
Cape Byron 116 *(7f,Asc,GS,May 11)*
Cape Cavalli 108 *(12f,Lei,GF,May 27)*
Cape Islay 109 *(12f,Chs,GF,Jun 29)*
Cape Of Good Hope 108 *(10f,Eps,G,Apr 24)*
Cape Victory 107 *(9f,Mus,GF,Sep 14)*
Capofaro 104 *(8f,Wdr,GF,May 27)*
Capri 110 *(14f,Cur,GF,Sep 15)*
Captain Jameson 104 *(7f,Yor,S,Oct 11)*
Caradoc 112 *(10f,Nmk,G,Jly 27)*
Caravan Of Hope 114 *(12f,Ffo,G,Aug 29)*
Carbon Dating 109 *(13f,Ham,GF,May 5)*
Cardano 110 *(10f,Nmk,GF,Aug 24)*
Cardaw Lily 104 *(6f,Thi,G,Aug 30)*
Cardsharp 114 *(7f,Lei,GF,Apr 27)*
Carey Street 103 *(8f,Ayr,G,Sep 19)*
Carnwennan 104 *(16f,Yor,GF,May 16)*
Carp Kid 106 *(12f,Chp,G,May 3)*
Cartmell Cleave 106 *(6f,Don,GF,Jun 29)*
Casanova 109 *(7f,Asc,S,Oct 5)*
Case Key 104 *(6f,Yar,GF,Jly 25)*
Casement 105 *(8f,Pon,GF,Apr 9)*
Caspian Prince 112 *(5f,Cur,G,Jly 21)*
Castletownshend 111 *(6f,Cur,G,Sep 15)*
Catch My Breath 106 *(10f,Yar,GF,Aug 8)*
Caustic Love 106 *(8f,Rip,GS,Aug 6)*
Cautious Approach 104 *(8f,Leo,GF,Aug 8)*
Cava 103 *(7f,Crl,GF,Jun 26)*
Celebrity Dancer 103 *(7f,Ayr,G,Jun 22)*
Celerity 109 *(5½f,Chs,G,Jly 12)*
Celestial Force 107 *(14f,Crl,GS,Aug 21)*
Celestial Spheres 112 *(12f,Mey,G,Feb 14)*
Celsius 105 *(5f,Hay,S,Jun 6)*
Celtic Classic 106 *(12f,Chp,G,Aug 26)*
Cent Flying 107 *(6f,Nmk,G,Aug 16)*
Central City 105 *(10f,Don,G,Mar 30)*
Century Dream 116 *(8f,Mey,G,Feb 21)*
Cerberus 105 *(8½f,Gal,G,Aug 3)*
Certain Lad 115 *(8f,Hay,GF,May 25)*
Chablis 103 *(10f,Cur,GF,Sep 15)*
Chairman Lo 121 *(7f,Sha,G,Mar 31)*
Chaleur 112 *(7f,Yor,G,Aug 22)*
Champagne Champ 104 *(18f,Nmk,GF,Sep 21)*
Champagne Marengo 110 *(16f,Asc,GF,Jly 12)*
Champagne Terri 110 *(12f,Gal,G,Aug 1)*
Champarisi 112 *(14f,Cat,GF,Sep 21)*
Champion Supreme 115 *(9f,Sha,G,Mar 31)*
Championship 114 *(7f,Mey,G,Jan 24)*
Champs De Reves 106 *(10f,Bat,F,May 6)*
Chance 106 *(8½f,Not,G,Jly 6)*
Channel 112 *(12f,Lon,G,Sep 15)*
Chaparral Dream 108 *(12f,Gal,G,Aug 1)*
Chapelli 106 *(6f,Chs,G,Jly 13)*
Chaplin Bay 103 *(7f,Ayr,HY,Aug 10)*
Charles Kingsley 112 *(12f,Bri,GF,Jun 3)*
Charles Molson 106 *(7f,Asc,GF,Jly 13)*
Charlie D 112 *(14f,Bat,F,Sep 15)*
Chartered 104 *(12f,Goo,S,Jun 14)*
Chatez 109 *(8f,Nby,GS,Apr 13)*
Chatham House 105 *(7f,Lei,GF,Sep 10)*
Chebsey Beau 103 *(14f,Cat,GF,Sep 10)*
Cheeky Bee 115 *(7f,Sha,G,Mar 31)*
Cheng Gong 104 *(11½f,Yar,HY,Oct 14)*
Cherry Cola 108 *(11½f,Yar,S,Jun 13)*
Chessman 112 *(6f,Cur,G,Jun 29)*
Chesterfield 105 *(11½f,Wdr,S,Oct 7)*
Cheval Grand 120 *(12f,Mey,G,Mar 30)*
Chickenfortea 103 *(6f,Red,G,Sep 25)*
Chief Ironside 111 *(8½f,Eps,GF,Jun 1)*
Chiefofchiefs 105 *(8f,Asc,HY,Oct 19)*
Chil Chil 110 *(6f,Wdr,GF,Sep 2)*
Chilean 103 *(8f,Asc,S,Jun 19)*
Chinese Alphabet 105 *(10f,Ffo,GF,Aug 1)*
Chinese Spirit 103 *(8f,Ayr,G,Jly 15)*
Chingachgook 108 *(11f,Crl,GF,Jun 26)*
Chitra 105 *(6f,Lin,GF,Sep 14)*
Chiu Chow Kid 103 *(8f,Sha,G,Jan 1)*
Chocolate Music 111 *(7f,Gal,G,Aug 1)*
Chynna 108 *(6f,Not,S,May 11)*
Ciao 104 *(12f,Cur,GY,Aug 23)*
Cimeara 108 *(14f,Cur,G,Jun 28)*
Circuit Three 112 *(9f,Sha,G,Mar 31)*
Circus Couture 108 *(8½f,Not,G,Jun 5)*
Circus Maximus 118 *(10½f,Chs,GS,May 9)*
Citron Major 107 *(6½f,Don,GF,Sep 13)*
Citta D'Oro 103 *(10½f,Chs,G,Jly 13)*
City Light 115 *(7f,Lon,G,Sep 15)*
City Wanderer 107 *(8f,Wdr,GF,Aug 24)*
Cityman 108 *(5f,Cur,GY,Jun 7)*
Claim The Lady 112 *(10f,Leo,GY,Jun 20)*
Claire Underwood 110 *(12½f,Mus,G,May 3)*
Clara Peeters 106 *(7f,Asc,GF,Sep 6)*
Classic Charm 109 *(8½f,Not,S,Aug 1)*
Clayton 104 *(10f,Red,GF,May 2)*
Clement Legend 105 *(9f,Sha,GF,Apr 22)*
Cleonte 116 *(16f,Asc,GF,May 1)*
Cliff 103 *(6f,Yar,S,Jun 12)*
Cliff Bay 103 *(7f,Ayr,G,Jly 15)*
Cliffs Of Capri 114 *(7f,Mey,G,Feb 7)*
Clon Coulis 113 *(8f,Asc,S,Jun 19)*
Club Wexford 111 *(8f,Ayr,G,Jun 22)*
Cnoc An Oir 109 *(8f,Leo,G,Jun 13)*
Coastline 106 *(8f,Yar,GF,Jly 4)*
Coby Boy 118 *(7f,Sha,G,Mar 31)*
Cockalorum 108 *(10f,Yor,S,Oct 12)*
Coeur Blimey 109 *(18f,Nby,S,Apr 12)*
Coeur D'amour 108 *(10f,Ayr,GF,May 22)*
Coeur De Lion 110 *(16½f,Nby,GS,Jly 20)*
Cogital 104 *(10f,Wdr,GF,Jun 30)*
Cold Stare 111 *(6f,Hay,HY,Jun 8)*
Colfer Me 105 *(8f,Lec,GF,Jly 11)*
Collide 106 *(12f,Yor,GF,May 15)*
Colonel Frank 109 *(5f,Not,HY,Nov 6)*
Colony Queen 108 *(10f,Nby,HY,Oct 25)*
Come On Leicester 107 *(6f,Not,S,May 11)*
Come September 104 *(7f,Leo,SH,Oct 26)*
Comedia Eria 103 *(5f,Lon,G,Sep 15)*
Comfort Life 117 *(7f,Sha,G,Jan 1)*
Comin' Through 113 *(7f,Mey,G,Jan 24)*
Commander Han 116 *(8f,Thi,G,May 4)*
Commes 109 *(10f,Lon,VS,Oct 6)*
Communique 113 *(12f,Eps,G,May 31)*
Concierge 110 *(5f,Asc,GF,Sep 7)*
Confessional 114 *(5f,Chs,GS,May 9)*
Confrontational 109 *(7f,Chs,S,Sep 28)*
Conga 103 *(6f,Ham,HY,Sep 30)*
Connect 109 *(9f,Mey,G,Feb 7)*
Conor Hogan 106 *(10f,Leo,GY,Apr 3)*
Conspiritor 103 *(8f,Bat,F,Jly 10)*
Constantinople 115 *(16f,Fle,GS,Nov 5)*
Conte 119 *(7f,Sha,G,Jan 1)*
Contingency Fee 103 *(12f,Bri,GF,Aug 20)*
Contrebasse 105 *(14f,Not,HY,Oct 2)*
Contrive 108 *(8f,Asc,GS,May 11)*
Conversant 112 *(6f,Cur,S,Oct 22)*
Cool Reflection 105 *(6f,Bat,F,Jly 3)*
Coolagh Forest 114 *(10f,Yor,S,Oct 12)*
Coolagh Magic 103 *(5f,Chs,S,Jun 15)*
Copper Knight 116 *(5f,Chs,GS,May 9)*
Coral Beach 116 *(8f,Leo,G,Sep 14)*
Corazon Espinado 104 *(8f,Wdr,G,May 6)*
Corelli 110 *(12f,Nmk,G,Aug 9)*
Corgi 106 *(12f,Yor,GF,May 15)*
Corinthia Knight 107 *(5f,Pon,G,Jly 19)*
Corncrake 107 *(10f,Not,G,Jly 6)*
Cornerstone Lad 107 *(16f,Cat,HY,Oct 29)*
Corton Lad 104 *(10f,Ayr,GF,May 22)*
Cosmic Horizon 108 *(8f,Leo,GF,Jly 11)*
Cosmic Law 106 *(6f,Yor,GS,Jun 15)*
Cosmic Ray 104 *(10f,Not,S,Oct 9)*
Cote D'Azur 107 *(10f,Yor,G,Sep 8)*
Cotton Club 106 *(14f,Bat,F,Sep 15)*
Couldn't Could She 111 *(10f,Chp,GF,May 23)*
Count D'orsay 114 *(5f,Cat,S,Oct 19)*
Count Of Carabass 104 *(7f,Leo,G,Jly 18)*
Count Otto 111 *(6f,Asc,GF,Sep 7)*
Country 109 *(10f,San,GF,Aug 31)*
Coviglia 105 *(7½f,Chs,G,Jly 12)*
Cowboy Soldier 107 *(5f,Yor,GF,May 16)*
Crafty Madam 110 *(7f,Yor,G,Aug 22)*
Craneur 106 *(10f,Sal,F,Jly 13)*
Credenza 111 *(9f,Cur,G,Aug 30)*
Creek Island 103 *(8f,Nmk,GS,Aug 16)*
Cristal Breeze 107 *(6f,Nmk,G,Jly 27)*
Cristal Spirit 105 *(16f,Nby,HY,Oct 25)*
Cross Counter 119 *(16f,Mey,G,Mar 30)*
Crossing The Line 104 *(7f,Nmk,GF,Jly 13)*
Crotchet 116 *(8f,Cur,GF,May 26)*
Crown Avenue 107 *(7f,Sha,G,Jan 1)*
Crowned Eagle 109 *(11½f,Wdr,GF,Aug 24)*
Crownthorpe 105 *(8f,Yor,S,Oct 11)*
Cruella Dovil 106 *(6f,Cur,Y,May 6)*
Crystal King 110 *(13f,Ayr,G,Jun 22)*
Crystal Moonlight 104 *(12f,Pon,G,Jun 23)*
Crystal Ocean 121 *(12f,Asc,GS,Jly 27)*
Crystal Tiara 105 *(10f,Not,S,Aug 6)*
Crystal Tribe 104 *(10f,Bri,GF,Jly 2)*
Cuba Ruba 104 *(12f,Thi,S,Aug 9)*
Cuban Hope 108 *(12f,Cur,GY,Jun 7)*
Cuban Surfer 104 *(12f,Cur,GY,Aug 23)*
Culture 108 *(10f,Chp,G,May 3)*
Cupid's Arrow 107 *(6f,Rip,GS,Jun 20)*
Cuppacoco 104 *(5f,Bev,GS,May 29)*
Curfewed 103 *(8f,Rip,G,Aug 27)*
Current Option 116 *(7f,Leo,G,Sep 14)*
Custard The Dragon 104 *(7f,Lei,GS,Jun 10)*
Cwynar 113 *(10f,Chp,GF,May 23)*
Cypress Creek 110 *(14f,Cur,GF,Sep 15)*
Cyrus Dallin 103 *(7f,Gal,G,Aug 3)*

D'bai 119 *(7f,Mey,G,Jan 24)*
Daddies Girl 104 *(8½f,Not,GS,Apr 30)*
Daddy's Daughter 106 *(7f,Sal,S,Jun 16)*
Daffy Jane 104 *(6f,Pon,GF,Jly 1)*
Daghash 109 *(16f,Chp,GF,May 14)*
Dahik 103 *(6f,Red,GF,Aug 24)*
Daimyo 106 *(7f,Lon,VS,Oct 6)*
Dakota Gold 116 *(5f,Asc,S,Oct 5)*
Dal Horrisgle 113 *(10½f,Hay,GF,Jly 4)*
Dalaalaat 107 *(10f,Goo,G,Aug 1)*
Dalgarno 103 *(10f,Nmk,S,Nov 1)*
Dalton 107 *(6f,Thi,G,May 18)*
Dalton Highway 104 *(16f,Cur,S,Oct 13)*
Dame Freya Stark 108 *(10f,Yar,GF,Aug 8)*
Dame Kyteler 103 *(8f,Cur,G,Jly 20)*
Dame Malliot 118 *(12f,Nmk,G,Jly 20)*
Damon Runyon 109 *(10f,San,GS,Jun 15)*
Dan's Dream 112 *(6f,Cur,GY,Jun 7)*
Dance Alone 108 *(8f,Leo,GF,Jly 11)*
Dance Diva 108 *(7f,Nby,HY,Oct 25)*
Dance Emperor 113 *(10f,Leo,GY,Jun 20)*
Dance King 106 *(11f,Crl,GF,Jun 26)*
Dance Legend 111 *(12f,Pon,G,Jun 23)*
Danceteria 111 *(10f,San,GF,Jly 6)*
Dancin Boy 104 *(10f,Red,GF,May 2)*
Dancing Doll 106 *(12f,Gal,G,Aug 1)*
Dancing Jo 104 *(8f,Wdr,G,Apr 8)*
Dancing Lilly 103 *(14f,Ffo,G,Aug 23)*
Dancing Mountain 107 *(5f,Cat,GS,Aug 6)*
Dancing On A Dream 108 *(7f,Gal,G,Jly 30)*
Dancing Rave 105 *(6f,Ayr,S,Oct 1)*
Dandhu 106 *(7f,Nby,GS,Apr 13)*
Dandy's Beano 103 *(5½f,Ayr,G,Sep 20)*
Dandys Gold 103 *(6f,Lei,GF,Aug 8)*
Danehill Kodiac 111 *(16f,Asc,GF,May 1)*
Danglydontask 104 *(16f,Chp,GF,Jly 26)*
Danielsflyer 108 *(6f,Don,GF,Mar 31)*
Dante's View 107 *(12f,Pon,G,Jun 23)*
Danzan 104 *(6f,Wdr,GS,Jun 17)*
Danzeno 113 *(5f,Asc,S,Oct 5)*
Dapper Man 113 *(5f,Ham,GF,Jun 27)*
Dark American 114 *(7f,Lon,VS,Oct 6)*
Dark Defender 104 *(6f,Rip,GS,May 10)*
Dark Devil 104 *(10½f,Chs,GS,Aug 4)*
Dark Intention 103 *(10f,Yor,GF,Jly 12)*
Dark Jedi 110 *(10½f,Chs,GS,May 9)*
Dark Lochnagar 109 *(10f,Don,HY,Oct 25)*
Dark Red 112 *(10f,Nmk,G,Jly 27)*
Dark Shadow 107 *(5f,Don,GF,Sep 11)*
Dark Shot 109 *(5f,Yor,GF,May 16)*
Dark Side Dream 106 *(5f,Yar,GF,Aug 20)*
Dark Vision 111 *(10f,Nmk,GF,Jly 12)*
Darkened 107 *(8½f,Gal,G,Aug 3)*
Darksideoftarnside 112 *(16f,Asc,S,Oct 4)*
Das Kapital 103 *(11½f,Yar,HY,Oct 14)*
Daschas 109 *(5f,Yar,GF,Sep 18)*
Dash D'or 105 *(5f,Cur,GY,Jun 27)*
Dashing Dart 103 *(8f,Sha,G,Jan 1)*
Dashing Poet 106 *(10f,Lin,S,May 11)*
Dashing Willoughby 113 *(14½f,Don,GF,Sep 14)*
Data Protection 111 *(8½f,Eps,G,Aug 26)*
Dave Dexter 109 *(5f,Hay,HY,Jun 8)*
Davydenko 111 *(8f,Nmk,GF,Aug 10)*
Dawaaleeb 112 *(8f,Thi,G,May 4)*
Dawn Breaking 104 *(8f,Pon,G,Aug 7)*
Dawn Hoofer 103 *(10f,Leo,GY,Jun 20)*
Dawn Treader 103 *(10f,Wdr,S,Oct 7)*
Days Of Glory 103 *(10f,Don,G,Apr 26)*
Dazzling Dan 111 *(6f,Asc,S,Oct 4)*
De Little Engine 103 *(7f,Bri,GF,Aug 8)*
De Name Escapes Me 113 *(12f,Cur,G,Jun 27)*
De Vegas Kid 106 *(8f,Bri,GF,Aug 7)*
Deal A Dollar 106 *(11f,Goo,GF,Aug 2)*
Dean Street Doll 116 *(8f,Cur,GF,May 26)*
Deansgate 103 *(7f,Thi,GF,Sep 16)*
Deauville 112 *(9f,Mey,G,Jan 24)*
December Second 108 *(12f,Hay,GF,Aug 8)*
Decrypt 114 *(8f,Cur,GF,May 25)*
Dedillon 108 *(7f,Gal,G,Jly 30)*
Dee Ex Bee 118 *(16f,Asc,GF,May 1)*
Dee Sprinter 105 *(5f,Cur,YS,Aug 9)*
Deemster 110 *(7f,Lon,G,May 16)*
Deep Intrigue 106 *(7f,Lei,GF,Jly 6)*
Defence Treaty 107 *(7f,Red,G,Aug 10)*
Defining Moment 112 *(7f,Sha,G,Jan 1)*
Defoe 118 *(12f,Eps,G,May 31)*
Deia Glory 107 *(5f,Yor,GF,Jly 13)*
Deinonychus 109 *(10f,Not,GS,Aug 13)*
Deirdre 118 *(10f,Goo,G,Aug 1)*
Delagate This Lord 107 *(6f,Bat,GS,Aug 17)*
Delaware 105 *(8f,Lon,GS,Apr 22)*
Delicate Kiss 103 *(8f,San,GF,Aug 31)*
Delph Crescent 105 *(10f,Don,GF,Jun 1)*
Delphinia 115 *(14½f,Don,GF,Sep 12)*
Derevo 114 *(10f,Pon,G,Jun 23)*
Desert Ace 104 *(5f,Bev,GF,Sep 18)*
Desert Doctor 105 *(6f,Rip,GS,Jun 5)*
Desert Encounter 114 *(10f,Wdr,GF,Aug 24)*
Desert Fire 119 *(8f,Mey,G,Jan 17)*
Desert Icon 113 *(10f,Nmk,GF,Aug 10)*
Desert Lion 104 *(8f,Thi,G,Apr 29)*
Desert Point 103 *(14f,Mus,GF,May 13)*
Desert Ruler 107 *(11f,Crl,GF,Jun 26)*
Desert Skyline 114 *(14f,Yor,GF,Aug 24)*
Desert Viper 106 *(7f,Gal,G,Jly 30)*
Designation 108 *(6f,Cur,Y,Aug 23)*
Desirous 106 *(8f,Asc,G,Jun 21)*
Destination 109 *(7f,Wet,GS,May 7)*
Destinys Rock 103 *(10f,Don,G,Jun 29)*
Destroyer 106 *(8f,Pon,GF,Sep 19)*
Devils Roc 103 *(6f,Bat,F,Sep 4)*
Dew Pond 106 *(14f,Cat,GF,Jly 1)*
Di Fede 109 *(8f,Pon,G,Jly 28)*
Diamond Dougal 109 *(6f,Rip,G,Apr 27)*
Diamond Lady 105 *(6f,Bri,GF,Apr 20)*
Diamond Rhyme 114 *(7f,Sha,G,Jan 1)*
Diocles Of Rome 107 *(7f,Don,GF,May 31)*
Diocletian 111 *(14½f,Chs,G,Sep 14)*
Diodorus 105 *(16f,Thi,G,Aug 30)*
Dirty Rascal 105 *(7f,Nmk,GF,Jly 12)*
Distant Chimes 109 *(16f,Chp,G,Aug 26)*
Divin Bere 103 *(14½f,Don,GF,Jun 1)*
Divine Approach 103 *(10f,Cur,GF,May 25)*
Divinity 106 *(8f,Hay,HY,Jun 12)*
Dizzy G 107 *(6f,Lin,GF,Sep 14)*
Doc Sportello 112 *(5f,San,G,Sep 18)*
Doctor Cross 106 *(12f,Yor,GF,Jun 29)*
Dominus 108 *(6f,Asc,S,Oct 4)*
Donjuan Triumphant 116 *(6f,Asc,HY,Oct 19)*
Donnachies Girl 106 *(14f,Red,GF,Jly 21)*
Donncha 105 *(8f,Rip,S,Aug 17)*
Donnelly's Rainbow 107 *(7f,Mus,G,Jly 23)*
Dono Di Dio 103 *(14f,Sal,GF,Jun 26)*

Doonard Prince 103 (6f,Cur,G,Jly 21)
Double Reflection 103 (10f,Bri,GF,Apr 30)
Doublet 114 (12f,Mey,G,Jan 19)
Dourado 107 (8f,Lei,GF,May 27)
Downdraft 112 (16f,Fle,GS,Nov 5)
Downforce 114 (6f,Cur,SH,Oct 13)
Dr Doro 105 (5f,San,G,Sep 13)
Dragon General 121 (7f,Sha,G,Mar 31)
Dragon Mountain 104 (10f,Ayr,GF,May 22)
Dragons Tail 108 (7f,Chs,S,Sep 28)
Dragons Voice 108 (12f,Thi,GS,Jun 18)
Dramatic Device 109 (12f,Nmk,G,Sep 26)
Dramatic Queen 118 (14f,Yor,GF,May 25)
Dramatise 103 (10f,Leo,GY,May 12)
Dream Ascot 109 (8f,Cur,G,Jun 29)
Dream Castle 118 (9f,Mey,G,Jan 24)
Dream Of Dreams 114 (6f,Asc,GF,Jun 22)
Dream Today 115 (7f,Mey,G,Feb 28)
Dream Walker 105 (8f,Pon,G,Aug 7)
Dream World 106 (7f,Nby,HY,Oct 25)
Dreamweaver 104 (10f,San,GF,Jly 6)
Drombeg Dream 103 (7f,Cur,GY,May 6)
Dubai Acclaim 110 (8f,Don,GF,Sep 11)
Dubai Discovery 110 (10f,Lin,GF,Sep 5)
Dubai Dominion 109 (7f,Hay,S,Sep 5)
Dubai Falcon 112 (12f,Lei,GF,May 27)
Dubai Icon 109 (10f,Yor,S,Oct 12)
Dubai Legacy 107 (8f,Nmk,GF,Aug 10)
Dubai Tradition 110 (12f,Pon,G,Jun 23)
Dubawi Fifty 106 (18f,Nmk,S,Oct 12)
Dubhe 118 (16f,Mey,G,Feb 7)
Dubious Affair 105 (10f,Lin,G,May 3)
Duckett's Grove 112 (11f,Goo,GF,May 24)
Ducky Mallon 113 (7f,Leo,G,Sep 14)
Dudley's Boy 103 (9f,Lin,HY,Jun 11)
Duke Of Alba 105 (12f,Thi,G,Apr 29)
Duke Of Firenze 107 (5f,Cur,GY,Jun 27)
Duke Of Hazzard 113 (8f,Hay,GF,May 25)
Duke Of Yorkshire 106 (14f,Cat,GF,Sep 10)
Duneflower 105 (8f,Asc,GF,Jly 26)
Dunkirk Harbour 112 (8f,Leo,GY,May 12)
Dupioni 106 (7f,Nmk,GS,Jun 21)
Durrell 105 (10f,San,G,Aug 8)
Durston 116 (12f,Goo,G,Jly 31)
Dutch Coed 106 (9f,Crl,GF,Jly 6)
Dutch Masterpiece 104 (5f,Mey,G,Jan 24)
Dutch Story 103 (7f,Yar,HY,Oct 22)
Dutch Uncle 105 (10f,Rip,GS,Jun 20)

Eagle Hunter 107 (8f,Lon,GS,Apr 22)
Eagles By Day 109 (12f,Asc,GS,Jun 21)
Early Summer 103 (16f,Goo,GS,Jun 9)
Earnshaw 114 (10f,Mey,G,Jan 17)
Earth And Sky 105 (10f,Yar,GF,Jly 17)
Earth Trilogy 104 (8f,Sha,G,Mar 31)
East 105 (8f,Cur,GF,May 26)
East Street Revue 105 (5f,Bev,GS,May 14)
Eastern Racer 108 (8f,Cur,S,Oct 22)
Ebbisham 104 (8f,Wet,GS,May 7)
Ebury 110 (8f,Asc,GF,Sep 6)
Echo 107 (14½f,Don,GF,Jun 1)
Echo Of Lightning 105 (7f,Mus,GF,Aug 27)
Eclipse Storm 105 (7f,Cur,GY,May 6)
Ecoeye 105 (6f,Cur,S,Oct 22)
Economic Crisis 107 (5f,Mus,S,Aug 9)
Eddystone Rock 112 (16f,Asc,G,Aug 10)
Edge 109 (10f,Chp,GF,May 23)
Edged Out 104 (5f,Bat,G,Jun 26)
Edification 103 (8f,Cur,GF,May 24)
Eeh Bah Gum 110 (5f,Yor,GF,May 16)
Effernock Fizz 109 (12f,Cur,GY,Aug 23)
Eightsome Reel 105 (10f,Asc,S,Jun 20)
Ekhtiyaar 112 (6f,Mey,G,Feb 21)
El Astronaute 115 (5f,Cur,GY,Jun 27)
El Picador 104 (10f,Chp,G,Jun 24)
El Tren 104 (12f,Cur,Y,Sep 28)
Elarqam 118 (10f,Yor,S,Jly 27)
Elector 109 (9f,Nmk,GF,May 4)
Electric Landlady 106 (7f,Lei,G,Apr 5)
Elegant Love 108 (10f,Ffo,GS,Aug 13)
Elerfaan 103 (7½f,Bev,GF,Jun 8)
Eleuthera 104 (7f,Ayr,GS,Jly 22)
Elhafei 109 (10f,Yar,GF,Jly 30)
Elite Icon 105 (16f,Mus,GF,Jly 3)
Elite Patch 116 (7f,Sha,GF,Apr 22)
Elleanthus 106 (8f,Cur,GF,May 24)
Elwazir 107 (10f,San,GF,May 23)
Elysian Flame 105 (14f,Yor,S,Oct 11)
Elysium Dream 104 (7f,Bri,GF,May 28)
Emaraaty Ana 116 (6f,Sal,GF,Sep 3)
Embour 109 (5f,Asc,GF,Jly 13)
Emenem 107 (12f,Eps,G,Apr 24)
Emily Goldfinch 105 (6f,Nmk,GF,May 17)
Eminence 114 (12f,Goo,G,Jly 31)
Eminent Authority 105 (14f,Asc,S,Jun 19)
Emirates Empire 110 (14½f,Don,GF,Jun 1)
Emirates Knight 107 (8f,Thi,GS,May 11)
Emma Point 108 (8f,Wdr,GF,Jun 30)
Empire Line 107 (5f,Cur,GY,Jun 7)
Employer 109 (12f,Thi,G,Sep 7)
Empoli 110 (12f,Mey,G,Jan 19)
Empress Ali 104 (10f,Not,HY,Aug 16)
Enable 123 (12f,Lon,VS,Oct 6)
Enbihaar 117 (14f,Yor,GF,May 25)
Encantador 104 (7f,Leo,Y,Apr 3)
Encapsulation 109 (8f,San,GF,Jly 6)
Encouraging 122 (7f,Sha,G,Mar 31)
Enhanced 103 (12f,Don,GF,May 31)
Enigmatic 106 (8f,Pon,GS,Jly 19)
Enjazaat 109 (6½f,Don,GF,Sep 13)
Enormous Honour 115 (7f,Sha,G,Apr 22)
Enough Already 107 (7f,Hay,GS,Jly 19)
Enough Said 105 (5f,Cur,S,Aug 9)
Enter The Red 107 (6f,Cur,S,Oct 22)
Enthaar 113 (5f,San,G,Sep 18)
Entrusting 108 (10f,Nby,G,Sep 20)
Envisaging 106 (7f,Yar,GF,Aug 8)
Enzemble 106 (9f,Lin,GF,May 30)
Epaulement 111 (12f,Hay,GF,Jly 6)
Epeius 107 (6f,Red,GF,Apr 22)
Epic Hero 109 (6f,Dea,G,Aug 4)
Eponina 107 (8f,Thi,GF,Sep 16)
Eqtidaar 111 (7f,Lei,GF,Apr 27)
Equiano Springs 106 (6f,Nmk,GF,Sep 21)
Equidae 107 (8f,Wet,GS,May 7)
Equilateral 110 (5f,Nmk,GF,May 4)
Equitant 107 (8f,Cur,GY,Aug 30)
Equitation 110 (6f,Asc,GF,Sep 6)
Er Faina 103 (8f,Lon,GS,Jly 14)
Erissimus Maximus 104 (5f,Asc,S,Oct 5)
Escapability 107 (11½f,Wdr,S,Oct 7)
Escape The City 107 (10f,Bri,GF,Sep 9)
Escobar 113 (8f,Asc,HY,Oct 19)
Eshtiraak 116 (7f,Mey,G,Feb 28)
Espresso Freddo 103 (8f,Nmk,HY,Nov 2)
Esprit De Corps 110 (7f,Ayr,GF,Jly 7)
Esspeegee 109 (12f,Bri,GF,Aug 20)
Estikmaal 104 (12f,Mey,G,Jan 19)
Estrela Star 103 (12f,Chp,G,Aug 26)
Euginio 113 (9f,Mey,G,Jan 24)
Eula Varner 103 (8f,Nmk,GF,Aug 3)
Euro Implosion 106 (12f,Ham,G,Jly 13)
Eva Maria 106 (8f,Thi,GS,Aug 3)
Evasive Power 103 (5f,Cur,GY,Jun 7)
Evening Attire 103 (7f,Lei,G,Apr 5)
Ever Laugh 106 (8f,Sha,G,Mar 31)
Everything For You 109 (12½f,Mus,G,May 3)
Excelcius 107 (10f,Leo,G,Aug 15)
Excellent George 106 (5f,Yar,G,Sep 17)
Excellent Times 113 (7f,Yor,G,Aug 22)
Exec Chef 108 (9f,Nmk,GF,May 4)
Exhort 114 (10f,Ayr,GF,May 22)
Extra Elusive 112 (10f,San,GF,Jly 5)
Eye Of The Storm 108 (13f,Ham,GF,May 5)
Eye Of The Water 106 (6f,Wdr,G,Aug 19)
Eyeoweyou 106 (8f,Leo,GF,Aug 8)
Eynhallow 108 (10f,Nmk,GF,Aug 10)
Ezanak 106 (12f,Bev,GS,Aug 15)

Faatinah 113 (5f,Mey,G,Feb 14)
Fabricate 110 (10f,Goo,GF,May 25)
Fabulist 105 (8f,Nmk,G,Jun 28)
Face Off 107 (5f,Cur,S,Aug 9)
Fairy Falcon 111 (5f,Bev,G,Jun 18)
Fairy Stories 110 (5f,Ham,S,Sep 23)
Fairyland 115 (8f,Cur,GF,May 26)
Falak 105 (13f,Leo,GF,Jly 11)
Falcon Eight 108 (16f,San,GF,Jly 6)
Falmouth Light 110 (10½f,Hay,HY,Jun 12)
Famous Dynasty 105 (11½f,Wdr,G,Apr 15)
Fanaar 107 (8f,Asc,GS,Jun 20)
Fannie By Gaslight 105 (10f,Nby,HY,Oct 25)
Fanny Logan 112 (10f,Sal,S,Aug 14)
Fantastic Blue 109 (11½f,Wdr,GF,Aug 24)
Fantastic Ms Fox 107 (14f,Red,GF,May 28)
Fantasy 104 (5f,Cur,G,Jly 21)
Fantasy Keeper 108 (5f,San,S,Jun 15)
Far Above 107 (7f,Nmk,G,May 18)
Farshad 112 (7f,Sha,GF,Apr 22)
Farzeen 111 (7f,Don,GF,Sep 13)
Fastman 106 (7f,Yor,GF,May 15)
Fayetta 111 (12f,Gal,G,Aug 1)
Fayez 110 (10f,Goo,G,Jly 30)
Faylaq 104 (12f,Nmk,G,Jun 27)
Fearless Warrior 104 (11½f,Bat,GF,Apr 19)
Feebi 103 (16f,Cat,S,Jun 17)
Feliciana De Vega 105 (8f,Hay,HY,Aug 10)
Felix 103 (10f,Don,G,Apr 26)
Fendale 105 (5f,Yor,GF,May 16)
Fennaan 114 (8f,Thi,G,May 4)
Ferretti 109 (8f,Cur,GF,May 25)
Field Of Vision 103 (7f,Lei,HY,Oct 8)
Fields Of Fortune 105 (12f,Bri,GF,Aug 8)
Fifth Position 116 (11f,Goo,GF,May 24)
Fighting Irish 103 (6f,Asc,GF,Jun 22)
Fighting Temeraire 107 (7f,Lin,G,Jun 22)
Filament Of Gold 105 (14f,Bat,F,Sep 15)
Final 104 (12f,Pon,G,Aug 18)
Final Endeavour 103 (8f,Cur,S,Oct 22)
Final Rock 108 (11½f,Lin,GF,Jun 1)
Final Venture 112 (5f,Bev,G,Jun 18)
Finche 116 (16f,Fle,GS,Nov 5)
Finding Nero 105 (10f,Leo,G,Aug 15)
Finniston Farm 110 (10½f,Hay,GF,May 25)
Finoah 106 (7f,Don,S,Aug 17)
Finsbury Square 105 (5f,Lon,VS,Oct 6)
Fire Diamond 108 (10f,Chp,GF,May 23)
Fire Fighting 104 (13f,Ayr,G,Jun 22)
Fire Fly 108 (7f,Gal,G,Aug 1)
Fire Jet 106 (14f,Mus,G,Apr 20)
Firenze Rosa 103 (5f,Bat,GS,Sep 30)
Firewater 107 (10f,Pon,G,Jly 28)
Firlinfeu 104 (10f,Cur,G,Jun 28)
Firmament 111 (7f,Yor,GS,Jun 15)
Firmdecisions 109 (6f,Crl,GF,May 20)
First Contact 115 (8f,Mey,G,Feb 21)
First Dance 103 (10f,Yor,GF,Jly 12)
First Eleven 108 (12f,Yor,GF,May 15)
First Flight 106 (12f,Cat,HY,Oct 29)
First In Line 108 (12f,Nmk,GS,Oct 11)
First Nation 119 (10f,Mey,G,Jan 17)
First Quest 104 (10f,Wdr,G,Apr 8)
First Response 104 (8f,Pon,GF,Sep 19)
First Sitting 103 (10f,Nmk,G,Jun 28)
Firsteen 106 (7f,Red,GF,Jly 21)
Fit For Function 109 (6f,Cur,GF,May 26)
Fitzrovia 107 (8½f,Not,S,Jun 17)
Fitzwilly 104 (16f,Chp,G,May 3)
Five Helmets 108 (10f,Ayr,GF,Jly 7)
Flag Of Honour 113 (10f,Cur,GY,May 6)
Flambeur 109 (10f,Lon,VS,Oct 5)
Flash Famous 110 (9f,Sha,G,Mar 31)
Flash Gordon 105 (7f,Cur,GY,May 6)
Flash Point 103 (16f,Mus,GF,Sep 14)
Flashcard 116 (8f,Asc,GS,Jly 27)
Flavius Titus 108 (6f,Nmk,G,May 5)
Fleeting 114 (12f,Lon,G,Sep 15)
Flight Risk 117 (8f,Leo,G,Jun 6)
Flint Hill 104 (10f,Red,G,Apr 8)
Flintrock 103 (16f,Asc,S,May 10)
Floating Artist 109 (12f,Goo,G,Aug 1)
Flood Defence 104 (11f,Crl,HY,Aug 13)
Florenza 105 (8f,Thi,GF,Sep 16)
Flower Power 103 (12f,Cat,GF,Sep 10)
Flowering Peach 106 (14f,Goo,GF,Aug 3)
Fly At Dawn 115 (8f,Mey,G,Jan 17)
Flying Dragon 109 (8f,Don,GF,Sep 11)
Flying Pursuit 109 (6f,Thi,G,Aug 30)
Flying Raconteur 108 (8f,Rip,G,Aug 27)
Flying Tiger 108 (10f,Chp,G,May 3)
Follow Intello 104 (12f,Nby,G,May 17)
Fool For You 111 (5f,Chs,GS,May 9)
Foolaad 111 (5f,Yor,GF,May 16)
For Your Eyes 104 (10f,Cur,G,Jun 27)
Forest Of Dean 114 (10f,Goo,G,Aug 1)
Forest Ranger 114 (10½f,Chs,S,May 10)
Forever In Dreams 114 (6f,Asc,HY,Oct 19)
Forewarning 106 (16f,Yor,G,Sep 8)
Forjatt 112 (8f,Mey,G,Feb 21)
Formula One 103 (10f,Cur,G,Jun 28)
Fortune And Glory 103 (8f,Nby,GS,Jly 19)
Forza Libranno 104 (6f,Cur,GY,Jun 7)
Four Kingdoms 107 (8f,Ham,GF,May 17)
Four Mile Bridge 105 (10f,Chp,GF,Jly 18)
Four Wheel Drive 113 (5f,Cat,S,Oct 19)
Fox Chairman 115 (10½f,Chs,GS,May 9)
Fox Champion 111 (6½f,Dea,G,Aug 4)
Fox Leicester 107 (8f,Nmk,G,May 4)
Fox Premier 112 (10f,Goo,G,Aug 1)
Fox Tal 107 (10f,Don,GF,Sep 11)
Fox Vardy 108 (12f,Sal,S,Jun 11)
Foxtrot Lady 111 (7f,Don,GF,Sep 13)
Foxtrot Liv 118 (8f,Cur,GF,May 26)
Foxy Forever 105 (5f,Yar,G,Sep 17)
Fragrant Belle 104 (12f,Bev,G,Jun 18)
Fragrant Dawn 106 (11½f,Yar,GF,Jly 25)
Framley Garth 111 (13f,Ham,GF,May 5)
Francis Xavier 107 (10f,Goo,GF,May 25)
Francophilia 105 (12f,Thi,GF,Jun 3)
Frankellina 107 (12f,Eps,G,May 31)
Franklyn 109 (8f,Leo,G,Jly 25)
Frankuus 106 (12f,Rip,G,Apr 27)
Frantical 106 (10f,Bat,F,Sep 4)
Franz Kafka 111 (8f,Bri,GF,May 28)
Fraser Island 108 (12f,Bri,GF,Aug 8)
Freckles 107 (8f,Bat,GF,May 1)
Free Love 106 (5f,Wdr,GF,Jly 8)
Freerolling 108 (10f,Don,G,Jly 20)
Freescape 115 (7f,Mey,G,Feb 7)
French King 104 (12f,Lon,VS,Oct 6)
French Mix 103 (12f,Eps,G,Jly 4)
French Pegasus 108 (7f,Lon,G,May 16)
Frequency Code 103 (12f,Don,G,Jly 20)
Fresh Power 115 (7f,Sha,G,Jan 1)
Fresnel 109 (9f,Cur,G,Aug 30)
Fridtjof Nansen 109 (6f,Cur,GY,Aug 30)
Friendly Advice 109 (5f,Bev,G,May 6)
Frontispiece 105 (10f,San,S,Jun 14)
Frontman 109 (8f,Wdr,GF,Jly 1)
Fugacious 110 (6f,Cur,S,Oct 22)
Fujaira Prince 107 (12f,Nmk,GF,Jly 12)
Full Of Chances 108 (9f,Sha,G,Mar 31)
Funny Man 110 (14f,Lin,S,Jly 27)
Furia Cruzada 115 (8f,Mey,G,Jan 17)
Furzig 107 (10f,Yor,GF,Aug 24)
Future Investment 109 (12f,Goo,G,Jly 31)
Futuristic 107 (6f,Yar,G,Sep 17)

G K Chesterton 106 (7f,Mey,G,Jan 19)
Gabrial 108 (7½f,Chs,G,May 25)
Gabrial The Devil 107 (6f,Hay,GF,Jly 6)
Gabrial The One 105 (12f,Chs,G,Sep 13)
Gabrial The Saint 113 (5f,Chs,GF,Jun 29)
Gabrial The Tiger 107 (7½f,Bev,GS,May 29)
Gabrial The Wire 105 (7f,Chs,GF,Jun 29)
Gabrials Boy 104 (10f,Rip,G,Aug 26)
Galactic Spirit 108 (11f,Goo,GF,Sep 3)
Gale Force Maya 114 (6f,Crl,GF,Aug 29)
Galeola 107 (12f,Cur,G,Jly 20)
Galileo Silver 105 (10f,San,GS,Jun 15)
Gallic 105 (8f,Nmk,GF,Jun 29)
Gallipoli 108 (7f,Asc,GS,May 11)
Galloway Hills 108 (6f,Red,GF,Apr 22)
Game Player 108 (7f,Lin,G,May 3)
Gamesters Icon 108 (8f,Bat,S,Oct 16)
Gantier 103 (11f,Nby,G,May 17)
Garden Oasis 105 (10½f,Chs,G,Sep 14)
Garrick 110 (8f,Thi,G,May 4)
Garrison Law 105 (10f,Chp,GF,Jly 18)
Garrus 113 (5f,Cur,G,Jly 21)
Gas Monkey 108 (11f,Nby,GS,Jun 25)
Gasta 110 (12f,Cur,G,Jun 27)
Gavroche 109 (12f,Mey,G,Jan 19)
Gealach 104 (12f,Cur,GY,Jun 7)
Geetanjali 106 (7f,Leo,Y,Aug 25)
Gemini 107 (17f,Bat,F,Aug 2)
Gemologist 104 (14f,Mus,GF,Sep 6)
Gendarme 108 (12f,Bri,GF,Jun 3)
General Allenby 104 (16f,Wet,GF,May 30)
General Brook 106 (12f,Chp,GS,Aug 15)
General Sherman 114 (7f,Sha,GF,Apr 22)
General Trump 109 (7f,Sha,G,Apr 22)
General Zoff 103 (14f,Ffo,GS,Aug 13)
Genetics 105 (12f,Asc,G,Aug 10)
Gentle Look 105 (7f,Don,GF,May 18)
Gentlewoman 104 (7f,Lei,GF,Jly 18)
Geological 104 (6f,Leo,GF,Aug 8)
George Bowen 104 (6f,Yor,GF,May 15)
George Mallory 103 (11f,Crl,GF,Jun 17)
George Of Hearts 108 (7f,Asc,GS,May 11)
George The Prince 107 (7f,Lon,VS,Oct 6)
George Villiers 108 (7f,Mey,G,Jan 19)
George William 108 (7f,Nmk,G,Jun 27)
Georgeville 112 (10f,Cur,G,Jun 29)
Geranium 106 (10f,San,G,Jly 24)
Gerry's Way 104 (8f,Leo,GF,Jly 11)
Get Knotted 109 (7f,Yor,S,Jly 27)
Get The Rhythm 105 (6f,Thi,G,Aug 30)
Getchagetchagetcha 107 (10f,Goo,HY,Sep 25)
Geyser 103 (14f,Red,GF,May 28)
Ghaiyyath 103 (12f,Lon,VS,Oct 6)
Ghalib 103 (9f,Ham,G,Jly 18)
Ghalyoon 106 (7f,Sal,F,Jly 13)
Ghayyar 104 (8½f,Bev,GF,Jly 16)
Gibbs Hill 108 (10f,Nby,GF,Sep 21)
Gifted Master 105 (6f,Nmk,GF,Apr 17)
Gifts Of Gold 115 (9f,Goo,GF,Aug 3)
Giga White 107 (8f,Leo,GF,Jly 11)
Gin In The Inn 105 (6f,Rip,G,Apr 27)
Gin Palace 109 (8f,Nby,GS,Aug 16)
Ginger Fox 110 (8f,Hay,GF,Jly 5)
Ginger Jam 107 (5f,Bev,G,Jly 30)
Ginvincible 105 (5f,Rip,GS,Jun 20)
Giuseppe Garibaldi 103 (12f,Leo,GF,Aug 8)
Give It Some Teddy 108 (10f,Yor,G,Sep 8)
Givepeaceachance 105 (11½f,Bat,GS,Jun 15)
Givinitsum 103 (7f,San,G,Aug 8)
Glan Y Gors 104 (12f,Thi,GS,May 11)
Glance 105 (10f,Yor,G,Jly 26)
Glass Slippers 117 (5f,Lon,VS,Oct 6)
Glasses Up 109 (10f,Pon,GF,Sep 19)
Glen Shiel 109 (8f,Asc,HY,Oct 19)
Glenamoy Lad 108 (6f,Asc,GF,Sep 7)
Glendevon 104 (10f,Goo,GF,May 25)
Glengarry 104 (7f,Mus,GF,Jly 3)
Glenn Coco 108 (7f,Lei,GF,Jly 6)
Global Falcon 104 (10f,Chp,G,May 3)
Global Giant 111 (10f,Cur,G,Jun 29)
Global Gift 109 (8f,Hay,HY,Jun 12)
Global Heat 108 (10f,Rip,G,May 19)
Global Hope 105 (6f,Yar,G,Sep 17)
Global Hunter 109 (8f,Wdr,GF,Jly 8)
Global Melody 103 (6f,Not,S,May 10)
Global Spirit 111 (7f,Ayr,GF,Jly 7)
Glorious Dane 104 (12f,Thi,GF,Jun 3)
Glorious Emaraty 105 (6f,Hay,HY,Jun 8)
Glorious Journey 115 (7f,Nby,S,Aug 17)
Glorious Lover 106 (7f,Nmk,G,May 18)
Gloweth 103 (9f,Goo,GS,Jun 7)
Glutnforpunishment 105 (12f,Nby,G,Aug 6)
Gm Hopkins 111 (10f,Mey,G,Feb 28)
Gnaad 109 (5f,Asc,GF,Sep 7)
Go Beauty Go 103 (8f,Sha,G,Jan 1)
Goddess 112 (9f,Cur,G,Aug 30)
Godspeed 105 (8f,Sha,G,Jan 1)
Gold Arrow 106 (6f,Crl,HY,May 31)
Gold At Midnight 103 (6f,Yar,GF,Sep 18)
Gold Filigree 106 (5½f,Ayr,G,Sep 20)
Gold Fleece 105 (12f,Bev,G,Jun 18)
Gold Hunter 103 (7f,Chp,GF,Jly 12)
Gold Mount 115 (14f,Yor,GS,Jun 15)
Gold Stick 109 (10f,Wet,G,May 7)
Gold Velvet 108 (8f,Sha,G,Jan 1)
Gold Vibe 108 (5f,Lon,G,Sep 15)
Gold Win 119 (7f,Sha,G,Mar 31)
Golden Apollo 111 (6f,Thi,G,Aug 30)
Golden Box 111 (15f,Lon,VS,Oct 5)

Golden Force 112 (7f,Lei,GF,Jly 24)
Golden Jaguar 113 (8f,Mey,G,Feb 28)
Golden Jeffrey 104 (15f,Ayr,G,Jun 21)
Golden Parade 105 (6f,Don,GF,Jly 25)
Gometra Ginty 106 (7f,Mus,G,Jly 23)
Good Birthday 114 (10f,Nby,G,May 18)
Good Business 104 (6f,Yar,S,Jun 12)
Good Effort 110 (7f,Mey,G,Feb 7)
Good Fit 111 (7f,Sha,GF,Apr 22)
Good Fortune 111 (7f,Mey,G,Jan 10)
Good Impression 106 (11f,Goo,GF,Sep 3)
Good Luck Fox 105 (5f,Rip,S,Jun 19)
Goodnight Girl 104 (6f,Sal,G,Sep 5)
Gopsies Daughter 107 (6f,Cur,GF,May 26)
Gordon Lord Byron 113 (6f,Cur,G,Sep 15)
Goring 107 (7f,Goo,G,May 4)
Goscote 103 (12f,Chp,GF,May 23)
Goshen 112 (14f,Not,S,Oct 30)
Gossamer Wings 104 (6f,Cur,G,Jun 29)
Gossip Column 107 (12f,Yor,GF,Jun 29)
Gossiping 112 (8½f,Eps,G,May 31)
Gowanbuster 103 (6f,Crl,GF,May 20)
Grace And Danger 110 (11½f,Wdr,GF,Aug 24)
Grace To Grace 107 (8f,Cur,S,Oct 22)
Graceful Act 104 (9f,Crl,GF,Jly 6)
Graceful Lady 112 (16f,Nmk,GF,Aug 10)
Gracious Ryder 105 (7f,Sha,G,Apr 22)
Graignes 113 (7f,Lon,G,Sep 15)
Grand Harbour 108 (7f,Sha,G,Apr 22)
Grand Inquisitor 105 (12f,Thi,GF,Jly 3)
Grand Vintage 110 (7f,Lon,GS,Apr 22)
Grandee 109 (13f,Ayr,G,Jun 22)
Grandfather Tom 108 (5f,Asc,GF,Sep 7)
Grandmaster Flash 109 (10f,Leo,GY,Apr 3)
Granite City Doc 103 (8f,Ham,GF,May 17)
Grapevine 105 (8f,Wdr,GS,Jun 17)
Graphite Storm 111 (7f,Lei,GF,Jly 6)
Gravistas 111 (12½f,Mus,GS,Jun 1)
Great Bear 106 (12f,Nmk,GF,Jun 8)
Great Example 111 (10f,Goo,G,Aug 25)
Great Grey 107 (10f,Leo,G,Aug 15)
Great Prospector 108 (7f,Yor,GS,Jun 15)
Great Scot 116 (7f,Nby,GS,Apr 13)
Great Shout 103 (6f,Yar,GF,Aug 15)
Great Trango 107 (18f,Nmk,S,Oct 12)
Great White Shark 105 (18f,Nmk,S,Oct 12)
Greeley 104 (10f,Bat,G,Aug 21)
Green Envy 112 (7f,Sha,G,Mar 31)
Green Power 107 (6f,Goo,G,Aug 23)
Greengage 104 (9f,Red,GF,Jly 21)
Greenside 113 (7f,Asc,S,Oct 5)
Greenview Paradise 106 (14f,Lin,GF,Sep 14)
Grenadier Guard 108 (12f,Pon,G,Jun 23)
Grey D'Ars 106 (11f,Goo,GF,Aug 2)
Grey Mist 103 (16f,Rip,GS,May 10)
Grey Spirit 105 (8½f,Eps,GF,Jly 11)
Grimsdyke 107 (6f,Red,G,Sep 25)
Groundworker 109 (5f,Ham,HY,Aug 30)
Group Stage 107 (12f,Nby,S,Jun 13)
Groveman 109 (11f,Crl,GF,Jun 26)
Growl 110 (6f,Ayr,G,Sep 21)
Guaranteed 112 (12f,Leo,GF,Aug 8)
Guinevere 104 (8f,Cur,G,Jly 20)
Gulf Of Poets 108 (10f,Rip,GS,Jun 20)
Gullane One 104 (6f,Rip,G,Aug 27)
Gulliver 114 (6f,Cur,G,Sep 15)
Gumball 110 (14f,Sal,GF,Apr 28)
Gunmetal 108 (6f,Asc,GF,Jun 22)
Guns Of Leros 104 (16f,Goo,GS,Jun 9)
Gustavus Weston 115 (6f,Cur,S,Aug 9)
Guvenor's Choice 106 (10½f,Hay,GF,Jly 5)
Gwafa 109 (16f,Nmk,GF,Aug 10)
Gyllen 104 (12½f,Dea,G,Aug 4)
Gylo 104 (12f,Cat,GF,Sep 10)
Gymkhana 107 (7½f,Chs,G,Jun 28)
Gypsy Spirit 103 (7f,Goo,G,Aug 2)

Hackbridge 103 (8f,Wdr,G,Apr 8)
Hackle Setter 108 (8½f,Eps,G,Aug 26)
Haddaf 104 (7f,Yar,F,Aug 25)
Hafeet Alain 111 (8f,Nmk,S,Nov 1)
Hajjam 110 (7f,Asc,GS,May 11)
Halimi 113 (12f,Cur,GF,Jly 21)
Hallalulu 107 (12f,Hay,GF,Jly 4)
Hamariyna 112 (8f,Leo,GY,May 12)
Hameem 104 (12f,Pon,G,Jun 23)
Hamish 108 (8f,Thi,G,Apr 29)
Hamley 107 (10f,Cur,G,Jun 28)
Hammer Gun 109 (8f,Don,GF,Sep 11)
Hammersmith 107 (6f,Cur,GF,May 25)
Han Solo Berger 107 (5f,Yar,G,Sep 17)
Hand On Heart 113 (8f,Leo,G,Jun 6)
Handiwork 105 (14f,Not,S,Oct 30)
Handsome Maverick 105 (6f,Cur,GY,Jun 7)
Handytalk 107 (6f,Ffo,GF,Jly 29)
Happen 109 (8f,Leo,G,Sep 14)
Happy Alumni 119 (7f,Sha,G,Mar 31)
Happy Company 104 (12f,Gal,G,Aug 1)
Happy Ending 103 (11½f,Bat,GS,Jun 15)
Happy Hiker 104 (12f,Nmk,G,Jly 20)
Happy Hour 114 (7f,Sha,G,Jan 1)
Happy Power 114 (7f,Nby,S,Apr 12)
Happy Sebring 114 (7f,Sha,G,Jan 1)
Happy Time 114 (5f,Sha,G,Apr 22)

Harbour Breeze 104 (10f,San,GF,Jly 5)
Harbour Spirit 104 (9f,Goo,GF,Aug 3)
Harbour Vision 104 (8f,Nmk,GF,Aug 3)
Hareeq 109 (13f,Ayr,G,Jun 22)
Harlan Strong 111 (10f,Mey,G,Jan 17)
Harlequin Rose 105 (8f,Bri,GF,Sep 1)
Harmonise 109 (12f,Chp,GS,Aug 15)
Harome 111 (5f,Asc,GF,Jly 13)
Harpo Marx 105 (14f,Asc,S,Jun 19)
Harriet's Force 109 (9f,Cur,G,Aug 30)
Harrogate 105 (6f,Eps,G,Jly 4)
Harrovian 109 (11f,Goo,GF,Aug 2)
Harry Hurricane 107 (5f,Goo,G,May 4)
Hart Stopper 110 (6f,Yar,GF,Jly 10)
Harvest Day 108 (8f,Thi,GF,Sep 16)
Harvestfortheworld 104 (8f,Leo,GY,Apr 3)
Harvey Dent 107 (9f,Ham,G,Jly 18)
Hasankey 110 (12f,Cur,G,Jun 27)
Hateya 103 (8½f,Not,GS,Apr 30)
Hathiq 109 (5f,Cur,GF,May 26)
Hats Off To Larry 110 (10f,Pon,G,Jun 23)
Hatsaway 110 (14f,Lin,GF,Sep 14)
Haveoneyerself 104 (5f,Yar,GF,Aug 7)
Hawaam 108 (5f,Pon,S,Oct 21)
Hayadh 117 (8f,Thi,G,May 4)
Hayyel 107 (12f,Cur,GY,Aug 23)
Hazapour 116 (8f,Leo,GY,May 12)
He's Amazing 105 (10f,Wdr,G,Apr 29)
Headman 115 (10f,Nby,G,May 18)
Healthy Treasure 107 (7f,Sha,G,Jan 1)
Healy's Double 110 (6f,Cur,Y,Aug 23)
Heart Of Soul 104 (10½f,Chs,GS,Aug 4)
Heartwarming 103 (5f,Bat,GF,Apr 19)
Heaven On Earth 103 (14f,Cur,G,Jun 28)
Heavenly Holly 105 (6f,Hay,GF,May 25)
Hector's Here 106 (8½f,Bev,GF,Jly 5)
Hee Haw 111 (6f,Cur,GF,May 26)
Hello Youmzain 117 (6f,Hay,S,Sep 7)
Hells Babe 112 (7f,Cat,S,Aug 12)
Helovaplan 106 (7½f,Bev,GF,Jly 22)
Herculean 113 (10f,Nmk,G,Jly 27)
Here Comes When 109 (10f,San,GF,May 23)
Hereby 109 (14f,Asc,S,Oct 4)
Heritage 111 (5f,Bat,F,Jly 5)
Hermocrates 108 (14f,Lin,S,Jly 27)
Hermosa 124 (8f,Cur,GF,May 26)
Hermoso Mundo 108 (16½f,Nby,GS,Jly 20)
Hero Hero 105 (7½f,Chs,G,May 25)
Hey Gaman 117 (7f,Lei,GF,Apr 27)
Hey Jonesy 108 (7f,Hay,GS,Jly 19)
Hidden Message 110 (8f,San,GF,Jly 6)
Hiella 110 (5f,Cur,YS,Aug 9)
Hieronymus 111 (5f,Not,S,Oct 30)
High Altitude 106 (8f,Leo,GF,Aug 8)
High Commissioner 107 (11f,Goo,GF,Aug 2)
High On Life 104 (6f,Mey,G,Feb 7)
High Rev 109 (9f,Sha,G,Mar 31)
Highfaluting 103 (10f,Wdr,G,Apr 8)
Highgarden 103 (12f,Hay,GF,Jly 6)
Highland Acclaim 105 (6f,Eps,G,Jly 4)
Highly Approved 106 (7f,Leo,G,Jly 18)
Highly Sprung 109 (6f,Pon,GS,Sep 26)
Hightime Hero 105 (7f,Lon,GS,Apr 22)
Hightimeyouwon 106 (6f,Cur,GF,May 24)
Highway Robbery 109 (14f,Lin,GF,Sep 14)
Highwaygrey 104 (8f,Thi,G,Apr 29)
Hillgrove Angel 105 (10f,Ayr,GF,May 28)
Himola 109 (11f,Lon,GS,Apr 22)
Hipster Boy 104 (12f,Mey,G,Jan 19)
Hiroshima 105 (11½f,Lin,S,May 11)
History Writer 105 (8f,San,GS,Jun 15)
Hit The Bid 113 (5f,Mey,G,Jan 24)
Hit The Silk 104 (6f,Cur,GF,May 25)
Ho Ho Feel 103 (9f,Sha,GF,Apr 22)
Hochfeld 106 (14f,Mus,G,Apr 20)
Hold Still 106 (8f,Wdr,GF,Aug 5)
Holdenhurst 103 (6f,Bat,F,Jly 10)
Hollywood Road 104 (12f,Bri,GF,Jly 9)
Holmeswood 107 (5f,Yar,GF,Sep 18)
Holy Kingdom 107 (12f,Nmk,GF,Jun 8)
Honest Albert 104 (8½f,Not,GS,Jun 27)
Honfleur 105 (11½f,Yar,GF,Sep 19)
Hope Is High 106 (14f,Bat,F,Sep 15)
Horatio Star 110 (17f,Bat,F,Aug 2)
Hornsby 116 (8f,Mey,G,Mar 2)
Hors De Combat 111 (8f,Mey,G,Jan 10)
Hortzadar 110 (8f,Pon,GF,Apr 15)
Hot Team 105 (8½f,Eps,HY,Sep 29)
Hotsy Totsy 108 (8f,Asc,G,Jun 21)
House Of Kings 107 (8f,Hay,HY,Aug 10)
Houtzen 107 (5f,Goo,GF,Aug 2)
How Bizarre 107 (7f,Mus,G,Jly 23)
Howzer Black 106 (7f,Ayr,G,Sep 21)
Htilominlo 111 (12f,Bri,GF,Aug 8)
Hugoigo 112 (15f,Ayr,G,Jun 21)
Hulcote 114 (10½f,Hay,HY,Jun 12)
Humanitarian 106 (12f,Eps,GF,Jun 1)
Humble Gratitude 108 (7½f,Chs,GS,Aug 4)
Hunni 104 (8f,Nmk,GF,Jun 29)
Hunting Horn 115 (12f,Asc,GS,Jly 27)
Hyanna 112 (10f,San,GF,Aug 31)
Hydroplane 107 (10f,Sal,F,Jly 13)
Hyperfocus 108 (6f,Thi,G,May 18)

I Am A Dreamer 106 (7f,San,G,Aug 8)
I Am Superman 111 (8f,Cur,GF,May 25)
I Can Fly 114 (8f,Leo,G,Sep 14)
I Could Do Better 103 (7f,Cat,GF,Jly 1)
I Do 104 (8f,Sha,G,Mar 31)
I Remember You 110 (7f,Gal,G,Aug 1)
I'll Be Good 104 (5f,Cat,S,Aug 19)
I'll Have Another 107 (14f,Nmk,G,Aug 17)
I'lletyougonow 108 (8f,Thi,G,Sep 7)
I'm Available 110 (8½f,Eps,HY,Sep 29)
Iballisticvin 103 (10f,Lin,GF,Jly 17)
Ibraz 109 (8f,Rip,G,Aug 26)
Ice Age 114 (6f,Sal,GF,Sep 3)
Ice Cold In Alex 115 (7f,Leo,G,Sep 14)
Ice Gala 104 (7f,Nmk,G,Jly 13)
Iconic Belle 104 (14f,Wet,GF,May 30)
Iconic Choice 109 (8f,Nmk,G,May 5)
Iconic Code 105 (8f,Ham,S,Sep 22)
Iconic Knight 107 (6f,Goo,GS,Jun 9)
Ideal Candy 105 (10f,Pon,GF,May 1)
Ideological 105 (12f,Rip,GF,Jly 8)
Ifton 103 (7f,Hay,GF,Jly 5)
Ignatius 110 (14f,Lin,GF,Sep 14)
Iiex Excelsa 109 (6f,Not,S,May 11)
Il Paradiso 117 (14½f,Don,GF,Sep 14)
Illumined 109 (10f,Goo,HY,Sep 25)
Imaging 110 (8f,Leo,GY,Apr 3)
Imhotep 103 (6f,Yar,G,Sep 17)
Imperial Court 103 (14f,Yar,S,Jun 13)
Imperial State 104 (7½f,Chs,G,Jun 28)
Imphal 105 (16f,Goo,GS,Jun 9)
Imprimis 109 (5f,Asc,G,Jun 18)
Impulsif 110 (8f,Lon,VS,Oct 5)
In Favour 116 (12f,Lon,GS,Jly 14)
Inclyne 104 (10f,Asc,GS,May 11)
Incredible 108 (7f,Sha,G,Jan 1)
Incredible Dream 107 (11½f,Yar,GF,Jly 30)
Incredulous 110 (10f,Nby,GF,Jly 25)
Indeed 112 (8f,Nmk,G,Jly 20)
Independent Missy 107 (6f,Cur,GF,May 24)
Indian Blessing 105 (7f,Mus,GS,Jun 1)
Indian Raj 108 (6f,Yar,GF,Jly 10)
Indian Tygress 105 (6f,Not,S,May 11)
Indianapolis 109 (12f,Hay,GF,Jly 6)
Indigenous Star 109 (8f,Sha,G,Mar 31)
Indomeneo 104 (10f,Don,G,Mar 31)
Inexes 103 (6f,Lei,HY,Jly 31)
Infanta Isabella 104 (10f,Asc,GS,May 11)
Inference 105 (10f,Wet,G,Apr 28)
Inflexiball 104 (10f,Not,GS,Aug 13)
Infrastructure 103 (11½f,Chs,G,Jly 12)
Infuse 109 (10f,Yar,GF,Jly 30)
Ingleby Hollow 107 (12f,Thi,GS,Jun 18)
Innamorare 116 (8f,Cur,GF,May 26)
Inner Circle 104 (7f,Ayr,G,Jly 15)
Inscribe 107 (12f,Cur,G,Jun 27)
Insignia Of Rank 108 (10f,Cur,GF,May 25)
Inspired Thought 105 (6f,Red,GF,May 28)
Intense Style 104 (8f,Don,S,Jun 16)
International Law 105 (8f,Pon,GF,Sep 19)
International Man 104 (7f,Cat,GS,Aug 6)
Intisaab 107 (6f,Rip,G,Apr 27)
Intrepidly 110 (8f,Thi,G,May 4)
Invictus Spirit 107 (10½f,Chs,G,Sep 13)
Invincible Army 113 (6f,Yor,GF,May 15)
Invincible Larne 106 (5f,Yar,GF,Aug 7)
Invitation 108 (12f,Gal,G,Aug 2)
Involved 109 (10½f,Chs,G,Sep 14)
Iridessa 122 (8f,Leo,G,Sep 14)
Irish Trilogy 113 (8f,Mey,G,Feb 28)
Iron Mike 104 (12½f,Mus,GF,Sep 6)
Irradiate 105 (12f,Gal,G,Aug 2)
Irreverent 110 (8f,Thi,G,Sep 7)
Irv 108 (8f,Yor,G,Jly 26)
Isaan Queen 104 (6f,Rip,G,May 19)
Isabella Brant 109 (12f,Sal,S,Jun 11)
Ishebayorgrey 104 (10f,Ayr,GF,May 28)
Iskanderhon 113 (15f,Lon,VS,Oct 5)
Island Brave 111 (13f,Ayr,G,Jun 22)
Island Of Life 104 (7f,Goo,G,Aug 2)
Isole Canarie 111 (8f,Wdr,GF,Jun 29)
Isomer 103 (8f,Don,G,Mar 30)
Isotope 105 (8f,Cur,GF,May 25)
Ispolini 118 (16f,Mey,G,Mar 30)
Istoria 107 (12f,Cur,GF,Jly 21)
Itizzit 111 (8f,Wdr,GF,Jun 30)

J Gaye 108 (10f,Lin,G,May 3)
Jaaref 115 (8f,Mey,G,Mar 2)
Jabalaly 103 (7f,Yor,S,Oct 11)
Jabbaar 111 (13f,Ham,GF,May 5)
Jabbarockie 109 (5f,Mus,G,Aug 2)
Jack's Point 106 (7f,Goo,GF,May 25)
Jackamundo 103 (14f,Yor,S,Oct 11)
Jackhammer 103 (9f,Crl,GS,Jun 11)
Jackstar 107 (7f,Hay,S,Sep 6)
Jacob Black 104 (7f,Mus,GF,May 13)
Jacob Cats 112 (16f,Chp,GS,Aug 15)
Jaleel 104 (7f,Nmk,G,Jun 22)
Jalmoud 119 (12f,Lon,GS,Jly 14)
James Park Woods 106 (7½f,Chs,S,Sep 28)
Jan De Heem 107 (14f,Red,G,Jun 22)
Janoobi 112 (8f,Mey,G,Feb 21)
Japan 122 (12f,Lon,VS,Oct 6)

Jash 111 (7f,Nmk,G,May 18)
Jassaar 116 (8f,Cur,GY,Aug 30)
Jawwaal 109 (6f,Yor,S,Jly 27)
Jazeel 110 (10f,Eps,G,May 31)
Jazz And Blues 106 (8f,Cur,G,Jly 20)
Jedhi 105 (13f,Nby,GS,Jly 19)
Jenerator 116 (7f,Sha,G,Mar 31)
Jerandme 106 (15f,Leo,G,Jun 13)
Jered Maddox 103 (7½f,Ffo,GF,Jly 29)
Jersey Wonder 105 (10f,San,GF,May 30)
Jewel Maker 104 (6f,Cat,HY,Oct 29)
Jill Rose 109 (6f,Thi,S,Aug 9)
Jimmy Greenhough 105 (8f,Lei,G,Jun 27)
Jimson The Famous 108 (7f,Sha,G,Apr 22)
Joe The Beau 105 (8f,Thi,G,Apr 29)
Joegogo 109 (5f,San,G,Sep 18)
John Clare 105 (7f,Lei,GF,Apr 27)
John Kirkup 112 (6f,Ayr,S,Oct 1)
Johni Boxit 104 (11½f,Yar,GF,May 22)
Johnny Cavagin 107 (5f,Bev,GF,Apr 25)
Johnny Drama 111 (10f,Yor,S,Oct 12)
Jolly Honour 104 (8f,Sha,G,Jan 1)
Jordan Electrics 108 (6f,Ham,G,Jly 2)
Joyful Mission 105 (10f,Goo,G,Aug 25)
Juanito Chico 111 (8½f,Not,GF,Apr 20)
Jubiloso 108 (7f,Goo,G,Aug 2)
Judicial 111 (5f,Bev,G,Aug 31)
Jukebox Jive 111 (16f,Mey,G,Feb 7)
Julia's Magic 106 (6f,Cur,G,Jun 29)
Jumira Bridge 106 (5f,San,GF,Jly 5)
Jumping Cats 106 (16f,Cat,GF,Jly 10)
Junderstand 103 (10f,Lei,G,Jun 27)
Jungle Juice 104 (7f,Chp,G,Jly 2)
Junius Brutus 106 (5f,Wdr,GF,Jun 30)
Junoesque 108 (10f,Lin,S,Jun 11)
Junooh 111 (10f,Not,HY,Oct 16)
Jupiter Road 108 (8f,Cur,GF,May 25)
Just Benjamin 113 (12½f,Mus,GS,Jun 1)
Just Glamorous 107 (5f,Goo,G,May 4)
Just Hiss 104 (8f,Yor,G,Jly 26)
Just Hubert 111 (14f,San,G,Jly 25)
Just Once 108 (10f,Ffo,GS,Aug 13)
Just Right 105 (10f,Chp,GF,May 23)
Just The Man 111 (10f,Nby,GF,Jly 25)
Just Wait 104 (12f,Don,GF,May 18)
Just Wonderful 121 (8f,Leo,G,Sep 14)
Justanotherbottle 107 (5f,San,GF,Aug 31)
Juthoor 105 (8f,Mey,G,Mar 2)

Ka Ying Legend 115 (7f,Sha,G,Jan 1)
Kaanoon 119 (8f,Mey,G,Mar 2)
Kachumba 104 (7f,Lin,GF,Sep 14)
Kachy 111 (6f,Asc,GF,Jun 22)
Kaeso 115 (7f,Asc,GS,May 11)
Kaftan 111 (7f,Gal,G,Aug 1)
Kafu 108 (8f,Leo,G,Jly 25)
Kaizer 107 (14f,Mus,G,Jly 23)
Kalagia 103 (9f,Ham,G,Jly 18)
Kalaya 103 (12f,Bev,GS,Aug 15)
Kaloor 109 (11f,Goo,GF,May 24)
Kangaroo Valley 105 (13f,Leo,GF,Jly 11)
Kannapolis 104 (8f,Don,GF,Sep 11)
Karasi 110 (8f,Cur,GF,May 25)
Karawaan 105 (8f,Cur,S,Sep 28)
Karnavaal 104 (7f,Yor,GF,May 15)
Kasaman 116 (12f,Lon,GS,Jly 14)
Kaser 105 (10½f,Chs,G,Sep 14)
Kashagan 104 (12f,Thi,GS,Aug 3)
Kastasa 110 (12f,Cur,GY,Aug 23)
Kasuku 107 (12f,Chp,G,Aug 26)
Katdar 109 (8f,Lon,GS,Jly 14)
Katiymann 108 (8f,Cur,GY,Aug 30)
Kattani 108 (8f,Cur,GY,Jun 27)
Keep Me Company 105 (8f,Lei,GS,Jun 10)
Keepup Kevin 106 (7f,Lei,GF,Jly 24)
Kelly's Dino 112 (12f,Hay,GF,Jly 6)
Ken's Sam's 105 (6f,Cur,GF,May 26)
Kenbaio 111 (6f,Dea,G,Aug 4)
Kenny The Captain 107 (6f,Red,G,Sep 25)
Kensington Art 108 (14f,Cat,G,Aug 28)
Kenstone 104 (8½f,Not,GF,Apr 20)
Kesia 104 (12f,Nmk,G,Jly 20)
Kew Gardens 117 (12f,Eps,G,May 31)
Key Player 107 (7f,Eps,GF,Aug 27)
Key Victory 117 (8f,Mey,G,Jan 17)
Keyser Soze 103 (7f,Asc,S,Oct 5)
Keystroke 112 (6f,Nmk,GF,Apr 17)
Khaadem 112 (6f,Goo,GF,Aug 3)
Khaan 103 (8f,Yar,GF,May 22)
Khafoo Shememi 113 (8f,Wdr,GF,Jun 29)
Kharbetation 105 (10f,Rip,GS,Jun 20)
Khismet 104 (14f,Bat,F,Sep 15)
Kick On 109 (8f,Nmk,G,May 4)
Kick On Kick On 107 (5f,Nby,S,Apr 12)
Kiefer 108 (12f,Sal,GF,Jun 26)
Kilbaha Lady 106 (10f,Red,G,Apr 8)
Kimifive 114 (7f,Goo,G,May 4)
Kindly 106 (6f,Crl,GF,Jly 11)
King Ademar 110 (8f,Wdr,GF,Jly 8)
King And Queen 108 (11f,Ham,G,Jly 13)
King Athelstan 104 (10f,Lin,S,May 11)
King Crimson 108 (6f,Bri,GF,May 28)
King Malpic 106 (6½f,Dea,G,Aug 4)
King Of Change 117 (8f,Asc,HY,Oct 19)

King Of Comedy 113 *(8f,San,GF,May 23)*
King Of The Sand 109 *(12f,Mey,GF,May 21)*
King Of Tonga 108 *(7f,Nmk,HY,Nov 2)*
King Opie 117 *(7f,Sha,G,Mar 31)*
King Oswald 106 *(8f,Yar,GF,May 22)*
King Ottokar 109 *(12f,Chs,GS,May 8)*
King Pellinor 105 *(10f,Leo,GY,Apr 3)*
King Power 103 *(11½f,Lin,S,May 11)*
King Robert 107 *(5f,San,S,Jun 15)*
King's Advice 110 *(12f,Thi,GF,Apr 13)*
King's Field 113 *(8f,Mey,G,Jan 10)*
King's Man 105 *(9f,Sha,GF,Apr 22)*
King's Pavilion 112 *(8f,Thi,G,May 4)*
King's Slipper 105 *(8f,Thi,G,May 4)*
King's Vow 106 *(12f,Gal,G,Aug 2)*
Kingfast 103 *(11½f,Lin,S,Jly 27)*
Kingson 104 *(10f,Don,S,Aug 17)*
Kingston Kurrajong 107 *(9f,Goo,GF,Aug 3)*
Kinks 110 *(6f,Nmk,G,Jly 27)*
Kinloch Pride 103 *(5f,Mus,GF,May 2)*
Kirkland Forever 109 *(11½f,Wdr,G,Apr 15)*
Kirtling 106 *(12f,Bri,GF,Sep 2)*
Kiseki 114 *(12f,Lon,G,Sep 15)*
Kitaabaat 103 *(12f,Don,GF,Sep 14)*
Kitty's Cove 107 *(14f,Mus,G,Jly 23)*
Klassique 109 *(12f,Hay,HY,Jun 8)*
Knight To Behold 114 *(10f,Yor,S,Jly 27)*
Knockabout Queen 106 *(6f,Bri,GF,Sep 2)*
Knowing 110 *(10f,Yar,GF,Aug 30)*
Knowing Glance 103 *(7f,Lei,GS,Jun 10)*
Kodiac Harbour 109 *(8f,Lei,GF,May 27)*
Kodimoor 104 *(7f,Ayr,G,Jly 15)*
Kodiqueen 105 *(6f,Cur,SH,Oct 13)*
Koditime 106 *(5f,Asc,GF,Jly 26)*
Koeman 108 *(12f,Hay,GF,Jly 6)*
Kolossus 104 *(7f,Red,GF,Jly 21)*
Komodo 107 *(7f,Lon,VS,Oct 6)*
Konchek 107 *(6f,Nmk,G,Jly 27)*
Konigin 104 *(10f,Yar,GF,Aug 7)*
Korcho 112 *(10f,Nmk,GF,Jly 12)*
Kosciuszko 105 *(12f,Goo,G,Jly 31)*
Kripke 107 *(8f,Hay,GS,Jun 22)*
Kronprinz 113 *(8f,Mey,G,Jan 10)*
Kupa River 108 *(7f,Mus,G,May 3)*
Kurious 111 *(5f,San,GF,Jly 6)*
Kuwait Currency 106 *(8f,Asc,GS,Jly 27)*
Kwanza 103 *(10f,Pon,GS,Jly 19)*
Kylie Rules 110 *(8f,Ayr,G,Sep 21)*
Kyllachy Warrior 108 *(5f,Bev,G,May 6)*
Kyllang Rock 106 *(5f,Not,GS,Aug 13)*
Kynren 115 *(7f,Asc,GS,May 11)*

L'Un Deux Trois 108 *(14f,Wet,G,Apr 28)*
La Canche 109 *(7f,Lon,G,May 16)*
La Derniere Fois 105 *(8f,Cur,G,Jly 20)*
La Lune 104 *(10f,Sal,GF,May 16)*
La Maquina 106 *(7f,Goo,GF,May 24)*
Laafy 110 *(16f,Asc,S,Oct 4)*
Ladies First 108 *(10f,Yor,S,Oct 12)*
Lady Alavesa 104 *(10f,Rip,S,Aug 17)*
Lady Bowthorpe 103 *(8f,San,G,Sep 18)*
Lady Calcaria 111 *(6f,Crl,HY,May 31)*
Lady Dancealot 105 *(6f,Nmk,GF,Sep 21)*
Lady Elysia 107 *(14f,Lin,GF,Sep 14)*
Lady First 115 *(7f,Sha,G,Jan 1)*
Lady In France 113 *(5f,Hay,HY,Jun 8)*
Lady Kaya 111 *(8f,Nmk,G,May 5)*
Lady Lizzy 104 *(8f,Thi,GF,Sep 16)*
Lady Mascara 110 *(10f,Lin,GF,Sep 5)*
Lady Monica 106 *(6f,Not,S,May 11)*
Lady Of Aran 106 *(6f,Pon,GF,Sep 19)*
Lady Of Shalott 105 *(12f,Nmk,GF,Jun 29)*
Lady Reset 113 *(10f,Chp,GF,May 14)*
Lady Stormborn 103 *(10f,Leo,SH,Oct 19)*
Lady Wannabe 111 *(10f,Cur,G,Jun 29)*
Lafilia 103 *(10f,Red,G,Apr 8)*
Lah Ti Dar 108 *(12f,Eps,G,May 31)*
Lahore 114 *(6f,Thi,G,Aug 30)*
Laieth 108 *(8f,Nmk,GF,May 17)*
Lake Volta 114 *(6f,Goo,GF,May 24)*
Lamloom 108 *(7f,Ayr,G,Jun 21)*
Lancaster House 115 *(8½f,Gal,G,Aug 3)*
Land Of Legends 110 *(7f,Nmk,G,Jun 27)*
Land Of Oz 115 *(14f,Sal,GS,Aug 15)*
Land Of Winter 106 *(11½f,Yar,S,Jun 13)*
Landa Beach 113 *(16f,Asc,S,Oct 4)*
Landing Night 106 *(5f,Cat,G,Sep 3)*
Langholm 107 *(10f,Bev,GF,Jly 16)*
Lansky 117 *(7f,Mey,G,Feb 28)*
Lapidary 104 *(6f,Lin,G,Jun 22)*
Laraaib 110 *(12f,Nby,G,May 18)*
Larchmont Lad 114 *(7f,Lei,GF,Apr 27)*
Lariat 105 *(12f,Chs,S,Jun 15)*
Last Empire 105 *(5½f,Ayr,G,Sep 20)*
Last Look 105 *(10f,Not,S,Aug 6)*
Latchet 105 *(8f,Cur,GF,May 24)*
Lathom 107 *(5f,Pon,S,Jun 10)*
Latoyah Of North 110 *(12f,Gal,G,Aug 2)*
Latrobe 113 *(12f,Leo,GF,Aug 8)*
Laugh A Minute 113 *(7f,Lei,GF,Apr 27)*
Laughifuwant 106 *(7f,Leo,SH,Oct 26)*
Laurens 119 *(8f,Leo,G,Sep 14)*
Lavender's Blue 111 *(8f,Nmk,GS,Oct 5)*
Lawmaking 105 *(8f,Hay,GS,Jun 22)*
Lawn Ranger 112 *(9f,Goo,G,Aug 24)*
Lawyersgunsn'money 103 *(10f,Bat,F,Sep 4)*
Le Brivido 114 *(8f,Nby,G,May 18)*
Le Don De Vie 112 *(12f,Goo,G,Jly 31)*
Le Musee 105 *(17f,Crl,GS,Jun 11)*
Le Panache 104 *(9f,Sha,GF,Apr 22)*
Leader Writer 108 *(8½f,Bev,GS,May 14)*
Leagan Gaeilge 107 *(8f,Cur,GF,May 24)*
Lean Perfection 123 *(7f,Sha,G,Mar 31)*
Ledham 103 *(8f,Hay,S,Apr 27)*
Legal Spin 107 *(12f,Gal,G,Aug 2)*
Lehoogg 109 *(8f,Don,G,May 4)*
Leo Davinci 104 *(7f,Red,GS,Jun 21)*
Leo De Fury 114 *(10f,Lon,VS,Oct 5)*
Leo Minor 106 *(5f,San,G,Sep 18)*
Leodis Dream 107 *(5f,Chs,GS,May 8)*
Leonio 110 *(7f,Lon,G,May 16)*
Leroy Leroy 111 *(10f,Red,GF,May 27)*
Leshlaa 115 *(9f,Mey,G,Jan 24)*
Lethal Angel 104 *(6f,Nmk,GF,May 17)*
Lethal Lunch 104 *(6f,Asc,GF,Sep 7)*
Lethal Missile 109 *(8f,Wdr,GF,May 27)*
Lethal Power 110 *(8f,Cur,GY,Aug 30)*
Lethal Promise 105 *(6f,Cur,GY,Jun 7)*
Lever Du Soleil 112 *(16f,Cat,GF,Jly 10)*
Lexington Law 106 *(12f,Thi,GF,Jly 3)*
Li Kui 103 *(8f,Pon,GF,Jly 9)*
Libbretta 107 *(10f,Lin,G,May 3)*
Libras Power 103 *(7f,Leo,G,Jun 6)*
Librisa Breeze 114 *(7f,Nby,S,Aug 17)*
Light And Dark 110 *(7f,Nmk,GF,Jly 12)*
Light Up Our Stars 106 *(10f,Don,GF,Sep 13)*
Lightening Dance 109 *(11½f,Wdr,G,May 13)*
Lightly Squeeze 106 *(11½f,Wdr,S,Oct 7)*
Lightning Attack 103 *(8f,Don,S,Jun 16)*
Ligne D'Or 114 *(12f,Lon,G,Sep 15)*
Lihou 109 *(6f,Asc,S,Oct 4)*
Lil Rockerfeller 103 *(20½f,Goo,G,Jly 31)*
Lilly Kafeine 109 *(7f,Lon,G,Sep 15)*
Lily's Prince 104 *(6f,Cur,GF,May 26)*
Lim's Cruiser 105 *(6f,Asc,GF,Jun 22)*
Limato 111 *(7f,Nmk,GF,Jun 29)*
Limerick Lord 103 *(8f,Bri,GF,Sep 1)*
Limit Long 107 *(7f,Gal,G,Jly 30)*
Lincoln Park 109 *(7f,Hay,S,Sep 6)*
Line Of Reason 109 *(5f,Bev,GF,Apr 17)*
Line Of Duty 115 *(10f,Lon,VS,Oct 5)*
Liquid Mercury 107 *(7f,Mey,G,Feb 28)*
Litigious 110 *(10f,Goo,GS,Jun 9)*
Litterale Ci 109 *(16½f,Nby,GS,Jly 20)*
Little Boy Blue 107 *(6f,Bri,GF,Jun 18)*
Little Clarinet 111 *(6f,Cur,GF,May 26)*
Little Fantasy 106 *(8f,Sha,G,Mar 31)*
Little General 117 *(7f,Sha,G,Apr 22)*
Little India 109 *(10½f,Hay,GF,Jly 5)*
Little Legs 106 *(5f,Cat,GF,Jly 17)*
Living Legend 114 *(10½f,Chs,GS,May 9)*
Lleyton 104 *(12f,Gal,G,Aug 1)*
Lobo's Legend 112 *(7f,Sha,G,Mar 31)*
Loch Ness Monster 106 *(8f,Hay,GF,May 25)*
Logi 105 *(7f,Ayr,G,Jun 21)*
Logician 120 *(14½f,Don,GF,Sep 14)*
London Eye 108 *(11f,Crl,HY,May 31)*
London Hall 111 *(9f,Sha,G,Mar 31)*
Long Call 106 *(10f,Bri,GF,Aug 8)*
Longroom 104 *(5f,Cat,G,Sep 3)*
Lonicera 104 *(8f,Ffo,G,Aug 29)*
Look Around 105 *(8f,Nmk,G,May 5)*
Look Closely 106 *(10f,Goo,GF,Sep 3)*
Look Surprised 105 *(5f,Wdr,G,Aug 19)*
Loolwah 105 *(8f,Asc,GF,Jly 13)*
Loose Chippings 105 *(12f,Bev,GS,Aug 15)*
Lord Glitters 118 *(8f,Asc,G,Jun 18)*
Lord Lamington 106 *(16f,Cat,GF,Jly 10)*
Lord North 110 *(8f,Asc,HY,Oct 19)*
Lord Oberon 108 *(6f,Hay,HY,Jun 8)*
Lord Of The Rock 105 *(8f,Thi,GS,Aug 3)*
Lord Riddiford 111 *(5f,Cur,GY,Jun 27)*
Lordsbridge Boy 103 *(6f,Nmk,GF,Aug 2)*
Lorelina 107 *(10f,Eps,G,May 31)*
Lorna Cole 103 *(5f,Asc,GF,Jly 26)*
Lorton 109 *(6f,Crl,HY,May 31)*
Loud And Clear 109 *(13f,Ham,GF,May 5)*
Louie De Palma 108 *(6f,Ayr,G,Sep 21)*
Love And Be Loved 107 *(11½f,Wdr,G,May 13)*
Love Dreams 112 *(7f,Goo,G,May 4)*
Love Explodes 103 *(8f,Thi,GF,Sep 16)*
Love So Deep 113 *(12f,Nmk,G,Jly 20)*
Love To Breeze 108 *(16f,Chp,GF,May 14)*
Lovee Dovee 105 *(8f,Cur,S,Sep 28)*
Lovely Acclamation 103 *(8f,Ffo,G,Aug 29)*
Loving Glance 106 *(8f,Nmk,GF,Aug 2)*
Loxley 106 *(12f,Nmk,G,Sep 27)*
Lucius Tiberius 111 *(12f,Hay,GF,Jly 6)*
Luck Of Clover 110 *(14f,Sal,GS,Aug 15)*
Lucky Deal 109 *(14f,Mus,G,Apr 20)*
Lucky Louie 107 *(7f,Don,GF,Jun 29)*
Lucky Lycra 103 *(15f,Lon,VS,Oct 5)*
Lucky Number 104 *(8f,Bat,GF,Aug 27)*
Lucky Violet 105 *(7f,Mus,G,Jly 23)*
Lucky's Dream 104 *(10f,Not,G,Jun 5)*
Lucy Lou 103 *(12f,Ffo,GS,Aug 13)*
Luis Vaz De Torres 107 *(7f,Cat,S,Aug 12)*
Luminent 105 *(8f,Leo,G,Jly 25)*
Lumsden 103 *(6f,Cur,G,Jly 21)*
Luna Magic 104 *(8½f,Bev,GS,Aug 15)*
Lunar Jet 111 *(10½f,Hay,HY,Jun 12)*
Lush Life 106 *(8f,Wdr,G,May 6)*
Lusis Naturea 110 *(12f,Gal,G,Aug 1)*
Luxuriant 104 *(9f,Leo,G,Jly 18)*
Lydiate Lady 109 *(5f,Not,S,Oct 30)*
Lyndon B 103 *(7f,Goo,G,Jly 31)*
Lyzbeth 108 *(7f,Yor,G,Aug 22)*

Maamora 113 *(8f,San,G,Jly 31)*
Maarek 110 *(5f,Cur,GY,Jun 27)*
Mabo 105 *(8f,Ffo,G,Aug 29)*
Mabs Cross 113 *(5f,Hay,GF,May 25)*
Mac Ailey 103 *(8f,Lei,G,Jun 27)*
Machine Learner 105 *(14f,San,G,Jly 24)*
Machree 106 *(5½f,Chs,G,Aug 31)*
Macquarie 105 *(10f,Cur,G,Jun 27)*
Macs Blessings 103 *(6f,Ayr,HY,Aug 10)*
Madam Seamstress 107 *(8f,Leo,GY,May 12)*
Madame Tantzy 103 *(10f,Nby,GF,Jly 25)*
Madeleine Bond 107 *(10f,Sal,S,Jun 11)*
Madeleine Must 109 *(8f,Nmk,GS,Oct 5)*
Madhmoon 114 *(10f,Leo,G,Sep 14)*
Madrinho 105 *(5½f,Chs,G,Jly 12)*
Maggies Angel 108 *(7f,Red,G,Aug 10)*
Magic Circle 108 *(13½f,Chs,S,May 9)*
Magic Legend 119 *(7f,Sha,G,Mar 31)*
Magic Shuffle 103 *(8f,Bat,G,Jun 26)*
Magic Wand 116 *(10f,Cur,G,Jun 28)*
Magical 118 *(12f,Lon,VS,Oct 6)*
Magical Effect 105 *(6f,Red,GF,Apr 22)*
Magical Rhythms 106 *(8f,Nmk,GF,Aug 2)*
Magical Ride 106 *(7f,Lin,G,Jun 22)*
Magical Spirit 104 *(6f,Red,GF,May 28)*
Magical Wish 106 *(6f,Yor,GS,Jun 15)*
Magna Grecia 115 *(8f,Nmk,G,May 4)*
Magnetic Charm 109 *(8f,Asc,G,Jun 21)*
Magnetic North 107 *(10f,Leo,GF,Jly 11)*
Magnetism 104 *(8f,Sha,G,Jan 1)*
Magnolia Springs 107 *(12f,Nmk,G,Jly 20)*
Maid For Life 104 *(8f,Hay,HY,Aug 10)*
Maid In India 116 *(5f,Hay,HY,Jun 8)*
Maid In Manhattan 108 *(16f,Thi,G,Aug 30)*
Maid Of Spirit 103 *(5f,Sal,S,Aug 14)*
Maid Up 110 *(14f,Yor,GF,May 25)*
Maiden Castle 113 *(10f,Chp,G,May 3)*
Maiden Voyage 104 *(10f,Bri,GF,Sep 9)*
Maifalki 106 *(12f,Mey,G,Feb 14)*
Mailshot 112 *(8f,Mey,G,Mar 2)*
Main Edition 115 *(7f,Red,HY,Oct 5)*
Majaalis 105 *(6f,Yar,GF,Sep 18)*
Majestic Dawn 112 *(10f,Not,HY,Oct 16)*
Majestic Endeavour 112 *(7f,Sha,G,Apr 22)*
Majestic Mac 103 *(7f,Nmk,G,Jun 22)*
Majestic Mambo 105 *(9f,Mey,G,Mar 30)*
Majestic Stone 104 *(11f,Crl,GS,Jun 17)*
Major Blue 103 *(5f,Pon,GF,Jly 9)*
Major Jumbo 112 *(6f,Chs,GS,Aug 4)*
Major Partnership 115 *(8f,Mey,G,Feb 21)*
Major Valentine 105 *(6f,Chp,GF,Jly 12)*
Makambe 103 *(10f,Yar,GF,Aug 7)*
Makanah 111 *(5½f,Yor,G,Aug 21)*
Makawee 114 *(12f,Yor,GF,May 25)*
Make A Challenge 120 *(6f,Cur,SH,Oct 13)*
Make A Wish 106 *(7f,San,GF,Jly 6)*
Make Good 109 *(16f,Chp,GS,Aug 15)*
Make Me 103 *(8f,Thi,G,May 18)*
Make Me Sway 106 *(8f,Cur,S,Sep 28)*
Make My Day 106 *(12f,Sal,S,Jun 11)*
Make The Switch 103 *(15f,Leo,G,Jun 13)*
Making Miracles 109 *(14f,Mus,G,Apr 20)*
Maksab 103 *(7f,Nmk,GF,Jly 12)*
Makzeem 108 *(7f,Nby,GS,Jly 20)*
Mallacoota 111 *(12f,Cur,G,Jun 27)*
Man On The Moon 107 *(8f,Lon,GS,Jly 14)*
Management Star 107 *(8f,Sha,G,Jan 1)*
Mancini 106 *(14f,Sal,GF,Apr 28)*
Mandalayan 106 *(12f,Lei,G,Apr 5)*
Mandarin 114 *(10f,Don,GF,Jun 1)*
Mandarin Monarch 106 *(12f,Cur,G,Jun 27)*
Mandocello 105 *(8f,Wdr,G,May 13)*
Manjaam 109 *(13f,Ayr,G,Jun 22)*
Mankayan 110 *(12f,Sal,S,Jun 11)*
Mannaal 109 *(10f,Goo,G,Jly 31)*
Manorah 103 *(12f,Nmk,GF,Jun 29)*
Mansfield 103 *(6f,Red,G,Jly 31)*
Manshood 113 *(5f,Cur,GY,Jun 27)*
Manuela De Vega 110 *(12f,Chs,G,Sep 14)*
Mapped 106 *(12f,Yor,GF,May 25)*
Maqsad 109 *(10f,Goo,G,Aug 1)*
Maquisard 104 *(16f,Goo,GS,Jun 9)*
Marengo 107 *(12f,Chp,GS,Aug 15)*
Marhaba Milliar 105 *(7f,Yar,GF,Jun 28)*
Marianafoot 112 *(7f,Lon,G,Sep 15)*
Marie's Diamond 110 *(8f,Pon,G,Jly 28)*
Marietta Robusti 104 *(5f,Ham,S,Sep 23)*
Marinaresco 112 *(7f,Mey,G,Jan 24)*
Marine One 108 *(12f,Gal,G,Aug 1)*
Mark's Choice 107 *(6f,Thi,G,Aug 30)*
Markazi 111 *(7f,Ayr,G,Sep 19)*
Marlborough Sounds 112 *(12f,Cur,G,Jun 27)*
Marmelo 112 *(12f,Eps,G,May 31)*
Marnie James 111 *(5f,Yor,GF,May 16)*
Maroon Bells 107 *(11½f,Yar,GF,May 22)*
Marronnier 113 *(8½f,Eps,HY,Sep 29)*
Marshal Dan 108 *(8f,Nmk,GS,Jun 21)*
Marshall Jennings 110 *(7f,Leo,G,Sep 14)*
Martineo 110 *(6f,Goo,GF,May 24)*
Mary Salome 109 *(6f,Crl,SH,Oct 13)*
Masaff 108 *(14f,Cur,G,Jun 28)*
Masar 108 *(12f,Nmk,GF,Jly 11)*
Masaru 107 *(7f,Asc,G,Jun 22)*
Masham Star 108 *(7½f,Chs,G,May 25)*
Masked Identity 105 *(8f,Asc,GF,Jly 12)*
Massa Lubrense 105 *(8f,Cur,S,Aug 9)*
Massif Central 110 *(12f,Cur,G,Jun 27)*
Massive Millennium 111 *(7f,Sha,G,Apr 22)*
Massive Power 106 *(7f,Sha,G,Apr 22)*
Master Archer 106 *(16f,Goo,GS,Jun 9)*
Master Bernini 109 *(7f,Sha,G,Apr 22)*
Master Grey 115 *(16f,Chp,GF,May 14)*
Master Matt 110 *(5f,Cur,S,Aug 9)*
Master Of Reality 116 *(16f,Fle,GS,Nov 5)*
Master Speaker 108 *(8f,Cur,GF,May 26)*
Master's Spirit 104 *(12½f,Dea,G,Aug 4)*
Match Maker 104 *(9f,Ayr,G,Jun 21)*
Matchmaking 107 *(16f,Nmk,GF,Aug 10)*
Material Girl 107 *(7f,Nmk,HY,Nov 2)*
Matewan 106 *(11f,Crl,GS,Jun 17)*
Matterhorn 119 *(8f,Leo,G,Sep 14)*
Maulesden May 107 *(10f,Ayr,GF,May 22)*
Mauricio 106 *(10f,Yar,GF,Aug 7)*
Max Dynamite 106 *(14f,Yor,GF,Aug 24)*
Max Zorin 105 *(8½f,Not,G,Jun 5)*
Maybe Today 107 *(12f,Don,GF,Sep 11)*
Maydanny 104 *(8½f,Not,HY,Jun 13)*
Mayfair Spirit 105 *(8f,Hay,GS,Jly 20)*
Maygold 109 *(5f,Asc,S,Oct 5)*
Mayne 105 *(10½f,Chs,G,Sep 13)*
Mazyoun 105 *(7½f,Chs,S,May 10)*
Mazzini 114 *(5f,Mey,G,Jan 24)*
Mazzuri 105 *(12f,Goo,G,Aug 25)*
Medahim 114 *(7f,Yor,S,Jly 27)*
Medal Winner 111 *(10f,Bri,GF,Jly 2)*
Medalla De Oro 106 *(10½f,Chs,G,Jly 13)*
Medicine Jack 108 *(6f,Cur,SH,Oct 13)*
Medieval 106 *(8f,Nby,GS,Aug 16)*
Mehdaayih 117 *(10f,Goo,G,Aug 1)*
Mekong 110 *(14f,Yor,GF,Aug 24)*
Melgate Majeure 104 *(10f,Bev,GF,Jly 16)*
Melicertes 109 *(8f,Lon,GS,Jly 14)*
Melting Dew 106 *(12f,Hay,GF,Jly 6)*
Memphis Bleek 103 *(9f,Ayr,G,Jun 21)*
Memyselfandmoi 110 *(7f,Gal,G,Aug 1)*
Menin Gate 109 *(12f,Don,G,Jly 20)*
Meqdam 103 *(10f,Bri,GF,Jly 2)*
Mer De Glace 116 *(16f,Fle,GS,Nov 5)*
Merdon Castle 106 *(10f,Bat,F,Sep 4)*
Merhoob 118 *(5f,Chs,GS,May 9)*
Merited 106 *(10f,Leo,G,Jun 13)*
Merry Banter 106 *(5f,Eps,G,Aug 26)*
Merry Vale 105 *(10f,Goo,GS,Jun 9)*
Merrygowin 109 *(8f,Sha,G,Jan 1)*
Message 103 *(12f,Don,GF,May 31)*
Met By Moonlight 105 *(6f,Bat,GS,Aug 17)*
Mi Manchi 103 *(11½f,Yar,S,Jun 13)*
Mia Maria 110 *(8f,Cur,G,Jly 20)*
Mia Mento 105 *(8f,Leo,GY,May 12)*
Mia Tesoro 111 *(9f,Mey,G,Feb 14)*
Miacomet 110 *(6f,Cur,SH,Oct 13)*
Michael's Mount 103 *(16f,Yor,GF,Jly 13)*
Michaels Choice 109 *(5f,San,G,Sep 18)*
Michele Strogoff 107 *(8f,San,G,Jly 31)*
Mickey 105 *(7f,Hay,GF,Jly 4)*
Micro Manage 116 *(12f,Cur,GY,Jun 7)*
Midnight Mood 103 *(12f,Nby,GF,Jly 25)*
Migration 111 *(10f,San,GF,Aug 31)*
Mikmak 108 *(10f,Rip,GF,Jly 8)*
Milan Reef 106 *(7f,Lei,HY,Oct 8)*
Mildenberger 105 *(14f,Yor,GF,May 17)*
Military Tactic 105 *(8f,Thi,GS,May 11)*
Militia 105 *(5f,Ayr,G,Sep 19)*
Militry Decoration 107 *(10f,Not,GS,Aug 13)*
Millfield 110 *(7f,Lon,VS,Oct 6)*
Mina Vagante 105 *(10f,Red,G,Jly 31)*
Mina Velour 107 *(6f,Crl,GF,Jly 11)*
Mind The Crack 112 *(12f,Goo,G,Jly 31)*
Ming 107 *(12f,Cur,G,Jun 27)*
Minnie Haha 108 *(8f,Leo,GF,Jly 11)*
Miracle Of Medinah 105 *(6f,Asc,GF,Sep 6)*
Miracle Works 106 *(5f,Bat,F,Aug 2)*
Mirage Dancer 114 *(16f,Fle,GS,Nov 5)*
Mirsaale 107 *(14f,Mus,G,Apr 20)*
Miss Blondell 107 *(10f,Bat,F,Sep 15)*
Miss Celestial 109 *(6f,Bat,GF,Jly 24)*
Miss Elsa 106 *(10f,Chp,G,Sep 17)*
Miss Jabeam 113 *(6f,Cur,G,Jly 21)*
Miss Latin 105 *(11½f,Yar,GF,Sep 19)*
Miss M 108 *(11½f,Bat,GS,Jun 15)*
Miss O Connor 109 *(8f,Hay,HY,Aug 10)*
Miss Ranger 106 *(14f,Red,G,Jun 22)*
Mister Chiang 111 *(14f,Cat,GF,Sep 21)*
Mister Musicmaster 104 *(8f,Bat,F,May 24)*
Mistiroc 104 *(10f,Don,G,Apr 27)*
Mistress Nellie 109 *(11½f,Yar,GF,May 22)*
Misty Breese 106 *(11½f,Yar,GF,May 22)*
Mitchum Swagger 111 *(7f,Red,HY,Oct 5)*
Mizaah 107 *(7f,Hay,S,Sep 5)*
Mizuki 103 *(10f,San,GF,May 30)*

Mobham 107 *(11½f,Wdr,G,Apr 15)*
Model Guest 107 *(8f,Asc,G,Jun 21)*
Moftris 108 *(8f,Wdr,GF,Jly 1)*
Mogsy 107 *(7f,Hay,GS,Jly 19)*
Mohaather 117 *(7f,Nby,GS,Apr 13)*
Mohareb 104 *(8f,Thi,GS,May 11)*
Mohawk 117 *(10½f,Chs,GS,May 9)*
Mojito 109 *(8f,Goo,GF,Aug 2)*
Mokaatil 114 *(5f,Chs,GS,May 9)*
Mokhalad 108 *(7f,Leo,G,Sep 14)*
Moktamel 112 *(12f,Cur,G,Jun 27)*
Moll Davis 109 *(12f,Ham,G,Jly 13)*
Molls Memory 112 *(7f,Hay,S,Sep 6)*
Moment Of Hope 107 *(10f,Goo,G,Jly 31)*
Momkin 112 *(7f,Lon,G,Sep 15)*
Monaco Rose 105 *(13f,Leo,G,Jun 6)*
Monarch Maid 103 *(5f,Yar,GF,Aug 20)*
Mondain 104 *(13f,Ham,G,Jly 2)*
Moneebb 103 *(6f,Cur,GF,May 26)*
Money Marshal 103 *(8f,Sha,G,Mar 31)*
Money Winner 105 *(8f,Sha,G,Jan 1)*
Mongolia 109 *(10f,Chp,GF,May 14)*
Monica 111 *(7f,Sha,G,Jan 1)*
Monica Sheriff 107 *(14f,Goo,HY,Sep 25)*
Monsieur Lambrays 107 *(12f,Nby,G,Aug 6)*
Monsieur Noir 107 *(7f,Lei,GF,Jly 6)*
Mont Kiara 103 *(6f,Bri,GF,May 28)*
Mont Kinabalu 104 *(8f,Pon,GF,Jly 1)*
Montatham 106 *(7f,Mus,S,Oct 14)*
Montys Angel 106 *(14f,Lin,GF,Sep 14)*
Monza 108 *(8f,Mey,G,Jan 17)*
Moon King 111 *(14f,Wet,G,Apr 28)*
Moonlight Spirit 114 *(15f,Lon,VS,Oct 5)*
Moonmeister 108 *(12f,Cur,G,Jly 20)*
Moonraker 104 *(5f,Asc,GF,Sep 7)*
Moqtarreb 105 *(8f,Nmk,GF,Jly 11)*
Moraawed 107 *(6f,Don,G,Apr 27)*
Morando 114 *(13½f,Chs,S,May 9)*
Mordin 110 *(8½f,Eps,GF,Jun 1)*
Mordred 108 *(11f,Goo,GF,Aug 2)*
More Than Likely 104 *(5f,Wdr,GF,Jun 30)*
Morethanlucky 118 *(7f,Sha,G,Jan 1)*
Moretti 103 *(7f,Yar,F,Aug 25)*
Morga 106 *(12f,Cur,GY,Aug 23)*
Morning Duel 105 *(8f,Rip,G,Aug 27)*
Morpho Blue 110 *(7f,Leo,G,Sep 14)*
Moss Gill 108 *(6f,Nmk,GF,Jly 11)*
Mostawaa 103 *(8f,Asc,S,Oct 4)*
Mot Juste 113 *(7f,Don,GF,Sep 13)*
Motafaawit 108 *(7f,Asc,S,May 10)*
Motakhayyel 104 *(7f,Yar,GF,Jun 28)*
Motamarris 110 *(11f,Lon,GS,Apr 22)*
Motawaj 107 *(8f,San,G,Jly 24)*
Moteo 105 *(14f,Leo,GF,Jly 11)*
Mother Vincent 110 *(8f,Cur,S,Oct 22)*
Mount Everest 114 *(12f,Leo,G,Sep 14)*
Mountain Angel 116 *(10f,Lon,VS,Oct 5)*
Mountain Hunter 125 *(12f,Mey,G,Feb 14)*
Mountain Peak 108 *(5f,Asc,GF,Sep 7)*
Mountain Rescue 110 *(8f,Nmk,GS,Jun 21)*
Mountain Rock 107 *(16f,Chp,GF,May 14)*
Move In Time 112 *(5f,Pon,G,Aug 7)*
Move Swiftly 112 *(8f,Asc,S,Jun 19)*
Movie Star 104 *(10f,Not,GS,Aug 13)*
Moxy Mares 104 *(7f,Gal,G,Jly 30)*
Moyassar 106 *(6f,Nmk,G,May 4)*
Mr Adjudicator 111 *(12f,Gal,G,Aug 2)*
Mr Buttons 103 *(6f,Wdr,GF,Sep 2)*
Mr Carbonator 103 *(8f,Pon,GF,Apr 9)*
Mr Coco Bean 110 *(10½f,Hay,GF,Jly 5)*
Mr Diamond 107 *(7f,Wet,GS,May 7)*
Mr Everest 107 *(18f,Nmk,S,Oct 12)*
Mr Greenlight 103 *(5f,Ayr,G,Sep 19)*
Mr Lumieres 112 *(5f,Sha,G,Apr 22)*
Mr Lupton 115 *(6f,Cur,GF,May 25)*
Mr Nice Guy 106 *(14f,Lin,GF,Sep 14)*
Mr Orange 106 *(6f,Pon,G,Aug 7)*
Mr Scaramanga 109 *(10f,Eps,G,May 31)*
Mr Shelby 104 *(6f,Ayr,HY,Aug 10)*
Mr Smith 106 *(17f,Crl,GS,Jun 11)*
Mr Top Hat 108 *(10f,San,GF,Aug 31)*
Mr Tyrrell 108 *(8f,Bat,F,May 6)*
Mr Wagyu 103 *(6f,Red,G,Aug 10)*
Mr Zoom Zoom 103 *(12f,Nmk,GF,Jun 8)*
Muatadel 104 *(6f,Red,GF,Apr 22)*
Mubakker 106 *(6f,Asc,S,Oct 4)*
Mubariz 110 *(10½f,Hay,GF,Jly 4)*
Mubhij 103 *(7f,Yar,GF,May 22)*
Mubtasim 120 *(7f,Mey,G,Feb 28)*
Mubtasimah 110 *(7f,Yor,G,Aug 22)*
Muchly 107 *(8f,San,GF,Jly 6)*
Mudlahhim 109 *(7f,Gal,G,Jly 30)*
Muette 112 *(15f,Lon,VS,Oct 5)*
Muftakker 107 *(14f,Red,G,Jun 22)*
Mugatoo 103 *(14f,Goo,S,Jun 14)*
Muhallab 105 *(7f,Red,GF,Jly 21)*
Mujassam 103 *(7f,Cat,GS,Aug 6)*
Mujid 108 *(12f,Gal,G,Aug 2)*
Mukha Magic 104 *(10f,Not,S,Jun 17)*
Mukhayyam 106 *(12f,Rip,G,Apr 27)*
Mullarkey 104 *(10f,Lin,S,May 11)*
Mulligatawny 105 *(10f,Ayr,GF,May 28)*
Multamis 107 *(10f,Eps,G,Jly 18)*
Multellie 107 *(12f,Rip,GS,Sep 28)*
Multigogo 112 *(7f,Sha,G,Jan 1)*
Mums Hope 109 *(8f,Asc,GF,Jly 13)*
Munfallet 106 *(8f,Leo,GF,Aug 8)*
Munhamek 118 *(8f,Hay,GF,May 25)*
Munitions 103 *(6½f,Dea,G,Aug 4)*
Muntadab 104 *(7f,Red,HY,Oct 5)*
Muqaatil 115 *(12f,Mey,G,Jan 19)*
Muraaqeb 111 *(7f,Mey,G,Feb 28)*
Musaddas 112 *(7f,Mey,G,Feb 28)*
Musicka 109 *(6f,Thi,G,May 18)*
Musharrif 104 *(6f,Pon,GF,Jly 9)*
Music Seeker 110 *(10f,Yor,S,Jun 14)*
Music Society 107 *(6f,Ayr,G,Sep 20)*
Musis Amica 115 *(12f,Lon,G,Sep 15)*
Mustaaqeem 104 *(16f,Chp,GF,May 14)*
Mustajeer 115 *(14f,Yor,GF,Aug 24)*
Mustarrid 110 *(8½f,Not,S,Oct 30)*
Mustashry 118 *(8f,Nby,G,May 18)*
Mutaabeq 108 *(10f,San,GF,Aug 31)*
Mutabaahy 106 *(6f,Rip,GS,Jun 20)*
Mutadaawel 104 *(8f,Cat,GF,May 24)*
Mutafani 106 *(8½f,Not,G,Jun 5)*
Mutamaasik 103 *(7f,Nmk,G,Aug 17)*
Mutamaded 109 *(11f,Crl,GF,Jun 26)*
Mutamakina 115 *(12f,Lon,G,Sep 15)*
Mutaraffa 105 *(7f,Red,G,Aug 10)*
Mutarakez 106 *(8½f,Not,GF,Apr 20)*
Mutasaamy 104 *(8f,Hay,GS,Jly 20)*
Mutawathea 110 *(8f,Mey,G,Feb 21)*
Muthmir 107 *(5f,Asc,GF,Jly 13)*
Muzdawaj 103 *(10f,Mey,G,Feb 21)*
My Boy Sepoy 109 *(10f,Lin,GF,May 3)*
My Reward 106 *(13f,Ayr,G,Jun 22)*
My Ukulele 104 *(8f,Thi,GS,Aug 3)*
My Valentino 107 *(8f,Ham,S,Sep 23)*
My Winner 119 *(7f,Sha,G,Mar 31)*
Myklachi 104 *(11½f,Lin,S,Jly 27)*
Mystic Meg 111 *(10f,Sal,S,Jun 11)*
Mystiquestar 111 *(10f,Chp,GF,May 14)*
Myth Creation 105 *(7f,Leo,SH,Oct 26)*
Mythical Madness 104 *(10f,Eps,G,Apr 24)*
Mythical Magic 119 *(8f,Mey,G,Feb 21)*

Naadirr 104 *(6f,Don,GF,Mar 31)*
Nabhan 105 *(14f,Ffo,G,Aug 29)*
Nagano Gold 107 *(12f,Lon,VS,Oct 6)*
Nahaarr 106 *(7f,Nmk,G,Jun 28)*
Naif 115 *(7f,Lon,GS,Apr 22)*
Najashee 106 *(8f,Ayr,GF,May 22)*
Nam 109 *(10f,Leo,G,Aug 15)*
Nantucket 103 *(8f,Wdr,GF,Jly 8)*
Napping 109 *(6f,Yar,S,Jun 12)*
Naqaawa 107 *(10f,Goo,G,Jly 31)*
Narak 103 *(7½f,Lin,GF,Sep 14)*
Narjes 110 *(10f,Lin,GF,May 3)*
Narynkol 103 *(10f,Rip,G,Aug 26)*
Nasee 110 *(11½f,Yar,GF,May 22)*
Nate The Great 109 *(11½f,Lin,S,May 11)*
National Glory 105 *(6f,Bri,GF,May 28)*
Natty Night 107 *(12f,Nby,GF,Jly 4)*
Nausha 106 *(10f,Cur,GF,Sep 15)*
Navajo Pass 108 *(14f,Crl,GS,Aug 21)*
Navigate By Stars 104 *(10f,Pon,GF,May 24)*
Nayef Road 118 *(14½f,Don,GF,Sep 14)*
Nayslayer 111 *(8f,Mey,G,Feb 28)*
Nazeef 110 *(8f,Nmk,GF,Sep 21)*
Nearly There 109 *(14f,Red,G,Jun 22)*
Nearooz 112 *(10f,Lin,GF,Sep 5)*
Ned Pepper 108 *(12f,Nby,G,Aug 6)*
Neff 107 *(10f,Lin,S,May 11)*
Neileta 103 *(10f,Ayr,GF,Jly 7)*
Nette Rousse 111 *(10f,San,GS,Jun 15)*
Neufbosc 112 *(16f,Fle,GS,Nov 5)*
Nevada 105 *(12f,Thi,G,Apr 29)*
Never Be Enough 108 *(8f,Ham,GF,May 17)*
Never Better 111 *(7f,Sha,G,Apr 22)*
Never Do Nothing 109 *(12f,Goo,G,Jun 21)*
Never No More 112 *(7f,Don,GF,Sep 14)*
Never Surrender 103 *(14f,Ffo,GS,Aug 13)*
New Arrangement 106 *(8f,Ham,G,Jly 18)*
New Asia Sunrise 117 *(7f,Sha,G,Mar 31)*
New Day Dawn 106 *(8f,Pon,GF,Jly 9)*
New Graduate 115 *(8f,Wdr,GF,Jun 29)*
New King 106 *(9f,San,GS,Jun 15)*
New Show 108 *(11½f,Wdr,G,Apr 29)*
Newmarket Warrior 103 *(8f,Hay,GS,Jun 22)*
Nezar 104 *(7f,Lei,GS,Jun 10)*
Nicconi Express 113 *(8f,Sha,G,Jan 1)*
Nice Kick 114 *(7f,Sha,G,Apr 22)*
Nicholas T 115 *(8f,Thi,G,May 4)*
Nickajack Cave 108 *(10f,Cur,G,Jun 28)*
Nicklaus 105 *(8f,Sal,GF,Jun 26)*
Nigg Bay 106 *(6f,Ffo,GF,Jly 29)*
Night Secret 103 *(6f,Wdr,GF,Jun 3)*
Nimitz 115 *(10f,Leo,GY,Jun 20)*
Ninjago 105 *(6f,Thi,GF,Jun 3)*
Nitro Boost 109 *(5f,Cur,GY,Jun 7)*
Njord 104 *(8f,Cur,SH,Oct 13)*
Nkosikazi 108 *(8f,Nmk,GF,Jly 11)*
No Nay Yellow 106 *(5f,Cur,YS,Aug 9)*
No Nonsense 104 *(7f,Nby,GS,Apr 13)*
Noble Account 104 *(10f,Bri,GF,Aug 8)*
Noble De Love 118 *(7f,Sha,G,Jan 1)*
Noble Expression 106 *(12f,Cur,G,Jun 27)*
Noble Music 103 *(12f,Hay,S,Sep 5)*
Noble Peace 104 *(8f,Pon,G,Aug 7)*
Noble Prospector 106 *(8f,Thi,G,Apr 29)*
Noble Steed 109 *(8f,Sha,G,Jan 1)*
Noirvento 112 *(6f,Cur,G,Jly 21)*
Nonchalance 103 *(8f,Hay,GF,May 24)*
Norab 111 *(16f,Chp,GS,Aug 15)*
Nordano 103 *(16f,Cat,S,Jun 17)*
Nordic Lights 115 *(10f,Mey,G,Jan 17)*
Normandel 110 *(8f,Cur,GF,May 25)*
Normandy Barriere 105 *(6f,Asc,GF,Jly 12)*
North Face 105 *(12f,Mey,G,Jan 24)*
Northern Lyte 105 *(8½f,Bev,GF,Aug 25)*
Northernpowerhouse 108 *(7f,Mus,G,Jly 23)*
Northwest Frontier 103 *(16f,Rip,G,Apr 27)*
Norway 116 *(12f,Leo,G,Sep 14)*
Not So Sleepy 110 *(18f,Nmk,S,Oct 12)*
Not Usual Talent 108 *(8f,Sha,G,Mar 31)*
Nubough 104 *(7f,Nmk,GF,Aug 24)*
Nuits St Georges 107 *(16f,Goo,GS,Jun 9)*
Numerian 115 *(8f,Cur,GY,Aug 30)*
Nyaleti 112 *(10f,Goo,G,Aug 1)*

Oasis Charm 108 *(10f,San,GF,Jly 5)*
Oasis Fantasy 110 *(11½f,Wdr,GF,Jun 29)*
Oasis Prince 110 *(10f,Nmk,GF,Jly 12)*
Obee Jo 105 *(6f,Not,S,May 11)*
Ocala 110 *(10f,Nby,S,Aug 17)*
Ocean Paradise 105 *(8½f,Not,HY,Jun 13)*
Ocean Reach 103 *(12f,Chp,G,Aug 22)*
Ocelot 105 *(6f,Hay,GF,May 25)*
Octave 104 *(7f,Nmk,GS,Jun 21)*
October Storm 106 *(16f,Goo,GS,Jun 9)*
Oeil De Tigre 103 *(6f,Wdr,G,Jun 24)*
Oh It's Saucepot 108 *(11½f,Yar,GF,Sep 19)*
Oh This Is Us 112 *(8½f,Eps,GF,Jun 1)*
Oi The Clubb Oi's 103 *(14f,Red,GF,Jly 21)*
Ojooba 108 *(10f,Not,HY,Aug 16)*
Old Glory 108 *(10f,Cur,GY,Jun 7)*
Old Persian 121 *(12f,Mey,G,Mar 30)*
Ollivander 104 *(7½f,Bev,GF,Jly 16)*
Olmedo 112 *(8f,Lon,VS,Oct 5)*
Olympic Honour 111 *(12f,Cur,G,Jun 27)*
Omotesando 104 *(16f,Chp,G,May 3)*
On A Session 107 *(8f,Cur,GY,Aug 30)*
On The Warpath 122 *(7f,Mey,G,Feb 28)*
One Cool Poet 112 *(12f,Gal,G,Aug 1)*
One Last Night 106 *(6f,Not,S,May 11)*
One Master 116 *(8f,Asc,G,Jun 18)*
One To Go 104 *(8½f,Bev,GF,Aug 25)*
Onebaba 103 *(8f,Wdr,GF,May 27)*
Oneiroi 104 *(6f,Cur,Y,Aug 23)*
Only Spoofing 113 *(5f,Asc,GF,Jly 26)*
Open Wide 112 *(5f,Ear,GF,Jly 13)*
Optimickstickhill 104 *(5f,Bev,GS,May 29)*
Optionality 103 *(5f,Cur,GF,May 26)*
Orange Blossom 103 *(6f,Eps,G,Aug 26)*
Orange Suit 109 *(10f,Bat,F,Sep 15)*
Orbaan 118 *(7f,Lon,GS,Apr 22)*
Oriental Lilly 105 *(7f,Red,GF,Sep 17)*
Oriental Splendour 105 *(5f,Bev,GS,May 29)*
Original Choice 111 *(10f,Mey,G,Feb 28)*
Orin Swift 106 *(16f,Goo,GS,Jun 9)*
Orion's Bow 106 *(5f,Ham,S,Jly 19)*
Ornate 114 *(5f,Bev,G,Jun 18)*
Orobas 105 *(8f,Ayr,GF,May 22)*
Orsino 104 *(16f,Thi,G,Aug 30)*
Orvar 111 *(5f,Cur,GY,Jun 27)*
Ostilio 107 *(8f,Nby,G,May 18)*
Oud Metha Bridge 103 *(8f,Yar,G,Apr 30)*
Our Little Pony 109 *(5f,Thi,S,Aug 16)*
Our Oystercatcher 109 *(5f,San,G,Sep 13)*
Our Place In Loule 104 *(5f,Mus,GF,Apr 2)*
Out On Friday 103 *(7f,Leo,G,Jly 18)*
Outbox 109 *(12f,Nmk,G,Aug 9)*
Outside Inside 110 *(8f,Ayr,GF,May 22)*
Ouzo 109 *(8f,Nmk,G,Jun 27)*
Overhaugh Street 108 *(12f,Chs,GF,Jun 29)*
Overtrumped 103 *(10f,Not,S,Jun 17)*
Oxted 111 *(6f,Don,GF,Sep 14)*
Oydis 107 *(14f,Sal,GF,Jly 27)*

Pablo Escobarr 110 *(11½f,Lin,S,May 11)*
Paddy Power 107 *(6f,Ham,G,Jly 2)*
Paddy The Chef 108 *(11½f,Yar,GF,Jly 30)*
Paddys Motorbike 108 *(14f,Goo,S,Jun 14)*
Pakistan Friend 109 *(8f,Sha,G,Jan 1)*
Pammi 110 *(15f,Ayr,G,Jun 21)*
Panatos 112 *(16f,Chp,GF,May 14)*
Paperback Writer 104 *(8f,Leo,GF,Jly 11)*
Paradise Boy 106 *(12f,Chs,GF,Jun 29)*
Park Row 108 *(10f,Leo,G,Jun 13)*
Parkers Hill 103 *(7f,Leo,G,Jly 18)*
Parsifal 111 *(12f,Mey,G,Jan 24)*
Party Playboy 112 *(18f,Nmk,S,Oct 12)*
Parys Mountain 107 *(7f,Hay,S,Sep 6)*
Pass The Gin 107 *(6f,Chs,G,Jly 13)*
Pass The Vino 109 *(6f,Nmk,GF,Jly 11)*
Passion And Glory 110 *(10f,Don,HY,Oct 25)*
Past Master 106 *(14f,Goo,G,Aug 24)*
Paths Of Glory 107 *(12f,Ffo,GF,Aug 1)*
Pattie 107 *(7f,Thi,G,Sep 7)*
Paved Paradise 110 *(6f,Cur,GF,May 26)*
Peace Prevails 108 *(12f,Eps,G,Aug 1)*
Peach Tree 107 *(12f,Cur,G,Jly 20)*
Pedro The First 110 *(7f,Lon,G,May 16)*
Peggie Sue 110 *(5f,Not,S,May 11)*
Pempie 110 *(10f,Sal,GF,May 25)*
Pendleton 110 *(6f,Crl,GF,Aug 29)*
Pendo 105 *(10f,Lin,S,May 11)*
Pennsylvania Dutch 108 *(6f,Goo,GS,Jun 9)*
Penwortham 104 *(7½f,Chs,G,Aug 31)*
Percy Prosecco 108 *(11½f,Yar,GF,Jly 30)*
Perfect Charm 103 *(5f,Ffo,GF,Aug 1)*
Perfect Grace 106 *(10f,Bat,F,Jly 10)*
Perfect Illusion 114 *(12f,Bri,GF,Jly 9)*
Perfect Match 122 *(7f,Sha,GF,Apr 22)*
Perfect Pair 120 *(7f,Sha,G,Mar 31)*
Perfect Swiss 103 *(6f,Red,G,Jly 31)*
Perfect Tapatino 107 *(12f,Cur,G,Jun 27)*
Perfect To Play 109 *(9f,Sha,G,Mar 31)*
Perfection 111 *(6f,Pon,G,Aug 18)*
Peri Lina 110 *(9f,Mey,G,Feb 14)*
Perla Blanca 103 *(13f,Ayr,GF,May 28)*
Persian Lion 109 *(12f,Cur,G,Jun 27)*
Persian Moon 115 *(11f,Goo,GF,May 24)*
Persian Sun 106 *(11½f,Wdr,G,Apr 29)*
Peshkova 109 *(6f,Cur,GF,May 26)*
Pete So High 104 *(10f,Ayr,GF,Jly 7)*
Petrastar 106 *(10f,Wdr,G,May 13)*
Petrus 111 *(8f,Bat,GF,Apr 19)*
Pettifogger 106 *(7f,Lin,G,May 3)*
Pettochside 104 *(5f,Goo,HY,Sep 25)*
Philipine Cobra 105 *(6f,Yor,S,Jun 14)*
Philonikia 107 *(12f,Don,G,Jly 20)*
Phoenix Of Spain 118 *(8f,Cur,GF,May 25)*
Phoenix Open 111 *(8f,Leo,GF,Jly 11)*
Piano Solo 104 *(7f,Cur,GY,May 6)*
Picken 119 *(7f,Sha,G,Jan 1)*
Pickett's Charge 104 *(7f,Bri,GF,Aug 8)*
Piedita 103 *(16f,Cat,GS,Aug 6)*
Pilaster 115 *(14f,Yor,GF,May 25)*
Pillmakers Hill 105 *(8f,Leo,G,Jun 6)*
Pincheck 117 *(8f,Leo,G,Sep 14)*
Pingwu Spark 115 *(7f,Sha,G,Jan 1)*
Pink Dogwood 115 *(10f,Cur,G,Jun 28)*
Pink Flamingo 107 *(5f,Asc,GF,Jly 26)*
Pinnata 103 *(8f,Nmk,GS,Aug 16)*
Pioneering 103 *(10f,Yor,S,Jun 14)*
Pipers Note 107 *(5f,Pon,GF,Apr 15)*
Pipes Of Peace 110 *(14f,Mus,G,Apr 20)*
Pirate King 104 *(12f,Yor,GF,Jun 29)*
Pivoine 108 *(12f,Nby,G,May 18)*
Placebo Effect 104 *(10f,Red,G,Jly 31)*
Platform Nineteen 107 *(16f,Yor,G,Sep 8)*
Platinum Warrior 110 *(16f,Mey,G,Mar 30)*
Platitude 111 *(16f,Asc,S,Oct 4)*
Play It By Ear 103 *(14f,Red,GF,May 28)*
Plough Boy 105 *(6f,Leo,GF,Aug 8)*
Plunger 107 *(8½f,Eps,G,Aug 26)*
Plutonian 105 *(10f,Goo,G,Jly 30)*
Pocket Dynamo 106 *(5f,Hay,GF,May 25)*
Poet's Dawn 109 *(10f,Yor,G,Sep 8)*
Poet's Prince 110 *(9f,Goo,GF,Aug 3)*
Poet's Society 117 *(7f,Mey,G,Feb 7)*
Poetic Charm 121 *(8f,Mey,G,Jan 17)*
Poetic Force 104 *(6f,Eps,G,Jly 4)*
Poetry 108 *(5f,Yor,GF,Jly 13)*
Pogo 111 *(8f,Nmk,G,May 4)*
Point In Time 104 *(13f,Nby,GS,Jly 19)*
Point Of Honour 104 *(14f,Red,G,Jun 22)*
Point Taken 103 *(12f,Hay,GF,Aug 8)*
Polly Douglas 112 *(6f,Cur,GF,May 26)*
Polydream 112 *(6½f,Dea,G,Aug 4)*
Polyphony 105 *(8½f,Not,G,Jly 16)*
Pondus 119 *(10½f,Hay,HY,Aug 10)*
Popping Corks 103 *(5f,Ham,HY,Aug 30)*
Port Lions 109 *(8f,Cur,G,Jun 29)*
Portamento 111 *(7f,Mey,G,Jan 24)*
Porth Swtan 110 *(7f,Mus,GF,Apr 2)*
Porto Ferro 105 *(5f,San,G,Sep 18)*
Post Var 112 *(7f,Lon,VS,Oct 6)*
Posted 112 *(7f,Don,GF,Sep 13)*
Potenza 108 *(8f,Lei,G,Jun 27)*
Poucor 103 *(11½f,Yar,HY,Oct 14)*
Pour Me A Drink 108 *(10f,Nby,S,Aug 17)*
Pouvoir Magique 115 *(8f,Mey,G,Mar 2)*
Power Of Darkness 107 *(8f,Nmk,GF,Apr 18)*
Power Of States 103 *(12f,Thi,GS,Aug 3)*
Power Player 103 *(8f,Hay,GS,Jly 20)*
Powerallied 113 *(5½f,Chs,G,Jly 12)*
Powerful Dream 104 *(5f,Bat,G,Jun 26)*
Powersville 105 *(6f,Cur,GF,May 26)*
Poyle Vinnie 106 *(6f,Goo,GF,Aug 3)*
Pradaro 110 *(7f,Lon,GS,Apr 22)*
Praxidice 104 *(6f,Crl,HY,May 31)*
Precioussship 115 *(7f,Sha,G,Mar 31)*
Preening 113 *(7f,Don,GF,Sep 13)*
Prefontaine 104 *(12f,Chs,S,Jun 15)*
Prejudice 104 *(10f,Nmk,G,Jun 28)*
Presidential 111 *(7f,Hay,S,Sep 6)*
Prestbury Park 110 *(5f,Pon,GS,Sep 26)*
Pretreville 111 *(7f,Lon,G,May 16)*
Pretty Baby 105 *(7f,Goo,G,Aug 2)*
Pretty Boy 106 *(6f,Dea,G,Aug 4)*
Pretty Pollyanna 120 *(8f,Cur,GF,May 26)*
Prevent 105 *(8f,Lei,GF,May 27)*
Price Range 109 *(8f,Lon,GS,Jly 14)*
Primo Uomo 106 *(6f,Cur,G,Sep 15)*

Primo's Comet 104 *(5f,Mus,GS,Jun 1)*
Prince Elzaam 105 *(7f,Mey,G,Jan 10)*
Prince Of Arran 116 *(16f,Fle,GS,Nov 5)*
Prince Of Harts 112 *(8f,Asc,GS,Jly 27)*
Prince Of Time 104 *(6f,Crl,GF,Jly 11)*
Princely 107 *(6f,Bat,GS,Aug 17)*
Princes Des Sables 109 *(6f,Hay,GF,Aug 8)*
Princess Palliser 103 *(6f,Thi,S,Aug 9)*
Princess Power 106 *(6f,Nmk,GF,Jly 11)*
Princess Way 104 *(10f,Bat,GF,Aug 7)*
Prisoner's Dilemma 103 *(8f,Cur,GY,Jun 27)*
Private Secretary 118 *(11f,Goo,GF,May 24)*
Production 104 *(8f,Don,G,May 4)*
Project Bluebook 108 *(17½f,Ayr,G,Sep 20)*
Projection 104 *(6f,Asc,GF,Jun 22)*
Promissory 106 *(14f,Goo,G,Aug 24)*
Promote 103 *(6f,Yar,GF,Aug 8)*
Proposed 106 *(12f,Mey,G,Jan 19)*
Proschema 109 *(16½f,Nby,GS,Jly 20)*
Prosecution 103 *(12f,Cur,Y,Sep 28)*
Proton 105 *(12f,Lei,HY,Oct 8)*
Proud Archi 108 *(6f,Crl,GF,May 20)*
Psychedelic Funk 109 *(7f,Leo,SH,Oct 26)*
Ptarmigan Ridge 110 *(7f,Hay,S,Apr 27)*
Pudding Chare 108 *(7f,Ayr,GF,Jly 7)*
Puds 111 *(6f,Goo,GF,May 24)*
Pulse Of Shanghai 109 *(6f,Cur,Y,Aug 23)*
Pure Shores 104 *(8f,Nmk,GF,Jun 29)*
Pythion 111 *(10f,Leo,GY,May 12)*
Pytilia 104 *(8f,Wdr,GF,Jun 30)*

Qaaraat 104 *(5f,Bev,GS,May 14)*
Qabala 111 *(8f,Cur,GF,May 26)*
Qarasu 110 *(10f,Goo,HY,Sep 25)*
Qaroun 108 *(7f,Goo,G,May 4)*
Qawamees 109 *(17½f,Ayr,G,Sep 20)*
Qaysar 110 *(7f,Asc,GS,May 11)*
Quanah 104 *(5f,Mus,S,Oct 15)*
Quantatmental 106 *(12f,Cur,G,Jun 27)*
Quarry Beach 105 *(7f,Nby,GF,Sep 21)*
Que Amoro 109 *(5½f,Yor,G,Jly 26)*
Queen 108 *(10f,Nmk,GS,Oct 11)*
Queen Amidala 106 *(8½f,Gal,G,Aug 3)*
Queen Jo Jo 112 *(6f,Not,S,May 11)*
Queen Of Burgundy 105 *(7f,Yar,GF,Aug 20)*
Queen Of Desire 106 *(6f,Yor,GF,Jly 12)*
Queen Of Time 103 *(10f,Not,G,Jun 2)*
Queen Penn 104 *(7f,Don,GF,Mar 31)*
Queen Power 109 *(10f,Wdr,GF,Aug 24)*
Queen's Sargent 104 *(7f,Don,GF,Mar 31)*
Queen's Soldier 103 *(12f,Eps,G,Jly 4)*
Queens Gift 109 *(5f,Bev,G,Aug 31)*
Quench Dolly 110 *(5f,Not,S,Oct 30)*
Quest The Moon 113 *(12f,Lon,G,Sep 15)*
Question Of Faith 111 *(15f,Ayr,G,Jun 21)*
Questionare 111 *(12f,Lei,GF,May 27)*
Quick 104 *(10f,Bri,GF,Sep 1)*
Quick Breath 104 *(7f,Nmk,GF,Aug 2)*
Quick Look 105 *(6f,Rip,GS,Jun 5)*
Quicksand 108 *(12f,Goo,G,Aug 25)*
Quizical 111 *(8f,Cur,GY,Aug 30)*
Quloob 110 *(16f,Asc,S,Oct 4)*
Quote 112 *(12f,Cur,GF,Jly 21)*
Qutob 103 *(7f,Nmk,G,Jly 20)*

Raa Atoll 110 *(14f,Cur,G,Jun 28)*
Raafid 104 *(6f,Mey,G,Mar 2)*
Raakib Alhawa 111 *(11½f,Wdr,GF,Aug 24)*
Race Day 118 *(8f,Mey,G,Jan 17)*
Racing History 115 *(9f,Mey,G,Jan 24)*
Raffaello 103 *(8f,Leo,GY,Jun 20)*
Rafiot 105 *(11f,Lon,GS,Apr 22)*
Ragnar 103 *(10f,San,S,Jun 14)*
Ragstone Cowboy 103 *(10f,Not,S,Aug 6)*
Raheen House 113 *(14f,Yor,GS,Jun 15)*
Railport Dolly 106 *(10f,Pon,G,Jly 28)*
Raincall 103 *(6f,Sal,GF,May 25)*
Raise You 118 *(10½f,Hay,HY,Aug 10)*
Raising Sand 114 *(7f,Asc,GS,May 11)*
Rakan 114 *(10f,Leo,GY,May 12)*
Rake's Progress 107 *(11f,Crl,GF,Jun 26)*
Ramatuelle 103 *(10f,Bri,GF,Sep 16)*
Rambaldi 103 *(8f,Nby,GF,Jly 4)*
Ramesses 106 *(7f,Lei,GF,Apr 27)*
Ramiro 104 *(6f,Cur,Y,Aug 23)*
Rampant Lion 105 *(8f,Bat,GF,Apr 19)*
Ranch Hand 106 *(11½f,Lin,S,May 11)*
Rangali Island 108 *(8f,Don,G,May 4)*
Raphael 112 *(8f,Leo,GF,Jly 11)*
Rapid Applause 103 *(6f,Ayr,G,Sep 21)*
Rapid Reaction 112 *(5f,Cur,GY,Jun 27)*
Rare Groove 114 *(13f,Ham,GF,May 5)*
Raselasad 110 *(7f,Mus,GF,Jly 3)*
Rasheeq 104 *(6f,Not,S,May 10)*
Rathbone 104 *(6f,Pon,GF,Apr 9)*
Rattan 117 *(7f,Sha,G,Jan 1)*
Rattling Jewel 104 *(6f,Cur,G,Jly 21)*
Raucous 112 *(6f,Yar,GF,Jly 10)*
Raven's Raft 104 *(12f,Chs,G,Jun 29)*
Rawdaa 116 *(10f,Goo,G,Aug 1)*
Raydiance 110 *(7f,Red,G,Jun 22)*
Raymond Tusk 116 *(16f,Asc,GF,May 1)*
Rayna's World 106 *(16f,Cat,HY,Oct 29)*
Rayounpour 109 *(12f,Cur,GF,Jly 21)*
Real Smooth 105 *(6f,Sal,GF,May 25)*
Reassurance 105 *(14f,Red,GF,Sep 17)*
Rebel Streak 105 *(5f,Mey,G,Jan 24)*
Reckless Endeavour 104 *(7f,Mus,GF,Apr 2)*
Recon Mission 109 *(6f,Yor,GS,Jun 15)*
Rectory Road 110 *(8f,Asc,GS,Jly 27)*
Red Alert 104 *(6f,Bat,G,Jun 26)*
Red Archangel 104 *(10f,Lin,GF,Jly 17)*
Red Armada 108 *(7f,Nby,G,May 17)*
Red Balloons 110 *(6f,Yor,GF,Jly 12)*
Red Force One 109 *(10½f,Hay,GF,May 25)*
Red Galileo 124 *(12f,Mey,G,Feb 14)*
Red Gerry 104 *(10f,Leo,G,Aug 15)*
Red Gunner 107 *(10f,Bat,F,Sep 4)*
Red Hot 103 *(10f,Not,HY,Aug 16)*
Red Impression 104 *(6f,Nby,G,May 18)*
Red Mist 103 *(9f,Rip,G,May 19)*
Red October 105 *(10f,Red,G,Apr 8)*
Red Pike 106 *(5f,Not,S,Oct 30)*
Red Sole Diva 106 *(8f,Leo,G,Jly 25)*
Red Starlight 111 *(8f,Don,G,Mar 30)*
Red Striker 109 *(12f,Cur,G,Jun 27)*
Red Stripes 110 *(5½f,Chs,G,Jly 12)*
Red Tea 113 *(8f,Cur,GF,May 25)*
Red Torch 105 *(7f,Lon,G,Sep 15)*
Red Verdon 113 *(14f,Yor,GF,Jly 13)*
Redarna 108 *(7f,Ayr,G,Sep 21)*
Redgrave 104 *(10½f,Chs,G,Jly 13)*
Redrosezorro 108 *(5½f,Chs,G,Jly 12)*
Reeves 108 *(7f,Nby,S,Apr 12)*
Regal Mirage 108 *(10f,Pon,G,Jly 28)*
Regal Reality 115 *(10f,San,GF,May 23)*
Regency Bo Bo 119 *(7f,Sha,G,Mar 31)*
Regency Gem 110 *(7f,Sha,G,Jan 1)*
Reggae Runner 112 *(8f,Hay,GF,May 25)*
Regimented 106 *(8f,Nmk,G,Jun 27)*
Regular Income 107 *(10f,Eps,G,May 31)*
Rehoboth Beach 105 *(10f,Leo,G,Aug 15)*
Reloaded 103 *(7f,Lin,GF,Sep 14)*
Remarkable 106 *(8f,Don,G,Mar 30)*
Remember Rocky 103 *(12f,Cat,GF,Sep 10)*
Remember The Days 105 *(14f,Mus,GF,Sep 6)*
Renardeau 105 *(10f,Ffo,GF,Jly 29)*
Reputation 113 *(6f,Rip,G,Apr 27)*
Reshoun 109 *(16½f,Nby,GS,Jly 20)*
Restive 105 *(8f,Ham,GF,May 17)*
Restless Rose 103 *(6f,Nmk,G,Sep 26)*
Restorer 104 *(12f,Asc,G,Aug 10)*
Reticent Angel 104 *(5f,San,S,Jun 15)*
Retirement Beckons 103 *(8f,Ham,G,Jly 18)*
Revich 112 *(6f,Asc,S,Oct 4)*
Rewaayat 108 *(5f,San,G,Sep 13)*
Rey De Oro 112 *(12f,Mey,G,Mar 30)*
Reynolds 108 *(7f,Nby,G,May 17)*
Rhythmic Intent 110 *(10f,Nby,GF,Jly 25)*
Rich Cummins 105 *(14f,Red,GF,May 28)*
Richenza 110 *(6f,Sal,S,Jun 16)*
Richmond Avenue 105 *(8f,Nmk,G,Sep 27)*
Rickyroadboy 103 *(5f,Not,S,May 11)*
Ricochet 103 *(5f,Lei,GF,Jly 24)*
Riflescope 105 *(6f,Mey,G,Feb 21)*
Right Action 106 *(7f,Don,GF,Mar 31)*
Rio Tigre 117 *(12f,Mey,G,Feb 14)*
Riogha 108 *(6f,Cur,Y,Aug 23)*
Rionach 107 *(7f,Cur,GY,May 6)*
Ripp Orf 112 *(7f,Asc,GS,May 11)*
Rips Dream 114 *(10f,Leo,GY,Jun 20)*
Rise Hall 114 *(10f,Nmk,G,Jly 27)*
Rita Levi 110 *(7f,Gal,G,Jly 30)*
Ritchie Valens 110 *(10f,Nby,G,May 18)*
Riven Light 108 *(10f,Asc,S,Jun 18)*
River Icon 104 *(14½f,Don,HY,Oct 25)*
Riviera Nights 109 *(7f,Asc,GF,Sep 6)*
Roar 105 *(11f,Crl,S,May 30)*
Roaring Forties 106 *(7f,Mus,G,May 3)*
Robeam 107 *(14f,Cat,GF,Jly 1)*
Robert Fitzroy 103 *(12f,Don,GF,May 31)*
Robin Of Navan 108 *(8f,Asc,GF,May 1)*
Roc Angel 111 *(8f,Asc,S,Jun 19)*
Rochester House 107 *(14f,Not,HY,Aug 16)*
Rock De Baune 103 *(16f,Cur,S,Oct 13)*
Rock Eagle 107 *(12f,Goo,GF,May 25)*
Rock On Baileys 107 *(6f,Nmk,GF,Aug 24)*
Rock The Cradle 107 *(10f,Yar,GF,Jly 17)*
Rockabill 111 *(12f,Cur,G,Jun 27)*
Rockage 108 *(7f,Sha,G,Apr 22)*
Rocket Power 118 *(7f,Mey,G,Jan 19)*
Rocques 107 *(7f,Goo,G,Aug 2)*
Roibeard 109 *(10f,Leo,G,Jun 13)*
Rolladice 103 *(7f,Cat,S,Oct 19)*
Roller 108 *(7½f,Chs,G,Jun 28)*
Roman Candle 118 *(12f,Lon,GS,Jly 14)*
Roman River 103 *(5f,Nmk,GF,Apr 18)*
Roman Stone 105 *(9f,Crl,HY,Aug 13)*
Romanised 116 *(7f,Cur,G,Jly 20)*
Romantic Touch 112 *(7f,Sha,G,Jan 1)*
Romantically 104 *(12f,Cur,GF,Jly 21)*
Romola 111 *(8½f,Not,HY,Aug 16)*
Rose Berry 104 *(6f,Chs,G,Jly 13)*
Rose Hip 107 *(5f,Bat,F,Aug 2)*
Roseman 110 *(8f,San,GF,May 23)*
Rosemay 103 *(8f,Ham,G,Jly 13)*
Rosie Royale 108 *(14f,Bat,F,Sep 15)*
Rotherwick 113 *(9f,Goo,GF,Aug 3)*
Roulston Scar 111 *(6f,Yor,G,Sep 8)*
Round The Island 104 *(6f,Pon,GF,Sep 19)*
Roundhay Park 109 *(6f,Thi,G,Aug 30)*
Rousayan 106 *(8½f,Bev,GS,May 14)*
Rovetta 103 *(12f,Cur,GY,Aug 23)*
Rowland Ward 107 *(12f,Thi,G,Sep 7)*
Royal Admiral 103 *(10f,Leo,G,Aug 15)*
Royal Birth 107 *(5f,Asc,GF,Sep 7)*
Royal Brave 103 *(6f,Rip,GS,Jun 5)*
Royal Canford 111 *(6f,Cur,S,Sep 28)*
Royal Cosmic 105 *(12f,Thi,GS,Jun 18)*
Royal Court 103 *(7f,Leo,Y,Apr 3)*
Royal Flag 103 *(12f,Bev,G,Jly 30)*
Royal Illusion 109 *(16f,Cur,S,Oct 13)*
Royal Intervention 116 *(6f,Yor,GF,Jly 12)*
Royal Line 110 *(10f,San,GF,Jly 5)*
Royal Marine 110 *(8f,Nmk,GF,Apr 17)*
Royal Prerogative 106 *(7f,Sha,G,Apr 22)*
Royal Prospect 108 *(6f,Red,GF,Jly 21)*
Royal Regent 104 *(10f,Ayr,HY,Aug 10)*
Royal Residence 105 *(6f,Don,G,May 4)*
Royal Welcome 103 *(7f,Red,GF,May 20)*
Roys Dream 103 *(6f,Bat,F,May 15)*
Rua Augusta 109 *(12f,Mey,G,Jan 19)*
Rufus King 109 *(8f,Hay,GF,Jly 5)*
Rum Baba 110 *(8f,Wdr,GF,Jly 1)*
Rum Runner 107 *(7f,Nmk,GF,Aug 2)*
Rumble Inthejungle 105 *(5f,San,GF,Jly 6)*
Ruminare 111 *(7f,Sha,G,Apr 22)*
Running Cloud 107 *(11½f,Wdr,G,Apr 29)*
Rux Ruxx 108 *(7f,Cat,GF,Jly 1)*
Rydan 105 *(14f,Goo,G,May 4)*

Saaheq 110 *(5f,Mus,G,Apr 20)*
Sabrina Fairchild 111 *(6f,Cur,G,Jly 21)*
Sacchoandvanzetti 104 *(5f,Cur,YS,Aug 9)*
Sadlers Beach 104 *(10f,Bat,F,Jly 3)*
Safe Voyage 114 *(7f,Cur,G,Jly 20)*
Saffran 106 *(10f,Chp,G,Jun 24)*
Saikung 108 *(8½f,Not,S,Aug 6)*
Saisons D'Or 105 *(8f,Rip,G,Jly 20)*
Salam Zayed 107 *(7½f,Chs,G,Jly 12)*
Salateen 107 *(7f,Hay,GS,Jly 19)*
Salayel 112 *(7f,Yor,G,Aug 22)*
Salouen 115 *(12f,Asc,GS,Jly 27)*
Salt Lake City 113 *(7f,Lon,VS,Oct 6)*
Salto Olimpico 109 *(7f,Sha,G,Jan 1)*
Saltonstall 111 *(8f,Cur,GY,Aug 30)*
Salute The Soldier 110 *(8f,Bat,GF,Apr 19)*
Saluti 107 *(6f,Red,GF,Apr 22)*
Sam Missile 104 *(8f,Leo,GY,Apr 3)*
Sam's Love 117 *(7f,Sha,G,Apr 22)*
Sambucca Spirit 105 *(5f,Cat,GS,Aug 6)*
Sameem 110 *(10f,Rip,GF,Jly 8)*
San Huberto 107 *(15f,Lon,VS,Oct 5)*
San Sebastian 105 *(10f,Yar,GF,Jly 30)*
Sanaadh 108 *(7f,Nmk,GF,Jly 13)*
Sand Share 106 *(10f,Sal,S,Aug 14)*
Sandra's Secret 103 *(5f,Pon,GF,Apr 15)*
Sandret 113 *(10f,Don,GF,Sep 13)*
Sands Chorus 103 *(10½f,Chs,G,May 25)*
Sandyman 108 *(10f,Lin,G,Aug 4)*
Sandyssime 104 *(7f,Lon,VS,Oct 6)*
Sangarius 109 *(8f,San,GF,May 23)*
Sapa Inca 111 *(12f,Nby,S,Jun 13)*
Sarasota Bay 103 *(6f,Crl,HY,May 31)*
Saroog 105 *(14½f,Don,GF,Sep 13)*
Sarvi 105 *(8f,Ham,S,Sep 22)*
Saryshagann 103 *(10½f,Hay,S,Apr 27)*
Sash 108 *(8f,Asc,GS,Jly 27)*
Sassie 110 *(17½f,Ayr,G,Sep 20)*
Sassoon 106 *(8f,Wdr,GF,May 27)*
Savalas 106 *(6f,Yor,GF,May 15)*
Savoir Aimer 105 *(11f,Lon,GS,Apr 22)*
Sawwaah 108 *(8f,Asc,S,Oct 4)*
Scaramanga 109 *(14f,Sal,GF,Apr 28)*
Scarlet Dragon 106 *(14f,Goo,GF,Aug 3)*
Scentasia 106 *(8f,Yar,GF,Sep 18)*
Scofflaw 108 *(10½f,Chs,G,Sep 14)*
Scorching Heat 107 *(6f,Cur,GY,Aug 30)*
Scottish Summit 104 *(10½f,Hay,GF,May 25)*
Screaming Gemini 103 *(8f,Bat,F,May 24)*
Sea Of Faith 114 *(12f,Sal,GS,Aug 15)*
Sea Of Mystery 106 *(10f,Lei,GF,Sep 10)*
Sea Tea Dea 105 *(8f,Ffo,G,Aug 29)*
Sea The Lion 112 *(12f,Cur,G,Jun 27)*
Sea's Aria 103 *(14f,Lin,GF,May 23)*
Seaborn 110 *(11f,Goo,GF,Sep 3)*
Seaborough 104 *(10f,Red,G,Apr 8)*
Seamster 103 *(5f,Cat,S,Aug 12)*
Search For A Song 115 *(14f,Cur,GF,Sep 15)*
Second Collection 104 *(6f,Wdr,G,May 13)*
Secret Potion 103 *(5f,Lei,GS,Aug 11)*
Secret Return 103 *(8f,Bat,GS,Aug 17)*
Secretarial 103 *(8f,Thi,GS,May 11)*
Secretfact 104 *(5f,San,S,Jun 15)*
Secretinthepark 108 *(5f,Bev,GF,Apr 25)*
Seductive Moment 105 *(8f,Wdr,GF,Jly 22)*
See Of Rome 107 *(12f,Gal,G,Aug 2)*
Seen The Lyte 109 *(5½f,Chs,G,Aug 31)*
Seinesational 110 *(17½f,Ayr,G,Sep 20)*
Self Assessment 104 *(7f,Cat,GF,Sep 10)*
Selino 107 *(14f,Red,GF,Aug 24)*
Sempre Presto 104 *(12f,Yor,S,Jun 14)*
Sendeed 103 *(10f,Not,HY,Oct 2)*
Sendmylovetoyou 111 *(6f,Cur,Y,Aug 23)*
Seniority 110 *(8f,Goo,GF,Aug 2)*
Sergei Prokofiev 107 *(5f,San,GF,Jly 6)*
Servalan 107 *(6f,Cur,S,Aug 9)*
Sestilio Jet 105 *(5f,Lon,G,Sep 15)*
Set In Stone 107 *(8f,Ham,GS,Jly 19)*
Set Piece 110 *(8f,Nmk,GF,Apr 17)*
Set Point Charlie 104 *(8f,Ffo,G,Aug 29)*
Setting Sail 109 *(10f,Goo,G,Jly 30)*
Settle For Bay 112 *(8f,Mey,G,Jan 17)*
Sevenna Star 103 *(16f,Nmk,G,Sep 26)*
Seventii 107 *(14f,Lin,GF,Sep 14)*
Severance 109 *(12f,Goo,G,Jly 31)*
Severnaya 109 *(8f,Nmk,S,Nov 1)*
Sextant 111 *(12f,Chs,G,Sep 14)*
Sh Boom 103 *(8f,Nmk,G,Sep 27)*
Sha La La La Lee 109 *(7½f,Chs,S,May 10)*
Shades Of Blue 115 *(6f,Yor,GF,Jly 12)*
Shadow Seven 103 *(12f,Cur,G,Jun 27)*
Shady McCoy 105 *(7f,Red,G,Jun 22)*
Shagalla 105 *(11½f,Wdr,G,May 13)*
Shailene 106 *(14f,Goo,GF,Aug 3)*
Shajjy 108 *(7f,Mey,G,Jan 19)*
Shallow Hal 105 *(7f,Nby,S,Apr 12)*
Shamad 110 *(12f,Gal,G,Aug 1)*
Shaman 111 *(8f,Lon,VS,Oct 5)*
Shambolic 108 *(12f,Nmk,GF,Aug 3)*
Shamshon 107 *(5f,Lei,GF,Sep 23)*
Shanghai Dragon 115 *(7f,Sha,G,Mar 31)*
Shanghai Grace 103 *(7f,Ayr,G,Jun 22)*
Shanty Star 113 *(8f,Mey,G,Feb 28)*
Shaqwar 105 *(7f,Red,G,Jly 31)*
Shareef Star 103 *(10f,Don,G,Mar 31)*
Shargiah 104 *(10f,Yor,GF,Jly 12)*
Sharja Bridge 113 *(8f,Don,G,Mar 30)*
Sharpalo 123 *(12f,Mey,G,Feb 14)*
Shawaaheq 103 *(7f,Asc,GF,Sep 6)*
Shawaamekh 112 *(7f,Leo,G,Sep 14)*
She Believes 111 *(10f,Lin,GF,May 3)*
She Can Boogie 108 *(5f,Chs,S,Jun 15)*
She's A Novelty 112 *(12f,Cur,G,Jun 27)*
She's Got You 108 *(8f,Nmk,G,Jun 22)*
Sheberghan 107 *(10f,Pon,GF,Sep 19)*
Sheisdiesel 106 *(10f,Cur,GF,May 25)*
Shekiba 109 *(8f,Cur,GF,May 25)*
Shelir 107 *(7f,Cur,GY,May 6)*
Shenanigans 116 *(10f,Ayr,GF,May 22)*
Shendam 114 *(8f,Lon,GS,Jly 14)*
Shepherd Market 104 *(7f,Asc,S,Oct 5)*
Shepherd's Purse 106 *(5f,Pon,S,Jun 10)*
Sherkali 106 *(8f,Leo,G,Jun 13)*
Shifting Gold 103 *(10f,Lin,GF,Aug 3)*
Shine So Bright 115 *(7f,Yor,GF,Aug 24)*
Shining Armor 105 *(7f,Mey,G,Jan 10)*
Shining Gem 112 *(7f,Sha,GF,Apr 22)*
Ship Of The Fen 108 *(16f,Nmk,GF,Aug 10)*
Shore Step 107 *(6f,Cur,G,Jly 21)*
Shortbackandsides 104 *(6f,Hay,HY,Jun 7)*
Shorter Skirt 104 *(6f,Nby,GF,Jly 4)*
Show Palace 109 *(5f,Not,S,Oct 30)*
Show Stealer 109 *(6f,Don,GF,Sep 14)*
Showboating 103 *(8f,Wet,GS,May 7)*
Showroom 103 *(12f,Lei,G,Apr 5)*
Shrewdness 111 *(10f,Lin,G,May 3)*
Shringara 104 *(10f,Leo,GY,May 12)*
Shufoog 107 *(12f,Nby,GF,Jly 25)*
Sicario 104 *(10f,Leo,G,Jun 13)*
Siglo Six 104 *(8f,San,GF,Aug 31)*
Signora Cabello 103 *(5f,Asc,G,Jun 18)*
Sigrid Nansen 106 *(12f,Eps,G,Aug 1)*
Silent Attack 114 *(8f,Mey,G,Jan 10)*
Silk Air 105 *(8f,Cur,G,Jly 20)*
Silk Forest 105 *(7f,Leo,Y,Apr 3)*
Silkstone 105 *(8f,Don,S,Jun 8)*
Silver Line 104 *(8f,San,G,Sep 18)*
Silver Quartz 105 *(8f,Don,G,Mar 30)*
Silver Service 107 *(6f,Cur,SH,Oct 13)*
Silverkode 108 *(7f,Leo,G,Sep 14)*
Silverwave 113 *(12f,Lon,G,Sep 15)*
Simbirsk 107 *(10f,Bat,F,May 6)*
Simoon 107 *(10f,Wdr,G,May 13)*
Simply Beautiful 110 *(12f,Nmk,G,Sep 27)*
Sincerity 109 *(10f,Ffo,GS,Aug 13)*
Singing Sheriff 103 *(10f,San,GF,May 23)*
Singing The Blues 109 *(14f,Bat,F,Sep 15)*
Singstreet 104 *(8f,Lon,GS,Apr 22)*
Sinjaari 114 *(10f,Nby,G,May 18)*
Sinndarella 104 *(12f,Chp,G,Aug 26)*
Sioux Frontier 105 *(11f,Crl,GS,Jun 17)*
Sir Busker 107 *(7½f,Chs,G,Aug 31)*
Sir Canford 107 *(10f,Lin,GF,Jun 1)*
Sir Chauvelin 108 *(14f,Mus,G,Apr 20)*
Sir Dancealot 114 *(7f,Don,GF,Sep 14)*
Sir Dragonet 118 *(14½f,Don,GF,Sep 14)*
Sir Jamie 107 *(8f,Yar,GF,May 22)*
Sir Maximilian 109 *(6f,Don,G,May 4)*
Sir Psycho 108 *(10f,Leo,GY,Apr 3)*
Sir Roderic 104 *(7f,Chp,G,Sep 2)*
Sir Ron Priestley 118 *(14½f,Don,GF,Sep 14)*
Sir Thomas Gresham 108 *(6f,Nmk,GF,Apr 17)*
Sir Titan 104 *(7f,Nmk,GF,Sep 21)*
Sirjack Thomas 111 *(8f,Cur,GY,Aug 30)*
Siyahamba 106 *(16f,Mus,GF,Jly 3)*
Siyarafina 105 *(8f,Lon,GS,Apr 22)*

Skalleti 117 *(10f,Lon,VS,Oct 5)*
Skardu 114 *(8f,Cur,GF,May 25)*
Skill Set 105 *(10f,Ayr,GF,May 22)*
Sky Defender 103 *(10f,Bat,F,May 6)*
Sky Seven 108 *(8f,Leo,G,Jun 13)*
Skygazer 109 *(12f,Mey,G,Jan 19)*
Skyman 109 *(10f,Not,HY,Oct 16)*
Skymax 110 *(14½f,Don,GF,Jun 1)*
Slalom 119 *(12f,Lon,GS,Jly 14)*
Sleep Education 118 *(7f,Sha,G,Mar 31)*
Sleeping Lion 109 *(14½f,Don,GF,Sep 13)*
Sloane Garden 106 *(8f,Thi,GF,Sep 16)*
Smart Champion 106 *(18f,Nmk,GF,Sep 21)*
Smart Patch 112 *(7f,Sha,G,Mar 31)*
Smarter 105 *(14f,Not,HY,Oct 2)*
Smash Williams 110 *(5f,Cur,GY,Jun 27)*
Smile A Mile 108 *(8f,Thi,G,Sep 7)*
Smiling Pride 111 *(8f,Sha,G,Jan 1)*
Smokey Lane 107 *(5f,Lei,HY,Oct 8)*
Smugglers Creek 106 *(7f,Mus,G,Aug 2)*
Snapraeceps 107 *(9f,Cur,G,Aug 30)*
Snazzy Jazzy 111 *(6f,Sal,S,Jun 16)*
Sneaky Getaway 106 *(18f,Nmk,S,Oct 12)*
Sneaky Peek 108 *(12f,Goo,G,Jun 21)*
So Beloved 110 *(8f,Asc,S,Jun 19)*
So Near So Farhh 111 *(16f,Chp,GS,Aug 15)*
So Perfect 113 *(5f,Cur,G,Sep 15)*
Socialites Red 103 *(5f,Pon,GF,Apr 15)*
Society Guest 104 *(7f,Nby,GF,Sep 21)*
Society Queen 103 *(5f,Chs,GS,May 8)*
Society Red 110 *(10f,Nmk,G,Jly 27)*
Sociologist 103 *(10f,Not,S,Oct 9)*
Sod's Law 106 *(8f,Lei,GF,May 27)*
Soffia 120 *(5f,Cur,G,Jly 21)*
Soft Light 117 *(12f,Lon,GS,Jly 14)*
Solage 108 *(9f,Cur,G,Aug 30)*
Solar Gold 111 *(7f,Nmk,GF,Jly 13)*
Solar Wave 107 *(8f,Cur,S,Aug 9)*
Soldier's Call 112 *(5f,Asc,G,Jun 18)*
Soldier's Minute 112 *(6f,Yor,GF,May 15)*
Solid Stone 112 *(8f,San,G,Jly 31)*
Soloist 105 *(11f,Crl,GS,Jun 17)*
Somewhat Sisyphean 104 *(12f,Thi,S,Aug 9)*
Somewhere Secret 105 *(6f,Hay,HY,Jun 7)*
Sonaiyla 108 *(6f,Cur,GF,May 24)*
Song Of The Isles 104 *(7f,Sal,G,Aug 23)*
Sonja Henie 106 *(6f,Eps,G,Aug 26)*
Sootability 106 *(10f,Eps,G,Sep 12)*
Sophosc 110 *(10f,Nby,GF,Jly 25)*
Soto Sizzler 110 *(12f,Eps,G,Apr 24)*
Sottsass 122 *(12f,Lon,VS,Oct 6)*
Sound 115 *(16f,Fle,GS,Nov 5)*
South Pacific 111 *(16f,Goo,G,Jly 30)*
South Sea Pearl 113 *(14½f,Don,GF,Sep 12)*
Southern France 113 *(16f,Fle,GS,Nov 5)*
Southern Horse 112 *(6f,Cur,G,Jun 29)*
Southern Legend 106 *(9f,Mey,G,Mar 30)*
Southern Rock 110 *(10½f,Hay,GF,Jly 4)*
Sovereign 115 *(10f,Leo,GY,May 12)*
Sovereign Duke 104 *(14f,Goo,GF,May 25)*
Space Blues 115 *(7f,Asc,G,Jun 22)*
Space Traveller 120 *(8f,Leo,G,Sep 14)*
Space Walk 109 *(14f,San,G,Jly 25)*
Spanish Archer 108 *(10f,Don,GS,Aug 3)*
Spanish Aria 103 *(8f,Asc,G,Jun 21)*
Spanish City 110 *(7f,Nmk,GF,Jly 13)*
Spanish Mission 117 *(11f,Goo,GF,May 24)*
Spanish Star 106 *(6f,Goo,G,May 23)*
Spark Of War 105 *(15f,Ayr,G,Jun 21)*
Sparkle Roll 114 *(12f,Nmk,G,Jly 20)*
Sparklealot 108 *(7f,Ayr,G,Sep 19)*
Speak In Colours 115 *(6f,Cur,S,Sep 28)*
Specialise 103 *(10f,Lin,GS,Jun 22)*
Speed Company 110 *(11½f,Wdr,GF,Jun 29)*
Speedo Boy 104 *(14f,Nmk,GF,Jun 8)*
Speedy Move 114 *(7f,Mey,G,Jan 19)*
Spinning Memories 114 *(6½f,Dea,G,Aug 4)*
Spirit Of Appin 114 *(12f,Nmk,G,Jly 20)*
Spirit Of May 104 *(6f,Nmk,GF,Sep 21)*
Spirit Of Wedza 104 *(5f,Ham,GF,May 5)*
Spirit Power 105 *(5f,Hay,GS,Jly 20)*
Spirit Ridge 108 *(12f,Nmk,G,Sep 26)*
Spirit Warning 105 *(8f,Wdr,GF,Jun 29)*
Spirited Guest 104 *(6f,Yar,G,Sep 17)*
Spoof 107 *(5f,Nby,S,Apr 12)*
Sporting Chance 114 *(8f,Mey,G,Feb 28)*
Spotify 118 *(12f,Mey,G,Jan 24)*
Spring Loaded 104 *(6f,Asc,GF,Jun 22)*
Spring Romance 104 *(6f,Not,GS,Jun 27)*
Spring Run 112 *(14f,Lin,GF,Sep 14)*
Springwood Drive 107 *(6f,Pon,G,Aug 18)*
Spruce Meadows 105 *(10f,Leo,G,Aug 15)*
Sputnik Planum 108 *(10f,Don,G,Jly 20)*
Squats 105 *(6f,Eps,GF,Jun 1)*
St Andrews 104 *(14f,Cat,GF,Sep 10)*
Stage Magic 115 *(12f,Mey,G,Feb 14)*
Stagehand 103 *(10f,Rip,G,Jly 20)*
Stake Acclaim 113 *(5f,Nby,S,Apr 12)*
Stallone 106 *(6f,Not,HY,Jun 13)*
Star Archer 108 *(12f,Thi,G,Sep 7)*
Star Catcher 116 *(12f,Lon,G,Sep 15)*
Star Of Athena 106 *(12f,Bat,GF,Aug 20)*
Star Of Bengal 109 *(10f,Wdr,GF,Aug 24)*
Star Of Southwold 108 *(8f,Pon,GS,Jly 19)*
Star Shield 106 *(7f,Lei,GS,Jun 10)*
Star Terms 111 *(14½f,Don,GF,Sep 12)*
Starcaster 109 *(12f,Thi,GF,Apr 13)*
Starczewski 108 *(12f,Hay,GF,Jly 4)*
Starfighter 107 *(10f,Sal,G,Sep 5)*
Starlight Romance 104 *(7f,Yor,G,Aug 22)*
Starship 103 *(8f,Sha,G,Mar 31)*
Start Time 105 *(7f,Ayr,S,Jly 29)*
State Of Affair 109 *(12f,Hay,GF,Jly 4)*
Statuario 104 *(12f,Thi,GS,Jun 18)*
Staxton 103 *(6f,Ham,S,Jly 19)*
Stay Classy 108 *(6f,Yor,GF,Jly 12)*
Stealth Fighter 107 *(10f,Eps,G,Aug 26)*
Steel Prince 116 *(16f,Fle,GS,Nov 5)*
Stivers 107 *(12f,Leo,G,Sep 14)*
Stone Mason 104 *(10f,Wet,G,May 7)*
Stone Of Destiny 109 *(5f,Asc,GF,Jly 13)*
Stoney Lane 103 *(5f,Crl,GS,Aug 21)*
Stonific 109 *(12f,Thi,G,Sep 7)*
Storm Ahead 110 *(8f,Don,S,Jun 16)*
Storm Melody 105 *(6f,Bat,GF,Jun 7)*
Storm Over 105 *(5f,Wdr,S,Jun 10)*
Storm Soldier 107 *(7f,Sha,G,Mar 31)*
Storm Steps 108 *(12f,Gal,G,Aug 1)*
Stormin Norman 103 *(17f,Crl,GS,Aug 5)*
Stormin Tom 107 *(14f,Cat,GF,Sep 21)*
Stormingin 104 *(10f,Lei,G,Jun 27)*
Stormy Antarctic 110 *(8f,Asc,G,Jun 18)*
Stormy Liberal 107 *(6f,Mey,G,Mar 30)*
Stormy Tale 107 *(10f,Leo,GY,May 12)*
Storting 112 *(10f,Don,GF,Sep 13)*
Stradivarius 116 *(16f,Goo,G,Jly 30)*
Straitouttacompton 103 *(12f,Cat,GF,Sep 10)*
Stranagone 103 *(8f,Leo,GF,Aug 8)*
Strategic 103 *(12½f,Mus,GF,Jly 3)*
Stratton Street 114 *(8f,Mey,G,Jan 17)*
Stratum 113 *(18f,Nmk,S,Oct 12)*
Strawberry Jack 103 *(8f,Thi,G,Apr 29)*
Street Parade 108 *(5f,Wdr,GF,May 27)*
Strict Tempo 103 *(7f,Sal,GF,Jly 27)*
Stringybark Creek 106 *(8½f,Bev,G,Jun 18)*
Strong Steps 110 *(8f,Ayr,GF,May 22)*
Stunning Spirit 109 *(7f,Lon,G,Sep 15)*
Stylehunter 111 *(8f,Asc,S,Jun 19)*
Suaimhneach 107 *(7f,Leo,G,Jly 18)*
Suave Richard 119 *(12f,Mey,G,Mar 30)*
Subaana 108 *(8f,Nmk,GF,Aug 2)*
Success Days 112 *(10½f,Chs,S,May 10)*
Sucellus 103 *(9f,Goo,G,May 23)*
Sudona 110 *(10f,Lin,GF,May 3)*
Suedois 116 *(8f,Leo,G,Sep 14)*
Suegioo 105 *(16f,Goo,GS,Jun 9)*
Sufficient 104 *(8f,Don,GF,Jly 11)*
Sufi 111 *(14f,Bat,F,Sep 15)*
Summer Flair 105 *(10f,Lin,G,May 3)*
Summer Moon 112 *(18f,Nmk,S,Oct 12)*
Summerghand 109 *(7f,Asc,S,Oct 5)*
Sumner Beach 104 *(8f,Pon,G,Aug 7)*
Sun Maiden 114 *(10f,Goo,G,Aug 1)*
Sun Sign 109 *(5f,Cur,YS,Aug 9)*
Sunday Star 110 *(6f,Dea,G,Aug 4)*
Sunny Boy 108 *(5f,Sha,G,Apr 22)*
Sunny Power 108 *(9f,Sha,G,Mar 31)*
Sunset Nova 105 *(6f,Cur,G,Sep 15)*
Sunsprite 106 *(6f,Asc,GF,Jly 12)*
Supaulette 103 *(7f,Thi,G,May 4)*
Super Elegance 120 *(7f,Sha,G,Mar 31)*
Super Fun 113 *(7f,Sha,G,Jan 1)*
Super Julius 105 *(5f,Cur,S,Aug 9)*
Super Kid 104 *(12f,Thi,GF,Apr 13)*
Super Treat 109 *(7f,Leo,G,Jly 18)*
Super Wise 124 *(7f,Sha,G,Mar 31)*
Surfman 104 *(10f,Yor,GF,May 16)*
Surprise Baby 116 *(16f,Fle,GS,Nov 5)*
Surrey Hope 113 *(8½f,Eps,G,Aug 26)*
Surrey Thunder 115 *(10½f,Hay,HY,Aug 10)*
Surrounding 116 *(8f,Leo,G,Sep 14)*
Suwaan 106 *(5f,Pon,G,Aug 7)*
Suyoof 110 *(8f,Mey,G,Jan 17)*
Suzi's Connoisseur 105 *(6f,Nmk,GF,Sep 21)*
Sweet Charity 107 *(8½f,Eps,G,Aug 26)*
Sweet Dime 105 *(12f,Cur,G,Jun 27)*
Sweet Forgetme Not 105 *(6f,Yar,GF,Jly 25)*
Sweet Promise 106 *(10f,Don,G,Jun 28)*
Sweet Pursuit 108 *(6f,Bat,GS,Aug 17)*
Swell Song 105 *(5f,Yar,GF,Aug 20)*
Swift Approval 108 *(7f,San,G,Aug 8)*
Swift Emperor 108 *(8½f,Bev,GS,May 14)*
Swift Rose 104 *(8f,Sal,GF,Jun 26)*
Swift Wing 103 *(12f,Hay,S,Sep 5)*
Swindler 113 *(6f,Asc,GF,Sep 7)*
Swiss Chill 104 *(5f,Lei,GF,Jly 24)*
Swiss Knight 106 *(6f,Yar,GF,Sep 19)*
Swissal 103 *(7f,Bri,GF,May 21)*
Switch Around 103 *(10f,Cur,G,Jun 27)*
Swordbill 108 *(14½f,Don,GF,Jun 1)*
Symbolization 110 *(9f,Mey,G,Feb 7)*
Syrena 109 *(6f,Cur,GF,May 26)*

Taamol 113 *(8f,Mey,G,Jan 10)*
Tabarrak 107 *(7f,Asc,GF,Sep 7)*
Tabou Beach Boy 104 *(14f,Wet,G,Apr 28)*
Tadaany 104 *(5f,Cat,GS,Aug 15)*
Tadaawol 107 *(7f,Cat,S,Aug 12)*
Tafaakhor 110 *(8f,Mey,G,Mar 2)*
Tailor Made 104 *(7f,Nby,GS,Apr 13)*
Tails I Win 104 *(10f,Not,S,Jun 17)*
Takarengo 105 *(12f,Leo,SH,Oct 19)*
Taking Aim 114 *(7f,Sha,G,Jan 1)*
Takumi 107 *(10f,Rip,G,May 19)*
Tamerlane 106 *(8f,Wdr,GF,Jly 15)*
Tammooz 110 *(12f,Rip,GS,Sep 28)*
Tammy Wynette 103 *(7f,Leo,Y,Apr 3)*
Tamok 105 *(12f,Chp,G,Aug 26)*
Tamreer 113 *(12f,Yor,GF,May 25)*
Tanasoq 104 *(5f,Mus,GF,Apr 2)*
Tang Fleming 111 *(7f,Sha,G,Mar 31)*
Tangmere 115 *(7f,Sha,GF,Apr 22)*
Tangramm 104 *(10f,San,GF,May 23)*
Tapisserie 106 *(7f,Sal,S,Jun 11)*
Tarboosh 110 *(5f,Hay,HY,Jun 8)*
Target Zone 103 *(8f,Asc,S,Oct 4)*
Tarnawa 110 *(10f,Cur,GF,Sep 15)*
Tarnhelm 105 *(6f,Crl,GF,Jly 6)*
Tartlette 103 *(10f,Chp,GF,May 14)*
Tauran Shaman 107 *(8f,Lon,VS,Oct 5)*
Tauteke 106 *(11½f,Lin,S,May 11)*
Tavus 109 *(12f,Lei,HY,Oct 8)*
Tawny Port 108 *(5f,Wdr,S,Jun 10)*
Tawseef 109 *(17½f,Ayr,GS,Jly 22)*
Te Akau Caliburn 106 *(12f,Pon,S,Jun 10)*
Team Talk 106 *(10f,Mey,G,Feb 21)*
Technician 116 *(14½f,Don,GF,Sep 14)*
Teepee Time 106 *(5f,Cat,S,Aug 19)*
Telecaster 109 *(10f,San,GF,Jly 6)*
Telekinetic 105 *(10f,Yar,GF,Aug 7)*
Tell William 105 *(8f,Bat,GF,Aug 27)*
Temple Church 107 *(16½f,Nby,GS,Jly 20)*
Ten Joys 108 *(6f,Cur,GF,May 26)*
Ten Sovereigns 113 *(6f,Nmk,GF,Jly 13)*
Tenax 112 *(6f,Crl,GF,Aug 29)*
Tennessee Wildcat 113 *(10f,Leo,GY,Jun 20)*
Teodora De Vega 109 *(12f,Rip,GS,Sep 28)*
Terebellum 108 *(10f,Lon,VS,Oct 6)*
Tertius 109 *(6f,Dea,G,Aug 4)*
Teruntum Star 113 *(5f,Bev,GF,Apr 17)*
Terzetto 107 *(8f,Cur,GF,May 26)*
Texas Rock 104 *(6f,Cur,G,Jly 20)*
Texting 112 *(5f,Asc,GF,Sep 7)*
Thanks Be 110 *(8f,Asc,G,Jun 21)*
That's Not Me 105 *(6f,Cur,G,Sep 15)*
The Armed Man 111 *(6f,Thi,G,Aug 30)*
The Broghie Man 103 *(6f,Cur,S,Aug 16)*
The Cashel Man 105 *(18f,Nby,S,Apr 12)*
The Chosen One 114 *(16f,Fle,GS,Nov 5)*
The Corporal 108 *(10f,Yar,GF,Jly 17)*
The Cruising Lord 107 *(5f,San,GF,Jly 6)*
The Daley Express 107 *(5f,Don,S,Aug 17)*
The Dancing Poet 103 *(10f,Eps,G,Sep 12)*
The Defiant 104 *(5f,Mus,GF,May 2)*
The Detainee 106 *(14f,Bat,F,Sep 15)*
The Emperor Within 105 *(8½f,Not,GF,Apr 10)*
The Fiddler 106 *(14f,Red,GF,Sep 17)*
The Game Is On 103 *(10f,Ffo,GF,Aug 1)*
The Grand Visir 109 *(16½f,Nby,GS,Jly 20)*
The Grey Zebedee 109 *(5f,Cat,S,Aug 19)*
The Jean Genie 109 *(10f,Don,GF,Sep 13)*
The King 113 *(10f,Cur,GY,May 6)*
The Lamplighter 106 *(6f,Goo,G,Aug 23)*
The Last Emperor 110 *(12f,Cur,G,Jun 27)*
The Lords Walk 105 *(10f,Lin,S,May 11)*
The Mouse Doctor 104 *(12f,Cur,G,Jun 27)*
The Night King 105 *(10f,Yar,GF,Jly 17)*
The Night Watch 103 *(6f,Hay,GS,Jly 19)*
The Pink'n 104 *(11½f,Wdr,G,Jun 24)*
The Resdev Way 113 *(15f,Ayr,G,Jun 21)*
The Revenant 117 *(8f,Lon,VS,Oct 5)*
The Throstles 109 *(10½f,Hay,GF,Jly 5)*
The Tin Man 116 *(6f,Hay,S,Sep 7)*
The Trader 111 *(10f,Nby,G,May 18)*
The Very Moon 103 *(10f,Don,G,Jun 28)*
Theatro 108 *(14f,Not,S,Oct 30)*
Thechildren'strust 104 *(9f,Goo,GF,Aug 3)*
Theglasgowwarrior 111 *(17½f,Ayr,G,Sep 20)*
Thegreatestshowman 109 *(5f,Asc,GF,Sep 7)*
Themaxwecan 111 *(14½f,Don,GF,Jun 1)*
Theodorico 103 *(7f,Don,GF,Mar 31)*
Thimbleweed 107 *(12f,Sal,GS,Aug 15)*
Third Time Lucky 106 *(8f,Don,G,Mar 30)*
Third World 105 *(12f,Cur,GY,Jun 7)*
This One's For You 106 *(7f,Sha,G,Apr 22)*
Thistimenextyear 113 *(10½f,Hay,HY,Jun 12)*
Thiswaycadeaux 109 *(7f,Gal,G,Aug 1)*
Thomas Cranmer 105 *(10f,Red,GF,May 27)*
Thomas Cubitt 107 *(14f,Red,GF,May 20)*
Thorn 103 *(8½f,Eps,G,Sep 12)*
Thornaby Nash 103 *(8f,Ham,GF,May 17)*
Thorntoun Care 103 *(10f,Bev,S,Sep 24)*
Thrave 110 *(8f,Nmk,G,Jly 20)*
Three Castles 106 *(10f,Ayr,HY,Aug 10)*
Three Comets 109 *(10f,Bev,G,Aug 31)*
Three Little Birds 107 *(5f,Asc,GF,Jly 26)*
Three Saints Bay 113 *(7f,Mus,G,Apr 20)*
Three Star General 105 *(16f,Chp,G,May 3)*
Thundering Blue 112 *(10f,Goo,GF,May 25)*
Tiar Na Nog 111 *(11½f,Wdr,G,May 13)*
Ticks The Boxes 103 *(6f,Pon,S,Jun 10)*
Tide Of Time 109 *(6f,Cur,G,Jun 29)*
Tiger Eye 106 *(8f,Goo,G,May 4)*
Tigerfish 109 *(11½f,Yar,GF,Jly 30)*
Tigerskin 109 *(12f,Ffo,GS,Aug 13)*
Tilsworth Lukey 105 *(10f,Not,GS,Aug 13)*
Tilsworth Sammy 103 *(16f,Chp,GF,May 14)*
Time Change 104 *(10f,Bat,GF,Aug 7)*
Time For A Toot 107 *(8f,Hay,S,Sep 7)*
Time For Mabel 104 *(13f,Leo,G,Jun 6)*
Time Stands Still 103 *(7f,Leo,Y,Apr 3)*
Time To Fly 113 *(7f,Lon,GS,Apr 22)*
Time To Study 103 *(14f,Hay,S,Sep 7)*
Time Tunnel 105 *(8½f,Gal,G,Aug 3)*
Timetodock 105 *(5f,Bev,G,May 6)*
Timoshenko 106 *(20½f,Goo,G,Jly 31)*
Tin Hat 103 *(6f,Bri,GF,Aug 9)*
Tinandali 110 *(10f,Leo,GY,Apr 3)*
Tinto 116 *(6f,Asc,S,Oct 4)*
Tintoretto 103 *(7f,Gal,G,Jly 30)*
Tip Two Win 103 *(6f,Asc,GF,Jun 22)*
Tipitena 106 *(10f,Cur,G,Jun 28)*
Tis Marvellous 116 *(5f,Asc,GF,Jly 13)*
Titanium Sky 113 *(7f,Gal,G,Aug 1)*
Tobouggaloo 104 *(12f,Nby,GF,Jly 25)*
Tom's Anna 104 *(8½f,Not,S,Jun 17)*
Tomily 105 *(5f,Cat,GS,Jly 24)*
Tommy G 106 *(7f,Mus,GF,Jly 3)*
Tommy Hallinan 104 *(12f,Cat,GF,Sep 21)*
Tommy Taylor 110 *(6f,Thi,G,Aug 30)*
Tomorrow's Angel 107 *(15f,Ayr,G,Jun 21)*
Tone The Barone 105 *(7f,Yar,GF,Jly 17)*
Toni's A Star 104 *(5f,Bri,GF,Sep 16)*
Tonkinese 104 *(7f,Leo,G,Jly 18)*
Tony The Gent 110 *(8f,Cur,G,Jun 29)*
Tonyx 107 *(10f,Sal,G,Sep 13)*
Too Darn Hot 115 *(8f,Cur,GF,May 25)*
Tooreen Legend 109 *(12f,Cur,G,Jun 27)*
Top Breeze 106 *(6f,Nmk,GF,Apr 17)*
Top Mission 103 *(8f,Asc,GF,Jly 12)*
Top Notch Tonto 107 *(11f,Crl,GF,Jun 26)*
Top Power 106 *(11½f,Wdr,S,Oct 7)*
Top Rank 109 *(8f,Nmk,G,Sep 26)*
Top Score 114 *(7f,Mey,G,Jan 24)*
Top Tug 107 *(12f,Nby,G,May 18)*
Topical 107 *(7f,Nby,S,Apr 12)*
Tor 106 *(14f,Mus,G,Apr 20)*
Torcello 111 *(10f,Nby,S,Aug 17)*
Tornado Twist 122 *(7f,Sha,G,Mar 31)*
Torochica 103 *(7f,Nmk,G,Jly 20)*
Toshima 106 *(16f,Ffo,GF,Jly 29)*
Tour To Paris 122 *(7f,Lon,GS,Apr 22)*
Town's History 108 *(12f,Mey,G,Jan 19)*
Toybox 106 *(8f,Wdr,GF,Jun 30)*
Trading Point 107 *(7f,Leo,G,Sep 14)*
Trais Fluors 108 *(10f,San,GF,Apr 26)*
Tranchee 103 *(7f,Gal,G,Jly 30)*
Trautmann 114 *(15f,Ayr,G,Jun 21)*
Travel On 105 *(10f,San,GF,Apr 26)*
Treasure Me 111 *(6f,Not,S,May 11)*
Treble Cone 104 *(8f,Cur,GF,May 24)*
Trelinney 107 *(10f,Chp,GF,Jly 18)*
Tresorier 103 *(6f,Cur,G,Sep 15)*
Trethias 110 *(9f,Cur,G,Aug 30)*
Tribal Craft 112 *(12f,Sal,GS,Aug 15)*
Tribal Warrior 112 *(7f,Mus,GF,Jly 3)*
Trickbag 104 *(7f,Mey,G,Feb 7)*
Tricky Dicky 106 *(6f,Yor,G,Jly 26)*
Triggered 105 *(6f,Don,G,May 4)*
Trinity Star 107 *(12f,Thi,G,Sep 7)*
Triple Distilled 104 *(6f,Pon,S,Jun 10)*
Tritonix 107 *(12f,Gal,G,Aug 2)*
Trolius 108 *(7f,Mey,G,Jan 10)*
Trossachs 118 *(12f,Cur,G,Jun 27)*
Trouble And Strife 108 *(14f,Cat,GF,Sep 21)*
Trouble Shooter 107 *(12f,Chp,G,Aug 22)*
True Blue Moon 107 *(5f,Cur,GY,Jun 27)*
True Destiny 105 *(20½f,Goo,G,Jly 31)*
True Mason 106 *(5f,Cur,G,Sep 15)*
True Romance 108 *(14f,Mus,G,Jly 23)*
True Self 113 *(14f,Yor,GF,Aug 24)*
Trueshan 116 *(12f,Ffo,G,Aug 29)*
Trulee Scrumptious 104 *(8f,Nmk,GS,Jun 21)*
Trulove 105 *(5f,Cat,S,Aug 19)*
Tudor City 109 *(10f,Cur,GF,Sep 15)*
Tukhoom 111 *(7f,Lei,GF,Jly 24)*
Tulfarris 111 *(8f,Don,G,May 4)*
Turf Sprint 105 *(8f,Sha,G,Jan 1)*
Turgenev 109 *(8f,Asc,GS,Jun 20)*
Turjomaan 110 *(8f,Goo,GF,Aug 2)*
Turnberry Isle 114 *(8f,Leo,G,Sep 14)*
Turning Gold 104 *(14f,Not,S,Oct 30)*
Turntable 103 *(8f,Bri,GF,Sep 16)*
Twenty Minutes 114 *(6f,Cur,G,Jun 29)*
Twentysixthstreet 108 *(5f,Ham,S,Sep 23)*
Twilight Payment 115 *(16f,Fle,GS,Nov 5)*
Twin Appeal 105 *(7½f,Bev,GF,Jly 16)*
Twin Star 104 *(14f,Goo,S,Jun 14)*
Twist 'N' Shake 104 *(8½f,Not,S,May 10)*
Two Bids 108 *(10f,San,GS,Jun 15)*
Twpsyn 104 *(10f,Ffo,GF,Jly 29)*
Typhoon Ten 105 *(6f,Lei,GS,Aug 11)*
Tyrconnell 109 *(6f,Cur,GF,May 26)*

UAE Jewel 110 *(8f,Nmk,G,Sep 27)*
UAE Prince 109 *(10f,Yor,GF,May 17)*
Ulshaw Bridge 109 *(7f,Red,G,Jun 22)*
Ulster 110 *(14f,Mus,G,Apr 20)*

Ultimate Glory 117 *(7f,Sha,G,Apr 22)*
Ultra Pride 103 *(10f,Cur,YS,Aug 16)*
Ummalnar 113 *(8f,Asc,GF,Jly 13)*
Uncertain Smile 104 *(10f,Not,S,Aug 6)*
Uncle Charlie 105 *(6f,Crl,GF,May 20)*
Uncle Jerry 103 *(7f,Asc,GF,Sep 6)*
Unicron Jewellery 107 *(8f,Sha,G,Mar 31)*
Union Rose 112 *(5f,San,G,Sep 13)*
Unique Treasure 105 *(5f,Sha,G,Apr 22)*
Unit Of Assessment 105 *(12f,Goo,S,Jun 7)*
Universal Gleam 112 *(8f,Ayr,GF,May 22)*
Up Helly Aa 110 *(9f,Leo,G,Jly 18)*
Up Ten Down Two 106 *(14f,Red,G,Jun 22)*
Upstaging 105 *(6f,Ayr,G,Sep 20)*
Urban Beat 112 *(6f,Cur,SH,Oct 13)*
Urban Icon 113 *(7f,Nby,GS,Apr 13)*
Urban Spirit 106 *(16f,Mus,GF,Jly 3)*
Uther Pendragon 104 *(10f,Bat,F,May 15)*
Utopia Life 112 *(5f,Sha,G,Apr 22)*

Valcartier 118 *(8f,Mey,G,Mar 2)*
Vale Do Sol 112 *(12f,Mey,G,Jan 19)*
Vale Of Kent 112 *(7f,Nmk,GF,Jly 13)*
Valence 103 *(10f,Bev,GS,May 14)*
Valkenburg 109 *(18f,Pon,GF,Apr 9)*
Vallambrosa 105 *(8f,Cur,GF,May 24)*
Valley Of Fire 103 *(7f,Don,GF,Mar 31)*
Van Beethoven 111 *(8f,Cur,GF,May 25)*
Vanbrugh 108 *(7f,Hay,S,Sep 5)*
Vasiliev 103 *(8f,Lei,GS,Jun 10)*
Vegas Boy 103 *(6f,Asc,S,May 10)*
Velorum 106 *(8f,Nmk,GF,May 17)*
Ventura Knight 109 *(10f,Red,GF,May 27)*
Ventura Ocean 104 *(7f,Don,G,Jly 20)*
Ventura Royal 107 *(8½f,Bev,S,Sep 24)*
Venturous 110 *(6f,Cur,G,Sep 15)*
Venusta 108 *(10f,Lin,GF,Sep 5)*
Veracious 113 *(8f,Nmk,GS,Oct 5)*
Verbal Dexterity 113 *(8f,Leo,GY,May 12)*
Verdana Blue 115 *(16f,Asc,GF,May 1)*
Verhoyen 110 *(6f,Cur,G,Jly 20)*
Verify 106 *(10f,Ffo,GF,Aug 1)*
Veronesi 114 *(12f,Lon,G,Sep 15)*
Very Talented 114 *(12f,Mey,G,Feb 14)*
Via Serendipity 104 *(8f,Nmk,G,Jly 20)*
Viadera 110 *(7f,Leo,G,Sep 14)*
Victoriano 114 *(14f,Sal,GS,Aug 15)*
Victorious Seeker 109 *(7f,Sha,G,Mar 31)*
Victory Angel 106 *(6f,Nmk,G,May 5)*
Victory Chime 109 *(10f,San,G,Jly 25)*
Victory Command 116 *(8f,Hay,GF,May 25)*
Victory Day 108 *(6f,Yor,GS,Jun 15)*
Victory Power 119 *(7f,Sha,G,Mar 31)*
Victory Rose 103 *(6f,Yar,G,Sep 17)*
Victory Wave 113 *(7f,Mey,G,Feb 7)*
Viking Way 108 *(6f,Yar,S,Jun 12)*
Villa Marina 114 *(12f,Lon,G,Sep 15)*
Villa Rosa 113 *(10f,Lon,VS,Oct 5)*
Vincy 112 *(8f,Sha,G,Jan 1)*
Vindolanda 107 *(12f,Nby,G,Aug 6)*
Vintage Brut 104 *(6f,Chs,GS,Aug 4)*
Vintager 110 *(10f,Goo,GF,May 25)*
Virtus Star 112 *(7f,Sha,G,Jan 1)*
Viscount Barfield 112 *(7f,Lon,GS,Apr 22)*
Vision Clear 106 *(11½f,Lin,GF,Jun 1)*
Visor 103 *(12f,Ffo,G,Sep 15)*
Vitralite 105 *(8f,Yor,GF,Aug 23)*
Vive La Difference 107 *(8f,Wet,GS,May 7)*
Vivianite 107 *(8f,Goo,G,May 4)*
Vivid Diamond 114 *(14½f,Don,GF,Sep 12)*
Vivionn 108 *(10f,Goo,G,Jly 31)*
Vivlos 114 *(9f,Mey,G,Mar 30)*
Vocal Queen 103 *(8f,Cur,S,Oct 22)*
Vocatus 109 *(6f,Cur,Y,Aug 23)*
Voi 106 *(10f,Yar,GF,Jly 30)*
Voice Of Calm 103 *(10f,Lin,G,Aug 10)*
Volcanic Sky 109 *(11f,Crl,GF,Jun 26)*
Voltaic 105 *(6f,Wdr,HY,Oct 21)*
Von Blucher 105 *(7f,Red,G,Jun 22)*
Vow And Declare 117 *(16f,Fle,GS,Nov 5)*
Voyage King 103 *(5f,Sha,G,Apr 22)*
Voyage Warrior 117 *(5f,Sha,G,Apr 22)*

Waarif 112 *(8f,Thi,G,May 4)*
Wadilsafa 115 *(10½f,Hay,HY,Aug 10)*
Wafy 105 *(8f,Asc,GF,Sep 6)*
Wahash 109 *(8f,Bat,GF,Apr 19)*
Wahoo 109 *(7f,Red,G,Aug 10)*
Waikuku 120 *(7f,Sha,G,Jan 1)*
Waitingfortheday 109 *(8f,Cur,G,Jly 20)*
Waldgeist 125 *(12f,Lon,VS,Oct 6)*
Waldpfad 113 *(6f,Hay,S,Sep 7)*
Waldstern 115 *(10f,Nmk,GF,Aug 10)*
Waleed 112 *(7f,Lon,GS,Apr 22)*
Walk It Talk It 103 *(10f,Wet,G,May 7)*
Walk On Walter 107 *(6f,Bat,F,Sep 14)*
Walking On Glass 104 *(13f,Leo,G,Jun 6)*
Walkinthesand 113 *(10f,Nmk,GF,Jly 12)*
Walton Street 123 *(12f,Mey,G,Feb 14)*
Wannie Mae 109 *(12f,Goo,G,Jun 21)*
Waqt 105 *(8f,Bat,F,May 24)*
War Diary 113 *(12f,Cur,G,Jun 27)*
War Eagle 106 *(12f,Chp,GS,Aug 15)*
War Glory 109 *(8f,Asc,S,Jun 19)*
War Hero 105 *(7f,Gal,G,Aug 3)*
War Of Succession 103 *(10f,Bat,F,Jly 10)*
War Room 118 *(7f,Sha,GF,Apr 22)*
War Whisper 108 *(5f,Bev,GF,Jly 6)*
Warning Fire 108 *(7f,Hay,GF,Jly 5)*
Wasim 119 *(7f,Mey,G,Feb 28)*
Wasmya 105 *(7f,Lon,VS,Oct 6)*
Watan 110 *(7f,Nmk,G,May 18)*
Watch Me 109 *(10f,Lon,VS,Oct 6)*
Watchable 111 *(6f,Eps,GF,Jun 1)*
Watchman 105 *(8f,Leo,GF,Aug 8)*
Waterlemon Bay 109 *(8f,Leo,GF,Aug 8)*
Way To Paris 114 *(12f,Lon,G,Sep 15)*
We Go 104 *(6f,Dea,G,Aug 4)*
We'll Go Again 105 *(8f,Cur,S,Oct 22)*
Wedding Blue 110 *(10f,Chp,G,May 3)*
Wedding Date 107 *(5f,Asc,GF,Jly 26)*
Weekender 111 *(14f,Yor,GF,Aug 30)*
Welcoming 108 *(8f,Ham,S,Sep 22)*
Weld Al Emarat 105 *(8½f,Bev,GS,May 14)*
Well Funded 107 *(14f,Red,GF,May 20)*
Wells Farhh Go 110 *(12f,Nmk,GF,Jun 29)*
Wentwood 105 *(10f,Cur,G,Jun 28)*
Wentworth Falls 109 *(6f,Don,GF,Sep 14)*
West End Charmer 118 *(10f,Don,GF,Jun 1)*
West Newton 104 *(12f,Don,GF,May 31)*
Westbrook Bertie 105 *(10f,Not,S,Oct 9)*
Western Australia 114 *(12f,Lon,GS,Jly 14)*
Western Duke 103 *(12f,Asc,GS,Jly 27)*
What A Welcome 109 *(16f,Asc,G,Aug 10)*
What About Carlo 104 *(10f,Eps,G,May 31)*
What Else But You 117 *(7f,Sha,G,Jan 1)*
What's The Story 108 *(8f,Asc,S,Jun 19)*
Whataguy 106 *(5f,Bri,GS,Jun 25)*
Whelans Way 106 *(6f,Asc,GF,Sep 6)*
Where's Jeff 110 *(12f,Thi,G,Sep 7)*
Whimbrel 105 *(8f,Asc,G,Jun 21)*
Whimsical Dream 105 *(10f,Lin,GF,Jly 17)*
Whinmoor 108 *(7f,Red,G,Aug 10)*
Whiskey And Water 105 *(16f,Mus,GF,Sep 14)*
Whisper Aloud 106 *(6f,Lin,GF,Sep 14)*
Whistler Bowl 114 *(14f,Sal,GS,Aug 15)*
Whitefountainfairy 111 *(7f,Hay,S,Sep 6)*
Who Dares Wins 110 *(16½f,Nby,GS,Jly 20)*
Wicker 107 *(7f,Sha,G,Jan 1)*
Wild Edric 106 *(5f,Chs,GF,Jun 29)*
Wild Hope 105 *(8f,Ayr,GF,Jly 8)*
Wild Illusion 114 *(10f,Cur,G,Jun 28)*
Wild Shot 107 *(10f,Ayr,GF,Jly 7)*
Wiley Post 103 *(5f,Bri,GF,Aug 8)*
Willie John 115 *(10f,Goo,GF,May 25)*
Wind N Grass 112 *(8f,Cur,G,Jun 29)*
Windsor Cross 104 *(8f,Ham,GF,May 17)*
Winged Spur 110 *(11½f,Lin,GF,Jun 1)*
Wings Of Time 109 *(8f,Nmk,GF,Jly 11)*
Winner's Way 115 *(7f,Sha,G,Jan 1)*
Winning Supreme 106 *(5f,Sha,G,Apr 22)*
Winston's Lad 115 *(7f,Sha,GF,Apr 22)*
Winter Snowdrop 104 *(10f,Yar,GF,Aug 8)*
Winwin Ruby 106 *(8f,Sha,G,Jan 1)*
Wisdom Mind 106 *(8f,Pon,GF,Jly 9)*
Wise Counsel 109 *(7f,Ayr,G,Sep 21)*
Wise Words 103 *(5f,San,S,Jun 15)*
Wish 104 *(8f,Cur,S,Oct 22)*
With You 107 *(10f,Lon,VS,Oct 6)*
Withhold 113 *(16½f,Nby,GS,Jly 20)*
Without Parole 110 *(9f,Mey,G,Mar 30)*
Witness Hunter 107 *(8f,Sha,G,Mar 31)*
Wolf Prince 105 *(12f,Cat,S,Aug 19)*
Woodside Wonder 105 *(7f,Cat,GF,Sep 10)*
Woody Creek 114 *(6f,Cur,S,Aug 9)*
Wootton 115 *(8f,Mey,G,Feb 21)*
World Famous 106 *(8f,Sha,G,Mar 31)*
World Record 118 *(7f,Sha,G,Mar 31)*
Worth Waiting 104 *(9f,Nmk,G,May 5)*
Woven 110 *(7f,Mey,G,Jan 10)*
Wrenthorpe 109 *(5f,Not,HY,Oct 16)*
Wufud 105 *(7f,Goo,GF,May 24)*
Wynford 104 *(17½f,Ayr,S,Jly 29)*

Xiang Bai Qi 104 *(8f,Sha,G,Mar 31)*
Xiang Huang Qi 107 *(7f,Sha,G,Apr 22)*
Xiang Yin 115 *(7f,Sha,G,Mar 31)*

Yaalail 116 *(8f,Mey,G,Mar 2)*
Yabass 105 *(16f,Rip,G,Apr 27)*
Yafordadoe 103 *(7f,Cur,S,Oct 22)*
Yafta 111 *(6f,Nmk,GF,Apr 17)*
Yale 103 *(6f,Cur,Y,Aug 23)*
Yee Cheong Lucky 117 *(7f,Sha,G,Mar 31)*
Yellow Tiger 107 *(12f,Asc,G,Aug 10)*
Yes You 103 *(6f,Yor,G,Jly 26)*
Yimou 108 *(6f,Nby,GF,Jly 11)*
Yolo Again 105 *(6f,Pon,G,Aug 18)*
Yonkers 106 *(12f,Cur,GY,Jun 7)*
You're Hired 113 *(9f,Goo,GF,Aug 3)*
Youceeyouceecee 105 *(6f,Cur,S,Oct 22)*
Youkan 107 *(6f,Goo,GS,Jun 9)*
Young Fire 113 *(7f,Hay,S,Sep 6)*
Young John 108 *(6f,Chp,GS,Sep 12)*
Young Legend 123 *(7f,Sha,G,Mar 31)*
Young Merlin 112 *(14f,Sal,GS,Aug 15)*
Youngstar 113 *(16f,Fle,GS,Nov 5)*
Yourtimeisnow 106 *(6f,Not,S,May 11)*
Yousini 104 *(6f,Nmk,GF,Apr 17)*
Yssingeaux 107 *(7f,Lon,VS,Oct 6)*
Yuften 113 *(7f,Cur,GF,May 26)*
Yulong Gold Fairy 111 *(8f,Leo,G,Jun 6)*
Yulong Prince 104 *(9f,Mey,G,Mar 30)*

Zaaki 113 *(8½f,Eps,GF,Jun 1)*
Zabeel Prince 110 *(9f,Nmk,GF,Apr 18)*
Zabriskie 107 *(10f,Cur,G,Jun 29)*
Zac Brown 106 *(5½f,Chs,G,Jly 12)*
Zainhom 113 *(8f,Mey,G,Jan 10)*
Zakouski 108 *(8f,Nmk,GF,Apr 17)*
Zamaam 112 *(12f,Mey,G,Jan 24)*
Zaman 119 *(12f,Mey,G,Feb 14)*
Zamjar 109 *(5f,Asc,GF,Sep 7)*
Zap 110 *(8f,Cur,GY,Aug 30)*
Zapper Cass 106 *(6f,Lei,HY,Oct 8)*
Zarafshan 105 *(10f,Leo,GY,Apr 3)*
Zavrinka 112 *(7f,Lon,VS,Oct 6)*
Zealous 104 *(9f,Crl,GS,Aug 5)*
Zeyzoun 103 *(6f,Not,GS,Jun 27)*
Zhui Feng 112 *(8f,Wdr,GF,Jun 29)*
Zig Zag Zyggy 105 *(5f,Ham,S,Jly 19)*
Zihba 113 *(8f,Leo,GY,May 12)*
Zillion 106 *(12f,Chp,GS,Aug 15)*
Zip 107 *(8f,Hay,HY,Jun 12)*
Zodiakos 109 *(8f,Wet,GS,May 7)*
Zofelle 105 *(8f,Nmk,G,Jun 22)*
Zoffalee 103 *(12f,Cur,G,Jly 20)*
Zoffee 107 *(11½f,Wdr,GF,Jly 29)*
Zoravan 105 *(8f,Ham,GS,Jly 19)*
Zoraya 103 *(7f,Lei,GS,Aug 11)*
Zorion 113 *(10f,Mey,G,Feb 28)*
Zuba 107 *(12f,Asc,G,Aug 10)*
Zuenoon 112 *(8f,Leo,GY,May 12)*
Zumurud 105 *(6f,Thi,G,Aug 30)*
Zwayyan 109 *(8f,Bat,GF,Apr 19)*
Zzoro 108 *(10f,Nby,S,Aug 17)*

THREE-YEAR-OLDS AND UPWARDS - AW

A Likely Story 108 *(6f,Dun,SD,Dec 13)*
A Sure Welcome 108 *(5f,Wol,SD,Mar 5)*
Abanica 103 *(6f,Dun,SD,Nov 20)*
Abe Lincoln 111 *(10f,Lin,SD,Feb 2)*
Abel Handy 109 *(5f,Ncs,SS,Nov 21)*
Able Dealer 103 *(8f,Dun,SD,Sep 20)*
Able Jack 107 *(8f,Dun,SD,Dec 13)*
Above The Rest 112 *(7f,Ncs,SD,Dec 14)*
Above Us Only Sky 111 *(8f,Dun,SD,Apr 5)*
Abstraction 109 *(5f,Dun,SD,Sep 20)*
Accessor 112 *(12½f,Ncs,SD,Dec 6)*
Accidental Agent 111 *(8f,Kem,SS,Nov 20)*
Acclaim The Nation 110 *(5f,Wol,SD,Jan 29)*
Across The Sea 106 *(6f,Cfd,SD,Sep 12)*
Active Approach 108 *(12f,Dun,SD,Mar 8)*
Ad Libitum 105 *(12½f,Ncs,SS,Sep 6)*
Addicted To You 105 *(16f,Kem,SS,Mar 13)*
Addis Ababa 103 *(10f,Ncs,SD,Apr 29)*
Admirality 105 *(7f,Cfd,SD,Aug 31)*
Admodum 109 *(11f,Dun,SD,Feb 22)*
Affluence 109 *(10f,Lin,SD,Mar 8)*
African Ride 109 *(8f,Mey,FT,Feb 28)*
Age Of Wisdom 108 *(16f,Kem,SS,Mar 11)*
Agent Gibbs 104 *(12f,Wol,SD,Jan 4)*
Agent Of Fortune 106 *(8f,Lin,SD,Dec 30)*
Agrotera 110 *(8f,Kem,SS,Apr 20)*
Aguerooo 104 *(6f,Lin,SD,Jan 26)*
Ahlan Bil Zain 107 *(7f,Dun,SD,Jan 4)*
Air Raid 103 *(6f,Ncs,SS,Jun 29)*
Aircraft Carrier 111 *(16½f,Wol,SD,Jan 14)*
Airglow 107 *(6f,Sth,SD,Oct 21)*
Ajman Prince 113 *(16f,Ncs,SD,Jan 8)*
Akavit 103 *(16f,Kem,SS,Mar 11)*
Akvavera 106 *(8f,Kem,SS,Oct 2)*
Al Barg 105 *(7f,Cfd,SD,May 9)*
Al Batal 104 *(8f,Dun,SD,Oct 4)*
Al Erayg 108 *(8f,Sth,SD,Oct 29)*
Al Hamdany 110 *(10f,Cfd,SD,May 23)*
Al Hayette 106 *(7f,Mey,FT,Jan 3)*
Al Jellaby 109 *(8f,Kem,SS,Sep 3)*
Al Kout 104 *(16f,Kem,SS,Jly 3)*
Al Reeh 108 *(8f,Kem,SS,Jan 4)*
Al Suil Eile 107 *(7f,Sth,SD,Dec 20)*
Alabaster 107 *(16f,Lin,SD,Mar 2)*
Albadr 103 *(8f,Kem,SS,Aug 20)*
Albernathy 110 *(8f,Mey,FT,Jan 19)*
Albuquerque 105 *(8f,Dun,SD,Mar 6)*
Alcander 106 *(12f,Dun,SD,Mar 6)*
Alda'iya 103 *(8f,Mey,FT,Nov 7)*
Alemagna 105 *(12f,Kem,SS,Aug 7)*
Alemaratalyoum 107 *(7f,Cfd,SD,Sep 24)*
Alexander James 112 *(8f,Sth,SD,Apr 29)*
Alfarqad 110 *(7f,Cfd,SD,Sep 24)*
Alfie Solomons 111 *(6f,Cfd,SD,Oct 26)*
Alfirak 103 *(7f,Dun,SD,Nov 22)*
Alfredo Arcano 112 *(6f,Dun,SD,Dec 13)*
Alhaazm 103 *(9f,Wol,SD,Oct 14)*
Alhajjaj 113 *(11f,Dun,SD,Feb 22)*
Alhakmah 103 *(7f,Kem,SS,Nov 6)*
Alice Milligan 103 *(11f,Dun,SD,Nov 6)*
Alicia Darcy 104 *(6f,Lin,SD,Nov 30)*
Alignak 109 *(11f,Kem,SS,Sep 23)*
Aljari 110 *(7f,Ncs,SD,Dec 14)*
Alkaraama 109 *(6f,Cfd,SD,Jly 23)*
All Points West 103 *(12f,Wol,SD,Oct 5)*
All Set To Go 105 *(12f,Wol,SD,Apr 27)*
All The King's Men 106 *(7f,Dun,SD,Oct 18)*
All The Mollies 110 *(8f,Dun,SD,Apr 5)*
All Yours 105 *(12f,Kem,SS,Sep 25)*
All's Quiet 112 *(16f,Dun,SD,Jan 11)*
Alla Mahlak 104 *(7f,Mey,FT,Mar 14)*
Allieyf 104 *(12f,Lin,SD,Mar 25)*
Allocator 104 *(10f,Lin,SD,Jan 18)*
Allux Boy 105 *(9f,Wol,SD,Jly 15)*
Alma Linda 107 *(12f,Kem,SS,Sep 6)*
Almanaara 116 *(7f,Mey,FT,Feb 21)*
Almashriq 105 *(8f,Cfd,SD,May 23)*
Almufti 106 *(8f,Lin,SD,Dec 30)*
Almurr 104 *(5f,Ncs,SD,Nov 1)*
Aloysius Lilius 105 *(6f,Lin,SD,Nov 30)*
Alpasu 107 *(12f,Lin,SD,Feb 22)*
Alpha Tauri 111 *(7f,Sth,SD,Mar 7)*
Alraased 109 *(6f,Mey,FT,Jan 5)*
Alrajaa 110 *(8f,Lin,SD,Nov 16)*
Alsvinder 109 *(6f,Lin,SD,Feb 16)*
Altair 104 *(7f,Dun,SD,Jan 25)*
Alwarda 107 *(11f,Dun,SD,Mar 8)*
Always A Drama 105 *(6f,Kem,SS,Feb 16)*
Always Amazing 103 *(5f,Wol,SD,Apr 13)*
Always Resolute 106 *(16f,Ncs,SS,Jun 29)*
Amade 111 *(16f,Kem,SS,Jan 5)*
Amadeus 105 *(16½f,Sth,SD,Mar 14)*
Amanaat 109 *(6f,Dun,SD,Feb 15)*
Amaretto 107 *(10f,Lin,SD,Mar 23)*
Amazing Amaya 105 *(5f,Sth,SD,Dec 5)*
Amazing Grazing 106 *(5f,Wol,SD,Feb 25)*
Amazing One 107 *(7f,Dun,SD,Feb 22)*
Amazing Red 108 *(12f,Wol,SD,Mar 4)*
Ambassadorial 109 *(7f,Cfd,SD,Jun 19)*
Ambient 103 *(8f,Lin,SD,Mar 1)*
Ambling 110 *(12f,Lin,SD,Aug 15)*
American Endeavour 105 *(9f,Wol,SD,Feb 20)*
American Graffiti 105 *(10f,Ncs,SS,Feb 20)*
Amitie Waltz 111 *(16½f,Sth,SS,Feb 13)*
Amjaady 106 *(10f,Cfd,SD,Sep 26)*
Amor Fati 105 *(9½f,Wol,SD,Feb 19)*
Amor Kethley 103 *(6f,Cfd,SD,Sep 21)*
Anapurna 108 *(10f,Lin,SS,Jan 30)*
Andaleep 103 *(10f,Cfd,SD,Nov 19)*
Aneczka 103 *(11f,Dun,SD,May 3)*
Anfaass 104 *(8f,Dun,SD,Nov 29)*
Angel Eyes 105 *(5f,Ncs,SS,Mar 29)*
Angel Lane 104 *(12f,Sth,SD,Dec 19)*
Angel Palanas 109 *(7f,Sth,SD,Jan 3)*
Angels 111 *(7f,Dun,SD,Nov 20)*
Anif 103 *(9½f,Wol,SD,Mar 26)*
Anna Jammeela 103 *(12f,Sth,SD,Jan 24)*
Annabelle Rock 108 *(5f,Dun,SD,Sep 20)*
Annie B 106 *(8f,Dun,SD,Dec 20)*
Another Angel 112 *(5f,Ncs,SD,Mar 8)*
Another Batt 104 *(8f,Cfd,SD,Aug 23)*
Another Dressin 108 *(11f,Dun,SD,Mar 8)*
Another Touch 115 *(8f,Lin,SD,Dec 31)*
Antilles 115 *(11f,Dun,SD,Sep 27)*
Anyonecanhaveitall 108 *(16f,Ncs,SD,Sep 20)*
Apache Blaze 106 *(10f,Cfd,SD,Mar 7)*
Apex King 109 *(8f,Lin,SD,Jan 12)*
Aphaea 104 *(14f,Sth,SD,May 2)*
Aqabah 112 *(7f,Mey,FT,Feb 21)*
Aquarium 109 *(10f,Cfd,SD,Apr 4)*
Aquarius 104 *(6f,Cfd,SD,Aug 9)*
Ar Saoirse 107 *(8f,Dun,SD,Mar 8)*
Arabic Culture 110 *(12½f,Ncs,SD,Oct 11)*
Arbalet 109 *(7f,Cfd,SD,Sep 14)*
Arcanada 106 *(7f,Wol,SD,Mar 9)*
Arcanears 111 *(6f,Dun,SD,Dec 13)*
Arch Gold 104 *(11f,Mey,FT,Jan 5)*
Archimedes 106 *(5f,Ncs,SD,Jan 31)*
Archive 107 *(16f,Ncs,SD,Jan 8)*
Arctic Sea 103 *(8f,Cfd,SD,Apr 1)*
Arecibo 107 *(6f,Ncs,SS,Jun 29)*
Areen Heart 110 *(7f,Ncs,SD,Jan 22)*
Argus 109 *(12f,Sth,SD,Mar 12)*
Argyle 104 *(16f,Lin,SD,Jan 23)*
Aridity 105 *(8f,Mey,FT,Apr 12)*
Arigato 107 *(8f,Kem,SS,Sep 7)*
Arishka 104 *(5f,Ncs,SS,Mar 22)*
Arlecchino's Arc 106 *(10f,Cfd,SD,Mar 2)*
Arnhem 103 *(7f,Dun,SD,Dec 13)*
Arnold 107 *(5f,Ncs,SD,Jun 4)*
Arroway 106 *(8f,Mey,FT,Mar 2)*
Art Of America 111 *(11f,Dun,SD,Dec 6)*
Art Of Unity 106 *(5f,Dun,SD,Sep 20)*
Artarmon 106 *(16f,Kem,SS,Jly 3)*
Asanda 105 *(11f,Dun,SD,Dec 20)*
Ascended 103 *(6f,Ncs,SD,Oct 18)*
Ascot Dreamer 109 *(6f,Dun,SD,Dec 3)*
Ashazuri 103 *(11f,Kem,SS,Oct 9)*
Ashqar 103 *(16f,Dun,SD,Jan 11)*
Asian Angel 104 *(12f,Sth,SD,Oct 4)*
Assimilation 106 *(9f,Wol,SD,Mar 26)*
Astonished 106 *(7f,Cfd,SD,Jly 6)*

Astromachia 106 *(16f,Kem,SS,Dec 11)*
At Your Service 104 *(6f,Cfd,SD,Jan 24)*
Athollblair Boy 111 *(6f,Ncs,SD,Apr 1)*
Atlas 107 *(8f,Dun,SD,Mar 15)*
Atletico 108 *(7f,Cfd,SD,Jun 6)*
Atomic Jack 108 *(16f,Lin,SD,Mar 2)*
Attain 104 *(10f,Lin,SD,Mar 1)*
Attainment 107 *(7f,Cfd,SD,Aug 24)*
Audible 113 *(10f,Mey,FT,Mar 30)*
Aussie Valentine 109 *(8f,Dun,SD,Feb 8)*
Austrian School 108 *(16f,Ncs,SS,Jun 29)*
Autretot 107 *(12½f,Ncs,SD,Oct 11)*
Avenue Of Stars 105 *(6f,Ncs,SS,Jan 12)*
Avigale 104 *(8f,Dun,SD,Feb 15)*
Awa Bomba 106 *(7f,Sth,SD,Oct 10)*
Aweedram 106 *(10f,Cfd,SD,Nov 7)*
Awesomedude 108 *(12f,Wol,SD,May 13)*
Awsaaf 105 *(5f,Wol,SD,May 31)*
Axelrod 109 *(10f,Mey,FT,Mar 30)*
Azari 110 *(16½f,Sth,SS,Feb 13)*
Azzeccagarbugli 105 *(7f,Wol,SD,Dec 3)*

Baasha 103 *(10f,Cfd,SD,Jan 3)*
Baashiq 109 *(8f,Kem,SS,Feb 28)*
Babbo's Boy 105 *(11f,Kem,SS,Sep 25)*
Baby Steps 104 *(7f,Wol,SD,Nov 30)*
Bacacarat 105 *(8f,Kem,SS,May 22)*
Badenscoth 107 *(8f,Kem,SS,Feb 28)*
Baghdad 108 *(12½f,Ncs,SD,Apr 19)*
Bahuta Acha 104 *(6f,Wol,SD,Nov 6)*
Baile An Roba 103 *(6f,Dun,SD,Mar 8)*
Balefire 103 *(8f,Dun,SD,Mar 29)*
Ballard Down 109 *(8f,Lin,SD,Jan 26)*
Ballistic 105 *(7f,Wol,SD,Mar 9)*
Ballycaines 112 *(8f,Dun,SD,Dec 3)*
Ballylemon 107 *(14f,Cfd,SD,Nov 2)*
Ballyquin 109 *(6f,Cfd,SD,Mar 7)*
Baltic Song 109 *(12f,Lin,SD,Feb 22)*
Bambari 107 *(5f,Dun,SD,Dec 18)*
Bandiuc Eile 107 *(8f,Dun,SD,Nov 1)*
Banksea 103 *(8f,Cfd,SD,Sep 4)*
Barbill 103 *(6f,Ncs,SS,Feb 20)*
Baron Bolt 103 *(6f,Cfd,SD,Apr 25)*
Barossa Red 106 *(8f,Sth,SD,Apr 4)*
Barrington 104 *(7f,Wol,SD,Dec 14)*
Barristan The Bold 108 *(7f,Ncs,SD,Jly 27)*
Bartholomeu Dias 111 *(10f,Cfd,SD,Sep 28)*
Barys 110 *(8f,Cfd,SD,Apr 11)*
Bashful Boy 107 *(11f,Dun,SD,Dec 6)*
Battered 109 *(7f,Ncs,SD,Jan 22)*
Battle Of Marathon 107 *(12f,Lin,SD,Dec 28)*
Battle Of Waterloo 104 *(7f,Cfd,SD,Jly 23)*
Battle of Paradise 103 *(8f,Kem,SS,Jan 16)*
Bay Of Naples 103 *(10f,Cfd,SD,Dec 12)*
Bayshore Freeway 109 *(14f,Cfd,SD,Jun 19)*
Bayston Hill 105 *(10f,Cfd,SD,Apr 1)*
Be Fair 104 *(12f,Lin,SD,Dec 4)*
Be Proud 109 *(5f,Ncs,SD,Dec 14)*
Be Thankful 105 *(10f,Ncs,SD,Jan 2)*
Beachcomber Bay 110 *(6f,Mey,FT,Mar 14)*
Bear Force One 110 *(8f,Kem,SS,Nov 19)*
Beat Of The Sea 107 *(11f,Dun,SD,Mar 8)*
Beau Satchel 104 *(8f,Dun,SD,Feb 15)*
Beau Warrior 114 *(6f,Dun,SD,Mar 15)*
Beaufort 104 *(12½f,Ncs,SS,Sep 20)*
Beauty Filly 104 *(7f,Cfd,SD,Aug 31)*
Beauvais 104 *(12f,Kem,SS,Nov 19)*
Bedouin's Story 112 *(8f,Ncs,SD,Jun 4)*
Bedtime Bella 103 *(7f,Sth,SD,Dec 20)*
Bee Machine 103 *(7f,Sth,SD,Nov 9)*
Behavioral Bias 109 *(8f,Mey,FT,Mar 9)*
Beleaguerment 104 *(6f,Lin,SD,Mar 15)*
Bellepower 106 *(11f,Dun,SD,Oct 11)*
Bellevarde 103 *(6f,Sth,SD,Jan 1)*
Bellick 108 *(6f,Dun,SD,Nov 15)*
Benedict Roezl 107 *(6f,Dun,SD,Oct 18)*
Bengali Boys 107 *(5f,Ncs,SD,Jan 8)*
Benny And The Jets 105 *(6f,Kem,SS,Nov 19)*
Berrahri 106 *(14f,Cfd,SD,Sep 28)*
Best Solution 107 *(12f,Kem,SS,Sep 7)*
Betancourt 112 *(16½f,Wol,SD,Jan 11)*
Beyond Dance 108 *(11f,Dun,SD,May 3)*
Beyond Equal 108 *(6f,Kem,SS,Oct 28)*
Beyond The Clouds 108 *(12½f,Ncs,SD,Oct 11)*
Bianca Minola 104 *(11f,Dun,SD,May 3)*
Big Brown Bear 109 *(11f,Mey,FT,Jan 19)*
Big Country 117 *(10f,Lin,SD,Feb 2)*
Big Daddy Kane 104 *(9½f,Wol,SD,Dec 14)*
Big Kitten 109 *(10f,Cfd,SD,May 2)*
Big Les 107 *(5f,Ncs,SD,Nov 22)*
Big Time Maybe 108 *(5f,Wol,SD,May 7)*
Billesdon Brook 110 *(7f,Cfd,SD,Jun 19)*
Billie Beane 105 *(10f,Cfd,SD,Sep 19)*
Billy Roberts 104 *(9f,Wol,SD,Feb 23)*
Billyfairplay 110 *(6f,Dun,SD,Feb 15)*
Billyoakes 105 *(6f,Wol,SD,Jan 30)*
Bin Battuta 115 *(10f,Cfd,SD,Sep 28)*
Bionic Tonic 104 *(8f,Dun,SD,Oct 4)*
Black Label 110 *(16f,Dun,SD,Mar 29)*
Blackcurrent 104 *(5f,Wol,SD,Dec 10)*
Blackheath 106 *(7f,Lin,SS,Oct 31)*
Blackstone Cliff 103 *(8f,Dun,SD,Nov 29)*
Blame Culture 104 *(7f,Cfd,SD,Apr 25)*
Blame It On Sally 106 *(16f,Ncs,SD,Sep 20)*

Blametheshady 107 *(7f,Dun,SD,Nov 8)*
Blastofmagic 103 *(5f,Dun,SD,Nov 22)*
Blaze Of Hearts 105 *(8f,Kem,SS,Jan 4)*
Blazing Dreams 103 *(8f,Ncs,SD,Sep 25)*
Blazon 104 *(16f,Kem,SS,Jan 5)*
Blenheim Palace 116 *(11f,Dun,SD,Sep 27)*
Blockchain 112 *(7f,Mey,FT,Mar 14)*
Blood Eagle 106 *(9½f,Wol,SD,Sep 30)*
Blowing Dixie 108 *(12f,Sth,SD,Sep 26)*
Blown By Wind 104 *(8f,Kem,SS,Sep 3)*
Blue De Vega 107 *(5f,Cfd,SD,Aug 16)*
Blue Medici 106 *(11f,Kem,SS,Oct 9)*
Blue Mist 106 *(7f,Cfd,SD,Aug 31)*
Blue Sovereign 107 *(9½f,Mey,FT,Oct 24)*
Blue Uluru 111 *(5f,Dun,SD,Oct 18)*
Blue Whisper 106 *(8f,Dun,SD,Feb 15)*
Blyton Lass 105 *(12f,Wol,SD,Sep 7)*
Bo Samraan 109 *(12f,Sth,SD,Nov 9)*
Bobby Biscuit 106 *(8f,Lin,SD,Oct 3)*
Bobby Joe Leg 108 *(6f,Ncs,SD,Jan 31)*
Bobby K 103 *(8f,Ncs,SD,Apr 29)*
Bochart 123 *(7f,Mey,FT,Jan 5)*
Bodacious Name 103 *(16½f,Sth,SD,Apr 21)*
Bodak 105 *(8f,Dun,SD,Nov 29)*
Boerhan 107 *(10f,Cfd,SD,May 9)*
Bois de Boulogne 107 *(11f,Mey,FT,Mar 14)*
Bold Approach 112 *(11f,Dun,SD,Oct 11)*
Bollihope 105 *(9½f,Wol,SD,Jan 7)*
Bond Angel 107 *(8f,Sth,SD,Apr 17)*
Boom The Groom 114 *(5f,Wol,SD,Feb 21)*
Born To Finish 104 *(6f,Cfd,SD,Nov 2)*
Bosham 104 *(5f,Cfd,SD,Apr 4)*
Boughtinthedark 106 *(6f,Dun,SD,Dec 3)*
Boutonniere 104 *(10f,Cfd,SD,Sep 26)*
Bowerman 107 *(8f,Ncs,SD,Apr 29)*
Bowson Fred 106 *(5f,Ncs,SD,Jan 22)*
Boy In The Bar 109 *(6f,Cfd,SD,Aug 10)*
Brandy Station 104 *(5f,Ncs,SD,Nov 1)*
Brasca 107 *(14f,Cfd,SD,Sep 5)*
Break The Rules 108 *(16f,Lin,SD,Aug 31)*
Break The Silence 107 *(7f,Sth,SD,Mar 7)*
Breaking Story 116 *(11f,Dun,SD,Dec 20)*
Breath Caught 108 *(10f,Cfd,SD,Sep 28)*
Breathless Times 105 *(7f,Cfd,SD,Sep 14)*
Breathtaking Look 105 *(8f,Lin,SS,Oct 31)*
Breden 108 *(8f,Lin,SD,Jan 12)*
Brexitmeansbrexit 106 *(10f,Lin,SD,Mar 1)*
Brian The Snail 111 *(6f,Ncs,SS,Jun 29)*
Brigham Young 103 *(7f,Kem,SS,Aug 14)*
Bright Eyed 104 *(11f,Dun,SD,Jan 4)*
Brittanic 105 *(8f,Cfd,SD,Mar 15)*
Brockagh Cailin 107 *(8f,Kem,SS,Jan 4)*
Brockey Rise 103 *(6f,Wol,SD,Apr 6)*
Brokopondo 104 *(12f,Dun,SD,Sep 27)*
Bronagh's Belle 111 *(16f,Dun,SD,Nov 29)*
Brother In Arms 103 *(10f,Cfd,SD,Dec 12)*
Brothers In Arms 109 *(8f,Dun,SD,Dec 3)*
Broughton Excels 104 *(6f,Cfd,SD,Sep 26)*
Broughtons Flare 103 *(6f,Cfd,SD,Aug 29)*
Bruinneall 106 *(12f,Dun,SD,Apr 17)*
Brushwork 112 *(6f,Ncs,SD,Dec 6)*
Bubble And Squeak 105 *(9f,Wol,SD,Dec 2)*
Buccaneers Vault 104 *(6f,Ncs,SD,Sep 27)*
Buckingham 105 *(7f,Cfd,SD,Jly 6)*
Buckman Tavern 109 *(14f,Cfd,SD,Aug 10)*
Bugler Bob 104 *(6f,Ncs,SD,Oct 18)*
Building Bridges 107 *(12f,Dun,SD,Sep 27)*
Buniann 108 *(5f,Ncs,SS,Sep 6)*
Burford Brown 103 *(5f,Ncs,SD,Apr 19)*
Buridan 105 *(6f,Ncs,SD,Oct 22)*
Burmese Waltz 104 *(6f,Dun,SD,Apr 14)*
Burren View Lady 104 *(6f,Dun,SD,Apr 24)*
Burtonwood 103 *(5f,Ncs,SD,Dec 14)*
Busby 109 *(7f,Cfd,SD,Sep 14)*
Busy Street 113 *(16f,Ncs,SD,Jan 22)*
Buzz 105 *(12½f,Ncs,SD,Apr 19)*
Buzz Killington 106 *(8f,Dun,SD,Oct 4)*
Bye Bye Hong Kong 116 *(8f,Cfd,SD,Apr 11)*
Bye Bye Lady 107 *(12f,Wol,SD,Oct 30)*

C Note 103 *(10f,Lin,SD,Feb 1)*
C'Est No Mour 107 *(11f,Kem,SS,Oct 9)*
Caballero 106 *(7f,Ncs,SD,Dec 14)*
Cachao 111 *(8f,Mey,FT,Nov 7)*
Cache Queen 106 *(11f,Dun,SD,Oct 25)*
Cacique Royale 109 *(12f,Dun,SD,Sep 27)*
Cadre Du Noir 106 *(8f,Kem,SS,Oct 2)*
Caesar's Comet 103 *(8f,Dun,SD,Oct 4)*
Calder Prince 107 *(9f,Wol,SD,Mar 16)*
California Jumbo 113 *(8f,Mey,FT,Dec 5)*
California Lad 106 *(12f,Wol,SD,May 31)*
California Love 107 *(8f,Lin,SS,Oct 31)*
Call Me Ginger 105 *(6f,Ncs,SS,Feb 20)*
Call Me Grumpy 107 *(7f,Kem,SS,Mar 11)*
Call Out Loud 105 *(7f,Lin,SD,Mar 13)*
Calling Out 106 *(10f,Cfd,SD,May 2)*
Calling The Wind 104 *(12f,Lin,SD,Dec 28)*
Calling Time 111 *(8f,Dun,SD,Dec 18)*
Camachess 105 *(6f,Ncs,SD,Mar 8)*
Camanche Grey 103 *(6f,Ncs,SD,Apr 30)*
Camelot Rakti 105 *(8f,Cfd,SD,Oct 26)*
Candelisa 104 *(8f,Lin,SD,Dec 30)*
Canford Bay 109 *(5f,Wol,SD,Dec 3)*
Canford Heights 105 *(16f,Ncs,SS,Jun 29)*

Cantiniere 108 *(11f,Kem,SS,Oct 31)*
Canvassed 105 *(8f,Kem,SS,Apr 3)*
Cape Agulhas 104 *(11f,Dun,SD,Mar 15)*
Cape Greco 107 *(7f,Cfd,SD,Feb 2)*
Cape Victory 109 *(9½f,Wol,SD,Aug 30)*
Capezzano 121 *(8f,Mey,FT,Jan 31)*
Capla Huntress 103 *(12f,Wol,SD,Oct 3)*
Caplin 109 *(12f,Wol,SD,Mar 28)*
Cappadocia 106 *(6f,Dun,SD,Apr 24)*
Cappananty Con 111 *(5f,Wol,SD,May 7)*
Capriolette 107 *(10f,Lin,SD,Dec 18)*
Captain Dion 103 *(6f,Sth,SD,Mar 27)*
Captain Joy 111 *(8f,Dun,SD,Jan 11)*
Captain Lars 110 *(5f,Lin,SD,Mar 2)*
Caradoc 105 *(10f,Lin,SD,Nov 16)*
Cardsharp 109 *(7f,Lin,SD,Mar 13)*
Carnwennan 112 *(16f,Ncs,SS,Jun 29)*
Caronda 108 *(11f,Dun,SD,Nov 6)*
Carried 112 *(11f,Dun,SD,Feb 22)*
Casa Comigo 106 *(16f,Lin,SD,Jan 23)*
Casa Romano 103 *(8f,Dun,SD,Apr 24)*
Casanova 109 *(9½f,Wol,SD,Aug 31)*
Cash N Carrie 103 *(10f,Cfd,SD,Sep 19)*
Cashel 104 *(8f,Kem,SS,Jan 16)*
Caspar The Cub 111 *(12f,Kem,SS,Feb 16)*
Castle Hill Cassie 106 *(7f,Wol,SD,Jan 2)*
Castle Quarter 103 *(7f,Ncs,SD,Aug 8)*
Castlelyons 109 *(16f,Kem,SS,Jan 5)*
Catapult 104 *(7f,Sth,SS,Feb 21)*
Cautious Approach 109 *(11f,Dun,SD,May 3)*
Cayirli 107 *(16f,Kem,SS,Jan 5)*
Celtic Prince 114 *(8f,Mey,FT,Dec 5)*
Cenotaph 113 *(6f,Lin,SD,Feb 2)*
Central City 105 *(10f,Lin,SD,Feb 1)*
Certain Lad 110 *(8f,Cfd,SD,Apr 11)*
Chablis 104 *(8f,Dun,SD,Nov 1)*
Chagall 106 *(8f,Dun,SD,Nov 29)*
Chairmanoftheboard 105 *(8f,Kem,SS,Oct 16)*
Chaleur 109 *(8f,Lin,SS,Oct 31)*
Champagne Marengo 109 *(14f,Cfd,SD,Aug 10)*
Champagne Rules 111 *(12½f,Ncs,SS,Mar 29)*
Champarisi 110 *(12f,Sth,SD,Mar 12)*
Champion Brogie 103 *(7f,Lin,SD,Dec 31)*
Champs De Reves 104 *(10f,Cfd,SD,Oct 31)*
Channel Packet 106 *(10f,Cfd,SD,Mar 7)*
Chaparral Dream 111 *(12f,Dun,SD,Mar 8)*
Chapelli 105 *(6f,Cfd,SD,May 2)*
Charcor 118 *(11f,Dun,SD,Dec 20)*
Charles Kingsley 107 *(12f,Wol,SD,Apr 22)*
Charles Molson 108 *(7f,Cfd,SD,Aug 31)*
Charlie D 106 *(12f,Wol,SD,Jly 17)*
Charming Guest 103 *(6f,Cfd,SD,Mar 7)*
Charming Kid 108 *(6f,Dun,SD,Jan 18)*
Chatham House 103 *(7f,Cfd,SD,Jly 23)*
Cheng Gong 104 *(12f,Wol,SD,Sep 7)*
Chess Grand Master 107 *(16f,Dun,SD,Feb 8)*
Chess Master 115 *(6f,Mey,FT,Apr 12)*
Chetwynd Abbey 103 *(16½f,Sth,SD,May 8)*
Chevallier 108 *(8f,Lin,SD,Jan 26)*
Chica De La Noche 107 *(6f,Cfd,SD,Mar 28)*
Chicago Doll 110 *(12f,Wol,SD,Aug 31)*
Chiefofchiefs 114 *(10f,Lin,SD,Feb 2)*
Chil Chil 107 *(6f,Kem,SS,Sep 6)*
Chitra 104 *(5f,Lin,SD,Dec 21)*
Chocco Star 106 *(5f,Wol,SD,Dec 2)*
Choice Encounter 107 *(6f,Ncs,SD,Apr 1)*
Chookie Dunedin 106 *(6f,Ncs,SS,Feb 18)*
Choosey 104 *(5f,Wol,SD,Oct 3)*
Chosen World 103 *(7f,Ncs,SS,Feb 20)*
Ciao 108 *(16f,Dun,SD,Dec 18)*
Circle Dream 107 *(6f,Mey,FT,Oct 24)*
Circus Couture 106 *(12f,Lin,SD,Dec 21)*
Cirque Royal 104 *(12f,Lin,SD,Mar 15)*
Citta D'Oro 106 *(9½f,Wol,SD,Feb 21)*
City Tour 108 *(11f,Kem,SS,Dec 11)*
Cityman 105 *(6f,Dun,SD,Nov 1)*
Claim The Roses 112 *(8f,Mey,FT,Jan 19)*
Claire Underwood 111 *(12½f,Ncs,SD,Jly 27)*
Clap Your Hands 113 *(12f,Wol,SD,Dec 26)*
Classic Design 108 *(9½f,Wol,SD,Dec 27)*
Classic Pursuit 105 *(6f,Ncs,SD,Apr 1)*
Clayton Hall 110 *(12½f,Ncs,SD,Dec 6)*
Cliara 103 *(11f,Dun,SD,Oct 11)*
Clifftop 106 *(8f,Dun,SD,Nov 29)*
Clipsham Tiger 105 *(8f,Sth,SD,Nov 9)*
Clonville 104 *(7f,Dun,SD,Oct 30)*
Cloudlam 110 *(10f,Ncs,SD,Jan 2)*
Cnoc An Oir 105 *(8f,Dun,SD,Nov 1)*
Coach Bombay 103 *(11f,Dun,SD,Jan 4)*
Coal Front 117 *(8f,Mey,FT,Mar 30)*
Coastal Cyclone 106 *(6f,Wol,SD,Jan 30)*
Coeur De Lion 109 *(16f,Ncs,SS,Jun 29)*
Cogital 110 *(16f,Lin,SD,Aug 31)*
Cold Harbour 107 *(12f,Sth,SD,Dec 29)*
Colfer Me 111 *(8f,Dun,SD,Mar 6)*
Collide 110 *(12f,Kem,SS,Dec 4)*
Colonel Slade 107 *(9f,Wol,SD,Oct 19)*
Colwood 109 *(16f,Lin,SD,Aug 31)*
Come Back And Stay 104 *(11f,Dun,SD,Oct 11)*
Come September 105 *(8f,Dun,SD,Nov 1)*
Comedia Eria 107 *(7f,Cfd,SD,Jun 19)*
Comhghairdeas 106 *(7f,Dun,SD,Dec 3)*
Comicas 113 *(6f,Mey,FT,Mar 9)*
Commander Cole 114 *(10f,Cfd,SD,Sep 28)*
Commander Han 108 *(6f,Ncs,SD,Dec 6)*

Compas Scoobie 106 *(6f,Kem,SS,Mar 9)*
Concierge 103 *(5f,Cfd,SD,Aug 16)*
Confident Kid 104 *(8f,Dun,SD,Nov 20)*
Confrontational 110 *(7f,Dun,SD,Jan 25)*
Conkering Hero 103 *(16f,Kem,SS,Jly 10)*
Consequences 105 *(6f,Cfd,SD,Aug 29)*
Contingency Fee 104 *(12f,Sth,SD,Apr 17)*
Continuum 109 *(16f,Lin,SD,Aug 31)*
Contrive 103 *(10f,Lin,SD,Nov 16)*
Convara 112 *(12f,Dun,SD,Sep 27)*
Coolagh Magic 103 *(5f,Sth,SS,Jan 31)*
Copper Knight 111 *(5f,Ncs,SS,Jun 28)*
Coral Beach 108 *(8f,Lin,SS,Oct 31)*
Corazon Espinado 107 *(7f,Lin,SD,Dec 31)*
Corinthia Knight 115 *(5f,Dun,SD,Oct 18)*
Corked 104 *(9f,Wol,SD,Feb 20)*
Coronation Cottage 103 *(5f,Wol,SD,Nov 16)*
Cosmeapolitan 108 *(11f,Kem,SS,Mar 30)*
Cosmelli 110 *(16f,Ncs,SD,Jan 22)*
Cosmic Landscape 108 *(11f,Kem,SS,Feb 28)*
Cosmic Law 113 *(6f,Ncs,SS,Jun 29)*
Cosmo Charlie 112 *(9½f,Mey,FT,Feb 7)*
Cote D'Azur 104 *(8f,Ncs,SD,Nov 8)*
Cotton Club 107 *(16f,Ncs,SS,Oct 2)*
Count Calabash 115 *(12f,Kem,SS,Feb 16)*
Count D'orsay 104 *(6f,Dun,SD,Mar 15)*
Count Of Carabass 108 *(7f,Dun,SD,Nov 6)*
Country'N'Western 105 *(12f,Sth,SS,Feb 13)*
Court House 115 *(10f,Lin,SD,Feb 2)*
Cowboy Soldier 111 *(5f,Kem,SS,Apr 20)*
Crafty Hugo 107 *(8f,Dun,SD,Nov 1)*
Creationist 110 *(11f,Kem,SS,Oct 31)*
Creative Talent 104 *(9½f,Wol,SD,Feb 19)*
Creek Harbour 106 *(6f,Cfd,SD,Aug 9)*
Creek Island 104 *(7f,Cfd,SD,Mar 28)*
Crest Of A Wave 106 *(7f,Dun,SD,Jan 25)*
Crimewave 105 *(9½f,Wol,SD,Dec 2)*
Croeso Cymraeg 104 *(12½f,Ncs,SS,Sep 6)*
Crosse Fire 110 *(5f,Sth,SD,Jan 13)*
Crossed Baton 112 *(10f,Lin,SD,Nov 16)*
Crossing The Line 109 *(7f,Kem,SS,Mar 23)*
Crossingoz 110 *(8f,Dun,SD,Feb 15)*
Crotchet 112 *(8f,Dun,SD,Nov 1)*
Crownthorpe 114 *(8f,Ncs,SD,Jun 4)*
Crystal King 109 *(12f,Wol,SD,Apr 27)*
Cuban Hope 108 *(8f,Dun,SD,Mar 15)*
Cuban Spirit 103 *(6f,Wol,SD,Jan 30)*
Cuillin 105 *(12f,Wol,SD,Nov 16)*
Cuppacoco 103 *(5f,Ncs,SS,Oct 2)*
Custard The Dragon 109 *(7f,Ncs,SD,Jan 31)*

Daddies Girl 104 *(8f,Lin,SD,Aug 31)*
Daffg 113 *(8f,Mey,FT,Mar 2)*
Dakota Gold 109 *(5f,Ncs,SS,Jun 28)*
Dalaalaat 106 *(8f,Cfd,SD,Jly 6)*
Dalgarno 110 *(10f,Lin,SD,Dec 21)*
Dalileo 112 *(12f,Dun,SD,Sep 27)*
Dalton 103 *(6f,Ncs,SS,Jun 29)*
Daltrey 103 *(7f,Mey,FT,Mar 14)*
Dame Freya Stark 103 *(8f,Lin,SD,Mar 15)*
Dance Alone 103 *(8f,Dun,SD,Sep 20)*
Dance Legend 103 *(13f,Lin,SS,Oct 31)*
Dancing Brave Bear 104 *(8f,Kem,SS,Apr 20)*
Dancing On A Dream 108 *(7f,Dun,SD,Oct 11)*
Dandhu 107 *(8f,Kem,SS,Nov 20)*
Dandilion 103 *(6f,Lin,SD,Aug 19)*
Dandy Belle 103 *(8f,Dun,SD,Mar 15)*
Dandy Highwayman 105 *(6f,Ncs,SD,Jan 17)*
Dandy's Beano 109 *(5f,Ncs,SD,Jun 28)*
Dandys Gold 106 *(6f,Dun,SD,Jan 28)*
Danehill Desert 103 *(5f,Ncs,SS,Mar 29)*
Danehill Kodiac 108 *(14f,Cfd,SD,May 9)*
Dante's View 105 *(10f,Cfd,SD,Jun 8)*
Danz Gift 104 *(5f,Dun,SD,Feb 1)*
Danzan 103 *(6f,Ncs,SS,Feb 18)*
Dapper Man 107 *(5f,Cfd,SD,Jly 5)*
Dargel 105 *(8f,Kem,SS,Nov 4)*
Daring Guest 103 *(6f,Cfd,SD,May 27)*
Dark Alliance 103 *(7f,Wol,SD,Jan 2)*
Dark Magic 107 *(7f,Dun,SD,Dec 18)*
Dark Miracle 113 *(12f,Wol,SD,May 13)*
Dark Red 112 *(10f,Cfd,SD,May 23)*
Dark Side Dream 103 *(5f,Wol,SD,Nov 16)*
Dark Vision 115 *(8f,Cfd,SD,Apr 11)*
Dash D'or 106 *(6f,Dun,SD,Nov 29)*
Dashing Poet 104 *(8f,Sth,SD,Jan 24)*
Davy Lamp 112 *(8f,Mey,FT,Dec 5)*
Dawaaween 103 *(7f,Kem,SS,Oct 16)*
Dawn Commando 104 *(8f,Kem,SS,Mar 27)*
Dawn Crusade 104 *(10f,Lin,SS,Jan 30)*
Dawn Delight 105 *(6f,Ncs,SS,Feb 15)*
Dayereh 109 *(11f,Dun,SD,Mar 8)*
Dazzling Rock 105 *(16f,Cfd,SD,Apr 30)*
Deal A Dollar 114 *(12½f,Ncs,SD,Sep 17)*
Deansgate 104 *(7f,Ncs,SD,Jan 31)*
Decision Maker 108 *(5f,Ncs,SD,Jun 4)*
Deeds Not Words 108 *(5f,Ncs,SD,Mar 8)*
Deep Intrigue 108 *(6f,Ncs,SS,Jun 29)*
Deference 105 *(8f,Lin,SD,Oct 3)*
Defilade 103 *(11f,Dun,SD,Oct 25)*
Dehbashi 109 *(10f,Mey,FT,Apr 12)*
Deia Glory 108 *(5f,Dun,SD,Oct 18)*
Deja 111 *(12f,Kem,SS,Jly 3)*
Delicate Kiss 107 *(8f,Lin,SD,Feb 1)*

Delilah Park 105 *(7f,Kem,SS,Sep 7)*
Delphinia 107 *(13f,Lin,SS,Oct 31)*
Denzille Lane 107 *(7f,Mey,FT,Jan 5)*
Deputise 103 *(6f,Lin,SD,Apr 19)*
Derek Duval 106 *(10f,Cfd,SD,Jan 26)*
Derevo 112 *(12½f,Ncs,SD,Jly 27)*
Derma Louvre 108 *(9½f,Mey,FT,Mar 30)*
Desert Caravan 104 *(9f,Wol,SD,Nov 18)*
Desert Doctor 112 *(6f,Cfd,SD,Jan 24)*
Desert Fire 111 *(10f,Cfd,SD,Sep 4)*
Desert Fox 106 *(6f,Cfd,SD,Aug 29)*
Desert Lion 107 *(8f,Cfd,SD,Oct 26)*
Desert Ruler 109 *(12½f,Ncs,SS,Feb 1)*
Desert Skyline 107 *(16f,Ncs,SD,Jun 29)*
Desert Wind 115 *(11f,Kem,SS,Mar 30)*
Diamond Lady 107 *(7f,Lin,SS,Apr 6)*
Diamond Reflection 104 *(11f,Kem,SS,Apr 10)*
Dilmun Dynasty 104 *(10f,Cfd,SD,Jun 8)*
Diocles Of Rome 107 *(7f,Cfd,SD,Sep 14)*
Dirchill 108 *(6f,Ncs,SD,Apr 1)*
Directory 106 *(8f,Sth,SD,May 1)*
Distant Chimes 107 *(12f,Wol,SD,Jly 17)*
Distant Mirage 105 *(6f,Lin,SD,Mar 15)*
Divine Approach 103 *(12f,Dun,SD,Nov 1)*
Divine Image 114 *(9½f,Mey,FT,Mar 9)*
Divine Messenger 108 *(8f,Kem,SS,Apr 12)*
Dizzy G 107 *(6f,Wol,SD,Oct 19)*
Dobrianka 105 *(12f,Kem,SS,Sep 6)*
Doc Sportello 104 *(6f,Ncs,SD,Dec 6)*
Doctor Sardonicus 105 *(5f,Wol,SD,Feb 21)*
Documenting 112 *(7f,Wol,SS,Feb 6)*
Dodgy Bob 106 *(6f,Wol,SD,Jan 30)*
Dolkong 116 *(10f,Mey,FT,Feb 28)*
Dollar Value 103 *(7f,Wol,SD,Jan 28)*
Dolly Dupree 103 *(8f,Sth,SD,Mar 7)*
Domagnano 103 *(10f,Cfd,SD,May 23)*
Dominus 105 *(7f,Cfd,SD,Oct 17)*
Dommersen 109 *(10f,Ncs,SS,Jan 6)*
Don Armado 105 *(6f,Kem,SS,Jan 4)*
Don't Do It 107 *(10f,Cfd,SD,Feb 14)*
Donncha 111 *(7f,Kem,SS,Mar 9)*
Dono Di Dio 106 *(11f,Kem,SS,Apr 3)*
Dotted Swiss 103 *(6f,Wol,SD,Jan 11)*
Double Legend 105 *(12f,Kem,SS,Mar 9)*
Double Talkin Jive 103 *(11f,Dun,SD,Dec 6)*
Double Up 103 *(6f,Wol,SD,Dec 19)*
Downdraft 107 *(12f,Dun,SD,May 3)*
Drafted 115 *(6f,Mey,FT,Mar 9)*
Dragon Mall 108 *(9½f,Wol,SS,Feb 6)*
Drakefell 109 *(5f,Wol,SD,Mar 9)*
Drakensberg 109 *(12f,Dun,SD,Mar 6)*
Dream Catching 105 *(6f,Kem,SS,Sep 11)*
Dream Focus 105 *(12f,Dun,SD,Mar 22)*
Dream Magic 111 *(12f,Wol,SD,Jan 30)*
Dream Of Dreams 109 *(6f,Cfd,SD,Apr 25)*
Dream Today 106 *(6f,Wol,SD,Oct 5)*
Dreamboat Dave 104 *(10f,Cfd,SD,Dec 12)*
Drombeg Duke 107 *(7f,Dun,SD,Oct 18)*
Dubai Blue 114 *(8f,Lin,SD,Aug 31)*
Dubai Future 107 *(12f,Kem,SS,Nov 19)*
Dubai Legacy 104 *(7f,Ncs,SD,May 3)*
Dubai Rainbow 111 *(8f,Dun,SD,Dec 3)*
Dubai Tradition 110 *(12f,Wol,SD,Oct 19)*
Dubai Warrior 114 *(10f,Lin,SD,Dec 21)*
Dubawi Fifty 113 *(16f,Ncs,SD,Dec 14)*
Dubious Affair 103 *(10f,Cfd,SD,Nov 28)*
Duckett's Grove 108 *(10f,Cfd,SD,May 2)*
Ducky Mallon 110 *(7f,Dun,SD,Nov 20)*
Duhallow Noelie 112 *(8f,Dun,SD,Apr 5)*
Duke Cosimo 109 *(6f,Ncs,SS,Jan 12)*
Duke Of Alba 105 *(9½f,Wol,SD,Feb 21)*
Duke Of Waspington 107 *(11f,Dun,SD,Jan 4)*
Dunkerron 109 *(6f,Kem,SS,Nov 29)*
Dunkirk Harbour 111 *(8f,Dun,SD,Apr 24)*
Durrell 108 *(10f,Cfd,SD,Jun 8)*
Dutch Treat 103 *(7f,Wol,SD,Nov 16)*
Dynamo Walt 110 *(5f,Wol,SD,Dec 19)*

Eacharn 107 *(7f,Dun,SD,Jan 25)*
Eardley Road 103 *(6f,Kem,SS,Feb 28)*
Earl Of Bunnacurry 104 *(12f,Dun,SD,Apr 17)*
Early Call 106 *(5f,Dun,SD,Dec 6)*
Early Strike 106 *(11f,Dun,SD,Nov 6)*
Earth And Sky 106 *(8f,Kem,SS,Nov 27)*
East Indies 103 *(16f,Kem,SS,Jan 5)*
East Street Revue 103 *(6f,Ncs,SD,Dec 18)*
Eastern Racer 107 *(8f,Dun,SD,Apr 24)*
Eastern Star 104 *(6f,Dun,SD,Oct 18)*
Easy Pass 103 *(11f,Dun,SD,Jan 4)*
Ebqaa 107 *(12f,Wol,SD,May 31)*
Echo 114 *(12½f,Ncs,SS,Mar 29)*
Ecoeye 104 *(7f,Dun,SD,Dec 3)*
Edaraat 103 *(8f,Kem,SS,Sep 23)*
Eddystone Rock 110 *(16f,Ncs,SD,Jan 22)*
Eden Gardens 105 *(10f,Cfd,SD,Nov 19)*
Eden Rose 111 *(16f,Lin,SD,Mar 25)*
Edification 112 *(12f,Dun,SD,Oct 4)*
Eeh Bah Gum 111 *(5f,Ncs,SS,Jun 28)*
Eesha My Flower 103 *(9½f,Wol,SD,Dec 2)*
Eirene 105 *(6f,Cfd,SD,Apr 25)*
El Borracho 108 *(14f,Cfd,SD,Aug 29)*
El Chapo 106 *(8f,Mey,FT,Mar 2)*
El Chico Mejor 103 *(11f,Dun,SD,Oct 25)*
El Ghazwani 110 *(10f,Cfd,SD,Sep 28)*
El Gumryah 104 *(8f,Kem,SS,Apr 20)*
El Hombre 111 *(6f,Ncs,SD,Dec 6)*
El Misk 111 *(12f,Wol,SD,Oct 19)*
Ela Katrina 104 *(12f,Kem,SS,Nov 19)*
Eldelbar 103 *(6f,Wol,SD,Oct 23)*
Elegiac 105 *(16f,Cfd,SD,Mar 7)*
Elenora Delight 103 *(8f,Kem,SS,Jan 23)*
Elerfaan 106 *(7f,Wol,SD,Apr 23)*
Eleuthera 104 *(5f,Dun,SD,Dec 18)*
Elite Trooper Grey 109 *(11f,Dun,SD,Oct 11)*
Elixsoft 104 *(8f,Sth,SD,Dec 29)*
Elizabeth Way 105 *(11f,Dun,SD,Oct 25)*
Eljaddaaf 103 *(7f,Lin,SD,Dec 31)*
Elusif 104 *(7f,Kem,SS,Feb 27)*
Elysees Palace 110 *(10f,Ncs,SS,Jan 6)*
Elzaam's Dream 105 *(7f,Wol,SD,Dec 2)*
Emadee 106 *(5f,Dun,SD,Apr 5)*
Ember's Glow 104 *(12f,Kem,SS,Jan 23)*
Embour 110 *(6f,Kem,SS,Apr 20)*
Emenem 107 *(12f,Kem,SS,Feb 16)*
Emily Goldfinch 108 *(6f,Cfd,SD,Apr 11)*
Eminence 112 *(11f,Dun,SD,Oct 11)*
Emirates Empire 106 *(12f,Wol,SD,Apr 13)*
Emirates Knight 105 *(9f,Wol,SD,Apr 27)*
Emphatic 107 *(11f,Dun,SD,Oct 25)*
Empire Line 113 *(6f,Dun,SD,Mar 15)*
Empire State 108 *(5f,Dun,SD,Apr 14)*
Enchanted Linda 105 *(5f,Wol,SD,Oct 23)*
Encoded 103 *(5f,Ncs,SD,Jan 2)*
Encore D'Or 115 *(5f,Ncs,SD,Jan 22)*
Encrypted 109 *(6f,Ncs,SS,Jun 29)*
Encryption 105 *(16f,Kem,SS,Jly 10)*
Enjazaat 105 *(6f,Kem,SS,Oct 9)*
Enough Said 108 *(5f,Dun,SD,Nov 15)*
Entangling 111 *(8f,Kem,SS,Nov 19)*
Enthaar 107 *(6f,Cfd,SD,Mar 7)*
Envisaging 104 *(7f,Cfd,SD,Nov 7)*
Envoy 103 *(16f,Kem,SS,Jan 5)*
Enzemble 107 *(8f,Kem,SS,Feb 2)*
Epeius 109 *(6f,Ncs,SD,Jan 31)*
Epitaph 112 *(12f,Wol,SD,Jan 30)*
Equiano Springs 111 *(6f,Ncs,SS,Feb 18)*
Equimou 106 *(5f,Cfd,SD,Apr 4)*
Equitant 103 *(7f,Dun,SD,Oct 18)*
Equitation 109 *(5f,Ncs,SD,Jan 8)*
Erissimus Maximus 107 *(6f,Kem,SS,Mar 9)*
Escapability 109 *(11f,Kem,SS,Feb 28)*
Espresso Freddo 103 *(9f,Wol,SD,Feb 23)*
Esprit De Corps 105 *(7f,Sth,SD,Oct 10)*
Essential 105 *(6f,Ncs,SS,Feb 15)*
Estihdaaf 110 *(9½f,Mey,SD,Jan 24)*
Estijmaam 109 *(16f,Dun,SD,Nov 29)*
Eternal Sun 105 *(5f,Sth,SD,Jan 10)*
Etijaah 110 *(9½f,Mey,FT,Feb 7)*
Etisalat 109 *(8f,Mey,FT,Mar 2)*
Everkyllachy 108 *(5f,Wol,SD,Dec 2)*
Every Breath 105 *(11f,Dun,SD,Jan 4)*
Everyhouronthehour 109 *(8f,Dun,SD,Nov 20)*
Exalted Angel 104 *(5f,Ncs,SD,Apr 19)*
Exceeding Power 108 *(11f,Kem,SS,Oct 31)*
Excelcius 107 *(8f,Dun,SD,Oct 11)*
Excellent George 106 *(6f,Cfd,SD,Sep 26)*
Exchequer 112 *(7f,Kem,SS,Mar 9)*
Exclusive Waters 109 *(11f,Dun,SD,Mar 22)*
Exec Chef 114 *(10f,Cfd,SD,May 23)*
Executive Force 111 *(10f,Kem,SS,Mar 6)*
Expressionism 107 *(12f,Kem,SS,Aug 7)*
Extra Elusive 114 *(10f,Kem,SS,Mar 30)*
Extra Large 108 *(7f,Mey,FT,Mar 14)*
Extrasolar 103 *(6f,Ncs,SD,Nov 4)*
Extreme Appeal 104 *(16f,Ncs,SS,Apr 11)*
Extrodinair 109 *(7f,Cfd,SD,Dec 13)*
Eyeoweyou 105 *(8f,Dun,SD,Mar 29)*
Ezanak 103 *(12f,Sth,SD,Jan 13)*

Fabricate 110 *(10f,Kem,SS,Mar 30)*
Fair Cop 107 *(5f,Ncs,SD,Mar 8)*
Fair Power 107 *(10f,Cfd,SD,Sep 19)*
Fairy Fort 103 *(8f,Dun,SD,Mar 29)*
Fairy Tale 103 *(11f,Kem,SS,Jun 26)*
Falcon Cliffs 105 *(16f,Lin,SD,Mar 2)*
Fame N Fortune 107 *(10f,Cfd,SD,Sep 19)*
Family Fortunes 110 *(8f,Kem,SS,Feb 2)*
Fanaar 109 *(8f,Cfd,SD,Apr 11)*
Fancy Footings 106 *(8f,Sth,SD,Nov 7)*
Fantastic Flyer 110 *(6f,Cfd,SD,Oct 26)*
Fantasy Justifier 103 *(6f,Wol,SD,Jan 30)*
Fantasy Keeper 105 *(5f,Sth,SD,Aug 26)*
Fard 103 *(7f,Ncs,SS,Aug 30)*
Farnese 107 *(8f,Dun,SD,Sep 20)*
Farnham 103 *(7f,Cfd,SD,Oct 24)*
Farook 104 *(7f,Mey,FT,Apr 5)*
Fascinating Spirit 105 *(8f,Dun,SD,Oct 4)*
Fashaar 104 *(8f,Dun,SD,Nov 6)*
Fastar 103 *(7f,Wol,SD,Dec 10)*
Fastidious 104 *(8f,Dun,SD,Feb 15)*
Fayez 109 *(10f,Cfd,SD,Jun 20)*
Faylaq 106 *(11f,Kem,SS,Sep 25)*
Fearless Warrior 105 *(11f,Kem,SS,Dec 11)*
Fearsome 110 *(12f,Wol,SD,Mar 4)*
Felix The Poet 105 *(8f,Cfd,SD,Jly 6)*
Fendale 111 *(6f,Ncs,SD,Dec 6)*
Fennaan 103 *(10f,Cfd,SD,Jun 20)*
Fern Owl 103 *(16½f,Sth,SD,Mar 30)*
Festina Plente 110 *(8f,Dun,SD,Nov 1)*
Festival Of Ages 110 *(16½f,Wol,SD,Jan 14)*
Fiannaiocht 104 *(11f,Dun,SD,Jan 4)*
Field Gun 109 *(7f,Cfd,SD,Feb 2)*
Fields Of Athenry 106 *(9f,Wol,SD,Oct 18)*
Fields Of Dreams 104 *(8f,Lin,SD,Dec 11)*
Fiesole 103 *(12f,Kem,SS,Oct 28)*
Fight Hero 109 *(6f,Mey,FT,Mar 30)*
Fighting Temeraire 110 *(7f,Cfd,SD,Dec 13)*
Film Noir 103 *(8f,Dun,SD,Mar 15)*
Final 103 *(12½f,Ncs,SD,Jly 27)*
Final Attack 104 *(9f,Wol,SD,Mar 25)*
Final Frontier 103 *(7f,Kem,SS,Oct 15)*
Final Go 105 *(6f,Ncs,SD,Sep 27)*
Final Orders 103 *(11f,Dun,SD,Dec 6)*
Finvarra 103 *(7f,Dun,SD,Jan 11)*
Fire Diamond 105 *(8f,Sth,SD,Apr 29)*
Fire Fighting 107 *(12f,Lin,SD,Mar 22)*
Firelight 103 *(6f,Kem,SS,Oct 28)*
Firmament 110 *(7f,Cfd,SD,Sep 14)*
Firnas 111 *(10f,Mey,FT,Dec 5)*
First Call 110 *(12½f,Ncs,SS,Mar 29)*
First Excel 104 *(5f,Ncs,SD,Jan 8)*
First Flight 103 *(10f,Ncs,SS,Jun 28)*
First In Line 110 *(14f,Cfd,SD,Nov 2)*
First Link 104 *(7f,Lin,SD,Apr 6)*
First Response 109 *(9½f,Wol,SD,Dec 27)*
Fivehundredmiles 110 *(8f,Dun,SD,Apr 5)*
Fizzy Feet 110 *(5f,Wol,SD,Oct 23)*
Flaming Marvel 109 *(12f,Wol,SD,Jan 11)*
Flamma Clarus 105 *(16f,Dun,SD,Mar 29)*
Flighty Almighty 104 *(9f,Wol,SD,Apr 6)*
Flood Defence 105 *(12f,Wol,SD,Jan 21)*
Florencio 106 *(8f,Kem,SS,Oct 10)*
Fly Lightly 104 *(10f,Lin,SD,Jun 4)*
Fly The Flag 104 *(10f,Cfd,SD,Jly 6)*
Fly True 103 *(7f,Sth,SD,Mar 12)*
Followthesteps 105 *(6f,Wol,SD,Apr 6)*
Fool For You 113 *(5f,Ncs,SS,Jun 28)*
Foolaad 109 *(5f,Ncs,SD,Jan 8)*
Footsteps At Dawn 108 *(8f,Dun,SD,Apr 5)*
Forbidden Dance 103 *(12f,Wol,SD,Nov 16)*
Forbidden Planet 118 *(11f,Kem,SS,Mar 30)*
Foreign Legion 103 *(6f,Cfd,SD,Feb 4)*
Forest View 109 *(12f,Dun,SD,Sep 27)*
Formal Order 105 *(8f,Dun,SD,Jan 11)*
Forseti 103 *(8f,Sth,SD,Dec 29)*
Four Mile Bridge 104 *(11f,Kem,SS,Oct 2)*
Fox Dream 106 *(8f,Dun,SD,Feb 15)*
Fox Power 103 *(8f,Cfd,SD,Dec 12)*
Fox Premier 112 *(10f,Cfd,SD,May 9)*
Foxrush Take Time 103 *(10f,Cfd,SD,Mar 2)*
Foxtrot Knight 106 *(5f,Wol,SD,Apr 2)*
Foxy Forever 108 *(5f,Wol,SD,Dec 19)*
Foza 103 *(11f,Dun,SD,Jan 25)*
Framley Garth 103 *(11f,Kem,SS,Apr 3)*
Francophilia 104 *(9½f,Wol,SD,Feb 1)*
Freebe Rocks 104 *(10f,Lin,SD,Jan 19)*
Freedom And Wheat 103 *(9f,Wol,SD,Dec 16)*
Freerolling 108 *(8f,Kem,SS,Sep 7)*
Freescape 117 *(8f,Dun,SD,Dec 6)*
Fresnel 114 *(11f,Dun,SD,Sep 27)*
Fridtjof Nansen 108 *(5f,Dun,SD,Sep 20)*
Frosty 104 *(8f,Dun,SD,Nov 1)*
Fujaira King 106 *(6f,Dun,SD,Oct 18)*
Full Intention 107 *(7f,Cfd,SD,Dec 13)*
Funny Kid 114 *(16f,Ncs,SD,Dec 14)*
Furia Cruzada 110 *(10f,Mey,FT,Apr 12)*
Furious 105 *(6f,Cfd,SD,Jun 20)*
Furni Factors 103 *(5f,Ncs,SD,Mar 1)*
Furzig 109 *(10f,Ncs,SD,Jly 27)*
Futuristic 108 *(6f,Ncs,SD,Oct 18)*
Fuwairt 107 *(7f,Kem,SS,Feb 6)*

Gabrial The Tiger 103 *(7f,Wol,SD,Mar 12)*
Gabrials Boy 108 *(9½f,Wol,SD,Dec 27)*
Galileo Silver 103 *(11f,Kem,SS,Jly 10)*
Galileo's Spear 106 *(16½f,Sth,SD,Mar 30)*
Galles 105 *(10f,Mey,FT,Apr 12)*
Gallic 107 *(10f,Cfd,SD,Aug 31)*
Gallipoli 108 *(7f,Lin,SD,Mar 13)*
Galvanize 112 *(8f,Mey,FT,Apr 12)*
Gantier 107 *(9½f,Wol,SD,Feb 21)*
Garbanzo 106 *(12f,Kem,SS,Aug 7)*
Garth Rockett 103 *(7f,Lin,SD,Nov 23)*
Gas Monkey 104 *(10f,Cfd,SD,Apr 1)*
Gasta 112 *(11f,Dun,SD,Feb 22)*
Gates Pass 104 *(10f,Cfd,SD,Mar 7)*
Gatsby Cap 104 *(8f,Dun,SD,Dec 3)*
Gavlar 108 *(16f,Lin,SD,Aug 31)*
Geetanjali 110 *(11f,Kem,SS,Oct 31)*
Geizy Teizy 103 *(8f,Cfd,SD,Nov 28)*
Gentlemen 109 *(6f,Cfd,SD,Feb 20)*
Geolai 105 *(11f,Dun,SD,Oct 25)*
Geological 115 *(7f,Dun,SD,Nov 20)*
George Bowen 110 *(6f,Kem,SS,Mar 30)*
George Dryden 103 *(5f,Wol,SD,Feb 19)*
George Villiers 117 *(8f,Mey,FT,Mar 2)*
George William 106 *(8f,Kem,SS,Oct 10)*
Georgian Bay 108 *(8f,Dun,SD,Jan 11)*
Geranium 107 *(11f,Kem,SS,Oct 9)*
Gervais 115 *(7f,Mey,FT,Mar 14)*
Getaway Queen 104 *(11f,Dun,SD,Nov 15)*
Getchagetchagetcha 103 *(12f,Wol,SD,Dec 7)*
Ghaith 105 *(6f,Kem,SS,Apr 12)*
Ghaziyah 105 *(8f,Cfd,SD,Jly 23)*
Gibbs Hill 106 *(12f,Kem,SS,Sep 7)*
Gifted Master 108 *(7f,Lin,SS,Oct 31)*
Ginger Fox 109 *(6f,Kem,SS,Nov 19)*
Ginger Jam 105 *(6f,Ncs,SS,Feb 15)*
Gino Wotimean 108 *(12f,Wol,SD,May 13)*
Giogiobbo 111 *(6f,Ncs,SS,Jun 29)*
Giorni Felice 104 *(8f,Dun,SD,Nov 29)*
Girolamo 114 *(12f,Dun,SD,Oct 4)*
Given Choice 103 *(14f,Wol,SD,Jan 7)*
Givepeaceachance 103 *(12f,Wol,SD,May 10)*
Glan Y Gors 105 *(16f,Ncs,SS,Jun 29)*
Gleaming Arch 105 *(5f,Ncs,SD,Sep 17)*
Glen Shiel 104 *(10f,Lin,SD,Dec 4)*
Glenamoy Lad 105 *(6f,Ncs,SD,Dec 6)*
Glendevon 109 *(8f,Kem,SS,Nov 19)*
Glengarry 104 *(7f,Ncs,SD,Jly 27)*
Glenn Coco 110 *(7f,Kem,SS,Mar 11)*
Global Academy 107 *(6f,Kem,SS,Mar 9)*
Global Art 104 *(10f,Cfd,SD,Jan 10)*
Global Falcon 104 *(14f,Cfd,SD,Aug 10)*
Global Gift 103 *(7f,Cfd,SD,Mar 28)*
Global Hope 104 *(6f,Kem,SS,Oct 22)*
Global Melody 105 *(6f,Sth,SD,Dec 19)*
Global Prospector 104 *(6f,Wol,SD,Mar 16)*
Global Tango 109 *(6f,Kem,SS,Mar 27)*
Global Wonder 107 *(10f,Lin,SD,Jan 19)*
Globe Theatre 107 *(11f,Dun,SD,Oct 25)*
Glorious Charmer 105 *(6f,Ncs,SD,Dec 6)*
Glorious Lover 103 *(7f,Ncs,SD,May 3)*
Glory 105 *(8f,Dun,SD,Dec 3)*
Glory Awaits 108 *(8f,Cfd,SD,Aug 23)*
Glory Of Paris 104 *(7f,Cfd,SD,Sep 24)*
Gm Hopkins 108 *(8f,Mey,FT,Mar 9)*
Gnaad 103 *(6f,Lin,SD,Nov 28)*
God Willing 103 *(10f,Ncs,SS,Jan 6)*
Godhead 104 *(8f,Kem,SS,Nov 29)*
Going Native 106 *(12f,Sth,SD,Dec 29)*
Gold Arch 103 *(12f,Wol,SD,Jly 9)*
Gold At Midnight 108 *(6f,Kem,SS,Sep 6)*
Gold Stone 109 *(5f,Ncs,SS,Feb 28)*
Gold Town 110 *(7f,Mey,FT,Feb 21)*
Golden Parade 103 *(6f,Wol,SD,Jly 17)*
Golden Salute 104 *(5f,Wol,SD,Jan 19)*
Golden Valour 112 *(11f,Dun,SD,Dec 20)*
Golden Wolf 103 *(8f,Kem,SS,Nov 19)*
Good Answer 107 *(6f,Kem,SS,Nov 29)*
Good Curry 118 *(8f,Mey,FT,Mar 9)*
Good Effort 112 *(5f,Ncs,SS,Nov 21)*
Good Tidings 110 *(11f,Kem,SS,Oct 31)*
Goodnight Girl 110 *(6f,Cfd,SD,Apr 11)*
Gordon Lord Byron 111 *(6f,Dun,SD,Nov 1)*
Gorgeous General 104 *(6f,Ncs,SD,Apr 29)*
Gorgeous Noora 116 *(6f,Lin,SD,Feb 2)*
Goring 113 *(8f,Lin,SD,Dec 31)*
Gossiping 108 *(8f,Kem,SS,Mar 27)*
Gougane Barra 110 *(8f,Dun,SD,Mar 15)*
Gowanbuster 112 *(5f,Ncs,SS,Mar 29)*
Graceful James 106 *(10f,Lin,SS,Jan 5)*
Gracious John 112 *(5f,Lin,SD,Mar 2)*
Grand Argentier 113 *(10f,Mey,FT,Dec 5)*
Grand Inquisitor 107 *(10f,Cfd,SD,May 31)*
Grandee 107 *(10f,Ncs,SS,Apr 11)*
Grandmaster Flash 114 *(16f,Dun,SD,Nov 29)*
Graphite Storm 105 *(8f,Kem,SS,Oct 16)*
Gravistas 111 *(12f,Wol,SD,May 13)*
Gravity Wave 110 *(12f,Wol,SD,Jan 30)*
Gray Magician 113 *(9½f,Mey,FT,Mar 30)*
Grazeon Roy 110 *(12f,Sth,SD,Nov 9)*
Great Esteem 105 *(9½f,Wol,SD,Aug 31)*
Great Example 105 *(10f,Cfd,SD,May 2)*
Great Suspense 105 *(5f,Wol,SD,Oct 30)*
Grecian Spirit 103 *(9½f,Mey,FT,Jan 19)*
Grey Britain 117 *(16f,Lin,SD,Feb 1)*
Grey D'Ars 104 *(12f,Kem,SS,Aug 21)*
Grey Destiny 104 *(7f,Wol,SD,Jan 28)*
Griffyndor 104 *(8f,Dun,SD,Dec 3)*
Griggy 104 *(5f,Wol,SD,Dec 2)*
Grisons 106 *(6f,Cfd,SD,Sep 24)*
Gronkowski 115 *(10f,Mey,FT,Mar 30)*
Groovy Jazz 109 *(11f,Dun,SD,Mar 22)*
Groupie 104 *(6f,Wol,SD,Oct 23)*
Guandi 104 *(12f,Wol,SD,Nov 16)*
Guardia Svizzera 104 *(5f,Wol,SD,Dec 2)*
Guernsey 111 *(7f,Mey,FT,Mar 2)*
Guiding 104 *(8f,Dun,SD,Nov 1)*
Gulliver 108 *(6f,Lin,SD,Feb 16)*
Gumball 105 *(12f,Lin,SD,Mar 25)*
Gundogdu 119 *(10f,Mey,FT,Mar 14)*
Gunmaker 106 *(6f,Ncs,SD,Apr 30)*
Gunnevera 113 *(10f,Mey,FT,Mar 30)*
Gurkha Friend 108 *(9f,Wol,SD,Mar 16)*
Guroor 108 *(11f,Kem,SS,Oct 2)*
Guvenor's Choice 104 *(9½f,Wol,SS,Feb 6)*

Habah 103 *(9½f,Mey,FT,Feb 21)*
Habub 111 *(7f,Cfd,SD,Sep 14)*
Hackbridge 103 *(10f,Lin,SD,Feb 23)*
Haddaf 109 *(7f,Cfd,SD,Dec 13)*
Hadfield 104 *(16f,Lin,SD,Mar 25)*
Hameem 110 *(12f,Kem,SS,Dec 4)*
Hamley 103 *(12f,Dun,SD,Nov 1)*
Hammer Gun 106 *(7f,Sth,SD,Jan 3)*

Handiwork 107 *(16f,Ncs,SS,Oct 2)*
Happaugue 104 *(8f,Dun,SD,Nov 6)*
Happy Escape 106 *(7f,Kem,SS,Jan 16)*
Haqeeba 107 *(6f,Dun,SD,Apr 24)*
Harbour Breeze 113 *(11f,Kem,SS,May 22)*
Harbour Quay 105 *(12f,Sth,SS,Feb 27)*
Harbour Spirit 106 *(9f,Wol,SD,Oct 18)*
Harbour Vision 108 *(7f,Cfd,SD,Feb 2)*
Hareem Queen 108 *(5f,Sth,SD,Dec 20)*
Harlow 103 *(9½f,Wol,SD,Feb 1)*
Harriet's Force 114 *(11f,Dun,SD,Sep 27)*
Harrovian 105 *(10f,Lin,SD,Jun 4)*
Harry Hurricane 112 *(5f,Lin,SD,Mar 2)*
Harry's Bar 111 *(5f,Ncs,SS,Nov 21)*
Hart Stopper 108 *(6f,Kem,SS,Nov 19)*
Harvey Specter 104 *(11f,Dun,SD,Nov 15)*
Hassaad 108 *(5f,Ncs,SD,Nov 1)*
Hasselnott 112 *(8f,Dun,SD,Mar 15)*
Hateya 110 *(8f,Lin,SD,Aug 31)*
Hathal 111 *(9f,Wol,SD,Feb 4)*
Hathiq 106 *(6f,Dun,SD,Apr 17)*
Havana Rocket 106 *(9f,Wol,SD,Mar 26)*
Have A Nice Day 105 *(7f,Dun,SD,Jan 25)*
Hazel Bay 109 *(11f,Dun,SD,Feb 15)*
He's Amazing 104 *(12f,Kem,SS,Oct 28)*
Healing Power 105 *(7f,Cfd,SD,Oct 17)*
Heart Of Soul 105 *(12f,Sth,SD,Mar 27)*
Heath Charnock 110 *(6f,Ncs,SD,Dec 6)*
Heavenly Holly 105 *(7f,Cfd,SD,Jun 19)*
Heavy Metal 116 *(8f,Mey,FT,Mar 9)*
Hee Haw 106 *(7f,Dun,SD,Jan 25)*
Helf 111 *(16½f,Wol,SD,Jan 11)*
Heliac 114 *(11f,Dun,SD,Oct 11)*
Helvetian 111 *(5f,Wol,SD,Oct 23)*
Hen 109 *(12f,Wol,SD,May 13)*
Heraldic 108 *(11f,Mey,FT,Jan 5)*
Heron 104 *(14f,Cfd,SD,Apr 4)*
Herringswell 108 *(6f,Ncs,SS,Nov 4)*
Hesslewood 104 *(8f,Kem,SS,Nov 4)*
Hey Jonesy 107 *(6f,Cfd,SD,Apr 25)*
Hey Pretty 105 *(7f,Dun,SD,Jan 25)*
Hic Bibi 105 *(7f,Cfd,SD,Apr 11)*
Hidden Spark 105 *(8f,Dun,SD,Sep 20)*
High Acclaim 105 *(9f,Wol,SD,Mar 5)*
High Command 108 *(16½f,Sth,SD,Apr 21)*
High Glory 104 *(12½f,Ncs,SD,Dec 6)*
Highbrow 112 *(10f,Cfd,SD,Sep 28)*
Higher Power 105 *(14f,Cfd,SD,May 9)*
Highest Mountain 103 *(7f,Cfd,SD,Mar 28)*
Highfaluting 103 *(7f,Kem,SS,Sep 23)*
Highgarden 108 *(14f,Cfd,SD,Jun 19)*
Highland Acclaim 105 *(6f,Lin,SD,Feb 2)*
Highly Approved 112 *(7f,Dun,SD,Nov 20)*
Highway One 104 *(10f,Lin,SD,Mar 1)*
Hindaam 103 *(10f,Lin,SS,Oct 31)*
Hiroshima 105 *(12f,Sth,SD,May 1)*
Hit The Bid 112 *(5f,Dun,SD,Oct 18)*
Hit The Silk 109 *(6f,Dun,SD,Dec 13)*
Holy Kingdom 109 *(14f,Cfd,SD,Nov 2)*
Holy Tiber 104 *(7f,Cfd,SD,Apr 11)*
Home Before Dusk 105 *(9½f,Wol,SD,Dec 14)*
Honest Albert 106 *(7f,Ncs,SD,Jly 27)*
Honey Gg 103 *(5f,Sth,SD,Mar 27)*
Honfleur 103 *(12f,Lin,SD,Aug 15)*
Hooflepuff 112 *(12½f,Ncs,SD,Dec 6)*
Hope Is High 103 *(14f,Cfd,SD,Sep 28)*
Hot Stuff 105 *(5f,Dun,SD,Dec 18)*
Houlton 107 *(14f,Cfd,SD,Aug 29)*
How Far 109 *(6f,Cfd,SD,Jan 24)*
Howzer Black 105 *(6f,Ncs,SD,Dec 6)*
Hucklebuck 111 *(8f,Mey,FT,Dec 5)*
Hugoigo 106 *(12½f,Ncs,SS,Mar 29)*
Hulcote 109 *(12f,Kem,SS,Dec 4)*
Human Nature 111 *(6f,Cfd,SD,Jan 24)*
Humbert 108 *(10f,Lin,SD,Dec 9)*
Hurricane Alert 105 *(5f,Lin,SD,Mar 2)*
Hurricane Hero 107 *(12f,Sth,SD,Apr 21)*
Hurricane Sky 103 *(12f,Dun,SD,Nov 8)*
Hussar Ballad 106 *(12f,Wol,SD,Jan 30)*
Hyanna 104 *(13f,Lin,SS,Oct 31)*
Hypnos 103 *(10f,Cfd,SD,Apr 1)*

I Can Fly 111 *(7f,Dun,SD,Mar 6)*
I Kirk 109 *(6f,Mey,FT,Mar 9)*
I'll Have Another 105 *(14f,Cfd,SD,Nov 2)*
I'm Available 103 *(9½f,Wol,SD,Nov 18)*
Ibn Malik 114 *(8f,Mey,FT,Mar 9)*
Ibraz 109 *(8f,Ncs,SD,Jun 4)*
Ice Canyon 107 *(12f,Wol,SD,Jan 4)*
Ice Cave 103 *(6f,Kem,SS,Nov 19)*
Ice Pyramid 105 *(10f,Ncs,SD,Jan 2)*
Iconic Girl 103 *(8f,Lin,SD,Feb 15)*
Iftiraaq 103 *(12f,Wol,SD,Jan 4)*
Iftitah 114 *(7f,Mey,FT,Mar 2)*
Ilhabela Fact 114 *(11f,Kem,SS,Feb 28)*
Illumined 106 *(12f,Kem,SS,Aug 7)*
Illusional 110 *(11f,Mey,FT,Mar 2)*
Illustrissime 106 *(9f,Wol,SD,Mar 16)*
Im Dapper Too 105 *(7f,Ncs,SS,Aug 30)*
Image Of The Moon 106 *(8f,Kem,SS,Aug 28)*
Immortalised 103 *(10f,Mey,FT,Oct 24)*
Imperial Act 105 *(9f,Wol,SD,May 31)*
Imperial Focus 110 *(12½f,Ncs,SD,Dec 6)*
Imperial Hint 115 *(6f,Mey,FT,Mar 30)*
Imperium 104 *(12f,Kem,SS,Sep 16)*
Important Message 112 *(11f,Dun,SD,Mar 8)*
Important Mission 114 *(7f,Mey,FT,Apr 5)*
Imprison 106 *(8f,Mey,FT,Apr 5)*
Improving 107 *(6f,Dun,SD,Dec 3)*
In The Lope 111 *(10f,Lin,SD,Feb 2)*
In The Red 104 *(8f,Lin,SD,Mar 1)*
Inaam 105 *(7f,Wol,SD,Jan 2)*
Inclyne 109 *(12f,Kem,SS,Aug 21)*
Incredulous 106 *(9½f,Wol,SD,Jly 9)*
Indeed 108 *(10f,Cfd,SD,Jun 19)*
India 104 *(12f,Lin,SD,Jan 19)*
Indian Affair 107 *(6f,Wol,SD,Jan 30)*
Indian Eye 105 *(11f,Dun,SD,Mar 8)*
Indian Tygress 109 *(6f,Kem,SS,Apr 20)*
Indian Viceroy 103 *(7f,Kem,SS,Aug 21)*
Indomeneo 105 *(9½f,Wol,SD,Dec 2)*
Indyco 112 *(8f,Lin,SD,Apr 19)*
Inference 114 *(10f,Cfd,SD,Aug 24)*
Infrastructure 111 *(16f,Ncs,SD,Dec 14)*
Ingelara 103 *(8f,Dun,SD,Apr 17)*
Ingleby Mackenzie 104 *(12f,Dun,SD,Sep 27)*
Inn The Bull 107 *(12f,Wol,SD,Apr 27)*
Innamorare 116 *(8f,Dun,SD,Nov 8)*
Inscribe 112 *(11f,Dun,SD,Oct 11)*
Insurgence 109 *(8f,Lin,SD,Jan 26)*
Insurplus 103 *(7f,Ncs,SS,Aug 30)*
International Law 106 *(9f,Wol,SD,Mar 5)*
Intisaab 108 *(6f,Wol,SD,Oct 5)*
Intransigent 105 *(7f,Lin,SD,Jan 11)*
Intrepidly 109 *(8f,Kem,SS,Feb 2)*
Intuitive 108 *(6f,Kem,SS,Apr 12)*
Invasion Day 107 *(8f,Dun,SD,Mar 22)*
Invincible Army 114 *(6f,Ncs,SS,Jun 29)*
Invincible Larne 103 *(6f,Cfd,SD,Sep 12)*
Invincible Queen 110 *(11f,Dun,SD,Mar 8)*
Invitation 104 *(13f,Lin,SS,Oct 31)*
Invitational 106 *(7f,Wol,SD,Apr 16)*
Involved 105 *(10f,Cfd,SD,Jan 26)*
Irene May 104 *(6f,Wol,SD,Oct 19)*
Irish Ambassador 103 *(8f,Dun,SD,Nov 29)*
Iron Mike 106 *(12f,Wol,SD,Oct 17)*
Ironclad 107 *(10f,Cfd,SD,Jun 8)*
Irradiate 115 *(16f,Dun,SD,Nov 29)*
Isaan Queen 106 *(6f,Cfd,SD,May 2)*
Iseebreeze 106 *(7f,Dun,SD,Feb 22)*
Ishebayorgrey 104 *(11f,Dun,SD,Mar 15)*
Island Brave 115 *(11f,Kem,SS,Mar 30)*
Island Of Life 110 *(6f,Ncs,SS,Jun 29)*
Isomer 105 *(10f,Lin,SD,Feb 1)*
Isotope 107 *(8f,Dun,SD,Mar 15)*
It Must Be Faith 108 *(7f,Cfd,SD,Feb 2)*
It's All A Joke 104 *(5f,Wol,SD,Jan 19)*
Itsalonglongroad 109 *(12f,Dun,SD,Mar 22)*

J Be Space 111 *(9½f,Mey,FT,Jan 19)*
Jaarim 103 *(6f,Mey,FT,Mar 2)*
Jabalaly 105 *(7f,Kem,SS,Sep 23)*
Jack The Truth 105 *(6f,Ncs,SS,Feb 15)*
Jack's Point 103 *(7f,Cfd,SD,Sep 21)*
Jackstar 107 *(7f,Wol,SD,Dec 14)*
Jacob Cats 105 *(16f,Lin,SD,Mar 25)*
Jadeerah 103 *(7f,Cfd,SD,Aug 10)*
Jafetica 103 *(10f,Lin,SD,Jan 9)*
Jahbath 110 *(8f,Sth,SD,Jan 24)*
Jai Hanuman 107 *(10f,Lin,SD,Apr 6)*
Jalaad 103 *(8f,Kem,SS,Nov 4)*
Jaleel 107 *(7f,Cfd,SD,Sep 24)*
Jamaican Jill 107 *(10f,Cfd,SD,Mar 7)*
James Street 108 *(6f,Wol,SD,Jan 29)*
Jan Van Hoof 111 *(5f,Ncs,SS,Mar 29)*
Javelin 104 *(7f,Cfd,SD,Apr 30)*
Jazz Hands 107 *(8f,Sth,SD,Dec 5)*
Jazz Legend 103 *(6f,Sth,SD,Mar 7)*
Jazzy J 104 *(12f,Dun,SD,Apr 17)*
Jedhi 105 *(14f,Cfd,SD,Jun 19)*
Jeffrey Harris 104 *(6f,Ncs,SD,Oct 7)*
Jem Scuttle 103 *(7f,Cfd,SD,Dec 13)*
Jered Maddox 104 *(7f,Dun,SD,Feb 1)*
Jersey Wonder 103 *(12f,Wol,SD,Oct 19)*
Jintshi 111 *(11f,Mey,FT,Mar 2)*
Joegogo 107 *(5f,Wol,SD,Jan 29)*
John Kirkup 105 *(6f,Ncs,SD,Oct 22)*
Johnny Cavagin 103 *(6f,Ncs,SS,Jan 12)*
Jomrok 105 *(10f,Cfd,SD,Jly 6)*
Jon Ess 103 *(12f,Dun,SD,Nov 8)*
Jonboy 104 *(6f,Ncs,SD,Nov 1)*
Juanito Chico 107 *(9½f,Wol,SD,Feb 26)*
Jubiloso 105 *(6f,Cfd,SD,Apr 25)*
Judicial 111 *(6f,Lin,SD,Nov 16)*
Julia's Magic 105 *(5f,Dun,SD,Oct 18)*
Jumellea 103 *(8f,Dun,SD,Nov 1)*
Jumira Bridge 106 *(5f,Cfd,SD,Aug 9)*
Jungle Jane 106 *(5f,Dun,SD,Nov 15)*
Junior Rip 108 *(10f,Cfd,SD,Sep 21)*
Junius Brutus 110 *(6f,Kem,SS,Nov 6)*
Jupiter Road 106 *(7f,Dun,SD,Feb 22)*
Jus Pires 103 *(12f,Sth,SD,Oct 4)*
Just Hubert 105 *(14f,Cfd,SD,Nov 2)*
Just That Lord 110 *(5f,Wol,SD,Apr 16)*
Just The Man 111 *(11f,Kem,SS,Oct 31)*
Justice Lady 108 *(5f,Ncs,SS,Feb 28)*
K Club 104 *(6f,Kem,SS,Jan 4)*
Kachy 121 *(6f,Lin,SD,Feb 2)*
Kadrizzi 109 *(7f,Cfd,SD,Jan 24)*
Kaftan 105 *(8f,Dun,SD,Nov 1)*
Kafu 115 *(8f,Dun,SD,Dec 6)*
Kamra 103 *(6f,Lin,SD,Dec 9)*
Kannapolis 103 *(10f,Ncs,SD,Oct 18)*
Kapono 106 *(6f,Ncs,SS,Jun 28)*
Karaginsky 103 *(7f,Mey,FT,Feb 7)*
Kareena Kapoor 103 *(6f,Ncs,SS,Jan 12)*
Karnavaal 103 *(7f,Cfd,SD,Aug 10)*
Kasbaan 112 *(8f,Kem,SS,Sep 7)*
Kasbah 109 *(7f,Dun,SD,Jan 25)*
Kaser 110 *(9½f,Wol,SD,Dec 27)*
Kashagan 108 *(9½f,Wol,SD,Sep 30)*
Katheefa 112 *(6f,Ncs,SS,Jun 29)*
Katie Gale 106 *(16½f,Sth,SD,Mar 30)*
Katie Lee 110 *(8f,Kem,SS,Jan 4)*
Katiymann 115 *(8f,Dun,SD,Nov 8)*
Kattani 110 *(11f,Dun,SD,Oct 11)*
Kelly's Dino 110 *(12f,Wol,SD,Mar 4)*
Ken's Sam's 108 *(6f,Dun,SD,Apr 24)*
Kendergarten Kop 103 *(7f,Kem,SS,Oct 31)*
Kenny The Captain 104 *(6f,Ncs,SD,Nov 22)*
Kentuckyconnection 109 *(6f,Ncs,SD,Apr 29)*
Kerosin 106 *(12f,Dun,SD,Jan 4)*
Kesia 105 *(12f,Wol,SD,Oct 30)*
Keswick 104 *(10f,Cfd,SD,Nov 19)*
Key Bid 104 *(10f,Mey,SD,Jan 24)*
Key Player 107 *(9½f,Wol,SD,Feb 26)*
Key To Power 105 *(5f,Dun,SD,Nov 15)*
Keyser Soze 109 *(7f,Lin,SD,Jan 11)*
Khabeerah 103 *(8f,Kem,SS,Aug 7)*
Khafaaq 105 *(7f,Dun,SD,Oct 18)*
Kheros 106 *(8f,Kem,SS,Sep 6)*
Khuzaam 113 *(8f,Kem,SS,Nov 20)*
Kick On Kick On 105 *(5f,Wol,SD,Nov 26)*
Kilbaha Lady 103 *(9½f,Wol,SD,Feb 21)*
Kimbear 113 *(8f,Mey,FT,Jan 10)*
Kimifive 105 *(7f,Kem,SS,Oct 9)*
Kindly 104 *(6f,Ncs,SD,Oct 22)*
King Cole 107 *(8f,Mey,FT,Mar 2)*
King Of Naples 104 *(9½f,Wol,SD,Feb 1)*
King Of The Sand 104 *(12f,Wol,SD,May 31)*
King Robert 109 *(6f,Cfd,SD,Jan 24)*
King's Advice 109 *(16f,Ncs,SS,Jun 29)*
King's Slipper 110 *(10f,Cfd,SD,Sep 28)*
King's Vow 113 *(11f,Dun,SD,Dec 20)*
Kingi Compton 103 *(5f,Kem,SS,Jan 18)*
Kings Highway 105 *(8f,Kem,SS,Jun 26)*
Kingsley Klarion 103 *(6f,Cfd,SD,Oct 3)*
Kingston Kurrajong 104 *(8f,Kem,SS,Jun 26)*
Kinver Edge 103 *(8f,Cfd,SD,Feb 21)*
Kirstenbosch 108 *(10f,Cfd,SD,Jun 20)*
Kitaabaat 107 *(14f,Cfd,SD,Sep 28)*
Kitcarina 103 *(8f,Kem,SS,Jun 5)*
Klass Action 106 *(6f,Lin,SD,Mar 15)*
Klopp 104 *(6f,Ncs,SD,Mar 8)*
Klute 103 *(7f,Dun,SD,Oct 18)*
Knight Crusader 109 *(16f,Kem,SS,Mar 11)*
Knockacullion 107 *(8f,Sth,SD,Sep 26)*
Knockout Blow 106 *(6f,Wol,SD,Jan 30)*
Kodiac Harbour 104 *(8f,Lin,SD,Feb 15)*
Kodiac Lass 104 *(7f,Wol,SD,Apr 5)*
Kodiline 103 *(7f,Lin,SS,Jan 5)*
Koeman 112 *(11f,Kem,SS,May 22)*
Koybig 109 *(11f,Dun,SD,Feb 22)*
Kraka 104 *(6f,Cfd,SD,Mar 2)*
Kupa River 106 *(6f,Ncs,SD,Dec 6)*
Kuwait Currency 112 *(8f,Lin,SD,Dec 31)*
Kwela 106 *(6f,Kem,SS,Sep 23)*
Kyllachy Gala 108 *(11f,Kem,SS,Oct 9)*
Kyllachy Warrior 108 *(5f,Ncs,SD,Nov 1)*
Kyllang Rock 110 *(5f,Wol,SD,Apr 16)*

La Derniere Fois 107 *(7f,Dun,SD,Oct 30)*
La Rav 104 *(8f,Ncs,SD,Nov 8)*
La Sioux 106 *(9f,Wol,SD,Mar 25)*
Laafy 106 *(12f,Kem,SS,Aug 5)*
Lady Adelaide 106 *(11f,Kem,SS,Dec 11)*
Lady Bergamot 108 *(14f,Cfd,SD,Jun 19)*
Lady Boomerang 104 *(8f,Dun,SD,Oct 4)*
Lady Dancealot 110 *(6f,Kem,SS,Nov 6)*
Lady De Vesci 105 *(12f,Dun,SD,Jan 4)*
Lady Godiva 104 *(8f,Dun,SD,Mar 22)*
Lady In France 105 *(5f,Ncs,SD,May 3)*
Lady In Lavender 107 *(8f,Dun,SD,Oct 30)*
Lady Lawyer 107 *(7f,Cfd,SD,Aug 10)*
Lady Madison 110 *(8f,Lin,SD,Aug 31)*
Lady Makfi 113 *(16½f,Wol,SD,Jan 11)*
Lady Of Authority 104 *(9½f,Wol,SD,Feb 19)*
Lady Rosebud 108 *(8f,Dun,SD,Apr 5)*
Lady Shanawell 104 *(12f,Wol,SD,Sep 7)*
Laethanta Saoire 105 *(8f,Dun,SD,Feb 15)*
Lafayette Hill 108 *(11f,Dun,SD,May 3)*
Lake Volta 106 *(7f,Cfd,SD,Sep 14)*
Lalania 103 *(6f,Cfd,SD,Nov 2)*
Lancelot Du Lac 111 *(5f,Wol,SD,Feb 21)*
Land Of Winter 105 *(12f,Sth,SD,Sep 26)*
Landa Beach 103 *(10f,Cfd,SD,May 2)*
Landing Night 109 *(5f,Ncs,SD,Nov 1)*
Landue 107 *(11f,Kem,SS,May 22)*
Lansky 104 *(6f,Mey,FT,Mar 9)*
Lapilli 106 *(6f,Dun,SD,Dec 3)*
Lappet 104 *(8f,Dun,SD,Feb 15)*
Laqab 103 *(9f,Wol,SD,Feb 23)*
Last Look 109 *(10f,Cfd,SD,Jly 6)*
Last Page 104 *(6f,Kem,SS,Nov 5)*
Last Winter 104 *(12f,Kem,SS,Nov 4)*
Latchet 112 *(11f,Dun,SD,Mar 22)*
Laubali 104 *(5f,Wol,SD,Oct 23)*
Lauberhorn Rocket 103 *(12f,Kem,SS,Aug 14)*
Laugh A Minute 111 *(6f,Ncs,SS,Jun 29)*
Laura Bullion 105 *(12f,Dun,SD,Oct 4)*
Lavaspin 114 *(6f,Mey,FT,Feb 14)*
Lawmaking 106 *(8f,Kem,SS,Oct 16)*
Lawn Ranger 110 *(11f,Kem,SS,Feb 28)*
Le Manege Enchante 103 *(6f,Wol,SD,Jan 30)*
Le Torrent 104 *(16f,Kem,SS,Jly 10)*
Le Vagabond 111 *(12f,Dun,SD,Mar 8)*
Leading Spirit 109 *(6f,Mey,FT,Apr 12)*
Lean And Keen 104 *(12f,Dun,SD,Apr 17)*
Lefortovo 106 *(7f,Wol,SD,Mar 12)*
Lennybe 103 *(8f,Sth,SD,Mar 7)*
Leodis Dream 111 *(5f,Dun,SD,Oct 18)*
Leroy Leroy 104 *(8f,Kem,SS,Apr 20)*
Lestrade 105 *(7f,Cfd,SD,Mar 15)*
Let Rip 104 *(10f,Cfd,SD,Aug 23)*
Lethal Angel 104 *(5f,Wol,SD,Nov 16)*
Lethal Lunch 112 *(7f,Kem,SS,Mar 9)*
Lethal Missile 103 *(8f,Kem,SS,Dec 4)*
Lethal Promise 107 *(5f,Dun,SD,Oct 18)*
Lever Du Soleil 113 *(16f,Dun,SD,Nov 29)*
Lexington Empire 111 *(10f,Cfd,SD,Jun 20)*
Lexington Law 107 *(12f,Kem,SS,Feb 16)*
Lexington Place 104 *(5f,Wol,SD,Apr 13)*
Liamba 106 *(6f,Sth,SD,Dec 19)*
Librisa Breeze 107 *(8f,Kem,SS,Nov 20)*
Lightning Charlie 104 *(6f,Sth,SD,Dec 19)*
Lihou 103 *(6f,Kem,SS,Nov 29)*
Lily Lily Rose 108 *(8f,Dun,SD,Nov 6)*
Lily's Prince 109 *(6f,Dun,SD,Apr 5)*
Limerick Lord 103 *(9f,Wol,SD,Jan 30)*
Line Of Reason 109 *(5f,Ncs,SS,Jun 28)*
Lion Hearted 107 *(7f,Wol,SD,Mar 12)*
Lippy Lady 103 *(7f,Kem,SS,Mar 11)*
Liquid Luck 107 *(11f,Dun,SD,Oct 25)*
Lissitzky 103 *(16f,Ncs,SS,Jun 29)*
Little Boy Blue 106 *(6f,Cfd,SD,Mar 2)*
Little Clarinet 104 *(6f,Dun,SD,Apr 5)*
Little Jo 104 *(8f,Ncs,SD,Nov 8)*
Little Palaver 105 *(6f,Kem,SS,Jan 16)*
Little Rock 105 *(8f,Sth,SS,Feb 27)*
Livvys Dream 106 *(10f,Cfd,SD,May 31)*
Lizard Point 112 *(11f,Dun,SD,Mar 8)*
Lleyton 106 *(16f,Dun,SD,Dec 18)*
Loaded 110 *(8f,Dun,SD,Nov 20)*
Logrado 106 *(8f,Mey,FT,Mar 30)*
Lomu 114 *(5f,Wol,SD,Dec 3)*
Long Arm 108 *(12f,Dun,SD,Oct 18)*
Longbourn 107 *(11f,Dun,SD,Dec 6)*
Longroom 107 *(5f,Ncs,SD,Nov 1)*
Lopes Dancer 110 *(12½f,Ncs,SD,Oct 11)*
Lord George 108 *(12f,Lin,SD,Jan 19)*
Lord Halifax 104 *(12f,Lin,SD,Dec 11)*
Lord Lamington 106 *(12½f,Ncs,SS,Mar 22)*
Lord Rapscallion 114 *(8f,Dun,SD,Dec 18)*
Lord Riddiford 107 *(5f,Cfd,SD,Jun 8)*
Lord Wimborne 107 *(8f,Dun,SD,Jan 11)*
Lordsbridge Boy 106 *(6f,Kem,SS,Nov 29)*
Los Camachos 104 *(7f,Lin,SD,Feb 1)*
Lost History 108 *(12f,Wol,SD,May 31)*
Lothario 105 *(8f,Kem,SS,Feb 28)*
Loud And Clear 114 *(16f,Ncs,SD,Jan 8)*
Loughanlea Lass 103 *(8f,Dun,SD,Nov 20)*
Loulin 106 *(5f,Ncs,SS,Mar 29)*
Love Dreams 113 *(7f,Kem,SS,Mar 9)*
Love Rat 105 *(12f,Lin,SD,Mar 6)*
Love Your Work 105 *(8f,Sth,SD,Mar 7)*
Lovely Approach 112 *(11f,Sth,SD,Apr 3)*
Loving Glance 104 *(7f,Wol,SD,Nov 26)*
Loxley 112 *(12f,Kem,SS,Dec 4)*
Loyalty 105 *(7f,Lin,SD,Feb 15)*
Lucky Lodge 112 *(6f,Ncs,SD,Apr 1)*
Lucky Turn 105 *(10f,Cfd,SD,Nov 28)*
Lucky's Dream 103 *(10f,Cfd,SD,Dec 12)*
Lucymai 108 *(7f,Ncs,SD,Jan 22)*
Lufricia 110 *(5f,Ncs,SD,Apr 19)*
Luis Vaz De Torres 106 *(6f,Lin,SD,Nov 30)*
Luna Magic 104 *(9½f,Wol,SD,Dec 16)*
Lunar Deity 105 *(10f,Lin,SD,Mar 22)*
Lush Life 106 *(8f,Kem,SS,Nov 20)*
Lusis Naturea 114 *(11f,Dun,SD,Mar 8)*
Lyford 103 *(12½f,Ncs,SS,Sep 6)*
Lyrical Attraction 105 *(8f,Dun,SD,Mar 15)*
Lytham St Annes 112 *(6f,Mey,FT,Mar 14)*

Maamora 110 *(8f,Cfd,SD,Sep 12)*
Maazel 110 *(7f,Sth,SD,Mar 7)*
Machiavelli 107 *(11f,Dun,SD,Mar 22)*
Machine Learner 105 *(14f,Cfd,SD,Sep 28)*
Madame Delavanti 105 *(8f,Dun,SD,Apr 5)*
Made Of Honour 104 *(7f,Ncs,SS,Jan 6)*
Madkhal 103 *(7f,Cfd,SD,Oct 17)*
Madrinho 106 *(6f,Kem,SS,Mar 27)*
Magi Gal 104 *(11f,Dun,SD,Nov 15)*
Magic Fountain 106 *(7f,Dun,SD,Nov 8)*
Magic Lily 109 *(10f,Lin,SD,Nov 16)*

Magic Mirror 110 (8f,Kem,SS,Feb 28)
Magic Sea 105 (12f,Dun,SD,Feb 8)
Magical Rhythms 104 (8f,Kem,SS,Aug 20)
Magical Spirit 106 (6f,Ncs,SD,Sep 27)
Magicinthemaking 103 (6f,Kem,SS,Sep 25)
Magnetic North 103 (12f,Dun,SD,Dec 6)
Maid For Life 106 (10f,Cfd,SD,Aug 31)
Maid Millie 103 (6f,Cfd,SD,Aug 9)
Main Street 109 (10f,Lin,SD,Feb 2)
Majestic Moon 104 (8f,Sth,SD,Apr 3)
Majestic Stone 104 (12½f,Ncs,SS,Sep 6)
Majestic Thunder 113 (8f,Mey,FT,Dec 5)
Major Power 103 (7f,Dun,SD,Dec 6)
Major Reward 105 (8f,Dun,SD,Mar 22)
Makambe 104 (8f,Kem,SS,Sep 3)
Makanah 103 (5f,Ncs,SS,Jun 28)
Make Good 105 (12f,Kem,SS,Feb 2)
Making Miracles 109 (16f,Ncs,SS,Jun 29)
Maksab 110 (7f,Kem,SS,Mar 9)
Makzeem 104 (8f,Kem,SS,Nov 20)
Malaysian Boleh 103 (6f,Ncs,SS,Feb 5)
Malbas 110 (12f,Dun,SD,Oct 4)
Mama Africa 104 (8f,Sth,SD,Jan 24)
Mamdood 109 (12½f,Ncs,SD,Dec 6)
Manguzi 113 (9½f,Mey,FT,Mar 30)
Manhunter 104 (8f,Mey,FT,Dec 5)
Manjaam 106 (14f,Cfd,SD,Sep 28)
Manjeer 108 (8f,Dun,SD,Mar 6)
Manomine 103 (12½f,Ncs,SS,Jan 12)
Manorah 104 (10f,Lin,SD,Aug 19)
Manshood 105 (6f,Ncs,SD,Apr 1)
Manton Grange 104 (8f,Kem,SS,May 22)
Maqaadeer 104 (8f,Lin,SD,Mar 15)
Marble Bar 108 (6f,Sth,SD,Mar 27)
Margie's Choice 106 (8f,Kem,SS,Mar 9)
Margub 110 (7f,Wol,SD,Apr 23)
Marhaban 105 (10f,Lin,SD,Jan 18)
Marine One 110 (16f,Dun,SD,Jan 11)
Mark Of Approval 115 (8f,Mey,FT,Oct 24)
Markhan 108 (12f,Dun,SD,Jan 4)
Markus Twain 103 (11f,Dun,SD,Mar 8)
Marshall Jennings 110 (8f,Dun,SD,Nov 8)
Martineo 113 (6f,Ncs,SD,Apr 1)
Marvel 107 (5f,Ncs,SS,Sep 6)
Masalai 107 (8f,Dun,SD,Feb 15)
Masham Star 106 (9f,Wol,SD,Mar 9)
Massa Lubrense 108 (8f,Dun,SD,Nov 8)
Massif Central 114 (11f,Dun,SD,Sep 27)
Master Archer 104 (16f,Kem,SS,Jly 3)
Master Diver 105 (7f,Dun,SD,Jan 25)
Master Matt 105 (6f,Dun,SD,Nov 1)
Master Speaker 107 (6f,Dun,SD,Feb 15)
Master The World 112 (10f,Kem,SS,Mar 30)
Matera Sky 116 (6f,Mey,FT,Mar 30)
Matewan 104 (12f,Lin,SD,Dec 11)
Matterhorn 121 (10f,Lin,SD,Apr 19)
Mawakib 105 (7f,Kem,SS,Jun 5)
Maximum Effect 103 (8f,Cfd,SD,Jly 23)
Maximum Power 104 (6f,Kem,SS,Feb 16)
May Peace Prevail 110 (11f,Dun,SD,Feb 15)
May Remain 109 (6f,Dun,SD,Dec 13)
Mayaadeen 110 (7f,Mey,FT,Mar 2)
Maybe Today 108 (12f,Lin,SD,Mar 22)
Mayfair Spirit 107 (10f,Cfd,SD,Sep 26)
Maygold 103 (6f,Lin,SD,Nov 16)
Mayne 103 (8f,Kem,SS,Aug 20)
Mazeed 115 (7f,Mey,FT,Jan 5)
Mcguigan 108 (11f,Dun,SD,Jan 18)
Media Deal 106 (11f,Dun,SD,Feb 15)
Medieval 104 (8f,Kem,SS,Apr 12)
Mehdaayih 112 (10f,Cfd,SD,Apr 18)
Mendoza 106 (7f,Kem,SS,Oct 31)
Menin Gate 104 (10f,Ncs,SD,Oct 7)
Mercenary Rose 107 (5f,Kem,SS,Oct 28)
Merchant Of Venice 107 (8f,Kem,SS,Mar 9)
Mercury 104 (7f,Dun,SD,Jan 25)
Merhoob 114 (6f,Wol,SD,Feb 25)
Merricourt 108 (8f,Dun,SD,Oct 30)
Merweb 104 (8f,Kem,SS,Dec 4)
Met By Moonlight 108 (7f,Lin,SD,Apr 6)
Michael's Mount 103 (16f,Ncs,SS,Jun 29)
Michele Strogoff 109 (7f,Cfd,SD,Sep 24)
Mickey 104 (7f,Lin,SD,Jan 11)
Midlander 114 (6f,Mey,FT,Oct 24)
Midnight Malibu 104 (5f,Sth,SD,Jan 24)
Midnight Sands 117 (7f,Mey,FT,Nov 7)
Midnight Wilde 105 (16f,Dun,SD,Dec 18)
Midnights' Gift 104 (12f,Lin,SD,Aug 15)
Midnitemudcrabs 103 (7f,Dun,SD,Oct 18)
Mildenberger 114 (16f,Ncs,SD,Dec 14)
Military Law 107 (8f,Ncs,SS,Jun 27)
Millicent Fawcett 107 (9f,Wol,SD,Dec 10)
Mininggold 108 (5f,Sth,SD,Jan 13)
Miracle Works 109 (5f,Cfd,SD,Aug 9)
Miss Crick 103 (12f,Kem,SS,Feb 13)
Miss Elsa 106 (11f,Kem,SS,Oct 2)
Miss Gradenko 103 (5f,Kem,SS,Oct 23)
Miss Jabeam 103 (7f,Dun,SD,Oct 4)
Miss Latin 105 (13f,Lin,SS,Oct 31)
Miss Liberty Belle 105 (6f,Cfd,SD,Sep 21)
Miss Louise 110 (11f,Dun,SD,Mar 22)
Miss Snossyboots 112 (11f,Dun,SD,May 3)
Mister Chiang 106 (14f,Cfd,SD,Aug 29)
Mister Music 109 (7f,Sth,SS,Feb 27)
Mistiroc 110 (10f,Cfd,SD,Jun 20)
Mistress Of Venice 106 (5f,Dun,SD,Apr 14)
Misty At Sea 105 (7f,Dun,SD,Nov 8)
Mixboy 104 (18½f,Sth,SD,Apr 3)
Mizbah 114 (11f,Mey,FT,Mar 2)
Mochalov 103 (7f,Cfd,SD,Feb 14)
Modakhar 103 (8f,Ncs,SD,Nov 8)
Mohareb 109 (7f,Lin,SD,Dec 31)
Mojave 106 (12f,Kem,SS,Aug 21)
Mokaatil 109 (5f,Wol,SD,Feb 21)
Mokarris 114 (6f,Lin,SD,Feb 2)
Moktamel 112 (12f,Dun,SD,Sep 27)
Molten Lava 106 (9f,Wol,SD,Mar 25)
Moment Of Silence 106 (7f,Wol,SD,Nov 16)
Mon Frere 103 (14f,Cfd,SD,Aug 3)
Monaadhil 103 (8f,Cfd,SD,Jly 23)
Mondain 107 (14f,Cfd,SD,Aug 10)
Mongolia 104 (12f,Sth,SD,Oct 16)
Mons Star 108 (10f,Cfd,SD,Nov 21)
Monsieur Lambrays 104 (12f,Wol,SD,Oct 5)
Monsieur Piquer 104 (11f,Dun,SD,Dec 20)
Mont Kiara 105 (6f,Kem,SS,Jan 16)
Mont Royal 107 (12½f,Ncs,SS,Mar 29)
Montatham 108 (8f,Kem,SS,Nov 19)
Montsarrat 109 (10f,Mey,FT,Apr 12)
Monumental Man 103 (6f,Wol,SD,Feb 19)
Moojib 113 (8f,Mey,FT,Apr 5)
Moon Trouble 110 (6f,Cfd,SD,Jun 6)
Moonbi Creek 103 (6f,Ncs,SS,Feb 5)
Moonmeister 108 (12f,Dun,SD,Mar 8)
Moonraker 112 (5f,Sth,SD,Feb 3)
Mootasadir 115 (10f,Kem,SS,Mar 30)
Moqarrab 118 (7f,Mey,FT,Feb 21)
Moqarrar 118 (8f,Mey,FT,Jan 19)
Moraawed 107 (6f,Kem,SS,Apr 12)
Moshaher 109 (8f,Mey,FT,Jan 5)
Moss Gill 104 (5f,Ncs,SD,May 3)
Motagally 113 (6f,Wol,SD,Oct 5)
Motahassen 104 (8f,Sth,SD,Nov 29)
Motajaasid 109 (7f,Lin,SD,Feb 22)
Motawaj 109 (8f,Kem,SS,Sep 7)
Moteo 103 (13f,Lin,SS,Oct 31)
Mount Wellington 106 (7f,Wol,SD,Dec 2)
Mountain Hunter 107 (12f,Kem,SS,Sep 7)
Mr Buttons 104 (6f,Kem,SS,Sep 23)
Mr Carbonator 108 (10f,Ncs,SS,Jan 6)
Mr Coco Bean 104 (8f,Sth,SS,Jan 31)
Mr Lupton 106 (6f,Ncs,SS,Jun 29)
Mr Scaramanga 111 (10f,Lin,SD,Nov 28)
Mr Scarlet 110 (6f,Dun,SD,Dec 13)
Mr Top Hat 106 (9½f,Wol,SD,Feb 26)
Muatadel 103 (6f,Ncs,SS,Feb 18)
Mubakker 104 (6f,Kem,SS,Sep 3)
Mubhij 104 (8f,Cfd,SD,Aug 16)
Muchly 105 (8f,Lin,SS,Oct 31)
Mudallel 112 (10f,Mey,FT,Apr 12)
Muhaarar's Nephew 105 (8f,Kem,SS,Aug 7)
Muhtaram 103 (7f,Mey,FT,Jan 5)
Mulfit 114 (9½f,Mey,FT,Oct 24)
Mulzamm 109 (8f,Dun,SD,Feb 15)
Munaajaat 107 (8f,Dun,SD,Nov 20)
Mundersfield 104 (16f,Lin,SD,Mar 2)
Munfallet 107 (8f,Dun,SD,Nov 6)
Muntazah 128 (8f,Mey,FT,Mar 9)
Muqarred 106 (8f,Sth,SD,Apr 3)
Muraad 106 (9f,Wol,SD,Apr 27)
Muraaqeb 105 (11f,Kem,SS,Apr 10)
Murdanova 103 (7f,Wol,SD,May 7)
Musawaat 117 (8f,Mey,FT,Mar 9)
Music Man 103 (16f,Lin,SD,Mar 25)
Mustarrid 104 (10f,Lin,SD,Dec 4)
Mutabaahy 109 (5f,Wol,SD,Dec 10)
Mutadaawel 108 (8f,Dun,SD,Dec 6)
Mutafani 105 (7f,Lin,SS,Oct 31)
Mutamaasik 103 (7f,Cfd,SD,Aug 3)
Mutasaamy 104 (8f,Kem,SS,Aug 5)
Muthmir 103 (5f,Cfd,SD,Aug 16)
Muzbid 111 (8f,Dun,SD,Dec 18)
My Boy Sepoy 107 (11f,Kem,SS,Dec 11)
My Brother Mike 103 (11f,Kem,SS,Jan 9)
My Catch 107 (6f,Mey,FT,Jan 3)
My Excelsa 108 (5f,Dun,SD,Oct 30)
My Good Brother 104 (6f,Dun,SD,Nov 15)
My Lark 105 (8f,Dun,SD,Apr 5)
My Target 108 (10f,Lin,SD,Dec 18)
Mystique Moon 103 (10f,Mey,SD,Jan 24)
Mythical Madness 110 (10f,Cfd,SD,May 2)

Naadirr 106 (6f,Kem,SS,Apr 20)
Naaeebb 111 (7f,Mey,FT,Mar 2)
Nafaayes 105 (16f,Lin,SD,Jan 23)
Nahaarr 104 (7f,Cfd,SD,Jly 5)
Nailed On Nina 105 (8f,Dun,SD,Nov 6)
Nam 107 (8f,Dun,SD,Nov 22)
Namazee 111 (11f,Dun,SD,Feb 22)
Name The Wind 108 (8f,Kem,SS,Apr 20)
Nampara 103 (6f,Dun,SD,Dec 16)
Nanning City 103 (8f,Dun,SD,Dec 20)
Napping 104 (6f,Cfd,SD,Sep 21)
Naqaawa 106 (10f,Cfd,SD,Jly 6)
Narjes 106 (10f,Lin,SD,Jan 19)
Narynkol 105 (11f,Dun,SD,Dec 6)
Nashirah 103 (7f,Mey,FT,Jan 3)
Nataleena 105 (16f,Ncs,SD,Oct 11)
Natch 104 (10f,Lin,SD,Jan 19)
National Glory 103 (6f,Kem,SS,Feb 16)
National Guard 111 (8f,Dun,SD,Mar 29)
Native Fighter 103 (12½f,Ncs,SS,Feb 1)
Natsovia 103 (12f,Wol,SD,Feb 26)
Natty Night 112 (12½f,Ncs,SD,Sep 17)
Navajo Ridge 107 (12f,Dun,SD,Sep 27)
Navajo Star 109 (16f,Lin,SD,Mar 2)
Nawar 104 (8f,Cfd,SD,Oct 26)
Nearly There 109 (12½f,Ncs,SD,Dec 6)
Ned Pepper 106 (12f,Wol,SD,Oct 17)
Nefarious 103 (7f,Kem,SS,Jun 5)
Nevada 112 (12½f,Ncs,SS,Mar 29)
Never Back Down 108 (7f,Dun,SD,Oct 18)
New Arrangement 106 (9f,Wol,SD,Oct 18)
New Trails 116 (9½f,Mey,FT,Feb 7)
New Vocation 113 (11f,Dun,SD,Mar 8)
New York Ballet 104 (8f,Dun,SD,Nov 1)
Nezar 104 (9f,Wol,SD,May 10)
Nibras Again 109 (5f,Ncs,SS,Feb 28)
Nicholas T 103 (8f,Ncs,SD,Apr 29)
Nick Vedder 108 (6f,Dun,SD,Feb 15)
Nicklaus 108 (8f,Cfd,SD,Aug 16)
Nigg Bay 107 (5f,Dun,SD,Nov 15)
Nightflight 105 (6f,Dun,SD,Dec 3)
Nimitz 112 (12f,Dun,SD,Oct 4)
Nine Below Zero 114 (7f,Mey,FT,Feb 21)
Nisior Donn 106 (7f,Dun,SD,Feb 8)
Nkosikazi 109 (8f,Lin,SD,Aug 31)
No Nay Yellow 103 (6f,Dun,SD,Oct 18)
No Nonsense 108 (6f,Kem,SS,Jan 4)
No Speed Limit 111 (7f,Dun,SD,Nov 20)
No Trouble 104 (11f,Dun,SD,Nov 15)
No Way Jack 103 (11f,Dun,SD,Jan 4)
Noble Expression 111 (16f,Dun,SD,Nov 29)
Noble Fox 103 (10f,Cfd,SD,Dec 12)
Noble Intention 105 (11f,Dun,SD,Feb 15)
Noble Lineage 108 (9½f,Wol,SD,Apr 5)
Noble Music 105 (11f,Kem,SS,Sep 23)
Noble Peace 104 (8f,Lin,SD,Dec 11)
Noble Prospector 103 (9f,Wol,SD,Aug 31)
Noirvento 107 (6f,Dun,SD,Dec 3)
Nonios 111 (10f,Cfd,SD,Jun 20)
Nonkono Yume 103 (8f,Mey,FT,Mar 30)
Nordic Passage 105 (6f,Dun,SD,Nov 1)
Normal Norman 105 (8f,Kem,SS,Dec 4)
Normandy Blue 111 (16½f,Wol,SD,Jan 11)
North America 122 (8f,Mey,FT,Jan 10)
North Face 105 (10f,Cfd,SD,May 2)
Northernpowerhouse 104 (7f,Ncs,SD,Dec 18)
Novabridge 105 (5f,Ncs,SS,Mar 29)
Novel Character 104 (16f,Dun,SD,Mar 29)
Nubough 103 (6f,Cfd,SD,Jan 26)
Numerian 115 (11f,Dun,SD,Sep 27)
Nylon Speed 106 (12f,Kem,SS,Mar 9)

Oasis Fantasy 105 (12f,Lin,SD,Mar 22)
Ode To Autumn 106 (8f,Mey,FT,Apr 12)
Offline 104 (6f,Dun,SD,Mar 15)
Oh It's Saucepot 103 (11f,Kem,SS,Jun 26)
Oh This Is Us 113 (8f,Lin,SD,Apr 19)
Ojooba 111 (10f,Lin,SD,Nov 16)
Olaudah 103 (6f,Cfd,SD,May 27)
Old Fashioned 114 (7f,Mey,FT,Jan 5)
Ollie Bang 104 (7f,Dun,SD,Nov 8)
Ollivander 104 (8f,Sth,SD,Oct 29)
Olly's Folly 105 (11f,Dun,SD,Mar 8)
Olympic Conqueror 107 (10f,Cfd,SD,Sep 21)
Omnivega 105 (11f,Kem,SS,Sep 23)
One Cool Daddy 104 (7f,Kem,SS,Oct 31)
One In All In 105 (12f,Dun,SD,Sep 27)
One More Chance 103 (9f,Wol,SD,Feb 20)
One One Seven 103 (6f,Wol,SD,Dec 3)
One Vision 103 (10f,Ncs,SS,Jan 6)
Onebaba 103 (7f,Wol,SD,Apr 5)
Oneiroi 105 (7f,Dun,SD,Feb 22)
Oneovdem 105 (9f,Wol,SD,Feb 23)
Only Spoofing 107 (5f,Cfd,SD,Aug 9)
Only The Brave 104 (8f,Dun,SD,Nov 29)
Orange Suit 106 (10f,Lin,SD,Dec 18)
Orchidia 105 (9½f,Wol,SD,Jly 9)
Oriental Lilly 106 (5f,Ncs,SS,Apr 19)
Original Choice 106 (10f,Cfd,SD,Sep 4)
Ornate 114 (5f,Ncs,SD,Jan 22)
Oromo 105 (12f,Dun,SD,Sep 27)
Orvar 108 (5f,Wol,SD,Feb 21)
Our Oystercatcher 103 (6f,Cfd,SD,Aug 9)
Outlaw Torn 103 (10f,Cfd,SD,Mar 2)
Outrage 113 (5f,Ncs,SD,Jan 22)
Outside Inside 112 (7f,Dun,SD,Nov 20)
Ouzo 107 (8f,Kem,SS,Nov 19)
Ozone 105 (12f,Dun,SD,Dec 13)

Pablo Escobarr 113 (12f,Kem,SS,Dec 4)
Pacific Fleet 104 (8f,Dun,SD,Feb 8)
Pacific Ocean 104 (8f,Dun,SD,Oct 11)
Pactolus 114 (10f,Lin,SD,Apr 19)
Paddy Power 105 (6f,Ncs,SD,Apr 1)
Paddyplex 103 (9½f,Wol,SD,Dec 27)
Paddytheirishman 103 (7f,Dun,SD,Jan 11)
Pak Army 110 (11f,Dun,SD,Nov 6)
Palladium 103 (12f,Wol,SD,Apr 13)
Panatos 105 (16½f,Sth,SD,Mar 30)
Papa Delta 104 (6f,Cfd,SD,Aug 9)
Papa Stour 103 (7f,Cfd,SD,Jun 19)
Para Mio 104 (12f,Wol,SD,Jan 4)
Paradise Boy 107 (12f,Wol,SD,Mar 28)
Paris Duvet 108 (8f,Dun,SD,Dec 20)
Park Row 110 (12f,Dun,SD,Mar 8)
Parkers Hill 106 (11f,Dun,SD,Dec 6)
Parklife 103 (11f,Mey,FT,Jan 5)
Parknacilla 103 (8f,Cfd,SD,Sep 19)
Pass The Vino 104 (6f,Kem,SS,Nov 6)
Passing Trade 112 (8f,Dun,SD,Dec 3)
Patchouli 104 (8f,Dun,SD,Dec 18)
Paths Of Glory 112 (12f,Wol,SD,Oct 19)
Patrick Joseph 103 (8f,Dun,SD,Jan 11)
Pattie 106 (7f,Cfd,SD,Jun 19)
Paved Paradise 106 (5f,Dun,SD,Mar 29)
Pavel 113 (10f,Mey,FT,Mar 30)
Pea Shooter 107 (5f,Ncs,SS,Feb 5)
Pearl Spectre 106 (7f,Cfd,SD,Jan 10)
Peckinpah 105 (9½f,Wol,SD,Apr 5)
Peddlers Pass 108 (7f,Dun,SD,May 3)
Pendo 106 (10f,Lin,SD,Apr 6)
Pennsylvania Dutch 108 (6f,Mey,FT,Nov 7)
Pentimento 103 (7f,Cfd,SD,Oct 17)
Pentland Lad 103 (7f,Kem,SS,Mar 11)
Pepperoni Pete 107 (11f,Dun,SD,Dec 6)
Perfect Refuge 104 (9½f,Wol,SD,Jan 28)
Perfect Symphony 104 (6f,Cfd,SD,May 27)
Perfect Tapatino 105 (12f,Dun,SD,Oct 18)
Persian Lion 110 (12f,Dun,SD,Sep 27)
Peshkova 108 (8f,Dun,SD,Nov 8)
Pesto 105 (8f,Kem,SS,Aug 21)
Petite Jack 106 (12f,Lin,SD,Dec 21)
Pharoh Jake 104 (5f,Lin,SD,Mar 2)
Pheidippides 106 (8f,Lin,SD,Mar 1)
Philamundo 108 (7f,Cfd,SD,Feb 2)
Phoenix Open 108 (8f,Dun,SD,Nov 22)
Phoenix Star 108 (6f,Kem,SS,Nov 29)
Pianissimo 110 (14f,Cfd,SD,Dec 13)
Picks Pinta 105 (6f,Ncs,SS,Feb 5)
Picture Poet 103 (10f,Cfd,SD,Sep 19)
Piece Of History 107 (7f,Cfd,SD,Sep 14)
Pike Corner Cross 106 (12f,Wol,SD,Jan 30)
Pillar 107 (6f,Dun,SD,Nov 15)
Pillar Of Society 116 (8f,Mey,FT,Mar 2)
Pinnata 112 (7f,Ncs,SD,Jan 22)
Piper Arrow 106 (8f,Cfd,SD,May 23)
Pipes Of Peace 116 (11f,Kem,SS,Mar 30)
Pirate King 108 (12f,Lin,SD,Dec 28)
Pirate's Cove 112 (6f,Mey,FT,Jan 5)
Pivoine 105 (12f,Kem,SS,Sep 7)
Pivotal Flame 104 (13f,Lin,SS,Jan 16)
Plait 106 (10f,Cfd,SD,Jan 26)
Plane Tree Fairy 103 (7f,Dun,SD,Oct 30)
Plata O Plomo 104 (8f,Mey,FT,Jan 17)
Playa Del Puente 114 (8f,Dun,SD,Mar 6)
Playfull Spirit 103 (7f,Ncs,SS,Feb 1)
Plough Boy 107 (6f,Dun,SD,Feb 15)
Plum Perfect 108 (8f,Dun,SD,Nov 20)
Plunger 105 (8f,Lin,SD,Oct 3)
Plus Que Parfait 114 (9½f,Mey,FT,Mar 30)
Pocotaligo 104 (8f,Dun,SD,Sep 20)
Poet's Prince 103 (10f,Cfd,SD,May 2)
Poeta Brasileiro 104 (6f,Cfd,SD,Aug 9)
Poetic Choice 105 (8f,Dun,SD,Apr 17)
Poetic Force 105 (7f,Kem,SS,Mar 27)
Poetic Legacy 110 (10f,Cfd,SD,Sep 19)
Point In Time 103 (12f,Wol,SD,Apr 29)
Poitin 105 (16f,Dun,SD,Mar 29)
Polish 103 (16f,Ncs,SS,Dec 15)
Political Policy 110 (16f,Dun,SD,Jan 11)
Politicise 109 (12f,Dun,SD,Sep 27)
Polly Douglas 103 (5f,Dun,SD,Nov 22)
Polybius 110 (6f,Kem,SS,Nov 29)
Pop The Hood 109 (6f,Mey,FT,Nov 7)
Popsicle 104 (8f,Lin,SD,Nov 20)
Porrima 105 (7f,Ncs,SS,Feb 1)
Port Lions 112 (8f,Dun,SD,Mar 15)
Portledge 108 (7f,Ncs,SD,Jan 31)
Power Drive 107 (12f,Dun,SD,Sep 27)
Power Link 110 (6f,Kem,SS,Aug 20)
Power Of States 107 (7f,Cfd,SD,Sep 21)
Powerful Dream 106 (5f,Wol,SD,Oct 23)
Poyle Vinnie 108 (5f,Cfd,SD,Apr 4)
Precious Plum 104 (5f,Cfd,SD,Mar 15)
Preening 109 (8f,Kem,SS,Apr 20)
Presence Process 103 (10f,Cfd,SD,Sep 19)
Prestbury Park 103 (5f,Wol,SD,Oct 3)
Presto 104 (12f,Dun,SD,Oct 18)
Pretty Little Liar 109 (11f,Dun,SD,Mar 8)
Pretty Smart 104 (6f,Dun,SD,Nov 15)
Pride's Gold 107 (8f,Cfd,SD,Mar 15)
Primero 108 (12f,Lin,SD,Jan 19)
Primo Uomo 108 (5f,Dun,SD,Oct 18)
Primo's Comet 111 (5f,Ncs,SS,Feb 28)
Prince Of Arran 107 (12f,Kem,SS,Sep 7)
Prince Of Harts 108 (9f,Wol,SD,Mar 26)
Prince Of Rome 108 (6f,Kem,SS,Nov 29)
Princely 104 (6f,Ncs,SS,Feb 15)
Princess Harley 108 (12f,Sth,SD,Dec 29)
Private Matter 108 (7f,Sth,SD,Dec 20)
Probability 104 (6f,Cfd,SD,Jun 20)
Proceeding 104 (8f,Ncs,SD,Nov 4)
Prominna 104 (5f,Lin,SD,Mar 2)
Promises Fulfilled 113 (6f,Mey,FT,Mar 30)
Promote 106 (6f,Cfd,SD,Oct 26)

Proschema 110 *(16f,Ncs,SS,Jun 29)*
Proton 107 *(12½f,Ncs,SD,Sep 17)*
Proud And Elated 103 *(8f,Dun,SD,Feb 1)*
Puds 110 *(6f,Cfd,SD,Mar 28)*
Pulsating 104 *(7f,Dun,SD,Nov 8)*
Punjab Mail 104 *(8f,Cfd,SD,Oct 26)*
Purdey's Gift 108 *(12f,Wol,SD,Oct 17)*
Purple Paddy 103 *(8f,Kem,SS,Nov 5)*
Purple Rock 110 *(12f,Sth,SS,Feb 27)*
Pushaq 108 *(8f,Dun,SD,Mar 15)*
Pushkin Museum 103 *(6f,Lin,SD,Jan 26)*

Qaaraat 110 *(5f,Ncs,SD,Nov 1)*
Qaffaal 106 *(9f,Wol,SD,Mar 9)*
Qaroun 106 *(8f,Cfd,SD,Sep 12)*
Quartier Francais 110 *(10f,Mey,FT,Oct 24)*
Queen Amidala 110 *(11f,Dun,SD,Oct 25)*
Queen Constantine 106 *(10f,Cfd,SD,Sep 21)*
Queen Guanhumara 104 *(8f,Dun,SD,Apr 24)*
Queen Of Kalahari 106 *(6f,Sth,SD,Sep 19)*
Queluz 103 *(11f,Dun,SD,Jan 18)*
Quick Breath 104 *(7f,Cfd,SD,Apr 11)*
Quiet Endeavour 103 *(7f,Lin,SD,Mar 2)*
Quila Saeda 106 *(11f,Sth,SD,Apr 3)*
Quintada 105 *(12f,Wol,SD,Aug 31)*
Quote 109 *(12f,Dun,SD,Oct 4)*

Raafid 108 *(6f,Mey,FT,Jan 5)*
Raayan 104 *(7f,Mey,FT,Mar 14)*
Ragtime Red 111 *(11f,Dun,SD,Mar 22)*
Rail Dancer 108 *(12f,Wol,SD,May 10)*
Rainbow Dreamer 113 *(16½f,Sth,SS,Feb 13)*
Raining Fire 106 *(12f,Wol,SD,Oct 30)*
Rakematiz 104 *(10f,Lin,SD,Feb 23)*
Rampant Lion 108 *(9f,Wol,SD,Oct 18)*
Ramsbury 103 *(10f,Cfd,SD,May 2)*
Ranch Hand 108 *(11f,Sth,SD,Apr 29)*
Rangali Island 108 *(8f,Kem,SS,Nov 4)*
Rangefield Express 104 *(5f,Ncs,SD,Nov 1)*
Raphael 113 *(8f,Dun,SD,Dec 6)*
Rapid Reaction 107 *(5f,Dun,SD,Oct 18)*
Rare 103 *(13f,Lin,SD,Jan 16)*
Rare Groove 110 *(16f,Ncs,SS,Jun 29)*
Rasaasy 105 *(12f,Sth,SD,Dec 19)*
Rashdan 107 *(16½f,Sth,SD,Apr 21)*
Rasima 107 *(12f,Kem,SS,Sep 7)*
Raucous 110 *(6f,Wol,SD,Feb 25)*
Raven's Corner 118 *(6f,Mey,FT,Jan 3)*
Rawdaa 108 *(8f,Kem,SS,Apr 20)*
Raydiance 109 *(7f,Ncs,SD,Dec 14)*
Raymond Tusk 115 *(16f,Ncs,SD,Dec 14)*
Razeena 104 *(9½f,Mey,FT,Feb 21)*
Real Estate 106 *(6f,Wol,SD,Dec 16)*
Reckless Endeavour 110 *(6f,Wol,SD,Feb 25)*
Reckless Lad 111 *(11f,Dun,SD,Feb 22)*
Recondite 105 *(8f,Lin,SD,Oct 3)*
Rectory Road 107 *(8f,Kem,SS,Sep 3)*
Red Alert 105 *(6f,Cfd,SD,Feb 20)*
Red All Star 106 *(6f,Dun,SD,Apr 5)*
Red Avenger 108 *(8f,Dun,SD,Nov 29)*
Red Bond 109 *(9½f,Wol,SD,Dec 27)*
Red Cymbal 105 *(6f,Dun,SD,Apr 5)*
Red Force One 105 *(11f,Kem,SS,Feb 6)*
Red Galileo 109 *(16f,Ncs,SS,Jun 29)*
Red Impression 106 *(5f,Ncs,SS,Nov 21)*
Red Royalist 103 *(16f,Kem,SS,Jan 5)*
Red Secret 103 *(11f,Kem,SS,Oct 2)*
Red Stripes 107 *(5f,Wol,SD,Dec 3)*
Red Tornado 109 *(16f,Ncs,SD,Jan 22)*
Reddiac 104 *(10f,Cfd,SD,Sep 19)*
Redicean 108 *(12f,Lin,SD,Jan 19)*
Reeves 111 *(7f,Cfd,SD,Nov 28)*
Reflektor 111 *(5f,Wol,SD,Apr 16)*
Regal Director 111 *(11f,Kem,SS,Oct 9)*
Regimented 103 *(7f,Cfd,SD,Apr 25)*
Regular Income 106 *(9½f,Wol,SD,Feb 1)*
Remmy D 108 *(10f,Ncs,SS,Feb 28)*
Renardeau 107 *(12f,Wol,SD,Dec 26)*
Reponse Exacte 105 *(10f,Lin,SD,Dec 18)*
Reputation 103 *(7f,Cfd,SD,Aug 31)*
Reshoun 103 *(16f,Kem,SS,Nov 20)*
Restive 111 *(12½f,Ncs,SS,Mar 29)*
Restless Rose 112 *(6f,Cfd,SD,Oct 26)*
Revich 104 *(7f,Lin,SS,Oct 31)*
Revolutionise 110 *(6f,Kem,SS,Sep 6)*
Rewaayat 103 *(6f,Ncs,SD,Apr 29)*
Rey Loopy 104 *(8f,Ncs,SS,Feb 5)*
Rhossili Down 103 *(6f,Cfd,SD,Oct 31)*
Right Flank 104 *(7f,Mey,FT,Mar 14)*
Ringo Kid 109 *(16f,Dun,SD,Mar 29)*
Rippling Waters 105 *(8f,Dun,SD,Nov 6)*
Rips Dream 114 *(11f,Dun,SD,Dec 20)*
Risaala 104 *(9f,Wol,SD,Apr 29)*
Rise Again 108 *(11f,Dun,SD,Mar 22)*
Ritchie Valens 109 *(10f,Cfd,SD,May 9)*
River Dart 110 *(16f,Ncs,SD,Jan 8)*
River Glades 111 *(16f,Ncs,SD,Jan 8)*
Riviera Nights 105 *(8f,Kem,SS,Apr 20)*
Robero 105 *(8f,Sth,SD,Dec 29)*
Robert Fitzroy 109 *(12f,Wol,SD,May 13)*
Robert L'Echelle 103 *(12f,Wol,SD,Jly 17)*
Robin Of Navan 106 *(10f,Kem,SS,Mar 30)*
Robin Weathers 113 *(7f,Mey,FT,Jan 5)*
Roc Angel 113 *(10f,Lin,SD,Apr 19)*
Rochester House 103 *(10f,Ncs,SD,Apr 1)*
Rock Bottom 104 *(5f,Wol,SD,Jan 11)*
Rock Boy Grey 104 *(6f,Wol,SD,Dec 27)*
Rock Force 104 *(11f,Kem,SS,May 22)*
Rock Hill 103 *(5f,Ncs,SS,Mar 29)*
Rock In Society 107 *(7f,Cfd,SD,May 23)*
Rock Of Estonia 105 *(7f,Sth,SD,May 2)*
Rock On Aidan 104 *(11f,Dun,SD,Nov 15)*
Rock On Baileys 104 *(7f,Lin,SD,Dec 21)*
Rock Sound 108 *(6f,Sth,SD,Nov 5)*
Rocket Action 112 *(5f,Wol,SD,Nov 6)*
Rockfish 107 *(12f,Dun,SD,Apr 17)*
Rockley Point 107 *(6f,Ncs,SS,Feb 15)*
Rockview Roman 107 *(11f,Dun,SD,Oct 11)*
Rockwood 105 *(10f,Ncs,SS,Feb 28)*
Rodaini 119 *(7f,Mey,FT,Feb 21)*
Roger That 103 *(6f,Dun,SD,Jan 4)*
Rogue 103 *(7f,Cfd,SD,Apr 18)*
Roman De Brut 103 *(9f,Wol,SD,Feb 23)*
Roman River 107 *(6f,Lin,SD,Feb 2)*
Roman Spinner 106 *(7f,Kem,SS,Feb 6)*
Roman Warrior 106 *(8f,Dun,SD,Sep 20)*
Romantically 111 *(16f,Dun,SD,Dec 18)*
Romola 107 *(8f,Kem,SS,Oct 2)*
Rose Berry 111 *(6f,Cfd,SD,Apr 11)*
Rousayan 105 *(8f,Kem,SS,Oct 2)*
Royal Admiral 113 *(11f,Dun,SD,Mar 8)*
Royal Birth 114 *(5f,Lin,SD,Mar 2)*
Royal Brave 107 *(5f,Wol,SD,Oct 23)*
Royal Cosmic 110 *(11f,Sth,SD,Apr 3)*
Royal Court 108 *(6f,Dun,SD,Mar 15)*
Royal Highness 107 *(7f,Dun,SD,Dec 13)*
Royal Intervention 103 *(6f,Cfd,SD,May 2)*
Royal Line 109 *(12f,Kem,SS,Sep 7)*
Royal Prospect 104 *(6f,Ncs,SD,Jan 2)*
Royal Sands 105 *(6f,Sth,SD,Oct 21)*
Rubenesque 108 *(16f,Ncs,SS,Oct 2)*
Rubensian 103 *(12f,Kem,SS,Feb 2)*
Rufus King 111 *(10f,Cfd,SD,Jun 20)*
Rule Of Honour 103 *(8f,Mey,FT,Dec 5)*
Rum Baba 104 *(10f,Lin,SD,Jun 4)*
Run After Genesis 104 *(7f,Kem,SS,Mar 11)*
Russian Realm 103 *(6f,Ncs,SS,Jan 25)*
Rux Power 110 *(7f,Cfd,SD,Mar 28)*

Saaheq 108 *(6f,Sth,SD,Apr 4)*
Sabrina Fairchild 106 *(6f,Dun,SD,Nov 15)*
Saga Bolton 108 *(11f,Dun,SD,Dec 6)*
Saint Equiano 109 *(7f,Sth,SD,Jan 1)*
Saint Mac 103 *(12f,Sth,SD,Jan 10)*
Saisons D'Or 103 *(7f,Wol,SD,Mar 12)*
Sajanji 106 *(10f,Ncs,SD,Jan 2)*
Salateen 109 *(8f,Lin,SD,Apr 19)*
Salt Whistle Bay 108 *(8f,Dun,SD,Dec 18)*
Saltarin Dubai 110 *(10f,Mey,SD,Jan 24)*
Salute The Soldier 109 *(9f,Wol,SD,Mar 16)*
Sam Missile 107 *(11f,Dun,SD,Oct 11)*
Samba Saravah 104 *(12½f,Ncs,SS,Jun 27)*
Samovar 105 *(5f,Sth,SD,Dec 20)*
Samphire Coast 107 *(8f,Kem,SS,Nov 19)*
San Andreas 108 *(7f,Dun,SD,Dec 20)*
Sanaadh 114 *(7f,Kem,SS,Mar 9)*
Sandret 106 *(9½f,Wol,SD,Nov 18)*
Sandridge Lad 113 *(6f,Cfd,SD,Oct 26)*
Sandy Steve 110 *(11f,Kem,SS,Oct 2)*
Santafiora 105 *(6f,Wol,SD,Oct 23)*
Santorini Sun 104 *(11f,Dun,SD,Nov 15)*
Sashenka 107 *(11f,Kem,SS,Dec 11)*
Sassie 103 *(16f,Kem,SS,Jly 3)*
Sauchiehall Street 103 *(12f,Kem,SS,Mar 9)*
Savaanah 106 *(8f,Kem,SS,Apr 20)*
Savalas 108 *(5f,Ncs,SS,Nov 21)*
Savitar 103 *(8f,Lin,SD,Aug 31)*
Sayesse 108 *(7f,Dun,SD,Dec 3)*
Scale Force 104 *(5f,Wol,SD,Aug 31)*
Scarlet Dragon 104 *(12f,Lin,SD,Dec 21)*
Scat King 112 *(8f,Sth,SD,Apr 4)*
Scentasia 113 *(10f,Lin,SD,Nov 16)*
Sceptical 108 *(6f,Dun,SD,Nov 20)*
Scheme 108 *(9½f,Wol,SD,Aug 30)*
Schindlers Ark 103 *(16f,Lin,SD,Jan 23)*
Scofflaw 107 *(7f,Cfd,SD,Jan 24)*
Scotts Honor 105 *(11f,Dun,SD,Dec 20)*
Scream 104 *(7f,Dun,SD,Oct 25)*
Scuzeme 108 *(6f,Ncs,SD,Apr 29)*
Sea Fox 107 *(8f,Lin,SD,Jan 26)*
Sea Sculpture 105 *(9f,Wol,SD,Apr 29)*
Sea Wings 103 *(9½f,Wol,SD,Sep 30)*
Sea's Aria 103 *(16f,Lin,SD,Jan 23)*
Seaborn 103 *(12f,Kem,SS,Sep 25)*
Seafarer 108 *(12f,Lin,SD,Jan 19)*
Seamour 109 *(16f,Ncs,SS,Jun 29)*
Search For Light 103 *(8f,Cfd,SD,May 23)*
Seasearch 104 *(12f,Sth,SS,Feb 27)*
Second Collection 107 *(6f,Kem,SS,Nov 29)*
Second Page 112 *(16½f,Sth,SS,Feb 13)*
Second Summer 105 *(9½f,Mey,FT,Feb 7)*
Secret Ambition 114 *(8f,Mey,FT,Mar 9)*
Secret Art 106 *(10f,Cfd,SD,Apr 4)*
Secret Potion 103 *(6f,Kem,SS,Oct 10)*
Secret Trade 112 *(10f,Mey,FT,Oct 24)*
Secret Wizard 113 *(11f,Dun,SD,Dec 20)*
Secretfact 107 *(5f,Wol,SD,Oct 23)*
Secretinthepark 104 *(5f,Ncs,SD,Oct 9)*
Seeking The Soul 109 *(10f,Mey,FT,Mar 30)*
Seeking Truth 105 *(8f,Dun,SD,Feb 15)*
Self Assessment 105 *(7f,Cfd,SD,Oct 24)*
Selino 106 *(12f,Kem,SS,Aug 5)*
Senior Investment 111 *(9½f,Mey,FT,Feb 7)*
Seniority 108 *(8f,Cfd,SD,Aug 23)*
Senorita Grande 104 *(6f,Cfd,SD,Sep 5)*
Senza Limiti 107 *(8f,Kem,SS,Apr 20)*
Seraphim 103 *(7f,Wol,SD,Dec 2)*
Serenely 104 *(8f,Dun,SD,Mar 15)*
Set Piece 114 *(8f,Kem,SS,Nov 20)*
Setting Sail 111 *(12f,Wol,SD,Apr 22)*
Seven Clans 104 *(12f,Sth,SD,Dec 19)*
Sevenleft 111 *(8f,Dun,SD,Feb 8)*
Severance 104 *(12f,Kem,SS,Aug 21)*
Sezim 107 *(10f,Lin,SD,Dec 9)*
Sh Boom 106 *(10f,Lin,SD,Nov 16)*
Sha La La La Lee 104 *(7f,Wol,SS,Feb 6)*
Shabeeb 105 *(16f,Ncs,SS,Jun 29)*
Shadow Seven 110 *(16f,Dun,SD,Jan 11)*
Shady McCoy 104 *(8f,Kem,SS,Oct 10)*
Shailene 107 *(12½f,Ncs,SD,Apr 19)*
Shake The Bucket 106 *(11f,Dun,SD,Mar 8)*
Shallow Hal 107 *(6f,Ncs,SD,Dec 6)*
Shamlahar 104 *(8f,Lin,SD,Jan 12)*
Shamshon 113 *(5f,Wol,SD,Feb 21)*
Shanaghai City 105 *(6f,Mey,FT,Mar 2)*
Shareef Star 104 *(10f,Ncs,SD,May 3)*
Sharg 105 *(8f,Dun,SD,Nov 6)*
Sharjah 112 *(11f,Dun,SD,Mar 8)*
Sharp Defence 104 *(6f,Dun,SD,Mar 1)*
Sharp Operator 103 *(10f,Lin,SD,Jan 12)*
Shawaaheq 103 *(7f,Cfd,SD,Jly 23)*
She's A Babe 113 *(8f,Dun,SD,Dec 6)*
She's Got You 108 *(8f,Lin,SS,Oct 31)*
Sheberghan 103 *(10f,Lin,SD,Jan 19)*
Sheila's Showcase 103 *(9f,Wol,SD,Oct 12)*
Sheisdiesel 116 *(11f,Dun,SD,Dec 20)*
Shekiba 107 *(11f,Dun,SD,Nov 15)*
Shenanigans 107 *(8f,Kem,SS,Apr 20)*
Shepherd's Purse 108 *(5f,Wol,SD,Oct 17)*
Sheriffmuir 103 *(8f,Kem,SS,Nov 29)*
Shimmering Dawn 107 *(6f,Cfd,SD,Jun 20)*
Shine Baby Shine 108 *(16½f,Sth,SD,Mar 30)*
Shoofly 104 *(12f,Dun,SD,Apr 17)*
Shore Step 105 *(6f,Dun,SD,Nov 29)*
Show Me The Bubbly 103 *(5f,Wol,SD,Oct 3)*
Show Stealer 112 *(6f,Kem,SS,Nov 6)*
Showboating 107 *(8f,Sth,SD,Jan 1)*
Shrewdness 104 *(10f,Cfd,SD,Aug 31)*
Shyron 105 *(8f,Kem,SS,Feb 2)*
Side Effect 105 *(8f,Sth,SD,Jan 24)*
Silent Attack 108 *(7f,Cfd,SD,Nov 28)*
Silent Echo 104 *(6f,Kem,SS,Dec 4)*
Silk Cravat 106 *(7f,Dun,SD,Apr 17)*
Silken Dancer 103 *(10f,Mey,FT,Oct 24)*
Silva 108 *(8f,Mey,FT,Jan 31)*
Silver Quartz 109 *(9f,Wol,SD,Feb 4)*
Silverturnstogold 106 *(7f,Sth,SD,Nov 29)*
Silvington 108 *(16½f,Wol,SD,Jan 11)*
Simoon 105 *(8f,Cfd,SD,Apr 1)*
Simply Beautiful 110 *(10f,Lin,SD,Nov 16)*
Simsir 117 *(11f,Dun,SD,Dec 20)*
Singing Sheriff 110 *(11f,Kem,SS,Oct 9)*
Sir Busker 104 *(8f,Kem,SS,Sep 23)*
Sir Chauvelin 113 *(16f,Ncs,SD,Dec 14)*
Sir Gnet 105 *(10f,Lin,SD,Apr 6)*
Sir Hector 109 *(5f,Wol,SD,Dec 2)*
Sir Ottoman 105 *(8f,Dun,SD,Dec 18)*
Sir Prize 105 *(12f,Kem,SS,Sep 6)*
Sir Thomas Gresham 113 *(6f,Lin,SD,Feb 2)*
Sirjack Thomas 114 *(8f,Dun,SD,Nov 8)*
Six Strings 103 *(6f,Cfd,SD,Sep 26)*
Sky Defender 110 *(10f,Lin,SD,Nov 28)*
Sky Moon 111 *(8f,Dun,SD,Dec 3)*
Sky Seven 109 *(11f,Dun,SD,Nov 15)*
Sleeping Lion 110 *(11f,Kem,SS,May 22)*
Sleepy Head 105 *(11f,Dun,SD,Jan 25)*
Smart Lass 103 *(12½f,Ncs,SS,Sep 6)*
Smarter 107 *(12f,Sth,SD,Apr 4)*
Smokey Lane 105 *(7f,Kem,SS,Feb 6)*
Smugglers Creek 103 *(7f,Wol,SD,Dec 3)*
Snapraeceps 107 *(10f,Lin,SD,Nov 16)*
Snow Ocean 108 *(9½f,Wol,SD,Dec 27)*
So Beloved 106 *(8f,Lin,SD,Nov 16)*
So Enjoy 105 *(11f,Dun,SD,Mar 22)*
Soar Above 104 *(6f,Kem,SS,Jly 3)*
Sociologist 104 *(12f,Sth,SD,Dec 29)*
Soghan 109 *(12f,Lin,SD,Jan 19)*
Solar Gold 108 *(7f,Cfd,SD,Jun 19)*
Solar Heat 104 *(12f,Dun,SD,Sep 27)*
Solar Heights 106 *(8f,Cfd,SD,Aug 29)*
Solar Park 103 *(6f,Wol,SD,Feb 4)*
Solar Shower 105 *(7f,Mey,FT,Mar 14)*
Soldier's Minute 110 *(6f,Kem,SS,Mar 23)*
Solomons Seal 105 *(8f,Dun,SD,Nov 20)*
Something Lucky 109 *(5f,Wol,SD,Feb 19)*
Sommer Katze 103 *(6f,Sth,SD,Dec 5)*
Son And Sannie 105 *(5f,Dun,SD,Oct 30)*
Sonja Henie 105 *(7f,Cfd,SD,Sep 14)*
Sonnet Rose 106 *(6f,Cfd,SD,Mar 28)*
Sophia Maria 106 *(7f,Ncs,SS,Aug 30)*
Sophosc 104 *(10f,Cfd,SD,Aug 23)*
Sosian 103 *(10f,Cfd,SD,Mar 2)*
Soto Sizzler 114 *(11f,Kem,SS,Mar 30)*
Sotomayor 103 *(12f,Lin,SD,Apr 6)*
Sovereigns Bright 109 *(11f,Dun,SD,Dec 6)*
Space Bandit 111 *(7f,Sth,SS,Feb 27)*
Space Walk 110 *(14f,Cfd,SD,Aug 10)*
Spanish Archer 103 *(10f,Cfd,SD,Jun 20)*
Spanish Dawn 108 *(11f,Dun,SD,Mar 8)*
Spanish Soprano 105 *(8f,Dun,SD,Feb 1)*
Spanish Tenor 106 *(8f,Dun,SD,Nov 8)*
Spark Of War 112 *(12½f,Ncs,SD,Dec 6)*
Spark Plug 106 *(16f,Lin,SD,Apr 19)*
Sparkalot 108 *(6f,Kem,SS,Nov 29)*
Specialise 105 *(10f,Cfd,SD,Jly 6)*
Speedy Move 117 *(7f,Mey,FT,Mar 14)*
Spelga 105 *(11f,Dun,SD,Nov 15)*
Spirit Of Angel 103 *(12f,Kem,SS,Sep 6)*
Spirit Of Appin 108 *(12f,Kem,SS,Nov 4)*
Spirit Of May 114 *(6f,Cfd,SD,Oct 26)*
Spirit Of Scotland 104 *(8f,Mey,FT,Mar 14)*
Spirited Guest 105 *(6f,Lin,SD,Nov 28)*
Splash Of Verve 107 *(12½f,Ncs,SS,Mar 29)*
Split Down South 106 *(7f,Cfd,SD,Dec 13)*
Spoof 106 *(6f,Kem,SS,Nov 29)*
Sporting Times 105 *(14f,Cfd,SD,Sep 28)*
Spruce Meadows 113 *(12f,Dun,SD,Sep 27)*
St Brelades Bay 109 *(6f,Dun,SD,Apr 5)*
Stagehand 109 *(12f,Wol,SD,Aug 31)*
Stake Acclaim 107 *(6f,Lin,SD,Nov 16)*
Stamford Raffles 105 *(10f,Lin,SD,Nov 28)*
Star Ascending 107 *(12f,Wol,SD,Jan 21)*
Star Cracker 104 *(6f,Ncs,SS,Feb 5)*
Star Of Bengal 115 *(10f,Cfd,SD,May 23)*
Star Of Southwold 112 *(10f,Cfd,SD,Jun 20)*
Star Of Valour 104 *(9f,Wol,SD,Dec 7)*
Star Shield 103 *(8f,Ncs,SD,Nov 8)*
Starczewski 112 *(14f,Cfd,SD,Aug 10)*
Stargazer 113 *(16f,Lin,SD,Feb 1)*
Starlight Romance 108 *(7f,Ncs,SD,Jan 22)*
State Of Affair 104 *(11f,Kem,SS,Oct 2)*
Staxton 115 *(6f,Ncs,SS,Jun 29)*
Stay Classy 104 *(7f,Lin,SD,Dec 11)*
Steal The Scene 105 *(9f,Wol,SD,Dec 16)*
Steelriver 106 *(6f,Ncs,SS,Feb 15)*
Stone Of Destiny 115 *(6f,Lin,SD,Feb 2)*
Storm Ahead 109 *(9½f,Wol,SD,Nov 18)*
Storm Over 112 *(5f,Wol,SD,Apr 16)*
Stormingin 103 *(10f,Lin,SD,Mar 22)*
Stormy Air 106 *(8f,Dun,SD,Mar 15)*
Stormy Blues 105 *(12f,Wol,SD,Jan 21)*
Straffan 103 *(5f,Dun,SD,Nov 1)*
Straight Right 110 *(7f,Ncs,SD,Jan 22)*
Stranagone 105 *(8f,Dun,SD,Mar 29)*
Stratification 104 *(10f,Cfd,SD,Aug 24)*
Stratum 108 *(16f,Ncs,SS,Jun 29)*
Strawberry Jack 103 *(7f,Cfd,SD,Nov 19)*
Strelka 110 *(10f,Cfd,SD,Aug 24)*
Stringybark Creek 103 *(7f,Kem,SS,Nov 19)*
Strong Johnson 107 *(5f,Dun,SD,Nov 15)*
Stronghold 106 *(11f,Dun,SD,Jan 18)*
Stubbins 106 *(9½f,Mey,FT,Mar 30)*
Subliminal 106 *(10f,Lin,SD,Mar 23)*
Sufi 103 *(12f,Kem,SS,Sep 25)*
Suitcase 'N' Taxi 107 *(7f,Sth,SD,Nov 27)*
Sulafaat 113 *(12½f,Ncs,SD,Dec 6)*
Summer Daydream 103 *(6f,Ncs,SD,Nov 8)*
Summerghand 108 *(6f,Wol,SD,Dec 26)*
Sun Maiden 107 *(12f,Kem,SS,Sep 7)*
Sunhill Lad 103 *(12½f,Ncs,SD,Dec 6)*
Suntory Times 107 *(8f,Dun,SD,Nov 6)*
Superior 108 *(9½f,Mey,FT,Mar 9)*
Sureyoutoldme 103 *(7f,Wol,SD,Apr 13)*
Surfman 109 *(10f,Ncs,SD,Apr 30)*
Surrounding 115 *(8f,Dun,SD,Nov 1)*
Survival Mode 103 *(8f,Dun,SD,Nov 6)*
Suzi's Connoisseur 111 *(5f,Ncs,SD,Jan 22)*
Sweet And Dandy 109 *(6f,Cfd,SD,Mar 28)*
Sweet Celebration 109 *(12f,Kem,SS,Oct 30)*
Sweet Charity 106 *(10f,Lin,SD,Apr 6)*
Sweet Dime 105 *(12f,Dun,SD,Nov 1)*
Swift Approval 111 *(7f,Kem,SS,Mar 9)*
Swift Rose 107 *(9½f,Mey,FT,Mar 30)*
Swiss Army Officer 106 *(8f,Dun,SD,Nov 29)*
Swiss Cheer 104 *(8f,Cfd,SD,Nov 19)*
Swiss Connection 104 *(5f,Ncs,SD,Sep 17)*
Swiss Knight 104 *(7f,Cfd,SD,Oct 24)*
Swiss Pride 104 *(6f,Kem,SS,Sep 11)*
Swiss Storm 109 *(9½f,Wol,SD,Feb 26)*
Switzerland 111 *(6f,Mey,FT,Mar 9)*
Sword Exceed 106 *(7f,Cfd,SD,May 27)*
Sylviacliffs 106 *(7f,Sth,SD,Apr 4)*
Syrena 105 *(8f,Dun,SD,Mar 22)*

Taamol 103 *(6f,Mey,FT,Feb 14)*
Tabarak 117 *(7f,Mey,FT,Feb 7)*
Tagur 106 *(8f,Sth,SD,Dec 5)*
Tahreek 106 *(7f,Cfd,SD,Jun 6)*
Tai Sing Yeh 105 *(6f,Dun,SD,Mar 8)*
Take The Helm 104 *(8f,Lin,SS,Jan 5)*
Take Two 103 *(16f,Kem,SS,Mar 11)*
Takeachancejimmy 106 *(8f,Dun,SD,Apr 5)*
Tallien 105 *(8f,Dun,SD,Mar 29)*
Tamerlane 107 *(8f,Kem,SS,Feb 28)*
Tammooz 109 *(14f,Cfd,SD,Nov 2)*
Tan 105 *(5f,Ncs,SS,Feb 28)*

Tarboosh 107 *(5f,Ncs,SS,Jun 28)*
Target Zone 106 *(8f,Kem,SS,Jan 16)*
Tartlette 104 *(11f,Dun,SD,Oct 11)*
Tathmeen 108 *(5f,Wol,SD,Feb 25)*
Tato Key 114 *(6f,Mey,FT,Mar 9)*
Taurean Star 106 *(7f,Kem,SS,Mar 9)*
Tavener 106 *(6f,Cfd,SD,Mar 7)*
Tawny Port 109 *(5f,Sth,SD,Dec 20)*
Technological 106 *(11f,Kem,SS,Feb 6)*
Tellovoi 104 *(6f,Ncs,SS,Feb 5)*
Templier 110 *(16½f,Wol,SD,Jan 11)*
Tempus 106 *(9f,Wol,SD,Oct 18)*
Temur Khan 104 *(12f,Sth,SD,Jan 24)*
Tennessee Wildcat 106 *(8f,Dun,SD,Dec 18)*
Tenth Amendment 105 *(11f,Dun,SD,Mar 8)*
Teodora De Vega 108 *(10f,Ncs,SD,Jly 27)*
Tesorina 104 *(12f,Lin,SD,Feb 15)*
Tetradrachm 107 *(12f,Wol,SD,Jan 19)*
Thammin 105 *(6f,Mey,FT,Mar 9)*
Thaqaffa 105 *(11f,Kem,SS,Feb 28)*
That Is The Spirit 110 *(7f,Cfd,SD,Jun 6)*
Thawry 111 *(12½f,Ncs,SD,Dec 6)*
The British Lion 105 *(7f,Wol,SD,Jan 28)*
The Bull 104 *(6f,Ncs,SD,Nov 4)*
The Daley Express 107 *(5f,Wol,SD,Dec 20)*
The Dancing Poet 105 *(9½f,Wol,SD,Sep 30)*
The Establishment 105 *(6f,Wol,SD,Feb 19)*
The Game Of Life 112 *(8f,Dun,SD,Feb 8)*
The Gill Brothers 104 *(8f,Cfd,SD,Dec 12)*
The Jean Genie 108 *(10f,Lin,SD,Dec 9)*
The King's Steed 104 *(7f,Wol,SD,Jan 28)*
The Last Emperor 103 *(8f,Dun,SD,Oct 11)*
The Lords Walk 105 *(10f,Lin,SD,Apr 6)*
The Met 105 *(7f,Wol,SD,Oct 23)*
The Mouse Doctor 112 *(16f,Dun,SD,Nov 29)*
The Night King 108 *(10f,Cfd,SD,Mar 7)*
The Perch 106 *(8f,Dun,SD,May 3)*
The Pinto Kid 108 *(14f,Cfd,SD,Sep 28)*
The Right Choice 108 *(7f,Sth,SD,Jan 3)*
The Throstles 106 *(9½f,Wol,SD,Dec 16)*
The Trader 111 *(10f,Cfd,SD,May 9)*
The Warrior 107 *(8f,Kem,SS,Jan 4)*
Thechildren'strust 103 *(8f,Lin,SD,Dec 11)*
Theglasgowwarrior 108 *(16f,Ncs,SD,Jun 29)*
Thegreatcollection 115 *(8f,Mey,FT,Apr 12)*
Thegreatestshowman 106 *(5f,Wol,SD,Nov 26)*
Theobald 114 *(8f,Dun,SD,Nov 8)*
These Days 108 *(8f,Dun,SD,Mar 29)*
Third Time Lucky 106 *(9f,Wol,SD,Mar 9)*
Three Card Trick 104 *(6f,Ncs,SD,Oct 18)*
Three Little Birds 104 *(5f,Wol,SD,Dec 3)*
Three Majors 106 *(8f,Dun,SD,Feb 15)*
Three Weeks 108 *(7f,Sth,SS,Feb 27)*
Thrifty One 106 *(8f,Dun,SD,Mar 22)*
Throckley 104 *(12f,Wol,SD,Apr 27)*
Thunder Buddy 105 *(7f,Sth,SS,Feb 21)*
Thunder Snow 116 *(10f,Mey,FT,Mar 30)*
Thundering Blue 104 *(12f,Kem,SS,Sep 7)*
Ticks The Boxes 108 *(6f,Dun,SD,Dec 3)*
Tiger Eye 106 *(7f,Cfd,SD,Jun 19)*
Tiger Lyon 103 *(5f,Wol,SD,May 31)*
Tigray 108 *(12f,Sth,SD,Apr 21)*
Tilsworth Sammy 103 *(16f,Lin,SD,Jan 23)*
Time Change 112 *(10f,Lin,SD,Nov 28)*
Time To Study 104 *(16f,Ncs,SS,Jun 29)*
Timemakesitfine 105 *(12f,Dun,SD,Sep 27)*
Tin Fandango 103 *(16f,Lin,SD,Apr 2)*
Tinto 108 *(6f,Lin,SD,Nov 16)*
Tio Esteban 103 *(9f,Wol,SD,Nov 6)*
Tipperary Jack 107 *(7f,Kem,SS,Nov 6)*
Tirmizi 110 *(16f,Dun,SD,Nov 29)*
Tis Marvellous 106 *(6f,Kem,SS,Apr 20)*
Titan Goddess 105 *(7f,Cfd,SD,Jan 10)*
Titanium Sky 108 *(8f,Dun,SD,Nov 1)*
To Be Wild 106 *(16f,Ncs,SD,Dec 14)*
To Dibba 104 *(8f,Mey,FT,Mar 2)*
Tobacco Road 105 *(10f,Cfd,SD,Feb 14)*
Togoville 113 *(6f,Dun,SD,Feb 15)*
Tomily 105 *(6f,Ncs,SD,Oct 22)*
Tommy G 108 *(5f,Ncs,SD,Mar 8)*
Tommy Taylor 112 *(6f,Cfd,SD,Oct 26)*
Toni's A Star 105 *(5f,Wol,SS,Feb 6)*
Tony The Gent 111 *(8f,Dun,SD,Jan 11)*
Too Precious 109 *(16f,Dun,SD,Jan 11)*
Tooreen Legend 108 *(12f,Dun,SD,Mar 6)*
Top Boy 103 *(6f,Kem,SS,Oct 10)*
Top Clearance 107 *(11f,Mey,FT,Mar 14)*
Top Rock Talula 103 *(12f,Lin,SD,Feb 15)*
Topology 103 *(11f,Kem,SS,Sep 11)*
Tor 104 *(12f,Wol,SD,Jan 4)*
Torno Subito 111 *(9½f,Mey,FT,Oct 24)*
Torochica 105 *(10f,Cfd,SD,Nov 19)*
Torolight 103 *(12f,Lin,SD,Apr 23)*
Total Commitment 107 *(6f,Kem,SS,Oct 22)*
Tough Remedy 108 *(9f,Wol,SD,Mar 16)*
Toy Theatre 106 *(7f,Kem,SS,Feb 16)*
Tracing 103 *(12f,Dun,SD,Oct 30)*
Tradesman 107 *(11f,Mey,FT,Mar 14)*
Trading Point 113 *(8f,Dun,SD,Nov 8)*
Trailboss 103 *(11f,Kem,SS,Oct 22)*
Train To Georgia 106 *(8f,Lin,SD,Mar 15)*
Tralee Hills 103 *(12f,Kem,SS,Oct 28)*
Transcendent 104 *(6f,Lin,SD,Apr 19)*
Travel On 103 *(12f,Kem,SS,Aug 21)*
Traveller 105 *(8f,Ncs,SD,Sep 25)*

Treacherous 108 *(6f,Kem,SS,Mar 9)*
Treasure Me 104 *(7f,Kem,SS,Feb 16)*
Trenchard 117 *(8f,Mey,FT,Nov 7)*
Trevena 109 *(12f,Dun,SD,Mar 8)*
Trevithick 104 *(8f,Ncs,SD,Apr 29)*
Tribal Path 109 *(6f,Dun,SD,Dec 3)*
Trickbag 109 *(7f,Mey,FT,Feb 21)*
Tried And True 107 *(10f,Mey,FT,Nov 7)*
Trinity Star 104 *(10f,Ncs,SS,Jun 28)*
Triple Nickle 103 *(9½f,Wol,SD,Dec 2)*
Trish's Company 106 *(8f,Dun,SD,Nov 22)*
Tritonix 110 *(16f,Dun,SD,Nov 29)*
Troop 105 *(8f,Ncs,SD,Sep 25)*
Tropics 111 *(5f,Wol,SD,Apr 16)*
Trouble Shooter 103 *(12½f,Ncs,SD,Oct 9)*
True Belief 107 *(6f,Kem,SS,Nov 29)*
True Destiny 104 *(16f,Cfd,SD,Apr 30)*
True Timber 104 *(8f,Mey,FT,Mar 30)*
Trueshan 103 *(12f,Wol,SD,Aug 2)*
Trump Card 105 *(12f,Dun,SD,Feb 8)*
Tsundoku 105 *(16½f,Sth,SD,Mar 30)*
Tudor City 108 *(11f,Dun,SD,Oct 11)*
Tukhoom 105 *(7f,Wol,SD,Dec 3)*
Turanga Leela 104 *(6f,Wol,SD,Jan 29)*
Turf Range 104 *(11f,Dun,SD,Nov 6)*
Turn 'n Twirl 107 *(7f,Cfd,SD,Sep 14)*
Turn To Rock 107 *(6f,Kem,SS,Oct 22)*
Twenty Minutes 108 *(8f,Dun,SD,Feb 8)*
Twist 103 *(10f,Lin,SD,Mar 22)*
Ty Rock Brandy 105 *(5f,Dun,SD,Nov 1)*
Tynamite 109 *(6f,Dun,SD,Apr 5)*
Tynecastle Park 109 *(16½f,Sth,SD,Mar 30)*
Typhoon Ten 105 *(7f,Lin,SD,Dec 4)*
Tyrconnell 103 *(7f,Dun,SD,Feb 22)*

U S S Michigan 113 *(8f,Cfd,SD,Apr 11)*
Ubla 107 *(9f,Wol,SD,Mar 25)*
Udontdodou 105 *(5f,Kem,SS,Apr 20)*
Ulshaw Bridge 110 *(8f,Ncs,SD,Jun 4)*
Ulster 107 *(14f,Cfd,SD,Sep 28)*
Ultimate Avenue 109 *(6f,Cfd,SD,Jan 24)*
Unabated 113 *(6f,Cfd,SD,Aug 10)*
Unabridged 107 *(8f,Dun,SD,Jan 11)*
Uncle Jerry 113 *(6f,Cfd,SD,Oct 26)*
Unforgiving Minute 106 *(7f,Wol,SD,Dec 3)*
Union Rose 107 *(5f,Wol,SD,Jan 19)*
Universal Gleam 113 *(10f,Lin,SD,Nov 28)*
Up Ten Down Two 110 *(12½f,Ncs,SS,Mar 29)*
Upavon 103 *(6f,Kem,SS,Jan 15)*
Urban Beat 110 *(6f,Dun,SD,Nov 1)*
Urban Spirit 103 *(16f,Ncs,SS,Apr 11)*
Ustath 104 *(6f,Wol,SD,Mar 28)*
Uther Pendragon 106 *(12f,Wol,SD,Dec 26)*

Vale Of Kent 107 *(7f,Cfd,SD,Aug 31)*
Valentino Dancer 112 *(11f,Kem,SS,Feb 28)*
Valley Of Fire 105 *(7f,Ncs,SD,Dec 6)*
Vampish 103 *(9f,Wol,SD,Feb 20)*
Van Beethoven 111 *(8f,Dun,SD,Mar 6)*
Van Gerwen 103 *(5f,Ncs,SD,Mar 1)*
Vandella 103 *(7f,Kem,SS,Jan 5)*
Vee Man Ten 106 *(6f,Cfd,SD,Oct 26)*
Velma Valento 111 *(10f,Lin,SD,Nov 16)*
Velvet Vision 103 *(10f,Cfd,SD,Apr 1)*
Ventura Knight 105 *(9f,Wol,SD,Mar 9)*
Venture 104 *(6f,Kem,SS,Nov 27)*
Venturous 108 *(5f,Wol,SD,Mar 26)*
Verhoyen 106 *(6f,Dun,SD,Feb 15)*
Verify 106 *(12f,Wol,SD,Oct 17)*
Verne Castle 109 *(5f,Lin,SD,Mar 2)*
Very Smart 106 *(7f,Dun,SD,Jan 25)*
Via Serendipity 110 *(8f,Kem,SS,Oct 10)*
Vibrance 105 *(16f,Kem,SS,Nov 29)*
Vibrant Chords 109 *(6f,Kem,SS,Apr 20)*
Victorious Secret 107 *(7f,Dun,SD,Jan 25)*
Victory Bond 113 *(10f,Lin,SD,Apr 19)*
Victory Command 109 *(10f,Cfd,SD,Aug 16)*
Victory Wave 109 *(6f,Kem,SS,Apr 20)*
View The Bay 111 *(6f,Dun,SD,Feb 15)*
Villette 106 *(11f,Kem,SS,Feb 28)*
Viola Park 103 *(7f,Kem,SS,Feb 27)*
Visionara 105 *(8f,Lin,SD,Aug 31)*
Visionary 108 *(6f,Ncs,SS,Feb 18)*
Vivacious Spirit 104 *(6f,Dun,SD,Mar 15)*
Vivax 103 *(11f,Dun,SD,May 3)*
Vivernus 104 *(12f,Sth,SD,Jan 13)*
Vivionn 104 *(10f,Cfd,SD,Jly 6)*
Voi 109 *(11f,Kem,SS,Feb 28)*
Voice Of A Leader 103 *(10f,Lin,SD,Mar 8)*
Volcanic Sky 105 *(12f,Kem,SS,Jun 5)*
Von Blucher 109 *(6f,Ncs,SS,Jun 29)*
Voyageofdiscovery 108 *(8f,Dun,SD,Feb 15)*

Waady 111 *(6f,Mey,FT,Nov 7)*
Wahash 103 *(9f,Wol,SD,Mar 9)*
Wait Forever 105 *(8f,Lin,SD,Nov 16)*
Waitaki 107 *(7f,Dun,SD,Jan 25)*
Walk In The Sun 106 *(10f,Mey,FT,Nov 7)*
Walk On Walter 110 *(6f,Cfd,SD,Mar 2)*
Walking Thunder 109 *(8f,Mey,FT,Jan 10)*
Wanaasah 104 *(12f,Wol,SD,Aug 12)*
War Advocate 104 *(7f,Dun,SD,May 3)*

War Glory 111 *(7f,Cfd,SD,Sep 14)*
War Hero 110 *(6f,Dun,SD,Dec 13)*
War Tiger 108 *(9½f,Wol,SD,Feb 21)*
Warning Fire 107 *(6f,Lin,SD,Mar 15)*
Warrior's Valley 105 *(5f,Sth,SD,Mar 14)*
Warsaw Road 104 *(6f,Ncs,SD,Oct 22)*
Wasntexpectingthat 107 *(6f,Ncs,SD,Nov 22)*
Watchable 113 *(5f,Ncs,SS,Nov 21)*
Water Diviner 103 *(7f,Cfd,SD,Jly 6)*
Water's Edge 104 *(9½f,Wol,SD,Feb 21)*
Waterboy 105 *(11f,Dun,SD,Mar 15)*
Watersmeet 116 *(16f,Lin,SD,Feb 1)*
Way Of Wisdom 118 *(6f,Mey,FT,Oct 24)*
Weekender 109 *(14f,Cfd,SD,May 9)*
Weld Al Emarat 112 *(7f,Sth,SS,Feb 27)*
Welford 113 *(11f,Mey,FT,Mar 14)*
Weloof 104 *(8f,Lin,SD,Dec 30)*
West Coast Flyer 109 *(12f,Kem,SS,Feb 16)*
Western Australia 113 *(8f,Dun,SD,Mar 6)*
Western Duke 107 *(11f,Kem,SS,May 22)*
What's The Story 103 *(7f,Ncs,SD,May 3)*
Whatharm 109 *(8f,Dun,SD,Nov 20)*
Whenapoet 103 *(8f,Sth,SD,Jan 24)*
Whimbrel 103 *(10f,Cfd,SD,Jun 6)*
Whisper Aloud 106 *(6f,Wol,SD,Oct 19)*
White Chocolate 107 *(14f,Cfd,SD,Jun 19)*
White Coat 106 *(7f,Cfd,SD,Mar 28)*
White Mountain 103 *(9f,Wol,SD,Nov 18)*
White Shaheen 104 *(12f,Wol,SD,Jan 11)*
Whitefountainfairy 105 *(6f,Kem,SS,Mar 30)*
Whitsunday Islands 103 *(12f,Dun,SD,Apr 24)*
Who Dares Wins 111 *(16f,Ncs,SS,Jun 29)*
Wiff Waff 103 *(5f,Wol,SD,Apr 2)*
Wild Edric 105 *(6f,Wol,SD,Jly 15)*
Wild Shot 114 *(11f,Dun,SD,Mar 22)*
Wiley Post 105 *(6f,Lin,SD,Nov 28)*
Will Be King 114 *(8f,Dun,SD,Dec 3)*
Wimpole Hall 108 *(11f,Kem,SS,May 22)*
Winged Spur 103 *(10f,Ncs,SS,Feb 28)*
Wise Ruler 112 *(12½f,Ncs,SD,Sep 17)*
Wise Words 104 *(5f,Ncs,SD,May 3)*
Wissahickon 118 *(10f,Lin,SD,Feb 2)*
With A Start 105 *(11f,Dun,SD,Feb 15)*
With Approval 104 *(7f,Ncs,SS,Aug 30)*
With Caution 108 *(6f,Cfd,SD,Sep 26)*
Woodditton 115 *(9½f,Mey,FT,Oct 24)*
Woven 103 *(6f,Cfd,SD,Sep 14)*

X Y Jet 118 *(6f,Mey,FT,Mar 30)*

Yale 109 *(5f,Dun,SD,Oct 30)*
Yamato 110 *(16f,Dun,SD,Dec 18)*
Yarraman 115 *(11f,Dun,SD,Mar 8)*
Yattwee 109 *(8f,Cfd,SD,Aug 16)*
Ydra 105 *(12f,Lin,SD,Feb 22)*
Yellow Tiger 107 *(12f,Wol,SD,Oct 19)*
Yimou 107 *(5f,Wol,SD,Nov 6)*
Yoshida 111 *(10f,Mey,FT,Mar 30)*
You Never Can Tell 103 *(7f,Lin,SD,Mar 2)*
You're Cool 107 *(5f,Cfd,SD,Apr 4)*
Young Fire 105 *(7f,Wol,SD,Nov 30)*
Young John 108 *(6f,Sth,SD,Oct 21)*
Young Rascal 111 *(12f,Kem,SS,Nov 4)*
Young Tiger 107 *(5f,Ncs,SD,Dec 14)*
Your Band 103 *(14f,Cfd,SD,Jan 10)*
Your Pal Tal 107 *(6f,Dun,SD,Mar 8)*
Yourartisonfire 104 *(8f,Dun,SD,Feb 15)*
Yuften 114 *(8f,Dun,SD,Dec 6)*
Yvette 108 *(11f,Kem,SS,Oct 2)*

Zaajer 106 *(6f,Mey,FT,Oct 24)*
Zac Brown 106 *(6f,Cfd,SD,Jun 6)*
Zack Mayo 105 *(12f,Wol,SD,Dec 26)*
Zafaranah 104 *(7f,Cfd,SD,Oct 31)*
Zalmi Star 104 *(7f,Mey,FT,Mar 14)*
Zamjar 107 *(6f,Ncs,SD,Oct 22)*
Zap 103 *(7f,Cfd,SD,Sep 14)*
Zapper Cass 109 *(5f,Ncs,SD,Mar 1)*
Zayriyan 107 *(11f,Dun,SD,Mar 8)*
Zeyzoun 106 *(7f,Cfd,SD,Aug 24)*
Zmhar 109 *(7f,Cfd,SD,Feb 20)*
Zorawar 106 *(10f,Cfd,SD,Feb 14)*
Zuba 107 *(12f,Kem,SS,Aug 5)*
Zubayr 110 *(16f,Ncs,SD,Jan 22)*
Zwayyan 108 *(9f,Wol,SD,Mar 9)*
Zylan 106 *(6f,Sth,SS,Feb 21)*

TWO-YEAR-OLDS - Turf

A New Dawn 104 *(7f,Leo,G,Jun 6)*
A'Ali 104 *(5f,Rip,GS,Jun 5)*
Aberama Gold 105 *(6f,Red,HY,Oct 5)*
Afraid Of Nothing 105 *(7f,Eps,HY,Sep 29)*
Agitare 108 *(8f,Leo,S,Oct 19)*
Ainsdale 109 *(5f,Not,S,Oct 30)*
Al Raya 106 *(5f,Asc,GS,Jun 19)*
Al Suhail 108 *(8f,Nmk,S,Oct 12)*
Albigna 116 *(8f,Lon,VS,Oct 6)*
Alix James 103 *(7f,Mus,S,Oct 15)*
Alpen Rose 106 *(8f,Don,GF,Sep 12)*
Alpine Star 114 *(7f,Gal,G,Aug 2)*
Always Fearless 106 *(7f,Hay,GS,Jly 20)*
Amaysmont 103 *(6f,Crl,GS,Aug 21)*
Amma Grace 113 *(8f,Leo,S,Oct 19)*
Ananya 104 *(8f,Don,GF,Sep 12)*
Areehaa 104 *(6f,Sal,GF,Sep 3)*
Arizona 115 *(6f,Cur,GF,May 26)*
Armory 105 *(7f,Cur,G,Sep 15)*
Art Power 104 *(5f,Yor,S,Oct 11)*
Astrozone 106 *(5f,Cat,G,Aug 28)*
Auchterarder 103 *(5f,Bev,GS,May 14)*
Auckland Lodge 108 *(5f,Cat,GF,Sep 3)*
Auxilia 105 *(7f,Leo,G,Jly 25)*
Azila 104 *(7f,Leo,SH,Oct 26)*

Back To Brussels 104 *(6f,Cur,GF,May 24)*
Band Practice 103 *(5f,Chp,G,Sep 2)*
Berlin Tango 105 *(7f,Don,GF,Sep 13)*
Bionic Woman 111 *(8f,Lon,VS,Oct 6)*
Blissful 103 *(6f,Cur,G,Jly 21)*
Bond's Boy 106 *(6f,Red,GF,Aug 24)*
Boomer 107 *(8f,Don,GF,Sep 12)*
Born With Pride 106 *(8f,Nmk,HY,Nov 2)*
Brad The Brief 108 *(6f,Nmk,S,Nov 1)*
Breathalyze 104 *(7½f,Chs,G,Sep 13)*
Breguet Boy 103 *(5f,Cat,G,Aug 28)*
Brook On Fifth 103 *(7f,Cur,S,Aug 16)*
Brunelle 105 *(6f,Cur,GY,Aug 30)*
Bushtucker Trial 105 *(5f,Lei,GF,May 20)*

C'Moi Cesar 103 *(8f,Lon,VS,Oct 5)*
Camachita 103 *(7f,Leo,SH,Oct 19)*
Captain Corcoran 103 *(6f,Cur,S,Aug 16)*
Cayenne Pepper 108 *(8f,Cur,GY,Aug 30)*
Ceinture Noire 104 *(8f,Lon,VS,Oct 5)*
Celestial Object 108 *(7f,Leo,SH,Oct 26)*
Celtic High King 110 *(8f,Leo,S,Oct 19)*
Champers Elysees 112 *(6f,Cur,HY,Sep 29)*
Chrysalism 108 *(6f,Cur,S,Aug 16)*
Classy Moon 107 *(5f,Crl,GS,Jun 11)*
Cloak Of Spirits 109 *(7f,Nmk,G,Sep 27)*
Coase 111 *(6f,Crl,S,May 30)*
Cobra Eye 103 *(6f,Hay,GS,Jly 19)*
Cognac 103 *(7f,Mus,GS,Aug 28)*
Cold Front 109 *(6½f,Nby,HY,Oct 25)*
Convict 107 *(8f,Yor,S,Oct 12)*
Cool Vixen 103 *(6f,Cur,GY,Aug 30)*

Daahyeh 110 *(7f,Nmk,G,Sep 27)*
Daily Times 103 *(5f,Not,S,Oct 30)*
Danyah 107 *(6f,Not,S,Aug 16)*
Dark Lady 106 *(6f,Sal,G,Sep 5)*
Degraves 108 *(9f,Leo,SH,Oct 26)*
Desert Safari 106 *(6f,Red,HY,Oct 5)*
Domino Darling 111 *(8f,Don,HY,Oct 25)*
Dr Simpson 104 *(5f,Ayr,G,Sep 20)*
Dragon Of Malta 104 *(6f,Cur,HY,Sep 29)*
Dubai Souq 114 *(10f,Not,S,Oct 9)*
Duesenberg 104 *(7f,Red,HY,Oct 5)*
Duke Of Condicote 106 *(10f,Not,S,Oct 9)*
Dylan De Vega 104 *(5f,Bev,G,May 6)*

Earthlight 108 *(6f,Nmk,G,Sep 28)*
Ellenor Gray 104 *(5f,Cat,G,Aug 28)*
Embolden 106 *(7f,Red,HY,Oct 5)*
Encipher 103 *(7f,Nby,GS,Jly 19)*
Epona Plays 110 *(8f,Leo,S,Oct 19)*
Exceptional 103 *(5f,Crl,S,May 30)*

Faakhirah 105 *(6f,Yar,F,Aug 25)*
Fee Historique 104 *(8f,Lon,VS,Oct 6)*
Feminista 105 *(7f,Leo,SH,Oct 26)*
Festival Day 104 *(7f,Chp,G,Sep 17)*
Final Song 110 *(5f,Asc,GS,Jun 19)*
Flaming Princess 106 *(5f,Asc,GS,Jun 19)*
Flight Of Thunder 106 *(5f,Cat,GF,Sep 3)*
Flighty Lady 113 *(8f,Lon,VS,Oct 6)*
Flippa The Strippa 105 *(5f,Asc,GS,Jun 19)*
Flower Garland 104 *(7f,Leo,SH,Oct 26)*
For The Trees 105 *(6f,Cur,S,Aug 16)*
Forbidden Land 106 *(8f,Don,GF,Sep 14)*
Fort Myers 108 *(6f,Cur,GY,Aug 30)*
Franklin Street 106 *(6f,Cur,HY,Sep 29)*
Fred 107 *(7f,Hay,GS,Jly 20)*
Free Solo 103 *(8f,Leo,G,Jly 25)*
French Rain 106 *(6f,Cur,G,Jly 21)*

Gallaside 105 *(6f,Crl,S,May 30)*
Genever Dragon 104 *(7f,Hay,GS,Jly 20)*
Gold Wand 110 *(8f,Don,HY,Oct 25)*
Golden Horde 107 *(6f,Nmk,G,Sep 28)*
Good Night Mr Tom 104 *(6f,Ham,GS,Aug 3)*
Gravity Force 105 *(7f,Nmk,HY,Nov 2)*
Green Book 106 *(10f,Not,S,Oct 9)*
Guildsman 109 *(6f,Cur,GY,Aug 30)*

Harpocrates 104 *(6f,Cur,GF,May 24)*
He's A Keeper 106 *(7f,Hay,GS,Jly 20)*
Helter Skelter 108 *(7f,Lon,GS,Jly 14)*
Highland Chief 104 *(7f,Asc,G,Jun 22)*
Holy Roman Empress 110 *(8f,Leo,S,Oct 19)*
Huboor 103 *(7f,Nmk,G,Sep 28)*

Iberia 105 *(7f,Leo,SH,Oct 19)*
Ickworth 104 *(5f,Ayr,G,Sep 20)*
Impressor 109 *(7f,Nmk,HY,Nov 2)*
In From The Cold 104 *(6f,Cur,S,Aug 16)*
Incinerator 104 *(8f,Wdr,GF,Sep 2)*
International Lion 106 *(8f,Yor,S,Oct 12)*
Into Faith 106 *(8f,Lon,VS,Oct 5)*
Isabeau 105 *(5f,Cur,S,Aug 16)*
Iva Go 103 *(5f,Bev,GF,Apr 25)*

Jamaheery 104 *(6f,Yar,GF,Sep 19)*
Jeanie B 104 *(6f,Nmk,S,Nov 1)*
Johan Zoffani 111 *(6f,Cur,HY,Sep 29)*
Jovial 107 *(6f,Yar,F,Aug 25)*
Juan Elcano 105 *(7f,Nmk,GF,Jly 13)*
Justifier 107 *(9f,Leo,SH,Oct 26)*

Kameko 107 *(7f,San,GF,Aug 31)*
Katiba 105 *(7f,Leo,SH,Oct 19)*
Katie Bo Kat 105 *(8f,Leo,S,Oct 19)*
Keep Busy 103 *(6f,Nmk,S,Nov 1)*
Kenzai Warrior 111 *(7f,Nmk,HY,Nov 2)*
Kimari 111 *(5f,Asc,GS,Jun 19)*
King Carney 104 *(8½f,Not,S,Oct 9)*
King Neptune 105 *(6f,Cur,GF,May 24)*
King Of Athens 104 *(6f,Cur,GF,May 26)*
King's Lynn 108 *(6½f,Don,GF,Sep 12)*
Kingbrook 106 *(8f,Don,GF,Sep 14)*
Kinross 110 *(7f,Nmk,GS,Oct 5)*
Know It All 103 *(7f,Cur,Y,Aug 23)*
Know No Limits 103 *(6f,Chs,S,Jun 15)*
Kuwait Direction 103 *(6f,Nmk,S,Nov 1)*

La Chica Lobo 103 *(5f,Cat,G,Aug 28)*
Lady G 105 *(8f,Don,HY,Oct 25)*
Lady Light 104 *(6f,Nmk,S,Nov 1)*
Lady Nectar 104 *(5f,Cat,GF,Sep 3)*
Lady Penelope 105 *(5f,Ayr,G,Sep 20)*
Ladysane 104 *(8f,Lon,VS,Oct 5)*
Laikaparty 104 *(6f,Bat,F,Sep 4)*
Lambeth Walk 103 *(5f,Asc,GS,Jun 19)*
Lampang 105 *(6f,Crl,GF,Aug 29)*
Lara Silvia 106 *(5f,Mus,GS,Sep 29)*
Letscrackon 109 *(5f,Wdr,HY,Oct 21)*
Liberty Beach 108 *(5f,Asc,GS,Jun 19)*
Lil Grey 105 *(6f,Cur,GY,Jun 7)*
Living In The Past 103 *(6f,Yor,G,Aug 22)*
Longclaw 108 *(7f,Gal,G,Aug 2)*
Lope Y Fernandez 111 *(6f,Cur,GY,Aug 30)*
Lord Of The Lodge 105 *(6f,Yor,GF,Aug 23)*
Lost In Time 107 *(6f,Sal,GF,Sep 3)*
Louganini 103 *(7f,Nmk,S,Nov 1)*
Love 110 *(7f,Leo,G,Jly 25)*
Lucander 108 *(8f,Yor,S,Oct 12)*
Luigi Vampa 104 *(8f,Lon,VS,Oct 5)*

Magical Journey 105 *(6f,Nmk,S,Nov 1)*
Magna Moralia 109 *(10f,Not,S,Oct 9)*
Majestic Sands 104 *(5f,Lei,G,May 28)*
Make It Rain 103 *(8f,Don,HY,Oct 25)*
Makyon 105 *(5f,Mus,S,Aug 9)*
Mambo Nights 108 *(7f,Nby,GS,Aug 16)*
Manigordo 106 *(6½f,Don,GF,Sep 12)*
Marieta 113 *(8f,Lon,VS,Oct 6)*
Max Vega 103 *(10f,Nmk,S,Oct 12)*
Megans Beau 106 *(6f,Cur,HY,Sep 29)*
Midnights Legacy 103 *(10f,Bat,S,Oct 16)*
Mighty Spirit 106 *(5f,Asc,GS,Jun 19)*
Mild Illusion 106 *(6f,Nmk,S,Nov 1)*
Military March 109 *(8f,Nmk,S,Oct 12)*
Millisle 107 *(6f,Nmk,G,Sep 28)*
Miss Molly T 103 *(7f,Leo,SH,Oct 26)*
Mogul 104 *(8f,Leo,G,Sep 14)*
Mogwli 104 *(6f,Cur,S,Oct 22)*
Mohican Heights 105 *(8f,Sal,G,Aug 23)*
Molatham 107 *(7f,Don,GF,Sep 13)*
Monarch Of Egypt 109 *(6f,Cur,S,Aug 9)*
Mount Fuji 103 *(6f,Cur,GY,Aug 30)*
Mums Tipple 113 *(6f,Yor,G,Aug 22)*
Myrcella 106 *(6f,Cur,HY,Sep 29)*
Mystery Power 107 *(7f,Nmk,GF,Jly 13)*

Nobel Prize 108 *(8f,Leo,S,Oct 19)*
Nope 104 *(7f,Nmk,GS,Oct 11)*
Not On Your Nellie 103 *(5f,Mus,GS,Sep 29)*

Ocasio Cortez 105 *(5f,Chs,GS,Jly 27)*
One Voice 109 *(7f,Leo,G,Jly 25)*
Ottoman Court 104 *(7f,Nby,GS,Aug 16)*
Owney Madden 104 *(6f,Yor,G,Aug 21)*

Panic Room 103 *(6f,Crl,GF,Aug 29)*
Peace Charter 108 *(6f,Cur,G,Jun 28)*
Peaceful 105 *(8f,Nmk,HY,Nov 2)*
Persia 107 *(9f,Leo,SH,Oct 26)*
Petite Mustique 106 *(7f,Cur,Y,Aug 23)*
Piece Of Paradise 107 *(5f,Ayr,G,Sep 20)*
Pierre Lapin 106 *(6f,Nby,GF,Sep 21)*
Pinatubo 116 *(7f,Cur,G,Sep 15)*
Pistoletto 104 *(6½f,Don,GF,Sep 12)*
Platinum Star 104 *(6f,Rip,G,Aug 26)*
Plegastell 110 *(8f,Lon,VS,Oct 6)*
Pop Dancer 113 *(5f,Pon,G,Jly 28)*
Positive 108 *(7f,San,GF,Aug 31)*
Powerful Breeze 108 *(8f,Don,GF,Sep 12)*
Praxeology 104 *(6f,Rip,G,Jun 6)*
Precious Moments 110 *(6f,Cur,G,Jun 28)*
Prince Of Naples 104 *(6f,Cur,GY,Aug 30)*
Proper Beau 103 *(5f,Bev,GF,Aug 25)*
Pyledriver 107 *(8f,Hay,S,Sep 7)*
Pyramid Rock 107 *(8f,Leo,S,Oct 19)*

Quadrilateral 109 *(7f,Nby,GS,Aug 16)*
Queen's Order 111 *(5f,Pon,G,Jly 28)*
Queens Blade 104 *(6f,Red,G,Aug 10)*

Raaeq 103 *(7f,Nby,GF,Sep 21)*
Raahy 103 *(5f,Lin,GF,Jun 29)*
Raasel 104 *(6f,Nmk,S,Nov 1)*
Raffle Prize 112 *(5f,Asc,GS,Jun 19)*
Raheeq 105 *(6f,Bat,G,Jun 26)*
Real Force 103 *(6f,Cur,G,Jun 29)*
Repartee 107 *(6f,Yor,GF,May 16)*
Rich Belief 105 *(8f,Yor,S,Oct 12)*
Road Rage 103 *(7f,Hay,S,Aug 9)*
Roca Roma 112 *(8f,Leo,S,Oct 19)*
Roman Turbo 103 *(6f,Cur,G,Jun 28)*
Romantic Vision 107 *(5f,Cat,G,Aug 28)*
Ropey Guest 110 *(7f,Nmk,HY,Nov 2)*
Rose Of Kildare 105 *(7f,Nmk,GS,Oct 11)*
Royal Crusade 104 *(7f,Don,GF,Sep 14)*
Royal Dornoch 107 *(8f,Nmk,G,Sep 28)*
Royal Lytham 108 *(6f,Cur,S,Aug 9)*
Run Wild 106 *(8f,Don,GF,Sep 12)*

Salsa 106 *(8f,Leo,S,Oct 19)*
San Pedro 103 *(7f,Leo,SH,Oct 26)*
Sand Diego 103 *(5f,San,G,Sep 13)*
Santiago 110 *(7f,Gal,G,Aug 2)*
Saphiri 105 *(6f,Cur,S,Oct 22)*
Savarin 103 *(8f,Lon,VS,Oct 6)*
Schroders Mistake 107 *(6f,Cur,SH,Oct 13)*
Separate 104 *(7f,Nmk,GS,Oct 11)*
Shadn 103 *(6f,Nby,GF,Sep 21)*
Shepherds Way 105 *(5f,Mus,GS,Sep 29)*
Silver Spear 105 *(6f,Cur,SH,Oct 13)*
Sinawann 106 *(8f,Cur,Y,Aug 23)*
Siskin 110 *(6f,Cur,G,Jun 29)*
Sky Storm 104 *(6½f,Nby,HY,Oct 25)*
So Wonderful 105 *(7f,Leo,G,Jly 25)*
Soineanta 103 *(7f,Leo,SH,Oct 26)*
Soul Search 106 *(7f,Cur,Y,Aug 23)*
Sound Of Cannons 105 *(8f,Hay,S,Sep 7)*
Spartan Fighter 105 *(5f,Rip,GS,Jun 5)*
Spring Bloom 103 *(5f,Lei,GF,May 20)*
Spygate 104 *(5f,Cat,GF,Sep 3)*
Star Alexander 103 *(5f,Bat,GS,Jun 15)*
Star In The Making 106 *(6f,Sal,GF,Sep 3)*
Stela Star 107 *(7f,Leo,SH,Oct 19)*
Stone Circle 103 *(6f,Cur,G,Sep 15)*
Stormy Girl 108 *(6f,Crl,GS,Sep 11)*
Strategic Fortune 106 *(6f,Cur,S,Oct 22)*
Stylistique 109 *(7f,Nmk,G,Sep 27)*
Subjectivist 103 *(8f,Sal,G,Aug 23)*
Summer Romance 104 *(6f,Nmk,GF,Jun 29)*
Summer Sands 111 *(6f,Red,HY,Oct 5)*

Tammani 104 *(8f,Hay,S,Sep 7)*
Tango 115 *(6f,Cur,SH,Oct 13)*
Tell Me All 105 *(7f,Hay,GS,Jly 20)*
The King Of Kells 108 *(6f,Cur,S,Oct 22)*
The New Marwan 104 *(8f,Yor,S,Oct 12)*
Threat 107 *(6f,Yor,GF,Aug 23)*
Three Coins 103 *(6f,Thi,S,Aug 16)*
Thunderous 103 *(7f,Red,GF,Jly 21)*
Tom Tulliver 103 *(5f,Bev,GF,Aug 25)*
Tomfre 104 *(7f,Nmk,HY,Nov 2)*
Top Buck 103 *(8f,Bat,F,Sep 14)*
Toro Strike 107 *(6½f,Don,GF,Sep 12)*
Treble Treble 106 *(6f,Hay,GS,Jly 19)*
Tritonic 106 *(7f,Hay,GS,Jly 20)*
Tropbeau 104 *(6f,Nmk,G,Sep 28)*
Troubador 107 *(6f,Red,HY,Oct 5)*

Under The Stars 108 *(7f,Nmk,G,Sep 27)*
Unforgetable 106 *(7f,Leo,G,Jly 25)*
Upstate New York 105 *(6f,Not,S,Aug 16)*

Valeria Messalina 104 *(7f,Nmk,GS,Oct 11)*
Vardon Flyer 105 *(6f,Crl,S,May 30)*
Ventura Flame 103 *(5f,Crl,GS,Jun 11)*
Ventura Lightning 107 *(6f,Cur,GY,Aug 30)*
Visinari 105 *(7f,Don,GF,Sep 13)*

War Storm 103 *(6f,Red,G,Jun 22)*
Waterville Lady 103 *(6f,Cur,HY,Sep 29)*
Well Of Wisdom 109 *(7f,Lon,GS,Jly 14)*
White Moonlight 105 *(8f,Nmk,GS,Oct 5)*
Wichita 109 *(7f,Nmk,G,Sep 26)*
Wild Thunder 107 *(8f,Don,GF,Sep 14)*
Winning Streak 103 *(6f,Wdr,G,Aug 19)*
With Respect 110 *(6½f,Nby,HY,Oct 25)*
Wonderful Tonight 106 *(8f,Don,HY,Oct 25)*

Xian Express 110 *(6f,Cur,HY,Sep 29)*

Year Of The Tiger 105 *(7f,Nmk,S,Oct 12)*
You're My Rock 104 *(7f,Hay,GS,Jly 20)*

Zarzyni 108 *(6f,Cur,GY,Aug 30)*
Zulu Zander 105 *(5f,Lei,G,Apr 5)*

TWO-YEAR-OLDS - AW

Above 103 *(7f,Wol,SD,Aug 16)*
Adamaris 104 *(8f,Dun,SD,Nov 29)*
Aerclub 105 *(8f,Dun,SD,Nov 22)*
Amarillo Star 103 *(6f,Kem,SS,Dec 5)*
Amelia Jane 103 *(8f,Dun,SD,Nov 29)*
Apricot Moon 108 *(8f,Dun,SD,Dec 13)*
Ascension 103 *(6f,Ncs,SS,Sep 6)*
Assurance 104 *(8f,Dun,SD,Nov 22)*
At War 103 *(8f,Dun,SD,Nov 15)*
Auchterarder 105 *(5f,Wol,SD,Nov 18)*
Auckland Lodge 104 *(5f,Ncs,SD,Nov 4)*

Balmari 105 *(8f,Dun,SD,Nov 8)*
Baltic State 103 *(5f,Ncs,SD,Nov 4)*
Barack Beach 112 *(6f,Mey,FT,Oct 24)*
Big Gossey 108 *(5f,Dun,SD,Dec 20)*
Bill The Butcher 109 *(7f,Sth,SD,Oct 10)*
Brinjal 105 *(8f,Dun,SD,Dec 13)*
Brunelle 109 *(5f,Dun,SD,Oct 4)*

Carlos Felix 103 *(8f,Kem,SS,Nov 5)*
Chanell Eclipse 103 *(5f,Dun,SD,Nov 15)*
Choice Of Mine 106 *(8f,Dun,SD,Dec 18)*
Clay Regazzoni 104 *(9f,Wol,SD,Oct 24)*
Colonel Whitehead 104 *(5f,Ncs,SS,Nov 21)*
Commanding 104 *(8f,Mey,FT,Dec 5)*
Cool Sphere 106 *(5f,Dun,SD,Oct 4)*
Corrienthes 111 *(5f,Dun,SD,Nov 1)*

Dance Fever 104 *(7f,Kem,SS,Nov 6)*
Dandizette 103 *(5f,Ncs,SD,Jun 4)*
Dark Vader 103 *(8f,Dun,SD,Dec 18)*
Dazzling Des 107 *(5f,Ncs,SD,Nov 4)*
Dr Simpson 117 *(5f,Dun,SD,Oct 18)*
Dream Shot 115 *(5f,Dun,SD,Sep 3)*
Dubai Souq 106 *(9f,Wol,SD,Aug 16)*
Dune Of Pilat 104 *(8f,Dun,SD,Nov 22)*

Eastern World 103 *(8f,Kem,SS,Dec 11)*
Electric Ladyland 104 *(5f,Cfd,SD,Sep 24)*
Emissary 107 *(9½f,Wol,SD,Oct 12)*
Enchanted One 105 *(8f,Dun,SD,Nov 29)*
Estepona Sun 103 *(7f,Dun,SD,Dec 3)*

First Receiver 104 *(8f,Kem,SS,Nov 5)*
First View 105 *(8f,Kem,SS,Nov 5)*
Fort Myers 105 *(7f,Dun,SD,Oct 4)*
Franconia 103 *(7f,Cfd,SD,Nov 8)*

George Cornelius 104 *(5f,Dun,SD,Apr 14)*
Get Boosting 105 *(5f,Ncs,SD,Nov 4)*
Glenties 105 *(9½f,Wol,SD,Oct 12)*
Gold Factory 104 *(8f,Dun,SD,Nov 15)*
Gypsy Dancer 103 *(8f,Dun,SD,Dec 13)*

Haifa 107 *(8f,Dun,SD,Dec 13)*
He's A Laddie 104 *(5f,Ncs,SD,Nov 4)*
Heer We Go Again 103 *(5f,Wol,SD,Dec 16)*
Helen De Pourtales 103 *(8f,Dun,SD,Dec 13)*
Hija De La Luna 103 *(5f,Dun,SD,Nov 15)*
Hukum 103 *(8f,Kem,SS,Nov 19)*
Huraiz 105 *(6f,Kem,SS,Sep 7)*
Hurcle 103 *(5f,Ncs,SS,Jun 29)*

Ickworth 110 *(5f,Dun,SD,Oct 18)*
Innisfree 109 *(8f,Ncs,SD,Nov 1)*
Island Hideaway 103 *(8f,Lin,SD,Dec 31)*

Jazzelle 104 *(8f,Dun,SD,Dec 13)*
Jeanie B 104 *(7f,Cfd,SD,Nov 8)*
Johan The Great 104 *(8f,Dun,SD,Nov 29)*
Justifier 103 *(7f,Dun,SD,Oct 4)*

Kameko 113 *(8f,Ncs,SD,Nov 1)*
Karbasann 104 *(8f,Dun,SD,Nov 22)*
King Of The Throne 103 *(8f,Dun,SD,Nov 22)*
Kinross 106 *(8f,Ncs,SD,Nov 1)*
Kuramata 103 *(8f,Kem,SS,Dec 11)*

Laa Baas 107 *(6f,Mey,FT,Oct 24)*
Lady Kermit 103 *(5f,Ncs,SD,Apr 19)*
Last Surprise 104 *(6f,Cfd,SD,Sep 12)*
Live In The Moment 104 *(7f,Sth,SD,Oct 10)*

Majhoola 107 *(7f,Mey,FT,Nov 7)*
Mambo Mischief 103 *(6f,Mey,FT,Oct 24)*
Maystar 103 *(6f,Wol,SD,Dec 7)*
Melodic Charm 103 *(6f,Kem,SS,Sep 7)*
Millionaire Waltz 103 *(7f,Wol,SD,Dec 12)*
Miss Cunning 105 *(6f,Dun,SD,Nov 20)*
Mogul 109 *(8f,Ncs,SD,Nov 1)*
Moll 107 *(8f,Dun,SD,Dec 13)*
Mrs Bouquet 106 *(5f,Ncs,SD,Jun 4)*

Numberoneson 105 *(8f,Dun,SD,Nov 8)*

Ocean Monarch 106 *(8f,Dun,SD,Nov 8)*
Odyssey Girl 103 *(7f,Lin,SD,Nov 30)*
Oh Purple Reign 105 *(6f,Kem,SS,Sep 7)*
Olcan 104 *(5f,Ncs,SD,Jun 4)*
On Tick 103 *(5f,Dun,SD,Oct 25)*
Ottoman Court 105 *(6f,Cfd,SD,Nov 8)*

Pepper Bay 103 *(5f,Ncs,SS,Nov 21)*
Phase After Phase 107 *(5f,Dun,SD,Oct 4)*
Point Reyes 105 *(8f,Dun,SD,Nov 15)*
Prince Of Naples 104 *(7f,Dun,SD,Dec 3)*
Psyche 105 *(8f,Dun,SD,Nov 22)*
Punita Arora 103 *(7f,Dun,SD,Oct 4)*

Qaaddim 103 *(8f,Lin,SD,Oct 3)*

Reassure 111 *(5f,Ncs,SD,Nov 4)*
Richard R H B 103 *(7f,Wol,SD,Nov 23)*
Rio Angie 113 *(7f,Mey,FT,Nov 7)*
Run Wild 106 *(8f,Kem,SS,Aug 28)*

Sampers Seven 104 *(5f,Dun,SD,Nov 15)*
Sebs Star 104 *(6f,Dun,SD,Nov 20)*
Second Love 103 *(6f,Cfd,SD,Sep 5)*
Sky Commander 103 *(7f,Kem,SS,Dec 5)*
St Just 105 *(8f,Lin,SD,Dec 31)*
Starcat 104 *(8f,Kem,SS,Dec 11)*
Streamline 107 *(6f,Kem,SS,Sep 7)*
Summeronsevenhills 105 *(9½f,Wol,SD,Dec 19)*

Tafish 103 *(7f,Sth,SD,Oct 4)*
Talap 103 *(9f,Wol,SD,Oct 24)*
Temple Of Heaven 106 *(6f,Ncs,SD,Oct 22)*
The King Of Kells 103 *(6f,Dun,SD,Nov 6)*

Unforgetable 103 *(7f,Dun,SD,Oct 4)*

Vivandiere 103 *(8f,Dun,SD,Dec 13)*

Windham Belle 103 *(5f,Dun,SD,May 3)*

Year Of The Tiger 109 *(8f,Ncs,SD,Nov 1)*

NOTES